2020

The International WHO'S WHO

2020

The International WHO'S WHO

83rd Edition

VOLUME 2: L–Z

Routledge
Taylor & Francis Group

LONDON AND NEW YORK

Eighty-third edition published 2019
by Routledge
2 Park Square, Milton Park, Abingdon, Oxon., OX14 4RN, United Kingdom

and by Routledge
52 Vanderbilt Avenue, New York, NY 10017, USA

www.routledge.com

Routledge is an imprint of the Taylor & Francis Group, an informa business

First published 1935

ISBN: 978-0-367-13558-4 (The Set)
ISBN: 978-0-367-27815-1 (Volume 2)
ISSN: 0074-9613

Typeset in Frome by Data Standards Limited

Editorial Director: Paul Kelly
Editorial Researchers: Denize Rodricks (Senior Team Leader), Shubha Banerjee (Team Leader), Meer Hussain (Senior Editorial Researcher), Nitya Arora (Editorial Researcher), Saumya Bhasin (Editorial Researcher), Aakanksha Saklani (Editorial Researcher), Sreerupa Sen (Editorial Researcher)
Consulting Editors: Sue Leckey, Justin Lewis
Editorial Assistant: Lucy Pritchard

PUBLISHER'S NOTE

The *International Who's Who* has been published annually since 1935 and provides biographical information on the most famous and talented men and women in the world today. We select the entries entirely on merit and our books are recognized by librarians in every country as a standard reference source in its field. We wish to make it clear that the Europa Biographical Reference Series has no connection with any other business purporting to produce a publication with the same title or a similar title to ours.

FOREWORD TO THE 83rd EDITION

This is the 83rd edition of THE INTERNATIONAL WHO'S WHO, which since its first publication in 1935 has become the standard reference work on the world's most famous and influential personalities. Now in two volumes, the current edition includes details of the lives and achievements of 25,000 of the world's leading men and women.

In compiling THE INTERNATIONAL WHO'S WHO, our aim is to create a reference work that answers the needs of readers seeking information on the lives of our most gifted and significant contemporaries. We choose the entries entirely on merit and for their continuing interest and importance, adding many hundreds to the selection on a regular basis. Some are household names in every continent. Others are noted for their contributions in specialized fields or for their role in the political, economic, social or cultural life of their particular countries. The scope and diversity of the work is reflected in the range of activities represented, which includes architecture, art, business, cinema, diplomacy, engineering, fashion, journalism, law, literature, medicine, music, photography, politics, science, sport, technology and theatre.

Entrants are sent questionnaires so that they may have an opportunity to make necessary additions and amendments to their biographical details. Supplementary research is continually conducted by the Editors and the Europa editorial department to ensure that the work is as up-to-date as possible upon publication. Valuable assistance is also provided by consultants and experts in particular fields or with specialized knowledge of certain countries.

The introduction contains a list of abbreviations and international telephone codes. The names of entrants whose death has been reported over the past year are included in the Obituary. There is also a section on Reigning Royal Families.

The biographical information contained in this 83rd edition, as well as information on past entrants, deceased entrants and entrants from the wide range of other Europa biographical sources, is provided online in WORLD WHO'S WHO. Using the product's sophisticated search functions, researchers can easily and quickly access the rich biographical data in the comprehensive Europa biographical database. As well, online users can take advantage of the quarterly updating cycle that ensures the data is as current as possible. Details of this resource are available at www.worldwhoswho.com.

Not many countries have their own who's who, and not all national who's whos are published annually. THE INTERNATIONAL WHO'S WHO 2020 represents a library of information from all countries that is not found elsewhere and is unrivalled in its balance and coverage.

May 2019

ALPHABETIZATION KEY

The list of names is alphabetical, with the entrants listed under surnames. If part of an entrant's first given name is in parentheses, this will not affect his or her alphabetical listing.

All names beginning Mc and Mac are treated as though they began Mac, e.g. McDowell before Mace, MacFarlane after McFadyen, Machen before McHenry.

Names with Arabic prefixes are normally listed after the prefix except when requested by the entrant. In the case of surnames beginning De, Des, Du, van or von the entries are normally found under the prefix. Names beginning St are listed as if they began Saint, e.g. St Arnaud after Sainsbury. As a general rule Chinese names are alphabetized under the last name.

In the case of an entrant whose name is spelt in a variety of ways, who is known by a pseudonym or best known by another name, a cross reference is provided, e.g.:

Fayrouz (see Fairuz).

Le Carré, John (see Cornwell, David John Moore).

Lloyd, Chris(tine) Marie Evert (see Evert, Chris(tine) Marie).

ABBREVIATIONS

AAA Agricultural Adjustment Administration
AAAS American Association for the Advancement of Science
AAF Army Air Force
AASA Associate of the Australian Society of Accountants
AB Bachelor of Arts; Aktiebolag; Alberta
ABA American Bar Association
AC Companion of the Order of Australia
ACA Associate of the Institute of Chartered Accountants
ACCA Associate of the Association of Certified Accountants
Acad. Academy; Académie
Accad. Accademia
accred accredited
ACIS Associate of the Chartered Institute of Secretaries
ACP American College of Physicians
ACS American Chemical Society
ACT Australian Capital Territory
ADC Aide-de-camp
Adm. Admiral
Admin(.) Administrative; Administration; Administrator
AE Air Efficiency Award
AERE Atomic Energy Research Establishment
AF Air Force
AFC Air Force Cross
ADB African Development Bank
affil. affiliated
AFL American Federation of Labor
AFM Air Force Medal
AG Aktiengesellschaft (Joint Stock Company)
Agric. Agriculture
a.i. ad interim
AIA Associate of the Institute of Actuaries; American Institute of Architects
AIAA American Institute of Aeronautics and Astronautics
AIB Associate of the Institute of Bankers
AICC All-India Congress Committee
AICE Associate of the Institute of Civil Engineers
AIChE American Institute of Chemical Engineers
AIDS Acquired Immune Deficiency Syndrome
AIEE American Institute of Electrical Engineers
AIME American Institute of Mining Engineers; Associate of the Institution of Mining Engineers
AIMechE Associate of the Institution of Mechanical Engineers
AIR All-India Radio
AK Alaska; Knight of the Order of Australia
Akad. Akademie
AL Alabama
Ala Alabama
ALS Associate of the Linnaean Society
Alt. Alternate
AM Alpes Maritimes; Albert Medal; Master of Arts; Member of the Order of Australia
Amb. Ambassador
AMICE Associate Member of the Institution of Civil Engineers
AMIEE Associate Member of the Institution of Electrical Engineers
AMIMechE Associate Member of the Institution of Mechanical Engineers
ANC African National Congress
ANU Australian National University
AO Officer of the Order of Australia
AP Andhra Pradesh
Apdo Apartado
APEC Asia and Pacific Economic Co-operation
approx. approximately
appt appointment
apptd appointed
apt apartment
AR Arkansas
ARA Associate of the Royal Academy
ARAM Associate of the Royal Academy of Music
ARAS Associate of the Royal Astronomical Society
ARC Agriculture Research Council
ARCA Associate of the Royal College of Art
ARCM Associate of the Royal College of Music
ARCO Associate of the Royal College of Organists
ARCS Associate of the Royal College of Science
ARIBA Associate of the Royal Institute of British Architects
Ariz. Arizona
Ark. Arkansas
ARSA Associate of the Royal Scottish Academy; Associate of the Royal Society of Arts
ASEAN Association of South-East Asian Nations
ASLIB Association of Special Libraries and Information Bureaux
ASME American Society of Mechanical Engineers
Asoc. Asociación
Ass. Assembly
Asscn Association
Assoc. Associate

ASSR Autonomous Soviet Socialist Republic
Asst Assistant
ATV Associated Television
Aug. August
autobiog. autobiography
AZ Arizona

b. born
BA Bachelor of Arts; British Airways
BAAS British Association for the Advancement of Science
BAFTA British Academy of Film and Television Arts
BAgr Bachelor of Agriculture
BAgrSc Bachelor of Agricultural Science
BAO Bachelor of Obstetrics
BAOR British Army of the Rhine
BArch Bachelor of Architecture
Bart Baronet
BAS Bachelor in Agricultural Science
BASc Bachelor of Applied Science
BBA Bachelor of Business Administration
BBC British Broadcasting Corporation
BC British Columbia
BCC British Council of Churches
BCE Bachelor of Civil Engineering
BChir Bachelor of Surgery
BCL Bachelor of Civil Law; Bachelor of Canon Law
BCom(m) Bachelor of Commerce
BCS Bachelor of Commercial Sciences
BD Bachelor of Divinity
Bd Board
BDS Bachelor of Dental Surgery
BE Bachelor of Education; Bachelor of Engineering
BEA British European Airways
BEcons Bachelor of Economics
BEd Bachelor of Education
Beds. Bedfordshire
BEE Bachelor of Electrical Engineering
BEM British Empire Medal
BEng Bachelor of Engineering
Berks. Berkshire
BFA Bachelor of Fine Arts
BFI British Film Institute
BIM British Institute of Management
biog. biography
BIS Bank for International Settlements
BL Bachelor of Laws
BLA Bachelor of Landscape Architecture
Bldg Building
BLit(t) Bachelor of Letters; Bachelor of Literature
BLL Bachelor of Laws
BLS Bachelor in Library Science
blvd boulevard
BM Bachelor of Medicine
BMA British Medical Association
BMus Bachelor of Music
Bn Battalion
BNOC British National Oil Corporation
BOAC British Overseas Airways Corporation
BP Boîte Postale
BPA Bachelor of Public Administration
BPharm Batchelor of Pharmacy
BPhil Bachelor of Philosophy
Br. Branch
Brig. Brigadier
BS Bachelor of Science; Bachelor of Surgery
BSA Bachelor of Scientific Agriculture
BSc Bachelor of Science
Bt Baronet
Bucks. Buckinghamshire

c. child; children; circa
CA California; Chartered Accountant
Calif. California
Cambs. Cambridgeshire
Cand. Candidate; Candidature
Cantab. of Cambridge University
Capt. Captain
Cards. Cardiganshire
CB Companion of the (Order of the) Bath
CBC Canadian Broadcasting Corporation
CBE Commander of the (Order of the) British Empire
CBI Confederation of British Industry
CBiol Chartered Biologist
CBIM Companion of the British Institute of Management
CBS Columbia Broadcasting System
CC Companion of the Order of Canada

CChem	Chartered Chemist
CCMI	Companion of the Chartered Management Institute (formerly CIMgt)
CCP	Chinese Communist Party
CD	Canadian Forces Decoration; Commander Order of Distinction
Cdre	Commodore
CDU	Christlich-Demokratische Union
CE	Civil Engineer; Chartered Engineer
CEAO	Communauté Economique de l'Afrique de l'Ouest
Cen.	Central
CEng	Chartered Engineer
CENTO	Central Treaty Organization
CEO	Chief Executive Officer
CERN	Conseil (now Organisation) Européen(ne) pour la Recherche Nucléaire
CFR	Commander of the Federal Republic of Nigeria
CGM	Conspicuous Gallantry Medal
CGT	Confédération Général du Travail
CH	Companion of Honour
Chair.	Chairman; Chairwoman; Chairperson
CHB	Companion of Honour of Barbados
ChB	Bachelor of Surgery
Chem.	Chemistry
ChM	Master of Surgery
CI	Channel Islands
CIA	Central Intelligence Agency
Cia	Compagnia (Company)
Cía	Compañía (Company)
CID	Criminal Investigation Department
CIE	Companion of the (Order of the) Indian Empire
Cie	Compagnie (Company)
CIEE	Companion of the Institution of Electrical Engineers
CIMgt	Companion of the Institute of Management (now CCMI)
C-in-C	Commander-in-Chief
CIO	Congress of Industrial Organizations
CIOMS	Council of International Organizations of Medical Science
CIS	Commonwealth of Independent States
CLD	Doctor of Civil Law (USA)
CLit	Companion of Literature
CM	Canada Medal; Master in Surgery
CMEA	Council for Mutual Economic Assistance
CMG	Companion of (the Order of) St Michael and St George
CNAA	Council for National Academic Awards
CNRS	Centre National de la Recherche Scientifique
CO	Colorado; Commanding Officer
Co.	Company; County
COI	Central Office of Information
Col	Colonel
Coll.	College
Colo	Colorado
COMECON	Council for Mutual Economic Assistance
COMESA	Common Market for Eastern and Southern Asia
Comm.	Commission
Commdg	Commanding
Commdr	Commander; Commandeur
Commdt	Commandant
Commr	Commissioner
CON	Commander of Order of Nigeria
Conf.	Conference
Confed.	Confederation
Conn.	Connecticut
Contrib.	Contributor; contribution
COO	Chief Operating Officer
Corp.	Corporate
Corpn	Corporation
Corresp.	Correspondent; Corresponding
CP	Communist Party; Caixa Postal (Post Office Box)
CPA	Certified Public Accountant; Commonwealth Parliamentary Association
CPhys	Chartered Physicist
CPP	Convention People's Party (Ghana)
CPPCC	Chinese People's Political Consultative Conference
CPSU	Communist Party of the Soviet Union
cr.	created
CSc	Candidate of Sciences
CSCE	Conference on Security and Co-operation in Europe
CSI	Companion of the (Order of the) Star of India
CSIRO	Commonwealth Scientific and Industrial Research Organization
CSSR	Czechoslovak Socialist Republic
CStJ	Commander of (the Order of) St John of Jerusalem
CT	Connecticut
Cttee	Committee
CUNY	City University of New York
CV	Commanditaire Vennootschap
CVO	Commander of the Royal Victorian Order
d.	daughter(s)
DArch	Doctor of Architecture
DB	Bachelor of Divinity
DBA	Doctor of Business Administration
DBE	Dame Commander of (the Order of) the British Empire
DC	District of Columbia
DCE	Doctor of Civil Engineering
DCL	Doctor of Civil Law; Doctor of Canon Law
DCM	Distinguished Conduct Medal
DCMG	Dame Commander of (the Order of) St Michael and St George
DCnL	Doctor of Canon Law
DComm	Doctor of Commerce
DCS	Doctor of Commercial Sciences
DCT	Doctor of Christian Theology
DCVO	Dame Commander of the Royal Victorian Order
DD	Doctor of Divinity
DDR	Deutsche Demokratische Republik (German Democratic Republic)
DDS	Doctor of Dental Surgery
DE	Delaware
Dec.	December
DEcon	Doctor of Economics
DEd	Doctor of Education
DEFRA	Department for Environment, Food and Rural Affairs
Del.	Delegate; Delegation; Delaware
Denbighs.	Denbighshire
DenD	Docteur en Droit
DenM	Docteur en Medicine
DEng	Doctor of Engineering
Dep.	Deputy
Dept	Department
DES	Department of Education and Science
Desig.	Designate
DèsL	Docteur ès Lettres
DèsSc	Docteur ès Sciences
Devt	Development
DF	Distrito Federal
DFA	Doctor of Fine Arts; Diploma of Fine Arts
DFC	Distinguished Flying Cross
DFM	Distinguished Flying Medal
DH	Doctor of Humanities
DHist	Doctor of History
DHL	Doctor of Hebrew Literature
DHSS	Department of Health and Social Security
DHumLitt	Doctor of Humane Letters
DIC	Diploma of Imperial College
DipAD	Diploma in Art and Design
DipAgr	Diploma in Agriculture
DipArch	Diploma in Architecture
DipEd	Diploma in Education
DipEng	Diploma in Engineering
DipMus	Diploma in Music
DipScEconSc	Diploma of Social and Economic Science
DipTh	Doctor of Theology
Dir	Director
Dist	District
DIur	Doctor of Law
DIurUtr	Doctor of both Civil and Canon Law
Div.	Division; divisional
DJur	Doctor of Law
DK	Most Esteemed Family (Malaysia)
DL	Deputy Lieutenant
DLit(t)	Doctor of Letters; Doctor of Literature
DLS	Doctor of Library Science
DM	Doctor of Medicine (Oxford)
DMD	Doctor of Dental Medicine
DMedSc	Doctor of Medical Science
DMilSc	Doctor of Military Science
DMunSci	Doctor of Municipal Science
DMS	Director of Medical Services
DMus	Doctor of Music
DMV	Doctor of Veterinary Medicine
DO	Doctor of Ophthalmology
DPH	Diploma in Public Health
DPhil	Doctor of Philosophy
DPM	Diploma in Psychological Medicine
DPS	Doctor of Public Service
Dr	Doctor
DrAgr	Doctor of Agriculture
DrIng	Doctor of Engineering
DrIur	Doctor of Laws
DrMed	Doctor of Medicine
DrOecPol	Doctor of Political Economy
DrOecPubl	Doctor of (Public) Economy
DrPhilNat	Doctor of Natural Philosophy
Dr rer. nat	Doctor of Natural Sciences
Dr rer. pol	Doctor of Political Science
DrSc(i)	Doctor of Sciences
DrScNat	Doctor of Natural Sciences
DS	Doctor of Science
DSC	Distinguished Service Cross
DSc(i)	Doctor of Sciences
DScS	Doctor of Social Science
DSM	Distinguished Service Medal
DSO	Companion of the Distinguished Service Order
DSocSc	Doctor of Social Science
DST	Doctor of Sacred Theology
DTech	Doctor of Technology
DTechSc(i)	Doctor of Technical Sciences
DTheol	Doctor of Theology
DTM	Diploma in Tropical Medicine
DTM&H	Diploma in Tropical Medicine and Hygiene
DUP	Diploma of the University of Paris
DUniv	Doctor of the University

E	East; Eastern
EBRD	European Bank for Reconstruction and Development
EC	European Commission; European Community
ECA	Economic Co-operation Administration; Economic Commission for Africa
ECAFE	Economic Commission for Asia and the Far East
ECE	Economic Commission for Europe
ECLA	Economic Commission for Latin America
ECLAC	Economic Commission for Latin America and the Caribbean
ECO	Economic Co-operation Organization
Econ.	Economic
Econs	Economics
ECOSOC	Economic and Social Council
ECSC	European Coal and Steel Community
ECWA	Economic Commission for Western Asia
ed	educated; edited
Ed.	Editor
ED	Efficiency Decoration; Doctor of Engineering (USA)
EdD	Doctor of Education
Edin.	Edinburgh
EdM	Master of Education
Edn	Edition
Educ.	Education
EEC	European Economic Community
EFTA	European Free Trade Association
eh	Ehrenhalben (Honorary)
EIB	European Investment Bank
EM	Edward Medal; Master of Engineering (USA)
Emer.	Emerita; Emeritus
Eng	Engineering
EngD	Doctor of Engineering
ENO	English National Opera
EPLF	Eritrean People's Liberation Front
ESA	European Space Agency
ESCAP	Economic and Social Commission for Asia and the Pacific
ESCWA	Economic and Social Commission for Western Asia
est.	established
ETH	Eidgenössische Technische Hochschule (Swiss Federal Institute of Technology)
Ets	Etablissements
EU	European Union
EURATOM	European Atomic Energy Community
Exec.	Executive
Exhbn	Exhibition
Ext.	Extension
f.	founded
FAA	Fellow of Australian Academy of Science
FAAS	Fellow of the American Association for the Advancement of Science
FAATS	Fellow of the Australian Academy of Technological Sciences
FACC	Fellow of the American College of Cardiology
FACCA	Fellow of the Association of Certified and Corporate Accountants
FACE	Fellow of the Australian College of Education
FACP	Fellow of American College of Physicians
FACS	Fellow of the American College of Surgeons
FAHA	Fellow Australian Academy of the Humanities
FAIA	Fellow of the American Institute of Architects
FAIAS	Fellow of the Australian Institute of Agricultural Science
FAIM	Fellow of the Australian Institute of Management
FAO	Food and Agriculture Organization
FAS	Fellow of the Antiquarian Society
FASE	Fellow of Antiquarian Society, Edinburgh
FASSA	Fellow Academy of Social Sciences of Australia
FBA	Fellow of the British Academy
FBI	Federal Bureau of Investigation
FBIM	Fellow of the British Institute of Management
FBIP	Fellow of the British Institute of Physics
FCA	Fellow of the Institute of Chartered Accountants
FCAE	Fellow Canadian Academy of Engineering
FCGI	Fellow of the City and Guilds of London Institute
FCIA	Fellow of the Chartered Institute of Arbitrators
FCIB	Fellow of the Chartered Institute of Bankers
FCIC	Fellow of the Chemical Institute of Canada
FCIM	Fellow of the Chartered Institute of Management
FCIS	Fellow of the Chartered Institute of Secretaries
FCMA	Fellow of the Chartered Institute of Management Accountants
FCO	Foreign and Commonwealth Office
FCSD	Fellow of the Chartered Society of Designers
FCT	Federal Capital Territory
FCWA	Fellow of the Institute of Cost and Works Accountants (now FCMA)
FDGB	Freier Deutscher Gewerkschaftsbund
FDP	Freier Demokratische Partei
Feb.	February
Fed.	Federation; Federal
FEng	Fellow(ship) of Engineering
FFCM	Fellow of the Faculty of Community Medicine
FFPHM	Fellow of the Faculty of Public Health Medicine
FGS	Fellow of the Geological Society
FGSM	Fellow of the Guildhall School of Music
FIA	Fellow of the Institute of Actuaries
FIAL	Fellow of the International Institute of Arts and Letters
FIAM	Fellow of the International Academy of Management
FIAMS	Fellow of the Indian Academy of Medical Sciences
FIAP	Fellow of the Institution of Analysts and Programmers
FIArb	Fellow of the Institute of Arbitrators
FIB	Fellow of the Institute of Bankers
FIBA	Fellow of the Institute of Banking Associations
FIBiol	Fellow of the Institute of Biologists
FICE	Fellow of the Institution of Civil Engineers
FIChemE	Fellow of the Institute of Chemical Engineers
FID	Fellow of the Institute of Directors
FIE	Fellow of the Institute of Engineers
FIEE	Fellow of the Institution of Electrical Engineers
FIEEE	Fellow of the Institute of Electrical and Electronics Engineers
FIFA	Fédération Internationale de Football Association
FIJ	Fellow of the Institute of Journalists
FilLic	Licentiate in Philosophy
FIM	Fellow of the Institute of Metallurgists
FIME	Fellow of the Institute of Mining Engineers
FIMechE	Fellow of the Institute of Mechanical Engineers
FIMI	Fellow of the Institute of the Motor Industry
FInstF	Fellow of the Institute of Fuel
FInstM	Fellow of the Institute of Marketing
FInstP	Fellow of the Institute of Physics
FInstPet	Fellow of the Institute of Petroleum
FIPM	Fellow of the Institute of Personnel Management
FIRE	Fellow of the Institution of Radio Engineers
FITD	Fellow of the Institute of Training and Development
FL	Florida
Fla	Florida
FLA	Fellow of the Library Association
FLN	Front de Libération Nationale
FLS	Fellow of the Linnaean Society
FMedSci	Fellow of the Academy of Medical Sciences
fmr(ly)	former(ly)
FNI	Fellow of the National Institute of Sciences of India
FNZIA	Fellow of the New Zealand Institute of Architects
FRACP	Fellow of the Royal Australasian College of Physicians
FRACS	Fellow of the Royal Australasian College of Surgeons
FRAeS	Fellow of the Royal Aeronautical Society
FRAI	Fellow of the Royal Anthropological Institute
FRAIA	Fellow of the Royal Australian Institute of Architects
FRAIC	Fellow of the Royal Architectural Institute of Canada
FRAM	Fellow of the Royal Academy of Music
FRAS	Fellow of the Royal Astronomical Society; Fellow of the Royal Asiatic Society
FRBS	Fellow of the Royal Society of British Sculptors
FRCA	Fellow of the Royal College of Anaesthetists
FRCM	Fellow of the Royal College of Music
FRCO	Fellow of the Royal College of Organists
FRCOG	Fellow of the Royal College of Obstetricians and Gynaecologists
FRCP	Fellow of the Royal College of Physicians
FRCPE	Fellow of the Royal College of Physicians, Edinburgh
FRCPGlas	Fellow of the Royal College of Physicians (Glasgow)
FRCPI	Fellow of the Royal College of Physicians of Ireland
FRCPath	Fellow Royal College of Pathologists
FRCR	Fellow Royal College of Radiology
FRCS	Fellow of the Royal College of Surgeons
FRCSE	Fellow of the Royal College of Surgeons, Edinburgh
FRCVS	Fellow of the Royal College of Veterinary Surgeons
FREconS	Fellow of the Royal Economic Society
FREng	Fellow of the Royal Academy of Engineering
FRES	Fellow of the Royal Entomological Society
FRFPS	Fellow of the Royal Faculty of Physicians and Surgeons
FRG	Federal Republic of Germany
FRGS	Fellow of the Royal Geographical Society
FRHistS	Fellow of the Royal Historical Society
FRHortS	Fellow of the Royal Horticultural Society
FRIBA	Fellow of the Royal Institute of British Architects
FRIC	Fellow of the Royal Institute of Chemists
FRICS	Fellow of the Royal Institute of Chartered Surveyors
FRMetS	Fellow of the Royal Meteorological Society
FRNCM	Fellow of the Royal Northern College of Music
FRPS	Fellow of the Royal Photographic Society
FRS	Fellow of the Royal Society
FRSA	Fellow of the Royal Society of Arts
FRSAMD	Fellow of the Royal Scottish Academy of Music and Drama
FRSC	Fellow of the Royal Society of Canada; Fellow of the Royal Society of Chemistry
FRSE	Fellow of the Royal Society of Edinburgh
FRSL	Fellow of the Royal Society of Literature
FRSM	Fellow of the Royal Society of Medicine
FRSNZ	Fellow of the Royal Society of New Zealand
FRSS	Fellow of the Royal Statistical Society
FRSSA	Fellow of the Royal Society of South Africa
FRTS	Fellow of the Royal Television Society
FSA	Fellow of the Society of Antiquaries
FSIAD	Fellow of the Society of Industrial Artists and Designers
FTI	Fellow of the Textile Institute
FTS	Fellow of Technological Sciences
FWAAS	Fellow of the World Academy of Arts and Sciences
FZS	Fellow of the Zoological Society
GA	Georgia
Ga	Georgia
GATT	General Agreement on Tariffs and Trade
GB	Great Britain

GBE	Knight (or Dame) Grand Cross of (the Order of) the British Empire	IPU	Inter-Parliamentary Union
GC	George Cross	ISO	Companion of the Imperial Service Order
GCB	Knight Grand Cross of (the Order of) the Bath	ITA	Independent Television Authority
GCIE	Knight Grand Commander of (the Order of) the Indian Empire	ITU	International Telecommunications Union
		ITV	Independent Television
GCMG	Knight (or Dame) Grand Cross of (the Order of) St Michael and St George	IUPAC	International Union of Pure and Applied Chemistry
		IUPAP	International Union of Pure and Applied Physics
GCSI	Knight Grand Commander of (the Order of) the Star of India		
GCVO	Knight (or Dame) Grand Cross of the Royal Victorian Order	Jan.	January
GDR	German Democratic Republic	JCB	Bachelor of Canon Law
Gen.	General	JCD	Doctor of Canon Law
GHQ	General Headquarters	JD	Doctor of Jurisprudence
GLA	Greater London Authority	JMK	Johan Mangku Negara (Malaysia)
Glam.	Glamorganshire	JP	Justice of the Peace
GLC	Greater London Council	Jr	Junior
Glos.	Gloucestershire	JSD	Doctor of Juristic Science
GM	George Medal	Jt(ly)	Joint(ly)
GmbH	Gesellschaft mit beschränkter Haftung (Limited Liability Company)	JUD	Juris utriusque Doctor (Doctor of both Civil and Canon Law)
		JuD	Doctor of Law
GOC	General Officer Commanding	JUDr	Juris utriusque Doctor (Doctor of both Civil and Canon Law);
GOC-in-C	General Officer Commanding-in-Chief		Doctor of Law
Gov.	Governor	Kan.	Kansas
Govt	Government	KBE	Knight Commander of (the Order of) the British Empire
GPO	General Post Office	KC	King's Counsel
Grad.	Graduate	KCB	Knight Commander of (the Order of) the Bath
GRSM	Graduate of the Royal School of Music	KCIE	Knight Commander of (the Order of) the Indian Empire
GSO	General Staff Officer	KCMG	Knight Commander of (the Order of) St Michael and St George
Hants.	Hampshire	KCSI	Knight Commander of (the Order of) the Star of India
hc	honoris causa	KCVO	Knight Commander of the Royal Victorian Order
HE	His Eminence; His (or Her) Excellency	KG	Royal Knight of the Most Noble Order of the Garter
Herefords.	Herefordshire	KGB	Committee of State Security (USSR)
Herts.	Hertfordshire	KK	Kaien Kaisha
HH	His (or Her) Highness	KLM	Koninklijke Luchtvaart Maatschappij (Royal Dutch Airlines)
HI	Hawaii	KNZM	Knight of the New Zealand Order of Merit
HIV	human immunodeficiency virus	KP	Knight of (the Order of) St Patrick
HLD	Doctor of Humane Letters	KS	Kansas
HM	His (or Her) Majesty	KStJ	Knight of (the Order of) St John of Jerusalem
HMS	His (or Her) Majesty's Ship	KT	Knight of (the Order of) the Thistle
Hon.	Honorary; Honourable	Kt	Knight
Hons	Honours	KY	Kentucky
Hosp.	Hospital	Ky	Kentucky
HQ	Headquarters		
HRH	His (or Her) Royal Highness	LA	Louisiana; Los Angeles
HSH	His (or Her) Serene Highness	La	Louisiana
HSP	Hungarian Socialist Party	Lab.	Laboratory
HSWP	Hungarian Socialist Workers' Party	Lancs.	Lancashire
Hunts.	Huntingdonshire	LDP	Liberal Democratic Party
		LDS	Licentiate in Dental Surgery
		Legis.	Legislative
IA	Iowa	Leics.	Leicestershire
Ia	Iowa	LenD	Licencié en Droit
IAAF	International Association of Athletics Federations	LèsL	Licencié ès Lettres
IAEA	International Atomic Energy Agency	LèsSc	Licencié ès Sciences
IATA	International Air Transport Association	LG	Lady of (the Order of) the Garter
IBA	Independent Broadcasting Authority	LHD	Doctor of Humane Letters
IBRD	International Bank for Reconstruction and Development (World Bank)	LI	Long Island
		LicenDer	Licenciado en Derecho
ICAO	International Civil Aviation Organization	LicenFil	Licenciado en Filosofía
ICC	International Chamber of Commerce	LicMed	Licentiate in Medicine
ICE	Institution of Civil Engineers	Lincs.	Lincolnshire
ICEM	Intergovernmental Committee for European Migration	LittD	Doctor of Letters
ICFTU	International Confederation of Free Trade Unions	LLB	Bachelor of Laws
ICI	Imperial Chemical Industries	LLC	Limited Liability Company
ICOM	International Council of Museums	LLD	Doctor of Laws
ICRC	International Committee for the Red Cross	LLL	Licentiate of Laws
ICS	Indian Civil Service	LLM	Master of Laws
ICSID	International Centre for Settlement of Investment Disputes	LLP	Limited Liability Partnership
ICSU	International Council of Scientific Unions	LM	Licentiate of Medicine; Licentiate Midwifery
ID	Idaho	LN	League of Nations
Ida	Idaho	LPh	Licentiate of Philosophy
IDA	International Development Association	LRAM	Licentiate of the Royal Academy of Music
IDB	Inter-American Development Bank	LRCP	Licentiate of the Royal College of Physicians
IEA	International Energy Agency	LSE	London School of Economics and Political Science
IEE	Institution of Electrical Engineers	Lt	Lieutenant
IEEE	Institution of Electrical and Electronic Engineers	Ltd	Limited
IFAD	International Fund for Agricultural Development	Ltda	Limitada
IFC	International Finance Corporation	LTh	Licentiate in Theology
IGAD	Intergovernmental Authority on Development	LVO	Lieutenant, Royal Victorian Order
IISS	International Institute for Strategic Studies		
IL	Illinois	m.	married; marriage; metre(s)
Ill.	Illinois	MA	Massachusetts; Master of Arts
ILO	International Labour Organization	MAgr	Master of Agriculture (USA)
IMCO	Inter-Governmental Maritime Consultative Organization	Maj.	Major
IMechE	Institution of Mechanical Engineers	MALD	Master of Arts in Law and Diplomacy
IMF	International Monetary Fund	Man.	Management; Manager; Managing; Manitoba
IMO	International Maritime Organization	MArch	Master of Architecture
IN	Indiana	Mass	Massachusetts
Inc.	Incorporated	Math.	Mathematics; Mathematical
Ind.	Indiana; Independent	MB	Bachelor of Medicine; Manitoba
Insp.	Inspector	MBA	Master of Business Administration
Inst.	Institute; Institution	MBE	Member of (the Order of) the British Empire
Int.	International	MBS	Master of Business Studies
INTERPOL	International Criminal Police Organization	MC	Military Cross
INTUC	Indian National Trades Union Congress	MCC	Marylebone Cricket Club
IOC	International Olympic Committee	MCE	Master of Civil Engineering

MCh	Master of Surgery
MChD	Master of Dental Surgery
MCL	Master of Civil Law
MCom(m)	Master of Commerce
MCP	Master of City Planning
MD	Maryland; Doctor of Medicine
Md	Maryland
MDiv	Master of Divinity
MDS	Master of Dental Surgery
ME	Maine; Myalgic Encephalomyelitis
Me	Maine
MEconSc	Master of Economic Sciences
MEd	Master in Education
mem.	member
MEng	Master of Engineering (Dublin)
MEP	Member of European Parliament
MFA	Master of Fine Arts
Mfg	Manufacturing
Mfrs	Manufacturers
Mgr	Monseigneur; Monsignor
MI	Michigan; Marshall Islands
MIA	Master of International Affairs
MICE	Member of the Institution of Civil Engineers
MIChemE	Member of the Institution of Chemical Engineers
Mich.	Michigan
Middx	Middlesex
MIEE	Member of the Institution of Electrical Engineers
Mil.	Military
MIMarE	Member of the Institute of Marine Engineers
MIMechE	Member of the Institution of Mechanical Engineers
MIMinE	Member of the Institution of Mining Engineers
Minn.	Minnesota
MInstT	Member of the Institute of Transport
Miss.	Mississippi
MIStructE	Member of the Institution of Structural Engineers
MIT	Massachusetts Institute of Technology
MJ	Master of Jurisprudence
MLA	Member of the Legislative Assembly; Master of Landscape Architecture
MLC	Member of the Legislative Council
MM	Military Medal
MLitt	Master in Letters
MM	Military Medal
MMus	Master of Music
MN	Minnesota
MNOC	Movement of Non-Aligned Countries
MO	Missouri
Mo.	Missouri
MOH	Medical Officer of Health
Mon.	Monmouthshire
Mont.	Montana
Movt	Movement
MP	Member of Parliament; Madhya Pradesh
MPA	Master of Public Administration (Harvard)
MPh	Master of Philosophy (USA)
MPhil	Master of Philosophy
MPolSci	Master of Political Science
MPP	Member of Provincial Parliament (Canada)
MRAS	Member of the Royal Asiatic Society
MRC	Medical Research Council
MRCP	Member of the Royal College of Physicians
MRCPE	Member of the Royal College of Physicians, Edinburgh
MRCS	Member of the Royal College of Surgeons
MRCSE	Member of the Royal College of Surgeons, Edinburgh
MRCVS	Member of the Royal College of Veterinary Surgeons
MRI	Member of the Royal Institution
MRIA	Member of the Royal Irish Academy
MRIC	Member of the Royal Institute of Chemistry
MRP	Mouvement Républicain Populaire
MS	Mississippi; Master of Science; Master of Surgery
MSc	Master of Science
MScS	Master of Social Science
MSP	Member Scottish Parliament
MT	Montana
MTS	Master of Theological Studies
MUDr	Doctor of Medicine
MusB(ac)	Bachelor of Music
MusD(oc)	Doctor of Music
MusM	Master of Music (Cambridge)
MVD	Master of Veterinary Medicine
MVO	Member of the Royal Victorian Order
MW	Master of Wine
N	North; Northern
NAS	National Academy of Sciences (USA)
NASA	National Aeronautics and Space Administration
Nat.	National
NATO	North Atlantic Treaty Organization
Naz.	Nazionale
NB	New Brunswick
NBC	National Broadcasting Corporation
NC	North Carolina
ND	North Dakota
NE	Nebraska; North East
NEA	National Endowment for the Arts
Neb.	Nebraska

NEDC	National Economic Development Council
NERC	Natural Environment Research Council
Nev.	Nevada
NF	Newfoundland
NGO	Non-Governmental Organization
NH	New Hampshire
NHS	National Health Service
NI	Northern Ireland
NIH	National Institutes of Health
NJ	New Jersey
NL	Newfoundland and Labrador
NM	New Mexico
Northants.	Northamptonshire
Notts.	Nottinghamshire
Nov.	November
NPC	National People's Congress
nr	near
NRC	Nuclear Research Council
NS	Nova Scotia
NSF	National Science Foundation
NSW	New South Wales
NT	Northern Territory
NU	Nunavut Territory
NV	Naamloze Vennootschap; Nevada
NW	North West
NWT	North West Territories
NY	New York (State)
NZ	New Zealand
NZIC	New Zealand Institute of Chemistry
O	Ohio
OAPEC	Organization of Arab Petroleum Exporting Countries
OAS	Organization of American States
OAU	Organization of African Unity
OBE	Officer of (the Order of) the British Empire
OC	Officer of the Order of Canada
Oct.	October
OE	Order of Excellence (Guyana)
OECD	Organisation for Economic Co-operation and Development
OEEC	Organization for European Economic Co-operation
OFS	Orange Free State
OH	Ohio
OHCHR	Office of the United Nations High Commissioner for Human Rights
OIC	Organization of the Islamic Conference
OJ	Order of Jamaica
OK	Oklahoma
Okla	Oklahoma
OM	Member of the Order of Merit
ON	Ontario; Order of Nigeria
Ont.	Ontario
ONZ	Order of New Zealand
OP	Ordo Praedicatorum (Dominicans)
OPCW	Organization for the Prohibition of Chemical Weapons
OPEC	Organization of the Petroleum Exporting Countries
OPM	Office of Production Management
OQ	Officer National Order of Québec
OR	Oregon
Ore.	Oregon
Org.	Organization
OSB	Order of St Benedict
OSCE	Organization for Security and Co-operation in Europe
Oxon.	of Oxford University; Oxfordshire
PA	Pennsylvania
Pa	Pennsylvania
Parl.	Parliament; Parliamentary
PC	Privy Councillor
PCC	Provincial Congress Committee
PdB	Bachelor of Pedagogy
PdD	Doctor of Pedagogy
PdM	Master of Pedagogy
PDS	Partei des Demokratischen Sozialismus
PE	Prince Edward Island
PEI	Prince Edward Island
Pembs.	Pembrokeshire
PEN	Poets, Playwrights, Essayists and Novelists (Club)
Perm.	Permanent
PGCE	Postgraduate Certificate in Education
PhB	Bachelor of Philosophy
PhD(r)	Doctor of Philosophy
PharmD	Docteur en Pharmacie
Phila	Philadelphia
PhL	Licentiate of Philosophy
PLA	People's Liberation Army; Port of London Authority
PLC	Public Limited Company
PLO	Palestine Liberation Organization
PMB	Private Mail Bag
pnr	partner
PO(B)	Post Office (Box)
POW	Prisoner of War
PPR	Polish Workers' Party
PPRA	Past President of the Royal Academy
PQ	Province of Québec
PR	Puerto Rico
PRA	President of the Royal Academy

ABBREVIATIONS

Pref.	Prefecture		SEC	Securities and Exchange Commission
Prep.	Preparatory		Secr.	Secretariat
Pres.	President		SED	Sozialistische Einheitspartei Deutschlands (Socialist Unity Party of the German Democratic Republic)
PRI	President of the Royal Institute (of Painters in Water Colours)		Sept.	September
PRIBA	President of the Royal Institute of British Architects		S-et-O	Seine-et-Oise
Prin.	Principal		SHAEF	Supreme Headquarters Allied Expeditionary Force
Priv Doz	Privat Dozent (recognized teacher not on the regular staff)		SHAPE	Supreme Headquarters Allied Powers in Europe
PRO	Public Relations Officer		SJ	Society of Jesus (Jesuits)
Proc.	Proceedings		SJD	Doctor of Juristic Science
prod.	producer		SK	Saskatchewan
Prof.	Professor		SLD	Social and Liberal Democrats
Propr	Proprietor		SM	Master of Science
Prov.	Province; Provincial		SOAS	School of Oriental and African Studies
PRS	President of the Royal Society		Soc.	Society; Société
PRSA	President of the Royal Scottish Academy		SpA	Societá per Azioni
PSM	Panglima Setia Mahota		SPD	Sozialdemokratische Partei Deutschlands
Pty	Proprietary		Sr	Senior
Publ.(s)	Publication(s)		SRC	Science Research Council
Publr	Publisher		SRL	Société a responsabilité
Pvt.	Private		SSM	Seria Seta Mahkota (Malaysia)
PZPR	Polish United Workers' Party		SSR	Soviet Socialist Republic
			St	Saint
QC	Québec; Queen's Counsel		Staffs.	Staffordshire
QGM	Queen's Gallantry Medal		STB	Bachelor of Sacred Theology
Qld	Queensland		STD	Doctor of Sacred Theology
QPM	Queen's Police Medal		STL	Licentiate of Sacred Theology
QSO	Queen's Service Order		STM	Master of Sacred Theology
q.v.	quod vide (to which refer)		str.	strasse
			Supt	Superintendent
RA	Royal Academy; Royal Academician; Royal Artillery		SW	South West
RAAF	Royal Australian Air Force		SWAPO	South West Africa People's Organization
RAC	Royal Armoured Corps			
RACP	Royal Australasian College of Physicians		TA	Territorial Army
RADA	Royal Academy of Dramatic Art		TD	Teachta Dála (member of the Dáil); Territorial Decoration
RAF	Royal Air Force		Tech.	Technical; Technology
RAFVR	Royal Air Force Volunteer Reserve		Temp.	Temporary
RAM	Royal Academy of Music		Tenn.	Tennessee
RAMC	Royal Army Medical Corps		Tex.	Texas
RAOC	Royal Army Ordnance Corps		ThB	Bachelor of Theology
RC	Roman Catholic		ThD	Doctor of Theology
RCA	Radio Corporation of America; Royal Canadian Academy; Royal College of Art		THDr	Doctor of Theology
			ThM	Master of Theology
RCAF	Royal Canadian Air Force		TN	Tennessee
RCM	Royal College of Music		Trans.	Translation; Translator
RCP	Romanian Communist Party		Treas.	Treasurer
RCP	Royal College of Physicians		TU(C)	Trades Union (Congress)
RCPI	Royal College of Physicians of Ireland		TV	television
Regt	Regiment		TX	Texas
REME	Royal Electric and Mechanical Engineers			
Rep.	Representative; represented		UAE	United Arab Emirates
Repub.	Republic		UAR	United Arab Republic
resgnd	resigned		UCLA	University of California at Los Angeles
retd	retired		UDEAC	L'Union Douanière et Economique de l'Afrique Centrale
Rev.	Reverend		UDR	Union des Démocrates pour la République
RI	Rhode Island		UED	University Education Diploma
RIBA	Royal Institute of British Architects		UK	United Kingdom (of Great Britain and Northern Ireland)
RMA	Royal Military Academy		UKAEA	United Kingdom Atomic Energy Authority
RN	Royal Navy		UMIST	University of Manchester Institute of Science and Technology
RNR	Royal Naval Reserve		UMNO	United Malays National Organization
RNVR	Royal Naval Volunteer Reserve		UN(O)	United Nations (Organization)
RNZAF	Royal New Zealand Air Force		UNA	United Nations Association
RP	Member Royal Society of Portrait Painters		UNCED	United Nations Council for Education and Development
RPR	Rassemblement pour la République		UNCHS	United Nations Centre for Human Settlements (Habitat)
RSA	Royal Scottish Academy; Royal Society of Arts		UNCTAD	United Nations Conference on Trade and Development
RSC	Royal Shakespeare Company; Royal Society of Canada		UNDCP	United Nations International Drug Control Programme
RSDr	Doctor of Social Sciences		UNDP	United Nations Development Programme
RSFSR	Russian Soviet Federative Socialist Republic		UNDRO	United Nations Disaster Relief Office
RSL	Royal Society of Literature		UNEF	United Nations Emergency Force
Rt Hon.	Right Honourable		UNEP	United Nations Environment Programme
Rt Rev.	Right Reverend		UNESCO	United Nations Educational, Scientific and Cultural Organisation
RVO	Royal Victorian Order			
RWS	Royal Society of Painters in Water Colours		UNFPA	United Nations Population Fund
			UNHCR	United Nations High Commissioner for Refugees
s.	son(s)		UNICEF	United Nations International Children's Emergency Fund
S	South; Southern		UNIDO	United Nations Industrial Development Organization
SA	Sociedad Anónima; Société Anonyme; South Africa; South Australia		UNIFEM	United Nations Development Fund for Women
			UNITAR	United Nations Institute for Training and Research
SAARC	South Asian Association for Regional Co-operation		Univ.	University
SADC	South African Development Community		UNKRA	United Nations Korean Relief Administration
SAE	Society of Aeronautical Engineers		UNRRA	United Nations Relief and Rehabilitation Administration
Salop.	Shropshire		UNRWA	United Nations Relief and Works Agency
SALT	Strategic Arms Limitation Treaty		UNU	United Nations University
Sask.	Saskatchewan		UP	United Provinces; Uttar Pradesh
SB	Bachelor of Science (USA)		UPU	Universal Postal Union
SC	Senior Counsel; South Carolina		Urb.	Urbanizacion
SCAP	Supreme Command Allied Powers		US	United States
ScB	Bachelor of Science		USA	United States of America
ScD	Doctor of Science		USAAF	United States Army Air Force
SD	South Dakota		USAF	United States Air Force
SDak	South Dakota		USAID	United States Agency for International Development
SDLP	Social and Democratic Liberal Party		USN	United States Navy
SDP	Social Democratic Party		USNR	United States Navy Reserve
SE	South East		USPHS	United States Public Health Service
SEATO	South East Asia Treaty Organization		USS	United States Ship
Sec.	Secretary		USSR	Union of Soviet Socialist Republics

ABBREVIATIONS

UT	Utah	WHO	World Health Organization
UWI	University of the West Indies	WI	Wisconsin
		Wilts.	Wiltshire
VA	Virginia	WIPO	World Intellectual Property Organization
Va	Virginia	Wis.	Wisconsin
VC	Victoria Cross	WMO	World Meteorological Organization
VI	(US) Virgin Islands	WNO	Welsh National Opera
Vic.	Victoria	Worcs.	Worcestershire
Vol.(s)	Volume(s)	WRAC	Women's Royal Army Corps
VSO	Voluntary Services Overseas	WRNS	Women's Royal Naval Service
VT	Vermont	WTO	World Trade Organization
Vt	Vermont	WV	West Virginia
		WVa	West Virginia
W	West; Western	WWF	World Wildlife Fund
WA	Washington (State); Western Australia	WY	Wyoming
Warwicks.	Warwickshire	Wyo.	Wyoming
Wash.	Washington (State)		
WCC	World Council of Churches	YMCA	Young Men's Christian Association
WCT	World Championship Tennis	Yorks.	Yorkshire
WEU	Western European Union	YT	Yukon Territory
WFP	World Food Programme	YWCA	Young Women's Christian Association
WFTU	World Federation of Trade Unions		

INTERNATIONAL TELEPHONE CODES

To make international calls to telephone and fax numbers listed in the book, dial the international code of the country from which you are calling, followed by the appropriate country code for the organization you wish to call (listed below), followed by the area code (if applicable) and telephone or fax number listed in the entry.

	Country code		Country code
Abkhazia	7	Egypt	20
Afghanistan	93	El Salvador	503
Åland Islands	358	Equatorial Guinea	240
Albania	355	Eritrea	291
Algeria	213	Estonia	372
American Samoa	1 684	Ethiopia	251
Andorra	376	Falkland Islands	500
Angola	244	Faroe Islands	298
Anguilla	1 264	Fiji	679
Antigua and Barbuda	1 268	Finland	358
Argentina	54	France	33
Armenia	374	French Guiana	594
Aruba	297	French Polynesia	689
Ascension Island	247	Gabon	241
Australia	61	Gambia	220
Austria	43	Georgia	995
Azerbaijan	994	Germany	49
Bahamas	1 242	Ghana	233
Bahrain	973	Gibraltar	350
Bangladesh	880	Greece	30
Barbados	1 246	Greenland	299
Belarus	375	Grenada	1 473
Belgium	32	Guadeloupe	590
Belize	501	Guam	1 671
Benin	229	Guatemala	502
Bermuda	1 441	Guernsey	44
Bhutan	975	Guinea	224
Bolivia	591	Guinea-Bissau	245
Bonaire	599	Guyana	592
Bosnia and Herzegovina	387	Haiti	509
Botswana	267	Honduras	504
Brazil	55	Hong Kong	852
British Indian Ocean Territory		Hungary	36
(Diego Garcia)	246	Iceland	354
British Virgin Islands	1 284	India	91
Brunei	673	Indonesia	62
Bulgaria	359	Iran	98
Burkina Faso	226	Iraq	964
Burundi	257	Ireland	353
Cabo Verde	238	Isle of Man	44
Cambodia	855	Israel	972
Cameroon	237	Italy	39
Canada	1	Jamaica	1 876
Cayman Islands	1 345	Japan	81
Central African Republic	236	Jersey	44
Ceuta	34	Jordan	962
Chad	235	Kazakhstan	7
Chile	56	Kenya	254
China, People's Republic	86	Kiribati	686
Christmas Island	61	Korea, Democratic People's Republic	
Cocos (Keeling) Islands	61	(North Korea)	850
Colombia	57	Korea, Republic (South Korea)	82
Comoros	269	Kosovo	381*
Congo, Democratic Republic	243	Kuwait	965
Congo, Republic	242	Kyrgyzstan	996
Cook Islands	682	Laos	856
Costa Rica	506	Latvia	371
Côte d'Ivoire	225	Lebanon	961
Croatia	385	Lesotho	266
Cuba	53	Liberia	231
Curaçao	599	Libya	218
Cyprus	357	Liechtenstein	423
Czech Republic	420	Lithuania	370
Denmark	45	Luxembourg	352
Djibouti	253	Macao	853
Dominica	1 767	Madagascar	261
Dominican Republic	1 809	Malawi	265
Ecuador	593	Malaysia	60

INTERNATIONAL TELEPHONE CODES

	Country code
Maldives	960
Mali	223
Malta	356
Marshall Islands	692
Martinique	596
Mauritania	222
Mauritius	230
Mayotte	262
Melilla	34
Mexico	52
Micronesia, Federated States	691
Moldova	373
Monaco	377
Mongolia	976
Montenegro	382
Montserrat	1 664
Morocco	212
Mozambique	258
Myanmar	95
Nagornyi Karabakh	374
Namibia	264
Nauru	674
Nepal	977
Netherlands	31
New Caledonia	687
New Zealand	64
Nicaragua	505
Niger	227
Nigeria	234
Niue	683
Norfolk Island	672
North Macedonia	389
Northern Mariana Islands	1 670
Norway	47
Oman	968
Pakistan	92
Palau	680
Palestinian Territories	970 or 972
Panama	507
Papua New Guinea	675
Paraguay	595
Peru	51
Philippines	63
Pitcairn Islands	872
Poland	48
Portugal	351
Puerto Rico	1 787
Qatar	974
Réunion	262
Romania	40
Russian Federation	7
Rwanda	250
Saba	599
Saint-Barthélemy	590
Saint Christopher and Nevis	1 869
Saint Helena	290
Saint Lucia	1 758
Saint-Martin	590
Saint Pierre and Miquelon	508
Saint Vincent and the Grenadines	1 784
Samoa	685
San Marino	378
São Tomé and Príncipe	239
Saudi Arabia	966
Senegal	221

	Country code
Serbia	381
Seychelles	248
Sierra Leone	232
Singapore	65
Sint Eustatius	1721
Sint Maarten	1721
Slovakia	421
Slovenia	386
Solomon Islands	677
Somalia	252
South Africa	27
South Ossetia	7
South Sudan	211
Spain	34
Sri Lanka	94
Sudan	249
Suriname	597
Svalbard	47
Swaziland	268
Sweden	46
Switzerland	41
Syria	963
Taiwan	886
Tajikistan	992
Tanzania	255
Thailand	66
Timor-Leste	670
Togo	228
Tokelau	690
Tonga	676
Transnistria	373
Trinidad and Tobago	1 868
Tristan da Cunha	290
Tunisia	216
Turkey	90
'Turkish Republic of Northern Cyprus'	90 392
Turkmenistan	993
Turks and Caicos Islands	1 649
Tuvalu	688
Uganda	256
Ukraine	380
United Arab Emirates	971
United Kingdom	44
United States of America	1
United States Virgin Islands	1 340
Uruguay	598
Uzbekistan	998
Vanuatu	678
Vatican City	39
Venezuela	58
Viet Nam	84
Wallis and Futuna Islands	681
Yemen	967
Zambia	260
Zimbabwe	263

* Mobile telephone numbers for Kosovo use either the country code for Monaco (377) or the country code for Slovenia (386).

Note: Telephone and fax numbers using the Inmarsat ocean region code 870 are listed in full. No country or area code is required, but it is necessary to precede the number with the international access code of the country from which the call is made.

REIGNING ROYAL FAMILIES OF THE WORLD

Biographical entries of most of the reigning monarchs and of certain other members of the reigning royal families will be found in their appropriate alphabetical order in the biographical section of this book. The name under which they can be found in the text of the book will be listed in this section in bold type.

BAHRAIN

Reigning King

HM SHEIKH HAMAD BIN ISA AL-**KHALIFA**; b. 28 January 1950; succeeded 6 March 1999 as Ruler of Bahrain on the death of his father, Sheikh Isa bin Sulman al-Khalifa; acceded as Amir 6 March 1999; proclaimed King 14 February 2002; married 9 October 1968, Shaikha Sabeeka bint Ibrahim al-Khalifa; three sons, one daughter; four sons, four daughters with his three other wives.

Crown Prince

HRH Sheikh Salman bin Hamad bin Isa al-**Khalifa**, b. 21 October 1969; married Hala bint D'aij al-Khalifa (died 2018); two sons, two daughters.

Parents of the King

Sheikh Isa bin Salman Al Khalifa, b. 3 June 1931, died 6 March 1999; succeeded to the throne December 1961, on the death of his father, Sheikh Salman bin Hamad Al Khalifa; married 8 May 1949, Shaikha Hessa bint Salman Al Khalifa (b. 1933); six sons, six daughters.

BELGIUM

Reigning King

HM KING **PHILIPPE** I; b. 15 April 1960; succeeded to the throne 21 July 2013, on the abdication of his father, King Albert II; married 4 December 1999, Mathilde Marie Christiane Ghislaine d'Udekem d'Acoz (Queen Mathilde) (b. 20 January 1973).

Children of the King

HRH Princess Elisabeth, Duchess of Brabant, b. 25 October 2001.

HRH Prince Gabriel, b. 20 August 2003.

HRH Prince Emmanuel, b. 4 October 2005.

HRH Princess Eléonore, b. 16 April 2008.

Brother and Sister of the King

Princess Astrid, b. 5 June 1962; married 22 September 1984, Archduke Lorenz; son, Prince Amedeo, b. February 1986; daughter, Princess Maria Laura, b. August 1988; son, Prince Joachim, b. December 1991; daughter, Princess Louisa-Maria, b. October 1995; daughter, Princess Laetitia Maria, b. 23 April 2003.

Prince Laurent, b. 19 October 1963; married 12 April 2003, Claire Coombs; daughter, Princess Louise, b. February 2004; son, Prince Aymeric, b. December 2005; son, Prince Nicolas, b. December 2005.

Parents of the King

King Albert II, b. 6 June 1934; succeeded to the throne 9 August 1993, on the death of his brother, King Baudouin I; married 2 July 1959, Donna Paola Ruffo di Calabria (Queen Paola) (b. 11 September 1937); abdicated 21 July 2013 in favour of his son, Crown Prince Philippe; three children.

BHUTAN

The Druk Gyalpo (Dragon King)

HM DASHO JIGME KHESAR NAMGYAL **WANGCHUCK**; b. 21 February 1980; succeeded to the throne 14 December 2006, on the abdication of his father, the Druk Gyalpo Jigme Singye Wangchuk.

Crown Prince

HRH Crown Prince Jigme Namgyel Wangchuck, Druk Gyalsey (Dragon Prince) of Bhutan, b. 5 February 2016.

Brothers and Sisters of the King

HRH Princess Chimi Yangzom Wangchuck, b. 10 January 1980.

HRH Princess Sonam Dechen Wangchuck, b. 5 August 1981.

HRH Princess Dechen Yangzom Wangchuck, b. 2 December 1981.

HRH Princess Kesang Choden Wangchuck, b. 23 January 1982.

HRH Prince Jigyel Ugyen Wangchuck, b. 16 July 1984.

HRH Prince Khamsum Singye Wangchuck, b. 6 October 1985.

HRH Prince Jigme Dorji Wangchuck, b. 14 April 1986.

HRH Princess Euphelma Choden Wangchuck, b. 6 June 1993.

HRH Prince Ugyen Jigme Wangchuck, b. 11 November 1994.

Parents of the King

King Jigme Singye **Wangchuck**, b. 11 November 1955; succeeded to the throne 24 July 1972; crowned 2 June 1974; abdicated 14 December 2006; married Queen Ashi Tshering Yandon Wangchuck (b. 21 June 1959); two sons, one daughter; three sons, four daughters with his three other wives.

BRUNEI

Reigning Sultan and Yang di-Pertuan

HM Sultan Haji HASSANAL **BOLKIAH MU'IZUDDIN WADDAULAH**; b. 15 July 1946; succeeded as 29th Sultan 5 October 1967, on the abdication of his father, Sultan Haji Omar Ali Saifuddien II; crowned 1 August 1968; married 29 July 1965, HM Raja Isteri Pengiran Anak Hajjah Saleha; two sons, four daughters; also married 28 October 1981, Mariam Abd Aziz (divorced 2003); two sons, two daughters; also married 19 August 2005, HRH Pengiran Isteri Azrinaz Mazhar Hakim (divorced 2010); one son, one daughter.

Crown Prince

HRH Prince Haji al-**Muhtadee Billah**, b. 17 February 1974; proclaimed Crown Prince 10 August 1998; married 9 September 2004, HRH Pengiran Anak Isteri Pengiran Anak Sarah binti Pengiran Salleh Ab Rahaman; two sons, one daughter.

Brothers of the Sultan

HRH Prince Mohamed **Bolkiah**, b. 27 August 1947.

HRH Prince Haji Sufri Bolkiah, b. 31 July 1951.

HRH Prince Haji Jefri **Bolkiah**, b. 6 November 1954.

CAMBODIA

Reigning King

KING **NORODOM SIHAMONI**; b. 14 May 1953; appointed King by the Royal Council of the Throne October 2004, following the abdication of his father, the late King Norodom Sihanouk.

Brothers and Sisters of the King

Princess Buppha Devi, b. 8 January 1943.

Prince Yuvaneath, b. 17 October 1943.

Prince **Norodom Ranariddh**, b. 2 January 1944.

Prince Ravivong, b. 1944, died 1973.

Prince Chakrapong, b. 21 October 1945.

Prince Naradipo, b. 10 February 1946, died 1976.

Princess Soriya Roeungsey, b. 1947, died 1976.

Princess Kantha Bopha, b. 1948, died 14 December 1952.

Prince Khemanourak, b. 1949, died 1975.

Princess Botum Bopha, b. 1951, died 1976.

Princess Socheata, b. 1953, died 1975.

Prince Narindrapong, b. 18 September 1954, died 8 October 2003.

Princess Arunrasmy, b. 2 October 1955.

Parents of the King

King Norodom Sihanouk, b. 31 October 1922, died 15 October 2012; elected King 1941; abdicated 1955; took oath of fidelity to vacant throne 1960; elected Head of State 1960, on the death of his father; deposed 1970; elected as King 24 September 1993; abdicated October 2004; married Queen Norodom Monineath Sihanouk.

DENMARK

Reigning Queen

HM QUEEN **MARGRETHE II**; b. 16 April 1940; succeeded to the throne 14 January 1972, on the death of her father, King Frederik IX; married 10 June 1967, Count Henri Marie Jean André de Laborde de Monpezat (HRH

Prince Consort Henrik, renounced title of Prince Consort to become HRH Prince Henrik of Denmark 1 January 2016) (b. 11 June 1934, died 13 February 2018).

Children of the Queen

HRH Crown Prince **Frederik André Henrik Christian**, b. 26 May 1968; married 14 May 2004, Mary Elizabeth Donaldson (HRH Crown Princess Mary Elizabeth) (b. 5 February 1972); son, HRH Prince Christian Valdemar Henri John, b. 15 October 2005; daughter, HRH Princess Isabella Henrietta Ingrid Margrethe, b. 21 April 2007; son, HRH Prince Vincent Frederik Minik Alexander, b. 8 January 2011; daughter, HRH Princess Josephine Sophia Ivalo Mathilda, b. 8 January 2011.

HRH Prince Joachim Holger Waldemar Christian, b. 7 June 1969; married 1st 18 November 1995, Alexandra Christina Manley (Alexandra Christina, Countess of Frederiksborg) (b. 30 June 1964) (divorced 2005); son, HH Prince Nikolai William Alexander Frederik, b. 28 August 1999; son, HH Prince Felix Henrik Valdemar Christian, b. 22 July 2002; married 2nd 24 May 2008, Marie Cavallier (Princess Marie of Denmark); son, HH Prince Henrik Carl Joachim Alain, b. 4 May 2009; daughter, HH Princess Athena Marguerite Françoise Marie, b. 24 January 2012.

Sisters of the Queen

HRH Princess Benedikte Astrid Ingeborg Ingrid, b. 29 April 1944; married 3 February 1968, Prince Richard zu Sayn-Wittgenstein-Berleburg (b. 29 October 1934); son, Prince Gustav, b. 12 January 1969; daughter, Countess von Pfeil und Klein-Ellguth (formerly Princess Alexandra), b. 20 November 1970, (married, two children); daughter, Princess Nathalie, b. 2 May 1975, (married, one son).

HM Queen Anne-Marie Dagmar Ingrid of the Hellenes, b. 30 August 1946; married 18 September 1964, HM King **Constantine II** of the Hellenes. 2 June 1940); daughter, Princess Alexia, b. 10 July 1965, (married, four children); son, Prince Pavlos, b. 20 May 1967, (married, five children); son, Prince Nikolaos, b. 1 October 1969, (married); daughter, Princess Theodora, b. 9 June 1983; son, Prince Philippos, b. 26 April 1986.

Parents of the Queen

King Frederik IX, b. 11 March 1899 (son of King Christian X and Queen Alexandrine), died 14 January 1972; married 24 May 1935, Princess Ingrid of Sweden (b. 28 March 1910, died 7 November 2000).

ESWATINI

Reigning Monarch

KING **MSWATI III**; b. 19 April 1968; proclaimed Crown Prince September 1983, following the death of his father the previous year; installed as head of state 25 April 1986.

Father of the King

King Sobhuza II, b. 22 July 1899, died 21 August 1982; 210 children with 70 wives.

JAPAN

Reigning Emperor

His Imperial Majesty EMPEROR **NARUHITO**; b. 23 February 1960; succeeded to the throne 1 May 2019, on the abdication of his father, Emperor Akihito; married 9 June 1993, Masako Owada (Empress Masako) (b. 9 December 1963).

Daughter of the Emperor

Princess Aiko (Toshi-no-miya), b. 1 December 2001

Brother and Sister of the Emperor

The Crown Prince **Fumihito**, b. 30 November 1965; married 29 June 1990, Kiko Kawashima (The Crown Princess Kiko) (b. 11 September 1966); daughter, Princess Mako, b. 23 October 1991; daughter, Princess Kako, b. 29 December 1994; son, Prince Hisahito, b. 6 September 2006.

Sayako Kuroda (fmrly Nori-no-miya, then Princess Sayako), b. 18 April 1969; married 15 November 2005 (relinquished Imperial claim), Yoshiki Kuroda (b. 17 April 1965).

Parents of the Emperor

Emperor Akihito, b. 23 December 1933; abdicated 30 April 2019; married 10 April 1959, Empress Michiko (b. 20 October 1934); three children.

JORDAN

Reigning King

KING **ABDULLAH II IBN AL-HUSSEIN**; b. 30 January 1962; succeeded to the throne 7 February 1999, on the death of his father, King Hussein Ibn Talal; married 10 June 1993, Rania al-Yassin (Queen **Rania al-Abdullah**) (b. 31 August 1970).

Children of the King

HRH Crown Prince Hussein, b. 28 June 1994.

HRH Princess Iman, b. 27 September 1996.

HRH Princess Salma, b. 26 September 2000.

HRH Prince Hashem, b. 30 January 2005.

Brothers and Sisters of the King

Princess Alia, b. 13 February 1956; married 1st 11 July 1977, Nasser Wasfi Mirza (divorced 1983); son, Prince Hussein Mirza, b. 12 February 1981; married 2nd 30 July 1988, Mohammad Farid as-Saleh; son, Talal as-Saleh, b. 12 September 1989; son, Abdel Hamid as-Saleh, b. 15 November 1991.

Prince Feisal, b. 11 October 1963; married 1st 10 August 1987, Alia at-Tabaa (Princess Alia) (divorced April 2008); daughter, Princess Ayah, b. 11 February 1990; son, Prince Omar, b. 22 October 1993; daughter, Princess Aisha, b. 27 March 1996; daughter, Princess Sarah, b. 27 March 1996; married 2nd 24 May 2010, Sara Qabbani (Princess Sara) (divorced 14 September 2013); married 3rd 4 January 2014, Zeina Lubbadeh (Princess Zeina); son, Prince Abdullah bin Feisal, b. 17 February 2016; son Prince Mohammad bin Feisal, b. 8 April 2017.

Princess Zein, b. 23 April 1968; married 3 August 1989, Majdi Farid as-Saleh; son, Jaafar as-Saleh, b. 9 November 1990; daughter, Jumana as-Saleh; adopted daughter, Tahani al-Shahwa.

Princess Aisha, b. 23 April 1968; married 1st 26 July 1990, Zeid Juma'a (divorced); son, Aoun Juma'a, b. 27 May 1992; daughter, Muna Juma'a, b. 18 July 1996; married 2nd 27 January 2016, Ashraf (fmrly Edward) Banayoti (divorced 1 July 2016).

Princess Haya bint al-Hussein, b. 3 May 1974; married 10 April 2004, Sheikh Muhammad bin Rashid al-Maktoum (Ruler of Dubai); daughter, Sheikha Al Jalila, b. 2 December 2007; son, Sheikh Zayed, b. 7 January 2012.

Prince Ali, b. 23 December 1975; married 23 April 2004, Rym Brahimi; daughter, Princess Jalilah, b. 16 September 2005; son, Prince Abdullah, b. 19 March 2007.

Prince Hamzah, b. 29 March 1980; named Crown Prince of Jordan 1999 (title rescinded by King Abdullah 2004); married 1st 29 August 2003 (official wedding 27 May 2004), Princess Noor bint Asem Ben Nayef (divorced 9 September 2009); daughter, Princess Haya, b. 18 April 2007; married 2nd 12 January 2012, Princess Basmah Bani Ahmad; daughter, Princess Zein, b. 3 November 2012; daughter, Princess Zein, b. 3 November 2012; daughter, Princess Noor, b. 5 July 2014; daughter, Princess Badiya, b. 8 April 2016; daughter, Princess Nafisa, b. 7 February 2018.

Prince Hashim, b. 10 June 1981; married 15 April 2006, Fahdah Mohammed Abu Neyan; daughter, Princess Haalah, b. 6 April 2007; daughter, Princess Rayet, b. 4 July 2008; daughter, Princess Fatima al-Alia, b. 5 November 2011; son, Prince Hussein Haidara, b. 15 June 2015.

Princess Iman, b. 24 April 1983; married 22 March 2013, Zaid Azmi Mirza; son, Omar Mirza, b. 8 October 2014.

Princess Raiyah, b. 9 February 1986.

Parents of the King

King Hussein ibn Talal, b. 14 November 1935, died 7 February 1999; married 1st Dina bint Abdelhamid (Queen Dina) (divorced), one child; married 2nd Antoinette Gardner (Princess Muna) (divorced 1972), four children; married 3rd Alia Toukan (Queen Alia) (deceased), two children; married 4th Lisa Najeeb Halaby (**Queen Noor**) (b. 23 August 1951), four children.

KUWAIT

Reigning Emir

SHEIKH SABAH AL-AHMAD AL-JABER AS-**SABAH**; b. 16 June 1929; married Fatuwah bint Salman as-Sabah (died 1990); four children (two deceased); succeeded as Emir 29 January 2006, following the abdication of Sheikh Saad al-Abdullah as-Salim as-Sabah.

Crown Prince

HH Sheikh Nawaf al-Ahmad al-Jaber as-**Sabah**, b. 25 June 1937; married Sharifa Sulaiman Al-Jasem Al-Ghanim; four sons, one daughter; proclaimed Crown Prince 20 February 2006.

Children of the Emir

Sheikh Nasser Bin Sabah Al-Ahmad Al-Sabah, b. 27 April 1948.

Sheikh Hamed Al-Ahmad Al-Sabah.

Sheikh Ahmed Al-Sabah, died 1969.

Sheikha Salwa Al-Sabah, died 23 June 2002.

Father of the Emir

Sheikh Ahmad Al-Jaber Al-Sabah, b. 1885, died 29 January 1950; appointed tenth ruler of Kuwait 1921, following the death of his uncle, the ninth ruler of Kuwait Sheikh Salem Al-Sabah.

LESOTHO

Reigning King

KING **LETSIE III**; b. 17 July 1963; installed as King 12 November 1990, abdicated 25 January 1995, reinstalled 7 February 1996, following the death of his father, King Moshoeshoe II on 15 January, crowned 31 October 1997; married 18 February 2000, Karabo Anna Mots'oeneng (Queen 'Masenate Mohato Bereng Seeiso).

Children of the King

Princess Senate Mary Mohato Seeiso, b. 7 October 2001.

Princess 'MaSeeiso Mohato Seeiso, b. 20 November 2004.

Crown Prince Lerotholi Mohato **Seeiso, b. 18 April 2007.**

Parents of the King

Moshoeshoe II, b. 2 May 1938, died 15 January 1996; married Tabitha 'Masentle Lerotholi Mojela (Queen 'Mamohato of Lesotho) (b. 28 April 1941), three children.

LIECHTENSTEIN

Reigning Prince

HSH PRINCE **HANS-ADAM II**, Duke of Troppau and Jägerndorf, Count of Rietberg; b. 14 February 1945; succeeded 13 November 1989, on the death of his father, Prince Franz Josef II; married 30 July 1967, Countess Marie Aglaë Kinsky von Wchinitz und Tettau (Princess Marie) (b. 14 April 1940).

Children of the Prince

Hereditary Prince **Alois Philipp Maria**, b. 11 June 1968; appointed permanent representative 15 August 2004, performing the duties of Head of State from that time; married 3 July 1993, Duchess Sophie of Bavaria (b. 28 October 1967); son, Prince Joseph Wenzel, b. 24 May 1995; daughter, Princess Marie Caroline, b. 17 October 1996; son, Prince Georg, b. 20 April 1999; son, Prince Nikolaus, b. 6 December 2000.

Prince Maximilian, b. 16 May 1969; married 29 January 2000, Angela Gisela Brown; son, Prince Alfons, b. 18 May 2001.

Prince Constantin, b. 15 March 1972; married 18 July 1999, Countess Marie Kalnoky; son, Prince Moritz, b. 27 May 2003; daughter, Princess Georgina, b. 23 July 2005; son Prince Benedikt, b. 18 May 2008.

Princess Tatjana, b. 10 April 1973; married 5 June 1999, Philipp von Lattorff; son, Lukas, b. 13 May 2000; daughter, Elisabeth, b. 25 January 2002; daughter, Marie Teresa, b. 18 January 2004; daughter, Camilla, b. 14 November 2005; daughter, Anna, b. 3 August 2007; daughter, Sophia, b. 30 October 2009; son, Maximilian, b. 17 December 2011.

Brothers and Sisters of the Prince

Prince Philipp, b. 19 August 1946; married 11 September 1971, Isabelle de l'Arbre de Malander; son, Prince Alexander, b. 19 May 1972; son, Prince Wenzeslaus, b. 12 May 1974; son, Prince Rudolf, b. 7 September 1975.

Prince Nikolaus, b. 24 October 1947; married 20 March 1982, Princess Margaretha of Luxembourg (b. 15 May 1957); son, Prince Leopold Emmanuel, b. 20 May 1984 (deceased); daughter, Princess Maria-Annunciata, b. 12 May 1985; daughter, Princess Marie-Astrid, b. 26 June 1987; son, Prince Joseph-Emmanuel, b. 7 May 1989.

Princess Nora, b. 31 October 1950; married 11 June 1988, Vicente Marques de Mariño (died 22 July 2002); daughter, María Teresa, b. 21 November 1992.

Prince Wenzel, b. 19 November 1962, died 28 February 1991.

LUXEMBOURG

Reigning Monarch

HRH GRAND DUKE **HENRI ALBERT FÉLIX MARIE GUILLAUME**; b. 16 April 1955; succeeded 7 October 2000, on the abdication of his father, Grand Duke Jean; married 14 February 1981, Maria Teresa Mestre y Batista-Falla, b. 22 March 1956.

Children of the Grand Duke

HRH Prince **Guillaume Jean Joseph Marie**, b. 11 November 1981; proclaimed Hereditary Grand Duke of Luxembourg 18 December 2000; married 20 October 2012, Countess Stéphanie de Lannoy, 18 February 1984.

Prince Félix Léopold Marie Guillaume, b. 3 June 1984; married 21 September 2013, Claire Margareta Lademacher (Princess Claire), b. 21 March 1985; daughter, Princess Amalia of Nassau, b. 15 June 2014.

Prince Louis Xavier Marie Guillaume, b. 3 August 1986; married 29 September 2006, Tessy Antony, b. 28 October 1985 (divorced 4 April 2019); son, Prince Gabriel, b. 12 March 2006; son, Prince Noah, b. 21 September 2007.

Princess Alexandra Joséphine Teresa Charlotte Marie Wilhelmine, b. 16 February 1991.

Prince Sébastien Henri Marie Guillaume, b. 16 April 1992.

Brothers and Sisters of the Grand Duke

Archduchess Marie-Astrid of Austria, b. 17 February 1954; married 6 February 1982, Carl Christian of Habsburg Lorraine, Archduke of Austria; daughter, Archduchess Marie-Christine Anne Astrid Zita Charlotte of Austria, b. 31 July 1983; son, Archduke Imre, b. 8 December 1985; son, Archduke Christophe, b. 2 February 1988; son, Archduke Alexander, b. 26 September 1990; daughter, Archduchess Gabriella, b. 26 March 1994.

Prince Jean, b. 15 May 1957; married 1st 27 May 1987, Hélène Suzanne Vestur (divorced 2004); daughter, Marie-Gabrielle, b. 8 December 1986; son, Constantin Jean Philippe, b. 22 July 1988; son, Wenceslas, b. 17 November 1990; son, Carl-Johann, b. 15 August 1992; married 2nd 18 March 2009, Diane de Guerre.

Princess Margaretha, b. 15 May 1957; married 20 March 1982, Prince Nikolaus of Liechtenstein (b. 24 October 1947); son, Prince Leopold Emmanuel, b. 20 May 1984 (deceased); daughter, Princess Maria-Annunciata, b. 12 May 1985; daughter, Princess Marie-Astrid, b. 26 June 1987; son, Prince Joseph-Emmanuel, b. 7 May 1989.

Prince Guillaume, b. 1 May 1963; married 24 September 1994, Sibilla Sandra Weiller (y Torlonia) (b. 12 June 1968); son, Prince Paul-Louis, b. 4 March 1998; son, Prince Léopold, b. 2 May 2000; daughter, Princess Charlotte, b. 2 May 2000; son, Prince Jean, b. 13 July 2004.

Parents of the Grand Duke

Grand Duke Jean Benoit Guillaume Marie Robert Louis Antoine Adolphe Marc d'Aviano, b. 5 January 1921, died 23 April 2019; married 9 April 1953, Joséphine Charlotte, Princess of Belgium (b. 11 October 1927, died 10 January 2005).

MALAYSIA

Yang di-Pertuan Agong (Supreme Head of State)

HM The Sultan of **Pahang**, Abdullah Ri'ayatuddin al-Mustafa Billah Shah ibni Sultan Ahmad Shah al-Musta'in Billah.; b. 30 July 1959; elected as 16th Yang di-Pertuan Agong 24 January 2019, took office 31 January 2019.

Timbalan Yang di-Pertuan Agong (Deputy Supreme Head of State)

HRH The Sultan of **Perak**, Tuanku Nazrin Muizzuddin Shah ibni al-Marhum Sultan Azlan Muhibuddin Shah.

The Hereditary Rulers

There are nine hereditary rulers who qualify for and elect the positions of Yang di-Pertuan Agong and Timbalan Yang di-Pertuan Agong.

The Yang di-Pertuan Besar of **Negeri Sembilan**, Tuanku Muhriz ibni al-Marhum Tunku Munawir.

HRH The Sultan of **Selangor**, Tuanku Sharafuddin Idris Shah Salahuddin Abdul Aziz Shah.

HRH Tuanku Syed Sirajuddin al-Marhum Syed Putra Jamalullail, The Raja of **Perlis**.

HRH The Sultan of **Terengganu**, Tuanku Mizan Zainal Abidin.

HRH The Sultan of **Kedah**, Tuanku Haji Abdul Halim Mu'adzam Shah ibni al-Marhum Sultan Badlishah.

HRH The Sultan of **Kelantan**, Tengku Muhammad Faris Petra ibni Sultan Ismail Petra, Sultan Muhammad V.

HRH The Sultan of **Johor**, Sultan Ibrahim Ismail ibni al-Marhum Sultan Mahmud Iskandar.

MONACO

Reigning Monarch

HSH PRINCE **ALBERT II**, Albert Alexandre Louis Pierre Grimaldi; b. 14 March 1958; succeeded 6 April 2005, on the death of his father, Prince Rainier III; daughter (Jazmin Grace Grimaldi, b. 4 March 1992) with Tamara Rotolo; son (Alexandre Coste, b. 24 August 2003) with Nicole Coste; married 2 July 2011, Charlene Lynette Wittstock (Charlene, Princess of Monaco), b. 25 January 1978; daughter, Princess Gabriella, b. 10 December 2014; son, Prince Jacques, b. 10 December 2014.

Sisters of the Prince

Princess Caroline Louise Marguerite, b. 23 January 1957; married 1st 28 June 1978, Philippe Junot (divorced 1980, marriage annulled 1992); married 2nd 29 December 1983, Stefano Casiraghi (died 3 October 1990); son, Andrea Albert Pierre, b. 8 June 1984; daughter, Charlotte Marie

Pomeline, b. 3 August 1986; son, Pierre Rainier Stefano, b. 5 September 1987; married 3rd 23 January 1999, Prince Ernst August of Hanover; stepson, Prince Ernst August of Hanover, b. 19 July 1983, stepson, Prince Christian of Hanover, b. 1 June 1985; daughter, Princess Alexandra of Hanover, b. 20 July 1999.

Princess Stéphanie Marie Elisabeth, b. 1 February 1965; married 1st 1 July 1995, Daniel Ducruet (divorced 1996); son, Louis Robert Paul, b. 26 November 1992; daughter, Pauline Grace Maguy, b. 4 May 1994; daughter, Camille Marie Kelly Gottlieb, b. 15 July 1998; married 2nd 10 September 2003, Adans Lopez Peres (divorced 2004).

Parents of the Prince

HSH Prince Rainier III, Rainier Louis Henri Maxence Bertrand Grimaldi, b. 31 May 1923, died 6 April 2005; married 18 April 1956, Grace Patricia Kelly (b. 12 November 1929, died 14 September 1982).

MOROCCO

Reigning King

HM KING **MOHAMMED VI**; b. 21 August 1963; succeeded to the throne 23 July 1999, on the death of his father, King Hassan II; married 21 March 2002, HRH Princess Lalla Salma Bennani (b. 10 May 1978).

Children of the King

HRH Crown Prince Moulay Hassan, b. 8 May 2003.

HRH Princess Lalla Khadija, b. 28 February 2007.

Brothers and Sisters of the King

HRH Princess Lalla Meryem, b. 26 August 1962; married 15 September 1984, Fouad Filali (divorced 1999); daughter, Lalla Soukaïna, b. 30 April 1986; son, Moulay Idriss, b. 11 July 1988.

HRH Princess Lalla Asma, b. 29 September 1965; married 5 November 1986, Khalid Bouchentouf; son, Moulay Yazid, b. 25 July 1988; daughter, Lalla Nuhaila, b. 29 May 1992.

HRH Princess Lalla Hasna, b. 19 November 1967; married 13 December 1991, Khalid Benharbit; daughter, Lalla Oumaïma, b. 15 December 1995; daughter, Lalla Oulaya, b. 20 October 1997.

HRH Prince Moulay Rachid, b. 20 June 1970; married 15 June 2014, Oum Kalthum Boufarès; son, Moulay Ahmed, b. 23 June 2016.

Parents of the King

HM King Hassan II, b. 9 July 1929, died 23 July 1999; married 1st 1961, Lalla Latifa Hammou (five children); married 2nd 1961, Lalla Fatima bint Qaid Amhourok.

THE NETHERLANDS

Reigning King

HM KING **WILLEM-ALEXANDER** CLAUS GEORGE FERDINAND; b. 27 April 1967; succeeded to the throne 30 April 2013, on the abdication of his mother, Queen Beatrix (now HRH Princess **Beatrix**); married 2 February 2002, Máxima Zorreguieta Cerruti (b. 17 May 1971); daughter, HRH Princess Catharina-Amalia Beatrix Carmen Victoria, b. 7 December 2003; daughter, HRH Princess Alexia Juliana Marcella Laurentien, b. 26 June 2005; daughter, HRH Ariane Wilhelmina Máxima Inés, b. 10 April 2007.

Brothers of the King

HRH Prince (Johan) Friso Bernhard Christiaan David, b. 25 September 1968, died 12 August 2013; married 24 April 2004 (relinquished right to the throne and membership of the Royal House), Mabel Wisse Smit; daughter, Countess Luana, b. 26 March 2005; daughter, Countess Zaria, b. 18 June 2006.

HRH Prince Constantijn Christof Frederik Aschwin, b. 11 October 1969; married 17 May 2001, Laurentien Brinkhorst (b. 25 May 1966); daughter, Countess Eloise, b. 8 June 2002; son, Count Claus-Casimir, b. 21 March 2004; daughter, Countess Leonore, b. 3 June 2006.

Parents of the King

HRH Princess **Beatrix** of The Netherlands, b. 31 January 1938; married 10 March 1966, Prince Claus George Willem Otto Frederik Geert Jonkheer van Amsberg (b. 6 September 1926, died 6 October 2002).

NORWAY

Reigning King

HM KING **HARALD V**; b. 21 February 1937; succeeded to the throne 17 January 1991, on the death of his father, King Olav V; sworn in 21 January 1991; married 29 August 1968, Sonja Haraldsen (HM Queen Sonja) (b. 4 July 1937).

Children of the King

Princess Märtha Louise, b. 22 September 1971; married 24 May 2002, Ari Mikael Behn (formerly Ari Mikael Bjørshol, b. 30 September 1972); daughter, Maud Angelica Behn, b. 29 April 2003; daughter, Leah Isadora Behn, b. 8 April 2005; daughter, Emma Tallulah Behn, b. 29 September 2008.

HRH Crown Prince **Haakon**, b. 20 July 1973; married 25 August 2001, Mette-Marit Tjessem Høiby (HRH Crown Princess Mette-Marit) (b. 19 August 1973); stepson, Marius Borg Høiby, b. 13 January 1997; daughter, HRH Princess Ingrid Alexandra, b. 21 January 2004; son, HH Prince Sverre Magnus, b. 3 December 2005.

Sisters of the King

Princess Ragnhild, b. 9 June 1930, died 16 September 2012; married 15 May 1953, Erling Lorentzen; three children.

Princess Astrid, b. 12 February 1932; married 12 January 1961, Johan Martin Ferner (b. Johan Martin Jacobsen, 22 July 1927, died 24 January 2015); five children.

Parents of the King

King Olav V, b. 2 July 1903, died 17 January 1991; married 21 March 1929 Princess Märtha of Sweden (b. 28 March 1901, died 5 April 1954).

OMAN

Reigning Sultan

SULTAN **QABOOS BIN SAID AS-SAID**; b. 18 November 1940; assumed power 23 July 1970, after deposing his father, Sultan Said bin Taimur (b. 13 August 1910, died 19 October 1972); married 1976, Sayyidah Nawwal bint Tariq (divorced 1977).

QATAR

Reigning Amir

HH SHEIKH TAMIM BIN HAMAD BIN KHALIFA ATH-**THANI**; b. 3 June 1980; proclaimed heir apparent 8 August 2003, succeeded to the throne 25 June 2013 on the abdication of his father; married 1st 8 January 2005, Sheikha Jawahar bint Hamad bin Sohaim ath-Thani; married 2nd 3 March 2009, Sheikha Anoud bint Mana Al-Hajri; married 3rd 25 February 2014, Sheikha Noora bint Hathal al-Dosari.

Children of the Amir by His First Wife

HE Sheikha Almayassa bint Tamim ath-Thani, b. 2006

HE Sheikh Hamad bin Tamim ath-Thani, b. 2008

HE Sheikha Aisha bint Tamim ath-Thani, b. 2010

HE Sheikh Jassim bin Tamim ath-Thani, b. 2012

Children of the Amir by His Second Wife

HE Sheikha Nayla bint Tamim ath-Thani, b. 27 May 2010

HE Sheikh Abdullah bin Tamim ath-Thani, b. 29 September 2012

HE Sheikha Rodha bint Tamim bin Hamad ath-Thani, b. January 2014

HE Sheikh Al-Qaqa bin Tamim bin Hamad ath-Thani, b. 3rd October 2015

Children of the Amir by His Third Wife

HE Sheikh Joa'an bin Tamim bin Hamad ath-Thani, b. 27 March 2015

HE Sheikh Mohammed bin Tamim bin Hamad ath-Thani, b. 17 July 2017

HE Sheikh Fahad bin Tamim bin Hamad ath-Thani, b. 16 June 2018

Parents of the Amir

HH Sheikh Hamad bin Khalifa ath-**Thani**, b. 1 January 1952; assumed power 27 June 1995, after deposing his father, Sheikh Khalifa bin Hamad ath-Thani (b. 17 September 1932), abdicated 25 June 2013 in favour of his son, HH Sheikh Tamim bin Hamad bin Khalifa ath-Thani; married 1st Sheikha Mariam bint Muhammad ath-Thani (two sons, six daughters); married 2nd Sheikha Mozah bint Nasser al-Missned (five sons, two daughters); married 3rd Sheikha Noora bint Khalid ath-Thani (four sons, five daughters).

SAMOA

O le Ao o le Malo (Head of State)

HH Tuimaleali'ifano Va'aletoa **Sualauvi II**; b. 29 April 1947; elected Head of State 30 June 2017; married HH Masiofo Fa'amausili Leinafo.

SAUDI ARABIA

Reigning King

HM KING SALMAN IBN ABD AL-AZIZ AS-**SA'UD**; b. 13 December 1935; succeeded to the throne, 23 January 2015, on the death of his half-brother, King Abdullah.

Crown Prince

HRH Muhammad ibn Salman ibn Abd al-Aziz as-**Sa'ud**, b. 31 August 1985; son of King Salman ibn Abd al-Aziz as-Sa'ud; married Sara bint Mashoodr bin Abdulaziz as-Sa'ud; appointed Deputy Crown Prince 29 April 2017; appointed Crown Prince 21 June 2017.

Brothers of the King include

King Saud ibn Abd al-Aziz as-Sa'ud, b. 15 January 1902, acceded 9 November 1953 (following the death of his father, King Abd al-Aziz as-Sa'ud), relinquished the throne 2 November 1964, died 24 January 1969.

King Faisal ibn Abd al-Aziz as-Sa'ud, b. April 1906, acceded 2 November 1964, died 25 March 1975; children include son, Prince Sa'ud al-Faisal as-**Sa'ud**, b. 1941; son, Prince Turki al-Faisal ibn Abd al-Aziz as-**Sa'ud**, b. 15 February 1945.

HRH Prince Mohammed ibn Abd al-Aziz as-Sa'ud, b. 4 March 1910, died 25 November 1988.

King Khalid ibn Abd al-Aziz as-Sa'ud, b. 13 February 1913, acceded 25 March 1975, died 13 June 1982.

King Fahd ibn Abd al-Aziz as-**Sa'ud**, b. 16 March 1921, acceded 13 June 1982, died 1 August 2005.

King Abdullah ibn Abd al-Aziz as-**Sa'ud**, b. 1 August 1924, acceded 1 August 2005, died 23 January 2015.

HRH Crown Prince Sultan ibn Abd al-Aziz as-**Sa'ud**, b. 5 January 1928, died 22 October 2011; children include son, HRH Prince Bandar ibn Sultan ibn Abd al-Aziz as-**Sa'ud**, b. 2 March 1949.

HRH Prince Talal ibn Abd al-Aziz as-**Sa'ud**, b. 15 August 1931, died 22 December 2018; children include son, Prince Walid ibn **Talal**.

HRH Prince Nayef ibn Abd al-Aziz as-**Sa'ud**, b. 1934, died 16 June 2012; children include son, Prince Muhammad ibn Nayef ibn Abd al-Aziz as-**Sa'ud**.

HRH Prince Muqrin ibn Abd al-Aziz as-**Sa'ud**, b. 15 September 1945.

SPAIN

Reigning King

HM KING **FELIPE VI**; b. 30 January 1968; succeeded to the throne 19 June 2014 on the abdication of his father; married 22 May 2004, HRH Princess Letizia Ortiz Rocasolano (HM Queen Letizia) (b. 15 September 1972).

Children of the King

HRH Princess Leonor, The Princess of **Asturias**, Princess of Viana, Princess of Girona, Duchess of Montblanc, Countess of Cervera and Lady of Balaguer, b. 31 October 2005.

HRH Princess (Infanta) Sofía, b. 29 April 2007.

Sisters of the King

HRH Princess (Infanta) Elena, b. 20 December 1963; married 18 March 1995, Don Jaime de Marichalar y Sáenz de Tejada (divorced 21 January 2010); son, Felipe Juan Froilán de Todos los Santos, b. 17 July 1998; daughter, Victoria Federica, b. 9 September 2000.

HRH Princess (Infanta) Cristina, b. 13 June 1965; married 4 October 1997, Iñaki Urdangarin (b. 15 January 1968); son, Juan Valentín, b. 29 September 1999; son, Pablo Nicolás Sebastián, b. 6 December 2000; son, Miguel, b. 30 April 2002; daughter, Irene, b. 5 June 2005.

Parents of the King

HM King **Juan Carlos I** b. 5 January 1938; succeeded to the throne 22 November 1975, abdicated 19 June 2014 in favour of his son HRH Prince Felipe, The Prince of Asturias; married 14 May 1962, Princess Sofía of Greece (HM Queen Sofía) (b. 2 November 1938, daughter of the late King Paul of the Hellenes and Queen Frederica).

SWEDEN

Reigning King

HM KING **CARL XVI GUSTAF**; b. 30 April 1946; succeeded to the throne 15 September 1973, on the death of his grandfather, King Gustaf VI Adolf; married 19 June 1976, Silvia Renate Sommerlath (HM Queen **Silvia**) (b. 23 December 1943).

Children of the King

HRH Crown Princess **Victoria Ingrid Alice Désirée**, Duchess of Västergötland, b. 14 July 1977; married 19 June 2010, Olof Daniel Westling Bernadotte (Prince Daniel, Duke of Västergötland), b. 15 September 1973; daughter, Princess Estelle, Duchess of Östergötland, b. 23 February 2012; son, Prince Oscar, Duke of Skåne, b. 2 March 2016.

HRH Prince Carl Philip Edmund Bertil, Duke of Varmland, b. 13 May 1979; married 13 June 2015, Sofia Kristina Hellqvist, b. 6 December 1984; son, Prince Alexander, Duke of Södermanland, b. 19 April 2016; son, Prince Gabriel, b. 31 August 2017.

HRH Princess Madeleine Thérèse Amelie Josephine, Duchess of Hälsingland and Gästrikland, b. 10 June 1982; married 8 June 2013, Christopher O'Neill, b. 27 June 1974; daughter, Princess Leonore, Duchess of Gotland, b. 20 February 2014; son, Prince Nicolas, Duke of Ängermanland, b. 15 June 2015; daughter, Princess Adrienne of Sweden, Duchess of Blekinge, b. 9 March 2018 .

Sisters of the King

Princess Margaretha, b. 31 October 1934; married 30 June 1964, John Ambler (b. 6 June 1924, died 31 May 2008); daughter, Sibylla Louise, b. 14 April 1965; son, Charles Edward, b. 14 July 1966; son, James Patrick, b. 10 June 1969.

Princess Birgitta, b. 19 January 1937; married 25 May 1961, Prince Johann Georg of Hohenzollern (b. 31 July 1932); son, Carl Christian, b. 5 April 1962; daughter, Désirée, b. 27 November 1963; son, Hubertus, b. 10 June 1966.

Princess Désirée, b. 2 June 1938; married 5 June 1964, Baron Nils-August Otto Carl Niclas Silfverschiöld (b. 31 May 1934, died 11 April 2017); son, Carl Otto Edmund, b. 22 March 1965; daughter, Kristina Louise Ewa Madeleine, b. 29 September 1966; daughter, Hélène Ingeborg Sibylla, b. 20 September 1968.

Princess Christina, b. 3 August 1943; married 15 June 1974, Tord Magnuson (b. 7 April 1941); son, Carl Gustaf Victor, b. 8 August 1975; son, Tord Oscar Fredrik, b. 20 June 1977; son, Victor Edmund Lennart, b. 10 September 1980.

Parents of the King

Prince Gustaf Adolf, Duke of Västerbotten, b. 22 April 1906, died 26 January 1947; married 20 October 1932, Sibylla, Princess of Saxe-Coburg and Gotha (b. 18 January 1908, died 28 November 1972).

THAILAND

Reigning King

HM KING **MAHA VAJIRALONGKORN**, (King Rama X); b. 28 July 1952; proclaimed Crown Prince 28 December 1972; succeeded to the throne 1 December 2016, shortly after the death of his father, King Bhumibol Adulyadej (Rama IX); crowned 4 May 2019; married 1st 3 January 1977, Mom Luang Soamsawali Kitiyakara (b. 13 July 1957) (divorced 1991); two daughters; married 2nd 1994 Yuvadhida Polpraserth (divorced 1996); four sons, one daughter (no royal claim); married 3rd 10 February 2001, Mom Srirasmi Mahidol na Ayudhya (HRH Princess Srirasmi, The Royal Consort) (b. 9 December 1971) (divorced December 2014); one son; married 4th 1 May 2019 Suthida Tidjai (b. 3 June 1978).

Children of the King

Princess Bajrakitiyabha, b. 7 December 1978

HRH Princess Siriwanwari Nariratana, b. 8 January 1987 (elevated status by royal command 15 June 2005).

HRH Prince Teepangkorn Rasmichoti, b. 29 April 2005.

Sisters of the King

Princess Ubol Ratana, b. 5 April 1951; married August 1972, Peter Ladd Jensen (relinquished royal claim) (divorced 1998); daughter, Khun Ploypailin, b. 12 February 1981; son, Khun Poomi, b. 16 August 1983, died 26 December 2004; daughter, Khun Sirikittiya, b. 18 March 1985.

HRH Princess Maha Chakri Sirindhorn, b. 2 April 1955.

HRH Princess **Chulabhorn**, b. 4 July 1957; married 7 January 1982, Flight Lieutenant Virayuth Didyasarin (divorced 1984); daughter, Princess Siribhachudabhorn, b. 8 October 1982; daughter, Princess Aditayadornkitikhun, b. 5 May 1984.

Parents of the King

HM King Bhumibol Adulyadej (King Rama IX), b. 5 December 1927, died 13 October 2016; succeeded to the throne 9 June 1946, on the death of his brother, King Ananda Mahidol; crowned 5 May 1950; married 28 April 1950, Mom Rajawongse Sirikit Kitiyakara (Queen Sirikit) (b. 12 August 1932).

TONGA

Reigning King

HM KING **Tupou VI**; b. 12 July 1959; proclaimed Crown Prince 11 September 2006; succeeded to the throne 18 March 2012, on the death of his elder brother, King George Tupou V; married 11 December 1982, Nanasipau'u Vaea (Princess Nanasipau'u).

Children of the King

Princess Latufuipeka Tuku'aho, b. 17 November 1983.

Crown Prince Tupouto'a 'Ulukalala, b. 17 September 1985, married 12 July 2012, Sinaitakala Fakafanua (b. 1987); son, Prince Taufa'ahau Manumataongo, b. 10 May 2013; daughter, Princess Halaevalu Mata'aho, b. 12 July 2014.

Prince Viliami Tuku'aho, The Prince Ata, b. 27 April 1988.

Brothers and Sister of the King

King George Tupuo V; b. 4 May 1948, died 18 March 2012; succeeded to the throne 10 September 2006; daughter 'Ilima Lei Fifita Tohi, b. 1974.

HRH Princess Salote Mafile'o Pilolevu Tuku'aho Tuita, Princess Regent, b. 17 November 1951; married 21 July 1976, Captain Ma'ulupekotofa Tuita (known as Honourable Tuita) (four daughters, one adopted son).

HRH Prince Fatafehi Alaivahamama'o Tuku'aho (known as Honourable Matu), b. 17 December 1954, died 17 February 2004; married (relinquished royal claim).

Parents of the King

King **Taufa'ahau Tupou IV**, b. 4 July 1918, died 10 September 2006; succeeded to the throne 15 December 1965; married 1947, Princess Halaevalu Mata'aho 'Ahome'e (Queen Halaevalu Mata'aho) (b. 29 May 1926, died 19 February 2017).

UNITED ARAB EMIRATES

Reigning Rulers

Ruler of Abu Dhabi: HH Sheikh KHALIFA BIN ZAYED AN-**NAHYAN**; b. 1948; succeeded to the throne 2 November 2004; married 1964 Sheikha Shamsa bint Suhail Al Mazrouei; two sons, six daughters.

Ruler of Dubai: HH Sheikh MUHAMMAD BIN RASHID AL-**MAKTOUM**; b. 15 July 1949; succeeded to the throne 4 January 2006; married 2nd 10 April 2004, HRH Princess Haya bint al-Hussein of Jordan; daughter, Al-Jalila, b. 2 December 2007; son, Zayed, b. 7 January 2012.

Ruler of Sharjah: HH Sheikh SULTAN BIN MUHAMMAD AL-**QASIMI**; b. 6 July 1939; succeeded to the throne 25 January 1972.

Ruler of Ras al-Khaimah: HH Sheikh SAUD IBN SAQR AL-**QASIMI**; b. 10 February 1956; succeeded to the throne 27 October 2010.

Ruler of Umm al-Qaiwain: HH Sheikh SAUD BIN RASHID AL-**MU'ALLA**; b. 1 October 1952; succeeded to the throne 2 January 2009.

Ruler of Ajman: HH Sheikh HUMAID BIN RASHID AN-**NUAIMI**; b. 1931; succeeded to the throne 6 September 1981.

Ruler of Fujairah: HH Sheikh HAMAD BIN MUHAMMAD ASH-**SHARQI**; b. 25 May 1948; succeeded to the throne 18 September 1974.

UNITED KINGDOM

Reigning Queen

HM QUEEN **ELIZABETH II**; b. 21 April 1926; succeeded to the throne 6 February 1952, on the death of her father, King George VI; crowned 2 June 1953; married 20 November 1947, HRH Prince Philip, Duke of **Edinburgh**, Earl of Merioneth, Baron Greenwich, KG, KT, OM, GBE, AC, QSO (b. 10 June 1921), son of Prince Andrew of Greece and Princess Alice of Battenberg (Mountbatten).

Children of the Queen

HRH Prince Charles Philip Arthur George, The Prince of **Wales**, Duke of Cornwall, Duke of Rothesay, Earl of Chester, Earl of Carrick, Baron Renfrew, Lord of the Isles and Great Steward of Scotland, KG, KT, GCB, OM, AK, QSO, ADC (heir-apparent), b. 14 November 1948; married 1st 29 July 1981, Lady Diana Frances Spencer (The Princess of Wales) (divorced 1996, died 31 August 1997); son, HRH Prince **William** Arthur Philip Louis of Wales (HRH The Duke of **Cambridge**), b. 21 June 1982; married 29 April 2011, Catherine Elizabeth Middleton (HRH The Duchess of **Cambridge**) (son, HRH Prince George Alexander Louis of Cambridge, b. 22 July 2013; daughter, HRH Princess Charlotte Elizabeth Diana, b. 2 May 2015); son, HRH Prince Louis Arthur Charles of Cambridge, b. 23 April 2018); son, HRH Prince Henry Charles Albert David of Wales (HRH The Duke of Sussex), b. 15 September 1984; married 19 May 2018, Rachel Meghan Markle (HRH The Duchess of Sussex) (son, HRH Archie Harrison Mountbatten-Windsor, b. 6 May 2019); married 2nd 9 April 2005, Camilla Parker Bowles (HRH The Duchess of **Cornwall**) (b. 17 July 1947).

HRH Princess Anne Elizabeth Alice Louise, The Princess **Royal**, KG, KT, GCVO, QSO, b. 15 August 1950; married 1st 14 November 1973, Captain Mark Phillips (divorced 1992); son, Peter Mark Andrew Phillips, b. 15 November 1977; daughter, Zara Anne Elizabeth Phillips, b. 15 May 1981; married 2nd 12 December 1992, Vice-Admiral Timothy Laurence, CB, MVO, ADC.

HRH Prince Andrew Albert Christian Edward, The Duke of **York**, Earl of Inverness, Baron Killyleagh, KS, KCVO, ADC, b. 19 February 1960; married 23 July 1986, Sarah Ferguson (The Duchess of York) (b. 15 October 1959) (divorced 1996); daughter, Princess Beatrice Elizabeth Mary of York, b. 8 August 1988; daughter, Princess Eugenie Victoria Helena of York, b. 23 March 1990; married 12 October 2018, Jack Christopher Stamp Brooksbank.

HRH Prince Edward Antony Richard Louis, The Earl of **Wessex**, KS, KCVO, ADC, b. 10 March 1964; married 19 June 1999, Sophie Rhys-Jones (HRH The Countess of Wessex) (b. 20 January 1965); daughter, Lady Louise Alice Elizabeth Mary Windsor, b. 8 November 2003; son, James Alexander Philip Theo, Viscount Severn, b. 17 December 2007.

Parents of the Queen

King George VI, b. 14 December 1895 (son of King George V and Queen Mary), died 6 February 1952; married 26 April 1923, Lady Elizabeth Angela Marguerite Bowes-Lyon (Queen Elizabeth The Queen Mother) (b. 4 August 1900, died 30 March 2002).

Sister of the Queen

Princess Margaret Rose, Countess of Snowdon, CI, GCVO, b. 21 August 1930, died 9 February 2002; married 6 May 1960, Antony Armstrong-Jones (Earl of Snowdon, GCVO) (divorced 1978, died 13 January 2017); son, David Albert Charles, Viscount Linley, b. 3 November 1961, (married, two children); daughter, Lady Sarah Frances Elizabeth Chatto (née Armstrong-Jones), b. 1 May 1964, (married, two children).

The full titles of Queen Elizabeth II are as follows:

United Kingdom
"Elizabeth the Second, by the Grace of God, of the United Kingdom of Great Britain and Northern Ireland and of Her other Realms and Territories Queen, Head of the Commonwealth, Defender of the Faith."

Canada
"Elizabeth the Second, by the Grace of God, of the United Kingdom, Canada and Her other Realms and Territories Queen, Head of the Commonwealth, Defender of the Faith."

Australia
"Elizabeth the Second, by the Grace of God, Queen of Australia and Her other Realms and Territories, Head of the Commonwealth."

New Zealand
"Elizabeth the Second, by the Grace of God, Queen of New Zealand and Her other Realms and Territories, Head of the Commonwealth, Defender of the Faith."

Jamaica
"Elizabeth the Second, by the Grace of God, Queen of Jamaica and of Her other Realms and Territories Queen, Head of the Commonwealth."

Barbados
"Elizabeth the Second, by the Grace of God, Queen of Barbados and of Her other Realms and Territories, Head of the Commonwealth."

The Bahamas
"Elizabeth the Second, by the Grace of God, Queen of the Commonwealth of The Bahamas and of Her other Realms and Territories, Head of the Commonwealth."

Grenada
"Elizabeth the Second, by the Grace of God, Queen of the United Kingdom of Great Britain and Northern Ireland and of Grenada and Her other Realms and Territories, Head of the Commonwealth."

Papua New Guinea
"Elizabeth the Second, Queen of Papua New Guinea and of Her other Realms and Territories, Head of the Commonwealth."

Solomon Islands
"Elizabeth the Second, by the Grace of God, Queen of the Solomon Islands and of Her other Realms and Territories, Head of the Commonwealth."

Tuvalu
"Elizabeth the Second, by the Grace of God, Queen of Tuvalu and of Her other Realms and Territories, Head of the Commonwealth."

Saint Lucia
"Elizabeth the Second, by the Grace of God, Queen of Saint Lucia and of Her other Realms and Territories, Head of the Commonwealth."

Saint Vincent and the Grenadines
"Elizabeth the Second, by the Grace of God, Queen of Saint Vincent and the Grenadines and of Her other Realms and Territories, Head of the Commonwealth."

Belize
"Elizabeth the Second, by the Grace of God, Queen of Belize and of Her other Realms and Territories, Head of the Commonwealth."

Antigua and Barbuda
"Elizabeth the Second, by the Grace of God, Queen of Antigua and Barbuda and of Her other Realms and Territories, Head of the Commonwealth."

Saint Christopher and Nevis
"Elizabeth the Second, by the Grace of God, Queen of Saint Christopher and Nevis and of Her other Realms and Territories, Head of the Commonwealth."

The Republics of India, Ghana, Cyprus, Tanzania, Uganda, Kenya, Zambia, Malawi, Singapore, Botswana, Guyana, Nauru, The Gambia, Sierra Leone, Bangladesh, Sri Lanka, Malta, Trinidad and Tobago,

Seychelles, Dominica, Kiribati, Vanuatu, Maldives, Namibia, Mauritius, South Africa, Fiji, Pakistan, Cameroon and Mozambique, together with the Federation of Malaysia, the Kingdom of Lesotho, the Kingdom of Eswatini, the Kingdom of Tonga, the Independent State of Samoa and the Sultanate of Brunei, recognize the Queen as "Head of the Commonwealth".

OBITUARY

Abalakin, Victor Kuz'mich	23 April 2018
Adji, Boukary	4 July 2018
Ahlmark, Per	8 June 2018
Alexander, Meena	21 November 2018
Alexeeva, Ludmilla	8 December 2018
Alferov, Zhores Ivanovich	1 March 2019
Allen, Paul Gardner	15 October 2018
Alsop, William Allen	12 May 2018
Ambartsumyan, Sergey Aleksandrovich	4 August 2018
Amissah-Arthur, Kwesi Bekoe	29 June 2018
Anderson, John Anthony	13 November 2018
Andersson, Bibi	14 April 2019
Annan, Kofi Atta	18 August 2018
Arens, Moshe	7 January 2019
Ashdown Of Norton Sub-Hamdon, Jeremy John Durham (Paddy) Ashdown	22 December 2018
Ashida, Jun	20 October 2018
Atiyah, Michael Francis	11 January 2019
Atkinson, Harry Hindmarsh	30 December 2018
Ayales Esna, Edgar	25 April 2018
Aznavour, Charles	1 October 2018
Azuma, Takamitsu	18 June 2015
Baker, Russell Wayne	21 January 2019
Barenblatt, Grigory Isaakovich	22 June 2018
Baring, Arnulf Martin	2 March 2019
Barnard, Eric Albert	23 May 2018
Beckett, Wendy	26 December 2018
Behmen, Alija	1 August 2018
Belotserkovsky, Oleg Mikhailovich	15 July 2015
Belshaw, Cyril Shirley	20 November 2018
Benetton, Carlo	10 July 2018
Bennet, Douglas (Doug) Joseph, Jr	10 June 2018
Bertolucci, Bernardo	26 November 2018
Betancur Cuartas, Belisario	7 December 2018
Billington, James Hadley	20 November 2018
Bitov, Andrei Georgevich	3 December 2018
Bjurström, Per Gunnar	4 September 2017
Blom-Cooper, Louis Jacques	19 September 2018
Bodman, Samuel Wright, III	7 September 2018
Bondurant, Stuart	26 May 2018
Bonner, John Tyler	7 February 2019
Bor, Naci	2018
Botha, Roelof Frederik (Pik)	12 October 2018
Bott, Martin Harold Phillips	20 October 2018
Bourgain, Jean	22 December 2018
Brenner, Sydney	5 April 2019
Briggs, Winslow Russell	11 February 2019
Broecker, Wallace (Wally) Smith	19 February 2019
Browne-Wilkinson, Nicolas Christopher Henry Browne-Wilkinson	25 July 2018
Brown, Harold	4 January 2019
Buldakov, Aleksey Ivanovich	3 April 2019
Bunin, Igor Mikhailovich	12 May 2018
Bush, George Herbert Walker	30 November 2018
Buthelezi, Manas	20 April 2016
Cagiati, Andrea	2018
Calder, John Mackenzie	13 August 2018
Campbell, Allan McCulloch	19 April 2018
Campbell, Roderick Samuel Fisher	22 March 2018
Caputo, Dante	20 June 2018
Carlsson, Arvid	29 June 2018
Carlucci, Frank Charles	3 June 2018
Carrick, John Leslie	18 May 2018
Carrington, Peter Alexander Rupert Carrington	10 July 2018
Casida, John Edward	30 June 2018
Castrillón Hoyos, Darío	18 May 2018
Cavalli-Sforza, Luigi Luca	31 August 2018
Chadwick, Peter	12 August 2018
Channing, Carol	15 January 2019
Chatterjee, Somnath	13 August 2018
Chen, Jinhua	2 July 2016
Chew, Geoffrey Foucar	11 April 2019
Chiladze, Tamaz	28 September 2018
Chisholm, Samuel Hewlings	9 July 2018
Cho, Yang-ho	7 April 2019
Chung, Sze-yuen	14 November 2018
Ciry, Michel	26 December 2018
Coates, Anne Voase	8 May 2018
Conway, Jill Ker	1 June 2018
Cortazzi, (Henry Arthur) Hugh	14 August 2018
Cox, Robert Warburton	9 October 2018

Daneliya, Georgiy Nikolayevich	4 April 2019
Danneels, Godfried	14 March 2019
Dassault, Serge	28 May 2018
De Cecco, Marcello	3 March 2016
Denholm, Ian (John Ferguson)	15 May 2018
Dewost, Jean-Louis	2 March 2019
Dianov, Evgeny Mikhailovich	30 January 2019
Djuhar, Sutanto	2 July 2018
Dlamini, Barnabas Sibusiso	28 September 2018
Donald, Alan (Ewen)	14 July 2018
Donen, Stanley	21 February 2019
Do, Muoi	1 October 2018
Dore, Ronald Philip	13 November 2018
Doruk, Mustafa	1 July 2017
Drach, Ivan Fyodorovich	19 June 2018
Dwurnik, Edward	28 October 2018
Eberle, James Henry Fuller	17 May 2018
Eibl-Eibesfeldt, Irenäus	2 June 2018
Eichelbaum, (Johann) Thomas	31 October 2018
Eigen, Manfred	6 February 2019
Elliott, Roger James	16 May 2018
Ellison, Harlan Jay	27 June 2018
Elverding, Peter A. F. W.	31 August 2017
Enwezor, Okwui	15 March 2019
Eskola, Antti Aarre	6 September 2018
Falcam, Leo A.	12 February 2018
Farquhar, John William	22 August 2018
Feast, Michael William	1 April 2019
Feher, George	28 November 2017
Feng, Lanrui	28 February 2019
Fernandes, George	29 January 2019
Fettweis, Günter Bernhard Leo	31 October 2018
Finney, Albert	7 February 2019
Fletcher, Neville Horner	1 October 2017
Fornés, María Irene	30 October 2018
Frängsmyr, Tore	28 August 2017
Franklin, Aretha	16 August 2018
Fraser, William Kerr	13 September 2018
Freeman, Michael Alexander Reykers	14 September 2017
Frère, Albert Pol Oscar Ghislain	3 December 2018
Froment-Meurice, Henri	2 July 2018
Funai, Tetsuro	4 July 2017
Galmot, Yves	3 October 2017
Ganz, Bruno	16 February 2019
Gaombalet, Célestin-Leroy	19 December 2017
García Pérez, Alan Gabriel Ludwig	17 April 2019
Gardner, Richard Newton	15 February 2019
Georgievski, Ljubiša	6 December 2018
Gidada, Negaso	27 April 2019
Giacconi, Riccardo	9 December 2018
Gibbs, Roger Geoffrey	3 October 2018
Gielen, Michael Andreas	8 March 2019
Gill, Anthony (Keith)	6 August 2018
Giri, Tulsi	18 December 2018
Gizenga, Antoine	24 February 2019
Glauber, Roy J.	26 December 2018
Glazer, Nathan	19 January 2019
Goldman, William	16 November 2018
Gomes, Daniel	11 December 2017
Govorukhin, Stanislav Sergeyevich	14 June 2018
Grassle, J. Frederick	6 July 2018
Greengard, Paul	13 April 2019
Gurirab, Theo-Ben	14 July 2018
Habgood, John Stapylton Habgood	6 March 2019
Hall, Donald Andrew	23 June 2018
Hanson, John Gilbert	13 January 2017
Hargrove, Roy Anthony	2 November 2018
Harkianakis, Stylianos	25 March 2019
Hasselmo, Nils	23 January 2019
Hercus, Luise Anna	15 April 2018
Hernández Colón, Rafael	2 May 2019
Hiller, Susan	28 January 2019
Hollings, Ernest (Fritz)	6 April 2019
Holtzman, Wayne Harold	23 January 2019
Hooley, Christopher	13 December 2018
Ho, Tao	29 March 2019
Hultqvist, Bengt Karl Gustaf	24 February 2019
Hurford, Peter John	3 March 2019
Hush, Noel Sydney	20 March 2019
Imry, Yoseph	29 May 2018
Indiana, Robert	19 May 2018

OBITUARY

Isayev, Alexander Sergeyevich	30 August 2018	Mroudjaé, Ali	2 May 2019
Ishizaka, Kimishige	6 July 2018	Munk, Walter Heinrich	8 February 2019
Islam, Syed Ashraful	3 January 2019	Murphy, Thomas (Tom)	15 May 2018
Ismail, Amat	16 October 2018	Murray, Leslie (Les) Allan	29 April 2019
Israelachvili, Jacob Nissim	20 September 2018	Mwape, Lupando Augustine Festus K.	21 January 2019
Jahn, Robert George	15 November 2017	Myerson, Jacob M.	7 July 2018
Jayawardena, Amarananda Somasiri	29 May 2018	Nagare, Masayuki	7 July 2018
Jean Benoît Guillaume Marie Robert Louis Antoine		Naipaul, V(idiadhar) S(urajprasad)	11 August 2018
Adolphe Marc D'Aviano, Grand Duke of Luxembourg	23 April 2019	Nakai, Hiroshi	22 April 2017
Jeffrey, Robin Campbell	4 November 2018	Nakanishi, Koji	28 March 2019
Jin, Yong	30 October 2018	Namphy, Henri	26 June 2018
Jory, Edward John	4 September 2016	Nanterme, Pierre	31 January 2019
Jowell, Tessa Jane Helen Douglas Jowell	12 May 2018	Neild, Robert Ralph	18 December 2018
Kalpokas, Donald Masike'Vanua	20 March 2019	Nekrošius, Eimuntas	20 November 2018
Kao, Charles K.	23 September 2018	Newton, John Oswald	26 September 2016
Karunanidhi, Muthuvel 'Kalaignar'	7 August 2018	Nishikawa, Koichiro	28 November 2018
Kashio, Kazuo	18 June 2018	Noakes, Michael	30 May 2018
Kates, Robert William	21 April 2018	Norwich, John Julius Cooper	1 June 2018
Khadjiev, Salambek Naibovich	2018	Nott, Peter John	20 August 2018
Kim, Jong-pil	23 June 2018	Novozhilov, Genrikh Vasilievich	28 April 2019
Kim, Yong-chun	16 August 2018	Obando Y Bravo, Miguel	3 June 2018
Kinkel, Klaus	4 March 2019	O'Brien Quinn, James Aiden	28 December 2018
Klug, Aaron	20 November 2018	Ollila, Esko Juhani	1 December 2018
Knussen, (Stuart) Oliver	8 July 2018	Olszewski, Jan Ferdynand	7 February 2019
Kobzon, Iosif Davydovich	30 August 2018	Omar, Abu Hassan Bin Haj	8 September 2018
Kok, Willem (Wim)	20 October 2018	Omar, Napsiah binti	16 April 2018
Koltai, Ralph	15 December 2018	Orrego Vicuña, Francisco	2 October 2018
Koo, Bon-moo	20 May 2018	Orszulik, Alojzy	21 February 2019
Kopelson, Arnold	8 October 2018	Osbaldeston, Gordon Francis	6 March 2019
Krauthammer, Charles	21 June 2018	Oz, Amos	28 December 2018
Krueger, Alan Bennett	16 March 2019	Parrikar, Manohar	17 March 2019
Kubuabola, Jone Yavala	16 September 2018	Peart, (William) Stanley	14 March 2019
Küçük, İrsen	10 March 2019	Pérez-Llorca, José Pedro	6 March 2019
Kutz, Kazimierz	18 December 2018	Peters, Wallace	December 2018
Labrie, Fernand	17 January 2019	Petkoff Malec, Teodoro	31 October 2018
Lacey, Richard Westgarth	3 February 2019	Petre, Zoe	1 September 2017
Lagerfeld, Karl Otto	19 February 2019	Piat, Jean	18 September 2018
Lance, James Waldo	20 February 2019	Pieronek, Tadeusz	27 December 2018
Lange, Hermann	28 July 2018	Pieroth, Elmar	31 August 2018
Lanzmann, Claude	5 July 2018	Pihl, Jüri	3 February 2019
Laqueur, Walter	30 September 2018	Pintilie, Lucian	16 May 2018
Lebed, Aleksey Ivanovich	27 April 2019	Powers, William C., Jr	10 March 2019
Lederman, Leon M.	3 October 2018	Previn, André George	28 February 2019
Lee, Stan	12 November 2018	Rabin, Oskar Yakovlevich	7 November 2018
Leibinger, Berthold	16 October 2018	Rajeswar, Thanjavelu	13 January 2018
Levi, Isaac	25 December 2018	Ramazani Baya, Raymond	1 January 2019
Levy, Andrea	14 February 2019	Reino, Fernando	15 April 2018
Lewis, Bernard	19 May 2018	René, (France) Albert	27 February 2019
Likhachev, Vasily Nikolayevich	8 April 2019	Rétoré, Guy	15 December 2018
Ling, Jiefang	15 December 2018	Reuber, Grant Louis	7 July 2018
Lin, Yu-Lin	9 June 2018	Reyes López, Juan Francisco	10 January 2019
Li, Rui	16 February 2019	Reynolds, Burt	6 September 2018
List, Roland	26 January 2019	Reynolds, Peter William John	19 October 2017
Liu, Dongdong	25 February 2015	Richter, Burton	18 July 2018
López-Ibor, Juan José	12 January 2015	Riddell, Clayton (Clay) H.	15 September 2018
Louly, Mohamed Mahmoud Ould Ahmed	16 March 2019	Rindler, Wolfgang	8 February 2019
Loutfy, Aly	27 May 2018	Ripa Di Meana, Carlo	2 March 2018
Lugar, Richard (Dick) Green	28 April 2019	Robuchon, Joël	6 August 2018
Lukianenko, Levko (Hryhorovych)	7 July 2018	Roche, (Eamonn) Kevin	1 March 2019
Mcbride, William Griffith	27 June 2018	Rodríguez Araque, Ali	19 November 2018
Mccain, John Sidney, III	25 August 2018	Roeg, Nicolas Jack	23 November 2018
Mcgee, Liam E.	13 February 2015	Rogers, James E., Jr	17 December 2018
Mccomb, Leonard William Joseph	19 June 2018	Rogers, T. Gary	2 May 2017
Macdonald, Donald Stovel	14 October 2018	Röller, Wolfgang	9 March 2018
Magowan, Peter Alden	27 January 2019	Rose, Clive (Martin)	17 April 2019
Manani Magaya, Alison	24 August 2015	Roth, Philip Milton	22 May 2018
Mao, Zhiyong	4 March 2019	Rowland, (John) David	18 February 2019
Marchionne, Sergio	25 July 2018	Rowlinson, John Shipley	15 August 2018
Marshall, (Carole) Penny	17 December 2018	Rozhdestvensky, Gennady Nikolayevich	16 June 2018
Martini-Urdaneta, Alberto	5 July 2017	Rubenstein, Edward	19 March 2019
Martre, Henri Jean François	3 July 2018	Ryman, Robert	8 February 2019
Masol, Vitaliy Andreyevich	21 September 2018	Sahnoun, Mohamed	20 September 2018
Matsushita, Yasuo	20 July 2018	Sakaiya, Taichi	8 February 2019
Maurício, Armindo Cipriano	28 September 2016	Salakhitdinov, Makhmud	27 April 2018
Medelci, Mourad	28 January 2019	Sanyal, Meera H.	11 January 2019
Medvedev, Zhores Aleksandrovich	15 November 2018	Sa'ud, Talal bin Abd al-Aziz al-	22 December 2018
Meinwald, Jerrold	23 April 2018	Schieffer, Rudolf	15 September 2018
Melchett, Peter Robert Henry Mond	29 August 2018	Schroder, Bruno Lionel	20 February 2019
Mendelsohn, John	7 January 2019	Screech, Michael Andrew	1 June 2018
Mensah, Joseph Henry	12 July 2018	Sebastián Aguilar, Fernando	24 January 2019
Merwin, W(illiam) S(tanley)	15 March 2019	Semikhatov, Mikhail Alexandrovich	28 November 2018
Metzger, Henry	20 November 2018	Sen, Mrinal	30 December 2018
Mirrlees, James Alexander	29 August 2018	Severino, Rodolfo	19 April 2019
Mitchell, Arthur Adam, Jr	19 September 2018	Shagari, Shehu Usman Aliu	28 December 2018
Mojaddedi, Sibghatullah	11 February 2019	Shahrudi, Sayed Mahmoud Hashemi	24 December 2018
Monory, Jacques	17 October 2018	Shange, Ntozake	27 October 2018
Moore, Gerald Ernest	24 March 2018	Sheng, Zhongguo	7 September 2018
Morley, Malcolm	2 June 2018	Shimogaichi, Yoichi	25 October 2017
Mosonyi, György	29 May 2018	Shimomura, Osamu	19 October 2018
Moureaux, Philippe	15 December 2018	Shipley, Walter Vincent	11 January 2019

Shmarov, Valery Nikolayevich	14 October 2018	Varda, Agnès	29 March 2019
Shock, Maurice	7 July 2018	Venturi, Robert	18 September 2018
Sidhu, Shivinder Singh	25 October 2018	Verba, Sidney	4 March 2019
Simms, David John	24 June 2018	Verstraete, Marc	16 August 2018
Simon, Neil	26 August 2018	Viénot, Marc	28 January 2019
Singh, Bhishma Narain	1 August 2018	Vincent of Coleshill, Richard (Frederick) Vincent	8 September 2018
Sioufas, Dimitris	11 January 2019	Virilio, Paul	10 September 2018
Skou, Jens Christian	28 May 2018	von der Dunk, Hermann Walther	22 August 2018
Smith, David Cecil	29 June 2018	Wald, Patricia McGowan	12 January 2019
Stanley, Eric Gerald	21 June 2018	Walker, Alan Cyril	20 November 2017
Starobinski, Jean	4 March 2019	Wang, Charles B.	21 October 2018
Stein, Elias M.	23 December 2018	Wang, Guangying	29 October 2018
Steitz, Thomas A.	9 October 2018	Wang, Ruilin	8 December 2018
Stepin, Vyacheslav Semenovich	14 December 2018	Ward, Ian Macmillan	5 November 2018
Stoltenberg, Thorvald	13 July 2018	Warnock, (Helen) Mary Warnock	20 March 2019
Street, Laurence Whistler	21 June 2018	Wasserman, Robert Harold	23 May 2018
Strunk, Klaus Albert	7 September 2018	Weatherall, David John	8 December 2018
Swinnerton-Dyer, (Henry) Peter Francis	26 December 2018	Wellershoff, Dieter	15 June 2018
Swire, Adrian (Christopher)	24 August 2018	White, Guy Kendall	22 May 2018
Sy, Henry, Sr	19 January 2019	Widjaja, Eka Tjipta	26 January 2019
Szabo, Denis	13 October 2018	Wilson, Michael H.	10 February 2019
Tadros, Tharwat Fouad	23 May 2018	Winkler, Hans Günter	9 July 2018
Talling, J(ohn) F(rancis)	20 June 2017	Winters, Robert Cushing	3 December 2018
Tauran, Jean-Louis Pierre	5 July 2018	Wofford, Harris Llewellyn	21 January 2019
Taylor, Paul B.	29 August 2018	Wolde-Giorgis, Girma	15 December 2018
Thacker, Charles (Chuck) P.	12 June 2017	Wolfe, Thomas (Tom) Kennerly, Jr	14 May 2018
Thomson, John Adam	3 June 2018	Xiao, Yang	19 April 2019
Thomson, Peter William	20 June 2018	Xing, Shizhong	11 March 2019
Thorne León, Jaime	5 April 2018	Yakovlev, Veniamin Fedorovich	24 July 2018
Thouless, David James	6 April 2019	Yang, Zhiguang	14 May 2016
Thurau, Klaus Walther Christian	1 November 2018	Yarrow, Eric Grant	22 September 2018
Tian, Congming	6 December 2017	Yasuoka, Okiharu	19 April 2019
Tiwari, Narayan Dutt	18 October 2018	Yemelyanov, Stanislav Vasilevich	15 November 2018
Tomlinson, Mel Alexander	5 February 2019	Yonekura, Hiromasa	16 November 2018
Tomur, Dawamat	19 December 2018	Yu, Min	16 January 2019
Tran, Dai Quang	21 September 2018	Yursky, Sergei Yurievich	8 February 2019
Ty, George S. K. (Siao Kian)	23 November 2018	Zachau, Hans G.	17 December 2017
Ullsten, Ola	28 May 2018	Zakharchenko, Aleksandr Vladimirovich	31 August 2018
Urbain, Robert	9 November 2018	Zhang, Shoucheng	1 December 2018
Vajpayee, Atal Bihari	16 August 2018	Zhu, Xu	15 September 2018
Van Caenegem, Raoul Charles	15 June 2018		

L

LA FOREST, Gerard V., CC, BCL, MA, LLD, JSD, DCL, FRSC; Canadian lawyer, academic and fmr judge; *Counsel, Stewart McKelvie Stirling Scales;* b. 1 April 1926, Grand Falls, NB; s. of J. Alfred La Forest and Philomene Lajoie; m. Marie Warner 1952; five d.; ed St Francis Xavier Univ., Univ. of New Brunswick, St John's Coll., Oxford, UK and Yale Univ., USA; called to Bar, New Brunswick 1949; QC 1968; practising lawyer, Grand Falls 1951–52; Advisory Counsel, Dept of Justice, Ottawa 1952–55; Legal Adviser, Irving Oil and associated cos 1955–56; Assoc. Prof. of Law, Univ. of New Brunswick 1956–63, Prof. 1963–68; Dean of Law, Univ. of Alberta 1968–70; Asst Deputy Attorney-Gen. of Canada (Research and Planning) 1970–74; Commr Law Reform Comm. of Canada 1974–79; Prof. and Dir Legis. Drafting Program, Faculty of Law (Common Law Section), Univ. of Ottawa 1979–81; Judge, Court of Appeal of New Brunswick 1981–85; Judge, Supreme Court of Canada 1985–97; Dir Canadian Pension Plan 1998–99; Counsel, Stewart McKelvie Stirling Scales 1998–; Distinguished Legal Scholar in Residence, Univ. of NB 1998–; Fellow, World Acad. of Art and Science; mem. Canadian Bar Asscn, Int. Law Asscn, Int. Comm. of Jurists; numerous hon. degrees and other distinctions; Queen Elizabeth II Diamond Jubilee Medal 2012. *Publications include:* Disallowance and Reservation of Provincial Legislation 1955, Extradition to and from Canada 1961, The Allocation of Taxing Power Under the Canadian Constitution 1967, Natural Resources and Public Property Under the Canadian Constitution 1969, Water Law in Canada 1973. *Address:* Stewart McKelvie Stirling Scales, Suite 600, Frederick Square, POB 730, Fredericton, NB E3B 5B4 (office); 320 University Avenue, Fredericton, NB E3B 4J1, Canada (home). *E-mail:* glaforest@stewartmckelvey.com (office). *Website:* www.stewartmckelvey.com (office).

LA GRENADE, Cécile Ellen Fleurette, OBE, GCMG, BChem, PhD; Grenadian food technologist and public servant; *Governor-General;* b. 30 Dec. 1952, Laborie, British Windward Islands (now Grenada); d. of Allan A. La Grenade and Sybil Sylvester-La Grenade; ed Univ. of the West Indies, Univ. of Maryland, USA; Man. Dir De La Grenade Industries (family food-processing co) 1992–; Chair. Public Service Comm. 2007–10; Gov.-Gen. of Grenada, Carriacou and Petite Martinique 2013–; Kt Grand Cross of Justice, Sacred Order of St George (Italy). *Address:* Office of the Governor-General, Government House, Bldg 5, Financial Complex, The Carenage, St George's, Grenada (office). *Telephone:* 440-6639 (office). *Fax:* 440-6688 (office). *E-mail:* pato@spiceisle.com (office).

LA PLANTE, Lynda, CBE; British television dramatist and novelist; *Chairman, La Plante Productions Ltd;* b. 15 March 1946, Formby; m. Richard La Plante (divorced); ed Royal Coll. of Dramatic Art; fmr actress; appeared in The Gentle Touch, Out, Minder; Founder and Chair. La Plante Productions 1994–. *Television includes:* Prime Suspect 1991, 1993, 1995, Civvies, Framed, Seekers, Widows (series), Comics (two-part drama) 1993, Cold Shoulder 2 1996, Cold Blood, Bella Mafia 1997, Trial and Retribution 1997–, Killer Net 1998, Mind Games 2000, The Warden 2001, Framed 2002, Widows (mini-series) 2002, The Commander 2003. *Publications include:* The Widows 1983, The Widows II 1985, The Talisman 1987, Bella Mafia 1991, Framed 1992, Civvies 1992, Prime Suspect 1992, Seekers 1993, Entwined 1993, Prime Suspect 2 1993, Lifeboat 1994, Cold Shoulder 1994, Prime Suspect 3 1994, She's Out 1995, The Governor 1996, Cold Blood 1996, Trial and Retribution 1997, Cold Heart 1998, Trial and Retribution 2 1998, Trial and Retribution 3 1999, Trial and Retribution 4 2000, Sleeping Cruelty 2000, Trial and Retribution 5 2002, Trial and Retribution 6 2002, Royal Flush 2002, Like a Charm (short stories) 2004, Above Suspicion (novel) 2004, The Red Dahlia 2006, Clean Cut 2007, Deadly Intent 2008, Silent Scream 2009, Blind Fury 2010, Bloodline 2011, Backlash 2012, Wrongful Death 2013, Twisted 2014, Tennison 2015, Hidden Killers 2016. *Address:* La Plante Productions Ltd, Paramount House, 162–170 Wardour Street, London, W1F 8ZX, England (office). *Telephone:* (20) 7734-6767 (office). *Fax:* (20) 7734-7878 (office). *E-mail:* admin@laplanteproductions.com (office). *Website:* www.laplanteproductions.com (office); www.lyndalaplante.com.

LA RUSSA, Ignazio; Italian lawyer and politician; b. 18 July 1947, Paternò; s. of Anthony La Russa; three s.; ed St Gallen, Switzerland, Univ. of Pavia; served in Italian mil.; early career in pvt. law practice; Regional Councillor, Lombardy 1985; mem. Camera dei Deputati (Parl.) for Liguria 1992–, Deputy Speaker 1994, Chair. Cttee on Parl. Immunity 1996–2001; Minister of Defence 2008–11; mem. Italian Socialist Movt 1992–95, Alleanza Nazionale (AN) 1995–2008, Chair. AN Parl. Group in Chamber of Deputies 2001, 2004–05, AN – Popolo della Libertà (PdL) 2008–12; Co-founder Fratelli d'Italia party (Brothers of Italy) 2012. *Address:* Fratelli d'Italia, Via Quattro Cantoni 16, 00184 Rome, Italy (office). *Telephone:* (06) 4880690 (office). *Fax:* (06) 48907931 (office). *E-mail:* info@fratelli-italia.it (office); larussa_i@camera.it. *Website:* www.fratelli-italia.it (office); www.ignaziolarussa .it.

LA TOURETTE, John Ernest, BA, MA, PhD; American economist and academic; b. 5 Nov. 1932, Perth Amboy, NJ; s. of John C. La Tourette and Charlotte R. Jones; m. Lillie (Lili) M. Drum 1957; one s. one d.; ed Rutgers Univ., NJ; served in USAF, rank of Capt. 1955–58; Instructor in Econs, Rutgers Univ. 1960–61; Asst Prof., Assoc. Prof., Prof., State Univ. of New York, Binghamton 1961–76, Chair. Dept of Econs 1967–75, Provost for Grad. Studies 1975–76; Vice-Provost for Research and Dean, Grad. School, Bowling Green State Univ., Ohio 1976–79; Vice-Pres. and Provost, Northern Illinois Univ. 1979–86, Pres. 1986–2000, Pres. and Prof. Emer. 2000; Ford Foundation Fellowship 1963; Brookings Inst. Research Professorship 1966–67; Univ. Research Fellowship, State Univ. of NY 1970; Sec. Yavapai Coll. Foundation Bd, Vice-Chair. West Yavapai Guidance Clinic Foundation, Prescott, Ariz. *Publications:* Pastor Pierre Peiret and Jean Latourette in America: A Comparative History of French Protestantism in America 2008; numerous articles and reviews in econs journals and to studies of Bearnais Protestantism (France), articles in the Bulletin du Centre d'Etude du Protestantisme Bearnais 2005–09. *Leisure interests:* genealogy, history of Protestantism in Bearn, France, travel, distance educ. *Address:* 218 S Deerview Circle, Prescott, AZ 86303, USA (home). *Telephone:* (928) 443-1151 (home). *E-mail:* jlatour7@commspeed.net (home).

LAAFAI, Monise; Tuvaluan politician; *Minister of Communications and Transport;* Gen. Man. Tuvalu Co-operative Soc. 1998–2010; Chef de mission, Tuvaluan Del. to Pacific Games, Samoa 2007; mem. Fale i Fono (Parl.) for Nanumaga constituency 2010–; Minister of Finance, Econ. Planning and Industries Sept.–Dec. 2010, Minister of Communications and Transport 2013–; fmr Pres. Tuvalu Athletics Asscn. *Address:* Ministry of Communications and Transport, PMB, Vaiaku, Funafuti, Tuvalu (office). *Telephone:* 20052 (office). *Fax:* 20772 (office). *E-mail:* tuvmet@tuvalu.tv (office).

LAANEOTS, Lt-Gen. Ants; Estonian army officer; b. 16 Jan. 1948, Kilingi-Nõmme, Pärnumaa; m. Natalia Laaneots; two c.; ed Higher Mil. School, Ukraine, Malinovsky Armoured and Mechanized Forces Acad., Moscow, NATO Defence Coll., Rome, Finnish Nat. Defence Coll.; Platoon Leader, then Co. Commdr, then Battalion Commdr, 300th Tank Regt for Soviet Army in Ukraine 1970–78; rank (Soviet) of Lt 1970, Sr Lt 1973, Capt. 1975, Maj. 1979, Lt Col 1982, Col 1987; posted to Soviet-Chinese border in Eastern Kazakhstan 1981–87, Exec. Officer, 96th Tank Regt 1981–83, Commdr 180th Tank Regt 1983–85, Deputy Commdr Chief of Staff, 78th Armoured Div. 1985–87; deployment to Ethiopia 1987–89, mil. advisor to infantry div. Commdr 1987, mil. advisor to Army Corps Gen. 1988–89; Chief of Regional Dept of Defence, Tartu, Estonia 1989–91; rank (Estonian) of Col 1992, Maj.-Gen. 1998, Lt Gen. 2008, Gen. (Kindral) 2011; Chief of Gen. Staff 1991–94, 1997–99; Insp. Gen. of Defence Forces 1997–2000; Head of Baltic Defence Research Centre 2000–01; Commdt, Estonian Nat. Defence Coll. 2001–06; C-in-C Estonian Defence Forces 2006–11; Advisor to the Prime Minister on defence matters 2011–14; mem. Estonian Nat. Defence League, Rotary Club; Commdr, Order of Merit Class Order, Order of the Red Star (USSR), Commemorative Medal '10 Years of the Restored Defence Forces', Rescue Badge, Border Guard Cross of Merit, Defence Medal of Merit, Order of the Ministry of Internal Affairs, Defence Badge, White Cross Order of Merit I Class, Order of the Cross of the Eagle, Class II 2000, Class I 2012. *Address:* Ministry of Defence, Sakala 1, Tallinn 15094, Estonia (office). *Telephone:* 717-0022 (office). *Fax:* 717-0001 (office). *E-mail:* info@ kaitseministeerium.ee (office). *Website:* www.kaitseministeerium.ee (office).

LAAR, Mart, MA, PhD; Estonian historian and politician; *Chairman of the Supervisory Board, Bank of Estonia;* b. 22 April 1960, Viljandi; s. of Tõnis Laar and Aime Laar; m. Katrin Kask 1982; one s. one d.; ed Tartu State Univ.; history teacher in Tallinn 1983–85; Head of Dept, Ministry of Culture of Estonia 1987–90; Deputy (Christian Democratic Party), Supreme Soviet of Estonia 1989–92; mem. Constitutional Ass. 1991–92; mem. Riigikogu (Estonian Parl.) 1992–; Founder and Chair. Pro Patria Union (Isamaaliit) Party 1992–95, Leader of Union of Pro Patria and Res Publica (Isamaa ja Res Publica Liit—IRL) following merger with Res Publica 2006–12; Prime Minister 1992–94, 1999–2002; Minister of Defence 2011–12; Chair. Supervisory Bd, Bank of Estonia 2013–; apptd mem. ISTAL by EC; mem. Advisory Bd Springfellow 2003; Founding mem. Foundation for the Investigation of Communist Crimes; fmr Pres. Council of Historians of Foundation of Estonia Inheritance, Soc. for Preservation of Estonia History, Soc. of Univ. Students of Estonia; Estonian Order of the Nat. Coat of Arms (Second Class), Cavaliere di Gran Groce dei Santi Maurizio e Lazzaro, Das Grosskreuz des Verdienstorderns des Bundesrepublik Deutschland, Nat. Order of Merit, Malta, Grand Cross, Ordre nat. du Mérite, France; Young Politician of the World (Jr Chamber Int.) 1993, European Tax Payer Asscn Year Prize 2001, European Bull, Davastoeconomic Forum, Global Link Award 2001, Adam Smith Award 2002, Milton Friedman Prize for Advancing Liberty, Cato Inst. 2006, Faith and Freedom Award, Acton Inst. 2007, Oskar Kallas Award 2016. *Publications include:* War in the Woods 1992, The Challenge for Europe 1994, Back to the Future: Ten Years of Freedom in Central Europe 2001, Estonia: Little Country that Could 2002, Estonia: A Land of Human Dimensions 2004, Estonia in World War II 2005, The Forgotten War 2005, Estonia's Way 2006, numerous other books in Estonian, Finnish, German, Hungarian, Latvian, Polish and Esperanto; several scientific papers. *Leisure interests:* tennis, squash, history. *Address:* Bank of Estonia, Estonia pst 13, 15095 Tallinn, Estonia (office). *Telephone:* 668-0719 (office). *E-mail:* info@eestipank.ee (office). *Website:* www.eestipank.ee (office).

LAÂRAYEDH, Ali; Tunisian politician; b. 15 Aug. 1955, Medenine; m. Wided Lagha; two s. one d.; trained as engineer in merchant navy; Founder mem. Hizb al-Nahdah/Ennahda Movt, political activist and Spokesman 1981–90, Sec.-Gen., Ennahda Party 2014–; arrested Dec. 1990, released 2004; Minister of the Interior 2011–13; Prime Minister March–Dec. 2013; mem. Première circonscription de Tunis (First Constituency of Tunis) 2014–; Insignia Of The Grand Cordon, Order of the Republic of Tunisia 2014. *Address:* cEnnahda Movement, 26 Khairi Building, Apartment 301, 3rd Floor, pl. du Gouvernement, La Kasbah, 1000 Tunis, Tunisia (office). *Telephone:* (71) 328-050 (office). *E-mail:* tunisdaf@nahdha.tn (office). *Website:* www.ennahdha.tn (office).

LABAKI, Nadine; Lebanese actress and director; b. 18 Feb. 1974, Baabdat; d. of Antoine Labaki and Antoinette Labaki; m. Khaled Mouzanar 2007; ed Saint Joseph Univ., Beirut; contestant on televised talent show Studio el in 'directing' category with music video Habeebi Ya for amateur singer called Carla early 1990s; first video, Tayr el Gharam, for Lebanese artist Pascale Machaalani; later made another two videos for Noura Rahal, followed by music video of the song Ma Fina with Katia Harb; breakthrough came with Nancy Ajram's video Akhasmak Ah 2003; further videos with Ajram followed; co-wrote, directed and starred in her first feature film Caramel 2007, premiered at Cannes Film Festival 2007, also shown at Toronto Int. Film Festival and American Film Inst. *Music videos include:* for Pascale Machaalani: Tayr el Gharam 2001; for Noura Rahal: Salemly Albak 2001, Shoflak Hall 2002; for Katia Harb: Ma Fina 2002; for Nancy Ajram: Akhasmak Ah 2003, Ya Salam 2003, Sehr Ouyounou 2003, Ah W Noss 2004, Lawn Ouyounak 2004, Enta Eih 2005, Yatabtab 2006, Fi Hagat 2010; for Carole Samaha: Habib Albi 2003, Tala' Fiyi 2004; for Guy Manoukian: Al-Urdun 2004; for Star Academy: Jayi el Hakika 2004; for Yuri Mrakadi: Bahebak Mot 2005; for Nawal Al Zoghbi: B'einak 2005; for Nicole Saba: Ya Shaghelny Beek 2005; for Magida El Roumi: I'tazalt El Gharam 2006. *Films:* Non métrage Libanais (short) 2003, Ramad (short) 2003, Seventh Dog (short) 2005, Bosta 2005, Caramel (also writer and dir) 2007, Stray Bullet 2010, The Father and the Foreigner 2010, The Smallest Red Carpet, But the Biggest Heart (documentary) 2011, Where Do We Go Now? (also writer, dir and producer) (People's Choice Award, Toronto Int. Film Festival) 2011, Rock the Casbah 2013, Mea culpa 2014, The Price of Fame 2014, Rio, I Love You (writer and dir) 2014, The Idol 2015, Capernaum (also writer and dir) (Jury Prize, Cannes Film Festival 2018) 2018. *E-mail:* nadine@nadinelabaki.com. *Website:* www.nadinelabaki.com.

LABARDAKIS, Augoustinos; Greek ecclesiastic; *Greek Orthodox Metropolitan of Germany and Exarch of Central Europe;* b. (Georges Labardakis), 7 Feb. 1938, Voukolies, Chania, Crete; s. of Emmanouil Labardakis and Eurydike Labardakis; ed theological schools in Chalki, Turkey, Salzburg, Austria, and Münster and West Berlin, Germany; ordained as priest, Greek Orthodox Metropolitanate of Germany 1964; served as priest, West Berlin 1964–72; elected Bishop of Elaia 1972; auxiliary bishop, Greek Orthodox Metropolitanate of Germany 1972–80; elected Greek Orthodox Metropolitan of Germany and Exarch of Cen. Europe 1980–; Chair. Bishops' Conf. in Germany 2010–; Great Fed. Cross of Merit (Germany) 1980, Order of Merit of Fed. State of North Rhine-Westphalia 1992, Grand Commdr, Order of Honour of the Hellenic Repub. 1994, Cross of Merit of Fed. State of Lower Saxony 2009; Hon. DTheol (Bonn) 2006. *Address:* Greek Orthodox Metropolitanate of Germany, Dietrich-Bonhoeffer-Strasse 2, 53227 Bonn (office); PO Box 300555, 53185 Bonn, Germany (office). *Telephone:* (228) 9737840 (office). *Fax:* (228) 97378424 (office). *E-mail:* metropolit@orthodoxie.net (office). *Website:* www.orthodoxie.net (office).

LABIS, Attilio; French ballet dancer, academic, choreographer and writer; b. 5 Sept. 1936, Vincennes; s. of Umberto Labis and Renée Labis (née Cousin); m. Christiane Vlassi 1959; two s.; ed Ecole de danse académique de l'Opéra, Paris; mem. Corps de Ballet at the Paris Opera 1952, Premier Danseur 1959, Premier Danseur Etoile Chorégraphe 1960–65, Maître de Ballet 1965–, Prof. of Dance, fmr Chief Choreographer; Prof. of Dance, Ecole de Danse; Prof. d'Adage et de Repertoire; Guest Dancer in London, Paris, Washington, Tokyo, Moscow, Kiev, Leningrad, Rome, Milan, Berlin, Munich, Stuttgart, Rio de Janeiro, Hong Kong, Singapore and Sydney; World Amb. for l'Ecole Française; devised choreography for productions including Rencontre (TV) 1961, Arcades 1964, Romeo and Juliet 1967, Spartacus 1973, Raymonda 1973; has created and interpreted numerous ballets, including Giselle, Sleeping Beauty, Swan Lake, Don Quixote, Pas de Dieux (Gene Kelly), Marines (Georges Skibine), Icare (Serge Lifar), Pas de danse (music by Gluck), Schéhérazade, Coppélia, Sarabande, The Nutcracker, Etudes (Harold Lander), Spartacus, Arcades, Romeo et Juliette, Raymonda, Spartacus, Romeo and Juliette, Arcades (Berlioz), Sarabande (Rossini); Chevalier des Arts et des Lettres, Légion d'honneur 2002; Prix Vaslaw Nijinsky. *Films:* Le spectre de la danse (documentary short) 1961, L'adage (short) 1964, Les cahiers retrouvés de Nina Vyroubova (documentary) 1996, Serge Lifar Musagète (documentary) 2005. *Television:* Discorama (series) 1959, L'âge en fleur (series) (actor) 1975. *Address:* Opéra de Paris, 8 rue Scribe, 75009 Paris (office); 13 Avenue Rubens, 78400 Chatou, France. *Telephone:* 1-30-53-48-07 (Paris) (home); 6-63781398 (mobile). *Fax:* 1-30-53-57-80 (Paris) (home). *E-mail:* attilio.labis.choregraphe@wanadoo.fr (home). *Website:* www.operadeparis.fr (office).

LABRO, Philippe; French screenwriter, director and actor; b. 27 Aug. 1936, Menthon-Saint-Bernard (Haute-Savoie); s. of Jean-François Labro and Henriette Labro; m. Françoise Labro; four c. (one from previous m.); ed Washington and Lee Univ., Va, USA; travelled across all of the USA; worked as radio and newspaper reporter on his return to Europe; soldier in Algeria 1960–62; began writing for Radio Télé Luxembourg (RTL), Paris Match, and for TF1 and Antenne 2 on short films; directed programmes on RTL 1985–2000, Ed.-in-Chief 1979, Vice-Pres. 1992, Vice-Chair. Bd of Dirs 2000, host, Mon RTL à moi 2011–12; Hon. Pres. Compagnie des Ecrivains de Tarn et Garonne à Montauban Écrivains; Officier, Légion d'honneur 2002, Commdr 2010. *Films include:* as actor: Le chat et la souris 1975; as writer and dir: Tout peut arriver (aka Don't Be Blue) 1969, Sans mobile apparent (Without Apparent Motive) (also actor, uncredited) 1971, L'héritier (The Inheritor, adaption) (also actor, uncredited) 1973, Le hasard et la violence (Chance and Violence) 1974, L'alpagueur (aka Hunter Will Get You, USA) 1976, La crime (aka Cover Up) 1983, Rive droite, rive gauche (Right Bank, Left Bank) 1984. *Television:* Les deux D: Marie Dubois, Françoise Dorléac (dir) 1966. *Publications include:* Des feux mal éteints (Poorly Extinguished Fires) 1967, L'Étudiant étranger (The Foreign Student) (Prix Interallié 1986) 1986, Le Petit Garçon (The Little Boy) 1988, Quinze ans (Fifteen) 1992, La Traversée (The Crossing) 1996, Tomber sept fois, se relever huit (Fall Seven Times, Get up Eight) 2003, Les Gens (People) 2009, Ce n'est qu'un début (This is Just the Beginning) 2018. *Address:* c/o Éditions Gallimard, 5 rue Gaston-Gallimard, 75328 Paris Cedex 07, France. *Telephone:* 1-49-54-42-00. *Fax:* 1-45-44-94-03. *Website:* www.gallimard.fr.

LABUS, Miroljub, MSc, PhD; Serbian economist, academic, lawyer and fmr politician; *Professor, Department of Economics, Faculty of Law, University of Belgrade;* b. 27 Feb. 1947, Mala Krsna; s. of Zdravko Labus and Draginja Labus (née Pavlovic); m. Olivera Labus (née Grabic); two d.; ed Belgrade Univ.; attorney in Belgrade 1970–71; Lecturer in Law, Belgrade Univ. 1971, Prof. of Econs, Faculty of Law 1971–; Fulbright Lecturer, Cornell Univ., USA 1983, Visiting Asst Prof. 1984; Sr Adviser, Fed. Statistics Office 1986–94; mem. Bd Ekonomska Misl i Ekonomske Analize journals; Fellow, Econ. Inst. 1993–99; Deputy Prime Minister and Minister of Foreign Econ. Relations, Fed. Repub. of Yugoslavia 1987–91, Deputy Prime Minister, with responsibility for econ. relations with the int. community 2001–03; unsuccessful presidential cand. 2002; Deputy Prime Minister in charge of European Integration, Repub. of Serbia 2004–06 (resgnd); mem. Fed. Parl. and Cttee on Monetary Policy; Vice-Pres. Democratic Party 1994–97; mem. Standing Cttee on Econ. Affairs, UNDPM Sarajevo 1996; with UNDP 1996–97; joined IBRD 1997; Ed. The Economic Trends, Fed. Statistics Office, Belgrade, The Economic Barometer, Econ. Inst., Belgrade 2000–; Pres. Admin. Bd G17 Plus movt (later G17 Plus party) 1999–2000, Pres. G17 Plus 2003–06 (resgnd). *Publications include:* Social and Collective Property Rights 1987, General Equilibrium Modelling (co-author) 1990, Contemporary Political Economy 1991, Foundations of Political Economy 1992, Foundations of Economics 1995, other books and numerous articles on econ. problems. *Leisure interests:* woodwork, skiing. *Address:* University of Belgrade, Faculty of Law, Bulevar kralja Aleksandra 67, 11000 Belgrade, Serbia (office); Gospodar Jevremova str. 13, Belgrade, Serbia (home). *Telephone:* (11) 3027700 (office). *Fax:* (11) 3221299 (office). *E-mail:* pravni@ius.bg.ac.rs (office). *Website:* www.ius.bg.ac.rs (office).

LaBUTE, Neil; American playwright, film writer and director; b. 19 March 1963, Detroit, Mich.; m.; two c.; ed Brigham Young Univ., Univ. of Kansas, New York Univ. *Films include:* In the Company of Men (writer, dir) (Sundance Film Festival Filmmakers' Trophy, Soc. of Tex. Film Critics Best Original Screenplay Award, New York Film Critics' Circle Best First Film) 1997, Your Friends and Neighbors (writer, dir) 1998, Tumble (writer) 2000, Nurse Betty (dir) 2000, Possession (screenplay writer, dir) 2002, The Shape of Things (writer, dir) 2003, The Wicker Man 2006, Lakeview Terrace 2008, Death at a Funeral (dir) 2010, Some Velvet Morning (writer, dir) 2013, My America 2014, Dirty Weekend 2015. *Theatre productions include:* Woyzeck, Dracula, Sangguinarians & Sycophants, Ravages, Rounder, Lepers, Filthy Talk For Troubled Times, In the Company of Men (Asscn for Mormon Letters Award for Drama 1993) 1992, Bash: Latterday Plays 2000, The Shape of Things 2001, The Distance From Here (Almeida, London) 2002, The Mercy Seat 2002, Merge 2003, Wrecks (Everyman Palace, Cork) 2005, This is How it Goes (New York, and Donmar Warehouse London) 2005, Some Girl(s) 2005, Land of the Dead/Helter Skelter 2007, Reasons to be Pretty 2008, Some White Chick 2009, The Purple Marmoset 2009, The Furies 2009, In a Forest Dark and Deep 2011, Lovely Head 2013, Reasons to Be Happy 2013, Money Shot 2014, The Way We Get By 2015, How To Fight Lonliness 2016. *Television includes:* Bash: Latter-Day Plays 2001, Full Circle (series) 2013, Ten X Ten (mini-series) 2014, Van Helsing (series) 2016–. *Publications include:* In the Company of Men 1998, Your Friends and Neighbors 1999, Bash: Latterday Plays 2000, The Shape of Things 2001, The Distance from Here 2003, The Mercy Seat 2003, Seconds of Pleasure (short stories) 2004.

LACALLE HERRERA, Luis Alberto; Uruguayan farmer, lawyer and fmr head of state; b. 13 July 1941, Montevideo; s. of Carlos Lacalle and María Hortensia de Herrera Uriarte; m. María Julia Pou Brito del Pino 1970; two s. one d.; ed Universidad de la República Oriental del Uruguay; journalist, Clarín daily newspaper 1961; currently contributor to El Debate of Montevideo; columnist, Correo de los Viernes, La Patria de Montevideo, Spanish newspaper ABC; joined Partido Nacional (Blanco) 1958; Deputy to Legis. Ass. 1971–73; elected Senator and Vice-Pres. 1984, mem. Cttee for Public Funds, for Transportation, for Public Works; cand. for Pres. for Partido Nacional (Blanco) 1989; Pres. of Uruguay 1990–95; presidential cand. 2004, 2009; Leader Nationalist sector, Herrerismo, mem. Party Directorate; Co-founder MERCOSUR 1991; mem. Club de Madrid; Gran Collar de la Orden Nacional del Mérito del Ecuador 1990, Gran Collar de la Orden al Mérito de Chile 1991, Collar de la Orden del Libertador Gral. San Martín de Argentina 1991, Gran Collar del Cóndor de los Andes de Bolivia 1991, Gran Cruz de la Orden Cruzeiro do Sul de Brasil 1991, Grand Cross of the Most Distinguished Order of St Michael and St George; Dr hc (Universidad Complutense de Madrid) 1992, (Hebrew Univ. of Jerusalem) 1992, (Autonomous Univ. of Guadalajara, Mexico) 1993, (Nat. Univ. of Paraguay) 1993; Gold Medal of the Xunta de Galicia (Spain) 1994, Jerusalem Award 1995. *Address:* Avda. de las leyes s/n Palacio Legislativo, Montevideo, Uruguay (office). *Telephone:* (2) 2000337 (office); (2) 6002757. *Fax:* (2) 9290255 (office). *E-mail:* lacalleherrera@parlamento.gub.uy (office); lacalleherrera@gmail.com. *Website:* www.parlamento.gub.uy (office).

LaCHAPELLE, David; American photographer; b. 1969, Fairfield, Conn.; s. of Philip LaChapelle and Helga LaChapelle; ed North Carolina School of the Arts, School of Visual Arts, New York, Art Student's League; began career by creating fine art images for Interview Magazine; photographer advertising campaigns for Keds, Estée Lauder, Prescriptives, Volvo, MasCosmetics, Diesel Jeans; widely published in fashion, music and entertainment magazines; photography prints and TV for clients including Jean Paul Gaultier, Giorgio Armani, MTV, Pepsi and Levis; fashion portraits of celebrities include Debbie Harry, Britney Spears, Madonna, David Bowie and Elton John; Best New Photographer of the Year, French Photo Magazine 1995, American Photo Magazine 1995, Photographer of the Year, VH1 Fashion Awards 1996, Best Cutting Edge Essay and Best Style Photography, Life magazine's Alfred Eisenstaedt Awards for Magazine Photography (the Eisies) 1998, Infinity Award, Int. Centre of Photography 1997, honoured in Cover of the Year category at the Eisies 1999, Best Video for Moby's Natural Blues, MTV Europe Music Awards 2000, Adult Contemporary Video of the Year for Elton John's This Train Don't Stop There Anymore, MVPA Awards 2003, Director of the Year (Best Rock Video of the Year) for No Doubt's It's My Life, MVPA Awards 2004, Special Jury Prize, Mountainfilm in Telluride 2004, Special Jury Recognition, Sundance Film Festival 2004, Best Documentary, Aspen Film Festival 2004. *Film:* Rize (dir) 2006. *Publications:* vols of photographic images: LaChapelle Land 1996, David LaChapelle Exhibition 1999, Hotel Lachapelle 1999, Portfolio 2000, David Lachapelle Photology 2001, Barbican Gallery 2002, Eros Fotografia 2003, If You Want Reality, Take The Bus! 2003, Taschen 25th Anniversary 2005, Artists and Prostitutes 2006, David LaChapelle 2006, Heaven to Hell 2006, David LaChapelle 2007, First Step 2008, Jesus is My Homeboy 2008, David LaChapelle 2008, Al Forte Belvedere 2008, Who Shot Rock and Roll 2009, Photo Wisdom 2009, Delirios de Razon 2009, The Rape of Africa 2009, Life 2010, Maybach: Going Places 2010, Atopia 2010, Divine Comedy 2010, Popular 2010, Bliss Amongst Chaos 2010, Taschen 30th Anniversary 2010, MOCA Taipei Catalogue 2010, Earth Laughs In Flowers 2011, Borders and Frontiers 2011, David LaChapelle: Lost and Found 2011, Nosotros: La humanidad al borde 2011, Thus Spoke LaChapelle 2011, LaChapelle 2012, Earth Laughs in Flowers 2012, David LaChapelle 2012, Burning Beauty 2012, Still Life 2013, Land Scape 2014. *Address:* c/o Steven Pranica, Creative Exchange Agency, 545 West 25th Street, 19th Floor, New York, NY 10001, USA. *Telephone:* (212) 414-4100; (212) 645-6100. *E-mail:* steven@cxainc.com; studio@davidlachapelle.com. *Website:* www.cxainc.com; www.davidlachapelle.com.

LACHMANN, Henri, Diplôme d'Expertise Comptable; French business executive; *Chairman of the Supervisory Board, Schneider Electric SA;* b. 13 Sept. 1938; m.; two c.; ed Ecole des Hautes Etudes Commerciales, Paris; Auditor and Dir, Arthur Andersen 1963–70; Dir, Pompey steel co. (later Strafor Facom) 1970–81, Chair. Strafor Facom 1981–98; Dir, Schneider Electric SA 1996–, Chair. and CEO 1999–2006, Chair. Supervisory Bd 2006–; Vice-Pres. Supervisory Bd Vivendi; Chair. Bd of Dirs Centre Chirurgical Marie-Lannelongue; Pres. Campaign Cttee

Fondation Université de Strasbourg; Founding mem. Foundation for Continental Law; Pres. l'Institut Télémaque; Vice-Pres. and Treas. l'Institut Montaigne; mem. Bd of Dirs AXA Group, CARMAT, Norbert Dentressangle; mem. Man. Cttee AXA Millésimes (SAS), Comité d'Orientation of Institut de l'Entreprise; Chair. Centre Chirurgical Marie Lannelongue; Officier, Légion d'honneur, des Palmes académiques, Commdr, Ordre nat. du Mérite; Dr hc (Ecole de Management de Grenoble). *Publication:* report: Bien-être efficacité au travail (co-author) 2010. *Leisure interests:* rugby, skiing. *Address:* Schneider Electric SA, 35 rue Joseph Monier, 92500 Rueil-Malmaison, France (office). *Telephone:* 1-41-29-70-52 (office). *Fax:* 1-41-29-71-28 (office). *Website:* www.schneider-electric.com (office).

LACHMANN, Sir Peter Julius, Kt, ScD, FRCP, FRCPath, FRS, FMedSci; British immunologist; *Sheila Joan Smith Professor Emeritus of Immunology, University of Cambridge;* b. 23 Dec. 1931, Berlin, Germany; s. of Heinz Lachmann and Thea Heller; m. Sylvia Stephenson 1962; two s. one d.; ed Trinity Coll., Univ. of Cambridge and Univ. Coll. Hosp., London; Research Student, Dept of Pathology, Univ. of Cambridge 1958–60, Research Fellow, Empire Rheumatism Council 1962–64, Asst Dir of Research, Immunology Div. 1964–71; Prof. of Immunology, Royal Postgraduate Medical School, Univ. of London 1971–75; Hon. Consultant Pathologist, Hammersmith Hosp. 1971–75; Dir MRC Research Group on serum complement 1971–75; Sheila Joan Smith Prof. of Immunology, Univ. of Cambridge 1977–99, Prof. Emer. 1999–; Hon. Dir, MRC Molecular Immunopathology Unit 1980–97; Hon. Consultant Clinical Immunologist, Cambridge Health Dist 1976–99; Pres. Royal Coll. of Pathologists 1990–93, Acad. of Medical Sciences 1998–2002; Biological Sec. and Vice-Pres. The Royal Soc. 1993–98; Visiting Investigator Rockefeller Univ., New York 1960–61, Scripps Clinic and Research Foundation, La Jolla, Calif. 1966, 1975, 1980, 1986, Basel Inst. for Immunology 1971; Meyerhof Visiting Prof., Weizmann Inst., Rehovot 1989; Visiting Prof., Collège de France 1993; Fellow, Christ's Coll. Cambridge 1962–71, 1976–, Royal Postgraduate Medical School 1995, Imperial Coll. London 2001; mem. Medical Advisory Cttee, British Council 1983–97, Scientific Advisory Bd SmithKline Beecham 1995–2000; Chair. Science Cttee Asscn Medical Research Charities 1988–92, Medical Research Cttee Muscular Dystrophy Group 1986–90, Research Cttee, CORE (Digestive Disorders Foundation) 2003–09; Pres. Fed. of European Acads of Medicine 2004–05 (Pres. Emer. 2006–07), Henry Kunkel Soc. 2003–05; Trustee, Arthritis Research Campaign 2000–06; mem. Academia Europaea 1992; Foreign mem. Norwegian Acad. of Science and Letters 1991; Foreign Fellow, Indian Nat. Acad. of Science 1997; Foundation Fellow, Univ. Coll. London Hosp. 1999; Hon. mem. Asscn of Physicians 1998; Hon. Foreign mem. Czech Acad. of Medicine 2012; Hon. Fellow, Faculty of Pathology, Royal Coll. of Physicians of Ireland 1993, Trinity Coll. Dublin 2007; Hon. DSc (Leicester) 2005; Gold Medal, European Complement Network 1997, Medicine and Europe Senior Prize, Inst. des Sciences de la Santé 2003; Foundation Lecturer, Royal Coll. of Pathologists 1983, Langdon Brown Lecturer, Royal Coll. of Physicians 1986, Heberden Orator, British Soc. of Rheumatology 1986, Charnock Bradley Memorial Lecturer 1992, Plenary Lecturer, Vienna 1993, Congress Lecturer, BSI 1993, Frank May Lecturer, Leicester 1994, Vanguard Medical Lecture, Univ. of Surrey 1998, Lloyd Roberts Lecturer, Medical Soc. of London 1999, Jean Shanks Lecturer, Acad. of Medical Sciences, London 2001. *Publications:* Jt Ed. Clinical Aspects of Immunology 1975, 1982, 1993. *Leisure interests:* keeping bees, walking in mountains. *Address:* Department of Veterinary Medicine, Madingley Road, Cambridge, CB3 0ES (office); 36 Conduit Head Road, Cambridge, CB3 0EY, England (home). *Telephone:* (1223) 766242 (office); (1223) 357842 (home). *Fax:* (1223) 766244 (office). *E-mail:* pjl1000@cam.ac.uk (office). *Website:* www.christs.cam.ac.uk/node/5900 (office).

LACHOUT, Karel, MusD; Czech composer, musicologist, writer, pianist and teacher; b. 30 April 1929, Prague; s. of Ing. Karel Lachout and Marie Lachoutová; m. (divorced); ed Charles Univ., Acad. of Musical Arts, Prague; teacher of music and English (approbation for grammar schools) 1952; Ed. Music Dept. Radio Prague 1953–79; freelance artist, composer and musicologist with specialization in Spanish and Latin American folk music 1979–; recognition from Queen Sofía of Spain for promotion of Spanish music 1995, from Pres. Eduardo Frei of Chile for promotion of Chilean music in Prague 1999. *Compositions include:* Such is Cuba orchestral suite 1962, Symphonietta for grand orchestra, America Latina orchestral suite (including 'Mar del Plata'), two string quartets, piano pieces. *Radio:* scripts for music programmes on Radio Prague of authentic music from Latin America, Spain and other countries, including Music From Cristóbal Colón's Land series 1974. *Publications include:* The Problem of Composer's Creation (dissertation) 1953, The World Sings (Czech Music Fund Prize) 1957, Music of Chile 1976, Music of Cuba (honoured by invitation from UNEAC to Music Festival, Havana 1986) 1979, Folk Music of Latin America (edn to commemorate 500th anniversary of discovery of S America, with two LPs and booklet) 1992, Folk Music of Spain (double LP and booklet) 1993. *Leisure interests:* languages (German, English, Spanish, Latin), travelling to explore origins of authentic folk music, relaxing in Spain at Costa Brava, philosophy of deeper sense of human life and belief in higher justice; active mem., Czech Hussite Church; big collection of folk music (books, instruments, recordings etc.) from all over the world; promotes int. summer folk music festival, Prague Fair every year. *Address:* Viklefova 11, 130 00 Prague 3, Czech Republic (home). *Telephone:* (2) 71770347 (home).

LACHOWSKI, Sławomir, BEcons, PhD; Polish banking executive and business consultant; *Founder, Consulting SL;* b. 1 Jan. 1958, Końskie; m. Marzena Lachowska; ed Univ. of Planning and Statistics, Warsaw (now Warsaw School of Econs), Gutenberg Univ., Mainz, Germany, Univ. of Zurich, Switzerland, Stanford Univ., USA, INSEAD, France; fmr Researcher, Inst. of Econ. Devt, Asst then Sr Asst 1983–90; Founder and Pres., INTEXIM Centre for Econ. Analysis 1987–92; fmr Deputy Pres., PKO BP and First Deputy Pres., PBG SA; Vice-Pres. Powszechny Bank Combined Econ. 1994–98, Universal Savings Bank State 1998–2000; mem. Bd of Man., BRE Bank SA 2000–01, Deputy Pres. in charge of retail banking 2001–04, Pres., Bd of Man. 2004–08; CEO FM Bank PBP SA 2013–15; Founder Consulting SL 2008–; Golden Cross of Merit 2007. *Publications include:* Droga innowacji 2010, Droga ważniejsza niż cel 2011, It's The Journey Not The Destination 2012, Od wartości do działania. Przywództwo w czasach przełomowych 2013, Acting on Values: Leadership in Turbulent Times 2015. *Leisure interests:* marathon running, mountaineering. *Address:* Consulting SL, Węgrzynowice 16, 97 212 Łódź, Poland (office). *Telephone:* 447102024 (office). *Website:* www.slawomirlachowski.pl.

LACINA, Ferdinand, MA; Austrian banker and fmr politician; b. 31 Dec. 1942, Vienna; s. of Ferdinand Lacina and Anna Lacina; m. Monika Lacina 1966; one s. one d.; ed Hochschule für Welthandel, Vienna; various posts in Kammer für Arbeiter und Angestellte, Vienna 1964; Beirat für Wirtschafts- und Sozialfragen 1974; Dir Dept of Financial Planning, Österreichische Industrieverwaltungs AG 1978; Dir Pvt. Office of Fed. Chancellor Kreisky 1980; Sec. of State, Fed. Chancellery 1982; Fed. Minister of Transport 1984–85, of Public Economy and Transport 1985–86, of Finance 1986–95; consultant, Montana AG, Vienna 1995, Erste Bank AG 1996; Chair. Man. Bd GiroCredit AG 1996; currently Counsellor, UniCredit Bank Austria AG (Bank Austria); Pres. WISE Forum, Vienna; mem. Vienna Chapter, American-Austrian Foundation, Inc.; Grand Cross, Order of Infante Dom Henrique (Portugal) 1984, Grand Gold Decoration, Honour for Services to the Republic of Austria 1987, Grand Decoration, Honour for Services to the City of Vienna 2004. *Publications include:* Auslandskapital in Österreich (with O. Grünwald); articles in trade union newspapers and political and econ. journals. *Leisure interests:* literature, walking. *Address:* UniCredit Bank Austria AG, Julius Tandler-Platz 3, 1090 Vienna, Austria (office). *Website:* www.bankaustria.at (office).

LACK, Andrew, BFA; American media industry executive; *Chairman and CEO, NBC News;* b. 16 May 1947, New York, NY; m. Betsy Kenny Lack; two s. one d.; ed Univ. of Paris (Sorbonne), France, Boston Univ.; joined CBS News division 1976, producer 60 Minutes 1977, Exec. Producer West 57th 1985–89, Sr Exec. Producer CBS Reports 1978–85, produced various documentaries, left CBS 1993; Pres. NBC News 1993–2001, Pres. and COO NBC 2001–03; Chair. and CEO Sony Music Entertainment Inc. 2003–04, CEO Sony BMG (following merger with Bertelsmann's BMG) 2004–06, Chair. Sony BMG Music Entertainment 2006; CEO Bloomberg Global Multimedia Group 2008–13, Chair. Bloomberg Media Group 2013; CEO and Dir Broadcasting Bd of Govs 2014–15; Chair. and CEO NBC News and MSNBC 2015–; Trustee Boston Univ. *Address:* NBC News, 30 Rockefeller Plaza, New York, NY 10112, USA (office). *Website:* www.nbcnews.com (office).

LACKIN, Winston G.; Suriname politician; b. 23 Dec. 1954, Nickerie; ed Anton de Kom Univ.; joined Ministry of Foreign Affairs 1983, Head of Europe Dept 1983–84, First Sec., Embassy in Brasilia 1991–94, Counsellor, Embassy in Brussels 1997–2000, Minister of Foreign Affairs 2010–15, Acting Finance Minister 2011; mem. Nationale Democratische Partij, Dir of Cabinet 2010; mem. Megacombinatie political alliance. *Address:* c/o Ministry of Foreign Affairs, Henck Aaronstraat 8, Paramaribo, Suriname.

LACLOTTE, Michel René; French museum director; b. 27 Oct. 1929, Saint-Malo; s. of Pierre Laclotte and Huguette de Kermabon; ed Lycée Pasteur, Neuilly, Inst. d'art et d'archéologie de l'Univ. de Paris and Ecole du Louvre; Insp. Inspectorate of Provincial Museums 1955–66; Chief Curator of Paintings, Musée du Louvre 1966–87, of collection Musée d'Orsay 1978–86, Dir Musée du Louvre 1987–92, Pres. de l'Etablissement Public (Musée du Louvre) 1992–94; Pres. Mission de préfiguration, Institut Nat. d'Histoire de l'Art 1994–98; Commdr, Légion d'honneur, Ordre nat. du Mérite, des Arts et des Lettres; Grand prix nat. des Musées 1993; Hon. CBE 1994. *Publications:* various works on history of art, catalogues and articles in reviews mainly on Italian and French painting (14th to 15th centuries) and the Louvre Museum. *Address:* 10 bis rue du Pré-aux-Clercs, 75007 Paris, France (home).

LACOSTE, Paul, OC, PhD; Canadian university administrator; b. 24 April 1923, Montréal, Québec; s. of Emile Lacoste and Juliette (née Boucher) Lacoste; m. 1st Louise Mackay (divorced), 2nd Louise Marcil 1973 (died 1995); one s. two d.; ed Univs of Montréal, Chicago and Paris; Vice-Pres., Montréal Univ. 1966–75; Prof., Dept of Philosophy, Montréal Univ. 1948–86; lawyer 1960–; Pres. Asscn des universités partiellement ou entièrement de langue française 1978–81, Fonds Int. de coopération universitaire 1978–81, Asscn of Univs and Colls of Canada 1978-79, Conf. of Rectors and Prins of Québec Univs 1977–80, mem. Bd Asscn of Commonwealth Univs 1977–80, Ecole polytechnique Montréal 1975–85, Clinical Research Inst. of Montréal 1975–, Ecole des hautes commerciales de Montréal 1982–85; Pres., Univ. of Montréal 1975–85; Chair. Comm. and Cttees of the Fed. Environmental Assessment Review to the Great-Whale Hydroelectric Project 1991–98; Chevalier, Légion d'honneur 1985; Hon. LLD (McGill Univ.) 1975, (Univ. of Toronto) 1978; Dr hc (Laval Univ.). *Publications:* Justice et paix scolaire 1962, A Place of Liberty 1964, Le Canada au seuil du siècle de l'abondance 1969, Principes de gestion universitaire 1970, Education permanente et potentiel universitaire 1977. *Leisure interests:* reading, music, travel. *Address:* Universite de Montréal, CP 6128, Cabinet du rectur, Montréal, Québec H3C 3J7, Canada (office). *Telephone:* (514) 343-6776 (office).

LACOTTE, Urs, MBA; Swiss international organization executive; *Special Adviser, International Olympic Committee;* m. France Lacotte; two c.; ed Univ. of Berne, Univ. of Bayreuth, Germany, Univ. of St Gallen; fmr tech. official for ski competitions in Switzerland; worked with Electrowatt Eng Co. in Asia and with forerunner to Swiss Sports Asscn; fmr planner, Ministry of Defence; Dir Gen. IOC 2003–11, Special Adviser 2011–. *Address:* International Olympic Committee, Château de Vidy, Case postale 356, 1001 Lausanne, Switzerland (office). *Telephone:* (21) 6216111 (office). *Fax:* (21) 6216216 (office). *Website:* www .olympic.org (office).

LACROIX, Christian Marie Marc; French fashion designer; b. 16 May 1951, Arles (Bouches-du-Rhône); s. of Maxime Lacroix and Jeannette Bergier; m. Françoise Roesenstiehl 1989; ed Lycée Frédéric Mistral, Arles, Univ. Paul Valéry, Montpellier, Univ. Paris-Sorbonne and Ecole du Louvre; Asst, Hermès 1978–79, Guy Paulin 1980–81; Artistic Dir Jean Patou 1981–87, Christian Lacroix 1987–2009 (purchased from LVMH by Falic Fashion Group 2005, business put into admin 2009, Autumn/Winter 2009 Haute Couture privately financed by himself), Emilio Pucci 2002–05; design for Carmen, Nîmes, France 1988, for L'as-tu revue? 1991, for Les Caprices de Marianne 1994; launched first line of floral perfume 1999; launched a children's line 2001; launched a perfume, Bazar 2002; launched a lingerie for women line as well as a menswear line 2004; decorated the TGV Méditerranée 2001; decorated Petit Moulin Hotel, Paris; Creative Dir Emilio Gucci 2002; has designed dresses for Hollywood stars, including Christina

Aguilera's wedding dress; designer of uniform of Air France staff and crew 2004; partnered with Avon cosmetics to launch Christian Lacroix Rouge fragrance for women and Christian Lacroix Noir for men 2007; released Christian Lacroix Absynthe 2009, Christian Lacroix Absynthe For Him 2009, Christian Lacroix Nuit 2011, Christian Lacroix Nuit For Him 2011; costume designs for the opera, theatre, dance and music displayed at exhbn Christian Lacroix Costumier, Nat. Museum of Singapore 2009; began collaborating with Barcelona-based clothing brand Desigual 2011; has completed interior design work at several hotels, including Hotel Le Petit Moulin 2005, Hotel Bellechasse, Saint-Germain-des-Prés, Paris 2007, Le Notre Dame hotel 2010; Commdr des Arts et des Lettres 1996; Chevalier, Légion d'honneur 2002; Dés d'or 1986, 1988, Council of Fashion Designers of America 1987, Prix Balzac 1989, Goldene Spinnrad Award (Germany) 1990, Prix Molière (for costumes in Phèdre) 1996. *Dance:* costumes for Opera Garnier (Paris), Stadt Oper (Vienna) and several ballets. *Plays:* costumes for Phèdre, Comédie Française (Paris) 1995. *Publications:* Pieces of a Pattern 1992, illustrations for albums Styles d'aujourd'hui 1995, Journal d'une collection 1996. *Address:* 2–4 place Saint Sulpice, 75006 Paris, France (office). *Telephone:* 1-42-68-79-00 (office); 1-46-33-48-95 (boutique) (office). *Fax:* 1-42-68-79-57 (office). *E-mail:* info@christian-lacroix.com (office). *Website:* www.christian-lacroix.com (office).

LACROIX, HE Cardinal Gérald Cyprien, BA, MA; Canadian ecclesiastic, academic and diplomatist; *Archbishop of Québec and Primate of Canada;* b. 27 July 1957, Saint-Hilaire de Dorset, Québec; ed Trinity High School, Saint Anselm Coll., USA, Laval Univ., Pius X Secular Inst.; Sec. Gen. Pius X Inst. 1982–95, Dir of the Gen. Council 1985–, Gen. Man. Christian Formation and Spiritual Centre 1985–87, worked in Colombia, opening new houses of the Inst. 1990–2000, Dir-Gen. Pius X Inst. 2001–10; ordained priest 1988; consecrated Titular Bishop of Hilta 2009; Auxiliary Bishop of Québec 2009–11, Archbishop of Québec and Primate of Canada 2011–; cr. Cardinal (Cardinal-Priest of San Giuseppe all'Aurelio) 2014–; Co-Chair. Cttee on Life and Family, Canadian Conf. of Catholic Bishops; Hon. DD (Saint Anselm Coll.) 2011. *Address:* Archdiocese of Québec, Chancellerie, 1073 boulevard René-Lévesque Ouest, Québec, PQ G1S 4R5, Canada (office). *Telephone:* (418) 688-1211 (office). *Fax:* (418) 688-2960 (office). *E-mail:* info@ecdq.org (office). *Website:* www.ecdq.org (office).

LACROIX, Hubert T., LLB, MBA; Canadian lawyer and broadcasting executive; *President and CEO, Canadian Broadcasting Corporation / Radio-Canada;* b. 13 July 1955, Montréal; ed Collège Jean-de-Brébeuf, Montréal, McGill Univ.; admitted to Quebec Bar 1977; lawyer with O'Brien, Hall, Saunders 1977–84; Pnr McCarthy Tétrault 1984–2000; Exec. Chair. Telemedia Corpn 2000–03, Sr Adviser, Telemedia Ventures Inc. 2003–05; Sr Adviser, Stikeman Elliott LLP 2003–07; Pres. and CEO CBC/Radio-Canada 2008–; Adjunct Prof., Faculty of Law, Univ. of Montreal; basketball commentator, Télévision de Radio-Canada during Summer Olympics 1984, 1988, 1996; fmr weekly contrib. to Hebdo-sports show, Radio Canada; mem. Bd of Dirs Zarlink Semiconductor Inc. 1992–, Transcontinental Inc., ITS Investments Ltd Partnership; Chair. SFK Pulp Fund; Dir Montreal Gen. Hosp. Foundation; fmr Dir Donohue Inc., Circo Craft Co. Inc., Adventure Electronics Inc., Cambior Inc., Secor Inc., Michelin Canada Inc.; Trustee Lucie and André Chagnon Foundation, Martlet Foundation (McGill Univ.). *Address:* Canadian Broadcasting Corporation, 181 Queen Street, Ottawa, ON K1P 1K9, Canada (office). *Telephone:* (613) 288-6000 (office). *E-mail:* liaison@cbc.ca (office). *Website:* www.cbc.ca (office).

LACROIX, Jean-Pierre, BA; French diplomatist and UN official; *Under-Secretary-General, UN Peacekeeping Operations;* b. 2 May 1960; ed École supérieure des sciences économiques et commerciales, Univ. Sciences-Po, Paris, École nat. d'admin; long career with Ministry of Foreign Affairs (MFA), including as First Sec., Perm. Mission to UN, New York 1990–93, Adviser, Cabinet of the Prime Minister 1993–95, First Sec. and Second Counsellor, Embassy in Washington, DC 1995–98, Second Counsellor and Deputy Chief of Mission, Embassy in Prague 1998–2002, Deputy Dir, UN and Int. Orgs Div., MFA 2002–06, Deputy Perm. Rep. of France to UN, New York 2006–09, Chief of Protocol, MFA 2009–10, Amb. to Sweden 2011–14, Dir for UN, Int. Orgs, Human Rights and La Francophonie, MFA 2014–17; Under-Sec.-Gen., Peacekeeping Operations, UN 2017–. *Address:* Department of Peacekeeping Operations, United Nations Secretariat, New York, NY 10017, USA (office). *Telephone:* (212) 963-4275 (office). *Fax:* (212) 963-3452 (office). *Website:* www.un.org/en/peacekeeping (office).

LACSON, Panfilo Morena 'Ping', BS (Eng), BS, MA; Philippine politician; b. 1 June 1948, Imus, Cavite; adopted s. of Cebu Lacson; m. Alice Perio de Lacson; three s.; ed High School, Imus Inst., Lyceum of the Philippines, Philippine Mil. Acad., Pamantasan ng Lungsod ng Maynila; joined Philippine Constabulary 1971, with Metrocom Intelligence and Security Group 1971–86, PC-INP Anti-Carnapping Task Force 1986–88; Prov. Commdr Prov. of Isabela 1988–89; Commdr Cebu Metrodiscom 1989–92; Prov. Dir Prov. of Laguna Feb.–July 1992; Chief, Presidential Anti-Crime Comm., Task Force Habagat 1992–95; Project Officer, Special Project Alpha 1996; Chief, Presidential Anti-Organized Crime Task Force 1998–2001, Chief, Philippine Nat. Police 1999–2001; mem. Laban ng Demokratikong Pilipino (LDP) Party; senatorial cand. Feb. 2001; elected Senator May 2001–13, 2016–; Asst Minority Floor Leader 2001–; Presidential Asst for Rehabilitation and Recovery 2013–15; presidential cand. 2004; One of Ten Outstanding Policemen of the Philippines 1988, Philippine Mil. Acad. Alumni Achievement Award 1988, Philippine Constabulary Metrodiscom Officer of the Year 1992, two Outstanding Achievement Medals, five Bronze Cross Medals, 17 Military Merit Medals, three Medalya ng Kadakilaan, three Medalya ng Kagalingan Awards. *Address:* Room 504, 5th Floor, Senate of the Philippines, GSIS Building, Financial Center, Roxas Blvd, Pasay City, The Philippines (office). *Telephone:* (2) 552-6601 (office). *Fax:* (2) 552-6743 (office). *E-mail:* costaff@pinglacson.ph (office); senlacson@pinglacson.ph. *Website:* www.senate.gov.ph (office).

LACUNZA MAESTROJUÁN, HE Cardinal José Luis, OAR; Panamanian (b. Spanish) ecclesiastic; *Bishop of David;* b. 24 Feb. 1944, Pamplona, Spain; ed Minor Seminary of San José of Augustinian Fathers, Spain, Nat. Univ. of Panama; ordained priest, Order of Augustinian Recollects (OAR) 1969; sent to Panama 1971; Auxiliary Bishop of Panamá 1985–94; consecrated Titular Bishop of Parthenia 1986; attained Panamanian nationality 1986; Bishop of Chitré 1994–99; Bishop of David 1999–; Pres. Episcopal Conf. of Panama 2000–04,

2007–13; cr. Cardinal (Cardinal-Priest of San Giuseppe da Copertino) 2015. *Address:* Obispado, Apartado 0426-00109, David, Chiriqui, Panamá (office). *Telephone:* 775-2916 (office). *Fax:* 774-3920 (office).

LACY, Alan J., BS, MBA; American business executive and financial analyst; ed Georgia Inst. of Tech., Emory Univ.; began career with Kraft Foods Inc., various sr financial positions at Dart and Kraft Inc., Sr Vice-Pres. Finance and Strategy Kraft General Foods; fmr Vice-Pres. Financial Services and Systems, Philip Morris Cos Inc.; fmr Pres. Philip Morris Capital Corpn; Sr Vice-Pres. Finance, Sears Roebuck and Co. 1994–95, Exec. Vice-Pres. and Chief Financial Officer 1995–97, Pres. Credit 1997–98, Pres. Credit and Chief Financial Officer 1998–99, Pres. Services 1999–2000, Chair. and CEO 2000–05, Vice-Chair. and CEO Sears Holding Corpn (formed from merger of Sears and Kmart Holding Corpn) 2005–06; mem. Bd Dirs Bristol-Myers Squibb Company, The Economic Club of Chicago, Lyric Opera of Chicago, Nat. Retail Fed.; mem. Civic Cttee Commercial Club of Chicago; Trustee, Fidelity Funds; mem. Bd Trustees, Field Museum of Natural History; Trustee and Past Chair. Nat. Parks Conservation Asscn.

ŁĄCZKOWSKI, Paweł Julian, DSoc; Polish politician and university teacher; *Head of Political Council, Alliance of Polish Christian Democrats;* b. 31 July 1942, Kielce; m. Maria Łączkowska; one s. three d.; ed Adam Mickiewicz Univ., Poznań; fmr scientific worker, Adam Mickiewicz Univ., Poznań 1966–90, 1994–; contract Prof., Collegium Polonicum, Słubice; mem. Solidarity Ind. Self-governing Trade Union 1980–; Deputy to Sejm (Parl.) 1989–93, 1997–2001, Deputy Chair. Civic Parl. Club 1989–90, Chair. Sejm Circle of Christian Democrats 1990–91, Chair. Parl. Club of Christian Democrats' Party (PChD) 1991–93, Parl. Comm. for Regulations and Deputies 1997–2001, mem. Solidarity Election Action Parl. Caucus 1997–2001; Co-founder Christian Democrats' Party (PChD) 1990, Leader 1992–99, merged with two other parties to form Alliance of Polish Christian Democrats 1999, currently Head of Political Council; Deputy Prime Minister 1992–93; Deputy Chair. Presidium Nat. Bd Solidarity Election Action 1999–2001; mem. Co-ordination Team Solidarity Election Action (AWS) 1996–99; Officer's Cross, Order of Polonia Restituta 2011. *Publications:* Circumstances for Stabilizing Worker Staff in Industrialized Districts 1977; numerous articles. *Leisure interest:* gardening. *Address:* Porozumienie Polskich Chrzescijanskich Demokratów, Sejm, ul. Wiejska 4/6, 00-902 Warsaw, Poland (office). *Telephone:* (61) 8520120 (home).

LADARIA FERRER, HE Cardinal Luis Francisco, DTheol; Spanish theologian and ecclesiastic; *Prefect of the Congregation for the Doctrine of the Faith;* b. 19 April 1944, Manacor, Mallorca; ed Univ. of Madrid, Comillas Pontifical Univ.; mem. Soc. of Jesus 1966–; ordained to the priesthood 29 July 1973; Prof. of dogmatic theology and the history of dogma, Comillas Pontifical Univ. 1975–, Pontifical Gregorian Univ., Rome 1984– (Vice-Rector 1986–94); Titular Archbishop of Thibica 2008–; cr. Cardinal 2018; mem. Int. Theological Comm. 1992–, Sec.-Gen. 2004–08, Pres. 2017–; Consultor to Congregation for the Doctrine of the Faith (CDF) 1995–, Sec. 2008–17, Prefect of CDF 2017–; Pres. Pontifical Biblical Comm. 2017–, Pontifical Comm.'Ecclesia Dei' 2017–; hon. degrees (Pontifical Univ. of Salamanca and Pontifical Univ. of Comillas, Madrid) 2014. *Address:* Palazzo del Sant'Uffizio, Piazza del Sant'Uffizio, 11, 00193 Rome, Italy (office). *Website:* www .vatican.va (office).

LADD, Paul, BSc, MSc; British economist and UN official; *Director, United Nations Research Institute for Social Development (UNRISD);* b. 18 July 1973, Stourport-on-Severn; ed Univ. of Warwick; Financial Adviser, Central Bank of Guyana 1995–97; Econ. Adviser for South Africa, Botswana, Lesotho, Namibia and Swaziland, UK Dept of Int. Devt, Pretoria 1997–2001; Chief Economist, Christian Aid (charity), London 2001–04; Policy Adviser, HM Treasury, London 2004–05; Sr Policy Adviser on Devt Finance, UNDP 2006–08, Sr Econ. Affairs Officer in Exec. Office of UN Sec.-Gen. 2008–09, led UNDP policy team on inclusive globalization and head of team that prepared UNDP's contribution to Sept. 2010 Review Summit on Millennium Devt Goals 2009–11, Dir, Team on Post-2015 Devt Agenda, UNDP –2015, Dir UN Research Inst. for Social Devt (UNRISD) 2015–; Hon. LLD. *Address:* United Nations Research Institute for Social Development (UNRISD), Palais des Nations, 1211 Geneva 10, Switzerland (office). *Telephone:* 229173020 (office). *Fax:* 229170650 (office). *E-mail:* paul.ladd@un.org (office). *Website:* www .unrisd.org (office).

LADER, Malcolm Harold, OBE, LLB, PhD, MD, DSc, FRCPsych, FMedSci; British professor of clinical psychopharmacology; *Professor Emeritus, Institute of Psychiatry, King's College London;* b. 27 Feb. 1936, Liverpool, England; s. of Abe Lader and Minnie Lader; m. Susan Packer 1961; three d.; ed Liverpool Inst. High School, Univ. of Liverpool, Univs of London; external mem. of scientific staff of MRC 1966–2001; Reader, King's Coll., Univ. of London 1973–78, Prof., Inst. of Psychiatry 1978, now Prof. Emer.; Consultant Psychiatrist, Bethlem Royal and Maudsley Hosps 1970–2001; mem. various UK Govt advisory bodies; Trustee, Psychiatry Research Trust 2002–; Hon. Fellow, American Coll. of Psychiatrists 1994, British Asscn for Psychopharmacology 1994, Soc. for the Study of Addiction 1998; Heinz Karger Memorial Foundation Prize 1974, Taylor Manor Award 1989. *Publications include:* Psychiatry on Trial 1977, Biological Treatments in Psychiatry 1990, Anxiety Panic and Phobias 1997; numerous articles on psychopharmacology. *Leisure interests:* antiques, paintings. *Address:* P 056, Institute of Psychiatry, Denmark Hill, London, SE5 8AF, England (office). *Telephone:* (20) 8650-0366 (office). *Fax:* (20) 7848-0818 (office). *E-mail:* malcolm.lader@kcl.ac.uk (office). *Website:* www.kcl.ac.uk/iop (office).

LADER, Philip, BA, MA, JD; American diplomatist, government official, business executive and lawyer; *Senior Advisor, Morgan Stanley International;* b. 17 March 1946, Jackson Heights, NY; m. Linda LeSourd 1980; two d.; ed Duke Univ., Univ. of Michigan, Univ. of Oxford, UK, Harvard Law School; Pres. Sea Pines Co. 1979–83, Winthrop Univ., SC 1983–85, Bond Univ., Gold Coast, Australia 1991–93, Business Execs for Nat. Security, 1991; Exec. Vice-Pres. Sir James Goldsmith's US Holdings 1986–89; Deputy Dir for Man., Office of Man. and Budget, Exec. Office of the Pres. 1993; Chair. Pres.'s Council for Integrity and Efficiency 1993, Pres.'s Man. Council, Policy Cttee, Nat. Performance Review 1993; Deputy Chief of Staff and Asst to Pres., White House 1993–94; Admin., US Small Business Admin. and mem. Pres.'s Cabinet 1995–97; Amb. to UK 1997–2001; Chair. WPP plc 2001–15; Sr Advisor, Morgan Stanley Int. 2001–; Partner, Nelson,

Mullins, Riley & Scarborough; Founder Renaissance Weekends 1981–; mem. Bd of Dirs, AES, WPP, Marathon Oil, UC Rusal Corpns, Smithsonian Museum of American History, Atlantic Council; mem. Council of Lloyds 2003–10, Council on Foreign Relations; mem. Chief Execs Org., Prince of Wales' Trust Advisory Bd; mem. Int. Advisory Council, Columbia Univ. 2007–, Advisory Bd, Yale Divinity School 2007–; Trustee, British Museum 2001–06, RAND Corpns 2001–11 (Vice-Chair. 2010–11), 21st Century Foundation, Windsor Leadership Trust, St Paul's Cathedral Foundation 2001–10, Bankinter Foundation for Innovation in Spain 2005–, Salzburg Global Seminar 2006–; Hon. Fellow, Pembroke Coll., Oxford, London Business School, John Moores Univ.; 14 hon. doctorates; RSA Benjamin Franklin Medal 2001, Urban Land Inst. Award for Excellence in Large scale Community Devt 1983, Nat. Gold Medal, Council for the Advancement and Support of Educ. 1986. *Leisure interests:* reading, tennis, walking. *Address:* Morgan Stanley International, 20 Bank Street, Canary Wharf, London, E14 4AD, England; 151 Meeting Street, Suite 600, Charleston, SC 29401, USA (home). *Telephone:* (20) 7425-6524 (London); (843) 534-4141 (home). *E-mail:* philip.lader@gmail.com. *Website:* www.morganstanley.com (office); www.nelsonmullins.com (office); www.renaissanceweekend.org (office).

LADREIT DE LACHARRIÈRE, Marc; French business executive; *President, Fimalac SA;* b. 6 Nov. 1940, Nice; s. of Pierre Ladreit de Lacharrière and Hélène Mora; m. Sibylle Lucet 1967 (divorced); one s. three d.; ed Ecole Nat. d'Admin; Asst Man. Banque de Suez et de l'Union des Mines 1970, Asst Dir 1971, Deputy Dir 1973; Vice-Pres. Masson Belfond Armand Colin 1974–95; Vice-Dir Banque de l'Indochine et de Suez 1975, Corp. Affairs Dir 1976; Financial Dir L'Oréal 1976, Man. Dir Admin. and Finance 1977, Vice-Pres. Man. Cttee 1978, mem. Strategic Cttee, Dir and Exec. Vice-Pres. 1984–91, Pres. of Finances 1987–91, mem. Bd Dirs L'Oréal Finance 1984–; Pres. La Revue des deux Mondes 1990–, Financière Marc de Lacharrière (Fimalac, holding co.) 1991–, Council Banque de la Mutuelle industrielle 1988; Vice-Pres. Sofres 1992–97; fmr Vice-Pres. Centenaire Blanzy, Pres. 1994–98; Pres. Financière Sofres 1992–97, Lille Bonnières & Colombe et Alspi 1993–96, Comptoir Lyon Allemand Louyot 1995–96; Chair. Geral, USA, Fitch Ratings, Inc., Fondation Culture & Diversité 2006, Agence France-Muséums (Louvre Abu Dhabi) 2007, Supervisory Bd Webedia 2013; Man. Dir Regefi and Holdilux, Luxembourg; Vice-Chair. L'Oréal (GB), Editions Masson; UNESCO Goodwill Amb. 2009; Dir Collection de l'Institut de l'Entreprise, France Télécom 1995–98, Air France 1996–97, Canal+ 1998–, Flo Group 1998–, Louvre Museum 1999–, Renault 2002–, Casino, Cassina; mem. Int. Council Renault Nissan 2000–; mem. Consultative Cttee, Banque de France; mem. Bd Conseil Arstistique des Musées Nationaux, Fondation Bettencourt Schueller, Soc. des Amis du Musée du Quai Branly, Fondation Nationale des Sciences Politiques, Musée du Louvre, Le Siècle, Strategic Cttee for French Econ. Attractiveness; Lecturer, Inst. d'Etudes Politiques, Paris 1971, then Prof.; Adviser, Foreign Trade of France; Hon. Pres. Inst. of Research and Study for Corp. Security (IERSE); mem. Académie des Beaux-Arts 2006; Grand Croix, Légion d'honneur, Officier, Ordre Nat. du Mérite, Officier des Arts et Lettres. *Publication:* Le droit de noter 2012. *Leisure interests:* tennis, skiing. *Address:* Fimalac, 97 rue de Lille, 75001 Paris, France (office). *E-mail:* contact@fimalac.com (office). *Website:* www.fimalac.com (office).

LADSOUS, Hervé; French diplomatist and UN official; b. 12 April 1950; m.; three c.; ed École nationale des langues orientales; Vice-Consul in Hong Kong 1973–75, with Econ. Affairs Div., Ministry of Foreign Affairs 1976–81, Second Counsellor, Embassy in Canberra 1981–83, Beijing 1983–86, Second Counsellor, Perm. Mission to UN, Geneva 1986–88, First Counsellor 1988–90, Asst Dir for the Americas, Ministry of Foreign Affairs 1990–92, Acting Chargé d'affaires a.i., Embassy in Port-au-Prince 1991–92, First Counsellor, Perm. Mission to UN, New York 1992–94, Minister Counsellor 1994–97, Perm. Rep. to OSCE, Vienna 1997–2001, Amb. to Indonesia 2001–03 (also accred to Timor Leste 2002–03), Communications Dir Ministry of Foreign Affairs 2003–05, Dir for Asia and Oceania 2005, Amb. to People's Repub. of China 2006–10, Chief of Staff to Minister for Foreign Affairs 2010–11; Under-Sec.-Gen. for Peacekeeping Operations, UN 2011–17; Chevalier, Légion d'honneur; Officier, Ordre nat. du Mérite.

LADUTSKA, Mikalay Alyaksandravich; Belarusian government official; b. 21 March 1959, Minsk; ed Belarusian Polytechnic Inst., Acad. of State Admin under Aegis of Pres. of Belarus; worked as a Foreman, Deputy Sec., Sec. Cttee of Leninist Young Communist League of Byelorussia, Dept 256, Minsk Production Asscn of Industrial House-Building, First Sec. Frunze Region Cttee of Leninist Young Communist League of Byelorussia, Minsk, Deputy Section Head, Cen. Cttee of Leninist Young Communist League of Byelorussia, Instructor, Frunze Region Cttee, Head of Section, Dept 256, Minsk Production Asscn of Industrial House-Building, Head of Section, Minsk Leasing Enterprise of Industrial House-Building 'Minskzhilstroy', Head of Construction Dept 101, Dir Communal Unitary Enterprise Dept of Capital Construction, Minsk City Exec. Cttee, Head of Frunze Region Admin of Minsk, Deputy Chair., First Deputy Chair., Acting Chair. Minsk City Exec. Cttee –2010, Chair. 2010–14; Merited Builder of Repub. of Belarus, Medal 'For Labour Merits'; Certificate of Honour, Council of Ministers of Repub. of Belarus. *Address:* c/o Minsk City Executive Committee, Nezavisimosti 8, 220030 Minsk, Belarus. *E-mail:* mgik@minsk.gov.by.

LADY GAGA; American singer and songwriter; b. (Stefani Joanne Angelina Germanotta), 28 March 1986, New York, NY; d. of Joseph Germanotta and Cynthia Germanotta (née Bissett); ed Convent of the Sacred Heart School, New York, Tisch School of the Arts, New York Univ.; learned to play piano aged four; wrote first piano ballad aged 13; began performing in New York clubs aged 14; began performing in rock music scene of New York City's Lower East Side 2003; signed with Streamline Records (imprint of Interscope Records); began solo professional singing career 2006–; has written songs for Britney Spears, the Pussycat Dolls; captured attention of Akon, who recognized her vocal abilities, and signed her to his own label, Kon Live Distribution; released her first fragrance, Lady Gaga Fame, in association with Coty, Inc. 2012; launched the Born This Way Foundation 2012; Billboard Rising Star Award 2009, Int. Dance Music Awards for Best Breakthrough Artist 2009, for Best Pop Dance Track (for Just Dance) 2009, MTV Europe Music Award for Best New Act 2009, MTV Video Music Award for Best New Artist 2009, Grammy Award for Best Dance Recording (for Poker Face) 2010, BRIT Awards for Best Int. Breakthrough Act 2010, for Best Int. Female Solo Artist 2010, eight MTV Video Music Awards 2010, Grammy Award for Best Female Pop Vocal Performance (for Bad Romance) 2011, MTV Europe Music Awards for Best Female 2011, 2016, for Biggest Fans 2011, for Best Look 2016, American Music Awards for Favorite Female Artist-Pop/Rock 2017, Golden Globe Award for Best Original Song (for Shallow) 2018, Grammy Award for Best Pop Solo Performance (for Joanne Where Do You Think You're Goin'?) 2019, for Best Pop Duo/Group Performance (for Shallow) (with Bradley Cooper) 2019, Academy Award for Music (Original Song) (for Shallow) (with Mark Ronson, Anthony Rossomando and Andrew Wyatt) 2019. *Tours include:* The Fame Ball Tour 2009, The Monster Ball Tour 2009–11, The Born This Way Ball Tour 2012–13, The Joanne Tour 2016–17. *Recordings include:* albums: The Fame (Grammy Award for Best Electronic/Dance Album 2010, BRIT Award for Best Int. Album 2010) 2008, The Fame Monster (Grammy Award for Best Pop Vocal Album 2011) 2009, Born This Way (two MTV Video Music Awards 2011, MTV Europe Music Award for Best Song, 2011, MTV Europe Music Award for Best Video 2011) 2011, Artpop 2013, Cheek to Cheek (with Tony Bennett) (Grammy Award for Best Traditional Pop Vocal Album 2015) 2014, Joanne 2016; singles: Til It Happens to You 2015, The Cure 2017. *Television includes:* American Horror Story: Hotel (Golden Globe Award for Best Actress – Miniseries or Television Film 2016) 2015–16. *Films:* Muppets Most Wanted 2014, Gaga: Five Foot Two (documentary) 2017, A Star is Born 2018. *Address:* Creative Artists Agency, 12 Hammersmith Grove, Hammersmith, London W6 7AP, England (office). *Telephone:* (20) 8846-3000 (office). *Fax:* (20) 8846-3090 (office). *Website:* www.caa.com (office); www.ladygaga.com.

LAERMANN, Karl-Hans, DrIng; German politician and academic; *Professor Emeritus of Statics, Bergische Universität Wuppertal;* b. 26 Dec. 1929, Kaulhausen, Kr. Heinsberg; s. of Johann Laermann and Elisabeth Laermann; m. Hilde Woestemeyer 1955; three s. one d.; ed Rhenish-Westphalian Coll. of Advanced Tech., Aachen; Lecturer in Experimental Statics, Rhenish-Westphalian Coll. of Advanced Tech. 1966–74; Prof. of Statics, Bergische Univ. G.H. Wuppertal, Head Lab. for Experimental Stress Analysis and Measurement 1974–, now Prof. Emer.; mem. FDP 1968–, mem. Fed. Exec. Cttee 1980–90, N Rhine-Westphalian Exec. Cttee 1978–94, Chair. Fed. Cttee on Research and Tech. of FDP 1981–96; mem. Bundestag (Parl.) 1974–98; Deputy Chair. working group of FDP Parl. Group on Educ. and Science, Research and Tech. 1980–94; Fed. Minister of Educ. and Science Feb.–Nov. 1994; mem. Bd Trustees Volkswagen Foundation 1984–94, Friedrich Naumann Foundation 1984–2010, Anglo-German Foundation for the Study of Industrial Society 1989–99; mem. Admin. Bd Inter Nationes 1995–99; Extraordinary mem. Goethe Inst. 1995–98; Corresp. mem. Accad. delle Scienze dell'Istituto Bologna; Hon. mem. VDI (Verein Deutscher Ingenieure, Asscn of German Engineers); Hon. CBE (UK) 1978, Commdr Order of Orange-Nassau (Netherlands) 1982, Great Cross with Star of Order of FRG 1996; Hon. DrIng (Magdeburg); Dr hc (Tech. Univ. Prague, Transilvania Univ. Braşov, Romania, Tech. Univ. Košice, Slovakia); Gold Medal of Honour, VDI 1999. *Publications:* Konstruktiver Ingenieurbau (Ed.) 1967, Experimentelle Plattenuntersuchungen-Theoretische Grundlagen 1971, Experimentelle Spannungsanalyse I, II 1972, 1977, Perspektiven – Ein Wissenschaftler in der Politik 1984, Optical Methods in Experimental Solid Mechanics (ed.) 2000, Inverse Problems in Experimental Structural Analysis 2008; about 240 publs on science and politics in int. journals. *Leisure interests:* painting, sailing. *Address:* Bergische Universität Wuppertal, FBD, Pauluskirche str. 7, 42285 Wuppertal (office); Am Tannenberg 19, 41189 Mönchengladbach, Germany (home). *Telephone:* (202) 4394249 (office); (2166) 58164 (home). *Fax:* (202) 4394078 (office); (2166) 958077 (home). *E-mail:* laermann.kh@t-online.de (home); laermann@uni-wuppertal.de (office). *Website:* www.uni-wuppertal.de (office).

LAFER, Celso, MA, PhD; Brazilian legal scholar, academic, international organization official and fmr government official; b. 7 Aug. 1941, São Paulo; s. of A. Jacob Lafer and Betty Lafer; m. Mary Macedo de Camargo Neves Lafer; two s. one d.; ed Faculty of Law, Univ. of São Paulo, Cornell Univ., USA; Prof. of Law, Univ. of São Paulo 1971–2011, now Prof. Emer.; Minister of Foreign Affairs 1992, 2001–02; Amb. to WTO and UN, Geneva 1995–98, Chair. WTO Gen. Council 1997, Dispute Settlement Body 1996; Minister of Devt, Industry and Commerce 1999–; mem. Consultative Bd to Dir Gen. WTO 2003–04; Chair. Panel of Dispute Settlement Body 1998–99, 2010; Pres. São Paulo Foundation for Advancement of Research (FAPESP) 2007–15; mem. Brazilian Acad. of Science 2004, Brazilian Acad. of Letters 2006; Hon. Fellow, Hebrew Univ. Jerusalem 2006; numerous decorations, including Grand Cross Rio Branco 1992, Grand Cross San Martin (Argentina) 1995, Grand Cross, Infante Dom Henrique (Portugal) 2001, Grand Cross Rio Branco (Brazil) 2002, Grand Officer, Légion d'honneur 2002, Grand Cross Scientific Merit (Brazil) 2002; Dr hc (Buenos Aires Univ.) 2001, (Cordoba Univ.) 2002, (Univ. Três de Febrero) 2011, (Univ. Jean Moulin Lyon 3) 2012, (Univ. of Haifa) 2014, (Univ. of Birmingham) 2014. *Address:* Avenida Brigadeiro Faria Lima 1306, Jardim Paulistano, 01451-914 São Paulo, Brazil (office). *Telephone:* (11) 3035-0060 (office). *E-mail:* c_lafer@uol.com.br.

LAFFAN, Brigid, PhD, MRIA; Irish political scientist and academic; *Director, Robert Schuman Centre for Advanced Studies and Director, Global Governance Programme, European University Institute;* b. 6 Jan. 1955, Co. Kerry; d. of Con Burns and Aileen Burns; m. Michael Laffan 1979; one s. two d.; ed Univ. of Limerick, Coll. of Europe, Bruges, Trinity Coll. Dublin; researcher, European Cultural Foundation 1977–78; Lecturer, Coll. of Humanities, Univ. of Limerick 1979–86; Lecturer, Inst. of Public Admin 1986–89; Newman Scholar, Univ. Coll. Dublin (UCD) 1989–90, Lecturer, Dept of Politics 1990–91, Jean Monnet Prof. of European Politics 1991–2013, Research Dir Dublin European Inst., UCD, Prin. Coll. of Human Sciences 2005–11, Prof. of European Politics, School of Politics and Int. Relations 2011–13; currently Dir, Robert Schuman Centre for Advanced Studies, also Dir, Global Governance Programme, European Univ. Inst.; Visiting Prof., Coll. of Europe, Bruges 1992–2004, European Univ. Inst., Florence, Italy 2011, Harvard Univ., USA 2012; adviser on EU enlargement, Oireachtas (Parl.) Foreign Affairs Cttee; mem. Council, Inst. of European Affairs, Dublin; mem. Irish Govt Asia Strategy Group 2005–10; Chevalier, Ordre nat. du Mérite 2010; Theseus Award for Outstanding Research on European Integration 2012, UACES Lifetime Achievement Award 2014. *Publications:* Ireland and South Africa 1988, Integration and Co-operation in Europe 1992, Constitution Building in the European Union (ed.) 1996, The Finances of the European Union 1997, Europe's Experimental Union: Re-thinking Integration (co-author) 1999, Renovation or Revolution: New Territorial Politics in Ireland and the United Kingdom (contributing co-ed. with J. Coakley and J. Todd) 2005, Ireland in the European Union (with Jane O'Mahoney) 2008, Core-periphery Relations in the European Union (co-ed. with J. M. Magone and C. Schweiger) 2016; numerous articles on Irish foreign policy, EC budgetary policy, insts, governance and political union. *Leisure interests:* theatre, reading, swimming. *Address:* Robert Schuman Centre for Advanced Studies, European University Institute, Via delle Fontanelle 18, 50014 San Domenico di Fiesole, Italy (office); 4 Willowbank, The Slopes, Dun Laoghaire, Co. Dublin, Ireland (home). *Telephone:* (055) 4685792 (office); (1) 2862617 (home). *E-mail:* brigid.laffan@eui.eu (office). *Website:* www.eui.eu/DepartmentsAndCentres/RobertSchumanCentre (office).

LAFFITTE, Pierre Paul; French engineer and politician; b. 1 Jan. 1925, St Paul, Alpes Maritimes; s. of Jean Laffitte and Lucie Fink; m. 1st Sophie Glikman-Toumarkine (deceased); m. 2nd Anita Garcia; ed Lycée de Nice, Ecole Polytechnique, Ecole des Mines de Paris; Dir Office of Geological, Geophysical and Mining Research 1953; Asst Dir-Gen. Office of Geological and Mining Research 1959–62, Deputy Dir 1963, Dir 1973–84; Gen. Engineer Mines 1973–; Pres. Conseil de Perfectionnement, Ecole Nat. Supérieure des Mines, Paris 1984–91; Founder Pres. Sophia-Antipolis 1969; Pres. Franco-German Asscn for Science and Tech., AFAST (German-French Asscn for Science and Tech.); Senator from Alpes Maritimes 1985–2008, now Hon. Senator; Pres. Rassemblement Democratique et Social Europeen 2008; Hon. Chair. Groupe européen de politique des clusters (pôles de compétence), EC 2009–; Officier, Légion d'honneur, Officier, Ordre nat. du Mérite, Commdr, Order of Polar Star (Sweden), Commdr, Order of Merit (Germany); Dr hc (Colorado School of Mines, USA) 1984, (Open Univ., England) 1990; De Gaulle-Adenauer Prize 1994, Prix du promoteur de la société de l'information 2004. *Publications:* works on mining and geology, science parks, the information age, local development. *Leisure interest:* gardening. *Address:* Sophia Antipolis, place Sophie Laffitte, 06560 Valbonne (office); Palais du Luxembourg, 75291 Paris Cedex 06; Ecole des Mines, 60 boulevard Saint Michel, 75006 Paris, France. *Telephone:* (4) 92-96-78-00 (office); (4) 93-32-85-90 (home). *Fax:* (4) 93-32-95-26 (home). *E-mail:* p.laffitte@senat.fr (office). *Website:* www.sophia-antipolis.com (office).

LAFFORGUE, Laurent, DèsSc; French mathematician and academic; *Permanent Professor of Mathematics, Institut des Hautes Etudes Scientifiques;* b. 6 Nov. 1966, Antony, Hauts-de-Seine; ed Ecole Normale Supérieure, Université de Paris-Sud XI; taught at École Spéciale Militaire, Saint-Cyr-Coëtquidan 1991–92; Research Fellow, CNRS 1990–2000, Research Dir 2000; Perm. Prof. of Math., Institut des Hautes Etudes Scientifiques, Bures-sur-Yvette 2000–; mem. Acad. des Sciences 2003–; mem. editorial cttee for Math. Publs, Institut des Hautes Etudes Scientifiques, editorial cttee Moscow Mathematical Journal; Chevalier, Légion d'Honneur; Prix Peccot and Cours Peccot, Collège de France 1996, Invited Lecturer, Int. Congress of Mathematicians, Berlin 1998, Bronze Medal, CNRS 1998, Clay Research Award 2 2000, Jacques Herbrand Prize in Math., Acad. des sciences, Paris 2001, Fields Medal, 24th Int. Congress of Mathematicians, Beijing (jtly) 2002. *Publications:* Chtoucas de Drinfeld et conjecture de Ramanujan-Petersson Astérisque 243 1997, Une compactification des champs classifiant les chtoucas de Drinfeld JAMS 1998, Chtoucas de Drinfeld et correspondance de Langlands Inventiones 147 2002, Chirurgie des Grassmanniennes CRM Monograph Series 19 2003, La Débâcle de l'école (with Liliane Lurçat) 2007; numerous articles in math. journals on number theory and analysis. *Address:* Institut des Hautes Etudes Scientifiques, Le Bois-Marie 35, route de Chartres, 91440 Bures-sur-Yvette, France (office). *Telephone:* 1-60-92-66-00 (office). *Fax:* 1-60-92-66-09 (office). *E-mail:* laurent@ihes.fr (office). *Website:* www.ihes.fr (office).

LAFLEY, Alan George, AB, MBA; American business executive; b. 13 June 1947, Keene, NH; ed Hamilton Coll., Harvard Business School; served with USN 1970–75; brand asst, Joy, Procter & Gamble Co. 1977–78, sales training, Denver Sales Dist 1978–80, Asst Brand Man. Tide 1978–80, Brand Man. Dawn & Ivory Snow 1980–81, Ivory Snow 1981–82, Cheer 1982–83, Assoc. Advertising Man. PS & D Div. 1983–86, Advertising Man. 1986–88, Gen. Man. Laundry Products PS & D Div. 1988–91, Vice-Pres. Laundry and Cleaning Products 1991–92, Group Vice-Pres., Pres. Laundry and Cleaning Products 1992–94, Group Vice-Pres. Far East Div. 1994–95, Exec. Vice-Pres., Pres. Asia Div. 1995–98, Exec. Vice-Pres. North American Div. 1998–99, Pres. Global Beauty Care and North America 1999–2000, Pres. and CEO Procter & Gamble Co. 2000–02, Chair., Pres. and CEO 2002–07, 2013–15, Chair. and CEO 2007–09, Chair. 2009–10, 2015–16; Sr Advisor, Clayton, Dubilier & Rice 2010–13; Chair. Cincinnati Center City Devt Corpn (3CDC); mem. Bd of Dirs General Electric Co., Dell, Inc., Grocery Mfrs of America, United Negro Coll. Fund; fmr mem. Bd Dirs General Motors Corpn; mem. The Business Council, The Business Roundtable, McKinsey Advisory Council, The Lauder Inst. Bd of Govs (Wharton School of Arts and Sciences), Harvard Business School Bd of Dean's Advisors; mem. American Soc. of Corp. Execs; fmr mem. American Chamber of Commerce in Japan, G100 (fmrly The M&A Group); Trustee, Hamilton Coll., US Council for Int. Business; fmr Trustee, Cincinnati Fine Arts Fund, Cincinnati Playhouse in the Park, Cincinnati Symphony Orchestra, Medical Center Fund of Cincinnati, The Seven Hills School, Xavier Univ. *Address:* c/o The Proctor & Gamble Co., 1 Procter & Gamble Plaza, Cincinnati, OH 43202-3315, USA. *E-mail:* info@pg.com.

LAFON, Jean-Pierre; French international organization official and fmr diplomatist; *Vice-President, Chirac Foundation;* b. 2 March 1941; ed Lycée Condorcet, Institut d'Etudes Politiques, Ecole Nationale d'Administration; mil. service in Germany 1964; Lecturer, Ecole Nationale d'Administration, Côte d'Ivoire 1964–66; joined Ministry of Foreign Affairs 1968, Second then First Sec., Embassy in London 1971–74, mem. Del. to Conf. on Security and Co-operation in Europe, Geneva 1973–74; with Econ. Affairs Div., Ministry of Foreign Affairs 1974–76; Adviser, Embassy in Iran 1977–79; Inspector of Foreign Affairs 1980–83, Head of Méthodes-Formation-Informatique Div. 1983–84; Consul in Arlit, Niger 1984–85; Adviser to Cabinet of Jacques Chirac 1986–88; Dir UN Div., Ministry of Foreign Affairs 1989–94; Amb. to Lebanon 1994–97; Pres. French Council for Protection of Refugees 1997–2002; Amb. to China 2002–04; Sec.-Gen. of Foreign Affairs 2004–06; Pres. Bureau int. des expositions, Paris 2007–12; Founding mem. and Vice-Pres. Chirac Fondation 2008–; Chevalier, Légion d'Honneur 1991, Officier, Ordre National du Mérite 2003, Commdr, Ordre National du Mérite 2008, Officer, Order of Saint Charles de Monaco 2011. *Telephone:* (7) 62-26-12-34 (office). *Website:* www.fondationchirac.eu (office).

LAFONT, Bruno; French business executive; *Co-Chairman, LafargeHolcim;* b. 1956; ed Hautes Etudes Commerciales, Paris, Ecole Nationale d'Admin, Paris; joined Lafarge SA as internal auditor in Finance Dept 1983, Chief Financial Officer Sanitaryware Div., Germany 1984, Chief Div. Finance Dept 1986–88, Int. Devt Dept 1988–89, Vice Pres. Lafarge Cement and Aggregates and Concrete operations, Turkey 1990–94, Group Exec. Vice-Pres., Finance and mem. Exec. Cttee 1994–98, Exec. Vice-Pres. Gypsum Div. 1998–2003, COO Lafarge SA 2003–06, mem. Bd of Dirs 2005–, CEO 2006–15, Chair. 2007–15 (co. merged with Holcim to become LafargeHolcim 2015), Co-Chair. LafargeHolcim 2015–; mem. Bd of Dirs, EDF 2008–, Arcelor Mittal 2011–; Co-Chair. World Business Council for Sustainable Devt's (WBCSD) Cement Sustainability Initiative, also Co-Chair. Energy Efficiency in Buildings initiative launched with United Technologies under aegis of WBCSD; Special Adviser to Mayor of Chongqing, China; Pres. Enterprises for the Environment Asscn 2009–. *Address:* LafargeHolcim Ltd, Zürcherstrasse 156, 8645 Jona, Switzerland (office). *Telephone:* (58) 8585858 (office). *Fax:* (58) 8585859 (office). *E-mail:* info@lafargeholcim.com (office). *Website:* www.lafargeholcim.com (office).

LAFONTAINE, Oskar; German politician; b. 16 Sept. 1943, Saarlouis; s. Catherine Lafontaine and Hans Lafontaine; m. Doris Vartan 1984; one step-d.; m. Sahra Wagenknecht; ed Univs of Bonn and Saarbrücken; Mayor of Saarbrücken 1976–85; mem. Saarland Landtag (Regional Parl.), Minister-Pres. 1985–98; Chair. SPD Regional Asscn, Saar 1977–96; mem. SPD Cen. Cttee; Vice-Chair. SPD 1987–96; Cand. for Chancellorship 1990; Leader SPD 1995–99 (resgnd); Minister of Finance 1998–99 (resgnd); Chair. Die Linke (The Left party) 2007–10 (resgnd). *Publications include:* Angst vor den Freunden 1983, Der andere Fortschritt 1985, Die Gesellschaft der Zukunft 1988, Das Lied vom Teilen 1989, Deutsche Wahrheiten 1990, Keine Angst vor der Globalisierung (jtly) 1998, Das Herz schlägt links (autobiog.) 2000, Portrait eines Rätselhaften 2013.

LAFONTANT, Jack Guy; Haitian physician, politician and fmr head of state; b. 4 April 1961, Port-au-Prince; m. 1st, one s. one d.; m. 2nd Marie-Nirva Blaise; one d.; ed State Univ. of Haiti; worked as gastroenterologist, Los Cayos Hosp. 1987–88; medical consultant, Ministry of Labour, Public Transport and Communications 1990; worked at Univ. Hosp. of Fort-de-France, Martinique 1992–94; Dir, Hôpital Sainte Croix, Léogâne 1995–2005; Prof. of gastroenterology, State Univ. of Haiti and Notre Dame Univ. in Haiti (UNDH) 2005; Prime Minister 2017–18; mem. Medical Asscn of Haiti, American Coll. of Gastroenterology; Leader, Mouvement Démocratique pour la Libération d'Haïti-Parti du Rassemblement Démocratique d'Haïti (MODELH-PRDH). *Address:* c/o Office of the Prime Minister, 33 blvd Harry S Truman, BP 6114, Port-au-Prince, Haiti (office).

LAGARDE, Christine Madeleine Odette, MA; French lawyer, government official and international organization official; *Madame Chairman of the Executive Board and Managing Director, International Monetary Fund;* b. 1 Jan. 1956, Paris; d. of Robert Lallouette and Nicole Lallouette; m. (divorced); two s.; partner Xavier Giocanti from 2006; ed Lycée Claude Monet, Le Havre, Holton-Arms School, Bethesda, Md, USA, Univ. Paris X, Institut d'études politiques d'Aix-en-Provence (Sciences Po Aix); worked as an intern at US Capitol, Washington, DC as William Cohen's congressional asst; started career as Lecturer at Univ. of Paris X; joined Baker & McKenzie LLP (law firm) 1981, apptd Partner 1987, Man. Partner 1991–95, elected to Global Exec. Cttee 1995, Chair. European Regional Council and Professional Devt Cttee 1995–98, Chair. Exec. Cttee 1999–2004, Chair. Global Policy Cttee 2004–05, f. European Law Centre, Brussels; Minister for Foreign Trade 2005–07, of Agric. 2007, of Economy, Finance and Industry 2007–11; Madame Chair. Exec. Bd and Man. Dir IMF 2011–; mem. Supervisory Bd, ING Group April–June 2005; mem. Int. Advisory Bd Escuela Superior de Administración y Dirección de Empresas (ESADE), Barcelona; mem. Int. Bd of Overseers, Illinois Inst. of Tech.; mem. Bd and Sec., Execs Club of Chicago; mem. Strategic Council on Attractivity of France; Co-Chair. US-Europe-Poland Action Comm., Center for Strategic and Int. Studies; mem. Int. Business Advisory Bd, Mayor of Beijing; ordered by Court of Justice of the Repub. to stand trial for alleged negligence in handling the Bernard Tapie arbitration approval Dec. 2015, found guilty of negligence but court declined to impose a penalty Dec. 2016; Chevalier, Légion d'honneur 2000, Officier 2012; Commdr, Ordre du Mérite agricole; Dr hc (Katholieke Universiteit Leuven, Belgium, Université de Montréal, Canada); ESADE Jaume Cordelles Award 2004, Richard Dimbleby Lecturer 2014. *Achievements include:* mem. French nat. synchronized swimming team as a teenager. *Leisure interests:* yoga, scuba diving, swimming, gardening. *Address:* International Monetary Fund, 700 19th Street NW, Washington, DC 20431, USA (office). *Telephone:* (202) 623-7000 (office). *Fax:* (202) 623-6278 (office); (202) 623-4661 (office). *E-mail:* publicaffairs@imf.org (office). *Website:* www.imf.org (office).

LAGARDE, Paul, DenD; French academic; *Professor Emeritus of Law, University of Paris I;* b. 3 March 1934, Rennes; s. of Gaston Lagarde and Charlotte Béquignon; m. Bernadette Lamberts 1962; two s. one d.; ed Univ. of Paris; Prof., Faculty of Law, Nancy 1961–69, Nanterre 1969–71; Prof. of Private Int. Law, Univ. of Paris I 1971–2001, now Prof. Emer.; Gen. Sec. Revue critique de droit international privé 1962, Ed.-in-Chief 1976, Dir 1990–2012; Pres. Comité Français de droit int. privé 1987–90; Conseiller d'Etat en service extraordinaire 1996–2001; Gen. Sec. Comm. Int. de l'Etat Civil 2000–09; Founder-mem. Groupe européen de droit int. privé (GEDIP); mem. Inst. of Int. Law; Chevalier, Légion d'honneur; Dr hc (Freiburg im Breisgau, Athens, Würzburg); Prize of Foundation Alexander von Humboldt 1992, Le droit int. privé: esprit et méthodes: Mélanges en l'honneur de Paul Lagarde (publ. in his honour) 2005, Hague Prize for Int. Law 2011. *Publications:* Recherches sur l'ordre public en droit international privé 1959, La réciprocité en droit international privé 1977, Le principe de proximité dans le droit international privé contemporain 1987, Traité de droit international privé (with Henri Batiffol) 1993, La nationalité française 2011, La reconnaissance des situations en droit international privé 2013. *Address:* 65 avenue Félix Faure, 75015 Paris, France. *Telephone:* 1-45-58-30-89. *E-mail:* paul.lagarde@orange.fr.

LAGARDÈRE, Arnaud; French media executive; *General and Managing Partner, Lagardère SCA;* b. 18 March 1961, Boulogne-Billancourt; s. of Jean-Luc Lagardère; m. Jade Foret; two c.; ed Lycée Janson-de-Sailly, Paris, Univ. of Paris

IX-Dauphine; Chair. Grolier Inc., USA 1994–98; Chair. and CEO Lagardère Media 1999–, Chair. Lagardère Active Broadcast (Europe 1) 2001–07, Gen. and Man. Partner, Lagardère SCA 2003–, Chair. Supervisory Bd, Lagardère Services, Lagardère Active, Chair. Exec. Cttee, Lagardère Sports and Entertainment, Chair. and CEO Lagardère Capital & Management; fmr Head, Dept of Emerging Activities and Electronic Media, Matra; mem. Bd of Dirs EADS NV 2003–13, Chair. (non-exec.) 2003–07, 2012–13; mem. Supervisory Bd, Daimler AG 2005–10; Dir, Hachette Livre; Chair. Jean-Luc Lagardère Foundation; Chevalier, Légion d'honneur 2008. *Address:* Lagardère SCA, 4 rue de Presbourg, 75116 Paris, France (office). *Telephone:* 1-40-69-16-00 (office). *E-mail:* secretariatal@lagardere.fr (office). *Website:* www.lagardere.com (office).

LAGAYETTE, Philippe Ernest Georges; French government official and business executive; *Honorary Chairman, Institut des Hautes Etudes Scientifiques (IHES);* b. 16 June 1943, Tulle (Corrèze); s. of Elie Lagayette and Renée Portier; m. Marie-Louise Antoni 1979; two s. two d.; ed Ecole Polytechnique and Ecole Nat. d'Admin, Paris; Eng Génie Maritime 1965; Insp. des Finances 1970; Deputy Dir Treasury Man., Ministry of Economy, Finance and Budget 1980; Dir Cabinet of Minister of Economy, Finance and Budget 1981–84; Deputy Gov. Banque de France 1984, First Deputy Gov. 1990; Insp.-Gen. des Finances 1988; Dir-Gen. Caisse des Dépôts et Consignations 1992–97; Chair. and CEO JP Morgan et Cie SA, JPMorgan Chase NA Group 1998–2008, apptd Vice-Chair. JPMorgan EMEA (Europe, Middle East and Africa) 2008, Man. Dir Paris Man. Cttee JP Morgan Chase Bank; Chair. Institut des Hautes Etudes Scientifiques (IHES) 1995–2014, now Hon. Chair.; Chair. French American Foundation 2003–, Fondation pour la recherche sur la maladie d'Alzheimer, PL Conseils; Bd mem. Comm. des Operations de Bourse (French Stock Market Regulator) 1989–92, Eurotunnel (now TNU PLC) 1993–2004, Club Mediterranee 1993–2003, PPR 1999–, Kering SA 1999–16, Fimalac 2003–, Renault 2007– (mem., Compensation Cttee, Audit, Risk and Ethics Cttee), Barclays PLC –2016, La Poste; mem. Council Institut Jacques Delors; Officier, Légion d'honneur, Commdr, Ordre nat. du Mérite. *Leisure interests:* hunting, tennis, skiing, cinema. *Address:* IHES, Le Bois-Marie, 35 rte de Chartres, 91440 Bures-sur-Yvette, France (office). *Telephone:* 1-60-92-66-00 (office). *E-mail:* comdev@ihes.fr (office). *Website:* www.ihes.fr (office).

LAGE DÁVILA, Carlos, MD; Cuban politician; b. 15 Oct. 1951, Havana; ed Univ. of Havana; trained as pediatrician 1970s; apptd Pres. Fed. of Univ. Students 1975; worked as physician at Hosp. Pediátrico d La Habana; sent to Ethiopia in charge of medical mission; apptd First Sec., UJOTAC 1981; mem. Grupo de Coordinación y Apoyo del Comandante en Jefe (Fidel Castro's inner staff) 1986; mem. Politburo; apptd Vice-Pres. and Exec. Sec., Council of Ministers 2009.

LAGHDAF, Moulaye Ould Mohamed, DèsSc; Mauritanian diplomatist and politician; *Secretary-General of the Presidency;* b. 1957, Nema; m.; four c.; ed Univ. of Liège, Univ. of Louvain; expert on Africa, The Caribbean and The Pacific, Centre for Industrial Devt 1991–97; Co-ordinator of devt project for Hodh Chargui region 2000–06; Amb. to Belgium and EU 2006–08, Prime Minister 2008–14; Sec.-Gen., the Presidency 2015–. *Publications include:* Enrichissement des minerais d'oxyde de cuivre 1983, Utilisation des schistes bitumineux en tant que matière minérale et organique en cimenterie 1984, Combustion des gaz dans un lit fluidisé 1992, Lutte contre les émissions d'oxyde d'azote 1992. *Address:* Office of the Secretary-General of the Presidency, BP 184, Nouakchott, Mauritania (office).

LAGO, Eduardo, MA, PhD; Spanish writer and academic; *Professor of Spanish and Latin American Literature, Sarah Lawrence College;* b. 1954, Madrid; ed Universidad Autónoma de Madrid, Grad. Center, City Univ. of New York; Prof. of Spanish and Latin American Literature, Sarah Lawrence Coll. 1993–; Exec. Dir Instituto Cervantes, New York 2006–; Co-founder Order of Finnegans; Bartolomé March Award for Excellence in Literary Criticism 2001. *Publications include:* Cuaderno de México 2000, Cuentos Dispersos 2000, Llámame Brooklyn (novel) (Premio Nadal Prize 2006, City of Barcelona Literary Prize for Literature 2007, National Critics Award 2007, Lara Foundation Award for Best Critical Reception 2007) 2006, Ladrón de mapas 2008; has translated work by Henry James, Hamlin Garland, William Howells, John Barth, Sylvia Plath, among others. *Address:* Sarah Lawrence College, 1 Mead Way, Bronxville/Yonkers, NY 10708, USA (office). *E-mail:* elago@sarahlawrence.edu (office). *Website:* /www.sarahlawrence.edu/faculty/lago-eduardo.html (office).

LAGOS ESCOBAR, Ricardo, PhD; Chilean economist, lawyer, politician and fmr head of state; *President, Fundación Democracia y Desarrollo (Foundation for Democracy and Development);* b. 2 March 1938, Santiago; m. Luisa Durán; five c.; ed Univ. of Chile, Duke Univ., USA; Prof., Univ. of Chile 1963–72, fmr Head School of Political and Admin. Sciences, fmr Dir Inst. of Econs, Gen. Sec. 1971; Visiting Prof., Univ. of N Carolina, Chapel Hill, USA 1974–75; Chair. Alianza Democrática 1983–84, Partido por la Democracia 1987–90; Minister of Educ. 1990–92, of Public Works 1994; Pres. of Chile 2000–06; Founder and Pres. Fundación Democracia y Desarrollo (Foundation for Democracy and Devt) 2006–; Pres. Club de Madrid 2006–09, mem. Bd of Dirs 2006–; UN Sec.-Gen.'s Special Envoy on Climate Change 2007–; Prof. at Large, Brown Univ., USA. *Publications:* Población, Pobreza y Mercado de Trabajo en América Latina 1997, numerous books and articles on econs and politics. *Address:* Fundación Democracia y Desarrollo, Roberto del Rio 1151, Providencia, Santiago, Chile (office). *Telephone:* (2) 333-80-98 (office); (2) 333-94-14 (office). *Fax:* (2) 334-23-61 (office). *E-mail:* cbudnik@fdd.cl (office). *Website:* www.fundaciondemocraciaydesarrollo.cl (office).

LAGRAVENESE, Richard, BFA; American screenwriter, director and producer; b. 30 Oct. 1959, Brooklyn, New York; s. of Patrick LaGravenese and Lucille LaGravenese; m. Ann Weiss LaGravenese 1986; one d.; ed Lafayette High School, Emerson Coll. and New York Univ.; Ind. Film Project Writer of the Year, Best Original Screenplay 2000, Distinguished Screenwriter Award, Austin Film Festival 2002, Ian McClellan Hunter Award for Career Achievement, Writers Guild Awards 2016. *Films include:* Rude Awakening 1989, The Fisher King (also actor) 1991, The Ref (also producer) 1994, A Little Princess 1995, The Bridges of Madison County 1995, Unstrung Heroes 1995, The Mirror Has Two Faces 1996, The Horse Whisperer 1998, Living Out Loud (also dir) 1998, Beloved 1998, The Legend of Bagger Vance 1999, Erin Brockovich (uncredited co-writer) 2000, Blow (actor) 2001, The Defective Detective 2002, A Decade Under the Influence (also producer and dir) 2003, Monster-in-Law 2005, Paris, je t'aime (dir) 2006, Freedom Writers (dir) 2007, P.S. I Love You (also dir) 2007, Conviction 2010, Water for Elephants 2011, Beautiful Creatures (also dir) 2013, Behind the Candelabra 2013, The Last Five Years (also dir and producer) 2014, Unbroken 2014, Pushing Dead (producer) 2016. *Television includes:* The Divide (creator, teleplay and producer) 2014, Dangerous Liaisons (film) (also exec. producer) 2014. *Leisure interests:* theatre, books, family. *Address:* c/o 3 Arts Entertainment, 9460 Wilshire Blvd, 7th Floor, Beverly Hills, CA 90212, USA (office). *Telephone:* (310) 888-3200 (office). *Fax:* (310) 888-3210 (office). *Website:* www.3arts.com (office).

LAGU, Lt-Gen. Joseph; South Sudanese politician, army officer and diplomatist; b. 21 Nov. 1931, Moli; s. of Yakobo Yanga and Marini Kaluma; ed Rumbek Secondary School, Mil. Acad. Omdurman; served in Sudanese Army 1960–63; joined South Sudan Liberation Movt 1963, Leader SSLM 1969; signed peace agreement with Govt of Sudan March 1972; Vice-Pres. of Sudan 1978–80, 1982–85; Pres. Supreme Exec. Council for the South 1978–80; fmr Perm. Rep. to UN; moved with his family to UK; Order of the Two Niles 1972. *Publication:* The Anya-Nya – What We Fight For 1972.

LAGUARTA, Ramon Luis, MBA; Spanish business executive; *President and CEO, PepsiCo, Inc.;* b. 1964, Barcelona; m. Maria Laguarta; three c.; ed ESADE Business School, Thunderbird School of Global Man.; began career with various int. roles in Asia, Europe, Middle East and USA with Chupa Chups, SA; joined PepsiCo, Inc. 1996, becoming Gen. Man. for Greece Snacks and Marketing Vice-Pres. for Spain Snacks 1999–2001, Gen. Man. for Iberia Snacks and Juices 2002–06, Commercial Vice-Pres., PepsiCo Europe 2006–08, Pres. Developing Markets Europe 2010–14, CEO PepsiCo Europe and Sub-Saharan Africa 2014–17, Pres. Pepsico, Inc. 2017–18, Pres. and CEO 2018–, also mem. Bd of Dirs (Oct. 2018–). *Address:* PepsiCo, Inc., 700 Anderson Hill Road, Purchase, Harrison, NY 10577, USA (office). *Telephone:* (914) 253-2000 (office). *Website:* www.pepsico.com (office).

LAGUMDŽIJA, Zlatko, MSc, PhD; Bosnia and Herzegovina politician; b. 26 Dec. 1955, Sarajevo; s. of Salko Lagumdžija; m. Amina Lagumdžija; three c.; ed Univ. of Sarajevo, Harvard Univ., USA; Visiting Prof., Univ. of Arizona, USA 1988–89; Prof. of Econ. and Electrical Eng, Univ. of Sarajevo 1989–, Dir Centre for Man. and Computer Tech. 1995; Vice-Chair. Council of Ministers of Bosnia and Herzegovina 1993–96, 2012–, Chair. 2001–02; mem. House of Reps of Parl. Ass. 1996–2014; Minister of Foreign Affairs and Treas. of the Insts of Bosnia and Herzegovina 2001–02, Minister of Foreign Affairs 2002–03, 2012–15; Co-founder Social and Democratic Party of Bosnia and Herzegovina (Socijaldemokratska Partija BiH) 1990, Chair. 1997–2014. *Address:* c/o Ministry of Foreign Affairs, 71000 Sarajevo, Musala 2, Bosnia and Herzegovina.

LAHHAM, Duraid, BSc; Syrian actor, comedian and director; b. 27 Jan. 1934, Damascus; m. 1st May al-Husayni two c.; m. 2nd Hala Bitar; one d.; ed Univ. of Damascus; Instructor, Chem. Dept, Univ. of Damascus 1955–60; stage roles 1960–; starred in mini-series Sahret Dimashq (Damascus Evening) on Syrian TV with Nihad Qali 1960, cr. duo called Duraid & Nihad, achieved dramatic success in Arab World until Qali retired from acting due to illness in 1976; joined cast of TV drama Abwab Al Rih (Gates of the Wind) to play role of Yousif Al Nahhas 2014–; Pres. Syrian Assoc. of Artists 1967; UNICEF Rep. in Syria for Children's Affairs 1990, UNICEF Amb. for Childhood in the Middle East and North Africa 1999–2004; Medal of the Syrian Repub. (Excellence Class) 1976, Medal of the Tunisian Repub. 1979, Medal of the Libyan Repub. 1991, Order of Merit of the Lebanese Repub. 2000. *Theatre includes:* Ukd al-Lulu (The Pearl Necklace) 1966, Masrah al-Shawk (The Thorn Theatre) 1968, Qadiyyah wa Haramiyya (A Cause and Thieves) 1972, Day'at Tishreen (October Village) 1974, Ghorba (Alienation) 1976, Kasak ya Watan (Cheers to the Homeland) 1978, Shaka'ik al-Nu'man (Anemones) 1987, Sani' al-Matar (The Rainmaker) 1992, Al-Asfura al-Sa'ida (The Happy Bird) 1992. *Films include:* Ghawar La'eb al-Kura (Ghawar the Football Player), Ukd al-Lulu (The Pearl Necklace) 1965, Al-Lus al-Zarif (The Nice Thief), Al-Sa'alik (The Crooks) 1968, Al-Sadikan (The Two Friends), Al-Sheridan (The Two Homeless Men), Al-Millionera (The Millionaire), Gharam fi Istanbul (Love Affair in Istanbul) 1967, Maqlab min al-Maksik (A Prank from Mexico), Lika' fi Tadmur (Rendezvous in Palmyra), Al-Rajul al-Munasib (The Right Man), Fundok al-Ahlam (The Dream Hotel) 1966, Khayyat lil Sayyidat (A Seamstress for Women) 1969, Wahid Za'ed Wahid (One plus One), Al-Nassaben al-Thalatha (The Three Crooks), Misk wa Anbar (Misk and Anbar), Al-Muzayafun (The Imposters), Al-Tha'lab (The Fox), Zawjati min al-Hippez (My Hippie Wife), Ana Antar (I am Antar), Imra'a Taskun Wahdiha (A Women Lives on Her Own), Sah al-Nawm (Good Morning), Abd al-Latiff Fathi, Ghawar James Bond, Indama Taghib al-Zawjat (When Wives are Absent), Samak bala Hasak (Fish with no Skeleton), Imbaratoriyyat Ghawar (The Empire of Ghawar), Al-Hudud (The Border), Al-Takrir (The Report), Kafroun. *Television includes:* Al-Ijaza al-Sa'ida (The Happy Holiday) 1960, Sahret Dimashq (Damascus Evening) 1960, Maqalib Ghawar (Ghawar's Pranks) 1966, Hammam al-Hana (Pleasant Bath) 1968, Sah al-Nawm (Good Morning) 1971, Sah al-Nawm (Part 2) 1972, Melh wa Sukkar (Salt and Sugar) 1972, Wayn al-Ghalat (Where is the Error?) 1980, Wadi al-Misk (Misk Valley) 1982, Al-Doghri (The Doghri) 1991, Ahlam Abu al-Hana (The Dreams of Abu al-Hana) 1994, Awdet Ghawar (The Return of Ghawar) 1999, A'ilati wa Ana (My Family and I) 2001, Ala Mas'uliyati (On My Responsibility) 2002, Alam Doreid (Doreid's World, Doreid haza al-Mas'a (Doreid this Evening). *Publications:* author of several comedies. *Leisure interest:* accordionist. *Address:* c/o Syrian Broadcasting Corporation, Omayya Square, Damascus, Syria. *E-mail:* info@duraidlahham.com. *Website:* www.duraidlahham.com.

LAHIRI, Susanta, MSc, PhD, DSc; Indian chemist and academic; *Senior Professor, Chemical Sciences Division, Saha Institute of Nuclear Physics;* b. 1 Aug. 1961, Darjeeling, West Bengal; mem. Faculty, Saha Inst. of Nuclear Physics, Kolkata 1997–, now Sr Prof., Chemical Sciences Div.; Prof., Homi Bhabha Nat. Inst.; Hevesy Medal, Int. Cttee on Activation Analysis of the Modern Trends in Activation Analysis Confs (ICAA-MTAA) (co-recipient) 2015. *Achievements include:* co-creator of element 117, Ununseptium (Uus). *Publications:* more than 210 papers in professional journals on heavy ion induced radioisotope production, converter targets, green chemistry and tracer packet techniques. *Address:* Chemical Sciences Division, Saha Institute of Nuclear Physics, 1/AF, Bidhannagar, Kolkata, 700064, West Bengal, India (office). *Telephone:* (33) 2337-5345 (office). *Fax;* (33) 2337-4637 (office). *E-mail:* susanta.lahiri@saha.ac.in (office). *Website:* www.saha.ac.in (office).

LAHLAIDI, Abdelhafid, PhD; Moroccan professor of medicine and cardiovascular specialist; *Chief, Department of Morphology, Université Mohammed V;* b. 20 May 1942, Essaouira; m.; three c.; ed Univ. of Paris, France, Univ. of Geneva, Switzerland; Professorial Asst, Faculty of Medicine, Univ. of Geneva, Switzerland 1973; Prof., Faculty of Medicine, Université Mohammed V 1973–, Chief, Dept of Morphology; Fellow, Islamic Acad. of Sciences 1990–; Fellow Académie Islamique des Sciences; mem. New York Acad. of Sciences; Grand Prix Scientifique, Morocco 1986, Prix Scientifique du Président de la République Tunisienne 1987, Prix Scientifique du Président de la République Algérienne 1989, Médaille d'or de l'Académie Nationale Française de Médecine 1990, Médaille de l'Académie des Sciences, Jordan 1991. *Publications:* Anatomie topographique, Applications, Anatom-Chirurgicles (five vols) 1986. *Leisure interests:* painting, writing. *Address:* Université Mohammed V, BP 6203, Rabat Institute, Rabat (office); Temara – Les Vieux Marocains, Allée 3, Maison 121, Rabat, Morocco (home). *Telephone:* (37) 77-04-21 (office); (37) 74-10-27 (home). *Fax:* (37) 77-37-01 (office); (37) 67-30-56 (home). *E-mail:* lahlaidi@online.fr (office); lahlaidi@gmail.com (home). *Website:* www.emi.ac.ma (office).

LaHOOD, Raymond (Ray) H., BS; American fmr politician and fmr government official; *Senior Policy Advisor, DLA Piper;* b. 6 Dec. 1945, Peoria, Ill.; m. Kathleen LaHood; two s. two d.; ed Canton Jr Coll., Bradley Univ.; began career as teacher 1971–77; Dist Admin. Asst to US Congressman Tom Railsback 1977–82; mem. Ill. State House of Reps 1982; Chief of Staff to US Congressman and House Minority Leader Bob Michels, Washington, DC 1982–94; mem. US House of Reps from 18th Ill. Dist 1995–2009; US Sec. of Transportation, Washington, DC 2009–13; Sr Policy Advisor, DLA Piper (law firm) 2014–; Co-Chair. Building America's Future 2014–; Republican; Dr hc (Lincoln Coll.) 2000, (Eureka Coll.) 2002, (Tri-State Univ.) 2004, (MacMurray Coll.) 2006. *Publication:* Seeking Bipartisanship: My Life in Politics 2015. *Address:* DLA Piper, 500 8th Street, NW, Washington, DC 20004, USA (office). *Telephone:* (202) 799-4000 (office). *Website:* www.dlapiper.com (office).

LAHOUD, Gen. Émile Jamil; Lebanese politician, naval officer and fmr head of state; b. 12 Jan. 1936, Baabdat; s. of Gen. Jamil Lahoud and Adrinée Badjakian; m. Andrée Amadouni 1967; two s. one d.; ed Brumana High School, also attended various courses at Naval Acads in UK and USA 1958–80; joined Mil. Acad. as cadet officer 1956, promoted to Sub-Lt 1959, Lt 1962, Lt Commdr 1969, Commdr 1974, Capt. 1980, Rear Adm. 1985, Vice-Adm. 1989, Commdr of Second Fleet 1966–68, of First Fleet 1968–70; Staff of Army Fourth Bureau 1970–72, Chief of Personal Staff of Gen. Commdr of Armed Forces 1973–79, Dir of Personnel, Army HQ 1980–83; Head of Mil. Office, Ministry of Defence 1983–89; C-in-C of Armed Forces 1989; Pres. of Lebanon 1998–2007; Lebanese Medal of Merit Gen. Officer 1989; War Medals 1991, 1992; Dawn of the South Medal 1993; Nat. Unity Medal 1993; Medal of Esteem 1994; Grand Cordon, Order of the Cedar 1993; numerous int. decorations, including Grand Cross (Argentina) 1998; Order of Merit Sr Officer Level (Italy) 1997; Order of Hussein ibn Ali (Jordan) 1999, King Abdul-Aziz Collar (Saudi Arabia) 2000, Great Collar of the Union (UAE) 2000, Great Collar of Mubarak (Kuwait) 2000, Great Collar of the Nile (Egypt) 2000, Great Collar of Independence (Qatar) 2000, Great Collar of the Khalifite Order (Bahrain) 2000, Great Cross, Légion d'honneur 2001, Al Muhammadi Decoration Extraordinary Grade (Morocco) 2001, Order of November 7th (Tunisia) 2001, Great Cross, Order of the Redeemer (Greece) 2001, Grand Cordon, Nat. Order of Oumaya (Syria) 2002, Nat. Order of Merit Al-Athir (Algeria) 2002, Order of the Repub. (Yemen) 2002, Grand Cross, Ipiranga Order (Brazil) 2004, Grand Cross with Chain, Order of Merit (Hungary) 2004, Grand Cross, Order of Merit (Poland) 2004, Kt Grand Cross of Merit with Gold Plate, Sacred Mil. Constantinian Order of St George 2005. *Publication:* Method and Style, Promise and Fulfilment. *Leisure interests:* diving, swimming, reading, music. *Address:* c/o Presidential Palace, Baabda, Beirut, Lebanon. *E-mail:* president_office@presidency.gov.lb.

LAI, Ching-te, (William Lai), BS, MD, MPH; Taiwanese politician and fmr physician; b. 6 Oct. 1959, Wanli; m. Wu Mei-ru; two s.; ed Nat. Taiwan Univ., Nat. Cheng Kung Univ., Harvard Univ.; Attending Physician, Nephrology Dept, Nat. Cheng Kung Univ. Hosp. and Sin-Lau Hosp. of the Presbyterian Church in Taiwan 1991–94; mem. Third Nat. Ass. (fmr parl.) 1996–99; mem. Legislative Yuan (parl.) 1999–2010; Mayor of Tainan 2010–17; Premier of Taiwan 2017–19; mem. Democratic Progressive Party. *Address:* c/o Executive Yuan, No.1, Sec. 1, Zhongxiao E. Road, Zhongzheng District, Taipei 10058, Taiwan (office).

LAI, Jimmy; Hong Kong business executive, journalist and publisher; b. (Lai Chee-Ying), 1948, Guangzhou, Guangdong, China; Propr Giordano (retail clothing chain) 1980–, Chair. 1980–94; Founder and Chair. Next Media, titles include Next Magazine 1990–2014, Apple Daily 1995, Sharp Daily 2006. *Address:* c/o Next Magazine, Next Media, 8 Chun Ying Street, T. K. O. Industrial Estate West, Tseung Kwan O, Kowloon, Hong Kong, Special Administrative Region, People's Republic of China (office).

LAI, Shin-yuan, MA, MPhil, DPhil; Taiwanese politician; *Ambassador of the Separate Customs Territory of Taiwan, Penghu, Kinmen and Matsu, World Trade Organization;* b. 9 Nov. 1956, Taichung; ed London School of Econs and Univ. of Sussex, UK; Dir and Research Fellow, Div. of Int. Affairs, Taiwan Inst. of Econ. Research 1996–2000; Dir Gen. Chinese Taipei Pacific Basin Econ. Cttee 1996–2000; Founder and Dir Chinese Taipei APEC Study Centre 1997–2000; Adjunct Assoc. Prof., Grad. School for Social Transformation Studies, Shih Hsin Univ. 1997–98; Adjunct Assoc. Prof., Dept of Int. Business Man., Tamkang Univ. 1997–2008; Dir Gen. Confed. of Asia-Pacific Chambers of Commerce and Industry 1999–2000; Sec.-Treas., Asian Bankers Asscn 1999–2000; Sr Adviser, Nat. Security Council 2000–04; chief negotiator for Taiwan's accession to WTO 2001; adviser to Taiwan WTO Centre, Chung-Hua Inst. for Econ. Research 2004; mem. Legis. Yuan 2005–08; Minister, Mainland Affairs Council, Exec. Yuan 2008–12; Amb. of the Separate Customs Territory of Taiwan, Penghu, Kinmen and Matsu to WTO 2012–. *Address:* Ministry of Foreign Affairs, 2 Kaitakeland Blvd, Taipei 10048, Taiwan (office). *Telephone:* (2) 23482999 (office). *Fax:* (2) 23805678 (office). *E-mail:* eyes@mofa.gov.tw (office). *Website:* www.mofa.gov.tw (office).

LAIDLAW, (William) Samuel (Sam) Hugh, MA, MBA, FRSA; British solicitor and energy industry executive; b. 3 Jan. 1956, Kensington, London; s. of Sir Christopher Laidlaw; m. Deborah (Debbie) Morris-Adams 1989; three s. one d.; ed Eton Coll., Gonville and Caius Coll., Cambridge, Institut Européen d'Admin des Affaires (INSEAD), Fontainebleu, France; solicitor, Macfarlanes, London 1977–79; Corp. Planner, Société Françaises Pétroles BP, Paris 1979–80; Man. of Corp. Planning, Amerada Hess Corpn, New York City, USA 1981–83, Vice-Pres. Amerada Hess Ltd, London 1983–85, Man. Dir 1986–95, Chair. 1995, Exec. Vice-Pres. Amerada Hess Corpn 1993–95, Pres. and COO, London 1995–2001; CEO Enterprise Oil 2001–03; Exec. Vice-Pres. Chevron Corpn 2003–06; Chief Exec. Centrica plc 2006–14, Chair. Exec. Cttee, Disclosure Cttee; Dir (non-exec.) Hanson plc 2003–07, HSBC Holdings plc 2008–; Lead Dir (non-exec.), Dept for Transport 2010–; mem. Bd of Dirs Business Council for Int. Understanding; mem. Prime Minister's Business Advisory Group 2010–12; Trustee, RAFT (medical charity); mem. UK Council of INSEAD; fmr Pres. UK Offshore Operators Asscn; fmr Chair. Petroleum Science and Tech. Inst., Abderdeen; fmr mem. UK Energy Advisory Panel; chaired a report on Business and Higher Educ. for the CBI 2010; led inquiry into West Coast Rail Franchise 2012. *Address:* c/o Centrica plc, Millstream, Maidenhead Road, Windsor, Berks., SL4 5GD, England. *E-mail:* info@centrica.co.uk.

LAIDLER, David Ernest William, PhD, LLD, FRSC; Canadian/British economist and academic; *Professor Emeritus, University of Western Ontario;* b. 12 Aug. 1938, Tynemouth, Tyne and Wear, England; s. of John Alphonse Laidler and Leonora Laidler (née Gosman); m. Antje Charlotte Breitwisch 1965; one d.; ed Tynemouth School, London School of Econs, Univs of Syracuse and Chicago, USA; Asst Lecturer, LSE 1961–62; Asst Prof., Univ. of Calif., Berkeley 1963–66; Lecturer, Univ. of Essex 1966–69; Prof., Univ. of Manchester 1969–75; Prof. of Econs, Univ. of Western Ont. 1975–2004, Bank of Montreal Prof. 2000–04, Prof. Emer. 2004–, Dept Chair. 1981–84; Special Adviser, Bank of Canada 1998–99; Scholar-in-Residence, CD Howe Inst., Toronto 1990–, Fellow-in-Residence 1999–, Canadian Bankers Asscn Fellow 2000–03; Visiting Economist, Reserve Bank of Australia 1977; Assoc. Ed. Journal of Money, Credit and Banking 1979–; mem. Editorial Bd Pakistan Devt Review 1987–, European Journal of the History of Econ. Thought 1993–; Co-Founder and mem. Exec. Cttee Money Study Group 1970–75; mem. Econs Cttee, CNAA 1971–75, Econs Cttee, SSRC 1972–75, Consortium on Macroeconomic Modelling and Forecasting, ESRC 1981–88, Econ. Advisory Panel to Minister of Finance, Canada 1982–84; Co-ordinator, Research Advisory Group on Econ. Ideas and Social Issues, Royal Comm. on Econ. Union and Devt Prospects for Canada (Macdonald Comm.) 1984–85; Dir Philip Allan Publrs Ltd 1972–99; Pres. Canadian Econs Asscn 1987–88; Distinguished Fellow, History of Econs Soc. 2009; Fellow, Canadian Econs Asscn 2012; Hon. mem. European Soc. for the History of Econ. Thought 2010; Canadian Econs Asscn Douglas Purvis Prize 1994, Hellmuth Prize, Univ. of Western Ontario 1999, Thomas Guggenheim Prize 2015. *Publications:* The Demand for Money 1969, Essays on Money and Inflation 1975, Monetarist Perspectives 1982, Taking Money Seriously 1990, The Golden Age of the Quantity Theory 1991, The Great Canadian Disinflation (co-author) 1993, Money and Macroeconomics: Selected Essays 1998, Fabricating the Keynesian Revolution 1999, Two Percent Target (co-author) (Donner Prize) 2004, Macroeconomics in Retrospect: Selected Essays 2004. *Leisure interests:* going to concerts, opera and theatre. *Address:* 45–124 North Centre Road, London, ON, N5X 4R3 (home); C.D. Howe Institute, 67 Yonge Street, Suite 300, Toronto, ON M5E 1J8 (office); Department of Economics, Room 4090, SSC, University of Western Ontario, London, ON, N6A 5C2, Canada (office). *Telephone:* (416) 865-1904 (C.D. Howe) (office); (519) 661-3400 (office); (519) 673-3014 (home). *Fax:* (416) 865-1866 (C.D. Howe) (office); (519) 661-3666 (office). *E-mail:* laidler@uwo.ca (office); cdhowe@cdhowe.org (office). *Website:* www.ssc.uwo.ca/economics/faculty/Laidler (office); www.cdhowe.org (office).

LAINE, Dame Clementina (Cleo) Dinah, DBE; British singer; b. 28 Oct. 1927, Southall, Middx; m. 1st George Langridge 1947 (dissolved 1957); one s.; m. 2nd John Philip William Dankworth 1958 (died 2010); one s. one d.; joined Dankworth Orchestra 1953; lead role in Seven Deadly Sins, Edinburgh Festival and Sadler's Wells 1961; acting roles in Edinburgh Festival 1966, 1967; f. Wavendon Stables Performing Arts Centre (with John Dankworth) 1970; numerous appearances with symphony orchestras performing Façade (Walton) and other compositions; Julie in Showboat, Adelphi Theatre 1971; title role in Colette, Comedy Theatre 1980; Desiree in A Little Night Music, Mich. Opera House, USA 1983; The Mystery of Edwin Drood, Broadway, New York 1986; Into the Woods (US Nat. Tour) 1989; frequent tours and TV appearances, Europe, Australia and USA; Freedom of Worshipful Co. of Musicians 2002; Hon. MA (Open Univ.) 1975, Hon. DMus (Berklee School of Music) 1982, (York) 1993, (Cambridge) 2004, Hon. DA (Luton) 1994; Melody Maker and New Musical Express Top Girl Singer Awards 1956, Moscow Arts Theatre Award for acting role in Flesh to a Tiger 1958, top place in Int. Critics' Poll of American Jazz magazine Downbeat 1965, Woman of the Year (9th annual Golden Feather Awards) 1973, Edison Award 1974; Variety Club of GB Show Business Personality Award (with John Dankworth) 1977, TV Times Viewers' Award for Most Exciting Female Singer on TV 1978, Grammy Award for Best Jazz Vocalist-Female 1985, Best Actress in a Musical (Edwin Drood), Theatre World Award for Edwin Drood 1986, Nat. Asscn of Recording Merchandisers (NARM) Presidential Lifetime Achievement Award 1990, Vocalist of the Year (British Jazz Awards) 1990, Lifetime Achievement Award (USA) 1991, ISPA Distinguished Artists Award 1999, Back Stage Bob Harrington Lifetime Achievement Award (with John Dankworth) 2001, BBC British Jazz Awards Lifetime Achievement Award (with John Dankworth) 2002. *Film:* Last of the Blonde Bombshells 2000. *Recordings include:* albums: Smilin' Through (with Dudley Moore) 2005, I Hear Music 2007. *Publications:* Cleo: An Autobiography 1994, You Can Sing If You Want To 1997. *Leisure interest:* painting. *Address:* The Old Rectory, Wavendon, Milton Keynes, MK17 8LT, England (home). *Fax:* (1908) 584414 (home). *Website:* www.quarternotes.com (office).

LAINE, Jermu Tapani, LLM; Finnish politician, lawyer and author; b. 17 Sept. 1931, Turku; s. of Johan Laine and Feb Emilia Heinonen; m. Terttu Anneli Rock 1954; three d.; ed Univ. of Helsinki, Univ. of Pennsylvania, USA; with Ministry of Trade and Industry 1955–65; Lecturer in Commercial Studies, Valkeakoski 1965–69; Rector, Commercial Inst., Mänttä 1969–78; municipal positions in Valkeakoski and Mänttä 1968–69; Political Sec. to Prime Minister Sorsa 1972–73; Minister for Foreign Trade 1973–75; mem. Parl. 1975–87; Minister, Ministry of Finance 1982–83; Minister for Foreign Trade 1983–87; Chair. Supervisory Bd

Valmet Og 1987–88; Dir-Gen. Finnish Customs Bd 1988–94; Chair. Finnish Nat. Theatres; mem. Social Democratic Party. *Plays:* Paniikkihäiriö 2001, Marie Curie, Puhdas käsi piirakassa, Mosan mamma, Äitini tunsi Kekkosen. *Publications:* Autobiography 1991, Alexis de Toqueville 1999, Finland in 1906 2006, Finnish Foreign Trade towards the West 2006. *Leisure interests:* literature, theatre, cinema.

LAING, Catriona, CB, MSc, MBA; British diplomatist and government official; *High Commissioner to Nigeria;* m. Clive David Bates; one d.; ed London School of Econs, Cranfield School of Man.; Planning Officer, Ministry of Works, Transports and Communication, Botswana 1986–89; Asst Economist, West Africa Dept, Overseas Devt Admin (ODA) 1989–90, Asst Economist, British Devt Div., East Africa 1990–91, Econ. Adviser, Aid Policy Dept 1992–93; Head of UN Devt Office, UN Mission, Somalia 1993–94, Econ. Adviser, Latin America, Caribbean and Atlantic Dept and Dept for Int. Devt (DFID) 1994–95, Team Leader EU and Int. Econ. Policy Dept 1996–98, Head of Eastern Europe, Western Hemisphere Policy Dept 1999–2000, mem. Globalization White Paper Team March–Dec. 2000; Deputy Dir Prime Minister's Strategy Unit, Cabinet Office 2001–05; Head of Int. Div. Advisory Dept 2005–06, Head of DFID, Sudan 2006–09; Dir Human Rights and Int., Ministry of Justice 2009–12; Sr Support Official for Russia/Ukraine Crisis and Communication, FCO Jan.–Aug 2014; Amb. to Zimbabwe 2014–18, High Commr to Nigeria 2018–. *Address:* British High Commission, Plot 1137, Diplomatic Drive, Central Business District, Abuja, Nigeria (office). *Telephone:* (9) 4623100 (office). *E-mail:* ppainformation.abuja@fco.gov.uk (office). *Website:* www.gov.uk/world/organisations/british-high-commission-abuja (office).

LAING, (John) Stuart, MA, MPhil; British academic and fmr diplomatist; b. 22 July 1948, Limpsfield, Surrey; s. of Denys Laing and Judy Dods; m. Sibella Dorman 1971; one s. two d.; ed Rugby School, Corpus Christi Coll., Cambridge; joined HM Diplomatic Service in 1970, served in Jeddah 1973–75, Brussels 1975–78, Cairo 1983–87, Prague 1989–92 and Riyadh 1992–95, High Commr in Brunei 1999–2002, Amb. to Oman 2002–05, to Kuwait 2005–08; Master, Corpus Christi Coll., Cambridge 2008–18; Pres., British Soc. for Middle Eastern Studies 2017–. *Publications:* Unshook till the End of Time – A History of Britain and Oman (with Robert Alston) 2012, Tippu Tip: Ivory, Slavery and Discovery in the Scramble for Africa 2017. *Leisure interests:* playing chamber music, hill walking, desert travel. *Address:* The Old Manor, West Overton, Marlborough, Wiltshire, SN8 4ER, England (office). *Telephone:* (16) 7286-1600 (office). *E-mail:* sl518@cam.ac.uk (office).

LAJČÁK, Miroslav, JUDr; Slovak diplomatist and politician; *Minister of Foreign Affairs;* b. 20 March 1963, Poprad, Czechoslovak Socialist Repub. (now Slovakia); m. Jarmila Lajčáková Hargašová; two d.; ed Comenius Univ., Bratislava, State Inst. of Int. Relations, Moscow, Russia, George C. Marshall European Center for Security Studies, Garmisch-Partenkirchen, Germany; joined Ministry of Foreign Affairs of Czechoslovakia 1988; served in Czechoslovak Embassy in Moscow, Russian Fed. 1991–93 (Embassy of Slovakia from 1 Jan. 1993); Dir Cabinet of Minister of Foreign Affairs 1993–94, 1998–2001; Dir Cabinet of Prime Minister of Slovakia 1993–94; Amb. to Japan 1994–98, to Yugoslavia (also accred to Albania and Fmr Yugoslav Repub. of Macedonia) 2001–05; Special Asst to UN Sec.-Gen.'s Special Envoy to the Balkans 1999–2001; Dir-Gen. of Political Affairs, Ministry of Foreign Affairs 2005–07; Special Rep. of EU for Common Foreign and Security Policy, Montenegro 2006; High Rep. of Int. Community and Special Rep. of EU, Mission in Bosnia and Herzegovina 2007–09; Minister of Foreign Affairs 2009–10, 2012–; Man. Dir for Russia, Eastern Neighbourhood and the Western Balkans, EU External Action Service, Brussels 2010–12; Deputy Prime Minister 2012–16; Pres. Gen. Ass., UN 2017–18; Person of the Year Award from two Bosnian daily newspapers: Nezavisne novine 2007 and Dnevni Avaz 2007. *Address:* Ministry of Foreign Affairs, Hlboká cesta 2, 833 36 Bratislava 37, Slovakia (office). *Telephone:* (2) 5978-1111 (office). *Fax:* (2) 5978-3333 (office). *E-mail:* info@mzv.sk (office); kami@mzv.sk (office). *Website:* www.mzv.sk (office).

LAJOLO, HE Cardinal Giovanni, BCL; Italian ecclesiastic and diplomatist; *President Emeritus, Governorate of Vatican City State;* b. 3 Jan. 1935, Novara; ordained priest of Novara 1960; entered Vatican diplomatic service 1970, served at Vatican Nunciature in Germany and in Secr. of State; Titular Archbishop of Caesariana and Sec. of Admin of Patrimony of the Apostolic See 1988–95; Apostolic Nuncio to Germany 1995–2003; Sec. for Relations with States 2003–06; Pres. Governorate of Vatican City State 2006–11, Pres. Emer. 2011–, Pontifical Comm. for Vatican City State 2006–11 (retd); cr. Cardinal (Cardinal-Deacon of Santa Maria Liberatrice a Monte Testaccio) 2007; participated in Papal Conclave 2013. *Publications:* I Concordati moderni 1968, Libertà di religione 1971, Le Sette Parole 2010, Maria Silenzi e Parole 2011, Passione Risurrezione 2013, Via Crucis 2013, Lettere alle Amiche 2014, Inviti a Casa Mia 2015, Maria: Ihre Worte, Ihr Schweigen 2015, La Chiesa: Sfide e Speranza 2016. *Address:* Città del Vaticano 00120, Italy. *Website:* www.vatican.va/vatican_city_state.

LAJUNEN, Samppa, MBA; Finnish professional skier and business executive; *CEO, Samla Capital Ltd;* b. 23 April 1979, Turku; ed Univ. of Jyväskylä; entered his first cross-country race aged two; was skiing 300 miles a year by age five; added ski jumping to pursuits aged nine; won overall World Cup title in Nordic combined 1997; Silver Medals, Individual and Team events, Winter Olympics, Nagano, Japan 1998; Gold Medals, Nordic Combined, Sprint and Team events, Winter Olympics, Salt Lake City, USA 2002; First Place, Individual Discipline, World Cup, Nayoro, Japan 2004; Second Place, Sprint Discipline, World Cup, Reit im Winkl, Germany 2004, Seefeld, Austria 2004, Individual Mass Start, Sapporo, Japan 2004, Sprint, Oslo, Norway 2004, Individual Discipline, Oslo 2004; Third Place, Individual Discipline, World Cup, Kuusamo, Finland 2003; Trainee, Man. and Leadership, OP Bank Group 2007–08; Business Controller, Kuiskaaja Oy 2008–10; Founder and Chair. Samla Sponsoring Man. 2010–, CEO Samla Capital Ltd Oy 2015–; f. Sports Club Ltd 2009; mem. Jyvaeskylaen Hiihtoseura Ski Club; now retd. *Address:* Sampa Capital Ltd., Kauppakatu 18 C 26, 40100 Jyväskylä, Finland (office). *Telephone:* (5) 552638 (office). *E-mail:* samppa.lajunen@Samla.fi (office). *Website:* www.samlacapital.fi (office).

LAKATANI, Sani; Niuean politician; b. 1936; Prime Minister of Niue March 1999–2001; Minister for External Affairs, Finance, Customs and Revenue, Econ. and Planning Devt and Statistics, Business and Pvt. Sector Devt, Civil Aviation, Tourism, Int. Business Co. and Offshore Banking, Niue Devt Bank March 1999–2001; fmr Leader Niue People's Party (NPP); Chancellor Univ. of the South Pacific, Fiji 2000–03; Deputy Premier and Minister for Planning, Econ. Devt and Statistics, the Niue Devt Bank, Post, Telecommunications and Information Computer Tech. Devt, Philatelic Bureau and Numismatics, Shipping, Investment and Trade, Civil Aviation and Police, Immigration and Disaster Man. 2002.

LAKE, (William) Anthony (Kirsopp), PhD; American academic, diplomatist, UN official and fmr government official; b. 2 April 1939, New York City; m.; three c.; ed Harvard Coll., Trinity Coll., Cambridge, UK, Woodrow Wilson School of Public and Int. Affairs, Princeton Univ.; joined Foreign Service 1962, Special Asst to Amb. Henry Cabot Lodge, Viet Nam; aide to Nat. Security Adviser Henry Kissinger 1969–70; Head of State Dept's policy planning operation 1977–81; Prof., Amherst Coll., Mass 1981–84, Mount Holyoke Coll. 1984–92; foreign policy adviser to fmr Pres. Clinton during presidential campaign 1992; Nat. Security Adviser 1993–97; served as US Pres.'s Special Envoy to Haiti as well as Ethiopia and Eritrea from 1997; worked with third Exec. Dir of UNICEF, James P. Grant, on org.'s presentation of its flagship publication, 'The State of the World's Children', at the White House, mem. Bd of US Fund for UNICEF 1998–2007, Chair. 2004–07, Perm. Hon. mem. 2007–, Exec. Dir UNICEF 2010–18; Int. Adviser to ICRC 2000–03; Distinguished Prof. in Practice of Diplomacy, Edmund A. Walsh School of Foreign Service, Georgetown Univ. –2010; fmr Chair. Marshall Legacy Inst.; has led Int. Voluntary Services; mem. Bd Save the Children 1975–77; fmr mem. Bd Overseas Devt Council; fmr mem. Bd of Trustees, Mount Holyoke Coll.; fmr mem. Advisory Council, Princeton Inst. for Int. and Regional Studies; has served on Governance Bd of Center for the Study of Democracy at St Mary's Coll. of Maryland; co-f. journal Foreign Policy; White House Samuel Nelson Drew Award 2000. *Publications include:* The 'Tar Baby' Option: American Policy Toward Southern Rhodesia 1976, Third World Radical Regimes: US Policy under Carter and Reagan 1985, Somoza Falling: A Case Study of Washington at Work 1990, Six Nightmares 2001. *Address:* c/o UNICEF House, 3 United Nations Plaza, New York, NY 10017, USA (office).

LAKE-TACK, Louise Agnetha; Antigua and Barbuda nurse, magistrate and government official; b. 26 July 1944, Long Lake Estate, Parish of St Phillips, Antiqua; two c.; ed Antigua Girls High School, Charing Cross Hosp., UK; worked as nurse at Nat. Heart Hosp. and Harley Street Clinic, UK; magistrate Marylebone and Horseferry Magistrate Courts 1995, also sat at Pocock Street Crown Court; Gov.-Gen. of Antigua and Barbuda (first woman) 2007–14; mem. Antigua and Barbuda Nat. Asscn.

LAKER, John, AO, BEcon (Hons), MSc, PhD; Australian business executive; *Chairman, Banking and Finance Oath Ltd;* ed Univ. of Sydney, Univ. of London, UK; worked in Commonwealth Treasury and IMF before joining Int. Dept of Reserve Bank of Australia (RBA) in 1982, held sr positions in econ., bank supervision and int. areas before becoming RBA's Chief Rep. in Europe, based in London 1991–93, Asst Gov. (Corp. Services) 1993–98, Asst Gov. (Financial System) 1998–2003; mem. Bd of Dirs Australian Prudential Regulation Authority (APRA) and Deputy Chair. Payments System Bd 1998–2003, Chair. APRA 2003–14, APRA's rep. on Payments System Board of RBA and APRA's rep. on Council of Financial Regulators; currently Chair. Banking and Finance Oath Ltd; Lecturer, Univ. of Sydney; advisor to IMF, Basel Cttee; mem. Council, Univ. of Tech., Sydney; mem. External Advisory Panel, Australian Securities and Investments Comm.; mem. Bd of Dirs Cancer Council NSW; Hon. DScEcon (Univ. of Sydney). *Address:* Banking and Finance Oath Ltd, Level 2, Legion House, 161 Castlereagh Street, Sydney, NSW 2000, Australia (office). *Website:* www.thebfo.org (office).

LAKERBAYA, Leonid; Georgian (Abkhaz) politician; b. 1 Jan. 1947, Kutaisi, Georgian SSR, USSR; ed Moscow Automobile and Road Inst., Russian SFSR; engineer with automotive enterprise in Abkhazia 1975–85; head of pilot plant of frozen foods co. in Gagra 1985–91; mem. Parl. 1991–96, 2000–02; First Deputy Prime Minister of Abkhazia 1992–95; Minister of Foreign Affairs 1995–96; nominated by People's Party to stand in 1999 presidential election but refused registration by Cen. Election Comm.; Chair. socio-political movt Aitaira (Revival) 2001–; Vice-Premier and First Vice-Premier in govt of Pres. Bagapsh 2005–11; Prime Minister of the 'Republic of Abkhazia' 2011–14 (resgnd). *Address:* c/o Office of the Prime Minister of the 'Republic of Abkhazia', 384900 Sukhumi, nab. Makhajirov 32, Georgia. *E-mail:* info@govabk.org.

LAKHANI, Amin Mohammed, BSc, MBA; Pakistani industrialist; *Managing Director, Lakson Group of Companies;* ed Stanford Univ. and Wharton School of Business, Univ. of Pennsylvania, USA; Man. Dir Lakson Group of Cos. 1983–, conglomerate with interests in computer software, cosmetics, insurance, fast food and textiles; CEO McDonald's Pakistan 1997–, SIZA Foods Pvt. Ltd, Tritex Cotton Mills Ltd, Clover Pakistan Ltd 2016– (also non-Exec. Dir); Founding mem. Pakistan Chapter, Young Presidents Org.; Dir (non-Exec.) Colgate-Palmolive (Pakistan) Ltd, Century Paper & Board Mills; Dir Merit Packaging Ltd, Century Insurance Co. Ltd; mem. Stanford Alumni Asscn, Wharton Alumni Asscn; mem. Exec. Cttee, ICC Pakistan; Hon. Consul-Gen. of Singapore in Pakistan; Public Service Star, Govt of Singapore 2007, Inst. Business Admin Award, Golden Arch Award, McDonald's Corpn. *Leisure interests:* polo, tennis, riding, weight lifting, travelling. *Address:* Lakson Group of Companies, Lakson Square Building, 2 Sarwar Shaheed Road, Karachi 74200, Pakistan (office). *Telephone:* (21) 5698000 (office). *Fax:* (21) 5683410 (office). *E-mail:* amin@cyber.net.pk (office). *Website:* www.lakson.com.pk (office).

LAKHANI, Iqbal Ali, BBA; Pakistani business executive; *Chairman, Lakson Group of Companies;* ed Univ. of California, Berkeley; one of four brothers controlling Lakson Group of Cos, with group since 1974, currently Chair.; CEO Century Paper & Board Mills Ltd, Tritex Cotton Mills Ltd, Merit Packaging, Cyber.Net (Pvt. Ltd); Charter mem. Indus Entrepreneurs; mem. Bd of Dir Pakistan Business Council; mem. Bd of Trustees Layton Rahmatullah Benevolent Trust; Hon. Consul-Gen. of Mexico in Pakistan. *Address:* Lakson Square, Bldg #2, Sarwar Shaheed Road, Karachi 74200, Pakistan (office). *Telephone:* (21) 5698000 (office). *Fax:* (21) 5683410 (office). *E-mail:* info@lakson.com.pk (office). *Website:* www.lakson.com.pk (office).

LAKHDAR, Zohra Ben, PhD; Tunisian physicist and academic; *Professor of Physics, University of Tunis;* b. 12 March 1943, Tunis; m.; two d.; ed Univ. of Tunis,

Univ. of Paris VI, France; fmr Head, Spectroscopy Lab., Supervisor, postgraduate students for Tunisian DEA Diploma, Co.-Chair. Molecular Spectroscopy Group for Master's Degree and PhD courses; Prof. of Physics, Univ. of Tunis 1978–, apptd Dir Laboratoire de Spectroscopie Atomique, Moléculaire et Applications (LSAMA) 1999; Founder mem. Tunisian Physics Soc., Tunisian Astronomy Soc.; Founding mem. and Pres. Tunisian Optical Soc.; mem. Islamic Acad. of Sciences 1994–; Sr Assoc. Abdus Salam Int. Centre for Theoretical Physics 2001–; Chevalier dans l'Ordre de la Légion d'honneur 2017; L'Oréal-UNESCO Women in Science Award 2005. *Publications:* numerous papers in scientific journals and contribs to textbooks. *Address:* Laboratory of Atomic-Molecular Spectroscopy and Applications, Faculté des Sciences de Tunis Département de Physique, Campus Universitaire, 1060 Tunis (office); 6 rue Manoubi Jarjar impasse 2, 1013 Tunis, Tunisia (home). *Telephone:* (22) 656-279 (office). *Fax:* (1)885-073 (office). *E-mail:* zohra.lakhdar@fst.rnu.tn (office).

LAKHERA, Lt-Gen. Madan Mohan, MSc; Indian army officer (retd) and government administrator; b. 21 Oct. 1937, Jakhand village, UP (now in Uttaranchal); s. of Jaya Nand Lakhera and Kalawati Lakhera; m. Pushpa Lakhera; four d.; ed Rashtriya Indian Mil. Coll., Dehra Dun, Nat. Defence Acad., Pune, Defence Services Staff Coll., Wellington, School of Artillery, Devlali, Coll. of Defence Man., Secundrabad; commissioned in Indian Army 1958; took part in Goa operation 1961, in Indo-Pakistan war, Jammu and Kashmir 1965, 1971; instructor School of Artillery 1967–81; commanded 4th Bn Kumaon Regt, Jammu and Kashmir 1975–78; Deputy Commdr brigade in Manipur 1981–82; rank of Brig. 1982; Commdr brigade in Kanpur 1984–85; Sub-Area Commdr in Kashmir valley 1985–90; rank of Maj.-Gen. 1990; Chief of Staff Kashmir valley-based Corps HQ 1990–92; rank of Lt-Gen. of Indian Army 1993; apptd Chief of Staff, Cen. Command HQ 1992, later Chief of Staff, Northern Command HQ; Adjutant Gen. of Indian Army 1993, Chair. Prin. Personnel Staff Officers' Cttee of three services; Col Commdt Kumaon Regt; following retirement, joined Indian Nat. Congress party, Chair. All India Congress Cttee Ex-Servicemen's Cell; Lt-Gov. of Pondicherry 2004–06, of Andaman and Nicobar Islands Feb.–Dec. 2006; Gov. of Mizoram 2006–11; Chief of Army Staff Commendation Card (twice) 1985, Vishisht Seva Medal 1990, Ati Vashisht Seva Medal 1991, Param Vishisht Seva Medal 1995. *Leisure interests:* golf, reading. *Address:* c/o Raj Bhavan, Aizawl 796 001, India (office).

LAKHOVA, Yekaterina Filippovna; Russian paediatrician and politician; b. 26 May 1948; m.; one d.; ed Sverdlovsk State Medical Inst.; Deputy Head of Div., Sverdlovsk (now Yekaterinburg) City Dept of Public Health, Deputy Head of Main Dept of Public Health, Sverdlovsk Regional Exec. Cttee 1972–90; RSFSR Peoples' Deputy, mem. Council of Repub. RSFSR Supreme Soviet, Chair. Cttee on Problems of Women, Motherhood and Childhood 1990–93; adviser to Russian Pres. on Problems of Family, Protection of Motherhood and Childhood 1992–94; Chair. Cttee on Problems of Women, Family and Demography of Russian Presidency 1992–; Founder and Chair. Women of Russia (political movt) 1993; mem. State Duma 1993–, head of State Duma Cttee on Women, Families and Children's Affairs; mem. Socialist Party of Russia 1996, Otechestvo (Homeland) political movt 1998–2000, Yedinaya Rossiya 2000–. *Address:* Committee on Women, Families and Children's Affairs, State Duma, 103265 Moscow, Okhotny ryad 1, Russia. *Telephone:* (495) 292-19-00 (office). *Fax:* (495) 292-94-64 (office). *E-mail:* www@duma.ru (office). *Website:* www.duma.ru (office).

LAKSACI, Muhammad, PhD; Algerian economist and fmr central banker; ed Louvain Univ., Belgium; fmr univ. prof.; joined Banque d'Algérie (central bank) in early 1990s, Gov. 2001–16, also Pres. Conseil de la Monnaie et du Crédit, Comm. Bancaire; apptd Chair. Asscn of African Central Banks 2012.

LAL, Deepak Kumar, MA, BPhil; British academic; *James S. Coleman Professor Emeritus of International Development Studies, Department of Economics, University of California, Los Angeles;* b. 3 Jan. 1940, Lahore, India; s. of Nand Lal and of Shanti Devi; m. Barbara Ballis 1971; one s. one d.; ed Doon School, Dehra Dun, St Stephen's Coll., India, Jesus Coll., Oxford, UK; served in Indian Foreign Service 1963–65; Lecturer, Christ Church, Oxford 1966–68; Research Fellow, Nuffield Coll., Oxford 1968–70; Lecturer, Univ. Coll. London 1970–79, Reader 1979–84, Prof. of Political Economy, Univ. of London 1984–93, Prof. Emer. 1993–; James S. Coleman Prof. of Int. Devt Studies, UCLA 1991–2010, Prof. Emer. 2010–; Consultant, Indian Planning Comm. 1973–74; Research Admin., World Bank, Washington, DC 1983–87; Dir Trade Policy Unit, Centre for Policy Studies 1993–96, Trade and Devt Unit, Inst. of Econ. Affairs 1997–2002; Pres. Mont Pelerin Soc. 2008–10; consultancy assignments ILO, UNCTAD, OECD, IBRD Ministry of Planning, Sri Lanka, Repub. of Korea 1970–2002; Dr hc (Univ. Paul Cézanne, Aix-Marseille III) 2009; Int. Freedom Award for Econs, Società Liberia (Italy) 2007. *Publications:* Wells and Welfare 1972, Methods of Project Analysis 1974, Appraising Foreign Investment in Developing Countries 1975, Unemployment and Wage Inflation in Industrial Economies 1977, Men or Machines 1978, Prices for Planning 1980, The Poverty of "Development Economics" 1983, Labour and Poverty in Kenya (with P. Collier) 1986, Stagflation, Savings and the State (co-ed. with M. Wolf) 1986, The Hindu Equilibrium (two vols) 1988, 1989, Public Policy and Economic Development (co-ed. with M. Scott) 1990, Development Economics (four vols) (ed.) 1991, The Repressed Economy 1993, Against Dirigisme 1994, The Political Economy of Poverty, Equity and Growth (with H. Myint) 1996, Unintended Consequences 1998, Unfinished Business 1999, Trade, Development and Political Economy (co-ed. with R. Snape) 2001, In Praise of Empires 2004, The Hindu Equilibrium 2005, Reviving the Invisible Hand: The Case for Classical Liberalism in the 21st Century 2006, Poverty and Progress: Reality and Myths about Third World Poverty 2012, Lost Causes: The Retreat from Classical Liberalism 2012. *Leisure interests:* opera, theatre, tennis, bridge. *Address:* Department of Economics, 8369 Bunche Hall, UCLA, Box 951477, Los Angeles, CA 90095-1477, USA (office); A30 Nizamuddin West, New Delhi 110013, India (home); 2 Erskine Hill, London, NW11 6HB, England (home). *Telephone:* (310) 825-1011 (office); (11) 41827013 (New Delhi) (home); (20) 8458-3713 (London) (home). *Fax:* (310) 825-9528 (office). *Website:* www.econ.ucla.edu/faculty/regular/Lal.html (office); www.econ.ucla.edu/lal (office).

LAL, Ganeshi, BA; Indian politician and academic; *Governor of Odisha;* b. 1 March 1942, Sirsa, Haryana; m. Sushila Devi; seven c.; fmr Prof. of Math. 1964–91; Chair., Disciplinary Cttee, Bharatiya Janata Party (BJP), Akhil Bharatiya Vidyarthi Parishad (ABVP, all-India student org.); Minister, Haryana Vikas Party–BJP Govt, Haryana 1996–99; mem. Haryana Legis. Ass. for Sirsa constituency 1996–99; fmr BJP State Pres., Haryana; mem., Rashtriya Swayamsewak Sangh (nationalist org.) 1962–; Gov. of Odisha 2018–. *Address:* Raj Bhavan, Bhubaneswar 751008, Odisha, India (office). *Telephone:* (0674) 2536699 (office); 9215604777 (home). *Fax:* (0674) 2536582 (office). *E-mail:* govodisha@nic.in (office); saraswatipoly.sirsa@yahoo.com (home). *Website:* www.rajbhavanodisha.gov.in (office).

LAL, Mahesh B., BS, MBA; Indian oil industry executive (retd); b. 1947; ed Indian Inst. of Tech., Kanpur, Indian Inst. of Man., Ahmedabad; trained as chemical engineer; fmr Adviser on Refineries, Ministry of Petroleum and Natural Gas; fmr Dir of Operations, Madras Refineries Ltd; Dir of Refineries, Bharat Petroleum Corpn Ltd –2002; Chair. and Man. Dir Hindustan Petroleum Corpn Ltd 2002–07; Adviser to Tech. Mission on Cotton 2003; Technical mem. (Petroleum and Natural Gas) Appellate Tribunal for Electricity 2007–12; fmr mem. Bd of Dirs Cochin Refineries, IBP Co. Ltd, Numaligarh Refineries Ltd, Kochi Refineries Ltd; Chair. Scientific Advisory Cttee, Review Cttee for Auto Fuel Policy, Ministry of Petroleum and Natural Gas; mem. Bd of Govs Indian Inst. of Man., Ahmedabad, Univ. of Petroleum and Energy Studies, Dehradun; Hon. Fellow, Energy Inst., London; Lifetime Achievement Award, Chemtech Foundation, UK, Strategy Award, Indira Group of Insts, Pune, HR Professional Award, ITM Business School.

LALEAU, Wilson; Haitian economist and politician; ed Centre de Techniques de Planification et d'Economie Appliquée, Haiti, Univ. Paris I (Sorbonne), France, Inst. Int. d'Admin Publique, Paris, Inst. of Social Studies (ISS), The Hague, Netherlands; Project Man., Commission Nationale à la Réforme Administrative (CNRA) 1997–2001; Nat. Coordinator, state modernization programme (UNDP/Govt of Haiti) 2000–01; Prof. at several insts including, Centre de Techniques de Planification et d'Economie Appliquée, Univ. of Quisqueya, Univ. d'Etat d'Haïti (UEH), also Vice-Rector for Academic Affairs, UEH 2003, 2007; fmr Econ. Adviser to Pres.; Minister of Trade and Industry 2011–15, of the Economy and Finance 2013–14, 2015–16; fmr consultant to Govt of Haiti and to several int. insts in Haiti including UNDP, IDB, World Bank, UNICEF. *Address:* c/o Ministry of the Economy and Finance, Palais des Ministères, rue Mgr Guilloux, Port-au-Prince, Haiti (office).

LALIBERTÉ, Guy, OC, OQ; Canadian entertainment industry executive; *Founder and Creative Guide, Cirque du Soleil Inc.;* b. 2 Sept. 1959, Québec City; s. of Gaston Laliberté and Blandine Laliberté; m. 1st Rizia Moreira 1990; m. Claudia Barilla; five c.; began career as musician and street performer; joined stiltwalker troupe Les Echassiers De Baie-Saint-Paul; est. summer festival La Fête Foriane, Baie-Saint-Paul 1982; created govt-sponsored event Le Grand Tour du Cirque Du Soleil 1984, show toured Canada for several years, began touring USA 1987, grew into major int. org. producing multiple shows worldwide as Cirque du Soleil, to date over 20 differently themed shows have been produced across five continents combining traditional circus skills with various other artistic and cultural elements, fmr CEO, now Creative Guide; Officier, Ordre de la Pléiade 2010; Dr hc (Université Laval) 2008; Great Montrealer, Académie des Grands Montréalais 2001, Ernst & Young Entrepreneur of the Year 2006, Lifetime Achievement Award, Canadian Marketing Asscn 2009, inducted into Canadian Business Hall of Fame 2011, American Gaming Asscn Gaming Hall of Fame 2012. *Publication:* Gaia 2011. *Address:* Cirque du Soleil, 8400 2nd Avenue, Montreal, PQ H1Z 4M6, Canada (office). *Telephone:* (514) 722-2324 (office). *Fax:* (514) 722-3692 (office). *E-mail:* contact@cirquedusoleil.com (office). *Website:* www.cirquedusoleil.com (office).

LALONDE, Brice; French politician and environmental consultant; *Advisor, United Nations Global Compact;* b. 10 Feb. 1946, Neuilly-sur-Seine; s. of Alain-Gauthier Lalonde and Fiona Lalonde (née Forbes); m. Patricia Raynaud 1986; two s. (one deceased) two d.; one s. one d. from previous m.; ed Univ. of Paris (Sorbonne); Pres. Union nationale des étudiants de france 1968; Chair. Friends of the Earth 1972, French br. 1978; cand. for Green Party, French presidential election 1981; Admin. European Environment Bureau 1983; Dir Paris Office Inst. for European Environmental Policy 1987; Sec. of State for the Environment 1988–89, for the Environment and the Prevention of Tech. and Natural Disasters 1989–90, Minister Del. 1990–91, Minister of the Environment 1991–92; Pres. Génération Ecologie (political movt) 1990–2002, Hon. Pres. 2002–; Mayor of Saint-Briac-sur-Mer 1995–2008; Chair. Cttee to Free Alexandr Nikitin 1996–; mem. Conseil Régional, Brittany 1998, Comité nat. de l'eau 1998–; Chair. Round Table on Sustainable Development, OECD 2007–08; Amb. responsible for Int. Negotiations on Climate Change 2007–10; Under-Sec. Gen. UN Exec. Co-ordinator, Rio 20 2011–12, Advisor to the UN Global Compact 2014; Chevalier, Légion d'honneur. *Publications:* L'écologie en bleu; Quand vous voudrez; Sur la vague verte. *Address:* 65 boulevard Arago, 75013 Paris, France (home). *E-mail:* lalonde@un.org (office).

LALONIU, Samuela, MA; Tuvaluan administrator and diplomatist; *Permanent Representative to United Nations;* b. 14 May 1969; m.Arataake Laloniu; two c.; ed Univ. of Otago, Dunedi, Victoria Univ., Wellington; Fisheries Research and Devt Officer, Ministry of Natural Resources 1994–96; Pacific Regional Project Assoc., FAO Office, Fiji 1997–98; Pvt. Sec. to Prime Minister 1998–2000; Asst Sec. Ministry of Communications and Transport 2000–04; Deputy High Commr to Fiji 2006–09; Deputy Perm. Rep. to UN 2009–10; Consul-Gen., Auckland 2010–14, High Commr to New Zealand 2015–17; Perm. Rep. to UN 2017–. *Address:* Permanent Mission of Tuvalu, 685 Third Avenue, Suite 1104, New York, NY 10017, USA (office). *Telephone:* (212) 490-0534 (office). *Fax:* (212) 808-4975 (office). *E-mail:* tuvalu.un@gmail.com (office).

LALOVAC, Boris, MSc; Croatian academic and politician; b. 16 Nov. 1976, Split; m.; ed Univ. of Dubrovnik, Univ. of Zagreb; Asst, Finance Dept, Auto-Hrvatska d.d. (finance co.), Zagreb 2001–03; Deputy Head of Control Dept, Karbon-Nova d.o.o (building materials firm), Zaprešić 2003–04; Head of Accounting, Finance and Reporting Dept, Raiffeisen Leasing 2005–11; Asst Lecturer, Univ. of Spilt (Zagreb br.) 2002–07; Lecturer, Libertas Business Coll., Zagreb 2008–; Lecturer, Business School for Law and Finance, Effectus Univ. Coll., Zagreb 2010–; Deputy Minister of Finance 2012–14, Minister of Finance 2014–16; mem. Social Democratic Party of Croatia. *Publication:* Poduzetnička ekonomija (Entrepreneurial Economy) (co-author) 2006. *Leisure interest:* basketball. *Address:* c/o Ministry of Finance, 10000 Zagreb, ul. Katančićeva 5, Croatia (office).

LALUMIÈRE, Catherine; French politician; *President, Fédération Française des Maisons de l'Europe;* b. 3 Aug. 1935, Rennes; m. Pierre Lalumière (deceased); fmr lecturer in public law, Univ. of Rennes and Univ. of Paris I; mem. Steering Cttee, Parti Socialiste 1979; mem. Nat. Ass. for Gironde 1986–89; Sec. of State for the Civil Service and Admin. Reforms May–June 1981, Minister for Consumer Affairs 1981–83, Sec. of State 1983–84, Minister for European Affairs 1984–86; Sec.-Gen. Council of Europe 1989–94; Urban Community Councillor, Bordeaux 1989–; Municipal Councillor, Talence 1989–95; MEP, Brussels 1994–2004, Vice-Pres. European Parl. 2001–04; Pres. Maison de l'Europe de Paris 2003–, Fédération Française des Maisons de l'Europe 2008–; Pres. European Asscn of the Schools of Political Studies, Council of Europe 2008–; Deputy Pres. Radical France 1996 (now Radical Socialist Party); apptd Pres. European Radical Alliance 1994; fmr Vice-Pres. Int. European Movt; Hon. DCL (Durham) 1995. *Address:* Fédération Française des Maisons de l'Europe, Maison de l'Europe de Paris, 35-37, rue des Francs Bourgeois, 75004 Paris, France (office). *Telephone:* 1-44-61-85-93 (office). *Website:* www.maisons-europe.eu (office).

LAM, Barry, MEng; Taiwanese electronics industry executive; *Chairman, Quanta Computer Inc.;* b. Shanghai; m.; two c.; ed Nat. Taiwan Univ.; Co-founder Kimpo (handheld calculator mfr) 1973; f. Quanta Computer Inc. (computer and components mfr) 1988, currently Chair.; Chair. Quanta Culture and Educ. Foundation; mem. Bd of Dirs Cloud Gate Theatre Group. *Address:* Quanta Computer Inc., 211 Wen Hwa Second Road, Kui Shan Hsiang, Taoyuan, Taiwan (office). *Telephone:* (3) 327-2345 (office). *Fax:* (3) 327-1511 (office). *E-mail:* campus@quantatw.com (office); qci.ir@quantatw.com (office). *Website:* www.quantatw.com (office).

LAM, Carrie, (Carrie Lam Cheng Yuet-ngor), JP; Hong Kong civil servant and politician; *Chief Executive;* b. 13 May 1957; m. Lam Siu-por; two s.; joined Admin. Service 1980, served in various bureaux and depts, including as Dir of Social Welfare Dept 2000–03, Perm. Sec. for Housing, Planning and Lands (Planning and Lands) 2003–04, Dir-Gen. Hong Kong Econ. and Trade Office, London, UK 2004–06, attained rank of Admin. Officer Staff Grade A1 2006, Perm. Sec. for Home Affairs 2006–07, Sec. for Devt 2007–12, Chief Sec. for Admin 2012–17; Chief Exec. (first female) 2017–; Gold Bauhinia Star 2010. *Address:* Office of the Chief Executive, Tamar, Hong Kong Special Administrative Region, People's Repub. of China (office). *Telephone:* 28783300 (office). *Fax:* 25090580 (office). *E-mail:* ceo@ceo.gov.hk. *Website:* www.ceo.gov.hk/eng/index.html (office).

LAMAMRA, Ramtane; Algerian diplomatist and politician; b. 15 June 1952, Amizour; m.; one c.; ed École nationale d'Admin; joined Ministry of Foreign Affairs (MFA) 1976, Amb. to Ethiopia and Djibouti 1989–91, to Austria and IAEA 1992–93, Perm. Rep. to UN, New York 1993–96, Amb. to USA 1996–99, to Portugal 2004–05, African Union (AU) Special Envoy to Liberia 2003, Sec.-Gen., MFA 2005–07, AU Commr for Peace and Security 2008–13, mem. Sec.-Gen.'s High-Level Advisory Bd Mediation, UN 2017–, Minister of Foreign Affairs 2013–17, March–April 2019, also Deputy Prime Minister March–April 2019; Minister of State 2013–15; mem. Bd of Dirs International Crisis Group (NGO) 2018–.

LAMANDA, Vincent; French judge (retd); b. 31 May 1946; Prosecutor, Evry-Corbeil 1972; fmr Deputy Public Prosecutor, Versailles; Tech. Advisor to Minister of Justice 1974; Lecturer, Univ. Paris II Panthéon-Assas 1977–94; Chief of Staff of Minister of Justice 1977; mem. Implementation Cttee of Report on Violence 1977; Tech. Advisor to Minister of Justice 1978–80; Counsellor, Court of Cassation 1979; Sec. Supreme Council of the Judiciary 1981, mem. 2002–06; Vice-Pres., Tribunal de grande instance de Paris (High Court of Paris) 1986; Presiding Judge, Bordeaux 1988; First Pres., Court of Appeal of Rouen 1992, Court of Appeal of Versailles 1996–2007; First Pres., Court of Cassation 2007–14 (retd); Vice-Pres. Network of Presidents of the Supreme Judicial Courts of the EU; Commdr, Ordre de la Légion d'honneur 2009. *Address:* c/o Cour de Cassation, Palais de Justice, 5 quai de l'Horloge, 75001 Paris Cedex 01, France.

LAMB, Allan Joseph; South African business executive and fmr professional cricketer; b. 20 June 1954, Langebaanweg, Cape Prov.; s. of Michael Lamb and Joan Lamb; m. Lindsay Lamb 1979; one s. one d.; ed Wynberg Boys' High School and Abbotts Coll.; middle-order right-hand batsman; teams: Western Prov. 1972–82, 1992–93, Northants. 1978–95 (Capt. 1989–95), Orange Free State 1987–88; qualified for England 1982 and played in 79 Tests 1982–92 (three as Capt.), scoring 4,656 runs (average 36.09, highest score 142) including 14 hundreds; toured Australia 1982–83, 1986–87, 1990–91; played in 122 One-Day Ints, scoring 4,010 runs (average 39.31, highest score 118) including four hundreds; scored 32,502 first-class runs (average 48.94, highest score 294) including 89 hundreds; scored 1,000 runs in a season on 15 occasions; Dir Allan Lamb Assocs Ltd (events man. co.), Grenada Sports Ltd; contrib. to Sky Sports Crickett; Wisden Cricketer of the year 1981. *Play:* Beef and Lamb in a stew (roadshow with Ian Botham) 1994–95. *Television:* contestant on a special Cricketers' Edn of the Weakest Link (voted off in second round). *Publication:* Silence of the Lamb (autobiography) 1995. *Leisure interests:* tennis, golf, cycling, rugby, horse racing, fly-fishing, shooting. *Address:* Allan Lamb Associates Ltd, First Floor, 4 St Giles Street, Northampton, NN1 1JB, England (office). *Telephone:* (1604) 231222 (office). *Fax:* (1604) 239930 (office). *E-mail:* info@lambassociates.co.uk (office). *Website:* www.lambassociates.co.uk (office).

LAMBECK, Kurt, AO, DPhil, DSc, FRS, FAA, FRSN; Australian (b. Dutch) geophysicist and academic; *Professor Emeritus, Australian National University;* b. 20 Sept. 1941, Netherlands; m. Bridget Marguerite Lambeck; one s. one d.; ed Univ. of New South Wales, Univ. of Oxford, UK; Geodesist, Smithsonian Astrophysical Observatory 1967–70; Dir of Research, Paris Observatory 1970–73; Prof. of Geophysics, Univ. of Paris 1973–77; Prof. of Geophysics, Research School of Earth Sciences, ANU 1977–2007, Prof. Emer. 2007–; Blaise Pascal Prof., École normale supérieure, Paris 2011–12; Visiting Prof. Nat. Inst. of Geophysics Volcanology, Italy 2018–19; Foreign mem. Royal Netherlands Acad. of Arts and Sciences 1993, Norwegian Acad. of Science and Letters 1998, Acad. des sciences (France) 2005, NAS 2009, American Acad. of Arts and Sciences 2010; Fellow, Australian Acad. of Science 1984–, Pres. 2006–10; Johannes Geiss Fellow, Int. Space Science Inst., Berne 2016–17; Fed. Medal; Chevalier, Légion d'honneur; Cavaliere, Ordine al merito della Repubblica Italiana; Hon. DEng (Nat. Tech. Univ. of Greece), Hon. DSc (Univ. of New South Wales), (Univ. of Wollongong); Macelwane Award, American Geophysical Union 1976, Whitten Medal, American Geophysical Union 1993, Jaeger Medal, Australian Acad. of Science 1995, Alfred Wegener Medal, European Union of Geosciences 1996, George Lemaître Prize 2002, Balzan Prize 2012, Wollaston Medal, Geological Soc. of London 2013, Flinders Medal, Australian Acad. of Science 2014, Prime Minister's Prize for Science 2018. *Publications include:* The Earth's Variable Rotation 1980, Geophysical Geodesy 1988; numerous papers on geodesy and geophysics. *Address:* Research School of Earth Sciences, Australian National University, Canberra, ACT 0200, Australia (office). *Telephone:* (2) 6125-5161 (office). *E-mail:* kurt.lambeck@anu.edu.au (office). *Website:* people.rses.anu.edu.au/lambeck_k/index.php (office).

LAMBERT, Christopher; American actor; b. (Christophe Guy Dénis Lambert), 29 March 1957, Great Neck, NY; m. 1st Diane Lane 1988 (divorced 1994); one d.; m. 2nd Jaimyse Haft 1999 (divorced 2006); m. 3rd Sophie Marceau 2012; ed L'Ecole Roche, Int. School, Lycée d'Annemasse, Coll. Floriment, Geneva, Florent School, Paris and Paris Conservatoire; left USA with family at age two; mil. service with Alpine Corps, Grenoble; trainee, Barclay's Bank, London 1976. *Films include:* Ciao, les mecs 1979, Le Bar du téléphone 1980, Asphalte 1981, Une sale affaire 1981, Putain d'histoire d'amour 1981, Légitime violence 1982, Greystoke: The Story of Tarzan, Lord of the Apes 1983, Paroles et Musiques 1984, Subway 1985, Highlander 1986, I Love You 1986, The Sicilian 1987, Love Dream 1988, To Kill A Priest 1988, Why Me? 1990, Highlander II: The Quickening 1991, Knight Moves 1992, Max & Jeremie 1992, Fortress 1993, Gunmen 1994, Road Killers 1994, Highlander III: The Sorcerer 1994, The Hunted 1995, Mortal Kombat 1995, Tashunga 1996, Adrenalin: Fear the Rush 1996, Hercule et Sherlock 1996, Nirvana 1997, Arlette 1997, Mean Guns 1997, Fortress 2 1999, Operation Splitsville 1999, Beowulf 1999, Resurrection 1999, Gideon 1999, Highlander: Endgame 2000, Aparté 2001, Vercingétorix 2001, The Point Men 2001, The Piano Player 2002, Absolon 2003, Janis et John 2003, À ton image 2004, Game of Swords 2006, Southland Tales 2006, Le lièvre de Vatanen 2006, Metamorphosis 2007, Trivial 2007, The Chauffeur 2008, White Material 2009, Cartagena 2009, The Gardener of God 2010, Ghost Rider: Spirit of Vengeance 2011, The Foreigner 2012, My Lucky Star 2012, Blood Shot 2013, Electric Slide 2014, 10 Days in a Madhouse 2015, Hail, Caesar! 2016, Everyone's Life 2017, Kickboxer Retaliation 2018, Bel Canto 2018. *Television includes:* Douchka 1981, La Dame de coeur 1982, King of Bandit Jing (mini-series) 2002, Dalida (film) 2005, Les associés (film) 2009, The Secret of the Whales (film) 2010, Very Bad Blagues (series) 2012, L'una e l'altra (film) 2012, NCIS: Los Angeles 2012–13, La source (series) 2013, Mata Hari (series) 2016. *Publications:* La fille porte-bonheur 2011, Le juge 2015. *E-mail:* info@delfuegomanagement.com (office). *Website:* www.delfuegomanagement.com (office).

LAMBERT, Phyllis, CC, GOQ, CAL, BA, MS (Arch), FRSC, FRAIC; Canadian architect and museum director; *Founding Director Emeritus, Centre Canadien d'Architecture/Canadian Centre for Architecture, Montréal;* b. 24 Jan. 1927, Montréal, Québec; d. of Samuel Bronfman and Saidye Bronfman (née Rosner); ed The Study, Montréal, Vassar Coll., New York, Illinois Inst. of Tech., Chicago; Adjunct Prof., School of Architecture, McGill Univ. 1986–; Assoc. Prof., Faculté de l'aménagement, École d'architecture, Univ. de Montréal 1989–; Bd Chair. and Prin., Ridgway Ltd, Architects/Developers, Los Angeles 1972–84; Founding Dir and Chair. Bd of Trustees, Centre Canadien d'Architecture (CCA), Montréal 1979–2013, Consulting Architect and Client CCA 1984–89, Founding Dir Emer. 2013–; Chair. Arthur Erickson Foundation 2011–, Pres. 2011–13; Pres. Institut de politiques alternatives de Montréal 2009–16, Hon. Pres. 2016–; cr. Fonds d'investissement de Montréal, pvt. fund for revitalization of Montréal neighbourhoods 1996; est. Int. Foundation for the Canadian Centre for Architecture Prize for Design of Cities 1999; jury mem. several cttees for architectural and urban design projects; numerous exhbns; mem. Bd of Trustees, Inst. of Fine Arts, New York Univ. 1973–, Bd of Advisors, Temple Hoyne Buell Center for the Study of American Architecture, Columbia Univ., New York 1984– (Founding Chair. 1984–89), Advisory Council School of Architecture, Princeton Univ. 1990–2003, 2006–, Bd Acquisitions Cttee Nat. Gallery of Canada 1991–, Provost's Advisory Bd Faculty of Architecture, Univ. of Toronto 1992–2004, Visiting Cttee Grad. School of Design, Harvard Univ. 1993–2005, and several other bodies; Founding mem. Bd Int. Confed. of Architectural Museums 1984– (Pres. 1984–87); fmr mem. Bd of Overseers, Coll. of Architecture and Planning, Ill. Inst. of Tech.; frequent guest lecturer at univs and professional orgs in N America and abroad; Academician, RCA 1977; Life mem. Council of the Ontario Asscn of Architects 2003; Fellow, Royal Architectural Inst. of Canada 1983, Soc. of Architectural Historians 2009; Foreign Hon. mem. American Acad. of Arts and Sciences 1995; Hon. FRIBA 2001; Hon. FAIA 2003; Chevalier, Ordre de la Pléiade, Assemblée parlementaire de la Francophonie 1998; Grand Officier, Ordre nat. du Québec 2005; Commdr, Ordre des Arts et des Lettres 2006; 27 hon. degrees from univs in N America and Europe; numerous awards and prizes, including Médaille de l'Acad. d'Architecture de France 1988, Gabrielle Léger Medal, Heritage Canada Foundation 1988, Prix d'excellence en architecture, Ordre des Architectes du Québec (for CCA) 1989, Médaille d'Honneur, Soc. Historique de Montréal 1990, RAIC Gold Medal 1991, AIA Inst. Honor (for CCA) 1992, Lescarbot Award, Govt of Canada 1992, Prix Gérard-Morisset, Gov. of Québec 1994, Hadrian Award, World Monuments Fund 1997, Montblanc Int. Arts Patronage Award 2001, Chrysler Design Award (as Design Champion) 2002, Prix Blanche Lemco van Ginkel, Ordre des Urbanistes du Québec 2003, Award of Excellence, Advocate for Architecture, RAIC 2005, Vincent J. Scully Prize, Nat. Building Museum 2006, Prix d'excellence de l'Opération patrimoine architectural de Montréal, Ville de Montréal et Héritage Montréal 2007, Pillar of New York Award, Preservation League of New York State 2007, Woodrow Wilson Award for Public Service, Canada Inst. of the Woodrow Wilson Int. Centre for Scholars 2007, Montréal Centre-Ville Tribute Award 2011, Golden Lion for Lifetime Achievement, 14th Int. Architecture Exhbn Fundamentals, Venice Biennale 2014, Bâtisseuse de la cité, Ville de Montréal 2014, Arnold W. Brunner Memorial Prize in Architecture, American Acad. of Arts and Letters 2016, Wolf Prize in Architecture, The Wolf Foundation 2016. *Projects include:* Seagram Bldg, New York (Dir of Planning) (AIA 25-Year Award 1984, New York Landmarks Conservancy Award 1989) 1954–58, Toronto-Dominion Centre, Toronto (consultant) 1962, Saidye Bronfman Centre, YM-YWHA, Montréal (architect) (RAIC Massey Medal 1970) 1963–68, Les Promenades St-Bruno Shopping Centre, St Bruno, Québec (consultant) 1974, Jane Tate House renovation, Montréal (architect) 1974–76, Biltmore Hotel renovation, Los Angeles (architect and developer) (AIA Award of Honor 1978) 1976, renovation of housing units, St-Hubert Street, Montréal (developer) 1978, 700-unit co-operative housing renovation project, Milton Park, Montréal (Pres.) 1979–85, Ben Ezra Synagogue Restoration Project, Cairo, Egypt (Dir) 1981–94. *Publications:* Court House: A Photographic Document 1978, Photography and Architecture: 1839–1939 1982, Architecture and its Image 1989, Canadian Centre for Architecture: Building and Gardens 1989, Opening the Gates of Eighteenth-Century Montréal (ed.) 1992, Fortifications and the Synagogue: The Fortress of Babylon and the Ben Ezra Synagogue, Cairo (ed.) 1994, Viewing Olmsted: Photographs by Robert Burley, Lee Friedlander and Geoffrey James (ed.) 1996, Autonomy and Ideology: Positioning an Avant-Garde in America 1997, Mies in America (ed.) 2001, Building Seagram 2013; numerous essays in architectural periodicals. *Address:* Centre Canadien d'Architecture, 1920 rue Baile, Montréal, PQ H3H 2S6, Canada (office). *Telephone:* (514) 939-7025 (office). *Fax:* (514) 939-7032 (office). *E-mail:* plambert@cca.qc.ca (office). *Website:* www.cca .qc.ca (office).

LAMBERT, Sir Richard Peter, Kt, BA; British journalist, organization official and university chancellor; *Chancellor, University of Warwick;* b. 23 Sept. 1944, Bucks., England; s. of Peter Lambert and Mary Lambert; m. Harriet Murray-Browne 1973; one s. one d.; ed Fettes Coll., Edinburgh, Balliol Coll., Oxford; mem. staff, Financial Times 1966–2001, Lex Column 1972, Financial Ed. 1978, New York Corresp. 1982, Deputy Ed. 1983, Ed. Financial Times 1991–2001; lecturer and contrib. to The Times 2001–; external mem. Bank of England Monetary Policy Cttee 2003–06; Dir-Gen. CBI, London 2006–11; Chancellor Univ. of Warwick 2008–; apptd to create Banking Standards Review Council 2013, interim Chair. 2013–15; Chair. Big Society Trust 2011–; Chair. (Non-Exec.) Bloomsbury Publishing PLC 2017–; currently Lead Non-Exec. Dir, FCO Supervisory Bd; mem. Bd of Dirs Nat. Centre for Universities and Business, Ernst & Young; fmr mem. Bd of Dirs (non-exec.) London Int. Financial Futures Exchange (LIFFE), AXA Investment Mans, Int. Rescue Cttee UK; Gov. Royal Shakespeare Co.; UK Chair. Franco-British Colloque; mem. UK-India Round Table; mem. Int. Advisory Bd British-American Business Inc.; Sr Ind. Adviser, Deutsche Bank 2012–; Trustee, British Museum 2003–11, Chair. 2014–; Hon. DLitt (City Univ. London) 2000; Hon. LLD (Warwick) 2004; Dr hc (Brighton, Exeter), (York) 2007; Princess of Wales Amb. Award 2001, World Leadership Forum Business Journalist Decade of Excellence Award 2001. *Address:* Office of the Chancellor, University of Warwick, Coventry, CV4 7AL, England (office). *Telephone:* (24) 7652-3523 (office). *Fax:* (24) 7646-1606 (office). *Website:* www2.warwick.ac.uk/about/management/chancellor (office).

LAMBERT, Yves Maurice; French international organization official and engineer; b. 4 June 1936, Nancy, Meurthe-et-Moselle; s. of André Arthur Lambert and Paulette Franck; m. Odile Revillon 1959; three s. two d.; ed Ecole Polytechnique, Paris, Nat. Civil Aviation School, Centre de Préparation à l'Admin des Entreprises; Dir Org. de Gestion et de Sécurité de l'Algérie (OGSA), Algeria 1965–68; Tech. Adviser to Minister of Transport, France 1969–72; Rep. of France to ICAO Council 1972–76; Sec.-Gen. ICAO Aug. 1976–88, Dir of Air Navigation, Ministry of Equipment and Housing, Transport and the Sea 1989–93; Dir-Gen. Eurocontrol 1994–2001; Fellow, Royal Aeronautical Soc. (UK); mem. Acad. Nat. de l'Air et de l'Espace; Officier, Légion d'honneur, Ordre nat. du Mérite; Médaille de l'Aéronautique, Glen Gilbert Award, Air Traffic Control Asscn 1997.

LAMBIN, Eric F., BA, MS, PhD; Belgian environmental scientist and academic; *George and Setsuko Ishiyama Provostial Professor, Stanford University;* b. 23 Sept. 1962, Brussels; m. Régine Geets; two d.; ed Université Catholique de Louvain; spent time as a doctoral student in sub-Saharan Africa mid-1980s; Asst Prof. of Geography, Boston Univ., USA 1991–93; Expert, Inst. for Remote Sensing Applications, Joint Research Centre, Ispra, Italy 1993–95; Asst Prof., Dept of Geology and Geography, Université Catholique de Louvain 1995–99, Assoc. Prof. 1999–2005, Prof. 2005–, Chair. of Dept 2000–02; Fellow, Center for Advanced Studies in the Behavioral Sciences, Stanford Univ. 2002–03, now George and Setsuko Ishiyama Provostial Prof., Co-Chair. Dept of Environmental Earth System Science 2013–, Sr Fellow, Stanford Woods Inst. for the Environment; Chair. Land Use and Land Cover Change (IGBP/IHDP LUCC) 1999–2005; contrib. to Millennium Ecosystem Assessment; involved in several European research projects; mem. Bd of Dirs, Beijer Inst. of Ecological Econs, Stockholm, Sweden 2011–, External Advisory Bd, Nat. Socio-Environmental Synthesis Center (SESYNC), USA 2012–13; Assoc. Ed., Ecology and Society: A journal of integrative science for resilience and sustainability 2005–; mem. Acad. Royale des sciences, des lettres et des beaux-arts de Belgique 2006, Academia Europaea 2010; Foreign Assoc. NAS 2009; Fellow, European Acad. of Sciences 2010; Francqui Prize in Sciences, Francqui Foundation 2009, Volvo Environment Prize 2014. *Publications:* numerous papers in professional journals. *Address:* Room 371, Y2E2 Building, 473 Via Ortega, Stanford, CA 94305-4216, USA (office). *Telephone:* (650) 724-9825 (office). *E-mail:* elambin@stanford.edu (office). *Website:* earth.stanford.edu/eric -lambin (office); woods.stanford.edu (office).

LAMBRINIDIS, Stavros, BA, JD; Greek lawyer, politician and diplomatist; *Special Representative for Human Rights, European Union;* b. 6 Feb. 1962, Athens; ed Amherst Coll. and Yale Univ. Law School, USA; attorney at Wilmer, Culter & Pickering, Washington, DC 1988–93; Special Advisor to the Under-Sec. of Foreign Affairs and subsequently the Minister of Educ., Giorgos Papandreou 1994–96; Head of Staff for Minister of Foreign Affairs, Theodoros Pangalos 1996; Sec.-Gen. for the Expatriate Greeks Section, Ministry of Foreign Affairs 1996–99; mem. PASOK Cttee for Expatriate Greeks 1996–99, PASOK Nat. Council; Amb. ad personam of the Hellenic Repub. 1999–2004; Dir-Gen. Int. Olympic Truce Centre (an IOC org.) 2000–05; fmr mem. Steering Cttee on the negotiation and implementation of nine bilateral agreements with Turkey; mem. European Parl. for the Panhellenic Socialist Movt (PASOK) 2004–11, Head of Greek Socialist Del. to European Parl., Vice-Chair. Cttee on Civil Liberties, Justice and Home Affairs, Rapporteur on the Integration of Immigrants in Europe and on the Protection of Critical Infrastructures; fmr Vice-Pres. Party of European Socialists; Minister of Foreign Affairs June–Nov. 2011; represented Greece on 66th UN Gen. Ass. Sept.

2011; EU Special Rep. for Human Rights 2012–; Ed.-in-Chief The Yale Journal of International Law 1998; Prof. Emer., Donetsk Univ. Inst. of Humanities, Ukraine 1999; Visiting Prof., Int. Olympic Acad., Greek Diplomatic Acad., Greek Police Acad. 1998–2004; Chair. DC (USA) Civil Rights Cttee 1990; Dr hc (Donetsk Nat. Univ., Ukraine); Award of Hellenic Leadership Conf. *Publications:* author of the Parl.'s reports on the 'Integration of Immigrants into the EU' and on 'Promoting Security and Fundamental Rights in the Electronic Age'. *Address:* European External Action Service, EEAS Building, 9A Rond Point Schuman, 1000 Brussels, Belgium (office). *Website:* eeas.europa.eu/policies/eu-special-representatives.

LAMBRON, Marc; French journalist and writer; b. 4 Feb. 1957, Lyon; s. of Paul Lambron and Jacqueline Lambron (née Denis); m. Sophie Missoffe 1983; one s. two d.; ed Ecole normale supérieure, Institut d'etudes politiques, Ecole nationale d'admin; columnist, Point 1986–, Madame Figaro; taught for some time at Ecole Supérieure de Commerce de Rouen and Ecole normale supérieure; mem. Conseil d'Etat 2006–; elected to Chair 38 of l'Acad. française June 2014; Commdr des Arts et des Lettres, Chevalier, Légion d'honneur 2004. *Publications include:* L'Impromptu de Madrid (Prix des Deux Magots 1989) 1988, La nuit des masques (Prix Colette 1991) 1990, Carnet de bal 1992, L'oeil du silence (Prix Fémina 1993) 1993, 1941 1997, Etrangers dans la nuit 2001, Carnet de bal II 2003, Les Menteurs 2004, Une saison sur la terre 2006, Mignonne, allons voir 2006, Eh bien, dansez maintenant 2008, Théorie du chiffon 2010, Carnet de bal III 2011, Nus vénitiens 2012, Tu n'as pas tellement changé 2014, Trésors du Quai d'Orsay 2014. *Leisure interests:* music, cinema. *Address:* 17 rue Lagrange, 75005 Paris, France (home). *Telephone:* 1-40-51-02-12 (home). *Fax:* 1-46-33-43-18 (home).

LAMEDA, Guaicaipuro, MA; Venezuelan business executive, engineer and army officer (retd); b. 6 Aug. 1954, Barquisimeto, Estada Lara; ed Mil. Acad. of Venezuela, Pacific Univ., USA, Inst. of Advanced Studies of Nat. Defense, Gen. Staff and Command School, USA; numerous managerial and educational posts in Venezuelan army and govt, including Chief Planning Officer, Venezuelan Co. of Mil. Industries (CAVIM) 1992, Dir of Budget Office, Ministry of Defence 1996, Dir Govt Cen. Budget Office 1998; Chair. Petróleos de Venezuela SA (PDVSA) 2000–02; Pres. of the Repub. Award, Nat. School for Advanced Defense Studies; 15 nat. and foreign distinctions; 3 mil. merit badges, 23 mil. honour awards.

LAMINE LOUM, Mamadou; Senegalese civil servant and politician; b. 3 Feb. 1952, Mboss; ed Faculty of Law, Univ. Cheikh Anta Diop, Ecole Nationale d'Admin et de Magistrature; Insp. at the Treasury 1977–84, Chief Treas. and Paymaster-Gen. 1984–91, Dir-Gen. of the Treasury 1991–93; Deputy Minister of Finance in charge of the Budget 1993–98, successfully negotiated debt rescheduling of Senegal with the Club of Paris, Minister of the Economy, Finance and Planning Jan.–July 1998; Prime Minister of Senegal 1998–2000; mem. Bd of Dirs, African Centre for Econ. Transformation; mem. Parti Socialiste (PS). *Address:* African Centre for Economic Transformation, Cantonments, PMB CT 4, 50 Liberation Road, Ridge Residential Area, Accra, Ghana. *Telephone:* (302) 210240. *E-mail:* info@acetforafrica.org. *Website:* acetforafrica.org.

LAMIZANA, Mariam, MA; Burkinabè politician and organization official; *Honorary President, Inter-African Cttee (IAC) on Traditional Practices;* b. 26 July 1951, Bobo-Dioulasso; m.; four c.; ed Univ. of Paris X–Nanterre and Institut de Service Social et de Recherches Sociales, Montrouge, France; Attaché d'Etudes, Soc. of African Studies and Devt, Ouagadougou 1976; Social Asst Bureau of Social Aid 1979–90; Prof. of Sociology, Institut Nat. d'Educ. 1981–84; Prov. Dir of Family Expansion and Nat. Solidarity, Houet—Bobo-Dioulasso 1984–86; Sec.-Gen. Ministry of Family Expansion and Nat. Solidarity 1986–88; Tech. Adviser to Minister of Social Action and the Family 1988–97; Pres. Inter-African Cttee (IAC) on Traditional Practices, Nat. Cttee of the Struggle against Circumcision (CNLPE) 1988–97, Perm. Sec. 1997–2000, now Hon. Pres.; mem. House of Reps 1996–99; Regional Councillor for Francophone Africa, RAINBO (Research, Action and Information Network for Bodily Integrity of Women), New York, USA 1997–2000; Dir-Gen. of Nat. Solidarity, Ministry of Social Action and Nat. Solidarity 2001, Minister for Social Action and Nat. Solidarity 2002–05; Pres. Voice of Women Asscn, Burkina Faso 2000; mem. Ind. Nat. Election Cttee 2001; chair. numerous govt cttees; del. to int. orgs. including UN, UNICEF, OAU, Inter-African Cttee; Chevalier Ordre du Mérite (Burkina Faso); Nathalie Masse Int. Prize, Centre Int. de l'Enfant 1995. *Publications include:* Développement Communautaire au Burkina Faso, Mémoire de Maîtrise 1980. *Address:* Inter-African Committee on Traditional Practices, c/o ECA, PO Box 3001, Addis Ababa, Ethiopia. *E-mail:* iac -htps@uneca.org. *Website:* www.iac-ciaf.net.

LAMM, Richard D., LLB, JD, CPA; American lawyer, academic and politician; *University Professor, Co-Director of the Institute for Public Policy Studies and Executive Director of the Center for Public Policy and Contemporary Issues, University of Denver;* b. 8 Aug. 1935, Madison, Wis.; s. of A. E. Lamm; m. Dottie Lamm; one s. one d.; ed Univ. of Wisconsin and Univ. of California, Berkeley; Certified Public Accountant, Ernst & Ernst, Denver 1961–62; lawyer, Colo Anti-Discrimination Comm. 1962–63; lawyer, Jones, Meiklejohn, Kilroy, Kehl & Lyons 1963–65; pvt. practice 1965–74; mem. Colo House of Reps 1966–74; Assoc. Prof. of Law, Univ. of Denver 1969–74, Univ. Prof., Co-Dir Inst. for Public Policy Studies and Exec. Dir Center for Public Policy and Contemporary Issues 1987–; Gov. of Colo 1975–87 (three terms); Chair. Advisory Bd Fed. for American Immigration Reform; Dir Diversity Alliance for a Sustainable America, Energy Literacy Advocates 2007–; Founding mem. Colo Trail Foundation; mem. Bd of Advisors, Foundation for Defense of Democracies; has continued to speak publicly on environmental, immigration reduction, and health care issues; Humanist of the Year Award, American Humanist Asscn 1993. *Publications include:* Population and the Law 1972, Some Reflections on the Balkanization of America 1978, Megatraumas: America at the Year 2000 1980, Energy Activities in the West 1980, The Angry West: A Vulnerable Land and Its Future (with Michael McCarthy) 1982, Campaign for Quality: An Education Agenda for the 80s 1983, Pioneers and Politicians: Ten Colorado Governors in Profile 1984, The American West: A Poem 1985, Immigration Time Bomb: The Fragmenting of America 1985, 1988 (novel) (with Arnie Grossman) 1985, The Immigration Time Bomb 1985, A California Conspiracy (with Arnold Grossman) 1988, Hard Choices 1989, Crisis: The Uncompetitive Society 1989, The Fall and Rise of the American Economy 1989, Indicators of Decline: An Article from The Futurist 1993, Health Care Workforce Reform: An Article from State Legislatures 1994, The West at Risk 1994, The Price of Modern Medicine 1997, Mountains of Colorado 1999, Vision for a Compassionate and Affordable Health System 2001, The Brave New World of Health Care 2004, The Challenge of an Aging Society: The Future of U.S. Health Care 2005, Two Wands, One Nation: An Essay on Race and Community in America 2006, Condition Critical: A New Moral Vision of Health Care 2007. *Leisure interests:* mountain climbing, reading, bicycling. *Address:* Institute for Public Policy Studies, University of Denver, Mary Reed Building 107, 2199 South University Blvd, Denver, CO 80208, USA (office). *Telephone:* (303) 871-2468 (office). *Fax:* (303) 871-3066 (office). *E-mail:* ipps@du.edu (office). *Website:* www.du.edu/ahss/ipps (office).

LAMM, Vanda Éva, PhD, DSc; Hungarian professor of international law and international legal official; *Director, Institute for Legal Studies, Hungarian Academy of Sciences;* b. 26 March 1945, Budapest; d. of Robert T. Lamm and Hedvig Lamm (née Vandel); ed Univ. of Budapest, Faculté int. pour l'enseignement du droit comparé, Strasbourg, France, Hague Acad. of Int. Law, Netherlands, Columbia Univ., USA; Research Fellow, Inst. for Legal Studies, Hungarian Acad. of Sciences, Dir 1991–; Prof. of Int. Law Univ. of Miskolc 1998, Univ. of Budapest-Győr; Head, Dept of Int. Law, Széchenyi István Univ.; mem. Perm. Court of Arbitration 1999–; Deputy mem. Court of Arbitration of OSCE; mem. UN CEDAW Cttee monitoring implementation of 1979 Convention on Elimination of Discrimination against Women; Pres. Int. Nuclear Law Asscn 2000–01, Hon. Pres. and mem. Bd of Man. 2004–05; Sec.-Gen. Hungarian Br., Int. Law Asscn; Vice-Chair. Group of Governmental Experts on Third Party Liability, OECD-NEA; Assoc. mem. Inst. of Int. Law 2001–; Ed.-in-Chief Állam-és Jogtudomány; Ed. Acta Juridica Hungarica; mem. European Acad. of Sciences and Arts. *Publications:* numerous publs on nuclear law and int. law. *Address:* Institute for Legal Studies, Hungarian Academy of Sciences, PO Box 25, I. Országház u. 30, 1250 Budapest (office); Department of International Law, Széchenyi István University, Egyetem tér 1, 9026 Győr, Hungary. *Telephone:* (1) 355-7384 (office); (96) 503-478. *Fax:* (1) 375-7858 (office); (96) 503-400/3535. *E-mail:* lamm@jog.mta.hu (office); lammv@mail.sze.hu. *Website:* www.mta-ius.hu (office).

LAMMERT, Norbert, PhD; German politician; b. 16 Nov. 1948; m. Gertrud Lammert, four c.; ed Univ. of Bochum, Univ. of Oxford; mem. CDU 1966–, Deputy Dist Chair. Bochum CDU 1977–85; deputy regional Chair. Junge Union, Westfalen-Lippe 1978–84; mem. Nat. Asscn Nordrhein-Westfalen CDU 1986–, Chair. 1996–2006; mem. City Council, Bochum 1975–80; Chair. Dist Asscn Ruhr CDU 1986–2008, Hon. Chair. 2008–; mem. Bundestag for Bochum 1980–2017, Vice-Pres. 2002–05, Pres. 2005–17; Deputy Chair. Cttee on Electoral Examinations, Immunity and Rules of Procedure 1983–89; Chair. German-Brazilian Parl. Group 1983–89; Parl. Sec. of State to the Fed. Minister for Educ. and Science 1989–94; for Economics 1994, for Transport 1997–98; Coordinator Fed. Govt for Aerospace 1995–98; cultural and media policy spokesman CDU/Christian Social Union Parl. Group 1998–2002; Deputy Chair. Konrad-Adenauer-Foundation 2001–. *Address:* c/o Bundestag, Pl. der Republik 1, 11011 Berlin, Germamy (office). *Telephone:* (30) 2270 (office). *Fax:* (30) 22736979 (office). *E-mail:* mail@bundestag.de (office). *Website:* www.bundestag.de (office).

LAMO DE ESPINOSA Y MICHELS DE CHAMPOURCÍN, Jaime, Marqués de Mirasol and Barón de Frignani y Frignestani; Spanish agronomic engineer, academic, national organization official and fmr politician; *Chairman, Asociación Nacional de Constructores Independientes;* b. 4 April 1941, Madrid; s. of Emilio Lamo de Espinosa y Enríquez de Navarra and María Luisa Michels de Champourcín; m. Carmen Rocamora 1965; four d.; ed Colegio de Nuestra Señora del Pilar, Escuela Técnica Superior de Ingenieros Agrónomos, Univ. of Madrid; Asst Engineer, Study Group, Servicio Nacional de Concentración Parcelaria 1964–69; Tech. Dir Fondo de Ordenación y Regulación de Productos y Precios Agrarios (FORPPA) 1969–73; Sub-commissar for Devt Plan 1973; Dir of Tech. Cttee, Ministry of Agric. 1974; Dir-Gen. Food Industries 1974–76; Under-Sec. of Agric. 1976; Asst to Third Vice-Pres. of Govt 1977–78; Minister of Agric. and Fisheries 1978–81; Minister Asst to Pres. Council of Ministers 1981–82; mem. Congress of Deputies for Castellón 1979–82; mem. Unión de Centro Democrático (UCD); Chief UCD spokesman in Congress 1981–82; briefly mem. Partido Liberal 1986; Pres. 20th FAO World Conf. 1979–81; Pres. Conf. of OECD Ministers of Agric. 1980; Prof., Int. Centre for Advanced Mediterranean Agronomic Studies, Montpellier, France (OECD) 1980; fmr Prof. of Econs, School of Agricultural Eng, Univ. of Valencia; fmr Prof. of Econs and Politics, School of Agricultural Eng, Polytechnic Univ. of Madrid; EC Jean Monnet Chair 1991; apptd adviser to the Pres. of the Generalidad Valenciana 1995; Chair. Asociación Nacional de Constructores Independientes 2004–; mem. Social Council of Universidad Jaime I de Castellón; mem. Bd of Dirs of several cos; Gran Cruz del Mérito Agrícola, Gran Cruz del Mérito Civil, Encomienda del Mérito Agrícola, Cross of Merit (FRG), Croix du Mérite Civil (France), Gran Cruz de la Orden de Isabel la Católica 2002; King Jaime I Prize for Econs 1999. *Publications:* Agricultura a tiempo parcial y minifundios, Reflexiones sobre la política de precios y su armonización con la política general agraria, Los latifundios y el desarrollo agrario, Interrelación de las políticas de precio y de estructura en la agricultura, La agricultura en una sociedad democrática, El sistema de cuotas lácteas (co-author) 1996, La década perdida: 1985–1996 (La agricultura española en la UE) 1998, La nueva política agraria común 1998, Agricultura sostenible 1999, Los problemas actuales de la contratación de obras públicas (co-author) 2000. *Leisure interests:* reading, music, painting. *Address:* Asociación Nacional de Constructores Independientes, Diego de León, 50, 5th floor, Madrid 28006 (office); José Abascal 46, Madrid, Spain. *Telephone:* (91) 5550539 (office); (91) 5554005 (office); 4413415. *E-mail:* anci@ancisa.com (office). *Website:* www.ancisa.com (office).

LAMONT, Donald Alexander, MA; British diplomatist (retd); b. 13 Jan. 1947; s. of Alexander Lamont and Alexa Lee Will; m. Lynda Margaret Campbell 1981; one s. one d.; ed Univ. of Aberdeen; with British Leyland Motor Corpn 1970; Second Sec., then First Sec. FCO 1974; First Sec., UNIDO/IAEA, Vienna 1977; First Sec. (Commercial), Embassy in Moscow 1980; First Sec., FCO 1982; Counsellor on secondment to IISS 1988; Political Adviser and Head of Chancery, British Mil. Govt, Berlin 1988–91; Amb. to Uruguay 1991–94; Head of Repub. of Ireland Dept, FCO 1994–97; Chief of Staff and Deputy High Rep., Sarajevo 1997–99; Gov. of Falkland Islands and Commr for S Georgia and S Sandwich Islands 1999–2002; Amb. to Venezuela 2003–07; CEO Wilton Park (FCO conference unit) 2007–09; mem. Bd of Dirs Sistema Scotland.

LAMONT, Edward Miner (Ned), Jr, BA, MBA; American politician; *Governor of Connecticut;* b. 3 Jan. 1954, Washington, DC; s. of Edward Miner Lamont and Camille Helene Lamont (née Buzby); m. Annie Huntress Lamont 1983; one s. two d.; ed Harvard Univ., Yale School of Man.; Reporter and Ed., Black River Tribune 1977–78; worked with Cablevision; founder and owner, Campus Televideo 1984–2015; f. Lamont Digital Systems 1985; cand. for US Senate 2006; Gov. of Connecticut 2019–; apptd Adjunct Prof. and Chair of the Arts and Sciences Public Policy Cttee, Central Connecticut State Univ., also Distinguished Prof. of Political Science and Philosophy. *Address:* Office of the Governor, 210 Capitol Avenue, Hartford, CT 06106, USA (office). *Telephone:* (860) 566-4840 (office). *Website:* www.portal.ct.gov/governor (office).

LAMONT OF LERWICK, Baron (Life Peer), cr. 1998, of Lerwick in the Shetland Islands; **Rt Hon. Norman Stewart Hughson Lamont,** PC; British politician and writer; b. 8 May 1942, Lerwick, Shetland, Scotland; s. of Daniel Lamont and Helen Irene Hughson; m. Alice Rosemary White 1971 (separated 1999); one s. one d.; ed Loretto School, Fitzwilliam Coll., Cambridge; personal Asst to Rt Hon Duncan Sandys MP 1965; mem. staff Conservative Research Dept 1966–68; MP for Kingston upon Thames 1972–97; Merchant Banker with NM Rothschild & Sons 1968–79, Dir Rothschild Asset Man.; Parl. Pvt. Sec. to Norman St John Stevas (Lord St John of Fawsley) 1974; Opposition Spokesman on Prices and Consumer Affairs 1975–76, on Industry 1976–79; Parl. Under-Sec. of State, Dept of Energy 1979–81; Minister of State, Dept of Trade and Industry 1981–85, of Defence Procurement 1985–86; Financial Sec. to Treasury 1986–89, Chief Sec. 1989–90; Chancellor of the Exchequer 1990–93; Chair. Conservatives Against a Fed. Europe 1998–99; Chair. East European Food Fund 1995; Chair. Bruges Group 2003, now Vice-Pres.; mem. House of Lords Select Cttee on EU 2001–03; Owner, Rocklea Ltd (consultancy); Chair. British-Iranian Chamber of Commerce; Pres. Econ. Research Council 2008–, British Romanian Chamber of Commerce; mem. Bd of Dirs Jupiter European Opportunities Trust plc (investment trust), Stanhope Gate Architecture & Urban Design Ltd, Compagnie Internationale de Participations Bancaires et Financieres (investment co.); mem. Bd of Dirs (non-exec.) N.M. Rothschild & Sons Ltd 1993–95; mem. Advisory Bd Halkin Investments, Abraaj Corpn (pvt. equity man.), Iran Heritage Foundation; mem. Advisory Council, Eurasian Council on Foreign Affairs; Adviser, Mutual Finance, Stanhope Capital LLP, Land Holdings Capital Ltd, BC Partners; Sr Advisor to Official Monetary and Financial Institutions Forum; Chair. Cambridge Univ. Conservative Asscn 1963; Pres., Cambridge Union 1964; Hon. Patron, Oxford Univ. History Soc. 2007. *Publications:* Sovereign Britain 1995, In Office 1999. *Leisure interests:* ornithology, theatre, literature. *Address:* House of Lords, Westminster, London, SW1A 0PW, England (office). *Telephone:* (20) 7219-5353 (office). *Fax:* (20) 7219-5979 (office).

LAMOTHE, Laurent Salvador, BSc, MBA; Haitian business executive and politician; b. 14 Aug. 1972, Port-au-Prince; s. of Louis G. Lamothe and Ghislaine Fortuney Lamothe; m.; two d.; ed Barry Univ., Miami, USA, St Thomas Univ.; co-f. Global Voice Group (int. telecoms co.) 1998, CEO –2011; mem. Interim Haiti Recovery Comm. 2011; Minister of Planning and External Co-operation Aug. 2010–; involved with electoral campaign of Michel Martelly 2011, Special Adviser to Pres. Michel Martelly 2011; Minister of Foreign Affairs 2011–12; Prime Minister of Haiti May 2012–14; Co-Chair. (with fmr US Pres. Bill Clinton) Presidential Advisory Council for Econ. Devt and Investment in Haiti 2011; Ernst and Young Entrepreneur of the Year Award 2008. *Leisure interest:* tennis (represented Haiti in Davis Cup 1994 and 1995). *Address:* Ministry of Planning and External Co-operation, avenue John Brown, route de Bourdon 347, Port-au-Prince, Haiti (office). *Telephone:* 2228-2512 (office). *Fax:* 2222-0226 (office). *E-mail:* info@mpce.gouv.ht (office). *Website:* www.mpce.gouv.ht (office); www.laurentlamothe.com.

LAMOUR, Jean-François; French politician and fmr fencer; b. 2 Feb. 1956, Paris; fmr sabre fencer; French Junior Champion 1971; Champion of France 1977–78, 1980–85, 1987–89, 1991–92; World Champion, Lausanne 1987; Silver Medal (team), Gold Medal (individual), Los Angeles Olympics 1984; Gold Medal (individual), Seoul Olympics 1988; Bronze Medal (team), Barcelona Olympics 1992; coached by Augustine Parent and László Szepesi; Adviser on Youth and Sports, Office of the Mayor of Paris 1993–95, to the Presidency 1995–2002; Minister of Sports 2002–04, of Youth, Sports and Social Asscns 2004–07; mem. Union pour un Mouvement Populaire (UMP) 2007–, joined group Rally UMP 2012, Vice-Pres. 2013–14; mem. Assemblée nationale for 13th Dist of Paris 2007–, mem. Finance Cttee; mem. Cttee, World Anti-Doping Agency 2004, Vice-Pres. 2006; Master of Sabre Prize 1988. *Address:* Assemblée nationale, 126 rue de l'Université, 75355 Paris 07 SP, France (office). *E-mail:* jflamour@assemblee-nationale.fr (office). *Website:* www.assemblee-nationale.fr/14/tribun/fiches_id/230329.asp (office).

LAMPERT, Edward (Eddie) S., BEcons; American retail executive; b. 1963, Greenwich, Conn.; s. of Floyd M. Lampert and Dolores Lampert; m. Kinga Keh 2001; three c.; ed Yale Univ.; sales and training internship Goldman Sachs & Co. 1984, held positions in Risk Arbitrage Dept 1985–88; Founding Chair. and CEO ESL Investments Inc. (pvt. investment fund), Greenwich, Conn. 1988–; Chair. Kmart Holding Corpn 2003–, Sears Holdings Corpn (after merger of Kmart Holding and Sears, Roebuck 2005) 2013–19, CEO 2013–18; mem. Bd of Dirs AutoNation Inc., AutoZone Inc. 1999–2006.

LAMPORT, Leslie B., BS, MA, PhD; American computer scientist; *Computer Scientist, Microsoft Corporation;* b. 7 Feb. 1941, New York; ed Bronx High School of Science, Massachusetts Inst. of Tech., Brandeis Univ.; worked part-time at Mitre Corpn 1962–65; computer scientist, Massachusetts Computer Assocs 1970–77, SRI International 1977–85, Digital Equipment Corpn/Compaq 1985–2001, Microsoft Corpn 2001–; mem. Nat. Acad. of Eng 1991, NAS 2011, American Acad. of Arts and Sciences 2014; Dr hc (Univ. of Rennes) 2003, (Christian Albrechts Univ. of Kiel) 2003, (École Polytechnique Fédérale de Lausanne) 2004, (Università della Svizzera Italiana, Lugano) 2006, (Université Henri Poincaré, Nancy) 2007, (Brandeis Univ., Waltham) 2017; Dijkstra Prize 2000, 2005, IEEE Emanuel R. Piore Award 2004, SIGOPS Hall of Fame Award, Asscn for Computing Machinery (ACM) 2007, 2012, 2013, LICS 1988 Test of Time Award 2008, IEEE John von Neumann Medal 2008, Jean-Claude Laprie Award in Dependable Computing 2013, 2014, Edsger W. Dijkstra Prize in Distributed Computing 2014, A.M. Turing Award, Asscn for Computing Machinery 2014. *Achievements include:* known for work in distributed systems and as initial developer of LaTeX document preparation system. *Publications include:* more than 170 papers in professional journals. *Address:* Microsoft Corporation, 1020 Enterprise Way, Sunnyvale, CA 94089, USA (office). *Telephone:* (650) 693-2725 (office). *E-mail:* lamport@microsoft.com (office). *Website:* www.lamport.org (office).

LAMY, Pascal Lucien Fernand, MBA; French civil servant and international organization official; *Honorary President, Jacques Delors Institute, Notre Europe;* b. 8 April 1947, Levallois-Perret (Seine); s. of Jacques Lamy and Denise Dujardin; m. Geneviève Luchaire 1972; three s.; ed Lycée Carnot, Paris, Ecole des Hautes Etudes Commerciales, Paris, Inst. d'Etudes Politiques, École Nationale d'Admin, Paris; Lt Commdr (navy); served in Inspection Générale des Finances 1975–79; Sec.-Gen. Mayoux Cttee 1979; Deputy Sec.-Gen., then Sec.-Gen. Inter-ministerial Cttee for the Remodelling of Industrial Structures (CIASI) Treasury Dept 1979–81; Tech. Adviser, then Deputy Dir Office of the Minister for Econ. and Financial Affairs 1981–82; Deputy Dir Office of the Prime Minister (Pierre Mauroy) 1983–84; Chef de Cabinet to Pres. of Comm. of EC (Jacques Delors) 1984–94; Dir-Gen. and mem. Exec. Cttee Crédit Lyonnais 1994–99; Commr for Trade, European Comm. 1999–2004; Pres. Jacques Delors Inst., Notre Europe 2004–05, Hon. Pres. 2005–; apptd Assoc. Prof., Institut d'Etudes Politiques, Paris 2004; Dir-Gen. WTO 2005–13; Officier, Légion d'honneur 1990, Kt Commdr's Cross (Badge and Star) of the Order of Merit (Germany) 1991, Commdr Order of Merit (Luxembourg) 1995, Officer of the Order of Merit (Gabon) 2000, Order of the Aztec Eagle (Mexico) 2003, Order of Merit (Chile) 2004, Commdr, Légion d'honneur 2013; Dr hc (Louvain) 2003, (Geneva) 2009, (Montreal) 2010, (Dhaka) 2012; Global Economy Prize, Kiel Inst. 2010. *Publications include:* Report on Welfare Assistance for Children (co-author) 1979, Report on "Monde-Europe" (XI Plan of the Commissariat Général au Plan) 1993, L'Europe en première ligne 2002, L'Europe de nos volontés (co-author) 2002, La démocratie monde 2004. *Leisure interests:* Nordic skiing, jogging, marathon running. *Address:* Jacques Delors Institute, Notre Europe, 19, rue de Milan, 75009 Paris, France (office). *Telephone:* 1-44-58-97-97 (office). *Fax:* 1-44-58-97-99 (office). *Website:* www.eng.notre-europe .eu (office).

LAN, Lijun, BA, MPA; Chinese diplomatist; b. 5 Dec. 1952, Jiangsu Prov.; m. Gu Langlin; one d.; ed Beijing Foreign Languages Inst., Queen's Univ. and McGill Univ., Canada, Kennedy School of Govt, Harvard Univ., USA; Deputy Dir-Gen. Dept of N American and Oceanian Affairs, Ministry of Foreign Affairs 1996–2000, Consul Gen., with rank of Amb., Consulate Gen. in Los Angeles and Minister at Embassy in Washington, DC 2002–05, Amb. to Indonesia 2005–08, to Canada 2009–11, to Sweden 2011–13.

LANBA, Adm. Sunil, ADC; Indian naval officer; *Chief of Naval Staff;* b. 17 July 1957, Mumbai; m. Reena Lanba; one s. two d.; ed Mayo Coll., Ajmer, Nat. Defence Acad., Royal Coll. of Defence Studies, UK; commissioned in Indian Navy 1978, has held various command, operational and staff positions, including Commdr of four warships, INS Kakinada (minesweeper), INS Himgiri (frigate), INS Ranvijay (destroyer) and INS Mumbai (destroyer), also served as Exec. Officer, aircraft carrier INS Viraat, staff positions included Chief of Staff, Southern Naval Command, Flag Officer of the Sea Training, Chief of Staff, Eastern Naval Command, Commdt, Nat. Defence Coll., Fleet Operations Officer of Western Fleet of Mumbai, Flag Officer Commdg-in-Chief, Southern Naval Command, Vice-Chief of Naval Staff 2014–16, apptd Flag Officer Commdg-in-Chief, Western Naval Command, Mumbai Jan. 2016, Chief of Naval Staff May 2016–; Chair. Chiefs of Staff Cttee Dec. 2016–; Hon. Aide-De-Camp to the Pres. of India; Param Vishist Seva Medal, Ati Vishist Seva Medal. *Address:* Office of the Chief of Naval Staff, Integrated Headquarters of the Ministry of Defence, New Delhi 110 011, India (office). *Telephone:* (11) 23019665 (office). *E-mail:* pronavy.dprmod@nic.in (office). *Website:* www.indiannavy.nic.in (office).

LANCASTER, (Christopher Ronald) Mark, BA; British/American artist and set designer; b. 14 May 1938, Holmfirth, W Yorks., England; s. of Charles Ronald Lancaster and Muriel Roebuck; m. David Bolger; ed Holme Valley Grammar School, Bootham School, York, Newcastle Univ.; asst to Andy Warhol, New York 1964; Lecturer, Newcastle Univ. 1965–66, Bath Acad. of Art 1966–68; Artist in Residence, King's Coll., Cambridge 1968–70; moved to USA permanently 1973; Pvt. Sec. to Jasper Johns, New York 1974–85; Resident Designer, Merce Cunningham Dance Co., New York 1975–80, Prin. Designer and Artistic Adviser 1980–84, designed sets, costumes and lighting for dance works including Sounddance 1975, Rebus 1975, Torse 1976, Squaregame 1976, Fractions (both video and stage versions) 1977, Tango 1978, Roadrunners 1979, Duets, 1980, Tens with Shoes 1981, Gallopade 1981, Trails 1982, Quartet 1982, Roaratorio 1983, Inlets 2 1983, Fielding Sixes 1983, Pictures 1984, Doubles 1984, also designed Duets for the American Ballet Theatre 1982, Fielding Sixes for Ballet Rambert 1983 and Ballet Royal de Wallonie 1983, returned in 1988 to design Five Stone Wind in Berlin, Avignon and New York (Bessie Award, New York Dance and Performance Awards 1989), Neighbors 1991, Touchbase for Rambert Dance Company 1992 and Cunningham Company 1992, CRWDSPCR 1993 and new versions of Sounddance and Rune 1994; US citizen 1999; New York Dance and Performance Award 1989. *Address:* c/o Robert Rogal, Rogallery.com, 47-15 36th Street, Long Island City, NY 11101, USA. *Telephone:* (718) 937-0901. *Fax:* (718) 937-1206. *E-mail:* art@rogallery.com. *Website:* www.rogallery.com/Lancaster/ Lancaster-hm.htm.

LANCE, Ryan M., BS; American oil engineer and business executive; *Chairman and CEO, ConocoPhillips Company;* ed Montana Tech, Butte; joined ARCO 1984, held various man., eng and operations positions, later Vice-Pres. of Western North Slope operations in Alaska (acquired by Phillips) –2001, Gen. Man. Lower 48 and Canadian operations for Phillips 2001–02, Vice-Pres. Lower 48 (upon merger with Conoco) 2002–03, Pres. Asia Pacific Exploration and Production 2003–05, Pres. Downstream Strategy, Integration and Specialty Functions 2005–06, Sr Vice-Pres. Tech. and Major Projects 2006–07, Sr Vice-Pres. Tech. 2007–09, Pres., Exploration and Production – Asia, Africa, Middle East and Russia/Caspian 2007–09, Sr Vice-Pres., Exploration & Production – International 2009–12, Chair. and CEO ConocoPhillips 2012–; mem. Bd of Dirs, Spindletop International, Montana Tech Foundation; mem. Energy Advisory Bd, Univ. of Houston; Chair. American Petroleum Inst. 2016; mem. Soc. of Petroleum Engineers. *Address:* ConocoPhillips Company, Conoco Center, 600 North Dairy Ashford, Houston, TX 77079-1175, USA (office). *Telephone:* (281) 293-1000 (office). *Fax:* (281) 293-1440 (office). *E-mail:* info@conocophillips.com (office). *Website:* www.conocophillips.com (office).

LANCELOT, Alain, DèsSc et LHum; French political scientist and academic; *Professor Emeritus, Institut d'Etudes Politiques;* b. 12 Jan. 1937, Chêne-Bougeries, Geneva, Switzerland; s. of Elisée Lancelot and Suzanne Perrin-Lancelot; m. Marie Thé Merlet 1958; one s. one d.; ed Inst. d'Etudes Politiques, Paris and Univ. of Paris-Sorbonne; Asst, French Political Science Assen 1959–62, Sec.-Gen. 1970–75; naval service 1962–63; Researcher, CNRS 1963–67; Prof., Inst. d'Etudes Politiques, Paris 1967–99, Prof. Emer. 1999–; Dir Centre for Study of French Political Life 1975–86; Dir Inst. d'Etudes Politiques de Paris and Exec. Officer Fondation Nat. des Sciences Politiques 1987–96, 2001–; Pres. Observatoire Interrégional du Politique; Chair. Int. Centre for Studies in Educ. 1987–96; Vice-Pres. Training Centre for Journalists 1987–96; mem. Conseil Constitutionnel 1996–2001, Strategic Cttee of the French Union of Electricity 2001–, Council for Democratic Elections of the Council of Europe 2002–, Bd Robert Schuman Foundation 2002–; Alt. mem. Venice Comm. for Democracy Through Law 2002–; Grand Officier, Légion d'honneur; Officier, Ordre nat. du Mérite, des Arts et des Lettres, des Palmes académiques; decorations from Germany and Italy. *Publications:* La participation des français à la politique 1961, Les attitudes politiques 1962, L'abstentionnisme électoral en France 1968, La vie politique en France depuis 1940 1975, Les élections sous la cinquième république 1983, Annuaire de la France politique 1984, 1985. *Leisure interest:* sailing. *Address:* Fondation Nationale des Sciences Politiques, 27 rue Saint-Guillaume, 75337 Paris Cedex 07 (office); 4 ter rue du Cherche-Midi, 75006 Paris, France (home). *Telephone:* 1-45-49-50-50 (office). *Website:* www.sciences-po.fr (office).

LANCI, Gianfranco; Italian business executive; *President and Chief Operating Officer, Lenovo Group;* b. 1954, Turin; m.; several c.; ed Politecnico of Turin; joined Texas Instruments (TI) Italia 1981, Country Man. for Portable Computers and Printers Div. in Italy, Middle East and Africa 1991–96, Pres. Europe, Middle East, Africa (EMEA) for TI's Personal Productivity Products Div. 1996–97, Man. Dir Acer Italy (following merger of TI's portable PC business with Acer in 1997) 1997–2000, Pres. Acer Europe 2000–02, Pres. Acer EMEA 2002–03, Pres. Acer's Int. Operations Business Group 2003–04, Pres. Acer Inc. 2005–11, CEO 2008–11; consultant, Lenovo 2011–12, Sr Vice-Pres. and Pres. EMEA 2012–14, COO and Exec. Vice-Pres. PC Group 2014–15, Pres. and COO, Lenovo Group 2015–. *Leisure interests:* reading, playing tennis. *Address:* Lenovo Group, 6 Shangdi West Roade, Haidan District, Beijing 100085, People's Republic of China (office). *Telephone:* (10) 58868888 (office). *E-mail:* info@lenovo.com (office). *Website:* www.lenovo.com (office).

LAND, Michael Francis, MA, PhD, FRS; British neurobiologist and academic; *Professor of Neurobiology, University of Sussex;* b. 12 April 1942, Dartmouth, Devon, England; s. of Prof. F. W. Land and Mrs N. B. Land; m. 1st Judith Drinkwater 1966 (divorced 1980), one s.; m. 2nd Rosemary Roper 1980; two d.; ed Birkenhead School, Jesus Coll. Cambridge, Univ. Coll. London and Univ. of California, Berkeley (Miller Fellowship); Asst Prof., Univ. of California, Berkeley 1969–71; Lecturer, School of Biological Sciences, Univ. of Sussex 1971–77, Reader 1977–84, Prof. of Neurobiology 1984–; Fellow, Univ. Coll. London 1998; Visiting Prof., Univ. of Ore. 1980; Sr Visiting Fellow, ANU 1982–84; Foreign mem. Royal Physiographical Soc., Sweden 1995; Frank Smart Prize in Zoology, Cambridge 1963, ALCON Prize for Vision Research 1996, Rank Prize for Opto-electronics 1998, Frink Medal, Zoological Soc. of London 1994. *Publications include:* Animal Eyes (with D. E. Nilsson) 2002 (revised edn 2012), Looking and Acting (with B. W. Tatler) 2009, The Eye – A Very Short Introduction 2014; 190 articles and papers on aspects of vision in animals from visual optics to behaviour. *Leisure interests:* gardening, music. *Address:* School of Life Sciences, University of Sussex, Brighton, BN1 9QG (office); Dart Cottage, 1 The Elms, Ringmer, BN8 5EZ, England (home). *Telephone:* (1273) 678505 (office); (1273) 813911 (home). *Fax:* (1273) 678433 (office). *E-mail:* m.f.land@sussex.ac.uk (office). *Website:* www.sussex.ac.uk/lifesci (office).

LANDAU, Igor, MBA; French business executive; *Chairman, Adidas AG;* b. 13 July 1944, Saint-Flour, Cantal; ed Hautes Etudes Commerciales, Institut Européen d'Admin des Affaires (INSEAD); Pres. La Compagnie du Roneo (German subsidiary), Frankfurt 1968–70; consultant, McKinsey Co., Paris 1971–75; Deputy to Pres. of Health Div., Rhône-Poulenc Inc. 1975, Exec. Vice-Pres. of Div. 1977–80, Chair. Health Sector 1987, mem. Exec. Cttee 1987, Group Pres. 1992, mem. Bd of Dirs 1998; mem. Man. Bd Aventis 1999–2002, Chair. Man. Bd 2000–, Chair. Supervisory Bd Aventis Pharma AG 1999–2002, mem. Bd of Dirs Sanofi-Aventis 2004–; mem. Supervisory Bd Adidas AG 2004–, Chair. 2009–; Pres. Supervisory Bd Centre Européen d'Educ. Perm.; mem. Institut pour le Développement Industrial; mem. Bd Dirs Essilor. *Address:* Adidas AG, Adi-Dassler-Strasse 1, 91074, Herzogenaurach, Germany (office). *Telephone:* (91) 32840 (office). *Fax:* (91) 32842241 (office). *Website:* www.adidas-group.com (office).

LANDAU, Jean-Pierre, MBA; French economist and academic; *Associate Professor, Department of Economics, Sciences Po;* b. 7 Nov. 1946, Paris; s. of André Landau and Andrée Pestre; m. Evelyne Dova 1979; ed École des Hautes Études Commerciales (HEC), Inst. d'études politiques de Paris, (Sciences Po), Ecole nat. d'admin; served in Ministry of Health and Social Security 1978–79; Assoc. Prof. of Econs, Sciences Po, Paris 1983–2011, Prof. of Public Policy 2007–11, Assoc. Prof., Dept of Econs 2013–, Dean, School of Public Affairs 2014–15; Asst Sec. for Trade Policy, Direction des Relations Économiques Extérieures 1986–89, various other positions in Ministry of Econ. and Finance; Exec. Dir IMF 1989–93; Dir Relations Economiques Extérieures (DREE) 1993–96; Dir-Gen. French Asscn of Banks 1999–2000; Financial Counsellor, French Embassy in UK 2001–06; Dir EBRD 2001–06; Second Deputy Gov. and mem. Gen. Council, Banque de France 2006–11; Lecturer, Woodrow Wilson School, Princeton Univ. 2012; Consultant, Bank of Korea 2012–13; mem. Ind. Panel Review of Doing Business Report, World Bank 2012–13; mem. Cttee on the Global Financial System, BIS 2006–11, mem. Bd of Dirs 2008–11; Chair. Int. Relations Cttee, Euopean Central Bank 2010–11; Visiting Prof., School for Advanced Int. Studies (SAIS), John Hopkins Univ. 1990–93. *Address:* Sciences Po, Département d'économie, 27, rue Saint Guillaume, 75337 Paris Cedex 07 (office); 13 rue de l'Odéon, 75006 Paris, France. *E-mail:* jeanpierre.landau@sciencespo.fr (office); jeanpierrelandau@hotmail.com. *Website:* www.econ.sciences-po.fr (office); www.jeanpierrelandau.com.

LANDAU, Peter, DJur; German professor of law and research institute director; *President, Stephan Kuttner Institute of Medieval Canon Law;* b. 26 Feb. 1935, Berlin; m. Angelika Linnemann 1971; one s. one d.; ed Univs of Berlin, Freiburg, Bonn and Yale Univ., USA; Prof., Univ. of Regensburg 1968–87; Prof. of Law, Univ. of Munich 1987–2003, Prof. Emer. 2003–, Pres. Stephan Kuttner Inst. of Medieval Canon Law; mem. Inst. for Advanced Study, Princeton, USA 1990–91; mem. Bayerische Akad. der Wissenschaften; Corresp. mem. Medieval Acad. of America, Accad. Senese degli Intronati; Hon. DrIur (Basel) 1981; Dr hc (Munich) 1997, (Paris) 2001, (Panthéon-Assas Univ.). *Publications include:* Die Entstehung des kanonischen Infamiebegriffs von Gratian bis zur Glossa ordinaria. Forschungen zur kirchlichen Rechtsgeschichte und zum Kirchenrecht Bd 5 1966, Ius Patronatus 1975, Strafrecht, Strafprozess und Rezeption (co-ed.) 1984, Officium und Libertas christiana 1991, Heinrich Mitteis nach hundert Jahren (1889–1989) 1991, Stufen der Gerechtigkeit 1995, Kanones und Dekretalen 1997, Karl von Amira zum Gedächtnis 1999, Große jüdische Gelehrte an der Münchener Juristischen Fakultät 2000, Magistri Honorii Summa 'De iure canonico tractaturus' I (Monumenta Iuris Canonici, Ser. A, Vol. 5) 2004, Die Lex Baiuvariorum. Entstehungszeit, Entstehungsort und Charakter von Bayerns ältester Rechts- und Geschichtsquelle 2004, Die Collectio Francofurtana: Eine französische Decretalensammlung. Analyse beruhend auf Vorarbeiten von Walther Holtzmann (Monumenta Iuris Canonici, Series B, Vol. 9) (co-ed.) 2007, Die Kölner Kanonistik des 12. Jahrhunderts; Ein Höhepunkt der europäischen Rechtswissenschaft. In: Kölner Rechtsgeschichtliche Vorträge, Heft 1 2008, Grundlagen und Geschichte des evangelischen Kirchenrechts und des Staatskirchenrechts 2010, Magistri Honorii Summa 'De iure canonico tractaturus', Tom. III (Monumenta Iuris Canonici, Series A, Corpus Glossatorum 5/III) (co-ed.) 2010, Canon Law, Religion and Politics. Liber Amicorum Robert Sommerville (co-ed.) 2012, Summa 'Omnis qui iuste iudicat' sive Lipsiensis', Tom. 7/II (co-ed.) 2012, Europäische Rechtsgeschichte und kanonisches Recht im Mittelalter 2013, Deutsche Rechtsgeschichte im Kontext Europas 2016; numerous essays and reviews. *Leisure interest:* art. *Address:* Stephan Kuttner Institute of Medieval Canon Law, Professor-Huber-Platz 2, 80539 Munich (office); Sperberstr. 21C, 81827 Munich, Germany (home). *Telephone:* (89) 21802122 (office); (89) 21801370 (office); (89) 4300121 (home). *Fax:* (89) 21802714 (office). *E-mail:* peter.landau@jura.uni-muenchen.de (office). *Website:* www.jura.uni-muenchen.de/personen/l/landau_peter/index.html (office); www.kuttner-institute.jura.uni-muenchen.de (office).

LANDAU, Uzi, PhD; Israeli systems analyst and politician (retd); b. 1943, Haifa; m.; three c.; ed Haifa Technion, Massachusetts Inst. of Tech., USA; served as paratrooper officer during mil. service; mem. Knesset (Likud Party) 1984–2006, (Israel Beytenu) 2008–15, Chair. Foreign Affairs and Defense Cttee, State Control Cttee; Knesset Observer at the European Council; mem. Israeli Del. to Madrid Peace Conf.; Observer at the European Council; Minister of Public Security 2001–03, of Nat. Infrastructure 2008–13, of Tourism 2013–15; fmr Minister in charge of overseeing the intelligence services and the US–Israel strategic dialogue in the Prime Minister's Office; Dir-Gen. Ministry of Transport; Lecturer, Israel Inst. of Tech. (Technion), Haifa; mem. Bd El-Al Airlines, Israel Port Authority, Israel Airport Authority, Soc. for the Protection of Nature, Si'ah Vasig (Israel Debating Soc.). *Publications:* articles in professional journals on transport planning, articles in the press on foreign policy, strategic and security affairs.

LANDEL, Michel; French (b. Moroccan) business executive; b. 7 Nov. 1951, Meknes, Morocco; m.; three c.; ed European Business School, Paris; Financial Analyst, Chase Manhattan Bank 1977–80; Gen. Man. Poliet Group (now Saint-Gobain) 1980–84; Chief Operating Man. for E and N Africa, Sodexho (now Sodexo SA) 1984–86, Pres. Group Remote Site Operations, Africa 1986–89, Head of N American Operations 1989–99, CEO Sodexho Inc. 1989–2000, Vice-Chair. Exec. Cttee, Sodexho Alliance SA 2000–03, COO Sodexho Alliance SA 2003–05, Group CEO 2005–18, Chair. Exec. Cttee 2005–18, mem. Bd of Dirs 2009–18, Pres. Sodexo STOP Hunger Asscn –2018; mem. Bd of Dirs Louis Delhaize SA, Catalyst Inc., Danone SA; Chevalier, Légion d'honneur; Golden Chain Award for Multi-Unit Food Service Operators 1997, Ivy Award for Restaurant & Institutions 1998, Penn State Hotel and Restaurant Soc. Hospitality Exec. of the Year 2002, Diversity Best Practice CEO Leadership Award, Asian Enterprise CEO Advocate of the Year 2004. *Leisure interests:* travel, relaxing in the kitchen preparing delicious and unique dishes for family and friends. *Address:* c/o Sodexo SA, 255 quai de la Bataille de Stalingrad, 92866 Issy-les-Moulineaux, France.

LANDER, Eric S., DPhil; American biologist and academic; *Director, The Broad Institute;* b. 3 Feb. 1957, Brooklyn, NY; ed Princeton Univ. and Univ. of Oxford, UK (Rhodes Scholar); taught econs to business students at Harvard Univ., Prof. of Systems Biology, Harvard Medical School; Fellow, Whitehead Inst. for Biomedical Research MIT 1985–89, f. Center for Genome Research at MIT 1990, fmr Assoc. Prof. of Biology, now Prof. of Biology and Dir Whitehead Inst. for Biomedical Research/MIT Center for Genome Research, Founding Dir The Broad Inst. 2003–; Co-Chair. Council of Advisors on Science and Technology in the Obama administration 2008–; mem. Advisory Bd USA Science and Eng Festival; serves on numerous govt advisory cttees; Founder and Dir Millennium Pharmaceuticals; fmr Chair. Jt Steering Cttee for Public Policy; Fellow, American Acad. of Arts and Sciences 1990; MacArthur Fellowship 1987, J. Allyn Taylor Int. Prize in Medicine, John P. Robarts Research Inst. (co-recipient) 2001, Harvey Prize, Technion Israel 2012, Dan David Prize 2012, Breakthrough Prize in Life Sciences 2013. *Publications:* In Wake of Genetic Revolution, Questions About Its Meaning 2000; numerous articles in scientific journals; led group of bioinformatics specialists who produced an analysis of draft human genome for publication in Nature 2001. *Address:* Office of the Provost, NE125-2246, The Broad Institute, 320 Charles Street, Cambridge, MA 02141-2023, USA (office). *Telephone:* (617) 252-1906 (office); (617) 258-5192 (Whitehead Inst.) (office). *Fax:* (617) 258-0903 (office). *E-mail:* lander@broad.mit.edu (office); lander@genome.wi.mit.edu (office). *Website:* biology.mit.edu/people/eric_lander (office); www.broad.mit.edu (office).

LANDER, Sir Stephen James, Kt, KCB, CB, MA, PhD; British public servant; m. Felicity Lander 1972; one s. (died 2002) one d.; ed Bishop's Stortford Coll., Herts., Queens' Coll., Cambridge Univ.; with Inst. of Historical Research, London Univ. 1972–75; joined Security Service (MI5) 1975, Dir 1992–96, Dir-Gen. 1996–2002; apptd Ind. Commr (overseeing complaints against solicitors), The Law Soc. 2002; mem. Bd of Dirs (non-exec.) HM Customs and Excise 2002–, Northgate Information Solutions 2004–; Chair. Serious and Organised Crime Agency (SOCA) 2004–09 (retd).

LANDGREN, Karin, BSc, LLM; Swedish UN official and academic; b. 13 Oct. 1957; two c.; ed London School of Econs, UK; grew up in Japan; spent nearly 20 years with UNHCR, worked extensively with Afghan, Iranian and Vietnamese asylum seekers as Protection Officer for UNHCR in India and as Deputy Rep. in the Philippines 1980s, headed UNHCR office in Bosnia-Herzegovina during the war 1990s, as well as offices in Eritrea and Singapore, later Chief of Standards and Legal Advice, UNHCR, Head of Child Protection, UNICEF 1998–2008, UN Deputy Special Rep. of Sec.-Gen. for Nepal 2008–09, UN Rep. for Nepal and Head of UN Mission in Nepal (UNMIN) 2009–10, Special Rep. and Head, UN Office in Burundi (BNUB) 2010, Special Rep. of Sec.-Gen. and Head of UN Mission in Liberia (UNMIL) 2012–15; Corresp. Ed. International Legal Materials; mem. Editorial Bd Sec.-Gen.'s Study on Violence against Children 2006; Adjunct Prof., School of Int. and Public Affairs, Columbia Univ., New York, USA. *Publications include:* has published widely on humanitarian, refugee and child protection issues.

LANDRIEU, Mary L., BA; American politician and foundation executive; b. 23 Nov. 1955, Arlington, Va; d. Moon Landrieu; m. E. Frank Snellings; two c.; ed Ursuline Academy, New Orleans and Louisiana State Univ.; Louisiana State Rep., Dist 90 1980–88; Louisiana State Treas. 1986–96; cand. for Democratic gubernatorial nomination 1995; Senator from Louisiana 1997–2015; strategic advisor, Walton Family Foundation 2015–; fmr mem. Women Execs in State Govt, Fed. of Democratic Women. *Address:* Walton Family Foundation, PO Box 2030, Bentonville, AR 72712, USA. *Website:* www.waltonfamilyfoundation.org.

LANDRY, Donald W., BS, PhD, MD; American professor of medicine; *Samuel Bard Professor of Medicine and Chairman, Department of Medicine, Columbia University College of Physicians and Surgeons;* b. 19 May 1954, Jersey City, NJ; s. of Donald O. Landry and Gloria A. Landry; m. Maureen O'Reilly Landry; two s.; ed Lafayette Coll., Harvard Univ., Columbia Univ.; Resident in Medicine, Massachusetts Gen. Hosp., Boston, Harvard Medical School 1983–85; Dir Div. of Experimental Therapeutics, Columbia Univ. Coll. of Physicians and Surgeons 1998–, Dir of Nephrology 2003–08, Chair. Dept of Medicine 2008–, currently Samuel Bard Prof. of Medicine; Physician-in-Chief, New York Presbyterian Hosp./Columbia; mem. Pres.'s Council on Bioethics 2008–09; mem. American Soc. for Clinical Investigation, American Asscn of Physicians, Nat. Acad. of Inventors; Presidential Citizen's Medal 2009. *Publications include:* more than 160 articles in learned journals. *Address:* Columbia University College of Physicians and Surgeons, Presbyterian Hospital, Room 8 East, 105 622 West 168th Street, New York, NY 10032, USA (office). *Telephone:* (212) 305-5839 (office). *E-mail:* dwl1@columbia.edu (office). *Website:* asp.cpmc.columbia.edu (office).

LANDSBERGIS, Gabrielius, BA, MA; Lithuanian diplomatist and politician; *Chairman, Tėvynės Sąjunga-Lietuvos Krikščionys Demokratai (Homeland Union-Lithuanian Christian Democrats);* b. 7 Jan. 1982, Vilnius, Lithuanian SSR, USSR; s. of Vytautas Landsbergis; m. Austėja Jasieniec; two s. two d.; ed Vilnius Univ. and its Inst. of Int. Relations and Political Science; adviser, Office of Foreign and European Affairs, Ministry of Foreign Affairs then adviser, Pres.'s Office of Protocol section 2002–07, posted to Embassy in Brussels 2007–11, Head of Regional Div., Chancellery 2011–14; mem. Tėvynės Sąjunga-Lietuvos Krikščionys Demokratai (Homeland Union-Lithuanian Christian Democrats), Chair. 2015–; mem. European Parl. (Group of the European People's Party, Christian Democrats) 2014–, Vice-Chair. Del. to EU-Kazakhstan, EU-Kyrgyzstan, EU-Uzbekistan and EU-Tajikistan Parl. Co-operation Cttees and for relations with Turkmenistan and Mongolia. *Address:* Tėvynės Sąjunga-Lietuvos Krikščionys Demokratai, L. Stuokos-Gucevičiaus g. 11, Vilnius 01122 (office); Room: I-466, Lietuvos Respublikos Seimas, Gedimino pr. 53, Vilnius 01109, Lithuania (office). *Telephone:* (5) 239-6721 (office). *E-mail:* sekretoriatas@tsajunga.lt (office); gabrielius.landsbergis@lrs (office). *Website:* www.tsajunga.lt (office).

LANDSBERGIS, Vytautas, (Jonas Zemkalnis); Lithuanian politician, musicologist, pianist and fmr head of state; b. 18 Oct. 1932, Kaunas; s. of Vytautas Landsbergis-Zemkalnis and Ona Jablonskytė-Landsbergienė; m. Grazina Ručyte; one s. two d.; ed J. Gruodis School of Music, Kaunas, Aušra Gymnasium, Kaunas, Lithuanian Acad. of Music, Vilnius; piano teacher, M.K. Čiurlionis Music School 1952–57; Accompanist, Lithuanian State Conservatoire 1955–57; Lecturer and Prof., Lithuanian Acad. of Music 1957–63, 1978–90; Lecturer and Assoc. Prof., Vilnius Pedagogical Inst. 1957–74; Assoc. Prof., then Prof., Affiliated Conservatoire Depts in Klaipeda 1974–78; Chair. M.K. Čiurlionis Soc. 1987–, Int. M.K. Ciurlionis Piano and Organ Competition 1995–2008; gave concert at Moscow Conservatoire with Russian Nat. Acad. Symphonic Orchestra 1999; piano recitals in Calw, Hanover, Helsinki, Guangzhou, Moscow, New York, Paris, Tokyo, Trieste, Uznam, Vilnius, Warsaw, etc.; fmr mem. Exec. Council and Secr. Composers' Union; elected to Initiative Group, Sajūdis Reform Movt, then to Sajūdis Seimas (Ass.) and Council 1988, Pres. Sajūdis Seimas Council 1988–90, Hon. Pres. Sajūdis Dec. 1991–; f. Lithuanian Conservative Party, Chair. 1993–2003; elected Deputy to USSR Congress of People's Deputies 1989–90; elected to Supreme Council of Lithuania Feb. 1990, Pres. Supreme Council (Head of State) 1990–91; mem. Seimas (Parl.) 1992–2004, Leader of Parl. Opposition 1992–96, Pres. Seimas 1996–2000; cand. for presidential elections 1997; mem. European Parl. 2004–14; mem. Lithuanian Composers' Union 1961; Academician, Lithuanian Catholic Acad. 1997; Paul Harris Fellow (Rotary) 1991; Int. Patron Henry Jackson Soc. 2005; Hon. Fellow, Univ. of Cardiff, UK 2000; Hon. Citizen of Turin, Italy 2007; numerous decorations including Grand Officer, European St Sebastian's Order of Kts 1995; Chevalier, Légion d'honneur 1997, Grand Croix 2016; Order of Grand Duke Vytautas, First Class (Lithuania) 1998; Grand Cross, Royal Norwegian Order of Merit 1998; Grand Cross, Order of the Repub. (Poland) 1999; Grand Cross, Order of Honour (Greece) 1999; Pléiade Ordre de la Francophonie (France) 2000; Three Stars Order (Second Class) (Latvia) 2001; Order of the Cross of St Mary's Land (First Class) (Estonia) 2002; Kt Grand Cross, Order of Orange-Nassau (Netherlands) 2008; Order of Merit of the Repub. of Hungary; Commdr's Cross, Order of the Cross of Vytis (Lithuania) 2012; Democracy Service Medal, Nat. Endowment for Democracy (USA) 2013; Hon. LLD (Loyola Univ., Chicago) 1991; Hon. PhD (Vytautas the Great Univ., Kaunas) 1992, (Klaipėda Univ., Lithuania) 1997; Hon. HD (Weber Univ., USA) 1992; Hon. DIur (Lithuanian Acad.

of Law) 2000; Dr hc (Helsinki) 2000, (Sorbonne) 2001, (Lithuanian Acad. of Art) 2003, (St Lucas Acad., Netherlands-Germany) 2004, (Ilia State Univ., Georgia) 2011, (Acad. of Public Admin, Azerbaijan) 2012, (Lithuanian Acad. of Music and Theatre) 2013, (Nat. Univ. of Music, Bucharest) 2015; Lithuanian State Award (for monograph on M. K. Ciurlionis) 1975; Norwegian People's Peace Prize (for role in restoration of Lithuanian independence; has used prize to establish Landsbergis Foundation to help disabled children and young musicians) 1991, Award of France Fund of Future 1991, Hermann-Ehlers Prize 1992, Catalan Ramon Llull IX Int. Prize 1994, Vibo Valentia Testimony Prize (Italy) 1998, Truman-Reagan Freedom Award (USA) 1999, Constitutional Medallion of Saxonian Parl. (Germany) 2003, Lithuanian Foundation Award 2004, Aschaffenburger Mutig-Preis, Germany 2004, Robert Schuman Medal, European Parl. 2005, Mérite Européen Medal (Luxembourg) 2006, Europa-Medaille Karls IV (Germany) 2007, Lithuanian Nat. Prize 2011, Gusi Int. Peace Prize (Philippines) 2014, Freedom Prize, Seimas of Republic of Lithuania 2017. *Recording:* Ciurlionis, Born of the Human Soul (works for solo piano) 1998. *Publications include:* over 20 books on musicology, art and music history (especially on artist and composer M. K. Ciurlionis) and politics, including M. K. Ciurlionis: Time and Content 1992, Lithuania Independent Again 2000; M. K. Ciurlionis – Thoughts, Pictures, Music (film script) 1965, Who Are We? (under pseudonym Jonas Zemkalnis) 2004, Glimmers of History 2006, Un peuple sort de prison 2007, Crossroad of Europe 2008, Guilt and Atonement: The Story of 13 January 2015, Ukraine's Golgotha 2015, On the Road to Damascus 2015, Astravyets' Coffin 2016, Blood of Medininkai 2016; poetry collections: Intermezzo 1991, Intermezzo non finito 2004, It's Serious, Children 2006; also numerous memoirs, essays and music scores. *Leisure interests:* history, poetry. *Address:* Traidenio Street 34-15, Vilnius 08116, Lithuania (office). *Telephone:* (52) 663676 (office); (52) 724466 (home). *Fax:* (52) 663675 (office); (52) 790505 (home). *E-mail:* vyland@lrs.lt (office). *Website:* www.landsbergis.lt.

LANE, (Alan) Piers, AO, BMus, ARCM, LMusA, AMusA; British/Australian pianist, artistic director and broadcaster; b. 8 Jan. 1958, London; s. of Peter Alan Lane and Enid Muriel Hitchcock; ed Queensland Conservatorium of Music, Royal Coll. of Music, London; broadcaster for BBC Radio 3; critic CD Review; has appeared with numerous orchestras, including London Philharmonic, Philharmonia, Royal Philharmonic, all BBC orchestras, City of Birmingham Symphony, Halle, Australian Chamber Orchestra, all ABC orchestras, New Zealand Symphony Orchestra, Auckland Philharmonic, Christchurch Symphony, Southern Sinfonia, Orchestra Ensemble Kanazawa (Japan), Orchestre National de France, Orchestre Philharmonique de Montpellier, American Symphony Orchestra, Czech Philharmonic, Warsaw Philharmonic, Gothenberg Symphony; has toured extensively in Australia, Africa, Europe, India, Japan, NZ, Russia, Scandinavia, S America, USA; has appeared at festivals including Aldeburgh, Arizona Chamber Music, Australian Festival of Chamber Music, Bard, Bath Mozartfest, BBC Promenade Concerts, Huntington, Husum Festival of Piano Rarities (Germany), Blair Atholl, Speedside, Toronto, Singapore Piano Festival, Newport Festival, Rhode Island, Duznicki Chopin Festival, Ruhr Piano Festival, Bergen Festival, Bridgewater Piano Festival, Prague Spring, Manchester 2003, Bagatelles Chopin Festival, Paris; La Roque d'Anthéron, Storioni Festival (Netherlands), El Paso Promusica, Sitka Summer Music Festival, Alaska; Int. Adjudicator Tbilisi and Sydney Int. Piano Competitions; Prof., RAM 1989–2011; Dir, Myra Hess Day Nat. Gallery 2006–14, Australian Festival of Chamber Music 2007–17, Sydney Int. Piano Competition 2015–; Dir and Trustee The Hattori Foundation; Patron, European Piano Teachers' Asscn (UK), The Old Granary Studio, Queensland Music Teachers' Asscn, Accompanists' Guild of Queensland, Youth Music Foundation of Australia, Tait Memorial Trust; Hon. ARAM 1994; Hon. DUniv (Griffith Univ.) 2007, Dr hc (James Cook Univ.) 2015; Bartók Special Prize, Liszt Int. Competition, Budapest 1976, Best Australian Pianist, Sydney Int. Piano Competition 1977, winner, Royal Overseas League Competition 1982. *Recordings include:* Moskowski, Paderewski Concertos 1990, Complete Etudes of Scriabin 1992, Piano Quintet by Brahms (New Budapest Quartet) 1992, Violin Virtuoso (with Tasmin Little) 1992, Cello Sonatas (with Alexander Baillie) by Shostakovich, Prokofiev, Schnittke and Rachmaninoff, d'Albert Concertos 1994, Vaughan-Williams and Delius Concertos plus Finzi Eclogue 1994, Elgar Piano Quintet (with Vellinger String Quartet) 1994, Delius Violin Sonatas (with Tasmin Little) (Diapason d'Or) 1997, d'Albert Solo Piano Works 1997, Saint-Saëns Complete Etudes 1998, Kullak & Dreyschock Concertos (with Niklas Willen) 1999, Complete Scriabin Preludes 2000, Grainger Piano Transcriptions 2001, Stanford Quintet (with Vanburgh Quartet) 2004, Delius and Ireland Piano Concertos 2005, Alnaes and Sinding Concertos 2005, Bloch Piano Quintets (with Goldner String Quartet) 2008, Bridge Piano Quintet (with Goldner String Quartet) 2008, Dvořák Piano Quintets (with Goldner String Quartet) 2009, Bach/d'Albert organ transcriptions 2010, Elgar Piano Quintet (with Goldner String Quartet) 2010, Harty Piano Quintet (with Goldner String Quartet) 2011, Strauss and Respighi Violin Sonatas (with Tasmin Little) 2012, Piers Lane Goes to Town 2013, Mozart Piano Concertos K482 and K491 (with Queensland Symphony) 2013, Walton and Ferguson Violin Sonatas (with Tasmin Little) 2013, Liszt/Berlioz Harold in Italy and Roger Viola Sonata (with Philip Dukes) 2013, Taneyev and Arensky Piano Quintets (with Goldner String Quartet) 2013, Pierné Piano Quintet (with Goldner String Quartet) 2014, Malcolm Williamson Complete Piano Concertos 2014, Schubert Chamber Works (with Tasmin Little and Tim Hugh) 2014, The Hour of Dreaming (flute works with Lorna McGhee) 2015, Bruch Piano Quintet (with Goldner String Quartet) 2015, Bliss, Bridge, Ireland Violin Sonatas (with Tasmin Little) 2015, Braunfels Konzertstück 2016, Borodin Piano Quintet and Cello Sonata (with Goldner String Quartet) 2016, Syzmanowski, Franck and Fauré Violin Sonatas (with Tasmin Little) 2017, Ries Piano Concertos 8, 9, Intro and Polonaise 2017, Brahms Violin Sonatas (with Tasmin Little) 2017. *Address:* c/o Hazard Chase, 25 City Road, Cambridge, CB1 1DP, England (office). *Telephone:* (1223) 312400 (office). *Fax:* (1223) 460827 (office). *E-mail:* sibylle.jackson@hazardchase.co.uk (office). *Website:* www.hazardchase.co.uk (office); www.pierslane.com.

LANE, Sir David Philip, Kt, PhD, FRS, FRSE, FRCPath, FRCSE, FMedSci; British oncologist and academic; *Professor of Molecular Oncology, University of Dundee;* b. 1 July 1952; s. of John Wallace Lane and Cecelia Frances Evelyn Wright; m. Prof. Ellen Birgitte Muldal 1975; one s. one d.; ed Univ. Coll., London; Research Fellow, Imperial Cancer Research Fund 1976–77, Staff Scientist 1985–90; Lecturer, Imperial Coll., London 1977–85; Prof. of Molecular Oncology,

Univ. of Dundee 1990–, Dir Transformation Research Group, Cancer Research Campaign 1990–; Exec. Dir Agency for Science, Tech. and Research (A*STAR) Inst. of Molecular and Cell Biology, Singapore 2004–07, Chief Scientist and NUS Dept of Medicine Adjunct Prof. 2009–; first Chief Scientist, Cancer Research UK 2007–10; CEO Experimental Therapeutics Centre, Singapore 2007–09; Chair. Biomedical Research Council, Singapore 2007–09, Chugai Pharmabody Research Pte Ltd, Singapore 2012–; Visiting Fellow, Cold Spring Harbor Labs, NY, USA 1978–80; Gibb Fellow, Cancer Research UK; mem. European Molecular Biology Org. 1990; Co-founder Acad. of Medical Sciences 1998; Hon. DSc (Abertay, Dundee) 1999, (Stirling) 2000, (Aberdeen) 2002, (Birmingham) 2002, (Nottingham) 2006, (University Paul Sabatier, France) 2007, (Liverpool) 2010; Doctor of Laws honoris causa 2011 University of Dundee/ United Kingdom 2011; Charles Rodolphe Brubacher Foundation Prize 1993, Joseph Steiner Foundation Prize 1993, Yvette Mayent Prize, Inst. Curie 1994, Swedish Soc. of Oncology Medal 1994, Meyenberg Foundation Prize 1995, Silvanus Thompson Medal, British Inst. of Radiology 1996, Henry Dryerre Prize 1996, Paul Ehrlich Prize 1998, Tom Conors Prize 1998, Bruce Preller Prize 1998, Soc. of Chemical Industry Medal 2003, Buchanan Medal, Royal Soc. 2004, Biochemistry Soc. Medal 2004, Anthony Dipple Carcinogenesis Award, EACR International 2004, Sergio Lombroso Award in Cancer Research, Weizmann Inst. of Science 2005, Int. Agency for Research on Cancer Medal (France) 2005, Inserm Award (France) 2006, David Hungerford Lecture Medal, Bangalore 2007, Asscn for Int. Cancer Research Colin Thomson Memorial Medal Lecturer, Beatson Inst. for Cancer Research, UK 2007, Gregor Mendel Memorial Medal, Brno, Czech Repub. 2007, Royal Medal, Royal Soc. of Edinburgh 2008, Datta Medal, Fed. of European Biochemical Socs 2009, Extraordinary Prof. to the TEFAF Oncology Chair (Netherlands) 2011, Lifetime Achievement Award, Cancer Research UK 2012. *Address:* Cancer Research UK, College of Life Sciences, University of Dundee, Dow Street, Dundee, DD1 5EH, Scotland (office). *E-mail:* dplane@p53Lab.a-star.edu.sg (office). *Website:* www .cancerresearchuk.org/science/research/who-and-what-we-fund/browse-by-location/dundee/university-of-dundee/david-lane-8 (office); www.a-star.edu.sg/p53lab (office).

LANE, Nathan; American actor and producer; b. (Joseph Lane), 3 Feb. 1956, Jersey City, NJ; s. of Daniel Lane and Nora Lane; m. Devlin Elliott 2015; ed St Peter's Preparatory High School, Jersey City; co-hosted Tony Awards 1995, 1996; GQ Man of the Year Award for Theater 1997, 2001, Trevor Project Hero Award 2007, Guild Hall Lifetime Achievement Award for the Performing Arts 2013, Eugene O'Neill Theater Center Monte Cristo Award 2015. *Plays include:* Lips Together, Teeth Apart 1991, The Nance (Drama League Award for Distinguished Performance 2013, Outer Critics Circle Award for Outstanding Actor in a Play 2013) 2013, It's Only a Play 2014, The Iceman Cometh 2015, White Rabbit, Red Rabbit 2016, Angels in America (Tony Award for Best Featured Actor in a Play 2018) 2017, 2018. *Musicals include:* Guys and Dolls, Broadway 1992, The Producers, Broadway (Tony Award for Best Actor in a Musical 2001) and Theatre Royal, London 2004, A Funny Thing Happened on the Way to the Forum (Tony Award for Best Actor in a Musical 1996) 1996. *Films include:* Ironweed 1987, Joe Versus the Volcano 1990, The Lemon Sisters 1990, He Said, She Said 1991, Frankie and Johnny 1991, Life with Mikey (aka Give Me a Break) 1993, Addams Family Values 1993, The Lion King (voice) 1994, Stand by Me 1995, Jeffrey 1995, The Birdcage (American Comedy Award for Funniest Lead Actor in a Motion Picture 1996) 1996, Timon and Pumbaa's Wild Adventure: Live and Learn (video, voice) 1997, Mousehunt 1997, Merry Christmas, George Bailey 1997, The Lion King II: Simba's Pride (video, voice) 1998, The Best Man 1999, At First Sight 1999, Stuart Little (voice) 1999, Isn't She Great 2000, Love's Labour's Lost 2000, Titan A.E. (voice) 2000, Trixie 2000, Stuart Little 2 (voice) 2002, Austin Powers in Goldmember 2002, Nicholas Nickleby 2002, Teacher's Pet (voice) 2004, Win a Date with Tad Hamilton! 2004, The Lion King 1½ (video, voice) 2004, Behind the Legend: Timon (video, voice) (uncredited) 2004, The Producers 2005, Swing Vote 2008, Astro Boy 2009, The Nutcracker 2010, Mirror Mirror 2012, The English Teacher 2013, Carrie Pilby 2016, The Vanishing of Sidney Hall 2017. *Television includes:* Jacqueline Susann's Valley of the Dolls (aka Valley of the Dolls) 1981, One of the Boys (series) 1982, Alice in Wonderland 1983, The Last Mile 1992, The Wizard of Oz in Concert: Dreams Come True 1995, Timon and Pumbaa (series) 1995, The Boys Next Door 1996, Encore! Encore! (series) (People's Choice Award for Favorite Male Performer in a New TV Series 1999) 1998, George and Martha (series) 1999, The Man Who Came to Dinner 2000, Teacher's Pet (series) (voice) 2000–02, One Saturday Morning (series) (voice) 2000, Laughter on the 23rd Floor 2001, Charlie Lawrence (series) (also producer) 2003, Modern Family (series) 2010–17, The Good Wife (series) 2012–14, The People v. O. J. Simpson: American Crime Story (series) 2016. *Address:* c/o International Creative Management, 10250 Constellation Blvd, Los Angeles, CA 90067, USA (office). *Telephone:* (310) 550-4000 (office). *Website:* www.icmpartners.com (office).

LANE, Neal Francis, BS, MS, PhD; American physicist and academic; *Malcolm Gillis University Professor and Senior Fellow in Science and Technology, James A. Baker III Institute for Public Policy, Rice University;* b. 22 Aug. 1938, Oklahoma; s. of Walter Lane and Harietta Hollander; m. Joni Sue Williams 1960; one s. one d.; ed Univ. of Oklahoma; NSF Postdoctoral Fellow 1964–65; Asst Prof. of Physics, Rice Univ. Houston 1966–69, Assoc. Prof. 1969–72, Prof. 1972–84, 1986–93, Prof. of Space Physics and Astronomy 1972–84, Chair. Dept of Physics 1977–82, Provost 1986–93; Dir Div. of Physics, NSF, Washington, DC 1979–80, Dir NSF 1993–98; Chancellor, Univ. of Colorado at Colorado Springs 1984–86; Asst to Pres. for Science and Tech., Dir Office of Science and Tech. Policy, Washington 1998–2001; Malcolm Gillis Univ. Prof. and Sr Fellow in Science and Tech., James A. Baker III Inst. of Public Policy, Rice Univ. 2001–; Visiting Fellow, Jt Inst. for Lab. Astrophysics, Univ. of Colo at Boulder 1965–66, 1975–76, non-resident Fellow 1984–93; Distinguished Visiting Scientist, Ky Univ., Lexington 1980; mem. Comm. on Physics, Science, Math. and Applications, Nat. Research Council 1989–93, Bd Overseers Superconducting Super Collider (SSC), Univs Research Asscn 1985–93, Advisory Cttee, Math. and Physical Sciences, NSF 1992–93; mem. American Inst. of Physics; Fellow, American Physics Soc., American Acad. of Arts and Sciences (Co-Chair. Governing Council 2010), AAAS, Asscn for Women in Science; Hon. DHL (Univ. of Oklahoma) 1995, (Marymount Univ.) 1995, (Illinois Inst. of Tech.) 1999; Hon. DSc (Univ. of Alabama) 1994, (Michigan State Univ.) 1995, (Ohio State Univ.) 1996, (Washington Coll.) 1998, (Univ. of Colorado) 1999, (Illinois Inst. of

Tech.) 1999, (Queen's Univ. Belfast) 2000, (North Carolina State Univ.) 2001, (Mt Sinai School of Medicine) 2002, (State Univ. of NY) 2002, (Univ. of Tulsa) 2006; Alfred P. Sloan Foundation Fellow 1967–71, Philip Hauge Abelson Award, AAAS 2000, William D. Carey Award, AAAS 2001, President's Award, ASME, ACS Public Service Award, Public Service Award, American Astronomical Soc./American Math. Soc./American Physical Soc., NASA Distinguished Service Award, Support of Science Award, Council of Science Socs Presidents, Distinguished Alumni Award, Univ. of Oklahoma, Public Welfare Medal, NAS 2009, K.T. Compton Medal for Leadership in Physics, American Inst. of Physics 2009, Gold Medal for service to Rice University, Asscn of Rice Alumni 20009, Distinguished Friend of Science Award, Southeastern Univs Research Asscn 2011, Vannevar Bush Award, Nat. Science Bd of NSF 2013. *Publications:* Quantum States of Atoms, Molecules and Solids, Understanding More Quantum Physics; several book chapters, and articles in professional journals. *Leisure interests:* tennis, squash. *Address:* Department of Physics and Astronomy, MS 108, Rice University, PO Box 1892, Houston, TX 77251-1892 (office); James A. Baker III Institute for Public Policy, MS 40, 6100 Main Street, Rice University, Baker Hall, Suite 120, Houston, TX 77005, USA (office). *Telephone:* (713) 348-2925 (office). *Fax:* (713) 348-5143 (office). *E-mail:* neal@rice.edu (office). *Website:* bakerinstitute.org/experts/neal-f-lane (office).

LANE, Philip R., BA, PhD; Irish economist, academic and central banker; *Governor, Central Bank of Ireland;* b. 27 Aug. 1969; ed Trinity Coll., Harvard Univ., USA; Asst Prof. of Econs and Int. Affairs, Trinity Coll. 1995–97, Lecturer in Econs 1997–2000, Asst Prof. of Econs 2000–04, Dir Inst. for Int. Integration Studies 2002–08, Prof. of Int. Macroeconomics 2004–12, Whately Prof. of Political Economy 2012–15; Gov., Central Bank of Ireland 2015–; Pres. Irish Econs Asscn 2012–14; Man. Ed., Econ. and Social Review 2004–07, Econ. Policy 2009–15; Visiting Fellow, Centre for Econ. Performance, London School of Econs 2004–05, Visiting Scholar, Harvard Univ. 2005, IMF 1997, 1998, 1999, 2000, 2001, 2002, 2004, 2005, Fed. Reserve Bank of New York 2001, 2003, 2009, Univ. of Wisconsin 2007; Eminent Visitor, Monetary Authority of Singapore 2013; Scientific Leader, EU Research Training Network 2000–04; apptd Research Fellow, Centre for Econ. Policy Research 2002, Int. Research Fellow, Kiel Inst. of World Econs 2005; European Econs Asscn Fellow 2013; mem. Royal Irish Acad. 2007–, Nat. Statistics Bd 2009–13; Barrington Prize 1997, German Bernacer Award in Monetary Econs 2001, Bhagwati Prize, Journal of Int. Econs 2010; numerous fellowships and grants. *Publications include:* The Dynamics of Asian Financial Integration: Facts and Analytics (co-ed) 2010; numerous articles in academic journals and book chapters. *Address:* Central Bank of Ireland, Dame Street, POB 559, Dublin 2, Ireland (office). *Telephone:* (1) 2246000 (office). *Fax:* (1) 6716561 (office). *E-mail:* enquiries@centralbank.ie (office). *Website:* www.centralbank.ie (office); www .philiplane.org.

LANE, Raymond J., BA; American business executive; *Managing Partner, GreatPoint Ventures;* b. 26 Dec. 1946, McKeesport, Pa; m. 1st Donna (divorced); m. 2nd Stephanie Herle; five c.; spent ten years with IBM in various product man., sales and marketing positions; Div. Vice-Pres., Electronic Data Systems Corpn (acquired by Hewlett-Packard 2008); Sr Partner, Booz-Allen & Hamilton (consulting co.), mem. Dirs and Exec. Man. Cttee; joined Oracle Corpn (software co.) as Pres. of Oracle USA 1992, Exec. Vice-Pres. and Pres. of Worldwide Operations 1993–97, mem. Bd of Dirs 1995–2000, Pres. and COO Oracle Corpn 1997–2000; Man. Partner, Kleiner Perkins Caufield & Byers (pvt. equity firm) 2000–14, GreatPoint Ventures 2015–; mem. Bd of Dirs Hewlett-Packard Co. 2010–, Chair. (non-exec.) 2010–11, Exec. Chair. 2011–13; Advisor, Meakem Becker Venture Capital, LLC; served as Interim CEO of V-Vehicle Inc.; Chair. Hara Software, Inc.; Chair. Exec. Cttee, Carnegie Mellon Univ. 2009–, mem. Bd of Trustees, co-creator of a High Dependability Computing Consortium with Carnegie Mellon and NASA; Chair. Elance Inc., SeeBeyond 2001, mem. Bd of Dirs 1998; mem. Bd of Dirs Quest Software Inc. 2000–11, Dir Emer. 2011–. mem. Compensation Cttee, fmr mem. Audit Cttee; mem. Bd of Dirs Kenandy, Inc., Enigma, Inc., MetaMatrix, Inc., Fisker Automotive, Inc., Visible Path Corpn, Xsigo Systems, SpikeSource, PodShow, Marimba Inc. 1997– (mem. Compensation Cttee), C-Bridge Internet Solutions Inc. 1999–, FreeMarkets Inc. 2001–; fmr mem. Bd of Dirs eXcelon Corporation, Sheer Networks, Asera, Inc.; fmr mem. Exec. Advisory Bd InSight Venture Partners; mem. Bd of Govs West Virginia Univ., mem. Acad. of Distinguished Grads of West Virginia Univ., mem. Univ.'s Foundation Bd; Vice-Chair. Special Olympics International, fmr mem. Int. Bd of Special Olympics; Hon. PhD (West Virginia Univ., Golden Gate Univ.); honoured by West Virginia Univ. with naming of Lane Dept of Computer Science and Electrical Eng 2011. *Address:* GreatPoint Ventures, 222 Third Street, Suite 2163, Cambridge, MA 02142 (office); Hewlett-Packard Co., 3000 Hanover Street, MS 1050, Palo Alto, CA 94304-1185, USA (office). *Telephone:* (617) 500-2676 (GreatPoint Ventures) (office); (650) 857-1501 (Hewlett-Packard) (office). *Fax:* (617) 376-1517 (GreatPoint Ventures) (office). *E-mail:* info@gpv.com (office); bod@hp.com (office). *Website:* www.gpv .com; www.hp.com (office).

LANE, Robert W., MBA; American business executive; b. 14 Nov. 1949, Washington, DC; m. Patricia Lane; three c.; ed Wheaten Coll., Ill., Univ. of Chicago Grad. School of Business; began career in corp. banking; joined Deere & Co. 1982, various positions in Worldwide Construction Equipment Div., Pres. and COO Deere Credit Inc., Sr Vice-Pres. World Agric. Equipment Div., Sr Vice-Pres. and Chief Financial Officer Deere & Co. 1996–97, Sr Vice-Pres. and Man. Dir for Operations Europe, Middle East, India and fmr USSR 1997–98, Pres. Worldwide Agric. Equipment Div. 1998–2000, Pres. and COO Jan.–Aug. 2000, Chair., Pres. and CEO Aug. 2000–09, Chair. 2009–10 (retd); mem. Bd of Dirs, BMW AG, General Electric Co. 2005– (also Audit, Man. Devt and Compensation Cttees), Verizon Communications Inc. 2004–15; Nat. Dir Lyric Opera of Chicago; mem. The Business Roundtable, Business Council, Council on Foreign Relations, New York; mem. Bd Trustees, Cttee for Devt, Univ. of Chicago; Hon. Dir, Lincoln Park Zoo, Chicago; Corporate Award, Univ. of Chicago Booth School of Business 2007, Order of Lincoln, The Lincoln Acad. of Ill. 2013. *Address:* c/o GE Corporate Headquarters, GE Shareowner Company, Fairfield, CT 06828, USA. *Telephone:* (203) 373-2211. *Website:* www.ge.com/about-us/leadership/profiles/robert-w-lane.

LANE-FOX OF SOHO, Baroness (Life Peer), cr. 2013, of Soho in the City of Westminster; **Martha Lane Fox,** CBE, BA; British entrepreneur and philanthropist; *Chairman, Go ON UK;* b. 10 Feb. 1973, Oxford; d. of Robin Lane Fox; ed

Oxford High School, Westminster School, Magdalen Coll., Oxford; Business Analyst, Spectrum Strategy Consultants 1994–96, Assoc. 1996–97; Business Devt Dir Carlton Communications 1997–98; Co-founder (with Brent Hoberman q.v.) and COO lastminute.com 1998–2003; co-f. Lucky Voice Private Karaoke 2005; Founder and Chair. Antigone (charity trust) 2008–; Dir (non-exec.) Channel 4 2005–11, Marks and Spencer 2007–, Mydeco.com 2008–; apptd Champion for Digital Inclusion by Prime Minister Gordon Brown 2009–10; f. the Race Online 2012 Campaign 2009–; re-apptd UK Digital Champion by Prime Minister David Cameron 2010–13; mem. Cabinet Office's Efficiency and Reform Bd 2010–13; Founder and Chair. Go ON UK (charity) 2012–; mem. (Crossbench), House of Lords (youngest female member) 2013–; Chancellor, Open Univ. 2014–; one of 200 public figures who were signatories to a letter to The Guardian opposing Scottish independence Aug. 2014; Patron, Reprieve, Camfed. *Address:* Go ON UK Ltd, 6th Floor, 20–24 Broadwick Street, London, W1F 8HT (office); House of Lords, Westminster, London, SW1A 0PW, England (office). *Telephone:* (20) 7440-5700 (office). *E-mail:* info@go-on.co.uk (office); contactholmember@parliament.uk (office). *Website:* www.go-on.co.uk (office); www.go-on.co.uk/about/board/martha.

LANG, Brian Andrew, CBE, MA, PhD, FRSE; British university vice-chancellor and management consultant; *Principal Emeritus, University of St Andrews;* b. 2 Dec. 1945, Edinburgh, Scotland; s. of Andrew Lang and Mary Lang; m. 1st 1975 (divorced 1982); m. 2nd 1983 (divorced 2000); two s. one d.; m. 3rd 2002; ed Royal High School, Edinburgh and Univ. of Edinburgh; social anthropological field research, Kenya 1969–70; Lecturer in Social Anthropology, Århus Univ., Denmark 1971–75; mem. scientific staff, Social Science Research Council 1976–79; Sec., Historic Building Br., Scottish Office 1979–80; Sec. Nat. Heritage Memorial Fund 1980–87, Deputy Chair. 2005–; Dir of Public Affairs, Nat. Trust 1987–91; Chief Exec. and Deputy Chair. British Library 1991–2000; Prin. and Vice-Chancellor Univ. of St Andrews 2001–08, now Prin. Emer.; Visiting Prof., Napier Univ., Edin. 1999–; Visiting Scholar, Getty Inst., Calif. 2000; Chair. European Nat. Libraries Forum 1993–2000, Heritage Lottery Fund Cttee for Scotland 2005–12, Royal Scottish Nat. Orchestra 2008–15, Edinburgh World Heritage Trust 2015–; Pres. Inst. of Information Scientists 1993–94; mem. Council, Nat. Trust for Scotland 2001–04, Council, St Leonard's School, St Andrews 2001–08, Bd Scottish Enterprise, Fife 2003–08, Scottish Exec. Cultural Cttee 2004–05; Trustee, Hopeton House Preservation Trust 2001–05, Newbattle Abbey Coll. 2004–08; Chair. Dovecot Tapestry Studios, Edinburgh; Hon. LLD (St Andrews), Hon. Dr (Edinburgh); Hon. Fellow, The Library Asscn 1997. *Leisure interests:* reading, music, museums, galleries, pottering. *Address:* 4 Manor Place, Edinburgh, EH3 7DD, Scotland (home). *Telephone:* (131) 260-9617 (home). *E-mail:* brian@lang-uk .com (office). *Website:* www.lang-uk.com (office).

LANG, David, PhD; American composer; b. 1 Aug. 1957, Los Angeles, Calif.; m.; three c.; ed Stanford Univ., Univ. of Iowa, Yale School of Music, studied with Jacob Druckman, Hans Werner Henze and Martin Bresnick; Jr Composer-in-Residence, Horizons Summer Festival 1980s; commissioned by Boston Symphony Orchestra, Cleveland Orchestra, St Paul Chamber Orchestra, BBC Singers, American Composers Orchestra and Santa Fe Opera and Settembre Musica Festival, Turin; co-f. (with Michael Gordon and Julia Wolfe) New York annual music festival Bang on a Can 1987–; composed album Brian Eno: Music for Airports 1998 for group Bang on a Can All-Stars; Carnegie Hall's Debs Composer's Chair for 2013–14; Composer-in-Residence, de Doelen centre, Rotterdam 2014–15, Carlsbad Music Festival Sept. 2014; Rome Prize, American Acad., Rome; BMW Prize, Munich Biennale for New Music Theatre; Friedheim Award, Kennedy Center; Revson Fellowship with New York Philharmonic, Musical America's Composer of the Year 2013; grants from Guggenheim Foundation, New York Foundation of Arts and Nat. Endowment for the Arts. *Recordings include:* The Little Match Girl Passion (Grammy Award for Best Small Ensemble Performance 2010) 2009, The Woodmans 2011, Love Fail 2012, Death Speaks 2013. *Compositions include:* chamber music: Frag 1984, Dance/Drop 1987, Burn Notice 1989, Music for Gracious Living 1992, Cheating, Lying, Stealing 1993, Face so Pale 1992, Wreck/Wed 1995, Slip 1996, Follow 1996, Little Eye 1999, My Very Empty Mouth 1999, Sweet Air 1999, Short Fall 2000, Birds of Minnesota 2000, Darker 2010, Man Made 2013; for chorus: By Fire 1984, Hecuba 1995, This Condition 2000, I Lie 2001, Again (After Ecclesiastes) 2005, Evening Morning Day 2007, The Little Match Girl Passion (Pulitzer Prize for Music 2008) 2007; opera: Judith and Holofernes 1989, Music for Gracious Living 1992, Modern Painters 1995, The Carbon Copy Building 1999, The Difficulty of Crossing a Field 2000, Lost Objects 2001; orchestral and large ensemble: Hammer Amour 1978, Eating Living Monkeys 1985, Spud 1986, Are You Experienced? 1987–89, Bonehead 1990, International Business Machine 1990, Fire and Forget 1992, My Evil Twin 1992, Slow Movement 1993, Under Orpheus 1994, Grind to a Halt 1996, The Passing Measures 1998, I Fought the Law 1998, Ariel's Version 1998, Haircut 2000, How to Pray 2002, Fur 2004, Loud Love Songs 2004, Pierced 2007, Every Ounce of Strength 2007, Mountain 2014. *Address:* c/o Amanda Ameer, First Chair Promotion, 331 West 57th Street, Suite 132, New York, NY 10019, USA (office). *E-mail:* info@davidlangmusic.com. *Website:* davidlangmusic.com.

LANG, Helmut; Austrian artist and fashion designer; b. 10 March 1956, Vienna; est. own studio in Vienna 1977; made-to-measure shop opened in Vienna 1979; development of ready-to-wear collections 1984–86; presented Helmut Lang women's wear, Paris fashion week from 1986, menswear from 1987; began licence business 1988; Helmut Lang Underwear 1994; Helmut Lang Protective Eyewear 1995; Prof. of Masterclass of Fashion, Univ. of Applied Arts, Vienna 1993–97; moved to New York 1997; sold a 51% stake in co. to the Prada Group 1999, retained control of design and advertising, Prada later developed a line of Helmut Lang accessories, including shoes, belts and bags and opened Helmut Lang stores in Hong Kong and Singapore; used unconventional materials including rubber, feathers and metallic fabrics and redefined the silhouette of the 1990s and early 2000s; first designer to stream his collection online; four different scents cr. by Lang in co-operation with Procter & Gamble, all discontinued with closing of the brand 2005; retd from fashion in 2005; collaborations with artists Jenny Holzer and Louise Bourgeois; recent works explore abstract sculptural forms and physical arrangements and space beyond the limitations of the human body; lives and works in New York and on Long Island; Österreichisches Ehrenzeichen für Wissenschaft u. Kunst 2009; Best Int. Designer of the Year, Council of Fashion Designers of America (CFDA) 1996, VH-1/Vogue Award for Best Menswear

Designer of the Year 1997, Fine Arts of Vienna 1997, Pitti Immagine Award for Best Designer of the Nineties 1998, New York Magazine Best Designer of the Year Award 1998, Design Distinction Award for Environments, I.D. Magazine 1998, Award for Interiors, New York City Chapter of AIA 1998, Architectural Record Award, Business Week 1999, AIA Award for Interior Architecture 1999, CFDA Menswear Designer of the Year 2000, GQ Designer of the Year 2004, 'The Imagineers of Our Time' Award, Fashion Group International 2004, LEAD Award 2005. *Publications:* has published excerpts from ongoing art projects, Long Island Diaries, and The Selective Memory Series, in several publs, including BUTT Magazine, Fannzine 137, Visionaire, The Travel Almanac. *E-mail:* helmutlangstudio@culture-edit.com. *Website:* www.helmutlangstudio.com.

LANG, Jack Mathieu Émile, DenD; French politician and UN official; *President, Arab World Institute;* b. 2 Sept. 1939, Mirecourt (Vosges); s. of Roger Lang and Marie-Luce Bouchet; m. Monique Buczynski 1961; two d. (one deceased); ed Lycée Henri-Poincaré, Nancy, Inst. of Political Studies, Paris; Founder and Dir World Festival of Univ. Theatre, Nancy 1963–77; Dir Théâtre du palais de Chaillot 1972–74; apptd Prof. of Int. Law 1976; apptd Dir Educ. and Research Unit for econ. and legal sciences, Nancy 1977; Councillor, Paris 1977–81; Deputy Nat. Ass. for Loir-et-Cher 1986–88, March–Dec. 1993, 1997–2000, Pres. Foreign Affairs Cttee 1997–2000, Deputy for Pas-de-Calais 6th constituency 2002–12; Special Adviser to First Sec., Parti Socialiste (PS) 1978–81, PS Nat. Del. for Culture 1979–81, Nat. Sec. 2005–07; Minister of Culture and Communications 1981–83, 1984–86, May–June 1988, 1991–92, of Educ. and Culture 1992–93, also Minister for Major Public Works and Bicentenary 1988–89, apptd Govt Spokesman 1991, Minister of Educ. 2000–02; Mayor of Blois 1989–2001; mem. European Parl. 1994–97; apptd Vice-Pres. Comité sur la réforme des institutions 2007; served as Pres. Nicolas Sarkozy's Special Envoy to Cuba Feb. 2009, to the Democratic People's Repub. of Korea Nov. 2009; Special Adviser to the Sec.-Gen. on Legal Issues related to Piracy off the Coast of Somalia, UN 2010–12; Pres. Arab World Inst. 2013–; Chevalier, Légion d'honneur; Commdr des Palmes académiques; Hon. DLitt (Nottingham) 1990; Dr hc (RCA) 1993; Prix Antonio de Sancha (Spain) 1997, Prix Wartburg (Germany) 1998. *Publications include:* L'État et le théâtre 1968, Le Plateau Continental de la mer du Nord: Arrêt de la Cour Internationale de Justice 1969, Demain les femmes 1995, Lettre à Malraux 1996, François Premier 1997, Les Araignées 2000, Anna au Muséum 2002, Une Ecole Elitaire pour tous 2003, Un Nouveau Régime Politique pour la France 2004, Nelson Mandela: Leçon de vie pour l'avenir 2005, Faire la Révolution Fiscale 2006, Demain Comme Hier (with Jean-Michel Helvig) 2009, La bataille du Grand Louvre 2010, Ce que je sais de François Mitterrand 2011, François Mitterrand: fragments de vie partagée 2011, Pourquoi ce vandalisme d'État Contre l'École: Lettre au Président de la République 2011. *Address:* 17 place des Vosges, 75004 Paris, France (home). *Telephone:* 6-68-54-54-88 (mobile) (home). *E-mail:* j.lang@wanadoo.fr (home).

LANG, Kathryn Dawn (k.d.); Canadian singer and songwriter; b. 2 Nov. 1961, Consort, Alberta; d. of Adam Lang and Audrey L. Lang; began playing guitar aged 10; formed band The Reclines in early 1980s, played N American clubs 1982–87; performed at closing ceremony, Winter Olympics, Calgary 1988, Winter Olympics, Vancouver 2010; performed with Sting, Bruce Springsteen, Peter Gabriel and Tracy Chapman in Amnesty Int. tour 1988; Hon. Fellow, The Royal Conservatory 2016; Canadian Country Music Asscn Awards for Best Entertainer of Year 1989, Best Album of Year 1990, Grammy Awards for Best Country Vocal Collaboration 1989, for Best Female Country Vocal Performance 1990, for Best Female Pop Vocal Performance 1993, American Music Awards, Favourite New Artist 1993, Songwriter of the Year (with Ben Mink) 1993, BRIT Award for Best Int. Female 1995. *Film appearances:* Salmonberries 1991, Teresa's Tattoo 1994, The Last Don 1997, Eye of the Beholder 1999; features on soundtrack to Dick Tracy. *Recordings include:* albums: A Truly Western Experience 1984, Angel With A Lariat 1987, Shadowland 1988, Absolute Torch And Twang 1989, Ingénue (Album of the Year 1993) 1992, Even Cowgirls Get The Blues (film soundtrack) 1993, All You Can Eat 1995, Drag 1997, Australian Tour 1997, Invincible Summer 2000, Live By Request 2001, A Wonderful World (with Tony Bennett; Grammy Award for Best Traditional Pop Vocal Album 2004) 2003, Hymns of the 49th Parallel 2004, Reintarnation 2006, Watershed 2008, Recollection 2010, Sing It Loud (with the Siss Boom Bang) 2011, case / lang / veirs 2016. *Address:* Direct Management Group, 8332 Melrose Avenue, Top Floor, Los Angeles, CA 90069, USA (office). *E-mail:* info@directmanagement.com (office). *Website:* directmanagement.com (office); www.kdlang.com.

LANG, Larry H. P., BA, MA, PhD; Taiwanese economist and academic; *Professor Emeritus, Chinese University of Hong Kong;* b. 21 June 1956; ed Tunghai Univ., Nat. Taiwan Univ., Wharton School of Business, Univ. of Pennsylvania, USA; fmr Lecturer, Wharton School of Business; fmr Prof. of Finance, Grad. School of Business, Michigan State Univ., Coll. of Business, Ohio State Univ., Stern School of Business, New York Univ.; fmr Visiting Prof. of Finance, Grad. School of Business, Univ. of Chicago; Chair Prof. of Finance, Faculty of Business Admin, Chinese Univ. of Hong Kong, now Prof. Emer.; Partner, GITIC-Lehman Infrastructure Fund, Lehman Brothers 1994–96; Consultant on Corp. Governance Projects to World Bank, Washington, DC 1998–2000, on WTO/Banking Issues to OECD 2000, on Corp. Governance to China Shenzhen Stock Exchange, Hong Kong Govt; presenter, half-hour talk show, Larry Lang Live 2004–06, show cancelled following criticism of Chinese Politburo. *Publications include:* numerous articles and research papers in professional journals. *Address:* Room 1208, 12/F, Cheng Yu Tung Building, Department of Finance, Chinese University of Hong Kong, No.12, Chak Cheung Street, Shatin, New Territories, Hong Kong Special Administrative Region, People's Republic of China (office). *Telephone:* 3943-7761 (office). *Fax:* 2603-6586 (office). *E-mail:* llang@baf.msmail.cuhk.edu.hk. *Website:* www.cuhk.edu.hk (office).

LANG, Laura, BA, MBA; American media executive; b. Warwick, RI; ed Tufts Univ., Univ. of Pennsylvania Wharton School of Business; began career with Quaker Oats Company in brand management in 1980; Dir Internal Consulting, Pfizer Pharmaceuticals 1983–85; Product Dir Bristol Myers 1986–89; Sr Vice-Pres. Yankelovich Clancy Shulman 1989–95; joined Marketing Corpn of America 1995, Pres. 1996–99; joined Digitas (digital agency) 1999, ran New York office for several years, CEO Digitas North America 2004–08, Worldwide CEO 2008–11, also headed parent co. Publicis Groupe's pure-play digital agencies, including Denuo, Big Fuel, Razorfish and Phonevalley; CEO Time Inc. 2011–13; Man. Dir Narragansett Ventures 2014–; mem. Bd of Dirs VF Corpn 2011–, Care.com, Inc, 2014–, Benchmark Electronics 2005–11, Nutrisystem 2010–12, Breast Cancer Research Foundation; Co-Chair. The One Hundred; mem. Advisory Bd Tufts Univ. Entrepreneurial Leadership Program; named by Advertising Age as one of its Women to Watch 2007. *Address:* Narragansett Ventures, LLC, 1250 Wallace Drive, Delray Beach, FL 33444, USA (office).

LANG, Hon. Otto, PC, OC, QC, BA, LLB, BCL, LLD; Canadian lawyer, politician, business executive and consultant (retd); b. 14 May 1932, Handel, Sask.; s. of Otto T. Lang and Maria Theresa Wurm; m. 1st Adrian Ann Merchant 1963 (divorced 1988); three s. four d.; m. 2nd Deborah J. McCawley 1989; one step-s. one step-d.; ed Univ. of Sask. and Oxford Univ., UK; admitted to Sask. Bar 1956, to Ont., Yukon and NWT Bars 1972, Manitoba Bar 1988; Asst Prof., Univ. of Sask., Faculty of Law 1956, Assoc. Prof. 1957, Prof. 1961, Dean of Law School 1961–68; MP for Saskatoon-Humboldt 1968–79; Minister without Portfolio 1968, with responsibility for Energy and Water Resources 1969, with responsibility for Canadian Wheat Bd 1969–79; Minister of Manpower & Immigration 1970–72, of Justice 1972–75, of Transport 1975–79, of Justice and Attorney-Gen. Aug.–Nov. 1978; Pres. Asscn of Canadian Law Teachers 1962–63; Vice-Pres. Sask. Liberal Asscn 1956–63; Fed. Campaign Chair. Liberal Party 1963–64; Past Pres. Saskatoon Social Planning Council; Exec. Vice-Pres. Pioneer Grain Co. Ltd 1979–88; mem. Bd of Dirs, Investor Group Trust Co. 1985–2009, Ind. Review Cttee 2009–; Co. Sec., Friends of Upper Fort Garry Gate 2007–; Chair. Transport Inst., Univ. of Manitoba 1988–93; Pres. and CEO Central Gas Manitoba Inc. 1993–99; consultant with GPC 2000–07; Vice-Chair. Winnipeg Airports Authority 1995–2008; Campaign Chair. Winnipeg United Way 1983; Chair. Royal Winnipeg Ballet Capital Campaign 1996–2000; Rhodes Scholar 1953; QC for Ont. 1972, for Sask. 1972; Hon. Consul-Gen. of Japan 1992–97. *Publication:* Contemporary Problems of Public Law in Canada (ed.) 1968. *Leisure interests:* tennis, bridge, golf. *Address:* 135 Ash Street, Winnipeg, Man. R3N 0P4, Canada. *Telephone:* (204) 334-9476. *E-mail:* ottolang@mts.net.

LANG, Rein, LLM; Estonian politician; b. 4 July 1957, Tartu; s. of Ants Lang and Ulve Lang; partner Ulvi Kuusk since 1979; one d.; ed 7th High School of Tallinn (now Tallinn English Coll.), Tartu State Univ.; previous positions include Deputy Man. Linnahall arena, Deputy Dir Muusik club, Chair., then Head of Supervisory Council, Trio media co.; apptd Deputy Mayor of Tallinn 2001; mem. Tallinn City Council 2002; Founding mem. Estonian Reform Party; mem. Parl. 2003–, First Deputy Speaker –2005; Minister of Foreign Affairs Feb.–April 2005, of Justice 2005–11, Acting Minister of the Interior May–June 2009, Minister of Culture 2011–13; mem. Rotary Club of Tallinn; Commdr, Ordre nat. du Mérite 2004, Pressivaenlane 2004, 2009, 2013, Order of the White Star, Fourth Class 2001, Second Class 2006; Estonian Police Award (Second Class) 2003. *Address:* Riigikogu, Lossi plats 1A, 15165 Tallinn, Estonia (office). *Telephone:* 6316565 (office). *Fax:* 6316334 (office). *E-mail:* rein.lang@riigikogu.ee (office). *Website:* www.riigikogu.ee (office); www.lang.ee.

LANG LANG; Chinese pianist; b. 14 June 1982, Shenyang; s. of Lang Guoren and Zhou Xiulan; ed Central Music Conservatory, Beijing, Curtis Inst. of Music, Philadelphia, USA; played the complete Chopin Etudes, Beijing Concert Hall 1995; performed as one of the soloists at the inaugural concert of the China Nat. Symphony 1996; US debut with Baltimore Symphony Orchestra 1998; last-minute substitution at the Ravinia Festival Gala of the Century, playing the Tchaikovsky Concerto with the Chicago Symphony Orchestra 1999; Carnegie Hall debut playing the Grieg Concerto with Baltimore Symphony under Yuri Temirkanov, April 2001; joined Philadelphia Orchestra and Wolfgang Sawallisch for the orchestra's 100th anniversary tour, including a performance in the Great Hall of the People, Beijing, June 2001; BBC Proms debut, playing Rachmaninov's Third Concerto, Aug. 2001; 2001/02 season included recital debuts at London's Wigmore Hall, Washington's Kennedy Center and the Paris Louvre, tour of Europe with the NDR Symphony Orchestra of Hamburg, and performance with the NHK Symphony Orchestra under Charles Dutoit; performed in five concerts at the Ravinia Festival 2002; season 2002/03 included performances with New York Philharmonic and Lorin Maazel in New York and a tour of Asia, concerts with the Cleveland Orchestra at Severance Hall, a tour of the Midwest with Franz Welser-Möst, appearances with Los Angeles Philharmonic, San Francisco Symphony, Pittsburgh Symphony, Philadelphia Orchestra; tour of China 2003; festival appearances 2003 included opening concert of BBC Proms, London, Mostly Mozart, Aspen, Tanglewood, Ravinia, Saratoga, Blossom, Verbier, Schleswig-Holstein and Ruhr Piano Festival; Carnegie Hall recital debut Nov. 2003; orchestral appearances with the Philadelphia, Los Angeles Philharmonic, London Philharmonic, Orchestre de Paris, Israel Philharmonic, Staatskapelle Berlin, Berliner Philharmoniker; guest soloist at Nobel Prize concert, Stockholm 2007; performed at opening ceremony for Summer Olympics, Beijing 2008; appeared at Carnegie Hall China Festival 2010, Queen's Diamond Jubilee Concert, London 2012, Latitude Festival, UK 2012; played with Korean artist PSY for opening ceremony of Asian Games in Incheon, South Korea 2014; performed 'Rhapsody in Blue' for US Independence Day televised celebration, Washington, DC 2015; UNICEF Int. Goodwill Amb. 2004–; Vice-Pres. All-China Youth Fed.; f. Lang Lang Int. Music Foundation, New York 2008; Global Amb. Leeds Int. Piano Competition 2013; Amb., Château de Versailles, Paris 2015; Hon. DMus (Royal Coll. of Music) 2011; First Prize, Shenyang Piano Competition 1987, First Prize, Fifth Xing Hai Cup Piano Competition, Beijing, First Prize and Outstanding Artistic Performance, Fourth Int. Young Pianists Competition, Germany, First Prize, Second Tchaikovsky Int. Young Musicians' Competition, Japan 1995, Leonard Bernstein Award 2002, 2007, Presidential Merit Award, Recording Acad. 2010, Crystal Award, World Econ. Forum 2010, Echo Klassik Instrumentalist of the Year Award 2010, 2015. *Recordings include:* Peter Tchaikovsky Piano Concerto No. 1 and Mendelssohn Piano Concerto No. 1, with Chicago Symphony Orchestra under Daniel Barenboim, Haydn, Rachmaninov, Brahms, recorded Live at Seiji Ozawa Hall, Tanglewood 2001, Rachmaninov Piano Concerto No. 3 and Scriabin Etudes, with St Petersburg Philharmonic under Yuri Temirkanov 2003, Lang Lang live at Carnegie Hall 2004, Lang Lang Memory 2005, Rachmaninov Piano Concerto No. 2 2005, Dragon Songs 2006, The Art of Lang Lang 2007, Chopin Piano Concerto No. 1 and No. 2 2008, Tchaikovsky and Rachmaninov Piano Trios 2009, Lang Lang Live 2010, Liszt: My Piano Hero 2015, The Chopin Album 2015, The Mozart Album 2016, Chopin Etudes 2016, Howard Shore: Two Concerti 2017, Piano Book 2019.

Publication: Journey of a Thousand Miles: My Story (with David Ritz) 2008. *Address:* c/o CAMI Music LLC, 1790 Broadway, New York, NY 10019-1412, USA (office). *Telephone:* (212) 841-9500 (office). *Fax:* (212) 841-9719 (office). *E-mail:* LangLang@columbia-artists.net (office). *Website:* www.camimusic.com (office); www.LangLang.com (office).

LANG OF MONKTON, Baron (Life Peer), cr. 1997, of Merrick and the Rhinns of Kells in Dumfries and Galloway; **Ian (Bruce) Lang,** OStJ, BA, PC, DL; British politician and businessman; *Chairman, Marsh & McLennan Companies Inc.;* b. 27 June 1940; s. of James F. Lang, DSC and Maude Stewart; m. Sandra Montgomerie 1971; two d.; ed Lathallan School, Kincardineshire, Rugby School and Sidney Sussex Coll. Cambridge; MP for Galloway 1979–83, for Galloway and Upper Nithsdale 1983–97; Asst Govt Whip 1981–83; a Lord Commr of HM Treasury 1983–86; Parl. Under-Sec. of State, Dept of Employment 1986, Scottish Office 1986–87; Minister of State, Scottish Office 1987–90; Sec. of State for Scotland and Lord Keeper of the Great Seal of Scotland 1990–95; Pres. Bd of Trade 1995–97; mem. House of Lords Select Cttee on the Constitution 2001–05, 2012–14, Chair. 2016–; Chair. Patrons of Nat. Galleries of Scotland 2001–08; Chair. Prime Minister's Advisory Cttee on Business Appointments 2009–14; Chair. Sustained Innovation Consulting LLP (man. consultants); mem. Bd of Dirs Marsh & McLennan Companies Inc. 1997– (Chair. 2011–), Lithgows Ltd 1997–2009, Charlemagne Capital Ltd 2006–; Ind. Advisor, Aquiline Capital Partners LLC (pvt. equity firm); Gov. Rugby School 1997–2007; mem. Queen's Bodyguard for Scotland (Royal Co. of Archers) 1974–; DL Ayrshire and Arran 1998–; mem. Conservative Party, Privy Council 1990–; mem. Council, The Rugbeian Soc.; Hon. Pres. St Columba's School, Renfrewshire 1999–2008. *Publication:* Blue Remembered Years 2002. *Address:* House of Lords, London, SW1A 0PW, England.

LANGAT, Nancy Jebet; Kenyan athlete; b. 22 Aug. 1981; m. Kenneth Cheruiyot; one s.; middle-distance runner; gold medallist 800m, World Junior Championships 2000, African Championships 2004; gold medallist 1500m, Olympic Games, Beijing 2008; gold medallist 1500m World Athletics Final 2009; gold medallist 800m, 1500m, Commonwealth Games, New Delhi, African Championships, Kenya 2010, Military World Games, Brazil 2011. *Address:* c/o Kenya Athletics Federation, PO Box 46722, Aerodrome Road, Riadha House, 00100 Nairobi West, Kenya. *Telephone:* (2) 605021. *Fax:* (2) 605020. *E-mail:* athleticskenya@gt.co.ke.

LÅNGBACKA, Ralf Runar, MA; Finnish theatre director and professor of theatre science; b. 20 Nov. 1932, Närpes; s. of Runar Emanuel Långbacka and Hulda Emilia Långbacka (née Backlund); m. Runa Birgitta Danielsson 1961; two s. one d.; ed Åbo Akademi, Munich Univ. and Freie Univ., Berlin; Ed. Finnish Radio literary programmes 1956; Asst and Dir Lilla Teatern, Helsinki 1958–60; Man. and Artistic Dir Swedish Theatre, Turku 1960–63; Dir Finnish Nat. Theatre 1963–65; Artistic Dir Swedish Theatre, Helsinki 1965–67; Dir Municipal Theatre, Gothenburg, Sweden; mem. Finnish State Comm. of Dramatic Art 1967–70; Artistic Dir Municipal Theatre, Turku 1971–77; Head Finnish Dirs Asscn 1978–82; Artistic and Man. Dir Municipal Theatre, Helsinki 1983–87, Artistic Prof. 1979–83, 1988–93; Prof. of Theatre Science, Åbo Akademi, Turku 1994–97; Pres. Finnish Centre, Int. Theatre Inst. (ITI) 1983–96, mem. Bd (Excom) of ITI 1991–95; Corresp. mem. Akad. der Künste, Berlin 1979; freelance dir in Finland, Sweden, Denmark, Germany, Norway, Russia, Estonia, USA, Chile, China 1960–2009; Academician, Finnish Acad. 2004–; Dr hc (Univ. of the Arts, Helsinki) 2018; The Critics Spurs 1963, Pro Finlandia 1973, Henrik-Steffens Award (Germany) 1994, Finland Prize, Swedish Acad., Sweden 1999, Finland Prize for Theatre 2001, Tollander Prize 2010. *Film:* Puntila 1979. *Music:* directed operas: Wozzeck (Berg) 1967, 2001, Carmen (Bizet) 1969, Don Giovanni (Mozart) 1973, 1984, Macbeth (Verdi) 1980, 1993, Don Carlos (Verdi) 1995, Rigoletto (Verdi) 2000, 2001. *Plays:* directed over 100 performances of plays, including Shakespeare, Chekhov, Brecht and Büchner. *Television:* Premiär (four-part feature) 1992. *Publications include:* Teatterikirja (The Theatre Book) (with Kalle Holmberg) 1977, Bland annat om Brecht (On Brecht and Others) 1981, Möten med Tjechov (Meetings with Chekhov) 1986, Denna långa dag, detta korta liv (This long day, This short life: poems) 1988, Krocketspelaren (The Croquet Player, play) 1990, Olga, Irina och jag (Olga, Irina and I, play) 1991, Brecht og det realistiske teater (Brecht and the Realistic Theatre) 1998, Att fånga ödets vindar (To Catch the Winds of Destiny), Memoirs 1 2009, På jakt efter en konstnärlig teater (Chasing an Artistical Theatre), Memoirs 2, 2011, Innan ridån faller (Before the Curtain Falls), Memoirs 3 2017; numerous articles. *Leisure interests:* music, mushrooms, sailing. *Address:* Laivalahdenkaari 42 B 31, 00810 Helsinki, Finland (home). *Telephone:* (40) 7323323 (home). *E-mail:* ralf.langbacka@gmail.com (home).

LANGBO, Arnold G.; Canadian business executive; b. 13 April 1937, Richmond, BC; s. of Osbjourn Langbo and Laura Marie Langbo (née Hagen); m. Martha M. Miller 1959; eight c.; ed Univ. of British Columbia, Vancouver; sales rep., Kellogg Canada Inc. 1956–67, Int. Div. 1967–69, Admin. Asst to Kellogg Co., Pres. 1969–70, Exec. Vice-Pres. 1970–71, Vice-Pres. of Kellogg Canada 1971–76, Salada Foods Ltd 1971–76, Pres. and CEO Kellogg Salada Canada Ltd Inc. 1976–78, Pres. US Food Products Div. of Kellogg Co. 1978–79, Corp. Vice-Pres. 1979–81, Exec. Vice-Pres. 1981–83, Group Exec. Vice-Pres., Kellogg Co. 1983–86, Pres. Kellogg International 1986–90, Pres., COO and Dir, Kellogg Co. 1990–91, Chair. and CEO 1992–99 (retd); mem. Bd of Dirs, Johnson & Johnson 1991–2010, Whirlpool Corpn 1994–2009, Atlantic Richfield Co. from 1998, Weyerhaeuser Co. 1999–2011, Int. Youth Foundation; Ind. Dir, Hershey Co. 2007–09; fmr mem. Bd of Dirs, Grocery Mfrs of America; fmr mem. Int. Advisory Council of CGI Group Inc.; mem. Advisory Bd J.L. Kellogg Grad. School of Man., Northwestern Univ.; Trustee, W.W. Kellogg Trust, Albion Coll.; Adrian Trimpe Distinguished Service Award, Haworth Coll. of Business, Western Mich. Univ. 2000. *Address:* c/o Board of Directors, Johnson & Johnson, 1 Johnson & Johnson Plaza, New Brunswick, NJ 08933; 7614 La Corniche Circle, Boca Raton, FL 33433, USA (home).

LANGDALE, Mark, BBA, LLB; American lawyer, business executive and fmr diplomatist; b. 1954; m. Patty Langdale 1982; one s. one d.; ed Univ. of Texas at Austin, Univ. of Houston School of Law; practised law in Houston, Tex. for ten years; Pres. Posadas USA, Inc. (US subsidiary of Grupo Posadas) 1989–2005, mem. Bd Dirs Grupo Posadas 1992–2004; Co-founder CapRock Communications Corpn; Chair. Texas Dept of Econ. Devt 1997–2001; Amb. to Costa Rica 2005–07; Pres. George W. Bush Foundation, Dallas 2008–13; mem. Young Presidents Org. 1992–2004; now engaged in real estate and investment man. in the Dallas/Fort Worth Area; YPO Legacy Award 2004.

LANGE, Hartmut; German author and dramatist; b. 31 March 1937, Berlin; s. of Karl Lange and Johanna Lange; m. Ulrike Ritter 1971; ed Babelsberg Film School; playwright at Deutsches Theater, Berlin 1961–65; freelance writer, W Berlin 1965–; Gerhart-Hauptmann-Preis 1968, Literatur Preis der Adenauer Stiftung 1998, Ehrengabe der Schiller-Stiftung von 1859 2000, Italo Svevo Preis 2003, Preis der LiteraTour Nord 2004. *Publications include:* Die Revolution als Geisterschiff 1974, Die Selbstverbrennung 1982, Deutsche Empfindungen 1983, Die Waldsteinsonate 1984, Das Konzert 1986, Die Ermüdung 1988, Vom Werden der Vernunft 1988, Gesammelte Theaterstücke (Collected Plays) 1988, Die Wattwanderung 1990, Die Reise nach Triest 1991, Die Stechpalme 1993, Schnitzlers Würgeengel 1995, Der Herr im Café 1996, Italienische Novellen 1998, Eine andere Form des Glücks 1999, Die Bildungsreise 2000, Das Streichquartett 2001, Irrtum als Erkenntnis 2002, Leptis Magna 2003, Der Wanderer 2005, Der Therapeut 2007, Der Abgrund des Endlichen 2009, Im Museum 2010, Das Haus in der Dorotheenstrasse 2012, Positiver Nihilismus 2012. *Leisure interest:* chess. *Address:* Hohenzollerndamm 197, 10717 Berlin, Germany (home); 06010 Niccone, Perugia, Italy (home).

LANGE, Jessica Phyllis; American actress; b. 20 April 1949, Cloquet, Minn.; d. of Albert John Lange and Dorothy Florence Lange (née Sahlman); m. Francisco (Paco) Grande 1970 (divorced 1981); one d. (with Mikhail Baryshnikov); one s. one d. (with Sam Shepard); ed Univ. of Minnesota; student of mime with Etienne DeCroux, Paris; Dancer Opéra Comique, Paris; model, Wilhelmina Agency, New York; Star Showtime TV production Cat On A Hot Tin Roof 1984; in summer stock production Angel On My Shoulder, NC 1980. *Theatre includes:* A Streetcar Named Desire, London (Theatre World Award, Golden Globe for TV performance 1996) 1992, Long Day's Journey into Night, London 2000, New York 2015 (Tony Award for Best Performance by an Actress in a Leading Role 2016), The Glass Menagerie 2005, 2007. *Films include:* King Kong 1976, All That Jazz 1979, How to Beat the High Cost of Living 1980, The Postman Always Rings Twice 1981, Frances 1982, Tootsie 1982 (Acad. Award for Best Supporting Actress 1982), Country (also producer) 1984, Sweet Dreams 1985, Crimes of the Heart 1986, Everybody's All American 1989, Far North 1988, Music Box 1989, Men Don't Leave 1989, Cape Fear 1991, Night and the City 1993, Blue Sky (Acad. Award for Best Actress 1995) 1994, Losing Isaiah 1995, Rob Roy 1995, A Thousand Acres 1997, Hush 1998, Cousin Bette 1998, Titus 1999, Prozac Nation 2001, Masked and Anonymous 2003, Great Performances 2003, Big Fish 2003, Don't Come Knockin' 2005, Broken Flowers 2005, Neverwas 2005, Bonneville 2006, The Vow 2012, The Big Valley 2012, Therese Raquin 2012, In Secret 2013, The Gambler 2015, Wild Oats 2015. *Television includes:* The Best Little Girl in the World 1981, Notre Dame of the Cross (documentary) 1981, Cat on a Hot Tin Roof 1985, O Pioneers! 1992, A Streetcar Named Desire 1995, Off the Menu: The Last Days of Chasen's (documentary) 1997, Normal (film) 2003, XXI Century (documentary) 2003, Peace by Peace: Women on the Frontlines (narrator) 2004, The Needs of Kim Stanley (documentary) 2005, Sybil (film) 2007, Grey Gardens (film) (Emmy Award for Outstanding Lead Actress in a Miniseries or Movie) 2009, American Horror Story (series) (Golden Globe Award for Best Supporting Actress in a Series, Mini-Series or Motion Picture Made for Television 2012, Emmy Award for Supporting Actress in a Mini-series or Movie 2012, Primetime Emmy Award for Outstanding Lead Actress in a Mini-series or a Movie 2014) 2011–15, Feud 2017. *Address:* c/o Toni Howard, ICM, Constellation Boulevard, Los Angeles, CA 90067, USA (office). *Telephone:* (310) 550-4000 (office). *Website:* www.icmtalent.com (office).

LANGELLA, Frank, BA; American actor; b. 1 Jan. 1940, Bayonne, NJ; s. of Frank A. Langella, Sr; m. Ruth Weil 1977 (divorced); ed Syracuse Univ. *Plays include:* numerous stage appearances on Broadway and elsewhere including Seascape (Tony Award for Best Featured Actor in a Play) 1975, Fortune's Fool (Tony Award for Best Featured Actor in a Play) 2002, Sherlock's Last Case 1987, Frost/Nixon (Tony Award for Best Leading Actor in a Play) 2007, A Man for All Seasons 2008, The Father (Tony Award for Best Performance by an Actor in a Leading Role 2016) 2015. *Films include:* Diary of a Mad Housewife 1970,The Twelve Chairs 1970, The Wrath of God 1972, The Mark of Zorro 1974, Dracula 1979, And God Created Woman 1988, Body of Evidence 1993, The Beast 2001, Now You See It 2005, Good Night and Good Luck 2005, Starting Out in the Evening (Boston Soc. of Film Critics Award) 2007, Frost/Nixon 2008, The Box 2009, Wall Street: Money Never Sleeps 2010, All Good Things 2010, Unknown 2011, Robot & Frank 2012, The Time Being 2012, Muhammad Ali's Greatest Fight 2013, Muppets Most Wanted 2014, Parts Per Billion 2014, Draft Day 2014, 5 to 7 2014, Grace of Monaco 2014, The Driftless Area 2015, Captain Fantastic 2016. *Television includes:* Sherlock Holmes 1981, Unscripted (series) 2005, Kitchen Confidential (series) 2005–06, The Miraculous Year (film) 2011, The Americans (series) 2015. *Publications include:* Dropped Names: Famous Men and Women As I Knew Them 2012. *Address:* CESD Talent Agency NY, 257 Park Avenue South, Suite 900, New York, NY 10010, USA (office). *Telephone:* (212) 477-1666 (office). *Fax:* (212) 979-2011 (office). *Website:* www.cesdtalent.com (office).

LANGER, Ivan, MD, MCL; Czech education administrator and fmr politician; *Chairman, CEVRO Institute;* b. 1 Jan. 1967, Olomouc; m. Markéta Vobořilová; two s. one d.; ed Univ. of Palacký, Charles Univ., Prague; Secr. Ministry for Justice of Czech Repub. 1993–96; mem. Council Olomouc 1994; mem. of Civic Democratic Party (ODS) 1991–, Vice-Chair. 1998–2002, 2004–10; mem. Parl. 1996–2010; Shadow Minister of the Interior 1999–2002; Vice-Chair. Chamber of Deputies (Parl.) 1998–2006; Minister of the Interior June–Oct. 2006 (resgnd), reinstated Jan. 2007–09, of Information 2007; Chair. of the Governing Bd, CEVRO Inst. (pvt. educational inst.), Prague 2010–; Hon. mem. Maltese Order of Help 1994–. *Publications include:* Rational Anti-drug Policy, After the Velvet Revolution. *Leisure interests:* tennis, music, theatre, film, golf. *Address:* CEVRO Institute, Jungmannova 17, 110 00 Prague 1, Czech Republic (office). *Fax:* 234707101 (home). *E-mail:* info@vsci.cz (office). *Website:* www.cevroinstitut.cz (office); www.langer.cz.

LANGER, Robert Samuel, Jr, ScD, BS; American chemical engineer and academic; *David H. Koch Institute Professor, Department of Chemical Engineering, Massachusetts Institute of Technology;* b. 29 Aug. 1948, Albany, NY; m. Laura Langer; three c.; ed Cornell Univ. and Massachusetts Inst. of Tech.; Chair. Math.

and Science Depts, The Group School, Cambridge, Mass 1972–73; Research Asst, MIT 1972–74, Visiting Asst Prof. of Nutritional Biochemistry, Dept of Nutrition and Food Sciences 1977–78, Asst Prof. of Nutritional Biochemistry 1978–81, Assoc. Prof. of Biochemical Eng, Dept of Nutrition and Food Sciences and the Whitaker Coll. of Health Sciences Tech. and Management, and the Harvard-MIT Div. of Health Sciences and Tech. 1981–85, Prof. of Biochemical Eng, Dept of Applied Biological Sciences etc. 1985–88, Germeshausen Prof. of Chemical and Biomedical Eng, Dept of Chemical Eng 1988–2005, Inst. Prof. 2005–09, David H. Koch Inst. Prof. 2009–; Research Assoc., Children's Hosp. Medical Center, Harvard Medical School, Boston 1974–, Sr Lecturer on Surgery, Harvard Medical School, Harvard Univ. 1999–; mem. SCIENCE Bd, US Food and Drug Admin 1995–2002, Chair. 1999–2002; mem. Bd of Dirs or Scientific Advisory Bd Wyeth, Alkermes, Mitsubishi Pharmaceuticals, Warner-Lambert, Momenta Pharmaceuticals, Puretech Ventures; has helped start 25 cos; mem. Inst. of Medicine (NAS) 1989, NAS, Nat. Acad. of Eng (NAE) 1992 (one of only a few people ever elected to all three US Nat. Acads and the youngest in history aged 43); Fellow, ACS 2011, AIChE 2012; Dr hc (ETH, Switzerland, Technion Univ., Israel, Hebrew Univ. of Jerusalem, Université Catholique de Louvain, Belgium, Univ. of Liverpool, UK, Univ. of Nottingham, UK, Albany Medical Coll., Pennsylvania State Univ., Uppsala Univ., Sweden, Yale Univ., Northwestern Univ., Yale Univ., Mount Sinai School of Medicine, Harvard Univ., Willamette Univ., Rensselaer Polytechnic Inst., Bates Coll., Ben Gurion Univ., Israel, Tel-Aviv Univ., Israel, Boston Univ.); more than 220 honours and major awards, ACS Award for Applied Polymer Science (Phillips Award) 1992, Gairdner Foundation Int. Award 1996, AIChE William Walker Award 1996, Lemelson-MIT Prize for Invention and Innovation 1998, ACS Award in Polymer Chem. 1999, NAE Charles Stark Draper Prize 2002, Dickson Prize for Science 2002, Heinz Award for Tech., Economy and Employment 2003, Harvey Prize 2003, John Fritz Award 2003, General Motors Kettering Prize for Cancer Research 2004, Dan David Prize in Materials Science 2005, Albany Medical Center Prize in Medicine and Biomedical Research 2005, Nat. Medal of Science 2006, inducted into Nat. Inventors Hall of Fame 2006, Millennium Tech. Prize 2008, Max Planck Research Award 2008, Prince of Asturias Award for Tech. and Scientific Research 2008, Nat. Medal of Tech. and Innovation 2011, Warren Alpert Foundation Prize 2011, Terumo Int. Prize 2012, ACS Priestley Medal 2012, Industrial Research Inst. Medal (co-recipient) 2013, Wolf Prize in Chem., Wolf Foundation 2013, Breakthrough Prize in Life Sciences (co-recipient) 2014, Kyoto Prize, Inamori Foundation (co-recipient) 2014, Cornell Entrepreneur of the Year 2015, Queen Elizabeth Prize for Eng 2015. *Publications:* more than 1,280 articles in scientific journals on drug delivery, biomaterials, tissue engineering, biotechnology, immobilized enzymes, biomedical engineering, and nearly 1,050 issued or pending patents world-wide. *Address:* Langer Lab, Massachusetts Institute of Technology, Room 76-661, The David H. Koch Institute Building, 77 Massachusetts Avenue, Cambridge, MA 02139-4307, USA (office). *Telephone:* (617) 253-3107 (office). *Fax:* (617) 258-8827 (office). *E-mail:* rlanger@mit.edu (office); langeroffice@mit.edu (office). *Website:* web.mit.edu/langerlab (office); be.mit.edu/directory/robert-langer (office).

LANGHOFF, Stephanie R., BS, MBA, PhD; American chemist; *Chief Scientist, NASA Ames Research Center;* ed Colorado Coll., Univ. of Washington, Massachusetts Inst. of Tech.; Post-Doctoral Fellow, Battelle Memorial Inst., Columbus, OH 1973–76; Nat. Research Council Fellow, NASA Ames Research Center 1976–78, Research Scientist, Computational Chem. Br. 1978–92, Br. Chief 1992–97, Chief Scientist 1998–, Chair. NASA Ames Basic Research Council 1999–2002; Sloan Fellow, MIT 1997–98; mem. American Physical Soc.; mem. US Dept of Energy Panel on Combustion Research, Panel on Innovative Concepts in Nuclear Propulsion. *Address:* NASA Ames Research Center, MS 230–3, Moffett Field, CA 94035, USA (office). *Telephone:* (650) 604-6213 (office). *Fax:* (650) 604-0350 (office). *E-mail:* stephanie.r.langhoff@nasa.gov (office). *Website:* www.nasa.gov/centers/ames (office).

LANGLANDS, Sir (Robert) Alan, Kt, FRSE, FRCPE; British university administrator and health care manager; *Vice-Chancellor, University of Leeds;* b. 29 May 1952, Glasgow, Scotland; s. of James Langlands and May Langlands (née Rankin); m. Elizabeth McDonald 1977; one s. one d.; ed Allan Glen's School, Univ. of Glasgow; grad. trainee Nat. Health Service Scotland 1974–76; with Argyll and Clyde Health Bd 1976–78; with Simpson Memorial Maternity Pavilion, Elsie Inglis Hosp. 1978–81; Unit Admin. Middx and Univ. Coll. Hosps and Hosp. for Women, Soho 1981–85; Dist Gen. Man. Harrow Health Authority 1985–89; Practice Leader Health Care, Towers Perrin 1989–91; Gen. Man. NW Thames Regional Health Authority 1991–92; Deputy Chief Exec. Nat. Health Service 1993–94, Chief Exec. 1994–2000; Prin. and Vice-Chancellor Univ. of Dundee 2000–09; Chief Exec. Higher Educ. Funding Council for England 2009–13; Vice-Chancellor Univ. of Leeds 2013–; mem. Cen. Research and Devt Cttee Nat. Health Service 1991–92, Inst. of Health Services Man., Nat. Forum for Research and Devt 1994–2000, Advisory Bd Centre for Corp. Strategy and Change, Univ. of Warwick 1995–2000, Nat. Advisory Bd, Healthcare Advisory Bd Institut Européen d'Admin des Affaires (INSEAD) 1998–2000; Chair. UK Biobank 2004–12, The Health Foundation 2009–17; Hon. Prof., Warwick Business School 1996–2016, Johns Hopkins Univ. 2000–04; Hon. FFPHM 1994; Hon. FIA 1999; Hon. FCGI 2000; Hon. CCMI CIMgt 2000; Hon. Fellow, Royal Coll. of Gen. Practitioners 2001; Hon. FRCP 2001; Hon. FRCSE 2001; Hon. FRCPSGlas 2002; Hon. FMedSci 2009; Hon. DUniv Glasgow 2001, (Sheffield Hallam) 2016; Hon. LLD (Dundee) 2010; Dr hc (Edinburgh) 2010. *Leisure interest:* walking in Yorkshire and Scotland. *Address:* Office of the Vice-Chancellor, University of Leeds, Leeds, LS2 9JT, England (office). *Telephone:* (113) 343-3000 (office). *E-mail:* vice-chancellor@leeds.ac.uk (office). *Website:* www.leeds.ac.uk/info/110000/senior_lay_officers_and_the_executive/212/sir_alan_langlands (office).

LANGLANDS, Robert Phelan, MSc, PhD, FRS, FRSC; Canadian/American mathematician and academic; *Hermann Weyl Professor Emeritus, School of Mathematics, Institute for Advanced Study, Princeton;* b. 6 Oct. 1936, New Westminster, BC; s. of Robert Langlands and Kathleen J. Phelan; m. Charlotte Cheverie 1956; two s. two d.; ed Univ. of British Columbia, Yale Univ., USA; Instructor, Assoc. Prof. Princeton Univ. 1960–67, Hermann Weyl Prof. Inst. for Advanced Study, Princeton 1972–2007, Prof. Emer. 2007–; Prof. Yale Univ. 1968–72; mem. NAS, Türk Bilim Akademisi, Russian Acad. of Science, American Philosophical Soc.; Fellow American Math. Soc. 2012; Wolf Prize 1995/96, Grande

Medaille d'Or, Paris 2000, Frederic Esser Nemmers Prize in Math. 2006, Shaw Prize 2007, Abel Prize, Norwegian Acad. of Science and Letters 2018. *Publications include:* Automorphic Forms on GL (2) (with H. Jacquet) 1970, Euler Products 1971, On the Functional Equations Satisfied by Eisenstein Series 1976, Base Change for GL (2) 1980, Les Débuts d'une Formule des Traces Stable 1983. *Leisure interests:* reading, travel. *Address:* School of Mathematics, Fuld Hall 115, Institute for Advanced Study, Einstein Drive, Princeton, NJ 08540 (office); 60 Battle Road, Princeton, NJ 08540, USA (home). *Telephone:* (609) 734-8115 (office); (609) 921-7222 (home). *E-mail:* rpl@math.ias.edu (office). *Website:* publications.ias.edu/rpl (office).

LANGLEY, Donna; British film industry executive and film producer; *Chairman, Universal Pictures;* b. Isle of Wight; m. Ramin Shamshiri; two s.; began career as asst at New Line Cinema, later served as Sr Vice-Pres. of Production; joined Universal Pictures as Sr Vice-Pres. of Production 2001, Pres. of Production –2009, Co-Chair. Universal Pictures (first British woman to run a Hollywood studio) 2009–13, Chair. 2013–; Global Amb. for Vital Voices Global; mem. Advisory Bd Chrysalis (charity), Co-Chair. Chrysalis' Annual Butterfly Ball; helped start The Hollywood Reporter's Women in Film Mentorship programme; Crystal Award for excellence in film-making, Women in Film 2010, Grace Kelly Award, March of Dimes 2011. *Films include:* exec. producer: Austin Powers: The Spy Who Shagged Me 1999, Drop Dead Gorgeous 1999, The Astronaut's Wife 1999, The Bachelor 1999, The Cell 2000, Lost Souls 2000, Highway 2002; other film roles: Summer School (production sec.) 1987, Born in East L.A. (production sec.) 1987, Austin Powers: International Man of Mystery (creative exec.) 1997, Northfork (office production asst) 2003. *Television includes:* Bakugan Battle Brawlers: Gundalian Invaders (series) (production exec.) 2010; other TV film roles: The Night Train to Kathmandu (film) (production office coordinator) 1988, Ancient Mysteries (series documentary) (production coordinator) 1996–97, Biography (series documentary) (post-production manager) 1998. *Leisure interest:* organic gardening. *Address:* Universal Pictures, 100 Universal City Plaza, Universal City, CA 91608-1002, USA (office). *Telephone:* (818) 777-1000 (office). *Fax:* (818) 866-3600 (office). *Website:* www.universalpictures.com (office).

LANGLOIS, HE Cardinal Chibly; Haitian ecclesiastic; *Bishop of Les Cayes;* b. 29 Nov. 1958, La Vallée; ed Grand Séminaire Notre-Dame, Port-au-Prince, Pontifical Lateran Univ., Rome; ordained priest of Diocese of Jacmel 1991; consecrated Bishop of Fort-Liberté 2004–11; Bishop of Les Cayes 2011–; cr. Cardinal (Cardinal-Priest of San Giacomo in Augusta) 2014–; Pres. Haiti's Bishops' Conf. *Address:* Diocese of Les Cayes, BP 43, Rue Toussaint-Louverture, Les Cayes, Haiti (office). *Telephone:* (5) 286-0131 (office).

LANGUETIN, Pierre; Swiss diplomatist and fmr central banker; b. 30 April 1923, Lausanne; m. Florentina Lobo 1951; one s. one d.; ed Univ. de Lausanne and LSE, UK; diplomatic career 1949–; in Div. of Exchange, OEEC, Paris; in Div. of Commerce, Fed. Dept of Public Economy 1955–76, Head of Secr. 1957–61, Chief of Section IA 1961–63; Chief of Subdiv. 1963; has been concerned with problems of European econ. co-operation; Asst Head of Bureau of Integration, Fed. Political Dept and Dept of Public Economy 1961; Swiss Del. to Trade Cttee, OECD, Paris 1961–76, Vice-Pres. 1963–76; mem. Swiss Del. to UNCTAD, Geneva 1964, New Delhi 1968; Swiss Rep. at various int. orgs 1965–66; Del. of Fed. Council for Trade Negotiations, title of Minister Plenipotentiary 1966–68; Head of Swiss Del. to EFTA Geneva 1967–76, title of Amb. 1968–76; Deputy Head of Swiss Negotiating Team with EEC 1970–72; Head of Swiss Del. to Exec. Cttee in special session OECD 1972–76; Head of Swiss Del. for accession negotiations to Int. Energy Agency 1974, Rep. for Switzerland to Governing Bd 1974–76; mem. Governing Bd of Swiss Nat. Bank 1976–81, Vice-Chair. 1981–84, Chair. 1985–88; mem. Bd of Dirs BIS 1985–88; Chair. Inst. for Public Admin. Studies, Lausanne 1988–97, Inst. for Bank and Financial Man., Lausanne 1990–96; Vice-Chair. Sandoz SA 1988–95; Chair. Rosbank (fmrly Unexim), Switzerland 1995–2009; mem. Bd of Dirs Ludwig Inst. 1987–2007, Swiss Reinsurance Co. 1988–93, Pargesa Holding SA 1988–2002, Paribas (Suisse) 1989–96 (Vice-Chair. 1992), Renault Finance 1989–99, Fin. Cpy Tradition 1995–; mem. Advisory Bd American Int. Group 1989–97, Arthur Andersen (Switzerland) 1991–97; mem. Bd of Dirs Chase Manhattan Pvt. Bank (Switzerland) 1991–2001, Dryden Bank (formerly Prumerica Pvt. Bank) (Switzerland) 2002–05; mem. Int. Red Cross Cttee 1988–93; Dr hc (Lausanne) 1979. *Address:* 33, Chemin des Roches 1470 Estavager-le-Lac, Switzerland (home). *Telephone:* (26) 6633325 (home). *Fax:* (26) 6633325 (home).

LANKESTER, Sir Timothy Patrick, Kt, KCB, BA, MA; British fmr government official and university administrator; *Chairman, Council, London School of Hygiene and Tropical Medicine;* b. 15 April 1942, Cairo, Egypt; s. of Robin P. A. Lankester and Jean D. Gilliat; m. Patricia Cockcroft 1968; three d.; ed Monkton Combe School, St John's Coll., Cambridge and Jonathan Edwards Coll., Yale; reacher with VSO, St Michael's Coll., British Honduras (now Belize) 1960–61; Faraday Fellow, St John's Coll. Oxford 1965–66; Economist, IBRD, Washington, DC 1966–69, New Delhi 1970–73; HM Treasury 1973–78, Under-Sec. 1983–85, Deputy Sec. 1988–89; Pvt. Sec. to Prime Minister Callaghan 1978–79, to Prime Minister Thatcher 1979–81; seconded to S.G. Warburg & Co. 1981–83; Econ. Minister, Washington, DC and UK Exec. Dir IMF and IBRD 1985–88; Perm. Sec., Overseas Devt Admin., FCO 1989–93, Dept for Educ. 1994–95; Dir SOAS, Univ. of London 1996–2000, Hon. Fellow 2002–; Pres. Corpus Christi Coll. Oxford 2001–10; Chair. Council of the London School of Hygiene and Tropical Medicine; mem. Jt Advisory Bd Georgetown University School of Foreign Service, Qatar; Dir European Investment Bank 1988–89, Smith and Nephew 1996–2003, London Metal Exchange 1997–2001, Mitchells and Butler plc 2003–, Actis 2004–; Gov. Asia-Europe Foundation 1997–; Deputy Chair. British Council 1998–2003; Trustee, Contemporary Dance Trust; Hon. Fellow, St John's Coll., Cambridge, Corpus Christi Coll., Oxford. *Address:* London School of Hygiene & Tropical Medicine, Keppel Street, London, WC1E 7HT, England (office). *Telephone:* (20) 7636-8636 (office). *Fax:* (20) 7436-5389 (office). *E-mail:* council@lshtm.ac.uk (office). *Website:* www.lshtm.ac.uk (office).

LANKFORD, James Paul, BS, MDiv; American politician; *Senator from Oklahoma;* b. 4 March 1968, Dallas, Tex.; m. Cindy Lankford; two d.; ed Univ. of Texas, Southwestern Baptist Theological Seminary; mem. staff, Baptist Gen. Convention, Okla 1996–2009; Dir Falls Creek Christian Summer Youth Camp, Davis, Okla 1996–2009; mem. US House of Reps from 5th Okla Dist, Washington,

DC 2011–15, mem. Transportation and Infrastructure Cttee, Budget Cttee, Oversight and Govt Reform Cttee, Chair. House Republican Policy Cttee 2013–15, House Energy, Policy, Health Care and Entitlements Sub-Cttee; Senator from Oklahoma 2015–; mem. Nat. Rifle Asscn, Heritage Foundation, Edmond Chamber of Commerce, Deer Creek Chamber of Commerce; Republican. *Leisure activities:* spending time with family, sport shooting, reading. *Address:* B40C Dirksen Senate Office Building, Washington, DC 20510, USA (office). *Telephone:* (202) 224-5754 (office). *Website:* www.lankford.senate.gov (office).

LANKHORST, Gertjan, AB; Dutch energy industry executive; *Chairman, VEMW;* b. 22 Dec. 1957, Amsterdam; ed Atheneum B, Amsterdam Free Univ.; held teaching position at Amsterdam Free Univ. 1982–86; joined Gen. Econ. Policy Dept, Ministry of Econ. Affairs 1986, becoming Dir of Oil and Gas 1996–99, Competition Dir 1999–2003, Dir-Gen. for Energy 2004–05; CEO GasTerra BV (fmrly Gasunie Trade & Supply BV) 2006–16; Chair. VEMW (Asscn for Energy Environment and Water) 2017–. *Address:* VEMW, Houttuinlaan 12, 3447 GM Woerden, Netherlands (office). *Telephone:* (34) 848-43-60 (office). *E-mail:* tr@vemw.nl (office). *Website:* www.vemw.nl (office).

LANOTTE, Johan Vande, MA, PhD; Belgian politician; *Mayor of Ostend;* b. 6 July 1955, Poperinge; one c.; ed Sint-Stanislascollege, Univ. of Antwerpen (UIA), Rijksuniversiteit Gent (RUG); Asst Dept of Political and Social Sciences, UIA 1982–83; Asst Special Admin. Law, RUG 1983–87; Head of Office for Minister of the Interior 1988–91; MP 1991–, Minister of the Interior and the Civil Service 1994–95; Deputy Prime Minister and Minister of the Home Dept 1995–98; Deputy Prime Minister and Minister of the Budget, Social Integration and Social Economy 1999; Deputy Prime Minister and Minister for the Budget and Public Enterprise, Deputy Prime Minister and Minister of Economy, Consumers and the North Sea 2011–14; Chair. Sociaal Progressief Alternatief (Socialist Party—Flemish wing) 2005–07; Mayor of Ostend 2015–. *Publications include:* Krachtlijnen van een vernieuwd gemeentebeleid 1983, Wonen in België. Mythen en werkelijkheid (co-author) 1985, Petitierecht 1987, De noodzakelijke decentralisatie 1988, De recente evolutie en de knelpunten in de ruimtelijke ordening en de stedebouw (co-author) 1988, De geschiedenis van de Provinciewet (co-author) 1990, De nieuwe gemeentelijke comptabiliteit (co-author) 1990, Inleiding tot het publiek recht 1994, Overzicht van het Belgisch Administratief Recht (co-author) 1996, Het Europees verdrag tot bescherming van de Rechten van de Mens: In Hoofdlijnen (co-author), 1997, België voor beginners: Wegwijs in het Belgisch labyrint (co-author) 1998, Handboek Europees Verdrag voor de Rechten van de Mens (co-author) 2004. *Leisure interest:* basketball. *Website:* www.oostende.be; www.johanvandelanotte.be.

LANOVOY, Vasiliy Semenovich; Russian actor; b. 16 Jan. 1934, Moscow; s. of Semion Petrovich Lanovoy and Agafia Ivanovna Yakubenko; m. 1st Tatyana Samoylova 1955 (divorced 1958); m. 2nd Tamara Zyablova 1963 (died 1970); m. 3rd Irina Petrovna Kupchenko 1972; two s.; ed Shchukin Theatre School; actor with Vakhtangov Theatre 1957–; also works as narrator; Prof., Faculty of Artistic Speech, Shchukin's Theatre School, Moscow 1995–; mem. CPSU 1968–90; Lenin Prize 1980, People's Artist of USSR 1985. *Television includes:* Brezhnev 2005, Bednye rodstvenniki 2012, Berega moey mechty 2013, Liniya Marty 2014. *Theatrical roles include:* Ognev in Korneichuk's Front, Prince Calaf in Gozzi's Princess Turandot, Caesar in Shaw's Antony and Cleopatra, Sagadeev in Abdullin's Thirteenth President, Don Juan in Pushkin's The Stone Guest, Trotsky in M. Shatrov's Peace of Brest, Oscar in La Bize's Murder at Lursin Street, Astrov in Uncle Vanya, J.B. Shaw in I. Kiltye's Dear Liar, King Henry in The Lion in Winter. *Films include:* War and Peace, Anna Karenina, The Strange Woman, Going in a Thunderstorm, The Picture, The Scarlet Sails, The Officers, Unknown War, The Colleges, Strategy for Victory, The Trifles of Life, Barin's Daughter, Tri mushketera 2013. *Leisure interests:* volleyball, badminton, hunting, skiing, dogs. *Address:* 121002 Moscow, Starokonyushenny per. 39, Apt 18, Russia. *Telephone:* (495) 203-94-03.

LANSBURY SHAW, Angela Brigid, (Angela Lansbury), DBE, CBE; British actress; b. 16 Oct. 1925, London, England; d. of Edgar Lansbury and Moyna Macgill (Charlotte Lillian McIldowie); m. 1st Richard Cromwell 1945 (divorced 1946); m. 2nd Peter Shaw 1949 (died 2003); one s. one d. one step-s.; ed Webber Douglas School of Singing and Dramatic Art, Kensington, Feagin School of Drama and Radio, New York; film debut in Gaslight 1944; numerous appearances on London and New York stages and on TV; Hon. DHumLitt (Boston) 1990; Silver Mask for Lifetime Achievement BAFTA 1991, Lifetime Achievement Award, Screen Actors' Guild 1997, Stephen Sondheim Award 2009, Hon. Acad. Award 2013, numerous other awards. *Stage appearances include:* Hotel Paradiso 1957, Dear World (Tony Award) 1969, The King and I 1978, A Little Family Business 1983, Deuce 2007, A Little Night Music 2009, Blithe Spirit 2014. *Films include:* Manchurian Candidate, In the Cool of the Day, Harlow, Moll Flanders, Bedknobs and Broomsticks, Death on the Nile, The Lady Vanishes 1980, The Mirror Cracked 1980, The Pirates of Penzance 1982, Company of Wolves 1983, Beauty and the Beast 1991, Anastasia (voice) 1997, Nanny McPhee 2005, Heidi 4 Paws (voice) 2009, Mr. Popper's Penguins 2011, Blithe Spirit (Olivier Award for Best Supporting Actress 2015) 2014. *Television includes:* Murder She Wrote 1984–96 (with special episodes thereafter, including Murder, She Wrote: The Celtic Riddle 2003), The Shell Seekers 1989, South by Southwest 1997, A Story to Die For 2000, Touched by an Angel (series) 2002, The Blackwater Lightship (film) 2004, Law & Order: Trial by Jury (series) 2005, Law & Order: Special Victims Unit (series) 2005, At the Paley Center (series) 2010. *Publication:* Angela Lansbury's Positive Moves (with Mimi Avins) 1990. *Address:* c/o WME Entertainment, 9601 Wilshire Boulevard, Beverly Hills, CA 90210-5213, USA (office). *Telephone:* (310) 285-9000 (office). *Fax:* (310) 285-9010 (office). *Website:* www.wma.com (office).

LANSING, Sherry, BS; American film producer and business executive; *CEO, Sherry Lansing Foundation;* b. (Sherry Lee Heimann), 31 July 1944, Chicago, Ill.; d. of Norton Lansing and Margot Lansing; m. 2nd William Friedkin 1991; ed Northwestern Univ.; math. and English teacher, Public High Schools, LA, Calif. 1966–69; model, TV commercials, Max Factor Co. and Alberto-Culver 1969–70; appeared in films Loving and Rio Lobo 1970; Exec. Story Ed., Wagner Int. 1970–73; Vice-Pres. for Production, Heyday Productions 1973–75; Exec. Story Ed., then Vice-Pres. for Creative Affairs, MGM Studios 1975–77; Vice-Pres., then Sr Vice-Pres. for Production, Columbia Pictures 1977–80; Pres. 20th Century-Fox

Productions 1980–83; Co-Founder Jaffe-Lansing Productions, LA 1982; Chair. Paramount Pictures 1992–2005; Founder and CEO Sherry Lansing Foundation 2005–; mem. Bd of Regents, Univ. of Calif. 1999–; mem. Bd of Dirs Encore.org, Entertainment Industry Foundation, W.M. Keck Foundation, Teach for America, American Film Inst., The Carter Center, DonorsChoose, American Asscn for Cancer Research, Friends of Cancer Research; Trustee Calif. Museum for History, Women and the Arts; Dr hc (American Film Inst.); Woodrow Wilson Award for Corporate Citizenship, Milestone Award from Producers Guild of America, Overcoming Obstacles Achievement Award for Business, YWCA Silver Achievement Award, Outstanding Woman in Business Award frome Women's Equity Action League, Distinguished Community Service Award from Brandeis Univ., Alfred P. Sloan, Jr. Memorial Award, Pioneer of the Year by Foundation of Motion Picture Pioneers 1996, first woman studio head to receive a star on Hollywood Walk of Fame 1996, Exemplary Leadership in Management Award, UCLA Anderson School of Man. 2005, Jean Hersholt Humanitarian Award 2007, Double Helix Medal, Cold Spring Harbor Laboratory 2008, Centennial Medal for Distinguished Public Service, American Asscn for Cancer Research 2009, Stem Cell Action Leadership Award, World Stem Cell Summit 2011, Lifetime Achievement Award, Israel Film Festival, Los Angeles 2013, Ellis Island Medal of Honor 2017. *Films produced include:* Racing with the Moon 1984, Firstborn 1984 (exec. producer), When the Time Comes (TV) (exec. producer), Fatal Attraction 1987, The Accused 1988, Black Rain 1989, School Ties 1992, Indecent Proposal 1993, The Untouchables: Capone Rising 2006. *Address:* Sherry Lansing Foundation, 2121 Avenue of the Stars, Suite 2020, Los Angeles, CA 90067, USA (office). *Telephone:* (310) 788-0057 (office). *E-mail:* slfasst@sherrylansingfoundation.org (office). *Website:* www.sherrylansingfoundation.org (office).

LANSLEY, Baron (Life Peer), cr. 2015; **Rt Hon. Andrew David Lansley,** CBE, BA; British politician; b. 11 Dec. 1956, Hornchurch, Essex, England; s. of Thomas Lansley; m. 1st Dr Marilyn Biggs (divorced 1997); three d.; m. 2nd Sally Low; one s. one d.; ed Brentwood School, Essex, Univ. of Exeter; fmr Pres. Guild for Students, Univ. of Exeter; began career as civil servant at Dept of Trade & Industry; Prin. Pvt. Sec. to Rt Hon. Norman Tebbit MP 1984–87; Deputy Dir-Gen. British Chambers of Commerce 1987–90; Dir Conservative Research Dept 1990–95; ran Conservative Party campaign for 1992 Gen. Election; Vice-Chair. Conservative Party (with responsibility for Policy Renewal) 1998–99; MP for South Cambridgeshire 1997–2010, for South Cambridgeshire (revised boundary) 2010–15; Shadow Minister for Cabinet Office and Policy Renewal 1999–2001, Shadow Chancellor of Duchy of Lancaster 1999–2001, Shadow Sec. of State for Health 2003–10; Sec. of State for Health 2010–12; Leader of the House of Commons and Lord Privy Seal 2012–14; mem. Health Select Cttee 1997–98, Trade and Industry Select Cttee 2001–04, House of Commons Comm. 2012–15, Speaker's Cttee for the Ind. Parl. Standards Authority 2012–15, Public Accounts Comm. 2012–15; mem. (Conservative), House of Lords 2015–; Vice-Pres. Local Govt Asscn 1996–; with Bain & Company 2015–; Conservative. *Leisure interests:* spending time with family, history, cricket, theatre, films, travel. *Address:* House of Lords, Westminster, London, SW1A 0PW, England (office). *Telephone:* (20) 7219-3000 (office). *E-mail:* lansleya@parliament.uk (office). *Website:* www.andrewlansley.co.uk.

LANTIGUA, José Rafael, BEd; Dominican Republic writer and politician; b. 17 Sept. 1949, Moca; ed Pedro Henríquez Ureña Nat. Univ.; Ed. Literary Section, Ultima Hora (newspaper) 1985–2000; Chair. Nat. Book Fair Standing Cttee 1996–2000; Sec. of State for Culture 2004–12; mem. Dominican Acad. of Language 2008–; Nat. Essay Prize 1976, Nat. Prize for Journalism 1988, Caonabo de Oro Prize 1999, Nat. Book Fair Prize 2016. *Publications:* poetry: Sobre un tiempo de esperanza 1982, Semblanzas del corazón 1985; essays: Domingo Moreno Jimenes: biografía de un poeta 1976, Hacia una revalorización del ideal duartiano 1985, La conjura del tiempo 1994, El oficio de la palabra 1995; anthology: del cuento cubano y dominicano 1999.

LANXADE, Adm. Jacques; French naval officer; *Chairman, Fondation Méditerranéenne d'Etudes stratégiques;* b. 8 Sept. 1934, Toulon; m. Loïse Rostan d'Ancezune 1959; one s. three d.; ed Ecole Navale, Institut d'Admin des Affaires (Université Dauphiné); Commdr destroyers Le Champenois 1970–72, La Galissonnière 1976–77, frigate Duguay-Trouin 1980–81; rank of Rear-Adm. 1984; Commdr Indian Ocean maritime zone 1984–86; Commdr French fleet in the Indian Ocean 1986; rank of Vice-Adm. 1987; Chef du Cabinet Militaire to Minister of Defence 1988–89; Chief of Staff, Elysée Palace 1989; Chief of Staff of French Armed Forces 1991–95; Amb. to Tunisia 1995–99; Chair. Fondation Méditerranéenne d'Etudes stratégiques; mem. Atomic Energy Cttee 1991–95, Initiative for a Renewed Transatlantic Partnership, Center for Strategic and Int. Studies 2003–, Acad. de Marine 2008–, Int. Cttee of Patronage of the French journal Politique américaine; Grand Officier Légion d'honneur, Officier, Ordre nat. du Mérite, Croix de la Valeur Militaire. *Publications:* Quand le monde a basculé 2001, Organizer la politique européenne et internationale de la France (report) 2002. *Leisure interests:* tennis, skiing. *Address:* Fondation Méditerranéenne d'Etudes stratégiques, Maison des technologies, place Georges Pompidou, 83000 Toulon, France (office); 41 rue Saint-André des Arts, 75006 Paris, France (home). *Telephone:* (4) 94-05-55-55 (office); 1-46-33-39-05 (home). *Fax:* (4) 94-05-55-59 (office). *E-mail:* info@fmes-france.org (office); jacqueslanxade@noos.fr (office). *Website:* fmes-france.org (office).

LANYON, Lance Edward, CBE, BVSc, PhD, DSc, FMedSci, MRCVS; British professor of veterinary anatomy and university administrator; b. 4 Jan. 1944; s. of Henry Lanyon and Heather Gordon (née Tyrrell); m. Mary Kear (divorced 1997); one s. one d.; ed Christ's Hosp., Univ. of Bristol; Lecturer, Univ. of Bristol 1967, Reader in Veterinary Anatomy 1967–79, currently Visiting Prof.; Assoc. Prof., Tufts School of Veterinary Medicine, Boston, USA 1980–83, Prof. 1983–84; Prof. of Veterinary Anatomy, Royal Veterinary Coll., Univ. of London 1984–89, personal title 1989–2004, Head of Dept of Veterinary Anatomy 1984–87, of Veterinary Basic Sciences 1987–88, Prof. Emer. 2004–, Prin. Royal Veterinary Coll. 1989–2004 (retd); Pro-Vice-Chancellor, Univ. of London 1997–99; Hon. Fellow, Royal Coll. of Veterinary Surgeons (RCVS) 2012; Hon. DSc (Bristol) 2004; RCVS Share Jones Lecturer 1989, Wooldridge Lecturer, British Veterinary Asscn 1996. *Publications include:* numerous articles in professional journals; chapters in books on osteoporosis, orthopaedics and athletic training. *Leisure interests:* building, home improvements, sailing.

LANZER, Toby, BA, MIA, DPhil; British UN official; *Deputy Special Representative, Assistance Mission in Afghanistan, United Nations;* b. 1965; m.; three c.; ed Univ. of Oxford, Columbia Univ. and Univ. of New Hampshire, USA; joined UNDP 1992, Jr Professional Officer, Angola 1992–93, Field Adviser, Angola, Dept of Humanitarian Affairs (DHA) 1994–95, Head of Office, Georgia 1996–98, Head of Office for Coordination of Human Affairs (OCHA) in Russian Fed. 1999–2003, Chief of Consolidated Appeals Process (CAP), UN, Geneva 2003–05, UNDP Resident Rep. in Cen. African Repub. 2006–12, Chief of Staff, UN Integrated Mission in Timor-Leste –2012, Deputy Resident Coordinator and Humanitarian Coordinator, UN Mission in Sudan 2012–15, Deputy Special Rep. of Sec.-Gen. 2012–15, UN Resident Coordinator, Humanitarian Coordinator and Resident Rep., UNDP 2012–15, 2017–, Regional Humanitarian Coordinator for the Sahel, UN Office for the Coordination of Humanitarian Affairs (UNOCHA) 2015–17, Deputy Special Rep. UN Assistance Mission in Afghanistan (UNAMA) 2017–. *Address:* United Nations Assistance Mission in Afghanistan (UNAMA), POB 5858, Grand Central Station, New York, NY 10163-5858, USA (office). *Telephone:* (831) 246000 (office). *Fax:* (831) 246069 (office). *E-mail:* spokesperson-unama@un.org (office). *Website:* unama.unmissions.org (office).

LAO, Chongpin; Chinese artist; b. 3 Nov. 1936, Xinxing City, Guangdong Prov.; s. of Lao Xianguang and Chen Ermei; m. Luo Yuzing 1956; two s. one d.; ed Fine Arts Dept, Cen. China Teachers' Coll.; has painted more than 1000 landscapes and human figures in Japan, Canada, France, Egypt, Yugoslavia, Democratic People's Repub. of Korea, Pakistan, Burma, Jordan, Hungary, USSR, Albania 1973–; Dir Poetry Inst. 1987–; mem. staff Chinese Exhbn Agency, Ministry of Culture; mem. Chinese Artists' Asscn, Advisory Cttee, Beijing Children's Fine Arts Research Acad., Chinese Poetry Asscn, Int. Biographical Asscn; Hon. Dir Hanlin Forest of Steles, Kaifeng, China Shaolin Research Inst. of Painting and Calligraphy 1989. *Major works:* Harvest Time, Spring Ploughing, Harbour, Riverside, Arashiyama in Rain, Mosque in Lahore, Golden Pagoda of Rangoon, Pyramid and Sphinx, Autumn in Amman, Morning Glory on Seine River, Niagara Falls; group exhbns include Seven Star Cliff, Japan 1979, Scenery on Xinghu Lake, Mexico 1980, Drum Beaters, Hong Kong 1982, Panda, Wulongtang Waterfall, Belgium 1982, Scenery on Huangshan Mountain, Jordan 1983, Light Boats on the Yangtze River (Nat. Arts Museum, Romania) 1986, Scenes of Petra (Sact City Museum, Jordan) 1987, Waterfall of Lushan Mountain (Zacheta Art Museum, Poland) 1987; one-man exhbns in many Chinese cities and provs 1979–, Hong Kong 1988, Philippines 1989, Jordan 1990, Singapore 1995, India 1996; Sixth Asian Art Biennale, Bangladesh 1993. *Publication:* An Album of Sketches of Life in Foreign Countries 1986. *Leisure interests:* travel, music. *Address:* 1-301 Building No. 43, Xidahe Dongli, Chaoyang Qu, Beijing 100028, People's Republic of China. *Telephone:* (10) 64672946.

LAOUROU, Grégoire; Benin politician; *President, Union pour la Majorité Présidentiel Plurielle;* Pres. Council of Ministers, W African Econ. and Monetary Union (UEMOA); mem. Minister of Finance and the Economy 2003–05; mem. Assemblée nationale (Force cauris pour un Bénin émergent—FCBE) 2007–, Pres. Union pour la Majorité Présidentiel Plurielle (UMPP) 2009–. *Address:* Assemblée nationale BP 371, Porto-Novo, Benin (office). *Telephone:* 20-21-22-19 (office). *Fax:* 20-21-36-44 (office). *E-mail:* assemblee.benin@yahoo.fr (office). *Website:* www.assembleebenin.org (office).

LAPANG, D. Dethwelson, BA; Indian politician; b. 10 April 1934; s. of Donwa War; m. Amethyst Lynda Jomes Blah 1958; one s. one d.; ed Shillong Govt High School, St Anthony's Coll., Shillong; mem. Meghalaya Legis. Ass. 1972, Minister of State for Co-operation, Jails, Educ. and Civil Defence 1978–79, Health and Family Welfare, Labour, Information and Public Relations 1979–83, Planning, Finance, Home, Revenue, Food & Civil Supply 1983–85, Finance, Planning, Evaluation, Home and Revenue 1985–87, Planning and Programme Implementation 1987–88, Home, Revenue and Excise 1987–88; Deputy Minister of Internal Affairs 1988–90; Chief Minister of Meghalaya 1992–93, 2003–06, 2007–08 (resgnd), 2009–10 (resgnd); Deputy Chief Minister 1998–2003; Chair. State Planning Board 1993–95, Comm. on Resources Mobilization 1995–97; Pres. Meghalaya State Council of Indo-Soviet Cultural Soc. 1979, Meghalaya State Indo-GDR Friendship Asscn; Founder Pres. Bhoi Student Asscn, Meghalaya State Basketball Asscn, Meghalaya Eds and Publrs Asscn, Affiliated State Olympic Asscn.

LAPHAM, Lewis H., BA; American writer and editor; *Editor, Lapham's Quarterly;* b. 8 Jan. 1935, San Francisco, Calif.; m.; three c.; ed Yale Univ., Univ. of Cambridge, UK; reporter, San Francisco Examiner newspaper 1957–59, New York Herald Tribune 1960–62; Ed. Harper's Magazine 1976–81, 1983–2006, Ed. Emer. and columnist 2006–; syndicated newspaper columnist 1981–87; univ. lecturer, including at Yale, Princeton, Dartmouth and Stanford Univs; Founder and Ed., Lapham's Quarterly magazine 2008–; appearances on American and British TV, broadcasts on Nat. Public Radio; mem. Council on Foreign Relations; Nat. Magazine Award for Essays 1995, Thomas Paine Journalism Award 2002, inducted into American Soc. of Magazine Editors' Hall of Fame 2007. *Publications include:* Fortune's Child (essays) 1980, Money and Class in America 1988, Imperial Masquerade 1990, Hotel America: Scenes in the Lobby of the Fin-de-Siècle 1995, Waiting for the Barbarians 1997, The Agony of Mammon 1999, Lapham's Rules of Influence 1999, Theater of War 2002, 30 Satires 2003, Gag Rule 2004, Pretensions to Empire: Notes on the Criminal Folly of the Bush Administration 2007; contrib. 'Notebook' monthly essay Harper's Magazine; also contrib. to Commentary, Nat. Review, Yale Literary Magazine, Elle, Fortune, Forbes, American Spectator, Vanity Fair, Parade, Channels, Maclean's, London Observer, New York Times, Wall Street Journal. *Address:* Lapham's Quarterly, 33 Irving Place, Eighth Floor, New York, NY 10003, USA (office). *E-mail:* editorial@laphamsquarterly.org (office). *Website:* www.laphamsquarterly.org (office).

LAPHEN, Michael W., MBA; American information technology executive; m.; ed Pennsylvania State Univ., Wharton School, Univ. of Pennsylvania; served in USAF and Pa Air Nat. Guard; joined Computer Sciences Corpn 1977, has held numerous man. positions, including Vice-Pres. Finance and Admin, Pres. Integrated Systems Div. 1992–98, Pres. Fed. Sector Civil Group 1998–2000, Pres. European Group 2000–03, Pres. and COO 2003–07, Chair., Pres. and CEO 2007–12; mem. Information Technology Asscn of America, Armed Forces Communications and Electronics Asscn, Nat. Defense Industrial Asscn. *Address:* c/o Computer Sciences Corporation, 3170 Fairview Park Drive, Falls Church, VA 22042, USA. *E-mail:* info@csc.com.

LAPID, Yair; Israeli politician, journalist, author, fmr television presenter and actor; *Chairman, Yesh Atid Party;* b. 5 Nov. 1963, Tel-Aviv; s. of fmr Deputy Prime Minister Yosef 'Tommy' Lapid and Shulamit Lapid; m. Lihi Lapid; three c.; one-time amateur boxer; began career in journalism as mil. corresp. for Israeli Defense Force's weekly magazine, Ba-Mahaneh (In the Camp); also wrote for daily Maariv; apptd Ed. of Tel-Aviv local newspaper published by the Yedioth Ahronoth group 1988; began writing weekly column, Where's the Money?, in a nat. newspaper's weekend supplement, at first for Maariv and later for its competitor, Yedioth Ahronoth 1991; hosted talk show on Israel TV's Channel 1 1994, talk show on Channel 3 1994, talk show on Channel 2 1999–2012; host of Ulpan Shishi (Friday Studio) on Channel 2 2008; left journalism to enter politics 2012; Founder and Chair. Yesh Atid party 2012–; Minister of Finance 2013–14. *Play:* The Right Age for Love, Cameri Theatre 2008. *Television includes:* Ha-Hofesh Ha'Acharon (series) (screenplay) 1989, Shevet Cohen (series) (writer) 1991, Me'ever Layam 1992, Shirat Ha'Sirena 1994, Sogrim Shavua (series) 1995, Yair Lapid Chai Be'Eser (series) (host) 1997, Yair Lapid (series) (host) 2000, Mischak Machur (series) 2005, Hadar Milhama (series) (actor and producer) 2005, Lemon Tree (played a TV presenter as himself) 2008. *Publications include:* The Double Head 1989, Yoav's Shadow (children's book) 1992, One-Man Play 1993, Elbi – A Knight's Story (children's book) 1998, The Sixth Riddle 2001, Standing in a Row (collection of newspaper columns) 2005, The Second Woman 2006, Sunset in Moscow 2007, Memories After My Death 2010. *E-mail:* english@yeshatid.org.il (office); ylapid@knesset.gov.il. *Website:* www.yeshatid.org.il (office).

LAPIERRE, Dominique; French journalist, writer and philanthropist; b. 30 July 1931, Châtelaillon, Charente-Maritime; s. of Jean Lapierre and Luce Lapierre (née Andreotti); m. 2nd Dominique Conchon 1980; one d. (by first m.); ed Lycée Condorcet, LaFayette Univ., USA; Ed. Paris Match Magazine 1954–67; Founder and Pres. Action Aid for Lepers' Children of Calcutta; Hon. Founder and Chair, City of Joy (NGO); Citizen of Honour of the City of Calcutta; Commdr, Confrérie du Tastevin 1990, Chevalier, Légion d'honneur 2000, Grand Cross of the Order of Social Solidarity (Spain) 2002, Padma Bhushan (India) 2008; Dr hc (Lafayette Univ.) 1982; Christopher Book Award 1986, 2002, Gold Medal of Calcutta, Int. Rainbow Prize, UN 2000, Vatican Prize for Peace 2000, Gold Medal of the City of Milan 2006. *Publications include:* Un dollar les mille kilomètres 1949, Honeymoon around the World 1953, En liberté sur les routes d'U.R.S.S. 1957, Russie portes ouvertes 1957, Les Caïds de New York 1958, Chessman m'a dit 1960, The City of Joy 1985, Beyond Love 1991, A Thousand Suns 1998, Five Past Midnight in Bhopal 2002, It Was Once the USSR 2006, Un Arc-en-Ciel dans la Nuit 2008, India mon amour 2010, Mountbatten And The Partition Of India 2015; with Larry Collins: Is Paris Burning? 1964, Or I'll Dress You In Mourning 1967, O Jerusalem 1971, Freedom at Midnight 1975, The Fifth Horseman 1980, Is New York Burning? 2004. *Leisure interests:* riding, tennis, collecting antiques, vintage cars. *Address:* 37 Rue Charles-Laffitte, 92200 Neuilly; Les Bignoles, Val de Rian, 83350 Ramatuelle, France. *Telephone:* 1-46-37-34-34 (Neuilly); (4) 94-97-17-31 (Ramatuelle). *Fax:* (4) 94-97-38-05. *E-mail:* D.Lapierre@wanadoo.fr (home).

LAPIS, Károly, PhD, DSci; Hungarian pathologist, clinical oncologist, cytopathologist and academic; *Professor Emeritus, Semmelweis University of Budapest;* b. 14 April 1926, Túrkeve; s. of Károly Lapis and Eszter Földesi; m. Ibolya Keresztes 1955; one s. one d.; ed Lóránd Eötvös Univ. Budapest; trainee, First Inst. of Pathology and Experimental Cancer Research, Eötvös Loránd Univ., Budapest 1950–51; Asst, Inst. of Pathology Medical Univ., Debrecen 1951–54; Scientific worker Oncopathological Research Inst. 1954–63; Prof. Postgraduate Medical School, Budapest 1963–68; Prof. 1st Inst. of Pathology and Experimental Cancer Research, Semmelweis Univ. of Budapest 1968–96, Prof. Emer. 1998– (Dir 1968–93); Gordon Jacob Fellow Chester Beatty Research Inst., London 1959–60; Eleanor Roosevelt Fellow, Paris 1963–64; Visiting Prof., Duke Univ. Medical School, Durham, NC 1972; Fogarty Scholar, Nat. Cancer Inst., Bethesda 1984–85; Corresp. mem. Hungarian Acad. of Sciences 1970, mem. 1979–; Foreign mem. Medical Acad. of the USSR (now Acad. of Medical Sciences of Russia) 1987, Serbian Acad. of Sciences and Arts 1989; Pres. 14th Int. Cancer Congress of the UICC, Budapest 1986; Vice-Pres. European Assoc. for Cancer Research 1979–85; Dir Metastasis Research Soc. 1986–90; Chief Ed. Acta Morphologica Hungarica 1985–94; mem. Exec. Cttee European Soc. of Pathology 1989–93, French Electron Microscope Soc., German Soc. of Pathology, Int. Gastro-Surgical Club, Hungarian Cancer Soc. (Pres. 1974–84), Hungarian Soc. of Gastroenterology, Hungarian Soc. of Pathologists, Int. Acad. of Pathology (Hungarian section), Hungarian Acad. of Sciences; Corresp. mem. American Asscn for Cancer Research; Foreign mem. Russian Medical Acad., Serbian Acad. of Science and Fine Arts; Hon. Citizen of Mezotur 1997; Labour Order of Merit 1978, 4th of April Order of Merit 1986; Krompecher Memorial Medal 1985, Semmelweis Memorial Medal 1987, Baló József Memorial Medal 1987, Hetényi Géza Memorial Medal 1990, 'Pro Optimo Merito in Gastroenterologia' Memorial Medal 1992, Golden seal ring of the Semmelweis University, Genersich Prize 1994, Széchenyi Prize 1996, George Weber Foundation Prize 1997. *Publications include:* Lymphknotengeschwülste (co-author) 1966, The Liver 1979, Sejtosztodas Szabalyozasa es Befolyasolasa (co-author) 1981, Mediastinal Tumors and Pseudotumors (co-author) 1984, Liver Carcinogenesis (co-ed.) 1979, Ultrastructure of Tumours in Man 1981, Regulation and Control of Cell Proliferation (co-author) 1984, Tumour Progression and Markers 1982, Models, Mechanisms and Etiology of Tumour Promotion 1984, Biochemistry and Molecular Genetics of Cancer Metastasis (co-author) 1986, Abstracts of Lectures, Symposia, and Free Communications (co-author) 1986, Lectures and Symposia of the 14th International Cancer Congress (co-author) 1987, Molecular Biology and Differentiation of Cancer Cells (Oncogenes, Growth Factors, Receptors) (co-author) 1987, Carcinogenesis and Tumour Progression (co-author) 1987, Radiotherapy, Paediatric Oncology, Neurooncology (co-author) 1987, Biological Response Modifiers, Leukaemias and Lymphomas (co-author) 1987, Medical Oncology (co-author) 1987, Morphological Diagnosis of Liver Diseases (in Russian) 1989, Pathology (textbook in Hungarian) 1989, Sincerely About Cancer for Men and Women (in Hungarian) 2001. *Leisure interests:* tennis, gardening. *Address:* First Institute of Pathology and Experimental Cancer Research, Semmelweis University, Üllői út 26, 1085 Budapest (office); Lónyay u. 25, 1093 Budapest, Hungary (home). *Telephone:* (1) 459-1500 (office); (1) 217-9699 (home).

Fax: (1) 317-1074 (office). *E-mail:* klapis@korb1.sote.hu (office); lapkar@t-online.hu (home).

LAPLI, Rev. Father Sir John Ini, Kt, GCMG, DipLicTheol; Solomon Islands Anglican priest and fmr government official; b. June 1955; s. of Christian Mekope and Ellen Lauai; m. Helen Lapli 1985; three s. one d.; ed Selwyn Coll., Guadalcanal, St John's Theological Coll., Auckland, New Zealand; Tutor, Theological Coll., Auckland 1982–83; Teacher, Catechist School, Rural Training Centre 1985; Parish Priest, Church of Melanesia 1986; Bible Translator 1987–88; Premier of Temotu Prov. 1988–99; Gov.-Gen. of Solomon Islands 1999–2004; taken hostage by rebels 2000, released after a few days when the Prime Minister and his govt promised to resign; Order of Propitious Clouds with Special Grand Cordon (ROC). *Leisure interests:* gardening, research and writing on oral local tradition and culture. *Address:* Luepe Village, Graciosa Bay, c/o Lata Post Office, Temotu Province, Solomon Islands. *Telephone:* 53111.

LAPOINTE, Carman L.; Canadian accountant, auditor and fmr UN official; b. 1951, Virden, Manitoba; three c.; ed Algonquin Coll., Colorado State Univ., USA; held chief oversight positions in several Canadian crown corpns, including Auditor, Bank of Canada 1993–98, Corp. Auditor, Canada Post Corpn 1998–2004, Vice-Pres. Internal Audit and Evaluation, Export Development Canada 1997–2004; Auditor Gen., World Bank Group 2004–09; Chair. and mem. OSCE Audit Cttee 2005–10; mem. UNRWA Audit Cttee 2007–10; Dir Office of Audit and Oversight, IFAD 2009–10; Under-Sec.-Gen., Office of Internal Oversight Services, UN, New York 2010–15; Chair. Inst. of Internal Auditors 1994–95; mem. Standards Task Force, Int. Fed. of Accountants; mem. Criteria of Control Bd, Canadian Inst. of Chartered Accountants. *Address:* c/o Office of Internal Oversight Services, United Nations, New York, NY 10017, USA (office).

LAPTHORNE, Sir Richard Douglas, Kt, CBE, BCom, FCMA, FCCA, FCT, CBIM; British business executive; *Chairman, Cable & Wireless Communications PLC;* b. 25 April 1943; m. Valerie Lapthorne; two s. two d.; ed Calday Grange Grammar School, West Kirby, Univ. of Liverpool; joined Unilever as trainee in Internal Audit Dept 1965–67, Financial Accountant for Lever Brothers Zambia Ltd 1967–69, returned to UK as Accountant of Unilever Pension Funds 1969–71, Accountant, Food Industries Ltd 1971–74, Commercial Officer, Urachem Div., Unilever Holland 1974–75; Commercial Dir Synthetic Resins Ltd 1975–77, Sheby SA, Paris 1977–80, Commercial mem., Urachem Div., London 1980–81, Commercial Dir Crosfield Chemicals Ltd 1981–83 (following acquisition of Urachem by DSM); Financial Controller, Courtaulds PLC 1983–86, Finance Dir 1986–92; Finance Dir British Aerospace PLC 1992–98, Vice-Chair. 1998–99; apptd mem. Bd of Dirs (non-exec.) Amersham Int. PLC 1998, Chair. Amersham PLC 1996–97, Nycomed Amersham (after merger) 1997–2003; Chair. Cable & Wireless PLC 2003–10, Cable & Wireless Communications PLC 2010–; Chair. PwC Public Interest Body; Chair. (non-exec.) New Look Group 2005–07, Morse PLC 1998–2008, McLaren Group 2009–10, Avecia PLC 1999–2005, Tunstall Holdings Ltd, TI Automotive 2001–03, Oasis Int. Leasing Co. (Abu Dhabi) 1997–2006, Foresight Group on UK Manufacturing 2012–13; mem. Bd of Dirs Sherritt Int. 2011–; HM's Trustee, Royal Botanic Gardens 2004–09; Trustee, Tommys Campaign 2002–. *Address:* Cable & Wireless Communications PLC, 62–65 Chandos Place, London, WC2N 4HG, England (office). *Telephone:* (20) 7315-4000 (office). *Website:* www.cwc.com (office).

LARA, Brian Charles; Trinidad and Tobago professional cricketer; b. 2 May 1969, Santa Cruz; s. of Bunty Lara and Pearl Lara; two d. with Leasel Rovedas; ed San Juan Secondary, Fatima Coll., Port of Spain; started playing cricket aged six; played football for Trinidad Under-14; played cricket for West Indies Under-19; captained a West Indies Youth XI against India, scoring 186; left-hand batsman; teams: Trinidad and Tobago 1987– (Capt. 1993–), Warwicks. 1994, 1998 (Capt.), making world record first-class score of 501 not out, including most runs in a day (390) and most boundaries in an innings (72) vs Durham, Edgbaston 3–4 June 1994; played in 131 Tests for West Indies 1990–2006 (37 as Capt.), scoring 11,953 runs (average 52.88) including 34 hundreds, highest score 400 not out (world record vs England, St John's, Antigua 10–12 April 2004; played in 299 One Day Ints, scoring 10,405 runs (average 40.48, highest score 169) including 19 hundreds; scored 22,156 first-class runs (average 51.88, highest score 501 not out) including 65 hundreds; scored 2,066 runs off 2,262 balls for Warwicks. 1994, with six hundreds in first seven innings; holds Test record of scoring most number of runs in a single over in a Test match, 28 runs off an over by Robin Peterson of S Africa 2003; only batsman to have ever scored a hundred, a double century, a triple century, a quadruple century and a quintuple century in First-class games over the course of a sr career; retd from int. cricket 19 April 2007; signed for breakaway Indian Cricket League 2007, currently Capt. Mumbai Champs; f. Pearl and Bunty Lara Foundation (charity); Amb. for Sport of Repub. of Trinidad and Tobago; Hon. AO 2009, Hon. Life membership MCC 2013; Dr hc (Univ. of Sheffield) 2007; Wisden Leading Cricketer in the World Award 1994, 1995, Wisden Cricketer of the Year 1995, Fed. of Int. Cricketers' Asscns Int. Cricketer of the Year 1999, BBC TV Overseas Sports Personality of the Year (one of only three cricketers). *Publication:* Beating the Field (autobiography) 1995. *Leisure interests:* golf, horse racing. *Address:* c/o West Indies Cricket Board, PO Box 616 W, St John's, Antigua. *Telephone:* 481-2450. *Fax:* 481-2498. *E-mail:* wicb@windiescricket.com. *Website:* www.windiescricket.com.

LARA CASTRO, Jorge, MA; Paraguayan diplomatist, sociologist, academic and government official; b. 5 Aug. 1945, Asunción; s. of Mariano Lara Castro and Carmen Casco; m.; ed Catholic Univ., Asunción, Latin American Faculty of Social Sciences, Mexico City; Prof., Autonomous Nat. Univ. of Mexico 1979–81; Prof., Catholic Univ., Asunción 1974–75; Prof., Centre for Econ. Research and Teaching, Mexico City 1980–91; Prof., Faculty of Philosophy and Human Sciences, Catholic Univ. of Asunción, Paraguay 1992–98, Dir Dept of Sociology 1997–99; Pres. Inst. of San Martín, Paraguay; Amb. and Perm. Rep. to UN, New York 2000–01; Minister of Foreign Affairs 2011–12. *Publications:* numerous publs on capitalism in Brazil, the birth of campesino movt, Latin American political systems and educ. and human rights in Paraguay. *Address:* c/o Ministry of Foreign Affairs, Edif. Benigno López, Palma, esq. 14 de Mayo, Asunción, Paraguay. *E-mail:* sistemas@mre.gov.py.

LARAKI, Moulay Ahmed; Moroccan politician, physician and diplomatist; b. 15 Oct. 1931, Casablanca; ed Univ. de Paris, France; with Ministry of Foreign Affairs 1956–57; Amb. and Perm. Rep. to UN, New York 1957–59; Head of Hosp. Services, Casablanca 1956–61; Amb. to Spain 1962–65, to Switzerland 1965–66, to USA (also accred to Mexico, Canada and Venezuela) 1966–67; Minister of Foreign Affairs 1967–69; Prime Minister 1969–71; Minister of Medical Affairs 1971–74; Minister of State for Foreign Affairs 1974–77; Minister of the Environment c. 1998; Pres. Soc. marocaine des sciences médicales. *Address:* c/o Office of the Prime Minister, Palais Royal, Touarga, Rabat, Morocco. *E-mail:* courrier@pm.gov.ma.

LARCOMBE, Brian, BCom; British business executive; b. 27 Aug. 1953; s. of John George Larcombe and Joyce Lucile Larcombe; m. Catherine Bullen 1983; ed Bromley Grammar School, Univ. of Birmingham, Advanced Management Program, Harvard Business School, USA; joined 3i Group PLC 1974, Local Dir 1982–88, Regional Dir 1988–92, Finance Dir and mem. Exec. Cttee 1992–2004, CEO 1997–2004; Chair. Bramdean Asset Management LLP, Aberdeen Private Equity Fund Ltd 2007–09; mem. Bd of Dirs, Gategroup Holding AG 2008–; Dir, Gallaher Group Ltd 2006–; Dir (non-exec.), Incisive Media Ltd, NXD Smith & Nephew PLC (also mem. Remuneration Cttee), F&C Asset Management plc 2005–11; Advisor, Lighthouse Advisors India Pvt. Ltd; fmr Chair. British Venture Capital Asscn. *Address:* Gategroup Holding AG, Balz-Zimmermannstrasse 7, Kloten, 8302 Zurich, Switzerland. *Telephone:* (43) 5337000. *Fax:* (44) 5337173. *E-mail:* communications@gategroup.com. *Website:* www.gategroup.com.

LARGE, Sir Andrew Mcleod Brooks, Kt, MA (Econ.), MBA; British banker and public policy adviser; *Founder-Partner, Systemic Policy Partnership;* b. 7 Aug. 1942, Goudhurst, Kent; s. of Maj.-Gen. Stanley Large and Janet Brooks Large; m. Susan Melville 1967; two s. one d.; ed Winchester Coll., Univ. of Cambridge, Institut Européen d'Admin des Affaires (INSEAD), France; British Petroleum 1964–71; Orion Bank Ltd 1971–79; Swiss Bank Corpn 1980–89, Man. Dir SBCI London 1980–83, Chief Exec. and Deputy Chair. SBCI London 1983–87, Group Chief Exec. SBCI London 1987–88, mem. Bd SBC 1988–90; Chair. Large, Smith & Walter 1990–92; Chair. Securities & Investments Bd (SIB) 1992–97; Deputy Chair. Barclays Bank 1998–2002, Dir 1998–2002; Chair. Euroclear 1998–2000; mem. Bd on Banking Supervision, Bank of England 1996–97, Deputy Gov. 2002–06; Chair. Risk Cttee, Axis 2006–, Sr Advisory Bd, Oliver Wyman 2009–, Supervisory Cttee, Marshall Wace 2009–; Sr Adviser, Hedge Fund Standards Bd 2009–; Founder-Partner Systemic Policy Partnership 2012–. *Publications:* The Future of Finance, an LSE Report 2010, Financial Stability Governance: A Job Half Done (G30) 2015. *Leisure interests:* skiing, walking, gardening, growing ancient apple varieties, photography, music. *Address:* Systemic Policy Partnership, 13th Floor, The Adelphi, 1–11 John Adam Street, London, WC2N 6HT, England (office). *Telephone:* (20) 7925-4826 (office). *Fax:* (20) 7316-2281 (office). *E-mail:* kw@the-spp.com (office). *Website:* www.the-spp.com (office).

LARGE, David Clay, PhD; American historian, academic and writer; *Senior Fellow, Institute of European Studies, University of California, Berkeley;* b. 13 Aug. 1945, Scott Field, Ill.; s. of H. R. Large, Jr; m. 1st Jacque Hambly 1968 (divorced 1977); one s.; m. 2nd Margaret Wheeler 1980; one d.; ed Univ. of Washington, Univ. of California, Berkeley; taught Modern European History, Smith Coll. 1973–78, Yale Univ. 1978–83, Dean, Pierson Coll. 1981–83; Prof. of European History, Mont. State Univ. 1983–2012; Sr Fellow, Inst. of European Studies, Univ. of California, Berkeley 2012–; Contrib. Ed. Military History Quarterly 1989; Woodrow Wilson Fellowship, Morse Fellowship (Yale), Nat. Endowment for the Humanities Fellowship, German Marshall Fund Fellowship. *Publications include:* The Politics of Law and Order: A History of the Bavarian Einwohnerwehr 1980, Wagnerism in European Culture and Politics 1984, Between Two Fires: Europe's Path in the 1930s 1990, Contending with Hitler: Varieties of German Resistance in the Third Reich 1991, Germans to the Front: West German Rearmament in the Adenauer Era 1996, Where Ghosts Walked: Munich's Road to the Third Reich 1997, Berlin 2000, And the World Closed Its Doors: One Family Abandoned to the Holocaust 2003, Nazi Games: The Olympics of 1936 2007, Munich 1972: Tragedy, Terror and Triumph at the Olympic Games 2012, The Grand Spas of Central Europe: A History of Intrigue, Politics, Art, and Healing 2015. *Leisure interests:* running, skiing, music, hiking. *Address:* Moses Hall, Institute of European Studies, University of California, Berkeley, CA 94720 (office); 995 Dolores Street, San Francisco, CA 94110, USA (home). *Telephone:* (415) 515-3529 (office); (415) 643-4584 (home). *E-mail:* largedavid3@gmail.com. *Website:* ies.berkeley.edu (office).

LARIJANI, Ali Ardashir, BSc, MS, PhD; Iranian politician; *Speaker, Majlis-e-Shura-e Islami (Parliament);* b. 1958, Najaf, Iraq; s. of Ayatollah Mirza-Hashem Amoli; ed Sharif Univ., Tehran Univ.; began career after 1979 revolution as dir of state TV; served in sr positions at Ministry of Revolutionary Guards, including Deputy Minister; Minister of Culture and Islamic Guidance 1992–94; Head, Islamic Repub. of Iran Broadcasting 1994–2004; Sec. Shura-ye Ali-ye Amniyyat-e Melli (Supreme Nat. Security Council) (one of two reps of Supreme Leader of Iran, Ayatollah Khamenei) 2005–07 (resgnd), roles included chief nuclear negotiator; mem. Majilis-e-Shura-e Islami (Parl.) from Qom Constituency, Speaker 2008–; unsuccessful presidential cand. 2005. *Address:* Office of the Speaker, Majlis-e-Shura-e Islami (Parliament), PO Box 11575-177, Baharestan Square, Tehran, 11576-12811, Iran. *Telephone:* (21) 39931 (office). *Fax:* (21) 33440309 (office). *E-mail:* en@parliran.ir (office). *Website:* www.parliran.ir (office).

LARIJANI, Hojatoleslam Sadeq Ardeshir; Iranian (b. Iraqi) cleric and government official; *Head of Judiciary;* b. 12 March 1961, Najaf, Iraq; s. of Ayatollah Hashem Amoli; brother of Ali Larijani, Speaker of Iranian Parl.; ed Qom Seminary, Tarbiat Modares Univ.; taught courses on Islamic ideology, both at seminary in Qom and at various Iranian Revolutionary Guard Corps bases around Iran; mem. Guardian Council 2001–09, oversaw Iran's disputed presidential election June 2009; Head of Judiciary 2009–; Chair. Expediency Discernment Council 2019–. *Address:* Office of the Head of the Judiciary, Tehran, Iran (office).

LARKINS, Richard Graeme, AO, BS, MD, PhD, FRACP, FTSE, FRCP, FRCPI, FAMMal, FAMSing; Australian endocrinologist, academic and university administrator; *Professor Emeritus, Monash University;* b. 17 May 1943; ed Univ. of London, UK, Univ. of Melbourne; James Stewart Chair of Medicine, Royal Melbourne Hosp. 1984–97; Dean of Medicine, Dentistry and Health Sciences, Univ. of Melbourne 1998–2003; Vice-Chancellor and Pres. Monash Univ. 2003–08 (retd), now Prof. Emer.; Chair. Victorian Comprehensive Cancer Centre –2016; Pres. National Stroke Foundation, Australian University Sport; Chair. Council of the European Molecular Biology Laboratory (Australia), Nat. Health and Medical Research Council of Australia 1997–2000; Pres. Endocrine Soc. of Australia 1982–84, Royal Australasian Coll. of Physicians 2000–02; Chair. Accreditation Cttee, Australian Medical Council 1991–95; mem. Nat. Aboriginal and Torres Strait Islander Health Council 1997–2000; mem. La Trobe Univ. Council 2014–; Eric Susman Prize 1982, Sir William Upjohn Medal 2002.

LAROCCO, James A., BA, MA, PhD; American diplomatist (retd); *Visiting Distinguished Lecturer, Near East South Asia Center for Strategic Studies, National Defense University;* b. Chicago, Ill.; m. Janet Larocco; three c.; ed Univ. of Portland, Johns Hopkins School of Advanced Int. Studies; entered Foreign Service 1973; Staff Asst Office of Congressional Relations, State Dept; Commercial Attaché, Jeddah 1975–77; Econ. Officer, Cairo 1978–81; Econ. Section Chief Kuwait 1981–83; Deputy Dir, Office of Pakistan, Afghanistan and Bangladesh Affairs, Near East Asia Bureau 1984; Minister-Counsellor for Econ. Affairs, Beijing; Kuwait Task Force Co-ordinator, State Operations Center, Operation Desert Storm 1990; Deputy Dir American Inst. in Taiwan 1991; Deputy Chief of Mission, Tel-Aviv 1993–96; Amb. to Kuwait 1997–2001; Prin. Deputy Asst Sec. Bureau of Near Eastern Affairs, Dept of State 2001–; Dir Gen. Sinai Multinational Force and Observers (ind. (non-UN) peacekeeping mission) 2004–09; Visiting Distinguished Lecturer, Near East South Asia Center for Strategic Studies, Nat. Defense Univ., Washington, DC 2009–; Congressional Fellowship 1983; US State Dept Distinguished Service Award and numerous other awards. *Address:* NESA Center for Strategic Studies, 2100 2nd Street, SW, Suite 4308, Washington, DC 20593, USA (office). *Telephone:* (202) 685-4131 (office). *Fax:* (202) 685-4999 (office). *Website:* nesa-center.org (office).

LAROCQUE, Irwin, MA; Dominican international organization official; *Secretary-General, Caribbean Community and Common Market (CARICOM);* m.; c.; ed Queen's Coll., New School for Social Research, New York Univ., USA; served in numerous civil service positions for more than 18 years in Dominica including as Perm. Sec. in Ministries of Trade, Industry, Enterprise Devt, Tourism, and Foreign Affairs, also Prin. Adviser to govt on regional integration and int. trade, Sr Policy Adviser on revision of Treaty of Chaguaramas; Asst Sec.-Gen. for Trade and Econ. Integration, Caribbean Community and Common Market (CARICOM) Secr. 2005–11, Sec.-Gen. CARICOM 2011–. *Address:* Caribbean Community and Common Market (CARICOM), PO Box 10827, Georgetown, Guyana (office). *Telephone:* (2) 222-0001 (office). *Fax:* (2) 222-0171 (office). *E-mail:* registry@caricom.org (office). *Website:* www.caricom.org (office).

LAROQUE, Michèle; French actress; b. 15 June 1960, Nice; d. of Claude Laroque and Doïna Trandabur; m. Dominique Deschamps (divorced); one d.; ed Univ. of Nice; f. own production co. PBOF (Please Buy Our Films); Chevalier des Arts et Lettres, Chevalier de l'Ordre de mérite. *Films include:* Suivez cet avion 1989, The Hairdresser's Husband 1990, Une époque formidable 1991, Max & Jeremie 1992, La Crise 1992, Paranoïa 1993, Tango 1993, Louis, enfant roi 1993, Chacun pour toi 1994, Personne ne m'aime 1994, Aux petits bonheurs 1994, Le Fabuleux destin de Madame Petlet 1995, Nelly & Monsieur Arnaud 1995, Pédale Douce 1995, Les Aveux de l'innocent 1996, Passage à l'acte 1996, Fallait pas! 1996, Le Plus Beau Métier du Monde 1996, Ma Vie en Rose 1996, Serial Lover 1997, Doggy Bag 1999, Epouse-moi 2000, Le Placard 2001, Malabar Princess 2003, Pedale Dure 2004, L'Anniversaire 2005, Comme t'y es belle! 2006, La Maison du bonheur 2006, L'Entente cordiale 2006, Enfin veuve 2007, The Neighbor 2007, Dans tes bras 2009, Oscar and the Lady in Pink 2009, Monsieur Papa 2010 2011, The Canterville Ghost 2016, Camping 3 2016, Alibi.com 2017, Kiss Me! 2017, Chouquette 2017, Brilliantissime 2018. *Theatre:* Silence en coulisses, Ornifle 1991, La Face cachée d'Orion, Une Folie 1993, Ils s'aiment 1996, Ils se sont aimés 2001, Faisons un rêve 2007, My Brilliant Divorce 2009, Ils se re-aiment 2012. *Television includes:* series: Vivement lundi 1988, Le Retour d'Arsène Lupin 1989, La Télé des inconnus 1990, Imogène 1990, C'est quoi ce petit boulot? 1992, Navarro 1993, Quatre pour un loyer 1995, Une femme dans mon coeur 1995, Le Nid tombé de l'oiseau 1995, Mouton noir 1995, Elvis Aziz 1996, L'Oiseau rare 2001, Mon voisin du dessus 2003, Petits secrets et gros mensonges 2006, Dans tes bras 2008, Oscar et la dame rose 2008, Hard 2015; films: Bébé express 1991, Les Cravates léopards 1992, B comme Bolo 1994, Le Mur 1998, Week-end 1998, Une femme neuve 2000, La Chose publique 2003, En marge des jours 2007, Faisons un rêve 2007, Moi à ton âge! 2011, En pères et contre tout 2014, Wicked Game 2016, Elles s'aiment depuis 20 ans 2017. *Leisure interests:* tennis, skiing, riding, golf. *Website:* www.monfilmavecmichele.com.

LAROSE, (Louis René) Peter, MBA, PhD; Seychelles accountant and politician; b. 14 Jan. 1954, Mahé; m.; three s.; ed Univ. of Birmingham, UK, Chartered Management Inst., UK; Trainee Accountant/Accountant, Duty Free Products Ltd (subsidiary of General Insurance Co. Ltd) 1975–80; Accountant, L'Union Cooperative des Seychelles 1980–82; Accountant, Mason's Travel (Pty) Ltd 1982–85; Sr Accountant, Seychelles Fishing Authority 1985–89; Gen. Man., Seychelles Marketing Bd (Fish Div.) 1993–95; Adviser, Ministry of Finance 2000–01; Gen. Man., Central Bank of Seychelles 2001–05; Man. Partner, Larose Int. Financial Services Consulting 2005–08; Adviser, World Bank Group 2008–10, Sr Adviser 2010–12, Alt. Exec. Dir 2012–14, Exec. Dir, Africa Group 1 2014–16; Minister of Finance, Trade and Econ. Planning 2016–18; Visiting Scholar, Central Taiwan Univ. of Science and Tech. 2005, Vanung Univ., Taiwan 2005, Nat. Taichung Inst. of Tech., Taiwan 2006; Dir Seychelles Nat. Bureau of Statistics 2006, Seychelles Savings Bank Ltd 2006–08, Seychelles Inst. of Man. 2006–08, Société Seychelles d'Investissement 2007–08; mem. American Econ. Asscn 2012.

LAROVERE, Joan Marie, BA, MD, MSc; British physician; b. 1966; ed St Andrews Univ., Harvard Univ. and Columbia Univ., USA; clinical training in paediatrics and paediatric intensive care, Great Ormond Street Hosp., London and Boston Children's Hosp., USA; fmr Dir Paediatric Cardiac Intensive Care Unit and Consultant Intensivist, Royal Brompton Hosp., London; Sr Lecturer, Imperial Coll. London School of Medicine and mem. Admissions Cttee; currently Attending Physician, Cardiovascular Critical Care, Boston Children's Hospital, also Asst Prof. of Pediatrics, Harvard Medical School; Co-founder and mem. Exec. Cttee Virtue Foundation (non-profit org.); Dir Int. Medical Educ. Trust 2000; mem. Chief Medical Officer for England's Working Group on Revalidation and Medical Educ.; Fellow, American Acad. of Pediatrics, American Coll. of Critical Care Medicine. *Address:* Boston Children's Hospital, Department of Cardiology, 300 Longwood Avenue, Bader, 6th Floor, Boston, MA 02115, USA (office). *Telephone:* (617) 355-7866 (office). *Website:* www.childrenshospital.org/doctors/joan-larovere (office); virtuefoundation.org.

LARQUIÉ, André Olivier, LenD; French civil servant; b. 26 June 1938, Nay; s. of Henri Larquié and Simone Tauziède; ed Lycée Louis-le-Grand, Univ. of Paris and Ecole nat. d'Admin.; Deputy Dir Musique Art lyrique et Danse, Ministry of Culture and Communications 1978–79, Official Rep. 1981–83, 1987; Govt Commr Centre nat. d'art et de Culture Georges Pompidou 1981–84; Pres. Paris Opera 1983–87; Tech. Adviser to the Prime Minister May 1988–89; Pres. Théâtre Contemporain de la Danse, Asscn pour le Dialogue entre les Cultures 1985; Pres. Radio France Int. 1989–95; Pres. Cité de la Musique, Paris –2002, Ballet de Nancy et Lorraine, Théâtre du Chatelet, Paris; Departmental Head, Gen. Inspectorate, Ministry of Culture and Communication 2001; Pres. Communication Cttee, French Comm. for UNESCO; apptd Pres. Palais Multisports Paris-Bercy 2004; Commdr des Arts et Lettres 1983 Officier, Légion d'honneur 1996 Chevalier, Ordre de la Pléïade 1997 Officier, Ordre du Mérite agricole 1998 Commdr, Ordre nat. du Mérite 2000 Commdr des Palmes académiques 2002–. *Publications:* official reports. *Leisure interests:* song, dance. *Address:* 26 blvd Raspail, 75007 Paris, France (home). *Fax:* 1-45-48-48-30 (home).

LARRAIN, Juan, BA; Chilean diplomatist, UN official and academic; *Visiting Assistant Professor, Center for Latin American Studies, University of Miami;* b. 29 Aug. 1941, Santiago; m. Mariel Cruchaga Belaunde; four c.; ed German School and Mil. Acad., Chile, Univ. of Chile, Diplomatic Acad., Ministry of Foreign Affairs; Asst Prof. School of Journalism, Catholic Univ. of Chile 1964–65; Prof. of Contemporary History Diplomatic Acad., Ministry of Foreign Affairs and Ed. Diplomacia (publ. of Acad.) 1978–79; Deputy Chief of Mission, OAS 1983–87, London 1988–90, Head of First Commercial Mission to Ireland 1991, Deputy Dir Multilateral Econ. Affairs 1991–92, Consul-Gen. New York 1992–94, Deputy Perm. Rep. to UN 1994–99, Perm. Rep. 1999–2001, also Deputy Perm. Rep. to UN Security Council 1996–97; fmr Head Monitoring Mechanism for Angola; Expert Adviser, UN Security Council Counter Terrorism Cttee Exec. Directorate 2003–07; week columnist, Estrategia 2008–, Diario Las Americas 2009–; Visiting Asst Prof., Center for Latin American Studies, Univ. of Miami, USA 2008–. *Leisure interests:* history, classical music, reading, golf. *Address:* 721 Biltmore Way, #602, Coral Gables, FL 33134, USA (home). *Telephone:* (305) 799-6419 (office); (305) 446-6280 (home). *E-mail:* december79@aol.com (home); j.larrain@miami.edu (office). *Website:* www.as.miami.edu/international-studies (office).

LARRAÍN BASCUÑÁN, Felipe, BA, MA, PhD; Chilean economist and politician; *Minister of Finance;* b. 14 Feb. 1958, Santiago; m. Francisca Cisternas Lira; five c.; ed Univ. Católica de Chile, Harvard Univ., USA; Prof. of Econs, Univ. Católica de Chile 2010–14; Visiting Prof., Robert Kennedy Chair of Latin American Studies, Harvard Univ., USA 2014–18; fmr consultant on macroeconomic issues to World Bank, UN, ECLAC, IDB; mem. Int. Advisory Bd Asian Devt Bank; Pres. Felipe Larraín & Associates (econ. consultancy); econ. adviser to several Latin American govts; Minister of Finance 2010–14, 2018–; mem. Bd of Dirs Antarchile SA; mem. UN Leadership Council, Sustainable Devt Solutions Network; Faculty Fellow, World Econ. Forum; several honours and awards including Premio Luis Cruz Martínez 1976, Premio Raúl Yver Oxley 1980. *Publications include:* ed. and author of 14 books including Desarrollo Económico en Democracia: Proposiciones para una Sociedad Libre y Solidaria 1987, Debt, Adjustment and Recovery: Latin America's Prospects for Growth and Development 1989, The Public Sector and the Latin American Crisis 1990, Chile Hacia el 2000 1995, Macroeconomics in the Global Economy (with Jeffrey Sachs) 2002, Chile: A developed nation 2007. *Address:* Ministry of Finance, Teatinos 120, 12°, Santiago, Chile (office). *Telephone:* (2) 2828-2000 (office). *Website:* www.hacienda.cl (office).

LARROULET VIGNAU, Christian, BBA, MA; Chilean academic and politician; b. 26 July 1953, Santiago; ed Univ. Católica de Chile, Univ. of Chicago, USA; Head of Planning Dept, Nat. Planning Office (Odeplan) 1980–82; Head, Antitrust Comm. 1982–84; Co-ordinator of Econ. Council, Ministry of Economy 1982–85; mem. Nat. Comm. for Privatization 1985–89; Chief of Staff to Finance Minister 1985–89; fmr Prof., Univ. Católica de Chile, Univ. de Chile; Visiting Researcher, Inst. of The Americas, Univ. of California, San Diego, USA; Dean and Prof. of Econs, Faculty of Business and Economy, Univ. del Desarrollo, Santiago; Co-founder and Exec. Dir Instituto Libertad y Desarrollo (private research and study centre) 1990–; Minister of the Presidency 2010–14; mem. The Mont Pelerin Soc. 1996, Academia Chilena de Ciencias Sociales, Políticas y Morales 2002; Premio Editorial Los Andes 1996, Premio Generación Empresarial 1997, Premio Ingeniero Comercial 2007, Premio Educación - Empresa 2007. *Publications include:* Soluciones privadas a problemas públicos (ed.) (Antony Fisher Award of the Atlas Economic Research Foundation 1995) 1993, El Gobierno de las Personas 1999, Chile 2010: el desafío del desarrollo. *Address:* c/o Office of the Minister, Secretary-General of the Presidency, Palacio de la Moneda, Santiago, Chile (office).

LARSEN, Esben Lunde, PhD; Danish politician; b. 14 Nov. 1978, Skjern; s. of Knud Helge Larsen and Anna Grethe Larsen; ed Univ. of Copenhagen; began career as school teacher, Sædding Continuation School 1998–99; political employee with Venstre (Liberal Party) Parl. Group 2001–07; mem. Ringkøbing-Skjern City Council 2006–13, Deputy Mayor 2009–13; mem. Folketing (Parl.) (Venstre) for Western Jutland 2011–, mem. Research, Innovation and Further Educ. Cttee, Food, Agric. and Fisheries Cttee, Rural Dists and Islands Cttee 2011–15, European Affairs Cttee and Environment Cttee 2013–15; Minister of Higher Educ. and Science 2015–16, of Environment and Food 2016–18; mem. Business Devt Centre, Ringkøbing Fjord Business Council 2009–13; Chair. Anker Fjord Hospice 2014–15; mem. Venstre. *Address:* c/o Ministry of Environment and Food, Slotsholmsgade 12, 1216 Copenhagen K, Denmark (office).

LARSEN, James Martin, BA, LLB; Australian lawyer and diplomatist; *Ambassador to Turkey;* m.; one s. two d.; ed Univ. of Melbourne; Commercial Solicitor for Minter Ellison 1988–91; grad. trainee, Dept of Foreign Affairs and Trade (DFAT) 1992–94, Second Sec., Embassy in Bangkok 1994–97, Dir, Admin. and Domestic Law Section, DFAT 1998–2000, Counsellor, Embassy in Brussels 2001–04, Asst Sec. and Legal Adviser, Legal Br., DFAT 2004–06, Amb. to Israel 2006–10, Australian Amb. for People Smuggling Issues 2010–12, Prin. Adviser to Minister for Foreign Affairs 2012–13, Amb. to Turkey 2013–. *Address:* Embassy of Australia, MNG Building, Uğur Mumcu Caddesi 88, 7th Floor, Gaziosmanpaşa 06700, Ankara (office); Embassy of Australia, PO Box 32, Çankaya 06552, Ankara, Turkey. *Telephone:* (312) 4599500 (office). *Fax:* (312) 4464827 (office). *E-mail:* ankara.embassy@dfat.gov.au (office). *Website:* www.turkey.embassy.gov.au (office).

LARSON, Alan P., BA, MA, PhD; American economist; *Senior International Policy Advisor, Covington & Burling LLP;* ed Univ. of Iowa; joined State Dept 1973, serving in sr positions covering Econs, trade, finance, energy, sanctions, transport, telecommunications; Amb. to OECD 1990–93; served in econ. sections of Embassies in Jamaica, Zaïre, Sierra Leone; Asst Sec. of State, Dept of State, Econ. and Business Affairs 1996–99; UnderSec. of State for Econ., Business and Agricultural Affairs 1999–2005; Sr Int. Policy Advisor, Covington & Burling LLP 2005–; Distinguished Fellow, Council on Competitiveness; consultant, World Econ. Forum; Chair. Transparency International (US chapter); mem. Bd of Dirs, Bread for the World, Helping Children Worldwide; mem. Bd of Counselors, McLarty Associates; Univ. of Iowa Distinguished Alumnus Award 2003, Career Amb., Dept of State 2004, Distlinguished Service Award, Dept of State 2005. *Address:* Covington & Burling LLP, One CityCenter, 850 Tenth Street, NW, Washington, DC 20001-4956, USA (office). *Telephone:* (202) 662-6000 (office). *E-mail:* alarson@cov.com (office). *Website:* www.cov.com (office).

LARSON, Gary, BA; American cartoonist; b. 14 Aug. 1950, Tacoma, Wash.; s. of Vern Larson and Doris Larson; m. Toni Carmichael 1988; ed Washington State Univ.; performed in jazz duo 1972–75; worked in a music store; sold first cartoons to Pacific Search magazine; subsequently sold cartoons to Seattle Times, San Francisco Chronicle, Chronicle Features Syndicate; f. FarWorks Inc., creator of The Far Side, a single-panel cartoon series that was syndicated internationally to more than 1,900 newspapers for 15 years; announced retirement Oct. 1994; Nat. Cartoonists Soc. Award for best syndicated panel of 1985, Outstanding Cartoonist of the Year Award 1991, 1994, Max and Moritz Prize for Best Int. Cartoon 1993, insect named after him: *Strigiphilus garylarsoni* (biting louse), also butterfly *Serratoterga larsoni*. *Films:* Gary Larson's Tales From The Far Side 1994 (Grand Prix, Annecy Film Festival 1995), Gary Larson's Tales From The Far Side II 1997. *Publications:* 23 books, including The Far Side, Beyond The Far Side, In Search of The Far Side, Bride of The Far Side, Valley of The Far Side, It Came From The Far Side, Hound of The Far Side, The Far Side Observer, Night of the Crash-test Dummies, Wildlife Preserve, Wiener Dog Art, Unnatural Selections, Cows of Our Planet, The Chickens Are Restless, The Curse of Madame "C", Last Chapter and Worse 1996; Anthologies: The Far Side Gallery 1, 2, 3, 4 and 5, The PreHistory of The Far Side, There's A Hair in my Dirt! A Worm's Story 1998; published a 2007 calendar with all author royalties donated to Conservation International. *Leisure interests:* jazz guitar, pickup basketball. *Address:* c/o Creators Syndicate, 737 3rd Street, Hermosa Beach, CA 90254; c/o Andrews McMeel Publishing, 1130 Walnut Street, Kansas City, MO 64106-2109, USA. *E-mail:* farside@creators.com; farside@amuniversal.com. *Website:* www.thefarside.com.

LARSON-GREEN, Julie, BBA, MS; American computer software industry executive; *Executive Vice-President, Devices and Studios Engineering Group, Microsoft Corporation;* m. Gareth Green; two c.; ed Western Washington Univ., Seattle Univ.; fmr Sr Devt Engineer on Adobe PageMaker desktop publishing software for Macintosh and Windows, Seattle; joined Microsoft Corpn 1993, joined Office team 1997, Corp. Vice-Pres. Windows Experience 2007, Exec. Vice-Pres. Devices and Studios Engineering Group 2013–; mem. Bd of Dirs Western Washington Univ. Foundation. *Address:* Microsoft Corporation, 1 Microsoft Way, Redmond, WA 98052-6399, USA (office). *Telephone:* (425) 882-8080 (office). *Fax:* (425) 936-7329 (office). *Website:* www.microsoft.com (office).

LARSSON, Commr Freda; British Salvation Army officer (retd); b. (Freda Turner), 1939, Scotland; m. Gen. John Larsson 1969; two s.; officer, Upper Kingston-upon-Thames Corps, Salvation Army 1965, served as Corps Officer, Area Youth Officer, Area Sec. 1965–69, Corps Officer, Territorial Guide Organiser in Scotland, Asst Youth Dept, Nat. HQ 1969–80; S America W Territorial Home League Sec. 1980–84; Coll. Librarian, Int. Training Coll. 1984; Coordinator of Married Women Officers, Int. HQ 1988–90; UK Territorial Pres. of Women's Org. 1990; served in NZ and Fiji Territory 1993–96, Sweden and Latvia Territory 1996–99; World Sec. for Women's Ministries and World Pres. Boy Scouts, Guides and Guards, Int. HQ 1999–2003, World Pres. of Women's Ministries 2003–06 (retd). *Address:* c/o Salvation Army HQ, 101 Newington Causeway, London, SE1 6BN, England.

LARSSON, Gen. (retd) John, BD; Swedish Salvation Army officer (retd); b. 2 April 1938; s. of Sture Larsson and Flora Larsson; m. Freda Turner 1969; two s.; ed Univ. of London, UK; commissioned as Officer, Upper Norwood Corps, The Salvation Army 1957; various appointments in UK including Corps Officer, Trainer, Territorial Youth Sec. for Scotland, British Territory Nat. Youth Sec.; apptd Chief. Sec., S America W 1980–84; Prin. William Booth Memorial Training Coll., London 1984–88; asst Admin. Planning to Chief of Staff for UK 1988–90; Territorial Commdr of UK and Repub. of Ireland Territory 1990–93, of NZ and Fiji Territory 1993–96, of Sweden and Latvia Territory 1996–99; Chief of Staff of the Salvation Army 1999–2002, 17th Gen. of the Salvation Army 2002–06 (retd). *Music includes:* co-author with Gen. John Gowans (retd) of 10 full-length musicals, Take-Over Bid 1967, Hosea 1969, Jesus Folk 1972, Spirit 1973, Glory 1975, White Rose 1977, The Blood of the Lamb 1978, Son of Man 1983, Man Mark II 1985, and The Meeting 1990. *Publications include:* Doctrine Without Tears 1974, Spiritual Breakthrough 1983, The Man Perfectly Filled with the Spirit 1986, How Your Corps Can Grow 1988, Saying Yes to Life 2006, '1929' 2009, Those Incredible Booths 2015. *Leisure interests:* music, reading, walking.

LARSSON, Per E.; Swedish business executive; *Chairman, Itiviti Group AB;* b. Feb. 1961, Harnosand; m.; four c.; ed Uppsala Univ.; fmr broker, Föreningssparbanken; Chief Exec. OM Group (Swedish trading tech. firm) 1985–2003 (resgnd after OM merger with HEX exchange); CEO Dubai Int. Financial Exchange (DIFX) 2006–07, CEO Borse Dubai 2007–12; mem. Bd of Dirs Orc Group 1997–2006, apptd Chair. Orc Group 2012, Chair. Itiviti Group AB (after merger of Orc Group and CameronTec), Stockholm 2016–; Global Leader for Tomorrow, World Econ. Forum 2001. *Leisure interests:* sport, spending time at second home in

France, tennis. *Address:* Itiviti Group AB, Kungsgatan 36, 111 35 Stockholm, Sweden (office). *Website:* www.itiviti.com (office).

LASHARI, Kamran, LLB, MSc; Pakistani civil servant and business executive; *Director-General, Walled City of Lahore Authority;* b. 7 July 1968, Sindh; ed Univ. of Punjab, Lahore, Virginia Commonwealth Univ., USA; Dir-Gen. Parks and Horticulture Authority 1998–2003; Chair. Capital Devt Authority 2003–08; Chief Commr of Islamabad and Environment Sec. 2009–10; mem. Dist Man. Group and head of various Prov. and Fed. Govt Depts and Ministries, apptd Sec. to Ministry of Petroleum and Natural Resources 2010; Chair. Oil & Gas Devt Co. Ltd–Sept. 2010; Dir-Gen. Walled City of Lahore Authority 2012–; fmr Chief Sec., Govt of Sindh, Officer on Special Duty, Establishment Div.; Pres. Govt Coll. Univ. Lahore; Chair. Alhamra Arts Council, Lahore; mem. Bd of Dirs Org. for Human Resource Devt; mem. Advisory Bd Fatima Foundation; Visiting Faculty, Civil Services Acad.; Pres. Pakistan Swimming Fed.; Pres. Old Ravians Unions. *Address:* Walled City of Lahore Authority, 54 Lawrence Road, Lahore 54000, Pakistan (office). *Telephone:* 3005001718 (mobile) (home); (42) 99204201 (ext. 114) (office). *Fax:* (42) 99204203 (office). *E-mail:* kamran.lashari@walledcitylahore.gop.pk (office); lashari-27@hotmail.com (home). *Website:* walledcitylahore.gop.pk (office).

LASKAWY, Philip A.; American business executive and management consultant; b. 1941; m.; two s.; Partner, Ernst & Whinney 1978–81, Man. Partner 1981–85; Vice-Chair., Regional Man. Partner, Ernst & Young (formed from merged cos Ernst & Whinney and Arthur Young) 1985–93, Deputy Chair. 1993, Chair. and CEO 1994–2001, Chair. Ernst & Young Int. 1997–2001; Chair. Fannie Mae (Fed. Nat. Mortgage Asscn) 2008–14 (retd); mem. Bd Dirs Henry Schein, Inc. 2002–, General Motors Corpn 2003–, Loews Corpn 2003–, Discover Financial Services 2007–, Lazard Ltd; Chair. of Trustees, Int. Accounting Standards Bd 2006–08; mem. Constitution Cttee, Int. Accounting Standards Cttee Foundation Trustee Cttee (Chair. 2006–07); mem. Bd Dance Theater Foundation (Alvin Ailey American Dance Theater), Educational Broadcasting Corpn (Thirteen WNET/New York), The Philharmonic Symphony Soc. of New York, Inc. *Address:* c/o Fannie Mae, 3900 Wisconsin Avenue NW, Washington, DC 20016-2892, USA. *E-mail:* headquarters@fanniemae.com.

LASKEY, Ronald Alfred, CBE, MA, DPhil, FRS, FMedSci, FLSW; British professor of molecular biology and embryology; *Professor Emeritus of Animal Embryology, University of Cambridge;* b. 26 Jan. 1945, High Wycombe, Bucks., England; s. of Thomas Leslie Laskey and Bessie Laskey; m. Margaret Anne Page 1971; one s. one d.; ed High Wycombe Royal Grammar School, Queen's Coll., Oxford; scientific staff mem., Imperial Cancer Research Fund 1970–73, Lab. of Molecular Biology, MRC 1973–83; Co-Dir Molecular Embryology Group, Cancer Research Campaign (CRC) 1983–91; Dir CRC, Wellcome CRC Inst. 1991–; Charles Darwin Prof. of Animal Embryology, Univ. of Cambridge 1983–2012, Prof. Emer. 2012–, Fellow, Darwin Coll. Cambridge 1982–; Hon. Dir MRC Cancer Cell Unit, Hutchison/MRC Research Centre, Cambridge 2001–10; Distinguished Visitor, Agency for Science, Tech. and Research (A*STAR), Singapore 2002; mem. Scientific Advisory Cttee, European Molecular Biology Lab., Heidelberg; Assoc. Ed. Cell; Pres. British Soc. of Cell Biology 1996–99, Biochemical Soc. 2012–; Vice-Pres. Acad. of Medical Sciences 2007–12, Scientific Cttee, Louis Jeantet Foundation 2010–; Trustee, Strangeways Research Lab. 1993–2009, Inst. of Cancer Research 2007–12; mem. Academia Europaea 1989; Fellow, Learned Soc. of Wales; Colworth Medal, Biochemical Soc. 1979, CIBA Medal, Biochemical Soc. 1997, Feldberg Foundation Prize 1998, Louis Jeantet Prize for Medicine, Jeantet Foundation, Geneva 1998, Medal of Medical Faculty, Charles Univ., Prague 1999, BBC Tomorrow's World Health Innovation Award for devt of new screening test for cancer 2000, Royal Medal, Royal Soc. 2009; his research papers have been listed amongst the 100 most highly cited papers in scientific literature, and two research papers were distinguished with the Citation Classics Honour 1983. *Recordings:* albums: Songs for Cynical Scientists, More Songs for Cynical Scientists, Selected Songs for Cynical Scientists. *Publications include:* articles on cell biology in professional journals. *Leisure interests:* music, mountains. *Address:* Department of Zoology, Downing Street, Cambridge, CB2 3EA, England (office). *Telephone:* (1223) 334106/7 (office). *E-mail:* ral19@cam.ac.uk (office). *Website:* www.zoo.cam.ac.uk/directory/professor-ron-laskey (office); www.darwin.cam.ac.uk (office).

LASORDA, Thomas (Tom) W., BA, MBA; Canadian automobile industry executive; b. 24 July 1954, Windsor, Ont.; ed Univ. of Windsor; with General Motors Corpn 1977–2000; Sr Vice-Pres. Powertrain Manufacturing, Chrysler Group, DaimlerChrysler Corpn 2000–02, Sr Vice-Pres. Production 2002–04, COO DaimlerChrysler Corpn, Auburn Hills, Mich. 2004–06, Pres. and CEO 2006–07, Pres. and CEO Chrysler LLC (after acquisition of Chrysler group by Cerberus Capital Man. LP) –Aug. 2007, Pres. and Vice-Chair. Aug. 2007–09; CEO Fisker Automotive Inc. 2011–12; Co-founder IncWell LP (venture capital firm) 2013; Deputy mem. Bd of Man. DaimlerChrysler AG 2004–05, mem. 2005–07.

LASSERRE, Bruno Marie André, MPL; French public servant; *Vice-President, Conseil d'Etat;* b. 4 Jan. 1954, Talence, Gironde; s. of Jacques Lasserre and Marie Garrigou-Lagrange de David de Lastours; m. Marie-Laure Sergent 1988; two d.; ed Bordeaux Faculty of Law, Inst. of Political Studies, Bordeaux, Ecole Nat. d'Admin, Paris; mem. Conseil d'Etat 1978–, Public Rapporteur, Litigation Chamber of Conseil d'Etat 1984–86, Deputy Pres. 2002–04, Pres. Interior Section 2016–18, Chair. Dispute Resolution and Sanctions Cttee of Energy Regulatory Comm. 2017–18, Vice-Pres., Conseil d'Etat 2018–; Pres. Superior Council, Admin. Tribunals and Admin. Courts of Appeal 2018–; Legal Counsel, becoming Head of Regulatory Directorate, then Dir-Gen. of Posts and Telecommunications, Ministry of Posts and Telecommunications 1986–97; consultant on int. telecommunications to Ministers for Industry and Foreign Affairs 1997–98; Pres. Comm. of Selection of Inspectors of Finance 1998–2000; Supervisor of Privatization, Soc. française de production 2001; Pres. Press Modernization Fund 1999–2004; Chair. École nationale d'administration (ENA) 2018–; mem. Comm. of Selection of Banks Advising the State 1998–2004; mem., later Pres. Conseil de la concurrence (Competition Council, regulatory body) 1998–2008 (renamed Autorité de la concurrence, Competition Authority 2008), Pres. Autorité de la concurrence 2009–14; mem. Comm. for the Liberation of French Econ. Growth 2007–08; Officier, Légion d'honneur, Commdr, Ordre nat. du Mérite. *Publications:* Open Government 1987, Government and Information Technologies 2000, Quality Regulation and Impact Assessment 2004. *Address:* Conseil d'Etat, 1, place du

Palais-Royal, 75100 Paris, France (office). *Telephone:* 1-40-20-81-00 (office). *E-mail:* greffe@conseil-etat.fr (office). *Website:* www.conseil-etat.fr (office).

LASSETER, John Alan, BFA; American animator and film industry executive; *Chief Creative Officer, Walt Disney and Pixar Animation Studios;* b. 12 Jan. 1957, Hollywood, Calif.; s. of Paul Eual Lasseter and Jewell Mae Lasseter (née Risley); m. Nancy Lasseter; five s.; ed Pepperdine Univ., California Inst. of the Arts; joined The Walt Disney Company as Jungle Cruise skipper at Disneyland, Anaheim, Calif., later animator at Walt Disney Feature Animation 1979–84; worked as 'interface designer' at Lucasfilm Computer Graphics Group 1984–86, worked on project that resulted in his first computer-animated short The Adventures of André and Wally B, later made first computer-animated feature Toy Story; Founding mem. and Exec. Producer, Pixar 1986 (bought by Disney 2006), Chief Creative Officer, Walt Disney and Pixar Animation Studios 2006–, Prin. Creative Advisor, Walt Disney Imagineering 2006–; also Exec. Producer, Disneytoon Studios' films; mem. Acad. of Motion Picture Arts and Sciences, Sec. 2009–; Fellow, American Acad. of Arts and Sciences; hon. degree from American Film Inst.; Dr hc (Pepperdine Univ.) 2009; Contribution to Cinematic Imagery Award, Art Dirs Guild 2004, Lifetime Achievement Award, Venice Film Festival 2009, Winsor McCay Award, ASIFA-Hollywood 2008, David O. Selznick Achievement Award, Producers Guild of America 2010, Extraordinary Contrib. to Filmmaking Award, Austin Film Festival 2011. *Films include:* as dir: Lady and the Lamp 1979, Luxo Jr. 1986, Red's Dream 1987, Tin Toy (Academy Award for Animated Short Film) 1988, Knick Knack 1989, Toy Story (Special Achievement Academy Award) 1995, A Bug's Life 1998, Toy Story 2 1999, Who Is Bud Luckey? 2004, Cars 2006, Mater and the Ghostlight 2006; as exec. producer: Geri's Game 1997, It's Tough to Be a Bug 1998, For the Birds 2000, Monsters, Inc. 2001, Sen to Chihiro no kamikakushi (aka Spirited Away) 2001, Finding Nemo 2003, Boundin' 2003, The Incredibles 2004, Hauru no ugoku shiro (aka Howl's Moving Castle) 2004, One Man Band 2005, Mater and the Ghostlight 2006, Lifted 2006, Meet the Robinsons 2007, Ratatouille 2007, How to Hook Up Your Home Theater 2007, Presto 2008, Glago's Guest 2008, Bolt 2008, Wall-E 2008, Ponyo 2008, Up 2009, Toy Story 3 (producer) 2010, Winnie the Pooh (producer) 2011, Cars 2 2011, The Muppets 2011, Brave (producer) 2012, Wreck-It Ralph 2012, Monsters University 2013, Planes 2013, Frozen (producer) 2013, The Pirate Fairy 2014, Planes: Fire & Rescue 2014, Big Hero 6 2014, Frozen Fever (Short) (exec. producer) 2014, Inside Out (producer) 2015, The Good Dinosaur (exec. producer) 2015, Zootropolis (exec. producer) 2016. *Address:* Pixar Animation Studios, 1200 Park Avenue, Emeryville, CA 94608 (office); Walt Disney Feature Animation, 500 South Buena Vista Street, Burbank, CA 91521, USA (office). *Telephone:* (510) 922-3000 (Emeryville) (office); (818) 560-1000 (Burbank) (office). *Fax:* (510) 922-3151 (Emeryville) (office); (818) 560-1930 (Burbank) (office). *E-mail:* info@pixar.com (office). *Website:* www.pixar.com (office); www.disneyanimation.com (office); waltdisneystudios.com/corp/unit/6/bio/245 (office).

LASSEZ, Jean-Louis, MSc, DEA, PhD; American (b. French) computer scientist and academic; b. 24 Dec. 1944, Bordeaux, France; m. Catherine Marcoussis 1968; one d.; ed Univ. of Paris; Lecturer, Acad. Commerciale Internationale 1968–70, Dept of Math., Sherbrooke Univ., Canada 1970–72; Research Fellow and Asst Prof., Dept of Computer Science, Purdue Univ., USA 1972–73; Adjunct Prof., Dept of Math., Univ. of Moncton, Canada 1974–79; Reader, Dept of Computer Science, Univ. of Melbourne, Australia 1976–85; Researcher, IBM T.J. Watson Research Center, Yorktown Heights, NY 1985–96; Prof., New York Univ. 1993–96; Visiting Prof., Dept of Computer Science, Brown Univ. 1996, 1997; Prof. of Computer Science, New Mexico Inst. of Tech. 1996–2002; Prof. of Computer Science and Information Systems, Coastal Carolina Univ., SC 2002–08, Chair. Dept 2003–08 (retd); Ed.-in-Chief, Journal of Logic Programming 1985–90; Area Ed., Journal of the Association for Computing Machinery 1991–96; Assoc. Ed., Series in Logic Programming, Logic Programming; mem. or fmr mem. Editorial Bd Journal of Symbolic Computation, Journal of Future Generation Computer Systems, New Generation Computing, Annals of Mathematics and Artificial Intelligence, Journal of Automated Reasoning, Constraints; 9th Asian Computer Science Conf., Chiang Mai, Thailand dedicated in his honour 2004. *Publications:* Logic Programming: The 4th International Conference (ed.) 1987, Computational Logic – Essays in Honor of Alan Robinson (co-ed.) 1991; numerous articles in scientific journals. *Address:* c/o Department of Computer Science and Information Systems, Coastal Carolina University, Coastal Science Center 111, Conway, SC 29528-6054, USA. *E-mail:* jlassez@coastal.edu.

LASVIGNES, Serge; French civil servant and museum administrator; *President, Centre National d'Art et de Culture Georges Pompidou;* b. 6 March 1954, Toulouse; ed Ecole Nat. d'Admin; taught French for seven years at Coll. Malesherbes, Loiret; Dir of Gen. and Int. Affairs and Cooperation, Ministry of Nat. Educ., Higher Studies, Research and Professional Integration 1995–96; Dir of Legal Affairs, Ministry of Nat. Educ., Higher Studies and Research 1996–97; Dir, Secr.-Gen. of the Govt 1997–2006, Sec.-Gen. of the Govt 2006–15; State Councillor 2005–; Pres., Centre Nat. d'Art et de Culture Georges Pompidou 2015–; Chair. Bd of Dirs Bibliothèque Publique d'Information (BPI), Institut de Recherche et de Coordination Acoustique/Musique (IRCAM), Centre Pompidou-Metz; Commdr, Légion d'honneur 2017. *Address:* Centre National d'Art et de Culture Georges Pompidou, Place Georges Pompidou, 75004 Paris, France (office). *Telephone:* (1) 44-78-12-33 (office). *Website:* www.centrepompidou.fr (office).

LÁSZLÓ, Géza, BEcons, PhD; Hungarian business executive; b. 1963; m.; three c.; ed Univ. of Econ. Sciences, Budapest, Princeton Univ., USA; Man., Budapest Bank Rt. 1992–93; Sr Economist, Investel Rt. 1993–96; Strategic and Business Devt Dir, MATÁV Rt. 1996–98; Chair. Antenna Hungária 1998–2002, CEO 1999–2008; mem. Bd VRAM Rt (Vodafone Hungary) 2000–04; mem. Hungarian Acad. of Sciences 1996. *Address:* c/o Petzvál József u. 31–33, 1119 Budapest, Hungary. *E-mail:* antennah@ahrt.hu.

LATASI, Sir Kamuta, KCMG, OBE; Tuvaluan politician; b. 4 Sept. 1936, Samoa; m. Naama Latasi; ed South Devon Technical Coll., UK; Lands Officer 1965–66; Minister of Natural Resources 1967, of Works and Utilities 1968–70; First High Commr to Fiji and Papua New Guinea and Perm. Rep. to S Pacific Comm. (currently Secr. of the Pacific Community), Noumea, New Caledonia and 1978–83; Sec. British Petroleum Co., Tuvalu 1983–93; Prime Minister of Tuvalu 1993–96, Minister of Foreign Affairs and Econ. Planning 1993–97; Speaker of Parliament 2006–14. *Leisure interests:* fishing, gardening. *E-mail:* klatasi@yahoo.com.

LATHAM, Mark, BEc; Australian politician; b. 28 Feb. 1961, Ashcroft, NSW; s. of Donald Charles Latham and Lorraine Lillian Latham; m. Janine Lacey; two s.; ed Univ. of Sydney; Councillor, Liverpool Council 1987–94; mem. Fed. Parl. (Australian Labour Party) for Werriwa 1994–2005; Shadow Minister for Urban Devt and Housing 2001–02, for Econ. Ownership and Community Security 2002–03; Leader Australian Labor Party and Leader of the Opposition in Fed. Parl. 2003–05 (resgnd due to ill health). *Publications:* Reviving Labor's Agenda 1990, Social Capital 1998, Civilising Global Capital 1998, What Did You Learn Today? 2001, The Enabling State (co-ed.) 2001, A Conga Line of Suckholes 2006. *Address:* c/o Australian Labor Party, 5/9 Sydney Avenue, Barton, ACT 2600, Australia. *E-mail:* info@alp.org.au. *Website:* www.alp.org.au.

LATHEEF, Mohamed, MEd, PhD; Maldivian diplomatist, politician and civil servant; *Chairman, Civil Service Commission;* m.; three c.; ed Univ. of Wales and postgraduate studies in Cardiff Univ., Wales, UK; Dir-Gen. Maldives Centre for Man. and Admin 1992–93; Nat. Dir Project for Public Admin. Reform 1992–93; Deputy Minister, Ministry of Atolls Admin 1993; Minister of Educ. 1993–2002; mem. and Deputy Speaker People's Special Majlis (Ass.) 1993–97; Vice-Chair. Nat. Educ. Council 1993–2002; mem. Parl. 2000–02; held posts at Ministry of Foreign Affairs and Embassy in Sri Lanka, Amb. and Perm. Rep. to UN 2002–07, Amb. to USA 2003–07; Commr, Civil Service Comm. 2007–, Chair. 2013–; mem. Judicial Service Comm. 2008–10, 2013–. *Address:* Civil Service Commissioners, Velaanaa Building, Ameeru Ahmed Magu, Malé, Maldives (office). *Telephone:* 330-3647 (office). *Fax:* 330-3648 (office). *E-mail:* admin@csc.gov.mv (office). *Website:* en.csc.gov.mv (office).

LATIFZODA, Rustam; Tajikistani engineer, government official and politician; *Chairman, Hizbi Agrari Tojikiston (HAT—Agrarian Party of Tajikistan);* b. (Rustam Latipov), 27 Nov. 1960, Vose Dist, Kulob (now Khatlon) Viloyat, Tajik SSR, USSR; m.; four c.; ed Agrarian Univ. of Tajikistan, St Petersburg Univ. of Geology, USSR; engineer, then head engineer, Mobilized Mechanical Unit #31 at construction agency, Tojik Vodstroi (Water Industry of Tajikistan) 1984–99; Head Specialist, then Head of Dept, Ministry of Nature Protection 1992–99; Specialist, then Head Specialist, Depts of Agro-Industries and Nature, and Emergency Situations, under Pres.'s Office 1992–2001; First Deputy Chair., Ministry of Nature Protection 2001–04; Deputy Chair. Nature and Forest Protection State Cttee 2004–06; Head of Science and Research Centre for Water Reserve Protection 2006–07; Head of Control Service for Use and Nature Protection 2007–08; Head of Dept of Water Resources, Science and Tech., Ministry of Land Reclamation and Water Resources 2008–09; mem. Majlisi Namoyandagon Majlisi Oli (Parl.) 2010–, Chair. Environmental Comm. 2010–13, Cttee on Agrarian Issues, Land and Water Resources 2015–; Head of Vose Dist, Khatlon Viloyat 2013–14; Chair. Hizbi Agrari Tojikiston (Agrarian Party of Tajikistan) 2014–. *Address:* Hizbi Agrari Tojikiston (Agrarian Party of Tajikistan), 734000 Dushanbe, Tajikistan (office).

LATOUR, Lamuré; Suriname lawyer and politician; b. 1953; m. Mona Gamboa; four c.; served as defence lawyer; Minister of Defence 2010–15; mem. Megacombinatie political alliance. *Address:* c/o Ministry of Defence, Kwattaweg 29, Paramaribo, Suriname.

LATULIPPE, Gérard, LLL, DSA; Canadian lawyer, politician and diplomatist; *High Commissioner to Trinidad and Tobago;* b. 5 Nov. 1944, Montréal; s. of Gérard Latulippe and Eugénie Dufort; m. Odette Dumontier; ed Université Sir George Williams (now Concordia Univ.), Univ. of Montréal, Univ. Libre de Bruxelles, Belgium; admitted to Québec Bar 1968; practised admin. and labour law with Malo, Wilhelmy et Associés 1968–76; Sr Assoc., Latulippe, L'Écuyer et Associés 1977–81, McDougall, Lemay et Associés 1981–85; Vice-Chair., Political Cttee, Québec Liberal Party 1984–85; mem. Québec Nat. Ass. 1985–89; Solicitor-Gen. of Québec 1985–87; Gen. Del. of Québec in Mexico 1989, in Brussels (responsible for relations with EU and Benelux) 1994–97; Deputy Minister, Québec Ministry of Int. Relations 1997; Exec. Vice-Pres. Société internationale des organismes de développement économique du Canada (SIODE) 1998–2002; joined Nat. Democratic Inst., Washington, DC 2003 as Morocco Country Dir and Sr Rep. in Maghreb region, becoming Resident Dir in Haiti –2010; Pres. Int. Centre for Human Rights and Democratic Devt (Rights & Democracy), Montréal 2010–12; High Commr to Trinidad and Tobago 2012–; mem. Bd of Dirs Saint-Luc Hosp., Montréal 1978–80. *Address:* Canadian High Commission, Maple House, 3–3a Sweet Briar Road, St Clair, POB 1246, Port of Spain, Trinidad and Tobago (office). *Telephone:* 622-6232 (office). *Fax:* 628-1830 (office). *E-mail:* pspan@international.gc.ca (office). *Website:* www.canadainternational.gc.ca/trinidad_and_tobago-trinite_et_tobago (office).

LAU, Andy; Hong Kong singer, actor, film producer and television presenter; b. (Liu Dehua), 27 Sept. 1961, Tai Po, Hong Kong; m. Carol Chu 2008; one d.; ed Band One Secondary School, Ho Lap Coll., San Po Kong, Kowloon, Ho Lap Coll., TVB Acad.; has performed in more than 160 films while maintaining a successful singing career; branded by the media as one of the 'Four Heavenly Kings' of Cantopop, along with Jacky Cheung, Aaron Kwok and Leon Lai 1990s; f. own film production co. Teamwork Motion Pictures Ltd (renamed Focus Group Holdings Ltd 2002); has own production house New Melody Production (renamed NMG 2000) 1992–; apptd Summer Paralympics Goodwill Amb. and sang theme song Flying with the Dream with Han Hong during Paralympics opening ceremony, Beijing 2008; involved with charity organizations Life Education Activity Program, Hong Kong Marrow Match Foundation, Ocean Park Conservation Foundation; f. Andy Lau Charity Foundation 1994; Hon. Fellow, Hongkong Acad. of Performing Arts; Medal of Honour (Hong Kong); Dr hc (Univ. of New Brunswick, Canada) 2010; Jade Solid Gold Top 10 Award, entered into Guinness World Records for Most Awards Won By A Cantopop Male Artist, Most Popular Male Artist 1990–92, 1994, 1999, 2004, Asia Pacific Most Popular Hong Kong Male Artist 1993, 1995–96, 2000–06, named of Ten Outstanding Young Persons of the World 1999, Honorary Award, Power Acad. Awards 2000, 2006, Performance Power Award, Power Acad. Awards 2001, 2005, Asian Filmmaker of the Year, Pusan Int. Film Festival 2006, Justice of Peace Award, Govt of Hong Kong Special Admin. Region 2008, World Outstanding Chinese Award 2010. *Recordings include:* albums: I Only Know I Love You 1985, Would It Be Possible (RTHK Top 10 Gold Songs Award 1990) 1990, Long Distance Companion 2009, Unforgettable 2010. *Films include:* Tau ban no hoi 1982, On the Wrong Track 1983, Ga joi Heung Gong 1983, Shanghai 13 1984, Ting bu liao de ai 1984, Xia ri fu xing 1985, Fat ngoi ching 1985, Zui jia fu xing 1986, Mo fei cui 1986, Ying hung ho hon 1987, Gan dan xiang zhao 1987, Gong woo ching 1987, Zhong Guo zui hou yi ge tai jian 1988, Qun long duo bao 1988, Long zhi jia zu 1988, Lie ying ji hua 1988, Fa nei qing 1988, Jing zhuong zhui nu zi zhi er 1988, Zui jia sun you 1988, As Tears Go By 1988, In the Blood 1988, Zui jia sun you chuang qing guan 1988, Shen xing tai bao 1989, Zhi zun wu shang 1989, Sheng gang qi bing di san ji 1989, Ren hai gu hong 1989, Juen diu daai ngok 1989, Fu gui bing tuan 1989, Fa nei qing da jie ju 1989, Tong gen sheng 1989, Biao cheng 1989, Zui jie nan peng you 1989, Ao qi xiong ying 1989, Di yi jian 1989, Xiao xiao xiao jing cha 1989, China White 1989, God of Gamblers 1989, Lang zhi yi zu 1989, Stars & Roses 1989, No Risk, No Gain: Casino Raiders – The Sequel 1990, Zai zhan jiang hu 1990, Forbidden Imperial Tales (singing voice) 1990, Island of Fire 1990, A Moment of Romance 1990, Ma deng ru lai shen zhang 1990, Yi daam hung sam 1990, Yu zhong long 1990, A Home Too Far 1990, Days of Being Wild 1990, Tian zi men sheng 1991, Tricky Brains 1991, God of Gamblers II 1991, Zhong Huan ying xiong 1991, The Last Blood 1991, Casino Raiders II 1991, Wu hu jiang zhi jue lie (Jin pai wu hu jiang) 1991, Ji dao zhui zong 1991, Lee Rock 1991, Lee Rock II 1991, Saviour of the Soul 1991, Xia sheng 1992, Lee Rock III 1992, Fan dou ma liu 1992, Do sing dai hang san goh chuen kei 1992, Do sing daai hang II ji ji juen mo dik 1992, Hua! ying xiong 1992, Long teng si hai 1992, Ji Boy xiao zi zhi zhen jia wai long 1992, Chuan dao fang zi 1992, Miu kai sup yi siu 1992, Handsome Siblings 1992, Zhan shen chuan shuo 1993, Chao ji xue xiao ba wang 1993, Ji jun sam sap lok gai ji Tau tin wun yat 1993, Sat sau dik tung wah 1994, Dao jian xiao 1994, Tian chang di jiu 1994, The Legend of Drunken Master 1994, Tian yu di 1994, Yu long gong wu 1994, Jui kuen III 1994, Da mao xian jia 1995, Full Throttle 1995, A Moment of Romance III 1996, Ding Lik (as Andy T. W. Lau), San Seung Hoi taan 1996, ½ Chi tung chong 1996, Qi yi lu cheng zhi: Zhen xin ai sheng ming 1996, Tin dei hung sam 1997, Kau luen kei 1997, Island of Greed 1997, A True Mob Story 1998, Du xia 1999 1998, Ai qing meng huan hao 1999, Hei ma wang zi 1999, Du xia da zhan Lasi Weijiasi 1999, Running Out of Time 1999, Century of the Dragon 1999, Kuet chin chi gam ji din 2000, Needing You... 2000, A Fu (also producer) 2000, Love on a Diet 2001, Fulltime Killer (also producer) 2001, Oi gwan yue mung (also producer) 2001, Kap sze moon yat goh gei kooi 2002, Fat Choi Spirit 2002, Wai See Lee ji lam huet yan 2002, Infernal Affairs 2002, Love Under the Sun (short) 2003, Lou she oi sheung mao 2003, Running on Karma 2003, Mou gaan dou III: Jung gik mou gaan 2003, Golden Chicken 2 2003, Moh waan chue fong 2004, House of Flying Daggers 2004, Gong wu (also exec. producer) 2004, McDull, Prince de la bun (voice) 2004, Yesterday Once More 2004, A World Without Thieves 2004, Wait 'Til You're Older 2005, The Shoe Fairy (voice) (also exec. producer) 2005, All About Love (also exec. producer) 2005, I'll Call You (also exec. producer) 2006, My Mother Is a Belly Dancer (also producer) 2006, Battle of Wits 2006, Protégé 2007, Brothers 2007, The Warlords (as Dehua Liu) 2007, Three Kingdoms: Resurrection of the Dragon 2008, Yau lung hei fung 2009, The Founding of a Republic 2009, Future X-Cops 2010, Detective Dee: Mystery of the Phantom Flame 2010, Shaolin 2011, What Women Want (also exec. producer) 2011, Beginning of the Great Revival 2011, A Simple Life (also exec. producer) 2011; exec. producer: Made in Hong Kong 1997, Runaway Pistol (uncredited) 2002, Invisible Waves 2006, Gallants 2010; producer: Hui nin yin fa dak bit doh 1998, Crazy Stone 2006. *Television includes:* Choi wan kuk 1982, Sou hat yi (series) 1982, Return of the Condor Heroes (series) 1983, Lao dong (series) 1983, Luk ding gei (series) 1984, The Last Performance (series) 1985, Yang ka cheung (series) 1986, Hao men ye yan (presenter) 1991, Shin chou kyou ryo: Condor Hero (series) (title theme, singing voice) 2001. *Leisure interest:* Chinese calligraphy. *Address:* Focus Films, Focus Group Holdings Ltd, 9/F, Tower A, Billion Centre, 1 Wang Kwong Road, Kowloon Bay, Kowloon, Hong Kong Special Administrative Region, People's Republic of China (office). *Telephone:* 3120-3388 (office). *Fax:* 3120-3328 (office). *Website:* www.focusgroup.cc (office).

LAU, John C. S., LLD; Hong Kong business executive; ed Univ. of Queensland, Australia; held several sr exec. roles with Cheung Kong (Holdings) Ltd and Hutchison Whampoa Ltd group of cos, Hong Kong; Pres. and CEO Husky Energy Inc. 2000–11; Fellow, Inst. of Chartered Accountants, Australian Soc. of Accountants, Hong Kong Soc. of Accountants, Taxation Inst. of Hong Kong, Inst. of Chartered Secs of Admins of UK; Guest Prof. and Hon. Dir Potential Gas Appraisal Centre, Univ. of Petroleum, Beijing; Queen's Golden Jubilee Medal, Centennial medals from Prov. of Alberta and Prov. Sask., Sask. Distinguished Service Award, Clearsight Wealth Management Friend of Educ. Award, Canadian Council for the Advancement of Educ., Champion of Public Educ. in Canada Award, Learning Partnership.

LAU, Joseph, BSc; Hong Kong real estate executive; b. (Lau Luen-hung), 21 July 1951, Hong Kong; m. Bo Wing-kam (divorced); six c.; ed Univ. of Windsor, Canada; family originated in Chaozhou, Guangdong Prov., China; more than 32 years' experience in corp. finance, manufacturing and property investment and devt; joined Chinese Estates Holdings Ltd 1989, Chair. and CEO –2014; Dir (non-exec.) Lifestyle Int. Holdings Ltd. *Leisure interest:* collecting art.

LAU, Lawrence J., BS, MA, PhD, JP; Chinese economist, academic, business executive and fmr university administrator; *Ralph and Claire Landau Professor of Economics, Chinese University of Hong Kong;* b. (Liu Zunyi), 12 Dec. 1944, Guizhou Prov.; s. of Shait-Tat Liu and Chi-Hing Yu Liu; m. Ayesha A. Macpherson; one s.; ed Stanford Univ. and Univ. of California, Berkeley, USA; Acting Asst Prof. of Econs, Stanford Univ., USA 1966–67, Asst Prof. of Econs 1967–73, Assoc. Prof. of Econs 1973–76, Prof. of Econs 1976–2006, Kwoh-Ting Li Prof. of Econ. Devt 1992–2006, Kwoh-Ting Li Prof. in Econ. Devt Emer. 2006–, Vice-Chair. Dept of Econs 1990–92, Co-Dir Asia/Pacific Research Center 1992–96, Dir Stanford Inst. for Econ. Policy Research 1997–99, Sr Fellow, Inst. for Int. Studies 1992–2004, Sr Fellow, Hoover Inst. on War, Revolution and Peace 1997–2004, Sr Fellow, Stanford Inst. for Econ. Policy Research 1997–2013; Visiting Asst Research Economist, Univ. of California, Berkeley 1968–69; Visiting Prof. of Econs, Harvard Univ. 1978–79; Prof. of Econs, Chinese Univ. of Hong Kong 2004–07, Ralph and Claire Landau Prof. of Econs 2007–, also Pres. (Vice-Chancellor) 2004–10; JP, Hong Kong Special Admin. Region (SAR) 2007–; Chair. CIC International (Hong Kong) Co. Ltd 2010–14; Vice-Chair. CITIC Capital Holdings Ltd 2010–13; mem. Bd of Dirs Far EasTone Telecommunications Co. Ltd, Taipei 2005–, CNOOC Ltd, Hong Kong 2005-, Shin Kong Life Insurance Co. Ltd, Taipei 2008–11, Semiconductor Manufacturing Int. Corpn, Shanghai 2011–14, 2018–, AIA Group Ltd 2014–, Hysan Development Co. Ltd 2014–; Non-official mem. Exec. Council, Govt of Hong Kong SAR 2009–12; mem. 11th Nat. Cttee, CPPCC, People's Repub. of China 2008–13, Vice-Chair. Sub-Cttee on Population, Resources and the Environment 2010–13; mem. 12th Nat. Cttee, CPPCC 2013–18, Vice-Chair. Econs Sub-cttee 2013–18; mem. editorial bds of several journals; Academician, Academia Sinica, Taipei 1982, Int. Eurasian Acad. of Sciences 1999; mem. American Econ. Asscn; Fellow, Econometric Soc.; Trustee, Hong Kong/Stanford Univ. Charitable Trust 1994–2004; Hon. Prof., Coll. of Man., Tsinghua Univ., Beijing 1987–, People's Univ. of China 1994–, Shantou Univ., 1994–, Inst. of Systems Science, Chinese Acad. of Sciences, Beijing 1996–, Nankai Univ., Tianjin 1998–, Nanjing Univ. 2000–, Southeast Univ., Nanjing 2000–; Hon. Research Fellow, Inst. of Quantitative and Tech. Econs, Chinese Acad. of Social Sciences, Beijing 1989–, Shanghai Acad. of Social Sciences 1998–; Hon. Mem. Chinese Acad. of Social Sciences, Beijing, 1997, Bd of Trustees, San Yuan Yu You-Ren Memorial Museum, San Yuan, Shaanxi, China 1997–; Gold Bauhinia Star; Hon. DScS (Hong Kong Univ. of Science and Tech.) 1999; Hon. LLD (Waseda Univ.) 2007, (Chinese Univ. of Hong Kong) 2014; Hon. DEcon (Fudan Univ.) 2011; Hon. Dr Man. Science (Nat. Cen. Univ.) 2010; Dr hc (Soka Univ.) 2007. *Publications include:* Farmer Education and Farm Efficiency (co-author) 1982, Models of Development: A Comparative Study of Economic Growth in South Korea and Taiwan (ed. and contrib.) 1986, Econometrics and the Cost of Capital: Essays in Honor of Dale W. Jorgenson (ed. and contrib.) 2000, North Korea in Transition: Prospects for Economic and Social Reform (co-ed. and contrib.) 2001, US Direct Investment in China (co-author) 2002, The China-U.S. Trade War and Future Economic Relations 2018; more than 200 articles and notes in professional journals. *Address:* 13/F Cheng Yu Tung Building, 12 Chak Cheung Street, Shatin, New Territories, Hong Kong Special Administrative Region, People's Republic of China (office). *Telephone:* 3943-1611 (office). *Fax:* 2603-5230 (office). *E-mail:* lawrence@lawrencejlau.hk (office). *Website:* www.igef.cuhk.edu.hk/index.php/en/professor-lawrence-j-lau (office).

LAU, Siu-Kai, JP, PhD; Chinese academic and political adviser; *Professor Emeritus of Sociology, Chinese University of Hong Kong;* b. 7 June 1947, Hong Kong; s. of Keng-por Lau and Wai-sin Fong; m. Sophie Lai-mui Kwok 1972; one s.; ed Univ. of Hong Kong, Univ. of Minnesota, USA; Assoc. Dir Hong Kong Inst. of Asia-Pacific Studies, Chinese Univ. of Hong Kong 1990–2002, Prof. of Sociology 1990–2007, Prof. Emer. 2007–, Chair. Dept of Sociology 1994–2002; mem., Preparatory Cttee for Hong Kong Special Admin. Region 1996–97; Head, Central Policy Unit, Hong Kong Special Admin. Region 2002–12; mem. CPPCC 2003–; Vice-Pres. Chinese Asscn of Hong Kong and Macao Studies; political commentator on Hong Kong issues on TV, radio and in newspapers and magazines; Gold Bauhinia Star. *Publications:* Society and Politics in Hong Kong 1982, The Ethos of the Hong Kong Chinese 1988, Governance and New Regime Building in Hong Kong after the Handover (in Chinese) 2012, The Practice of One Country Two Systems in Hong Kong 2015. *Leisure interests:* reading, walking. *Address:* Department of Sociology, Chinese University of Hong Kong, Shatin, NT, Hong Kong Special Administrative Region (office); Flat B3, 8/F Cloudview Mansion, 8 Lok Fung Path, Fotan, NT, Hong Kong Special Administrative Region, People's Republic of China (home). *Telephone:* 3943-6631 (office); 2603-6438 (home). *Fax:* 2603-5213 (office); 2603-6438 (home). *E-mail:* siukailau@cuhk.edu.hk (office). *Website:* www.cuhk.edu.hk (office).

LAUDA, Andreas-Nikolaus (Niki); Austrian fmr racing driver; *Non-Executive Chairman, Mercedes AMG Petronas Formula One Team;* b. 22 Feb. 1949, Vienna; s. of Ernst Peter Lauda and Elisabeth Lauda; m. 1st Marlene Knaus 1976 (divorced 1991); two s. one d. and one s. from another relationship; m. 2nd Birgit Lauda 2008; one s. one d. (twins); competed in hill climbs 1968, later in Formula 3, Formula 2 and sports car racing; winner John Player British Formula 2 Championship 1972; started Formula 1 racing 1971; World Champion 1975, 1977, 1984, runner-up 1976; retd 1979; returned to racing 1981, won US Formula 1 Grand Prix, British Grand Prix 1982, Dutch Grand Prix 1985 171 starts, 25 wins, 54 podiums; retd again 1985; f. LaudaAir 1979, Chair. –2000, ceased operations 2013; commentator on Grands Prix for Austrian and German TV on RTL 1996–; CEO Ford Motor Co. Premier Performance Div. 2001–02; Head of Jaguar Racing Team 2001–02; f. FlyNiki airline 2003 (acquired by Air Berlin 2011); Chair. (non-exec.) Mercedes AMG Petronas Formula One Team 2012–; winner Victoria Sporting Club's Int. Award for Valour following recovery from near-fatal crash in 1976 German Grand Prix at Nürburgring 1977, Austrian Sportsman of the Year 1977, BBC Overseas Sports Personality of the Year 1977, Autosport Int. Racing Driver Award 1984, inducted into Int. Motorsports Hall of Fame 1993, stamp honouring him issued by Austrian post office 2005, ranked 22nd by ESPN TV network on their top drivers of all-time 2008. *Grand Prix wins:* Spanish (Ferrari) 1974, Dutch (Ferrari) 1974, Monaco (Ferrari) 1975, Belgian (Ferrari) 1975, Swedish (Ferrari) 1975, French (Ferrari) 1975, US (Ferrari) 1975, Brazilian (Ferrari) 1976, South African (Ferrari) 1976, Belgian (Ferrari) 1976, British (Ferrari) 1976, South African (Ferrari) 1977, German (Ferrari) 1977, Dutch (Ferrari) 1977, Swedish (Brabham-Alfa Romeo) 1978, Italian (Brabham-Alfa Romeo) 1978. *Film:* cameo appearance in Rush (which portrayed the 1976 F1 battle between Niki Lauda and James Hunt) 2013. *Publications:* The Art and Science of Grand Prix Driving (also titled Formula 1: The Art and Technicalities of Grand Prix Driving) 1975, My Years with Ferrari 1978, The New Formula One: A Turbo Age 1984, Meine Story (also titled To Hell and Back) 1986, Das dritte Leben 1996. *Leisure interests:* music, skiing. *Address:* Mercedes AMG Petronas Formula One Team, Operations Centre, Brackley, Northants., NN13 7BD, England. *E-mail:* enquiries@mercedes-amg-f1.com. *Website:* www.mercedesamgf1.com.

LAUDER, Leonard Alan; American business executive and philanthropist; *Chairman Emeritus, The Estée Lauder Companies Inc.;* b. 19 March 1933, New York, NY; s. of Joseph Lauder and Estée Lauder (née Mentzer); m. Evelyn Hausner 1959; two s.; ed Wharton School, Univ. of Pennsylvania, Columbia Univ. Grad. School of Business; served as Lt in USN; with Estée Lauder Inc. (cosmetics and fragrance co.) New York 1958–, Exec. Vice-Pres. 1962–72, Pres. 1972–82, Pres. and CEO 1982–99, Chair. 1995–2009, Chair. Emer. 2009–; Gov. Joseph H. Lauder Inst. of Man. and Int. Studies 1983–; Chair. Emer. Bd of Trustees, Whitney Museum of American Art; Trustee, The Aspen Inst. for Humanistic Studies 1978– (Chair. Int. Cttee); Charter Trustee, Univ. of Pennsylvania 1977–; Pres. Whitney Museum of American Art 1977–; Co-founder and Chair. Alzheimer's Drug

Discovery Foundation; mem. Council on Foreign Relations, Pres.'s Council of Memorial Sloan-Kettering Hosp.; donated collection of 78 pieces of Cubist painting (Pablo Picasso, Georges Braque, Fernand Léger and Juan Gris) to Metropolitan Museum of Art, New York 2013. *Address:* The Estée Lauder Companies Inc., 767 Fifth Avenue, New York, NY 10153, USA (office). *Telephone:* (212) 572-4200 (office). *Fax:* (212) 893-7782 (office). *E-mail:* mediarequests@estee.com (office). *Website:* www.elcompanies.com (office).

LAUDER, Ronald Stephen, BS; American business executive, diplomatist and art collector; *President, World Jewish Congress;* b. 26 Feb. 1944, New York, NY; s. of Joseph Lauder and Estée Lauder (née Mentzer); m. Jo Carole Knopf 1967; two d.; ed Bronx High School of Science, Wharton School of the Univ. of Pennsylvania, Univ. of Paris (Sorbonne), France, Univ. of Brussels, Belgium; Estée Lauder NV Belgium 1965–67, Estée Lauder SA France 1967, Estée Lauder Sales Promotion Dir 1968–69, Vice-Pres. Sales Promotion, Clinique 1969–72, Exec. Vice-Pres., Gen. Man. Clinique, Inc. 1972–75, Exec. Vice-Pres. Estée Lauder Int. 1975–78, Exec. Vice-Pres. Estée Lauder Inc., Chair. Estée Lauder Int. 1978–83; Deputy Asst Sec. of Defense for European and NATO Policy 1983–86; Amb. to Austria 1986–87, pvt. investment man. New York 1987–, now E and Cen. Europe; Trustee, Museum of Modern Art 1975– (Chair. 1995–), Mt. Sinai Medical Center 1981–; Chair. and Pres. Lauder Investments; Chair. (non-exec.) Cen. European Devt Corpn (now Cen. European Media Enterprises Ltd); Pres. Jewish Nat. Fund 1997–; Pres. Ronald S. Lauder Foundation; Pres. World Jewish Congress 2007–; Founder Ronald S. Lauder Foundation 1987, Neue Galerie, New York (also Pres.) 2001–, RWL Water, LLC (also Chair.) 2010; Co-Pres. and Dir Inst. for the Study of Aging; mem. New York Landmarks Conservancy's Advisory Bd, Bd of Govs Joseph H. Lauder Inst. of Man. and Int. Studies at Univ. of Pennsylvania, Visiting Cttee Wharton School, Int. Soc. for Yad Vashem, Int. Bd of Govs Tel-Aviv Museum, Chair. Bd Trustees Sakharov Archive at Brandeis Univ., Chair. Jewish Heritage Program, World Monuments Fund, Co-Chair. Alzheimer's Drug Discovery Foundation, Clinique Laboratories, LLC, US Holocaust Memorial Council, Bd Dirs Jewish Theological Seminary, Bd Dirs American Jt Jewish Distribution Cttee, Bd Trustees Anti-Defamation League Foundation, Bd Trustees Abraham Fund; Chevalier, Ordre nat. du Mérite, Great Cross of the Order of Aeronautical Merit with White Ribbon (Spain), Dept of Defense Medal for Distinguished Public Service; Dr hc (Ben-Gurion Univ. of the Negev); ranked 12 on ArtReview magazine's Power 100 list 2005, Andrey Sheptytsky Medal 2018. *Address:* World Jewish Congress, 9th Floor, 501 Madison Avenue, New York, NY 10022 (office); Lauder Investments Inc., 767 Fifth Avenue, Suite 4200, New York, NY 10153, USA. *Telephone:* (212) 755-5770 (office). *Fax:* (212) 755-5883 (office). *E-mail:* info@worldjewishcongress.org (home). *Website:* www.worldjewishcongress.org (office); lauderfoundation.com.

LAUDER, William P., BA, MBA; American business executive; *Executive Chairman, The Estée Lauder Companies Inc.;* b. 11 April 1960, son of Leonard A. Lauder and Evelyn Lauder (née Hausner); grandson of co-founder Estée Lauder; m.; several c.; ed Wharton School, Univ. of Pennsylvania and Univ. of Grenoble, France; completed Macy's exec. training program, New York, later Assoc. Merchandising Man. New York Div./Dallas 1985; Regional Marketing Dir Clinique USA, The Estée Lauder Companies 1986, Vice-Pres./Gen. Man., later Pres. of Origins Natural Resources Inc. 1990–98, Pres. Clinique Laboratories 1998–2001, Pres. Clinique Worldwide and Group Pres. The Estée Lauder Companies 2001–03, COO The Estée Lauder Companies Inc. 2003–04, Pres., CEO and mem. Bd of Dirs 2004–09, Exec. Chair. and Chair. Bd of Dirs 2009–; mem. Bd of Dirs, Univ. of Pennsylvania, The Fragrance Foundation, The Fresh Air Fund, The 92nd Street Y, The Partnership For New York City, Inc., True Temper Sports, Inc. 2004–, GLG Partners, Inc. 2006–, Breast Cancer Research Foundation Inc., Freedom Acquisition Holdings Inc. 2006–, Jarden Corpn 2011–; mem. Exec. Council, Golub Capital LLC; mem. Bd of Trustees, The Trinity School. *Leisure interests:* golf, skiing, mountain biking, hiking. *Address:* The Estée Lauder Companies Inc., 767 Fifth Avenue, New York, NY 10153, USA (office). *Telephone:* (212) 572-4200 (office). *Fax:* (212) 893-7782 (office). *E-mail:* mediarequests@estee.com. *Website:* www.elcompanies.com (office); www.esteelauder.com (office).

LAUER, Reinhard, DPhil; German philologist and academic; *Professor Emeritus of Slavonic Philology, University of Göttingen;* b. 15 March 1935, Bad Frankenhausen; s. of Erich Lauer and Rose Fischer; m. Stanka Ibler 1962; one d.; ed Univs of Marburg, Belgrade and Frankfurt and Freie Univ. of Berlin; Reader in German Language, Univ. of Zagreb, Yugoslavia 1960–62; Research Fellow, Univ. of Frankfurt 1962–69; Prof. of Slavonic Philology and Head of Dept of Slavonic Philology, Univ. of Göttingen 1969–, now Prof. Emer.; Head of Göttingen br., Southeast Europe Asscn 1973–; mem. Göttingen Acad. of Sciences 1980, Chair. Comm. for Interdisciplinary Southeastern Europe Research 1987–; Corresp. mem. Serbian Acad. of Sciences and Arts 1987, Croatian Acad. of Sciences and Arts 1989, Austrian Acad. of Sciences 1995, Slovenian Acad. of Sciences and Arts 2003; Hon. mem. Bulgarian Philology Soc.; Valjavec Prize 1960, Yugoslav Flag with Golden Garland 1989. *Publications:* Heine in Serbien 1961, Gedichtform zwischen Schema und Verfall 1975, Europäischer Realismus (ed.) 1980, M. Krleža und der deutsche Expressionismus 1984, Sprachen und Literaturen Jugoslaviens (ed.) 1985, Poetika i ideologija 1987, Sprache, Literatur und Folklore bei Vuk St Karadžić (ed.) 1989, Kulturelle Traditionen in Bulgarien (co-ed.) 1989, Künstlerische Dialektik und Identitätssuche (ed.) 1990, Die Moderne in den Literaturen Südosteuropas (ed.) 1991, Höfische Kultur in Südosteuropa (co-ed.) 1994, Serbokroatische Autoren in deutscher Übersetzung (ed.) 1995, Slavica Gottingensia (ed.) 1995, Die Kultur Griechenlands in Mittelalter und Neuzeit (co-ed.) 1996, Die russische Seele 1997, Geschichte der russischen Literatur 2000, Deutsche und Slovakische Literatur (ed.) 2000, A. S. Puškins Werk und Wirkung (co-ed.) 2000, Philologie in Göttingen (ed.) 2001, Die literarische Avantgarde in Südosteurope und ihr politische und gesellschaftliche Bedeutung (ed.) 2001, Studije i rasprave 2002, Kleine Geshichte der russischen Literatur 2005. *Leisure interests:* music, painting, ornithology. *Address:* Seminar für Slavische Philologie, Universität Göttingen, Humboldtallee 19, 37073 Göttingen (office); Allensteiner Weg 32, 37120 Bovenden, Germany. *Telephone:* (551) 394197 (office); (551) 81375 (home). *E-mail:* rlauer@uni-goettingen.de (office). *Website:* www.uni-goettingen.de/en/51177.html (office).

LAUGHLIN, Robert Betts, BA, PhD; American theoretical physicist and academic; *Anne T. and Robert M. Bass Professor of Physics, Stanford University;* b. 1 Nov. 1950, Visalia, Calif.; m. Anita Rhona Perry 1979; two s.; ed Univ. of California, Berkeley, Massachusetts Inst. of Tech.; mil. service, US Army 1972–74; Postdoctoral Fellow, Bell Telephone Labs 1979–81; Research Scientist, Lawrence Livermore Nat. Lab. 1981–2004; Assoc. Prof. of Physics, Stanford Univ. 1985–89, Prof. of Physics 1989–, Prof. of Applied Physics (dual appointment with Physics) 1993–2007, Anne T. and Robert M. Bass Prof. of Physics and Applied Physics –2004, 2006–; Pres. Korea Advanced Inst. of Science and Tech. (KAIST), Daejon 2004–06; Pres. Asia-Pacific Centre for Theoretical Physics 2004–06; mem. Bd Science Foundation Ireland 2002–03; mem. NAS 1994; Fellow, AAAS, American Physics Soc., American Acad. of Arts and Sciences; Hon. DLitt (Univ. of Maryland) 2005; E.O. Lawrence Award for Physics 1985, Oliver E. Buckley Prize 1986, Benjamin Franklin Medal for Physics, Franklin Inst. 1998, Nobel Prize in Physics (shared with Horst L. Störmer and Daniel C. Tsui for discovery of a new form of quantum fluid with fractionally charged excitations—fractional quantum Hall effect) 1998, Golden Plate Award, Acad. of Achievement 1999, Onsager Medal 2007. *Publications:* A Different Universe: Reinventing Physics from the Bottom Down 2005, Looking for a Hero 2006, The Crime of Reason: And the Closing of the Scientific Mind 2008, Mente y materia. ¿Qué es la vida? Sobre la vigencia de Erwin Schrödinger (co-author) 2010, Powering the Future: How We Will (Eventually) Solve the Energy Crisis and Fuel the Civilization of Tomorrow 2011; numerous papers in scientific journals. *Address:* Department of Physics, Stanford University, McCullough 301, Stanford, CA 94305, USA (office). *Telephone:* (650) 723-4563 (office). *Fax:* (650) 724-3681 (office). *E-mail:* rbl@large.stanford.edu (office). *Website:* large.stanford.edu (home).

LAUGHTON, Sir Anthony Seymour, Kt, PhD, FRS; British oceanographic scientist; b. 29 April 1927, London; s. of Sydney T. Laughton and Dorothy (Chamberlain) Laughton; m. 1st Juliet A. Chapman 1957 (dissolved 1962), one s.; m. 2nd Barbara C. Bosanquet 1973, two d.; ed Marlborough Coll. and King's Coll. Cambridge; RNVR 1945–48; John Murray Student, Columbia Univ., New York 1954–55; Nat. Inst. of Oceanography, later Inst. of Oceanographic Sciences 1955–88, fmr Dir; mem. Jt IOC/IHO Guiding Cttee GEBCO (ocean charts) 1974–2003, Chair. 1986–2003; mem. Council, Univ. Coll. London 1983–93; mem. Co-ordinating Cttee for Marine Science and Tech. 1987–91; Pres. Challenger Soc. for Marine Science 1988–90, Soc. Underwater Tech. 1995–97, Hydrographic Soc. 1997–99; mem. Governing Body Charterhouse School 1981–2000, Chair. 1995–2000; Trustee Natural History Museum 1990–95; Hon. DSc (Southampton Univ.); Royal Soc. of Arts Silver Medal 1958, Prince Albert 1er Monaco Gold Medal 1980, Founders Medal, Royal Geographical Soc. 1987, Murchison Medal, Geological Soc. 1989, Pres.'s Award, Soc. for Underwater Tech. 1998. *Publications:* papers on marine geophysics. *Leisure interests:* music, gardening, sailing, woodwork. *Address:* Okelands, Pickhurst Road, Chiddingfold, Surrey, GU8 4TS, England (home). *Telephone:* (1428) 683941 (home). *E-mail:* aslaughton@googlemail.com (home).

LAUNDER, Brian Edward, ScD, DSc (Eng), DEng, FRS, FREng, FCGI, FIMechE, FRAeS; British engineer, academic and editor; *Research Professor (part-time), University of Manchester;* b. 20 July 1939, London; s. of Harry Edward Launder and Elizabeth Ann Launder (née Ayers); m. Dagny Simonsen 1968; one s. one d.; ed Enfield Grammar School, Imperial Coll., London, Massachusetts Inst. of Tech., USA; Lecturer, then Reader, Mechanical Eng Dept, Imperial Coll. London 1964–76; Prof. of Mechanical Eng, Univ. of California, Davis 1976; Prof. of Mechanical Eng, UMIST (now Univ. of Manchester) 1980–98, Head, Mechanical Eng Dept 1983–85, 1993–95, Research Prof. 1998–; Dir Environmental Strategy Group 1998–2004; Regional Dir Tyndall Centre for Climate Change Research 2001–06; Ed.-in-Chief International Journal of Heat and Fluid Flow 1987–2013; mem. Scientific Advisory Bd CERFACS, Toulouse 1992–2013; assessor, Center for Turbulence Research, Stanford Univ., Calif. 1996–2004; Hon. Prof., Nanjing Aerospace Inst. 1993; Dr hc (Inst. Nat. Polytechnique, Toulouse) 1999, (Univ. Paul Cézanne, Aix-en-Provence) 2008; Hon. DSc (Aristotle Univ., Thessaloniki, Greece) 2005; Hon. Diploma, Russian Acad. of Sciences (Novosibirsk Br.) 2013; Busk Prize, Royal Aeronautical Soc. 1995, Computational Mechanics Award, Japan Soc. of Mechanical Engineers 1995, Daniel & Florence Guggenheim Award, Int. Council of Aeronautical Sciences 2000, Nusselt-Reynolds Prize, Council of World Confs in Fluid Mechanics, Heat Transfer and Thermodynamics 2013. *Publications include:* Mathematical Models of Turbulence 1972, Turbulent Shear Flows, Vols 1–9 (ed.), Computational Strategies for Turbulent and Transitional Flows (ed.) 2002, Geoengineering Climate Change: Environmental Necessity or Pandora's Box? 2009, Modelling Turbulence in Engineering and the Environment 2011; more than 300 papers on measurement and modelling of turbulent flow. *Leisure interests:* French culture and cuisine, countryside walking, photography. *Address:* C31, George Begg, School of Mechanical, Aerospace and Civil Engineering, University of Manchester, Manchester, M13 9PL, England (office). *Telephone:* (161) 306-3801 (office). *E-mail:* brian.launder@manchester.ac.uk (office). *Website:* www.manchester.ac.uk (office).

LAUNSKY-TIEFFENTHAL, Peter; Austrian diplomatist and UN official; b. 30 Nov. 1957, Vienna; fmrly worked for Int. Finance Corpn, London, UK and Investkredit Bank, Vienna; Deputy Chief of Mission, Embassy in New Delhi 1996–2000, Consul-Gen. in Los Angeles, USA 2000–04, Head, Dept for Crisis Man. and Citizens Services, Federal Ministry for Foreign Affairs 2005–07, Spokesperson and Head, Dept for Communication and Information, Federal Ministry for European and Int. Affairs, later Head, Dept for Press and Information 2007–12; Under-Sec.-Gen. for Communications and Public Information, UN 2012–15, also Coordinator for Multilingualism, UN Secr. *Address:* c/o Department of Public Information, United Nations, New York, NY 10017, USA.

LAURA, Ernesto Guido; Italian film director, film critic and fmr film festival director; b. 4 May 1932, Villafranca, Veronese; s. of Manuel Laura and Pia Romei Laura; m. Anna Maria Vercellotti 1958; two s.; ed Dept of Law, Catholic Univ., Milan; Co-Nat. Sec. Centri Universitari Cinematografici 1953–54; Admin. Nat. Sec. Federazione Italiana Circoli del Cinema 1954–55; Chief Ed. Bianco e Nero 1956–58, Filmlexicon 1968; Film Critic, Il Veltro from 1958; mem. Editorial Bd Rivista del Cinematografo from 1967; Pres. Immagine, Centro Studi Iconografici from 1968, now Hon. Pres.; Dir Venice Film Festival 1969–70; Premio Charlie Chaplin (co-recipient) 2012. *Films include:* Diario di Una Dama Veneziana (documentary) 1958, Riscoperta di un Maestro (documentary) 1960, Alla Ricerca di

Franz Kafka (documentary) 1964, Spielberg (documentary) 1964, Don Minzoni (documentary) (Special Award) 1967, I mari della mia fantasia (short, also writer) 1971, La caduta del fascismo (documentary, also writer) 1983, Le Stagioni Dell'Aquila (Years of the Eagle) (documentary, writer) 1997. *Publications:* Il Film Cecoslovacco 1960, La Censura Cinematografica 1961, Ladri di Biciclette 1969, Immagine del Fascismo. Volume primo: La conquista del potere (1915–1925) 1973, Comedy Italian Style 1980, Teleconfronto: IV Mostra internazionale del telefilm, 23 maggio-1 giugno 1986 1986, L'immagine bugiarda: mass-media e spettacolo nella Repubblica di Salo (1943–1945) 1986, Quando Los Angeles si chiamava Hollywood. Cinema americano tra le due guerre 1996, Le stagioni dell'aquila: Storia dell'Istituto Luce (Immagini allo specchio) 2000, Hitchcock e il surrealismo. Il filo inesplorato che lega il maestro del cinema all'arte del Novecento 2005, La gola (Piemme Shots) (co-author) 2012.

LAURANCE, Dale R., BS, MS, PhD; American chemical engineer and business executive; *Chairman, Ingram Micro Inc.;* m.; ed Oregon State Univ., Univ. of Kansas; worked at E.I. DuPont de Nemours 1967–77; with Olin Corpn 1977–83; served in various man. and exec. positions with Occidental Petroleum Corpn 1983–96, mem. Bd of Dirs 1990–2004, Pres. 1996–2004; Owner, Laurance Enterprises LLC (pvt. advisory services co.), Nightingale Properties LLC (Hawaiian real estate devt co.); mem. Bd of Dirs, Ingram Micro Inc. 2001–, Chair. 2007–; Chair. Advisory Bd, Dept of Chemical Eng, Univ. of Kansas 1985–97; mem. Oregon State Univ. Coll. of Eng Acad. of Distinguished Engineers 1999–; mem. Bd of Dirs Jacobs Engineering Group 1994–, Saint John's Health Center; mem. Advisory Bd Hancock Park Assocs; mem. Bd of Trustees Polytechnic School, Children's Bureau; mem. Advisory Bd Golden West Humanitarian Foundation; mem. American Chem. Council; Hon. mem. Oregon State Univ.'s Chemical Eng Advisory Bd 1997–; mem. Hall of Fame, Dept of Chemical Eng, Univ. of Kansas. *Publications:* several US patents. *Address:* Ingram Micro Inc., 1600 East St Andrew Place, PO Box 25125, Santa Ana, CA 92799-5125, USA (office). *Telephone:* (714) 566-1000 (office). *E-mail:* info@ingrammicro.com (office). *Website:* www .ingrammicro.com (office).

LAURANCE, William (Bill) F., BSc, PhD; American/Australian biologist, environmental scientist and academic; *Distinguished Research Professor, James Cook University;* b. 12 Oct. 1957; m. Dr Susan G. Laurance; two c.; ed Boise State Univ., Univ. of California, Berkeley; Dir S.F.S. Centre for Rainforest Studies, Yungaburra, Qld, Australia 1989–91; Sr Prin. Scientist, Wet Tropics Man. Authority, Qld 1992–94; Wet Tropics Postdoctoral Fellow, CSIRO Tropical Forest Research Centre, Atherton, Qld 1994–96; Sr Scientist, Biological Dynamics of Forest Fragments Project, Smithsonian Inst. and Nat. Inst. for Amazonian Research (INPA), Manaus, Brazil 1996–2000; Sr Staff Scientist, Smithsonian Tropical Research Inst., Balboa, Panamá 2000–; Distinguished Research Prof., School of Marine and Tropical Biology, James Cook Univ., Australia 2009–; Prince Bernhard Chair in Int. Nature Conservation, WWF-Netherlands and Univ. of Utrecht, Netherlands 2010–14; Founder and Dir Alliance of Leading Environmental Researchers and Thinkers–ALERT 2015–; Research Assoc., Arnold Arboretum, Harvard Univ. 2009; John A. Erskine Fellow, Univ. of Canterbury, NZ 2005; Pres. Asscn for Tropical Biology and Conservation 2006; mem. Editorial Bd, Biotropica 1998–2000, Biological Conservation 1998, Ecology Letters 2002–04, Natureza e Conservação 2002, Trends in Ecology and Evolution 2003, Tropical Conservation Science 2007, Environmental Conservation 2009, Research and Reports in Biodiversity Studies 2010; Fellow, AAAS 2003, Australian Acad. of Science 2015; Hon. Fellow, World Innovation Foundation 2005; Silver and Gold Award for Outstanding Contribs, Boise State Univ. 1981, Biology Dept Scholarship, Boise State Univ. 1982, National Dean's List 1982, Outstanding Teaching Asst, Dept of Instruction in Biology, Univ. of California, Berkeley 1985, American Soc. of Mammalogists Award 1989, Award for Outstanding Scientist in the 25-year History of the Biological Dynamics of Forest Fragments Project, Manaus, Brazil 2004, John L. Boething Award for Conservation Research, Stanford Univ. 2005, BBVA Frontiers in Ecology and Conservation Biology Award 2008, Distinguished Alumni Award, Boise State Univ. 2010, Australian Laureate Award 2010–15, Distinguished Service Award, Soc. for Conservation Biology 2011, Australia's Best Science Writing Prize 2012, Winner, Faculty of 1000 Selection for Outstanding Articles 2012, Dr A.H. Heineken Prize for Environmental Sciences, Royal Netherlands Acad. of Arts and Sciences 2012, Outstanding Achievements in Conservation Award by Royal Zoological Soc. of London 2015, Cassowary Prize for Tropical Research and Conservation 2017. *Publications:* five books and more than 400 scientific and popular articles on the impacts of intensive land-uses, such as habitat fragmentation, logging, and wildfires, on tropical forests and species, as well as climate change and conservation policy. *Address:* Centre for Tropical Environmental & Sustainability Science (TESS), School of Marine and Tropical Biology, James Cook University, Cairns, Qld 4870, Australia (office). *Telephone:* (7) 4042-1819 (office); (7) 4038-1518 (home). *E-mail:* bill.laurance@jcu.edu.au (office). *Website:* research.jcu.edu.au/portfolio/bill.laurance (office); laurancelab .org/prof-william-laurance (office).

LAUREDO, Luis J., BA; American diplomatist, lawyer and business executive; m. Maria Regina Lauredo; two d.; ed Columbia Univ., Univ. of Madrid, Spain and Georgetown Univ.; Commr, Fla Public Service Comm. 1992–94; Chair. Int. Relations Cttee, Nat. Asscn of Regulatory Utility Commrs 1992–94; Nat. Co-ordinator Summit of the Americas 1994–95; Pres. Greenberg Taurig Consulting Inc. 1995–99; Perm. Rep. to OAS 1999–2001; consultant, Hunton & Williams law firm 2001–; mem. Presidential Advisory Cttee for Trade Promotion Negotiations 2003–; Exec. Dir FTAA Ministerial and American Business Forum 2003; Sr Vice-Pres., Export-Import Bank of the USA; Chair. Miami Int. Press Center; Dir, Rica Foods Inc. 1996–99, 2001–07, Colonial Bank of South Florida 2001–; Founding Dir, Hispanic Council on Foreign Affairs, Washington, DC; mem. Int. Advisory Bd, Baptist Health South Florida Inc. 2008–; Trustee, Pan-American Devt Foundation; represented US Pres. as Special US Amb. to the inaugurations of the Presidents of Colombia, Venezuela, Brazil and Costa Rica. *Address:* Baptist Health South Florida Inc., 6855 Red Road, Suite 600, Coral Gables, Miami, FL 33143-3632, USA (office). *Telephone:* (786) 662-6000 (office). *Fax:* (786) 662-6000 (office). *E-mail:* corporatepr@baptisthealth.net. *Website:* baptisthealth.net (office).

LAUREN, Ralph; American couturier and business executive; *Chairman, Ralph Lauren Corporation;* b. (Ralph Lifshitz), 14 Oct. 1939, Bronx, New York; s. of Frank Lifschitz and Frida Lifschitz; m. Ricky Anne Loew-Beer 1964; two s. one d.; ed DeWitt Clinton High School, the Bronx, New York; Baruch Coll., City Coll. of New York; changed name from Lifschitz to Lauren aged 16; served in US Army 1962–64; salesman, Bloomingdale's, New York, Brooks Bros, New York (cr. Polo label for them); Asst Buyer, Allied Stores, New York; Rep., Rivetz Necktie Mfrs, New York; neckwear designer, Polo Div., Beau Brummel, New York 1967–69; est. Polo Menswear Co., New York 1968–, Ralph Lauren's Women's Wear, New York 1971–, Polo Leathergoods 1978–, Polo Ralph Lauren Luggage 1982–, Ralph Lauren Home Collection 1983–; Chair. and CEO Polo Ralph Lauren Corpn (now Ralph Lauren Corpn), announced creation of Office of the Chairman led by Ralph Lauren 2013, resgnd as CEO 2015, now Chief Designer; cr. other brands, including Chaps, Club Monaco, Purple Label, Polo Jeans Co., Big & Tall, Golf sportswear 1998, Blue Label 2002, Ralph Lauren Rugby 2004, Black Label, Purple Label, RLX 2008, RRL, Denim & Supply, Ralph Lauren Childrenswear, Baby Ralph Lauren, Ralph Lauren Home, Ralph Lauren Paints, American Living; outfitter of US Olympic Team 2008, 2010, 2012; co-f. Nina Hyde Center for Breast Cancer Research, Georgetown Univ. 1989; launched Polo Ralph Lauren Foundation 2001; launched Pink Pony Fund; partnered with The Royal Marsden NHS Foundation Trust to fund a new breast cancer research facility 2014; Chevalier, Legion d'honneur 2010; numerous fashion awards, including American Fashion Award 1975, Council of Fashion Designers of America Award 1981, CFDA Lifetime Achievement Award 1992, CFDA American Fashion Legend Award 2007, James Smithson Bicentennial Medal 2014. *Publication:* Ralph Lauren 2007. *Leisure interest:* collecting and showing classic automobiles. *Address:* Ralph Lauren Corporation, 625 Madison Avenue, New York, NY 10022, USA (office). *Telephone:* (212) 318-7000 (office); (212) 813-7868 (office). *Fax:* (212) 888-5780 (office). *Website:* www.ralphlauren.com (office).

LAURÉN, Reidunn, BA, DIur; Swedish lawyer and politician; b. 11 Aug. 1931; m.; three c.; fmr Judge Admin. Court of Appeal, Stockholm; fmr Deputy Sec. Parl. Standing Cttee on Social Affairs; Legal Adviser Ministry of Labour; Perm. Under-Sec. Ministry of Housing and Physical Planning; Justice of the Supreme Admin. Court; Chair. Labour Court; Chair. Equal Opportunities Tribunal; Minister for Constitutional and Civil Law 1991–93; Pres. Admin. Court of Appeal 1994–97; Chair. Queen Sophia's Hosp. 1995–2002; King's Medal for distinguished legal service 2000. *Publications:* Equal Opportunities at Work for Women and Men; numerous articles on legal matters.

LAURENT, Jean, MSc, CE; French banking executive and administrator; *Vice-Chairman, Supervisory Board, Eurazeo Service Actionnaires;* b. 31 July 1944, Mazamet; m.; five c.; ed École Nat. Supérieure d'Aéronautique, Wichita State Univ., USA; Dir, AMACAM Co. 1994, Indocam 1996, Indosuez Bank of Pvt. Man. 1998, Crédit Lyonnais 1999; apptd Chair. Segespar 1999 (Dir 1994), Union of Studies and Investments 1999 (Dir 1996); fmr CEO Crédit Agricole SA; apptd Vice-Pres. Banca Intesa and Bank Espirito Santo 1999, Bd of Trustees Crédit Agricole Indosuez 2000; Pres. Fédération Bancaire Française, AFECEI 2001–; Chair. Calyon (formed from merger of Crédit Agricole and Crédit Lyonnais 2003) 2005–07; Chair. Institut Europlace de Finance, Paris Europlace from 2003; Chair. Financière des Régions; currently Vice-Chair. (Ind.), Supervisory Bd Eurazeo Service Actionnaires; Chevalier, Légion d'honneur; Officier, Ordre du Mérite agricole. *Address:* Eurazeo Service Actionnaires, 32 rue de Monceau, 75008 Paris, France (office). *Telephone:* 1-44-15-01-11 (office). *E-mail:* info@@eurazeo.com (office). *Website:* www.eurazeo.com (office).

LAURENT, Mélanie; French actress, director, model, singer and writer; b. 21 Feb. 1983, Paris; d. of Pierre Laurent and Annick Laurent; career began when Gérard Depardieu gave her a part in The Bridge 1999; abandoned plans to direct her first play, Mi-cuit cœur pistache at Théâtre Marigny, Paris, when she was cast as Shosanna Dreyfus in the Quentin Tarantino film Inglourious Basterds 2009; hostess of opening and closing ceremonies of 64th Cannes Film Festival 2011; a Climate Amb. for Kofi Annan's Global Humanitarian Forum 'Tck Tck Tck' Campaign; co-recipient (with Belgian actor Jérémie Renie) Romy Schneider and Jean Gabin Prizes for "most promising actor and actress" 2006. *Theatre includes:* Promenade de santé by Nicolas Bedos 2010. *Films include:* The Bridge 1999, Ceci est mon corps 2001, Summer Things 2002, La faucheuse (short) 2003, Snowboarder 2003, Une vie à t'attendre 2004, Rice Rhapsody 2004, The Last Day 2004, The Beat That My Heart Skipped 2005, Days of Glory 2006, Dikkenek (Étoiles d'Or for Best Female Newcomer) 2006, Don't Worry, I'm Fine (César Award for Most Promising Actress, Lumière Award for Most Promising Young Actress, NRJ Ciné Award for Best Young Talent in a Debut Film, Étoiles d'Or for Best Female Newcomer) 2006, Hidden Love 2007, Beluga 2007, Le tueur 2007, La chambre des morts 2007, Paris 2008, Inglourious Basterds (Austin Film Critics Asscn Award for Best Actress, Best Actress, Online Film Critics Soc.) 2009, Jusqu'à toi 2009, The Concert 2009, The Round Up 2010, Beginners 2010, Requiem pour une tueuse 2011, Et soudain tout le monde me manque 2011, The Adopted 2011, Night Train to Lisbon 2013, Now You See Me 2013, Enemy 2013, Aloft 2014; as writer and director: De moins en moins (short) 2008. *Television includes:* acted in; Route de nuit (film) 2000, Jean Moulin, une affaire française (film) 2003; writer and director: X Femmes (series) (À ses pieds) 2008. *Recording:* En t'Attendant (debut album) 2011. *Address:* c/o Cécile Felsenberg, UBBA, 6 rue de Braque, 75003 Paris, France.

LAUREY, Nuihau; French Polynesian politician; *Vice-President;* b. 1964, Tahiti; ed Univ. of Nice Sophia Antipolis, France; several years working in information tech. and financial sectors; fmr teacher of econs and finance; consultant in renewable energy and natural gas; tech. adviser to Minister of Energy, Teva Rohfritsch 2010; Man. Dir SARL INTIA (renewable energy co.) 2011–13; Municipal Councillor, Punaauia; Minister of the Economy, Finance and the Budget, and Public Service, with responsibility for Enterprise and Industry, the Promotion of Exports and the Fight against Inflation 2013–17; Vice-Pres. 2013–, Acting Pres. 5–12 Sept. 2014; mem. French Senate for French Polynesia 2015–; mem. Tahoera'a Huiraatira (People's Rally) –2015. *Publication:* Plaidoyer pour une véritable politique de l'énergie en Polynésie Française 2009. *Address:* Sénat, Casier de la Poste, 15 rue de Vaugirard, 75291 Paris, Cedex 06, France (office). *E-mail:* n.laurey@senat.fr (office). *Website:* www.senat.fr (office).

LAURI, Maris, MSc; Estonian economist and government official; b. 1 Jan. 1966, Kiviõli; ed Univ. of Tartu; mem. staff, Econ. Analysis Dept, Bank of Estonia

1994–96; Econ. Analyst, Bank of Tallinn 1996; Econ. Analyst, Swedbank Estonia 1998–2011; f. Oeconomia LLC 2011; Econ. Adviser to the Prime Minister April–Nov. 2014; Minister of Finance 2014–15, Minister of Educ. and Research Sept.–Nov. 2016; fmr mem. Academic Supervisory Cttee, Univ. of Tartu, Tallinn Univ. of Tech., EBS, Audentes Int. Univ., Veritas Coll.; mem. Estonian Reform Party.

LAURIE, (James) Hugh Callum, CBE, OBE; British actor, writer and musician; b. 11 June 1959, Oxford; s. of (William George) Ranald (Mundell) Laurie and Patricia Laurie (née Laidlaw); m. Jo Green 1989; two s. one d.; ed Eton Coll., Univ. of Cambridge; fmr Pres. Footlights, Univ. of Cambridge. *Films include:* Peter's Friends 1992, A Pin for the Butterfly 1994, Sense and Sensibility 1995, 101 Dalmatians 1996, The Snow Queen's Revenge 1996, The Borrowers 1997, Spice World 1997, The Ugly Duckling 1997, The Man in the Iron Mask 1998, Cousin Bette 1998, Stuart Little 1999, Carnivale 2000, Maybe Baby 2000, Lounge Act 2000, The Piano Tuner 2001, Chica de Río 2001, Stuart Little 2 2002, Flight of the Phoenix 2004, Valiant (voice) 2005, Street Kings 2008, Monsters vs Aliens (voice) 2009, The Oranges 2011, Mr. Pip 2012, Tomorrowland 2015, Holmes and Watson 2018, The Personal History of David Copperfield 2019. *Television appearances include:* Alfresco (series, also writer) 1983, The Crystal Cube (also writer) 1983, Mrs Capper's Birthday (film) 1985, Saturday Live (writer) 1986, A Bit of Fry and Laurie (series, also writer) 1986–95, The Laughing Prisoner (also writer) 1987, Blackadder the Third (series) 1987, Up Line 1987, Blackadder: The Cavalier Years 1988, Les Girls (series) 1988, Blackadder's Christmas Carol 1988, Blackadder Goes Forth (series) 1989, Hysteria 2! 1989, Jeeves and Wooster (series) 1990–92, Treasure Island (series) 1993, All or Nothing at All 1993, Look at the State We're In! (series, also dir) 1995, The Adventures of Mole 1995, The Best of Tracey Takes On. . . 1996, The Place of Lions 1997, Blackadder Back & Forth 1999, Santa's Last Christmas (voice) 1999, Little Grey Rabbit (series) 2000, Preston Pig (series) 2000, Life with Judy Garland: My and My Shadows 2001, Second Star to the Left 2001, Family Guy (series) 2001–09, Spooks (series) 2002, Stuart Little (series) 2003, Fortysomething (series, also dir) 2003, The Young Visiters [sic] 2003, House (Satellite Award for Outstanding Actor in a Series, Drama 2005, 2006, Television Critics Association Award for Individual Achievement in Drama 2005, 2006, Golden Globe Award for Best Performance in a Drama TV Series 2006, Golden Globe Award for Best Actor in a Drama TV Series 2007, Screen Actors' Guild Award for Outstanding Performance by a Male Actor in a Drama Series 2007, 2009, Teen Choice Award for TV Actor: Drama 2007, People's Choice Award for Favourite Male TV Star 2008, 2009, for Favourite TV Drama Actor 2010, 2011, for Favourite TV Doctor 2011) 2004–12, Monsters vs Aliens: Mutant Pumpkins from Outer Space (film) 2009, The Simpsons (voice) 2010, Fry and Laurie Reunited 2010, Veep (series) 2015–17, The Night Manager (Golden Globe Award for Best Supporting Actor in a Series 2017) 2016, Chance (series) 2016–17, Catch-22 (mini-series) 2019. *Recordings:* albums: Let Them Talk 2011, Didn't It Rain 2013. *Publications include:* Fry and Laurie 4 (with Stephen Fry) 1994, The Gun Seller 1996, The Paper Soldier 2009. *Leisure interest:* motorcycle enthusiast. *Address:* c/o Christian Hodell, Hamilton Hodell Ltd, 20 Golden Square, London, W1F 9JL, England (office). *Telephone:* (20) 7636-1221 (office). *Fax:* (20) 7636-1226 (office). *E-mail:* info@hamiltonhodell.co.uk (office). *Website:* www.hamiltonhodell.co.uk (office); hughlaurieblues.com.

LAURIE, Robert Stephen, AM, BA; Australian diplomatist (retd); b. 5 Nov. 1936, Sydney, NSW; s. of William Robert Laurie; m. Diana Victoria Mary Doyne 1969; one s. one d.; ed Knox Grammar School and Univ. of Sydney; joined Dept of External Affairs (now Dept of Foreign Affairs and Trade) 1958; served in Colombo 1960, Moscow 1960–63; First Sec., Washington, DC 1965–68; Counsellor, Hong Kong 1968–69; Deputy High Commr in India 1969–71; Amb. to Burma 1975–77, to Poland 1977–80; High Commr in Canada 1985–89, in NZ 1989–92; First Asst Sec., South Pacific, Middle East and Africa Divs, Dept of Foreign Affairs and Trade 1993–97; High Commr in India 1997–2001. *Leisure interests:* tennis, cricket, golf, music. *Address:* 31 Arthur Circle, Manuka, Griffith, ACT 2603; c/o Department of Foreign Affairs and Trade, R.G. Casey Building, John McEwen Crescent, Barton ACT 0221, Australia.

LAURISTIN, Marju, PhD; Estonian politician, sociologist and academic; *Professor Emerita of Social Communication, Tartu University;* b. 7 April 1940, Tallinn; d. of Johannes Lauristin and Olga Lauristin; m. Peeter Vihalemm 1978; two d.; ed Tartu Univ.; Head of Dept of Journalism, Tartu Univ. –1989, Prof. 1993, Prof. of Social Communication 2003, now Prof. Emer.; mem. CPSU –1990; f. Popular Front of Estonia 1988–92; Chair. Estonia Social-Democratic Party 1990–94; USSR People's Deputy 1989–90; Deputy Speaker of Estonian Supreme Soviet (now Parl.) 1990–92; mem. Estonian Parl. 1992–95, 1999–2003; Minister of Social Affairs 1992–94; MEP 2014–17; mem. Advisory Cttee for the Protection of Nat. Minorities, Council of Europe 2004–08; mem. Bd European Sociological Asscn 2007–11; mem. United Nations Univ. Council 2004–10; Order of Nat. Coat of Arms, Third Class 1998, Second Class 2003, Kt, Order of the White Rose, First Class, Finland 2003; Dr hc (Univ. of Helsinki) 2006; Democracy and Civil Soc. Award, USA and EU 1998. *Publication:* Return to the Western World: Cultural and Political Perspectives on the Estonian Post-Communist Transition (ed. with P. Vihalemm), The Challenge of the Russian Minority: Emerging Multicultural Democracy in Estonia (jt ed.) 2002. *Leisure interest:* literature. *Address:* Siili 6, Apt 35, Tartu 50104, Finland (home). *Telephone:* (7) 471-532 (home). *E-mail:* marju.lauristin@ut.ee (home).

LAUTENS, Mark, OC, BS, PhD, FRSC; Canadian chemist and academic; *J.B. Jones Distinguished Professor of Organic Chemistry, University of Toronto;* b. 9 July 1959, Hamilton, Ont.; s. of Trevor Lautens and Audrey Lane Lautens; ed Guelph Univ., Univ. of Wisconsin, Harvard Univ., USA; Research Assoc., Harvard Univ. 1985–87; Asst Prof. of Chem., Univ. of Toronto 1987–92, Assoc. Prof. 1992–94, Prof. 1994–, AstraZeneca Prof. of Organic Synthesis 1998–, NSERC/ Merck Industrial Research Chair in New Medicinal Agents via Catalytic Reactions 2003–13, Univ. Prof. 2012–, J.B. Jones Distinguished Prof. of Organic Chem. 2013–; mem., Canadian Soc. of Chem.; Fellow, Alfred P. Sloan Foundation 1991; Killam Research Fellowship, Canada Council for the Arts 2013, CIC Catalysis Award 2016; Eli Lilly Award 1992, Rutherford Memorial Medal in Chem., Royal Soc. of Canada 1994, Pedler Award 2011, Chemical Inst. of Canada Medal 2013, Henry Marshall Tory Award, RSC 2018. *Address:* Department of Chemistry,

University of Toronto, Davenport Chemical Laboratories, 80 St George Street, Toronto, ON M5S 3H6, Canada (office). *Telephone:* (416) 978-6083 (office). *Fax:* (416) 946-8185 (office). *E-mail:* mark.lautens@utoronto.ca (office). *Website:* www.chem.utoronto.ca/staff/ML (office).

LAUTMANN, Rüdiger, DPhil, DJur; German sociologist and academic; b. 22 Dec. 1935, Koblenz; s. of Kurt Lautmann and Sibylle Lautmann; m. Heiko Hinrichs 2005; ed Univs of Bonn, Berlin, Würzburg and Munich; Research Asst, Univ. of Bielefeld and Dortmund 1968–71; Prof. of Sociology, Law School, Univ. of Bremen 1971–82, Dept of Sociology 1982–2001; Ed. Journal of the German Sociological Asscn 1995–99; mem. Advisory Council, Kriminologisches Journal 2008–09; Pres. Inst. of Research in Security and Prevention, Hamburg 2002–09; Co-Ed. Invertito 2017–. *Publications include:* Wert und Norm 1969, Die Funktion des Rechts in der modernen Gesellschaft (co-ed.) 1970, Die Polizei (co-ed.) 1971, Soziologie vor den Toren der Jurisprudenz 1971, Seminar Gesellschaft und Homosexualität 1977, Der Zwang zur Tugend 1984, Die Gleichheit der Geschlechter und die Wirklichkeit des Rechts 1990, Das pornographierte Begehren (co-author) 1990, Männerliebe im alten Deutschland (co-ed.) 1992, Homosexualität (ed.) 1993, Vom Guten, das noch stets das Böse schafft (co-ed.) 1993, Die Lust am Kind 1994, Der Homosexuelle und sein Publikum 1997, Ausgrenzung macht krank (co-author) 2000, Soziologie der Sexualität 2002, NS-Terror gegen Homosexuelle (co-ed.) 2002, Punitivität (co-ed.) 2004, Fremde als Ordnungshüter (co-author) 2010, Justiz–die stille Gewalt 2011, Lexikon zur Soziologie (co-ed.) 2011, Was ist Homosexualität? (co-ed.) 2014, Capricen. Momente schwuler Geschichte (ed.) 2014, Soziologie des Strafrechts (co-ed.) 2014, Homosexualität – en und Altern (co-ed.) 2016, Sexualität und Strafe (co-ed.) 2016. *Leisure interests:* theatre, e-music. *Address:* Lindauer Str. 7, D- 10781 Berlin, Germany (home). *E-mail:* lautmann@uni-bremen.de (home). *Website:* www.lautmann.de.

LAUVERGEON, Anne Alice Marie; French government official and business executive; *Chairman, SIGFOX;* b. 2 Aug. 1959, Dijon; d. of Gérard Lauvergeon and Solange Martellière; m. Jean-Eric Molinard 1986; ed Lycées Lakanal, Sceaux, Lycée Voltaire, Orléans, Ecole Normale Supérieure and Ecole Nat. Supérieure des Mines, Paris; began professional career in iron and steel industry, first in Canada, then with Usinor 1983–84; Eng Inst. for Protection and Nuclear Safety, Centre d'Energie Atomique and Head of Div. Direction Régionale de l'Industrie et de la Recherche, Ile-de-France 1985–88; Asst to Head of Service of Conseil-Général des Mines 1988–89; Adviser on int. econ. and foreign trade, Presidency of Repub. 1990; Deputy Sec.-Gen. Presidency of Repub. 1990–95; Partner and Man. Lazard Frères & Cie 1995–98; Deputy Dir-Gen. Alcatel Alsthom 1997, mem. Exec. Cttee Alcatel Group 1998; Pres., Dir-Gen. Compagnie générale des matières nucléaires (Cogema) 1999–2001, Chair. Exec. Bd and CEO Areva Group (formed by merger of Cogema, CEA-Industrie, Framatome) 2001–11, also Dir Areva Enterprises Inc.; Chair. Supervisory Bd, Libération (daily newspaper) 2011–; Chair. SIGFOX (cellular network) 2014–; Chair. Ecole Nationale Superieure des Mines de Nancy; Vice-Pres. Bd of Dirs Société d'applications générales d'électricité et de mécanique (Sagem) 2000; mem. Strategy, Ethics and Environment Cttees, Suez Lyonnaise Group 2000; mem. Bd of Dirs Pechiney 1996–, Framatome 1998, Total Fina Elf 2000–, GDF-SUEZ, Vodafone Group Plc, EADS 2013–; Officier, Légion d'honneur. *Publication:* Sur les traces des dirigeants ou la vie du chef dans les grandes entreprises (co-author) 1988. *Address:* SIGFOX HQ, Bâtiment E-volution, 425 rue Jean Rostand, 31670 Labège (office). Libération, 11 rue Béranger, 75154 Paris Cedex 03, France. *Telephone:* 1-42-76-17-89 (Paris). *Fax:* 1-42-72-94-93 (Paris). *E-mail:* info@sigfox.com (office). *Website:* www.sigfox.com (office); www.liberation.com.

LAVADOS MONTES, Hugo, MA; Chilean economist, government official, academic and university administrator; *Rector, Universidad San Sebastián;* b. Aug. 1949, Talca; m.; two c.; ed Univ. of Chile, Boston Univ., USA; Prof. of Econs, Univ. of Chile 1976–81; Gen. Man. Manpower Chile 1983–90; Supervisor, Valores y Seguros 1990–94; mem. Anti-Trust Comm. 1990–94; Gen. Man. Banco BHIF 1994–98; with Ernst & Young 1999–2003; Dir ProChile (govt agency to promote exports) 2003–06; Minister of the Economy, Econ. Promotion and Reconstruction 2008–10; Dean, Faculty of Economics and Business, Universidad San Sebastián 2010–14, Rector Universidad San Sebastián 2014–. *Website:* www.uss.cl.

LAVAGNA, Roberto; Argentine politician and economist; b. 24 March 1942, Buenos Aires; m. Claudine Marechal; ed Univ. of Buenos Aires, Univ. of Brussels, Belgium; fmr mem. Radical Party; Sec. of Industry and Foreign Trade –1987; mem. Justicialist Party; Visiting Researcher, Center for Int. Affairs, Harvard Univ., USA 1995; fmr Prof., Univ. of Buenos Aires; Dir Ecolatina consulting firm 1995; Amb. to EU 2000–02; Minister of the Economy 2002–05; formed a front (Una Nacion Avanzada—An Advanced Nation) to run against the govt's cand., Cristina Fernández de Kirchner, in the presidential elections Oct. 2007; co-f. Unidos Para Cambiar (United for Change) 2013; Konex Award 2006. *Address:* c/o Ministry of the Economy and Public Finance, Hipólito Yrigoyen 250, C1086AAB Buenos Aires, Argentina. *E-mail:* ciudadano@mecon.gov.ar. *Website:* www.planlavagna.com.

LAVANT, Denis; French actor; b. 17 June 1961, Neuilly-sur-Seine, Hauts-de-Seine. *Films include:* Les Misérables 1982, Paris ficelle 1983, Coup de foudre 1983, L'homme blessé (The Wounded Man) 1983, Viva la vie! (Long Live Life) 1984, Boy Meets Girl 1984, Partir, revenir (Going and Coming Back) 1985, Mauvais sang (Bad Blood) 1986, L'étendu 1987, Un tour de manège (Roundabout) 1989, Mona et moi (Mona and I) 1989, C'est merveilleux 1991, Les amants du Pont-Neuf (The Lovers on the Bridge, USA) 1991, Drôle d'immeuble 1992, Fuis la nuit 1993, De force avec d'autres (Forced to Be with Others) 1993, La partie d'échecs (The Chess Game) 1994, L'ennemi 1995, Visiblement je vous aime (Obviously I Need You) 1995, Yasaeng dongmul bohoguyeog (Wild Animals) 1996, Don Juan 1998, Le monde à l'envers 1998, Cantique de la racaille (Melody for a Hustler, USA) 1998, Beau travail (Good Work) 1999, Tuvalu 1999, Promenons-nous dans les bois (Deep in the Woods) 2000, La squale (The Squale) 2000, Married/Unmarried 2001, Affaire Libinski 2001, La merveilleuse odyssée de l'idiot Toboggan (voice) 2002, Luminal 2004, Un long dimanche de fiançailles (A Very Long Engagement) 2004, Camping sauvage 2005, Mister Lonely 2006, Holy Motors 2012, Marussia 2013, Age of Uprising: The Legend of Michael Kohlhaas 2013, Journey to the West 2014, Graziella 2015, History's Future 2016. *Television includes:* L'ombre sur la plage 1982, Hôtel du siècle (series) 1985, Oscar et Valentin 1986, Les petits meurtres d'Agatha Christie (series) 2009, Marcel Dassault, l'homme au pardessus (film) 2014, Midnight Sun (series) 2016.

LAVAUDANT, Georges; French theatre director; b. 18 Feb. 1947, Grenoble (Isère); first production Lorenzaccio by Musset, Théâtre Partisan, Grenoble 1975; Co-Dir Centre Dramatique Nat. des Alpes 1976–, Maison de la Culture de Grenoble 1981, Théâtre nat. populaire de Villeurbanne (Rhône) 1986–96; Dir Odéon-Théâtre de l'Europe, Paris 1996–2007. *Productions include:* Le Régent by Jean-Christophe Bailly 1987, texts of Denis Roche (Louve basse), Pierre Bourgeade (Palazzo Mentale), Jean-Christophe Bailly (Les Céphéïdes and Pandora), Michel Deutsch (Féroé, la nuit...), Le Clézio (Pawana), Veracruz, Les Iris, Terra Incognita, Ulysse/Matériaux, interspersed with productions of works by Musset, Shakespeare, Chekhov, Brecht, Labiche, Pirandello, Genet and others; Comédie Française: Lorenzaccio, Le Balcon, Hamlet; Opéra de Paris: Roméo et Juliette by Gounod; Opéra de Lyon: L'enlèvement au sérail by Mozart, Malcolm by Gérard Maimone, Rodrigue et Chimène by Debussy; in Mexico City: Le Balcon, Pawana; in Montevideo: Isidore Ducasse/Fragments; in Bhopal: Phèdre; in Hanoi: Woyzeck; in St Petersburg: Reflets, Lumières (I) 'Près des ruines' 1995, Lumières (II) 'Sous les arbres' 1996, Théâtre Maly de St Petersburg in Russian adapation of Lumières: Reflets 1997, Prova d'orchestra by Giorgio Battistelli, Opéra du Rhin 1997; Odéon-Théâtre de l'Europe: Le Roi Lear by Shakespeare 1996, Bienvenue by Lavaudant 1996, Reflets by Jean-Christophe Bailly 1997, Ajax et Philoctète by Sophocle (Petit Odéon) 1997, Histoires de France (in collaboration with Michel Deutsch) 1997, Un chapeau de paille d'Italie by Eugène Labiche 1997, La dernière nuit by Lavaudant (Petit Odéon) 1997, Pawana by Jean-Marie Le Clézio 1997, La noce chez les petits bourgeois et Tambours dans la nuit by Bertolt Brecht 1998, L'Orestie by Aeschylus 1999, Les Géants de la Montagne by Pirandello (in Catalan) 1999, Fanfares 2000, Un fil à la patte by Feydeau 2001, La mort de Danton by Büchner 2002, El Pelele by Jean-Christophe Bailly 2003, The Cherry Orchard by Chekhov 2004, La rose et la hache 2004, Les Cenci 2007; Ateliers Berthier, Paris: Cassandre 2006; Centre dramatique nat. de Montreuil: Troïlus et Cressida 2007; various theatres: La Mort d'Hercule, after the tragedies Les Trachiniennes by Sophocles and Héraklès furieux by Euripides 2007, 20e/ PREMIERES, École nationale supérieure des arts du cirque, La Villette 2009, Allegro ricordando by Ami Flammer 2009, La Nuit de l'iguane by Tennessee Williams 2009, Roberto Zucco by Bernard-Marie Koltès 2009, La Tempête by William Shakespeare 2010, Macbeth Horror Suite by Carmelo Bene 2010, État civil, after António Lobo Antunes, with the junior students of École Supérieure de Théâtre de Montpellier 2011, Fado Alexandrino by António Lobo Antunes 2011, La mort de Danton by Georg Büchner 2012; abroad: Le Balcon in Mexico, Pawana in Mexico, Phèdre by Racine, with Jean-Christophe Bailly, in Hindi in Bhopal 1990, Isidore Ducasse/Fragments after Les Chants de Maldoror by Lautréamont, Montevideo 1993, Woyzeck, Hanoi, Otsviety (Reflets), Theatre Maly, St Petersburg 1997, Els gegants de la muntanya (Les géants de la montagne) by Luigi Pirandello, in Catalan, Nat. Theatre of Catalonia, Barcelona 1999, Impressions d'Afrique, Goldoni Theatre, Florence 2000, Coriolà (Coriolanus) by William Shakespeare, in Catalan, Nat. Theatre of Catalonia 2002, Començaments sense fi after Franz Kafka, in Catalan, Nat. Theatre of Catalonia 2003, Play Strindberg by Friedrich Dürrenmatt, in Spanish, Madrid and Barcelona 2006, 2007, Hay que purgar a Totó (On purge bébé) after Georges Feydeau, in Spanish, Madrid 2008, El misantrop (Le misanthrope) by Molière, in Catalan, Nat. Theatre of Catalonia 2011, Cyrano de Bergerac by Edmond Rostand, premiered at Maly Theatre, Moscow 2013. *Opera productions:* Prova d'orchestra compositeur by Giorgio Battistelli after the film by Federico Fellini 1995, Impressions d'Afrique, libretto by Georges Lavaudant and Daniel Loayza, Théâtre Goldoni, Florence, Opéra national du Rhin 2000, Roméo et Juliette by Charles Gounod, Opéra de Paris, L'Enlèvement au sérail by Mozart, Opéra de Lyon, Malcolm by Gérard Maimone, Rodrigue et Chimène by Claude Debussy, Tristan et Isolde by Richard Wagner, Corum Opéra Berlioz de Montpellier 2006, Scènes de chasse after Penthésilée by Heinrich von Kleist, Opéra Berlioz 2008, Andromaque by André-Ernest-Modeste Grétry, libretto by Louis-Guillaume Pitra, Opéra national de Montpellier Languedoc-Roussillon 2010, La Cerisaie by Philippe Fénelon, libretto by Alexei Parine after Chekhov, Palais Garnier 2012, Eine florentinische Tragödie (Une tragédie florentine) by Alexander von Zemlinsky, Opéra de Lyon 2012. *Films:* Spécial police (actor) 1985, Régime sans pain (producer) 1985, The Birth of Love (actor) 1993. *Publications:* Veracruz (novel) 1989, Les Iris (novel) 1992, Terra Incognita (novel) 1992, Ulysse/ Matériaux, Théâtre et histoire contemporains III (with Jean-Christophe Bailly) 2004. *Address:* c/o Union of the Theatres of Europe, 1 boulevard Lénine, 93000 Bobigny, France. *Telephone:* 1-57-14-84-65. *E-mail:* ute.heynen@ymail.com.

LAVELLI, Jorge; French theatre and opera director; b. 1932, Buenos Aires, Argentina; s. of Italian immigrants in Argentina; ed Ecole Charles Dullin et Jacques Lecoq, Paris, Université du Théâtre des Nations; has lived in France since early 1960s, French citizenship 1977; Dir Théâtre Nat. de la Colline 1987–96; fmr Pres. Centre français de l'Institut Int. du Théâtre (UNESCO); Chevalier, Légion d'honneur 1992, Commdr 1994; Chevalier, Ordre nat. du Mérite, Officier 2002; Commdr des Arts et des Lettres 1993; Commdr's Cross, Order of Merit (Poland); theatrical prizes in France, Spain and Italy, Prix du brigadier for Macbeth 1993, Grand Prix des arts de la scène, City of Paris 1996, ACE Award for Six Characters in Search of an Author 1999, ACE Award for Mein Kampf 2000, Prix Plaisir du théâtre 2004, SACD Prize 2008. *Plays include:* Le Mariage, Paris 1963, Berlin Festival (Grand Prix at Concours nat. des jeunes compagnies) 1964, Jeux de Massacre, Paris (Prix de la Critique) 1970, Le Roi se meurt, Paris (Prix Dominique de la mise en scène, Prix de la Critique) 1976, Doña Rosita La Soltera, Madrid, Jerusalem and Caracas Festivals and Paris 1980; at Théâtre Nat. de la Colline: Une Visite inopportune by Copi (Prix de la meilleure création française, Syndicat de la Critique) 1988, Réveille-toi Philadelphie (Prix de la meilleure création d'une pièce française, Syndicat de la Critique) 1988, La Veillée 1989, Greek (Molière Prize for Best Production) 1990, La Nonna 1990, Heldenplatz 1991, 1992, Le Désarroi de Monsieur Peters 2002, La Hija del aire 2004, Merlin ou la terre dévastée 2005, Himmelweg (by Juan Mayorga) 2007, Oedipus the King (by Sophocles), Festival of Mérida, Spain 2008, The Boy in the Last Row (by Juan Mayorga), Théâtre de la Tempête 2009, The Miser of Molière, Centro Nacional dramático, Teatro María Guerrero, Madrid 2010 (and Spanish tour –2012), Love Letters to Stalin (by Juan Mayorga), Théâtre de la Tempête 2011, Le prix des boites (by Frédéric Pommier), Athénée Théâtre Louis Jouve 2013. *Operas include:* The Trial (by Von Einem), Vienna State Opera 1970, Idomeneo, Angers 1975, Faust, Opéra de Paris 1975, L'Heure Espagnole and L'Enfant et les Sortilèges, La Scala Milan 1975, La Traviata, Aix-en-Provence Festival 1976, Faust, Metropolitan Opera, New York, Kennedy Center, Washington 1976, Pelléas et Mélisande, Opéra de Paris 1977, Fidelio, Toulouse 1977, Madame Butterfly, La Scala, Milan and Opéra de Paris 1978, Alcina, Aix-en-Provence Festival 1978, Carmen, Strasbourg, Brussels 1978, Oedipus Rex, Opéra de Paris 1979, Le Nozze di Figaro, Aix-en-Provence Festival, Liège 1979, Dardanus (by Rameau), Opéra de Paris 1980, Les Arts Florissants (by Charpentier), Versailles 1982, Norma, Bonn 1983, Salome, Zürich 1986, La Clemenza di Tito, Hamburg 1986, The Makropoulos Affair, Buenos Aires 1986, Die Zauberflöte, Aix-en-Provence Festival 1989, Die Entführung aus dem Serail, Aix-en-Provence Festival 1990, Cecilia 2000, Siroe (by Handel) 2000, Ariodante 2001 Faust, Paris Opera, Opéra Bastille 2001–03, Medea, Paris Opera 2001–02, L'Enfant et les sortilèges, Teatro Real, Madrid 2002–03 (Grand Teatre del Liceu, Barcelona 2004), The Flying Dutchman (by Wagner), Teatro San Carlo in Naples 2003, Siroe, Brooklyn Acad. of Music, New York 2004, Cécilia (by Charles Chaynes), Theatre Opera d'Avignon 2005, Simon Boccanegra (by Giuseppe Verdi), Capitol Theatre (Halle aux Grains), Toulouse 2009, Polieukt (by Zygmunt Krauze), Warsaw Chamber Opera 2010, 2013 (Théâtre du Capitole, Toulouse 2011), The Merry Widow (by Franz Lehár), Paris Opera, Palais Garnier 2012, Rienzi (by Richard Wagner), Théâtre du Capitole, Toulouse 2012; several opera productions for TV. *Address:* c/o Théâtre National de la Colline, 15 rue Malte Brun, 75020 Paris, France.

LAVENIR, Frédéric; French business executive; *CEO, CNP Assurances SA;* b. 1960; ed École des Hautes Études Commerciales, École Nationale d'Admin; Finance Insp. 1986–90; joined the French Treasury, initially as Head of Banking Regulations, then as Dir of Insurance Co. Office, Sec.-Gen. of Interministerial Cttee for Industrial Restructuring (CIRI) 1995–97, Deputy Dir Office of Minister of Economy and Finance 1997–2000; joined BNP Paribas 2001, COO BNP Paribas Lease Group 2001–02, Chair. and CEO 2002–07, Head of Group Human Resources, BNP Paribas and mem. Exec. Cttee 2007–12; CEO CNP Assurances SA 2012–; Vice-Pres. Asscn for Right to Econ. Initiative (ADIE). *Address:* CNP Assurances SA, 4 place Raoul Dautry, 75716 Paris Cedex 15, France (office). *Telephone:* 1-42-18-88-88 (office). *Fax:* 1-42-18-93-66 (office). *E-mail:* edmond .alphandery@cnp.fr (office). *Website:* www.cnp.fr (office).

LAVER, Rod(ney) George, MBE, OBE; Australian fmr tennis player; b. 9 Aug. 1938, Rockhampton, Queensland; s. of R. S. Laver; m. Mary Benson 1966; one s.; ed Rockhampton Grammar and High Schools; turned professional 1963; Australian Champion 1960, 1962, 1969; Wimbledon Champion 1961, 1962, 1968, 1969; USA Champion 1962, 1969; French Champion 1962, 1969; only player to win two Grand Slams 1962, 1969; played Davis Cup for Australia 1958, 1959, 1960, 1961, 1962 and 1973 (first open Davis Cup); in a 23-year career won 47 professional titles; Int. Tennis Hall of Fame 1981; Melbourne Park centre court renamed Rod Laver Arena in his honour 2000. *Publications:* How to Play Winning Tennis 1964, Education of a Tennis Player 1971, A Memoir 2012. *Leisure interests:* golf, fishing, skiing. *Address:* c/o Tennis Australia, Private Bag 6060, Richmond South, Vic. 3121, Australia (office); 3009 Via Conquistador, Carlsbad, CA 92009, USA (home). *Telephone:* (760) 476-0658 (home). *E-mail:* rglaver@gmail.com (home).

LAVEUMAAU, Tevita Lotoaatu, BA; Tongan financial advisor and politician; b. Mataika, Vava'U; m.; ed Tupou Coll.; Financial Advisor, MV 'Onemato (ferry service) 2010–14; fmr acting Dir, Land Transport Div., Ministry of Infrastructure; mem. Legis. Ass. for 'Eua No. 11 constituency 2014–; Minister of Revenue and Customs 2014; Minister of Finance and Nat. Planning June–Sept. 2017.

LAVIER, Bertrand; French artist; b. 14 June 1949, Châtillon-sur-Seine; s. of Jean Lavier and Geneviève Duteil; m. Gloria Friedmann 1989; ed Ecole Nat. Supérieure d'Horticulture; landscape artist and town planner, Marne Lavallée New Town 1971–72; at Centre de Recherches et d'Etudes sur le Paysage, Paris 1973–75; artist 1974–; First Prize (Sculpture), Biennale, Budapest 1984, Grand Prix Nat. de la Sculpture 1994. *Publication:* Bertrand Lavier présente la peinture des Martin de 1603 à 1984 1984. *Leisure interests:* hunting, motor-racing, tennis. *Address:* Galerie Durand-Dessert, 28 rue de Lappe, 75011 Paris (office); rue La Demoiselle, 21510 Aignay-le-Duc, France (home).

LAVILLENIE, Renaud; French pole vaulter; b. 18 Sept. 1986, Barbezieux-Saint-Hilaire; vaulted 5.81 m. in Aulnay-sous-Bois 2008; bronze medal, World Championships 2009, 2011, 2015, silver medal 2013; gold medal, European Indoor Championships 2009, 2011, 2013, 2015; silver medal, Continental Cup 2010; gold medal, European Championships 2010, 2012, 2014, 2016; gold medal, Int. Asscn of Athletics Feds. (IAAF) World Indoor Championships 2012, 2016, gold medal, Olympic Games, London 2012 (new Olympic record), Olympic Games, Rio 2016; mem. Clermont Athletisme Auvergne club; French Legion of Honour 2014; Best Male Athlete Award, Asscn Internationale De La Presse Sportive (AIPS) 2012, Men's European Athlete of the Year 2014. *Website:* www.renaud-lavillenie.com.

LAVIN, Franklin L., BSc, MSc, MA, MBA; American business executive, fmr government official and fmr diplomatist; *CEO, Export Now;* b. Canton, Ohio; m. Ann Lavin; three c.; ed Georgetown Univ., Johns Hopkins Univ., Wharton School, Univ. of Pennsylvania; served as Deputy Exec. Sec., Nat. Security Council and Dir Office of Political Affairs during Reagan Admin; Deputy Asst Sec. of Commerce for Asia and Pacific during George H. W. Bush Admin; Sr Man. positions Citibank and Bank of America in Hong Kong and Singapore 1996–2001; Amb. to Singapore 2001–05; Under-Sec. of Commerce for Int. Trade, US Int. Trade Admin, Washington, DC 2005–07; Man. Dir and COO Cushman & Wakefield Investors Asia, Hong Kong 2007–09; Chair. Public Affairs Practice, Edelman Asia Pacific 2009–; CEO and Chair., Export Now 2010–; mem. Bd of Dirs Consistel, Globe Specialty Metals; fmr Lt Commdr in USNR; fmr mem. Council on Foreign Relations, IISS. *Publication:* Export Now 2011. *Address:* Export Now, 526 South Main Street, Akron, OH 44311, USA (office). *Telephone:* (330) 510-1069 (office). *E-mail:* info@exportnow.com (office). *Website:* www.exportnow.com (office).

LAVÍN INFANTE, Joaquín José; Chilean economist and politician; b. 23 Oct. 1953, Santiago; s. of Joaquín Lavín Pradenas and Carmen Infante Vial; m. María Estela León Ruiz; seven c.; ed Pontificia Univ. Católica de Chile, Univ. of Chicago; econ. adviser, ODEPLAN (Ministry for Planning) 1975–77, Dean Faculty of Econ. and Admin. Sciences, Concepción Univ. 1979–81; Econ. Ed. El Mercurio 1986–88;

fmr Sec.-Gen. UDI (Ind. Democratic Union); Dean Faculty of Econs and Business, Univ. del Desarrollo 1996–98; Mayor Las Condes 1992–96, 1996–2000; presidential cand. 1999, 2005; Mayor of Santiago 2000–04; Minister of Educ. 2010–11 of Social Devt 2011–13; Founder La Vaca (NGO); mem. Opus Dei. *Publications:* Miguel Kast: Pasión de Vivir 1986, Chile Revolución Silenciosa 1987.

LAVIZZO-MOUREY, Risa, MBA, MD; American physician and foundation executive; *President and CEO, The Robert Wood Johnson Foundation;* b. 1954, Seattle, Wash.; m. Dr Robert Lavizzo-Mourey; two c.; ed State Univ. of NY at Stony Brook, Harvard Medical School and Wharton School, Univ. of Pennsylvania; residency in internal medicine, Brigham and Women's Hosp., Boston, Mass; fmr Robert Wood Johnson Clinical Scholar, Univ. of Pennsylvania; fmr Deputy Admin. Agency for Health Care Policy and Research (now Agency for Health Care Research and Quality), Dept of Health and Human Services; fmr Co-Chair. Working Group on Quality of Care, White House Task Force on Health Care Reform; Sylvan Eisman Prof. of Medicine and Health Care Systems and Dir Inst. on Aging, Univ. of Pennsylvania –2001; Sr Vice-Pres. and Dir Health Care Group, The Robert Wood Johnson Foundation 2001–03, Pres. and CEO (first woman and first African-American) 2003–; mem. or fmr mem. several cttees, including Nat. Cttee for Vital and Health Statistics (Chair. Sub-cttee on Minority Populations), Pres.'s Advisory Comm. on Consumer Protection and Quality in the Health Care Industry, Bd of Dirs American Bd of Internal Medicine, Bd of Regents American Coll. of Medicine; Co-Dir Inst. of Medicine study on racial disparities in health care, resulting in the publication of Unequal Treatment, Confronting Racial and Ethnic Disparities in Health Care 2004; mem. Inst. of Medicine (NAS); two hon. doctorates; numerous awards, including those from Harvard School of Public Health, Dept of Health and Human Services, NAS, American Coll. of Physicians, Nat. Library of Medicine, American Medical Women's Asscn, Nat. Medical Asscn, Univ. of Pennsylvania. *Publications:* several books and numerous articles. *Address:* The Robert Wood Johnson Foundation, PO Box 2316, College Road East and Route 1, Princeton, NJ 08543, USA (office). *Telephone:* (888) 631-9989 (office). *Website:* www.rwjf.org (office).

LAVROV, Sergei Viktorovich; Russian diplomatist and politician; *Minister of Foreign Affairs;* b. 21 March 1950, Moscow, Russian SFSR, USSR; m. Mariya Lavrova; one d.; ed Moscow State Inst. of Int. Relations; has served in diplomatic service since 1972; attaché, USSR Embassy in Sri Lanka 1972–76, Sec., Dept of Int. Econ. Orgs, Ministry of Foreign Affairs 1976–81, Sec. and Counsellor, Perm. Mission of USSR to UN, New York 1981–88; Deputy Chair., then Chair. Dept of Int. Econ. Relations, Ministry of Foreign Affairs 1988–90; Dir Dept of Int. Orgs and Global Problems, Ministry of Foreign Affairs 1990–92, Deputy Minister of Foreign Affairs 1992–94, Perm. Rep. to UN, New York 1994–2004, Minister of Foreign Affairs 2004–; Order of Heydär Äliyev, Order of Honour 1996, Order of Service to the Nation 1997, Order of Merit for the Fatherland (Fourth Class) 1998, (Third Class) 2005, (Second Class) 2010; Honoured Worker of the Diplomatic Service of the Russian Fed. 2004, Order of the Holy Prince Daniel of Moscow (Second Class) (Russian Orthodox Church), (First Class) 2010; Hon. Medal, UN Asscn of Russia 2005, Order of Friendship (Kazakhstan) 2005, Order of Friendship of Peoples (Belarus) 2006, Grand Cross of the Order of the Sun (Peru) 2007, Order of Friendship (Viet Nam) 2009, Order of Friendship (Laos), Medal of Honour (South Ossetia) 2010, Order of St Mashtots (Armenia) 2010, Order of Service to the Fatherland (First Class) 2015, Order of the Serbian Flag, First Class 2016; Hon. Dr in Diplomacy (Univ. of Piraeus, Greece) 2016; Gold Medal, Yerevan State Univ., Armenia 2007. *Leisure interests:* white-water rafting, playing the guitar, writing songs and poetry, supports FC Spartak Moscow. *Address:* Ministry of Foreign Affairs, 119200 Moscow, Smolenskaya-Sennaya pl. 32/34, Russia (office). *Telephone:* (499) 244-16-06 (office). *Fax:* (499) 244-34-48 (office). *E-mail:* ministry@mid.ru (office). *Website:* www.mid.ru (office); www.mid.ru/bul_ns_en.nsf/kartaflat/en03.01 (office).

LAVROVA, Olga V.; Kyrgyzstani economist and politician; b. 14 May 1956, Barnaul, Altai Region; ed Kyrgyz State Univ.; started career as economist, Pervomaisky Br., State Bank of USSR, Frunze City (now Bishkek); Economist, later Sr Economist and Lead Economist, Ministry of Finance 1978–85; Deputy Divisional Dir, later Dir, Frunze City Dept of Finance 1985–93; Inspector, Divisional Dir, Jogorku Kenesh (Supreme Council, Parl.) Control Chamber 1983–96; Auditor, Adviser to Chair. of Accounts Chamber of Kyrgyz Repub. 1996–2004; Deputy Minister of Finance 2004–05, Minister of Finance 2005–07, 2012–15; Chair. Social Security Fund of the Kyrgyz Repub. 2005–07; Dir, Gazpromneft Asia Ltd 2007–12; mem. Dignity Political Party (Ar-Namys); Certificate of Merit of the Kyrgyz Repub. *Address:* c/o Ministry of Finance, 720040 Bishkek, bul. Erkindik 58, Kyrgyzstan.

LAVROVSKY, Mikhail Leonidovich, MA; Russian ballet dancer, choreographer and academic; *Choreographer, Bolshoi State Theatre;* b. (Mikhail Ivanov-Lavrovsky), 29 Oct. 1941, Tbilisi, Georgia; s. of Leonid Lavrovsky and Elena Chikvaidze; m. Dolores García Ordonyez 1958; one s.; ed Moscow Choreographic School (now the Moscow State Choreographic Acad.), studied under O. Khodot, N. Tarassov and G. Evdokimo, studied ballet under Alexei Ermolaev, Moscow State Acad. of Theatre Art (now the Russian Univ. of Theatrical Arts—GITIS); Artistic Dir, Tbilisi State Academic Opera and Ballet Theatre Z. Paliashvili 1983–85, left the troupe 1988; Ballet Master/Repetiteur, Bolshoi State Theatre 1987–; Artistic Dir, Moscow Academic Music Theatre K.S. Stanislavsky and Vl.I. Nemirovich-Danchenko ballet co. 2005–08; Artistic Dir, Moscow State Acad. of Choreography 2010–; repertoire as a dancer includes: Slave (A. Khachaturian's Spartacus) 1962, Georgy's Son (The Pages of Life, A. Balanchivadze 1961, Philippe (Boris Asfiev's The Flames of Paris) 1962, Prince (Cinderella by S. Prokofiev) 1963, Vatslav (Boris Asafiev's The Fountain of Bakhchisaray) 1963, Albrecht (Giselle by A. Adam) 1963, Bluebird (The Sleeping Beauty by Tchaikovsky) 1963, Coral (Rodion Shchedrin's The Humpbacked Horse) 1963, Frondoso (Laurencia by A. Crain) 1964, Qays (Majnun) (Layla and Majnun by S. Balasanyan) 1965, Ferkhad (Arif Melikov's A Legend of Love) 1965, The Nutcracker-Prince (Nutcracker by Tchaikovsky) 1966, Basil (Don Quixote by L. Minkus) 1967, Spartacus (A. Khachaturian's Spartacus) 1968, Romeo (Romeo and Juliet by Prokofiev) 1969, Prince (Swan Lake by Tchaikovsky) 1970, Viktor (Angara by A. Eshpai) 1976), cr. role of Ivan the Terrible (Ivan the Terrible, to music by Prokofiev) 1978, Paganini (Paganini to music of Rachmaninov) 1979, Claudio (Love for Love, music by Tikhon Khrennikov) 1979, Artynov (Anyuta to music of V. Gavrilin) 1986, Fantasy on the Theme of Casanova (to music by W.A. Mozart) 1993, cr. role of Capulet at the Bolshoi Theatre (Romeo and Juliet, music by Prokofiev) 2003; starred in the original TV ballets: Romeo and Juliet (music by Prokofiev) 1968, White Nights (after the novel by F. Dostoevsky, to music by Schoenberg) 1972, Fedra (music by A. Lokshin, performed part of Ippolit) 1972, Three Cards (after Pushkin's story The Queen of Spades, music by K. Molchanov) 1983, staged the ballets: Romeo and Juliet (after L. Lavrovsky, Tbilisi Theatre Z. Paliashvili, danced Romeo) 1983, Saratov Academic Opera and Ballet Theatre 2004, Porgy and Bess (jazz-ballet, to music by Gershwin, Tbilisi Theatre Z. Paliashvili, danced Porgy) 1983, Choreographic novellas to music by J.S. Bach, Franz Liszt and others, Arizona Ballet, Phoenix, USA 1987, Suite No. 2 for Flute by J.S. Bach, Arizona Ballet 1989, Casanova to music by W.A. Mozart, Atlanta Ballet, USA 1989, Revelations to music by V. Kikta, theatre-studio A Group of Citizens (premier took place on the stage of the Moscow Academic Musical Theatre K.S. Stanislavsky and VI.I. Nemirovich-Danchenko) 1991, Mziri D. Toradze, Houston Ballet, USA 1992, More Powerful than Gold and Death, to music by Wagner, Russian Chamber Ballet 'Moscow' 1996, Café-Block, to music by Gershwin (Moscow Operetta Theatre) 1995, Nijinsky, to music by Rachmaninov (with the participation of the Bolshoi Theatre dancers, danced part of Sergei Diaghilev, Maly Theatre) 2000, Richard III, to music by Ravel (danced the title role, Concert Hall P.I. Tchaikovsky) 2000, Matador, to music by de Falla (with the participation of the Bolshoi Theatre dancers, Bolshoi Theatre) 2001; revived Giselle for the troupe of the Russian Chamber Ballet 'Moscow' 1996; staged original TV ballets: Mziri (to music by D. Toradze, dir Z. Kakabadze, danced title role, Georgian TV films studio) 1977 (won Grand Prix at Int. Festival of the Dance-Video Films Asscn, New-York 1978), Prometheus (to music by Scriabin, dir Z. Kakabadze, danced title role, Georgian TV films studio) 1981, Choreographic novellas 1986, A Dreamer (video version of jazz ballet Blues, danced title role, dir V. Bunin, Mosfilm) 1989; staged dance and stage movement at drama theatres: Anna Karenina (one-person production after the novel by Tolstoy, Theatre Agency BOGIS) 1998, The Last Night of the Last Tsar (after the play by E. Radzinsky, BOGIS) 1998, Evgeny Onegin... Pushkin (BOGIS) 2000, An Excellent Cure for Melancholy (after the play by S. Zlotnikov, School of the Modern Play) 2001, Le Petit Prince (after the story by A. de Saint-Exupéry) 2001; actively engaged in pedagogical activities, conducts workshops; took part in seminars in Germany, USA (Houston Ballet), Japan (Tokyo Ballet), Italy (Nat. Dance Acad. of Rome), Yugoslavia (Ballet Co. of the Serbian Nat. Theatre, Novi Sad); est. Choreographic School L.M. Lavrovsky, Moscow; People's Artist of the USSR, Honour Order 2002; prizewinner, Int. Competition in Varna, Bulgaria 1965, Lenin Prize 1970, Nizhinsky Prize, Paris Acad. of Dance 1972, USSR People's Artist 1976, USSR State Prize 1977. *Films include:* choreography and lead role Ali Baba and the Forty Thieves (Dir Kakhagadze), Fantasior (Dir Bunin). *Publication:* From Myself to My Friends. *Leisure interests:* sport, fencing, reading, painting, philosophy, drama, cinema. *Address:* Bolshoi Theatre, 125009 Moscow, Teatralnaya pl. 1 (office); 125009 Moscow, Voznesensky per. 16/4, Apt 7, Russia (home). *Telephone:* 916-576-24-43 (Russia, mobile) (office); (495) 455-55-55 (office); (495) 505-95-61 (home). *E-mail:* pr@bolshoi.ru (office); lavrovsky@mail.ru (office). *Website:* www.bolshoi.ru (office); www.lavrovsky.ru (office).

LAW, Jude; British actor; b. 29 Dec. 1972, London; s. of Peter Law and Maggie Law; m. Sadie Frost 1997 (divorced 2003); one step-s. two s. one d.; fmrly with Nat. Youth Music Theatre; co-f. Natural Nylon (production co.), Dir 2000–03; Chevalier, Ordre des Arts et des Lettres 2007; Hon. César Award 2007. *Stage appearances include:* Joseph and the Amazing Technicolor Dreamcoat, Les Parents Terribles 1994, Ior 1995, Tis A Pity She's A Whore 1999, Doctor Faustus 2002, Hamlet (Donmar Warehouse, London) 2009. *Film appearances include:* Shopping 1994, I Love You I Love You Not 1996, Wilde 1997, Gattaca 1997, Midnight in the Garden of Good and Evil 1997, Bent, Music From Another Room 1998, Final Cut 1998, The Wisdom of Crocodiles 1998, eXistenZ 1999, The Talented Mr Ripley (BAFTA Award for Best Supporting Actor) 1999, Enemy at the Gates 2000, Love Honour and Obey 2000, AI: Artificial Intelligence 2001, Road to Perdition 2002, Cold Mountain 2003, Sky Captain and the World of Tomorrow 2004, Alfie 2004, I Heart Huckabees 2004, The Aviator 2004, Lemony Snicket's A Series of Unfortunate Events (voice) 2004, Breaking and Entering 2006, All the King's Men 2006, The Holiday 2006, My Blueberry Nights 2007, Sleuth 2007, The Imaginarium of Doctor Parnassus 2009, Sherlock Holmes 2009, Repo Men 2010, Sherlock Holmes: A Game of Shadows 2011, Anna Karenina 2012, The Grand Budapest Hotel 2014, Spy 2015, Genius 2016, King Arthur: Legend of the Sword 2017, Vox Lux 2018, Fantastic Beasts: The Crimes of Grindelwald 2018, Captain Marvel 2019. *Address:* c/o WME, Centre Point, 103 New Oxford Street, London, WC1A 1DD, England (office). *Telephone:* (20) 7534-6800 (office). *Fax:* (20) 7534-6900 (office). *Website:* www.wma.com (office).

LAWRENCE, Carmen Mary, PhD; Australian politician and fmr psychologist; b. 2 March 1948, Morawa, WA; d. of Ern Lawrence and Mary Lawrence; m. 1979; one s.; ed Santa Maria Coll., Perth and Univ. of Western Australia; Sr Tutor, Dept of Psychiatry and Behavioural Science, Univ. of Western Australia 1979, Lecturer and Course Controller in Behavioural Science applied to Medicine 1980–83; Lecturer and Tutor, Curtin Univ., Univ. of Melbourne; Research Psychologist in Research and Evaluation Unit, Psychiatric Services, Health Dept of WA 1983–86; mem. (for Subiaco) Western Australia State Ass. 1986–89, Glendalough 1989, apptd Minister for Educ. 1988, fmr Minister for Educ. and Aboriginal Affairs, Premier of WA 1990–93, also Treas., Minister for the Family and for Women's Interests; Leader of the Opposition, Shadow Treas., Shadow Minister for Employment, for Fed. Affairs 1993–94; Fed. Shadow Minister of Health 1994–96, on Status of Women and on Environment and the Arts 1996–97; mem. Fed. Parl. for Fremantle 1994–2007 (retd); Minister for Human Services and Health and Minister Assisting the Prime Minister for the Status of Women 1994–97; Shadow Minister for the Environment, the Arts and Asst to the Leader of the Opposition on the Status of Women 1996–97; Shadow Minister for Industry, Innovation and Tech. 2000, for the Status of Women 2000–02, for Reconciliation, Aboriginal and Torres Strait Islander Affairs 2000–02; Professorial Fellow, School of Psychology, Univ. of Western Australia 2008–, mem. Faculty Advisory Bd, Faculty of Arts, Humanities and Social Sciences; Benjamin Rosenstamm Prize in Econs, British Psychological Soc. Prize for Psychology, Australian Psychological Soc. Prize for Psychology, H. I. Fowler Prize for Research in Psychology, J. A. Wood

Memorial Prize and other awards and prizes. *Publications:* several academic papers on psychology. *Leisure interests:* reading, theatre, classical music, cooking. *Address:* School of Psychology, University of Western Australia, 35 Stirling Highway, Crawley, Perth, WA 6009 (office); Unit 7, Queensgate Mall, William Street, Fremantle, WA 6160, Australia (office). *E-mail:* carmen.lawrence@uwa.edu.au (office). *Website:* www.uwa.edu.au/people/carmen.lawrence (office).

LAWRENCE, Jennifer Shrader; American actress; b. 15 Aug. 1990, Louisville, Ky; d. of Gary Lawrence and Karen Lawrence. *Films include:* Garden Party 2008, The Poker House 2008, The Burning Plain 2008, Winter's Bone (Detroit Film Critics Soc. Award for Best Actress, San Diego Film Critics Soc. Award for Best Actress, Stockholm Int. Film Festival Award for Best Actress, Toronto Film Critics Asscn Award for Best Actress) 2010, Like Crazy 2011, The Beaver 2011, X-Men First Class 2011, The Hunger Games 2012, Silver Linings Playbook (Golden Globe Award for Best Actress in a Motion Picture – Comedy or Musical 2013, Academy Award for Best Actress 2013) 2012, House at the End of the Street 2012, The Devil You Know 2013, The Hunger Games: Catching Fire 2013, American Hustle (Best Supporting Actress, Nat. Soc. of Film Critics 2014, Golden Globe Award for Best Supporting Actress in a Motion Picture 2014, BAFTA Award for Best Supporting Actress 2014) 2013, Serena 2014, X-Men: Days of Future Past 2014, The Hunger Games: Mockingjay – Part 1 2014, The Hunger Games: Mockingjay – Part 2 2015, Joy (Golden Globe Award for Best Actress in Motion Picture – Musical or Comedy 2016) 2015, X-Men: Apocalypse 2016, Passengers 2016. *Television includes:* Company Town (film) 2006, Monk (series) 2006, Cold Case (series) 2007, Not Another High School Show (film) 2007, Medium (series) 2007–08, The Bill Engvall Show 2007–09. *Address:* c/o Creative Artists Agency, 2000 Avenue of the Stars, Los Angeles, CA 90067, USA (office). *Telephone:* (424) 288-2000 (office). *Fax:* (424) 288-2900 (office). *Website:* www.caa.com (office).

LAWRENCE, Peter Anthony, PhD, FRS; British biologist; *Scientist Emeritus, Medical Research Council Laboratory of Molecular Biology and Department of Zoology, University of Cambridge;* b. 23 June 1941, Longridge, Lancs.; s. of Ivor D. Lawrence and Joy Liebert; m. Birgitta Haraldson 1971; ed Univ. of Cambridge; Commonwealth Fellowship, USA 1965–67; Dept of Genetics, Univ. of Cambridge 1967–69, Staff Scientist, MRC Lab. of Molecular Biology, Zoology Dept 1969–2007, Jt Head, Cell Biology Div. 1984–87, Scientist Emer. 2007–; Foreign mem. Swedish Royal Acad. of Sciences 2000; Medal of Zoological Soc. of London 1977, Darwin Medal, Royal Soc. 1994, Prize Vinci d'Excellence Moët et Chandon, Paris 1996, Waddington Medal, British Soc. of Developmental Biology 2006, Prince of Asturias Award for Scientific and Tech. Research, Oviedo (co-recipient) 2007. *Publications include:* The Making of a Fly 1992; numerous scientific papers. *Leisure interests:* garden, golf, trees, fungi, ascalaphidae, theatre. *Address:* Department of Zoology, University of Cambridge, Downing Street, Cambridge, CB2 3EJ (office); MRC Laboratory of Molecular Biology, Hills Road, Cambridge, CB2 0QH (office); 9 Temple End, Great Wilbraham, CB1 5JF, England (home). *Telephone:* (1223) 769015 (office); (1223) 880505 (home). *E-mail:* pal38@cam.ac.uk (office). *Website:* www.zoo.cam.ac.uk (office); www.making-of-a-fly.me (office).

LAWRENCE, Robert Swan, BA, MD; American physician and academic; *Center for a Livable Future Professor Emeritus, Bloomberg School of Public Health, Johns Hopkins University;* b. 6 Feb. 1938, Philadelphia, Pa; s. of Thomas George Lawrence and Catherine Swan Lawrence; m. Cynthia Starr Cole 1960; three s. two d.; ed Harvard Coll. and Medical School; Internal Medicine Residency, Mass Gen. Hosp. 1964–66, 1969–70; Medical Epidemiologist, Center for Disease Control, US Public Health Service, Atlanta 1966–69; Asst to Assoc. Prof. of Medicine, Dir Div. of Community Medicine, NC Univ. School of Medicine 1970–74; Dir Div. of Primary Care, Asst to Assoc. Prof. of Medicine, Harvard Medical School 1974–91, Charles Davidson Assoc. Prof. of Medicine 1981–91; Assoc. Chief of Medicine, Cambridge Hosp. 1974–77, Chief of Medicine, Dir Dept of Medicine 1980–91; Dir Health Sciences, Rockefeller Foundation 1991–95; Adjunct Prof. of Medicine, New York Univ. 1991–95; Prof. of Health Policy, Assoc. Dean for Professional Educ. and Dir Center for a Livable Future, Bloomberg School of Public Health, Johns Hopkins Univ., 1995–2006, Prof. of Medicine, Johns Hopkins School of Medicine 1996–, Edyth Schoenrich Prof. of Preventive Medicine 2000–06, Prof. of Environmental Health Sciences 2006–, apptd inaugural Center for a Livable Future Prof. 2008, now Prof. Emer.; Chair. US Preventive Services Task Force, Dept of Health and Human Services, US Govt 1984–89, mem. 1990–95; Ed. American Journal of Preventive Medicine 1990–92; Pres. Physicians for Human Rights 1998–2002, Chair. Bd Trustees 2007–13; mem. Nat. Acad. of Medicine, NAS 1978; Trustee, Teachers' Coll., Columbia Univ. 1991–97; Fellow, American Coll. of Preventive Medicine; Master, American Coll. of Physicians; Maimonides Prize 1964, John Atkinson Ferrell Prize, UNC 1998, Special Recognition Award, American Coll. of Preventive Medicine 1988, Duncan Clark Lecturer, Asscn of Teachers of Preventive Medicine 1993, Leadership Award, Soc. for Gen. Internal Medicine 1996, Albert Schweitzer Humanitarian Award 2002, Sedgwick Memorial Medal, American Public Health Asscn 2009. *Publications:* Co-Ed. Preventing Disease: Beyond the Rhetoric 1990, Health Promotion and Disease Prevention in Clinical Practice 1996, International Perspectives on Environment, Development and Health 1997; 110 articles in scientific journals. *Address:* Johns Hopkins Bloomberg School of Public Health, 615 N Wolfe Street, Room W7010, Baltimore, MD 21205 (office); 82 Pascal Avenue, Rockport, ME 04856, USA (home). *Telephone:* (410) 223-1811 (office); (207) 230-8162 (home). *Fax:* (410) 223-1829 (office). *E-mail:* rlawrenc@jhsph.edu (office). *Website:* www.jhsph.edu/clf (office).

LAWRENCE, Walter Nicholas Murray, MA; British underwriting agent; b. 8 Feb. 1935, London, England; s. of Henry Walter Neville Lawrence and Sarah Schuyler Lawrence (née Butler); m. Sally Louise O'Dwyer 1961; two d.; ed Winchester Coll., Trinity Coll., Oxford; with C.T. Bowring & Co. Ltd 1957–62, 1976–84, Treaty Dept 1957–62, Dir 1976–84; with Harvey Bowring and Others 1962–84, Asst Underwriter 1962–70, Underwriter 1970–84; Dir C.T. Bowring (Underwriting Agencies) Ltd 1973–84; Chair. Fairway Underwriting Agencies Ltd 1979–85; mem. Lloyd's Underwriter's Non-Marine Asscn, Deputy Chair. 1977, Chair. 1978; served Cttee of Lloyd's 1979–82, 1991, Deputy Chair. 1982, mem. Council of Lloyd's 1984–91, Deputy Chair. 1984–87, Chair. 1988–90; Dir, Chair. Murray Lawrence Holdings Ltd 1988–94, Murray Lawrence Members Agency Ltd 1988–92, Murray Lawrence & Partners Ltd (now Amlin Underwriting Ltd) 1989–93; Dir, Cbs Services No 1 Ltd 1991–95, Amlin Underwriting Ltd 1991–96,

Amlin Corporate Services Ltd 1992–97, Amlin Dedicated Ltd 1994–96, Amlin Corporate Member Ltd 1994–96, Asta Management Services Ltd 1993–96, Benenden School (Kent) Ltd 1992–98, The Benenden School Trust 1998–2008. *Leisure interests:* golf, opera, travel. *Address:* c/o Amlin Underwriting Ltd, St Helen's, 1 Undershaft, London, EC3A 8ND, England.

LAWSON, Lesley (Twiggy); British model, singer and actress; b. 19 Sept. 1949, London; d. of William Hornby and Helen Hornby (née Reeman); m. 1st Michael Whitney Armstrong 1977 (died 1983); one d.; m. 2nd Leigh Lawson 1988; ed Brondesbury and Kilburn Grammar School; model 1966–70; f. Twiggy Enterprises Ltd 1966; f. Twiggy & Co. 1998; launched Twiggy skin care range 2001; as designer has her own clothing line for HSN and M&S; two Golden Globe Awards 1970. *Recordings include:* several albums including Twiggy 1976, Please Get My Name Right 1977, Best of Twiggy 1999, Gotta Sing, Gotta Dance 2009, Romantically Yours 2011. *Films include:* The Boy Friend 1971, W 1974, There Goes the Bride 1980, The Doctor and the Devils 1985, Club Paradise 1986, Madame Sousatzka 1988, Istanbul 1989, Edge of Seventeen 1998, Woundings 1998. *Plays include:* Cinderella 1976, Captain Beaky 1982, My One and Only 1983–84, Blithe Spirit, Chichester 1997, Noel and Gertie, USA 1998, If Love Were All, New York 1999, Blithe Spirit, New York 2002, Play What I Wrote 2002, Mrs Warren's Profession 2003. *Television includes:* Twiggy (musical series) 1975–76, Young Charlie Chaplin (series) 1989, Princesses (series) 1991, has appeared in numerous TV dramas in UK and USA; chat shows include Twiggy's People 1998, Take Time with Twiggy 2001, This Morning 2001. *Publications include:* Twiggy: An Autobiography 1975, An Open Look 1985, Twiggy in Black and White 1997, A Guide to Looking and Feeling Fabulous over Forty 2008. *Leisure interests:* music, design. *Address:* Peters, Fraser and Dunlop, Drury House, 34-43 Russell Street, London, WC2B 5HA, England (office). *E-mail:* info@twiggylawson.co.uk. *Website:* www.twiggylawson.co.uk.

LAWSON, Sonia, MA, RA, RWS; British artist; b. 2 June 1934, Darlington, Co. Durham; d. of Frederick Lawson and Muriel Metcalfe; m. Charles William Congo 1969; one d.; ed Royal Coll. of Art, London; travelling scholarship to France 1956–60; one of four young artists for John Schlesinger's BBC TV documentary 1960; Visiting Lecturer, Royal Acad. Schools 1985–; Lorne Scholarship, Univ. of London 1986–87; works in collections including Arts Council, Great Britain, Belfast Art Gallery, Bolton Art Gallery, Carlisle Art Gallery, Cartwright Hall, Bradford, Chatsworth Collection, Graves Art Gallery, Sheffield, Harrogate Art Gallery, Huddersfield Art Gallery, Imperial War Museum, Leeds Univ., Middlesbrough Art Gallery, Nuffield Collection, Rochdale Art Gallery, RCA Collection, Royal Acad. of Arts Collection, Univ. of Birmingham, The Vatican, Rome, Wakefield Art Gallery; works commissioned by Imperial War Museum, BAOR 1984, Lambeth Palace for the Pope 1989, drawings for Look at it This Way! (collection of poems) by James Kirkup 1993, two related works for Univ. Centre, Birmingham 1994, New Year's Eve (short story) by Fay Weldon 1995, Barclays Capital Paris 1998; Rowney Drawing Prize 1984, Eastern Arts Drawing Prize 1984, 1989, Lorne Award 1987, Eastern Art Drawing Prize 1990. *Address:* c/o Royal Academy of Arts, Burlington House, Piccadilly, London, W1V 0DS, England. *Telephone:* (20) 7300-5680 (Academicians' Affairs Office). *Fax:* (20) 7300-5812. *E-mail:* art@sonialawson.co.uk (home). *Website:* www.sonialawson.co.uk.

LAWSON OF BLABY, Baron (Life Peer), cr. 1992, of Newnham in the County of Northamptonshire; **Nigel Lawson,** PC, BA (Hons PPE), MA; British politician and business executive; b. 11 March 1932, London, England; s. of Ralph Lawson and Joan Elisabeth Lawson (née Davis); m. 1st Vanessa Salmon 1955 (divorced 1980); m. 2nd Thérèse Mary Maclear 1980 (divorced 2012); two s. four d. (one deceased); ed Westminster School and Christ Church, Oxford (Scholar); Sub-Lt, RNVR 1954–56, CO HM MTB Gay Charger; mem. editorial staff, Financial Times 1956–60; City Ed. Sunday Telegraph 1961–63; Special Asst to Prime Minister Sir Alec Douglas-Home 1963–64; Financial Times columnist and BBC broadcaster 1965; Ed. The Spectator 1966–70; regular contributor to Sunday Times and Evening Standard 1970–71, The Times 1971–72; Fellow, Nuffield Coll. Oxford 1972–73; Special Political Adviser, Conservative Party HQ 1973–74; MP for Blaby, Leics. 1974–92; Opposition Whip 1976–77; Opposition spokesman on Treasury and Econ. Affairs 1977–79; Financial Sec. to the Treasury 1979–81; Sec. of State for Energy 1981–83, Chancellor of the Exchequer 1983–89; mem. (Conservative) House of Lords 1992–, House of Lords Econ. Affairs Cttee 2004–08, 2010–15; Dir (non-exec.), Barclays Bank 1990–98; Chair. Central Europe Trust Co. Ltd 1990–2012; Chair. Oxford Investment Partners (OXIP) 2006–13; Founding Chair. Global Warming Policy Foundation 2009–; Chair. Vote Leave Feb.–March 2016, mem. Campaign Cttee 2016; Pres. British Inst. of Energy Econs 1995–2003; Dir Inst. for Int. Econs, Wash. 1991–2001; Founding Chair. Global Warming Policy Forum 2016–; mem. Governing Body, Westminster School 1999–2005, Fellow 2005–; Hon. Student, Christ Church, Oxford 1996; Hon. DSc (Buckingham) 2011; Finance Minister of the Year, Euromoney Magazine 1988, IEA Nat. Free Enterprise Award 2008, Mousquetaire d'Armagnac 2010. *Publications include:* The Power Game (with Jock Bruce-Gardyne) 1976, The View from No. 11 1992 (revised edn as Memoirs of a Tory Radical 2010), The Nigel Lawson Diet Book (with Thérèse Lawson) 1996, An Appeal to Reason: A Cool Look at Global Warming 2008, Memoirs of Tory Radical 2010; various pamphlets. *Address:* House of Lords, Westminster, London, SW1A 0PW, England (office). *Telephone:* (20) 7219-3000 (office). *E-mail:* rathbonea@parliament.uk (office).

LAWTON, Sir John Hartley, Kt, CBE, BSc, PhD, FRS; British ecologist and academic; *President, Institution of Environmental Sciences;* b. 24 Sept. 1943, Preston, Lancs.; s. of Frank Hartley and Mary Lawton; m. Dot (Lady Dorothy) Lawton; one s. one d.; ed Univ. of Durham; Lecturer in Zoology, St Anne's and Lincoln Coll., Univ. of Oxford 1968–71; Lecturer, Sr Lecturer, Reader then Prof. of Biology, York Univ. 1972–89; Founding Dir Centre for Population Biology, Natural Environment Research Council (NERC), Imperial Coll. London, Silwood Park 1989–99, Chief Exec. Natural Environment Research Council 1999–2005; Adviser to Royal Comm. on Environmental Pollution 1986–89, mem. 1990–96, Chair. 2005–11; Chair. Royal Soc. for the Protection of Birds 1993–98, currently Vice-Pres.; Pres. Council of British Ecological Soc. 2005–07; Vice-Pres. British Trust for Ornithology 2002–08; Pres. and Chair., York Museums Trust 2012–; Pres., Inst. of Environmental Sciences 2015–; Trustee, WWF-UK 2002–08, currently Fellow; Chair. Yorkshire Wildlife Trust 2009–14; Scientific Adviser and Presenter, The

300 Million Years War, BBC 1985 and The State of the Planet 2000; Foreign mem. American Acad. of Arts and Sciences, Nat. Acad. of Sciences; Patron, Inst. of Ecology and Environmental Man. 2011; Hon. Fellow, Royal Entomological Soc. 2001, Zoological Soc. of London 2007, British Ecological Soc. 2009, Inst. of Environmental Sciences 2011, Soc. for the Environment 2013; Hon. DSc (Lancaster), (Birmingham), (East Anglia), (York), (Aberdeen), (Imperial Coll.); Pres.'s Gold Medal, British Ecological Soc. 1987, Frink Medal, Zoological Soc. of London 1998, La Roe Award, Soc. for Conservation Biology 2002, Japan Prize for Science and Tech. for Conservation of Biodiversity 2004, Ramon Margalef Prize in Ecology and Environmental Science 2006, RSPB Medal 2011. *Publications:* author or ed. of five books and more than 320 papers, articles and book chapters. *Leisure interests:* bird watching, gardening, natural history, walking, cooking, playing with his grandchildren.

LAX, Peter David, AB, PhD; American mathematician and academic; *Professor Emeritus of Mathematics, Courant Institute of Mathematics, New York University;* b. 1 May 1926, Budapest, Hungary; s. of Henry Lax and Klara Kornfeld; m. Anneli Cahn 1948 (died 1999); two s.; ed New York Univ.; with Los Alamos Scientific Lab., Manhattan Project 1945–46; Asst Prof., New York Univ. 1951, Prof. 1957–99, Prof. Emer. 1999–, Dir AEC Computing and Applied Math. Center 1964–72, Courant Inst. of Math. Sciences 1972–80, Courant Math. and Computing Lab. 1980–; Fulbright Lecturer in Germany 1958; Visiting Lecturer, Univ. of Oxford 1969; Vice-Pres. American Math. Soc. 1969–71, Pres. 1978–80; mem. Nat. Science Bd 1980–86; mem. American Acad. of Arts and Sciences 1982, NAS 1982, American Philosophical Soc. 1996, Moscow Math. Soc. 1995, Norwegian Acad. of Science and Letters; Foreign Assoc. French Acad. of Sciences 1982, Academia Sinica 1993, Hungarian Acad. of Sciences 1993; Foreign mem. Soviet (now Russian) Acad. of Sciences 1989; Fellow, American Math. Soc.; Hon. Life mem. New York Acad. of Sciences 1982; Dr hc (Kent State) 1975, (Paris) 1979, (Tech. Univ. of Aachen) 1988, (Heriot Watt) 1990, (Tel-Aviv) 1992, (Univ. of Maryland, Baltimore) 1993, (Brown) 1993, (Beijing) 1993, (Texas A&M) 2000; Lester R. Ford Award 1966, 1973, Von Neumann Lecturer, S.I.A.M. 1969, Hermann Weyl Lecturer 1972, Hedrick Lecturer 1973, Chauvenet Prize, Math. Asscn of America 1974, Norbert Wiener Prize, American Math. Soc. and Soc. of Industrial and Applied Math. 1975, NAS Award in Applied Math. and Numerical Sciences 1983, Nat. Medal of Science 1986, Wolf Prize 1987, Steele Prize, American Math. Soc. (co-winner) 1992, Distinguished Teaching Award, New York Univ. 1995, Abel Prize, Norwegian Acad. of Arts and Letters 2005, Gibbs Lecturer, American Math. Soc. 2007, Lomonosov Gold Medal, Russian Acad. of Sciences (co-recipient) 2013. *Publications:* Recent Advances in Partial Differential Equations, Mathematical Aspects of Production and Distribution of Energy, Nonlinear Partial Differential Equations in Applied Science, Decay of Solutions of Systems of Nonlinear Hyperbolic Conservation Laws (co-author) 1970, Calculus with Applications and Computing (co-author) 1979, Hyperbolic Systems of Conservation Laws and the Mathematical Theory of Shock Waves 1987, Scattering Theory (co-author) 1989, Recent Mathematical Methods in Nonlinear Wave Propagation (co-author) 1996, Scattering Theory for Automorphic Functions (co-author) 2001, Functional Analysis 2002, Selected Papers. Vol. I 2005, Vol. II 2005, Hyperbolic Partial Differential Equations 2006, Linear Algebra and Its Applications (second edn) 2007; numerous papers in learned journals. *Address:* Courant Institute of Mathematics, New York University, Warren Weaver Hall, Room 912, 251 Mercer Street, New York, NY 10012, USA (office). *Telephone:* (212) 998-3232 (office). *Fax:* (212) 995-4121 (office). *E-mail:* lax@cims.nyu.edu (office). *Website:* www.math.nyu.edu (office).

LAXMAN, V(angipurappu) V(enkata) S(ai); Indian professional cricketer; b. 1 Nov. 1974, Hyderabad, AP; s. of Dr Shantaram Laxman and Dr Satyabhama Laxman; m. G. R. Sailaja 2004; one s. one d.; ed Little Flower High School, St John's School, studied medicine at univ.; right-handed batsman; occasional right-arm off-break bowler; plays for Hyderabad 1992–, India 1996–2012, Lancs. 2007, 2009, Deccan Chargers 2008–10 (Capt. 2008), Kochi Tuskers Kerala 2011; First-class debut: 1992/93; Test debut: India v S Africa, Ahmedabad 20–23 Nov. 1996; One-Day Int. (ODI) debut: India v Zimbabwe, Cuttack 9 April 1998; has played in 134 Tests, scored 8,781 runs (17 centuries, 56 half-centuries), highest score 281, average 45.97, best bowling 1/2; ODIs: 86 matches, 2,338 runs, highest score 131, average 30.76; First-class: 267 matches, 19,730 runs, highest score 353, average 52.64, took 22 wickets, best bowling 3/11; announced retirement from int. cricket 18 Aug. 2012; Arjuna Award, Govt of India 2001, Wisden Cricketer of the Year 2002, Padma Shri 2011, Northern Stand at Rajiv Gandhi Int. Cricket Stadium named after him 2012. *Address:* c/o Honorary Secretary, Hyderabad Cricket Association, Gymkhanna Grounds, Secunderabad, Hyderabad Urban 500 039; Hyderabad Cricket Association, Rajiv Gandhi International Cricket Stadium, Uppal, Hyderabad 500 039, India.

LAYARD, Baron (Life Peer), cr. 2000, of Highgate in the London Borough of Haringey; **Peter Richard Grenville Layard,** BA, MSc, FBA; British economist and academic; *Director, Wellbeing Programme, Centre for Economic Performance, London School of Economics;* b. 15 March 1934, Welwyn Garden City, Herts.; s. of John Willoughby Layard and Doris Layard; m. Molly Meacher 1991; ed Univ. of Cambridge, London School of Econs; school teacher, London Co. Council 1959–61; Sr Research Officer, Robbins Cttee on Higher Educ. 1961–64; Deputy Dir Higher Educ. Research Unit, LSE 1964–74, Lecturer, LSE 1968–75, Reader 1975–80, Prof. of Econs 1980–99, Prof. Emer. 1999–, Hon. Fellow 2000–, Head, Centre for Labour Econs 1974–90, Co-Dir Centre for Econ. Performance 1990–2003, currently Dir Wellbeing Programme; Consultant, Centre for European Policy Studies, Brussels 1982–86; mem. Univ. Grants Cttee 1985–89; Chair. Employment Inst. 1987–92; Co-Chair., World Economy Group of the World Inst. for Devt Econs Research 1989–93; Econ. Adviser to Russian Govt 1991–97; Fellow, Econometric Soc. 1986, European Econ. Asscn 2004; mem. (Labour) House of Lords 2000–; W.W. Leontief Medal, Russian Acad. of Natural Sciences for "achievements in economics" 2005, IZA Prize in Labor Econs (co-recipient with S. Nickell), Inst. for the Study of Labor 2008. *Publications include:* Cost Benefit Analysis 1973, Causes of Poverty (with D. Piachaud and M. Stewart) 1978, Microeconomic Theory (with A. A. Walters) 1978, More Jobs, Less Inflation 1982, The Causes of Unemployment (co-ed.) 1984, The Rise in Unemployment (co-ed.) 1986, How to Beat Unemployment 1986, Handbook of Labor Economics (co-ed.) 1987, The Performance of the British Economy (co-author) 1988, Unemployment: Macroeconomic Performance and the Labour Market (co-author) 1991 (second edn 2005), East-West Migration: the alternatives (co-author) 1992, Post-Communist Reform: Pain and Progress 1993 (co-author), Macroeconomics: A Text for Russia 1994, The Coming Russian Boom 1996 (co-author), What Labour Can Do 1997, Tackling Unemployment 1999, Tackling Inequality 1999, What the Future Holds (co-ed.), Happiness: Lessons from a New Science 2005 (second edn 2011), A Good Childhood (with J. Dunn) 2009, Thrive 2014. *Leisure interests:* walking, tennis. *Address:* Centre for Economic Performance, London School of Economics, Houghton Street, London, WC2A 2AE (office); 45 Cholmeley Park, London, N6 5EL, England (home). *Telephone:* (20) 7955-7048 (office). *Fax:* (20) 7955-7595 (office). *E-mail:* r.layard@lse.ac.uk (office). *Website:* cep.lse.ac.uk/layard (office).

LAYDEN, Anthony Michael, CMG, LLB (Hons); British diplomatist (retd); *Chairman, Centre des Etudes Euro-Méditerranéennes et Africaines (CEMAS);* b. 27 July 1946; m. Josephine Layden; three s. one d.; ed Holy Cross Acad., Edinburgh, Univ. of Edinburgh; Lt 15th (Scottish Volunteer) Batallion, Parachute Regiment 1966–69; joined British Diplomatic Service 1968, Desk Officer, Atomic Energy and Disarmament Dept, FCO 1968–69; at Middle East Centre for Arab Studies 1969–71; Second Sec., Jedda 1971–73, First Sec. and Head of Chancery, Rome 1973–77, Desk Officer, Middle East Dept 1977–79, Rhodesia Dept 1979–80, Personnel Operations Dept 1980–82, Head of Chancery, Jedda 1982–85, Deputy Head of Hong Kong Dept, FCO 1985–87, Deputy Head of Mission, Muscat 1987–91, Counsellor, later Deputy Head of Mission, Copenhagen 1991–95, Head of W European Dept, FCO 1995–98, Amb. to Morocco 1999–2002, to Libya 2002–06; Foreign Sec.'s Special Rep. for Deportation with Assurances 2006–13; Chair. The British Moroccan Soc. 2007–14, Hon. Life Pres. 2014–; Chair. Centre des Etudes Euro-Méditerranéennes et Africaines (CEMAS) 2015–; Pres. Soc. for Libyan Studies 2009; Chair. Travellers Club 2010–14. *Leisure interests:* sailing, hill walking, bridge. *Address:* Centre des Etudes Euro-Méditerranéennes et Africaines, City Business Centre, Unit 17, Lower Road, London, SE16 2XB, England (office). *Telephone:* (20) 7252-3000 (office). *E-mail:* cemas-london@gmail.com (office). *Website:* www.cemas.org.uk (office); www.britishmoroccansociety.org (office).

LAYNE, Kingsley, BA; Saint Vincent and the Grenadines civil servant and diplomatist; b. 1949; ed Univ. of the West Indies, Univ. of British Columbia, Inst. for Applied Behavioural Sciences; economist, Ministry of Trade, Agric. and Tourism 1973–74; Sr Official, Econ. Affairs Secr., Org. of Eastern Caribbean States, St John's, Antigua 1982–86; Perm. Sec., Ministry of Trade, Agric. and Industry 1986–87, Tourism, Aviation and Culture 1987–89, Trade and Tourism 1989–90; Amb. and Perm. Rep. to UN, New York 1990–94, Amb. to USA 1991–2000, Perm. Rep. to OAS, Vice-Chair. –1999; mem. New Democratic Party. *Publications:* several publs on staff devt and man. training.

LAYTON, Donald H., BS, MS, MBA; American business executive; *CEO, Freddie Mac (Federal Home Loan Mortgage Corporation);* ed Massachusetts Inst. of Tech., Harvard Business School; joined predecessor of JPMorgan Chase as a trainee 1980s, responsible for Treasury & Securities Services (operating services unit of the co.) 1999–2004, responsible for Chase's worldwide capital markets and trading activities prior to merger of Chase Manhattan and J.P. Morgan 2000, Co-CEO J.P. Morgan (investment bank of the co.) 2000–02, responsible for Chase Financial Services 2002–04, Vice-Chair. and mem. of three-person Office of the Chair., retd 2004; Chair. and then CEO E*TRADE Financial 2007–09; mem. bds of several financial services firms; Sr Advisor, Securities Industry and Financial Markets Asscn 2006–08; CEO Freddie Mac (Fed. Home Loan Mortgage Corpn) 2012–; Chair. Partnership for the Homeless, New York City. *Address:* Freddie Mac, 8200 Jones Branch Drive, McLean, VA 22102-3110, USA (office). *Telephone:* (703) 903-2000 (office). *E-mail:* info@freddiemac.com (office). *Website:* www.freddiemac.com (office).

LAZAR, Philippe; French scientist and administrator (retd); b. 21 April 1936, Paris; s. of Maximilien Lazar and Françoise Lazar; m. Monique Lazar 1960; one s. one d.; ed Ecole Polytechnique, Paris; researcher, Nat. Inst. of Hygiene 1960, Dir of Research Institut Nat. de la Santé et de la Recherche Médicale (INSERM) 1964, Dir Environmental Health Research Unit 1977, Chair. Scientific Council 1981, Dir-Gen. INSERM 1982–96; Chair. European Medical Research Councils (EMRC) 1994–96; Chair. Bd Research Inst. for Devt (IRD) 1997–2001; with Cour des Comptes 2001–05; Visiting Prof. Harvard School of Public Health 1975; Officier, Légion d'honneur 1994, Chevalier, Ordre des Arts et des Lettres 1994, Commdr, Ordre nat. du Mérite 1999. *Publications:* Eléments de probabilités et statistiques 1967, Méthodes statistiques en expérimentation biologique 1974, Les explorateurs de la santé 1989, L'éthique biomédicale en question 1995, La République a-t-elle besoin de savants? 1998, Autrement dit laïque 2003, Court traité de l'âme 2008. *Leisure interests:* arts, literature. *Address:* 9 rue Friant, 75014 Paris, France. *Telephone:* (6) 81-11-80-67. *E-mail:* philippe.lazar@orange.fr.

LAZĂR, Valeriu, BEng; Moldovan politician; b. 20 May 1968, Mingir, Hînceşti Dist; m.; two c.; ed Agrarian State Univ. of Moldova, Inst. Int. d'Admin Publique, Paris, France, European Inst. of Public Admin, Bruges, Belgium; joined Ministry of Devt 1994, Special Co-ordinator, Nat. Agency for Promoting Foreign Investment 1994, Dir Foreign Econ. Relations Dept 1994–96, Adviser to Minister of Economy 1996–98, Adviser to Deputy Prime Minister 1998–99, Deputy Prime Minister 1999, Deputy Minister of Economy 2004–05, Deputy Prime Minister and Minister of the Economy 2009–13; Rep. for Moldova to EBRD and Multilateral Investment Guarantee Agency 2005–06; Exec. Dir Business Intelligent Services SRL 2000–04, 2006–09; Exec. Dir BIS-Capital Investment House Ltd 2007–09; mem. Parl. 2009–; mem. Democratic Party of Moldova (Partidului Democrat din Moldova), currently Sec.-Gen. *Address:* Democratic Party of Moldova (PDM—Partidul Democrat din Moldova) 2001 Chişinău, str. Tighina 32, Moldova. *Telephone:* (22) 27-82-29. *Fax:* (22) 27-82-30. *E-mail:* pdm@mtc.md. *Website:* www.pdm.md.

LAZARAN, Frank, BSc; American retail executive; *Founder, Galazarano Investments & Consulting;* b. 1957; ed California State Univ.-Long Beach, Univ. of Southern Calif.; joined Ralphs Grocery Co., Compton, Calif. 1974, various positions including Group Vice-Pres. of Sales, Advertising and Merchandising –1997; Sr Vice-Pres. of Sales, Merchandising and Logistics, Randalls Food Markets, Inc., Houston, Tex. 1997–99, Pres. 1999–2002; Exec. Vice-Pres. and COO Winn-Dixie Stores Inc., Jacksonville, Fla 2002–03, Pres., CEO and Dir 2003–04; Chair. City Markets 2003–04; Chair., Pres. and CEO Marsh Supermarkets, Inc. 2006–11; Founder Galazarano Investments & Consulting 2012–; mem. Gov.'s Advisory Bd, State of Tex. 1999–2002, Greater Houston Partnership 1999–2002; mem. Gator Bowl Cttee Asscn 2003–04, 2004 Super Bowl Host Cttee 2004; mem. Bd Jacksonville Zoo and Gardens 2003–04; mem. Advisory Bd NGB Markets 2012–, Magical Brands 2013–. *Address:* NGB Markets, 555 Bryant Street, #237, Palo Alto, CA 94301, USA. *Telephone:* (650) 646-4931. *E-mail:* info@ngbmarkets.com. *Website:* www.ngbmarkets.com.

LAZARIDIS, Mike, OC, FRSC; Canadian engineer, inventor and business executive; b. Istanbul, Turkey; s. of Nick Lazaridis and Dorothy Lazaridis; m. Celia Lazaridis; one s. one d.; ed Univ. of Waterloo; emigrated to Canada with family aged five 1966; awarded industrial automation contract by General Motors 1984; Founder, Co-Chair., Pres. and Co-CEO Research in Motion Ltd (name changed to BlackBerry 2013) (designer and manufacturer of wireless electronic products) 1984–2012 (resgnd), mem. Bd of Dirs 1984–; est. Perimeter Inst. for Theoretical Physics, Univ. of Waterloo 2000; Chancellor Univ. of Waterloo 2003–; inventor of BlackBerry wireless e-mail pager device 1991; Order of Ont.; Hon. DEng (Waterloo), Dr hc (McMaster, Windsor, Laval); numerous industry and community awards for innovations for wireless radio tech. and software, including Academy Award for Tech. Achievement for invention of digital barcode reader for film editing 1999; named by readers of newspaper The Globe and Mail as Canada's Nation Builder of the Year 2002, Ernest C. Manning Principal Award. *Publications:* more than 30 patents. *Leisure interests:* cinema, cars. *Address:* c/o Board of Directors, BlackBerry, 295 Phillip Street, Waterloo, ON N2L 3W87, Canada.

LAZARUS, Henry (see SLAVITT, David Rytman).

LAZARUS, Rochelle (Shelly), BA, MBA; American advertising executive; *Chairman Emeritus, Ogilvy & Mather Worldwide;* b. 1 Sept. 1947, New York; m. George Lazarus; three c.; ed Smith Coll., Columbia Univ. Business School; with Clairol 1970; with Ogilvy & Mather 1971–74, 1976–, Pres. Ogilvy & Mather Direct US 1989–91, Pres. Ogilvy & Mather Advertising, New York 1991–94, Pres. Ogilvy N America 1994–95, Pres. and COO Ogilvy & Mather Worldwide 1995–96, CEO 1996–2009, Chair. 1997–2012, Chair. Emer. 2012–; mem. Bd of Dirs General Electric, New York Presbyterian Hosp., World Wildlife Fund, Merck & Co. 2004–, The Blackstone Group, FINRA; mem. Bd of Dirs Partnership for New York City, Lincoln Center for Performing Arts; mem. Bd Overseers Columbia Business School, Cttee to Encourage Corp. Philanthropy; mem. Council on Foreign Relations, Business Council, Advertising Women of New York, Cttee of 200, Women's Forum, American Asscn of Advertising Agencies' Advisory Council, Yale Pres.'s Council on Int. Activities, Advisory Bd Judge Inst. of Man. Studies, Cambridge Univ. (UK); fmr Chair. American Asscn of Advertising Agencies, Bd Trustees Smith Coll.; Distinguished Leadership Award in Business, Columbia Business School (first woman recipient), Lifetime Achievement Award, Advertising Educational Foundation, inducted into Direct Marketing Asscn Hall of Fame, American Advertising Fed. Hall of Fame 2013, numerous advertising, communications, and business leadership awards. *Address:* Ogilvy & Mather Worldwide, 636 11th Avenue, New York, NY 10036, USA (office). *Telephone:* (212) 237-4000 (office). *Fax:* (917) 475-3628 (office). *Website:* www.ogilvy.com (office).

LAZENBY, Alec, AO, ScD, FIBiol; Australian/British agronomist and university administrator (retd); b. 4 March 1927, UK; s. of G. Lazenby and E. Lazenby; m. Ann J. Hayward 1957; one s. two d.; ed Univ. Coll. of Wales and Univ. of Cambridge, UK; Scientific Officer, Welsh Plant Breeding Station 1949–53; Demonstrator, Agricultural Botany, Univ. of Cambridge 1953–58, Lecturer in Agricultural Botany 1958–65, Fellow and Asst Tutor, Fitzwilliam Coll. 1962–65; Foundation Prof. of Agronomy, Univ. of New England, NSW 1965–70, Vice-Chancellor 1970–77; Dir Grassland Research Inst. 1977–82; Visiting Prof., Reading Univ. 1978–82; Hon. Professorial Fellow, Univ. of Wales 1979–82; Vice-Chancellor, Univ. of Tasmania 1982–91; consultant in higher educ. and agricultural research and man. 1991–2012; Fellow, Australian Acad. of Technological Sciences, Australian Inst. of Agricultural Science and Tech.; Hon. Prof., Victoria Univ. of Tech. 1992; Hon. DRurSci (New England) 1981; Hon. LLD (Tasmania) 1992; Centenary Medal for contrib. to Rural Science and Tech. 2003. *Publications include:* Intensive Pasture Production (co-ed.) 1972, Australian Field Crops (co-ed.), Vol. I 1975, Vol. II 1979, Australia's Plant Breeding Needs 1986, The Grass Crop (co-ed.) 1988, The Story of IDP 1999, Competition and Succession in Pastures (co-ed.) 2001; papers on pasture plant breeding, agronomy and weed ecology in various scientific journals. *Leisure interests:* golf, gardening, current affairs. *Address:* 16/99 Groom Street, Hughes, ACT 2605, Australia (home). *Telephone:* (2) 6281-2898 (home). *Fax:* (2) 6281-0451 (home). *E-mail:* alazenby@netspeed.com.au (home).

LAZIO, Enrico (Rick) Anthony, AB, JD; American lawyer, business executive and politician; *Partner, Jones Walker LLP;* b. 13 March 1958, Amityville, Suffolk Co., NY; s. of Anthony Lazio and Olive E. Lazio (née Christensen); m. Patricia Moriarty; two d.; ed Vassar Coll., American Univ. Washington Coll. of Law; called to New York Bar 1984; Asst Dist Attorney, Suffolk Co. Rackets Bureau, Hauppage, NY 1983–88, Exec. Asst Dist Attorney, Suffolk Co. 1987–88, Village Attorney, Village of Lindenhurst, NY 1988–93; Man. Partner, Glass, Lazio & Glass, Babylon, NY 1989–93; mem. Suffolk Co. Legis. from 11th Dist, NY 1989–93, mem. House of Reps, Deputy Majority Whip, then Asst Majority Leader 1993–2000; cand. for Senate, New York State 2000; Pres. and CEO Financial Services Forum 2001–05; Exec. Vice-Pres. Global Govt Affairs and Public Policy, JPMorgan Chase & Co.; unsuccessful cand. for New York Republican gubernatorial nomination 2010; Sr Advisor, Dynasty Financial Partners 2011–12; Partner, Jones Walker LLP; Sr Dir, Alliantgroup; Dir, United Guaranty Corpn, Polaroid Holding Co., TB Woods Co.; mem. Enterprise Community Partners, Bretton Woods Cttee, Tomorrow's Hope Foundation, Int. Conservation Caucus Foundation, Dean's Advisory Cttee of American Univ. Washington Coll. of Law, Pres.'s Advisory Council, Vassar Coll. *Leisure interests:* numismatics, guitar. *Address:* Jones Walker, 350 5th Avenue, Suite 5200, New York, NY 10118, USA (office). *Telephone:* (212) 759-7025 (office). *E-mail:* lazioadvisors@gmail.com. *Website:* lazio.com.

LAZOVIĆ, Vujica, PhD; Montenegrin economist, academic and politician; b. 10 March 1963, Plav; m.; one d.; ed Univ. of Podgorica; fmr mem. Faculty of Econs, Univ. of Montenegro, Vice-Dean 1998–2000, Dean 2001–06; currently Prof. of Econs and Dean of Faculty of Econs, Univ. of Podgorica; Deputy Prime Minister,

responsible for Econ. Policy 2006–09, Deputy Prime Minister, responsible for Econ. Policy and the Financial System and Minister of the Information Society and Telecommunications 2009–16; several awards, including 19 December Liberation of Podgorica Award, Veljko Vlahović Univ. Award for the best success in final year of study. *Publications include:* numerous books and articles on economics; conducted several studies in UK and USA. *Address:* c/o Office of the Chairman of the Government, 81000 Podgorica, Karađorđeva bb, Montenegro. *E-mail:* kabinet@mfa.gov.me (office).

LAZRAQ, Alami; Moroccan business executive; *President and Director-General, Groupe Alliances;* m.; three c.; ed Ecole Speciale d'Architecture, France; started career as Head of Studies and Realization Dept, Ministry of Habous (Islamic land legislation) 1976; Man. Dir Etablissement Regional d'Amenagement et de Construction du Tensift 1978; joined Groupe Omnium Nord Africain 1989; f. Groupe Alliances 1994, currently Pres. and Dir-Gen.; Chair. Al Maaden Golf Resort. *Address:* Groupe Alliances, 16, rue Ali Abderazak, Casablanca, Morocco (office). *Telephone:* (522) 993480 (office). *Fax:* (522) 993481 (office). *Website:* www.alliances.co.ma (office).

LAZUTKIN, Valentin Valentinovich, CandPhil; Russian politician and journalist; b. 10 Jan. 1945, Kraskovo, Moscow Region; m.; one s. one d.; ed Moscow State Univ., Acad. of Social Sciences Cen. Cttee CPSU; Head Div. of Press and Information Cttee of Youth Orgs 1967–73; Deputy Head, Head Dept of Int. Relations, mem. Exec. Bd, Deputy Chair. USSR State Cttee on Radio and TV 1974–91; First Deputy Chair. 1991, Deputy Chair., Dir-Gen. of Int. Relations, Russian State TV-Radio Broadcasting Co. Ostankino 1991–93; First Deputy Chair. Feb.–Dec. 1993, First Deputy Head Russian Fed. Service on TV and Radio Broadcasting, concurrently Dir-Gen. Russian State TV-Radio Broadcasting Co. Ostankino 1993–95; Head Russian Fed. Service on TV and Radio Broadcasting 1995–98; Rector Humanitarian Inst. of Television and Radio Broadcasting 1998–; Chair. Interstate TV Service, Union of Russia and Belarus 1998–, Coordinating Bd Soyuz (Union) Media Group 2001–, Moscow TV Center Channel –2005; Deputy Head Exec. Cttee Union of Russia and Belarus 2000–; Dir Nat. TV Broadcasters Asscn, Russian CATV Asscn; mem. Bd Dirs Moscow CableCom 2004–; mem. Russian TV Acad., Int. TV Acad., Russia Acad. of Natural Sciences; Officier des Arts et Lettres, Peter the Great Prize and other decorations. *Leisure interests:* history, military heraldry. *Address:* c/o M. Sufott, Porzio, Bromberg & Newman, 156 West 56th Street, New York, NY 10019, USA; Humanitarian Institute of Television and Radio Broadcasting, Brodnikov per. 3, 109186 Moscow, Russia (office). *Telephone:* (495) 238-19-75 (office).

LE, Duc Thuy, PhD; Vietnamese government official and fmr central banker; b. 30 June 1948, Ha Tinh Prov.; ed Nat. Econs Univ., Hanoi, postgraduate studies in USSR; mem. Party Cen. Cttee; Asst in Econs to Prime Minister and to Gen. Sec. of CP early 1990s; joined State Bank of Viet Nam 1996, Deputy Gov. –1999, Gov. 1999–2007, Gov. for Viet Nam, IMF, Washington, DC; Vice-Chair. Nat. Financial, Monetary Policy Advisory Council 2007–11; Visiting Scholar, Harvard Inst. for Int. Devt, USA 1991–92.

LE, Hon. Hieu Van, AC, BEcons, MBA; Australian (b. Vietnamese) accountant and government official; *Governor of South Australia;* b. 1954, Quang Tri, South Vietnam; m. Lan T. Phuong Le; two s.; ed Dalat Univ., Viet Nam, Univ. of Adelaide; fled Viet Nam 1977, came by boat via Malaysia to Darwin as a refugee; Sr Investigator, later Sr Man.– Financial Services Regulation, Australian Securities and Investments Comm. 1991–2009; mem. South Australian Multicultural and Ethnic Affairs Comm. 1995–, Deputy Chair. 2001–07, Chair. 2007–14; Lt-Gov. of South Australia 2007–14, Gov. 2014–; mem. Australian Soc. of Certified Practising Accountants; Fellow mem. Financial Services Inst. of Australasia (Finsia); Australia Day Medal 1996, Australian Centenary of Fed. Medal 2001; Dr hc (Adelaide) 2008, (Flinders) 2011. *Address:* Government House, GPO Box 2373, Adelaide, SA 5001, Australia (office). *Telephone:* (8) 8203-9800 (office). *Fax:* (8) 8203-9899 (office). *E-mail:* governors.office@sa.gov.au (office). *Website:* www.governor.sa.gov.au (office).

LE, Gen. Kha Phieu; Vietnamese army officer and politician; b. 27 Dec. 1931, Dong Khe Commune, Dong Son Dist, Thanh Hoa Prov.; ed Viet Nam Mil. Coll.; joined CP 1949, served in several positions 1964–93 including Regt's Political Commissar and Commdr of the Regiment, Deputy Chief Army Political Dept of Second Army Corps, Deputy Political Commissar and Chief Political Dept of Ninth Mil. Zone, Maj.-Gen., Chief of Political Dept and Deputy Political Commdr of 719 Front, Lt-Gen., Deputy Chief and then Sr Lt-Gen. and Chief Gen. Political Dept Vietnamese People's Army; Gen. Sec. CP of Viet Nam 1997–2001, mem. Politburo, Politburo Standing Bd.

LE, Luong Minh, MA; Vietnamese diplomatist and international organization official; b. 1 Sept. 1952, Thanh Hoa; m.; two d.; ed Inst. of Int. Relations, Hanoi, Jawaharlal Nehru Univ., New Delhi; joined Ministry of Foreign Affairs 1975, has served in several sr positions including Deputy Dir-Gen., Dir-Gen. for Int. Orgs, Dir-Gen. for Multilateral Econ. Co-operation; Amb. and Perm. Rep. to UN and other Int. Orgs, Geneva 1995–97, Deputy Perm. Rep. to UN, New York 1997–99, Amb. and Perm. Rep. to UN 2004–11, Pres. UN Security Council July 2008–09; Asst Minister for Foreign Affairs 2007–08, Deputy Minister for Foreign Affairs 2008–11; Sec.-Gen. ASEAN 2013–17. *Address:* c/o Association of Southeast Asian Nations (ASEAN), 70a Jalan Sisingamangaraja, POB 2072, Jakarta 12110, Indonesia (office).

LE, Minh Hung; Vietnamese politician and central banker; *Governor, State Bank of Vietnam;* b. 11 Dec. 1970, Huong Son dist, Ha Tinh Prov.; s. of Le Minh Huong; ed Saitama Univ., Japan; IMF Specialist, Int. Relations Dept, State Bank of Vietnam 1993–96, Deputy Dir-Gen. and Head of Dept of Int. Cooperation 2002–09, mem. Party Comm., Dept of Organization and Personnel 2010–11, Deputy Gov. 2011–14, Gov. 2016–; Deputy Head, later Head, Asian Devt Bank 1998–2002; Deputy Chief, Gen. Office, CP of Viet Nam 2014–16, mem. Central Cttee Jan.–April 2016. *Address:* State Bank of Vietnam, 49 Ly Thai To Street, Hoan Kiem District, Hanoi, Viet Nam (office). *Telephone:* (84) 9343327 (office). *E-mail:* thuongtrucweb@sbv.gov.vn (office). *Website:* www.sbv.gov.vn (office).

LE, Yucheng; Chinese diplomatist; *Executive Vice-Minister of Foreign Affairs;* b. June 1963, Jiangsu Prov.; m.; one s.; staff mem. and Attaché, Dept of Soviet and

East European Affairs, Ministry of Foreign Affairs (MFA) 1986–90, Attaché, Embassy in Moscow, USSR 1990–91, Third Sec., then Second Sec., Embassy in Moscow, Russian Fed. 1991–93, Deputy Dir, then Dir Dept of East European and Cen. Asian Affairs, MFA 1993–98, Counsellor, Perm. Mission to UN, New York 1998–2001, Counsellor and Deputy Dir Gen., Dept of East European and Cen. Asian Affairs, MFA 2001–04, Minister Counsellor, then Minister, Embassy in Moscow 2004–08, Deputy Dir Gen., then Dir Gen., Policy Research Dept, MFA 2008–09, Dir Gen., Policy Planning Dept 2009–11, Asst Minister of Foreign Affairs 2011–13, Deputy Dir of Office of Cen. Leading Group for Foreign Affairs (also of Cen. Comm. for Foreign Affairs) 2016–18, Exec. Vice-Minister of Foreign Affairs 2018–, Amb. to Kazakhstan 2013–14, to India 2014–16. *Address:* Ministry of Foreign Affairs, 2 Chaoyangmen Nan Dajie, Chaoyang Qu, Beijing 100701, People's Republic of China (office). *Telephone:* (10) 65961114 (home). *Fax:* (11) 26885486 (office). *E-mail:* webmaster@mfa.gov.cn (office). *Website:* www.fmprc.gov.cn (office).

LE BLANC, Bart, PhD; Dutch banker and academic; *Chairman, APG Asset Management;* b. 4 Nov. 1946, Bois-le-Duc; s. of Christian Le Blanc and Johanna Bogaerts; m. Gérardine van Lanschot; one s. two d.; ed Leyden and Tilburg Univs; Special Adviser, Prime Minister's Office, Deputy Sec. to Cabinet 1973–79; Deputy Dir-Gen. for Civil Service at Home Office 1979–80; Dir-Gen. for Budget at Treasury 1980–83; Deputy Chair. Man. Bd F. van Lanschot Bankiers NV, 's-Hertogenbosch 1983–91; Sec.-Gen. EBRD, London 1991–94, Vice-Pres. of Finance 1994–98; Dir Int. Finance, Caisse des Dépôts et Consignations, Paris 1998; Chief Financial Officer, Urenco Ltd 2004–11; Chair. ETC, UK 2006–13, Andreas Capital Group SA (Luxembourg) 2010–; Chair. APG Asset Management 2014–; Chair. Investment Cttee, UN Office For Project Services; Kt, Order of Netherlands Lion 1986. *Publications:* books and contribs on econ. and fiscal policy to nat. and int. journals. *Leisure interest:* farming in France. *Address:* Nutfield Corner, Fairmile, Henley-on-Thames, RG9 2JU, England (office). *Telephone:* (14) 9157-2083 (office). *E-mail:* ljcmleblanc@gmail.com (office).

LE BRIS, Raymond-François; French professor of law and fmr university administrator; b. 18 Sept. 1935, Gouesnou; s. of François Le Bris and Bernadette Le Bris (née Lunven); m. Jacqueline Pareau 1964; one s. two d.; ed Coll. Notre-Dame-de-Bon-Secours, Brest, Univ. of Rennes; Asst Lecturer, Law Faculty, Univ. of Rennes 1958–63, Lecturer 1963–65; Prof., Univ. of Bordeaux 1965–68; Asst Dir Institut Henry-Vizioz des Antilles-Guyanne 1966; Prof., Univ. of Bretagne Occidentale 1969, 1976–77, Pres. 1971; Dir Institut de droit et des sciences économiques, Brest 1969; Deputy Dir for higher educ. and research, Ministry of Nat. Educ. 1972, Dir-Gen. 1972–74; Dir de Cabinet of Sec. of State for Univs 1974–76; Préfet, L'Ariège 1977–79, L'Ain 1979–81, Seine-Saint-Denis 1986–90; Prof. Univ. of Paris IX – Dauphiné 1981–86; Sec.-Gen. Conseil pour l'avenir de la France 1982–86; Dir-Gen. Chambre de commerce et d'industrie de Paris 1990–95; Dir Ecole Nat. d'Admin 1995–2000; expert consultant to Tekelec Airtronic, Sociovision CoFremca, NN France, Tilder Associates; mem. Bd MIT France, Bd of Trustees, Int. Council for Educational Devt; apptd a chosen expert in the field of environment and sustainable devt, Conseil économique, social et environnemental (CESE—Econ., Social and Environmental Council) 2010; Préfet Honoraire; Hon. mem. Autonomous Univ. of Santo Domingo, Dominican Repub.; Officier, Légion d'honneur; Commdr, Ordre nat. du Mérite, des Palmes académiques; Grand Officier, Ordre de Castello Branco (Brazil); Dr hc (Loyola Univ. of New Orleans). *Publications:* La Relation du travail entre époux 1965, Les Universités à la loupe: prof, préfet 1986, Réforme de l'ENA et réforme de l'État 2000, L'Etat, quand même (with Michel Schifres) 2005, Réflexion et propositions sur l'organisation et le fonctionnement des services de l'État à l'étranger: rapport au Premier Ministre 2005, Une modernisation interrompue: Regard sur le septennat de Valéry Giscard d'Estaing 2013. *Leisure interest:* cross-country and marathon running. *Address:* Tekelec Airtronic, 5 rue Carle Vernet, Sèvres 92 (office); CoFremca, 16 rue d'Athènes, 75009 Paris (office); 34 rue des Vignes, 75007 Paris, France (home); Tilder Associates, 57 boulevard de Montmorency, 75026 Paris. *Telephone:* 1-46-90-23-50 (office); 1-59-70-60-00 (office); 1-45-25-14-32 (home). *Fax:* 1-46-90-23-92 (office). *E-mail:* raymond-francois.lebris@temex.fr (office).

LE BRUN, Christopher Mark, MA, DFA, RA; British artist; *President, Royal Academy of Arts;* b. 20 Dec. 1951, Portsmouth; s. of John Le Brun, BEM and Eileen B. Le Brun (née Miles); m. Charlotte Verity 1979; two s. one d.; ed Portsmouth Southern Grammar School, Slade School of Fine Art and Chelsea School of Art; Visiting Lecturer, Brighton Polytechnic 1975–82, Slade School of Fine Art 1978–83, Wimbledon School of Art 1981–83; Prof. of Drawing RA 2000–02; mem. Advisory Cttee, Prince of Wales's Drawing Studio 2000–; Chair. Educ. Cttee RA 2000, Pres. Royal Acad. of Arts 2011–; work in numerous public collections including Tate Gallery, London and Museum of Modern Art, New York, Metropolitan Museum of Art, New York, Art Gallery, New South Wales, Sydney; major comms include Liverpool Anglican Cathedral 1996, Monument to Victor Hugo, St Helier 2012, City Wing, London 2013; Pres. Artists' General Benevolent Inst. (AGBI), London 2012–; Chair. Academic Advisory Bd, Prince of Wales Drawing School 2004–; Trustee, Tate Gallery 1990–95, Nat. Gallery 1996–2003, Dulwich Picture Gallery 2000–05, Trustee, Princes' Drawing School (now The Royal Drawing School) 2004–, Nat. Portrait Gallery, London 2012–; Patron, Turner's House Trust, London, Gainsborough's House, Suffolk, PRA; Hon. Fellow, Univ. of the Arts London 2010, RWS, Royal Birmingham Soc. of Artists; Gulbenkian Printmakers Award 1983, DAAD Award, West Berlin 1987–88 and other prizes. *Publication:* Christopher Le Brun 2001, New Paintings 2014. *Address:* The Royal Academy of Arts, Burlington House, Piccadilly, London, W1V 0DS, England (office). *Telephone:* (20) 7300-8000 (office). *E-mail:* press.office@royalacademy.org.uk (office). *Website:* www.royalacademy.org.uk (office); christopherlebrun.co.uk.

LE CARRÉ, John (see CORNWELL, David John Moore).

LE CLÉZIO, J(ean) M(arie) G(ustave); British/French writer; b. 13 April 1940, Nice; s. of Raoul Le Clézio and Simone Le Clézio; m. 1st Rosalie Piquemal 1961; one d.; m. 2nd Jemia Jean 1975; ed Bristol Univ., Univ. de Nice, Univ. de Provence, Univ. de Perpginan; lived in Nigeria as a child 1948–50; has taught at univs in Bangkok, Mexico City, Boston, Austin, Albuquerque, Seoul; Chevalier des Arts et Lettres, Chevalier, Légion d'honneur 1991, Officier, Ordre national du Mérite 1996, Officier, Légion d'honneur 2009; Prix Larbaud 1972, Grand Prix Paul Morand (Acad. française) 1980, Grand Prix Jean Giono 1997, Prix Prince de Monaco 1998, Stig Dagermanpriset 2008, Nobel Prize for Literature 2008. *Publications include:* Le procès-verbal (The Interrogation) (Prix Renaudot) 1963, Le jour où Beaumont fit connaissance avec sa douleur 1964, La fièvre (Fever) 1965, Le procès 1965, Le déluge 1966, L'extase matérielle 1967, Terra amata 1967, Le livre des fuites 1969, La guerre 1970, Haï 1971, Conversations 1971, Les géants 1973, Mydriase 1973, Voyages de l'autre côté 1975, Mondo et autres histoires 1978, L'inconnu sur la terre 1978, Vers les Icebergs 1978, Voyages au pays des arbres 1978, Désert 1980, Trois villes saintes 1980, Lullaby 1980, Celui qui n'avait vu la mer suivi de la Montagne du dieu vivant 1982, La ronde et autres faits divers 1982, Journal du chercheur d'or 1985, Balaabilou 1985, Villa Aurore 1985, Voyage à Rodrigues 1986, Le rêve mexicain ou la pensée interrompue 1988, Printemps et autres saisons 1989, La Grande Vie 1990, Sirandanes, Suivi de Petit lexique de la langue créole et des oiseaux (jtly) 1990, Onitsha 1991, Étoile errante 1992, Pawana 1992, Diego et Frida 1993, La Quarantaine 1995, Le Poisson d'or 1997, La Fête chantée 1997, Hasard et Angoli Mala 1999, Coeur brûlé et autres romances 2000, Révolutions 2003, L'Africain 2004, Ourania 2005, Raga: approche du continent invisible 2006, Ballaciner 2007, Ritornelle de la faim 2008. *Address:* c/o Editions Gallimard, 5 rue Gaston-Gallimard, 75328 Paris, France. *Website:* www.gallimard.fr.

LE DRIAN, Jean-Yves; French politician; *Minister of Foreign Affairs;* b. 30 June 1947, Lorient (Morbihan); s. of Jean Le Drian and Louisette Le Drian; m. 2nd Maria Vadillo; ed Univ. of Rennes 2 Haute Bretagne; mem. Socialist Party (Parti socialiste—PS) 1974–2018 (resgnd); Deputy to Nat. Ass. for Fifth Dist of Morbihan 1978–86, 1988–91, 1997–2007; Deputy Mayor of Lorient 1977–81, Mayor of Lorient 1981–98, mem. City Council 1998–2004; Sec. of State for Maritime Affairs under Edith Cresson 1991–92; mem. Regional Council of Brittany 1998–2004, Pres. 2004–12; Pres. Conf. of Peripheral Maritime Regions 2010–; Minister of Defence 2012–17, of Foreign Affairs 2017–; Hon. Insp.-Gen. for National Education 1993–; Grand Cross, Order of Isabella the Catholic (Spain) 2015, Order of Merit (Germany) 2017, Grand Cordon, Order of the Republic (Egypt) 2017. *Address:* Ministry of Foreign Affairs, 37 quai d'Orsay, 75700 Paris, France (office). *Telephone:* 1-43-17-53-53 (office). *Fax:* 1-43-17-47-53 (office). *Website:* www.diplomatie.gouv.fr (office).

LE FLOCH-PRIGENT, Loïk; French business executive; b. 21 Sept. 1943, Brest; s. of Gérard Le Floch and Gabrielle Julienne; nephew of Breton poet Maodez Glanndour; m.; one s. two d.; ed Institut Nat. Polytechnique, Grenoble and Univ. of Missouri, USA; scientific and tech. research, DGRST 1969–81; Dir of Cabinet of Industry Minister, Pierre Dreyfus 1981–82; Chair. and CEO Rhône-Poulenc 1982–86, Elf Aquitaine 1989–93, Société Nationale des Chemins de fer Français (SNCF) 1995–96; Chair. Gaz de France 1993–95, Asscn Europe et Entreprises 1994–, Club des présidents d'université et entreprise, Ecole Nat. Supérieure de Création Industrielle 1992–95; Dir Crédit Nat. 1985–97, Compagnie Général des Eaux 1990–96, Banco Cen. Hispano Americano 1990–94, Pallas from 1991, Pinault Printemps Redoute from 1991, Entrepose-Montalev from 1994; int. consultant 1997–2003; imprisoned for involvement in Elf Affair (financial scandal) May 2001, sentenced to five years in prison Nov. 2003, released in April 2004 for health reasons, ordered to return to prison to serve remainder of his sentence June 2007; travelled, on behalf of Pilatus and as part of its mining expertise, to Repub. of the Congo, Mali, Democratic Repub. of the Congo, Benin, Tanzania, Egypt, Syria, Turkey, Iraq, Oman, UAE, Qatar, Canada, USA 2005–10; Supreme Court ordered his imprisonment for six months Jan. 2010, detained in Fresnes prison; charged with being an accessory to fraud whilst in Togo Sept. 2012, extradited to Ivory Coast and appeared before a judge where he was questioned in Lomé, released from prison and sent to French authorities Feb. 2013; Officier, Légion d'honneur (medal withdrawn), Ordre nat. du Mérite. *Publications:* Pour des fonds de pension Européens 1998, Affaire Elf, affaire d'État, entretiens avec Éric Decouty 2001, La Crevette et le Champignon 2005, Une incarcération ordinaire 2006, Granit rosse 2012, Le Mouton Noir: 40 ans dans les coulisses de la République 2014.

LE FOLL, Stéphane, DEA (Econ); French politician; b. 9 Feb. 1960, Le Mans; ed Nat. Conservatory for Industrial Arts and Crafts; econs teacher 1987–91; Head of the Office of First Sec. of the Socialist Party (Parti socialiste—PS) 1997–2004; Vice-Chair. Le Mans Urban Community Council and mem. Le Mans Municipal Council 2002–04; mem. (PS) European Parl. for the West of France (Group of the Progressive Alliance of Socialists and Democrats in the European Parl.) 2004–12, mem. Cttee on Agric. and Rural Devt, Del. for relations with the Palestinian Legis. Council; mem. Nat. Ass. (Parl.) for Sarthe no. 4 constituency June-July 2012, 2017–; Minister of Agric. and Food 2012–17, also Govt Spokesman 2014–17; Chevalier du Mérite agricole. *Address:* Parti Socialiste, 10 rue de Solférino, 75333 Paris Cedex 07, France (office). *Telephone:* 1-45-56-77-00 (office). *Fax:* 1-47-05-15-78 (office). *E-mail:* interps@parti-socialiste.fr (office). *Website:* www.parti-socialiste.fr (office).

LE FUR, Gérard; French physician and pharmaceuticals industry executive; b. 22 Aug. 1950; trained as doctor of pharmacy and science with specialisation in area of cen. nervous system disorders; Head of Lab., Dept of Pharmacological Biochemistry, Pharmuca 1973–82; Dir of Biology Dept, Rhône-Poulenc 1982–86; Assoc. Dir of Research and Devt, Sanofi 1986–95, Dir of Research and Devt 1995–98, Man.-Dir in charge of Scientific Depts 1998, Dir of Research, Sanofi-Synthélabo (following merger of Sanofi and Synthélabo 1998) 1999–2002, Group Man.-Dir 2002–04; Chair. Man. Bd Aventis 2004–06, CEO Sanofi-Aventis SA (following merger of Sanofi-Synthélabo and Aventis) 2006–08; mem. Acad. des Sciences 1999–2003, Corresp. mem. 2003–04; Order of Pharmacists Prize 2004; Galien Prize 1983, 2000. *Publications include:* more than 300 scientific papers in int. publs.

LE GREW, Daryl John, MArch; Australian university administrator and professor of architecture; *Vice-Chancellor Professorial Fellow, Monash University;* b. 17 Sept. 1945, Melbourne, Vic.; s. of A. J. Le Grew; m. Josephine Le Grew 1971; one s. two d.; ed Trinity Grammar School, Kew and Univ. of Melbourne; Lecturer, Dept of Town and Regional Planning, Univ. of Melbourne 1969–73, Lecturer and Sr Lecturer, Dept of Architecture and Building 1973–85; Prof. of Architecture, Deakin Univ. 1986–98, Dean Faculty of Design and Tech. 1992–93, Chair. Academic Bd 1992–98, Pro-Vice-Chancellor (Academic) 1993–94, Deputy Vice-Chancellor and Vice-Pres. (Academic) 1994–98; Vice-Chancellor Univ. of Canterbury, New Zealand 1998–2002; Vice-Chancellor and Pres. Univ. of Tasmania 2003–11; Vice-Chancellor Professorial Fellow, Univ. of Melbourne 2010–, Monash Univ. 2010–; Senate Pres., Australian Acad. of Design 2010–; Dir LeGrew Design Pty Ltd 2010–; Sr Consultant Gehl Architects, Copenhagen 2010–; Consultant, UK Science Research Council Training Programme; Architectural Consultant and Adviser to Dir and Trustees of Nat. Gallery of Victoria, Melbourne for redevelopment of gallery site, to Dir and Council Museum of Victoria, Melbourne for its redevelopment, mem. Council; several sr appointments in business and higher educ.; Life Fellow, Museum of Vic. 1997; Visiting Fellow, Bartlett School of Architecture and Planning, Univ. Coll. London; Fellow, Australian Inst. of Man.; Hon. Fellow, Certified Practising Accountant of Australia; Hon. DLitt (Univ. of Tasmania). *Leisure interests:* swimming, music, poetry, philosophy. *Address:* Office of the Vice-Chancellor, Monash University, Clayton, Vic., Australia (office); PO Box 118, Aireys Inlet, Vic. 3231, Australia. *Telephone:* (3) 9903-2709 (office); (3) 6289-6354. *E-mail:* daryl.legrew@monash.edu (office); daryllegrew@gmail.com. *Website:* www.monash.edu (office); www.legrew.com.

LE HOUÉROU, Philippe, MBA, PhD; French economist, banker and international organization official; *Executive Vice-President and CEO, International Finance Corporation;* b. 1957, Montpellier; ed Institut d'Etudes politiques de Paris, Columbia Univ., USA; began career in private banking sector; joined World Bank Group as part of Young Professional program 2006, has worked in East Asia, Latin America, Africa, Europe and Central Asia, becoming Regional Vice-Pres. for South Asia Region, World Bank –2014; Vice-Pres. for Policy and Partnerships, EBRD, London 2015–16; Exec. Vice-Pres. and CEO, Int. Finance Corpn (IFC), Washington, DC 2016–. *Address:* International Finance Corporation (IFC), 2121 Pennsylvania Avenue, NW, Washington, DC 20433, USA (office). *Telephone:* (202) 473-3800 (office). *Fax:* (202) 974-4384 (office). *E-mail:* information@ifc.org (office). *Website:* www.ifc.org (office).

LE MAIRE, Bruno; French politician; *Minister of the Economy;* b. 15 April 1969, Neuilly-sur-Seine (Hauts-de-Seine); s. of Maurice Le Maire and Viviane Fradin de Belabre; ed École nationale d'admin, Paris; Adviser to Dominique de Villepin, Ministry of Foreign Affairs 2002–04, Adviser, Ministry of the Interior 2004–05, Political Adviser to Prime Minister (Dominique de Villepin) 2005–06, Head of PM's Cabinet 2006–07; mem. Assemblée nationale (Parl.) for Eure 2007–09, 2012–; mem. Municipal Council, Évreux (Eure) 2008–; Regional Councillor, Haute-Normandie 2010–16; Sec. of State in charge of European Affairs 2008–09; Minister of Food, Agric. and Fisheries 2009, of Agric., Food, Fisheries, Rural Affairs and Town and Country Planning (Regional Devt) 2009–12, of the Economy 2017–; mem. Union pour un Mouvement Populaire (UMP), Political Adviser 2008–09, Regional Sec. for Eure 2008–; mem. election campaign team of François Fillon –2017. *Publications:* Le Ministre 2004, Des hommes d'État (Prix Edgar Faure 2008) 2007, Sans mémoire, le présent se vide 2010, Musique absolue: Une répétition avec Carlos Kleiber (Prix Pelléas du Festival de Nohant 2013, Prix de la Ville de Deauville 2013) 2012, Jours de Pouvoir (Prix du Livre Politique 2013) 2013, À nos enfants 2014, Ne vous résignez pas! 2016. *Address:* Ministry for the Economy and Finance, 139 rue de Bercy, 75572 Paris Cedex 12, France (office). *Telephone:* 1-40-04-04-04 (office). *Website:* www.economie.gouv.fr (office); www .brunolemaire.fr.

LE PEN, Jean-Marie, LenD; French politician; b. 20 June 1928, La Trinité-sur-Mer, Morbihan; s. of Jean Le Pen and Anne-Marie Hervé; m. 1st Pierrette Lalanne, 1960 (divorced); three d.; m. 2nd Jeanne-Marie Paschos 1991; ed Coll. des Jésuites Saint-François-Xavier, Vannes, Lycée de Lorient, Univ. de Paris; Pres. Corpn des étudiants en droit de Paris 1949–51; Sub-Lt 1st foreign Bn of paratroopers, Indochina 1954–55; Political Ed. Caravelle 1955, Nat. Del. for Union de défense de la jeunesse française, then Deputy 1st Sector, La Seine; mem. Groupe d'union et de fraternité at Nat. Ass., independent Deputy for la Seine 1958–62; Gen. Sec. Front Nat. Combattant 1956, of Tixier Vignancour Cttee 1964–65; Dir Soc. d'études et de relations publiques 1963–; Pres. Front Nat. 1972–2011, Front Nat. Provence-Alpes-Côte d'Azur 1992–2000; mem. Nat. Ass. 1986–88; mem. European Parl. 1984–2000, Pres. groupe des droites européennes 1984–2000; presidential cand. 1988, 2002, 2007; convicted of physical assault and banned from holding or seeking public office for two years, given three-month suspended prison sentence April 1998, appeal upheld by EU Court of First Instance 2003; expelled from Front Nat. party May 2015; launched Blue White and Red Rally party Sept. 2015; Croix de la Valeur militaire. *Publications:* Les Français d'abord 1984, La France est de retour 1985, L'Espoir 1986, J'ai vu juste 1998. *Address:* Serp, 6 rue de Beaune, 75007 Paris (office); 8 parc de Montretout, 92210 St-Cloud, France (home).

LE PEN, Marine; French lawyer and politician; *President, Front National;* b. 5 Aug. 1968, Neuilly-sur-Seine; d. of Jean-Marie Le Pen and Pierrette Lalanne; m. 1st Franck Chauffroy (divorced); three c.; m. 2nd Eric Iorio (divorced); ed Faculté d'Assas, Univ. of Paris II; practised as lawyer in Paris 1992–98; Dir Legal Service, Front National 1998–2004, mem. Bureau Politique 2000–, Vice-Pres. (one of eight) 2003–06, Exec. Vice-Pres. 2006–10, Pres. 2011–; mem. European Parl. for Île-de-France 2004–09, for North-West 2009–; Pres. Générations Le Pen 2002–; Regional Councillor, Nord-Pas-de-Calais 1998–2004, 2010–; Regional Councillor, Île-de-France 2004–10, also Group Chair. Regional Council 2004–10; Municipal Councillor, Hénin-Beaumont (Pas-de-Calais) 2008–11; unsuccessful cand. French presidential elections 2012 (eliminated in first round with 17.9% of votes cast), 2017 (21.3% in first round, 33.9% in second round); mem. Nat. Ass. for Pas-de-Calais 11th constituency 2017–. *Address:* 1 rue Jean-Jacques Rousseau, 62110 Hénin-Beaumont; Front National, 76-78, rue des Suisses, 92000 Nanterre, France (office). *Telephone:* 1-41-20-20-00 (office). *Fax:* (2) 284-97-09 (Brussels) (office). *E-mail:* marinelepen@frontnational.com (office). *Website:* www.frontnational.com (office); www.marinelepen.com.

LE PENSEC, Louis; French politician; b. 8 Jan. 1937, Mellac (Finistère); s. of Jean Le Pensec and Marie-Anne Hervé; m. Colette Le Guilcher 1963; one s.; Personnel Officer, Soc. nationale d'étude et de construction de moteurs d'aviation 1963–66, Soc. anonyme de véhicules industriels et d'équipements mécaniques 1966–69; Teacher of Personnel Man., Legal Sciences Teaching and Research Unit, Univ. of Rennes 1970–73; Mayor of Mellac 1971–97; Deputy (Finistère) to Nat. Ass. 1973–81, 1983–88, 1993; Councillor for Finistère 1976–, Senator 1998–; mem. Steering Cttee, Parti Socialiste 1977, Exec. Bureau 1979; Minister for the Sea 1981–83, 1988, of Overseas Depts and Territories 1988–93; Govt Spokesperson 1989–91; Vice-Pres. for Europe, Council of European Communities 1983–; Minister of Agric. and Fisheries 1997–98; Vice-Pres. County Council (Finistère) 1998–2008; Head ASEAN Mission for External Trade; mem. Senate Del. for EU 1999–; Vice-Pres. Council of European Municipalities and Regions 2007–; Commdr du Mérite maritime, du Mérite agricole, Order du Mérite (Côte d'Ivoire), Grand-croix du Royaume (Thailand). *Publication:* Ministre à Babord 1997. *Leisure interest:* golf. *Address:* Kerviguennou, 29300 Mellac (home); Hôtel du département, 32 quai Dupleix, 29196 Quimper Cedex, France (office). *Telephone:* (2) 98-76-20-24 (office); (2) 98-35-08-00 (home). *Fax:* (2) 98-76-21-96 (office); (2) 98-35-08-09 (home). *E-mail:* louis.le-pensec@wanadoo.fr (office). *Website:* www.senat.fr/senateur/le_pensec_louis98051u.html.

LE PICHON, Xavier, PhD; French geologist and academic; *Honorary Professor of Geodynamics, Collège de France;* b. 18 June 1937, Quinhon, Viet Nam; s. of Jean-Louis Le Pichon and Hélène Tyl; m. Brigitte Barthélemy 1962; five c.; ed Sciences Physiques, Strasbourg; Research Asst Columbia Univ., New York 1963; Scientific Adviser, Centre Nat. pour l'Exploitation des Océans 1968, 1973; Head, Dept of Oceanography, Centre Océanologique de Bretagne, Brest 1969; Prof. Univ. P. & M. Curie, Paris 1978; Dir Dept of Geology, Ecole Normale Supérieure, Paris 1984–91, Dir Lab. of Geology 1984–2000; Prof. and Chair. of Geodynamics, Collège de France 1986–2008, Hon. Prof. 2009–; Pres. Ifremer Scientific Council 1991–2000, Sr Jury Inst. Universitaire de France 1997; Visiting Prof. Oxford Univ. 1994, Univ. of Tokyo 1995, Rice Univ. Houston 2002; mem. Acad. des Sciences; Founder mem. Acad. Europaea 1988, NAS 1995, Catholic Acad. of France 2008; Officier, Légion d'Honneur, Commdr Ordre Nat. du Mérite; Dr hc (Dalhousie Univ.) 1989, (ETH, Zürich) 1992; Maurice Ewing Medal, American Geophysical Union 1984, Huntsman Award (Canada) 1987, Japan Prize 1990, Wollaston Medal (Geological Soc. of London) 1991, Balzan Prize 2002, Wagener Medal 2003. *Publications include:* Plate Tectonics (with others) 1973, Expédition Famous, à 3000m sous l'Atlantique (with C. Riffaud) 1976, Kaiko, voyage aux extrémités de la mer 1986, Aux racines de l'homme, De la Mort à l'Amour 1997, La Mort, Desclée de Brouwer 1999. *Address:* Collège de France, 11, place Marcelin-Berthelot, 75231 Paris, Cedex 05, France (office). *Website:* www.college-de-france.fr (office).

LE PORS, Anicet; French politician, economist and jurist; b. 28 April 1931, Paris; s. of François Le Pors and Gabrielle Croguennec; m. Claudine Carteret 1959; one s. two d.; ed Collège Arago, Paris, Ecole de la Météorologie, Univ. of Paris, Centre d'étude des programmes économiques; Meteorological Eng, Marrakesh, Morocco 1953, Paris 1957–65; trade union official (CGT) 1955–77; Consultant, World Meteorological Org., Léopoldville, Congo (now Kinshasa, Democratic Repub. of Congo) 1960; Sec. Communist section of Metropolitan Office 1962; Head of Dept, Ministry of Economy and Finance 1965; Sec. Cttee of Cen. Admin., Parti Communiste Français (PCF) 1976–77, Head of Nationalizations, Industrial Policy and Insts Dept, then of Int. Dept, PCF 1978, mem. Cen. Cttee 1979; Head of Interministerial Comm., Univ. of Paris XIII 1976–77 and Ecole supérieure des Sciences Economiques et Commerciales 1978; Senator (Hauts-de-Seine) 1977–81; Minister-Del. for the Civil Service and Admin. Reforms, attached to Prime Minister 1981–83; Sec. of State in charge of Public and Admin. Reform 1983–84; apptd Sr mem. Council of State 1985; mem. Higher Council for Integration; Councillor-Gen. from Hauts-de-Seine 1985–98; Vice-Pres. Nat. Council of Tourism 2000–13; Chair. Youth Employment Programme, Cttee de pilotage pour l'égal accès des femmes et des hommes (cttee for equal rights for men and women); Section Pres. Comm. de recours des réfugiés (now Cour nationale du droit d'asile, Nat. Court of Asylum) 2000–13; Officier, Légion d'honneur; Officier, Ordre nat. du mérite. *Publications include:* Les transferts Etats-industries en France et dans les pays occidentaux 1976, Les béquilles du capital 1977, Marianne à l'encan 1980, Contradictions 1984, L'état efficace 1985, Pendant la mue, le serpent est aveugle 1993, Le Nouvel Age de la citoyenneté 1997, La Citoyenneté 1999, Eloge de l'échec 2001, Le droit d'asile 2005. *Leisure interests:* swimming, sailing. *Address:* 189 boulevard de la République, 92210 St-Cloud, France (home).

LE ROUX, Bruno; French politician; b. 2 May 1965, Gennevilliers, Hauts-de-Seine; ed Univ. Paris West Nanterre La Défense; Deputy Mayor of Epinay-sur-Seine 1989–95, Mayor 1995–2001; Municipal Councillor, Épinay-sur-Seine 2001–08; Gen. Counsel, Seine-St-Denis 1992–97; mem. Nat. Ass. for Seine-St-Denis 1997–2017, Leader of Parl. Socialist Group 2012–16, mem. Nat. Defence Cttee 2006, 2012–17, Constitutional Cttee 1997–2012; Minister of the Interior Dec. 2016–March 2017 (resgnd). *Publication:* La Sécurité pour tous: une exigence de justice sociale 2001. *Address:* c/o Ministry of the Interior, place Beauvau, 75008 Paris, France (office).

LE ROY, Alain; French diplomatist and UN official; *Secretary-General, European External Action Service;* b. 5 Feb. 1953; m.; one s.; ed Ecole nationale supérieure des Mines, Paris, Paris 1 (Sorbonne) Univ.; early career as petroleum engineer for Total 1980–90; Sous-préfet, Dir Office of the Prefect of Eure-et-Loir 1990–91; Sous-préfet d'Avallon 1991–92; Cabinet Chief, Ministry of Agric. 1992–93; Counsellor, Cour des comptes 1993–95, 1995–99; Deputy to UN Special Co-ordinator for Sarajevo and Dir of Operations for restoration of essential public services March–Sept. 1995; UN Regional Admin. in Kosovo (Western Region) 1999–2000; Nat. Co-ordinator for Stability Pact for SE Europe, Ministry of Foreign Affairs 2000; fmr EU Special Rep. in Fmr Yugoslav Repub. of Macedonia; fmr Asst Sec. for Econ. and Financial Affairs, Ministry of Foreign Affairs; Amb. to Madagascar 2006–07; Conseiller Maître, Cour des comptes and Amb. in charge of Union for Mediterranean Initiative 2007–08; UN Under-Sec.-Gen. for Peacekeeping Operations 2008–11; Amb. to Italy 2012–14; Sec.-Gen. European External Action Service 2015–; Commdr, Ordre nat. de Madagascar. *Address:* European External Action Service, 1046 Brussels, Belgium (office). *Telephone:* (2) 584-11-11 (office). *E-mail:* info@eeas.europa.eu (office). *Website:* www.eeas.europa.eu (office).

LE ROY LADURIE, Emmanuel, DèsSc; French historian and academic; *Professor Emeritus of History of Modern Civilization, Collège de France;* b. 19 July 1929, Les Moutiers en Cinglais (Calvados); s. of Jacques Le Roy Ladurie and Léontine Dauger; m. Madeleine Pupponi 1956; one s. one d.; ed École Normale Supérieure; taught at Lycée de Montpellier 1955–57; research attaché, CNRS 1957–60; Asst Faculté des Letters, Montpellier 1960–63; Asst Lecturer and Dir of Studies, École des Hautes Études 1963; Lecturer, Univ. of the Sorbonne 1970–71, Univ. of Paris VII 1971–73; Prof. of History of Modern Civilization, Collège de France 1973–99, Prof. Emer. 1999–; Gen. Admin. Bibliothèque Nat. 1987–94, Pres.

Scientific Council 1994–; mem. Conseil scientifique de l'École Normale Supérieure 1998–; mem. Acad. des Sciences morales et politiques; writes for Le Nouvel Observateur, L'Express, Le Monde newspapers; appears on French TV; Foreign Hon. mem., Acad. des Sciences américaines 1974; Grand-Croix d'Ordre national du Mérite 2018, Commdr, Légion d'honneur, Ordre des Arts et des Lettres; 15 hon. degrees; Medal of Center for French Civilization and Culture, New York Univ. 1985. *Publications include:* Les paysans de Languedoc 1966, Histoire du climat depuis l'an mil 1967, Le territoire de l'historien Vol. I 1973, Vol. II 1978, Montaillou, village occitan de 1294 à 1324 1975, Le carnaval de Romans 1579–80 1980, L'argent, l'amour et la mort en pays d'oc 1980, Histoire de la France urbaine, Vol. III 1981, Paris-Montpellier PC-PSU 1945-1963 1982, La Sorcière de Jasmin 1983, Parmi les historiens 1983, The French Peasantry 1450–1680, Pierre Prion, scribe 1987, Monarchies 1987, L'Histoire de France de: L'Etat Royal 1460–1610 (co-author) 1987, L'Ancien Régime 1610–1770 (co-author) 1991, The Royal French State 1460–1610 1994, Le Siècle des Plaeter (1499–1628) 1995, The Ancien Régime: A History of France 1610–1774 1996, Mémoires 1902–1945 1997, L'Historien, le chiffre et le texte 1997, Saint-Simon, le système de la Cour 1997, Le Voyage de Thomas Plaeter 2000, Histoire de France des Régions 2001, Histoire des paysans français de la Peste Noire à la Revolution 2002, Histoire humaine et comparée du climat 2004, Abrégé d'Histoire du climat 2007. *Leisure interests:* cycling, swimming. *Address:* Collège de France, 11 place Marcelin-Berthelot, 75005 Paris (office); 88 rue d'Alleray, 75015 Paris, France (home). *Telephone:* 1-44-27-10-38 (office); 1-48-42-01-27 (home). *Fax:* 1-44-27-12-40 (office). *E-mail:* e.m.ladurie@wanadoo.fr (home).

LEA, Ruth Jane, CBE, BA, MSc; British economist; *Economic Adviser, Arbuthnot Banking Group;* b. 22 Sept. 1947, Cheshire, England; d. of Thomas Lea and Jane Lea (née Brown); ed Lymm Grammar School, Univs of York and Bristol; asst statistician, Sr Econ. Asst, HM Treasury 1970–73, statistician 1977–78; Lecturer in Econs, Thames Polytechnic 1973–74; statistician, Civil Service Coll. 1974–77, Cen. Statistics Office 1978–84; briefing and policy posts, Dept of Trade and Industry 1984–88; with Mitsubishi Bank 1988–93, Chief Economist 1990–93; Chief UK Economist, Lehman Brothers 1993–94; Econs Ed. Ind. TV News 1994–95; Head of Policy Unit, Inst. of Dirs 1995–2003; Dir Centre for Policy Studies 2004–07; Ind. Dir (non-exec.), Arbuthnot Banking Group 2005–16, Econ. Adviser 2007–; Dir Global Vision 2007–10; mem. Retail Prices Advisory Cttee 1992–94, Nat. Consumer Council 1993–96, Rowntree Foundation Income and Wealth Inquiry Group 1993–94, Nurses' Pay Review Body 1994–98, Research Centres Bd ESRC 1996, Research Priorities Bd 1996–97, Statistics Advisory Cttee Office of Nat. Statistics 1996–97; Trustee, New Europe Research Trust 1999–2005; Council mem. Univ. of London 2001–06; Gov. LSE 2003–08; Freeman, City of London; Hon. DBA (Greenwich) 1997, (BPP Univ. Coll.) 2010, (Chester) 2015. *Publications:* numerous publs on business and econ. topics and the EU including Stamps as Witnesses of History: A Guide to Political Philately 2018. *Leisure interests:* music, philately, natural history and countryside, heritage. *Address:* Arbuthnot Banking Group, Arbuthnot House, 7 Wilson Street, London, EC2M 2SN (office); 25 Redbourne Avenue, Finchley, London, N3 2BP, England (home). *Telephone:* 7800-608674 (mobile) (office); (20) 8346-3482 (home). *E-mail:* ruth.lea@btinternet.com (home); ruthlea@arbuthnot.co.uk (office). *Website:* www.arbuthnotgroup.com (office).

LEACH, James Albert Smith (Jim), BA, MA; American politician; *Chair in Public Affairs, Visiting Professor of Law and Senior Scholar, University of Iowa;* b. 15 Oct. 1942, Davenport, Ia; m. Elisabeth 'Deba' Leach; one s. one d.; ed Princeton Univ., Johns Hopkins Univ., London School of Econs, UK; staffer for then US Rep. Donald Rumsfeld 1970s; entered US Foreign Service, del. to Geneva Disarmament Conf. and UN Gen. Ass., New York –1973 (resgnd); returned to Iowa to head family business 1973–76; mem. US House of Reps from Iowa's 2nd Congressional Dist (numbered as 1st Dist 1977–2003) 1977–2007, Chair. House Cttee on Banking and Financial Services 1995–2001, Sr mem. House Cttee on Int. Relations (Chair. Sub-cttee on Asian and Pacific Affairs 2001–06), Founder and Co-Chair. Congressional Humanities Caucus; John L. Weinberg Visiting Prof. of Public and Int. Affairs, Woodrow Wilson School, Princeton Univ. 2007–09; Interim Dir Inst. of Politics, John F. Kennedy School of Govt, Harvard Univ. 2007–08; Chair. Nat. Endowment for the Humanities 2009–13; Chair in Public Affairs, Visiting Prof. of Law and Sr Scholar, Univ. of Iowa 2013–; Vice-Chair. Century Foundation; mem. Council on Foreign Relations; fmr Chair. Ripon Soc., Republican Mainstream Cttee; fmr Pres. Parliamentarians for Global Action; fmr mem. Bd Social Science Research Council, Carnegie Endowment for Int. Peace, Kettering Foundation; fmr Trustee, Princeton Univ.; mem. American Acad. of Arts and Sciences, Council on Foreign Relations; Republican; decorations from two foreign govts; 13 hon. degrees; Wayne Morse Integrity in Politics Award, Woodrow Wilson Award, Johns Hopkins, Univ., Adlai Stevenson Award, UNA, Edger Wayburn Award, Sierra Club, elected to Wrestling Hall of Fame, Stillwater, Okla, Int. Wrestling Hall of Fame, Waterloo, Ia. *Achievements include:* won state wrestling championship at 138-pound weight class for Davenport High School 1960. *Address:* 414 Boyd Law Building, University of Iowa, Melrose & Byington, Iowa City, IA 52242-1113, USA (office). *Telephone:* (319) 335-9034 (office). *E-mail:* james-leach@uiowa.edu (office). *Website:* law.uiowa.edu/jim_leach (office).

LEADSOM, Rt Hon. Andrea Jacqueline; British financial services executive and politician; *Lord President of the Council and Leader of the House of Commons;* b. (Andrea Salmon), 13 May 1963; m. Ben Leadsom; two s. one d.; ed Univ. of Warwick; Trainee Broker, EF Hutton, Commodities/London Metals Exchange 1985–87; Debt Trader, Barclays de Zoete Wedd/Barclays 1987–97; Man. Dir, De Putron Fund Man. (hedge fund) 1997–99; Sr Investment Officer and Head of Corp. Governance, Invesco Perpetual 1999–2009; MP (Conservative) for S Northamptonshire 2010–, mem. Treasury Cttee 2010–14, Public Accounts Cttee 2014–15; Econ. Sec. (HM Treasury) 2014–15, Minister of State (Dept of Energy and Climate Change) 2015–16, Sec. of State for Environment, Food and Rural Affairs 2016–17, Lord Pres. of the Council and Leader of the House of Commons 2017–. *Address:* Office of the Leader of the House of Commons, 1 Horse Guards Road, London, SW1A 2HQ (office); House of Commons, London, SW1A 0AA, England (office). *Telephone:* (20) 7276-1005 (office). *Fax:* (20) 7276-1006 (office). *E-mail:* commonsleader@cabinetoffice.gov.uk (office); andrea.leadsom.mp@parliament.uk (office). *Website:* www.gov.uk/government/organisations/the-office-of-the-leader-of-the-house-of-commons (office); www.andrealeadsom.com.

LEAHY, Patrick Joseph, BA, JD; American politician and lawyer; *Senator from Vermont;* b. 31 March 1940, Montpelier, Vt; s. of Howard Francis Leahy and Alba Leahy (née Zambon); m. Marcelle Pomerleau 1962; two s. one d.; ed St Michael's Coll., Colchester, Vt and Georgetown Univ. Law Center, Washington, DC; admitted to practise law, State of Vt 1964, US Supreme Court, Second Circuit Court of Appeals, New York, US Fed. Dist Court of Vt, State Attorney, Chittenden Co., Vt 1966–74; Senator from Vt 1975–, Vice-Chair. Intelligence Cttee 1985–86, Chair. Agric. Cttee 1987–95, Judiciary Cttee 2001, 2007–15, Sr mem. Appropriations Cttee, Co-Chair. Senate Nat. Guard Caucus, Ranking mem. Appropriations Sub-cttee on State Dept, Foreign Operations and Related Programs, Pres. Pro Tempore 2012–15, Pres. Pro Tempore Emer. 2015–; mem. Vt Bar Asscn 1964–; Vice-Pres. Nat. Dist Attorneys' Asscn 1971–74; Democrat; Distinguished Service Award of Nat. Dist Attorneys' Asscn 1974, inducted into Freedom of Information Act Hall of Fame 1996, Harry S. Truman Award, Nat. Guard Asscn 2003, Champion of Freedom Award, Electronic Privacy Information Center 2004, Bi-Partisan Leadership Award 2005, John Peter Zenger Press Freedom Award, US Senator John Heinz Award for Greatest Public Service 2013, Silver Mouse Award 2013. *Leisure interests:* photography, reading, hiking, cross-country skiing, comic books (especially Batman), fan of the Grateful Dead. *Address:* 437 Russell Senate Office Building, Washington, DC 20510, USA (office). *Telephone:* (202) 224-4242 (office). *Website:* www.leahy.senate.gov (office).

LEAHY, Sir Terence Patrick, Kt, BSc; British business executive; *Senior Advisor, Clayton, Dubilier & Rice, Inc.;* b. 28 Feb. 1956, Belle Vale, Liverpool, England; m. Alison Leahy; two s. one d.; ed St Edward's Coll., Liverpool, Univ. of Manchester Inst. of Science and Tech.; mem. staff, Co-op supermarket group 1977–79; joined Tesco plc 1979, held several sr positions including Marketing Dir 1992–95, Deputy Man. Dir 1995–97, Chief Exec. 1997–2011; Sr Advisor, Clayton, Dubilier & Rice, Inc. 2011–; Chair. B&M Retail Ltd 2012–; Chancellor UMIST 2002–04, Co-Chancellor Univ. of Manchester 2004–; Special Adviser, Everton Football Club 2004–; mem. Bd of Dirs Motor Fuel Group, Anatwine Ltd, Blackcircles.com Ltd 2014–, Purple WiFi Ltd 2015–; mem. Liverpool Vision Regeneration Bd; Freeman of the City of Liverpool 2002; Hon. DSc (Cranfield Univ.) 2007; Outstanding Alumni Award, Alliance Manchester Business School 1996, Business Leader of the Year 2003, Fortune European Businessman of the Year 2004, selected as Britain's most admired business leader by Management Today 2005. *Publications include:* Management in 10 Words 2012. *Leisure interests:* sport, reading, theatre, architecture. *Address:* Clayton, Dubilier & Rice, Inc., Cleveland House, 33 King Street, London, SW1Y 6RJ, England (office). *Telephone:* (20) 7747-3800 (office). *Fax:* (20) 7747-3801 (office). *Website:* www.cdr-inc.com (office).

LEAKEY, Louise Nicol, BS, PhD; Kenyan palaeontologist and academic; *Director, Turkana Basin Institute;* b. 21 March 1972, Kenya; d. of Richard Leakey and Meave Leakey (née Epps); grand-d. of Louis Leakey; m. Emmanuel de Merode; two d.; ed Univ of Bristol, Univ Coll. London, UK; worked with parents from early age in Turkana Basin, Kenya; currently Dir Turkana Basin Inst.; Research Prof., Dept of Anthropology, Univ. of Stony Brook, NY; named (with mother) Nat. Geographic Soc. Explorer-at-Large 2002–; Chair. Nat. Museums of Kenya 2014. *Achievements include:* discovery of *Kenyanthropus platyops*, a new human species that extended diversity in hominid family record back to 3.5 million years. *Address:* Turkana Basin Institute, PO Box 24467, Nairobi 00502, Kenya (office); Department of Anthropology, University of Stony Brook, N507 Social and Behavioural Sciences, Stony Brook, NY 11794-4364, USA (office). *Telephone:* (631) 632-5800 (Stony Brook) (office). *Fax:* (631) 632-5810 (Stony Brook) (office). *E-mail:* louise.leakey@stonybrook.edu (office). *Website:* www.turkanabasin.org (office); www.stonybrook.edu/anthro/staff.shtml (office); www.leakey.com; www.africanfossils.org.

LEAKEY, Richard Erskine Frere, FRAI; Kenyan politician, palaeontologist and conservationist; b. 19 Dec. 1944, Nairobi; s. of Louis Leakey and Mary Leakey; m. 1st Margaret Cropper 1965; m. 2nd Meave Gillian Epps 1970; three d.; ed Duke of York School (later known as Lenana School), Nairobi; trapper of primates for research 1961–65; co-leader of research expeditions to Lake Natron 1963–64, Omo River 1967; Dir Root & Leakey Safaris (tour co.) 1965–68; archaeological excavation, Lake Baringo 1966; Admin. Dir Nat. Museums of Kenya 1968–74, Dir and Chief Exec. 1974–89; research in Nakali/Suguta Valley 1978; leader of research projects, Koobi Fora 1979–81, W Turkana 1981–82, 1984–89, Buluk 1983; Dir Wildlife Conservation and Man. Dept 1989–90; Dir Kenya Wildlife Service 1990–94, 1998–99; Man. Dir Richard Leakey & Assocs Ltd 1994–98; Co-Founder and Gen. Sec. Safina Party 1995–98; nominated MP Nat. Ass. –1999; Perm. Sec., Sec. to the Cabinet, Head of the Public Service, Office of the Pres., Rep. of Kenya 1999–2001; interim Chair. Transparency International (Kenya br.) 2007; numerous hon. positions including Chair. Wildlife Clubs of Kenya 1969–80 (Trustee 1980–), Foundation for Research into the Origins of Man (USA) 1971–85, Kenya Nat. Cttee of the United World Colls 1982–, E African Wildlife Soc. 1984–89, SAIDIA 1989–; Chair. Bd of Trustees, Nat. Museums of Kenya 1989–94; Co-founder and mem. Bd Dirs Wildlife Direct 2004–; Life Trustee, L.S.B. Leakey Foundation; Trustee, Nat. Fund for Disabled in Kenya 1980–95, Agricultural Research Foundation, Kenya 1986–; has given more than 750 public and scholarly Lectures; Foreign Hon. mem. American Acad. of Arts and Sciences 1998; Order of the Burning Spear, Kenya 1993; nine hon. degrees; numerous awards and honours, including James Smithsonian Medal, USA 1990, Gold Medal, Royal Geographical Soc., UK 1990, World Ecology Medal, Int. Centre for Tropical Ecology, USA 1997. *TV documentaries:* Bones of Contention, Survival Anglia 1975, The Making of Mankind, BBC 1981, Earth Journal (presenter), NBC 1992. *Publications include:* numerous articles on finds in the field of palaeontology in scientific journals, including Nature, Journal of World History, Science, American Journal of Physical Anthropology, etc.; contrib. to General History of Africa (Vol. I), Perspective on Human Evolution and Fossil Vertebrates of Africa; Origins (book, with R. Lewin) 1977, People of the Lake: Man, His Origins, Nature and Future (book, with R. Lewin) 1978, The Making of Mankind 1981, Human Origins 1982, One Life 1983, Origins Reconsidered (with R. Lewin) 1992, Origins of Humankind (with R. Lewin) 1995, The Sixth Extinction (with R. Lewin) 1995, Wildlife Wars: My Fight to Save Africa's Natural Treasures (with V. Morrell) 2001, Wildlife Wars: My Battle to Save Kenya's Elephants 2011. *Leisure interests:* sailing and cooking. *Address:* Africa Conservation Fund, PO Box 24926, Karen 00502,

Nairobi, Kenya (office). *Telephone:* (3) 865120 (office). *E-mail:* info@wildlifedirect.org (office); leakey@wananchi.com (home). *Website:* www.leakey.com; www.leakeyfoundation.org; richardleakey.wildlifedirect.org.

LEAL, Guilherme Peirão; Brazilian business executive; *Co-Chairman, Natura Cosméticos SA;* b. 22 Feb. 1950, Santos; five c.; ed Univ. of São Paulo, Harvard Business School, USA, Advanced Man. Management Programme, Fundação Dom Cabral/Institut Européen d'Admin des Affaires (INSEAD); joined Natura Cosméticos SA 1979, mem. Bd of Dirs 1998–, Co-Chair. 2001–; f. Instituto Ethos 1998, currently Pres. and mem. Admin. Council; mem. Superior Council on Social Responsibility, (FIESP), Nat. Council on Food Security; mem. Bd of Dirs Brazilian Fund for Biodiversity; mem. Admin. Council, Grupo 'O Estado de São Paulo', WWF Brasil; Founder Movimento Nossa São Paulo 2007, Instituto Arapyaú 2008; unsuccessful Green Party cand. for Vice-Pres. alongside Marina Silva in presidential election 2010; helped found Rede de Ação Política pela Sustentabilidade (Action Network for Sustainability Policy) 2012; Citizen of the State of Rio de Janeiro 2004. *Address:* Natura Cosméticos SA, Rodavia Régis Bittencourt, s/nº, km 293, Potuverá, 06882-700 Itapecerica da Serra, São Paulo, Brazil (office). *Telephone:* (11) 3074-1504 (office). *E-mail:* guilhermeleal@natura.net (office). *Website:* www.natura.net (office).

LEANCĂ, Iurie, MA; Moldovan diplomatist and politician; *Deputy Prime Minister, responsible for European Reintegration;* b. 20 Oct. 1963, Orașul, Cimișlia Dist, Moldovan SSR, USSR; m. Aida Leancă; two c.; ed Moscow State Inst. of Int. Relations; joined Ministry of Foreign Affairs 1986, served in several positions including Minister-Counselor, Embassy in Washington, DC 1993–97, Amb.-at-Large for European Integration 1998, Deputy Minister of Foreign Affairs 1998–99, First Deputy Minister of Foreign Affairs 1999–2001; Deputy CEO Ascom Group (oil co.) 2001–05, 2007–09; Sr Adviser to OSCE High Commr on Nat. Minorities 2005–07; Vice-Pres. Foreign Policy Asscn of Moldova 2005–09; mem. Parl. 2009–; Deputy Prime Minister 2009–13, Minister of Foreign Affairs and European Integration 2009–13, Acting Prime Minister April–May 2013, Prime Minister of Moldova May 2013–15; Deputy Prime Minister, responsible for European Reintegration 2017–; mem. Alliance for Democracy and Reforms 1998–99, Alliance for European Integration 2009–13, Liberal Democratic Party of Moldova (Partidul Liberal Democrat din Moldova) 2009–15, Pro-European Coalition 2013–15, European People's Party of Moldova (also Founder and Leader) 2015–. *Address:* Office of the Council of Ministers, 2033 Chișinău, Piața Marii Adunări Naționale 1 (office); Partidul Popular European din Moldova (European People's Party of Moldova), 2019 Chișinău, Vasile Alecsandri 87, Moldova (office). *Telephone:* (22) 25-01-01 (office); 787-81000 (mobile) (office). *Fax:* (22) 24-26-96 (office). *E-mail:* petitii@gov.md (office); echipa@ppe.md (office). *Website:* www.gov.md (office); www.ppe.md (office); www.facebook.com/IurieLeancaUE.

LEAPE, James P., AB, PhD; American lawyer, international organization official and academic; *Consulting Professor, Stanford Woods Institute for the Environment, Stanford University;* b. 1956; ed Harvard Coll. and Harvard Law School; began career as environmental lawyer, working on environmental protection cases in USA, advising UNEP, Nairobi, Kenya and co-authoring a text on environmental law; Trial Attorney, US Dept of Justice 1980–82; Counsel for Wildlife Programs, Nat. Audubon Soc., Washington, DC 1983–86; Assoc. Prof., College of Law, Univ. of Utah 1987–89; joined WWF-US 1989, Exec. Vice-Pres. of world-wide conservation programmes 1991–2001, Dir-Gen. WWF International 2005–14; Consulting Prof., Stanford Woods Inst. for the Environment, Stanford Univ. 2014–, Cox Consulting Prof., School of Earth, Energy & Environmental Sciences; Dir conservation and science initiatives, David and Lucile Packard Foundation 2001–05; fmr Advisor, World Econ. Forum; fmr mem. Bd of Dirs Int. Civil Soc. Center, China Council for Int. Cooperation in Environment and Devt. *Publication:* Environmental Regulation: Law, Science, and Policy (Aspen Casebook) (co-author) 2013. *Address:* Stanford Woods Institute for the Environment, 473 Via Ortega, Room 347, Stanford, CA 94305, USA (office). *Telephone:* (650) 498-0916 (office). *E-mail:* jleape@stanford.edu (office). *Website:* woods.stanford.edu (office).

LÉAUD, Jean-Pierre; French actor; b. 28 May 1944, Paris; s. of Pierre Léaud and Jacqueline Pierreux; m. Brigitte Duvivier; debut as Antoine Doinel in Truffaut's The 400 Blows 1959, first of a series of Doinel films directed by Truffaut over 20 years; Hon. César Award 2000, Hon. Palme d'Or, Cannes Film Festival 2016. *Films include:* Les quatre cents coups (The Four Hundred Blows) 1959, La Tour, prends garde! (aka Killer Spy) 1960, Boulevard 1960, Le testament d'Orphée, ou ne me demandez pas pourquoi! (The Testament of Orpheus) (uncredited) 1962, L'amour à vingt ans (Love at Twenty) 1962, Les mauvaises fréquentations (Bad Company) 1963, La peau douce (The Soft Skin) (asst dir; uncredited) 1964, L'amour à la mer (Love at Sea) 1963, Une femme mariée: Suite de fragments d'un film tourné en 1964 (asst dir) 1964, Mata-Hari (also asst dir; uncredited) 1964, Alphaville, une étrange aventure de Lemmy Caution (Alphaville, a Strange Case of Lemmy Caution) (also asst dir; uncredited) 1965, Pierrot le fou (also asst dir; uncredited) 1965, Le Père Noël a les yeux bleus (Santa Claus Has Blue Eyes) 1966, Masculin, féminin: 15 faits précis (Silver Bear for Best Actor, Berlin Int. Film Festival) 1966, Made in U.S.A. (also asst dir) 1966, Le plus vieux métier du monde (The Oldest Profession in the World) (uncredited) 1967, Le départ 1967, La chinoise 1967, Week End 1967, Dialóg 20-40-60 1968, La Concentration 1968, Baisers volés (Stolen Kisses) 1968, Paul 1969, Der Leone have sept cabeças (The Lion Has Seven Heads) 1969, Le gai savoir (Joy of Learning) 1969, Porcile (Pigsty) 1969, Domicile conjugal (Bed & Board) 1970, Os herdeiros (The Heirs) 1970, Une aventure de Billy le Kid (aka A Girl Is a Gun, USA) 1971, Out 1, noli me tangere 1971, Les deux anglaises et le continent (Two English Girls and the Continent) 1971, Out 1: Spectre 1972, Last Tango in Paris 1972, La nuit américaine (aka Day for Night) 1973, La maman et la putain (The Mother and the Whore) 1973, De quoi s'agit-il? (dir) 1974, Umarmungen und andere Sachen 1975, Les lolos de Lola 1976, L'amour en fuite (Love on the Run) 1979, Parano 1980, La cassure 1981, Aiutami a sognare (Help Me Dream) 1981, Rebelote 1983, Paris vu par… vingt ans après (Paris Seen By… 20 Years After) 1984, Treasure Island 1985, Csak egy mozi 1985, Détective 1985, Boran – Zeit zum Zielen 1986, Corps et biens (Lost with All Hands) 1986, Ossegg oder Die Wahrheit über Hänsel und Gretel 1987, Jane B. par Agnès V. 1987, Les keufs (Lady Cops) 1987, 36 fillette (Junior Size 36) 1988, La couleur du vent (The Colour of the Wind) 1988, Bunker Palace Hôtel 1989, I Hired a Contract Killer 1990, Paris s'éveille (Paris Awakens) 1991, C'est la vie 1991, La vie de bohème (Bohemian Life) 1992, La naissance de l'amour (The Birth of Love) 1993, Personne ne m'aime (Nobody Loves Me) 1994, Les cent et une nuits de Simon Cinéma (A Hundred and One Nights of Simon Cinema) 1995, Mon homme (My Man) 1996, Le journal du séducteur (Diary of a Seducer) 1996, Irma Vep 1996, Pour rire! (Best Actor, Thessaloniki Film Festival) 1996, Elizabeth (uncredited) 1998, Innocent 1999, Une affaire de goût (A Question of Taste) 2000, L'affaire Marcorelle (The Marcorelle Affair) 2000, Ni neibian jidian (What Time Is It There?) 2001, Le Pornographe (The Pornographer) (FIPRESCI Prize 2001) 2001, La guerre à Paris (The War in Paris) 2002, Folle embellie 2004, Léaud de Hurledents (writer) 2004, J'ai vu tuer Ben Barka 2005, Visage 2009, Le Havre 2011, Camille Rewinds 2012, La mort de Louis XIV 2016. *Television includes:* L'éducation sentimentale (mini-series) 1973, Le petit pommier 1981, Mersonne ne m'aime 1982, Le tueur assis 1985, L'herbe rouge 1985, Néo Polar (series; episode Des choses qui arrivent) 1985, Grandeur et décadence 1986, Sei delitti per padre Brown (mini-series) 1988, Femme de papier (Front Woman) 1989, L'homme aux cercles bleus 2009.

LEAVER, Sir Christopher, Kt, GBE, KStJ, JP; British business executive; b. 3 Nov. 1937, London, England; s. of Dr Robert Leaver and Audrey Kerpen; m. Helen Mireille Molyneux Benton 1975; one s. two d.; ed Eastbourne Coll.; commissioned, Royal Army Ordnance Corps 1956–58; mem. Retail Food Trades Wages Council 1963–64; JP, Inner London 1970–83, City 1974–93; mem. Council, Royal Borough of Kensington and Chelsea 1971–74; Alderman, Court of Common Council (Ward of Dowgate), City of London 1974–2002, Sheriff, City of London 1979–80, Lord Mayor of London 1981–82; Chair. London Tourist Bd Ltd 1983–89; Deputy Chair. Thames Water PLC 1989–93, Chair. 1993–94, Vice-Chair. 1994–2000; mem. Bd of Brixton Prison 1975–78, Comm. of Lt for City of London 1982–2002, Finance Cttee of London Diocesan Fund 1983–86, Council of Mission to Seamen 1983–93; Adviser to Sec. of State on Royal Parks 1993–96; Gov. Christ's Hosp. School 1975–2002, City of London Girls' School 1975–78, City Univ. 1978–2002 (Chancellor City Univ. 1981–82), City of London Freemen's School 1980–81, Music Therapy Trust 1981–89; Chair. Young Musicians' Symphony Orchestra Trust 1979–81, London Tourist Bd 1983–89, Eastbourne Coll. 1988–2006; Pres. City of London Bowling Club 1981; Vice-Pres. Nat. Playing Fields Asscn 1983–99, Bridewell Royal Hosp. 1983–89; Chair. Pathfinder Properties PLC 1997; Dir (non-exec.) Bath & Portland Group PLC 1983–85, Thermal Scientific PLC 1985–88, Unionamerica Holdings 1994–97, Pathfinder Minerals PLC 1997–2002, Pathfinder Repossessions II Ltd 1998–2002, The Turkish Earthquake Disaster Relief Fund 1999; Trustee, Chichester Festival Theatre 1982–97, London Symphony Orchestra 1983–90; Church Warden, St Olave's Hart Street 1975–89, Church Commr 1982–93, 1996–99; Hon. mem. Guildhall School of Music 1982; Hon. Col 151 Regt RCT(V) 1983–89; Hon. Col Commdt RCT 1988–91; Hon. Liveryman, Worshipful Co. of Farmers 1980, Worshipful Co. of Environmental Cleaners; Freeman, Worshipful Co. of Watermen and Lightermen, Liveryman Co. of Water Conservators; Master Worshipful Co. of Carmen 1987–88; KStJ 1982; Order of Oman; Hon. DMus (City Univ.) 1982. *Leisure interests:* gardening, music, travel.

LEAVER, Christopher John, CBE, BSc, MA, PhD, DIC, ARCS, FRS, FRSE; British scientist and academic; *Emeritus Professor of Plant Sciences, University of Oxford;* b. 31 May 1942, Bristol; s. of Douglas P. Leaver and Elizabeth C. Leaver; m. Anne Huggins 1971; one s. one d.; ed Imperial Coll. of Science, London, Univ. of Oxford; Fulbright Scholar, Purdue Univ., Ind., USA 1966–68; Scientific Officer, ARC Unit of Plant Physiology, Imperial Coll. London 1968–69; Lecturer, Univ. of Edinburgh 1969–80, Reader 1980–86, Science and Eng Research Council Sr Research Fellow 1985–90, Prof. of Plant Molecular Biology 1986–90; Sibthorpian Prof. of Plant Sciences, Univ. of Oxford 1990–2007, Head of Dept of Plant Sciences 1991–2007, Chair. Technology Transfer Advisory Group 1996–2000, Prof. Emer. 2008–; Royal Soc. Commonwealth Bursary, CSIRO, Canberra 1975; European Molecular Biology Org. Sr Fellowship, Biozentrum, Basle 1980; Trustee and mem. Governing Council, John Innes Centre, Norwich 1984–; Trustee, Nat. History Museum, London 1997–2006 (mem. Audit Cttee 1997–06); mem. Council, Agric. and Food Research Council 1990–93, Co-ordinator, Plant Molecular Biology Programme 1989–92; Scientific Advisory Bd, Arable Crops Research 1995–2000; mem. Priorities Bd for Research and Devt, Ministry of Agric., Fisheries and Food Priorities, Chair. Arable Crops Advisory Sectoral Group 1990–94; mem. Royal Soc. Council 1992–94; mem., Council Biochemical Soc. 1995–99, Vice-Chair. 2002–04, Chair. and Trustee 2005–07, Chair. Nucleic Acids and Molecular Biology Group 1995–2000, of Educ. Cttee 2005–12; mem. European Molecular Biology Org. (Fellowship Council 1984–88, Council mem. 1992–97, Vice-Chair. and then Chair. 1996–97); mem. UK Govt Advisory Council on Science and Tech. 1992–93; Dir Isis Innovation Ltd, Univ. of Oxford 1996–2002; Visiting Prof., Univ. of Western Australia 2001–15; Visiting Lecturer, Royal Soc./Acad. des Sciences 1994; Del. Oxford Univ. Press 2002–07; mem. Biotechnology and Biological Sciences Research Council 2000–03, mem. Individual Merit Promotion Panel 1996–2005, Chair. Personal Merit Promotion Panel 2005–11; Chair. External Scientific Advisory Bd, Inst. of Molecular and Cell Biology, Univ. of Oporto; mem. Scientific Advisory Bd, Inst. of Molecular and Cellular Biology, Singapore, ITQB Advisory Cttee, Univ. of Lisbon, Science Advisory Panel, Royal Inst. of Great Britain 2002–, Scientific Advisory Bd Australian Research Council Centre of Excellence in Plant Energy Biology, WA 2005–14 (Chair. 2010), Scientific Planning and Review Cttee, ICSU 2006–12, Int. Advisory Panel, A*Star Grad. Acad., Singapore 2006– (Chair. 2009–); mem. Academia Europaea 1988; corresponding mem., American Soc. of Plant Biologists 2003; Fellow, St John's Coll. Oxford 1990–; Huxley Gold Medal, Imperial Coll. 1970; Tate & Lyle Award, Phytochemical Soc. of Europe 1984, Humboldt Prize 1997, Sibthorp Medal, Univ. of Oxford 2007. *Publications:* ed. several books; numerous papers in int. scientific journals. *Leisure interests:* walking and talking in Upper Coquetdale. *E-mail:* chris.leaver@plants.ox.ac.uk (office).

LEAVER, Peter Lawrence Oppenheim, QC; British lawyer; b. 28 Nov. 1944; s. of Marcus Isaac Leaver and Lena Leaver (née Oppenheim); m. Jane Rachel Pearl 1969; three s. one d.; ed Aldenham School, Elstree, Trinity Coll., Dublin; called to Bar, Lincoln's Inn 1967, QC 1987, Recorder 1994–, Bencher 1995; Chief Exec. Football Asscn Premier League 1997–99; Chair. Bar Cttee 1989, Int. Practice Cttee 1990; mem. Cttee on Future of the Legal Profession 1986–88, Council of Legal Ed. 1986–91, Gen. Council of the Bar 1987–90; Dir Investment Man. Regulatory Org. 1994–2000; Deputy High Court Judge; Deputy Chair. Financial Services Authority

Regulatory Decisions Cttee; mem. Chartered Inst. of Arbitrators, Soc. of Legal Scholars; mem. Dispute Resolution Panel for Winter Olympics, Salt Lake City 2002. *Publication:* Pre-Trial and Pre-Hearing Procedures Worldwide (contrib.) 1990. *Leisure interests:* sport, theatre, wine, opera. *Address:* The Chambers of Lord Grabiner QC, 1 Essex Court, Temple, London, EC4Y 9AR (office); 5 Hamilton Terrace, London, NW8 9RE, England (home). *Telephone:* (20) 7583-2000 (office); (20) 7286-0208 (home). *Fax:* (20) 7520-4837 (office). *E-mail:* pleaver@oeclaw.co.uk (office). *Website:* www.oeclaw.co.uk (office).

LEAVEY, Thomas Edward, MA, PhD; American international postal official (retd); b. 10 Nov. 1934, Kansas City, Mo.; m. Anne Roland 1968; ed Josephinum Coll., Inst. Catholique, Paris, France, Princeton Univ.; Prof., Farleigh Dickinson Univ. and George Washington Univ. 1968–70; various man. and exec. positions in US Postal Services (USPS) in Los Angeles, Chicago and Washington, DC 1970–87, Asst Postmaster-Gen. for Int. Postal Affairs, USPS HQ 1987–94; Chair. Exec. Council, Universal Postal Union (UPU) 1989–94, Dir-Gen. Int. Bureau of UPU 1995–2004; Chevalier, Légion d'honneur 2004; American Soc. for Training and Devt Award 1973, John Wanamaker Award 1991, Heinrich von Stephan Medal, German Ministry of Post and Telecommunication 1997. *Leisure interests:* golf, tennis.

LEAVITT, Michael (Mike) Okerlund, BS; American insurance industry executive, fmr politician and fmr government official; *Founder and Chairman, Leavitt Partners;* b. 11 Feb. 1951, Cedar City, Utah; s. of Dixie Leavitt and Anne Okerlund; m. Jacalyn Smith; four s. one d.; ed Southern Utah Univ.; Sales Rep., Leavitt Group, Cedar City 1972–74, Account Exec. 1974–76, Man. Underwriting, Salt Lake City 1976–82, COO 1982–84, Pres. and CEO 1984–92; Gov. of Utah 1993–2003; Admin. US Environmental Protection Agency, Washington, DC 2003–05; US Sec. of Health and Human Services 2005–09; Founder and Chair., Leavitt Partners 2009–; mem. Bd of Dirs Pacificorp, Portland, Ore., Utah Power and Light Co., Salt Lake City, Great Western Thrift & Loan, Salt Lake City; mem. staff, Reagan–Bush '84 campaign; fmr Chair. Republican Govs Asscn, Western Govs Asscn, Nat. Govs Asscn 1999–2000; mem. Bd of Dirs Midwestern Regional Medical Center, Inc., Cancer Treatment Centers of America, Inc., HealthEquity, Inc. 2010–, Cogent Healthcare, Inc. 2011–, Ind. Living Systems, LLC 2012–, American Express Co. 2015–; China Public Health Award. *Publication:* Finding Allies, Building Alliances (co–author) 2014. *Leisure interest:* golf. *Address:* Leavitt Partners, 299 South Main Street, Suite 2300, Salt Lake City, UT 84111-2278, USA (office). *Telephone:* (801) 538-5082 (office). *E-mail:* info@leavittpartners.com (office). *Website:* leavittpartners.com (office).

LeBARON, Joseph Evan, BS, PhD; American diplomatist (retd); *Senior Advisor, Squire Patton Boggs LLP;* b. Ore.; m. Elinor Drake; one d.; ed Portland State Univ., American Univ. of Beirut, Princeton Univ., Seminar XXI on Int. Relations, Massachusetts Inst. of Tech.; served in USAF during Vietnam War as TV newscaster and radio broadcaster in Thailand and Turkey for American Forces Radio and TV Service (AFRTS), helped produce 'Air Force Now' while at AFRTS HQ, Calif.; Doctoral Research Fellow, Univ. of Khartoum, Sudan 1978–79; career mem. Foreign Service since 1980, Vice-Consul, Embassy in Doha, Qatar 1980–82, later assignments included rotational assignment (political and econ.-commercial officer), Embassy in Amman 1982–84, Staff Asst to Amb., Embassy in Ankara 1984–85, Political Officer, Consulate Gen. in Istanbul 1985–87, Desk Officer for Lebanon, Bureau of Near Eastern Affairs, State Dept 1987–89, detailed to US Senate to serve on nat. security and foreign affairs staff of Majority Leader, George J. Mitchell 1989–90, Persian language studies at Foreign Service Inst., Consul Gen., Dubai, UAE 1990–91, Deputy Chief of Mission, Embassy in Manama, Bahrain 1994–96, Deputy Dir Office of Iran and Iraq, Bureau of Near Eastern Affairs 1996–98, Deputy Asst Sec., Bureau of Intelligence and Research –2003, Amb. to Mauritania 2003–06, to Qatar 2008–11; Sr Advisor, Squire Patton Boggs LLP (law firm), Washington, DC 2011–; Founder and CEO Gulfscape Arabia LLC, Washington, DC 2011–; Vice-Chair. Daruna (real estate devt firm in Qatar) 2014–; mem. Bd of Advisors, Lagoon Capital Partners 2013–; part-time mem. Grad. Faculty, Elliott School for Int. Affairs, George Washington Univ. 2001–03; Commdr, Nat. Order of Merit (Mauritania) 2006; numerous State Dept Sr Performance, Superior and Meritorious Honor Awards, Sinclaire Language Award for the distinguished study of Persian, Presidential Meritorious Service Award 2003. *Address:* Squire Patton Boggs LLP, 2550 M Street, NW, Washington, DC 20037, USA (office). *Telephone:* (202) 457-5134 (office). *E-mail:* joseph.lebaron@squirepb.com (office); LeBaron@gulfscape-arabia.com (office). *Website:* www.squirepattonboggs.com (office); www.gulfscape-arabia.com (office).

LEBEDEV, Aleksander Yevgenyevich, PhD; Russian banker; *President, National Reserve Bank;* b. 16 Dec. 1960; m.; one s.; ed Moscow Inst. of Int. Relations; staff mem., Inst. of Econs of World Socialist System, USSR Acad. of Sciences 1982–83; joined Ministry of Foreign Affairs 1983, First, then Second Sec., Embassy in UK 1987–92; Rep. Swiss Bank in Russia 1992–93; Founder and Chair. of Bd Russian Investment Finance Co. 1993–; Pres. Nat. Reserve Bank (NRB) 1995–, mem. Bd of Dirs 2008–, Chair. 2010–, mem. Bd of Dirs Nat. Reserve Corpn (parent co. of NRB) 2014–, Chair. 2016–; Chair. Nat. Investment Bd 1999–; Pres. Charitable Reserve Foundation; f. Raisa Gorbachev Foundation (with Mikhail Gorbachev) 2006; Deputy Head Sloboda Regional Duma, Kirov 2011–14; Order For Merit to the Fatherland, 2nd degree, Medal For Merits, 3rd Degree (Ukraine); St Innokenty Award by Russian Orthodox Church, St Vladimir Award by Ukrainian Orthodox Church, Medal of UNESCO Dialogue of Cultures. *Publications:* contrib. to various publications. *Address:* National Reserve Bank, 117036 Moscow, 10A Prospekt 60–Letiya, Oktyabra, Russia (office). *Telephone:* (495) 213-32-20 (office); (495) 234-48-50 (office). *Website:* www.nrb.ru (office); www.alebedev.ru.

LEBEDEV, Pavlo Valentynovych; Ukrainian economist, business executive and politician; b. 12 July 1962, Novomikhailovskii, Krasnodar Krai, Russia; m.; five d.; ed Yaroslavl Higher Mil. Financial School; began career as locksmith, Orlyatko 1979–80; performed mil. service in Chernivtsi garrison, becoming Head, Bn Financial Service, later Deputy Head of Div. Financial Service and Inspector-Auditor 1984–92; Chair. Prestige-Inter (leather goods co.) 1992–99; Councillor, Chernivtsi Municipal Council 1994–2000, also Chair. of Budget Comm. and Chair. of Privatization Comm.; Financial Dir Tytan PJSC (chemical plant), Armyansk 1999–2002; Chair. Supervisory Bd Kremenchuk Steel Plant, Kremenchuk and Dniprovagonmash Co., Dnipropetrovsk 2002–05; Pres. Inter Car Group (investment group) 2005–06, Hon. Pres. 2006–; Pres. Sevastopol Econ. Devt Fund 2006–12; mem. Verkhovna Rada (Supreme Council, Parl.) 2006–13 (parl. mandate annulled by Parl.); Minister of Defence 2012–14 (dismissed); Medal of Distinction in Mil. Service, 1st Class, Crimean Autonomous Repub. State Prize in Industry, Merited Economist of Ukraine 2011. *Address:* c/o Ministry of Defence, 01021 Kyiv, vul. M. Hrushevskoho 30/1, Ukraine. *E-mail:* webmaster@mil.gov.ua.

LEBEDEV, Army Gen. Sergei Nikolayevich; Russian international organization official and fmr intelligence officer; *Executive Secretary, Commonwealth of Independent States;* b. 9 April 1948, Jizzax, Uzbek SSR; m. Vera Mikhailovna; two s.; ed Kyiv Polytechnic Inst., Ukrainian SSR, Diplomatic Acad. of USSR; staff mem., Chernihiv br., Kyiv Polytechnic Inst. 1970; army service 1971–72; with state security bodies 1973–75, Foreign Intelligence Service 1975–78; Rep. of Foreign Intelligence Service to USA 1998–2000; Dir Fed. Foreign Intelligence Service (SVR) 2000–07; Exec. Sec. Commonwealth of Ind. States (CIS) 2007–; numerous state awards. *Leisure interests:* travelling, Greco-Roman wrestling, shooting. *Address:* Office of the Executive Secretary, Commonwealth of Independent States, 220000 Minsk, vul. Kirova 17, Belarus (office). *Telephone:* (17) 222-35-17 (office). *Fax:* (17) 227-23-39 (office). *E-mail:* anna@cis.minsk.by (office). *Website:* www.cis.minsk.by (office).

LEBEDEVA, Tatyana Romanovna; Russian athlete; b. 21 July 1976, Sterlitamak, Volgograd; m.; two d.; joined Russian Army 1997, currently Lt-Col; specialises in triple jump and long jump; set two world records at 2004 World Indoor Championships in Budapest, finished with leap of 15.36m; produced best-ever series of triple jumps prior to 2000 Olympic Games, of 15.14m, 15.32m, 15.15m, 15.16m, 14.86m; personal best of 7.33m in long jump, Tula 2004; winner Gold Medal for triple jump, European Cup, Gateshead 2000, Bremen 2001, European Indoor Championships, Ghent 2000, Goodwill Games, Brisbane 2001, World Championships, Edmonton 2001, World Championships, Paris 2003, Russian Indoor Championships 2003, World Indoor Championships, Budapest 2004, European Championships, Gothenburg 2006; winner Gold Medal for long jump, World Indoor Championships, Budapest 2004, Olympic Games, Athens 2004, World Championships, Osaka 2007, Olympic Games, Beijing 2008; winner Silver Medal for triple jump, Int. Asscn of Athletics Feds (IAAF) World Cup, Johannesburg 1998, Goodwill Games, NY 1998, Olympic Games, Sydney 2000, World Indoor Championships, Lisbon 2001, World Championships, Osaka 2007, Olympic Games, Beijing 2008; winner Silver Medal for long jump, Olympic Games, Beijing 2008, World Championships, Berlin 2009; winner Bronze Medal for triple jump, World Jr Championships 1994, Olympic Games, Athens 2004; only athlete to record six wins in six Golden Leagues, winning Golden League jackpot 2005; mem. Volgograd Army Club, RUS. *Website:* www.lebedeva.ru.

LEBÈGUE, Daniel Simon Georges, BL; French independent financial director; *Chairman, Observatoire sur la Responsibilité Sociétale des Enterprises;* b. 4 May 1943, Lyon; s. of Robert Lebègue and Denise Lebègue (née Flachet); m. Chantal Biron 1970; one s. one d.; ed Univ. of Lyon, Inst. for Political Sciences and Nat. School for Admin., Paris; civil servant, Ministry of Economy and Finance 1969–73; Financial Adviser, Embassy in Japan 1974–76; Head of Balance of Payments Section, Treasury 1976–79, Head of Monetary Funds Section 1979–80; Deputy Dir of Savings and Financial Market 1980–81; Counsellor in charge of Economy and Finance, Prime Minister's Office 1981–83; Head of Dept of Financial and Monetary Affairs at Treasury 1983–84, Head of Treasury 1984–87; Pres. and COO Banque Nat. de Paris 1987–96, Vice-Chair. 1996–97; Pres. and CEO Caisse des dépôts et consignations (CDC) 1997–2002, Chair. CDC Ixis (formed after merger of CDC and CNCE) 2001–02; Dir SCOR SE 2003–; Chair. Institut Français des Administrateurs (French Inst. of Dirs) 2003–14, Observatoire sur la Responsibilité Sociétale des Enterprises 2008–; currently Chair. Transparency International (France); Chevalier, Légion d'honneur, Ordre nat. du Mérite. *Publications:* Le Trésor et la politique financière 1988, La fiscalité de l'épargne dans le marché unique européen 1988. *Leisure interests:* opera, cinema, hiking. *Address:* Observatoire sur la Responsibilité Sociétale des Enterprises, 25 rue du Charolais, 75012 Paris, France (office). *Telephone:* 1-43-46-02-22 (office). *Fax:* 1-43-46-86-99 (office). *E-mail:* contact@orse.org (office). *Website:* www.orse.org (office).

LEBEL, The Hon. Denis, PC, BA; Canadian politician (retd); *President and General Manager, Conseil de l'industrie forestière du Québec;* b. 26 May 1954, Roberval, Quebec; m. Danielle Girard; two c.; Mayor of Roberval 2000–07; mem. House of Commons for Roberval-Lac-Saint-Jean 2007–15, for Lac-Saint-Jean 2015–17; Minister of State for the Econ. Devt Agency of Canada for the Regions of Quebec 2008–15, Minister of Transport, Infrastructure and Communities 2011–13, of Infrastructure, Communities and Intergovernmental Affairs 2013–15; Pres. and Gen. Man. Conseil de l'industrie forestière du Québec 2017–; mem. Bd of Dirs Union des municipalités du Québec; fmr Chair. Caucus des municipalités voisines des Premières Nations; fmr Dir Infrastructure Québec; fmr Vice-Pres. Société d'aide au développement des collectivités Lac-Saint-Jean Ouest, Agence régionale de santé du Saguenay–Lac-Saint-Jean; mem. Conservative Party of Canada, Deputy Leader 2015–17. *Address:* Conseil de l'industrie forestière du Québec, 1175 Avenue Lavigerie, Québec, QC G1V 4P1, Canada. *Telephone:* (418) 657-7916 (office). *Fax:* (418) 657-7971 (office). *Website:* www.cifq.com.

LEBEL, Jean-Jacques; French artist, art critic and translator; b. 1936, Neuilly-sur-Seine; s. Robert Lebel; one s.; ed Accad. delle Belle Arti, Florence, Italy; first solo show Galleria Numero, Florence 1955; has exhibited in many galleries and museums in Europe, USA and Japan; ran Front Unique (poetry, art and politics magazine); worked with American Happening artists, Claes Oldenburg 1962 and Allan Kaprow 1963; involved in NO!art and took part in Involvement Show and Doom Show 1960–61, March Gallery, New York; has produced more than 80 Happenings (Direct Poetry actions or performances worldwide); set up Festival de la Libre Expression, American Center in Paris (an int. exchange of experimental arts); directed Picasso's Desire Caught by the Tail 1967; Co-founder (with son) and mem. Bd of Dirs Fonds de dotation Jean-Jacques Lebel 2013–. *Works include:* 8m high Monument to Felix Guattari (open-ended motorized multi-media desiring machine, including live performances and videos by poets, philosophers, musicians, anti-psychiatrists and artists close to Guattari and Lebel), Off Limits Exhbn, Centre Georges Pompidou, Paris 1994, large installation entitled Reliquaire pour un Culte de Venus. *Publications include:* Happening (The Burial of Tinguely's

Chose) 1960; has published 10 books of essays on culture and politics, including Poesie Directe, Happenings and Interventions, Paris 1994; trans of Ginsberg, Corso, Burroughs, Ferlinghetti were the first to appear in French. *Website:* fondsdedotationjjlebel.org.

LeBLANC, Dominic, PC, BA, LLB, LLM; Canadian lawyer and politician; *Minister of Intergovernmental and Northern Affairs and Internal Trade;* b. 14 Dec. 1967, Ottawa; s. of Roméo LeBlanc (fmr Gov. Gen. of Canada) and Joslyn Carter; m. Jolène Richard 2003; ed Trinity Coll., Univ. of Toronto, Univ. of New Brunswick, Harvard Law School, USA; began career as barrister and solicitor with Clark Drummie (law firm), Shediac and Moncton; Special Adviser to Prime Minister Jean Chrétien 1993–96; mem. House of Commons for Beauséjour 2000–, Parl. Sec. to Leader of the Govt in the House of Commons 2004–06, Parl. Sec. to Minister of Nat. Defence Jan.–Dec. 2003, Liberal Party House Leader 2012–, Leader of the Govt in the House of Commons 2015–, Minister of Fisheries, Oceans, and Canadian Coast Guard 2016–18, of Intergovernmental and Northern Affairs and Internal Trade 2018–; Pres. Queen's Privy Council for Canada 2018–; mem. Liberal Party of Canada. *Address:* Department of Intergovernmental Affairs, Privy Council Office, Rm 1000, 85 Sparks St, Ottawa, ON K1A 0A3, Canada (office). *Telephone:* (613) 957-5153 (office). *Fax:* (613) 957-5043 (office). *E-mail:* info@pco-bcp.gc.ca (office). *Website:* www.pco-bcp.gc.ca/aia (office).

LeBLANC, Matthew (Matt) Steven; American actor; b. 25 July 1967, Newton, Mass; son of Paul LeBlanc and Patricia LeBlanc; m. Melissa McKnight 2003 (divorced 2006); one d.; ed Newton North High School; trained as a carpenter; appeared in TV commercials for a variety of products, New York 1987; began formal acting training 1988; f. Fort Hill Productions (production co.). *Films include:* Anything to Survive 1990, Grey Knight (int. title The Killing Box) 1993, Red Shoe Diaries 3: Another Woman's Lipstick 1993, Lookin' Italian 1993, Ed 1996, Red Shoe Diaries 7: Burning Up 1997, Lost in Space 1998, Charlie's Angels 2000, All the Queen's Men 2001, Charlie's Angels: Full Throttle 2003, Lovesick 2014. *Television includes:* series: TV 101 (as Chuck Bender) 1988, Top of the Heap 1991, Vinnie & Bobby 1992, Red Shoe Diaries, Rebel Highway, Friends (as Joey Tribbiani) (Screen Actors Guild Award for Outstanding Performance by an Ensemble in a Comedy Series 1995, TV Choice Actor, Teen Choice Awards 2002, Favorite Male Television Star, People's Choice Awards 2005) 1994–2004, Joey 2004–06, Episodes (Golden Globe Award for Best Performance by an Actor in a Television Series – Comedy or Musical 2012) 2011–16, Web Therapy (series) 2013, Man with a Plan 2016–18; films: Anything to Survive 1990, Reform School Girl 1994, The Prince (dir) 2006, Jonah Hex (exec. producer) 2010; host: Top Gear (with Chris Evans) 2016–18. *Leisure interest:* landscape photography.

LEBONA, Sentje Leonard; Lesotho politician; *Minister of Defence and National Security;* fmr Sr Superintendent, Mohale's Hoek Correctional Inst.; mem. Nat. Ass. (Parl.) (ABC) for Mohale's Hoek constituency no. 58 2015–; Minister of Defence and Nat. Security 2017–; mem. All Basotho Convention (ABC). *Address:* Ministry of Defence and National Security, Kingsway, opp. National Library, Private Bag A166, Maseru 100, Lesotho (office). *Telephone:* 22326651 (office). *Fax:* 22310444 (office). *E-mail:* pglerotholi@gmail.com (office). *Website:* www.gov.ls/defence (office).

LEBOUDER, Jean-Pierre; Central African Republic politician; b. 1944; ed Ecole nationale supérieure agronomique, Toulouse, France; Dir Research Centre, Union cotonnière centrafricaine 1971–72, Dir-Gen. 1974–76; Minister of Rural Devt 1976, of Planning, Statistics and Int. Co-operation 1978–80; Prime Minister 1980–81; Minister of State, responsible for Planning, the Economy, Finance, the Budget and Int. Co-operation 2003–05.

LEBOUTHILLIER, Diane, PC, MP, BSc; Canadian politician and fmr social worker; *Minister of National Revenue;* three s.; ed Univ. de Moncton; more than 23 years as social worker with Rocher Percé Health and Social Services Centre; mem. House of Commons (Parl.) for Gaspésie–Les Îles-de-la-Madeleine 2015–; Minister of Nat. Revenue 2015–; fmr mem. Bd of Govs Cégep de la Gaspésie et des Îles (gen. and vocational coll.); fmr Chair. Réseau collectif Gaspésie Les Îles, Transport adapté et collectif des Anses; fmr Vice-Chair. Les Ateliers Actibec 2000 Inc.; mem. Liberal Party of Canada. *Address:* Office of the Minister of National Revenue, Canada Revenue Agency, 7th Floor, 555 McKenzie Avenue, Ottawa, ON K1A 0L5, Canada (office). *Telephone:* (613) 952-9184 (office). *Website:* www.cra-arc.gc.ca (office); dianelebouthillier.liberal.ca.

LEBOWITZ, Joel L., MS, PhD; American mathematician and academic; *George William Hill Professor of Mathematics and Physics, Rutgers University;* b. 10 May 1930, Taceva, Czechoslovakia; m. 1st Estelle Mandelbaum 1953 (died 1996); 2nd Ann K. Beneduce 1999; ed Brooklyn Coll. and Syracuse Univ.; Nat. Science Foundation Postdoctoral Fellow, Yale Univ. 1956–57; Asst Prof., Stevens Inst. of Tech. 1957–59; Asst Prof., Belfer Grad. School of Science, Yeshiva Univ. 1959–60, Assoc. Prof. 1960–65, Prof. of Physics 1965–77, Chair. Dept of Physics 1968–76; apptd Dir Center for Mathematical Sciences Research and Prof. of Math. and Physics, Rutgers Univ. 1977, currently George William Hill Prof. of Math. and Physics; Ed.-in-Chief, Journal of Statistical Physics 1975–; mem. NAS 1980–, AAAS, New York Acad. of Sciences, American Physical Soc.; Foreign mem. Accademia Nazionale dei Lincei; Fellow, American Math. Soc. 2012; Dr hc (Ecole Polytechnique Fédérale, Lausanne, Clark Univ.) 1999; Guggenheim Fellowship 1976–77, Boltzmann Medal 1992, Max Planck Research Award 1993, Delmar S. Fahrney Medal, Franklin Inst. 1994, AAAS Scientific Freedom and Responsibility Award 1999, Max Planck Medal, German Physical Soc. 2007, Henri Poincaré Prize, IAMP 2000, Grande Medaille de l'Academie des sciences 2014 and other awards. *Publications:* more than 450 scientific papers. *Address:* Room 612, Hill Center, Center for Mathematical Sciences Research, Rutgers University, 110 Frelinghuysen Road, Piscataway, NJ 08854-8019, USA (office). *Telephone:* (848) 445-3117 (office). *E-mail:* lebowitz@math.rutgers.edu (office). *Website:* www.math.rutgers.edu (office).

LEBRANCHU, Marylise; French politician and academic; *Minister of Reform of the State, Decentralization and Public Service;* b. 25 April 1947, Loudéac (Côtes-d'Armor); d. of Adolphe Perrault Lebranchu and Marie Epert; m. Jean Lebranchu 1970; three c.; ed Rennes Univ.; began career as researcher, semi-public co., Nord-Finistère 1973–78; joined Parti Socialiste Unifié (PSU) 1972, Parti Socialiste (PS) 1977; Parl. Asst to MP Marie Jacq 1978–93; Municipal Councillor, Morlaix (Finistère) 1983, Mayor 1995–97; Regional Councillor, Brittany 1986–; mem. Assemblée nationale (Parl.) for Finistère 1997, 2002–12; Minister of State attached to Minister for the Economy, Finance and Industry, with responsibility for small and medium-sized enterprises, trade and artisan activities 1997–2000, Minister of Justice and Keeper of the Seals 2000–02, Minister of Reform of the State, Decentralization and Public Service 2012–; Jr Lecturer in Econs, Univ. of Brest 1990–; Trombinoscope Politician of the Year Award 2000. *Publications:* Etre Juste, Justement, Brèves de campagne. *Leisure interest:* music. *Address:* Ministry of Reform of the State, Decentralization and Public Service, 80 rue de Lille, 75007 Paris Cedex 07, France (office). *Telephone:* 1-43-19-23-50 (office). *Fax:* 1-43-19-23-97 (office). *E-mail:* sec-mredfp-sp@action-publique.gouv.fr. *Website:* www.fonction-publique.gouv.fr (office).

LeBRETON, Marjory; Canadian politician; b. 1940, Nepean, Ont.; m. Douglas LeBreton; one s. one d. (deceased); ed Ottawa Business Coll.; worked for Progressive Conservative Party of Canada (PC) nat. campaign group 1962, 1963 general elections; worked in office of John G. Diefenbaker 1963–67, in office of Robert L. Stanfield 1967–75, office of Joe Clark 1976–79; mem. Senate 1993–2015, fmr Chief Opposition Whip, fmr mem. several Standing Cttees including Social Affairs, Human Rights, Forestry and Agric., Internal Economy, Banking, currently Co-Chair Senate Standing Cttee on Health, Leader of the Govt in the Senate 2006–13, Sec. of State for Seniors 2007–13; Chair. Mothers Against Drunk Drivers, Canada.

LECHLEITER, John C., BSc, MSc, PhD; American pharmaceutical industry executive; b. 17 Aug. 1952, Louisville, Ky; s. of John H. Lechleiter and Jeanne Lechleiter; m. Sarah Lechleiter; two s. one d.; ed Xavier Univ., Cincinnati, OH, Harvard Univ., Mass (NSF Fellow); joined Eli Lilly as sr organic chemist in process research and devt 1979, Pharmaceutical Product Devt Dir, Lilly Research Centre, Windlesham, UK 1983–86, Man. European Research and Devt, USA 1986–88, Dir Devt Projects Man. 1988–91, Exec. Dir Pharmaceutical Product Devt 1991–93, Vice-Pres. 1993, Vice-Pres. Regulatory Affairs 1994–96, Vice-Pres. Lilly Research Labs 1996–98, Sr Vice-Pres. Pharmaceutical Products 1998–2001, Exec. Vice-Pres. Pharmaceutical Products and Corporate Devt 2001–04, Exec. Vice-Pres. Pharmaceutical Operations 2004–05, mem. Bd of Dirs, Pres. and COO 2005–08, Pres. and CEO 2008–16, Chair. 2008–17; mem. Bd of Dirs, Ford Motor Co., United Way of Cen. Indiana, Fairbanks Inst. (also mem. Exec. Cttee), Cincinnati, Indianapolis Downtown, Inc., Pharmaceutical Research and Mfrs of America (PhRMA), Nike, Inc.; mem. Business Roundtable, Business Council; mem. Visiting Cttee, Harvard Business School 2004–, Health Policy and Man. Council, Harvard School of Public Health 2004–, Dean's Advisory Bd, Indiana Univ. School of Medicine; Distinguished Advisor, The Children's Museum of Indianapolis, Bd United Way Worldwide, Bd Life Sciences Foundation, Bd Central Indiana Corp. Partnership, 2012 Indianapolis Super Bowl Host Cttee; mem. Bd of Trustees Xavier Univ.; mem. ACS; Dr hc (Univ. of Indianapolis) 2012, (Nat. Univ. of Ireland) 2012, (Indiana Univ., Franklin Coll., Purdue Univ., Butler Univ.), Hon. DBA (Marian Coll., Indianapolis); Project HOPE Global Health Partner Award 2012, Int. Citizen of the Year Award 2015.

LECLERCQ, Patrick; French diplomatist; b. 2 Aug. 1938, Lille; m. 2nd Marie-Alice Berard; two s.; one s. from previous m.; ed Institut d'Etudes Politiques, Paris, Ecole Nat. d'Admin; joined Diplomatic Service 1966; Consul-Gen. Montréal, Canada 1982–85; Amb. to Jordan 1985–89, to Egypt 1991–96, to Spain 1996–99; Minister of State and Dir of External Relations for Monaco 2000–05; Dir Société des Bains de Mer; Officier, Légion d'honneur, Commdr, Ordre nat. du Mérite, several foreign decorations, including Orden del Merito and Isabel la Católica, Spain, Ordre de Saint-Charles, Monaco 2002. *Address:* 3 rue Francisque Sarcey, 75116 Paris, France. *Telephone:* 1-40-72-65-28. *E-mail:* leclercq_patrick@hotmail.fr.

LECOINTRE, Gen. François Gérard Marie; French army officer; *Chief of Staff of the Armed Forces;* b. 6 Feb. 1962, Cherbourg; m.; four d.; ed École spéciale mil. de Saint-Cyr, École de l'infanterie, Inter-arm Defence Coll., Morbihan, Centre des hautes études militaires, Paris; Combat Platoon Commdr, 3rd Marine Infantry Regt (3e RIMa) 1988–91, Combat Co. Commdr, 3e RIMa, Vannes 1993–96, Instructor, École spéciale mil. de Saint-Cyr, Morbihan 1996–99, Speechwriter and later Desk Officer (programme), Office of Chief of Staff of French Army 2001–05, Commanding Officer, 3e RIMa, Vannes 2005–07, Commdr, 9th Marine Infantry Brigade, Poitiers 2011–13, Commdr, EU Training Mission, Mali Jan.–July 2013, Chargé de Mission, Gen. Staff HQ of French Army, becoming Deputy Chief of Gen. Staff HQ 2014–16, Head of Prime Minister's mil. cabinet 2016–17, Chief of Staff of the Armed Forces 2017–; deployed abroad to Iraq during Opération Daguet (Desert Storm), Kuwait 1991, Opération Oryx, Somalia 1992, Opération Turquoise, Rwanda 1994, Battle of Vrbanja Bridge, Sarajevo 1995, Opération Licorne, Côte d'Ivoire 2005; rank of Second Lt 1986, Lt 1987, Capt. 1991, Maj. 1996, Lt Col 2000, Col 2003, Brig.-Gen. 2011, Maj.-Gen. 2015, Lt Gen. 2017, Gen. 2017; Commdr, Légion d'honneur, Commdr, ordre nat. du Mérite, Croix de la Valeur militaire, Commdr, ordre nat. du Mali; Kuwait Liberation Medal. *Address:* Ministry of Defence, Hôtel de Brienne, 14 rue St Dominique, 75007 Paris, France (office). *Website:* www.defense.gouv.fr/terre (office).

LECONTE, Patrice; French film director and screenwriter; b. 12 Nov. 1947, Tours; m. Agnès Béraud; two c.; ed Institut des Hautes Etudes Cinématographiques. *Films include:* L'Espace vital 1969, Le Laboratoire de l'angoisse 1971, La Famille heureuse (Famille Gazul) 1973, Les Vécés étaient fermés de l'interieur 1976, Les Bronzés 1978, Les Bronzés font du ski 1979, Viens chez moi, j'habite chez une copine 1981, Ma femme s'appelle reviens 1982, Circulez y'a rien à voir 1983, Les Spécialistes 1985, Tandem 1987), Monsieur Hire 1989, Le Mari de la coiffeuse 1990, Contre l'oubli 1991, Le Batteur du boléro 1992, Tango 1993, Le Parfum d'Yvonne 1994, Lumière et compagnie 1996, Les Grands ducs 1996, Ridicule 1996, Une chance sur deux 1998, La Fille sur le pont 1999, La Veuve de Saint-Pierre 2000, Félix et Lola 2001, Rue des plaisirs 2002, L'Homme du train 2002, Confidences trop intimes 2004, Dogora-Ouvrons les yeux 2004, Les Bronzés 3: amis pour la vie 2006, Mon meilleur ami 2006, La Guerre des miss 2008, Voir la mer 2011, The Suicide Shop 2012, A Promise 2013, Do Not Disturb 2014.

LECOURTIER, Christophe; French civil servant, business executive and diplomatist; *CEO, Business France;* ed Ecole Nat. d'Admin and Ecole Normale

Supérieure; long career working for Ministry of Economy, Finances and Industry, including as adviser in charge of int. econ. relations, worked as Chief of Staff for Minister for Trade, François Loos, and as Adviser to Minister for Economy, Finances and Industry, Francis Mer, held position of First Asst Sec. in charge of Continental Asia, Div. of External Econ. Relations, Ministry of Economy, Finance and Industry, also served in Prime Minister's Office, responsible for External Relations with EU, fmr Chief of Staff and Special Adviser to Christine Lagarde; CEO Ubifrance (French agency for int. business devt) –2014, Business France 2017–; Amb. to Australia 2014–17; Chevalier, Légion d'honneur, Ordre nat. du Mérite. *Address:* Business France, 77 blvd Saint-Jacques, 75014 Paris, France (office). *Telephone:* 1-40-73-30-00 (office). *E-mail:* accueilexport@businessfrance.fr (office). *Website:* www.businessfrance.fr (office).

LEDER, Philip, MD, FAAS; American geneticist and academic; *John Emory Andrus Professor Emeritus of Genetics and Head, Department of Genetics, Harvard Medical School;* b. 19 Nov. 1934, Washington, DC; ed Harvard Coll. and Harvard Medical School; Intern and Resident in Medicine, Univ. of Minnesota Hosps 1960–62; Research Assoc., Biochemical Genetics, NIH Nat. Heart Inst., Bethesda, Md 1962, joined lab. of Marshall Nirenberg 1963, Research Medical Officer, Biosynthesis, Lab. of Biochemistry, Nat. Cancer Inst. 1966–69; Chair. Dept of Biochemistry, Grad. Program of Foundation for Advanced Educ. in the Sciences 1968–73, mem. Bd of Dirs 1968–74 (Vice-Pres. Foundation 1970–71, Pres. 1973); Head, Section on Molecular Genetics, Lab. of Molecular Genetics, Nat. Inst. of Child Health and Human Devt 1969–71, Dir Lab. for Molecular Genetics 1972–80; John Emory Andrus Prof. of Genetics and Head Dept of Genetics, Harvard Medical School 1980–2008, Prof. Emer. 2008–, Dir Harvard Inst. of Human Genetics 1995–2008; Sr Investigator, Howard Hughes Medical Inst. 1986–2004; Visiting Scientist, Weizmann Inst., Rehovot, Israel 1965–66; Dir Pharmacia (fmrly Monsanto Co.) 1990, Genome Therapeutics, Inc. 1994, Schering-Plough Corpn 2003; mem. NAS 1979, American Acad. of Arts and Sciences 1981, Inst. of Medicine 1982; Trustee and Chair. Bd Charles A. Revson Foundation; Trustee Foundation for Advanced Educ. in the Sciences, Hadassah Medical Org. 1996–; Hon. Trustee, Massachusetts Gen. Hosp.; Hon. DSc (Yale Univ.) 1984, (Mount Sinai Medical Center) 1985, (Univ. of Guelph) 1986, (Hebrew Univ. of Jerusalem) 1996; Detur Award for Academic Excellence 1954, NIH Director's Award 1976, Drew Award in Biomedical Research, CIBA-Geigy Ltd 1978, Award in Biological and Medical Sciences, New York Acad. of Sciences 1978, Warren Triennial Prize, Massachusetts Gen. Hosp. 1980, Dickson Prize, Univ. of Pittsburgh School of Medicine 1980, NAS Richard Lounsberry Award 1981, Harvey Prize in Human Health, Technion-Israel Inst. of Tech. 1983, Award for Distinguished Research in the Biomedical Sciences, American Asscn of Medical Colls 1983, Steven C. Beering Award for Advancement of Biomedical Science, Indiana Univ. School of Medicine 1984, Bristol-Meyers Award for Distinguished Achievement in Cancer Research (co-recipient) 1985, Giovanni Lorenzini Foundation Prize for Basic Biomedical Research 1987, Albert Lasker Basic Medical Research Award 1987, Cancer Research Award in Basic Sciences Milken Family Medical Foundation 1988, V.D. Mattia Award, Roche Inst. of Molecular Biology 1988, Nat. Medal of Science 1989, Dr H.P. Heinekin Prize for Biochemistry, Royal Netherlands Acad. of Arts and Sciences 1990, Lee Kuan Yew Distinguished Visitorship, Repub. of Singapore 1990, Ernst W. Bertner Award, Univ. of Texas M.D. Anderson Cancer Center 1991, City of Medicine Award, City of Durham, NC 1991, American Coll. of Physicians Award 1991, Distinguished Alumnus Award, NIH Nat. Inst. of Child Health and Human Devt 1994, William Allan Award for Exceptional Contributions in the Field of Human Genetics, American Soc. of Human Genetics 1997, Albert Einstein Lecturer, Israel Acad. of Sciences and Humanities 2000. *Publications:* more than 240 articles in scientific journals. *Address:* Department of Genetics, Harvard Medical School, New Research Building, Room 358d, 77 Avenue Louis Pasteur, Boston, MA 02115, USA (office). *Telephone:* (617) 432-7667 (office). *Fax:* (617) 432-7944 (office). *E-mail:* leder@receptor.med.harvard.edu (office). *Website:* genetics.med.harvard.edu/faculty/leder (office).

LEDEZMA CORNEJO, Jorge; Bolivian lawyer, diplomatist and politician; *Minister of National Defence;* b. 24 Aug. 1963; Vice-Pres. Irrigation Users Departmental Fed. of Cochabamba 1997; Dir Irrigation Users Asscn, Sacaba 1998; Chair. Supervisory Cttee, Municipality of Sacaba 1998; mem. Municipal Council, Sacaba 1999, Mayor of Sacaba 2000–01; mem. Bolivian Nat. Congress (Parl.) for Sacaba and Chapare constituency 2002–08; Acting Prefect of Cochabamba 2008–10; Amb. to Peru 2011–15; Minister of Nat. Defence 2015–. *Address:* Ministry of National Defence, Calle 20 de Octubre 2502, esq. Pedro Salazar, La Paz, Bolivia (office). *Telephone:* (2) 243-2525 (office). *Fax:* (2) 243-3153 (office). *E-mail:* utransparencia@mindef.gob.bo (office). *Website:* www.mindef.gob.bo (office).

LEDINGHAM, John Gerard Garvin, MA, DM, FRCP; British medical scientist and academic; *Professor Emeritus of Clinical Medicine, University of Oxford;* b. 19 Oct. 1929, London; s. of John Ledingham and Una C. Garvin; grandson of J. L. Garvin; m. Dr Elaine Maliphant 1962; four d.; ed Rugby School, New Coll. Oxford and Middlesex Hosp. London; Registrar, Middlesex Hosp. 1960–62; Sr Registrar in Medicine, Westminster Hosp. 1962–64; Visiting Fellow, Columbia Univ., New York 1965–66; Consultant Physician, United Oxford Hosps 1966–74; May Reader in Medicine, Univ. of Oxford 1974–95, Prof. of Clinical Medicine 1989–95, Prof. Emer. 1995–, Dir of Clinical Studies 1977–81, 1990–95; Fellow, New Coll. Oxford 1974–95, Emer. Fellow 1995–, Hon. Fellow 2001–, Sub-Warden 1994–95; Hon. Clinical Dir Biochemical and Clinical NMR Unit, Medical Research Council 1988–95; mem. Nuffield Council on Bioethics 2001–03; Trustee, Nuffield Trust 1978–2002, Beit Trust 1988–2008; Hon. Fellow, New Coll. Oxford, Distinguished Friend of Oxford 2011; Osler Memorial Medal 2000. *Publications:* Oxford Textbook of Medicine (co-ed.) 1983, Concise Oxford Textbook of Medicine 2000, We Hope to Get Word Tomorrow – The Garvin Family Letters 1914–1916 (co-ed.) 2009; contribs to medical journals. *Leisure interests:* music, reading, golf. *Address:* 124 Oxford Road, Cumnor, Oxford, OX2 9PQ, England (home). *Telephone:* (1865) 865806 (home). *Fax:* (1865) 865806 (home). *E-mail:* jeled@btopenworld.com (home).

LEE, Allen Peng-Fei, CBE, OBE, BS, JP; Chinese business executive; b. 24 April 1940, Chefoo; m. Maria Choi Yuen Ha; two s. one d.; ed Univ. of Michigan, USA; joined Lockheed Aircraft Ltd 1966, Test Eng Supervisor 1966–67, Test Eng Man. 1968–70; Eng Operations Man. Fabri-Teck Ltd 1967; Test Man., Ampex Ferrotec Ltd 1970–72, Man. Dir 1974–79; Gen. Man. Dataproducts Hong Kong Ltd 1972–74; Man. Dir Ampex World Operations SA 1979–83, Ampex Far East Operations 1983–; Dir, consultant Elec & Eltek Co. Ltd 1984; Chair. Hong Kong Productivity Council 1982; Chair. Hong Kong Liberal Party 1994–98; Deputy NPC 1997–2004; Chair. Pacific Dimensions Consultants Ltd; Dir Sam Woo Holdings Ltd 2003–; mem. Industry Devt Bd 1983, Hong Kong Gen. Chamber of Commerce (Cttee and Council mem.), Fed. of Hong Kong Industries, Broadcasting Review Bd 1984, Political Section of Preparatory Cttee for Hong Kong Special Admin. Region; Outstanding Young Persons of Hong Kong Award 1977. *Leisure interests:* fishing, swimming, tennis. *Address:* c/o Liberal Party, Shun Ho Tower, 2/F, 24–30 Ice House Street, Central Energy Plaza, Tsimshatsui East, Kowloon, Hong Kong Special Administrative Region, People's Republic of China (office).

LEE, Ang, BA, MA, MFA; American (b. Taiwanese) film director; b. 23 Oct. 1954, Chaochou, Pingtung; m. Jane Lin 1983; two s.; ed Nat. Taiwan Coll. of Arts, Univ. of Illinois, Urbana-Champaign, Tisch School of the Arts, New York Univ.; moved to USA 1978; classmate of Spike Lee at NYU; finished a 16mm short film, Shades of the Lake that won Best Drama Award in Short Film in Taiwan 1982; winner of nat. script-writing contest (Taiwanese Govt) 1990. *Films:* Pushing Hands 1992, The Wedding Banquet (Asia-Pacific Film Festival Best Film) 1993, Eat Drink Man Woman (Asia-Pacific Film Festival Best Film) 1995, Sense and Sensibility 1996, The Ice Storm 1998, Ride with the Devil 1998, Crouching Tiger, Hidden Dragon (Acad. Award for Best Foreign Film, David Lean Award for Best Dir, BAFTA Award 2001, Golden Globe for Best Dir 2001) 1999, Chosen 2001, Hulk 2003, Brokeback Mountain (Venice Film Festival Golden Lion, Critics' Choice Award for Best Film and Best Dir, Golden Globe for Best Dir and Best Drama, Dirs Guild of America Best Dir 2006, BAFTA David Lean Award for Achievement in Direction 2006, Acad. Award for Best Dir 2006) 2005, Sè, Jiè (Lust, Caution) (Golden Lion, Venice Film Festival 2007) 2007, Taking Woodstock 2009, Life of Pi (Academy Award for Best Dir 2013) 2012, Billy Lynn's Long Halftime Walk 2016. *Address:* c/o Creative Artists Agency, 2000 Avenue of the Stars, Los Angeles, CA 90067, USA (office). *Telephone:* (424) 288-2000 (office). *Fax:* (424) 288-2900 (office). *Website:* www.caa.com (office).

LEE, Bill, BS; American business executive and politician; *Governor of Tennessee;* b. 9 Oct. 1959, Franklin, Tenn.; m. 1st Carol Ann Lee 1984 (died 2000); m. 2nd Maria Lee 2008; two s. two d.; ed Auburn Univ.; Pres. Lee Co. 1992–2016, Chair. 2016–19; Gov. of Tenn. 2019–; fmr Chair. YMCA, Middle Tenn.; fmr Pres. Associated Builders and Contractors, Tennesseans for Econ. Growth; mem. Bd, Hope Clinic for Women, Men of Valor Prison Ministry; mem. Bd of Trustees, Belmont Univ.; Most Admired CEO, Nashville Business Journal 2015. *Address:* Office of the Governor, State Capitol, 1st Floor, 600 Dr Martin L. King, Jr Blvd, Nashville, TN 37243, USA (office). *Telephone:* (615) 741-2001 (office). *Website:* www.tn.gov/governor (office).

LEE, Brett; Australian professional cricketer and television commentator; b. 8 Nov. 1976, Wollongong, NSW; s. of Bob Lee and Helen Lee (née Buxton); m. Elizabeth Kemp 2006 (divorced 2009); one s.; m. Lana Anderson 2014; one d.; ed Balarang Public School, Oak Flats High School; bowler; lower order right-handed batsman; right-arm fast bowler; plays for NSW 1995–2012, Australia 1999–2012, Kings XI Punjab 2008–10, Kolkata Knight Riders 2011–13, Wellington 2011, Sydney Sixers 2011–15; First-class debut: 1994/95; Test debut: Australia v India, Melbourne 26–30 Dec. 1999; One-Day Int. (ODI) debut: Australia v Pakistan, Brisbane 9 Jan. 2000; T20I debut: NZ v Australia, Auckland 17 Feb. 2005; played in 76 Tests, took 310 wickets and scored 1,451 runs, highest score 64, average 20.15, best bowling (innings) 5/30, (match) 9/171; ODIs: 221 matches, scored 1,176 runs, highest score 59, average 17.81, took 380 wickets, average 23.36, best bowling 5/22; First-class: 116 matches, 2,120 runs, highest score 97, average 18.59, took 487 wickets, average 28.22, best bowling 7/114; retd from Test cricket Feb. 2010, from int. cricket July 2012; retd from all forms of the game 2015; ranked with Pakistani bowler Shoaib Akhtar as the fastest bowler in contemporary cricket during most of decade 2000–09; first player in Twenty20 Int. cricket to take a hat-trick; launched own fashion label 'BL' 2001; cricket commentator for Channel Nine; f. Mewsic Foundation in India 2011; apptd Cochlear's Global Hearing Amb. by 2015–; mem. (with brother Shane and fmr NSW cricketers Brad McNamara, Gavin Robertson and Richard Chee Quee) rock band Six & Out; Hon. mem. Lord's Cricket Ground 2013; inaugural Donald Bradman Young Player of the Year Award 2000, Wisden Young Cricketer of the Year 1999–2000, VB Series Player of the Series 2002–03, VB Series Player of the Series 2004–05, chosen in Australia's Greatest ODI XI (selected by fmr and current Australian ODI reps), chosen in ODI Team of the Year at ICC (Int. Cricket Council) Awards 2005, chosen in Test Team of the Year at ICC Awards 2006, chosen in ODI Team of the Year at ICC Awards 2006, Wisden Cricketer of the Year 2006, DLF Cup Player of the Tournament 2006, Warne-Muralitharan Trophy Player of the Series 2007, Border-Gavaskar Trophy Player of the Series 2007–08, McGilvray Medallist for ABC's Australian Test Player of the year 2007, Australian Test Player of the Year 2008, Allan Border Medallist 2008, chosen in ODI Team of the Year at ICC Awards 2008, chosen in Test Team of the Year at ICC Awards 2008, Champions League Twenty20 Player of the Series 2009. *Film:* UnIndian 2016. *Television:* fmr Host, Personal Best. *Music:* recording: You're the One For Me (duet with Asha Bhosle). *Publication:* My Life (with James Knight) (autobiog.) 2011. *Address:* Mewsic Foundation, Khar West, Mumbai 400052, India. *E-mail:* emily.r.menon@innovaid.co.in; mark@brettlee.com.au. *Website:* www.mewsic.in; www.brettlee.com.au.

LEE, C. Y., MArch; Taiwanese (b. Chinese) architect; *Principal, C. Y. Lee & Partners Architects/Planners;* b. 30 Dec. 1938, Guangdong, China; ed Nat. Cheng Kung Univ., Princeton Univ., USA; Prin. C. Y. Lee & Partners Architects/Planners, Taiwan 1978–; Prof., Dept of Architecture, Waseda Univ., Japan 2003–06; architect of Taipei 101, world's tallest building 2004–10; first China Outstanding Architect Award 1995, winner, Architecture Category, Nat. Awards for Arts 2008. *Major works include:* in Taiwan: Hung Kuo Building, Taipei 1989, Grand 50 Tower, Kaohsiung (Taiwan's tallest building 1992–93), Far Eastern Plaza I & II, Taipei 1994, Tuntex Sky Tower, Kaohsiung (Taiwan's tallest building 1997–2004), Grand Formosa, Taichung 1997, Taiwan Taoyuan Int. Airport-Terminal 2, Taoyuan (Buddhist temple, tallest Buddhist Building in the world

2001–06), New Chien-Cheng Circle, Taipei 2003, Taipei 101, Taipei (Taiwan's tallest building 2004–, world's tallest skyscraper 2004–10), W Taipei; in China: Post & Telecommunications Centre, Tianjin 1998, Yuda International Trade Centre, Zhengzhou 1999, Fangyuan Mansion, Shenyang 2001, Jinsha Plaza, Shenyang 2001, Pangu 7 Star Hotel, Beijing 2008. *Address:* C.Y. Lee & Partners Architects/Planners, 13th Floor, No. 178, Sec. 3, Ming-Quan East Road, Taipei, 10542, Taiwan (office). *Telephone:* (2) 2719-8288 (office). *Fax:* (2) 2719-8808 (office). *E-mail:* info@cyleearchitect.com (office). *Website:* www.cyleearchitect.com (office).

LEE, Chang-hee; South Korean accountant, academic and business executive; *Chairman, POSCO;* Certified Public Accountant, Min, Sohn & Kim, Samil PricewaterhouseCoopers; Prof., Coll. of Law, Seoul Nat. Univ.; Ind. Dir (non-exec.), Pohang Iron and Steel Co. (POSCO) 2009–, Chair. 2014–; Int. Dir, Tax Law Asscn. *Address:* POSCO Head Office, 1 Goedong-dong, Nam-gu, Pohang, Kyongsangbuk-do, 790-600, Republic of Korea (office). *Telephone:* (54) 220-0114 (office). *Fax:* (54) 220-6000 (office). *E-mail:* info@posco.com (office). *Website:* www .posco.com (office).

LEE, Datuk Chong Wei; Malaysian badminton player; b. 21 Oct. 1982, Bagan Serai, Perak; m. Wong Mew Choo 2012; two c.; began playing badminton at age 11; winner Asian Badminton Championships 2006, Silver Medal, Olympic Games, Beijing 2008, Gold Medal, Commonwealth Games, Delhi 2010, Silver Medal, Asian Games 2010, Winner All-England Open Men's Singles 2010, 2011, Malaysia Open Grand Prix Gold 2011, India Open 2011, Indonesian Open 2011, Malaysia Masters 2016, Malaysia Open 2016, Indonesia Open 2016; apptd Amb. KDU Univ. Coll. 2011; several awards including Penang Sportsman 2005, 2007, 2008, 2009, Malaysia's Male Olympian 2008, BWF Player of the Year Award 2013, Most Popular Icon on Television Award 2013. *Publication:* Dare to be a Champion (autobiography) 2012. *Website:* www.leechongwei.com.

LEE, David Morris, AB, MS, PhD; American physicist and academic; *Professor of Physics, Texas A&M University ;* b. 20 Jan. 1931, Rye, NY; s. of Marvin Lee and Annette Lee (née Franks); m. Dana Thorangkul 1960; two s.; ed Harvard Univ., Univ. of Connecticut, Yale Univ.; served in US Army 1952–54; Instructor in Physics, Cornell Univ., Ithaca, NY 1959–60, Asst Prof. 1960–63, Assoc. Prof. 1963–68, Prof. 1968–97; James Gilbert White Distinguished Prof. of Physical Sciences 1997–2007, now Prof. Emer.; Prof. of Physics, Texas A&M Univ. 2009–; Visiting Scientist, Brookhaven Nat. Lab., Upton, NY 1966–67; Visiting Prof., Univ. of Fla 1974–75, 1994, Univ. of Calif., San Diego 1988; Visiting Lecturer, Peking Univ., Beijing, China 1981; Chair. Joseph Fourier Univ., Grenoble, France 1994; mem. American Acad. of Arts and Sciences, NAS; Foreign mem. Russian Acad. of Sciences 2007–; Fellow, AAAS, American Physical Soc., ACS, British Inst. of Physics, Japan Soc. for Promotion of Sciences 1977; John Simon Guggenheim Fellow 1966–67, 1974–75; Dr hc (Univ. of Connecticut, Polytechnic Inst. of New York Univ. of Florida, Univ. of Buenos Aires, Joseph Fourier Univ., Lancaster Univ.); Sir Francis Simon Memorial Prize, British Inst. of Physics 1976, Oliver Buckley Prize, American Physical Soc. 1981, Nobel Prize for Physics (jtly) 1996, Wilber Cross Medal, Yale Univ. 1998. *Achievements include:* co-discoverer superfluid 3He, tricritical point of 3He-4He mixtures; co-observation of spin waves in spin polarized hydrogen gas. *Address:* MPHY 572B, Texas A&M University, Department of Physics and Astronomy, College Station, TX 77843-4242, USA (office). *Telephone:* (979) 458-7938 (office). *Fax:* (979) 845-2590 (office). *E-mail:* dmlee@physics.tamu.edu (office). *Website:* physics.tamu.edu (office).

LEE, David Tawei, PhD; Taiwanese editor, academic, government official and diplomatist; b. 15 Oct. 1949, Taipei; m.; one s. one d.; ed Nat. Taiwan Univ., Univ. of Virginia, USA; Man. Ed. Asia and the World Forum 1976–77; staff consultant, Co-ordination Council for N American Affairs, Washington, DC 1982–88; Prin. Asst to Minister of Foreign Affairs 1988–89; Adjunct Assoc. Prof. of Int. Politics, Grad. School of Social Science, Nat. Taiwan Normal Univ. 1988–93; Deputy Dir Dept of Int. Information Services, Govt Information Office 1989–90; Deputy Dir Dept of N American Affairs, Ministry of Foreign Affairs 1990–93, Dir 1996, Deputy Minister of Foreign Affairs 1998–2001, Minister of Foreign Affairs 2016–18; Assoc. in Research, Fairbank Center for E Asian Research, Harvard Univ. 1993–96; Dir-Gen. Taipei Econ. and Cultural Office, Boston 1993–96; Deputy Dir-Gen. Govt Information Office, Exec. Yuan 1996–97; Dir-Gen. Govt Information Office, Exec. Yuan and Govt Spokesman 1997–2000; Rep. to Belgium, Luxembourg and EU, Brussels 2001–04; to USA 2004–07; to Canada 2007–12; Chair. Co-ordination Council for N American Affairs, Taipei 2012–14; Rep., Taipei Econ. and Cultural Office in Australia 2014–16. *Address:* c/o Ministry of Foreign Affairs, 2 Kaitakeland Blvd, Taipei 10048, Taiwan (office).

LEE, Gang-yon, BA (Econ), MBA; South Korean business executive; *Senior Advisor, Lee International IP & Law Group;* m.; one s. one d.; ed Yonsei Univ., New York Univ. Grad. School of Business Admin, Manufacturers Hanover Trust Co.'s Exec. Training Program, IMF's Balance of Payments Methodology Course, US Dept of State's AID Int. Capital Markets Program; began career in public admin at Ministry of Finance serving as Deputy Dir Foreign Exchange Control Div., Int. Finance Div. and Treasury Div. 1969–75, Foreign Investment Promotion Officer, then Dir of Insurance Div., Securities Div. and Foreign Fund Div. 1976–80, Dir Gen. augmented to US Customs Service and Customs Counsellor of Korean Embassy in Washington, DC 1984–90, additionally, Dir Gen. Korea Customs Service's Int. Co-operation and Valuation Bureau 1991–95, Investigation Bureau 1995–97, Korea Customs Service's Deputy Commr 1997–99, Chair. Ministry of Finance's Advisory Cttees of the Task Force for the Establishment of the Korean Financial Intelligence Unit 2000–01, Ministry of Finance & Economy's Prevention of Money Laundering Cttee 2002–05; Adjunct Prof., Grad. School of Industry and Business, Dankook Univ. 2001–07; Sr Advisor, Lee International IP & Law Group 2000–05, 2013–; Sr Advisor, Samjong KPMG 2005–12; Chair. Korea Gas Corpn (KOGAS) 2006–09; Chair. Sejong Trade & Customs Advisory Services, Inc. 2008–12, Asia Pacific Trade & Customs Advisory Services 2012–; Corp. Advisor, Fila Korea Ltd 2012–; Outside Dir (and mem. Audit Cttee) Hyundai Heavy Industries Co. Ltd 2003–06, Shin Dong-Ah Fire & Marine Insurance Co. 2002–07, CJ Freshway 2012–; Research Advisor, Korea Inst. for Int. Econ. Policy 1999–2007; mem. Asia Pacific Advisory Bd of Deutsche Bank 2008–13; Vice-Chair. Korean-American Asscn 2013–; Order of Service Merit Red Stripe 1992. *Publication:* Money Laundering (third edn). *Leisure interests:* playing golf, hiking. *Address:* Lee International IP & Law Group, 14F Poongsan Building, 23

Chungjeongro, Seodaemun-Gu, Seoul, 120-837, Republic of Korea (office). *Telephone:* (2) 2189-3605 (office). *E-mail:* gylee@leeinternational.com (office). *Website:* www.leeinternational.com (office).

LEE, Hae-chan; South Korean politician; *Chairman, Democratic Party of Korea (Minjoo Party of Korea);* b. 10 July 1952, Cheongyang County; one c.; fmr Vice-Mayor of Seoul; fmr chief policy-maker for Millennium Democratic Party; mem. Nat. Ass. 1988–2008, 2012–16; Minister for Educ. 1998–99; Prime Minister 2004–06 (resgnd); Leader, Uri Party 2003–07, party merged with Democratic Party 2007, now Minjoo Party of Korea, interim Leader –2016, Chair. 2018–. *Address:* Democratic Party of Korea (Minjoo Party of Korea), 14, Gukhoe-daero 68-gil, Youngdeungpo-gu, Seoul 150-036, Republic of Korea (office). *Telephone:* (2) 1577-7667 (office). *Fax:* (2) 2630-0000 (office). *Website:* theminjoo.kr (office).

LEE, Han-dong, BA; South Korean politician; b. 5 Dec. 1934, Gyeonggi-do; m. Nam Sook Cho; one s. two d.; ed Kyungbok High School, Seoul Nat. Univ.; Mil. Prosecutor, Rep. of Korea Army 1959, Staff Judge Advocate with 5th Corps 1961; Judge, Seoul Dist Court 1963, Prosecutor 1969, Prosecutor, Seoul High Prosecutor's Office and Deputy Dir of Legal Affairs Training, Ministry of Justice 1974; Sr Prosecutor, Daejeon Dist Prosecutor's Office 1975, Pusan Dist Prosecutor's Office 1977, Seoul Dist Prosecutor's Office 1980; elected mem. Nat. Ass. 1981, Deputy Floor Leader for Democratic Justice Party (DJP) 1981, Floor Leader, Democratic Liberal Party (DLP) 1986, 1993, Vice-Speaker 1995; Chief Sec. to Party Pres. 1982, DJP Sec.-Gen. 1984, mem. Cen. Exec. Council 1990; Minister of Home Affairs 1988; Sr Adviser to Party Pres. 1996; Chief Exec. and Chair. New Korea Party 1997, Grand Nat. Party 1997, Vice-Pres. 1998, Acting Pres. 1998; Acting Pres. United Liberal Democrats 2000, apptd Pres. 2000; Prime Minister of Repub. of Korea 2000–02; unsuccessful presidential cand. 2002; Service Merit Medal 1976.

LEE, Dame Hermione, DBE, CBE, MA, FBA, FRSL; British writer, broadcaster and academic; *Professor Emeritus, Oxford University;* b. 29 Feb. 1948, Winchester, Hants.; d. of Dr Benjamin Lee and Josephine Lee; m. John Barnard 1991; ed Univ. of Oxford; Instructor, Coll. of William and Mary, Williamsburg, Va, USA 1970–71; Lecturer, Dept of English, Univ. of Liverpool 1971–77; Lecturer, Dept of English, Univ. of York 1977–87, Sr Lecturer 1987–90, Reader 1990–93, Prof. 1993–98; Goldsmiths' Chair of English Literature and Fellow of New Coll., Oxford 1998–2008, Pres. Wolfson Coll., Oxford 2008–17; now Prof. Emer. of English Literature, Oxford Univ.; presenter of Book Four on Channel Four TV (UK) 1982–86; Chair. of Judges, Man Booker Prize for Fiction 2006; Mel and Lois Tukman Fellow, Dorothy and Lewis B. Cullman Center for Scholars and Writers, New York Public Library 2004–05; Foreign Hon. mem. American Acad. of Arts and Sciences; Hon. Fellow, St Hilda's Coll. Oxford 1998, St Cross Coll. Oxford 1998; Hon. DLitt (Liverpool) 2002, (York) 2007. *Publications include:* The Novels of Virginia Woolf 1977, Elizabeth Bowen 1981 (2nd ed. 1999), Philip Roth 1982, The Secret Self I 1985 and II 1987, The Mulberry Tree: Writings of Elizabeth Bowen 1986, Willa Cather: A Life Saved Up 1989, Virginia Woolf 1996, Virginia Woolf: Moments of Being (ed.) 2002, Body Parts: Essays on Life-Writing 2005, Virginia Woolf's Nose 2005, Edith Wharton (biog.) 2007, Biography: A Very Short Introduction 2009, Penelope Fitzgerald: A Life (biog., James Tait Black Prize 2014, Plutarch Award 2015) 2013; Co-Ed. (with David Constantine and Bernard O'Donoghue): Oxford Poets 2000: An Anthology, Oxford Poets 2001: An Anthology, Oxford Poets 2002: An Anthology; Consultant Ed., The Good Fiction Guide 2001, 2002; Assoc. Ed., The Oxford Companion to English Literature (seventh edn). *Leisure interests:* reading, music, countryside. *Address:* c/o United Agents, 12–26 Lexington Street, London, W1F 0LE, England (office). *Telephone:* (20) 3214-0800 (office). *Fax:* (20) 3214-0801 (office). *E-mail:* info@unitedagents.co.uk (office). *Website:* unitedagents.co.uk (office).

LEE, Hoesung, BA, PhD; South Korean economist and international organization official; *Chairman, Intergovernmental Panel on Climate Change (IPCC);* b. 31 Dec. 1945; ed Seoul Nat. Univ., Rutgers Univ., USA; Economist, Exxon USA 1975–78; Sr Fellow, Korea Devt Inst. 1978–81; Founding Dir, Korea Energy Econs Inst. 1986–95; Special adviser to Minister of Environment 1994–96; Bd mem., Hyundai Corporation 1996–99, Inst. for Global Environmental Strategies, Japan 1998–2005; Prof. in econs of climate change, energy and sustainable devt, Korea Univ. Graduate School of Energy and Environment; Prof. and Dean, Coll. of Environment, Keimyung Univ. 2003–11; fmr Co-Chair. Working Group III, Intergovernmental Panel on Climate Change (IPCC), Vice-Chair. IPCC 2008–15, Chair. 2015–; fmr Pres. Council on Energy and Environment, S Korea; Pres. Int. Asscn for Energy Econs (IAEE) 1999; lead author in many major policy projects, including response strategies to climate change, energy, industry, privatization, and rationalization of energy and environment investment. *Publications include:* The Income and Welfare Effects of Farm Price Supports 1971, Climate Change 1994: Radiative Forcing of Climate Change and an Evaluation of the IPCC 1992 IS92 Emission Scenarios (co-author) 1995, Climate Change 1995: Economic and Social Dimensions of Climate Change: Contribution of Working Group III to the Second Assessment Report of the Intergovernmental Panel on Climate Change (co-author) 1996. *Address:* Intergovernmental Panel on Climate Change, World Meteorological Organization, 7 bis, avenue de la Paix, CP 2300, 1211 Geneva 2, Switzerland (office). *Telephone:* 227308208 (office). *E-mail:* IPCC-Sec@wmo.int (office); IPCC-Media@wmo.int (office). *Website:* www.ipcc.ch (office).

LEE, Hoi-chang, BA; South Korean politician; b. 2 June 1935, Sohung, Hwanghae Prov.; m.; two s. one d.; ed Kyonggi High School, Seoul Nat. Univ., Harvard Univ., USA; service in AF, attained rank of Capt.; Judge, Incheon and Seoul Dist Court 1960–65; apptd Judge, Seoul High Court 1965, Sr Judge 1977; Prof., Judicial Research and Training Inst. 1971; Dir Planning and Co-ordination Office, Ministry of Court Admin 1980; Justice, Supreme Court 1981–86, 1988–93; practised law 1986–88, 1994–; Head of Nat. Election Comm. 1988–93; Head of Bd of Audit and Inspection 1993; Prime Minister of Repub. of Korea 1993; cand. of ruling New Korea Party in presidential elections 1997; mem. Nat. Ass. 1999–2002, 2008–12; Pres. Grand Nat. Party (GNP) 2000–02; cand. of GNP in presidential elections 2002, ind. cand. 2007; Founder and Leader, Liberty Forward Party 2007–11. *Leisure interest:* listening to classical music. *Address:* c/o Liberty Forward Party, Yeongsan Bldg, 3rd Floor, 14-14, Yeouido-dong, Yeoungdeungpo-gu, Seoul (office); 10-1401 Asia Seonsuchon Apt, Jamsil-7-dong, Songpa-gu, Seoul, Republic of Korea (home). *Telephone:* (2) 780-3988 (office); (2) 3432-2030 (home).

Fax: (2) 780-3983 (office). *E-mail:* webmaster@jayou.or.kr (office). *Website:* www.jayou.or.kr (office).

LEE, Hong-koo, PhD; South Korean politician and political scientist; b. 9 May 1934, Seoul; m.; one s. two d.; ed Oxford Coll., Seoul Nat. Univ., Emory and Yale Univs, USA; Asst Prof., Emory Univ. 1963–64, Case Western Reserve Univ. 1964–67; Asst Prof., Assoc. Prof., Prof. of Political Science, Seoul Nat. Univ. 1968–88, Dir Inst. of Social Sciences 1979–82; Fellow Woodrow Wilson Int. Center for Scholars, Smithsonian Inst. 1973–74, Harvard Law School 1974–75; Minister of Nat. Unification 1988–90; Special Asst to Pres. 1990–91; Amb. to UK 1991–93; Sr Vice-Chair. Advisory Council for Unification; Chair. Seoul 21st Century Cttee, The World Cup 2002 Bidding Cttee 1993–94; Deputy Prime Minister and Minister of Nat. Unification April–Dec. 1994, Prime Minister of Republic of Korea 1994–95; mem. Comm. on Global Governance 1991–95; Chair. New Korea Party May 1996; Amb. to USA 1998–2001; fmr Pres. Seoul Forum for Int. Affairs; mem. Club of Madrid 1995–; Trustee, The Asia Foundation 2003–13, Trustee Emer. 2013–; Sheth Distinguished Int. Alumni Award from Emory Univ. 2002. *Publications:* An Introduction to Political Science, One Hundred Years of Marxism, Modernization. *Address:* c/o The Asia Foundation, PO Box 193223, San Francisco, CA 94119-3223, USA. *Telephone:* (415) 982-4640. *Fax:* (415) 392-8863. *E-mail:* info@asiafound.org. *Website:* asiafoundation.org.

LEE, Brig.-Gen. (retd) Hsien Loong, (BG Lee); Singaporean politician and fmr military officer; *Prime Minister;* b. 10 Feb. 1952; s. of Lee Kuan Yew and Kwa Geok Choo; m. 1st Wong Ming Yang 1978 (died 1982), one s. one d.; m. 2nd Ho Ching 1985; two s.; ed Catholic High School, Nat. Junior Coll., Trinity Coll., Cambridge, UK, Kennedy School of Govt, Harvard Univ., USA; nat. service 1971; Sr Army course at Fort Leavenworth, USA; Asst Chief of Gen. Staff (Operations) 1981–82, Chief of Staff (Gen. Staff), Singapore Army 1982–84; resgnd as Brig.-Gen. Aug. 1984, Nat. Reserves –2002; Political Sec. to Minister of Defence; MP for Teck Ghee SMC 1984–91, for Ang Mo Kio GRC 1991–; Chair. Comm. for Restructuring of the Economy 1985; Minister of State for Defence and for Trade and Industry 1985–86, for Trade and Industry 1986–93; Deputy Prime Minister 1990–2004, also Minister of Finance, Minister of Defence 1993–95, Second Minister of Defence (Services), Head Monetary Authority of Singapore; Prime Minister of Singapore and Minister of Finance 2004–07, Prime Minister 2007–; Chair. Govt of Singapore Investment Corpn 2011–; Second Asst Sec.-Gen., People's Action Party 1989–2004, Sec.-Gen. 2004–; Orden El Sol del Perú en el grado de Gran Cruz con Brillantes (Order of the Sun of Peru) 2008, Olympic Order (Gold) 2010. *Leisure interests:* reading, walking, listening to classical music, tinkering with computers. *Address:* Office of the Prime Minister, The Istana, Orchard Road, Singapore City, Singapore 238823 (office). *Telephone:* 63327200 (office). *Fax:* 68356621 (office). *E-mail:* lee_hsien_loong@pmo.gov.sg (office). *Website:* www.pmo.gov.sg (office); www.parliament.gov.sg/mp/lee-hsien-loong.

LEE, Hun-jai, MA, MBA; South Korean government official and financial analyst; b. 17 April 1944, Shanghai, China; ed Seoul Nat. Univ., IMF Inst., Boston Univ. and Harvard Business School, USA; Dir Financial Policy Div., Ministry of Finance 1974–78, Deputy Dir-Gen. Office of Public Finance and Monetary Policy 1978–79; Exec. Man. Dir and CEO Daewoo Semiconductor Co. Ltd 1984–85; Pres. and CEO Korea Investors Service Co., Ltd 1985–91; Head of Secr. to Jt Presidential Cttee for Econ. Policy 1997–98; Chair. Financial Supervisory Comm. 1998–2000; Minister of Finance and Economy 2000, Acting Prime Minister May 19–22 2000; Deputy Prime Minister and Minister of Finance and the Economy 2004–05 (resgnd), Acting Prime Minister 25 May–30 June 2004; Chair. Korean Inst. of Dirs 2002–04; Chair. Bd of Govs Asian Devt Bank; mem. Advisory Bd, Cen. Cttee of Agric. Cooperative Union 1993–97; mem. Citizens Advisory Cttee, City of Seoul 1995–97. *Publication:* Development of the Credit Rating System in Korea 1988.

LEE, Hyoung-keun (Hank), BEng; South Korean automotive company executive; *Vice-Chairman and Co-CEO, Kia Motors Corporation;* ed Seoul Nat. Univ.; joined Hyundai Motor Group 1977, has held numerous positions including Sr Exec. Vice-Pres. and COO Int. Business Div. –2009, Pres. Kia Motors Europe and Pres. and CEO Dongfeng Yueda Kia (joint venture in China), served as a Co-Pres. Kia Motors Corpn in charge of overseas business operations 2009–10, Vice-Chair. Kia Motors Corpn 2010–, CEO 2011–14, Co-CEO 2014–. *Address:* Kia Motors Corporation, Hyundai Kia Buillding, Seoul 137130, Republic of Korea (office). *Telephone:* (2) 3464-1114 (office). *E-mail:* info@kia.com (office). *Website:* www.kia.com/worldwide (office).

LEE, Hyung-koo; South Korean banker and government official; b. 30 Aug. 1940; m. 1969; ed Seoul Nat. Univ.; Deputy Dir Planning and Man. Office, Budget Bureau, Econ. Planning Bd (EPB) 1964; Sec. for Econ. Affairs, Presidential Secr. 1969–70; Dir and Dir-Gen. EPB 1971–81; Parvin Fellow, Woodrow Wilson School of Public Admin., Princeton Univ. 1978–79; Asst Minister, Ministry of Finance 1982; Vice-Minister, Ministry of Construction 1986, Ministry of Finance 1988, EPB 1988; Gov. Korea Devt Bank 1990–96. *Publications:* Economic Development in Korea, The Korean Economy, The Korean Economy Looks to the 21st Century. *Leisure interests:* golf, tennis.

LEE, In-ho, BA; South Korean banking executive; b. 2 Nov. 1943; ed Yonsei Univ.; joined Shinhan Bank as incorporator 1982, Dir and Deputy Pres. (Exec. Vice-Pres.) 1991–99, Pres. and CEO 1999–2003, Dir (non-exec.) Shinhan Financial Group Co. Ltd, CEO 2005–09, Corp. Advisor, Shinhan Bank 2009–11; Ind. Dir, Samsung Electronics Co. Ltd 2010–. *Address:* Samsung Electronics Building, 1320-10 Seocho-2-dong, Seocho-gu, Seoul 137-857, Republic of Korea (office). *Telephone:* (2) 2255-0114 (office). *Fax:* (2) 2255-0117 (office). *E-mail:* j-npr@samsung.co.kr (office). *Website:* www.samsung.com (office).

LEE, Jae-joung; South Korean academic and politician; b. 1 March 1944, Jincheon, N Chungcheong prov.; m.; one d.; ed Korea Univ. and Univ. of Manitoba and Trinity Coll., Canada; ordained Anglican priest 1972; teacher then Pres. Sung Kong Hoe Univ., Seoul 1994–2000; mem. Nat. Ass. 2000–04; Chief Campaign Man. for Pres. Roh during 2002 presidential campaign; co-f. Uri Party, now Adviser; worked at House of Shalom (shelter for migrant workers) 2004; Sr Vice Chair. Nat. Unification Advisory Council and presidential advisor on N Korea policy 2004–06; Minister of Unification 2006–08; arrested for accepting illegal political funds during the 2002 presidential campaign 2004, sentenced to a fine, received

presidential pardon 2006; Co-founder and fmr Pres. People's Participation Party 2010 (merged into United Progressive Party 2011).

LEE, Jai-seong; South Korean business executive; fmr Chief Financial Officer Hyundai Heavy Industries Co. Ltd, later Chief of Admin and Assistance HQ, Sr Exec. Vice-Pres. –2010, mem. Bd of Dirs, Pres. and Co-CEO 2010–13, Chair. and CEO 2013–14 (resgnd). *Address:* c/o Hyundai Heavy Industries Co. Ltd, 1, Jeonha-dong, Dong-gu, Gyeonsang nam-do, Ulsan 682-792, Republic of Korea. *E-mail:* ir@hhi.co.kr.

LEE, Jang-moo, BSc, PhD; South Korean engineer, university administrator and academic; *President Emeritus, Seoul National University;* b. 14 May 1945, Seoul; ed Seoul Nat. Univ., Iowa State Univ., USA, Babes-bolyai Univ., Romania, Hokkaido Univ., Japan; Prof., Coll. of Eng, Seoul Nat. Univ. 1976–, Dean Coll. of Eng 1997–2002, Pres. Seoul Nat. Univ. 2006–10, Pres. Emer. 2010–; Visiting Scholar, MIT, USA 1982–83; Chair. Univ. Educ. Section Cttee, Educational Policy Council, Korean Ministry of Educ. 1998–2000, Industrial Tech. Evaluation Inst., Korean Ministry of Industry and Resources 1999–2005, Founding Cttee for the Nat. Science Museum 2001–06, Climate Change Center of Korea 2010–13; Pres. Korean Soc. for Precision Eng 1996–99, Nat. Asscn of Deans of Eng Colls 1998–2000, Korean Soc. of Mechanical Engineers 2000, Korean Soc. for New and Renewable Energy 2004–06; Vice-Pres. Asscn of Korean Socs of Science and Tech. 2005–07; mem. Nat. Presidential Advisory Cttee on Science and Tech. 1998–99, Nat. Cttee for Innovation of Science and Tech. 2004–06; Fellow, American Soc. of Mechanical Engineers, Int. Acad. of Production Research, Korean Acad. of Science and Tech.; mem. Korean Acad. of Eng; mem. Int. Advisory Bd Hong Kong Polytechnic Univ.; Order of Service Merit (Blue Stripe); Dr hc (several); Korean Acad. of Science Award. *Address:* Office of the 24th President Emeritus, Seoul National University, San 56-1, Sillim-dong Gwanak-gu, Seoul 151-742, Republic of Korea (office). *Telephone:* (2) 880-7137 (office). *Fax:* (2) 889-7515 (office). *E-mail:* leejm@snu.ac.kr (office). *Website:* www.snu.ac.kr (office).

LEE, Jay Y., (Lee Jae-yong), BA, MBA, DBA; South Korean business executive; *Vice-Chairman, Samsung Electronics Company;* b. 23 June 1968, Seoul; s. of Lee Kun-hee (Chair. Samsung Electronics Co.) and Hong Ra-hee; m. Im Se-ryung (divorced); two c.; ed Seoul Nat. Univ., Keio Univ., Japan, Harvard Business School, USA; joined Samsung Electronics Co. 1991, becoming Vice-Pres. of Strategic Planning, later Chief Customer Officer, mem. Exec. Man. Team 2003, Chief Operating Officer and Exec. Vice-Pres. 2009–10, COO and Pres. 2010–12, Vice-Chair. 2012–; Chair. Samsung Foundation of Culture 2015–, Samsung Life Public Welfare Foundation 2015–. *Address:* Samsung Electronics Building, 1320-10 Seocho-2-dong, Seocho-gu, Seoul 137-857, Republic of Korea (office). *Telephone:* (2) 2255-0114 (office). *Fax:* (2) 2255-2133 (office). *Website:* www.samsung.com (office).

LEE, Jenny, BSc, MSc, MBA; Singaporean venture capitalist and fmr electrical engineer; *Managing Partner, GGV Capital;* b. 1972; m.; ed Cornell Univ. and Northwestern Univ. Kellogg School of Man., USA; Assoc., Morgan Stanley 2001–02; Vice-Pres. JAFCO Asia 2002–05; Asst Prin. Engineer, ST Aerospace 2005–09; Man. Partner, GGV Capital, Shanghai 2005–; mem. Bd of Dirs hiSoft Technology International Ltd 2004–, China Talent Group 2006–, 21ViaNet Group Ltd 2008–, YY Inc. 2009–, Chukong Technologies 2012–. *Address:* GGV Capital, Unit 3501, Two IFC 8 Century Avenue, Pudong District, Shanghai 200120, People's Republic of China (office). *Telephone:* (21) 61611720 (office). *Fax:* (21) 54035580 (office). *Website:* www.ggvc.com (office).

LEE, Jeong-gwan; South Korean Diplomatist; *Ambassador to Brazil;* m.; one s. one d.; ed Seoul Nat. Univ., Georgetown Univ. Grad. School, USA; joined Ministry of Foreign Affairs 1981, various posts as Sec. in Embassies in Tokyo 1989–92, Sofia 1992–96, Washington, DC 1996–2000, served in Presidential Office 2000–02, 2007–08, Dir, North American Affairs Bureau 2002–07, Dir Gen., Bureau for Overseas Koreans and Consular Affairs 2008–10, Consul-Gen. in San Francisco 2010–15, Amb. to Brazil 2015–. *Address:* Embassy of Republic of Korea, SEN, Av. das Nações, Lote 14, 70800-915 Brasília, DF, Brazil (office). *Telephone:* (61) 3321-2500 (office). *Fax:* (61) 3321-2508 (office). *E-mail:* emb-br@mofa.go.kr (office). *Website:* bra-brasilia.mofa.go.kr (office).

LEE, John Joseph, MA, MRIA; Irish historian and academic; *Glucksman Professor of Irish Studies and Director, Glucksman Ireland House, New York University;* b. 9 July 1942, Tralee, Co. Kerry; s. of Thomas P. Lee and Catherine Burke; m. Anne Marie Mitchell 1969; one s. two d.; ed Franciscan Coll. Gormanston, Univ. Coll. Dublin, Inst. for European History, Mainz, Germany, Peterhouse, Cambridge, UK; Admin. Officer, Dept of Finance, Dublin 1963; Asst in History, Univ. Coll. Dublin 1963–65; Research Fellow, Peterhouse, Univ. of Cambridge 1968–70, Official Fellow, Lecturer, Tutor 1970–74; Prof. of Modern History, Univ. Coll. Cork (UCC) 1974–93, Prof. of History 1993–2002, Dean Faculty of Arts 1976–79, Vice-Pres. UCC 1982–85; Visiting Mellon Prof., Univ. of Pittsburgh, USA 1979; Visiting Prof., European Univ. Inst., Florence, Italy 1981; Guest Fellow, Austrian Acad. 1989; Eisenhower Fellow, USA 1989, Distinguished Slick Visiting Prof. of World Peace, L.B.J. School, Univ. of Texas, Austin 1989–90; Visiting Prof. of Govt, Colby Coll. 1991; Visiting Sr Parnell Fellow, Magdalene Coll., Cambridge 1992–93, Visiting Arbuthnot Fellow, Univ. of Edinburgh 1996; Visiting Prof. of Irish Studies, New York Univ. 1999–2000, Glucksman Prof. of Irish Studies, Prof. of History and Dir Glucksman Ireland House 2002–; Distinguished Visiting Fellow, Queen Mary, Univ. of London 2007; Visiting Research Fellow, Trinity Coll. Dublin 2009, 2015, mem. External Advisory Bd, Long Room Hub 2007–; columnist, Sunday Tribune 1996–2002; Chair. Irish Scholarship Exchange Bd 1980–92, Irish Fulbright Comm. 1992–96; mem. Irish Senate 1993–97; mem. British-Irish Parl. Body 1993–97; Hon. DLitt (Nat. Univ. of Ireland) 2006, Hon. DJur (Univ. Coll. Dublin) 2016; Irish Life/Sunday Independent Arts Award 1991, Aer Lingus/Irish Times Prize for Literature 1992, Donnelly Prize for History and Social Sciences, American Conf. for Irish Studies 1992. *Publications:* The Modernization of Irish Society 1848–1918 1973 (revised edn 2008), Labour in German Industrialisation, in Cambridge Economic History of Europe, VII 1978, Ireland 1912–1985: Politics and Society 1989, Europe and America in the 1990s (co-ed.) 1991, The Shifting Balance of Power, Exploring the 20th Century 2000, Making the Irish American (co-ed.) 2006. *Leisure interests:* sport, reading. *Address:* Glucksman Ireland House, One Washington Mews, New

York, NY 10003, USA (office). *Telephone:* (212) 998-3950 (office). *Fax:* (212) 995-4373 (office). *E-mail:* jl91@nyu.edu (office). *Website:* irelandhouse.fas.nyu.edu (office).

LEE, Joon-sik, BS, MS, PhD; South Korean mechanical engineer, academic and government official; *Deputy Prime Minister for Social Affairs and Minister of Education;* b. Busan; ed Seoul Nat. Univ., Univ. of California, Berkeley, USA; joined Faculty, School of Mechanical and Aerospace Eng, Seoul Nat. Univ. 1985, Full-time Prof., also Eng Research Affairs Office 2011, Chair, Eng Educ. Innovations Cttee, Vice-Pres. for Research Affairs 2012–14; Deputy Prime Minister for Social Affairs and Minister of Educ. 2016–; fmr Chair., Cttee for Reform of Eng Colls, Ministry of Science, ICT and Future Planning; fmr Head, Presidential Advisory Council on Science and Tech.; mem. Science Advisory Cttee, Int. Inst. for Applied Systems Analysis (IIASA) 2011–16. *Address:* Ministry of Education, 77-6, Sejong-no, Jongno-gu, Seoul 110-760, Republic of Korea (office). *Telephone:* (2) 6222-6060 (office). *Fax:* (2) 2100-6133 (office). *E-mail:* webmaster@moe.go.kr (office). *Website:* www.moe.go.k (office).

LEE, Ju-yeol, BA, MA; South Korean academic, economist and central banker; *Governor, Bank of Korea;* b. 24 July 1952, Wonju; m. Young Ja Kyung; one s. one d.; ed Yonsei Univ., Pennsylvania State Univ., USA; joined Bank of Korea 1977, apptd Team Head, Statistics Dept 1990, Research Dept 1991, Int. Dept 1993, Foreign Exchange Dept 1993, Research Dept 1994, then Deputy Dir-Gen. Research Dept 1995, Dir Int. Econs Office 1998–99, Sr Economist, New York Rep. Office 1999–2002, Dir Overseas Econ. Information Office 2002–03, Deputy Dir-Gen. Research Dept 2003–05, Dir-Gen. Monetary Policy Dept 2005–07, Deputy Gov. 2007–09, Sr Deputy Gov. 2009–12 (retd), Gov. Bank of Korea 2014–; Advisor, Hana Inst. of Finance 2012–14; Distinguished Prof., Grad. School of Econs, Yonsei Univ. 2013–14. *Leisure interest:* playing tennis. *Address:* Bank of Korea, 110, 3-ga, Namdaemun-no, Jung-gu, Seoul 100-794, Republic of Korea (office). *Telephone:* (2) 759-4114 (office). *Fax:* (2) 759-4060 (office). *E-mail:* bokdplp@bok.or.kr (office). *Website:* www.bok.or.kr (office).

LEE, Jye; Taiwanese naval officer (retd) and fmr government official; b. 6 June 1940, Tianjin City; m.; three d.; ed ROC Naval Acad., Navy Command and Staff Coll., Naval War Coll., USA; served as Submarine Commdg Officer, Submarine Squadron Commdr, Antisubmarine Warfare Commdr, Taiwan Navy 1992–94, Chief of Staff Navy GHQ 1994–95, Commdg Gen. of Fleet Command 1995–96, Deputy C-in-C Navy GHQ 1996–97, C-in-C 1999–2002; Vice-Chief of Gen. Staff, Ministry of Nat. Defence Taiwan 1997–99, Chief of Gen. Staff 2002–04, Minister of Nat. Defence 2004–05, 2006–07 (retd); mem. Kuomintang (KMT, Nationalist Party of China) –2007.

LEE, Kai-Fu, BS, PhD, FIEEE; Chinese (b. Taiwanese) computer software executive and entrepreneur; *Chairman and CEO, Sinovation Ventures;* b. 3 Dec. 1961, Taipei, Taiwan; s. of Li Tianmin; m. Shen Ling Hsieh 1983; two d.; ed high school, Oak Ridge, Tenn., Columbia Univ., New York, Carnegie Mellon Univ., Pittsburg, Pa, USA; emigrated to USA 1973; Asst Prof., Carnegie Mellon Univ. 1988–90, developed Bill (Bayesian learning-based system for playing board game Othello that won US nat. tournament of computer players 1989); joined Apple Computer as research and devt exec. 1990, Vice-Pres. Interactive Media Group 1990–96, mem. of team that developed PlainTalk, the Apple Newton and several versions of QuickTime and QuickTime VR; Vice-Pres. and Gen. Man., Silicon Graphics Inc. (SGI) 1996–98, also Pres. Cosmo Software; joined Microsoft Corpn and moved to China to found and head up Microsoft Research Asia, Beijing 1998–2000, returned to USA 2000, Corp. Vice-Pres. Natural Interactive Services Div. 2000–05; Vice-Pres. Google and Founding Pres. Google Greater China 2005–09, responsible for launching Google.cn regional website; Founder, Chair. and CEO Innovation Works (renamed Sinovation Ventures 2016, business creation platform for creating new Chinese high-tech cos and for mentoring next generation of Chinese entrepreneurs) 2009–; Co-founder, LightInTheBox Co., Ltd 2009, mem. Bd of Dirs 2013–; Chair. Advisory Bd, WI Harper Group 2009–; Vice-Chair. Committee of 100; mem. Bd of Dirs Shangri-La Asia Ltd 2015–, Hon Hai Precision Industry Co., Ltd, Meitu, Inc. 2016–, Fosun International Limited 2017–; Fellow, IEEE; Dr. hc Hon. Doctorate (Univ. of Hong Kong) 2011. *Achievements:* Sphinx (first large-vocabulary, speaker-independent, continuous speech-recognition system) selected by Business Week as the "Most Important Innovation of 1988". *Publications:* Automatic Speech Recognition: The Development of the Sphinx Recognition System, Readings in Speech Recognition (co-ed.) 1990, Making a World of Difference (autobiog.) 2011, AI Superpowers: China, Silicon Valley, and the New World Order 2018; four best-selling books in China; more than 60 papers in computer science. *Address:* Sinovation Ventures, Dinghao Tower Block A, No. 3, Haidian District, Beijing 10080, People's Republic of China (office). *Telephone:* (10) 57525200 (office). *Website:* www.sinovationventures.com (office); en.chuangxin .com (office); www.kaifulee.com.

LEE, Ku-taek, BE; South Korean business executive; b. 1946; ed Kyunggi High School, Seoul, Seoul Nat. Univ.; joined POSCO (Pohang Iron and Steel Co.) 1969, various positions including steel specialist Pohang Works, Gen. Man. Export Dept, Gen. Man. Corp. Strategic Planning Dept, Sr Exec. Vice-Pres. 1996–98, Pres. 1998–2003, Chair. and CEO POSCO 2003–09 (resgnd); fmr Pres. Korea Iron and Steel Asscn; apptd mem. Exec. Cttee, Int. Iron and Steel Inst. (renamed World Steel Asscn 2008) 2004, apptd Vice-Chair. 2007; sr positions, Korea-US Econ. Council (KUSEC), Korea Inst. of Tech. (KITECH); Hon. AC (Australia) 2006.

LEE, Kun-hee, BCom, MBA; South Korean business executive; *Chairman, Samsung Electronics;* b. 9 Jan. 1942, Uiryung, Kyongnam Prov.; s. of Lee Byung-chull and Park Doo-eul; m. Hong Ra-hee 1967; one s. two d.; ed Waseda Univ., Tokyo, Grad. School of Business, George Washington Univ., USA; Exec. Dir Joong-Ang Daily 1968–78, Tong-Yang Broadcasting Corpn 1968–78; Vice-Chair. Samsung Group 1979–87, Chair. 1987–98, Chair. and CEO Samsung Electronics Co. Ltd 1998–2008 (resgnd), Chair. 2010–; Vice-Chair. Korea-Japan Econ. Comm. 1981–, Fed. of Korean Industries 1987–; Pres. Korean Amateur Wrestling Fed. 1982–97, now Hon. Pres.; Vice-Pres. Korean Olympic Cttee 1993–96, now Hon. Pres.; mem. IOC 1996–2017; Order of Sport Merit, Maengho Medal 1984, Order of Sport Merit, Cheongryong Medal 1986, IOC Olympic Order 1991, Chevalier, Légion d'honneur 2004; Hon. DBA (Seoul Nat. Univ.) 2000, Hon. PhD (Korea Univ.) 2005, Hon. LLD (Waseda Univ.) 2010; Margaret Mead Award 1997, James

A. Van Fleet Award 2006. *Publications include:* Read the World, With Your Own Thinking 1997. *Leisure interests:* horse riding, golf. *Address:* Samsung Electronics Building, 1320-10 Seocho-2-dong, Seocho-gu, Seoul 137-857, Republic of Korea (office). *Telephone:* (2) 2255-0114 (office). *Fax:* (2) 2255-2133 (office). *Website:* www .samsung.com (office).

LEE, Kyung-shik; South Korean politician and fmr central banker; ed Korea Univ.; joined Bank of Korea; Econ. Planning Bd 1961–72; served in Office of Pres. 1972–74; later Vice-Minister of Communications and mem. Monetary Bd of Korea; Pres. Daewoo Motor Co. 1988–93, Korea Gas Corpn –1993; Deputy Prime Minister and Minister of Econ. Planning 1993; Gov. Bank of Korea 1995–98.

LEE, Kyung-soo; South Korean diplomatist; *Ambassador to Germany;* ed Univ. of Cambridge, UK; joined Ministry of Foreign Affairs (MFA) 1981, apptd Consul in Sydney 1986, apptd Dir Foreign Language Training Div., Inst. of Foreign Affairs and Nat. Security 1998, First Sec., Embassy in Singapore 1992–95, Korean Embassy in Tokyo 1995–2000, Counsellor, Embassy in Budapest 2000–02, Counsellor, Embassy in Vienna, also at Perm. Mission to Int. Orgs 2002–04, Deputy Dir-Gen. for Asian and Pacific Affairs Bureau, MFA 2004–06, Minister-Counsellor, Embassy in Beijing 2006–07, Dir-Gen. for South Asian and Pacific Affairs Bureau 2007–09, Amb. to Cambodia 2009–10, Minister, Embassy in Tokyo 2010–13, Deputy Minister for Political Affairs, MFA 2013–15, Amb. to Germany 2015–. *Address:* Embassy of Republic of Korea, Stülerstr. 8–10, 10787 Berlin, Germany (office). *Telephone:* (30) 260650 (office). *Fax:* (30) 2606551 (office). *E-mail:* koremb-ge@mofat.go.kr (office). *Website:* www.koreaemb.de (office).

LEE, Martin Chu Ming, QC, JP, BA; Chinese barrister; b. 8 June 1938, Hong Kong; m. Amelia Lee 1969; one s.; ed Univ. of Hong Kong; Chair. Hong Kong Bar Asscn 1980–83; mem. Hong Kong Legis. Council 1985–2008, Hong Kong Law Reform Comm. 1985–91, Basic Law Drafting Cttee 1985–90 (expelled for criticism of People's Repub. of China); Chair. Hong Kong Consumer Council 1988–91; formed United Democrats of Hong Kong, party opposed to Chinese mil. suppression of Tiananmen Square demonstrators in 1989, Leader 1990–94 (merged with Meeting Point party to become Democratic Party of Hong Kong), Chair. 1994–2002; Goodman Fellow, Univ. of Toronto 2000; Bencher, Hon. Soc. of Lincoln's Inn 2000; Hon. LLD (Holy Cross Coll.) 1997, (Amherst Coll., USA) 1997, (Warwick Univ.) 2006; Prize for Freedom, Liberal Int. 1996, Int. Human Rights Award (American Bar Asscn) 1995, Democracy Award, Nat. Endowment for Democracy, USA 1997, Statesmanship Award, Claremont Inst., USA 1998, Schuman Medal, European Parl. 2000, Rutgers Coll. Brennan Human Rights Award 2004. *Publication:* The Basic Law: some basic flaws (with Szeto Wah) 1988. *Address:* Admiralty Centre, Room 704A, Tower I, 18 Harcourt Road, Hong Kong Special Administrative Region, People's Republic of China (office). *Telephone:* 25290864 (office). *Fax:* 28612829 (office). *E-mail:* oml@martinlee.org.hk (office). *Website:* www.martinlee.org.hk (office).

LEE, Michael (Mike) Shumway, BS, JD; American lawyer and politician; *Senator from Utah;* b. 4 June 1971, Mesa, Ariz.; s. of Rex E. Lee and Janet Lee (née Griffin); m. Sharon Burr 1993; three c.; ed Timpview High School, Provo, Utah, Brigham Young Univ. J. Reuben Clark Law School; served mission for Church of Jesus Christ of Latter-day Saints in Tex. Rio Grande Valley 1990–92; Pres. Student Body, Brigham Young Univ. 1993–94; admitted to Bar Utah 1998, DC 1999; law clerk to Judge Dee V. Benson of US Dist Court for Dist of Utah 1997–98, to Judge Samuel A. Alito, Jr of US Court of Appeals for the Third Circuit Court, Newark, NJ 1998–99; attorney, Sidley & Austin LLP, Washington, DC 2000–02, specialized in appellate and Supreme Court litigation; Asst US Attorney, Salt Lake City 2002–05; Gen. Counsel to Gov. of Utah, Jon M. Huntsman, Jr 2005–06; clerk at US Supreme Court with Justice Alito, Washington, DC 2006–07; Partner, Howrey LLP (law firm), Salt Lake City 2007–10; Senator from Utah 2011–, mem. Judiciary Cttee, Energy and Natural Resources Cttee, Armed Services Cttee, Jt Economic Cttee; mem. J. Reuben Clark Law Soc., Federalist Soc. for Law and Public Policy Studies; fmr mem. Alumni Bd Brigham Young Univ., Alumni Bd Brigham Young Univ. Law School; Republican. *Address:* 316 Hart Senate Office Building, Washington, DC 20510, USA (office). *Telephone:* (202) 224-5444 (office). *Fax:* (202) 228-1168 (office). *Website:* lee.senate.gov (office).

LEE, Myles, BE, FCA; Irish civil engineer, accountant and business executive; b. 1953; ed Univ. Coll. Cork; worked in professional accountancy practice and in oil industry –1982; joined CRH plc 1982, Gen. Man. Finance 1988–2003, Finance Dir and mem. Bd of Dirs CRH plc 2003–09, Group Chief Exec. 2009–13 (retd); mem. Bd of Dirs Ingersoll Rand 2015–, Babcock International Group plc 2015–.

LEE, Myung-bak, BA; South Korean business executive, politician and fmr head of state; b. 19 Dec. 1941, then-Korean residential dist of Nakakawachi-gun, Osaka Pref., Japan (now Hirano-ku, Osaka City); s. of Lee Cheung-u and Chae Taewon; m. Kim Yun-ok; one s. three d.; ed Korea Univ., Seoul Nat. Univ., Yonsei Univ.; worked for Hyundai Group 1977–92, fmr Pres. Hyundai Construction; Assembly-man, 16th Nat. Ass. 1996–2001; Mayor of Seoul City 2002–06; Founder and Exec. Chair. Anguk Forum 2006; Pres. Republic of Korea 2008–13; Chair., Korea Atomic Industry Forum Inc. 1980; Chair. Int. Contractors Asscn of Korea 1980; Pres. Korea Amateur Swimming Fed. 1981–92; Exec. mem. Korean Olympic Cttee 1982–92; Chief, Construction Div., Econ. Cooperation Cttee in SE Asian Countries 1982; Deputy Chair. Korea Chamber of Commerce 1982; Vice Pres., Korea Man. Asscn 1983; Bureau mem. FINA 1984; Deputy Chair., Korea-USSR Econ. Asscn 1989; Exec. Dir, Korea Electric Asscn 1990; mem. NE Asia Econ. Cttee 1991; Vice-Chair., World Fed. of Korean Asscn of Commerce 1993; Founder East Asia Foundation, Chair. 1994–2002; Pres. Asian Pacific Foundation, Korea 2000–02; Commr, Sub-cttee on Future Competitiveness, Nat. Cttee, Grand Nat. Party 2001–02; Adviser, Overseas Korean Traders Asscn 2001–07; Econ. Adviser to Hun Sen, Prime Minister of Kingdom of Cambodia 2000–07; Hon. Consul-Gen. of Kingdom of Bhutan to Korea 1986–99; Hon. Amb. of Arkansas State 1992–2007; Hon. Instructor, Undergraduate School of Business Admin, Korea Univ. 1993–; Hon. Instructor, Grad. School of Political Science, Kookmin Univ. 1995–, Hon. Instructor, Grad. School of Business Admin, Korea Univ. 1997–; Order of Civil Merit 1984, Order of Industrial Service Merit, Gold Tower 1985; Hon. DSc (Korea Nat. Univ. of Physical Educ.) 1998; Hon. DBA (Sogang Univ.) 2004; Hon. DEcon (Nat. Univ. of Mongolia) 2005, (Mokpo Nat. Univ.) 2005; Dr hc (Eurasia Univ., Astana, Kazakhstan) 2004; Excellent Enterprise Award by Pres. 1979, Excellent

Enterprise Award, Business Admin Center, Korea Univ. 1983, selected as one of top 50 business leaders contributing to Nat. Devt, Daily Chosun 1998, selected as one of the top 30 business leaders in Korea in 20th century, Daily Maekyung and Fed. of Korean Industries 1999, Personality of the year 2005 awarded by fDi Magazine, affiliate magazine of the Financial Times 2005, Time magazine Hero of the Environment 2007, Zayed Int. Prize for the Environment (Category 1) 2011. *Publications include:* History of June 3rd Student Movement 1994, There Is No Such Thing as a Myth 1995, See Hope When Everyone Else Talks of Despair 2002, Cheonggyecheon Flows to the Future 2005, Unwavering Promise 2007, My Mother 2007. *Leisure interests:* tennis, swimming. *Address:* Saenuri Party, 14-31, Yeouido-dong, Yeongdeungpo-gu, Seoul 156-768, Republic of Korea (office). *Telephone:* (2) 3786-3000 (office). *Fax:* (2) 3786-3610 (office). *Website:* www.saenuriparty.kr (office).

LEE, Nak-yon, LLB; South Korean fmr journalist and politician; *Prime Minister;* b. 20 Dec. 1952, Yeonggwang County, South Jeolla Prov.; m. Kim Suk-hee; one s.; ed Seoul Nat. Univ.; journalist, Dong-A Ilbo (daily newspaper) 1979–2000, including as Tokyo Corresp. 1989, Ed.-in-Chief, Dong-A Ilbo Editorial Cttee 1997–99; mem. Nat. Ass. 2000–14, mem. Nat. Ass. Steering Cttee 2004–06, Chair. Agric., Forestry and Fisheries Food Cttee 2008–10, fmr Vice Chair. Nat. Ass. Korean–Japanese Parl. League; Sec. Nat. Defense Comm. 2002–03; Gov. South Jeolla Prov. 2014–17; Prime Minister 2017–; mem. Minjoo Party of Korea (Democratic Party of Korea), Sec.-Gen. 2010–11. *Address:* Prime Minister's Office, 55, Sejong-no, Jongno-gu, Seoul 110-760, Republic of Korea (office). *Telephone:* (2) 2100-2114 (office). *Fax:* (2) 739-5830 (office). *E-mail:* webmaster@pmo.go.kr (office). *Website:* www.pmo.go.kr (office).

LEE, Pal-seung, BL, MBA; South Korean business executive; b. 2 Feb. 1944, Kyongsangnam-do Hadong; three d.; ed Jinkyo High School, Korea Univ., Advanced Information Man. Program, Korea Advanced Inst. of Science and Tech.; fmr Dir of Work Integration Div., Hanmi Bank, fmr Head of Busan and Gyeongnam HQ of Hanmi Bank; fmr Man. Dir Hanvit Bank; fmr Pres. and CEO Woori Securities, Hanvit Securities, CEO Woori Investment & Securities and Exec. Man. Dir Hanil Bank 1999–2008, Chair. and CEO Woori Finance Holdings Co. Ltd 2008–13, Chair. Woori Bank; Chair. KOFICE, Woori Multicultural Scholarship Foundation; CEO Seoul Philharmonic Orchestra 2005–08; Hon. PhD (Chungnam Nat. Univ.).

LEE, Patrick A., PhD; American physicist and academic; *William and Emma Rogers Professor of Physics, Massachusetts Institute of Technology;* b. 8 Sept. 1946, British Hong Kong; ed Massachusetts Inst. of Tech.; Gibbs Instructor, Yale Univ. 1970–72; mem. tech. staff, Theoretical Physics Dept, Bell Labs 1972–73, 1974–81, Head, Theoretical Physics Dept 1981–82; Asst Prof., Univ. of Washington 1973–74; Prof. of Physics, MIT 1982–, William and Emma Rogers Prof. of Physics 1990–, fmr Div. Head, Atomic, Biological, Condensed Matter and Plasma Physics, affiliated with Quantum-Effects Devices Group of Research Lab. of Electronics; Co-Chair. Gordon Research Conf. 1984; Guest Ed. Special Issue on Disordered Solids, Physics Today 1988; mem. Editorial Bd, Chinese Physics 1980–85; mem. Proposal Review Bd, Stanford Synchrotron Radiation Lab. 1977–80, Bd of Trustees, Aspen Center for Physics 1981–87, Advisory Bd, Inst. for Theoretical Physics 1992–95; mem. NAS, American Acad. of Arts and Sciences, Academia Sinica (Taiwan); Fellow, American Physical Soc.; Oliver Buckley Prize, American Physical Soc. 1990, Dirac Medal, Int. Centre for Theoretical Physics 2005. *Publications:* numerous articles in scientific journals. *Address:* Department of Physics, Building 6C-347, Massachusetts Institute of Technology, 77 Massachusetts Avenue, Cambridge, MA 02139-4307, USA (office). *Telephone:* (617) 253-8325 (office). *Fax:* (617) 253-2562 (office). *E-mail:* palee@mit.edu (office). *Website:* web.mit.edu/physics/people/faculty/lee_patrick.html (office).

LEE, Sang-dae; South Korean business executive; *Executive Vice-President and Head of Retail Division, Samsung Securities Co. Ltd;* ed Korea Univ.; has held numerous sr man. positions with Samsung Corpn including Exec. Vice-Pres. Samsung Training Inst., Exec. Vice-Pres. Planning and Man. Office, Pres. and CEO Housing Devt Div., Pres. and CEO Construction and Devt Div., Vice-Chair. and CEO Samsung C&T Corpn –2011, fmr Pres. and CEO Construction Group, Housing Group, Exec. Vice-Pres. Office of Strategic Planning, Exec. Dir and Vice-Pres. Samsung Human Resources Devt Centre, Man. Dir HQ for Planning and Man., Samsung E&C Ltd, currently Exec. Vice-Pres. and Head of Retail Division, Samsung Securities Co. Ltd. *Address:* Samsung Securities Co. Ltd, Samsung Main Bldg. 67, Sejong-daero, Jung-gu, Seoul 04514, Republic of Korea (office). *Telephone:* (2) 2020-8000 (office). *Website:* www.samsungsecurities.com (office).

LEE, Gen. Sang-hee; South Korean army officer (retd) and politician; b. 12 Aug. 1945, Wonju, Gangwon Prov.; m. Kim Sun Young; one s. one d.; ed Kyung-Gi High School, Seoul, Repub. of Korea (ROK) Mil. Acad., Coll. of Liberal Arts and Science, Seoul Nat. Univ., Center for Int. Security Studies, Univ. of Maryland, USA; Commdr 29th Regt, 9th Infantry Div. 1989–91, Chief of Mil. Strategy, J-5 Directorate, Jt Chiefs of Staff 1991–92, Advisor to the Pres. for Nat. Defense Policy, Office of the Presidential Secr. 1992–94, Chief of Force Planning, G-5 Directorate, ROK Army HQ 1995–96, Commanding Gen., 30th Infantry Div. (Mechanized) 1996–98, Dir Policy Planning Bureau, Ministry of Nat. Defense 1998–99, Commanding Gen. 5th Corps 1999–2001, Chief Dir Strategy and Plans (J5), Jt Chiefs of Staff 2001–02, Chief Dir Operations (J3), Jt Chiefs of Staff 2002–03, promoted to four-star Gen. and Commanding Gen., Third ROK Army 2003, 32nd Chair. Jt Chiefs of Staff 2005–06 (retd); Minister of Nat. Defense 2008–09; Visiting Fellow, Brookings Inst., Washington, DC 2007; Presidential Citation, Order of Nat. Security 'Samil' Medal, Order of Nat. Security 'Chonsu' Medal, Order of Nat. Security 'Gukson' Medal, Armed Forces Merit Award (Turkey), Legion of Merit, Commdr and Officer Grade (USA).

LEE, Seong-tae, BA, MA; South Korean fmr central banker; b. 20 June 1945; ed Seoul Nat. Univ., Univ. of Illinois, USA; joined Bank of Korea 1968, Chief of Monetary Policy Dept 1981–83, Chief of Research Dept 1983–86, Deputy Dir Research Dept 1986–89, Deputy Gen. Man. Pusan Br. 1989–91, Deputy Dir Monetary Policy Dept 1991–94, Gen. Man. Changwon Br. 1994–95, Dir Public Information Dept 1995–96, Dir Support Services and Properties Dept 1996–97, Dir Budget and Man. Dept 1997–98, Dir Research Dept 1998–2000, Deputy Gov. 2000–03, Sr Deputy Gov. 2003–04, Sr Deputy Gov. and mem. Monetary Policy Cttee 2004–06, Gov. Bank of Korea 2006–10.

LEE, Shau Kee; Hong Kong real estate executive; *Chairman and Managing Director, Henderson Land Development Company Ltd;* b. 1928, Guangdong; m. (divorced); five c.; Founder Henderson Land Development Co. Ltd, Chair. and Man. Dir 1976–; Founder, Chair. and Man. Dir Henderson Investment Ltd; Chair. Henderson Cyber Ltd; Exec. Dir Henderson China Holdings Ltd; Chair. Hong Kong and China Gas Co. Ltd; Vice-Chair. Sun Hung Kai Properties Ltd; Dir Hong Kong Ferry (Holdings) Co. Ltd, The Bank of East Asia Ltd, Miramar Hotel and Investment Co. Ltd, Rimmer (Cayman) Ltd, Riddick (Cayman) Ltd, Hopkins (Cayman) Ltd, Henderson Development Ltd, Believegood Ltd, Cameron Enterprise Inc.; Grand Bauhinia Medal 2007; Hon. DBA, Hon. DSSc, Hon. LLD. *Address:* Henderson Land Development Co. Ltd, 6th Floor, World-Wide House, 19 Des Voeux Road, Central, Hong Kong Special Administrative Region, People's Republic of China (office). *Telephone:* 29088888 (office). *Fax:* 29088838 (office). *E-mail:* corpcomm@hld.com (office). *Website:* www.hld.com (office).

LEE, Tan Sri Dato' Shin Cheng; Malaysian business executive and real estate executive; *Executive Chairman, IOI Group;* b. 3 June 1939; m. Puan Sri Hoong May Kuan; two s. four d.; became field supervisor at palm oil co. aged 22; controlled small co. by 1981, bought Industrial Oxygen Inc. 1981 (name changed to IOI 1995), served as CEO, currently Exec. Chair. IOI Group (operator of palm oil plantations, refineries and related mfg activities), also Exec. Chair. IOI Properties Group Berhad; Council mem. East Coast Econ. Region Devt Council 2008–14; mem. Council Malaysian Palm Oil Asscn, Malaysia-China Business Council; Adviser to KL & Selangor Chinese Chamber of Commerce and Industry; mem. Bd Universiti Putra Malaysia; Hon. Fellowship, Malaysian Oil Scientists and Technologists Asscn 2008; Hon. Pres. Asscn of Eng Choon Socs of Malaysia, Fed. of Hokkien Asscn of Malaysia, Associated Chinese Chambers of Commerce; Dr hc (Universiti Putra Malaysia) 2002; FIABCI Malaysia Property Man of the Year Award 2001, Malaysian Palm Oil Asscn Recognition Award 2011, Palm Oil Industry Leadership Award 2015. *Address:* IOI Corporation Berhad, 2 IOI Square, IOI Resort, 62502 Putrajaya, Malaysia (office). *Telephone:* (3) 8947-8888 (office). *Fax:* (3) 8943-2266 (office). *E-mail:* corp@ioigroup.com (office). *Website:* www.ioigroup.com (office).

LEE, Si-chen, BS, MS, PhD; Taiwanese engineer, academic and fmr university administrator; *Distinguished Professor, Department of Electrical Engineering, National Taiwan University;* b. 13 Aug. 1952, Gon-Shan; ed Nat. Taiwan Univ., Stanford Univ., USA; Researcher, Energy Conversion Devices, Inc., Troy, Mich., USA 1980–82; Visiting Assoc. Prof., Dept of Electrical Eng, Nat. Taiwan Univ. 1982–85, Prof. of Electrical Eng, Coll. of Electrical Eng and Computer Science 1985–, now Distinguished Prof., Chair. Dept of Electrical Eng 1988–92, Dean of Academic Affairs 1996–2002, Pres. Nat. Taiwan Univ. 2005–13; Asst to Minister of Nat. Defence 1993–94; Chair. University Mobility in Asia and the Pacific 2005–; Pres. Asscn of Nat. Univs of Taiwan 2006–; Leader Bioenergy Field Group, Biology Dept, Nat. Science Council 1992–98, Microelectronics Group, Eng Dept 1988–93; mem. Directorate, Asscn of Chinese Electrical Engineers 1992–94; consultant, Electronics Research and Service Org., Industrial Tech. Research Inst. 1986–89, 1991–92; mem. Directorate, Chinese Asscn of Electromagnetism in Life Science 1999–2004; Assoc. Ed. Materials Chemistry and Physics 1992–2004, Journal of Chinese Engineers 1996–2000; Fellow, IEEE 2002 (mem. Vice-Directorate, IEEE Taipei section 2001–02); mem. Chinese Inst. of Electrical Eng, Asia-Pacific Acad. of Materials 1997; Dr hc (Kansai Univ.) 2005, (Exeter Univ.) 2012; five consecutive Outstanding Research Awards from Nat. Science Council 1986–96, Sun Yat-San Academic Award (Eng) 1987, Young Distinguished Engineer, Chinese Engineer Asscn 1987, Special Contracted Researcher, Nat. Science Council 1996–2002, IEEE Third Millennium Medal 2000, Annual Medal, Chinese Asscn of Electrical Engineers 2002, 47th Academic Award, Ministry of Educ. 2003. *Publications:* numerous scientific papers in professional journals. *Address:* Department of Electrical Engineering, EE Building 2 R440, National Taiwan University, Taipei 106, Taiwan (office). *Telephone:* (2) 23635251 (office). *Fax:* (2) 23675509 (office). *E-mail:* sclee@cc.ee.ntu.edu.tw (office). *Website:* www.ee.ntu.edu.tw/e_profile?id=6 (office).

LEE, Soo-chang; South Korean insurance executive; *Chairman and CEO, Korea Life Insurance Association;* b. 1949, Yecheon, Gyeongsangbuk-do; m. three c.; ed Daechang High School, Coll. of Veterinary Medicine, Seoul Nat. Univ.; joined Samsung Life Insurance Co. Ltd 1973, Dir Cheil Jedang (subsidiary co.) 1990, Dir Shipbuilding Dept, Samsung Heavy Industries 1990–92, Dir Heavy Machinery Dept, Samsung Heavy Industries Jan.–Dec. 1993, Man. Dir Samsung Life Insurance Co. 1993–95, Man. Dir Samsung Fire 1995–95, Sr Man. Dir 1996–98, Vice-Pres. 1998–99, Vice-Pres. and CEO 1999–2001, Pres. and CEO 2001–06, Pres. and CEO Samsung Life Insurance Co. Ltd 2006–10; Chair. and CEO Korea Life Insurance Asscn 2014–; Iron Tower Order of Industrial Service 2000; 1st Nat. Country Love-Leader Award 2006, Forbes Korea Excellence in Leadership Award 2007. *Leisure interests:* reading, go, golf. *Address:* Korea Life Insurance Association, 16th Floor, 173 Toegyero, Jung-gu, Seoul, 04554, Republic of Korea (office). *Telephone:* (2) 2262-6600 (office). *Website:* www.klia.or.k (office).

LEE, Soo-ho, BA; South Korean business executive; b. 8 Feb. 1944, Jinju, Kyungnam Prov.; m. Young-Sook Park; one s. one d.; ed Jinju High School, Yonsei Univ.; began career with trading co. 1968–78; joined Bando International (renamed LG International) 1978, Sr Man. Gen. Merchandise Dept 1980–81, with Br. Office, Jakarta, Indonesia 1981–84, Overseas Man. Div./Resources 1985–88, Br. Offices, Singapore and Hong Kong 1988–92, Man. Dir Sales Group/Support 1992–95, Sr Man. Dir Support 1995–96, Vice-Pres. Business Operations 1996–97, CEO LG International Corpn 1997–2003; Pres. Korea Gas Corpn (KOGAS) 2005–08; Order of Merit for Industrial Service 1997.

LEE, Soo-sung, LLB, LLM, LLD; South Korean legal scholar and politician; b. 10 March 1939; Lecturer, Law Research Inst., Seoul Nat. Univ. 1967–69, Asst Prof., Law Research Inst. 1969–73, Assoc. Prof., Law Research Inst. 1973–74, Assoc. Prof., Dept of Law, Coll. of Law 1974–78, Prof., Dept of Law, Coll. of Law 1978–82, Dean, Office of Student Affairs 1980, Dept Head, Coll. of Law 1985–86, Dean, Coll. of Law 1988–90, Pres. Seoul Nat. Univ. 1995, Prof. Emer. 2004–; Prime Minister of Repub. of Korea 1995–97; co-f. Democratic Nat. Party 2000; co-f. Education Forum for Asia; Pres. Nat. Council of Saemaul-Undong Movement; Head, Screening Cttee, Asscn for Enhancing and Practising the Spirit of Manhae.

LEE, Spike; American filmmaker and actor; b. (Shelton Jackson Lee), 20 March 1957, Atlanta, Ga; s. of Bill Lee and Jacquelyn Shelton; m. Tonya Lewis 1993; one d.; ed Morehouse Coll., New York Univ. Inst. of Film and Television; wrote scripts for Black Coll.: The Talented Tenth, Last Hustle in Brooklyn; produced, wrote, Dir Joe's Bed-Stuy Barbershop: We Cut Heads; has directed music videos, TV commercials and other short projects; f. Forty Acres and a Mule Filmworks; Commdr des Arts et des Lettres 2003; Dr hc (New York Univ.) 1998; Cannes Film Festival Best New Dir 1986, LA Film Critics' Asscn Awards 1986, 1989, Chicago Film Festival Critics' Awards 1990, 1992, Golden Satellite Best Documentary 1997; inducted into Nat. Asscn for the Advancement of Colored People (NAACP) Hall of Fame 2003, Gov.'s Award (Hon. Oscar), Acad. of Motion Picture Arts and Sciences 2015. *Films include:* She's Gotta Have It 1985 (Cannes Film Festival Prize for Best New Film), School Daze 1988, Do the Right Thing 1989, Love Supreme 1990, Mo' Better Blues 1990, Jungle Fever 1991, Malcolm X 1992, Crooklyn, Girl 6, Clockers 1995, Get on the Bus, He Got Game 1998, Summer of Sam 1999, Tales from the Hood 1995 (exec. producer), Bamboozled 2000, The Original Kings of Comedy 2000, Lisa Picard is Famous 2001, A Huey P. Newton Story 2001, The 25th Hour 2003, CSA: Confederate States of America (exec. producer) 2004, She Hate Me 2004, Inside Man 2006, Miracle at St. Anna 2008, Red Hook Summer 2012, Da Sweet Blood of Jesus 2014, Chi-Raq 2015, BlacKkKlansman (Cannes Film Festival Grand Prix 2018) 2018. *Television:* Sucker Free City 2004. *Documentaries:* Four Little Girls 1997, When the Levees Broke 2006, Michael Jackson's Journey from Motown to Off the Wall 2016. *Publications:* Spike Lee's Gotta Have It: Inside Guerrilla Filmmaking 1987, Uplift the Race 1988, The Trials and Tribulations of the Making of Malcolm X 1992, Girl 6 1996, Get on the Bus 1996. *Leisure interest:* basketball. *Address:* Forty Acres and a Mule Filmworks, 124 De Kalb Avenue, Suite 2, Brooklyn, New York, NY 11217, USA. *Telephone:* (718) 624-3703. *Fax:* (718) 624-2008.

LEE, Sun-jin; South Korean diplomatist and academic; *Professor, Institute of East Asian Studies, Sogang University;* m.; one s. one d.; ed Seoul Nat. Univ.; joined Ministry of Foreign Affairs 1975, overseas postings include Second Sec., Embassy in Beirut 1980, First Sec., Embassy in Washington, DC 1985, Counsellor, Embassy in Beijing 1992, Minister-Counsellor, Embassy in Tokyo, fmr Vice-Consul in Seattle, Wash., USA, Deputy Dir-Gen., Int. Trade Bureau, Ministry of Foreign Affairs and Trade 1996, Dir-Gen. for Policy Planning, Office of Policy Planning and Int. Orgs 2001, Deputy Minister for Policy Planning and Int. Orgs 2003, Amb. to Indonesia 2005–08; currently Prof., Inst. of East Asian Studies, Sogang Univ., Seoul. *Publications include:* The Rise of China and Responses from Southeast Asia: An Ambassador's Review 2011, Korean Ambassadors on an Asia Strategy 2013. *Address:* Institute of East Asian Studies, Sogang University, 35 Baekbeom-ro, Sinsu-dong, Mapo-gu, Seoul 04107, Republic of Korea (office). *Telephone:* (2) 705-8227 (office). *Website:* www.eastasia.kr (office).

LEE, Teng-Hui, PhD; Taiwanese politician; b. 15 Jan. 1923, Taiwan; m. Tseng Wen-fui; two d.; ed Kyoto Imperial Univ., Japan, Nat. Taiwan Univ., Iowa State and Cornell Univs, USA; Asst Prof., Nat. Taiwan Univ. 1949–55, Assoc. Prof. 1956–58; Research Fellow, Taiwan Co-operative Bank 1953; Specialist and Econ. Analyst, Dept of Agric. and Forestry, Taiwan Prov. Govt 1954–57; Specialist, Joint Comm. on Rural Reconstruction (JCRR) 1957–61, Sr Specialist and Consultant 1961–70, Chief, Rural Economy Div. 1970–72; Prof. Nat. Chengchi Univ. 1958–78; Minister without Portfolio 1972–78; Mayor of Taipei City 1978–81; Gov. Taiwan Province 1981–84; Vice-Pres. of Repub. of China (Taiwan) 1984–88, Pres. 1988–2000; co-f. Taiwan Solidarity Union 2001; expelled from KMT (Kuomingtang) Party 2001; Hon. LLD (Southern Methodist Univ., USA) 1994; Int. Distinguished Achievement Citation, Iowa State Univ., USA and other awards. *Publications:* several works on agricultural development in Taiwan. *Leisure interests:* art, music and sport.

LEE, Gen. (retd) Tien-yu; Taiwanese air force officer (retd) and government official; b. 23 May 1946, Nanjing; served in Tactical Fighter Wing, Armed Forces of Taiwan 1990–92, Commdr Combat Air Command 1998–2001, Commdr of Air Force 2002–04, Chief of Gen. Staff 2004–2007; Strategic Adviser to Pres. Chen Shui-bian Feb.–May 2007; Minister of Nat. Defense 2007–08 (resgnd); Order of Blue Sky and White Sun with Grand Cordon 2007.

LEE, Tsung-Dao, PhD; American (b. Chinese) physicist; *University Professor Emeritus, Columbia University;* b. 25 Nov. 1926, Shanghai; s. of Tsing-Kong Lee and Ming-Chang Chang; m. Jeanette H. C. Chin 1950 (died 1995); two s.; ed Nat. Chekiang Univ., Nat. Southwest Univ., China and Univ. of Chicago, USA; Research Assoc. in Astronomy, Univ. of Chicago 1950; Research Assoc. and Lecturer in Physics, Univ. of California 1950–51; mem. Inst. for Advanced Study, Princeton, NJ 1951–53; Asst Prof. of Physics, Columbia Univ., New York 1953–55, Assoc. Prof. 1955–56, Prof. 1956–60, 1963, Enrico Fermi Prof. of Physics 1964, Univ. Prof. 1984–2012, Univ. Prof. Emer. 2012–; Prof. Princeton Inst. for Advanced Study 1960–63; mem. NAS; naturalized as American citizen 1962; Order of the Rising Sun, Gold and Silver Star (Japan) 2007; shared Nobel Prize in Physics 1957 with Prof. Yang Chen-ning for work on elementary particles; Albert Einstein Award in Science 1957; numerous other awards including New York Acad. of Science Award 2000. *Publications:* articles in physical journals. *Address:* Department of Physics, Columbia University, Building 538, Morningside Heights, W 120th Street, New York, NY 10027 (office); 25 Claremont Avenue, New York, NY 10027, USA (home). *Telephone:* (212) 854-1759 (office). *Fax:* (212) 932-0418 (office). *E-mail:* tdl@phys.columbia.edu (office). *Website:* www.columbia.edu (office).

LEE, Ufan; South Korean painter; b. 1936, Gyeonsang Nam-do; ed Seoul Nat. Univ. and Nihon Univ., Tokyo, Japan; Leader Mono-Ha group (Japanese avant-garde art movt) 1969; Prof., Tama Art Univ., Tokyo 1973–2007; Invited Prof., Ecole Nat. Supérieure des Beaux-Arts, Paris 1997; Artists Summit, Kyoto 2005; Cultural Decoration 1990, Chevalier des Arts et des Lettres 1991, Order of the Rising Sun, Gold Rays with Rosette 2009; prize for critical writing for From Object to Being 1969, UNESCO Prize, Shanghai Biennale, Paris-Shanghai 2000, Praemium Imperiale Award (Painting), Japan Art Asscn 2001, Ho-Am Prize in the Arts 2001. *E-mail:* info@studioleeufan.org. *Website:* www.studioleeufan.org.

LEE, Virginia M.-Y., BSc, MSc, PhD, MBA; American biochemist, neuroscientist and academic; *John H. Ware III Endowed Professor in Alzheimer's Research, Department of Pathology and Laboratory Medicine, University of Pennsylvania;* b. Chongqing, SW China; m. John Trojanowski 1979; ed Royal Acad. of Music and Imperial Coll. London, UK, Univ. of California, San Francisco and Wharton School, Univ. of Pennsylvania, USA; moved to Hong Kong aged five, then to London 1962; worked at Univ. of California, San Francisco, USA, then at Univ. of Utrecht, The Netherlands 1973; Postdoctoral Fellow, Boston Univ. 1974; researcher, Smith, Kline & French (now GlaxoSmithKline), Philadelphia 1980; joined Univ. of Pennsylvania 1980, currently John H. Ware III Endowed Prof. in Alzheimer's Research, Dept of Pathology and Lab. Medicine, Perelman School of Medicine, Co-Dir Marian S. Ware Alzheimer Drug Discovery Program, Dir Center for Neurodegenerative Disease Research; J. Allyn Taylor Int. Prize in Medicine (co-recipient) 2014. *Publications:* numerous papers in professional journals. *Address:* Center for Neurodegenerative Disease Research, 3rd Floor, Maloney Building, 3600 Spruce Street, Philadelphia, PA 19104-4283, USA (office). *Telephone:* (215) 662-6427 (office). *Fax:* (215) 349-5909 (office). *E-mail:* vmylee@mail.med.upenn.edu (office). *Website:* www.med.upenn.edu (office).

LEE, Wan-koo, BA, MA, PhD; South Korean politician; b. 2 June 1950, Hongseong, South Chungcheong Prov.; ed Sung Kyun Kwan Univ., Dankook Univ., Michigan State Univ., USA; Deputy Dir, Hongseong District Office, Chungnam Provincial Govt 1974; Deputy Dir, Econ. Planning Bd 1975–77; Chief, Hongseong Police Station 1981–82; Consul, Korean Consulate-Gen., Los Angeles 1986–89; Chief, Chungbuk Police Agency March–Sept. 1993; Sr Superintendant Gen., Planning and Management Office, Nat. Police Agency 1993–94; Chief, Chungnam Police Agency 1994–95; mem. Nat. Ass. 1996–, mem. Agric., Forestry and Fisheries Cttee 1996–98, Special Cttee on Budget and Accounts 1996–98, Finance and Economy Cttee 2000–02, Sec., Agric., Forestry and Maritime Cttee 1998–2000; Prime Minister Feb.–April 2015; Gov., South Chungcheong Prov. 2006–09; Visiting Prof., UCLA 2004–06; mem. Saenuri Party (New Frontier Party), Chair. Saenuri Party Emergency Cttee 2014, Saenuri Party Floor Leader 2014–15; Hon. Pres. South Korea Regional Newspaper Asscn 2008; Hon. LLD (Chungnam Nat. Univ.) 2008, Hon. DBA (Kongju Nat. Univ.) 2009. *Address:* c/o Prime Minister's Office, 55, Sejong-no, Jongno-gu, Seoul 110-760, Republic of Korea (office).

LEE, Won-gul, BPA; South Korean business executive; b. 1959, Busan; ed Sungkyunkwan Univ.; Asst to Dir of Small Business Burea, Ministry of Trade, Industry and Energy 1980–83, later Dir Aerospace Industry Div., Basic Industry Bureau; Vice-Minister of Commerce, Industry and Energy –2006; Pres. and CEO Korea Electric Power Corpn (KEPCO) 2006–08.

LEE, Yeh Kwong Charles, OBE, JP, LLM, ACIS; Chinese lawyer; *Pro-Chancellor, Open University of Hong Kong;* b. 16 July 1936, Shanghai; m. Nancy Lee 1960; one s. one d.; ed London School of Econs, UK; audit asst, Li Kwan Hung 1954–57, Peat Marwick Mitchell & Co., Hong Kong 1957–60; Asst Registrar, Registrar-Gen.'s Dept 1960–65; articled clerk, Nigel, Wallis & Apfel, Solicitors, UK 1965–68; solicitor, Registrar-Gen.'s Dept 1968–70, Johnson Stokes & Master 1970–72, Partner 1972–73; Partner Charles Lee & Stephen Lo 1973, Woo Kwan Lee & Lo 1973–; Sec. Companies Law Revision Cttee 1968–73; non-official mem. Exec. Council of Hong Kong 1997–2002, 2005–12; mem. Council, Stock Exchange of Hong Kong Ltd 1988–91, Chair. 1991–94; Chair. Council of the Open University of Hong Kong 1998–2009, apptd Pro-Chancellor 2013–; Chair. Mandatory Provident Fund Schemes Authority 1998–2007, Hong Kong Exchange and Clearing Ltd 1999–2006; Chair. Exec. Cttee, Hong Kong Arts Festival Soc. Ltd 2003–12, Hong Kong-Taiwan Economic and Cultural Co-operation and Promotion Council 2010–15, Audit Profession Reform Advisory Group, Hong Kong Inst. of Certified Public Accountants 2010–; Dir several listed cos including Hutchison Whampoa 2013–, Cheung Kong (Holdings) Ltd 2013–; mem. Gov.'s Business Council 1992–97, Court of Hong Kong Polytechnic Univ. 1995–2002, Equal Opportunities Comm. of Hong Kong 1996–2003; Adviser Hong Kong Affairs 1993–97; mem. Hong Kong Univ. of Science and Tech. 1998–, Hon. mem. 2004–; Fellow, Chartered Asscn of Certified Accountants; Gov., Bd of Govs., Our Hong Kong Foundation 2015–; Hon. DIur (Univ. of Santo Tomas) 2000, DBA (Hong Kong Polytechnic Univ.) 2001, DScS (Open Univ. of Hong Kong) 2003, (Univ. of Hong Kong) 2005; Gold Bauhinia Star 2000, Grand Bauhinia Medal 2006. *Leisure interests:* boating, scuba diving. *Address:* Open University of Hong Kong, 30 Good Shepherd Street, Ho Man Tin, Hong Kong Special Administrative Region (office); Woo Kwan Lee & Lo, 26/Fl. Jardine House, 1 Connaught Place, Hong Kong Special Administrative Region, People's Republic of China (office). *Telephone:* 27112100 (Open University of Hong Kong) (office); 28477999 (office). *Fax:* 27150760 (Open University of Hong Kong) (office); 28459225 (office). *E-mail:* info@ouhk.edu.hk (office); wkll@wkll.com (office). *Website:* www.ouhk.edu.hk (office); www.wkll.com (office).

LEE, Yock Suan, BSc; Singaporean politician; b. 30 Sept. 1946, Singapore; m. Adeline Oh Choon Neo; one s. one d.; ed Queenstown Secondary Technical School, Raffles Institution, Imperial Coll., Univ. of London, UK, Univ. of Singapore; Div. Dir (Projects), Econ. Devt Bd 1969–80; MP 1980–2006; Deputy Man. Dir Petrochemical Corpn of Singapore (Pte.) Ltd Jan.–Sept. 1981; Minister of State (Nat. Devt) 1981–83, (Finance) 1983–84, Sr Minister of State and Acting Minister for Labour 1985–86, Minister for Labour 1987–91, Second Minister of Educ. 1991–92, Minister of Educ. 1992–97, of Trade and Industry 1998–99, for Information and the Arts 1999–2001, of Environment 1999–2000, Minister in Prime Minister's Office and Second Minister of Foreign Affairs 2001–04; Deputy Chair. People's Asscn 1984–91. *Leisure interest:* badminton. *Address:* 9 Bishopsgate, 249988, Singapore. *Telephone:* 62381600. *E-mail:* leeyocksuan2004@yahoo.com.sg. *Website:* www.parliament.gov.sg.

LEE, Yong-joon, BA; South Korean diplomatist; *Ambassador to Italy;* b. 13 Nov. 1956; m.; one s. one d.; ed Seoul Nat. Univ.; joined Ministry of Foreign Affairs (MFA), Third Sec., Embassy in Paris 1984–89, apptd First Sec., Embassy in Bangkok 1989, held various roles within Office of Pres., including as Asst Sec. for Foreign Affairs and Nat. Security and Sr Dir for Policy Co-ordination, Dir, North American Affairs Bureau, MFA 1996–97, Counsellor, Embassy in Hanoi 1997–2002, apptd Deputy Dir Gen. for North American Affairs and Head of Jt Task Force for the Improvement of Status of Forces Agreement, MFA 2002, also served as Dir Gen. for Strategic Planning on Cttee of NE Asian Co-operation Initiative, Deputy Minister for Foreign Affairs 2008–10, Amb. to Malaysia 2010–13, Amb. for Int. Relations of Gyeonggi Prov. of Korea 2013–15, Amb. to Italy (also accred to Malta) 2015–. *Address:* Embassy of Republic of Korea, Via Barnaba Oriani 30, 00197 Rome, Italy (office). *Telephone:* (06) 802461 (office). *Fax:* (06) 802462259 (office). *E-mail:* koremb-it@mofa.go.kr (office). *Website:* ita.mofa.go .kr (office).

LEE, Yong-kyung, BS, MS, PhD; South Korean telecommunications executive; b. 11 June 1943, Anyang; m.; two c.; ed Seoul Nat. Univ., Univ. of Oklahoma, Univ. of California, Berkeley, USA; Asst Prof. of Information Eng, Univ. of Illinois, Chicago 1975–77; sr researcher, Exxon Enterprises 1977–79; sr researcher, AT&T Bell Labs 1979–91; Vice-Pres. Outside Plant T Lab., Korea Telecom 1991–94, Vice-Pres. Telecommunication Systems Lab. and Software Lab. 1994–95, Vice-Pres. Wireless Tech. Lab. 1995–96, Exec. Vice-Pres. Research and Devt Group 1996–2000; CEO KT Freetel Co. 2000–02, Pres. and CEO KT Corpn (telecommunications service provider) 2002–05 (retd); participant on the future of communications panel, World Econ. Forum, Davos 2004; Exec. Leader in Residence, Kellogg School of Man., USA 2007; Adjunct Prof., KAIST Grad. School of Information and Media Man.; Visiting Scholar, Institut Européen d'Admin des Affaires (INSEAD) 2014; mem. Korea Nat. Ass. 2008–12, mem. Standing Cttee on Culture, Sports, Tourism, Broadcasting, and Telecommunications; Distinguished Eng Alumnus, Univ. of California, Berkeley 2003, Forbes magazine's Man. Leadership Award 2004, Industrial Gold Medal Korean Govt 2005. *Address:* c/o KT Corporation, 206 Jungja-dong, Bundang-gu, Sungnam, Kyonggi 463-711, Republic of Korea (office); c/o INSEAD, boulevard de Constance 77305 Fontainebleau, France. *Telephone:* 1-60-72-48-41 (Fontainebleau). *E-mail:* yongkyun.lee@insead.edu.

LEE, Yoon-woo, BSEE; South Korean business executive; b. 26 April 1946; ed Seoul Nat. Univ.; joined Display Device Business, Samsung Electronics 1968, Products Man., Semiconductor Business 1976–87, Man. Dir, Giheung Plant, Semiconductor Business 1987–92, mem. Bd of Dirs Samsung Electronics 1988–, Exec. Vice-Pres., Semiconductor Business 1992–96, Exec. Vice-Pres. and CEO 1993–96, Pres. and CEO 1996–2004, Vice-Chair., Global Collaboration, Samsung Electronics and CEO Samsung Advanced Inst. of Tech. 2004–05, Vice-Chair., Corp. Chief Tech. Officer and Global Collaboration, Samsung Electronics and Vice-Chair., Samsung Advanced Inst. of Tech. 2005–08, Vice-Chair. and CEO Samsung Electronics 2008–09, Vice-Chair., CEO and DS Business Pres. 2009–10, Vice-Chair. and Chair. Bd of Dirs 2010, Vice-Chair. 2010–12; apptd Chair. Korea Semiconductor Industry Asscn 2000, Korea AV Equipment Research Asscn 2001, Korea Engineers' Club 2004, Joong Dong Foundation 2004, Korea Inst. of Patent Information 2005; Vice-Chair. Korea Industrial Tech. Asscn 2003, Seoul Chamber of Commerce and Industry, Korea Fed. of Science and Tech. Socs 2005; Dir, Korea Int. Trade Asscn 2003; Technology and Science Award, Invention of 256K DRAM 1985, Order of Industrial Service Merit Award, Silver Tower 1993, Grand Prize of Korean Productivity Award 1995, Grand Prize of Korean Environment Man. Award 1998, Best TPM CEO Award, TPM World Conf. 1998, Order of Industrial Service Merit Award, Gold Tower 1999, Proud Korean Award, Journalist Fed. of Korea 2003, 34th CEO of the Year Award, Korea Man. Asscn 2005.

LEE, Young-sun; South Korean business executive; fmr Pres. Hallym Univ.; fmr Prof. of Econs and Head of Inst. of State Governance Studies, Yonsei Univ.; Ind. Dir (non-exec.), POSCO (f. as Pohang Iron and Steel Co.), Chair. POSCO 2012–14, Ind. Dir (non-exec.) 2014–. *Address:* POSCO Head Office, 1 Goedong-dong, Nam-gu, Pohang, Kyongsangbuk-do, 790-600 (office); POSCO, POSCO Centre, 892 Daechi-4-dong, Kangnam-ku, Seoul 135-777, Republic of Korea (office). *Telephone:* (54) 220-0114 (Head Office) (office); (2) 3457-0114 (POSCO Centre) (office). *Fax:* (54) 220-6000 (Head Office) (office); (2) 3457-6000 (POSCO Centre) (office). *E-mail:* info@posco.com (office). *Website:* www.posco.com (office).

LEE, Yuan-Tseh, PhD; Taiwanese scientist and academic; *Professor Emeritus, Department of Chemistry, University of California, Berkeley;* b. 19 Nov. 1936, Hsinchu; s. of Tse Fan Lee and Pei Tasi; m. Bernice Wu 1963; two s. one d.; ed Nat. Taiwan Univ., Univ. of California, Berkeley, USA; Asst Prof., James Franck Inst. and Dept of Chem., Univ. of Chicago 1968–71, Assoc. Prof. 1971–72, Prof. of Chem. 1973–74; Prof. of Chem., Univ. of California, Berkeley 1974–94, Prof. Emer. 1994–, also Prin. Investigator, Lawrence Berkeley Lab. 1974–97; Distinguished Research Fellow, Inst. of Atomic and Molecular Sciences, Academia Sinica, Taiwan 1994–2006, Pres. 1994–2006; Sloan Fellow 1969; Guggenheim Fellow 1976; Miller Professorship 1981–82; mem. Int. Council for Science 1993–, Pres. 2011–14, mem. Standing Cttee on Freedom in the Conduct of Science 1996–2005, elected Pres. 2008 to take up office 2010; mem. American Acad. of Arts and Sciences, NAS, American Physical Soc. and numerous other scholarly socs; Hon. Prof., Inst. of Chem., Chinese Acad. of Sciences, Beijing 1980–, Hon. Foreign Mem. Indian Nat. Science Acad. 1997, Hon. Mem. Chemical Soc. of Japan 2002–; E.O. Lawrence Award (US Dept of Energy) 1981, Harrison Howe Award, Rochester Section, ACS, 1983, Nobel Prize for Chem. (jtly) 1986, Nat. Medal of Science 1986, Peter Debye Award of Physical Chem., ACS 1986, Faraday Medal, Royal Soc. of Chem., UK 1992, Clark Kerr Award, Univ. of California, Berkeley 1999, Jawaharlal Nehru Centenary Medal, Indian Nat. Science Acad. 2004, and many other awards and prizes. *Publications:* articles in professional journals. *Address:* Department of Chemistry, 419 Latimer Hall, University of California, Berkeley, CA 94720-1460, USA (office). *Telephone:* (510) 642-5882 (office). *Fax:* (510) 642-9675 (office). *Website:* chem.berkeley.edu/faculty/emeriti/lee.php (office).

LEE, Yung-San, MA, PhD; Taiwanese economist, banking executive, company director and fmr politician; b. 7 Dec. 1938; m.; three d.; ed Nat. Taiwan Univ., Univ. of Wisconsin, Madison, USA; joined as Asst, Inst. of Econs, Academia Sinica, served successively as Asst Research Fellow, Assoc. Research Fellow, Research Fellow 1962–70, Deputy Dir 1985–87, Dir 1988–90; Prof. of Econs, Nat. Taiwan Univ. 1973–94; Visiting Scholar, Harvard Univ., USA 1976–77; Dir Econ. Research Dept, Cen. Bank of China 1977–85; Pres. Chiao Tung Bank 1990–94; Chair. Farmers Bank of China 1994–98, Int. Commercial Bank of China 1998–2002, Bankers Asscn of Taiwan 2000–02, Asian Bankers Asscn 2000–02; Minister of Finance 2002; fmr Man. Dir Chang Hwa Commercial Bank Ltd, Chair. 2007; Ind. Dir, Nan Ya Plastics Corpn; fmr Dir, International Bills Financial Corpn, Micron Memory Taiwan Co. Ltd, Rexchip Electronics Corpn. *Address:* Nan Ya Plastics Corpn, No. 35-1, Zhongshan 3rd Road, Kaohsiung City, Taiwan. *Telephone:* (2) 2712-2211. *Fax:* (2) 2717-8533. *E-mail:* nanya@npc.com.tw. *Website:* www.npc.com.tw.

LEE-CHIN, Michael, OJ, BSc; Canadian/Jamaican investment industry executive; *Executive Chairman and CEO, Portland Holdings Inc.;* b. 1951, Port Antonio, Jamaica; m. Vera Lee-Chin 1974; three c.; partner Sonya Hamilton; two c.; ed McMaster Univ.; emigrated to Canada 1970, began career in financial services in 1977, positions included Financial Advisor, Investors Group and Regional Br. Man., Regal Capital Planning; est. Berkshire Group (financial services co.) 1985, purchased Advantage Investment Council 1987 (renamed AIC), CEO –2006, then Chair., AIC acquired majority shares of Nat. Commercial Bank of Jamaica 2002, established AIC Caribbean Fund 2004, AIC sold to Manulife 2009; Founder and currently Exec. Chair. and CEO Portland Holdings Inc. (investment firm); Chair. Government of Jamaica's Econ. Growth Council 2016–; Chancellor, Wilfrid Laurier Univ. 2011–16; Dr hc (McMaster Univ.) 2003, (Northern Caribbean Univ.), (Wilfrid Laurier Univ.), (Univ. of the West Indies), (York Univ.); Hon. LLD, Univ. of Toronto 2007; Harry Jerome Award for Business Leader of the Decade 2002, one of Time magazine's 'Canada's Heroes' 2004. *Address:* Portland Holdings Inc., 1375 Kerns Road, Suite 100, Burlington, ON L7P 4V7, Canada (office). *Telephone:* (905) 331-4292 (office). *Website:* www.portlandholdings.com (office).

LEE HANG, Susuga Hon. Papliitele Niko; Samoan accountant and politician; *Minister of Works, Transport and Infrastructure;* b. 15 Nov. 1954; m. Doris Ruth Lee; four c.; ed St Joseph Coll., Univ. of New Zealand, Univ. of Waikato, NZ; Asst Gen. Man. 1990–97; Accountant and Public Trustee 1997–2000; mem. Parl. elected to one of two seats reserved for Individual Voters 2001–, Deputy Chair. Labour Cttee 2001–06, mem. Public Accounts Cttee and Trade, Commerce and Industries Cttee 2001–06, mem. Electoral Cttee 2002–06, House Cttee 2006–11, Chair. Finance and Expenditure Cttee 2011–; Parl. Under-Sec. to Minister of Justice 2002–04, to Minister of Revenue 2004–06; nominated to a Cabinet post by the Prime Minister; Minister of Finance 2006–11; Assoc. Minister of Communications and Information Tech. 2011; Minister of Works, Transport and Infrastructure 2016–; mem. Human Rights Protection Party. *Leisure interests:* Association football, tennis. *Address:* Ministry of Works, Transport and Infrastructure, TATTE Building, Level 4, Sogi, Samoa (office). *Telephone:* 23700 (office). *E-mail:* enquiries@mwti.gov.ws (office). *Website:* www.mwti.gov.ws (office).

LEEBRON, David W., BA, JD; American lawyer and university administrator; *President, Rice University;* b. 1956, Philadelphia, Pa; s. of Norman D. Leebron; m. Y. Ping Sun; one s. one d.; ed Harvard Coll., Harvard Law School; began career as clerk, US Ninth Circuit Court of Appeals; Acting Asst Prof. of Law, UCLA 1980; Assoc., Cleary, Gottlieb, Steen & Hamilton (law firm), New York 1981–83; Prof. of Law, New York Univ. (NYU) 1983, also Dir NYU Int. Legal Studies Program 1983–89; joined faculty, Columbia Univ. Law School 1989, Dean of Law School and Lucy G. Moses Prof. of Law 1996–2004; Pres. Rice Univ. 2004–, also Prof., Dept of Political Science; Jean Monnet Visiting Prof., Universität Bielefeld, Germany 1992–93; mem. Bd of Dirs IMAX Corpn, Jacobs Univ. Bremen, KIPP Foundation, Council on Foreign Relations; mem. Comm. on Federal Election Reform 2005–06; mem. NY State Bar; mem. American Law Inst., Council on Foreign Relations, American Soc. of Int. Law; fmr mem. Editorial Bd Foundation Press; mem. Bd of Trustees Internet2 2010–; Commdr, Ordre Nat. du Mérite 2006; Dr hc (Nankai Univ.) 2008. *Address:* Office of the President, Rice University, 6100 Main Street, Houston, TX 77005, USA (office). *Telephone:* (713) 348-5050 (office). *E-mail:* president@rice.edu (office). *Website:* www.professor.rice.edu/professor/Office_of_the_President.asp (office).

LEENHARDT, Jacques, PhD; French sociologist and academic; *Director of Studies, School of Advanced Studies in Social Sciences, École des Hautes Études en Sciences Sociales;* b. 17 April 1942, Geneva, Switzerland; s. of Franz J. Leenhardt and Antoinette Chenevière; m. 1st Françoise Warnod 1964 (divorced 1970); one s.; m. 2nd Sabine Wespieser 2006; contrib. to Le Journal de Genève 1963–98, to Le Temps 1998–; Fellow, Inst. for Advanced Study, Princeton, NJ 1979–80; Visiting Prof. to Univs in Brazil, Chile, Germany, Mexico, Portugal, Puerto Rico, USA 1974–; now Dir of Studies, School of Advanced Studies in Social Sciences, École des Hautes Études en Sciences Sociales, Paris; Pres. French Art Critics Asscn 1981–90, Crestet Centre d'Art 1987–2002, Int. Art Critics Asscn 1990–96, Art in Nature 1991–; mem. European Acad. of Arts and Sciences 1992–; curator of various exhbns in France and Brazil; Chevalier des Arts et des Lettres 1983, Ordre nat. du Mérite 1987; Oficial, Ordem Nacional do Cruzeiro do Sul (Brazil) 1998; Edra-Place Award 2000. *Publications include:* Lecture politique du roman 1973, Lire la lecture 1982, La force des mots 1982, Au Jardin des Malentendus 1990, Les Amériques latines en France 1992, Dans les jardins de Roberto Burle Marx 1994, Villette-Amazone 1996, Bienal do Mercosur 1998, Michel Corajoud, Paysagiste 2000, Erico Veríssimo. O romance da História 2001, Conscience du paysage: Le passant de Montreuil 2002, Reinventar o Brasil: Gilberto Freyre entre historia e ficçao 2006, monography on Wifredo Lam, exhbn catalogue on Iberê Camargo, new edn of J.-B. Debret's Voyage pittoresque et historique au Brésil (1834–1839) with notes and Introduction 2014. *Address:* École des Hautes Études en Sciences Sociales, 13 rue de l'Abbé Grégoire, 75006 Paris, France (office). *Telephone:* (9) 66-95-66-49 (office). *Fax:* (9) 66-95-66-49 (office). *E-mail:* jacques.leenhardt@ehess.fr (office). *Website:* cral.ehess.fr (office).

LEES, Sir David (Bryan), Kt, CBIM, FCA, FRSA; British chartered accountant and business executive; b. 23 Nov. 1936, Aberdeen, Scotland; s. of Rear-Adm. D. M. Lees, CB, DSO, and C. D. M. Lees; m. Edith M. Bernard 1961; two s. one d.; ed Charterhouse, Godalming, Surrey; 2nd Lt, Royal Artillery 1955–57; articled clerk, Binder Hamlyn & Co. (Chartered Accountants) 1957–62, Sr Audit Clerk 1962–63; Chief Accountant, Handley Page Ltd 1964–68; Financial Dir Handley Page Aircraft Ltd 1969; Chief Accountant, GKN Sankey Ltd 1970–72, Deputy Controller 1972–73, Dir, Sec., Controller 1973–76; Group Finance Exec. GKN Ltd 1976–77, Gen. Man. Finance 1977–82; Finance Dir GKN PLC 1982–87, Group Man. Dir 1987–88, CEO 1988–96, Chair. 1988–2004; Chair. Courtaulds 1996–98 (Dir (non-exec.) 1991–98); Deputy Chair. Brambles Industries Ltd and Brambles Industries PLC 2001–; Chair. Tate & Lyle PLC 1998–2009; Dir (non-exec.), Bank of England 1991–99, Chair. of the Court 2009–14; Dir Royal Opera House 1998–2008, QinetiQ Group plc 2005– (Deputy Chair. 2005–12); Pres. Eng Employers' Fed. (EEF) 1990–92, Soc. of Business Economists 1994–99; mem. CBI Council 1988–, Chair. CBI Econ. Affairs Cttee 1988–94, mem. CBI Pres.'s Cttee 1988–96; Commr, Audit

Comm. 1983–90; mem. Listed Cos Advisory Cttee 1990–97, Nat. Defence Industries Council 1995–2004, European Round Table 1995–2002, Panel on Takeovers and Mergers 2001– and other bodies; Gov. Shrewsbury School from 1986 (Chair. Governing Body 2004–07), Sutton's Hosp. in Charterhouse 1995–; DL, Shropshire 2007; Hon. Patron Shrewsbury Town Football Club 2010–; Officer's Cross, Order of Merit (FRG) 1996; ICAEW Award for Outstanding Achievement 1999. *Leisure interests:* walking, golf, opera, music. *Address:* c/o Bank of England, Threadneedle Street, London, EC2R 8AH, England.

LEES, Martin, BMechEng; British engineer, international official and university administrator; *Rector Emeritus, United Nations University for Peace;* b. 1941; m.; four c.; ed Fettes Coll., Edinburgh, Univ. of Cambridge, Coll. of Europe, Belgium; joined OECD 1971; Special Adviser to Bradford Morse, Admin. UNDP 1978, Exec. Dir UN Financing System for Science and Tech. for Devt 1979–84, Asst Sec.-Gen. UN 1984; Exec. Dir InterAction Council of Former Heads of State and Govt 1983; Dir Gen. Int. Cttee for Econ. Reform and Cooperation, Bonn 1991–96; Founder mem. Toyota Int. Advisory Bd, Moderator 1995–2008; Rector and CEO UN Univ. for Peace, Costa Rica 2001–05, Rector Emer. 2005–; Sr Adviser to Chinese Govt on climate change and sustainable devt 2005–09; Sec.-Gen. Club of Rome, Winterthur, Switzerland 2008–10; currently Int. Affairs Expert, Climate Change Task Force. *Website:* www.climatechangetaskforce.org.

LEEVES, Jane; British actress; b. 18 April 1963, Ilford, Essex; d. of Colin Leeves and Ruth Leeves; m. Marshall Coben 1996; two c.; co-f. (with Frasier co-star Peri Gilpin) Bristol Cities Production Co. 1998. *Films:* Monty Python's The Meaning of Life 1983, The Hunger 1983, To Live and Die in LA 1985, Mr Write 1994, Miracle on 34th Street 1994, James and the Giant Peach (voice) 1996, Hercules (voice) 1998, Don't Go Breaking My Heart 1998, Music of the Heart 1999, The Adventures of Tom Thumb and Thumbelina (voice) 2000, The Event 2003, Garfield: A Tail of Two Kitties (voice) 2006, Endless Bummer 2009. *Television includes:* The Benny Hill Show 1983–85, Double Trouble 1984, Throb (series) 1986–88, Murphy Brown (series) 1989–93, Seinfeld (series) 1992, 1998, Frasier 1993–2004, Pandora's Clock 1996, Hercules (series) 1998, Misconceptions (series) 2006, Phineas and Ferb (series) 2009–13, Hot in Cleveland (series) 2010–15, The Resident 2018. *Theatre:* Cabaret, Broadway 2002. *Leisure interests:* reading, cooking, sports, dance classes.

LEFEBVRE, Dominique; French cereal farmer and business executive; *Chairman, Crédit Agricole SA;* b. 1961; has held numerous positions within professional agricultural orgs; became involved in Crédit Agricole's working bodies 1990s, elected Chair. Crédit Agricole de la Beauce et du Perche (Crédit Agricole Val de France since 1997) 1995, also holds several nat. offices; elected mem. Bureau de la Fédération Nationale du Crédit Agricole 2004–, Deputy Chair. 2008–10, Chair. 2010–15, Chair. SAS Rue La Boétie (Crédit Agricole SA's majority shareholder), Chair. Caisse régionale Val de France, Chair. Crédit Agricole SA 2015–. *Address:* Crédit Agricole SA, 91–93 blvd Pasteur, 75015 Paris, France (office). *Telephone:* 1-43-23-52-02 (office). *Fax:* 1-43-23-34-48 (office). *E-mail:* info@credit-agricole-sa.fr (office). *Website:* www.credit-agricole-sa.fr (office).

LEFEBVRE, Georges; French postal service executive; b. 1952; ed Ecole Nationale Supérieure des PTT; joined La Poste 1970, Head of Personnel Dept at Regional Directorate of Post North 1981–83, Regional Dir La Poste's Nord-Pas-de-Calais 1983–86, Departmental Dir of the Marne 1987–90, in charge of man. of cadre leaders of La Poste with Dir-Gen. of the Post Office 1990–94, Dir of Human Resources at territorial del. of La Poste Ile de France 1994–97; joined office of Christian Pierret, Sec. of State for Industry 1997, served as advisor in charge of post and telecommunications; returned to La Poste Group, Dir of Human Resources 1998–2001, Deputy Dir-Gen. 2001–02, Man. Dir 2002–10, Gen. Del., Dir of Human Resources and Social Relations 2010–12, Deputy CEO 2012–16; Officier, Ordre national du Mérite 2005, Officier, Ordre national de la Légion d'honneur 2009.

LEFÈVRE, Brigitte; French ballet dancer and ballet director; b. 15 Nov. 1944; m. Olivier Meyer; entered Paris Opera Ballet School aged eight and corps de ballet aged 16, studied with Yvette Chauviré, Gérard Mulys, Serge Peretti, Yves Brieux, Rita Thalia, Janine Schwarz, Serge Perrault and Raymond Franchetti, dancing in ballets by George Balanchine, Roland Petit, Maurice Béjart, Michel Descombey and Gene Kelly, as well as in the major classical works; studied jazz with Gene Robinson and participated in numerous courses given by Alwin Nikolaïs, Merce Cunningham and Paul Taylor; choreographed first work, Mikrocosmos (to music by Bartók), for Jacques Garnier, Michaël Denard and herself 1970, presented at Avignon Festival in the Cour d'honneur; has also worked for the theatre and for musical comedy, in productions by Jean-Michel Ribes, Jean Mercure and Serge Peyrat at the Théâtre de la Ville; cr. choreography for La Révolution Française at the Palais des Sports, Paris; debut as actress in the role of Lisa, in Dostoïevsky's The Possessed, at Théâtre de la Ville, Paris; left the Paris Opera 1972; co-f., with Jacques Garnier, Théâtre du Silence, La Rochelle 1974–85, toured 21 countries world-wide, gave both classical and contemporary classes within the company and acted as sole dir from 1980; Prin. Insp. of Dance, Ministry of Culture 1985–87, Gen. Insp. and Chief Dance Delegate 1987–92; Gen. Admin. Paris Opéra-Garnier 1992–94, Assoc. Dir and Head of Dance 1994–95, Dir of Dance, Paris Opera 1995–2014; Vice-Pres. Conservatoire nat. supérieur de musique et de danse de Paris; Admin. Centre Nat. de la Danse 1998–, La Soc. Radio France 2004–; Pres. Bd of Dir Orchestre de chambre de Paris 2013; Officier, Ordre nat. du Mérite, Légion d'honneur; Commdr des Arts et des Lettres.

LEFKOWITZ, Robert J., BA, MD; American biologist/biochemist and academic; *James B. Duke Professor of Medicine, Professor of Biochemistry and Chemistry Investigator, Howard Hughes Medical Institute, Duke University Medical Center;* b. 15 April 1943, New York, NY; ed Columbia Univ.; Intern, Dept of Medicine, Columbia-Presbyterian Medical Center 1966–67, Asst Resident 1967–68; Clinical and Research Assoc., US Public Health Service, NIH, Bethesda, Md 1968–70; Sr Resident, Dept of Medicine, Mass Gen. Hosp., Boston 1970–71, Clinical and Research Fellow, Dept of Cardiology 1971–73; Teaching Fellow, Harvard Medical School, Dept of Medicine, Boston 1971–73; Assoc. Prof. of Medicine, Duke Univ. Medical Center Durham, NC 1973–77, Asst Prof. of Biochemistry 1973–85, Prof. of Medicine 1977–82, James B. Duke Prof. of Medicine 1982–, Prof. of Biochemistry 1985–, Chem. Investigator, Howard Hughes Medical Inst. 1976–; George Thorn Visiting Prof., Brigham and Women's Hosp. 1984; Sterling Drug Visiting Prof. of Pharmacology, Univ. of Mich. Medical School 1986; Sterling Drug-Maurice L. Tainter Professorship, Stanford Univ. School of Medicine 1988; Bulfinch Visiting Prof., Mass Gen. Hosp. 1999; Sec./Treasurer American Fed. for Clinical Research 1980–83; Pres. American Soc. for Clinical Investigation 1987–88; Treasurer Asscn of American Physicians 1989–94, Vice-Pres. 1999–2000, Pres. 2000–01; mem. Bd of Dirs Lexicon Pharmaceuticals 2001–; mem. American Fed. for Clinical Research, American Soc. of Biological Chemists, American Soc. for Clinical Investigation, American Heart Asscn Councils on Basic Science, Clinical Cardiology and Hypertension, American Soc. for Pharmacology and Experimental Therapeutics, Endocrine Soc., Asscn of American Physicians, American Physiological Soc.; mem. Editorial Bd Journal of Clinical Investigation 1990–, Proceedings of the Asscn of American Physicians 1995–, Molecular Biology of the Cell 1996–, Physiological Genomics 1999–, Molecular Interventions 2000–, Circulation 2000–, Fellowship, Int. Acad. of Cardiovascular Sciences 2002; Hon. mem. Japanese Biochemical Soc. 1990; Hon. DSc (Medical Univ. of South Carolina) 2004, (Mount Sinai School of Medicine, New York Univ.) 2004; numerous awards including Roche Prize for Excellence in Medical Studies 1962, Janeway Prize 1966, John J. Abel Award in Pharmacology, American Soc. for Pharmacology and Experimental Therapeutics 1978, George W. Thorn Award for Scientific Excellence, Howard Hughes Medical Inst. 1979, Gordon Wilson Lecture and Award, American Clinical and Climatological Asscn 1982, Ernst Oppenheimer Memorial Award, Endocrine Soc. 1982, Award for Outstanding Research, Int. Soc. for Heart Research 1985, Steven C. Beering Award for Outstanding Achievement in Biomedical Science, Indiana Univ. School of Medicine 1986, H.B. van Dyke Award for Excellence in Medical Research, Columbia Univ. Coll. of Physicians and Surgeons 1986, Goodman and Gilman Award, American Soc. for Pharmacology and Experimental Therapeutics 1986, Gairdner Foundation Int. Award 1988, American Heart Asscn Basic Research Prize (co-recipient) 1990, Asscn of American Medical Colls Biomedical Research Award 1990, Giovanni Lorenzini Prize for Basic Biomedical Research 1992, Bristol-Myers Squibb Award for Distinguished Achievement in Cardiovascular Research 1992, Columbia Univ. Coll. of Physicians and Surgeons Alumnus Award for Distinguished Achievements in Medicine 1992, Joseph Mather Smith Prize, Columbia Univ. Coll. of Physicians and Surgeons 1993, Glorney-Raisbeck Award in Cardiology, The New York Acad. of Medicine 1997, F.E. Shideman-Sterling Award 2000, Novartis/Drew Award in Biomedical Research 2000, Francis Gilman Blake Award, Asscn of American Physicians 2001, Peter Harris Distinguished Scientist Award, Int. Soc. for Heart Research 2001, NAS Jessie Stevenson Kovalenko Medal 2001, Louis and Artur Lucian Award for Research in Circulatory Disease 2001, Pasarow Cardiovascular Research Award 2002, Medal of Merit, Int. Acad. of Cardiovascular Sciences 2003, IPSEN Endrocrinology Prize, France 2003, Grand Prix for Science, Fondation Lefloulon-Delalande, Institut de France 2003, Founding Distinguished Scientist Award, American Heart Asscn, Distinguished Faculty Award, Duke Univ. Medical Center 2004, Albany Medical Center Prize in Medicine and Biomedical Research 2007, The Shaw Prize in Life Science and Medicine 2007, Nat. Medal of Science 2007, Research Achievement Award, American Heart Asscn 2009, BBVA Frontiers of Knowledge Award (Biomedicine Category) 2009, Nobel Prize in Chem. (jtly with Brian K. Kobilka) 2012. *Publications:* more than 800 articles in scientific and medical journals. *Address:* Department of Medicine, Howard Hughes Medical Institute, Duke University Medical Center, PO Box 3821, Durham, NC 27710, USA (office). *Telephone:* (919) 684-2974 (office). *Fax:* (919) 684-8875 (office). *E-mail:* lefko001@receptor-biol.duke.edu (office). *Website:* www.lefkolab.org (office).

LEFRANÇOIS, Jacques Roger; Belgian accountant; *Secretary-General, Conseil mondial de crise;* b. 1 March 1929, Eu, Seine Maritime, France; s. of Roger Lefrançois and Simone Boussy; m. Rosa Van Laer Londerzeel 1952; one s. one d.; ed Coll. d'Eu, Inst. Nat. de Comptabilité; second accountant (Sogeco mar) 1948–52; publicity agent (Publi-Buro) 1952–68; Spokesman, Union pour le contrôle de la democratie 1960; mem. Congress of European People (EFB-MFE) 1961–65; confidential employee 1966–78; World Citizen for Peace through Human Rights 1965; proposed UN Day for World Peace and the Environment 1970; mem. Professional Union of Int. School of Detective Experts 1950–75, Belgium Comm. World Political Union, The Hague 1978–; First Sec. Universal Charter for Survival (UFOS) 1978; Pres. Group 'L'Homme Planétaire' 1970–2012; Founder and Sec.-Gen. Conseil mondial de crise 1998–; mem. Flemish Asscn of Journalists of Periodical Press 1970–94; Ed. L'Indépendant Schaerbeek 1964–, Het Watervlietje 1975–2001; Sec. Flemish Regions, Parti Progressiste Belge 1989–93, Pres. 1985–89; Belgian Ombudsman/Médiateur Belge 1986–88; Pres. Flemish Progressive Party, European Flemish Programme 1989–92; Vice-Pres. European Progressive Party 1990–94; Hon. Pres. and Public Relations Ombudsman Parti Mondial du Coeur 1993–97; mem. Assemblée consultative du congrès des peuples 2007–; Citoyen d'honneur de la ville mondialisée de Dison 2004; Prize for Action to Promote European Federalism 1967, Diploma for services to Brussels tradition and folklore, Ordre des Amis de Manneken-Pis 1986, Action for Handicap International 1998, Action for Alzheimer 2006. *Address:* 9 Rue Leo Baekelandstraat, 2030 Antwerp, Belgium. *Telephone:* (3) 542-04-58.

LEGGESE, Addisu; Ethiopian politician; Pres. Amhara Nat. Regional State 1992–2000; mem. Parl. for Belessa 2005–10; Deputy Prime Minister 2005–10, Minister of Agric. and Rural Devt 2005–08; Chair. Amhara Nat. Democratic Movt—ANDM (branch of EPRDF) –2010; Chair. Ethiopian Airlines 2011–14; Pres. Meles Zenawi Leadership Acad. –2015.

LEGGETT, Sir Anthony J., Kt, PhD, KBE, FRS; British/American physicist and academic; *John D. and Catherine T. MacArthur Professor of Physics and Professor, Center for Advanced Study, University of Illinois at Urbana-Champaign;* ed Balliol, Merton and Magdalen Colls, Oxford; Postdoctoral Research Assoc., Univ. of Illinois, USA 1964–65, Visiting Research Assoc. 1967; Lecturer in Physics, Univ. of Sussex 1967–71, Reader 1971–78, Prof. 1978–83; Fellow, Magdalene Coll. Oxford 1965–67; John D. and Catherine T. MacArthur Prof. of Physics and Prof., Center for Advanced Study, Univ. of Illinois at Urbana-Champaign 1983–; Mike and Ophelia Lazaridis Distinguished Visiting Prof., Univ. of Waterloo, Ont. 2006–; mem. American Philosophical Soc. 1991–, American Acad. of Arts and Sciences 1996–; Foreign Assoc. NAS 1997–; Foreign mem. Russian Acad. of Sciences 1999–; Fellow, American Physical Soc., American Inst. of Physics; Hon. FInstP 1999; Prize Fellowship, Magdalene Coll., Oxford 1963–64; Inst. of Physics (UK) Maxwell Medal and Prize 1975, Inst. of Physics Simon Memorial Prize 1981, Fritz London

Memorial Award 1981, Inst. of Physics Paul Dirac Medal and Prize 1992, John Bardeen Prize (jt recipient) 1994, Wolf Prize (jt recipient) 2003, Nobel Prize in Physics (shared with Alexei Abrikosov and Vitaly Ginzburg) 2003. *Publications include:* The Problems of Physics 1986, Quantum Liquids: Bose Condensation and Cooper Pairing in Condensed Matter Systems 2006; numerous articles on superconductivity, superfluidity and theoretical condensed matter physics in scientific journals. *Address:* Department of Physics, University of Illinois at Urbana-Champaign, 1110 West Green Street, Urbana, IL 61801-3080, USA (office). *Telephone:* (217) 333-2077 (office). *Fax:* (217) 333-9819 (office). *E-mail:* aleggett@uiuc.edu (office). *Website:* www.physics.uiuc.edu (office).

LÉGLISE-COSTA, Philippe; French civil engineer and diplomatist; *Permanent Representative, European Union;* ed Ecole polytechnique, École des ponts ParisTech, Institut d'études politiques, Ecole nat. d'admin; contrib., Le Monde 1991–92; joined Ministry of Foreign Affairs, Quai d'Orsay 1992, assigned to Sub-Dept of Foreign Affairs, European and Econ. Affairs 1992–95, Counsellor for External Relations, Perm. Representation of France to EU, Brussels 1995–99, Tech. Adviser to Foreign Minister, Hubert Védrine 1999–2002, Special Adviser to Minister responsible for European Affairs 2001–02, assigned to Perm. Mission to UN, New York 2002–06, Deputy Dir for Econ. and Financial Affairs, Ministry of Foreign Affairs 2006–07, Dir of Cabinet of Jean-Pierre Jouyet, Sec. of State for European Affairs June–Sept. 2007, Deputy Perm. Rep., Perm. Representation of France to EU, Brussels 2008–12, Deputy Diplomatic Adviser for European Affairs to Pres. François Hollande 2012–17, Sec.-Gen. for European Affairs 2014–17, Amb. and Perm. Rep. to EU, Brussels 2017–. *Address:* Permanent Mission of France to the European Union, Place de Louvain 14, 1000 Brussels, Belgium (office). *Telephone:* (2) 229-82-09 (office). *Fax:* (2) 229-82-82 (office). *E-mail:* courrier .bruxelles-dfra@diplomatie.gouv.fr. *Website:* www.rpfrance.eu (office).

LEGQOG; Chinese politician; b. Oct. 1944, Gyangze Co., Tibet; ed CCP Cen. Cttee Cen. Party School; teacher, Gyangze Co., Tibet Autonomous Region 1964–71; Political Cadre, Gyangze Co., Tibet Autonomous Region 1971–73; joined CCP 1972; Sec. Gyangze Co. Autonomous Co. Cttee, CCP Communist Youth League 1973–75; mem. Standing Cttee CCP Communist Youth League Autonomous Prefectural Cttee, Xigaze Prefecture, Tibet Autonomous Region 1973–75; Sec. Org. Dept (Supervisory and Org. Divs) CCP Tibet Autonomous Regional Cttee 1975–80, Deputy Head Org. Dept and Deputy Chief Org. Div. 1980–86, Exec. Deputy Head Org. Dept 1986–91, mem. Standing Cttee CCP Tibet Autonomous Regional Cttee 1991–2010, Deputy Sec. CCP Tibet Autonomous Regional Cttee 1994–2010; Sec. CCP Lhasa City Cttee 1991–94; Vice-Chair. Tibet Autonomous Region People's Govt 1995–98, Chair. 1998–2004; Chair. Standing Cttee Tibet Autonomous Regional People's Congress 2003–10; Alt. mem. CCP 15th Cen. Cttee 1997–2002, mem. CCP 16th Cen. Cttee 2002–07, mem. CCP 17th Cen. Cttee 2007–12. *Address:* c/o People's Government of Tibetan Autonomous Region, Lhasa, Tibet, People's Republic of China.

LEGRAS, Guy; French diplomatist and international organization official; b. 19 July 1938, Angers; s. of René Legras and Pauline Legras; m. Borka Oreb 1971; one s. one d.; ed Faculté de Droit, Paris, Inst. d'Etudes Politiques, Paris and Ecole Nat. d'Admin; joined Ministry of Foreign Affairs 1967; Cabinet of Sec. of State for Foreign Affairs 1968–71; Sec.-Gen. of Interministerial Cttee (SGCI) for European Affairs (Prime Minister) 1971–74; Cabinet of Sec.-Gen. of OECD 1974–77; Counsellor, Perm. Rep. of France at European Communities, Brussels 1977–80; Asst Sec.-Gen. SGCI 1980-82; Head, Dept of Econ. Affairs, Ministry of Foreign Affairs 1982–85; Dir-Gen. for Agricultural Comm. of European Communities (now EC), Brussels 1985–99, for External Affairs 1999–2003 (retd); Adviser to Croatia for EU accession talks from 2004; Minister Plenipotentiary 1988; Officier, Ordre nat. du Mérite; Chevalier, Légion d'honneur; Order of Duke Branimir with Necklace (Croatia) 2012. *Leisure interest:* tennis.

LEGRIS, Manuel Christophe; French ballet dancer and ballet company director; *Director, Wiener Staatsballett;* b. 19 Oct. 1964, Paris; s. of Michel Legris and Raymonde Gazave; ed Paris Opera School of Dancing; mem. corps de ballet, Opéra de Paris 1980, 'Danseur Etoile' 1986–2009; repertoire included lead roles in works by Frederick Ashton, George Balanchine, Patrice Bart, Maurice Béjart, Trisha Brown, August Bournonville, Vladimir Burmeister, John Cranko, Nacho Duato, Mats Ek, Mikhail Fokin, William Forsythe, Jiří Kylián, Pierre Lacotte, Harald Lander, Serge Lifar, Kenneth MacMillan, John Neumeier, Rudolf Nureyev, Roland Petit, Angelin Preljocaj, Jerome Robbins, Twyla Tharp, Antony Tudor and Rudi van Dantzig; major roles at Paris Opéra include Arepo (Béjart) 1986, In the Middle Somewhat Elevated (Forsythe) 1987, Magnificat (Neumeier) 1987, Rules of the Game (Twyla Tharp) 1989, The Sleeping Beauty (Nureyev) 1989, Manon (MacMillan) 1990, Dances at the Gathering (Robbins) 1993, Variations sur Carmen (Roland Petit) 2003, Phrases de Quatuor (Maurice Béjart) 2003; in Hamburg created Cinderella Story and Spring and Fall (Neumeier); has also appeared at Bolshoi Ballet, Moscow, La Scala, Milan, Royal Ballet, London, New York City Ballet, Tokyo Ballet, Stuttgart Ballet and others; danced at Burgtheater as part of ImPulsTanz 2005, performed in ImPulsTanz ballet gala 2008; presented the gala Manuel Legris & Guests 2012; also appeared with his own ensemble, Manuel Legris et ses Étoiles; danced solo at Vienna Philharmonic's New Year's Concert 2001; guest performances at Paris Opéra and at other theatres in Europe, Asia and N America 2009–; Dir Wiener Staatsballett and Artistic Dir Ballet School of the Vienna State Opera 2010–; productions include Rudolf Nureyev's version of Don Quixote, Pierre Lacotte's La Sylphide, Rudolf Nureyev's The Nutcracker; as dancer, appeared at Wiener Staatsoper at opening ceremony of the Vienna Opera Ball 2011, and at Nureyev Galas 2011, 2012, 2013; toured with Wiener Staatsballett to Japan 2012 (cr. title role in Patrick de Bana's Ludwig II – The Swan King and also danced in Roland Petit's The Bat); Chevalier des Arts et des Lettres 1993, Officier 1998, Commdr 2009; Chevalier, Ordre nat. du Mérite 2002, Légion d'honneur 2006; Gold Medal, Osaka Competition 1984, Prix du Cercle Carpeaux 1986, Nijinsky Prize 1988, Prix Benois de la danse 1998, Nijinsky Award (Best Dancer in the World) 2000, Prix Positano 2001, Prix Léonide Massine 2001, Prix Danza & Danza 2002, People's Choice Award (Dance Open Int. Ballet Festival, St Petersburg) 2016. *Film appearances include:* Romeo and Juliet, Le Spectre de la Rose, Notre Dame de Paris, L'Arlésienne, The Sleeping Beauty, Don Quixote. *Address:* Wiener Staatsoper GmbH, Opernring 2, 1010 Vienna, Austria (office). *Telephone:* (1) 51444 (office). *E-mail:* information@wiener-staatsoper.at (office). *Website:* www.wiener-staatsoper.at (office).

LEGWAILA, Legwaila Joseph, MA; Botswana diplomatist; b. 2 Feb. 1937, Mathathane; s. of Madume Legwaila and Morongwa Legwaila; m. Pholile Matsebula 1975; three d.; ed Bobonong School, Brussels School, SA, Serowe Teacher Training Coll., Univs of Calgary and Alberta, Canada; early career as primary school teacher; Asst Prin. External Affairs, Govt of Botswana 1973–74, Sr Pvt. Sec. to Pres. of Botswana 1974–80; apptd Perm. Rep. to UN 1980; High Commr to Guyana 1981–2001, concurrently High Commr to Jamaica 1982–2001, Amb. to Cuba 1983–2001; Deputy Special Rep. of the UN Sec.-Gen. for Namibia 1989–90, Head of UN Mission in Ethiopia and Eritrea (UNMEE) 2000–06, Sec.-Gen.'s Special Adviser on Africa 2006–08. *Publication:* Safari to Serowe (co-author) 1970. *Leisure interests:* music, cycling. *Address:* c/o Office of the Secretary General, United Nations, New York, NY 10017, USA.

LEHMAN, Ronald (Ron) Frank, II, PhD; American security expert and government official; *Director, Center for Global Security Research, Lawrence Livermore National Laboratory;* b. 25 March 1946, Napa, Calif.; s. of Ronald Lehman and Esther Suhr; m. Susan Young 1979; ed Claremont Men's Coll. and Claremont Grad. School; served in US Army in Viet Nam 1969–71; Legis. Asst US Senate 1976–78; mem. professional staff, US Senate Armed Services Cttee 1978–82; Deputy Asst Sec. of Defense, Office of Int. Security Policy 1982–83; Sr Dir Defense Programs and Arms Control, Nat. Security Council 1983–86; Deputy US Negotiator for Strategic Nuclear Arms, Dept of State, Washington, DC 1985–86, Chief US Negotiator Geneva 1986–88; Deputy Asst to Pres. for Nat. Security Affairs 1986; Asst Sec. Dept of Defense 1988–89; Dir Arms Control and Disarmament Agency, Washington, DC 1989–93; Asst to Dir Lawrence Livermore Nat. Lab. 1993–, Dir Center for Global Security Research 1996–; mem. Presidential Advisory Bd on Arms Proliferation Policy 1995–96; Adjunct Prof. Georgetown Univ. 1982–89; mem. Bd Dirs US Inst. of Peace 1988–93, Keck Center for Int. and Strategic Studies (now Chair.), Claremont McKenna Coll.; mem. Int. Advisory Bd Inst. of Global Conflict and Cooperation, Univ. of Calif. San Diego 1994–; mem. IISS, Council on Foreign Relations, Atlantic Council. *Address:* Center for Global Security Research, Lawrence Livermore National Laboratory, PO Box 808, L-1, Livermore, CA 94551 (office); 693 Encina Grande Drive, Palo Alto, CA 94306, USA (home). *Telephone:* (925) 422-6141 (office). *Fax:* (925) 422-5252 (office). *E-mail:* lehman3@llnl.gov (office). *Website:* cgsr.llnl.gov (office).

LEHMANN, Klaus-Dieter; German librarian and institute director; *President, The Goethe Institute;* b. 29 Feb. 1940, Breslau (now Wrocław, Poland); ed Max-Planck-Institut für Chemie, Mainz; University Librarian, Darmstadt 1970–73; worked at Municipal Library and Univ. Library, Frankfurt am Main 1973–88, Man. Dir 1978–88; Dir-Gen. Univ. Library, Frankfurt 1988–90; following re-unification, Dir-Gen. united German Library Leipzig, Frankfurt, Berlin (subsequently the German National Library) 1990–98; Pres. Prussian Cultural Heritage Foundation, Berlin 1998–2008; Vice-Pres. Goethe Inst. 2002–08, Pres. and mem. Bd of Trustees 2008–; Chair. Supervisory Bd Germanic National Museum Nürnberg, German Museum in Munich; mem. Acad. of Sciences and Literature, Mainz, Berlin-Brandenburg Acad. of Science; mem. Bd of Trustees German Acad. for Language and Poetry, Federal Cultural Foundation, Bertelsmann Foundation, Acad. of Sciences and Literature, Mainz, Peace Prize of German Publrs and Booksellers Asscn; Hon. Prof., Univ. of Frankfurt am Main 1986, Humboldt Univ. 2006; Hon. Senator, Humboldt Univ. 2010; Hon. mem. Bavarian Acad. of Fine Arts, Asscn of German Librarians, German Publishers and Booksellers Asscn (Börsenvereins des Deutschen Buchhandels); Ordre des Palmes académiques, Bundesverdienstkreuz (First Class), Order of Merit of the Land Berlin 2006, Austrian Honorary Cross for Science and Art (First Class) 2007, Culture of the German Cultural Council groschen 2008, Großes Verdienstkreuz 2011, Order of the Rising Sun (Japan) 2015; Dr hc (Ludwig-Maximilians Univ., Munich) 2001; Gutenberg Prize, City of Mainz and Gutenberg Soc. 2016. *Publications include:* Treasures of the World Cultures in the Collections of the Stiftung Preussischer Kulturbesitz 2004, Digital Resources from Cultural Institutions for Use in Teaching and Learning 2004, Science and Culture in Libraries, Museums and Archives 2005, Phoenix Bird 2007, Picture Book and Archetypes 2008. *Address:* Goethe-Institut, Head Office, Dachauer Strasse 122, 80637 Munich, Germany (office). *Telephone:* (89) 15921-0 (office). *Fax:* (89) 15921-450 (office). *E-mail:* praesident@goethe.de (office). *Website:* www.goethe.de (office).

LEHN, Jacques André, LèsL; French business executive; b. 15 July 1944, Lausanne, Switzerland; s. of François-Xavier Lehn and Geneviève Jaeger; ed lycées in Rabat, Morocco and Sceaux, Sorbonne, Paris, Inst. d'Etudes Politiques, Paris and Ecole des Hautes Etudes Commerciales; Man. Consultant, Arthur Andersen 1969–76; Finance Dir Warner Lambert France 1976–79; Dir-Gen. Adams' France 1979–80; Dir Matra, Médias Br. 1980–81; Dir Hachette Group 1981–84, Deputy Dir-Gen. 1984–90, Dir-Gen. 1990; Dir-Gen. Matra-Hachette 1993–; Vice-Pres. Europe I Communication 1986–94, Deputy Pres. 1994–99; Pres., Dir-Gen. Europe développement int. 1996–; Pres. Supervisory Bd Europa Plus, France 1996–, Holpa 1996–; Chair. and CEO Go Mass Media, Go Outdoor Holdings Systems 1999–; Chair. Supervisory Bd Giraudy 1999–; Founding mem. ORMA (Ocean Racing Multihull Asscn) 1993–, Pres. 1993–2004; Vice-Chair. Oceanic Sub-cttee, Int. Sailing Fed. (ISAF) 2005–09, Chair. Offshore and Oceanic Cttee 2009–, mem. ISAF Council 2012–; numerous other business affiliations; Chevalier, Ordre nat. du Mérite, Chevalier, Légion d'honneur. *Leisure interest:* yachting. *Address:* ORMA, 9 rue Royale, 75008 Paris (office); ISAF UK (Ltd), Ariadne House, Town Quay, Southampton, Hants., SO14 2AQ, England; 47 blvd Lannes, 75116 Paris, France (home). *Telephone:* 1-53-30-86-07 (office); (23) 8063-5111. *Fax:* (23) 8063-5789; 1-47-42-32-14 (office). *E-mail:* secretariat@isaf.co.uk (office); jacques.lehn@libertysurf.fr (office). *Website:* www.sailing.org (office).

LEHN, Jean-Marie Pierre, DèsSc, PhD; French chemist and academic; *Director, Laboratoire de Chimie Supramoléculaire, University of Strasbourg;* b. 30 Sept. 1939, Rosheim, Bas-Rhin; s. of Pierre Lehn and Marie Lehn (née Salomon); m. Sylvie Lederer 1965; two s.; ed Univ. of Strasbourg; various posts, CNRS 1960–66; post-doctoral Research Assoc. with Prof. R. B. Woodward, Harvard Univ., USA 1963–64; Asst Prof., Univ. of Strasbourg 1966–70, Assoc. Prof. 1970, Prof. 1970–79, f. Institut de Science et d'Ingénierie Supramoléculaires 2002, currently Dir Laboratoire de Chimie Supramoléculaire, Chair. Chimie des Systèmes Complexes,

Institut d'Études Avancées; Visiting Prof. of Chem., Harvard Univ. 1972, 1974, ETH, Zurich 1977, Univ. of Cambridge 1984, Barcelona Univ. 1985; Prof., Collège de France, Paris 1979–; Pres. Scientific Council of Rhône-Poulenc 1992–, of Ministry of Nat. Educ., Youth and Sport 1989–93; mem. Research Strategy Cttee 1995, Inst. de France, Deutsche Akad. der Naturforscher Leopoldina, Accad. Nazionale dei Lincei; Foreign assoc. NAS; Foreign mem. Royal Netherlands Acad. of Arts and Sciences, Royal Soc. and many others; Foreign Hon. mem. American Acad. of Arts and Sciences; Commdr, Légion d'honneur, Officier, Ordre nat. du Mérite, mem. Order 'Pour le Mérite' 1990, Österreichisches Ehrenkreuz für Wissenschaft und Kunst, Erste Klasse 2001; shared Nobel Prize in Chem. 1987, Gold, Silver and Bronze Medals of CNRS, Gold Medal, Pontifical Acad. of Sciences 1981, Paracelsus Prize, Swiss Chemical Soc. 1982, von Humboldt Prize 1983, Karl Ziegler Prize (German Chemical Soc.) 1989, Davy Medal (Royal Soc.) 1997, Lavoisier Medal 1997, A.R. Day Award 1998, numerous others. *Publications:* about 900 scientific publs. *Leisure interest:* music. *Address:* Laboratoire de Chimie Supramoléculaire, ISIS, Allée Gaspard Monge 8, 67000 Strasbourg Cedex (office); 6 rue des Pontonniers, 67000 Strasbourg, France (home). *Telephone:* (3) 68-85-51-45 (office); (88) 37-06-42 (home). *Fax:* (3) 68-85-51-40 (office). *E-mail:* lehn@unistra.fr (office). *Website:* www.usias.fr/en/chairs/jean-marie-lehn (office).

LEHNER, Ulrich; German business executive; *Chairman of the Supervisory Board, Deutsche Telekom AG;* b. 1 May 1946, Düsseldorf; m. Johanna Ewers 1970; two s. one d.; mem. Bd of Man., Henkel KGaA 1995–2000, Chair. Exec. Bd, Pres. and CEO 2000–08, mem. Stockholder Cttee 2008–; Chair. Supervisory Bd, Dial Corpn, Deutsche Telekom AG, ThyssenKrupp AG 2013– (mem. 2008–); mem. Supervisory Bd, E.ON AG, Porsche Automobil Holding SE; mem. Advisory Bd, Novartis AG (Switzerland), Dr August Oetker KG; Pres. Verbandes der Chemischen Industrie 2007–10; Hon. Prof., Univ. of Münster. *Address:* Deutsche Telekom AG, Friedrich-Ebert-Allee 140, 53113 Bonn, Germany (office). *Telephone:* (228) 1814949 (office). *Fax:* (228) 18194004 (office). *E-mail:* info@deutschetelekom.com (office). *Website:* www.deutschetelekom.com (office); www.telekom.com (office).

LEHOHLA, Archibald Lesao, BSc, BA, MA; Lesotho politician; b. 28 July 1946, Mafeteng; m.; two s. one d.; ed Mafeteng Secondary School, Basutoland High School, Univ. of Botswana, Lesotho and Swaziland, Roma, Univ. of Oxford, UK; Teaching Asst in Math., Univ. of Botswana, Lesotho and Swaziland 1971–72; Asst Teacher, Bereng High School 1975–76, Headmaster 1977–93; elected mem. Parl. for Mafeteng 1993; Deputy Prime Minister 2003–12, Minister of Home Affairs (Local Govt, Rural and Urban Devt) 1993–95, of Transport, Posts and Telecommunications 1995–96, of Educ. and Manpower Devt 1996–2004, of Home Affairs and Public Safety 2004–12, and of Parl. Affairs 2007–12; Chair. Scott Hosp. Comm. of Inquiry 1990; fmr Chair. Mafeteng Tractor Owners' Cooperative; Church Elder and mem. Mafeteng LEC consistory; fmr mem. Lesotho Headmasters' and Headmistresses' Asscn, Lesotho Evangelical Church Law Review Comm., LEC Educational Sec.'s Advisory Cttee on Educ.; rep. Lesotho at Commonwealth Seminar on Educational Admin and Supervision, Univ. of Nairobi, Kenya 1977; UNESCO Fellowship to Univ. of Oxford 1975. *Leisure interests:* gardening, singing, crop farming.

LEHR, Ursula M., DrPhil (Habil.); German government official, psychologist and academic; *Deputy Chairman, German National Association of Senior Citizens Organizations;* b. (Ursula M. Leipold), 5 June 1930, Frankfurt am Main; d. of Georg-Josef Leipold and Gertrud Jendorff; m. 1st Helmut Lehr 1950 (died 1994); two s.; m. 2nd Hans Thomas 1998 (died 2001); Research Asst, Univ. of Bonn 1955–60, Research and Teaching Asst, Inst. of Psychology 1960–68, mem. perm. staff 1968–69, Additional Prof. and Head Dept of Developmental Psychology 1969–72, Chair. Dept of Psychology and Dir Inst. of Psychology 1976–86, Hon. Prof. 1987–; Chair. of Pedagogics and Pedagogical Psychology, Albertus Magnus Univ., Cologne 1972; Dir Inst. of Gerontology, Ruprecht Karls Univ., Heidelberg 1986–88, 1991–96; Academic Dir, Deutsches Zentrum für Alternsforschung (DZFA—German Centre for Research on Aging), Heidelberg 1996–98; Fed. Minister of Youth, Families, Women and Health 1988–91; mem. Families Advisory Bd, Fed. Ministry of Youth, Families and Health 1972–80, WHO Expert Advisory Panel on Health of Elderly Persons 1983–87; mem. Parl. 1990–94; Pres. Asscn of Fmr Mems of the German and European Parl. 2002–08; Chair. German Nat. Asscn of Senior Citizens Orgs (BAGSO) 2009–15, Deputy Chair. 2015–; Vice-Pres. German Gerontological Soc. 1973–78, 1980–84, Pres. 1997–99; Founder mem. Acad. of Sciences, Berlin 1987–91; Corresp. mem. Acad. of Sciences, Austria 1994–, Sächsische Akad. der Wissenschaften 1998–; mem. European Acad. of Yuste, Spain 2000–; Hon. mem. Socs of Gerontology of Switzerland, Spain, Mexico, Hon. Pres. BAGSO (German Nat. Asscn of Senior Citizens' Orgs) 2009–; Grosses Bundesverdienstkreuz 1996; Hon. PhD (Fribourg, Switzerland, Univ. of Vechta); Landesverdienstmedaille Baden-Württemberg 1999, Lifetime award Bund Deutscher Psychologen 2003. *Publications:* more than 900 scientific texts. *Leisure interests:* art (paintings of the Middle Ages), history of art. *Address:* Am Büchel 53B, 53173 Bonn, Germany. *Telephone:* (228) 352849. *Fax:* (228) 352741. *E-mail:* ursula.lehr@t-online.de. *Website:* www.bagso.de.

LEHRER, James (Jim) Charles, AA, BJ; American writer and fmr broadcast journalist; b. 19 May 1934, Wichita, Kan.; m. Kate Lehrer (née Staples); three d.; ed Victoria Coll., Tex., Univ. of Missouri; served as infantry officer, US Marine Corps 1956–58; reporter, Dallas Morning News (daily newspaper) 1959–61; reporter and columnist Dallas Times-Herald 1961–70; Exec. Dir of Public Affairs, on-air host, and Ed., nightly news program KERA–TV, Dallas 1970–72; Public Affairs Coordinator, Public Broadcasting Service (PBS), Washington, DC 1972–73, also mem. Journalism Advisory Bd and Fellow, Corpn for Public Broadcasting, Corresp. Nat. Public Affairs Center for TV (NPACT) 1973, co-hosted PBS coverage of US Senate Watergate hearings and US House Judiciary Cttee Nixon impeachment inquiry, Washington corresp., Robert MacNeil Report 1975, co-anchor MacNeil/Lehrer Report 1975–83, co-anchor MacNeil/Lehrer NewsHour 1983–96, Exec. Ed. and Anchor, The News Hour with Jim Lehrer 1996–2011; served as moderator for several US presidential election debates; Fellow, American Acad. of Arts and Sciences; Hon. Bd Mem., The Writer's Center; Dr hc (McDaniel Coll.) 2004; numerous awards for journalism including two Emmys, Fred Friendly First Amendment Award, George Foster Peabody Broadcast Award, William Allen White Foundation Award for Journalistic Merit, Medal of Honor, Univ. of Missouri School of Journalism; Nat. Humanities Medal 1999; inducted (with Robert MacNeil) TV Hall of Fame, Silver Circle of Washington, DC Chapter of Nat. Acad. of TV Arts and Sciences, Fourth Estate Award, Nat. Press Club 2011. *Plays:* Chili Queen 1987, Church Key Charlie Blue 1988, The Will and Bart Show 1992. *Publications include:* We Were Dreamers 1975, Kick the Can 1988, Crown Oklahoma 1989, The Sooner Spy 1990, Lost and Found 1991, Short List 1992, A Bus of My Own 1992, Blue Hearts 1993, Fine Lines 1994, The Last Debate 1995, White Widow 1997, Purple Dots 1998, The Special Prisoner 2000, No Certain Rest 2002, Flying Crows 2004, The Franklin Affair 2005, The Phony Marine 2006, Super 2010, Tension City 2011, Top Down: A Novel of the Kennedy Assassination 2013.

LEHTOMÄKI, Paula Ilona, MSc; Finnish politician; *Secretary-General, Nordic Council of Ministers;* b. 29 Nov. 1972, Kuhmo; m. Jyri Sahlsten; three c.; acting head teacher 1995; research asst 1998; mem. Kuhmo Town Council 1997–2004; mem. Parl. (Centre Party) 1999–2015; mem. Finnish Del. to Nordic Council 1999–2003, to Council of Europe 2003; Minister for Foreign Trade and Devt and Minister at the Prime Minister's Office 2003–07, of the Environment 2007–11, State Sec. to Prime Minister 2015–; mem. Kainuu Regional Council 2005–08; Vice-Chair. Centre Party 2002–10; Pres. Finland-Russia Soc. 2014–15; Sec.-Gen., Nordic Council of Ministers 2019–; mem. Supervisory Bd VR-Group Ltd 2000–03, Exec. Cttee Lasten Keskus Publishing House 2000–01, Finnish 4H Fed. Cttee 2001–03, Man. Bd Finland Soc. 2013–15; mem. Bd Audiator Oy 2000–03, UKK Soc. 2010–; Commdr of the White Rose; Military Merit Medal, War Veterans Asscn's Medal of Merit. *Leisure interest:* fitness training, singing. *Address:* Nordic Council of Ministers Secretariat, Ved Stranden 18, 1061 Copenhagen K, Denmark (office). *Telephone:* 21-71-71-29 (office). *E-mail:* hejo@norden.org (office); nmr@norden.org (office). *Website:* www.norden.org/en/nordic-council-ministers (office).

LEI, Lt-Gen. (retd) Mingqiu; Chinese army officer; b. June 1942, Jiangjiaqiao, Qidong Co., Hengyang City, Hunan Prov.; ed Zhuzhou Aeronautical Acad. Hunan and PLA Political Acad.; joined PLA 1962, CCP 1964; platoon leader and Deputy Political Instructor, Mortar Bn 1965–69; Deputy Section Chief of Org., Div. Political Dept 1969–71, Dir Div. Political Dept 1982–83; clerk and Deputy Chief (later Chief) of Youth Affairs Section, Political Dept, Guangzhou City, PLA Guangzhou Mil. Region 1971–80; Deputy Political Commissar, 42nd Army, Army (or Ground Force), PLA Services and Arms 1983–85, Political Commissar 1985–92; Dir Political Dept, Guangzhou Mil. Region 1992–94; Deputy Political Commissar, Nanjing Mil. Region 1994–2000 (Sec. Comm. for Discipline Inspection, CCP Party Cttee 1994–99), apptd Political Commissar 2000; mem. 13th CCP Cen. Cttee 1987–92, 14th CCP Cen. Cttee 1992–97, 15th CCP Cen. Cttee 1997–2002, 16th CCP Cen. Cttee 2002–07.

LEIBINGER-KAMMÜLLER, Nicola, DrPhil; German business executive; *President and Chairwoman of the Management Board, TRUMPF Group;* b. 15 Dec. 1959, Wilmington, Ohio, USA; d. of Beithold Leibinger; ed studied German, English and Japanese language and literature in Freiburg, Germany, Middlebury, Vt, USA and Zurich, Switzerland; worked in Press and Public Relations Office, TRUMPF Group 1984–88, for TRUMPF Corpn, Japan 1988–90, Man. Dir Berthold Leibinger Foundation, GmbH 1992–2003, Exec. Vice-Pres. TRUMPF GmbH & Co. KG (man. holding co. of TRUMPF Group) 2003–05, Pres. 2005–, Pres. and Chair. Man. Bd TRUMPF Group 2008–, responsible for strategic devt, corp. communication and real estate and facilities; mem. Supervisory Bd CLAAS KGaA mbH 2006–, Siemens AG 2008–, Voith AG, Axel-Springer-Verlag; mem. Advisory Bd Landesbank Baden-Wuerttemberg; previously served with Claas Kommanditgesellschaft auf Aktien mgh and Deutsche Lufthansa AG from 2008. *Address:* TRUMPF Group, TRUMPF GmbH & Co. KG, Johann-Maus-Str. 2, 71254 Ditzingen, Germany (office). *Telephone:* (7156) 303-0 (office). *Fax:* (7156) 303-30309 (office). *E-mail:* info@trumpf.com (office). *Website:* www.trumpf.com (office).

LEIBLER, Kenneth (Ken) Robert, BA; American business executive; b. 21 Feb. 1949, New York, NY; s. of Max Leibler and Martha Leibler (née Dales); m. Marcia Kate Reiss 1973; one s. one d.; ed Syracuse Univ. and Univ. of Pennsylvania; Options Man. Lehman Bros 1972–75; Vice-Pres. Options, American Stock Exchange, New York 1975–79, Sr Vice-Pres. Admin. and Finance 1979–81, Exec. Vice-Pres. Admin. and Finance 1981–85, Sr Exec. Vice-Pres. 1985–86, Pres. 1986–90; Pres. and COO Liberty Financial Cos 1990–95, Pres. and CEO 1995–2000; Chair. and CEO Boston Stock Exchange 2001–05; Chair. and CEO NASDAQ OMX BX, Inc. 2001–05; Founder Partner and Chair. Boston Options Exchange Group, LLC 2004–07; Vice-Chair. Beth Israel Medical Center 2009–12; Instructor, New York Inst. of Finance; Dir, Securities Industry Automation Corpn, Beth Israel Deaconess Care Org.; Lead Dir and Dir, The Ruder Finn Group 2005–10; mem. Finance Execs Inst. of Securities Industry Asscn, American Stock Exchange Clearing Corpn; Trustee, Northeast Utilities 2006–, Putnam Investment Management, LLC 2006–, Beth Israel Deaconess Hosp., Boston 2006–; Dir/Trustee, Optimum Funds in Fund Complex 2003–06; Ind. Trustee of various funds in the fund complex of Putnam Funds (except Putnam Investment Management) 2006–, Chair. Audit and Compliance Cttee 2012–. *Publication:* Handbook of Financial Markets: Securities, Options, Futures (contrib.) 1981. *Address:* Northeast Utilities, Prudential Building, Boston, MA 02199, USA (office). *Telephone:* (860) 665-3249 (office). *E-mail:* info@nu.com (office). *Website:* www.nu.com (office).

LEIBOVITZ, Annie; American photographer; b. 2 Oct. 1949, Westport, Conn.; ed San Francisco Art Inst. and studies with photographer Ralph Gibson; lived on a kibbutz in Israel and participated in archaeological dig at site of King Solomon's temple 1969; photographed rock 'n' roll stars and other celebrities for Rolling Stone magazine 1970–83; served as concert-tour photographer for The Rolling Stones band 1975; Chief Photographer, Vanity Fair 1983–; Propr Annie Leibovitz Studio, New York; official photographer Olympic Games, Atlanta 1996; advertising campaigns for American Express 2005, Disney 2007; celebrity portraits include John Lennon, Mick Jagger, Bette Midler, Louis Armstrong, Ella Fitzgerald, Jessye Norman, Mikhail Baryshnikov, Arnold Schwarzenegger, Tom Wolfe 1991, HM Queen Elizabeth II 2007; Photographer of the Year Award, American Soc. of Magazine Photographers 1984, Innovation in Photography Award, American Soc. of Magazine Photographers 1987, Clio Award 1987, Campaign of the Decade Award, Advertising Age magazine 1987, Infinity Award for applied photography, Int. Center for Photography 1990, Lifetime Achievement Award, Int. Center of Photography 2008, Award to Distinguished Women in the Arts, Museum of

Contemporary Art, Los Angeles 2012, Prince of Asturias Award for Communication and Humanities 2013. *Film:* Annie Leibovitz Life through a Lens 2006. *Publications:* Photographs 1970–90 1992, Women (with Susan Sontag) 2000, A Photographer's Life 1990–2005 2006, Annie Leibovitz at Work 2008. *Address:* Annie Leibovitz Studio, 443 West 18th Street, Suite 4, New York, NY 10011-3817 (office); c/o Jim Moffat, Art and Commerce, 755 Washington Street, New York, NY 10014, USA. *Telephone:* (212) 594-3817 (office). *E-mail:* als@leibovitzstudio.com (office). *Website:* www.leibovitzstudio.com (office).

LEIFERKUS, Sergey Petrovich; Russian singer (baritone); b. 4 April 1946, Leningrad; ed Leningrad Conservatory with Barsov and Shaposhnikov; stage debut in Leningrad Theatre of Musical Comedy 1972; soloist Maly Theatre of Opera and Ballet 1972–78, sang in Eugene Onegin, Iolanta, Il Barbiere di Siviglia and Don Giovanni; Kirov (now Mariinsky) Theatre of Opera and Ballet 1977–85, joined Mariinsky Opera Co. 1979; has appeared frequently at Royal Opera House, Covent Garden, Vienna State Opera, Opera Bastille, La Scala, San Francisco Opera, Metropolitan Opera, Netherlands Opera, Teatro Colon; has also appeared with other orchestras including London Symphony, Boston Symphony, New York Philharmonic and Philadelphia Orchestra under numerous conductors including Claudio Abbado, Valery Gergiev, James Levine, Bernard Haitink, Zubin Mehta, Riccardo Muti, Seiji Ozawa and Sir Georg Solti; prizewinner, All-Union Mikhail Glinka Vocalists' Competition, Vilnius 1971. *Recordings include:* Songs of Borodin and Dargomizhsky 1996, Mahler's Symphony No. 8 1997, Mahler's Das klagende Lied 1997, Verdi, Tenor Arias 2001, Mussorgsky's Chansons 2003, Shostakovich's Songs and Waltzes 2006. *Address:* Mariinsky Opera Company, Mariinsky Theatre, 190000 St Petersburg, Theatre Square, 1, Russia. *Website:* www.mariinsky.ru/en/company/opera_guest/leiferkus_serg.

LEIGH, Irene May, CBE, OBE, BSc, MB BS, MD, DSc (Med), FRCP, FRSE, FMedSci; British dermatologist, cell biologist and academic; *Professor Emeritus of Cellular and Molecular Medicine, University of Dundee;* b. 25 April 1947, Liverpool; d. of A. Allen and M. L. Allen; m. 1st Nigel Leigh 1969 (divorced 1999); one s. three d.; m. 2nd J. E. Kernthaler 2000; two step-s. one step-d.; ed Merchant Taylors' Girls' School, London Hosp. Medical Coll.; Dir Cancer Research UK Skin Tumour Lab. 1989–2016; Prof. of Dermatology, Barts and London School of Medicine and Dentistry (BLSMD) 1992–98, Research Dean 1996–2001, Prof. of Cellular and Molecular Medicine 1998–2006, now Prof. Emer.; Vice-Prin. and Head of the Coll. of Medicine, Dentistry and Nursing, Univ. of Dundee 2006–11, Vice-Pres. Research, Univ. of Dundee 2009–11, Prof. of Cellular and Molecular Medicine 2006–16; Research Dir UK, I-PRI, Lyon 2011–13; Archibald Gray Medal 2012. *Publications:* more than 300 peer-reviewed publs in biomedical literature. *Leisure interests:* baroque music, opera, theatre, cinema, children, grandchildren. *Address:* College of Medicine, Dentistry and Nursing, University of Dundee, Dundee, DD1 4HN, Scotland (office); 14 Oakeshott Avenue, London, N6 6NS, England (home). *Telephone:* 7989-344212 (mobile) (office); (20) 8340-4761 (home). *E-mail:* i.m.leigh@dundee.ac.uk (office).

LEIGH, Jennifer Jason; American actress; b. 5 Feb. 1962, Los Angeles, Calif.; d. of Vic Morrow and Barbara Turner; m. Noah Baumbach (divorced); one s.; ed Palisades High School; appeared in Walt Disney TV movie The Young Runaways aged 15; other TV films include The Killing of Randy Webster 1981, The Best Little Girl in the World 1981. *Films include:* Eyes of a Stranger 1981, Fast Times at Ridgemont High 1982, Grandview, USA 1984, Flesh and Blood 1985, The Hitcher 1986, The Men's Club 1986, Heart of Midnight 1989, The Big Picture 1989, Miami Blues 1990, Last Exit to Brooklyn 1990, Crooked Hearts 1991, Backdraft 1991, Rush 1992, Single White Female 1992, Short Cuts 1993, The Hudsucker Proxy 1994, Mrs Parker and the Vicious Circle 1994, Georgia 1995, Kansas City 1996, Washington Square 1997, eXistenZ 1999, The King is Alive 2000, The Anniversary Party 2001, Crossed Over 2002, Road to Perdition 2002, In the Cut 2003, The Machinist 2004, Childstar 2004, The Jacket 2005, Palindromes 2005, Rag Tale 2005, Margot at the Wedding 2007, Synecdoche, New York 2008, Greenberg 2010, Kill Your Darlings 2013, The Spectacular Now 2013, The Moment 2013, Hateship Loveship 2013, Jake Squared 2013, Alex of Venice 2014, Welcome to Me 2014, Me 2014, The Hateful Eight 2015. *Television includes:* Weeds (series) 2009–12, Revenge (series) 2012, Open (film) 2014. *Stage appearances include:* Sunshine, Off-Broadway 1989. *Address:* c/o CAA, 2000 Avenue of the Stars, Los Angeles, CA 90067, USA (office).

LEIGH, Sir Michael, Kt, KCMG, PhD; British fmr European Union official and international consultant; *Senior Fellow, German Marshall Fund of the United States;* ed Univ. of Oxford, Massachusetts Inst. of Tech., USA; Lecturer in Int. Relations, Univ. of Sussex 1974–76; Asst Prof. of Int. Relations, Johns Hopkins Univ., USA 1976–77, Moderator and Coordinator, Distinguished Lecture Series, European and Eurasian Studies Program, Paul H. Nitze School of Advanced Int. Studies 2015, 2016; with Directorate-Gen. for External Relations, Secr.-Gen., Council of the European Communities 1977–80, Int. Fisheries Negotiations, bilateral and multilateral, Directorate-Gen. for Fisheries, EC, Brussels 1980–82, Desk Officer for UK Ireland and Denmark, Press and Information, Directorate-Gen. for Information 1982–85, Directorate-Gen. for External Relations, Horizontal unit North–South Relations 1985–88, mem. Cabinet of Vice-Pres. Lord Cockfield 1988–89, mem. Cabinet of Vice-Pres. Frans Andriessen 1989–92, 1993–98, mem. Cabinet of Commr Hans van den Broek 1999, Negotiator for Czech Repub., Task Force for the Accession Negotiations 1998–2000, Dir, Directorate-Gen., Enlargement, Turkey, Cyprus, Bulgaria, Malta, Romania 2000–03, Deputy Dir-Gen., Directorate-Gen., External Relations, responsible for European Neighbourhood Policy, relations with Eastern Europe, Southern Caucasus and Cen. Asia, Middle East and S Mediterranean 2003–05, Dir-Gen. for Enlargement 2006–11; consultant and Sr Fellow to The German Marshall Fund of the US, Brussels 2012–; also Sr Advisor, EU Public Policy Practice Group, Covington; Erskine Fellow, Nat. Centre for Research on Europe, Univ. of Canterbury 2017. *Address:* The German Marshall Fund of the United States, Résidence Palace, Rue de la Loi 155 Wetstraat, 1040 Brussels, Belgium (office). *Telephone:* (2) 238-52-70 (office); 2 545-75-06 (Covington) (office). *Fax:* (2) 238-52-99 (office). *E-mail:* mleigh@gmfus.org (office); mleigh@cov.com (office). *Website:* www.gmfus.org (office); www.cov.com (office).

LEIGH, Mike, OBE; British dramatist and film and theatre director; b. 20 Feb. 1943, Salford, Lancs., England; s. of A. A. Leigh and P. P. Leigh (née Cousin); m. Alison Steadman (q.v.) 1973 (divorced 2001); two s.; ed Royal Acad. of Dramatic Art, Camberwell School of Arts and Crafts, Cen. School of Art and Design, London Film School; Chair. Govs London Film School 2001–; BAFTA Fellowship 2015; Officier des Arts et des Lettres; Hon. MA (Salford) 1991, (Northampton) 2000, Hon. DLitt (Staffs.) 2000, (Essex) 2002. *Plays include:* The Box Play 1965, My Parents Have Gone to Carlisle, The Last Crusade of the Five Little Nuns 1966, Nenaa 1967, Individual Fruit Pies, Down Here and Up There, Big Basil 1968, Epilogue, Glum Victoria and the Lad with Specs 1969, Bleak Moments 1970, A Rancid Pong 1971, Wholesome Glory, The Jaws of Death, Dick Whittington and His Cat 1973, Babies Grow Old, The Silent Majority 1974, Abigail's Party 1977 (also TV play), Ecstasy 1979, Goose-Pimples (London Evening Standard and London Drama Critics' Choice Best Comedy Award 1981) 1981, Smelling A Rat 1988, Greek Tragedy 1989 (in Australia), 1990 (in UK), It's a Great Big Shame! 1993, Two Thousand Years (Cottlesloe Theatre, London) 2005, Grief 2011. *Feature films include:* Bleak Moments (Golden Leopard, Locarno Film Festival, Golden Hugo, Chicago Film Festival 1972) 1971, High Hopes (Int. Critics' Prize, Venice Film Festival 1989, London Evening Standard Peter Sellers Best Comedy Film Award 1990) 1989, Life is Sweet 1991, Naked (Best Dir Cannes Film Festival 1993) 1993, Secrets and Lies (winner Palme d'Or) 1996, (Alexander Korda Award, BAFTA 1997), Career Girls 1997, Topsy-Turvy 1999 (London Evening Standard Best Film 1999, Los Angeles Film Critics' Circle Best Film 1999, New York Film Critics' Circle Best Film 1999), All or Nothing 2002, Vera Drake (Best British Ind. Film, Best Dir, British Ind. Film Awards, Best Film, Evening Standard British Film Awards 2005, David Lean Award for Achievement in Direction, BAFTA Awards 2005) 2004, Happy-Go-Lucky 2008, Another Year 2010, A Running Jump (short) 2012, Mr. Turner 2014. *Radio play:* Too Much of a Good Thing 1979. *Television films include:* A Mug's Game 1972, Hard Labour 1973, The Permissive Society, The Birth of the 2001 F.A. Cup Final Goalie, Old Chums, Probation, A Light Snack, Afternoon 1975, Nuts in May 1976, Knock for Knock 1976, The Kiss of Death 1977, Abigail's Party 1977, Who's Who 1978, Grown-Ups 1980, Home Sweet Home 1981, Meantime 1984, Four Days in July 1984, The Short and Curlies 1987, A Sense of History 1992. *Publications include:* Abigail's Party and Goose-Pimples 1982, Ecstasy and Smelling a Rat 1989, Naked and other Screenplays 1995, Secrets and Lies 1997, Career Girls 1997, Topsy-Turvy 1999, All or Nothing 2002, Two Thousand Years 2006, Vera Drake 2008, Mike Leigh on Mike Leigh 2008. *Address:* c/o United Agents, 12–26 Lexington Street, London, W1F 0LE, England (office). *Telephone:* (20) 3214-0800 (office). *Fax:* (20) 3214-0801 (office). *E-mail:* info@unitedagents.co.uk (office). *Website:* unitedagents.co.uk (office).

LEIGHTON, Allan Leslie; British business executive; *Chairman, Entertainment One;* b. 12 April 1953; m.; two s. one d.; ed Magdalen Coll. School, North Oxon. Polytechnic, A.M.P. Harvard; with Mars Confectionery 1974–91, rising to Business Sector Man. UK Grocery Div.; Sales Dir Pedigree Petfoods 1991–92; joined ASDA Stores Ltd as Group Marketing Dir 1992, then successively Retail Dir, Deputy Chief Exec.; Chief Exec. 1996; Pres. and CEO Wal-Mart Europe 1999–2000; Dir (non-exec.) Wilson Connolly Holdings PLC 1995 (Deputy Chair. 2000, interim CEO 2001–02); Dir (non-exec.) BSkyB PLC 1999–, Dyson Ltd –2004, Cannons –2004, Scottish Power PLC 2001, George Weston Ltd 2001 (currently Deputy Chair.), Consignia PLC 2001; Chair. (non-exec.) lastminute.com 2000–04, Cannons Group Ltd 2001; apptd Dir (non-exec.) Royal Mail Holdings PLC 2001, Chair. 2002–14; Chair. Race for Opportunity 2000, BHS Ltd 2000–; Chair. Pandora 2010–13, CEO 2013–; Chair. Entertainment One 2014–; Deputy Chair. (non-exec.) Leeds Sporting PLC 1998, Loblaw Companies Ltd, Selfridges & Co. *Publication:* On Leadership 2007. *Address:* Entertainment One, 45 Warren Street, London, W1T 6AG, England (office). *Telephone:* (20) 3691-8600. *Website:* www.entertainmentone.com (office).

LEIGHTON, Sir John, Kt; British art historian and museum director; *Director-General, National Galleries of Scotland;* b. 1959, Belfast, Northern Ireland; ed Univ. of Edinburgh, Edinburgh Coll. of Art, Courtauld Inst. of Art; trained as art historian and taught art history at Univ. of Edinburgh; Curator of 19th Century Paintings, Nat. Gallery, London 1987–97; Dir Van Gogh Museum, Amsterdam 1997–2005, organized exhbn 'Van Gogh and Gauguin' in conjunction with Chicago Art Inst. 1997–2002; Dir-Gen. Nat. Galleries of Scotland 2006–; mem. Supervisory Bd, Rijksmuseum, Amsterdam 2016–. *Publications:* has contributed to catalogues for the above exhbns; has published and lectured on various aspects of 19th and 20th century art. *Address:* The Dean Gallery, 73 Belford Road, Edinburgh, EH4 3DS, Scotland (office). *Telephone:* (131) 624-6200 (office). *E-mail:* enquiries@nationalgalleries.org (office). *Website:* www.nationalgalleries.org (office).

LEIJONHUFVUD, Baron Axel Stig Bengt, PhD; Swedish economist and academic; *Professor Emeritus, University of Trento;* b. 9 June 1933, Stockholm; s. of Erik G. Leijonhufvud and Helene A. Neovius; m. 1st Marta E. Ising 1955 (divorced 1977), 2nd Earlene J. Craver 1977; one s. two d.; ed Univ. of Lund, Univ. of Pittsburgh and Northwestern Univ., USA; Acting Asst Prof. of Econs, UCLA 1964–67, Assoc. Prof. 1967–71, Prof. of Econs 1971–94, now Prof. Emer., Chair. Dept of Econs 1980–83, 1990–92, Dir Center for Computable Econs 1991–97; Prof. of Monetary Econs, Univ. of Trento 1995–2008, Prof. Emer. 2008–; Visiting Prof., Stockholm School of Econ. and Commerce 1979–80, 1986, 1987, 1996, Inst. for Advanced Studies, Vienna 1976, 1987, Inst. for Advanced Studies, Jerusalem 1987, Nihon Univ. Tokyo 1980, European Univ. Inst., Florence 1982, 1986–87, 1989, Istituto Torcuato di Tella, Buenos Aires 1989, 1995; Ständiger Gastprofessor Univ. of Konstanz 1982–85; mem. Econ. Export Cttee of Pres. of Kazakhstan 1991; other professional appointments, Cttee memberships etc.; Brookings Inst. Fellow 1963–64; Marshall Lecturer, Univ. of Cambridge 1974; Overseas Fellow, Churchill Coll. Cambridge 1974; Inst. for Advanced Study Fellow 1983–84; Dr hc (Lund) 1983, (Nice, Sophia Antipolis) 1995; Macroeconomics in the Small and the Large: Essays on Microfoundations, Macroeconomic Applications and Economic History in Honour of Axel Leijonhufvud (ed. by Roger E. A. Farmer) 2008, Inflation, Institutions and Information: Essays in Honour of Axel Leijonhufvud (co-ed. by Daniel Vaz and Kumaraswamy Velupillai) 2010. *Publications:* On Keynesian Economics and the Economics of Keynes: A Study in Monetary Theory 1968, Keynes and the Classics: Two Lectures 1969, Information and Coordination: Essays in Macroeconomic Theory 1981, High Inflation (co-author) 1995, Macroeconomic Instability and Coordination 2000, Monetary Theory as a Basis for Monetary Policy (ed.) 2001, Monetary Theory and Policy Experience (ed.) 2001, Informazione, coordinamento e instabilità macroeconomica (a cura di Elisabetta De Antoni) 2004, Organización e inestabilidad económica: Ensayos elegidos 2006;

contribs to professional journals. *Telephone:* (805) 474-1540 (office). *Fax:* (805) 474-9896 (office). *E-mail:* stigaxel33@gmail.com (office); axel@ucla.edu (office); axel@economia.unitn.it (office). *Website:* www-ceel.economia.unitn.it/staff/leijonhufvud (office).

LEIMAN, Ricardo, BComm, MBA; Brazilian business executive; *Member, Global Management Committee and Partner, BTG Pactual SA;* ed Univ. of São Paulo, Univ. of Rochester, NY, USA, Univ. of Nyenrode, The Netherlands; began career with Credit Lyonnais Bank in Brazil followed by man. positions with Louis Dreyfus in Brazil, Eximcoop in The Netherlands and Trader Classified Media in London and Paris; rejoined Louis Dreyfus as COO, North America, EMEA (Europe, Middle East, Africa and Asia) 2002, later COO, Soft Commodities; joined Noble Resources Ltd 2006, COO Noble Group Ltd 2006–09, mem. Bd of Dirs 2009–12, CEO 2010–12; mem. Global Man. Cttee and Partner, BTG Pactual SA, London 2013–; mem. Bd of Dirs Gloucester Coal Ltd 2009–; Dir (non-exec.) Windimurra Vanadium Ltd (alternatively, Precious Metals Australia Ltd) 2006–09. *Address:* BTG Pactual SA, 6th Floor, Berkeley Square House, Berkeley Square, London, W1J 6BR, England (office). *Telephone:* (20) 7647-4900 (office). *E-mail:* info@btgpactual.com (office). *Website:* www.btgpactual.com (office).

LEINEN, Margaret, BS, MS, PhD; American oceanographer, academic and research institute director; *Director, Scripps Institution of Oceanography, Vice-Chancellor for Marine Sciences and Dean, School of Marine Sciences, University of California, San Diego;* b. 1946; ed Univ. of Illinois, Oregon State Univ., Univ. of Rhode Island; Vice-Provost for Marine and Environmental Programs and Dean of Grad. School of Oceanography, Univ. of Rhode Island 1991–2000; Asst Dir for Geosciences and Co-ordinator of Environmental Research and Educ., NSF 2000–07; Chief Science Officer, Climos, Inc. 2007–08; CEO The Climate Response Fund 2009–11; Vice-Provost for Marine and Environmental Initiatives and Exec. Dir Harbor Br. Oceanographic Inst., Florida Atlantic Univ. 2011–13; Prof., Geosciences Research Div., Univ. of California, San Diego and Dir Scripps Inst. of Oceanography 2013–, also Vice-Chancellor for Marine Sciences and Dean, School of Marine Sciences; Pres. American Geophysical Union 2014–16; Vice-Chair. Research Bd, Gulf of Mexico Research Initiative; fmr Vice-Chair. Int. Geosphere-Biosphere Programme; fmr Pres. The Oceanography Soc.; fmr Chair. Atmospheric and Hydrospheric Science Section of AAAS; mem. Bd Nat. Council for Science and the Environment; fmr mem. Bd on Global Change of Nat. Research Council/NAS; fmr mem. Nat. Ecological Observatory Network; Fellow, AAAS, Geological Soc. of America; Distinguished Alumni Awards, Univ. of Illinois, Oregon State Univ. and Univ. of Rhode Island. *Publications:* numerous papers in professional journals on ocean sediments and their relationship to global biogeochemical cycles and the history of Earth's ocean and climate. *Address:* Scripps Institution of Oceanography, University of California, San Diego, 9500 Gilman Drive, #0210, La Jolla, CA 92093-0210, USA (office). *Telephone:* (858) 534-2827 (office). *Fax:* (858) 534-0167 (office). *E-mail:* mleinen@ucsd.edu (office). *Website:* scripps.ucsd.edu/about/leadership/director (office); scrippsscholars.ucsd.edu/mleinen/biocv (office).

LEINONEN, Tatu Einari, MSc, DTech; Finnish engineer and academic; *Professor of Machine Design, University of Oulu;* b. 21 Sept. 1938, Kajaani; s. of Aate Leinonen and Aili Leinonen (née Nieminen); m. Tuula Tuovinen 1968; one s. two d.; Lecturer, Tech. Inst. of Helsinki 1963; Researcher, Tech. Research Centre of Finland 1965; Design Engineer, State Railway Co. 1966; Prof. of Machine Design, Univ. of Oulu 1968–; Visiting Prof., Univ. of Vt, USA 1976, Mich. Tech. Univ., USA 1977, 1981–82, 1991, Univ. of Fla, USA 1991, Lakehead Univ., Canada 1991, 2000, Toin Univ. of Yokohama, Japan 1994, Yanshan Univ., China 2000; fmr Sec.-Gen. IFToMM. *Publications include:* more than 300 papers and books 1966–. *Leisure interests:* cross-country skiing, golf. *Address:* Department of Mechanical Engineering, PO Box 4900, University of Oulu, 9014 Oulu (office); Tuulastie BA6, 90550 Oulu, Finland (home). *Telephone:* (8) 5532050. *Fax:* (8) 5532026. *E-mail:* tatu.leinonen@oulu.fi (office). *Website:* www.oulu.fi (office).

LEIPER, Quentin John, CBE, MSc, PhD, CEng, CEnv, FICE; British civil engineer, academic and business executive; m. Dorothy Leiper; three c.; ed Univ. of Glasgow; spent 16 years working for specialist sub-contractors in foundations, ground treatment and geotechnical eng; joined Carillion plc 1991, fmr Dir for Eng and the Environment, Group Chief Engineer 1991–2014 (retd), major projects include Canary Wharf and Canada Water stations, Tees Barrage and Copenhagen Metro; Chair. British Geotechnical Asscn 1999–2001, UK Ground Forum 1977–99; Pres. ICE 2006–07, then Chair. Exec. Bd; Vice-Pres. Inst. of Civil Engineers 2003–06, Pres. 2006–07, now Fellow; fmr Dir and Council mem. Construction Industry Research and Information Asscn; fmr mem. two British Standards cttees, two working groups set up by Sustainable Procurement Task Force and UK Construction Industry Sustainability Forum, Eng and Physical Sciences Research Council's Built Environment Coll. and several research steering groups; Founding Ed. ICE's Proceedings journal, Engineering Sustainability, fmr mem. ICE Proceedings journal, Geotechnical Engineering editorial panel; Visiting Prof., School of Eng, Univ. of Edinburgh 1998–, Chair. School Advisory Bd; fmr mem. Civil Eng Advisory Bds, Univs of Nottingham, Southampton, City Univ.; fmr Judge, Science, Eng and Tech. Student of the Year Award; Fellow, Royal Acad. of Eng 2011–; Gov. The Royal School, Wolverhampton;, Council mem., Soc. for the Environment. *Publications:* about 50 papers and articles on a range of subjects, including sustainability, environmental and supply chain management, the training and development of engineers, earthworks, construction, foundations, piling, reinforced soil and ground radar. *Leisure interests:* hockey, flying kites, playing tenor sax and clarinet. *Address:* School of Engineering, University of Edinburgh, Sanderson Building, Robert Stevenson Road, The King's Buildings, Edinburgh, EH9 3FB, Scotland (office). *Website:* www.eng.ed.ac.uk (office).

LEIPOLD, Gerd, PhD; German academic and environmentalist; b. 1 Jan. 1951, Rot an der Rot; two c.; ed Max Planck Inst. for Meteorology, Hamburg; trained as scientist; joined Greenpeace Germany as volunteer 1980, joined full-time 1983, later mem. Exec. Cttee and Trustee, Int. Co-ordinator Nuclear Free Seas Campaign 1987, fmr Chair. Bd Green Peace Nordic, mem. Bd Greenpeace USSR, Dir Greenpeace Nuclear Disarmament Campaign, London, Acting Int. Exec. Dir Greenpeace International Feb.–June 2001, Int. Exec. Dir June 2001–09; f. consultancy, GEM Partners Ltd, London, Dir 1993–2001; mem. Bd of Dirs Global Climate Forum 2010–15, Head, Earth League research process; Trustee, Humboldt-Viadrina School of Governance 2014–. *Leisure interests:* playing piano, literature, soccer, history. *Address:* Humboldt-Viadrina Governance Platform, Paris Platz 6, 10117 Berlin (office); Im Hebsack 4, 88430 Rot, Germany (home). *E-mail:* gerd.leipold@gmail.com (office). *Website:* www.governance-platform.de (office).

LEIRNER, Sheila Anne; Brazilian journalist, art critic, curator and writer; b. (Sheila Anne Klinger), 25 Sept. 1948, São Paulo; d. of Abraham L. Klinger and Giselda Leirner Klinger; m. 1st Décio Tozzi 1970 (divorced 1972); one s.; m. 2nd Gustavo Halbreich 1974 (divorced 1988); one s.; m. 3rd Jean-Louis Andral 1991 (divorced 2000); m. 4th Patrick Corneau 2007; ed Univ. of Vincennes, Ecole Pratique des Hautes Etudes, Sorbonne, Paris; art critic, O Estado de São Paulo 1975–90; Gen. Curator, 18th and 19th São Paulo Biennial 1985, 1987; curator of various exhbns in Brazil and abroad; now ind. curator and art critic; apptd to Ile-de-France regional comm. to examine projects of the "1% artistic", French Ministries of the Interior and Educ.; mem. French and Brazilian sections, Int. Asscn of Art Critics; mem. juries and invited lecturer in Latin America, Africa, USA, Asia and Europe; corresp. for nat. and foreign publs; lives and works in Paris; Chevalier, Ordre des Arts et des Lettres; Critic of the Year Award, Brazilian Asscn of Art Critics and Sec. of Culture of the State of São Paulo, Artistic Personality of the Year in Latin America, Argentine Asscn of Art Critics. *Publications include:* selected works of art criticism, anthologies and monographies, including Leopoldo Nóvoa, Art as Measure 1982, Art and Its Time 1991, Ars in Natura 1996, Lateinamerikanische Kunst 1993, Sky Above – A Tombeau for Haroldo de Campos 2005, The Surrealism (with J. Guinsburg) 2009. *Leisure interests:* literature, music, collecting miniatures and dolls houses. *Address:* c/o Editora Perspectiva, Avenida Brigadeiro Luis Antônio 3025–3035, 01401-000 São Paulo, Brazil. *E-mail:* sheila.leirner@estadao.com.br; sheila.leirner@gmail.com (home). *Website:* sheila.leirner.pagesperso-orange.fr.

LEISINGER, Klaus Michael, Dr rer. pol; German sociologist, academic, foundation executive and UN official; b. 6 July 1947, Lörrach; ed Univ. of Basel, Switzerland; Prof. of Devt Sociology, Univ. of Basel; fmr Man. of Ciba Pharmaceuticals, East Africa, headed co.'s Dept for Developing-country Relations, Basel; Exec. Dir and Del. of Novartis Foundation's Bd of Trustees –2002, Chair. –2013, Pres. and Man. Dir Novartis Foundation 1996–2012; Special Advisor on the Global Compact, UN, New York 2005–06; adviser to various nat. and int. orgs dealing with sustainable devt, including UNDP, World Bank (CGIAR), Asian Devt Bank, and ECLA; mem. Exec. Cttee German Soc. for UN; mem. Advisory Council of Mary Robinson's Ethical Globalization Initiative; mem. European Acad. of Science and Arts 1994; mem. Bd of Trustees German Network Business Ethics; Hon. DTheol (Univ. of Fribourg, Switzerland) 2004; Republic of Korea Hansen Grand Award 2012. *Publications:* Unternehmensethik. Globale Verantwortung und modernes Manageme 1997, Die sechste Milliarde. Weltbevölkerungswachstum und nachhaltige Entwicklung 1999; several articles. *Address:* c/o Novartis Foundation for Sustainable Development, Schwarzwaldallee 215, 4058 Basel, Switzerland (office).

LEITE, Arcangelo; Timor-Leste politician; ed IIP Depdagri Jakarta, Indonesia, National Education Univ., Bali; has held several govt posts including Dir Nat. Directorate for State Admin, Acting Dir (Territories), Ministry of State, Minister for State Admin and Territorial Planning 2007–12; Advisor, Office of Minister of State for Coordinating Social Affairs 2015–.

LEITER, Michael E., BA, JD; American naval officer, lawyer, business executive, security consultant and fmr government official; *Executive Vice-President for Business Development and Strategy, Leidos Holdings, Inc.;* ed Columbia Univ., Harvard Law School; Naval Flight Officer, USN 1991–97, served on US, NATO and UN missions in the Fmr Yugoslavia and Iraq; fmr Harvard Law School Human Rights Fellow, Int. Criminal Tribunal for the Fmr Yugoslavia, The Hague; fmr law clerk to Assoc. Justice Stephen G. Breyer, US Supreme Court, and to Chief Judge Michael Boudin of US Court of Appeals for the First Circuit; Asst US Attorney, Eastern Dist of Virginia, US Dept of Justice 2002–05; Deputy Gen. Counsel and Asst Dir, Pres.'s Comm. on Intelligence Capabilities of the US Regarding Weapons of Mass Destruction (Robb-Silberman Comm.) 2005; Deputy Chief of Staff, Office of Dir of Nat. Intelligence 2005–07; Prin. Deputy Dir Nat. Counterterrorism Center Feb.–Nov. 2007, Acting Dir 2007–08, Dir 2008–11; Sr Counsellor to the CEO, Palantir Technologies, Inc. 2011–; counterterrorism, cybersecurity and nat. security analyst for NBC News 2011–; Exec. Vice-Pres. for Business Devt and Strategy, Leidos Holdings, Inc. 2014–. *Address:* Leidos Holdings, Inc., 11951 Freedom Drive, Reston, VA 20190, USA (office). *Telephone:* (571) 526-6000 (office). *E-mail:* info@leidos.com (office). *Website:* www.leidos.com (office).

LEITH, Prudence Margaret (Prue), CBE, OBE, DL, FRSA; British caterer and author; b. 18 Feb. 1940, Cape Town, South Africa; d. of Stewart Leith and Margaret Inglis; m. 1st Rayne Kruger (died 2002); one s. one d.; m. 2nd John Playfair; ed Haywards Heath, Sussex, St Mary's, Johannesburg, Cape Town Univ., Sorbonne, Paris and Cordon Bleu School, London; started Leith's Good Food (commercial catering co.) 1965, Leith's restaurant 1969; cookery corresp. Daily Mail 1969–73; Man. Dir Prudence Leith Ltd 1972–94, Chair. Leith's Ltd 1994–96; opened Leith's School of Food and Wine 1975; added Leith's Farm 1976; Cookery Corresp., Daily Express 1976–80; Cookery Ed., The Guardian 1980–85, columnist 1986–90; subject of TV documentaries by BBC and Channel 4; presented series Tricks of the Trade, BBC One; judge, Great British Menu, BBC Two 2006–16, My Kitchen Rules, Channel 4 2016, The Great British Bake Off, Channel 4 2017–; Vice-Pres. Restaurateurs' Asscn of GB; Gov. Nat. Inst. of Econ. and Social Research; Vice-Patron Women in Finance and Banking; Chair. UK Cttee New Era Schools' Trust 1994–2000, Royal Soc. of Arts 1995–97 (Deputy Chair. 1997–2000), The British Food Heritage Trust 1997–2006; Dir (non-exec.) Halifax PLC 1992–99, Whitbread PLC 1995–2005, Argyll Group 1989–96, Woolworths 2001–06, Orient Express Hotels 2006–15; Hon. Fellow, Univ. Salford 1992; Chancellor, Queen Margaret Univ. 2017–; Visiting Prof., Univ. of North London 1993–; Chair. School Food Trust 2006–10; mem. Nat. Council for Vocational Qualifications and UK Skills, Stamp Cttee 1997–2003; Gov. Kingsmead City Tech. Coll., Ashridge Man. Coll.; Reader for Queen's Anniversary Prizes; Patron Prue Leith Chefs Academy, Johannesburg 1997–, Prue Leith Group; Chair. 3Es Enterprises 1998–2006, King's Coll. 1998–2007; Trustee, Forum for the Future 1998–2003; Training for Life 1999–2006, Places for People 1999–2003; DL Greater London 1998; Freeman, City of London 1994; Dr hc (Open Univ.) 1997; Hon. DUniv (Oxford Brookes) 2000;

Business Woman of the Year 1990. *Publications include:* Leith's All-Party Cook Book 1969, Parkinson's Pie 1972, Cooking for Friends 1978, The Best of Prue Leith 1979, Leith's Cookery Course (with J. B. Reynaud) 1979–80, The Cook's Handbook 1981, Prue Leith's Pocket Book of Dinner Parties 1983, Dinner Parties 1984, Leith's Cook Book 1985, Leith's Cookery School (with Caroline Waldegrave) 1985, Entertaining with Style (with P. Tyrer) 1986, Confident Cooking (part-work) 1989–90, Leith's Cookery Bible (with Caroline Waldegrave) 1991, Leith's Complete Christmas 1992, Sunday Times Slim Plan: The 21-Day Diet for Slimming Safely 1992, Leith's Baking (with Caroline Waldegrave) 1993, Leith's Vegetarian Cookery 1993, Leith's Step by Step Cookery 1993, Salads 1993, Chicken Dishes 1993, Starters 1993, Fruit 1993, Quick and Easy 1993, Leith's Contemporary Cooking (with Caroline Yates and Alison Cavaliero) 1994, Leith's Guide to Wine (with Richard Harvey) 1995, Leaving Patrick (novel) 1999, Sisters (novel) 2001, A Lovesome Thing (novel) 2004, Choral Society (novel) 2009, A Serving of Scandal (novel) 2010, Relish: My Life on a Plate (memoir) 2012, The Food of Love (novel) 2015, The Prodigal Daughter (novel) 2016, Prue: My All-Time Favourite Recipes 2018, The Lost Son (novel) 2019. *Leisure interests:* travelling, walking, fishing, gardening, old cookbooks, kitchen antiques, Trollope. *Address:* c/o Hilary Knight Management, Grange Farm, Church Lane, Old, Northampton, Northants., NN6 9QZ, England (office); The Office, Chastleton Glebe, Chastleton, Moreton-in-Marsh, Glos., GL56 0SZ, England (home). *Telephone:* (1604) 781818 (office); (1608) 674908 (office). *E-mail:* hilary@hkmanagement.co.uk (office); pmleith@prue-leith.com (office). *Website:* www.hkmanagement.co.uk (office); www.prue-leith.com. *Fax:* (1608) 674083 (office).

LEKHANYA, Maj.-Gen. Justin Metsing; Lesotho politician and army officer; b. 7 April 1938, Thaba-Tseka; Commdr of Lesotho Army; overthrew Prime Minister Leabua Jonathan in a mil. coup 1986; Head Mil. Council and Council of Ministers 1986–91, Minister of Defence and Internal Security 1986–91, also Minister of Public Service, Youth and Women's Affairs, Food Man. Units and Cabinet Office; deposed King of Lesotho in mil. coup 1990, later restored; Lekhanya ousted in coup 1991; elected mem. Nat. Ass. 2002; fmr Leader, Basotho Nat. Party.

LEKISHVILI, Niko Mikhailovich; Georgian politician; b. 20 April 1947, Tbilisi; m.; two d.; ed Tbilisi Polytech. Inst., Moscow Acad. of Nat. Econ.; Sr Lab. Asst, Georgian Polytechnic Inst. 1971–72; Komsomol functionary 1972–77; Second Sec., Chair. Dist Exec. Cttee, First Sec., Pervomay Dist CP Cttee, Tbilisi 1977–89; Second Sec., then First Sec., Tbilisi City CP Cttee 1989–90; Chair. Tbilisi City Soviet 1990; Deputy, Supreme Soviet Georgian SSR 1990–91; Chief State Counsellor, Georgian Cabinet of Ministers Jan.–Nov. 1992; mem. Parl. Repub. of Georgia 1992–95, 1999–2004; Deputy Prime Minister Sept.–Oct. 1993; Mayor of Tbilisi 1993–95; State Minister of Georgia 1995–98; Chair. Union of Tax-Payers. *Leisure interests:* music, football, travel. *Address:* Kargareteli Str. 3a, 380064 Tblisi (home); Ingorokva str. 7, 380034, Tbilisi, Georgia.

LEKO, Josip; Croatian lawyer and politician; b. 19 Sept. 1948, Plavna, Bač, Serbia; m.; two c.; ed Faculty of Law, Univ. of Zagreb; legal admin. in Slavonija DI, Slavonski Brod 1975–76; volunteer at Municipality Court, Zagreb 1976, 1977; legal adviser, Novi Zagreb Municipality 1976–82; Sec. Exec. Bd, Novi Zagreb Municipality 1982–86; State Ombudsmen for Self-Man. 1986–89; Dir Working Community and Vice-Gen. Dir Zagrepčanka co. for trade, production and catering 1989–91; mem. Socijaldemokratska Partija Hrvatske (SDP—Social Democratic Party of Croatia), Business Dir SDP 1991–2000, Pres. Standing Cttee of SDP 2008–; mem. (SDP) Parl. 2000–, Chair. Legislation Cttee 2000–03, mem. Cttee on the Constitution, Standing Orders and Political System 2000–03, Judiciary Cttee 2000–03, Pres. Supervisory Bd Croatian Radiotelevision 2000–03, Pres. Comm. for Conflict of Interest of the Repub. of Croatia 2003–07, Chair. then Deputy Chair. Legislation Cttee 2003–07, mem. Judiciary Cttee 2003–07, Deputy Chair. Cttee on the Constitution, Standing Orders and Political System 2007–11, mem. Legislation Cttee and Judiciary Cttee 2007–11, mem. State Judiciary Council, Nat. Water Council and Comm. for Conflict of Interest 2007–11, Chair. Cttee on the Constitution, Standing Orders and Political System 2011–12, Deputy Speaker of the Ass. (Sabor, Parl.) 2011–12, Interim Speaker 1–10 Oct. 2012, Speaker 10 Oct. 2012–15. *Address:* Sabor, 10000 Zagreb, trg sv. Marka 6–7, Croatia (office). *Telephone:* (1) 4569313 (office); (1) 6303065 (office). *Fax:* (1) 1 4569535 (office). *E-mail:* klubsdp@sabor.hr (office). *Website:* www.sabor.hr/Default.aspx?sec=6346 (office).

LEKOTA, Mosiuoa Gerard Patrick; South African politician; *President, Congress of the People (COPE);* b. 13 Aug. 1948, Senekal, Orange Free State; s. of Mapiloko Lekota and Mamosiuoa Lekota; m. Cynthia Lekota 1975; two s. two d. (deceased); ed Univ. of the North (Turfloop); perm. organizer, South African Students' Org. (SASO) 1972–74; charged under Terrorism Act 1974; tried and imprisoned on Robben Island 1976–82; Nat. Publicity Sec. United Democratic Front (UDF) 1983–91; fmrly with African Nat. Congress (ANC) in Natal; organizer for ANC in Northern Free States 1990; apptd mem. ANC Working Cttee 1991, Nat. Chair. ANC Nat. Exec. Cttee 1991, Chair. Southern OFS of Nat. Exec. Comm. 1991, Sec. Elections Comm. 1992–94; Nat. Chair. ANC 1997–2007, detained 1983, 1984, 1985; on trial with 21 others charged with treason and murder in Delmas case 1986, convicted 1988, sentenced to 12 years imprisonment after being held in custody for four years; conviction overturned by Appeal Court 1989; in exile, returned to S Africa 1990; Premier, Free State Prov. Legislature 1994; Chair. Nat. Council of Provinces 1997–99; Minister of Defence 1999–2008 (resgnd); Co-founder and Pres. Congress of the People party 2008–; mem. Nat. Ass. 2010–. *Leisure interests:* cycling, reading, soccer, rugby and studying wildlife. *Address:* National Assembly, Parliament Bldg, Room E118, Parliament Street, Cape Town 8000 (office); Congress of the People (COPE), Marks Bldg, 4th Floor, 90 Plein Street, Cape Town, South Africa. *Telephone:* (21) 4032595 (office). *Fax:* (21) 4619462 (office). *E-mail:* mlekota@parliament.gov.za (office); copemedia2014@gmail.com. *Website:* www.parliament.gov.za (office); www.congressofthepeople.org.za.

LELEU, Romain; French trumpeter; b. 1983, Lille; ed Paris Conservatoire, Karlsruhe Hochschule fur Musik, Germany; numerous performances at music festivals and in concert halls world-wide; soloist with Orchestre Nat. de Lille, Orchestre Nat. d'Ile de France, Orchestre Nat. de Lorraine, Ensemble Orchestral de Paris, Orchestre de Bretagne, Orchestre Régional de Cannes PACA, Orchestre Philharmonique de l'Opéra de Marseille, Orchestre d'Auvergne, Orchestre des Concerts Colonne, Württembergisches Kammerorchester Heilbronn, Baltic Chamber Orchestra, Slovak Sinfonietta in France and abroad in Switzerland, Belgium, Spain, Portugal, Athenaeum Concert Hall, Romania, in Turkey, Algeria, Israel, Cuba, Egypt, Japan, USA; has collaborated with Karol Beffa (premiere of Subway and Nuit Etoilée), Philippe Hersant (premiere of Folk Tunes), Martin Matalon and others; f. Feeling Brass Quintet 2000; Laureate of the Fondation Meyer 2002–, of French Academie des Beaux Arts 2011, of French Victoires de la Musique Classique 2009–; currently trumpet teacher, Aubervilliers Regional National Conservatory; also Dir Trumpet Collection, Editions Billaudot, Paris; regularly invited to perform on radio and TV, including France 2, France 3, Direct 8 TV, France Musique, France Inter, Radio Suisse Romande, Radio Romania Muzical; gives numerous master-classes in France, Korea, Japan, USA and elsewhere; winner, Festival Musical d'Automne de Jeunes Interprètes, Special Interpretation Prize, Finnish Int. Competition, Lieksa Brass Week 1999, Adami's Classical Revelation, First Prize for Trumpet, Paris Conservatoire 2003, First Prize for Chamber Music 2003, Third Prize, Int. Competition of Chamber Music, Lyon 2005, Victoires de la Musique (category Revelation) 2009, Prix Del Duca, Acad. des Beaux Arts 2011. *Recordings include:* Famous Trumpet Sonatas 2008, Outrageously French – Wind Music from France 2008, L'école française des vents 2009, Classical Concertos with Baltic Chamber Orchestra (St Petersburg Philharmonic) 2011, Oeuvres de Bartok, Piazzolla, Tchaïkovky, Bellini, Michel Legrand, Nino Rota 2013. *Address:* c/o M. Jérémie Barret, Musicaglotz, 29 rue Violet, 75015 Paris, France (office). *Telephone:* 1-42-34-53-44 (office). *E-mail:* jeremie.barret@musicaglotz.com (office); contact@romainleleu.com. *Website:* www.musicaglotz.com (office); www.romainleleu.com.

LELONG, Pierre Alexandre; French administrative official; b. 22 May 1931, Paris; s. of Prof. Marcel Lelong; m. Catherine Demargne 1958; four s. one d.; ed Coll. Stanislas, Paris, Univ. of Paris and Ecole Nat. d'Admin.; Ministry of Finance and Econ. Affairs 1958–62; Econ. Adviser to Prime Minister Pompidou 1962–67; Gen. Man. Fonds d'Orientation et de Régularisation des Marchés Agricoles (FORMA) 1967–68; MP for Finistère 1968–74; Sec. of State for Posts and Telecommunications 1974–75; Judge, Court of Accounts 1975–77; mem. European Court of Auditors 1977–84, Pres. 1981–84; Pres. of Section (Defence) at Court of Accounts 1990–94, Pres. of Chamber (European Affairs) 1994–97; Pres. Interministerial Cttee for Mil., Aeronautic and Mechanical State Procurements 1997–2004; Pres. Consultative Cttee on Secret Defence Affairs 1999–2005; Pres. Commission des Marchés Publics de l'Etat 2005–08; Commdr, Légion d'honneur, Officier, Ordre nat. du Mérite, Grand Cross, Ordre de la Couronne de Chêne (Luxembourg). *Publications:* Une experience française, 50 ans au coeur de la Republique 2012. *Address:* 130 rue de Rennes, 75006 Paris, France (home). *Telephone:* 1-45-44-12-49 (home). *Fax:* 1-45-44-12-49 (home). *E-mail:* lelongdemargne@gmail.com (home).

LELOUCH, Claude; French film director, producer and writer; b. 30 Oct. 1937, Paris; s. of Simon Lelouch and Charlotte Abeilard; m. 1st Christine Cochet 1968 (divorced); m. 2nd Evelyne Bouix 1980 (divorced 1985); m. 3rd Marie-Sophie Pochat 1986 (divorced 1992); m. 4th Alessandra Martines 1993 (separated 2009); two s. five d.; Pres. and Dir-Gen. Soc. Les Films 13 1966–; Pres. Jury, 18th Moscow Int. Film Festival 1993; Chevalier, Ordre nat. du Mérite, Officier des Arts et des Lettres, Grand Prix Nationaux 1993; Dr hc (UMIST) 1996; Palme d'or, Cannes 1966, Acad. Award 1966. *Films include:* L'amour des si... (In the Affirmative) 1962, La femme-spectacle (Night Women) 1964, Une fille et des fusils 1964, Les grands moments 1965, ...pour un maillot jaune (For a Yellow Jersey) 1965, Jean-Paul Belmondo 1965, Un homme et une femme (A Man and a Women) (uncredited) 1966, Loin du Vietnam (Far from Vietnam) 1967, Vivre pour vivre (Live for Life) 1967, 13 jours en France (aka Challenge in the Snow) 1968, Un homme qui me plaît (A Man I Like) 1969, La vie, l'amour, la mort (Life Love Death) 1969, Le voyou (The Crook) 1970, Smic Smac Smoc 1971, L'Aventure c'est l'aventure (aka Money Money Money) 1972, La bonne année (Happy New Year) 1973, Visions of Eight (also co-dir) 1973, Toute une vie (also producer, dir, author) 1974, Mariage 1974, Le chat et la souris (Cat and Mouse) 1975, C'était un rendez-vous 1976, Le bon et les méchants (The Good Guys and the Bad Guys) 1976, Si c'était à refaire (If I Had to Do It All Over Again) 1976, Un autre homme, une autre chance (Another Man, Another Chance) 1977, Robert et Robert 1978, A nous deux (Us Two) 1979, Les uns et les autres (aka Within Memory) 1981, Edith et Marcel 1983, Viva la vie! 1984, Partir, revenir (Going and Coming Back) 1985, Un homme et une femme, 20 ans déjàs (A Man and a Woman: 20 Years Later) 1986, Attention bandits 1986, Itinéraire d'un enfant gâté 1988, Il y a des jours... et de lunes 1990, La belle histoire (The Beautiful Story) 1992, Tout ça... pour ça! (All That... for This?!) 1993, Les Misérables (Golden Globe 1996, Ephèbe d'or 1996) 1995, Lumière et compagnie 1996, Hommes, Femmes, mode d'emploi (Men, Women: A User's Manual) 1996, Hasards ou coïncidences 1998, Une pour toutes (One 4 All) 1999, And Now... Ladies and Gentlemen... 2002, 11'09"01 – September 11 2002, Le genre humain – 1ère partie: Les parisiens 2004, Le courage d'aimer 2005, Chachun son cinéma 2007, Roman de Gare 2007, Ces amours là 2010, D'un film à l'autre (documentary) 2011, Salaud, on t'aime! 2014. *Television includes:* Les uns et les autres (mini-series) 1983. *Publication:* Itinéraire d'un enfant très gâté (autobiog.) 2000. *Address:* 15 avenue Hoche, 75008 Paris, France. *Telephone:* 1-42-25-00-89.

LEMANN, Jorge Paulo; Swiss/Brazilian business executive; *Principal, 3G Capital;* b. 26 Aug. 1939, Rio de Janeiro; m. Susanna Lemann; five c.; ed Harvard Univ., USA; trainee at Credit Suisse 1961–62; co-f. Banco de Investimentos Garantia 1971, Sr Pnr 1971–98, bought control of a Brazilian brewery that eventually became AmBev; CEO Brahma 1990–99, mem. Bd of Dirs, Companhia de Bebidas das Américas/Ambev (formed after merger of Brahma and Antarctica) 1999–2004, mem. Admin. Council, InBev NV/SA (after merger of Interbrew and Ambev) 2004–08 (following acquisition of Anheuser-Busch); Co-founder and Prin., 3G Capital, New York 2004–, bought Burger King 2010, acquired H.J. Heinz Co. and Warren Buffet's Berkshire Hathaway 2013; mem. Admin. Council, Gillette Corpn 1998–2005, Lojas Americanas SA; mem. Advisory Cttee, New York Stock Exchange 1998–2005, Chair. Latin American Advisory Cttee; mem. Int. Advisory Bd, Credit Suisse, DaimlerChrysler AG; Founder and mem. Advisory Council, Fundação Estudar; mem. Bd of Deans Advisors, Harvard Business School; est. Lemann Scholarships 2005; has lived in Switzerland since 1999 following an attempted kidnapping of his children. *Sporting achievements:* Swiss nat. tennis champion 1963, played at Wimbledon. *Leisure interest:* tennis. *Address:* 3G Capital, 600 Third Avenue, 37th Floor, New York, NY 10016, USA (office).

Telephone: (212) 893-6727 (office). *E-mail:* ir@3g-capital.com (office). *Website:* www.3g-capital.com (office).

LEMANN, Nicholas Berthelot, BA; American journalist and academic; *Dean Emeritus and Joseph Pulitzer II and Edith Pulitzer Moore Professor of Journalism, Columbia University;* b. 11 Aug. 1954, New Orleans, La; m. 1st Dominique Alice Browning 1983; two s.; m. 2nd Judith Anne Shulevitz 1999; one s. one d.; ed Harvard Coll.; Assoc. Ed. and Man. Ed., Washington Monthly magazine 1976–78; Assoc. Ed. and Exec. Ed. Texas Monthly magazine 1978–79, Exec. Ed. 1981–83; Nat. Staff Reporter, Washington Post 1979–81; Nat. Corresp. The Atlantic Monthly magazine 1983–99; staff writer, The New Yorker magazine 1999, Washington Corresp. 2000–03, currently Contrib.; Joseph Pulitzer II and Edith Pulitzer Moore Prof. of Journalism, Columbia Univ. 2003–, Dean Grad. School of Journalism 2003–13, now Dean Emer.; fmr contrib. to numerous publs including New York Times, New York Review of Books, New Republic, Slate, American Heritage; mem. Bd of Dirs Authors Guild, Center for Humanities, CUNY Grad. Center, Soc. of American Historians, Acad. of Political Science; mem. New York Inst. for Humanities; Fellow, American Acad. of Arts and Sciences 2010; Helen B. Bernstein Award for Excellence in Journalism 1991. *Television:* documentary projects for Blackside Inc., Frontline, Discovery Channel, BBC. *Publications:* The Fast Track: Texans and Other Survivors 1981, Out of the Forties 1983, The Promised Land: The Great Black Migration and How It Changed America (Pen Award 1992) 1991, The Big Test: The Secret History of the American Meritocracy 1999 (Washington Monthly Political Book Award), Redemption: The Last Battle of the Civil War 2006. *Address:* Columbia University Graduate School of Journalism, Pulitzer Hall, MC 3801, 2950 Broadway, New York, NY 10027, USA (office). *Telephone:* (212) 854-6056 (office). *E-mail:* nl2124@columbia.edu (office). *Website:* www.journalism.columbia.edu (office).

LEMBERGS, Aivars; Latvian politician and business executive; *Mayor of Ventspils;* b. 26 Sept. 1953, Jēkabpils, Latvian SSR, USSR; m. 1st Ināra Lemberga; one s. one d.; m. 2nd Kristīne Krasovska; one s.; ed Latvian State Univ. (now Univ. of Latvia); worked in various positions in CP of Latvia; Mayor of Ventspils 1988–; Founder and Leader, Latvijai un Venstpilij (For Latvia and Ventspils) local political party 1994–, formed alliance with Zaļo un Zemnieku Savienība (Greens' and Farmers' Union); fmr business partner of Ainars Gulbis; unsuccessful cand. for post of Prime Minister; detained on charges of money laundering, abuse of public office, and bribery charges March 2007, spent several months in Matisa Prison, later placed under house arrest 2008, subject of court proceedings Feb. 2009; Order of Three Stars (Third Class) 2008. *Address:* Office of the Mayor, Ventspils City Council, Jūras iela 36, 3601 Ventspils, Latvia (office). *Telephone:* 6360-1113 (office). *Fax:* 6360-1118 (office). *E-mail:* atbalsts@ventspils.gov.lv (office). *Website:* www.ventspils.lv (office); www.aivarslembergs.lv.

LEMERCIER GEORGES, André; Haitian lawyer and politician; served in pvt. legal practice; fmr consultant, Domus Conseil; Minister of the Economy and Finance 2011–14. *Address:* c/o Ministry of the Economy and Finance, Palais des Ministères, rue Mgr Guilloux, Port-au-Prince, Haiti. *E-mail:* mef@mefhaiti.gouv.ht.

LEMIERRE, Jean; French international civil servant and international business consultant; *Chairman, BNP Paribas Group;* b. 6 June 1950, Sainte-Adresse, Seine-Maritime; m.; three c.; ed Institut d'Etudes Politiques de Paris, Ecole Nationale d'Admin; Inspection Générale des Finances 1976; various positions, Tax Policy Admin 1980–87, Head 1987–89; Directeur Général des Impôts 1989–95; Directeur de Cabinet, French Pvt. Office, Minister of Economy and Finance, Paris 1995; Head of Treasury 1995–2000; mem. European Monetary Cttee 1995–98; Chair. European Econ. and Finance Cttee 1999–2000, Paris Club 1999–2000; Pres. EBRD 2000–08; Sr Advisor to the Chair., BNP Paribas Group 2008–14, Chair. 2014–; mem. negotiating cttee representing pvt. creditors holding Greek debt Jan. 2012; mem. Bd of Dirs, Bank Gospodarki Zywnosciowej - BGZ (Poland), TEB Holding AS (Turkey), Total 2016–. *Address:* BNP Paribas SA, 3 rue d'Antin, 75002 Paris, France (office). *Telephone:* 1-42-98-12-34 (office). *Fax:* 1-40-14-45-46 (office). *E-mail:* pressoffice.paris@bnpparibas.com (office). *Website:* www.bnpparibas.com (office).

LEMIEUX, Mario, OC, CQ; Canadian ice hockey executive and fmr ice hockey player; *Co-Owner and Chairman, Pittsburgh Penguins;* b. 5 Oct. 1965, Montreal; m. Nathalie Asselin; four c.; picked first overall in 1984 Nat. Hockey League (NHL) Entry Draft by Pittsburgh Penguins; winner of Stanley Cup 1991, 1992, 2009 (as owner); retd 1997; led group that acquired Penguins 1999, returned as player 2000, retd 2006, currently Co-Owner and Chair.; played for Canadian nat. team in Canadian Cup 1988, gold medal, Olympic Games, Salt Lake City 2002; est. Mario Lemieux Foundation 1993; regular competitor at the American Century Championship, Edgewood Tahoe Golf Course, Lake Tahoe, NV, won tournament 1998; Chevalier, Ordre nat. du Québec; CHL Player of the Year 1984, Calder Memorial Trophy 1985, NHL All-Rookie Team 1985, Chrysler-Dodge/NHL Performer of the Year 1985, 1986, 1987, NHL All-Star Game MVP 1985, 1988, 1990, Dapper Dan Athlete of The Year 1986, 1989, Lester B. Pearson Award 1986, 1988, 1993, 1996, NHL Second All-Star Team 1986, 1987, 1992, 2001, Art Ross Trophy 1988, 1989, 1992, 1993, 1996, 1997, NHL First All-Star Team 1988, 1989, 1993, 1996, 1997, Hart Memorial Trophy 1988, 1993, 1996, Conn Smythe Trophy 1991, 1992, Bill Masterton Memorial Trophy 1993, Lou Marsh Trophy 1993, NHL Plus/Minus Award 1993, ESPY Award NHL Player of the Year 1993, 1994, 1998, inducted into Hockey Hall of Fame 1997, ranked No. 4 on The Hockey News' list of the 100 Greatest Hockey Players (highest-ranking French-Canadian player) 1998, Lester Patrick Trophy 2000, ESPN Hockey Player of the Decade 2000, featured as the cover athlete on EA Sports' 2002 edn of its popular NHL series for multiple platforms, inducted into Canada's Walk of Fame 2004. *Leisure interest:* golf. *Address:* Pittsburgh Penguins, CONSOL Energy Center, 1001 Fifth Avenue, Pittsburgh, PA 15219, USA (office). *Telephone:* (412) 642-1300 (office). *Fax:* (412) 255-1980 (office). *E-mail:* info@penguins.nhl.com (office). *Website:* penguins.nhl.com (office).

LEMINE, Mohamed Mahmoud Ould Mohamed, DEcon; Mauritanian politician; *Chairman, Union for the Republic;* b. 1952, Hodh El Gharbi, Mauritania, French West Africa; m.; ed Univ. of Cairo, Egypt; fmr Prof. of Econs, Univ. of Nouakchott –1996; Dir-Gen. Ecole Nationale d'Admin, Nouakchott 1996–2007; Minister of Interior, Posts and Telecommunications March–April 2007, of Nat. Defence 2007–08; Chair. Union pour la République (Union for the Republic) 2009–. *Address:* Union for the Republic, Nouakchott, Mauritania (office). *E-mail:* campagne2013@upr.mr (office). *Website:* www.upr.mr (office).

LeMOND, Gregory (Greg) James; American motor racing driver, fmr professional road racing cyclist and entrepreneur; b. 26 June 1961, Lakewood, Calif.; m. Kathy Morris 1981; two s. one d.; began professional competitive cycling career 1980; won Coors Classic stage race 1981, 1985; World Road Race Champion 1983, 1989; won Tour de France 1986, 1989, 1990; retd from cycling due to injury 1994; currently designer of bicycles; also leads cycling tours; now engaged in auto racing, professional series debut 1997 (with US F2000); Sports Illustrated Sportsman of the Year 1989, ABC Wide World of Sports Athlete of the Year 1989, 1990, World's Most Outstanding Athlete, Jesse Owens Int. Trophy Awards 1991, twice winner of the Pernod Trophy (for best cyclist in the world), inducted into Cycling Hall of Fame. *Publication:* The Science of Fitness 2014. *Leisure interests:* outdoor enthusiast, fly fishing. *E-mail:* info@greglemond.com. *Website:* greglemond.com.

LEMPER, Ute; German singer, dancer and actress; b. 4 July 1963, Münster; partner Todd Turkisher; three s. one d.; ed Dance Acad., Cologne, Max Reinhardt Seminary for Dramatic Art, Austria; leading role in Viennese production of Cats 1983; appeared in Peter Pan, Berlin, Cabaret, Düsseldorf and Paris (recipient of Molière Award 1987), Chicago (Laurence Olivier Award) 1997–99 and in London and New York, Life's a Swindle tour 1999, Punishing Kiss tour 2000, The Last Tango in Berlin tour 2009; Die sieben Todsünden (Weill) at Covent Garden Festival, London 2000; collaborations with Michael Nyman, Paulo Coelho; French Culture Prize 1993. *Recordings include:* Life is a Cabaret 1987, Ute Lemper Sings Kurt Weill 1988, (Vol. 2) 1993, The Threepenny Opera 1988, Mahagonny Songspiel 1989, Crimes of the Heart 1989, The Seven Deadly Sins 1990, Songbook (with Michael Nyman) 1992, Illusions 1992, Espace Indécent 1993, Portrait of Ute Lemper 1995, City of Strangers 1995, Berlin Cabaret Songs 1996, Nuits Étranges 1997, All that Jazz/The Best of Ute Lemper 1998, Punishing Kiss 2000, But One Day 2002, Blood and Feathers 2006, Between Yesterday and Tomorrow 2008, Paris Days/Berlin Nights (with Vogler String Quartet) 2012, Ute Lemper Sings Weill, Vol.2 2013, Punishing Kiss 2013, Forever: The Love Poems of Pablo Neruda 2013, The 9 Secrets 2015. *Television appearances include:* L'Affaire Dreyfus (Arte), Tales from the Crypt (HBO), Illusions (Granada) and The Look of Love (Gillian Lynne). *Film appearances include:* L'Autrichienne 1989, Moscou Parade 1992, Coupable d'Innocence 1993, Prêt à Porter 1995, Bogus 1996, Combat de Fauves, A River Made to Drown In, Appetite 1997. *Address:* Dispeker Artists, 59 East 54th Street, Suite 81, New York, NY 10022, USA (office). *Telephone:* (212) 421-7678 (office). *E-mail:* emmy@dispeker.com (office). *Website:* www.utelemper.com.

LENAERTS, Baron; **Koen,** Lic.iuris, LLM, MPA, PhD; Belgian judge; *President, Court of Justice of the European Union;* b. (Koenraad Lenaerts), 20 Dec. 1954, Mortsel; m. Kris Grimonprez; six d.; ed Univs of Namur and Leuven, Belgium and Harvard Univ., USA; Asst Prof., Leuven Univ. 1979–82, Assoc. Prof. 1982–83, Prof. of EC Law 1983–; Prof. of European Insts, Coll. of Europe, Bruges 1984–89; law clerk to Judge R. Joliet, Court of Justice of the European Communities 1984–85; Visiting Prof. of Law, Univ. of Burundi 1983, 1986, Univ. of Strasbourg 1986–89, Harvard Univ. 1988–89; mem. Brussels Bar 1986–89; Dir, Inst. of European Law, Leuven Univ. 1990–2009; Judge, Court of First Instance of the European Communities, Luxembourg 1989–2003; Judge, Court of Justice of the European Union 2003–, Vice-Pres. 2012–15, Pres. 2015–; numerous academic distinctions, fellowships and prizes. *Publications include:* 'The Negative Implications' of the Commerce Clause and 'Preemption' Doctrines as Federalism Related Limitations on State Power: a Historical Review 1978, Constitutie en rechter 1983, International privaatrecht (with G. Van Hecke) 1986, Le juge et la constitution aux Etats-Unis d'Amérique et dans l'ordre juridique européen 1988, European Union Law (co-author) 1999 (third edn 2011), Procedural Law (co-author) 2014; articles and contribs to reviews etc. *Address:* Court of Justice of the European Union, rue du Fort Niedergrünewald, 2925 Luxembourg (office). *Telephone:* 4303-3553 (office). *Fax:* 4303-3541 (office). *E-mail:* koen.lenaerts@curia.europa.eu (office). *Website:* www.curia.europa.eu (office).

LENDL, Ivan; American (b. Czech) fmr professional tennis player; b. 7 March 1960, Ostrava, Czechoslovakia; s. of Jiri Lendl and Olga Lendlova; m. Samantha Frankel 1989; five d.; Davis Cup player 1978–85, winner 1980; winner, Italian Jr Singles 1978, French Jr Singles 1978, Wimbledon Jr Singles 1978, Spanish Open Singles 1980, 1981, S. American Open Singles 1981, Canadian Open Singles 1980, 1981, WCT Tournament of Champion Singles 1982, WCT Masters Singles 1982, WCT Finals Singles 1982, Masters Champion 1985, 1986, French Open Champion 1984, 1986, 1987, US Open Champion 1985, 1986, 1987, US Clay Court Champion 1985, Italian Open Champion 1986, Australian Open Champion 1989, 1990; finalist Wimbledon 1986; held World No. 1 ranking for a record 270 weeks 1985–87, 1989; won 94 singles titles and six doubles; named World Champion (Int. Tennis Fed.) 1985, 1986, 1990; competed in 19 Grand Slam singles finals; retd Dec. 1994; coach to Andy Murray 2011–14; mem. Laureus World Sports Acad.; granted US citizenship 1992; ATP Most Improved Player 1981, ITF World Champion: 1985, 1986,1987, 1990, ATP Player of the Year 1985, 1986, 1987, inducted into Int. Tennis Hall of Fame 2001. *Publication:* Ivan Lendl's Power Tennis. *Leisure interests:* golf, collecting art. *Address:* StarGames LLC, 40 Salem Street, Suite 7, Lynnfield, MA 01940, USA. *E-mail:* ivan@stargamesinc.com. *Website:* www.ivanlendl.net.

LENDLEIN, Andreas, DrScNat; German scientist and academic; *Deputy Director and Co-ordinator of Research Field 'Bio-Engineering', Berlin-Brandenburg School for Regenerative Therapies;* ed Univ. of Technology (RWTH), Aachen, Johannes Gutenberg-Universität Mainz; Postdoctoral Fellow, Dept for Material Science, ETH, Zurich, Switzerland 1996–97; Visiting Scientist, Dept of Chemical Eng, MIT, USA 1997–98; Head of Dept, Devt and Eng of Biocompatible Polymer Systems, German Wool Research Inst., Univ. of Tech. (RWTH), Aachen 1997–2002; Man. Dir Nemoscience GmbH, Aachen 1998–2003; Prof., Materials in Life Sciences, Faculty of Math. and Natural Sciences, Univ. of Potsdam 2002–; Dir Inst. of Polymer Research, Helmholtz-Zentrum Geesthacht Research Centre, Teltow 2002–13, Co-Dir Joint Laboratory for Biomaterials and Regenerative Medicine 2009–; Dir Inst. for Tech. and Devt, Medical Devices (ITEMP), RWTH 2004–06; Prof., Medical Faculty, RWTH 2004–06; Deputy-Dir and Co-ordinator of Research Field 'Bio-Engineering', Berlin-Brandenburg School for Regenerative Therapies, Virchow Charité, Berlin 2006–, mem. Medical Faculty Bd 2006–; Guest Prof., Tianjin Univ., People's Repub. of China 2006; Authorised Officer for Health Sciences, Health Capital Network, Berlin-Brandenburg 2006; Scientific Amb. of Brandenburg 2008; Speaker, Research Programme 'Regenerative Medicine', Helmholtz Asscn of German Research Centres 2003–08, Cross-Program Activity 'Regenerative Medicine and Active Biomaterials' 2009–, Innovation Nucleus 'Polymers for Biomedicine' 2010–, Portfolio Topic 'Technology and Medicine: Multimodale Imaging of polymer-based Biomaterials' 2012–; Hon. Prof. of Chem., Free Univ., Berlin 2008–; Hon. mem. Israel Chemical Soc. 2009; World Tech. Award in Health and Medicine, The World Tech. Network 2005. *Publications:* numerous scientific papers in professional journals on biomaterials for clinical applications in regenerative medicine. *Address:* Berlin-Brandenburg School for Regenerative Therapies, Charité Campus Virchow Klinikum, Augustenburger Platz 1, 13353 Berlin (office); Kantstraße 55, 14513 Teltow-Seehof, Germany (home). *Telephone:* (30) 450539417 (office). *Fax:* (30) 450539918 (office). *E-mail:* coordination_office@bsrt.de (office). *Website:* www.bsrt.de (office).

LENG, James (Jim) W.; British business executive; b. 1945; served in several roles with Low & Bonar PLC (packaging and performance materials co.) 1984–95, including as Group Chief Exec. 1992–95; CEO Laporte PLC 1995–2001; apptd Dir (non-exec.) Corus Group PLC (fmrly British Steel) 2001, Deputy Chair. and Sr Ind. Dir 2002–03, Chair. 2003–09; mem. Bd of Dirs HSBC Bank plc 2010–13 (Chair. 2012–13); currently European Chair. and Chair. European Advisory Bd, AEA Investors Ltd (pvt. equity group); mem. Bd of Dirs Genel Energy plc, Alston 2003–, AON PLC 2014–; fmr mem. Bd of Dirs Pilkington PLC, IMI PLC, JP Morgan Fleming Mid Cap Investment Trust PLC, Hanson PLC, TNK–BP, Doncasters (fmr Chair.); fmr Lead Non-Exec. Dir, UK Ministry of Justice; Gov. Nat. Inst. of Econ. and Social Research; Trustee, Guyll-Leng Charitable Trust. *Address:* AEA Investors Ltd, 78 Brook Street, London, W1K 5EF, England (office). *Telephone:* (20) 7659-7800 (office). *Fax:* (20) 7491-2155 (office). *Website:* www.aeainvestors.com (office).

LENG, Rongquan, MSc; Chinese telecommunications industry executive (retd); b. 1949, Liaoning Prov.; ed Beijing Inst. of Posts and Telecommunications; Chief Engineer, Beijing Long Distance Telephone Bureau 1989–94, Deputy Chief Engineer, Telecommunications Bureau, Ministry of Posts and Telecommunications 1994–99; Vice-Pres. China Telecom Group 2000–02; apptd Vice-Pres. China Netcom Group 2002; apptd Deputy Dir Gen., China Telecommunications Corpn Ltd, then Exec. Dir, Pres. and COO 2004–08, also deputy Party sec., also Deputy Gen. Man., China Network Communications Group Corpn 2002–04, Vice-Chair. China Netcom Group Corpn (HK) Ltd –2004; mem. Bd of Dirs Alcatel-Lucent Shanghai Bell Co. Ltd, China Finance Online Co. Ltd 2012–15, Beijing Digital Telecom Co., Ltd 2010–15; Vice-Chair. China Inst. of Communications, Internet Society of China.

LENGKON, Bruno; Ni-Vanuatu politician; b. 3 March 1972, Ambrym; ed Lycée Louis Antoine de Bougainville, Vanuatu Nat. Inst. of Tech.; fmr accountant, Hebrida; worked for several years with Vanuatu Broadcasting and Television Corpn (VBTC), including as radio presenter, Radio Vanuatu and Deputy Gen. Man., VBTC; MP (NUP) for Ambrym constituency 2012–; fmr Legal Adviser to Minister of Trade; Minister of Foreign Affairs, Int. Co-operation and External Trade 2016–17; represented Vanuatu at ACT/EU Jt Parl. Ass. 2013; mem. Nat. United Party (NUP). *Address:* c/o Ministry of Foreign Affairs, International Co-operation and External Trade, PMB 9051, Port Vila, Vanuatu (office). *Telephone:* 27045 (office). *Fax:* 27832 (office).

LENK, Hans Albert Paul, PhD; German fmr rower and academic; *Professor Emeritus of Philosophy, Karlsruhe Institute of Technology;* b. 23 March 1935, Berlin; s. of Albert Lenk and Annemarie Lenk; m. Ulrike Reincke; two s. one d.; ed Lauenburgische Gelehrtenschule, Ratzeburg, Freiburg and Kiel Univs, Tech. Univ. of Berlin; early career as rower (competed for Unified Team of Germany in 1960 Summer Olympics); Asst Prof., Tech. Univ. of Berlin 1962, Assoc. Prof. 1966, Prof. 1969; Chair. and Prof. of Philosophy, Karlsruhe Univ. (now Karlruhe Inst. of Tech.) 1969, now Prof. Emer., Dean, Coll. of Humanities and Social Sciences 1973–75; Dean and Prof. Philosophy of Social Sciences and Theory of Planning, European Faculty of Land Use and Devt, Strasbourg 1983–2006; Visiting Prof. numerous foreign univs; Hon. Prof. Tech. Univ., Budapest 1992; Green Honors Prof., Tex. Christian Univ., Fort Worth 1987; Pres. Int. Philosophic Soc. for Study of Sport 1980–81, Int. Olympic Union 1980–90, European Forum, Baden 1980–; Vice-Pres. European Acad. of Sciences and Philosophy of Law 1986–; Pres. Gen. Soc. for Philosophy in Germany 1991–93; Pres. Argentine-German Soc. of Philosophy 1992–, German-Hungarian Soc. of Philosophy 1993–2005, Chilean-German Soc. of Philosophy 1995–, German-Romanian Soc. of Philosophy 2000–, German-Russian Soc. for the Philosophy of Science and Technology 2002–, Int. Inst. of Philosophy (World Acad.) 2005–08; Vice-Pres. Féd. Int. des Sociétés de Philosophie 1998–2003; mem. American Acad. of Kinesiology and Physical Educ., Russian Acad. of Science 2003, Nat. Olympic Cttee for Germany –1992, German UNESCO Comm. –1992, Inst. Int. de Philosophie 1994 (mem. Bd 1996–2000, Pres. 2005–08), Int. Acad. of Philosophy of Science 1995–; Hon. mem. Int. Olympic Acad., Romanian Acad. of Science, Dept of Philosophy 2001; Dr hc (Deutsche Sporthochschule, Cologne) 1986, (Córdoba/Argentina) twice 1992, (Tech. Univ. Budapest) 1993, (Univ. Pécs) 1994, Moscow (Univ. of Humanistic Studies) 1995, (Int. Ind. Univ. for Ecology and Politology) 2001, Rostov 2002; four German, two European and one Olympic title for rowing, Silver Leaf of Fed. Pres. 1959, 1960, Scientific Diem Plaque 1962, Sievert Award (Olympian Int.) 1973, Noel Baker Prize (UNESCO) 1978, Fed. Pres. of Germany's Great Merit Cross 2005, Ethics Prize (German Olympic Sports Confed.) 2010, Hall of Fame of German Sports 2012. *Achievements include:* Olympic Champion, Eight Oar Crew 1960, two European championships in rowing, Amateur Coach World Champion Eight Oar Crew 1966. *Publications:* more than 140 books, including Kritik der logischen Konstanten 1968, Pragmatische Vernunft 1979, Social Philosophy of Athletics 1979, Zur Sozialphilosophie der Technik 1982, Zwischen Wissenschaftstheorie und Sozialwissenschaft 1985, Zwischen Sozialpsychologie und Sozialphilosophie 1987, Kritik der kleinen Vernunft 1987, Das Prinzip Fairness 1989, Prometheisches Philosophieren zwischen Praxis und Paradox 1991, Zwischen Wissenschaft und Ethik 1992, Philosophie und Interpretation 1993, Macht und Machtbarkeit der Technik 1994, Interpretation und Realität 1995, Einführung in die angewandte Ethik 1997, Einführung in die Erkenntnistheorie 1998, Konkrete Humanität 1998, Praxisnahes Philosophieren 1999, Erfassung der Wirklichkeit 2000, Albert Schweitzer – Ethik als Konkrate Humanität 2000, Advances and Problems in the Philosophy of Technology (ed.) 2001, Das Denken und sein Gehalt 2001, Kleine Philosophie des Gehirns 2001, Erfolg oder Fairness? 2002, Natur-Umwelt-Ethik 2003, Wittgenstein y el giro pragmático en la Filosofía (co-author) 2005, Veranwortung und Gewissen des Forschers 2006, Das Gefass 2006, Ethics Facing Globalization (co-ed.) 2006, Kant Today (chief ed.) 2006, Bewusstsein Kreativität und Leistung 2007, Global Technoscience and Responsibility 2007, Filosofía pragmática y humanidad concreta 2007, Land Development Strategies: Patterns, Risks and Responsibilities (co-ed.) 2009, Umweltverträglichkeit und Menschenzuträglichkeit 2009, Aesthetics in Contemporary Philosophy (co-ed.) 2009, Comparative and Intercultural Philosophy (ed.) 2009, Acción, Responsabilidad, Tolerancia y Humanidad 2010, Das flexible Vielfachwesen 2010, Sport von Kopf bis Fuss(ball) 2010, Responsabilidad, Ciencia, Tecnología y Bioética 2012, S.O.S. – Save Olympic Spirit: Toward a Social Philosophy of the Olympics (co-ed.) 2012, Mala Filosofija Mozga 2012, Kreative Pluralität 2013; more than 2,000 articles. *Address:* Karlsruhe Institute of Technology (Universität Karlsruhe Institut für Philosophie), Kollegium am Schloss, Bau 2, 76128 Karlsruhe (office); Neubrunnenschlag 15, 76337 Waldbronn, Germany (home). *Telephone:* (721) 60842149 (office); (7243) 67971 (home). *Fax:* (721) 60843084 (office). *E-mail:* sekretariat@philosophie.kit.edu (office); hans.lenk@kit.edu (home). *Website:* www.philosophie.kit.edu (office).

LENNOX, Annie, OBE, ARAM; British rock singer and lyricist; *Chancellor, Glasgow Caledonian University;* b. 25 Dec. 1954, Aberdeen, Scotland; d. of Thomas A. Lennox and Dorothy Lennox (née Ferguson); m. 1st Rahda Raman 1984 (divorced); m. 2nd Uri Fruchtmann; one s. two d.; m. 3rd Mitch Besser 2012; ed Aberdeen High School for Girls, Royal Acad. of Music; Founder-mem. (with Dave Stewart q.v.) The Catch 1977, renamed The Tourists 1979–80, Eurythmics 1980–89, 1999–; numerous Eurythmics tours world-wide; solo artist 1988–; f. The Circle (charity) 2008; apptd Patron, Elton John Aids Foundation 2010, UNAIDS Goodwill Amb. 2010, Amb. for Oxfam, Amb. for Amnesty International, Amb. for British Red Cross, Special Evoy for HIV/AIDS in Scotland, London Amb. for HIV/AIDS; Chancellor, Glasgow Caledonian Univ. 2017–; Dr hc (Royal Scottish Acad. of Music and Drama, Glasgow) 2006, (Berklee Coll. of Music) 2013; American Soc. of Composers Award, BPI Award for Best Female Vocalist 1982/83, 1987/88, 1989/90, 1992/93, Grammy Award for Best Female Performance (for Sweet Dreams) 1983, Ivor Novello Award for Best Pop Song (for Sweet Dreams, with Dave Stewart) 1983, MTV Music Award for Best New Artist Video (for Sweet Dreams (Are Made Of This)) 1984, Ivor Novello Award for Best Song (for It's Alright (Baby's Coming Back, with Dave Stewart) 1987, Ivor Novello Award for Best Song (for Why) 1992, BRIT Award for Best Female Solo Artist 1996, Grammy Award for Best Female Pop Vocals (for No More I Love Yous) 1996, BRIT Award for Outstanding Contrib. to Music 1999, Tartan Cleff Award 2001, Acad. Award for Best Song (for Into the West and Use Well the Days, from the film Lord of the Rings: The Two Towers) 2004, ASCAP Founders Award 2006, Special Award of Merit, American Music Awards 2008, Red Cross Humanitarian Award 2008, Youth Aids Award 2008, Inspirational Woman Of The Year, Glamour Magazine 2008, Woman of Peace Award, World Summit of Nobel Peace Prize Laureates 2009, Save the Children Amigo de los Niños Award 2009, Harper Women of the Year (for Outstanding Achievement) 2010, Nordoff Robbins Silver Clef Award 2011, Humanitarian Award, NARM 2011, Women For Women International Making a Difference Award 2011, Jonny Walker Charity Award 2011, Music Industry Trust Award 2013, Lovie Person of the Year Award 2016, Harper's Bazaar Philanthropy Award 2016, Fashion4Development Award 2016. *Film:* Revolution 1985. *Recordings include:* albums: with The Tourists: The Tourists 1979, Reality Affect 1980, Luminous Basement 1980; with Eurythmics: In The Garden 1981, Sweet Dreams (Are Made of This) (Grammy Award for Best Video Album) 1982, Touch 1983, 1984 (For The Love of Big Brother) 1984, Be Yourself Tonight 1985, Revenge 1986, Savage 1987, We Too Are One 1989, Peace 1999, The Ultimate Collection 2005; solo: Diva (BPI Award for Best Album) 1992, Medusa 1995, Train In Vain 1995, Bare 2003, Songs of Mass Destruction 2007, A Christmas Cornucopia 2010, Nostalgia 2014. *Address:* c/o XIX Management, Unit 5B, The Albion Riverside, London, SW11 4AX, England (office); Glasgow Caledonian University, Cowcaddens Road, Glasgow, Scotland, G4 0BA, England (office). *Telephone:* (141) 331-3000 (office). *Fax:* (141) 331-3005 (office). *E-mail:* ukroenquiries@gcu.ac.uk (office). *Website:* www.gcu.ac.uk (office); www.annielennox.com; www.eurythmics.com.

LENNOX-BOYD, Simon Ronald Rupert (see BOYD OF MERTON, 2nd Viscount).

LENO, Jay, BA; American comedian and TV presenter; b. (James Douglas Muir Leno), 28 April 1950, New Rochelle, NY; m. Mavis Nicholson; ed Emerson Coll.; started career as stand-up comedian and comedy writer in 1970s; named one of several guest hosts Tonight Show (NBC) 1986, exclusive guest host 1987–92, Host 1992–2009, 2010–14; host, The Jay Leno Show (NBC) 2009–10; Emmy Award 1995, Mark Twain Prize for American Humor 2014, inducted into Television Hall of Fame 2014. *Films include:* American Hot Wax 1978, Silver Bears 1978, Americathon 1979, What's Up, Hideous Sun Demon (voice) 1983, Collision Course 1989, We're Back! A Dinosaur's Story (voice) 1993, The Flintstones 1994, Robots (voice) 2005, Ice Age: The Meltdown (voice) 2006, Cars (voice) 2006, Ice Age 2: The Meltdown (voice) 2006, Christmas is Here Again (voice) 2007, Unstable Fables: Tortoise vs. Hare (voice) 2008, Igor (voice) 2008, Scooby-Doo and the Goblin King (voice) 2008. *Leisure interests:* classic cars and motorcycles. *Address:* ICM, 10250 Constellation Boulevard, Los Angeles, CA 90067, USA (office). *Telephone:* (310) 550-4000 (office). *Website:* www.icmtalent.com (office); www.nbc.com/jay-lenos-garage.

LENZ, Carl Otto, DJur; German lawyer; b. 5 June 1930, Berlin; s. of Dr Otto Lenz and Marieliese Pohl; m. Ursula Heinrich 1960; two s. three d.; ed schools in Germany and Switzerland, Univs of Bonn, Freiburg and Munich, Germany, Univ. of Fribourg, Switzerland, and Harvard and Cornell Univs, USA; Sec.-Gen. Christian Democratic Group, European Parl. 1956–66; mem. Bundestag 1965–84; Advocate-Gen. European Court of Justice 1984–97; Hon. Prof. of European Law, Saarland Univ. 1990–; Grosses Bundesverdienstkreuz 1976,

Grosseskreuz des Verdienstordens (Grand Duchy of Luxembourg) 1998 and numerous other honours. *Publications:* Die Notverstandsverfassung des GG 1971, EG Handbuch Recht im Binnenmarkt 1994, EG-Vortrag Kommentar 1994. *Address:* Baker & McKenzie LLP, Bethmannstrasse 50-54, 60311 Frankfurt am Main (office); Rodensteinstrasse 22, 64625 Bensheim, Germany. *Telephone:* (69) 29908-189 (office). *Fax:* (69) 29908-108 (office). *E-mail:* otto.c.lenz@bakernet.com (office). *Website:* www.bakernet.com.

LENZ, Guy; Luxembourg army officer; b. 28 Jan. 1946, Pétange; s. of Louis Lenz and Hélène Ludovicy; m. Liliane Wetz; two d.; ed Belgian Infantry School, Armed Forces Staff Coll., Norfolk, Va, USA; rank of Lt 1973, Capt. 1976, Maj. 1982, Lt-Col 1986, Col 1998; Chief of Staff of the Luxembourg Army 1998–2002; served as Head of Operations and Training, Deputy Commdr of the Mil. Training Centre; Head of GIVO at HQ, Mil. Councillor at NATO; Mil. Rep. at SHAPE; Perm. Rep. to NATO Mil. Cttee; Mil. Del. WEU Perm. Council; Commdr, Ordre de Mérite, Cross for 25 years service; Kt, Order of Civilian and Mil. 'Mérite de Adolphe de Nassau', Meritorious Service Medal (USA), Commdr, Ordre de la Couronne de Chêne (Belgium); Kt, Order of Orange Nassau (Netherlands). *Address:* Headquarters of the Armed Forces, BP 1873, 1018 Luxembourg (office); 50 rue um Böchel, 9017 Ettelbruck, Luxembourg (home). *Telephone:* (26) 848-1 (office); 819680 (home). *Fax:* (26) 845601 (office); 819680 (home). *E-mail:* info@armee.lu (office). *Website:* www.armee.lu (office).

LEO, Melissa; American actress; b. 14 Sept. 1960, New York, NY; d. of Arnold Leo and Peggy Leo; one s. with John Heard; ed Mountview Theatre School, London, UK. *Films include:* Always 1985, A Time of Destiny 1988, The Ballad of Little Jo 1993, 21 Grams 2003, Hide and Seek 2005, American Gun 2006, The Cake Eaters 2007, One Night 2007, Frozen River (several awards including Central Ohio Film Critics Asscn Award for Best Actress, Central Ohio Film Critics Asscn Award for Best Breakthrough Film Artist, Florida Film Critics Circle Award for Best Actress, Gotham Independent Film Award for Breakthrough Actor, Independent Spirit Award for Best Female Lead, San Sebastián Int. Film Festival Award for Best Actress) 2008, Lullaby 2008, Righteous Kill 2008, Welcome to the Rileys 2010, The Dry Land 2010, Conviction 2010, The Fighter (several awards including Broadcast Film Critics Asscn Award for Best Supporting Actress, Dallas-Fort Worth Film Critics Asscn Award for Best Supporting Actress, Denver Film Critics Soc. Award for Best Supporting Actress, Florida Film Critics Circle Award for Best Supporting Actress, New York Film Critics Circle Award for Best Supporting Actress, Academy Award for Actress in a Supporting Role 2011) 2010, Red State 2011, Lost Revolution 2011, Francine 2011, The Sea Is All I Know (short) 2011, Seven Days in Utopia 2011, Francine 2012, Prisoners 2013, The Equalizer 2014. *Television includes:* The Young Riders (series) 1989–90, Homicide: Life on the Street (series) 1993–97, In the Line of Duty: Hunt for Justice 1995, Legacy 1998, Homicide: The Movie 2000, The L Word (series) 2005, Treme (series) 2010–13, Mildred Pierce (mini-series) 2011, Wayward Pines (series) 2015. *Address:* c/o Untitled Entertainment, 1801 Century Park East, Suite 700, Los Angeles, CA 90067, USA (office). *Telephone:* (310) 601-2100 (office). *Fax:* (310) 601-2344 (office).

LEÓN GROSS, Bernardino; Spanish diplomatist, politician and fmr UN official; *Director-General, Emirates Diplomatic Academy;* b. 20 Oct. 1964, Málaga; s. of Bernardino León Diaz and Cristina Gross; m. Regina Reyes Gallur; three c.; ed Univ. of Málaga, Univ. of Barcelona, King's Coll. London, UK, Univ. of Paris (Sorbonne), France; joined Diplomatic Corps 1990, becoming Head of Coordination, Office of Sec. of State for Int. Cooperation and Latin America 1989–90, Deputy Head of Mission, Embassy in Liberia 1990–91, Chief of Staff to Pres. Nat. Comm. for V Centenary (religious anniversary comm.) 1991–92, Consul of Spain in Algiers 1992–95, Minister Counselor, Embassy in Athens 1995–98, Head of Cabinet and Spokesman of Special Rep. of EU for peace process in Middle East 1998–2001; Coordinator, Three Cultures Foundation, Seville 2001–04; Sec. of State for Foreign Affairs 2004–08; Sec.-Gen. of Spanish Presidency 2008–11; Special Rep. of EU for S Mediterranean Region 2011–14; UN Special Rep. and Head of UN Support Mission in Libya 2014–15; Dir-Gen. Emirates Diplomatic Acad. 2015–; mem. Partido Socialista Obrero Español (PSOE) 1998–; decorations from Ministry of Foreign Affairs 1991, 1995, 2001; Navy Cross of Merit 1998. *Address:* Emirates Diplomatic Academy, POB 3556, Behind Falcon Tower on Hamdan Bin Mohammed Street, Al Hosn Palace District, Abu Dhabi, United Arab Emirates (office). *Telephone:* 59-59-53 (office). *Website:* eda.ac.ae (office).

LEON GUERRERO, Lourdes (Lou) Aflague, BSc, MPH; Guam politician, fmr banking executive and nurse; *Governor of Guam;* b. 8 Nov. 1950; d. of Jesus Sablan Leon Guerrero and Eugenia Calvo Aflague Leon Guerrero; m. Jeffrey Cook; two c.; ed California State Univ., Los Angeles, Univ. of California, Los Angeles, Univ. of Washington; worked as staff nurse, Santa Monica Hosp., California –1980; nurse, Guam Memorial Hosp. from 1980, later becoming Staff Devt Coordinator and Asst Nursing Dir; Nursing Supervisor, Assoc. Operations Man. and Dir of Operations, FHP Inc. 1984–94; Dir Bank of Guam 1991, CEO and Pres. 2011–18, also Chair. BankGuam Holding Co. 2011–18; Senator, Legislature of Guam 1995–2005; Gov. of Guam (first female) 2019–; Founding Pres. Guam Women's Chamber of Commerce; Democrat. *Address:* Office of the Governor, POB 2950, Hagåtña, GU 96932, Guam (office). *Telephone:* 472-8931 (office). *Fax:* 477-4826 (home). *E-mail:* governor@mail.gov.gu (office). *Website:* governor.guam.gov (office).

LEÓN PORTILLA, Miguel, PhD; Mexican anthropologist and historian; b. 22 Feb. 1926, Mexico City; s. of Miguel León Ortiz and Luisa Portilla Nájera; m. Ascensión Hernández Triviño 1965; one d.; ed Loyola Univ. of Los Angeles and Nat. Univ. of Mexico; Sec.-Gen. Inter-American Indian Inst. 1955–59, Asst Dir 1959–60, Dir 1960–66; Asst Dir Seminar for Náhuatl Culture, Nat. Univ. of Mexico 1956, Dir Inst. of Historical Research 1963–78, Prof. Emer. 1988–; Dir América Indígena 1960; Adviser, Int. Inst. of Different Civilisations 1960; Perm. Rep. of Mexico to UNESCO, Paris 1987; mem. Bd Govs Nat. Univ. Mexico 1976; mem. American Anthropological Asscn 1960–, Mexican Acad. of Language 1962–, Société des Américanistes de Paris 1966–, Mexican Acad. of History 1969–, Nat. Coll. of Mexico 1971–; Corresp. mem. Royal Spanish Acad. of History 1969–; Guggenheim Fellow 1969; Fellow, Portuguese Acad. of History, Lisbon 1995; Hon. mem. American Historical Asscn 1991, NAS 1995; Commendatore Repub. Italiana 1977, Great Cross of Alfonso X el sabio (Spain) 1998, Ordre des Palmes académiques 2000, Orden del Mérito Civico (en grado de Gran Cruz) (Spain) 2003; Hon. PhD (Southern Methodist Univ., Dallas, Tex.) 1980, (California) 1986, (Tel-Aviv) 1987,

(Toulouse) 1990, (Colima) 1993, (San Andrés, Bolivia) 1994, (Brown Univ.) 1996, (Carolina Univ., Prague) 2000; Fifth Distinguished Lecturer, American Anthropological Asscn 1974, Serra Award 1978, Nat. Prize in the Social Sciences (Mexico) 1981, Manuel Gamio Anthropological Award 1983, Nat. Univ. of Mexico Prize 1994, Belisario Domínguez Medal (Mexico) 1997, Bartolomé de las Casas Prize (Spain) 2001, Investigador Nacional de Excelencia (Mexico) 2002, Presea 'Estado de Mexico 2001' 2002, Universidad Latinoamericana Prize, 2003, Veracruz Prize 2003, Medalla Ignacio de la Llave 2003, recognized for his historical investigations over 46 years by UNAM 2003, Toltecáyod Prize, Universidad de Tula Hidalgo 2005, Tlamatili Prize, Universidad Iberoamericana, Mexico 2005, Fundación México Unido Prize 2005, Chiapas Prize 2006, US Library of Congress Living Legend Award 2013. *Publications include:* La Filosofía Náhuatl 1956, Visión des los Vencidos 1959, Los Antiguos Mexicanos 1961, The Broken Spears, Aztec Account of the Conquest of Mexico 1962, Aztec Thought and Culture 1963, Literaturas Precolombinas de México 1964, Imagen del México Antiguo 1964, Trece Poetas del Mundo Azteca 1967, Pre-Columbian Literatures of Mexico 1968, Tiempo y Realidad en el Pensamiento Maya 1968, De Teotihuacan a los Aztecas 1971, The Norteño Variety of Mexican Culture 1972, The Voyages of Francisco de Ortega to California 1632–1636 1972, Time and Reality in the Thought of the Maya 1973, Historia Natural y Crónica de la Antigua California 1973, Aztecs and Navajos 1975, Endangered Cultures: The Indian in Latin America 1975, L'Envers de la conquête 1977, Los Manifestos en Náhuatl de Emiliano Zapata 1978, Toltecayotl, Aspectos de la Cultura Náhuatl 1980, Mesoamerican Spirituality 1980, Literaturas de Anahuac y del Imcario 1982, Mesoamerica before 1519 1984, La Pensée Aztèque 1985, Libro de los Coloquios 1986, Das Alte Mexiko: Religion 1986, Huehuehtlahtolli, Testimonies of the Ancient Word 1988, Mesoamerica in 1492 and on the eve of 1992, 1988, Poésie Náhuatl d'amour et d'amitié 1991, Fifteen Poets of the Aztec World 1992, The Aztec Image of Self and Society 1992, Raíces indígenas, presencia hispánica 1993, La flecha en el blanco 1995, Tonantzin Guadalupe 2000, La Visión de los Vencidos (published in English as The Broken Spear), La Filosofía Náhuatl (published as Aztec Thought and Culture), In the Language of Kings – An Anthology of Mesoamerican Literature Pre-Columbian to the Present 2001, México an 1554, Ordenanzas de Tema Indígena en Castella y náhuatl – Expedidas par Maximiliano de Habsburgo 2003, Pueblos Indígenas de México – Autonomía y Diferencia Cultural 2003, Obras de Miguel León-Portillo – En torno a la Historia de Mesoamérica 2004, Aztecas-Mexicas – Desarrollo de una civilización originaria 2005. *Leisure interests:* scouting and gardening. *Address:* Instituto de Investigaciones Históricas, Circuitro Mtro. Mario de la Cueva, Zona Cultural, Ciudad Universitaria, UNAM, 04510 México, DF (office); Alberto Zamora 131 antes 103, Col. Coyoacán, 04520 Delegación, México, DF, Mexico (home). *Telephone:* (5) 665-44-17 (office); (55) 54-08-02 (home). *Fax:* (5) 665-0070 (office). *E-mail:* portilla@servidor.unam.mx (office).

LEONARD, Brian Edmund, BSc, PhD, DSc, MRIA; Irish pharmacologist and academic; *Professor Emeritus of Pharmacology, National University of Ireland, Galway;* b. 30 May 1936, Winchester, Hants., England; s. of Harold E. Leonard and Dorothy Coley; m. Helga F. Mühlpfordt 1959; two d.; ed Univ. of Birmingham; Dept of Medical Biochemistry, Univ. of Birmingham 1956–62; Lecturer in Pharmacology, Univ. of Nottingham 1962–68; Tech. Officer, CNS Research, ICI Pharmaceuticals Div. Alderley Park, Cheshire 1968–71; Group Leader, CNS Pharmacology, Organon International BV, Oss, Netherlands 1971–74; Prof. of Pharmacology, Univ. Coll. (now Nat. Univ. of Ireland) Galway 1974–, Prof. Emer. 1999–; Councillor, CINP 1996–2000, Treas. 1992–96, Pres. Elect 2002–04, Pres. 2004–06; Visiting Prof., Brain and Behaviour Research Inst., Maastricht Univ. 2002–; Deputy Chair. Lundbeck Inst. for Neuropsychiatric Research 2004–; Pres. British Asscn Psychopharmacology 1988–90; Past Pres. Int. Soc. for the Investigation of Stress; Assoc. mem. Royal Coll. of Psychiatrists; Foreign Corresp. mem. American Coll. Neuropsychopharmacology; Visiting Fellow, Magdalen Coll. Oxford 1990–91; mem. Royal Irish Acad.; Hon. Prof., Faculty of Medicine, Queen's Univ. Belfast, NI, Dept of Psychiatry, Univ. of Hong Kong 2004–06, Dept of Psychiatry and Psychotherapy, Ludwig Maximilian Univ., Munich 2007–; Hon. mem., S African Asscn of Psychiatrists, British Asscn of Psychopharmacology, Egyptian Psychiatric Asscn; Silver Medal, Royal Irish Acad. 1996, Lifetime Achievement Award, British Asscn for Psychopharmacology 2008. *Publications include:* Fundamentals of Psychopharmacology 1992, Fundamentals of Psychoimmunology 2000; over 400 articles in int. scientific journals. *Leisure interests:* entomology, classical music, political science. *Address:* Pharmacology Department, National University of Ireland, University Road, Galway (office); Currabhaitia, Tullykyne, Moycullen, Co. Galway, Ireland (home). *Telephone:* (91) 524411 (ext. 3837) (office); (91) 555292 (home). *Fax:* (91) 525700 (office). *E-mail:* belucg@iol.ie. *Website:* www.nuigalway.ie/pharmacology (office).

LEONARD, Hugh Terence; New Zealand broadcasting executive; b. 20 July 1938, Greymouth; s. of Michael James Leonard and Elizabeth Leonard (née Storey); m. Pauline Lobendahn 1965; one s. two d.; joined NZ Broadcasting Service 1956, Fiji Broadcasting Comm. 1960, Gen. Man. 1973–85; Sec.-Gen. Asia-Pacific Broadcasting Union 1985–2002, Special Adviser to the Pres. 2002–03 (retd); Fiji Independence Medal 1970. *Leisure interests:* classic motorcycles, remote-controlled model aircraft, computers.

LEONARD, Jason, OBE; British fmr professional rugby football player (rugby union); *President, Rugby Football Union;* b. 14 Aug. 1968, Barking, Essex; s. of Frank Leonard and Maria Leonard; two s. one d.; ed Warren Comprehensive, Chadwell Heath, Essex; prop forward (usually loose-head); teams: Barking, Saracens, Harlequins 1990– (264 appearances, five tries), England Under-21, England A (2 caps), England 1990– (debut versus Argentina); 114 Tests (world record) for England (2 as Capt.), one try, to 31 March 2004; mem. Grand Slam winning squads 1991, 1992, 1995, 2003, Five Nations Championship winners 1999, Six Nations Championship winners 2000, 2001, World Cup winning squad 2003, runners-up 1991, 4th place 1995; mem. British Lions' team, New Zealand (2 Tests) 1993, South Africa (1 Test), 1997 Australia (2 Tests) 2001; Pres. Rugby Football Union 2015–; Freeman, City of Greater London; inducted into Int. Rugby Hall of Fame 2007. *Address:* Rugby House, Twickenham Stadium, 200 Whitton Road, Twickenham, TW2 7BA, England (office). *Telephone:* (87) 1222-2120 (office). *Website:* www.englandrugby.com (office).

LEONARD, Ray Charles ('Sugar Ray'); American fmr professional boxer; b. 17 May 1956, Wilmington, NC; s. of Cicero Leonard and Getha Leonard; m. 1st Juanita Wilkinson 1980 (divorced 1990); two s.; m. 2nd Bernadette Robi 1993; four c.; ed Palmer Park High School, Md; amateur boxer 1970–77; won 140 of 145 amateur fights; world amateur champion 1974, US Amateur Athletic Union champion 1974, Pan-American Games gold medallist 1975, Olympic gold medallist 1976; guaranteed record purse of US $25,000 for first professional fight Feb. 1977; won North American welterweight title from Pete Ranzany August 1979; won World Boxing Council version of world welterweight title from Wilfred Benitez Nov. 1979; retained title against Dave Green March 1980, lost title to Roberto Durán (q.v.), Montréal, June 1980, regained it from Durán, New Orleans, Nov. 1980; world jr middleweight title, World Boxing Asscn (WBA) June 1981; won WBA world welterweight title from Tommy Hearns to become undisputed world champion Sept. 1981, drew rematch June 1989; 36 professional fights, 33 wins, lost two, drawn one; retd from boxing Nov. 1982; returned to the ring April 1987; won World middleweight title, lost to Terry Norris 1991, retd from boxing 1991; returned to ring March 1997; lost Int. Boxing Council middleweight title fight to Hector Camacho 1997; boxing promoter (Sugar Ray Leonard Boxing); commentator for Home Box Office TV Co.; commentator, ABC, ESPN; co-host Prime Time Boxing, PBC on NBC; Founder Sugar Ray Leonard Foundation 2009; Ring magazine's Fighter of the Decade for the 1980s, inducted into Boxing Hall of Fame 1997. *Films:* The Fighter 2010. *Television:* The Contender 2005, Dancing with the Stars 2011. *Publication:* The Big Fight: My Life In and Out of the Ring 2011. *Address:* Suite 206-B, 4401 East West Highway, Bethesda, MD 20814, USA. *Telephone:* (310) 471-3100 (office). *Website:* sugarrayleonard.com; www.sugarrayleonardfdn.org.

LEONARDO, Anne Itto; South Sudanese politician; d. of Leonardo Tongun Itto; Deputy Sec. Gen., Sudan People's Liberation Movt (southern sector); Chair. Political Cttee, Jt Nat. Transitional Team 2005–; Minister of State for Agric. and Forestry, Govt of Nat. Unity, Sudan 2005–10; mem. Nat. Ass. 2005–; Minister of Agric. and Forestry, Govt of South Sudan 2011. *Address:* c/o Ministry of Agriculture and Forestry, Juba, South Sudan (office).

LEONG, Alan, LLB, LLM; Chinese barrister and politician; b. 22 Feb. 1958, Hong Kong; m.; three c.; ed Wah Yan Coll., Kowloon, Univ. of Hong Kong, Univ. of Cambridge, UK; called to Hong Kong Bar 1983, to Inner Bar 1998 (first to be apptd after establishment of Hong Kong Special Admin. Region; f. Alan Leong's SC Chambers; mem. Legis. Council (Civic Party) representing Kowloon East 2004–10 (resgnd); unsuccessful Civic Party cand. in 2007 election for Chief Exec.; Chair. Special Cttee on Mainland Practice and Relations; Chair. Asscn of Heads of Secondary Schools of Tsuen Wan, Kwai Chung and Tsing Yi Dist 1998; Chair. Water Pollution Control Appeal Bd 2001–07; Dir Applied Research Council 2000–06; mem. Cttee of Bilingual Legal System in Hong Kong 1997–2004, Criminal and Law Enforcement Injuries Compensation Bd 2000–06, Ind. Police Complaints Council 2000–04 (Vice-Chair. 2005–06), Hong Kong Bar Asscn 2000– (Chair. 2001–03), Central Policy Unit Panel on Social Cohesion 2002–03, Professional Services Advisory Cttee Hong Kong Trade Devt Council 2002–06, Chief Justice's Steering Cttee on Implementation of Use of Chinese in the Courts 1996–2003, Task Group on Promotion of English Standards in the Workplace, Standing Cttee on Language Educ. and Research 1999–2000, Cen. Policy Unit Panel on Social Cohesion 2002–03, Cttee of Bilingual Legal System in Hong Kong 1998–2004; Pres. Kwai Tsing Lions Club 1998–99; Chair. Task Force on Accreditation re Internship, Advisory Cttee on Teacher Educ. and Qualification 2003; mem. Hong Kong Housing Authority 2009–; Bar's Rep. on the Working Group on Review of Legal Educ. and Training 1999–2002; Hon. Lecturer, Dept of Professional Legal Educ., Univ. of Hong Kong 2002–. *Address:* Room 1324A, Prince Building, 10 Chater Road, Central, Hong Kong Special Administrative Region, People's Republic of China (office). *Telephone:* 25266182 (office). *Fax:* 25093101 (office). *E-mail:* enquiries@alsc-chambers.com (office); al@alanleong.net; contact.kitgor@gmail.com (office). *Website:* www.alanleong.net; alsc-chambers.com/alan.html (office).

LEONG, Lampo, BFA, MFA, PhD; American (b. Chinese) artist and academic; *Professor of Art, University of Missouri-Columbia;* b. (Liang Lanbo), 3 July 1961, Guangzhou, Guangdong Prov., People's Repub. of China; ed Guangzhou Acad. of Fine Arts, California Coll. of the Arts, San Francisco and Univ. of California, Berkeley, USA, Cen. Acad. of Fine Arts, Beijing; Instructor, California Coll. of Arts and Crafts 1986–87, Chabot Coll., Hayward, Calif. 1989–94, Univ. of California, Berkeley 1989–99, Diablo Valley Coll., Pleasant Hill, Calif. 1998–99; Visiting Asst Prof., San Francisco State Univ. 1996–2001; Prof. of Art, Univ. of Missouri-Columbia 2001–, Chair. Art Dept 2007–09; Weiner Distinguished Prof., Missouri Univ. of Science and Tech. 2012; Assoc. Dir, The Fine Arts and Design Educ. Devt Alliance of the Guangdong-Hong Kong-Macao Greater Bay Area 2018–; Distinguished Prof. of Art, Doctoral Adviser, Assoc. Chair., Dept of Communication and Dir of Centre for Arts & Design, Univ. of Macau 2018–, also works as Art Ed., Review of Culture magazine, Univ. of Macau & Cultural Affairs Bureau 2018–; Guest Speaker, Asian Art Museum of San Francisco 1985, 1990, 1992, 1994, 1996–2001, Univ. of California, Berkeley, Dept of Art History 1997, 1998, 2001, 2006, Stanford Univ. Inst. for Int. Studies 1999, 2000, Univ. of Minnesota 2005, 2006, Univ. of California, Davis 2010, Luxun Acad. of Fine Arts, People's Repub. of China 2010, Guangzhou Acad. of Fine Arts 2008, 2009, 2011, 2012, Harbin Inst. of Tech. 2012, Guangxi Acad. of Arts 2012; Visiting Prof., Wuhan Univ. of Tech. 2016, Sichuan Univ. 2016–17, Guangdong Univ. of Tech. 2017, Central China Normal Univ. 2017–; works in 15 museums and more than 70 public collections worldwide, including Japan, China, Hong Kong, Macao, Taiwan, Indonesia, Canada, France, Germany; mem. Advisory Cttee for Establishment of Faculty of Design, Univ. of Macau 2013–15; Summer Research Fellowship, Univ. of Missouri, Columbia 2017; Hon. Visiting Prof., Guangzhou Acad. of Fine Arts 2009–, South China Normal Univ. 2011–, Huazhong Normal Univ., Wuhan 2012–, Hon. Master Painter, Guangzhou Painting Acad. 2011–; numerous awards, including Gold Medal Award, XV Exposição Colectiva dos Artistas de Macau 1998, Mayoral Proclamation: Lampo Leong Day (Nov. 19th), City of San Francisco 1999, Best of Show, 42nd Annual Int. Exhbn, Sumi-e Soc. of America 2005, Diploma of Excellence, Medial 1.Art Biennial, Medial Museum, London 2005, Top Ten Award, Exposição Annual de Artes Visuais, Instituto Cultural do Governo da Macao 2007, 2009, 2011, 2012, Faculty-Alumni Awards, Univ. of Missouri-Columbia 2007, Cover Award, New Art International, New York 2009, Gold Medal Award, Creative Quarterly (No. 18), New York 2010, Best of Show, 48th Annual Int. Exhbn, Sumi-e Soc. of America 2011, Research Council Grant, Univ. of Missouri-Columbia 2012, 2013, Foundation Macau Grant 2014–17. *Publications:* contrib. to numerous art books and journals, including 50 essays and more than 900 reviews and publs internationally. *Leisure interests:* photography, film, travel, ballroom dancing. *Address:* Department of Art, A129 Fine Arts, University of Missouri-Columbia, Columbia, MO 65211, USA (office); University of Macau, Avenida da Universidade, Taipa, Macao, The People's Republic of China (office). *Telephone:* (573) 882-9446 (office); (53) 88228833 (office). *Fax:* (573) 884-6807 (office). *E-mail:* leongl@missouri.edu (office); LampoLeong@um.edu.mo (office). *Website:* web.missouri.edu/~leongl (office); www.lampoleong.com; www.comm.fss.um.edu.mo/people/academic-staff/lampo-leong.

LEONI, Téa; American actress; b. 25 Feb. 1966; m. 1st Neil Tardio; m. 2nd David Duchovny (q.v.) 1997 (divorced 2014); two c. *Films include:* Switch 1991, A League of Their Own 1992, Wyatt Earp 1994, Bad Boys 1995, Flirting with Disaster 1996, Deep Impact 1998, There's No Fish Food in Heaven 1999, Life in the Fast Lane 1999, The Family Man 2000, Jurassic Park III 2001, Hollywood Ending 2002, People I Know 2003, House of D 2004, Spanglish 2004, Fun with Dick and Jane 2005, You Kill Me 2007, Ghost Town 2008, The Smell of Success 2009, Tower Heist 2011. *Television:* Flying Blind 1992–93, The Naked Truth 1995–98, Madam Secretary (political drama series) 2014–. *Address:* ICM, 8942 Wilshire Boulevard, Beverly Hills, CA 90211, USA (office).

LEONI SCETI, Elio; Italian business executive; *Chairman, LSG Holdings;* b. Rome; m.; four c.; began career in brand man., Proctor & Gamble 1988–92; Marketing Man., Reckitt Benckiser 1992–93, Marketing Dir, Benckiser USA 1993–95, Gen. Man., Benckiser Germany 1995–97, Gen. Man., Benckiser Italy 1997–99, Sr Vice-Pres. and Regional Dir, North America 1999–2001, Exec. Vice-Pres., Category Devt 2001–06, Exec. Vice-Pres., Europe 2001–08; CEO, EMI Music 2008–10, also Pres., New Music Div.; CEO Iglo Foods Group Ltd 2013–15, Dir Nomad Foods (following purchase of Iglo Foods) 2015–; Dir Anheuser-Busch InBev 2014–; Co-Founder and Chair. LSG Holdings. *Address:* LSG Holdings, Dudley House, 169 Piccadilly, London, W1J 9EH, England (office). *Telephone:* (20) 7491-7103 (office). *E-mail:* info@lsgholdings.com (office). *Website:* www.lsgholdings.com (office).

LEONOV, Maj.-Gen. Aleksey Arkhipovich; Russian fmr cosmonaut and banking executive; *Advisor to the First Deputy Chairman, Alfa Bank;* b. 30 May 1934, Listvianka, Kamerovo Region; s. of Arkhip Leonov and Yevdokia Leonova; m. Svetlana Leonova; two d.; ed Kremenchug Air Force School for Pilots, Chuguev Air Force School for Pilots and Zhukovsky Air Force Eng Acad.; pilot 1956–59; mem. CPSU 1957–91; cosmonaut training 1960; first man to walk in space 18 March 1965: took part in flight of space-ship Voskhod 2 and spent 12 minutes and 9 seconds outside the spaceship, connected by a 5.35-m tether; Deputy Commdr Gagarin Cosmonauts Training Centre 1971; took part in joint flight Soyuz 19–Apollo 1975; rank of Maj.-Gen. 1975; Chair. Council of Founders of Novosti Press Agency 1969–90; Deputy Head, Centre of Cosmonaut Training 1975–92, Commdr of Cosmonauts 1976–92; Dir Cheteck-Cosmos Co. 1981–92, Pres. Investment Fund Alfa-Capital 1993–; Vice-Pres. Alfa Bank from 1998, currently Advisor to the First Deputy Chair.; Co-Chair. Int. Asscn of Cosmonauts; mem. Int. Acad. of Astronauts, Soviet Artists Union; Acting mem. and Academician, Russian Acad. of Arts; Acting mem. New York Acad. of Arts; Hon. Citizen of Belgorod, Vologda, Kaliningrad, Kaluga, Kemerovo, Nalchik, Perm, Arkalyk (Kazakhstan), Kremenchug (Ukraine), Veliko Tarnovo, Vidin, Svishtov (Bulgaria), Usti nad Labem (Czech Repub.), San Antonio (Chile); Hon. mem. Russian Acad. of Fine Arts; Order for Service to the Homeland in the Armed Forces of the USSR, 3rd Class, five Jubilee Medals, Order of the Red Star 1961, Hero of the Soviet Union 1965, 1975, Hero of Socialist Labour (Bulgaria) 1965, Hero of Viet Nam, Hero of Labour (Viet Nam) 1966, Order of Karl Marx (DDR) 1966, Order 'For Merit', 1st Class (Syria) 1966, Order of Georgi Dimitrov (Bulgaria), Order of the Banner of the Hungarian People's Repub., Pilot-Cosmonaut of USSR 1966, Yuri Gagarin Gold Medal 1965, Hero of Bulgaria 1965, Hero of Vietnam 1965, Master of Sports 1965, Order of Lenin 1965, 1975, USSR State Prize 1981, Order for Merit to the Fatherland, 4th Class 2000, Order the 'Pride of Russia', Foundation for the 'Pride of the Fatherland' 2007, Order 'The Glory of the Fatherland', 2nd Class 2008, Order of Friendship 2011, Order of Merit, 3rd Class (Ukraine) 2011, Commdr, Order of St Anne, II Degree, Head of the Russian Imperial House Maria Vladimirovna Romanova 2011; Hon. DrScEng 1981; Honoured Master of Sport of the USSR 1965, Lenin Komsomol State Prize 1979, USSR State Prize 1981, Ludwig Nobel Prize 2007, Nat. Award 'To the Glory of the Fatherland' in the 'Glory to Russia', Int. Acad. of Social Sciences and Int. Acad. of Patronage 2008. *Publications:* Two Sides of the Moon: Our Story of the Cold War Space Race (with David Scott) 2006, Into That Silent Sea (contrib.) 2007; numerous books, papers and articles, notably on the psychological activity of cosmonauts. *Leisure interests:* painting, shooting movies. *Address:* Alfa Bank, 27 Kalanchevskaya Street, 107078 Moscow, Russia (office). *Telephone:* (495) 620-91-91 (office). *E-mail:* mail@alfabank.ru (office). *Website:* alfabank.com (office).

LEONTYEV, Leopold Igorevich, DrTechSci; Russian metallurgist; b. 1 Dec. 1934, Sverdlovsk (now Yekaterinburg); m.; two s.; ed Urals Polytechnic Inst.; researcher, Head of Lab., then Deputy Dir Inst. of Metallurgy, Ural br. of USSR (now Russian) Acad. of Sciences 1957–93, Deputy Chair. 1993, currently mem. Presidium, also mem. Russian Acad. of Sciences 1997, mem. Presidium 2000; First Deputy Minister of Science and Tech. 1993–96, 1997–2000; First Deputy Chair. State Cttee on Science and Tech. 1996–97; mem. editorial bds of seven journals; Russian Federation Government Award, Labor Red Star Medal 1987, Medal of Honour 1999, Balkin IP Award, Russian Acad. of Sciences 2005. *Publications:* more than 400 scientific publs on the devt of physical and chemical fundamentals and processes of complex use of metallurgic raw materials; more than 80 patents. *Address:* Presidium of Ural Branch of Russian Academy of Sciences, Yekaterinburg, Pervomayskaya str. 91, 620219 Yekaterinburg, Russia (office). *Telephone:* (495) 237-39-31 (Moscow) (office); (3432) 74-53-85 (Yekaterinburg) (office).

LEOPHAIRATANA, Prachai, BE, MSEE; Thai business executive; *CEO, TPI Polene Public Co. Ltd;* b. 28 Aug. 1944; s. of Phorn Leophairatana and Boonsri Leophairatana; m. Orapin Leophairatana 1974; ed Canterbury Univ., New

Zealand, Univ. of California, Berkeley, USA, Directors Accreditation Program, Thai Inst. of Dirs; CEO International Plastic Trading Co. Ltd 1981–2006; CEO Thai Petrochemical Industry Public Co. Ltd (PCL) (now IRPC PCL) 1988–2006, TPI Group of Cos 1988–2006, TPI Polene PCL 2001–; Man. Dir Hong Yiah Seng Co. Ltd 1986–; mem. Senate; Chair. United Grain Industry Co. Ltd from 1986, Bangkok Union Insurance PCL from 1986, Thai Industrial Estate Corp. Ltd from 1988, Exec. Bd Thai Caprolactam PCL from 1989, Uhde (Thailand) Co. Ltd from 1990, Thai Int. Tankers Co. Ltd from 1994; Vice-Chair. Thai Alliance Textile Co. Ltd from 1986; Dir, Bangkok Union Insurance Public Co. Ltd 2012–; Dir Rice Export Asscns, Thai–Chinese Friendship Asscn, Thai–Chinese Promotion of Investment and Trade Asscn, Bd of Trade of Thailand; Sec.-Gen. Environment for Better Life Foundation; Kt Grand Cross, Most Noble Order of the Crown of Thailand, Kt Grand Cross (1st Class), Exalted Order of the White Elephant, Kt Grand Cordon (Special Class), Most Noble Order of the Crown of Thailand, Companion (4th Class), Most Admirable Order of the Direkgunabhom. *Address:* TPI Polene Public Co. Ltd, TPI Tower, 26/56 Chan Tat Mai Road, Tungmahamek, Sathorn, Bangkok 10120, Thailand (office). *Telephone:* (2) 2855090 (office). *Fax:* (2) 2131035 (office). *E-mail:* info@tpipolene.co.th (office). *Website:* www.tpipolene.co.th (office).

LÉOTARD, François Gérard Marie; French politician, diplomatist and civil servant; b. 26 March 1942, Cannes; s. of André Léotard and Antoinette Tomasi; m. 1st France Reynier 1976; m. 2nd Ysabel Duret 1992; one s. one d.; ed Lycées Charlemagne and Henri IV, Paris, Faculté de Droit and Inst. d'Etudes Politiques, Paris and Ecole Nat. d'Admin; Sec. of Chancellery, Ministry of Foreign Affairs 1968–71; Admin. Town Planning 1973–75; Sous-préfet 1974–77; Mayor of Fréjus 1977–92, 1993–97, Municipal Councillor 1992; Deputy to Nat. Ass. (UDF-PR) 1978–86, 1988–92; Conseiller-Gen., Var 1980–88; Sec.-Gen. Parti Républicain 1982–88, Pres. 1988–90, 1995–97, Hon. Pres. 1990–95; Vice-Pres. Union pour la Démocratie Française (UDF) 1983–84, Pres. 1996–98; Minister of Culture and Communications 1986–88, of Nat. Defence (oversaw peace-keeping operations in Bosnia) 1993–95; Deputy for Var 1988–92, 1995–97, 1997–2002; apptd EU Special Envoy to Macedonia 2001; Insp. Gen. des Finances pour l'extérieur 2001; convicted of money-laundering and illegal party funding, received ten month suspended sentence Feb. 2004; Chevalier, Ordre nat. du Mérite. *Publications include:* A Mots Decouverts 1987, Culture: Les Chemins de Printemps 1988, La Ville aimée: mes chemins de Fréjus 1989, Pendant la Crise, le spectacle continue 1989, Adresse au Président des Républiques françaises 1991, Place de la République 1992, Ma Liberté 1995, Pour l'honneur 1997, Je vous hais tous avec douceur 2000, Paroles d'immortels 2001, La Couleur des Femmes 2002, À mon frère qui n'est pas mort 2003, Ça va mal finir 2008. *Leisure interests:* running, tennis, parachuting.

LEPAGE, Corinne Dominique Marguerite; French lawyer and politician; *President, CAP 21 LRC;* b. 11 May 1951, Boulogne-Billancourt; d. of Philippe Lepage and Jacqueline Schulmann; m. 1st Christian Jessua, one d.; m. 2nd Christian Huglo, one s.; ed Lycée Molière, Univ. of Paris II and Inst. d'Etudes Politiques, Paris; in legal partnership 1971–76; barrister, Paris 1978–; Dir of Studies, Univ. of Paris II 1974–77; Dir of Educ. Univ. of Metz 1978–80; Deputy Mayor of Cabourg 1989–2001; Lecturer, Inst. d'Etudes Politiques, Paris 1979–87, 1989–94; Course Dir Univ. of Paris II 1982–86, Univ. of Paris XII 1987–92; mem. Bar Council 1987–89; Vice-Pres. then Pres. Asscn of Admin. Law Advocates 1989–95; Minister of the Environment 1995–97; Pres. Asscn nationale des docteurs en droit 1998–2003, Asscn Women Engage for a Common Future, Asscn 2° Investing, Friends of Humankind Rights; MEP 2009–14; Vice-Pres. Environnement sans frontières 1998–, Modem; Pres. Comité de Recherche Indépendante et d'Information sur le Génie Génétique (CRII-GEN), now Hon. Pres.; Leader CAP 21 – Citoyenneté Action Participation pour le 21è siècle 1996–2014, Pres. CAP 21 LRC 2014–; Prof., Inst. d'Etudes Politiques de Paris 1994–; Pres. Observatoire de vigilance et d'alerte écologique; Pres. New Economy Entrepreneurs' Movement; Chevalier, Légion d'honneur. *Publications:* Code annoté des procédures administratives contentieuses 1990, Les audits de l'environnement 1992, On ne peut rien faire, Madame le ministre 1998, Bien gérer l'environnement, une chance pour l'entreprise 1999, La Politique de Précaution 2001, Oser l'Espérance, Robert Jauze 2002, De l'Écologie, Hors de l'Imposture et l'Opportunisme 2003, Santé et Environnement, l'Abécédaire 2005, Ecoresp I et II, Et si c'était elle? 2006, La vérité sur le nucléaire: le choix interdit 2011, La vérité sur les OGM, c'est notre affaire!: Editions Charles Léopold Mayer 2012, Les femmes au secours de la République, de l'Europe et de la planéte 2015, Atlas Mondial du Nucléaire, Librairie Autrement 2015, A bout de confiance, de la morale en politique, Librairie Autrement 2017; numerous articles in La Gazette du Palais. *Leisure interests:* cinema, reading, tennis, skiing, swimming. *Address:* Huglo-Lepage Avocats, 42 rue de Lisbonne, 75008 Paris, France (office). *Telephone:* 1-42-90-98-01 (office). *Fax:* 1-42-90-98-10 (office). *E-mail:* corinne.lepage@huglo-lepage.com (home). *Website:* lerassemblementcitoyen.fr (office); www.huglo-lepage.com (home).

LePAGE, Paul Richard, BS, MBA; American business executive, politician and fmr state governor; b. 9 Oct. 1948, Lewiston, Me; s. of Gerard A. LePage and Theresa B. LePage (née Gagnon); eldest s. of 18 c.; m. 1st Ann S. Crabbe 1971 (divorced 1980); two d.; m. 2nd Ann M. Derosby 1984; two c. one adopted s.; ed Husson Coll. (now Husson Univ.), Bangor, Me, Univ. of Maine; left home aged 11 and lived on streets of Lewiston for two years, various jobs including shining shoes, washing dishes and loading boxes aged 13, later worked at a rubber co., a meat packing plant, and was a short order cook and bartender; ed. of coll. newspaper as a student; Treas. and Gen. Man. Arthurette Lumber Co., Canada 1971–77; Task Force Leader, Town of Perth-Andover, Canada 1976–77; Vice-Pres. Mid-Maine United Way Program, Waterville 1985–86; Dir of Finance, Maine State Housing Authority, Augusta 1977–79; Controller, Scott Paper Co., Winslow 1979–83; Dir of Finance and Admin, Interstate Food Processing Corpn, Fort Fairfield 1983–84; Chief Financial Officer, Forster Manufacturing Co., Inc., Wilton 1984–85; Pres. Paul LePage Assocs, Inc., Waterville 1985–; teacher, Kennebec Vallery Vocational Inst., Waterville 1986–; Gen. Man. Marden's Surplus and Salvage 1996–; Head of LePage & Kasevich (pvt. consultancy); served two terms as City Councillor, Waterville –2003, Mayor of Waterville 2003–10; Gov. of Maine 2011–18; mem. Maine Forest Products Council, American Asscn Council, Nat. Asscn of Accountants, Mid-Maine Chamber of Commerce, Maine Chamber of Commerce and Industry, Toastmasters, Rotary, Elks; Republican; Dr hc (Thomas Coll., Waterville) 2012; voted Mid-Maine Chamber of Commerce's Businessman of the Year 2006, named by Nat. Fed. of Ind. Business as Maine Business Champion 2007. *Leisure interests:* furniture making, softball, racquetball, ice hockey. *Address:* c/o Office of the Governor, 1 State House Station, Augusta, ME 04333, USA (office).

LEPAGE, Robert, CC; French-Canadian actor and theatre and opera director; *Artistic Director, Ex Machina;* b. 1957, Quebec City; ed Conservatoire d'Art Dramatique Québec, Canada; Artistic Co-Dir Théatre Repère 1986–89; Founder and Pres. Robert Lepage Inc. 1988–; Artistic Dir Nat. Arts Centre Ottawa, Canada 1989–93; Artistic Dir Ex Machina 1994–; Founder, Pres. and Artistic Dir In Extremis Inc. 1995–2004; Founder La Caserne Dalhousie 1997–; Officier, Order nat. du Québec 1999; Chevalier, Légion d'honneur 2002; Compagnon des Arts et des Lettres du Québec 2015; Hon. PhD (Laval) 1994, Hon. DLitt (Toronto, McGill) 1997, Hon. LLD (Concordia) 1999; Evening Standard Award for Best Play 2001, Herbert Whittaker Drama Bench Award 2002, Denise Pelletier Prize 2003, Hans Christian Andersen Prize 2004, Samuel de Champlain Prize 2005, Stanislavski Award 2005, Europe Theatre Prize 2007, Gov.-Gen's Performing Arts Award 2009, Eugene McDermott Award, MIT 2012, Glenn Gould Prize 2014, Herald Archangel Award 2015. *Films:* (scriptwriter, dir): The Confessional 1995, The Polygraph 1996, Nô 1998, Possible Worlds 2000, The Far Side of the Moon 2003, Triptych 2013, Michelle (short) 2014, Marie (short) 2014, Thomas (short) 2014. *Operas:* (dir): Bluebeard's Castle 1993, Erwartung 1993, The Damnation of Faust 1999, The Busker's Opera 2004, 1984 2005, The Rake's Progress 2007, The Nightingale an Other Short Fables 2008, Der Ring des Nibelungen (Das Rheingold) 2010, (Die Walküre and Siegfried) 2011, (Götterdämmerung) 2012, The Tempest 2012, L'Amour de Loin 2015, The Magic Flute 2018. *Productions include:* Circulations 1984, Dragon's Trilogy (co-writer, dir and actor) 1985, Vinci (writer, dir and actor) 1986, Polygraph (writer, dir and actor) 1987, Tectonic Plates (co-writer, dir and actor) 1988, Needles and Opium (dir) 1991, A Midsummer Night's Dream (dir) 1992, Coriolanus (dir) 1992, Macbeth (dir) 1992, The Tempest (dir) 1992, The Seven Streams of the River Ota (writer and dir) 1994, Elsinore (writer and dir) 1995, The Geometry of Miracles (co-writer and dir) 1998, Zulu Time (writer and dir) 1999, The Far Side of the Moon (writer, dir and actor) 2000, La Casa Azul (writer and dir) 2001, The Andersen Project (writer and dir) 2005, Lipsynch (writer and dir) 2007, The Blue Dragon (writer and dir) 2008, Eonnagata (co-writer, dir and actor) 2009, La Tempête (dir) 2011, Playing Cards: Spades (co-writer and dir) 2012, Playing Cards: Hearts (co-writer and dir), Needles and Opium (second adaptation) (dir) 2013, 887 (writer, dir and actor) 2015, Quills (actor) 2016, Frame by Frame (dir) 2018, Coriolanus (dir and set designer) 2018, SLĀV (dir and design) 2018, Kanata (co-writer and dir) 2018, The Seven Streams of the River Ota (second adaptation) (writer and dir) 2019. *Publications:* Connecting Flights 1995; (in French): La Trilogie des Dragons 2005, Le Projet Andersen 2007, La Face cachée de la Lune 2007, Chantiers d'écriture scénique 2007, The Image Mill 2008, The Blue Dragon 2011, Le Rossignol, Renard et autres fables 2011, 887 2016. *Address:* 103 Dalhousie, Quebec City, PQ G1K 4B9, Canada (office). *Telephone:* (418) 692-0055 (home). *Fax:* (418) 692-2390 (office). *E-mail:* rli@exmachina.ca (office). *Website:* www.lacaserne.net (office).

LEPAON, Thierry; French trade union official; *President, Agence Nationale de Lutte contre l'Illettrisme;* b. 31 Jan. 1960, Caen (Calvados); entered work force aged 17; worked as welder at factory, Caterpillar Inc., near Caen; employed at Spie Batignolles (metallurgical co.), Caen region –1983; worked for Moulinex SA, Cormelles-le-Royal from 1983; joined Confédération Générale du Travail (CGT, trade union), elected to Exec. Cttee of Fed. of CGT Metalworkers 1986–90, Sec. of CGT union in Caen 1990–2001, Gen. Sec., Calvados Departmental Union 2001–06, elected to Exec. Cttee of Cen. Trade Union Part of CGT Fed. of Metallurgy 2006–08, apptd by CGT to Conseil d'orientation pour l'emploi est. under Prime Minister 2006–11, Regional Head of CGT for Basse-Normandie 2008–12, also led del. of CGT in negotiations for the reform of vocational training 2008, Sec.-Gen., CGT 2013–15; Pres., Agence Nationale de Lutte contre l'Illettrisme (Nat. Agency for the Fight against Illiteracy) 2016–. *Publication:* La vie continue 2015. *E-mail:* sec.president@anlci.fr (office). *Website:* www.anlci.gouv.fr (office).

LERNER, Randolph (Randy) David, LLB; American lawyer and business executive; b. 21 Feb. 1962, Brooklyn, NY; s. of Alfred Lerner and Nancy Wolkoff; ed Columbia Coll., Clare Coll., Cambridge, UK, Columbia Univ. Law School; mem. New York and DC Bar Asscns; began career as Investment Analyst, Progressive Corpn; Founder and Man.-Dir Securities Advisors Inc. 1991–2001; apptd Dir MBNA Corpn 1993, Chair. 2002–06, involved in its sale to Bank of America 2006, also Dir MBNA America Bank 1993–2006; Chair. New York Acad. of Arts 1998–2003; Owner Cleveland Browns Football Club, Nat. Football League (NFL) 2002–12, mem. NFL Business Ventures Cttee; Owner/Chair. Aston Villa Football Club, Premier League, UK 2006–14; Trustee, Hosp. for Special Surgery, New York City 1996–; fmr Trustee, Corcoran Museum, Washington, DC. *Address:* Aston Villa Football Club, Villa Park, Birmingham, B6 6HE, England (office). *Telephone:* (121) 327-2299 (office). *Fax:* (121) 322-2107 (office). *E-mail:* info@avfc.co.uk (office). *Website:* www.avfc.co.uk (office).

LERNER, Richard A., BS, MD, PhD; American chemist and academic; *Lita Annenberg Hazen Professor of Immunochemistry, Institute Professor and Professor, Department of Cell and Molecular Biology, Scripps Research Institute;* b. 28 Aug. 1938, Chicago, Ill.; m. 1st Diana Pickett; two s. one d.; m. 2nd Nicola Green 1981; ed Northwestern Univ., Stanford Medical School; fmr intern, Palo Alto Stanford Hosp.; Postdoctoral Research Fellow, Scripps Clinic and Research Foundation, later Chair., Dept of Molecular Biology, Scripps Research Inst. 1982–86, Pres. Scripps Research Inst. 1986–2012, also Lita Annenberg Hazen Prof. of Immunochemistry, Inst. Prof. and fmr Cecil H. and Ida M. Green Chair. in Chem., mem. Skaggs Inst. for Chemical Biology 1996–; Staff mem., Wistar Inst., Phila 1970–; mem. Scientific Advisory Bd, Dyadic Group 2004–, Senomyx; mem. Scientific Policy Advisory Cttee, Uppsala Univ., Sweden 1991; mem. Scientific Advisory Bd, Econ. Devt Bd, Singapore 1991; mem. ETH Inst. of Biotechnology Advisory Bd, Zurich, Switzerland 1994; mem. Stanford Linear Accelerator Center Scientific Policy Cttee, Stanford, Calif. 1995–98; mem. Center for Nanoscale Science and Tech. Scientific Advisory Bd 1996; mem. Bd of Dirs, Calif. Council on Science and Tech. 1996–97; mem. Advisory Steering Group for Chem., Calif. State Univ. 1996; mem. Academic Cttee, Bd of Govs, Technion Israel Inst. of Tech., Haifa, Israel 1998; Sr Contributing Ed. PNAS, Chem. and Biology, Bioorganic and Medicinal Chem., Molecular Medicine, Catalysis Technology, Angewandte

Chemie; mem. Editorial Bd Journal of Virology, Molecular Biology and Medicine, Vaccine, Bioorganic and Medicinal Chemistry Letters, Drug Targeting and Delivery, Bioorganic and Medicinal Chemistry, Molecular Medicine, Catalysis Technology, Angewandte Chemie; mem. Advisory Bd Chemical and Engineering News 1994–96; mem. NAS 1991, American Acad. of Arts and Sciences 2000, American Soc. for Experimental Pathology, American Soc. of Microbiology, New York Acad. of Sciences, Biophysical Soc., Pluto Soc.; Foreign mem. Royal Swedish Acad. of Sciences 1985; AAAS Fellow 2005; Trustee, Neurosciences Research Foundation, Inc. 1992–; Distinguished Visiting Scientist, IBM T.J. Watson Research Center, NY 2006; Hon. DSc (Technion Israel Inst. of Tech.) 2001, (Northwestern Univ.) 2002, (Oxford) 2006; Hon. DHumLitt (Florida Atlantic Univ.) 2004; Dr hc (Ben-Gurion Univ. of the Negev, Israel) 2004; Parke Davis Award 1978, John A. Muntz Memorial Prize 1990, San Marino Prize 1990, Arthur C. Cope Scholar Award 1991, Jeanette Piperno Memorial Award 1991, CIBA-GEIGY Drew Award in Biomedical Research 1992, Humboldt Research Award 1994, Wolf Prize in Chem. 1994, Calif. Scientist of the Year Award 1996, Coley Award for Distinguished Research in Basic and Tumor Immunology 1999, Univ. of Calif. Presidential Medal 2002, Scientist of the Year Award, ARCS Foundation, Inc. 2002, Paul Ehrlich and Ludwig Darmstaedter Prize, Frankfurt, Germany 2003, Pres.'s Medal, Univ. of California 2003, DART/NYU Biotechnology Achievement Award in Basic Biotechnology, New York 2005. *Address:* Scripps Research Institute, 10550 North Torrey Pines Road, La Jolla, CA 92037, USA (office). *Telephone:* (858) 784-8265 (office). *Fax:* (858) 784-9899 (office). *E-mail:* rlerner@scripps.edu (office). *Website:* www.scripps.edu/research/faculty/lerner (office); www.scripps.edu/lerner (office).

LERNMARK, Åke, PhD; Swedish/American medical scientist, biologist and academic; *Professor of Experimental Diabetes, Lund University;* b. 11 Aug. 1945, Stockholm; ed Univ. of Umeå; Instructor, Dept of Histology, Univ. of Umeå 1968–70, Research Assoc. 1970–73, Asst Prof. (Docent) of Histology 1973–79; Visiting Scientist, Dept of Biochemistry, Univ. of Chicago 1974–75, Visiting Asst Prof., Dept of Biochemistry and Univ. of Chicago Diabetes Research and Training Center 1977–78; Dir of Research, Hagedorn Research Lab., Gentofte, Denmark 1979–87; Robert H. Williams Prof. in Medicine, Dept of Medicine, Univ. of Washington, Seattle, Wash. 1988–92, 1995–2008, Adjunct Prof., Dept of Pathology 1991–93, Affiliate Prof., Dept of Medicine 1993–94, Adjunct Prof., Dept of Immunology 1995–2007, mem. Grad. Faculty 1997–; Prof. of Experimental Endocrinology, Dept of Molecular Medicine (Chair.), Karolinska Inst., Stockholm 1993–94, Adjunct Prof., Experimental Endocrinology, Dept of Molecular Medicine 1995–2001; Adjunct Prof. of Medical Cell Biology, Lund Univ., Malmö, Sweden 1984–89, Prof. in Diabetes Research, Malmö Gen. Hosp. (leave of absence) 1989–91, Adjunct Prof., Dept of Endocrinology 1998–2005, Adjunct Prof., Dept of Clinical Sciences 2006–08, Prof. of Experimental Diabetes, Dept of Clinical Sciences 2009–; C.C. Sturgis Visiting Prof., Univ. of Michigan Medical School 1985; Visiting Prof., Vrije Universiteit Brussel, Belgium 1990–2000; David Pyke Prof., King's Coll., London, UK 1994; Hillblom Visiting Prof., UCLA 2007; Enz Visiting Prof., Univ. of Kansas, Lawrence 2007; Assoc. Ed. Diabetologia 1989–94; Co-Ed.-in-Chief Hormone and Metabolic Research 1996–2003; mem. Editorial Bd Diabetes 1982–89, Diabetes Research 1984–89, Regional Immunology 1990–99, Diabetes Research and Clinical Practice 1989–2006, Diabetes Technology & Therapeutics 2000–06, Endocrine Reviews 2006–; mem. Editorial Advisory Bd Journal of Clinical Investigation 1998–2002; mem. Advisory Bd Autoimmunity 2002–; mem. Scandinavian Soc. for the Study of Diabetes 1969, European Asscn for the Study of Diabetes 1970 (Hon. Sec. 1986–88), American Diabetes Asscn 1979, AAAS 1980, Danish Acad. of Natural Sciences 1981, Bd Swedish Endocrine Soc. 1986–89, Immunology and Diabetes Workshops 1988–91 (Chair. 1989–91), Juvenile Diabetes Foundation International 1992, Immunology of Diabetes Soc. 1996 (Pres. 1996–98), Asscn of American Immunologists 2001, Royal Physiographic Soc. in Lund 2002; Fellow, American Coll. of Physicians 2008; CIBA Fellow, Swedish Soc. of Endocrinology 1974, C.G. Bergstrand Lecturer, Swedish Pediatric Soc. 1982, Minkowski Award, European Asscn for the Study of Diabetes 1984, David Rumbough Award, Juvenile Diabetes Foundation International 1985, Kellion Medal, Australian Diabetes Foundation 1985, Paul E. Lacy Award, Nat. Diabetes Research Interchange 1985, E.F.F. Copp Lecturer, California Metabolic Research Foundation and Los Angeles Co. Medical Asscn 1986, Nordisk Lecturer, McGill Univ. 1986, Pehr Dubb Lecturer, Göteborgs Läkaresällskap 1986, Jacob E. Poulsen Grant, Scandinavian Soc. for the Study of Diabetes 1991, Arnold Lazarow Memorial Lecturer, Univ. of Minnesota 1993, API-Novo Nordisk Lecturer, Madras, India 1995, Kroc Lecturer, Baylor Coll., Houston, Tex. 1996, Dorothy Hodgkin Lecturer, British Diabetes Asscn 1998, John K. Davidson Diabetes Lectureship, Emory Univ., Atlanta, Ga 1999, Hamdan Award for Medical Science Excellence, Dubai, UAE 2002, J. Allyn Taylor Int. Prize in Medicine 2002, Langerhans-Virchow Lecturer, Pacific Northwest Research Inst., Seattle, Wash. 2006. *Publications:* 50 book chapters and more than 400 articles in peer-reviewed journals on genetic causes of diabetes. *Address:* Department of Clinical Sciences, Lund University, CRC, Entrance 72, 20502 Malmö, Sweden (office). *Telephone:* (40) 391901 (office); 70-6164779 (mobile). *Fax:* (40) 337042 (office). *E-mail:* ake .lernmark@med.lu.se (office). *Website:* www.lu.se/lucat/user/endo-ale (office).

LEROI, Armand Marie, BSc, PhD; Dutch evolutionary biologist; *Professor of Evolutionary Developmental Biology, Department of Life Sciences, Imperial College London;* b. 16 July 1964, Wellington, New Zealand; ed Dalhousie Univ., Canada, Univ. of California, Irvine, USA; postdoctoral work at Albert Einstein Coll. of Medicine, New York; Lecturer, Department of Life Sciences, Imperial Coll. London 1996–2001, apptd Reader in Evolutionary Developmental Biology 2001, currently Prof. of Evolutionary Developmental Biology. *Television:* Mutants (three-part series, Channel 4) 2004, Alien Worlds (Channel 4) 2005, What Makes Us Human (Channel 4) 2006, What Darwin Didn't Know (documentary) (BBC 4) 2009, Aristotle's Lagoon (documentary) (BBC 4) 2010. *Publications include:* Mutants: On the Form, Varieties and Errors of the Human Body (Guardian First Book Award 2004) 2003, The Lagoon: How Aristotle Invented Science 2014; contrib. to London Review of Books; numerous research papers. *Address:* Department of Life Sciences, Division of Ecology and Evolutionary Biology, Imperial College London, South Kensington Campus, London, SW7 2AZ, England. *Telephone:* (20) 7589-5111 (office). *E-mail:* a.leroi@imperial.ac.uk (office). *Website:* www.imperial.ac.uk/people/a.leroi (office); www.armandmarieleroi.com.

LEROY, Maurice; French economist and politician; *President, Departmental Council of Loir-et-Cher;* b. 2 Feb. 1959, Paris; m.; three c.; Head of Cabinet for Mayor of Orly 1982–84; Sec. Gen., Communist Group in Senate 1984–90; Mayor of Poislay 1989–2001; Head of Cabinet of Pres., Val-de-Marne Gen. Council 1990–91; Head of Cabinet of Mayor of Nanterre, then of Mayor of Colombes 1991–93; Chargé de Mission for Charles Pasqua (Minister of State) 1993–97; Gen. Councillor, canton of Droué 1994–; Chargé de Mission of Éric Raoult, responsible for Urban Affairs 1995–97; mem. Assemblée nationale (Parl.) for Vendôme 1997–2010, Vice Pres. Assemblée nationale 2009–10; Pres. Loir-et-Cher Departmental Council 2004–; Vice-Pres. Union des conseillers généraux de France 1998–2001, Pres. 2001–08; mem. Nouveau Centre (Nouveau Centre), also Spokesman; Minister of Urban Affairs 2010–12; Vice-Pres. Assemblée des départements de France 2015. *Address:* Conseil départemental de Loir-et-Cher, Place de la République, 41020 Blois Cedex, France (office). *Telephone:* (2) 54-58-41-41 (office). *Fax:* (2) 54-58-42-13 (office). *E-mail:* mleroy.depute@wanadoo.fr (office). *Website:* www.le-loir-et-cher.fr (office).

LEŞ, Gabriel-Beniamin, MA; Romanian politician; *Minister of National Defence;* b. 23 Dec. 1975, Satu Mare; m.; three c.; ed Univ. de Vest Timişoara, Univ. de Vest "Vasile Goldiş", Arad, Nat. Defence Coll.; Assoc., SC Expert Design SRL, Satu Mare 1990–2010; Designer, SC Tipo-les SRL, Satu-Mare 1994–2000; Municipal Councillor, Satu Mare 2000–04, Vice-Mayor of Satu Mare 2004–08; Prefect, Satu Mare Prefecture 2009; Advisor on European projects, Racşa Village, Satu Mare 2010–13; CEO, Agency for Payments and Intervention in Agriculture, Satu Mare County 2013–15; Sec. of State, Armaments Dept, Ministry of Defence 2015–16; mem. Senatul (upper house of parl.) for Satu Mare 2016–; Minister of Nat. Defence Jan.–June 2017, 2018–; mem. Partidul Social Democrat (PSD, Social Democratic Party) 2003–, Head of Education, Youth and Social Dept, Satu Mare PSD Br. 2005–07, Dir election campaign for European elections, Satu Mare PSD Br. 2007, mem. PSD Nat. Council 2007–09. *Address:* Ministry of National Defence, 050561 Bucharest 5, Str. Izvor 110 (office); Partidul Social Democrat, 011346 Bucharest 1, Şos. Kiseleff 10, Romania (office). *Telephone:* (21) 4104040 (office); (31) 4135147 (PSD) (office). *Fax:* (21) 3195689 (office); (21) 2223171 (PSD) (office). *E-mail:* secretariat_general@mapn.ro (office); psd@psd.ro (office). *Website:* www.mapn.ro (office); www.psd.ro (office).

LESAR, David J., BS, MBA; American business executive; *Executive Chairman of the Board, Halliburton Company;* b. 1954, Madison, Wis.; ed Univ. of Wisconsin-Madison; Partner and Commercial Group Dir, Arthur Anderson Co., Dallas, Tex. –1993; Exec. Vice-Pres. Finance and Admin, Halliburton Energy Services 1993–95, Exec. Vice-Pres. and Chief Financial Officer, Halliburton Co. 1995–96, Pres. and Chief Operating Officer 1997–2000, Chair., Pres. and CEO 2000–17, Exec. Chair. of the Bd 2017–; Pres. and CEO Brown & Root Inc. 1996–97; mem. Bd of Dirs Lyondell Chemical Co. 2000–07, Mirant Corpn Agrium, Inc. 2010–15; mem. Upstream Cttee, American Petroleum Inst., Bd of Dirs American Iranian Council. *Address:* Halliburton Company, 3000 North Sam Houston Parkway East, Houston, TX 77032, USA (office). *Telephone:* (281) 871-4000 (office). *E-mail:* info@halliburton.com (office). *Website:* www.halliburton.com (office).

LESCHLY, Jan, BSc, MSc; Danish business executive and fmr professional tennis player; *Partner and Chairman, Care Capital, LLC;* b. 11 Sept. 1940; m. Lotte Enngelbred 1963; four s.; ed Copenhagen Coll. of Pharmacy, Copenhagen School of Econ. and Business Admin, Princeton Univ., USA; tour tennis professional 1960s and early 1970s, participated in nine Wimbledon Championships 1959–71, best result reaching fourth round of singles event and quarterfinals of doubles with Jorgen Ulrich 1966, reached semifinals of US Open 1967; ranked World No. 10 for 1967 by Lance Tingay of The Daily Telegraph; Novo Industries A/S 1972–79; Vice-Pres. Commercial Devt, Squibb Corpn 1979, US Pres. 1981, Group Vice-Pres. and Dir 1984, Exec. Vice-Pres. 1986, Pres. and COO 1988–90; Chair. SmithKline Beecham Pharmaceuticals 1990, CEO 1994–2000; Founding Partner and Chair. Care Capital LLC 2000–; Chair. Epigenesis Pharmaceuticals, LLC; Dir, Dampskibsselskabet AF 1912 AS, Inotek Pharmaceuticals Corpn, LifeTecNet, Vaxart, Squibb Corpn 1984–90, SmithKline Beecham Ltd 1990, Inc., American Express Co. 1997–2013, CBS Corpn 1998, A.P. Møller – Mærsk A/S (fmrly Dampskibsselskabet Svendborg A/S) 2000–, APM-Maersk Group, Viacom 2000–, D-pharm Ltd 2001–, Dynavax Technologies Corpn 2004–06; mem. Int. Advisory Bd DaimlerChrysler AG, Emory Univ. Goizueta Business School Dean's Advisory Council; mem. pharmaceutical asscns and educational bodies; Chair. Int. Tennis Hall of Fame. *Address:* Care Capital LLC, 47 Hulfish Street, Suite 310, Princeton, NJ 08542, USA. *Telephone:* (609) 683-8300. *Fax:* (609) 683-5787. *E-mail:* info@carecapital.com. *Website:* www.carecapital.com.

LESCURE, Pierre François Amar; French business executive and actor; *President, Cannes Film Festival;* b. 2 July 1945, Paris; s. of François Lescure and Paulette Baudoin; m. Frédérique Fayles-Bernstein 1996; ed Lycée Turgot, Paris, Centre de formation des journalistes; reporter and newsreader, Radio Télé Luxembourg 1965–68; with Radio Caroline and Radio Monte Carlo 1968–72; newsreader and presenter, Office de radiodiffusion télévision française (ORTF) 1973–77, Deputy Ed., weekend programmes 1977–80, Dir Programmes Europe 1 1980–81; Ed.-in-Chief Antenne 2 1982–84, Head of Programmes 1984–86; Dir-Gen. Canal+ 1986–94, Chair. and Man. Dir 1994–2000, Chair. 2000–02; Chair. Canal Jimmy 1991–2002; Chair. and Man. Dir Paris Saint-Germain Football SA 1994–, Le Studio Canal+ 1991–2002, Le Monde Presse 1994–; Chair. UGCDA (audiovisual rights co.) 1997–, CanalPro 1997–2002, Multithématiques 2001–; Deputy Chair. Exec. Cttee Havas 1997–; Co-CEO Vivendi Universal 2000–02; Dir and mem. Strategic Cttee, Havas Group 1993–; mem. Advisory Bd, Lagardère Group 2000–; mem. Bd Dirs, Kudelski Group 2004–; Pres. of the Jury, American Film Festival, Deauville 2002, mem. Bd 2013–; Producer and Dir of Operations, Marigny Theatre 2008–; Perm. mem. of the jury, Prix des prix littéraires 2011–; Pres. Cannes Film Festival 2014–; Chevalier, Ordre nat. du Mérite, Officier des Arts et Lettres; Homme de la décennie de la télévision, CB News 1996, Manager of the Year, le Nouvel économiste 1996, Le Laurier d'Or d'honneur de la télévision 2014 and other awards. *Films include:* 5% de risques (voice) 1980, Le quart d'heure américain 1982, La Cité de la peur 1994, Mon petit doigt m'a dit… 2005, Le Grand appartement 2006, Musée haut, musée bas 2009. *Television includes:* 24½ (presenter) 2003, Graffiti 60 (mini-series) (presenter and screenplay) 2004, Graffiti 70 2005, Ça balance in Paris (Paris Première) 2006–10, Master classe (France 4)

2012. *Publications:* A nous la radio, In the baba (memoir) 2012. *Address:* Association française du festival international du film, 3 rue Amélie, 75007 Paris, France (office). *Telephone:* 1-53-59-61-00 (office). *Fax:* 1-53-59-61-10 (office). *E-mail:* info@festival-cannes.fr (office). *Website:* www.festival-cannes.fr (office); www.festival-cannes.org (office).

LESIN, Mikhail Yuryevich; Russian politician, journalist and media executive; *Director General, JSC Gazprom-Media Holding;* b. 11 July 1958, Moscow; m.; one s.; ed Kuibyshev Construction Eng Inst., Moscow; fmr eng constructor; organised commercial programmes for the KVN humour competitions from 1987; f. Igrotechnika (later Intelleks) Co-operative 1989–91; Founder and Chair. Video International (advertising co.) 1990–94; Minister of Antiquities for Russian Museum of Ethnography 1993–95; mem. of staff, RIA Novosti, Dir-Gen. Novosti-TV Co. 1993–96; Head of Dept of Public Relations, Russian Presidency 1996–97 (resgnd); First Deputy Chair. All-Russian State TV Co. 1997–99; Minister of Press, TV, Broadcasting and Telecommunications (subsequently the Press, Broadcasting and Mass Media) 1999–2004; credited as the creator of the RT television news network (previously known as Russia Today) "to establish a news channel that would counter CNN and BBC– with a Moscow spin"; Adviser to the Pres. of the Russian Fed. 2004–09; Dir Gen. JSC Gazprom-Media Holding 2013–; mem. Bd of Dirs Pervyi Kanal 2004–10, National Telecommunications 2010–12; Order 'For Service to the Motherland', IV Degree; Hon. Diploma of the Pres. of the Russian Fed. *Address:* OAO Gazprom-Media Holding, Krasnopresnenskaya nab. 12, CMT-2, 123610 Moscow, Russia (office). *Telephone:* (495) 789-65-00 (office). *Fax:* (495) 981-29-55 (office). *E-mail:* info@gazprom-media.com (office). *Website:* www .gazprom-media.com (office).

LESJAK, Catherine A. (Cathie), BS, MBA; American business executive; *Executive Vice-President and Chief Financial Officer, Hewlett Packard Company;* b. 1959; m.; ed Stanford Univ., Univ. of California, Berkeley; joined Hewlett Packard Co. 1986, Controller and Credit Man., Commercial Customer Org. 2000–02, Vice-Pres. of Finance for Enterprise Marketing and Solutions and Vice-Pres. of Finance for Software Global Business Unit 2002–03, Group Controller, Software Solutions Org. and Sr Vice-Pres. 2003–06, Treas. 2003–07, Exec. Vice-Pres. and Chief Financial Officer (CFO) 2007–Aug. 2010, Oct. 2010–, Interim CEO and CFO Aug.–Oct. 2010. *Address:* Hewlett Packard Company, 3000 Hanover Street, Palo Alto, CA 94304-1185, USA (office). *Telephone:* (650) 857-1501 (office). *Fax:* (650) 857-5518 (office). *Website:* www.hp.com (office).

LESNIC, Cristina, LLD, PhD; Moldovan politician; *Deputy Prime Minister;* b. 28 March 1982, Chişinău, Moldovan SSR, USSR; ed Moldova State Univ.; long career with Ministry of Internal Affairs, including as Prin. Specialist, Directorate for Int. Cooperation 2004–10, Head of European Integration Section 2010–13, Chief of Gen. Directorate of Foreign Affairs and European Integration 2013–17, Head of Policy Analysis, Monitoring and Evaluation Div. 2017–18; Deputy Prime Minister, responsible for Reintegration 2017–. *Address:* Office of the Council of Ministers, 2033 Chişinău, Piaţa Marii Adunări Naţionale 1, Moldova (office). *Telephone:* (22) 25-01-01 (office). *Fax:* (22) 24-26-96 (office). *E-mail:* petitii@gov.md (office). *Website:* www.gov.md (office).

LESOURNE, Jacques François; French newspaper editor, economist and academic; *President, Futuribles International;* b. 26 Dec. 1928, La Rochelle; s. of André Lesourne and Simone Lesourne (née Guille); m. Odile Melin 1961; one s. two d.; ed Lycée Montaigne, Bordeaux, École Polytechnique, École Nationale Supérieure des Mines de Paris; Head Econ. Service of French Collieries 1954–57; Dir Gen., later Pres. METRA Int. and SEMA 1958–75; Prof. of Econs École des Mines de Saint-Étienne 1958–61; Prof. of Industrial Econs École Nationale Supérieure de la Statistique 1960–63; Pres. Asscn Française d'Informatique et de Recherche Operationnelle 1966–67; mem. Council Int. Inst. of Applied Systems Analysis, Vienna 1973–79, Inst. of Man. Science 1976–79; Prof. Conservatoire Nat. des Arts et Métiers 1974–; Dir Projet Interfuturs OECD 1976–79; Dir of Studies, Inst. Auguste Comte 1979–81; Pres. Comm. on Employment and Social Relations of 8th Plan 1979–81; mem. Comm. du Bilan 1981, Council European Econ. Asscn 1984–89; Pres. Asscn Française de Science Économique 1981–83, Int. Federation of Operational Research Socs 1986–89; Dir and Man. Ed. Le Monde 1991–94; Pres. Futuribles Int. 1993–, Centre for Study and Research on Qualifications 1996–; Bd mem. Acad. des Technologies; Officier, Légion d'honneur 1993, Commdr 2009, Commdr, Ordre nat. du Mérite, Officier des Palmes académiques. *Publications include:* Economic Technique and Industrial Management 1958, Du bon usage de l'étude économique dans l'entreprise 1966, Les systèmes du destin 1976, L'entreprise et ses futurs 1985, Éducation et société, L'après-Communisme, de l'Atlantique à l'Oural 1990, The Economics of Order and Disorder 1991, Vérités et mensonges sur le chômage 1995, Le Modèle français: Grandeur et Décadence 1998, Un Homme de notre Siècle 2000, Ces Avenirs qui n'ont pas eu lieu 2001, Leçons de Microéconomie évolutionniste (with André Orléan and Bernard Walliser) 2002, Democratie: Marché et Gouvernance, Quels Avenirs? 2004, Evolutionary Microeconomics (with André Orléan and Bernard Walliser) 2006, La recherche et l'innovation en France (with Denis Radet) 2007, 2008, 2009, Les crises et le XXIème siècle 2009, L'humanité face au changement climatique (with R. Dautray) 2009. *Leisure interest:* piano. *Address:* 52 rue de Vaugirard, 75006 Paris, France. *Telephone:* 1-43-25-66-05. *Fax:* 1-56-24-47-98. *E-mail:* jolesourne@wanadoo.fr. *Website:* www.futuribles.com.

LESSARD, Claude; Canadian business executive; *Chairman and CEO, Vision7 International;* b. 29 July 1949, Notre Dame du Portage; s. of Jean-Luc Lessard and Carmen Cerat; m. Marie Lortie 1971; three s.; ed Univ. Laval, Québec; joined Groupe Cossette Communication 1972, Chair. and CEO 1980–, also of Vision7 International (holding co.) 2010–; Dir Canam-Manac, Inst. de cardiologie de Québec, Opéra de Québec, Faculté des Sciences de l'Admin, Univ. Laval, Fondation Communautaire du Grand Québec, DiagnoCure Inc., Ronald McDonald Children's Charities of Canada, Faculté des sciences de l'admin at l'Université Laval; Co.-Chair. Canadian Congress of Advertising 1995; Hermes Prize (Univ. of Laval) 1984, Dimensions Prize 1987, 'Spiess' Bessies Award 1993, ACA Gold Medal 1994. *Leisure interests:* golf, skiing, riding. *Address:* Vision7 International, 300 St Paul Street, Suite 300, Québec, PQ, G1K 7R1, Canada (office). *Telephone:* (418) 647-2727 (office). *Fax:* (418) 647-2564 (office). *E-mail:* information@ v7international.com (office). *Website:* vision7international.com (office).

LESSELS, Norman, CBE, CA; British chartered accountant; b. 2 Sept. 1938, Edinburgh, Scotland; s. of John Clark Lessels and Gertrude Margaret Ellen Lessels (née Jack); m. 1st Gillian Durward Clark 1960 (died 1979); one s. (and one s. one d. deceased); m. 2nd Christine Stevenson Hitchman 1981; ed Melville Coll., Edin., Edin. Acad.; apprentice with Graham Smart & Annan, Edin. 1955–60, with Thomson McLintock & Co., London 1960–61; Pnr, Wallace & Somerville, Edin., subsequently merged with Whinney Murray & Co., latterly Ernst & Whinney 1962–80; Pnr, Chiene & Tait, CA 1980–93, Sr Pnr 1993–98; Dir (non-exec.) The Standard Life Assurance Co. 1978–2002 (Chair. 1988–98), Cairn Energy PLC 1988–2002 (Chair. 1995–2002), Bank of Scotland 1988–97, General Surety & Guarantee Co. Ltd 1988–97, Havelock Europa PLC –1998 (Chair. 1993–98), NWS Bank PLC 1989–97, Robert Wiseman Dairies PLC 1994–2003, Martin Currie Portfolio Investment Trust PLC 1999–2001; Pres. Inst. of Chartered Accountants of Scotland 1987–88; Chair. Tilney & Co. 1993–98. *Leisure interests:* golf, bridge, music. *Address:* 15 India Street, Edinburgh, EH3 6HA, Scotland (home).

LESSER, Richard (Rich), BS, MBA; American business executive; *President and CEO, Boston Consulting Group;* b. 1962; s. of Edward A. Lesser and Arlene Wagner; m. Gabrielle Del Sesto; three c.; ed Univ. of Michigan, Harvard Business School; worked in product devt, Procter & Gamble Co. 1983–86; joined Boston Consulting Group (BCG) as Consultant 1988, becoming Head, BCG New York Metro Office 2000–09, mem. Exec. Cttee 2006–, Chair., BCG North and South America 2009–12, Pres. and CEO, Boston Consulting Group 2013–; mem. World Econ. Forum Int. Business Council, US Business Roundtable. *Address:* Boston Consulting Group, 10 Hudson Yards, New York, NY 10001, USA (office). *Telephone:* (212) 446-2800 (office). *Website:* www.bcg.com (office).

LESSIG, Lawrence (Larry), BA, BS, MA, JD; American professor of law and institute director; *Professor of Law, Harvard Law School and Director, Edmond J. Safra Foundation Center for Ethics, Harvard University;* b. 3 June 1961, Rapid City, SDak; m. Bettina Neuefeind; two s. one d.; ed Univ. of Pennsylvania, Trinity Coll., Cambridge, UK, Yale Univ. Law School; grew up in Williamsport, Pa; active Teenage Republican, serving as Youth Gov. for Pennsylvania through YMCA Youth & Govt Program 1978; law clerk for Judge Richard Posner, 7th Circuit Court of Appeals, Chicago, Ill. 1989–90, for Justice Antonin Scalia, US Supreme Court, Washington, DC 1990–91; Asst Prof. of Law, Univ. of Chicago Law School 1991–95, Prof. of Law 1995–97; Visiting Prof. of Law, Yale Law School 1995; Fellow, Program on Ethics and the Professions, Harvard Univ. 1996–97, Visiting Prof. of Law, Harvard Law School 1997, Prof. of Law 1997–2000, Jack N. and Lillian R. Berkman Prof. for Entrepreneurial Legal Studies 1998, Prof. of Law and Dir Edmond J. Safra Foundation Center for Ethics, Harvard Univ. 2009–; joined Stanford Law School 2000, Co-Dir Center for Internet and Society 2000–, Wilson Faculty Scholar 2002, Prof. of Law 2000–02, John A. Wilson Distinguished Faculty Scholar 2003–05, C. Wendell and Edith M. Carlsmith Prof. of Law 2005–09; Lecturer in LLM programme for Eastern and Cen. European lawyers, Legal Studies Programme, CEU Budapest Coll., Budapest, Hungary 1992, 1993, 1995, Moscow 1994; Moderator, Constitutional Law Discussion Group, Lexis Counsel Connect, Miamisburg, Ohio 1994–95; Chair. Creative Commons, San Francisco 2001–07, mem. Bd 2007–; mem. Bd of Dirs Public Library of Science, San Francisco 2003–07; mem. Bd Red Hat Center for the Public Domain, Durham, NC 2000–01, Electronic Frontier Foundation, San Francisco 2002–07, Public Knowledge, Washington, DC 2002–07, Free Software Foundation, Cambridge, Mass 2004–07, Software Freedom Law Center, New York 2005–08, iCommons, London, UK 2005–, Brave New Films Foundation, Los Angeles 2007–08 (Chair. 2008–), Free Press, Washington, DC 2007–09, Change Congress, San Francisco 2008–, American Acad. in Berlin, Germany 2008–, MAPLight.org, Berkeley, Calif. 2008–, Freedom House, Washington, DC 2008–; mem. Editorial Advisory Bd Lexis-Nexis Electronic Authors Press 1995–97; mem. Advisory Bd LifeJournal, San Francisco 2008–09, Sunlight Foundation, Washington, DC 2008–, Journal of Academic Legal Studies 2008–; Comm. mem. Pennsylvania Nat. Comm. on Soc., Culture and Community, Philadelphia 1997–98; columnist, The Industry Standard, San Francisco 1998–2001, Red Herring 2002–03, CIO Insight, New York 2002–03, Wired Magazine 2003–07; Fellow, Wissenschaftskolleg zu Berlin 1999–2000, Business Law Center, Tokyo Univ., Japan 2002, American Acad. in Berlin 2007–08, American Acad. of Arts and Sciences 2006, American Philosophical Soc. 2007; announced candidacy for Democratic nomination for US Pres. 2015; Dr hc (Amsterdam) 2010; hon. degrees from Athabasca Univ., Georgian-American Univ.; Award for the Advancement of Free Software, Free Software Foundation 2003, National Law Journal 100 Most Influential Lawyers in America 2000, 2006, BusinessWeek 25 Top eBiz Leaders 2000, 2001, World Technology Award for Law 2001, 2009, named as one of Scientific American's Top 50 Visionaries 2002, Editors' Choice, Best Non-Technical Book, Linux Journal 2002, Monaco Media Prize 2008. *Achievements include:* a proponent of reduced legal restrictions on copyright, trademark and radio frequency spectrum, particularly in technology applications; has served as lead counsel in several key cases marking boundaries of copyright law in digital age, including Eldred v. Ashcroft, a challenge to the 1998 Sonny Bono Copyright Term Extension Act, and Golan v. Holder. *Publications:* Code and Other Laws of Cyberspace 2000, The Future of Ideas: The Fate of the Commons in a Connected World 2001, Free Culture: The Nature and Future of Creativity 2004, Code: Version 2.0 2006, Remix: Making Art and Commerce Thrive in the Hybrid Economy 2008; numerous articles in professional journals. *Address:* Edmond J. Safra Center for Ethics, Harvard University, Areeda 235, 124 Mount Auburn Street, Suite 520N, Cambridge, MA 02138 (office); 20 Amory Street, Brookline, MA 02446, USA. *Telephone:* (617) 496-8853 (office); (617) 487-5307. *Fax:* (617) 496-6104 (office). *E-mail:* sgray@law.harvard.edu (office); ethics@harvard.edu (office). *Website:* www.ethics.harvard.edu (office); www.lessig.org.

LESTER, Adrian Anthony, OBE; British actor; b. 14 Aug. 1968, Birmingham; m. Lolita Chakrabarti; two d.; ed Royal Acad. of Dramatic Art; mem. Council, Royal Acad. of Dramatic Art, Artistic Bd Royal Nat. Theatre; Amb., The Prince's Foundation for Children and the Arts; Time Out Award 1992, Olivier Award 1996, Carlton Theatre Award 2001. *Theatre appearances include:* Cory in Fences, Garrick 1990, Paul Poitier in Six Degrees of Separation (Time Out Award), Royal Court and Comedy Theatre 1992, Anthony Hope in Sweeney Todd, Royal Nat. Theatre 1994, Rosalind in As You Like It (Time Out Award), Albery and Bouffes du Nord 1995, Company (Olivier Award), Albery and Donmar 1996, Hamlet, Bouffes du Nord and Young Vic 2001, Henry V, Royal Nat. Theatre 2003, Brick, Cat on a

Hot Tin Roof, Novello, Red Velvet, Tricycle Theatre, Othello, Royal Nat. Theatre. *Films include:* Les Soeurs Soleil 1997, Primary Colors 1997, Storm Damage, Love's Labour's Lost 2000, Best 2000, Maybe Baby 2000, Born Romantic 2000, Dust 2001, The Final Curtain 2002, The Day After Tomorrow 2004, As You Like It 2006, Scenes of a Sexual Nature 2006, Starting Out in the Evening 2007, The Key (video) 2007, Doomsday 2008, Case 39 2009, All is by My Side 2013. *Radio:* The Making of Slavery (BBC Radio 4) 2007. *Television includes:* The Affair 1995, Company 1996, Storm Damage 1998, Jason and the Argonauts 2000, The Tragedy of Hamlet 2002, Girlfriends (episodes) 2002–03, Hustle (as Mickey Stone) 2004–12, Afterlife (episode) 2005, The Ghost Squad (episode) 2005, Beyond (film) 2006, Empire's Children (film) 2007, Ballet Shoes (film) 2007 Being Human (series) 2008, Bonekickers (series) 2008, Merlin (series) 2009, Sleep with Me (film) 2009, Robot Chicken (series) 2013. *Leisure interests:* Tae Kwon Do (Black Belt 2nd Dan), music. *Address:* c/o Tina Price Consultants, Bay Tree House, Haywards Lane, Child Okeford, Dorset, DT11 8DX (office); c/o Artists Rights Group (ARG), 4 Great Portland Street, London, W1W 8PA, England (office). *Telephone:* (1258) 861221 (Tina Price) (office); (20) 7436-6400 (ARG) (office). *Fax:* (20) 7436-6700 (ARG) (office). *E-mail:* tina@tinapriceconsultants.com (office); latimer@argtalent.com (office). *Website:* www.argtalent.com (office).

LESTER, Richard; American film director and producer; b. 19 Jan. 1932, Philadelphia, Pa; s. of Elliott Lester and Ella Young; m. Deirdre V. Smith 1956; one s. one d.; ed William Penn Charter School, Univ. of Pennsylvania; TV Dir, CBS 1952–54, ITV 1955–59; composer 1954–57; film director 1959–; Grand Prix, Cannes Festival 1965, Best Dir, Rio de Janeiro Festival 1966, Gandhi Peace Prize, Berlin Festival 1969, Best Dir, Tehran Festival 1974, MTV Video Vanguard Award 1994. *Films directed:* The Running, Jumping and Standing Still Film 1959, It's Trad, Dad 1962, The Mouse on the Moon 1963, A Hard Day's Night 1963 (re-release 2000), The Knack 1965, Help! 1965, A Funny Thing Happened on the Way to the Forum 1966, How I Won the War 1967, Petulia 1969, The Bed Sitting Room 1969 (also producer), The Three Musketeers 1973, Juggernaut 1974, The Four Musketeers 1974, Royal Flash 1975, Robin and Marian 1976, The Ritz 1976, Butch and Sundance: The Early Days 1979, Cuba 1979, Superman II 1980, Superman III 1983, Finders Keepers 1984, The Return of the Musketeers 1989, Get Back (documentary) 1991. *Television includes:* as dir and producer: Son of Fred 1956, A Show Called Fred 1956, After Hours 1958, Room at the Bottom 1964. *Leisure interests:* tennis, music.

LESTER OF HERNE HILL, Baron (Life Peer), cr. 1993, of Herne Hill in the London Borough of Southwark; **Anthony Paul Lester,** QC, BA, LLM; British barrister; b. 3 July 1936, London, England; s. of Harry Lester and Kate Lester; m. Catherine Elizabeth Debora Wassey 1971; one s. one d.; ed City of London School, Trinity Coll. Cambridge, Harvard Law School; called to the Bar, Lincoln's Inn 1963, Bencher 1985; Special Adviser to Home Sec. 1974–76; QC 1975; Special Adviser to Northern Ireland Standing Advisory Comm. on Human Rights 1975–77; Recorder, South-Eastern Circuit 1987–93; Hon. Visiting Prof., Univ. Coll. London 1983–; mem. Bd of Dirs Salzburg Seminar 1996–2000; mem. Bd of Overseers, Univ. of Pa Law School 1977–90, Council of Justice; mem. Court of Govs, LSE 1980–94; Pres. Interights 1983–; UK legal expert EEC Comm. Network Cttee on Equal Pay and Sex Discrimination 1983–93; mem. House of Lords Select Cttee on European Communities Sub-cttee E (Law and Insts) 2000–Jan. 2004, rejoined Dec. 2004, Sub cttee on 1996 Inter-Governmental Conf., Sub-cttee F (Social Affairs, Educ. and Home Affairs) 1996–2000; Co-Chair. of Bd European Roma Rights Centre, Budapest 1999–2001; Gov. British Inst. of Human Rights; Chair. Bd of Govs, James Allen's Girls' School 1987–93; Chair. Runnymede Trust 1990–93; mem. Advisory Cttee Centre for Public Law, Univ. of Cambridge 1999–, Int. Advisory Bd, Open Soc. Inst. Justice Initiative 2000–, Parl. Jt Human Rights Comm. 2001–04, 2005–; Vice-Chair. All-Party Parl. Group on Genocide Prevention 2005–; Ind. Adviser to Justice Sec. on Constitutional Reform 2007–08; Patron, Family Planning Asscn; Foreign Hon. mem. American Acad. of Arts and Sciences 2002, Foreign mem. American Philosophical Soc. 2003; Hon. Adjunct Prof. of Law, Univ. Coll. London 2007; Chevalier de l'Ordre de la Légion d'Honneur 2009; hon. degrees/fellowships from Open Univ., Univ. Coll., London Univ., Ulster Univ., South Bank Univ., Stirling Univ.; Liberty Human Rights Lawyer of the Year 1997, Liberty and Justice Judges Award for Lifetime Achievement 2007. *Publications:* Justice in the American South (Amnesty International) 1964, Race and Law (co-author) 1972, Five Ideas to Fight For: How Our Freedom is Under Threat and Why it Matters 2016; Ed.-in-Chief Butterworths Human Rights Cases; Consultant Ed. and Contrib. Halsbury's Laws of England Title Constitutional Law and Human Rights (4th edn 1996), Human Rights Law and Practice (co-ed.) 1999 (3rd edn 2009), and articles on race relations, public affairs and int. law. *Leisure interests:* painting, walking. *Address:* Blackstone Chambers, Blackstone House, Temple, London, EC4Y 9BW, England (office). *Telephone:* (20) 7583-1770 (office). *E-mail:* anthonylester@blackstonechambers.com (office). *Website:* www.blackstonechambers.com (office).

LETERME, Yves Camille Désiré, LLB, BSc, LLM, MPA; Belgian politician and international organization official; *Secretary-General, International Institute for Democracy and Electoral Assistance (International IDEA);* b. 6 Oct. 1960, Wervik, West Flanders; two s. one d.; ed Catholic Univ. of Leuven, Ghent Univ.; served as auditor at Court of Auditors (Rekenhof/Cour des Comptes); Deputy Sec.-Gen., then Sec.-Gen. CVP, resgnd to become civil servant with EU, indefinite leave 1997, apptd mem. Belgian Parl. (House of Reps) 1997–, elected 1999, 2003; mem. City Council of Ypres 1995–2016, Alderman of Ypres 1995–2001; Chair. Christen-Democratisch en Vlaams (Christian Democratic and Flemish party—CD&V) 2003–04; Minister-Pres. of Flanders 2004–07; fmr Flemish Minister of Agric. and Fisheries; fmr Deputy Prime Minister and Minister of Budget, Institutional Reforms, Transport and the North Sea in Belgian Fed. Govt; Prime Minister of Belgium March–Dec. 2008, 2009–11; Minister of Foreign Affairs July–Nov. 2009; Deputy Sec. Gen., OECD 2011–14; Sec.-Gen. Int. Inst. for Democracy and Electoral Assistance (International IDEA) 2014–; Dir TeleColumbus AG; Chief Investigator, Financial Fair Play (UEFA); Vice-Chair. Cttee on Electoral Integrity in the Digital Age, Kofi Annan Foundation; Co-Chair. ToJoy Group; mem. Global Sustainability Council, Volkswagen Group AG; hon. lifetime title of Minister of State for Belgium. *Address:* International Institute for Democracy and Electoral Assistance (International IDEA), Strömsborg, 103 34 Stockholm, Sweden (office); Kapelstraat 109/502, 8450 Bredene, Belgium (home). *Telephone:* 46-704293701 (mobile) (office). *E-mail:* y.leterme@idea.int (office). *Website:* www.idea.int (office).

LETH, Jørgen; Danish filmmaker and writer; b. 14 June 1937, Århus; one d. three s.; has also written, produced, edited, filmed, designed production for and acted in many of his own films; cycling commentator, Tour de France on Danish TV2; Thomas Mann Award 1972, Danish Acad. Special Prize 1983, Paul Hammerich Award 1992, Robert Award, Danish Film Acad. 1996, 2000, Prix de France 1997, Danish State Art Foundation Special Award 1999, Grand Prix for Best Feature, Odense Int. Film Festival 2004, Grand Prix for Best Feature Film, Odense Int. Film Festival 2004. *Films include:* as Dir (English titles): Stop for Bud 1963, Look Forward to a Time of Security 1964, The Perfect Human 1967, Ophelia's Flowers 1968, Near Heaven, Near Earth, 1968, Jens Otto Krag 1969, The Deer Garden 1969, Without Kin 1970, Teatret i de grønne bjerge 1970, Motional Picture 1970, The Search 1970, Life in Denmark 1971, Chinese Ping-Pong 1972, Eddy Merckx in the Vicinity of a Cup of Coffee (TV) 1973, The Impossible Hour 1974, Stars and the Water Carriers 1974, Klaus Rifbjerg 1974, The Good and the Bad 1975, Sunday in Hell 1976, Peter Martins: A Dancer 1978, A Midsummer's Play (TV) 1979, Kalule 1979, At danse Bournonville 1979, Step on Silence 1982, 66 Scenes from America 1982, Haiti Express 1983, Pelota 1984, Notebook from China 1986, Moments of Play 1986, Composer Meets Quarter 1987, Notes on Love 1989, Dansk litteratur 1989, Traberg 1992, Michael Laudrup: A Football Player 1993, Haiti, Untitled 1996, I Am Alive 1999, Dreamers 2002, New Scenes from America 2003, The Five Obstructions 2003, Aarhus 2005, Erotic Man 2010, I Am Talking To You 2013, Pelota II 2015. *Publications include:* The Movie Machine: Selected Stories about Films 1965-78 1979, Collected Poems 2002, The Imperfect Man: Scenes from My Life (memoir) 2005. *Address:* c/o Zentropa Production, Filmbyen 22, 2650 Hvidovre, Denmark (office).

LETO, Jared Joseph; American singer, songwriter, musician (guitar) and actor; b. 26 Dec. 1971, Bossier City, La; s. of Constance Leto; ed Emerson Preparatory School, Washington, DC, Univ. of the Arts, Philadelphia, New York City School of Visual Arts; TV and film actor 1992–; Founder-mem. 30 Seconds to Mars 1998–; MTV2 Award at MTV Video Music Awards 2006, MTV Australia Video Music Awards for Best Rock Video and Video of the Year 2007, Kerrang! Awards for Best Int. Newcomer 2007, for Best Single 2007, 2008, 2011, for Best Int. Band 2008, 2010, 2011, TRL Award for Best New Artist 2007, Bandit Rock Award for Best Int. Breakthrough 2008, Los Premios MTV Award for Best Int. Rock Artist 2008, MTV Europe Music Rock Out Award 2008, MTV Europe Music Video Star Award 2008, MTV Video Music Award for Best Rock Video 2010, 2013, MTV Europe Music Award for Best Rock Act 2010, for Best Alternative Act 2013, 2014, 2017. *Recordings include:* with 30 Seconds to Mars: 30 Seconds to Mars 2002, A Beautiful Lie (MTV Asia Video Star Award 2008) 2005, This is War 2009, Love, Lust, Faith and Dreams 2013, America 2018. *Films include:* How to Make an American Quilt 1995, The Last of the High Kings 1996, Switchback 1997, Prefontaine 1997, Basil 1998, Urban Legend 1998, The Thin Red Line 1998, Black and White 1999, Girl, Interrupted 1999, Fight Club 1999, American Psycho 2000, Sunset Strip 2000, Requiem for a Dream (Boston Society of Film Critics Award for Best Actor 2000, Stockholm Film Festival Award for Best Actor 2000) 2000, Highway 2002, Panic Room 2002, Phone Booth 2002, Alexander 2004, Lord of War 2005, Hubert Selby Jr.: It'll Be Better Tomorrow (documentary) 2005, Lonely Hearts 2006, Chapter 27 2007, Mr. Nobody (Puchon International Fantastic Film Festival Award for Best Performance 2009, Sitges Film Festival Award for Best Actor 2009) 2009, Dallas Buyers Club (Golden Globe Award for Best Supporting Actor in a Motion Picture, Screen Actors Guild Award for Outstanding Performance by a Male Actor in a Supporting Role, Academy Award for Best Supporting Actor 2014) 2013, Suicide Squad 2016, Blade Runner 2049 2017, The Outsider 2018. *Television includes:* Camp Wilder (series) 1992, Almost Home (series) 1993, Rebel Highway (series) 1994, Cool and the Crazy (film) 1994, My So-Called Life (series) 1994. *Website:* jaredleto.com/thisiswhoireallyam; www.thirtysecondstomars.com.

ŁĘTOWSKA, Ewa Anna, MA, LLD; Polish lawyer and judge; b. 22 March 1940, Warsaw; m. Janusz Łętowski (deceased); ed Faculty of Law, Warsaw Univ.; scientific worker, Inst. of Legal Sciences, Polish Acad. of Sciences, Warsaw 1962–, Corresp. mem. 1997–2010, Full mem. 2010–, mem. Legal Science Cttee 2011–15; Lecturer, Dept of Law, Warsaw Univ. 1963–83; first Commr for Civil Rights Protection 1987–92; lecturer and author of educational material, Helsinki Foundation for Human Rights, Warsaw 1992–99; mem. Expert Cttee, ILO 1993–2002; Judge, Supreme Administrative Court 1999–2002; Judge, Polish Constitutional Tribunal 2002–11; mem. Int. Comm. of Jurists 1995–, mem. Exec. Cttee 1995–98, Vice-Pres. 1998–2001; fmr mem. Bd of Stichting European Human Rights Foundation, Legis. Council at Chair. of Council of Ministers, Codifying Comm. for the Reform of Civil Law; Corresp. mem. Acad. of Comparative Law, Paris; mem. Polish Helsinki Cttee 1991–, Académie de Droit Comparé; Kt's Cross, Order of Polonia Restituta; Friedrich Ebert Stiftung Award, Hon. Medal of the 1st degree, Polish Red Cross Soc. 2011; recipient of many scientific awards. *Publications:* 19 books on civil law, consumer protection and constitutional law; co-author of three books about music; introductions to theatre programmes, concerts and opera reviews; over 30 articles. *Leisure interests:* classical music, vocalism.

LETSIE III, King of Lesotho, BLL; b. (David Mohato Bereng Seeiso), 17 July 1963, Morija; s. of King Moshoeshoe II and Queen Mamohato Berenc Seeiso; m. Anna Karabo Motšoeneng (now Queen 'Masenate Mohato Seeiso) 2000; children: Princess Mary Senate Mohato Seeiso, b. 7 Oct. 2001, Princess 'M'aSeeiso, b. 20 Nov. 2004, Prince Lerotholi David Mohato Bereng Seeiso, b. 18 April 2007; ed Ampleforth Coll., UK, Nat. Univ. of Lesotho, Univs of Bristol, Cambridge and London, UK; Prin. Chief of Matsieng 1989; installed as King Nov. 1990, abdicated Jan. 1995, reinstated following his father's death Feb. 1996–; apptd FAO Special Amb. for Nutrition 2016; Patron, Prince Mohato Award (Khau Ea Khosana Mohato); Grand Master of the Most Dignified Order of Moshoeshoe, Grand Master of the Most Meritorious Order of Mohlomi, Grand Master of the Most Loyal Order of Ramatseatsane, Outstanding Service Medal; Bailiff Kt Grand Cross of Justice of the Two Sicilian Royal Sacred Mil. Constantinian Order of St George 2013. *Leisure interests:* visiting family cattle posts, arable farming and country life, horse riding, squash, tennis, rugby, classical and traditional music. *Address:* The Royal Palace

Secretariat, PO Box 527, Maseru, Lesotho. *Telephone:* (22) 322170; (22) 312776. *E-mail:* sps@palace.org.ls. *Website:* www.gov.ls/king.

LETTA, Enrico, PhD; Italian politician; *President, Jacques Delors Institute;* b. 20 Aug. 1966, Pisa; m. Gianna Letta; three s.; ed Univ. of Pisa, Sant'Anna School of Advanced Studies; researcher, Agency for Research and Legislation, Rome 1991–94, Sec.-Gen. 1994–; Chair. European Young Christian Democrats 1991–95; Head of Secr. of Foreign Minister Beniamino Andreatta 1993–94; Sec.-Gen. Cttee for the Euro, Ministry of the Treasury, the Budget and Econ. Planning 1996–97; Deputy Sec. Italian People's Party 1997–98; Minister for Community Policies 1998–99, for Industry, Trade and Crafts Jan.–April 2000, for Industry and Foreign Trade 2000–01; nat. official of Margherita party responsible for the economy 2001–07; mem. Chamber of Deputies 2001–04, 2006– (Olive Tree coalition); mem. Partito Democratico 2007–; mem. European Parl. for NE Italy 2004–06, part of Alliance of Liberals and Democrats for Europe, mem. Cttee on Econ. and Monetary Affairs, mem. Del. for relations with the Maghreb countries and the Arab Maghreb Union (including Libya); Under-Sec. of State to the Presidency of the Council of Ministers 2006–08; Shadow Minister for Welfare 2008–13; Prime Minister 2013–14 (resgnd), Minister of Agric. Jan.–Feb. 2014; Vice-Pres. Aspen Inst. Italy 2004–; Prof. under contract, Libera Università Cattaneo 2001–03, la Scuola superiore S. Anna di Pisa 2003, Haute école de commerce, Paris 2004, 2005; Pres. Jacques Delors Inst. 2016–; mem. Trilateral Comm. *Publications include:* Passaggio a Nord-Est 1994, Euro sì – Morire per Maastricht 1997, La Comunità competitiva 2001, Dialogo intorno all'Europa (with L. Caracciolo) 2002, L'allargamento dell'Unione europea 2003, Viaggio nell'economia italiana (with P. Bersani) 2004, L'Europa a Venticinque 2005. *Address:* Jacques Delors Institute, 19, rue de Milan, 75009 Paris, France (office). *Telephone:* 1-44-58-97-97 (office). *E-mail:* info@delorsinstitute.eu (office). *Website:* www.delorsinstitute.eu (office).

LETTE, Kathy; Australian author and playwright; b. 11 Nov. 1958, Sydney; d. of Mervyn Lette and Val Lette; m. Geoffrey Robertson (q.v.) 1990; one s. one d.; fmr columnist, Sydney and New York; fmr satirical news writer and presenter, Willasee Show, Channel 9; fmr TV sitcom writer, Columbia Pictures, Los Angeles; fmr guest presenter, This Morning with Richard and Judy, ITV; Writer-in-Residence, The Savoy, London 2003; Australian Literature Board Grant 1982. *Plays include:* Wet Dreams 1985, Perfect Mismatch 1985, Grommits 1986, I'm So Happy For You, I Really Am 1991. *Films include:* Puberty Blues 1982, Mad Cows 2001. *Publications include:* Puberty Blues (with G. Carey) 1979, Hit and Ms 1984, Girls' Night Out 1987, The Llama Parlour 1991, Foetal Attraction 1993, Mad Cows 1996, She Done Him Wrong (essays), The Constant Sinner by Mae West (introduction) 1995, Altar Ego 1998, Nip 'n Tuck 2001, Dead Sexy 2003, How to Kill Your Husband 2005, A Stitch in Time 2005, To Love, Honour, and Betray 2009, The Boy Who Fell to Earth 2012, Love is Blind 2013, Courting Trouble 2014; contribs to Sydney Morning Herald, The Bulletin, Cleo Magazine. *Leisure interests:* scuba diving, opera, feminism. *Address:* c/o Ed Victor, 6 Bayley Street, London, WC1B 3HB, England. *Telephone:* (20) 7304-4100 (office). *Fax:* (20) 7304-4111 (office). *E-mail:* kathy.lette@virgin.net. *Website:* www.kathylette.com.

LETTERMAN, David Michael; American comedian, talk show host and producer; b. 12 April 1947, Indianapolis, Ind.; s. of Joseph Letterman and Dorothy Letterman; m. 1st Michelle Cook 1969 (divorced 1977); m. 2nd Regina Lasko 2009; one s.; ed Ball State Univ.; began career as radio talk show host on WNTS (AM) and on Indianapolis TV station WLWI (now WTHR) as anchor and weatherman; radio and TV announcer in Indianapolis 1970–75; performer, The Comedy Store, LA 1975; frequent guest host on The Tonight Show with Johnny Carson; host, David Letterman Show 1980, Late Night with David Letterman (NBC) 1982–93; Late Show with David Letterman (CBS, also writer and producer) 1993–2015; Host of the Academy Awards 1995; Founder and Chair. Worldwide Pants Inc. (production co.) 1993–; TV scriptwriter including Bob Hope Special, Good Times, Paul Lynde Comedy Hour, John Denver Special; Co-owner Rahal Letterman Lanigan Racing 1996–; Emmy Awards for Outstanding Host or Hostess in a Variety Series 1981, Outstanding Individual Achievement – Writers 1981, Outstanding Writing in a Variety or Music Program 1984, 1985, 1986, 1987, Outstanding Variety, Music or Comedy Series 1994; American Comedy Awards for Funniest Male Performer in a TV Special (Leading or Supporting) Network, Cable or Syndication 1989, 1995, Funniest Male Performer in a TV Series (leading role) Network, Cable or Syndication 1994, 2001, Kennedy Center Honor 2012, Mark Twain Prize for American Humour 2017. *Publications include:* The Late Night with David Letterman Book of Top Ten Lists 1990, An Altogether New Book of Top Ten Lists 1991, David Letterman's Book of Top Ten Lists 1996. *Leisure interests:* baseball, basketball, running, auto racing. *Address:* Worldwide Pants Inc., 1697 Broadway, Suite 805, New York, NY 10019, USA. *Telephone:* (212) 975-5300. *Fax:* (212) 975-4780. *Website:* www.rahal.com.

LETTINGA, Gatze, DrIr; Dutch chemical engineer and academic; *Adviser to Board, Lettinga Associates Foundation;* b. 4 Jan. 1936, Dongjum, Friesland; ed RHBS High School, Harlingen, Tech. Univ., Delft, Inter Univ. Reactor Inst., Delft; began his work on devt and implementation of anaerobic treatment systems in 1971, developed Upflow Anaerobic Sludge Bed Reactor system 1972, succeeded in implementing it in sugar beet industry for treatment of wastewater; joined Dept of Environmental Tech., Wageningen Agricultural Univ. 1970, Prof. in Environmental Tech. 1988–2001 (retd); currently Advisor to Bd Lettinga Associates Foundation (LeAF—fmrly Environmental Protection and Resources Conservations Foundation, Chair. 1997–2002); has served on organizing or scientific cttees of several nat. and int. confs, including Second Int. AD-Symposium 1981, Third Int. AD-Symposium, Boston 1983; organized yearly int. courses on Anaerobic Digestion for developing countries; fmr mem. Editorial Bd Agricultural Wastes (now Bioresources Technology), Re/Views in Environmental Science and Bio/Technology, Journal of Environmental Science and Health; mem. Dutch Asscn of Water Pollution Control (NVA), Dutch Asscn of Biotechnology (NBV), Int. Water Asscn; Dr hc (Univ. of Valladolid, Spain) 2001; NVA Prize, Dutch Asscn on Wastewater Treatment 1979, Medaille d'argent de la Ville de Paris 1981, Karl Imhoff Award, Int. Asscn of Water Pollution Research Control 1992, Royal Shell Prize for Sustainable Devt and Energy 2001, Tyler Prize for Environmental Achievement 2007, Singapore Lee Kuan Water Prize 2009. *Achievements include:* was involved in more than 15 eng projects on anaerobic wastewater treatment plants in developing countries, including Cuba, Brazil, Indonesia, India and Viet Nam 1980s, Morocco present day. *Publications include:* more than 500 scientific papers in professional journals on anaerobic digestion and treatment of solid and liquid wastewater in modern high-rate treatment systems under psychrophilic, mesophilic and thermophilic conditions for remediation and energy production. *Address:* Lettinga Associates Foundation, PO Box 500, 6700 AM Wageningen, Netherlands (office). *Telephone:* (317) 484208 (office). *Fax:* (317) 482108 (office). *E-mail:* gatze.lettinga@wur.nl (office). *Website:* www.lettinga-associates.wur.nl (office).

LETWIN, Rt Hon. Sir Oliver, Kt, PC, MA, PhD, FRSA; British politician; b. 19 May 1956, Hampstead, London, England; s. of Prof. William Letwin and Shirley R. Letwin; m. Isabel Grace Davidson 1984; one s. one d. (twins); ed Eton Coll., Trinity Coll., Cambridge, London Business School; procter and visiting research fellow, Princeton Univ. 1980–81; research fellow, Darwin Coll. Cambridge 1981–82; special adviser, Dept of Educ. and Science 1982–83; mem. Prime Minister's Policy Unit 1983–86; Dir N.M. Rothschild and Sons Ltd 1987–2004; MP (Conservative) for West Dorset 1997–; Opposition Front Bench Spokesperson on Constitutional Affairs 1998–99; Shadow Financial Sec. to Treasury 1999–2000; Shadow Chief Sec. to Treasury 2000–01; Shadow Sec. of State for Home Affairs 2001–02; Privy Councillor 2002; Shadow Sec. of State for Econ. Affairs and Shadow Chancellor of the Exchequer 2003–05; Shadow Sec. of State for Environment, Food and Rural Affairs May–Dec. 2005; Chair. of Policy Review and Chair. of Conservative Research Dept 2005–10; Minister for Govt Policy (Cabinet Office) 2010–14; Minister for Govt Policy and Chancellor of the Duchy of Lancaster 2014–16; Minister in Overall Charge of the Cabinet Office 2015; Vice-Pres. Great Britain China Centre 2017–; Sr Fellow, Legatum Inst.; Sr Adviser, Faraday Inst. *Publications include:* Ethics, Emotion and the Unity of Self 1984, Privatising the World 1987, Aims of Schooling 1988, Drift to Union 1990, The Purpose of Politics 1999, Hearts and Minds 2017; numerous articles in professional and popular journals. *Leisure interests:* philosophy, walking, skiing, tennis. *Address:* House of Commons, Westminster, London, SW1A 0AA (office); Constituency Office, Chapel House, Dorchester Road, Maiden Newton, DT2 0BG, England (office). *Telephone:* (20) 7219-0826 (Westminster) (office); 1308 456891 (Maiden Newton) (office). *E-mail:* letwino@parliament.uk (office). *Website:* www.parliament.uk/biographies/commons/mr-oliver-letwin/247 (office); www.oliverletwinmp.com.

LEUENBERGER, Moritz; Swiss politician and lawyer; b. 21 Sept. 1946, Biel/Bienne; s. of Robert Leuenberger and Ruth Leuenberger; m. Gret Loewensberg 2003; two s.; ed Univ. of Zürich; pvt. practice as lawyer 1972–91; joined Social Democratic Party (SP) 1969, Leader Zürich SP 1972–80; mem. Zürich City Council 1974–83; Pres. Swiss Tenants' Asscn 1986–91; elected to Nat. Council 1979; elected to Zürich Cantonal Council 1991, Dir of Justice and Internal Affairs 1991–95; Fed. Councillor 1995–2010; Minister, Fed. Dept of Transport, Communications and Energy 1995–2010, Head of Fed. Dept of Environment, Transport, Energy and Communications (subsequently Transport, Energy and Communications) 2001–10; Vice-Pres. Swiss Federal Council 2000, 2005, 2010, Pres. 2001, 2006. *Website:* www.moritzleuenberger.net.

LEUNG, C. C., BSc; Taiwanese business executive; *Vice-Chairman and President, Quanta Computer Inc.;* ed Nat. Taiwan Univ.; co-f. Quanta Computer Inc. 1988, Pres. 1993–2006, 2007–, also Vice-Chair., Gen. Man. and Chief Research and Devt Officer; Pres. Quanta Research Inst. *Address:* Quanta Computer Inc., 211 Wen Hwa Second Road, Kui Shan Hsiang, Taoyuan City 333, Taiwan (office). *Telephone:* (3) 327-2345 (office). *Fax:* (3) 327-1511 (office). *E-mail:* qci.invest@quantatw.com (office). *Website:* www.quantatw.com (office).

LEUNG, Hon. Chun-ying, JP; Chinese civil servant; b. 1954, Hong Kong; m. Regina Tong Ching Yee; three c.; ed Hong Kong Univ. of Science and Tech., Bristol Polytechnic and King's Coll. London, UK; fmr Sec.-Gen. Basic Law Consultative Cttee; Vice-Chair. Preparatory Cttee, Hong Kong Special Admin. Region 1995–96; Convenor Exec. Council, Non-Official Mem. 1997–2012; Chief Exec., Exec. Council of Hong Kong 2012–17; Chair. DTZ Debenham Tie Leung Ltd, One Country Two Systems Research Inst. Ltd; mem. Nat. Cttee and Standing Cttee, 10th CPPCC 2008–08, 11th CPPCC 2008–13; Chancellor The Chinese Univ. of Hong Kong; Fellow, Hong Kong Inst. of Surveyors; Gold Bauhinia Star; Hon. DBA. *Leisure interests:* gardening, sports. *Address:* C/O Office of the Chief Executive, 5/F, Main Wing, Central Government Offices, Lower Albert Rd, Central, Hong Kong Special Administrative Region, People's Republic of China (office).

LEUNG, Oi Sie (Elsie), GMB, LLM, JP; Chinese politician, solicitor and legal official; *Vice-Director, Hong Kong Basic Law Committee, National People's Congress Standing Committee;* b. 24 April 1939, Hong Kong; ed Univ. of Hong Kong, Coll. of Law, England; admitted as solicitor of Hong Kong 1968, registered as overseas solicitor, UK Supreme Court 1976; Notary Public 1978; admitted as solicitor and barrister of Vic., Australia 1982; Founding mem. Hong Kong Fed. of Women Lawyers 1975, Hong Kong Fed. of Women 1993; Pres. Int. Fed. of Women Lawyers 1994; del. 7th People's Congress of Guangdong Prov. 1989–93, 8th Nat. People's Congress, People's Repub. of China 1993–97; Sec. for Justice of Hong Kong Special Admin. Region 1997–2005, also Chief Legal Adviser and Ex-Officio mem. Exec. Council of Hong Kong 1997–2005; resumed practice as solicitor 2006–; Vice-Dir Hong Kong Basic Law Cttee, Nat. People's Congress Standing Cttee, People's Repub. of China 2006–; Hon. LLD (China Univ. of Political Science and Law) 2004, (Warwick) 2005, (Hong Kong Shue Yan Univ.) 2010, (Univ. of Science and Tech., Hong Kong) 2011, Hon. DScS (Hong Kong Univ.) 2016, Hon. DLitt (Open Univ., Hong Kong) 2017; Grand Bauhinia Medal (Hong Kong) 2002. *Address:* 2201–2202 Admiralty Centre, Tower 1, 18 Harcourt Road, Hong Kong Special Administrative Region, People's Republic of China (office). *Telephone:* 25249995 (office). *Fax:* 25372609 (office). *E-mail:* elsie.leung@iulaili.com (office).

LEUNG, Tony Chiu Wai; Hong Kong actor; b. 27 June 1962, *Films include:* Feng kuang ba san (Mad Mad 83) 1983, Qing chun chai guan (Young Cops) 1985, Din lo jing juen (The Lunatics) 1986, Deiha tsing (Love Unto Waste) 1986, Yan man ying hung (The People's Hero) 1987, Sha shou hu die meng (My Heart is that Eternal Rose) 1987, Kai xin kuai huo ren (Happy Go Lucky) 1987, Tie jia wu di Ma Li A (I Love Maria) 1988, Beiqing chengshi (City of Sadness) 1989, Zhong yi qun ying (Seven Warriors) 1989, Liang ge you qi jiang (Two Painters) 1989, Die xue jie tou (Bullet in the Head) 1990, A Fei jing juen (Days of Being Wild) 1991, Hoyat gwan tsoi loi (Au revoir mon amour) 1991, Sinnui yauman III (Chinese Ghost Story 3) 1991, Zhong huan ying xiong (Don't Fool Me) 1991, Wu hu jiang zhi jue lie (The Tigers) 1991, Sha Tan-Zi yu Zhou Shih-Nai (Royal Scoundrel) 1991, Qian Wang (The Great Pretenders) 1991, Haomen yeyan (The Banquet) 1991, Lashou shentan (Hard Boiled) 1992, Ya Fei yu Ya Ji (The Days of Being Dumb) 1992, Ti dao bao (Lucky Encounter) 1992, Fan dou ma liu (Come Fly the Dragon) 1992, Yi yu zhi mo lu ying xiong (End Of The Road) 1993, Xin xian hao shen zhen (The Magic Crane) 1993, Ge ge de qing ren (Three Summers) 1993, Xin nan xiong nan di (He Ain't Heavy, He's My Father) 1993, Xin liu xing hu die jian (Butterfly and Sword) 1993, Wei Xiao Bao zhi feng zhi gou nu (Hero Beyond The Boundary Of Time) 1993, Seidu yinghung tsun tsi dung sing sai tsau (The Eagle Shooting Heroes) 1993, Mo hua qing (Fantasy Romance) 1993, Feng chen san xia (Tom, Dick, and Hairy) 1993, Chong qing sen lin (Chungking Express) 1994, Dung che sai duk (Ashes of Time) 1994, Shen long du sheng zhi qi kai de sheng (Always Be the Winners) 1994, Dun jeuk nai guay loy (The Returning) 1994, Xich lo (Cyclo) 1995, Ming yat tin aai (Tomorrow) 1995, Liu mang yi sheng (Dr Mack) 1995, Jushi shengun (Heaven Can't Wait) 1995, Tou tou ai ni (Blind Romance) 1996, Hong xing zi zhi jiang hu da feng bao (War of the Underworld) 1996, Cheun gwong tsa sit (Happy Together) 1997, Zui jia pai dang zhi zui jie pai dang (97 Aces Go Places) 1997, Aau dut (The Longest Nite) 1998, Hai shang hua (Flowers of Shanghai) 1998, Mooi tin oi lei siu shut (Your Place or Mine) 1998, Hei yu duan chang ge zhi qi sheng zhu rou (Chinese Midnight Express) 1998, Chiu si hung yiu oi (Timeless Romance) 1998, Bor lei jun (Gorgeous) 1999, Dong jing gong lue (Tokyo Raiders) 2000, Fa yeung nin wa (In the Mood for Love) (Best Actor Cannes Film Festival) 2000, Tung gui mat yau (Fighting for Love) 2001, Hap gwat yan sam (Healing Hearts) 2001, Yau ching yam shui baau (Love Me, Love My Money) 2001, Tian xia wu shuang (Chinese Odyssey 2002) 2002, Ying xiong (Hero) 2002, Wu jian dao (Infernal Affairs) 2002, Xing yun chao ren (My Lucky Star) 2003, Wu jian Dao 3 (Infernal Affairs III) 2003, Dei gwong tit 2003, Di xia tie 2003, 2046 (Best Actor Hong Kong Film Critics' Society 2005) 2004, Han chang gong lue 2005, Seung sing (Confession of Pain) 2006, Se, jie (Lust, Caution) 2007, Chi bi (Red Cliff) 2008, Red Cliff: Part 2 2009, Ashes of Time Redux 2009, The Great Magician 2011, The Silent War 2012, The Grandmaster 2013, The Ferryman 2015, Hema Hema: Sing Me a Song While I Wait 2016. *Television includes:* Wut lik sap jat 1982, Heung sing long ji 1982, But dou san hung 1983, Luk ding gei 1984, San jaat si hing-juk jaap 1985, Yang ka cheung 1986, The Seasons (Mini-Series) 1987, Two Most Honorable Knights 1988, Dak ging 90 III-Zi ming jat tin ngaai (film) 1995, Nature Is Speaking 2015. *Address:* c/o Jet Tone Productions Limited, Flat E, 3/F, Kalam Court 9, Grampion Road, Kowloon, Hong Kong Special Administrative Region, People's Republic of China (office).

LEUNG KAM CHUNG, Antony, BSc; Hong Kong government official and financial services industry executive; *CEO, Nan Fung Group;* b. 29 Jan. 1952, Hong Kong; m. 1st Sophie Leung; m. 2nd Fu Mingxia 2002; one d.; ed Univ. of Hong Kong, Harvard Business School, USA; Man. Dir and Regional Man. for Greater China and the Philippines, Chase Manhattan Bank; Chair. Univ. Grants Cttee 1993–98; Dir Hong Kong Futures Exchange 1987–90, Hong Kong Policy Research Inst. 1996–; Arbitrator, China Int. Econ. and Trade Arbitration Comm. 1994–; mem. Exec. Council Hong Kong Special Admin. Region 1997–2001; Financial Sec. of Hong Kong 2001–03 (resgnd); Chair. Blackstone Greater China, Blackstone Group HK Ltd, Hong Kong 2007–13, now mem. Int. Advisory Bd; CEO Nan Fung Group 2013–; Chair., Heifer Int. Hong Kong and Food Angel, Harvard Business School Asscn of Hong Kong; mem. Industrial Devt Bd 1985, Univ. and Polytechnic Grants Cttee 1990–93, Bd Provisional Airport Authority 1990–95, Bd Airport Authority 1995–99, Cen. Policy Unit 1992–93, Bd Hong Kong Community Chest 1992–94, Educ. Comm. 1993–98 (Chair. 1998), Standing Council Chinese Soc. of Macroeconomics, State Planning Comm. 1994, Exchange Fund Advisory Cttee 1993, Prep. Cttee of Hong Kong Special Admin. Region 1996–97; mem. Bd of Dirs China Merchants Bank; Trustee, Queen Mary Hosp. Charitable Trust 1993–, Hong Kong Centre for Econ. Research 1995–98; Hong Kong Affairs Adviser 1994–97. *Leisure interest:* golf. *Address:* Nan Fung Group, 23rd Floor, Nan Fung Tower, 88 Connaught Road C, Central, Hong Kong Special Administrative Region, People's Republic of China (office). *Website:* www.nanfung.com (office).

LEUNG KWAN-YUEN, Andrew, GBS, MBE, BSc, JP; Chinese (b. British) politician and business executive; *President, Legislative Council of Hong Kong;* b. 24 Feb. 1951; m. Susana Cheong Suk-hing; ed Univ. of Leeds, UK; Founder and Chair. Sun Hing Knitting Factory; Chair. Fed. of Hong Kong Industries 2003–04; Chair. Hong Kong Productivity Council 2003–09; Council mem., Hong Kong Trade Devt Council 2010–16; Chair. Business and Professionals Alliance for Hong Kong 2012–16; mem. Legis. Council, Hong Kong 2004–, Pres. 2016–; mem. Econ. Devt Comm. 2013–17; Hon. Chair. Textile Council of Hong Kong; Gold Bauhinia Star 2010; Hon. DBA Coventry Univ., UK. *Address:* Legislative Council, Room 710, Legislative Council Complex, 1 Legislative Council Road, Central, Hong Kong Special Administrative Region, People's Republic of China (office). *Telephone:* 2537 1339 (office). *Fax:* 2697 8482 (office). *E-mail:* andrewleunglegco@outlook.com (office). *Website:* www.andrewkyleung.hk.

LEUTHARD, Doris; Swiss politician; b. 10 April 1963; m. Roland Hausin; ed Univ. of Zurich; mem. Swiss Nat. Council 1999–2006; Grossrätin, Aragau Canton 1997–2000; Vice-Pres. Christian Democratic Party 2001–04, Pres. 2004–06; mem. Fed. Council 2006–18, Head of Fed. Dept of Econ. Affairs 2006–10, also responsible for Agric., Veterinary Affairs, Consumer Affairs, Housing, Vocational Training, European Integration, Vice-Pres. Fed. Council 2009, 2016–17, Pres. 2010, 2017, Head of Fed. Dept of the Environment, Transport, Energy and Communications 2010–18; mem. Parti Démocrate-Chrétien Suisse (PDC). *Address:* c/o Federal Department of the Environment, Transport, Energy and Communications, Kochergasse 10, 3003 Bern, Switzerland (office).

LEVADA, HE Cardinal William Joseph, STD; American ecclesiastic; *Prefect Emeritus, Congregation for the Doctrine of the Faith;* b. 15 June 1936, Long Beach, Calif.; s. of Joseph Levada, Jr and Lorraine Nunez Levada; ed St Anthony's High School, Long Beach, Our Lady Queen of Angels Seminary, San Fernando, St John's Seminary, Camarillo, North American Coll. and Pontifical Gregorian Univ., Rome, Italy; ordained priest 1961; Assoc. Pastor, St Louis of France Parish, San Gabriel Valley community of La Puente 1962; Assoc. Pastor, St Monica's Church, Santa Monica 1963–67, where he served as high school religion teacher and chaplain of

local Community Coll. Newman Center; taught theology at St John's Seminary School of Theology, Los Angeles 1970–76; served as first Dir Continuing Educ. for the Clergy, Archdiocese of Los Angeles 1973; Pres. Senate of Priests 1975–76; official of Congregation for the Doctrine of the Faith, Vatican City 1976–82; part-time Instructor, Pontifical Gregorian Univ. 1976–82; Exec. Dir California Catholic Conf. of Bishops, Sacramento 1982–84; Auxiliary Bishop of Los Angeles (Titular Bishop of Capri) 1983–86; Episcopal Vicar for Santa Barbara Co. 1984–86; Chancellor and Moderator of the Curia 1986; Archbishop of Portland, Ore. 1986–95; Coadjutor Archbishop of San Francisco Aug.–Dec. 1995, Archbishop of San Francisco 1995–2005, currently Archbishop Emer.; Apostolic Admin. Diocese of Santa Rosa 1999–2000; Bishop Co-Chair. Anglican–Roman Catholic Dialogue in the US 2000–05; mem. Congregation for the Doctrine of the Faith 2000–05, Prefect 2005–12, Prefect Emer. 2012–; cr. Cardinal (Cardinal-Deacon of Santa Maria in Domnica) 2006, elevated to Cardinal-Priest 2016; participated in Papal Conclave 2013; Chair. US Conf. of Catholic Bishops' Cttee on Doctrine 2003–05; Pres. Int. Theological Comm. 2005–12, Pres. Emer. 2012–; Pres. Pontifical Biblical Comm. 2005–12, Pres. Emer. 2012–; Pres. Pontifical Comm. 'Ecclesia Dei' 2009–12, Pres. Emer. 2012–. *Address:* Congregation for the Doctrine of the Faith, Palazzo del Sant'Uffizio, Piazza del S. Uffizio 11, 00193 Rome, Italy (office). *Website:* www.vatican.va/roman_curia/congregations/cfaith (office).

LEVEAUX, David; British theatre director; b. 13 Dec. 1957, Leicester, England; s. of Michael Leveaux and Eve Powell; ed Univ. of Manchester; Assoc. Dir Riverside Studios 1981–85; Artistic Dir Theatre Project Tokyo from 1993; has directed productions for Nat. Theatre, RSC, ENO, Almeida Theatre, Donmar Warehouse (Assoc. Dir) and on Broadway. *Productions include:* Broadway: A Moon for the Misbegotten 1984, Anna Christie 1993, Electra (Sophocles) 1998, The Real Thing 2000, Betrayal 2000, Nine 2003, Fiddler on the Roof 2004, Jumpers 2004, The Glass Menagerie 2005, Cyrano de Bergerac 2007, Arcadia 2011, Romeo and Juliet 2013; Almeida Theatre: Betrayal 1991, Moonlight 1993, No Man's Land 1992 (transferred to Comedy Theatre 1993), The Distance From Here 2002; Theatre Project Tokyo: Electra 1995, Lulu 1999, Modern Noh Plays, The Changeling, Hedda Gabler, Two Headed Eagle; Donmar Warehouse: Nine 1996, Electra 1997, The Real Thing 1999 (transferred to the Albery Theatre 2000); Duke of York's Theatre: Backbeat 2011. *Address:* c/o Simpson Fox Associates, 6 Beauchamp Place, London, SW3 1NG, England (office). *Telephone:* (20) 7434-9167 (office). *E-mail:* david.bingham@simpson-fox.com (office). *Website:* www.simpson-fox.com (office).

LEVELT, Willem Johannes Maria (Pim), PhD; Dutch psychologist, psycholinguist and academic; *Director Emeritus, Max-Planck-Institute for Psycholinguistics;* b. 17 May 1938, Amsterdam; s. of Dr W. H. Levelt and J. Levelt-Berger; m. Elisabeth C. M. Jacobs 1963; two s. one d.; ed Univ. of Leiden; mem. staff, Inst. for Perception, Soesterberg 1962–65; Research Fellow, Center for Cognitive Studies, Harvard Univ., USA 1965–66; Visiting Asst Prof., Univ. of Illinois, USA 1966–67; Prof. of Experimental Psychology, Groningen Univ. 1967–70; Prof. of Experimental Psychology, Nijmegen Univ. 1971–79, Leader Max-Planck Project Group for Psycholinguistics 1976–79, Prof. of Psycholinguistics (special Max Planck Soc. Chair) 1980–2006; Dir Max-Planck-Inst. for Psycholinguistics, Nijmegen 1980–2006, Dir Emer. 2006–; Visiting Prof., Univ. of Louvain 1967–70; mem. Inst. for Advanced Study, Princeton, NJ, USA 1971–72; mem. Royal Netherlands Acad. of Sciences (Pres. 2002–05), Holland Soc. of Sciences, Academia Europaea, Royal Flemish Acad. of Belgium for Sciences and Arts, American Philosophical Soc., NAS, Deutsche Akademie der Naturforscher Leopoldina, Bayerische Akad. der Wissenschaften, Österreichische Akad. der Wissenschaften; Foreign Assoc., NAS, Fellow, Cognitive Science Soc. 2007; Hon. mem. World Innovation Foundation, Linguistic Soc. of America 1998, De Jonge Akademie, Royal Netherlands Acad. of Arts and Sciences 2006; Kt, Order of the Dutch Lion 1998; Ordre pour le mérite 2010; Bundesverdienstkreuz mit Stern 2012; Dr hc (Maastricht) 2000, (Antwerp) 2003, (Padua) 2004, (Catholic Univ. of Louvain) 2005; Radboud Stichting Award 1968, Hendrik Muller Award for the Social and Behavioral Sciences, Royal Netherlands Acad. of Sciences 1993, Heymans Award, Dutch Psychology Asscn 1996, Silver Medal, Univ. of Nijmegen 2004, Medal of Honour, Netherlands Psychonomic Soc. 2006, Patrick Suppes Prize in the History of Science, American Philosophical Soc. 2013. *Publications:* On Binocular Rivalry 1968, Formal Grammars in Linguistics and Psycholinguistics (three vols) 1974, Psycholinguistic Applications 1974, Speaking: From Intention to Articulation 1989, A History of Psycholinguistics: The Pre-Chomskyan Era 2012. *Leisure interest:* playing the traverso. *Address:* Max-Planck-Institute for Psycholinguistics, PO Box 310, 6500 AH Nijmegen, The Netherlands (office). *Telephone:* (24) 352-1317 (office). *Fax:* (24) 352-1213 (office). *E-mail:* pim.levelt@mpi.nl (office). *Website:* www.mpi.nl/Members/PimLevelt (office).

LEVELT SENGERS, Johanna (Anneke) Maria Henrica; American (b. Dutch) physicist; *Scientist Emerita, National Institute of Standards and Technology;* b. 4 March 1929, Amsterdam, The Netherlands; d. of Wilhelmus Levelt and Josephine Berger; m. Jan V. Sengers 1963; two s. two d.; ed Univ. of Amsterdam, Univ. of Wisconsin, Madison; joined Nat. Bureau of Standards (now Nat. Inst. of Standards and Tech.) 1963, Group Leader, Chemical Science and Tech. Lab. (Physical and Chemical Properties Div.) 1978–87, Sr Fellow 1984, Scientist Emer. 1995–; Lecturer, Catholic Univ. Louvain, Belgium 1971; Research Assoc., Inst. of Theoretical Physics, Univ. of Amsterdam 1974–75; Regents Prof., Dept of Chemistry, UCLA 1982; Fellow, American Physical Soc., AAAS, Int. Asscn for the Properties of Water and Steam (IAPWS); mem. NAS, Nat. Acad. of Eng; Corresp. mem. Royal Netherlands Acad. of Arts and Sciences, Koninklijke Holland Maatschappij der Wetenschappen; fmr Pres. IAPWS and US nat. rep. to IAPWS on behalf of ASME; Jt Organizer first NATO Summer School on Supercritical Fluids 1994; co-Chair., Women for Science Working Group, InterAmerican Network of Acads of Sciences (IANAS) 2010–; Dr hc (Tech. Univ. of Delft, Netherlands); Dept of Commerce Silver Medal 1972, Gold Medal 1978, Alexander Von Humboldt Research Award, Germany 1991, N American recipient of L'Oréal-UNESCO Women in Science Award 2003, ASME Yeram S. Touloukian Award 2006. *Publications include:* How Fluids Unmix 2002; numerous papers and reviews on thermodynamics and properties of fluids and fluid mixtures near their critical points, 14 book chapters. *Leisure interests:* swimming, hiking, travelling, reading. *Address:* Physical and Chemical Properties Division, Chemical Science and Technology Laboratory, National Institute of Standards and Technology,

Gaithersburg, MD 20899-8380 (office); 110 N. Van Buren Street, Rockville, MD 20850, USA (home). *Telephone:* (301) 975-2463 (office). *Fax:* (301) 869-4020 (office). *E-mail:* johanna.sengers@nist.gov (office). *Website:* www.nist.gov/mml/properties/Levelt-Sengers.cfm (office).

LEVENE OF PORTSOKEN, Baron (Life Peer), cr. 1997, of Portsoken in the City of London; **Peter Keith Levene,** KBE, BA (Econ); British business executive; *Chairman, Starr Underwriting Agents Limited;* b. 8 Dec. 1941, Pinner, Middx, England; s. of Maurice Levene and Rose Levene; m. Wendy Ann Levene 1966; two s. one d.; ed City of London School and Univ. of Manchester; joined United Scientific Holdings 1963, Man. Dir 1968, Chair. 1982; Personal Adviser to Sec. of State for Defence 1984; Chief of Defence Procurement, Ministry of Defence 1985–91; mem. SE Asia Trade Advisory Group 1979–83, Council, Defence Mfrs Asscn 1982–85, Vice-Chair. 1983–84, Chair. 1984–85; Chair. European NATO Nat. Armaments Dirs 1990–91, Docklands Light Railway Ltd 1991–94; Special Adviser to Sec. of State for the Environment 1991–92; Adviser to Prime Minister on Efficiency 1992–97; Special Adviser to Pres. of the Bd of Trade 1992–95; mem. Nat. Security Strategy (Jt Cttee) 2013–; Chair. Public Competition and Purchasing Unit, HM Treasury 1991–92; Deputy Chair. Wasserstein Perella & Co. Ltd 1991–94; Chair. and CEO Canary Wharf Ltd 1993–96; Sr Adviser Morgan Stanley & Co. Ltd 1996–98; Chair. Bankers Trust Int. 1998–99, Investment Banking Europe, Deutsche Bank AG 1999–2001 (Vice-Chair. Deutsche Bank UK 2001–02), General Dynamics UK Ltd 2001–, Lloyd's 2002–11, NBNK Investments plc 2011–13; Vice-Chair. Starr International Co. Inc. –2015; currently Chair. Starr Underwriting Agents Ltd; Chair. Ministry of Defence Reform Group 2010–; mem. Bd of Dirs, Haymarket Group Ltd 1997–, J. Sainsbury PLC 2001–04, China Construction Bank 2006–11; mem. Supervisory Bd Deutsche Boerse AG 2004–05; Alderman, City of London 1984–, Sheriff 1995–96, Lord Mayor of London 1998–99; Fellow, Queen Mary and Westfield Coll., Univ. of London 1995; Hon. Col Commdt, Royal Corps of Transport 1991–93, Royal Logistics Corps 1993; Master, Worshipful Co. of Carmen 1992–93; KStJ 1998; Commdr, Order nat. du Mérite 1996; Kt Commdr, Order of Merit (Germany) 1998; Middle Cross Order of Merit (Hungary) 1999; Hon. DSc (City Univ.) 1998, (Univ. of London) 2005. *Publication:* Send for Levene (autobiog.) 2018. *Leisure interests:* skiing, travel, watching Association football. *Address:* 30 Fenchurch Avenue, London, EC3M 5AD, England (office). *Telephone:* (20) 7398-5087 (office). *E-mail:* peter.levene@starrcompanies.com (office). *Website:* www.starrcompanies.com (office).

LEVENS, Marie E.; Suriname politician and international organization official; *Director, Department of Human Development and Employment, Organization of American States;* b. 1950; fmr Sr Policy Adviser, Higher Educ. Devt Scholarship and Exchange Programs, Ministry of Educ. and Community Devt; Consultant, Inter-American Devt Bank 1998; Minister of Foreign Affairs 2000–05; mem. Suriname Nat. Party (NPS-Nationale Partij Suriname); currently Dir Dept of Human Devt and Employment, OAS, Washington, DC. *Address:* Organization of American States, General Secretariat Building (GSB), Office 760, 1889 F Street NW, Washington, DC 20006, USA (office). *Telephone:* (202) 370-9771 (office). *Website:* www.oas.org (office).

LÉVÊQUE, Didier; French business executive; *Chairman and CEO, Finatis SA;* ed Ecole des Hautes Etudes Commerciales; Research Analyst, Finance Dept, Roussel-UCLAF Group 1985–89; joined Euris as Deputy Sec.-Gen. 1989, later Sec.-Gen. Euris SAS, CEO Finatis SA 2008–, Chair. 2010–, CEO Euris North America Corpn (ENAC), Euris Real Estate Corpn (EREC), Pres. Montech cos, Parantech, 2 and By-Bel, Matignon Diderot, Co. CEO Carpinienne of Participations (listed co.), Admin. Carpinienne Participations (listed co.), Park Street Investments International Ltd, Euris Ltd, Perm. Rep. to Bd of Finatis, Bd of Dirs of Foncière Euris (listed co.); Perm. Rep. of Comm. of Omnium Trade and Investments to Bd of Dirs of Casino, Guichard-Perrachon (listed co.); Perm. Rep. of Matignon Corbeil co. to Bd of Dirs to Rallye (listed co.); Perm. Rep. of L'Habitation Moderne de Boulogne on Bd of Dirs, Colosseum Finance II Soc.; Dir, Casino, Guichard-Perrachon SA (also known as Casino Guichard Perrachon & Cie SA) 2003–, Rallye SA (also known as Rallye Group) 2008–, Cnova NV 2014–. *Address:* Finatis SA, 83 rue du Faubourg Saint Honoré, 75008 Paris, France (office). *E-mail:* contact-finatis@euris.fr (office). *Website:* www.finatis.fr (office).

LEVER, Sir Jeremy Frederick, Kt, KCMG, MA, QC, FRSA; British lawyer; b. 23 June 1933, London; s. of Arnold Lever and Elizabeth Cramer (née Nathan); ed Bradfield Coll., Berks., University Coll. Oxford, Nuffield Coll., Oxford; Fellow, All Souls Coll. Oxford 1957–, Sub-Warden 1982–84, Sr Dean 1988–2011; QC (England and Wales) 1972, (Northern Ireland) 1988; Bencher, Gray's Inn 1986; Dir (non-exec.) Dunlop Holdings Ltd 1973–80, The Wellcome Foundation 1983–94; mem. arbitral tribunal, US/UK Arbitration concerning Heathrow Airport user charges 1989–94, Univ. of Portsmouth Ind. Inquiry 1995; Chair. Oftel Advisory Body on Fair Trading in Telecommunications 1996–2000, Performing Rights Soc. Appeals Panel 1997–2001; Visiting Prof., Wissenschaftszentrum Berlin für Sozialforschung Jan.–March 1999; Pres. Oxford Union Soc. 1957, Trustee 1972–77, 1988–2014; mem. Council British Inst. of Int. and Comparative Law 1987–2005; Africa Gen. Service Medal 1953. *Publications:* The Law of Restrictive Trading Agreements 1964, Comparative Law Casebook, Torts (with W. van Gerven) and other legal works. *Leisure interests:* porcelain, music. *Address:* All Souls College, Oxford, OX1 4AL; Monckton Chambers, 1–2 Raymond Buildings, Gray's Inn, London, WC1R 5NR, England (office). *Telephone:* (1865) 279379 (Oxford); (20) 7405-7211 (office). *Fax:* (1865) 279299 (Oxford); (20) 7405-2084 (office). *E-mail:* chambers@monckton.co.uk (office). *Website:* www.monckton.co.uk (office).

LEVER, Sir Paul, KCMG, CMG, MA; British diplomatist (retd) and business executive; *Vice-President of the Council, Royal United Services Institute;* b. 31 March 1944; s. of John Morrison Lever and Doris Grace Lever (née Battey); m. Patricia Anne Ramsey 1990; ed St Paul's School, Queen's Coll., Oxford; Third Sec. FCO 1966–67; Third, then Second Sec., Embassy in Helsinki 1967–71; Second, then First Sec., UK Del. to NATO 1971–73; with FCO, London 1973–81; Asst Pvt. Sec. to Sec. of State for Foreign and Commonwealth Affairs 1978–81; Chef de Cabinet to Vice-Pres. of EEC 1981–85; Head of UN Dept, FCO 1985–86, Head of Defence Dept 1986–87, Security Policy Dept 1987–90; Amb. and Head of UK Del. to Conventional Arms Control Negotiations, Vienna 1990–92; Asst Under-Sec. of State, FCO 1992–94, Deputy Sec. Cabinet Office and Chair. Jt Intelligence Cttee 1994–96; Deputy Under-Sec. of State (Dir for EU and Econ. Affairs), FCO 1996–97; Amb. to Germany 1998–2003; Global Devt Dir RWE Thames Water PLC 2003–06 (co. sold to Kemble Water Ltd); mem. Bd of Dirs Königswinter 2003–; Chair. Royal United Services Inst. for Defence and Security Studies 2004–09, now Vice-Pres. of the Council; Hon. LLD (Birmingham) 2001. *Leisure interests:* walking, art deco pottery, the music of Sandy Denny. *Address:* Royal United Services Institute, 61 Whitehall, London, SW1A 2ET, England (office). *Telephone:* (20) 7747-2600 (office). *E-mail:* info@rusi.org (office). *Website:* www.rusi.org (office).

LEVETE, Amanda, CBE; British architect; *Founder and Principal, AL_A;* b. 17 Nov. 1955, Bridgend; d. of Michael Levete and Gina Levete (née Seagrim); m. 1st Jan Kaplicky 1991; one s.; m. 2nd Ben Evans; ed St Paul's Girls School, London, Hammersmith School of Art, Architectural Asscn, London; worked with Alsop & Lyall 1980–81, YRM Architects 1982–84, Powis & Levete 1983–86, Richard Rogers & Partners 1984–89; Dir Future Systems 1989–2009; Founder and Prin., AL_A (formerly known as Amanda Levete Architecture) 2009–; Visiting Prof., Bartlett School of Architecture 2017; mem. Bd ARB 1997–2000, Architecture Foundation 1997–, Artangel 2000–13; Gov. Fox School 2002–04; Judge, Designs of the Year Award; Jane Drew Prize (The Architects' Journal and The Architectural Review) 2018. *Work includes:* Space Station Wardroom Table 1989 (NASA Certificate of Recognition), Museum of the Moving Image (MOMI) Tent 1992 (Bovis Royal Acad. Award), Hauer/King House, London 1992 (British Construction Industry Award), Stonehenge Visitor Centre 1993, Floating Bridge, London 1994, West India Quay Bridge, London 1998, NatWest Media Centre, Lords Cricket Ground 1999 (RIBA Stirling Prize, Civic Trust Award, World Architecture Awards, Aluminium Imagination Architectural Award), Selfridges Dept Store, Birmingham 2003, M-Pavilion, Melbourne 2015, Museum of Art, Architecture and Tech. (MAAT), Lisbon 2016, Central Embassy tower block, Bangkok 2017, Victoria and Albert Museum Exhibition Road Quarter 2017. *Exhibitions include:* Future Systems, RIBA 1982, Future Systems: Architecture, RIBA 1991, Future Systems: Recent Work, Storefront, RA Summer Show, London 1990, 1993, 1995, 1996, 2001, 2002, Future Systems, Inst. of Contemporary Arts, London 1998, Future Systems Originals, Faggionato Fine Arts Gallery, London 2001, La Biennale di Venezia 2002, La Triennale di Milano 2003, Max Protech Gallery, New York 2003. *Address:* AL_A, 14A Brewery Road, London, N7 9NH, England (office). *Telephone:* (20) 7243-7670 (office). *E-mail:* info@ala.uk.com (office). *Website:* www.ala.uk.com (office).

LEVETT, Michael (Mike) John, BComm, FIA, FFA, FASSA; South African insurance industry executive; b. 6 June 1939, Cape Town; m. Mary Gillian Aston 1966; two s. one d.; ed Christian Brothers Coll., Cape Town, Univ. of Cape Town; joined Old Mutual Life Assurance Soc. 1959, Gen. Man. 1981–85, Man. Dir 1985–2001, Exec. Chair. 1990–2001, Chair. (non-exec.) 2001–05; Chair. South African Mutual Life Assurance Soc. 1990–99, Mutual & Federal Insurance Co. Ltd 1993–99, South Africa Growth Equities 1995–; Deputy Chair. Mutual & Federal Insurance Co. Ltd –2005; Dir, Central Africa Building Soc. 1985–2005, South African Breweries (now SABMiller) 1999–2004; Dir (non-exec.), Barloworld Ltd 1985–2009, Mutual & Federal Insurance Co. Ltd –2005, Nedbank Group Ltd (fmrly Nedcor Ltd) 1987–2004, Sasol 1991–2000, Old Mutual South Africa Trust plc 1994–; Trustee, World Wide Fund for Nature (South Africa) 1990–, Nelson Mandela Children's Fund 1994–, The Coll. of Medicine Foundation 1995–; Patron Free Market Foundation 1990–; Founding Patron The Children's Hospital Trust 1996–; Hon. DEconSc (Cape Town) 1997; Businessman of the Year, Sunday Times Business Times Top 100 Companies 1999. *Leisure interests:* skiing, tennis.

LEVEY, Gerald Saul, AB, MD; American physician and academic; *Dean Emeritus, David Geffen School of Medicine, University of California, Los Angeles;* b. 9 Jan. 1937, Jersey City, NJ; m. Barbara Ann Levey (née Cohen) 1961; two c.; ed Univ. of Medicine and Dentistry of New Jersey; intern, Jersey City Medical Center 1961–62, resident 1962–63; Postdoctoral Fellow, Dept of Biological Chem., Harvard Univ. Medical School 1963–65; Medical Resident, Mass Gen. Hosp., Boston 1965–66; Clinical Assoc., Clinical Endocrinology Br., Nat. Inst. of Arthritis and Metabolic Diseases, NIH, Bethesda, Md 1966–68; Clinical Assoc., Nat. Heart and Lung Inst. 1968–69, Sr Investigator 1969–70; Assoc. Prof. of Medicine, Univ. of Miami School of Medicine 1970–73, Prof. of Medicine 1973–79, also Howard Hughes Medical Inst. Investigator; Prof. and Chair. Dept of Medicine, Univ. of Pittsburgh School of Medicine 1979–91, also Physician-in-Chief, Presbyterian Univ. Hosp.; Sr Vice-Pres. for Medical and Scientific Affairs, Merck and Co. 1991–94; apptd Prof. and Vice Chancellor, Medical Sciences, David Geffen School of Medicine, UCLA 1994, also Provost of Medical Sciences and Dean, now Dean Emer. and Consultant, currently Lincy Foundation Distinguished Service Chair Distinguished Professor, Dept of Medicine; Co-Chair. Nat. Study of Internal Medicine Manpower; Fellow, ACP; fmr Pres. Asscn of Profs of Medicine; mem. Bd of Govs American Bd of Internal Medicine; mem. American Medical Asscn, Asscn of American Physicians, Soc. of Gen. and Internal Medicine, Southern Soc. for Clinical Investigation, Endocrine Soc., American Soc. for Clinical Investigation, American Fed. for Clinical Research, American Thyroid Asscn; Trustee, Metzler/Payden Investment Group; Medical Visionary Award 2010. *Address:* Office of the Dean, David Geffen School of Medicine, 12-138 CHS, Los Angeles, CA 90095-1722, USA. *Telephone:* (310) 825-5687 (office). *Fax:* (310) 206-2142 (office). *E-mail:* glevey@mednet.ucla.edu (office). *Website:* dgsom.healthsciences.ucla.edu (office).

LEVI, Arrigo, PhD; Italian journalist and political writer; b. 17 July 1926, Modena; s. of Enzo Levi and Ida Levi (née Donati); m. Carmela Lenci 1952; one d.; ed Univs of Buenos Aires and Bologna; refugee in Argentina 1942–46; Negev Brigade, Israeli Army 1948–49; BBC European Services 1951–53; London Corresp. Gazzetta del Popolo and Corriere d'Informazione 1952–59; Moscow Corresp. Corriere della Sera 1960–62; news anchorman on Italian State Television 1966–68; special corresp. La Stampa 1969–73, Ed. in Chief 1973–78, Special Corresp. 1978; columnist on int. affairs, The Times 1979–83; Leader Writer, Corriere della Sera 1988–2007; Adviser for External Relations to Italian Pres. Carlo Azeglio Ciampi and Pres. Giorgio Napolitano 1998–2007; Commendatore Ordine al Merito della Repubblica Italiana 1991, Cavaliere Di Gran Croce Ordine Al Merito Della Repubblica Italiana 1999; Premio Trento 1987, Premio Luigi Barzini 1995, Premio Ischia Internazionale di Giornalismo 2001, Guidarello Prize 2006, Premio Pulcinella Mente Sant Arpino 2012. *Publications include:* L'economia degli Stati Uniti oggi 1966, Il potere in Russia 1965, La televisione all'italiana 1969, Viaggio fra gli economisti 1970, PCI, la lunga marcia verso il potere 1971, Un'idea dell'Italia 1983, La Democrazia nell'Italia che cambia 1984, Intervista sulla Dc 1986, Noi: gli italiani 1988, Tra Est e Ovest 1990, Yitzhak Rabin 1996, Le due fedi 1996, La vecchiaia può attendere 1997, Rapporto sul Medio Oriente 1998, Russia del '900 1999, Dialoghi di fine Millennio 1999, Dialoghi sulla fede 2000, America Latina: Memorie e ritorni 2004, Cinque discorsi tra due secoli 2004, America latina: Memorie e ritorni 2004, Un paese non basta 2009, Gente, luoghi, vita 2013.

LEVI, Noel, CBE, BA; Papua New Guinea fmr politician and fmr diplomatist; b. (Wasangula Noel Levi), 6 Feb. 1942, Nonopai, Kavieng; m. Josepha Muna Levi; two s. two d.; ed Scots Coll., Queensland, Papua New Guinea Admin. Coll., Cromwell Coll. Univ. of Queensland and Univ. of Papua New Guinea; patrol officer Dept of Dist Admin., Papua New Guinea 1967, later Asst Dist Commr; Asst Sec. Dept of Chief Minister 1973; Sec. Dept of Defence 1974; Minister of Foreign Affairs 1980; Amb. to People's Repub. of China 1987; High Commr to UK (also accred to Israel, Zimbabwe and Egypt) 1991; Sec., Dept of the Prime Minister and Nat. Exec. Council 1995; Sec.-Gen. Pacific Islands Forum Secr. 1998–2003; fmr Chair. New Ireland Tourism Bureau. *Leisure interests:* reading, walking, watching rugby. *Address:* House No. 4, Forum Secretariat Compound, Ratu Sukuna Road, Suva, Fiji (home).

LEVIN, Carl, JD; American politician; b. 28 June 1934, Detroit, Mich.; s. of Saul R. Levin and Bess Levin (née Levinson); m. Barbara Halpern 1961; three d.; ed Detroit Central High School, Swarthmore Coll., Harvard Law School; Mich. Asst Attorney Gen. and Gen. Counsel for Mich. Civil Rights Comm. 1964–67; Special Asst Attorney Gen. and Chief Appellate Attorney for Defender's Office of Legal Aid and Defender Assoc. of Detroit 1968–69; elected to Detroit City Council 1969, re-elected as City Council Pres. 1973; Senator from Michigan 1979–2015 (retd), Chair. Armed Services Cttee 2001–03, 2007, mem. Governmental Affairs Cttee; joined Honigman Miller Schwartz and Cohn LLP Attorneys and Counselors, Detroit 2015; Democrat; Christian A. Herter Award, WorldBoston 2002, Distinguished Public Service Award, Sec. of the Navy 2003, Harry S. Truman Award, Nat. Guard Asscn 2004, Stewardship Award, Nat. Marine Sanctuary 2005, one of TIME's 10 Best Senators 2006, Four Freedoms Medal, Franklin and Eleanor Roosevelt Foundation 2007, Global Service Award, World Affairs Council 2007. *Address:* Honigman Miller Schwartz and Cohn LLP Attorneys and Counselors, 2290 First National Building, 660 Woodward Avenue, Detroit, MI 48226, USA (office). *Website:* www.honigman.com (office).

LEVIN, Gerald Manuel, BA, LLB; American fmr media executive; *Presiding Director, Moonview Sanctuary;* b. 6 May 1939, Philadelphia, Pa; s. of David Levin and Pauline Schantzer; m. 1st Carol S. Needleman 1959 (divorced 1970), two s. (one deceased), one d.; m. 2nd Barbara Riley 1970, one s. one d.; m. 3rd Laurie Perlman 2005; ed Haverford Coll. and Univ. of Pennsylvania; Assoc., Simpson, Thatcher & Bartlett, New York 1963–67; Gen. Man. and COO, Devt and Resources Corpn, New York 1967–71; Rep., Int. Basic Economy Corpn, Tehran 1971–72; Vice-Pres. Programming, Home Box Office, New York 1972–73, Pres. and CEO 1973–76, Chair. and CEO 1976–79; Group Vice-Pres. (Video), Time Inc. New York 1979–84, Exec. Vice-Pres. 1984–88, Vice-Chair. 1988–90, Vice-Chair. Time-Warner Inc. 1990–92, Jt CEO 1992–93, CEO and Chair. 1992–2001, CEO AOL Time Warner (created after merger of Time Warner and American Online 2000) 2001–02 (retd); Presiding Dir Moonview Sanctuary (spiritual healing firm) 2004–; Chair. StartUp Health 2011–; mem. Bd of Dirs Organized Wisdom; Hon. LLD (Texas Coll.) 1985, (Middlebury Coll.) 1994, Hon. LHD (Univ. of Denver) 1995; Media Person of the Year Award, Cannes Lions Int. Advertising Festival 2001. *Leisure interests:* reading, jogging. *Address:* Moonview Sanctuary, PO Box 1518, Santa Monica, CA 90406, USA (office). *Telephone:* (866) 601-0601 (office). *E-mail:* glevin@moonviewsanctuary.com (office). *Website:* www.moonviewsanctuary.com (office).

LEVIN, Richard Charles, BA, BLitt, PhD; American economist, academic and fmr university administrator; *CEO, Coursera Inc.;* b. 7 April 1947, San Francisco, Calif.; s. of Derek Levin and Phylys Goldstein; m. Jane Aries 1968; two s. two d.; ed Lowell High School, San Francisco, Stanford and Yale Univs and Merton Coll., Oxford, UK; Asst Prof. of Econs, Yale Univ. 1974–79, Assoc. Prof. 1979–82, Prof. of Econs and Man. 1982–92, Dir Grad. Studies in Econs 1984–86, Chair. Dept of Econs 1987–92, Frederick William Beinecke Prof. of Econs 1992–, Dean, Grad. School 1992–93, Pres. Yale Univ. 1993–2013; CEO Coursera Inc. (online learning co.) 2014–; Fellow, Merton Coll. Oxford 1996; mem. Yale-New Haven Hosp. Bd of Trustees 1993, Yale-New Haven Health Services Corpn Inc. 1993; mem. Bd of Dirs Hewlett Foundation, Lucent Technologies, Satmetrix; Trustee, Hewlett Foundation, Univs Research Asscn 1994–99; mem. American Econ. Asscn, Econometric Soc.; Fellow, American Acad. of Arts and Sciences; Hon. LLD (Princeton) 1993, (Harvard) 1994; Hon. DCL (Oxford) 1998. *Publication:* The Work of the University 2003. *Address:* Coursera Inc., 1975 El Camino Real West, Mountain View, CA 94040, USA (office). *Website:* www.coursera.org (office).

LEVIN, Richard I., BS, MD, FACP, FACC, FAHA; American physician, academic, university administrator and foundation president; *President and CEO, Arnold P. Gold Foundation;* b. 28 July 1948, Long Branch, NJ; s. of Jack Levin and Sally Stark; m. Jane Bressman 1970; two c.; ed Peddie School, Yale Univ., New York Univ. (NYU) School of Medicine, Cornell Univ. Medical Coll.; Postdoctoral Fellowship, Cornell Univ. Medical Coll. 1979–83; Founder, Vice-Pres. and Medical Dir Q-Med, Inc. 1983–2008; practised and taught medicine for 35 years at NYU and Bellevue Hosp. Center, New York City; Prof. of Medicine, NYU 1996–2006, Prof. Emer. 2006–, also Vice-Dean for Educ., Faculty and Academic Affairs, NYU School of Medicine; Vice-Prin. (Health Affairs), McGill Univ., Montreal, also Dean, Faculty of Medicine 2006–11, Prof. Emer. 2013–; Pres. and CEO Arnold P. Gold Foundation 2012–; Clinical Investigator, Nat. Heart, Lung, and Blood Inst.; consultant to Liposome Co., Princeton 1988–; mem. American Fed. for Medical Research (Councillor 1986–88), Harvey Soc., New York Heart Asscn, Fed. of American Socs for Experimental Biology; Fellow, American Coll. of Physicians, American Coll. of Cardiology, American Heart Asscn (AHA, Clinician Scientist), Canadian Acad. of Health Science 2011, NY Acad. Medicine, Gold Humanism Honor Soc.; Hon. DSc (Wake Forest Univ.) 2016; AHA Beller Research Award, AHA Mission Achievement Award, David L. Johnston Award, McGill Univ., Aaron Diamond Res Award, Dana Award. *Publications:* more than 85 publs in int. journals. *Address:* APGF, 619 Palisade Avenue, Englewood Cliffs, NJ 07632, USA (office). *Telephone:* (201) 567-7999 (office). *Fax:* (201) 567-7880 (office). *E-mail:* rlevin@gold-foundation.org (office). *Website:* www.humanism-in-medicine.org (office).

LEVIN, Simon Asher, PhD; American mathematician, ecologist and academic; *George M. Moffett Professor of Biology, Department of Ecology and Evolutionary Biology and Director, The Center for BioComplexity, Princeton University;* b. 22 April 1941, Baltimore, Md; s. of Theodore S. Levin and Clara G. Levin; m. Carole Lotte Leiffer; one s. one d.; ed Johns Hopkins Univ., Baltimore, Univ. of Maryland, College Park; Asst Prof., Cornell Univ. 1965–70, Assoc. Prof. 1971–77, Chair. Section of Ecology and Systematics, Div. of Biological Sciences 1974–79, Prof. of Applied Math. and Ecology 1977–92, Charles A. Alexander Prof. of Biological Sciences 1985–92, Adjunct Prof. 1992–, Dir Ecosystems Research Center 1980–87, Dir Center for Environmental Research 1987–90; Affiliated Faculty, Program in Applied and Computational Math., Princeton Univ. 1992–, George M. Moffett Prof. of Biology 1992–, Affiliated Faculty, Princeton Environmental Inst. 1993–, Dir Princeton Environmental Inst. 1992–98, Dir The Center for BioComplexity 2001–, Participating Faculty, Biophysics Program 2009–; numerous visiting positions including Univ. of Maryland, College Park 1968, Univ. of British Columbia, Vancouver 1979–80, Weizmann Inst., Rehovot, Israel 1977, 1980, Univ. of Kyoto, Japan 1983–84, Colorado State Univ. (Visiting Distinguished Ecologist) 1987, Stanford Univ., Calif. 1988, All Souls Coll., Oxford, UK (Visiting Fellow) 1988, Inst. for Advanced Study, Princeton 1999, 2008–09, Univ. of Miami 2004–05, Univ. of California, Irvine 2007, 2009; Visiting Miller Research Prof., Univ. of California, Berkeley 2003, Univ. of Miami 2004–05; Chair. Council Int. Inst. for Applied Systems Analysis (IIASA), Laxenburg, Austria 2003–08, (Vice-Chair. 2009–12), US Nat. Cttee for IIASA, The Nat. Academies 2003–; mem. numerous advisory bds including Biodiversity Science and Educ. Initiative (BSEI), Smithsonian Inst. 2005–, DIMACS, Rutgers Univ. 2008–11, Center for Social and Econ. Dynamics, Brookings Inst. 2008–, Miller Inst. for Basic Research in Science, Univ. of California, Berkeley 2009–12; mem. Science Bd Inst. for Medical BioMathematics, Bene Ataroth, Israel 1999–, Santa Fe Inst., NM 1991–99, 2001–; Ed.-in-Chief Encyclopedia of Biodiversity, Online Edn 2005–; Co-Man. Ed. Monographs in Population Biology 1992–, Complexity Series 1992–; mem. Editorial Bd numerous journals including Evolutionary Theory 1976–, Mathematical and Computer Modelling 1979–, Applied Mathematics Letters 1987–, Mathematical Biosciences 1987–, Conservation Ecology 1995–, Issues in Ecology 1995–, Journal of Biomathematics (China) 1999–, Journal of Mathematical Biology 1995–; mem. Advisory Bd severala journals including Journal of Environmental and Ecological Statistics 1992–, Ecological Research 1996–, Ecological Complexity 2004–, Mathematical Biosciences and Engineering 2004–; Fellow, American Acad. of Arts and Sciences 1992, AAAS 1992, Ecological Soc. of America 2012; mem. American Inst. of Biological Sciences, American Soc. of Naturalists, British Ecological Soc., Ecological Soc. of America (Pres. 1990–91), Soc. for Industrial and Applied Math., Soc. for Math. Biology (Pres. 1987–89, Past Pres. and Vice-Pres. 1989–91), Soc. for the Study of Evolution, NAS 2000, American Philosophical Soc. 2003; Foreign mem. Istituto Veneto di Scienze, Lettere ed Arti, Venice 2008; Beijer Fellow 2007; Fellow, Soc. for Industrial and Applied Math. 2009; Hon. Ed. several journals; Hon. mem. Lund (Sweden) Ecological Soc. 1999, Eastern Europe Soc. of Math. Ecology 1995, Asian Math. Ecology Soc. 1995, World Innovation Foundation 2003; Hon. DSc (Eastern Michigan Univ.) 1990, (Michigan State Univ.) 2009; Hon. DHumLitt (Whittier Coll.) 2004; numerous awards including MacArthur Award, Ecological Soc. of America 1988, Distinguished Statistical Ecologist Award, Int. Asscn for Ecology 1994, Distinguished Service Citation, Ecological Soc. of America 1998, First Okubo Lifetime Achievement Award, Soc. for Math. Biology and Japanese Soc. for Theoretical Biology 2001, Medallion of Université de Montpellier 2004, Dr A.H. Heineken Prize for Environmental Sciences, Royal Netherlands Acad. of Arts and Sciences 2004, Kyoto Prize in Basic Sciences, Inamori Foundation, Japan 2005, SIAM I.E. Block Community Lecture Award 2006, Distinguished Scientist Award, American Inst. of Biological Sciences 2007, Margalef Prize for Ecology 2010, Eminent Ecologist Award, Ecological Soc. of America 2010, Tyler Prize for Environmental Achievement, Univ. of Southern California 2014. *Publications:* numerous publs on modelling of ecological systems, dynamics of populations and communities, spatial heterogeneity and problem of scale, evolutionary, math. and theoretical ecology. *Address:* Department of Ecology and Evolutionary Biology, 203 Eno Hall, Princeton University, Princeton, NJ 08544-1003, USA (office). *Telephone:* (609) 258-6880 (office). *Fax:* (609) 258-6819 (office). *E-mail:* slevin@princeton.edu (office). *Website:* www.eeb.princeton.edu/~slevin (office).

LEVINE, Alan J., BS, JD; American lawyer, entertainment industry executive and lecturer; *Managing Partner, Canon Media Partners, LLC;* b. 8 March 1947, Los Angeles, Calif.; s. of Phil Levine and Shirley Lauber; m. Judy Birnbaum 1973; two c.; ed Univ. of Southern California (USC); called to the California Bar 1972, US Dist Court (South Dist), Calif. 1972; Partner, Pacht, Ross, Warne, Bernhard & Sears, LA 1971–78, Schiff, Hirsch & Schreiber, Beverly Hills, Calif. 1978–80, Armstrong, Hirsch & Levine, LA 1980–89; Pres. and COO SONY Pictures Entertainment Inc., Culver City, Calif. 1989–96, Chair. 1994–96, entertainment and media consultant 1996–99; Of Counsel, Ziffren, Brittenham, Branca & Fischer (now Ziffren, Brittenham, Branca, Fischer, Gilbert-Lurie, Stiffleman & Cook LLP), LA from 1999; Founder J.P. Morgan Entertainment Advisors 2007 (became Canon Media Partners, LLC), Man. Partner 2010–; mem. Bd of Councilors, School of Cinema-TV; fmr mem. Bd of Dirs, DreamWorks Studios, Castle Rock Entertainment, and several other civic, charitable and education bds and cttees, including Frank Sinatra Foundation, Bd Govs, Cedars-Sinai Medical Center, Los Angeles, Bd of Councilors, USC School of Cinematic Arts and USC Law School, Roundtable of the Museum of Radio & Television; has lectured at numerous entertainment and media confs at Harvard Business School, Howard Univ., UCLA and USC; mem. Acad. of Motion Picture Arts & Sciences, Acad. of Television Arts & Sciences. *Address:* Gould School of Law, University of Southern California, 699 Exposition Boulevard, Los Angeles, CA 90089 (office); Canon Media Partners, LLC, 100 North Crescent Drive, Suite 300, Beverly Hills, CA 90210, USA. *Telephone:* (213) 740-7331 (Los Angeles) (office); (310) 385-3676 (Beverly Hills). *Fax:* (310) 432-5000 (Beverly Hills). *E-mail:* alevine@law.usc.edu (office). *Website:* weblaw.usc.edu/contact/contactInfo.cfm?detailID=71043 (office); www.canonmp.com.

LEVINE, James; American musician, conductor and pianist; b. 23 June 1943, Cincinnati, Ohio; s. of Lawrence M. Levine and Helen Levine (née Goldstein); ed Walnut Hills High School, Cincinnati, The Juilliard School; Asst Conductor,

Cleveland Orchestra 1964–70; Prin. Conductor, Metropolitan Opera, New York 1973–, Music Dir 1976–2016, Emer. 2016–18 (dismissed), Artistic Dir 1986–2004; Music Dir Ravinia Festival 1973–93, Cincinnati May Festival 1974–78; Chief Conductor, Munich Philharmonic 1999–2004; Music Dir UBS Verbier Festival Youth Orchestra 2000–04; Music Dir Boston Symphony Orchestra 2004–11; Guest Conductor, Philadelphia Orchestra 2015; regular appearances as conductor and pianist in Europe and the USA with orchestras including Vienna Philharmonic, Berlin Philharmonic, Chicago Symphony, Philadelphia Orchestra, Philharmonia, Dresden Staatskapelle, Boston Symphony, New York Philharmonic, Israel Philharmonic, Salzburg and Bayreuth Festivals; conducted Metropolitan Opera premieres of I Vespri Siciliani, Stiffelio, I Lombardi (Verdi), The Rise and Fall of the City of Mahagonny (Weill), Lulu (Berg), Porgy and Bess (Gershwin), Oedipus Rex (Stravinsky), Idomeneo, La Clemenza di Tito (Mozart), Erwartung, Moses und Aron (Schönberg), La Cenerentola (Rossini), Benvenuto Cellini (Berlioz), The Ghosts of Versailles (Corigliano) (world premiere), The Great Gatsby (Harbison) (world premiere); Conductor of Salzburg Festival premieres of Offenbach's Les contes d'Hoffmann 1980 and Schönberg's Moses und Aron 1987; conducted Munich Philharmonic Orchestra at the BBC Proms 2002, Boston Symphony 2007; led more than a dozen concerts on the Three Tenors World Tour 1996–2000; Dr hc (Univ. of Cincinnati, New England Conservatory, Northwestern Univ., The Juilliard School); Grammy Awards for audio recordings of Orff's Carmina Burana, Mahler's Symphony No. 7, Brahms' A German Requiem, Verdi's La Traviata (film soundtrack), Wagner's Das Rheingold, Die Walküre, Götterdämmerung, Strauss' Ariadne auf Naxos, Ravel's Daphnis et Chloé; Cultural Award of New York City 1980, Smetana Medal 1987, Musical America's Musician of the Year Award, Gold Medal, Nat. Inst. of Social Sciences 1996, Nat. Medal of Arts 1997, Anton Seidl Award 1997, Lotus Award 1997, Kennedy Center Honors 2002, World Econ. Forum Crystal Award 2003, Metropolitan Opera Guild Opera News Award 2006, Nat. Endowment for the Arts Opera Award 2008, Award in the Vocal Arts, Bard Coll. 2009, Ditson Conductors Award, Columbia Univ. 2009, George Peabody Medal, Johns Hopkins's Peabody Conservatory 2010. Recordings include: over 100 albums of symphonic works, chamber music, lieder and song recitals, solo piano music and 36 complete operas, including Wagner: Der Ring Des Nibelungen (Grammy Award for Best Opera Recording 2013), The Art of James Levine 2015, Jessye Norman - Lieder 2016.

LEVINE, Marne; American business executive; *Chief Operating Officer, Instagram;* b. 1 Oct. 1970, Ohio; d. of Dr Mark Levine and Teri Levine (née Ladmer); m. Phillip Deutch; two s.; ed Miami Univ., Ohio, Harvard Business School; worked for US Treasury Dept 1993–2000; Chief of Staff to Larry Summers, Harvard Univ. 2000–02; Dir of Product Man., Revolution Money 2006–08; Chief of Staff and Special Asst for Econ. Policy, White House Nat. Econ. Council 2009–10; Vice-Pres., Global Public Policy, Facebook 2010–14; COO, Instagram 2014–; Dir Women for Women Int. *Address:* Instagram, 181 South Park Street, San Francisco, CA 94107, USA (office). *Telephone:* (415) 857-3369 (office). *Website:* instagram.com (office).

LEVINSOHN, James, BA, MPA, PhD; American economist and academic; *Charles Goodyear Professor of Global Affairs, Professor of Economics and Management and Director, Jackson Institute of Global Affairs, Yale University;* ed Williams Coll., Woodrow Wilson School, Princeton Univ.; joined faculty of Univ. of Michigan 1987, becoming Assoc. Dean, Gerald R. Ford School of Public Policy 2003–07, also J. Ira and Nicki Harris Family Prof. of Public Policy and Prof. of Econs; Visiting Prof., Cowles Foundation, Yale Univ. 2008, Charles W. Goodyear Prof. of Global Affairs, Prof. of Econs and Man. and Founding Dir, Jackson Inst. of Global Affairs, Yale Univ. 2010–; Research Assoc., Nat. Bureau of Econ. Research 1992–; Visiting Prof., Tel-Aviv Univ. 1994, Univ. of Cape Town 2009; Visiting Fellow, Inst. for Int. Econ. Studies, Stockholm 1989, 1991; Nat. Fellow, Hoover Inst., Stanford Univ. 1990–91; served on editorial bds of numerous econs publs, including American Economic Review 2006–09, Review of Economics and Statistics 2003–, Journal of Economic Literature 2004–; consultant to Presidency of South Africa 2004–08; Founding Partner, ApplEcon LLC, MightyGoodCoffee.com. *Address:* Office of the Director, Jackson Institute of Global Affairs, Yale University, Rosenkranz Hall, 115 Prospect Street, PO Box 208206, New Haven, CT 06520-8206, USA (office). *Telephone:* (203) 432-6610 (office). *E-mail:* james .levinsohn@yale.edu (office). *Website:* jackson.yale.edu (office); levinsohn.commons .yale.edu (office).

LEVINSON, Arthur D., BS, PhD; American biochemist and business executive; *Chairman, Apple Inc.;* b. 31 March 1950, Seattle, Wash.; s. of Sol Levinson and Malvina Levinson (née Lindsay); m. Rita May Liff 1978; two c.; ed Univ. of Washington, Princeton Univ.; Postdoctoral Fellow, NIH 1972–77, Univ. of California, San Francisco 1977, American Cancer Soc. 1978–80; Sr Scientist, Genentech Inc. 1980–83, Staff Scientist 1983–87, Dir Cell Genetics Dept 1987–89, Vice-Pres. Research Tech. 1989–90, Vice-Pres. Research 1990–92, Sr Vice-Pres. Research 1992–93, Sr Vice-Pres. Research & Devt 1993–95, Pres. and CEO Genentech Inc. 1995–99, Chair. and CEO 1999–2009, Chair. 2009–14; Chair. Apple Inc. 2011–; CEO Calico 2013–; mem. Bd of Dirs, F. Hoffmann-La Roche 2010–14, NGM Biopharmaceuticals 2009–14, Amyris Biotechnologies 2009–14; mem. Bd of Scientific Consultants, Memorial Sloan Kettering Cancer Center, Industrial Advisory Bd, California Inst. for Quantitative Biosciences (QB3), Advisory Council for the Princeton Univ. Dept of Molecular Biology, Advisory Council for the Lewis-Sigler Inst. for Integrative Genomics; mem. Editorial Bd Virology 1984–87, Molecular Biology and Medicine 1986–89, Molecular and Cellular Biology 1987–96, Journal of Virology 1988–91; mem. AAAS, New York Acad. of Sciences, Pharmaceutical Research & Mfrs of America (Dir 1997–2001), Biotechnology Industry Org. 1995–2000, American Soc. of Biochemistry & Molecular Biology, American Soc. of Microbiology; Fellow, American Acad. of Arts and Sciences; numerous awards, including Salk Translational Medicine Award, Univ. of California, San Diego 1999, James Madison Medal, Princeton Univ. 2006, Biotechnology Heritage Award, Chemical Heritage Foundation/ Biotechnology Industry Org. 2010, Margaret Foti Award, American Asscn for Cancer Research 2011, Cold Spring Harbor Laboratory Double Helix Medal Honoree 2012, Alumnus Summa Laude Dignatus Award, Univ. of Washington 2014. *Publications include:* author or co-author of more than 80 scientific articles; named inventor on 11 US patents. *Address:* Apple Inc., 1 Infinite Loop, Cupertino,

CA 95014, USA (office). *Telephone:* (408) 996-1010 (office). *Fax:* (408) 974-2113 (office). *E-mail:* media.help@apple.com (office). *Website:* www.apple.com (office).

LEVINSON, Barry; American screenwriter, film director and film producer; b. 6 April 1942, Baltimore, Md; m. 1st Valerie Curtin 1975 (divorced); m. 2nd Diana Rhodes; ed American Univ.; fmrly wrote and acted on TV comedy show in Los Angeles; later worked on network TV; wrote and appeared, The Carol Burnett Show; worked on film scripts for Silent Movie and High Anxiety (with Mel Brooks q.v.); f. Baltimore Pictures, Inc. and The Levinson/Fontana Co. (Exec. Producer); Hon. DFA (American Univ.) 1999; ShoWest Director of the Year Award 1998, named one of Variety Winners 'Billion Dollar Directors' 1998, Creative Achievement Award, 13th Annual American Comedy Awards 1999, ACE Golden Eddie Filmmaker of the Year Award 2002, Distinguished Screenwriter Award. Austin Film Festival 2004, Laurel Award for Screenwriting Achievement 2010, Crystal Globe For Outstanding Artistic Contrib. To World Cinema, Karlovy Vary Int. Film Festival 2018. *Actor:* High Anxiety 1977, Rain Man 1988, Quiz Show 1994, Bee Movie (voice) 2007. *Writer:* Diner, Tin Men, Avalon; co-wrote screenplays (with Valerie Curtin) for And Justice for All, Inside Moves, Best Friends, Unfaithfully Yours, Toys, Liberty Heights. *Films directed:* Diner 1982, The Natural 1984, Young Sherlock Holmes 1985, Tin Men 1987, Good Morning Vietnam 1987, Rain Man (Academy Award for Best Picture 1988, Academy Award for Best Dir 1988, Directors Guild Award for Best Dir 1988) 1988, Disclosure 1994; directed and produced Avalon (Writers Guild Award for Best Screenplay 1989) 1990, Bugsy (Golden Globe Award for Best Picture 1991) 1991, Toys 1992, Jimmy Hollywood (dir, writer) 1994, Sleepers 1996, Wag the Dog 1997, Sphere 1998, Liberty Heights 2000, An Everlasting Piece 2001, Bandits 2001, Envy 2004, Man of the Year 2006, What Just Happened? 2008, What Just Happened (producer) 2008, The Bay (producer) 2012, The Last Act (producer) 2014. *Television includes:* writer for Tim Conway Comedy Hour, The Marty Feldman Comedy Machine, The Carol Burnett Show (Emmy Awards for TV Comedy Writing 1974, 1975); exec. producer: Harry, 30 Minutes of Investigative Ticking, Diner, Homicide: Life on the Street (series) (Emmy Award for Best Dir 1993, Peabody Award 1993, 1995, 1997, Writers Guild Award 1994, 1995, The Nancy Susan Reynolds Award for Outstanding Portrayal of Sexual Responsibility in a Dramatic Series 1996, The Prism Commendation from the Nat. Inst. Inst. on Drug Use and The Entertainment Industries Council 1997, DGA Award for Outstanding Directorial Achievement for Dramatic Series 1998, TCA Award for Program of the Year and Drama of the Year 1998, Emmy Award for Best Male Actor in a Drama Series 1998, Emmy Award for Best Casting in a Drama Series 1998, Humanitas Award 1999), Oz, The Beat 2000, Shot in the Heart 2001, Baseball Wives 2002, Possession 2002, Analyze That 2002, Deliver Us from Eva 2003, Strip Search 2004, Envy 2004, The Jury (series) 2004, The Bedford Diaries (series) 2006, M.O.N.Y. 2007, The Philanthropist (series) 2009, You Don't Know Jack 2010, Phil Spector 2013, Copper (series) 2012–13, Borgia (series) 2011–14, Shades of Blue (series) 2016, Killing Fields (series) 2016. *Publications:* Levinson on Levinson 1992, Sixty-Six (novel) 2003. *Website:* www.levinson.com (office).

LEVITIN, Igor Yevgenyevich; Russian politician and government official; *Presidential Aide;* b. 21 Feb. 1952; m.; one d.; ed Mil. Acad. of Rear Services and Transportation; served in Soviet armed forces in Odessa 1970–80, with Armies Southern Div. 1980–83, Mil. Commdt of Urgal station and Baikal 1983–85, Mil. Commdt and Deputy Head of Moscow Mil. Railway Communications Service 1985–94; Head of Transport Dept, Phoenix-Trans Co. 1995–98; Head of Railway Dept, worked for Severstaltrans 1996–2004, Deputy Dir 1998–2004; Minister of Transport 2004–12; Presidential Aide 2012–; Order 'For Merit to the Fatherland', 4th Class, then 3rd Class, Medal 'For the Development of Railways'. *Address:* c/o Presidential Executive Office, 103132 Moscow, Staraya Square 4, Russia (office). *Telephone:* (495) 925-35-81 (office). *Fax:* (495) 206-07-66 (office). *E-mail:* president@gov.ru (office). *Website:* www.kremlin.ru (office); www.state.kremlin.ru (office).

LEVITIN, Mikhail Zakharovich; Russian stage director and writer; *Artistic Director, Hermitage Theatre;* b. 27 Dec. 1945, Odessa, Ukraine; m.; two d. one s.; ed Moscow Inst. of Theatre Arts; Founder and Artistic Dir Moscow Hermitage Theatre 1981–; People's Artist of Russia, Order of Honour 2006; Moscow State Prize Laureate 2010. *Stage productions include:* Wanderings of Pilgrim Billy, Faryatyev's Fantasies in Moscow Theatre of Soviet Army, Alice Behind the Mirror, Moscow Theatre of Young Spectators, Harm! Harms! Shardam! or Clowns' School 1981, Pauper or Zanda's Death 1986, Evening in a Lunatic Asylum 1991, Maria, Hermitage Theatre 1996, New Year Tree at Ivanovs', Omsk Drama Theatre 1996; Hermitage Theatre: Fiend 2003, Suyer-Viyer 2005, Rescue Cantata 2005, Dissecting Room of Engineer Evno Azef 2005, A Feast in the Time of Plague 2005–06, Erendira and Her Grandmother 2006, Under the Bed 2006, Golden Calf or Back to Odessa 2007, The Secret Notes of a Secret Counselor 2009, Kapnist Round Trip 2009, These Bitches Wanted to Kill Me 2011, Wedding Krechinsky 2016, Don Quijote 2017. *Television:* series of broadcasts '…and others' 2011–12, Happy Generation 2012, Under the Theatre's Sky 2013, Star of Nonsense 2016. *Publications include:* Other Man's Spectacle, My Friend Believes, Bolero, Sheer Indecency, Plutodrama, Dog's Shit, Dissecting Room of Engineer Evno Azef, Clowns' School, Tairov, The Book About Petr Fomenko. *Address:* Moscow Hermitage Theatre, Karentny Ryad 3, 103006 Moscow, Russia (office). *Telephone:* (495) 209-20-76 (office). *E-mail:* info@ermistage.ru (office). *Website:* ermitazh .theatre.ru/people/levitin (office).

LEVITIS, Yefim Zavelyevich; Russian religious leader; b. 29 Nov. 1930; m.; one s.; ed Moscow Inst. of Aviation, Jewish seminary at Moscow Choral Synagogue, Higher Rabbis' School, Budapest; Scientific Sec. Moscow Jewish community 1975–80; Rabbi, St Petersburg 1980–91, Chief Rabbi, Grand Choral Synagogue 1991–97; Deputy Chief Rabbi of Russia responsible for co-operation with non-Jewish orgs; mem. Jewish Conf. of Rabbis; mem. Working Group, Consultative Council of Confession Heads, St Petersburg. *Address:* c/o Grand Choral Synagogue, 2 Lermontovsky pr., St Petersburg, Russia.

LEVITT, Arthur, Jr; American business executive and fmr government official; *Senior Advisor, The Carlyle Group;* b. 3 Feb. 1931, Brooklyn; s. of Arthur Levitt and Dorothy Wolff; m. Marylin Blauner 1955; one s. one d.; ed Williams Coll.; Asst Promotion Dir Time Inc. New York 1954–59; Exec. Vice-Pres., Dir Oppenheimer Industries Inc. Kansas City 1959–62; with Shearson Hayden Stone Inc. (later

Shearson Lehman Bros Inc.), New York 1962–78, Pres. 1969–78; Chair., CEO, Dir American Stock Exchange, New York 1978–89; Chair. Levitt Media Co. New York 1989–93, New York City Econ. Devt Corpn 1990–93; Chair. SEC 1993–2001; Sr Advisor, The Carlyle Group 2001–, Promontory Financial Group, LLC; fmr Owner, Roll Call, Inc.; Advisor, Goldman Sachs Group, Inc. 2009–; mem. Bd of Dirs Bloomberg LP; mem. Advisory Bd Gold Bullion International LLC; mem. American Acad. of Arts and Sciences; Hon. LLD (Williams Coll.) 1980, (Pace) 1980, (Hamilton Coll.) 1981, (Long Island) 1984, (Hofstra) 1985; Award for Distinguished Leadership in Global Capital Markets, Yale School of Man. 2001. *Publications:* Take on the Street: What Wall Street and Corporate America Don't Want You to Know 2002. *Address:* The Carlyle Group, 520 Madison Avenue, New York, NY 10022, USA (office). *Telephone:* (212) 813-4900 (office). *Fax:* (212) 813-4901 (office). *Website:* www.carlyle.com (office).

LEVITT, Brian Michael, BASc, LLB; Canadian business executive; *Chairman, TD Bank Financial Group;* b. 26 July 1947, Montreal; s. of Eric Levitt and Rya Levitt; m. Claire Gohier 1992; two d.; ed Univ. of Toronto; Special Asst to Provost, Univ. of Toronto 1969–73; called to Bar, Ont. 1974; Dir Interpretation, Prices and Profits Branch, Anti-Inflation Bd, Govt of Canada 1975–76; Assoc., Osler, Hoskin & Harcourt LLP, Toronto 1976–79, Partner 1979–91, Counsel, Montreal office 2001–; Pres. IMASCO Ltd, Montreal 1991–2000, also COO, CEO 1995–2000; mem. Bd of Dirs TD Bank Financial Group 2008–, Chair. 2011–; mem. Bd of Dirs Domtar Corpn (Chair. until merger with Weyerhauser's –2007), Bell Canada, BCE Inc.; Chair. Bd of Trustees, Montreal Museum of Fine Arts; Vice-Chair. C.D. Howe Inst.; apptd to five-person Competition Policy Review Panel cr. by Govt of Canada 2007; Chair. Judicial Compensation and Benefits Comm. of Canada; Chancellor Bishop's Univ. 2013–. *Publications:* various articles on business law. *Leisure interests:* skiing, riding, sailing. *Address:* TD Bank Financial Group, Toronto-Dominion Centre, King Street West and Bay Street, Toronto, ON M5K 1A2, Canada (office). *Telephone:* (416) 982-8222 (office). *Fax:* (416) 982-5671 (office). *E-mail:* td.capa@td.com (office). *Website:* www.td.com (office).

LEVITT, Michael, PhD, FRS; American/British/Israeli biologist and academic; *Robert W. and Vivian K. Cahill Professor in Cancer Research in the School of Medicine and Professor, by courtesy, of Computer Science, Stanford University;* b. 9 May 1947, Pretoria, South Africa; s. of Gertrude Levitt; m. Rina Levitt (died 2017); three s.; ed King's Coll. London, Peterhouse, Cambridge, UK; Postdoctoral Fellow, Weizmann Inst. of Science, Israel 1972–74, Assoc. Prof. of Chemical Physics 1979–84, Full Prof. 1984–87, Chair. of Dept 1980–83; Staff Scientist, MRC Lab. of Molecular Biology, Cambridge 1974–79; Visiting Scientist, Salk Inst., Calif. 1977–79; Prof. of Structural Biology, Stanford Univ. School of Medicine 1987–, Chair., Dept of Structural Biology 1993–2004, currently Robert W. and Vivian K. Cahill Prof. in Cancer Research and Prof., by courtesy, of Computer Science; Blaise Pascal Prof. of Research, Fondation de l'Ecole Normale Superieure, Paris, 2002–04; mem. NAS 2002, American Acad. of Arts and Sciences 2010–; Nobel Prize in Chemistry (jtly with Martin Karplus and Arieh Warshel) 2013. *Address:* Stanford University, Department of Structural Biology, Fairchild Science Building D 100, 99 Campus Drive Street, Stanford, CA 94305-5126, USA (office). *Telephone:* (650) 276-0500 (office). *Fax:* (650) 723-8464 (office). *E-mail:* michael.levitt@stanford.edu (office). *Website:* med.stanford.edu/profiles/michael-levitt (office); csb.stanford.edu/levitt (office).

LEVITZKI, Alexander, PhD; Israeli biochemist and academic; *Wolfson Family Professor of Biochemistry and Director, Institute for Advanced Studies, Hebrew University of Jerusalem;* ed Hebrew Univ. of Jerusalem, Weizmann Inst. of Science, Rehovot and Univ. of California, Berkeley, USA; Fulbright-Hayes Fellow 1968–71; Sr Scientist, Dept of Biophysics, Weizmann Inst. of Science 1970, Assoc. Prof. 1974–76; Assoc. Prof., Hebrew Univ. of Jerusalem 1974, Prof. 1976–, Wolfson Family Prof. of Biochemistry 1985–, Dir Inst. for Advanced Studies 1998–2001, currently with Dept of Biological Chem., Alexander Silberman Inst. of Life Sciences; Visiting Prof. of Chem. and Research Assoc., Inst. of Molecular Biology, Univ. of Ore. Eugene 1974; Visiting Prof. of Biochemistry, Univ. of California, Berkeley 1974, Visiting Miller Research Professor, Miller Inst. for Basic Research in Science 2008; Visiting Scientist, Nat. Cancer Inst., NIH, Bethesda, Md 1979–80; Fogarty Scholar-in-Residence, NIH, Bethesda, Md 1984–85; Visiting Scholar, Stanford Univ., Calif. 1993–94; Visiting Prof., Comprehensive Cancer Center, Univ. of California, San Francisco 2001–03; Edward Rotan Visiting Prof., The M.D. Anderson Cancer Center, Houston, Tex. 2002–, John H. Blaffer Endowed Professorship 2005; Sr Consultant, Biotechnology Research Consultants, Tel-Aviv 1982–86, Rorer Biotechnology, King of Prussia, Pa, USA 1987–92; consultant and mem. Bd of Dirs Int. Diagnostic Labs, Jerusalem 1984–88; consultant, Eldan-Tech 1987–91; mem. Scientific Advisory Bd SUGEN, Inc., Redwood City, Calif. 1993–97, Vice-Pres. Research 1993–94; Chief Scientific Advisor and mem. Scientific Advisory Bd Peptor Ltd 1997–2003; Co-founder TK Signal, Israel 2000, UnResto 2001; Founder Algen Biopharmaceuticals, Israel and USA 2001; mem. Scientific Advisory Bd, ProteoLogics, Rehovot 2002–05, Teva Pharmaceutical Industries Ltd 2008; Founder NovoTyr Pharmaceuticals 2005; Vice-Pres. Fed. of Israeli Socs of Experimental Biology 1999, Pres. 2002–05; mem. Bd Govs, Israel Cancer Asscn 2007–; Ed. Current Topics in Cellular Regulation 1987–91; Assoc. Ed. Cellular Signalling 1987–; mem. Editorial Bd European Journal of Biochemistry 1975–81, Molecular Physiology 1982–85, Journal of Cyclic Nucleotide Research 1982–94, Pharmacology 1991–, Science 1993–96, Anti-cancer Drug Design 1995–2002, Molecular Biology Research Communications 1998–2001, European Journal of Chemical Biology (ChemBiochem) 2000, Oncology Research 2002, Journal of Biological Chemistry 2003, Current Signal Transduction Therapy 2006; mem. European Molecular Biology Org. 1978, Israel Acad. of Sciences 1999 (Chair. Div. of Natural Sciences 2004), Academia Europea 2010; Hon. mem. American Soc. of Biological Chemists 1985; Hon. Scholar, Tel-Hai Academic Coll., Tel Hai, Israel 2006; Dr hc (Ben-Gurion Univ.) 2006; Bi-Annual Shlomo Hestrin Prize, Israel Biochemical Soc. 1975, Bronze Medal for Biochemistry, Free Univ. of Brussels 1983, Israel Prize in Biochemistry 1990, Rothschild Prize in Biology 1990, Lectureship Award, Fed. of European Biochemical Socs 1991, Schender Prize for Pharmacology and Drug Research 1998, Lichtenstein Memorial Lecturer 1998, Hamilton-Fairley Award, European Soc. of Medical Oncology 2002, Medal of the Univ., Univ. of Helsinki 2003, Al Wolf Lectureship (IRSC), Australia 2003, Wolf Prize for Medicine 2005 (jt winner), Research Award, The Jacqueline Seroussi Memorial Foundation for Cancer, Tel-Aviv 2006, Research Award, Prostate Cancer Foundation 2006, 2007, Paul Ehrlich Magic Bullet Lifetime Achievement Award in Oncology, 100th Anniversary Paul Ehrlich meeting, Nuremberg, Germany 2008, Karl Friedrich Bonhöffer Lecturer, Max Plank Inst. for Biophysical Chemistry, Göttingen 2011, The Nauta Award in Pharmacochemistry, European Fed. of Medicinal Chem. 2012, Award for Outstanding Achievement in Chem. in Cancer Research, American Asscn for Cancer Research 2013. *Publications:* numerous articles in scientific journals on developing techniques for targeted destruction of cancer cells through biochemical means. *Address:* The Levitzki Lab, Unit of Cellular Signalling, Department of Biological Chemistry, The Alexander Silberman Institute of Life Sciences, The Hebrew University of Jerusalem, 91904 Jerusalem, Israel (office). *Telephone:* (2) 6585404 (office). *Fax:* (2) 6512958 (office). *E-mail:* alex.levitzki@mail.huji.ac.il (office). *Website:* biolchem.huji.ac.il/levitzki/levitzki.html (office).

LEVY, Alain M., BASc, MBA; French entertainment industry executive; *Executive Chairman, Algean Group;* b. 19 Dec. 1946; ed Ecole des Mines and Wharton Business School, Univ. of Pennsylvania, USA; Asst to the Pres. CBS Int., New York 1972–73, Vice-Pres. Marketing for Europe, Paris 1973, Vice-Pres. of Creative Operations for Europe, also Man. CBS Italy 1978; Man. Dir CBS Disques, France 1979–84, CEO PolyGram France 1984–88, Exec. Vice-Pres. PolyGram Group, France and FRG 1988–90, Man. US Operations PolyGram Group 1990–98, Pres., CEO, mem. Bd Man. PolyGram USA 1991–98; mem. Group Man. Cttee Philips Electronics, majority shareholder PolyGram USA 1991–98; Chair. Bd EMI Group PLC 2001–07, Chair. and CEO EMI Recorded Music 2001–07; Sr Advisor to Banijay 2008–09; Exec. Chair., Algean Group 2013–; mem. advisory bd Film Business Academy 2006–. *Address:* Algean Group, 19 Portland Place, London, W1B 1PX (office). *E-mail:* info@algeangroup.com (office). *Website:* www.algeangroup.com (office).

LÉVY, Bernard-Henri; French writer and philosopher; b. 5 Nov. 1948, Beni-Saf, Algeria; s. of André Lévy and Ginette Lévy; m. 1st Isabelle Doutreluigne; one d.; m. 2nd Sylvie Bouscasse 1980; one s. one d.; m. 2nd Arielle Sonnery 1993; ed Ecole Normale Supérieure (rue d'Ulm); War Corresp. for Combat 1971–72; Lecturer in Epistemology, Univ. of Strasbourg, in Philosophy, Ecole Normale Supérieure 1973; mem. François Mitterrand's Group of Experts 1973–76; joined Editions Grasset as Ed. 'nouvelle philosophie' series 1973; Ed. Idées section, Quotidien de Paris; Contrib. to Nouvel Observateur and Temps Modernes 1974; Co-founder Action International contre la Faim 1980, Radio Free Kabul 1981, SOS Racisme; Founder-Dir La Règle du jeu (journal) 1990–; apptd Pres. Supervisory Council Sept-Arte 1993; apptd by French Govt to head fact-finding mission to Kabul, Afghanistan 2002. *Film:* directed: Le Jour la Nuit 1997. *Publications include:* Bangladesh: Nationalisme dans la révolution 1973, Les Indes rouges 1973, La barbarie à visage humain (Prix d'honneur) 1977, Le testament de Dieu 1979, L'idéologie française 1981, Questions de principe 1983, Le diable en tête (Prix Médicis) 1984, Impressions d'Asie 1985, Questions de principe II 1986, Eloge des intellectuels 1987, Les derniers jours de Charles Baudelaire (Prix Interallié) 1988, Questions de principe III 1990, Frank Stella: Les années 80 1990, Les bronzes de César 1991, Les aventures de la liberté 1991, Piet Mondrian 1992, Piero Della Francesca 1992, Le jugement dernier (play) 1992, Questions de principe IV 1992, Les hommes et les femmes (jtly) 1993, Un jour dans la mort de Sarajevo (screenplay, jtly) 1993, Bosna! (screenplay, jtly) 1994, La pureté dangereuse 1995, Questions de principe V 1995, Le lys et la cendre 1996, Comédie 1997, The Rules of the Game 1998 (revised edn What Good Are Intellectuals?: 44 Writers Share Their Thoughts 2000), Le siècle de Sartre 2000, Réflexion sur la guerre, Le mal et la fin de l'histoire 2001, Mémoire vive 2001, Qui a tué Daniel Pearl? 2003, American Vertigo 2006, Ce grand cadavre à la renverse 2007, Ennemis publics (with Michel Houellebecq) 2008, Left in Dark Times: A Stand Against the New Barbarism 2009, Pièces d'identité 2010, La Guerre sans l'aimer 2011. *Leisure interests:* skiing, judo, water-skiing. *Website:* www.laregledujeu.org (office); www.bernard-henri-levy.com.

LEVY, David; Israeli politician; b. 21 Dec. 1938, Morocco; emigrated to Israel 1957; construction worker; joined Histadrut (trade union); mem. Knesset (Parl.) representing Herut (Freedom) group of Gahal 1969–2006 (subsequently of Likud Bloc); Likud cand. for Sec.-Gen. of Histadrut 1977, 1981; Minister of Immigrant Absorption 1977–78, of Construction and Housing 1978–90, of Foreign Affairs 1990–92, 1996–97, 1999–2000, Deputy Prime Minister 1981–84, 1988–92, Minister without portfolio April–July 2002; f. Gesher Party 1996 (merged with Likud 2003); Israel Prize for Lifetime Achievement 2018.

LÉVY, Jean-Bernard; French business executive; *Chairman and CEO, EDF Group;* b. 18 March 1955; m.; four c.; ed École Polytechnique, École Nationale Supérieure des Télécommunications; engineer with France Telecom 1978–86; Tech. Adviser to Minister for Postal Services and Telecommunications 1986–88; Gen. Man. Communication Satellites, Matra Marconi Space 1988–93; Chief of Staff to Minister for Industry, Postal Services, Telecommunications and Foreign Trade 1993–94; Chair. and CEO Matra Communication (Lagardère Group) 1995–98; Man. Partner, Corp. Finance, Oddo Pinatton (equities broker) 1998–2002; COO Vivendi Universal (now Vivendi) 2002–05, Chair. Man. Bd and CEO 2005–12 (resgnd); Chair. and CEO, Thales Group 2012–14; Chair. and CEO EDF Group 2014–; mem. Bd of Dirs, Société Générale, Institut Pasteur; Officier, Légion d'honneur, Ordre nat. du Mérite. *Address:* EDF Group, 22–30 avenue Wagram, 75382 Paris, Cedex 8, France (office). *Telephone:* 1-40-42-22-22 (office). *Fax:* 1-40-42-89-00 (office). *E-mail:* info@edf.fr (office). *Website:* www.edf.fr/groupe-edf (office).

LEVY, Joaquim Vieira Ferreira, BEng, PhD, MEcons; Brazilian economist, politician and fmr naval engineer; *Managing Director and Chief Financial Officer, World Bank Group;* b. 1961, Rio de Janeiro; ed Universidade Federal do Rio de Janeiro, Univ. of Chicago, USA, Getúlio Vargas Foundation; began career in Eng and Operations Dept, Flumar S/A Navegação (shipping co.) 1984; course teacher, Getúlio Vargas Foundation 1990; Economist with IMF 1992–99, several positions in W Hemisphere Dept 1992, Europe I Dept 1993–97, Capital Markets and Research 1997–98; Visiting Economist, Capital Markets and Monetary Strategy Divs, European Central Bank 1999–2000; Asst Sec. for Econ. Policy, Ministry of Finance 2000–01, Chief Economist, Ministry of Planning 2001–03, Sec. of the Treasury 2003–06; Vice-Pres. of Finance and Admin, IDB 2006; Financial Sec., Dept of Finance, State of Rio de Janeiro 2007–10; Man. Dir, Bradesco Asset

Management (banking and financial services co.) 2010–14; Minister of Finance 2014–15; Man. Dir and Chief Financial Officer, World Bank Group 2016–. *Address:* The World Bank, 1818 H Street, NW Washington, DC 20433, USA (office). *Telephone:* (202) 458-2624 (office). *E-mail:* Ykobayashi2@worldbankgroup.org (office). *Website:* www.worldbank.org (office).

LÉVY, Maurice; French advertising executive; *Chairman of Supervisory Board, Publicis Omnicom Group;* b. 18 Feb. 1942, Oudja, Morocco; m.; three s.; joined Publicis Groupe SA and given responsibility for data processing and information tech. systems 1971, apptd Corp. Sec. 1973, Man. Dir 1976, Chair. and CEO Publicis Conseil 1981, Vice-Chair. Publicis Groupe SA 1986, Vice-Chair. Man. Bd 1988, Chair. Man. Bd and CEO 1987, Chair. and CEO Publicis Group 1988–2013, Co-CEO Publicis Omnicom Group (following merger with Omnicon) 2013–17, Chair. Supervisory Bd 2017–, launched Viva Technology 2016; French Pres. French-American Business Council; Dir Musée des Arts Décoratifs, Paris, Council on Foreign Relations, New York; mem. Foundation Bd World Econ. Forum, Supervisory Bd Deutsche Bank; Commdr, Légion d'honneur, Grand Officier, Ordre nat. du Mérite. *Address:* Publicis Groupe SA, 133 avenue des Champs Elysées, 75008 Paris, France (office). *Telephone:* 1-44-43-70-00 (office). *E-mail:* contact@publicisgroupe.com (office). *Website:* www.publicisgroupe.com (office).

LEVY, Baron (Life Peer), cr. 1997, of Mill Hill in the London Borough of Barnet; **Michael Abraham Levy,** FCA, CA; British consultant; b. 11 July 1944, London; s. of Samuel Levy and Annie Levy; m. Gilda Altbach 1967; one s. one d.; ed Hackney Downs Grammar School; Chartered Accountant, Lubbock Fine 1961–66; Prin. M. Levy & Co. 1966–69; Partner, Wagner, Prager, Levy & Partners 1969–73; Chair. Magnet Group of Cos 1973–88, D & J Securities Ltd 1988–92, M & G Records 1992–97; Vice-Chair. Phonographic Performance Ltd 1979–84, British Phonographic Industry Ltd 1984–87; Chair. British Music Industry Awards Cttee 1992–95, Patron 1995–; Nat. Campaign Chair. United Jt Israel Appeal 1982–85, Hon. Vice-Pres. 1994–2000, Hon. Pres. 2000–; Special Envoy of Prime Minister and Adviser on Middle East 1997–2007; mem. (Labour), House of Lords 1997–; Chair. Jewish Care 1992–97, Pres. 1998–; fmr Chair. Jewish Care Community Foundation, Foundation for Educ.; Vice-Chair. Cen. Council for Jewish Community Services 1994–, Chair. Chief Rabbinate Awards for Excellence 1992–2007; mem. Jewish Agency World Bd of Govs 1990–95, World Chair. Youth Aliyah Cttee 1991–95; mem. Keren Hayesod World Bd of Govs 1991–95, World Comm. on Israel–Diaspora Relations 1995–, Int. Bd of Govs, Peres Centre for Peace 1997–2009, Advisory Council of the Foreign Policy Centre 1997–2006, Nat. Council of Voluntary Orgs Advisory Cttee 1998–2011, Community Legal Service Champions Panel 1999–2010, Hon. Cttee Israel, Britain and the Commonwealth Asscn 2000–11; Pres. Volunteering Matters (fmrly known as CSV—Community Service Volunteers) 1998–, Jewish Lads & Girls Brigade 2006–; Chair. Wireart Ltd and Chase Music Ltd (fmrly M & G Music Ltd) 1992–2008, International Standard Asset Management 2008–11; Chair. Bd of Trustees, New Policy Network Foundation 2000–07; Vice-Pres. JLC 2010–11; mem. Devt Bd, British Library 2008–11, Exec. Cttee of Chai-Lifeline 2001–02, Advisory Council, Set Up To Serve 2013–, World Bd of Dirs of Int. Peace Inst. 2014–; Gov. Jewish Free School 1990–95, Pres. 2001–; Trustee, Holocaust Educ. Trust 1998–2007; Patron Prostate Cancer Charitable Trust 1997–2011, Friends of Israel Educ. Trust 1998–2011, Save a Child's Heart Foundation 2000–, Simon Mark's Jewish Primary School Trust 2002–, Mathilda Marks-Kennedy Jewish Primary School 2011–; Hon. Patron, Cambridge Univ. Jewish Soc. 2002–; Hon. PhD (Middlesex Univ.) 1999; B'nai B'rith First Lodge Award 1994, Scopus Award Hebrew Univ. of Jerusalem 1998, Israel Policy Forum Special Recognition Award (USA) 2003. *Publication:* A Question of Honour (memoir) 2008. *Leisure interests:* tennis, swimming. *Address:* House of Lords, Westminster, London, SW1A 0PW, England (office). *Telephone:* (20) 7487-5174 (office). *Fax:* (20) 7486-7919 (office). *E-mail:* ml@lordlevy.com (office). *Website:* www.parliament.uk/biographies/lords/lord-levy/2033 (office).

LEVY, Yitzhak; Israeli rabbi and politician (retd); b. 6 July 1947, Morocco; s. Daniel-Yitzhak Levy; m.; five c.; ed Kerem B'Yavne and Yeshivat Hakotel; emigrated to Israel in 1957; ordained rabbi; served in Israeli Defence Forces, to rank of Maj.; mem. Knesset (Parl.) (Nat. Religious Party, now Jewish Home—HaBayit HaYehudi) 1988–2009 (retd), mem. Knesset House Cttee, Cttees on Finance, on Constitution, Law and Justice, on Labour and Social Welfare 1988–92, on Knesset House Cttee and Cttee on Constitution, Law and Justice 1992–96; Minister of Transport 1996–98, of Educ. 1998–99 (also Minister of Religious Affairs), of Housing and Construction 1999–2000, without Portfolio 2002, of Tourism 2002–03; Deputy Prime Minister 2003–04; mem. Bnei Akiva Exec. and World Secr.; Leader Nat. Religious Party 1998–2002; Chair. Israel–Argentina Parl. Friendship League.

LEW, Jacob (Jack), AB, JD; American government official; b. 29 Aug. 1955, New York; ed Harvard Coll., Georgetown Univ.; began career as legislative aide to US Rep. Joe Moakley, Washington, DC 1973–75; Prin. Domestic Policy Advisor to US House Speaker Tip O'Neill 1979–87, Asst Dir US House Democratic Steering and Policy Cttee, later Exec. Dir; Partner, Van Ness, Feldman and Curtis (law firm), Washington, DC 1988–93; Special Asst to Pres. Clinton 1993–94, Deputy Dir Office of Program Analysis, Office of Man. and Budget (OMB) 1995–98, Dir of OMB 1998–2001, 2010–12, mem. Nat. Security Council 1998–2001; Exec. Vice-Pres. and Prof. of Public Admin, Wagner School of Public Service, New York Univ. 2001–06; Man. Dir and COO, Citi Global Wealth Man., Citigroup 2006–08, Citi Alternative Investments 2008–09; Deputy Sec. of State for Man. and Resources, Dept of State 2009–10; Chief of Staff to Pres. 2012–13; Sec. of the Treasury 2013–17; Exec. Dir Center for Middle East Research; Issues Dir Democratic Nat. Cttee's Campaign 88; Chair. Corpn for Nat. and Community Service Bd, Man., Admin and Govt Cttee 2004–08; Co-Chair. Advisory Bd for City Year New York; Co-leader Quadrennial Diplomacy and Devt Review; mem. Council on Foreign Relations, Brookings Inst. Hamilton Project Advisory Bd, Nat. Acad. of Social Insurance; mem. Massachusetts and District of Columbia Bar; Hon. DHumLitt (Georgetown) 2014.

LEWANDOWSKI, Janusz Antoni, MA, DEcon; Polish politician, economist and fmr EU official; b. 13 June 1951, Lublin; s. of Karol Lewandowski and Halina Lewandowska; m. Lidia Talewska Lewandowska 1997; one d.; ed Gdańsk Univ.; Lecturer, Gdańsk Univ. 1974–84 (dismissed); econ. adviser, Solidarity Trade Union, Gdańsk 1980–81; Lecturer, Harvard Univ., USA; with Polish Ocean Lines, then consulting firm 1984–85; Assoc., journal Przegląd Polityczny (pen-name Jędrzej Branecki) 1984–89; Co-Founder pvt. Gdańsk Inst. of Market Econs 1989, Chair. Programme Bd 1993–94; Minister of Proprietary Transformations 1991–93; Co-Founder and Pres. Liberal-Democratic Congress 1990–94; Deputy to Sejm (Parl.) 1991–93, 1997–2004, Vice-Chair. Parl. Cttee for Treasury, Affranchisement and Privatization 1997–2004, Parl. Cttee on Europe 2001–04; mem. Freedom Union (UW) 1994–2001, Civic Platform (PO) 2001–; Observer to European Parl. 2003–04; mem. European Parl. (Group of the European People's Party—Christian Democrats and European Democrats) 2004–10, Chair. Cttee on Budgets 2004–07, Vice-Chair. Cttee on Budgets 2007–09, Vice-Chair. Del. for Relations with Japan 2009–10, mem. Conf. of Cttee Chairmen 2004–07, Substitute mem. Temporary Cttee on Policy Challenges and Budgetary Means of the Enlarged Union 2007–; Commr for Financial Programming and Budget, EC, Brussels 2010–14; Chair. Athletics Club of Sopot 2000–. *Publications include:* Samorząd w dobie 'Solidarności' (Local Government in the Era of 'Solidarity') 1984, Neoliberałowie wobec współczesności (Neoliberals until the Present Day) 1989, Strategia rozwoju województwa gdańskiego (Strategic Development of Gdansk Voivodship) (co-author) 1997. *Leisure interests:* sport, mountain hiking. *Address:* Biuro Poselskie w Gdyni, ul. Świetojawska 60/2, 81-393 Gdynia, Poland (office). *Telephone:* (58) 699-36-00 (office). *E-mail:* janusz.lewandowski@januszlewandowski.pl (office). *Website:* www.januszlewandowski.pl.

LEWIN, Ben; Australian/American film director and screenwriter; b. 6 Aug. 1946, Poland; m. Judi Levine; ed Univ. of Melbourne, Nat. Film and Television School, UK; f. Such Much Films. *Films include:* Welcome to Britain (documentary) 1975, Georgia 1988, The Favour, the Watch and the Very Big Fish 1991, Lucky Break 1994, Hollywood Gold (documentary) 2003, The Sessions (also writer and producer) 2012. *Television includes:* ITV Playhouse (series) – The Case of Cruelty to Prawns 1979, Destination Australia: The Migrant Experience Since 1788 (series documentary) 1984, The Dunera Boys (film) 1985, Rafferty's Rules (series) 1987, A Matter of Convenience (film) 1987, Georgia 1988, The Favour, the Watch and the Very Big Fish 1991, Paperback Romance 1994, Ally McBeal (series) – Let's Dance 1999, SeaChange (series) 2000, Touched by an Angel (series) – The Good Earth 2003, The Sessions 2012, Please Stand By 2017, The Catcher Was a Spy 2017. *Website:* www.suchmuchfilms.com (office).

LEWIN, Harris A., BS, MS, PhD; American geneticist, immunologist, academic and university administrator; *Robert and Rosabel Osborne Endowed Chair in Evolution and Ecology and Distinguished Professor of Evolution and Ecology, University of California, Davis;* b. 1957, Brooklyn, NY; ed Cornell Univ., Univ. of California, Davis; Asst Prof. of Immunogenetics, Dept of Animal Sciences, Univ. of Illinois, Urbana, Ill. 1984–89, Assoc. Prof. of Immunogenetics 1989–94, Prof. of Immunogenetics 1994–2011, Dir Univ. of Illinois Biotechnology Center 1996–98, Founding Dir W. M. Keck Center for Comparative and Functional Genomics 1998–2003, Sr Scientist, Nat. Center for Supercomputing Applications 1998–2003, E.W. and J.M. Gutgsell Endowed Chair 1999–2011, Resident Assoc., Center for Advanced Study 2001–02, Research Prof., Microelectronics Lab. 2002–11, Founding Dir Inst. for Genomic Biology 2003–11, Affiliate, Micro and Nanotechnology Lab. 2008–11, Prof., Center for Advanced Study 2009–11; Vice-Chancellor of Research and Prof. of Evolution and Ecology, Univ. of California, Davis 2011–16, Robert and Rosabel Osborne Endowed Chair in Evolution and Ecology and Distinguished Prof. of Biological Sciences 2016–; Visiting Scientist, Dept of Animal Genetics, Nat. Veterinary Inst., Oslo, Norway Aug. 1989; Visiting Assoc. Prof., Section of Molecular Biology, Univ. of Southern California, Los Angeles 1991; mem. Bd of Dirs Stormont Laboratories, Woodland, Calif. 1984–2006; Founder and Scientific Dir Midwest Molecular Diagnostics, Champaign 1987–89; consultant, American Cyanamid Co., Princeton, NJ 1990–94, Applied Biosystems, Inc., Foster City, Calif. 1993–98, Protiva/Monsanto Chesterfield, Mo. 1997–99, ELANCO, Greenfield, Ia 2000–02, Pfizer Inc., New York, NY 2007, Hebrew Univ. of Jerusalem, Israel 2009, Washington Advisory Group, Washington, DC 2010; mem. External Advisory Cttee, Food Animal Biotechnology Center, Univ. of Minnesota 1994–2001; Chair. Scientific Advisory Bd, GenoMar AS, Norway 1997–2003; mem. Scientific Advisory Bd, Burrill & Co., Animal Health Venture Fund, San Francisco 1999–2003; Founder-mem. Scientific Advisory Bd, Pyxis Genomics, Inc., Chicago 2000–07; Assoc. Ed. Animal Biotechnology 1990–; Man. Ed. National Animal Genome Research Program (NAGRP) Newsletter 1993–96; Founding Ed. Annual Reviews of Animal and Veterinary Biosciences; Section Ed. Encyclopedia of Genetics, Genomics, Proteomics and Bioinformatics 2002; mem. Editorial Bd Physiological Genomics 1999–, Faculty of 1000, Genomics Section, Genetics and Genomics Faculty, BioMed Central 2002–03; mem. Editorial Cttee, Annual Reviews of Genomics and Human Genetics 2009–; mem. American Asscn of Immunologists, American Asscn of Veterinary Immunologists, Int. Soc. for Animal Genetics, American Asscn of Animal Science; Foreign mem. Royal Swedish Acad. of Agric. and Forestry 2007; Fellow, AAAS 2004; American Asscn of Veterinary Immunologists Travel Award, William and Flora Hewlett Foundation Int. Travel Award 1989, Young Faculty Award for Excellence in Research, Coll. of Agric., Univ. of Illinois 1992, Univ. Scholar, Univ. of Illinois 1993–96, H.H. Mitchell Award for Grad. Teaching and Research 1995, Paul A. Funk Recognition Award, Coll. of Agricultural, Consumer and Environmental Sciences, Univ. of Illinois 1996, Arnold O. Beckman Research Award, Univ. of Illinois 1997, Wellcome Visiting Professorship in Basic Biomedical Sciences, Washington State Univ. 1999–2000, C.R. Henderson Lecturer in Animal Breeding and Genetics, Cornell Univ. 2000, Pres.'s Distinguished Speakers, Univ. of Illinois 2000-01, Sir Frederick McMaster Fellowship (declined after award) 2001, ACES Team Award for Excellence in Research 2003, Alltech Distinguished Lecturer in Nutrigenomics, Univ. of Kentucky, Lexington 2009, Wolf Prize in Agric. (with R. James Cook) 2011. *Publications:* Gene Mapping: Techniques and Applications (co-ed.) 1991, Comparative Analysis and Phylogeny (Section Ed.). In, S. Subramaniam (ed.) Encyclopedia of Genetics, Genomics, Proteomics and Bioinformatics 2005, Earth BioGenome Project: Sequencing life for the future of life (Lead Author) 2018; 21 book chapters and more than 160 papers in professional journals on mammalian comparative and functional genomics. *Address:* Genome Center, 4321 GBSF, University of California, Davis, CA 95616, USA (office). *Telephone:* (530) 754-5098 (office). *E-mail:* lewin@ucdavis.edu (office). *Website:* genomecenter.ucdavis.edu/people/faculty/name/harris-lewin (office).

LEWINTON, Sir Christopher, Kt, CEng, FEng, FIMechE; British/American engineer and industrialist; *Chairman, Camper & Nicholsons Marina Investments*

Limited; b. 6 Jan. 1932, London; s. of Joseph Lewinton and Elizabeth Lewinton; m. 1st Jennifer Alcock (divorced); two s.; m. 2nd Louise Head 1979; two step-s.; ed Acton Tech. Coll.; commissioned army service in REME; Pres. Wilkinson Sword, N America 1959–71, CEO Wilkinson Sword Group 1970–85; Pres. Int. Group, Allegheny Int. 1978–85; Chief Exec. TI Group 1986–99, Chair. and CEO 1989–2000; Dir Reed Elsevier 1993–99, Messier-Dowty 1994–1998, Y&R/WPP 1996–2003; mem. Supervisory Bd Mannesmann AG 1995–99; mem. Exec. Bd, J. F. Lehman & Co. 2001–; Adviser to Booz Allen Hamilton Inc. 2000–03, to Morgan Stanley Capital Partners (now Metalmark Capital) 2000–, Compass Advisers 2004–10; Chair. Camper & Nicholsons Marina Investments Ltd 2008–; Hon. FRAeS 1993; Hon. DTech (Brunel) 1997. *Leisure interests:* golf, tennis, travel, reading. *Address:* Camper & Nicholsons Marina Investments Ltd, Fifth Floor, Cording House, 34–35 St James's Street, London, SW1A 1HD, England (office). *Telephone:* (20) 7201-5490 (office). *Fax:* (20) 7201-5499 (office). *E-mail:* clewinton@cl-partners.co.uk (office). *Website:* www.cnmarinas.com (office).

LEWIS, Aylwin B., BA, MBA; American business executive; *President and CEO, Potbelly Corporation;* ed Univ. of Houston; started career as Dist Man. of Operations Jack in the Box restaurants in Tex.; held various exec. positions at food retailers including KFC Corpn, COO Pizza Hut 1996–2000, Exec. Vice Pres. of Operations and New Business Devt Tricon Global Restaurants Inc. then Pres., Chief Multibranding and Operating Officer YUM! Brands Inc. (fmrly Tricon) 2000–03; Pres. and CEO Kmart Holdings Corpn 2004, Pres. and CEO Sears Holding Corpn (after merger of Kmart and Sears, Roebuck) 2005–08, also mem. Bd of Dirs 2004–08; Pres. and CEO Potbelly Corpn 2008–, also mem. Bd of Dirs; mem. Bd of Dirs Halliburton Co., Walt Disney Co. 2004–, World Business Chicago, Starwood Hotels & Resorts 2013–; Trustee, Rush Univ. Medical Center 2009–. *Address:* Potbelly Sandwich Works, LLC, 222 Merchandise Mart Plaza, 23rd Floor, Chicago, IL 60654, USA (office). *Website:* potbelly.com (office).

LEWIS, Brandon, BSc, LLB, LLM; British barrister and politician; *Chairman, Conservative Party;* b. 20 June 1971; m. Justine Rappolt; two c.; ed Univ. of Buckingham, King's Coll. London; mem. Brentwood Borough Council 1998–2009, Leader 2004–09; Dir Woodlands Schools Ltd 2001–12; MP for Great Yarmouth (Conservative) 2010–; Parl. UnderSec. of State at Dept for Communities and Local Govt 2012–14, Minister of State for Housing and Planning 2014–16, Minister of State for Policing and Fire Service 2016–17, Minister of State for Immigration 2017–18, Minister without Portfolio 2018–; mem. Conservative Party, Chair. 2018–. *Address:* Conservative Party, 30 Millbank, London, SW1P 4DP, England (office). *Telephone:* (20) 7222-9000 (office). *Fax:* (20) 7222-1135 (office). *E-mail:* chairman@conservatives.com (office). *Website:* www.conservatives.com (office).

LEWIS, Dave; British business executive; *Group Chief Executive, Tesco plc;* b. 1965; ed Trent Polytechnic (now Nottingham Trent Univ.), Advanced Man. Program, Harvard Univ., USA; joined Unilever 1987, began as a Unilever Cos Man. Devt Scheme trainee for Lever Brothers, Kingston, held a variety of marketing (local/European) and customer man. roles, launched Dove brand in UK 1992, Marketing Operations Man. 1993–96, moved to South America as Marketing Dir of River Plate (Argentina, Uruguay and Paraguay) 1996–99, moved to Indonesia as Man. Dir Unilever Indonesia's personal care business and personal care SE Asia 1999–2002, Sr Vice-Pres. for Home and Personal Care, Cen. and Eastern Europe 2002–05, returned to UK as Man. Dir UK Home and Personal Care business 2005–07, Chair. Unilever UK and Ireland 2007–10, Pres., Americas 2010–11, Pres., Personal Care 2011–14; Group Chief Exec. Tesco plc 2014–. *Leisure interest:* sport and fitness (has participated in London Marathon and Unilever's annual triathlon). *Address:* Tesco plc, New Tesco House, PO Box 18, Delamare Road, Cheshunt, Herts., EN8 9SL, England (office). *Telephone:* (1992) 632222 (office). *Fax:* (1992) 644962 (office). *E-mail:* philip.clarke@tesco.com (office). *Website:* www.tesco.com (office).

LEWIS, Hon. Douglas (Doug) Grinslade, PC, LLB, FCA, QC; Canadian lawyer, chartered accountant and fmr politician; b. 17 April 1938, Toronto, Ont.; s. of Horace Grinslade and Brenda Hazeldine Lewis (née Reynolds); m. Linda Diane Haggans 1962; two s. three d.; ed Univ. of Toronto, Osgoode Hall Law School; Progressive Conservative MP for Simcoe N 1979–93; Parl. Sec. to Minister of Supply and Services 1979; Deputy Opposition House Leader 1981, Opposition House Leader 1983; Parl. Sec. to Pres. of Treasury Bd 1984, to Pres. of Privy Council 1985, to Deputy Prime Minister and Pres. of Queen's Privy Council for Canada 1986–87; Minister of State (Deputy House Leader) and Minister of State (Treasury Bd) 1987–88; Acting Pres. Treasury Bd 1988; Minister of Justice, Attorney-Gen. and Govt House Leader 1989–90; Minister of Transport 1990–91; Solicitor-Gen. 1991–93; currently practising law with Lewis Downey Tornosky Lassaline & Timpano Professional Corpn; Chair. Fed. Govt Panel on Railway Safety in Canada 2007; currently Chair. Audit Cttee, Ministry of the Attorney Gen.; Bencher, Law Soc. of Upper Canada 2007–11; mem. Orillia Soldiers' Memorial Hosp. Foundation Bd 2001–06; Orillia Citizen of the Year 1972, 2002. *Address:* Lewis Downey Tornosky Lassaline & Timpano Professional Corporation, PO Box 851, Orillia, ON L3V 6K8, Canada (office). *Telephone:* (705) 327-2600 (office). *Fax:* (705) 327-7532 (office). *Website:* www.greatlaw.ca (office).

LEWIS, Frederick Carlton (Carl); American fmr professional athlete; b. 1 July 1961, Birmingham, Ala; s. of William Lewis and Evelyn Lawler Lewis; ed Univ. of Houston; bronze medal for long jump, Pan-American Games 1979; won World Cup competition 1981, first World Championships (with 8.55m); achieved world record 8.79m jump 1983; gold medals at Olympic Games 1984 for 100m, 200m., long jump and 4×100m; athlete in fields of sprints and long jump; silver medal for 200m, gold medal for 100m, Olympic Games 1988; jumped 8.64m New York 1991; world record for 100m 9.86 seconds Aug. 1991 (surpassed 1994); gold medal, long jump Olympic Games 1992; gold medal for long jump (8.50m), Olympic Games 1996; only man to defend an Olympic long jump title successfully; retd 1997; has won a total of nine Olympic gold medals; revealed in 2003 to have failed a drugs test at Seoul Olympics 1988, disqualified at the time, but case dismissed after an appeal; f. Carl Lewis Fund to help disadvantaged youths; official supporter of Ronald McDonald House Charities, mem. Friends of RMHC celebrity bd; appeared in several TV and film projects produced by the Carl Lewis Entertainment Group; nominated a Goodwill Amb. for the UN FAO 2009; filed petitions to run as a Democrat for NJ Senate 2011, disqualified by Lt Gov. for failing to meet state's residency requirements, appeal to Third Circuit Court of Appeals eventually rejected; Hon. Chair. Negro Coll. Fund; Track and Field News Athlete of the Decade 1980–89, World Athlete of the Year 1982, 1983, 1984, Athlete of the Century, Int. Asscn of Athletics Feds 1999, voted Sportsman of the Century by IOC 1999, named Olympian of the Century by Sports Illustrated 1999, Univ. of Houston named the Carl Lewis Int. Complex in his honour 2000. *Films:* has appeared in numerous films, including playing himself in cameos in Perfect Strangers, Speed Zone!, Alien Hunter and Material Girls. *Television:* appeared on The Weakest Link; played Stu in TV film Atomic Twister and appeared in short documentary Challenging Impossibility 2011; guest on ESPN TV show College GameDay 2011. *Address:* c/o Cleve Lewis Management, 5170 Pinyon Jay Road, Parker, CO 80134 (office); c/o Carl Lewis Foundation, 3350 Wilshire Blvd, Suite 675, Los Angeles, CA 90010, USA. *Telephone:* (303) 531-4469 (office); (310) 578-1885. *Fax:* (303) 531-5340 (office). *E-mail:* carl@clevelewis.com. *Website:* www.iaaf.org/athletes/united-states/carl-lewis-1622; www.carllewis.com.

LEWIS, Geoffrey David, MA, FSA, FMA; British museum director, museum consultant and university teacher; b. 13 April 1933, Brighton, Sussex; s. of David Lewis and Esther Lewis; m. Frances May Wilderspin 1956; three d.; ed Varndean Grammar School, Brighton, Univ. of Liverpool; Asst Curator, Worthing Museum and Art Gallery 1950–60; Deputy Dir (and Keeper of Antiquities) Sheffield City Museum 1960–65; Dir Sheffield City Museums 1966–72, Liverpool City Museums 1972–74, Merseyside Co. Museums 1974–77; Dir of Museum Studies, Univ. of Leicester 1977–89, Assoc. Teacher 1989–92; Fellow, Museums Asscn London 1966, Pres. 1980–81, Pres. Int. Council of Museums 1983–89, Chair. Documentation Cttee 1971–77, Chair. Advisory Cttee 1974–80, Chair. Ethics Cttee 1996–2004; currently a museum consultant; mem. Bd of Trustees, Royal Armouries 1990–99, Chair. Design Cttee 1995–99; Chair. Printing Matters (Bude) Ltd 1991–96; Deputy Chair. The Genesis Agendum 1996–2008; Gov. Wolvey School 1993–2003, Chair. of Govs 1998–2003; Hon. Lecturer in British Prehistory, Univ. of Sheffield 1965–72; Hon. Fellow, Museums Asscn 1989; Hon. mem. Int. Council of Museums 2004. *Publications include:* The South Yorkshire Glass Industry 1964, Prehistoric and Roman Times in the Sheffield Area (co-author) 1968, For Instruction and Recreation: A Centenary History of the Museums Association 1989, Manual of Curatorship (co-ed.) 1984, 1992; contrib. to Encyclopaedia Britannica 2010 and Britannica Online 2018; numerous articles on archaeology, museum history, management and professional ethics. *Leisure interests:* reading, music. *Address:* 4 Orchard Close, Wolvey, Hinckley, Warwicks., LE10 3LR, England (home). *E-mail:* mail@geoffreylewis.co.uk (home). *Website:* www.geoffreylewis.co.uk (home).

LEWIS, Gwyneth, MA, DPhil, FRSL; British poet and writer; b. 1959, Cardiff, Wales; d. of Gwilym Lewis and Ann Eryl James; m. Leighton Denver Davies; ed Girton Coll., Cambridge, Harvard and Columbia Univs, USA, Balliol Coll., Oxford; fmr freelance journalist in New York, USA and documentary producer and dir, BBC Wales; composed bilingual inscription on front of Cardiff's Wales Millennium Centre, opened in 2004; Nat. Poet of Wales 2005–06; Writer-in-Residence, School of Physics and Astronomy, Cardiff Univ. 2006; Harkness Fellow 1982–84, Nat. Endowment for Science, Tech. and the Arts Fellowship 2002–07; Fellow, Radcliffe Inst. for Advanced Studies, Harvard Univ. 2008–09, Stanford Humanities Center 2009–10; Bain-Swiggett Visiting Lecturer of Poetry and English, Princeton Univ. 2014; mem. faculty, Bread Loaf School of English, Vt, USA, Robert Frost Chair of Literature 2016; Mary Amelia Cummins Harvey Visiting Fellow Commonership, Girton Coll., Cambridge 2011; Royal Literary Fund Fellow, Swansea Univ. 2012–13; Writing Fellow, Centre for New Writing, Univ. of Manchester 2012; Hon. Fellow, Univ. of Cardiff 2005, Univ. of Liverpool 2011, Bangor Univ. 2012; Dr hc (Glamorgan) 2012; Eric Gregory Award 1987, Aldeburgh Festival Prize 1996, Wellcome Trust Sciart Award, Creative Wales Award, Cholmondeley Award 2010. *Plays include:* Clytemnestra (Sherman Cymru), Y Streic a Fi (The Strike and Me) (screenplay) (BAFTA Wales for Best Drama 2015). *Radio:* Sunbathing in the Rain (BBC Radio 4), Stardust: A Love Story (BBC Radio 4). *Television:* Zero Gravity (BBC 2). *Publications include:* Llwybrau bywyd (poetry) 1977, Ar y groesffordd (poetry) 1978, Sonedau Redsa a Cherddi Eraill 1990, Parables and Faxes (poetry) (Aldeburgh Poetry Festival Prize) 1995, Cyfrif Un ac Un yn Dri (poetry) 1996, Zero Gravity (poetry) 1998, Y Llofrudd Iaith (poetry) (Welsh Arts Council Book of the Year) 2000, Sunbathing in the Rain: A Cheerful Book About Depression (non-fiction) 2002, Keeping Mum (poetry) 2003, Redflight/Barcud (libretto) 2005, The Most Beautiful Man from the Sea (oratorio) 2005, Two in a Boat: A Marital Voyage 2005, Tair mewn Un (poetry) 2005, Chaotic Angels (poetry) 2005, Dolffin (libretto) 2006, The Hospital Odyssey (poetry) 2010, The Meat Tree (stories) 2010, Sparrow Tree (Roland Mathias Poetry Award 2012) 2011, Y Storm (trans. of The Tempest) 2012. *Address:* c/o James Macdonald Lockhart, Antony Harwood Ltd, 103 Walton Street, Oxford, OX2 6EB, England (office). *Telephone:* (18) 6555-9615 (office). *E-mail:* james@antonyharwood.com (office).

LEWIS, Jerry Lee; American rock singer and musician (piano); b. 29 Sept. 1935, Ferriday, La; m. 6th Kerrie Lynn McCarver Lewis 1984 (divorced 2005); two s. (one deceased); one d.; m. 7th Judith Brown 2012; ed Waxahachie Bible Inst., Texas; numerous concert tours, festival appearances. *Films include:* Jamboree 1957, High School Confidential 1958, Be My Guest 1965. *Theatre includes:* Iago in Catch My Soul. *Recordings include:* albums: Jerry Lee Lewis 1957, Jerry Lee's Greatest 1961, Live At The Star Club 1965, The Greatest Live Show On Earth 1965, The Return Of Rock 1965, Whole Lotta Shakin' Goin' On 1965, Country Songs For City Folks 1965, By Request – More Greatest Live Show On Earth 1967, Breathless 1967, Together (with Linda Gail Lewis) 1970, Rockin' Rhythm And Blues 1971, Sunday Down South (with Johnny Cash) 1972, The Session (with Peter Frampton and Rory Gallagher) 1973, Jerry Lee Lewis 1979, When Two Worlds Collide 1980, My Fingers Do The Talking 1983, I Am What I Am 1984, Keep Your Hands Off It 1987, Don't Drop It 1988, Great Balls of Fire! (film soundtrack) 1989, Rocket 1990, Young Blood 1995, Keep Your Eyes Off Of It 2000, By Invitation Only 2000, Last Man Standing 2006, Mean Old Man 2010. *Address:* The Lewis Ranch, Box 384, Nesbit, MS 38651, USA. *E-mail:* phoebemedia@aol.com. *Website:* www.jerryleelewis.com.

LEWIS, Joseph C. (Joe); British business executive; b. 5 Feb. 1937, Bow, London, England; s. of Charles Lewis; m. 1st Esther Browne (divorced); one s. one d.; m. 2nd Jane Lewis; joined father's small catering business 1958; with father ran Hanover Grand chain of banqueting suites, London 1970s; moved to New Providence, Bahamas 1979 (tax exile); moved into currency trading 1980s and

1990s; teamed up with George Soros to bet on pound crashing out of European Exchange Rate Mechanism (Black Wednesday) Sept. 1992; Founder and Owner Tavistock Group of financial services, property and retail businesses (more than 200 cos in 15 countries); shareholder Rapallo Ltd, London, English Nat. Investment Corpn, Tamarind Int., Hong Kong, auction house Christie's, London. *Leisure interest:* art collection includes works by Picasso, Matisse, Lucian Freud and Francis Bacon and sculptor Henry Moore. *Address:* PO Box N7776, Lyford Cay, New Providence, Bahamas. *E-mail:* info@tavistock.com. *Website:* www.tavistock.com.

LEWIS, Juliette; American film actress and musician; b. 21 June 1973, Los Angeles, Calif.; d. of Geoffrey Lewis and Glenis Batley Lewis; m. Steve Berra 1999 (divorced 2005); f. band Juliette & The Licks 2003–09; Chicago Film Critics' Asscn Most Promising Actress 1991, NATO/ShoNest Female Star of Tomorrow 1993, Venice Film Festival Pasinetti Prize 1994. *Films include:* My Stepmother is an Alien 1988, Meet the Hollowheads 1989, National Lampoon's Christmas Vacation 1989, Cape Fear 1991, Crooked Hearts 1991, Husbands and Wives 1992, Kalifornia 1993, One Hot Summer, That Night 1993, What's Eating Gilbert Grape 1993, Romeo is Bleeding 1994, Natural Born Killers 1994, Mixed Nuts 1994, The Basketball Diaries 1995, Strange Days 1995, From Dusk Till Dawn 1996, The Evening Star 1996, The Audition, Full Tilt Boogie 1997, The Other Sister 1999, The 4th Floor 1999, Way of the Gun 2000, My Louisiana Sky 2002, Hysterical Blindness 2002, Enough 2002, Gaudi Afternoon 2003, Old School 2003, Cold Creek Manor 2003, Blueberry 2004, Starsky and Hutch 2004, Aurora Borealis 2005, Daltry Calhoun 2005, Lightfield's Home Videos 2006, The Darwin Awards 2006, Grilled 2006, Catch and Release 2006, Whip It! 2009, Sympathy for Delicious 2010, The Switch 2010, Conviction 2010, Due Date 2010, Hick 2011, August: Osage County 2013, Helion 2014, Kelly and Cal 2014, Jem and the Holograms 2015, Nerve 2016. *Television appearances include:* Homefires (mini-series), I Married Dora 1988, Too Young To Die (film) 1989, A Family For Joe 1990, The Firm (series) 2012, Secrets and Lies (series) 2015–16, Wayward Pines (series) 2015. *Theatre:* Fool for Love (Apollo Theatre, London) 2006. *Recordings include:* albums: You're Speaking My Language 2005, Four on the Floor 2006, Terra Incognita 2009, Future Deep 2016; singles: Hello Hero 2016. *Address:* c/o Lizzie Hardy, Three Six Zero, 7175 Willoughby Avenue, Los Angeles, CA 90046, USA. *Website:* www.juliettelewis.com.

LEWIS, Kenneth D., BA; American banking executive (retd); b. 9 April 1947, Meridian, Miss.; s. of Vernon Kenneth Lewis and Alice Byrdine Lewis; m. Donna Lewis 1980; two c.; ed Georgia State Univ., Stanford Univ.; credit analyst, North Carolina Nat. Bank (NCNB, predecessor to NationsBank and Bank of America), Charlotte, NC 1969–77, Man. NCNB Int. Banking Corpn, NY 1977–79, Sr Vice-Pres. and Man. US Dept 1979–83, Middle Market Group Exec. (following creation of Bank of America group) 1983–86, Pres. Fla Div. 1986–88, Pres. Tex. Div. 1988–90, Pres. Consumer and Commercial Banking 1990–99, Pres. and COO Bank of America Corpn 1999–2001, Pres. and CEO 2001–09, Chair. 2001–09; fmr Chair. Nat. Urban League; Vice-Chair. Corp. Fund Bd of The John F. Kennedy Center for the Performing Arts; mem. Financial Services Roundtable, Financial Services Forum, Cttee to Encourage Corporate Philanthropy; Fifth Dist's Rep. on Fed. Advisory Cttee; mem. Bd, Exec. Cttee and past Chair. United Way of Central Carolinas, Inc.; mem. Bd of Dirs Health Man. Assocs Inc., Homeownership Educ. and Counseling Inst., Lowe's Cos Inc., Presbyterian Hosp. Foundation (fmr Chair.), Homeownership Educ. and Counseling Inst., Clearing House LLC., FIA Card Services; Banker of the Year, American Banker 2002, 2008, Top CEO, US Banker 2002.

LEWIS, Lennox, CBE; British/Canadian professional boxer; b. 2 Sept. 1965, London; s. of Violet Blake; m. Violet Chang; four c.; defeated Jean Chanet to win European heavyweight title, Crystal Palace 1990; defeated Gary Mason to win British heavyweight title, Wembley 1991; Commonwealth heavyweight; WBC heavyweight 1992; defeated Frank Bruno 1993; WBC world champion 1993–94, 1997–2001; defended WBC title and challenged for World Boxing Asscn (WBA) and Int. Boxing Fed. (IBF) titles against Evander Holyfield (q.v.) March 1999, bout declared a draw; undisputed world heavyweight champion 1999–2001 (lost WBC and IBF titles when defeated by Hasim Rahman April 2001); regained title of world heavyweight champion from Hasim Rahman Nov. 2001; retained title of undisputed world heavyweight champion June 2002 (after beating Mike Tyson q.v.) and June 2003 (after beating Vitali Klitschko); 41 professional wins (32 knockouts), two defeats, one draw; announced retirement Feb. 2004; f. Lennox Lewis Coll., Hackney 1994; Dr hc (Univ. of London) 1999, (Wilfrid Laurier Univ.) 2011; inducted into Canadian sports Hall of Fame 2008, Int. Boxing Hall of Fame 2009. *Film:* Ocean's Eleven 2002. *Publications include:* Lennox Lewis (autobiog.) 1993, Lennox 2002. *Leisure interests:* action movie watching, urban music, cross training, golf, chess. *Website:* www.lennoxlewis.com.

LEWIS, Mark; Canadian filmmaker and photographer; b. 1958, Hamilton, Ont.; ed Harrow Coll. of Art, London, Polytechnic of Central London; studied with artist and writer Victor Burgin and worked with film theorist Laura Mulvey 1980s; started as photographer and creator of public installation works, later began making film-based installations mid-1990s; noted for film installations; represented Canada at Venice Biennale 2009; Co-Editorial Dir Afterall (cultural journal publr); works held in numerous collections including Nat. Gallery of Canada, Museum of Modern Art New York, Musée d'art contemporain de Montréal, Centre Pompidou, Paris; Gov. Gen.'s Award in Visual and Media Arts 2016. *E-mail:* info@marklewisstudio.com (office). *Website:* marklewisstudio.com (office).

LEWIS, Michael, BA, MA; American author and journalist; b. 15 Oct. 1960, New Orleans, La; s. of J. Thomas Lewis and Diana Monroe Lewis; m. 1st Diane de Cordova Lewis (divorced); m. 2nd Kate Bohner (divorced); m. 3rd Tabitha Soren; one s. two d.; ed Princeton Univ., London School of Econs, UK; worked as bond salesman for Salomon Brothers, London –1988; worked for The Spectator, The New York Times Magazine; fmr columnist, Bloomberg; fmr Sr ed. The New Republic; Contributing Ed. Vanity Fair 2009–; Visiting Fellow, Univ. of California, Berkeley; Distinguished Achievement Award, Soc. of American Business Eds and Writers 2014. *Publications include:* Liar's Poker 1989, Pacific Rift 1991, The Money Culture 1991, Trail Fever 1997, The New New Thing: A Silicon Valley Story 2000, Next: The Future Just Happened 2000, Moneyball: The Art of Winning an Unfair Game 2003, Coach: Lessons on the Game of Life 2005, The Blind Side: Evolution of a Game 2006, Panic: The Story of Modern Financial Insanity 2009, Home Game: An Accidental Guide to Fatherhood 2009, The Big Short: Inside the Doomsday Machine 2010, Boomerang: Travels in the New Third World 2011, Flash Boys: A Wall Street Revolt 2014, The Undoing Project: A Friendship That Changed Our Minds 2016. *Address:* c/o Elizabeth Riley, W. W. Norton & Company Inc, 500 Fifth Avenue, New York, NY 10110, USA (office). *Telephone:* (212) 354-5500 (office). *Fax:* (212) 869-0856 (office). *E-mail:* eriley@wwnorton.com (office). *Website:* michaellewiswrites.com.

LEWIS, Patrick Albert, PhD; Antigua and Barbuda historian and fmr diplomatist; b. 27 Nov. 1938, St John's; m. Michele Lewis; two c.; ed Hampton Inst. and Univ. of Cincinnati; Asst Prof. Univ. of Cincinnati 1971–73, Asst Prof., Assoc. Prof., Prof. of History, Hampton Univ. 1973–84; Adviser to Deputy Prime Minister of Antigua and Barbuda 1984–87, Minister-Counsellor, Perm. Mission to the UN 1987–91, apptd Amb. to UN 1995, to Brazil 1999. *Leisure interests:* cricket, movies, theatre, music.

LEWIS, Peter, CB, BA; British fmr prosecutor and international organization official; *Registrar, International Criminal Court;* ed City of Birmingham Polytechnic; Articled Clerk, Dudley Metropolitan Borough Council, West Midlands 1979–81; Solicitor Supreme Court of England & Wales 1981; Prosecuting Solicitor, West Midlands County Council 1981–86; Sr Crown Prosecutor, Crown Prosecutor Service (CPS), West Midlands 1986–91, Branch Crown Prosecutor CPS, Kent 1991–93, Asst Chief Crown Prosecutor CPS, East Midlands 1993–95, Head of Casework Services, London 1996–99, Chief Crown Prosecutor, Nottinghamshire 1999–2003, Dir of Business Devt, London 2003–06, CEO CPS 2007–16, mem. Strategic Bd 2016–; UK del. to UN Preparatory Comm., Int. Criminal Court (ICC) 1999–2000, Registrar ICC 2018–; Leader of Delegation to UAE and Spain to increase recovery of Proceeds of Crime 2013; UK del. to Consultative Forum of Eurojust 2014. *Address:* International Criminal Court, Oude Waalsdorperweg 10, 2597 AK The Hague, Netherlands (office). *Telephone:* (70) 5158515 (office). *Fax:* (70) 5158555 (office). *E-mail:* otp.informationdesk@icc-cpi.int (office). *Website:* www.icc-cpi.int (office).

LEWIS, Roger Charles, BMus, FRWCMD; British sports executive and fmr broadcasting executive; *Chairman, Cardiff International Airport;* b. 24 Aug. 1954, Bridgend, Glamorgan, Wales; s. of Griffith Charles Job Lewis and Dorothy Lewis (née Russ); m. Christine Trollope 1980; two s.; ed Cynffig Comprehensive School, Bridgend, Univ. of Nottingham; freelance musician 1976–80; Music Officer Darlington Arts Centre 1980–82; presenter Radio Tees 1981–84; producer Capital Radio 1984–85; BBC Radio 1 1985–87, Head of Music Radio 1 1987–90; Dir Classical Div. EMI Records 1990–95, Man. Dir 1995, Man. Dir EMI Premier 1995–97; Pres. Decca Record Co. 1997–98; Man. Dir and Programme Controller Classic FM 1998–2004; Man. Dir ITV Wales 2004–06; Group CEO Welsh Rugby Union (WRU) 2006–15; Chair. Classic FM Charitable Trust 1998–2004, Music and Dance Scheme Advisory Group, Dept for Educ. and Skills 2000–04, Barchester Group 2001–06, Royal Liverpool Philharmonic 2003–06, Int. Advisory Bd Cardiff Univ. Business School 2008–, Yes for Wales Referendum Campaign 2010–11, Cardiff Capital Region Bd 2013–15, Churchill Lines Charitable Fund 2014–; currently Chair. Cardiff Int. Airport; Deputy Chair. Boosey & Hawkes 2004–06; Pres. Bromley Youth Music Trust 2000–05; Vice-Pres. London Welsh Male Voice Choir 2004–; mem. Bd of Dirs GWR PLC 1998–2004, The Radio Corpn Ltd 1999–2004, Digital One 2003–04, Liverpool Capital of Culture 2003–06 (mem. Bd Liverpool Culture Co.), Wales Millennium Centre 2004–06, ERC Ltd 2006–14, Celtic Rugby Ltd 2006–15, RMG Ltd 2012–, British and Irish Lions 2014–15; mem. British Phonographic Inst. (Classical Cttee 1990–98, Chair. 1996–98), Six Nations Council 2012–15; mem. Advisory Bd D Group 2008–; Chair. of Trustees, Ogmore Centre 1996–2008; Trustee, Masterprize (Int. Composers' Competition) 1995–2010, Masterclass Charitable Trust 2000–04, Inst. of Welsh Affairs 2014–; Hon. Fellow, Royal Welsh Coll. of Music and Drama, Cardiff Univ.; Hon. mem. Royal Coll. of Music; Order of St John; Dr hc (Nottingham), (Glamorgan); Sony Radio Award 1987, 1988, 1989, Grand Award Winner and Gold Medal, New York Radio Festival 1987, One World Broadcasting Trust Award 1989, NTL Commercial Radio Programmer of the Year 2002. *Leisure interests:* music, rugby, walking, skiing, country pursuits.

LEWIS, Stephen, CC; Canadian international advocate and humanitarian; *Co-Director, AIDS-Free World;* b. 11 Nov. 1937, Ottawa, Ont.; s. of David Lewis and Sophie Lewis; m. Michele Landsberg 1963; three c.; ed Univs of Toronto and British Columbia; spent one year teaching and travelling in Africa; MPP for Scarborough W, Ont. Legis. 1963–78; Prov. Leader, New Democratic Party (NDP) 1970–77; Canadian Amb. to UN 1984–88; Special Adviser to UN Sec.-Gen. on Africa 1986–91; Special Rep. to UNICEF 1990, Deputy Exec. Dir UNICEF 1995–99; mem. Int. Panel of Eminent Personalities to investigate genocide in Rwanda 1998; UN Special Envoy for HIV/AIDS in Africa 2001–06; Co-founder and Chair. Stephen Lewis Foundation 2003–; Co-founder and Co-Dir AIDS-Free World 2007–; served on Global Comm. on HIV and the Law 2010–12; Social Sciences Scholar-in-Residence, McMaster Univ. 2006, Prof. in Global Health 2007–09; Prof. of Distinction, Ryerson Univ. 2010–18; Prof. of Practice in Global Governance, Inst. for the Study of Int. Devt, McGill Univ. 2014–16; Kt Commdr of Most Dignified Order of Moshoeshoe (Lesotho) 2007; Hon. LLD from 42 univs; Gordon Sinclair ACTRA Award 1982, Maclean's Magazine Canadian of the Year 2003, Bonham Centre Award 2013. *Publications:* Art Out of Agony 1983, Race Against Time 2005. *Address:* c/o Stephen Lewis Foundation, 260 Spadina Avenue, Suite 501, Toronto, ON M5T 2E4, Canada (office). *Telephone:* (416) 533-9292 (office). *E-mail:* stephen.lewis@ryerson.ca (office); info@stephenlewisfoundation.org (office); info@aidsfreeworld.org (office). *Website:* www.stephenlewisfoundation.org (office); www.aidsfreeworld.org (office).

LEWIS, Vaughan Allen, PhD, CBE; Saint Lucia politician and academic; *Professor Emeritus of International Relations, University of the West Indies;* b. 17 May 1940; m. Shirley May Lewis; two d.; ed Univ. of Manchester, UK; temporary Asst Lecturer, Dept of Political Theory, Univ. Coll. Swansea, Wales 1963–64; Asst Lecturer, Dept of Politics, Univ. of Liverpool 1964–66; Research Fellow Dept of Govt, Univ. of Manchester 1966–68; Lecturer, Dept of Govt, Univ. of the West Indies, Mona, Jamaica 1968–72, Part-time Lecturer, Inst. of Int. Relations, Univ. of the West Indies, St Augustine, Trinidad 1974–80, Acting Dir Inst. of Social and Econ. Research, Univ. of the West Indies 1974, Dir (rank of Full Prof.) 1977–82;

Dir-Gen. Org. of Eastern Caribbean States, Castries, St Lucia 1982–95; Prime Minister of Saint Lucia 1996–97; Prof. of Int. Relations, Inst. of Int. Relations, Univ. of the West Indies 1999, now Prof. Emer.; Visiting Prof., Fla Int. Univ. 1980, Ford Foundation Visiting Fellow, Yale Univ. 1981. *Publications:* numerous books, papers and articles on int. relations, particularly concerning the Caribbean. *Address:* Institute of International Relations, University of the West Indies, St Augustine Campus, St Augustine, Trinidad and Tobago. *E-mail:* iirt@sta.uwi.edu (office). *Website:* sta.uwi.edu/iir (home).

LEWIS, W. Joe, BS, MS, PhD; American entomologist and government scientist; b. Miss.; ed Mississippi State Univ.; Research Entomologist, Crop Protection and Man. Research Unit, Agricultural Research Service (ARS), US Dept of Agric. (USDA), Tifton, Ga 1967–2006; Charter Ed. Biological Control: Theory and Applications in Pest Management 1991; fmr Research Scientist, Coll. of Agricultural & Environmental Sciences, Univ. of Georgia Tifton; Fellow Entomological Soc. of America 2008–; Founders' Memorial Lecturer Award, Entomological Soc. of America 1990, USDA-ARS Outstanding Scientist of the Year Award 1999, Special Congressional Recognition for Outstanding Achievement, Service and Public Distinction 2000, Jean-Marie Delwart Prize for Science of Chemical Communications (co-recipient) 2003, Invitational Fellowship for Research, Japan Soc. for Promotion of Science 2003, Wolf Prize in Agric. (Israel) (co-recipient) 2008. *Publications:* several book chapters and more than 200 peer-reviewed papers in professional journals. *Address:* c/o Crop Protection and Management Research Unit, USDA-ARS, PO Box 748, Tifton, GA 31793, USA (office).

LEWIS, William; British journalist, newspaper editor and newspaper executive; *CEO, Dow Jones;* b. 2 April 1969; m. Rebecca Lewis; four c.; worked on financial section of Mail on Sunday (UK) 1991–94; Global News Ed., later Mergers and Acquisitions Ed. (based in New York), later Investment Corresp., Financial Times 1994–2002; Business Ed. Sunday Times 2002–05; Jt Deputy Ed. Daily Telegraph 2005–06, Man. Dir (Editorial) 2006, Ed. 2006–09, Ed.-in-Chief 2007–09, also of Sunday Telegraph 2007–09, Digital Man. Dir 2009–10; Group Gen. Man., News International (now News UK) 2010–13, Exec. mem. Man. and Standards Cttee 2011–14, Chief Creative Officer, News Corporation 2013–14, CEO Dow Jones 2014–; Hon. LLD (Bristol) 2010; Hon. DLitt (Lincoln) 2011; several awards, including Wincott Young Financial Journalist of the Year, Journalist of the Year, British Press Awards 2010. *Address:* Dow Jones, News Corporation, 1211 Avenue of the Americas, New York, NY 10036, USA (office). *Telephone:* (212) 426-3400 (office). *Website:* newscorp.com/leader/will-lewis (office).

LEWONTIN, Richard (Dick) Charles, AB, BA, BSc, BS, MA, MSc, MPhil, MS, PhD, DPhil, MD, FRS; American evolutionary biologist, geneticist and academic; *Professor Emeritus of Biology and Alexander Agassiz Professor Emeritus of Zoology, Museum of Comparative Zoology, Harvard University;* b. 29 March 1929, New York, NY; m. Mary Ann Lewontin; ed Forest Hills High School, École Libre des Hautes Études, New York, Harvard Coll., Columbia and Harvard Univs; held faculty positions at North Carolina State Univ., Univ. of Rochester, Univ. of Chicago; Alexander Agassiz of Zoology and Prof. of Biology, Harvard Univ. 1973–98, Research Prof. 2003–, now Prof. Emer.; mem. NAS 1970s (later resgnd); Fulbright Fellowship 1961, NSF Sr Postdoctoral Fellow 1961, Sewall Wright Award 1994, Crafoord Prize in Biosciences (Ecology), Royal Swedish Acad. of Sciences (co-recipient) 2015. *Publications:* numerous papers in professional journals on the mathematical basis of population genetics and evolutionary theory. *Address:* Museum of Comparative Zoology, Harvard University, 26 Oxford Street, Cambridge, MA 02138, USA (office). *Telephone:* (617) 495-2419 (office). *Fax:* (617) 495-5667 (office). *E-mail:* lewontin@oeb.harvard.edu (office). *Website:* www.mcz.harvard.edu (office).

LEXDEN, Baron (Life Peer), cr. 2010, of Lexden in the County of Essex and of Strangford in the County of Down; **Alistair Basil Cooke,** OBE; British political historian; b. 20 April 1945, Colchester, Essex, England; s. of Dr Basil Cooke and Nancy Cooke (née Neal); ed Peterhouse, Cambridge; spent majority of career in cen. org. of Conservative Party; taught and researched modern British and Irish history at Queen's Univ., Belfast 1971–77; political adviser to Airey Neave, Conservative Spokesman on NI 1977–79; Asst Dir, then Deputy Dir Conservative Research Dept 1983–97, consultant 2004–, Dir Conservative Political Centre 1988–97; Gen. Sec. Independent Schools Council 1997–2004; Official Historian and Archivist, Carlton Club 2007–; Official Historian, Conservative Party 2009–, Vice-Chair. Conservative Policy Forum 2010–; mem. (Conservative), House of Lords 2010–; historical consultant to Conservative Party Archive; Pres. NI Schools Debating Competition; has reviewed history books for The Daily Telegraph, Northern Ireland magazine Fortnight and for academic journals; obituarist for several nat. newspapers. *Publications include:* as author: Ulster: The Unionist Options, Ulster: The Origins of the Problem, Making Unionism Positive A Party of Change: A Brief History of the Conservatives (co-author), Government and Party Politics in Britain 1885–86, The Governing Passion: Cabinet (with John Vincent), The Carlton Club 1832–2007 (with Sir Charles Petrie) 2007, A Party of Change: A Brief History of the Conservatives 2008, Tory Heroine: Dorothy Brant and the Rise of Conservative Women 2008, Tory Policy-Making: The Conservative Research Department 1929–2009 2009, A Gift from the Churchills: The Primrose League 1883–2004 2010; as editor of historical series: The Conservative Party: Seven Historical Studies 1680 to the 1990s, A Conservative Party Leader in Ulster: Sir Stafford Northcote's Diary of a Visit to the Province, October 1883, The Conservative Research Department 1929–2004, Ireland and Party Politics, 1885–87: An Unpublished Conservative Memoir, The Ashbourne Papers 1869–1913 (co-ed.); as editor of party publs: The Campaign Guide, Seven Volumes, 1987–2005, Collected Speeches: Margaret Thatcher, John Major and David Cameron, Conservative Political Centre: 120 pamphlets, 1988–97, Politics Today, published 12 times a year by the Research Dept 1986–97; frequent letters on historical subjects in nat. press. *Address:* House of Lords, Westminster, London, SW1A 0PW, England (office). *Telephone:* (20) 7219-8216 (office). *Fax:* (20) 7219-5979 (office). *E-mail:* lexdena@parliament.uk (office). *Website:* www.alistairlexden.org.uk.

LEY, Steven Victor, CBE, BSc, PhD, FRS, FRSC, FMedSci; British chemist and academic; *Head of Organic Chemistry, University of Cambridge;* b. 10 Dec. 1945, Stamford, Lincs., England; ed Loughborough Univ.; Postdoctoral Fellow, Ohio State Univ., USA 1972–74; Postdoctoral Fellow, Imperial Coll., London 1974–75, Probationary Lecturer 1975–76, Lecturer 1976–83, Prof. of Organic Chem. 1983–92, Head of Dept 1989–92, Fellow 2001–; BP (1702) Prof. of Organic Chem., Univ. of Cambridge 1992–2014, Head of Organic Chem. 1992–, Fellow, Trinity Coll. 1993–; numerous hon. lectureships including at univs in USA, Canada, Japan, Australia; Pres. RSC 2002–03; Hon. Fellow, Chemical Research Soc. of India 2001; Hon. DSc (Loughborough) 1994, (Salamanca, Spain) 2000, (Huddersfield) 2003; 29 major prizes and awards, including Corday-Morgan Medal and Prize, Royal Inst. of Chem. 1980, Davy Medal, Royal Soc. 2000, Gesellschaft Deutscher Chemiker August-Wilhelm-von Hofmann Medal 2001, Wolfson Merit Award 2003, ACS Ernest Guenther Award in the Chem. of Natural Products 2003, RSC Teamwork in Innovation Award 2004, iChemE Award for Innovation in Applied Catalysis 2004, Alexander-von-Humboldt Award 2004, Innovation of the Year Award (jtly with AstraZeneca, Avecia and Syngenta), Chemical Industries Asscn 2004, Messel Medal Lecture, Soc. of Chemical Industry 2004, Yamada-Koga Prize 2005, RSC Robert Robinson Award and Medal 2006, Nagoya Gold Medal, Banyu Life Science Foundation International, Japan 2006, ACS Award for Creative Work in Synthetic Organic Chem. 2007, SCI Innovation Award 2007, Hans Herloff Inhoffen Medal, Helmholtz Zentrum für Infektionsforschung, Germany 2008, Prous Inst.-Overton and Meyer Award for New Technologies in Drug Discovery, European Fed. of Medicinal Chem. 2008, RSC High Throughput Drug Discovery Methodologies Award 2008, U.R. Ghatak Endowment Lecture and Gold Medal, Indian Asscn for the Cultivation of Science 2009, first recipient of the RSC Perkin Prize for Organic Chem. 2009, Heinrich Wieland Prize, Boehringer Ingelheim 2009, Tetrahedron Prize for Creativity in Organic Chem. 2009, Paracelsus Prize, Swiss Chemical Soc. 2010, Royal Medal, Royal Soc. 2011, included by The Times in its list of the "100 most important people in British science" 2011, Franco Brittanique Prize, Soc. Chimie de France 2013, RSC Longstaff Prize 2013. *Publications:* more than 770 papers in scientific journals. *Address:* Department of Chemistry, University of Cambridge, Lensfield Road, Cambridge, CB2 1EW, England (office). *Telephone:* (1223) 336398 (office). *E-mail:* svl1000@cam.ac.uk (office). *Website:* www.leygroup.ch.cam.ac.uk (office).

LEYSEN, Thomas; Belgian business executive; *Chairman, KBC Group NV;* b. 1960; ed Univ. of Leuven; began career in maritime business in Hamburg, London and Tokyo; managed Transcor group 1983–88; managed restructuring of General Trading Cy (subsidiary of Société Générale de Belgique) 1989; joined Umicore as mem. Exec. Cttee 1993, successively managed several industrial divisions, Exec. Vice-Pres. 1998–2000, CEO 2000–08, Chair. 2008–; Chair. Fed. of Belgian Enterprises 2008–11; Chair. KBC Group NV 2011–; Chair. Corelio (newspaper publishing group); Chair. Fed. of Belgian Enterprises 2008–11, Belgium-Japan Asscn, Rubenianum Fund, Heritage Fund of the Fondation Roi Baudouin, European Friends of Versailles; Vice-Pres. Vrienden van het Rubenshuis; mem. Supervisory Bd Bank Metzler, Frankfurt, Global Advisory Council of Toyota Motor Corpn (Japan); mem. Trilateral Comm., European Round Table of Industrialists. *Address:* KBC Group NV, Havenlaan 2, Brussels 1080, Belgium (office). *Telephone:* (2) 429-50-45 (office). *Fax:* (2) 429-63-40 (office). *E-mail:* thomas.leysen@kbc.be (office). *Website:* www.kbc.be (office).

LHENDUP, Kesang; Bhutanese politician; *President, Druk National Congress;* joined Druk Nat. Congress 1994, served as Gen. Sec. and Vice-Pres., Pres. 2011–; also worked in Dept of Revenue and Custom. *Address:* Druk National Congress, Boudha 6, POB 5754, Kathmandu, Nepal (office). *Telephone:* (1) 2298060 (office). *E-mail:* dnc@bhutandnc.com (office); dnc2006@gmail.com (office). *Website:* www.bhutandnc.com (office).

LHENDUP, Dasho Shera; Bhutanese lawyer and government official; *Attorney-General;* ed Yangchenphug High School, Sherbutse Coll., George Washington Univ. Law School, USA; spent nine years as child at Buddhist monastery in Rawabi, Lhuentse; early career as music performer, composed hit song Jyalam Jaylam Gi Ashi 1981; sat for Royal Civil Service Comm. examination 1991, joined High Court 1992; went to Mumbai, India to study law 1994–96; joined Nat. Environment Comm. 1998; Dragpon (judge), Wangduephodrang 2005–09; Founder and Prin., Sayang Law Chambers, Thimphu 2009–12; Chief Exec. Counsel, Bhutan Law Services 2013–15; Attorney-General 2015–; mem. Bd of Dirs Galinkha Group of Companies 2011–12. *Address:* Office of the Attorney-General, POB 1045, Thori Lam, Lower Motithang, Thimphu, Bhutan (office). *Telephone:* (2) 326889 (office). *Fax:* (2) 324606 (office). *E-mail:* oag@oag.gov.bt (office). *Website:* oag.gov.bt (office).

LHO, Shin-yong; South Korean politician and diplomatist; b. 28 Feb. 1930, S Pyongyang Prov.; ed Law Coll. of Seoul Nat. Univ., Kentucky State Univ., USA; joined diplomatic service 1956, Dir Planning and Man. Office, Ministry of Foreign Affairs 1967; Consul-Gen., Los Angeles, USA 1969–72; Amb. to India 1973, to Geneva 1976; Vice-Foreign Minister 1974, Foreign Minister 1980–82; Acting Prime Minister Feb.–May 1985, Prime Minister May 1985–87; Head, Agency of Nat. Security Planning 1982–85; mem. Democratic Justice Party (later New Korea Party to be merged with Democratic Party to form Grand Nat. Party); elected Chair. Lotte Foundation 1995. *Publications:* The U.S.–Korea Success Story (The Heritage Lectures) 1969, Forging an Asia Pacific Community: The East-West Center's Role in the 21st Century 1969, No Sin-yong hoegorok 2000. *Address:* Lotte Foundation, 24th Floor, Lotte Building, 81 Namdaemun-ro, Jung-Gu, Seoul 100-721 Republic of Korea. *Telephone:* (2) 776-6723. *Fax:* (2) 318-4823. *E-mail:* scholarship@lotte.net; welfare@lotte.net. *Website:* www.lottefoundation.or.kr.

LI, Arthur K. C., GBS, BChir, MA, MD, JP; British surgeon and academic; *Secretary for Education and Manpower, Hong Kong Special Administrative Region;* b. 23 June 1945, Hong Kong; ed St Paul's Co-educational Coll., King's Coll., Cambridge, Middlesex Hosp. Medical School, Harvard Medical School, USA; house physician, Addenbrooke's Hosp., Cambridge 1969–70, Rotational Sr House Officer 1970–71; house surgeon, Middx Hosp., London 1970; Rotational Surgical Registrar, Queen Elisabeth II Hosp. 1971–72, Hillingdon Hosp., Uxbridge 1972–73; Surgical Registrar, St Mary's Hosp., London 1973–75; Lecturer in Surgery and Sr Surgical Registrar, Royal Free Hosp., London 1975–77, Chair. Div. of Jr Hosp. Doctors 1975–77, Consultant Surgeon and Sr Lecturer in Surgery 1980–82; Stanley Thomas Johnson Foundation Research Fellow, Harvard Medical School, Massachusetts Gen. Hosp. and Shriners Burns Inst., Boston 1977–78, Clinical and Research Fellow 1978–79, Surgical Staff and Instructor in Surgery 1979–80; Foundation Prof. of Surgery and Chair. of Surgical Services, Chinese Univ. of

Hong Kong and the Prince of Wales Hosp. 1982–95, Assoc. Dean, Faculty of Medicine 1986–92, Dean 1992–96, Prof. of Surgery 1995, Vice-Chancellor (Pres.) and mem. Univ. Council 1996–2002; Chair. Hosp. Gov. Cttee, United Christian Hosp. 1987–97; mem. Exec. Council and Sec. for Educ. and Manpower, Hong Kong Special Admin. Region 2002–; Visiting Prof., Royal Australian Coll. of Surgeons 1984, 1986, Nat. Univ. of Singapore 1986, Yale Univ. 1989; Pearce Gould Visiting Prof. in Surgery, Univ. Coll. London and Middlesex School of Medicine 1993; Edward Tooth Prof., Royal Brisbane Hosp. 1995; mem. Bd United Christian Medical Services 1987–; fmr mem. Bd Dirs Hong Kong Science and Tech. Parks Corpn, Hong Kong Applied Science and Tech. Research Inst.; mem. Int. Advisory Panel Ministry of Health, UAE 1993–; fmr Vice-Pres. Asscn of Univ. Pres of China; Hon. Prof. of Surgery, Sun Yat-sen Univ. of Medical Sciences, Guangzhou 1986, People's Hosp., Beijing Medical Univ. 1987, Mil. Postgraduate Medical School and Chinese PLA Gen. Hosp., Beijing 1994; Hon. Prof., Peking Union Medical Coll. 1996, Shanghai Medical Univ.; Hon. Fellow, Sidney Sussex Coll. Cambridge, Philippines Coll. of Surgeons 1994, Asscn of Surgeons of GB and Ireland 1998; Hon. FRCS (Glasgow) 1995; Hon. FRCS (Ireland); Hon. FRSM 1997; Hon. FACS 2000; Hon. FRCP; Hon. DSc (Hull) 1999; Hon. DLitt (Hong Kong Univ. of Science and Tech.) 1999; Dr hc (Soka Univ., Tokyo) 1999; European Soc. for Surgical Research Prize 1980, Moynihan Medal 1982, Royal Coll. of Surgeons Gordon Watson Medal 1987, Stanford Cade Memorial Medal 1988, Royal Marsden Surgical Soc. Ernest Miles Memorial Medal 1990, Edward Hallaran Bennett Lecturer, Trinity Coll. Dublin 1995, Pres.'s Gold Medal Royal Coll. of Surgeons of Edin. 1996, Sir Edward Dunlop Memorial Lecturer, Royal Australian Coll. of Surgeons 2000, Gold Bauhinia Star, Govt of Hong Kong Special Admin. Region 2000, Shaw Prize 2004. *Publications:* numerous research papers in learned journals. *Leisure interests:* reading, skiing, scuba diving. *Address:* Education and Manpower Bureau, 15/F, Wu Chung House, 213 Queen's Road East, Wan Chai, Hong Kong Special Administrative Region, People's Republic of China (office). *Telephone:* (852) 28910088 (office). *Fax:* (852) 28930858 (office). *E-mail:* embinfo@emb.gov.hk (office). *Website:* www.emb.gov.hk (office).

LI, Baomin; Chinese economist and business executive; ed Faculty of History, Jiangxi Teachers' Univ., Corp. Man. Coll. of Fudan Univ., Postgraduate Programme of Econs of Jiangxi Prov. Party Cttee Coll.; fmr Deputy Sec. of Party Cttee, Jiangxi Copper Co. Ltd, now Sec., Supervisor, Jiangxi Copper Co. Ltd 2003–, has held several man. positions, Exec. Dir and Vice-Chair. 2007–13, Chair. 2013–17 (resgnd). *Address:* c/o Jiangxi Copper Co. Ltd, 15 Yejin Avenue, Guixi 335424, People's Republic of China (office). *Telephone:* (701) 3777070 (office). *E-mail:* webmaster@jxcc.com (office). *Website:* www.jxcc.com (office).

LI, Baotian; Chinese actor; b. 28 Nov. 1946, Xuzhou, Jiangsu Prov.; one s.; ed Cen. Acad. of Drama; taught at Cen. Acad. of Drama 1981; China Golden Eagle Award for Most Popular Actor 2000. *Films include:* From Place to Place 1983, The Wanderer and The Swan 1985, Woman, Demon, Human (China Golden Eagle Award for Best Supporting Actor 1988) 1987, Killer in the Wild 1988, Ju Dou 1990, Country Teachers (Hundred Flowers Award for Best Actor 1994, China Golden Eagle Award for Best Actor 1994) 1994, Shanghai Triad 1995, Keep Cool (Hundred Flowers Award for Best Supporting Actor 1998) 1997, Courthouse on Horseback 2006, The Nightingale 2013, Forever Love 2015. *Television includes:* Liu Luoguo 1995, Policeman: Li Jiuping 2000, The Great Doctor: Xi Laile 2001, Dragon Gate 2002, Never Again 2009, Clown Dad 2010, Legend of the Great Doctor: Xi Laile 2013.

LI, Bin, BA, DEcon; Chinese government official; b. 1954, Fushun City, Liaoning Prov.; ed Jilin Univ.; joined CCP 1981; Asst to Gov., Jilin Prov. 2000–01, mem. People's Govt 2001–07, Vice-Gov. 2001–07; Deputy Dir, Nat. Population and Family Planning Comm. 2007–08, Dir 2008–11, also Sec., CCP Leading Party Group 2007–11; Vice-Gov., Anhui Prov. 2011–12, Gov. 2012–13, also mem. and Deputy Sec., CCP Prov. Standing Cttee 2011–13; Minister, Nat. Health and Family Planning Comm. 2013–18; mem. 17th CCP Cen. Cttee 2007–12, 18th CCP Cen. Cttee 2012–17 19th CCP Cen. Cttee 2017–, also mem. CCP Cen. Cttee Central Guidance Cttee on Ethical and Cultural Construction 2008–11. *Address:* National Population and Family Planning Commission, 1 Xizhinenwai Nan Lu, Xicheng Qu, Beijing 100044, People's Republic of China (office). *Telephone:* (10) 68792114 (office). *Fax:* (10) 64012369 (office).

LI, Boyong; Chinese state official and engineer; b. 1932, Tianjin City; ed Air Force Inst. of Mil. Eng, fmr USSR; Vice-Minister, Labour and Personnel 1986–93; mem. 14th CCP Cen. Cttee 1992–97; Minister of Labour 1993–98; Vice-Chair. Legal Affairs Cttee of 9th NPC 1998–2003.

LI, Chang'an; Chinese party and state official; b. 1935, Tai'an Co., Liaoning Prov.; ed Shandong Tech. Coll.; joined CCP 1961; Alt. mem. 12th CCP Cen. Cttee 1982, mem. 1985; Deputy Sec. CCP Cttee, Shandong Prov. 1983–88; Gov. of Shandong 1985–88; Deputy Sec.-Gen. CCP State Council 1987; Deputy Head State Flood Control HQ 1988, Cen. Forest Fire Prevention 1987; Deputy Head Leading Group for Comprehensive Agricultural Devt 1990–; Vice-Chair. State Tourism Cttee 1988; Exec. Vice Chair. China Poly Group Corpn 1993–2001; Chair. China Orient Telecomm Satellite Co. Ltd 1995–2003; Dir (non-exec.) PYI Corpn 2007.

LI, Changchun; Chinese party and government official (retd); b. Feb. 1944, Dalian City, Liaoning Prov.; m. Zhang Shurong; ed Harbin Inst. of Tech.; joined CCP 1965; at Harbin Inst. of Tech. 1966–68; technician, Shenyang Switchgear Plant, Liaoning Prov. 1968–75; Deputy Man. later Man. Shenyang Electrical Equipment Co. 1975–80 (Vice-Chair. CCP Revolutionary Cttee, mem. Standing Cttee and Deputy Sec. CCP Party Cttee 1975–80); Deputy Dir Bureau of Mechanical and Electrical Industry, Shenyang City 1980–81 (Deputy Sec. CCP Party Cttee 1980–81); Deputy Sec.-Gen. CCP Municipal Cttee, Shenyang City 1981–82; Vice-Mayor Shenyang City 1982–83, Mayor 1983–85; Sec. Shenyang Municipal CCP Cttee 1983–86 (Chair. Econ. Cttee 1982–83); Deputy Sec. Liaoning Prov. CCP Cttee 1985–90; Vice-Gov. (also Acting Gov.) of Liaoning Prov. 1986–87, Gov. 1987–90; Vice-Gov. (also Acting Gov.) of Henan Prov. 1990–91, Gov. 1991–92; Sec. CCP 5th Henan Prov. Cttee 1992–98; Chair. Standing Cttee Henan Prov. People's Congress 1993–98; Alt. mem. 12th CCP Cen. Cttee 1981–82, mem. 13th CCP Cen. Cttee 1987–92, 14th CCP Cen. Cttee 1992–97, 15th CCP Cen. Cttee 1997–2002, Politburo 15th CCP Cen. Cttee 1997–2002, 16th CCP Cen. Cttee 2002–07, Politburo 16th CCP Cen. Cttee 2002–07, Standing Cttee Politburo 16th CCP Cen. Cttee 2002–07, 17th CCP Cen. Cttee 2007–12, Standing Cttee Politburo 17th CCP Cen. Cttee 2007–12; Sec. CCP Guangdong Prov. Cttee 1998–2002; Chair. CCP Central Guidance Comm. for Building Spiritual Civilization 2002–12. *Address:* c/o Standing Committee of the Politburo, Chinese Communist Party Central Committee, Beijing, People's Republic of China (office).

LI, Changjin, MEng; Chinese railway industry executive; *Chairman, President and Executive Director, China Railway Group;* ed Changsha Railway Inst., Southwest Jiaotong Univ.; Vice-Pres. The Fourth Survey and Design Inst., MOR Jan.–Dec. 1995, Deputy Dir and Sr Engineer, The Second Eng Bureau of MOR (predecessor of China Railway No. 2 Engineering Group Co. Ltd) 1996–98, Vice-Chair. and Gen. Man. China Railway No. 2 Engineering Group Co. Ltd 1998–2002, also Chair. and Sec. to CCP Cttee, Deputy Gen. Man. China Railway Engineering Corpn (CRECG) 2002–06, mem. Bd of Dirs 2006–, Pres. and Exec. Dir China Railway Group Ltd –2010, Chair. and Exec. Dir 2010–13, Chair., Pres. and Exec. Dir 2013–; recognized as prof.-level sr engineer by Ministry of Personnel 2003. *Address:* China Railway Group Ltd, 26 Lianhuachi Nanli, Beijing 100055, People's Republic of China (office). *E-mail:* info@crecg.com (office). *Website:* www.crecg.com (office); www.crec.cn/en (office).

LI, Changyin; Chinese engineer and business executive (retd); apptd Chair. China Shipbuilding Industry Co. Ltd 2008, fmr Deputy Gen. Man. China Shipbuilding Industry Corpn, currently Gen. Man. and Pres. –2015.

LI, Chunting; Chinese provincial governor; b. Oct. 1936, Luotang village, Zhaili, Qixia Co., Shandong Prov.; joined CCP 1958; worked as farmer; assumed leading posts at village, township, co., prefectural and city level; fmr Deputy Sec. CCP Qixia Co. Cttee, Deputy Sec. CCP Yantai Prefectural Cttee, Head Prov. Metallurgical Dept; Vice-Gov. Shandong Prov. 1988–95, Gov. 1995–97; Deputy Sec. CCP Shandong Prov. Cttee 1992–2001; mem. 15th CCP Cen. Cttee 1997–2002; Vice-Chair. NPC Agric. and Rural Affairs Cttee 2001–. *Address:* National People's Congress, Tiananmen, Beijing, People's Republic of China.

LI, Dadong; Chinese engineer; b. 24 Feb. 1938, Beijing; ed Peking Univ.; joined Research Inst. of Petroleum Processing (RIPP) 1962, becoming Group Leader, Dir, Research Dept, Deputy Chief Engineer 1987–88, Vice-Pres. 1988–91, Pres. 1991–2003, Dir Science Cttee 2004–; Fellow Chinese Acad. of Eng 1994–, Chair. Standing Cttee of Chemical Eng, Metallurgy and Material Eng Dept; many nat., prov. and ministerial prizes. *Publications:* published 70 research papers. *Address:* Petrochemical Science Research Institute, 18 Xueyuan Road, Beijing 100083, People's Republic of China (office). *Telephone:* (10) 62310757 (office). *Fax:* (10) 62311290 (office). *E-mail:* ripp@mimi.cnc.ac.cn (office).

LI, Daoyu; Chinese diplomatist; b. 7 Aug. 1932, Shanghai; m. Ye Zhao Lie 1956; two s.; ed Univ. of Shanghai; joined Foreign Service 1952; held various posts Dept of Int. Orgs and Confs; Deputy Perm. Rep. to UN at Geneva 1983–84; Dir Dept of Int. Orgs, Foreign Ministry 1984–88; Asst Foreign Minister 1988–90; Perm. Rep. to UN, New York 1990–93, Amb. to USA 1993–98; led Chinese Del. to ESCAP session 1989; fmr Vice-Chair. Chinese Nat. Comm., UNESCO, Nat. Cttee for Pacific Econ. Co-operation, Preparatory Cttee of China for Int. Space Year 1992, Nat. Cttee for Int. Decade for Natural Disaster Reduction; fmr rep. of China on Comm. on Human Rights, ECOSOC and UNCTAD; Vice-Chair. Overseas Chinese Affairs Cttee of 9th NPC 1998; mem. Standing Cttee NPC 1998–2003; Prof. School of Int. Studies, Beijing Univ., Inst. of Int. Studies, Tsinghua Univ., Foreign Affairs Coll., Center for American Studies, Fudan Univ., Pacific Inst., Tongji Univ.; Pres. China Int. Public Relations Asscn 1999–, Chinese Asscn of Arms Control and Disarmament 2001–; Vice-Pres. China Int. Friendship Exchange Asscn, China Women Devt Fund; mem. Council Chinese People's Inst. of Foreign Affairs; Sr Adviser China Inst. of Int. Strategic Studies; Adviser China Int. Law Soc., Centre for Across-the-Straits Relationship Studies, Shanghai WTO Affairs Consulting Centre. *Address:* China International Public Relations Association, Room 918, 7 Fuchengmenwai Street, Beijing, 100037, People's Republic of China (office). *Telephone:* (10) 68095777 (office). *Fax:* (10) 68095775 (office). *E-mail:* info@cipra.org.cn (office). *Website:* www.cipra.org.cn (office).

LI, Dezhu, (Li Dek Su); Chinese party and government official; b. 1943, Wangqing Co., Jilin Prov.; ed Yanbian Univ.; joined CCP 1965; Vice-Gov. of Jilin Prov. 1988–93; Deputy Head United Front Work Dept 1992; Pres. Chinese Asscn of Ethnic Minorities for External Exchanges 1992–98; Minister State Comm. of Ethnic Affairs 1998–2008; mem. 14th CCP Cen. Cttee 1992–97, 15th CCP Cen. Cttee 1997–2002, 16th CCP Cen. Cttee 2002–07.

LI, Dongsheng; Chinese electronics industry executive; *Chairman, TCL–Thomson Electronics Company Limited (TTE);* b. July 1957; ed Huanan Tech. Inst.; started career as technician with TTK Home Appliances Co. Ltd 1982, later Deputy Workshop Dir, Business Man.; Gen. Man. TCL Communication Equipment Co. 1985–93, Gen. Man. TCL Corpn 1993–96, Chair. and Pres. 1996–2004, Chair. TCL–Thomson Electronics Co. Ltd (TTE) 2004–; mem. 16th CCP Cen. Cttee 2002–07; Special Contributor to China Household Appliance Industry 1994, Nat. Excellent Young Entrepreneur 1995, Nat. Model Worker 2000, Meritorious Figure of Chinese Brands 2009. *Address:* TCL Corporation, East Yunshan Road, Jiangbei Huizhou, Guangdong 516003, People's Republic of China (office). *Telephone:* (752) 2803898 (office). *Fax:* (752) 2803188 (office). *Website:* (office).

LI, Fanghua, BS; Chinese physicist; *Professor, Institute of Physics, Chinese Academy of Sciences;* b. 6 Jan. 1932, Hong Kong; d. of Jiong Li and Jiqing Liu; m. Haifu Fan 1960; one s. one d.; ed Beijing Furen and Peidao High Schools, Lingnan and Zhongshan Univs, Guangzhou, Wuhan Univ., Hubei Prov., Leningrad (now St Petersburg) Univ., USSR; Research Asst, Inst. of Physics, Chinese Acad. of Sciences 1956–61, Research Assoc. 1962–78, Assoc. Prof. 1979–86, Prof. 1986–; Visiting Scientist, Osaka Univ. 1982–83; Visiting Prof., City Univ. of Hong Kong 1998–99; Pres. Chinese Electron Microscopy Soc. 1996–2000; mem. Chinese Acad. of Sciences 1993, Third World Acad. of Science (now named TWAS, the academy of sciences for the developing world) 1998; Asia-Pacific recipient, L'Oréal-UNESCO For Women in Science Award (first Chinese woman) 2003, State Natural Science Awards (Second Class) 2005, Ho Leung Ho Lee Prize for Scientific and Technological Progress 2009. *Publications include:* Electron Crystallography and Image Processing (in Chinese) 2009; numerous articles in scientific journals. *Leisure interest:* singing. *Address:* Institute of Physics, Chinese Academy of Sciences, PO

Box 603, Beijing, 100190, People's Republic of China (office). *Telephone:* (10) 82649361 (office). *Fax:* (10) 82649531 (office). *E-mail:* lifh@iphy.ac.cn (office). *Website:* www.iphy.ac.cn (office).

LI, Fanrong, BSc, MBA; Chinese engineer and oil industry executive; *Deputy Director, National Energy Administration (NEA);* b. Oct. 1963; ed Jianghan Petroleum Univ., Cardiff Business School, UK; joined China Nat. Offshore Oil Corpn (CNOOC) 1984, engaged in well testing, CNOOC Nanhai East Corpn 1984–89, Production Supervisor and Platform Man., ACT (Agip-Chevron-Texaco) Operators Group 1990–95, becoming Production Dept Man., Liuhua Oilfield Jt Operation Org., Gen. Man., Lufeng 22-1 Oilfield Jt Operation Org., Deputy Gen. Man., CNOOC (China) Ltd-Shenzhen Br. and concurrently Chinese Chief Rep. at CACT (CNOOC-Agip-Chevron-Texaco) Operators Group 1995–2005, Gen. Man., Devt and Production Dept, CNOOC Ltd 2005–07, Gen. Man., CNOOC (China) Ltd-Shenzhen Br. 2007, Asst Pres., CNOOC 2009, also Gen. Man. CNOOC Energy Technology & Services Ltd 2009, Vice-Pres. and Party Leadership Group mem., CNOOC 2010–, Pres. CNOOC Ltd 2010–16, CEO CNOOC Ltd 2011–16; Deputy Dir Nat. Energy Administration 2016–. *Address:* National Energy Administration, 38 Yuetan South Street, Xicheng District, Beijing 100824, People's Republic of China (office). *E-mail:* nea@nea.gov.cn (office). *Website:* www.nea.gov.cn (office).

LI, Furong; Chinese sports administrator and fmr table tennis player; b. 1942, Shanghai City; fmr mem. Chinese Nat. Table Tennis Team; Deputy, 5th NPC 1978–83; Deputy Dir Training Bureau under the Comm. for Physical Culture and Sports 1983, Dir 1986–; Vice-Chair. Youth Fed. 1983; Vice-Minister of the Physical Culture and Sports Comm. 1987; Sec.-Gen. Chinese Olympic Team, Seoul 1988; Vice-Pres. Chinese Olympic Cttee 1989–; apptd Vice-Minister in charge of State Gen. Admin for Sports 1999; Pres. Asian Table Tennis Union 2001–09, Hon. Life Pres. 2010–; Head of Chinese Delegation, World Univ. Games 2008. *Address:* 9 Tiyuguan Road, Beijing 100763, People's Republic of China.

LI, Fushan; Chinese artist and engraver; b. June 1940, Quinhuangdao, Hebei; s. of Li Yinchang and Wang Lihui; m. Lei Suoxia 1961; one s. two d.; worked at Quinhuangdao Cultural Centre 1959–62, at Shanhaiguan Cultural Centre 1962, apptd deputy researcher 1994; works are in pvt. collections in Canada, USA, Italy, NZ and countries in SE Asia; Dir Quinhuangdao Arts Asscn; mem. Hebei Br. China Arts Asscn, Hebei Prov. Research Asscn of Etched Plates. *Leisure interests:* classical literature, photography.

LI, Genshen, DSc; Chinese party official and engineer; b. 1 July 1930, Huzhou City, Zhejiang Prov.; s. of Li Xin-pei and Zhang Zhu-bao; m. Xu Ying; one s. two d.; ed Jiaotong Univ., Shanghai and in USSR; Dir and Chief Engineer, No. 3 Research Inst., No. 7 Research Acad., China Shipbuilding Industrial Corpn; Chair. Bd Harbin Power Equipment Co. 1993–97, Dir (non-exec.) 1997–; mem. Standing Cttee Heilongjiang Prov. CCP Cttee 1983–92, Sec.-Gen. 1984, Deputy Sec. 1985–86; Vice-Chair. Heilongjiang Prov. 8th People's Congress 1993–96; Sec. Harbin Mun. CCP Cttee 1985, Chair. 1983–; Standing Cttee CCP Heilongjiang Prov. Cttee 1988; mem. 13th CCP Cen. Cttee 1987–92; mem. Standing Cttee 1988. *Publication:* Principles, Design and Testing of Marine Steam and Gas Turbines. *Leisure interest:* reading. *Address:* 1 Guomin Street, Nangang District, Harbin 150001, Heilongjiang Province, People's Republic of China (office). *Telephone:* (451) 84616291 (office); (451) 53624054 (home).

LI, Gong; Chinese/Singaporean actress; b. 31 Dec. 1965, Shenyang, Liaoning; m. Ooi Hoe-Seong 1996 (divorced 2010); apptd Global Environmental Amb., UN 2008; Pres. jury of numerous film festivals; Rep., Shanghai Tang (clothing line); Beauty Amb., L'Oréal; first ever Chinese actress to appear on the cover of TIME magazine; Ordre des Arts et des Lettres 1998, Commdr, Legion of Honor 2010; Festival Trophy, Cannes Film Festival 2004, Chinese World Influence Award 2007. *Films include:* Red Sorghum 1987, Evil Empress 1988, Operation Cougar (Hundred Flowers Award for Best Supporting Actress 1989) 1988, The Terracotta Warrior 1989, Ju Dou 1990, The Banquet 1991, God of Gamblers II: Back to Shanghai 1991, Raise the Red Lantern (Hundred Flowers Award for Best Actress 1993) 1991, The Story of Qiu Ju (Golden Rooster Awards for Best Actress, 1993, Venice Film Festival Volpi Cup for Best Actress1992) 1991, Mary from Beijing 1992, Farewell, My Concubine (New York Film Critics Circle Award 1993) 1993, Flirting Scholar 1993, To Live 1994, La Peintre 1994, The Great Conqueror's Concubine 1994, Semi-Gods and Semi-Devils 1994, Shanghai Triad 1995, Temptress Moon 1996, The Empress and the Assassin 1997, Chinese Box 1998, Breaking the Silence (Golden Rooster Awards for Best Actress 2000, Montreal World Film Festival for Best Actress 2000, Hundred Flowers Award for Best Actress 2000, Hundred Flowers Award for Best Actress 2001) 1999, Zhou Yu's Train (Students' Choice Award for Favourite Actress, Beijing Student Film Festival 2003) 2002, Eros 2004, 2046 2004, Memoirs of a Geisha 2005, Miami Vice 2006, Man cheng jin dai huang jin jia (Curse of the Golden Flower) (Hong Kong Film Awards for Best Actress, Golden Bauhinia Award for Best Actress 2007) 2006, Hannibal Rising 2007, Shanghai 2010, What Women Want 2011, Coming Home (Hundred Flowers Award for Best Actress 2014, China Film Directors' Guild Award for Best Actress 2015) 2014, The Monkey King 2 2016.

LI, Guixian; Chinese party official; b. 23 Aug. 1937, Gaixian Co., Liaoning Prov.; ed Chinese Univ. of Science and Tech., Mendeleyev Chemical Tech. Inst., Moscow, USSR; joined CCP 1962; worker, Research Inst., Ministry of Public Security 1966–67; technician, later Workshop Dir, later Deputy Dir, later Chief Engineer, No. 777 Factory 1967–77 (Deputy Sec. CCP Party Cttee 1967–77); Deputy Dir, Chief Engineer Jinzhou City Bureau of Electronics Industry 1977–79; Deputy Dir Liaoning Provincial Bureau of Electronics Industry 1979–82 (Deputy Sec. CCP Leading Party Group 1979–82); Vice-Gov. Liaoning Prov. 1982–85; Chair. Science and Tech. Comm. CCP Liaoning Prov. Cttee, CCP Leading Party Group 1982–83; Sec. CCP Cttee, Liaoning Prov. 1985–86, Anhui Prov. 1986–87; Gov. People's Bank of China 1988–93 (resgnd); State Councillor 1988–98; mem. 12th CCP Cen. Cttee 1982–87, 13th CCP Cen. Cttee 1987–92, 14th CCP Cen. Cttee 1992–97, 15th CCP Cen. Cttee 1997–2002, 16th CCP Cen. Cttee 2002–07; Vice-Chair. Nat. Cttee of 9th CPPCC 1998–2003, Nat. Cttee of 10th CPPCC 2003–08; Pres. Chinese Asscn for Int. Understanding 1999; fmr Dir China Cttee of Int. Decade for Natural Disaster Reduction.

LI, Guohua; Chinese business executive; *President, China Post Group;* Vice-Pres. China Post Group –2012, Pres. and Deputy Sec. CCP Cttee of China Post Group 2012–. *Address:* China Post Group, 3 Financial Street, Beijing, 100080, People's Republic of China (office). *E-mail:* info@chinapost.com.cn (office). *Website:* www.chinapost.com.cn (office).

LI, Guorui; Chinese engineer and business executive; b. 1950; ed Southwest Jiaotong Univ.; Sec. to CCP Cttee, China Railway Engineering Corpn 1996–97; joined China Railway Construction Corpn (CRCC) Ltd 1997, Sec. to CRCC CCP Cttee 1997–2007, Deputy Gen. Man. CRCC 2002–05, Chair. 2005–10, also Gen. Man. 2007–10; Chair. Nanjing Changjiang Tunnel Co. Ltd; mem. 17th CCP Congress. *Address:* c/o China Railway Construction Corporation Ltd, 40 Fuxing Road, Haidian District, Beijing 100855, People's Republic of China. *E-mail:* ir@crcc.cn.

LI, Hongzhi; Chinese spiritual leader; b. 13 May 1951, Jilin Prov.; m.; one d.; fmr stud farm worker, trumpeter in police band and grain clerk; Leader, Falun Gong spiritual movt 1992–; lives in exile in New York, USA. *Publication:* Zhuan Falun (Law of the Wheel) 1996. *Address:* c/o The Universe Publishing, PO Box 193, Gillette, NJ 07933, USA (office). *Telephone:* (888) 353-2288 (office). *Fax:* (888) 214-2172 (office).

LI, Huaji; Chinese artist; b. 16 Feb. 1931, Beijing; s. of Li Jue-Tian and Zhang Yun-Zheng; m. Quan Zhenghuan 1959; two d.; mem. Acad. Cttee and Dir Mural Painting Dept, Cen. Acad. of Fine Arts; Vice-Dir Mural Painting Cttee, Artists' Asscn of China; mem. Oil Painting Research Asscn; important murals include Hunting (Harbin Swan Hotel), 5,000 Years of Culture (Beijing Nat. Library). *Leisure interests:* classical music, Beijing opera.

LI, Hui; Chinese diplomatist; *Ambassador to the Russian Federation;* b. Feb. 1953, Heilongjiang Prov.; m.; one d.; Asst, USSR and Eastern Europe Dept, Ministry of Foreign Affairs 1975–81, Attaché, becoming Third Sec., later Second Sec., Embassy in Moscow 1981–85, Second Sec., later Deputy Head of Dept, First Sec., USSR and Eastern Europe Dept, Ministry of Foreign Affairs 1985–90, First Sec., Embassy in Moscow 1990–92, First Sec., Counsellor, Embassy in Almaty 1992–95, Counsellor, later Deputy Dir, Eastern European and Central Asian Affairs Dept 1995–97, Amb. to Kazakhstan 1997–99, Dir Eastern European and Central Asian Dept 1999–2003, Asst Minister of Foreign Affairs 2003–08, Deputy Minister of Foreign Affairs 2008–09, Amb. to the Russian Fed. 2009–; Deputy to 12th NPC 2013–; Deputy Chair. Nat. Soc. of Philatelists (6th convocation); Dr hc (Inst. of Far Eastern Studies, Moscow State Linguistic Univ.). *Address:* Embassy of the People's Republic of China, 117330 Moscow ul. Druzhby 6, Russia (office). *Telephone:* (495) 783-08-67 (office). *Fax:* (499) 956-11-69 (office). *E-mail:* chiemb@microdin.ru (office). *Website:* ru.china-embassy.org (office).

LI, Jennifer, BA, MBA; Chinese business executive; *CEO, Baidu Capital;* m.; two c.; ed Tsinghua Univ., Univ. of British Columbia, Canada; held several finance positions at General Motors in Canada, USA and Singapore 1994–2001, worked at General Motors China, responsible for overseeing finance functions of General Motors' wholly owned and joint venture businesses in China 2001–04, later Chief Financial Officer; Controller, General Motors Acceptance Corpn North American Operations 2005–08; Chief Financial Officer, Baidu, Inc. 2008–17, CEO Baidu Capital 2017–; mem. Bd of Dirs Philip Morris International, Inc. 2010–. *Address:* Baidu, Inc., Baidu Campus, No. 10, Shangdi 10th Street, Haidian District, Beijing 100085, People's Republic of China (office). *Telephone:* (10) 59928888 (office). *Fax:* (10) 59920000 (office). *E-mail:* info@baidu.com (office). *Website:* www.baidu.com (office).

LI, Jet; Chinese actor, producer and martial artist; b. 26 April 1963, Beijing; m. 1st Qiuyan Huang 1987 (divorced 1990); two d.; m. 2nd Nina Li Chi 1999; two d.; began training at Wu Shu (martial arts) Acad., Beijing aged nine; winner of five gold medals in Chinese Wu Shu Championships aged 11; world Wu Shu champion on several occasions; became Wu Shu nat. coach age 20; film debut in Shao Lin tzu (The Shaolin Temple) 1979. *Films include:* Shao Lin tzu 1979, Shao Lin xiao zi 1983, Zhong hua ying xiong 1986, Nan bei Shao Lin 1986, Long zai tian ya 1988, Once upon a Time in China 1991, The Legend (also producer) 1993, Lord of the Wu Tang (also producer) 1993, Claws of Steel (also producer) 1993, Tai-Chi (also producer) 1993, The Legend 2 (also producer) 1993, The Defender (also producer) 1994, High Risk 1995, The Enforcer 1995, Adventure King 1996, Lethal Weapon 4 1998, Romeo Must Die 2000, Kiss of the Dragon (also producer) 2001, The One 2001, Ying xiong 2002, The Contract Killer 2002, Legend of the Red Dragon (also producer) 2002, Legend of the Swordsman 2002, Rise to Honor 2003, Danny the Dog 2005, Huo Yuan Jia 2006, War 2007, The Warlords 2007, The Forbidden Kingdom 2008, The Mummy: Tomb of the Dragon Emperor 2008, The Founding of a Republic 2009, Ocean Heaven 2010, The Expendables 2010, The Expendables 2 2012, Badges of Fury 2013, The Expendables 3 2014, League of Gods 2016. *Website:* www.jetli.com.

LI, Jianguo; Chinese politician; b. April 1946, Juanchen Co., Shandong Prov.; ed Shandong Univ., joined CCP 1971; joined CCP 1971; worker, Culture and Educ. Bureau, Ninghe Co., Shandong Prov., Publicity Dept, CCP Co. Cttee, Ninghe Co., Publicity Div., Agricultural Cttee, Tianjin Municipality, Gen. Office CCP Tianjin Municipal Cttee (Deputy Office Dir 1981, Dir 1983, Deputy Sec.-Gen. CCP Tianjin Municipal Cttee 1988, Sec.-Gen. 1989, Deputy Sec. 1992–97); Sec. CCP Heping Dist Cttee, Tianjin 1991–92; Vice-Sec. CCP Tianjin Mun. Cttee 1992; apptd Sec. CCP Shaanxi Prov. Cttee 1997–98, elected Sec. 1998–2002, Chair. Standing Cttee of Shaanxi Prov. People's Congress 1998–; Alt. mem. 14th CCP Cen. Cttee 1992–97, mem. 15th CCP Cen. Cttee 1997–2002, 16th CCP Cen. Cttee 2002–07, 17th CCP Cen. Cttee 2007–12, 18th CCP Cen. Cttee 2012–17, 18th CCP Cen. Cttee Politburo 2012–17; Sec.-Gen. and Vice-Chair. 11th NPC Standing Cttee 2008–13; Vice-Chair. 12th NPC Standing Cttee 2013–. *Address:* Chinese Communist Party, Zhongnanhai, Beijing, People's Republic of China (office). *Website:* cpc.people.com.cn (office).

LI, Jianhong, MA, MBA; Chinese economist and business executive; *Chairman, China Merchants Bank Company Limited;* ed Wuhan Univ. of Water Transportation Eng, Jilin Univ., Univ. of East London, UK; joined Cosco Pacific Ltd 1989, Gen. Man. and Factory Dir, Nantong Shipyard and Gen. Man. Nantong Steel Co. 1995, Pres. Asst, Chief Economist and Vice-Pres., China Ocean Shipping (Group) Co. (holding co. of Cosco Pacific Ltd) from 2000, Exec. Dir, Cosco International Holdings Ltd 2002–08, Dir (non-exec.) 2008–10, Chair. China International

Marine Containers Group Co. Ltd (CIMC) 2004–07, Chair. Cosco Corpn (Singapore) Ltd 2008–10, Chair. Sino-Ocean Land Holdings Ltd 2008–10; Dir and Pres. China Merchants Group 2010–14, Dir (non-exec.) and Chair. China Merchants Bank Co. Ltd 2014–, Chair. China Merchants Group, China Merchants Holdings (International) Co. Ltd, China Merchants Energy Shipping Co. Ltd, China International Marine Containers (Group) Co. Ltd, China Merchants Huajian Highway Investment Co. Ltd, China Merchants Capital; Nat. Role Model, Nat. Outstanding Youth Entrepreneur. *Address:* China Merchants Group Ltd, 40th Floor, China Merchants Building, 168–200 Connaught Road, Central, Hong Kong Special Administrative Region (office); China Merchants Bank Co. Ltd, 7088 Shen Nan Road, Futian District, Shenzhen 518040, Guangdong, People's Republic of China (office). *Telephone:* 25428288 (Hong Kong) (office); (755) 83198888 (Shenzhen) (office). *Fax:* 25448851 (Hong Kong) (office); (755) 83195109 (Shenzhen) (office). *E-mail:* cmhk@cmhk.com (office). *Website:* www.cmhk.com (office); www.cmbchina.com (office).

LI, Jiating; Chinese politician; b. April 1944, Shiping, Yunnan Prov.; ed Tsinghua Univ.; joined CCP 1964; cadre CCP Heilongjiang Prov. Cttee; Vice-Dir Office of Heilongjiang Prov. Econ. Comm. then Vice-Dir of Comm.; Vice-Mayor then Mayor of Harbin; Asst Gov. of Heilongjiang Prov. 1968–93; Vice-Gov. Yunnan Prov. 1993–98, Gov. 1998–2001; Alt. mem. CCP 14th and 15th Cen. Cttees 1992–2002; arrested and detained pending trial on corruption charges 2002, convicted of corruption, received suspended death sentence 2003.

LI, Ji'nai; Chinese army officer; b. July 1942, Tengzhou City, Shandong Prov.; ed Harbin Acad. of Mil. Eng; joined CCP 1965; joined PLA 1967; various posts, 2nd Artillery; Dir Cadre Dept PLA Gen. Political Dept 1987–90, Deputy Dir 1990–92, Dir 2004–12; Deputy Political Commissar, State Comm. of Science, Tech. and Industry for Nat. Defence 1992–95, Political Commissar 1995, PLA Gen. Equipment Dept 1998–2002; rank of Maj.-Gen. 1988, Lt-Gen. 1993, Gen. 2000; Alt. mem. 14th CCP Cen. Cttee 1992–97, mem. 15th CCP Cen. Cttee 1997–2002, 16th CCP Cen. Cttee 2002–07; mem. 16th CCP Cen. Cttee Cen. Military Comm. 2002–07, 17th CCP Cen. Cttee Cen. Military Comm. 2007–12.

LI, Jinbin, MA; Chinese party official; b. Feb. 1958, Chengdu; ed Jilin Univ.; joined CCP Sept. 1978; spent much of his career in Jilin Prov., including as Officer and Deputy Dir, Personnel Office, Jilin Educ. Dept 1982–85, Deputy Dir and later Dir, Cadre Office 1985–92, also Deputy Dir of Jilin Provincial Educ. Cttee 1985–92; Deputy Party Chief, Changchun CCP 1994–95; Mayor of Tonghua city 1995–98; CCP Party Chief, Liaoyuan city 2001–02; Vice-Gov., Jilin Prov. 2002–07; Dir of Organization Dept, CCP Provincial Cttee, Shaanxi Prov. 2007–13; Deputy CCP Sec., Anhui Prov. 2013–16; Gov., Anhui Prov. 2015–16; Rep to 9th Nat. People's Congress 1998–2003; Rep to 16th CCP Nat. Congress 2002, 17th 2007, 18th 2012; mem. 19th CCP Cen. Cttee 2017–. *Address:* People's Government of Anhui Province, 23000 Hefei, Anhui, People's Republic of China (office). *Telephone:* (551) 62602130 (office). *Website:* english.ah.gov.cn (office).

LI, Adm. Jing; Chinese naval officer and party official; b. 1930, Tengzhou, Shandong Prov.; ed Air Force Aviation Acad. of China; joined PLA 1946, CCP 1949; Deputy Chief PLA Navy Staff 1973–80; Deputy Commdr Naval Air Force 1980–82; Deputy Commdr PLA Navy 1982–92 and concurrently Commdr Naval Air Force 1985–90; Deputy Chief of PLA Gen. Staff HQ 1992–95; rank of Vice-Adm. 1988, Adm. 1994; mem. 7th NPC 1987–92; mem. 14th CCP Cen. Cttee 1992–97; mem. Standing Cttee, Vice-Chair. Foreign Affairs Cttee, 9th Nat. Cttee of CPPCC 1998–2003; mem. Standing Cttee 9th NPC 1998–2008; apptd Sr Adviser Int. Strategy Soc. 1998.

LI, Jinhua; Chinese politician (retd); b. July 1943, Rudong Co., Jiangsu Prov.; ed Cen. Inst. of Finance and Banking, CCP Cen. Cttee Cen. Party School; joined CCP 1965; teacher, Northwest China Inst. of Finance and Banking, Shaanxi Prov. 1966; Deputy Dir later Dir Factory, Ministry of Aeronautics Industry (Deputy Sec. CCP Party Cttee) 1971–85; Dir Econ. and Trade Dept of Shaanxi Prov. 1985; Deputy Auditor Gen. Nat. Audit Office 1985–98, Auditor-Gen. 1998–2008; mem. 14th CCP Cen. Cttee for Discipline Inspection 1992–97, 15th CCP Cen. Cttee 1997–2002, 16th CCP Cen. Cttee 2002–07; Vice-Chair. 11th CPPCC Nat. Cttee 2008–13; Chair. Environmental Auditing Cttee (and mem. Governing Bd), Asian Org. of Supreme Audit Insts; Hon. Prof. Peking Univ., Nankai Univ., Cen. Univ. of Finance and Banking, Nanjing Audit Inst. *Leisure interests:* calligraphy, bridge, swimming, climbing. *Address:* c/o China National Audit Office, No. 17, Jin Zhong Du Nan Jie, Fengtai District, Beijing 100073, People's Republic of China.

LI, Jinping; Chinese business executive; *Chairman and President, Shanxi Lu'An Mining Industry (Group) Company Limited;* Chair. Shanxi Lu'an Environmental Energy Development Co. Ltd 2011–, fmr Deputy Gen. Man. and Dir, Shanxi Lu'an Mining Industry (Group) Co. Ltd, currently Chair. and Pres. *Address:* Shanxi Lu'An Mining Group, Houbu Town, Changzhi 046204, People's Republic of China (office). *Telephone:* (355) 5922-114 (office). *Website:* www.chinaluan.com (office).

LI, Jinyuan, MBA; Chinese business executive; *Chairman and President, Tiens Group;* b. June 1958, Changzhou, Hebei Prov.; ed Nankai Univ.; left school at 14 and worked in oil field and plastics factory for seven years before starting own business in 1985, set up printing co., flour mill and fodder factory; Chair. and Pres. Tiens Group 1995–, also Chair. and CEO Tiens Bio-Tech Group (USA) Inc. 2010–; numerous awards for philanthropy including title of Patriotic Entrepreneur by Patriotic Chinese Businessmen New Year Gathering and Forum of Econ. and Business Cooperation 2005, named as one of Top 10 Philanthropists in Mainland China 2005, honoured with title of State Advanced Individual in Nat. Unity 2005, named as one Top 10 Econ. Talents in China 2005, named China's Top Business Education Leader 2008, China Most Philanthropic Entrepreneur 2010. *Address:* Tiens Group, No. 18, Xinyuan Road, Wuqing Development Zone, Tianjin Hi-Tech Industrial Park, Tianjin 301700, People's Republic of China (office). *Telephone:* (22) 82124400 (office). *Fax:* (22) 821372804 (office). *E-mail:* zcfw@tiens.com.cn (office). *Website:* www.tiens.com (office).

LI, Jun, MA; Chinese economist and banking executive; ed Huazhong Univ. of Science and Tech.; joined Bank of Communications 1990, Deputy Gen. Man. and Gen. Man. Wuhan Branch 1990–98, Controller Gen. 1998–2001, Exec. Dir 2000–09, Exec. Vice-Pres. 2000–06, Vice-Chair. and Pres. 2006–09; Chair. Bd of Supervisors, Bank of China Ltd 2010–16, Vice-Party Sec. 2009–. *Address:* c/o Bank of China Ltd, 1 Fuxingmen Nei Dajie, Beijing 100818, People's Republic of China (office). *Telephone:* (10) 6659-6688 (office). *Fax:* (10) 6659-3777 (office). *E-mail:* info@boc.cn (office). *Website:* www.boc.cn (office).

LI, Ka-shing, KBE, JP; Chinese entrepreneur and business executive; *Adviser, Cheung Kong Hutchison (Holdings) Ltd;* b. 1928, Chaozhou, Guangdong Prov.; m. Chong Yuet-ming (deceased); two s.; moved with family from mainland to Hong Kong 1940; worked in watch-strap co. 1942; salesman, later Man. then Gen. Man., for watch strap co. 1945–47; est. Cheung Kong Plastics Co. 1950; est. Cheung Kong Real Estate Co. Ltd 1971; listed Cheung Kong (Holdings) Ltd in Hong Kong 1972, Chair. 1971–2018; acquired Hutchison Whampoa Ltd 1979; Chair. Cheung Kong Hutchison (Holdings) Ltd 1981–2018, Adviser 2018–; est. Li Ka Shing Foundation 1980; f. Shantou Univ. 1981; acquired Hongkong Electric Holdings Ltd (later renamed Power Assets Holdings Ltd) 1985, Cheung Kong Infrastructure Holdings Ltd spun off in listing 1996, Tom.com (later renamed TOM Group) listed on GEM Stock Exchange 2000, CK Life Sciences International (Holdings) Inc. listed on GEM Stock Exchange 2002, TOM Group advanced to Main Bd of Hong Kong Stock Exchange (HKSE) 2004, CK Life Sciences International (Holdings) Inc. advanced to Main Bd of HKSE 2008; has investments in 52 countries; mem. Drafting Cttee for Basic Law of Hong Kong Special Admin. Region (HKSAR) 1985–90; Hong Kong Affairs Adviser 1992–97; mem. Preparatory Cttee for the HKSAR 1995–97, mem. Selection Cttee of Govt of HKSAR 1996–; mem. Int. Business Advisory Council of the UK 2006; Hon. Citizen of a number of cities in People's Repub. of China (PRC) and overseas; Grand Officer, Order Vasco Nuñez de Balboa (Panama) 1982, Commdr, Order of the Crown (Belgium) 1986, Hon. KBE 2000, Commdr, Order of Leopold (Belgium) 2000, Grand Bauhinia Medal (HKSAR) 2001, Commdr, Légion d'honneur 2005; Hon. LLD (Univ. of Hong Kong) 1986, (Univ. of Calgary, Canada) 1989, (Chinese Univ. of Hong Kong) 1997, (Univ. of Cambridge, UK) 1999; Hon. DScS (Hong Kong Univ. of Science and Tech.) 1995, (City Univ. of Hong Kong) 1998, (Open Univ. of Hong Kong) 1999; Dr hc (Peking Univ.) 1992; Entrepreneur of the Millennium Award, The Times newspaper and Ernst & Young, UK 1999, Int. Distinguished Entrepreneur Award (Univ. of Manitoba, Canada) 2000, Malcolm S. Forbes Lifetime Achievement Award 2006, Special Hon. Award for Econ. Contrib., China Central Television 2007, Lifetime Achievement Award for Philanthropy, PRC Ministry of Civil Affairs 2007, Presidential Award, Teachers of English to Speakers of Other Languages, Inc. 2007, The Robert H. Alway Lifetime Achievement Award, Stanford Univ., USA 2010, Lifetime Achievement Award, DHL/SCMP Hong Kong Business Awards 2010, Carnegie Medal of Philanthropy, Carnegie Corpn 2011, Berkeley Medal, Univ. of California, Berkeley 2011. *Address:* 22/F, Hutchison House, 10 Harcourt Road, Hong Kong Special Administrative Region, People's Republic of China (office). *Telephone:* (852) 21281188 (office). *Fax:* (852) 2128 1705 (office). *E-mail:* info@ckh.com.hk (office). *Website:* www.ckh.com.hk (office).

LI, Keqiang, MA, PhD; Chinese economist and politician; *Premier;* b. July 1955, Dingyuan Co., Anhui Prov.; m. Cheng Hong; ed Beijing Univ.; sent to do manual labour, Dongling Production Brigade, Damiao Commune early 1970s (Sec. CCP Party Br. 1976–78); joined CCP 1976; Head, Beijing Univ. Students' Fed. 1978–82; Sec. Communist Youth League, Beijing Univ. 1978–82; fmr Deputy Dir Dept of Schools and Colls of Communist Youth League Cen. Cttee; Sec.-Gen. All-China Students' Fed. 1982, Vice-Chair. 1990; Sec. Secr. of Communist Youth League Cen. Cttee 1982–93, First Sec. 1993–98; Pres. China Youth Political Coll. 1993; Deputy Sec. CCP Henan Prov. Cttee 1998–2002 (mem. Standing Cttee 2001–04), Sec. 2002–04; Deputy Gov. Henan Prov. 1998, Acting Gov. 1998–99, Gov. 1999–2003; Chair. Standing Cttee Henan Prov. People's Congress 2003–04, Standing Cttee Liaoning Prov. People's Congress 2004–07; Sec. CCP Liaoning Prov. Cttee 2004–07; mem. Standing Cttee of NPC 1993–98; mem. 15th CCP Cen. Cttee 1997–2002, 16th CCP Cen. Cttee 2002–07, 17th CCP Cen. Cttee 2007–12, 17th CCP Politburo 2007–12 and Politburo Standing Cttee 2007–12; mem. 18th CCP Cen. Cttee 2012–17, also mem. 18th CCP Cen. Cttee Politburo 2012–17 and Politburo Standing Cttee 2012–17; mem. 19th CCP Cen. Cttee Politburo 2017– and Politburo Standing Cttee 2017–; First Vice-Premier 2008–13, Premier 2013–; Deputy Sec. State Council Leading Party mems group 2008–13; Party Sec., State Council; Dir State Council Leading Group for Western Region Devt 2013–; Deputy Dir State Energy Comm. 2008–13, Dir 2013–. *Address:* Office of the Premier, Great Hall of the People, West Edge, Tiananmen Square, Beijing, People's Republic of China (office). *Telephone:* (10) 88050813 (office). *Fax:* (10) 63070900 (office). *Website:* english.gov.cn/2008-03/16/content_921792.htm (office).

LI, Keyu; Chinese fashion and costume designer; b. 15 May 1929, Shanghai; m. Yuan Mao 1955; ed Cen. Acad. of Fine Arts; Chief Costume Designer of Cen. Ballet; Deputy Dir Chinese Soc. of Stage Design; mem. Bd All-China Artists' Asscn, Chinese Dancers' Asscn; Deputy Dir China Export Garments Research Centre; Prof. and Sr consultant, Beijing Inst. of Fashion Tech. and Head Apparel Research Inst.; has designed costumes for many works, including Swan Lake, Le Corsaire, The Maid of the Sea, The Fountain of Bakhchisarai, La Esmeralda, The Red Detachment of Women, The East is Red, The New Year Sacrifice (Ministry of Culture costume design prize), Zigeunerweisen (Ministry of Culture costume design prize), Othello (for Peking Opera, Beijing's costume design prize), Tang Music and Dance, Zheng Ban Qiao (Houston Ballet), Fu (Hongkong Ballet), La Péri (Houston Ballet); winner sole costume design prize, 4th Japan World Ballet Competition, Osaka 1984. *Publications:* two vols of sketches. *Address:* 21 Gongjian Hutong, Di An-Men, Beijing 100009, People's Republic of China. *Telephone:* 4035474.

LI, Hon. Kwok Nang Andrew, CBE, MA, LLM, QC, JP; Chinese fmr judge; b. 12 Dec. 1948, Hong Kong; s. of Li Fook Kow and Edith Kwong Li; m. Judy Mo Ying Li; two d.; ed St Paul's Co-Educational Coll., Hong Kong, Repton School, Univ. of Cambridge, UK; called to the Bar, Middle Temple 1970, Hong Kong 1973; practised at Hong Kong Bar 1973–97; QC 1988, Chief Justice, Court of Final Appeal Hong Kong 1997–2010; Hon. Bencher Middle Temple 1997; Hon. Fellow, Fitzwilliam Coll. Cambridge 1999; Hon. Prof., Univ. of Hong Kong, Chinese Univ. of Hong Kong, City Univ. of Hong Kong 2010; Grand Bauhinia Medal 2008; Dr hc (Hong Kong Univ. of Science and Tech.) 1993, (Baptist Univ.) 1994, (Open Univ. of Hong Kong) 1997, (Univ. of Hong Kong), (The Griffith Univ.) 2001, (Univ. of NSW) 2002, (Univ. of Tech., Sydney) 2005, (Chinese Univ. of Hong Kong) 2006, (Hong Kong Shue Yan Univ.) 2009, (Lingnan Univ. Hong Kong) 2010, (City Univ. of Hong

Kong) 2010, (Univ. of Oxford) 2013; Grand Bauhinia Medal 2008. *Leisure interests:* reading, tennis, hiking.

LI, Gen. Laizhu; Chinese army officer and party official; b. 1932, Shen Co., Shandong Prov.; ed PLA Mil. and Political Acad.; joined PLA 1947, CCP 1948; Deputy Commdr of Beijing Mil. Area Command 1985; rank of Lt-Gen., PLA 1988; gave verbal order to send in troops to clear student protests, Tiananmen Square June 1989; Commdr Beijing Mil. Region 1994–97; Gen. mem. 14th CCP Cen. Cttee 1992–97; rank of Gen. 1994–.

LI, Lanqing; Chinese government and party official (retd); b. 22 May 1932, Zhengjiang Co., Jiangsu Prov.; ed Fudan Univ., Shanghai; joined CCP 1952; worker, No. 1 Automobile Works, Changchun City Jilin Prov. 1952, Chief of Planning Section 1957–59; trainee, Liharchev and Gorky Automobile Factories, USSR 1956–57; worker, First Ministry of Machine-Building Industry 1959–81, State Econ. Comm. 1959–81, No. 2 Automobile Works 1959–81, No. 3 Automobile Factory 1959–81; Chief, Govt Loan Office, State Admin Comm. on Import and Export Affairs 1981–82; Dir Foreign Investment Admin. Bureau, Ministry of Foreign Econ. Relations and Trade 1982; Vice-Mayor Tianjin 1983–85; Vice-Minister of Foreign Econ. Relations and Trade 1986–90, Minister 1990–92; Vice-Premier, State Council 1993–2003; Head Nat. Leading Group for Foreign Investments (State Council) 1994–2003; Deputy Head Cen. Leading Group for Party Bldg Work 1994; Chair. Academic Degrees Cttee 1995–; Dir Nat. Cttee for the Patriotic Public Health Campaign 1998–; Deputy Head, State Steering Group of Science, Tech. and Educ. 1998–; mem. 8th NPC 1993–98; Alt. mem. 13th CCP Cen. Cttee 1987–92, mem. 14th CCP Cen. Cttee 1992–97 (mem. Politburo 1992–97), 15th CCP Cen. Cttee 1997–2002 (mem. Standing Cttee of Politburo 1997–2002); retired 2003; Hon. DH (Hong Kong Baptist Univ.) 2011.

LI, Liguo; Chinese government official; b. Nov. 1953, Yutian County, Tangshan, Hebei Prov.; ed Northeastern Univ.; joined CCP 1974; Chinese Communist Youth League Prov. Deputy Sec., Liaoning Prov. 1985–90; Vice-Mayor of Panjin, Liaoning Prov. 1990–93; Sec.-Gen., CCP Autonomous Regional Cttee, Tibet Autonomous Region 1993–2001, Deputy Sec. 1999–2003; Vice-Chair., CPPCC Autonomous Regional Cttee, Tibet Autonomous Region 2003; Vice-Minister of Civil Affairs 2003–05, Exec. Vice-Minister of Civil Affairs 2005–10, Minister of Civil Affairs 2010–16; Deputy Dir, Nat. Cttee for Disaster Reduction 2013–; mem. 18th CCP Cen. Cttee 2012–17. *Address:* Ministry of Civil Affairs, 147 Beiheyan Dajie, Dongcheng Qu, Beijing 100721, People's Republic of China (office). *Telephone:* (10) 58123114 (office). *Website:* www.mca.gov.cn (office).

LI, Lihui, DEcon; Chinese banker; *Chairman, Bohai Industrial Investment Fund Management Company Limited;* b. 1952, Fujian Prov.; ed Xiamen Univ., Guanghua School of Man. at Peking Univ.; with People's Bank of China, Fujian Br. 1977–84; joined Industrial and Commercial Bank, Fujian Br. 1984, served in several positions 1989–94, including Deputy Gen. Man. Fujian Br., Chief Rep. of Singapore Rep. Office and Gen. Man. Int. Business Dept, Exec. Vice-Pres. Industrial and Commercial Bank 1994–2002; Deputy Gov. Hainan Prov. 2002–04; Vice-Chair. and Pres. Bank of China Ltd 2004–14, Vice-Chair. Bank of China (Hong Kong) Ltd 2009–14; Chair. BOCI International Holdings Ltd 2005–14; Chair. Bohai Industrial Investment Fund Management Co. Ltd 2006–. *Address:* Bohai Industrial Investment Fund Management Co. Ltd, 26th Floor, Tower B, ICTC, 59 Machang Road, Hexi District, Tianjin 300203, People's Republic of China (office). *Telephone:* (22) 8386-7800 (office). *Fax:* (22) 8386-7810 (office). *E-mail:* info@bohaicapital.cn (office). *Website:* www.bohaicapital.com (office).

LI, Lingwei; Chinese sports administrator and fmr badminton player; b. 7 Jan. 1964; ed Beijing Sport Univ.; won women's singles title at 3rd World Badminton Championships, Copenhagen 1982; elected 7th in list of 10 best Chinese athletes 1984; won women's singles and women's doubles (co-player Wu Dixi) at 5th ALBA World Cup, Jakarta 1985; won women's singles, at World Badminton Grand Prix finals, Tokyo 1985, at Dunhill China Open Badminton Championships, Nanjing 1987, at Malaysian Badminton Open, Kuala Lumpur 1987, at World Grand Prix, Hong Kong 1988, at China Badminton Open 1988, at Danish Badminton Open, Odense 1988, at All-England Badminton Championships 1989, at 6th World Badminton Championships, Jakarta; coached Chinese women's singles players; Rep. Chinese People's Congress 1998–2003; mem. CPPCC 2003–08; Deputy Dir Int. Relations Dept, Organising Cttee for Games of the XXIX Olympiad, Beijing 2003–08; Deputy Dir-Gen. Table Tennis and Badminton Administrative Center of Gen. Admin of Sport of China 2008–10, Deputy Dir-Gen. Tennis Administrative Center 2010–; Vice-Pres. Chinese Badminton Asscn 2002–; mem. Exec. Bd Badminton World Fed. (BWF) 2002–, Deputy Chair. Int. Relations Comm. 2009–, Vice-Chair. Women's Comm. 2009–; mem. Exec. Bd Chinese Olympic Cttee 2004–; mem. Beijing Olympic City Development Asscn 2009–; mem. IOC 2012–; inducted into IBF Hall of Fame 1998, Int. Olympic Cttee Women and Sport Trophy for Asia 2008, elected to The Top Ten Athletes in China (four times), on list of The Top Ten Coaches in China (two times); Distinguished Service Award, World Badminton Federation (BWF), inducted into BWF Hall of Fame, Medal of Honor of the World Labor Day in China, Medal of Honor of the Women's Day in China, Women and Sport Award, IOC. *Address:* International Olympic Committee, Château de Vidy, Case postale 356, 1001 Lausanne, Switzerland. *Website:* www .olympic.org.

LI, Luye; Chinese diplomatist (retd); b. Aug. 1938, Hefei, Anhui Prov.; ed Univ. of Shanghai; joined Ministry of Foreign Affairs 1952, Dir Dept of Int. Orgs 1980, Perm. Rep. to UN, New York 1990–93, Amb. to USA 1993–98, also served as Chair Chinese People's Asscn for Friendship with Foreign Countries, Dir Chinese Int. Studies Centre, Vice-Chair. Foreign Affairs Cttee and Pres. China Nat. Cttee for Pacific Econ. Co-operation; mem. Standing Cttee of 8th NPC 1993–98. *Address:* c/o Ministry of Foreign Affairs, No. 2, Chaoyangmen Nandajie, Chaoyang District, Beijing 100701, People's Republic of China.

LI, Ming, MS, MS, PhD, FRSC; Canadian/Chinese computer scientist and academic; *University Professor and Canada Research Chair in Bioinformatics, University of Waterloo;* ed Inst. of Computing Tech., Chinese Acad. of Sciences, Wayne State Univ., Cornell Univ.; farmer, Su Jia Tuo Village, Beijing, People's Repub. of China 1974–76; Computer Programmer, Cen. Weather Bureau of China 1976–78; Asst Prof., Dept of Computer Science and Information, Ohio State Univ.,

USA 1985–86; Postdoctoral Fellow, Harvard Univ. 1986–87, Visiting Asst Prof., Aiken Computational Lab. 1987–88; Asst Prof., Computer Science Dept, York Univ. 1988–89; Assoc. Prof., Computer Science Dept, Univ. of Waterloo 1989–94, Prof., School of Computer Science 1994– (on leave 2000–02), Canada Research Chair in Bioinformatics, Tier I 2002–, Univ. Prof. 2009–; Prof., Computer Science Dept, Univ. of California, Santa Barbara 2000–02; Guest Prof., Academia Sinica 1995–, Univ. of Science and Tech. of China 1995–, Peking Univ. 1995–; Visiting Prof., City Univ. of Hong Kong 1996–97, 2004–05; Chang Jiang Prof., Tsinghua Univ., China 2003–; Co-Ed.-in-Chief Journal of Bioinformatics and Computational Biology 2002–; Assoc. Ed.-in-Chief Journal of Computer Science and Technology 2003–, Journal of Computer and System Sciences 1992–, SIAM Journal on Computing 2002–08, Information and Computation 1997–2006, Journal of Combinatorial Optimization 1995–, International Journal of Foundation of Computer Science 1999–2003, Journal of Software 2001–; Fellow, IEEE 2006, Asscn for Computing Machinery 2006; First-class Prize, China's Nat. Excellent Science and Tech. Book Prize 1999, Best Paper Awards: Genome Informatics Workshop, Tokyo, Japan 1999, Genome Informatics Workshop, Singapore 2007, CSB 2007, San Diego 2007, COLING 2010, Beijing 2010; E.W.R. Steacie Memorial Fellowship, NSERC 1996, Award of Merit, Fed. of Chinese Canadian Professionals 1997, Killam Research Fellowship, Canada Council for the Arts 2001, Pioneer Award, IEEE GrC Conf. 2006, Premier's Discovery Award (Innovation Leadership) 2009, Outstanding Contrib. Award, IEEE Granular Computing, San Jose 2010, Killam Prize in Engineering, Canada Council for the Arts 2010. *Publications:* An Introduction to Kolmogorov Complexity and Its Applications (with P. Vitányi) 1993 (third edn 2008), A Course on Java Programming (with H. A. Li) (in Chinese) 1997, Descriptional Complexity (with P. Vitányi) (in Chinese) 1999; numerous papers in professional journals on bioinformatics algorithms and software, Kolmogorov complexity and its applications, analysis of algorithms, computational complexity, and computational learning theory; five US patents. *Address:* Davis Center 3355, David R. Cheriton School of Computer Science, University of Waterloo, Waterloo, ON N2L 3G1, Canada (office). *Telephone:* (519) 888-4659 (office), (519) 591-3578 (mobile). *Fax:* (519) 885-1208 (office). *E-mail:* mli@ uwaterloo.ca (office). *Website:* www.cs.uwaterloo.ca/~mli (office).

LI, Na, BA; Chinese fmr professional tennis player; b. 26 Feb. 1982, Wuhan, Hubei; d. of Li Shengpeng; m. Jiang Shan 2006; ed Huazhong Univ. of Science and Tech.; mem. China's Nat. Tennis Team 1997–2002; turned professional 1999; winner, Tashkent Open doubles title, Uzbekistan 2000, Guangzhou Int. Women's Open singles title 2004, AEGON Classic doubles title, Birmingham, UK 2006, Gold Coast Tournament singles title 2008, AEGON Classic singles title, Birmingham, UK 2010, Medibank Int. Sydney tournament singles title, Australia 2011, Shenzhen Gemdale Open, Shenzhen, China 2013; Grand Slam results: quarter-finalist, Wimbledon 2006, 2010, 2013, US Open 2009, finalist, Australian Open 2011 (first Asian player to appear in a Grand Slam singles final), 2013, winner, French Open 2011 (first Asian player to win a Grand Slam singles title), Australian Open 2014, semi-finalist, US Open 2013; announced retirement following injury Sept. 2014; Laureus China Sportswoman of the Year 2011. *Address:* c/o Max Eisenbud, IMG, 1360 East 9th Street, Suite 100, Cleveland, OH 44114, USA.

LI, Peigen, BSc, MSc, PhD; Chinese engineer, academic and university administrator; ed Shanghai Textile Inst. of Tech., Huazhong Univ. of Science and Tech., Univ. of Wisconsin, USA; Dean, School of Mechanical Science and Eng, Huazhong Univ. of Science and Tech. (HUST) 1995–2002, Vice Pres. HUST 2002–05, Pres. 2005–14; mem. Chinese Acad. of Eng 2003–; Govt of Hubei Prov. Outstanding Professionals Award 2001. *Publications:* three books and over 100 papers. *Address:* c/o Huazhong University of Science and Technology, 1037 Luoyu Road, Wuchang, Wuhan, People's Republic of China (office). *Telephone:* (27) 87544088 (office). *Website:* www.hust.edu.cn/english (office).

LI, Peng; Chinese politician; b. Oct. 1928, Chengdu City, Sichuan Prov.; s. of Li Shuoxun and Zhao Juntao; m. Zhu Lin 1958; two s. one d.; ed Yan'an Inst. of Natural Sciences, Zhangjiakou Vocational School of Industry, Moscow Power Inst., USSR; joined CCP 1945; technician, Shanxi-Chahar-Hebei Power Co. 1946–48; Asst Man. Harbin Grease Co. 1946–48 (Sec. CCP Party Cttee 1946–48); Chief Engineer and Deputy Dir Fengman Hydroelectric Power Plant, Jilin Prov. 1955; fmr Deputy Chief Engineer, Northeast China Power Admin, later Dir Electricity Dispatch Dept; fmr Dir Fuxin Power Plant, Liaoning Prov. (Deputy Sec. CCP Party Cttee); Acting Sec. Beijing Power Supply Bureau, CCP Party Cttee 1966–76 (Chair. CCP Revolutionary Cttee 1966–76); Deputy Sec. Power Admin, CCP Party Cttee, Beijing 1966–76; Chair. Power Admin, CCP Revolutionary Cttee, Beijing 1966–76; Dir Power Admin, Beijing 1966–76 (Sec. CCP Leading Party Group 1966–76); Vice-Minister of Electric Power Industry 1979–81, Minister 1981–82; Vice-Minister of Water Conservancy and Electric Power 1982–83 (Deputy Sec. CCP Leading Party Group); Vice-Premier of State Council 1983–87; Minister in Charge of State Educ. Comm. 1985–88; Acting Premier, State Council 1987–88, Premier 1988–98; Minister, State Comm. for Restructuring the Economy 1988–90; Chair. Standing Cttee 9th NPC 1998–2003; mem. 12th Cen. Cttee of CCP 1982–87, 13th CCP Cen. Cttee 1987–92, 14th CCP Cen. Cttee 1992–97, 15th CCP Cen. Cttee 1997–2002; mem. Political Bureau 1985–2002, Standing Cttee 1987–2002; mem. Secr. CCP Cen. Cttee 1985–87; announced retirement 2003. *Publication:* The Critical Moment – Li Peng Diaries 2010. *Address:* c/o Zhongguo Gongchan Dang (Chinese Communist Party), Zhongnanhai, Beijing, People's Republic of China (office).

LI, Qiang; Chinese politician; *Communist Party Secretary, Shanghai;* b. 1959, Rui'an, Zhejiang Prov.; ed Zhejiang Agricultural Univ., CCP Central Party School; joined CCP 1986; CCP Sec., Wenzhou City 2003–04, also Dir Standing Cttee, Wenzhou City People's Congress 2003–04; Sec.-Gen. and mem. Standing Cttee, Zhejiang CCP Provincial Cttee 2004–11; Sec., Political and Legal Affairs, Zhejiang Prov. 2011–16; Acting Gov., Zhejiang Prov. 2012–13, Gov. 2013–16; CCP Sec., Jiangsu Prov. 2016–17; CCP Sec., Shanghai 2017–; alt. mem. 18th CCP Cen. Cttee 2012–17, mem. 19th CCP Cen. Cttee 2017–, also mem. 19th Politburo 2017–. *Address:* CPC Municipal Committee, Shanghai 200000, People's Republic of China (office). *Website:* www.shanghai.gov.cnl (office).

LI, Lt-Gen. Qianyuan; Chinese army officer (retd); b. 12 March 1942, Linzhou, Henan Prov.; ed Zhengzhou Textile Machinery Inst., Mil. Acad. of the Chinese PLA; joined PLA 1961; joined CCP 1963; Regimental Commdr, PLA 1976; Div.

Chief of Staff, PLA 1982–83, Deputy Chief of Staff 1st Army, Army (or Ground Force), PLA Services and Arms 1983–85, Army Commdr Group Army, PLA Services and Arms 1985–90 (Deputy Sec. CCP Party Cttee 1985–90); Deputy Chief of Staff, Guangzhou Mil. Command 1990–94; rank of Maj.-Gen. 1997, Lt-Gen. 1996; Chief of Staff, Lanzhou Mil. Region 1994–99, Commdr 1999–2007; Alt. mem. 14th CCP Cen. Cttee 1992–97, 15th CCP Cen. Cttee 1997–2002, mem. 16th CCP Cen. Cttee 2002–07.

LI, Qingkui, MBA; Chinese engineer and business executive; *Chairman, China Southern Power Grid Company Ltd;* b. March 1956, Dingtao Co., Shandong Prov.; ed North China Electric Power Univ. and Shandong Univ.; Deputy Gen. Man. China Huadian Corpn (state-owned power generator) 2008–13, Chair. 2014–16, Sec. CCP Leading Party Group 2008–16; Chair. China Southern Power Grid Co. Ltd 2016–. *Address:* China Southern Power Grid Co. Ltd, 6 Huasui Road, Zhujiang Xincheng, Tianhe District, Guangzhou 510623, People's Republic of China (office). *Telephone:* (20) 3812-1958 (office); (20) 3812-1080 (office). *Fax:* (20) 3886-5670 (office); (20) 3812-0189 (office). *E-mail:* international@csg.cn (office). *Website:* www .csg.cn (office); eng.csg.cn (office).

LI, Renjie, BA; Chinese economist and business executive; fmr Dir of Planning Div., Fujian Br. of People's Bank of China; fmr Exec. Dir Hong Kong Jiang Nan Finance Ltd; fmr Chair. Great Wall Securities Co. Ltd; worked as Head of Preparatory Team, Pres. of Shenzhen Br. of Industrial Bank, later Vice-Pres. of Industrial Bank Co. Ltd, mem. Bd of Dirs 2007–16, Pres. 2013–16. *Address:* c/o Industrial Bank Co. Ltd, 154 Hudong Road, Fuzhou 350003, People's Republic of China. *E-mail:* webmaster@cib.com.cn.

LI, Richard; Hong Kong computer engineer and business executive; *Chairman, Pacific Century Group Holdings Ltd;* b. (Li Tzar Kai), 1966; s. of Li Ka-shing; ed Stanford Univ., USA; cr. Star TV (first satellite cable TV network in Asia) 1992, sold to Rupert Murdoch's News Corp 2003; Founder, Chair. and CEO Pacific Century Group 1993–, Pacific Century CyberWorks (PCCW) Ltd 1999– (PCCW merged with Cable & Wireless HKT 2000), PCCW Japan 2000–, Chair. Pacific Century Regional Devts Ltd, Singapore, Pacific Century Premium Devts Ltd, acquired asset management business of American International Group, Inc. 2010 (renamed PineBridge Investments), acquired ING Group N.V.'s Hong Kong, Macau and Thailand insurance business 2013 (renamed FWD); cr. Network of the World (NOW—internet and digital TV content service) 2000, NOW Japan 2001; Gov. World Econ. Forum for Information Technologies and Telecommunications; mem. Int. Councillors' Group, Center for Strategic and Int. Studies, Washington, DC, Global Information Infrastructure Comm., Panel of Advisors to UN Information and Communication Technologies Task Force, Hong Kong Computer Soc.; Lifetime Achievement Award, Cable & Satellite Broadcasting Association of Asia 2011. *Address:* Pacific Century Group Holdings Ltd, 38/F. Citibank Tower, Citibank Plaza, 3 Garden Road, Central, Hong Kong Special Administrative Region (office); Pacific Century CyberWorks Ltd, Floor 39, PCCW Tower, Taikoo Place, 979 Kings Road, Quarry Bay 070, Hong Kong Special Administrative Region, People's Republic of China (office). *Telephone:* 28882888 (office). *Fax:* 28778877 (office). *Website:* www.pccw.com (office); www.richardli.com.

LI, Robin, BS, MS; Chinese business executive and entrepreneur; *Co-founder, Chairman and CEO, Baidu, Inc.;* b. (Li Yanhong), 17 Nov. 1968, Yangquan, Shanxi Prov.; m. Ma Dongmin 1995; one d.; ed Yangquan First High School, Peking Univ., State Univ. of New York, Buffalo, NY, USA; joined Dow Jones & Co., NJ, USA 1994, served as sr consultant for IDD Information Services, USA (a NJ div. of Dow Jones & Co.) 1994–97; staff engineer, Infoseek 1997–99; Co-founder Baidu, Inc. (internet search engine) 2000, Chair. 2000–, CEO 2004–; ASEAN Youth Award 2005, named by American Business Weekly as World's Best Business Leader 2006. *Publications:* Business War in Silicon Valley 1998; received a US Patent for the RankDex site-scoring algorithm used for search engine results page ranking 1999. *Address:* Baidu, Inc., Baidu Campus, 10 Shangdi 10th Street, Haidian District, Beijing 100085, People's Republic of China (office). *Telephone:* (10) 59928888 (office). *Fax:* (10) 59920000 (office). *E-mail:* ir@baidu.com (office). *Website:* www .baidu.com (office); ir.baidu.com (office).

LI, Rongrong; Chinese economist and state official; b. Dec. 1944, Suzhou, Jiangsu Prov.; ed Tianjin Univ.; workshop chief, Wuxi Oil Pump and Oil Throttle Factory, Deputy Dir, then Dir 1968–86; Vice-Chair. Wuxi Municipal Econ. Comm. 1986, later Dir Wuxi Municipal Light Industry Bureau and Chair. Wuxi Municipal Planning Comm.; Vice-Chair. Jiangsu Prov. Planning and Econ. Comm. 1986–91; Production Planning Bureau, State Council Production Office 1992; Dir Foreign Econ. Cooperation Dept, State Council 1994–95; Deputy Dir, State Econ. and Trade Comm. (SETC) 1999–2001, Dir 2001–03; Dir State-Owned Assets Supervision and Admin Comm. (SASAC) 2003–10; joined CCP 1983, mem. 16th CCP Cen. Cttee 2002–07, 17th CCP Cen. Cttee 2007–12; Vice-Chair. 11th CPPCC, Nat. Cttee, Econs Cttee 2010–13; ranked 61st by Forbes magazine amongst The World's Most Powerful People 2009.

LI, Ruihuan; Chinese party and government official (retd); b. 17 Sept. 1934, Baodi Co., Tianjing; ed part-time studies at an architecture eng inst.; construction worker, Beijing No. 3 Construction Co. 1951–65; Joined CCP 1959; Deputy Sec. Beijing Building Materials Co. CCP Party Cen. 1965–66; Vice-Chair. Beijing Municipal Trade Union Fed. 1971; Vice-Chair. All-China Youth Fed. 1971–80; Dir-Gen. Work Site for Mao Zedong Memorial Hall, Beijing 1977; Deputy for Beijing, 5th NPC 1978; Sec. Communist Youth League 1979–81; mem. Standing Cttee, 5th NPC 1978–83; Deputy Mayor Tianjin 1981, Acting Mayor 1982, Mayor Tianjin 1982–89; Sec. CCP Municpal Cttee, Tianjin 1982–84; mem. 12th CCP Cen. Cttee 1982–87, 13th CCP Cen. Cttee 1987–92, 14th CCP Cen. Cttee 1992–97, 15th CCP Cen. Cttee 1997–2002; mem. Politburo 1987–2002, Standing Cttee Politburo 1989, Perm. mem. Politburo 1992–2002; Chair. 8th Nat. Cttee CPPCC 1993–98, 9th Nat. Cttee CPPCC 1998–2003; Hon. Pres. Chinese Fed. for the Disabled 1993–; Hon Pres. Chinese Table Tennis Asscn 1990–; named Nat. Model Worker 1979.

LI, Sanli, PhD; Chinese computer scientist; *Professor, Department of Computer Science & Technology, Tsinghua University;* b. 24 Aug. 1935, Shanghai; ed Tsinghua Univ., Acad. of Sciences, USSR; Co-Chair. Accreditation Cttee Computer Discipline of State Academic Comm. of the State Council; Deputy Chief Ed. China Computer Encyclopaedia; Exec. Dir of China Computer Fed.; Pres. IEEE in China; Dir EUROMICRO Europe 1984–97; fmr Dir Research Inst. of Computer Sciences

and Eng, Tsinghua Univ., Prof., Dept of Computer Science & Tech. 1995–; currently Jt Dean and Prof., School of Computer Eng and Science, Shanghai Univ.; mem. Chinese Acad. of Engineering 1995–; many awards including State Scientific and Technological Progress Award, First Class (Govt of Shanghai) 2001, (Govt of Shenzhen) 2004, Second Class (Govt of Guangdong Province) 2005, (Govt of Shanghai) 2006. *Publications:* more than 11 books including RISC – Single and Multiple Issue Architecture and more than 100 research papers. *Address:* Department of Computer Sciences and Technology, Tsinghua University, Beijing 100084, People's Republic of China (office). *Telephone:* (10) 62782530 (office). *Fax:* (10) 62773281 (office). *E-mail:* lsl-dcs@mail.tsinghua.edu.cn (office). *Website:* www .tsinghua.edu.cn (office).

LI, Shaozhu, BEng, MBA; Chinese engineer and business executive; *Executive Director and Chairman, Dongfeng Motor Corporation;* b. Dec. 1960; ed Tsinghua Univ., Zhongnan Univ. of Finance and Econs; joined Dongfeng Motor Corpn 1983, began as Head of No. 2 Foundry Plant, Deputy Gen. Man. Dongfeng Motor Corpn 1997–99, Gen. Man. Dongfeng Automobile Co. Ltd 1999–2001, Vice-Pres. Dongfeng Motor Co. Ltd 2003–05, mem. Bd of Dirs 2004–, Chair. Dongfeng Design Inst. Co. Ltd 2011, Chair. Dongfeng Motor City Logistics Co. Ltd 2011, Exec. Dir and Chair. Dongfeng Motor Group Co. Ltd 2016–; Chair. Dawnpro Information & Technologies Ltd 2001; apptd mem. Nat. Master in Eng Educ. Cttee by the Second Academic Degrees Cttee of the State Council 2004; honoured as Sr Engineer 1997. *Address:* Dongfeng Motor Corporation, 29 Baiye Road, Wuhan 430015, Hubei Province, People's Republic of China (office). *Telephone:* (719) 8226-962 (office). *Fax:* (719) 8226-845 (office). *E-mail:* info@dfmc.com.cn (office). *Website:* www.dfmc.com.cn (office).

LI, Shenglin; Chinese politician; b. Nov. 1946, Nantong Co., Jiangsu Prov.; ed Zhejiang Coll. of Agricultural Machinery 1970; joined CCP 1973; fmr Planner, Tools Workshop, Tianjin Tractor Plant (Clerical Sec., later Deputy Sec., later Sec. CCP Communist League, later Sec. CCP Party Br.); fmr Deputy Man. Chemical Industry Machinery Co., Tianjin, later Deputy Office Dir; fmr Deputy Section Chief, Tractor Industry Co., Tianjin; fmr Cadre, Planning Div., People's Govt, Tianjin Municipality, later Deputy Sec.-Gen. People's Govt; fmr Dir CCP Party Cttee, Tianjin Municipality; fmr Dir Textile Industry Bureau, Tianjin Municipality (Deputy Sec. CCP Party Cttee); Dir Planning Cttee, Tianjin Municipality 1983; Deputy Sec. Work Cttee, CCP Tianjin Municipal Cttee 1983, Deputy Sec. Municipal Cttee 1993–98, mem. Standing Cttee of Municipal Cttee 2002–05; Vice-Mayor of Tianjin 1991–93, Mayor 1993–98; Vice-Sec. CCP Tianjin Mun. Cttee 1993; mem. 15th CCP Cen. Cttee 1997–2002, 16th CCP Cen. Cttee 2002–07, 17th CCP Cen. Cttee 2007–12; Minister of Transport 2005–13; Deputy, 9th NPC 1998–2003.

LI, Shufu, MSc; Chinese motor company executive; *Founder and Chairman, Zhejiang Geely Holding Group Company, Ltd;* b. 25 June 1963, Taizhou, Zhejiang Prov.; m. Li Wang; ed Harbin Polytechnic Univ., Yan Shan Univ.; Pres. Geely Guorun and Maple Guorun (jt ventures of Geely Automobile Holdings Ltd); Owner of Zhejiang Geely Merrie Automobile Co. Ltd; Founder and Chair. Zhejiang Geely Holding Group Co. Ltd (also known as Geely Group Co. Ltd) 1986–; Chair. Shanghai Maple Guorun Automobile Co. Ltd 2005–; purchased Volvo Cars from Ford Motor Co. 2010, Chair. Volvo Car Corpn 2010–; mem. 9th and 10th CPPCC; honours include Operation and Management Master, one of Top 10 Private Entrepreneurs, Man of the Automobile Industry in China, Heroes of China's Automobile Industry (for 50 Years), Man of the Year of Zhejiang Merchants, Top 25 People Contributing to Chinese Brands, Top 10 Philanthropists in China, Top 10 Figures of Chinese Automobiles in 2006, Heroes Contributing to Independent Innovation of Chinese Automobile Brands, Innovation Grand Prize of Zhejiang Merchants 2007, accredited as one of 50 of 50 (Fifty Influential Persons for the Fiftieth Anniversary of the China Automobile Industry) from pertinent insts in China. *Leisure interests:* poetry. *Address:* Zhejiang Geely Holding Group Co., Ltd, 1760 Jiangling Road, Binjiang District, Hangzhou, Zhejiang Prov. 310051, People's Republic of China (office); Volvo Car Corporation, VAK building, Assar Gabrielssons väg, 405 31 Göteborg, Sweden (office). *Telephone:* (571) 28001111 (Hangzhou) (office); (46) 31-59-00-00 (Göteborg) (office). *Fax:* (571) 87766217 (Hangzhou) (office); (46) 31-59-40-64 (Göteborg) (office). *E-mail:* ash@geely.com (office). *Website:* www.zgh.com (office); www.geely.com (home); www.volvocars .com (office).

LI, Sush-der, BBA, MBA; Taiwanese government official; *Chairman, Taiwan Stock Exchange;* b. 29 Nov. 1951, Taipei; ed Tamkang Univ., Minnesota State Univ., USA; Section Chief and Sr Specialist, Nat. Treasury Agency, Ministry of Finance 1980–88, Chief Sec., Nat. Treasury Agency 1988–91, Chief Sec., Taipei Nat. Tax Admin 1991–93, Deputy Dir Nat. Tax Admin of N Taiwan Prov. 1993–94, Deputy Dir-Gen. Nat. Treasury Agency 1994–96, Dir-Gen. Kaohsiung Nat. Tax Admin 1996–98; Commr, Dept of Finance, Taipei City Govt 1998–2006; Sec.-Gen. Taipei City Govt 2006–08; Minister of Finance 2008–12; Chair. Taiwan Stock Exchange 2012–. *Address:* Taiwan Stock Exchange, 3F, 9-12F, No. 7, Sec. 5, Xinyi Road, Taipei 11049, Taiwan (office). *Telephone:* (2) 8101310 (office). *Website:* www .twse.com.tw/en (office).

LI, Tieying; Chinese fmr state official; b. Sept. 1936, Changsha City, Hunan Prov.; s. of Li Weihan; m. Qin Xinhua; ed Charles Univ., Czechoslovakia; joined CCP 1955; worker, Research Inst., Ministry of Electronics Industry 1961, Chief Engineer and Dir 1976; Deputy Dir Science and Tech. Cttee, Shenyang City, Liaoning Prov. 1976; Sec. CCP Shenyang City Cttee 1981–83, CCP Liaoning Prov. Cttee 1983–86; Minister of Electronics Industry 1985–88; Minister in charge of State Comm. for Econ. Restructuring 1987–88, 1993–98, of State Educ. Comm. 1988–93; Chair. Cen. Patriotic Public Health Campaign Cttee; State Councillor 1988–98; Head Leading Group for the Reform of the Housing System 1991–; Deputy Head Nat. Leading Group for Anti-Disaster and Relief Work 1991–; Dir Nat. Cttee for the Patriotic Public Health Campaign; Vice-Chair. NPC 10th Standing Cttee 2003–08; Pres. Chinese Acad. of Social Sciences 1998–2003; Del., World Conf. on Educ., Bangkok 1990, visited India, Laos 1992; Alt. mem. 12th CCP Cen. Cttee 1982, mem. 1985, mem. 13th CCP Cen. Cttee 1987–92, 14th CCP Cen. Cttee 1992–97, 15th CCP Cen. Cttee 1997–2002, mem. Politburo of CCP 1992–2002; Hon. Pres. Mao Zedong Acad. of the Arts 1997–, Athletics Asscn, Soc. of Nat. Conditions; Nat. Science Conf. Prize 1978. *Publications include:* Enrich Series on China's Economic Reform: Vol. 1 Reforming China: Theoretical

Framework, Vol. 2 Reforming China: Experiences and Lessons, Vol. 3 Reforming China: Major Events (1978–1991), Vol. 4 Reforming China: Major Events (1992–2004), Vol. 5 Reforming China: International Comparisons and Reference. *Address:* Chinese Academy of Social Sciences, 5 Jianguomen Nei Da Jie, Beijing 100732, People's Republic of China (office). *Telephone:* (10) 65137744 (office).

LI, Victor Tzar Kuoi, BSc, MSc; Hong Kong business executive; *Chairman, CK Hutchison Holdings Ltd;* s. of Li Ka-Shing; joined Cheung Kong (Holdings) Ltd 1985, Deputy Man. Dir 1993–98, apptd Deputy Chair. 1994, apptd Man. Dir 1999, Chair. Exec. Cttee 2013–, Man. Dir, Deputy Chair. and Exec. Dir Cheung Kong Property Holdings Ltd 2015–18; Exec. Dir Hutchison Whampoa Ltd 1995–2018, Deputy Chair. 1999–2018, Chair. CK Hutchison Holdings Ltd 2018–; mem. Bd of Dirs Husky Energy Inc. 2000–, currently Co-Chair.; Chair. Cheung Kong Infrastructure Holdings Ltd, CK Life Sciences International (Holdings) Inc.; Exec. Dir Hongkong Electric Holdings Ltd; Dir Hongkong and Shanghai Banking Corpn Ltd, Continental Realty Ltd, Honourable Holdings Ltd, Winbo Power Ltd, Polycourt Ltd, Well Karin Ltd; Vice-Chair. Hong Kong Gen. Chamber of Commerce; mem. Comm. on Strategic Devt, Council for Sustainable Devt of the Hong Kong Special Admin. Region; mem. Standing Cttee 11th Nat. Cttee CPPCC; Hon. Consul of Barbados in Hong Kong; Hon. LLD. *Address:* Husky Energy Inc., 707-8th Avenue SW, Box 6525, Station 'D', Calgary, Alberta, T2P 3G7, Canada (office); CK Hutchison Holdings Ltd, 22nd Floor, Hutchison House, 10 Harcourt Road, Hong Kong Special Administrative Region, People's Republic of China (office). *Telephone:* (403) 298-6111 (Calgary) (office); 2128-1188 (Hong Kong) (office). *Fax:* (403) 298-7464 (Calgary) (office); 2128-1705 (Hong Kong) (office). *E-mail:* info@huskyenergy.com (office); info@ckh.com.hk (office). *Website:* www.huskyenergy.com (office); www.ckh.com.hk (office).

LI, Weikang; Chinese opera singer; b. Feb. 1947, Beijing; ed China Acad. of Traditional Operas; Dir Troupe No 2, China Peking Opera Co., performer Beijing Peking Opera Co. 1987–; Prof. Nat. Acad. of Chinese Theatre Arts; Plum Blossom Award 1984, Gold Album Award for Lead Role at Nat. Theatrical Performance Ass., Gold Prize at Nat. Mei Lanfang Grand Competition, Gold Eagle Award for Best Actress. *Recordings include:* Selected Arias of Li Weikang 1995, Battle on the Plain, Unicorn Trapping Purse. *Address:* c/o Beijing Opera Company, Beijing, People's Republic of China.

LI, Wenke; Chinese business executive; *President and CEO, China Railway Materials Company Ltd;* Deputy Gen. Man. China Railway Materials Commercial Corpn (now China Railway Materials Co. Ltd) 2007–11, Pres. and CEO 2011–. *Address:* China Railway Materials Co. Ltd, 17 Fuxing Street, Haidian District, Beijing 100036, People's Republic of China (office). *Telephone:* (10) 51898888 (office). *Fax:* (10) 51895028 (office). *E-mail:* crm@crmsc.com.cn (office). *Website:* www.crmsc.com.cn (office).

LI, Xi; Chinese politician; *Communist Party Secretary, Guangdong Province;* b. Oct. 1956, Liangdang County, Gansu Prov.; ed Northwest Normal Univ.; joined CCP 1982; Sec., CCP Yan'an City Cttee, Shaanxi Prov. 2006–14; mem. 18th CCP Cen. Cttee Cen. Comm. for Discipline Inspection 2012–17; Deputy CCP Sec. of Shanghai 2013–14; Gov., Liaoning Prov. 2014–15; CCP Sec., Liaoning Prov. 2015–17; CCP Sec., Guangdong Prov. 2017–; alt. mem. 17th CCP Cen. Cttee 2007–12, 18th CCP Cen. Cttee 2012–17, mem. 19th CCP Cen. Cttee 2017–, also mem. 19th Politburo 2017–. *Address:* CPC Provincial Committee, Guangdong Province, Guangzhou 510000, People's Republic of China (office).

LI, Xiaolin, ME; Chinese business executive; *Vice-President China Datang Corporation;* b. 1961; d. of Li Peng, fmr Premier, People's Repub. of China, and Zhu Lin; ed Tsinghua Univ.; worked as engineer at Equipment Introduction Office, Beijing Power Supply Bureau; fmr Assoc. Dir Int. Econ. and Trade Dept, Ministry of Energy; fmr Dir Int. Econ. and Trade Dept, Ministry of Electric Power; joined China Power Int. Devt Ltd (CPI) as Gen. Man. 1996, CEO, Vice-Chair. and mem. Exec. Bd 2004, CEO and Chair. 2008–15, fmr Vice-Pres. CPI Group and mem. Exec. Bd CPI Holding; Vice-Pres. China Datang Corpn 2015–; mem. Bd of Dirs Companhia de Electricidade de Macao; mem. Copenhagen Climate Council; fmr Visiting Scholar, Sloan School of Man., MIT. *Address:* China Datang Corporation, 1 Guangningbo Street, Xicheng District, Beijing, People's Republic of China (office).

LI, Gen. Xinliang; Chinese army officer and party official; b. 1936, Laiyang Co., Shandong Prov.; joined PLA 1953, CCP 1956; Commdr Autonomous Region Mil. Dist, Guangxi Prov. 1983–88; Party Cttee Sec. PLA Guangxi Mil. Area Command 1986–89; mem. 13th CCP Cen. Cttee 1987–92; Deputy Commdr Guangzhou Mil. Region 1989–94; Political Commissar Shenyang Mil. Region 1994–95, Commdr Shenyang Mil. Area Command 1995–97; Commdr Beijing Mil. Area Command 1997–2002; mem. 15th CCP Cen. Cttee 1997–2002; rank of Lt-Gen. 1993, Gen. 1998.

LI, Xu'e; Chinese politician and aerospace industry executive; b. 1928, Hanyang, Hubei Prov.; ed Tsinghua Univ.; joined CCP 1955; apptd Deputy Chief Designer, Chinese submarine-launched missile system 1980; Vice-Minister of Space Industry 1982–85; Minister of Astronautics (Space) Industry 1985–88; Vice-Minister State Science and Tech. Comm. 1988–93; apptd Chair. Bd of Dirs China Science and Tech. Consultant Corpn 1983; apptd Vice-Chair. China Environmental Protection Cttee 1988, Co-ordination Group for Weather Change 1990, China Cttee of Int. Decade for Nat. Disaster Reduction 1991; apptd Pres. Soc. of Social Devt Science 1992, China Soc. of Geographic Information System 1994; mem. 12th CCP Cen. Cttee 1982–87, 8th NPC 1993–98, 9th NPC 1998–2003; Vice-Chair. Educ., Science, Culture and Public Health Cttee; Head Dels to Poland, Finland, India.

LI, Yining; Chinese economist; *Professor and Dean Emeritus, Guanghua School of Management, Peking University;* b. 22 Nov. 1930, Yizheng City, Jiangsu Prov.; ed Beijing Univ.; Prof., Dean Economy Admin. Dept, Beijing Univ. 1955–; joined CCP 1984; Vice-Chair. 8th Chinese Democratic League Cen. Cttee 1997; mem. Standing Cttee 7th NPC, 8th NPC; Vice-Chair. Finance and Econ. Cttee of 9th NPC 1998; apptd Dean Guanghua School of Man., Peking University 1993, currently Prof. and Dean Emer. *Publications include:* Economics of Education 1984, System, Objective, and Human-Challenges Faced by Economics 1986, Political Economy of Socialism 1986, Ideas on China's Economic Reform 1989, China's Economic Reform and Share-holding System 1992, Share-holding System and Modern Market Economy 1994, Development Theory of Transformation 1996, Transcending Market and Transcending Government: Role of Moral Power in Economy 1999, The Origin of Capitalism: Comparative Studies of Economic History 2003. *Address:* Guanghua School of Management, Peking University, 5 Yiheyuan Road, Hai Diau, Beijing 100871, People's Republic of China (office). *Telephone:* 62752114 (office). *Fax:* 627517207 (office). *Website:* www.pku.edu.cn (office).

LI, Yiyi; Chinese metallurgist; b. 20 Oct. 1933, Beijing; m. Ke Wei; one s. one d.; ed Beijing Univ. of Iron and Steel Tech.; China's first female workshop chief in charge of a blast furnace late 1950s; researcher, Metal Research Inst., Chinese Acad. of Sciences 1962–, Vice-Dir 1986, Dir 1990–98; mem. Chinese Acad. of Sciences 1993–, mem. Fourth Presidium 2000–; Vice-Pres. Chinese Soc. for Metals, Chinese Materials Research Soc.; mem. Third World Acad. of Sciences 1999–; mem. Bd Int. Cryogenic Materials Conf. 1985–; mem. Editorial Bd, Modelling of Simulation in Materials Science and Eng 2002–; developed five series of hydrogen-resistant steels and alloys; Nat. Science and Tech. Advancement Award (five times), Chinese Acad. of Sciences Award for Advancement in Science and Tech. (seven times). *Publications:* more than 200 research papers. *Address:* Metal Research Institute, Chinese Academy of Sciences, 72 Wenhua Road, Shenyang 110016, People's Republic of China (office). *Telephone:* (24) 23881881 (office). *Fax:* (24) 23891320 (office). *E-mail:* yyli@imr.ac.cn (office). *Website:* english.imr.cas.cn (office).

LI, Yong, BA, MA; Chinese government official and UN official; *Director-General, United Nations Industrial Development Organization (UNIDO);* b. 1951, Zhejiang Prov.; m.; one s.; ed Nankai Univ., Grad. School of the Research Inst. for Fiscal Science, Ministry of Finance; joined CCP 1973; internship at Ernst & Whinney (Ernst & Young), USA 1981–82; Deputy Dir Research Inst. for Fiscal Science, Foreign Fiscal Research Office, Ministry of Finance 1984–85, Dir World Bank Dept, Ministry of Finance 1989–90; Sr Adviser to Exec. Dir for China, World Bank Group 1990–92; Deputy Dir-Gen., then Dir-Gen. World Bank Dept, Ministry of Finance 1992–96; Exec.-Dir for China, World Bank Group 1996–98; Asst Minister, Ministry of Finance 2000–03, Vice-Minister of Finance 2003–13, also mem. Central Bank Monetary Policy Cttee, Alt. Gov. for China, World Bank Group 2003–12, Alt. Gov. for China, Asian Devt Bank 2003–12, Gov. for China, Int. Fund for Agricultural Devt 2004–11; Second Sec., later First Sec., Perm. Mission to UN, New York 1985–88; Dir-Gen. UNIDO 2013–; Sec.-Gen. Chinese Inst. of Certified Public Accountants 1999–2002; Pres. Confed. of Asian and Pacific Accountants 2001–02. *Publications include:* numerous articles and contribs to academic journals. *Address:* United Nations Industrial Development Organization (UNIDO) Headquarters, Vienna International Centre, Wagramerstr. 5, PO Box 300, 1400 Vienna, Austria (office). *Telephone:* (1) 260-26 (office). *Fax:* (1) 269-26-69 (office). *Website:* www.unido.org (office).

LI, Yuanchao, MS, PhD; Chinese politician; b. 1950, Lianshui Co., Jiangsu Prov.; ed Shanghai Fudan Univ., Beijing Univ., Cen. Party School; joined CCP 1978; Sec. Shanghai Municipal Cttee Communist Youth League (CCYL) 1983; mem. Sec. Youth League Cen. Cttee 1983–90; Dir Nat. Cttee for Young Pioneers' work 1984; Vice-Chair. Nat. Youth Fed. 1986–96; Dir First Bureau, Int. Publicity Leading Group 1990–93, Vice-Minister Int. Publicity Office under CCP Cen. Cttee 1993–96, Vice-Minister of Culture 1996–2000; Deputy Sec. CCP Jiangsu Prov. Party Cttee 2000–02, Sec. 2002–07, Chair. Standing Cttee 2003–07; Sec. CCP Party Cttee Nanjing City 2001–03; Head, CCP Central Org. Dept 2007–12; Vice-Pres. People's Republic of China 2013–18; mem. CPPCC 7th Nat. Cttee 1988–93, 8th Nat. Cttee 1993–98, 9th Nat. Cttee 1998–2003; Alt. mem. 16th CCP Cen. Cttee 2002–07; mem. 17th CCP Cen. Cttee 2007–12, 18th CCP Cen. Cttee 2012–17, mem. 18th CCP Politburo 2012–17. *Address:* c/o Office of the Vice-President, Great Hall of the People, West Edge, Tiananmen Square, Beijing, People's Republic of China (office). *Website:* www.gov.cn (office).

LI, Yue, BEng, MBA, DBA; Chinese telecommunications industry executive; *Executive Director, President and CEO, China Mobile Communications Corporation;* ed Correspondence Coll. of Beijing Univ. of Posts and Telecommunications, Tianjin Univ., Hong Kong Polytechnic Univ.; began career with China Mobile Communications Corpn 1976, later Deputy Dir Gen. and Chief Engineer of Tianjin Long-Distance Telecommunications Bureau, Deputy Dir Gen. of Tianjin Posts and Telecommunications Admin, Pres. Tianjin Mobile Communications Co., Deputy Head of Preparatory Team and Vice-Pres. China Mobile Communications Corpn, Exec. Dir, Pres. and CEO 2003–; Chair. Aspire Holdings Ltd, Union Mobile Pay Ltd; Dir (non-exec.) Phoenix Satellite Television Holdings Ltd; numerous nat., prov. and ministerial-level scientific and technological progress awards. *Address:* China Mobile Communications Corpn, 29 Financial Street, Xicheng District, Beijing 100032, People's Republic of China (office). *Telephone:* (10) 3121-8888 (office). *Fax:* (10) 2511-9092 (office). *E-mail:* info@chinamobile.com (office). *Website:* www.chinamobileltd.com (office); www.chinamobile.com (office).

LI, Yunpeng, MA; Chinese engineer and business executive; *President, China Ocean Shipping (Group) Company (COSCO);* ed Tianjin Univ.; served as fourth engineer, then third engineer, then second engineer on China Ocean Shipping (Group) Company (COSCO)'s vessels, also served in COSCO Tianjin as Deputy Man. and Gen. Man. Human Resources Dept, Gen. Man. Admin Dept and Party Sec. Office, various posts including Deputy Gen. Man. Exec. Div., Deputy Sec. of Party Disciplinary Inspection Office, Gen. Man. Supervisory Div., Dir of Org. Div., Gen. Man. Human Resources Div., Asst to Pres., Party Cttee mem., Dir of Party Disciplinary Inspection Office and Exec. Vice-Pres. COSCO Group, mem. Bd of Dirs and Pres. COSCO 2013–. *Address:* China Ocean Shipping (Group) Company (COSCO), Ocean Plaza, 158 Fuxingmennei Street, Beiing 100031, People's Republic of China (office). *Telephone:* (10) 66493388 (office). *Fax:* (10) 66492266 (office). *Website:* www.cosco.com (office).

LI, Zehou; Chinese philosopher; b. 13 June 1930, Hankou; ed Hu'an No. 1 Prov. Normal School, Peking Univ.; Asst Research Fellow, Assoc. Research Fellow then Research Fellow Philosophy Inst., Chinese Acad. of Sciences 1955; Vice-Chair. Aesthetics Soc. of China; confined to house arrest for criticism of the government 1989–91; moved to USA 1991; academic positions at Colorado Coll., Univ. of Michigan, Univ. of Wisconsin, Swarthmore Coll., Univ. of Colorado Boulder; mem. Exec. Council Chinese Writers Asscn and Soc. of Sun Yat-sen Studies. *Publica-*

tions: The Course of Beauty 1988, History of Chinese Aesthetics 2006, Critique of Critical Philosophy 2010, essays on China's Ancient Intellectual History.

LI, Zemin; Chinese party official; b. 1934, Cangxi Co., Sichuan Prov.; ed People's Univ. of China; joined PLA 1950, soldier in Korean War 1952; joined CCP 1954; Deputy Dir Marxism-Leninism Teaching and Research Centre, Shenyang Agricultural Coll., Liaoning Prov. 1973–78 (Sec. CCP Party Br. 1973–78); Deputy Sec. Shenyang Mun. CCP Cttee, Liaoning Prov. 1983–85, Sec. 1986–88; Deputy Sec. Liaoning Prov. CCP Cttee 1985–86; First Sec. CCP Party Cttee, Zhejiang Mil. Dist, PLA Nanjing Mil. Region 1988; Sec. CCP Zhejiang Prov. Cttee 1988–98; Chair. Standing Cttee of Zhejiang Prov. People's Congress 1993; mem. 13th CCP Cen. Cttee 1987–92, 15th CCP Cen. Cttee 1997–2002; Deputy, 8th NPC 1993–98.

LI, Zhanshu; Chinese politician; *Chairman, Standing Commitee, National People's Congress;* b. 1950, Pingshan County, Hebei Prov.; ed Harbin Inst. of Tech.; joined CCP 1975; Staff mem., Document Dept, Gen. Office, CCP Prefectural Cttee, Shijiazhuang Prefecture, Hebei Prov. 1976–83; Sec., Wuji County CCP Cttee, Hebei Prov. 1983–85, Deputy Sec., Shijiazhuang City CCP Cttee 1985–86, also Commr, Shijiazhuang Prefectural Admin. Office 1985–86; Sec., Communist Youth League of China, Hebei Prov. 1986–90; Deputy Sec., CCP Dist Cttee, Chengde Prefecture 1990–93; Sec.-Gen., CCP Prov. Cttee, Hebei Prov. 1993–97; Deputy, 8th NPC 1993–98; Commr, Prov. Admin. Office, Hebei Prov. 1998–2002; Sec., Xi'an City CCP City Cttee 2002–04; Chair., Standing Cttee, Xi'an City People's Congress 2002–04; Deputy Sec., Heilongjiang Prov. CCP Prov. Cttee 2003–10; Vice-Gov., Heilongjiang Prov. 2004–07, Acting Gov. 2007–08, Gov. 2008–10; Sec., CCP Prov. Cttee, Guizhou Prov. 2010–12; Dir, CCP Cen. Cttee Gen. Office 2012–17; Chair., Standing Cttee, Nat. People's Congress 2018–; alt. mem. 16th CCP Cen. Cttee 2002–07, mem. 17th CCP Cen. Cttee 2007–12, 18th CCP Cen. Cttee 2012–17, also mem. Politburo and Secr. 2012–17; mem. 19th CCP Cen. Cttee 2017–, also mem. 19th CCP Cen. Cttee Politburo 2017– and Politburo Standing Cttee 2017–. *Address:* Zhongguo Gongchan Dang (Chinese Communist Party), Zhongnanhai, Beijing, People's Republic of China (office). *Website:* cpc.people.com .cn (office).

LI, Zhaoxing, MA; Chinese politician and diplomatist; b. Oct. 1940, Jiaonan, Shandong Prov.; m. Qin Xiaomei; one s.; ed Beijing Univ., Beijing Foreign Languages Inst.; joined CCP 1965; on staff, Chinese People's Inst. of Foreign Affairs 1967–70; attaché, Embassy, Nairobi, Kenya 1970–77; Third Sec., later Second Sec., later Deputy Div. Chief, Information Dept, Ministry of Foreign Affairs 1977–83, Deputy Dir-Gen., later Dir-Gen. 1985–90 (also Spokesman, Ministry of Foreign Affairs 1985–90), Asst to Vice-Minister of Foreign Affairs 1990–93; First Sec. Embassy, Maseru, Lesotho 1983–85; Chinese Rep. and Amb. to UN 1993–95; Vice-Minister of Foreign Affairs 1995–98; Amb. to USA 1998–2001; Vice-Minister of Foreign Affairs in charge of American and Latin American Affairs 2001–03, Minister of Foreign Affairs 2003–07; Alt. mem. 15th CCP Cen. Cttee 1997–2002, mem. 16th CCP Cen. Cttee 2002–07; Chair. 11th NPC Foreign Affairs Cttee 2008–13. *Address:* c/o Ministry of Foreign Affairs, 225 Chaoyangmen Nan Dajie, Chaoyang Qu, Beijing 100701, People's Republic of China (office).

LI, Zhaozhuo; Chinese politician; b. Sept. 1944, Pingguo, Guangxi Zhuang Autonomous Region; ed Guangxi Univ., Nanning, CCP Guangxi Zhuang Autonomous Regional Cttee Party School, CCP Cen. Cttee Cen. Party School; sent to do manual labour, Army Farms, Guangxi Zhuang Autonomous Region and Hunan Prov. 1968–70; technician, Du'an Commune, Debao Co., Guangxi Zhuang Autonomous Region 1970–74; joined CCP 1974; technician, Sec., later Deputy Dir Debao Co. Hydroelectric Power Bureau, Guangxi 1975–80; Deputy Dir Capital Construction Bureau, Debao Co., Guangxi Zhuang Autonomous Region 1980–83, Deputy Dir Planning Cttee 1980–83; Dir Econ. Cttee, CCP Autonomous Co. Cttee, Debao Co., Guangxi Zhuang Autonomous Region 1983–84 (also mem. Standing Cttee), Sec. CCP Autonomous Co. Cttee 1984–85; Deputy Sec. CCP Autonomous Prefectural Cttee, Bose Prefecture, Guangxi Zhuang Autonomous Region 1985–92 (Sec. 1992–93), Commr, Prefectural Admin. Office 1985–93; Sec. CCP Fangchenggang Autonomous City Cttee, Guangxi Zhuang Autonomous Region 1993–95, Chair. Autonomous Regional People's Congress 1993–95; Sec. Nanning Autonomous City Cttee, Guangxi Zhuang Autonomous Region 1994–96; Deputy Sec. Guangxi Zhuang Autonomous Regional Cttee 1996–2002 (mem. Standing Cttee 1996–2002); Chair. People's Govt of Guangxi Zhuang Autonomous Region 1997–2003; mem. 15th CCP Cen. Cttee 1997–2002, 16th CCP Cen. Cttee 2002–07, 17th CCP Cen. Cttee 2007–12; Vice-Chair. 10th CPPCC Nat. Cttee 2003–08, 11th CPPCC Nat. Cttee 2008–13. *Address:* c/o People's Government of Guangxi Zhuang Autonomous Region, 1 Minle Road, Nanning 530012, Guangxi, People's Republic of China (office).

LI, Zhengwu; Chinese physicist; b. Nov. 1916; Pres. Soc. of Nuclear Fusion and Plasma 1980; mem. Chinese Acad. of Sciences 1980–; mem. Nat. Cttee 7th CPPCC 1988–93; Hon. Dir Southwestern Inst. of Physics; mem. Ed. Bd Plasma Science and Technology (journal). *Address:* c/o Chinese Academy of Sciences, 52 Sanlihe Road, Xicheng District, Beijing 100864, People's Republic of China.

LI, Zhensheng; Chinese geneticist; *Senior Research Fellow, Institute of Genetics and Developmental Biology;* b. 25 Feb. 1931, Zibo, Shandong Prov.; ed Shandong Agricultural Coll.; Dir Northwest Botanical Research Inst.; Vice-Chair. China Science and Tech. Asscn; currently Sr Research Fellow Inst. of Genetics and Developmental Biology, Chinese Acad. of Sciences; mem. 4th Presidium, Chinese Acad. of Sciences 2000–; Fellow, Chinese Acad. of Sciences, fmr Vice-Pres.; mem. Third World Acad. of Sciences 1990–; bred super wheat varieties Xiaoyan Nos. 4, 5 and 6; created the blue-grained wheat monosomic system (BGM); pioneered 'the nullisomic backcrossing method' for fast breeding alien substitution lines of wheat and laid a foundation for wheat chromosome eng breeding; awarded title of Nat. Model Worker 1980, Nat. Supreme Scientific and Technological Award 2006. *Publications:* Outline of Distant Hybridisation of Plants, Distant Hybridisation of Wheat. *Address:* Institute of Genetics and Developmental Biology, Datun Road, Andingmenwai, Beijing 100101, People's Republic of China (office). *Telephone:* (10) 64889331 (office). *Fax:* (10) 64856610 (office). *E-mail:* zsli@genetics.ac.cn (office). *Website:* www.genetics.ac.cn (office).

LI SHAN, Most Rev. Joseph; Chinese ecclesiastic; *Archishop of Beijing;* b. March 1965, Beijing; ed Chinese Catholic Acad. of Theology and Philosophy, Beijing Theological Seminary; among first priests ordained after Cultural Revolution 1989; taught the Bible at Beijing Theological Seminary; Vice-Chair. Beijing Church Affairs Cttee; Deputy to Beijing Municipal People's Congress (local parl.); cr. Bishop 2007, Archbishop of Beijing 2007–. *Address:* Catholic Mission, Si-She-Ku, Hebei Prov., Beijing, People's Republic of China (office).

LI YAN, (Zhuang Bei); Chinese painter; b. Nov. 1943, Beijing; s. of Li Ku Chan and Li Hui Wen; m. Sun Yan Hua 1972; one d.; Prof., Cen. Inst. of Arts and Crafts and of Shandong; fmr Vice-Pres. Li Ku Chan Museum; mem. Chinese Artists' Asscn; Prof., Acad. of Arts, Tsinghua Univ.; Deputy Dir of Li Kuchan Memorial; Vice-Pres. Int. Soc. Yi Jing, Research Fellow Research Soc. Yi Jing; Specialist, Appraising Cttee of Chinese Arts of Calligraphy and Painting; specializes in painting figures, animals and mountains and water scenes and in calligraphy; over 10,000 sketches and paintings from life, 3,000 exercises in Chinese painting 1956; mem. 9th CPPCC 1998–2003, 10th CPPCC 2003–08; mem. Beijing PCCC; works have been exhibited in Sweden, USA, Canada, Japan, Singapore, Philippines, Hong Kong, Tanzania; gave lectures at Hong Kong Univ. 1980; held lectures and exhbn in India 1989, in Malaysia 1991, in Indonesia 1993; subject of TV films by Shen Zhen TV 1986 and Swedish TV 1986, presenter of CCTV's The Wind of China 1995; important works include Chinese Emperor, Zhou Wen Emperor, Lao Zi, Confucian Worry about Taoism, Lao Zi and Einstein, Five-Colour Earth, Start Sailing, A Swarm of Monkeys, Cat and Chrysanthemum, Tiger Cub. *Publications:* Yi Jing Album 1993; several magazine articles on art. *Leisure interests:* writing poetry, Qigong, The Book of Changes.

LIANG, Dongcai, PhD; Chinese molecular biophysicist and protein crystallographer; b. 29 May 1932, Guangzhou, Guangdong Prov.; ed Zhongshan Univ., Inst. of Organo-Element Compounds, USSR Acad. of Sciences, Royal Inst., UK, Univ. of Oxford, UK; Prof., Inst. of Biophysics, Chinese Acad. of Sciences (Dir 1983–86), currently Principal Investigator, Nat. Lab. of Biomacromolecules; mem. Chinese Acad. of Sciences 1980–, Dir Biology Div.; Vice-Chair. Nat. Natural Science Foundation of China 1986–95, adviser 1995–98, Chair. Inspection Cttee 1998–2001; mem. Cttee on Biomacromolecule Crystallography of Int. Soc. of Crystallography 1981–84; mem. Council of Int. Soc. of Biophysics 1993–99, 4th Presidium of Depts, Chinese Acad. of Sciences 2000–; Pres. Chinese Biophysics Soc. 1983–86, 1990–98; Vice-Pres. Chinese Biochemistry Soc. 1987–90; Fellow, Third World Acad. of Sciences 1985–; Alt. mem. 12th CCP Cen. Cttee 1982–87; mem. 13th CCP Cen. Cttee 1987–92; Chinese Nat. Scientific Prize (2nd Rank) 1982, 1989, Scientific Prize (2nd Rank), Chinese Acad. of Sciences 1986, 1992, Scientific Prize (1st Rank), Chinese Acad. of Sciences 1987, Wang Danping Science Award 1992, Ho Leung Ho Lee Prize 1994, Scientific and Technological Prize of Beijing, (1st Rank) 2004, Beishizhang Award 2009. *Publications:* more than 140 papers in scientific journals. *Address:* Institute of Biophysics, Chinese Academy of Sciences, Beijing 100101, People's Republic of China (office). *Telephone:* (10) 64888506 (office). *Fax:* (10) 64871293 (office). *E-mail:* dcliang@sun5.ibp.ac.cn (office).

LIANG, Gen. Guanglie; Chinese army officer and government official; b. Dec. 1940, Santai Co., Sichuan Prov.; ed Xinyang Infantry Acad. 1963, PLA Mil. Acad., Nat. Defence Univ., Henan Univ.; joined CCP 1958, PLA 1959; Vice-Div. Commdr and then Div. Commdr 1979–82; Vice-Army Commdr then Army Commdr, Vice-Commdr PLA Beijing Mil. Area Command 1983–97; rank of Lt-Gen. 1995, Gen. 2002; Commdr PLA Shenyang Mil. Area Command 1997–2000; Commdr PLA Nanjing Mil. Area Command 2000–03; Alt. mem. 13th CCP Cen. Cttee 1982–87, 14th CCP Cen. Cttee 1987–92, mem. 15th CCP Cen. Cttee 1997–2002, 16th CCP Cen. Cttee 2002–07, 17th CCP Cen. Cttee 2007–12 (mem. Cen. Mil. Comm. 2002–12); Chief, HQ of Gen. Staff, PLA 2002–07; Minister of Nat. Defence 2008–13; State Councillor 2008–13. *Address:* c/o Ministry of National Defence, 20 Jingshanqian Jie, Beijing 100009, People's Republic of China (office).

LIANG, Xiaosheng; Chinese writer; b. 22 Sept. 1949, Harbin; ed Fudan Univ.; worker on land reclamation project; elementary school teacher; local newspaper reporter; Ed. New Harbor (now Tianjin Literature); became Film Script Ed., Beijing Film Studio 1982, later Chinese Children's Film Studio 1990; mem. Chinese Writers' Asscn, Chinese Filmmakers' Asscn; mem. and official of Chinese Film Scriptwriters' Asscn. *Publications include:* works include: The Masters of Borderland (short story) 1975, Bitter Love (film script) 1979, The Snowstorm is Coming Tonight (novella and TV play) (All-China TV Playscript Grand Prize, National Novella Award) 1983, Meijing chi (The Jet Ruler) (novel) 1983, If Heaven Had Mercy (short story) 1984, For the Harvest (short story) 1984, Father (short story) (Nat. Short Story Award) 1984, Zhe shi yipian shenqi de tudi (This Is A Mystical Land) (short story) (Nat. Short Story Award) 1985, From Fudan University to Beijing Film Studio (novel) 1987, A Monologue of a Red Guard (novel) 1988, Snow City (novel) 1988, The Floating City (novel) 1992, Broken Heart Bar (novel) 2004, This is a Strange Land, Father (short story), Growth Rings (TV series), The Depressed Chinese (novel).

LIAO, Fan; Chinese film and theatre actor; b. 14 Feb. 1974, Hunan Prov.; ed Shanghai Theatre Acad. *Films include:* Chicken Poets 2002, No Lonely Angels 2002, Baober in Love 2004, The Game of Killing 2004, Green Hat 2004, Gimme Kudos 2005, Curiosity Kills the Cat 2006, Getting Home 2007, Assembly 2007, Ocean Flame 2008, Showtime 2010, Let the Bullets Fly 2010, If You Are the One 2 2010, Beginning of the Great Revival 2011, The Founding of a Party 2011, Love on Credit 2011, Love is Not Blind 2011, Full Circle 2012, Chinese Zodiac 2012, Black Coal, Thin Ice (Silver Bear for Best Actor, Berlin Int. Film Festival) 2014, A Bed Affair 2 2014, Hidden Man 2018. *Television includes:* I'm Looking Forward to Being Loved (series) 2004, Meng's Palace (series) 2013, Beiping wu zhan shi (series) 2014.

LIAO, Hui; Chinese government official; b. 1942, Huiyang Dist, Guangdong Prov.; s. of Liao Chengzhi and Jing Puchum; ed Mil. Eng Inst. of Chinese PLA; joined CCP 1965; fmr technician, Air Force, PLA Services and Arms (Rep. in charge of Mil. Inspection); fmr Staff Officer, HQ of the Gen. Staff, PLA Beijing Mil. Region; Dir Overseas Chinese Affairs Office, State Council 1984–, Dir Leading Party Group 1984–87, Sec. Leading Party Group 1984–97; Dir Hong Kong and Macao Affairs Office of the State Council 1997–; Vice-Chair. Macao Special Admin. Region Preparatory Cttee 1998–99; Vice-Chair. 10th CPPCC Nat. Cttee 2003–08, 11th CPPCC Nat. Cttee 2008–13; mem. 12th CCP Cen. Cttee 1982–87, 13th CCP Cen. Cttee 1987–92, 14th CCP Cen. Cttee 1992–97, 15th CCP Cen. Cttee 1997–2002,

16th CCP Cen. Cttee 2002–07, 17th CCP Cen. Cttee 2007–12; Vice-Pres. China Overseas Exchanges Asscn 1991–97; mem. 21st Century Comm. for Sino-Japanese Friendship 1985–; Hon. Vice-Chair. Zhonghai Inst. of Agricultural Tech. 1987–. *Address:* c/o State Council, Zhong Nan Hai, Beijing, People's Republic of China.

LIAO, Gen. (retd) Xilong; Chinese army officer; b. June 1940, Sinan Co., Guizhou Prov.; ed Mil. Acad. of Chinese PLA; joined PLA 1959, CCP 1963; served as Platoon Commdr 1966–67, Co. Commdr 1969–71, Deputy Chief of a regimental combat training section 1971–73, Deputy Chief of a div. mil. affairs section 1973–78, Deputy Regt Commdr 1978–79, Regt Commdr 1979–80, Deputy Div. Commdr 1981–83, Div. Commdr 1983, Army Commdr 1984–85, Deputy Commdr Chengdu Mil. Region 1985–95, Commdr 1995–2003; rank of Maj.-Gen. 1988–93, Lt-Gen. 1993–2000, Gen. 2000; Dir Logistics Dept, PLA 2002; mem. 15th CCP Cen. Cttee 1997–2002, 16th CCP Cen. Cttee 2002–07, 17th CCP Cen. Cttee 2007–12 (mem. Cen. Mil. Comm. 2002).

LIAO, Yongyuan, MA; Chinese fmr oil industry executive; professor-level sr engineer; has worked in oil and gas industry since 1980s; Deputy Dir New Zone Exploration and Devt Dept, China Nat. Petroleum Corpn (CNPC) 1996–99, Standing Deputy Commdr, then Commdr Tarim Petroleum Exploration and Devt HQ 1996–99, Gen. Man. PetroChina Tarim Oilfield Co. 1999–2001, Deputy Dir Gansu Prov. Econ. and Trade Cttee 2001–04, Asst to Gen. Man. of CNPC 2004–05, concurrently Head of Co-ordination Team for Oil Enterprises in Sichuan and Chongqing and Dir Sichuan Petroleum Admin 2004–05, Vice-Pres. PetroChina 2005–15, Deputy Gen. Man. and Vice-Pres. CNPC Feb. 2007–13, Safety Dir July 2007–08, Dir 2008–15, Gen. Man. and Pres. 2013–15, Vice-Chair. PetroChina 2014–15; placed under investigation by the CCP's anti-corruption agency March 2015; expelled from CCP June 2015; sentenced to 15 years prison Jan. 2017.

LIBAI, David, LLD; Israeli lawyer and politician; b. 22 Oct. 1934, Tel-Aviv; m.; one s. one d.; ed Ironi Alef High School, Hebrew Univ. of Jerusalem, Tel-Aviv Univ., Univ. of Chicago, USA; served as Deputy Chief Mil. Prosecutor, discharged with rank of Maj.; certified as a lawyer 1960; apptd Chief Asst to Attorney Gen. Colin Gillon and Chief Prosecutor of the State Workers' Disciplinary Court; opened a private law office 1964; Deputy Attorney-Gen.; Assoc. Prof. and Dir Inst. of Criminology and Criminal Law, Tel-Aviv Univ., fmr Dean of Students; Chair. Labour Party Constitution Cttee 1977, Israel-Britain Parl. Friendship Asscn, Public Audit (Control) Cttee 1984–92; mem. Knesset (Alignment) 1984–91, (Labour Party) 1991–99, served on various cttees; Spokesman, Ministry of Justice, then Minister of Justice 1992–96; Minister of the Interior 1995; Assoc. Prof., Herzliya Interdisciplinary Center; fmr mem. Nat. Comm. of Inquiry on Prison Conditions, Press Council; mem. Israel Labour Party; Head of Israel Bar Asscn 1983–85; Pinchas Rosen Award, Ethics Award from Minister of Justice 2005. *Publications:* Imprisonment Law 1978; numerous articles on legal issues. *Address:* c/o Israel Labour Party, PO Box 62033, Tel-Aviv, 61620, Israel. *Telephone:* 3-6899444. *Fax:* 3-6899420. *E-mail:* inter@havoda.org.il. *Website:* www.havoda.org.il.

LIBANIO CHRISTO, Carlos Alberto (Frei Betto); Brazilian Dominican friar and writer; b. 25 Aug. 1944, Belo Horizonte, Minas Gerais; s. of Antônio Carlos Vieira Christo and Maria Stella Libanio Christo; ed Univ. of Brazil, Escola Dominicana de Teologia and Seminário São Leopoldo; Vice-Pres. High School Municipal Union of Belo Horizonte 1961; Nat. Leader Catholic Young Students 1961–64; political prisoner 1964; newspaper and magazine ed. 1966–69; political prisoner held in São Paulo, accused of carrying out subversive activities 1969–73; organizer of basic Church communities 1973–79; writer and teacher with Workers' Pastoral 1979–; was sued, under the Media Law, by São Paulo Mil. Police for denouncing the violent acts of some its mems 1992, absolved by court 1993; Dir América Libre (magazine) 1993–2003; mem. Council Swedish Foundation for Human Rights 1991–96, Inst. for Critical Research, Amsterdam, Cajamar Inst., São Paulo, 'Sedes Sapientiae' Centre for Popular Educ., São Paulo; Consultant, Movimento dos Trabalhadores Rurais Sem Terra (MST); mem. and consultant Inst. Cidadania –2003; consultant to Itau Cultural Inst.; Special Assessor of the Presidency of the Repub., acting as Co-ordinator of Social Mobilization for the Zero Hunger Programme 2003–04; mem. Strategic Bd Faca Parte (Join In); assisted the Popular Movts Cen. Bd Workers Pastoral in the ABC area, São Paulo, Centre of Popular Movts, Ecclesiastical Base Communities; Co-ordinator ANAMPOS (Nat. Articulation for Popular and Union Movts Sindicais); consultant to Rural Landless Workers Movt; Hon. Citizen of Brasilia 2007; Intellectual of the Year Prize, Brazilian Writers' Union 1985, Human Rights Prize, Bruno Kreisky Foundation, Vienna 1987, Human Rights Prize, Bruno Kreisky Foundation 1988, Crea de Meio Ambiente Prize, Conselho Regional de Engenharia e Arquitetura, Rio de Janeiro, Paolo E. Borsellino Award (Italy) for work in human rights 1998, Award of Rio de Janeiro Regional Council for Architecture and Eng 1998, Chico Mendes de Resistência Medal, Grupo Tortura Nunca Mais, Rio de Janeiro 1998, Solidarity Medal (Cuba) 2000, Prêmio Abogados de Atocha (Spain), Paulo Freire Trophy for Social Commitment, Brazilian Psychology Council 2000, Medal of Merit 2006, José Martí Int. Award, UNESCO 2013. *Publications include:* Cartas da Prisão (Letters from the Prison) 1974, Das Catacumbas 1976, Oração na Ação (Prayers in the Action) 1977, Natal, a ameaça de um menino pobre (Christmas, a Threat of a Poor Boy) 1978, A Semente e o Fruto, Igreja e Comunidade (The Seed, the Fruit, Church and the Community) 1981, Diário de Puebla (Diary of Puebla) 1979, A Vida Suspeita do Subversivo Paul Parelo (The Suspect Life of Paul Parelo – short stories) 1979 (re-published with the title O Aquária Negro – The Black Fishbowl) 1986), Puebla para o Povo (Puebla for the People) 1979, Nicarágua Livre, o Primeiro Passo (Nicaragua Free, First Step) 1980, O que é Comunidade Eclesial de Base (What is an Ecclesiastical Base Community) 1981, O Fermento na Massa (The Baking Powder in the Dough) 1981, CEBs, Rumo à Nova Sociedade (EBC – A Step to a New Society) 1981, Batismo de Sangue, Os dominicanos e a morte de Carlos Marighella (Blood Baptism, The Dominican Friars and the Death of Carlos Marighella) (Jabuti Prize, Brazilian Book Asscn 1983) 1982, Fogãozinho, culinária em histórias infantis (Cooking in Children's Stories) (with Maria Stella Libanio Christo) 1984, Fidel e a Religião, Conversas com Frei Betto (Fidel and Religion – Talks with Frei Betto) 1985, OSPB, Introdução à Politica Brasileira (Social and Political Organization of Brazil - Introduction to Brazilian Politics) 1985, O Dia de Angelo (Angelo's Day) (romance) 1987, Cristianismo & Marxismo (Christianity and Marxism) 1988, Sinal de contradição (Sign of Contradiction) (with Afonso Borges Filho) 1988, Essa escola chamada vida (A School Called Life) (with Paulo Freire and Ricardo Kotscho) 1988, Lula – Biografia Politica de um Operário (Lula - Political Biography of a Worker) 1989, A Proposta de Jesus (Jesus' Proposal) (Popular Catechism, Vol. I) 1989, A Comunidade de Fé (The Faith Community) (Popular Cathecism, Vol. II) 1989, Militantes do Reino (Militants of the Kingdom) (Popular Catechism, Vol. III) 1990, Viver em Comunhão de Amor (Living in a Communion of Love) (Popular Catechism, Vol. IV) 1990, A Menina e o Elefante (The Girl and the Elephant) (teenage book) 1990, Fome de Pão e de Beleza (Hunger of Bread and Beauty) 1990, Uala, o Amor (Uala and Love) (teenage literature) 1991, Popular Catechism (condensed version) 1992, Alucinado Som de Tuba (Allucinated Sound of Tuba) (romance) 1993, O Paraiso Perdido – nos bastidores do socialismo (The Lost Paradise – In the Backstage of Socialism) 1993, Por que Eleger Lula Presidente da República (Why Elect Lula President of the Republic?) 1994, Mistica e espiritualidade (Mystic and Spirituality) (with Leonardo Boff) 1994, O Desafio Ético (The Ethical Challenge) (with Eugenio Barba and Jurandir Freire Costa) 1995, A Obra do Artista – uma visão holistica do Universo (The Artist's Work – A Holistic Vision of the Universe) 1995, Comer como um frade – divinas receitas para quem sabe por que temos um céu na boca (Eating like a Fries – Divine Recipes) 1996, Cotidiano & Mistério (Everyday Stories and Mystery) 1996, O Vencedor (The Winner) (romance) 1996, Sinfonia Universal, a cosmovisão de Teilhard de Chardin (Universal Symphony – The Cosmovision of Teilhard de Chardin) 1997, Entre todos os homens (Amongst All Men) (novel) 1997, Talita abre a porta dos evangelhos (Talita Opens the Doors of the Gospels) 1998, A noite em que Jesus nasceu (The Night when Jesus was Born) (Best Young Readers' Book, Art Critics Asscn of São Paulo 1998) 1998, Hotel Brasil (detective story) 1999, Mysterium Creationes – Um olhar interdisciplinar sobre o Universo (Jabuti Prize 2000) 2000, Brasil 500 Anos: trajetórias, identidades e destinos (Brazil 500 Years: Routes, Identities and Destinies) 2000, O Decálogo (The Commandments) (short stories in partnership with Moacyr Scliar, Luiz Vilela, Ivan Angelo, José Roberto Torero and others) 2000, A mula de Balaão (Balaao's Mule) 2001, Os dois irmãos (The Two Brothers) 2001, A mulher Samaritana (The Samaritan) 2001, Alfabetto – Autobiografia Escolar (Alfabetto – An Educational Self-Biography) 2002, Gosto de Uva – Textos selecionados (Taste of Grapes – Selected Articles) 2003, Típicos Tipos – Coletânea de Perfis Literários (Typical Types – Collective of Literary Profiles) 2004, Uma saborosa viagem pelo Brasil – Limonada e sua turma em historias e receitas a bordo do Fogãozinho (A Tasteful Journey in Brazil – Lemonade and his Gang with Their Stories and Recipes on Board a Cooker) 2004, Treze contos diabólicos e um angélico 2005, A Mosca Azul 2006; numerous articles in Brazilian newspapers and magazines, including Diário Popular, O Globo, Folha de S. Paulo, O Estado de Minas, Correio Braziliense, O Dia, Caros Amigos, Brasileira, Chronica Brasil. *Leisure interests:* cooking, swimming.

LIBBRECHT, Kenneth G., BS, PhD; American physicist and academic; *Professor of Physics, California Institute of Technology;* b. 9 June 1958, Fargo, ND; m. Rachel Wing; two c.; ed California Inst. of Tech., Princeton Univ.; Asst Prof. of Astrophysics, California Inst. of Tech. 1984–89, Assoc. Prof. 1989–95, Prof. of Physics 1995–, Exec. Officer for Physics Dept 1997–; Fellow, AAAS 1996; Fisher Prize for Physics, California Inst. of Tech. 1979, NSF Presidential Young Investigator Award 1987, Newton Lacy Pierce Prize in Astrophysics, American Astronomical Soc. 1991, US Postal Service Stamp Set (using KGL photographs) 2006, Emile Chamot Award, State Microscopical Soc. of Ill. 2009, Swedish Postal Service Stamp Set (using KGL photographs) 2010, Lennart Nilsson Award 2010, several website awards. *Publications:* The Snowflake: Winter's Secret Beauty (with Patricia Rasmussen photography) 2003 (Benjamin Franklin Book Award 2004, Nat. Outdoor Book Award 2004), The Little Book of Snowflakes (Runner-up, Benjamin Franklin Book Award 2005) 2004, The Magic of Snowflakes 2005, Ken Libbrecht's Field Guide to Snowflakes 2006, The Art of the Snowflake: A Photographic Album 2007, Snowflakes 2008, The Secret Life of a Snowflake 2010; numerous research papers and articles in learned journals. *Address:* Physics Department, California Institute of Technology, Caltech 264–33, Pasadena, CA 91125, USA (office). *Telephone:* (626) 395-3722 (office). *Fax:* (626) 395-3814 (office). *E-mail:* kgl@caltech.edu (office). *Website:* www.its.caltech.edu/~atomic (office).

LIBBY, Peter, BA, MD; American cardiologist, medical researcher and academic; *Mallinckrodt Professor of Medicine, Harvard Medical School;* b. 13 Feb. 1947, Berkeley, Calif.; s. of Henry Libby and Vivian Libby (née Green); m. Beryl Rica Benacerraf 1975; one s. one d.; ed Université de Bordeaux, France, Univ. of California, Berkeley, Univ. of California, San Diego School of Medicine; Intern, Peter Bent Brigham Hosp., Boston, Mass 1973–74, Residency in Internal Medicine 1974–76; Fellow, Harvard Medical School, Boston 1976–79, Brigham and Women's Hosp., Boston 1979–80; Asst Prof., Tufts Univ. School of Medicine, Boston 1980–86, Assoc. 1986–90; Asst Physician, New England Medical Center, Boston 1980–87, Physician 1987–90; Assoc. Prof. of Medicine, Harvard Medical School, Boston 1990–96, apptd Prof. of Medicine 1996, Mallinckrodt Prof. of Medicine 1998–; Dir Vascular Medicine and Atherosclerosis Unit, Brigham and Women's Hosp., Boston 1990–97, Physician 1992–, Chief of Cardiovascular Medicine 1998–; mem. Asscn of Profs of Cardiology, Int. Soc. and Fed. of Cardiology, N American Vascular Biology Org., American Asscn of Immunologists, American Soc. of Cell Biology, Asscn of American Physicians, American Physiological Soc., American Soc. for Clinical Investigation; Past Pres. Asscn of Univ. Cardiologists; Fellow, American Coll. of Cardiology; Hon. mem. British Atherosclerosis Soc., Japan Circulation Soc., Japanese Coll. of Cardiology; Hon. MA (Harvard Univ.) 1996; Dr hc (Université Lille II); highest basic research awards from American Heart Asscn, American Coll. of Cardiology, Gold Medal, European Soc. of Cardiology, Anitchkow Award, European Atherosclerosis Soc., S.A. Levine Fellow, American Heart Asscn 1976–77, Established Investigator Award, American Heart Asscn 1986–91, MERIT Award, Nat. Heart, Lung, and Blood Inst. 1993, Ernst Jung Gold Medal for Medicine, Ernst Jung Foundation 2016. *Publications:* Braunwald's Heart Disease (Ed.-in-Chief of eighth edn); more than 370 peer-reviewed papers in professional journals. *Address:* Division of Cardiovascular Medicine, Brigham and Women's Hospital, 75 Francis Street, Boston, MA 02115 (office); 111 Perkins Street, Jamaica Plain, MA 02130-4313, USA (home). *Telephone:* (617) 525-4351 (office). *Fax:* (617) 525-4400 (office). *E-mail:* plibby@partners.org (office). *Website:* www.brighamandwomens.org (office).

LIBERADZKI, Bogusław Marian, DEcon; Polish politician, economist and academic; b. 12 Sept. 1948, Sochaczew; m.; two s.; ed Main School of Planning and

Statistics, Warsaw and Univ. of Illinois, USA; Scientist, Main School of Planning and Statistics (now Warsaw School of Econs) Warsaw 1971–75, Asst 1971–75, Tutor 1975–82, Asst Prof. 1982–99, Prof. of Econs 1999–, Head, Dept of Transport; Dir Transport Econs Research Centre, Warsaw 1986–89; Prof., Maritime Univ., Szczecin 1998–; Deputy Minister of Transport 1989–93; mem. Transport Comm., Polish Acad. of Sciences 1988–96, European Rail Congress Council, Brussels; Chair. Supervisory Bd Polish LOT Airways –1993; Minister of Transport and Maritime Economy 1993–97; mem. Sojusz Lewicy Demokratycznej-Unia Pracy (SLD-UP—Democratic Left Alliance) Parl. Club; Deputy to Sejm (Parl.) 1997–2004, Vice-Chair. Infrastructure Cttee 2001–04, European Cttee 2003–04, Polish-Nordic Group 2001–04, Chair. Perm. Sub-cttee on Transport 2001–04, Perm. Sub-cttee for Monitoring the Utilization of EU Funds 2001–04; Observer to European Parl. 2003–04; mem. European Parl. (Group of the Progressive Alliance of Socialists and Democrats in the European Parl.) 2004–, mem. Parl.'s Bureau, Quaestors, Cttee on Transport and Tourism 2004–, Cttee on Budgetary Control, Del. to the EU-Ukraine Parl. Co-operation Cttee, Substitute mem. Del. for relations with the Arab Peninsula; Gold and Silver Cross of Merit 1978; Medal of the Nat. Educ. Comm., Fulbright Scholarship 1986, recognized as the most industrious MEP (MEP Awards) in the category of Transportation 2008. *Publications:* Economics of Railways 1980, Supply of Railroad Services 1981, Transport: Demand, Supply, Equilibrium 1999. *Leisure interests* biographies, gardening. *Address:* European Parliament, Bât. Altiero Spinelli 13G154, 60 rue Wiertz, 1047 Brussels, Belgium (office); Biuro Poselskie, ul. Garncarska 5, 70-402 Szczecin, Poland. *Telephone:* (2) 284-54-23 (office); (91) 4341918. *Fax:* (2) 284-9423 (office). *Website:* www.europarl.europa.eu (office).

LIBERIA-PETERS, Maria; Curaçao politician; b. 20 May 1941, Willemstad; m. Neils Liberia; two adopted c.; fmr kindergarten teacher; mem. Curaçao Island Council 1975–82; elected mem. Staten (legislature of Netherlands Antilles) 1982–2010; Minister of Economic Affairs, Netherlands Antilles 1982–84; mem. Nat. Volkspartij (Nat. People's Party), fmr Pres.; Prime Minister of Netherlands Antilles 1984–86, 1988–94; Leader of the Opposition 1986–88, 1994; mem. Council of Women World Leaders. *Address:* c/o Partido Nashonal di Pueblo, Winston Churchillweg 133, Willemstad, Curaçao (office).

LIBESKIND, Daniel, BArch, MA; American architect; *Owner and Architect, Studio Daniel Libeskind;* b. 1946, Łódź, Poland; s. of Nachman Libeskind and Dora Blaustein; m. Nina Lewis 1969; two s. one d.; ed Cooper Union School of Architecture, New York, Univ. of Essex, UK; fmr Head, Dept of Architecture, Cranbrook Acad. of Art, Bloomfield Hills, Mich. fmr Sr Scholar, John Paul Getty Centre; fmr Visiting Prof., Harvard Univ.; fmr Bannister Fletcher Prof., Univ. of London, UK; fmr holder Davenport Chair, Yale Univ.; Owner, Studio Daniel Libeskind (architectural practice), Berlin 1989–; apptd lead architect for rebuilding of World Trade Center site 2003; Prof., Hochschule für Gestaltung, Karlsruhe; holder of Creative Chair, Univ. of Pennsylvania, USA; mem. Akad. der Kunst 1990–, European Acad. of Arts and Letters, American Acad. of Arts and Letters; Hon. RA 2002; Dr hc (Humboldt Univ.) 1997, (Univ. of Essex) 1999, (Technion, Israel); Hon. DHumLitt (De Paul Univ.) 2002, (Brandeis) 2007; Hon. DScS (Edinburgh) 2002; Hon. LLD (Toronto) 2004; Commander's Cross, Order of Merit (Germany); numerous awards including Lion d'Or, Venice Biennale 1985, Berlin Cultural Prize 1996, Award for Architecture, American Acad. of Arts and Letters 1996, Goethe Medallion 2000, Hiroshima Art Prize 2001, Holocaust Educational Trust Award, Leo Baeck Inst. Award, Trebbia European Award, Prague 2006, Gold Medal Award for Architecture, Genoa, Italy, Nat. Arts Club Gold Medal for Architecture 2007, Penn State IAH Medal for Distinguished Contribution to Public Advancement of Arts and Humanities, Yivo Inst. for Jewish Research 'Lifetime Achievement' Award, New York City. *Opera:* stage sets: Tristan und Isolde (also costume design), Saarbrücken, Germany 2001, Saint Francis of Assisi, Berlin, Germany 2002. *Projects include:* (architectural) Felix-Nussbaum-Haus, Osnabrück, Germany 1998, Jewish Museum, Berlin 1999 (German Architecture Prize 1999, Art Forum Int. Best of 1998), Imperial War Museum North, Manchester 2001 (RIBA Award 2004, British Construction Industry Building of the Year), Eighteen Turns (summer pavilion) Serpentine Gallery, London 2001, Weil Gallery, Majorca 2001, Jewish Museum, Copenhagen 2002, CUBE Bar and Restaurant, Manchester 2002, London Metropolitan Univ. Graduate Centre 2004 (RIBA Award), Wohl Centre, Bar-Ilan Univ., Israel 2005 (RIBA Int. Award), Denver Art Museum Residences 2006 (American Inst. of Architects Award of Honor 2008, CNBC Americas Property Awards 2008), Royal Ontario Museum, Canada 2007 (Award of Merit for innovative steel design), Ascent at Roebling's Bridge, Ky 2008 (CNBC Americas Property Awards 2008), Jewish Museum, San Francisco 2008; Univ. Guadalajara, Mexico, Creative Media Centre, Hong Kong, Złota 44 (apartment tower), Warsaw, Poland, Reflections at Keppel Bay, Singapore. *Publications:* Radix—Matrix: Architecture and Writings 1997, The Space of Encounter 2001, Breaking Ground (with Sarah Crichton) 2004, Counterpoint: Daniel Libeskind in Conversation with Paul Goldberger 2008. *Address:* Studio Daniel Libeskind, 2 Rector Street, 19th Floor, New York, NY 10006, USA (office); Studio Libeskind Zurich, Ankerstrasse 3, 8004 Zürich, Switzerland (office). *Telephone:* (212) 497-9100 (New York) (office); (44) 540-4700 (Zürich) (office). *Fax:* (212) 285-2130 (New York) (office). *E-mail:* info@daniel-libeskind.com (office). *Website:* libeskind.com (office).

LICITRA, Karen, BS; American business executive; *Worldwide Chairman, Global Medical Solutions, Johnson & Johnson;* b. Bridgewater, NJ; ed Rider Coll.; joined Johnson & Johnson as sales rep. with Ethicon, Inc. 1984, advanced through positions in sales and marketing, Dir of Marketing, Ethicon Endo-Surgery, Inc. 1991–96, Vice-Pres., Product Man. 1996–97, Vice-Pres., Breast Care Man. (following acquisition of Biopsys Medical business 1997) 1997–2000, Vice-Pres. and Gen. Man. Ethicon Endo-Surgery, Inc. 2000, Pres. Dec. 2000–02, Co. Group Chair. for Johnson & Johnson and Worldwide Franchise Chair. for Ethicon Endo-Surgery, Inc., including Advanced Sterilization Products business and Johnson & Johnson Medical, Canada 2002–12, Worldwide Chair., Global Medical Solutions, Johnson & Johnson 2012–; mem. Bd of Trustees, Rider Univ., St Peter's Healthcare System Inc.; mem. Bd Campaign to End Obesity. *Address:* Johnson & Johnson, 1 Johnson & Johnson Plaza, New Brunswick, NJ 08933, USA (office). *Telephone:* (732) 524-0400 (office). *Fax:* (732) 214-0332 (office). *E-mail:* info@jnj.com (office). *Website:* www.jnj.com (office).

LICK, Dale Wesley, BS, MS, PhD; American mathematician, academic, fmr university administrator, business executive and author; *President Emeritus and Professor Emeritus, Florida State University;* b. 7 Jan. 1938, Marlette, Mich.; s. of John R. Lick and Florence May Lick (née Baxter); m. Marilyn Kay Foster 1956; one s. three d.; ed Michigan State Univ., Univ. of California, Riverside; Instructor and Chair. Dept of Math., Port Huron Jr Coll. (later St Clair Co. Community Coll.), Port Huron, Mich. 1959–60; Asst to Comptroller, Line and Staff Man., Michigan Bell Telephone Co., Detroit, Mich. 1961; Instructor of Math., Univ. of Redlands, Calif. 1961–63; Teaching Asst in Math., Univ. of Calif., Riverside, Calif., 1964–65; Asst Prof. of Math., Univ. of Tenn. 1965–67, Assoc. Prof. 1968–69; textbook and manuscript reviewer for several publrs 1966–; Visiting Research Mathematician, Applied Math. Dept, Brookhaven Nat. Lab., Upton, New York 1967–68; Consultant, Computing Tech. Center, Union Carbide Corpn, Oak Ridge, Tenn., under auspices of US Atomic Energy Comm. 1966–71; Adjunct Assoc. Prof., Dept of Pharmacology (Biomathematics), Temple Medical School, Temple Univ. 1969–72; Head and Assoc. Prof., Dept of Math., Drexel Univ., Philadelphia, Pa 1969–72; Vice-Pres. for Academic Affairs, Russell Sage Coll., Troy, New York 1972–74; Dean, School of Sciences and Health Professions and Prof. of Math. and Computing Sciences, Old Dominion Univ., Norfolk, Va 1974–78; Pres. and Prof. of Math. and Computer Sciences, Georgia Southern Coll., Statesboro, Ga 1978–86; Pres. and Prof. of Math., Univ. of Maine 1986–91; Co-founding Leader, American Univ. in Bulgaria 1991; Pres. and Prof. of Math., Florida State Univ., Tallahassee 1991–94, Univ. Prof., Learning Systems Inst. and Dept of Educ. Leadership 1993–2008, Pres. and Prof. Emer. 2008–; Co-Developer and Chair. HyLighter, LLC 2000–; mem. Editorial Bd, Innovate (journal), International Journal for the Scholarship of Teaching and Learning; mem. American Asscn of Univ. Admins, American Asscn of Univ. Profs, American Math. Soc., Math. Asscn of America, Asscn Study of Higher Educ., Nat. Staff Devt Council, American Educ. Research Asscn; mem. Bd of Trustees, Graceland Univ. 2015–; Pres.'s Award, US Baseball Fed. 1985, Man of the Year Award, Rotary Club of Statesboro 1985, Certificate of Appreciation, US Dept of Educ. 1985, Silver Beaver Award, Coastal Empire Council of Boy Scouts of America 1986, Medallion of Merit, US Govt Printing Office 1988, Athletic Hall of Fame, Georgia Southern Univ. 1990, Renaissance Award for Leadership and Enlightenment, Southeast Georgia, Black Image Steering Cttee 1993, Circle of Gold, Florida State Univ. Alumni Asscn, Rosa Parks Servant Leader Award, Florida State Univ. 1996, Distinguished Alumni Award, Michigan State Univ. 2006, named by Univ. of California, Riverside "One of 40 Alumni Who Make a Difference" 2006, Int. Peace Prize, United Cultural Convention 2010. *Publications:* Fundamentals of Algebra 1970, Whole-Faculty Study Groups: A Powerful Way to Change School and Enhance Learning (co-author) 1998, New Directions in Mentoring: Creating a Culture of Synergy (co-author) 1999, Whole-Faculty Study Groups: Creating Student-Based Professional Development (co-author) 2001, Whole-Faculty Study Groups: Creating Professional Learning Communities That Target Student Learning (co-author) 2005, The Whole-Faculty Study Group Fieldbook: Improving Schools and Enhancing Student Learning (co-author) 2005, The Whole-Faculty Study Groups Fieldbook: Lessons Learned and Best Practices from Classrooms, Districts, and Schools (with Murphy) 2007, Schoolwide Action Research for Professional Learning Communities: Improving Student Learning Through the Whole-Faculty Study Groups Approach (co-author) 2008, Schools Can Change: A Step-by-Step Change Creation System for Building Innovative Schools and Increasing Student Learning (co-author) 2013; more than 100 book chapters, papers and articles in learned journals and 300 newspaper columns. *Leisure interests:* sports, reading, writing, the arts, church work. *Address:* 348 Remington Run Loop, Tallahassee, FL 32312-1402, USA (home). *Telephone:* (850) 284-3219 (office); (850) 553-4080 (home). *Fax:* (850) 553-4081 (office). *E-mail:* dwlick@comcast.net (home); dlick@lsi.fsu.edu (office).

LIDDELL OF COATDYKE, Baroness (Life Peer), cr. 2010, of Airdrie in Lanarkshire; **Helen Lawrie Liddell,** PC; British economist, politician and diplomatist; b. (Helen Reilly), 6 Dec. 1950, Coatbridge, Lanarkshire, Scotland; d. of Hugh Reilly and Bridget Lawrie Reilly; m. Alistair Henderson Liddell 1972; one s. one d.; ed St Patrick's High School, Coatbridge, Univ. of Strathclyde; Head, Econ. Dept Scottish TUC 1971–75, Asst Sec. 1975–76; Econ. Corresp. BBC Scotland 1976–77; Scottish Sec. Labour Party 1977–88; Dir Personnel and Public Affairs, Scottish Daily Record and Sunday Mail Ltd 1988–92; Chief Exec. Business Venture Programme 1993–94; MP for Monklands E 1994–97, for Airdrie and Shotts 1997–2005, Opposition Spokeswoman on Scotland 1995–97; Econ. Sec. HM Treasury 1997–98, Minister of State Scottish Office 1998–99; Minister of Transport 1999, Minister for Energy and Competitiveness in Europe 1999–2001; Sec. of State for Scotland 2001–03; High Commr to Australia 2005–09; Commr, BBC Privacy Comm. 2011; mem. Inquiry into the Mull of Kintyre Helicopter Accident 2010–11; currently mem. Bd of Dirs, VisitBritain; Trustee, Northcote Trust; Hon. LLD (Strathclyde). *Publication:* Elite (novel) 1990. *Leisure interests:* cooking, hill-walking, music, writing. *Address:* House of Lords, Westminster, London, SW1A 0PW, England (office). *Telephone:* (20) 7219-6960 (office). *E-mail:* liddellh@parliament.uk (office).

LIDDY, Edward (Ed) Michael, BA, MBA; American business executive; b. 28 Jan. 1946; m. Marcia Liddy; three c.; ed Catholic Univ. of America, George Washington Univ.; joined G.D. Searle & Co. 1979, Sr Vice-Pres. and COO –1986; Exec. Vice-Pres. ADT 1986–88; sr financial and operation positions Sears, Roebuck & Co. 1988–91, Chief Financial Officer 1991–94; Pres. and COO The Allstate Corpn 1994–99, Chair. 1999–2008, also Pres. and CEO 1999–2005, CEO 1999–2006; Interim Chair. and CEO American International Group (AIG), Inc. 2008–09; Partner, Clayton Dubilier & Rice, LLC 2008, 2010–15; fmr Chair. ServiceMaster Global Holdings Inc.; mem. Bd of Dirs Goldman Sachs 2003–08, The Kroger Co. 1996–2006, 3M 2000–,The Boeing Co. 2007–08, 2010–, Museum of Science and Industry; Chair. and Nat. Gov. Boys & Girls Clubs of America (BGCA); mem. Civic Cttee Commercial Club, Financial Services Forum, Business Roundtable, Catalyst; Trustee, Northwestern Univ.

LIDEGAARD, Martin; Danish politician; b. 12 Dec. 1966; s. of Mads Lidegaard and Else Lidegaard; m. Sniff Andersen Nexø; one d.; ed Roskilde Univ.; Bank Asst, Bikuben 1985; worked at Danish Red Cross Asylum Centre 1986–87; Ed. 'RUCNyt' (Roskilde Univ. News) 1988–92; freelance consultant, Int. Forum of the Labour Movt 1992–93; Information Officer and Man., Municipalities Mutual Insurance Co. 1993–96; Information Officer and Deputy Sec.-Gen., Danish Asscn for Int.

Cooperation 1996–2001; mem. Folketing (Parl.) for W Copenhagen constituency 2001–05, for Roskilde Co. constituency 2005–07; Co-founder and Chair. CONCITO (think-tank) 2008–11; Communications Consultant, RelationPeople 2008–11; Minister for Climate, Energy and Buildings 2011–14, for Foreign Affairs 2014–15; mem. Det Radikale Venstre (Social Liberals). *Address:* c/o Ministry of Foreign Affairs, Asiatisk Pl. 2, 1448 Copenhagen K, Denmark (office).

LIDINGTON, Rt Hon. David Roy, CBE; British politician; *Minister for Cabinet Office and Chancellor of the Duchy of Lancaster;* b. 30 June 1956, London; m. Helen Lidington; four s.; ed Haberdashers' Aske's Boys' School, Sidney Sussex Coll., Cambridge; began career with BP and RTZ; Special Adviser to Home Sec. Douglas Hurd 1987–90; MP (Conservative) for Aylesbury 1992–, mem. Educ. Cttee 1993–96, House of Commons Comm. 2015–, Public Accounts Comm. 2016–, Speaker's Cttee for the Ind. Parl. Standards Authority 2016–; Shadow Spokesperson (Home Affairs) 1999–2001, Shadow Financial Sec. 2001–02, Shadow Sec. of State for Environment, Food and Rural Affairs 2002–03, Shadow Minister (Food, Farming and Environment) Sept.–Dec. 2002, Shadow Sec. of State for N Ireland 2003–07, Shadow Minister (Foreign and Commonwealth Affairs) 2007–10, Minister of State (Foreign and Commonwealth Office) (European issues and NATO) 2010–16, Lord Pres. of the Council and Leader of the House of Commons 2016–17, Lord Chancellor and Sec. of State for Justice 2017–18, Minister for Cabinet Office and Chancellor of the Duchy of Lancaster 2018–; mem. Conservative Party. *Address:* Cabinet Office, 70 Whitehall, London, SW1A 2AS (office); House of Commons, Westminster, London, SW1A 0AA, England. *Telephone:* (20) 7276-1234 (Cabinet); (20) 7219-7151 (Westminster). *E-mail:* david.lidington.mp@parliament.uk (office); publiccorrespondence@cabinetoffice.gov.uk (office). *Website:* www.gov.uk/government/organisations/cabinet-office (office); www.davidlidington.com.

LIDSTRÖM, Nicklas Erik; Swedish fmr professional ice hockey player; b. 28 April 1970, Västerås, Västmanland; s. of Jan-Eric Lidström; m. Annika Lidström; four s.; defenseman; played for Skogsbo SK youth team, Västerås IK sr team 1988–91; played entire Nat. Hockey League (NHL) career with Detroit Red Wings (picked 53rd overall in NHL draft in 1989) Capt. 2006–12 (retd); won Stanley Cup 1997, 1998, 2002, 2008, played for Swedish nat. team 1990–2010: gold medal, World Championships 1991, Winter Olympics, Turin 2006, silver medal, World Championships 2004, bronze medal, World Championships 1994; Sr Adviser, Swedish men's nat. hockey team; winner, Norris Trophy (best defensive player) 2001, 2002, 2003, 2006, 2007, 2008, 2011, Conn Smythe Trophy (most valuable player during playoffs) 2002; NHL All-Rookie Team 1992, NHL All-Star Team 1996, 1998, 1999, 2000, 2001, 2002, 2003, 2004, 2007, 2008, 2009, 2011, 17th, mem. Olympic All-Star Team 2006, Viking Award (best Swedish ice hockey player in North America) 2000, 2006, selected by The Hockey News as the Best European-trained player ever in the NHL, selected by The Sporting News and Sports Illustrated as the NHL Player of the Decade, inducted into Hockey Hall of Fame 2015. *Publications:* Captain Fantastic 2016. *Leisure interests:* tennis, golf, boating.

LIEBENBERG, Christo Ferro, MPA; South African politician and banker (retd); b. 2 Oct. 1934, Touwsrivier; s. of Christiaan Liebenberg and Helene Griessel; m. Elly Liebenberg 1959; two s.; ed Worcester Boys' High School, Harvard Univ., USA, Institut Européen d'Admin des Affaires, Paris and Cranfield Polytechnic, UK; joined Nedbank, Cape Town 1952, Man. Dir Nedbank Group Ltd, Johannesburg 1988–90, CEO Nedcor 1990–94, Chair. 1997–2004; fmr Chair. Credit Guarantee Insurance Corpn of Africa Ltd, Syfrets Ltd, Cape Town; fmr Deputy Chair. NedPerm Bank; Pres. Inst. of Bankers in S Africa 1991; Minister of Finance 1994–96; fmr Dir, Mutual and Federal Insurance Co., Oceana Fishing Group; fmr mem. Policy Bd for Financial Services and Regulation, Council of Univ. of Stellenbosch School of Business; fmr Chair. Salvation Army Nat. Advisory Bd. *Leisure interests:* music, photography, theatre, ballet, reading, golf. *Address:* c/o National Treasury, 40 Church Square, Pretoria 0002, South Africa.

LIEBER, Charles Michael, BA, PhD; American chemist and academic; *Mark Hyman, Jr Professor of Chemistry, Harvard University;* b. 9 April 1959, Philadelphia, Pa; s. of Robert Lieber and Marlene Lieber; m. Jennifer Karas Lieber; one s. one d.; ed Franklin and Marshall Coll., Stanford Univ., California California Inst. of Tech.; Asst Prof. of Chem., Columbia Univ., New York 1987–90, Assoc. Prof. 1990–91; Prof. of Chem., Harvard Univ. 1991–99, holds jt appointment in Dept of Chem. and Chemical Biology, as Mark Hyman, Jr Prof. of Chem., and John A. Paulson School of Eng and Applied Sciences 1999–, Chair. Dept of Chem. and Chemical Biology; Co-Ed. Nano Letters; Consulting Ed. International Journal of Biomedical Nanoscience and Nanotechnology; mem. Editorial or Advisory Bd of numerous journals; f. Nanosys, Inc. 2001, Vista Therapeutics 2007; mem. American Physical Soc. 1996, AAAS 1996, NAS 2004, American Acad. of Arts and Sciences 2002, IEEE, Int. Soc. for Optical Eng, Optical Soc. of America, Materials Research Soc.; Foreign mem., Chinese Acad. of Science; Fellow, Materials Research Soc. 2008, ACS (Inaugural Class); Hon. Prof., Zhejiang Univ. 2002, Fudan Univ. 2002, Univ. of Science and Tech. of China 2002, Peking Univ. 2008, Univ. of Science and Tech., Beijing 2011, Inst. of Chem., Chinese Acad. of Sciences 2014, Nankai Univ. 2014; Hon. Fellow, Chinese Chemical Soc.; Wilson Prize 1990, ACS Award in Pure Chem. 1992, MRS Outstanding Young Investigator Award 1993, George Ledlie Prize, Harvard Univ. 1994–95, ACS Leo Hendrik Baekeland Award 1995, NSF Creativity Award 1996, ranked No. 1 in Chem. by Thomson Reuters for the decade 2000–10, Breakthrough of the Year, Science Magazine 2002, Feynman Prize in Nanotechnology 2001, MRS Medal 2002, Harrison Howe Award, Univ. of Rochester 2002, American Physical Soc. McGroddy Prize for New Materials 2003, New York Intellectual Property Law Asscn Inventor of the Year 2003, Scientific American 50 Award in Nanotechnology and Molecular Electronics 2003, World Tech. Award in Materials, The World Tech. Network 2003, 2004, ACS Award in the Chem. of Materials 2004, Nanotech Briefs Nano 50 Award 2005, NBIC Research Excellence Award, Univ. of Pennsylvania 2007, Einstein Award, Chinese Acad. of Sciences 2008, recognised as the leading chemist in the world by Thomson Reuters for the decade 2000–10 for the impact of his scientific publs 2011, NIH Pioneer Award 2008, Wolf Foundation Prize in Chem. (shared with Paul Alivisatos) 2012, Willard Gibbs Medal, ACS Chicago Section 2013, IEEE Nanotechnology Pioneer Award 2013, Nano Research Award, Tsinghua University Press/Springer 2013, Remsen Award 2016, MRS Von Hippel Award 2016. *Publications:* more than 380 papers in peer-reviewed journals on the synthesis of a broad range of nanoscale materials, and the demonstration of applications of these materials in nanoelectronics, nanocomputing, biological and chemical sensing, neurobiology and nanophotonics; prin. inventor on more than 40 patents. *Address:* Department of Chemistry and Chemical Biology, Harvard University, 12 Oxford Street, Cambridge, MA 02138, USA (office). *Telephone:* (617) 496-3169 (office). *Fax:* (617) 496-5442 (office). *E-mail:* cml@cmliris.harvard.edu (office). *Website:* cmliris.harvard.edu (office).

LIEBERMAN, Avigdor, BA; Israeli politician; b. 5 June 1958, Kishinev, USSR (now Chisinau, Moldova); m. Ella Tzipkin; three c.; ed Hebrew Univ. of Jerusalem; emigrated to Israel aged 20; attained rank of corporal during mil. service; worked for Likud party as party Dir Gen. 1993–96; head of Prime Minister Benjamin Netanyahu's office 1997; Founder and Chair. Israel Beytenu Party 1999–, mem. Knesset (Israel Beytenu Party, Ihud Leumi-Israel Beytenu Party) 1999–2012, 2013–, mem. Foreign Affairs and Defence Cttee; Minister of Nat. Infrastructure 2001–02, of Transport 2003–04, Deputy Prime Minister and Minister of Strategic Affairs 2006–08, Deputy Prime Minister and Minister of Foreign Affairs 2009–12, 2013–15, Minister of Defence 2016–18 (resgnd); Sec. Nat. Workers' Union; Chair. Bd of Dirs of Information Industries; Dir, Econ. Corpn of Jerusalem 1983–88; Dir Likud Movt 1993–96; Dir Prime Minister's Office 1996–97; f. Zionist Forum. *Leisure interests:* football, tennis. *Address:* Israel Beytenu, 78 Yirmiyahu Street, Jerusalem 94467, Israel (office). *Telephone:* 2-5012999 (office). *Fax:* 2-5377188 (office). *E-mail:* gdv7191@hotmail.com (office). *Website:* www.beytenu.org.il (office).

LIEBERMAN, Joseph (Joe) I., BA, JD; American lawyer and fmr politician; *Senior Counsel, Kasowitz Benson Torres & Friedman LLP;* b. 24 Feb. 1942, Stamford, Conn.; s. of Henry Lieberman and Marcia Lieberman (née Manger); m. Hadassah Freilich 1983; two s. two d.; ed Yale Univ.; called to the Bar, Conn. 1967; mem. Conn. Senate 1971–81, Senate Majority Leader 1975–81; Pnr, Lieberman, Segaloff & Wolfson, New Haven, Conn. 1972–83; Attorney Gen., State of Conn., Hartford 1983–88, Senator for Connecticut 1989–2013 (retd), Chair. Governmental Affairs Cttee 2001–03, Homeland Security Cttee 2007–13; Sr Counsel, Kasowitz Benson Torres & Friedman LLP, New York 2013–; Co-Chair. American Internationalism Project, American Enterprise Institute 2013–; Chair. Democratic Leadership Council 1995–2001; cand. for Vice-Pres. of Democratic Party 2000; sought Democratic Party presidential candidacy 2004; rt; Democrat –2006, Ind. Democrat; Ewald von Kleist Award 2012, Order of Diplomatic Service Merit Gwanghwa Medal (South Korea) 2012. *Publications include:* The Power Broker 1966, The Scorpion and the Tarantula 1970, The Legacy 1981, Child Support in America 1986. *Address:* Kasowitz Benson Torres & Friedman LLP, 1633 Broadway, New York, NY 10019, USA (office). *Telephone:* (212) 547-1417 (office). *E-mail:* jlieberman@kasowitz.com (office). *Website:* www.kasowitz.com (office); www.aei.org/scholar/joseph-lieberman.

LIEBLEIN, Grace D., BEng, MA; Brazilian automotive industry executive; *Vice-President of Global Purchasing and Supply Chain, General Motors Company;* ed Kettering Univ., Michigan State Univ.; joined General Motors Co. (GM) 1978 as cooperative eng student at Gen. Ass. Div., Los Angeles, Calif., later Vehicle Chief Engineer, Front Wheel Drive Trucks for Product Devt, Detroit, Pres. and Man. Dir GM de Mexico 2008–11, Pres. and Man. Dir GM do Brasil 2011–12, Vice-Pres. of Global Purchasing and Supply Chain, GM 2012–; mem. Bd GM Hispanic Initiative Team; mem. Bd Honeywell International, Inc.; Professional Achievement Award, Hispanic Eng Nat. Achievement Awards Conf., Latino Executive of the Year, Urban Wheels Awards 2006. *Address:* General Motors Co., Renaissance Center, Detroit, MI 48265, USA (office). *Telephone:* (313) 556-5000 (office). *Website:* www.gm.com (office); www.chevrolet.com (office).

LIEDTKE, Kurt W., Dr jur.; German lawyer and business executive; *Chairman, Board of Trustees, Robert Bosch Stiftung GmbH;* b. 23 March 1943, Darmstadt; m. 1966; three c.; ed Goethe School, Dieburg, Univ. of Frankfurt am Main, Univ. of Lausanne, Switzerland; began career as lawyer specializing in tax law, Frankfurt 1972–74; Gen. Counsel, Laufenberg Power Station, Switzerland 1974–77; Sr Consultant, Corp. Law and Contracts Dept, Robert Bosch GmbH, Stuttgart 1977–81, various positions, Marketing Dept, Fàbrica Española Magnetos SA, Spain 1981–82, Man.-Dir Robert Bosch Comercial Española Magnetos SA, Spain 1982–89, Man.-Dir Robert Bosch Ltd, London, UK 1989–96, Pres. Robert Bosch Australia Pty Ltd, Melbourne 1996–2001, Assoc. mem. Bd of Man. Robert Bosch GmbH 2001–02, mem. 2002–, Pres., Chair. and CEO Robert Bosch Corpn, USA 2001–05, Partner and mem. Bd of Trustees Robert Bosch Stiftung GmbH 2006–, Chair. 2007–; Deputy Chair. Royal Winter Foundation; mem. Advisory Bd Baden-Württemberg Film Acad., Bd Tanja Liedtke Foundation, German Sponsors of the Univ. of Haifa eV, Friends of the Museum Asscn eV; Trustee, Foundation of the Int. Charlemagne Prize of Aachen; Patron Asscn for the Municipal Theatre; Officier, Légion d'honneur 2012. *Leisure interests:* sports, opera, classical music. *Address:* Robert Bosch Stiftung GmbH, Postfach 10 06 28, 70005 Stuttgart, Germany (office). *Telephone:* (711) 46084-0 (office). *Fax:* (711) 46084-94 (office). *Website:* www.bosch-stiftung.de (office).

LIEN, Chan, MSc, PhD; Taiwanese politician; b. 27 Aug. 1936, Sian, Shansi; s. of Chen Tung Lien and Chao Lan-Kun Lien; m. Yui Fang; two s. two d.; ed Nat. Taiwan Univ. and Univ. of Chicago, USA; Assoc. Prof. Nat. Taiwan Univ. 1968–69, Prof. and Chair. Dept of Political Science and Dir Graduate Inst. of Political Science 1969–75; Amb. to El Salvador 1975–76; Dir Dept of Youth Affairs, Cen. Cttee Kuomintang 1976–78; Deputy Sec.-Gen. Cen. Cttee Kuomintang 1978, mem. Cen. Standing Cttee 1983, Chair. 2000–05, Chair. Emer. 2005–; Chair. Nat. Youth Comm., Exec. Yuan 1978–81; Minister of Communications 1981–87; Vice-Premier 1987–88; Minister of Foreign Affairs 1989–90; Gov. Taiwan Provincial Govt 1990–93; Premier of Taiwan 1993–97; Vice-Pres. of Taiwan 1997–2000; unsuccessful presidential cand. 2000; Pres. Chinese Asscn of Political Science 1979–82; Special Envoy, Asia-Pacific Econ. Cooperation 2008–12. *Publications include:* The Foundation of Democracy, Taiwan in China's External Relations, Western Political Thought. *Leisure interests:* golf, swimming, music.

LIEN, Siaou-Sze, MSc; Singaporean business executive; *Senior Executive Coach, Mobley Group Pacific Ltd;* b. Singapore; one d.; ed Nanyang Univ., Imperial Coll. of Science and Tech., Univ. of London, UK; joined Hewlett-Packard (HP) as systems engineer 1978, later Vice-Pres. and Man. Dir HP Asia Pacific, Sr Vice-Pres. HP Services Asia Pacific (following merger with Compaq; first woman vice-pres. in region) 2002–06 (retd); Sr Exec. Coach, Mobley Group Pacific Ltd 2006–; mem. Bd of Dirs Luvata Ltd, Huhtamäki Oyj 2009–; Deputy Chair. Bd Govs Republic Polytechnic (Chair. Admin. Cttee); fmr Dir PSA (Port of Singapore Authority) Int.; fmr adviser, Gov. of Guangdong Prov., People's Repub. of China; Trustee Nanyang Technological Univ. *Leisure interests:* sports, jogging, dancing, hot-air ballooning. *Address:* Mobley Group Pacific Ltd, Room 2006-2008, 20/F, One Corporate Avenue, 222 Hu Bin Road, Shanghai 200021, People's Republic of China (office). *Telephone:* (21) 63406222 (office). *Fax:* (21) 63406226 (office). *Website:* www .mobleygrouppacific.com (office).

LIEPA, Andris; Russian/Latvian ballet dancer and choreographer; b. 6 Jan. 1962, Moscow; s. of Marius Liepa and Margarita Zhigunova; brother of Ilze Liepa (q.v.); m. Yekaterina Liepa; one d.; ed Moscow Choreographic School of Bolshoi Theatre; with Bolshoi Ballet 1980–87; Golden Medal, Moscow int. competition 1981, Silver Medal 1985, Jackson, USA (Grand Prix) 1986; has lived in the West 1987–; appeared with New York City Ballet, subsequently with American Ballet Theater; danced in Raymonda Variations, Swan Lake (Baryshnikov), Romeo and Juliet (Macmillan), Violin Concerto (Balanchine); worked with Nina Ananiashvili, Carla Fracci and other partners; choreographer 1993–, restored Fokin's masterpieces Petrushka, Scheherazade and The Firebird; has adapted Fokine ballets for film, including Return to the Firebird; guest artist with Kirov (now Mariinsky) Ballet, London tour 1990; staged The Legend of the Invisible City of Kitezh by Rimsky-Korsakov at the Mariinsky Theatre 1994, Edinburgh Festival 1995; est. Liepa Charity Foundation 1997; premiered production of Scheherazade at Latvian Nat. Opera 1998; performed with Katya Liepa the leading parts in The Firebird with the Mariinsky Theatre in Munich 1999; organized Ballet Evenings in commemoration of Maris Liepa at Moscow Operetta Theatre 2000; gala-concert for participants of Int. Conf. 'Teenagers and Youth in Changing Society' 2001; organized performance of The Firebird and Scheherazade ballets by Mariinski Co. at State Kremlin Theatre, Moscow 2002; stage director of concert to mark 300th anniversary of St Petersburg 2003; stage director for world premiere of ballet Sapphires 2004; mem. Jury, Golden Mask Contest 2004; staged The Firebird and Petrushka ballets for Dresden Opera and Ballet Theatre 2005; stage director for ballets Petrushka and The Firebird performed by Rome Opera at music festival in Aspendos, Turkey 2005; produced opening nights of ballets Petrushka and The Firebird for Opera and Ballet Theatre of Marseille, France 2006; mem. Bd of Trustees, Church of the Great Martyr Catherine, Cherry-Tree Forest Festival; works in USA, Russia and Latvia; People's Artist of Russia 2009. *Address:* Maris Liepa Charity Foundation, ul. Ilyinka 4, 103132 Moscow, Russia. *Telephone:* (495) 956-76-76; (495) 698-12-43. *E-mail:* andris@liepa.ru. *Website:* www.liepa.ru.

LIEPA, Ilze; Russian/Latvian ballerina; b. 22 Nov. 1963; d. of Maris Liepa and Margarita Zhigunova; sister of Andris Liepa (q.v.); m. 1st Sergey Stadler (divorced); m. 2nd Vladislovas A. Paulius; ed Russa Academic Choreography Coll. (studied with N. V. Zolotariova), Pedagogic Faculty of Moscow Theatre Art Acad.; joined Bolshoi ballet 1982, then First Soloist; danced on various stages of Europe and America performing parts of classic repertoire, including Legend about Love, Romeo and Juliet, Firebird, Don Quixote, Corsair, Raimonda, Prince Igor; début in England concert Stars of World Ballet, Covent Garden (Firebird), tours with Bolshoi Theatre in most countries of Europe and America, independently toured in Argentina, Greece, Taiwan, Japan; Artistic Dir Golden Age Asscn 1994–98; f. Maris Liepa Foundation; Prize of Russian Trade Unions, Hon. Artist of Russian Fed. 1996, People's Artist of Russia 2002, Gold Mask (Best Female Ballet Role) 2003. *Films include:* The Shining World 1983, Bambi's Childhood 1984, Lermontov 1985, Lomononov 1987, Return of the Firebird 1994. *Plays include:* Your Sister and Captive 1999, The Empress's Dream 2000. *Publication:* Circle of the Sun (play) 2000. *Address:* Ilynka st. 4, Moscow, Russia. *Telephone:* (495) 956-76-76. *Website:* www.ilze-liepa.ru; www.liepa.ru.

LIÈS, Michel M.; Luxembourg business executive; *Chairman, Zurich Insurance Group;* b. 1954; ed Fed. Inst. of Tech. (ETH), Zurich; joined Swiss Re 1978, Head of Latin America Div. 1998–2000, Head of Europe Div. 2000–05, Head of Client Markets in charge of all client relationships world-wide, and mem. Group Exec. Cttee 2005–11, Chair. Global Partnerships 2011–12, Group CEO Suisse Reinsurance (Swiss Re) 2012–16, mem. Swiss Re Advisory Panel; Chair. Zurich Insurance Group 2018–; mem. Supervisory Bd CNP Assurances SA, Bd of Dirs Swiss American Chamber of Commerce. *Address:* Zurich Insurance Group, Austrasse 46, 8045 Zürich, Switzerland (office). *Telephone:* 446252299 (office). *Fax:* 446250299 (office). *E-mail:* investor.relations@zurich.com (office). *Website:* www.zurich.com (office).

LIEVONEN, Matti, BSc (Eng); Finnish business executive; *President and CEO, Neste Oil;* b. 1958; with ABB –1986; held several sr positions at UPM-Kymmene Corpn 1986–2008, including Pres. Fine and Speciality Papers Div., mem. Exec. Bd 2002–08; Pres. and CEO Neste Oil 2008–; Vice-Chair. CEPIFINE; Chair. Supervisory Bd Ilmarinen Mutual Pension Insurance Co.; Chair. Advisory Bd Excellence Finland; mem. Advisory Bd Nat. Emergency Supply Agency; Hon. DTech (Aalto Univ.) 2016. *Address:* Neste Oil Oyj, Keilaranta, PO Box 95, 00095 Espoo (office); Neste Oil Oyj, Keilaranta 21, Espoo, Finland (office). *Telephone:* (10) 45811 (office). *Fax:* (10) 458-4442 (office). *E-mail:* info@nesteoil.com (office). *Website:* www.nesteoil.com (office).

LIÈVREMONT, Marc; French rugby union coach and fmr professional rugby union player; b. 28 Oct. 1968, Dakar, Senegal; raised in Argelès-sur-Mer; began rugby career with amateur club Étoile sportive catalane 1974–88; played for Perpignan 1988–97, Stade Français 1997–2000 (Top 14 1998, 2000), Biarritz Olympique 2000–02; played as a back-row forward for France, gaining 25 caps 1995–99; selected in France's Rugby World Cup squad 1999; also played with French Rugby Sevens team and with French Barbarians; coach of France Under 21 team 2003–; following retirement from playing rugby, turned to coaching at US Dax 2005–07, guided team to promotion to the Top 14 2007; Head Coach of French Nat. Rugby Union Team following Rugby World Cup 2007–11; coached France to win Six Nations Championship and Grand Slam beating England 12–10 2010; guided France to Rugby World Cup final where they played New Zealand, losing 7–8 at Eden Park, Auckland 2011; Giuseppe Garibaldi Trophy 2008, 2009, 2010, Grand Slam 2010, Eurostar Trophy. *Publication includes:* Frames and Overflows 2012.

LIEW, Datuk Vui Keong, LLB, JP; Malaysian lawyer and politician; b. 18 Jan. 1960, Kota Belud, Sabah; s. of Ping-Hon Liew and Yet Liew Wong; m. Dr Lindai Lee; four c.; ed Diploma in Business and Finance, Univ. of North London, Lincoln's Inn, London, UK; active legal practitioner in criminal law and jurisdiction in Malaysia; called to Malayan Bar 1990, Borneo Bar 1992; est. own legal practice 1997; legal adviser to the Sabah United Chinese Chamber of Commerce, United Sabah Sze Yip Asscn, Sabah Motion Picture & Entertainment Asscn, Sabah Sze Yip Asscn (West Coast), Sabah Women Asscn, Kota Belud Chinese Chamber of Commerce, Kota Kinabalu Journalists Asscn, Sabah Law Asscn; joined LDP 1994, Head, Usukan Div., Kota Belud 1994–2004, Kapayan Div. 2004, Asst Sec.-Gen. LDP 1999–2004, Sec.-Gen. 2005–06, Pres. 2006–14; Vice-Pres. Barisan Nasional, Malaysia. *Leisure interests:* swimming, reading. *Address:* c/o Liberal Democratic Party, Tingkat 1, No. 33, Karamunsing Warehouse, PO Box 16033, 88868 Kota Kinabalu, Sabah, Malaysia.

LIEZIETSU, Shurhozelie, BA, MA; Indian teacher, writer and politician; *President, Naga People's Front;* b. 20 Nov. 1936; s. of Krusietsu Liezietsu; four s.; ed Guwahati Univ.; began career as Upper Division Asst, Nagaland Secr. 1962; Asst Teacher, Baptist English School, Kohima 1962–63; Founder and Headmaster, Thinuovicha Memorial School, Kohima 1963–67; mem., Nagaland Legis. Ass. 1969–74, 1982–88, 1993–98; Minister of State for Educ. 1974–75, 1977–82, Minister of Planning and Coordination, Urban Devt and Higher Educ. 2003–08, of Higher and Technical Educ. and Urban Devt 2008–13; Treas., Naga People's Council 1978–97, Sec.-Gen. 1986–97; Pres., Naga People's Front (NPF) 2005–; Chair., Democratic Alliance of Nagaland (DAN) and NPF Political Affairs Cttee 2013–; Chief Minister of Nagaland Feb.–July 2017; mem. Commonwealth Parl. Asscn, Red Cross Soc. of India; DLit hc (Nagaland Univ.) 2003; Gov.'s Award for outstanding achievement and contribution in the field of literature 2005. *Publications include:* more than 40 books including poetry, novels, history, drama and translations; novels: Puo A Meho Tha Zo (She is looking at me), A Puo Kekhrie (The love of my father), Methuophemia (Name of a village), Telhe Mote (Not long after); poetry collections: Üca (Old Poems), U teiki Geizo (Modern Poems), Thenou –rutso (Modern Poems). *Address:* Naga People's Front, P.R. Hill, Above Academy Hall, Kohima 797001, Nagaland, India (office). *Website:* www.npfweb.org (office).

LIFTON, Richard P., BA, MD, PhD; American biochemist, geneticist and academic; *Sterling Professor of Genetics and Professor of Medicine (Nephrology) and Chairman, Department of Genetics, Yale University;* b. 1953; ed Dartmouth Coll., Stanford Univ.; Resident in Internal Medicine, Brigham and Women's Hosp., Boston, Mass 1983–86, Chief Medical Resident 1986–87, Instructor in Medicine, Brigham and Women's Hosp. and Harvard Medical School 1987–91, Asst Prof. 1991–93; Asst Prof. of Medicine and Genetics, Yale Univ. 1993–94, Assoc. Prof. 1994–97, Prof. 1997–, currently Sterling Prof. of Genetics and Prof. of Medicine (Nephrology), Chair. Dept of Genetics, Dir Yale Center for Human Genetics and Genomics; Asst Investigator, Howard Hughes Medical Inst. 1994–96; mem. Transatlantic Network on Hypertension-Renal Salt Handling in the Control of Blood Pressure (France) 2007, Jt Strategy Cttee for the Yale-UCL Collaborative 2011; mem. NAS Inst. of Medicine; Fellow, AAAS; Young Investigator Award, Int. Soc. of Hypertension 1994, The Basic Science Prize, American Heart Asscn, Homer Smith Award, American Soc. of Nephrology 1998, MSD Int. Award, Int. Soc. of Hypertension, Alfred Newton Richards Award, Int. Soc. of Nephrology 2007, Wiley Prize in Biomedical Sciences 2008, Breakthrough Prize in Life Sciences (co-recipient) 2014. *Publications:* numerous papers in professional journals. *Address:* Department of Genetics, Yale University School of Medicine, PO Box 208005, 333 Cedar Street, New Haven, CT 06520-8005, USA (office). *Telephone:* (203) 785-2649 (Dept) (office). *Fax:* (203) 785-7227 (office). *E-mail:* richard.lifton@yale.edu (office). *Website:* medicine.yale.edu/genetics (office).

LIGACHEV, Yegor Kuzmich; Russian politician; b. 29 Sept. 1920; m.; one s.; ed Moscow Inst. of Aviation and CPSU Higher Party School; engineer 1943–49; joined CPSU 1944; Party and Local Govt Official Novosibirsk 1949–55; Vice-Chair. Novosibirsk Regional Soviet of Working People's Deputies 1955–58; Sec. Novosibirsk Regional Cttee CPSU 1959–61, mem. Cen. Cttee CPSU 1961–65; First Sec. Tomsk Regional Cttee CPSU 1965–83; Cand. mem. Cen. Cttee CPSU 1966–76, mem. 1976–90, mem. Politburo 1985–90; Deputy to Supreme Soviet 1966–89; Sec. Cen. Cttee in Charge of Personnel and Ideology 1983–88; in Charge of Agric. 1988–90; People's Deputy of the USSR 1989–91; active in Russian nat. and communist movt; Vice-Chair. Union of Communist Parties of fmr USSR 1995–; mem. State Duma (Parl.) 1999–2003. *Publication:* Inside Gorbachev's Kremlin 1993.

LIGEARD, Cynthia; New Caledonian politician; *Minister for Public Service and Road Safety;* b. 26 June 1962, Nouméa; ed Lycée Blaise Pascal; several years as civil servant working in office of Mayor of Nouméa, including in Cultural and Festival Dept, becoming Chef de Cabinet to Mayor Jean Lèques 2002; mem. Assemblée de la Province Sud (regional Ass.), Vice-Pres. 2011–12, Pres. 2012–14; mem. Congress of New Caledonia (Parl.) 2004–, Pres. of RPCR parl. group 2007–08, Pres. Finance and Budget Cttee 2007–09, Vice-Pres. Infrastructure and Energy Cttee 2007–09, Transport and Communication Cttee 2007–09; Pres. Council of Ministers (Prime Minister) 2014–15; Minister for Public Service and Road Safety 2015–; mem. del. to signing of Nouméa Accord (on political status of New Caledonia), Paris 2007; mem. Rassemblement pour la Calédonie dans la République (RPCR)/ Rassemblement-UMP. *Address:* c/o Présidence du Gouvernement, 8 route des Artifices, Artillerie, BP M2, 98849 Nouméa Cedex, New Caledonia (office). *Telephone:* 246565 (office). *Fax:* 246580 (office). *Website:* www .gouv.nc (office).

LIGHT, Jay Owen, BA, PhD; American academic and university administrator; *George F. Baker Professor Emeritus of Administration, Harvard Business School;* b. Ohio; m. Judy Light; two c.; ed Cornell Univ., Harvard Univ.; early career in data communications and satellite guidance at Jet Propulsion Lab. –1970; mem. of Faculty, Harvard Business School 1970–, Dwight P. Robinson, Jr. Prof. of Business Admin 1979–, held various sr positions including Chair. Finance Area 1985–88, Sr Assoc. Dean and Dir of Faculty Planning 1988–92, Sr Assoc. Dean and Dir of Planning and Devt 1998–2005, Interim Dean, Harvard Business School 2005–06, Dean 2006–10 (retd), took leave of absence from Harvard to serve as Dir of Investment and Financial Policies, Ford Foundation 1977–79, now George F. Baker Prof. Emer. of Administration; mem. Bd of Dirs Harvard Man. Co., Partners

HealthCare, also Chair. Investment Cttee; Trustee, Groton School. *Publications:* The Financial System (with W.L. White) 1979; numerous articles in professional journals and more than 70 cases and notes. *Address:* c/o Office of the Dean, Harvard Business School, Soldiers Field, Boston, MA 02163, USA. *Telephone:* (617) 495-6358.

LIGHTFOOT, Edwin N., BS, PhD; American scientist and academic; *Hilldale Professor Emeritus of Chemical and Biological Engineering, University of Wisconsin;* m.; five c.; ed Cornell Univ., New York; joined Faculty of Univ. of Wisconsin-Madison 1953, became one of the country's first profs in biochemical eng, now Hilldale Prof. Emer. of Chemical and Biological Eng; mem. Nat. Acad. of Eng 1979, Royal Norwegian Soc. of Sciences and Letters 1985, NAS 1995; Hon. DrTech (Tech. Univ. of Norway) 1985; Fulbright Research Scholar, Tech. Univ. of Norway 1962, AIChE William H. Walker Award 1975, AIChE Warren K. Lewis Award 1991, Nat. Medal of Science (jt recipient) 2004. *Publications:* Transport Phenomena 1960 (second edn 2002), Transport Phenomena and Living Systems: Biomedical Aspects of Momentum and Mass Transport 1974; numerous scientific papers in professional journals. *Address:* Department of Chemical and Biological Engineering, 3639 Engineering Hall, 1415 Engineering Drive, Madison, WI 53706, USA (office). *Telephone:* (608) 262-6934 (office). *Fax:* (608) 262-5434 (office). *E-mail:* lightfoot@engr.wisc.edu (office). *Website:* directory.engr.wisc.edu/che/Faculty/Lightfoot_Edwin (office).

LIGHTHIZER, Robert Emmet, BA, JD; American lawyer and government official; *US Trade Representative;* b. 11 Oct. 1947, Ashtabula, Ohio; ed Georgetown Univ.; called to the Bar, Dist of Columbia; fmr Chief of Staff, US Senate Cttee on Finance; Deputy US Trade Rep. (with rank of Amb.) during Reagan admin; Nat. Treas., Republican Presidential Campaign 1996; Partner, Skadden, Arps, Slate, Meagher & Flom LLP (law firm), Washington, DC; US Trade Rep. 2017–; fmr Vice-Chair., Overseas Private Investment Corpn (OPIC). *Address:* Office of the United States Trade Representative, Winder Bldg, 600 17th Street, NW, Washington, DC 20508, USA (office). *Telephone:* (202) 395-3230 (office). *Fax:* (202) 395-6121 (office). *E-mail:* correspondence@ustr.eop.gov (office). *Website:* www.ustr.gov (office).

LIGHTING, Jane, FRSA; British television executive; two c.; ed Oakdene School; began career with Crown Cassette Communications 1976; fmr marketing exec. for Video Arts (training film co.), then with its sister co., later worked in int. sales and distribution; Founder and Man. Dir, Minotaur International (distribution co.) 1995, acquired by Flextech (part of UK cable group Telewest) 1999; Man. Dir of Broadcast and TV, Flextech, oversaw five TV channels: Bravo, Living, Trouble, Challenge and Freeview entertainment channel FTN as well as 10-channel jt venture with BBC, including UK Gold and UK History 1999–2002, CEO Flextech 2002–03; CEO Channel 5 2003–08; Chair. Royal TV Soc. 2006–10, Trustee 2008–; Dir (non-exec.) Trinity Mirror PLC 2008–, Paddy Power 2009–13, Countrywide Plc 2014–; fmr Gov. Nat. Film and Television School; mem. British Screen Advisory Council; Olswang Business Award, Carlton Women in Film and TV Awards 2001.

LIGHTMAN, Alan Paige, AB, PhD; American physicist, writer and academic; *Professor of the Practice of the Humanities, Massachusetts Institute of Technology;* b. 28 Nov. 1948, Memphis, Tenn.; s. of Richard Lightman and Jeanne Lightman (née Garretson); m. Jean Greenblatt 1976; two d.; ed Princeton Univ., California Inst. of Technology; Postdoctoral Fellow, Cornell Univ. 1974–76; Asst Prof., Harvard Univ. 1976–79; staff scientist, Smithsonian Astrophysical Observatory, Cambridge 1979–88; Prof. of Science and Writing, MIT 1988–2002, John E. Burchard Chair 1995–2001, f. Grad. Program in Science Writing 2001, Adjunct Prof. of Humanities, Creative Writing, Physics 2002–12, Prof. of the Practice of the Humanities 2012–; Founding Dir Harpswell Foundation to empower women leaders in Cambodia 2003; Fellow, American Acad. of Arts and Sciences, American Physical Soc.; mem. American Astronomical Soc.; Hon. DLitt (Bowdoin Coll.) 2005, Hon. DFA (Memphis Coll. of Arts) 2006; Hon. Dr of Humanities (Univ. of Maryland) 2006, Hon. DHumLitt (Univ. of Massachusetts) 2010; Asscn of American Publishers Most Outstanding Science Book in the Physical Sciences Award 1990, Boston Globe Winship Book Prize 1993, American Inst. of Physics Andrew Gemant Award 1996, Nat. Public Radio Book of the Month 1998, Distinguished Alumnus Award, California Inst. of Tech. 2003, Sigma Xi John P. McGovern Award, 2006, Gold Medal for Humanitarian Service, Govt of Cambodia 2008, Sydney Award for Best Essays 2011. *Publications include:* fiction: Einstein's Dreams 1993, Good Benito 1994, The Diagnosis 2000, Reunion 2003, Ghost 2007, Song of Two Worlds 2009, Mr g 2012; non-fiction: Problem Book in Relativity and Gravitation 1974, Radiative Process in Astrophysics (with George B. Rybicki) 1976, Time Travel and Papa Joe's Pipe 1984, A Modern Day Yankee in a Connecticut Court and Other Essays on Science 1986, Origins: The Lives and Worlds of Modern Cosmologists (with Roberta Brawer) 1990, Ancient Light: Our Changing View of the Universe (adapted from Origins) 1991, Great Ideas in Physics 1992, Time for the Stars: Astronomy in the 1990s 1992, The World is Too Much with Me: Finding Private Space in the Wired World 1992, Dance for Two: Selected Essays 1996, A Sense of the Mysterious: Science and the Human Spirit (essays) 2005, The Discoveries 2005, The Accidental Universe (essays) 2014; editor: Revealing the Universe: Prediction and Proof in Astronomy (with James Cornell) 1982, The Best American Essays 2000; contrib. to professional journals and literary magazines. *Address:* Massachusetts Institute of Technology, Room 14E-303, 77 Massachusetts Avenue, Cambridge, MA 02139, USA (office). *Telephone:* (617) 253-2308 (office). *Website:* www.harpswellfoundation.org (office); www.alanlightman.com.

LIGI, Jürgen, BA, MBA; Estonian economist and politician; b. 16 July 1959, Tartu; s. of Herbert Ligi and Reet; m.; two s.; ed Tartu Second High School, Tartu State Univ., Estonian Business School; Economist, Estonian SSR Planning Inst. 1982–89; Chief Specialist, Saaremaa Agro-Industrial Asscn 1989–90; Head, Saaremaa Dept, Chamber of Commerce and Industry 1990–91; consultant on entrepreneurial activities 1991–92; Econ. Adviser, Kaarma Rural Municipal Govt 1992–93; Head of Br. Office, EVEA Bank, Kuressaare 1993–95; joined Reform Party 1994; mem. Riigikogu (Parl.) for Harju and Rapla Dist 1995–2005, 2007–09, Chair. Parl. Cttee for Budget Control 2007–09; Minister of Defence 2005–07, of Finance 2009–14 (resgnd), of Educ. and Research 2015–16, of Foreign Affairs Sept.–Nov. 2016; Chair. Compensation Fund Supervisory Bd; mem. Estonian Athletic Asscn; Trustee, Tallinn Tech. Univ. *Publications:* articles in newspapers. *Address:* c/o Ministry of Foreign Affairs, Iceland Square 1, Tallinn 15049, Estonia (office).

LIGON, Glenn, BA; American artist; b. 1960, Bronx, New York; ed Wesleyan Univ.; worked a proofreader at a law firm in the early 1980s and constantly practised painting in his free time; currently lives and works in New York; Fletcher Fellowship 2005, Skowhegan Medal for Painting 2006, US Artists Fellowship Award 2010. *Website:* www.glennligonstudio.com (office).

LIGRESTI, Giulia Maria; Italian business executive; ed Università Commerciale Luigi Bocconi, Milan, Queen Mary Coll., London, UK; apptd Pres. and CEO Premafin Finanziaria SpA 2002, Chair. and Man. Dir Premafin Finanziaria Holding di Partecipazioni SpA; Deputy Chair. Fondiaria SAI SpA, mem. Bd of Dirs several subidiary cos; Chair. Gilli Srl, Fondazione FON-SAI, Saifin SpA; Man. Dir SAI Holding Italia SpA; mem. Bd of Dirs Finadin SpA, Sailux SA, Sainternational SA, Saifin SpA, Filarmonica della Scala di Milano, Helm Finance SGR SpA, ATA Hotels SpA, Istituto Europeo di Oncologia Srl.

LIIKANEN, Erkki Antero, BA, MPolSci (Econ); Finnish politician and central banker; *Governor, Bank of Finland;* b. 19 Sept. 1950, Mikkeli; m. Hanna-Liisa Issakainen 1971; two d.; ed Univ. of Helsinki; mem. Parl. 1972–90; Minister of Finance 1987–90; mem. Social Democratic Party (SDP) Cttee 1978–, Gen. Sec. 1981–87; Amb. to EU 1990–95; EC Commr for Budget, Personnel and Admin 1995–99, for Industry and Information (subsequently Enterprise, Competitiveness, Innovation and the Information Society) 1999–2004; Gov. Bank of Finland (cen. bank) 2004–, also mem. Governing Council, European Cen. Bank 2004–, IMF Gov. for Finland 2004–; Chair. Finnish Red Cross 2008–14; Hon. DSc (Tech.) (Univ. of Tech.), Hon. DSc (Econ) (Aalto/Helsinki School of Econs and Business Admin). *Address:* Bank of Finland, Snellmaninaukio, PO Box 160, 00101 Helsinki, Finland (office). *Telephone:* (10) 8312001 (office). *Fax:* (10) 8312022 (office). *E-mail:* erkki.liikanen@bof.fi (office). *Website:* www.bof.fi (office).

LIKA, Hazbi, DPhil; Macedonian philologist and politician; *Deputy Prime Minister, responsible for the Implementation of the Ohrid Framework Agreement;* b. 19 April 1972, Tetovo, Socialist Repub. of Macedonia, Socialist Fed. Repub. of Yugoslavia; ed Univ. of Prishtina, Kosovo; fmr mem. Ushtria Çlirimtare e Kosovës (Kosovo Liberation Army) and Ushtria Çlirimtare Kombëtare (Nat. Liberation Army—Macedonia); commdr in Tetovo during the conflict in Macedonia 2001; apptd Deputy Minister of the Interior 2003; Mayor of Tetovo 2005–09; mem. Bashkimi Demokratik për Integrim (Democratic Union for Integration), Chair. party br. in Tetovo; Deputy Prime Minister, responsible for the Implementation of the Ohrid Framework Agreement 2017–. *Address:* Office of the Prime Minister, 1000 Skopje, Ilindenska b.b. 2, North Macedonia (office). *Telephone:* (2) 3118022 (office). *Fax:* (2) 3112561 (office). *E-mail:* primeminister@primeminister.gov.mk (office). *Website:* www.vlada.mk (office).

LIKENS, Gene Elden, BS, MS, PhD; American ecologist, academic and research institute director; *Distinguished Senior Scientist, Ecologist, Founding Director and President Emeritus, Cary Institute of Ecosystem Studies;* b. 6 Jan. 1935, Pierceton, Indiana; s. of Colonel and Josephine Likens; m. Phyllis C. Likens (deceased); three c.; ed Univ. of Wisconsin, Madison; joined faculty of Dartmouth Coll. 1961; Co-founder Hubbard Brook Ecosystem Study at Hubbard Brook Experimental Forest, White Mountains of NH; Founder Cary Inst. of Ecosystem Studies (fmrly Inst. of Ecosystem Studies), Millbrook, NY (part of New York Botanical Garden) 1983, inst. became ind. 1993, Dir and Pres. 1993–2007, Distinguished Sr Scientist, Ecologist, Founding Dir 1993, Pres. Emer. 2007–, also Distinguished Sr Scientist Emer. 2012–; holds faculty positions at Yale, Cornell, Rutgers Univs, State Univ. of NY, Albany and Univ. of Connecticut, Jinan Univ., Chinese Acad. of Science, Uppsala Univ., Sweden; fmr Pres. Int. Soc. of Theoretical and Applied Limnology, American Inst. of Biological Sciences, Ecological Soc. of America, American Soc. of Limnology and Oceanography; mem. American Acad. of Arts and Sciences 1979, NAS 1981, American Philosophical Soc. 2006; Foreign mem. Royal Swedish Acad. of Sciences 1988, Royal Danish Acad. of Sciences and Letters 1994, Austrian Acad. of Sciences 2000; Flagship Fellowship in Water for a Healthy Country Flagship, CSIRO, Australia 2007–08; Einstein Prof., Chinese Acad. of Science 2010; Fellow, AAAS 1965, Timothy Dwight Coll., Yale Univ. 1985; Hon. Prof., Jinan Univ., China; Hon. mem. British Ecological Soc.; 11 hon. doctorate degrees; Guggenheim Fellowship 1972, Tyler Prize, The World Prize for Environmental Achievement (with F. H. Bormann) 1993, Australia Prize for Science and Tech. 1994, Naumann-Thienemann Medal, Societas Internationalis Limnologiae 1995, Eminent Ecologist Award, Ecological Soc. of America 1995, Nat. Medal of Science 2001, Blue Planet Prize (with F. H. Bormann), Asahi Glass Foundation 2003, Miegunyah Fellowship, Melbourne, Australia 2004, BBVA Frontiers of Knowledge Award 2006. *Achievements include:* best known for his discovery of acid rain in N America. *Publications:* author, co-author or ed. 25 books, including Pattern and Process in a Forested Ecosystem (co-author) 1979, Limnological Analyses (co-author) 1979, Biogeochemistry of a Forested Ecosystem (co-author) 1995, The Ecosystem Approach: Its Use and Abuse. Excellence in Ecology, Vol. 3 1992, Mirror Lake: Interactions among Air, Land and Water (co-author) 2009, Effective Ecological Monitoring (co-author) 2010; more than 600 scientific papers in professional journals. *Leisure interests:* basketball, fishing. *Address:* Cary Institute of Ecosystem Studies, 2801 Sharon Turnpike, PO Box AB, Millbrook, NY 12545, USA (office). *Telephone:* (845) 677-5343 (office). *Fax:* (845) 677-5976 (office). *E-mail:* likensg@caryinstitute.org (office). *Website:* www.caryinstitute.org/science-program/our-scientists/dr-gene-e-likens (office).

LILIĆ, Zoran; Serbian politician and government official; b. 27 Aug. 1953, Brza Palanka, Serbia; s. of Sokol Lilić and Dobrila Lilić; m. Ljubica Brković-Lilić 1980; one s.; ed Belgrade Univ.; several posts as grad. engineer, then man., with state-owned Rekord enterprise, Belgrade; fmr Pres. Exec. Bd Yugoslav Tyre Makers Business Asscn, mem. Presidency of Belgrade Chamber of Economy, Pres. Man. Bd of Belgrade Airport, mem. Council of Faculty of Tech.; mem. Serbian League of Communists, subsequently Socialist Party of Serbia (SPS); Deputy to Nat. Ass. of Repub. of Serbia 1990, Chair. Cttee on Industry, Energy, Mining and Construction, Chief of Group of SPS Deputies; re-elected Deputy and also Pres. of Nat. Ass. 1992; Pres. of Fed. Repub. of Yugoslavia 1993–97; Vice-Prime Minister of Yugoslavia 1997–2000; Vice-Pres. Socialist Party of Serbia (SPS) 1995–2000; apptd Chair. Upravnog odbora JP Putevi Srbije (Bd of Public Roads of Serbia)

2008; testified against successor Slobodan Milosevic at Int. Criminal Tribunal for Fmr Yugoslavia, The Hague, Netherlands 2002. *Leisure interests:* fishing, football, chess.

LILIUS, (Percy Henrik) Mikael, BSc, MSc, BBA; Finnish business executive; *Chairman, Ambea AB;* b. 3 Dec. 1949, Helsinki; m.; three c.; ed Helsinki School of Econs; Marketing Dir Huhtamäki Oy Polarpak, Helsinki 1981–84, Pres. 1984–85, Pres. Packing Div. 1985–89, Chair. 2005–13; Pres. and CEO KF Industri AB (Nordico), Stockholm 1989–90; Pres. and CEO Incentive AB, Stockholm 1990–98; Pres. and CEO Gambro AB (medical supply co.), Stockholm 1998–2000; Pres. and CEO Fortum (Finnish state-owned energy co.), Espoo 2000–09; Chair. Ambea AB 2011–, Wärtsilä Oyj Abp 2011–, Sanitec Oy, Mehiläinen Oy; Chair. Supervisory Bd Teollisuuden Voima Oy; Vice-Chair. Ahlstrom Oyj 2001–05, OAO Lenenergo, Lite-On Mobile Oyj (fmrly Perlos Oyj); Deputy Chair. Aker Solutions ASA; Dir Gambro AB, Sweden-Japan Foundation, Huhtamäki Van Leer Oyj, Instrumentarium Oy, Perlos Oy, A. Ahlstrom Corpn, Wärtsilä Oyj Abp 2010–, Aker Solutions ASA 2011–, Metso Corpn 2013–, Aker Kvaerner Subsea AS; mem. Advisory Bd EQT; mem. Supervisory Bd Finnish Fair Corpn, Kemijoki Oy; Chair. Asscn of Finnish Energy Industries. *Address:* Ambea AB, Holländargatan 21A 4 Floor, 111 60 Stockholm, Sweden (office). *Telephone:* (8) 617-39-00 (office). *Fax:* (8) 617-39-80 (office). *E-mail:* info@ambea.com (office). *Website:* www.ambea.com (office).

LILL, John Richard, CBE, FRCM; British pianist and academic; *Professor, Keyboard Faculty, Royal College of Music;* b. 17 March 1944, London; s. of George Lill and Margery Lill (née Young); m. Jacqueline Clifton Smith; ed Leyton County High School and Royal Coll. of Music; London debut at Royal Festival Hall 1963; plays regularly throughout Europe, USA and Far East, as recitalist and as soloist with most prin. orchestras; currently Prof., Keyboard Faculty, Royal Coll. of Music; Hon. DSc (Univ. of Aston); Hon. DMus (Exeter Univ.); Hon. FTCL, FLCM; First Prize, Royal Overseas League Competition 1963, Int. Tchaikovsky Competition, Moscow 1970, Dinu Lipatti Medal, Chappell Gold Medal. *Recordings include:* complete Beethoven piano sonatas, concertos and bagatelles, complete piano works of Rachmaninov (with BBC Nat. Orchestra of Wales/Otaka), Brahms piano concertos, Tchaikovsky Piano Concerto No. 1 (with London Symphony Orchestra), complete Prokofiev sonatas 1991. *Leisure interests:* chess, amateur radio, walking. *Address:* Keyboard Faculty, Royal College of Music, Prince Consort Road, London, SW7 2BS, England (office). *Telephone:* (20) 7591-4300 (office). *Fax:* (20) 7591-4737 (office). *E-mail:* info@rcm.ac.uk (office). *Website:* www.rcm.ac.uk/keyboard (office).

LILLEE, Dennis Keith, MBE; Australian fmr professional cricketer; b. 18 July 1949, Perth, WA; s. of K. Lillee; m. Helen Lillee 1970; two s.; ed Belmay State School, Belmont High School; right-arm fast bowler, lower-order right-hand batsman; played for WA 1969–84, Tasmania 1987–88, Northants. 1988; Test debut: Australia v England, Adelaide 29 Jan.–3 Feb. 1971; One-Day Int. debut: England v Australia, Manchester 24 Aug. 1972; played in 70 Tests for Australia 1970–84, taking then world record 355 wickets (average 23.92), including record 167 wickets in 29 Tests against England, and scoring 905 runs (average 13.71, highest score 73 not out), best bowling (innings) 7/83, (match) 11/123; toured England 1972, 1975, 1980, 1981, 1983 (World Cup), took 882 First-class wickets (average 23.46), best bowling (innings) 8/29; Coach Western Australian Cricket Asscn 2000; coaching fast bowlers, MRF Pace Foundation, Chennai, India 2001, Dennis Lillee Fast Bowling Acad. (est. June 2002) 2002–; continued playing cricket, bowling for the Australian Cricket Bd Chair.'s XI –2000; Pres. Western Australian Cricket Asscn 2004–15; Wisden Cricketer of the Year 1973, inducted into Australian Cricket Hall of Fame 1996, named mem. of Australia's Test Team of the Century. *Publications include:* Back to the Mark 1974, The Art of Fast Bowling 1977, Dennis Lillee's Book of Family Fitness 1980, My Life in Cricket 1982, Over and Out 1984. *Leisure Interests:* music, philately.

LILLEY, Rt Hon. Peter Bruce, PC, MA; British politician; b. 23 Aug. 1943, Kent; s. of S. Arnold Lilley and Lilian Lilley (née Elliott); m. Gail Ansell 1979; ed Dulwich Coll., Clare Coll., Cambridge; Chair. Bow Group 1973; MP for St Albans 1983–97, for Hitchin and Harpenden 1997–; Econ. Sec. to Treasury 1987–89, Financial Sec. 1989–90; Sec. of State for Trade and Industry 1990–92, for Social Security 1992–97; Opposition Front Bench Spokesman for Treasury 1997–98; Deputy Leader of the Opposition 1998–99; fmr Dir Greenwell Montagu (Oil Analyst); Dir (non-exec.) JP Morgan Fleming Claverhouse Investment 1997–2008, IDOX PLC 2002–, Melchior Japan Investment Trust 2006–10, Tethys Petroleum Ltd 2006–14; mem. Advisory Bd Yihei Capital 2013–. *Publications:* The Delusion of Incomes Policy (with Samuel Brittan) 1977, The End of the Keynesian Era 1980, Thatcherism: The Next Generation 1990, Winning the Welfare Debate 1996, Patient Power 2000, Common Sense on Cannabis 2001, Taking Liberties 2002, Save Our Pensions 2003, The Case Against ID Cards 2004, Too Much of a Good Thing? 2005, In it Together (Report of Global Poverty Group) 2007, Paying for Success (Policy Exchange) 2008, What is Wrong with Stern: the Failings of the Stern Review of the Economics of Climate Change 2012. *Leisure interest:* France (and most things French). *Address:* House of Commons, Westminster, London, SW1A 0AA, England (office). *Website:* www.peterlilley.co.uk (office).

LILLIKAS, Yiorgos, MA; Cypriot politician and consultant; b. 1 June 1960, Pafos; m. Barbara Petropoulou; one s.; ed Inst. of Political Science, Lyon, France, Inst. of Political Science, Grenoble; mem. Historic Politology Research Team, Nat. Scientific Research Centre of France 1985–87; Special Adviser to Pres. of Repub. of Cyprus 1988–90; Gen. Sec. Secr. for New Generation 1990–93; consultant in public relations, strategic marketing and advertising 1993–2001; mem. House of Reps from Nicosia 1996–2006, fmr mem. Parl. Cttees on Finance, Foreign and European Affairs, Educ., Trade, fmr Chair. Environment Cttee; Minister of Commerce, Industry and Tourism 2003–06, of Foreign Affairs 2006–07; fmr Head of Del. to Parl. Ass. of OSCE; Vice-Pres. OSCE Political Affairs and Security Cttee Jan.–June 2006; cand. in presidential election Feb. 2013; fmr mem. Anorthotiko Komma Ergazomenou Laou (Progressive Party of the Working People); Pres. Citizen's Alliance 2013–; f. BlueTree Consultants (advises on international investment) 2008. *Address:* House of Representatives, 8, John Kennedy Avenue, 1087 Nicosia, Cyprus (office). *Telephone:* 22407231 (office). *Fax:* 22282200 (office). *E-mail:* yiorgos@lillikas.com (office).

LIM, C(hwen) J(eng), AA Dip; British architect, urban designer and academic; *Director, Studio 8 Architects;* b. 1964, Ipoh, Malaysia; s. of Kar Sun Lim and Yoke Kheng Leong; ed St Michael's Inst., Ipoh, Malaysia, Ashville Coll., Harrogate, Architectural Asscn School of Architecture, London; Prof. of Architecture and Urbanism, Bartlett School of Architecture, Univ. Coll. London (UCL) 1993–, Dir Bartlett Architecture Research Lab. 1999–2007, UCL Pro-Provost of N America 2008–11, Bartlett Vice-Dean 2011–13; Sr Lecturer Univ. of E London 1990–93, Univ. of N London 1991–99; Dir Studio 8 Architects, London 1994–; Visiting Prof., Curtin Univ., Perth, Australia 1996, Stadelschule, Frankfurt 1997–98, 2000–01, Technological Univ., Lund, Sweden 2001–, MacKintosh School of Architecture, Glasgow 2001–11, School of Architecture, Århus, Denmark 2002, Chiba Inst. of Tech., Japan 2004, Royal Danish Acad. of Fine Arts, Denmark 2006, The Univ. of Girona, Spain 2008, Seoul Nat. Univ., South Korea 2012, RMIT Australia 2012; RIBA External Examiner 2000–; numerous exhbns Europe, Japan, Canada, USA, Australia; RIBA Pres.'s Medals for Academic Contrib. in Architecture 1997, 1998, 1999; several prizes for architectural research projects including First Prize Bldg Centre Trust Competition 'Housing: a demonstration project' 1987, UCL Cultural Centre Int. Competition 1996, Cen. Glass Int. Competition Japan: Glasshouse 2001, 2nd Prize Japanese/NCE Competition: an image of the bridge of the future 1987, Concept House 2000 (Int.) Ideal Home Exhbn 1999, Tangshan Earthquake Memorial Landscape China 2007, NanYu Shopping Park China 2008, Great Places: Environmental Design Research Asscn Int. Competition, USA 2009. *Achievements:* represented UK at the Venice Biennale 2004. *Publications:* 441/10. . . We'll Reconfigure the Space When You're Ready 1996, Sins + Other Spatial Relatives 2000, Realms of Impossibility: Water 2002, Realms of Impossibility: Ground 2002, Realms of Impossibility: Air 2002, How Green is Your Garden? 2003, Museums (Work in Process) 2004, Devices 2005, Neoarchitecture 2005, Virtually Venice 2006, Smartcities and Eco-warriors 2010, Short Stories: London in Two-and-a-half Dimensions 2011, Food City 2014, Inhabitable Infrastructures: Science Fiction or Urban Future? 2017. *Address:* Studio 8 Architects, 95 Greencroft Gardens, London, NW6 3PG, England (office). *Telephone:* (20) 7679-4842 (office). *E-mail:* mail@cjlim-studio8.com (office). *Website:* www.cjlim-studio8.com (office).

LIM, Dong-won; South Korean politician and diplomatist; b. 25 July 1934; ed Korea Mil. Acad., Seoul Nat. Univ.; Asst Prof., Korean Mil. Acad. 1964–69; with Armed Forces, attained rank of Maj.-Gen. 1980, now retd; apptd Amb. to Nigeria 1981, to Australia 1984; Chancellor Inst. of Foreign Affairs and Nat. Security, Ministry of Foreign Affairs 1988–92; Chair. Presidential Comm. on Arms Control 1990; Del. South–North High-Level Talks 1990–92; apptd Chair. Asscn for Nat. Unification of Korea 1993; mem. Unification Policy Evaluation Cttee 1993; Sec.-Gen. Kim Dae Jung Peace Foundation for the Asia-Pacific 1995; Sr Sec. for Nat. Security and Foreign Affairs, Pres. Sec. 1998; Minister for Unification (involved in reconciliatory Sunshine Policy towards North Korea) 1999–2001; Dir-Gen. Nat. Intelligence Service 1999–2001; Special Envoy to North Korea April 2002; fmr staff mem. Sejong Inst., Chair. Sejong Foundation 2004–08. *Publication:* Peacemaker (memoir) 2012.

LIM, Guan Eng, BEcons; Malaysian politician; *Minister of Finance;* b. 8 Dec. 1960, Johor Bahru, Johor; s. of Lim Kit Siang (fmr leader of the opposition) and Neo Yoke Tee; m. Betty Chew Gek Cheng; three s. one d.; ed Monash Univ., Australia; fmr banker and chartered accountant; mem. Dewan Rakyat (Parl.) for Melaka City 1986–99, for Bagan 2008–; mem. Penang State Ass. for Air Putih 2008–; Chief Minister of Penang 2008–18; Minister of Finance 2018–; mem. Democratic Action Party (DAP), Sec.-Gen. 2004–. *Address:* Ministry of Finance, 5 Persiaran Perdana, Presint 2, Pusat Pentadbiran Kerajaan Persekutuan, 62592 Putrajaya, Malaysia (office). *Telephone:* (3) 80008000 (office). *Fax:* (3) 88823893 (office). *E-mail:* pro@treasury.gov.my (office). *Website:* www.treasury.gov.my (office); www.limguaneng.com.

LIM, Hng Kiang, BSc, MPA; Singaporean government official; *Minister of Trade;* b. 9 April 1954; m. Lee Ai Boon (died 2014); two s.; ed Raffles Inst., Univ. of Cambridge, UK, Kennedy School, Harvard Univ., USA; with Singapore Armed Forces 1976–85, Ministry of Defence 1986; Deputy Sec. Ministry of Nat. Devt 1987; CEO Housing and Devt Bd 1991; mem. Parl. 1991–; Minister of State for Nat. Devt 1991–94, Acting Minister for Nat. Devt and Sr Minister of State for Foreign Affairs 1994–95, Minister for Nat. Devt 1995–99, Second Minister for Foreign Affairs 1995–98, Second Minister for Finance 1998–2004, Minister of Health 1999–2003, Minister, Prime Minister's Office 2003–04, Minister of Trade and Industry 2004–15, of Trade 2015–, also Deputy Chair. Monetary Authority of Singapore; mem. Bd of Dirs Govt of Singapore Investment Corpn. *Leisure interests:* swimming, golf. *Address:* Ministry of Trade and Industry, 100 High Street, 09-01 The Treasury, 179434 Singapore (office). *Telephone:* 62259911 (office). *Fax:* 63327260 (office). *E-mail:* mti_email@mti.gov.sg (office). *Website:* www.mti.gov.sg (office).

LIM, Dato Jock Hoi, BSc, PGCE; Brunei public servant and international organization official; *Secretary-General, ASEAN;* b. 5 Dec. 1951; m.; two s.; ed City of London Polytechnic, Keele Univ.; entered Govt Service as Educ. Officer 1977, Secondary School Prin. 1981–85; Special Duties Officer, Int. Relations and Trade Devt Dept, Ministry of Industry and Primary Resources 1989–96, Dir 1996–2001, Dir-Gen. 2001–05; Deputy Perm. Sec., Ministry of Foreign Affairs and Trade 2005, Perm. Sec. 2006–17; Chair. Governing Bd, Econ. Research Inst. for Asscn of Southeast Asian Nations (ASEAN) and East Asia 2011–17; Brunei Darussalam's chief negotiator for numerous trade deals, including Trans-Pacific Partnership Agreement (TPP); Sec.-Gen. ASEAN 2018–; Order of Loyalty to the State of Brunei (Fourth Class) 1990, (Third Class) 2000, Order of the Crown of Brunei (Third Class) 1995, (Second Class) 2007. *Address:* Association of Southeast Asian Nations, 70a Jalan Sisingamangaraja, POB 2072, Jakarta 12110, Indonesia (office). *Telephone:* (21) 7262991 (office). *Fax:* (21) 7398234 (office). *E-mail:* www.asean.org (office). *Website:* www.asean.org (office).

LIM, Kitack, MSc; South Korean maritime administrator and international organization official; *Secretary-General, International Maritime Organization (IMO);* b. 22 Jan. 1956, Masan, Gyeongsangnam-do; m. Jung-ae Do; ed Korea Maritime and Ocean Univ., Busan, Graduate School of Admin, Yonsei Univ., World Maritime Univ.; naval officer rising to sub-lieutenant, Korean Navy 1977–99; Second Officer, then Chief Officer, Sanko Shipping Co. 1979–83; Man. Maritime Affairs, Chunkyung Shipping 1983–85; joined Korea Maritime and Port

Admin 1985; attended IMO meetings as part of South Korean del. 1986; Maritime Attaché, IMO 1998–2001; Dir Maritime Tech. Div., Maritime Safety Bureau, Ministry of Maritime Affairs and Fisheries 2001–02, Dir Shipping Policy, Shipping and Logistics 2002–03, Dir-Gen. for Public Relations and Spokesman 2005–06; Maritime Attaché and Minister-Counsellor, Embassy in London 2006–09; Deputy Perm. Rep. of South Korea to IMO –2009; Dir-Gen. for Maritime Safety Policy Bureau, Ministry of Land, Transport and Maritime Affairs 2009–11; led South Korean del. to IMO Ass. 2009; Commr, Korean Maritime Safety Tribunal 2011–12; Pres., Busan Port Authority 2012–15; Sec.-Gen., IMO 2016–. *Leisure interests:* golf, tennis, reading. *Address:* Office of the Secretary-General, International Maritime Organization, 4, Albert Embankment, London, SE1 7SR, England (office). *Telephone:* (20) 7735-7611 (office). *Fax:* (20) 7587-3210 (office). *E-mail:* secretary-general@imo.org (office). *Website:* www.imo.org (office).

LIM, Pin, MA, MD, FRCP, FRCPE, FRACP, FACP; Singaporean medical scientist, endocrinologist and academic; *Professor Emeritus of Medicine, National University of Singapore;* b. 12 Jan. 1936, Penang, Malaysia; m. Shirley Loo Ngai Seong 1964; two s. one d.; ed Raffles Inst., Singapore and Cambridge Univ.; Registrar, King's Coll. Hosp., London 1965; Medical Officer, Ministry of Health, Singapore 1965–66; Lecturer in Medicine, Nat. Univ. of Singapore 1966–70, Sr Lecturer 1971–73, Assoc. Prof. of Medicine 1974–77, Prof. and Head of Dept 1978–81, Deputy Vice-Chancellor 1979–81, Vice-Chancellor 1981–2000, now Prof. Emer.; apptd Prof. of Medicine and Sr Consultant Endocrinologist, Nat. Univ. Hosp. 2000, now Consultant Emer.; Commonwealth Medical Fellow, The Royal Infirmary, Edin. 1970; Chair. Nat. Wages Council, Bio-ethics Advisory Cttee, Tropical Marine Science Inst., Nat. Longevity Insurance Cttee 2007–, Singapore-MIT Alliance for Research & Tech. 2007–, Special Needs Trust Co. 2008 (apptd), Singapore Millennium Foundation Ltd 2008–; apptd Deputy Chair., Lee Kuan Yew Water Prize Council 2009; Dir United Overseas Bank; apptd mem. Chinese Heritage Council 1995; Patron Mensa Singapore, Eisenhower Fellow 1982, Dir Raffles Medical Group; Hon. Fellow, Coll. of General Practitioners, Singapore 1982, Royal Australian Coll. of Obstetricians and Gynaecologists 1992, Royal Coll. of Physicians and Surgeons of Glasgow 1997, Royal Coll. of Surgeons of Edin. 1997, Int. Coll. of Dentists, USA 1999 (Dental Surgery), Royal Coll. of Surgeons of Edin. 1999; Officier, Ordre des Palmes académiques 1988, Singapore Distinguished Service Order 2000; Hon. DSc (Univ. of Hull) 1999; Rep. of Singapore Public Admin. Medal (Gold) 1984, Meritorious Service Medal 1990, Friend of Labour Award, NTUC 1995, Gordon Arthur Ransome Orator 2000, Lee Foundation–NHG Lifetime Achievement Award 2002, Nat. Univ. of Singapore Outstanding Service Award 2003. *Publications include:* numerous articles in medical journals. *Leisure Interest:* swimming. *Address:* Department of Medicine, National University of Singapore/National University Hospital, 5 Lower Kent Ridge Road, 119074 Singapore (office). *Telephone:* 67724976 (office). *Fax:* 67735627 (office). *Website:* www.nus.edu.sg (office).

LIM, Sung-nam, BA, MA, AM; South Korean diplomatist and government official; *First Vice-Minister of Foreign Affairs;* b. 28 Dec. 1958, Seoul; m. Lim Jung-mi; ed Seoul Nat. Univ., Harvard Univ., USA; career diplomat since 1980s, served at Perm. Mission to UN during South Korea's term as a non-perm. mem. of Security Council 1996–97, held two posts at Embassy in Washington, DC, served in Taipei late 1990s, Deputy Chief of Mission and Political Minister, Embassy in Beijing, has held various positions in Foreign Ministry dealing with a wide range of issues related with USA, China, Japan and North Korea, seconded to Office of Pres. twice, Special Rep. for Korean Peninsula Peace and Security Affairs, Ministry of Foreign Affairs –2013, Amb. to UK 2013–15, First Vice-Minister of Foreign Affairs 2015–; Visiting Research Scholar, Univ. of Tokyo 2008–09; Hon. KCVO 2011. *Leisure interests:* visiting museums, opera. *Address:* Ministry of Foreign Affairs and Trade, 37 Sejong-no, Seoul, 110-787, Republic of Korea (office). *Telephone:* (2) 2100-2114 (office). *Fax:* (2) 2100-7999 (office). *E-mail:* web@mofat.go.kr (office). *Website:* www.mofat.go.kr (office).

LIMA, Adriana Francesca; Brazilian fashion model and actress; b. 12 June 1981, Salvador, Bahia; m. Marko Jarić 2009; two d.; finished first in Ford's Supermodel of Brazil model search 1995, finished second in Ford's Supermodel of the World contest 1996; moved to New York City and signed with Elite Model Management 1999; best known for work with Victoria's Secret; was the face of Telecom Italia Mobile (mobile phone carrier) 2005; appeared at Givenchy fashion show 2009; carries out charitable work with orphanage, Caminhos da Luz (Ways of Light), Salvador, Bahia. *Film:* first acting role in The Follow (short film in BMW's series The Hire) 2001. *Television includes:* Pista Dupla (series) 1996, hosted What Is Sexy? programme for E! Entertainment Network 2008, appeared as guest playing herself in series How I Met Your Mother 2007, appeared on US TV series Ugly Betty playing herself 2008, appeared on Var mısın? Yok musun? (Turkish version of Deal or No Deal) 2009, Access Hollywood (series) 2009, Today (series) 2009–12, The Victoria's Secret Fashion Show (film) 2010, 2011, Super Bowl's Greatest Commercials 2012 (film) 2012, Late Night with Jimmy Fallon (series) 2012. *Address:* c/o The Society Model Management Inc., 156 5th Avenue, Suite #800, New York, NY 10010, USA (office). *Telephone:* (212) 377-5025 (office). *Fax:* (212) 377-5024 (office). *E-mail:* info@thesocietymanagement.com (office). *Website:* www.thesocietymanagement.com (office); adrianalima.com.

LIMA, Cássio Casseb, BE; Brazilian banking executive; b. 8 Aug. 1955; m.; two c.; ed Univ. of São Paulo; began career with Leading and Credit Dept, Bank of Boston 1976–79; Account Officer, Chief Financial Officer then Commercial Officer NW Region, Banco Francês & Brasileiro (Credit Lyonnaise) 1979–88; Chief Financial Officer then Exec. Vice-Pres. Banco Mantrust SRL 1988–92; Coordinator Industrial Restructuring Vila Romana Group 1992–93; Vice-Pres. Finance (Treas.) Citibank 1993–97; Pres. Credicard SA 1997–99; apptd Head Industrial Strategy Vichuna Textil, Fibra Dupont, Fibrasil, Companhia Siderúrgica Nacional, Vale do Rio Doce, Maxitel, Banco Fibra 1999; Pres. Banco do Brasil 2003–05; CEO Cia. Brasileira de Distribuição (Grupo Pão de Açúcar) 2006–07; mem. Bd Nat. Assn Open Market Insts. (ANDIMA), Brazilian Banking Science Inst. (IBCB) 1993–97; mem. Bd of Dirs Vicunha, Banco Fibra, Solpart 1999, Brasilprev –2005, Aliança do Brasil –2005, Localiza SA –2006, Localiza Rent SA –2006, Sadia SA 2008–; Ind. Dir, Marisa Lojas SA 2008–, mem. Fiscal Council; Man. Inst. Reciclar; mem. Superior Econ. Council, Fed. of Industry for São Paulo (FIESP) 2006–. *Address:* Marisa Lojas SA, Rua James Holland, nº 422, 01138-909 São Paulo, Brazil. *Telephone:* (11) 2109-3121. *Fax:* (11) 3392-4276. *E-mail:* info@marisa.com.br. *Website:* www.marisa.com.br.

LIMA DA VEIGA, Maria de Fátima; Cabo Verde diplomatist; b. 22 June 1957, São Vicente; m.; two c.; ed Univ. of Aix-ex-Provence, France, post-univ. training in devt and diplomacy at German Foundation in Berlin, training in Praia by Foreign Affairs Ministry in cooperation with the UN Inst. for Training and Research and Rio Branco Inst. of Brazil; joined Ministry of Foreign Affairs 1980, subsequently adviser, Chief of Staff, Office of Minister for Foreign Affairs 1995–99, Amb. to Cuba 1999–2001, Sec. of State for Foreign Affairs 2001–02, Minister of Foreign Affairs, Co-operation and Communities 2002–04, Amb. and Perm. Rep. to UN, New York 2004–07, Amb. to USA (also accred to Canada and Mexico) 2007–14; fmr Vice-Chair. and Acting Chair. Alliance of Small Island Developing States (OASIS), New York; fmr mem. Nat. Comm. Interstate Cttee for Drought Control in the Sahel, Nat. Comm. of La Francophonie, Network of Women Ministers and Parliamentarians; Medalla de la Amistad (Cuba); Gran Cruz de la Orden del Mérito Civil (Spain). *Address:* Ministry of Foreign Affairs, Palácio das Comunidades, Achada de Santo António, CP 60, Praia, Santiago, Cabo Verde (office). *Telephone:* (260) 7853 (office). *Fax:* (261) 9270 (office). *E-mail:* info@mirex.gov.cv (office). *Website:* www.mirex.gov.cv (office).

LIMONOV, Eduard; Russian/French writer, poet and politician; b. (Eduard Venyaminovich Savenko), 22 Feb. 1943, Dzerzhinsk, Gorkii (now Nizhnii Novgorod) Oblast; m. 1st Yelena Limonova Shchapova 1971 (divorced); m. 2nd Natalya Medvedeva (divorced); m. 6th Yekaterina Volkova 2006; one s. one d.; first wrote poetry at age of 15; in Kharkov 1965–67, moved to Moscow in 1967, worked as a tailor; left USSR 1974; settled in New York, USA 1975; moved to Paris, France 1982; participant in Russian nationalist movt 1990–; returned to Russia 1991; Chair. Nat. Radical Party 1992–93, then Chair. Nat. Bolshevik Party (banned political party) –2010, leader Other Russia party 2010–; arrested on terrorism and conspiracy charges 2001, sentenced by Saratov Oblast Court to four years' imprisonment for illegal acquisition and possession of arms April 2003, released June 2003; f. Russia without Putin movt Jan. 2004. *Publications include:* verse and prose in Kontinent, Ekho, Kovcheg, Apollon –1977 (in trans. in England, USA, Austria and Switzerland); over 40 books including It's Me – Eddie (novel) 1979, Russian (Russkoye) (verse) 1979, Diary of a Failure 1982, Teenager Savenko: Memoir of a Russian Punk 1983, The Young Scoundrel (memoir) 1986, The Death of Contemporary Heroes 1993, The Murder of the Sentry 1993, Selected Works (three vols) 1999, The eXile: Sex, Drugs and Libel in the New Russia (with Mark Ames and Matt Taibbi) 2000, My Political Biography; articles in Russian Communist and nationalist newspapers 1989–. *Website:* drugoros.ru.

LIN, Cho-Liang, BMus; American violinist and academic; *Professor of Violin, Shepherd School of Music, Rice University;* b. 29 Jan. 1960, Taiwan; s. of Kuo-Jing Lin and Kuo-Ling Yu; m. Deborah Lin; ed Juilliard School, Sydney Conservatoire, Australia; soloist with leading orchestras including London Symphony Orchestra, Philharmonia, Concertgebouw, Orchestre de Paris, Chicago Symphony Orchestra, Philadelphia Orchestra and Boston Symphony Orchestra; played Tchaikovsky's Concerto at London Proms 1999; Founder and Dir Taipei Int. Music Festival; Music Dir La Jolla Music Society's SummerFest 2001–; Artistic Dir Hong Kong Int. Chamber Music Festival, Nat. Taiwan Symphony Orchestra's Youth Music Summer Camp; mem. Faculty, Juilliard School 1991–; also Prof. of Violin, Shepherd School of Music, Rice Univ.; Gramophone Record Award 1989, Musical American's Instrumentalist of the Year 2000. *Recordings include:* standard violin concerti from Mozart to Stravinsky, chamber music from Brahms to Ravel and contemporary music from Chen Yi to Christopher Rouse. *Leisure interests:* tennis, wine. *Address:* Opus 3 Artists, 470 Park Avenue South, 9th Floor North, New York, NY 10016, USA (office); Shepherd School of Music, 2201 Alice Pratt Brown Hall, Rice University, Houston, TX 77005, USA (office). *Telephone:* (713) 348-3818 (office). *E-mail:* cllin@rice.edu (office). *Website:* music.rice.edu (office); cholianglin.com.

LIN, Chuan, PhD; Taiwanese economist and politician; b. 13 Dec. 1951, Kaohsiung; m.; two d.; ed Fu Jen Catholic Univ., Nat. Chengchi Univ., Univ. of Illinois, USA; Assoc. Research Fellow, Chung Hua Inst. for Econ. Research 1994–89; Assoc. Prof., Dept of Public Finance, Nat. Chengchi Univ. 1989–90, Prof. 1990–95, 1998–2000; Dir Bureau of Finance, Taipei City Govt 1995–98; Dir-Gen. Directorate-Gen. of Budget, Accounting and Statistics 2000–02; Minister of Finance 2002–06; CEO New Frontier Foundation (think-tank) –2016; Premier (head of Exec. Yuan) 2016–17; Instructor (part-time), Dept of Econs, National Taiwan Univ.

LIN, Dan; Chinese badminton player; b. 14 Oct. 1983, Longyan, Fujian; m. Xie Xingfang 2010; one s.; ed Huaqiao Univ.; began playing badminton at age five; took part in winning Chinese nat. team, Asian Junior Championships 2000; began professional career 2001; mem. Chinese nat. badminton team 2001–; has won all major titles in world badminton (Olympic Games, World Championships, World Cup, Thomas Cup, Sudirman Cup, All England Open, Asian Games, Asia Championships); highest world ranking No. 1 (Feb. 2004); Gold Medals (men's singles): Olympic Games, Beijing 2008, London 2012, World Championships, Madrid 2006, Kuala Lumpur 2007, Hyderabad 2009, World Cup, Yiyang 2005, 2006, Asian Games, Doha 2006, Guangzhou 2010, Incheon 2014, Asian Championships, New Delhi 2010, Chengdu 2011; winner Men's Singles, All England Open Badminton Championship 2012, Men's Singles German Open 2004–05, 2007, 2011–12, 2016, Yonex Open Japan Superseries 2015, Swiss Open Champion 2017, New Zealand Open 2018, Malaysia Open 2019; Laureus China Sportsman of the Year 2011. *Publication:* Until the End of the World 2012. *Website:* www.cba.org.cn.

LIN, David Yung-lo, BCom, MSFS; Taiwanese diplomatist and government official; b. March 1950; ed Nat. Chengchi Univ., Taipei, Georgetown Univ., USA; Sec., Embassy in South Africa 1980–87, Chief of Section, Dept of African Affairs and Personnel Dept, Ministry of Foreign Affairs (MFA) 1987–92, Deputy Dir Gen., Dept of European Affairs 1992–95, Dir Gen., Taipei Econ. and Cultural Office (TECO), Houston, Tex., USA 1995–97, Amb. to Grenada and Saint Vincent 1997–2001, Dir Gen., Dept of European Affairs, MFA 2001–03, Rep., Taipei Econ. and Trade Office, Indonesia 2003–07, Dir Gen., Dept of Int. Orgs, MFA 2007–08, Vice-Minister of Foreign Affairs 2008–10, Rep., Taipei Rep. Office in EU and

Belgium 2010–12, Minister of Foreign Affairs 2012–16. *Address:* c/o Ministry of Foreign Affairs, 2 Kaitakeland Blvd, Taipei 10048, Taiwan (office).

LIN, Hsin-i, BSc; Taiwanese politician and business executive; b. 2 Dec. 1946; m.; three c.; ed Taiwan Prov. Cheng Kung Univ., Oklahoma City Univ., USA; engineer, China Motor Corpn, later Deputy Man. Eng Div. 1972–76, Deputy Man. Marketing Div. 1976–79, Man. Yangmei Plant 1980–82, Vice-Pres. 1982–87, Exec. Vice-Pres. 1987–90, Pres. 1991–96, Vice-Chair. 1997–2000; Chair. Sino Diamond Motors Ltd 1993–2000, Automotive Research and Testing Centre 1996–2000, Newa Insurance Co. Ltd 1999–2000; Minister of Econ. Affairs 2000–02; Vice-Premier and Chair. Council of Econ. Planning and Devt 2002–04 (resgnd); Chair. Industrial Tech. Research Inst. 2004–08; Sr Presidential Adviser 2005; fmr Man. Dir Nan Ya Plastics Corpn; Ind. Dir, E.Sun Commercial Bank Ltd 2008–, E.Sun Financial Holdings Co. Ltd, Sinyi Realty Inc., Xin-I Property; Dir, Acer Inc. 2011–, Yulon Motor Co. Ltd, China Motor Corpn; Chair. Formosa Ha Tinh Steel Corpn, Guang Yuan Investment Co. Ltd. *Address:* Acer Inc., 7F-5, 369 Fuxing North Road, Songshan District, Taipei 105, Taiwan (office). *Telephone:* (2) 2719-5000 (office). *E-mail:* stock.affairs@acer.com (office). *Website:* www.acer-group.com (office).

LIN, Join-sane, LLD; Taiwanese politician; *Chairman, Foundation for the Development of the Chinese Nation;* b. 17 Dec. 1944; ed Nat. Chengchi Univ.; Assoc. Specialist, later Specialist, Ministry of the Interior 1970–77; Section Chief, later Sr Specialist and Sr Exec. Officer, Dept of Land, Taipei City Govt 1977–83; Deputy Dir, later Dir, Dept of Land, Kaohsiung City Govt 1983–90, Sec.-Gen., Kaohsiung City Govt 1990–94, Deputy Mayor, Kaohsiung City 1995–98; Admin. Deputy Minister, later Political Deputy Minister, Ministry of the Interior 1998–2009; Sec.-Gen., Exec. Yuan (Cabinet) 2009–12; Sec.-Gen. Kuomintang (KMT) (Nationalist Party of China) Feb.–Sept. 2012; Chair. Straits Exchange Foundation 2012–16, Foundation for the Development of the Chinese Nation 2016–.

LIN, Justin Yifu, MBA, MA, PhD; Chinese (b. Taiwanese) economist and international organization official; *Honorary Dean and Professor, National School of Development, Peking University;* b. (Lin Zhengyi), 15 Oct. 1952, Yilan Co., Taiwan; m. Yunying Chen; one s. one d.; ed Nat. Chengchi Univ., Taipei (defence scholarship), Peking Univ., People's Repub. of China, Univ. of Chicago, USA; returned to Army of Repub. of China (ROC) following his MBA 1978, achieved rank of Capt., swam from Jinmen to mainland China 16 May 1979; Research Asst, Dept of Econs, Univ. of Chicago 1984–86; Postdoctoral Fellow, Econ. Growth Center, Yale Univ., USA 1986–87; Assoc. Prof. of Econs, Peking Univ., Beijing 1987–93, Prof. of Econs 1993, Founding Dir China Centre for Econ. Research (now Nat. School of Devt) 2005–, Hon. Dean and Prof. 2012–, Founding Dir Center for New Structural Econs 2015–; Deputy Dir Inst. of Devt Research, Research Center for Rural Devt, State Council 1987–89; fmr Prof. of Econs, Hong Kong Univ. of Science and Tech.; Chief Economist and Sr Vice-Pres., Devt Econs, World Bank Group, Washington, DC (first developing country citizen to hold post) 2008–12; served as a Deputy of China's People's Congress and Vice-Chair. All-China Fed. of Industry and Commerce; has served on several nat. and int. cttees, leading groups and councils on devt policy, tech. and environment, including UN Millennium Task Force on Hunger, Eminent Persons Group of Asian Devt Bank, Nat. Cttee on US-China Relations, Hong Kong-US Business Council, Working Group on the Future of the OECD, Reinventing Bretton Woods Cttee; Vice-Chair. All-China Fed. of Industry and Commerce; mem. editorial bds of several int. academic econs journals; Fellow, Acad. of Sciences for the Developing World 2005; Corresp. Fellow, British Acad. 2010; Nat. Labour Medal, State Council of China (highest civil honour conferred by Chinese government) 2005, Labour Medal, Beijing Municipality Govt 2005; Commdr, Ordre nat. du Mérite de la République du Sénégal 2014; Dr hc (Université D'Auvergne) 2004, (Univ. of Nottingham) 2009, (City Univ. of Hong Kong) 2009, (Fordham Univ.) 2009, (LSE) 2012, (Hong Kong Univ. of Science and Tech.) 2012, (Univ. of British Columbia) 2014, (Katholieke Universiteit Leuven) 2014, (Open Univ. of Hong Kong) 2015; Sun Yefang Prize (highest honour for economists in China) 1993, 2001, Policy Article Prize, Centre for Int. Food and Agricultural Policy, Univ. of Minnesota 1993, Sir John Crawford Award, Australian Agricultural and Resource Econs Soc. 1997, Cai Yuanpei Medal (highest honour awarded by Peking Univ.) 2006, Marshall Lecturer, Univ. of Cambridge, UK 2007, Professional Achievement Award, Univ. of Chicago 2011, First Prize and Bao Steel Award for Distinguished Teacher in China 2005, Marshall Lecturer, Univ. of Cambridge 2007, Simon Kuznets Lecturer, Yale Univ. 2011, Bernard Fain Lectruer, Brown Univ. 2011, Leonard White Lecturer, Univ. of Chicago 2012, David Finch Lecturer, Univ. of Melbourne 2013, Arndt Memorial Lecturer, ANU 2013. *Publications:* 25 books, including Institution, Technology and Agricultural Development in China, II (First Prize, Outstanding Research Publication, Ministry of Education), The China Miracle: Development Strategy and Economic Reform; Fiscal Decentralization and Economic Growth in China (First Prize, Eighth Philosophy and Social Science Award of Peking Univ.) 2002; Economic Development and Transition: Thought, Strategy, and Viability; Viability, Economic Development and Transition: Theories and Empirical Testing (Wu Yuzhang Prize, First Prize, Outstanding Research Publication, Ministry of Education 2006, First Prize, Outstanding Research Publication, 10th Philosophy and Social Science Award of Peking University and Zhang Peigang Prize 2006) 2007; The Quest for Prosperity: How Developing Economies Can Take Off 2012, Against the Consensus 2013, New Structural Economics: A Framework for Rethinking Development and Policy (Pushan Prize, International Economics Association 2012, National Publication Book Award 2014), Going Beyond Aid: Development Cooperation for Structural Transformation 2016, Beating the Odds: Jump-Starting Developing Countries 2017; more than 110 articles in refereed int. journals and collected vols on history, devt and transition. *Address:* National School of Development, Peking University, Beijing 100871, People's Republic of China (office). *Telephone:* (10) 62751475 (office). *Fax:* (10) 62751474 (office). *E-mail:* justinlin@nsd.pku.edu.cn (office). *Website:* en.nsd.edu.cn/article .asp?articleid=6948 (office).

LIN, Liyun; Chinese state official; b. 1933, Taizhong, Taiwan; ed Minatogawa High School, Kyoga Prefecture, Japan, Beijing Univ.; teacher, Chinese School, Kobe, Japan 1952; Bureau Chief, CCP Cen. Cttee Int. Dept 1953–78; joined CCP 1963; council mem. Sino-Japanese Friendship Asscn 1973–; mem. Standing Cttee 4th NPC 1975–78, Standing Cttee 5th NPC 1978–83, Standing Cttee 6th NPC 1983–88 (mem. Presidium 6th NPC 1986–88, mem. Credentials Cttee NPC 1984–88)), Standing Cttee 7th NPC 1988–93, Standing Cttee 8th NPC 1993–98; Deputy for Taiwan to 5th NPC 1978, 6th NPC 1983; Deputy Sec. CCP Langfang Prefectural Cttee, Hebei Prov. 1981; Vice-Chair. Exec. Cttee All-China Women's Fed. 1978 (mem. Secr. and Leading Party Group 1978); Vice-Chair. All-China Sports Asscn 1979; Pres. All-China Fed. of Taiwan Compatriots 1981–; mem. Overseas Chinese Affairs Cttee NPC 1988–98 (now Vice-Chair.); mem. Working Group for Unification of the Motherland 1984–; Vice-Pres. China Int. Cultural Exchange Centre 1984–; adviser Asscn for the Promotion of the Peaceful Reunification of China 1988–; Vice-Pres. All China Fed. of Returned Overseas Chinese 1994–; adviser, Asscn for Relations Across the Taiwan Straits; mem. 10th CCP Cen. Cttee 1972–77, 11th CCP Cen. Cttee 1977–82, 12th CCP Cen. Cttee 1982–87, 13th CCP Cen. Cttee 1987–92, 14th CCP Cen. Cttee 1992–97, 15th CCP Cen. Cttee 1997–2002.

LIN, Maw-Wen; Taiwanese business executive; ed Shanghai Jiao Tong Univ.; Vice-Pres. CPC Corpn –2010, Pres. 2010–12; Dir Taiwan Stock Exchange Corpn.

LIN, Maya, MArch, PhD; American artist and architect; b. 5 Oct. 1959, Athens, Ohio; d. of Prof. Henry H. Lin and Prof. Julia Lin (née Chang); m. Daniel Wolf; two c.; ed Yale Univ.; architectural designer, Pers Forbes & Assocs, New York 1986–87; pvt. practice, New York 1987–; mem. Batey & Mack, San Francisco 1983, Fumihiko Maki Assoc., Tokyo 1985; f. Maya Lin Studio, New York 1986; William A. Bernoudy Resident in Architecture, American Acad., Rome, Italy 1998–99; artwork rep. by Pace Wildenstein; mem. Bd Nat. Resources Defense Council; subject of Acad. Award-winning documentary Maya Lin: A Strong Clear Vision 1995; mem. Bd of Trustees, Natural Resources Defense Council; mem. American Acad. of Arts and Letters, American Acad. of Arts and Sciences; fmr mem. Yale Corpn, Energy Foundation; William A. Bernoudy Resident in Architecture Fellowship, American Acad., Rome; inducted into National Women's Hall of Fame 2005; Dr hc (Yale), (Harvard), (Williams Coll.), (Smith Coll.); American Acad. of Arts and Letters Award in Architecture, Finn Juhl Architecture Award 2003; Presidential Design Award, Artist Award from National Endowment for the Arts; AIA Honor Award, Finn Juhl Prize, Nat. Medal of Arts 2009, Presidential Medal of Freedom 2016. *Major projects include:* Vietnam Veterans' Memorial, Washington, DC 1982; Peace Chapel, Juniata Coll., Pennsylvania; Langston Hughes Library, Clinton, Tennessee; Civil Rights Memorial, Montgomery, AL 1989; The Women's Table, Yale Univ., CT 1993; Groundswell, Wexner Center for the Arts, Columbus, OH 1993, Museum for African Art, New York 1993, Eclipsed Time, Pennsylvania Station, New York 1994, The Wave Field, Univ. of Michigan Coll. of Eng, Ann Arbor 1995, Langston Hughes Library, Clinton, Tenn. 1999, Federal Courthouse, Manhattan, New York, Ecliptic, Grand Rapids, Mich. 2000, the character of a hill, under glass, American Express Financial Advisors, Minneapolis, Minn., Aveda HQ, Manhattan 2002, Where the Land Meets the Sea 2005, Confluence Project 2006, Maya Lin: Systematic Landscapes 2006, Storm King Wavefield 2008, What is Missing? 2009. *Publications:* Maya Lin: Public/Private 1994, Boundaries 2000, Maya Lin: Systematic Landscape Catalogue 2006. *Address:* 52 East 78th Street, New York, NY 10075-1810, USA. *Website:* www .mayalin.com.

LIN, See-Yan, MA, MPA, PhD, CStat, FIB, FRSS, FIBM; Malaysian banker and financial consultant; *Chairman and CEO, Lin & Associates;* b. 3 Nov. 1939, Ipoh; ed Univ. of Malaya in Singapore, Harvard Univ., USA; Tutor in Econs, Univ. of Malaya 1961–63, Harvard Univ. 1970–72, 1976–77; Statistician, Dept of Statistics 1961–63; Econ. Adviser, Minister of Finance 1966–69; Dir Malaysian Rubber Exchange and Licensing Bd 1974–85; mem. Council on Malaysian Invisible Trade 1981–85, Econ. Panel of the Prime Minister 1982–87, Capital Issues Cttee 1985–86; Chief Economist, Bank Negara Malaysia (Cen. Bank of Malaysia) 1973–77, Econ. Adviser 1977–80, Deputy Gov. 1980–94; Chair., Pres. and CEO Pacific Bank Group 1994–98; Chair. Credit Guarantee Corpn Malaysia Berhad, Malaysian Insurance Inst.; Deputy Chair. Industrial Bank of Malaysia Berhad (Bank Industri); Dir Malaysia Export Credit Insurance Berhad, Govt Officers Housing Corpn, Seacen Research and Training Centre, Malaysian Wildlife Conservation Foundation; mem. Malaysia Program Advisory Council, US-ASIAN Centre for Tech. Exchange, Commonwealth Group of Experts on the Debt Crisis 1984, IMF Working Party on Statistical Discrepancy in World Currency Imbalances 1985–87, IMF Cttee of Balance of Payments Compilers 1987; Chair. and CEO Lin & Associates; Pres. Malaysian Econ. Asscn; mem. Nat. Econ. Action Council Working Group, Asian Financial Regulatory Shadow Committee, USA; Econ. Adviser, Associated Chinese Chambers of Commerce and Industry of Malaysia; Trustee Malaysia Univ. for Science and Tech.; Chair. (non-Exec.) Krisassets Holdings Berhad 2004– (also Dir), Kris Components BHD 2004–, Igb Reit Management Sdn Bhd 2012–; Dir (non-Exec.) Jobstreet Corp. Bhd 2004–15, Top Glove Corpn Bhd 2010–15, Sunway Berhad 2015–; Dir Fraser & Neave Holdings Bhd 1996–2013, Great Eastern Holdings 1999–2012, Genting Malaysia Berhad 2002–10, mem. Bd Dirs Monash Univ. (Sunway Campus) Malaysia; Gov. Asian Inst. of Man., Manila; mem. bds several publicly listed and pvt. cos in Malaysia, Singapore and Indonesia; Chair. Emer. Harvard Grad. School Alumni Asscn Council, Harvard Univ., Regional Dir for Asia, Harvard Alumni Asscn, mem. Visiting Cttee for Asian Studies; Pres. Harvard Club of Malaysia; Pro-Chancellor Universiti Sains Malaysia –2011; Adjunct Prof. of Econs, Universiti Utara Malaysia; Trustee Tun Ismail Ali Foundation (PNB), Harvard Club of Malaysia Foundation, Malaysian Econ. Asscn Foundation, MAKNA (Nat. Cancer Council); Eisenhower Fellow 1986, mem. Eisenhower Fellowships' International Advisory Council, Phila, USA; Distinguished Fellow, Inst. of Strategic and Int. Studies; Fellow, Inst. of Statisticians, Malaysian Inst. of Man., Malaysian Econ. Asscn; Hon. PhD (Universiti Utara Malaysia); Hon. Fellow, Malaysian Insurance Inst. *Publications:* numerous articles in academic, banking and business journals. *Address:* Lin and Associates, B-610, First Floor, Jalan Air Putih, Pusat Komersial Air Putih, 25300 Kuantan, Pahang, Malaysia (office).

LIN, Sheng-chung, PhD; Taiwanese politician and business executive; ed Nat. Taiwan Univ., Univ. of Arizona; fmr Taiwan Rep. at WTO, Zurich, Switzerland; also worked at Taiwanese office in Boston and at Taipei City Govt; fmr Chief Exec. Dir, Chung-Hua Inst. for Econ. Research; fmr Vice-Minister of Econs; Chair. CPC Corpn, Taiwan (state-run oil co.) 2012–16. *Address:* c/o CPC Corporation, 3 Songren Road, Sinyi Chiu, Taipei 11010, Taiwan.

LIN, Simon; Taiwanese computer industry executive; *Chairman and CEO, Wistron Corporation;* ed Nat. Chiao Tung Univ.; fmr Pres. Acer Inc.; currently Chair. and CEO Wistron Corpn, Chair. and CSO Wistron NeWeb Corpn, Wistron Information and Technology Services Corpn, Chair. AOpen Inc.; mem. Bd of Dirs Gamania Digital Entertainment Co. Ltd, TICP Neo Solar Power Corpn; Outstanding Man. of the Repub. of China Award, Govt of Taiwan 1989, named Outstanding Alumnus, Nat. Chiao Tung Univ. 1996. *Address:* Wistron Corporation, 20 Park Avenue II, Hsinchu Science Park, Hsinchu 308, Taiwan. *Telephone:* (3) 6667799. *E-mail:* info@wistron.com (office). *Website:* www.wistron.com (office).

LIN, Zhaohua, BA; Chinese theatre director; *Senior Director, Beijing People's Art Theatre;* b. 1 July 1936, Tianjin; s. of Lin Baogui and Zhang Shuzhen; m. He Binzhu 1964; one s. one d.; ed Cen. Acad. of Drama, Beijing; Vice-Pres. and Dir Beijing People's Art Theatre 1984–, Chair. Art Cttee 1984–; Artistic Dir Lin Zhaohua Drama Studio 1990–; mem. Standing Cttee, China Theatre Asscn 1984–; Chair. Peking Univ. Theatre Research Inst. 2005–; Lin Zhaohua Theatre Arts Festival 2010–. *Theatre productions include:* The Red Heart 1978, Just Opinion 1980, Absolute Signal 1982, Bus Stop 1983, Festivities of Marriage and Funeral 1984, Wildman 1985, Schweyk in the Second World War 1986, Uncle Doggie's Nirvana 1986, Peace Lake 1988, Filed...Filed 1989, Peking Man 1989, Chinese Orphan 1990, Hamlet 1990, Countryside Anecdote 1990, A Report from Hu-Tuo River 1991, Birdman, Romulus the Great 1992, Ruan Lingyu 1994, Faust 1994, Chessman 1995, Fisherman 1997, The Three Sisters Waiting For Godot (adapted from Chekhov's Three Sisters and Beckett's Waiting for Godot) 1998, The Teahouse 1999, Boundless Love 2000, A Parody 2000, Richard III 2001, Cai Wen Ji (Anhui Opera) 2002, Zhao's Orphan 2003, Toilet 2004, The Cherry Orchard 2004, The Dream Play 2005, Bird People, Antiques, Tea House, Frameless Wind and Moon, Beijingers, The Master Builder 2006, Coriolanus 2007, The Assassin 2008, The Lobbyist 2010, Ivanov 2011, The Book of Mountains and Sea 2012. *Beijing Opera productions include:* Mountain Flower 1991, Turandot, The Humpbacked Prime Minister Liu 2000, The Minister Liu Luoguo I 2000, The Minister Liu Luoguo II 2001, The Minister Liu Luoguo III 2002, The Bravest and Cleverest Soldier Sun Wu 2002, Farewell My Concubine 2003, The Very Best Zhangxie 2003. *Videos:* The Ape and His Six Roars – An Anthology of Lin Zhaohua Drama 2003, The Anthology of Lin Zhaohua Drama Studio (eight dramas and interview with Lin Zhaohua) 2004. *Publications:* Stage Art of Absolute Signal (ed.) 1985, Stage Art of Marriage and Funeral 1997, Lin Zhaohua on Theatrical Directing 1992. *Leisure interests:* Chinese yoga, swimming, music, playing the erhu. *Address:* Beijing People's Art Theatre, 22 Wangfujing Street, Beijing (office); 3-7-503, East Block, Ditan Beili, Heping li, Beijing, People's Republic of China (home). *Telephone:* (10) 65254346 (office); (10) 84043339 (home). *Fax:* (10) 62753253 (office). *E-mail:* linzhaohua1936@hotmail.com (home); lzh@linzhaohua .org (office). *Website:* www.linzhaohua.org (home).

LIN, Zuoming, PhD; Chinese aviation industry executive; *Chairman, Aviation Industry Corporation of China (AVIC);* b. 1957, Zhangzhou City, Fujian Prov.; ed Nanjing Aeronautical Inst., Beijing Univ. of Aeronautics and Astronautics; began career 1976, successively, mem. staff and Deputy Dir Human Resource Div., Deputy Dir of Eng and Tech. Div., Deputy Dir Gen. Tech. Research Inst., Deputy Chief Engineer, Deputy Gen. Man., Gen. Man. and Chair. Chengdu Engine Co. Ltd; Gen. Man. Shenyang Liming Aero-Engine (Group) Corpn Ltd 1998–2001; Vice-Pres. and mem. Leading Party Group of CCP, Aviation Industry Corpn of China (AVIC) 2001–06, Sec. 2006–, Pres. and CEO Aviation Industry Corpn of China 2008–12, Chair. 2012–; Chair. AVIC I Commercial Aircraft Co. Ltd, AVIC I Investment Co. Ltd, AVIC I Consultant Co. Ltd, AviChina 2008–; Vice-Chair. Commercial Aircraft Corpn of China Ltd; Alt. mem. 16th CCP Cen. Cttee 2002–07, 17th CCP Cen. Cttee 2007–12, mem. 18th CCP Cen. Cttee 2012–17. *Address:* Aviation Industry Corporation of China, PO Box 2399, AVIC Plaza, 128 Jianguo Road, Chaoyang District, Beijing 100022, People's Republic of China (office). *Telephone:* (10) 58356511 (office). *Fax:* (10) 58356516 (office). *E-mail:* overseascrm@avic.com (office). *Website:* www.avic.com.cn (office); www.avic2.com (office).

LINCOLN, Blanche Meyers Lambert, BA; American consultant and fmr politician; *Principal, Lincoln Policy Group;* b. 30 Sept. 1960, Helena, Ark.; d. of Jordan Bennett Lambert and Martha Lambert (née Kelly); m. Dr Steve Lincoln; two s. (twins); ed Central High School, Helena, Randolph-Macon Woman's Coll., Univ. of Arkansas; served as staff asst to US Rep. Bill Alexander (Democrat from Ark.'s 1st Congressional Dist) 1982–84; mem. US House of Reps 1993–97; Senator from Ark. 1999–2011, mem. Senate Finance Cttee 2001–11, also mem. Agric., Nutrition and Forestry Cttee (Chair. 2009–11), Special Cttee on Aging, Select Cttee on Ethics, Social Security Task Force, Rural Health Caucus, Chair. of Rural Outreach for Senate Democratic Caucus; currently Founder and Prin., Lincoln Policy Group (consultancy); mem. Bd of Dirs Entergy Corpn 2011–; Democrat. *Address:* Lincoln Policy Group, 1110 Vermont Avenue, NW, Suite 1000, Washington, DC 20005, USA (office). *Telephone:* (202) 530-4869 (office). *E-mail:* michaelasinclair@lincolnpolicygroup.com (office). *Website:* www .lincolnpolicygroup.com (office).

LINDAHL, George, III, BS; American petroleum industry executive; ed Univ. of Alabama, Tulane Univ., Advanced Man. Program at Harvard Business School; began career as geologist and Man. Amoco Production Co.; Exec. Vice-Pres., Dir and Partner Walker Energy Partners of Houston –1987; joined Union Pacific Resources (UPR) Group, Inc. 1987, Pres. and COO 1996–99, Chair., Pres. and CEO 1999–2000; Dir Anadarko Petroleum Corpn, Vice-Chair. 2000–01; Man. Partner, Sandefer Capital Partners 2001–07; Dir, EV Energy Partners LP 2006–; mem. or fmr mem. Advisory Bd NAPE (fmrly North American Prospect Expo), True North Energy Corpn; mem. Pres.'s Council, Univ. of Ala; mem. Visiting Cttee, Petroleum and Geosystems Engineering Dept, Univ. of Texas at Austin; mem. Texas Hall of Fame Foundation; fmr Pres. Fort Worth Petroleum Club; mem. All-American Wildcatters 1999. *Address:* EV Energy Partners LP, 1001 Fannin Street, Houston, TX 77002 (office); c/o Sandefer Capital Partners, 515 Congress Avenue, Suite 1875, Austin, TX 78701-3518, USA. *Telephone:* (713) 651-1144 (office); (512) 495-9925. *Fax:* (713) 651-1260 (office). *E-mail:* info@evenergypartners.com (office). *Website:* www.evenergypartners.com (office).

LINDAHL, Tomas Robert, MD, FRS, FMedSci; Swedish medical scientist; *Emeritus Group Leader, Francis Crick Institute;* b. 28 Jan. 1938, Stockholm; ed Karolinska Inst., Stockholm; postdoctoral research at Princeton Univ. and Rockefeller Univ., USA; joined Imperial Cancer Research Fund (now Cancer Research UK) 1981, Deputy Dir of Research, Cancer Research UK, London Research Inst., later Researcher, Mutagenesis Lab., Dir Clare Hall Laboratories, Francis Crick Inst. 1986–2005, Dir Emer. 2005–09, now Emer. Group Leader; INSERM (French Nat. Inst. for Health and Medical Research) Prix Etranger 2007, Royal Medal, Royal Soc. 2007, Copley Medal, Royal Soc. 2010, Nobel Prize in Chem. (co-recipient with Paul Modrich and Aziz Sancar) 2015. *Address:* Francis Crick Institute, 1 Brill Place, London NW1 1BF, England (office). *E-mail:* tomas .lindahl@cancer.org.uk (office). *Website:* www.cancerresearchuk.org/science (office).

LINDBÆK, Jannik, Jr; Norwegian banker and petroleum industry executive; b. 23 March 1939, s. of Jannik Lindbæk, Sr and Ellen Margrethe Lund; m. Grete Schjøttelvig 1963; ed Norwegian School of Econs and Business Admin, Bergen, Univ. of Kansas (Fulbright Scholar), USA; began career at Vesta 1962, promoted to Vice-Chief Exec.; Pres. and CEO Storebrand Group (Storebrand-Norden from 1982) 1975–85 (resgnd); Pres. and CEO Nordiska Investeringsbanken (Nordic Investment Bank), Helsinki 1986–94; Exec. Vice-Pres. Int. Finance Corpn (World Bank Group), Washington, DC, USA 1994–99; Chair. Den norske Bank 1999–2003; Chair. Statoil ASA 2003–07 (until merger with Norsk Hydro ASA to form StatoilHydro ASA, name changed again to Statoil ASA 2009); Sr Vice-Pres. of Corp. Communications, Aker Solutions ASA 2007–10; Ind. Dir (non-exec.) Valiant Petroleum Plc 2011–, Ithaca Energy Inc. 2013–; Advisor, Voxtra Foundation, Investment Arm; Chair. Bergen Int. Festival, Transparency Int. Norge, Plan International Norge, Gearbulk; fmr Chair. Gaz de France Norge, Saga Petroleum, Den Norske Bank; mem. Bd of Dirs Kristian Gerhard Jebsen Skipsrederi (shipping co.). *Address:* Ithaca Energy (UK) Ltd, 8 Rubislaw Terrace, Aberdeen, AB10 1XE, Scotland (office); Ithaca Petroleum Norge AS, Trelastgata 3, 0191 Oslo, Norway (office). *Telephone:* (1224) 638582 (Aberdeen) (office); 20-00-30-50 (Oslo) (office). *Fax:* (1224) 635795 (Aberdeen) (office); 22-00-30-51 (Oslo) (office). *E-mail:* info@ ithacaenergy.com (office). *Website:* www.ithacaenergy.com (office).

LINDBECK, Assar, PhD; Swedish economist and academic; *Professor of International Economics, Institute for International Economic Studies, University of Stockholm;* b. 26 Jan. 1930, Umeå; s. of Carl Lindbeck and Eugenia Lindbeck (née Sundelin); m. Dorothy Nordlund 1953; one s. one d.; ed Univs of Uppsala and Stockholm; Asst Prof., Univ. of Michigan, USA 1958; with Swedish Treasury 1953–56; Asst Prof. of Econs, Univ. of Stockholm 1962–63, Prof., Stockholm School of Econs 1964–71, Prof. of Int. Econs 1971–, Dir Inst. of Int. Econs 1971–94; Visiting Prof., Columbia Univ., USA 1968–69, Univ. of California, Berkeley 1969, ANU 1970, Yale Univ. 1976, Stanford Univ. 1977; Research Fellow, Research Inst. of Industrial Econs, Stockholm, CESifo, Munich, Kiel Inst. of World Econs, Kiel; Consultant, World Bank 1986–87; mem. Nobel Prize Cttee on Econs 1969–94 (Chair. 1980–94). *Music:* Sonata for Clarinet and piano: Fantasi i folkton 1948, performed in City Hall, Luleå 1948. *Publications:* A Study in Monetary Analysis 1963, The Political Economy of the New Left 1971, Economics of the Agricultural Sector 1973, Swedish Economic Policy 1975, The Insider-Outsider Theory (with Dennis Snower) 1988, Unemployment and Macroeconomics 1993, The Swedish Experiment 1997. *Leisure interest:* painting. *Address:* Institute for International Economic Studies, Stockholm University, 106 91 Stockholm (office); Karlavägen 78, 114 59 Stockholm, Sweden (home). *Telephone:* (8) 16-30-78 (office); (8) 21-23-37 (home). *Fax:* (8) 16-29-46 (office); (8) 21-23-37 (home). *E-mail:* assar@iies.su.se (office). *Website:* people.su.se/~alind.

LINDBLOM, Seppo Olavi, LicPolSc; Finnish bank executive and politician; b. 9 Aug. 1935, Helsinki; s. of Olavi Lindblom and Aura Lindblom (née Sammal); m. Anneli Johanson 1958; four d.; ed Univ. of Helsinki; Man. br. office, Finnish Workers' Savings Bank 1958–60; Economist, Bank of Finland 1960–68; Sec. to Prime Minister 1968–70; Head, Labour Inst. for Econ. Research 1970–72; Minister in Ministry of Trade and Industry 1972; Head, Dept of Nat. Econ. Ministry of Finance 1973–74; Nat. Conciliator for Incomes Policy 1973–74; Dir Bank of Finland 1974–82, mem. Bd of Man. 1982–87; Minister of Trade and Industry 1983–87; Chair. and Chief Exec. Postipankki Ltd 1988–96. *Publications:* (in Finnish): SAK's Remuneration Policy is the Main Principle of the Second World War 1959, Investment Theory of Investment Surveys Theoretical Basis 1966, Political Negotiation Process Problems in the Industrialized Market Economy Countries 1967, Left Qualm 1970, Finland and the European Economy 1992, People's Home Beyond – The Welfare State Accountability Review 2002, Policy on the Run 2007, Manu in the Ointment 2009, Wobbly Republic 2013. *Leisure interests:* music, chess.

LINDE DE CASTRO, Luis María, BEcons; Spanish economist and central banker; b. 15 May 1945, Madrid; ed Univ. Complutense de Madrid; Head, Directorate-Gen. for Foreign Trade, Ministry of Trade 1969–71, Head, Balance of Payments Office 1971–73; Head, Spanish Trade Office, Moscow 1974–78; Technical Sec.-Gen., Ministry of Economy and Trade 1978–82; Deputy Dir-Gen., Foreign Dept, Banco de España (central bank) 1983–87, Dir-Gen. of Int. Affairs 1987–2000, Dir, Country Risk Dept 2001–04, Adviser to Assoc. Directorate-Gen. of Int. Affairs 2009–11, mem. Council 2012, Gov. Banco de España 2012–18; Dir Official Credit Inst. 1989–92; Exec. Dir for Spain, IDB 2005–08; Econs Coordinator, Revista de Libros (magazine) of Fundación Caja Madrid 1998–2012; Founding mem. and sponsor, Fundación Transición Española (Spanish Transition Foundation) 2007–. *Publications include:* Don Pedro Girón, Duque de Osuna: La hegemonía española en Europa a comienzos del siglo XVII 2005.

LINDEGAARD, Jørgen, MEng; Danish business executive; *Vice-Chairman, Zealand Pharma A/S;* b. 7 Oct. 1948; ed Tech. Univ. of Denmark; worked as exec. in telecommunications eng; with Philips Telekommunikation (subsidiary of the Dutch Philips conglomerate) –1977; Pres. Fyns Telefon A/S 1977–91, Københavns Telefon A/S 1991–95; fmr mem. Exec. Bd Tele Danmark; Chair. Sonofon Holding A/S 1996–2004; Pres. and CEO GN Store Nord 1997–2001; Pres. and CEO SAS Group 2001–06; CEO ISS A/S (world's largest facilities man. co.) 2006–10, Dir 2010–11; Vice-Chair. and mem. Remuneration and Nomination Cttee, Zealand Pharma A/S 2011–; mem. Bd of Dirs Cimber Sterling Group A/S 2011–; Fellow, Norwegian Acad. of Technological Sciences. *Address:* Zealand Pharma A/S, Smedeland 36, 2600 Glostrup Copenhagen, Denmark (office). *Telephone:* 88-77-

36-00 (office). *Fax:* 88-77-38-98 (office). *E-mail:* info@zealandpharma.com (office). *Website:* www.zealandpharma.com (office).

LINDEMAN, Fredrik Otto, DPhil; Norwegian academic; *Professor Emeritus of Indo-European Linguistics, University of Oslo;* b. 3 March 1936, Oslo; s. of Carl Fredrik Lindeman and Agnes Augusta Lindeman; m. Bente Konow Taranger 1960; one s. one d.; ed Univ. of Oslo, Sorbonne, Paris; Prof. of Indo-European Linguistics, Univ. of Copenhagen 1970–76; Prof. of Indo-European Linguistics, Univ. of Oslo 1976–2005, now Emer.; Visiting Prof., Dublin Inst. for Advanced Studies, School of Celtic Studies 1982–83; Dals Prize for Outstanding Achievement, Univ. of Oslo 1997. *Publications include:* Les Origines Indo-Européennes de la 'Verschärfung' Germanique 1964, Einführung in die Laryngaltheorie 1970, The Triple Representation of Schwa in Greek and some related problems of Indo-European Phonology 1982, Studies in Comparative Indo-European Linguistics 1996, Introduction to the 'Laryngeal Theory' 1997, Våre Arveord Etymologisk Ordbok (with Harald Bjorvand) 2000 (enlarged and revised edn) 2007. *Leisure interest:* music. *Address:* Abbedikollen 13, 0280 Oslo 2 (home); Institutt for lingvistiske og nordiske studier, Universitetet i Oslo, PB 1102 Blindern, 0317 Oslo, Norway (office). *Telephone:* 22-50-92-78 (home). *E-mail:* bente.lindeman@c2i.net (home).

LINDENSTRAUSS, Elon, BSc, MSc, PhD; Israeli mathematician and academic; *Professor, Einstein Institute of Mathematics, Hebrew University of Jerusalem;* b. 1 Aug. 1970, Jerusalem; s. of Joram Lindenstrauss and Naomi Lindenstrauss; ed Hebrew Univ. Secondary School, Hebrew Univ. of Jerusalem; fmr mem. Inst. for Advanced Study, Princeton, NJ, USA; fmr Szego Asst Prof., Stanford Univ., USA; Long Term Prize Fellow, Clay Math. Inst. 2003–05; Prof., Princeton Univ., USA 2004–; Prof., Einstein Inst. of Math., Hebrew Univ. of Jerusalem 2009–; apptd Visiting Miller Prof., Univ. of California, Berkeley 2014; represented Israel at Int. Math. Olympiad and won a bronze medal 1988, Israel Defense Prize, Israel Defense Forces, Salem Prize (co-recipient) 2003, European Math. Soc. Prize 2004, Michael Bruno Memorial Award 2008, Erdős Prize 2009, Fermat Prize 2009, Fields Medal (co-recipient) 2010. *Publications:* more than 40 papers in professional journals on ergodic theory and its applications to number theory. *Address:* Einstein Institute of Mathematics, Edmond J. Safra Campus, Givat Ram, Manchester House 103, Hebrew University of Jerusalem, Jerusalem 91904, Israel (office). *Telephone:* 2-6586834 (office). *Fax:* 2-6537266 (office). *E-mail:* elon@math.huji.ac.il (office). *Website:* www.math.princeton.edu/~elonl.

LINDERBERG, Jan Erik, FD; Danish chemist and academic; *Professor Emeritus of Theoretical Chemistry, Aarhus University;* b. 27 Oct. 1934, Karlskoga, Sweden; s. of David Linderberg and Sara Bäckström; m. Gunnel Björstam 1957; two s.; ed Uppsala Univ.; Docent, Uppsala Univ. 1964–68; Prof. of Theoretical Chem., Aarhus Univ., Denmark 1968–, now Prof. Emer.; Adjunct Prof. of Chem., Univ. Florida, Gainesville and Univ. of Utah, USA; mem. Royal Danish Soc. of Sciences and Letters, Int. Acad. of Quantum Molecular Science, Royal Soc. of Science (Uppsala). *Publications:* Role of Correlation in Electronic Systems 1964, Propagators in Quantum Chemistry (co-author), Quantum Science (with others) 1976; more than 100 papers in refereed journals. *Leisure interest:* orienteering. *Address:* Aarhus University, Department of Chemistry, Langelandsgade 140, 8000 Aarhus C (office); Janus la Cours gade 20, 8000 Aarhus C, Denmark (home). *Telephone:* 87-15-53-45 (office); 86-12-02-41 (home). *Fax:* 86-19-61-99 (office). *E-mail:* jan@chem.au.dk (office). *Website:* pure.au.dk/portal/da/persons/id(aff9b4bb-2f80-47d3-a4a5-59efc1370df0).html (office).

LINDNER, Christian; German business executive and politician; *Chairman, Free Democratic Party;* b. 7 Jan. 1979, Wuppertal; s. of Wolfgang Lindner; m. Dagmar Rosenfeld-Lindner; ed Rheinischen Friedrich-Wilhelms-Univ.; freelance business consultant 1997–99, 2002–04; Partner, Knüppel Lindner Communications GmbH 1999–2002; co-f. Moomax GmbH (internet co.) 2000; mem. North Rhine-Westphalia Landtag (State Parl.) 2000–09, 2012–; mem. Bundestag (Parl.) 2009–12; mem. Freie Demokratische Partei (FDP, Free Democratic Party) 1995–, mem. Exec. Bd, FDP North Rhine-Westphalia 1998–, Sec.-Gen. 2004–10, mem. Exec. Bd, FDP (Fed. level) 2007–, Sec.-Gen. 2009–11, Chair. 2013–. *Address:* Freie Demokratische Partei, Reinhardtstr. 14, 10117 Berlin, Germany (office). *Telephone:* (30) 28495820 (office). *Fax:* (30) 28495822 (office). *E-mail:* fdp-point@fdp.de (office). *Website:* www.fdp-bundespartei.de (office); www.christian-lindner.de.

LINDNER, Walter Johannes; German diplomatist; *State Secretary, Federal Foreign Office;* b. 25 Nov. 1956, Munich; m. Laura Sustersic; one d.; ed Ludwig Maximilian Univ. of Munich; non-mil. nat. service followed by music studies in Munich, Graz and Boston 1976–80; undergraduate studies 1980-86; practical legal training in Munich and work as translator for Spanish and Portuguese agencies 1986–88; joined Diplomatic Service 1988, Attaché, Legal Gen., Fed. Foreign Office, Bonn 1988–90, Desk Officer for Press and Political Affairs, Embassy in Ankara 1990–92, Deputy Head of Mission, Embassy in Managua, Nicaragua 1992–95, Desk Officer/Spokesperson, Press Division, Fed. Foreign Office 1995–98, Counsellor, Perm. Mission to UN, New York 1998–2001, Deputy Head of Div., Task Force for Human Rights, Fed. Foreign Office, Berlin 2001–02, Fed. Foreign Office Spokesperson and Spokesman for Foreign Minister Joschka Fischer, Berlin 2002–06, Amb. to Kenya (also accred to Somalia, Burundi and the Seychelles) 2006–09, Crisis Man. Commr, Fed. Foreign Office 2009–10, Dir for Sub-Saharan Africa and the Sahel 2010–12, Amb. to Venezuela 2012–14, Special Rep. of Fed. Govt for the Ebola Crisis 2014–15, Amb. to South Africa (also accred to Lesotho and Swaziland) 2015–17, State Sec., Fed. Foreign Office 2017–. *Leisure interests:* music. *Address:* Federal Foreign Office, Auswärtiges Amt, 11013 Berlin, Germany (office). *Telephone:* (30) 18170 (office). *Fax:* (30) 18173402 (office). *E-mail:* poststelle@auswaertiges-amt.de (office). *Website:* www.auswaertiges-amt.de (office).

LINDSAY, Most Rev. and Hon. Orland Ugham, OD, OJ, BD, DD; Jamaican/Antiguan ecclesiastic (retd); b. 24 March 1928, Jamaica; s. of Hubert Lindsay and Ida Lindsay; m. Olga Daphne Wright 1959; three s.; ed Mayfield Govt School, Southfield, Jamaica, Culham Coll. Oxford, England, St Peter's Theological Coll., Jamaica, Montréal Diocesan Theological Coll. at McGill Univ., Canada; served in RAF 1944–49; teacher Franklin Town Govt School 1949–52; Asst Master Kingston Coll. 1952–53, 1958–63; ordained Deacon, Jamaica 1956; Asst Curate St Peter's Vere Cure 1956–57; ordained Priest 1957; Chaplain Kingston Coll. 1958–63; Asst Curate in charge of Manchioneal Cure 1960–63; Sec. Jamaica Diocesan Synod 1962–70; Chaplain Jamaica Defence Force 1963–67; Prin. Church Teachers' Coll., Mandeville, Jamaica 1967–70; Bishop of Antigua, latterly of NE Caribbean and Aruba 1970–98; Archbishop of the West Indies 1986–98; Order of Distinction (Antigua) 1996, Order of Jamaica 1997; Hon. DD (Berkeley Divinity School, Yale Univ.) 1978, (St Paul's Coll., S Va) 1998; Hon. STD (Diocesan Theological Coll., Montreal) 1997. *Leisure interests:* swimming, listening to music, reading, photography. *Address:* Crosbies, PO Box 3456, Antigua, West Indies (home). *Telephone:* 560-1724 (home). *Fax:* 462-2090 (home). *E-mail:* orland@candw.ag (home).

LINDSAY, Robert; British actor; b. (Robert Lindsay Stevenson), 13 Dec. 1949, Ilkeston, Derbyshire; s. of Norman Stevenson and Joyce Stevenson; m. 1st Cheryl Hall (divorced); m. 2nd Rosemarie Ford; two s.; one d. by actress Diana Weston; ed Royal Acad. of Dramatic Art; began career as dialect coach with repertory company in Exeter, later joined regional theatre group, then moved on to West End and to television roles; first became household name in UK as Wolfie in sitcom Citizen Smith 1977; stage career commenced at Manchester Royal Exchange; Patron of New Arts Course, NCN (fmrly Clarendon Coll.) – Robert Lindsay Theatre; Hon. Fellow, Univ. of Manchester; Freedom of the Borough of Erewash 2016; Dr hc (Nottingham, Derby). *Theatre includes:* Hamlet, Royal Exchange, Manchester (then tour of UK) 1983, Bill Snibson in Me and My Girl, Adelphi Theatre, London, Broadway and LA (Laurence Olivier Award for Outstanding Performance by an Actor in a Musical, Tony Award for Best Actor in a Musical, Drama Desk Best Actor Award, Outer Critics' Best Actor Award, Fred Astaire Award for Best Dancer on Broadway) 1985–87, Henry II in Anouilh's Beckett, West End, London (Variety Club Best Theatre Actor) 1991, Cyrano de Bergerac, Theatre Royal, London 1992, Oliver! (Laurence Olivier Award for Best Actor), Beaux Stratagem/Philoctetes, Royal Exchange, Manchester (Manchester Evening News Award), Richard III, tour by RSC then at Stratford-upon-Avon then at Savoy Theatre, London 1998, The Changeling, Riverside Studios, London, The Cherry Orchard, The Roundhouse, London, Godspell, Wyndhams Theatre, How I Got That Story, Hampstead Theatre, Octavius in Julius Caesar, Royal Exchange, Manchester, Leaping Ginger, Royal Exchange, Manchester, Lower Depths, The Roundhouse, London, Power, Royal Nat. Theatre, London, D'Artagnan in Three Musketeers, Royal Exchange, Manchester, Trelawny of The Wells, Old Vic, London, The Entertainer, Old Vic, London. *Films include:* That'll Be the Day 1973, Three for All 1974, Adventures of a Taxi Driver 1976, Bert Rigby, You're a Fool 1989, Strike It Rich (aka Loser Takes All; Money Talks) 1990, Goodbye My Love 1996, Fierce Creatures 1997, Remember Me? 1997, The Canterbury Tales (voice) 1998, Divorcing Jack 1998, Wimbledon 2004; training videos: The Dreaded Appraisal, The Helping Hand, I Wasn't Prepared For That, Meeting Breaks – Bosses From Hell, From 'No' To 'Yes', Sell It To Me!. *Radio includes:* Puttin' On The Style (BBC Radio 2), Peer Gynt (BBC Radio 4) (Sony Award), Oedipus (Radio 4), Frankenstein (BBC World Service), Nineteen Ninety Four, (Radio 4) Nobody Will Laugh (Milan R3), as Iago with Robert Stephens as Othello (Prince's Trust CD); audiobooks: Pinocchio, Fortysomething, Falling, Tom Jones, Virgin And The Gypsy, Sherlock Holmes, Mary Shelley's 'Frankenstein', Can't You Sleep Little Bear?. *Television includes:* Get Some In! (series) 1975–77, Wolfie in Citizen Smith (series) 1977, Twelfth Night 1980, Seconds Out (series) 1981, All's Well That Ends Well 1981, A Midsummer Night's Dream 1981, Cymbeline 1982, Give us a Break (series) 1983, Edmund in King Lear (Granada) 1984, Much Ado About Nothing 1984, Confessional 1989, Nightingales (series) 1990, Michael in GBH (mini-series; Channel 4) (BAFTA Award for Best Actor, Royal Television Soc. Award for Best Actor) 1991, Genghis Cohn 1993, The Wimbledon Poisoner (mini-series) 1994, Jake's Progress (mini-series) 1995, The Office 1996, Brazen Hussies 1996, In Your Dreams (series; voice) 1998, Capt. Pellew in Hornblower: The Even Chance 1998, Hornblower: The Examination for Lieutenant 1998, Hornblower: The Duchess and the Devil 1999, Hornblower: The Frogs and the Lobsters 1999, Oliver Twist (mini-series) 1999, My Family (series) 2000–11, Hawk (mini-series) 2001, The Heat Is On (series) 2001, Hornblower: Mutiny 2001, Hornblower: Retribution 2001, Don't Eat the Neighbours (series) 2001, Hornblower: Duty 2003, Hornblower: Loyalty 2003, Friends and Crocodiles 2005, A Very Social Secretary 2005, Jericho (series) 2005, Friends and Crocodiles 2006, Gideon's Daughter 2006, The Trial of Tony Blair 2007, Spy (series) 2011–12, Atlantis (series) 2013–15, Bull (series) 2015, Galavant (series) 2016. *Address:* c/o Christian Hamilton, Hamilton Hodell Ltd, 5th Floor, 66–68 Margaret Street, London, W1W 8SR, England (office). *Telephone:* (20) 7636-1221 (office). *Fax:* (20) 7636-1226 (office). *E-mail:* lorraine@hamiltonhodell.co.uk (office). *Website:* www.hamiltonhodell.co.uk (office); www.robertlindsay.net.

LINDSEY, Lawrence B., AB, MA, PhD; American economist and fmr government official; *President and CEO, Lindsey Group;* b. 18 July 1954, Peekskill, NY; s. of Merritt Lindsey and Helen Hissam; m. Susan Lindsey 1982; three c.; ed Bowdoin Coll., Harvard Univ.; on staff of Pres. Reagan's Council of Econ. Advisers; Special Asst for Policy Devt to Pres. George H.W. Bush; fmr Prof. of Econs, Harvard Univ.; mem. Bd of Govs Fed. Reserve System 1991–97; Man. Dir Econ. Strategies Inc. 1997–2001; Econ. Adviser to Pres. 2001–02; Dir Nat. Econ. Council 2001–02; Pres. and CEO Lindsey Group 2003–; Chair. Bd Neighborhood Reinvestment Corpn 1993–97; Resident Scholar and holder Arthur C. Burns Chair., American Enterprise Inst. 1997–2001, now Visiting Scholar; mem. Bd of Dirs Aozora Bank, Ltd 2004–; CitiCorp Wriston Fellow for Econ. Research, Manhattan Inst. 1988; Hon. JuD (Bowdoin Coll.) 1993; Outstanding Doctoral Dissertation Award, Nat. Tax Asscn 1985, Distinguished Public Service Award, Boston Bar Asscn 1994. *Publications:* The Growth Experiment: How the New Tax Policy is Transforming the US Economy 1990, Econ. Puppermasters: Lessons From the Halls of Power 1998, What A President Should Know: An Insider's View on How to Succeed in the Oval Office 2008, The Growth Experiment Revisited: Why Lower, Simpler Taxes Really Are America's Best Hope for Recovery 2013, Conspiracies of the Ruling Class: How to Break Their Grip Forever 2016; numerous articles in professional publs. *Address:* The Lindsey Group, 11320 Random Hills Road, Suite 650, Fairfax, VA 22030, USA (office). *Telephone:* (703) 621-1170 (office). *Fax:* (703) 218-3956 (office). *E-mail:* info@thelindseygroup.com (office). *Website:* www.thelindseygroup.com (office).

LINDSTEN, Jan Eric, PhD, MD; Swedish geneticist and academic; *Professor Emeritus of Medical Genetics, Karolinska Institute;* b. 23 Jan. 1935, Stockholm; s. of Carl-Eric Lindsten and Lisa M. Hallberg; m. Marianne E. Östling 1960; two s. one d.; ed Uppsala Univ., Karolinska Inst., Stockholm; Prof. of Human Genetics,

Århus 1968–70; Prof. of Medical Genetics, Karolinska Inst. 1969–2000, Prof. Emer. 2000–, Head, Dept of Clinical Genetics 1970–90; Chief Medical Officer, Karolinska Hosp. 1987–90, Man. Dir 1990–94; Man. Dir Nat. Univ. Hosp. Copenhagen 1994–96; Dean of Medical Faculty, Karolinska Inst. 1996–98; Sec., Nobel Ass. and Medical Nobel Cttee, Karolinska Inst. 1979–90; Pres. Royal Swedish Acad. of Sciences 2003–06. *Publications include:* more than 300 publs in the field of medical genetics, especially clinical genetics. *Address:* Council of Cultural Affairs, Karolinska Institutet, 17177 Stockholm, Sweden (office). *Telephone:* (8) 52-48-39-29 (office). *Fax:* (8) 31-67-74 (office). *E-mail:* jan.lindsten@ki.se (office).

LINEHAN, Fergus; Irish theatre director; *Director and Chief Executive, Edinburgh International Festival;* began career in Dublin, producing numerous shows and then directing Dublin Theatre Festival; Chief Exec. and Artistic Dir Sydney Festival 2004–09; Head of Music, Sydney Opera House 2010–12; Dir (part-time), Edinburgh Int. Festival 2013–14, Dir and Chief Exec. 2014–; Festival Dir Vivid LIVE. *Address:* Edinburgh International Festival, The Hub, Castlehill, Edinburgh, EH1 2NE, Scotland (office). *Telephone:* (131) 473-2099 (office). *E-mail:* marketing@eif.co.uk (office). *Website:* www.eif.co.uk (office).

LINEKER, Gary Winston, OBE; British television presenter, journalist and fmr professional footballer; *Presenter, Match of the Day, British Broadcasting Corporation;* b. 30 Nov. 1960, Leicester, Leics., England; s. of Barry Lineker and Margaret Patricia Morris Lineker (née Abbs); m. 1st Michelle Denise Cockayne 1986 (divorced 2006); four s.; m. 2nd Danielle Bux 2009; ed City of Leicester Boys' Grammar School; striker; youth player, Leicester City 1976–78, sr team 1978–85 (won Football League Second Div. 1979/80); played for Everton 1985–86 (won FA Charity Shield 1985), Barcelona 1986–89 (won Copa del Rey 1988, European Cup Winners' Cup 1989), Tottenham Hotspur 1989–92 (won FA Cup 1991, shared FA Charity Shield 1991), Nagoya Grampus Eight, Japan 1992–94 (retd); mem. England team 1984–92, scoring 48 goals in 80 appearances (won Rous Cup 1986, 1988, 1989, 1991, England Challenge Cup 1991), rep. England World Cup, Mexico 1986, World Cup, Italy 1990, Capt. of England 1990–92; never booked in 16-year career; began working as football pundit on BBC Radio 5 Live and on BBC TV's Match of the Day, went on to present show, has also worked on other programmes; began working for NBC Sports Network as part of their Premier League coverage 2013–; contributes to US version of Match of the Day; columnist for The Mail on Sunday –2010; led consortium that invested in Leicester City FC, saving it from bankruptcy 2002, now Hon. Vice-Pres.; has featured in several TV commercials for Walkers Crisps 1994–; Freeman of City of Leicester 1995; Hon. MA (Leicester) 1992, (Loughborough) 1992; English league top scorer 1985, 1986, 1990, only English player to win Golden Boot Award (for scoring most goals in a World Cup) 1986, Football Writers' Asscn Player of the Year 1986, 1992, Professional Footballers' Asscn Players' Player of the Year 1986, Runner-up, European Footballer of the Year 1986, FIFA Fair Play Award 1990, Third Place, FIFA World Player of the Year 1991, inducted into English Football Hall of Fame 2003, TRIC Awards Sports Presenter/Reporter of the Year 2003, 2006, 2007, 2009, 2010, 2011, north stand of Leicester City Football Club's Walkers Stadium named in his honour, voted by Leicester City fans as club's greatest ever player in poll by Sky Sports 2009. *Television includes:* presenter, Match of the Day, BBC TV 1995–, team capt. They Think It's All Over (quiz show) 1995–2003, presenter for BBC's golf coverage, co-presenter BBC Sports Personality of the Year, presented six-part BBC series called Golden Boots 1998, co-hosted, with wife Danielle, series of BBC's Northern Exposure 2009, main presenter of London Olympics for the BBC 2012, Who Do You Think You Are? 2013, presenter of FIFA World Cup in Brazil for BBC 2014, Commonwealth Games, Glasgow for BBC 2014. *Leisure interests:* cricket, golf, snooker. *Address:* c/o Diana van Bunnens, Jon Holmes Media Ltd, 3 Wine Office Court, London, EC4A 3BY, England (office). *Telephone:* (1582) 469233 (office). *E-mail:* diana@jonholmesmedia.com (office). *Website:* www.jonholmesmedia.com (office).

LINFIELD, Edmund Harold, MA, PhD; British electrical engineer and academic; *Professor of Terahertz Electronics and Director of Research, University of Leeds;* ed Univ. of Cambridge; currently Prof. of Terahertz Electronics and Dir of Research, Univ. of Leeds; Dream Fellowship, Eng and Physical Sciences Research Council 2011–13; Faraday Medal, Inst. of Physics (co-recipient) 2014. *Publications:* numerous papers in professional journals on the devt of terahertz science and tech. and the use of biological processes for nanotechnology. *Address:* Room 458, School of Electronic and Electrical Engineering, University of Leeds, Leeds, LS2 9JT, England (office). *Telephone:* (113) 343-2015 (office). *Fax:* (113) 343-7265 (office). *E-mail:* e.h.linfield@leeds.ac.uk (office). *Website:* www.engineering.leeds.ac.uk (office).

LING, Jihua, MBA; Chinese party official; b. 1956, Shanxi Prov.; m. Gu Liping; one s. (deceased); ed China Youth Univ. for Political Sciences, Beijing, Hunan Univ.; joined CCP 1976; Cadre, Propaganda Dept, Communist Youth League of China (CYLC) Cen. Cttee 1979–83, Deputy Dir 1985–88, Dir 1994–95; Dir Gen. Office, CYLC Cen. Cttee Secr. 1988–90, Deputy Dir-Gen. 1990–94; Ed.-in-Chief, Youth League Journal 1990–94; Deputy Dir CCP Cen. Cttee Investigation and Research Office 1997–99, Dir 1999–2003, Dir, CCP Cen. Cttee Research Office 1998–2007, Deputy Dir, CCP Cen. Cttee Org. Dept 2000–12, Dir CCP Cen. Cttee Gen. Office 2007–12; Alt. mem. 16th CCP Cen. Cttee 2002–07, mem. 17th CCP Cen. Cttee 2007–12, also mem. 17th CCP Cen. Cttee Politburo Secr. 2007–12, mem. 18th CCP Cen. Cttee 2012–, also Head, CCP Cen. Cttee United Front Work Dept 2012–14; Vice-Chair. 12th CPPCC Nat. Cttee 2012–14; expelled from CCP July 2015; put on trial, charged with taking bribes, illegally obtaining State secrets and abusing power, People's Court of Tianjin May 2016; sentenced to life imprisonment July 2016.

LING, Tun Liong Sik, MB, BS; Malaysian university administrator and fmr politician; *Chairman, University Council, Tunku Abdul Rahman University;* b. 18 Sept. 1943, Kuala Kangsar, Perak; m. Datin Ee Nah Ong 1968; two c.; ed King Edward VII School, Royal Mil. Coll. and Univ. of Singapore; Parl. Sec., Ministry of Local Govt and Fed. Territory 1976–77; Deputy Minister of Information 1978–82, of Finance 1982–84, of Educ. 1985–86; Minister of Transport 1986–2003; Deputy Pres. Malaysian Chinese Asscn 1985–87, Pres. 1987–2003; currently Chair. Univ. Council, Tunku Abdul Rahman Univ.; Grand Commdr, Order of Loyalty to the Crown of Malaysia 2004. *Leisure interests:* reading, golf. *Address:* Office of the Chairman, Tunku Abdul Rahman University, 13, Jalan 13/6, 46200, Petaling Jaya, Selangor, Malaysia (office). *Telephone:* (3) 79582628 (office). *Fax:* (3) 79561923 (office). *E-mail:* info@utar.edu.my (office). *Website:* www.utar.edu.my (office).

LING, Sergei Stepanovich; Belarusian politician, diplomatist and agronomist; *Chairman, State Committee on Economics and Planning;* b. 7 May 1937; m.; three c.; ed Belarus Agricultural Acad., Higher CPSU School, CPSU Cen. Cttee; agronomist sovkhoz, Lesnoye Kopylsk Dist, Chief Agronomist Sovkhoz, Krynitsa Kopylsk Dist, Chief Agronomist, Deputy Dir Lyuban Production Co., Chief Soligorsk Production Agric. Admin; Deputy Chair. then Chair. Slutsk Dist Exec. Cttee, Sec. Smolevichi Dist CPSU Cttee 1960–72; Chief Agric. Div., Sec. Minsk Regional Belarus CP Cttee 1972–82; First Deputy Chair. then Chair. Exec. Cttee Minsk Regional Soviet 1982–86; Chair. Belarus State Cttee on Prices, Deputy Chair. State Planning Cttee 1986–90; Head Agric. Div., Sec. Cen. Cttee Belarus CP 1990–91; Deputy Chair. Belarus Council of Ministers; Chair. State Cttee on Econs and Planning 1991–; Deputy Prime Minister of Belarus 1994–96, Acting Prime Minister 1996–97, Prime Minister 1997–2000; Amb. and Perm. Rep. to UN 2000–02. *Address:* Ministry of Economy, 220050 Minsk, vul. Bersona 14, Belarus. *Telephone:* (17) 200-53-16. *Fax:* (17) 200-37-77. *E-mail:* minec@economy.gov.by. *Website:* www.economy.gov.by.

LING, Wen, PhD; Chinese academic and business executive; *Vice-Chairman and General Manager, Shenhua Group Corporation Limited;* b. Feb. 1963; ed Shanghai Jiao Tong Univ., Harbin Inst. of Tech.; conducted postdoctoral research at Shanghai Jiao Tong Univ., Dept of Automation 1992–94; fmr Lecturer, Harbin Inst. of Tech.; fmr Deputy Dir of Industry and Communication, Loan Dept, Industrial and Commercial Bank of China (ICBC) and Asst Gov. Div. Bank of Shenyang; fmr Deputy Gen. Man. ICBC (Asia) and Deputy Gen. Man. Int. Business Dept, ICBC; mem. CCP Leading Group and Pres. and CEO Shenhua Group Corpn Ltd, Exec. Dir and Chair. China Shenhua, Exec. Dir, Pres. and CEO China Shenhua Energy Co. Ltd 2006–14, Deputy Gen. Man. Shenhua Group Corpn 2010–14, Vice-Chair. and Gen. Man. 2014–; Prof., School of Man., Harbin Inst. of Tech.; mem. Inst. of Financial Accountants of the UK; Fellow-Professional Accountant, Nat. Inst. of Accountants of Australia. *Address:* Shenhua Group Corporation Ltd, Guohua Investment Plaza, 3 Dongzhimen South Street, Dongcheng District, Beijing 100007, People's Republic of China (office). *Telephone:* (10) 58133113 (office); (10) 58132001 (office); (10) 58132114 (office). *E-mail:* shjt@shenhuagroup.com.cn (office). *Website:* www.shenhuagroup.com.cn (office).

LINGFIELD, Baron (Life Peer), cr. 2010, of Lingfield in the County of Surrey; **Robert George Alexander Balchin,** Kt; English educationalist; *Chairman, The Chartered Institution for Further Education;* b. 31 July 1942, Dulverton, Somerset; m. Jennifer Kinlay; two s. (one deceased); ed Bec School, Univ. of London, Univ. of Hull; teacher 1964–69; researcher, Inst. of Educ., Univ. of Hull 1969–71; Chair. Grant-Maintained Schools Centre (fmrly Foundation) 1989–99, Centre for Educ. Man. (now Centre for Educ. and Finance Man.) 1995–; Asst Dir-Gen. St John Ambulance 1982–84, Dir-Gen. 1984–90; Founding Chair. Balchin Family Soc. 1993–; Chair. St John Nat. Schools Project 1990–95, ARNI Inst. 2000–, Educ. Comm. 2003–10, Maritime Heritage Foundation 2012–, Cadet Vocational Qualifications Org. 2012–; Chair. The Chartered Inst. for Further Educ. 2014–; Pres. English Schools Orchestra 1997–, League of Mercy 1999–; mem. Court of Univ. of Leeds 1995–2001, Council of Goldsmiths Coll., London 1997–2005 (Deputy Chair. 1999–2005); Pro-Chancellor Brunel Univ. 2006–12; mem. Council Imperial Soc. of Kts Bachelor 1995–, Kt Registrar 1998–2006, Kt Prin. 2006–12, Kt Pres. 2012–; mem. Funding Agency for Schools 1994–97; Deputy Patron Nat. Asscn for Gifted Children 1998–2010; DL of Greater London 2001–; Liveryman, Worshipful Co. of Goldsmiths 1987 (Freeman 1981); Liveryman, Worshipful Soc. of Apothecaries 2015 (Freeman 2013); Hon. Fellow, Coll. of Preceptors 1987 (Fellow 1971), Hon. Fellow, Heraldry Soc. 1987, Hon. FCGI 1997; Hon. Col, Humberside and S Yorks. Army Cadet Force 2004–12; KStJ 1984, Commdr's Cross (Pro Merito Melitensi SMOM) 1987, Grand Cross Order of Eagle of Georgia 2014; Hon. DLitt (Hull) 2006, Hon. EdD (Brunel) 2013. *Publications:* Emergency Aid in Schools 1984, Choosing a State School (co-author) 1989), Emergency Aid at Work (co-author) 1990, Lingfield Report on Professionalism in Further Education (Dept of Business, Innovation and Skills) 2012; numerous articles on education and politics. *Leisure interest:* restoring an ancient house. *Address:* House of Lords, Westminster, London, SW1A 0PW, England (office). *Telephone:* (20) 7219-5353 (office). *Fax:* (20) 7219-5979 (office).

LINGHU, An; Chinese politician; b. Oct. 1946, Pinglu Co., Shanxi Prov.; ed Beijing Eng Inst.; joined CCP 1965; fmr Deputy Dir City Machin-Building Industry Bureau, Dalian City, Liaoning Prov., City Instrument, Meter and Electronics Bureau, Dalian City (later Deputy Gen. Man.); fmr Deputy Sec. CCP Dalian City Cttee; fmr Chair. Dalian Fed. of Trade Unions; fmr Vice-Chair. Comm. for Restructuring the Economy, Dalian City; Exec. Vice-Mayor Dalian City 1988; fmr mem. CCP Standing Cttee, Dalian City Cttee; fmr Dir Gen. Office, People's Govt, Dalian City; fmr Dir Retired Cadres Bureau, Ministry of Labour; Vice-Minister of Labour 1989–93; Deputy Sec. CCP Yunnan Prov. Cttee 1993–97, Sec. 1997–2001; Chair. Yunnan Prov. People's Political Consultative Conf. 1998–2001; apptd Deputy Auditor-Gen. Nat. Audit Office 2001; mem. 15th CCP Cen. Cttee 1997–2002; Del., 14th CCP Nat. Congress 1992–97.

LINGWOOD, James Peter Boyce, MBE; British gallery curator; *Co-Director, Artangel Media Ltd;* b. 28 May 1959; s. of Robert Neville Garrard Lingwood and Patricia Lingwood; m. Jane Hamlyn; one s. two d.; Exhbns Curator, Inst. of Contemporary Arts, London 1986–90; Co-Dir (with Michael Morris) Artangel 1991–, Artangel Media Ltd 2000–; has curated exhbns for numerous nat. and int. arts insts, including Juan Muñoz's Double Bind in Tate Modern's Turbine Hall 2001, Field Trips – Robert Smithson and Bernd and Hilla Becher at Museu Serralves, Porto and Douglas Gordon's exhbn What Have I Done at Hayward Gallery, London 2002, Susan Hiller's exhbn at Baltic, Gateshead 2004; has organized major survey exhbns with Vija Celmins, Juliao Sarmento, Thomas Struth and Thomas Schütte; Trustee, Paul Hamlyn Foundation 2003–, Art Fund 2008–, Cubitt Studios, London; mem. Int. Advisory Bd Museu Serralves, Porto, Atelier Calder, Saché, France, Capc, Bordeaux; adviser, Oslo Biennale 2016. *Publications include:* Juan Muñoz: Double Bind at Tate Modern 2001, Robert Smithson, Bernd and Hilla Becher: Field Trips 2001, Off Limits – 40 Artangel

Projects 2002, Susan Hiller: Recall 2004. *Address:* Artangel, 31 Eyre Street Hill, London, EC1R 5EW, England (office). *Telephone:* (20) 7713-1400 (office). *Fax:* (20) 7713-1401 (office). *E-mail:* info@artangel.org.uk (office). *Website:* www.artangel.org.uk (office).

LINI VANUAROROA, Ham; Ni-Vanuatu politician; *Minister of Climate Change Adaptation, Meteorology, Geo-Hazards, Environment, Energy and Disaster Management;* b. 8 Dec. 1951; m. Ruth Lini; mem. Nat. United Party (NUP), Pres. 1999–, leader 2004, 2013–14, apptd Deputy Leader 2015; MP, Pentecost Constituency 1998–; Deputy Prime Minister 2003–04, also Minister of Home Affairs, of Infrastructure and Public Utilities and of Civil Aviation; Prime Minister of Vanuatu 2004–08; Minister of Public Works and Utilities 2008, Deputy Prime Minister and Minister of Justice and Social Welfare 2008–09, Deputy Prime Minister and Minister of Trade, Industry and Tourism 2010–11, 2011–13, Deputy Prime Minister and Minister of Trade, Commerce and Ni-Vanuatu Business 2014–15, Minister of Climate Change Adaptation, Meteorology, Geo-Hazards, Environment, Energy and Disaster Man. 2016–. *Address:* Ministry of Climate Change Adaptation, Meteorology, Geo-Hazards, Environment, Energy and Disaster Management, Port Vila, Vanuatu.

LJINIĆ, Slavko; Croatian economist and politician; b. 19 Sept. 1949, Grobnik (Čavle); ed Univ. of Rijeka; began career with Avtotehna, Ljubljana 1972; worked in Viktor Lenac naval shipyard, Rijeka 1974–76; Chief Financial Officer, Gradšped 1976–78; Chief Financial Officer, Kvarnertrans 1979; Dir of Financial Accounting Services, Rijeka Oil Refinery 1979–90; Mayor, City of Rijeka 1990–2000; mem. Sabor (Parl.) 1997–2000, 2004–, mem. Tourism Cttee, Maritime Affairs Cttee, Transportation and Communications Cttee, Planning and Building Cttee; Deputy Prime Minister 2000–03, Minister of Finance 2011–14; mem. Social Democratic Party of Croatia (Socijaldemokratska partija Hrvatske) 1990–. *Leisure interest:* skiing. *Address:* c/o Ministry of Finance, 10000 Zagreb, ul. Katančićeva 5, Croatia (office).

LINK, Christoph, DJur; German/Austrian legal scholar and academic; *Professor Emeritus of State, Administration and Church Law, University of Erlangen;* b. 13 June 1933, Dresden; s. of Hellmuth Link and Gerda Link; m. 1st Eva Link 1957; m. 2nd Sibylle Obermayer 1991; two s. one d.; ed Kreuzschule, Dresden and Univs of Marburg, Cologne and Munich; Prof. Vienna 1971–77, Salzburg 1977–79, Hon. Prof. 1979–, Göttingen 1979–86; Prof. of State Admin and Church Law, Univ. of Erlangen 1986, now Prof. Emer.; Dir Hans-Liermann-Inst. für Kirchenrecht 1986–2001; mem. Akad. der Wissenschaften, Göttingen; DTheol hc (Vienna), (Tübingen); Österreichisches Ehrenkreuz für Wissenschaft und Kunst, 1st Klasse 2004. *Publications:* Die Grundlagen der Kirchenverfassung im lutherischen Konfessionalismus des 19ten Jahrhunderts 1966, Herrschaftsordnung und bürgerliche Freiheit 1979, Hugo Grotius als Staatsdenker 1983, Kirchen und privater Rundfunk (with A. Pahlke) 1985, Staat und Kirche in der neueren deutschen Geschichte 2000, Kirchliche Rechtsgeschichte 2009. *Address:* Hans-Liermann-Institut für Kirchenrecht, 91054 Erlangen, Hindenburgstrasse 34 (office); Ruehlstrasse 35, 91054 Erlangen, Germany (home). *Telephone:* (9131) 8522242 (office); (9131) 209335 (home). *Fax:* (9131) 8524064 (office); (9131) 534566 (home). *E-mail:* hli@jura.uni-erlangen.de (office); linkerta@t-online.de (home). *Website:* www.jura.uni-erlangen.de (office).

LINKEVIČIUS, Linas Antanas; Lithuanian politician and diplomatist; *Minister of Foreign Affairs;* b. 6 Jan. 1961, Vilnius, Lithuanian SSR, USSR; m. Danguolė Linkevičienė 1982; two d.; ed Kaunas Polytechnical Inst.; worked in technical insts 1983–92; reviewer, newspaper Tiesa 1992–93; mem. Council of Lietuvos Demokratinė Darbo Partija (Lithuanian Democratic Labour Party) 1991–96; mem. Seimas (Parl.) 1992–96; Chair. Parl. Del. to N Atlantic Ass. 1992–93; Deputy Chair. Parl. Comm. on Foreign Affairs 1992–93; Chair. Lietuvos Leiboristų Jaunimo Unija (Lithuanian Labour Youth Union) 1992–93; Observer, Lithuanian daily 'Tiesa'; Minister of Nat. Defence 1993–96, 2000–04; Amb. and Head of Lithuanian Mission to NATO and WEU 1997–99; Amb. for Special Missions, Ministry of Foreign Affairs 2004–05; Amb. and Perm. Rep. to NATO, Brussels 2005–11; Minister of Foreign Affairs Dec. 2012–; mem. Exec. Bd European Leadership Network for Multilateral Nuclear Disarmament and Non-proliferation; Order of Three Stars, Third Class (Latvia) 2001; Cross of Commdr, Order of the Grand Duke Gediminas 2003; Cross of Commdr, Order of the Cross of Vytis 2004; Order of the Cross of Terra Mariana, Second Class (Estonia) 2005; Order of Honour (Georgia) 2011, Hon. Order of the Republic of Moldova 2014, Grand Cross of Commdr, Order of Vytautas the Great 2015, Order of the North Star (Sweden) 2015. *Address:* Ministry of Foreign Affairs, J. Tumo-Vaižganto g. 2, Vilnius 01511, Lithuania (office). *Telephone:* (5) 236-2444 (office). *Fax:* (5) 231-3090 (office). *E-mail:* urm@urm.lt (office). *Website:* www.urm.lt (office).

LINKLATER, Richard; American film director and screenwriter; b. 30 July 1960, Houston, Tex.; f. Detour Films, Austin, Tex.; Founder and Artistic Dir Austin Film Soc.; Founder's Directing Award, San Francisco Int. Film Festival 2014, Sonny Bono Visionary Award, Palm Springs Int. Film Festival 2015. *Films include:* Slacker 1991, Dazed and Confused 1993, Before Sunrise (Berlin Int. Film Festival Silver Bear for Best Dir 1995) 1995, Suburbia 1997, The Newton Boys 1998, Waking Life 2001, Tape 2001, Live from Shiva's Dance Floor 2003, School of Rock 2003, Before Sunset 2004, Bad News Bears 2005, A Scanner Darkly 2006, Fast Food Nation 2006, Me and Orson Welles 2009, Bernie 2011, Before Midnight 2013, Boyhood (New York Film Critics Award for Best Film 2014, Berlin Int. Film Festival Silver Bear for Best Dir 2014, Fed. of Film Critics (Fipresci) Grand Prix 2014, Best Film, Los Angeles Film Critics Asscn 2014, Best Film, Boston Soc. of Film Critics 2014, New York Film Critics Circle 2014, Best Int. Ind. Film, British Ind. Film Awards 2014, Golden Globe for Best Dir and for Best Motion Picture (Drama) 2015, Best Film and Best Dir, Critics' Choice Movie Awards, Broadcast Film Critics Asscn 2015, Film of the Year and Dir of the Year, London Critics' Circle 2015, BAFTA Award for Best Film and Best Director 2015) 2014, Everybody Wants Some! 2016, Last Flag Flying 2017. *Television includes:* Up to Speed (series) 2012. *Address:* c/o Creative Artists Agency, Inc., 9830 Wilshire Blvd, Beverly Hills, CA 90212-1825, USA (office).

LINNEY, Laura, BFA; American actress; b. 5 Feb. 1964, New York; m. 1st David Adkins 1995 (divorced 2000); m. 2nd Marc Schauer 2009; one s.; ed Northfield Mount Hermon School, Northwestern Univ., Brown Univ., Juilliard School; Theatre World Award 1992, Calloway Award 1994, Best Actress, Toronto Film Critics Asscn 2000, Best Actress, Nat. Soc. Film Critics 2000, Best Actress, NY Film Critics Circle 2000, Best Actress, Boston Soc. Film Critics 2000, Emmy Award, Outstanding Lead Actress 2002, Best Supporting Actress, Nat. Bd of Review 2004, Desert Palm Award for Best Actress, Palm Springs Int. Film Festival 2004, Emmy Award, Best Guest Actress in a Comedy Series 2004, Special Civil Rights Award, Pride Awards 2004, Best Supporting Actress, Broadcast Film Critics Asscn 2004. *Plays include:* The Seagull, Six Degrees of Separation, Sight Unseen, Hedda Gabler, Holiday 1995, Honour 1998. *Films include:* Lorenzo's Oil 1992, Dave 1993, Blind Spot 1993, Searching for Bobby Fischer 1993, A Simple Twist of Fate 1994, Congo 1995, Primal Fear 1996, Absolute Power 1997, The Truman Show 1998, You Can Count on Me 2000, The House of Mirth 2000, Lush 2000, Maze 2000, Running Mates 2000, The Laramie Project 2001, The Mothman Prophecies 2002, The Life of David Gale 2003, Mystic River 2003, Love, Actually 2003, P.S. 2004, Kinsey 2004, The Squid and the Whale 2005, The Exorcism of Emily Rose 2005, Driving Lessons 2006, Jindabyne 2006, The Hottest State 2006, Man of the Year 2006, The Savages 2007, Breach 2007, The Nanny Diaries 2007, The Other Man 2008, The City of Your Final Destination 2009, Sympathy for Delicious 2010, Morning 2010, The Details 2011, Hyde Park on Hudson 2012, The Fifth Estate 2013, Mr Holmes 2015, Genius 2016, Sully 2016, Nocturnal Animals 2016, The Dinner 2017. *Television includes:* Armistead Maupin's Tales of the City 1993, Class of '61 1993, More Tales of the City 1998, Love Letters 1999, Wild Iris 2001, Further Tales of the City 2002, Frasier (series) 2003–04, John Adams (mini-series, HBO) (Golden Globe Award for Best Performance by an Actress in a Mini-Series 2009) 2008, The Big C (series) (Golden Globe Award for Best Performance by an Actress in a TV Series – Comedy or Musical 2011, Emmy Award for Best Actress in a mini-series 2013) 2010–13. *Address:* c/o Toni Howard, ICM, Constellation Boulevard, Los Angeles, CA 90067, USA (office). *Telephone:* (310) 550-4000 (office). *Website:* www.icmtalent.com (office).

LIONS, Pierre-Louis, DèsSc; French mathematician and academic; *Professor of Partial Differential Equations and Applications, Collège de France;* b. 11 Aug. 1956, Grasse, Alpes-Maritime; s. of Jacques-Louis Lions and Andrée Olivier; m. Lila Laurenti 1979; one s.; ed Lycée Pasteur and Lycée Louis-le-Grand, Paris, Ecole Normale Supérieure, Paris, Univ. of Paris VI; Researcher, CNRS 1979–81, Dir of Research 1995–; Prof. of Math., Univ. of Paris-Dauphine 1981–2003; part-time Prof. of Applied Math., Ecole Polytechnique, Palaiseau 1995–2001, 2002–; Prof. of Partial Differential Equations and Applications, Collège de France 2002–; mem. Editorial Bd 45 int. journals; mem. Acad. des sciences, Paris, Naples Acad., Academia Europaea; Chevalier, Légion d'honneur 1995, Officier 2008, Commdr 2014; Grand Cross, Nat. Order of Scientific Merit (Brazil) 2007; Dr hc (Heriot-Watt Univ., Edinburgh, UK) 1995, (Univ. of Hong Kong) 1999, (École polytechnique fédérale de Lausanne) 2010; Doistau-Blutet Foundation Prize, Acad. des sciences 1986, IBM Prize 1987, Philip Morris Prize 1991, Ampère Prize, Acad. des sciences 1992, Fields Medal, Int. Congress of Mathematicians, Zurich 1994, Prix du meilleur article en Finance Mathématique, Institut de Finance Europlace 2003, Thomson Prize 2004, Grand Prix INRIA 2012. *Publications:* numerous articles in math. journals on theory of nonlinear partial differential equations. *Leisure interests:* cinema, reading, rugby, swimming. *Address:* Collège de France, 11 place Marcelin Berthelot, 75005 Paris, France (office). *Telephone:* 1-44-27-12-11 (office). *Fax:* 1-44-05-49-08 (office). *E-mail:* lions@dmi.ens.fr (office). *Website:* www.college-de-france.fr/site/en-pierre-louis-lions/#course (office).

LIOTTA, Ray, BFA; American actor; b. 18 Dec. 1955, Newark, NJ; s. of Alfred Liotta and Mary Liotta; m. Michelle Grace 1997; one d.; ed Univ. of Miami. *Films include:* The Lonely Lady 1983, Something Wild 1986, Arena Brains 1987, Dominick and Eugene 1988, Field of Dreams 1989, Goodfellas 1990, Article 99 1992, Unlawful Entry 1992, No Escape 1994, Corrina, Corrina 1994, Operation Dumbo Drop 1995, Unforgettable 1996, Turbulence 1997, Phoenix 1997, Copland 1997, The Rat Pack 1998, Forever Mine 1999, Muppets From Space 1999, Blow 2001, Heartbreakers 2001, Hannibal 2001, John Q. 2002, A Rumor of Angels 2002, Narc 2002, Identity 2003, Last Shot 2004, Control 2004, Happy Endings 2005, Slow Burn 2005, Revolver 2005, Take the Lead 2006, Even Money 2006, Local Color 2006, Comeback Season 2006, Smokin' Aces 2006, Wild Hogs 2007, Battle in Seattle 2007, Bee Movie (voice) 2007, Hero Wanted 2008, Chasing 3000 2008, La Linea 2008, Powder Blue 2009, Crossing Over 2009, Observe and Report 2009, Youth in Revolt 2010, Date Night 2010, The River Sorrow 2010, Killing Them Softly 2012, Breathless 2012, The Iceman 2012, The Place Beyond the Pines 2012, Yellow 2012, Bad Karma 2012, The Devil's in the Details 2013, Suddenly 2013, Better Living Through Chemistry 2014, Muppets Most Wanted 2014, The Identical 2014, Sin City: A Dame to Kill For 2014, Revenge of the Green Dragons 2014, Kill the Messenger 2014, Stretch 2014, Kill the Messenger 2014, Blackway 2015, Sticky Notes 2016, Flock of Dudes 2016. *Television appearances include:* Another World, NBC 1978–80, Hardhat & Legs (CBS movie) 1980, Crazy Times (ABC pilot) 1981, Casablanca, NBC 1983, Our Family Honor, NBC 1985–86, Women & Men 2–In Love There Are No Rules 1991, The Rat Pack 1998, Point of Origin 2002, Smith (series) 2006, The Money (film) 2014, Shades of Blue 2016–18.

LIPENGA, Ken, BEd, PhB; Malawi journalist, editor and politician; b. 14 Feb. 1952; ed Univ. of Malawi, Univ. of New Brunswick; fmr Asst Lecturer, Univ. of Malawi; Ed.-in-Chief Blantyre Newspapers Ltd and Gen. Man. Blantyre Printing and Publishing Co. 1986–92; Founding Ed.-in-Chief The Malawi Nation 1993–95; apptd Special Asst to Pres. 1995; Minister of Educ., Sports and Culture 1999–2004, of Labour and Vocational Training 2005–06, Deputy Minister of Finance 2006–08, Minister of Econ. Planning and Devt 2008–11, of Finance and Devt Planning 2011–13; mem. Parl. for Phalombe East 2004–; mem. Democratic Progressive Party.

LIPIČ, Maj.-Gen. Ladislav, BSc; Slovenian army officer and diplomatist; b. 30 Nov. 1951, Murska Sobota; ed Univ. of Ljubljana; Asst for Organizational and Mobilization Affairs, Murska Sobota Municipal Territorial Defence HQ 1987–90; Chief of Logistics, Territorial Defence Regional Command (Vzhodna Štajerska Region) 1990–94, Commdr 1994–97; Chief of Logistics, Slovenian Armed Forces Gen. Staff 1997–2000, Deputy Chief of Gen. Staff 2000–01, Chief of Gen. Staff 2001–06; Amb. to Bulgaria (also accred to Hungary) 2006–08; Adviser to the Pres. of Slovenia on defence matters 2008–12; Co-Dir CAE 98 Exercise (Jt NATO and PfP mem. countries exercise), Slovenia 1998; rank of Brig. 1998, Maj.-Gen. 2003;

guest lecturer, Faculty of Social Sciences, Univ. of Ljubljana; Gold Medal of Gen. Master with Swords, Gold Medal of General Master, Gold Medal of the Slovenian Armed Forces, Golden Order for Services in Mil. or Security Field of Repub. of Slovenia; Chevalier, Légion d'honneur; Kt, Hungarian Culture 2003; Legion of Merit (USA) 2004. *Address:* Ministry of Defence, General Staff of the Slovenian Armed Forces Vojkova cesta 55, 1000 Ljubljana, Slovenia (office). *Telephone:* (1) 471-22-11 (office). *Fax:* (1) 471-16-50 (office). *E-mail:* glavna.pisarna.gssv@mors.si (office). *Website:* www.slovenskavojska.si (office).

LIPMAN, David J., BA, MD; American biologist, biochemist and academic; *Director, National Center for Biotechnology Information, National Institutes of Health;* ed Brown Univ., Univ. at Buffalo, State Univ. of NY; Founding Dir Nat. Center for Biotechnology Information, Nat. Library of Medicine, NIH, Bethesda, Md 1989–, cr. GenBank (world's largest public database of DNA data), introduced PubMed Central to provide free, permanent electronic access to articles from participating journals 2000; one of the originators of the Influenza Genome Sequencing Project; Ed.-in-Chief Biology Direct online journal; mem. NAS 2005; Fellow, American Coll. of Medical Informatics 2001; Asscn of Biomolecular Resource Facilities Award 1996, Accomplishment by a Sr Scientist Award, Int. Soc. for Computational Biology 2004. *Publications:* numerous articles in scientific journals on sequence comparison methods, comparative genomics and molecular evolution. *Address:* National Center for Biotechnology Information, Building 38A, Room N807, 8600 Rockville Pike MSC 6075, Bethesda, MD 20894-6075, USA (office). *Telephone:* (301) 496-2475 (office). *Fax:* (301) 480-2288 (office). *E-mail:* lipman@ncbi.nlm.nih.gov (office). *Website:* www.ncbi.nlm.nih.gov/research/staff/lipman (office).

LIPP, Robert I., BA, MBA, JD; American insurance industry executive; *Senior Advisor, Stone Point Capital LLC;* m. 1st Bari Lipp (deceased); m. 2nd Martha Berman; five c.; ed Williams Coll., Harvard Univ., New York Univ.; various positions with Chemical NY Corpn (now JPMorgan Chase & Co.) 1963–86; joined Citigroup 1986, Chair. and CEO CitiFinancial Credit Co. 1991–93, Co-Chair. Citigroup Inc. 1998–99, Vice-Chair. and mem. Office of Chair. 2000, Chair. and CEO Global Consumer Business 1999–2000; Vice-Chair. and Dir Travelers Group Inc. 1991–98; Chair. and CEO Travelers Insurance Group Inc. 1993–2000; CEO and Pres. Travelers Insurance Group Holdings Inc. 1996–98, Chair. 1996–2000, 2001, Chair. and CEO Travelers Property Casualty Corpn 2001–04, Chair. The St Paul Travelers Cos Inc. (following merger of The St Paul Co. and Travelers Insurance Group 2004) 2004–05; Sr Advisor, Brysam Global Partners, LLC 2008–09; Sr Advisor, Stone Point Capital LLC and Exec. Chair. StoneRiver Group, LP 2009–; mem. Bd of Dirs The Travelers Cos, Inc. 2001–10, Accenture Ltd 2001–, Bank One Corpn 2003–, JPMorgan Chase & Co. 2005–08, GENEX Services, Inc.; Pres. New York City Ballet; Chair. Bd Trustees, Williams Coll.; Founder Bari Lipp Foundation; Treas. Massachusetts Museum of Contemporary Art; Trustee Carnegie Hall. *Address:* Stone Point Capital LLC, 20 Horseneck Lane, Greenwich, CT 06830-6327, USA (office). *Telephone:* (203) 862-2900 (office). *Fax:* (203) 625-8357 (office). *E-mail:* info@stonepoint.com (office). *Website:* www.stonepoint.com (office); www.stoneriver.com (office).

LIPPARD, Stephen J., BA, PhD, MRIA; American chemist and academic; *Arthur Amos Noyes Professor of Chemistry, Massachusetts Institute of Technology;* b. 12 Oct. 1940, Pittsburgh, Pa; m. Judith Ann Lippard 1964 (died 2013); two s.; ed Haverford Coll., Haverford, Pa, Massachusetts Inst. of Tech.; Asst Prof. of Chem., Columbia Univ. 1966–69, Assoc. Prof. 1969–72, Prof. 1972–82; Prof. of Chem., MIT 1983–89, Arthur Amos Noyes Prof. of Chem. 1989–, Head, Dept of Chem. 1995–; mem. NAS 1989, Nat. Inst. of Medicine 1993, Italian Chemical Soc. 1996, Deutsche Akad. der Naturforscher Leopoldina 2004; Scientific mem. Max-Planck-Gesellschaft 1996; Fellow, Alfred P. Sloan Foundation 1968–70, John Simon Guggenheim Foundation 1972, John E. Fogarty Int. Center 1979, AAAS 1980, American Acad. of Arts and Sciences 1986; Hon. Fellow, Woodrow Wilson Foundation 1962; Hon. mem. Italian Chemical Soc. 1996; Hon. DSc (Texas A&M Univ.) 1995, (Haverford Coll.) 2000; Int. Precious Metals Inst. Henry J. Albert Award 1985, ACS Award in Inorganic Chem. 1987, Remsen Award 1987, Alexander von Humboldt Sr US Scientist Award 1988, John C. Bailar, Jr Award, Univ. of Illinois 1993, ACS Award for Distinguished Service in Inorganic Chem. 1994, William H. Nichols Medal 1995, Frontiers in Biological Chem. Award, Max-Planck-Institut für Strahlenchemie 1995, Basolo Medal 2002, Richards Medal 2002, ACS Alfred Bader Award in Bio-organic or Bio-inorganic Chem. 2004, Nat. Medal of Science 2004, Linus Pauling Medal 2009, Breslow Award for Achievement in Biomimetic Chem. 2010, RSC Centenary Medal 2010, Sacconi Medal, Italian Chemical Soc. 2012, James R. Killian Jr Faculty Achievement Award, MIT 2013, ACS Priestley Medal 2014, Welch Award in Chem. (co-recipient) 2016. *Publications:* Progress in Inorganic Chemistry, Vols 11–40 (co-ed.) 1970–92, Platinum, Gold, and Other Metal Chemotherapeutic Agents, ACS Symposium Series 209 (co-ed.) 1983, Principles of Bioinorganic Chemistry (co-author) 1994, Bioinorganic Chemistry (co-ed.) 1994, Medicinal Inorganic Chemistry (co-ed.) 2005; numerous papers in scientific journals. *Leisure interests:* playing the harpsichord, supporting Boston Red Sox baseball team. *Address:* Department of Chemistry, Massachusetts Institute of Technology, Room 18-498, Cambridge, MA 02139, USA (office). *Telephone:* (617) 253-1892 (office). *Fax:* (617) 258-8150 (office). *E-mail:* lippard@mit.edu (office). *Website:* chemistry.mit.edu/people/lippard-stephen (office); lippardlab.mit.edu (office).

LIPPE, Stefan, PhD; German/Swiss insurance industry executive; b. 11 Oct. 1955, Mannheim; ed Univ. of Mannheim; joined Bavarian Re 1983, Head of Non-proportional Underwriting Dept 1986, Deputy Mem. Bd of Dirs 1988–91, Full Mem. Bd of Dirs 1991–93, Chair. Bd of Man. 1993, mem. Exec. Cttee Swiss Reinsurance Co. (Swiss Re; as Head of Bavarian Re Group) 1995–, Head of Property and Casualty Business Group, Swiss Re Co. 2001–05, Head of Reinsurance Products 2005–08, COO and Deputy CEO 2008–09, CEO 2009–12; co-f. Paperless Inc. (now Yes.com) 2013; mem. Bd of Dirs Acqufin AG 2011, AXA SA 2012–, CelsiusPro AG 2013–; mem. Supervisory Bd Commerzbank AG 2014–18; Kurt Hamann Foundation Prize 1982. *Address:* AXA Group, Investor Relations Department, 25 avenue Matignon, 75008 Paris, France (office). *Telephone:* 1-40-75-46-85 (office). *Website:* www.axa.com (office).

LIPPERT, Mark W., BA, MA; American government official and diplomatist; ed Stanford Univ., Beijing Univ., China; Foreign and Defense Policy Advisor to Senator Tom Daschle and Senate Democratic Policy Cttee 1999–2000, Professional Staff Mem. on Senate Appropriations Cttee, State-Foreign Operations Sub-cttee, adviser to Senator Patrick Leahy on foreign aid and security assistance issues 2000–05; Foreign Policy Advisor for then-Senator Obama 2005–08, managed the Senator's work on Senate Foreign Relations Cttee; took leave of absence to act as Intelligence Officer with Seal Team One in support of Operation Iraqi Freedom 2007–08; Deputy Dir for Foreign Policy on Obama-Biden Transition Team and Sr Foreign Policy Advisor on Obama for America campaign 2008; Deputy Asst to the Pres. and Chief of Staff for Nat. Security Council 2009; mobilization on active duty in USN 2009–12, deployed to Afghanistan and served as an Intelligence Officer for Naval Special Warfare Devt Group, Virginia Beach, Va 2009–11; held sr positions in Dept of Defense 2012–14, including Chief of Staff to Sec. of Defense and Asst Sec. of Defense for Asian and Pacific Security Affairs, Prin. Advisor to Sec. of Defense; Amb. to South Korea 2014–17; mil. awards and decorations include Bronze Star Medal, Defense Meritorious Service Medal, Basic Parachutist Badge.

LIPPONEN, Paavo Tapio, MA; Finnish writer, international affairs scholar, business consultant and fmr politician; *Chairman, Cosmopolis Oy;* b. 23 April 1941, Turtola (now Pello); s. of Orvo Lipponen and Hilkka Lipponen; m. Päivi Lipponen 1998; three d.; ed Univ. of Helsinki, Dartmouth Coll., USA; journalist 1963–67; Research and Int. Affairs Sec. and Head Political Section Finnish Social Democratic Party (SDP) 1967–79; Pvt. Sec. (Special Political Adviser) to Prime Minister 1979–82; Political Sec. to Minister of Labour 1983; Man. Dir Viestintä Teema Oy 1988–95; Head Finnish Inst. of Int. Affairs 1989–91; Chair. Supervisory Bd Outokumpu Oy 1989–90; mem. Helsinki City Council 1985–95; MP 1983–87, 1991–2007 (retd); mem. SDP Party Cttee 1987–90, Chair. SDP Helsinki Dist 1985–92, Chair. SDP 1993–2005; Speaker of Parl. March–April 1995, 2003–07; Prime Minister of Finland 1995–2003; SDP cand. (unsuccessful) in presidential election 2012; writer-columnist; consultant to Pohjolan Voima Oy (Finland) on nuclear energy 2007–, to Nord Stream 2008–; currently Chair. Cosmopolis Oy, Protagon Oy; Dr hc (Dartmouth Coll., USA) 1997, (Finlandia Univ.) 2000, (Acad. of Arts and Design, Helsinki) 2008, (Åbo Akademi, Turku) 2007, (Univ. of Joensuu) 2007, (Univ. of Helsinki) 2012; Theodor Aue Prize 2007, Konstsamfundet 2008, Östersjöfondens Prize 2013, High-North Hero Prize, Nord Univ., Norway 2015, Svenska Akademiens Finlandspris 2017. *Publications:* Muutoksen suunta 1986, Kohti Eurooppaa 2001, Järki voittaa 2008, Muistelmat I 2009, Muistelmat II 2014, Die Vernunft siegt 2014. *Leisure interests:* architecture, swimming, collecting medals. *Address:* Cosmopolis Oy, Töölönkatu 4, 00100 Helsinki, Finland (office). *Telephone:* 230441. *E-mail:* paavo.t.lipponen@gmail.com (office).

LIPŠIC, Daniel, LLM, JUDr; Slovak lawyer and politician; *Chairman, Nová väčšina-Dohoda (NOVA);* b. 8 July 1973, Bratislava; m. Beáta Oravcová; ed Comenius Univ., Bratislava, Harvard Law School, USA; Chair. Civil Democratic Youth 1991–95; Project Leader Advisory Centre for Slovak Businesses and Banks 1996–97; with Dist Mil. Prosecutor, Prešov 1997–98, Ernest Valko legal firm 1998; Deputy Chair. for Internal Policy, Christian Democratic Movt 2000–12; Head, Office of Ministry of Justice 1998–2002; Deputy Prime Minister and Minister of Justice 2002–06; mem. Nat. Council of the Slovak Repub. 2006–10, 2012–16 (resgnd); Minister of the Interior 2010–12; Founder and Chair. Nová väčšina-Dohoda (New Majority—Agreement) party 2012–. *Address:* Nová väčšina-Dohoda (New Majority—Agreement), Ružová dolina 6, 821 08 Bratislava, Slovakia (office). *Telephone:* (2) 3211-6655 (office). *E-mail:* nova@nova.sk (office). *Website:* www.nova.sk (office); www.lipsic.sk.

LIPSKA, Ewa; Polish poet; b. 8 Oct. 1945, Kraków; ed Acad. of Fine Arts, Kraków; Co-Ed. Pismo 1981–83; mem. editorial Bd Dekada Literacka 1990–92; First Sec., Polish Embassy, Vienna 1991–95, Adviser 1995–97; Deputy Dir Polish Inst., Vienna 1991–95, Dir 1995–97; mem. Asscn of Polish Writers, Polish and Austrian PEN Club; Koscielscy Foundation Award (Switzerland) 1973, Robert Graves PEN Club Award 1979, Ind. Foundation for Polish Culture, Polcul Foundation Award 1990, PEN Club Award 1992, Alfred Jurzykowski Foundation Award (USA) 1993, City of Kraków Award 1995, Andrzej Bursa Award 1997, Literary Laurel 2002, Samuel Bogumil Linde Twin Cities Göttingen-Toruń 2007, Zlatni Kljuc Smederevа 2009, Naim Frasheri Prize 2010, Cape of Good Hope Award, Ministry of Culture, Repub. of Kosovo 2010, Gdynia Literary Award 2011. *Publications include:* Wiersze (Poems) 1967, Drugi zbiór wierszy (Second Vol. of Poems) 1970, Trzeci zbiór wierszy (Third Vol. of Poems) 1972, Czwarty zbiór wierszy (Fourth Vol. of Poems) 1974, Piaty zbiór wierszy (Fifth Vol. of Poems) 1978, Zywa smierc (Living Death) 1979, Dom Spokojnej Mlodosci (House of the Quiet Youth) 1979, Nie o smierc tutaj chodzi, lecz o bialy kordonek 1982, Przechowalnia ciemnosci 1985, Utwory wybrane (Selected Poems) 1986, Strefa ograniczonego postoju 1990, Wakacje Mizantropa (Misanthrope's Holidays) 1993, Stypendysci czasu 1994, Wspólnicy zielonego wiatraczka 1996, Ludzie dla poczatkujacych (People for Beginners) 1997, Zycie zastepcze (Substitute Life) (Polish-German edition 1998), Godziny poza godzinami (After-hours Hours) 1999, Biale truskawki (White Strawberries) 2000, Sklepy zoologiczne (Pet Shops) 2001, Uwaga stopien 2002, Ja 2003, Gdzie indziej 2005, Drzazga 2006, Pomarańcza Newtona 2007, Sefer (prose) 2009; selections of poems translated include Versei (Hungary) 1979, Vernisaz (Czechoslovakia) 1979, Such Times (Canada) 1981, Huis voor een vredige jeugd 1982, Auf den Dächern der Mausoleen (Germany) 1983, En misantrops ferie (Denmark) 1990, Meine Zeit. Mein Leib. Mein Leben (Austria) 1990, Poet? Criminal? Madman? (UK) 1991, Wakancitie na mizantropa (Bulgaria) 1994, Zon (Sweden) 1997, Stipiendisti Wremiena (Yugoslavia) 1998, Mennesker for Begyndere (Denmark) 1999, Mesohu me vdekjen (Albania) 2000, Menseen voor beginners (Netherlands) 2000, Sedemnast cervenych vevericiek (Slovakia) 2001, Selection of Poems (Israel) 2001, Fresas Blancas (Spain) 2001, Pet Shops (UK) 2002.

LIPSKY, John, BA, MA, PhD; American academic, business executive and fmr international organization official; *Peter G. Peterson Distinguished Scholar, Henry A. Kissinger Center for Global Affairs, Johns Hopkins University;* b. 1947; s. of Abbott Lipsky and Joan Lipsky; m.; one s. two d.; ed Wesleyan and Stanford Univs; spent a decade at IMF, where he helped manage exchange rate surveillance procedure and analysed devts in int. capital market, also participated in negotiations with several mem. countries and served as IMF Resident Rep. in Chile 1978–80; joined Salomon Brothers Inc. 1984, directed European Econ. and Market Analysis Group, London, UK 1989–92, Chief Economist 1992–97; Chief

Economist and Dir of Research, Chase Manhattan Bank 1997; fmr Chief Economist, JPMorgan, later Vice-Chair. JPMorgan Investment Bank; Chair. Financial Sector Review Group, IMF 2000, First Deputy Man. Dir IMF 2006–11, Acting Man. Dir (following resignation of Dominique Strauss-Kahn) May–July 2011, Special Advisor to Man. Dir Sept.–Nov. 2011; apptd Distinguished Visiting Scholar, Paul H. Nitze School Advanced International Studies, Johns Hopkins Univ. 2012, currently Peter G. Peterson Distinguished Scholar, Henry A. Kissinger Center for Global Affairs and Sr Fellow, Foreign Policy Inst.; Co-Dir Program on Global Economy, Aspen Inst.; mem. Bd of Dirs HSBC Holdings PLC 2012–18; mem. Bd of Dirs and Vice-Chair., Nat. Bureau of Econ. Research (NBER); Life mem., Council on Foreign Relations; fmr Trustee, Stanford Inst. for Econ. Policy Research, now mem. Advisory Bd. *Address:* Henry A. Kissinger Center for Global Affairs, School of Advanced International Studies, Johns Hopkins University, 1740 Massachusetts Avenue, NW, Washington, DC 20036, USA (office). *Telephone:* (202) 663-5813 (office). *E-mail:* jlipsky@jhu.edu (office). *Website:* www.sais-jhu.edu (office); www.kissinger.sais-jhu.edu (office).

LIPSTOK, Andres; Estonian politician and fmr central banker; b. 6 Feb. 1957, Haapsalu; s. of John Lipstok; m.; one s. one d.; ed Haapsalu Secondary School No. 1, Univ. of Tartu; Deputy Head, Finance Dept, Exec. Cttee of Haapsalu Dist 1980–83, Head 1983–86; Chair. Planning Comm. 1986–89; apptd Deputy Minister of Finance, Estonian SSR 1989; mem. Council of Lääne Co. 1989–93, Gov. Lääne Co. 1989–94; Minister of Finance 1994–95, of Econ. Affairs 1995–96; mem. Riigikogu (Parl.) 1995–2005; Gov. Bank of Estonia 2005–12; Advisor to the Rector, Tallinn Univ. 2013–; mem. Estonian Liberal Democratic Party 1993–94, Estonian Reform Party 1994–2005; mem. Bd Eesti Vehklemisliit (Estonian Fencing Fed.); mem. Congress of Lions Club 1992; Vice-Pres. Estonian Olympic Cttee 2004–08; IV Class Order of the Nat. Coat of Arms.

LIPTON, David, BA, MA, PhD; American economist, government official and international organization official; *First Deputy Managing Director, International Monetary Fund;* ed Wesleyan Univ., Harvard Univ.; economist, IMF, Washington, DC 1981–89; econ. advisor (with Harvard Univ. Prof. Jeffrey Sachs) to govts of Russia, Poland, Slovenia 1989–92; Fellow, Woodrow Wilson Center of Scholars 1992–93; Under-Sec. for Int. Affairs, US Treasury Dept, Washington, DC 1993–98; Man. Dir Moore Capital Strategy Group, Moore Capital Management 2000–05; Man. Dir and Head of Global Country Risk Man. Citigroup 2005–08; Special Asst to US President Obama, Sr Dir for Int. Econ. Affairs, Nat. Econ. Council and Nat. Security Council, The White House 2008–11; Special Advisor to Man. Dir, IMF July–Nov. 2011, First Deputy Man. Dir 2011–; mem. Nat. Advisory Bd, Merage Foundation for the American Dream. *Address:* International Monetary Fund, 700 19th Street NW, Washington, DC 20431, USA (office). *Telephone:* (202) 623-7000 (office). *Fax:* (202) 623-4661 (office). *Website:* www.imf.org/external/np/omd/bios/dl.htm (office).

LIPTON, Stuart A., MD, PhD; American neuroscientist and academic; *Professor and Scientific Director, Del E. Webb Center for Neuroscience and Aging, The Burnham Institute;* b. 11 Jan. 1950, Danbury, Conn.; ed Cornell and Harvard Univs, Univ. of Pennsylvania; Intern in Medicine, Beth Israel Hosp., Boston, Mass 1977–78, Chief Resident in Neurology 1980, Asst in Neurology 1981–86, Assoc. in Neurology 1986–93, Sr Assoc. in Neurology, Beth Israel Deaconess Medical Center 1993–99; Jr and Sr Asst Resident, Longwood Area Neurology Program, Harvard Medical School, Boston 1978–80, Instructor in Neurology 1981–83, Asst Prof. of Neurology (Neuroscience) 1983–87, Assoc. Prof. of Neurology (Neuroscience) 1987–97, Assoc. Prof. of Neuroscience (Neurosurgery) 1997–2001; Chief Resident in Neurology, Children's Hosp. 1980, Asst in Neurology 1981–88, Dir Lab. of Cellular and Molecular Neuroscience 1987–97, Assoc. in Neurology 1988–97; Chief Resident in Neurology, Brigham and Women's Hosp. 1980, Assoc. in Neurology 1988–97, Chief, CNS Research Inst. 1997–99; Clinical Asst in Neurology, Massachusetts Gen. Hosp. Boston 1991–92, Clinical Assoc. in Neurology 1992–97; Prof. and Scientific Dir, Del E. Webb Center for Neuroscience and Aging, The Burnham Inst., La Jolla, Calif. 1999–; Attending Neurologist, Medical Center, Univ. of California, San Diego, La Jolla 1999–, Adjunct Prof., Depts of Neurosciences and Psychiatry 1999–; Adjunct Prof., Dept of Neuropharmacology and Molecular and Experimental Medicine, Scripps Research Inst., La Jolla 1999–; Adjunct Prof. of Neuroscience, Salk Inst., La Jolla 2002–; Established Investigator, American Heart Asscn 1988–93; mem. Asscn for Research in Vision and Ophthalmology 1974–, American Acad. of Neurology 1979–98 (Fellow 1998–), AAAS 1980–, Soc. for Neuroscience 1982–, Biophysical Soc. 1986–; mem. Scientific Advisory Bd, HIV Neurobehavioral Research Center, School of Medicine, Univ. of California, San Diego 1995–99, Center for Neurovirology and Neurodegenerative Disorders, Univ. of Nebraska and Creighton Univ. 1997–, AIDS Research Center, Scripps Research Inst. 1997–; Assoc. Ed. Neuron 1995–; Reviewing Ed. Cell Death and Differentiation 2000–; mem. Editorial Bd several journals on neuroscience; Hon. mem. British Brain Research Association 1982–, European Brain and Behaviour Soc. 1982–; Ford Foundation Scholarship 1968–72, NIH MD-PhD Fellowship 1972–77, Mary Ellis Bell Prize for Research, Univ. of Pennsylvania School of Medicine 1973, Baluin-Lucke Memorial Prize for Research 1976, Von L. Meyer Research Award, Children's Hosp., Boston 1979, Hartford Foundation Fellowship 1981–84, NIH Teacher-Investigator Development Award 1984–89, Pattison Award in Neuroscience, Research Inst. for Child Devt Research, Inc. 1989, Nobel Foundation Lectureship, Karolinska Institutet, Stockholm 1994, Grass Foundation Lectureship 1995, San Diego Health Hero Award, American Parkinson's Disease Asscn 2002, Ernst Jung Prize for Medicine 2004. *Publications:* more than 520 articles in scientific and medical journals. *Address:* Center for Neuroscience and Aging, The Burnham Institute, 10901 Torrey Pines Road, La Jolla, CA 92037, USA (office). *Telephone:* (858) 713-6261 (office). *Fax:* (858) 713-6262 (office). *E-mail:* slipton@burnham.org (office). *Website:* www.burnham.org (office).

LIPTON, Sir Stuart Anthony, Kt; British property developer; *Partner, Lipton Rogers Developments LLP;* b. 9 Nov. 1942; s. of Bertram Green and Jeanette Lipton; m. Ruth Marks 1966; two s. one d.; ed Berkhamsted School; Dir Sterling Land Co. 1971–73, First Palace Securities Ltd 1973–76; Man. Dir Greycoat PLC 1976–83; Founder and Chair. Stanhope Properties PLC 1983–95, Stanhope PLC 1995–2006; Deputy Chair. Chelsfield Partners LLP 2006; Partner, Lipton Rogers Devts LLP, London 2013–; Chair. Comm. for Architecture and the Built Environment 1999–2005; adviser, Glyndebourne Opera House 1989–94; Dir Nat. Gallery Trust Foundation 1998–; mem. Bd of Dirs PCCW Planning and Development Ltd, National Gallery Trust Foundation Ltd 1998–; mem. Bd Royal Nat. Theatre 1988–98, Royal Opera House 1998–2006; mem. Advisory Bd Hampton Site Co, National Gallery 1985–91, Tate Gallery Museum of Modern Art 1994–2005; mem. Barbican Centre Advisory Council 1997–2007; mem. Governing Body Imperial Coll. 1987–2000, Royal Fine Art Comm. 1988–99, LSE 2000–06; Fellow, Royal Inst. of Chartered Surveyors 2008; Edward Bass Visiting Fellow, Yale School of Architecture 2006; Trustee, Whitechapel Art Gallery 1987–94, Millennium Bridge Trust 1998–2002; Life Trustee, Urban Land Inst. 2009–; Hon. FRIBA; Hon. Fellow, Imperial Coll.; Hon. LLD (Bath) 2005; Dr hc (London Metropolitan) 2007; Hon. DSc (Univ. Coll. London) 2009. *Address:* Lipton Rogers Developments LLP, 33 Cavendish Square, London, W1G 0PW, England (office). *Website:* www.liptonrogers.com (office).

LIPWORTH, Sir (Maurice) Sydney, Kt, QC, BCom, LLB; British barrister and business executive; b. 13 May 1931, Johannesburg, South Africa; s. of Isidore Lipworth and Rae Lipworth; m. Rosa Liwarek 1957; two s.; ed King Edward VII School, Johannesburg, Univ. of the Witwatersrand; practising barrister, Johannesburg 1956–64; Dir (non-exec.) Liberty Life Asscn of Africa Ltd 1956–64; Exec. Pvt. Trading Cos. 1964–67; Exec. Dir Abbey Life Assurance PLC 1968–70; Vice-Pres. and Dir Abbey Int. Corpn Inc. 1968–70; one of co-founders and Dir Allied Dunbar Assurance PLC 1970–88, Deputy Man. Dir 1977–79, Jt Man. Dir 1979–84, Deputy Chair. 1984–88; Dir J. Rothschild Holdings PLC 1984–87, BAT Industries PLC 1985–88; Deputy Chair., Dir (non-exec.) Nat. Westminster Bank 1993–2000; Chair., Dir (non-exec.) Zeneca Group PLC 1995–99 (Dir 1994–99); Dir (non-exec.), Carlton Communications PLC 1993–, Centrica PLC 1999–2002; Chair. Monopolies and Mergers Comm. 1988–92, Bar Asscn for Commerce, Finance and Industry 1991–92 (Vice-Pres. *c.* 2012), Financial Reporting Council 1993–2001; Arbitrator/Mediator, One Essex Court (The Chambers of Lord Grabiner QC) 2004–; mem. Sr Salaries Review Body 1994–, Panel of Conciliators and of Arbitrators, Int. Centre for Settlement of Investment Disputes, Int. Advisory Bd, SOAS 2004–, Constitution Committee, Int. Accounting Standards Cttee Foundation Trust 2000–, European Policy Forum; Vice-Chair. of Trustees, Philharmonia Orchestra 1986–93, Chair. 1993–; Trustee, South Bank Ltd 1996–; Hon. QC 1993; Hon. LLD (Witwatersrand) 2003. *Publications:* The Monopolies and Mergers Yearbook: March 1989–December 1990 Vol. 1 1991, Major Issues in Regulation: Regulation Lectures (co-author) 1992. *Leisure interests:* music, theatre, tennis. *Address:* One Essex Court, Temple, London, EC4Y 9AR (office); International Accounting Standards Board, 30 Cannon Street, EC4M 6XH, England. *Telephone:* (20) 7583-2000 (office); (20) 7726-1000. *Fax:* (20) 7583-0118 (office); (20) 7726-1038 (office). *E-mail:* clerks@oeclaw.co.uk (office). *Website:* www.oeclaw.co.uk (office); www.ifrs.org.

LISH, Gordon Jay, BA; American editor and writer; b. 11 Feb. 1934, Hewlett, New York; s. of Philip Lish and Regina Lish (née Deutsch); m. 1st Loretta Frances Fokes 1956 (divorced 1967), three c.; m. 2nd Barbara Works 1969 (died 1994), one s.; ed Univ. of Arizona, San Francisco State Univ.; began career as English teacher, Mills High School, Millbrae, Calif.; Ed.-in-Chief, Chrysalis Review 1959–61; Editorial Dir, Genesis West 1961–65; Ed.-in-Chief, also Dir of Linguistic Studies, Behavioral Research Laboratories, Menlo Park, Calif. 1963–66; with Educational Development Corpn, Palo Alto 1966–69; Fiction Ed., Esquire magazine 1969–77; Sr Ed., Alfred A. Knopf, Inc. 1977–95; Lecturer, Yale Univ. 1970–74, Guest Fellow 1974–80; Teacher, fiction writing, Columbia Univ. 1980–97; Founding Ed.-in-Chief, The Quarterly 1987–97; fmr Prof., New York Univ. Coll. of Arts and Sciences; ran fiction writing seminars, Center for Fiction in Manhattan 2009 and 2010; Guggenheim Fellowship 1984; Hon. DLitt (State Univ. of New York) 1994; American Soc. of Magazine Eds award for distinguished editing in fiction 1971, Columbia School of Journalism Awards for distinguished editing in fiction 1971 and in nonfiction 1975, Antioch Review Award for Distinguished Prose 2005; named one of the 200 major writers of our time by Le Nouvel Observateur 1995. *Publications include:* non-fiction: English Grammar 1964, The Gabbernot 1965, Why Work 1966, A Man's Work 1967, New Sounds in American Fiction 1969, The Secret of Life of Our Times (Ed.) 1973, All Our Secrets Are the Same (Ed.) 1976, Self-Imitation of Myself 1997; novels: Dear Mr Capote 1983, Peru 1986, Extravaganza 1989, My Romance 1991, Zimzum 1993, Epigraph 1996; short stories: What I Know So Far 1981, Mourner at the Door 1988, The Selected Stories of Gordon Lish 1996; published several other short stories in the Antioch Review including 'For Jeromé—with Love and Kisses' (O. Henry Prize) 1984.

LISIN, Vladimir Sergeyevich, PhD; Russian business executive; *Chairman, Novolipetsk Steel (NLMK);* b. 7 May 1956, Ivanovo, USSR; m.; three c.; ed Siberian Metallurgic Inst., Russian Foreign Trade Acad., Russian Presidential Acad. of Nat. Economy and Public Admin; started career as coalmine mechanic 1975; apptd Deputy Chief Engineer, Karaganda Steel Plant, Kazakhstan 1986, apptd Deputy CEO 1989; mem. Bd of Dirs Novolipetsk Steel (NLMK) 1996–, Chair. 1998–; Pres. Int. Shooting Sports Fed. 2018–, also mem. Exec. Cttee; Prof., Russian Presidential Acad. of Nat. Economy and Public Admin; mem. Bd Dirs Zenit Bank, Novolipetskii Metallurgical Combine, JSC Chernomorneftegaz; mem. Russian Union of Industrialists and Entrepreneurs (RSPP); Trustee, Inst. of Social Devt Foundation; Hon. Metallurgist of the Russian Fed. 1999; Kt, Order of Honour 2000, Order of St Sergiy Radonezhsky 2001; USSR Council of Ministers Prize for Science and Tech. 1989. *Publications include:* numerous research papers in professional journals. *Address:* NLMK Group, 119017 Moscow, 40 Bolshaya Ordynka Ulitsa, Building 3, Russia (office). *Telephone:* (495) 504-05-04 (office). *E-mail:* info@nlmk.com (office). *Website:* nlmk.com (office).

LISITSYN, Aleksander Petrovich; Russian marine geologist, geophysicist and geochemist; *Head of Department, P.P. Shirshov Institute of Oceanology, Russian Academy of Sciences;* b. 3 July 1923; m.; two c.; ed Moscow Geological Prospecting Inst.; Jr, Sr Researcher, Head of Lab., Head of Div., P.P. Shirshov Inst. of Oceanology, USSR (now Russian) Acad. of Sciences 1953–81, Head of Dept 1981–; Corresp. mem. USSR (now Russian) Acad. of Sciences 1974, mem. 1994–; research in marine geology, geophysics and geochemistry of seas and oceans; USSR State Prize, F. Shepard Award. *Publications include:* Sedimentation in the World Ocean 1972, Processes of Oceanic Sedimentation 1978, Geological History of Oceans 1980, Biogeochemistry of Oceans 1983, Avalanche Sedimentation and Gapes in

Sedimentation in Seas and Oceans 1988, Marine Glacial and Marine Ice Sedimentation 1994, Oceanic Sedimentation, Lithography and Geochemistry 1996, Litology of Lithospheric Plates 2001, Sea-Ice and Iceberg Sedimentation in the Ocean 2002; numerous journal contribs. *Address:* P.P. Shirshov Institute of Oceanology, Russian Academy of Sciences, Nachimovsky Prospect 36, 117851 Moscow (office); Ivanovskaya 8A, 1 127434 Moscow, Russia (home). *Telephone:* (495) 124-85-28 (office); (495) 977-97-02 (home). *Fax:* (495) 124-85-28 (office). *Website:* www.ocean.ru (office).

LISITSYN, Anatoly Ivanovich; Russian politician; b. 26 June 1947, Bolshiye Smenki, Kalinin Region; m.; one c.; ed Leningrad Acad. of Forest Tech.; Rybinsk furniture factory 1987, also Chair., Rybinsk City Dist Exec. Cttee 1987–90; Chair. Rybinsk City Exec. Cttee 1990–91; Deputy Head, Head, Yaroslavl Regional Admin 1991–92; mem. Council of Fed. 1993–; mem. Movt Our Home is Russia (resgnd); mem. People's Democratic Party 1995; Gov. Yaroslavl Region 1995–2007; Chair. Interregional Asscn Cen. Russia 1994–97; mem. Council of Russian Fed. 1996–2000; apptd mem. Presidium State Council 2001; mem. State Duma 2007–; mem. Bd Union of Russian Govs 1992; Hon. Citizen, Rybinsk 2002, Yaroslavl 2006; Order of Friendship 1996, Order of Honour 2000, Order of Merit for the Fatherland, 3rd class 2004, Order of the Badge of Honour, Order of Holy Prince Daniel of Moscow, 2nd class, Order of St Blessed Prince Dimitry, Order of St Sergius, 1st and 2nd class; Gov. of the Year 2001, Medal of Honour (Belarus) 2002, Russian Nat. Olympus. *Address:* State Duma, 103265 Moscow, Okhotnyi ryad 1, Russia (office). *Telephone:* (495) 692-62-66 (office). *Fax:* (495) 697-42-58 (office). *E-mail:* stateduma@duma.gov.ru (office). *Website:* www.duma.gov.ru (office).

LIŠKA, Juraj; Slovak politician; b. 29 Nov. 1964, Trenčin; m.; two c.; ed Slovak Tech. Univ., Univ. of Transport, Žilina; employed in State Forest 1982–84; TOS Trenčin 1989–91; entrepreneur in wood production, Finnish saunas 1991–; Chair. Regional Asscn, Slovak Democratic Christian Union 2000; elected mem. Národná rada Slovenskej republiky (Parl.) 2002, mem. Finances, Budget and Currency Cttee, Standing Del. to Parl. EU Cttee; Mayor of Trenčin Dec. 2002–Oct. 2003; Minister of Defence 2003–06 (resgnd); resgnd as Deputy Chair. Slovak Democratic and Christian Uniion (SDKÚ) 2008. *Address:* Národná rada Slovenskej republiky (National Council of the Slovak Republic), nám. Alexandra Dubčeka 1 1, 812 80 Bratislava, Slovakia (office). *Telephone:* (2) 5972-1111 (office). *Fax:* (2) 5441-9529 (office). *E-mail:* info@nrsr.sk (office). *Website:* www.nrsr.sk (office).

LISKOV, Barbara H., BA, MS, PhD; American computer scientist and academic; *Institute Professor, Department of Electrical Engineering and Computer Science, Massachusetts Institute of Technology;* b. 7 Nov. 1939, Calif.; m. Nathan Liskov; one s.; ed Univ. of California, Berkeley, Stanford Univ.; Applications Programmer, The Mitre Corpn, Bedford, Mass 1961–62, mem. of Tech. Staff, Computer Science Research and Devt 1968–72; Programmer, Language Trans. Project, Harvard Univ. 1962–63; Grad. Research Asst in Artificial Intelligence, Stanford Univ. 1963–68; Asst Prof., Dept of Electrical Eng and Computer Science, MIT 1972–76, Assoc. Prof., 1976–80, Prof. 1980–, NEC Prof. of Software Science and Eng 1986–97, Ford Prof. of Eng 1997–2008, Inst. Prof. 2008–, Assoc. Head for Computer Science 2001–04, Assoc. Provost for Faculty Equity 2007–; fmr Assoc. Ed. ACM, Transactions on Programming Languages and Systems; served as a consultant to numerous orgs. including Bolt, Beranek, and Newman, Cadence, Digital Equipment Corpn, Hewlett-Packard, Intermetrics, NCR, Prime Computer; mem. American Acad. of Arts and Sciences, Nat. Acad. of Eng, IEEE; Fellow, Asscn for Computing Machinery (ACM); Dr hc (ETH Zurich) 2005; Achievement Award, Soc. of Women Engineers 1996, named by Open Computing magazine amongst the top 100 women in computing 1996, named by Discover magazine amongst the 50 most important women in science 2003, ACM SIGPLAN Programming Languages Lifetime Achievement Award 2007, ACM SIGSOFT Impact Paper Award 2007, IEEE John von Neumann Medal 2004, ACM A.M. Turing Award 2008, inducted into Nat. Inventors Hall of Fame 2012, Computer Pioneer Award 2018. *Publications:* CLU Reference Manual (co-author) 1984, Abstraction and Specification in Program Development (co-author) 1986, Program Development in Java: Abstraction, Specification, and Object-Oriented Design 2001; 137 papers in professional journals and 102 reports. *Address:* Computer Science and Artificial Intelligence Laboratory, Massachusetts Institute of Technology, Room 32-G942, 32 Vassar Street, Cambridge, MA 02139, USA (office). *Telephone:* (617) 253-5886 (office). *Fax:* (617) 253-8460 (office). *E-mail:* liskov@csail.mit.edu (office). *Website:* www.pmg.csail.mit.edu/~liskov (office).

LISOV, Yevgeny Kuzmich; Russian politician and lawyer; b. 1940, Ivanovo Region; ed Saratov State Univ.; investigator, Dist Prosecutor's Office, Kursk Region, Sr Investigator, Head of Div., Deputy Head, Investigation Dept, RSFSR Prosecutor's Office; Deputy Gen. Prosecutor of Russian Fed. 1991–93; investigated coup d'état 1991; Deputy Prosecutor of Moscow 1993–95; attorney, Moscow Regional Coll. of Barristers; expert, magazine Ogonyok 1995–98; Deputy Head, Admin of Russian Presidency, Head, Main Control Dept, Admin of Russian Presidency 1998–2004. *Publications include:* Kremlin Conspiracy (with V.G. Stepankov); articles in magazines and newspapers.

LISSAKERS, Karin Margareta, MA; American economist and fmr government official; b. 16 Aug. 1944; m.; two c.; ed Ohio State Univ. and Johns Hopkins Univ.; mem. staff, Cttee on Foreign Relations, US Senate, Washington, DC 1972–78; Deputy Dir Econ. Policy Planning Staff, US Dept of State 1978–80; Sr Assoc. Carnegie Endowment for Int. Peace, New York 1981–83; Lecturer in int. banking, Dir int. business and banking programme, School of Int. Public Affairs, Columbia Univ. 1985–93; US Exec. Dir IMF 1993–2001; mem. Council on Foreign Relations; Chief Adviser to George Soros on globalization issues, Soros Fund Management LLC 2001–06; Dir Revenue Watch Inst. (now Natural Resource Governance Inst.) 2006–12 (retd), currently mem. advisory council. *Publications:* Banks, Borrowers and the Establishment 1991; articles in professional journals. *Address:* c/o Natural Resource Governance Institute, 80 Broad Street, Suite 1801, New York, NY 10004, USA (office). *Telephone:* (646) 929-9750 (office). *E-mail:* nrgi@resourcegovernance.org (office). *Website:* resourcegovernance.org (office).

LISSNER, Stéphane Michel; French theatre director; *Director-General, Opéra National de Paris;* b. 23 Jan. 1953, Paris; s. of Georges Lissner and Elisabeth Landenbaum; two s. one d.; ed Coll. Stanislas and Lycée Henri IV, Paris; f. his first theatre, Théâtre Mécanique 1971; Sec.-Gen. Centre dramatique, Aubervilliers 1977–78; Co-Dir Centre dramatique, Nice 1978–83; Admin., Théâtre du Châtelet, Paris 1983–88, Gen. Man. 1988–98; Dir-Gen. Orchestre de Paris 1993–95; Artistic Dir Teatro Real de Paris 1996–97; Dir Aix-en-Provence Int. Festival 1998–2006; Co-Dir (with Peter Brook) Théâtre des Bouffes du Nord, Paris 1998–2005; Dir Théâtre de la Madeleine, Paris 2002–11; Music Dir Wiener Festwochen 2005–13; Supt and Artistic Dir Teatro alla Scala, Milan 2005–14; Dir-Gen. Desig. Opéra Nat. de Paris 2012–14, Dir-Gen. 2014–; Chevalier, Légion d'honneur, Officier, Ordre nat. du Mérite, Ufficiale Ordine al Merito della Repubblica Italiana. *Publication:* Métro Chapelle 2000. *Address:* Opéra National de Paris, Palais Garnier, 8 rue Scribe, 75009 Paris, France. *Website:* www.operadeparis.fr.

LISSOUBA, Pascal, DèsSc; Republic of the Congo fmr head of state; b. 15 Nov. 1931, Tsinguidi, Congo (Brazzaville); s. of Albert Lissouba and Marie Bouanga; m. 2nd Jocelyne Pierrot 1967; one s. six d.; ed secondary education in Nice, France and Ecole Supérieure d'Agric., Tunis, Tunisia; fmr agricultural specialist; Prime Minister of Congo (Brazzaville) 1963–66, concurrently Minister of Trade and Industry and Agric.; Prof. of Genetics, Brazzaville 1966–71, concurrently Minister of Planning 1968, Minister of Agric., Waterways and Forests 1969; Dir Ecole Supérieure des Sciences, Brazzaville 1970; sentenced to life imprisonment for complicity in assassination of Pres. Ngouabi 1977, subsequently released and exiled; Dir African Bureau for Science and Tech., Nairobi from 1981; Leader Union panafricaine pour la Démocratie sociale (UPADS); Pres. Repub. of the Congo 1992–97; living in exile in London, UK; convicted *in absentia* on charges of treason and corruption and sentenced to 30 years by high court in Brazzaville 2001. *Leisure interests:* geology, music.

LISSOWSKI, Antoine; French business executive; *Chief Executive Officer, CNP Assurances SA;* b. 1956; ed Institut d'Études Politiques de Paris, École Nationale d'Admin; began career at Caisse des Dépôts et Consignations as Head of the Treasury and currency eurocredits; Special Adviser to Securities and Exchange Comm. 1985–88; returned to Caisse des Dépôts 1988, Head of Business Devt activities on money and bond markets 1988–90, Man. Dir Fund Autonomous Refinancing (CAR-Groupe Caisse des Dépôts) and Chief Financial Officer (CFO) Banking and Financial Deposit 1990–2000; CFO CDC IXIS 2000–03, mem. Exec. Bd 2002–03; mem. Bd of Dirs CNP Assurances SA 2003–07, Deputy CEO (Finance) 2007–18, Deputy Dir Gen. and CFO CNP Assurances SA 2007–12, Acting CEO and CFO June–Sept. 2012, CEO 2018–; Chair. Econ. and Financial Plenary Cttee, FSSA 2003–, Pres. (Solvency), Centre Européen des Assurances 2003–; currently Chair. Strategic Investment Fund (FSP) 2018–; fmr mem. Supervisory Bd Groupe Caisse d'Epargne SA. *Address:* CNP Assurances SA, 4 place Raoul Dautry, 75716 Paris Cedex 15, France (office). *Telephone:* 1-42-18-88-88 (office). *E-mail:* info@cnp.fr (office). *Website:* www.cnp.fr (office).

LIST, Benjamin, PhD; German chemist and academic; *Director, Max Planck Institute for Coal Research;* b. 1968, Frankfurt; ed Free Univ., Berlin, Univ. of Frankfurt; postdoctoral researcher, Scripps Research Inst., La Jolla, Calif., USA 1997–98, Asst Prof. (Tenure Track) 1999–2003; Group Leader, Max-Planck-Institut für Kohlenforschung, Mülheim (Max Planck Inst. for Coal Research) 2003–05, Dir 2005–, Man. Dir 2012–14; Visiting Prof., Gakushuin Univ., Tokyo, Japan 2005, Sungkyunkwan Univ., Korea 2008; Hon. Prof., Univ. of Cologne 2004–; NaFöG-Award from City of Berlin 1994, Feodor-Lynen Fellowship, Alexander von Humboldt Foundation 1997, Synthesis-Synlett Journal Award 2000, Carl-Duisberg-Memorial Award, German Chemical Soc. 2003, Degussa Prize for Chiral Chem. 2004, Lecturer's Award, Fonds der Chemischen Industrie 2004, Lieseberg Prize, Univ. of Heidelberg 2004, Lectureship Award, Soc. of Synthetic Chem., Japan 2005, AstraZeneca European Lecturer 2005, Novartis Young Investigator Award 2005, JSPS Fellowship Award (Japan) 2006, 100 Masterminds of Tomorrow (Germany) 2006, Award of the Fonds der Chemischen Industrie (Silver) 2007, OBC-Lecture Award 2007, AstraZeneca Award in Organic Chem. 2007, Boehringer-Ingelheim Lectureship (Canada) 2009, Organic Reactions Lectureship (USA) 2009, ERC Advanced Grant 2011, Boehringer-Ingelheim Lectureship, Harvard Univ., USA 2011, Otto Bayer Award 2012, Ruhr Prize for Art and Science 2013, Cope Scholar Award 2014, Gottfried Wilhelm Leibniz Prize 2016. *Publications include:* more than 120 papers in professional journals on new synthetic methodologies, asymmetric catalysis, organocatalysis, bio-organic chemistry and natural product synthesis. *Address:* Max-Planck-Institut für Kohlenforschung, Kaiser-Wilhelm-Platz 1, 45470 Mülheim an der Ruhr, Germany (office). *Telephone:* (208) 306-2410 (office). *Fax:* (208) 306-2999 (office). *E-mail:* list@mpi-muelheim.mpg.de (office); list@kofo.mpg.de (office). *Website:* www.kofo.mpg.de/de/forschung/homogene-katalyse (office).

LISTER, Gwen, BA; Namibian journalist; *Chairperson, Namibia Media Trust;* b. 5 Dec. 1953, East London, S Africa; one s. one d.; ed Univ. of Cape Town, South Africa; began career as journalist with Windhoek Advertiser 1975; Co-founder (with Hannes Smith) Windhoek Observer 1978, Political Ed. 1978–84 (S African authorities banned newspaper during coverage of independence talks 1984, ban defeated, resgnd because of accusations by newspaper sr staff 1984); Founder The Namibian newspaper 1985, Ed. 1985–2011 (copies confiscated by authorities, advertising boycott by business community, office bldg burned down 1988, prohibition of govt advertising in newspaper 2001); currently Chair. Namibia Media Trust; Exec. Dir Free Press of Namibia (Pty) Ltd (publishes The Namibian); Co-founder Media Inst. of Southern Africa, fmr Chair. Governing Council and mem. Trust Funds Bd; mem. UNESCO Press Freedom Council, African Advisory Bd Int. Women's Media Foundation, Advisory Bd Int. Consortium of Investigative Journalists; various speeches on media freedom/democracy and ethics worldwide, including at several UNESCO confs; Namibian nat. colours for squash, Inter Press Service Int. Journalism Award 1988, S African Soc. of Journalists Pringle Prize for Journalism 1988, Cttee to Protect Journalists Int. Journalism Award 1991, Nieman Fellowship, Harvard Univ. 1995–96, Media Inst. of S Africa Press Freedom Award 1997, named Int. Press Inst. Press Freedom Hero 2000, Int. Women's Media Foundation Courage in Journalism Award 2004. *Publications:* several book chapters. *Address:* The Namibian, PO Box 20783, 42 John Meinert Street, Windhoek, Namibia (office). *Telephone:* (61) 279600 (office). *Fax:* (61) 279602 (office). *E-mail:* gwen@namibian.com.na (office). *Website:* www.namibian.com.na (office).

LISTER OF BURTERSETT, Baroness (Life Peer), cr. 2011, of Nottingham in the County of Nottinghamshire; **Ruth Lister,** CBE, BA (Hons), MA, FBA, FAcSS;

British sociologist and academic; *Professor Emerita of Social Policy, Loughborough University;* b. (Margot Ruth Aline Lister), 3 May 1949, Huddersfield, W Yorks.; d. of Werner Bernard Lister and Daphne Lister; ed Univs of Essex and Sussex; worked for Child Poverty Action Group 1971–87, Dir 1979–87; Prof. and Head of Dept of Applied Social Studies, Univ. of Bradford 1988–94; Prof. of Social Policy, Dept of Sociology, Loughborough Univ. 1994–2010, Prof. Emer. of Social Policy 2010–; consultant on a Joseph Rowntree Foundation funded project, Living through Change in Challenging Neighbourhoods, Sheffield Hallam Univ.; mem. Social Policy Asscn; Chair. Jt Univ. Council Social Policy Cttee 1994–96; Founding Academicians, Acad. of Social Sciences; first Donald Dewar Visiting Prof. of Social Justice, Univ. of Glasgow 2005–07; Chair. Editorial Bd Social Policy & Administration 2003–09; mem. several journal editorial bds; mem. Bd, Smith Inst.; fmr mem. Comm. on Social Justice, Opsahl Comm. on the future of Northern Ireland, Comm. on Poverty, Participation and Power (est. by UK Coalition against Poverty as part of their Voices for Change consultation project), Fabian Comm. on Life Chances and Child Poverty, Nat. Equality Panel, task group on social protection as part of Sir Michael Marmot's Strategic Review of Health Inequalities in England, Post 2010; Trustee, Community Devt Foundation 2000–10; Chair Compass Management Cttee 2011–; sits on various other voluntary sector and research advisory cttees; mem. (Labour), House of Lords 2011–; Hon. Pres. Child Poverty Action Group 2010–, Social Policy Asscn 2016–; Hon. LLD (Manchester), (Brighton) 2012, (Bath) 2014; Hon. DLitt (Glasgow Caledonian), (Essex) 2012, (Loughborough) 2015; Hon. DSc (Lincoln) 2013; Eleanor Rathbone Memorial Lecturer 1989, Queen's Anniversary Prize for Higher and Further Educ. (co-recipient) 2005, 2006 Jill Vickers Prize, Canadian Political Science Asscn (co-recipient) 2006, Lifetime Achievement Award, Social Policy Asscn 2010. *Publications:* Social Justice. Strategies for National Renewal (report co-author) 1994, Citizenship: Feminist Perspectives 1998 (second edn 2003, translated into Chinese), Listen Hear: The Right to be Heard (report co-author) 2000, Young Peoples Voices. Citizenship Education (with S. Middleton and N. Smith) 2002, Poverty 2004 (translated into Polish, Macedonian and Japanese), Narrowing the Gap (report co-author) 2006, Why Money Matters (co-ed.) 2008, Understanding Theories and Concepts in Social Policy (Understanding Welfare series) 2010, An Anatomy of Economic Inequality in the UK (report co-author) 2010; numerous book chapters and articles in academic journals. *Leisure interests:* walking, watching tennis, music, films and theatre, meditation, Tai Chi. *Address:* House of Lords, Westminster, London, SW1A 0PW, England (office). *Telephone:* (20) 7219-5353 (office); (20) 7219-8984 (office). *E-mail:* m.r.lister@lboro.ac.uk (office); listerr@parliament.uk (office).

LITHERLAND, Albert Edward, PhD, DSc, FRS, FRSC; Canadian physicist and academic; *University Professor Emeritus, University of Toronto;* b. 12 March 1928, Wallasey, Merseyside, England; s. of Albert Litherland and Ethel Clement; m. Anne Allen 1956; two d.; ed Wallasey Grammar School and Univ. of Liverpool; Scientific Officer, Atomic Energy of Canada 1955–66; Prof. of Physics, Univ. of Toronto 1966–79, Univ. Prof. 1979–93, Univ. Prof. Emer. 1993–, Dir Isotrace Lab. 1982–2008; Guggenheim Fellow 1986; Hon. DSc (Toronto) 1998; Gold Medal, Canadian Asscn of Physicists 1971, Rutherford Medal and Prize, Inst. of Physics 1974, Silver Medal, Journal of Applied Radiation and Isotopes 1981, Henry Marshall Tory Gold Medal, Royal Soc. of Canada 1993. *Publications:* numerous scientific papers. *Leisure interests:* reading, travel. *Address:* Apartment 509, 111 Avenue Road, Toronto, ON M5R 3J8, Canada (home). *Telephone:* (416) 978-3785 (office); (416) 923-5616 (home). *E-mail:* ted.litherland@utoronto.ca (office).

LITHGOW, John Arthur; American actor; b. 19 Oct. 1945, Rochester, New York; s. of Arthur Lithgow and Sarah Jane (née Price); m. 1st Phoebe Jean Taynton 1966; m. 2nd Mary Yeager 1981; ed Harvard Univ., London Acad. of Music and Dramatic Art, UK; Broadway debut in The Changing Room 1973; also writes children's literature. *Films include:* Obsession 1976, All That Jazz 1979, The World According to Garp 1982, Terms of Endearment 1983, The Day After 1983, Footloose 1984, Harry and the Hendersons 1987, Raising Cain 1992, The Pelican Brief 1993, A Civil Action 1998, Don Quixote 2000, Shrek (voice) 2001, Orange County 2002, The Life and Death of Peter Sellers 2004, Kinsey 2004, Dreamgirls 2006, Leap Year 2010, Shrek Forever After 2010, The Campaign 2012, This Is 40 2012, Love Is Strange 2014, The Homesman 2014, Interstellar 2014, Miss Sloane 2016, Beatriz at Dinner 2017. *Theatre includes:* The Changing Room (Tony Award for Best Featured Actor in a Play) 1973, Boy Meets Girl 1976, Comedians 1976, Division Street 1980, Requiem for a Heavyweight 1985, M. Butterfly 1988, Sweet Smell of Success (Tony Award for Best Actor in a Musical) 2002, Dirty Rotten Scoundrels 2005, All My Sons 2008, Mr & Mrs Fitch 2010. *Television includes:* 3rd Rock from the Sun (Primetime Emmy Award for Outstanding Lead Actor in a Comedy Series 1996, 1997, 1999) 1996–2001, Twenty Good Years 2006, Dexter (series) (Golden Globe Award) 2009, How I Met Your Mother (series) 2011–14, Once Upon a Time in Wonderland (series) 2013–14, The Crown (SAG Award for Outstanding Performance by a Male Actor in a Drama Series 2017, Emmy Award for Outstanding Supporting Actor in a Drama Series 2017) 2016–17, Trial and Error 2017. *Publications include:* children's stories: Remarkable Farkle Mcbride 2000, Marsupial Sue 2001, Micawber 2002, I'm a Manatee 2003, A Lithgow Palooza 2004, Carnival of the Animals 2004, Mahalia Mouse Goes to College 2007, I Got Two Dogs 2008; Drama: An Actor's Education 2011. *Address:* Brady, Brannon & Rich, 5670 Wilshire Blvd, Suite 820, Los Angeles, CA 90036, USA (office). *Telephone:* (323) 852-9559 (office). *Fax:* (323) 852-9579 (office). *Website:* www.bbrtalentagency.com (office).

LITTLE, Brad, BS; American politician; *Governor of Idaho;* b. 15 Feb. 1954, Emmett, Ida; m. Teresa Little (née Soulen); two s.; ed Univ. of Idaho; Owner and Gen. Partner, Little Land and Livestock Co. 1979–; mem. Senate, Ida 2001–09, mem. Cttees on Resources and Environment Affairs 2002, Agricultural Affairs 2002, State Affairs 2003–09; Lt-Gov. of Ida 2009–19, Gov. 2019–; Chair. Ida Asscn of Commerce and Industry 1981–2001, Ida Wool Growers Asscn; Vice-Chair. Ida Community Foundation 2004, Emmett Public School Foundation 2004; mem. Bd of Dirs, Univ. of Idaho Foundation; mem. Bd, Home Federal Bank, Performance Design Inc.; mem. Nat. Rifle Asscn, Ida Petroleum Storage Tank, Endowment Investment Bd. *Address:* Office of the Governor, State Capitol, PO Box 83720, Boise, ID 83720, USA (office). *Telephone:* (208) 334-2100 (office). *Fax:* (208) 854-3036 (office). *E-mail:* governor@gov.idaho.gov (office). *Website:* www.gov.idaho.gov (office).

LITTLE, (Robert) Alastair, MA; British restaurateur and chef; b. 25 June 1950, Colne, Lancs., England; s. of R. G. Little and M. I. Little; m. 1st Kirsten Pedersen 1981; one s. one d.; m. 2nd Sharon Jacob 2000; ed Kirkham Grammar School, Downing Coll., Cambridge; self-taught chef; Head Chef, Old Compton Wine Bar 1974–76; Chef/Propr, Le Routier Wrentham Suffolk 1976–79, Simpsons, Putney, London 1979–81; Chef, L'Escargot, London 1981–82, 192 Kensington Park Road 1982–85; Chef/Propr, Alastair Little, Frith Street 1985–2002, Lancaster Road 1996–2002; Propr Tavola (delicatessen), Westbourne Grove, London 2003–; food columnist, Daily Mail 1993–; mem. Acad. Culinaire; Times Restaurant of Year 1993. *Publications:* Keep it Simple 1993, Mediterranean Redefined (with Richard Whittington) 1995, Alastair Little's Italian Kitchen 1996, Soho Cooking 2000. *Leisure interests:* jigsaws, trashy novels, travel, wine, reading, mycology, watching sport. *Address:* Tavola, 155 Westbourne Grove, Notting Hill, London, W11 2RS, England. *Telephone:* (20) 7229-0571.

LITTLE, Tasmin E., OBE, ARCM (Hons), FGSM; British violinist; b. 13 May 1965, London; d. of George Little and Gillian Little; one s. one d.; ed Yehudi Menuhin School, Guildhall School of Music, studied privately with Lorand Fenyves in Canada; has performed with New York Philharmonic, Berlin Philharmonic, Leipzig Gewandhaus, Cleveland Orchestra, Berlin Symphony, London Symphony, London Philharmonic, Philharmonia, Royal Philharmonic, New Japan Philharmonic, Royal Stockholm Philharmonic, Adelaide Symphony, Tasmanian Symphony, Hong Kong Philharmonic, BBC Symphony, Royal Liverpool Philharmonic, European Community Chamber, Royal Danish and Stavanger Symphony Orchestras; has played with orchestras conducted by Gustavo Dudamel, Kurt Masur, Vladimir Ashkenazy, Leonard Slatkin, Tadaaki Otaka, Sir Charles Groves, Sir Andrew Davis, Vernon Handley, Yan Pascal Tortelier, Sir Edward Downes, Yehudi Menuhin and Sir Simon Rattle; played at the BBC Promenade Concerts on 20 occasions since 1990; concerto and recital performances in UK, Europe, Scandinavia, S America, Hong Kong, Oman, Zimbabwe, Australia, NZ, USA and Japan; numerous TV appearances, including BBC Last Night of the Proms 1995, 1998, Wallace and Gromit Prom 2012; Hon. RAM; Hon. DLitt (Bradford) 1996; Hon. DMus (Leicester) 2002; Hon. DArts (Hertfordshire) 2007, (City) 2008. *Recordings include:* works by Bruch, Dvořák, Brahms, Sibelius, Delius, Rubbra, Saxton, George Lloyd, Ravel, Debussy, Poulenc, Delius, Elgar, Bax, Finzi; Dohnányi violin sonatas, Bruch Scottish Fantasy, Lalo Symphonie Espagnole, Pärt Spiegel im Spiegel and Fratres, The Naked Violin (Gramophone/Classic FM Award for Innovation 2008) 2007, Elgar Violin Concerto (Classic BRIT Award, Critic's Choice 2011) 2010, Strauss and Respighi sonatas, British Violin Sonatas 2013, Moeran Concerto, Lark Ascending 2013, Schubert Complete Works for violin and Piano 2015, Beethoven: Complete Sonatas 2016, A Violin For All Seasons 2016. *Publication:* paper on Delius' violin concerto. *Leisure interests:* theatre, cinema, swimming, languages. *Address:* 67 Teignmouth Road, London, NW2 4EA, England (office). *Telephone:* (20) 8208-2480 (office). *Fax:* (20) 8208-2490 (office). *E-mail:* dkantor.kaydar@gmail.com (office). *Website:* www.tasminlittle.net.

LITTLE RICHARD; American rock singer and songwriter; b. (Richard Wayne Penniman), 5 Dec. 1932, Macon, Ga; adopted s. of Enotris Johnson and Ann Johnson; R&B singer in various bands, including own band The Upsetters; gospel singer 1960–62; worldwide tours and concerts; announced retirement 2002; Dr hc (Mercer Univ.) 2013; inducted into Rock and Roll Hall of Fame 1986, Grammy Lifetime Achievement Award 1993, American Music Award of Merit 1997, inducted into Songwriters Hall of Fame 2003. *Recordings include:* albums: Cast A Long Shadow 1956, Little Richard Vol. 1 1957, Little Richard Vol. 2 1957, Little Richard Vol. 3 1957, Here's Little Richard 1957, The Fabulous Little Richard 1959, Clap Your Hands 1960, Pray Along With Little Richard Vol. 1 1960, Pray Along With Little Richard Vol. 2 1960, King Of The Gospel Singers 1962, Sings Spirituals 1963, Sings the Gospel 1964, Little Richard Is Back 1965, The Wild and Frantic Little Richard 1965, The Explosive Little Richard 1967, Rock 'n' Roll Forever 1967, Good Golly Miss Molly 1969, Little Richard 1969, Right Now 1970, Rock Hard Rock Heavy 1970, Little Richard 1970, Well Alright! 1970, Mr Big 1971, The Rill Thing 1971, The Second Coming 1971, Dollars 1972, The Original 1972, You Can't Keep A Good Man Down 1972, Rip It Up 1973, Talkin' 'Bout Soul 1974, Recorded Live 1974, Keep A Knockin' 1975, Sings 1976, Little Richard Live 1976, Now 1977, Lucille 1988, Shake It All About 1992, Shag On Down By The Union Hall 1996. *Films include:* Don't Knock the Rock 1956, Mr Rock 'n' Roll 1957, The Girl Can't Help It 1957, Keep On Rockin' 1970, Down and Out in Beverly Hills 1986, Mother Goose Rock 'n' Rhyme (Disney Channel) 1989.

LITTLECHILD, Stephen Charles, PhD; British economist and public servant; *Fellow, Judge Business School, University of Cambridge;* b. 27 Aug. 1943, Wisbech, Cambs.; s. of Sidney F. Littlechild and Joyce M. Littlechild; m. Kate Crombie 1974 (died 1982); two s. one d.; ed Wisbech Grammar School, Univ. of Birmingham, Univ. of Texas, USA; Harkness Fellow 1965–67; Sr Research Lecturer in Econs, Graduate Centre for Man. Studies, Birmingham 1970–72; Prof. of Applied Econs and Head of Econs, Econometrics, Statistics and Marketing Subject Group, Aston Man. Centre, Birmingham 1972–75; Prof. of Commerce, Univ. of Birmingham 1975–94, Head, Dept of Industrial Econs and Business Studies 1975–89, Hon. Prof. 1994–2004, Prof. Emer. 2004–; Visiting Scholar, Dept of Econs, UCLA, USA 1975; Visiting Prof., New York, Stanford and Chicago Univs and Virginia Polytechnic 1979–80; mem. Monopolies and Mergers Comm. 1983–89, Sec. of State for Energy's Advisory Council on Research and Devt 1987–89; Dir-Gen. of Electricity Supply 1989–98; Prin. Research Fellow, Judge Business School, Univ. of Cambridge 2000–04, Fellow 2004–; mem. Postcomm 2006–11; Hon. DSc (Birmingham) 2001; Hon. DCL (East Anglia) 2004. *Publications:* Operational Research for Managers 1977, (with M. F. Shutler) 1991, The Fallacy of the Mixed Economy 1978, 1986, Elements of Telecommunications Economics 1979, Energy Strategies for the UK (with K. G. Vaidya) 1982, Regulation of British Telecommunications' Profitability 1983, Economic Regulation of Privatised Water Authorities 1986; approx. 200 articles in learned journals. *Leisure interest:* family history. *E-mail:* sclittlechild@tanworth.mercianet.co.uk (office).

LITTLEWOOD, Peter Brent, BA, PhD, FInstP; British/American physicist and academic; *Director, Argonne National Laboratory;* b. 18 May 1955, Pembury, Kent, England; m. Elizabeth Littlewood 1978; one s. one d.; ed Cavendish Lab., Univ. of Cambridge; worked at Bell Labs, Murray Hill, NJ, USA 1980–97, Head of

Theoretical Physics Research Dept 1992–97; Prof. of Physics, Cavendish Lab., Univ. of Cambridge 1997–2005, Head of Theory of Condensed Matter Group, Cavendish Lab. 1997–2005, Head of Dept of Physics, Cavendish Lab. 2005–11, Head of Cavendish Lab. 2005–11, Fellow, Trinity Coll.; Assoc. Lab. Dir for Physical Sciences and Engineering, Argonne Nat. Lab., USA 2011–14, Dir Argonne Nat. Lab. 2014–; Prof. of Physics, James Franck Inst., Univ. of Chicago 2011–; Matthias Scholar, Los Alamos Nat. Lab. 2003–04; has served as consultant to Los Alamos Nat. Lab., Nat. High Magnetic Field Lab., Defense Advanced Research Projects Agency; mem. Royal Soc. 2008–; Fellow, American Physical Soc. 1989, Inst. of Physics 2005. *Address:* Argonne National Laboratory, 9700 South Cass Avenue, Argonne, IL 60439, USA (office). *Telephone:* (630) 252-2000 (office). *E-mail:* pblittlewood@anl.gov (office). *Website:* www.anl.gov (office).

LITTON, Andrew, MM; American conductor and pianist; *Music Director, New York City Ballet;* b. 16 May 1959, New York; ed Fieldston High School, New York, Mozarteum, Austria, Juilliard School; Asst Conductor, La Scala, Milan 1980–81; Exxon/Arts Endowment Asst Conductor, then Assoc. Conductor, Nat. Symphony Orchestra, Washington, DC 1982–86; Prin. Guest Conductor, Bournemouth Symphony Orchestra 1986–88, Prin. Conductor and Artistic Adviser 1988–94, Conductor Laureate 1994–; Prin. Conductor and Music Dir Dallas Symphony Orchestra 1994–2006, Music Dir Emeritus 2006–; Prin. Conductor, Bergen Philharmonic Orchestra 2002–15, Music Dir 2005–15; apptd Prin. Guest Conductor and Artistic Adviser, Colorado Symphony Orchestra 2002, Music Dir 2013–15, Prin. Guest Conductor and Artistic Adviser 2016–; Artistic Dir Minnesota Orchestra's Sommerfest 2003–; Music Dir New York City Ballet 2015–; guest conductor with numerous orchestras world-wide, including Chicago Symphony, Philadelphia, Los Angeles Philharmonic, Pittsburgh Symphony, Toronto Symphony, Montréal Symphony, Vancouver Symphony, London Philharmonic, Royal Philharmonic, London Symphony, English Chamber Orchestra, Leipzig Gewandhaus, Moscow State Symphony, Stockholm Philharmonic, RSO Berlin, RAI Milan, Orchestre Nat. de France, Suisse Romande, Tokyo Philharmonic, Melbourne Symphony and Sydney Symphony orchestras; debut at Metropolitan Opera, New York with Eugene Onegin 1989; also conducted at St Louis Opera, LA Opera, Royal Opera House, Covent Garden and ENO; music consultant to film The Chosen; Royal Order of Merit (Norway); Hon. DMus (Bournemouth) 1992; winner, Bruno Walter Conducting Fellowship 1981, William Kapell Memorial US Nat. Piano Competition 1978, BBC/Rupert Foundation Int. Conductors Competition 1982, Yale Univ. Sanford Medal, Elgar Soc. Medal. *Recordings include:* Mahler Symphony No. 1 and Songs of a Wayfarer, Elgar Enigma Variations, complete Tchaikovsky symphony cycle, complete Rachmaninov symphony cycle, Shostakovich Symphony No. 10, Gershwin Rhapsody in Blue, Concerto in F and Ravel Concerto in G (as piano soloist and conductor), Bernstein Symphony No. 2, Brahms Symphony No. 1, Walton's Belshazzar's Feast (with Bryn Terfel and Bournemouth Symphony) (Grammy Award), Rachmaninov Piano Concertos (with Stephen Hough and Dallas Symphony Orchestra) (Classical BRIT Critics' Award 2005) 2004. *Address:* c/o Ron Merlino, Musicvine, 2576 Broadway, Suite 239, New York, NY 10025, USA (office); New York City Ballet, David H. Koch Theater, 20 Lincoln Center, New York, NY 10023, USA (office). *Telephone:* (646) 825-9585 (office). *E-mail:* merlino@musicvinearts.com (office); info@nycballet.com (office). *Website:* www.nycballet.com (office); www.andrewlitton.com.

LITVINOVA, Renata Muratovna; Russian actress and scriptwriter; b. 11 Jan. 1968, Moscow; d. of Murat Vergazov and Alissa Litvinova; m. Mikhail Dobrovsky; ed All-Union State Inst. of Cinematography; mem. Union of Theatre Workers; mem. jury, Moscow International Film Festival 2007; Honoured Artist of the Russian Fed. 2003, Nat. Award of Public Recognition, Russian Acad. of Business and Entrepreneurship 2007, Pushkin Medal 2012. *Films include:* The Border-Taiga Romance, Dve strely. Detektiv kamennogo veka (Two Arrows: The Crime Story from the Stone Age) (State Prize of Russia 2001) 1989, Uvlecheniya (Passions) (Best Acting Debut, Kinotavr Film Festival, "Woman-style" Film Award) 1994, Tri istorii (Three Stories) (Best Actress, Yekaterinburg Film Festival, Best Supporting Actress, Int. Film Festival) 1997, 8½ $ (voice) 1999, Aprel (April) 1992, Nebo. Samolyot. Devushka. (Sky. Plane. Girl.) (also writer and producer) (Best Actress, RKF "Literature and Cinema", Gatchina 2003) 2002, Net smerti dlya menya (There is No Death for Me) (dir) (Laurel Branch) 2002, The Tulse Luper Suitcases, Part 3: From Sark to the Finish 2003, Nastroyshchik (The Tuner) (Best Actress for CF "Viva Cinema of Russia" 2005) 2004, Boginya: kak ya polyubila (Goddess: How I Felt in Love) (also writer and dir and producer) 2004, Zhmurki 2005, Vokaldy paralelder 2005, Zhest 2006, Mne ne bolno (Best Actress, Kinotavr Film Festival) 2006, Dva v odnom 2007, Zhestokost 2007, Wow! (Generation P) 2011, Heart's Boomerang 2011, Poslednyaya skazka Rity 2012, The Girl and Death 2012, Vechnoye vozvrashcheniye 2012, Psevdonim dlya geroya 2014, Gena Beton 2014, About Love 2015, Peterburg. Tolko po lyubvi 2016, Rorrim Bo and the Magic Goblet 2016, ANGST 2018, Last Prince of Atlantis (voice) 2018. *Scriptwriter for films:* Leningrad, November, Nelyubov (No Love) 1991, Traktoristy (Tractor Drivers) 1992, Muzhskiye otkroveniya (Revelations of Men) 1995, Principal and Compassionate Eye, Tri istorii (Three Stories) 1997, Strana glukhikh (The Country of Deaf People) 1998. *Television includes:* Granitsa. Tayozhnyy roman (mini-series) 2001, Diversant (mini-series) 2004, Prikazano unichtozhit. Operatsiya 'Kitayskaya shkatulka (series) 2009, Pedistal krasoty. Istoriya obuvi s Renatoy Litvinovoy (mini-series) 2013. *Publications:* Prize of Film Festival Centaurs for Passions. *Leisure interests:* antiques, cats. *E-mail:* info@renatalitvinova.ru. *Website:* renatalitvinova.ru.

LIU, Andong; Chinese business executive; b. 1946, Fengcheng Co., Liaoning Prov.; ed Beijing Inst. of Posts and Telecommunications; joined CCP 1966; technician, Petrochemical Research Inst., Ministry of Petroleum Industry 1970–85, Assoc. Engineer 1970–85; technician, Computer Bureau, Ministry of Foreign Trade and Econ. Cooperation 1970–85; Office Sec., Work Group for Special Econ. Zones, Gen. Office of the State Council 1970–85, Deputy Div. Head, Open City Group 1985–88, Deputy Div. Head, Foreign Investment Dept 1985–88, Deputy Dir Foreign Investment Dept 1988–98, Deputy Dir Open Zones Dept 1988–98, Deputy Dir Open Coastal Regions Dept 1988–98, Dir Foreign Investment Dept 1988–98, Dir Open Zones Dept 1988–98, Dir Coastal Regions Dept 1988–98; Vice-Pres. China Post Group 1998–2003, Pres. 2003–12.

LIU, Benren; Chinese engineer and business executive; b. Nov. 1942, Pinghu, Zhejiang Prov.; ed Wuhan Int. of Metallurgy, Training Dept of Party School of CCP; joined Wuhan Iron & Steel Corpn 1965, fmr Man. Wuhan Hot Rolling Plant, later Vice-Chief Eng, then Vice-Gen. Man. and Party Cttee mem. Wuhan Iron and Steel Plant, Gen. Man. 1965–86, also Party Cttee mem. and Vice-Sec. Party Cttee Wuhan Iron and Steel Group Corpn (WISCO) 1993–2004; Chair. and External Dir China Metallurgical Group Corpn 2004–10; Deputy Chair. Prosperity Int. Holdings (H.K.) Ltd 2010–13; mem. Bd of Dirs Wuhan Iron and Steel Co. 1983–93, China Classification Soc. 1994–97, Shenhua Group Corpn Ltd 2005–, China Shenhua Energy Co. Ltd 2010–12, Fosun Int. Ltd 2007–12; mem. 8th, 9th and 10th Nat. Cttee CPPCC; Nat. May 1 Labor Medal. *Address:* c/o China Metallurgical Group Corpn, No. 28 Shuguangxili, Chaoyang, Beijing 100000, People's Republic of China (office).

LIU, Bosu; Chinese artist and academic; b. Nov. 1935, Nanchang City, Jiangxi Prov.; ed Cen. Inst. of Fine Arts; Assoc. Prof. Cen. Inst. of Fine Arts 1981–83, apptd Prof. 1983, Vice Dir 1986; Dir Chinese Painting Acad. 1993; mem. 7th CPPCC 1988–93, 8th CPPCC 1993–98.

LIU, Chao-shiuan, BS, MS, PhD; Taiwanese academic and politician; b. 10 May 1943; ed Nat. Taiwan Univ., Univ. de Sherbrooke and Univ. of Toronto, Canada; Assoc. Prof., Nat. Tsing Hua Univ. 1971–75, Prof. 1975–79, Dean, Coll. of Science 1982–84, Pres., Nat. Tsing Hua Univ. 1987–93, Chair Prof. 2000; Dir-Gen. Dept of Planning and Evaluation, Nat. Science Council, Exec. Yuan 1979–82, Deputy Minister 1984–87, Minister 1996–97; Minister of Transportation and Communications 1993–96; Vice Premier 1997–2000, Premier 2008–09 (resgnd); Pres. Soochow Univ. 2004–08; Pres. Gen. Asscn of Chinese Culture 2009–16, Asscn of Pvt. Univs and Colls 2006–08; Vice-Chair. Nat. Policy Foundation 2000–04; Chair. Monte Jade Science and Tech. Asscn of Taiwan 2001–05, K.T. Li Foundation for Devt of Science and Tech. 2000–08; Pres. Chemical Soc. 1986–87; Rose Wolfe Distinguished Alumni Award, Univ. of Toronto 1999.

LIU, Christina Yi-ru, BA, MBA, PhD; Taiwanese economist, academic and politician; b. 7 April 1955, Taipei; m. Johnsee Lee (divorced 1995); ed Nat. Taiwan Univ., Univ. of Chicago, USA; Lecturer, Dept of Econs, Univ. of Chicago 1983–86; Asst Prof. of Econs and Finance, CUNY 1987–92, Assoc. Prof. 1992–93; Visiting Prof., Coll. of Business and Econs, ANU 1992–98; Prof., Dept of Finance, Nat. Taiwan Univ. 1993–97, Adjunct Prof. 1997–, Chair., Dept and Graduate Inst. of Finance 1994–96; mem. Securities Listing Review Cttee, Taiwan Stock Exchange Corpn 1994–2001, mem. Public Interest Bd 1995–2001; mem. Ministry of Finance Financial Reform Comm. 2001–03; Adjunct Prof. of Business Admin, Tsinghua Univ., Beijing, Chinese Univ. of Hong Kong 2001–09; mem. and Convenor, Legis. Yuan Finance Cttee 2002–07, Commr, Exec. Yuan Tax Reform Comm. 2008–09, Chief Economist, Exec. Yuan 2009–10; Chief Econ. Adviser, Daiwa Inst. of Research 2008–09; Adviser, Chinese Nat. Fed. of Industries 2009–10; Chief Econ. Adviser, Chinatrust Financial Holding Co. Ltd 2009–10; Minister for Council for Econ. Planning and Devt 2010–12, Minister of Finance Feb.–May 2012. *Address:* c/o Ministry of Finance, 2 Ai Kuo West Road, Taipei 10066, Taiwan. *E-mail:* mof@mail.mof.gov.tu.

LIU, Chuanzhi; Chinese computer scientist and business executive; *Chairman, Legend Holdings Ltd;* b. 29 April 1944, Zhenjiang, Jiangsu Prov.; m.; three c.; ed Xi'an Mil. Telecommunications Inst.; researcher, Research Inst. No. 10 of State Science and Tech. Comm., Chengdu 1967–70; researcher, Computational Science Research Inst. of Chinese Acad. of Sciences 1970–83, later Dir; Cadre, Cadre Bureau, Chinese Acad. of Sciences 1983; Founder and Pres. Computational Science Research Inst. Inc. 1984; Founder, Chair. and Pres. Legend Holdings Group Inc., Hong Kong Special Admin. Region 1984–2012 (largest computer co. in China and parent co. of Lenovo), Chair. 2012–, Chair. and Pres. Lenovo Group Ltd 1994–2005, Chair. 2009–11, Hon. Chair. 2011–; Deputy, 10th NPC 2003–08; Vice-Chair. Exec. Cttee All-China Fed. of Industry and Commerce 2002; Dir, Computer Tech. Research Inst. of Chinese Acad. of Sciences 2004–; elected one of China's Top Ten Econ. Figures 2000, Businessman of the Year, CCTV 2009, Entrepreneur for the World Award 2010, Distinguished Exec. Award 2012, Thinkers 50 Leadership Award 2013. *Address:* Legend Holdings Ltd, 10/F, Tower A, Raycom Info Tech Park, No. 2 Ke Xue Yuan Nanlu, Zhongguancun, Haidian District, Beijing 100190, People's Republic of China (office). *Telephone:* (10) 62572078 (office). *Fax:* (10) 62561056 (office). *Website:* www.legendholdings.com.cn (office); www.lenovo.com (office).

LIU, Chunhong; Chinese weightlifter; b. 29 Jan. 1985, Yantai, Shandong Prov.; ed Yantai Sports School; switched from judo to weightlifting at Sports School 1996; mem. Shandong Prov. Weightlifting Team 1998–; mem. nat. team 2002–; competes in 63–69kg weight div.; silver medal at clean and jerk World Championships, Warsaw 2002; gold medals at snatch (with world record weight of 120kg), clean and jerk (world record 150kg) and combined (world record 270kg) World Championships, Vancouver 2003; gold medal, Olympic Games, Athens 2004, broke world records at snatch (122.5kg), clean and jerk (152.5kg), combined (275kg); gold medal, Olympic Games, Beijing 2008; gold medal (69kg weight div.) Nat. Games 2009; gold medal (69kg weight div.) Asian Games 2010; broke world records at snatch (128kg), clean and jerk (158kg), combined (286kg); has set 27 world records (12 jr, 15 sr) throughout career. *Leisure interests:* music, reading, painting. *Address:* 9 Tiyuguan Road, Beijing, 100763, People's Republic of China (office).

LIU, Dehai; Chinese musician and university professor; b. May 1937, Cangxian Co., Hebei Prov.; ed Centre Music Inst.; began learning Pipa and other traditional Chinese instruments (including Erhu and Sanxian) at age 13; toured extensively abroad and performed with many famous orchestras including Boston Symphony Orchestra, Berlin Symphony Orchestra; Prof., Centre Music Inst. 1984–; mem. 7th CPPCC Nat. Cttee 1988–93, 8th 1993–98. *Address:* c/o CRC Jianian, Inc., No. 18, Jianguo Mennei Street, Rm 1706–08, Henderson Center, Dongcheng District, Beijing 100005, People's Republic of China.

LIU, Deshu, BEng, EMBA; Chinese petrochemical industry executive; b. Nov. 1952; ed Tsinghua Univ., China-Europe Int. Business School; active in foreign trade for more than 20 years; Vice-Gen. Man., later Gen. Man. China Nat. Machinery Import and Export Corpn –1998; Pres. and CEO Sinochem Group 1998–2014, Chair. 2014–15 (retd); Pres. Sinofert Holdings Ltd, Sinochem

Quanzhou Petrochemical Co. Ltd, Far East Horizon Ltd; mem. 10th CPPCC, 11th CPPCC; del., 16th CCP Nat. Cttee 2002–07, 17th CCP Nat. Cttee 2007–12; Del. to 12th NPC, Vice-Chair. Environment Protection and Resources Conservation Cttee; Dir, Int. Acad. of Man. 2003–; one of the "Top 30 Economic Figures over the 30-year Reform and Opening-up in China", ranked by Fortune China amongst the Top 10 of "China's Most Influential Business Leaders" for four consecutive years. *Address:* c/o Sinochem Group, 11/F Central Tower, Chemsunny World Trade CCentre 28 Fuxingmennei Street, 100031 Beijing, People's Republic of China. *E-mail:* webmaster@sinochem.com.

LIU, Fang, LLM, PhD; Chinese aviation industry official and international organization official; *Secretary-General, International Civil Aviation Organization (ICAO);* ed Wuhan Univ., Leiden Univ., Netherlands; Legal Counsel, Dept of Int. Affairs and Cooperation, Civil Aviation Admin of China, later Deputy Dir, Dir and Deputy Dir-Gen. 1987–2007; Dir, Bureau of Admin and Services, ICAO 2007–15, Sec.-Gen., ICAO (first woman) 2015–; fmr Chair. Security Advisory Group and Vice-Chair., Security Man. Team for all UN orgs in Canada; fmr Chair. of group of aviation experts and Airline Services Group, Asia-Pacific Econ. Cooperation. *Address:* International Civil Aviation Organization, 999 University Street, Montreal, PQ H3C 5H7, Canada (office). *Telephone:* (514) 954-8219 (office). *Fax:* (514) 954-6077 (office). *E-mail:* icaohq@icao.int (office). *Website:* www.icao.int (office).

LIU, Fangren; Chinese party official; b. Jan. 1936, Wugong, Shaanxi Prov.; ed Shenyang Building Materials Eng Coll.; joined CCP 1954; worker, later technician, later Deputy Workshop Head, later Deputy Chief Engineer, later Deputy Factory Dir, Ministry of Ordnance Industry; fmr Deputy Sec., later Sec. CCP Jiujiang City Cttee, Jiangxi Prov.; Deputy Sec. Jiangxi Prov. CCP Cttee 1985–93; First Sec. CCP Party Cttee Guizhou Mil. Dist, PLA Chengdu Mil. Region 1993; Sec. CCP 7th Guizhou Prov. Cttee 1993–2001; Chair. Standing Cttee Guizhou Prov. People's Congress 1998; Alt. mem. 13th CCP Cen. Cttee 1987–92, 14th CCP Cen. Cttee 1992–97, mem. 15th CCP Cen. Cttee 1997–2002; Deputy, 8th NPC 1993–98, 9th NPC 1998–2003 (Vice-Chair. Agriculture and Rural Affairs Cttee 1998–2003); expelled from CCP following accusations of corruption 2003; sentenced to life imprisonment for taking bribes 2004.

LIU, Fuchun; Chinese business executive; b. 1949; ed Beijing Foreign Trade Junior Coll., Beijing Foreign Trade Inst.; several years' work experience in N America and Europe, including as Deputy Consul, Chinese Consular Section, Vancouver 1981–85; Deputy Division Dir, Division Dir, Oils and Fats Division, Cereals, Oils & Foodstuffs Import and Export Corpn (COFCO) 1985–91, Exec. Dir and Man. Dir COFCO 2000–07, also Pres. and Vice-Chair. 2000, Man. Dir COFCO HK; Gen. Man. Top Glory (London) Ltd 1989–91, Exec. Dir Top Glory Int. Holdings Ltd 2002–; Pres., Vice Chair. and Exec. Dir, China Foods Ltd 2000–07; mem. Bd of Dirs China Aviation Oil (Singapore) Corpn Ltd 2006–14, DaChan Food (Asia) Ltd 2007–14, China Mengniu Dairy Co. Ltd 2009–14, China Modern Dairy Holdings Ltd 2013.

LIU, Gang, MS; Chinese dissident; b. 30 Jan. 1961, Liaoyuan city, Jilin; m. Yinghua Guo (divorced); one d.; ed Peking Univ., Columbia Univ., USA; leader of Tiananmen Square pro-democracy demonstrations 1989; f. Beijing Students' Autonomous Fed.; imprisoned 1989–95; fled China; granted temporary asylum in USA 1996; trader with Morgan Stanley, New York 2009–11.

LIU, Guchang; Chinese diplomatist; b. 1946, Jiangsu Prov.; entered Foreign Ministry 1973, assigned to Embassy in Bucharest 1973–80, Third Sec. 1986–90, First Sec. 1986–90, Deputy Chief, Soviet Union and E European Affairs Dept 1980–86, Chief 1990–92, Chief, Europe-Asia Dept, Ministry of Foreign Affairs 1992–95, Amb. to Romania 1996–99, Asst to Minister of Foreign Affairs 1999–2002, Vice-Minister of Foreign Affairs 2002–03, Amb. to Russia 2003–09, Advisor, Ministry of Foreign Affairs 2009–. *Address:* Ministry of Foreign Affairs, 2 Chaoyangmen, Nan Dajie, Chao Yang Qu, Beijing 100701, People's Republic of China (office). *Telephone:* (10) 65961114 (office). *Fax:* (10) 65962146 (office). *E-mail:* webmaster@mfa.gov.cn (office). *Website:* www.fmprc.gov.cn (office).

LIU, Guoguang; Chinese economist; *Special Invited Consultant, Chinese Academy of Social Sciences;* b. 23 Nov. 1923, Nanjing; s. of Liu Zhihe and Zhiang Shulang; m. Liu Guoshiang 1948; two s. one d.; ed Southwest China United Univ., Kunming and Moscow State Inst. of Econs, USSR; joined CCP 1961; Deputy Dir-Gen. Nat. Bureau of Statistics 1980–82; Dir Inst. of Econs, Chinese Acad. of Social Sciences 1982–85, Vice-Pres. Chinese Acad. of Social Sciences 1982–93, Special Invited Consultant 1993–; Prof., Beijing Univ.; Alt. mem. 12th Cen. Cttee, CCP 1982–87, 13th Cen. Cttee 1987–92; mem. 8th NPC Standing Cttee 1993–98, mem. Financial and Econ. Cttee; mem. State Academic Degree Comm. 1988–95; mem. State Council Project Review Cttee for Three Gorges Project 1990–93; China Econs Award 2005. *Publications include:* The Problem Concerning the Reform of the Management System of the National Economy, Problems Concerning China's Strategy of Economic Readjustment, Economic Reform and Economic Readjustment, Developing Marxist Theory in the Practice of Reform, Reform, Stability and Development: Macroeconomic Management under the Dual-Track System, New Stage of China's Economic Reform and Development, Two Fundamental Transformations in China's Economy. *Leisure interest:* music. *Address:* Chinese Academy of Social Sciences, Beijing, People's Republic of China (office). *Telephone:* (10) 85195012 (office); (10) 87752681 (home). *Fax:* (10) 65137435 (office); (10) 87752680 (home). *E-mail:* liugg2005@yahoo.com.cn (home).

LIU, Haibin, BA; Chinese editor and business executive; b. 1952; fmr Deputy Ed.-in-Chief; fmrly worked as Special Commr of State Audit Bureau to Nanjing, Special Commr to Shanghai from State Audit Bureau; Chair. Supervisory Bd, Shanghai Pudong Development Bank Co. Ltd –2015; mem. Bd of Dirs, Shanghai International Group Co. Ltd. *Address:* c/o Shanghai Pudong Development Bank Co. Ltd, 12 Zhongshan Dong Yi Road, Shanghai 200002, People's Republic of China. *E-mail:* webmaster@spdb.com.cn.

LIU, He, BEcons, MEcon, MPA; Chinese economist and politician; *Vice Premier;* b. 25 Jan. 1952, Beijing; s. of Liu Zhiyan; ed Renmin Univ., Harvard Univ. John F. Kennedy School of Govt; worked at Beijing Wireless Factory 1974–78; Teacher, Renmin Univ. of China 1978–87; Researcher, Devt Research Centre, State Council 1987–88, Deputy Dir 2011–13; Deputy Dir, Policy Research Office, Nat. Devt and

Reform Comm. 1988–98; f. Chinese Economists 50 Forum 1998; Worker, State Information Centre 1998–2003, Exec. Deputy Dir 2003–11; Chair., China Econ. Information Network Data Co. Ltd 2003–11, also Chair., China Social Devt Network and Chair., IBASE Software Co. 2003–11; Prof., Beihang Univ. 2003–11; Vice-Chair., China Information Industry Asscn 2003–11; Deputy Dir, Nat. Devt and Reform Comm. 2013–; Dir, CCP Leading Group for Finance and Econ. Affairs 2013–; mem. State Council 2018–; Vice Premier 2018–; mem. 18th CCP Cen. Cttee 2012–17; mem. 19th CCP Cen. Cttee 2017–, also mem. 19th CCP Cen. Cttee Politburo 2017– and Politburo Secr. 2017–. *Publications:* more than 200 articles on economic subjects. *Address:* Leading Group for Financial and Economic Affairs, Communist Party of China Central Committee, Zhongnanhai, Beijing, People's Republic of China (office). *Website:* cpc.people.com.cn (office).

LIU, Hongliang; Chinese scientist; b. 20 June 1932, Dalian, Liaoning Prov.; s. of Liu Changchun (China's first Olympic athlete); ed Tsinghua Univ., Beijing; Fellow, Chinese Acad. of Eng 1994–; Pres. and Prof., Chinese Research Acad. of Environmental Sciences (CRAES) 1982, now Research Fellow; Chair. Agric., Textile and Environment Eng Div., Chinese Acad. of Eng; Deputy Dir, Consultant Cttee on Science and Tech., Ministry of Environmental Protection; Chief Ed. Environmental Science Research journal (Huanjing Kexue Yanjiu); travelled to Greece to take part in Olympic torch handover procession 2008; environmental consultant to Beijing Organizing Cttee for Olympic Games; pioneer in research on water environment. *Publications:* over 20 research papers and a number of monographs. *Address:* Chinese Research Academy of Environmental Sciences (CRAES), Dayangfang, Beiyuan, Andingmen Wai, Beijing 100012, People's Republic of China (office). *Telephone:* (10) 64232542 (office). *Fax:* (10) 64232542 (office). *E-mail:* engach@mail.cae.ac.cn (office).

LIU, Hongru, PhD; Chinese business executive; b. 1930, Yushu, Jilin; ed Northeast Mil. Coll., Chinese People's Univ., Moscow Univ., Moscow Financial Coll., USSR; joined CCP 1948; Vice-Gov. Agricultural Bank of China 1979–80; Vice-Gov. People's Bank of China 1981–89, Vice-Pres. Council People's Bank of China 1980; Vice-Minister State Economic Restructuring Comm. 1988–93; Vice-Gov. People's Bank of China 1981–89; Vice-Chair. Securities Comm. of the State Council 1992–95; Part-time Prof., Beijing, Qinghua and Nankai Univs; apptd Pres. Financial and Banking Inst. of China, China Monetary Coll. 1989, China Finance and Economics Univ.; Deputy Head Leading Group for the Reform of the Housing System 1991–; Chair. China Securities Regulatory Comm. 1992–95; Alt. mem. 13th CCP Cen. Cttee 1987–92; Vice-Chair. Econ. Sub-cttee 8th and 9th Nat. Cttees. of CPPCC 1993–2003; Ind. Supervisor PetroChina 1999–2002, Ind. Dir (non-exec.) 2002–; Chair. Chinese Financial Educ. Devt Foundation, Capital Market Research Inst.; currently Vice-Pres. China Finance and Banking Soc., China Nat. Debt Asscn; Hon. Pres. Securities and Futures Coll., Univ. of Hanzhou 1995–; Hon. Chair. Oriental Patron (ind. financial services group); Dr hc (City Univ. of Hong Kong) 1966. *Publications include:* Questions on Socialist China's Currency and Banking, Questions on Socialist Credit.

LIU, Huan; Chinese singer; b. 26 Aug. 1963, Tianjin; m. Lu Lu 1988; one d.; ed Beijing Int. Relations Inst.; solo artist; teacher, Univ. of Int. Relations, Beijing; currently teaching at Beijing Univ. of Int. Business and Econs; performed official theme song "You and Me" at Summer Olympic Games Opening Ceremony, Beijing, August 2008. *Stage production:* Sister Liu (opera) 2003. *Television:* The Voice of China (judge) 2012. *Compositions include:* themes to TV dramas: Plainclothes Cop 1986, The Water Margin, A Native of Beijing in New York, Snow City, Sun Rises in the East and Rain Drops in the West; songs: Asking Myself a Thousand Times for That, Helpless Love. *Address:* University of International Business and Economics, No. 10 Huixin Dongjie, Chaoyang District, Beijing 100029, People's Republic of China (office). *Telephone:* (10) 64492131 (office). *Fax:* (10) 64493860 (office). *Website:* english.uibe.edu.cn (office).

LIU, Huanzhang; Chinese sculptor; b. 30 Dec. 1930, Leting County, Hebei Province; m. Shen Chaohui 1968; one d.; ed Beijing Yuying Pvt. School, Beijing Cen. Acad. of Fine Arts; Assoc. Prof., Sculpture Studio, Beijing Cen. Acad. of Fine Arts 1956–; works at Tangshan No. 1 Middle School, Chen Jinlun Middle School, Beijing, Meixian, Guangdong Prov., Lanzhou Inst., Gansu Prov.; Ministry of Culture's Lifetime Achievement Award for Plastic Arts 2004. *Publications:* Liu Huanzhang Carre Works Selection 1984, Sculpture Works Selection 1985, Seals Selection 1988. *Leisure interests:* sports, gardening. *Address:* Building No. 3, 1-102, Hong Miao Beili Chao Yang, Beijing, People's Republic of China.

LIU, Huaqiu; Chinese diplomatist; b. Nov. 1939, Wuchuan Co., Guangdong Prov.; ed Foreign Affairs Inst., Beijing; joined CCP 1965; Second Sec., Embassy, Accra, Ghana 1973–81; Clerk, Gen. Office of State Council 1981; Counsellor then Minister, Embassy, Sydney, Australia 1984–86; Dir Dept of Affairs of the Americas and Oceania, Ministry of Foreign Affairs 1986–87; Asst Minister of Foreign Affairs 1987–89; Vice-Minister of Foreign Affairs 1989–98; Dir Foreign Affairs Office, State Council 1994–1998; Alt. mem. 14th CCP Cen. Cttee 1992–97, mem. 15th CCP Cen. Cttee 1997–2002, 16th CCP Cen. Cttee 2002–07; apptd Dir Cen. Foreign Affairs Office, CCP Cen. Cttee 1998; fmr Deputy Dir China Cttee of the Int. Decade for Natural Disaster Reduction; fmr Vice-Chair. Chinese Preparatory Committee, UN World Summit on Social Devt.

LIU, Jianfeng; Chinese politician and government official; b. 1936, Ninghe Co., Hebei Prov.; ed Kiev Eng Coll., USSR; joined CCP 1956; Deputy Dir, later Dir No. 1425 Research Inst., 4th Ministry of Machine-Building Industry 1968–84 (Acting Sec. CCP Party Cttee 1968–84); Vice-Minister of Electronics Industry 1984–88; Sec. Work Cttee, CCP Hainan Prov. Cttee 1988; Deputy Sec. CCP Hainan Prov. Cttee 1988–93; Gov. Hainan Prov. 1989–93; Vice-Minister of Electronics Industry 1993–98; Vice-Minister of Information Industry 1998–2003; Dir, Gen. Admin, Civil Aviation Admin of China 1998–2008; mem. 14th CCP Cen. Cttee 1992–97, 15th CCP Cen. Cttee 1997–2002, 16th CCP Cen. Cttee 2002–07; Del., 13th CCP Nat. Congress 1987–92; Pres. Electronics Br., China Council for the Promotion of Int. Trade; Chair. CPPCC Subcommittee of Foreign Affairs 2003–. *Address:* c/o Civil Aviation Administration of China, 155 Four East West Main Streets, Dongcheng District, Beijing, People's Republic of China (office).

LIU, Jiang; Chinese government official; b. 1940, Beijing; m.; two d.; ed Shihezi Agricultural Coll., Xinjiang Uygur Autonomous Region, CCP Cen. Cttee Cen. Party School; technician, later Chief, Mil. Farm, Tibet Autonomous Region; Farm

Head, later Dir Animal Husbandry Bureau, Beijing 1972–84 (Sec. CCP Party Cttee 1972–84); joined CCP 1978; Vice-Minister of Agric., Animal Husbandry and Fishery 1986–90; Vice-Chair. State Planning Comm. 1990–93; Minister of Agric. 1993–98; Chair. Beijing Greening Cttee 1997; apptd Vice-Chair. Nat. Devt and Reform Comm. 1998; Deputy Head State Working Group for Comprehensive Agricultural Devt, Leading Group, Aid-the-Poor Projects 1998–; mem. 15th CCP Cen. Cttee 1997–2002; Vice-Chair. China Council for Int. Cooperation on Environment and Devt.

LIU, Jianzhong; Chinese business executive; *CEO, Shanxi Coal Transportation and Sales Group Company Ltd;* Sec., Party Cttee, Shanxi International Electricity Group Co. Ltd, currently CEO Shanxi Coal Transportation and Sales Group Co. Ltd. *Address:* Shanxi Coal Transportation and Sales Group Co. Ltd, 82 Kaihuasi Street, Taiyuan 030002, Shanxi Province, People's Republic of China (office). *Telephone:* (351) 4924076 (office). *Fax:* (351) 4924061 (office). *E-mail:* sxct@jmxs .com (office). *Website:* www.jmxs.com (office).

LIU, Jiayi; Chinese government official; *CCP Secretary, Shandong Province;* b. 1956, Chongqing Municipality, Kaixian County; ed CCP Cen. Cttee Cen. Party School; joined CCP 1976; Staff mem., Finance Dept, Supervision Div., Sichuan Prov. 1984–88; Cadre, Nat. Audit Office, Special Correspondent Office, Chengdu 1988–89, Deputy Special Commr 1989–92; Deputy Dir-Gen., Trade Audit Dept, Nat. Audit Office 1992–93, Dir-Gen. 1993–96, Deputy Auditor-Gen. 1996–2008, Auditor-Gen. 2008–17 Chair., UN Bd of Auditors 2011–; CCP Sec., Shandong Prov. 2017–; mem. 16th CCP Cen. Cttee 2002–07, 17th CCP Cen. Cttee 2007–12, 18th CCP Cen. Cttee 2012–17, 19th CCP Cen. Cttee 2017–. *Address:* CCP Provincial Committee, Jinan, Shandong Province, People's Republic of China (office).

LIU, Jibin; Chinese politician; b. Dec. 1938, Longkou, Shandong Prov.; ed Beijing Aeronautics Inst.; joined CCP 1966; engineer, Section Dir then Vice-Man. Shenyang Songling Machinery Factory 1981–85; Deputy Chief Engineer, Ministry of Aeronautics Industry 1985; Minister of Aeronautics Industry 1985–88; Dir State Admin of State Property 1985–88; Vice-Minister of Finance 1988–98; Minister in Charge of Comm. of Science, Tech. and Industry for Nat. Defence 1998–2003; Del., 14th CCP Nat. Congress 1992–97; mem. Cen. Comm. for Discipline Inspection, CCP Cen. Cttee 1992–2002, Nat. Narcotics Control Comm. 1993, State Academic Degrees Cttee 1995–97, Hong Kong Special Admin. Region Preparatory Cttee 1995–97 (mem. Govt Del., Hong Kong Hand-Over Ceremony 1997), State Steering Group of Science, Tech. and Educ. 1998–; Vice Chair., Sr Advisory Cttee, Great Wall Securities Co. Ltd. *Address:* Great Wall Securities Co., Ltd., 6008 Shennan Road, Shenzhen 518034, Guangdong Province, People's Republic of China (office).

LIU, Jie; Chinese business executive; *President of the Board of Supervisors, China State Construction Engineering Corporation;* b. 22 Nov. 1943, Shucheng, Anhui Prov.; ed Wuhan Iron and Steel Inst., E.M. Beijing Iron and Steel Inst.; technician, Wuhan Iron and Steel Co. 1968; Chair. and Gen. Man., Anshan Iron and Steel Group Inc. 1994–2007 (retd); Pres. Bd of Supervisors China State Construction Eng Corpn 2008–; Alt. mem. 15th CCP Cen. Cttee 1997–2002, 16th CCP Cen. Cttee 2002–07; Fellow, Chinese Acad. of Eng 1996–; State Science and Tech. Progress, Ministry of Metallurgical Industry of China: First Prize, Third Prize and Special Class Prize 1985, Third Prize 1987, Special Class Prize 1990, Second Prize 1997. *Publications:* more than 10 specialized articles, treatises and tech. reports. *Address:* China State Construction Engineering Corporation, CSCEC Mansion, 15 Sanlihe Road, Haidian District, Beijing 100037, People's Republic of China (office). *Telephone:* (10) 8808-2888 (office). *E-mail:* info@cscec .com (office). *Website:* www.cscec.com (office); english.cscec.com (office).

LIU, Jingsheng; Chinese writer; b. 5 Jan. 1954, Beijing; m. Jin Yanming; one c.; ed Middle School; factory worker; pro-democracy campaigner; Co-founder and fmr Co-ed. Tansuo (Explorations) journal during late 1970s; joined Democracy Wall movt 1978, this involvement leading to theft charge and arrest for producing and distributing the journal, released from prison and resumed job as bus driver; helped establish China Freedom and Democracy Party after Tiananmen Square incident 1989; detained incommunicado for two years in 1992, trial July 1994, found guilty of membership in counter-revolutionary orgs, most notably Chinese Progressive Alliance, Liberal Democratic Party of China, and Free Labour Union of China; sentenced to eight years' imprisonment for "organising and leading a counter-revolutionary organisation" and a further eight years for "inciting counter-revolutionary subversion" 1994, combined into 15-year prison sentence and four years' deprivation of political rights, sentence reduced by one year and three months in 2000 and 2001 for "good behaviour"; released early from prison 27 Nov. 2004; est. Beijing Huaxia Gongwei Consultation Center April 2005, forcefully locked out by govt; est. Jingsheng Work House Sept. 2005; Hon. mem. UK, German, NZ, Netherlands and Swedish PEN Centres; PEN/Barbara Goldsmith Freedom to Write Award 1998. *Address:* Zhongguan Village A21-203, Haidan District, Beijing 100080, People's Republic of China (home). *Telephone:* (10) 82591379 (home). *E-mail:* ljs6454@hotmail.com (home).

LIU, Gen. Jingsong; Chinese army officer; b. 1933, Shishou, Hubei Prov.; ed PLA 7th Infantry Acad.; joined CCP 1954; platoon leader, Training Bn, First Mechanized Div., PLA Services and Arms, later Commdr Artillery Gun Co., Tank Regt; Regimental Staff Officer, Operations and Training Dept, PLA Regimental Office, later Div. Staff Officer; Deputy Commdr, later Chief of Staff, Artillery Gun Regt, PLA Services and Arms; Div. Commdr, later Div. Chief of Staff, later Army Commdr, PLA; Commdr, Shenyang Mil. Region, PLA 1985–; rank of Lt-Gen., PLA 1988, Gen. 1994; Commdr Lanzhou Mil. Region 1992–97; Pres. PLA Acad. of Mil. Sciences 1997–99; mem. 12th CCP Cen. Cttee 1985–87, 13th CCP Cen. Cttee 1987–92, 14th CCP Cen. Cttee 1992–97, 15th CCP Cen. Cttee 1997–2002.

LIU, Jinsong, BEcons, MA; Chinese diplomatist; *Ambassador to Afghanistan;* b. 1972, Zhejiang Prov.; m.; one s.; ed Inst. of Regional Econs, Renmin Univ. of China, Fletcher School of Law and Diplomacy, Tufts Univ., USA; Staff mem., Attaché, Third Sec., later Deputy Dir, Dept of Asian Affairs, Ministry of Foreign Affairs (MFA) 1993–2000; Deputy Dir, Dept of Policy Research, MFA 2000–01; Second Sec., Dir of Political Section and Spokesperson, Embassy in Bangkok 2001–03; First Sec., Dept of Asian Affairs, MFA 2003–04; First Sec., later Political Counselor, Embassy in Tokyo 2004–07; Political Counselor, Embassy in London 2007–09; Deputy Dir-Gen., Dept of Research, State Council Taiwan Affairs Office

2010–11; Deputy Dir-Gen., Dept of Hong Kong, Macao and Taiwan Affairs, MFA 2011–12; Deputy Dir-Gen., Policy Planning Dept, MFA 2012–15; Deputy Chief of Mission and Minister, Embassy in New Delhi 2015–17; Amb. to Afghanistan 2018–. *Address:* Embassy of the People's Republic of China, Sardar Shah Mahmoud Ghazi Wat, Kabul, Afghanistan (office). *Telephone:* (20) 2102548 (office). *Fax:* (20) 2102728 (office). *E-mail:* chinaemb_af@mfa.gov.cn (office). *Website:* af.china-embassy.org (office).

LIU, Kun; Chinese politician; *Minister of Finance;* b. Dec. 1956, Raoping Co., Guangdong Prov.; ed Xiamen Univ.; sent to work in factory during Cultural Revolution, Yunxiao Co. 1973; joined CCP 1984; Deputy Dir, Gen. Office, People's Govt, Guangdong Prov. 1982–2001, Sec.-Gen., People's Govt, Guangdong Prov. 2001–02; Dir, Finance Dept, Guangdong Prov. 2002–10; Deputy, 10th NPC 2003–08, 11th NPC 2008–13, Dir, NPC Budgetary Affairs Comm. 2016–18; Vice-Gov. of Guangdong 2010–13; Vice-Minister of Finance 2013–16, Minister of Finance 2018–; mem. Central Comm. for Discipline Inspection 2017–. *Address:* Ministry of Finance, 3 Nansanxiang, Sanlihe, Xicheng Qu, Beijing 100820, People's Republic of China (office). *Telephone:* (10) 68551114 (office). *E-mail:* webmaster@mof.gov.cn (office). *Website:* www.mof.gov.cn (office).

LIU, Liehong, MBA; Chinese business executive; *President, China Electronics Corporation;* b. Oct. 1968; ed Automation Control Dept, East China Univ. of Science and Tech., School of Man., Xi'an Jiaotong Univ.; Researcher and Sr Engineer; Deputy Dir No. 29 Research Inst.; Dir and Party Sec. No. 2 Research Inst.; Deputy Gen. Man., China Electronics Technology Group Corpn; fmr Pres. China Center for Information Industry Group and Beijing CCID Consulting Co. Ltd; Dir, Pres. and mem. Party Leadership Group, China Electronics Corpn 2008–; mem. 12th CCPCC Nat. Cttee; mem. Bd of Dirs Singapore Exchange Ltd, TPV Technology Ltd; winner, Special Govt Allowance from the State Council. *Address:* China Electronics Corporation, 66, Zhongguancun East Road, Beijing 100084, People's Republic of China (office). *Telephone:* (10) 68218529 (office). *Fax:* (10) 68213745 (office). *Website:* www.cec.com.cn (office).

LIU, Lucy; American actress and artist; b. 2 Dec. 1968, Jackson Heights, Queens, NY; ed Brooklyn Technical High School, Stuyvesant High School, New York Univ., Univ. of Mich.; UNICEF Amb. 2005–; Asian Excellence Award. *Films include:* Bang 1995, Jerry Maguire 1996, Payback 1999, Play it to the Bone 1999, Shanghai Noon 2000, Charlie's Angels 2000, Cypher 2002, Chicago 2002, Charlie's Angels: Full Throttle 2003, Kill Bill Vol. 1 2003, Domino 2005, Lucky Number Slevin 2005, 3 Needles 2005, Rise 2005, The Year of Getting to Know Us 2007, Code Name: The Cleaner 2007, Rise: Blood Hunter 2007, Watching the Detectives 2007, Kung Fu Panda (voice) 2008, The Year of Getting to Know Us 2008, Tinker Bell 2008, Tinker Bell and the Lost Treasure 2009, Tinker Bell and the Great Fairy Rescue 2010, Nomads 2011, East Fifth Bliss 2011, Detachment 2011, Tinker Bell and the Mysterious Winter Woods 2011, Kung Fu Panda 2 2011, Someday This Pain Will Be Useful to You 2011, The Man with the Iron Fist 2011, Detachment 2011, Secret of the Wings 2012, Future World 2018; as producer: Freedom's Fury 2006, Code Name: The Cleaner 2007. *Television:* Beverly Hills 90210 1991, L.A. Law 1993, Coach 1994, Home Improvement 1995, ER 1995, Pearl 1996, The X-Files 1996, Nash Bridges 1996, NYPD Blue 1997, Ally McBeal (series) 1998–2002, Futurama (voice) 2001–02, Joey 2004–05, Game Over 2004, Ugly Betty 2007, Cashmere Mafia 2008, Dirty Sexy Money 2008–09, Afro Samurai Resurrection 2009, Marry Me (mini-series) 2010, Ni Hao, Kai-Lan 2010, Pixie Hollow Games (film) 2011, Southland (series) 2012, Kung Fu Panda: Legends of Awesomeness 2011–14, Elementary (series) 2012. *Address:* Creative Artists Agency, 2000 Avenue of the Stars, Los Angeles, CA 90067, USA. *Telephone:* (424) 288-2000. *Fax:* (424) 288-2900. *Website:* www.caa.com.

LIU, Mingkang, MBA; Chinese banker and public servant; b. 28 Aug. 1946, Fuzhou, Fujian Prov.; m.; two s.; ed City Univ., London, UK, Cass Business School; Vice-Pres. Bank of China Fujian Branch 1988–92, Pres. 1992–93, Chair. and Pres. Bank of China 2000–03; Deputy Gov. Fujian Prov. 1993–94; Deputy Gov. State Devt Bank of China 1994–98; First Deputy Gov. People's Bank of China and Vice-Chair. Monetary Policy Cttee 1998–99; Chair. China Everbright Group, Hong Kong 1999–2000; Chair. China Banking Regulatory Comm. 2003–11; Alt. mem. 16th CCP Cen. Cttee 2002–07, mem. 17th CCP Cen. Cttee 2007–12; Distinguished Fellow, Fung Global Inst.; mem. Bd of Dirs Int. Centre for Leadership in Finance, Bank Negara Malaysia; mem. Consultant Cttee for Chair. of Financial Stability Forum, BIS; mem. Int. Advisory Council, Faculty of Business Admin, Chinese Univ. of Hong Kong; Sr Fellow, Hong Kong Inst. of Bankers; Distinguished Research Fellow, Inst. of Global Econs and Finance, Chinese Univ. of Hong Kong; Hon. Dir Fudan Univ. Int. Financial Centre, Hon. Prof. Chinese Univ. of Hong Kong, Hon. Dean Lingnan College of Sun Yat-Sen Univ.; Dr hc (City, Univ. London); Lifetime Achievement Award, The Asian Banker Magazine 2012. *Leisure interests:* jogging, swimming.

LIU, Mingzhong, DEng; Chinese engineer and business executive; *Chairman, Xinxing Cathay International Group Company Ltd;* Vice-Chair. Xinxing Ductile Iron Pipes Co. Ltd 1997–2000, Chair. and Gen. Man. 2000–05, Chair. 2005–, Chair. Wuhu Xinxing Ductile Iron Pipes Co. Ltd 2003–05, currently Chair. Xinxing Cathay International Group Co. Ltd (fmrly Xinxing Ductile Iron Pipes Co. Ltd), Sec. of the Party Cttee. *Address:* Xinxing Cathay International Group, 27F Office Tower, Beijing Fortune Plaza, 7 Dongsanhuan Zhong Road, Beijing 100020, People's Republic of China (office). *Telephone:* (10) 59290000 (office). *Fax:* (10) 59290029 (office). *E-mail:* service@xxpgroup.com (office). *Website:* english.xxcig .com (office).

LIU, Mingzu; Chinese fmr party official; b. Sept. 1936, Weihai City, Shandong Prov.; joined CCP 1959; fmr Deputy Dir Office of CCP Weihai City Cttee, later Deputy Sec. then Sec. Weihai City Cttee; fmr Sec. CCP Rushan Co. Cttee, Shandong Prov.; fmr Deputy Sec. CCP Yantai Prefectural Cttee, Shandong Prov.; fmr Sec. CCP Linyi Prefectural Cttee, Shandong Prov.; Chair. Guangxi Regional People's Congress 1993–94; Deputy Sec., Standing Cttee and mem. CCP Guangxi Regional Cttee 1988–94; mem., Standing Cttee, mem. and Sec. CCP Inner Mongolia Autonomous Region Cttee 1994–2000; Chair. Inner Mongolia Regional People's Congress 1997–99; Alt. mem. 14th CCP Cen. Cttee 1992–97, mem. 15th CCP Cen. Cttee 1997–2002; Deputy, 8th NPC 1993–98, 9th NPC 1998–2003, Vice-

Chair. Ethnic Affairs Cttee 2002, Chair. Agric. and Rural Affairs Cttee 2003; Del., 12th CCP Nat. Congress 1982–87, 13th CCP Nat. Congress 1987–92.

LIU, Nianqu; Chinese composer; b. 24 Nov. 1945, Shanghai; s. of Liu Jin Chuang and Wang Yun Cong; m. Cai Lu 1973; one d.; ed Shanghai Conservatory of Music; Art Inspector Gen. Shanghai Int. Arts Festival 1987; Art Dir Shanghai Creation Centre; Vice Sec.-Gen. Org. Cttee 1990, Shanghai Art Festival; Vice-Chair. Exec. Cttee 1991, Shanghai Spring Arts Festival; Vice-Chair. Shanghai Musicians' Asscn; Councillor China Musicians' Asscn. *Compositions include:* Phoenix Singing at Qi San Mountain (dance drama) 1983, 1989, Spring of Life and Universe (oratorio) 1989 (1st Prize Shanghai Art Festival). *Leisure interests:* table tennis, football.

LIU, Qi; Chinese government official; b. 3 Nov. 1942, Wujin Co., Jiangsu Prov.; ed Beijing Inst. of Iron and Steel Eng; joined CCP 1975; gas controller, furnaceman and founder, No. 2 Blast Furnace, Steel Works, Wuhan Iron and Steel Co. 1968–78, technician and Deputy Head, No. 3 Blast Furnace 1978–83, Deputy Dir Steel Works and Head Production Dept 1983–85, First Deputy Man. Wuhan Iron and Steel Co. 1985–90 (mem. Standing Cttee, CCP Party Cttee 1985–93), Man. 1990–93; Minister of Metallurgical Industry 1993–98 (Sec. CCP Leading Party Group at Ministry 1993–98); Deputy Sec. CCP Beijing Municipal Cttee 1998–2002, Sec. 2002–12; Vice-Mayor of Beijing 1998–99, Mayor of Beijing 1999–2002; Alt. mem. 14th CCP Cen. Cttee 1992–97, mem. 15th CCP Cen. Cttee 1997–2002, 16th CCP Cen. Cttee 2002–07 (mem. Politburo 2002–07), 17th CCP Cen. Cttee 2007–12 (mem. Politburo 2007–12); Chair. Chinese Olympic Cttee, Beijing Municipality 2007; Deputy Dir CCP Central Guidance Cttee on Ethical and Cultural Construction 2012–. *Address:* c/o CCP Central Guidance Committee Ethical and Cultural Construction, Beijing, People's Republic of China (office).

LIU, Qibao; Chinese government official; b. 1953, Susong, Anhui Prov.; ed Anhui Normal Univ., Jilin Univ.; sent to countryside during Cultural Revolution 1968–72; joined CCP 1971, Worker, Publicity Dept, CCP Prov. Cttee, Anhui Prov. 1974–77; Deputy Dir, Publicity Dept, Communist Youth League of China (CYLC), Anhui Prov. 1980–82, Dir 1982–83; Deputy Sec., CYLC, Anhui Prov. 1982–83; Deputy Sec., CCP City Cttee, Suzhou City 1984–85, Mayor of Suzhou City 1984; Sec., CYLC Cen. Cttee 1985–93; Deputy Ed.-in-Chief, People's Daily 1993–94; Deputy Sec.-Gen., State Council 1994–2000; Deputy, 10th NPC 2003–08; Sec., CCP Autonomous Regional Cttee, Guangxi Zhuang Autonomous Region 2006–07; Sec., CCP Prov. Cttee, Sichuan Prov. 2007–12, Chair. Standing Cttee, Sichuan Prov. People's Congress 2008–12; Dir CCP Cen. Cttee Propaganda Dept 2012–17; alt. mem. 16th CCP Cen. Cttee 2002–07, 17th CCP Cen. Cttee 2007–12, 18th CCP Cen. Cttee 2012–17, also mem. Politburo 2012–17, Secr. 2012–17. *Address:* c/o CCP Central Committee Propaganda Department, Zhongnanhai, Beijing, People's Republic of China (office). *Website:* cpc.people.com.cn (office).

LIU, Qitao; Chinese business executive; *Executive Director and Chairman, China Communications Construction Company Limited;* ed Dalian Inst. of Tech. (now known as Dalian Univ. of Tech.); worked at Sinohydro Bureau 13 1982–98, Deputy Head of Bureau 1995–98; held positions as Asst to Gen. Man. and Deputy Gen. Man. with China Nat. Water Resources and Hydropower Engineering Corpn, Gen. Man. Dept of Overseas Operations 1997–2003; Deputy Gen. Man. Sinohydro Corpn 2003–09, Chair. Sinohydro International Engineering Co. Ltd 2004–06, Dir and Gen. Man. Sinohydro Group Ltd 2009–10; Pres. China Communications Construction Co. Ltd 2010–14, Exec. Dir 2011–, Chair. 2013–; Top Ten Young and Middle-Aged Leaders of Technical Expertise, China Nat. Water Resources and Hydropower Engineering Corpn 1995. *Address:* China Communications Construction Co. Ltd, B88 Andingmenwai Dajie, Beijing 100011 (office); China Communications Construction Co. Ltd, 85 Deshengmenwai Street, Xicheng District, Beijing 100088, People's Republic of China (office). *Telephone:* (10) 82016655 (office). *Fax:* (10) 82016500 (office). *E-mail:* info@ccgrp.com.cn (office). *Website:* www.ccgrp.com.cn (office).

LIU, Shahe; Chinese poet; b. (Wu Xuntan), 11 Nov. 1931, Chengdu, Sichuan Prov.; m. 1st 1966; one s. one d.; m. 2nd 1992; ed Sichuan Univ.; mem. editorial staff, The Stars (poetry magazine) –1957, 1979–; satirical poem Verses of Plants (1957) led to condemnation as 'bourgeois rightist'; in labour camp during Cultural Revolution 1966–77, rehabilitated 1979. *Publications include:* Night on the Farm 1956, Farewell to Mars 1957, Liu Shahe Poetic Works (Nat. Prize) 1982, Travelling Trace 1983, Farewell to my Home 1983, Sing Alone 1989, Selected Poems of Seven Chinese Poets 1993, Random Notes by Liu Shahe 1995, River of Quicksand (poetry) 1995, River of Quicksand (short texts) 2001. *Address:* 30 Dacisi Road, Chengdu, Sichuan Province, People's Republic of China (home). *Telephone:* (28) 6781738 (home).

LIU, Shaohui; Chinese artist; b. 27 Aug. 1940, Szechuan; s. of Liu Veizheng and Xiong Wenying; m. Yang Yijing 1968; one s. one d.; ed Cen. Inst. of Applied Arts, Beijing; fmr Dir Art Layout Office, Yunnan People's Publishing House; Assoc. Prof., Pedagogical Inst., Guilin Pref.; mem. Chinese Artists Asscn; Assoc. Pres. Guilin Chinese Painting Acad. 1995–; engaged in design and research; exhbns in USA, Japan, Bulgaria, Hong Kong, Italy, Taiwan; works at Guilin Arts Garden; main designer for film Fire Boy (1st Prize, Int. Animated Film Festival, Japan 1984); Prize of Nat. Art Works of Excellence 1981, 1983, Japanese Int. Fine Arts Exhbn Prize of the Highest Honour. *Works include:* Zhaoshutun – Legend of a Dai Prince, An Elementary Theory on Binding and Layout of Books, The Candlewick Fairy 1985, Cowrie and a Little Girl 1986, Fine Arts Collection 1989. *Publications:* Yunnan School – A Renaissance in Chinese Painting 1988, Selected Paintings by Liu Shaohui 1989, The Third Sister Liu 1993, Selected Paintings of Guilin Chinese Painting Academy 1995. *Leisure interests:* music, travel, table-tennis. *Address:* Pedagogical Institute, Guilin Prefecture, 45 Xing Yi Road, Guilin, People's Republic of China (office).

LIU, Shaoyong, MBA; Chinese airline industry executive; *Chairman, President and Deputy Party Secretary, China Eastern Airlines Holding Company;* b. Nov. 1958; ed Civil Aviation Flight Univ. of China, Tianjin Univ. of Finance and Econs; Deputy Fleet Leader and Fleet Leader, Taiyuan fleet of China General Aviation Corpn 1993–95, Deputy Gen. Man. China General Aviation Corpn and Deputy Dir Civil Aviation Admin of China (CAAC) Shanxi Bureau 1995–97; Gen. Man. Shanxi branch, China Eastern Airlines Corpn Ltd (state-owned airline) 1997–99; Dir CAAC Dept of Flight Standards 1999–2000; Pres. China Eastern Airlines Co. Ltd 2000–02; Vice-Minister CAAC 2002–04; Pres. China Southern Air Holding Co. 2004–08, Chair. China Southern Airlines Co. Ltd 2004–08; Pres. and Deputy Party Sec., China Eastern Airline Holding Co. 2008–, Chair. 2009–; Vice-Chair. Supervisory Cttee China's Listed Cos Asscn; mem. Bd of Dirs Int. Air Transport Asscn, Asscn for Relations across Taiwan Straits. *Address:* China Eastern Air Holding Company, No. 212 Jiangning Road, Shanghai, People's Republic of China (office). *Website:* www.en.ceair.com (office).

LIU, Shiyu, MA; Chinese banking executive; *Chairman, China Securities Regulatory Commission;* b. Nov. 1961, Guanyun Co., Jiangsu; ed Tsinghua Univ.; worked successively in Econ. System Restructuring Cttee of Shanghai Municipal Govt, State Econ. System Restructuring Cttee, China Construction Bank 1987–96; Deputy Dir Gen. and Adviser, Banking Supervision Dept II, People's Bank of China (PBC) 1996–98, Dir Gen. and Deputy Dir Gen., Banking Supervision Dept II 1998–2002, Dir Gen., Gen. Admin Dept PBC 2002–04, Asst Gov. PBC 2004–06, Vice-Gov. 2006–14; Exec. Chair. Agricultural Bank of China (ABC) Ltd and Sec. ABC Party Cttee 2014–16; Chair. China Securities Regulatory Comm. (CSRC) and Sec. CSRC Party Cttee 2016–; Dir (non-exec.), China Investment Corpn; mem. 19th CCP Cen. Cttee 2017–. *Address:* China Securities Regulatory Commission, Focus Place 19, Jin Rong Street, West District, Beijing 100033, People's Republic of China (office). *Fax:* (10) 6621-0205 (office). *E-mail:* consult@csrc.gov.cn (office). *Website:* www.csrc.gov.cn (office).

LIU, Shunda; Chinese engineer and business executive; mem. CCP; fmr Deputy Head of Gen. Services Dept, Electric Power Div., Ministry of Energy; fmr Deputy Dir Office of the Minister of Electricity; fmr Party Cttee mem. and Asst to the Chief and Deputy Chief (Deputy Gen. Man.) Electric Power Bureau (Power Co.), Hunan Prov.; fmr Party Cttee mem. and Deputy Chief (Deputy Gen. Man.) East China Power Adm. Bureau (Power Corpn); fmr Party Sec. and Chief (Chair./Gen. Man.) Electric Power Bureau (Power Co. Ltd), Fujian Prov.; fmr Party Cttee mem. and Deputy Gen. Man. China Datang Corpn, Chair. Datang Huayin Electric Power Co. Ltd 2006–10, Chair. and Party Sec. China Datang Corpn 2010–13, Chair. Datang International Power Generation Co. Ltd 2010–13; Chair. China Nat. Machinery Industry Corpn Ltd (Sinomach) –2015.

LIU, Lt-Gen. Shutian; Chinese army officer; b. 1940, Tengzhou Co., Shandong Prov.; ed Nanjing Political Coll. of the Chinese PLA; joined PLA 1958, CCP 1960; platoon leader, later staff mem., later Deputy Section Head, later Section Head, Cadre Section, Div. Political Dept; Political Commissar, Regt 1983; Political Commissar, 8th Div., Artillery Force, PLA Services and Arms 1983–86; Dir 26th Army (Political Dept), Army (or Ground Force), PLA Services and Arms 1986–88, Political Commissar 26th Army 1988–92; Deputy Political Commissar, Guangzhou Mil. Area Region 1994–98, Political Commissar 1998, Political Commissar, Chengdu Military Command –2012; mem. 15th CCP Cen. Cttee 1997–2002, 16th CCP Cen. Cttee 2002–07. *Address:* c/o Chengdu Military Area Command Headquarters, Chengdu, People's Republic of China (office).

LIU, Wei; Chinese artist; b. 1972, Beijing; ed China Acad. of Art; Hon. mention, Chinese Contemporary Art Award 2006, Best Artist, Chinese Contemporary Art Award 2008, Credit Suisse Today Art Award 2011, Martell Artist of the Year Award 2012, Artist of the Year Atron AAC Award 2016. *Address:* c/o Tilton Gallery, 8 E 76 Street, New York, NY 10021, USA. *Telephone:* (212) 737-2221. *Fax:* (212) 396-1725. *E-mail:* info@jacktiltongallery.com. *Website:* www.jacktiltongallery.com.

LIU, Weiping; Chinese business executive; *Chairman, Tianjin Material and Equipment Group Corporation (Tewoo Group Company Limited);* Gen. Man. Tianjin Material and Equipment Group Corpn (Tewoo Group Co. Ltd) –2014, Chair. 2014–. *Address:* Tewoo Group Co. Ltd, 4 Yingkoudao Road, Heping District, Tianjin 300041, People's Republic of China (office). *Telephone:* (22) 23030779 (office). *Fax:* (22) 23315316 (office). *E-mail:* office@tewoo.com (office). *Website:* www.tewoo.com (office).

LIU, Xiang; Chinese athlete (retd); b. 13 July 1983, Shanghai; m. Ge Tian (divorced 2015); ed Jr Sports School, Putuo District, Shanghai, East China Normal Univ., Shanghai; began competitive athletics career as a high jumper, switched to 110m. hurdles in 1998; set world jr and Asian records for 110m. hurdles Lausanne, 2001; won titles at World Univ. Games, Asian Games and Asian Championships in 2001–02; bronze medal 110m. World Indoor Championships, Birmingham, UK 2003; silver medal 110m. World Indoor Championships, Budapest 2004; bronze medal 110m. hurdles World Championships, Paris 2003; three Grand Prix victories in 2004; gold medal 110 m. hurdles Olympic Games, Athens 2004 in world-record equalling time of 12.91 seconds; set world-record time of 12.88 seconds, Lausanne 2006; first Chinese man to win Olympic track and field gold medal; 1st place, 60m. hurdles, IAAF World Indoor Championships, Valencia 2008; 1st place, 110m. hurdles, Asian Games China 2010, Asian Championships Japan 2011, IAAF Diamond League 2012; forced to withdraw from Beijing Olympics due to injury 2008 and from London Olympics 2012; retd 2015; elected as Deputy Sec., China Communist Youth League Shanghai Sports Bureau Cttee 2011; Male Athlete of the Year 2003 by Chinese Sports Journalists, Laureus China Most Popular Sportsman of the Year 2011. *Leisure interests:* music, video games, karaoke.

LIU, Xiaoming; Chinese diplomatist and government official; *Ambassador to UK;* m. Hu Pinghua; one s.; ed Dalian Univ. of Foreign Languages, Fletcher School of Law and Diplomacy, Tufts Univ., USA; Desk Officer, Ministry of Foreign Affairs 1974–75; Political Officer, Embassy in Lusaka, Zambia 1975–78; Desk Officer, Div. of US Affairs, Dept of American and Oceanian Affairs, Ministry of Foreign Affairs 1978–82, Deputy Dir, Div. of US Affairs 1983–89; Second Sec., Embassy in Washington, DC 1989–90, First Sec. 1990–93; Dir, Div. of US Affairs, Dept of N American and Oceanian Affairs, Ministry of Foreign Affairs 1993–94, Counsellor 1994–95, Deputy Dir-Gen. 1995–98; Minister (Deputy Chief of Mission), Embassy in Washington, DC 1998–2001; Amb. to Egypt 2001–03; Amb., Ministry of Foreign Affairs 2003–04; Deputy Sec.-Gen., Govt of Gansu Prov. 2004, Asst Gov. 2004–05; Vice-Minister, Cen. Foreign Affairs Office of China 2005–06; Amb. to North Korea 2006–09, to UK 2009–; mem. Eighth Nat. Cttee of the All-China Youth Fed., First and Second Cttee of the Youth Fed. of the Cen. Govt of China; The Fletcher Dean's Medal, Fletcher School of Law and Diplomacy, Tufts Univ. 2007, First Class Friendship Medal (N Korea) 2010. *Address:* Embassy of the People's Republic of

China, 49–51 Portland Place, London, W1B 4JL, England (office). *Telephone:* (20) 7299-4049 (office). *Fax:* (20) 7636-5578 (office). *E-mail:* press_uk@mfa.gov.cn (office). *Website:* www.chinese-embassy.org.uk/eng (office).

LIU, Xiaoqing; Chinese actress and business executive; b. 30 Oct. 1955, Chengdu City, Sichuan Prov.; d. of Ran Changru and Liu Huihua; m. Chen Guojun (divorced 1991); ed Sichuan Music Coll. Affiliated High; joined Chengdu's Army Performing Group 1973; head of business empire ranging from film production to real estate (45th richest person in China), including Xiaoqing Cultural Arts Ltd, Beijing. *Films include:* Great Wall of South China Sea 1976, Spring Song 1978, Wedding 1978, Little Flower 1979, Look at this Family (3rd Hundred Flowers (Baihua) Best Actress Award) 1980, Burning Down Yuan Ming Yuan 1983, Furong Zhen (Lotus Town) (10th Hundred Flowers Best Actress Award, 7th Golden Cock Best Actress Award 1986) 1986, Loveless Lover 1986, Hibiscus Town 1986, Yuanye (11th Hundred Flowers Best Actress Award) 1988, A Woman For Two 1988, Evil Empress 1988, Dream of Red Mansion 1, 1988, 2 1988, 3, 1989, 4 1989, 5 1989, 6 1989, Chuntao (12th Hundred Flowers Best Actress Award) 1989, Li Lianying, the Imperial Eunuch 1991, Town of Furong (Baihua Best Actress Award), Plastic Flowers 2004. *Television includes:* Wu Ze Tian 1995, Huo Shao E Pang Gong 1998, Tian Gui Hua 2000, Huo Feng Huang 2001, Lotus Lantern 2005. *Plays:* The Last Night of Taipan Chin, Taipei 2008. *Publication:* My Way, My Eight Years, From a Movie Star to Billionaire. *Address:* PO Box 38, Asia Sport Village, Beijing, People's Republic of China. *Telephone:* (10) 4915988. *Fax:* (10) 4915899.

LIU, Xinwu; Chinese writer; b. 4 June 1942, Chengdu, Sichuan Prov.; s. of Liu Tianyan and Wang Yuntao; m. Lu Xiaoge 1970; one s.; ed Beijing Teachers' Coll.; lived in Beijing 1950–; school teacher 1961–76; Ed. Beijing Publishing House 1976–80; professional writer 1980–87; Ed.-in-Chief, People's Literature 1987–89; mem. Council, Chinese Writers' Asscn. *Publications include:* Class Counsellor (Nationwide Short Story Prize) 1977, The Position of Love 1978, I Love Every Piece of Green Leaves (Nationwide Short Story Prize) 1979, Ruyi (As You Wish) 1980, Overpass 1981, Black Walls 1982, Drum Tower (Mao Dun Literature Prize) 1984, A Scanning over the May 19th Accident 1985, Wind Passing through the Ear 1992, Four Decorated Archways 1993, Liu Xinwu Collected Works (eight vols) 1993, Phoenix Perched Building 1996, Construction and Environment in My Eyes 1998, A Small Block of Wood 1999, The Beauty of Material 2004, Standing on the Ice 2004, Liu Xinwu explores The Dream in Red Mansions 2005–07, The Destiny to Meet Each Other 2010, Liu Xinwu Collected Works (forty vols) 2012, Bay Window 2014, Liu Xinwu Literature Collections (twenty-six vols) 2016. *Leisure interests:* reading, travelling, painting, stamp collecting, music, gardening, football. *Address:* 8 Building No. 1404, Anding Menwai Dongheyan, Beijing 100011, People's Republic of China (home). *Telephone:* (10) 64263965 (home).

LIU, Xinyi, MA; Chinese banking executive; *Vice-Chairman and President, Shanghai Pudong Development Bank Company Ltd;* b. 1965; ed Tongji Univ.; fmr Deputy Gen. Man. Airport Sub-br., Shanghai Pudong Development Bank Co. Ltd (SPDB) and fmr Deputy Gen. Man. SPDB Shanghai Br., served as Vice-Pres., Dir of Financial Insts Dept, Asst Dir Gen. Financial Office, Shanghai Financial Service Office 2002–05, temporarily transferred to Shanghai Municipal Finance Service Office as Section Chief of Financial Insts Dept and later as Asst to the Office Dir, Chief Financial Officer and Exec. Vice-Pres. SPDB –2014; Chair. First Sino Bank –2014; Ind. Dir, Shanghai International Airport Co. Ltd. *Address:* Shanghai Pudong Development Bank Co. Ltd, 12 Zhongshan Dong Yi Road, Shanghai 200002, People's Republic of China (office). *Telephone:* (21) 61618888 (office). *E-mail:* webmaster@spdb.com.cn (office). *Website:* www.spdb.com.cn (office).

LIU, Yandong; Chinese politician; b. 1945, Nantong City, Jiangsu Prov.; d. of Liu Ruiling; m. Yang Yuanxing; one d.; ed Jilin Univ.; joined CCP 1964; Sec. Org. Dept, CCP Beijing Municipal Cttee 1980–81; Deputy Sec. CCP Chaoyang Dist Cttee, Beijing 1980–81; mem. Secr. CCP Communist Youth League of China 1982–87; Vice-Pres. All-China Youth Fed. 1982, later Pres.; mem. Standing Cttee, CPPCC Nat Cttee 1983–2003; Deputy Dir Youth Ideological Educ. Research Centre 1988–93; Deputy Head United Front Work Dept 1991–2002; Alt. mem. 15th CCP Cen. Cttee 1997–2002, mem. 16th CCP Cen. Cttee 2002–07, 17th CCP Cen. Cttee 2007–12 (mem. Politburo 2007–12), 18th CCP Cen. Cttee 2012–17 (mem. Politburo 2012–17); Vice-Chair. 10th CPPCC Nat. Cttee 2003–08; State Councillor 2008–13; Vice-Premier 2013–18; fmr Pres., later Sec.-Gen. China Youth Devt Foundation; Vice-Pres. China Inventors' Asscn 1988–93; mem. Sino-Japanese Friendship Asscn. *Address:* c/o State Council, 22 Xi'anmen Avenue, Beijing, People's Republic of China (office). *Telephone:* (10) 66036884 (office).

LIU, Yang, BEcons; Chinese business executive; *Chairman and Chief Investment Officer, Atlantis Investment Management Group;* ed Central Univ. of Finance and Investment, Beijing, Grad. Diploma in Applied Finance and Investment, Securities Inst. of Australia; joined CITIC Group, Beijing 1988; joined CMG CH China Investment Ltd 1993, later Chief Investment Officer CMG CH China Fund (later renamed New Era PRC Fund); Head of China equities at First State Investment Management (HK) 2001–02; joined Atlantis 2002, later Fund Man. of Atlantis China Fund, Atlantis New China Fortune Fund and Atlantis China Healthcare Fund, Chair. and Chief Investment Officer Atlantis Investment Management Ltd and Atlantis Investment Management (HK) Ltd 2011–; Dir (non-Exec.) VCREDIT Holdings Ltd 2016–; Co-founder China Times Investments; Man. Dir Riverwood Asset Management (Cayman) Ltd. *Address:* Atlantis Investment Management (Hong Kong) Ltd, Room 3501, The Centrium, 60 Wyndham Street, Central, Hong Kong Special Administrative Region, People's Republic of China (office). *Telephone:* (852) 21106320 (office). *Fax:* (852) 21109378 (office). *E-mail:* investment@atlantis-investment.com (office). *Website:* www.atlantis-investment.com (office).

LIU, Yonghao; Chinese business executive; *Director, New Hope Liuhe Company;* b. 1951, Xinjin, Sichuan Prov; brother of Liu Yongxing; m.; one d.; fmr Lecturer, Cadres' Inst., Sichuan Machinery Ministry; co-f. New Hope Group 1982 (restructured in 1995), Pres. New Hope Group 1993–2013, Chair. New Hope Liuhe Co. Ltd 1998–2013, Dir 2013–; Vice-Chair. Chinese Minsheng Bank Co. Ltd 1996–2003, 2009–; Deputy Pres. Chinese Feed Industry Asscn, Chinese Dairy Industry Asscn, Chinese Glory Undertaking Enhance Asscn; mem. 9th CPPCC Standing Cttee 1998–2003, Deputy Dir Econ. Cttee 2003–, fmr mem. 8th, 10th and 11th CPPCC Standing Cttee; named as one of Top Ten Private Entrepreneurs of China, Man of China's Reform, Top Ten Poverty-fighters, The Most Outstanding Enterprise Admin Talent, Man of China Real Estate and Star of Asia (Business Weekly) 2000, Ernst & Young Entrepreneur of the Year 2007. *Address:* New Hope Group, 24th Floor, Building 2, No. 366 Jinshi Road, Jinjiang District, Chengdu 610023, People's Republic of China (office). *Telephone:* (28) 65721666 (office). *E-mail:* contact@newhope.cn (office). *Website:* www.newhopegroup.com (office).

LIU, Yongxing, BS; Chinese business executive; *Chairman, East Hope Group;* b. June 1948, Xinjin, Sichuan Prov.; brother of Liu Yonghao; m.; one s.; started family business, Hope Group, raising quail and chickens in Sichuan with his three brothers 1982, grew into second largest animal feed producer in China, co. later restructured into four entities each owned by one of the brothers; East Hope Group relocated from Sichuan to Shanghai 1999; Chair. East Hope Group 1995–; apptd Exec. Dir China Guangcai Business Council 2010; maintains portfolio interests in MinSheng Bank, MinSheng Insurance, Bright Dairy; mem. Shanghai Pudong New Area CPPCC Standing Cttee; awarded hon. title of "30 Rural People in 30-Year China's Reform and Opening-up" 2008, Outstanding Contribution to Post-disaster Reconstruction in Dujiangyan City, Shanghai 2011. *Address:* East Hope Group, 57 Songlin Road, Pudong, Shanghai 200120, People's Republic of China (office). *Telephone:* (21) 5831-2099 (office). *Fax:* (21) 6876-8702 (office). *Website:* www.easthope.cn (office).

LIU, Gen. Yuan; Chinese army officer and government official; *Political Commissar, PLA General Logistics Department;* b. 1951, Beijing; s. of Liu Shaoqi and Wang Guangmei; joined CCP 1982; Vice-Mayor Zhengzhou City, Henan Prov. 1985–88, Vice-Gov. Henan 1988–92; Second Political Commissar, PRC Police Force 1992–98; rank of Maj.-Gen. 1992, Lt-Gen. 2003, Gen. 2009; Deputy Political Commissar, PLA Gen. Logistics Dept 2003–05, Political Commissar 2011–; Political Commissar, Acad. of Military Sciences 2005–11; mem. 17th CCP Cen. Cttee 2007–12, 18th CCP Cen. Cttee 2012–17. *Address:* People's Liberation Army Academy of Military Sciences, Beijing, People's Republic of China.

LIU, Yuan, BEcons; Chinese economist and business executive; *Chairman of the Board of Supervisors, China Merchants Bank Company Limited;* ed Renmin Univ.; Head of Banking Cases Inspection Bureau, Head of Banking Consumers Protection Bureau, Office Dir, China Banking Regulatory Comm. (CBRC), Shenzhen, Office Dir, CBRC, Shanxi, Deputy Dir Banking Supervision Dept II, CBRC 2003–14; Chair. Bd of Supervisors China Merchants Bank Co. Ltd 2014–; Special Cttee Chair. under Supervisory Bd of China Asscn for Public Companies. *Address:* China Merchants Group Ltd, 40th Floor, China Merchants Building, 168–200 Conaught Road, Central, Hong Kong Special Administrative Region (office); China Merchants Bank Co. Ltd, 7088 Shen Nan Road, Futian District, Shenzhen 518040, Guangdong, People's Republic of China (office). *Telephone:* 25428288 (Hong Kong) (office); (755) 83198888 (Shenzhen) (office). *Fax:* 25448851 (Hong Kong) (office); (755) 83195109 (Shenzhen) (office). *E-mail:* cmhk@cmhk.com (office). *Website:* www.cmhk.com (office); www.cmbchina.com (office).

LIU, Yunshan; Chinese politician; *President, CCP Central Party School;* b. July 1947, Xinzhou, Shanxi Prov.; ed Jining Normal School, Inner Mongolia, CCP Cen. Cttee Cen. Party School; teacher, Baishi School, Inner Mongolia 1968; sent to do manual labour, Sobugai People's Commune, Inner Mongolia 1968–69; clerk, Publicity Dept, CCP Inner Mongolia Autonomous Prefectural Cttee 1969–75; joined CCP 1971; reporter, Div. Head, Xinhua News Agency, Inner Mongolia Autonomous Region 1975–82; Deputy Sec. Communist Youth League Inner Mongolia Autonomous Regional Cttee 1982–84; Deputy Head Publicity Dept CCP Inner Mongolia Autonomous Regional Cttee 1984–86, Head 1986–87 (mem. Standing Cttee 1986–92), Sec.-Gen. CCP Inner Mongolia Autonomous Regional Cttee 1987–91 (Sec. Insts of Higher Learning Work Cttee 1987–91), Deputy Sec. 1992–93; Sec. CCP Chifeng Municipal Cttee, Inner Mongolia Autonomous Region 1991–93; Sec. CCP Inner Mongolia Autonomous Regional Cttee; Vice-Dir Propaganda Dept of CCP Cen. Cttee 1993; Pres. CCP Central Party School 2013–; alt. mem. 12th CCP Cen. Cttee 1987–92, 14th CCP Cen. Cttee 1992–97, mem. 15th CCP Cen. Cttee 1997–2002, 16th CCP Cen. Cttee 2002–07 (mem. Politburo 2002–07, Secr. of Politburo 2002–07), 17th CCP Cen. Cttee 2007–12 (mem. Politburo 2007–12); Deputy Head, Publicity Dept CCP Cen. Cttee 1993–97, Head 1997–2002; Head, Office of Spiritual Civilization Steering Cttee, Offices Under Cen. Cttee CCP Cen. Cttee 2002–07; mem. 18th CCP Cen. Cttee 2012–17, Politburo 2012–17, Politburo Standing Cttee 2012–17; First Sec., CCP Cen. Secr. 2012–. *Address:* CCP Central Party School, Beijing, People's Republic of China (office). *E-mail:* tgwww@ccps.gov.cn (office). *Website:* www.ccps.gov.cn (office).

LIU, Zhenmin, LLM; Chinese diplomatist; *Under-Secretary-General for Economic and Social Affairs, United Nations;* b. 1955, Shanxi Prov.; m.; ed Peking Univ.; joined Foreign Service 1982, staff mem., Dept of Treaty and Law 1982–84, Attaché then Third Sec., Perm. Mission to UN, New York 1984–88, Third Sec. then Deputy Div. Dir, Dept of Treaty and Law 1988–92, Second Sec. then First Sec., Perm. Mission to UN, Geneva 1992–95, First Sec., Dept of Treaty and Law 1996, Counsellor 1996–98, Deputy Dir-Gen. 1998–2003, Dir-Gen. 2003–06, Amb. and Deputy Perm. Rep. to UN, New York 2006–09, Asst Minister of Foreign Affairs 2009–11, Amb. and Perm. Rep. to UN, Geneva 2011–13, Vice-Minister of Foreign Affairs 2013–17, Under-Sec.-Gen. for Econ. and Social Affairs 2017–. *Address:* United Nations Headquarters, 405 E 42nd Street, New York, NY 10017, USA (office). *Telephone:* (212) 963-1234 (office). *Fax:* (212) 963-4879 (office). *Website:* www.un.org (office).

LIU, Gen. (retd) Zhenwu; Chinese army officer (retd); b. Aug. 1944, Nanxian Co., Hunan Prov.; joined PLA 1961; squad leader, later platoon leader, 42nd Army (124 Div., 370 Regt, 4th Co.), Army (or Ground Force), PLA Services and Arms, Deputy Army Commdr and Chief of Staff 42nd Army 1983–92, Army Commdr 1992–94; Commdr PLA Hong Kong Garrison 1994–99; fmr staff mem., later Head, Regimental Combat Training Br., PLA Guangzhou Mil. Region, Guangdong Prov., later Section Head, Combat Training Dept, later Deputy Dir Mil. Training Dept, Deputy Commdr PLA Guangzhou Mil. Region 1999–2002, Commdr 2002–07; Alt. mem. 15th CCP Cen. Cttee 1997–2002, 16th CCP Cen. Cttee 2002–07; Deputy Chief of Gen. Staff, PLA 2007–09; Deputy Dir, 11th NPC Foreign Affairs Cttee 2010–13; rank of Maj.-Gen. 1990, Lt-Gen. 1997, Gen. 2004.

LIU, Zhenya; Chinese energy industry executive; b. 1952, Shandong Prov.; ed Electric Power Dept, Shandong Eng and Tech. Inst.; several positions at Shandong Linyi Power Supply Utility 1984–91 including Section Chief, then Vice-Dir, then

Dir; Vice-Pres. then Pres. Shandong Electric Power Bureau 1997–2004, renamed State Grid Corpn of China, Man. State Grid Corpn of China 1997–2004, Pres. and CEO 2004–13, Chair. 2013–16 (retd); joined CCP 1984; Alt. mem. 17th CCP Cen. Cttee 2007–12. *Address:* c/o State Grid Corporation of China, 86 West Chang'an Street, Xicheng District, Beijing 100031, People's Republic of China. *E-mail:* sgcc -info@sgcc.com.cn.

LIU, Zhongli; Chinese state official (retd); b. 1934, Ningbo City, Zhejiang Prov.; joined CCP 1954; Deputy Div. Chief, Vice-Chair., Chair. Heilongjiang Prov. Planning Comm. 1973–84, Chair. Planning and Econ. Comm. 1984–95; Vice-Gov. Heilongjiang Prov. 1985–88; Vice-Chair. State Cttee for Enterprise Man. 1988; Vice-Minister of Finance 1988–92, Minister 1992–98; Deputy Sec.-Gen. State Council 1990, Dir Econ. System Reform Office of State Council 1998–2000; Dir State Gen. Admin. of Taxation 1994–98; Deputy Head Cen. Financial and Econ. Leading Group; mem. 14th CCP Cen. Cttee 1992–97, 15th CCP Cen. Cttee 1997–2002; Pres. Nat. Social Security Fund Council 2000–04; Chair. CPPCC Sub-Cttee of Economy 2003–; Pres. Chinese Inst. of Certified Public Accountants. *Address:* c/o Chinese Institute of Certified Public Accountants, Building B, No. 16 Xisihuanzhonglu, Haidian District, Beijing 100039, People's Republic of China (office).

LIU, Zhongyi; Chinese administrator; b. 1930, Wuchang City, Hubei Prov.; ed Zhongyuan Univ., Hainan Prov.; squad leader, Sub-Regional Training Unit, PLA Cen. China Mil. Command 1949; joined CCP 1954; fmr Dir Agriculture, Forestry and Water Conservancy Planning Bureau, State Devt and Reform Comm.; Vice-Minister, State Planning and Reform Comm. 1985–90; Minister of Agric. 1990–93; Research Fellow and Deputy Dir Environmental Protection Cttee of the State Council 1992; Deputy Dir-Gen. Devt Research Centre of the State Council 1993–98; State Leading Group for Comprehensive Agricultural Devt 1990; mem. 14th CCP Cen. Cttee 1992–97; Del., 15th CCP Nat. Congress 1997–2002; mem. Standing Cttee 9th NPC 1998–2003, Vice-Chair. Agric. and Rural Affairs Cttee 1998–2003; Chair. Sino-Finnish Friendship Asscn.

LIVADIOTTI, Massimo; Italian painter and sculptor; b. 20 Nov. 1959, Zavia, Libya; s. of Mario Livadiotti and Giovanna Mattera; ed Accad. di Belle Arti, Rome; major shows Rome 1987, 1989, 1994, 2000, Milan 1990, 1992, Bologna 1994; retrospectives, Petőfi Museum, Budapest 1997, Sociedade Nacional de Belas Artes, Lisbon 2000; numerous group exhbns; work inspired by San Filippo Neri acquired by the Vatican 1995. *Publications:* Monograph 1987, Anthology Monographs to accompany exhbns at Centro Ausoni, Rome, Petőfi Museum, Budapest, Sociedade Nacional de Belas Artes, Lisbon 2001, Kalós Arte Contemporanea 2001, Le anime del bosco 2009. *Leisure interests:* gardening and light exercise. *Address:* Piazza Vittorio Emanuele II, N 31, 00185 Rome, Italy. *Telephone:* (06) 49382757. *E-mail:* maxlivadia@gmail.com (office).

LIVELY, Dame Penelope Margaret, DBE, CBE, OBE, FRSL; British writer; b. (Penelope Margaret Low), 17 March 1933, Cairo, Egypt; d. of Roger Low and Vera Greer; m. Jack Lively 1957 (died 1998); one s. one d.; ed St Anne's Coll., Oxford; mem. Bd British Library 1993–99, Bd British Council 1998–; Vice-Pres. Friends of the British Library; mem. Soc. of Authors (fmr Chair.), PEN; Hon. Fellow, Swansea Univ. 2002, St Anne's Coll., Oxford 2007; Hon. DLitt (Tufts Univ.) 1993, (Warwick) 1998. *Publications include:* juvenile fiction: Astercote 1970, The Whispering Knights 1971, The Wild Hunt of Hagworthy 1971, The Driftway 1972, Going Back 1973, The Ghost of Thomas Kempe (Carnegie Medal) 1973, The House in Norham Gardens 1974, Boy Without a Name 1975, Fanny's Sister 1976, The Stained Glass Window 1976, A Stitch in Time (Whitbread Award) 1976, Fanny and the Monsters 1978, The Voyage of QV66 1978, Fanny and the Battle of Potter's Piece 1980, The Revenge of Samuel Stokes 1981, Uninvited Ghosts and Other Stories 1984, Dragon Trouble, Debbie and the Little Devil 1984, A House Inside Out 1987, The Cat, the Crow and the Banyan Tree 1994, Good Night, Sleep Tight 1995, Two Bears and Joe 1995, Staying with Grandpa 1995, A Martian Comes to Stay 1995, Heatwave 1996, Lost Dog 1996, One, Two, Three... Jump! 1998, Beyond the Blue Mountains: Stories 1997, Spiderweb 1998, In Search of a Homeland: The Story of the Aeneid 2001; adult fiction: The Road to Lichfield 1977, Nothing Missing but the Samovar and Other Stories (Southern Arts Literature Prize) 1978, Treasures of Time (Nat. Book Award) 1979, Judgement Day 1980, Next to Nature, Art 1982, Perfect Happiness 1983, Corruption and Other Stories 1984, According to Mark 1984, Moon Tiger (Booker-McConnell Prize 1987) 1986, Pack of Cards: Stories 1978–86 1986, Passing On 1989, City of the Mind 1991, Cleopatra's Sister 1993, The Photograph 2003, Making It Up 2005, Consequences 2007, Family Album 2009, How It All Began 2011; non-fiction: The Presence of the Past: An Introduction to Landscape History 1976, Oleander, Jacaranda: A Childhood Perceived (autobiog.) 1994, A House Unlocked (memoir) 2001, Ammonites and Leaping Fish 2013, Life in the Garden 2017; TV and radio scripts; contrib. to numerous journals and magazines. *Leisure interests:* gardening, landscape history, talking, listening. *Address:* c/o David Higham Associates, 5–8 Lower John Street, Golden Square, London, W1F 9HA, England (office). *Telephone:* (20) 7434-5900 (office). *Fax:* (20) 7437-1072 (office). *E-mail:* dha@davidhigham.co.uk (office). *Website:* www.davidhigham.co.uk (office); www .penelopelively.net.

LIVERIS, Andrew N., BSc, FIChemE, FAATS; Australian chemical industry executive; b. Darwin, Northern Territory; m. Paula Liveris; three c.; ed Univ. of Queensland, Brisbane; chartered engineer; joined Dow Chemical Co. 1976, Gen. Man. Thailand 1989–92, Group Business Dir Midland, Mich. 1992–93, Gen. Man. 1993–94, Vice-Pres. 1994–95, Pres. Dow Chemical Pacific Hong Kong 1995–98, Vice-Pres. Specialty Chemicals, Midland 1998–2000, Business Group Pres. 2000–04, Pres. Dow Chemical 2003–16, COO 2003–04, mem. Bd of Dirs and CEO 2004–18, Chair. 2006–18, mem. Bd of Dirs, Dow Corning Corpn; mem. Bd of Dirs, Citigroup, IBM, Special Olympics; Chair. US Business Council; Vice-Chair. Business Roundtable; Pres. Int. Council of Chemical Asscn; Co-Chair. Pres. Obama's Advanced Manufacturing Partnership 2011–16; Chair. Pres. Trump's American Manufacturing Council Jan.–Aug. 2017; fmr Chair. US-China Business Council, American Chem. Council, Soc. of Chemical Industry America Int. Group; mem. Pres.'s Export Council, US-India CEO, Peterson Inst. for Int. Econs, Int. Council of Chemical Asscns, United States Climate Action Partnership, American Australian Asscn, Detroit Econ. Club, Nat. Petroleum Council, Soc. de Chimie Industrielle; Trustee, Tufts Univ., The Herbert H. and Grace A. Dow Foundation,

US Council for Int. Business; Inaugural Chair. The Univ. of Queensland in America Foundation 2011–; Co-founder and Chair. The Hellenic Initiative (to support economic renewal in Greece) 2012–; Hon. DSc (Univ. of Queensland) 2005; Officer, Order of Australia 2014; University Medal for year of graduation, Alumnus of the Year 2005, named by ICIS Chemical Business magazine as the greatest influential person in the global chemical markets 2010, Distinguished Performance Award for Excellence in Public Policy, Cttee for Econ. Devt 2011, Int. Leadership Award, US Council for Int. Business 2011, Legend in Leadership, Yale Chief Exec. Leadership Inst. 2011, named Platts Global Energy Awards CEO of the Year 2011, named as one of the most influential people in the global chemical markets, ICIS Chemical Business magazine 2010–12, George E. Davis Medal, Inst. of Chemical Engineers 2011, Int. Palladium Medal, Soc. de Chimie Industrielle 2012, Vanguard Award, Chemical Educ. Foundation, Inspired Leadership Award, The Performance Theater 2012, Aristeio Award in Business, American Hellenic Council 2012, Archbishop Iakovos Leadership 100 Award for Excellence 2012, named a BOSS True Leader by the Australian Financial Review 2012, BENS Eisenhower Award, Business Execs for Nat. Security 2013, Chemical Industry Medal, Soc. of Chemical Industry 2013. *Publication:* Make It in America 2011. *Leisure interests:* science, maths, astronomy, sports.

LIVERMORE, Ann Martinelli, BA, MBA; American computer company executive; b. 23 Aug. 1958, Greensboro, N Carolina; ed Univ. of N Carolina at Chapel Hill and Stanford Univ., Calif.; joined Hewlett-Packard in 1982, held several man. positions in Marketing, Sales, Research and Devt, Business Man. before being elected a Corp. Vice-Pres. in 1995, CEO Enterprise Computing Solutions Org. 1996, Exec. Vice-Pres. HP Services 2001–04, Exec. Vice-Pres. HP Enterprise Business 2004–11, mem. Bd Dirs 2011–; mem. Bd Dirs United Parcel Service Inc. 1997–; mem. Bd of Visitors Kenan-Flagler Business School at Univ. of N Carolina at Chapel Hill, Bd of Advisors at Stanford Business School. *Address:* HP, 3000 Hanover Street, Palo Alto, CA 94304-1185, USA (office).

LIVINGSTON OF PARKHEAD, Baron (Life Peer), cr. 2013; **Ian Paul Livingston,** BA; British chartered accountant, business executive and government official; b. 28 July 1964; ed Kelvinside Acad., Univ. of Manchester; held sr man. positions at 3i Group and Bank of America International; joined Dixons in 1991, held several operational and financial roles, both in UK and abroad, Group Finance Dir Dixons Group 1997–2002; Group Finance Dir BT Group plc 2002–05, Chief Exec. BT Retail 2005–08, Chief Exec. BT Group plc 2008–13; mem. (Conservative), House of Lords 2013–; Minister of State for Trade and Investment 2013–15; Dir (non-exec.) Ladbrokes plc 2003–07, Celtic plc 2007–. *Address:* c/o Department for Business, Innovation and Skills, 1 Victoria Street, London, SW1H 0ET, England (office). *Telephone:* (20) 7215-5000 (office). *Website:* www.gov.uk/ government/organisations/department-for-business-innovation-skills (office).

LIVINGSTONE, Catherine B., AO, BA (Hons), FCA, FTSE, FAICD, FAA; Australian business executive; *Chairman, Commonwealth Bank of Australia;* b. 17 Sept. 1955; ed Macquarie Univ.; has held several finance and Gen. Man. roles, predominantly in medical devices sector; Chief Exec. Cochlear Ltd 1994–2000; Dir Telstra Corpn Ltd 2000–16, Chair. 2009–16, Chair. Nomination and NBN Cttees, mem. Remuneration, Audit and Tech. Cttees; mem. Bd of Dirs Sydney Inst. 1998–2005, Goodman Fielder Ltd 2000–03, Rural Press Ltd 2000–03, Macquarie Bank Ltd 2003–13, Macquarie Grad. School of Man. Pty Ltd 2007–08, Macquarie Group Ltd 2007–13, WorleyParsons Ltd 2007–, Future Directions International Pty Ltd 2007–, Saluda Medical Pty Ltd 2013–, Commonwealth Bank of Australia 2016– (Chair. 2017–); Chair. CSIRO 2001–06, Australian Business Foundation 2000–05; Chancellor Univ. of Technology Sydney 2016–; mem. Dept of Accounting and Finance Advisory Bd, Macquarie Univ., Business/Industry/Higher Educ. Collaboration Cttee (BIHECC), New South Wales Innovation and Productivity Council 2007–, Fed. Govt's Nat. Innovation System Review Panel 2008, Advisory Bd for the John Grill Centre for Project Leadership at Univ. of Sydney 2013–; Pres. Australian Museum Trust 2012–, Business Council of Australia 2014–16; Dir, The George Inst. 2012–; mem. Royal Inst. of Australia 2009–; Fellow, Australian Acad. of Technological Sciences, Australian Inst. of Co. Dirs; Hon. DSc (Murdoch Univ.); Hon. DBus (Macquarie Univ.). *Address:* Commonwealth Bank of Australia, Ground Floor, Tower 1, 201 Sussex St, Sydney, NSW 2000, Australia (office). *Telephone:* (2) 9378-2000 (office). *Fax:* (2) 9118-7192 (office). *Website:* www .commbank.com.au (office).

LIVINGSTONE, Kenneth (Ken) Robert; British politician and presenter; b. 17 June 1945, London; s. of Robert Moffat Livingstone and Ethel Ada Kennard; m. Christine Pamela Chapman 1973 (divorced 1982); ed Tulse Hill Comprehensive School, Phillipa Fawcett Coll. of Educ.; technician, Cancer Research Unit, Royal Marsden Hosp. 1962–70; Councillor, Borough of Lambeth 1971–78, of Camden 1978–82, of Greater London Council 1973–86 (Leader 1981–86); MP for Brent East 1987–2001; Mayor of London 2000–08; joined Labour Party 1969–2000, 2003–18, mem. Regional Exec. 1974–86, Nat. Exec. Cttee 1987–89, 1997–98, NI Select Cttee 1997–99; consultant to Venezuelan Pres., Hugo Chavez 2008; mem. Council, Zoological Soc. of London 1994–2000 (Vice-Pres. 1996–98); joined LBC 97.3 as radio presenter 2008–16, Co-host (with David Mellor) Ken and David radio show. *Publications:* If Voting Changed Anything They'd Abolish It 1987, Livingstone's Labour 1989, You Can't Say That (memoirs) 2011, Being Red 2016. *Leisure interests:* science fiction, cinema, natural history, thinking while gardening.

LIVINGSTONE, Marco Eduardo, MA; American/British art historian, writer and curator; b. 17 March 1952, Detroit, Mich., USA; s. of Leon Livingstone and Alicia Arce Fernández; partner Stephen Stuart-Smith; ed Univ. of Toronto, Courtauld Inst. of Fine Art, Univ. of London; Asst Keeper of British Art, Walker Art Gallery, Liverpool 1976–82; Deputy Dir Museum of Modern Art, Oxford 1982–86; Area Ed. for 20th Century The Dictionary of Art 1986–91, Deputy Ed. for 19th and 20th Centuries 1987–91; UK adviser to Art Life, Tokyo 1989–98; freelance writer and ind. curator 1991–. *Publications include:* Sheer Magic by Allen Jones 1979, Allen Jones Retrospective 1979, David Hockney 1981, Patrick Caulfield 1981, Peter Phillips Retrovision 1982, Duane Michals 1984, Stephen Buckley: Many Angles 1985, R. B. Kitaj 1985 (revised edn 2010), Arthur Tress: Talisman 1986, Stephen Farthing: Mute Accomplices 1987, David Hockney: Faces 1987, Michael Sandle 1988, Pop Art: A Continuing History 1990, Tim Head 1992, Tom Wesselmann 1993, Duane Hanson 1994, David Hockney in California 1994, Jim Dine: Flowers and Plants 1994, Allen Jones Prints 1995, Jim Dine: The Body and its Metaphors 1996, George Segal 1997, The Pop '60s: Transatlantic Crossing 1997, The Essential Duane Michals 1997, R. B. Kitaj: An American in Europe 1998, Jim Dine: The Alchemy of Images 1998, David Hockney: Space and Line 1999, Signature Pieces: Contemporary British Prints and Multiples 1999, Patrick Caulfield 1999, Photographics 2000, Jim Dine: Subjects 2000, Encounters: New Art from Old (contrib.) 2000, Kienholz Tableau Drawings 2001, Callum Innes: Exposed Paintings 2001, Langlands & Bell: The Language of Places 2002, David Hockney: Egyptian Journeys 2002, Clive Barker Sculpture (with Ann Fermon) 2002, Maurice Cockrill (with Nicholas Alfrey) 2002, Blast to Freeze (contrib.) 2002, Tony Bevan: Paintings 2000–2003 2003, David Hockney's Portraits and People (with Kay Heymer) (Sir Bannister Fletcher Award for Best Book on the Arts 2004) 2003, Pop Art UK: British Pop Art 1956–1972 2004, R. B. Kitaj: Portrait of a Hispanist 2004, Patrick Caulfield: Paintings 2005, British Pop 2005, Tom Wesselmann (contrib.) 2005, British Pop 2005, Richard Woods 2006, Tilson 2007, Tony Bevan Monotypes 2007, Gary Hume: Prints 2007, Tony Bevan (contrib.) 2007, Seeing Double: The Poetic Focus of Claes Oldenburg and Coosje van Bruggen 2007. Gilbert & George: Major Exhibition (contrib.) 2007, Peter Blake: A Retrospective (contrib.) 2007, Paula Rego 2007, Antony Donaldson: French Paintings 2008, John Wesley: Works on Paper & Paintings 2008, Paula Rego: Human Cargo 2008, Colin Self: Art in the Nuclear Age (contrib.) 2008, Jim Dine: Talking about Aldo 2008, Peter Blake: One Man Show 2009, Peter Blake: Venice Fantasies (with Peter Blake) 2009, David Hockney: Just Nature (contrib.) 2009, Peter Kinley (with Catherine Kinley) 2010, Paula Rego 2010, Peter Blake: Paris Escapades 2011, David Hockney: My Yorkshire 2011, David Hockney: A Bigger Picture (contrib.) 2012, Paula Rego (contrib.) 2012, Tom Wesselmann: Beyond Pop (contrib.) 2012, Allen Jones: Off the Wall (contrib.) 2012, Pop Art Design (contrib.) 2012, Peter Blake: Rock, Paper, Scissors 2012, David Mach 2012, Joe Tilson: A Survey 2013, Patrick Caulfield 2013, Pop Imagery 2013, Clive Barker: Objects for Contemplation 2013, When Britain Went Pop (contrib.) 2013, Caroline Walker: In Every Dream Home (contrib.) 2013, Tom Wesselmann. Still Life, Nude, Landscape: The Late Prints 2013, Post Pop: East Meets West (ed.), Touch: Figure Drawings by Allen Jones 1958–2010 2014, Allen Jones (contrib.) 2014–15, Tom Wesselmann: A Line to Greatness 2015, Inside Out: Sculptures by Allen Jones 2015, Peter Blake: Portraits and People 2015, Jim Dine: About the Love of Printing (contrib.) 2015, Michael Craig-Martin: Transience (contrib.) 2015, Robert Rauschenberg: Transfer Drawings from the 1960s and 1970s (contrib.) 2016, David Hockney (contrib.) 2017, Gerald Laing: Catalogue Raisonné (contrib.) 2017, David Hockney: The Complete Early Etchings 1961–1964 2017, David Mach: Alternative Facts 2017, Source and Stimulus: Polke, Lichtenstein, Laing 2018, Caroline Walker: Picture Window 2018, Uptown/Downtown: The Early Paintings of Richard Smith 1959–63 2018. *Leisure interests:* music, languages, travel, collecting art, drawing and painting. *Telephone:* (20) 7607-0282 (office).

LIVNAT, Limor; Israeli politician (retd); b. 22 Sept. 1950, Haifa; m.; two c.; ed Tel-Aviv Univ.; in Israel Defense Forces, served in Educ. and Social Welfare Unit; worked in advertising and public relations; mem. Knesset (Parl.) 1992–2015, mem. Knesset Educ. and Culture Cttee, Labour and Social Affairs Cttee 1991–96, Chair. Knesset Cttee for Advancement of Status of Women 1993–94, Sub-Cttee on Women's Representation, Parl. Comm. of Inquiry into domestic violence 1995; Chair. of Likud and of Benjamin Netanyahu's election campaign 1996; Minister of Communications 1996–99, of Educ. 2001–06 (resgnd), Minister of Culture and Sport 2002–06 (resgnd), 2009–15; fmr Vice-Chair. World Likud Movt, fmr mem. Educ. and Cultural Cttee, Labour and Social Affairs Cttee, Comm. for Commercial TV. *Address:* c/o Knesset, Kiryat Ben-Gurion, Jerusalem 91950, Israel (office).

LIVNI, Tzipi, LLB; Israeli lawyer and fmr politician; b. 5 July 1958, Tel Aviv; d. of Eitan Livni and Sara Rosenberg; m.; two c.; ed Bar-Ilan Univ.; with Mossad 1980–84; practised law in pvt. firm for ten years before entering public life; Gen. Man. Govt Cos Authority 1996–99; mem. Knesset 1999–, served as mem. Constitution, Law and Justice Cttee, Cttee on the Status of Women, Chair. Sub-cttee responsible for legislation of the Prevention of Money Laundering Law; Minister of Regional Co-operation March–Aug. 2001, without Portfolio 2001–02, of Agric. and Rural Devt Dec. 2002–Feb. 2003, of Immigrant Absorption 2003–06; Acting Minister of Housing and Construction 2004, Minister of Housing and Construction 2004–05; Acting Minister of Justice 2004–05, 2006–07, Minister of Justice 2005–06, of Foreign Affairs 2006–09, Vice-Premier 2006–09; mem. Likud Party 1999–2005; Co-founder and mem. Kadima Party 2005–12, Leader 2008–12; Co-founder Hatnuah party 2012–, Leader 2018–19, Co-leader Zionist Union (alliance of Hatnuah party) 2014–19; Chubb Fellowship, Yale Univ. 2009; Abirat Ha-Shilton (Champion of Good Govt Award) 2004.

LJAJIĆ, Rasim; Serbian physician and politician; *Deputy Prime Minister and Minister of Trade, Tourism and Telecommunications;* b. 28 Jan. 1964, Novi Pazar; m.; two c.; ed Medical Faculty, Sarajevo Univ.; journalist for various newspapers and periodicals across fmr 1989–2000; Founder and Pres. Coalition of Sandzak 1994–2007 (now Sandzak Democratic Party); Pres. Social Democratic Party of Serbia 2007–; Minister of Nat. and Ethnic Communities 2000–06; also Pres. Co-ordinating Body for Municipalities of Presevo, Bujanovac and Medvedja 2000–03, 2005–07; Vice-Pres. Co-ordination Centre for Kosovo and Metohija 2001–03; Minister of Human and Minority Rights of Serbia-Montenegro 2003–06; Minister of Labour and Social Policy 2007–12; Deputy Prime Minister and Minister of Foreign and Domestic Trade and Telecommunications 2012–14, Deputy Prime Minister and Minister of Trade, Tourism and Telecommunications 2014–; Co-Pres. Jt Cttee for co-operation with Arab countries 2003–06; Pres. Nat. Council for Co-operation with the Int. Criminal Tribunal for the fmr Yugoslavia (ICTY) 2004–07; mem. Forum for Int. Relations, Belgrade, East-West Inst., Prague. *Address:* Ministry of Trade, Tourism and Telecommunications, 11070 Belgrade, bul. Mihaila Pupina 2 (office); Social Democratic Party of Serbia (Socijaldemokratska Partija Srbije), 11000 Belgrade, Terazije 16, Serbia. *Telephone:* (11) 3113432 (office); (11) 2656442. *Fax:* (11) 3114650 (office); (11) 2656333. *E-mail:* potpredsednik@mtt.gov.rs (office); kabinet@mtt.gov.rs (office); info@sdpsrbije.org.rs. *Website:* mtt.gov.rs (office); www.sdpsrbije.org.rs.

LJUNGQVIST, Bengt, BA; Swedish business executive and lawyer; b. 13 Aug. 1937, Stockholm; s. of Gunnar Ljungqvist and Solveig Ljungqvist; m. 1st Sylvia Elmstedt 1961 (divorced 1977); m. 2nd Christina (née Hedén) Ljungqvist 1978; two s. two d.; ed Stockholm Univ.; joined Malmström and Malmenfelt Advokatbyrå, Stockholm 1967, Partner 1971–; Solicitor-Royal 1995–; Pres. Bd of City Planning, Danderyd 1976–85, Chair. City Council, Danderyd 1986–; mem. Council, Swedish Bar Asscn 1983–, apptd Vice-Pres. 1985; Pres. Swedish Bar Asscn 1989–92; mem. Council Int. Bar Asscn 1984–90; Pres. JP-Bank Stockholm, Swedish Real Property Owners Assn 1991–96; Vice-Pres. Union Int. de la Propriété Immobilière 1993–96; mem. Bd, Länsförsäkringar-Stockholm 1993–, Pres. 1995–.

LLEWELLYN OF STEEP, Baron (Life Peer) cr. 2016, of Hampshire; **Edward David Gerard Llewellyn,** PC, OBE; British diplomatist; *Ambassador to France;* b. 23 Sept. 1965; ed New Coll., Univ. of Oxford; mem. Research Dept, Conservative Party 1988–92; Pvt. Sec. to fmr Prime Minister Margaret Thatcher 1990–91; Personal Adviser to Gov., Hong Kong 1992–97; mem. Office of the High Rep. to Bosnia and Herzegovina 1997–99, Chief of Staff 2002–05; mem. Cabinet of EU Commr for External Relations 1999–2002; Chief of Staff to Leader of HM's Opposition 2005–10, to Prime Minister 2010–16; Amb. to France 2016–. *Address:* British Embassy, 35 rue du Faubourg St Honoré, 75383 Paris Cedex 08, France (office). *Telephone:* 1-44-51-31-00 (office). *Fax:* 1-44-51-31-09 (office). *E-mail:* France.Enquiries@fco.gov.uk (office). *Website:* www.gov.uk/world/france (office).

LLEWELLYN-SMITH, Sir Chris(topher) Hubert, Kt, DPhil, FRS; British theoretical physicist and academic; b. 19 Nov. 1942, Giggleswick, W Yorks.; s. of John Clare Llewellyn Smith and Margaret Emily Frances Crawford; brother of Elizabeth Llewellyn-Smith (q.v.) and Sir Michael Llewellyn-Smith (q.v.); m. Virginia Grey 1966; one s. one d.; ed Wellington Coll. and New Coll. Oxford; Royal Soc. Exchange Fellow, Lebedev Inst., Moscow 1967–68; Fellow, CERN, Geneva 1968–70, Staff mem. 1972–74, Chair. Scientific Policy Cttee 1990–92, Dir-Gen. CERN European Lab. for Particle Physics 1994–98; Research Assoc., Stanford Linear Accelerator Center (SLAC), Calif., USA 1970–72; Univ. Lecturer in Theoretical Physics, Univ. of Oxford and Fellow, St John's Coll. 1974–98, Reader in Theoretical Physics 1980–87, Prof. 1987–98 (on leave of absence 1994–98), Chair. of Physics 1987–92, Sr Research Fellow in Theoretical Physics 2002–03, Visiting Prof. 2004–, Dir of Energy Research 2011–17; Pres. and Provost Univ. Coll., London 1999–2002; mem. various advisory bodies for SLAC, CERN, DESY (Deutsches Elektronen-Synchrotron, Hamburg), Science and Eng Research Council, CCLRC, Princeton Plasma Physics Lab., Max Planck Inst. for Plasma Physics, Forschung Zentrum Karlsruhe, Saclay; mem. Advisory Council on Science and Tech. 1989–92; Dir United Kingdom Atomic Energy Authority (UKAEA) Culham Division 2003–08; Chair. Consultative Cttee for Euratom on Fusion 2004–09, Council of Int. Tokamak Experimental Reactor (ITER) 2007–09; Pres. Council of Synchrotron-light for Experimental Science and its Applications in the Middle East (SESAME) 2008–11; mem. Academia Europaea 1989; Fellow, American Physical Soc. 1994; Foreign Fellow, Indian Nat. Science Acad. 1998; Hon. Fellow, Univ. of Wales 1998, St John's Coll. Oxford 2000, New Coll. Oxford 2002; Hon. FInstP 2008; Hon. DSc (Bristol), (Shandong), (Granada), (York), (Guelph); Maxwell Medal 1979, US Dept of Energy Distinguished Assoc. Award 1998, US NSF Distinguished Service Award 1998, Medal of Japanese Assoc. of Medical Sciences 1997, Gold Medal, Slovak Acad. of Science 1998, Glazebrook Medal, Inst. of Physics 1999, Royal Medal, Royal Soc. 2015, AAAS Award for Science Diplomacy 2019. *Publications:* numerous articles in scientific journals including Nuclear Physics, Physics Letters, Physical Review. *Leisure interests:* books, travel, opera. *Address:* Theoretical Physics,Beecroft Building, Parks Road, Oxford, OX1 3PU, England (office). *E-mail:* c.llewellyn-smith@physics.ox.ac.uk (office). *Website:* www-thphys.physics.ox.ac.uk/people/ChrisLlewellynSmith (office).

LLEWELLYN-SMITH, Elizabeth, CB, BA, MA; British public servant and college principal (retd); b. 17 Aug. 1934, Upshire, Essex; d. of John Clare Llewellyn-Smith and Margaret Emily Frances Crawford; sister of Sir Michael John Llewellyn-Smith (q.v.) and Sir Chris Llewellyn-Smith (q.v.); ed Christ's Hosp., Univ. of Cambridge and Royal Coll. of Defence Studies; fmr civil servant; Deputy Dir-Gen. of Fair Trading 1982–87; Deputy Sec. Dept of Trade and Industry 1987–90; Dir European Investment Bank 1987–90; Prin. St Hilda's Coll., Oxford 1990–2001; mem. Council Consumers' Asscn 2002–08, Accountancy Investigation and Disciplinary Bd 2003–09; Hon. Fellow, Girton Coll., Cambridge 1994, St Mary's Coll., Durham Univ. 1999, St Hilda's Coll., Oxford 2001. *Publications:* articles in Dictionary of National Biography. *Leisure interests:* travel, books, entertaining. *Address:* Brook Cottage, Taston, nr Charlbury, Oxon., OX7 3JL, England (home). *Telephone:* (1608) 811874 (home). *E-mail:* e.llewellynsmith@btopenworld.com (home).

LLEWELLYN-SMITH, Sir Michael John, Kt, KCVO, CMG, MA, DPhil; British diplomatist (retd) and writer; b. 25 April 1939, Tunbridge Wells, Kent, England; s. of John Clare Llewellyn Smith and Margaret Emily Frances Crawford; brother of Elizabeth Llewellyn-Smith (q.v.) and Sir Chris Llewellyn-Smith (q.v.); m. Colette Gaulier 1967; one s. one d.; ed Wellington Coll., Berks., New Coll. and St Antony's Coll., Oxford; at Embassy, Moscow 1973–75, at Embassy, Paris 1976–78; at Royal Coll. of Defence Studies 1979; at Embassy, Athens 1980–83; Head, Western European Dept, FCO 1984–85, Head of Soviet Dept 1985–88; Minister, Embassy, Paris 1988–91; Amb. to Poland 1991–96, to Greece 1996–99; Vice-Chair. Cathedrals Fabric Comm. for England 1999–2006; Dir (non-exec.), Coca-Cola Hellenic Bottling Co. SA 2000–16, Sr Ind. Dir 2013–16; Vice-Pres. British School at Athens 2009–; Council mem. Anglo-Hellenic League 1999–; Hon. Fellow, St Antony's Coll., Oxford 2007; John D. Criticos Prize 1999. *Publications:* The Great Island: A Study of Crete 1965, Ionian Vision: Greece in Asia Minor 1919–22 1973, The British Embassy Athens 1998, Olympics in Athens 1896: The Invention of the Modern Olympic Games 2004, Athens: A Cultural and Literary History 2004, Scholars, Travels, Archives: Greek History and Culture through the British School at Athens (ed.) 2009. *Leisure interest:* music. *Website:* www.michaelllewellynsmith.co.uk.

LLOYD, Chris(tine) Marie Evert (see EVERT, Chris(tine) Marie).

LLOYD, Christopher; American actor; b. 22 Oct. 1938, Stamford, Conn.; ed Neighborhood Playhouse, New York. *Plays include:* Red White & Madox, Possessed, Midsummer Night's Dream, Kaspar (Drama Desk and Obie Awards 1973), Unexpected Man 2002, Mornings at 7 (Broadway) 2002, Twelfth Night (Shakespeare in the Park) 2002. *Films include:* One Flew Over the Cuckoo's Nest

1975, Three Warriors 1978, Goin' South 1978, Butch and Sundance: The Early Days 1979, The Onion Field 1979, The Black Marble 1980, The Legend of the Lone Ranger 1981, Mr Mom 1983, To Be or Not To Be 1983, Star Trek III: The Search for Spock 1984, The Adventures of Buckaroo Banzai Across the 8th Dimension 1984, Back to the Future 1985, Clue 1985, Walk Like a Man 1987, Who Framed Roger Rabbit? 1988, Track 29 1988, Eight Men Out 1988, The Dream Team 1989, The Real Blonde, Back to the Future Part II 1989, Why Me? 1990, Back to the Future Part III 1990, The Addams Family 1991, Twenty Bucks (Independent Spirit Award for Best Dramatic Actor) 1993, Dennis the Menace 1993, Addams Family Values 1993, Angels in the Outfield 1994, The Pagemaster 1994, Camp Nowhere 1994, Radioland Murders 1994, Things To Do in Denver When You're Dead 1995, Cadillac Ranch 1996, Changing Habits 1997, Anastasia 1997, Dinner at Fred's 1999, Baby Geniuses 1999, My Favorite Martian 1999, Man on the Moon 1999, Wish You Were Dead 2002, Interstate 60 2002, Hey Arnold! The Movie (voice) 2002, Haunted Lighthouse 2003, Merry Christmas Space Case (voice) 2003, Admissions 2004, A Fate Totally Worse Than Death 2005, Enfants terribles 2005, Flakes 2007, Fly Me to the Moon (voice) 2007, Call of the Wild 2009, Adventures of Serial Buddies 2011, Dorothy and the Witches of Oz 2012, Super Athlete 2013, Sin City: A Dame to Kill For 2014. *Television includes:* The Word (mini-series) 1978, Taxi (series) (two Emmy Awards including Best Supporting Actor) 1978–83, Road to Avonlea (Emmy Award for Best Supporting Actor) 1992, Dead Ahead: The Exxon Valdez Disaster 1992, Stacked (series) 2005–06, A Perfect Day 2006, Granite Flats (series) 2014–15. *Address:* c/o The Gersh Agency, 9465 Wilshire Blvd, 6th Floor, Beverly Hills, CA 90212, USA (office).

LLOYD, Clive Hubert, AO, CBE; Guyanese sports administrator and fmr professional cricketer; b. 31 Aug. 1944, Georgetown, British Guiana (now Guyana); s. of Arthur Christopher Lloyd and Sylvia Thelma Lloyd; cousin of Lance Gibbs; m. Waveney Benjamin 1971; one s. two d.; ed Chatham High School, Georgetown; left-hand batsman; right-arm medium-paced bowler; played for British Guiana/Guyana 1963–83, Lancashire 1968–86 (Capt. 1981–83, 1986); played in 110 Tests for W Indies 1966–85, record 74 as Capt., scoring 7,515 runs (average 46.67, highest score 242 not out) including 19 hundreds; scored 31,232 First-class runs (average 49.26) including 79 hundreds; W Indies Team Man. 1988–89, 1996–99; Int. Cricket Council (ICC) Referee 1992–95, Match Referee 2001–06, apptd Chair. ICC Cricket Cttee and Ex-Officio mem. ICC Chief Execs' Cttee 2008; apptd Exec. Promotions Officer, Project Fullemploy 1987; Dir Red Rose Radio PLC 1981; Patron Nat. Lottery Charities Bd, Major League Cricket for inaugural Interstate Cricket Cup (named the Sir Clive Lloyd Cup), USA 2005; Hon. Fellow, Manchester Polytechnic, Lancs. Polytechnic 1986; Hon. MA (Manchester, Hull); Hon. DLitt (Univ. of W Indies, Jamaica); Golden Arrow of Achievement (Guyana) 1975, Wisden Cricketer of the Year 1971. *Publications include:* Living for Cricket (with Tony Cozier) 1980, Winning Captaincy (with Mihir Bose) 1995.

LLOYD, David Robert, MA, PhD, ScD, MRIA, FInstP; British chemist and academic; *Fellow Emeritus, Department of Chemistry, Trinity College Dublin;* b. 19 May 1937, Derby, England; s. of George Lloyd and Effie Lloyd; m. Heidi Hoffman 1964; one s. one d.; ed Halesowen Grammar School, Worcs. and Selwyn Coll., Cambridge; temporary Lecturer, Chem. Dept, Northwestern Univ., USA 1963–65; Lecturer in Chem., Univ. of Birmingham 1965–78; Prof. of Chem., Trinity Coll. Dublin, Ireland 1978–2000, now Fellow Emer., Head of Chem. Dept 1978–85, 1992–94; A. von Humboldt Fellowship 1962–63; mem. Royal Irish Acad. *Publications:* approx. 118 papers on aspects of chemistry and physics, three on Plato's view of the elements. *Leisure interests:* music, hill walking, domestic chores, theology, classical Greek. *Address:* Department of Chemistry, University of Dublin, Trinity College, Dublin 2, Ireland (office). *Telephone:* (1) 8961000 (office). *E-mail:* copleym@tcd.ie (office). *Website:* chemistry.tcd.ie (office).

LLOYD, Sir Geoffrey Ernest Richard, Kt, PhD, FBA; British academic; *Professor Emeritus of Ancient Philosophy and Science, University of Cambridge;* b. 25 Jan. 1933, London, England; s. of William Ernest Lloyd and Olive Irene Neville Lloyd; m. Janet Elizabeth Lloyd 1956; three s.; ed Charterhouse and King's Coll., Cambridge; Asst Lecturer in Classics, Univ. of Cambridge 1965–67, Lecturer 1967–74, Reader in Ancient Philosophy and Science 1974–83, Prof. 1983–2000, Prof. Emer. 2000–; Master, Darwin Coll., Cambridge 1989–2000, Hon. Fellow 2000–; Fellow, King's Coll. 1957–89, Hon. Fellow 1990–; A. D. White Prof.-at-Large, Cornell Univ., USA 1990–96; Chair. East Asian History of Science Trust 1992–2002; mem. Japan Soc. for Promotion of Science, Int. Acad. of History of Science; Zhu Kezhen Visiting Prof., Inst. for History of Natural Science, Beijing 2002; Foreign Hon. mem. American Acad. of Arts and Sciences 1995; Hon. LittD (Athens) 2003; Sarton Medal 1987, Kenyon Medal 2007. *Publications include:* Polarity and Analogy 1966, Aristotle, the Growth and Structure of his Thought 1968, Early Greek Science: Thales to Aristotle 1970, Greek Science after Aristotle 1973, Hippocratic Writings (ed.) 1978, Aristotle on Mind and the Senses (co-ed. with G. E. L. Owen) 1978, Magic, Reason and Experience 1979, Science, Folklore and Ideology 1983, Science and Morality in Greco-Roman Antiquity 1985, The Revolutions of Wisdom 1987, Demystifying Mentalities 1990, Methods and Problems in Greek Science 1991, Adversaries and Authorities 1996, Aristotelian Explorations 1996, Greek Thought (ed.) 2000, The Ambitions of Curiosity 2002, The Way and the Word (with N. Sivin) 2002, In the Grip of Disease, Studies in the Greek Imagination 2003, Ancient Worlds, Modern Reflections 2004, The Delusions of Invulnerability 2005, Principles and Practices in Ancient Greek and Chinese Science 2006, Cognitive Variations, Reflections on the Unity and Diversity of the Human Mind 2007, Disciplines in the Making, Cross-Cultural Perspectives on Elites, Learning and Innovation 2009. *Leisure interest:* travel. *Address:* 2 Prospect Row, Cambridge, CB1 1DU (home); Needham Research Institute, 8 Sylvester Road, Cambridge, CB3 9AF, England (office). *Telephone:* (1223) 311545 (office); (1223) 355970 (home). *E-mail:* eahost1@hotmail.com (office); gel20@cam.ac.uk (office).

LLOYD, John Nicol Fortune, MA; British journalist and academic; *Contributing Editor, Financial Times;* b. 15 April 1946; s. of Christopher Lloyd and Joan A. Fortune; m. 1st Judith Ferguson 1974 (divorced 1979); m. 2nd Marcia Levy 1983 (divorced 1997); one s.; ed Waid Comprehensive School and Univ. of Edinburgh; Ed. Time Out 1972–73; reporter, London Programme 1974–76; Producer, Weekend World 1976–77; industrial reporter, labour corresp., industrial and labour ed., Financial Times 1977–86; Ed. New Statesman 1986–87, Assoc. Ed. 1996–2003; with Financial Times 1987–, posts include East Europe Ed., Financial Times Magazine Ed., Moscow Corresp. 1991–95, currently Contributing Ed.; columnist, Reuters.com, La Repubblica, Rome; Sr Research Fellow, Reuters Inst. for the Study of Journalism, Univ. of Oxford; Supernumerary Fellow, St Anne's Coll., Oxford, also Assoc. Mem. Nuffield Coll.; Chair. Advisory Council, Moscow School of Political Studies; Journalist of the Year, Granada Awards 1984, Specialist Writer of the Year, IPC Awards 1985, Rio Tinto David Watt Memorial Prize 1997, Biagio Agnes Int. Journalist of the Year 2014. *Publications include:* The Politics of Industrial Change (with Ian Benson) 1982, The Miners' Strike: Loss Without Limit (with Martin Adeney) 1986, In Search of Work (with Charles Leadbeater) 1987, Counterblasts (contrib.) 1989, Rebirth of a Nation: An Anatomy of Russia 1998, Re-engaging Russia 2000, The Protest Ethic 2001, What the Media are Doing to Our Politics 2004, Scandal! 2011. *Leisure interests:* opera, Italy. *Address:* Reuters Institute for the Study of Journalism, 13 Norham Gardens, Oxford, OX2 6PS, England (office). *Telephone:* (1865) 611080 (office). *E-mail:* john.lloyd@ft.com (office). *Website:* reutersinstitute.politics.ox.ac.uk (office).

LLOYD HOLLINS, Carli Anne; American professional footballer; b. 16 June 1982, Delran, NJ; d. of Stephen Lloyd and Pamela Lloyd; m. Brian Hollins 2016; ed Delran High School, Rutgers Univ.; midfielder; began playing soccer at aged five; played for Rutgers Univ. Scarlet Knights 2001–04; played for Central Jersey Splash 1999, New Brunswick Power 2000, South Jersey Banshees 2001, New Jersey Wildcats 2004; started sr career with Chicago Red Stars 2009, Sky Blue FC 2010, Atlanta Beat 2011, Western New York Flash 2013–14, Houston Dash 2015–, Manchester City (short-term contract) 2017–; mem. US Under-21 team 2002–05, US women's nat. team 2005–, Olympic Gold Medal 2008, 2012, FIFA Women's World Cup Champion 2015; Co-Chair. President's Council on Fitness, Sports and Nutrition; Jt US Soccer Athlete of the Year 2008, CONCACAF Women's Player of the Year 2015, Golden Ball, Silver Boot, FIFA Women's World Cup 2015, Women's Sports Foundation Sportswoman of the Year Team Sport Award 2015, FIFA World Player of the Year 2015, Best FIFA Women's Player 2016, inducted into NJ Hall of Fame 2017. *Publication:* When Nobody Was Watching (memoir) 2016. *Address:* c/o Universal Academy LLC, 63 East Main Street, Moorestown, NJ 08057, USA. *E-mail:* office@carlilloyd.com. *Website:* www.carlilloyd.com.

LLOYD-JONES, David Mathias, BA; British musician and conductor; b. 19 Nov. 1934, London; s. of Sir Vincent Lloyd-Jones and Margaret Alwena Mathias; m. Anne Carolyn Whitehead 1964; two s. one d.; ed Westminster School, Magdalen Coll., Oxford; Repetiteur, Royal Opera 1959–61; Chorus Master, New Opera Co. 1961–64; conducted at Bath Festival 1966, City of London Festival 1966, Wexford Festival 1967–70, Scottish Opera 1968, Welsh Nat. Opera 1968, Royal Opera, Covent Garden 1971, Sadler's Wells Opera Co. (now ENO) 1969; Asst Music Dir ENO 1972–78; Artistic Dir Opera North 1978–90; also conductor for TV operas (Eugene Onegin, The Flying Dutchman, Hansel and Gretel) and has appeared with most British symphony orchestras and conducted worldwide; Chair. Delius Trust 1997–, Gen. Ed. William Walton Edn 1996–2014; Hon. mem. Royal Philharmonic Soc. 2007; Hon. DMus (Leeds) 1986. *Music includes:* many acclaimed recordings of British and Russian music; has edited works by composers, including Mussorgsky, Bizet, Walton, Berlioz, Elgar and Sullivan. *Publications include:* Boris Godunov–Translation, Vocal Score, Eugene Onegin–Translation, Vocal Score, Boris Godunov–Critical Edition of Original Full Score, numerous contribs to publs including Grove's Dictionary of Music and Musicians, Musik in Geschichte und Gegenwart, Music and Letters, The Listener. *Leisure interests:* theatre, French cuisine, rose growing. *Address:* 94 Whitelands House, Cheltenham Terrace, London, SW3 4RA, England (home). *Telephone:* (20) 7730-8695.

LLOYD WEBBER, Baron (Life Peer), cr. 1997, of Sydmonton in the County of Hampshire; **Andrew Lloyd Webber,** FRCM; British composer; *Chairman, The Really Useful Group Ltd;* b. 22 March 1948, Kensington, London; s. of William Southcombe Lloyd Webber and Jean Hermione Johnstone; brother of Julian Lloyd Webber (q.v.); m. 1st Sarah Jane Tudor (née Hugill) 1971 (divorced 1983); one s. one d.; m. 2nd Sarah Brightman 1984 (divorced 1990); m. 3rd Madeleine Astrid Gurdon 1991; two s. one d.; ed Westminster School, Magdalen Coll. Oxford, Royal Coll. of Music; Chair. The Really Useful Group Ltd; owner of six London theatres including Theatre Royal Drury Lane and The London Palladium; seven Tony Awards, four Drama Desk Awards, seven Laurence Olivier Awards, 14 Ivor Novello Awards from British Acad. of Songwriters, Composers and Authors, Triple Play Award from ASCAP 1988, Star on the Hollywood Walk of Fame for live theatre 1993, Praemium Imperiale Award 1995, four Grammy Awards, Golden Globe Award, Academy Award 1996, Richard Rodgers Award for Excellence in Musical Theatre 1996, Kennedy Center Honor 2006, Woodrow Wilson Award for Public Service 2008, Classic BRITs Special Recognition Award for Musical Theatre & Education 2018, American Songwriters Hall of Fame; Commdr's Cross of the Order of Merit (Hungary) 2005. *Works:* musicals: Joseph and the Amazing Technicolor Dreamcoat (lyrics by Tim Rice) 1968 (revised 1973, 1991), Jesus Christ Superstar (lyrics by Tim Rice) 1970 (revised 1996, 2012), Jeeves (lyrics by Alan Ayckbourn) 1975 (revised as By Jeeves 1996), Evita (lyrics by Tim Rice) 1976 (stage version 1978), Tell Me on a Sunday (lyrics by Don Black) 1980 (revised 2003), Cats (based on T. S. Eliot's Old Possum's Book of Practical Cats) (Tony Awards for Best Score and Best Musical 1983) 1981, Song and Dance (lyrics by Don Black) 1982, Starlight Express (lyrics by Richard Stilgoe) 1984, The Phantom of the Opera (lyrics by Richard Stilgoe and Charles Hart) (Tony Award for Best Musical 1988) 1986, Aspects of Love (lyrics by Don Black and Charles Hart) 1989, Sunset Boulevard (lyrics by Christopher Hampton and Don Black) (Tony Award for Best Score and Best Musical 1995) 1993, Whistle Down the Wind (lyrics by Jim Steinman) 1996, The Beautiful Game (lyrics by Ben Elton) (London Critics' Circle Best Musical 2000) 2000, The Woman in White (lyrics by David Zippel) 2004, Love Never Dies (lyrics by Glenn Slater) 2010, Stephen Ward (lyrics by Christopher Hampton and Don Black) 2013, School of Rock 2015; other compositions: Variations (based on A minor Caprice No. 24 by Paganini) 1977 (symphonic version 1986), Requiem Mass 1985, Amigos Para Siempre (official theme for 1992 Olympic Games), UK Eurovision entry, It's My Time (co-written with Diane Warren), Moscow 2009; film scores: Gumshoe 1971, The Odessa File 1974. *Producer:* Joseph and the Amazing Technicolor Dreamcoat 1973, 1974, 1978, 1980, 1991, Jeeves Takes Charge 1975, Cats 1981, Song & Dance 1982, Daisy Pulls it Off 1983, The Hired Man 1984, Starlight Express 1984, On Your Toes 1984, The

Phantom of the Opera 1986, Café Puccini 1986, The Resistible Rise of Arturo Ui 1987, Lend Me a Tenor 1988, Aspects of Love 1989, Shirley Valentine (Broadway) 1989, La Bête 1992, Sunset Boulevard 1993, By Jeeves 1996, Whistle Down the Wind 1996, 1998, Jesus Christ Superstar 1996, 1998, The Beautiful Game 2000, Bombay Dreams 2002, Tell Me On A Sunday, 2003, The Woman in White 2004, The Sound of Music 2006 and others. *Film:* The Phantom of the Opera (dir Joel Schumacher) 2004. *Publications:* Evita (with Tim Rice) 1978, Cats: the book of the musical 1981, Joseph and the Amazing Technicolor Dreamcoat (with Tim Rice) 1982, The Complete Phantom of the Opera 1987, The Complete Aspects of Love 1989, Sunset Boulevard: from movie to musical 1993, Unmasked (autobiography) 2018. *Leisure interests:* architecture, art. *Address:* c/o The Really Useful Group Ltd, 17 Slingsby Place, London, WC2E 9AB, England (office). *Telephone:* (20) 7240-0880 (office). *Fax:* (20) 7240-1204 (office). *Website:* www.reallyuseful.com (office); www.andrewlloydwebber.com.

LLOYD WEBBER, Julian, FRCM; British cellist (retd), music educationist and writer; *Principal, Birmingham Conservatoire;* b. 14 April 1951, London; s. of William Southcombe Lloyd Webber and Jean Hermione Johnstone; brother of Baron Andrew Lloyd Webber (q.v.); m. 1st Celia M. Ballantyne 1974 (divorced 1989); m. 2nd Zohra Mahmoud Ghazi 1989 (divorced 1999); one s.; m. 3rd Kheira Bourahla 2001 (divorced 2007); m. 4th Jiaxin Cheng 2009; one d.; ed Univ. Coll. School, Royal Coll. of Music (scholar), studied with Pierre Fournier in Geneva; debut with first London performance of Bliss Cello Concerto at Queen Elizabeth Hall 1972; debut, Lincoln Center, New York 1980; debut with Berlin Philharmonic Orchestra 1984; appeared at major int. concert halls and on concert tours throughout Europe, N and S America, S Africa, Australasia, Singapore, Japan, China, Hong Kong and S Korea; numerous radio and TV appearances and broadcasts in UK, Netherlands, Africa, Germany, Scandinavia, France, Belgium, Spain, Australasia and USA; retired from performing 2014; Patron Jacqueline du Pré Charity Concerts 2006–, BSO (Bournemouth Symphony Orchestra) Vibes 2012–; Chair. Sistema England charity 2008–; Prin. Royal Birmingham Conservatoire 2015–; Pres. Elgar Soc. 2009; Dr hc (Hull) 2003, (Thames Valley) 2004, (Plymouth) 2014; Suggia Gift 1968, Brit Award for Elgar Cello Concerto recording 1987, Crystal Award, World Economic Forum (Switzerland) 1998, Classic FM Red Award for outstanding services to music 2005, ISM Distinguished Musician Award 2014. *Television:* Classic Cellists at the BBC 2016. *Recordings include:* world premiere recordings of Britten's 3rd Suite for Solo Cello, Bridge's Oration, Rodrigo's Cello Concerto (Spanish Ministry of Culture Award for world premiere recording 1982), Holst's Invocation, Gavin Bryars' Cello Concerto, Michael Nyman's Cello and Saxophone Concerto, Sullivan's Cello Concerto, Vaughan Williams' Fantasia on Sussex Folk Tunes, Andrew Lloyd Webber's Variations (Gold disc 1978), Elgar's Cello Concerto (British Phonographic Industry Award for Best Classical Recording 1986), Dvořák Concerto, Saint-Saëns Concerto, Lalo Concerto, Walton Concerto, Britten Cello Symphony; Philip Glass Cello Concerto, And the Bridge is Love 2015. *Publications:* Classical Cello 1980, Romantic Cello 1981, French Cello 1981, Frank Bridge, Six Pieces 1982, Young Cellist's Repertoire (three vols) 1984, Holst's Invocation 1984, Travels with my Cello 1984, Song of the Birds 1985, Recital Repertoire for Cellists (four vols) 1986, Short Sharp Shocks 1990, The Great Cello Solos 1992, The Essential Cello 1997, Cello Moods 1999, String Quartets, 2003; Made in England 2003; columnist, Daily Telegraph 2003–; contrib. to The Times, The Sunday Times, USA Today. *Leisure interests:* topography (especially British), football (Leyton Orient), turtles. *Website:* sistemaengland.org.uk; www.julianlloydwebber.com.

LO, Vincent Hong Sui; Chinese business executive; *Chairman and Chief Executive, Shui On Group;* b. 18 April 1948, Hong Kong; m. Jean Lo 1981; one s. one d.; ed Univ. of New South Wales, Australia; f. Shui On Group 1971, now Chair. and Chief Exec., also Chair. and Chief Exec. Shui On Land Ltd, Chair. Shui On Construction And Materials Ltd, China Xintiandi Ltd; Chair. Hong Kong Gen. Chamber of Commerce 1991–92; mem. Exec. Cttee Basic Law Consultative Cttee 1985–90; mem. Bd Land Devt Corpn 1988–90; mem. Hong Kong Trade Devt Council 1991–92, Hong Kong Baptist Coll. 1987–89; mem. Council, Exec. Cttee Hong Kong Man. Asscn 1984–94; Vice-Chair. All-China Fed. of Industry and Commerce; Pres. Business and Professionals Fed. of Hong Kong, currently Hon. Pres.; Pres. Shanghai-Hong Kong Council for the Promotion and Devt of Yangtze; Econ. Advisor, Chongqing Municipal Govt; mem. Preparatory Cttee for the Hong Kong Special Admin. Region 1996–97; Hong Kong Affairs Adviser, People's Repub. of China State Council's Office of Hong Kong and Macao Affairs/Xinhua News Agency, Hong Kong Br. 1994–97; Adviser China Soc. of Macroeconomics, Peking Univ. China Centre for Econ. Research; mem. Gov.'s Business Council 1992–97, Airport Authority 1990–99, Hong Kong/United States Econ. Co-operation Cttee, Tenth Nat. Cttee of Chinese People's Political Consultative Conf.; mem. Nat. Cttee, 12th CPPCC 2013–; Dir The Real Estate Developers Asscn of Hong Kong, The Community Chest of Hong Kong 1990–95, Great Eagle Holdings Ltd, Airport Authority Hong Kong 2013–15 (Chair. 2014–15); Dir (non-exec.) China Telecom Corp. Ltd 2002–08, .Hang Seng Bank Ltd, New World China Land Ltd; Chair. Council Hong Kong Univ. of Science and Tech.; JP 1999; Advisory Professorship (Shanghai Tongji Univ.) 1996, (Shanghai Univ.) 1998; Hon. Citizen of Shanghai 1998; Gold Bauhinia Star 1998, Chevalier des arts et des lettres (France) 2005; Hon. DBA (Hong Kong Univ. of Science and Tech.) 1996; World Chinese Economic Forum Lifetime Achievement Award for Leadership in Property Sector 2012, Grand Bauhinia Medal, Hong Kong 2018. *Address:* 34/F Shui On Centre, 6–8 Harbour Road, Hong Kong Special Administrative Region, People's Republic of China. *Website:* www.shuion.com (office).

LO, Yuk-ming Dennis, BA (Hons), MB BS, MA, DPhil, MD, FRCP, FRCPE, FRCPath; Hong Kong physician, pathologist and academic; *Professor of Chemical Pathology, Li Ka Shing Professor of Medicine and Associate Dean for Research, Faculty of Medicine, Chinese University of Hong Kong;* b. Hong Kong; ed Univs of Cambridge and Oxford, UK; Jr Research Fellow in Natural Sciences, Hertford Coll., Oxford 1990–93, Wellcome Career Devt Fellow in Clinical Medicine 1993–94, Univ. Lecturer in Clinical Biochemistry and Fellow of Green Coll., Oxford 1994–97, Hon. Consultant Chemical Pathologist, John Radcliffe Hosp., Oxford Medical School; returned to Hong Kong 1997; mem. Faculty of Medicine, Chinese Univ. of Hong Kong (CUHK) 1997–, Full Prof. 2003–, Prof. of Chemical Pathology, Li Ka Shing Prof. of Medicine, Dir Li Ka Shing Inst. of Health Sciences, Chair. and Chief-of-Service, Dept of Chemical Pathology, CUHK and Prince of Wales Hosp., Assoc. Dean for Research, CUHK Faculty of Medicine; Past Pres. Hong Kong Soc. of Clinical Chem.; mem. Editorial Bd, Clinical Chemistry, Disease Markers; Trustee, Croucher Foundation, Hong Kong; Hon. Prof., Nanjing Medical Univ., Sun Yat-sen Univ.; Hon. Fellow, Hong Kong Coll. of Pathologists 2011, Hong Kong Coll. of Obstetrics and Gynaecology 2013; State Natural Science Award, State Council of China 2005, Abbott Award for Outstanding Contrib. to Molecular Diagnostics, Int. Fed. of Clinical Chem. and Lab. Medicine 2006, Distinguished Scientist Award, US Nat. Acad. of Clinical Biochemistry 2006, Croucher Sr Medical Research Award 2006, King Faisal Int. Prize in Medicine 2014, Future Science Prize (for developing a prenatal test for detecting Down's syndrome in fetuses) 2016. *Publications include:* author or co-author of more than 350 publs in scientific journals; holds numerous patents in molecular diagnostics on the study of cell-free DNA molecules in human plasma. *Address:* Li Ka Shing Institute of Health Sciences, Li Ka Shing Medical Sciences Building, The Chinese University of Hong Kong, Prince of Wales Hospital, Shatin, New Territories, Hong Kong Special Administrative Region, People's Republic of China (office). *Telephone:* 3763-6003 (office). *Fax:* 3763-6333 (office). *E-mail:* loym@cuhk.edu.hk (office). *Website:* www.cpy.cuhk.edu.hk (office).

LOACH, Kenneth, BA; British film director; b. 17 June 1936, Nuneaton; s. of John Loach and Vivien Loach (née Hamlin); m. Lesley Ashton 1962; three s. (one deceased) two d.; ed King Edward VI School, Nuneaton, St Peter's Hall (now St Peter's Coll.), Oxford; BBC trainee, Drama Dept 1963; Hon. DLitt (St Andrews), (Staffs. Univ., Bristol); Dr hc (Royal Coll. of Art) 1998; Hon. Fellow, St Peter's Coll. Oxford; Praemium Imperiale 2003, Léopard d'honneur for Lifetime Achievement, Locarno Film Festival 2003, London Film Critics' Circle Award for Outstanding Contrib. to Cinema 2005, Hon. Golden Bear, Berlin Film Festival 2014. *Films include:* Poor Cow 1967, Kes 1969, In Black and White 1970, Family Life 1971, Black Jack 1979, Looks and Smiles 1981, Fatherland 1986, Hidden Agenda 1990, Riff-Raff 1991, Raining Stones 1993, Ladybird, Ladybird 1994, Land and Freedom 1995, Carla's Song 1996, My Name is Joe 1998, Bread and Roses 2000, 11.09.01 UK Segment 2002, Sweet Sixteen 2003, A Fond Kiss 2004, Tickets (with others) 2005, The Wind That Shakes the Barley (Palme d'Or, Cannes Film Festival 2006, Best Film, Irish Film and TV Awards 2007) 2006, It's a Free World 2007, Looking for Eric 2009, Route Irish 2010, The Angels' Share (Jury Prize, Cannes Film Festival 2012) 2012, The Spirit of '45 (documentary) 2013, Jimmy's Hall 2014, I, Daniel Blake (Palme d'Or, Cannes Film Festival 2016, BAFTA for Outstanding British Film 2017) 2016. *Television includes:* Diary of a Young Man 1964, Three Clear Sundays 1965, The End of Arthur's Marriage 1965, Up the Junction 1965, Coming Out Party 1965, Cathy Come Home 1966, In Two Minds 1966, The Golden Vision 1969, The Big Flame 1970, After a Lifetime 1971, The Rank and File 1972, Days of Hope (four films) 1975, The Price of Coal 1977, The Gamekeeper 1979, Auditions 1980, A Question of Leadership 1980, The Red and the Blue 1983, Questions of Leadership 1983, Which Side are You on? 1984, The View from the Woodpile 1988, Time to Go 1989, Dispatches: Arthur Scargill 1991, The Flickering Flame 1996, Another City 1998, The Navigators 2001. *Address:* Sixteen Films, 2nd Floor, 187 Wardour Street, London, W1F 8ZB, England. *Telephone:* (20) 7734-0168. *Website:* www.sixteenfilms.co.uk.

LOADER, Danyon Joseph, ONZ; New Zealand fmr swimmer; b. 21 April 1975, Timaru; s. of Peter Loader and Daphne Loader; ed Otago Polytechnic; world short-course record in 200m butterfly 1991; silver medallist, Olympic Games, Barcelona 1992; gold, silver (three times) and bronze medallist, Commonwealth Games, Victoria, BC 1994; gold medallist, 200m and 400m freestyle, Olympic Games, Atlanta 1996; est. over 40 NZ records; retd 2000; motivational speaker with Speakers New Zealand; apptd Olympic Amb. by NZ Olympic Cttee 2007; Asst Coach and Squad Coach, North Shore Swim Club 2011–13; Programme Coach, Nat. High Performance Centre 2013–14; Asst Man., Belgravia Leisure Ltd 2015–16; Global Mobility Co-ordinator SIRVA, Worldwide Relocation and Moving 2016–18; NZ Sportsman of the Decade (1990s), Lonsdale Cup. *Leisure interests:* reading, films, surfing, scuba diving, socializing. *Address:* 9 Prince Albert Road, St Kilda, Dunedin, New Zealand. *Telephone:* (3) 455-2486.

LOBATO, Edson, MS; Brazilian agronomist and administrator; b. 1940; ed Nat. School of Agronomy (now Coll. of Agricultural Sciences), Southern Illinois Univ., USA; began career in soil fertility research through programme sponsored by IRI Research Inst., USAID and Brazilian Ministry of Agric. 1964; received USAID fellowship to study soil fertility in USA 1972–73; hired as researcher, Brazilian Corpn of Agricultural Research (EMBRAPA) 1973, responsible for coordinating several programmes, including outlining plan for Cerrado Agricultural Research Centre, served in variety of positions at EMBRAPA Cerrado Centre, including Tech. Dir 1975–2004; World Food Prize (co-recipient) 2006. *Publications:* Cerrado: Soil Correction and Fertilization; more than 80 publs in professional journals. *Address:* c/o Embrapa, Parque Estação Biológica - PqEB s/nº, Brasília, DF - 70770-901, Brazil. *Telephone:* (61) 3448-4433. *Fax:* (61) 3347-1041. *Website:* www.embrapa.br.

LOBKOWICZ, Michal; Czech business executive and fmr politician; *Partner, Corsum Group;* b. 20 July 1964, Prague; m.; one s.; ed Charles Univ., Prague; mem. Parl. for Civic Democratic Party (ODS) 1992–98, for Freedom Union (FU) 1998–2002; Chef de Cabinet for Minister of Foreign Affairs 1993–96; Minister of Defence Jan.–July 1998; mem. Cttee for European Integration 1998–2002, Cttee for Defence and Security 1998–2002; left parl. functions following elections in 2002; Partner, Corsum Group 2002–; mem. Supervisory Bd Massag Bílovec, SK Slavia Prague soccer club. *Address:* Corsum Group s.r.o. Opatovická 4, 110 00 Prague 1, Czech Republic (office). *Telephone:* (2) 24934707 (office). *Fax:* (2) 24934701 (office). *E-mail:* corsum@corsum.cz (office). *Website:* www.co (office).

LOBKOWICZ, Prince; **Nicholas,** DPhil; American philosopher, political scientist and academic; *Director, Institute of Central and Eastern European Studies, Catholic University of Eichstätt-Ingolstadt;* b. 9 July 1931, Prague, Czechoslovakia (now Czech Repub.); s. of Prince Jan Lobkowicz and Countess Marie Czernin; m. 1st Countess Josephine Waldburg-Zeil 1953; three s. two d.; m. 2nd Aleksandra N. Cieślińska 1999; ed Collegium Maria Hilf, Switzerland, Univs of Erlangen and Fribourg; Assoc. Prof. of Philosophy, Univ. of Notre Dame, Ind. 1960–67; Prof. of Political Theory and Philosophy, Univ. of Munich 1967–90, Dean School of Arts and Letters 1970–71, Rector Magnificus 1971–76, Pres. Univ. of Munich 1976–82; Pres. Catholic Univ. of Eichstätt 1984–96, Founder and Dir Inst. of Cen. and

Eastern European Studies 1994–; mem. Bd of Dirs Fed. Inst. of Int. and E European Studies, Cologne 1972–75, Senate, West German Rectors' Conf. 1976–82, Perm. Cttee European Rectors' Conf. 1979–84, Council Int. Fed. of Catholic Univs 1984–91; Founding mem. Int. Metaphysical Asscn; mem. Cen. Cttee of German Catholics 1980–84; mem. Ukrainian Acad. of Arts and Science (USA) 1979–; mem. W Europe Advisory Cttee to Radio Free Europe/Radio Liberty 1980–2002, Chair. 1994–2002; Founder-mem., Vice-Pres. European Acad. of Sciences and Arts 1990–; Pres. Freier Deutscher Autorenverband 1985–91; mem. Pontifical Council for Culture 1982–93; Pres. Czechoslovak Christian Acad. in Rome 1983–90; Administrator of Faculty of Catholic Theology, Charles Univ. Prague 2002–03; Hon. Citizen of Dallas, Tex.; Hon. DHL (Wayne State Univ.); Hon. DLL (Univ. of Notre Dame); Hon. DrPhil (Seoul and Ukrainian Univ., Munich, Catholic Univ. of America); Hon. DTheol (Charles Univ., Prague). *Publications:* Theory and Practice 1967, Ende aller Religion? 1976, Marxismus und Machtergreifung 1978, Wortmeldung zu Staat, Kirche, Universität 1981, Irrwege der Angst 1983, Das europäische Erbe 1984, Das Konzil 1986, Zeitwende 1993, Czas przelomu 1996, Rationalität und Innerlichkeit 1997, Duše Evropy 2001, Večnaja filosofia 2007. *Address:* Oskar-von-Miller-Strasse 20, 82319 Starnberg (home); Katholische Universität, 85071 Eichstätt, Germany. *Telephone:* (8421) 931717 (office). *Fax:* (8421) 931780 (office). *E-mail:* zimos@ku-eichstaett.de (office); nikolaus.lobkowicz@t-online.de (home). *Website:* www.ku.de/forschung/forschungseinr/zimos/mitarbeiter/nikolaus-lobkowicz (office).

LOBO ANTUNES, António, MD; Portuguese novelist; b. 1 Sept. 1942, Lisbon; s. of João Alfredo Lobo Antunes and Maria Margarida Almeida Lima; m. 1st Maria José Xavier da Fonseca e Costa (divorced); m. 2nd Maria João Espírito Santo Bustorff Silva (divorced); m. 3rd Cristina Ferreira de Almeida 2010; three d.; ed higher educ. in Portugal; fmr doctor and psychiatrist, now full-time writer (his experience of the Portuguese colonial war in Angola being a major influence); Commdr, Ordre des Arts et des Lettres 2008, Grand Cross of Order of Saint James of the Sword; Prize of Portuguese Writers' Asscn 1985, 1999, French Culture Prize 1996, 1997, Prix du Meilleur Livre Etranger, Rosália de Castro Prize 1999, European Literature Prize of Austria 2000, Latin Union Int. Prize 2003, Ovid Prize 2003, Jerusalem Prize 2005, Premio Camões 2007, Juan Rulfo Premio de Literatura en Lengua Romances 2008, Int. Nonino Prize 2014. *Publications include:* novels: Memória de Elefante 1979, Os Cus de Judas 1979, Conhecimento do Inferno 1980, Explicação dos Pássaros 1981, Fado Alexandrino 1983, Auto dos Danados 1985, As Naus 1988, Tratado das Paixões da Alma 1990, A Ordem Natural das Coisas 1992, A Morta de Carlos Gardek 1994, O Manual dos Inquisidores 1996, O Esplendor de Portugal 1997, Exortação aos Crocodilos 1999, Não Entres Tão Depressa Ness Noite Excura 2000, Que Farei Quando Tudo Arde? 2001, Boa Tarde ás Coisas Aqui em Baixo 2003, Eu Hei-de Amar Uma Pedra 2004, Ontem Não Te Vi em Babilónia 2006, O Meu Nome é Legião 2007, O Arquipélago da Insónia 2008, Que Cavalos São Aqueles Que Fazem Sombra no Mar? 2009, Sôbolos Rios Que Vão 2010, Comissão das Lágrimas 2011, Não é Meia-Noite quem quer 2012, Caminha Como Numa Casa em Chamas 2014, Da Natureza dos Deuses 2015, Para Aquela que Está Sentada no Escuro à Minha Espera 2016; collections: Livro de Crónicas 1998, Segundo Livro de Crónicas 2002, Terceiro Livro de Crónicas 2006, Quarto Livro de Crónicas 2011, Quinto Livro de Crónicas 2013; short stories: A História do Hidroavião 1994–2005 2005, The Fat Man and Infinity and Other Writings (in trans.) 2009; other: Letrinhas de Cantigas 2002, Apontar com o dedo o centro da terra 2002, D'este Viver Aqui Neste Papel Descripto 2005, Quem me assassinou para que eu seja tão doce? 2008. *Address:* c/o Publicações Dom Quixote, Rua Cidade de Códova 2, 2610-038 Alfragide, Portugal. *Website:* www.dquixote.pt.

LOBO MORENO, Ramón Augusto, MBA; Venezuelan economist and politician; *President, Banco Central de Venezuela;* b. 24 April 1967, La Azulita, Andrés Bello, Mérida State; s. of Ramón Lobo Albarrán and Silvina Moreno de Lobo; m. Carolina Marín de Lobo; two d.; ed Univ. of the Andes, Fermín Toro Univ.; fmr Asst Admin. and Budget Analyst, Faculty of Pharmacy, Univ. of the Andes; fmr Lecturer in Accounting, Econs and Financial Math., Antonio José de Sucre Univ. Inst.; Finance Coordinator, Municipality of Andrés Bello 1998–2007; Mayor of Andrés Bello 2000–08; mem. Nat. Ass. (Parl.) for Mérida State 2011–17; Vice-Pres. of Economy and Minister of Economy and Finance Jan.–Oct. 2017; Pres. Banco Central de Venezuela 2017–; mem. Partido Socialista Unido de Venezuela (PSUV). *Address:* Banco Central de Venezuela, Avda Urdaneta, esq. de Carmelitas, Caracas 1010, Venezuela (office). *Telephone:* (212) 801-5111 (office). *Fax:* (212) 861-0048 (office). *E-mail:* info@bcv.org.ve (office). *Website:* www.bcv.org.ve (office).

LOBO SOSA, Porfirio (Pepe); Honduran politician, lawyer and fmr head of state; b. 22 Dec. 1947, Trujillo; ed Univ. of Miami, USA; Deputy, Nat. Congress 1990; Head, Honduran Corpn for Forestry Devt 1990–94; presidential cand. 2005; Pres. Partido Nacional; Pres., Repub. of Honduras 2010–14. *Address:* c/o Office of the President, Palacio José Cecilio del Valle, Blvd Juan Pablo II, Tegucigalpa, Honduras (office).

LOCHHEAD, Liz; British poet, playwright, screenwriter and teacher; b. 26 Dec. 1947, Motherwell; d. of John Lochhead and Margaret Forrest; fmr art school teacher, Glasgow and Bristol; Lecturer, Univ. of Glasgow; Scots Makar (Nat. Poet of Scotland) 2011–16; Dr hc (Edinburgh) 2000; BBC Scotland Prize 1971, Scottish Arts Council Award 1972, Queen's Gold Medal for Poetry 2015. *Television includes:* Damages (BBC). *Publications include:* poetry: Memo for Spring 1972, The Grimm Sisters 1981, Dreaming of Frankenstein and Collected Poems 1984, True Confessions and True Clichés 1985, Bagpipe Muzak 1991, Cuba/Dog House (with Gina Moxley) 2000, The Colour of Black and White: Poems 1984–2003 2003, A Choosing: The Selected Poems of Liz Lochhead 2011; plays: Blood and Ice 1982, Silver Service 1984, Dracula (adaptation) 1989, Mary Queen of Scots Got Her Head Chopped Off 1989, Molière's Tartuffe (Scots trans. in rhyming couplets), Perfect Days 1998, Medea (adaptation) 2000, Misery Guts (adaptation) 2002, Thebans 2003, Good Things 2006, Five Plays 2012; screenplay: Now and Then 1972; anthology contribs: Penguin Modern Poets Vols 3 and 4, Shouting It Out 1995; other: Alasdair Gray: Now and Then (co-author) 2008. *Address:* Knight Hall Agency Ltd, Lower Ground Floor, 7 Mallow Street, London, EC1Y 8RQ, England (office). *E-mail:* office@knighthallagency.com (office). *Website:* www.knighthallagency.com/client/liz-lochhead (office).

LOCHTE, Karin, MSc, PhD (Habil.); German oceanographer, environmental scientist, academic and research institute director; *Director, Alfred Wegener Institute for Polar and Marine Research;* b. 20 Sept. 1952, Hanover; ed Tech. Univ., Hanover, Marine Science Labs, Menai Bridge, Univ. Coll. of N Wales, Bangor, UK, Univ. of Bremen; Post-doctoral researcher, Inst. of Oceanography, Kiel 1985–90; mem. Scientific Staff, Alfred Wegener Inst. for Polar and Marine Research, Bremerhaven, Germany 1990–94, Scientific Advisor 1999–2003, Dir 2007–; Head of Section, Biological Oceanography and Prof. of Biological Oceanography, Inst. for Baltic Sea Research, Univ. of Rostock 1995–2000; Prof. of Biological Oceanography, Leibniz Inst. for Marine Sciences, Christian-Albrechts Univ., Kiel 2000–07; Project Co-ordinator for ADEPD (Atlantic Data Base for Exchange Processes at the Deep Sea Floor —EU-funded marine research project) 1998–2000; Chair. Governing Bd Jacobs Univ., Bremen 2007–; mem. ECOPS Working Group 'Deep Sea Floor Instrumentation Development' 1991–92, Scientific Steering Cttee Jt Global Ocean Flux Studies 1995–2001, Bd of Trustees Terramare Research Centre, Wilhelmshaven 1996–98, Nat. Cttee for Global Change Research (Co-Chair. 2000–05), Scientific Cttee Int. Geosphere-Biosphere Programme (Vice-Chair. 2001-06), DFG Fachkollegiums 313 'Atmosphären- und Meeresforschung' 2004–05, Senate Cttee Deutsche Forschungsgemeinschaft for Oceanography 1995– (Chair. 2004–), Jury for Science Prize of WGL 'Society Needs Science' 2002–, Science Council 2004 (Chair. Scientific Comm. 2006–), Grant Cttee of Excellence Initiative 2005–, Exec. Cttee Acad. of Sciences, Hamburg 2005–; Scientific Advisor, Royal Netherlands Inst. for Sea Research (NIOZ), Texel 1998–2004, Instituts Chemie und Biologie des Meeres, Universität Oldenburg 1998–2006 (Chair. 2003–), Potsdam Instituts für Klimafolgenforschung 2002–05, Max Plank Inst. for Marine Microbiology, Bremen 2006–; Consultant, Third World Aid Programme to S America, Deutscher Akademischer Austausch Dienst 2003–; Mentor, Advancement Programme for Young Scientists, Univ. of Bremen 2005–07. *Publications:* numerous scientific papers in professional journals. *Address:* Alfred Wegener Institute, Building E-3226, Am Handelshafen 12, 27570 Bremerhaven, Germany (office). *Telephone:* (471) 4831-1101 (office). *E-mail:* karin.lochte@awi.de (office). *Website:* www.awi.de (office).

LOCHTE, Ryan Steven; American swimmer; b. 3 Aug. 1984, Rochester, New York; s. of Steven R. Lochte and Ileana M. Lochte; m. Kayla Rae Reid 2018; one s.; ed Spruce Creek High School, Port Orange, Univ. of Florida; raised in Daytona Beach, Fla where his parents were swimmers who coached him up until coll.; mem. Florida Gators swimming and diving team; NCAA Swimmer of the Year twice, seven-time NCAA champion, seven-time SEC champion, 24-time All-American; won individual titles in three individual events at NCAA Men's Swimming and Diving Championships 2006, set US Open and American records in 200-yard individual medley and 200-yard backstroke; also broke NCAA record in 400-yard individual medley; currently trains under Coach Gregg Troy at Univ. of Florida; Pan American Games, Santo Domingo 2003: gold medal, 4×200m freestyle; Olympic Games, Athens 2004: gold medal, 4×200m freestyle, silver medal, 200m medley, Beijing 2008: gold medal, 200m backstroke, 4×200m freestyle, bronze medal, 200m medley, 400m medley, London 2012: gold medal, 400m individual medley, 4×200m. freestyle relay, silver medal, 4×100m. freestyle relay, 200m individual medley, bronze medal, 200m. backstroke; World Championships (short course), Indianapolis 2004: gold medal, 4×200m freestyle, silver medal, 200m medley, bronze medal, 200m freestyle, Shanghai 2006: gold medal, 200m backstroke, 200m medley, 400m medley, silver medal, 4×100m medley, bronze medal, 4×100m freestyle, 4×200m freestyle, Manchester 2008: gold medal, 100m medley, 200m medley, 400m medley, 4×100m freestyle, silver medal, 200m backstroke, 4×100m medley, Dubai 2010: gold medal, 200m backstroke, 200m freestyle, 100m medley, 200m medley, 400m medley, 4×100m medley, silver medal, 4×200m freestyle; World Championships (long course), Montreal 2005: gold medal, 4×200m freestyle, bronze medal, 200m backstroke, 200m medley, Melbourne 2007: gold medal, 200m backstroke, 4×200m freestyle, silver medal, 100m backstroke, 200m medley, 400m medley, Rome 2009: gold medal, 200m medley, 400m medley, 4×100m freestyle, 4×200m freestyle, bronze medal, 200m backstroke, Shanghai 2011: gold medal, 200m backstroke, 200m freestyle, 200m medley, 400m medley, 4×200m freestyle, bronze medal, 4×100m freestyle, Barcelona 2013: gold medal, 200m backstroke, 200m medley, 4×200m freestyle, silver medal, 4×100m freestyle; Pan Pacific Championships, Victoria 2006: gold medal, 4×200m freestyle, silver medal, 100m backstroke, 200m medley, Irvine 2010: gold medal, 200m backstroke, 200m freestyle, 200m medley, 400m medley, 4×100m freestyle, 4×200m freestyle; holds world record in 200m individual medley (long and short course) and 400m individual medley (short course); as part of US team, holds world record in 4×200m freestyle relay (long course); swims for Daytona Beach Swimming and Univ. of Florida; suspended May 2018 for taking illegal intravenous infusion; Golden Goggles Male Swimmer of the Year 2010, Male Race of the Year for 200m individual medley at Mutual of Omaha Pan Pacific Championships 2010, Swimmer of the Year 2010–11, American Swimmer of the Year 2010–11, FINA Swimmer of the Year 2010–11. *Leisure interests:* surfing, skate boarding, drawing, volleyball, basketball, drawing. *Address:* c/o Jeff Ostrow, Proplayer Sports LLC, 1 West Las Olas Blvd, Suite 500, Fort Lauderdale, FL 33301, USA (office). *E-mail:* ostrow@proplayersports.com (office). *Website:* www.proplayersports.com (office); ryanlochte.com.

LOCK, Margaret, PhD, FRSC, OC; Canadian (b. British) anthropologist and academic; *Marjorie Bronfman Professor Emerita in Social Studies in Medicine, McGill University;* b. 26 Feb. 1936, Bromley, England; m.; one s. one d.; ed Univ. of California, Berkeley; Research Assoc., Dept of Biochemistry, Univ. of Toronto 1961–62, Univ. of California 1962–64, Dept of Psychiatry, Mount Zion Hospital, San Francisco 1975–76; Asst Prof., Dept of the History of Medicine, McGill Univ., Montréal 1977–81, Dir East Asian Studies 1981–83, Assoc. Prof., Dept of Humanities and Social Studies in Medicine and Dept of Anthropology 1981–87, Chair 1988–93, Prof. 1987–, Marjorie Bronfman Prof. in Social Studies in Medicine, affiliated with Dept of Social Studies of Medicine and Dept of Anthropology 2002–07, Prof. Emer. 2007–; Visiting Prof., Kyoto Univ., Japan, 1983–84, Univ. of Vienna 1999, Slovenian Acad. of Sciences and Arts 2005, 2009; mem. Canadian Inst. of Advanced Research, Population Programme 1993–2002, Research Program "Humans and the Microbiome" 2015–; Hon. mem. Golden Key Int. Honor Soc. 2011–; Officier, Ordre nat. du Québec 2004, L'Ordre de Montréal 2017; Canada Council Killam Fellowship 1993–95, Prix du Québec, domaine

Sciences Humaines 1997, Molson Prize, Canada Council for the Arts 2002, Robert B. Textor Prize 2003, Killam Prize, Canada Council for the Arts 2005, Trudeau Foundation Fellowship 2005, named a Grande Montréalaise, Secteur Social 2005, Career Achievement Award, Soc. of Medical Anthropology, American Anthropological Asscn 2008, McGill Univ. Medal for Exceptional Academic Achievement 2011, Queen Elizabeth II Diamond Jubilee Medal 2012. *Publications:* East Asian Medicine in Urban Japan: Varieties of Medical Experience 1980, Health and Medical Care in Japan: Cultural and Social Dimensions (co-ed.) 1987, Biomedicine Examined (co-ed.) 1988, La santé mentale et ses visages: Un Québec pluriethnique au quotidien (co-author) 1992, Knowledge, Power and Practice: The Anthropology of Medicine and Everyday Life (co-ed.) 1993, Encounters With Aging: Mythologies of Menopause in Japan and North America (six prizes, including Staley Prize, School of American Research, Canada-Japan Book Prize, Wellcome Medal, Royal Anthropological Soc. of GB 1997) 1993, Social Suffering (co-ed.) 1997, Pragmatic Women and Body Politics (co-ed.) 1998, Living and Working with the New Medical Technologies: Intersections of Inquiry (co-ed.) 2000, Remaking a World: Violence, Social Suffering, and Recovery (co-ed.) 2001, Twice Dead: Organ Transplants and the Reinvention of Death (several awards) 2002, New Horizons in Medical Anthropology: A Festschrift in Honor of Charles Leslie (co-ed.) 2002, Remaking Life and Death: Towards an Anthropology of the Biosciences (co-ed.) 2003, An Anthropology of Medicine (with Vinh-Kim Nguyen) (American Publishers Asscn PROSE Award for Archeology and Anthropology 2010) 2010, The Alzheimer Conundrum: Entanglements of Dementia and Aging 2013, Can Science Resolve the Nature/Nurture Debate? 2016 (with Gisli Palsson); numerous scholarly articles. *Address:* Department of Social Studies of Medicine, Room 103, McGill University, 3647 Peel Street, Montréal, PQ H3A 1X1, Canada (office). *Telephone:* (514) 398-6033 (office). *Fax:* (514) 398-1498 (office). *E-mail:* margaret.lock@mcgill.ca. *Website:* www.mcgill.ca/ssom (office); www.mcgill.ca/ssom/staff/lock (office).

LOCK, Thomas Graham, BSc, CEng, CBIM, FIMMM; British business executive; b. 19 Oct. 1931, Cardiff, Wales; s. of Robert H. Lock and Morfydd Lock (née Thomas); m. 1st Janice O B. Jones 1954 (divorced 1992); two d.; m. 2nd Judith Elizabeth Lucy 2004 (divorced 2010); ed Whitchurch Grammar School, Univ. Coll. of S. Wales, Monmouthshire Coll. of Advanced Tech. (Aston) and Harvard Business School, USA; Instructor Lt RN 1953–56; joined Lucas Industries Ltd 1956; Production Foreman, Lucas Electrical Ltd 1957–59, Factory Man. 1959–61; Dir Girling Bremsen GmbH 1961–66; Overseas Operations Dir Girling Ltd 1966–73; Gen. Man. and Dir Lucas Service Overseas Ltd 1973–79; Man. Dir Industrial Div. Amalgamated Metal Corpn PLC 1979–83, Chief Exec. 1983–91; Dir (non-exec.) Evode Group PLC 1985–91, Marshalls Universal PLC 1983–86; Liveryman Co. of Gold and Silver Wyre Drawers 1988–; Freeman, City of London. *Leisure interests:* sailing, music, skiing. *Address:* Parolas Villa, 4520 Pareklisia, nr Limassol, Cyprus (home). *Telephone:* (25) 634965 (home). *Fax:* (25) 634965 (home). *E-mail:* brython@cytanet.com.cy (home).

LOCKE, Gary F., BA, JD; American lawyer, diplomatist and fmr government official; b. 21 Jan. 1950; s. of James Locke and Julie Locke; m. Mona Lee 1994; one s. two d.; ed Yale Univ., Boston Univ.; Deputy Prosecuting Attorney, State of Washington, King Co.; mem. State House of Reps 1982–93; Chief Exec. King Co. 1994–97; Gov. of Washington 1996–2005; Pnr, Davis Wright Tremaine LLP (law firm), Seattle 2005–09; US Sec. of Commerce, Washington, DC 2009–11; Amb. to People's Repub. of China 2011–14; fmr mem. Bd of Dirs Digital Learning Commons, Pacific Health Summit Sr Advisory Group 2004, Fred Hutchinson Cancer Research Center, Safeco, Inc. *Address:* US Department of State, 2201 C Street NW, Washington, DC 20520, USA (office). *Telephone:* (202) 647-4000 (office). *Fax:* (202) 647-6738 (office). *Website:* www.state.gov (office).

LOCKHART, Albert; Antigua and Barbuda banking executive; currently Country Dir Antigua and Barbuda Office, Eastern Caribbean Cen. Bank. *Address:* Eastern Caribbean Central Bank-Antigua and Barbuda Office, Sagicor Financial Centre, Factory Road, POB 741, Saint John's Antigua and Barbuda (office). *Telephone:* 462-2489 (office). *Fax:* 462-2490 (office). *E-mail:* eccbanu@candw.ag (office). *Website:* www.eccb-centralbank.org (office).

LOCKHART, James, BMus, FRCM, FRCO (CHM); British conductor and music director; b. 16 Oct. 1930, Edinburgh, Scotland; s. of Archibald C. Lockhart and Mary B. Lawrence; m. Sheila Grogan 1954; two s. one d.; ed George Watson's Coll., Edin., Univ. of Edin. and Royal Coll. of Music; Asst Conductor, Yorkshire Symphony Orchestra 1954–55; Repetiteur and Asst Conductor, Städtische Bühnen Münster 1955–56, Bayerische Staatsoper, Munich 1956–57, Glyndebourne Festival Opera 1957–59; Dir Opera Workshop, Univ. of Texas 1957–59; Repetiteur and Asst Conductor, Royal Opera House, Covent Garden 1959–60, Conductor 1962–68; Asst Conductor, BBC Scottish Orchestra 1960–61; Conductor, Sadler's Wells Opera 1961–62; Prof. Royal Coll. of Music 1962–72; Musical Dir Welsh Nat. Opera 1968–73; Generalmusikdirektor, Staatstheater Kassel 1972–80, Koblenz and Theater der Stadt, Koblenz 1981–88, Rheinische Philharmonie 1981–91; Prin. Guest Conductor, BBC Concert Orchestra 1982–87; Dir of Opera, Royal Coll. of Music 1986–92, London Royal Schools' Vocal Faculty 1992–96, Opera Consultant 1996–98; Guest Prof. of Conducting, Tokyo Nat. Univ. of Fine Arts and Music (Tokyo Geidai) 1998–2001, Prof. Emer. 2001–; freelance conductor 2001–; Guest Prof. of Conducting, Sydney Conservatorium of Music 2005–; Hon. RAM 1993. *Leisure interests:* travel, swimming, hill-walking. *Address:* 5 The Coach House, Mill Street, Fontmell Magna, Shaftesbury, Dorset, SP7 0NU, England (home). *Telephone:* (1747) 811980 (home). *E-mail:* lockgrog@zen.co.uk (home).

LOCKYER, Darren; Australian rugby league player (retd); b. 24 March 1977, Brisbane, Queensland; s. of David Lockyer and Sharon Lockyer; m. Loren Pollock 2007; ed ed Wandoan State School, Roma, Queensland; fullback, five-eighth; player for Brisbane Broncos 1995–2011, Queensland Maroons 1998–11 (Capt. of Series Winning Sides 2001, 2006, 2007), Australia 1998–11 (Capt. 2003–11), NRL All Stars 2010–11; mem. Australian World Cup winning team 2000; mem. Australian Tri-Nations winning team 2004, 2006, 2009; Brisbane Broncos Rookie of the Year 1995, Clive Churchill Medal 2000, Brisbane Broncos Player of the Year 2002, 2003, Rugby League World Golden Boot Award 2003, 2006, Dally M. Medal Five-Eighth of the Year 2007, named in list of Australia's 100 Greatest Players (1908–2007) commissioned by NRL and ARL to celebrate the code's centenary year in Australia (only current player to make the list) 2008, chosen in Queensland Rugby League's Team of the Century at fullback 2008.

LOCSIN, Teodoro Lopez, Jr, LLM; Philippine politician, lawyer, diplomatist and fmr journalist; *Secretary of Foreign Affairs;* b. 15 Nov. 1948, Manila; s. of Teodoro Locsin, Sr; m. Maria Lourdes Barcelon; four c.; ed Ateneo de Manila Univ., Harvard Univ.; Editorial Writer 1967–72; Dir-Gen. Office of Media Affairs 1986–88; Legal Counsel to Pres. Corazon J. Aquino 1987–92; Speechwriter to Pres. Joseph Ejercito Estrada 1998, to Pres. Gloria Macapagal-Arroyo 2002–06; Publr The Daily Globe 1998–93; Publr and Ed.-in-Chief Today 1993–2003; mem. House of Reps 2001–10; Pres. Mga Kalalakihang Hindi Nakakaintindi sa Konsepto ng Panggagahasa Foundation 2013–15; Prof. of Law, San Beda Coll. 2014–17; Perm. Rep. to UN 2017–18; Sec. of Foreign Affairs 2018–. *Television:* Host ABS-CBN 1994–2001. *Address:* Department of Foreign Affairs, DFA Building, 2330 Roxas Blvd, Pasay City, 1330 Metro Manila, Philippines (office). *Telephone:* (2) 8344000 (office). *Fax:* (2) 8321597 (office). *E-mail:* webmaster@dfa.gov.ph (office). *Website:* www.dfa.gov.ph (office).

LODDER, Celsius Antônio, MSc; Brazilian economist and international administrator; b. 28 May 1944, Nova Lima, Minas Gerais; s. of Ary Lodder and Maria van Krimpen Lodder; m. Denise Lodder; three d.; ed Fed. Univ. of Minas Gerais, Belo Horizonte, Getúlio Vargas Foundation, Rio de Janeiro and Inst. of Social Studies, The Hague; researcher, Applied Econs Research Inst. Ministry of Econ., Finance and Planning 1970–80; subsequently held appointments with State of Minas Gerais and Fed. Govt of Brazil; Sec. for Commercial Policy, Ministry of Finance, later at Ministry of Industry, Commerce and Tourism; Supt Nat. Supply Authority, Ministry of Finance; Chief Adviser, State Bank of Minas Gerais 1983–84; Co-ordinator, Intergovernmental Relations Office, Civil Cabinet of Pres. of Brazil; Lecturer in Econs at various Brazilian univs; Exec. Dir Int. Coffee Org. 1994–2002; mem. Bd of Dirs American School of Brasília. *Publications include:* books and reports on matters related to regional planning and devt. *Leisure interests:* reading, walking.

LODGE, David John, CBE, PhD, FRSL; British writer and academic; *Professor Emeritus of English Literature, University of Birmingham;* b. 28 Jan. 1935, London; s. of William F. Lodge and Rosalie M. Lodge (née Murphy); m. Mary Frances Jacob 1959; two s. one d.; ed St Joseph's Acad., Blackheath and Univ. Coll., London; asst, British Council, London 1959–60; Asst Lecturer in English, Univ. of Birmingham 1960–62, Lecturer 1963–71, Sr Lecturer 1971–73, Reader 1973–76, Prof. of English Literature 1976–87, Hon. Prof. 1987–2000, Prof. Emer. 2001–; Chair. Booker Prize Cttee 1989; Harkness Commonwealth Fellow, 1964–65; Visiting Assoc. Prof. Univ. of Calif. at Berkeley 1969; Henfield Writing Fellow, Univ. of E Anglia 1977; Fellow, Univ. Coll. London 1982, Goldsmith's Coll. 1992; Chevalier des Arts et des Lettres 1997; Yorkshire Post Fiction Prize 1975, Hawthornden Prize 1976, RTS Award for Best Drama Serial 1990. *Plays:* The Writing Game 1991, Home Truths 1999, Secret Thoughts 2011. *Publications:* fiction: The Picturegoers 1960, Ginger, You're Barmy 1962, The British Museum is Falling Down 1965, Out of the Shelter 1970, Changing Places: A Tale of Two Campuses 1975, How Far Can You Go? (aka Souls and Bodies) (Whitbread Book of Year) 1980, Small World: An Academic Romance 1984, Nice Work (Sunday Express Book of the Year) 1988, Paradise News 1991, Therapy 1995, Home Truths (novella) 1999, Thinks… (novel) 2001, Author, Author 2004, Deaf Sentence (novel) 2008, A Man of Parts 2011; non-fiction: Language of Fiction 1966, Graham Greene 1966, The Novelist at the Crossroads and Other Essays on Fiction and Criticism 1971, Evelyn Waugh 1971, Twentieth-Century Literary Criticism: A Reader (ed.) 1972, The Modes of Modern Writing: Metaphor, Metonymy and the Typology of Modern Literature 1977, Working with Structuralism: Essays and Reviews on Nineteenth- and Twentieth Century Literature 1981, Write On: Occasional Essays 1986, Modern Criticism and Theory: A Reader (ed.) 1988, After Bakhtin: Essays on Fiction and Criticism 1990, The Art of Fiction: Illustrated from Classic and Modern Texts 1992, The Practice of Writing: Essays, Lectures, Reviews, and a Diary 1996, Consciousness and the Novel 2002, The Year of Henry James 2006, Lives in Writing: Essays 2014, Quite a Good Time to Be Born: A Memoir 1935–1975 2015. *Leisure interests:* television, cinema. *Address:* c/o Jonny Geller, Curtis Brown, Haymarket House, 28–29 Haymarket, London, SW1Y 4SP, England (office). *Telephone:* (20) 7393-4492 (office). *E-mail:* gelleroffice@curtisbrown.co.uk (office). *Website:* www.curtisbrown.co.uk (office).

LODGE, Matthew James, BA (Hons); British diplomatist; b. 3 June 1968, Crosby, Lancs.; s. of David James Lodge MBE and Helen Mary Lodge (née Hutchison); m. Alexia Lodge; two s.; ed Abingdon School, Oxon., Univ. of Birmingham; Desk Officer, Bosnia Section, FCO 1996–97, Entry Clearance Officer, Tbilisi and Yerevan Oct.–Dec. 1997, Second Sec., Embassy in Athens 1998–2000, Desk Officer, Czech Repub. and Slovakia, FCO Nov.–Dec. 2000, Second Sec., Embassy in Paris Jan.–Aug. 2001, Second Sec., Embassy in Brussels 2001–03, Head of Cyprus and Greece Section, Europe Directorate, FCO 2003–04, Pvt. Sec., Perm. UnderSec.'s Office 2004–07, Deputy Head of Mission, Embassy in Baghdad Mar.–Nov. 2007, Career Devt Attachment, UK Defence Acad., Shrivenham Jan.–April 2008, Head of Afghanistan Group, FCO 2008–10, Amb. to Finland 2010–13, to Kuwait 2014–17; Minister, British Embassy in Paris 2017–.

LODGE, Michael W., LLB, MSc; British lawyer and international organization official; *Secretary-General, International Seabed Authority;* ed Univ. of East Anglia, London School of Econs; Barrister, Gray's Inn, London 1991–95; Legal Counsel, South Pacific Forum Fisheries Agency 1991–95; Legal Counsel, Int. Seabed Authority (ISA) 1996–2003, Deputy Sec.-Gen. and Legal Counsel 2007–16, Sec.-Gen. 2016–; Consultant, MacAlister Elliott & Partners (fisheries consultancy) 1996–97; Head, Interim Secr., Western and Central Pacific Fisheries Comm. (WCPFC) 1997–2004; Counsellor, Round Table on Sustainable Devt, Org. for Econ. Cooperation and Devt (OECD) 2004–07; Ind. Adjudicator, Marine Stewardship Council 2006–16; Adviser, Pew Charitable Trust Marine Program 2008–11; mem. World Econ. Forum Global Agenda Council on Oceans 2011–16; Assoc. Fellow, Chatham House, London 2007, Visiting Fellow, Somerville Coll., Oxford 2012–13. *Publications:* more than 25 published books and articles on law of the sea, oceans policy and related issues. *Address:* International Seabed Authority, 14–20 Port Royal Street, Kingston, Jamaica (office). *Telephone:* (876) 922-9105 (office). *Fax:* (876) 922-0195 (office). *Website:* www.isa.org.jm (office).

LODHA, Rajendra Mal, BSc, LLB; Indian lawyer and judge (retd); b. 28 Sept. 1949, Jodhpur; s. of Justice S.K. Mal Lodha; ed Univ. of Jodhpur; enrolled with Bar Council of Rajasthan 1973, Central Govt Standing Counsel in charge of litigation of Union of India, Jaipur Bench 1990–92, Perm. Judge, Rajasthan High Court 1994; transferred to Bombay High Court as Judge 1994–2007, various positions include Sr Admin. Judge, Chair. Rules Cttee, E-Cttee, Monitoring Cttee; Visitor, Bd of Visitors, Judicial Officers Training Inst., Nagpur; transferred to Rajasthan High Court as Admin. Judge 2007; Chief Justice, Patna High Court 2008; Judge, Supreme Court 2008–14, Chief Justice April–Sept. 2014 (retd); fmr Chair., State Judicial Acad., Rajasthan, Nat. Legal Services Authority; Exec. Mem. Nat. Law Univ., Jodhpur.

LODHI, Maleeha, BSc, PhD; Pakistani diplomatist, journalist and academic; *Permanent Representative, United Nations;* b. Lahore; m. (divorced); one s.; ed Univ. of Oxford and London School of Econs, UK; Lecturer, Dept of Public Admin, Quaid-i-Azam Univ., Islamabad 1977–78; Lecturer in Politics and Sociology, LSE 1980–85; Assoc. Ed. The Muslim 1985–87, Ed. 1987–90; Founding Ed. The News (daily newspaper) 1990–94, Ed. 1997–99; Amb. to USA 1994–97 (with rank of Minister of State), 1999–2002, High Commr to UK 2003–08, Perm. Rep. to UN, New York 2015–; Visiting Faculty, Nat. Defence College 2002–03; Special Int. Affairs Adviser, Jang Group, Geo Television Network 2011–; mem. UN Sec.-Gen.'s Advisory Bd on Disarmament 2001–05, Global Agenda Council of World Economic Forum, Senate of Pakistan's Nat. Defence Univ.; mem. Advisory Bd Middle East Center; Fellow, Inst. of Politics, Harvard Univ.; Public Policy Scholar, Woodrow Wilson Center; Hon. Fellow, LSE 2004; Hon. DLit (London Metropolitan Univ.) 2005; award from All Pakistan Newspaper Soc. 1994, named by Time Magazine as one of 100 global pacesetters and leaders who would define the 21st century 1994, Hilal-e-Imtiaz Presidential Award for public service 2002. *Publications include:* Pakistan's Encounter with Democracy, The External Dimension (ed) 1994, Pakistan: Beyond the Crisis State 2010; numerous contribs to int. journals. *Address:* Pakistan Mission to United Nations, New York, 8 East 65th Street, New York, NY 10065, USA (office). *Telephone:* (212) 879-8600 (office). *Fax:* (212) 744-7348 (office). *E-mail:* pakistan@un.int (office). *Website:* www.pakun.org (office).

LODIN, Maj.-Gen. Per Gustaf; Swedish army officer and UN official; *Chief Military Observer and Head of Mission, United Nations Military Observer Group in India and Pakistan (UNMOGIP);* b. 18 March 1956, Stockholm; s. of Gustaf Lodin; m. Anitha Lodin 1982; one s. one d.; ed Nat. Defence Coll., Stockholm, Graduate Inst. of Int. Studies, Geneva; joined Swedish Army 1978, becoming Commdr, Norrbotten Regt 1999–2003, Deputy Chief of Staff, Swedish Armed Forces 2005–06, Head of Multinational Task Force Centre, KFOR, Kosovo 2006–07, Head of Strategies, Research and Devt and Business Devt 2007, Dir of Strategic Planning and Devt 2008, Deputy Dir of Nat. Armaments for Sweden 2012–14, Dir of Procurement and Logistics for Swedish Armed Forces 2014–16; Chief Mil. Observer and Head of Mission, UN Mil. Observer Group in India and Pakistan (UNMOGIP) 2016–; rank of Lt 1978, Capt. 1981, Maj. 1986, Col 1997, Brig.-Gen. 2003, Maj.-Gen. 2008; mem. Royal Acad. of Military Sciences 2001–; Mil. Service Medal in bronze, Armed Forces Medal for Int. Efforts in bronze, NATO Non-Article 5 Medal for Operations in the Balkans. *Leisure interests:* skiing, golf. *Website:* www.un.org/en/peacekeeping/missions/unmogip/ (office).

LOEAK, Christopher Jorebon; Marshall Islands politician and fmr head of state; b. 11 Nov. 1952, Ailinglaplap Atoll; m. Anono Lieom Loeak; three c.; ed Hawaii Pacific Coll., Gonzaga Univ. School of Law, Spokane, USA; mem. Nitijela (Parl.) for Ailinglaplap constituency 1985–; Minister of Justice 1988–92, of Social Services 1992–96, of Educ. 1996–98, for Ralik Islands 1998–99, in Assistance to Pres. 1999, 2008–11; Pres. of the Marshall Islands 2012–16. *Address:* c/o Office of the President, Government of the Republic of the Marshall Islands, PO Box 2, Majuro, MH 96960, Marshall Islands (office).

LOEHNIS, Anthony David, CMG, MA; British banker (retd); b. 12 March 1936, London; s. of Sir Clive Loehnis and Rosemary Loehnis (née Ryder); m. Jennifer Forsyth Anderson 1965; three s.; ed Eton Coll., New Coll. Oxford, Harvard School of Public Admin; in Diplomatic Service 1960–66; with J. Henry Schroder Wagg and Co. Ltd 1967–80 (seconded to Bank of England 1977–79); Assoc. Dir Bank of England 1980–81, Exec. Dir (Overseas Affairs) 1981–89; Group Exec. Dir, Vice-Chair. S. G. Warburg and Co. 1989–92; Exec. Dir UK–Japan 21st Century Group 1999–2002; Dir (non-exec.) St James's Place Capital PLC 1993–2005, Alpha Bank London Ltd 1994–2015 (Chair. 2005–15), Tokyo-Mitsubishi Int. PLC 1996–2007, AGCO Corpn (USA) 1997–2005, VTB Capital PLC 2007–13; Chair. Public Works Loan Bd 1997–2005. *Telephone:* 7595-760424 (mobile) (home). *E-mail:* antloehnis@gmail.com (home).

LÖSCHER, Peter, MA, MBA; Austrian business executive; *Chairman, Sulzer Limited;* b. 17 Sept. 1957, Villach; m.; four c.; ed Vienna Univ., Chinese Univ. of Hong Kong and Harvard Business School, USA; began career at Kienbaum and Partner (man. consultants), Germany 1985; mem. Strategic Planning Man. Team, Hoechst AG 1988–89, Dir Business Devt 1989–91, Man. Dir Hoechst Roussel Veterinaria AIE, Spain 1991–94, Vice-Pres. 1994–95, Project Leader 1996–97, Pres. and CEO Hoechst Marion Roussel Ltd, UK 1999; Chair., Pres. and CEO Aventis Pharma Ltd, Japan 2000–02; Pres. Amersham Health (life sciences co.), UK 2002–04, COO 2004; Pres. and CEO General Electric Healthcare Bio-Sciences and mem. Corp. Exec. Council 2004–05; Pres. Global Human Health Div. and mem. Exec. Cttee, Merck and Co. Inc. 2006–07; Pres. and CEO Siemens AG 2007–13, Chair. Bd of Trustees Siemens Stiftung Germany 2008–14, also Head of Corp. Devt; CEO and Del. of Bd of Dirs, Renova Management AG 2014–16; Chair. Sulzer Ltd 2014–, also mem. Bd of Dirs; Chair. Supervisory Bd OMV Group 2016–19; Founding Partner Medical Tech. Venture Partners; Chair. Asia-Pacific Cttee of German Business; Vice-Chair. European Round Table of Industrialists; Co-Chair. EU-Russia Industrialists' Round Table; mem. Bd of Dirs Telefónica 2016–; mem. Supervisory Bd Münchener Rückversicherungs-Gesellschaft AG; Hon. Prof., Tongji Univ. 2011; Grand Decoration of Honour in Gold for Services to the Repub. of Austria 2010, Order of Friendship of Russian Federation 2012; Hon. DEng (Michigan State Univ.) 2008, Dr hc (Slovak Univ. of Engineering). *Address:* Sulzer Limited, Neuwiesenstrasse 15, 8401 Winterthur, Switzerland (office). *Telephone:* 522623000 (office). *Website:* www.sulzer.com (office).

LÖWE, Jan, FRS, BSc, PhD; German biochemist; *Director, MRC Laboratory of Molecular Biology;* b. 14 July 1967; ed Univ. of Hamburg, Max-Planck Inst., Martinsried; joined MRC Lab. of Molecular Biology (LMB), Cambridge 1996, becoming Group Leader 1998, European Molecular Biology Org. (EMBO) Young Investigator 2001, Jt Head, Structural Studies Div. 2010–, Deputy Dir LMB 2016–18, Dir 2018–; mem. EMBO 2004; Fellow, Darwin Coll., Cambridge 2012, Nat. Akademie der Wissenschaften Leopoldina 2013; Leverhulme Prize for Biochemistry 2002, EMBO Gold Medal 2007, Wellcome Trust Sr Investigator Award 2011. *Address:* MRC Laboratory of Molecular Biology, Francis Crick Avenue, Cambridge Biomedical Campus, Cambridge CB2 0QH, England (office). *Telephone:* (1223) 267000 (office). *Fax:* (1223) 268300 (office). *E-mail:* jyl@mrc-lmb.cam.ac.uk (office). *Website:* www2.mrc-lmb.cam.ac.uk/ (office).

LÖFGREN, Lars, PhD; Swedish theatre, film and television director, playwright, poet and court official; b. 6 Sept. 1935, The Arctic Circle; m. Anna-Karin Gillberg 1963; one s. two d.; ed Gustavus Adolphus Coll., USA, Stanford Univ., USA, Univ. of Paris (Sorbonne), France, Uppsala Univ.; Dir Royal Dramatic Theatre of Sweden 1985–97, Nordic Museum 1997–2001; Lord Chamberlain to HM King Carl XVI Gustaf 1999; Lord-in-Waiting to His Majesty the King; Commdr, Légion d'honneur 2001; Royal Prize of Swedish Acad. 1996, Prix Italia 1997. *Publications include:* various plays, filmscripts, TV scripts, poetry, novels, including Svensk Teater 2003, Himlens Fäste 2011. *Telephone:* (8) 855822 (home). *E-mail:* lars.lofgren@pof.se (home).

LÖFVEN, (Kjell) Stefan; Swedish trade union official and politician; *Prime Minister;* b. 21 July 1957, Stockholm; foster parents Ture Melander (deceased) and Iris Melander; m. Ulla Löfvén 2003; ed Sollefteå High School, AMU, Kramfors, Umeå Univ.; began career as a welder at Hägglunds, Örnsköldsvik 1979, chosen as group's union rep. 1981, went on to hold a succession of union posts; ombudsman in Swedish Metalworkers' Union, working on contract negotiations 1995–98, Int. Sec., Int. Affairs 1998–99, Head of Unit 1999–2002, Deputy Fed. Chair. 2002–05; Chair. IF Metall 2006–12; Leader Social Democratic Party 2012–; Prime Minister of Sweden 2014–18, 2019–, Caretaker Prime Minister 25 Sept. 2018–16 Jan. 2019; mem. Bd Olof Palme Int. Centre 2002–06; Vice-Pres. Trade Council 2004–12; Deputy Dir and mem. Exec. Cttee Social Democrats 2005–12; Chair. and Group Counsel, Welfare 2007–09; mem. Bd Royal Inst. of Tech. 2010–12. *Address:* Prime Minister's Office, Rosenbad 4, 103 33 Stockholm, Sweden (office). *Telephone:* (8) 405-10-00 (office). *Fax:* (8) 723-11-71 (office). *E-mail:* sb.registrator@regeringskansliet.se (office). *Website:* www.government.se (office); www.socialdemokraterna.se/Stefan-Lofven.

LOGAN, Lara, BCom; South African journalist and broadcaster; *Chief Foreign Affairs Correspondent, CBS News;* b. 1971, Durban; m. 1st Jason Siemon (divorced); m. 2nd Joseph Burckett 2008; one s.; ed Univ. of Natal, Univ. de l'Alliance Française, Paris, France; news reporter, Sunday Tribune, Durban 1988–89, then with Daily News, Durban 1990–92; Sr Producer, Reuters TV Africa 1992–96; freelance journalist 1996–2000, worked as reporter and ed./producer with ITN and Fox/SKY, CBS News, ABC News (London), NBC, European Broadcast Union; corresp., GMTV (breakfast show), London 2000–02; joined CBS News 2002, corresp. and contrib. to 60 Minutes II 2002–04, corresp. for 60 Minutes 2006–, Chief Foreign Affairs Corresp., CBS News 2006–; Emmy Award, Overseas Press Club Award and Murrow Award (for Ramadi: On the Front Line) 2006, five American Women in Radio and Television Gracie Awards, Asscn of International Broadcasters' Best International News Story Award (for report on the Taliban) 2007, David Bloom Award, Radio and Television Correspondents Asscn 2008. *Address:* CBS News, 2020 M Street, NW, Washington, DC 20036, USA (office). *Website:* www.cbsnews.com/team/lara-logan (office).

LOGAN, Malcolm (Mal) Ian, AC, DipEd, PhD, MBA; Australian geographer, academic and fmr university administrator; b. 3 June 1931, Inverell, NSW; s. of A. J. Logan; m. Antoinette Lalich 1954; one d.; ed Tamworth High School, New England Univ. Coll., Sydney Teachers' Coll., Univ. of Sydney; Lecturer in Geography, Sydney Teachers' Coll. 1956–58; Lecturer in Geography, Univ. of Sydney 1959–64, Sr Lecturer 1965–67; Prof. of Geography and Urban and Regional Planning, Univ. of Wisconsin, Madison, USA 1967–71; Prof. of Geography, Monash Univ. 1971–86, Pro-Vice-Chancellor 1982–85, Deputy Vice-Chancellor 1986, Vice-Chancellor 1987–96, also fmr Pres.; Deputy Chair. Int. Devt Program of Australian Univs 1991–93; Chair. Australian Centre for Contemporary Art 1990, Open Learning Agency of Australia 1993–96, Monash International Pty Ltd 1994–96, TENTAS Pty Ltd 1998–, Australia Educ. Gateway Pty Ltd 1998–; Dir Australia Communications Computing Inst. 1998–, Job Scene Pty Ltd 2000–; Chair. and Dir Pinnacle Pty Ltd 2000–; mem. Comm. for the Future 1995–; Visiting Prof., Univ. of Ibadan, Nigeria 1970–71, LSE, UK 1973, Nanyang Univ., Singapore 1979; Hon. DLitt (Monash) 1997. *Publications:* co-author: Studies in Australian Geography 1968, New Viewpoints in Urban and Industrial Geography 1971, Urban and Regional Australia 1975, Urbanisation, The Australian Experience 1980, The Brittle Rim 1989, Reconstructing Asia: The Economic Miracle That Never Was, The Future That Is 1998. *Leisure interests:* golf, reading. *Address:* 1/50 Bourke Street, Melbourne, Vic. 3000; c/o Monash University, Wellington Road, Clayton, Vic. 3168, Australia.

LOGAN, William, BA, MFA; American poet and critic; *Professor of Creative Writing, University of Florida;* b. 1950, Boston, Mass; s. of W. Donald Logan, Jr. and Nancy Damon Logan; m. Debora Greger; ed Yale Univ., Univ. of Iowa; Dir of Creative Writing, English Dept, Univ. of Florida 1983–2000, Prof. of Creative Writing 2000–; Amy Lowell Poetry Travelling Scholarship 1980, Peter I. B. Lavan Award, Acad. of American Poets 1989, J. Howard and Barbara M.J. Wood Prize 2003, Corrington Award for Literary Excellence 2004, Aiken Taylor Award in Modern American Poetry 2012. *Publications include:* poetry: Sad-faced Men 1982, Difficulty 1985, Sullen Weedy Lakes 1988, Vain Empires 1998, Night Battle 1999, Macbeth in Venice 2003, The Whispering Gallery 2005, Strange Flesh 2008, Madame X 2012; criticism: All the Rage 1998, Reputations of the Tongue 1999, Desperate Measures 2002, The Undiscovered Country (Nat. Book Critics Circle Award for Criticism 2005, Randall Jarrell Award in Criticism 2005) 2005, Our Savage Art 2009, Guilty Knowledge, Guilty Pleasure: The Dirty Art of Poetry 2014; as co-ed.: Certain Solitudes 1997. *Address:* Department of English, Turlington Hall 4211H, PO Box 117310, Gainesville, FL 32611-7310, USA (office). *Telephone:* (352) 294-2883 (office). *Fax:* (352) 392-0860 (office). *E-mail:* wlogan@ufl.edu (office). *Website:* www.english.ufl.edu/faculty/wlogan (office).

LÖGER, Hartwig; Austrian politician and fmr insurance executive; *Federal Minister for Finance;* b. 15 July 1965, Selzthal, Styria; m.; one s. one d.; ed Vienna

Univ. of Econs, Univ. of St Gallen; Client Relationship Man., AON Jauch & Hübener Versicherungsmakler GmbH, Graz 1985–86; Sales Man., Allianz Versicherung AG, Graz 1989–96; Asst to the Bd, Grazer Wechselseitige Versicherung AG 1996–97, Head of Sales, Donau Versicherung AG (parent co.), Vienna 1997–2002; Man. Dir UNIQA International Versicherungs-Holding GmbH, Vienna 2002–05, Head of Exclusive Sales Group, UNIQA Versicherungen AG 2005–11, Chair. Man. Bd UNIQA Österreich Versicherungen AG 2013–17; Fed. Minister for Finance 2017–; fmr Vice-Pres. Insurance Asscn Austria; mem. Österreichische Volkspartei (ÖVP—Austrian People's Party); mem. (ex-officio) Bd of Govs. EIB 2018–, European Stability Mechanism 2018–, EBRD 2018–, Asian Devt Bank 2018–, Asian Infrastructure Investment Bank 2018–, Multilateral Investment Guarantee Agency 2018–, World Bank 2018–, Inter-American Investment Corpn 2018–. *Address:* Federal Ministry of Finance, Johannesgasse 5, 1010 Vienna, Austria (office). *Telephone:* (1) 514-33 (office). *E-mail:* hartwig.loeger@bmf.gv.at (office). *Website:* www.bmf.gv.at (office).

LOGSDAIL, (Christopher) Nicholas Roald, OBE; British gallery owner; *Founder, Lisson Gallery;* ed Slade School of Art; co-f., with Fiona Hildyard, the Lisson Gallery 1967, represents artists including Marina Abramović, Ai Weiwei, Allora and Calzadilla, Art & Language, Cory Arcangel, Carl Andre, Daniel Buren, Gerard Byrne, James Casebere, Angela de la Cruz, Nathalie Djurberg & Hans Berg Spencer Finch, Ceal Floyer, Ryan Gander, Rodney Graham, Dan Graham, Carmen Herrera, Christian Jankowski, Peter Joseph, John Latham, Tim Lee, Lee Ufan, Sol LeWitt, Liu Xiaodong, Richard Long, Robert Mangold, Jason Martin, Haroon Mirza, Tatsuo Miyajima, Jonathan Monk, Tony Oursler, Giulio Paolini, Florian Pumhösl, Rashid Rana, Pedro Reyes, Fred Sandback, Santiago Sierra, Sean Snyder, Donald Judd, Robert Ryman and Lawrence Weiner, exhibited many of the artists who came to be known under the term New British Sculptors, including Tony Cragg, Richard Deacon, Shirazeh Houshiary, Anish Kapoor, Shirazeh Houshiary, Julian Opie, Richard Wentworth and Bill Woodrow; opened gallery in Milan 2010, office in New York 2011, also galleries in New York and Singapore. *Address:* Lisson Gallery, 27 Bell Street, Lisson Grove, London, NW1 5BY (office); Lisson Gallery, 67 Lisson Street, London, NW1 5DA, England (office). *Telephone:* (20) 7724-2739 (office). *Fax:* (20) 7724-7124 (office). *E-mail:* contact@lissongallery.com (office). *Website:* www.lissongallery.com (office).

LOHANI, Prakash Chandra, MBA, PhD; Nepalese economist, politician and academic; b. 21 April 1944; ed Indiana Univ., Univ. of California, Los Angeles, USA; fmr Lecturer, Univ. of Calif.; fmr Minister of Foreign Affairs and of Finance; Minister of Finance, Interim Govt 2003–04; fmr Jt Gen. Sec. Rashtriya Jana Shakti Party (National People's Power Party); Adjunct Faculty and Chair. Bd of Regents, South Asian Inst. of Man. *Address:* South Asian Institute of Management, Lagankhel, Lalitpur, PO Box 23955, Kathmandu; Rashtriya Jana Shakti Party (National People's Power Party), Ramalphokhari, Kathmandu, Nepal (office). *Telephone:* (1) 4437063 (office). *Fax:* (1) 4437064 (office). *E-mail:* pclohani@saim.edu.np; rjpnepal@info.com.np (office). *Website:* www.rjpnepal.org (office); www.saim.edu.np.

LOHELA, Maria, BA; Finnish politician; b. 11 June 1978; m. Samppa Mattila 2015; ed Univ. of Turku; mem. City Council, Turku 2009–12; mem. The Finns Party Parliamentary Group 2011–17, 1st Vice-Chair. 2014–15; MP 2011–, Speaker Parl. 2015–18, mem. Audit Cttee 2018–; mem. Int. Affairs Forum 2011–; Finnfund's Supervisory Bd 2013–; mem. Finns Party –2017, Blue Reform 2017–19, Liike Nytt-Movement 2019–. *Leisure interests:* gym, walking, floorball, badminton, horse riding, reading novels, movies, theatre, console games. *Address:* Eduskunta (Parliament of Finland), 00102, Helsinki, Finland (office). *Telephone:* (9) 4323092 (office). *E-mail:* maria.lohela@eduskunta.fi (office); maria@marialohela.fi. *Website:* www.eduskunta.fi (office); www.marialohela.fi.

LOHIA, Aloke, BCom; Indian business executive; *Vice-Chairman and Group CEO, Indorama Ventures PCL;* b. 1958; m. Suchitra Lohia; three c.; ed Univ. of Delhi; Finance Dir PT Indo Rama Synthetics, Indonesia 1979–87; f. Indorama Ventures PCL, Thailand 1988, currently Vice-Chair. and Group CEO; Dr hc (Rajamangala Univ. of Technology Thanyaburi). *Address:* Indorama Ventures PCL, 75/102 Ocean Tower 2, 37th Floor, Soi Sukhumvit 19 (Wattana), Bangkok 10110, Thailand (office). *Telephone:* (2) 661-6661 (office). *Fax:* (2) 661-6664 (office). *Website:* www.indorama.net (office).

LOHSE, Martin J., DrMed; German pharmacologist and academic; *Professor and Chair, Institute for Pharmacology and Toxicology, Julius Maximilians University of Würzburg;* b. 26 Aug. 1956, Mainz; s. of Prof. Eduard Lohse and Roswitha Lohse; m. Friederike Lohse; three s.; ed Univ. of Göttingen, Univ. of London, UK and Univ. of Paris, France; worked at Pharmacological Insts in Bonn and Heidelberg; Asst Prof., Duke Univ., USA 1988–90; Group Leader, Gene Center, Univ. of Munich/Max-Planck Inst. for Biochemistry, Martinsried 1990–93; Prof. and Chair, Inst. for Pharmacology and Toxicology, Julius Maximilians Univ. of Würzburg 1993–, Chair. Graduate School 2003–, Vice-Pres. for Research 2009–; Chair. Rudolf-Virchow-DFG Research Center for Experimental Biomedicine 2001–; project man. several European research programmes; mem. Bavarian Acad. of Science 1998, Leopoldina German Acad. of Science 2000– (Vice-Pres. 2009), Northrhine-Westfalia Acad. of Science 2004, Nat. Ethics Council 2001–08, Senate and Excellence Comm., German Research Foundation 2001–10; mem. Editorial Bd Nature, Science, The EMBO Journal; mem. Advisory Bd numerous scientific foundations; Fed. Order of Merit (1st class) 2002, Bavarian Order of Merit 2006; Gerhard Hess Prize, FRG 1990, Research Prize, Fed. Dept of Health 1991, William Vaillant Prize 1996, Gottfried Wilhelm Leibniz Prize, Deutschen Forschungsgemeinschaft 1999, Ernst Jung Prize in Medicine 2000, Research Achievement Award, Int. Soc. of Heart Research 2007, Jakob Henle Medal 2010, Svedberg Lecturer, Univ. of Uppsala 2012, Visiting Professorship, Vallee Foundation, Harvard Medical School 2012. *Publications:* numerous articles in scientific journals. *Address:* Julius-Maximilians-Universität Würzburg, Institut für Pharmakologie und Toxikologie, Versbacher Straße 9, 97078 Würzburg, Germany (office). *Telephone:* (931) 201-48400 (office). *Fax:* (931) 201-48411 (office). *E-mail:* lohse@toxi.uni-wuerzburg.de (office). *Website:* www.pharmakologie.uni-wuerzburg.de (office).

LOIZAGA, Eladio, LLB; Paraguayan diplomatist, civil servant and politician; b. 17 March 1949, Asunción; m.; two c.; ed Catholic Univ. and Nat. Univ., Asunción; joined Ministry of Foreign Affairs 1967, various posts with Dept of Int. Orgs Treaties and Instruments 1981, Dir of Dept 1983–88, Rep. to Yacyretá Binational Agency 1989–92, Adviser to Minister; elected to Nat. Chamber of Deputies 1989, mem. cttees concerning constitutional and legis. issues; Pvt. Sec. to Pres. of Paraguay and Minister Exec. Br. 1989–92; mem. Perm. Cttee of Congress 1992–93; Amb. and Perm. Rep. to UN, WTO and other specialized agencies, Geneva 1995–98; served with Embassy in Washington, DC and Alt. Rep. to OAS; Amb. and Perm. Rep. to UN, New York 2001–09, Pres. High-level Cttee of South–South Co-operation of UN Gen. Ass. 2005–07; Advisor, Ministry of Foreign Affairs 2009–10, Minister of Foreign Affairs 2013–18. *Address:* c/o Ministry of Foreign Affairs, Edif. Benigno López, Palma, esq. 14 de Mayo, Asunción, Paraguay (office).

LØJ, Ellen Margrethe, MPolSci; Danish diplomatist and UN official; b. 17 Oct. 1948, Gedesby; ed Univ. of Copenhagen; joined staff of Ministry of Foreign Affairs 1973, Sec., Perm. Mission to UN, New York 1977–80, Counsellor, Perm. Representation of Denmark to EC, Brussels 1982–85, Head of Dept, Ministry of Foreign Affairs 1986–89, Amb. to Israel 1989–92, Under-Sec., South Group (Multilateral, later Bilateral Affairs), Ministry of Foreign Affairs, State Sec. 1996–2001, Perm. Rep. to UN, New York 2001–06, Co-Chair. Gen. Ass. Working Cttee on the Peace-building Comm., Amb. to Czech Repub. –2007; UN Sec.-Gen.'s Special Rep. for Liberia 2007–12, Special Rep. of the UN Sec.-Gen. and Head of UN Mission in Repub. of South Sudan (UNMISS) 2014–16 (retd); Chair. Plan International (charity) 2012; mem. Advisory Bd Industrialization Fund for Developing Countries 1994–96, Investment Fund for Cen. and Eastern Europe 1994–96; mem. Supervisory Bd Scandlines AG and Scandlines A/S 1998–2001; mem. Bd of Dirs Centre for Humanitarian Dialogue 2012–14; Dame Grand Commdr, Humane Order of African Redemption (Liberia) 2012.

LOKHORST, Wim; Dutch business executive; m.; three c.; ed Technische Universiteit Delft; worked for more than 20 years at Royal Dutch Shell; Man. Dir Oiltanking GmbH –2003, mem. Bd of Dirs Marquard & Bahls AG (parent co.) 1996–, CEO 2003–10, mem. Supervisory Bd 2010–; mem. Asia Cttee, Hamburg Chamber of Commerce. *Address:* Marquard & Bahls AG, Koreastraße 7, 20457 Hamburg, Germany (office). *Telephone:* (40) 37004-0 (office). *Fax:* (40) 37004-141 (office). *E-mail:* office@marquard-bahls.com (office). *Website:* www.marquard-bahls.com (office).

LOKUBANDARA, W(ijesinghe) J(ayaweera) M(udiyanselage), BA; Sri Lankan attorney, politician, poet and songwriter; *Governor of Sabaragamuwa Province;* b. 5 Aug. 1941, Haputale; s. of W. J. M. Gunesekara Bandara and R. M. Loku Manike; m. Malathi Lokubandara; three s.; ed Yahala-Bedda School, Bandarawela Cen. Coll., Univ. of Peradeniya, Univ. of London, UK (external degree); worked as an assistant legal draftsman; mem. Parl. (United Nat. Party) for Badulla 1977–, Chief Opposition Whip 1994–2001, Speaker of the Parl. 2004–10, mem. Cttee of Selection, House Cttee, Cttee on Standing Orders, Cttee on Parl. Business; fmr non-cabinet Minister of Indigenous Medicine; Minister of Cultural Affairs, Educ. and Media 1989–94; Minister for Justice, Law Reform and Nat. Integration and Minister for Buddha Sasana 2001–04; Gov. of Sabaragamuwa Prov. 2010–. *Publications include:* The Mystique of Sigiriya, Sigiri Gee Siri, Rasadipani, Sastriya Vadalipi, Garu Kathanayakanumani: Mati Sabaye Kala Kata. *Address:* Office of the Governor, Ratnapura, Sabaragamuwa Province (office); 14 Samagi Mawatha, Gangodawila, Nugegoda, Colombo, Sri Lanka (home). *Website:* www.sabaragamuwapc.com (office).

LOLLOBRIGIDA, Gina; Italian actress, photographer and sculptor; b. 4 July 1927, Sibiaco; d. of Giovanni Mercuri and Giuseppina Mercuri; m. 1st Milko Skofic 1949; one s.; ed Liceo Artistico, Rome; fmr model; first screen role in Pagliacci 1947; currently photographer and sculptor. *Films include:* Campane a Martello 1948, Cuori senza Frontiere 1949, Achtung, Banditi! 1951, Enrico Caruso 1951, Fanfan la Tulipe 1951, Altri Tempi 1952, The Wayward Wife 1952, Les belles de la nuit 1952, Pane, amore e fantasia 1953, La Provinciale 1953, Pane, amore e gelosia, La Romana 1954, Il Grande Gioco 1954, La Donna più bella del Mondo 1955, Trapeze 1956, Notre Dame de Paris 1956, Solomon and Sheba 1959, Never So Few 1960, Go Naked in the World 1961, She Got What She Asked For 1963, Woman of Straw 1964, Le Bambole 1965, Hotel Paradiso 1966, Les Sultans 1966, Le Piacevoli Notti 1966, Cervantes 1966, La Morte Fatto L'uovo (A Curious Way to Love) and (Death Laid an Egg) 1967, Stuntman 1968, Buona Sera Mrs Campbell 1968, Un Bellissimo Novembre (That Splendid November) 1968, The Private Navy of Sgt O'Farrell 1968, Peccato Mortale (Mortal Sin also known as The Lonely Woman also known as Roses and Green Peppers) 1972, King, Queen, Knave 1972, Le Avventure Di Pinocchio 1972, Bad Man's River 1972, The Bocce Showdown 1990, Les Cent et Une Nuits (A Hundred and One Nights) 1995, Plucked, XXL 1997. *Television:* Falcon Crest (series) 1984, Deceptions (TV film) 1985. *Publications:* Italia Mia (photography) 1974, The Philippines. *Leisure interest:* photography. *Address:* Via Appia Antica 223, 00178 Rome, Italy.

LOMAIA, Alexander, PhD; Georgian engineer, government official and diplomatist; b. 1963, Tbilisi; m.; two s.; ed Georgian Tech. Univ., Moscow Construction Eng Inst.; engineer, Tbilhihroproekti Inst. 1985–87; fmr Ed., Argumenti Newspaper; mem., Georgian Community Hall, Moscow 1989–92; apptd Deputy Rep. of Govt to Moscow 1991, later Acting Rep.; Co-ordinator, Eurasia Fund Civil Public and Media Program 1995–2000; Dir, Georgia Representation to Eurasia Fund 2000–02; Regional Dir Democracy Coalition in post-Soviet states 2002–03; Exec. Dir Open Soc. Georgia 2003–; active in 'rose revolution' of 2003; Minister of Educ. and Sciences 2004–07; Nat. Security Adviser to Pres. 2007–09; Amb. and Perm. Rep. to UN, New York 2009–13. *Address:* Ministry of Foreign Affairs, 0108 Tbilisi, Sh. Chitadze str. 4, Georgia (office). *Telephone:* (32) 294-50-50 (office). *Fax:* (32) 294-50-01 (office). *E-mail:* inform@mfa.gov.ge (office). *Website:* www.mfa.gov.ge (office).

LOMAX, (Janis) Rachel, MA, MSc; British economist and civil servant; b. 15 July 1945; d. of William Salmon and Dilys Salmon; m. Michael Acworth Lomax 1967 (divorced 1990); two s.; ed Cheltenham Lady's Coll., Girton Coll., Cambridge, London School of Econs; Econ. Asst, HM Treasury 1968, Econ. Adviser 1972, Sr Econ. Adviser 1978, Prin. Pvt. Sec. to Chancellor of the Exchequer 1985–86, Under-Sec. 1986–90, Deputy Chief Econ. Adviser 1990–92, Deputy Sec. Financial Insts and Markets 1992–94, Deputy Sec. Cabinet Office 1994–95; Vice-Pres. and Chief of Staff, IBRD 1995–96; Perm. Sec. Welsh Office 1996–99, Dept of Social

Security, then Dept for Work and Pensions 1999–2002; Perm. Sec. Dept for Transport 2002–; Deputy Gov. (responsible for monetary policy) Bank of England July 2003–08; Chair. UK Selection Cttee, Harkness Fellowships 1995–97; mem. Council Royal Econ. Soc. 1989–94; Gov. De Montfort Univ. 1997–2007, Henley Coll. of Man. 2000–03, LSE 2003–; Pres. Council, Inst. of Fiscal Studies 2007–; mem. Bd of Dirs Royal Nat. Theatre 2002–, HSBC Holdings PLC 2008–, BAA Ltd 2010–, Arcus European Infrastructure Fund GP LLP, Scottish American Investment Co. PLC, Reinsurance Group of America Inc., Serco Group plc; Trustee, Centre for Economic Policy Research, Ditchley Foundation; Dr hc (Univ. of Glasgow, City Univ., Univ. of Glamorgan). *Address:* The Institute for Fiscal Studies, 7 Ridgmount Street, London, WC1E 7AE, England.

LOMBARD, Didier; French business executive; *Chairman, Technicolor SA;* b. 27 Feb. 1942; m.; three s.; ed École Polytechnique, École Nationale Supérieure des Télécommunications; with CNET (now Research and Devt Div., France Telecom) 1967; Scientific and Tech. Dir, Ministry of Research and Tech. 1988–90; Gen. Man. of Industrial Strategy, Ministry of Economy 1991–98, Chair. Agence Française for International Investment 1991–98; Founder, Chair. and Deputy Amb. for Int. Investment, Agency for Int. Investment 1999–2003; apptd Exec. Vice-Pres., in charge of Technologies, Strategic Partnerships and New Usages, France Telecom SA (now Orange SA) 2003, Chair. and CEO 2005–10, Chair. (non-exec.) 2010–11; mem. Bd of Dirs Technicolor SA 2010–, Chair. 2014–; Chair. Supervisory Bd STMicroelectronics NV 2011–14, Vice-Chair. 2014–. *Address:* Technicolor SA, 1, Rue Jeanne d'Arc, Issy Les Moulineaux 92443, France (office). *Telephone:* 1-41-86-50-00 (office). *Fax:* 1-41-86-58-59 (office). *Website:* www.technicolor.com (office).

LOMBARD, Marie-Christine, MBA; French business executive; *CEO, Geodis;* b. 1958, Paris; m.; two c.; ed ESSEC Business School, Paris; began career at Lord & Taylor, New York, USA; fmr banking exec. with Chemical Bank, Paris, Paribas Bank, Lyon; Chief Financial Officer, Jet Services, France 1993–97, Man. Dir 1997–99, co. acquired by TNT Express (Dutch postal and logistics group) in 1999, Chair. and Man. Dir TNT Express France 1999–2004, Group Man. Dir TNT Express and mem. Bd of Man. 2004–12, Chair. and CEO TNT Express NV 2011–12 (resgnd); CEO Geodis 2012–; mem. Supervisory Bd Groupe Banques Populaire 2010–, Royal Wessanen NV 2006–09, Metro Group 2008–11; mem. Bd of Dirs Postnl NV; Chair. Lyon Ville de l'Entrepreneuriat; Chevalier, Légion d'honneur 2005. *Address:* SNCF Geodis, Cap West, 7/9 allées de l'Europe, Clichy 92110, France (office). *Telephone:* 1-56-76-26-00 (office). *Website:* www.geodis.com (office).

LONDOÑO PAREDES, Julio; Colombian politician and diplomatist; *Professor and Director, Centro de Estudios Políticos e Internacionales (CEPI), Universidad de Rosario;* b. 10 June 1938, Bogotá; m.; ed San Isidro Hermanos Maristas School, El Carmen Inst. and Mil. Cadet School, Bogotá; Prof. of Int. Politics, Univ. of Jorge Tadeo Lozano, Bogotá; Prof. of Int. Public Law, Univ. of El Rosario, Bogotá, currently Prof., Dept of Political Science, also Dir Centro de Estudios Políticos e Internacionales; served in army, retd 1981 with rank of Lt-Col; Head of Frontier Div., Ministry of Foreign Affairs 1969–79, Sec.-Gen. 1979–82, Vice-Minister 1982–83, Amb. to Panama 1983–86, Amb. to OAS, Washington, DC 1990–94, Amb. and Perm. Rep. to UN, New York 1994–99, Amb. to Cuba 1998–2010; Dr hc (Universidad Nueva Granada). *Publications:* History of the Colombo-Peruvian Conflict of 1932, Colombian Territorial Law, Colombian Border Issues. *Address:* Centro de Estudios Políticos e Internacionales (CEPI), Facultades de Ciencia Política y Gobierno y de Relaciones Internacionales, Universidad de Rosario, Carrera 6ª No. 14–13, Of. 206, Bogotá, Colombia (office). *E-mail:* julio.londono@urosario.edu.co (office). *Website:* www.urosario.edu.co/cpg-ri/Investigacion-CEPI (office).

LONERGAN, Kenneth; American film director, playwright and screenwriter; b. 16 Oct. 1962, Bronx, New York; m. J. Smith-Cameron 2000; one d.; ed Walden School, New York, New York Univ., Wesleyan Univ.; fmr speechwriter, New York office of US Environmental Protection Agency; wrote industrial shows for corp. clients; worked with Off-Broadway co. Naked Angels; PEN/Mike Nichols Award for Performance Writing 2019. *Plays include:* The Rennings Children 1982 (selected for Young Playwright's Festival 1982), This is Our Youth 1996, Waverly Gallery 1999, Lobby Hero 2002, The Starry Messenger 2009, Medieval Play 2012, Hold On to Me Darling 2016. *Films include:* as screenwriter: Analyze This 1999, The Adventures of Rocky and Bullwinkle 2000; as screenwriter and dir: You Can Count On Me 2000 (Writers Guild of America Award for Best Original Screenplay 2000, Nat. Soc. of Film Critics Award for Best Screenplay 2000, New York Film Critics Circle Award for Best Screenplay 2000, Grand Jury Prize, Sundance Film Festival), Margaret 2011, Manchester by the Sea (Acad. Award for Best Original Screenplay 2017, BAFTA for Original Screenplay 2017) 2016. *Television:* Howards End (series) 2017. *Address:* c/o WME Speakers (office). *Telephone:* (212) 903-1400 (office). *E-mail:* info@wmespeakers.com (office). *Website:* www.wmespeakers.com (office).

LONFERNINI, Giovanni; San Marino lawyer and politician; b. 12 May 1976; Co-Capt.-Regent (Jt Head of State and Govt) of San Marino 2003–04, 2012–13; Sec. of State for Culture 2005–06, for Tourism and Relations with the Azienda Autonoma di Stato per i Servizi Pubblici 2013; fmr Sec.-Gen. San Marino Christian Democrat Party (Partito Democratico Cristiano Sammarinese); f. Gruppo dei Democratici di Centro 2007.

LONG, David H.; American business executive; *Chairman, President and CEO, Liberty Mutual Holding Company Inc.;* joined Liberty Mutual 1985, held various positions of increasing responsibility and authority principally in the Commercial Markets and Agency Markets business units –2005, Exec. Vice-Pres. and Man. Dir Commercial business unit 2005–06, Exec. Vice-Pres. Liberty Mutual Group Commercial Markets business unit 2006–09, Pres. Liberty International 2009–, Pres. Liberty Mutual Holding Co. Inc. 2010–, CEO 2011–, Chair. 2013–; Dir, QUINN Insurance Ltd 2011–; Chair. Aspire (fundraiser); Dir, Massachusetts Gen. Hosp.'s Pres.'s Council; mem. Bd, Tamarack Technologies, Greater Boston Chamber of Commerce, Jobs for Massachusetts, Inc., Massachusetts Competitive Partnership, Ford's Theatre; mem. Bd Govs's for the Boston Coll. Chief Execs' Club of Boston; mem. Pres.'s Advisory Cttee for Trade Policy and Negotiations. *Address:* Liberty Mutual Holding Co. Inc., 175 Berkeley Street, Boston, MA 02116, USA (office). *Telephone:* (617) 357-9500 (office). *Fax:* (617) 574-6688 (office). *E-mail:* info@libertymutual.com (office). *Website:* www.libertymutualgroup.com (office); www.libertymutual.com (office).

LONG, Guillaume, BA, MPolSci, PhD; Ecuadorean politician; b. 1977, Sucy-en-Brie, Val-de-Marne, France; m. 1st (divorced); one c.; m. 2nd; one c.; ed School of Oriental and African Studies, Univ. of London and Inst. for the Study of the Americas, Univ. of London, UK; int. affairs corresp., Diario El Telégrafo (daily newspaper), Guayaquil 2008–13; Adviser to Nat. Sec. of Planning and Devt 2010–11; Chair., Bd of Evaluation, Accreditation and Quality Assurance in Higher Educ. (CEAACES) 2011–13; Coordinating Minister for Knowledge and Human Talent 2013–15, Minister of Culture and Heritage 2015–16, of Foreign Relations and Migration 2016–17; fmr lecturer in int. relations and history at several Ecuadorian univs; mem. Alianza País (AP), Pres., AP Int. Relations Cttee.

LONG, Malcolm William, AM, LLB, MAICD; Australian broadcasting executive; *Principal, Malcolm Long Associates Proprietary Limited;* b. 13 April 1948, Fremantle, WA; s. of William Long and Dorothy Long; m. Helen Trotter 1973; two d.; ed Univ. of Western Australia; Dir Radio Talks and Documentaries, ABC 1978–82; Man. (Radio) Victorian ABC 1982–84; Dir ABC Radio 1985–92; Deputy Man. Dir Australian Broadcasting Corpn 1992–93; Dir PAN TV Ltd 1996–; Man. Dir SBS Corpn 1993–97; Prin., Malcolm Long Assocs Pty Ltd 2000–; Pres. Australian Museum Trust 1995–2000; Chair. Nat. Inst. of Dramatic Art, Advisory Cttee of Australian Centre for Broadband Innovation; Dir, Macquarie Communications Infrastructure Group 2001–07, Australian Film Television and Radio School 2003–07, Broadcast Australia Pty Ltd 2011–; fmr Dir, Pan TV Ltd; fmr Chair. Exec. Cttee Int. Inst. of Communications; mem. Australian Broadcasting Authority 2000–05, Australian Communications and Media Authority 2005–10. *Publications:* Marx & Beyond 1973, Beyond the Mechanical Mind (with P. Fry) 1977; numerous articles on broadcasting policy and culture. *Leisure interests:* music, reading, running. *Address:* Broadcast Australia, PO Box 1212, Crows Nest, NSW 1585, Australia (office). *Telephone:* (2) 8113-4666 (office). *Fax:* (2) 8113-4646 (office). *E-mail:* info@broadcastaustralia.com.au (office). *Website:* www.broadcastaustralia.com.au (office).

LONG, Sir Richard, Kt, CBE, RA; British artist; b. 2 June 1945, Bristol; s. of Maurice Long and Frances Carpenter; m. Denise Johnston 1969 (divorced 1999); two d.; pnr Denise Hooker; ed West of England Coll. of Art, Bristol and St Martin's School of Art, London; has exhibited widely since mid-1960s; work exhibited in Städtisches Museum, Mönchengladbach 1970, Museum of Modern Art, New York 1972, Stedelijk Museum, Amsterdam 1973, Scottish Museum of Modern Art, Edin. 1974, Kunsthalle, Berne 1977, Nat. Gallery of Canada, Ottawa 1982, Solomon R. Guggenheim Museum, New York 1986, Tate Gallery 1990, Hayward Gallery, London (retrospective) 1991, ARC, Paris 1993, Palazzo delle Esposizioni, Rome 1994, São Paulo Bienal 1994, Nat. Modern Art Museum of Kyoto 1996, Kunstverein Hanover 1999, Guggenheim, Bilbao 2000, Museum Kurhaus Kleve 2001, Tate St Ives 2002, Galleria Lorcan O'Neill Roma 2003, Haunch of Venison 2003, 2006, Galeria Mário Sequeira, Braga 2004, Kulge Gallery, Seoul 2004, Sperone Westwater, New York 2004, Synagogue Stommeln 2004, Galerie Tschudi, Glarus 2005, Museum of Modern Art, San Francisco 2006, Lismore Castle, Waterford 2006, Scottish Nat. Gallery of Modern Art 2007; Chevalier des Arts et des Lettres 1990; Hon. DLit (Bristol) 1995; Turner Prize 1989, Wilhelm Lembruck Prize 1995, Praemium Imperiale 2009. *Publications include:* South America 1972, River Avon Book 1979, Twelve Works 1981, Countless Stones 1983, Stone Water Miles 1987, Old World New World 1988, Nile 1990, Walking in Circles 1991, Mountains and Waters 1992, River to River 1993, Mirage 1997, A Walk Across Across England 1997, From Time to time 1997, Every Grain of Sand 1999, Midday 2001, A Moving World 2002, Walking the Line 2002. *Address:* c/o James Cohan Gallery, 533 West 26th Street, New York, NY 10001, USA. *Telephone:* (212) 714-9500. *E-mail:* info@jamescohan.com. *Website:* www.richardlong.org.

LONG, Ziping; Chinese engineer and business executive; *Chairman, Jiangxi Copper Company Limited;* ed Jiangxi Inst. of Metallurgy, Central South Univ.; served at various operating and man. positions with Jiangxi Copper, including Deputy Chief and Factory Head of Guixi Smelter, Man. of JCC Guixi Smelter, Head of Smelting Dept in Guixi Smelter, Exec. Dir, Jiangxi Copper Co. Ltd 2007–09, Vice-Pres., Deputy Gen. and Chief Legal Adviser 2009–13, Gen. Man. 2013–, Exec. Dir, Vice-Chair. and Pres. 2013–17, Chair. 2017–, also Deputy Party Sec. *Address:* Jiangxi Copper Co. Ltd, 15 Yejin Avenue, Guixi 335424, People's Republic of China (office). *Telephone:* (701) 3777070 (office). *E-mail:* webmaster@jxcc.com (office). *Website:* www.jxcc.com (office).

LONGO, Jeannie Michèle Alice; French cyclist; b. 31 Oct. 1958, Annecy; d. of Jean Longo and Yvette Longo; m. Patrice Ciprelli 1985; ed Inst. d'Etudes Commerciales (Grenoble), DESS droit et economie, Univ. of Limoges; French cycling champion 1979–2011; French cycling master champion 2014–18; winner of over 13 world titles, including world champion (road) 1979–89, 1992, 1995, 1998, 1999, 2000, runner up 1981, world champion (track) 1984, 1985, world champion (pursuit) 1986, 1988, 1989, world champion (against the clock) 1995–97, 2001; winner, Tour of Colorado 1985, 1986, 1987, Tour of Colombia 1987, 1988, Tour of Norway 1987, Tour de France 1987, 1988, 1989; silver medal, World Track Race 1984, 1985, 1987, UCI Masters World Champion 2015, 2017, 2018; holder of 38 world records, including 11-hour world record; silver medallist, Olympic Games, Barcelona 1992, gold and silver medallist Road Race, Olympic Games, Atlanta 1996, bronze medallist, Olympic Games, Sydney 2000; achieved over 1,450 career wins, more than any other cyclist in history; Hon. Citizen of Texas; Commdr, Légion d'honneur, Ordre nat. du Mérite; Officer, Sovereign Order of Malta; Le Mérite sportif (Colombia); Médaille d'Or, La Jeunesse et les Sports, Médaille d'Or, Acad. des Sports, Médaille du mérite et dévouement Français 2002. *Address:* BP 17, 38950 Saint Martin le Vinoux, France. *E-mail:* jeannielongo@free.fr. *Website:* www.jeannielongo.fr.

LONGORIA, Eva Jacqueline, BS; American actress and producer; b. 15 March 1975, Corpus Christi, Nueces Co., Tex.; d. of Enrique Longoria, Jr and Ella Eva Mireles; m. 1st Tyler Christopher 2002 (divorced 2004); m. 2nd Tony Parker 2007 (divorced 2011); m. 3rd José Antonio Bastón 2016; one s.; ed Texas A&M Univ.-Kingsville, California State Univ., Northridge; won Miss Corpus Christi, USA title 1998; entered talent contest that led her to Los Angeles; later spotted and signed by a theatrical agent; guest starred in episode of Beverly Hills, 90210; began TV career in role of Isabella Braña on CBS soap opera The Young and the Restless 2001–03; has appeared on cover of Vogue, Marie Claire and Harper's Bazaar magazines; f. Eva's Heroes charity 2006; nat. spokesperson for PADRES Contra El Cancer; appointed to bi-partisan comm. given task of determining feasibility of creating Nat. Museum of the American Latino 2009; Co-Chair. Barack Obama's re-election campaign 2012, f. Latino Victory Project, Eva Longoria Foundation; ALMA Award for Person of the Year 2006. *Films include:* Snitch'd (video) 2003, Señorita Justice (video) 2004, Carlita's Secret (video) (also co-producer) 2004, Hustler's Instinct (short) 2005, Harsh Times 2005, The Sentinel 2006, The Heartbreak Kid 2007, Over Her Dead Body 2008, Lower Learning 2008, Foodfight! (voice) 2009, Without Men 2011, Arthur Christmas (voice) 2011, For Greater Glory: The True Story of Cristiada 2012, Long Time Gone 2012, The Truth 2012, The Baytown Outlaws 2013; exec. producer: Hot Tamales Live: Spicy, Hot and Hilarious (video) (producer) 2003, Latinos Living the American Dream (documentary) (also writer and dir) 2010, The Harvest (documentary) 2011; dir: A Proper Send-Off (short) 2011, For Greater Glory: The True Story of Cristiada 2012, Frontera 2014, Any Day 2015, Lowriders 2016, Un Cuento de Circo & A Love Song 2016, Overboard (Imagen Award for Best Actress Feature Film 2018) 2018, Dog Days 2018. *Television includes:* The Young and the Restless (series) (ALMA Award for Outstanding Actress in a Daytime Drama 2002) 2001, Dragnet (series) 2003–04, The Dead Will Tell (film) 2004, Desperate Housewives (series) (Choice TV Breakout Performance – Female, Teen Choice Awards 2005, Outstanding Performance by an Ensemble in a Comedy Series, Screen Actors Guild Awards (shared with cast) 2005, 2006, Bambi Award for TV Series International 2007, Favorite Female TV Star, People's Choice Awards 2007) 2004–12, Children's Hospital (series) 2008; exec. producer: 2006 ALMA Awards (special) (producer) 2006, 2007 ALMA Awards (film) 2007, The Philanthropist (film) 2008, 2009 Alma Awards (film) 2009, 2011 ALMA Awards (film) 2011, Devious Maids (series) 2012, Ready for Love (series) 2012, Mother Up! 2013, Brooklyn Nine-Nine 2014–15, Telenovela (series) (also producer) 2015–16. *Address:* Eva Longoria Foundation, 2708 Wilshire Blvd, #369, Santa Monica, CA 90403, USA. *E-mail:* info@evalongoriafoundation.org. *Website:* www.evalongoriafoundation.org; www.evalongoria.com.

LONGRIGG, Anthony (Tony) James, CMG; British diplomatist; b. 21 April 1944; m. Jane Rosa Cowlin 1968; three d.; joined FCO 1972, with Research Unit 1973; First Sec. Chancery, Moscow 1975–78; with E African Dept FCO 1978–80, Conf. for Security and Co-operation in Europe, FCO 1980–81; First Sec., Brasilia 1981–85; with Soviet Dept FCO 1985–87; Counsellor, Moscow 1987–91; Counsellor Econ./EU Affairs, Madrid 1991–95; Head S Atlantic/Antarctic Dept FCO 1995–97; Minister and Deputy Head of Mission, Moscow 1997–2000; Gov. of Montserrat 2001–04 (retd).

LONGUET, Gérard Edmond Jacques; French politician; b. 24 Feb. 1946, Neuilly-sur-Seine; s. of Jacques Longuet and Marie-Antoinette Laurent; m. Brigitte Fossorier 1967; four d.; ed Paris Univ., Ecole Nationale d'Admin; Pvt. Sec. to Prefect of Eure's Office 1973–74, to Prefect of Somme's Office 1974–76, to Sec. of State (attached to Prime Minister's Office) 1977–78; Deputy of Meuse 1978–81, 1988–93, Vice-Pres. Gen. Councillor's Office 1982–92; Gen. Councillor, Seuil d'Argonne 1979–92, Town Councillor 1983; Municipal Councillor, Bar-le-Duc 1983–89; mem. European Parl. 1984–86; Sec. of State March–Aug. 1986, then Minister at Ministry of Industry 1986–88; Minister of Industry, Posts and Telecommunications and Foreign Trade 1993–94, of Defence and Veterans' Affairs 2011–12; Sec.-Gen. Union pour la Démocratie Française (UDF) 1989; Regional Councillor of Lorraine 1992–2010 (resgnd), Pres. Regional Council 1992–2004; Pres. Republican Party 1990–95; Senateur de la Meuse 2001–11, Pres. of UMP Group in Senate 2009–11; Collection Dir, France Empire publrs; Pres. Sokrates Group, ETD 2003, Asscn des Régions de France. *Publications:* L'Epreuve de vérité 1995, L'Espoir industriel 1995. *Leisure interest:* skiing. *Address:* Sokrates Group, 56 rue de Chateaudun, 75009 Paris, France (office).

LONSDALE, Anne Mary, CBE, BA (LitHum), BA (OrientStud); British university administrator (retd); *Chairman, Council for At-Risk Academics;* b. 16 Feb. 1941, Huddersfield, Yorks., England; d. of A. C. G. Menzies and Molly Menzies; m. 1st Geoffrey Griffin 1962 (died 1962); m. 2nd Roger Lonsdale 1964 (divorced 1994); one s. one d.; ed St Anne's Coll., Oxford; Lecturer in Classical Chinese, St Anne's Coll. Oxford 1965–73; Univ. Admin. 1973–86; Dir External Relations Office, Univ. of Oxford 1986–93; Sec.-Gen. Cen. European Univ. 1993–96; Pres. New Hall (now Murray Edwards Coll.) Cambridge 1996–2008, Pro-Vice-Chancellor, Univ. of Cambridge 1998–2004, Deputy Vice-Chancellor 2004–08, Deputy High Steward 2010–; mem. Commonwealth Scholarship Comm. 1996–2003; fmr Trustee, Moscow School of Social and Econ. Sciences, LEAD Int. UK, European Humanities Univ., Vilnius/Minsk; Chair. Council for At-Risk Academics; fmr Chair. Camfed International; Cavaliere del'Ordine al Merito della Repubblica Italiana 1992; Officier des Palmes académiques 2003; Dr hc (Tashkent Oriental Studies Univ., Uzbekistan) 2001; Dostyk Award (Kazakhstan) 2016. *Publications:* publs on Chinese literature and univ. admin. *Leisure interests:* travel, film, contemporary art. *E-mail:* al213@cam.ac.uk (office).

LOOMBA, Baron (Life Peer), cr. 2011, of Moor Park in the County of Hertfordshire; **Raj Loomba,** CBE, FRSA; British business executive; *Executive Director, Rinku Group;* b. 13 Nov. 1943, Dhilwan, Punjab, British India; s. of Pushpa Wati Loomba; m. Veena Chaudhry; one s. two d.; ed D.A.V. Coll., Jalandhar, State Univ. of Iowa, USA; began in business on a market stall in Widnes, Cheshire 1964; Founder and Exec. Chair. Rinku Group (fashion and clothing co.), London, group designs and produces Tigi-Wear, Viz-A-Viz and iZ brands; longstanding supporter of business and cultural relations between India and UK; chaired Organizing Cttee for British Indian Golden Jubilee Banquet, Grosvenor House Hotel, London to celebrate 50th anniversary of India's independence 1997; Chair. British Indian Golden Jubilee Banquet Fund; Founder-Chair. and Trustee, Dr L.M. Singhvi Foundation; Chair. India First PLC; initiated Chatham House Prize (awarded annually to a world statesman) 2004; est. (with his wife) Shrimati Pushpa Wati Loomba Trust as a charitable trust to pioneer widows' rights 1997; launched 23 June as Int. Widows Day 2005; Vice-Pres. for Europe, Global Org. of People of Indian Origin; Vice-Pres. Safer London Foundation, Barnardo's; Chair. Friends of the Three Faiths Forum, UK; mem. Bd London First 2000–04, Council of Royal Soc. of Int. Affairs (Chatham House) (first Indian) 2002–, Pres.'s Council 2004–06, Inst. of Int. of Dirs, Rotary Club of London, Bd of Govs Univ. of East London; Trustee, Maharajah Ranjit Singh Trust, India; Patron, RSA in India, Children In Need Inst.; Founding Patron, World Punjabi Org.; Vice-Patron, Gates; Paul Harris Fellow, Rotary International; Freeman of the City of London; Hind Rattan Award 1991, Int. Excellence Award 1991, Asian of the Year Award 1997, Pride of India Gold Medal 1998, Into Leadership Award 2000, Judges' Special Commendation, Worldaware Business Awards 2001, Highly Commended New Initiative, Beacon Prize 2004, Leadership Memento for The Loomba Trust, Prime Minister of India 2004, Neville Shulman Charity Cup, Life Time Achievers Award, Chief Minister of Punjab, Priyadarshni Acad. Global Award 2006, Charity of the Year Award, Asian Who's Who 2006, NRI Inst. of India Achievers Award, on behalf of Loomba Trust 2008, Distinguished Non-Resident Philanthropist (Forbes India Philanthropy Awards) 2012. *Address:* Rinku Group Ltd, 622 Western Avenue, London, W3 0TF (office); House of Lords, Westminster, London, SW1A 0PW, England. *Telephone:* (20) 8102-0351 (office); (20) 7219-5353. *Fax:* (20) 8896-9977 (office); (20) 7219-5979. *E-mail:* loombar@parliament.uk; raj@loomba.com; safdar@theloombafoundation.org. *Website:* www.loombagroup.co.uk.

LOONE, Eero, PhD; Estonian philosopher and academic; *Professor Emeritus, University of Tartu;* b. 26 May 1935, Tartu; s. of Nikolai Loone and Leida Loone (née Rebane); m. 1st Halliki Uibo 1965; m. 2nd Leiki Sikk 1971; two d.; ed Moscow Univ. and Acad. of Sciences, Moscow; mem. CPSU 1965–90; teacher, Dept of Gen. History, Univ. of Tartu 1963–66, Sr Lecturer 1966–69, Assoc. Prof. and Sr Researcher 1969–85, Prof. 1985–2000, Head, Dept of Philosophy 1986–89, 1993–94, 1998–2000, Head, Dept of Philosophy and Political Science 1989–93, Prof. Emer. 2000–; Prof. of Political Theory, Tallinn Univ. of Tech. 2008–09, apptd Sr Research Fellow 2009; Visiting Prof., British Acad. 1993, Ashby Lecturer 1994; Founding mem. Estonian Union of Scientists 1989–2009, Estonia Foreign Policy Inst. 1991, Estonian Political Science Asscn 1993–; mem. Int. Political Science Asscn 1994–; NATO Democratic Insts Fellow 1993–94; Life mem. Clare Hall, Cambridge, UK 1990–; Fulbright Scholar, Columbia Univ., USA 1997. *Publications include:* Contemporary Philosophy of History 1980 (trans. into English as Soviet Marxism and Analytical Philosophies of History 1990); numerous articles in scholarly journals. *Leisure interest:* science fiction. *Address:* Faculty of Arts and Humanities, University of Tartu, Ulikooli 18, 50090 Tartu (office); Vabaduse pst. 168-5, 10917 Tartu, Estonia (home). *Telephone:* (7) 375317 (office); (6) 778685 (home). *Fax:* (7) 375345 (office). *E-mail:* eero.loone@ut.ee (office). *Website:* www.fl.ut.ee (office).

LOOSLI, Hansueli, CFA; Swiss accountant and business executive; *Chairman, Coop-Gruppe Genossenschaft;* b. 4 Nov. 1955, Bern; m.; two c.; Controller, Deputy Dir, Mövenpick Produktions AG, Adliswil 1982–85; Man. Dir Waro AG, Volketswil 1985–92; Dir of Non-Food Product Procurement, Coop Switzerland, Wangen 1992–96, Man. Dir Coop Zurich, Zurich 1992–97, Chair. Exec. Cttee and Coop Group Exec. Cttee, Coop Switzerland, Basle 1997–2000, Chair. Exec. Cttee and CEO, Coop-Gruppe Genossenschaft, Basle 2001–11, Chair. Bd of Dirs 2011–; Chair. Coop Immobilien AG, Berne, Bell AG, Basel, Swisscom AG, Ittigen, Transgourmet Holding AG, Basel, Coop Mineraloel AG, Allschwil. *Address:* Coop-Gruppe Genossenschaft, Güterstrasse 190, 4053 Basel, Switzerland (office). *Telephone:* 613366666 (office). *E-mail:* info@coop.ch (office). *Website:* www.coop.ch (office).

LOPARDO, Frank; American singer (tenor); b. 23 Dec. 1957, Brentwood, NY; m. Carolyn J. Montalbano 1982; two s.; ed Queen's Coll., City Univ. of New York and Juilliard School of Music, studied with Dr Robert White, Jr; professional debut as Tamino in The Magic Flute, Opera Theater of St Louis 1984; European debut as Fenton at Teatro di San Carlo in Naples; debut at La Scala, Milan 1987, Glyndebourne Festival 1987, Metropolitan Opera as Almaviva in Il Barbiere di Siviglia 1989–90; has appeared as Tamino, Rodolfo in La bohème, Alfredo in La traviata, the Duke in Rigoletto, Edgardo in Lucia di Lammermoor, Tonio in La fille du régiment, Nemorino in L'elisir d'amore, Don Ottavio in Don Giovanni, Idreno in Semiramide, Ferrando in Così fan tutte, Fenton in Falstaff; appearances with various North American opera cos, including Lyric Opera of Chicago, Los Angeles Opera, Houston Grand Opera, Dallas Opera, Canadian Opera Co., San Francisco Opera, Santa Fe Opera; In Europe, has sung as Edgardo, Rodolfo, the Duke, and Lenski in Eugene Onegin at Opéra Nat. de Paris; at Royal Opera House, Covent Garden, has sung as Lindoro in L'Italiana in Algeri; performances at other major European theatres include Vienna State Opera, Grand Théâtre de Genève, Teatro alla Scala, Milan, Teatro Comunale, Florence, Teatro Real, Madrid; has appeared at the Salzburg Festival, Glyndebourne Opera Festival, and Aix-en-Provence Festival, and has sung with De Nederlandse Opera; has sung with orchestras world-wide, including performances of Verdi's Requiem with London Symphony Orchestra and Montreal Symphony Orchestra, Mozart's Requiem with Berlin Philharmonic Orchestra at La Scala, Berlioz's Requiem and Orff's Carmina Burana with Boston Symphony Orchestra, Beethoven's Ninth Symphony with San Francisco Symphony Orchestra, Rossini's Stabat Mater with Philadelphia Orchestra and Dvořák's Requiem with Danish Radio Symphony Orchestra; Hon. DMus (Aaron Copland School of Music) 1992; First Prize, Liederkranz Foundation competition 1983. *Recordings include:* Requiem (Mozart), with Riccardo Muti 1987, L'Italiana in Algeri (Rossini), with Claudio Abbado 1987, Don Giovanni (Mozart), with Riccardo Muti 1990, Great Mass in C minor (Mozart), with Leonard Bernstein 1991, Falstaff (Verdi), with Sir Colin Davis 1991, Il signor Bruschino (Rossini), with Ion Marin 1991, Il barbiere di Siviglia (Rossini), with Claudio Abbado 1992, Semiramide (Rossini), with Ion Marin 1992, Carmina Burana (Orff), with André Previn 1992, Don Pasquale (Donizetti), with Roberto Abbado 1993, Idomeneo (Mozart), with James Levine 1993, Così fan tutte (Mozart), with Sir George Solti 1993, La traviata (Verdi), with Sir George Solti 1994, Berlioz Requiem, with Atlanta Symphony Orchestra and Chorus, conducted by Robert Spano (Grammy Award for Best Choral Performance) 2005, Imelda de' Lambertazzi (Donizetti), with Mark Elder 2006, Ninth Symphony (Beethoven), with Franz Welser-Möst 2007. *Leisure interest:* golf. *E-mail:* mail@franklopardo.com. *Website:* www.franklopardo.com.

LOPATKINA, Ulyana Vyacheslavovna; Russian fmr ballerina; b. 23 Oct. 1973, Kerch, Ukraine; m. Vladimir Kornev 2001 (divorced 2010), one d.; ed Vaganova Acad. of Russian Ballet (studied with Natalya Dudinskaya); soloist, Kirov Ballet/Mariinsky Theatre 1991–95, Prin. Dancer 1995–16; performed in the closing ceremony of Winter Olympics 2010, 'Swan Lake' at Opera de Paris 2010; retd 2017; numerous performances, masterclasses and workshops; winner Int. Vaganova-prix Competition, St Petersburg 1991, Golden Sofit 1995, 2015, Golden Mask 1997, Baltika Prize 1997, 2001, State Prize of Russian Fed. 1999, 2015, Honoured Artist of Russia 2000, Peoplés Artist of Russia 2005,. *Repertoire includes:* leading roles in Giselle, Sleeping Beauty, Anna Karenina, Fountain of Bakhchisarai, Raimonda, Sheherazade, Swan Lake, Bayadera, Le Corsaire, The Sound of the Blank Pages, The Swan, Grand pas from Paquita, The Legend of Love, Pas de Quatre, Serenade, Piano Concerto No. 2, La Valse, Leningrad Symphony, Symphony in C, Waltz, Kiss of a Fairy, The Legend of LoveJewels, In the Night, The Nutcracker, The Imperial, La Baiser de la Fée, Le Poeme de l'Extase, In the Middle, La Rose Malade, Magruerite and Armand; performed in Goya-Divertissement; tours with Mariinsky Theatre in Europe, N and S America. *Website:* www.uliana-lopatkina.com.

LOPES, Carlos, PhD; Guinea-Bissau economist, diplomatist and UN official; *Executive Secretary, United Nations Economic Commission for Africa;* b. 7 March 1960; ed Univ. of Geneva, Univ. of Paris 1 Panthéon-Sorbonne; taught at univs in Lisbon, Coimbra, Zurich, Uppsala, Mexico, São Paulo and Rio de Janeiro; fmr consultant for UNESCO, Swedish Int. Devt Cooperation Agency, UN Econ. Comm. for Africa, Research and Technological Exchange Group, Ruraltec Switzerland; Devt Economist, UNDP 1988, then Deputy Dir Office of Evaluation and Strategic Planning, Resident Rep. in Zimbabwe, Deputy, then Dir Bureau for Devt Policy, Asst Admin. UNDP, UN Resident Coordinator and UNDP Resident Rep. in Brazil 2003–05; apptd Dir Exec. Office of Sec.-Gen. in charge of Political, Peacekeeping and Humanitarian affairs 2005; Exec. Dir UNITAR 2007–12; Exec. Sec., UN Econ. Comm. for Africa 2012–; fmr Dir UN System Staff Coll.; elected to Lisbon Acad. of Sciences, Portugal 2008; mem. Instituto Ethos, Ecôle Polytechnique Fédérale de Lausanne, King Baudouin International Development Prize Selection Committee; mem. Advisory Bd Kofi Annan Foundation, UNESCO Int. Inst. for Educational Planning, Bonn Int. Center for Conversion, Swiss Network for Int. Studies; mem. Editorial Cttee Géopolitique Africaine, African Sociological Review, African Identities, Cooperation South Journal; Hon. PhD (Univ. of Cândido, Brazil). *Address:* United Nations Economic Commission for Africa, PO Box 3001, Addis Ababa, Ethiopia (office). *Telephone:* (11) 5443336 (office). *Fax:* (11) 5514416 (office). *E-mail:* ecaweb@uneca.org (office). *Website:* www.uneca.org (office).

LOPÈS, Henri Marie Joseph; Republic of the Congo author, politician and diplomatist; b. 12 Sept. 1937, Léopoldville, Belgian Congo (now Kinshasa, Democratic Repub. of the Congo); s. of Jean-Marie Lopès and Micheline Vulturi; m. Nirva Pasbeau 1961; one s. three d.; ed France; Minister of Nat. Educ. 1968–71, of Foreign Affairs 1971–73; mem. Political Bureau, Congolese Labour Party 1973; Prime Minister and Minister of Planning 1973–75, of Finance 1977–80; UNESCO Asst Dir-Gen. for Programme Support 1982–86, UNESCO Asst Dir-Gen. for Culture and Communication 1986–90, for Culture 1990–94, for Foreign Affairs 1994–95, Deputy Dir-Gen. 1996–98; apptd Amb. to France (also accred to Portugal, Spain, UK and The Holy See (Vatican City)) 1998; mem. Haut Conseil de la Francophonie; Chevalier, Légion d'honneur, Commdr du Mérite Congolais, etc., Officier de la Légion d'honneur 2015; Dr hc (Univ. of Paris XII) 2002, (Univ. of Quebec) 2002, (Univ. of Sonfoniah, Guinea) 2013; Prix littéraire de l'Afrique noire 1972, Prix SIMBA de littérature 1978, Prix de littérature du Président (Congo), Prix de l'Acad. de Bretagne et des Pays de la Loire 1990, Grand Prix de la Francophonie de l'Acad. française 1993. *Publications:* Tribaliques (short stories), La Nouvelle Romance (novel), Learning to be (with others), Sans tam-tam (novel) 1977, Le Pleurer Rire (novel) 1982, Le Chercheur d'Afriques (novel) 1990, Sur l'autre Rive (novel) 1992, Le Lys et le flamboyant (novel) 1997, Dossier classé 2002, Une enfant de Poto-Poto 2012, Le Méridonal 2015.

LÓPEZ, Carlos Ricardo Henríquez; Panamanian banker; *President, Banco Nacional de Panamá;* fmr Vice-Pres., Banco Comercial de Panamá SA Bancomer; currently Pres., Banco Nacional de Panamá (govt-owned bank); fmr Dir FDR Investments Corpn. *Address:* Office of the President, Banco Nacional de Panamá, Casa Matriz, Vía España, Apdo 5220, Panamá 5, Panama (office). *Telephone:* 505-2000 (office). *Fax:* 269-0091 (office). *E-mail:* sugerencia@banconal.com.pa (office). *Website:* www.banconal.com.pa (office).

LOPEZ, Eugenio, III, BA, MBA; Philippine broadcasting executive; *Chairman Emeritus, ABS-CBN Corporation;* b. 13 Aug. 1952; s. of Eugenio Lopez Jr and Conchita La'O Lopez; m. Panjee Gonzales; four c.; ed Bowdoin Coll. and Harvard Business School, USA; Dir of Finance, ABS-CBN Broadcasting Corpn 1986, Gen. Man. 1987, Pres. –1996, Chair. 1996–2018, Chair. Emer. 2018–, CEO (company renamed ABS-CBN Corpn) 2010–12; Treas. Lopez Holdings Corpn (parent co., fmrly Benpres Holdings Corpn); Tanglaw ng Araw Award 2014, Lifetime Achievement Award, Kapisanan ng mga Brodkaster ng Pilipinas (KBP) Golden Dove Awards 2014. *Address:* ABS-CBN Corporation, Sgt Esguerra Avenue, corner Mother Ignacia Street, Quezon City, Metro Manila, Philippines (office). *Telephone:* (2) 4152272 (office). *Fax:* (2) 4319368 (office). *Website:* www.abs-cbn.com (office).

LOPEZ, Jennifer, (J.Lo); American actress, singer, dancer and business executive; b. (Jennifer Lynn Lopez), 24 July 1969, Bronx, New York; m. 1st Ojani Noa 1997 (divorced 1998); m. 2nd Chris Judd 2001 (divorced 2003); m. 3rd Marc Anthony 2004–14 (divorced); one s. one d. (twins); ed Baruch Coll., City Univ. of New York; began career as a Fly Girl on TV programme In Living Color and as a back-up dancer for Janet Jackson; gained recognition in film Money Train 1995; first leading role in biographical film Selena 1997; released debut album On the 6 1999; second album J.Lo reached No. 1 on Billboard 200 the same week her film The Wedding Planner led the box office 2001; released remix album J To Tha L-O! The Remixes 2002; released first full Spanish album Como Ama una Mujer 2007; collaborations with Ja Rule, Big Pun, Fat Joe; Dance Again World Tour 2012; est. clothing and lingerie lines and various perfumes with her celebrity endorsement; current residency 'Jennifer Lopez: All I Have' at Planet Hollywood Resort & Casino, Las Vegas; Golden Globe 1998, MTV Movie Award 1999, Billboard Latin Award for Hot Latin Track of the Year 2000, MTV Video Music Award for Best Dance Video 2000, VH1/Vogue Fashion Versace Award 2000, MTV Europe Music Award for Best Female Act 2001, MTV Award for Best Female 2002, American Music Award for Favorite Pop/Rock Female Artist 2003, American Music Award for Favorite Latin Artist 2007, 2011, Vanguard Award, Glaad Media Awards 2014. *Films include:* My Little Girl 1986, My Family, Mi Familia 1995, Money Train 1995, Jack 1996, Blood and Wine 1996, Selena (ALMA Award for Outstanding Actress) 1997, Anaconda 1997, U Turn 1997, Out of Sight (ALMA Award) 1998, Antz (voice) 1998, The Cell 2000, The Wedding Planner 2001, Angel Eyes 2001, Enough 2002, Maid in Manhattan 2002, Gigli 2003, Jersey Girl 2004, Shall We Dance? 2004, Monster-in-Law 2005, An Unfinished Life 2006, El Cantante 2006, Bordertown (Artists for Amnesty Prize 2007) 2006, The Back-Up Plan 2010, Scrat's Continental Crack-Up: Part 2 (short) (voice) 2011, What to Expect When You're Expecting 2012, Ice Age: Continental Drift (voice) 2012, Parker 2013, The Boy Next Door 2015, Lila & Eve 2015, Ice Age: Collision Course (voice) 2016. *Television includes:* In Living Color 1990, Nurses on the Line: The Crash of Flight 7 1993, Second Chances (series) 1993–94, South Central (series) 1994, Hotel Malibu (series) 1994, How I Met Your Mother (series) 2010, judge, American Idol 2010–12, Shades of Blue (series) 2016–17. *Recordings include:* albums: On The 6 1999, J.Lo 2001, J To Tha L-O! (remixes) 2002, This Is Me... Then 2002, Rebirth 2005, Como Ama una Mujer 2007, Brave 2007, Love? 2011, Dance Again... The Hits 2012, AKA 2014. *Publication:* True Love 2014. *Address:* c/o WME Entertainment, 9601 Wilshire Boulevard, Beverly Hills, CA 90210, USA (office). *Telephone:* (310) 285-9000 (office). *Fax:* (310) 285-9010 (office). *Website:* www.wma.com (office); www.jenniferlopez.com.

LÓPEZ, Martin (Mark) L., MBA; Philippine business executive; *Chairman, ABS-CBN Corporation;* ed Menlo Coll., California, Asian Inst. of Man.; Man. Dir Manila Electric Co. (MERALCO) 2001–06, becoming Chief Information Officer, later Vice-Pres., Pres. and CEO e-Meralco Ventures, Inc. (subsidiary of MERALCO) –2010; held several positions at ABS-CBN Corpn including Chief Tech. Officer, Chief Information Officer, Dir, mem. Advisory Bd, Chair. 2018–; Dir Soluziona Philippines Inc. 2007–08. *Address:* ABS-CBN Corporation, Sgt. E.A. Esguerra Avenue, Quezon City 1103, Philippines (office). *Telephone:* (2) 4152272 (office). *Website:* corporate.abs-cbn.com.

LOPEZ, Oscar, MPA; Philippine business executive; *Chairman Emeritus, Lopez Group;* b. 1930, Manila; s. of Eugenio H. Lopez; m. Consuelo R. Lopez; three s. five d.; ed Littauer School of Public Admin (now Kennedy School of Govt), Harvard Univ., USA; began career as Publr, Manila Chronicle 1960–66; joined Meralco Securities Corpn (now First Philippine Holdings Corpn) 1965, CEO 1986; Chair. and CEO Benpres Holdings Corpn (now Lopez Holdings Corpn) 1999–2004, Chair. Lopez Group 1999, currently Chair. Emer., Chair. and Trustee Lopez Group Foundation Inc.; Chair. and CEO Metro Pacific Tollways Corpn 2007–08; Chair. Energy Devt Corpn 2007–, Bayan Telecommunications Holdings Corpn, Bayan Telecommunications Inc.; Dir ABS-CBN Corpn (formerly ABS-CBN Broadcasting) 1966–, Manila Electric Co. (Meralco), Maynilad Water Services Inc.; mem. Man. Asscn of the Philippines; Bundesverdienstkreuz (FRG) 2005; Man. Man of the Year, Man. Asscn of the Philippines 2000, Philippine Mil. Acad. Distinguished Citizen Award 2008, TOFIL Outstanding Filipino Award 2009. *Leisure interest:* mountain climbing. *Address:* Lopez Group Foundation Inc., 5/F Benpres Building, Meralco Avenue, corner Exchange Road, Ortigas Center, Pasig City 1600, Philippines (office). *Telephone:* (2) 4900779 (office). *Website:* www.lopezgroup.org (office).

LÓPEZ ÁLVAREZ, Patxi; Spanish politician; b. 4 Oct. 1959, Portugalete; m. Begoña Gil; joined Young Basque Socialists 1975, Sec.-Gen. 1985–88; mem. Basque Socialist Party-Basque Left (PSE-EE/PSOE) 1977–, mem. Exec. Cttee 1988–, Sec. PSE-EE/PSOE 1991–95, Sec.-Gen. 2002–14; mem. Congreso de los Diputados (Congress of Deputies) 1987–89, 2016–, Pres. Jan.–July 2016, Chair. Cttee on Health and Social Services; mem. Basque Parl. 1991–2014; Lehendakari (Pres.) of Basque Govt 2009–12. *Address:* Congress of Deputies (Congreso de los Diputados), Carrera de Floridablanca s/n, 28071 Madrid, Spain (office). *Telephone:* (91) 3906000 (office). *Fax:* (91) 4298707 (office). *E-mail:* informacion@congreso.es (office). *Website:* www.congreso.es (office); www.patxilopez.com.

LÓPEZ BENÍTEZ, Benigno María, LLM; Paraguayan politician and lawyer; *Minister of Finance;* ed Universidad Católica Nuestra Señora de la Asunción, Georgetown Univ., USA; Gen. Counsel Cen. Bank of Paraguay 1998–2002, mem. Bd of Dirs 2007–12; Pnr Parquet and Associates Law Firm 2002–07; Sr Adviser to the Exec. Dir, IMF 2012–13; Exec. Legal Dir Itaipu Binacional 2013–; Pres. Instituto de Previsión Social (IPS) 2014–18; Minister of Finance 2018–; mem. Colorado Party. *Address:* Ministry of Finance, Chile 252, 1220 Asunción, Paraguay (office). *Telephone:* (21) 440-010 (office). *Fax:* (21) 448-283 (office). *E-mail:* info@hacienda.gov.py (office). *Website:* www.hacienda.gov.py (office).

LÓPEZ CHARRETON, Susana, BSc, MSc PhD; Mexican virologist and academic; *Professor of Developmental Genetics and Molecular Physiology, National Autonomous University of Mexico;* ed Nat. Autonomous Univ. of Mexico (UNAM); Asst Prof. of Molecular Biology, Centre for Research on Genetic Eng and Biotechnology, Cuernavaca 1989–93; Fogarty Fellow, Div. of Biology, California Inst. of Tech. 1992–93; currently Prof. of Developmental Genetics and Molecular Physiology, Dept of the Inst. of Biotechnology, UNAM; Howard Hughes Medical Inst. Int. Research Scholar 2005–10; Nat. Science Award, Mexican Acad. of Sciences 1993, Premio Bienal FUNSALUD en Infecciones Gastrointestinales Fundación Mexicana para la Salud 2000, Carlos J. Finlay Prize for Microbiology, UNESCO (co-recipient with her husband, Carlos Arias Ortiz) 2001, Premio Bienal Funsalud en Enfermedades Gastrointestinales (NADRO), Fundación Mexicana para la Salud 2002, Sor Juana Ines de la Cruz Medal, Nat. Autonomous Univ. of Mexico 2004, L'Oréal-UNESCO For Women in Science Award (Latin America) (for elucidating the mechanisms of rotavirus infections) 2012. *Publications:* numerous papers in professional journals. *Address:* Instituto de Biotecnología/UNAM, Avenida Universidad #2001, Col. Chamilpa CP 62210 Cuernavaca, Morelos Apdo Postal 510-3, CP 62250, Mexico (office). *Telephone:* (777) 329-1615 (office). *Fax:* (777) 331-14701 (office). *E-mail:* susana@ibt.unam.mx (office). *Website:* www.ibt.unam.mx (office).

LOPEZ-COLOMÉ, Ana Maria, PhD; Mexican neuroscientist, biochemist and academic; *Professor of Neuroscience and Biochemistry, Institute of Cellular Physiology, National Autonomous University (UNAM);* b. Mexico City; one s. one d.; ed Nat. Autonomous Univ. of Mexico (UNAM); fmr Lecturer, Faculty of Sciences, UNAM, Mexico City, currently Prof. of Neuroscience and Biochemistry, Inst. of Cellular Physiology; Univ. Councilor, UNAM; mem. Soc. for Neuroscience, Int. Soc. for Neurochemistry, American Soc. for Neurochemistry, ISDN, Mexican Soc. for Biochemistry, Mexican Soc. for Physiological Sciences, Academia de la

Investigación Científica; Regional Ed. Molecules; works on retinal biochemistry in health and diseases leading to blindness; L'Oreal-UNESCO For Women in Science Award 2002. *Publications:* numerous articles in scientific journals. *Address:* Instituto de Fisiología Celular, UNAM, División de Neurociencias, Apartado postal 70-253, 04510 Mexico City, DF, Mexico (office). *Telephone:* (525) 622-5617 (office). *Fax:* (525) 622-5607 (office). *E-mail:* acolome@ifc.unam.mx (office). *Website:* www.ifisiol.unam.mx (office).

LÓPEZ CONTRERAS, Carlos; Honduran lawyer, notary, academic, politician and diplomatist; *National Consultant, Ministry of Foreign Affairs;* b. 31 Jan. 1942, Marcala, La Paz; m. Armida María Villela de López; one s. one d.; ed Nat. Univ. of Honduras, Univ. Complutense of Madrid, Spain, Acad. of American and Int. Law, Dallas, Tex., USA; authorized as Attorney at Law and Notary Public by Supreme Court of Justice of Honduras 1974; Prof. of Law, Univ. of San Pedro Sula 1977–79, Nat. Univ. of Honduras 1981–85; Vice-Minister of Foreign Affairs 1979–80, Minister of Foreign Affairs 1986–90, 2009; Founding Partner, Aczalaw (law firm), Sr Partner 2002–; Rep. for Honduras and mem. Perm. Court of Arbitration, Int. Court of Justice, The Hague, Netherlands; 1980–; mem. Bd of Dirs for Honduras to Cen. American Bank for Econ. Integration 1990–91; consultant to Armed Forces and Ministry of Economy of Honduras; National Consultant, Ministry of Foreign Affairs; mem. Nat. Acad. of Law and Social Sciences; Founder and Pres. Honduran Foundation of Human Culture, Funadación para el Museo del Hombre Hondureño; mem. Hispanic-Portuguese-American Inst. for Int. Law, El Escorial, Spain 2002–; mem. Partido Nacional; 25 decorations from foreign and nat. govts, cultural and social orgs; Honrar la Toga Gold, Nat. Coll. of Honduras Attorneys 2015. *Leisure interests:* reading, walking, music, travel. *Address:* Aczalaw, Colonia Tepeyac, Calle Yoro, 2403 Tegucigalpa, Honduras (office). *Telephone:* 2232-6502 (office). *E-mail:* clopez@aczalaw.com (office). *Website:* aczalaw.com (office).

LÓPEZ GARCÍA, Antonio; Spanish painter, draughtsman and sculptor; b. 6 Jan. 1936, Tomelloso, La Mancha; m. María Moreno 1961; two d.; ed Escuela de Bellas Artes de San Fernando, Madrid; his art evolved from primitivist and surrealist influences to a strict realism; formed friendships with Francisco Lopez Hernandez, Amalia Avia and Isabel Quintanilla, out of which nucleus a realist group, the New Spanish Realists, was formed in Madrid; travelled to Italy on a scholarship with Francisco Lopez and studied Italian painting from the Renaissance 1955; gave classes at Escuela de Bellas Artes de San Fernando 1964–69; works in public collections including Museum of Fine Arts, Boston, Reina Sofía Nat. Museum, Madrid; Hon. mem. Acad. of Arts and Letters, New York 2004; Prize of Diputación de Jaén 1957, Prize of Fundación Rodríguez Acosta 1958, Molino de Oro Prize of Exposición Regional de Valdepeñas 1959, Darmstadt Prize 1974, Medalla de Oro, Castilla-La Mancha 1986, Medalla de Oro, Comunidad de Madrid 1990, Velázquez Prize for Fine Arts 2006. *Film:* his painting was the subject of the film El Sol del Membrillo (The Quince Tree Sun, directed by Victor Erice and written by both) 1992. *Address:* c/o Galería Marlborough SA, Orfila 5, 28010 Madrid (office); Poniente 3, 28036 Madrid, Spain (home). *Telephone:* (91) 3191414 (office). *Fax:* (91) 3084345 (office). *E-mail:* info@galeriamarlborough.com (office). *Website:* www.galeriamarlborough.com (office); www.artnet.com/artists/antonio-l%C3%B3pez+garc%C3%ADa.

LÓPEZ OBRADOR, Andrés Manuel; Mexican politician and head of state; *President;* b. 13 Nov. 1953, Tepetitán, Tabasco; m. 1st Rocio Beltran (died 2003); three s.; m. 2nd Beatriz Gutiérrez Müller 2006; ed Universidad Nacional Autónoma de México; Dir Instituto Indigenista de Tabasco 1984; Dir of Social Promotion, Instituto Nacional del Consumidor 1985; joined Corriente Democrática 1986; joined Frente Democrático Nacional and stood for Gov. of Tabasco; joined Partido de la Revolución Democrática 1989 and led party in Tabasco, stood for Gov. and lost 1994, left the party 2012; Pres. Partido de la Revolucíon Democrática 1996–99; Mayor of Mexico City 2000–05 (resgnd to work on his unsuccessful 2006 campaign for Pres.); runner-up in 2012 presidential election; Leader, Movimiento Regeneración Nacional (Morena) 2012–; Pres. of Mexico 2018–. *Address:* Office of the President, Los Pinos, Col. San Miguel Chapultepec, 11850 México, DF, Mexico (office). *Telephone:* (55) 5093-5300 (office). *Fax:* (55) 5277-2376 (office). *E-mail:* felipe.calderon@presidencia.gob.mx (office). *Website:* www.presidencia.gob.mx (office).

LÓPEZ RODRIGUEZ, HE Cardinal Nicolás de Jesús, DScS; Dominican Republic ecclesiastic; *Archbishop Emeritus of Santo Domingo;* b. 31 Oct. 1936, Barrancas; ed Pontifical Seminary 'Santo Tomas de Aquino', Santo Domingo, Int. Center for the Sociological Formation of the Clergy, Rome, Italy, Pontifical St Thomas Univ. and Pontifical Gregorian Univ., Rome; ordained priest 1961; pastoral work in diocese of La Vega 1961–64, 1966–68; Diocesan Counsellor, La Vega, 1969–78; Ecclesiastical Assessor Christian Family Movt and Cursillo Movt; Diocesan Vicar, later Pro-Vicar General, Gen. later Vicar Gen.; Bishop of San Francisco de Macoris 1978; Rector Nordestana di San Francisco de Macorís Univ. 1979–84; Metropolitan and Primate of Santo Domingo 1981–2016, then Archbishop Emer.; cr. Cardinal (Cardinal-Priest of San Pio X alla Balduina) 1991; participated in Papal Conclave 2005, 2013; Grand Chancellor Catholic Univ. of Santo Domingo 1982; Mil. Ordinary for the Dominican Repub. 1982; Del. to Dominican Bishops' Conf. 1979–81, Pres. Bishops' Justice and Peace Comm., mem. (currently Pres.) Perm. Comm., Nat. Chaplain to the Christian Renewal of the Holy Spirit, Pres. Dominican Bishops' Conf. 1984–2002; attended Sixth Ordinary Ass. World Synod of Bishops, Vatican City 1983, Second Extraordinary Ass. World Synod of Bishops, Vatican City 1985; Pres. Latin American Episcopal Council 1991; Grand Cross of Isabella the Catholic (Spain) 1989; hon. degrees from Univ. of Santo Domingo and Creighton Univ., Neb., USA. *Address:* Calle Pellerano Alfau 1, Ciudad Colonial, Santo Domingo, Dominican Republic (office). *Telephone:* 221-8430 (office). *Fax:* 685-0227 (office).

LÓPEZ SUÁREZ, Guillermo; Salvadorean banker and politician; ed Inst. of Tech. and Higher Studies, Monterrey, Mexico, N Dakota State School of Science, USA; Asst to Dir-Gen., Empresa Cocotera and Empresa Cafetalera Sol Mollet 1978–81; Head of Finance, Granjero and Sello de Oro 1983–84; Dir-Gen. Grupo Lotisa, Maquilishuat, and Cumbres de Cuscatlán 1984–97; Financial Dir Grupo Avicola Salvadoreña and Grupo La Sultana 1987–95, apptd Dir-Gen. 1995; Dir-Gen. Grupo Pollo Campero 1994–2004; Minister of the Treasury 2004–06 (resgnd); Pres. Comisión Ejecutiva Portuaria Autónoma (CEPA) –2010; Minister of Agriculture and Livestock 2010–12 (resgnd); fmr Adviser to Nat. Asscn of Pvt. Commerce, Asscn of Poultry Farmers of El Salvador, Fed. of Poultry Farmers of Cen. America and the Caribbean; fmr mem. Bd of Govs World Bank, IBRD, Int. Finance Corpn, IDA.

LORAN, Oleg Borisovich, DrMed; Russian surgeon and urologist; b. 24 June 1943, Moscow; s. of Boris Yulievich Loran and Irina Donatovna Loran; m. Irina Petrovna Grebennikova; one s. two d.; ed Moscow Sechenov Inst. of Medicine; surgeon, Salda City Hosp., Sverdlovsk Region 1966–69; intern, urologist, Moscow Botkin Hosp. of Urgent Medicine 1969–72; Asst, Head Div. of Urology, Prof., Moscow Medical Inst. of Stomatology (now Moscow State Medical and Stomatological Univ.) 1972–; Chief Urologist, Ministry of Public Health of Russian Fed.; Chief Scientific Sec., Russian Soc. of Urologists 1978; mem. Exec. Bd East European Soc. of Urologists, Bd Russian Asscn of Oncological Urology; mem. Editorial Bd journals Urology and Nephrology, Annals of Surgery; mem. Higher Attestation Comm. of Russian Fed.; mem. European Asscn of Urologists 1992; Diplomas of American Asscn of Urologists and American Urological Foundation. *Publications:* more than 230 scientific works including nine books on problems of urology, ten patents. *Leisure interests:* music, theatre. *Address:* Moscow State Medical Stomatological Institute, Delegatskaya str. 20/1, 127473 Moscow, Russia (office). *Telephone:* (495) 281-65-13 (office). *Website:* www.msmsu.ru (office).

LORCH, George A., BS; American business executive; ed Virginia Polytechnic Inst. and State Univ.; joined Armstrong Holdings Inc. 1963, held various marketing positions 1963–83, Group Vice-Pres. for Carpet Operations 1983–88, Exec. Vice-Pres. 1988–93, Pres. and CEO 1993–94, Chair. May–Aug. 2000, mem. Bd of Dirs Armstrong World Industries Inc. (subsidiary) 1988–2000, Pres. and CEO 1993–2000, Chair. 1994–2000, Chair. Emer. Armstrong Holdings Inc. 2000–; mem. Bd of Dirs Pfizer Inc. 2000–15, Chair. (non-exec.) 2010–11, Lead Ind. Dir 2011–15; Ind. Dir, Autoliv Inc. 2003–14, Lead Ind. Dir 2014–; mem. Bd of Dirs Dir HSBC Finance Corpn 1994–, HSBC North America Holdings Inc., JPM Naples Event, Warner-Lambert Co. 1997, RR Donnelley & Sons Co. 2001–11, The Williams Cos Inc. 2001–11, WPX Energy, Inc. 2011–, Masonite International, Inc. 2009–.

LORD, Hon. Bernard, BA, QC; Canadian politician; *CEO, Medavie Blue Cross;* b. 27 Sept. 1965, Roberval, Quebec; s. of Ralph Frank Lord and Marie-Emilie; m. Diane Lord 1990; two c.; ed Université de Moncton; Leader, Progressive Conservative Party of NB 1997; MLA for Moncton East (becoming Leader of the Official Opposition) 1998–2007; Premier of NB 1999–2006, also Pres. of Exec. Council, Minister of Intergovernmental Affairs, Minister responsible for NB Advisory Council on Youth, Minister responsible for Premier's Council on Status of Disabled Persons; apptd Chair. Ontario Power Generation 2014; Pres. and CEO Canadian Wireless Telecommunication Asscn of Canada; CEO Medavie Blue Cross (not-for-profit health services provider and insurance co.) 2016–; Order of New Brunswick 2007, Grand Officier, Ordre de la Pléiade, Int. Asscn of Francophone Parliamentarians; Dr hc (Univ. of New Brunswick), (Université de Moncton); Alumni of the Year from the Université de Moncton. *Address:* Medavie Blue Cross, 644 Main Street, Moncton, NB E1C 1E2, Canada (office). *Website:* web.medavie.bluecross.ca (office).

LORD, Winston, BA, MA; American civil servant and diplomatist; *Chairman Emeritus, International Rescue Committee;* b. 14 Aug. 1937, New York; s. of Oswald Bates Lord and Mary Lord (née Pillsbury); m. Bette Bao 1963; one s. one d.; ed Yale Univ., Fletcher School of Law and Diplomacy; mem. Staff Congressional Relations, Politico-mil. and Econ. Affairs, US Dept of State, Washington, DC 1961–65, Geneva 1965–67; mem. staff Int. Affairs, US Dept of Defense, Washington, DC 1967–69; mem. staff Nat. Security Council 1969–73, Special Asst to Asst to Pres. on Security Affairs 1970–73; Dir Policy Planning Staff, US Dept of State 1973–77; Pres. Council on Foreign Relations 1977–85; Amb. to People's Repub. of China 1985–89; freelance lecturer, writer New York 1989–93; Asst Sec. of State for East Asian and Pacific Affairs 1993; Chair. Carnegie Endowment Nat. Comm. on America and the New World 1991–92, Nat. Endowment for Democracy 1992–93; Vice-Chair. Int. Rescue Cttee 1991–93, Co-Chair. 1997–2005, Chair. Emer. 2005–; fmr mem. Bd of Dirs Fletcher School of Law and Diplomacy, Nat. Cttee on US–China Relations, Nat. Endowment for Democracy, US–Japan Foundation; mem. Global Advisory Council, WTA Tour, Inc.; several hon. degrees; Freedom Award, Int. Rescue Cttee, Pentagon's Outstanding Performance Award, State Department's Distinguished Service Award, National Cttee on US-China Relations Award, Hotchkiss and Fletcher Alumni Awards. *Leisure interests:* sports, literature, arts. *Address:* International Rescue Committee, 122 East 42nd Street, New York, NY 10168-1289, USA.

LORDKIPANIDZE, Vazha Giorgevich, DEcon; Georgian politician, sociologist, demographer and academic; *Head of Demography Department, Tbilisi State University;* b. 29 Nov. 1949, Tbilisi; m. Irina Khomeriki 1983; two d.; ed Tbilisi State Univ., Moscow Acad. of Social Sciences; joined Faculty, Tbilisi State Univ. 1975, Head, Demography Dept 2000–; Sec., Second, First Secr. Cen. Comsomol Cttee of Georgia 1980–86, First Sec., Tbilisi Dist CP Cttee 1986–88, Head, Dept of Culture and Ideology Cen. Cttee, CP of Georgia 1988–90; Sr Researcher, Inst. of Demography and Sociology, Georgian Acad. of Sciences 1991–92; Chief State Counsellor, State Council of Georgia 1992; Head of Personnel, Eduard Shevardnadze Admin. 1992–95; Amb. to Russia 1995–98; Minister of State 1998–2000; mem. Parl. 2000–04; apptd Pres. Demographers Asscn of Georgia 2000, Vice-Pres. Int. Research Centre for East–West Relationships 2000; mem. Georgian Acad. of Econs 1996–, UN Int. Acad. of Informatics; Pres. Special Olympic Cttee 2001; Head of Christian Democrat Party of Georgia 2002. *Publications include:* various scientific articles, monographs and books. *Leisure interest:* football. *Address:* Demography Department, Tbilisi State University, Building/block 6, Ilia Chavchavadze Avenue no.14, 380079 Tbilisi (office); 5 Larsi Street, Flat 9, Tbilisi, Georgia (home). *Telephone:* (32) 25-02-61 (office); (32) 23-20-70 (home). *Fax:* (32) 25-12-39 (office); (32) 233259 (office); (32) 99-05-13 (home). *E-mail:* ikhomeriki@hotmail.com.

LOREN, Sophia; Italian actress; b. (Sofia Villani Scicolone), 20 Sept. 1934, Rome; d. of Riccardo Scicolone and Romilda Villani; m. 1st the late Carlo Ponti 1957 (marriage annulled 1962), m. again 1966 (died 2007); two s.; ed Scuole Magistrali Superiori; first screen appearance as extra in Quo Vadis; Chair. Nat. Alliance for Prevention and Treatment of Child Abuse and Maltreatment; Goodwill Amb. for

Refugees 1992; Chevalier, Légion d'honneur; numerous awards including Hon. Acad. Award for Lifetime Achievement 1990, Praemium Imperiale 2010. *Films include:* E Arrivato l'Accordatore 1951, Africa sotto i Mari (first leading role), La Tratta delle Bianche, La Favorita 1952, Aida 1953, Il Paese dei Campanelli, Miseria e Nobiltà, Il Segno di Venere 1953, Tempi Nostri 1953, Carosello Napoletano 1953, L'Oro di Napoli 1954, Attila 1954, Peccato che sia una canaglia, La Bella Mugnaia, La Donna del Fiume 1955, Boccaccio 1970, Matrimonio All'Italiana; and in the following American films: The Pride and the Passion 1955, Boy on a Dolphin, Legend of the Lost 1956, Desire Under the Elms 1957, That Kind of Woman 1958, Houseboat 1958, The Key 1958, The Black Orchid (Venice Festival Award 1958) 1958, It Started in Naples, Heller in Pink Tights 1960, The Millionairess 1961, Two Women (Cannes Film Festival Award for Best Actress 1961) 1961, El Cid 1961, Madame Sans Gêne 1962, Yesterday, Today and Tomorrow 1963, The Fall of the Roman Empire 1964, Lady L 1965, Operation Crossbow 1965, Judith 1965, A Countess from Hong Kong 1965, Arabesque 1966, More than a Miracle 1967, The Priest's Wife 1970, Sunflower 1970, Hot Autumn 1971, Man of La Mancha 1972, Brief Encounter (TV) 1974, The Verdict 1974, The Voyage 1974, The Cassandra Crossing 1977, A Special Day 1977, Firepower 1978, Brass Target 1979, Blood Feud 1981, Mother Courage 1986, Two Women 1989, Prêt à Porter 1994, Grumpier Old Men 1995, Between Strangers 2002, Peperoni ripieni e pesci in faccia 2004, Nine 2009, My House Is Full of Mirrors 2010. *Publications:* Eat with Me 1972, Sophia Loren on Women and Beauty 1984, Yesterday, Today, Tomorrow: My Life as a Fairy Tale 2014. *Address:* Case Postale 430, 1211 Geneva 12, Switzerland.

LORENTZ, Francis; French business executive; *Executive Chairman, LD&A Jupiter;* b. 22 May 1942, Mulhouse; s. of Paul Lorentz and Lucienne Lorentz (née Biechy); m. Laure Doumenc; three c.; ed Lycée Kléber, Strasbourg, Ecole des Hautes Etudes Commerciales, Ecole Nat. d'Admin; with Ministry of Economy 1970–80; Exec. Vice-Pres. Société Lyonnaise des Eaux 1980–82; joined Honeywell-Bull as CEO 1982, Chair. and CEO Groupe Bull 1987–92; Chair. Dir-Gen. Régie autonome des transports parisiens (RATP) 1992–94; Prof., Univ. of Paris-Dauphine 1994–2000; Chair. Etablissement public de financement et de restructuration (EPFR) 1996–2000; Head of French Nat. e-Business Task Force 1997–2000; Dir Gen. Laser (groupe Galeries Lafayette) 2000–04; CEO e-LaSer and LaSer Informatique 2000–04; Chair. Institut de l'audiovisuel et des télécommunications en Europe (IDATE) 2000–11, Digiworld Inst. 2012–; Exec. Chair. Lorentz, Deschamps et Associés (now LD&A Jupiter) 2004–; Chevalier du mérite nat., Chevalier, légion d'honneur. *Publications:* several publs on devt admin, state-owned cos, industrial policy and future of e-commerce. *Leisure interests:* skiing, mountaineering, contemporary art, wine tasting, diving, tennis. *Address:* LD&A Jupiter, 8 rue Halévy, 75009 Paris, France (office). *Telephone:* 1-58-18-39-00 (office). *Fax:* 1-53-43-09-76 (office). *E-mail:* florentz@ldajupiter.com (office). *Website:* www.ldajupiter.com (office).

LORENZ, Hans-Walter, Dr rer. pol; German economist; *Professor of Economics, Friedrich Schiller University Jena;* b. 3 Aug. 1951, Bielefeld; s. of Walter Lorenz and Lieselotte Lorenz; m. Karin Hottmann 1987; ed Univ. of Göttingen; Research Asst, Univ. of Göttingen 1977–82, Asst Prof. 1984–91, Privatdozent 1991–94; Prof. of Econs, Friedrich Schiller Univ. 1994–; Visiting Scholar, Univ. of California, Berkeley, USA 1982–83; Visiting Prof., Univ. of Tech., Sydney, Australia 1999. *Publications include:* Business Cycle Theory (with G. Gabisch) 1987 (second edn 1989), Nonlinear Dynamical Economics and Chaotic Motion 1989 (second edn 1993, Japanese edn 2001), Determinismus, nicht-lineare Dynamik und wirtschaftliche Evolution 1990, Studien zur Evolutorischen Ökonomik III. Schriften des Vereins für Socialpolitik (co-ed.) 1995, Studien zur Evolutorischen Ökonomik IV. Schriften des Vereins für Socialpolitik (co-ed.) 2001; numerous articles in professional journals; several book reviews. *Address:* Room 4.149, Wirtschaftswissenschaftlichen Fakultät, Friedrich-Schiller-Univerität, Carl-Zeiß-Str. 3, 07743 Jena (office); Hermann-Föge-Weg 1A, 37073 Göttingen, Germany (home). *Telephone:* (3641) 943210 (office); (551) 44317 (home). *Fax:* (3641) 943212 (office); (551) 44974 (home). *E-mail:* H.W.Lorenz@wiwi.uni-jena.de (office). *Website:* www.wiwi.uni-jena.de/Makro/index.html (office).

LORENZANA, Maj.-Gen. (retd) Delfin; Philippine government official and fmr army officer; *Secretary of National Defense;* b. Banga, South Cotabato; ed Philippine Mil. Acad.; commissioned as Second Lt in Philippine Army 1973, military roles included Commdr, Scout Ranger Co., Scout Ranger Bn and Light Armor Brigade, Instructor, Scout Ranger School and Philippine Army Training Command, Commdr of Special Operations Command (SOCOM), Defense and Armed Forces Attaché, Embassy in Washington, DC, retd from army 2004; Presidential Rep. and Head, Office of Veterans Affairs, Embassy in Washington, DC 2004–09, 2013; Sec. of Nat. Defense 2016–; Philippine Legion of Honor. *Address:* Department of National Defense, DND Bldg, 3rd Floor, Camp Aguinaldo, Quezon City, 1110 Metro Manila, Philippines (office). *Telephone:* (2) 9116402 (office). *Fax:* (2) 9111651 (office). *E-mail:* webmaster@dnd.gov.ph (office). *Website:* www.dnd.gov.ph (office).

LORENZINO, Hernán Gaspar, LLB, MEconSc; Argentine lawyer, politician and diplomatist; b. 5 March 1972, La Plata; ed Nat. Univ. of La Plata, Torcuato di Tella Univ.; Prov. Dir of Funding Policy and Public Credit, Prov. of Buenos Aires 2004–07; Financial Rep. for Argentina, Washington, DC 2007–08; Sec. of Finance, Ministry of the Economy 2008–11, Minister of the Economy and Public Finance 2011–13; fmr mem. La graN maKro (econ. and social policy think-tank); Amb. to EU, Brussels 2013–16. *Address:* Ministry of Foreign Affairs, International Trade and Worship, Esmeralda 1212, C1007ABR Buenos Aires, Argentina (office). *Telephone:* (11) 4819-7000 (office). *E-mail:* info@cancilleria.gob.ar (office). *Website:* www.cancilleria.gov.ar (office).

LORENZO ESTEFAN, Fernando, LicEcon, PhD; Uruguayan economist and politician; b. 31 Jan. 1960, Montevideo; ed Univ. de la República, Montevideo, Univ. de Paris IX-Dauphine, France, Univ. Carlos III de Madrid, Spain; Prof. of Econs, Univ. ORT, Montevideo 1998–, Univ. de la República 2001–; Researcher, Centro de Investigaciones Económicas (CINVE-Uruguay) 1995–97, Dir 1997–2004; fmr Dir, Commercial Policy Consultancy, Ministry of Economy and Finance, Dir Macroeconomic and Financial Consultancy 2005–08, Minister of Economy and Finance 2010–13; consultant on nat. and int. econ. affairs; Pres. Mercosur Econ. Investigation Network; mem. Asamblea Uruguay. *Publications include:* numerous research papers and publs on macroeconomic issues, int. trade and finance. *Address:* Asamblea Uruguay, Carlos Quijano 1273 Montevideo, Uruguay (office). *Telephone:* (2) 9032121 (office). *Fax:* (2) 9241147 (office). *E-mail:* info@2121.org.uy (office). *Website:* www.2121.org.uy (office).

LORGAT, Haroon, BCom; South African accountant, business executive and sports administrator; b. 26 May 1960, Port Elizabeth; m. Farah Ebrahim 1985; one s. one d.; ed Rhodes Univ.; leading cricket all-rounder in SA, played in 76 First-class games 1977–91; qualified as CA 1985; worked briefly in man. at IBM before founding professional services firm, built large ind. firm through a series of mergers over 15 years before successfully merging with Ernst & Young, apptd Man. Partner for Ernst & Young Western Cape and served on Nat. Exec. Cttee 2002–07; f. Kapela Investment Holdings (pvt. equity firm), Cape Town and Johannesburg 2006; Chief Exec. Int. Cricket Council 2008–12; has served in various capacities in South African cricket, including as Chair. Western Prov. Professional Cricket and as non-exec. Bd mem. Western Prov. Cricket Asscn, served as a non-exec. Dir for Cricket South Africa overseeing finance, Chair. Nat. Selectors for the South Africa cricket team 2004–07, CEO Cricket South Africa 2013–17; mem. South African Inst. of Chartered Accountants. *Leisure interests:* golf, travel.

LORIMER, George Huntly, BSc, MS, PhD, FRS; British/American scientist and academic; *Distinguished University Professor, University of Maryland, College Park;* b. 14 Oct. 1942, Edinburgh, Scotland, UK; s. of Gordon Lorimer and Ellen Lorimer; m. Freia Schulz-Baldes 1970; one s. one d.; ed George Watson's Coll., Edinburgh, Univ. of St Andrews and Univ. of Illinois and Michigan State Univ., USA; scientist, Max-Planck Soc., Berlin 1972–74; Research Fellow, Inst. for Advanced Studies, Canberra 1974–77; Prin. Investigator, then Research Leader, Cen. Research Dept, E.I. Du Pont de Nemours & Co. 1978–91, Dupont Fellow 1991–97; currently Distinguished Univ. Prof., Univ. of Maryland, College Park; scientist, Soc. for Environmental Research, Munich 1977; mem. Editorial Bd Journal of Biological Chemistry 1998; mem. NAS 1997; Resident Scholar, Rockefeller Foundation Bellagio, Italy 1992, Research Award, Alexander von Humboldt Foundation 1997. *Publications include:* Osmotically Induced Water Movements in Corn Mitochondria 1969, The Role of Oxygen in Photorespiration 1972, Molecular Chaperones (Methods in Enzymology Vol. 290) 1998. *Leisure interests:* philately, music. *Address:* Department of Chemistry and Biochemistry, University of Maryland, 2121-Biomolecular Sciences Building, 2300 Symons Hall, College Park, MD 20742-3281 (office); 7705 Lake Glen Drive, Glen Dale, MD 20769, USA (home). *Telephone:* (301) 405-1828 (office). *Fax:* (301) 314-9121 (office). *E-mail:* glorimer@umd.edu (office). *Website:* www.chem.umd.edu/faculty-staff-directory/facultydirectory/george-lorimer (office); www.biochem.umd.edu/faculty/lorimer.htm (office).

LORING, Jeanne, BS, PhD; American biologist and academic; *Director, Center for Regenerative Medicine, Scripps Research Institute;* ed Univ. of Washington, Univ. of Oregon; Asst Prof. of Embryology, Univ. of Calif., Davis 1982–87; Sr Staff Scientist, Parkinson's Disease Research Program, HanaBiologics Inc. 1987–89; Sr Scientist, GenPharm Int. Inc. 1989–95; Sr Research Fellow, Molecular Dynamics Inc. 1995–97; Sr Dir (Transgenics and Neurobiology), Incyte Genomics Inc. 1997–2001; Founder and Chief Scientific Officer, Arcos BioScience Inc. 1997–2004; Adjunct Prof. of Stem Cells and Regenerative Medicine and Co-Dir NIH Exploratory Center for Human Embryonic Stem Cell Research, Burnham Inst. for Medical Research 2004–, also Dir Human Embryonic Stem Cell Training Course 2004–; Prof. of Developmental Neurobiology, Scripps Research Inst. 2007–, Dir Center for Regenerative Medicine 2008–, currently Prof., Kellogg School of Science and Tech.; currently also Adjunct Prof., Dept of Reproductive Medicine, School of Medicine, Univ. of California; mem. numerous scientific advisory bds; Educational Award, Clinical Research Professionals (San Diego chapter) 2006, Leadership Award, Burnham Inst. for Medical Research 2007, Stem Cell Research Award, Millipore Foundation 2008, 2009, Stem Cell Research Award, Esther O'Keefe Foundation 2009, 2010, Marie and Jimmy Mayer Award 2009. *Publications:* Human Stem Cell Manual: A Laboratory Guide 2007; numerous scientific papers. *Address:* Scripps Research Institute, 10550 North Torrey Pines Road, La Jolla, CA 92037, USA (office). *Telephone:* (858) 784-7767 (office). *E-mail:* jloring@scripps.edu (office). *Website:* www.scripps.edu (office).

LORING, John Robbins, BA; American artist, designer and author; *Design Director Emeritus, Tiffany & Co.;* b. 23 Nov. 1939, Chicago, Ill.; s. of Edward D'Arcy and China Robbins Loring (née Logeman); ed Yale Univ., Ecole des Beaux Arts, Paris; Distinguished Visiting Prof., Univ. of Calif., Davis 1977; Bureau Chief Architectural Digest magazine, New York 1977–78; Design Dir Tiffany and Co., New York 1979–2009, now Design Dir Emer., Exec. Vice-Pres., 1981–84, Sr Vice-Pres. Design and Merchandising 1984–; mem. acquisitions comm. Dept of prints and illustrated books, Museum of Modern Art, New York 1990–; Contributing Ed. Arts magazine 1973–; work in perm. collections Museum of Modern Art, New York, Whitney Museum of American Art, Chicago Art Inst., Boston Museum of Fine Arts, RI School of Design, Baltimore Museum of Art, Yale Univ. Art Gallery, NY Historical Soc.; works commissioned by US Customhouse, New York, Prudential Insurance Co., Woodbridge, NJ, City of Scranton, Pa; mem. Acquisitions Cttee, Dept of Prints and Illustrated Books, Museum of Modern Art; Hon. DrArts (Pratt Inst.) 1996; Edith Wharton Award, Design and Art Soc. 1988, Distinction in Design Award, Fashion Group Int. 1996, Pratt Inst. Legends Award 2002, Dallas Fashion Award 2004, Lifetime Achievement Award, Museum of Art and Design 2005, Artistic Achievement Award, American Cancer Soc. 2010. *Publications:* The New Tiffany Table Settings 1981, Tiffany Taste 1986, Tiffany's 150 Years 1987, The Tiffany Wedding 1988, Tiffany Parties 1989, The Tiffany Gourmet 1992, A Tiffany Christmas 1996, Tiffany's 20th Century 1997, Tiffany Jewels 1999, Paulding Farnham, Tiffany's Last Genius 2000, Magnificent Tiffany Silver 2001, Louis Comfort Tiffany at Tiffany & Co. 2002, Tiffany in Fashion 2003, Greetings from Andy Warhol 2004, Tiffany Timepieces 2004, Tiffany's Palm Beach 2005, Tiffany Diamonds 2005, Tiffany Pearls 2006, Tiffany Colored Gems 2007, Tivoli Gardens 2007, Tiffany Style 2008. *Leisure interests:* collecting 20th-century decorative arts, writing on design and lifestyle, cooking. *Address:* 621 Avon Road, West Palm Beach, FL 33401, USA (home). *Telephone:* (561) 659-3452 (home). *Fax:* (561) 651-7009 (home).

LORIUS, Claude, LèsSc, DèsSc, PhD; French glaciologist, academic and research institute director; b. 27 Feb. 1932, Besançon; ed Univ. of Besançon; joined CNRS, Grenoble 1953, apptd Research Dir 1987, Assoc. Dir 1979–83, Dir Laboratoire de glaciologie et geophysique de l'environnement 1984–89, Pres. Institut Français pour la Recherche et la Technologie polaires (IFRTP) 1992–98, Dir Emer. of Research, CNRS 1998–2008; responsibilities at Ministries of Research and the Environment, French Nat. Cttee on Antarctic Research 1987–94, mem. World Climate Research Programme (OMM-ICSU) 1980–84, Exec. Cttee Past Global Changes (IGBP) 1989–98, European Cttee on Oceanography and Polar Sciences (European Science Foundation (ESF) and EC) 1989–97, Exec. Cttee Greenland Ice Core Project 1989–93; contributed to work of Scientific Cttee on Antarctic Research, Int. Council for Science (Pres. 1986–90), Int. Arctic Science Cttee 1991–98; led a working group on glaciology, ESF 1985–93; presided over European Program for Ice Coring in Antarctica project 1993–95; has helped organize many int. collaborations, notably the Vostok ice core; Corresp. mem. Acad. des Sciences (mem. 1994), Acad. des Technologies 2000; Foreign mem. Russian Acad. of Sciences 1994; mem. Academia Europaea 1989; Fellow, European Geophysical Soc. 1999; Officier, Légion d'honneur 1998, Grand Officier, Ordre national du Mérite 2015; Humbold Prize 1989, Belgica Medal 1989, Italgas Prize 1994, Tyler Prize for Environmental Achievement 1996, Balzan Prize for climatology (jtly with Jean Jouzel) 2001, Medaille d'or du CNRS 2002, Vernadsky Medal, European Geosciences Union 2006, Blue Planet Prize, Asahi Glass Foundation (co-recipient) 2008. *Achievements include:* was instrumental in discovery and interpretation of palaeo-atmosphere information within ice cores; took part in 22 polar expeditions, mostly to Antarctica, led several French polar expeditions 1984–87. *Publications include:* Glaces de l'Antarctique: une mémoire, des passions 1991, L'Antarctique (with R. Gendrin) 1997; more than 100 scientific papers in professional journals. *Website:* www.claude-lorius.com.

LORTIE, Marc, BA; Canadian diplomatist; b. 1948, Beauport, Québec; m. Patricia Dunn; ed Séminaire de Québec, Laval Univ.; joined Dept of External Affairs 1971, overseas postings include in Tunisia 1973–75, in USA 1979–83; Head, Int. Media Relations, Office of Prime Minister, Ottawa 1985–87, Press Sec. 1987–89; Minister-Counsellor for Political Affairs, Embassy in Paris and Personal Rep. of Prime Minister for La Francophonie 1989–93; Sr Coordinator for Fed.-Prov. Relations, Dept of Foreign Affairs and Int. Trade 1998–2000, Asst Deputy Minister of Americas 2001; apptd Personal Rep. of Prime Minister, Third Summit of the Americas 2000; Amb. to Chile 1993–97, to Spain 2004–07, to France 2007–12; fmr Fellow, Centre for Int. Affairs, Harvard Univ. *Address:* Foreign Affairs, Trade and Development Canada, Lester B. Pearson Building, 125 Sussex Drive, Ottawa, ON K1A 0G2, Canada (office). *Telephone:* (613) 944-4000 (office). *Fax:* (613) 996-9709 (office). *E-mail:* enqserv@international.gc.ca (office). *Website:* www.international.gc.ca (office).

LOSANG, Jamcan (Gyaltsen); Tibetan politician; *Chairman, People's Congress, Tibet Autonomous Region;* b. 1957, Zhag'yab County, Tibet Autonomous Region; ed Tibet Nationality Coll., CCP Cen. Cttee Party School; joined CCP 1978; Teacher, Tibet Inst. of Nationalities 1979–84; Sec., Communist Youth League of China (CYLC) Student Dept, Tibet Autonomous Region (TAR) 1984–86, Sec. CYLC, TAR 1986–92; Commr, Prefectural Admin. Office, Nagchu Prefecture, TAR 1992–95, also Sec., CCP TAR Autonomous Prefectural Cttee 1992–95; Deputy Sec., CCP Autonomous City Cttee, Lhasa 1995–2003, Deputy Mayor of Lhasa 1995–96, Mayor 1996–2003; Vice-Chair., TAR People's Govt 2002–10, 2010–12, Chair. 2012–17; mem. Standing Cttee, CCP Autonomous Regional Cttee, TAR 2006–, Deputy Sec. 2016–; Chair., People's Congress, TAR 2017–; mem. Standing Cttee, CCP Autonomous Regional Cttee, TAR 2006–; Deputy, 11th Nat. People's Congress 2008–13; Alt. mem., 18th CCP Cen. Cttee 2012–17, 19th CCP Cen. Cttee 2017–. *Address:* Tibet Autonomous Region People's Congress, 85000 Lhasa, Tibet, People's Republic of China.

LÖSCHNAK, Franz, DJur; Austrian jurist and politician; b. 4 March 1940, Vienna; m.; one s.; ed Univ. of Vienna; employed with Vienna City Council 1959–77, Dir of Personnel Affairs and Admin. Org. 1977; Under-Sec. Fed. Chancellery 1977; Minister, Fed. Chancellery 1985–87; Minister of Health and the Civil Service 1987–89; Minister of the Interior 1989–95; formed legal base of the Austrian Holocaust Memorial Service 1992; Pres. Vienna Athletic Sports Meeting 1982; Vice-Pres. Fed. Athletic Sports Meeting 1983, Pres. 1989; Pres. Austrian Sports Meeting 1995; Pres. Org. to Support the Austrian and Chinese Econ. Co-operation *c.* 2007; Decoration of Honour for Services to the Repub. of Austria; Order of Leopold II. *Publication:* Menschen aus der Fremde: Fluchtlinge, Vertriebene, Gastarbeiter (Themen der Zeit) 1993.

LØSETH, Øystein, BEcon, MSc; Norwegian energy industry executive; *Chairman, Statoil ASA;* b. 1958; m.; three c.; ed Bedriftsøkonomisk Institutt Norwegian School of Man., Bergen, Norwegian Univ. of Science and Tech.; held various positions at Statoil 1984–93; Planning Man., Alliance Gas, London, UK 1993–94; Commercial Dir Naturkraft, Oslo 1994–97; Man. Dir Statkraft Energy Europe, Dir, Head of Strategy Div. and M&A, mem. Bd responsible for Production, Business Devt and R&D, Statkraft, Norway and the Netherlands 1997–2003; Man. Dir Nuon Energy Sourcing and CEO Nuon NV, Amsterdam, Netherlands 2003–09, mem. Bd of Dirs 2008–09; First Exec. Sr Vice-Pres. and Head of Business Group Benelux, Vattenfall AB 2009–10, Pres. and CEO Vattenfall AB 2010–14; mem. Bd of Dirs, Statoil ASA 2014–, Chair. 2015–; Chair. Eidsiva Energi AS. *Leisure interests:* trekking, cross-country skiing and mountain biking. *Address:* Statoil ASA, Forusbeen 50, 4035 Stavanger, Norway (office). *Telephone:* 51-99-00-00 (office). *Fax:* 51-99-00-50 (office). *E-mail:* statoil@statoil.com (office). *Website:* www .statoil.com (office).

LOSHCHININ, Valery Vassilyevich; Russian diplomatist; b. 11 Sept. 1940, Gomel Region, Byelorussia; m.; two s. two d.; ed Belarus State Univ., Diplomatic Acad. of USSR Ministry of Foreign Affairs; with Ministry of Foreign Affairs, Belarus SSR, then USSR Ministry of Foreign Affairs 1965–77; with Perm. Mission to Russia 1977–89, Deputy Perm. Rep. to Int. Orgs, Geneva 1989–95, Dir Second European Dept, Russian Ministry of Foreign Affairs 1995–96, Amb. to Belarus 1996–99, Amb. and Perm. Rep. to UN and other Int. Orgs, Vienna 1999–2001, Deputy Minister of Foreign Affairs (responsible for relations with CIS countries) 2001–02, First Deputy Minister of Foreign Affairs 2002–05, Amb. and Perm. Rep. to UN and other Int. Orgs, Geneva 2006–11. *Address:* Ministry of Foreign Affairs, 119200 Moscow, Smolenskaya-Sennaya pl. 32/34, Russia (office). *Telephone:* (499) 244-16-06 (office). *Fax:* (499) 244-34-48 (office). *E-mail:* ministry@mid.ru (office). *Website:* www.mid.ru (office).

LOTT, Dame Felicity Ann Emwhyla, DBE, CBE, BA, LRAM, FRAM; British singer (soprano); b. 8 May 1947, Cheltenham, Glos.; d. of John A. Lott and Whyla Lott (née Williams); m. 1st Robin Golding 1973 (divorced); m. 2nd Gabriel Woolf 1984; one d.; ed Pate's Grammar School for Girls, Cheltenham, Royal Holloway Coll., Univ. of London and Royal Acad. of Music; debut with ENO as Pamina in Die Zauberflöte 1975; prin. roles at Glyndebourne, Covent Garden, ENO, WNO, New York Metropolitan Opera, Vienna, La Scala, Paris Opéra, Brussels, Hamburg, Munich, Chicago, San Francisco, Dresden; wide recital repertoire; Founder-mem. Songmakers Almanac; mem. Equity, Inc. Soc. of Musicians; Hon. Fellow, Royal Holloway Coll., Hon. FRCM; Officier des Arts et des Lettres 2000, Chevalier, Légion d'honneur 2001; Dr hc (Sussex) 1990, Hon. DLitt (Loughborough) 1996, Hon. DMus (London) 1997, (Royal Scottish Acad. of Music and Drama) 1998, (Oxford) 2001, (Leicester) 2010, (Gloucester) 2010, (Paris Sorbonne) 2010; Kammersängerin, Bayerische Staatsoper, Munich 2003, Wigmore Hall Medal 2010, Inc. Soc. of Musicians Distinguished Musician Award 2015, Int. Classical Music Award for Lifetime Achievement 2016. *Roles include:* Countess in Le Nozze de Figaro, Ellen Orford in Peter Grimes, Fiordiligi in Così fan Tutte, Elvira in Don Giovanni, Xiphares in Mitridate, Marschallin in Der Rosenkavalier, Countess in Capriccio (Richard Strauss), many recitals with Graham Johnson and duets with Ann Murray, DVD of Offenbach's Hélène in La Belle Hélène and La Grande Duchesse. *Publications:* Il nous faut de l'amour (with Olivier Bellamy). *Leisure interests:* reading, gardening. *Address:* Askonas Holt Ltd, 15 Fetter Lane, London, EC4A 1BW, England (office). *Telephone:* (20) 7400-1710 (office). *Fax:* askona-sholt.co.uk (office). *E-mail:* mail@felicitylott.de. *Website:* www.felicitylott.de.

LOTT, (Chester) Trent, BPA, JD; American lawyer and fmr politician; *Senior Counsel, Squire Patton Boggs;* b. 9 Oct. 1941, Grenada, Miss.; s. of Chester P. Lott and Iona Lott (née Watson); m. Patricia E. Thompson 1964; one s. one d.; ed Univ. of Mississippi; called to Miss. Bar 1967; Assoc., Bryan & Gordon, Pascagoula, Miss. 1967; Admin. Asst to Congressman Colmer 1968–73; mem. US House of Reps from 5th Dist Miss. 1973–89, House Minority Whip 1981–89; Senator from Miss. 1989–2007 (resgnd), Senate Majority Whip 1995–96, Senate Majority Leader 1996–2001, Nov.–Dec. 2002, Minority Leader 2001–02, Minority Whip Jan.–Dec. 2007, mem. Senate Republican Policy Cttee; named as observer from House to Geneva Arms Control talks; Co-founder Breaux Lott Leadership Group (lobbying firm) 2008, firm subsequently acquired by Squire Patton Boggs, now Sr Counsel, Co-Chair. Public Policy practice; mem. American Bar Asscn; Republican; Golden Bulldog Award, Guardian of Small Business Award. *Publication:* Herding Cats: A Life in Politics 2005. *Address:* Squire Patton Boggs, 2550 M Street, NW, Washington, DC 20037, USA (office). *Telephone:* (202) 457-5290 (office). *Website:* www.squirepattonboggs.com (office).

LOU, Jiwei, BA, MEcon; Chinese politician and financial executive; b. Dec. 1950, Beijing; ed Tsinghua Univ., Chinese Acad. of Social Sciences; joined CCP 1973; following postgraduate studies, worked as Deputy Head of financial and banking office group of Gen. Office of State Council from 1982; Dir Inst. of Finance and Trade, Chinese Acad. of Social Sciences mid-1980s; apptd Deputy Dir Econ. System Reform Office, Beijing Municipality 1992; Dir Macro-Control Dept, State Comm. for Restructuring the Economy 1992–95; Vice-Gov. Guizhou Prov. 1995–98; Vice-Minister of Finance 1998–2007, Deputy Sec. CCP Leading Party Group 1998–2007; mem. Academic Affairs Cttee of State Council 1999–, Deputy Sec.-Gen. of State Council 2007; Chair. and CEO China Investment Corpn 2007–13; Minister of Finance 2013–16; Alt. mem. 17th CCP Cen. Cttee 2007–12, mem. 18th CCP Cen. Cttee 2012–. *Address:* c/o Ministry of Finance, 3 Nansanxiang, Sanlihe, Xicheng Qu, Beijing 100820, People's Republic of China (office).

LOUBOUTIN, Christian; French footwear designer; b. 7 Jan. 1964, Paris 12th arrondissement; s. of Roger Louboutin and Irene Louboutin; apprenticeship at Folies Bergères 1980–86; worked freelance for Chanel, Yves Saint Laurent, Maud Frizon and other fashion houses 1986–89; turned to garden design 1989; cr. Christian Louboutin brand and opened first boutique in Paris 1992; opened first boutique in New York 1994; began contributing for couture and ready-to-wear seasons for Jean-Paul Gaultier, Chloé, Azzaro, Diane Von Furstenberg, Victor & Rolf, Givenchy and Lanvin 1995; partnership with landscape architect Louis Benech 1997–; collaborated with film dir David Lynch on exhbn 'Fetish' 2007, partnered with Batallure Beauty LLC to launch Christian Louboutin Beauté 2012; FFANY Award, Int. Fashion Group 1996, 2008, honoured by Fashion Inst. of Tech., New York including retrospective of his work 2008, Star Honouree, Int. Fashion Group 2008. *Publication:* Christian Louboutin. *Leisure interest:* trapeze flying. *Address:* 19 rue Jean-Jacques Rousseau, 75001 Paris, France (office). *Telephone:* 1-42-36-05-31 (office). *E-mail:* info@christianlouboutin.fr (office). *Website:* www.christianlouboutin.com (office).

LOUCKS, Vernon R., Jr, BA, MBA; American business executive; *Chairman, The Aethena Group, LLC;* b. 24 Oct. 1934, Evanston, Ill.; s. of Vernon Reece Loucks and Sue Burton; m. Linda Olson; six c.; ed Yale Univ. and Harvard Graduate School of Business Admin.; served as First Lt US Marine Corps; fmr Sr Man. Consultant, George Fry & Assocs; joined Baxter Int. Inc. 1966, mem. Bd of Dirs 1975, Pres. and COO 1976–80, CEO 1980–98, Chair. 1987–99, retd as Asst to the Pres. and the CEO; Chair. InLight, Inc. 1998–2000; Co-founder and Chair. The Aethena Group, LLC (pvt. equity group) 2000–; CEO Segway LLC Jan.–Nov. 2003; Chair. Proton Therapy Global Management; mem. Advisory Bd, PAX Scientific, Inc., Five9 Technologies, LLC, Metalmark Capital LLC, Pain Therapeutics Inc. 2007– (Dir 2003–07); fmr Special Advisor, NIH; mem. Bd of Dirs, Emerson Electric Co. 1979–2011, Quaker Oats Co. 1981–2001, Affymetrix, Inc. 1993–2009, GeneSoft Pharmaceuticals 1998–2004, Anheuser-Busch Cos 1998, Edwards Lifesciences Corpn 2000–08, Oscient Pharmaceuticals Corpn 2004–05, MedAssets Inc. 2007–; mem. Business Advisory Bd, Bay City Capital LLC; Dir, Harvard Business School Bd of Assocs; Trustee, Rush Univ., Rush Univ. Medical Center, The Lawrenceville School; several awards, including Chicago Inst. of Medicine Citizen Fellowship Award 1982, Yale Medal 1997. *Address:* The Aethena Group LLC, 100 Woodbrook Lane, Baltimore, MD 21212, USA (office). *E-mail:* info@aethena.us (office). *Website:* aethena.us (office).

LOUDIYI, Abdellatif; Moroccan politician; *Minister-delegate to the Prime Minister, in charge of the Administration of National Defence;* Dir of the Treasury and of External Finance, Ministry of Economy and Finance –2003, Sec.-Gen., Ministry of Economy and Finance 2003; Minister-del. to Prime Minister, in charge of the Admin of Nat. Defence 2010–; Ind. *Address:* Office of the Prime Minister, Palais Royal, Touarga, Rabat, Morocco (office). *Telephone:* (53) 7219400 (office). *Fax:* (53) 7768656 (office). *E-mail:* courrier@pm.gov.ma (office). *Website:* www.pm.gov.ma (office).

LOUDON, Jonkheer Aarnout Alexander, LLM; Dutch fmr business executive; b. 10 Dec. 1936, The Hague; m. Talitha Adine Charlotte Boon 1962; two s.; ed Univ. of Utrecht; joined Bank Mees & Hope 1964, Head, New Issues Dept 1967; joined Akzo Group 1969, Dir Financial Affairs Akzo, Arnhem 1971; Finance Dir Akzo Coatings, France 1972; Pres. Akzo, Brazil 1975–77; mem. Man. Bd, Akzo NV 1977, Deputy Chair. 1978, Chair. 1982–94, Chair. Supervisory Bd, Akzo Nobel NV 1994–2006; Chair. Supervisory Bd, ABN AMRO Holding NV 1994–2006; mem. Supervisory Bd, Royal Dutch Petroleum Co. 1997–2003, NED Royal Dutch Shell; Sr Adviser, Cinven PLC 2006–13; mem. Senate, Dutch Parl. 1995–99; Commdr, Order of Orange Nassau. *Leisure interest:* horse riding. *Address:* Houtweg 71, 2514 BN The Hague, Netherlands (home). *Telephone:* (70) 3463260 (home). *E-mail:* aarnout@loudon.nu.

LOUDON, Rodney, DPhil, FRS; British theoretical physicist; *Professor Emeritus, University of Essex;* b. 25 July 1934, Manchester; s. of Albert Loudon and Doris Helen Loudon (née Blane); m. Mary A. Philips 1960; one s. one d.; ed Bury Grammar School, Oxford Univ.; Postdoctoral Fellow, Univ. of California at Berkeley, USA 1959–60; Scientific Civil Servant, RRE, Malvern 1960–65; mem. Tech. Staff, Bell Laboratories, Murray Hill, NJ, USA 1965–66, 1970, RCA, Zürich, Switzerland 1975, British Telecom Research Labs 1984, 1989–95; Prof. of Theoretical Physics, Univ. of Essex 1967–2007, Prof. Emeritus 2008–; Visiting Prof., Yale Univ. 1975, Univ. of Calif., Irvine 1980, Ecole Polytechnique, Lausanne 1985, Univ. of Rome 1987, 1996; Fellow, Optical Soc. of America 1994; Thomas Young Medal and Prize (Inst. of Physics) 1987, Max Born Award (Optical Soc. of America) 1992, Humboldt Award 1998. *Publications:* The Quantum Theory of Light 1973, 1983, 2000, Scattering of Light by Crystals (with W. Hayes) 1978, 2004, Surface Excitations (Ed. with V.M. Agranovich) 1984, An Introduction to the Properties of Condensed Matter (with D. Barber) 1989. *Leisure interest:* classical music. *Address:* 3 Gaston Street, East Bergholt, Colchester, Essex, CO7 6SD, England (home). *Telephone:* (1206) 298550 (home).

LOUEKOSKI, Matti Kalevi, LLM; Finnish politician, business executive and lawyer; b. 14 April 1941, Oulu; m. Pirjo Hiltunen 1969; one s. one d.; Sec.-Gen. Union of Finnish Student Corpns 1967–69; official at Ministry of Finance and Ministry of Interior 1969–70; Counsellor of Higher Educ. 1970–72; Special Adviser, Office of the Council of State 1975–76; established own law firm 1978; Dir Finnish Workers' Savings Bank 1979–83; mem. Parl. 1976–79, 1983–96; Minister of Educ. 1971–72; Minister without Portfolio Feb.–Sept. 1972; Minister of Justice 1972–75, of Justice and Nordic Co-operation 1987–90, of Finance 1990–91; Vice-Speaker of Parl. 1985–87, 1995–96; mem. Bd Bank of Finland 1996–2000, Deputy Gov. 2001–07, Alt. Gov. IMF 2000–07; mem. Financial Supervision Authority, Vice-Chair. 1996–97, Chair. 1998–2007; mem. Social Democratic Party.

LOUEMBÉ, Blaise; Gabonese government official and business executive; *Minister of Youth and Sport;* b. 20 Feb. 1960, Koulamoutou; m.; six c.; ed Université des Sciences sociales de Grenoble, France; served in several positions at Treasury, including Head of Customs Directorate 1988–90, Deputy Dir 1990–92, Gen. Man. Disbursement Services; Treas.-Paymaster Gen., Ministry of Economy, Finance, Budget and Privatization 2000–08, of the Budget, Public Accounts and the Civil Service, responsible for State Reform 2008–11, Minister of Housing, Town Planning, the Environment and Sustainable Devt 2011–12, Minister of the Digital Economy, Communication and Posts 2012–14, of Youth and Sport 2014–; owns a restaurant, estate and a private channel called Kanal 7. *Address:* Ministry of Youth and Sport, BP 2150, Libreville, Gabon (office). *Telephone:* 01-74-00-19 (office). *Fax:* 01-74-65-89 (office). *Website:* www.kanal7gabon.com.

LOUGHRAN, James, CBE, FRNCM, FRSAMD; British conductor; b. 30 June 1931, Glasgow, Scotland; s. of James Loughran and Agnes Loughran (née Fox); m. 1st Nancy Coggon 1961 (divorced 1983); two s.; m. 2nd Ludmila Navratil 1985; ed Glasgow, Bonn, Amsterdam and Milan; Assoc. Conductor, Bournemouth Symphony Orchestra 1962–65; debut Royal Opera House, Covent Garden 1964; Prin. Conductor, BBC Scottish Symphony Orchestra 1965–71; Prin. Conductor and Musical Adviser, Hallé Orchestra 1971–83, Conductor Laureate 1983–91; debut New York Philharmonic with Westminster Choir 1972; Prin. Conductor, Bamberg Symphony Orchestra 1979–83; Chief Guest Conductor BBC Welsh Symphony Orchestra 1987–90; Guest Perm. Conductor, Japan Philharmonic Symphony Orchestra 1980, Hon. Conductor 2006–; Chief Conductor, Århus Symphony Orchestra, Denmark 1996–2003, Chief Guest Conductor 2003–11; BBC Proms 1965–89 including The Last Night five times 1977–85; Liveryman, Worshipful Co. of Musicians 1992; Hon. DMus (Sheffield) 1983, (Royal Scottish Acad. of Music and Drama) 2005; First Prize, Philharmonia Orchestra Conducting Competition 1961, Mancunian of the Year 1981, Gold Disc, EMI 1983. *Recordings include:* recorded complete Beethoven Symphonies with London Symphony Orchestra as contribution to European Broadcasting Union Beethoven Bicentenary Celebrations 1969–70; recordings with Hallé, London Philharmonic, Philharmonia, BBC Symphony, Århus Symphony, Scottish Chamber Orchestra, Japan Philharmonic. *Leisure interests:* unwinding, golf. *Address:* 18 Hatfield Drive, Glasgow, G12 0YA, Scotland (home). *Telephone:* (141) 337-2091 (home). *E-mail:* jamesloughran@btinternet.com (home).

LOUIS, Jean-Victor, DenD; Belgian lawyer and academic; *Professor Emeritus, Université Libre de Bruxelles;* b. 10 Jan. 1938, Uccle; m. Maria Rosa Moya Benavent 1963; three s.; ed Univ. Libre de Bruxelles; Sec. Inst. d'Etudes Européennes, Univ. Libre de Bruxelles 1967–71, Dir 1971–72, Dir of Research 1977–80, Pres. 1980–92; Lecturer, Univ. Libre de Bruxelles 1970–73, Prof. 1973–2003, Prof. Emer. 2003–; Prof. European Univ. Inst. 1998–2002; Adviser, Nat. Bank of Belgium 1972–80, Head, Legal Dept 1980–97, Adviser to Bd of Dirs 1990–97; Pres. Belgian Asscn for European Law 1983–85; legal expert, Institutional Cttee, European Parl. 1992–94; Pres. Initiative Cttee 96, Int. European Movt 1995–98; mem., Monetary Cttee of Int. Law Asscn; Ed. Cahiers de Droit Européen 1977–; Exec. Dir Philippe Wiener-Maurice Anspach Foundation 1971–2002, Pres. 2002–13; mem. European Constitutional Law Network; Francqui Chair 2007–08; Commdr, Order of Belgian Crown; Dr hc (Univ. Paris 2) 2001; Emile Bernheim Prize 1969, P.H. Spaak Prize 1979. *Publications include:* Les règlements de la Communauté économique européenne 1969, Le Droit de la Communauté économique européenne (dir and co-author), 15 vols 1970–, The European Community Legal Order 1979, Implementing the Tokyo Round (with J. Jackson and M. Matsushita) 1984, Vers un Système européen de banques centrales (ed.) 1989, From the EMS to the Monetary Union 1990, Banking Supervision in the EC (ed.) 1995, L'Union européenne et l'avenir de ses institutions 1996, The Euro and European Integration (ed.) 1999, The Euro in the National Context (ed.) 2002, The Euro: Law, Politics, Economics (co-ed. with A. Komninos), L'Ordre juridique de l'Union européenne (with T. Ronse) 2005, L'Europe, sortir du doute 2006, L'Union européenne et sa monnaie 2009; many articles on EC law, especially in field of monetary cooperation and integration. *Address:* 524 avenue Louise, Boîte 9, 1050 Brussels, Belgium.

LOUIS-DREYFUS, Julia Scarlett Elizabeth; American actress and producer; b. 13 Jan. 1961, New York City; d. of Gérard Louis-Dreyfus and Judith LeFever Bowles; m. Brad Hall 1987; two s.; ed Holton-Arms School, Bethesda; Dr hc (Northwestern Univ.) 2007; Mark Twain Prize for American Humor 2018. *Films include:* Troll 1986, Hannah and Her Sisters 1986, Soul Man 1986, National Lampoon's Christmas Vacation 1989, Jack the Bear 1993, North 1994, Fathers' Day 1997, Deconstructing Harry 1997, A Bug's Life 1998, Picture Paris 2012, Planes 2013, Enough Said 2013. *Television includes:* Saturday Night Live 1982–85, Family Ties 1988, Day by Day 1988–89, Seinfeld (American Comedy Awards for Funniest Supporting Female Performer in a TV Series 1993, 1994, 1995, 1997, 1998, Golden Globe Award 1994, Screen Actors Guild Award 1994, 1996, 1997, Primetime Emmy Award 1996) 1990–98, Dinosaurs 1992, The Single Guy 1995, London Suite 1996, Dr. Katz, Professional Therapist 1997, Hey Arnold! 1997, Animal Farm 1999, Geppetto 2000, Curb Your Enthusiasm 2000–01, 2009, The Simpsons 2001, 2007, 2008, Watching Ellie (also producer) 2002–03, Arrested Development 2004–05, The New Adventures of Old Christine (also producer) (Primetime Emmy Award 2006) 2006–10, Saturday Night Live 2006, 2007, 2016, 30 Rock 2010, Web Therapy 2012, Veep (also exec. producer) (Primetime Emmy Award 2012, 2013, 2014, 2015, 2016, 2017, Critics' Choice Award 2013, 2014, Screen Actors Guild Award 2013, 2016, 2017, Television Critics Association Award 2014) 2012–, Inside Amy Schumer 2015. *Address:* c/o Bryan Lourd or Michael Katcher, Creative Artists Agency, 2000 Avenue Of The Stars, Los Angeles, CA 90067, USA (office). *Telephone:* (424) 288-2000 (office). *Website:* www.caa.com (office).

LOUIS-DREYFUS, Margarita, LLB; Russian/Swiss business executive; *Chairperson of the Supervisory Board, Louis Dreyfus Holding BV;* b. (Margarita Bogdanova), 1 June 1962, Leningrad (now St Petersburg); m. 2nd Robert Louis-Dreyfus 1992 (died 2009); three s.; partner Philipp Hildebrand; twin d.; ed Moscow State Univ.; Chair. Louis Dreyfus and Louis Dreyfus SAS 2009–13, Chair. Supervisory Bd, Louis Dreyfus Holding BV 2013–, Deputy Chair. Louis Dreyfus Commodities Holdings BV 2013–16, Chair. 2016–; majority shareholder of Olympique de Marseille; Capitalist of the Year Award, Le Nouvel Economist 2011. *Address:* Louis Dreyfus Commodities BV, Westblaak 92, 3012 Rotterdam, The Netherlands (office). *E-mail:* DRH-Paris@louisdreyfus.fr (office). *Website:* www.ldcom.com (office); www.louisdreyfus.com (office).

LOUISY, Dame (Calliopa) Pearlette, GCMG, DStJ, GCSL, BA, MA, PhD; Saint Lucia government official and academic; b. 8 June 1946, Laborie, Saint Lucia; d. of Rita Louisy; ed St Joseph's Convent Secondary School, Univ. of the West Indies (UWI), Université Laval, Québec, Canada, Univ. of Bristol, UK; grad. teacher, St Joseph's Convent 1969–72, 1975–76; tutor, Saint Lucia 'A' Level Coll. 1976–81, Prin. 1981–86; Dean Sir Arthur Lewis Community Coll. 1986–94, Vice-Prin. 1994–95, Prin. 1996–97; Gov.-Gen. of Saint Lucia 1997–2017; Commonwealth Scholar 1972; Hon. Distinguished Fellow, UWI 2003; Grand Cross, Order of St Lucia 1997, Dame of the Most Venerable Order of St John of Jerusalem 2001, Dame of the Equestrian Order of St Gregory the Great 2002; Hon. LLD (Bristol) 1999, (Sheffield) 2003, (UWI) 2011; Int. Woman of the Year 1998, 2001, Paul Harris Fellow, Rotary International 2001–10, Caribbean Luminary, American Foundation of the Univ. of the West Indies 2007, Woman of Distinction, Celebrating Women Int. 2016. *Publications:* A Guide to the Writing of Creole 1985, The Changing Role of the Small State in Higher Education 1993, Dilemmas of Insider Research in a Small Country Setting 1997, Higher Education in the Caribbean: Issues and Strategies 1999, Expanding the Horizons of Creole Research 1999, Globalisation and Comparative Education: A Caribbean Perspective 2001, Nation Languages and National Development in the Caribbean 2002, Whose Context for What Quality? – Informing Educational Strategies for the Caribbean 2004, Global Trends in Education – The Cultural Dimension 2007, Tertiary Education in Saint Lucia: Challenges and Priorities within the Evolving Global Environment 2011. *Leisure interests:* the performing arts, culture, gardening. *Address:* Marisule, Gros Islet, Castries, Saint Lucia, West Indies (office). *Telephone:* 450-2025 (office). *E-mail:* govgenslu@candw.lc (office).

LOUKAL, Mohamed; Algerian banking executive and fmr central banker; *Minister of Finance;* b. 19 July 1950; held several positions with State Holdings 1996–2000; apptd Chair. and CEO Bank Intercontinental Arabic, Paris 2005; CEO Banque Exterieur d'Algérie (BEA) 2001–16; apptd Co-Chair. Cttee Bancassurance 2011; apptd Chair. Union of Maghreb Banks (UBM), Tunis 2015; Gov. Banque d'Algérie (cen. bank) 2016–19; Minister of Finance 2019–; mem. Bd of Dirs and Exec. Cttee Union of Arab and French Banks (UBAF), Paris 2005–16; mem. Bd of Dirs British Arab Commercial Bank (BACB), London 2005–, Bank BIA Paris 2000–05, Arab Bank for Investment and Foreign Trade, Abu Dhabi 2004–11, Bank Arab Maghreb Investment and Trade (BAMIC) 2005–. *Address:* Ministry of Finance, Immeuble Ahmed Francis, Ben Aknoun, Algiers, Algeria (office). *Telephone:* (21) 59-51-51 (office). *E-mail:* mfmail@mf.gov.dz (office). *Website:* www.mf.gov.dz (office).

LOUSTAU-LALANNE, Maurice; Seychelles civil aviation official, administrator and politician; *Minister of Finance, Trade, Investment and Economic Planning;* ed studied aviation in UK; Dir-Gen. Civil Aviation 1981–82; Exec. Dir Int.

Operations, Air Seychelles 1983, Exec. Chair. –1988; Prin. Sec., Ministry of Tourism and Transport 1988–98, Ministry of Environment 1998–2003, Ministry of Health 2004–06; Chair. and CEO Seychelles Tourism Bd 2006–10; Amb./Prin. Sec. for Foreign Affairs, Ministry of Foreign Affairs and Transport 2010–16; Sec. of State for Health June–Dec. 2016; Minister of Tourism, Civil Aviation, Ports and Marine 2016–18, of Finance, Trade, Investment and Econ. Planning 2018–. *Leisure and interests:* golf, big game fishing, environmental protection. *Address:* Ministry of Finance, Trade, Investment and Economic Planning, Liberty House, PO Box 313, Victoria, Seychelles (office). *Telephone:* 4382000 (office). *Fax:* 4325161 (office). *E-mail:* minister@finance.gov.sc (office). *Website:* www.finance.gov.sc (office).

LOUSTEAU, Martín, BSc, MSc; Argentine economist, banker, government official and fmr diplomatist; *Member of Chamber of Deputies for Buenos Aires;* b. 8 Dec. 1970, Buenos Aires; m. Carla Peterson; one s.; ed Univ. of San Andres, London School of Econs, UK; worked at Ministry of Economy and Public Works 1996–97; Chief Economist and Dir, APL Economia (business consulting firm) 1997–2002; Adviser to Pres. of Cen. Bank and mem. Cttee on Inflation Targets 2003–04; Chief of Staff, Ministry of Production 2004–05, Minister of Production for Buenos Aires Prov. 2005; Pres. Banco de la Provincia de Buenos Aires 2005–07; Minister of the Economy 2007–08 (resgnd); Amb. to USA 2015–17 (resgnd); mem. Chamber of Deputies (Unión Cívica Radical, Buenos Aires) 2017–. *Address:* Chamber of Deputies, Av. Rivadavia 1864, Buenos Aires, C1033AAV, Argentina. *Telephone:* (11) 4127-7100. *E-mail:* mlousteau@hcdn.gob.ar. *Website:* www .evolucionenlaciudad.com.

LOUVIER, Alain; French composer, conductor and harpsichordist; b. 13 Sept. 1945, Paris; s. of René Louvier and Marthe Louvier (née Fournier); m. Marie-Paule Siruguet; one s. one d.; ed Centre Nat. de Télé-Enseignement, Conservatoire Nat. Supérieur de Musique, Paris; Dir Conservatoire Nat. de Région, Boulogne-Billancourt 1972–86, 2009–13; Dir Conservatoire Nat. Supérieur de Musique, Paris 1986–91, Prof. of Musical Analysis 1991–2010; Prix de Rome 1968, Arthur Honegger Award 1975, Paul Gilson Award 1981, Prix de la SACEM 2009. *Works include:* Chant des limbes for orchestra 1969, 3 Atmosphères for clarinet and orchestra 1974, Canto di Natale 1976, Le Clavecin non tempéré 1978, Messe des Apôtres 1978, Casta Diva (with Maurice Béjart) 1980, Poèmes de Ronsard for voice ensemble and chamber orchestra 1984, Envol d'écailles for flute, viola and harp 1986, Le Jeu des 7 Musiques for sax quartet 1986, Chant des aires for 25 flutes 1988, Agrexandrins pour piano 1992, L'Isola dei Numeri for piano 1992, Concerto for alto 1996, Météores for two pianos and orchestra 1998, String Quartet 1999, Eclipse for flute and string trio 2000, Une cloche de feu rose dans les nuages for piano and 11 voices 2000, Nuit de feu, Rumeur d'espace 2001, Herbier 2 for guitar, harp and mandolin 2004, Heptagone 2004, Solstices for children voices and piano 2005, Archimède for wind orchestra 2006, Etudes pour Agresseurs (six books for piano, clavecin, orgue) 1964–82, Etudes pour Agresseurs (book seven for piano, harpsichord, organ and orchestra) 2007, L'harpenteur étrange for harp 2009, Herbier 4 for piano and harpsichord 2011, Sonata for two violas 2013. *Publications:* L'Orchestre 1997, Louvier, Les claviers de lumière, par P.A. Castanet 2002, Messiaen et le Concert de la nature 2011. *Leisure interests:* botany and entomology. *Address:* 53 avenue Victor Hugo, 92100 Boulogne-Billancourt, France. *Telephone:* 6-85-41-53-59 (mobile). *E-mail:* alainlouvier@yahoo.fr. *Website:* alain-louvier-com.

LOUVRIER, Franck, DEng; French public relations officer and civil servant; *President, Publicis Events;* b. 30 May 1968, Nantes; ed Ecole Superieure de Gestion, Paris; Chief of Staff to Mayor of Neuilly, Nicolas Sarkozy 1999–2002; press and communications adviser to Sarkozy at Interior Ministry 2002–04, 2005–07, Finance Ministry 2004; apptd Dir of Communications, Union pour un mouvement populaire (UMP) 2004, presidential campaign of Nicolas Sarkozy 2005–06, Office of the Pres. of the Repub. 2007; elected Regional Councillor of Loire 2010; Pres. Publicis Events 2012–, Vice-Pres. Publicis Consultants 2013–; elected Advisor, City of La Baule Escoublac 2014, elected regional adviser 2015, Pres. Regional Cttee for Tourism 2016. *Address:* Publicis Events France, MSL Group, 5, rue Feydeau, 75002 Paris, France (office). *Telephone:* 1-44-82-44-68 (office). *E-mail:* franck.louvrier@publicis.com (office). *Website:* www.publicisevents.com (office); www.francklouvrier.fr.

LOUW, Eugene, BA, LLB; South African politician and lawyer; b. 15 July 1931, Cape Town; s. of Anath Louw and Johanna de Jager; m. Hantie Phyfer 1964; three s. one d.; ed Bellville High School and Univ. of Stellenbosch; Chair. Students' Council, Univ. of Stellenbosch 1957; attorney, pvt. practice, Durbanville 1964–79, 1993–; Mayor of Durbanville 1967–72; mem. Parl. for Durbanville 1974–79, Malmesbury 1972–74, Paarl 1989–94; Admin. of Cape Prov. 1979–89; Minister of Home Affairs 1989–92, of Defence and Public Works 1992–93; apptd Chair. and Sr Partner, Louw and Coetzee 1994; Chair. Nat. Huguenot Tercentenary Festival Cttee 1988, Capab 1982–88, Nat. Dias Quincentenary Festival Cttee 1988, Constitutional Investigation Cttee into Regional Local Govt; Patron Western Prov. Rugby Union 1979–89; Abe Bailey Travel Bursary Holder; Alumnus of the Year Award (Stellenbosch Univ.) 1993; recipient of seven hon. citizenships; four public buildings named after him. *Leisure interests:* politics, legal profession, sport. *Address:* 10 Watsonia Close, Plattekloof, 7500 Parow (home); PO Box 15432, 7506 Panorama, South Africa. *Telephone:* (21) 9305620 (home). *Fax:* (21) 9305621 (home).

LOUW, Raymond; South African media consultant; b. 13 Oct. 1926, Cape Town; s. of George K. E. Louw and Helen K. Louw (née Finlay); m. Jean Ramsay Byres 1950; two s. one d.; ed Parktown Boys' High School, Johannesburg, Univ. of Cape Town; reporter on Rand Daily Mail 1946–50, Worthing Herald 1951–52, North-Western Evening Mail (Barrow-in-Furness) 1953–54, Westminster Press Provincial Newspapers (London) 1955–56; Night News Ed. Rand Daily Mail 1958–59, News Ed. 1960–65, Ed. 1966–77; News Ed. Sunday Times 1959–60; Chair. SA Morning Newspaper Group 1975–77; Gen. Man. SA Associated Newspapers 1977–82, City Press, Johannesburg 1982–84; mem. Man. Cttee, South African Press Asscn 1977–82; Chair. South African Newspaper Press Conciliation Bd 1979–82; Ed. and Publr Southern Africa Report 1982–2011; Rapporteur, Five Freedoms Forum mission to Lusaka to meet banned African Nat. Congress leaders 1989; Chair. Media Defence Fund 1989–94, Campaign for Open Media 1985–94 (now merged as Freedom of Expression Inst., Chair. 1994–96); Chair. New Era

Schools Trust 1989–2007, currently mem.; Co-chair. Campaign for Independent Broadcasting 1991–94; Dir Media Business Training Foundation 1992–94; Trustee, Inst. for Advancement of Journalism 1992–; Africa Consultant, World Press Freedom Cttee 2003–09; mem. Task Group on Govt Communications 1996; mem. Exec. Bd, International Press Inst., London, 1979–87, Fellow 1994; mem. Independent Media Comm. 1994; chosen by International Press Inst. to travel to Cameroon to make plea for release from jail of the late Pius Njawe (Ed. of Le Messager) 1998, Njawe freed six months later; mem. IPI delegations to Pres. of Indonesia 2000, Zimbabwean Govt 2001, Israeli Govt 2003, Ethiopian Govt 2004 on media freedom issues; Founder and council mem. South African Nat. Editors' Forum 1996–; Vice-Pres. South African PEN 2005–, as mem. of FXI, described role of South African press between 1960 and 1994 to Truth and Reconciliation Comm. 1997; Chair. SA Chapter Media Inst. of Southern Africa 2012–; Chair. Press Council of South Africa 2007–13; Hon. DLitt (Rhodes Univ.) 2012; Pringle Medal for services to journalism 1976, 1992, Media Freedom Award, Media Inst. of Southern Africa 2005, Wrottesley Award, South African Nat. Editors' Forum 2006, 2008, 2010, Mondi-Shanduka Newspaper Lifetime Achiever Award 2007, Vodacom Journalist of the Year Lifetime Achiever Award 2010, Award for Press Freedom Campaigning, Int. Press Inst. 2010, World Press Freedom Hero Award, Int. Press Inst. 2011. *Publications include:* Four Days in Lusaka – Whites from 'Home' in talks with the ANC 1989, Report on the media situation in South Africa (for UNESCO) 1994, narrative for Nelson Mandela, Man of Destiny: A Pictorial Biography (by Peter Magubane) 1996, Undue Restriction: Laws Impacting on Media Freedom in the SADC (ed.); numerous papers and articles on the media and press freedom. *Leisure interests:* sailing, walking, travel, wildlife. *Address:* 23 Duncombe Road, Forest Town, Johannesburg 2193, South Africa (home). *Telephone:* (11) 646-8790 (home). *Fax:* (11) 646-8790 (home). *E-mail:* rlouw@sn.apc.org (office).

LOVASZ, László, CandMathSci, Dr rer. nat, DrMathSci; Hungarian/American mathematician and computer scientist; *Professor, Mathematical Institute, Eötvös Loránd University;* b. 9 March 1948, Budapest; m.; four c.; ed Eötvös Loránd Univ., Budapest; Adjunct Prof., Univ. of Waterloo, Canada 1980–90; A.D. White Prof.-at-Large, Cornell Univ., Ithaca, NY 1982–87; John von Neumann Prof., Univ. of Bonn 1985; William K. Lanman Prof. of Computer Science and Math., Yale Univ., New Haven, Conn. 1993–2000; Sr Researcher, Theory Group, Microsoft Research, Redmond, Wash. 1999–2006; Dir Math. Inst., Eötvös Loránd Univ. 2006–11, Prof. 2011–; Pres. Int. Math. Union 2007–10; Visiting Prof., Inst. for Advanced Study, Princeton, NJ 2011–12; mem. Exec. Cttee Int. Math. Union 1987–94, Abel Prize Cttee 2004–06; Ed.-in-Chief Combinatorica; Ed. 12 other journals; Corresp. mem. Hungarian Acad. of Sciences 1979 (Full mem. 1985), mem. Presidium 1990–93, 2008–, Pres. 2014–; mem. Rheinland-Westphalische Akad. der Wissenschaften 1993, European Acad. of Sciences, Arts and Humanities 1981, Academia Europaea 1991, Deutsche Akad. der Naturforscher Leopoldina 2002, Russian Acad. of Sciences 2006. Royal Dutch Acad. of Science 2006, Royal Swedish Acad of Sciences 2007, NAS 2012; affiliated with Budapest Semesters in Math. (programme in English for American and Canadian undergraduates); Hon. Prof., Univ. of Bonn 1984, Academia Sinica 1988; Hon. mem. London Math. Soc. 2009; Hungarian Nat. Order of Merit 1998; Dr hc (Univ. of Waterloo) 1992, (Univ. of Szeged, Hungary) 1999, (Budapest Univ. of Tech.) 2002, (Univ. of Calgary) 2006; Grünwald Geza Prize, Bolyai Soc. 1970 George Pólya Prize, Soc. for Industrial and Applied Math. 1979, Best Information Theory Paper Award, IEEE 1981, Ray D. Fulkerson Prize, American Math. Soc.-Math. Programming Soc. 1982, Hungarian State Prize 1985, Tibor Szele Medal, Bolyai Soc. 1992, Brouwer Medal, Dutch Math. Soc. 1993, Bolzano Medal, Czech Math. Soc. 1998, Wolf Prize (Israel) 1999, Knuth Prize, Asscn for Computing Machinery 1999, Corvin Chain Award (Hungary) 2001, Goedel Prize, Asscn for Computing Machinery-European Asscn for Theoretical Computer Science 2001, IEEE John von Neumann Medal 2005, John von Neumann Theory Prize, INFORMS 2006, Bolyai Prize (Hungary) 2007, Széchenyi Grand Prize (Hungary) 2008, Kyoto Prize, Inamori Foundation (co-recipient) 2010, Ray D. Fulkerson Prize, American Math. Soc.-Math. Prog. Soc. 2012, Barcelona Hypatia European Science Prize for Science and Tech. 2019. *Publications:* Combinatorial Problems and Exercises 1979, Algorithmic Theory of Numbers, Graphs, and Convexity 1986, Geometric Algorithms and Combinatorial Optimization 1993, Combinatorial Optimization: Papers from the Dimacs Special Year (co-author) 1995, Graph Theory and Combinatorial Biology (co-author) 1999, Computation Complexity (co-author) 2002, Discrete Mathematics: Elementary and Beyond (co-author) 2003, Handbook of Combinatorics (co-author) 2003, Discrete Mathematics and Computation 2004, Large Networks and Graph Limits 2012; more than 200 articles in math. journals and four monographs on discrete math., theory of computing and combinatorial optimization. *Address:* Eötvös Loránd Tudományegyetem, Számítógéptudományi Tanszék, Pázmány Péter sétány 1/C, 1117 Budapest, Hungary (office). *Telephone:* (1) 381-2183 (office); (1) 381-8083 (office). *E-mail:* lovasz@cs.elte.hu (office). *Website:* www.cs.elte.hu/~lovasz (office).

LOVE, Courtney; American rock musician, singer and actress; b. (Love Michelle Harrison), 9 July 1964, San Francisco, Calif.; d. of Hank Harrison and Linda Carroll; m. 1st James Moreland; m. 2nd Kurt Cobain (deceased); one s. one d.; began career as occasional actress and mem. of bands Faith No More and Babes in Toyland; Founding singer and guitarist, rock band Hole 1989–2002, 2010–12; solo artist 2003–. *Films include:* Sid and Nancy 1986, Straight To Hell 1987, Tapeheads 1988, Basquiat 1996, Feeling Minnesota 1996, The People vs Larry Flynt 1996, 200 Cigarettes 1999, Man on the Moon 1999, Beat 2000, Julie Johnson 2001, Trapped 2002, Straight to Hell Returns 2010. *Television includes:* Sons of Anarchy (series) 2014, Empire (series) 2015, Revenge (series) 2015. *Recordings include:* albums: with Hole: Retard Girl 1990, Pretty On The Inside 1991, Live Through This 1994, Celebrity Skin 1998, Nobody's Daughter 2010; solo: America's Sweetheart 2004; singles: with Hole: Beautiful Son 1993, Doll Parts 1994, Ask for It 1995, Celebrity Skin 1998, Malibu 1998, Awful 1999; solo: Mono 2004. *Publication:* Dirty Blonde (autobiog.) 2006.

LOVE, Mike; American singer and songwriter; b. 15 March 1941, Baldwin Hills, Calif.; m. Jacquelyne Love; eight c.; mem. Beach Boys 1961–; mem. own band, Endless Summer 1981; numerous tours, concerts and festival appearances; band est. Brother Records label (also now holding co.) 1967; American Music Awards Special Award of Merit 1988, Grammy Lifetime Achievement Award 2001, Ella Award, Soc. of Singers 2014. *Recordings include:* albums: with The Beach Boys:

Surfin' Safari 1962, Surfer Girl 1963, Little Deuce Coupe 1963, Shut Down Vol. 2, All Summer Long 1964, Christmas Album 1964, The Beach Boys Today! 1965, Summer Days (and Summer Nights) 1965, Beach Boys Party 1966, Pet Sounds 1966, Smiley Smile 1967, Wild Honey 1968, Friends 1968, 20/20 1969, Sunflower 1970, Surf's Up 1971, Carl and the Passions – So Tough 1972, Holland 1973, The Beach Boys in Concert 1973, Endless Summer 1974, 15 Big Ones 1976, The Beach Boys Love You 1977, M.I.U. 1978, LA (Light Album) 1979, Keepin' The Summer Alive 1980, The Beach Boys 1985, Still Cruisin' 1989, Two Rooms 1991, Summer in Paradise 1992, The Sounds of Summer: The Very Best of The Beach Boys 2003, That's Why God Made the Radio 2012; solo: Looking Back With Love 1981. *Publication:* Good Vibrations: My Life as a Beach Boy 2016. *Website:* mikelove .com.

LØVEID, Cecilie Meyer; Norwegian playwright and poet; b. 21 Aug. 1951, Mysen; d. of Erik Løveid and Ingrid Meyer; m. Bjørn H. Ianke 1978; one s. two d.; ed arts and crafts school in Bergen and studies in graphic design, theatre history and drama; mem. editorial staff, Profil (magazine) 1969; Sec. Norsk Forfattersentrum, Vestlandsardelingen 1974; Teacher, Writing Arts Centre, Bergen 1986; mem. Literary Council, Den norske Forfatterforening 1987; Prix Italia 1982, Aschehoug Prize 1984, Donbloug Prize (shared with Johannes Heggland) 1990, Ibsen Prize 1999, Gyldendal Prize 2001. *Plays:* Dobbel nytelse 1978, Måkespisere (radio play) 1982, Måkespisere 1983, Vift (radio play) 1985, Balansedame 1985, Fornuftige dyr 1986, Dobbel nytelse 1988, Tiden mellom tidene 1991, Barock Friise 1993, Maria Q. 1994, Rhindøtrene 1996, Osterrike 1998, Den riktige vind (Play for children) 1999, Visning 2005. *Publications:* poetry: Mørkets muligheter 1976, Fanget villrose 1977, Badehuset 1990, Mykt glass 1999, Spilt 2001, Gartnerløs 2007, Nye ritualer (New rituals) 2008, Svartere bunader 2010, Flytterester 2012, Straff (Punishment) 2013; prose: Most 1972, Tenk om isen skulle komme 1974, Alltid skyer over Askøy 1976, Sug 1979; children's books: Lille Pille og Lille Fille i Den dype skogs teater 1990, Hund får besøk 1992, Den riktige vind 1996, Fars ansikt 2000. *Leisure interests:* old wooden toys, walking in the mountains, swimming. *Address:* c/o Colombine Theatre Agency, Gaffelgränd 1A, 11130 Stockholm, Sweden (office); Aller house, Elsesro 28A, 5095 Bergen, Norway (home). *Telephone:* (8) 411-70-85 (office). *Fax:* (8) 411-72-85 (office). *E-mail:* info@colombine.se (office); cecilieloveid@gmail.com. *Website:* www.colombine.se (office); www.cecilieloveid.com.

LOVEJOY, Thomas Eugene, III, BS, PhD; American biologist, conservationist and academic; *Biodiversity Chair, H. John Heinz III Center for Science, Economics and the Environment;* b. 22 Aug. 1941, New York, NY; m. Charlotte Seymour 1966 (divorced 1978); three d.; ed Yale Univ.; has worked in Brazilian Amazon since 1965; directed conservation programme at World Wildlife Fund-US 1973–87; Asst Sec. for Environmental and External Affairs, Smithsonian Inst., Washington, DC 1987–98, Counsellor to Sec. for Biodiversity and Environmental Affairs 1994–2000; Science Advisor to US Sec. of the Interior 1993; Scientific Advisor to Exec. Dir UNEP 1994–97; Chief Biodiversity Advisor to Pres. World Bank and Lead Specialist for Environment for Latin America and the Caribbean 1998–2002; Sr Adviser to Pres. UN Foundation 2001–02; Pres. H. John Heinz III Center for Science, Econs, and the Environment 2002–08, Biodiversity Chair 2008–; Chair. Yale Inst. for Biospheric Studies; fmr Chair. US Man and Biosphere Program; Past Pres. American Inst. of Biological Sciences, Soc. for Conservation Biology; conceived idea for Minimum Critical Size of Ecosystems project (jt project between Smithsonian Inst. and Brazil's Instituto Nacional de Pesquisas da Amazônia); Vice-Chair. Woods Hole Research Center; mem. Bd of Dirs World Wildlife Fund; mem. External Advisory Bd Chicago Climate Exchange, Inc.; Fellow, AAAS, American Acad. of Arts and Sciences, American Philosophical Soc., Linnaean Soc. of London, American Ornithologists Union; Order of Rio Branco (Brazil), Grand Cross of the Order of Scientific Merit (Brazil) 1998; Tyler Prize for Environmental Achievement 2001, Lindbergh Award 2002, BBVA Foundation Frontiers of Knowledge Award in the Ecology and Conservation Biology category (co-recipient) 2008, Blue Planet Prize 2012. *Achievements include:* developed 'debt-for-nature swaps' for purchase of biologically sensitive tracts of land in debtor nations for purposes of environmental protection; has also supported Forests Now Declaration, calling for new market-based mechanisms to protect tropical forests; played key role in establishing conservation biology through First Int. Conf. on Research in Conservation Biology, La Jolla, Calif. Sept. 1978, introduced terms 'conservation biology' and 'biological diversity' to scientific community; serves on numerous scientific and conservation bds and advisory groups; drew up first projections of global extinction rates for Global 2000 Report to the President, predicted in 1980 extinction of 10%–20% of all species by 2020. *Television:* started public TV series Nature. *Publications:* Ecology, Conservation, and Management of Southeast Asian Rainforests 1995, Global Warming and Biological Diversity (ed.) 1994, Climate Change and Biodiversity (ed.) 2006; numerous books and articles. *Address:* H. John Heinz III Center for Science, Economics and the Environment, 900 17th Street, NW, Suite 700, Washington, DC 20006, USA (office). *Telephone:* (202) 737-6307 (office). *Fax:* (202) 737-6410 (office). *E-mail:* lovejoy@heinzctr.org (office). *Website:* www.heinzctr.org (office).

LOVELL, Harold Earl Edmund, Jr, BA, MJ; Antigua and Barbuda politician and barrister; b. 27 Sept. 1955, St John's; ed Antigua Grammar School, Univ. of the West Indies, Thames Valley Univ., Middle Temple and Univ. of Birmingham, UK; fmr teacher, Antigua Grammar School, Antigua State Coll.; Minister of Foreign Affairs, Tourism, Int. Travel and Trade 2004–05, of Tourism, Civil Aviation, Culture and the Environment 2005–09, of Finance, the Economy and Public Admin 2009–14; fmr Vice-Pres. Guild of Undergraduates, Univ. of the West Indies; fmr Gen. Sec., then Vice-Chair. Antigua Caribbean Liberation Movement; fmr Gen. Sec. Antigua and Barbuda Union of Teachers; Vice-Chair. United Progressive Party; mem. BBC Advisory Council for Leicestershire 1990–92. *Address:* United Progressive Party (UPP), UPP Headquarters Bldg, Upper Nevis St, POB 2379, St John's, Antigua and Barbuda (office).

LOVELOCK, James Ephraim, CH, CBE, PhD, DSc, FRS; British scientist, inventor, writer and academic; *Honorary Visiting Fellow, Green College, Oxford;* b. 26 July 1919, Letchworth Garden City, Herts.; s. of Tom Arthur Lovelock and Nellie Ann Elizabeth Lovelock (née March); m. 1st Helen Mary Hyslop 1942 (died 1989); two s. two d.; m. 2nd Sandra Jean Orchard 1991; ed Strand School, Univ. of Manchester, London School of Hygiene and Tropical Medicine; staff scientist, Nat. Inst. for Medical Research, London 1941–61; Prof. of Chem., Baylor Univ. Coll. of Medicine, Tex., USA 1961–64; ind. scientist 1964–; Hon. Visiting Fellow, Green Coll., Oxford 1994–; Rockefeller Travelling Fellowship in Medicine, Harvard Univ., USA 1954; Visiting Scientist, Yale Univ. Medical School 1958–59; Visiting Prof., Univ. of Reading 1967–90; Pres. Marine Biology Asscn 1986–90; Arne Naess Chair (jtly), Global Justice and the Environment, Univ. of Oslo 2007; mem. Environmentalists for Nuclear Energy; Hon. DSc (Univ. of East Anglia) 1982, (Plymouth Polytechnic) 1988, (Univ. of Exeter) 1988, (Stockholm Univ.) 1991, (Univ. of Edinburgh) 1993, (Univ. of Kent) 1996, (Univ. of East London) 1996, (Univ. of Colorado) 1997; CIBA Foundation Award for Research in Ageing 1955, three NASA Certificates of Recognition for: Gas Chromatograph Interface System and Method, Vapor Phase Detectors, Combined Carrier Gas Separator and Generator for Gas Chromatographic Systems 1972, Tswett Medal for Chromatography 1975, ACS Chromatography Award 1980, Stephen Dal Nogare Award 1985, Norbert Gerbier Prize, Silver Medal and Prize, Plymouth Marine Lab. 1986, World Meteorological Asscn 1988, Dr A. H. Heineken Prize for the Environment, Royal Netherlands Acad. of Arts and Sciences 1990, Rosenstiel Award in Oceanographic Science 1990, Nonino Prize 1996, Volvo Environment Prize 1996, The Blue Planet Prize 1997, Goi Peace Prize 2000, Discovery Lifetime Award, Royal Geographical Soc. 2001, Wollaston Medal, Geological Soc. 2006. *Achievements include:* inventor of the electron capture detector (which made possible the detection of CFCs and other atmospheric nano-pollutants) and of the microwave oven; originator of the 'Gaia hypothesis' during 1960s as a result of work for NASA concerned with detecting life on Mars; hypothesis proposes that living and non-living parts of the Earth form a complex interacting system that can be thought of as a single organism; named after Greek goddess Gaia, hypothesis postulates that biosphere has a regulatory effect on the Earth's environment that acts to sustain life. *Publications:* Gaia: A New Look at Life on Earth 1979, The Great Extinction (co-author) 1983, The Greening of Mars (co-author) 1984, The Ages of Gaia 1988, Gaia: The Practical Science of Planetary Medicine 1991, Homage to Gaia: The Life of an Independent Scientist 2000, Gaia: Medicine for an Ailing Planet 2005, The Revenge of Gaia: Why the Earth is Fighting Back: and How We Can Still Save Humanity 2006, The Vanishing Face of Gaia 2009, A Rough Ride to the Future 2014. *Leisure interests:* walking, reading novels, music. *Address:* Matthew Cottage, The Old Coastguards, Abbotsbury, Dorset, DT3 4LB, England. *Website:* www.jameslovelock.org.

LOVETT, Lyle; American singer, songwriter and actor; b. 1 Nov. 1957, Klein, Tex.; m. Julia Roberts 1993 (divorced 1995); backing singer for Nanci Griffith 1985; solo singer, songwriter 1986–; numerous TV appearances, regular tours; two Grammy Awards, four Country Music Awards. *Film appearances include:* The Player 1992, Short Cuts 1993, Prêt-à-Porter 1994, Bastard Out of Carolina 1996, Breast Men 1997, Fear and Loathing in Las Vegas 1998, The Opposite of Sex 1998, Cookie's Fortune 1999, The New Guy 2002, Three Days of Rain 2003, The Open Road 2009, Angels Sing 2013. *Television includes:* The Bridge (series) 2013–14. *Recordings include:* albums: Lyle Lovett 1986, Pontiac 1988, Lyle Lovett and his Large Band 1989, Joshua Judges Ruth 1992, Leap of Faith (soundtrack) 1992, I Love Everybody 1994, Road to Ensenada 1996, Step Inside This House 1998, Live in Texas 1999, Can't Resist It 1999, Dr T and the Women 2000, My Baby Don't Tolerate 2003, It's Nor Large It's Big 2007, Natural Forces 2009, Release Me 2012, Best of Lyle Lovett Live 2015. *Address:* c/o Steve Macklam, Macklam Feldman Management, #200–1505 West 2nd Avenue, Vancouver, BC V6H 3Y4, Canada (office). *Telephone:* (604) 630-3199 (office). *E-mail:* findlay@mfmgt.com (office). *Website:* www.mfmgt.com (office); www.lylelovett.com.

LOVINS, Amory B., MA, PhD, FRSA; American physicist, environmentalist and academic; *Chairman Emeritus and Chief Scientist, Rocky Mountain Institute;* b. 13 Nov. 1947, Washington, DC; m. Hunter Lovins; ed Harvard Univ., Univ. of Oxford, UK; spent two years at Harvard Univ., then transferred to Univ. of Oxford, UK; fmr spokesman for Friends of the Earth (UK); has been Regents' Lecturer in Energy and Resources and in Econs at Univ. of California; Grauer Lecturer, Univ. of British Columbia; Luce Visiting Prof., Dartmouth Coll.; Distinguished Visiting Prof., Univ. of Colorado; Oikos Visiting Prof., Business School, Univ. of St Gallen; an Eng Visiting Prof., Peking Univ.; MAP/Ming Prof., Stanford Univ. 2007; Co-founder (with his wife), Rocky Mountain Inst. (non-profit applied research centre) 1982, now Chair. Emer. and Chief Scientist; co-f. E SOURCE (information source on advanced electric efficiency) (sold to Financial Times Group 1999); Founder and Chair. RMI's fourth spinoff, Fiberforge, Inc. (eng firm); mem. US Dept of Energy's Sr Advisory Bd 1980–81, Defense Science Bd task force on mil. energy strategy 1999–2001, 2006–07; occasional adviser to Nat. Asscn of Regulatory Utility Commrs, World Business Council for Sustainable Devt, Kleiner Perkins Caufield & Byers; Foreign mem. Royal Swedish Acad. of Eng Sciences 2007; Fellow, AAAS 1984, World Acad. of Arts and Sciences 1988; World Business Acad. 2001; MacArthur Fellow 1993, Ashoka Fellow 2009; Hon. Mem. AIA 2007; Hon. Sr Fellow, Design Futures Council 2007; 10 hon. doctorates; shared with Hunter Lovins: Mitchell Prize 1982, Right Livelihood Award 1983, Lindbergh Award 1999, Time magazine's Heroes for the Planet 2000; winner of first DELPHI Prize, Onassis Foundation 1989, Blue Planet Award, Shingo Prize, Jean Meyer Prize, Nissan Prize 1993, Heinz Award 1997, World Tech. Award (Environment) 1999, Happold Medal, Construction Industry Council (UK) 2000, Benjamin Franklin Medal, Royal Soc. of Arts 2005, Volvo Environment Prize, Volvo Environment Foundation 2007, National Geographic Energy and Environment Award for Individual Thought Leadership 2008, National Design Award 2009. *Publications:* 29 books, including Soft Energy Paths: Towards a Durable Peace 1977, Non-Nuclear Futures: The Case for an Ethical Energy Strategy 1980, A Golden Thread: 2500 Years of Solar Architecture & Technology 1980, Energy/War, Breaking the Nuclear Link 1981, Least-Cost Energy: Solving the CO 2 Problem 1982, Brittle Power: Energy Strategy for National Security 1982, 2001, Energy Unbound: A Fable for America's Future 1986, Consumer Guide to Home Energy Savings 1991, Reinventing Electric Utilities: Competition, Citizen Action, and Clean Power 1996, Factor Four: Doubling Wealth – Halving Resource Use: A Report to the Club of Rome 1997, Natural Capitalism: Creating the Next Industrial Revolution 2000, Small is Profitable: The Hidden Economic Benefits of Making Electrical Resources the Right Size 2003, Winning the Oil Endgame: Innovation for Profit, Jobs and Security 2005; several hundred papers in professional journals as well as poetry, landscape photography, music (fmr pianist and composer) and an electronics patent. *Address:* Rocky Mountain Institute, 2317 Snowmass Creek Road, Snowmass, CO 81654, USA (office). *Telephone:* (970) 927-3851 (office). *E-mail:* info@rmi.org (office). *Website:* www.rmi.org (office); www.fiberforge.com (office).

LOVRIN, Ana, LLB; Croatian lawyer and politician; b. 2 Dec. 1953, Zagreb; m. Miodrag Lovrin; four d.; ed Faculty of Law, Univ. of Zagreb; legal officer in Tankerska plovidba, Zadar 1978–80; Man. Legal Dept, Zadar Airport 1980; mem. Zadar City Council, Zadar 1993; mem. Croatian Democratic Union (Hrvatska demokratska zajednica—HDZ) 1993–, Vice-Pres. 1999–2001, Pres. 2003–05, mem. Cen. Cttee 2003–; State Sec. of Zadar, in charge of legal affairs 1993–2001; Deputy Mayor of Zadar 2001–04, Mayor 2004–05; mem. Zadar local govt in charge of property rights and local govt matters 2005–06; Deputy in Sabor (Ass.) 2005–, Chair. Legislation Cttee, mem. Cttee for the Constitution, Rules of Procedure and Political System, Cttee for Tourism, Chair. Judiciary Cttee; Minister of Justice 2006–08. *Leisure interests:* reading, classical music. *Address:* Croatian Parliament, 10000 Zagreb, trg sv. Marka 6, Croatia (office). *Telephone:* (1) 4569477 (office). *E-mail:* klubhdz@sabor.hr (office). *Website:* www.sabor.hr (office).

LOW, Jan, BA, MS, PhD; American plant scientist; *Principal Scientist and Leader of the Sweetpotato for Profit and Health Initiative, International Potato Center;* b. 1955, Denver, Colo; ed Pomona Coll., Univ. of Nairobi, Kenya, Cornell Univ.; as an undergraduate, lived with Kenyan family for two months and studied at Univ. of Nairobi, followed by three months in a coastal village researching vector-borne diseases of mosquitoes; joined the Peace Corps and worked in Zaïre in fisheries and aquaculture for four years; joined Int. Potato Center (Centro Internacional de la Papa—CIP) and studied sustainability of production systems in southwestern Uganda, Regional Leader for Africa and Leader of Sweetpotato for Profit and Health Initiative 2009–14, Prin. Scientist 2014–; World Food Prize (co-recipient) 2016. *Address:* Centro Internacional de la Papa, Avenida La Molina 1895, La Molina, Apartado Postal 1558, Lima, Peru (office). *Telephone:* 3496017 (office). *E-mail:* cip@cgiar.org (office). *Website:* cipotato.org (office).

LOW, Dato' Tuck Kwong; Indonesian (b. Singaporean) coal mining executive; *President Commissioner, PT Bayan Resources;* b. 1948; s. of Low Sum; m.; one s. one d.; ed Japan Inst. of Energy; began working for father's building co. in Singapore; moved to Indonesia 1972; f. PT Jaya Sumplies Indonesia 1973; f. PT Bayan Resources (coal mining co.) 1997, Pres. Dir 2004–08, Pres. Commr 2008–; fmr Pres. Dir PT Nirmala, PT Muji Inti Utama, PT Graha Balikpapan Pratama, PT Dinamika Energi Nusantara, PT Kaltim Kariangau Industry, PT Kariangau Power; fmr Dir Bayan Int., PT Kalimantan Citra Bara, Carbonic, Manhattan Investment Pte Ltd, Manhattan Kalimantan Investment Pte Ltd; Dr hc (Univ. of Notre Dame, Dadiangas) 2012. *Address:* Bayan Resources Tbk, Floor 12, Graha Irama Building, Block X-1, HR Rasuna Said Road, Lot 1-2, Jakarta 12950, Indonesia (office). *Telephone:* (21) 5269868 (office). *Fax:* (21) 5269866 (office). *Website:* www.bayan.com.sg (office).

LOWASSA, Edward Ngoyai, MSc; Tanzanian politician; b. 1953; m. Regina Lowassa; four c.; ed Univ. of Dar es Salaam, Univ. of Bath; Minister for Environment and Poverty 1988–2000; Man. Dir Arusha Int. Conference Centre 1989–90; Minister for Judiciary and Parliamentary Affairs 1990–93; Minister of Lands and Human Settlement Devt 1993–95; Minister of Water and Livestock Devt 2000–05; Prime Minister 2005–08 (resgnd); cand. in presidential election 2015; mem. Chama Cha Mapinduzi (CCM) 1977–2015, CHADEMA 2015–. *Address:* c/o Office of the Prime Minister, POB 980, Dodoma, Tanzania (office).

LOWCOCK, Sir Mark Andrew, KCB, MSc; British diplomatist and UN official; *Under-Secretary-General for Humanitarian Affairs and Emergency Relief Coordinator, Office for the Co-ordination of Humanitarian Affairs (OCHA);* b. 25 July 1962; m. Julia Watson; two s. one d.; ed Oxford Univ., Birkbeck Coll., Univ. of London; joined Overseas Devt Admin (now Dept for Int. Devt—DFID) 1985, Head Regional Office for East Africa 1991–2001, Pvt. Sec. to Minister for Overseas Devt 1992–94, Deputy Head and later Head, Regional Office for Cen. Africa, Dept for Int. Devt (DFID) 1994–97, Head EU Dept 1997–99, Dir Finance and Corporate Performance 2001–03, Dir-Gen. Finance, Corporate Performance and Knowledge Sharing 2003–06, Policy and Int. Finance 2006–08, Country Programmes 2008–11, Perm. Sec. DFID 2011–17; Under-Sec.-Gen. for Humanitarian Affairs and Emergency Relief Coordinator, Office for Co-ordination of Humanitarian Affairs (OCHA) 2017–. *Address:* Office for the Co-ordination of Humanitarian Affairs (OCHA), United Nations Plaza, New York, NY 10017, USA (office). *Telephone:* (212) 963-1234 (office). *Fax:* (212) 963-1312 (office). *E-mail:* unocha@un .org (office). *Website:* unocha.org (office).

LOWE, Hon. Douglas Ackley, AM; Australian fmr politician and administrator; b. 15 May 1942, Hobart, Tasmania; s. of Ackley Reginald Lowe and Dulcie Mary Lowe; m. Pamela June Grant 1963; two s. two d.; ed St Virgil's Coll.; worked as electrical fitter, Electrolytic Co.; State Sec. Tasmanian Section, Australian Labour Party 1965–69, State Pres. 1974–75; mem. Tasmania House of Ass. for Franklin 1969–81, Ind. 1981–86; Minister for Housing 1972–74; Chief Sec. 1974–76; Deputy Premier 1975–77; Minister for Planning and Reorganization 1975–76, for Industrial Relations 1976–79, for Planning and Environment 1976, for Health 1976–77; Premier of Tasmania 1977–81; Minister for Manpower Planning 1977–79, for Econ. Planning and Devt 1979–80, for Energy 1979, Treas. 1980–81; mem. Tasmanian Legis. Council 1986–92; Deputy Govt Leader Tasmanian Legis. Council 1989–92; Exec. Officer, Tasmanian Br., Australian Medical Asscn 1992–; Del. to Australian Constitutional Convention; State Pres., Tasmanian Swimming Inc. 1991–98, Life mem. 2000–; Queen's Silver Jubilee Medal 1977, Australian Sports Medal 2000, Centenary Medal 2000, President's Award, Australian Medical Asscn 2004. *Publications:* Directions for Future Development in Tasmania 1979, The Price of Power 1984. *Leisure interests:* swimming, tennis, fishing, football. *Address:* AMA Tasmania State Office, 147 Davey Street, Hobart, Tasmania 7000 (office); 1 Michele Court, Berriedale, Tasmania 7010, Australia (home). *Telephone:* (3) 6223-2047 (office). *Fax:* (3) 6223-6469 (office). *Website:* www.amatas.com.au (office).

LOWE, Sir Frank Budge, Kt, FRSA; British fmr business executive; b. 23 Aug. 1941; s. of Stephen Lowe and Marion Lowe; m. Dawn Lowe 1991; two s. one d.; ed Westminster School; Man. Dir Collett Dickenson Pearce 1972–79; Founder and Chair. Lowe Agency 1981–2003 (retd), Emer. Chair. 2003–; Founder and Chair. Octagon 1997–2003; Dir Interpublic 1990–2003; Founder and Chair. The Red Brick Road 2006–09; Visiting Prof., Univ. Coll. London 1990; Dir Sir Frank Lowe Football Trust 2010–; The President's Award, Design and Art Dirs Asscn of London 1985. *Leisure interests:* tennis, skiing, shooting. *Address:* Sir Frank Lowe Football Trust, 10 New Square, Lincoln's Inn, London, WC2A 3QG, England.

LOWRY, Glenn David, MA, PhD; American museum director; *Director, Museum of Modern Art;* b. 28 Sept. 1954, New York; s. of Warren Lowry and Laure Lowry (née Lynn); m. Susan Chambers 1974; three s.; ed Williams Coll., Harvard Univ.; Asst Curator Fogg Art Museum, Harvard Univ. 1978–80; research asst in archaeological survey, Amalfi, Italy 1980; Curator (Oriental art) Museum of Art, Providence, RI 1981–82; Dir Joseph and Margaret Muscarelle Museum of Art, Williamsburg, Va 1982–84; Curator (Near Eastern Art) Freer Gallery, Smithsonian Inst., Washington 1984–90, Curatorial Co-ordinator 1987–89; Dir Art Gallery of Ont., Toronto 1990–95; Dir Museum of Modern Art, New York 1995–; Fellow, American Acad. of Arts and Sciences 2006; Chevalier des Arts et des Lettres 1994, Officier 2004; Chevalier, Ordre nat. du Mérite 2000; Hon. DFA (Pennsylvania Acad. of Fine Arts) 2000; hon. degrees from Coll. of William and Mary 2009, Pratt Univ. 2010; Karl E. Weston Prize for Distinction in the Arts, Williams Coll. 1976, Travel Award, Inst. of Turkish Studies 1988, Scholarly Studies Award, Smithsonian Inst. 1990, Bicentennial Medal, Williams Coll. 2005. *Publications include:* Fatehpursikri: A Source Book 1985, Akbar's India: Art from the Mughal City of Victory 1986, From Concept to Context: Approaches to Asian and Islamic Calligraphy 1986, Asian Art in the Arthur M. Sackler Gallery: The Inaugural Gift 1987, Jeweler's Eye: Islamic Arts of the Book from the Vever Collection 1988, Timur and the Princely Vision: Persian Art and Culture in the Fifteenth Century (Special Exhibitions Fund Award 1987) 1989, Governor Nelson A. Rockefeller Empire State Plaza Art Collection and Plaza Memorials 2002, (Introduction for) Duveen: The Story of the Most Spectacular Art Dealer of All Time 2003, Whose Muse?: Art Museums and the Public Trust 2003, The Museum of Modern Art in this Century 2009, Oil and Sugar: Contemporary Art and Islamic Culture 2009, Abodes of the Muses: Theorising the Modern Art Museum 2011, Design for the New Museum of Modern Art 2004; articles in ARTnews and The Economist. *Address:* Museum of Modern Art, 11 West 53rd Street, New York, NY 10019-5498, USA (office). *Website:* www.moma.org (office).

LOWY, Sir Frank, AC; Australian business executive; *Chairman, Westfield Group;* b. 22 Oct. 1930, Czechoslovakia; m.; three s.; spent World War II years in Budapest, then moved to Palestine where he fought in underground Zionist army Haganah; immigrated to Australia 1952; Co-founder and Exec. Chair. Westfield Group (shopping centre co.) 1959–2011, Chair. (non-exec.) 2011–; Founder and Chair. Lowy Inst. for Int. Policy; mem. Int. Advisory Council, Brookings Inst.; Chair. Football Fed. Australia; fmr Pres. Art Gallery of New South Wales; mem. Bd of Dirs Reserve Bank of Australia 1995–2005; Dir Daily Mail and General Trust, UK; Dr hc (Univ. of New South Wales), (Tel-Aviv Univ.); Australian Grad. School of Man. Financial Times Global Business Leader Award 2005, Woodrow Wilson Award for Corp. Citizenship, Woodrow Wilson Int. Center for Scholars 2005, Henni Friedlander Award for the Common Good, Bowdoin Coll. 2007. *Address:* Westfield Group, Westfield Towers, 100 William Street, Sydney 2011, Australia (office). *Telephone:* (2) 9358-7000 (office). *Fax:* (2) 9358-7079 (office). *Website:* www.westfield.com (office).

LOZANČIĆ, Niko; Bosnia and Herzegovina politician and lawyer; b. 1957, Kakanj; mem. Croatian Democratic Union (HDZ), Leader 2001, Vice-Pres. 2001–; fmr municipal councillor; mem. House of Peoples and state-level House of Reps; Pres. Fed. of Bosnia and Herzegovina 2003–07; charged by Croatian Govt that he illegally received three years of privileged pensions, lawsuit still pending. *Address:* c/o HDZ BiH (Croatian Democratic Union of Bosnia and Herzegovia), Kneza Domagoja bb, 88000 Mostar, Bosnia and Herzegovia (office). *E-mail:* niko .lozancic@parlament.ba (office). *Website:* www.hdzbih.org (office).

LOZOYA AUSTIN, Emilio Ricardo, BA (Econ), LLB, MPA; Mexican business executive; s. of Emilio Lozoya Thalmann; ed Instituto Tecnológico Autónomo de México (ITAM) and Universidad Nacional Autónoma de México, Mexico City, Harvard Univ., USA; analyst, office in charge of investing int. reserves in securities, Banco de México (Cen. Bank of Mexico) 1999–2001; mem. of several bds of dirs of cos in the infrastructure, concessions, financial and information tech. sectors, as well as of Qualitas Asscn 2003–06; Investment Officer, Inter-American Investment Corpn 2006–10; Dir and Head of Latin America, World Econ. Forum 2010–12; Exec. Dir and Co-founder JFH SA investment fund; responsible for int. affairs during the transition period of elected Pres. Enrique Peña Nieto 2012; CEO Petróleos Mexicanos (PEMEX) 2012–16. *Address:* c/o Petróleos Mexicanos (PEMEX), Avenida Marina Nacional 329, Col. Huasteca, 11311 Mexico City DF, Mexico.

LU, (Hsiu-lien) Annette; Taiwanese fmr politician; b. 7 June 1944, Taoyuan; ed Taiwan Prov. Taipei First Girls' High School, Nat. Taiwan Univ., Univ. of Illinois and Harvard Univ., USA; fmr Sr Specialist, Section Chief Exec. Law and Regulations Cttee of Exec. Yuan; participated in street demonstrations; sentenced to twelve years' imprisonment 1979, released after five years and four months on medical parole; f. North American Taiwanese Women's Asscn, Clean Election Coalition 1985–90; mem. Democratic Progressive Party 1990–2018; organized and led Alliance for the Promotion of UN Membership for Taiwan 1991; fmr mem. Legis. Yuan for Taoyuan (Democratic Progressive Party), mem. Foreign Affairs Cttee 1992–95; Nat. Policy Adviser to Pres. 1996; Magistrate for Taoyuan Co. 1996–99; Vice-Pres. of Taiwan 2000–08; Chair. Third Global Summit of Women, Taiwan 1994; f. Centre for Women's and Children's Safety; World Peace Prize 2001. *Publications:* novels: These Three Women, Empathy; non-fiction: New Feminism, I Love Taiwan, Viewing Taiwan from Abroad, Retrying the Formosa Case.

LU, Daopei; Chinese medical scientist; *Honorary Director, Peking University Institute of Hematology;* b. 30 Oct. 1931, Shanghai; ed Tongji Medical Coll.; doctor, Doctor-in-Charge, Chief Doctor, Prof. and Dir of Internal Medicine, People's Hosp. of Beijing Medical Coll. 1955; Dir Blood Disease Research Inst. and Inst. of Hematology, Beijing Medical Univ. 1981–2005; Dir of Internal Medicine, Peking Univ. People's Hosp. 1985–2005, currently Hon. Dir Peking Univ. Inst. of Hematology; joined Chinese Peasants and Workers Democratic Party 1992, Chair. Beijing Municipal Cttee 1992–; Vice-Chair. CPPCC Beijing Municipal Cttee 1998–, mem. Standing Cttee 9th CPPCC Nat. Cttee 1998–2003; Vice Pres. Asian Hematology Association 2002–; Distinguished Prof., Fudan Univ. 2005–; Founder, Lu Daopei Hospitals Group 2006–; Vice-Chair. Chinese Medical Soc.; Chair. Soc. of Hematological Malignancies, Chinese Anti-Cancer Asscn; f. Chinese Soc. of Blood and Marrow Transplantation (CSBMT); mem. Int. Bd Bone Marrow Transplantation Authority 1995–; Fellow, Chinese Acad. of Eng 1996–; initiator of bone-marrow transplants in China; Scientific and Technological Progress Award, Ho Leung Ho Lee Foundation 1997, Chen Jia-gen Prize for Promotion in Medicine & Pharmacy 1997, Tan Kah Kee Prize 1997, Distinguished Service Award, Center for Int. Blood & Marrow Transplant Research 2016, Lifetime Achievement Award, China Anti-Cancer Asscn 2016. *Publications include:* more than 360 papers in professional journals. *Address:* Peking University Peoples Hospital, No. 11 Xizhimen South Street, Xicheng District, Beijing 100044 (office); Beijing Lu Daopei Hospital, 22 Tongji South Road, Yizhuang Ecomonic and Technological Development Zone, Daxing District, Beijing 102600, People's Republic of China (office). *Telephone:* (10) 88325965 (Peking University Peoples Hospital) (office); 13488699771 (mobile) (office). *Fax:* (10) 88324775 (Peking University Peoples Hospital) (office). *E-mail:* iao@pkuph.edu.cn (office); bryan_liu@ludaopei.com (office). *Website:* english.pkuph.cn (office); www.ludaopei.com (office).

LU, Dongliang, BEcons, CPA; Chinese accountant and business executive; *President and Executive Director, Aluminum Corporation of China Limited;* b. 1974; ed North China Univ. of Tech.; more than 20 years' work experience in financial man. in non-ferrous metals industry; fmr Cadre, Audit Dept, China Non-ferrous Metals Industry Corpn; fmr Officer-in-charge of Capital Div., Finance Dept, China Copper Lead & Zinc Group Corpn; fmr Head of Accounting and Capital Divs, Finance Dept, Aluminum Corpn of China (CHALCO), becoming Man., Gen. Man. Office, Deputy Gen. Man. and later Gen. Man., Finance Dept, Exec. Dir 2015–, Sr Vice Pres. –2018, Pres. 2018–; fmr Exec. Dir, Chief Financial Officer and Pres., Chalco Gansu Aluminum Electricity Co., Ltd; Dir, Jiaozuo Wanfang Aluminum Manufacturing Co., Ltd 2012–; mem. Bd of Dirs International Aluminium Inst., Chinalco Qingdao Light Metal Co., Ltd. *Address:* Aluminium Corporation of China Ltd (CHALCO), 62 Xizhimen Bei Dajie, Haidian Qu, Beijing 100082, People's Republic of China (office). *Telephone:* (10) 82298080 (office). *Fax:* (10) 82298081 (office). *E-mail:* webmaster@chalco.com.cn (office). *Website:* www.chinalco.com.cn (office).

LU, Gongxun; Chinese party official; b. Nov. 1933, Shuozhou City, Shanxi Prov.; joined CCP 1950; worker, Org. Dept, CCP Yanbei Prefectural Cttee, Shanxi Prov. 1956–57; Deputy Dir, Rural Work Dept, Shuoxian Co., Shanxi Prov. 1957–65; Deputy Sec. CCP Youyu Co. Cttee, Shanxi Prov. 1965–70; Deputy Sec. CCP Zuoyun Co. Cttee, Shanxi Prov. 1970–82, Sec. 1982–83; Head, Org. Dept, CCP Shanxi Prov. Cttee 1983–89; mem. Standing Cttee, CCP Shuozhou City Cttee, Shanxi Prov. 1983–89, Deputy Sec. 1988–93; Pres. Party School, CCP Shanxi Prov. Committee 1988–93; Chair. Standing Cttee of People's Congress, Shanxi Prov. 1993–2003; Alt. mem. 12th CCP Cen. Cttee 1982–87, 13th Cen. Cttee 1987–92; Del., 14th CCP Nat. Congress 1992–97, 15th CCP Nat. Congress 1997–2002; Deputy, 8th NPC 1993–98, 9th NPC 1998–2003.

LU, Hao; Chinese politician; b. April 1947, Changli, Hebei Prov.; ed Shenyang School of Chemical Eng, Dalian Eng Coll., Lanzhou Univ.; technician, Research Inst., Group Army, PLA Services and Arms 1968–71; technician, No. 5266 Factory 1971–78, Personnel Sec. 1971–75; joined CCP 1981; teaching asst, political tutor, Lanzhou Univ. 1982; Deputy Dir then Dir, Gen. Office of CCP Gansu Prov. Cttee (Sec. Div.) 1982–85; Deputy Dir then Dir Org. Dept of CCP Gansu Prov. 1985–96; Sec. CCP Lanzhou City Cttee, Gansu Prov. 1996–2000; Gov. Gansu Prov. 2001–06; Deputy Sec. CCP Gansu Prov. Cttee 2002; Deputy Dir, NPC Foreign Affairs Cttee 2011; Alt. mem. 15th CCP Cen. Cttee 1997–2002, mem. 16th CCP Cen. Cttee 2002–07, 17th CCP Cen. Cttee 2007–12.

LU, Lay Sreng; Cambodian politician; b. 10 March 1937, Phnom Penh; ed California State Univ., Long Beach, USA; mem. resistance movt against Vietnamese occupation of Cambodia 1982–91; Minister of Information 1993–2003, apptd Deputy Prime Minister and Minister of Rural Devt 2003; fmr First Vice-Pres. United Nat. Front for an Ind., Neutral, Peaceful and Co-operative Cambodia Party (Funcinpec).

LU, Liangshu; Chinese agronomist; b. 3 Nov. 1924, Shanghai; s. of Lu Zezhi and Hu Lian; m. Yin Xueli 1950; three s.; deputy to 3rd NPC 1965, 5th NPC 1978; Deputy to 13th CCP 1988; Deputy Dir Science and Tech. Committee, Ministry of Agric. 1983; Pres. Chinese Acad. of Agricultural Sciences 1982–87; Pres. Chinese Asscn of Agricultural Science Socs 1982–92, now Hon. Pres.; mem. Chinese Acad. of Eng (Vice-Pres. 1994). *Publications:* Food Composition and Development Strategy in China, Compilation on China's Agricultural Devt Strategy and the Progress of Science and Tech. *Leisure interests:* swimming, music. *Address:* Chinese Academy of Agricultural Sciences, 30 Baishiqiao Road, Beijing 100081, People's Republic of China (office). *Telephone:* (10) 68975516 (office). *Fax:* (10) 62174142 (office). *E-mail:* xujm@mail.caas.net.cn (office).

LU, Peijian; Chinese banking executive (retd); b. Aug. 1928, Hongze Co., Jiangsu Prov.; m. Sheng Lixia 1985; three c.; joined CCP 1944, New 4th Army 1944; accountant, Cen. China and E China Mil. Commands 1944–49; Section Chief, later Div. Chief, later Deputy Dir Gen. Office, Ministry of Finance 1949–78, Vice-Minister of Finance 1978–82; Pres. People's Bank of China 1982–85; Auditor-Gen. Nat. Audit Office of China 1985–94; Chair. Governing Bd ASOSAI (Asian Org. of Supreme Audit Insts) 1991–94; Chair. Bd of Supervisors, China Devt Bank 1994–2008; mem. 12th CCP Cen. Cttee 1982–87, 13th CCP Cen. Cttee 1987–92, 14th CCP Cen. Cttee 1992–97; mem. Standing Cttee 9th CPPCC Nat. Cttee 1998–2003.

LU, Qihui; Chinese sculptor; *Professor, Shanghai Oil Painting and Sculpture Institute;* b. 8 April 1936, Shanghai; d. of Ren Jin; m. Fang Zengxian 1960; one s. one d.; ed Sculpture Dept, Cen. Art Acad., East China Branch 1955–61; teacher, Shanghai Art College 1961–65; professional sculptor, Shanghai Oil Painting and Sculpture Inst. 1965–, Prof. 1988–; mem. Chinese Artists' Asscn. *Works include:* Transplanting rice seedlings, workers group statues, Nat. Industrial Exhibition 1960, Statue of Child Labourers 1974, Sculpture for Chairman Mao Memorial Hall 1977, Statue of Lu Xun 1979, Angrily Seeking Verses against Reign of Terror 1980, Plateau in the Morning Sun 1986, Bada, an ancient Chinese Artist 1987 (exhibited New York in Contemporary Oil Painting from the PRC), The Emotion at Plateau 1989, Zhang Zhong-Jingi a Pioneer of Chinese Medical Science 1990 (bronze), Song Jie-Cai Rang of a Tibetan 1990 (stone), Hawk-dancing 1991 (statue), Wang Ge-Ji memorial (bronze) 1992, Magic painter Mar-Lang (bronze) 1993, Wu Chan-Shu memorial (bronze), one for Shanghai Memorial Hall 1994, one for Japanese Fakuoka 1995, Xia-Qiu-Son (bronze) 1995, Balzac Memorial (bronze), Garden of Famous People, Shanghai 1996, Sampan (bronze), for Shanghai Stadium 1997, Wu Fu-Zhi memorial (bronze) 1998, The Sound of Spring (forging) 2001, Liu Kai-Qu memorial (bronze) 2004. *Leisure interests:* Chinese painting, sport. *Address:* 278, 333 Alley, Chang-Dong Road, Xin-Qiao Town, Song Jiang, Shanghai, People's Republic of China (home). *Telephone:* (21) 67644032 (home).

LU, Qizhou; Chinese engineer and fmr business executive; ed Nanjing Tech Univ.; fmr Man. Jianbi Power Plant (now Jianbi power station); fmr Vice-Gen. Man. and Party mem., Jiangsu Electric Power (co-ed.); later Vice-Gen. Man. State Grid; mem. Bd State Nuclear Power Technology Corpn; President and Gen. Man. China Power Investment Corpn –2015 (retd), later Party mem.

LU, Rongjing; Chinese politician; b. 1933, Lujiang Co., Anhui Prov.; joined CCP 1954; Dir Tongguanshan Mine, Anhui Prov. 1968–76 (Sec. CCP Party Cttee 1968–76); fmr Deputy Sec. CCP Tongling City Cttee and Ma'anshan City Cttee, Anhui Prov.; Deputy Dir Industrial and Communications Office, Anhui Prov. 1978, Prov. Econ. Cttee 1979; Head, Org. Dept, CCP Anhui Prov. Cttee 1983–84, Deputy Sec. CCP Anhui Prov. Cttee 1985–88, Sec. 1988–98; Vice-Gov. Anhui Prov. 1987, Acting Gov. 1987–93; Chair. CPPCC Anhui Prov. Cttee 1996; mem. 13th CCP Cen. Cttee 1987–92, 14th CCP Cen. Cttee 1992–97, 15th CCP Cen. Cttee 1997–2002.

LU, Ruihua, MA; Chinese politician; b. Nov. 1938, Chaozhou City, Guangdong Prov.; ed Zhongshan Univ., Guangdong Prov.; joined CCP 1972; fmrly engineer, Deputy Dir, Dir Foshan Analytical Instrument Factory; fmrly Mayor of Foshan, Vice-Chair. Foshan City Econ. Cttee, mem. Standing Cttee CCP Guangdong Prov. Cttee, mem. then Deputy Sec. Standing Cttee CCP Foshan City Cttee; Vice-Gov. Guangdong Prov. 1991–96, Gov. 1996–2003; Deputy Sec. CCP Guangdong Prov. Cttee 1996– (mem. Standing Cttee 2002–); Alt. mem. 14th CCP Cen. Cttee 1992–97, mem. 15th CCP Cen. Cttee 1997–2002; Deputy, 7th NPC 1988–93, 8th NPC 1993–98, 9th NPC 1998–2003. *Address:* c/o People's Government of Guangdong, Guangzhou, Guangdong Province, People's Republic of China.

LU, Shengzhong, MA; Chinese artist; *Professor, Folk Arts Department, Central Academy of Fine Arts;* b. 4 Jan. 1952, Pingdu Co., Shandong Prov.; s. of Lu Wanjin and Jiang Yongzhen; m. Liu Guangjun 1980; one s.; ed Cen. Acad. of Fine Arts; specializes in Chinese folk arts; currently Prof., Folk Arts Dept, Cen. Acad. of Fine Arts; Deputy Sec.-Gen. Chinese Asscn of Fine Artists. *Works include:* When Heaven and Earth are in Harmony, All Living Things, Thrive, Life, Solitary Walking, Magic and Acrobatics. *Publications include:* Chinese Folk Papercut, Chinese Folk New Year Paintings, Arts from My Mother, Solitary Walk on the Holy Road, Outline of Chinese Folk Woodcut Print, Words of Calling the Souls, Farewell Tradition I-IV. *Address:* Central Academy of Fine Arts, No.8 Hua Jia Di Nan St., Chao Yang District, Beijing 100102, People's Republic of China (office). *Website:* www.cafa.edu.cn (office).

LU, Shih-Peng, BA; Taiwanese historian and academic; b. 16 Sept. 1928, Kao-yu, Chiang Su; s. of Lu Chun-tai and Lu Chia Chu-yin; m. Julia Wei-chun; one s. one d.; ed Nat. Taiwan Univ., Taipei, Harvard Univ., USA; Teaching Asst, Nat. Taiwan Univ., Taipei 1953–55; Research Asst, Academia Sinica, Taipei 1955–58; Lecturer, Tunghai Univ., Taichung 1958–63, Assoc. Prof. 1963–67, apptd Prof. of History 1967, Dir Evening School 1972–81, Chair. Dept of History 1981–87, Dean Coll. of Arts 1988–94; Visiting Scholar, Harvard Univ. 1961–63; Outstanding Youth, China Youth Corps 1952; Ed. Chinese Culture Monthly 1979–; Outstanding Prof., Ministry of Educ. 1992. *Publications include:* Vietnam during the period of Chinese Rule 1964, The Modern History of China 1979, The Contemporary History of China 1992. *Leisure interests:* reading, classical music, ping pong/table tennis, jogging, Chinese opera.

LU, Shumin; Chinese diplomatist; b. 24 Feb. 1950, Xi'an, Shanxi Province; m. Gao Shuqing; one d.; staff mem. Dept of N American and Oceanian Affairs, Ministry of Foreign Affairs 1976–77, Embassy in Canada 1977–79, Diplomatic Personnel Services Bureau, Beijing 1979–85; Third Sec., Embassy in Australia 1985; Second Sec. –1989; various staff positions at Ministry of Foreign Affairs including Deputy Div. Chief, Div. Chief, Counsellor –1993, Deputy Dir-Gen 1993–94, Counsellor, Embassy in USA 1994, Minister Counsellor –1998; Dir-Gen 1998–2002; Amb. to Indonesia 2002–05, to Canada 2005–08; Commr of Ministry of Foreign Affairs, Macao Special Admin. Region 2008–11.

LU, Yimin, BSc, MPA; Chinese engineer and business executive; *President and Vice-Chairman, China United Network Communications Group Company Limited (China Unicom);* ed Shanghai Jiao Tong Univ., John F. Kennedy School of Govt, Harvard Univ., USA; fmr mem. Sec. Bureau of Gen. Office of CCP Cen. Cttee, served as Deputy Dir and Dir Information Processing Office 1992–2001, Sec. at Deputy Dir-Gen. level 2001–05, Sec. at Dir-Gen. level 2005–07; Sr Man. and Exec. Dir, China Netcom Group Corpn (Hong Kong) Ltd (acquired by China Unicom 2008) 2007–09, Pres., Vice-Chair. and Deputy Sec. Party Leadership Group, China United Network Communications Group Co. Ltd (China Unicom) 2009–, mem. Bd of Dirs Nov. 2009–; Dir and Pres. A Share Co., CUCL; Dir (non-exec.) PCCW Ltd 2008–. *Address:* China Unicom Ltd 75th Floor, The Center, 99 Queen's Road Central, Hong Kong Special Administrative Region (office); China United Telecommunications Corpn Ltd, No. 133A, Xidan North Street, Xicheng District, Beijing 100032 (office); China United Telecommunications Corpn Ltd, 29/F, Lian Tong Tower, 1033 Chang Ning Road, Shanghai 200050, People's Republic of China (office). *Telephone:* 2126-2018 (Hong Kong) (office); (10) 66505588 (Beijing) (office); (21) 52732228 (Shanghai) (office). *Fax:* 2126-2016 (Hong Kong) (office); (21) 52732220 (Shanghai) (office). *E-mail:* info@chinaunicom.com.hk (office). *Website:* eng.chinaunicom.com (office); www.chinaunicom.com.hk (office); www.chinaunicom-a.com (office); www.chinaunicom.com.cn (office).

LU, Yongxiang; Chinese university professor and government official; b. 28 April 1942, Ningbo City, Zhejiang Prov.; s. of Lu Zhau and Lee Feng; m. Diao Linlin 1966; one s. one d.; ed Zhejiang Univ., Tech. Univ. of Aachen, Germany; Asst Lecturer, Dept of Mechanical Eng, Zhejiang Univ. 1964–79, Assoc. Prof. 1981–83,

Full Prof., Dir Inst. of Fluid Power Transmission and Control 1981–, Vice-Pres. Inst. of Science and Tech. 1985–88, Pres. and Deputy Dir 1988–95; Academician, Chinese Acad. of Sciences 1991, Vice-Pres. 1993–97, Pres. 1997–2011, mem. 4th Presidium of Depts 2000–; Vice-Chair. China Asscn for Science and Tech. 1986–96; mem. Academic Degrees Comm. of State Council 1986– (Vice-Chair. 1999), State Steering Group of Science, Tech. and Educ. 1998; mem. Third World Acad. of Sciences 1990 (Vice-Pres. 1998–), Chinese Acad. of Eng 1993, Nat. Natural Sciences Foundation of China; Del. NPC 1983–91; joined CCP 1964; mem. 14th CCP Cen. Cttee 1992–97, 15th CCP Cen. Cttee 1997–2002, 16th CCP Cen. Cttee 2002–07, 17th CCP Cen. Cttee 2007–12; Vice-Chair. 10th NPC Standing Cttee 2003–08, 11th NPC Standing Cttee 2008–13; Vice-Pres. First Council, China Overseas Friendship Asscn 1997; Foreign mem. German Acad. of Natural Scientists Leopoldina 2005, Russian Acad. of Sciences 2006; Hon. DEng (The Hong Kong Univ. of Science and Tech.) 1996; Second Prize for Nat. Invention 1988, Third Prize 1989, Higher Eng Educ. Prize of Nation 1989, Gao Hua Super Prize 1993, Rudolf Diesel Gold Medal (Germany) 1997, Abdus Salam Medal, Acad. of Sciences for the Developing World 2006, Max-Planck-Gesellschaft Harnack-Medaille (Germany) 2006, and many other awards and prizes. *Publications:* Electrohydraulic Proportional Technique 1988; more than 160 published papers and over 20 patents. *Leisure interests:* model aeroplanes, playing football. *Address:* Chinese Academy of Sciences, 52 Sanlihe Road, Beijing 100864, People's Republic of China (office). *Telephone:* (10) 68597289 (office). *Fax:* (10) 68512458 (office). *E-mail:* engach@mail.cae.ac.cn (office). *Website:* english.cas.ac.cn (office).

LU, Youmei; Chinese hydraulic engineer; *Honorary Chairman, Chinese National Committee on Large Dams;* b. 1934, Shanghai; ed East China Water Conservancy Coll. (now Hohai Univ.); mem. CCP 1956–; engineer, Bureau for Construction of Liujia Gorge Hydropower Station of Yellow River –1970; posts in various bureaux of Ministry of Water Conservancy and Electric Power 1978–84; Vice-Minister of Water Conservancy and Electric Power 1984–88; Vice-Minister, Ministry of Energy Resources 1988–93; Pres. China Yangtze Three Gorges Project Construction; Vice Chair. Three Gorges Project Construction Cttee 1993–; Prof., Tsinghua Univ. and Hohai Univ.; fmr Chair. Chinese Nat. Cttee on Large Dams (CHINCOLD), currently Hon. Chair.; mem. Chinese Acad. of Eng 2003–. *Publications include:* numerous papers for professional journals. *Address:* Chinese National Committee on Large Dams, Room 1266, Block A, Chinese Academy of Water Sciences, No. 1 Fuxing Road, Beijing 100038, People's Republic of China (office). *Telephone:* (10) 68435228 (office). *Fax:* (10) 68712208 (office). *E-mail:* chincold@iwhr.com (office). *Website:* www.chincold.org.cn (office).

LU, Zhaoxi (Jonathan); Chinese business executive; b. 1969, Guangzhou; ed Guangzhou Univ.; began career in hotel industry, working as lobby man., room man. and restaurant man. –1997; joined Alibaba e-commerce group 2000, leading roles in several key divs including Dir Alibaba South China Sales Region 2000–04, Pres. Alipay (online payment service) 2004–08, Gen. Man. Taobao (online marketplace) 2008, CEO 2010, Chief Data Officer Aliyun (mobile operating service) and Head, Alibaba.com (business-to-business e-commerce platform) 2011, CEO Alibaba Group 2013–15, remains mem. Bd of Dirs. *Address:* Alibaba.com, 6th Floor Chuangye Mansion, East Software Park, No. 99 Huaxing Road, Hangzou, Zhejiang Province, 310012 (office); Alibaba.com Technology Corpn Ltd, Room 408, Fanli Building, 22 Chaoyangwai Street, Chaoyang District, Beijing, 100020, People's Republic of China (office). *Telephone:* (571) 85022088 (Hangzhou) (office); (10) 6588-9698 (office). *Fax:* (571) 88157866 (Hangzhou) (office); (10) 6588-9699 (office). *Website:* www.alibaba.com (office).

LUBCHENCO, Hon. Jane, BA, MS, PhD; American environmental scientist, academic and government official; *Distinguished University Professor and Adviser in Marine Studies, Oregon State University;* b. 4 Dec. 1947, Denver, Colo; m.; two c.; ed Colorado Coll., Univ. of Washington, Harvard Univ.; Asst Prof. of Ecology, Harvard Univ. 1975–77; Research Assoc. Smithsonian Inst. 1978–84; Asst Prof., Oregon State Univ. 1977–82, Assoc. Prof. 1982–88, Prof. of Zoology 1988–2009, Distinguished Prof. of Zoology 1993–2009, Wayne and Gladys Valley Prof. of Marine Biology 1995–2009, 2013–14, Distinguished Univ. Prof. and Adviser in Marine Studies 2013–; US Under-Sec. of Commerce for Oceans and Atmosphere and Admin. Nat. Oceanic and Atmospheric Admin, Washington, DC 2009–13; Mimi and Peter E. Haas Distinguished Visitor, Haas Center for Public Service, Stanford Univ. March–June 2013; Fellow, AAAS, Pres. 1997–98, Ed.-in-Chief Science 1999–2000; Pres. Ecological Soc. of America 1992–94; mem. Bd of Trustees David and Lucile Packard Foundation, Environmental Defense, Monterey Bay Aquarium 2001–04, Trustee Emer. 2004–; Commr Pew Oceans Comm.; mem. Bd of Dirs, Royal Swedish Acad. of Sciences' Beijer Inst. of Environmental Econs; Pres. ICSU 2001–05; Founder and Co-Chair. Aldo Leopold Leadership Program; US Science Envoy for the Ocean; mem. NAS 1996, American Acad. of Arts and Sciences, American Philosophical Soc., Nat. Science Bd; MacArthur Fellow and Pew Scholar in Conservation and the Environment; Dr hc (Drexel Univ.) 1992, (Colorado Coll.) 1993, (Bates Coll.) 1997, (Unity Coll.) 1998, (Southampton Coll.) 1999, (Long Island Univ.) 1999, (Princeton Univ.) 2001, (Plymouth State Coll.) 2002, (Michigan State Univ.) 2003; numerous awards, including Scientist of the Year, Oregon Acad. of Sciences and American Philosophical Asscn 1994, David B. Stone Award 1999, Golden Plate Award 2001, Howard Vollun Award 2001, Heinz Award in the Environment 2002, Ed Ricketts Memorial Award, Monterey Bay Nat. Marine Sanctuary 2002, Nierenberg Prize for Science in the Public Interest, Scripps Inst. of Oceanography 2003, Distinguished Service Award, Soc. for Conservation Biology 2003, Distinguished Scientist Award, American Inst. of Biological Sciences 2004, Environmental Law Inst. Award 2004, Zayed Int. Prize for the Environment (Category 2) 2008, Peter Benchley Ocean Award for Excellence in Policy 2010, named by Nature journal Newsmaker of the Year 2010, Blue Planet Prize 2011, Public Understanding of Science Award, The Exploratorium 2011, Sailors for the Sea's Ocean Hero Award 2012, Presidential Citation for Science and Society, American Geophyiscal Union 2012, BBVA Foundation Frontiers of Knowledge Award in Ecology and Conservation Biology category 2012, inducted into Women in Science and Tech. Hall of Fame 2012, Prince Albert II of Monaco Foundation Climate Change Award 2013, Distinguished Public Service Award 2013, Tyler Prize for Environmental Achievement, Univ. of Southern California (co-recipient) 2015. *Publications include:* 50 publs on ecology, biodiversity, climate change, sustainability science and the state of the oceans. *Address:* Department of Integrative Biology, Oregon State University, 3029 Cordley Hall, 2701 SW Campus Way, Corvallis, OR 97331, USA (office). *Telephone:* (541) 737-2993 (office). *Fax:* (541) 737-0501 (office). *E-mail:* ib@science.oregonstate.edu (office). *Website:* gordon.science.oregonstate.edu/lubchenco (office).

LUBIMOV, Alexey Borisovich; Russian pianist and academic; *Professor, Moscow Conservatory;* b. 16 Sept. 1944, Moscow; m. Aza Lubimova; one d.; ed Moscow State Conservatory; soloist, chamber musician, pianist, harpsichordist, organist; organizer and artistic dir of chamber ensembles and festivals of experimental character; well-known performer on historical keyboard instruments 1980–; teacher, Moscow Conservatory 1968–75, Prof. 1997–; Prof., Univ. Mozarteum, Salzburg 1999–2010; Honoured Artist of Russia 2003; winner, int. competitions in Rio de Janeiro (First Prize) 1965 and Montreal 1968. *Recordings:* more than 40 CDs (classical, Baroque and contemporary music) 1990–2004, Mozart Complete Sonatas on historical pianos 1991, Silvestrov: Metamusik 2003, Pärt's Lamentate 2005. *Leisure interests:* collecting ancient keyboard instruments. *Address:* c/o Helge R. Augstein, Artist Management Augstein & Hahn, 80331 Munich, Germany (office); Klimentovskiy per. 9, Apt 12, Moscow, Russia (home). *Telephone:* (89) 2602-4333 (office); (495) 951-62-51 (home). *Fax:* (89) 2602-4344 (office); (495) 629-51-45 (office); (495) 951-62-51 (home). *E-mail:* mail@augstein.info (office); alexeilubimov@mail.ru (home). *Website:* www.augstein.info (office).

LUBIN, Steven, BA, MS, PhD; American pianist and academic; *Professor Emeritus, Conservatory of Music, Purchase College, State University of New York;* b. 22 Feb. 1942, New York, NY; s. of Jack Lubin and Sophie Lubin; m. Wendy Lubin 1974; two s.; ed Harvard Coll., Juilliard School, New York Univ.; piano studies with Lisa Grad, Nadia Reisenberg, Seymour Lipkin, Rosina Lhevinne, Beveridge Webster; recital and concert tours in USA, Canada, Mexico, UK, France, Netherlands, Spain, Italy, Germany, Austria, Finland, Australia, Taiwan, Japan and Ukraine; f. The Mozartean Players 1978–; mem. Faculty, Juilliard School 1964–65, Aspen Music School 1967, Vassar Coll. 1970–71, Cornell Univ. 1971–75; Prof., Conservatory of Music, Purchase Coll., State Univ. of New York (SUNY) 1975–2016, now Prof. Emer.; Hon. mem., Harvard Phi Beta Kappa Soc. 2013; Martha Baird Rockefeller Grant 1968, Stereo Review Recording of the Year Award 1988, Kempner Distinguished Professor Award, SUNY, Purchase 2001. *Film:* soloist in Man and Music (British documentary) 1987. *Recordings include:* complete Beethoven Piano Concertos, Mozart and Schubert Trios, six Mozart Concertos as soloist and conductor and other solo and chamber music; recorded for Decca, Harmonia Mundi USA, Arabesque, Classical Soundings. *Publications:* articles in The New York Times, Keynote, Ovation, Keyboard Classics and Historical Performance, Early Music America Magazine, Brahms Soc. Newsletter 1999; contrib. to A Companion to Schubert's Schwanengesang 2000. *Leisure interests:* reading about relativity and quantum mechanics. *Address:* c/o John Gingrich Management, Inc., PO Box 1515, New York, NY 10023, USA (office); Conservatory of Music, School of the Arts, State University of New York, Purchase, NY 10577, USA (office). *Telephone:* (212) 799-5080 (office). *E-mail:* gingarts@verizon.net (office); steven.lubin@gmail.com (office). *Website:* www.gingarts.com (office); www.stevenlubin.com.

LUBINDA, Given; Zambian politician; *Minister of Justice;* b. 15 May 1963; mem. Nat. Ass. for Kabwata constituency, Lusaka; Minister of Information, Broadcasting and Tourism –2012, Minister of Foreign Affairs 2012–13; mem. Patriotic Front; Minister of Justice 2016–. *Address:* Ministry of Justice, Fairley Road, POB 50106, 15101 Ridgeway, Lusaka, Zambia (office). *Telephone:* (21) 1255763 (office); 977863244 (mobile). *Fax:* (21) 1292252 (office). *E-mail:* glubinda@parliament.gov.zm (office); lubinda2014@gmail.com. *Website:* www.moj.gov.zm (office).

LUBOVITCH, Lar; American choreographer; *Artistic Director, Lar Lubovitch Dance Company;* b. 9 April 1943, Chicago, Ill.; ed Univ. of Iowa, Juilliard School; danced in numerous modern, ballet and jazz cos; Founder and Artistic Dir Lar Lubovitch Dance Co. 1968–; has choreographed more than 110 dances for the co.; his works are included in repertoires of most major int. dance cos including New York City Ballet, American Ballet Theater, Paris Opera Ballet, Royal Danish Ballet, Stuttgart Ballet, Mikhailovsky Ballet, Alvin Ailey American Dance Theater, Martha Graham Dance Co. and Netherlands Dance Theatre; has created dances for ice-skaters including John Curry; Distinguished Prof., Univ. of California, Irvine 2016–; Distinguished Prof., Univ. of California, Irvine; Dr hc (Juilliard School) 2014; Guggenheim Fellowship 1971, Astaire Award 1994, Elan Award 2004, Ford Fellow 2011, Dance/USA Honors 2011, Prix Benois 2012, American Dance Guild 2013, America's Irreplaceable Dance Treasures (Dance Heritage Coalition) 2016, Scripps/American Dance Festival 2016, Dance Magazine 2016, Martha Graham Award 2018. *Dances created include:* Whirligogs (music by Luciano Berio) 1969, The Time Before the Time After (After the Time Before) (Stravinsky) 1971, Les Noces (Stravinsky) 1976, Marimba (Steve Reich) 1976, Exultate, Jubilate (Mozart) 1977, Scriabin Dances (Scriabin) 1977, North Star (Philip Glass) 1978, Cavalcade (Reich) 1980, Beau Danube (Strauss) 1981, Big Shoulders (no music) 1983, A Brahms Symphony 1985, Concerto Six Twenty-Two (Mozart) 1986, Sleeping Beauty (Tchaikovsky); full-length televised ice-dancing version starring Robin Cousins and Rosalynn Sumners) 1987, Into the Woods (Sondheim) 1987, Musette (Poulenc) 1988, Rhapsody in Blue (Gershwin) 1988, Fandango (Ravel) 1989, Waiting for the Sunrise (Les Paul and Mary Ford) 1991, American Gesture (Charles Ives) 1992, The Red Shoes (Jule Styne; Astaire Award, Theater Devt Fund 1994) 1993, The Planets (Holst) (Emmy Award 1995, Grammy Award 1995) 1994, Oklahoma! (Rodgers and Hammerstein) 1994, The King and I (Rodgers and Hammerstein) 1996, Adagio (Bach) 1996, Othello (Goldenthal) 1997, Meadow (Schubert, etc.) 1999, The Hunchback of Notre Dame (Menken) 1999, Men's Stories (Marshall) 2000, My Funny Valentine (Rodgers) 2001, Smile With My Heart (Laird) 2002, Artemis (Chris Theofanidis) 2003, Pentimento (Richard Woodbury) 2004, Love Stories (Kurt Elling) 2005, Elemental Brubeck (Brubeck) 2005, Recordare (Goldenthal) 2005, Little Rhapsodies (Schumann; solo version) 2006, (trio version) 2007, Serenade (Dvorak) 2007, Cryptoglyph (Monk) 2007, Angel's Feet (montage) 2007, Jangle (Bartók) 2008, Coltrane's Favorite Things (Coltrane) 2010, Dogs of War (Prokofiev) 2010, Histoire du Soldat (Stravinsky) 2010, Lamentation Variation (Beethoven) 2010, The Legend of Ten (Brahms) 2010, Crisis Variations (Sharlat) 2011, Transparent Things (Debussy) 2012, As Sleep Befell (Prestini) 2013, Vez (Woolf) 2013, Crazy 8's (Woolf) 2013, Artemis in Athens (Chris Theofanidis) 2014, The Black Rose (Scott Marshall) 2014, The Bronze

Horseman (Reinhold Gliere) 2016, Something About Night (Franz Schubert) 2018. *Film:* The Company (Robert Altman) 2003. *Television:* The Sleeping Beauty 1987, Concerto Six Twenty-Two and North Star/Dancemaker 1988, Fandango/Pictures From the Edge 1989, The Planets 1995, Othello 2003. *Address:* Lar Lubovitch Dance Company, 229 West 42nd Street, 8th Floor, New York, NY 10036, USA (office). *Telephone:* (212) 221-7909 (office). *Fax:* (212) 221-7938 (office). *E-mail:* lubovitch@aol.com (office). *Website:* www.lubovitch.org.

LUCAS, Sir Colin Renshaw, Kt, MA, DPhil, FRHistS; British academic; b. 25 Aug. 1940; s. of Frank Renshaw Lucas and Janine Charpentier; m. 1st Christiane Berchon de Fontaine Goubert 1964 (divorced 1975); one s.; m. 2nd Mary Louise Hume 1990; ed Sherborne School, Lincoln Coll., Oxford; Asst Lecturer, then Lecturer, Univ. of Sheffield 1965–69; Visiting Asst Prof., Indiana Univ., USA 1969–70; Lecturer, Univ. of Manchester 1970–73; Fellow, Balliol Coll. Oxford and Lecturer in Modern History, Univ. of Oxford 1973–90; Prof., Univ. of Chicago, USA 1990–94, Dean Div. of Social Sciences 1993–94; Master of Balliol Coll., Oxford 1994–2001, Pro-Vice-Chancellor, Univ. of Oxford 1995–97, Vice-Chancellor 1997–2004, Univ. Officer Fellow, All Souls Coll. 2001–04, Two-Year Fellow, All Souls Coll. 2004–06, Warden, Rhodes House, Oxford 2004–09, Quondam Fellow, All Souls Coll. 2006–; Chair. British Library 2006–10; Officier des Arts et des Lettres 1990, Chevalier, Ordre nat. du Mérite 1994, Chevalier, Légion d'honneur 1998, Officier, Légion d'honneur 2005; Hon. DLitt (Lyon) 1989, (Sheffield) 2000, (Univ. of WA) 2000, (Glasgow) 2001, (Princeton) 2002, (Beijing) 2002, (Francis Xavier) 2003, (Oxford) 2003, (Oxford Brookes) 2004, (Warwick) 2006; Dr hc (Heidelberg Univ.) 2013. *Publications:* The Structure of the Terror 1973, Beyond the Terror (with G. Lewis) 1983, The Political Culture of the French Revolution (ed.) 1988; contribs to academic journals. *Address:* All Souls College, Oxford, OX1 4AL, England.

LUCAS, George Walton, Jr, BA; American screenwriter and film director and producer; *Creative Consultant, Lucasfilm Ltd;* b. 14 May 1944, Modesto, Calif.; s. of George Walton Lucas, Sr and Dorothy Ellinore Lucas (née Bomberger); m. 1st Marcia Lou Griffin 1969 (divorced 1983); one adopted s. two adopted d.; m. 2nd Mellody Hobson 2013; ed Univ. of Southern California School of Cinema-TV; apprenticeship at Warner Brothers Studios; Co-founder (with Francis Ford Coppola) American Zoetrope (film production co.) 1969; f. Lucasfilm Ltd 1971, currently Creative Consultant, group includes Lucasfilm Animation Ltd, Lucas Digital (Industrial Light & Magic and Skywalker Sound), LucasArts Entertainment Co., Lucas Licensing (Lucasfilm sold to Disney 2012); Founder and Chair. George Lucas Educational Foundation; mem. Bd of Councilors Univ. of Southern California School of Cinema-TV; Dr hc (Univ. of Southern California) 1994; Irving Thalberg Award 1991, American Film Inst. Lifetime Achievement Award 2005, Inaugural Filmmaker's Award from Motion Picture Sound Editors 2005, named amongst the 100 Greatest Americans by the Discovery Channel 2005, inducted into the Science Fiction Hall of Fame 2006, served as Grand Marshal for the Tournament of Roses Parade 2007, one of 13 California Hall of Fame inductees in The California Museum's yearlong exhibit 2009, Nat. Medal of Arts 2012. *Films include:* writer and dir: Look at Life 1965, Herbie 1966, Freiheit 1966, The Emperor 1967, Anyone Lived in a Pretty How Town 1967, Filmmaker 1968, American Graffiti 1973; producer: Kagemusha 1980, Body Heat 1981, Twice Upon a Time 1983, Howard the Duck 1986; writer and producer: Star Wars Episode V: The Empire Strikes Back 1980, Raiders of the Lost Ark 1981, Star Wars Episode VI: Return of the Jedi 1983, Indiana Jones and the Temple of Doom 1984, Captain Eo 1986, Willow 1988, Indiana Jones and the Last Crusade 1989, Radioland Murders 1994; writer, producer and dir: THX 1138 1971, Star Wars Episode IV: A New Hope 1977, Star Wars Episode I: The Phantom Menace 1999, Star Wars Episode II: Attack of the Clones 2002, Star Wars Episode III: Revenge of the Sith 2005; writer or producer or exec. producer: Indiana Jones and the Kingdom of the Crystal Skull 2008, Red Tails 2012. *Television includes:* The Young Indiana Jones Chronicles (series) 1992–93, The Adventures of Young Indiana Jones: The Perils of Cupid (film) 2007, Robot Chicken: Star Wars Episode II (film) 2008, Star Wars: The Clone Wars (series) 2008–14, Star Wars: Detours (series) 2012, Star Wars: Underworld (series) 2013. *Address:* Lucasfilm Ltd, 5858 Lucas Valley Road, Nicasio, CA 94946 (office); George Lucas Educational Foundation, PO Box 3494, San Rafael, CA 94912, USA. *Telephone:* (415) 662-1800 (office). *Fax:* (415) 448-2495 (office). *E-mail:* george.lucas@lucasfilm.com (office). *Website:* www.lucasfilm.com (office); www.edutopia.org.

LUCAS, Jonathan, BA, MA, PhD; Seychelles international organization official; ed Univ. of Lyon, France, Univ. of Newcastle-upon-Tyne, UK, Acadia Univ., Canada, Grad. Inst. for Int. Studies, Switzerland; Consultant, ILO, Switzerland 1982; Assoc. Social Affairs Officer, Div. of Narcotic Drugs, UN 1984, later positions include Legal and First Officer, UN Int. Drug Control Programme, Sr Programme Man. Officer, Office of Exec. Dir, Dir-Gen., Office on Drug Control and Crime Prevention, UN, Vienna, Chief, Commissions Secr. Section 1998–2004, Rep. Regional Office for Southern Africa, UN Office on Drugs and Crime 2004–10, Sec., Int. Narcotics Control Bd (INCB) and Chief, INCB Secr. 2010–11, Dir UN Interregional Crime and Justice Research Inst. 2011–15. *Address:* c/o United Nations Interregional Crime and Justice Research Institute, Viale Maestri del Lavoro, 10, 10127 Turin, Italy (office).

LUCAS, Michel; French banking executive; b. 4 May 1939, Lorient; ed Industrial Inst. of the North; joined Confédération Nationale du Crédit Mutuel 1971, several exec. positions, Pres. 1971–2016; Gen. Man. Banque Federative du Crédit Mutuel, Caisse Centrale du Crédit Mutuel, Crédit Mutuel Centre Est Europe; Pres. and Chair. Man. Bd CIC Crédit Industriel & Commercial SA 1998–2016; Pres. Assurances du Crédit Mutuel; Pres. Europay France SA –2004, apptd Vice-Pres. 2004; apptd Dir Regional Bd MasterCard Europe 1992, apptd Vice-Chair. 2002, apptd Dir MasterCard Int. Inc. 2004; mem. Bd of Dirs Banque de Luxembourg, Banque de Tunisie, Banque Marocaine du Commerce Extérieur, Caisses Desjardins, Banque Transatlantique; Officer, Ordre national de la Légion d'honneur 2005, Commdr Ordre national de la Légion d'honneur 2011.

LUCAS, Robert Emerson, Jr, BA, PhD; American economist and academic; *Professor Emeritus, Department of Economics, University of Chicago;* b. 15 Sept. 1937, Yakima, Wash.; ed Univ. of Chicago; Asst Prof. of Econs, Carnegie Inst. of Tech. 1963–67; Assoc. Prof. of Econs, Carnegie-Mellon Univ. 1967–70, Prof. 1970–74; Ford Foundation Visiting Research Prof. of Econs, Univ. of Chicago 1974–75, Prof. of Econs 1975–80, John Dewey Distinguished Service Prof. of Econs 1980–, now Prof. Emer., Vice-Chair. Dept of Econs 1975–83, Chair. 1986–88; Visiting Prof. of Econs, Northwestern Univ. 1981–82; Assoc. Ed. Journal of Economic Theory 1972–78, Journal of Monetary Economics 1977–81; Ed. Journal of Political Economy 1988–2002, Review of Economic Dynamics 2002–08; mem. American Econ. Asscn (mem. Exec. Cttee 1980–82, Vice-Pres. 1987, Pres. 2002), American Acad. of Arts and Sciences 1980 (Council mem.), Econometric Soc. (Fellow 1975, Pres. 1997), NAS 1981; Fellow, AAAS 1980, American Finance Asscn 2004; Dr hc (Université Paris-Dauphine) 1992, (Athens Univ. of Econs and Business) 1994, (Univ. of Montreal) 1998; Nobel Prize for Econs 1995, Phoenix Prize 2015. *Publications:* Rational Expectations and Econometric Practice (co-ed.) 1981, Studies in Business-Cycle Theory 1981, Models of Business Cycles (Yrjo Jahnsson Lectures, Oxford) 1985, Recursive Methods in Economic Dynamics (co-author) 1989, Lectures on Economic Growth 2002; numerous articles in professional journals. *Address:* Department of Economics, University of Chicago, 1126 E 59th Street, Chicago, IL 60637 (office); 320 West Oakdale Avenue, #1903, Chicago, IL 60657, USA (home). *Telephone:* (773) 702-5079 (office). *E-mail:* relucas@midway.uchicago.edu (office). *Website:* economics.uchicago.edu/facstaff/lucas.shtml (office).

LUCAS, Sarah, BA; British artist; b. 1962, London; d. of Irene Lucas; ed Working Men's Coll., London, London Coll. of Printmaking, Goldsmiths Coll., London; emerged as one of the major Young British Artists during the 1990s; works with a variety of materials and media, including photographs, sculpture and installations that use humour and visual puns to explore gender; represented Britain at 56th Venice Int. Art Biennale 2015. *Dance:* Before and After: The Fall, The Michael Clark Co. (set design for a new work performed on tour) 2001. *Television:* Two Melons and a Stinking Fish (Illuminations for BBC TV/Arts Council) 1996, This Is Modern Art (Channel 4 six-part series) 1999, The History of Britart (BBC) 2001. *Address:* c/o Sadie Coles HQ, 69 South Audley Street, London, W1K 2QZ, England. *Telephone:* (20) 7493-8611. *Fax:* (20) 7499-4878. *E-mail:* info@sadiecoles.com. *Website:* www.sadiecoles.com.

LUCE, Baron (Life Peer), cr. 2000, of Adur in the County of West Sussex; **Richard Napier Luce,** Kt, KG, PC, GCVO, DL; British fmr politician; b. 14 Oct. 1936, London; s. of Sir William Luce, GBE, KCMG and Lady Luce (née Margaret Napier); m. Rose Helen Nicholson 1961; two s.; ed Wellington Coll. and Christ's Coll., Cambridge, Wadham Coll. Oxford; Subaltern, Wilts. Regiment, Nat. Service 1955–57; Dist Officer, Kenya 1961–63; Marketing Man. Gallaher Ltd 1963–65; Marketing Man. Spirella Co. of GB 1965–67; Dir Nat. Innovation Centre 1967–71; mem. European Advisory Bd Corning Glass Int. 1976–79; Dir (non-exec.) Booker Tate 1991–96, Meridian Broadcasting 1991–97; MP for Arundel and Shoreham 1971–74, for Shoreham 1974–92; Opposition Whip 1974–75; Opposition Spokesman, Foreign and Commonwealth Affairs 1977–79; Parl. Under-Sec. of State 1979–81; Minister of State, FCO 1981–82, 1983–85; Minister of State (Minister for the Arts) and Minister of State for Civil Service, Privy Council Office 1985–90; Gov. and C-in-C Gibraltar 1997–2000; Lord Chamberlain of her Majesty's Household 2000–06; High Steward, Westminster Abbey 2011–; Vice-Chancellor Univ. of Buckingham 1992–96; Chancellor, Univ. of Gibraltar 2015; Chair. Atlantic Council of UK 1991–96, Commonwealth Foundation 1992–96; mem. Royal Mint Advisory Cttee, Bd Trustees, Royal Collection Trust 2000–06; Pres. Voluntary Arts Network, Royal Overseas League, King George V Fund for Actors and Actresses 2006–11, Commonwealth Youth Orchestra 2010–13; Trustee Geographers' Map Trustees Ltd (A–Z); Trustee Emer. Royal Acad. of Arts; Vice-Patron Harambee and Langalanga Trusts; Parl. Crossbencher (Independent) in the House of Lords; Chair. Crown Nominations Comm. for the See of Canterbury 2012–; Hon. Vice-Pres. Overseas Pensioners' Asscn; Hon. Fellow, Christ's Coll. Cambridge; Hon. Fellow, Atlantic Council of the UK; KStJ. *Publication:* Ringing the Changes: A Memoir 2007. *Leisure interests:* walking, swimming, painting, reading, piano. *Address:* c/o House of Lords, Westminster, London, SW1A 0PW, England.

LUCIANO, Juan R., BEng, MEng; Argentine business executive; *Chairman, President and CEO, Archer Daniels Midland Company;* b. 1961; ed Buenos Aires Inst. of Technology; with The Dow Chemical Co. 1986–2011, including as Exec. Vice-Pres. and Pres., Performance Div.; Exec. Vice-Pres. and COO Archer Daniels Midland 2011–14, mem. Bd of Dirs and Pres. 2014–, CEO 2015–, Chair. 2016–; Gov. Boys and Girls Clubs of America, Midwest Chair. of its Nat. Trustees Bd. *Address:* Archer Daniels Midland Company, 4666 Faries Parkway, Decatur, IL 62526, USA (office). *Telephone:* (217) 424-5200 (office). *Fax:* (217) 424-6196 (office). *E-mail:* media@adm.com (office). *Website:* www.adm.com (office).

LUCIE-SMITH, (John) Edward (McKenzie), MA, FRSL; British art critic and poet; b. 27 Feb. 1933, Kingston, Jamaica; s. of John Dudley Lucie-Smith and Mary Lushington; ed King's School, Canterbury, Merton Coll., Oxford; officer in RAF 1954–56; fmrly worked in advertising and as freelance journalist and broadcaster; contributes to The Times, Sunday Times, Independent, Mail on Sunday, Spectator, New Statesman, Evening Standard, Encounter, London Magazine, Illustrated London News, La Vanguardia (Barcelona); now works as a freelance art historian and exhbn curator; John Llewellyn Rhys Memorial Prize. *Solo photographic exhibitions include:* Zlato Oko, Novi Sad, Vojvoidina, Serbia 1998, Adonis Art, London 1998, Art Kiosk, Brussels 1999, Rivington Gallery, London 1999, Toni Berini Gallery, Barcelona 2000, Rosenfeld Gallery, Tel-Aviv 2001, Plus 1, Plus 2 Gallery, London 2001, Il Politico, Rome 2002, D-137 Gallery, St Petersburg 2002, Butler Inst. of Art, Youngstown, Ohio 2003, Valentine Willie Fine Art, Kuala Lumpur 2003, Albemarle Gallery, London 2003, Art Gallery, Univ. of Buckingham 2003, Labiola Gallery, Ljubljana 2003, O'Connor, A Gallery, Toronto 2004, Museu de Arte Moderna, Rio de Janeiro 2004, Wunderkammer, Valencia 2005, Museum of Contemporary Art, Skopje, Macedonia 2005, Galerija Svetega Donalda, Piran, Slovenia 2006, O'Connor, A Gallery, Toronto 2007, City Art Museum, Helsinki 2007, Gallery Kontrast, Stockholm 2007, Piramid Sanat, Istanbul 2007, Galleria Forni, Bologna 2007, Grafiki Kolektiv, Belgrade 2008, Nat. Gallery, Kingston, Jamaica 2010. *Publications include:* A Tropical Childhood and Other Poems 1961, Confessions and Histories 1964, What is a Painting? 1966, Thinking About Art 1968, Towards Silence 1968, Movements in Art Since 1945 1969, Art in Britain 69–70 1970, A Concise History of French Painting 1971, Symbolist Art 1972, Eroticism in Western Art 1972, The First London Catalogue 1974, The Well Wishers 1974, The Burnt Child (autobiography) 1975, The Invented Eye (early photography) 1975, World of the Makers 1975, Joan of Arc 1976, Fantin-Latour 1977, The Dark Pageant (novel) 1977, Art Today 1977, A Concise History of Furniture 1979, Super Realism 1979, Cultural Calendar of the Twentieth Century 1979, Art in the Seventies 1980, The Story of Craft 1981, The Body 1981, A History of Industrial Design 1983, Art Terms: An Illustrated Dictionary 1984, Art in the Thirties 1985, American Art Now 1985, Lives of the Great Twentieth Century Artists 1986, Sculpture Since 1945 1987, Art in the Eighties 1990, Art Deco Painting 1990, Fletcher Benton 1990, Jean Rustin 1991, Harry Holland 1992, Art and Civilisation 1992, Andres Nagel 1992, Wendy Taylor 1992, Alexander 1992, British Art Now 1993, Race, Sex and Gender: Issues in Contemporary Art 1994, American Realism 1994, Art Today 1995, Visual Arts in the Twentieth Century 1996, Arts Erotica: an Arousing History of Erotic Art 1997, Adam 1998, Stone 1998, Zoo 1998, Sean Henry – The Centre Of The Universe (with Beatrice F. Buscaroli) 1999, Judy Chicago: an American Vision 2000, Flesh and Stone 2000, Changing Shape (poems) 2002, Censoring the Body 2008, Byzantium & Beyond: The Paintings of Dave Pearson (with Margaret Mytton) 2012; has edited numerous anthologies. *Leisure interest:* surfing the internet. *Address:* 104, West Kensington Court, Edith Villas, London, W14 9AB, England (home). *E-mail:* edward@edwardlucie-smith.com; jemls_uk@yahoo.com. *Website:* www.edwardlucie-smith.info.

LUCINSCHI, Petru Chiril, CandPhilSc, PhD; Moldovan politician and fmr head of state; *Head, Foundation for Strategic Studies and Development of International Relations;* b. 27 Jan. 1940, Rădulenii Vechi village, Soroca Co. (now Floreşti dist); s. of Chiril Lucinschi and Parascovia Lucinschi; m. Antonina Georgievna Lucinschi 1965 (died 2006); two s.; ed Kishinev (Chişinău) Univ. and CPSU Cen. Cttee Higher Party School; served in Soviet Army 1962–63; Komsomol work for Cen. Cttee of Moldavian CP 1963–71; mem. CPSU 1964–91; First Sec. of Bălti City Komsomol Cttee 1964–65; Head of Section, Second Sec., First Sec. of Cen. Cttee of Moldavian Komsomol 1965–71; Sec. of Cen. Cttee of Moldavian CP 1971–76, First Sec. Nov. 1989–91; First Sec. of Kishinev City Cttee 1976–78; Deputy Head, Propaganda Dept of CPSU Cen. Cttee 1978–86; Second Sec. of Cen. Cttee of Tadzhik CP 1986–89; Cand. mem. of CPSU Cen. Cttee 1986–89, mem. 1989–91, Sec. 1990–91; Deputy to USSR Supreme Soviet 1986–89; USSR People's Deputy 1989–91; mem. CPSU Politburo 1990–91; Moldovan Amb. to Russia 1992–93; fmr Leader Agrarian Democratic Party; Chair. Moldovan Parl. 1993–96; Pres. of Moldova 1996–2001; Head, Foundation for Strategic Studies and Devt of Int. Relations 2001–; mem., Russian Fed. Social Sciences Acad.; Grand Croix, Légion d'honneur 1998, Order of Redeemer (Greece) 1999, Grand Order of the Kts of the Holy Sepulchre (Greek Orthodox Church, Jerusalem) 2000, Order 'Steaua Romaniei' (Star of Romania), Sash rank 2000, Order of Repub. of Moldova; Dr hc (Minsk, Baku); numerous awards, including Int. Pilgrim of Peace Award, Assisi (Italy). *Publications:* The Last Days of the USSR 1998, The Life and Death 2003, Moldova and Moldavians 2007. *Leisure interests:* sports, travelling, reading, theatre, hunting. *Address:* 76 Bucuresti str., Chişinău, Moldova (home). *Telephone:* (22) 237979 (office). *Fax:* (22) 237981 (office). *E-mail:* office@ipa.dnt.md (office). *Website:* www.president.md/eng/petru-lucinschi.

LUCK, Edward C., BA, MA, MIA, MPhil, PhD; American political scientist, academic and UN official; *Professor, Joan B. Kroc School of Peace Studies, University of San Diego;* b. 17 Oct. 1948; m.; one d.; ed Dartmouth Coll., Columbia Univ.; Founder and Exec. Dir Center for the Study of Int. Org. (research centre jointly est. by School of Law, New York Univ. and Woodrow Wilson School of Public and Int. Affairs, Princeton Univ.) –2001; Prof. in the Professional Practice of Int. Affairs, School of Int. and Public Affairs, Columbia Univ. and Dir Center on Int. Org. 2001– (currently on public service leave); Vice-Pres. and Dir of Studies, Int. Peace Acad. 2008–09; Sr Consultant, Dept of Admin and Man., UN 1995–97, Staff Dir Gen. Ass.'s Open-ended High-level Working Group on the Strengthening of the United Nations System 1995–97, Adviser to Pres. of Gen. Ass., Razali Ismail, on proposals for Security Council reform 1995–97, fmr sr consultant to Sec.-Gen.'s Special Rep. for Children and Armed Conflict, fmr mem. Sec.-Gen.'s Policy Working Group on the UN and Terrorism, Special Adviser at Asst Sec.-Gen. level to Sec.-Gen., UN 2008–12; Prof., Joan B. Kroc School of Peace Studies, Univ. of San Diego 2012–; served in several research and man. capacities, UNA of the USA 1974–84, Pres. and CEO 1984–94, Pres. Emer. 1994–98; fmr Visiting Prof., Sciences-Po, Paris; fmr consultant to numerous pvt. foundations and research centres. *Publications include:* Mixed Messages: American Politics and International Organization, 1919–1999 1999, International Law and Organization: Closing the Compliance Gap (co-ed.) 2004, The UN Security Council: Practice and Promise 2006; has published numerous articles in Foreign Policy, Washington Quarterly, Current History, Disarmament, and other scholarly journals, as well as in the New York Times, Washington Post, Los Angeles Times, Christian Science Monitor, International Herald Tribune, USA Today, Newsday, and other newspapers. *Address:* Joan B. Kroc School of Peace Studies, KIPJ Room 113, 5998 Alcala Park, San Diego, CA 92110, USA (office). *Telephone:* (619) 260-7919 (office). *E-mail:* luck@sandiego.edu (office). *Website:* www.sandiego.edu/peacestudies (office).

LUCKE, Lewis W., BA, MBA; American diplomatist (retd) and business executive; *Chairman, Fuelie Systems, Inc.;* b. 1951, Austin, Tex.; m.; three c.; ed Univ. of North Carolina, Thunderbird, Garvin School of Int. Man.; joined Foreign Service in 1978, career mem. Sr Foreign Service with rank of Minister-Counsellor, has served in Mali, Senegal, Costa Rica, Tunisia, Bolivia, Jordan, Haiti and Iraq, served for 25 years with USAID, including as Mission Dir in Bolivia, Jordan and Haiti, as first Mission Dir in Iraq and as Deputy Asst Admin. USAID in charge of Iraq 2002–04, Amb. to Swaziland 2005–07, then Special Coordinator for Relief and Reconstruction, Dept of State; Pres. Lewis Lucke, LLC 2008–; Exec. Dir Daroke Resources 2013–; Sr Vice-Pres. Emerging Market Access Group 2015–; Chair. Fuelie Systems Inc. 2015–; Presidential Merit Award 2001, Admin. Distinguished Career Award, USAID 2001, Award for Heroism, USAID 2004, named Distinguished Alumnus of the Year, Thunderbird, Garvin School of Int. Man. 2003. *Publication:* Waiting for Rain: Life and Development in Mali, West Africa. *Address:* Fuelie Systems, Inc., 11744 Hwy 15/501 South, Suite 200, Chapel Hill, NC 27517, USA (office). *Website:* www.fueliesystems.com (office).

ŁUCZAK, Aleksander Piotr, PhD; Polish politician and historian; *Vice-President, National Broadcasting Council;* b. 10 Sept. 1943, Legionowo; m. Janina Zakrzewska; one d.; ed Warsaw Univ. and Adam Mickiewicz Univ., Poznań; mem. United Peasants' Party (ZLS) 1966–91; mem. Polish Peasants' Party (PSL) 1991–; lecturer, Dept of History of the Peasant Movt Cen. Cttee ZSL until 1976; mem. Faculty, Univ. of Warsaw 1976–, Asst Prof. 1983–91, Prof. 1991; Adviser to Pres. of Cen. Cttee ZSL 1976–79; Head, Dept of Ideology, Press and Propaganda, Cen. Cttee PSL 1986, Vice-Chair., Head Council PSL 1991–97; Deputy Minister of Nat. Educ. 1986–87; Head, Office of Council of Ministers June–Oct. 1992; Deputy Prime Minister and Minister of Educ. 1993–94; Deputy Prime Minister, Minister and Head of Scientific Research Cttee 1994–96; Minister and Head of Scientific Research Cttee 1996–97; Deputy to Sejm (Parl.) 1989–2001; Chair. Polish Asscn of Adult Educ. 1995–2001; Pres. World Scout Parl. Union 1997–2000; mem. Nat. Broadcasting Council (KRRiT) 2001–, Vice-Pres. 2003–. *Publications:* more than 30 publs on recent history of Poland and the peasant movt. *Leisure interest:* tennis. *Address:* National Broadcasting Council, Skwer Ks. Kard. S. Wyszyńskiego 9, 01-015 Warsaw, Poland (office). *Telephone:* (22) 5973042 (office). *Fax:* (22) 5973180 (office). *E-mail:* luczak@krrit.gov.pl (office). *Website:* www.krrit.gov.pl (office).

LUDER, Owen (Harold), CBE, FRSA, PP RIBA; British architect, planner, environmentalist and writer; *Founder, Owen Luder Consultancy;* b. 7 Aug. 1928, London; s. of Edward Charles Luder and Ellen Clara Luder; m. 1st Rose Dorothy (Doris) Broadstock 1951 (divorced 1988), one s. (deceased) four d.; m. 2nd Jacqueline Ollerton 1989 (died 2008); ed Brixton School of Building, Regent St Polytechnic Evening School of Architecture (now Univ. of Westminster), Brixton School of Architecture; f. Owen Luder Partnership 1957, Sr Partner 1965–78 (when partnership became unlimited co.), Chair. and Man. Dir 1978–87; f. Owen Luder Consultancy, Communication in Construction 1988–2003; Dir (non-exec.) Jarvis PLC 1995–2003; Council mem. RIBA 1967–97, 2010–16, Hon. Treas. 1975–78, Pres. 1981–83, Sr Vice-Pres. 1994–95, Pres. 1995–97, Architect mem. Architects' Registration Bd and Vice-Chair. 1997–2002, Chair. 2002–03; Pres. Norwood Soc. 1982–92; Sec.-Treas. Commonwealth Asscn of Architects 1985–87; Pres. UIA Congress 1986; Vice-Pres. Membership Communications 1989–90; Dir Communication in Construction Ltd 1990–2003; Consultant to Nat. Coal Bd for environmental, architectural and planning issues on Vale of Belvoir Coal Mining Project, UK 1975–87; Architect/Planner for revitalization schemes for British Rail Eng Works at Shildon, Co. Durham and Swindon; consultant and architect for many commercial devt schemes in UK, Saudi Arabia, Nigeria, UAE and USA 1959–2003; Little Rock Arkansas, architectural consultant and qualified mediator; mem. Acad. of Experts 1992–, Vice-Chair. 1997–98; Freeman, US State of Arkansas 1970, Freeman of the Worshipful Company of Architects 1994, Freeman, City of London 2010; RIBA Architecture Bronze Medal 1963, Town Planning and Housing Council Silver Jubilee Award 'Housing in the 80s', Business Consultant of the Year 1985, and various other architectural, design and civic trust awards and commendations. *Film:* Get Luder (documentary) 2003. *Radio:* numerous interviews and contribs. over the years. *Publications:* Adventure in Architecture – A Portrait of the Owen Luder Partnership 1976, Promotion and Marketing for Building Professionals 1988, Sports Stadia After Hillsborough 1990, Keeping Out of Trouble 1999; frequent contribs to nat. and tech. publs. *Leisure interests:* photography, writing, Arsenal Football Club, swimming. *Address:* Owen Luder Consultancy, Apartment 702, Romney House, 47 Marsham Street, London, SW1P 3DS, England; Craig-y-Don, Cliff Road, Laugharne, Carmarthen, Wales (home). *Telephone:* (20) 7222-0198 (home). *E-mail:* owenluder@gmail.com (home).

LUDEWIG, Johannes, MSc, PhD; German civil servant and business executive; b. 6 July 1945, Hamburg; m.; three c.; ed Univ. of Hamburg, Stanford Univ., USA, Ecole Nat. d'Admin., Paris, France; worked on energy, econ. and business policy, Fed. Ministry of Econs 1975–83; joined Office of the Fed. Chancellor 1983, Ministerial Dir, Dept of Econ. and Financial Policy 1991–94; fmr State Sec., Fed. Ministry of Econs; fmr Commr of Fed. Govt for New German Fed. States; mem. Exec. Bd Deutsche Bahn AG 1997–99, Chair. 1997–99; apptd Chair. Nat. Regulatory Control Council 2006; Exec. Dir Community of European Railways and Infrastructure Cos (CER) 2001–11; Verdienstkreuz 1st Klasse 2005, Merit of the State of Saxony-Anhalt 2015.

LUDFORD, Baroness (Life Peer), cr. 1997, of Clerkenwell in the London Borough of Islington; **Sarah Ludford,** MSc; British politician; b. 14 March 1951, Halesworth; d. of Joseph Campbell Ludford and Valerie Kathleen Ludford (née Skinner); m. Steve Hitchins; ed Portsmouth High School for Girls, London School of Econs; barrister, called to the Bar Gray's Inn 1979; official, Secr.-Gen. and Directorate Gen. Competition, EC 1979–85; European and UK policy adviser, Lloyds of London 1985–87; Vice-Pres. Corp. External Affairs, American Express European 1987–90; freelance Euro consultant 1990–99; mem. Liberal Democrat Party; Councillor (Liberal Democrat) Islington Borough Council 1991–99; Vice-Chair. Liberal Democrat Federal Policy Cttee 1991–98; Vice-Pres. Gay and Lesbian Lib Dems (DELGA); MEP (Liberal Democrat) for London 1999–; mem. Council European Liberal Democrat and Reform (ELDR) Party; mem. Cttee on Citizens' Freedoms and Rights, Justice and Home Affairs, Foreign Affairs, Human Rights, Common Security and Defence Policy; mem. Inter-Parl. dels: Cyprus, South-East Europe (also Vice-Pres.); ELDR spokeswoman on Justice and Home Affairs; rapporteur on Anti-Racism, European Parl. 2000, on Legal Rights for EU-resident foreign nationals 2001–02; Vice-Pres. European Parl. Inter-Group on Anti-Racism, co-ordinating European Parl. Kurdish Network; mem. Royal Inst. of Int. Affairs, European Movt. *Publications include:* The EU: From Economic Community to Human Rights Community (article); contrib. to To the Power of Ten 2000. *Leisure interests:* theatre, ballet, gardening. *Address:* European Parliament, Office 10G165, Rue Wiertz, 1047 Brussels, Belgium (office); Constituency Office, 36B St Peter's Street, London, N1 8JT, England (office). *Telephone:* (2) 284-71-04 (office); (20) 7288-2526 (office). *Fax:* (2) 284-91-04 (office); (20) 7288-2526 (office). *E-mail:* office@sarahludfordmep.org.uk (office); sarah.ludford@europarl.europa.eu (office). *Website:* www.europarl.europa.eu (office); www.sarahludfordmep.org.uk (office).

LUDWIG, Christa; Austrian/French singer (mezzo-soprano); b. 16 March 1928, Berlin, Germany; d. of Anton Ludwig and Eugenie Besalla-Ludwig; m. 1st Walter Berry 1957 (divorced 1970, died 2000); one s.; m. 2nd Paul-Emile Deiber 1972; opera debut aged 18, guest appearance at Athens Festival in Epidauros 1965; joined Vienna State Opera 1955, Hon. mem. 1981; appearances at festivals in Salzburg, Bayreuth, Lucerne, Holland, Prague, Saratoga, Stockholm; guest appearances in season in Vienna, New York, Chicago, Buenos Aires, Milan, Berlin, Munich; numerous recitals and soloist in concerts; Hon. mem. Vienna Konzerthaus, Vienna Philharmonic; Commdr des Arts et des Lettres 1989, Grosses Ehrenzeichen 1994, Commdr, Ordre pour le Mérite 1997, Commdr, Légion d'honneur 2010; winner, Bach-Concours, record award for Fricka in Walküre and Des Knaben Wunderhorn, awarded title of Kammersängerin by Austrian Govt 1962, Prix des Affaires Culturelles (for recording of Venus in Tannhäuser), Paris 1972, Silver Rose (Vienna Philharmonic) 1980, Golden Ring (Staatsoper, Vienna) 1980, Golden Gustav Mahler Medal 1980, Hugo Wolf Medal (Austria) 1980, Gold Medal (City of Vienna) 1988, Midem Classical Lifetime Achievement Award 2008, Hugo Wolf Medal (Germany) 2010, Gramophone Lifetime Achievement Award 2016. *Recordings include:* Lieder and complete operas including Norma (with Maria Callas), Lohengrin, Così fan tutte, Der Rosenkavalier, Carmen, Götterdämmerung, Die Walküre, Bluebeard's Castle, Don Giovanni, Die Zauberflöte, Le Nozze di Figaro, Capriccio, Fidelio. *Publication:* In My Own Voice (biog.) 1994. *Leisure interests:* music, archaeology, reading, home movie making, cooking, sewing, fashion, shopping, weaving, rug knitting and travelling. *Address:* c/o Ingpen & Williams, 7 St George's Court, 131 Putney Bridge Road, London, SW15 2PA, England (office). *Website:* www.ingpen.co.uk/artist/christa-ludwig (office).

LUERS, William Henry, MA, FAAS; American diplomatist, museum administrator and academic; *Director, Iran Project;* b. 15 May 1929, Springfield, Ill.; s. of Carl U. Luers and Ann L. Luers; m. Wendy Woods Turnbull 1979; three s. one d. by previous marriage and two step-d.; ed Hamilton Coll., Columbia and Northwestern Univs; fmr USN officer; Foreign Service Officer, Dept of State 1957, Vice-Consul, Naples, Italy 1957–60, Second Sec. Embassy in Moscow 1963–65, Political Counsellor, Embassy in Caracas 1969–73, Deputy Exec. Sec., Dept of State 1973–75, Deputy Asst Sec. for Inter-American Affairs 1975–77, Deputy Asst Sec. for Europe 1977–78, Amb. to Venezuela 1978–82, to Czechoslovakia 1983–86; Pres. Metropolitan Museum of Art, New York 1986–99; Pres. and CEO UN Asscn of USA 1999–2009; currently Dir The Iran Project; also currently Adjunct Prof. of Int. and Public Affairs, School of Int. and Public Affairs, Columbia Univ.; Dir's Visitor, Princeton Inst. for Advanced Studies 1982–83; mem. Bd Rockefeller Brothers Fund, AOL-Latin America, Scudder Funds, Wickes Corpn; mem. Council on Foreign Relations, American Acad. of Arts and Sciences, American Acad. of Diplomacy; Hon. LLD (Hamilton Coll.) 1982; American Foreign Service Cup 1988. *Address:* International Affairs Building, 13th Floor, Columbia University, 420 West 118th Street, New York, NY 10027 (office); 419 East 57th Street, Apt 14A, New York, NY 10022, USA (home). *Telephone:* (212) 854-3213 (office); (212) 593-0586 (home). *E-mail:* whl39@columbia.edu (office); iranproject@fcsny.org (office). *Website:* iranprojectfcsny.org (office); sipa.columbia.edu/faculty/william-h-luers (office).

LUGANSKY, Nikolai L.; Russian pianist; b. 26 April 1972, Moscow; s. of Lev Borisovich Lugansky and Anna Nikolayevna Luganskaya; m. Lada Borisovna Luganskaya; two s. one d.; ed Moscow State Conservatory; repertoire includes more than 40 piano concertos and music from Bach to modern composers; ensemblist and interpreter of chamber music; performances in Russia and abroad in Australia, Austria, Belgium, Brazil, Canada, England, France, Germany, Italy, Japan and elsewhere, including at Royal Festival Hall and Wigmore Hall in London, Salle Gaveau and Louvre in Paris, Conservatoria Verdi in Milan, Gasteig in Munich, Concertgebouw in Amsterdam, Alte Oper in Frankfurt; First Prize, All-Union student competition Tbilisi Georgia 1988, Silver Medal, Bach Int. Competition, Leipzig, Germany 1988, Second Prize, Rachmaninov Competition, Moscow 1990, First Prize, Tchaikovsky Int. Competition, Moscow 1994, Terence Judd Award for the most promising pianist of a generation 1995, Honoured Artist of the Russian Fed. 2005, Echo Klassik Award 2005, 2007, 2013, BBC Music Magazine Award 2011, People's Artist of Russia 2013, Int. Classical Music Award for Solo Instrument 2013. *Recordings include:* numerous albums including Rachmaninov piano concertos, Tchaikovsky's Piano Concerto No. 1 2004, Liszt 2011, Prokofiev's Piano Concerto No. 3 and Grieg's Piano Concerto with Deutsches-Symphonie Orchester Berlin and Kent Nagano 2013, Chopin Piano Concertos with Sinfonia Varsovia and Alexander Vedernikov 2014, Rachmaninov's 24 Preludes in 2018, Debussy works for Solo Piano 2018. *Leisure interests:* chess, table tennis, reading. *Address:* c/o HarrisonParrott, The Ark, 201 Talgarth Road, London, W6 8BJ, England (office); Moscow 119334, Kosygina str. 2, apt 2, Russia (home). *E-mail:* lydia.connolly@harrisonparrott.co.uk (office). *Website:* www.harrisonparrott.com/artist/profile/nikolai-lugansky (office); www.facebook.com/NikolaiLugansky. *Telephone:* (495) 137-18-36 (home).

LUGO MÉNDEZ, Fernando Armindo; Paraguayan politician, fmr ecclesiastic and fmr head of state; b. 30 May 1951, San Solano; s. of William and Maximina Lugo Mendez Fleitas; one s.; ed Catholic Univ. of Our Lady of the Assumption, Pontifical Gregorian Univ., Rome; ordained priest of Soc. of the Divine Word 1977; moved to Ecuador as missionary in Bolivar prov., then studied in Rome; returned to Paraguay, apptd Bishop of San Pedro 1994–2005 (resgnd), resgnd from priesthood 2006; Leader, Movimiento Popular Tekojoja; Pres. of Paraguay 2008–12; mem. Senate 2013–. *Address:* Senate, National Congress, May 14 e / Avda. Republic, Asunción, Paraguay (office). *Telephone:* (414) 5000 (office). *Website:* www.senado.gov.py (office).

LUHABE, Wendy Yvonne Nomathemba, BA, BComm; South African business executive, fmr university chancellor and social entrepreneur; b. 29 May 1957, Johannesburg, Gauteng Prov.; d. of Stanley Garfield Luhabe and Adelaide Boniwe Bulana; m. Mbhazima Shilowa; two s.; ed Univ. of Lesotho; marketing professional with Vanda Cosmetics, BMW South Africa & N America 1981–91; Founder Bridging the Gap (human resources and recruitment firm) 1992–2001; Foundermem. Women Investment Portfolio Holdings 1994, Women Private Equity Fund 1996, Women in Infrastructure Devt and Energy 2014; social entrepreneur, Wendy Luhabe Foundation for the educ. and leadership devt of women; Chair. Alliance Capital –2009, Vodacom Group –2009, Vendome SA, Industrial Devt Corpn, Int. Marketing Council; mem. Consultative Network of the Helsinki Process on Globalization and Democracy; Int. Trustee, The Duke of Edinburgh's Award Int. Foundation for Young People; Chancellor, Univ. of Johannesburg 2006–12; Hon. LVO 2014; Dr hc (Univ. of Fort Hare) 2005, (Stellenbosch Univ.) 2006; recognized by World Econ. Forum as a Global Leader for Tomorrow 1997, Leadership in Practice, Unisa Business Leadership School 1997, Outstanding

Young Person, Osaka Jr Chamber of Commerce (Japan) 1997. *Publication:* Defining Moments 2002. *Leisure interests:* travel, spirituality, decoupage, nature, culture, music. *Address:* PO Box 91413, Auckland Park, Johannesburg 2006, South Africa (office). *Telephone:* (11) 8807117 (office). *Fax:* (11) 8803767 (office). *E-mail:* wendy@definingmoments.co.za (office). *Website:* www.wendyluhabe.org.

LUHRMANN, Bazmark (Baz) Anthony; Australian writer, producer and director; b. 17 Sept. 1962, NSW; s. of Leonard Luhrmann and Barbara Luhrmann; m. Catherine Martin 1997; one d.; ed Narrabeen High School, Sydney; theatre work with Peter Brook (q.v.); owns Bazmark Inq. production co., Sydney; acting roles in films Winter of Our Dreams 1981, The Dark Room 1982. *Recording:* Something for Everybody (concept album, including track Everybody's Free To Wear Sunscreen) (Platinum Album, Australia, Gold Album, USA). *Plays:* Strictly Ballroom, Haircut. *Operas directed:* La Bohème, Sydney 1990, New York 2002–03, San Francisco 2002, A Midsummer Night's Dream, Sydney 1993. *Films directed:* Strictly Ballroom (Cannes Film Festival Prix de la Jeunesse, Toronto Film Festival People's Choice Award, Chicago Film Festival Award for Best Feature Film) 1992, Romeo + Juliet (also producer) 1996, Moulin Rouge! (also producer) (numerous awards, including Golden Globe, Producers' Guild of America Film of the Year, Hollywood Film Festival Best Movie) 2001, Australia (also producer) 2008, Waist Up/Waist Down (short) 2012, Ugly Chic (short) 2012, The Surreal Body (short) 2012, The Exotic Body (short) 2012, The Classical Body (short) 2012, Schiaparelli & Prada: Impossible Conversations (short) 2012, Naïf Chic (short) 2012, Hard Chic (short) 2012, The Great Gatsby (also producer) 2013. *Screenplays:* Strictly Ballroom 1992, Romeo + Juliet 1996, Moulin Rouge (also story) 2001, Australia (also story) 2008, The Great Gatsby 2013. *Television includes:* A Country Practice (actor) 1981–82, La Bohème (film) 1993. *Address:* c/o Robert Newman, WME, 9601 Wilshire Blvd, 10th Floor, Beverly Hills, CA 90212, USA (office); Bazmark Inq., PO Box 430, Kings Cross, NSW 1340, Australia (office). *Website:* www.bazmark.com (office).

LÜHRMANN, Reinhard, Dr rer. nat; German biochemist and academic; *Director, Department of Cellular Biochemistry, Max Planck Institute of Biophysical Chemistry;* ed Univ. of Münster; Research Group Leader, Max Planck Inst. for Molecular Genetics, Berlin 1981–88; Prof. of Biochemistry and Molecular Biology, Univ. of Marburg 1988–99; Dir, Dept of Cellular Biochemistry, Max Planck Inst. for Biophysical Chem., Göttingen 1999–; Hon. Prof., Philipps Univ. of Marburg 2000–, Georg August Univ. of Göttingen 2007–; Max Planck Research Award 1990, Gottfried Wilhelm Leibniz Prize 1996, Feldberg Foundation Prize Lecturer 2002, Ernst Jung Prize 2003. *Publications:* numerous articles in scientific journals. *Address:* Max-Planck-Institut für biophysikalische Chemie, Abteilung Zelluläre Biochemie, Am Faßberg 11, 37077 Göttingen, Germany (office). *Telephone:* (551) 201-1407 (office). *Fax:* (551) 201-1197 (office). *E-mail:* reinhard.luehrmann@mpibpc.mpg.de (office). *Website:* www.mpibpc.mpg.de/luehrmann (office).

LUI, Frank Fakaotimanava, CNZM; Niuean politician; b. 1945, Alofi; m. Iris Lui; Premier of Niue 1993–99, also Minister for External Relations, Niueans Overseas, Police and Immigration, Civil Aviation and Public Service Comm.; Ind.; Companion, NZ Order of Merit 1999. *Address:* c/o Office of the Secretary to Government, PO Box 40, Alofi, Niue. *E-mail:* richard.hipa@mail.gov.nu.

LUIK, Jüri; Estonian diplomatist, politician and journalist; *Minister of Defence;* b. 17 Aug. 1966, Tallinn, Estonian SSR, USSR; m. Ruth Lausma Luik; one s.; ed Tallinn 7th High School, Tartu Univ. and postgraduate research, Carnegie, USA; Political Ed. Vikerkaar (monthly) 1988–90, Ed. 1990; specialist on Anglo-Saxon Countries, Estonian Inst. 1989–91; mem. Pro Patria (Isamaaliit) Party 1989–2006, 2018–, Isamaa ja Res Publica Liit (Union of Pro Patria and Res Publica) 2006–18; attaché, Embassy of Estonia, UK 1991; Head, Political Dept, Ministry of Foreign Affairs 1991–92; mem. Riigikogu (Parl.) 1992–95; Minister without portfolio responsible for Estonian-Russian Negotiations 1992–93; Minister of Defence 1993–94, 1999–2001, 2017–, of Foreign Affairs 1994–95; Sr Research Fellow, Carnegie Foundation 1995–96; Amb. to NATO and Benelux States, Brussels 1996–99; head of govt del. for accession talks with NATO 2002–03; Amb. to USA (also accred to Canada) 2003–07, Amb. and Perm. Rep. to NATO, Brussels 2007–12, Amb. to the Russian Fed. 2013–15; Head, International Center for Defense and Security, Tallinn 2015–17; Order of the Nat. Coat of Arms (Third Class) 2004. *Leisure interests:* theatre, films, tennis. *Address:* Ministry of Defence, Sakala 1, Tallinn 15094, Estonia (office). *Telephone:* 717-0022 (office). *Fax:* 717-0001 (office). *E-mail:* info@kaitseministeerium.ee (office). *Website:* www.kaitseministeerium.ee (office).

LUJAN GRISHAM, Michelle, BS, JD; American politician; *Governor of New Mexico;* b. 24 Oct. 1954, Los Alamos, NM; d. of Llewellyn 'Buddy' Lujan and Sonja Lujan; m. Gregory Grisham (died 2004); two d.; ed Univ. of NM; Dir State Agency on Aging, NM 1991–2002; Sec., Aging and Long Term Services, New Mexico 2002–04; Sec., Dept of Health, NM 2004–07; Commr Bernalillo Co. 2011–12; cofounder and co-owner, Delta Consulting Group 2013–17; mem. US House of Reps 2013–18; Gov. of NM 2019–; Attorney, Lawyer Referral for the Elderly Program, State Bar of NM; Vice-Chair. Hispanic Caucus; mem. of numerous congressional caucuses including Women's Issues, Financial Protection and Life Insurance, House Science and Nat. Labs. *Address:* Office of the Governor, 490 Old Santa Fe Trail, Room 400, Santa Fe, NM 87501, USA (office). *Telephone:* (505) 476-2200 (office). *Website:* www.governor.state.nm.us (office).

LUK, Kam-Biu, BSc, PhD; American (b. Hong Kong) physicist and academic; *Professor of Physics, University of California, Berkeley;* ed Univ. of Hong Kong, Rutgers Univ.; postdoctoral research, Univ. of Washington, Seattle 1983–86; Assoc. Scientist and R.R. Wilson Fellow, Fermilab 1986–89; jt appointment as Faculty Scientist at Lawrence Berkeley Nat. Lab. and Univ. of California, Berkeley 1989–, Miller Prof. 2001, currently Prof. of Physics, Univ. of California, Berkeley and Sr Faculty mem. Physics Div., Lawrence Berkeley Nat. Lab.; Dept of Energy Outstanding Jr Investigator Award 1990, Sloan Fellowship 1990–94, Panofsky Prize (co-recipient) 2014, Breakthrough Prize in Fundamental Physics (co-recipient) 2016. *Publications:* numerous papers in professional journals. *Address:* Room 427 LeConte, Department of Physics, University of California, Berkeley, Berkeley, CA 94720-7300, USA (office). *Telephone:* (510) 642-8162 (office); (510) 486-7054 (office). *E-mail:* k_luk@berkeley.edu (office). *Website:* physics.berkeley.edu (office); neutrino.physics.berkeley.edu (office).

LUKAČ, Col Dragan, BA, MA; Bosnia and Herzegovina police officer and government official; *Minister of the Interior, Republika Srpska;* b. 1968, Krnjeuša, Bosanski Petrovac Municipality, Socialist Repub. of Bosnia and Herzegovina, Socialist Fed. Repub. of Yugoslavia; m.; four c.; ed Faculty of Internal Affairs, Univ. of Banja Luka; worked in the SUP, Socialist Repub. of Bosnia and Herzegovina, in the Ministry of Interior, Sarajevo Canton and in Bihać Canton, and in Ministry of Internal Affairs, Republika Srpska 1992–2005, various capacities, including as a police officer and in various managerial positions; during the Bosnian War, commanded special police units; promoted to rank of Col of the Police; mem. City Admin of Banja Luka 2005–14, Head of Dept of Communal Police, Admin of City of Banja Luka; Minister of the Interior, Republika Srpska 2014–; Order of Milos Obilic Medal for Bravery; Karađorđeva Zvezda. *Address:* Ministry of the Interior of Republika Srpska, 78000 Banja Luka, trg Republike Srpske 1, Bosnia and Herzegovina (office). *Telephone:* (51) 338478 (office). *Fax:* (51) 338844 (office). *E-mail:* mup@mup.vladars.net (office). *Website:* www.mup.vladars.net (office).

LUKAS, D. Wayne, EdM; American race horse trainer; b. 2 Sept. 1935, Antigo, Wis.; s. of Ted Lukas and Bea Lukas; m. Laura Lukas; one s.; ed Univ. of Wisconsin; began career as Asst Basketball Coach, Univ. of Wisconsin, then Head Basketball Coach, LaCrosse High School; later spent more than ten years training quarter horses, with a record 150 wins; switched to training thoroughbreds 1978; six consecutive Triple Crown race wins: Tabasco Cat–Preakness 1994, Belmont 1994, Thunder Gulch–Derby 1995, Belmont 1995, Timber Country–Preakness 1995, Grindstone–Kentucky Derby 1996; has trained 17 Breeders' Cup winners; all-time leading money winner; four-time Eclipse Award winner–Trainer of the Year, Outstanding Trainer, New York Turf Writers Asscn 1985, C.V. Whitney Achievement Award (with Michael Tabor), New York Turf Writers Asscn 1995, Big Sport of Turfdom Award, Turf Publicists of America 1999, inducted into Thoroughbred Racing Hall of Fame 1999. *Address:* D. Wayne Lukas Racing Stable, 5242 Katella Avenue, Suite 103B, Los Alamitos, CA 90720, USA. *Website:* www.lukasracing.com.

LUKASHENKA, Alyaksandr Rygorovich; Belarusian politician, economist and head of state; *President;* b. 30 Aug. 1954, Kopys, Vitebsk (Viciebsk) Oblast, Belarusian SSR, USSR; m. Halyna Rodionovna Lukashenka 1975 (estranged); two s.; one s. with Irina Abelskaya; ed Mogilev (Mahiloŭ) State Univ. and Belarus Agric. Acad.; served in Soviet Army 1975–77, 1980–82; Sec. Komsomol Cttee, Shklov, instructor Political Div. Komsomol Cttee W Border 1975–77; Sec. Komsomol Cttee Mogilev City Food Dept; instructor regional Exec. Cttee 1977–80; Deputy Commdr of Co. 1980–82; Deputy Chair. Udarnik collective farm 1982–83; Deputy Dir Enterprise of Construction Materials 1983–85; Sec. CP Cttee Collective Farm of V.I. Lenin, Shklov Dist 1985–87; Dir Gorodets state farm 1987–94; elected Deputy, Supreme Council of Belarus SSR 1990–94; Chair. Parl. Comm. on Struggle against Corruption 1993–94; Pres. of Belarus 1994–; C-in-C Armed Forces of Belarus 1994–; Chair. Higher Council of Belarus and Russia Union 1997–; Chair. Supreme State Council of the Union State of Belarus and Russia 2000–; Hon. Academician, Russian Acad. of Sciences 1995, Hon. Citizen of Yerevan, Armenia 2001; Order of the Holy Cross of the Kts of the Holy Sepulchre 2000, José Martí Order (Cuba) 2000, Order of the Revolution (Libya) 2000, Order 'For Services to the Fatherland', (Second Class) (Russia) 2001, Order of St Dmitry Donskoy (First Degree) 2005, Order of St Cyril (Belarusian Orthodox Church) 2006, Order of St Vladimir (First Class) (Russian Orthodox Church) 2007, Keys to the City of Caracas, Venezuela 2010, Order of Distinguished Citizen, Caracas 2010, Order of the Repub. of Serbia 2013, Order of Alexander Nevsky 2014; Honour Diploma of Eurasian Econ. Community 2006; Int. Andrey Pervozvanny (St Andrew) Prize 'For Faith and Loyalty' 1995, M. Sholokhov Int. Award 1997, Special Prize of IOC 'Gates of the Olymph' 2000, Medal of the Int. Fed. of Festival Orgs 2005. *Address:* Office of the President, 220016 Minsk, vul. K. Marksa 38, Dom Urada, Belarus (office). *Telephone:* (17) 222-35-03 (office). *Fax:* (17) 222-30-20 (office). *E-mail:* press@president.gov.by (office). *Website:* www.president.gov.by (office).

LUKE, Hon. Justice Desmond Edgar Fashole, BL, MA; Sierra Leonean chief justice (retd), diplomatist and politician; b. 6 Oct. 1935, Freetown; s. of Sir Emile Fashole-Luke and Lady Christina Fashole-Luke; one s. one d.; ed Prince of Wales School, Freetown, King's Coll., Taunton, UK, Keble Coll., Oxford, UK, Magdalene Coll., Cambridge, UK, Georgetown Univ., Washington, DC, USA; admitted to Bar of England and Wales 1962, of Sierra Leone 1963; in pvt. practice, barrister and solicitor 1963–69; Legal Adviser to Mobil Oil, British Petrol, Bata Shoe Co., Barclays Bank, Diamond Corpn, Allen & Elliot (SL) Ltd, Singer Sewing Machine Co. Ltd, Trade Marks Owners' Asscn, Adams and Adams Patent Attorneys and other industrial and commercial cos 1963–69; UN Human Rights Fellow, India 1964; Amb. to FRG (also accred to Netherlands, Belgium and Luxembourg 1970–73) 1969–73, to France, Italy and Perm. Rep. to EEC 1971–73; Deputy Leader Del. to Heads of State Summit of OAU, Addis Ababa, Non-Aligned Summit, Algeria 1969, Commonwealth Prime Minister's Conf., Ottawa 1973, Abidjan Peace Talks 1996, ECOWAS Conf., Abuja 1997, UN Gen. Ass., NY 1997; Leader Del. to IAEA Conf., Vienna 1970, to African Econ. Conf., Milan 1971, to Council of Ministers of OAU, Addis Ababa 1973–75, to UN Gen. Ass., NY 1973–74; Minister of Foreign Affairs 1973–75 (resgnd), of Health 1977–78; Man. Dir Africa Int. Ltd 1975; Chair. Comm. for Consolidation of Peace 1996–97; Chief Justice of Sierra Leone 1998–2002; Special Envoy of Pres. Kabbah to Pres. Kuffour of Ghana 2002; Grand Cross, Order of Merit (FRG) 1973; Grand Cordon, Order of Menelik II (Ethiopia) 1973; Oxford Blues Athletic Awards 1955–58, finalist (long jump), Commonwealth Games, Cardiff 1958, Oxford and Cambridge Freshman's Champion and Record Holder (high jump) 1954, Men in Action Certificate of Merit for Contrib. to Restoration of Democracy in Sierra Leone 1999, Jarwlee Lewis Meritorious Award for Services to State 2001. *Publications include:* Republican Constitution: What Form?. *Leisure interests:* sports, art, music. *Address:* c/o Office of the Chief Justice, Supreme Court, Freetown (office); Luke House, PO Box 214, Freetown, Sierra Leone (home). *Telephone:* (22) 231863 (office). *Fax:* (22) 225670 (office). *E-mail:* fasholeluke@yahoo.com (home).

LUKIN, Vladimir Petrovich, PhD, DSc; Russian politician and diplomatist; *President, Russian Paralympic Committee;* b. 13 June 1937, Omsk; m.; two s.; ed Moscow State Pedagogical Inst., USSR Acad. of Sciences; researcher, Museum of Revolution, Inst. of World Econs and Int. Relations, USSR Acad. of Sciences 1959–65; on staff of journal World Review, Prague until Aug. 1968 when he was recalled to USSR for protesting against Soviet invasion of Czechoslovakia; Research Fellow, Inst. of US and Canadian Studies, USSR Acad. of Sciences 1969–87; Deputy Dir Dept of Assessment and Planning of the USSR Ministry of Foreign Affairs 1987–90; People's Deputy of RSFSR (now Russia) 1990–93; Chair. Foreign Affairs Cttee of the Russian Supreme Soviet 1990–92; Amb. to USA 1992–93; Co-Founder and Leader, pre-election bloc (later political movt) Yabloko (with G. Javlinsky) 1993; mem. State Duma (Parl.) 1993–2003, Chair. Cttee for Foreign Affairs 1994–99, Deputy Chair. State Duma 2000–02; Commr for Human Rights of Russian Fed. (Fed. Ombudsman) 2004–14; Pres. Russian Paralympic Cttee 1996–; two decorative orders, one medal. *Publications include:* Centres of Power: Conceptions and Reality, China's Place in US Global Policy, With Concern and Hope: Russia and the West. *Leisure interests:* sport. *Address:* Russian Paralympic Committee, 101000 Moscow, 6th Floor, Turgenevskaya Square, 2 (office); c/o Yabloko Party, 119034 Moscow, M. Levshinskii per. 7/3, Russia. *E-mail:* pkr@paralymp.ru (office); info@yabloko.ru. *Website:* paralymp.ru (office); www.yabloko.ru.

LUKŠIĆ, Igor, MA, PhD; Montenegrin politician; b. 14 June 1976, Bar, Montenegrin SR, SFR Yugoslavia; m. Nataša Lukšić; two d.; ed Univ. of Montenegro, Podgorica; asst on implementation of Obnova assistance programmes of EC, Ministry of Foreign Affairs 1998–2000; Adviser on int. relations, Demokratska Partija Socijalista Crne Gore (DPS—Democratic Party of Socialists of Montenegro) 2000–01; performed duties of Sec. in Ministry of Foreign Affairs Jan.–May 2001; elected mem. Parl. of Montenegro 2001, 2002, 2006, 2008; mem. Parl. of Serbia and Montenegro 2003–06; Adviser on Public Relations to the Prime Minister Jan.–April 2003; Deputy Minister of Foreign Affairs of Serbia and Montenegro 2003–04; Minister of Finance 2004–10, Gov. on behalf of Montenegro at World Bank and EBRD 2006; Deputy Prime Minister 2008–10; Prime Minister 2010–12; Deputy Prime Minister, responsible for European Integration and Minister of Foreign Affairs and European Integration 2012–16; Assoc. Prof., Economy and Devt and Market Process, Faculty of Int. Econs, Finance and Business, Podgorica, Asst to course on Entrepreneurship, Faculty of Econs summer terms 2004, 2005, 2006; mem. Cttee for ECO Sciences, Montenegrin Acad. of Arts and Science; mem. Presidency of DPS, Presidency of Basketball Asscn of Montenegro 2010–11. *Publications include:* several academic works as well as a book of poetry and prose, Book of Laughter, Book of Fear; publishes regular blogposts in both Montenegrin and English. *Leisure interests:* music, reading, basketball, tennis. *Address:* Demokratska Partija Socijalista, 81000 Podgorica, Jovana Tomaševića, Montenegro. *Telephone:* (20) 243952 (office). *Fax:* (20) 243347 (office). *E-mail:* office@dps.me (office). *Website:* www.dps.me (office); igorluksic.wordpress.com (home).

LUKŠIČ, Igor, PhD; Slovenian political scientist, academic and politician; *President, Social Democrats;* b. 3 Dec. 1961, Novo mesto, Slovenian SR, SFR Yugoslavia; ed Univ. of Ljubljana; Teaching Asst, Faculty of Social Sciences, Univ. of Ljubljana 1986, later Asst Prof., Prof. of Political Science 2003–, Chair. Dept of Political Science 1997–99, 2007–, Vice-Dean, Faculty of Social Sciences 1999–2001, Dean 2001–03, fmr Pres. Union of Slovenian Sports Socs; Ed.-in-Chief Teorija in praksa magazine 1995–2008; has lectured at several int. univs, including Michigan State Univ. and Univ. of California, Davis, USA and Univ. of Genoa, Italy; Vice-Pres. Social Democrats (Socialni demokrati—SD) 2005–09, Pres. 2012–; mem. Nat. Ass. (Parl.) 2008–; Minister of Educ. and Sport 2008–12. *Publications:* five books, including: Demokracija v pluralni družbi – Preverjanje veljavnosti konsociativne teorije (Democracy in a Plural Society) 1991, Liberalizem versus korporativizem (Liberalism versus Corporativism) 1994, Politični sistem Republike Slovenije (The Political System of the Republic of Slovenia) 2001; articles on political culture, the history of political ideas and political systems, and analysis of policies, published in Slovene, German, English, Czech and Serbo-Croatian. *Address:* Socialni demokrati, Levstikova 15, 1000 Ljubljana (office); Room C208, Faculty of Social Sciences, University of Ljublana, Kardeljeva ploščad 5, PO Box 2547, 1001 Ljubljana, Slovenia (office). *Telephone:* (1) 2444100 (SD) (office); (1) 5805181 (Faculty) (office). *Fax:* (1) 2444111 (SD) (office). *E-mail:* info@socialnidemokrati.si (office); igor.luksic@fdv.uni-lj.si (office). *Website:* www.socialnidemokrati.si (office); www.fdv.uni-lj.si (office).

LULA DA SILVA, Luiz Inácio; Brazilian trade union official, politician and fmr head of state; b. 27 Oct. 1945, Caetés (then a dist of Garanhuns), Pernambuco; s. of Aristides Inácio da Silva and Eurídice Ferreira de Mello; m. Marisa Leticia 1974; five c.; qualified as mechanic; started working at Indústrias Villares steelworks 1966; Assoc. mem. Exec. Cttee, São Bernardo do Campo and Diadema Metalworkers' Union 1969–72, First Sec. (responsible for social security) 1972–75, Pres. 1975–80; led steelworkers' strikes 1978, 1979; Pres. Partido dos Trabalhadores (Labour Party) 1980–87, 1993; a leader of the 'Elections Now' campaign for direct presidential elections 1984; a leader of campaign to impeach Pres. Collor de Mello 1992; Fed. Deputy 1986–; presidential cand. 1989, 1994, 2002; f. a 'Parallel Govt' (to prepare an alternative set of policies for the country) 1990; Councillor, Citizenship Inst. 1992–; Pres. of Brazil 2003–11; apptd Chief of Staff to Pres. Dilma Rousseff March 2016, appointment suspended immediately by Supreme Court Judge Gilmar Mendes; found guilty on corruption charges July 2017, sentenced to nine and a half years in prison; began serving sentence April 2018; Brazilian Order of Merit, Brazilian Orders of Mil., Naval and Aeronautical Merit, Brazilian Order of Scientific Merit, Mexican Order of the Aztec Eagle, Norwegian Order of Royal Merit, First Class, Order of Prince Yaroslav the Wise (Ukraine) 2003, Order of Liberty (Ukraine) 2009; Dr hc (Inst. of Political Studies, Paris) 2011; Prince of Asturias Award for Int. Co-operation 2003, chief guest at India's Repub. Day celebration 2004, Jawaharlal Nehru Award 2006, UNESCO Félix Houphouët-Boigny Peace Prize 2008, Chatham House Prize 2009, O.P. Dwivedi Public Service Award, Int. Asscn of Schools and Insts of Admin 2009, chosen as Man of the Year by El País and Le Monde newspapers 2009, Indira Gandhi Prize for Peace, Disarmament and Development 2010, Global Statesman, World Econ. Forum 2010, World Food Prize (co-recipient) 2011.

LULLA, Kishore, BA; Indian film industry executive; *Group Executive Chairman, Eros International Ltd;* b. 4 Sept. 1964; s. of Arjan Lulla; ed Mumbai Univ.; co-f. Eros UK (br. of family-owned film distribution co. Eros Int.) 1988, apptd Chair. Eros Int. 2005, Group Exec. Chair. 2010–, CEO 2011–12, Exec. Dir Eros International Media Ltd 2009–; mem. BAFTA, Young Pres.'s Org.; mem. Exec. Bd UCLA School of Theater, Film and Television; Trustee Eros International Foundation; BDO Stoy Hayward Business of the Year, Eastern Eye Asian Business Award 2007, India Splendour Award 2007, Indian Film Acad. Award 2007, Entrepreneur of the Year, GG2 Leadership and Diversity Awards 2010. *Address:* Eros International Ltd, 9th Floor, Supreme Chambers, Off Veera Desai Road, Mumbai 400053, Maharashtra, India (office). *Telephone:* (22) 66021500 (office). *Fax:* (22) 66021540 (office). *Website:* www.erosintl.com (office).

LULU-BRIGGS, High Chief O.B.; Nigerian business executive; *Chairman, Moni Pulo Ltd;* b. 1930, Abonnema, Kalabari; m. Seinye Lulu Briggs; Founder-Chair. Moni Pulo Ltd (oil co.) 1992–; Dir (non-exec.) Transnational Corpn of Nigeria Plc 2007–, also mem. Nomination and Governance Cttee; Co-founder O.B Lulu-Briggs Foundation 2001–; Officer, Order of the Niger. *Address:* Moni Pulo Limited, 5, Odoni Street, Amadi Flats, Port Harcourt, Nigeria (office). *Telephone:* (8) 4462827 (office). *Fax:* (8) 4464017 (office). *E-mail:* info@monipulo.com (office). *Website:* www.monipulo.com (office).

LUM, Olivia, BSc; Malaysian business executive and fmr chemist; *Head of Research and Development, President and Group CEO, Hyflux Group;* b. Kampar, Perak; adopted at birth; ed Tiong Bahru Secondary School, Hwa Chong Jr Coll., Nat. Univ. of Singapore; chemist, Glaxo Pharmaceutical 1986–89; f. Hydrochem (now Hyflux Group) 1989, manufacturer of water filters and treatment chemicals, Head of Research and Devt, Pres. and Group CEO; mem. Parl. (nominated) 2002–05; mem. Bd of Dirs International Enterprise Singapore; Pres. Singapore Water Asscn; mem. Singapore-Tianjin Economic and Trade Council, Singapore-Jiangsu Cooperation Council, Singapore-Zhejiang Economic and Trade Council, Singapore-Oman Business Council, Singapore Business Federation Council; Ind. Dir (non-exec.) Singapore Exchange –2008 (resgnd); mem. Bd SPRING Singapore, National Univ. Singapore Council; mem. UNESCAP Business Advisory Council, Singapore Green Plan 2012; Int. Man. Action Award 2003, Global Female Invent and Innovate Award 2004, Ernst & Young World Entrepreneur Of The Year 2011. *Address:* Hyflux Ltd, Hyflux Building, 202 Kallang Bahru, Singapore City, 339339, Singapore (office). *Telephone:* 6214-0777 (office). *Fax:* 6214-1211 (office). *E-mail:* contact_us@hyflux.com (office). *Website:* www.hyflux.com (office).

LUMLEY, Joanna Lamond, OBE, FRGS; British actress; b. 1 May 1946, Kashmir, India; d. of Maj. James Rutherford Lumley and Thyra Beatrice Rose Lumley; m. 1st Jeremy Lloyd (divorced); m. 2nd Stephen Barlow 1986; one s.; ed Army School, Malaysia, Mickledene, Kent, St Mary's St Leonards on Sea; Hon. DLitt (Kent) 1994; Hon. DUniv (Oxford Brookes) 2000; Dr hc (Queen's Univ. Belfast) 2008, (St Andrews) 2009; BAFTA Award 1992, 1994, Special BAFTA 2000. *Stage appearances include:* Noël Coward's Blithe Spirit 1986, Vanilla 1990, Revengers Comedies 1991, The Letter 1995, Hedda Gabler, Private Lives, An Ideal Husband, The Cherry Orchard 2007, La Bête (Broadway) 2010, The Lion in Winter 2011. *Films include:* Some Girls Do, Tam Lin, The Breaking of Bumbo, Games That Lovers Play, Don't Just Lie There Say Something, The Plank, On Her Majesty's Secret Service, Trail of the Pink Panther, Curse of the Pink Panther, Satanic Rites of Dracula 1978, Shirley Valentine, Innocent Lies 1995, James and the Giant Peach 1996, Cold Comfort Farm 1996, Prince Valiant 1997, Parting Shots 1998, The Tale of Sweeney Todd 1998, Mad Cows 1999, Maybe Baby 1999, The Cat's Meow 2000, EuroTrip 2004, Ella Enchanted 2004, The Magic Roundabout (voice) 2005, The Corpse Bride (voice) 2005, Stories of Lost Souls 2006, Dolls 2006, Boogie Woogie 2009, Animals United (voice) 2010, The Snowman: The Live Stage Show (video) (narrator) 2010, Late Bloomers 2011, The Wolf of Wall Street 2013, Me Before You 2016, Absolutely Fabulous: The Movie 2016. *Television includes:* Release, Mark II Wife, Comedy Playhouse, It's Awfully Bad for Your Eyes Darling, Coronation Street, The Protectors, General Hospital 1974–75, The New Avengers 1976–77, Steptoe & Son, Are You Being Served?, The Cuckoo Waltz, Up The Workers, That was Tori, Sapphire and Steel 1978, Absolutely Fabulous (series) 1992–2012, Class Act 1994, Girl Friday (documentary) 1994, White Rajahs of Sarawak (documentary), Joanna Lumley in the Kingdom of the Thunder Dragon (documentary) 1997, Coming Home 1998, A Rather English Marriage 1998, Nancherrow, Dr Willoughby, MD, Mirrorball 1999, Giraffes on the Move (documentary) 2001, Up in Town 2002, Agatha Christie's Marple 2004, Sensitive Skin 2005–07, Jam & Jerusalem 2006–08, In the Land of the Northern Lights 2007, Lewis (series) 2009, Mistresses 2010, Marple: The Mirror Crack'd from Side to Side 2010, Joanna Lumley's Nile 2010, Comic Relief: Uptown Downstairs Abbey (film) 2011, Joanna Lumley's Greek Odyssey 2011, three Absolutely Fabulous Specials (Identity 2011, Job 2012, Olympics 2012), Joanna Lumley: In Search of Noah's Ark 2012, Little Crackers (series) 2012, The Making of a Lady (film) 2012, Jonathan Creek 2013, Joanna Lumley's Japan 2016; co-producer The Cazalets (BBC 1) 2001. *Publications include:* Stare Back and Smile (autobiography) 1989, Forces' Sweethearts 1993, Girl Friday 1994, Joanna Lumley in the Kingdom of the Thunder Dragon 1997, No Room for Secrets (autobiog.) 2004, Joanna Lumley Absolutely 2009. *Leisure interests:* walking, gardening, collecting things, painting, music, travelling. *Address:* c/o John Grant, Conway van Gelder, 3rd Floor, 8/12 Broadwick Street, London, W1F 8HW, England (office). *Telephone:* (20) 7287-0077 (office). *E-mail:* john@conwayvg.co.uk (office).

LUMSDEN, Andrew Gino Sita, MA, PhD, FRS, FMedSci; British neurobiologist and academic; b. 22 Jan. 1947, Beaconsfield, Bucks., England; m. (divorced, remarried); two d.; ed Kingswood School, Bath, St Catharine's Coll., Cambridge, Yale Univ., USA, Univ. of London; Lecturer in Anatomy, Sr Lecturer, then Reader, Guy's Hosp. Medical School; Prof. of Developmental Neurobiology, King's Coll. London 1989–, Dir MRC Centre for Developmental Neurobiology 2000–15; Howard Hughes Int. Research Scholar 1993–98; Visiting Prof., Univ. of California, Berkeley, USA 1994; mem. European Molecular Biology Org. 2008; Fulbright Scholar 1968–70, W. Maxwell Cowan Prize for Developmental Neuroscience 2007. *Publications:* The Developing Brain (co-author) 2001, Principles of Development (co-author) 2015; more than 150 scientific publs. *Leisure interests:* mechanical eng, natural history. *Address:* Medical Research Council Centre for Developmental Neurobiology, King's College London, New Hunts House, Guy's Campus, London, SE1 1UL (office); 16 Elephant Lane, London, SE16 4JD, England (home). *Telephone:* (20) 7848-6520 (office); (20) 7640-0187 (home). *Fax:* (20) 7848-6550 (office). *E-mail:* andrew.lumsden@kcl.ac.uk (office). *Website:* www.kcl.ac.uk/ioppn/depts/devneuro/Research/groups/lumsden.aspx (office); kclpure.kcl.ac.uk/portal/andrew.lumsden.html (office).

LUMSDEN, Sir David James, Kt, MusB, MA, DPhil; British musician (retd); b. 19 March 1928, Newcastle-upon-Tyne; s. of Albert Lumsden and Vera May Lumsden (née Tate); m. Sheila Daniels 1951; two s. two d.; ed Dame Allan's School, Newcastle-upon-Tyne, Selwyn Coll., Cambridge (Organ Scholar); Asst Organist, St John's Coll. Cambridge 1951–53; Organist and Choirmaster St Mary's, Nottingham and Univ. Organist 1954–56; Founder and Conductor Nottingham Bach Soc. 1954–59; Rector Chori Southwell Minster 1956–59; Dir of Music, Keele 1958–59; Prof. of Harmony, RAM 1959–61; Fellow and Organist, New Coll. Oxford and Lecturer, Faculty of Music, Univ. of Oxford 1959–76; Prin., Royal Scottish Acad. of Music and Drama, Glasgow 1976–82, RAM 1982–93; Conductor Oxford Harmonic Soc. 1961–63; Organist, Sheldonian Theatre 1964–76; Harpsichordist to the London Virtuosi 1972–75; Pres. Inc. Asscn of Organists 1966–68; Visiting Prof., Yale Univ., USA 1974–75; Conductor Oxford Sinfonia 1967–70; Choragus, Univ. of Oxford 1968–72; Pres. Inc. Soc. of Musicians 1984–85, Royal Coll. of Organists 1986–88; Chair. Nat. Youth Orchestra 1985–94, Nat. Early Music Asscn 1986–89; mem. Bd Scottish Opera 1978–83, ENO 1984–89; Hon. Fellow, Selwyn Coll. Cambridge, New Coll. Oxford, King's Coll., London; Hon. RAM; Hon. FRCO; Hon. GSMD; Hon. FRCM; Hon. FRSAMD; Hon. FRNCM; Hon. FTCL; Hon. FLCM; Hon. FRSCM; Hon. FGCM 2005; Hon. DLitt (Reading) 1989. *Music includes:* recordings of organ, choral and chamber music; recitals world-wide. *Publications include:* An Anthology of English Lute Music 1954, Thomas Robinson's Schoole of Musicke 1603 1971, Music for the Lute (Gen. Ed.) 1965–82. *Leisure interests:* reading, walking, theatre, photography, travel. *Address:* 26 Wyke Mark, Dean Lane, Winchester, SO22 5DJ, England. *Telephone:* (1962) 877807. *E-mail:* lumsdendj@aol.com.

LUNA MENDOZA, Ricardo V., AB, MIA; Peruvian diplomatist; b. 19 Nov. 1940, Lima; s. of Ricardo Luna and Victoria Mendoza de Luna; m. Margarita Proaño 1969; one d.; ed Princeton Univ., NJ and Columbia Univ., USA, Diplomatic Acad. of Peru; joined Diplomatic Service 1967, posts held include Third Sec., Div. of Econ. Affairs, Foreign Ministry 1967, Third Sec., Embassy in UK 1968–70, Second Sec., Embassy in Israel 1970–71, First Sec., Perm. Mission of Peru to UN Office at Geneva, Head, UN Dept, Foreign Ministry 1975–77, Counsellor, Washington, DC 1978, Chef du Cabinet of Minister for Foreign Affairs 1979, Minister Counsellor, Mission of Peru to UNESCO 1980, Quito 1987, Minister, Perm. Mission to UN 1984, Under-Sec. for Multilateral Policy, Ministry of Foreign Affairs 1987–89, Perm. Rep. to UN 1989–92, Amb. to USA 1992–99, to UK 2006–10, Minister of Foreign Affairs 2016–18; Fellow, Center for Int. Affairs, Harvard Univ., USA 1980–81; Adjunct Prof. of Latin American Affairs, The Fletcher School, Tufts Univ. 1999–2006; fmr Lecturer, Woodrow Wilson School of Public and Int. Affairs, Princeton Univ.; Founding mem. Peruvian Centre for Int. Studies; mem. Peruvian Soc. of Int. Law; Order de Mayo (Argentina), Order Río Branco (Brazil), Panamerican Foundation Pan American Order. *Leisure interests:* art, art history, jazz, cinema, mountain climbing, hiking. *Address:* c/o Ministry of Foreign Affairs, Jirón Lampa 535, Lima 1, Peru (office).

LUND, Helge, MBA; Norwegian oil industry executive; *Chairman, BG Group;* b. 16 Oct. 1962, Oslo; m. Else-Cathrine Lund; two c.; ed Norwegian School of Econs and Business Admin (NHH), Bergen, Institut Européen d'Admin des Affaires (INSEAD), Fontainebleu, France; fmr Political Adviser to Conservative Parl. (Storting) Group; consultant with McKinsey & Co. –1993; joined Hafslund Nycomed 1993, Deputy Man.-Dir Nycomed Pharma AS 1997–99; Deputy Chief Exec. and COO Aker RGI Holding ASA 1999–2002; Deputy Chair. Aker Martitime 2001; apptd mem. Bd Kværner ASA 2001, CEO Aker Kværner ASA (following merger between Aker and Kværner) 2002–04; CEO Statoil ASA (renamed StatoilHydro in 2007 following merger between Statoil and Norsk Hydro's oil and gas business) 2004–14; Chief Exec. BG Group 2015–16, Chair. 2019–; mem. Bd of Dirs Nokia Corpn 2011–14, Schlumberger Ltd 2016–18, BP Global 2018–; mem. Bd of Trustees International Crisis Group. *Address:* BG Group plc, 1 St James's Square, London, SW1Y 4PD, England (office). *Telephone:* (20) 7496-4000 (office). *Fax:* (20) 7496-4630 (office). *E-mail:* careline@bp.com (office). *Website:* www.bg.com (office).

LUND, Henning, DrPhil; Danish chemist and academic; *Professor Emeritus of Chemistry, University of Aarhus;* b. 15 Sept. 1929, Copenhagen; s. of Prof. Hakon Lund and Bergljot I. G. Lund (née Dahl); m. Else Margrethe Thorup 1953; one s. three d.; ed Aarhus Katedralskole and Tech. Univ. of Copenhagen; Research Chemist, Leo Pharmaceutical Products 1952–60; Research Fellow, Harvard Univ. 1954–55; Asst Prof. of Chem., Univ. of Aarhus 1960, Prof. 1964–99, Prof. Emer. 1999–; Visiting Prof., Japan 1976, France 1981; Chair. UNESCO workshop for European Co-operation in Organic Electrochemistry 1976–81; Section Co-Chair. Int. Soc. of Electrochemistry 1973–78, 1986–90, Nat. Sec. 1986–90; Pres. Learned Soc., Univ. of Aarhus 1973–79; mem. Danish Research Council for Tech. Sciences 1977–82, Vice-Chair. 1980–82; mem. Royal Danish Acad. of Sciences and Letters 1979–; Dr hc (Rennes) 1998; Bjerrums Gold Medal 1969, M. M. Baizer Award (Electrochemical Soc.) 1996. *Publications include:* Elektrodereaktioner i Organisk Polarografi og Voltammetri 1961, Encyclopaedia of Electrochemistry of the Elements, Vols 11–15 (co-ed.) 1978–84, Organic Electrochemistry (co-ed.) 1983, 1991, 2000; contrib. of about 300 papers to scientific journals. *Leisure interests:* music, literature, jogging. *Address:* Department of Chemistry, University of Aarhus, 8000 Aarhus (office); Vinkelvej 8A, 8240 Risskov, Denmark (home). *Telephone:* (45) 87-15-59-49 (office); (45) 86-17-90-27 (home). *Fax:* (45) 86-19-61-99 (office). *E-mail:* hlund@chem.au.dk (office). *Website:* www.chem.au.dk (office).

LUND, Maj.-Gen. Kristin; Norwegian army officer and UN official; *Head of Mission and Chief of Staff, United Nations Truce Supervision Organization (UNTSO);* b. 16 May 1958; ed United States Army War Coll., Norwegian Defence Univ. Coll.; joined Norwegian Army 1979, Deputy Commdr Norwegian Army Forces Command 2007–09, promoted to Maj.-Gen. 2009, apptd Chief of Staff Norwegian Home Guard 2009; deployed to UN Interim Force in Lebanon (UNIFIL) 1986, to UN Protection Force (UNPROFOR) 1992–93, 1994–95, to HQ Int. Security Assistance Force, NATO Afghanistan 2003–04, Force Commdr UN Peacekeeping

Force in Cyprus (UNFICYP) 2014–16, Head of Mission and Chief of Staff UN Truce Supervision Org. (UNTSO) 2017–; Adviser Norwegian Defence Univ. Coll.; mem. Nordic Women Mediation Network 2015–; UN Women Champion 2017; Norwegian Armed Forces Equality Award 2004. *Address:* Department of Peacekeeping Operations, Room S-3727B, United Nations, New York, NY 10017, USA (office). *Telephone:* (212) 963-8077 (office). *Fax:* (212) 963-9222 (office). *Website:* peacekeeping.un.org (office).

LUND, Kristin Skogen, BA, MBA; Norwegian business executive; *Executive Vice-President and Head of Digital Services, Telenor Group;* b. 1966; ed Univ. of Oregon, USA, Institut Européen d'Admin des Affaires (INSEAD), Fontainebleau, France; worked as man. in Lever Europe 1992–95; hired by Coca-Cola Co. 1995, Dir of Coca-Cola Beverages Sweden 1997–98; CEO Scandinavia Online 1998–2002, CEO Scanpix 2003–04; moved to Aftenposten AS (newspaper owned by Schibsted) 2004, CEO 2007–09, held various bd memberships within Schibsted Group; Dir of Nordic activities, Telenor Group 2009–10, Exec. Vice-Pres. and Head of Digital Services 2010–; mem. Bd Orkla Group, Norwegian Chamber Orchestra (Pres.); Vice-Pres. Confed. of Norwegian Enterprise (Næringslivets Hovedorganisasjon—NHO) 2008–10, Acting Pres. 2010–; mem. Council Civita (think tank). *Address:* Telenor ASA, Snarøyveien 30, 1331 Fornebu, Norway (office). *Telephone:* 81-07-70-00 (office); 67-89-00-00 (office). *E-mail:* info@telenor.com (office). *Website:* www.telenor.com (office).

LUND, Peter Anthony; American broadcasting executive; *Chairman, EOS International Inc.;* b. 12 Jan. 1941, Minneapolis, Minn.; s. of Arthur H. Lund and Elizabeth Rohan; m. Theresa M. Kessel 1960; two s.; ed St Thomas Coll.; announcer, sales rep., Station KCCR, Pierce, SD 1961–62; sales rep., Station KELO TV, Sioux Falls, SD 1962–64; sales rep., sales man., Station WTTC, Minneapolis 1964–66; Gen. Sales Man. Westinghouse Broadcasting Co. 1966–71; Vice-Pres., Man. Station KSDO, San Diego, Calif. 1972–75, Station WTOP, Washington, DC 1976–77; Vice-Pres. CBS-owned AM Stations, New York 1977–80; Vice-Pres., Gen. Man. WBBM-TV, Chicago 1980–83, WCBS-TV, New York 1983–84; Exec. Vice-Pres. CBS Sports, New York 1984–85, Pres. 1985–87; Pres. Multimedia Entertainment 1987–90; Exec. Vice-Pres., Pres. Marketing, CBS 1990–94; Broadcast Group Pres. CBS Pres. 1995–97, Exec. Vice-Pres. CBS TV Network 1994–95, CEO CBS 1995–97, Pres. CEO CBS TV and Cable 1997; mem. Bd of Dirs DIRECTV Group Inc. 2000–, Crown Media Holdings, Inc., Emmis Communications Corpn; currently Chair. EOS International Inc. *Address:* EOS International Inc., 2292 Faraday Avenue, Carlsbad, CA 92008-7208, USA (office). *Telephone:* (760) 431-8400 (office). *Fax:* (760) 431-8448 (office). *E-mail:* info@eosintl .com (office). *Website:* www.eosintl.com (office).

LUNDGREEN-NIELSEN, Flemming Torkild Jacob, DPhil; Danish academic; b. 24 Jan. 1937, Hellerup; s. of Otto Nielsen and Edith Mortensen; ed Frederiksborg Statsskole and Univ. of Copenhagen; teaching posts at Univ. of Copenhagen 1965–2007, Lecturer 1972–88, Prof., DIS Study Div. 1970–90, Docent 1988–2007 (retd); mem. Danish Soc. of Language and Literature, Royal Acad. of Sciences and Letters. *Publications include:* Grundtvig. Skaebne og forsyn 1965, Den nordiske fortaelling i det 18. årh. 1968, Det handlende ord I-II 1980, CC Lyschanders digtning I-II 1989, Jens Bielke: Relation om Grønland 1990, Grundtvig og danskhed, in Dansk identitetshistorie 3 1992, På sporet af dansk identitet 1992, København laest og påskrevet 1997, Svøbt i mår. Dansk Folkevisekultur 1550–1700 I-IV (Ed. and Contrib.) 1999–2002, N.F.S. Grundtvig: Schriften in Auswahl !-III (Ed. and Contrib.) 2010; articles on Danish and Scandinavian literary subjects. *Address:* Upsalagade 22, 2100 Copenhagen Ø, Denmark. *E-mail:* fln@royalacademy.dk; fln@privat.tele.dk.

LUNDGREN, Dolph, MA; American (b. Swedish) actor, director and screenwriter; b. 3 Nov. 1959, Stockholm, Sweden; m. Anette Lundgren 1994; two d.; ed Washington State Univ., Massachusetts Inst. of Tech. and Royal Inst. of Tech. Stockholm; f. Thor Pictures (production co.) 1992. *Films include:* A View to a Kill 1985, Rocky IV 1985, Masters of the Universe 1987, Red Scorpion 1989, The Punisher 1989, Dark Angel 1990, Cover Up 1991, Showdown in Little Tokyo 1991, Universal Soldier 1992, The Joshua Tree 1993, Pentathlon (also producer) 1994, Men of War 1994, Johnny Mnemonic 1995, The Shooter 1995, Silent Trigger 1996, The Peacekeeper 1997, The Minion 1998, Sweepers 1998, Storm Catcher 1999, Bridge of Dragons 1999, Jill the Ripper 2000, The Last Patrol 2000, Agent Red 2000, Hidden Agenda 2001, Detention 2003, Direct Action 2004, Fat Slags 2004, Retrograde 2004, The Defender (also dir) 2004, The Mechanik (also writer and dir) 2005, The Inquiry 2006, Diamond Dogs (also exec. producer and dir) 2007, Missionary Man (also writer and dir) 2007, Direct Contact 2009, Command Performance (also writer and dir, performer: 'Breakdown', 'Girl') 2009, Universal Soldier: Regeneration 2009, Icarus (also dir) 2010, The Expendables 2010, The Expendables 2 2012, Legendary 2013, Battle of the Damned 2013, Blood of Redemption 2013, Puncture Wounds 2014, The Expendables 3 2014, War Pigs 2015, Hail, Caesar! 2016, Female Fight Club 2016, Larceny 2016. *Website:* www .dolphlundgren.com.

LUNDGREN, Johan Peter; Swedish travel industry executive and fmr trombonist; *Chief Executive Officer, EasyJet PLC;* b. 4 Oct. 1966; m. Maria Lundgren; one s. one d.; ed Stockholm School of Econs, Int. Inst. for Man. Devt, Lausanne, Switzerland; studied classical trombone in Sweden, UK and USA 1982–85; Guide, Fritidsresor (travel operator) 1986–88; Marketing Man., Swedish/Soviet Travel Agency 1988–90; Sales Man., Always Tour Operations 1990–93, Dir, Sales and Marketing 1993–96, Man. Dir 1996–99; Pres., MyTravel, Canada 1999–2002, Man. Dir, MyTravel, Sweden 2002–03; Man. Dir and CEO TUI Nordic 2003–07, Man. Dir (Northern Europe), TUI Travel PLC 2007–11, Man. Dir (UK & Ireland), TUI Travel PLC 2010–11, Group Deputy CEO, TUI Travel PLC 2011–14, mem. Exec. Bd TUI AG 2014–15, Group Deputy CEO & CEO of Mainstream, TUI AG 2014–15; CEO EasyJet PLC 2017–. *Address:* Hangar 89, London Luton International Airport, Luton, LU2 9PF, Bedfordshire, England (office). *Telephone:* (1582) 525330 (office). *Fax:* (1582) 443355 (office). *E-mail:* press.office@easyjet.com (office). *Website:* www.easyjet.com (office).

LUNDGREN, Terry J., BA; American retail executive; b. 1953, Long Beach, Calif.; m. Nancy Lundgren; two c.; ed Univ. of Arizona; joined Bullock Div., Federated Dept Stores Inc. (FDSI), LA 1975, Pres. Bullock Wilshire Security Operations –1988, Chair. and CEO Neiman Marcus 1988–94, Head, Federated

Merchandising Group, New York 1994–95, COO and Chief Merchandising Officer, FDSI (renamed Macy's, Inc. 2007) 1997–2003, Pres. 1997–2018, CEO 2003–17, Chair. 2004–18. *Address:* c/o Macy's Inc., 7 West Seventh Street, Cincinnati, OH 45202, USA (office). *Telephone:* (513) 579-7000 (office). *Fax:* (513) 579-7555 (office). *E-mail:* info@macysinc.com (office); info@fds.com (office). *Website:* www.macysinc .com (office); www.fds.com (office).

LUNDIN, Jan, BA; Swedish diplomatist and international organization official; m.; two d.; ed Univ. of Uppsala, Univ. of Stockholm; several years with Swedish Ministry of Foreign Affairs (MFA), served at Embassy in Yugoslavia 1984–86, First Sec., Embassy in Lithuania 1992–94, Counsellor, Embassy in Russian Fed. 1994–96, Counsellor and Deputy Head of Mission, Embassy in Serbia, Deputy Head of Mission and Head of Political Dept, Embassy in Germany 1996–2000, Coordinator, Stability Pact for SE Europe, Ministry of Foreign Affairs 1999; Researcher, Stockholm Inst. for Soviet and E European Econs and Politics, Uppsala Univ. 1987–88; European Exec. Dir Russian–European Centre for Econ. Policy 1998–99; Dir Gen. Council of the Baltic Sea States Secr. 2010–16. *Address:* c/o Council of the Baltic Sea States Secretariat, PO Box 2010, Slussplan 9, 103 11 Stockholm, Sweden (office). *Telephone:* (8) 440-19-21 (office). *Fax:* (8) 440-19-20 (office). *E-mail:* jan.lundin@cbss.org (office). *Website:* www.cbss.org (office).

LUNDSTEDT, Martin, MSc; Swedish motor industry executive; *President and CEO, Volvo Group;* b. 28 April 1967, Mariestad; m.; two c.; ed Chalmers Univ. of Tech.; joined Scania as a trainee 1992, Project Leader Scania do Brasil 1995–96, Man. Industrial Eng, Scania Engine Production 1996–97, Production Man. Scania Engine Production 1997–99, Head of Basic Engine Devt 1999–2001, Man. Dir Scania Production, Angers, France 2001–05, Head of Product Marketing and mem. Exec. Team 2005–06, Head of Trucks 2006–07, Head of Franchise and Factory Sales 2007–12, Pres. and CEO Scania Group 2012–15; mem. Group Exec. Bd, Pres. and CEO Volvo Group 2015–; Chair. Partex Marking Systems AB, Permobil AB, ACEA Commercial Vehicles; Co-Chair. UN Sec.-Gen.'s High-Level Advisory Group on Sustainable Transport; mem. Bd Concentric AB, Royal Swedish Acad. of Eng Sciences. *Address:* Volvo Group, 405 08 Gothenburg, Sweden (office). *Telephone:* (31) 66-00-00 (office). *Fax:* (31) 54-57-72 (office). *Website:* www.volvogroup.com (office).

LUNDY, Victor Alfred, MArch, FAIA; American architect; b. 1 Feb. 1923, New York, NY; s. of Alfred Henry Lundy and Rachel Lundy; m. 1st Shirley Corwin 1947 (divorced 1959); one s. one d.; m. 2nd Anstis Manton Burwell 1960; one s.; ed New York Univ. Coll. of Architecture, Harvard Univ.; mil. service 1943–46; pvt. practice, Sarasota, Fla 1951–59, New York 1960–75, projects include St Paul's Lutheran Church, Sarasota 1959, US Tax Court Bldg and Plaza, Washington, DC, US Embassy in Colombo, Sri Lanka, Recreation Shelters for Smithsonian Inst., travelling air-supported Exhbn Bldg and exhibit for US Atomic Energy Comm. and commercial, religious and govt bldgs throughout the USA and overseas; pvt. practice, Houston, Tex. 1976–87, Design Prin. and Vice-Pres. HKS Inc., Dallas, Tex. 1984–90, visiting professorships and lectureships, Harvard, Yale, Columbia, Calif. (Berkeley) and Houston Univs and Univ. of Rome, Italy; work included in many exhbns, including São Paulo Int. Biennial Exhbn of Architecture 1957, America Builds, Berlin 1957, Fifth Congress of Union Internationale des Architectes, Moscow 1958, Expo '70, Osaka, Japan 1970; Purple Heart Medal, US Combat Infantry Badge; numerous prizes and awards, honoured by the Smithsonian Inst. on his 90th birthday 2013. *Projects include:* GTE Telephone Operations World HQ, Irving, Tex., Greyhound Corp. (now Dial Corp.) Center, Phoenix, Ariz., Mack Center II, Tampa, Fla, Walnut Glen Tower (now Dr Pepper Bldg), Dallas, Tex. Austin Centre-Radisson Hotel and One Congress Plaza, Austin, Tex., Stahl Residence, Siesta Key, Fla 1953, Drive-In Church, Nokomis, Fla 1954, Greater Sarasota Chamber of Commerce (Pagoda Bldg) 1956, Alta Vista Elementary School, aka The Butterfly Wing 1957, 25 South Osprey Avenue 1957, Herron House, Venice, Fla 1957, Bee Ridge Presbyterian Church, Sarasota, Fla 1957, 533 S. US 301 1958, Warm Mineral Springs Motel, North Port 1958, St Paul's Lutheran Church, Sarasota 1958, Galloways Furniture Showroom, Sarasota (today, Visionworks), south of US 41 and 301 1959, Bubble Pavilions, for the New York World's Fair of 1964–65 (The Brass Rail Snack Bars), Church of the Resurrection, Harlem, New York City 1966 (now demolished), IBM branch office, Cranford, NJ, First Unitarian Church, Westport, Conn., US Tax Court Bldg, Washington, DC, Lundy home, Aspen, Colo 1972, The Sierra Blanca (NM) Ski Apache Ski Resort Lodge. *Film:* of his life and work: Victor Lundy: Sculptor of Space 2014. *Address:* HKS Inc., 1111 Plaza of the Americas North, Suite LB 307, Dallas, TX 75201 (office); 701 Mulberry Lane, Bellaire, TX 77401, USA (home). *Telephone:* (214) 969-3396.

LUNENFELD, Bruno, MD, PhD, FRCOG; Israeli endocrinologist; *President, International Society for the Study of the Aging Male;* b. 11 Feb. 1927, Vienna, Austria; s. of David Lunenfeld and Ernestine Lunenfeld; m. Pnina Buyanover 1996; two s.; ed British Inst. of Eng Tech., Medical School, Univ. of Geneva, Switzerland; Acting Chief, Endocrine Research and Devt, Tel-Hashomer 1962–64; Scientist, Weizman Inst. of Science 1961–66; Assoc. Prof. and Head Dept of Biology, Bar-Ilan Univ. 1964–69, Prof. Ordinarius and Head Dept of Life Sciences 1969–71, Prof. of Life Sciences 1971; Dir Inst. of Endocrinology, Sheba Medical Centre 1964–92, Chair. Div. of Labs 1977–81, Chair. Research and Ethical Cttee 1977–81; mem. Expert Cttee on Biological Standardization, WHO 1967–87; Counsellor, External Relations to Minister of Health and Head Dept of Int. Relations, Ministry of Health 1981–85; Acting Chief Scientist, Ministry of Health 1984–86; mem. Nat. Council for Research and Devt 1985–87; Visiting Prof., Yale School of Medicine, USA 1986–87; mem. Nat. Council for Health and Social Affairs 1985–87; Pres. Israel Fertility Asscn 1979–83, Israel Endocrine Soc. 1992–95; Founder and Pres., International Soc. for the Study of the Aging Male (ISSAM) 1997–; Medical Dir International Fertility Inst., Ranana 1996–99; Vice-Pres. Scientific Council of Israel Medical Asscn; mem. Exec. Bd Scientific Council, Exec. Council of Int. Cttee for Research in Reproduction, Exec. Council Medical Examination Bd, Exec. Council of International Andrology Soc., Exec. Council of International Soc. of Gynaecological Endocrinology (Treas. 1992–2014); Ed.-in-Chief The Aging Male 1997–; Founder and Sec.-Gen. Asia Pacific Initiative on Reproduction 2004–; Hon. Fellow, American Coll. of Obstetricians and Gynaecologists; Hon. mem. Int. Fed. of Fertility Socs, European Soc. of Human Reproduction and Embryology, German Endocrine Soc. of Reproduction, Austrian Soc. of

Fertility and Sterility, Asian Soc. of Andrology, Deutsche Gesellschaft für Gynäkologie und Geburtshilfe; Verdienstkreuz First Class (Germany) 1995; Pliskin Prize, Israel Trade Union Sick Fund 1962, Yaffeh Prize, Ministry of Health 1963, US Public Health Service Special Recognition Award 1983, Jacob Henle Medal (Georg Augustus Univ., Göttingen) 1993, Bertarelli Foundation Award 2002, World Fertility Awareness Month Lifetime Achievement Award 2005. *Achievements include:* discovered the clinical use of Human Menopausal Gonadotropin for the treatment of female and male hypogonadism and infertility; induction of ovulation with GnRH; pioneer in the study of gender-specific aging. *Publications include:* 21 books including, Infertility, Diagnosis and Treatment of Functional Infertility 1978, Ovulation Induction 1982, Diagnosis and Management of Male Infertility 1984, Ovulation Induction and In Vitro Fertilization 1986, Infertility in Male and Female 1986, 1993, Textbook of Men's Health 2002; 25 chapters in books; 495 papers in scientific journals; 120 published lectures and abstracts. *Leisure interests:* opera, sociology, photography. *Address:* 7 Rav Ashi Street, 69395 Tel-Aviv, Israel (home). *Telephone:* (561) 8867943 (office); 3-6425434 (home). *Fax:* 3-6424454 (home). *E-mail:* blunenfeld@gmail.com. *Website:* www.issam.ch (office).

LUNGIN, Pavel Semenovich, (Pavel Loungine); Russian scriptwriter and director; b. 12 July 1949, Moscow; m. Yelena Lungina; ed Moscow State Univ.; debut as scriptwriter 1976, as film dir 1990; mem. Jury, Moscow Int. Film Festival 1993, Pres. 2009; People's Artist of Russia 2008; Special Prize, Cannes Film Festival. *Libretti:* librettist for Nikolai Karetnikov's opera Till Eulenspiegel (written 1983), Karetnikov's oratorio The Mystery of St Paul. *Films include:* The Problem is Brother 1976, The End of Taiga Emperor 1978, Invincible 1983, Fellow Traveller 1987, Oriental Romance 1992, Queen of Spades 2014; dir: Taxi-Blues (Best Dir Prize, Cannes Film Festival) 1990, Luna Park 1992, Lifeline 1996, The Wedding 2000, Tycoon 2002, Bednye Rodstvenniki 2005, The Island 2006, Lilacs 2007, Tsar 2009, The Conductor 2012. *Television includes:* Delo o myortvykh dushakh (mini-series) 2005, La maison haute (film documentary) 2005. *Address:* Novy Arbat str. 31, Apt 8, 121009 Moscow, Russia. *Telephone:* (495) 205-04-32. *E-mail:* info@lunginstudio.ru. *Website:* www.lunginstudio.ru.

LUNGU, Edgar Chagwa, LLB; Zambian lawyer, politician and head of state; *President;* b. 11 Nov. 1956; m. Esther Lungu; six c.; ed Univ. of Zambia; fmr lawyer with Ministry of Justice, Barclays Bank Zambia Ltd and Zambia Consolidated Copper Mines; mem. Nat. Ass. (Parl.) (PF) for Chawama constituency –2015; Jr Minister in Office of Vice-Pres. 2011; Minister of Defence and of Justice 2014–15; Pres. of Zambia Jan. 2015–; mem. Patriotic Front, Sec.-Gen. –2014, Pres. 2014–. *Address:* Office of the President, POB 30135, Lusaka 10101, Zambia (office). *Telephone:* (21) 1260317 (office). *Fax:* (21) 1254545 (office). *Website:* www.statehouse.gov.zm (office); www.edgar-lungu.com.

LUNGU, Effron, BA, PhD; Zambian politician; b. 25 Dec. 1952; m.; fmr teacher; mem. Nat. Ass. (Parl.) for Chama South constituency 2011–; Deputy Minister of Foreign Affairs 2011–13, Minister Feb.–Aug. 2013; mem. Patriotic Front (PF). *Leisure interests:* football, music. *Address:* National Assembly of Zambia, Parliament Buildings, POB 31299, Lusaka, Zambia (office). *Telephone:* (21) 1292425 (office). *Fax:* (21) 1292252 (office). *E-mail:* ecglungu@parliament.gov.zm (office); galamalalungu@yahoo.com. *Website:* www.parliament.gov.zm (office).

LUO, Gan, DipEng; Chinese state official, party official (retd) and engineer; b. 14 July 1935, Jinan, Shandong Prov.; m. He Zuozhi 1965; one s. one d.; ed Beijing Inst. of Iron and Steel Eng, Karl Marx Univ. and Freiburg Inst. of Mining and Metallurgy, Leipzig, GDR, May 7th Cadre School; worker, Leipzig Iron and Steel Plant and Leipzig Metal Casting Plant 1955–56; joined CCP 1960; Project Group Leader and Technician, Mechanical Eng Research Inst., First Ministry of Machine-Building Industry, Zhengzhou City, Henan Prov. 1962–69, Deputy Dir, later Dir Luohe Preparatory Office 1970–80; Chair. Science and Tech. Cttee, Henan Prov. 1980–81; Vice-Gov. Henan Prov. 1981–83; Sec. CCP Henan Prov. Cttee 1981–83; Minister of Labour and Social Services 1988; Sec.-Gen. of State Council 1988–98, State Councillor 1993–2003, Vice-Premier of State Council 1998–2003; Sec. Work Cttee for Cen. Govt Organs 1989–; Alt. mem. 12th CCP Cen. Cttee 1982–87, mem. 13th Cen. Cttee 1987–92, 14th Cen. Cttee 1992–97, 15th CCP Cen. Cttee 1997–2002, 16th CCP Cen. Cttee 2002–07; mem. CCP Politburo, Sec. Secr. CCP Cen. Cttee 1997–2002; mem. Standing Cttee, CCP Politburo 2002–07; Deputy Sec. Political and Legis. Affairs Cttee, Offices Under Cen. Cttee, 14th CCP Cen. Cttee 1993–98, Sec. 1998–2007; mem. Secr. and Vice-Pres. All-China Fed. of Trade Unions 1983–88 (Deputy Sec. CCP Leading Party Group 1983–88). *Address:* c/o State Council, Zhong Nan Hai, Beijing, People's Republic of China (office).

LUO, Jianchuan, PhD; Chinese mining executive; ed Kunming Univ. of Science and Tech., Cen. South Univ. of Industry; served as engineer with Lead and Zinc Bureau of China Non-ferrous Metals Industry Corpn; fmr Man. Haikou Nanxin Industry and Commerce Corpn; fmr Asst to Gen. Man. Jinpeng Mining Devt Corpn; fmr Vice-Pres. Beijing Xinquan Tech-trading Corpn; fmr Asst to Pres. of China Non-ferrous Metals Industry Trading Group Corpn; fmr Deputy Chief of Trading Div. of China Copper, Lead and Zinc Group Corpn; fmr Gen. Man. China Aluminum International Trading Corpn Ltd; joined Aluminum Corpn of China (CHALCO) 2001, later Gen. Man. Operations and Sales Div., Vice-Pres. from 2003, Sr Vice-Pres. –2007, Pres. 2007–09, Exec. Dir and Pres. 2013–15. *Address:* c/o Aluminum Corporation of China (CHALCO), 62 North Xizhimen Street, Haidian District, Beijing 100082, People's Republic of China (office). *Telephone:* (10) 8229-8103 (office). *Fax:* (10) 8229-8081 (office). *E-mail:* webmaster@chalco.com.cn (office); info@chinalco.com.cn (office). *Website:* www.chalco.com.cn (office); www.chinalco.com (office).

LUO, Pingan; Chinese artist; b. 12 April 1945, Xian; s. of Luo Deyu and Tian Cuilan; m. Qi Juyan 1969; two s.; ed Xian Acad. of Fine Arts; mem. China Artists' Asscn, Shaanxi Br.; Artist of Shaanxi Imperial Art Gallery (traditional Chinese painting); Vice-Pres. Changan Imperial Art Acad.; Dir Artistic Cttee of China Artistic Asscn, Shaanxi br.; Excellent Works Prize, Beijing 1988, Copper Medal of 7th Nat. Artistic Works-Exhbn 1989, Tabei City, Taiwan. *Publications:* The Collection of Luo Pingan's Painting, Collected Landscapes by Luo Pingan. *Leisure interests:* literature, folk art, countryside and music. *Address:* 32 North Street, Xian, Shaanxi Province, People's Republic of China. *Telephone:* 25333; 7251984 (home).

LUO, Tao; Chinese economist and business executive; *President and General Manager, China Nonferrous Metal Mining (Group);* ed Beijing Radio and Television Univ.; joined CCP 1973; fmr Vice-Dir and Vice-Sec. Party Cttee, Beijing Gen. Research Inst. for Nonferrous Metals; fmr Vice-Pres. and Sec. Comm. for Discipline Inspection, Vice-Chief of Dept of Personnel Educ., China Nonferrous Metal Industry Corpn; fmr Dir Dept of Personnel, Nat. Bureau for Nonferrous Metal Industry; Deputy Dean of Beijing Gen. Research Inst. for Non-ferrous Metals 1993–97; Deputy Dir Dept of Human Resources and Training, China Nonferrous Metal Industry Corpn 1997–98; Dir Dept of Human Resources, State Bureau of Non-ferrous Metals Industry 1998–2000; participated in establishment of Aluminium Corpn of China Ltd (Chinalco) 2000–01, Deputy Gen. Man. Aluminium Corpn of China Ltd 2001, fmr Chair. Bd of Supervisors; Dir, Ord River Resources Ltd 2004–12, Deputy Chair. (non-exec.) 2005–09, Chair. 2009–12; Chair. China Nonferrous Metals International Mining Co. Ltd and China Nonferrous Mining Corpn Ltd 2010–15; Pres., Gen. Man. and Deputy Party Sec., China Nonferrous Metal Mining (Group) Co. Ltd 2012–; Chair. China Nonferrous Metal Industry's Foreign Engineering and Construction Co. Ltd, Zambia-China Economic and Trade Co-operation Zone Development Co. Ltd, China Nonferrous Metals Foreign Engineering and Construction Inc.; fmr Chair. (non-exec.) Kryso Resources PLC; Dir, Chaarat Gold Holdings Ltd, CNMIM. *Address:* China Nonferrous Metal Mining (Group), 10 Anding Road, Beijing 100029, People's Republic of China (office). *Telephone:* (10) 84426826 (office). *Fax:* (10) 84426699 (office). *E-mail:* webmaster@cnmc.com.cn (office). *Website:* www.cnmc.com.cn (office).

LUO, Xi, MA (Econ); Chinese economist and business executive; *Vice-Chairman and General Manager, China Resources (Holdings) Company Ltd;* b. 6 Dec. 1960; ed Grad. School of the People's Bank of China; fmr Vice-Chair. and Gen. Man. China Export & Credit Insurance Corpn; Gen. Man., Int. Dept, Agricultural Bank of China 2002, Sr Exec. Vice-Pres. 2004, later Exec. Dir and Vice-Pres. and Asst to the Pres. of Agricultural Bank of China; fmr Exec. Dir and Vice-Pres. Industrial and Commercial Bank of China Ltd, later Sr Exec. Vice-Pres.; Vice-Chair. and Gen. Man. China Resources (Holdings) Co. Ltd 2016–. *Address:* China Resources (Holdings) Co. Ltd, Floor 49, CRC Building, 26 Harbour Road, Wanchai, Hong Kong Special Administrative Region, People's Republic of China (office). *Telephone:* 28797888 (office). *Fax:* 28275774 (office). *E-mail:* crc@crc.com.hk (office). *Website:* www.crc.com.hk (office).

LUO, Zhaohui, MA; Chinese diplomatist; *Ambassador to India;* b. Feb. 1962, Hubei Prov.; m.; one d.; Attaché, then Third Sec., Dept of Asian Affairs, Ministry of Foreign Affairs (MFA) 1985–89, Third Sec., then Second Sec., Embassy in Delhi 1989–93, Second Sec., then Deputy Div. Dir, Dept of North American and Oceania Affairs, MFA 1993–96, Second Sec., then First Sec., Embassy in Washington, DC 1996–2000, Counsellor, Dept of Asian Affairs, MFA 2000–03, Minister Counsellor, Embassy in Singapore 2003–04, Deputy Dir Gen., Dept of Asian Affairs, MFA 2004–06, Amb. to Pakistan 2006–10, Dir Gen., Dept of External Security Affairs, MFA 2010–11, Dir-Gen., Dept of Asian Affairs 2011–14, Amb. to Canada 2014–16, to India 2016–. *Address:* Embassy of the People's Republic of China, 50D Shanti Path, Chanakyapuri, New Delhi 110 021, India (office). *Telephone:* (11) 26112345 (office). *Fax:* (11) 26885486 (office). *E-mail:* chinaemb_in@mfa.gov.cn (office). *Website:* in.china-embassy.org (office).

LUO, Zhongli, MFA; Chinese artist; b. 1948, Chongqing; ed Sichuan Fine Arts Inst., Royal Acad. of Fine Arts, Antwerp; worked in an iron factory in Chongqing –1978; created his famous painting "Father" while still a student 1980; currently Prof., Sichuan Fine Arts Inst. *Address:* Sichuan Fine Arts Institute, Huangjueping Main St, HuangJuePing, Jiulongpo Qu, Chongqing 400060, People's Republic of China (office). *Telephone:* (23) 86181008 (office). *E-mail:* info@scfai.edu.cn (office). *Website:* www.scfai.edu.cn (office).

LÜPERTZ, Markus; German painter, sculptor, writer and academic; b. 25 April 1941, Reichenberg (now Liberec), Bohemia; ed Werkkunstschule, Krefeld, Kunstakademie, Düsseldorf, Villa Romana, Florence, Italy; worked mainly in Berlin 1960s; Prof., State Acad. of Fine Arts, Karlsruhe 1976; Prof. and Dir Kunstakademie Düsseldorf 1988–2009; works include The Fallen Warrior, Bonn 1994; Villa Romana Prize 1970, Prize of Deutschen Kritikerverband, Esslingen Artists' Guild 1990. *Publications:* Selected Poems 1961–83; editing own journal since 2003, called Frau und Hund of which two edns in other languages have appeared (Signora e cane, in Italian, and Femme et Chien, in French). *Address:* c/o Galerie Michael Werner, Gertrudenstrasse 24–28, 50667 Cologne, Germany. *Telephone:* (221) 77899950. *Fax:* (221) 77899952. *E-mail:* galeriewerner@michaelwerner.de. *Website:* www.michaelwerner.de.

LUPO, L. Patrick, BA, LLB; American business executive; *Chairman, Bunge Limited;* ed Seattle Univ., Univ. of San Francisco; joined DHL Worldwide Express (DHL) 1976, served as CEO The Americas and Gen. Counsel, Chair. and CEO DHL 1986–97, Exec. Chair. 1997–2001; mem. Bd of Dirs, Bunge Ltd 2006–, fmr Deputy Chair. and Lead Ind. Dir, Chair. Bunge Ltd 2014–; mem. Supervisory Bd, Cofra, AG; fmr Dir, O2 plc, Ladbrokes plc (fmrly Hilton Group plc). *Address:* Bunge Ltd, 50 Main Street, 6th Floor, White Plains, NY 10606, USA (office). *Telephone:* (914) 684-2800 (office). *Fax:* (914) 684-3499 (office). *E-mail:* info@bunge.com (office). *Website:* www.bunge.com (office).

LUPOLIANSKI, Uri; Israeli politician; b. 1951, Haifa; s. of Jacob Lupolianski and Sarah Lupolianski; m. Michal Lupolianski (née Schneller); twelve c.; school teacher, Jerusalem 1970s; Founder and Chair. Yad Sarah (charitable foundation) 1976–; Deputy Mayor of Jerusalem –2003, Acting Mayor, then Mayor 2003–08; mem. United Torah Judaism; sentenced to six years' imprisonment after being convicted of bribery 2014, sentence reduced to six-month sentence of community service due to poor health 2015; Knesset Speaker's Award, Kaplan Prize, The Israel Prize 1994.

LUPU, Marian Ilie, PhD; Moldovan economist and politician; *Chairman, Partidul Democrat din Moldova (Democratic Party of Moldova);* b. 20 June 1966, Bălţi, Moldovan SSR, USSR; s. of Prof. Ilie Ion Lupu; m. 1992; one s. one d.; ed Gheorghe Asachi Lyceum, Chişinău, Moldova State Univ., Plekhanov Moscow Inst. of the Nat. Economy, Moscow, Int. Monetary Fund Inst., Washington, DC, USA, World Trade Org. Inst., Geneva, Switzerland; mem. Komsomol 1980–88; mem. CP Soviet Union 1988–91; worked in Dept for External Econ. Relations,

Chişinău 1991–97, Dir 1997; Exec. Dir TACIS (EU aid programme) in Moldova 1992–2000; Deputy Minister of the Economy 2001–03, Minister of the Economy 2003–05; mem. Partidul Comuniştilor din Republica Moldova (PCRM—Party of Communists of the Repub. of Moldova) –2009, mem. Partidul Democrat din Moldova (PDM—Democratic Party of Moldova) 2009–, currently Chair.; mem. Parl. (PCRM) 2005–09, (PDM) 2009–, Chair. (Speaker) 2005–09, 2010–13; selected as Alianţa pentru Integrare Europeană (Alliance for European Integration) cand. for Pres. of Moldova 2009; Acting Pres. of Moldova 30 Dec. 2010–23 March 2012. *Address:* Partidul Democrat din Moldova (Democratic Party of Moldova) 2001 Chişinău, str. Tighina 32 (office); Parlamentul (Parliament), 2073 Chişinău, bd Ştefan cel Mare 105, Moldova. *Telephone:* (22) 54-17-22 (office); (22) 23-33-52. *Fax:* (22) 27-70-08 (office); (22) 23-30-12. *E-mail:* pdm@mtc.md (office); inform@parlament.md. *Website:* www.pdm.md (office); www.parlament.md.

LUPU, Radu, CBE, MA; Romanian pianist; b. 30 Nov. 1945, Galaţi; s. of Meyer Lupu and Ana Gabor; ed High School, Braşov, Moscow Conservatoire, USSR; first piano lessons 1951; won scholarship to Moscow 1961; entered Moscow Conservatoire 1963, graduated 1969; has toured Eastern Europe with London Symphony Orchestra; has appeared numerous times with Berlin Philharmonic since his debut with that orchestra at Salzburg Festival under Herbert von Karajan 1978; American debut 1972 with Cleveland Orchestra under Daniel Barenboim in New York and then with Chicago Symphony under Carlo Maria Giulini; frequent concerts with New York Philharmonic, Royal Concertgebouw Orchestra, Vienna Philharmonic; several tours of Japan; gave world première of André Tchaikowsky Piano Concerto, London 1975; Artist-in-Residence, Dresden Staatskapelle 2014; performances with Cleveland Orchestra at Teatro alla Scala, Milan and Gasteig, Munich 2015–16; First Prize, Van Cliburn Competition 1966, Enescu Int. Competition, Bucharest 1967, Leeds Int. Competition 1969, Abbiati Prize, Italian Critics' Asscn 1989, 2006, Premio Internazionale Arturo Benedetti Michelangeli Award 2006. *Recordings include:* complete Beethoven cycle (with Israel Philharmonic and Zubin Mehta), complete Mozart sonatas for violin and piano (with Szymon Goldberg), Brahms piano concerto No. 1 (with Edo de Waart and London Philharmonic Orchestra), Mozart piano concerto K467 (with Uri Segal and English Chamber Orchestra), various Beethoven and Schubert sonatas, Mozart and Beethoven wind quintets in E flat, Mozart concerto for 2 pianos and concerto for 3 pianos transcribed for 2 pianos (with Murray Perahia and English Chamber Orchestra), Schubert Fantasie in F minor and Mozart sonata in D for 2 pianos (with Murray Perahia), Schubert Lieder (with Barbara Hendricks), Schubert Piano Duets (with Daniel Barenboim); Schubert's Sonatas, D. 960 and 664 (Grammy Award 1995), Schumann Kinderszenen, Kreisleriana and Humoresque (Edison Award 1995). *Leisure interests:* history, chess, bridge. *Address:* c/o Opus 3 Artists, 470 Park Avenue South, 9th Floor North, New York, NY 10016, USA (office). *Telephone:* (212) 584-7500 (office). *Fax:* (646) 300-8200 (office). *E-mail:* info@opus3artists.com (office). *Website:* www.opus3artists.com/artists/radu-lupu (office).

LUQMAN, Ahmad Mohammad; Egyptian international organization executive; Dir-Gen. Arab Labour Org. (ALO) 2008–15.

LURIE, Alison, AB; American novelist and academic; *Frederic J. Whiton Professor Emerita of American Literature, Cornell University;* b. 3 Sept. 1926, Chicago, Ill.; d. of Harry Lawrence Lurie and Bernice Stewart Lurie; m. 1st Jonathon Peale Bishop 1948 (divorced 1985); three s.; m. 2nd Edward Hower 1996; ed Radcliffe Coll.; Editorial Asst, Oxford Univ. Press 1946; worked as receptionist and sec.; Lecturer in English, Cornell Univ. 1969–73, Adjunct Assoc. Prof. 1973–76, Assoc. Prof. 1976–79, Frederic J. Whiton Prof. of American Literature 1979–98, now Emer.; mem. American Acad. of Arts and Sciences 2005; Fellow, Yaddo Foundation 1963, 1964, 1966, 1984, Rockefeller Foundation 1967, Guggenheim Fellow 1965; Dr hc (Univ. of Oxford) 2007, (Univ. of Nottingham) 2007; American Acad. of Arts and Letters Literature Award 1978, Prix Femina Étranger 1989, Parents' Choice Foundation Award 1996. *Publications include:* fiction: Love and Friendship 1962, The Nowhere City 1965, Imaginary Friends 1967, Real People 1969, The War Between the Tates 1974, Only Children 1979, Clever Gretchen and Other Forgotten Folktales (juvenile) 1980, The Heavenly Zoo (juvenile) 1980, Fabulous Beasts (juvenile) 1981, Foreign Affairs 1984 (Pulitzer Prize in Fiction 1985), The Man with a Shattered World 1987, The Truth about Lorin Jones 1988, Women and Ghosts 1994, The Last Resort 1998, Truth and Consequences 2005; non-fiction: V. R. Lang: A Memoir 1959, The Language of Clothes 1981, Don't Tell the Grown Ups, Subversive Children's Literature (essays) 1990, Familiar Spirits: A Memoir of James Merrill and David Jackson 2001, Boys and Girls Forever: Reflections on Children's Classics (essays) 2003, The Language of Houses 2014; other: Garland Library of Children's Classics (co-ed.). *Leisure interests:* gardening, collecting of contemporary folklore and ghost stories. *Address:* Department of English, Cornell University, 250 Goldwin Smith Hall, 232 East Avenue, Ithaca, NY 14850, USA (office). *E-mail:* al28@cornell.edu (office). *Website:* english.cornell.edu (office); www.alisonlurie.com.

LURIE, Jacob Alexander, BSc, PhD; American mathematician and academic; *Professor of Mathematics, Harvard University;* b. 7 Dec. 1977, Washington, DC; ed Harvard Coll., Massachusetts Inst. of Tech.; Assoc. Prof., MIT 2007; Prof. of Math., Faculty of Arts and Sciences, Harvard Univ. 2009–; Morgan Prize 2000, Breakthrough Prize in Math. 2015. *Achievements include:* participated in Int. Mathematical Olympiad 1994 (gold medal); research focuses on topology and algebraic geometry. *Address:* Department of Mathematics, FAS, Harvard University, One Oxford Street, Cambridge, MA 02138, USA (office). *Telephone:* (617) 495-2171 (office). *Website:* www.math.harvard.edu (office).

LURIE, Ranan Raymond; American/Israeli political cartoonist and journalist; *CEO, Lurie Studios LLC;* b. 26 May 1932, Port Said, Egypt; s. of Joseph Lurie and Rose Lurie (née Sam); m. Tamar Fletcher 1958; two s. two d.; ed Herzelia High School, Tel Aviv, Jerusalem Art Coll.; Israel Air Force intelligence officer and spokesman 1949–50; trained as Parachute Officer, French Foreign Legion 1955, British Paratroopers 1956, US 101 Airborne Div. 1962, served as Combat Paratroop Maj., Israeli Army Reserve 1950–67; Corresp. Maariv Daily 1950–52; Features Ed. Hador Daily 1953–54; Ed.-in-Chief Tavel (weekly news magazine) 1954; staff political cartoonist The Times of Cyprus 1954–56, Yedioth Aharonot Daily 1957–66; went to USA (invited by Life Magazine) 1968, naturalized 1974; political cartoonist, Life Magazine, New York 1968–73; Contrib. New York Times 1970–; weekly political cartoon page, Newsweek Int. 1974–77; Ed., political cartoonist, Vision Magazine of S America 1974–76, Honolulu Advertiser 1979; political cartoonist interviewer Die Welt, Bonn 1980–81; syndicated by United Features Syndicate 1971–73; syndicated nationally by Los Angeles Times and internationally by New York Times to over 260 newspapers 1973–75; syndicated nationally by King Features Syndicate, internationally by Editors Press Syndicate (345 newspapers) 1975–83, in USA by Universal Press Syndicate 1982–86; Lecturer, Univ. of Hawaii, American Program Bureau, Boston; political cartoonist, The Times, London 1981–83; Sr Political Analyst and cartoonist, The Asahi Shimbun, Tokyo 1983–84; Sr Analyst and political cartoonist, US News and World Report, Washington 1984–85; political cartoonist Time Magazine 1994–97; Ed.-in-Chief Cartoon News 1996–99; Chief Editorial Dir Editors' Press Service 1985; currently CEO Lurie Studios LLC; inventor of first animated electronic TV news cartoon; joined MacNeil/Lehrer News Hour as daily political cartoonist/analyst, appearing on 275 TV stations; Nightline (ABC TV network programme) and ZDF (German nat. TV); cr. Taiwan's official new nat. cartoon symbol 'Cousin Lee', Japan's nat. cartoon symbol 'Taro San'; Sr Adjunct Fellow, Center for Strategic and Int. Studies, Washington, DC; mem. Asscn of Editorial Cartoonists, Nat. Cartoonists' Soc. of America; syndicated internationally to 1,098 papers in 104 countries; listed in Guinness Book of World Records as 'most widely syndicated political cartoonist in the world' (Certificate of Merit for 20 years as consecutive title holder); Chief Judge Seoul Int. Cartoon Competition 1996; Hon. Assoc. mem. Asahi Shimbun; Sokolov Prize (highest Israeli journalism award – first recipient) 1954, US Headliners Award 1972, named Outstanding Editorial Cartoonist of Nat. Cartoonist Soc. 1972–78, Salon Award, Montréal Cartoon 1971, New York Front Page Award 1972, 1974, 1977, Certificate of Merit of US Publication Designers 1974, John Fischetti Political Cartoon Award 1982, Toastmasters' Int. and Leadership Award 1985, UN Soc. of Writers Award for Excellence 1995, Hubert H. Humphrey First Amendment Freedoms Prize 1996, Cartoon Award, UN 2000; Nat. Fed. of Hispanic-owned Papers est. Ranan R. Lurie Political Cartoon Award 1994, UN established an annual int. award in his honour (LurieUNaward.com) 1999. *Publications include:* Among the Suns 1952, Lurie's Best Cartoons (Israel) 1961, Nixon Rated Cartoons (New York Times) 1973, Pardon Me, Mr President (New York Times) 1974, Lurie's Worlds (USA) 1980, So sieht es Lurie (Germany) 1981, Lurie's Almanac (UK) 1982, (USA) 1983, Taro's International Politics, Taro-San No Kokusai Seijigaku (Japan) 1984, Lurie's Middle East 1986, Lurie's Mideast Almanac (Israel) 1986, Lurie's Far East Views (China) 1987, The Cartoonist's Mask (novel) 2004; creator The Expandable Painting 1969, The Uniting Painting, Nixon Rated Cartoons 1974, Pardon me, Mr. President! 1975. *Address:* Cartoonews International, 375 Park Avenue, Suite 1301, New York, NY 10152, USA (office). *Telephone:* (212) 980-0855 (office). *Fax:* (212) 980-1664 (office). *Website:* cartoonews.com (office).

LUSCOMBE, David Edward, MA, PhD, LittD, FBA, FSA, FRHistS; British historian and academic; *Professor Emeritus of Medieval History, University of Sheffield;* b. 22 July 1938, London; s. of Edward Dominic Luscombe and Nora Luscombe; m. Megan Phillips 1960; three s. one d.; ed St Michael's Convent School, Finchley Catholic Grammar School, London and King's Coll. Cambridge; Fellow, King's Coll. 1962–64, Churchill Coll. Cambridge 1964–72; Prof. of Medieval History, Univ. of Sheffield 1972–95, Leverhulme Personal Research Prof. of Medieval History 1995–2000, Research Prof. of Medieval History 2000–03, Prof. Emer. of Medieval History 2003–, Dean of Faculty of Arts 1985–87, Pro-Vice-Chancellor 1990–94, Chair. Humanities Research Inst. 1992–2003, Dir for Research in the Humanities Div. of Grad. School 1994–2003; mem. Governing Body, later the Asscn of St Edmund's House, Cambridge 1971–84; Visiting Prof., Royal Soc. of Canada 1991, Univ. of Conn. at Storrs 1993; Visiting Fellow, All Souls Coll. Oxford 1994; Raleigh Lecturer, British Acad. 1988; British Acad. Exchange Visitor to Japan Acad. 1996; mem. Council, British Acad. 1989–97, Chair. Publs Cttee 1990–97, Medieval Texts Editorial Cttee 1991–2004 (mem. 1982–91, 2004–), mem. Humanities Research Bd 1994–96; mem. Cttee, Soc. for Study of Medieval Languages and Literature 1991–96, Council, Royal Historical Soc. 1981–85, Cttee, Ecclesiastical History Soc. 1976–79, Supervisory Cttee British Acad./Oxford Univ. Press for New Dictionary of Nat. Biography 1992–99, Assoc. Ed. 1993–98; Vice-Pres. Soc. int. pour l'étude de la philosophie médiévale 1987–97, Pres. 1997–2002; mem. Commonwealth Scholarships Comm. in UK 1994–2000; Auditor, Higher Educ. Quality Council, Div. of Quality Audit 1994–97; mem. Council Worksop Coll. and Ranby House School 1996–2008; Fellow, Woodward Corpn 2000–08, Hon. Fellow 2008; Hon. LittD (Sheffield) 2013; Medal for Outstanding Achievement, British Acad. 2014, J. Franklin Jameson Award, American Historical Asscn 2015. *Publications:* The School of Peter Abelard 1969, Peter Abelard's Ethics 1971, Church and Government in the Middle Ages (co-ed.) 1976, Petrus Abaelardus (1079–1142): Person, Werk, und Wirkung (co-ed.) 1980, The Evolution of Medieval Thought by David Knowles (co-ed. revised edn with C. Brooke) 1988, David Knowles Remembered (co-author) 1991, Anselm, Aosta, Bec and Canterbury (co-ed.) 1996, Medieval Thought 1997; Cambridge Studies in Medieval Life and Thought, 4th series (Advisory Ed.) 1983–88, (Gen. Ed.) 1988–2004; The New Cambridge Medieval History, *c.* 1024–*c.* 1198, IV, 1–2 (co-ed.) 2004, Peter Abelard, Expositio in Hexameron (co-ed.) 2004, Peter Abelard, Sententie (co-ed.) 2006, Beauchief Abbey Cartulary (co-ed.) 2011, Rulership and Rebellion in the Anglo-Norman World, c.1066–c.1216 (co-ed.) 2015; articles in learned journals. *Leisure interests:* family, using libraries, walking, cooking for two. *Address:* Department of History, University of Sheffield, Jessop West, 1 Upper Hanover Street, Sheffield, S3 7RA (office); 28 Endcliffe Hall Avenue, Sheffield, S10 3EL, England (home). *Telephone:* (114) 222-2555 (office). *Fax:* (114) 222-2576 (office). *E-mail:* d.luscombe@sheffield.ac.uk (office). *Website:* www.shef.ac.uk/history (office).

LÜST, Reimar, Dr rer. nat; German physicist; *Professor of Physics, University of Hamburg;* b. 25 March 1923, Barmen; s. of Hero Lüst and Grete Lüst (née Strunck); m. 1st Dr Rhea Kulka 1953; two s.; 2nd Nina Grunenberg 1986; ed Univs of Frankfurt am Main and Göttingen; Research Physicist, Max Planck Inst. (MPI), Göttingen and Munich 1950–60, Enrico Fermi Inst., Univ. of Chicago 1955–56, Princeton Univ. 1956; Head, Dept for Extraterrestrial Physics, MPI for Physics and Astrophysics 1960, Dir Inst. of Extraterrestrial Physics 1963–72, later Scientific Mem. for Extraterrestrial Physics, MPI; Visiting Prof., Univ. of New York 1959, MIT 1961, Calif. Inst. of Tech. 1962, 1966; Chair. German Research Council 1969–72, Deutsche Gesellschaft für Luft- und Raumfahrt 1968–72; Pres.

Max-Planck-Gesellschaft 1972–84; Dir-Gen. European Space Agency 1984–90; Prof. of Physics, Univ. of Hamburg 1992–; Pres. Alexander von Humboldt Foundation 1989–99, Hon. Pres. 1999; Chair. Bd Int. Univ. Bremen 1999–2004, Hon. Chair. 2005–; mem. Int. Acad. of Astronautics, Royal Astronomical Soc., Bavarian Acad. Sciences; Corresp. mem. Real Acad. de Ciencias Exactas, Físicas y Naturales de Madrid; Fellow, Imperial Coll. of Science and Tech., London; Hon. Prof., Inst. for Theoretical Physics, Chinese Acad. of Sciences, Beijing 1997, Beijing Univ. 1997; Hon. Foreign mem. American Acad. of Arts and Sciences, Austrian Acad. of Sciences; Hon. mem. Heidelberg Acad. of Sciences, Senat Max-Planck-Gesellschaft, Deutsche Gesellschaft für Luft- und Raumfahrt; Hon. Citizen of State of Texas 1999; Hon. Citizen of Freie Hansestadt Bremen 2001; Officier, Ordre des Palmes Académiques; Officier, Légion d'honneur; Bayerischer Maximiliansorden für Wissenschaft und Kunst; Grosses Verdienstkreuz mit Stern und Schulterband; Distinguished Service Cross (Poland) 1997; Dr hc (Sofia) 1991, (Birmingham) 1993, (Slovak Acad. of Sciences) 1995 and several other hon. degrees from int. univs; Planet 4386 named Lüst 1991; Daniel and Florence Guggenheim Int. Astronautics Award, Personality of the Year 1986, Tsiolkowsky Medal (USSR Fed. of Cosmonauts) 1987, Harnack Medal of Max Planck Soc. 1993 and numerous other awards; shared Adenauer-de Gaulle Prize 1994. *Publications:* articles on space research, astrophysics and plasmaphysics. *Leisure interests:* history, tennis, skiing. *Address:* Max-Planck-Institut für Meteorologie, Bundesstrasse 53, 20146 Hamburg (office); Bellevue 49, 22301 Hamburg, Germany (home). *Telephone:* (40) 41173300. *Fax:* (40) 41173390. *E-mail:* cornelia.sengbusch@mpimet.mpg.de (office).

LUSZTIG, George, MA, PhD, FRS; American mathematician and academic; *Abdun Nur Professor of Mathematics, Massachusetts Institute of Technology;* b. (Gheorghe Lusztig), 20 May 1946, Timişoara, Romania; m. 1st Michal-Nina Abraham 1972 (divorced 2000); two d.; m. 2nd Gongqin Li 2003; ed Univ. of Bucharest and Princeton Univ.; Visiting mem. Inst. for Advanced Study, Princeton, NJ 1969–71; Research Fellow, Dept of Math., Univ. of Warwick 1971–72, Lecturer 1972-74, Prof. 1974–78; Prof. of Math., MIT 1978–, Norbert Wiener Prof. 1999–2009, Abdun Nur Prof. 2009–; mem. NAS; Guggenheim Fellowship 1982; Cole Prize in Algebra, American Math. Soc. 1985, Brouwer Medal, Dutch Math. Soc. 1999, Steele Prize for Lifetime Achievement, American Math. Soc. 2008, Shaw Prize in Math. Sciences 2014. *Publications:* The Discrete Series of GLn over a Finite Field, 1974, Characters of Reductive Groups over a Finite Field 1984, Introduction to Quantum Groups 1993, Hecke Algebras with Unequal Parameters 2003. *Leisure interest:* yoga. *Address:* Department of Mathematics, Massachusetts Institute of Technology, Room 2-365, 77 Massachusetts Avenue, Cambridge, MA 02139, USA (office). *Telephone:* (617) 253-4398 (office). *Fax:* (617) 253-4358 (office). *E-mail:* gyuri@math.mit.edu (office). *Website:* www-math.mit.edu/~gyuri (office).

LUTCHMEENARAIDOO, Vishnu Seetanah, MBA; Mauritian politician; b. 24 May 1944; m. Susanne Lutchmeenaraidoo; three s.; ed Aix-Marseilles Univ., France, Ecole Supérieure de Commerce, Marseilles; Minister of Economy and Finance 1983–91, of Finance and Econ. Devt 2014–16, of Foreign Affairs, Regional Integration and Int. Trade 2016–19 (resgnd); Chair. State Bank 1998–2001; mem. Nat. Ass. for Constituency No. 7 (Piton and Rivière du Rempart) 2014–; mem. Mouvement Militant Mauricien –2014, mem. Alliance Lepep 2014–; Exec. Chair. Net Mauritius; Grand Commdr, Order of the Star and the Key of the Indian Ocean; Dr hc (Dauphine Univ., Paris). *Address:* c/o Ministry of Foreign Affairs, Regional Integration and International Trade, Newton Tower, 9th–11th Floors, Sir William Newton Street, Port Louis, Mauritius (office).

LUTE, Jane Holl, PhD, JD; American government official, UN official and fmr army officer; *Special Coordinator on Improving United Nations Response to Sexual Exploitation and Abuse;* m. Lt. Gen. Douglas Lute; three d.; ed Stanford Univ., Georgetown Univ.; career Officer, US Army (retd 1994); fmr teacher of Political Science, West Point Mil. Acad.; served in Europe, Persian Gulf during Operation Desert Storm 1991; mem. of Staff, Nat. Security Council, Dir of European Affairs 1991–94; Head of Carnegie Comm. on Preventing Deadly Conflict 1994–99; Sr Public Policy Fellow, Woodrow Wilson Centre for Int. Scholars 1994–99; Exec. Dir Asscn of US Army Project on role of American mil. power 2000; Exec. Vice-Pres. and COO UN Foundation and Better World Fund 2000–03; Asst Sec.-Gen. for Mission Support, UN Dept Peace-keeping Operations 2003–09; Deputy Sec., US Dept of Homeland Security, Washington, DC 2009–13; Special Adviser to UN Sec.-Gen. for Relocation of Camp Hurriya Residents Outside of Iraq 2014–16; Special Coordinator on Improving UN Response to Sexual Exploitation and Abuse 2016–; mem. of Va Bar. *Address:* Office of the Secretary-General, United Nations, New York, NY 10017, USA (office). *Telephone:* (212) 963-1234 (office). *Fax:* (212) 963-4879 (office). *Website:* www.un.org/sg (office).

LÜTKESTRATKÖTTER, Herbert Hermann, Dr-Ing; German business executive; b. 1950; ed Aachen Tech Univ. and its Inst. of Hydraulic Eng and Water Resources Man.; held planning and man. roles at Lahmeyer International 1978–99, becoming Man. Dir and also mem. Exec. Bd, Lahmeyer AG; Int. Business Man. Philipp Holzmann AG 1999, Labour Relations Dir 2000; fmr Chair. Exec. Bd Dussmann AG & Co. KGaA; joined Hochtief AG 2003, mem. Exec. Bd 2003–11, Deputy Chair. 2006–07, Chair. 2007–11, responsible for the Americas and Europe divs, for Corp. Devt, Corp. Communications and Corp. Governance; mem. Bd of Dirs Aecon Group Inc. 2005–; mem. Supervisory Bd ThyssenKrupp Elevator AG; Alt. Dir Leighton Holdings Ltd 2004–07, apptd Dir (non-exec.) 2007.

LUTON, Jean-Marie; French engineer; *Honorary President, Starsem;* b. 4 Aug. 1942, Chamalières; s. of Pierre Luton and Marie Luton; m. Cécile Robine 1967; three s.; ed Lycée Blaise Pascal, Clermont-Ferrand, Lycée St Louis, Paris, Faculté des Sciences, Paris and Ecole Polytechnique; with CNRS 1964–71; Ministry of Industrial and Scientific Devt 1971–73; Head of Research, Centre Nat. d'Etudes Spatiales 1974–75, Head of Planning 1975–78, Dir of Programmes and Planning 1978–84, Deputy Dir-Gen. 1984–87, Dir-Gen. 1989–90; Dir of Space Programmes, Aérospatiale 1987–89; Dir-Gen. European Space Agency 1990–97; Pres., Dir-Gen., then Chair. Arianespace 1997–2006; Chair. and CEO Starsem 2002–06, Hon. Pres. 2006–; Chevalier, Légion d'honneur, Officier, Ordre nat. du Mérite; Prix de l'Astronautique; Prix de l'Innovateur industriel, Society of Satellite Professionals (USA) 1998. *Leisure interests:* tennis, sailing. *Address:* c/o Starsem, 2 rue François Truffaut, 91042 Evry Cedex, France (office).

LUTSENKO, Yuriy Vitaliyovych; Ukrainian engineer and politician; *Prosecutor-General;* b. 14 Dec. 1964, Rivne, Rivne Oblast, Ukrainian SSR, USSR; s. of Vitaliy Ivanovych Lutsenko and Vira Mikhailivna Lutsenko; m. Irina; two s.; ed Lviv Polytechnical Inst.; mil. service in army 1984–86; Chief Constructor and Head, Tech. Workshop, Gazotron, Rivne 1989–94; Deputy Head, Rivne Oblast Council of People's Deputies 1994–96; Head, Rivne Oblast Admin Econs Cttee 1996–97; Deputy Minister of Science and Tech. 1997–98; adviser to Prime Minister 1998–99; adviser to Leader of Sotsialistychna Partiya Ukrainy (SPU—Socialist Party of Ukraine) 1999–2002; Deputy, Verkhovna Rada (Parl.) 2002–05; Minister of Internal Affairs 2005–06, 2007–10; mem. SPU 1996–2006, Sec., Political Council 1996–98, later held number of sr positions; mem. Construction, Transportation, Communal Services and Communications Cttee, Verkhovna Rada 2002–05; active in Ukraina bez Kuchmy! (Ukraine Without Kuchma!) campaign 2000–01, 'Orange Revolution' 2004; Chief-Ed. Grani 2000–05; Founder Narodna Samooborona Yuriya Lutsenka (NSYuL—Yuriy Lutsenko People's Self Defence) movt 2007 (registered as political party 2010); charged with abuse of office and forgery, imprisoned Lukyanivska Prison from Dec. 2010–Aug. 2012, went on hunger strike April–May 2011, sentenced to four years' imprisonment for embezzlement and abuse of office Feb. 2012, protests against sentence made by EU, US Dept of State, Canada and other Int. Orgs and human rights orgs; appealed against sentence March 2012, lost appeal April 2013, pardoned and released from prison for health reasons April 2013; held at Menska Colony Aug. 2012–April 2013; NSYuL absorbed into Blok Yulii Tymoshenko (Yuliya Timoshenko Bloc) 2012; f. new non-parl. org. Tretya Respublika (Third Repub.) 2013; one of the organizers of Euromaidan (wave of demonstrations, civil unrest and revolution with public protests demanding closer European integration) Nov. 2013; Tretya Respublika transformed into political party Tretya Ukrainska Respublika (Third Ukrainian Repub.) July 2014, absorbed into Blok Petra Poroshenka 'Solidarnist' (BPP—S—Solidarity—Petro Poroshenko Bloc) Aug. 2014, Leader, BPP—S Aug. 2014; Prosecutor-Gen. 2016–; Commdr, Order of Prince Yaroslav the Wise (Fifth Class) 2006. *Address:* Office of the Prosecutor-General, 01011 Kyiv, vul. Riznytska 13–15, Ukraine (office). *Telephone:* (44) 288-84-71 (office). *Fax:* (44) 280-28-51 (office). *E-mail:* interel@gp.gov.ua (office); lutsenko_pressa@ukr.net (office). *Website:* www.gp.gov.ua (office).

LUTTER, Marcus Michael, PhD; German professor of law; *Professor Emeritus and Dean, Zentrum für Europäisches Wirtschaftsrecht, University of Bonn;* b. 11 Dec. 1930, Munich; s. of Michael Lutter; m. Rebecca Garbe 1957; one s. two d.; ed Univs of Munich, Paris and Freiburg; notary, Rockenhausen 1957–60; research scholarship, Deutsche Forschungsgesellschaft, Brussels, Strasbourg, Paris, Rome, Utrecht 1961–63; notary, Rockenhausen and external lecturer, Univ. of Mainz 1964–65; Prof. Inst. for Civil Law, German and European Trade and Econ. Law, Univ. of Bochum 1966–79; fmr Prof. and Dir Inst. for Trade and Econ. Law, Univ. of Bonn, now Prof. Emer. and Dean of the Zentrum für Europäisches Wirtschaftsrecht (Centre for European Econ. Law); Visiting Prof., Univ. of California, Berkeley 1972, Techno Univ., Tokyo 1982, Univ. of Oxford 1997; Publr Zeitschrift für Unternehmens-und Gesellschaftsrecht; Pres. German Lawyers' Asscn 1982–88; Hon. PhD (Vienna, Warsaw, Jena). *Publications:* Information and Confidentiality in the Supervisory Board 1984, 2006, European Company Law 1996, The Letter of Intent 1998, Duties and Rights of Board Members 2002; various monographs and treatises especially on participation, jt stock cos and supervisory bds. *Address:* Zentrum für Europäisches Wirtschaftsrecht der Universität Bonn, Adenauerallee 24–42, 53113 Bonn (office); Auf der Steige 6, 53129 Bonn, Germany (home). *Telephone:* (228) 739559 (office); (228) 231722 (home). *Fax:* (228) 737078 (office). *E-mail:* marcus.lutter@jura.uni-bonn.de (office). *Website:* www.jura.uni-bonn.de (office).

LUTTWAK, Edward Nicolae, PhD; American academic, international consultant and writer; *Senior Associate, Center for Strategic and International Studies;* b. 4 Nov. 1942, Arad, Romania; s. of Joseph Luttwak and Clara Baruch; m. Dalya Iaari 1970; one s. one d.; ed Carmel Coll., Wallingford and London School of Econs, UK, Johns Hopkins Univ.; Lecturer, Univ. of Bath, UK 1965–67; Consultant, Walter J. Levy SA (London) 1967–68; Visiting Prof., Johns Hopkins Univ. 1974–76; Sr Fellow, Center for Strategic and Int. Studies, Washington, DC 1977–87, Burke Chair. of Strategy 1987–92, Sr Fellow 1992, now Sr Assoc. (non-resident); Consultant to Office of US Sec. of Defense 1975, to Policy Planning Council, US Dept of State 1981, Nat. Security Council, The White House 1987, US Dept of Defense 1987, to Govts of Italy, Korea, Spain; Prin., Edward N. Luttwak Inc. Int. Consultants 1981–; Pres. Servicios Agricolas Tupinamba, Bolivia; Int. Assoc. Inst. of Fiscal and Monetary Policy, Japan Ministry of Finance (Okurasho); mem. editorial Bd The American Scholar, Journal of Strategic Studies, The National Interest, Géopolitique, The Washington Quarterly, Orbis; Hon. LLD (Bath) 2004; Nimitz Lectureship, (Univ. of Calif.) 1987, Tanner Lecturer, (Yale Univ.) 1989, Rosenstiel Lecturer, (Grinner Coll.) 1992. *Publications include:* Coup d'Etat 1968, Dictionary of Modern War 1972, The Israeli Army 1975, The Political Uses of Sea Power 1976, The Grand Strategy of the Roman Empire 1978, Strategy and Politics: Collected Essays 1979, The Grand Strategy of the Soviet Union 1983, The Pentagon and the Art of War 1985, Strategy and History: collected essays 1985, International Security Yearbook 1984/85 (with Barry M. Brechman) 1985, On the Meaning of Victory 1986, Strategy: The Logic of War and Peace 1987, The Dictionary of Modern War (with Stuart Koehl) 1991, The Endangered American Dream 1993, Il Fantasma della Povertà (co-author) 1996, Cose è davvero la Democrazia 1996, La Renaissance de la puissance aérienne stratégique 1998, Turbo-Capitalism 1999, Il Libro della Libertà 2000, Strategy: The Logic of War and Peace (ed.) 2002, The Grand Strategy of the Byzantine Empire 2010; books have been translated into 16 languages. *Leisure interest:* ranching in the Amazon. *Address:* Center for Strategic and International Studies, 1616 Rhode Island Avenue, NW, Washington, DC 20036, USA (office). *Website:* www.csis.org (office).

LUTZ, Robert (Bob) A., BS, MBA; American automotive industry executive; b. 12 Feb. 1932, Zürich, Switzerland; s. of Robert H. Lutz and Marguerite Lutz; m. 1st Betty D. Lutz 1956 (divorced 1979); m. 2nd Heide-Marie Schmid 1980 (divorced 1993); m. 3rd Denise Ford 1994; four d. from 1st marriage; ed Univ. of California, Berkeley; Capt. in US Marine Corps 1954–59; Research Assoc. IMEDE, Lausanne 1962–63; Sr Analyst, Forward Planning, General Motors Corpn (GM), New York 1963–65, Staff Asst, Man. Dir's Staff, Adam Opel AG (GM) 1965–66, various man. positions at GM France 1966–69, Asst Domestic Gen. Sales Man., Merchandising,

Adam Opel AG 1969, Dir of Sales and mem. Man. Bd 1969–70; Vice-Pres. (Sales) and mem. Man. Bd, BMW AG 1970–74; Gen. Man. Ford of Germany 1974–76, Vice-Pres. (Truck Operations), Ford of Europe 1976–77; Pres. Ford of Europe 1977–79, Vice-Pres. Ford Motor Co. and Chair. of Bd Ford of Europe 1979–82; Exec. Vice-Pres. Ford Int. Automotive Operations, Dearborn, Mich. 1982–86, Exec. Vice-Pres. North American Truck Operations 1986; Head of, Int. Operations, Pres. and COO Chrysler Corpn 1988–96, Vice-Chair. 1996–98; Chair., CEO and Pres. Exide Corpn 1998–2001, Chair. 2001–02; Vice-Chair. of Product Devt, General Motors (GM) 2001–09, Chair. GM North America 2001–09, Vice Chair. and Sr Advisor to CEO 2009–10, Special Advisor 2010–; f. Lutz Communications (consultancy), Ann Arbor, Mich.; Chair. Silicon Graphics, ASCOM, Switzerland, New Common School Foundation; mem. Bd of Dirs Transonic Combustion, Inc. 2010–; Vice-Chair. Bd of Trustees, Marine Mil. Acad.; mem. Bd of Trustees, US Marine Corps Univ. Foundation. *Publications:* Guts: The Seven Laws of Business That Made Chrysler the World's Hottest Car Company 1999, Guts: 8 Laws of Business from One of the Most Innovative Business Leaders of Our Time 2003, Car Guys vs. Bean Counters 2011, Icons and Idiots: Straight Talk on Leadership 2013. *Address:* Lutz Communications, Ann Arbor, MI 48103-9628, USA (office). *Telephone:* (866) 476-3931 (office). *E-mail:* info@boblutzsez.com (office). *Website:* www.boblutzsez.com (office).

LUU, Jane, BS, PhD; Vietnamese/American astronomer and academic; *Senior Scientist, Lincoln Laboratory, Massachusetts Institute of Technology;* b. July 1963, Saigon, South Viet Nam; m. Ronnie Hoogerwerf; ed Stanford Univ., Univ. of California, Berkeley, Massachusetts Inst. of Tech.; emigrated to USA as a refugee 1975; Postdoctoral Fellow, Harvard-Smithsonian Center for Astrophysics, Univ. of California, Berkeley and Stanford Univ. 1990–94; Asst Prof., Harvard Univ. 1994–98; Prof., Leiden Univ., The Netherlands 1998–2001; Sr Scientist, Lincoln Laboratory, MIT 2001–; Annie J. Cannon Award in Astronomy, American Astronomical Soc. 1991, Hubble Fellowship, Space Telescope Science Inst., asteroid 5430 Luu named in her honour, Shaw Prize in Astronomy (co-recipient) 2012, Kavli Prize (co-recipient) 2012. *Publications:* numerous papers in professional journals. *Leisure interests:* playing cello, travelling. *Address:* Lincoln Laboratory, Massachusetts Institute of Technology, 244 Wood Street, Lexington, MA 02421-6426, USA (office). *Telephone:* (781) 981-5500 (office). *E-mail:* llwebmaster@ll.mit.edu (office). *Website:* www.ll.mit.edu (office).

LUXTON, John, BAgrSc; New Zealand politician; b. 14 Sept. 1946; m. Mary Scholtens; three c.; ed Massey Univ.; Nat. Party MP for Matamata 1987–96, for Karapiro 1996–99; Minister of Housing and Energy, Assoc. Minister of Educ. 1990–93, Assoc. Minister of Maori Affairs 1991–97; Minister of Maori Affairs, Police and Assoc. Minister of Educ. 1993–97, Minister of Commerce, Fisheries, Lands and Biosecurity, for Industry and Assoc. Minister for Agric. 1997–98; Minister of Food, Fibre, Biosecurity and Border Control, Assoc. Minister of Immigration and Assoc. Minister for Int. Trade 1998–99; Nat. Party Spokesperson on Int. Trade Negotiations and Inward Investment and Regional Devt, Assoc. Foreign Affairs 2000–01; Nat. Party Spokesman for Tourism, Communications, Inward Investment 2001; fmr Chair. Tatua Industry Co-operative Dairy Co. Ltd, Deputy Chair. Wallford Meats Ltd; Dir Wallace Corpn Ltd, Tatua Co-operative Dairy Co., Asia 2000 Foundation; int. agric. consultant and farmer; AC Cameron Memorial Award 1987.

LUZHKOV, Yurii Mikhailovich; Russian politician; b. 21 Sept. 1936, Moscow; m. Marina Bashilova 1958 (died 1989); two s.; m. 2nd Yelena Baturina 1991; two d.; ed Gubkin Inst. of Oil and Gas, Moscow; researcher, Research Inst. of Plastic Materials 1958–64; Head of Div. Ministry of Chemical Industry 1964–87; First Deputy Chair. Exec. Cttee, Moscow City Council and Chair. Moscow Agric. Industry Dept 1987–90; Chair. Exec. Cttee, Moscow City Council 1990–91; Vice-Mayor of Moscow and Premier, Moscow City Govt 1991–92, Mayor and Head of City Govt 1992–2010, re-elected 1996, 1999, 2003, apptd 2007–10; mem. Russian Council of Fed. 1996–2001; Founder and Co-Chair. Fatherland (Otechestvo) Movt 1998–2001, formed alliance with All Russia party in 1999, subsequently merged with pro-Putin Unity party to create Unity and Fatherland-United Russia party (UF-UR) 2001, later simply United Russia (Yedinaya Rossiya); Co-Chair. Supreme Council, UF-UR; Chair. Int. Fund Assistance to Free Enterprise; Pres. Moscow Int. Business Asscn 2002; Hon. Prof., Acad. of Labour and Social Relations; Lenin Order, Red Banner Order, Order in the Name of Russia 2004; Hon. DSc (Lomonosov State Univ. Moscow); Golden Mask Prize for support of the arts. *Publications include:* 72 Hours of Agony 1991, The Quietist Negotiations 1994, We Are Your Children, Moscow 1996, The Renewal of History: Mankind in the 21st Century and the Future of Russia 2003, Russian Parkinson's Law 2005, The Kazakhstan Way 2008. *Leisure interests:* football, tennis, skiing, equestrian sport, fishing, bee-keeping.

LUZÓN LÓPEZ, Francisco; Spanish banker; b. 1 Jan. 1948, Cañavate, Cuenca; ed Univ. of Bilbao; trainee, Banco de Vizcaya 1972, Regional Man. Seville 1974, Man. of Planning and Man. Control, Bilbao 1975–78, Int. Div. Madrid 1978–80, Man. London 1980–81; mem. Bd and Gen. Man. Banco de Crédito Comercial 1981–82; mem. Bd and Gen. Man. Banco Occidental 1982–85; Gen. Man. Commercial Banking Network 1985–87; mem. Bd and Gen. Man. Banco de Vizcaya 1987–88, Banco Bilbao-Vizcaya 1988; Chair. Banco Exterior de España 1988–99; Vice-Pres. Banco Atlántico and mem. Bd Teneo 1991–94; Chair. and CEO Argentaria 1991–96; Chair. Caja Postal SA 1991–, Banco de Crédito Local 1994–99, Banco Hipotecario de España 1994–, Corporación Bancaria de España SA; mem. Bd of Dirs, Banco Santander Central Hispano 1997–2012, Exec. Vice-Pres. for Latin America 1999–2012; Worldwide Vice-Pres. Universia SA 1999–2012; Dir, Inditex-Zara SA 1997–2012, LATAM Airlines Group SA 2012–; adviser, IDB; Leader-Guest Prof., School of Business China-Europe (CEIBS), Shanghai; Lecturer, Univ. of Deusto, Bilbao. *Address:* c/o Ciudad Grupo Santander, Avenida de Cantabria s/n, 28660 Boadilla del Monte, Madrid (office); Paseo de Recoletos 10, 28001 Madrid, Spain; LATAM Airlines Group, Pdte. Riesco 5711, 20th Floor, Las Condes, Santiago, Chile. *Telephone:* (91) 2890000 (office). *E-mail:* investor.relations@lan.com (office). *Website:* www.santander.com (office).

LUZZATTO, Lucio, FRCPath, FRCP; Italian geneticist and haematologist; *Scientific Director, Istituto Toscano Tumori;* b. 28 Sept. 1936, Genoa; s. of Aldo Luzzatto and Anna Luzzatto Gabrielli; m. Paola Caboara 1963; one s. one d.; ed Liceo D'Oria, Genoa, Univ. of Genoa Medical School, Univ. of Pavia; Sr Lecturer in

charge of Sub-Dept of Haematology, Univ. of Ibadan, Nigeria 1967–68, Prof. of Haematology 1968–74, Consultant Haematologist, Univ. Coll. Hosp. Ibadan, Nigeria 1967–68; Dir Int. Inst. of Genetics and Biophysics, CNR, Naples 1974–81; Prof. of Haematology (Univ. of London) and Dir of Haematology Dept Royal Postgrad. Medical School, Consultant Haematologist Hammersmith Hosp., London, UK 1981–94, Hon. Dir MRC/LRF Leukaemia Unit, London 1987–93; Chair. Dept of Human Genetics, Courtney Steel Chair., Attending Physician in Genetics and Haematology, mem. Cell Biology Program, Memorial Sloan-Kettering Cancer Center, New York, Prof. of Medicine and Human Genetics, Cornell Univ. Medical Coll., New York 1994–2000; Scientific Dir Nat. Inst. of Cancer Research (IST), Genoa, Italy 2000–04, personal Chair of Haematology 2002–; currently Scientific Dir Istituto Toscano Tumori, Florence; Founding Pres. Nigerian Soc. for Haematology; fmr Pres. Italian Asscn of Genetics; fmr Chair. Ethics Cttee American Soc. for Gene Therapy; mem. European Molecular Biology Org. 1979, Human Genome Org. (HUGO) 1990, American Asscn of Physicians; Foreign mem. American Acad. of Arts and Sciences 2004; Hon. mem. American Soc. of Hematology; Hon. DSc (Ibadan) 1990; Dr hc of Pharmacy (Urbino) 1990; William Dameshek Medal 1975, Pius XI Medal 1976, Sanremo Int. Prize for Human Genetics 1982, Int. Chiron Award for Biomedical Research 1995, Premio Napoli 1995, Jose Carreras Medal 2002. *Publications:* more than 330 articles in scientific journals and scientific and medical textbooks. *Address:* Istituto Toscano Tumori, Via T. Alderotti 26N, 50139 Florence, Italy (office). *Telephone:* (55) 4385213 (office). *Fax:* (55) 4385252 (office). *E-mail:* lucio.luzzatto@regione.toscana .it (office). *Website:* www.ittumori.it (office).

LY, Oumar Tatam, MA; Malian economist and politician; b. 28 Sept. 1963, Paris, France; s. of Ibrahima Ly and Madina Tall Ly; m.; two c.; ed Ecole Normale Superieure de Lyon, Univ. Paris–1 (Sorbonne), Ecole supérieure des Sciences économiques et commerciales, Cergy-Pontoise, France; began career as economist, World Bank 1990; Project Man., Gen. Secr. of Pres. of Mali 1992–93, Technical Adviser 1993–94; Analyst, Central Man. Studies and Forecasting Dept, Banque centrale des États de l'Afrique de l'Ouest (BCEAO), Dakar 1994–96, Deputy Dir of Studies 1996, Chief Financial Officer 2000–06, Dir, Dept of Issue, Accounting and Finance 2007–09, Nat. Dir for Mali, BCEAO 2008, Special Adviser to Gov. –2013; Prime Minister 2013–14. *Leisure interests:* reading, cinema, tennis. *Address:* c/o Office of the Prime Minister, Quartier du Fleuve, BP 790, Bamako, Mali.

LYAKHOV, Col Vladimir Afanasyevich; Russian cosmonaut (retd); b. 20 July 1941, Antratsit, Voroshilovgrad Oblast, Ukrainian SSR; m.; two c.; ed Kharkov Aviation School for Pilots, Chuguyev, Kharkov Oblast, Gagarin Mil. Acad.; mem. CPSU 1963–91; served in fmr Soviet Air Force 1964–; mem. Cosmonaut team 1967–94; Commdr of space-ship Soyuz-32 1979 and Soyuz T-9 which connected up with orbital station Salyut-7; Commdr Soyuz TM-6 1988; space-walked 1983; spent 333 days, 7 hours, 47 minutes in space; worked in Yuri Gagarin Centre 1995–99; Hero of Soviet Union (twice), Pilot-Cosmonaut of the USSR, Order of Lenin (two), Order of the October Revolution, Medal 'For Merit in Space Exploration' (Russian Fed.), Order of Sukhbaatar (Mongolia), Order 'The Sun of Liberty' (Afghanistan), Order of Merit, Third Class (Ukraine); K. Tsiolkovski Gold Medal. *Leisure interest:* hockey. *Address:* c/o Yuri Gagarin Research & Test Training Centre, 141160 Star City, Moscow Region, Russia. *Telephone:* (495) 526-34-07. *Fax:* (495) 526-26-12.

LYALL, John Adrian, RIBA, FRSA; British architect; *Co-Director, Lyall Bills & Young Architects Ltd;* b. 12 Dec. 1949, Daws Heath, Essex; s. of Keith Lyall and Phyllis Lyall (née Sharps); m. Sallie Jean Davies 1991; one s. one d.; ed Southend High School for Boys, Essex, Architectural Asscn School of Architecture; worked for Cedric Price, Piano & Rogers, Bahr, Vermeer & Haecker, Rock Townsend 1996–79; Founder Multimatch Design Group 1970–73; in practice with Will Alsop as Alsop & Lyall, later Alsop, Lyall & Störmer 1980–91; Man. Dir John Lyall Architects (now Lyall Bills & Young Architects) 1991–2011, Co-Dir 2011–; RIBA Vice-Pres. of Cultural Affairs 1997, of Future Studies 1999–2000, Chair. of Validation Task Force, RIBA 2001; Bannister Fletcher Prof. Univ. Coll. London 1998; design teaching and lecturing at Architectural Asscn and Bartlett Schools, London and univs in USA, UK, Russia, Chile, Colombia and Ecuador; design adviser to Cardiff Bay Devt Corpn and English Partnerships; apptd as enabler for CABE 2001 and Chair. of RIBA's Educ. Validation Task Force 2001–02; Chair. Peterborough Design Panel 2009; mem. CABE Design Review Panel 2008; created Polyark II project 2009–10; award-winning bldgs include: The Corn Exchange, Leeds (Ironbridge Award, British Archaeological Soc. 1990, 1998, Leeds Award for Architecture 1990, Europa Nostra Award, 1991, RIBA National Award, 1991, RIBA White Rose Award 1991, Civic Trust Commendation 1991, British Council of Shopping Centres Award 1991, Design Week Award 1991, Royal Inst. of Chartered Surveyors Urban Renewal Award 1995) 1991, White Cloth Hall, Leeds (Leeds Award for Architecture 1992, The Minerva Award 1993) 1992, Tottenham Hale Overground Station, London (Aluminium Imagination Award 1993) 1992 (Tottenham Hale London Underground Station and Station Forecourt 1999), Harry Ramsden's Restaurant, Cardiff Bay 1996, North Greenwich Jubilee Line Station, London (RIBA Regional Award 1999, RIBA Nat. Category Award 1999, Civic Trust Commendation 2000) 1999, Crystal Palace Park, London 2003, Silver House, Carnaby Street, London 2003–04, Regeneration of Cranfields Mills, Ipswich 2004–09, Hammersmith Pumping Station (residential conversion and new-build affordable housing block) 2004–08, Jerwood Dance House, Ipswich 2005, Goldsmiths Centre, Clerkenwell, London 2007–; Pumping Stations, Olympic site, London 2009–. *Television:* contrib. to Masterclass – Denys Lasdun; panel mem. BBC Knowledge 2000–01. *Dance:* design collaborator with Rosemary Butcher Dance Co. on various performances 1990–96. *Music:* production designer for Opera 80 travelling opera 1980–83. *Publications include:* John Lyall: Contexts and Catalysts 1999; contrib. to A Guide to Recent Architecture: London 1993, A Guide to Recent Architecture: England 1995, Context – New Buildings in Historic Settings 1998. *Leisure interest:* choral singing, gardening. *Address:* Lyall Bills & Young Architects Ltd, Studio D2, 400 Caledonian Road, London, N1 1DN, England (office); Newlands, Gandish Road, East Bergholt, Suffolk, CO7 6TP, England (home). *Telephone:* (20) 7253-1630 (office). *E-mail:* john.lyall@lbyarchitects.com (office). *Website:* www.lbyarchitects.com (office).

LYASHKO, Oleh Valeriovich; Ukrainian journalist and politician; *Leader, Radikalna Partiya Oleha Lyashka (RPL—Radical Party of Oleh Lyashko);* b. 12 March 1972, Chernihiv, Ukrainian SSR, USSR; m. Rosita Lyashko; one d.; ed H.S.

Skovoroda Kharkiv Nat. Pedagogical Univ.; attended coll. for tractor operator studies; corresp. and Head of Moloda Hvardiya (Young Guard) newspaper, Kyiv 1990–92; Ed. Komertsiyni Visti (Business News), Ministry of Foreign Econ. Relations 1992; arrested and indicted for embezzlement 1993, found guilty by Criminal Coll. of Kyiv City Court, sentenced to six years' imprisonment and to sequestration of property, sentenced reduced by Supreme Court to four years, released under amnesty 1995, criminal case erased 1998; Ed. Politika (Politics) newspaper, Pravda Ukrainy (Truth of Ukraine) 1995–96, Chief Ed. 1996–99 (newspaper closed down by Moscow Dist court in Kyiv for "divulging state secrets"); Chief Ed. Svoboda (Freedom) newspaper 2000–06; Deputy (for Blok Yulii Tymoshenko—Yuliya Tymosehnko Blok 2006–10, Radikalna Partiya Oleha Lyashka—RPL—Radical Party of Oleh Lyashko 2010–) to Verkhovna Rada (Parl.) 2006–; Leader, RPL 2011–; went on hunger strike in support of jailed opposition leader Yuliya Tymoshenko Nov. 2012; unsuccessful cand. in presidential election 2014; elected to Kyiv City Council but decided not to become a deputy June 2014. *Address:* Radikalna Partiya Oleha Lyashka (Radical Party of Oleh Lyashko), 01008 Kyiv, vul. Hrushevskogo 5, Ukraine (office). *Telephone:* (44) 255-27-48 (office). *E-mail:* liashko.oleh@rada.gov.ua (office); liashko.press@gmail.com (office); info@liashko.ua (office). *Website:* liashko.ua (office).

LYDON, Nicholas B., BSc, PhD, FRS; British/American biochemist, entrepreneur and academic; *CEO, Granite Biopharma, LLC;* b. 27 Feb. 1957, England; ed Strathallan School, Perth, Scotland, Univs of Leeds and Dundee; researched interferon at Schering-Plough, Paris and Lyon, France 1982–85; Leader of Protein Kinase Inhibitor Programme, Ciba-Geigy Pharmaceuticals (now Novartis, cr. through merger with Sandoz 1996), Basel, Switzerland 1985–97; introduced to oncologist Brian J. Druker late 1980s, both scientists successful in developing the drug Gleevac at Novartis 1996; Founder, Pres. and CEO Kinetix Pharmaceuticals, Inc., Boston, Mass 1997–2000 (acquired by Amgen, Inc. 2000), Vice-Pres. for Small Molecule Drug Discovery 2000–02; Founder, Granite Biopharma, LLC (consulting co.), Jackson Hole, Wyo.; Co-founder and Dir AnaptysBio, San Diego, Calif., Blueprint Medicines, Cambridge, Mass; mem. Bd of Dirs and Scientific Advisory Bd Ambit Biosciences (Avalon VI), AnaptysBio, Inc. Biosciences (Avalon VII); Hon. LLD (Dundee) 2011; Warren Alpert Foundation Prize 2000, AACR-Bruce F. Cain Memorial Award 2002, Charles F. Kettering Prize, General Motors Cancer Research Foundation 2002, Lasker-DeBakey Clinical Medical Research Award (co-recipient) 2009, Japan Prize (co-recipient) 2012, GlaxoSmithKline Prize and Lecturer, Royal Soc. 2014. *Achievements include:* developed, with Brian J. Druker and Charles L. Sawyers, imatinib (or Gleevac) and dasatinib - targeted treatments for chronic myeloid leukemia. *Publications:* numerous papers in professional journals. *Address:* AnaptysBio, Inc., 10421 Pacific Center Court, Suite 200, San Diego, CA 92121, USA (office). *Telephone:* (858) 362-6295 (office). *Fax:* (858) 362-6296 (office). *E-mail:* corpdev@anaptysbio.com (office). *Website:* www.anaptysbio.com (office).

LYKKETOFT, Mogens; Danish politician; b. 9 Jan. 1946, Copenhagen; s. of Axel Lykketoft and Martha Lykketoft; m. Mette Holm; two d.; ed Univ. of Copenhagen; worked at Econ. Council of the Labour Movt 1966–81, Head of Dept 1975–81; mem. Folketing (Parl.) 1981–, Political Spokesman for Social Democratic Party 1991–93, 2001–02, Leader 2002–05, Spokesman on Foreign Affairs 2005–09, Vice-Pres. of Parl. and Vice-Chair. Foreign Policy Cttee 2009–11, Speaker of the Parl. 2011–15; Minister for Inland Revenue 1981–82, of Finance 1993–2000, of Foreign Affairs 2000–01; Pres. UN Gen. Ass. 2015–16. *Publications include:* ed. of several books and numerous articles in magazines, periodicals and newspapers. *Address:* Folketinget, Christiansborg, 1218 København K (office); Trepilevej 1 B, 2930 Klampenborg, Denmark (home). *Telephone:* 61-62-35-75 (office). *E-mail:* smoly@ft.dk (office). *Website:* www.lykketoft.dk.

LYNAM, Desmond (Des) Michael, OBE, ACII; British sports broadcaster; b. 17 Sept. 1942, Ennis, Co. Clare, Repub. of Ireland; s. of Edward Lynam and Gertrude Veronica Malone; m. Susan Eleanor Skinner (divorced 1974); one s.; ed Varndean Grammar School, Brighton, Brighton Business Coll.; career in insurance –1967; freelance journalist and reporter local radio 1967–69; reporter, presenter and commentator BBC Radio 1969–78; presenter and commentator BBC TV Sport 1978–99 (including Grandstand, Sportsnight, Match of the Day, Commonwealth and Olympic Games and World Cup coverage); presenter, Holiday (BBC) 1988–89, How Do They Do That? (BBC) 1994–96, The Des Lynam Show (BBC Radio) 1998–99, ITV Sport 1999–2004, BAFTA TV Awards (ITV) 2000, The Premiership (ITV) 2001–04, Des Meets 2004, Countdown (Channel 4) 2005–06, Britain's Favourite View (ITV) 2007, Setanta Sports (Setanta) 2007–08, Sport Mastermind (BBC TV) 2008, Touchline Tales (BBC Radio 4) 2010–13; columnist for The Daily Telegraph; Assoc., Chartered Insurance Inst.; TV Sports Presenter of the Year, TRIC 1985, 1987, 1988, 1993, 1997, Radio Times Male TV Personality 1989, RTS Sports Presenter of the Year 1994, 1998, Richard Dimbleby Award, BAFTA 1994, Variety Club of GB Media Award 1997. *Publications include:* Guide to the Commonwealth Games 1986, The 1988 Olympics 1988, The 1992 Olympics 1992, Sport Crazy 1998, I Should Have Been At Work! (autobiog.) 2005. *Leisure interests:* golf, tennis, Brighton and Hove Albion, reading, theatre. *Address:* c/o Jane Morgan Management, Argentum, 2 Queen Caroline Steet, London, W6 9DX, England (office). *Telephone:* (20) 3178-8071 (office). *E-mail:* enquiries@janemorganmgt.com (office). *Website:* www.janemorganmgt.com (office).

LYNCH, Christopher S.; American business executive; *Non-Executive Chairman, Freddie Mac (Federal Home Loan Mortgage Corporation);* held several positions with KPMG LLP, including Nat. Partner in Charge – Financial Services, chaired KPMG's Americas Financial Services Leadership team, mem. of Global Financial Services Leadership and US Industries Leadership teams, led Banking & Finance practice, also served as a partner in Dept of Professional Practice and as Practice Fellow at Financial Accounting Standards Bd, retd 2007; Chair. (non-exec.) Freddie Mac (Fed. Home Loan Mortgage Corpn) 2011–; mem. Bd of Dirs American International Group, Inc.; mem. Nat. Audit Cttee Chair Advisory Council, Nat. Asscn of Corp. Dirs. *Address:* Freddie Mac, 8200 Jones Branch Drive, McLean, VA 22102-3110, USA (office). *Telephone:* (703) 903-2000 (office). *E-mail:* info@freddiemac.com (office). *Website:* www.freddiemac.com (office).

LYNCH, David; American film director and photographer; b. 20 Jan. 1946, Missoula, Mont.; m. 1st Peggy Reavey 1967 (divorced); one d.; m. 2nd Mary Fisk 1977 (divorced); one s.; m. 3rd Mary Sweeney 2006 (divorced); one s.; m. 4th Emily Stofle 2009; ed Hammond High School, Alexandria, Corcoran School of Art, School of Museum of Fine Arts, Boston and Pennsylvania Acad. of Fine Arts; Guest Artistic Dir AFI Fest 2010; Fellow, Center for Advanced Film Studies, American Film Inst. 1970; Founder and Chair. Bd of Trustees, David Lynch Foundation for Consciousness-Based Educ. and World Peace 2005–; Officier, Légion d'Honneur 2007; Dr hc (Royal Coll. of Art) 1991; Stockholm Int. Film Festival Lifetime Achievement Award 2003, Venice Film Festival Golden Lion 2006. *Films include:* The Grandmother 1970, Eraserhead 1977, The Elephant Man 1980, Dune 1984, Blue Velvet 1986 (Golden Palm, Cannes), Wild at Heart 1990 (Golden Palm, Cannes 1990), Storyville 1991, Twin Peaks: Fire Walk With Me 1992, Lost Highway 1997, Crumb (presenter), The Straight Stay 1999, Mullholland Drive (Best Dir, Cannes Film Festival) 2001, Darkened Room 2002, Rabbits 2002, Inland Empire 2006; numerous shorts and documentaries. *Television includes:* Twin Peaks (series) 1990–91, 2017. *Music includes:* album: Crazy Clown Time 2011, The Big Dream 2013; singles: Cannes Memory (with John Neff 2002), Blurred Dancer Music 2011, Bad The John Boy 2013. *Soundtracks include:* Twin Peaks 1990, Love Heritage 2002, Coachella 2006, Surveillance 2008, Psych 2010. *Website:* davidlynch.com; www.davidlynchfoundation.org.

LYNCH, John H., BA, MBA, JD; American business executive, academic and fmr politician; *Senior Lecturer, Tuck School of Business, Dartmouth College;* b. 25 Nov. 1952, Waltham, Mass; s. of William Lynch and Margaret Lynch; m. Dr Susan Lynch 1977; one s. two d.; ed Univ. of New Hampshire, Harvard Business School, Georgetown Univ. Law Center; Dir of Admisssions, Harvard Business School 1982–86; ind. consultant 1987–94; Pres. and CEO Knoll, Inc. 1994–2001; Pres. The Lynch Group 2001–04; Gov. of New Hampshire 2005–13; Perkins Bass Distinguished Visitor, Nelson A. Rockefeller Center, Dartmouth Coll. 2012–13, Sr Lecturer and Sr Fellow, Center for Global Business and Government, Tuck School of Business 2013–; apptd to Univ. System of New Hampshire's Bd of Trustees 2000, Chair. 2001–04; fmr Pres. Univ. of New Hampshire Alumni Asscn; mem. Bd Catholic Medical Center 1997–2003, Citizens Bank of New Hampshire, Capitol Center for the Arts; Democrat; Lifetime of Service Award, City Year New Hampshire 2006, Granite State Legacy Award, New Hampshire Union Leader 2013. *Address:* Tuck School of Business, 100 Tuck Hall, Hanover, NH 03755, USA (office). *E-mail:* john.h.lynch@tuck.dartmouth.edu (office). *Website:* www.tuck.dartmouth.edu (office).

LYNCH, Loretta Elizabeth, BA, JD; American lawyer and government official; b. 21 May 1959, Durham, North Carolina; m. Stephen Hargrove; two step-c.; ed Harvard Coll., Harvard Law School; Litigation Assoc., Cahill, Gordon & Reindel 1984–90; Fed. Prosecutor, US Attorney's Office (Eastern Dist), New York, US Dept of Justice 1990–2001, Chief, Long Island Offices 1994–98, Chief Asst US Attorney (Eastern Dist), New York 1998–99, US Attorney 1999–2001, 2010–15; Partner, Hogan & Hartson LLP, New York City 2002–10; US Attorney-Gen. 2015–17; mem. Bd Federal Reserve Bank of New York 2003–05; mem. ABA, Eastern Dist Cttee on Civil Litigation, Federal Bar Council. *Leisure interests:* reading, tennis.

LYNCH, Michael Francis, AM, CBE; Australian arts administrator; b. 6 Dec. 1950, Sydney; s. of Wilfred Brian Lynch and Joan Margaret Lynch; m. 1st Jane Scott 1967 (divorced 1987); one d.; m. 2nd Irene Hannan; two step s.; m. 3rd Christine Josephine Lynch; ed Marcellin Coll., Randwick, Univ. of Sydney; began career with Australian Council for the Arts 1973; fmr Gen. Man. King O'Malley Theatre Co., Australian Theatre for Young People; Admin. Australian Nat. Playwrights Conf.; Gen. Man. Nimrod Theatre 1976–78; Casting Dir and Man. Partner Forcast Pty Ltd 1981–89; Gen. Man. Sydney Theatre Co. 1989–94, Australia Council 1994–98; Chief Exec. Sydney Opera House 1998–2002; Chief Exec. South Bank Centre, London 2002–09; fmr Chair. Australia Asia Pacific Performing Arts Centres; apptd CEO West Kowloon Cultural District 2011; fmr mem. Performing Arts Centres Consortium of N America. *Films:* Crocodile Dundee (Casting Dir) 1986, Raw Nerve (producer) 1988, Crocodile Dundee in Los Angeles (Casting Dir) 2001. *Leisure interests:* film, theatre, racing, beach.

LYNCH, Peter; American investor; *Vice-Chairman, Fidelity Management and Research Company;* b. 19 Jan. 1944; m. Carolyn Lynch; three d.; intern, Fidelity Investments 1966, Man. Fidelity Magellan Fund, Boston 1977–90, Trustee Fidelity Investments 1990–, currently Vice-Chair. Fidelity Man. and Research Co.; Chair. Inner-City Scholarship Fund; f. Lynch Foundation; Pres. Catholic Schools Foundation; mem. Univ. Bd of Trustees, Boston Coll.; 14 hon. degrees; Hon. Chair. Boston Coll. Ever to Excel campaign; Mother Seton Award, Interfaith Relations Award. *Publications include:* One Up on Wall Street 1989, Beating the Street 1993, Learn to Earn 1996 (all with John Rothchild). *Address:* Fidelity Investments Institutional Services Company Inc., 82 Devonshire Street, Boston, MA 02109, USA. *Telephone:* (617) 563-7000. *Fax:* (617) 476-3876. *Website:* www.401k.com.

LYNCH, Philip F., CBE; American business executive; *Founder, Stem Capital Partners;* ed Yale Univ.; fmrly with Lehman Brothers, held various man. positions in New York before moving to London in 1977 to become Br. Man., Sr Vice-Pres. and then Man. Dir 1987–2000, Co-head of Asia-Pacific Investment Banking 2000–02, Head of Global Finance, Europe, the Middle East and Africa 2002–06, Co-head of European Equities 2006–08, CEO Middle East and Africa, Nomura International plc (following acquisition of European and Asian arms of Lehman Brothers) 2008–10, CEO Asia (ex-Japan) and Middle East 2010–12; Founder Stem Capital Partners 2013–; Chair. (non-exec.), Int. Petroleum Exchange of London Ltd 1989–95; Chief Exec. Exchange Clearing House (ECHO) 1996–97, COO and Dir of Shareholder Affairs, CLS Services Ltd (after acquisition of ECHO) 1997–2000; Dir (non-exec.), Earthport plc 2006. *Address:* Stem Capital Partners, 2203–04, 22/F ManYee Building, 68 Des Voeux Road Central, Hong Kong Special Administrative Region, People's Republic of China (office). *Telephone:* 2503-5698 (office). *E-mail:* info@stemcapitalpartners.com (office). *Website:* www.stemcapitalpartners.com (office); stemcapital.net (office).

LYNE, Adrian; British film director; b. 4 March 1941, Peterborough; m. Samantha Lyne; one d.; ed Highgate School; joined J. Walter Thompson (advertising agency) in post room, later became asst producer of commercials; with two pnrs est. Jennie & Lyne 1971; dir of commercials; Palme d'Or, Cannes Commercial Film Festival 1976, 1978. *Films include:* Mr. Smith 1976, Foxes 1980,

Flashdance 1983, 9¹/₂Weeks 1986, Fatal Attraction 1987, Jacob's Ladder (also co-writer) 1990, Indecent Proposal 1993, Lolita 1997, Unfaithful 2002.

LYNE, Rt Hon, Sir Roderic Michael John, KBE, CMG, BA; British diplomatist (retd) and business consultant; *Deputy Chairman of the Council, Chatham House;* b. 31 March 1948; s. of Air Vice-Marshal Michael Lyne and Avril Joy Buckley; m. Amanda Mary Smith 1969; two s. one d.; ed Eton Coll., Univ. of Leeds; joined Diplomatic Service 1970, served at Embassy in Moscow 1972–74, in Senegal 1974–76, with Eastern Europe and Soviet Dept, FCO 1976–78, Rhodesia Dept 1979, Asst Pvt. Sec. to Foreign and Commonwealth Sec. 1979–82, with Perm. Mission to UN, New York 1982–86, Visiting Research Fellow, Royal Inst. of Int. Affairs (Chatham House) 1986–87 (mem. Council 2008), Head of Chancery and Political Section, Embassy in Moscow 1987–90, Head of Soviet Dept, FCO 1990–91, of Eastern Dept 1992–93; Pvt. Sec. to Prime Minister for Foreign Affairs, Defence and Northern Ireland 1993–96; Dir of Policy Devt for CIS, Middle East and Africa, British Gas PLC 1996; Perm. Rep. to WTO, UN and Other Int. Orgs, Geneva 1997–2000, Amb. to Russia 2000–04; Special Adviser, BP plc 2004–09, HSBC Bank plc 2004–07; Chair. Int. Advisory Bd Altimo 2006–07; mem. Council, Royal Inst. of Int. Affairs (Chatham House) 2008, Deputy Chair. 2009–; mem. Bd of Dirs Aricom 2006– (acquired by Petropavlovsk PLC 2009), Accor 2006–09, Russo-British Chamber of Commerce 2006–09; Sr Adviser, JPMorgan Chase Bank 2007–10; Visiting Prof., Kingston Univ. Business School 2005–10, mem. Bd of Govs Kingston Univ. 2007–, Chair. 2011–; mem. cttee, The Iraq Inquiry 2009–; Gov Ditchley Foundation; mem. Privy Council 2009; Hon. Prof., Moscow Higher School of Social and Econ. Studies 2001; Dr hc (Leeds) 2002; Hon. DBA (Kingston) 2004; Hon. DLitt (Heriot-Watt) 2004; Stephen Roskill Memorial Lecturer, Churchill Coll., Cambridge 2016. *Publications include:* Engaging with Russia: The Next Phase – Report to the Trilateral Commission (co-author) 2006 (updated edns in Japanese and Russian) 2007, The Imaginary Curtain in Russia: The Challenges of Transformation (co-eds Dutkiewicz and Trenin) 2011. *Leisure interests:* sport, grandchildren. *Address:* 39 Richmond Park Road, London, SW14 8JU, England (home). *E-mail:* Roderic.Lyne@btinternet.com (home). *Website:* www.chathamhouse.org (office).

LYNGSTAD, Anni-Frid (Frida); Norwegian singer; b. 15 Nov. 1945, Ballangen, Narvik, Norway; m. 1st Ragnar Fredriksson 1964 (divorced 1970); m. 2nd Benny Andersson 1978 (divorced 1981); m. 3rd Prince Reuss of Plauen 1992 (died 1999); one s. one d. (from previous relationship); leader of own dance band Anni-Frid Four; mem. pop group ABBA 1972–82; winner, Eurovision Song Contest 1974; world-wide tours; concerts include Royal Performance, Stockholm 1976, Royal Albert Hall, London 1977, UNICEF concert, New York 1979, Wembley Arena 1979; reunion with ABBA, Swedish TV This Is Your Life 1986; solo artist 1983–; World Music Award, Best Selling Swedish Artist 1993. *Film:* ABBA: The Movie 1977. *Recordings include:* albums: with ABBA: Ring Ring 1973, Waterloo 1974, ABBA 1975, Greatest Hits 1976, Arrival 1977, The Album 1978, Voulez-Vous 1979, Greatest Hits Vol. 2 1979, Super Trouper 1980, The Visitors 1981, The Singles: The First Ten Years 1982, Thank You For The Music 1983, Absolute ABBA 1988, ABBA Gold 1992, More ABBA Gold 1993, Forever Gold 1998, The Definitive Collection 2001; solo: Frida Alone 1976, Something's Going On 1982, Shine 1983, Djupa Andetag 1996, Frida 1967–72 1998, Frida: The Mixes 1998, Svenska Popfavoriter 1998. *Website:* www.abbasite.com.

LYNTON, Michael, BA, MBA; American media executive; *Chairman, Snap Inc.;* b. 1 Jan. 1960, London, UK; s. of Mark O. L. Lynton and Marion Sonnenberg; m. Elizabeth Jane Alter; three d.; ed Harvard Coll., Harvard Business School; Assoc., The First Boston Corpn 1982–85; Sr Vice-Pres. Disney Publishing Group 1987–93, Pres. Hollywood Pictures, The Walt Disney Co. 1993–96; Chair. and CEO The Penguin Group 1996–2000; Pres. AOL International 2000–03, also Pres. for Int. Efforts and Exec. Vice-Pres. AOL Time Warner Inc. 2002–03; Chair. and CEO Sony Pictures Entertainment 2004–17, CEO Sony Corpn of America 2012–17, Sony Entertainment, Inc. 2012–17; Chair. Snap Inc. 2017–; Chair. (non-Exec.) Warner Music Group Inc. 2019–; mem. Harvard Bd of Overseers 2012–; mem. Bd of Dirs Marvel Entertainment, LLC 1998, Samsonite International SA 2003–05, EA Mobile, LLC 2005–, USC School of Cinematic Arts 2013–, RAND Corpn, Snapchat 2013–, Ares Management Corporation 2014–, IEX Group, Inc. 2017–, Pearson PLC 2018–, Los Angeles County Museum of Art; mem. Advisory Bd Modern Times Group (MTG) 2013–; mem. Council on Foreign Relations. *Address:* Snap Inc., 2772 Donald Douglas Loop North, Santa Monica, CA 90405, USA (office). *Telephone:* (310) 399-3339 (office). *E-mail:* ir@snap.com (office). *Website:* www.snap.com (office).

LYONS, Jenna; American fashion designer and retail executive; *President and Executive Creative Director, J. Crew Group, Inc.;* b. 1969, Boston, Mass; m. Robert Mazeau (divorced); one s.; ed Parsons The New School For Design; Intern, Donna Karan (designer womenswear label) 1990; Asst Designer, J. Crew Group, Inc. 1990–94, Designer 1994–95, Design Dir 1996–98, Sr Design Dir 1999, Vice-Pres. Women's Design 1999–2005, Sr Vice-Pres. 2005–07, Creative Dir 2007–10, Pres. and Exec. Creative Dir 2010–. *Address:* J Crew Group, Inc, 770 Broadway, New York, NY 10003, USA (office). *Telephone:* (203) 682-8200 (office). *E-mail:* jlyons@jcrew.com (office). *Website:* www.jcrew.com (office).

LYONS, Sir Michael, Kt, KBE, PhD; British economist and media executive; *Chairman, English Cities Fund;* b. 1950; m.; three c.; ed Stratford Grammar School, Middlesex Univ. and Queen Mary Coll., Univ. of London; worked as part-time street trader at Bell Street Market, London to fund higher educ.; furthered career as economist in public sector; fmr Lecturer in Econs, Univ. of Nottingham, Wallbrook Coll., London; mem. (Labour) Birmingham City Council 1980–83; Chief Exec. Wolverhampton Borough Council 1985–90, Notts. County Council 1990–94, Birmingham City Council 1994–2001; Prof. of Public Policy, Birmingham Univ. 2001–06; responsible for Lyons Inquiry into Local Govt, commissioned by Deputy Prime Minister and Chancellor of the Exchequer 2004–07; Chair. BBC Trust 2007–11; Chair. English Cities Fund 2002–; SQW Ltd, City of Birmingham Symphony Orchestra 2001–07, Regional Advisory Council, ITV –2006; Deputy Chair. and Acting Chair. The Audit Comm. 2003–06; strategic adviser on public asset man. and regeneration to CBRE (commercial property and real estate services consultancy); mem. Bd of Dirs (non-exec.) Redrow plc 2015–; Bd Mentor, Criticaleye; fmr mem. Bd of Dirs and Gov. Royal Shakespeare Co.; fmr mem. Bd of Dirs Wragge and Co., Mouchel Parkman plc, Central Television 2003–06; Hon.

LLD (Birmingham Univ.) 2009; Dr hc (Middlesex Univ.). *Address:* English Cities Fund, Anchorage One, Anchorage Quay, Salford Quays, Manchester, M50 3YJ, England (office). *Telephone:* (16) 1877-0016 (office). *Fax:* (16) 1848-8748 (office). *Website:* www.englishcitiesfund.co.uk (office).

LYONS, Richard Kent, BS, PhD; American economist, academic and university administrator; *William & Janet Cronk Chair in Innovative Leadership, University of California, Berkeley;* b. 10 Feb. 1961, Palo Alto, Calif.; s. of J. Richard Lyons and Ida P. Lyons; m. Jennifer Lyons; two c.; ed Univ. of California, Berkeley, Massachusetts Inst. of Tech.; Research Analyst, Financial Industries Div., SRI Int., Menlo Park, Calif. 1983–84; Assoc. and Asst Prof., School of Business and School of Int. Affairs, Columbia Univ. 1987–93; Asst Prof., Haas School of Business, Univ. of California, Berkeley 1993–96, Assoc. Prof. 1996–2000, Prof. 2000–04, Acting Dean 2004–05, Exec. Assoc. Dean 2005–06, Bank of America Dean 2008–18, William & Janet Cronk Chair in Innovative Leadership 2018–; Chief Learning Officer, Goldman Sachs, New York 2006–08; consultant to IMF, World Bank, US Fed. Reserve System, EC, UN, Citibank; mem. Council on Foreign Relations; Trustee, Matthews Asian Funds, Syntax Funds, Ashesi Univ. Foundation; fmr Trustee, iShares; NSF Grad. Fellowship 1984–87, Int. Affairs Fellowship, Council on Foreign Relations 1993, NSF grants 1994–97, 1997–2000, 2000–03; Distinguished Teaching Award, Univ. of Calif., Berkeley 1998. *Publications:* The Microstructure Approach to Exchange Rates 2001; numerous articles and papers. *Leisure interests:* guitar, skiing. *Address:* Office of the Dean, Haas School of Business, University of California, Berkeley, CA 94720-1900, USA (office). *Telephone:* (510) 643-2027 (office). *Fax:* (510) 642-5630 (office). *E-mail:* lyons@haas.berkeley.edu (office). *Website:* faculty.haas.berkeley.edu/lyons (office).

LYOVOCHKIN, Serhiy; Ukrainian government official; b. 17 Aug. 1972; s. of Volodymyr Lyovochkin; m. Zinaida Lihacheva; three c.; fmr police Col; adviser to Pres. Leonid Kuchma 1997–2002, First Aide to Pres. Kuchma 2002–05; head of Prime Minister Viktor Yanukovych's office 2006–07; mem. Verkhovna Rada (Supreme Council) (Parl.) 2007–; Head of Presidential Secr. to Viktor Yanukovych 2010–14 (resgnd); fmr mem. Party of the Regions (fmr Deputy Chair.), f. Party of Development of Ukraine 2014, then merged with several other parties opposed to Euromaidan events to form Opozytsiyny Blok (Opposition Bloc); Co-Owner, Inter Media Group. *Address:* Verkhovna Rada (Supreme Council), 01008 Kyiv, vul. M. Hrushevskoho 5, Ukraine (office). *Telephone:* (44) 255-21-15 (office). *Fax:* (44) 253-32-17 (office). *E-mail:* umz@rada.gov.ua (office). *Website:* www.rada.gov.ua (office); opposition.org.ua.

LYSSARIDES, Vassos, MD; Cypriot politician and physician; *Honorary President, Movement for Social Democracy;* b. 13 May 1920, Lefkara; s. of Michael Lyssarides and Eleni Lyssanides; m. Barbara Cornwall 1963; ed Univ. of Athens; mem. House of Reps 1960–, Pres. 1985–91; Pres. Socialist Party of Cyprus (originally founded as United Democratic Union of Centre—EDEK) (now Movt for Social Democracy) 1969–2002, Hon. Pres. 2002–; Sec.-Gen. Int. Cttee of Solidarity with the Struggle of the Peoples of Southern Africa; Vice-Pres. Presidium, Afro-Asian Peoples' Solidarity Org.; Hon. Citizen of numerous Greek municipalities, Hon. Pres. Nicosia Medical Asscn Hippocrates; Dr hc (Univ. of Athens), (Panteion Univ.); Highest Honour of Distinction, Palestinian Authorities. *Leisure interests:* poetry, painting. *Address:* PO Box 21064, 1096 Nicosia, Cyprus (home). *Telephone:* (22) 666763 (office); (22) 665385 (home). *Fax:* (22) 666762 (office). *E-mail:* edek@mtnmail.com.cy (office). *Website:* www.lyssarides.com.

LYTH, Ragnar Vilhelm, BA; Swedish theatre director, screenwriter and academic; *Head of Theatre Directing, Swedish Dramatic Institute;* b. 2 April 1944, Karlstad; s. of Arne Lyth and Reidunn Eleonore; m. 1st Karin Falk 1967; m. 2nd Kerstin Österlin 1996; two s.; ed Nat. Film School, Swedish Dramatic Inst.; theatre and TV dir in Sweden, Norway and Denmark; represented Sweden at int. TV festival 'INPUT', Philadelphia, Banff, Montreal 1985, 1989, 1993; Head of Stage Dirs, Swedish Dramatic Inst. 1984–86, currently Head of Theatre Directing; Chair. Swedish Dirs' Union; Prof. of Theatre Direction; Dir-in-Residence, Nat. Theatre, Oslo, Norway, Stockholm City Theatre; Sweden Art Award. *Plays directed include:* The Wild Duck 1997, Hedda Gabler 1998, Faust (I and II) 1999, Temperance 2000, The General Inspector 2001, Twelfth Night 2002, The Visit 2003, Endgame 2004, Tartuffe 2005, Dirty Hands 2007, During åpen sky 2008, Mephisto: A Career 2010, The Dance of Death 2011, A Doll's House 2013. *Television:* Death Dance 1981, Hamlet 1985, Don Juan 1988, Maclean 1991. *Publication:* Theatre Life 2003. *Leisure interest:* nature. *Address:* Sjöbjörnsvägen 25, 11767 Stockholm, Sweden. *Telephone:* (8) 19-88-93. *E-mail:* ragnar.lyth@draminst.se (office); ragnar@ragnarlyth.se (home).

LYTHGOE, Nigel Bruce, OBE; British choreographer, film director and television producer; b. 9 July 1949, Wirral, Merseyside, England; s. of George Percival Lythgoe and Gertrude Emily Lythgoe; m. Bonnie Shawe 1974 (divorced 2010); two s.; ed Hylton-Bromley School of Dance and Drama and Perry Cowell School of Dance, Wallasey, Merseyside, trained in London under Joanne Steuer and Molly Molloy; began tap dancing aged ten; studied classical ballet, modern jazz, ballroom, character, classical Greek and nat. dance of various countries; first professional job in Corps de Ballet for nat. tour of The Merry Widow; fmr dancer with BBC's Young Generation dance troupe 1969; danced, choreographed, produced and directed a Royal Variety Performance; producer of Pop Idol and American Idol and creator and exec. producer and judge of So You Think You Can Dance; also cr. Superstars of Dance 2009; owns a vineyard in Paso Robles, Calif.; Governors Award 2007, Int. Emmy: Founders Award 2011, Ellis Island Int. Medal of Honor 2014. *Television includes:* producer of numerous series, including Popstars (series) (exec. producer) 2000, 2001, Pop Idol (series) (exec. producer) 2001, American Idol (series) (exec. producer) 2002–14, All American Girl (series) (exec. producer) 2003, American Juniors (series) (exec. producer) 2003, So You Think You Can Dance (series) (exec. producer) 2005–12, The Next Great American Band (series) (exec. producer) 2007, Superstars of Dance (series) (exec. producer) 2009, Every Single Step (series) (exec. producer) 2015, Easiest Game Show Ever (series) (exec. producer) 2016. *Address:* Nigel Lythgoe Productions, 9000 Sunset Blvd, Suite 1560, West Hollywood, CA 90069, USA (office). *Telephone:* (310) 432-0330 (office). *Fax:* (310) 432-0331 (office). *E-mail:* info@nigellythgoeproductions.com (office). *Website:* www.nigellythgoeproductions.com (office).

LYTVYN, Volodymyr Mykhaylovych, DrHis; Ukrainian academic and politician; b. 28 April 1956, Sloboda, Zhytomyr Oblast; s. of Mykhaylo Klymovych Lytvyn and Olga Andriivna Lytvyn; m. Tetyana Kostyantynivna; one s. one d.; ed Kyiv T. Shevchenko State (now Nat.) Univ.; researcher, Docent, Vice-Rector, Kyiv State Univ. 1978–86, Docent and Prof. 1991–94; Head of Dept, Ukrainian Ministry of Higher Educ. 1986–89; Lecturer, consultant, Asst to Sec., Cen. Cttee of Ukrainian Komsomol 1989–91; Adviser to Ukrainian Pres. 1994–2002, Deputy Head, Admin. to the Pres. 1995–96, Head Admin. 1999–2002; apptd to Nat. Security and Defence Council 1999; mem. Co-ordination Cttee on Problems of Foreign Policy 1996–; elected to Verkovna Rada (Parl.) 2002, Chair. 2002–06, 2008–12; currently Leader, People's Party (Narodna Partiya); mem. Ukrainian Acad. of Sciences 1997, Academician 2003. *Publications include:* Political Arena of Ukraine 1995; more than 200 articles on contemporary politics. *Leisure interests:* reading, football, taking care of Dalmatian dogs. *Address:* Verkhovna Rada, 01008 Kyiv, vul. M. Hrushevskoho 5 (office); People's Party (Narodna Partiya), 01034 Kyiv, vul. Reitarska 6a, Ukraine (office). *Telephone:* (44) 255-21-15 (Verkhovna Rada) (office); (44) 270-61-86 (Narodna Partiya (office). *Fax:* (44) 253-32-17 (Verkhovna Rada) (office); (44) 270-65-91 (Narodna Partiya (office). *E-mail:* umz@rada.gov.ua (office); info@narodna.org.ua (office). *Website:* www.rada.gov.ua (office); www.narodna.org.ua (office); www.lytvyn-v.org.ua.

LYU, Joseph Jye-Cherng; Taiwanese government official and banker; b. 1956; m. Cathie Lyu; one d.; ed Nat. Chengchi Univ., Kellogg Grad. School of Man., Northwestern Univ., USA; fmr Assoc. Prof., Nat. Chengchi Univ.; Vice-Pres. Bank of New York, Taipei Br. and New York Head Office –1981; fmr Vice-Pres. Banque Nationale de Paris, Taiwan; Pres. Land Bank of Taiwan –2004; Chair. Bank of Taiwan 2004–06; Minister of Finance 2006; Minister without Portfolio from 2006; fmr Chair. Bankers Asscn of Taiwan; fmr Man. Dir Bd Trust Asscn; fmr Dir Mega Financial Holding Co., Financial Information Service Co. Ltd, Taiwan Futures Exchange; Chair. Central Taiwan Theological Seminary; Dir, Hsu Wen-Lung Art & Culture Foundation. *Address:* c/o Ministry of Finance, 2 Ai Kuo West Road, Taipei 10066, Taiwan. *E-mail:* mof@mail.mof.gov.tu.

LYUBSHIN, Stanislav Andreyevich; Russian actor; b. 6 April 1933; m.; two s.; ed Shchepkin Theatre School; worked with various Moscow theatres: Sovremennik, Taganka, Yermolova, Malaya Bronnaya 1959–80; one of prin. actors with Moscow Arts Theatre 1980–, Anton Chekhov Arts Theatre 1987–; film debut 1959; RSFSR People's Artist 1981, People's Actor of Russia, Order of Service to Fatherland, Order of Friendship 2014. *Films include:* Segodnya uvolneniya ne budet (There Will Be No Leave Today) 1959, Tretya raketa (The Third Missile) 1963, Esli ty prav… 1963, Mne dvadtsat let (I am Twenty) 1964, Kakoe ono, more? 1964, Bolshaya ruda (The Big Ore) 1964, Alpiyskaya ballada 1965, Shchit i mech (The Shield and the Sword) 1968, Krasnaya ploshchad (Red Square) 1970, Pechki-lavochki (Happy Go Lucky, aka The Ship Crowd) 1972, Moya zhizn 1972, Monolog 1972, Slovo dlia zashchity (Speech for the Defence) 1976, Sentimentalnyy roman (Sentimental Romance) 1976, Pozovi menya v dal' svetluyu (Call Me from Afar) 1976, Step (The Steppe) 1977, Vstrecha (The Meeting) 1979, Tema (The Theme) 1979, Pyat vecherov (Five Evenings) 1979, My vesely, schastlivy, talantlivy! (We Are Cheerful, Happy, Talented!) 1986, Kin-Dza-Dza 1986, Zabavy molodykh (Joys of the Youth) 1987, Chyornyy monakh (The Black Monk) 1988, Vechnyy muzh 1989, Kanuvshee vremya 1989, Shkura (Skin) 1991, Nelyubov (No Love) 1991, Uvidet Parizh i umeret (To See Paris and Die) 1992, Bolshoy kapkan, ili solo dlya koshki pri polnoy lune (Big Trap, or Solo for Cat Under Full Moon) 1992, Tsar Ivan Groznyy (Tsar Ivan the Terrible) 1993, Mechty idiota (Idiot Dreams) 1993, Terra incognita 1994, Tsarevich Aleksei 1996, Kino pro kino 2002, The Country Estate 2004, Prodayotsya detektor lzhi 2005, Antikiller D.K: Lyubov bez pamyati 2009. *Television includes:* Pervaya lyubov (First Love) 1968, Ne strelyayte v belykh lebedey 1980, Dym (mini-series) 1992, The Country Estate (series) 2004, The Chess Player (series) 2004, Umnozhayushchiy pechal (mini-series) 2005, Rieltor (series) 2005, Kruzheva (series) 2008, Pyataya strazha (series) 2013. *Address:* 117571 Moscow, Vernadskogo prosp. 123, Apt 171, Russia. *Telephone:* (495) 433-35-14.

LŽICAR, Josef, DIur; Czech lawyer and actor; b. 6 June 1944, Švábenice; s. of Josef Lžicar and Anna Lžicar; m. Zdenka Lzicarová; one s.; ed Charles Univ., Prague; lawyer and advocate 1967–; Chief of Office of Pres. of Czechoslovak Repub. 1989–90; mem. Czech Chamber of Advocates 1990–, Czech Helsinki Cttee 1990–. *Film:* Kajinek (also consultant) 2010. *Television series:* known for his work on Private Traps 2008, Top star magazín 2009. *Leisure interest:* ornithology. *Address:* c/o Czech Helsinki Committee, Stefánikova 21, 150 00 Prague 5 (office); Sokolovská 24–37, 18600 Prague 8, Czech Republic (office). *Telephone:* (2) 22325334 (office). *E-mail:* sekr@helcom.cz (office). *Website:* www.helcom.cz/en (office).

M

MA, Fucai, BEng; Chinese oil industry executive; b. 1947; ed Beijing Petroleum Inst.; Deputy Dir, later Dir Shengli Petroleum Admin Bureau 1990–96; Asst to Pres., China Nat. Petroleum Corpn (CNPC) Nov.-Dec. 1996, Vice-Pres. 1996–98, Pres. 1998–2004 (resgnd); Chair. PetroChina 1999–2004; apptd Vice-Dir State Energy Office 2005; Dir Daqing Petroleum Admin Bureau 1997–98; Alt. mem. 16th CCP Cen. Cttee 2002–07.

MA, Huateng, (Pony Ma), BSc; Chinese telecommunications executive; *Chairman and CEO, Tencent;* b. 29 Oct. 1971, Chaoyang, Guangdong; ed Shenzhen Univ.; began career in research and devt dept for internet paging systems and internet calling systems, Shenzhen Runxun Communications Co. Ltd; fmrly in charge of research and devt for internet paging systems, China Motion Telecom Development Ltd; Co-founder Tencent 1998–, currently Exec. Dir, Chair. and CEO; f. instant messaging service QQ 1999. *Address:* Tencent Building, Kejizhongyi Avenue, Hi-techPark, Nanshan District, Shenzhen 518057, People's Republic of China (office). *Telephone:* (755) 86013388 (office). *Fax:* (755) 86013399 (office). *Website:* www.tencent.com (office).

MA, Jack, (Ma Yun), BA; Chinese business executive; *Founder, Alibaba Group;* b. 15 Nov. 1964, Hangzhou, Zhejiang Prov.; m. Zhang Ying; two c.; ed Hangzhou Teacher's Inst.; began as English teacher, Hangzhou Electronics and Eng Inst.; f. China Pages (chinapages.com), regarded to be China's first internet-based co. 1995; Head, Information Dept China Int. Electronic Commerce Center (CIECC) 1998–99; f. Alibaba Group (China's largest e-commerce co.), Hangzhou, Chair. and CEO 1999–2013, Exec. Chair. 2013–18, Pres. Rookie Network Technology div. 2013–; Hon. DS (De La Salle Univ., Manila) 2017, Hon. DScS (Univ. of Hong Kong) 2018, Dr hc (Tel Aviv Univ., Israel) 2018; chosen by World Econ. Forum as one of Young Global Leaders, Asian Awards Entrepreneur of the Year 2015. *Address:* Alibaba.com, 6th Floor Chuangye Mansion, East Software Park, No. 99 Huaxing Road, Hangzou, Zhejiang Province, 310012 (office); Alibaba.com Technology Corpn Ltd, Room 408, Fanli Building, 22 Chaoyangwai Street, Chaoyang District, Beijing 100020, People's Republic of China (office). *Telephone:* (571) 85022088 (Hangzhou) (office); (10) 6588-9698 (office). *Fax:* (571) 88157866 (Hangzhou) (office); (10) 6588-9699 (office). *Website:* www.alibaba.com (office).

MA, Kai; Chinese politician; b. June 1946, Shanghai, Jinshan; ed People's Univ. of China; fmr Deputy Dir State Comm. of Reform for Econ. Systems; Deputy Dir State Planning Comm. 1995–98; Minister of Nat. Devt and Reform Comm. (f. as State Planning Comm. 1952, renamed State Devt Planning Comm. 1998, renamed Nat. Devt and Reform Comm. 2003) 2003–08; mem. State Council 2008–18, Sec.-Gen. 2008–13; Vice-Premier 2013–18; Dir State Council Leading Group for Migrant Workers 2013–; Pres. Chinese Acad. of Governance (fmrly Nat. School of Admin) 2007–12; mem. 16th CCP Cen. Cttee 2002–07, 17th CCP Cen. Cttee 2007–12; mem. 18th CCP Cen. Cttee 2012–17, mem. 18th CCP Politburo 2012–17. *Address:* c/o State Council, Great Hall of the People, West Edge, Tiananmen Square, Beijing, People's Republic of China (office).

MA, Mary, BA; Chinese business executive; *Non-Executive Vice-Chair, Lenovo Group Holdings;* b. (Ma Xuezheng), Tianjin; ed Capital Normal Univ. and King's Coll., London, UK; began career as English trans. at Chinese Acad. of Sciences; Exec. Dir and Sr Vice-Pres. Legend Holdings Ltd (name changed to Lenovo Group Holdings 2003), Chief Financial Officer 2000–07, Non-Exec. Vice-Chair. 2007–; ind. Dir (non-exec.) Standard Chartered Bank (Hong Kong) Ltd, Sohu.com Inc. 2000–; mem. Hong Kong Dirs' Soc. *Address:* Lenovo Group Holdings, No. 6 Chuang Ye Road, Shangdi Information Industry Base, Haidan District, Beijing 100085, People's Republic of China (office). *Telephone:* (10) 58868888 (office). *E-mail:* cmk@lenovo.com (office). *Website:* www.lenovo.com (office).

MA, Mingzhe, PhD; Chinese business executive; *Chairman and CEO, Ping An Insurance (Group) Company of China Limited;* b. 1960; ed Zhongnan Univ. of Econs and Law; fmr Deputy Man. China Merchants Shekou Industrial Zone Social Insurance Co.; f. Shekou Ping An Insurance Co. (precursor to Ping An Insurance Group Co.) 1988, later Pres., Chair. Ping An Insurance (Group) Co. of China Ltd 1994–, CEO 2001–; mem. 11th CPPCC Nat. Cttee. *Address:* Ping An Insurance (Group) Co. of China Ltd, 15–18 Floors, Galaxy Development Centre, Fu Hua No. 3 Road, Fu Tian District, Shenzhen 518048, Guangdong (office); Ping An Insurance (Hong Kong) Co. Ltd, 11th Floor, Dah Sing Financial Centre, 108 Gloucester Road, Wanchai, Hong Kong Special Administrative Region, People's Republic of China (office). *Telephone:* (400) 8866338 (Shenzhen) (office); 28271883 (Hong Kong) (office). *Fax:* (755) 82431029 (Shenzhen) (office); 28020018 (Hong Kong) (office). *E-mail:* IR@paic.com.cn (office). *Website:* www.pingan.com (office); ir.pingan.com/en/index.shtml (office); www.pingan.com.cn (office).

MA, Qingyun, MArch; Chinese architect and academic; *Professor, School of Architecture, US-China Institute, University of Southern California;* b. 1965, Xi'an; ed Tsinghua Univ., Grad. School of Fine Arts, Univ. of Pennslyvania, USA; Architect, Kohn Pederson and Fox, New York 1991–95, Kling Lindquist 1997–99; Assoc. Prof. and Asst Dean of Architecture, Shenzhen Univ. 1995–96; Founding Pnr and Chair. MADA s.p.a.m., New York 1995–, Beijing and Shanghai 1999–, Los Angeles 2007–; Lecturer, Architecture Dept, Univ. of Pennsylvania 1997–2000; Visiting Lecturer, Tongji Univ., Shanghai 2001–, Nanjing Univ. 2002–, Berlage Inst., Netherlands 2003, ETH 2004, Tech. Univ., Berlin 2004; Dean, School of Architecture, Univ. of Southern California 2007–17, Della and Harry MacDonald's Dean Chair. in Architecture 2007–, currently Prof., School of Architecture, US-China Inst.; fmr Visiting Prof., Harvard Univ., Columbia Univ., Universität Karlsruhe, Ecole Speciale d'Architecture, Paris; invited by Disney Headquarters to be a consultant for Shanghai Disney Project 2010; Frank Miles Day Memorial Prize, Design Vanguard Award, Architectural Record, Phaidon's Emerging Design Talents designation, New Trends of Architecture designation, Euro-Asia Foundation. *Buildings designed include:* Longyang Residential Complex, Shanghai, Silk Tower, Xi'an, Qingpu Community Island, Shanghai, Centennial TV and Radio Center, Xi'an, Tianyi City Plaza, Ningpo. *Address:* US-China Institute, School of Architecture, University of Southern California, 3502 Watt Way, ASC G24, Los Angeles, CA 90089-0281, USA (office). *Telephone:* (213) 740-2723 (office). *Fax:* (213) 821-2382 (office). *E-mail:* qingyunm@usc.edu (office). *Website:* china.usc.edu (office); www.madaspam.com.

MA, Qizhi; Chinese politician; b. Nov. 1943, Jingyuan, Ningxia Hui Autonomous Region; ed Cen. Univ. for Nationalities; teacher, Yucheng Middle School, Anshan Iron and Steel Works, Yinchuan City No. 2 Middle School, Ningxia Hui Autonomous Region; joined CCP 1972; Gen. Sec. Communist Youth League, Ningxia Hui Autonomous Region 1973–82, Deputy Dir 1973–82, Deputy Sec. 1982–83; Deputy Sec. CCP Guyuan Pref. Cttee 1983–85; Deputy Dir Autonomous Regional Cttee, Ningxia Hui Autonomous Region 1985–88, Head, Publicity Dept 1991–97, apptd Deputy Sec. 1993; Cttee Vice-Sec., then Dir-Gen. CCP Yinnan Pref.; Dir Propaganda Dept of CCP Ningxia Hui Autonomous Region Cttee 1969–93, Vice-Sec. 1993–98; Vice-Chair. Ningxia Hui Autonomous Regional People's Govt 1995–96, Chair. 1996–2008; Alt. mem. 14th CCP Cen. Cttee 1992–97, 15th CCP Cen. Cttee 1997–2002, mem. 16th CCP Cen. Cttee 2002–07; Chair. 11th Nationalities Cttee of NPC 2008–13.

MA, Wanfan, (Mayi); Chinese business executive; b. 1930, Longkou Co., Shandong Prov.; Chair. China Nat. Chemicals Corpn 1989; mem. 7th CPPCC Nat. Cttee 1987–92, 8th Nat. Cttee 1993–98, 9th Nat. Cttee 1998–2003.

MA, Weihua, BA, PhD; Chinese economist and business executive; *Chairman China Global Philanthropy Institute;* b. 1949; ed Jilin Univ., Southwest Finance and Economics Univ.; Deputy Section Dir and Deputy Sec.-Gen. Liaoning Prov. Planning Economy Comm. 1982–85, transferred to Gen. Office of Liaoning Prov. Govt 1985–86; worked in Gen. Office of Anhui Prov. Govt 1986–88; Deputy Dir Gen. Office, People's Bank of China 1988–90, Deputy Dir of Planning and Cash Dept 1990–92, Pres. Hainan Prov. Br., People's Bank of China and Dir of State Foreign Exchange Regulatory Bureaux, Hainan Br. 1992–98; Dir and CEO China Merchants Bank Co. Ltd 1999–2013, Pres. 2004–13; Chair. Wing Lung Bank Ltd 2008–15; Chair. CMB International Capital Corpn Ltd, China Merchants Cigna Life Insurance Co. Ltd; Chair. Shenzhen Domestic Bankers' Asscn; currently Chair. China Global Philanthropy Inst.; Ind. Dir (non-exec.) TOM Online Inc. 2003–, China Petrochemical International Co. 2010–, Fujian Petrochemical Co. Ltd 2010–, China Petroleum & Chemical Corpn 2010–15, Winox Holdings Ltd 2011–15, Postal Savings Bank of China Co., Ltd 2013–, China Resources Land Ltd 2013–, China Eastern Airlines Corpn Ltd 2013–, Legend Holdings Corpn 2015–, Guotai Junan Securities Co., Ltd –2016, Roadshow Holdings Ltd 2017–; Ind. Dir Shenyang Dongruan Software Co. Ltd; Dir Sinopec Corpn; mem. Standing Council of China Finance Acad., Shenzhen Soft Science Devt Foundation; Deputy Gov. China Industrialists Asscn; Trustee, China United Devt Research Inst.; Guest Prof., Peking Univ., Jilin Univ., Southwest Finance and Economics Univ., Yunnan Univ., Northwest Univ., Grad. School of the People's Bank of China; Rep. to 10th NPC; Standing Cttee mem. China Finance Insts, 8th Council of Red Cross Soc. of China; Order of the Star of Itay; Dr hc (Univ. of Southern California, USA); Compassion Award 2017. *Address:* China Global Philanthropy Institute, Room. 207, Building 6, Qianhai Shenzhen-Hong Kong Youth Innovation and Entrepreneur Hub, Shenzhen 518052, People's Republic of China (office). *Telephone:* (755) 23961890 (office). *E-mail:* info@cgpi.org.cn (office). *Website:* www.cgpi.org.cn (office).

MA, Wen; Chinese government official; b. 1948, Hebei Prov.; m. Yu Zhenqi; one d.; ed Nankai Univ.; sent to countryside during Cultural Revolution, Inner Mongolia Autonomous Region 1968; Deputy Head of commune brigade and of revolutionary cttee 1972–78; Teacher, Nankai Univ. 1982–87; Sec., Nat. Population and Family Planning Comm. CCP Cttee 1989–95, Deputy Dir, Publicity and Educ. Dept 1989–97; mem. 15th CCP Cen. Cttee Cen. Comm. for Discipline Inspection 1997–2002, 16th CCP Cen. Cttee Cen. Comm. for Discipline Inspection 2002–07, Deputy Sec. 2004–07, 2007–12; mem. 17th CCP Cen. Cttee 2007–12; Minister of Supervision 2007–13; Dir, Nat. Bureau of Corruption Prevention 2007–13; mem. CCP Cen. Cttee Public Security Comm. 2007–12. *Address:* c/o Chinese Communist Party Public Security Commission, Zhongnanhai, Beijing, People's Republic of China (office).

MA, Xinsheng; Chinese economist, engineer and business executive; ed Univ. of Shanghai, Shanghai Nat. Accounting Inst.; Deputy Party Sec., then Party Sec. and Factory Man., Shanghai Rectifier Factory 1979–81; Deputy Gen. Man. Shanghai Electric Group Co. Ltd 1989–95; Gen. Man. and Party Sec., Shanghai Jidian Maoyi Building 1995–96; Chair. of Labour Union, Pres. and Deputy Party Sec., Shanghai Electric (Group) Corpn 1996–2003; Deputy Party Sec. Shanghai State-owned Assets Supervision and Admin Comm. 2003–07; apptd Chair. and Party Sec., Bailian Group Co. Ltd 2008; Chair. Shanghai Friendship Group Inc. Co., Lianhua Supermarket Holdings Co. Ltd 2009; Chair. China Bailian (Hong Kong) Ltd; Dir, Shanghai Pudong Development Bank Co. Ltd 2008; CEO Award, Robert A. Mundel World Executive Awards 2004.

MA, Ying-jeou, LLB, LLM, SJD; Taiwanese politician, academic and fmr head of state; b. 13 July 1950, Hong Kong; m. Chow Mei-ching; two d.; ed Nat. Taiwan Univ., New York Univ. Law School, Harvard Univ. Law School, USA; with Marine Corps, Navy 1972–74; Legal Consultant, First Nat. Bank of Boston, USA 1980–81; Research Consultant, Univ. of Maryland Law School 1980–81; Assoc., Cole and Deitz (law firm), New York 1981; Deputy Dir First Bureau, Office of the Pres. of Taiwan 1981–88; Adjunct Assoc. Prof., Grad. School of Law, Nat. Chengchi Univ. 1981, Assoc. Prof. of Law, Nat. Chengchi Univ. Law School 1997–98; Deputy Sec.-Gen. Cen. Cttee, Kuomintang (KMT) 1984–88, Vice-Chair. 2004–05, Chair. 2005–07 (resgnd), 2009–; Chair. Research, Devt and Evaluation Comm., Exec. Yuan 1988–91, Sr Vice-Chair. Mainland Affairs Council 1991–93; Minister of Justice 1993–96; Minister of State without Portfolio 1996–97; Mayor of Taipei 1998–2006; Pres. of Taiwan 2008–16. *Publications include:* Legal Problems of Seabed Boundary Delimitation in the East China Sea 1984, The Diauyutai (Senkaku) Islets and the Maritime Boundary Problems in the East China Sea (Chinese) 1986, Cross-Straits Relations at a Crossroad: Impasse of Breakthrough 2001; articles and 17 academic papers. *Leisure interests:* jogging, music, charity.

MA, Yo-Yo, BA; American cellist; b. 7 Oct. 1955, Paris, France; of Chinese parentage; m. Jill A. Hornor 1978; one s. one d.; ed Harvard Univ. and cello studies with his father, with Leonard Rose and at Juilliard School of Music, New York; first public recital aged five; performed under numerous conductors with all major orchestras of the world, including Berlin Philharmonic, Boston Symphony, Chicago Symphony, Israel Philharmonic, London Symphony and New York Philharmonic; regularly participates in festivals of Tanglewood, Ravinia, Blossom, Salzburg and Edinburgh; also appears in chamber music ensembles with artists including Isaac Stern, Emanuel Ax, Leonard Rose, Pinchas Zukerman, Gidon Kremer and fmrly Yehudi Menuhin; premiered the Concerto by H. K. Gruber, Tanglewood 1989; recital tour with Emanuel Ax celebrating 20th anniversary of their partnership 1995–96; performed Bach's suites for solo cello at the Barbican Hall, London 1995; est. The Silk Road Project to promote study of cultural, artistic and intellectual traditions of the route 2001; Smithsonian Folklife Festival 2002; Judson and Joyce Green Creative Consultant, Chicago Symphony Orchestra 2010–; apptd Messenger of Peace by UN Sec.-Gen. 2006; mem. Pres.'s Cttee on the Arts and Humanities 2009–; Dr hc (Northeastern Univ.) 1985 and from other colls and univs, including Harvard, Yale, Tufts and Juilliard, Chinese Univ. of Hong Kong; Hon. DMA (Princeton) 2005; Avery Fisher Prize 1978, Glenn Gould Prize 1999, Nat. Medal of the Arts 2001, Dan David Prize 2006, Sonning Prize 2006, Award of Distinction, Int. Cello Festival 2007, World Econ. Forum Crystal Prize 2008, Musical America Award for Musician of the Year 2009, Presidential Medal of Freedom 2010, 15 Grammy Awards, two Emmy Awards, 19 Canadian Gemini Awards, Honoree, Kennedy Center Honors 2011, Polar Music Prize (Sweden) 2012, Vilcek Prize in Contemporary Music 2013, Midwest Young Artists Golden Baton Award 2014, Fred Rogers Legacy Award 2014. *Recordings include:* Portrait of Yo-Yo Ma 1989, The Japanese Album 1989, A Cocktail Party 1990, Hush 1992, Made in America 1993, The New York Album 1994, King Gesar 1996, From Ordinary Things 1997, Seven Years in Tibet 1997, Liberty! 1997, Piazzolla: Soul of the Tango 1997, The Protecting Veil and Wake Up...and Die 1998, John Williams Greatest Hits 1969–1999 1999, My First 79 Years 1999, Solo 1999, Brahms: Piano Concerto No.2, Cello Sonata Op. 78 1999, Lulie the Iceberg 1999, Songs and Dances 1999, Franz Joseph Haydn 1999, Simply Baroque 1999, Crouching Tiger, Hidden Dragon (film soundtrack) 2000, Corigliano: Phantasmagoria 2000, Simply Baroque II 2000, Appalachian Journey 2000, Dvorak: Piano Quartet No. 2, Sonatina in G, Romantic Pieces 2000, Classic Yo-Yo 2001, Classical Hits 2001, Heartland: An Appalachian Anthology 2001, Yo-Yo Ma Plays Bach 2002, Isaac Stern: In Tribute and Celebration 2002, Mozart: Piano Quartets 2002, Naqoyqatsi (film soundtrack) 2002, Yo-Yo Ma Plays the Music of John Williams 2002, Silk Road Journeys—When Strangers Meet 2002, Obrigado Brazil 2003, Classics for a New Century 2003, Paris—La Belle Époque 2003, Vivaldi's Cello 2004, The Dvorák Album 2004, Silk Road Journeys—Beyond the Horizon 2005, Essential Yo-Yo Ma 2005, R. Strauss: Don Quixote 2005, Memoirs of a Geisha (film soundtrack) 2005, Yo-Yo Ma plays Ennio Morricone 2006, Bach: Unaccompanied Piano Suites 2006, Appassionato 2007, Songs of Joy and Peace (Grammy Award for Best Classical Crossover Album 2010) 2008, 'Cinema Paradiso' on Chris Botti in Boston 2009, The Goat Rodeo Sessions 2011, Songs Of Joy And Peace 2015, Hush (with Bobby McFerrin) 2015, Yo-Yo Ma Plays Ennio Morricone 2016, Sing Me Home (with The Silk Road Ensemble) (Grammy Award for Best World Music Album 2017) 2016. *Address:* Opus 3 Artists, 470 Park Avenue South, 9th Floor North, New York, NY 10016, USA (office). *Telephone:* (212) 584-7500 (office). *Fax:* (646) 300-8200 (office). *E-mail:* info@opus3artists.com (office). *Website:* www.opus3artists.com (office); www.yo-yoma.com.

MA, Yongwei; Chinese banker; b. 1942, Rongcheng, Shandong Prov.; ed Liaoning Inst. of Finance and Econs; joined CCP 1965; fmr Gov. Agric. Bank of China (Sec. CCP Leading Party Group); Exec. mem. and Vice-Chair. Int. Confed. for Agricultural Credit 1993–98; mem. Monetary Policy Comm., People's Bank of China 2000; Chair., Pres. People's Insurance Co. of China 1994–95, Chair. and Pres. China Insurance Group Co. 1995–98; Chair. China Insurance Regulatory Comm. 1998–2003; Ind. Dir (non-exec.) China Life Insurance Co. 2006–12; Dir (non-exec.) Mingyuan Medicare Devt Co. Ltd 2008–12; Ind. Dir Cninsure Inc. 2008–12; Del., 13th CCP Nat. Congress 1987–92, 14th CCP Nat. Congress 1992–97, 15th CCP Nat. Congress 1997–2002; mem. Standing Cttee of Nat. Cttee of CPPCC 2003–08.

MA, Yuan; Chinese judge; b. 30 June 1930, Xinmin Co., Liaoning Prov.; two s.; ed Chinese People's Univ., Beijing; joined CCP 1953; teacher, Dept of Law, Beijing Univ. and part-time lawyer 1955–62, part-time Prof. 1990; Asst Judge, Judge Supreme People's Court 1963–82, Deputy Dir Civil Dept 1982–85, Vice-Pres. Supreme People's Court 1985–98; mem. Standing Cttee All China Women's Fed.; Vice-Pres. China Marriage and Family Research Inst. 1983–; Pres. Chinese Asscn of Women Judges 1994, now Hon. Pres.; Asst Sec.-Gen. Civil and Econ. Law Cttee, China Law Soc. 1983; Hon. Prof., Renmin Univ. of China School of Law. *Address:* The School of Law, Renmin University of China, 59 Zhongguancun Ave, Beijing 100872, People's Republic of China (office).

MA, Zehua, LLM; Chinese economist and business executive; *Chairman, China Ocean Shipping (Group) Company (COSCO);* b. 1953; ed Shanghai Maritime Univ.; successive positions as Exec. Vice-Pres. and Sec. CCP Party Cttee, China Shipping (Group) Co., Exec. Vice-Pres. China Ocean Shipping (Group) Co. (COSCO), Gen. Man. COSCO Qingdao, Deputy Gen. Man. COSCO Guangzhou, Pres. COSCO America Inc., Gen. Man. Devt Div. and Asst Pres. COSCO, Pres. COSCO (UK) Ltd –2011, mem. Bd of Dirs, Pres. and Deputy Sec. CCP Party Cttee COSCO 2011–13, Chair. and Sec. CCP Party Cttee 2013–; mem. Foreign Cttee, Nat. People's Congress. *Address:* China Ocean Shipping (Group) Company (COSCO), Ocean Plaza, 158 Fuxingmennei Street, Beiing 100031, People's Republic of China (office). *Telephone:* (10) 66493388 (office). *Fax:* (10) 6649288 (office). *E-mail:* internet@cosco.com (office). *Website:* www.cosco.com (office).

MA, Zhaoxu, PhD; Chinese diplomatist; *Permanent Representative, United Nations;* b. Sept. 1963, Heilongjiang Prov.; m.; one; ed London School of Econs, UK; Attaché, Dept of Int. Orgs and Confs, Ministry of Foreign Affairs (MFA) 1987–90, Attaché and Third Sec., Perm. Mission to UN, New York 1990–93, Third Sec. and Deputy Dir, Dept of Int. Orgs and Confs, MFA 1993–94, completed advanced studies 1994–95, Deputy Dir Dept of Int. Orgs and Confs, MFA 1995–96, Deputy Dir, Dir, Counsellor, State Council Foreign Affairs Office 1996–99, Deputy Dir-Gen., Cen. Foreign Affairs Office, CCP 1999–2001, Counsellor, Embassy in London 2001–02, Minister Counsellor, Embassy in Brussels and Perm. Mission to EU 2002–04, Deputy Dir-Gen., then Dir Gen. Policy Research Dept, MFA 2004–09, Dir-Gen. Information Dept 2009–11, Asst Minister of Foreign Affairs 2011–13, Amb. to Australia 2013–16, Amb. and Perm. Rep. to UN Office and Other Int. Orgs in Geneva, Switzerland 2016–18; Perm. Rep. of China to UN, NY 2018–. *Address:* 350 East 35th Street, Manhattan, New York, NY 10016, USA (office). *Telephone:* (212) 655-6100 (office). *Fax:* (212) 634-7626 (office). *E-mail:* chinamission_un@mfa .gov.cn (office); ChinaMissionUN@gmail.com (office). *Website:* www.china-un.org (office).

MA, Zhengang; Chinese diplomatist; b. 9 Nov. 1940, Shandong; m. Chen Xiaodong; one s.; ed Beijing Foreign Languages Univ., Ealing Tech. Coll., London, LSE; staff mem., Attaché, Embassy in Yugoslavia 1970–74; Attaché N American and Oceanic Affairs Dept, Ministry of Foreign Affairs, Beijing 1974–81, Deputy Dir, then Dir N American and Oceanic Affairs Dept 1985–90, Deputy Dir-Gen., then Dir-Gen. N American and Oceanic Affairs Dept 1991–95; Vice-Consul, Consul, Consulate-Gen., Vancouver 1981–85; Counsellor, Embassy in Washington, DC 1990–91; Vice-Minister of Foreign Affairs 1995–97; Amb. to UK 1997–2002; Vice-Chair. 10th CPPCC Nat. Cttee 2003–; Amb., Ministry of Foreign Affairs 2002–04; Pres. China Inst. of Int. Studies (CIIS) 2004, Chair. China Nat. Cttee, Council for Security Cooperation in Asia Pacific (CSCAP), Chair. editorial bd International Studies, Chair. of Academic Cttee. *Leisure interests:* literature, bridge, table tennis. *Address:* c/o China Institute of International Studies, No.3, Toutiao, Taijichang, Beijing 100005, People's Republic of China.

MA, Zhongchen; Chinese party official; b. Sept. 1936, Tai'an, Shandong Prov.; joined CCP 1956; Deputy Sec. CCP Tai'an Co. Cttee, Shandong Prov. 1966–76, Sec. 1978–83; Sec. CCP Zhangqiu Co. Cttee, Shandong Prov. 1976–78; Sec. CCP Tai'an City Cttee, Shandong Prov. 1983–86; Vice-Gov. Shandong Prov. 1986–88; Sec.-Gen. People's Govt, Shandong Prov. 1986–88; Deputy Sec.-Gen. State Council 1987; Deputy Sec. CCP Shandong Prov. Cttee 1988–90; Vice-Minister of Agric. 1990–92; Vice-Gov. Henan Prov. 1992, Acting Gov. 1992–93, Gov. 1993–98; Deputy Sec. CCP Henan Prov. Cttee 1995–98, Sec. 1998–2000; Alt. mem. 12th CCP Cen. Cttee 1982–87, 13th Cen. Cttee 1987–92, 14th Cen. Cttee CCP 1992–97, mem. 15th CCP Cen. Cttee 1997–2002.

MA, Zonglin; Chinese business executive; mem. Bd of Dirs and Pres. Power Construction Corpn of China (PowerChina, state-owned corpn) 2011–16. *Address:* c/o Power Construction Corporation of China, No. 7 & 8 Building, Beijing Xiyuan Hotel, 1 Sanlihe Road, Haidian District, Beijing 100040, People's Republic of China. *E-mail:* infocenter@powerchina.cn.

MA SI-HANG, Frederick, GBS, BA, JP; Hong Kong business executive and fmr government official; b. 22 Feb. 1952, Hong Kong; ed New Method Coll., Tai Hang, Univ. of Hong Kong; fmrly with J. P. Morgan Private Bank, Chase Manhattan Bank, Kumagai Gumi (HK) Ltd, RBC Dominion Securities Ltd, Hong Kong Exchanges and Clearing Ltd, Hong Kong Securities and Futures Comm.; Group Chief Financial Officer, Exec. Dir, mem. Exec. Cttee PCCW Ltd –2002; Sec. for Financial Services and the Treasury, Hong Kong Special Admin. Region 2002–07, for Commerce and Econ. Devt 2007–08; mem. Int. Advisory Council, China Investment Corpn 2009; Chair. (non-exec.) China Strategic Holdings Ltd 2009–12; Dir, Husky Energy Inc. 2010–, Agricultural Bank of China Ltd 2011–; Ind. Dir (non-exec.), China Resources Land Ltd 2010–, Hutchison Port Holdings Management Pte Ltd (also Trustee-Man., Hutchison Port Holdings Trust) 2011–, Aluminum Corpn of China Ltd 2013–, MTR Corpn Ltd 2013–; Dir, Hong Kong International Theme Parks Ltd, Mandatory Provident Fund Schemes Authority, Hong Kong Inst. for Monetary Research; Hon. Prof., School of Econs and Finance, Univ. of Hong Kong 2008; Hon. Fellow, School of Accountancy, Central Univ. of Finance and Econs 2010; Grand Bauhinia Star 2009. *Address:* Hutchison Port Holdings Trust, 50 Raffles Place, Singapore City 048623, Singapore (office). *Website:* www.hphtrust.com (office).

MA TAO-LI, Hon. Geoffrey, LLB, QC; Hong Kong barrister and judge; *Chief Justice, Court of Final Appeal of Hong Kong;* b. 11 Jan. 1956, Hong Kong; m. Madam Justice Maria Candace Yuen Ka-ning; one d.; ed in Altrincham and at Univ. of Birmingham, UK; called to the Bar, Gray's Inn, London, UK 1978, commenced practice as a barrister in England and Wales; called to the Bar in Hong Kong 1980, Vic., Australia 1983, Singapore 1990; QC 1993; fmr legal consultant to Messrs David Chong & Co., Singapore, Advocates & Solicitors; Head of Chambers, Temple Chambers, Hong Kong –2001; Recorder, Court of First Instance of the High Court 2000–01, Judge of the Court of First Instance of the High Court 2001–02, Justice of Appeal of the Court of Appeal of the High Court 2002–03, Chief Judge of the High Court 2003–10; Chief Justice of the Court of Final Appeal of Hong Kong 2010–; Chair. Appeal Tribunal Panel (Buildings) 1994–2001, Steering Cttee on Civil Justice Reform 2004–09, Monitoring Cttee on Civil Justice Reform 2009–; Deputy Chair. Bd of Review (Inland Revenue) 1997–2000, Securities and Futures Comm. (SFC) Appeals Panel 1999–2001, SFC Takeovers Appeal Cttee 1999–2001; mem. Bar Council of the Hong Kong Bar Asscn 1982–84, 1992–96; Adjudicator, Registration of Persons Tribunal, Hong Kong 1987–96; mem. Criminal and Law Enforcement Injuries Compensation Bd 1991–2001, Steering Cttee for the 11th Int. Congress of Maritime Arbitrators 1992–94, Civil Court Users Cttee of the Judiciary 1993–2001, Hong Kong Futures Exchange Disciplinary Appeal Tribunal 1994–2001, Man. Cttee of the Consumer Legal Action Fund 1994–98 (later Vice-Chair.), Appointment Advisory Bd of the Hong Kong Int. Arbitration Centre (HKIAC) 1997–, HKIAC Arbitration Ordinance Review Cttee 1998–, Working Party on Civil Justice Reform 2000–01; Hon. Lecturer, Dept of Professional Legal Educ., Univ. of Hong Kong 1987–; Hon. Bencher of Gray's Inn 2004; Hon. Fellow, Harris Manchester Coll., Oxford 2012; Hon. Bencher of the Middle Temple 2016; Hon. LLD (Birmingham) 2011, (Chinese Univ. of Hong Kong) 2016. *Publications:* Hong Kong Civil Procedure (contributing ed.) 2002, Litigation in the Commercial List: 2002 Law Lectures for Practitioners (contrib.) 2002, Arbitration in Hong Kong: A Practical Guide (Ed.-in-Chief) 2003, Professional Conduct and Risk Management in Hong Kong (Ed.-in-Chief) 2007. *Address:* Court of Final Appeal of Hong Kong, 8 Jackson Road, Central, Hong Kong Special Administrative Region, People's Republic of China (office). *Telephone:* 2123-0011 (office). *Fax:* 2121-0310 (office). *E-mail:* enquiry@judiciary.gov.hk (office). *Website:* www.hkcfa.hk (office).

MA'AFU, Lord; **Siosa'ia Lausi'i (Ma'afu Tukui'aulahi);** Tongan politician and fmr military officer; b. 1955; s. of Tevita 'Ungamotangitau Lausi'i and Peti Lausi'i; m. HRH Princess Lavinia Mata-'o-Taone Tuku'aho; two c.; ed Wanganui Collegiate School, New Zealand, Naval Staff Coll., USA; enrolled in Tonga Defence Services March 1975, becoming Platoon Commdr, Tonga Royal Guards 1975, ADC to HM King Taufa'ahau Tupou IV 1977, 1983–89, Mil. Liaison Officer for Foreign Affairs 1980, Commanding Officer of Land Force 1991, 2000; retd from army 2000; Private Sec. to HM King Taufa'ahau Tupou IV 2001–06; mem. Legis. Ass. as Nobles' Rep. for Tongatapu 2008–; Minister for Environment and Climate Change 2009–11, Minister for Lands, Survey, Natural Resources, Environment and Climate Change 2011–18, Deputy Prime Minister 2017, Minister of HM Armed Forces Jan.–March 2018; installed with noble title 10th Ma'afutukui'aulahi 30 Oct. 1997; King Taufa'ahau Silver Jubilee Medal, Long Service and Good Conduct Medal, Gen. Service Medal (Bougainville), US Army Commendation Medal.

MAAIT, Mohamed Ahmed, BA, M.Phil, MSc, PhD; Egyptian academic, financial executive and politician; *Minister of Finance;* b. 31 Aug. 1962; ed Cairo Univ., City Univ., London; Asst Lecturer for Statistics, Quantitative Methods and Insurance, Faculty of Commerce, Open Univ. of Cairo 1988–95; Prof. in Quantitative Pathology and Dir of Programme of Financial and Actuarial Math., City Univ., London 1997–2003; Sr Lecturer of Actuarial Science and Financial Math., Univ. of Glasgow, Scotland 2007–, then Dir; apptd Exec. Dir Egyptian Insurance Inst. 2007; Sr Pension and Social Insurance Reform Advisor to Minister of Finance 2007–09, Deputy to Minister of Finance for Pension and Social Insurance 2009–13, Chair. Egyptian Governmental Actuarial Dept, Ministry of Finance 2010–13, First Deputy to Minister of Health & Population for Financial & Admin. Affairs 2014–15, First Deputy to Minister of Finance 2015, Deputy Minister of Finance for Gen. Treasury Affairs and Head of Econ. Justice Unit 2016–18; Minister of Finance 2018–; Consultant, Egyptian Financial Supervisory Authority 2012–; Chair. Nat. Org. for Social Insurance 2011–12; Vice-Chair. Egyptian Financial Supervisory Authority 2013–15; Chair. Audit and Investment Cttee African Reinsurance Co., Nigeria 2013–; mem. Inst. of Actuaries London 1996–2003; mem. Bd of Dirs, Gen. Authority for Health Insurance 2008–, Egypt Aviation Holding Co. 2017–, Alexandria Bank 2017–, Inst. of Nat. Planning 2017–, Financial Supervisory Authority 2018–; Fellow Royal Statistical Soc., London 1997–2007. *Address:* Ministry of Finance Towers, Cairo (Nasr City), Egypt (office). *Telephone:* (2) 23428830 (office). *Fax:* (2) 26861561 (office). *Website:* www.mof.gov.eg (office).

MAALIM, Mahboub M., BSc, MSc; Kenyan engineer and international organization official; *Executive Secretary, Intergovernmental Authority on Development (IGAD);* b. Garissa; ed Univ. of Texas, USA; Dist Water Engineer, Ministry of Water 1985–94; Nat. Coordinator Arid Lands Resource Man. Project 1996–2004; Perm. Sec. Ministry of Water and Irrigation 2006–08; Exec. Sec. IGAD 2008–; Chair. Kenya Power 2018–; Assoc. mem. American Soc. of Civil Engineers. *Address:* Office of the Executive Secretary, IGAD Secretariat, Avenue Georges Clemenceau, PO Box 2653, Djibouti, Republic of Djibouti (office). *Telephone:* 356452 (office). *Fax:* 353520 (office). *E-mail:* info@igad.int (office). *Website:* www.igad.int (office).

MAALOUF, Amin, Maîtrise en Sociologie; Lebanese/French writer; b. 25 Feb. 1949, Beirut, Lebanon; s. of Ruchdi Maalouf and Odette Ghossein; m. Andrée Abouchdid 1971; three c.; ed Univ. Saint-Joseph, Beirut, Univ. de Lyon; journalist, an-Nahar 1971–76, Economia 1976–77; Ed. Jeune Afrique 1978–79, 1982–84; mem. Acad. française Fauteuil 29 2011–; Grand Cordon, Ordre du Cèdre (Lebanon), Commdr, Ordre nat. du Mérite, Chevalier, Légion d'honneur, Commdr des Arts et des Lettres, Kt, Order of the Lion of Finland; Dr hc (Univ. Catholique de Louvain, Belgium), (American Univ. of Beirut, Lebanon), (Tarragona Univ., Spain), (Evora Univ., Portugal); Prix France-Liban 1986, Grand Prix de l'UNICEF 1991, Prix Goncourt 1993, Premio Nonino 1997, Premio Elio Vittorini 1997, Prix européen de l'essai 1998, Premio Grinzane Cavour 2001, Premio Antonio de Sancha 2003, Prix Méditerranée 2004, Premio Grupo de Compostela 2009, Prix du livre des Droits de l'Homme 2009, Premio Príncipe de Asturias 2010, Sheikh Zayed Book Award for Cultural Personality of the Year 2016. *Publications include:* Les Croisades vues par les Arabes 1983, Léon l'Africain 1986, Samarcande 1988, Les Jardins de lumière 1991, Le premier siècle après Béatrice 1992, Le Rocher de Tanios 1993, Les Echelles du Levant 1996, Les Identités meurtrières 1998, Le Périple de Baldassare 2000, L'Amour de Loin (opera libretto) 2001, Origines 2004, Adriana Mater (opera libretto) 2006, Origins: A Memoir 2008, Le Dérèglement du monde 2009, Émilie (opera libretto) 2010, Les désorientés 2012, Un fauteuil sur la Seine 2016. *Address:* Académie française, 23 quai de Conti, 75006 Paris, France (home).

MAALOUF, Maria; Lebanese journalist, television presenter and media executive; ed Sainte Famille Maronites Coll., Univ. of Lebanon; presenter, Bila Rakib (Without Censorship) 2002–04, Maa Maria Maalouf (NBN TV) 2006; Founder, Gulf Printing and Publishing Co.; Owner, Arrouwad (newspaper); mem. Syrian Nat. Soc. Party. *Publication:* A Woman Looking for a Homeland. *Website:* www.mariamaalouf.com/maria.

MAAMAU, Taneti; I-Kiribati politician and head of state; *President;* b. Onotoa; fmr Perm. Sec., Public Service Office; fmr Perm. Sec., Ministry of Finance and Econ. Devt; mem. House of Ass. (Parl.) for Onotoa; Beretitenti (Pres.) of Kiribati 2016–; mem. Tobwaan Kiribati Party. *Address:* Office of the President, POB 68, Bairiki, Tarawa, Kiribati (office). *Telephone:* 21183 (office). *Fax:* 21145 (office). *E-mail:* info@ob.gov.ki (office). *Website:* www.president.gov.ki (office).

MAAS, Heiko; German lawyer and politician; *Federal Minister of Foreign Affairs;* b. 19 Sept. 1966, Saarlouis; m.; two c.; ed Univ. des Saarlandes; began career with Ford Werke GmbH, Saarlouis 1988; mem. Saarland Landtag (State Parl.) 1994–96, 1999–; Sec., Ministry of Environment, Energy and Transport 1996–98; Minister for Environment, Energy and Transport in Saarland 1998–99, Minister for Econs, Labour, Energy and Transport and Deputy Prime Minister in Saarland 2012–13; Fed. Minister of Justice and Consumer Protection 2013–18, of Foreign Affairs 2018–; mem. Sozialdemokratische Partei Deutschlands (SPD), Chair. SPD Parl. Group 1999–2012, mem. SPD Party Exec. 2001–; mem. Bd of Supervisory Dirs, KfW 2018–; Chair. Bd of Trustees, Aktion Deutschland Hilft 2018–; mem. Bd of Trustees, RAG-Stiftung 2015–. *Address:* Federal Ministry of Foreign Affairs, Werderscher Markt 1, 10117 Berlin, Germany (office). *Telephone:* (30) 18170 (office). *Fax:* (30) 18173402 (office). *E-mail:* poststelle@auswaertiges-amt.de (office). *Website:* www.auswaertiges-amt.de (office); www.heiko-maas.de.

MAASIKAS, Matti; Estonian government official and diplomatist; *Deputy Minister for European Union Affairs, Ministry of Foreign Affairs;* b. 12 June 1967, Tallinn; m.; two c.; ed Tartu Univ.; Consultant, Ministry of Defence 1993–94; Int. Sec., Pro Patria Union (Estonian Conservative Party) 1994–96; Head of Foreign Relations Dept, Chancellery of Riigikogu (Parl.) 1996–99; Head of Prime Minister Mart Laar's Pvt. Office 1999–2001; Amb. to Finland 2001–05; Sec.-Gen., Ministry of Foreign Affairs 2005–08, currently Deputy Minister for EU Affairs; mem. of Cabinet, European Commr for Enlargement and Econ. and Monetary Affairs 2009–10; Adviser, Bureau of European Policy Advisers, EC 2010–11; Amb. and Perm. Rep. to EU, Brussels 2011–15. *Address:* Ministry of Foreign Affairs of Estonia, Islandi Väljak 1, Tallinn 15049, Estonia (office). *Telephone:* 637-7000 (office). *Fax:* 637-7099 (office). *E-mail:* vminfo@vm.ee (office). *Website:* vm.ee (office).

MABILANGAN, Felipe H., MA; Philippine diplomatist and international organization official; *Senior Foreign Affairs Adviser;* m. Ada Kalaw Ledesma; three c.; ed Univs of Oxford, UK and Geneva, Switzerland; various positions, Dept of Foreign Affairs 1971–79, Dir Gen. for European Affairs 1988, Amb. to France (also accred to Portugal) 1979–87, to China (also accred to Mongolia) 1989–95, Amb. and Perm. Rep. to UN, New York 1995–2001, currently Sr Foreign Affairs Adviser, Dept of Foreign Affairs; mem. UN Advisory Cttee on Admin. and Budgetary Questions 2001–04; del. to numerous int. confs; Chevalier, Ordre nat. du Mérite; Gawad Mabini (Philippines). *Leisure interests:* golf, tennis. *Address:* Department of Foreign Affairs, DFA Building, 2330 Roxas Blvd, Pasay City, 1330 Metro Manila, The Philippines (office). *Telephone:* (2) 8344000 (office). *Fax:* (2) 8321597 (office). *E-mail:* webmaster@dfa.gov.ph (office). *Website:* www.dfa.gov.ph (office).

MABUS, Hon. Raymond (Ray) Edwin, Jr, BA, MA, JD; American government official, lawyer, consultant and fmr politician; b. 11 Oct. 1948, Ackerman, Miss.; s. of Raymond Edwin Mabus, Sr and Lucille C. Mabus; m. (divorced); two d.; ed Univ. of Mississippi, Johns Hopkins Univ., Harvard Univ. Law School; Surface Warfare Officer, USS Little Rock, US Navy 1970–72; called to Texas Bar 1976, Washington, DC 1978, Miss. 1982; law clerk, US Circuit Court of Appeals, Montgomery, Ala 1976–77; Legal Counsel to House of Reps, DC 1977–78; Assoc. Fried, Frank et al., Washington, DC 1979–80; Gov.'s Legis. Aide, State of Miss., Jackson 1980–83; State Auditor, State of Miss. 1984–88; Gov. of Miss. 1988–92; Amb. to Saudi Arabia 1994–96; Counsel, Baker Donaldson Bearman & Caldwell 1996–; Chair. and CEO Foamex International, Inc. 2006–07; Sec. of the Navy 2009–17; fmr Chair. Southern Govs' Asscn, Southern Regional Educ. Bd; mem. Bd of Dirs, EnerSys 2009–; Woodrow Wilson Scholarship, Johns Hopkins Univ. 1969; Democrat; Distinguished Lecturer on the Middle East, Univ. of Mississippi; King Abdul Aziz Award, Saudi Arabia 1996, Distinguished Public Service Award, US Dept of Defense, Martin Luther King Social Responsibility Award, Nat. Wildlife Fed. Conservation Achievement Award, Friend of Educ. Award, Mississippi Asscn of Educators. *Television:* numerous appearances as an expert on the Middle East, including 60 Minutes and Nightline; cameo appearances on TV drama NCIS 2009, 2014 and NCIS: New Orleans 2015. *Leisure interests:* spectator sports, walking, reading, photography, scuba diving.

MABUZA, David, BA; South African politician and fmr teacher; *Vice-President;* b. 25 Aug. 1960, Brondal, Mathafeni; m. 1st Ruth Funi Silinda (divorced); m. 2nd Nonhlanhla Patience Mnisi; ed Univ. of South Africa; Teacher, KaNgwane Dept of Educ. 1986–88; Prin., Lungisani Secondary School 1989–93; mem. Mpumalanga Prov. Exec. Council for Educ. 1994–98, for Housing 1999–2001, for Roads and Transport 2007–08, for Agric. and Land Admin 2008–09; mem. Mpumalanga Prov. Legislature 1999–2001, 2004–07; Premier of Mpumalanga 2009–18; mem. Nat. Ass. (parl.) for Mpumalanga constituency 2001–04, 2018–; mem. African Nat. Congress (ANC), Regional ANC Chair. 1994–98, mem. ANC Prov. Exec. Cttee 1998–2006, mem. ANC Nat. Exec. Cttee 2007–, Deputy Pres. ANC 2017–; Vice-Pres. of South Africa 2018–. *Address:* The Presidency, Union Bldgs, West Wing, Government Ave, Pretoria 0001, South Africa (office). *Telephone:* (12) 3005200 (office). *Fax:* (12) 3238246 (office). *E-mail:* president@presidency.gov.za (office). *Website:* www.thepresidency.gov.za (office).

McADAM, Lowell C., BEng, MBA; American engineer and telecommunications industry executive; *Chairman and CEO, Verizon Communications Inc.;* ed Cornell Univ., Univ. of San Diego; spent six years in USN Civil Engineer Corps; held various exec. positions with Pacific Bell, including Area Vice-Pres. of Bay Area Marketing and Gen. Man. of South Bay Customer Services 1983–93; joined AirTouch as Exec. Dir of Int. Applications and Operations 1993, served as Vice-Pres. of Int. operations for AirTouch Communications and was Lead Tech. Partner for Cellular Ventures in Spain, Portugal, Sweden, Italy, Korea and Japan, later Pres. and CEO PrimeCo Personal Communications (jt venture owned by Bell Atlantic and Vodafone AirTouch), later COO; Exec. Vice-Pres. and COO Verizon Wireless 2000–07, Pres. and CEO 2007–10, Pres. and COO Verizon Communications Inc. 2010–11, Pres. and CEO Aug.–Dec. 2011, Chair. and CEO 2012–, Chair. Verizon Wireless Bd of Reps, mem. Bd of Dirs; past Chair. CTIA – The Wireless Asscn; Dir, Nat. Acad. Foundation. *Address:* Verizon Communications Inc., 140 West Street, New York, NY 10007, USA (office). *Telephone:* (212) 395-2121 (office). *Fax:* (212) 571-1897 (office). *E-mail:* info@verizon.com (office). *Website:* www.verizon.com (office).

MACAIRE, Robert Nigel Paul, CMG; British diplomatist; *Ambassador to Iran;* b. 19 Feb. 1966; m. Alice Muriel Macaire; two d.; ed St Edmund Hall, Oxford; Ministry of Defence, Procurement Policy, Special Forces Secr., Policy Studies Secr. 1987–97, Falklands Islands Dept, FCO 1990, Second Sec. (Know How Fund), Embassy in Bucharest 1991–95, Head, Levant Section, NE and North Africa Dept, FCO 1995–96, Head, MEPP Section, NE and North Africa Dept 1996–97, Head, Southern Africa Section, Africa Directorate 1997–98, Head, Sierra Leone Unit 1998, First Sec., Middle East and Counter-terrorism, Embassy in Washington, DC 1998–2002, Head, Counter Terrorism Policy Dept, FCO 2002–04, Political Counsellor, High Comm. in New Delhi 2004–06, Dir Consular Services, FCO 2006–08, High Commr to Kenya 2008–11; Dir Govt and Public Affairs and Political Risk, BG Group plc 2011–16; Amb. to Iran 2018–. *Address:* Embassy of the UK, 198

Ferdowsi Ave, Tehran, 11316–91144, Iran (office). *Telephone:* (21) 64052000 (office). *E-mail:* chancery.tehran@fco.gov.uk. *Website:* ukiniran.fco.gov.uk (office).

McALEESE, Mary Patricia, LLB, MA, FRSA, MRIA; Irish academic, journalist and fmr head of state; *Distinguished Professor in Irish Studies, St Mary's University;* b. 27 June 1951, Belfast, Northern Ireland; d. of Patrick J. Leneghan and Claire McManus; m. Martin McAleese 1976; one s. two d.; ed Queen's Univ. Belfast, Inn of Court of Northern Ireland, King's Inns, Dublin and Trinity Coll., Dublin; called to Northern Ireland Bar 1974; Reid Prof. of Criminal Law, Criminology and Penology, Trinity Coll., Dublin 1975–79, 1981–87; current affairs journalist and presenter, Radio Telefís Éireann 1979–85; Dir Inst. of Professional Legal Studies 1987–97; Pro-Vice-Chancellor, Queen's Univ., Belfast 1994–97; Pres. of Ireland 1997–2011; Visiting Prof., Boston Coll., USA 2011–14; Distinguished Prof. in Irish Studies, St Mary's Univ., London 2015–; Dir (non-exec.) Northern Ireland Electricity 1992–97, Channel 4 TV 1993–97, fmr Dir Royal Group of Hosps Trust; Founder mem. Irish Comm. for Prisoners Overseas; mem. Catholic Church Episcopal Del. to the New Ireland Forum 1984, Catholic Church Del. to the North Comm. on Contentious Parades 1996; Del. to White House Conf. on Trade and Investment in Ireland 1995, and to the follow-up Pittsburgh Conf. 1996; Hon. Fellow, Trinity Coll. Dublin, Inst. of Engineers of Ireland, Royal Coll. of Surgeons, Coll. of Anaesthetists, Liverpool John Moore's Univ., Royal Coll. of Physicians and Surgeons, Glasgow; Hon. Bencher, King's Inns, Inn of Court of Northern Ireland; Freeman, City of Kilkenny 2009; Hon. LLD (Univ. of Otago, NZ) 2007, (Mount Holyoke Coll., Mass) 2009, (Fordham Univ., NY) 2010, (Nat. Univ. of Ireland, Vic. Univ. of Tech., Australia, Saint Mary's Univ., Canada, Loyola Law School, LA, Univ. of Aberdeen, Univ. of Surrey, Queen's, Belfast), (Nottingham) 1998, (Trinity Coll. Dublin, Metropolitan Univ., Manchester, Univ. of Delaware, Univ. of Bristol), Hon. DHumLitt (Rochester Inst. of Tech., New York, USA), Hon. DLitt (Univ. of Ulster); Silver Jubilee Commemoration Medal, Charles Univ., Prague, Great Gold Medal, Comenius Univ., Bratislava, The American Ireland Fund Humanitarian Award 2007. *Publications:* The Irish Martyrs 1995, Reconciled Being 1997. *Leisure interests:* hillwalking, theology. *Address:* Centre for Irish Studies, St Mary's University, Waldegrave Road, Strawberry Hill, Twickenham, London, TW1 4SX, England (office). *Website:* www.stmarys.ac.uk/irish-studies (office).

McALLISTER, Sir Ian Gerald, Kt, CBE, BSc (Econs); British transport industry executive; b. 17 Aug. 1943, Glasgow, Scotland; m. Susan Mitchell; three s. one d.; ed Thornleigh Salesian Coll., Bolton, Univ. Coll., London; grad. economist, Ford Motor Co. Ltd 1964, responsible for German Operations 1980s, Man. Dir Ford of Britain 1991, Chair. 1992–2002; Chair. (non-exec.), Network Rail Ltd 2002–09; Chair. Carbon Trust 2001–11, Greater Essex Prosperity Forum 2007; Dir (non-exec.), Scottish & Newcastle, Energy Saving Trust 2001–, UCL Business PLC 2007–; Dr hc (Loughborough) 1999. *Leisure interest:* Manchester United Football Club. *Address:* UCL Business PLC, The Network Building, 97 Tottenham Court Road, London, W1T 4TP, England (office). *Telephone:* (20) 7679-9000 (office). *Fax:* (20) 7679-9838 (office). *E-mail:* info@uclb.com (office). *Website:* www.uclb.com (office).

MACAN, Tom, BA; British diplomatist (retd); b. 14 Nov. 1946, Manchester, England; s. of Dr Thomas Townley Macan and Zaida Bindloss Macan (née Boddington); one s. one d.; ed Shrewsbury School, Univ. of Sussex; joined HM Diplomatic Service 1969, served in Bonn, Brasília and FCO; Press Sec. Embassy at Bonn 1981; Head Commonwealth Co-ordination Dept, FCO 1986–88, Head Training Dept 1988–90; Deputy Head of Mission at Lisbon 1990–95; Amb. to Lithuania 1995–98; seconded to BOC Group 1998–99; Minister at New Delhi 1999–2002; Gov. of the Virgin Islands 2002–06; mem. Inst. of Linguists. *Leisure interests:* sailing, steamboats, church architecture. *Address:* Stevney, Outgate, Ambleside, Cumbria, LA22 0NH, England (home). *Telephone:* (1539) 436978 (office). *E-mail:* ttm@mailcan.com (office).

McANUFF, Des; American/Canadian producer, director and writer; b. 19 June 1952, Princeton, Ill.; m. 1st Susan Berman 1984 (divorced 2009); one d.; m. 2nd Bryna McAnuff 2012; ed Woburn Collegiate; trained under drama coach Basya Hunter, Toronto; raised in Scarborough, Toronto; worked with Toronto Free Theatre as dir of several plays; moved to New York City, where he co-f. Dodger Theatre Co. 1978, directed first production, Gimme Shelter; directed for American Repertory Theatre at Harvard, also Yale Rep; fmr faculty mem. Juilliard School; Artistic Dir La Jolla Playhouse (revived 1983) –2007, directed Romeo and Juliet, A Mad World, My Masters, Big River, As You Like It, The Seagull, The Matchmaker, A Walk in the Woods, Two Rooms, 80 Days, Macbeth, A Funny Thing Happened on the Way to the Forum, Twelfth Night, Three Sisters, Elmer Gantry, Much Ado About Nothing, The Who's Tommy, How to Succeed in Business Without Really Trying; Co-Artistic Dir Stratford Shakespeare Festival 2006–08, Artistic Dir 2008–12; also produced Tony award-winning revivals of Broadway classics, including Guys and Dolls, The Music Man, Into the Woods, 42 Street, The King and I, and many others. *Productions include:* Big River (Tony Award for Best Dir (Musical) 1985) 1985, A Walk in the Woods 1988, The Gospel at Colonus 1988, Dangerous Games 1989, The Grapes of Wrath 1990, Prelude to a Kiss 1990, The Who's Tommy (Tony Award for Best Dir (Musical) 1993, Laurence Olivier Theatre Award for Best Dir of 1996 at Shaftesbury Theatre 1997) 1993, How to Succeed in Business Without Really Trying 1995, I Am My Own Wife 2003, Dracula, The Musical 2004, 700 Sundays 2004, Good Vibrations 2005, Jersey Boys 2005, The Farnsworth Invention 2007, Cry-Baby 2008, Guys & Dolls 2009, A Funny Thing Happened on the Way to the Forum 2009, As You Like It 2010, The Tempest 2010, Jesus Christ Superstar 2011, Twelfth Night 2011, A Word or Two 2012, Henry V 2012, The Who's Tommy 2013, 700 Sundays 2014. *Films:* Cousin Bette 1998, The Iron Giant (producer) 1999, The Adventures of Rocky and Bullwinkle 2000, Quills (exec. producer) 2000. *Address:* 375 Greenwich Street, New York, NY 10003, USA (office). *Telephone:* (212) 941-3867 (office). *E-mail:* mfrank@skunkincorporated .com (office).

MACAPAGAL ARROYO, Gloria, PhD; Philippine politician, economist, journalist and fmr head of state; *Speaker, House of Representatives;* b. 5 April 1947, San Juan; d. of Diosdado Pangan Macapagal (fmr Pres. of the Philippines) and Dr Evangelina Macaraeg Macapagal; m. Jose Miguel Tuason Arroyo 1968; two s. one d.; ed Assumption Convent, Georgetown Univ., Assumption Coll., Ateneo de Manila Univ., Univ. of the Philippines; Asst Prof., Ateneo de Manila Univ. 1977–87; Chair. Econs Dept, Assumption Coll. 1984–87; Prof., Univ. of the Philippines School of Econs 1977–87; Prof., Mary Knoll Coll., St Scholastica's Coll.; Asst Sec., Dept of Trade and Industry 1987–89, Under-Sec. 1989–92; Exec. Dir Garments and Textile Export Bd 1988–90; Senator 1992–98; mem. House of Reps., Pampanga 2nd Dist 2010–, Deputy Speaker 2016–17, Speaker 2018–; Sec. Dept of Social Welfare and Devt 1998–2000; Vice-Pres. of Repub. 1998–2001, Pres. of the Philippines 2001–10 (re-elected 2004); Chair. and Pres. Univ. of the Philippines Health Maintenance Org. 1989–98; Exec. Dir Philippine Center for Econ. Devt 1994–98; Chair. Univ. of the Philippines Econ. Foundation 1994–98; Chair. ASEAN Jan. 2007–Nov. 2007; mem. Presidential Task Force on Tax and Tariff Reforms 1994–98, Tech. Working Group of the Philippine Nat. Devt Plan for the 21st Century (Cttee on Nat. Framework for Regional Devt and Macroeconomics Framework for Devt Financing); mem. or fmr mem. Asscn for Philippines-China Understanding, Philippine Econs Soc., Georgetown Club of the Philippines, Concerned Women of the Philippines; arrested on corruption charges 2012, released on bail 2012, arrested on allegations of plunder 2012 (detained in hospital for four years), charges dismissed 2016; mem. Bd of Dirs, Boao Forum for Asia 2018–; Hon. LLD (La Trobe Univ.) 2000, (Waseda Univ.) 2002, (Fordham Univ.) 2003, (Old Dominion Univ.) 2003; Hon. DEcon (Tsinghua Univ.) 2001; Hon. DH (Mapua Inst. of Tech.) 2004; Hon. Community Coll. Assoc. Degree in Int. Relations (City Coll. of San Francisco) 2003; UPSE Fellowship 1970–71, Japan Foundation Grant 1976–77, Rockefeller Foundation Scholarship 1978–83. *Address:* House of Representatives, Room MB-2F, Quezon City, Philippines (office). *Telephone:* (2) 9315001 (office). *Website:* www.congress.gov.ph (office); www.gloriamarroyo.ph.

MACÁRIO DO NASCIMENTO CLEMENTE, HE Cardinal Manuel José, (His Beatitude Manuel III, Patriarch of Lisbon), DrHistTheol; Portuguese ecclesiastic and academic; *Patriarch of Lisbon;* b. 16 July 1948, Torres Vedras; ed Major Seminary of Christ the King of the Groves, Univ. of Lisbon, Catholic Univ. of Portugal; taught Church History at Catholic Univ. of Portugal from 1975; ordained priest, Archdiocese of Lisbon 1979; assigned as Parochial Vicar of Runa, Torres Vedras; Canon of Lisbon Cathedral and Vice-Rector of Major Seminary of Christ the King of the Groves 1989–97, Pres. 1997; Co-ordinator of Patriarchate 1996, of Preparatory Comm. of Presbytery Assembly for Jubilee 2000; consecrated Auxiliary Bishop of Lisbon 1999 and Titular Bishop of Pinhel 2000; Dir Centre for Study of Religious History 2000–07; Head of Foundation for Science and Tech.'s projects: Church and Social Movements: Catholic Organizations in Portugal in Twentieth Century 1993–95, The Catholic Movement and Presence Church in Portuguese Soc. 1996–98; Bishop of Porto 2007–13; Patriarch of Lisbon 2013–; cr. Cardinal (Cardinal-Priest of Sant'Antonio in Campo Marzio) 2015; mem. Scientific Soc. of Catholic Univ. of Portugal 1993; Assoc. Academic Corresp., Portuguese Acad. of History 1996; Hon. Citizen of Porto 2011, Vila Nova de Gaia 2013; Grand Cross, Mil. Order of Christ 2010; Grand Cross pro Merito Melitensi, Sovereign Mil. Order of Malta 2012; Medal of Honour from Marco de Canaveses 2010, Medal of Honour from Valongo 2011, Medal of Honour of Porto 2011, Medal of Honour of the City-Grade Gold from Gondomar 2012, Key Honour from Melres 2012, Medal of Honour of the City of Vila Nova de Gaia 2013; Hon. Dr of Political Science and Int. Relations Citizenship (Lusophone Univ. of Porto) 2012; Pessoa Prize 2009. *Publications include:* Portugal and the Portuguese and a Single Purpose 2009, Portuguese Church and Society, the Republic of Liberalism. *Address:* Archdiocese of Lisbon, Mosteiro de São Vicente de Fora, Campo de Santa Clara, 1100-472 Lisbon (office); Casa Patriarcal, Seminário dos Olivais, Quinta do Cabeço, 1800 Lisbon, Portugal (home). *Telephone:* (218) 810500 (office); (219) 457310 (home). *Fax:* (218) 810555 (office); (219) 457329 (home). *E-mail:* info@patriarcado-lisboa.pt (office). *Website:* www.patriarcado-lisboa.pt (office).

MacARTHUR, Dame Ellen Patricia, DBE, MBE; British yachtswoman; *Chair of Trustees, Ellen MacArthur Foundation;* b. 8 July 1976, Derby, Derbyshire; d. of Ken MacArthur and Avril MacArthur; ed Anthony Gell School, Wirksworth; circumnavigated UK single-handed (youngest person to pass Yachtmaster Offshore Qualification) 1995; took part in Mini Transat race 1997; Class Winner Route du Rhum race 1999, 2002; second place in Vendée Globe Race (94 days' solo sailing, fastest woman and youngest sailor to circumnavigate the globe single-handedly) 2001; set non-stop round the world record of 71 days, 14 hours, 18 minutes and 33 seconds 2005; f. Ellen MacArthur Cancer Trust 2003, Ellen MacArthur Foundation 2009 (Chair of Trustees); Chevalier, Légion d'honneur; BT/YJA Young Sailor of the Year 1995, Sailing's Young Hope (France) 1998, BT/YJA Yachtsman of the Year 1999, Cable Industry Outstanding Achievement Award, Women of the Year Awards 2001, Royal Geographical Soc. Discovery Award 2001, Walpole Medal of Excellence 2001, Pride of Britain Award 2001, Royal Inst. of Navigation Award 2001, Times Sportswoman of the Year 2001, Runner-up Sports Personality of the Year 2001, Int. Sailing Fed. World Sailor of the Year 2001. *Publications:* Taking on the World 2002, Race Against Time 2005, Full Circle 2010. *Address:* Ellen MacArthur Foundation, The Sail Loft, 42 Medina Road, Cowes, Isle of Wight, PO31 7BX, England (home). *E-mail:* info@ellenmacarthur.com (home). *Website:* www.ellenmacarthurfoundation.org (home); www .ellenmacarthurcancertrust.org (home); www.ellenmacarthur.com (home).

McASLAN, John Renwick, CBE, MA, RIBA, FRSA, FRIAS, FRICS, FICE, FRSE; British architect; *Executive Chairman, John McAslan + Partners;* b. 16 Feb. 1954, Glasgow, Scotland; s. of Prof. T. Crawford and Jean Renwick McAslan; m. Dava Sagenkahn 1981; one s. two d.; ed Dunoon Grammar School, Dollar Acad., Univ. of Edin.; trained with Cambridge Seven Assocs, Boston, Mass. 1978–80; Richard Rogers and Partners, London 1980–84; Founding Partner and Dir Troughton McAslan (later John McAslan + Partners) 1984–96, Exec. Chair. 1996–; extensive int. teaching experience at architectural schools including Glasgow, Belfast, Cardiff, Dublin, Beijing, London, Edin., Mexico City, Sydney, Helsinki, Seoul, Tokyo 1990–; Chair. of numerous architectural award juries in UK 1990–; Visiting Prof., Univ. of Wales 1998–2001; mem. Bd of Regents, Univ. of Edinburgh 2013; Foundation Trustee, Whitechapel Art Gallery 1989–97; Founder John McAslan Family Trust, London 1997, Volubilis Foundation, Morocco 2001, RIBA/ICE McAslan Bursary 2004; External Examiner, various univs; Assoc. Int. mem. AIA; mem. Architectural Inst. of Japan; Hon. Consul, Repub. of Haiti, London 2012–13; Dr hc (Univ. of Edinburgh) 2015; , RIBA Award for Architecture 2011, Civic Trust Award 2013, European Heritage Award 2013, Architect of the Year Award 2015, Int. Property Award 2016, Int. Region Design Award, American Inst. of Architects 2017, Building Award for Int. Project of the Year 2018, Int.

Architecture Award 2018, Int. Brunel Award, Structural Steel Design Award, Royal Acad. of Arts Award, Architectural Inst. of Japan Award, AIA Merit Award. *Publications include:* more than 500 int. publs on architectural work, including monographs and profiles. *Leisure interests:* travel, sport, jazz, blues and opera, spending time with family. *Address:* John McAslan + Partners, 7–9 William Road, London, NW1 3ER, England (office). *Telephone:* (20) 7313-6000 (office). *Fax:* (20) 7313-6001 (office). *E-mail:* j.mcaslan@mcaslan.co.uk (office). *Website:* www.mcaslan.co.uk (office).

MacAULAY, Lawrence, PC; Canadian politician and fmr farmer; *Minister of Veterans Affairs and Associate Minister of National Defence;* b. 9 Sept. 1946, St Peter's Bay, Prince Edward Island; m. Frances Elaine O'Connell 1972; three d.; worked as seed potato and dairy farmer before entering politics; mem. House of Commons (Parl.) for Cardigan 1988–; Sec. of State for Veterans 1993–97, Official Opposition Critic for Seniors 1990–93, 2008–09, for Fisheries and Oceans 2011–15; Minister of Labour 1997–98; Solicitor Gen. of Canada 1998–2002; Minister of Agric. and Agri-Food 2015–19, Minister of Veterans Affairs and Assoc. Minister of Nat. Defence 2019–; mem. Liberal Party of Canada. *Address:* Veterans Affairs Canada, 161 Grafton Street, PO Box 7700, Charlottetown, PE C1A 8M9, Canada (office). *Telephone:* (866) 522-2122 (office). *E-mail:* information@vac-acc.gc.ca (office). *Website:* www.vac-acc.gc.ca (office).

McAULIFFE, Terence (Terry) Richard, JD; American lawyer and politician; b. 9 Feb. 1957, Syracuse, New York; m. Dorothy Swann; five c.; ed Catholic Univ. of America, Georgetown Law Center; mem. staff, Carter-Mondale Re-election Cttee; Chair. Federal City National Bank 1988; mem. Democratic Party, served in various positions including Finance Dir Democratic Nat. Cttee (DNC), Finance Dir Democratic Congressional Campaign Cttee, Nat. Finance Chair. presidential nomination campaign of Dick Gephardt 1988, Nat. Co-Chair. Presidential Campaign Clinton–Gore 1996, Co-Chair. Presidential Inaugural Cttee 1997, Chair. DNC Convention, LA 2000, Chair. DNC 2001–05; Gov. of Virginia 2014–18; Vice-Chair. Nat. Governors Association 2015–16, Chair. 2016–; cr. Hispanic Project, Women's Vote Center, Voting Rights Inst.; est. many cos in fields of banking, insurance, marketing and real estate; practising attorney. *Publication:* What a Party! My Life Among Democrats 2007.

McAVOY, James; British actor; b. 21 April 1979, Glasgow, Scotland; s. of James McAvoy and Elizabeth McAvoy; m. Anne Marie Duff 2006; ed Royal Scottish Acad. of Music and Drama; BAFTA Orange Rising Star Award 2006. *Films include:* Regeneration 1997, Bright Young Things 2003, Inside I'm Dancing 2004 (Edinburgh Int. Festival Audience Award), Wimbledon 2004, Strings 2004, The Chronicles of Narnia: The Lion, the Witch and the Wardrobe 2005, The Last King of Scotland 2006, Penelope 2006, Burns 2006, Starter for Ten 2006, Becoming Jane 2007, Atonement 2007, Wanted 2008, The Last Station 2009, The Conspirator 2010, X-Men: First Class 2011, Welcome to the Punch 2013, Trance 2013, Filth (British Independent Film Award for Best Actor) 2013, X-Men: Days of Future Past 2014, The Disappearance of Eleanor Rigby: Them 2014, Victor Frankenstein 2015, X-Men: Apocalypse 2016, Atomic Blonde 2017, Deadpool 2 2018, Glass 2019. *Television includes:* An Angel Passes By 1997, The Bill 1997, Lorna Doone 2000, Murder in Mind 2001, Band of Brothers 2001, Payment in Blood 2002, White Teeth 2002, Foyle's War 2002, Bollywood Queen 2002, Children of Dune 2003, State of Play 2003, Early Doors 2003, Shameless 2005, Macbeth 2005, Watership Down 2018. *Theatre includes:* The Reel of the Hanged Man, Edinburgh 2000, Out in the Open, Hampstead Theatre 2001, Privates On Parade, Donmar Warehouse 2001–02, Breathing Corpses, Royal Court Theatre 2005, Three Days of Rain, Apollo Theatre 2009. *Address:* United Agents, 12–26 Lexington Street, London, W1F 0LE, England (office). *Telephone:* (20) 3214-0800 (office). *Fax:* (20) 3214-0801 (office). *E-mail:* info@unitedagents.co.uk (office). *Website:* unitedagents.co.uk (office).

McBRIDE, Christian; American jazz bass player; b. 31 May 1972, Philadelphia, Pa; s. of Lee Smith; m. Melissa Walker; ed High School for the Creative and Performing Arts, Philadelphia, Juilliard School, New York; began playing electric bass aged nine, followed by acoustic bass two years later; tour to Europe with Philadelphia Youth Orchestra 1989; travelling USA with classical jazz fusion group, Free Flight 1989; played with Bobby Watson, Freddie Hubbard 1990–93, Ray Brown and Jay Clayton 1991, Benny Green, Roy Hargrove, Joshua Redman, Diana Krall, Pat Metheny 1992, Joe Henderson, D'Angelo, Kathleen Battle, Herbie Hancock, Quincy Jones, Natalie Cole and Milt Jackson; signed to Verve Records 1994; joined George Duke's band 2002; f. own groups, including Christian McBride Band; soloist; Co-Dir The Jazz Museum, Harlem 2005–; Creative Chair for Jazz, Los Angeles Philharmonic Orchestra 2005–10; mem. Heaven on Earth 2009–; Scholarship to Juilliard School, named by Rolling Stone magazine "Hot Jazz Artist" of 1992, Jazz Journalists' Asscn Award for Bassist of the Year 2013, 2015, 2016, 2017, Grammy Award for Best Improvised Jazz Solo 2016. *Commissions include:* Bluesin' in Alphabet City by Jazz at Lincoln Center, performed by Wynton Marsalis with Lincoln Center Jazz Orchestra, The Movement, Revisited by the Portland (ME) Arts Soc. and Nat. Endowment for the Arts, written and arranged for quartet and 30-piece gospel choir 1998. *Films include:* Café Society 1995, Kansas City 1996. *Recordings include:* albums: Ray Brown's Super Bass 1989, Roy Hargrove's Public Eye 1990, Kenny Kirkland 1991, Joshua Redman 1993, Fingerpainting: The Music of Herbie Hancock 1997, Introducing Joshua Redman 1999, Bobby Hutcherson's Skyline 1999, Don Braden's Fire Within 1999, Sting's All This Time (CD, DVD and tour) 2001, George Duke's Face the Music 2002, The Good Feeling (Grammy Award for Best Large Jazz Ensemble Album 2012) 2011, People Music 2013, Out Here 2013, Bringin' It (Grammy Award for Best Large Jazz Ensemble Recording 2018) 2017; with Heaven on Earth: Heaven on Earth 2009; solo albums include: Gettin' To It 1994, Number Two Express 1996, A Family Affair 1998, Sci-Fi 2000, The Philadelphia Experiment 2001, Vertical Vision (with electrical quartet) 2003, Live at Tonic 2006, Conversations with Christian 2009, Kind of Brown (with Inside Straight) 2009. *Address:* c/o Andre Guess, GuessWorks, Inc., 89 Elm Street, Montclair, NJ 07042, USA (office). *Telephone:* (212) 863-9824 (office). *Fax:* (917) 591-5216 (office). *E-mail:* andre@guessworks.org (office); info@christianmcbride.com. *Website:* www.guessworksinc.com (office); www.christianmcbride.com.

McBRIDE, Patricia Lee; American ballet dancer (retd) and dance teacher; *Associate Artistic Director, Charlotte Ballet;* b. 23 Aug. 1942, Teaneck, NJ; m. Jean-Pierre Bonnefoux; one s. one d.; ed School of American Ballet; enrolled in ballet lessons aged seven; joined New York City Ballet 1959, becoming the company's youngest prin. dancer at age 18 1961, 28 years as prin. dancer, dancing more than 100 roles; danced many roles with partners Edward Villella, Mikhail Baryshnikov and Helgi Tomasson; fmr teacher of dance, Indiana Univ.; numerous roles created for her by George Balanchine including Hermia in A Midsummer Night's Dream, Tarantella, Colombine in Harlequinade, ballerina role in Intermezzo of Brahms–Schoenberg Quartet, Rubies, Who Cares?, Divertimento from Le Baiser de la Fée, Swanilda in Coppélia, Pavane, paper ballerina in The Steadfast Tin Soldier, Pearly Queen in Union Jack; joined North Carolina Dance Theatre (now Charlotte Ballet) 1996, currently Assoc. Artistic Dir and Master Teacher; Arts and Science Council Honors Lifetime Achievement Award in the Field of Arts (with Jean-Pierre Bonnefoux) 2008, Kennedy Center Honor 2014. *Address:* Charlotte Ballet, 701 North Tryon Street, Charlotte, NC 28202, USA (office). *Telephone:* (704) 372-3900 (office). *Website:* charlotteballet.org (office).

McBRIDE, William James (Willie-John), MBE; British fmr bank manager and fmr rugby union player; b. 6 June 1940, Toomebridge, Northern Ireland; s. of William James McBride and Irene Patterson; m. Penny Michael 1966; one s. one d.; ed Ballymena Acad.; first played rugby for Ireland against England 1962; six Lions tours of South Africa 1962, NZ 1966, South Africa 1968, NZ 1971, South Africa 1974, Capt. unbeaten Lions 1974, Man. Lions in NZ 1983; holder of 63 int. caps; 17 Test appearances for Lions (record); toured Australia 1967 and Argentina 1970 for Ireland; fmr Bank Man.; Pres. Ballymena Rugby Football Club; Pres. Wooden Spoon Soc. (Ulster); Vice-Pres. Northern Ireland Riding for Disabled; Freeman, Borough of Newtownabbey; inducted into Int. Rugby Hall of Fame 1997, Rugby Personality of the Century 2004; Dr hc (Nat. Univ. of Ireland) 2004. *Leisure interests:* golf, gardening, after-dinner speaking. *Address:* Gorse Lodge, 105 Ballycorr Road, Ballyclare, Co. Antrim, BT39 9DE, Northern Ireland. *Telephone:* (28) 9335-2710. *Fax:* (28) 9335-2710.

McCABE, Eamonn Patrick; British photographer; b. 28 July 1948; s. of James McCabe and Celia McCabe; m. 1st Ruth Calvert 1972 (divorced 1993); one s.; m. 2nd Rebecca Smithers 1997; one d.; ed Challoner School, Finchley and San Francisco State Coll., USA; began career as photographer with Physics Dept, Imperial Coll., London; fmr freelance photographer for local papers and The Guardian for one year; staff photographer, The Observer 1977–86, 1987–88; Official Photographer, Pope's Visit to Britain 1982; Picture Ed. Sportsweek 1986–87, The Guardian 1988–2001; freelance photographer 2001–; Dir, Newscast 2001–, Fairfield House Gardens Man. Co. Ltd; Fellow in Photography, Nat. Museum of Photography and TV, Bradford 1988; Hon. Prof., Thames Valley Univ. 1994; Sports Photographer of the Year, Royal Photographic Soc. and Sports Council 1978, 1979, 1981, 1984, News Photographer of the Year, British Press Awards 1985, Picture Ed. of the Year, Nikon Press Awards (six times from 1992). *Publications:* Sports Photographer 1981, Eamonn McCabe, Photographer 1987, Emerald Gems of Ireland 2001, Making of Great Photographs 2005, Artists and Their Studios 2008. *Leisure interests:* playing tennis, squash, cinema. *Telephone:* (20) 3137-9137 (office). *E-mail:* photo@newscast.co.uk (office). *Website:* www.newscast.co.uk (office).

McCAFFREY, Gen. (retd) Barry R., MA; American army officer (retd), academic, news analyst and consultant; *President, BR McCaffrey Associates LLC;* b. 17 Nov. 1942, Taunton, Mass.; m. Jill Ann Faulkner 1964; one s. two d.; ed Phillips Acad., Mass, US Mil. Acad., American Univ., Harvard Univ., Western Behavioral Science Inst., Nat. Defense Univ., Command and Gen. Staff Coll., Army War Coll.; commissioned into US Army 1964, served in Viet Nam 1966–67, 1968–69; Asst Prof. of Social Sciences, Dept of Social Sciences, US Mil. Acad. 1972–75; 3rd Infantry Div., Germany 1979–83, Div. Chief of Staff 9th Infantry Div. 1982–86, Asst Commandant US Army Infantry School 1986–88, US Deputy Mil. Rep. to NATO 1988–89, Prin. Staff Asst to Chair. of Jt Chiefs of Staff, Chief of Strategic Planning 1989–90, 24th Infantry Div. 1990–92, led div. into Iraq in Operation Desert Storm 1991, C-in-C US Armed Forces Southern Command 1994–96, at retirement youngest four-star Gen. in Army and most highly decorated combat officer; Dir White House Office of Nat. Drug Control Policy 1996–2001; Bradley Distinguished Prof. of Int. Security Studies, US Mil. Acad. 2001–05, Adjunct Prof. of Int. Security Studies 2005–10; fmr mem. prin. negotiation team START II Nuclear Arms Control Treaty; mem. Nat. Security Council, Council on Foreign Relations, Nat. Asscn for Advancement of Colored People; Pres. B. R. McCaffrey Associates; currently NBC News analyst on terrorism; decorations from France, Brazil, Argentina, Colombia, Peru, and Venezuela; Distinguished Service Cross (twice), Silver Star (twice), Distinguished Service Medal, Combat Infantry Badge, US Health and Human Services Lifetime Achievement Award For Extraordinary Achievement in the Field of Substance Abuse Prevention 2004, US Dept of State Superior Honor Award for the Strategic Arms Limitation Talks, US Coast Guard Distinguished Public Service Award, NAACP Roy Wilkins Renown Service Award 1991, Norman E. Zinberg Award of the Harvard Medical School 1997, James Cardinal Gibbons Medal (Highest Honor), Catholic Univ. of America 2004, Federal Law Enforcement Foundation Nat. Service Award 2000, CIA Great Seal Medallion 2000, Community Anti-Drug Coalitions of America Lifetime Achievement Award 2000, Nat. Leadership Award by Community Anti-Drug Coalitions of America 2007, Golden Eagle, Soc. of American Mil. Engineers (SAME) 2007, inducted into US Army Ranger Hall of Fame 2007, American Red Cross Lifetime of Achievement Award 2008, Air Force Asscn W. Stuart Symington Award 2008, J Dennis Hastert Lifetime Achievement Award, Nat. Narcotics Officers Asscn 2009, Distinguished Grad., West Point Asscn of Graduates, US Mil. Acad. 2010, Footsie Britt Award, Soc. of the 30th Infantry Regiment 2010, Extraordinary Leadership and Service in Homeland Security Award, Government Security News 2010. *Publications:* Proceedings of the Twenty-Fifth Student Conference on United States Affairs 1973, We Are Soldiers All: An Analysis of Possible Roles for Women in the Army 1973, numerous articles on mil. subjects, drugs law enforcement and money laundering. *Leisure interests:* hunting, reading military history. *Address:* BR McCaffrey Associates LLC, 211 North Union Street, Suite 100, Arlington, VA 22314, USA (office). *Telephone:* (703) 519-1250 (office). *Fax:* (703) 683-4707 (office). *E-mail:* brm@mccaffreyassociates.com (office). *Website:* www.mccaffreyassociates.com (office).

McCALL, Dame Carolyn Julia, DBE, OBE, BA, MA; British business executive; *CEO, ITV plc;* b. 13 Sept. 1961, Bangalore, India; m.; three c.; ed Univs of Kent and London; teacher, Holland Park School 1982–84; Risk Analyst, Costain Group PLC 1984–86; Planner, Guardian Newspapers Ltd (GNL) 1986–88, Advertisement Exec. 1988–89, Advertisement Man. 1989–91, Product Devt Man. 1991–92, Display Advertisement Man. 1992, Advertisement Dir Wired UK 1992–94, Deputy Advertisement Dir 1994–95, Advertisement Dir 1995–97, Commercial Dir 1997–98 (with responsibility for internet strategy – launched Guardian Unlimited 1999), Deputy Man. Dir 1998–2000, CEO of GNL 2000–06, and mem. Bd of Dirs Guardian Media Group PLC (GMG) 2000–10, Chief Exec. GMG 2006–10; CEO easyJet plc 2010–18; CEO ITV plc (first female) 2018–; Dir (non-exec.), New Look Group PLC 1999–2005, Tesco PLC 2005–08, Lloyds TSB 2008–09; Chair. Opportunity Now (gender equality and diversity org.) 2005–08; UK Business Amb. 2014–; fmr Pres. Women in Advertising and Communications London; Trustee, Tools for Schools (educational charity) 2000–05; Hon. DSc (Cranfield) 2014; Veuve Clicquot Business Woman of the Year 2008. *Address:* ITV plc, The London Television Centre, Upper Ground, London, SE1 9LT, England (office). *Website:* www.itvplc.com (office).

McCALL SMITH, Alexander, CBE; British writer and academic; *Professor Emeritus of Medical Law, University of Edinburgh;* b. 1948, Southern Rhodesia (now Zimbabwe); m. Elizabeth Parry; two d.; currently Emer. Prof. of Medical Law, Univ. of Edinburgh; fmr mem. Human Genetics Comm. (fmr Vice-Chair.), UNESCO Int. Bioethics Comm., British Medical Journal Ethics Cttee (fmr Chair.), Roslin Inst. Ethics Cttee (fmr Chair.); Hon. DIur (Edinburgh) 2007; British Book Awards Author of the Year 2004, Booksellers' Asscn Author of the Year 2004, Waterstones Author of the Year 2004. *Publications:* fiction: The No. 1 Ladies' Detective Agency 1998, Tears of the Giraffe 2000, Morality for Beautiful Girls 2001, The Kalahari Typing School for Men 2002, The Full Cupboard of Life (Saga Award for Wit) 2003, At the Villa of Reduced Circumstances 2003, Portuguese Irregular Verbs 2003, In the Company of Cheerful Ladies 2004, 44 Scotland Street (serialized in The Scotsman) 2004, The Sunday Philosophy Club 2004, The 2½ Pillars of Wisdom 2004, Friends, Lovers, Chocolate 2005, Blue Shoes and Happiness 2006, Dream Angus: The Celtic God of Dreams 2006, Love Over Scotland 2007, The World According to Bertie 2007, The Right Attitude to Rain 2007, The Careful Use of Compliments 2007, The Miracle at Speedy Motors 2008, Corduroy Mansions 2008, Tea Time for the Traditionally Built 2009, The Unbearable Lightness of Scones 2009, La's Orchestra Saves the World 2009, The Comfort of Saturdays 2009, The Lost Art of Gratitude 2010, The Double Comfort Safari Club 2010, The Charming Quirks of Others 2010, The Forgotten Affairs of Youth 2011, The Dog Who Came in From the Cold 2012, The Great Cake Mystery 2012, The Limpopo Academy of Private Detection 2012, Fatty O'Leary's Dinner Party (Bollinger Everyman Wodehouse Prize 2015) 2014, Emma: A Modern Retelling 2015, My Italian Bulldozer 2016; non-fiction: Law and Medical Ethics (with J. K. Mason) 1983, The Duty to Rescue: The Jurisprudence of Aid (with Michael A. Menlowe) 1993, Forensic Aspects of Sleep (with C. Shapiro) 1997, Justice and the Prosecution of Old Crimes: Balancing Legal, Psychological, and Moral Concerns (with Daniel W. Shuman) 2000, The Criminal Law of Botswana, A Work of Beauty: Alexander McCall Smith's Edinburgh 2014; children's fiction includes: White Hippo 1980, The Perfect Hamburger 1982, Jeffrey's Joke Machine 1990, The Five Lost Aunts of Harriet Bean 1990, Marzipan Max 1991, Uncle Gangster 1991, The Spaghetti Tangle 1992, Harriet Bean and the League of Cheats 1991, The Ice-Cream Bicycle 1992, Akimbo and the Lions 1992, The Doughnut Ring 1992, Springy Jane 1992, The Princess Trick 1992, The Cowgirl Aunt of Harriet Bean 1993, My Chameleon Uncle 1993, The Muscle Machine 1993, Paddy and the Ratcatcher 1994, The Banana Machine 1994, Akimbo and the Crocodile Man 1995, Billy Rubbish 1995, The Watermelon Boys 1996, Calculator Annie 1996, The Bubblegum Tree 1996, Bursting Balloons Mystery 1997, The Popcorn Pirates 1999, Chocolate Money Mystery 1999, Precious and the Puggles 2010; short story collections: Children of Wax: African Folk Tales 1991, Heavenly Date and Other Stories (revised edn as Heavenly Date: And Other Flirtations) 1995, The Girl Who Married a Lion (short stories) 2004, One City (contrib.) 2006. *Address:* c/o David Higham Associates, 7th Floor, Waverley House, 7–12 Noel Street, London, W1F 8GQ, England (office). *E-mail:* contact@ alexandermccallsmith.co.uk. *Website:* www.alexandermccallsmith.co.uk.

McCALLISTER, Michael (Mike) B., BA, MBA; American business executive; b. 1952, Shreveport, La; ed Pepperdine Univ., Louisiana Tech. Univ.; joined Humana Inc. 1974, various positions including finance specialist, Vice-Pres. Health Plans and Hosps, Ariz. 1989–92, Vice-Pres. Health Plans and Hosps, Tex. 1992–96, Pres. Tex., Fla and Puerto Rico Div. 1996–97, Sr Vice-Pres. Health Plan Div. 1997–99, apptd to Office of the Chair. 1999–2000, Pres. and CEO 2000–10, Chair. and CEO 2010–12, Chair. 2013; Founding Chair. World Wellness Alliance 2010–; mem. Bd Greater Louisville Health Enterprises Network, Louisville Fund for the Arts, Business Roundtable, American Asscn of Health Plans; mem. Advisory Bd Coll. of Admin and Business, Louisiana Tech. Univ.; Tower Medallion Award, Louisiana Tech. Univ. 2003. *Address:* c/o Humana Inc., 500 West Main Street, Louisville, KY 40202, USA. *E-mail:* info@humana.com.

McCALLUM, John, PC, BA, DEcon; Canadian politician, fmr professor of economics and diplomatist; b. 9 April 1950, Montréal; s. of Alexander Campbell McCallum and Joan McCallum (née Patteson); m. Nancy Lim; three s.; ed Queens' Coll., Cambridge, UK, Univ. of Paris, France, McGill Univ.; Prof. of Econs, Univ. of Manitoba 1976–78, Simon Fraser Univ. 1978–82, Univ. du Québec à Montréal 1982–87; Prof. of Econs McGill Univ. 1987–94; fmr Dean, Faculty of Arts; mem. House of Commons (Parl.) for Markham 2000–04, for Markham–Unionville 2004–15, for Markham–Thornhill 2015–17; Minister of Nat. Defence 2002–03, Minister of Veterans Affairs 2003–04, of Nat. Revenue 2004–06, of Immigration, Refugees and Citizenship 2015–17; Amb. to People's Repub. of China 2017–19; fmr Sr Vice-Pres. and Chief Economist, Royal Bank of Canada; Chair. Expenditure Review Cttee; mem. Liberal Party of Canada; Hon. mem. Royal Mil. Coll. of Canada. *Publications:* Unequal Beginnings: Agriculture and Economic Development in Quebec and Ontario until 1870 1980, Unemployment and Inflation: The Canadian Experience (with Clarence Barber) 1980, Controlling Inflation: Learning from Experience in Canada, Europe and Japan (with Clarence Barber) 1982, Parting as Friends: The Economic Consequences for Quebec 1991, Global Disequilibrium in the World Economy 1992.

McCALLUM, Martin, FRSA; British theatre producer; b. 6 April 1950, Blackpool, Lancs., England; s. of Raymond McCallum and Jessie McCallum; m. 1st Lesley Nunnerley 1971 (divorced); one s. one d.; m. 2nd Julie Edmett (divorced); one d.; m. 3rd Mary Ann Rolfe (divorced); two s.; ed Barfield School, Surrey, Frensham Heights School, Surrey; began career as student Asst Stage Man., Castle Theatre, Farnham Surrey 1967; worked as actor, stage man., lighting and sound technician; Production Man. Nat. Theatre at Old Vic (with Laurence Olivier and later Peter Hall) 1971–78, Founder Production Office West End 1978–84, productions included Filumena, Evita, Sweeney Todd; consultant to Glyndebourne Festival Opera, Arts Council's Regional Theatre Scheme; Man. Dir Cameron Mackintosh Ltd 1981–2000, Vice-Chair. 2000–03; Dir Donmar Warehouse Theatre 1992–2006, Chair. 1996–2004; initiated Wyndham Report 1998; est. New Writing Symposium 1999; Pres. Soc. of London Theatre 1999–2002; initiated inaugural jt Theatre Conf. of SOLT/TMA/ITC Theatre 2001 Future Directions; mem. League of American Theatres and Producers 1988–2010, Drama Panel, Arts Council of England 1999–2004, Cultural Strategy Group London 2000–04; mem. V&A Theatre Museum Cttee 1999–2004; consultant on design projects including Old Fire Station Theatre, Oxford (new build), Prince Edward Theatre (restoration) 1993, Musical Hall, Stuttgart (new build) 1994, Capital Theatre, Sydney (restoration) 1995, Musical Theatre, Duisberg (new build) 1996, Theatre Royal, Sydney (restoration) 1998, Wales Millennium Centre, Lyric Theatre (new build study) 1998, Auditorium Theatre, Chicago (restoration) 2001, Schaumburg Village Theatre, Illinois (new build) 2003, Fine Arts Building Theatre, Chicago (restoration study) 2003, Prince of Wales Theatre, London (restoration) 2003, Montecasino Theatre, Johannesburg, SA 2007 (new build scheme); Dir Sydney Theatre Co. 2005–; Co-Producer Matthew Bourne's dance production of Edward Scissorhands, London 2005, The Cripple of Inishmaan, Broadway 2014, Hughie, Broadway 2016; Exec. Producer Spider-Man Broadway 2010; Producer Dirty Dancing, Australia 2015; New York Drama Desk Award 2007. *Leisure interests:* performing arts, music, art, gardens. *Telephone:* 401-279464 (mobile) (office). *E-mail:* martin@ sunriseroad.com (office).

McCANN, Renetta, BS; American advertising executive; *Chief Talent Officer (US), Leo Burnett Group;* b. 8 Dec. 1956, Chicago, Ill.; d. of Aditha Lorraine Collymore Walker; m.; two c.; ed Aquinas Dominican High School and Northwestern Univ.; joined Leo Burnett advertising agency as client service trainee 1978–79, Media Supervisor 1979–88, Vice-Pres. 1988–89, Media Dir 1989–95, Sr Vice-Pres. 1995–98, Man. Dir Starcom 1998, CEO Starcom MediaVest Group Americas (following merger with D'Arcy) –2005, CEO Starcom MediaVest Group Worldwide 2005–08, Head of Talent Devt Platform, VivaKi (subsidiary of Publicis Groupe) 2008, Chief Talent Officer (US), Leo Burnett Group 2012–; mem. Bd of Dirs Chicago Shakespeare Theater 2011–, Women's Initiative 2011–; mem. Advisory Bd Genius in Motion 2011–, Center for Excellence in Advertising 2011–; Trustee, Ancona School 2011; winner of numerous Effies and Cannes Lions, chosen as 'Media Maven' by Advertising Age 1991, selected as one of Ebony magazine's 57 Most Intriguing Blacks, named by Black Enterprise as Executive of the Year 2002, selected by Women's Advertising Club of Chicago as Advertising Woman of the Year 2002. *Address:* Leo Burnett Group, 35 West Wacker Drive, Chicago, IL, 60601, USA. *Telephone:* (312) 220-5959 (office). *Website:* www .leoburnett.us/chicago (office).

McCARRICK, Theodore Edgar, BA, MA, DD, PhD; American fmr ecclesiastic; b. 7 July 1930, New York City; s. of Theodore Egan McCarrick and Margaret McCarrick (née McLaughlin); ed Fordham Univ., St Joseph's Seminary, Yonkers, New York, Catholic Univ. of America; ordained priest 1958; served as an Asst Chaplain, Catholic Univ. of America, later Dean of Students and Dir of Devt 1963–65, Chancellor 2001–06; Pres. Catholic Univ. of Puerto Rico 1965–69; rank of Domestic Prelate of HH 1965; Assoc. Sec. for Educ. and Asst Priest, Blessed Sacrament Parish 1969–71; Sec. to Cardinal Terence Cooke 1971–77; Auxiliary Bishop of New York and Titular Bishop of Rusibisir 1977–81; Bishop of Metuchen 1981–86; Archbishop of Newark 1986–2000; Archbishop of Washington 2001–06, Archbishop Emer. 2006–18; cr. Cardinal (Cardinal-Priest of Santi Nereo ed Achilleo) 2001–18; mem. Pontifical Council for Promoting Christian Unity, Pontifical Council for Justice and Peace, Pontifical Council for the Pastoral Care of Migrants and Itinerant Peoples, Pontifical Comm. for Latin America and the Admin of the Patrimony of the Holy See; Head, Cttee on Migration, US Conf. of Catholic Bishops 1986, 1992, Cttee for Aid to the Church in Cen. and Eastern Europe 1992; Chair. Cttee on Int. Policy 1996, Domestic Policy Cttee 2001; mem. US Sec. of State's Advisory Cttee on Religious Freedom Abroad 1996–99, US Comm. for Int. Religious Freedom 1999–2001; mem. Bd, Catholic Relief Services; Pres. Papal Foundation 1997–; Pres. Bd of Trustees, Basilica of the Nat. Shrine of the Immaculate Conception 2001–06; Counsellor, Center for Strategic and Int. Studies 2007–; Distinguished Visiting Scholar, Library of Congress 2011–; laicized after church trial found him guilty of sexually abusing minors 2019; Order of Cedars of Lebanon 2000; 35 hon. degrees 1976–2010; Eleanor Roosevelt Award for Human Rights 2000.

McCARTHY, Sir Callum, Kt, MA, MS, PhD; British civil servant, economist and banker; *Non-Director Chairman, Promontory Financial Group (UK) Limited;* b. 29 Feb. 1944, Brentwood, Essex, England; s. of Ralph McCarthy and Agnes Graham; m. Penelope Ann Gee 1966; two s. one d.; ed Univs of Oxford and Stirling, Business School, Stanford Univ., USA; econ. and operations researcher ICI 1965; Prin. Pvt. Sec. to Roy Hattersley (q.v.) and Norman Tebbit (q.v.), Dept of Trade and Industry 1972–85, also Under-Sec.; Dir of Corp. Finance, Kleinwort Benson 1985–89; Man. Dir, Head of Corp. Finance, BZW 1989–93; CEO Barclays Bank Group Japan and N America 1993–98; Dir-Gen. of UK Gas Supply 1998–2003; Dir-Gen. of UK Electricity Supply 1999–2003; Chair. Gas and Electricity Markets Authority 2000–03; Chief Exec. Ofgem 2000–03; Chair. Financial Services Authority 2003–08; currently Chair. (non-dir) Promontory Financial Group (UK) Ltd; Chair. (non-exec.) Castle Trust; mem. Bd of Dirs, HM Treasury 2008, Industrial and Commercial Bank of China; Sloan Fellow, Grad. School of Business, Stanford Univ., Intercontinental Exchange; Hon. Fellow, Merton Coll., Oxford 2006; Freeman, City of London 2008; Dr hc (Stirling) 2004. *Publication:* Introduction to Technological Economics (with D. S. Davies) 1967. *Leisure interests:* walking, reading, bee-keeping. *Address:* Promontory Financial Group, LLC, 801 17th Street, NW, Suite 1100, Washington, DC 20006, USA (office). *Telephone:* (20) 7997-

3403 (office). *E-mail:* cmccarthy@promontory.com (office). *Website:* www.promontory.co.uk (office).

McCARTHY, Cormac; American writer; b. 20 July 1933, Rhode Island; s. of Charles Joseph McCarthy and Gladys McGrail; m. 1st Lee Holleman 1961 (divorced 1962); one s.; m. 2nd Annie DeLisle 1967 (divorced 1981); m. 3rd Jennifer Winkley 1997 (divorced 2006); ed Univ. of Tennessee; served in USAF 1953–57; Guggenheim Fellowship 1969; MacArthur Fellowship 1981; Rockefeller Fellowship; PEN/Saul Bellow Award for Lifetime Achievement 2009. *Plays:* The Stonemason 1994, The Sunset Limited 2006. *Screenplays:* The Gardener's Son 1996, The Counselor 2013. *Publications:* novels: The Orchard Keeper 1965, Outer Dark 1968, Child of God 1973, Suttree 1979, Blood Meridian 1985, All the Pretty Horses (Vol. 1 of The Border Trilogy) (Nat. Book Award for Fiction 1992, Nat. Book Critics Circle Award 1992) 1992, The Crossing (Vol. 2 of The Border Trilogy) 1994, Cities of the Plain (Vol. 3 of The Border Trilogy) 1998, No Country for Old Men 2005, The Road (James Tait Black Memorial Prize for Fiction 2007, Pulitzer Prize for Fiction 2007, Quill Award for General Fiction 2007) 2006. *Address:* c/o Amanda Urban, International Creative Management, 730 Fifth Avenue, New York, NY 10019, USA (office); c/o Santa Fe Institute, 1399 Hyde Park Road, Santa Fe, NM 87501, USA. *Telephone:* (212) 556-5600 (office). *Website:* www.cormacmccarthy.com.

McCARTHY, Gina, BA, MS; American government official; b. 3 May 1954, Boston, Mass; m. Kenneth McCarey; one s. two d.; ed Univ. of Massachusetts, Tufts Univ.; mem. Hazardous Waste Facility Site Safety Council, Mass Exec. Office of Environmental Affairs 1985–90, Council Chair. 1990–94, Exec. Dir, Admin. Council 1994–99, Asst Sec. for pollution prevention, environmental business and tech. 1999–2003, Under-Sec. for Policy 2003; Deputy Sec. for Operations, Mass Office of Commonwealth Devt 2003–04; Commr, Conn. Dept of Environmental Protection 2004–09; Asst Admin. for air and radiation, Environmental Protection Agency (EPA), Washington, DC 2009–13, Admin., EPA 2013–17; Chair. The Climate Registry.

McCARTHY, James J., BS, PhD; American oceanographer and academic; *Professor of Biological Oceanography and Alexander Agassiz Professor of Biological Oceanography, Harvard University;* ed Gonzaga Univ., Scripps Inst. of Oceanography; Dir Museum of Comparative Zoology, Harvard Univ. 1982–2002, Acting Curator Malacology Dept, currently Prof. of Biological Oceanography and Alexander Agassiz Prof. of Biological Oceanography, holds faculty appointments in Dept of Organismic and Evolutionary Biology and Dept of Earth and Planetary Sciences, Head Tutor for degrees in Environmental Science and Public Policy, Master of Pforzheimer House; Chair. Int. Cttee that establishes research priorities and oversees implementation of Int. Geosphere-Biosphere Program 1986–93; has served and serves on numerous nat. and int. planning cttees, advisory panels and comms relating to oceanography, polar science and study of climate and global change; involved in two int. assessments on climate impacts; Co-Chair. Intergovernmental Panel on Climate Change (IPCC), Working Group II, for Third IPCC Assessment 2001; a lead author on Arctic Climate Impact Assessment; Vice-Chair. Northeast Climate Impacts Assessment 2007; fmr Chair. Union of Concerned Scientists, now Chair. Emer.; mem. US Arctic Research Comm. 2012–; Founding Ed. American Geophysical Union's Global Biogeochemical Cycles 1986–89; Fellow, AAAS (Pres. 2008–09), American Acad. of Arts and Sciences; Foreign mem. Royal Swedish Acad. of Sciences; Tyler Prize for Environmental Achievement 2018, David B. Stone Award, New England Aquarium, Museum of Science Walker Prize. *Publications:* numerous scientific papers in professional journals on the regulation of plankton productivity in the sea. *Address:* 503 MCZ Labs, Museum of Comparative Zoology, Harvard University, 26 Oxford Street, Cambridge, MA 02138, USA (office). *Telephone:* (617) 495-2330 (office). *Fax:* (617) 496-4079 (office). *E-mail:* jmccarthy@oeb.harvard.edu (office). *Website:* mccarthylab.oeb.harvard.edu (office).

McCARTHY, John Philip, AO, MA, LLB; Australian lawyer and diplomatist; b. 29 Nov. 1942, Washington, DC, USA; s. of Edwin McCarthy and Marjorie McCarthy; two d.; ed Univ. of Cambridge, UK; practised as barrister in London, UK 1965–66; with Shearman and Sterling (law firm), New York, USA 1966–67; joined Dept of Foreign Affairs 1968; Second Sec., Vientiane 1969–72; First Sec., Washington, DC 1973–75; Chargé d'affaires a.i., Damascus 1977–78; Sr Pvt. Sec. to Minister for Foreign Affairs 1979–80; Amb. to Viet Nam 1981–83, to Mexico 1985–87, to Thailand 1992–94, to USA 1995–97, to Indonesia 1997–2000, to Japan 2001–05; High Commr in India and Amb. to Bhutan 2005–09, Special Rep. to Sri Lanka 2010; Deputy Sec. Dept of Foreign Affairs and Trade, Canberra 1994–95; Fellow, Australian Inst. of Int. Affairs 2009, Nat. Pres. 2010–15. *Leisure interests:* skiing, Asian art, walking, travel.

McCARTHY, Paul, BFA, MFA; American artist; b. 4 Aug. 1945, Salt Lake City, Utah; ed Univ. of Utah, San Francisco Art Inst., Univ. of Southern California; early work includes series of black paintings 1967–68; became known for visceral performances and film works 1970s; extended practice into stand-alone sculptural figures, installations and a series of large, inflatable sculptures 1990s; Tate Gallery Modern commissioned outdoor inflatable sculptures for North Landscape, London 2003. *Works include:* Blockhead, Tate Modern 2003, Daddies Bighead, Tate Modern 2003. *Solo exhibitions include:* Museum of Contemporary Art, LA 2000, Retrospective, New Museum of Contemporary Art, New York 2001, Villa Arson (France) 2001, Tate Liverpool (UK) 2001, Stor retrospektiv, Museet for Samtidskunst, Oslo (Norway) 2003, Inaugural Show, Hauser & Wirth, London (UK) 2003, Herzliya Museum of Art, Herzeliyya (Israel) 2004, Brain Box Dream Box, Stedelijk Van Abbemuseum (Netherlands) 2004, Moderna Museet, Stockholm 2006, Stedelijk Museum voor Actuele Kunst, Ghent, Belgium 2007, Whitney Museum of American Art, New York 2008, Hauser & Wirth, New York 2009, 2011, 2013, Fondazione Nicola Trussardi, Milan 2010, Kukje Gallery, Seoul 2012, Galleri F15, Moss, Norway 2014, Schinkel Pavillon, Berlin 2015, Henry Art Gallery, Seattle 2016. *Group exhibitions include:* Stunt Videos, Tennis Palace City Art Museum, Helsinki (Finland) 2003, Spiritus, Magasin 3 Stockholm Konsthall (Sweden) 2003, Apparation, Kettle's Yard, Cambridge (UK) 2003, Spiritus, Douglas Hyde Gallery, Dublin (Ireland) 2003, Twilight, Gimpel Fils, London 2003, Sphere, Presentation House Gallery, Vancouver (Canada) 2003, From East to West, Gas Art Gallery, Torino (Italy) 2003, C'est arrive demain, Musée d'Art Contemporain, Lyon (France) 2004, Spiritus, Sundsvalls Museum, (Sweden) 2004, Partners, Haus der Kunst, Munich (Germany) 2004, Playlist, Palais de Tokyo, Paris (France) 2004, Point of View, Museum of Contemporary Art, New York 2004, Speaking with Hands, Guggenheim New York 2004, I am the Walrus, Chelm & Reid, New York 2004, Monument to Now, Deste Foundation Centre for Contemporary Art, Athina 2004, Wattis Inst. for Contemporary Arts, San Francisco 2009. *Address:* c/o Hauser & Wirth, 32 East 69th Street, New York, NY 10021, USA. *Telephone:* (212) 794-4970. *Fax:* (212) 794-4971. *E-mail:* newyork@hauserwirth.com. *Website:* www.hauserwirth.com/artists/20/paul-mccarthy/biography/#top.

McCARTNEY, Rt Hon. Ian; British fmr politician; b. 25 April 1951; s. of Hugh McCartney; m. 1st Jean McCartney (divorced); two d. one s. (deceased); m. 2nd Ann Parkes; joined Labour Party 1966, Labour Party Organizer 1973–87; Councillor for Wigan Borough 1982–87; MP (Labour) for Makerfield 1987–2010; Opposition Spokesperson on NHS (Nat. Health Service) 1992–94, on Employment 1994–96, Chief Spokesperson on Employment 1996–97; Minister of State Dept of Trade and Industry 1997–99, Cabinet Office 1999–2001; Minister for Pensions Dept for Work and Pensions 2001–03; Minister without Portfolio, Chair. Labour Party 2003–06; Minister for Trade, FCO and Dept of Trade and Industry 2006–07; Minister to Watch, Spectator Awards 1999. *Leisure interest:* Rugby League (supports Wigan Warriors). *E-mail:* ianmccartney@1makerfield.freeserve.co.uk.

McCARTNEY, Sir (James) Paul, Kt, CH, MBE, FRCM; British singer, songwriter and musician (guitar, bass, piano, organ); b. 18 June 1942, Liverpool; s. of James McCartney and Mary McCartney; m. 1st Linda Eastman 1969 (died 1998); one s. two d. one step-d.; m. 2nd Heather Mills 2002 (divorced 2008); one d.; m. 3rd Nancy Shevell 2011; ed Stockton Wood Road Primary School, Speke, Joseph Williams Primary School, Gateacre and Liverpool Inst.; wrote first song 1956, wrote numerous songs with John Lennon; joined pop group The Quarrymen 1956; appeared under various titles until formation of The Beatles 1960; appeared with The Beatles for performances in Hamburg 1960, 1961, 1962, The Cavern, Liverpool 1960, 1961; worldwide tours 1963–66; attended Transcendental Meditation Course at Maharishi's Acad., Rishikesh, India Feb. 1968; formed Apple Ltd, parent org. of The Beatles Group of Cos 1968; left The Beatles after collapse of Apple Corpn Ltd 1970; formed MPL Group of Cos 1970; first solo album McCartney 1970; formed own pop group Wings 1971–81, tours of Britain and Europe 1972–73, UK and Australia 1975, Europe and USA 1976, UK 1979, World Tour 1989–90, World Tour 1993, US Tour 2002, World Tour 2003, European Tour 2004, US Tour 2005, US and European Tours 2009, World Tour 2010–11, World Tour 2011–12, World Tour 2013–15; also records as The Fireman, dance music duo with Youth 1994–; numerous collaborations including Elvis Costello, Dave Grohl and Krist Novoselic, Michael Jackson, Rihanna, Kanye West, Stevie Wonder; solo performances at Party at the Palace, Buckingham Palace 2002, Opening Ceremony, Summer Olympic Games, London 2012; Fellow, British Acad. of Composers and Songwriters 2000; Freeman of the City of Liverpool 1984, Hon. Fellow, Liverpool John Moores Univ. 1998; Dr hc (Sussex) 1988, Hon. DMus (Yale) 2008; two Grammy Awards for Band on the Run (including Best Pop Vocal Performance) 1975, Ivor Novello Award for Best Selling British Record 1977–78 for single Mull of Kintyre, for Int. Hit of the Year 1982 for single Ebony and Ivory, for Outstanding Services to British Music 1989, Guinness Book of Records Triple Superlative Award (43 songs each selling more than 1m copies, holder of 60 gold discs, estimated sales of 100m albums and 100m singles) 1979, Lifetime Achievement Award 1990, Polar Music Prize 1992, Lifetime Achievement Award People for the Ethical Treatment of Animals (with Linda McCartney) 1996, Radio Acad. Lifetime Achievement Award 2007, Q Icon Award 2007, BRIT Award for Outstanding Contribution to Music 2008, ASCAP Award for Songwriter of the Year 2009, Gershwin Prize for Popular Song, US Library of Congress 2010, Kennedy Center Honor 2010, Grammy Award for Best Rock Song (for Cut Me Some Slack, with Dave Grohl, Krist Novoselic and Pat Smear) 2014, Wolf Prize for Music 2018. *Recordings include:* albums: with The Beatles: Please Please Me 1963, A Hard Day's Night 1964, Beatles for Sale 1965, Help! 1965, Rubber Soul 1966, Revolver 1966, Sgt Pepper's Lonely Hearts Club Band 1967, Magical Mystery Tour 1967, The Beatles (White Album) 1968, Yellow Submarine 1969, Abbey Road 1969, Let It Be 1970, 1962–1966 (Red Album) 1973, 1967–1970 (Blue Album) 1973, Past Masters Vol. One 1988, Past Masters Vol. Two 1988, The Beatles Anthology: 1 1995, The Beatles Anthology: 2 1996, The Beatles Anthology: 3 1996, 1 2000; with Wings: Wild Life 1971, Red Rose Speedway 1973, Band On The Run (Grammy Award for Best Historical Album 2012) 1973, Venus and Mars 1975, Wings at the Speed of Sound 1976, Wings Over America 1976, London Town 1978, Wings Greatest 1978, Back To The Egg 1979, Wingspan 2001; solo: McCartney 1970, Ram 1971, McCartney II 1980, Tug of War 1982, Pipes of Peace 1983, Give My Regards to Broad Street 1984, Press To Play 1986, All the Best! 1987, CHOBA B CCCP 1988, Flowers in the Dirt 1989, Tripping the Live Fantastic 1990, Unplugged: The Official Bootleg 1991, Paul McCartney's Liverpool Oratorio (with Carl Davis) 1991, Off the Ground 1993, Paul is Live 1993, Flaming Pie 1997, Standing Stone (symphonic work) 1997, Run Devil Run 1999, Working Classical 1999, A Garland for Linda (with eight other composers for a cappella choir) 2000, Driving Rain 2001, Back in the US: Live 2002, Back in the World 2003, Chaos and Creation in the Back Yard 2005, Ecce Cor Meum (classical) (Classical BRIT Award for Best Album 2007) 2006, Memory Almost Full 2007, Kisses on the Bottom (Best Traditional Pop Vocal Album 2013) 2012, New 2013, Egypt Station 2018; with The Fireman: Strawberries Oceans Ships Forest 1994, Rushes 1998, Electric Arguments 2008; film soundtracks: The Family Way 1966, James Paul McCartney 1973, Live and Let Die 1973, The Zoo Gang (TV series) 1973. *Ballet:* Ocean's Kingdom (orchestral score, written for the New York City Ballet) 2011. *Films:* A Hard Day's Night 1964, Help! 1965, Magical Mystery Tour (TV film) 1967, Yellow Submarine (animated colour cartoon film) 1968, Let it Be 1970, Wings Over the World (TV) 1979, Rockshow 1981, Give My Regards to Broad Street (wrote and directed) 1984, Rupert and the Frog Song (wrote and produced) (BAFTA Award Best Animated Film) 1985, Press to Play 1986, Get Back (concert film) 1991, Live Kisses (concert film) (Grammy Award for Best Music Film 2014) 2012. *Publications include:* Paintings 2000, The Beatles Anthology (with George Harrison and Ringo Starr) 2000, Sun Prints (with Linda McCartney) 2001, Many Years From Now (autobiography) 2001, Blackbird Singing: Poems and Lyrics 1965–1999 2001, High in the Clouds (juvenile, with Philip Ardagh and Geoff Dunbar) 2005. *Address:* c/o MPL Communications Ltd, 1 Soho Square, London, W1D 3BQ, England (office). *Website:* www.paulmccartney.com.

McCARTNEY, Stella, OBE, BA; British fashion designer; b. (Stella Nina McCartney), 13 Sept. 1971, Lambeth, London, England; d. of Sir Paul McCartney (q.v.) and Linda McCartney; m. Alasdhair Willis 2003; two s. one d.; ed Bexhill Coll., Central St Martin's Coll. of Art and Design; work with Christian Lacroix at age 15 and later with Betty Jackson; work experience in Fashion Dept, Vogue magazine; set up own clothing line, London 1995; Creative Dir Chloe, Paris 1997–2001; designed collection for Gucci 2001; est. own fashion house, in partnership with Gucci Group 2001–; launched first perfume, Stella 2003; designed costumes for film Sky Captain and the World of Tomorrow 2004; designed clothes for Madonna's Re-Invention Tour, Annie Lennox's summer tour 2004; launched a skincare line, CARE 2007; designed sportswear ranges for Adidas 2007–; launched a new lingerie line 2008; Stella McCartney Kids collection launched 2010; apptd Team GB's Creative Dir for the 2012 Olympics by Adidas 2010; designed costumes for the New York City Ballet's Ocean's Kingdom which premiered in New York 2011; VH1/Vogue Fashion and Music Designer of the Year 2000, Woman of Courage Award 2003, Glamour Award for Best Designer of the Year 2004, Designer of the Year, British Fashion Awards 2007, Glamour magazine Woman of the Year 2009, Red Carpet Award, British Fashion Council 2011. *Address:* Peake House, 92 Golborne Road, London, W10 5PS, England (office). *Telephone:* (20) 7518-3111. *Fax:* (20) 7518-3112. *E-mail:* press@stellamccartney.com. *Website:* www.stellamccartney.com (office).

McCASKILL, Claire, BS; American lawyer and politician; b. 24 July 1953, Rolla, Mo.; d. of William Y. McCaskill and Betty Anne McCaskill; m. 1st David Exposito (divorced 1995); one s. two d.; m. 2nd Joseph Shepard 2002; four step-c.; ed Hickman High School, Columbia, Univ. of Missouri-Columbia; worked in public sector 1978–; spent one year as a law clerk on Mo. Court of Appeals for Western Dist, Kansas City; fmr Asst Prosecutor, Jackson Co. Prosecutor's office, specializing in arson cases; attorney in pvt. practice 1989–91; mem. Mo. House of Reps for Brookside neighbourhood of Kansas City 1983–88; elected to Jackson Co. Legislature 1990–92; Jackson Co. Prosecutor (first woman) 1993–98; State Auditor 1999–2006; defeated Gov. Bob Holden in Democratic primary race 2004 (first person to defeat an incumbent gov. in state history); Senator from Missouri 2007–19; Ranking mem. Senate Cttee on Homeland Security and Governmental Affairs 2017–; mem. Armed Services, Commerce, Homeland Security Cttee, Indian Affairs Cttee, Special Cttee on Aging; Democrat. *Address:* c/o United States Senate, Washington, DC 20510, USA (office).

McCAW, Richard (Richie) Hugh, ONZ; New Zealand professional rugby union player (retd); b. 31 Dec. 1980, Oamaru, North Otago; ed Otago Boys' High School, Dunedin, Lincoln Univ., Christchurch; plays as loose forward (openside flanker); began playing seriously at Otago Boys' High School 1994, selected in New Zealand Under 19 squad that won world championship in Wales 1999; selected in New Zealand Under 21 squad 2000, debut for Canterbury in Nat. Prov. Championship (NPC) against North Harbour 2000; plays for Canterbury 1999–, Crusaders 2001–15 (retd); Super Rugby debut with Crusaders against Hurricanes 2001; played full season with NPC champions Canterbury and captained New Zealand Under 21s; selected for New Zealand Nat. Rugby Team (All Blacks)'s end-of-year tour 2001, debut for All Blacks against Ireland (Man of the Match); selected as New Zealand's first choice open-side flanker for World Cup 2003; named Capt. of All Blacks 2006–15, led team at World Cup 2007; captained All Blacks to victory in Rugby World Cup held in NZ defeating France 8–7 in final at Eden Park, Auckland 2011, against Australia in Rugby World Cup held in England winning 34–17 in final at Twickenham 2015; captained All Blacks to win The Rugby Championship 2012, 2013 (replaced after round 3 by Kieran Read following injury), 2014; with Canterbury, won NPC (later ITM Cup) five times and with Crusaders reached Super Rugby semifinals nine times, going on to win the final on four of these occasions; with All Blacks, won ten Tri Nations/Rugby Championship titles, completed three successful Grand Slam tours and won Bledisloe Cup eight times; played his 100th Super Rugby game, made a record-equalling 94th test appearance for NZ and became most capped All Blacks capt., leading the side in 57 test matches 2010; first All Black to reach 100 caps (in World Cup Pool game against France) 2011; first rugby union player to win 100 tests 2012; first rugby union player to achieve 100 caps as capt. 2014; 148 Test caps (world record) to Oct. 2015; Amb. Air New Zealand 2010, apptd Goodwill Amb. AIG Inc. 2015; Hon. Squadron Leader, Royal NZ Air Force; Dr hc (Lincoln Univ.) 2012; New Zealand Under 21 Player of the Year 2001, Int. Rugby Board (IRB) Newcomer of the Year Award 2001, voted Newcomer of the Year by Int. Rugby Players Asscn 2002, Air New Zealand NPC Div. One Player of the Year 2002, 2004, Kelvin Tremain Memorial Trophy for Player of the Year 2003, 2006, New Zealand Player of the Year, Steinlager Rugby Awards 2003, 2006, 2009, 2012, IRB Int. Player of The Year 2006, 2009, 2010, New Zealand Sportsman of the Year 2010, 2011. *Publication:* Richie McCaw: The Open Side (autobiog., with Greg McGee) 2012. *Leisure interest:* flying.

McCHRYSTAL, Gen. (retd) Stanley A., BS, MA, MS; American army officer (retd); *Senior Fellow, Jackson Institute for Global Affairs, Yale University;* b. 14 Aug. 1954; ed US Mil. Acad., West Point, NY, US Naval War Coll., Newport, RI, Salve Regina Univ., Newport, RI; commissioned as 2nd Lt in US Army 1976; initial assignment as Weapons Platoon Leader to C Co., 1st Bn, 504th Parachute Infantry Regt, 82d Airborne Div. 1976–78, as Rifle Platoon Leader Feb.–July 1978, as Exec. Officer July–Nov. 1978; enrolled as student in Special Forces Officer Course, Special Forces School, Fort Bragg, NC 1978–79, remained at Fort Bragg as Commdr Detachment A, A Co., 1st Bn, 7th Special Forces Group (Airborne) 1979–80; attended Infantry Officer Advanced Course, Infantry School, Fort Benning, Ga 1980–81; Intelligence and Operations Officer (S-2/S-3) for UN Command Support Group–Jt Security Area, S Korea 1981–82; serve as training officer in Directorate of Plans and Training, A Co., HQ Command, Fort Stewart, Ga March–Nov. 1982; Commdr A Co., 3rd Bn, 19th Infantry, 24th Infantry Div. (Mechanized) 1982–84, Bn Operations Officer (S-3) 1984–85, April 1988–June 1989, Bn Liaison Officer, 3rd Bn, 75th Ranger Regt Sept. 1985–Jan. 1986, May 1987–April 1988, Commdr A Co. Jan. 1986; student in Command and Staff Course, Naval War Coll. 1989–90; Army Special Operations Action Officer, J-3, Jt Special Operations Command 1990–93, deployed to Saudi Arabia for Operations Desert Shield and Desert Storm; Commdr 2nd Bn, 504th Parachute Infantry Regt, 82nd Airborne Div. April 1993–Nov. 1994, 2nd Bn, 75th Ranger Regt Nov. 1994–June 1996; Sr Service Coll. Fellow, John F. Kennedy School of Govt, Harvard Univ. 1996–97; Commdr 75th Ranger Regt 1997–99; Mil. Fellow, Council on Foreign Relations 1999–2000; promoted to Brig. Gen. 2001; Asst Div. Commdr (Operations), 82d Airborne Div., including duty as Commdr Coalition/Jt Task Force Kuwait, Camp Doha, Kuwait 2000–01; Chief of Staff, XVIII Airborne Corps, including duty as Chief of Staff of Combined Jt Task Force 180, HQ formation contributed by XVIII Airborne Corps to direct all Operation Enduring Freedom operations in Afghanistan 2001–02; Vice-Dir of Operations and mem. Jt Staff, J-3, Pentagon, Washington, DC 2002–03, selected to deliver nationally televised Pentagon briefings on US mil. operations in Iraq; Commdr Jt Special Operations Command 2003–08, served first as Commdg Gen. Jt Special Operations Command 2003–06, then as Commdr Jt Special Operations Command/Commdr Jt Special Operations Command Forward 2006–08; promoted to Lt-Gen. 2006; Dir Jt Staff and Commdr NATO operations 2008–09; promoted to Gen. 2009; Commdr Int. Security Assistance Force (ISAF), NATO 2009–10 (resgnd); Commdr US Forces Afghanistan (USFOR-A) 2009–10 (resgnd and retd); Sr Fellow, Jackson Inst. for Global Affairs, Yale Univ. 2010–; Co-Founder and Partner, McChrystal Group LLC, Alexandria, Va; Defense Distinguished Service Medal, Defense Superior Service Medal (with one Oak Leaf Cluster), Legion of Merit (with two Oak Leaf Clusters), Bronze Star, Defense Meritorious Service Medal, Meritorious Service Medal (with three Oak Leaf Clusters), Army Commendation Medal, Army Achievement Medal, Expert Infantryman Badge, Parachutist Badge (US), Ranger Tab, Special Forces Tab, Jt Chiefs of Staff Identification Badge. *Publication:* My Share of the Task: A Memoir 2013. *Address:* McChrystal Group LLC, 333 North Fairfax Street, Suite 100, Alexandria, VA 22314 (office); Jackson Institute for Global Affairs, Rosenkranz Hall, 115 Prospect Street, Yale University, New Haven, CT 06511, USA (office). *Telephone:* (203) 432-6253 (Yale) (office). *E-mail:* jackson.institute@yale.edu. *Website:* jackson.yale.edu (home); www.mcchrystalgroup.com (office).

McCLEAN, Maxine, BPA, MA, MBA; Barbadian management consultant and politician; ed Univ. of the West Indies; fmr Lecturer in Man. Studies, Univ. of the West Indies; Founder Strategic Interventions Inc. (consultancy firm) 1991; mem. Senate 2008–; Leader of Govt Business and Minister in the Prime Minister's Office Jan.–Dec. 2008; Minister of Foreign Affairs, Foreign Trade and Int. Business 2008–18; fmr Pres., Vice-Pres. and mem. Supervisory Cttee City of Bridgetown Cooperative Credit Union Ltd; currently Pres. Univ. of the West Indies Cave Hill Campus Alumni Asscn; fmr Chair. Bd of Dirs Bridgetown Cruise Terminals Inc., Need Trust Fund of the Pinelands Creative Workshop, Dir Goddards Enterprises Ltd, RBTT Bank Barbados Ltd, Barbados Stock Exchange Inc.; OAS Fellowship, Univ. of Ohio 1979, Fulbright Fellowship, Louisiana State Univ. 1986.

McCLELLAN, Scott; American business executive and fmr government official; *Vice-President for Communications, Seattle University;* b. 14 Feb. 1968, Austin, Tex.; s. of Carole Keeton Strayhorn; m. Jill Martinez 2003; two s.; ed Univ. of Texas; Deputy Communications Dir for Texas Gov. George W. Bush 1999; served as Travelling Press Sec. during 2000 presidential campaign; Deputy Press Sec., The White House 2001–03, Press Sec. 2003–06; public affairs consulting 2006–12; Vice-Pres. for Communications, Seattle Univ. 2012–. *Publication:* What Happened: Inside the Bush White House and Washington's Culture of Deception 2008. *Address:* Marketing Communications, Seattle University, 715 13th Avenue, Seattle, WA 98122, USA (office). *Telephone:* (206) 296-2104 (office). *E-mail:* mcclells@seattleu.edu (office). *Website:* www.seattleu.edu/marcom (office).

McCLELLAND, Robert, LLM; Australian lawyer and politician; *Judge, Family Court of Australia;* b. 26 Jan. 1958, Sydney; s. of Douglas McClelland; m. Michelle McClelland; one s. three d.; ed Univ. of New South Wales, Univ. of Sydney; worked as assoc. to Hon. Justice Philip Evatt, Fed. Court of Australia 1980–82; Solicitor, Turner Freeman Solicitors 1982–88, Partner 1988–96; MP (Australia Labor Party) for Barton, NSW 1996–2013; Shadow Attorney-Gen. 1998–2001, Shadow Minister for Workplace Relations 2001–03, for Justice and Community Security 2003, for Homeland Security 2003, for Defence and Homeland Security 2004, for Defence 2005, for Foreign Affairs 2006–07, Attorney-Gen. 2007–11; Vice-Pres. Exec. Council 2010–12; Judge, Family Court of Australia, Sydney 2015–. *Publications include:* numerous legal essays. *Leisure interests:* Australian history, surfing, sailing, rugby league (St George). *Address:* Family Court of Australia, Lionel Bowen Building, 97-99 Goulburn Street, Sydney, NSW 2000, Australia (office). *Website:* www.familycourt.gov.au (office).

McCLUSKEY, Leonard (Len) David; British trade unionist; *General Secretary, Unite;* b. 23 July 1950, Liverpool; s. of Leonard McCluskey and Margaret Fulton; m. Ann P. Doyle 1969 (divorced 1997); one s.; ed Cardinal Godfrey School, Anfield; worked for Mersey Docks and Harbour Co. as a teenager and remained there for the next 11 years; trade unionist since 1968; became a shop steward aged 19; officer of Transport and Gen. Workers Union (TGWU) 1979, campaign organizer for TGWU in Merseyside during 1980s; supported Liverpool Militant during 1980s though not a mem.; mem. Labour Party (UK) 1970–; Nat. Sec. TGWU's Gen. Workers group 1990, moved to London to work in union HQ, TGWU's Nat. Organizer for the service industries 2004–10; Asst Gen. Sec. for Industrial Strategy, Unite –2010, Gen. Sec. Unite 2011–. *Address:* Unite, 128 Theobald's Road, Holborn, London, WC1X 8TN (office); Unite, 35 King Street, Covent Garden, London, WC2E 8JG, England (office). *Telephone:* (20) 7611-2500 (Holborn) (office); (20) 7420-8900 (Covent Garden) (office). *Fax:* (20) 7611-2555 (Holborn) (office); (20) 7420-8998 (Covent Garden) (office). *E-mail:* info@unitetheunion.org (office). *Website:* www.unitetheunion.org (office).

McCOLGAN, Ellyn, BA, MBA, LLD; American business executive; *Executive Advisor, Aquiline Capital Partners LLC;* b. 16 Jan. 1954, Jersey City, NJ; ed Montclair State Coll.; with Shearson Lehman Brothers, New York 1983, later with Bank of New England; joined Fidelity 1990, fmrly with Fidelity Accounting and Custody Services, Pres. Fidelity Investments Tax-Exempt Services Co. 1996–2000, Fidelity Investments Institutional Retirement Group 2000–01, Fidelity Financial Intermediary Services (FFIS) 2001–02, Fidelity Brokerage Co. 2002–07 (resgnd); Pres. and COO Global Wealth Man. Group, Morgan Stanley 2008–09, mem. Man. Cttee; Exec. Advisor to Aquiline Capital Partners LLC, New York 2010–; mem. Bd of Dirs NASDAQ OMX Group, Inc 2012–, Primerica 2010–11; Trustee Museum of Fine Arts, Boston; mem. Boston Club. *Address:* Aquiline Capital Partners LLC, 535 Madison Avenue, 24th Floor, New York, NY 10022 (office); 91 Central Park West, 8A, New York, NY 10023-4600, USA. *Website:* www.aquiline-llc.com (office).

McCOLL OF DULWICH, Baron (Life Peer), cr. 1989, of Bermondsey in the London Borough of Southwark; **Rt Hon Ian McColl,** CBE, MS, FRCS, FRCSE, FACS; British professor of surgery; b. 6 Jan. 1933; s. of Frederick George McColl and Winifred Edith McColl; m. Jean Lennox McNair 1960 (died 2012); one s. two d.; ed Hutchesons' Grammar School, Glasgow, St Paul's School, London, Guy's Hosp. Medical School, Univ. of London; Moynihan Fellowship, Asscn of Surgeons 1967; Reader in Surgery, St Bartholomew's Hosp., London 1967–71, Sub-Dean, St Bartholomew's Hosp. Medical Coll. 1969–71; Prof. of Surgery, Guy's Hosp., London 1971–98, Consultant Surgeon 1971–98, Dir of Surgery 1985–98, currently Part-time Lecturer; Chair. Dept of Surgery, United Medical and Dental Schools, St Thomas' Hosps 1985–92; Hon. Consultant to British Army 1976–98; Parl. Pvt. Sec. (Lords) to Prime Minister 1994–97; mem. (Conservative), House of Lords 1989–, Deputy Speaker 1994–2002, mem. Draft Modern Slavery Bill 2014; Chair. Bd of Govs, Mildmay Mission Hosp. 1984–; Vice-Chair. Disablement Services Authority for England 1987–91; Chair. Bd Dirs, Vice-Chair. Int. Bd Mercy Ships 1998–, Consultant Surgeon 2000–; mem. Council, Royal Coll. of Surgeons 1986–94, Council, Imperial Cancer Research Fund 1986–94; Pres. Nat. Asscn of Limbless Disabled, Soc. of Minimally Invasive Surgery, Leprosy Mission; Vice-Pres. John Grooms Asscn for the Disabled; mem. Bd Govs, American Coll. of Surgeons 1982–88; Fellow, King's Coll. London 2001; Hon. Fellow of Dental Surgery, Royal Coll. of Surgeons; George and Thomas Hutcheson's Award 2000, Nat. Maritime Historical Soc. Award 2002, Great Scot Award 2002. *Eponymous lectures:* Arris and Gale (2), Erasmus Wilson, Haig Gudenian Memorial, Colles, Letsomian, Lord Cohen Memorial. *Publications:* Intestinal Absorption in Man 1976, NHS Data Book 1984, Govt Report on supply of artificial legs and wheelchairs for England; articles on colonic diseases, medical audit and amputations. *Leisure interest:* forestry, ornithology. *Address:* House of Lords, Westminster, London, SW1A 0PW, England (office). *Telephone:* (20) 7219-5141 (office). *Fax:* (20) 7219-5979 (office). *E-mail:* mccolli@parliament.uk (office).

McCOMB, William (Bill) L., BA (Econ), MBA; American business executive; b. Columbia, Mo.; m.; three s.; ed Miami Univ., Ohio, Univ. of Chicago Grad. School of Business; held several positions with Leo Burnett advertising firm in Chicago, working on advertising for The Procter & Gamble Co. 1989–92; Asst Product Dir for Johnson & Johnson Consumer Products Co. 1992–94, joined Johnson & Johnson-Merck as Group Product Dir 1995–96, Vice-Pres. Marketing, McNeil Consumer Products Co. 1996–2001, Pres. McNeil Consumer Healthcare, with additional responsibilities as Pres. McNeil Consumer & Specialty Pharmaceuticals and Ortho Women's Health & Urology 2001–05, Co. Group Chair. DePuy Companies 2005–06; CEO and mem. Bd of Dirs, Liz Claiborne, Inc. (later Fifth & Pacific Cos, Inc., then Kate Spade & Co.) 2006–14; Vice-Chair. on Exec. Cttee and mem. Bd of Dirs, Consumer Healthcare Products Asscn 2001–05; fmr mem. Bd, GS1, OREF, INROADS of Philadelphia, American Apparel & Footwear Asscn, Nat. Retail Fed.; mem. Business Roundtable.

McCONAUGHEY, Matthew; American actor; b. 4 Nov. 1969, Ulvade, Tex.; m. Camila Alves 2012; one s. one d.; ed Univ. of Texas at Austin. *Films include:* Dazed and Confused, The Return of the Texas Chainsaw Massacre, Boys on the Side, My Boyfriend's Back 1993, Angels in the Outfield 1994, Scorpion Spring, Submission 1995, Glory Daze, Lone Star, A Time to Kill 1996, Larger Than Life 1997, Amistad, Contact, Making Sandwiches, Last Flight of the Raven, Newton Boys, South Beach, EdTV 1999, U-571 2000, The Wedding Planner 2001, Frailty 2001, Reign of Fire 2002, How to Lose a Guy in Ten Days 2003, Tiptoes 2003, Sahara 2005, Two for the Money 2005, Failure to Launch 2006, We Are Marshall 2006, Fool's Gold 2008, Tropic Thunder 2008, Surfer, Dude 2008, Ghosts of Girlfriends Past 2009, The Lincoln Lawyer 2011, Bernie 2011, Killer Joe 2011, The Paperboy 2012, Magic Mike 2012, Mud 2013, Dallas Buyers Club (Golden Globe Award for Best Actor in a Motion Picture, Screen Actors Guild Award for Outstanding Performance by a Male Actor in a Leading Role, Academy Award for Best Actor in a Leading Role 2014) 2013, The Wolf of Wall Street 2013, Interstellar 2014, The Sea of Trees 2015, Kubo and the Two Strings 2016, The Dark Tower 2017, White Boy Rick 2018, The Beach Bum 2019. *Television includes:* Freedom: A History of Us 2003, Eastbound & Down (series) 2012, True Detective 2014. *Address:* c/o Creative Artists Agency, 2000 Avenue of the Stars, Los Angeles, CA 90067, USA. *Telephone:* (424) 288-2000. *Fax:* (424) 288-2900. *Website:* www.caa.com.

McCONNELL, Addison Mitchell (Mitch), Jr, BA, JD; American politician and lawyer; *Senator from Kentucky;* b. 20 Feb. 1942, Tuscumbia, Ala; s. of Addison Charles McConnell and Julia McConnell (née Shockley); m. 1st Sherrill Redmon (divorced); three d.; m. 2nd Elaine L. Chao (q.v.) 1993; ed Univ. of Louisville Coll. of Arts and Sciences, Univ. of Kentucky Coll. of Law; served in US Army Reserve 1967; admitted to the Bar, Ky 1967; worked as intern on Capitol Hill for Senator John Sherman Cooper; Chief Legis. Asst to Senator Marlow Cook, Washington, DC 1968–70; est. legal practice, Louisville 1970; Deputy Asst US Attorney-Gen. 1974–75; Judge-Exec, Jefferson Co., Louisville 1978–85; Senator from Kentucky 1985–, Majority Whip 2003–07, Minority Leader 2007–15, Majority Leader 2015–, Chair. Ethics Cttee 1995–97, Rules Cttee 1999–2001, Sr mem. Appropriations, Agric. and Rules Cttees; Chair. Jefferson Co. Republican Cttee 1973–74, Nat. Republican Senatorial Cttee 1997–2001; Co-Chair. Nat. Child Tragedies Coalition 1981; Founding Chair. Ky Task Force on Exploited and Missing Children 1982; Founder James Madison Center for Free Speech, Washington, DC 1997; mem. Pres.'s Partnership on Child Safety; mem. Ky Asscn of Co. Judge Execs (Pres. 1982), Nat. Inst. of Justice (mem. Advisory Bd 1982–84), Bd of Selectors, Jefferson Awards for Public Service; Republican; Commendation, Nat. Trust in Historical Preservation in the US 1982, Conservationist of the Year Award, League of Ky Sportsmen 1983, Certificate of Appreciation, American Correctional Asscn 1985, inducted into Sons of the American Revolution 2013. *Leisure interests:* cooking, fishing. *Address:* 317 Russell Senate Office Building, Washington, DC 20510, USA (office). *Telephone:* (202) 224-2541 (office). *Fax:* (202) 224-2499 (office). *Website:* www.mcconnell.senate.gov (office).

McCONNELL, David John, PhD, MRIA; Irish geneticist and academic; *Fellow Emeritus in Genetics, Trinity College Dublin;* b. 15 May 1944, Dublin; s. of John J. McConnell and Joan Warwick; m. Janet Overend 1966; two s.; ed Zion Nat. Schools, Rathgar, Dublin, Sandford Park School, Ranelagh, Dublin, Trinity Coll. Dublin and California Inst. of Tech.; Lecturer in Genetics, Trinity Coll. Dublin (TCD) 1970–85, Fellow of TCD 1978, Assoc. Prof. of Genetics 1985–90, Head, Dept of Genetics 1987–98, Prof. of Genetics 1990–2014, Sr Fellow of TCD 2007–14, Fellow Emer. in Genetics 2014–, Vice-Provost, Trinity Coll. 1990–91, Pres. Coll. Historical Soc. 2003–; Eleanor Roosevelt Fellow, Int. Union Against Cancer, Lab. of Prof. Wally Gilbert, Dept of Biochem. and Molecular Biology Harvard Univ. 1976–77; Visiting Prof., Univ. of California, Davis 1979; consultant in genetic eng and biotechnology, UNIDO 1982–; UNDP Star consultant, Beijing Agric. Univ. 1987; Chair. Adelaide Hosp. 1988–94, Pres. 1995–2001; Pres. Royal Zoological Soc. of Ireland (ZSI) 1992–96, Fellow, ZSI 1996; other professional appointments; Chair. Irish Times Trust 2001–10; Co-Vice-Chair. European Action on Global Life Sciences (EAGLES) 2004–09; mem. Irish Council for Science, Tech. and Innovation 1997–2003; mem. Exec. Bd, European Fed. of Biotechnology 2004–09; mem. European Molecular Biological Org. (EMBO) 1976; Hon. Pres. Humanist Asscn of Ireland 2009–. *Publications:* more than 100 papers in scientific journals. *Leisure interests:* windsurfing, Kerry, gardening. *Address:* Department of Genetics, Smurfit Institute of Genetics, Trinity College, Dublin 2, Ireland (office). *Telephone:* (1) 702-2008 (office); (1) 702-1140 (office). *Fax:* (1) 671-4968 (office). *E-mail:* david.mcconnell@tcd.ie (office). *Website:* www.tcd.ie/Genetics (office).

McCONNELL, Vice-Adm. John Michael (Mike), MPA; American consultant and naval officer (retd) and fmr government official; *Senior Executive Advisor, Booz Allen Hamilton Inc.;* b. 26 July 1943, Greenville, SC; m. Terry McConnell; two c. two step-c.; ed Furman Univ., George Washington Univ., Nat. Defense Univ.; commissioned as line officer in USN 1967, served a tour in Viet Nam and became intelligence officer, served as intelligence officer for Jt Chiefs Chair. Colin Powell during first Gulf War; Dir Nat. Security Agency 1992–96; Sr Vice-Pres. Booz Allen Hamilton Inc., McLean, Va 1996–2007, Exec. Vice-Pres. 2009–11, Vice-Chair. 2011–14, Sr Exec. Advisor 2014–; Dir of Nat. Intelligence, Washington, DC 2007–09 (resgnd); mem. Pres.'s Intelligence Advisory Bd 2009–; fmr Chair. and CEO Intelligence and Nat. Security Alliance; mem. Bd of Dirs, CompuDyne Corpn 2004–07; mem. Advisory Bd, Council on CyberSecurity 2013; Dr hc (George Washington Univ.) 2008; William Oliver Baker Award, Intelligence and Nat. Security Alliance 2011. *Address:* Booz Allen Hamilton Inc., 8283 Greensboro Drive, McLean, VA 22102, USA (office). *Telephone:* (703) 902-5000 (office). *E-mail:* communications@bah.com (office). *Website:* www.boozallen.com (office).

McCONNELL OF GLENSCORRODALE, Baron (Life Peer), cr. 2010, of the Isle of Arran in Ayrshire and Arran; **Jack Wilson McConnell,** BSc, DipEd, PC; British politician, diplomatist and teacher; b. 30 June 1960, Irvine, Ayrshire, Scotland; s. of William Wilson McConnell and Elizabeth McEwan McConnell; m. Bridget Mary McLuckie 1990; one s. one d.; ed Arran High School, Isle of Arran, Stirling Univ.; math. teacher, Alloa 1983–92; Labour mem. Stirling Dist Council 1984–92, Treas. 1988–92, Leader 1990–92; Gen. Sec. Scottish Labour Party 1992–98, Leader 2001–07 (resgnd); co-ordinated Labour's Yes Yes Referendum Campaign 1997; mem. Scottish Constitutional Convention 1989–98; Minister for Finance, Scottish Exec. 1999–2000, for Educ. and External Affairs 2000–01; First Minister of Scotland 2001–07; Head, Clinton Hunter Devt Initiative on developing educ. in Malawi and Rwanda; currently mem. House of Lords, Prime Minister's Special Rep. for Peacebuilding 2008–10; currently Chair. McConnell Int. Foundation, All Party Group on African Great Lakes Region; mem. Convention of Scottish Local Authorities (COSLA) 1988–92; currently mem. Amnesty International, Advisory Bd to Inst. of Cultural Diplomacy, Berlin, Advisory Bd, PricewaterhouseCoopers; Hon. DUniv (Stirling) 2008. *Leisure interests:* golf, music, watching football. *Address:* The House of Lords, Westminster, London, SW1A 0PW, England (office). *Telephone:* (20) 7219-8913 (office). *Fax:* (20) 7219-5979 (office). *E-mail:* mcconnellj@parliament.uk (office). *Website:* www.jackmcconnell.org.

McCORMACK, Michael Francis; Australian politician and fmr journalist; *Deputy Prime Minister;* b. 2 Aug. 1964, Wagga Wagga, New South Wales; s. of Lance McCormack and Eileen Margaret McCormack (née Margosis); m. Catherine Shaw 1986; three c.; fmr journalist, news editor and publisher; campaign Dir for Kay Elizabeth Hull (fmr politician) 2004, 2007; mem. House of Reps (Parl.) (Nationals) for Riverina constituency 2010–; Minister assisting the Prime Minister for Centenary of ANZAC 2012–18; Parl. Sec. to Minister of Finance 2013–15; Asst Minister to Deputy Prime Minister 2015–16; Asst Minister for Defence Feb.–July 2016; Minister for Small Business 2016–17, for Veterans' Affairs 2017–18, for Defence Personnel 2017–18; Deputy Prime Minister and Minister for Infrastructure and Transport 2018–; mem. Nat. Party of Australia, mem. Nationals State Cen. Council 2010, Fed. Parl. Leader 2018–. *Leisure interest:* cricket. *Address:* The Nationals, 7 National Circuit, John McEwen House, Barton, ACT 2600 (office); Wagga Wagga Electorate Office, Suite 2 11-15, Fitzmaurice Street, Wagga Wagga NSW 2650, Australia (office). *Telephone:* (2) 6273-3822 (office); (2) 6921-4600 (office). *Fax:* (2) 6273-1745 (office); (2) 6921-5900 (office). *E-mail:* federal.nationals@org.au (office); michael.mccormack.mp@aph.gov.au (office). *Website:* www.nationals.org.au (office); www.aph.gov.au (office); www.michaelmccormack.com.au (home).

McCORMICK, Richard D., BS; American business executive; *Chairman Emeritus, United States Council for International Business;* b. 4 July 1940, Fort Dodge, Ia; s. of Elmo Eugene McCormick and Virgilla McCormick (née Lawler); m. Mary Patricia Smola 1963; four c.; ed Iowa State Univ.; engineer with AT&T, Kansas City, Mo. 1961–69, Northwestern Bell 1969–85, Pres. 1982–85; Exec. Vice-Pres. US West, Inc. (now part of Qwest Communications) 1985–86, Pres. and COO 1986–90, CEO 1990–98, Chair. 1992–98, Chair. (non-exec.) 1998–99, Chair. Emer. 1999–; Vice-Pres. ICC 1998–2000, Pres. 2001–03, Hon. Chair. 2003–; Chair. US Council for Int. Business 1995–2001, Vice-Chair. 2001–03, Chair. Emer. 2003 also Sr Trustee; mem. Bd United Airlines, Wells Fargo & Co. 1983–2010, Nortel Networks Corpn, United Technologies Corpn, Concept Five Technologies, Health Trio, Inc.; mem. Bd Creighton Univ., Omaha; mem. George W. Bush for President, Bush-Cheney '04, John McCain 2008, Freedom and Free Enterprise Political Action Cttee; Trustee, Denver Art Museum. *Address:* United States Council for International Business, 1212 Avenue of the Americas, New York, NY 10036, USA (office). *Telephone:* (212) 354-4480 (office). *Fax:* (212) 575-0327 (office). *E-mail:* info@uscib.org (office). *Website:* www.uscib.org (office).

McCORMICK, Richard Levis, BA, PhD; American historian, fmr university administrator and academic; *President Emeritus, Rutgers University;* b. 26 Dec. 1947, New Brunswick, NJ; s. of Richard Patrick McCormick and Katheryne Levis McCormick; m. 1st Suzanne Lebsock; one s. one d.; m. 2nd Joan Barry McCormick;

one d.; ed Piscataway Township High School, NJ, Amherst Coll., Yale Univ.; Asst Prof. of History, Rutgers Univ. 1976–81, Assoc. Prof. 1981–85, Prof. 1985–92, Chair. Dept of History 1987–89, Founding Dir Rutgers Center for Historical Analysis 1988–89, Dean Faculty of Arts and Sciences 1989–92, Pres. Rutgers Univ. 2002–12, Pres. Emer. and Univ. Prof. 2012–; Exec. Vice-Chancellor, Provost and Vice-Chancellor for Academic Affairs, Univ. of North Carolina 1992–95; Pres. Univ. of Washington 1995–2002; Gov. James E. McGreevey's Comm. on Jobs, Growth, and Econ. Devt 2003–04, James E. McGreevey's Review, Planning, and Implementation Steering Cttee 2003–04, James E. McGreevey's Comm. to Support and Enhance New Jersey Mil. and Coast Guard Installations 2004–; mem. Asscn of American Univs 1995–, Business-Higher Educ. Forum 1999–, Council of Presidents, Asscn of Governing Bds of Univs and Colls 2001–, Interdisciplinary Task Force of Asscn of American Univs 2002–, Capital Planning Task Force of Comm. on Higher Educ. 2005–; mem. Bd of Dirs, New Jersey Tech. Council 2003–, Robert Wood Johnson Univ. Hosp., New Brunswick, NJ 2003–; mem. Bd Overseers, Robert Wood Johnson Medical School, Univ. of Medicine and Dentistry of NJ 2003–; mem. Bd Trustees, State Theatre, New Brunswick 2003–, New Jersey Network Foundation 2003–, New Jersey Historical Soc. 2005–; George Washington Egleston Prize, Yale Univ. 1977, Visiting Fellowship, Shelby Cullom Davis Center for Historical Studies, Princeton Univ. 1981–82, John Simon Guggenheim Memorial Foundation Fellowship 1985, Woodrow Wilson Int. Center for Scholars Fellowship 1985. *Publications:* From Realignment to Reform: Political Change in New York State, 1893–1910 1981, Progressivism (co-author) 1983, The Party Period and Public Policy: American Politics from the Age of Jackson to the Progressive Era 1986, Public Life in Industrial America, 1877–1917 1997, Raised at Rutgers: A President's Story 2014; numerous articles. *Address:* The State University of New Jersey, 4 Huntington Street, New Brunswick, NJ 08901-1071, USA (office). *Telephone:* (848) 932-7705 (office). *Fax:* (732) 932-6185 (office). *E-mail:* rlm@rutgers.edu (office). *Website:* www.rutgers.edu (office).

McCOURT, Jamie D., BS, MS, JD, MBA; American lawyer, business executive and diplomatist; *Ambassador to France;* b. 5 Dec. 1953, Baltimore, Md; d. of Jack Luskin and Jean Luskin; m. Frank McCourt 1979 (divorced 2011); four s.; ed Georgetown Univ., Univ. of Maryland School of Law, MIT Sloan School of Man.; 14 years in private legal practice, engaged in int. and securities law in Mass and New York; Vice Pres. and Gen. Counsel, McCourt Co. (family real estate devt firm), Boston 1994–2004; Co-Owner, Los Angeles Dodgers (professional baseball team) 2004–12, Vice Chair. 2004, Pres. 2005, CEO 2009–12; Visiting Prof., UCLA Anderson School of Man. 2005–11; Founder and CEO Jamie Enterprises (venture capital firm) 2011–; Amb. to France 2017–; mem. Bd, Los Angeles County Museum of Art, Museum of Contemporary Art; mem. Bd of Dirs Wallis Annenberg Center for the Performing Arts; Republican. *Address:* Embassy of the USA, 2 ave Gabriel, 75382 Paris Cedex 08, France (office). *Telephone:* 1-43-12-22-22 (office). *Fax:* 1-42-66-97-83 (office). *Website:* fr.usembassy.gov (office); www.jamiemccourt.com.

McCOY, Sir A(nthony) P(eter) (Tony), Kt, OBE, MBE; Irish professional jockey (retd); b. 4 May 1974, Moneyglass, Co. Antrim, NI; s. of Peadar McCoy; apprentice to Jim Bolger 1989; won first race riding Legal Steps at Thurles March 1992; Champion Hurdle Winner, Make a Stand 1997; Cheltenham Gold Cup Winner, Mr Mulligan 1997; 1,000th winner Majadou, Cheltenham 1999; 1,500th winner Celtic Nave, Exeter 2001; 2,000th winner Magical Bailiwick, Wincanton 2004; 3,000th winner Restless D'Artaix, Plumpton 2009; 4,000th winner Mountain Tunes, Towcester 2013; 4,348 career jumps winners; nine flat race wins; Champion Jump Jockey for 20 successive seasons 1995/96–2014/15; winners included Cheltenham Gold Cup, Champion Hurdle, Queen Mother Champion Chase, King George VI Chase and 2010 Grand National, riding Don't Push It on his 15th attempt; greatest number of career winners by any jockey 2002; greatest number of winners in any season by any jockey (289) 2001/02 (broke 55-year old record); Official Horse Racing Amb., Eventmasters Ltd 2014–; retd April 2015; Lester Awards: Conditional Jockey of the Year 1995, Jump Jockey of the Year 1996, 1997, 1998, 1999, 2000, 2001, 2002, 2003, 2004, 2005, 2006, 2007, 2008, 2009, 2010, 2011, 2012, 2013, Jockey of the Year 1997 (award discontinued after 1997), Jump Ride of the Year 2009, 2012; named Sportsman of the Year at British Sports Awards in London, voted for by Sports Journalists Asscn 2010, BBC Sports Personality of the Year (first jockey to win the award) 2010, 'Jump Off the Sofa Moment' Award, Jaguar Acad. of Sport Annual Awards 2010, RTÉ Sports Person of the Year 2013, BBC Sports Personality of the Year Lifetime Achievement Award 2015. *Publications include:* Real McCoy: My Life So Far 1999, McCoy: The Autobiography 2003. *Address:* c/o Claire Burns, Director of Lloyd Burns Management, 483 Green Lanes, London, N13 4BS, England (office). *Telephone:* (207) 642-3330 (office). *E-mail:* claire@lloydburnsmangement.com (office); ap@apmccoy.com. *Website:* www.lloydburnsmanagement.com (office).

McCOY, Sherilyn (Sheri) S., BS, MS, MBA; American cosmetics industry executive; *Director, Novocure;* b. Quincy, Mass; m.; three s.; ed Univ. of Massachusetts, Princeton Univ., Rutgers Univ.; Assoc. Research Scientist, Personal Products Co., Johnson & Johnson 1982–96, Vice-Pres. Research and Devt, Personal Products Worldwide 1996–2000, Vice-Pres. for Marketing, Skin Care Franchise, Johnson & Johnson Consumer Cos Inc. 2000–02, Global Pres. Baby and Wound Franchise 2002–05, Co. Group Chair. and Worldwide Franchise Chair. Ethicon Inc. 2005–08, Worldwide Chair. Surgical Care Group 2008–09, Worldwide Chair. Pharmaceuticals Group 2009–11, mem. Exec. Cttee 2009–12, Vice-Chair. Exec. Cttee and mem. Office of the Chair., with responsibility for Pharmaceutical and Consumer business segments 2011–12; CEO Avon Products, Inc. 2012–18; Dir Novocure 2018–; Vice-Pres. Montgomery Township Educ. Foundation; Bd mem. Bd FIRST (charity); mem. Rutgers Univ. Pres.'s Business Leaders Cabinet. *Publications:* four US patents. *Address:* Novocure, Second Floor No.4, The Forum Grenville Street, St. Helier, Jersey, NJ JE2 4UF, USA (office). *E-mail:* generalinfo@novocure.com (office). *Website:* www.novocure.com (office).

McCREEVY, Charlie, BComm, FCA; Irish accountant and politician; *Chairman, Murray & Spelman Ltd;* b. 30 Sept. 1949, Sallins, Co. Kildare; m. Noeleen Halligan, three s., one s. three d. from previous m.; ed Univ. Coll. Dublin; Pnr, Tynan Dillon & Co. (chartered accountants), Dublin, Naas and Ballyhaunis; mem. Kildare Co. Council 1979–85; mem. Dáil 1977–2002; Minister for Social Welfare 1992–93, for Tourism and Trade 1993–94, for Finance 1997–2004; fmr Fianna Fáil Spokesperson on Finance; EU Commr for Internal Market and Services, Brussels 2004–10; Chair. Murray & Spelman Ltd 2016–; mem. Bd of Dirs Ryanair 2010–, Sports Direct International plc 2011–, Sentenial 2011–. *Address:* Murray & Spelman Ltd, G.F.S.C, Tuam Road, Galway Ireland (office). *Telephone:* (1) 759500 (office). *E-mail:* insurances@murrayspelman.ie (office). *Website:* www.murrayspelman.ie (office).

McCRORY, Patrick (Pat) Lloyd, BA, MA; American business executive and politician; b. 17 Oct. 1956, Columbus, Ohio; s. of Rollin 'Mac' McCrory and Audrey McCrory; m. Ann Gordon 1988; ed Ragsdale High School, Jamestown, Catawba Coll., Salisbury; received NC teaching certificate 1978; worked full-time for Duke Energy 1978–2008, first on man. training programme, later promoted to sr adviser with Business and Econ. Devt Group; mem. Bd of Trustees, Catawba Coll.; Partner, McCrory & Co. (sales consulting firm), Charlotte, NC 2009–12; Sr Dir of Strategic Initiatives, Moore & Van Allen PLLC law firm, Charlotte 2010–12; began political career in Charlotte when elected as an At-Large City Councilman 1989, re-elected 1991, 1993, served as Mayor Pro Tempore 1993–95; Mayor of Charlotte 1995–2009; fmr Chair. Republican Mayors Asscn; apptd by Pres. George W. Bush to US Homeland Security Advisory Council 2002–06; unsuccessful cand. for Gov. of NC 2008; f. Mayor's Mentoring Alliance 1995, NC Metropolitan Mayors Asscn 2001; paid adviser to transit tax campaigns 2008–12; Gov. of NC 2013–17; Republican; fmr Hon. Chair. Charlotte chapter of Alzheimer's Foundation and Arthritis Foundation; Dr hc (Catawba Coll.) 2001; Nat. Home-ownership Hero Award 2003.

McCULLAGH, Peter, PhD, FRS; Northern Irish statistician; *John D. MacArthur Distinguished Service Professor, University of Chicago;* b. 8 Jan. 1952, Plumbridge, Northern Ireland; s. of John A. McCullagh and Margaret B. McCullagh; m. Rosa Bogues 1977; one s. three d.; ed St Columb's Coll., Derry, Univ. of Birmingham, Imperial Coll., London; Asst Prof., Dept of Statistics, Univ. of Chicago 1977–79, Prof. 1985–, now John D. MacArthur Distinguished Service Prof.; Lecturer, Imperial Coll. London 1979–85; Fellow, American Acad. of Arts and Sciences 2002; Guy Medal (Bronze), Royal Statistical Soc. 1983, Presidents' Award, Cttee of Presidents of Statistical Socs (COPSS) 1990, Notable Alumni Award, St Columb's Coll. 2007. *Achievements include:* known for McCullagh's parametrization of the Cauchy distributions. *Publications:* Generalized Linear Models (with J. A. Nelder) 1983 (second edn 1989), Tensor Methods in Statistics 1987; more than 75 articles in professional journals and about 35 other publs. *Address:* Department of Statistics, University of Chicago, Eckhart 119, 5734 South University Avenue, Chicago, IL 60637 (office); 5039 Ellis Avenue, Chicago, IL 60615, USA (home). *Telephone:* (773) 702-8340 (office). *Fax:* (773) 702-9810 (office). *E-mail:* pmcc@galton.uchicago.edu (office). *Website:* galton.uchicago.edu/faculty/mccullagh.shtml (office); www.stat.uchicago.edu/~pmcc (office).

McCULLIN, Sir Donald (Don), Kt, CBE; British photographer; b. 9 Oct. 1935, London; s. of Frederick McCullin and Jessica McCullin; m. 1st Christine Dent 1959 (divorced 1987); two s. one d. and one s. by Laraine Ashton; m. 2nd Marilyn Bridges 1995 (divorced 2001); m. 3rd Catherine Fairweather 2002; one s.; ed Tollington Park Secondary Modern, Hammersmith Art and Crafts School; RAF Nat. Service; photographer with Observer for four years; photographer with Sunday Times, London for 18 years; freelance 1980–; has covered ten wars (Viet Nam, Cambodia, Biafra, Congo, Israel, Cyprus, Chad, Lebanon, Iraq, Syria) and many famine areas; has travelled to 64 countries; in addition to war reportage has done advertising work for a variety of brands; Patron, Ian Parry Awards, Faith through a Lens Awards; FRPS 1977; Hon. FRPS 2003; Hon. Fellow, Hereford Coll. of Arts 2009; Dr hc (Bradford) 1993, (Open) 1994, (Lincoln) 2005; Hon. DLitt (Gloucestershire) 2008; Hon. Dr of Arts (Bath) 2011, (Bath Spa) 2015, (Hereford); World Press Photographer 1964, Warsaw Gold Medal 1964, Granada TV Award 1967, 1969, Designers and Art Directors Asscn Gold Award for Photography 1968, First Prize, World Press Photo Foundation 1969, 1977, Photokina Prize for Overall Achievement, Cologne 1972, American Soc. of Magazine Photographers Award 1978, German Soc. of Photography Erich Salomon Prize for Outstanding Use of Photography in Press, Berlin 1992, Two Gold, One Silver Art Director Awards, UK, Special 150th Anniversary Medal, Royal Photographic Soc. 2003, Cornell Capa Award 2006. *Television:* films: Beautiful, Beautiful 1968, Just One More War 1977, Homefront 1986, The Redundant Warrior 1991, Contacts: Don McCullin 1992, Words Are Not Enough 2005. *Publications:* The Destruction Business 1971, The Concerned Photographer II 1972, Is Anyone Taking Notice? 1973, Hearts of Darkness 1980, Battle Beirut–A City in Crisis 1983, Perspectives 1987, Skulduggery 1987, Open Skies 1989, Unreasonable Behaviour (autobiog.) 1990, Sleeping with Ghosts 1995; A Life's Work in Photography 1995, India 1999, Don McCullin A Retrospective 2001, Don McCullin 2004, Don McCullin in Africa 2005, Don McCullin in England 2007, Southern Frontiers 2011, Shaped by War 2011. *Leisure interests:* walking, collecting Victorian children's books, antiques.

McCULLOUGH, David Gaub, BA; American historian and writer; b. 7 July 1933, Pittsburgh, Pa; m. Rosalee Ingram Barnes 1954; three s. two d.; ed Yale Univ.; Ed., Time Inc., New York 1956–61, US Information Agency, Washington, DC 1961–64, American Heritage Publishing Co., New York 1964–70; Scholar-in-Residence, Univ. of New Mexico 1979, Wesleyan Univ. 1982, 1983; Visiting Prof., Cornell Univ. 1989; Marian McFadden Memorial Lecturer, Indianapolis-Marion County Public Library 2002; mem. Jefferson Legacy Foundation, Nat. Trust for Historic Preservation, Soc. of American Historians, Harry S. Truman Library Inst.; Officier, Ordre nat. de la Légion d'honneur 2014; awarded more than 50 hon. doctorates; New York Public Library Literary Lion Award 1981, Washington Irving Medal for Literary Excellence 1993, Nat. Endowment for the Humanities Charles Frankel Prize 1995, Presidential Medal of Freedom 2006, Aspen Inst. Public Service Award 2006, Living Legend of Library of Congress Award 2008, Nat. Arts Club Medal of Honor for Literature 2010, Lafayette Prize, French-American Cultural Foundation 2011, Gold Medal for Biography, American Acad. of Arts and Letters 2012, Arthur M. Schlesinger, Jr. Award, Soc. of American Historians 2012, American Ireland Fund Chairman's Award 2014, among numerous others. *Television:* host, Smithsonian World 1984–88, The American Experience 1988– (both PBS). *Publications include:* The Johnstown Flood 1968, The Great Bridge 1972, The Path Between the Seas (Nat. Book Award for History 1978, Samuel Eliot Morison Award 1978, Cornelius Ryan Award 1978, Francis Parkman Prize 1978) 1977, Mornings on Horseback (Nat. Book Award) 1981,

Brave Companions 1991, Truman (Pulitzer Prize in Biography 1993, Harry S. Truman Public Service Award 1993) 1992, John Adams (Pulitzer Prize 2002) 2001, 1776 2005, The Course of Human Events 2005, In the Dark Streets Shineth: A 1941 Christmas Eve Story 2010, The Greater Journey 2011, Great Bridge 2012, The Wright Brothers 2015. *Address:* Janklow & Nesbit Associates, 445 Park Avenue, New York, NY 10022, USA (office). *Website:* www.davidmccullough.com.

McCULLUM, Brendon Barrie, ONZ; New Zealand professional cricketer; b. 27 Sept. 1981, Dunedin, Otago; s. of S. J. McCullum (fmr first-class player for Otago); Ellissa Arthur; one s. one d.; ed King's High School, Dunedin; wicketkeeper batsman; right-handed batsman; plays for Otago 1999–2003, 2007–, New Zealand 2002–16, Canterbury 2003–06, Glamorgan 2006, Kolkata Knight Riders 2008–10, 2012–13, NSW 2009, Sussex 2010, Kochi Tuskers Kerala 2011, Brisbane Heat 2011–15, 2016–, Chennai Super Kings 2014–15, Warwicks. 2015, Middlesex 2016, Gujarat Lions 2016–; First-class debut: 1999/2000; Test debut: NZ v S Africa, Hamilton 10–14 March 2004; One-Day Int. (ODI) debut: Australia v NZ, Sydney 17 Jan. 2002; T20I debut: NZ v Australia, Auckland 17 Feb. 2005; played in 100 Tests, took 1 wicket and scored 6,283 runs (11 centuries, 31 half-centuries), highest score 302, average 38.07, best bowling (innings) 1/1, (match) 1/13; ODIs: 260 matches, scored 6,083 runs, highest score 166, average 30.41; T20Is: 71 matches, scored 2,140 runs, highest score 123, average 35.66; retd from int. Cricket Feb. 2016; Sitara-i-Imtiaz, Pakistan 2018. *Achievements include:* set new World Cup record by smashing 50 runs from 20 balls against Canada in Saint Lucia 21 March 2007; scored 158 not out in inaugural match of Indian Premier League (then the world highest score by a batsman in a Twenty20 match) 18 April 2008; first player to score 1000 T20I runs, playing against Zimbabwe in ICC World Twenty20 in Guyana 28 June 2010; scored 123 runs against Bangladesh at Pallekele, setting a new record for the highest T20I innings, and becoming the first player to score two T20I centuries Sept. 2012; posted the fastest ever Test century, in 54 balls, in his final Test match against Australia, beating record jointly held by Viv Richards and Misbah-ul-Haq, and scoring a total of 145 off 79 balls Feb. 2016. *Address:* c/o Otago Cricket Association Inc., University Oval, Grandstand, Logan Park Drive, PO Box 1419, Dunedin, New Zealand. *Telephone:* (3) 477-9056. *Fax:* (3) 477-3056. *E-mail:* info@otagocricket.co.nz. *Website:* www.otagocricket.co.nz.

McCULLY, Murray, LLB; New Zealand politician; b. 19 Feb. 1953, Whangarei; MP for East Coast Bays 1987–99, 2002–17, for Albany 1999–2002, mem. Māori Affairs Select Cttee 2002–03, Foreign Affairs, Defence and Trade Cttee 2005–08; Minister of Customs 1991–96, of Housing 1993–96, of Tourism 1996–99, for Sport, Fitness and Leisure 1996–99, for Accident Rehabilitation and Compensation Insurance 1997–99, for Housing Corpn 1998–99, for Housing New Zealand 1998–99, for Accident Insurance 1999, of Foreign Affairs and for Sport and Recreation 2008–14, of Foreign Affairs 2014–17; Assoc. Minister of Tourism 1991–96, of Immigration 1998–99, for Sport and Recreation 2014–; Spokesman for Infrastructure 1999–2005, for Local Govt 1999–2002, for Sport, Fitness and Leisure 1999–2002, for Immigration 2002–03, for State Services 2002–05, for Conservation 2005–06; Parl. Asst to Leader of the Opposition 2003–05; mem. New Zealand Nat. Party.

McCUTCHEON, Stuart, BAgrSc, PhD; New Zealand physiologist, endocrinologist, academic and university administrator; *Vice-Chancellor, University of Auckland;* b. Wellington; ed Massey Univ.; Lecturer, Massey Univ. while undertaking a PhD in metabolic physiology; Post-doctoral Fellow (Harkness Fellowship), Cornell Univ., USA 1982–84; Head of Dept of Animal Science, Massey Univ. 1990–94, Asst Vice-Chancellor (Research) 1994–99, Deputy Vice-Chancellor 1999–2001; Vice-Chancellor Victoria Univ. of Wellington 2000–05; Vice-Chancellor Univ. of Auckland 2005–; has served as adviser to several govt agencies and producer bds; Chair. NZ Vice-Chancellors' 2004–05, Universities NZ Research Cttee; fmr Dir or Bd mem. New Zealand Dairy Research Inst., Wellington Regional Econ. Devt Trust, Wellington Coll. of Educ., Malaghan Inst. of Medical Research, Universitas 21, U21 Global, Univ. of Auckland Foundation, UK and US Friends of Univ. of Auckland. *Publications:* numerous papers in professional journals on endocrinology and metabolic physiology. *Address:* Office of the Vice-Chancellor, The University of Auckland, Private Bag 92019, Auckland Mail Centre, Auckland 1142, New Zealand (office). *Telephone:* (9) 373-7599 (ext. 87751) (office). *Fax:* (9) 373-7591 (office). *E-mail:* s.mccutcheon@auckland.ac.nz (office). *Website:* www.auckland.ac.nz (office).

McDAID, James, MB, BCh, BAO; Irish politician and medical doctor; b. 3 Oct. 1949, Termon, Co. Donegal; m. 1st Marguerite McLoughlin; three s. one d.; m. 2nd Siobhán McDaid; one s.; ed St Eunan's Coll., Letterkenny, Nat. Univ. of Ireland, Galway; Sr Surgical House Officer, Letterkenny Gen. Hosp. 1974–79; Gen. Practitioner, Letterkenny 1979; Founder and Pres. Donegal Hospice Movt 1988; mem. Dáil Éireann for Donegal NE 1989–2010; mem. Dáil Cttee on Women's Rights 1992, Cttee of Public Accounts 1993, Cttee on Foreign Affairs and NI Sub-Cttee 1995; Spokesperson on North/South Devts 1995, for Equality and Law Reform 1996–97; Minister (desig.) for Defence 1991 (resgnd), Minister for Tourism, Sport and Recreation 1997–2002, Minister of State at Dept of Transport with special responsibility for road traffic including road haulage 2002–04. *Leisure interests:* football, horse racing, golf. *Address:* Pearse Road, Letterkenny, Co. Donegal, Ireland (home). *Telephone:* (74) 25132 (home).

McDIARMID, Ian, MA; British actor and artistic director; b. 11 Aug. 1944, Carnoustie, Scotland; s. of Frederick McDiarmid and Hilda Emslie; ed Univ. of St Andrews, Royal Scottish Acad. of Music and Dramatic Art, Glasgow; Actor; Assoc. Dir Royal Exchange, Manchester; Jt Artistic Dir (with Jonathan Kent) Almeida Theatre 1990–2002; Gold Medal Royal Scottish Acad. of Music and Dramatic Art 1968. *Films include:* The Awakening 1980, Dragonslayer 1981, Gorky Park 1983, Return of the Jedi 1983, Dirty Rotten Scoundrels 1988, Restoration 1995, Little Orphan Annie 1995, Star Wars: Episode I: The Phantom Menace 1999, Sleepy Hollow 2000, Star Wars Episode II: Attack of the Clones 2002, Star Wars Episode III: Revenge of the Sith 2005, The Odds 2009, The Lost City of Z 2016. *Plays include:* Almeida Theatre: Volpone, Ivanov, Tartuffe, School for Wives, Creditors, Kurt Weill Concerts, Government Inspector, The Jew of Malta, The Tempest, Faith Healer (Olivier Award for Best Actor, Critics Circle Award for Best Actor 2001); Merchant of Venice 2014; RSC: Henry V, The Merchant of Venice, The Party, Crimes in Hot Countries, The Castle, Life of Galileo 2013; Royal Court: Hated Nightfall, Love of a Good Man, Insignificance; The Faith Machine 2011,

Emperor and Galilean 2011; Barbican: The Soldier's Tale; Royal Exchange, Manchester: Edward II, The Country Wife; Aldwych: The Black Prince; Oxford Playhouse: Peer Gynt, Mephisto; Booth Theater, New York: Faith Healer (Tony Award for Best Featured Actor) 2006; Donmar Warehouse: Pirandello's Henry IV 2005, Ibsen's John Gabriel Borkman 2007, The Prince of Homburg 2010; What Shadows, Birmingham Repertory Theatre 2016. *Plays directed include:* Almeida Theatre: Scenes from an Execution, Venice Preserved, Siren Song, A Hard Heart, Lulu, The Possibilities, The Rehearsal; Royal Exchange: Don Juan; Donmar Warehouse: Pirandello's Henry IV, Be Near Me 2009; Chichester Festival/Gielgud Theatre: Six characters in search of an author 2008. *Television includes:* Richard's Things 1981, Chernobyl: The Final Warning 1991, Heart of Darkness 1994, Hillsborough 1996, Rebecca, Karaoke, Creditors, The Nation's Health, The Professionals, Great Expectations 1999, All the King's Men 1999, Crime and Punishment 2001, Charles II 2004, Elizabeth I 2005, Our Hidden Lives 2005, City of Vice 2008, Margaret 2009, 37 Days 2014, Utopia 2014. *Radio:* numerous plays and readings, including Volpone (title role), The Cocktail Party (as The Uninvited Guest). *Appearances:* Aldeburgh Festival, Scottish Chamber Orchestra, London Symphony Orchestra (The Soldier's Tale), Royal Opera House, Covent Garden (The King goes forth to France). *Publications:* Be Near Me (adapted from the novel by Andrew O'Hagan) 2009. *Address:* c/o Conor McCaughan, Troika Talent, 180 Great Portland Street, London, W1W 5QZ England (office). *Telephone:* (20) 7336-7868 (office). *Website:* www.troikatalent.com (office).

McDONAGH, Bobby, BA, MA; Irish diplomatist; b. 29 June 1954, Washington, DC, USA; m. Mary McDonagh; four d.; ed Gonzaga Coll., Dublin, Balliol Coll., Oxford, UK; joined Dept of Foreign Affairs 1977, has held numerous EU-related posts including mem. Secr. European Parl. 1983–85, based at Perm. Mission to EU 1987–90, joined Cabinet of Farm Commr 1990, served as Deputy Chef de Cabinet to Commr for Social Affairs, fmr Deputy to IGC Rep., Treaty of Amsterdam negotiations, Dir-Gen. EU Div., Dept of Foreign Affairs 2001–05, fmr Alt. mem. Convention on Future of Europe, Perm. Rep. to EU 2005–09, Amb. to UK 2009–13, to Italy 2013–17, returned to Dublin 2017. *Publication:* Original Sin in a Brave New World: The Paradox of Europe 1998. *Address:* Department of Foreign Affairs and Trade, 80 St Stephen's Green, Dublin 2, D02 VY53, Ireland (office). *Telephone:* (1) 4082000 (office). *Website:* www.dfa.ie (office).

McDONAGH, Enda; Irish theologian and academic; b. 27 June 1930, Co. Mayo; s. of Patrick McDonagh and Mary Kelly; ed St Jarlath's Coll., Tuam, St Patrick's Coll., Maynooth, Gregorian Univ., Rome and Univ. of Munich; priest, Archdiocese of Tuam 1955–; Prof. of Moral Theology (and Canon Law), St Patrick's Coll. 1958–95, Dir Postgraduate Studies in Theology 1970–76, Dean of Faculty of Theology 1973–79; Lecturer in Irish School of Ecumenics, Dublin 1970–; Husking Prof. of Theology, Univ. of Notre Dame, USA 1979–81; McKeever Prof. of Theology, New York 1990–92; Chair. Governing Body, Univ. Coll. Cork 1999–2007; Leverhulme Research Fellow, Univ. of Cambridge, UK 1978; Hon. LLD (Nat. Univ. of Ireland) 2000, Hon. DD (Trinity Coll. Dublin) 2001; Ferguson Lecturer, Univ. of Manchester 1978. *Publications include:* Roman Catholics and Unity 1963, Religious Freedom 1967, Invitation and Response: Essays in Christian Moral Theology 1972, Gift and Call: Towards a Christian Theology of Morality 1975, Social Ethics and the Christian: Towards Freedom in Communion 1979, Doing the Truth: The Quest for Moral Theology (co-author) 1979, Church and Politics: From Theology to a Case History of Zimbabwe 1980, The Making of Disciples: Tasks of Moral Theology 1982, Between Chaos and New Creation 1985, Between Chaos and New Creation: Doing Theology at the Fringe (Theology and Life Series, No. 19) 1987, Small Hours of Belief 1989, The Gracing of Society 1989, Survival or Salvation?: A Second Mayo Book of Theology 1994, Faith in Fragments 1997, Religion and Politics in Ireland at the Turn of the Millennium: Essays in Honour of Garret Fitzgerald on the Occasion of His Seventy-Fifth Birthday (co-author) 2004, Vulnerable To The Holy: In Faith, Morality And Art 2005; ed. and contrib. The Meaning of Christian Marriage 1963, Moral Theology Renewed 1965, Truth and Life 1968, Faith and the Hungry Grass 1989, The Gracing of Society 1990, Salvation or Survival 1993, Faith in Fragments 1995, Vulnerable to the Holy 2005, Immersed in Mystery 2007. *Leisure interests:* theatre, poetry and the visual arts.

McDONALD, Arthur Bruce, OC, BSc, MSc, PhD, FRS, FRSC; Canadian astrophysicist and academic; *Professor Emeritus, Queen's University;* b. 29 Aug. 1943, Sydney, Nova Scotia; s. of A. Bruce and Valerie McDonald; m.; four c.; ed California Inst. of Tech., Pasadena, Dalhousie Univ., Halifax, NS; Postdoctoral Fellow, Atomic Energy of Canada, Chalk River, Ont. 1969–70, Asst Research Officer 1970–75, Sr Research Officer 1980–82; Prof., Princeton Univ. 1982–89; Prof., Queen's Univ. 1989–2013, Prof. Emer. 2013–; Univ. Research Chair 2002–06, Gordon and Patricia Gray Chair in Particle Astrophysics 2006–13, Dir Sudbury Neutrino Observatory (SNO) 1989–, Dir Inst. 1991–2003, 2006–09, Assoc. Dir SNOLAB Inst. 2009–13; Visiting positions: Univ. of Washington, Seattle 1978, Los Alamos Nat. Lab. 1981, Queen's Univ. 1988, Univ. of Oxford, UK 2003, 2009, CERN, Geneva, Switzerland 2004, Univ. of Hawaii 2004, 2009, Affiliate Grad. Faculty, Univ. of Hawaii 2010–17; mem. Princeton Univ. Physics Dept Advisory Council 2009–15, Scientific Advisory Bd Max-Planck-Institut für Kernphysik, Heidelberg, Germany 2010–12; mem. Bd Perimeter Inst. Waterloo, Canada 2011–18, Kavli Inst. for Cosmological Physics, Chicago, USA 2011–13; mem. Fed. Advisory Bd, Fundamental Science Review 2016–17; CIAR Cosmology and Gravity Program Assoc. 2000– (Chair. Advisory Bd 2000–05); mem. Canadian Asscn of Physicists 1964, American Physical Soc. 1969 (Fellow 1983); Certified mem. Professional Engineers of Ontario 2003; Hon. Life mem. Science North, Sudbury, Ont. 1997, Foreign Assoc., NAS 2016; Order of Ont. 2012, Order of Nova Scotia 2016; Hon. LLD (Dalhousie) 1997, (Univ. Coll. of Cape Breton) 1999, (St Francis Xavier Univ.) 2009; Hon. DSc (Royal Mil. Coll.) 2001, (Univ. of Chicago,) 2006, (Univ. of Alberta) 2011, (Univ. of Waterloo) 2012, (McGill Univ.) 2017, (Queen's Univ.) 2017, (Univ. of Toronto) 2017, (Laurentian Univ.) 2018; numerous awards, including Gov. Gen.'s Gold Medal, Dalhousie 1964, Rutherford Memorial Fellowship 1969–70, Killam Research Fellowship 1998, T.W. Bonner Prize in Nuclear Physics, American Physical Soc. 2003, Canadian Asscn of Physicists Medal for Lifetime Achievement in Physics 2003, Award of Excellence, Natural Sciences and Eng Research Council of Canada (NSERC) 2003, Gerhard Herzberg Canada Gold Medal for Science and Eng 2003, UK-Canada Rutherford Lecturer, Royal Soc. 2003, Bruno Pontecorvo Prize in Particle Physics, JINR, Dubna 2005, NSERC John C. Polanyi Award to SNO team 2006, Benjamin Franklin Medal in

Physics (co-recipient) 2007, Donald R. Hamilton Lecturer, Princeton Univ. 2008, Huggins Science Lecturer, Acadia Univ. 2008, inducted into Canadian Science and Eng Hall of Fame 2009, Killam Prize in the Natural Sciences 2010, inducted into Nova Scotia Discovery Centre Hall of Fame 2010, E. Segre Lecturer, Univ. of California, Berkeley 2010, Henry Marshall Tory Medal, Royal Soc. of Canada 2011, Giuseppe and Vanna Cocconi Prize, HEP Div., European Physics Society 2013, Nobel Prize in Physics (co-recipient with Takaaki Kajita) 2015, Breakthrough Prize in Fundamental Physics (co-recipient) 2016, W.B. Lewis Medal, Canadian Nuclear Soc. 2017, Distinguished Alumni Award, California Inst. of Tech. 2018. *Publications:* more than 150 papers in professional journals. *Address:* Department of Physics, Engineering Physics and Astronomy, Queen's University, Kingston, ON K7L 3N6, Canada (office). *Telephone:* (613) 533-2702 (office). *Fax:* (613) 533-6813 (office). *E-mail:* art@snolab.ca (office). *Website:* www.queensu.ca/physics/arthur-mcdonald (office); www.sno.phy.queensu.ca (office).

MacDONALD, Brian P., BS, MBA; American business executive; ed Mount Allison Univ., McGill Univ., Canada; worked at General Motors Corpn and held a variety of positions in Financial Management, including Deputy Chief Financial Officer (CFO) for Isuzu Motors Ltd, Treas. GM Canada 1998–2000; Vice-Pres. and Treas. Dell International, Inc. 2002–09, CFO Commercial Business Unit Dell, Inc. 2008–09, also Chair. Dell Financial Services; joined Sunoco Inc. 2009, Dir, Sunoco Partners LLC (Gen. Partner of Sunoco Logistics Partners LP) 2009–, CFO and Sr Vice-Pres. Sunoco Inc. 2009–10, CFO and Sr Vice-Pres. Sunoco Partners LLC 2010–12, Vice-Pres. –2012, mem. Bd of Dirs, Chair., Pres. and CEO ETP Holdco Corpn 2012–; Interim CEO Hertz Corpn Sept.–Nov. 2014, Pres. and CEO Hertz Equipment Rental Corpn 2014–15; mem. Bd of Dirs, Southeastern Pa Chapter of American Red Cross, SunCoke Energy Inc. 2010–12, Computer Sciences Corpn, CDK Global, Inc. 2015– (Chair. 2016–18), Suncor Energy, Inc 2018–. *Address:* CDK Global, Inc., 1950 Hassell Road, Hoffman Estates, IL 60169-6308, USA (office). *Telephone:* (888) 672-2140 (office). *E-mail:* investor.mail@cdk.com (office). *Website:* www.cdkglobal.com (office).

McDONALD, Donald Benjamin, AC, BCom; Australian business executive; b. 1 Sept. 1938, Sydney, NSW; s. of Benjamin McDonald and Maida Hands; m. Janet Isabel McDonald AO 1964; one s. one d.; ed Fort Street Boys' High School and Univ. of New South Wales; Finance Dir, Vogue Publs 1965–68; with Australian Opera 1968–72 (Gen. Man. 1987–96), Musica Viva Australia 1972–78; Gen. Man. Sydney Theatre Co. 1980–86; Dir Australian Tourist Comm. 1993–96; Chair. State Opera Ring Corpn, SA 1996–98, Australian Broadcasting Corpn 1996–2006, Constitutional Centenary Foundation 1997–2000, The Really Useful Company (Aust) Pty Ltd; Dir Festival, Perth 1998–, Univ. of New South Wales Foundation 1998–, Focus Publishing Pty Ltd 1999–2000, Australian Classification Bd 2007–; fmr Dir Sydney 2000 Olympic Bid Ltd, Chair. Sydney 2000 Bid Cultural Cttee; fmr mem. Bd Sydney Organising Cttee for the Olympic Games (SOCOG), Chair. SOCOG's Cultural Comm.; mem. Bd Welsh Nat. Opera, Cardiff, UK 1997–2000, Opera Australia Capital Fund, Perth Int. Festival; Visiting Fellow, Univ. of Edin., UK 1992; Fellow, Senate of Univ., Sydney 1994–97; AO 1991. *Publication:* The Boyer Collection (ed.) 2001. *Leisure interests:* reading, swimming. *Address:* c/o Australian Classification Board, Classification Branch, Attorney-General's Department, 3–5 National Circuit, Barton, ACT 260, Australia.

McDONALD, Gabrielle Kirk, LLB; American judge and fmr professor of law; b. 12 April 1942, St Paul, Minn.; d. of James G. Kirk and Frances R. Kirk; one s. one d.; ed Boston Univ., Hunter Coll., Howard Univ. School of Law (First in Class Grad.); Counsel, Legal Defense and Educ. Fund, Nat. Asscn for the Advancement of Colored People; Partner and Attorney-at-Law, McDonald & McDonald, PC, Matthews Branscomb PC; Judge, US Dist Court for the Fed. Dist Court; Of Counsel, Walker, Bright & Whittenton; Prof. of Law, Texas Southern Univ., Thurgood Marshall School of Law, St Mary's Univ. School of Law; Int. Criminal Law Judge, Int. Criminal Tribunal for the Fmr Yugoslavia (ICTY), Pres. ICTY; Arbitrator, Iran-US Claims Tribunal (retd 2013); Special Counsel to the Chair. on Human Rights, Freeport-McMoRan Copper & Gold, Inc.; mem. Exec. Bd, ABA Center for Human Rights; mem. Bd of Dirs American Arbitration Asscn; mem. Bd, Int. Jury of the Félix Houphouët-Boigny Peace Prize, ABA Human Rights Center and Genocide Prevention Task Force; mem. Bd of Trustees, Howard Univ.; mem. American Acad. of Diplomacy, US Inst. of Peace, Horatio Alger Asscn of Distinguished Americans; Hon. DJur (Georgetown Univ. Law Center), (Univ. of Notre Dame), (Howard Univ. School of Law), (Stetson Coll. of Law), (Jewish Theological Seminary), (Amherst Coll.), (Univ. of Hartford); Leadership Award, Cen. Eastern European Law Initiative, First Equal Justice and Ronald Brown Int. Law Awards, Nat. Bar Asscn, Goler Teal Butcher Award for Human Rights, American Soc. of Int. Law, Human Rights Award, Minnesota Advocates for Human Rights, Margaret Brent Women Lawyers of Achievement Award, ABA Comm. on Women in the Profession, Congressman Mickey Leland Legacy Award, First Women Ground Breakers in Int. Justice Award, Open Soc. Inst., Dorothy I. Height Lifetime Achievement Award, inducted into Texas Women's Hall of Fame. *Publications:* Substantive and Procedural Aspects of International Criminal Law, The Experience of International and National Courts (co-ed.) 2000; several published addresses and articles in int. law reviews.

MACDONALD, Henry Leonard, LLM; Suriname diplomatist; *President, World Development Foundation;* b. 3 Aug. 1963, NW Nickerie; m. Hyacinth MacDonald; five c.; ed Anton de Kon Univ., American Univ., Washington, DC, USA; Coordinator for Int. Affairs and Human Rights, Ministry of Justice and Police 1989–98; Deputy Chief of Mission to OAS 1998–2000; Chargé d'affaires a.i., Embassy in Washington, DC 2000, Deputy Chief of Mission, 2001–07, also Alt. Rep. to OAS; Coordinator to Summit of Americas Implementation Process 2004–07; Amb. and Perm. Rep. to UN, New York 2007–17; Pres. World Devt Foundation, Inc. 2017–; UNITAR Fellowship 1994, Law Fellowship, Univ. of Amsterdam 1998. *Address:* World Development Foundation, 353 West 48th Street, Suite 353, New York, NY 10036, USA (office). *E-mail:* wdf@globalwdf.org (office). *Website:* www.globalwdf.org (office).

MACDONALD, (Hugh) Ian, OC, BCom, BPhil, LLD, MA; Canadian economist, academic and university administrator; *President Emeritus and Professor Emeritus of Economics and Public Policy, York University;* b. 27 June 1929, Toronto; five c.; ed Univ. of Toronto, Univ. of Oxford, UK; Chief Economist, Govt of Ontario 1965–67, Deputy Treas. 1967–68, Deputy Minister of Treasury and Econs

1968–72, Deputy Minister of Treasury, Econs and Intergovernmental Affairs 1972–74; Pres. York Univ., Toronto 1974–84, Pres. Emer. 1984–, Dir York International 1984–94, Prof. of Econs and Public Policy 1984–, currently Prof. Emer., Dir Master of Public Admin. Program 1994–; Chair. McGraw-Hill Ryerson 1996–2014; Chair. Commonwealth of Learning, Vancouver 1994–2003, Fellow 2004; mem. The AGF Funds 1979–2014; Hon. Life mem. Canadian Olympic Asscn 1997–, Hon. Prof. (Hunan Univ.) 2007; Kt of Grace, Order of St Lazarus of Jerusalem 1978, Southeastern Conf. Public Admin Senator Boorsma Medal, USA 2006; Hon. LLD (Toronto) 1974, DUniv (Open Univ., UK) 1998, Hon. DLitt (Open Univ., Sri Lanka) 1999, (The B.R. Ambedkar Open Univ., Hyderabad, India) 2002, (York Univ.) 2007; Gov.-Gen.'s Medal 1952, Centennial Medal 1967, Queen's Silver Jubilee Medal 1977, Canadian Confed. Medal for the 125th Anniversary 1992, Award of Merit, Canadian Bureau for Int. Educ. 1994, Vanier Medal 2000, Senator Boorsma Medal 2006, Queen's Golden Jubilee Medal 2002, Queen's Diamond Jubilee Medal 2012, honored as one of the eight 'Legends of the Ontario Public Service', Govt of Ontario 2013, honored as one of ten 'Alumni of Influence', Univ. Coll., Univ. of Toronto 2013, Special Award, Commonwealth Asscn for Public Admin and Man. 2014. *Publications include:* numerous articles, essays and contribs to books. *Leisure interests:* ice hockey and tennis. *Address:* York University, Room N207, Schulich School of Business, 4700 Keele Street, Toronto, ON M3J 1P3, Canada (office). *Telephone:* (416) 736-5632 (office). *Fax:* (416) 736-5643 (office). *E-mail:* yorkmpa@yorku.ca (office). *Website:* www.schulich.yorku.ca (office).

McDONALD, Jackson Chester, BS, MA; American diplomatist; *President, Jefferson Waterman International;* b. Fla; m.; three c.; ed School of Foreign Service, Georgetown Univ., Washington, DC, Institut d'Etudes Politiques and Ecole Nationale d'Admin, Paris, France; career mem. Sr Foreign Service since 1980, Third Sec. and Vice-Consul, Embassy in Dhaka 1980–82, Country Officer for Bangladesh, Dept of State 1982–84, Second Sec. for Political Affairs, Embassy in Beirut 1984–86, studies at Ecole Nationale d'Admin 1986–87, First Sec. for Political Affairs, Embassy in Paris 1987–89, Russian language training 1989–90, First Sec. for Political Affairs, Embassy in Moscow 1990–91, Chargé d'affaires a.i., then Deputy Chief of Mission, Embassy in Almaty, Kazakhstan 1992–94, Consul-Gen. in Marseille (also accred to Monaco) 1994–97, mem. Senior Seminar exec. devt program 1997–98, Deputy Chief of Mission, Embassy in Abidjan, Côte d'Ivoire 1998–2001, Amb. to The Gambia 2001–04, to Guinea 2004–07; currently Pres. Jefferson Waterman Int.; mem. Africa Advisory Bd; Hon. Officer, Nat. Order of the Repub. of The Gambia; six Superior Honor Awards. *Address:* Jefferson Waterman International, 1401 K Street, North West, Suite 400, Washington, DC 20005, USA (office). *Telephone:* (202) 216-2200 (office). *Fax:* (202) 216-2999 (office). *E-mail:* info@jwidc.com (office). *Website:* www.jwidc.com (office).

McDONALD, John W., AB, JD; American lawyer and diplomatist (retd) and international organization executive; *Chairman and CEO, Institute for Multi-Track Diplomacy;* b. 18 Feb. 1922, Koblenz, Germany; s. of John Warlick McDonald and Ethel Mae Raynor; m. 1st Barbara Jane Stewart 1943 (divorced); one s. three d.; m. 2nd Christel Meyer 1970; ed Univ. of Illinois, Nat. War Coll., Washington, DC; admitted to Ill. Supreme Court Bar 1946, to US Supreme Court 1951; Legal Div., US Office of Mil. Govt, Berlin 1947; Asst District Attorney, US Mil. Govt Courts, Frankfurt 1947–50; Sec. Law Cttee, Allied High Comm., Petersburg, Germany 1950–52; mem. Mission to NATO and OECD, Paris Marshal Plan 1952–54; Office of Exec. Sec. Dept of State 1954–55; Exec. Sec. to Dir of Int. Co-operation Admin. 1955–59; US Econ. Co-ordinator for CENTO Affairs, Ankara 1959–63; Chief, Econ. and Commercial Sections, Embassy in Cairo 1963–66; Deputy Dir Office of Econ. and Social Affairs, Dept of State 1967–68, Dir 1968–71; Co-ordinator, UN Multilateral Devt Programmes, Dept of State 1971–74, Acting Deputy Asst Sec. of State for Econ. and Social Affairs 1971, 1973; Deputy Dir-Gen. ILO, Geneva, Switzerland 1974–78; Pres. Int. Telecommunications Satellite Org. (INTELSAT) Conf. on Privileges and Immunities 1978; Amb. to UN Conf. on TCDC 1978; Sec.-Gen. 27th Colombo Plan Ministerial Meeting 1978; US Co-ordinator for UN Decade on Drinking Water and Sanitation 1979; rep. to UN Confs with rank of Amb. 1978–; Amb. to UNIDO III 1979–80; Chair. Fed. Cttee for UN Int. Year of Disabled Persons; Amb. to UN World Ass. on Ageing 1981–82; Co-ordinator for Multilateral Affairs, Center for the Study of Foreign Affairs, US Dept of State 1983–87; Pres. Iowa Peace Inst. 1988–92, People-to-People Cttee for the Handicapped, Countdown 2001, World Cttee: UN Decade of Disabled Persons; del. to many int. confs; Bd of Dirs Global Water 1982–; Chair. American Asscn for Int. Ageing 1983–; Law School Prof., George Washington Univ., Washington, DC 1987–88; Adjunct Prof. of Political Science, Grinnell Coll. 1989–92; Distinguished Visiting Prof., George Mason Univ., Fairfax, Va 1992–93; Adjunct Prof., Union Inst. 1995–98, George Mason Univ. 1998–2000; Co-founder, Chair. and CEO Inst. for Multi-Track Diplomacy, Washington, DC 1992–; mem. Cosmos Club, American Foreign Service Asscn, US Asscn for the Club of Rome, DKE; Hon. PhD (Mount Mercy Coll.) 1989, (Teiko Mary Crest Univ.) 1991, (Salisbury State Univ.) 1993; Hon. LLD (St John's Univ.) 2007; Superior Honour Award, Dept of State 1972, Presidential Meritorial Service Award 1984, Alumni Asscn Award, Univ. of Illinois School of Liberal Arts 2004, Alumni of the Year Award, Univ. of Illinois 2006, Amb. John W. McDonald Award for Leadership and Innovation in Global Governance and Conflict Resolution, Univ. of Massachusetts, Boston Campus 2011. *Publications:* The North-South Dialogue and the United Nations 1982, How To Be a Delegate 1984, International Negotiations 1985, Perspectives on Negotiation: Four Case Studies 1986, Conflict Resolution: Track Two Diplomacy 1987, US-Soviet Summitry 1987, US Base Rights Negotiations 1989, Multi-Track Diplomacy 1991, Defining a US Negotiating Style 1996, The Shifting Grounds of Conflict and Peacebuilding 2008. *Leisure interests:* reading, tennis, fencing, skiing. *Address:* Institute for Multi-Track Diplomacy, 1901 North Fort Myer Drive, Suite 405, Arlington, VA 22209, USA (office). *Telephone:* (703) 528-3863 (office); (703) 525-9755 (home). *Fax:* (703) 528-5776 (office). *E-mail:* jmcdonald@imtd.org (office). *Website:* www.imtd.org (office).

MacDONALD, Julien, OBE, MA; British fashion designer; b. 19 March 1972, Merthyr Tydfil, Wales; ed Cyfarthfa High School, Merthyr Tydfil, Faculty of Arts and Architecture, Brighton, Royal Coll. of Art; worked for Alexander McQueen and Koji Tatsuno as a student; knitwear designer for Chanel Ready-to-Wear, Chanel Couture and Karl Lagerfeld; has had four shows in his own right; Art Dir Max Factor Spring/Summer 1999 advertising campaign (including TV commercial);

Chief Designer, Givenchy 2001–04; selected by British Airways to redesign their flight attendants' uniforms 2001; consultant, Boots PLC 2001–; creations have been worn by Joely Richardson, Dannii Minogue, Geri Halliwell, Dame Shirley Bassey, Carmen Electra, Naomi Campbell, Beyoncé Knowles, Bonnie Tyler and Selena Gomez; London Fashion Award for Glamour, named British Fashion Designer of the Year 2001. *Television:* judge on UK version of Project Runway, known as Project Catwalk (Sky One) 2008, judge on Britain & Ireland's Next Top Model 2010, celebrity contestant on Strictly Come Dancing 2013. *Telephone:* (20) 3542-0270 (office). *E-mail:* gemma@julienmacdonald.com (office). *Website:* www .julienmacdonald.com (office).

McDONALD, Mary Lou; Irish politician; *President, Sinn Féin;* b. 1 May 1969, Dublin; m. Martin Lanigan; two c.; ed Trinity Coll., Dublin, Univ. of Limerick, Dublin City Univ.; fmr consultant, Irish Productivity Centre; fmr researcher, Inst. of European Affairs; fmr trainer, Partnership Unit, Educational and Training Services Trust; mem. European Parl. (Sinn Féin) for Dublin 2004–09; mem. Dáil (parl.) for Dublin Central 2011–, mem. Public Accounts Cttee 2011–17; mem. Fianna Fáil 1997–98; mem. Sinn Féin 1998–, Vice-Pres. 2009–18, Pres. 2018–. *Address:* Sinn Féin, 53 Falls Rd, Belfast BT12 4PD, Northern Ireland (office). *Telephone:* (28) 9034-7350 (office). *Fax:* (28) 9022-3001 (office). *E-mail:* marylou@ sinnfein.ie (office). *Website:* www.sinnfein.ie (office).

McDONALD, Robert (Bob) A., BS, MBA, FRSA; American business executive and government official; b. 20 June 1953, Gary, Ind.; m. Diane McDonald; one s. one d.; ed US Mil. Acad., West Point, Univ. of Utah; Capt., US Army 1975–80; joined P&G 1980, Brand Asst, Solo, PS&D Advertising 1980–81, Sales Training, Oklahoma City Sales Dist 1981, Asst Brand Man., Dawn, PS&D Advertising 1981–82, Asst Brand Man., Cascade, PS&D Advertising 1982–83, Brand Man., Cascade 1983–84, Brand Man., Tide, PS&D Advertising 1984–86, Brand Man., Tide 1986–87, Assoc. Advertising Man., Laundry Products, PS&D Div. 1987–89, Man., Laundry Products, P&G Canada 1989–91, Gen. Man., Philippines, Asia/ Pacific-South, P&G Far East 1991–94, Vice-Pres., Gen. Man., Philippines, Asia/ Pacific-South, P&G Far East 1994–95, Vice-Pres., Gen. Man., Laundry and Cleaning Products, P&G Asia, and Beauty Care Products-Japan, P&G Asia 1995–96, Regional Vice-Pres. Japan, Procter & Gamble Asia 1996–99, Vice-Pres. Northeast Asia 1999, Pres. Northeast Asia 1999–2001, Pres. Global Fabric Care 2001, Pres. Global Fabric & Home Care 2001–04, Vice-Chair. Global Operations, Procter & Gamble Co. 2004–07, COO Procter & Gamble Co. 2007–09, Pres. and CEO 2009–13, Chair. 2010–13; Sec. for Veterans Affairs 2014–17; mem. Bd of Dirs Xerox Corpn, McKinsey Advisory Council; Chair. GS1, Fuqua Global Partnerships Cttee, Duke Univ.; Vice-Chair. US-China Business Council; Special Amb., Hyogo Pref. and Kobe City, Japan; mem. US Advisory Cttee for Trade Policy and Negotiations, Asscn of Grads, US Mil. Acad., West Point, Singapore Int. Advisory Council of Econ. Devt Bd; Mentor, Nat. Conf. on Ethics in America; mem. Advisory Bd Northwestern Integrated Marketing Communications, David Eccles School of Business, Univ. of Utah, Grad. School of Man., St Petersburg State Univ., Russia; mem. Bd of Visitors and Exec. Cttee, Fuqua School of Business, Duke Univ.; fmr Dir, Procter & Gamble and Clorox Jt Venture; fmr Chair. Soap and Detergent Asscn; fmr Gov. American Chamber of Commerce in Japan; fmr Moderator, Kobe Union Church Council; Inaugural Leadership Excellence Award, Stockdale Center for Ethical Leadership at US Naval Acad. and Harvard Business Review 2007, Pres.'s Leadership Award, Far East Council Boy Scouts.

MacDONALD, Hon. Rodney, BS; Canadian politician and education administrator; *CEO, Colaisde na Gàidhlig / The Gaelic College;* b. 2 Jan. 1972, Inverness, Nova Scotia; s. of Alex Angus and Elizabeth Ann MacDonald; m. Lori-Ann MacDonald; one s.; ed St. Francis Xavier Univ.; teacher, Strait Regional School Board 1994–99; MLA for Inverness 1999–2009; Premier of Nova Scotia 2006–09; Leader, Nova Scotia Progressive Conservative Party 2006–09; Founder and CEO RMD Development Inc. (consultancy) 2010–; CEO Colaisde na Gàidhlig/The Gaelic Coll. 2011–; mem. Bd of Dirs Canada Nova Scotia Offshore Petroleum Board 2010–16. *Address:* Colaisde na Gàidhlig/The Gaelic College, PO Box 80, 51779 Cabot Trail, Englishtown, NS B0C 1H0, Canada (office). *Telephone:* (902) 295-3411 (office). *E-mail:* ceo@gaeliccollege.edu (office). *Website:* www.gaeliccollege.edu (office).

McDONALD, Sir Trevor, Kt, OBE; British broadcast journalist; b. 16 Aug. 1939, Trinidad; m.; two s. one d.; worked on newspapers, radio and TV, Trinidad 1960–69; Producer BBC Caribbean Service and World Service, London 1969–73; reporter Ind. TV News 1973–78, sports corresp. 1978–80, diplomatic corresp. 1980–87, newscaster 1982–87, Diplomatic Ed. Channel Four News 1987–89, newscaster News at 5.40 1989–90, News at Ten 1990–99, ITV Evening News 1999–2000, ITV News at Ten 2001–04, 2008, News at 10.30 2004–05; Chair. Better English Campaign 1995–97, Nuffield Language Inquiry 1998–2000; apptd Gov. English-Speaking Union of the Commonwealth 2000; Pres. European Year of Languages 2000; Chancellor London South Bank Univ. 1999–2009; Hon. Fellow, Liverpool John Moores Univ. 1998, Hon. Vice-Pres. Vision Aid Overseas; Hon. DLitt (South Bank) 1994, (Plymouth) 1995, (Southampton Inst.) 1997, (Nottingham) 1997, Dr hc (Surrey) 1997, (Open Univ.) 1997, Hon. LLD (Univ. of West Indies) 1996; Gold Medal, Royal TV Soc. 1998, Richard Dimbleby Award for outstanding contrib. to TV, BAFTA 1999, Royal Television Soc. Lifetime Achievement Award 2005, BAFTA Fellowship, British Acad. Television Awards 2011. *Publications include:* Clive Lloyd: A Biography 1985, Vivian Richards: A Biography 1987, Queen and Commonwealth 1989, Fortunate Circumstances (autobiography) 1993, Favourite Poems 1997, World of Poetry 1999. *Leisure interests:* tennis, golf, cricket. *Address:* c/o ITN, 200 Gray's Inn Road, London, WC1X 8XZ, England.

MACDONALD OF RIVER GLAVEN, Baron (Life Peer), cr. 2010, of Cley-next-the-Sea in the County of Norfolk; **Ken Macdonald,** BA, QC; British barrister; *Founder-Member, Matrix Chambers;* b. 4 Jan. 1953; s. of Kenneth Macdonald and Maureen Sheridan Hacker; m. Linda Zuck 1980; two s. one d.; ed St Edmund Hall, Oxford; called to the Bar 1978, QC 1997; part-time judge, Crown Court 2001–; Dir of Public Prosecutions and Head of Crown Prosecution Service 2003–08; Chair. Criminal Bar Asscn; Founder-mem. Matrix Chambers; Bencher of the Inner Temple 2003–; mem. Sentencing Guidelines Council 2003–08; mem. Criminal Procedure Rule Cttee 2003–08. *Leisure interests:* Arsenal Football Club, crime thrillers, film noir, 20th century history. *Address:* Matrix Chambers, Griffin

Buildings, Gray's Inn, London, WC1R 5LN, England (office). *Telephone:* (20) 7404-3447 (office). *Website:* www.matrixlaw.co.uk (office).

McDONNELL, Robert (Bob) Francis, BBA, MBA, MA, JD; American lawyer and fmr politician; b. 15 June 1954, Philadelphia, Pa; s. of John McDonnell and Emma McDonnell; m. Maureen Patricia Gardner 1976; two s. three d.; ed Bishop Ireton High School, Alexandria, Va, Univ. of Notre Dame, Boston Univ., Regent Univ. School of Law; served as medical supply officer in US Army for four years, and in Army Reserve 1981–97 (retired with rank of Lt-Col), ran medical clinic in Germany 1976–79, in Newport News, Va 1979–81, various positions American Hosp. Supply Corpn 1981–85; policy intern, Republican Policy Cttee 1988; law clerk, Office of Commonwealth Attorney, Chesapeake, 1989, Asst Commonwealth Attorney, Virginia Beach 1990–91; represented 84th Dist in Virginia Beach in Virginia House of Dels 1992–2005, Co-Chair. Cttee on the Chesapeake and its Tributaries 2000–01, Chair. Courts of Justice Cttee 2003, also served on Rules Cttee 2000–05, Asst Majority Leader 2002–06; Pnr, Huff, Poole & Mahoney, Professional Corpn, Virginia Beach 1992–2006; Attorney-Gen., State of Virginia 2006–09; Gov. of Virginia 2010–14; fmr Chair. Republican Govs Asscn, Southern Growth Policies Bd, Southern Regional Educ. Bd, Legal Affairs Cttee of the Nat. Govs Asscn; Republican; convicted of 11 charges including wire fraud and receiving property based on his official duties while Gov. of Virginia and sentenced to two years in prison 2015; named Legislator of Year, Network of Victims of Crime 1996, Family Foundation 1998, 2001, Nat. Legislator of Year, Nat. Child Support Enforcement Asscn 1998, Legislator of Year, Virginia Sheriff's Asscn 2005.

McDONOUGH, Denis R., BA, MSFS; American government official; b. 2 Dec. 1969, Stillwater, Minn.; s. of William McDonough and Kathleen McDonough; ed St John's Univ., Collegeville, Minn., Edmund A. Walsh School of Foreign Service, Georgetown Univ., Washington, DC; following graduation, travelled extensively throughout Latin America and taught high school in Belize early 1990s; worked as an aide to Int. Relations Cttee, US House of Reps, Washington, DC 1996–99; Sr Foreign Policy Advisor to Senator Tom Daschle 1999–2004; Legis. Dir for Senator Ken Salazar 2004–05; Sr Fellow, Center for American Progress 2004; Chief Foreign Policy Advisor to Senator Barack Obama 2007–09; Head of Strategic Communication, Nat. Security Council 2009–10, also served as Nat. Security Council Chief of Staff; Deputy Nat. Security Advisor to Pres. Barack Obama 2010–13; Chief of Staff, The White House 2013–17.

McDONOUGH, William Andrews, BA, MArch, FAIA, Int. FRIBA; American architect and business executive; *Founding Principal, William McDonough + Partners;* b. 21 Feb. 1951, Tokyo, Japan; ed Dartmouth Coll., Yale Univ.; Founding Prin. William McDonough + Partners, New York City 1981– (moved to Charlottesville, Va 1994); first major comm. Environmental Defense Fund HQ 1985; Dean of School of Architecture, Univ. of Virginia 1994–99; several large corp. projects for The Gap, Nike and Herman Miller; commissioned in 1991 to write The Hannover Principles: Design for Sustainability as guidelines for the City of Hannover's EXPO 2000; commissioned for 20-year, US $2 billion environmental re-eng of Ford Motor Co.'s River Rouge Plant, Dearborn, Mich., including world's largest 'living roof'; Co-founder and Prin., MBDC; Venture Partner and Sr Advisor, VantagePoint Venture Partners 2004–; Chair. Bd of Councilors, China-US Center for Sustainable Devt 1999–2009, Chair. Emer. 2009–; Chair. Meta-Council on the Circular Economy, World Econ. Forum 2014–; mem. Advisory Bd, Dow Jones Sustainability Index 2004–, Cherokee Sustainability Advisory Council 2004–, External Advisory Council Walmart 2009–13, SAP CEO Sustainability Advisory Panel 2011–; Co-founder not-for-profit orgs GreenBlue 2000, Cradle to Cradle Products Innovation Inst. 2009; contributing author on Huffington Post since 2013; Charter mem. US Green Buidling Council 1993–; Dean, School of Architecture and Edward E. Elson Prof. of Architecture, Univ. of Virginia 1994–99, Alumni Research Chair, Visiting Exec. Lecturer, Darden School of Business 1999–; Consulting Prof., Dept of Civil and Environmental Eng 2004–; Founding mem. Sustainability Leadership Council, Univ. of Cambridge, UK 2007–; Fellow, Urban Land Inst. 1999; Hon. Prof. Tongji Univ., Shanghai 2004–; Hon. mem. American Soc. of Landscape Architects 2008; first and only individual recipient of Presidential Award for Sustainable Devt 1996, named by TIME magazine as a Hero for the Planet 1999, named by Interiors Magazine as Designer of the Year 1999, I.D. Forty Design Award 2001, Benjamin Botwinick Prize for Ethical Practice in the Professions 2003, first US EPA Presidential Green Chem. Challenge Award 2003, Nat. Design Award, Smithsonian Cooper-Hewitt Nat. Design Museum 2004, Presidential Green Chem. Challenge Award 2004, 21st Century Visionary Science Leadership Award 2008, Rachel Carson Environmental Award 2013, J.N. 'Ding' Darling Conservation Award 2015. *Projects include:* Herman Miller 'GreenHouse' Factory and Offices 1995, 901 Cherry, Offices for Gap Inc. 1997, Oberlin Coll.'s Adam Joseph Lewis Center for Environmental Studies 2000. *Publication:* Cradle to Cradle: Remaking the Way We Make Things (co-author) 2002, The Upcycle: Beyond Sustainability: Designing for Abundance (co-author) 2013. *Address:* William McDonough + Partners, 700 East Jefferson Street, Charlottesville, VA 22902, USA (office). *Telephone:* (434) 979-1111 (office). *Fax:* (434) 979-1112 (office). *E-mail:* info@mcdonoughpartners.com (office); media@mcdonough.com. *Website:* www.mcdonoughpartners.com (office); live-mcdonoughpartners.gotpantheon.com/ williammcdonough (office); www.mcdonough.com.

McDORMAND, Frances, BA, MFA; American actress; b. 23 June 1957, Chicago, Ill.; d. of Veron McDormand and Noreen McDormand; m. Joel Coen (q.v.) 1994; one s.; ed Bethany Coll., Yale Univ. School of Drama; Screen Actors' Guild Award 1996, London Film Critics' Circle Award 1996, Ind. Spirit Award 1996, American Comedy Award 1997. *Films include:* Blood Simple 1984, Raising Arizona 1987, Mississippi Burning 1988, Chattahoochee 1990, Darkman 1990, Miller's Crossing 1990, Hidden Agenda 1990, The Butcher's Wife 1991, Passed Away 1992, Short Cuts 1993, Beyond Rangoon 1995, Fargo 1996 (Acad. Award for Best Actress), Primal Fear 1996, Lone Star 1996, Paradise Road 1997, Johnny Skidmarks 1997, Madeline 1998, Talk of Angels 1998, Wonder Boys (Best Supporting Actress, Broadcast Film Critics Asscn, Florida Film Critics Circle, LA Film Critics Asscn 2000) 1999, Almost Famous 2000, The Man Who Wasn't There 2001, Upheaval 2001, Laurel Canyon 2002, City By the Sea 2002, Something's Gotta Give 2003, North Country 2005, Friends with Money (Independent Spirit Award for Best Supporting Female) 2006, Miss Pettigrew Lives for a Day 2007, Burn After Reading 2008, Transformers: Dark of the Moon 2011, Moonrise Kingdom 2012,

Promised Land 2012, Every Secret Thing 2014, The Good Dinosaur 2015, Three Billboards Outside Ebbing, Missouri (Golden Globe Award for Best Performance By An Actress In A Motion Picture, Drama 2018, Academy Award for Best Actress in a Leading Role 2018) 2017. *Stage appearances include:* Awake and Sing 1984, Painting Churches 1984, The Three Sisters 1985, All My Sons 1986, A Streetcar Named Desire 1988, Moon for the Misbegotten 1992, Sisters Rosensweig 1993, The Swan 1993, Good People (Tony Award for Best Actress in a Play) 2011. *Television includes:* Olive Kitteridge (Outstanding Performance by a Female Actor in a Television Movie or Mini-Series, Screen Actors' Guild Awards 2015, Primetime Emmy Award for Outstanding Lead Actress in a Limited Series or a Movie and Outstanding Limited Series 2015) 2014. *Address:* c/o WME, 9601 Wilshire Blvd, Beverly Hills, CA 90212, USA (office). *Website:* www.wma.com (office).

MacDOUALL-GAYE, Neneh; Gambian broadcaster, journalist and government official; b. 8 April 1957, Banjul; m.; ed Radio and TV Training Inst., Maspero-Cairo, Egypt, Nat. Film and TV Inst., Accra, Ghana, Radio Netherlands Training Centre, Netherlands; Presenter/Producer, Radio Gambia 1979; Producer and Head of Media Unit, Worldview International Foundation 1993; Prin. Producer, Documentary, Drama and Youth Dept, Gambia Radio and TV Services (GRTS) 1996–2001, Man. TV Programmes 2001–02, Deputy Dir-Gen. GRTS 2002–05; Sec. of State, Dept of State for Trade, Industry and Employment 2005, Sec. of State for Communication, Information and Information Tech. 2005–08; Man. Dir Daily Observer (newspaper) 2008–09; Amb. to USA May–Aug. 2009; Founder and host, Talking Point Africa USA (TV programme) 2011–; Minister of Foreign Affairs 2015–17 (resgnd).

McDOUGALL, Douglas, OBE; British business executive; b. 1944; ed Univ. of Oxford; joined Baillie Gifford & Co. 1965, Partner 1969–89, Jt Sr Partner 1989–99; Chair. Scottish Investment Trust PLC 2003–16; fmr Chair. Investment Man. Regulatory Org. Ltd (IMRO), Asscn of Investment Trust Cos, Institutional Fund Mans Asscn; Chair. Law Debenture Corpn PLC 2000–13, 3i Bioscience Investment Trust PLC, Foreign & Colonial Eurotrust PLC, The Independent Investment Trust PLC, Pacific Horizon Investment Trust PLC; Dir The Herald Investment Trust PLC 2002, The Monks Investment Trust PLC (also Sr Ind. Dir) 1999. *Address:* c/o The Scottish Investment Trust, 6 Albyn Place, Edinburgh, EH2 4NL, Scotland.

MacDOWELL, Andie; American actress; b. 21 April 1958, S. Carolina; d. of Marion MacDowell and Pauline MacDowell; m. 1st Paul Qualley; two d. one s.; m. 2nd Rhett DeCamp Hartzog 2001 (divorced 2004). *Television appearances include:* Secret of the Sahara 1987, Women and Men 2, In Love There Are No Rules 1991, Jo 2002, Riding the Bus with My Sister 2005, The Prince of Motor City 2008, Lone Star 2010, Jane by Design (series) 2012, Cedar Cove (series) 2013–15. *Films include:* Greystoke 1984, St Elmo's Fire 1985, Sex, Lies and Videotape 1989, Green Card 1990, Hudson Hawk 1991, The Object of Beauty 1991, The Player 1992, Ruby 1992, Groundhog Day 1993, Short Cuts 1993, Bad Girls 1994, Four Weddings and a Funeral 1994, Unstrung Heroes 1995, My Life and Me 1996, Multiplicity 1996, The End of Violence 1997, Town and Country 1998, Shadrack 1998, The Scalper 1998, Just the Ticket 1998, Muppets From Space 1999, The Music 2000, Town and Country 2001, Harrison's Flowers 2002, Crush 2002, Ginostra 2002, The Last Sign 2004, Beauty Shop 2005, Tara Road 2005, Barnyard (voice) 2006, Inconceivable 2008, The 5th Quarter 2009, Daydream Nation 2010, Monte Carlo 2011, Footloose 2011, Mighty Fine 2012, Breaking at the Edge 2013, Love After Love 2017. *Address:* c/o ICM, 10250 Constellation Blvd, Los Angeles, CA 90067, USA.

McDOWELL, David Keith, MA; New Zealand diplomatist, conservationist and environmental consultant; b. 30 April 1937, Palmerston North; s. of Keith McDowell and Gwen McDowell; m. Jan Ingram 1960; one s. three d.; ed Victoria Univ. of Wellington; joined Ministry of Foreign Affairs 1959, seconded to Prime Minister's Dept, Western Samoa 1962–63, Head, UN and African and Middle East Divs 1973, Dir of External Aid 1973–76, Head, Econ. Div. 1980–81, Special Asst to Sec.-Gen., Commonwealth Secr., London 1969–72; High Commr in Fiji 1977–80, in India, Nepal and Bangladesh 1983–85; Asst Sec. of Foreign Affairs for Asia, Australia and the Americas 1981–85; First Sec., Perm. Mission to UN 1964–68, Perm. Rep. 1985–88; Dir-Gen. Dept of Conservation 1988–89; CEO Dept of Prime Minister and Cabinet 1989–91; Amb. to Japan 1992–94; Dir-Gen. Int. Union for Conservation of Nature (IUCN—World Conservation Union), Switzerland 1994–99; pvt. consultant 1999–; mem. Review Panel, Environmental Performance of World Bank 2002, Ministerial Advisory Group on Oceans Policy 2002–03 (NZ), Strategic Advisory Group, Office of the Compliance Advisor/Ombudsman (CAO), Int. Finance Corpn 2003–; currently environmental consultant, Panel of Experts, Nam Theun Multi-Purpose Project, Ministry of Mines and Energy, Laos. *Leisure interests:* fishing, boating, tennis, conservation, gardening, music. *Address:* 86 Waerenga Road, Otaki, New Zealand (home). *Telephone:* (6) 364-6296 (office). *E-mail:* jan.david.mcdowell@xtra.co.nz (office).

McDOWELL, John Henry, MA, FBA, FAAS; British academic; *Distinguished University Professor, University of Pittsburgh;* b. 7 March 1942, Boksburg, South Africa; s. of Sir Henry McDowell and Norah McDowell (née Douthwaite); m. Andrea Lehrke 1977; ed St John's Coll. Johannesburg, Univ. Coll. of Rhodesia and Nyasaland, New Coll., Oxford; Fellow, Praelector in Philosophy, Univ. Coll., Oxford 1966–86; Prof. of Philosophy, Univ. of Pittsburgh 1986–88, Distinguished Univ. Prof. 1988–; Hon. DHumLitt (Chicago) 2008; Distinguished Achievement Award, Andrew W. Mellon Foundation 2010. *Publications include:* Ed. (with Gareth Evans) Truth and Meaning, Ed. (with Philip Pettit) Subject, Thought and Context, Mind and World, Mind, Value and Reality, Meaning, Knowledge and Reality, Having the World in View, The Engaged Intellect; trans of Plato, Theaetetus. *Leisure interests:* gardening, reading. *Address:* Department of Philosophy, University of Pittsburgh, 1001 Cathedral of Learning, Pittsburgh, PA 15260 (office); 947 Heberton Street, Pittsburgh, PA 15206, USA. *Telephone:* (412) 624-5792 (office); (412) 361-3784. *E-mail:* jmcdowel@pitt.edu (office). *Website:* www.philosophy.pitt.edu (office).

McDOWELL, Malcolm; British actor; b. (Malcolm Taylor), 13 June 1943, Leeds, Yorks., England; m. 1st Mary Steenburgen 1980; one s. one d.; m. 2nd Kelley Kuhr 1992; began career with the RSC at Stratford 1965–66; early television appearances in such series as Dixon of Dock Green, Z Cars. *Stage appearances:* RSC, Stratford 1965–66, Entertaining Mr. Sloane, Royal Court 1975, Look Back in Anger, New York 1980, In Celebration, New York 1984, Holiday Old Vic 1987, Another Time, Old Vic 1993. *Films include:* If... 1969, Figures in a Landscape 1970, The Raging Moon 1971, A Clockwork Orange 1971, O Lucky Man 1973, Royal Flash 1975, Aces High 1976, Voyage of the Damned 1977, Caligula 1977, The Passage 1978, Time After Time 1979, Cat People 1981, Blue Thunder 1983, Get Crazy 1983, Britannia Hospital 1984, Gulag 1985, The Caller 1987, Sunset 1987, Sunrise 1988, Il Maestro 1989, Moon 44, Double Game, Class of 1999, Assassin of the Tsar 1991, Star Trek: Generations 1995, Tank Girl 1995, Mr Magoo 1998, Class of 1999, Gangster No 1 2000, Island of the Dead 2000, Just Visiting 2001, The Void 2001, Dorian 2001, The Barber 2001, Between Strangers 2002, Superman: Shadow of Apokolips 2002, I Spy 2002, I'll Sleep When I'm Dead 2003, Tempo 2003, Inhabited 2003, Red Roses and Petrol 2003, The Company 2003, Hidalgo 2004, Evilenko 2004, Bobby Jones, Stroke of Genius 2004, Tempesta 2004, Pinocchio 3000 (voice) 2004, Rag Tale 2005, Dinotopia: Quest for the Ruby Sunstone (voice) 2005, Cut Off 2006, Bye Bye Benjamin 2006, Exitz 2007, The List 2007, Halloween 2007, Doomsday 2008, The Evening Journey 2008, Blue Gold: World Water Wars 2008, Halloween II 2009, Suck 2009, The Book of Eli 2010, Golf in the Kingdom 2010, Easy A 2010, The Artist 2011, Psych 2011, Suing the Devil 2011, Silent Hill: Revelation 3D 2012, The High Fructose Adventures of Annoying Orange 2012, Antiviral 2012, Metalocalypse 2012, The Employer 2013, Some Kind of Beautiful 2014, Tbilisi, I Love You 2014, Kids vs Monsters 2015, The Black Hole 2016, Culture of Fear 2017, Dreams I Never Had 2018, The Player, Chain of Desire, East Wind, Night Train to Venice, Snake Eyes, Schweitzer, Kids of the Round Table, Where Truth Lies. *Television includes:* Our Friends in the North, Entourage, Heroes 2007–08, Robot Chicken: Star Wars 2007, War and Peace 2007, The Mentalist 2010–13, Franklin & Bash 2011–14, CSI: Miami 2010, 2012, Community 2013, Mozart in the Jungle 2014–18. *Address:* c/o Markham, Froggatt and Irwin, 4 Windmill Street, London, W1T 2HZ, England (office). *Telephone:* (20) 7636-4412 (office). *E-mail:* admin@markhamfroggattirwin.com (office). *Website:* www.markhamfroggattandirwin.com/cv/client_malcolm-mcdowell_id_100165.htm (office).

McDOWELL, Michelle, MBE, BSc, CEng, FREng, FICE; British civil engineer; *Chair of Civil and Structural Engineering, BDP;* b. 6 April 1963, Co. Londonderry, Northern Ireland; d. of Ronald McDowell and Doris McDowell; partner Jason Fox; two s.; ed Univ. of Bristol; joined BDP (design consultancy) 1997, currently Chair. Civil and Structural Eng; Vice-Chair. Asscn for Consultancy and Eng 2009, Chair. 2010; fmr Vice-Pres. Inst. of Civil Engineers; mem. British Construction Industry Awards Nat. Judging Panel 2011–; Fellow, Royal Acad. of Eng 2010–; Hon. DEng (Bristol) 2012; First Woman of Property Award 2010, Veuve Clicquot Business Woman of Award 2011, ACE Eng Amb. of the Year 2012. *Projects include:* Royal Albert Hall, BBC Mailbox, Birmingham, Roche HQ, Chatham Historic Dockyard, Royal Alexandra Children's Hosp., All England Lawn Tennis Club, Wimbledon, Palace of Westminster Restoration and Renewal. *Address:* BDP, 16 Brewhouse Yard, Clerkenwell, London, EC1V 4LJ, England (office). *Telephone:* (20) 7812-8000 (office). *E-mail:* michellejmcdowell@gmail.com (home). *Website:* www.bdp.com (office).

MACE, Dame Georgina, DBE, CBE, OBE, BSc, PhD, FRS; British ecologist and academic; *Professor of Biodiversity and Ecosystems and Head of the Centre for Biodiversity and Environment Research, University College London;* b. 12 July 1953, London, England; m. Roderick O. Evans; one s. two d.; ed Univs of Liverpool and Sussex; fmr Researcher, Smithsonian Inst., USA; Research Fellow, Inst. of Zoology, London 1991–2000, Scientific Dir 2000–06; Dir Natural Environment Research Council (NERC) Centre for Population Biology, Imperial Coll., London 2006–12; Prof. of Biodiversity and Ecosystems and Dir Centre for Biodiversity and Environment Research, Univ. Coll., London 2012–; Pres. Soc. for Conservation Biology 2007–09, British Ecological Soc. 2011–13; Chair. DIVERSITAS int. programme on biodiversity science 2012–14 (merged into Future Earth Programme 2014); Chair. Royal Soc. science policy report on 'Resilience to Extreme Weather' 2014; mem. UK Govt's Natural Capital Cttee 2012–15, NERC Council, Council of Royal Soc.; Academic Ed. PLOS Biology; Hon. DSc (Sussex) 2007; Int. Cosmos Prize (Japan) 2007, Dr A.H. Heineken Prize for Environmental Sciences 2016, Linnean Medal, Linnean Soc. 2016. *Publications:* numerous papers in professional journals. *Address:* Centre for Biodiversity & Environment Research, Department of Genetics, Evolution and Environment, University College London, Gower Street, London, WC1E 6BT, England (office). *Telephone:* (20) 3108-1125 (office). *E-mail:* g.mace@ucl.ac.uk (office). *Website:* www.ucl.ac.uk/cber/mace (office); iris.ucl.ac.uk (office).

MACEL, Christine; French gallery curator; *Chief Curator, Musée national d'art moderne – Centre Pompidou;* Chief Curator, Musée nat. d'art moderne – Centre Pompidou, Paris 2000–, Dir Département de création contemporaine et prospectif; has curated numerous exhbns, including Raymond Hains, Sophie Calle, Philippe Parreno, Gabriel Orozco, Dionysiac, Airs de Paris and The Promises of the Past; art critic for various magazines, including artpress, Flash Art and Artforum; mem. Jury, 54th Int. Art Exhbn, Venice Biennale 2011; Artistic Dir Venice Biennale 2017. *Publications include:* 315 Livre: No. 3 (ed.) 2004, Time taken, the work of time in the work of art (essay on contemporary art) 2007, Airs de Paris (with Daniel Birnbaum) 2007, Damian Ortega: 315 Livre Numero 17 (with Anna Hiddleston and Sinziana Ravini) 2008, Promises of the Past – A Discontinuous History of Art in Former Eastern Europe, Parreno (co-ed.) 2009, Ralph Samuel Grossman (with Laurent Salomé and Ralph Samuel Grossmann) 2010, Gabriel Orozco 2010, Danser sa vie – Anthologie (with Emma Lavigne) 2011, Danser sa vie – Album (with Emma Lavigne, Anna Hiddleston and Florencia Chernajovsky) 2011, Danser sa vie: Art et danse de 1900 à nos jours (with Emma Lavigne and Alain Seban) 2011. *Address:* Musée national d'art moderne, Centre Pompidou, place Georges Pompidou, 75004 Paris, France (office). *Telephone:* 1-44-78-12-33 (office). *E-mail:* info@centrepompidou.fr (office). *Website:* www.centrepompidou.fr (office).

McENERY, Peter Robert; British actor; b. 21 Feb. 1940; s. of Charles McEnery and Ada Mary Brinson; m. 1978; one d.; Founder-mem. and Assoc. Artist with RSC. *Theatre roles include:* Eugene in Look Homeward Angel 1962, Rudge in Next Time I'll Sing to You 1963, Konstantin in The Seagull 1964, Edward Gover in Made in Bangkok 1986, Trigorin in The Seagull 1975, Frederick Treves in The Elephant Man (Royal Nat. Theatre) 1980, Fredrick in A Little Night Music 1990, Torvald in A Doll's House 1994, Hector in Heartbreak House 1997, Claudius in Hamlet (Royal Nat. Theatre) 2000–01, Laertes, Clarence, Tybalt, Silvius, Patroclus, Bassanio,

Orlando, Pericles, Brutus, Antipholus, Albie Sachs, Lorenzaccio (with RSC). *Plays directed:* Richard III 1971, The Wound 1972. *TV:* Clayhanger 1976, The Aphrodite Inheritance 1979, The Jail Diary of Albie Sachs 1980, Japanese Style 1982, The Collectors 1986, The Mistress 1986, Witchcraft 1991, Reach for the Moon 2000. *Films:* Tunes of Glory 1961, Victim 1961, The Moonspinners 1963, Entertaining Mr Sloane 1970, La Curée, J'ai tué Raspoutine, Le Mur d'Atlantique, Le Montreur de Boxe. *Leisure interests:* steam railway preservation, skiing, American football. *Address:* United Agents, 12–26 Lexington Street, London, W1F 0LE, England. *Telephone:* (20) 3214-0800. *Fax:* (20) 7323-0101.

McENROE, John Patrick; American broadcaster and fmr professional tennis player; b. 16 Feb. 1959, Wiesbaden, then Fed. Repub. of Germany; s. of John P. McEnroe I and Katy McEnroe; brother of Patrick McEnroe, fmr professional tennis player; m. 1st Tatum O'Neal (q.v.) 1986; two s. one d.; 2nd Patty Smyth; two c.; one step-d.; ed Trinity High School, NJ and Stanford Univ.; amateur player 1976–78 (including NCAA singles championship 1978), professional 1978–93; winner of 77 singles titles during professional career, ranked world number one 1981–84; US Open Singles Champion 1979, 1980, 1981, 1984; US Open Doubles Champion 1979, 1981, 1989; Wimbledon Champion (doubles) 1979, 1981, 1983, 1984, 1992, (singles) 1981, 1983, 1984; WCT Champion 1979, 1981, 1983, 1984, 1989; Grand Prix Champion 1979, 1983, 1984; played Davis Cup for USA 1978–85, Capt. 1999–2000; only player to have reached the Wimbledon semifinals as pretournament qualifier 1977; tennis sportscaster, USA Network 1993–, CBS 1994–, ESPN; mem. Men's Sr Tours Circuits 1994–, winner numerous titles including Quality Challenge 1997, 1998, 1999, Honda Challenge 2003; returned to ATP Tour to play two doubles tournaments 2006; won at French Open with his brother Patrick for the over-45 legends doubles competition 2012; Owner John McEnroe Gallery, New York; coach, British Lawn Tennis Asscn 2003–; ATP Most Improved Player 1978, ITF World Champion 1981, 1983, 1984, ATP Player of the Year 1981, 1983, 1984, Nat. Father of the Year Award 1996, Int. Tennis Hall of Fame 1999, Davis Cup Commitment Award. *Television:* presenter, The Chair (ABC game show) 2002, McEnroe (talk show) CNBC 2004. *Publications:* You Cannot Be Serious (autobiog. with James Kaplan) 2002. *Leisure interest:* music. *Address:* The John McEnroe Gallery, 41 Greene Street, New York, NY 10013, USA. *Telephone:* (212) 219-0395. *Fax:* (212) 219-0399. *E-mail:* macgallery@earthlink.net. *Website:* johnmcenroegallery.com.

McENTEE, Andrew, BA, LLB, MA, LLM; British lawyer and international relations analyst; b. 2 July 1957, Glasgow, Scotland; s. of Shaun McEntee and Margaret McEntee (née O'Neill); ed Univ. of Stirling, Univ. of Wolverhampton, Univ. of North London, London Metropolitan Univ., School of Slavonic and East European Studies, Univ. Coll., London; Case Worker, Citizens' Advice Bureau 1982–83, Scottish Council for Civil Liberties (now Scottish Human Rights Centre) 1983–84; community care worker, Strathclyde Social Work Dept 1985–86; Gen. Sec. Chile Cttee for Human Rights/South American Human Rights Coordination 1986–91; Gen. Sec. Cen. America Human Rights Cttee 1993–96; UK-apptd Chair. Amnesty International Lawyers Network 1994–2001, Chair. Amnesty International UK 1998–2001; Sr Consultant, Atlantic Celtic Films Co. 1996–2002; Founder and UK Chair. Coalition for an Int. Criminal Court 1997–2002; adviser to Spanish and Chilean lawyers and victims and coordinator of Amnesty International case during extradition proceedings against Gen. Augusto Pinochet in London 1998–2000; Human Rights Adviser to OSCE mission to Serbia and Montenegro, Belgrade 2002–06; election observer in Latin America, Cen. and Eastern Europe, Russia, the Balkans, the Caucasus and Cen. Asia for FCO, OSCE and EU 2003–; Consultant/Assoc. Producer, Clover Films 2006–; Expert mem. UK Foreign Sec.'s Team of Experts for preventing sexual violence in armed conflict (Preventing Sexual Violence Initiative) 2012–; field worker, writer, lecturer and media commentator on human rights, security and int. relations; First Aid 'First Responder'. *Leisure interests:* gardening, bread-making by hand, hill walking, arts galleries, fmr Bellahouston Harrier. *Address:* Clover Films, 7 Alma Road, Windsor, Berks., SL4 3HU, England (office). *Telephone:* (1753) 850500 (office). *E-mail:* humanrightsresearch@yahoo.com (office). *Website:* www.clover-films.com (office); andrewmcentee.blogspot.com; andymcentee.wordpress.com.

McEWAN, Angus David, BE, MEngSc, PhD, FAA, FTSE; Australian (b. British) oceanographer; b. 20 July 1937, Alloa, Scotland; s. of David Nichol Rei McEwan and Anne Marion McEwan; m. Juliana R. Britten 1961 (divorced 1982); two d.; ed Upwey High School, Melbourne High School, Caulfield Tech. Coll., Melbourne Univ., Univ. of Cambridge; engineer, Aeronautical Research Labs, Melbourne 1956–58, Research Scientist 1961–62, 1966–69; Research Scientist, Program Leader, Chief Research Scientist, Div. of Atmospheric Research, CSIRO, Aspendale, Vic. 1972–81, Foundation Chief, Div. of Oceanography, Hobart 1981–95; Sr Scientific Adviser (Oceanographer) to CSIRO and Commonwealth Bureau of Meteorology 1995–2005; Australian Del. to UNESCO Intergovernmental Oceanographic Comm. (IOC) 1982–2004; mem. IOC Cttee on Climatic Changes and the Ocean 1982–90, Chair. 1987–90; Rep. of the Global Ocean Observing System (GOOS) Steering Cttee 1995–2003, Chair. Intergovernmental GOOS Cttee 1998–2001; Chair. Oceanographic Data Exchange Policy Group 2001–02; mem. numerous other nat. bodies and cttees concerning marine science; Rossby Fellow, Woods Hole Oceanographic Inst., USA 1975; Fellow, Australian Acad. of Technological Sciences and Eng; Hon. Research Prof., Univ. of Tasmania 1988–; Queen Elizabeth Fellow 1969–71, Australian Centenary Medal 2003. *Publications:* scientific articles on geophysical fluid dynamics. *Leisure interests:* sailing, sketching, woodwork. *Address:* 300 Sandy Bay Road, Sandy Bay, Tasmania 7005, Australia. *Telephone:* (3) 6221-2090. *Fax:* (3) 6221-2089. *E-mail:* oceans@iprimus.com.au.

McEWAN, Ian Russell, CBE, MA, FRSL; British writer; b. 21 June 1948, Aldershot, Hants.; s. of David McEwan and Rose Moore; m. 1st Penny Allen 1982 (divorced 1995); two s. and two step-d.; m. 2nd Annalena McAfee 1997; ed Woolverstone Hall, Univs of Sussex and East Anglia; Hon. Fellow, American Acad. of Arts and Sciences 1997; Hon. DPhil (Sussex) 1989, (East Anglia) 1993, (London) 1998; Primo Letterario, Prato 1982, Shakespeare Prize, Germany 1999, British Book Award for Author of the Year 2008, Jerusalem Prize 2011. *Screenplays:* The Imitation Game & Other Plays 1981, The Ploughman's Lunch 1985, Sour Sweet 1989, The Good Son 1993, On Chesil Beach 2017, The Children Act 2017. *Publications:* novels: The Cement Garden 1978, The Comfort of Strangers 1981,

Rose Blanche (juvenile) 1985, The Child in Time (Whitbread Novel of the Year 1987, Prix Fémina Etranger 1993) 1987, The Innocent 1989, Black Dogs 1992, The Daydreamer (juvenile) 1994, Enduring Love 1997, Amsterdam (Booker Prize for Fiction 1998) 1998, Atonement (WHSmith Literary Award 2002, Nat. Book Critics Circle Fiction Award 2002, Los Angeles Times Prize for Fiction 2003, Santiago Prize for the European Novel 2004) 2001, Saturday (James Tait Black Memorial Prize 2006) 2005, On Chesil Beach (British Book Award for Book of the Year 2008) 2007, Solar (Bollinger Everyman Wodehouse Prize for Comic Fiction) 2010, Sweet Tooth 2012, The Children Act 2014, Nutshell 2016, Machines Like Me 2019; short stories: First Love, Last Rites (Somerset Maugham Award 1976) 1975, In Between the Sheets 1978, My Purple Scented Novel 2018; librettos: Or Shall We Die? (oratorio) 1983, For You (opera) 2008. *Leisure interest:* hiking. *Address:* c/o Peter Straus Rogers, Coleridge & White Ltd, 20 Powis Mews, London, W11 1JN, England. *E-mail:* info@rcwlitagency.com. *Website:* www.rcwlitagency.com; www.ianmcewan.com.

McEWAN, Ross, BBS; New Zealand banking executive; *Chief Executive, Royal Bank of Scotland Group;* b. 16 July 1957; m. Stephanie McEwan; two c.; ed Massey Univ., Stanford Univ., USA; began career in Personnel Dept at Unilever and Dunlop; later worked in both insurance and investment industries in Australia and NZ for more than 25 years; held sr positions at First NZ Capital Securities; fmr Chief Exec. National Mutual Life Asscn of Australasia/AXA NZ; Exec. Gen. Man., later Group Exec. for Retail Banking Services, Commonwealth Bank of Australia –2012, Exec. Dir 2012–; UK Retail CEO Royal Bank of Scotland 2012–13, Group Chief Exec. and Exec. Dir Royal Bank of Scotland Group plc 2013–; currently CEO Nat. Westminster Bank plc, also Exec. Dir 2013–; mem. Bd of Dirs Preferred Capital Ltd 2007, ASB Bank 2008. *Leisure interests:* water skiing, cycling, reading, spending time with his family. *Address:* Royal Bank of Scotland Group plc, Group Secretariat, Business House F Gogarburn, Edinburgh, EH12 1HQ, Scotland (office). *Telephone:* (131) 556-8555 (office). *Fax:* (131) 557-6565 (office). *Website:* www.rbs.com (office).

McFADDEN, Daniel L., BS, PhD; American economist and academic; *Presidential Professor of Health Economics, University of Southern California;* b. 29 July 1937, Raleigh, NC; m. Beverlee Tito Simboli McFadden; one d. two s.; ed Univ. of Minnesota; Instructor in Physics, Univ. of Minnesota 1957–58, Research Asst in Social Psychology 1959–60, Instructor in Econs 1961–62; Asst Prof. of Econs, Univ. of Pittsburgh 1962–63; Asst Prof. of Econs, Univ. of Calif., Berkeley 1963–66, Assoc. Prof. 1966–68, Prof. of Econs 1968–79, 1990, E. Morris Cox Chair 1990, Dir Econometrics Lab. 1991–95, 1996, now Prof. of the Graduate School, Chair. Dept of Econs 1995–96; Prof. of Econs, Mass Inst. of Tech. 1978–91, James R. Killian Chair, 1984–91, Dir Statistics Center 1986–88; currently Presidential Prof. of Health Econs, Univ. of Southern California with jt appointments at Sol Price School of Public Policy and Dept of Econs, Dornsife Coll.; Visiting Assoc. Prof., Univ. of Chicago 1966–67; Irving Fisher Research Prof., Yale Univ. 1977–78; Sherman Fairchild Distinguished Scholar, Calif. Inst. of Tech. 1990; Pres. American Econ. Asscn 2005; mem. American Acad. of Arts and Sciences, NAS 1981–, American Philosophical Soc. 2006–; Dr hc (Univ. Coll. London) 2003, (North Carolina State Univ.) 2006; Econometrics Soc. Frisch Medal 1986, Nemmers Prize in Econs 2000, Nobel Prize for Econs (jt recipient) 2000, Richard Stone Prize in Applied Econometrics 2000. *Publications include:* Lectures on Longitudinal Analysis (Underground Classics in Economics) (jt author), Handbook of Econometrics IV (with R. Engle) 1994. *Address:* USC Sol Price School of Public Policy, University of Southern California, Lewis Hall 312, Los Angeles, CA 90089-0626, USA (office). *Telephone:* (213) 821-7955 (office). *E-mail:* daniel.mcfadden@usc.edu (office). *Website:* priceschool.usc.edu (office).

McFADDEN, Mary; American fashion designer; b. 1 Oct. 1938, New York; d. of Alexander Bloomfield McFadden and Mary Josephine Cutting; m. 1st Philip Harari 1964 (divorced); one d.; m. 2nd Frank McEwen 1968 (divorced); m. 3rd Armin Schmidt (divorced); m. 4th Kohle Yohannan (divorced); m. 5th Vasilios Calitsis 1996 (divorced); ed École Lubec, Univ. of Paris (Sorbonne), France, Traphagen School of Design, Columbia Univ., New School for Social Research; Dir of Public Relations, Christian Dior, New York 1962–64; Merchandising Ed. Vogue, SA 1964–65; political and travel columnist, Rand Daily Mail, SA 1965–68; Founder, Vukutu Sculpture Workshop, Rhodesia 1968–70; freelance ed. My Fair Lady, Cape Town and French Vogue 1968–70; Special Projects Ed. American Vogue 1970–73; fashion and jewellery designer (noted for tunics made from African and Chinese silks), New York 1973–; Chair. Mary McFadden Inc. 1976–; Pres. Council of Fashion Designers of America 1982–83; launched McFadden Knitwear Co. 1981, McFadden Studio 1995; Partner, MMcF Collection by Mary McFadden 1991–; fmr Pres. Council of Fashion Designers of America; numerous awards, including Coty Award 1976, Neiman Marcus Award 1979, Best Dressed List Hall of Fame 1979, Coty American Fashion Critics' Hall of Fame Award 1979, Woman of the Year, Police Athletic League 1990, New York Landmarks Conservancy 1994, Designer of the Decade and Beyond, Fashion Group Int. and Philadelphia Breast Health Inst. 1997, Legends Award, Pratt Inst., Lifetime Achievement in Fashion Award, Fashion Week of the Americas 2002, Pres.'s Fellows Award, Rhode Island School of Design. *Films:* Zooni –The Last Chak Empress, Sufism in India. *Television:* QVC, Worldly Accessories. *Publications:* Mary McFadden: A Lifetime of Design, Collecting, and Adventure 2012; contribs to Vogue and House & Garden. *Leisure interests:* tennis, squash, travelling the world, lecturing. *Address:* Mary McFadden Inc., 240 West 35th Street, Floor 17, New York, NY 10001, USA (office). *Telephone:* (212) 736-4078 (office). *Fax:* (212) 239-7259 (office).

MACFADYEN, Air Marshal Sir Ian David, Kt, KCVO, CB, OBE; British government official and air force officer (retd); b. 19 Feb. 1942, Maidenhead, Berks.; s. of Air Marshal Sir Douglas Macfadyen and Lady Macfadyen (née Rowan); m. Sally Harvey 1967; one s. one d.; ed Marlborough, RAF Coll. Cranwell, RAF Staff Coll., Royal Coll. of Defence Studies; joined RAF 1960, Cranwell cadet 1960–63, fighter pilot, 19 Squadron 1965–68, HQ, RAF Strike Command 1969; Flying Instructor RAF Coll. Cranwell 1970–73, RAF Staff Coll. 1973, 111 Squadron 1974–75; Flight Commdr 43 Squadron 1976, HQ 2ATAF RAF Germany 1976–79, Command 29 Squadron 1980–83, 23 Squadron 1983; with Ministry of Defence 1983–85, 1989–90; with Command RAF Leuchars, Fife 1985–87, Royal Coll. of Defence Studies 1988; Chief of Staff then Commdr HQ British Forces

Middle East, Riyadh 1990–91, Asst Chief of Defence Staff, Operational Requirements (Air Systems) 1991–94; Dir-Gen. Saudi Arabia Armed Forces Project 1994–98; retd 1999; Lt-Gov. Isle of Man 2000–05; Nat. Pres. The Royal British Legion 2006–09; Constable and Gov. Windsor Castle 2009–14 (retd); Chair. Bd of Trustees, Geoffrey de Havilland Flying Foundation 2003–; Trustee, RAF Museum 1999–2002; Trustee Bentley Priory Battle of Britain Trust 2006–14; Pres. Windsor Festival 2010–15, Dawn to Dusk Challenge 2010–16; Patron, Manx TT Riders Asscn 2005–, Alexander Devine Children's Hospice Service 2009–, Guillain-Barré Syndrome Asscn (GAIN) 2010–; Liveryman, Guild of Air Pilots and Navigators (GAPAN) 1999, Hon. Air Cdre 606 (Chiltern) Squadron, Royal Auxiliary Air Force 2006–19; Hon. Inspector Gen. Royal Auxiliary Air Force 2009, Worshipful Company of Lightmongers 2011; Sword of Honour, Cranwell 1963; Queen's Commendation for Valuable Service in the Air (QCVSA) 1973; Officer, Order of St John of Jerusalem 2001. *Publication:* Gulf War contrib. to Imperial War Museum Book of Modern Warfare 1945–2000 2002. *Leisure interests:* golf, shooting, watercolour painting, gliding, history.

McFADYEN, Jock, RA, MA; British artist; b. 18 Sept. 1950, Paisley, Scotland; s. of James Lachlan McFadyen and Margaret McFadyen; m. 1st Carol Hambleton 1972 (divorced 1987); one s.; m. 2nd Susie Honeyman 1991; one s. one d.; ed Chelsea School of Art; has made works about London, New York, Belfast, Berlin, Orkney and France; represented in 30 public collections including Tate and in numerous pvt. and corp. collections; artist in residence Nat. Gallery, London 1981; part-time Lecturer Slade School of Fine Art 1985–2004; designed sets and costumes for The Judas Tree, Royal Opera House, Covent Garden 1992; Arts Council Major Award 1979, Prizewinner, John Moores Liverpool Exhbn 1991. *Publications:* numerous exhbn catalogues. *Leisure interests:* cycling, motorcycling, walking, swimming, greyhounds. *Address:* c/o The Grey Gallery (office). *Telephone:* 7910-359087 (mobile) (office). *E-mail:* info@thegreygallery.com (office).

McFARLAND, Susan Reese; American business executive; ed Texas A&M Univ., Stanford Univ. Exec. Program; started career as Sr Auditor, Deloitte & Touche; Chief Financial Officer (CFO), Capital One Financial Corpn 2002–04, Exec. Vice-Pres. and Controller 2004–11, Exec. Vice-Pres., Finance and Prin. Accounting Officer March–July 2011; Exec. Vice-Pres. and CFO Fannie Mae (Fed. Nat. Mortgage Asscn), Washington, DC 2011–13, mem. Exec. Cttee; mem. Bd of Dirs Exeter Finance Corpn 2013–; Outstanding Alumna, Mays Business School, Texas A&M Univ. 2014. *Website:* www.exeterfinance.com.

MACFARLANE, Alan Donald James, MA, DPhil, PhD, FBA; British anthropologist and academic; *Professor Emeritus of Anthropological Sciences, University of Cambridge;* b. 20 Dec. 1941, Assam, India; s. of Donald Macfarlane and Iris Macfarlane; m. 1st Gillian Ions 1965; m. 2nd Sarah Harrison 1981; one d.; ed Sedbergh School, Worcester Coll., Oxford, London School of Econs and School of Oriental and African Studies, London; Sr Research Fellow in History, King's Coll., Cambridge 1971–75, Fellow 1981–, Life Fellow 2008–, Lecturer in Social Anthropology, Univ. of Cambridge 1975–81, Reader in Historical Anthropology 1981–91, Prof. of Anthropological Science 1991–2009, Prof. Emer. 2009–; Life Fellow, King's Coll., Cambridge 2009–; Rivers Memorial Medal 1984, Radcliffe-Brown Memorial Lecturer, British Acad. 1992, Huxley Memorial Lecturer 2012. *Television series:* The Day the World Took Off (adviser and participant), Channel 4 2000. *Publications include:* Witchcraft in Tudor and Stuart England 1970, Family Life of Ralph Josselin 1970, The Diary of Ralph Josselin (ed.) 1976, Resources and Population 1976, The Origins of English Individualism 1977, The Justice and the Mare's Ale 1981, Marriage and Love in England 1986, The Culture of Capitalism 1987, The Nagas: Hill Peoples of North India (co-author) 1990, The Cambridge Database System Manual 1990, The Savage Wars of Peace 1997, The Riddle of the Modern World: Of Liberty, Wealth and Equality 2000; ed. and trans. (with Sarah Harrison) of Bernard Pignède, The Gurungs of Nepal 1993, The Making of the Modern World: Visions from West and East 2002, The Glass Bathyscaphe: How Glass Changed the World (with Gerry Martin) 2002, Green Gold: The Empire of Tea (with Iris Macfarlane) 2003, Letters to Lily: On How the World Works 2005, Japan through the Looking Glass 2007, Reflections on Cambridge 2009, Dorset Days 2012, Dragon Days 2012, Invention of the Modern World 2012, Master's Letters to Young Chinese (nine vols 2014–17, Japan, China, Europe and the Anglos-Sphere 2018. *Leisure interests:* gardening, walking, music, travel. *Address:* King's College, Cambridge, CB2 1ST, England (office). *Telephone:* (1223) 811976 (office). *Website:* www.alanmacfarlane.com.

MacFARLANE, Sir Alistair George James, Kt, CBE, DSc, PhD, ScD, FRS, FREng, FRSE, FIET; British professor of engineering and vice-chancellor (retd); b. 9 May 1931, Edinburgh, Scotland; s. of George R. MacFarlane and Mary MacFarlane; m. Nora Williams 1954 (died 2005); one s.; m. Anwen Tudor Davies 2008; ed Hamilton Acad., Univs of Glasgow, London and Manchester; with Metropolitan-Vickers, Manchester 1953–58; Lecturer, Queen Mary Coll., Univ. of London 1959–65, Reader 1965–66; Reader in Control Eng, UMIST 1966–69, Prof. 1969–74; Prof. of Eng, Univ. of Cambridge 1974–89; Fellow, Selwyn Coll., Cambridge 1974–89, Vice-Master 1980–88; Prin. and Vice-Chancellor, Heriot-Watt Univ., Edin. 1989–96, Emer. Research Fellow 1997–99; Chair. Cambridge Control Ltd 1985–89; mem. Council Science and Eng Research Council (SERC) 1981–85, Computer Bd 1983–88; Chair. Scottish Council for Research in Educ. 1992–98, Scottish Library and Information Council 1994–98, Advisory Body on High Performance Computing 1994–98, BT Advisory Forum 1997–2000; Academic Adviser Univ. of Highlands and Islands Project 1997–2001; Trustee Scottish Library and Information System Council 1994–98; mem. Royal Soc. Council 1997–99, Vice-President Educ. Cttee 1997–99, Chair. 2000–04; Fellow, Royal Acad. of Eng, Inst. of Eng and Tech.; Hon. Fellow, Selwyn Coll. 1989; Hon. mem. Chartered Inst. of Library and Information Professionals (Scotland) 1998; Hon. DEng (Glasgow) 1995; Hon. DUniv (Heriot-Watt) 1997, (Paisley) 1997; Hon. DSc (Abertay Dundee) 1998; Hon. DLitt (Lincolnshire and Humberside) 1999; Centennial Medal, ASME 1980, Sir Harold Hartley Medal 1982, IEE Achievement Medal 1992, Oldenburger Medal 2004. *Publications:* Engineering Systems Analysis 1964, Dynamical System Models 1970, (with I. Postlethwaite) A Complex Variable Approach to the Analysis of Linear Multivariable Feedback Systems 1979, Frequency-Response Methods in Control Systems (ed.) 1979, Complex Variable Methods for Linear Multivariable Feedback Systems (ed.) 1980, (with S. Hung) Multivariable Feedback: a quasi-classical approach 1982, (co-author) An Expert Systems Approach to Computer-Aided Design of Multivariable Systems 1987. *Leisure interest:* computing. *Address:* Tregarth, 2 Marine Parade, Barmouth, Gwynedd, LL42 1NA, Wales. *Telephone:* (1341) 280445. *E-mail:* alistair .macfarlane@btinternet.com.

MacFARLANE, Ian John, AC, FASSA; Australian fmr central banker; b. 22 June 1946, Sydney; ed Monash Univ.; taught at Monash Univ.; with Inst. of Econs and Statistics, Univ. of Oxford, UK, then in various positions at OECD, Paris 1973–78; joined Reserve Bank of Australia (Research Dept) 1979, Head of Research 1988, Asst Gov. (Econ.) 1990–92, Deputy Gov. 1992–96, Gov. 1996–2006 (retd), Chair. Payments System Bd 1998–2006, Australian Council of Financial Regulators 1998–2006; Dir (ind. and non-exec.) Australia and New Zealand Banking Group Ltd 2007–16, fmr Chair. Risk Cttee, mem. Governance Cttee, Audit Cttee; Dir Lowy Inst. for Int. Policy 2004–, CIMIC Group Ltd 2007–13, Leighton Holdings Ltd 2007–13, Woolworths Ltd 2007–15; mem. Int. Advisory Bd, CHAMP Pvt. Equity 2007–15, Council of Int. Advisors, China Banking Regulatory Comm. 2009–15; Hon. DSc, Hon. DLitt.

McFARLANE, John, OBE, MA, MBA, FRSA; Australian/British financial services executive; *Executive Chairman, Barclays plc;* b. 14 June 1947, Dumfries, Scotland; ed Dumfries Acad., Univ. of Edinburgh, Cranfield School of Man., London Business School; with Ford Motor Co. 1969–74; with Citibank 1975–93, including as Man. Dir Citicorp Investment Bank Ltd, Man. Dir Citicorp and Citibank UK; Group Exec. Dir Standard Chartered Bank plc 1993–97; CEO Australia and New Zealand Banking Group Ltd 1997–2007; Exec. Chair. Aviva plc July–Dec. 2012, Chair. (non-exec.) 2013–15; Chair. FirstGroup plc –2015; Dir (non-exec.), Barclays plc Jan. 2015–, Chair. (non-exec.) April–July 2015, Exec. Chair. July 2015–; Dir, London Stock Exchange 1989–91, The Securities Asscn 1989–90, Auditing Practices Bd 1991–97, Capital Radio PLC 1995–98, Royal Bank of Scotland Group plc 2008–12; Dir (non-exec.), Westfield Holdings 2008–, Old Oak Holdings 2008–; fmr Chair. Australian Bankers Asscn; fmr Pres. Int. Monetary Conf.; Fellow, Hong Kong Inst. of Bankers (FHKIB) 1995; Sr Fellow, Financial Services Inst. of Australasia (SFFIN) 1997; Fellow, Chartered Inst. for Securities and Investment (FCSI) 2009; Hon. DSc (Cranfield) 2012; MSI, The Securities Inst. (UK) 1993, Australian Centenary Medal 2003, inaugural Distinguished Alumnus Award, Cranfield 2003. *Address:* Barclays plc, One Churchill Place, Canary Wharf, London, E14 5HP, England (office). *Telephone:* (20) 7116-1000 (office). *Website:* www.barclays.com (office).

MacFARLANE, Robert, PhD, FRSL; British writer and academic; *Reader in Literature and the Geohumanities, Faculty of English, Emmanuel College;* b. 15 Aug. 1976, Halam, Nottingham; ed Pembroke Coll., Emmanuel Coll., Cambridge, Magdalen Coll., Oxford; Fellow, Emmanuel Coll., Cambridge 2002–, University Senior Lecturer in Post-WWII Literature in English, Reader in Literature and the Geohumanities, Faculty of English 2016–; judge, Man Booker Prize for Fiction 2007, 2013; Founding Trustee, Action For Conservation; Dr hc (Univ. of Aberdeen), (Univ. of Gloucestershire). *Publications include:* Mountains of the Mind: A History of a Fascination (Guardian First Book Award, Somerset Maugham Award 2004) 2003, Wild Eyed 2005, Original Copy: Plagiarism and Originality in Nineteenth-Century Literature 2007, The Wild Places (Boardman Tasker Prize, Scottish Arts Council Non-Fiction Book of The Year Award, Grand Prize Banff Mountain Festival) 2007, The Old Ways: A Journey On Foot (Dolman Best Travel Book Award 2013) 2012, Holloway 2013, Landmarks (Hay Festival Medal for Prose) 2015, The Lost Words (with Jackie Morris) (Children's Book of the Year, British Book Awards 2018) 2017, Underland: A Deep Time Journey 2019; contrib. to Granta, The Guardian, The New York Times, The Sunday Times, The Observer, TLS, The Spectator, Evening Standard. *Address:* c/o Jessica Woollard, The Marsh Agency Ltd, 50 Albemarle Street, London, W1S 4BD (office); Emmanuel College, St Andrew's Street, Cambridge, CB2 3AP, England (office). *Telephone:* (20) 7493-4361 (office); (22) 3334-200 (office). *Fax:* (20) 7495-8961 (office). *Website:* www.marsh -agency.co.uk (office); www.emma.cam.ac.uk (office).

McFARLANE, Hon. Robert Carl (Bud), MS; American fmr government official; *Principal, Energy and Communications Solutions LLC;* b. 12 July 1937, Washington, DC; s. of William McFarlane and Alma Carl; m. Jonda Riley 1959; one s. two d.; ed US Naval Acad. and Inst des Hautes Etudes, Geneva; US Marine Corps, Second Lt rising to Lt-Col 1959–79; White House Fellow, Exec. Asst Council to Pres. for Legis. Affairs 1971–72; Mil. Asst to Henry Kissinger (q.v.) 1973–75; Exec. Asst to Asst to Pres. for Nat. Security Affairs 1975–76; Special Asst to Pres. 1976–77; Research Fellow Nat. Defense Univ., Washington, DC 1977–78; mem. Professional Staff Senate Comm. on Armed Services 1979–81; Counselor Dept of State 1981–82; Deputy Asst to Pres., Nat. Security Affairs 1982–83; Personal Rep. of US Pres. in Middle East July–Oct. 1983; Asst to Pres. for Nat. Security Affairs 1983–85 (resgnd); pleaded guilty to four misdemeanour counts of withholding information from Congress as part of the Iran-Contra cover-up 1988, sentenced to two years' probation and a $20,000 fine, pardoned by Pres. George H. W. Bush Dec. 1992; Co-founder and fmr CEO Global Energy Investors; currently Prin., Energy and Communications Solutions LLC, Washington DC; mem. Bd of Dirs Aegis Defence Services; Chair. and CEO McFarlane Asscn 1986–; adviser to the John McCain presidential campaign 2008; Co-founder (with Henry Kissinger) and Vice-Chair. America-China Soc.; Co-founder US Energy Security Council 2011; mem. Bd of Advisors, Washington Inst. for Near East Policy, Set America Free Coalition (Founding mem.), Partnership for a Secure America; Pres. Inst. for the Analysis of Global Security; lobbyist for Macedonia 1992; has been working in southern region of Sudan and Darfur on inter-tribal relations and devt projects 2009–; Navy Distinguished Service Medal, Bronze Star with Valor device, Meritorious Service Medal, Navy Commendation Medal with Valor device, Army Commendation Medal, Combat Action Ribbon, Sec. of State Distinguished Service Award, Sec. of the Navy Medal for Distinguished Public Service, Presidential Service Badge; Alfred Thayer Mahan Award for Literary Achievement 1979, American-Swiss Friendship Man of the Year Award 1985. *Publications:* At Sea Where We Belong 1971, Crisis Resolution (co-author) 1978, The Political Potential of Parity 1979. *Address:* Partnership for a Secure America, 1775 K Street NW, Suite 400, Washington, DC 20240, USA (office). *Telephone:* (202) 293-8580 (office). *E-mail:* info@psaonline.org (office); media@iags.org. *Website:* www.psaonline.org (office); www.usesc.org/energy_security.

MacFARLANE, Seth Woodbury, BFA; American actor, voice actor, animator and screenwriter, comedian, producer, director and singer; b. 26 Oct. 1973, Kent, Conn.; s. of Ronald Milton MacFarlane and Ann Perry MacFarlane (née Sager); ed Kent School, Rhode Island School of Design; began career as animator and writer for Hanna-Barbera TV shows, including Johnny Bravo, Cow and Chicken, Dexter's Laboratory and I Am Weasel; helped create Disney series Jungle Cubs; Exec. Producer of sitcom The Winner (Fox); cr. own YouTube series, Seth MacFarlane's Cavalcade of Cartoon Comedy 2008; has performed as a singer at Carnegie Hall, Royal Albert Hall, London; f. Fuzzy Door Productions (production co.); Webby Award for Film & Video Person of the Year 2009, Harvard Humanist of the Year 2011. *Films include:* Hellboy II: The Golden Army (voice) 2008, Futurama: Into the Wild Green Yonder (video) (singing voice) 2009, Tooth Fairy 2010, The Drawn Together Movie: The Movie! (video) (voice) 2010, Ted (dir, writer, voice) 2012. *Television includes:* The What a Cartoon Show (series) (voice) 1997, Family Guy (series) (Primetime Emmy Award 2000, 2002, Annie Award 2006, Teen Choice Award for Choice Animated Series 2010) 1999–, 3-South (series) (voice) 2002, Complete Savages (series) 2004, Star Trek: Enterprise (series) 2004–05, Robot Chicken (series) (voice) 2005–10, American Dad! (series) 2005–, The War at Home (series) 2006, Help Me Help You (series) 2007, Robot Chicken: Star Wars (film) (voice) 2007, Robot Chicken: Star Wars Episode II (film) (voice) 2008, Cavalcade of Cartoon Comedy (series) (voice) 2008–10, The Cleveland Show (series) 2009–13, Phineas and Ferb (series) (voice) 2010, Robot Chicken: Star Wars Episode III (film) (voice) 2010, Lovin' Lakin (mini-series) 2012, The Orville 2017. *Recordings:* albums: Music Is Better Than Words 2011, Holiday for Swing 2014. *Address:* c/o WME Entertainment, 9601 Wilshire Boulevard, Beverly Hills, CA 90210-5213, USA (office). *Website:* www.wma.com (office).

MacFARLANE, (Stephen) Neil, MA, DPhil; Canadian political scientist and academic; *Lester B. Pearson Professor of International Relations, St Anne's College, University of Oxford;* b. 7 March 1954; ed Dartmouth Coll., NH, USA and Univ. of Oxford, UK; Research Assoc., IISS, London 1981–82; Postdoctoral Fellow, Centre for Int. Affairs, Harvard Univ. 1982–83; Research Assoc., Inst. for Int. Relations, Univ. of British Columbia 1983–84; Asst Prof. of Govt and Foreign Affairs, Univ. of Virginia 1984–87, Assoc. Prof. of Govt and Foreign Affairs 1987–91, Grad. Co-ordinator 1987–89, Dir Centre for Russian and East European Studies 1989–91; Research Assoc., Center for Slavic and East European Studies, Univ. of California, Berkeley 1986–87; Prof. of Politics, Queen's Univ., Kingston, Ont. 1991–96, Co-ordinator, Post-Soviet Studies Program, Centre for Int. Relations 1992–97, Grad. Admissions Co-ordinator, Dept of Political Studies 1993–94, Chair. Skelton Clark Cttee for Visiting Scholars, Dept of Political Studies 1993–96, Dir Centre for Int. Relations 1995–96; Lester B. Pearson Prof. of Int. Relations, Univ. of Oxford and Fellow, St Anne's Coll. 1996–, Dir Centre for Int. Studies 1997–, Head of Dept of Politics 2005–10, Deputy Head of Social Sciences Div. 2008–10; Adjunct Prof. of Political Science, Dalhousie Univ., Halifax, NS 1996–; Visiting Prof. in Int. Relations, Coll. of Europe, Bruges, Belgium 2007–08; Visiting Prof., S. Rajaratnam Prof. of Strategic Studies, Nanyang Technological Univ., Singapore 2008; Visiting Prof. of Int. Relations, Tbilisi State Univ., Georgia 2010–; mem. Bd Faculty of Social Studies, Univ. of Oxford 1997–, mem. Social Sciences Divisional Bd 2004–10; mem. Econ. and Social Research Council Research Grants Bd 2007–10. *Publications:* Western Engagement in the Caucasus and Central Asia 1999, Politics and Humanitarian Action 2000, Humanitarian Action: The Conflict Connection 2001, Intervention in Contemporary World Politics 2002, US Hegemony and International Organizations (co-author) 2003, The UN and Human Security: A Critical History (co-author) 2006. *Address:* St Anne's College, University of Oxford, Oxford, OX2 6HS, England (office). *Telephone:* (1865) 274891 (office). *Fax:* (1865) 274899 (office). *E-mail:* neil.macfarlane@politics.ox.ac.uk (office). *Website:* www.politics.ox.ac.uk (office).

MACFARLANE OF BEARSDEN, Baron (Life Peer), cr. 1991, in the District of Bearsden and Milngavie; **Norman Somerville Macfarlane,** KT, FRSE; British business executive; *Honorary Life President, United Distillers PLC;* b. 5 March 1926; s. of Daniel Robertson Macfarlane and Jessie Lindsay Somerville; m. Marguerite Mary Campbell 1953; one s. four d.; ed Glasgow High School; f. N. S. Macfarlane and Co. Ltd 1949, Chair. Macfarlane Group (Clansman) PLC 1973–98, Man. Dir 1973–90; Chair. Scottish Industrialists Council 1975–; Dir Glasgow Chamber of Commerce 1976–79; Chair. The Fine Art Soc. PLC 1976–98 (Hon. Pres. 1998); Underwriting mem. of Lloyds 1978–97; Dir American Trust PLC 1980–97, Chair. 1984–97; Dir Clydesdale Bank PLC 1980–96, Deputy Chair. 1993–96; Dir Edin. Fund Mans PLC 1980–98; Dir Gen. Accident Fire and Life Assurance Corpn PLC 1984–96; Chair. Guinness Co. 1987–89, Jt Deputy Chair. 1989–92; Chair. United Distillers PLC 1987–96, Hon. Life Pres. 1996–; Chair. Arthur Bell Distillers 1989; mem. Council CBI Scotland 1975–81; mem. Bd Scottish Devt Agency 1979–87; Chair. Glasgow Devt Agency 1985–92; Vice-Chair. Scottish Ballet 1983–87, (Dir 1975–87), Pres. 2001–; Pres. Stationers' Asscn of GB and Ireland 1965, Co. of Stationers of Glasgow 1968–70, Glasgow High School Club 1970–72, Royal Glasgow Inst. of the Fine Arts 1976–87; Hon. Pres. Charles Rennie Mackintosh Soc. 1988–; Regent Royal Coll. of Surgeons, Edin. 1997–; Dir Scottish Nat. Orchestra 1977–82, Third Eye Centre 1978–81; Gov. Glasgow School of Art 1976–87; Scottish Patron, Nat. Art Collection Fund 1978–; Patron, Scottish Licensed Trade Asscn 1992–; Chair. Govs, High School of Glasgow 1979–92, Hon. Pres. 1992–; mem. Royal Fine Art Comm. for Scotland 1980–82; Lord High Commr Gen. Ass., Church of Scotland 1992, 1993, 1997; mem. Court, Glasgow Univ. 1979–87; Trustee, Nat. Heritage Memorial Fund 1984–97, Nat. Galleries of Scotland 1986–97; DL Dunbartonshire 1993; Vice-Pres. Professional Golfers Asscn; f. Scotvec.; Hon. Patron, Queen's Park F.C.; Hon. FRIAS, FRCPS (Glas); Hon. Fellow, Glasgow School of Art 1993; Hon. Patron Queen's Park Football Club; Freeman Dumfries & Galloway 2006, City of Glasgow 2007; Hon. LLD (Strathclyde) 1986, (Glasgow) 1988, (Glasgow Caledonian) 1993, (Aberdeen) 1995; Hon. DUniv (Stirling) 1992; Dr hc (Edin.) 1992; St Mungo Award 2005, Goodman Award for Art and Business 2007. *Leisure interests:* golf, cricket, theatre, art. *Address:* Macfarlane Group PLC, Clansman House, 21 Newton Place, Glasgow, G3 7PY (office); 50 Manse Road, Bearsden, Glasgow, G61 3PN, Scotland. *Telephone:* (141) 333-9666 (office). *Fax:* (141) 333-1988 (office).

McFAUL, Michael Anthony, BA, MA, PhD; American political scientist, foreign policy analyst, academic and fmr diplomatist; *Professor of Political Science and Peter and Helen Bing Senior Fellow, Hoover Institution, Stanford University;* b. Mont.; ed Stanford Univ., Univ. of Oxford, UK; Research Fellow, Center for Int. Security and Arms Control, Stanford Univ. 1988–90, Research Assoc. 1992–94, Visiting Research Fellow, Hoover Inst. 1990–91, Research Fellow 1995–2003, Asst Prof., Dept of Political Science 1995–2001, Assoc. Prof. 2001–05, Prof. 2007–, Peter and Helen Bing Sr Fellow, Hoover Inst. 2003–, Co-Dir Iran Democracy Project 2003–09, Freeman Spogli Inst. (FSI) for Int. Studies, Dir FSI Center on Democracy, Devt and Rule of Law 2005–09, Deputy Dir FSI 2006–09 (Acting Dir 2007), Dir 2015–; Visiting Scholar, Moscow State Univ. 1990–91; Sr Assoc., Carnegie Endowment for Int. Peace 1994–2009, Moscow Carnegie Center 1994–95, resident in Washington, DC 1998–2001; Sr Consultant and Commentator (Russian Parl. Elections), CBS News 1995, CNN 1996, 1999, 2000; Special Asst to the Pres. and Sr Dir Russia and Eurasia Affairs, Nat. Security Council, The White House 2009–12; Amb. to Russia 2012–14; Research Assoc., Center for Int. Security and Arms Control; Sr Adviser to Nat. Democratic Inst.; mem. Bd of Dirs Eurasia Foundation, Firebird Fund, Freedom House, Int. Forum for Democratic Studies of Nat. Endowment for Democracy, Int. Research and Exchange Bd; mem. Steering Cttee Europe and Eurasia Div., Human Rights Watch; mem. Editorial Bd Current History, Journal of Democracy, Demokratizatsiya, Perspectives on European Politics and Society; consultant to several govt agencies and cos; mem. American Political Science Asscn, American Asscn for the Advancement of Slavic Studies, Council on Foreign Relations, Int. Forum for Democratic Studies, Pacific Council, Soc. for Comparative Research; Best Paper, Democratization Section of the American Political Science Asscn National Convention 2001, Dean's Award for Distinguished Teaching, Stanford Univ. 2005, Class Day Speaker, Stanford Univ. 2007. *Publications include:* The Troubled Birth of Russian Democracy: Political Parties, Programs and Profiles (co-author) 1993, Post-Communist Politics: Democratic Prospects in Russia and Eastern Europe 1993, Privatization, Conversion and Enterprise Reform in Russia (co-author) 1995, Russia's 1996 Presidential Election: The End of Bi-Polar Politics 1997, Rossiya v izbiratel'nom tsikle: 1999–2000 godov (Russia in the Electoral Cycle, 1999–2000) (co-ed.) 2000, Russia's Unfinished Revolution: Political Change from Gorbachev to Putin (Hon. Mention, Vucinich Prize for Best Book in Slavic Studies 2002) 2001, Popular Choice and Managed Democracy: The Russian Elections of 1999 and 2000 (co-author) 2003, Power and Purpose: American Policy toward Russia after the Cold War (co-author) (Lepgold Prize for Best Book in Int. Relations 2004) 2003, After the Collapse of Communism: Comparative Lessons of Transitions (co-ed.) 2004, Between Dictatorship and Democracy: Russian Postcommunist Political Reform (co-author) 2004, Revolution in Orange: The Origins of Ukraine's Democratic Breakthrough (co-ed.) 2006, Advancing Democracy Abroad: Why We Should and How We Can 2009, American Versus European Approaches to Democracy Promotion (co-ed.) 2009, Waves and Troughs of Democratization in the Post-communist World (co-ed.) 2009; contribs to New York Times, LA Times, Chicago Tribune, Moscow Times, Washington Post; numerous articles in professional journals. *Address:* Stanford University, Encina Hall West 307, Stanford, CA 94305-6055, USA (office). *Telephone:* (650) 723-1806 (office). *Fax:* (650) 723-1808 (office); mcfaul@stanford.edu (office). *Website:* politicalscience.stanford.edu/faculty/michael-mcfaul (office); fsi.stanford.edu/mediaguide/michaelamcfaul (office).

McGAHN, Donald (Don) F., BA, JD; American lawyer and government official; *White House Counsel;* b. 16 June 1968; s. of Donald McGahn and Noreen McGahn (née Rogan); m. Shannon McGahn; two s.; ed US Naval Acad., Univ. of Notre Dame, Widener Univ. School of Law, Georgetown Univ.; Assoc., Patton Boggs LLC (law firm) 1995–99, Pnr 2013–14; Gen. Counsel, Nat. Republican Congressional Cttee 1999–2008; Man. Pnr, McGahn and Assocs (law firm) 2005–08; Chair. Fed. Election Comm. July–Dec. 2006, Commr 2009–12, Vice-Chair. June–Sept. 2013; Pnr, Jones Day (law firm) 2014–17; White House Counsel 2017–. *Address:* The White House, 1600 Pennsylvania Avenue, NW, Washington, DC 20500, USA (office). *Telephone:* (202) 456-1414 (office). *Fax:* (202) 456-2461 (office). *E-mail:* vice_president@whitehouse.gov (office). *Website:* www.whitehouse.gov (office).

McGAUCHIE, Donald G., AO; Australian telecommunications industry executive; *Chairman and Director, Australian Agricultural Co.;* b. 29 Jan. 1959, Sydney, NSW; Partner, C&E McGauchie-Terrick W Estate; Pres. Nat. Farmers' Fed. 1994–98; Chair. Woodstock Australia Ltd 1999–2002; apptd Dir Telstra Corpn Ltd 1998, Chair. 2004–09 (resgnd); Chair. Rural Finance Corpn 2003–04, Advisory Bd Telstra Country Wide; Deputy Chair. Ridley Corpn Ltd 1998–2004; Dir Australian Wool Testing Authority Limited 1999–, Chair. 2005–; Dir Nufarm Limited 2003–, Chair. 2010–; Chair. and Dir Australian Agricultural Co. 2010–; mem. Bd Dirs Reserve Bank of Australia, Nat. Foods Ltd 2000–05, James Hardie Industries NV (Deputy Chair, Jt Bd and Supervisory Bd and mem. Remuneration Cttee), Sinclair Knight Merz (SKM) Consulting 2001–04; fmr mem. Foreign Affairs Council, Trade Policy Advisory Council; fmr Adviser to Prime Minister's Supermarket to Asia Council; fmr mem. Int. Policy Council on Agric., Food and Trade, Washington DC; Fellow, Australian Inst. of Co. Dirs. *Address:* Australian Agricultural Co., GPO Box 587, Brisbane, Queensland 4001, Australia (office). *Telephone:* (7) 3368-4400 (office). *E-mail:* reception@aaco.com.au (office). *Website:* aaco.com.au (office).

MacGIBBON, Ross; British film director, producer, photographer and fmr ballet dancer; b. 29 Jan. 1955, Bromley, England; s. of Prof. Iain MacGibbon and Dawn MacGibbon; m. Julie Kavanagh; two s.; ed Royal Ballet School; dancer with Royal Ballet 1973–86; began working as dance filmmaker for TV 1986; currently dir of live cinema performances. *Films:* more than 75 films, including White Man Sleeps (Channel 4), Wyoming (1st Prize, IMZ DanceScreen competition) 1989, The Far End of the Garden 1991, Should Accidentally Fall (Special Jury Prize 1994, Video-Dance Grand Prix, Vancouver), Echo 1996 (Special Jury Prize), Swan Lake (Mariinsky Ballet) 1996, Explosive Dance: Live from the Royal Albert Hall 1998, Maurice Béjart's der Nussknacker (Béjart Ballet Lausanne) 2000, La Belle Hélène (Theatre Musical de Paris) 2000, The Firebird & Les Noces 2001, Gianni Schicci (producer) 2004, Cloud Gate Dance Theatre of Taiwan: Cursive II 2005, Romeo & Juliet (The Royal Ballet) 2007, Swan Lake (video) 2007, Spartacus: The Bolshoi Ballet (video) 2008, Swan Lake (The Royal Ballet) 2009, Mayerling (The Royal Ballet) 2009, La Bayadère (Royal Ballet) 2009, Ondine (The Royal Ballet) 2009, The Nutcracker (The Royal Ballet) 2009, Manon (The Royal Ballet) 2009, Three Ballets by Kenneth MacMillan: Elite Syncopations/The Judas Tree/Concerto 2010, Swan Lake 2012, Swan Lake 3D – Live from the Mariinsky Theatre 2013, The Railway Children 2016. *Television:* Dance for the Camera (series) 1994, Swinger (BBC 2) 1996, Peter and the Wolf (BBC 1) 1997, The Judas Tree (Channel 4) (Int.

Emmy Award for Performing Arts 1998), Explosive Dance (special) 1998, A Midsummer Night's Dream (film) 1999, Coppélia, A Ballet in Three Acts (film) 2000, La belle Hélène (film) 2000, The Car Man (film) 2001, Great Performances (series) – The Nutcracker 2001, Bourne to Dance (film documentary) 2001, Swan Lake (Royal Swedish Ballet) (also exec. producer) 2002, est. Petersburg 300th Anniversary Gala (special) 2003, Nutcracker! (film) 2003, Faust (film) (exec. producer) 2004, Die Fledermaus (Glyndebourne Festival Opera) 2004, Riot at the Rite (film) (exec. producer) 2005, Giselle (film) 2006, Pinocchio (film) (exec. producer) 2006, The Sleeping Beauty (film) 2007, Sylvia (film) 2007, For Art's Sake: The Story of Ballets Russes (film documentary) 2009, Frederick Ashton: Les Patineurs/Divertissements/Scènes de Ballet 2011, The Most Incredible Thing (film) 2011, Peter and the Wolf (film) 2011, Matthew Bourne's Sleeping Beauty: A Gothic Romance 2012, Matthew Bourne's Swan Lake in 3D 2013, Matthew Bourne's Christmas (Channel 4) (Prix Italia 2013), The Winter's Tale from the Royal Ballet (film) 2014, 1984 a ballet by Jonathan Watkins (film) 2016, The Royal Ballet: Woolf Works (film) 2017. *Telephone:* (20) 7821-1117; 7855-240617 (mobile). *E-mail:* rossmacgibbon@btinternet.com. *Website:* rossmacgibbon.com.

McGILLIS, Kelly; American actress; b. 9 July 1957, Newport Beach, Calif.; m. 1st Boyd Black 1979 (divorced 1981); m. 2nd Fred Tillman 1988 (divorced 2002); two d.; pnr Melanie Leis; ed Pacific School of Performing Arts and Juilliard School of Music. *Films include:* Reuben, Reuben 1983, Witness 1985, Top Gun 1986, Ha-Holmim 1987, Made in Heaven 1987, The House on Carroll Street 1988, The Accused 1988, Winter People 1989, Cat Chaser 1989, Grand Isle 1991, The Babe 1992, North 1994, Painted Angels 1998, Ground Control 1998, The Settlement 1999, Morgan's Ferry 1999, At First Sight 1999, The Monkey's Mask 2000, No One Can Hear You 2001, 1 a Minute 2010, Stake Land 2010, The Innkeepers 2011, What Could Have Been 2011, We Are What We Are 2013, Tio Papi 2013, Grand Street 2014, Blue 2015. *Television includes:* In the Best of Families: Marriage, Pride & Madness 1994, Dark Eyes (series) 1995, Remember Me 1995, We the Jury 1996, The Third Twin 1997, Perfect Prey 1998, Storm Chasers: Revenge of the Twister 1998, Cold Shoulder 2006, Black Widower 2006, The L Word 2008, Love Finds You in Sugarcreek (film) 2014, An Uncommon Grace (film) 2017, Maternal Secrets (film) 2018. *Plays include:* The Graduate 2004.

McGINN, Colin, MA, BPhil; British academic; *Professor, Department of Philosophy, University of Miami;* b. 10 March 1950; s. of Joseph McGinn and June McGinn; one s.; ed Univ. of Manchester, Univ. of Oxford; Lecturer, Univ. Coll. London 1974–85; Wilde Reader in Mental Philosophy, Univ. of Oxford 1985–90; Prof., Rutgers Univ., USA 1990–2005, Dept of Philosophy, Univ. of Miami 2005–; John Locke Prize 1973. *Publications include:* The Character of Mind 1981, The Subjective View 1982, Wittgenstein on Meaning 1984, Mental Content 1989, The Problem of Consciousness 1991, Moral Literacy 1992, The Space Trap 1992, Problems in Philosophy 1993, Minds and Bodies: Philosophers and their Ideas 1997, Ethics, Evil and Fiction 1997, Knowledge and Reality 1998, The Mysterious Flame 1999, Logical Properties 2000, The Making of a Philosopher 2002, Consciousness and its Objects 2004, Mindsight: Image, Dream, Meaning 2004, The Power of Movies 2005, Shakespeare's Philosophy 2006, Mindfucking 2008, The Meaning of Disgust 2011. *Leisure interest:* fitness. *Address:* Department of Philosophy, University of Miami, Ashe Building, Room 705, PO Box 248054, Coral Gables, FL 33124-4670 (office); 270 West End Avenue, Apartment 9E, New York, NY 10023, USA. *Telephone:* (305) 284-4757 (office). *E-mail:* cmg124@aol.com (office). *Website:* www.as.miami.edu/phi (office); www.colinmcginn.net.

McGINN, Richard A., BA; American telecommunications executive; *General Partner, RRE Ventures LLC;* b. 1947; m.; one d.; ed Grinnell Coll., Iowa; with Illinois Bell 1969; exec. positions, int. and computer systems groups, AT&T 1978, CEO network systems; CEO, Pres. Lucent Technologies 1997–2000, Chair. and CEO –2000; Gen. Partner, RRE Ventures LLC (investment advisory and venture capital firm) 2001–; Chair. (non-exec.) VeriFone Systems, Inc. 2012–March 2013, Interim CEO March–Sept. 2013; mem. Bd of Dirs American Express Co. 1998–, Viasystems Group, Inc. 2003–, Roundbox Inc. 2005–, VeriFone Systems, Inc. 2008–14, Certeon Inc., Enpirion Inc., Taqua Systems Inc., VeriFone Inc., Mintera Corpn, Mountain Top Foundation; Ind. Dir, Nexsan Technologies Inc. 2003–; mem. Advisory Bd Roundbox Inc.; fmr mem. Bd of Dirs Lucent Technologies, Oracle Corpn; mem. Business Council. *Leisure interests:* adventure sports, deep-sea fishing. *Address:* RRE Ventures LLC, 130 East 59th Street, 17th Floor, New York, NY 10022, USA (office). *Telephone:* (212) 418-5100 (office). *E-mail:* info@rre.com (office). *Website:* www.rre.com (office).

McGLADE, Jacqueline M., BSc, MA, PhD, FLS, FRSA; British/Canadian environmental scientist, academic and international organization official; *Frank Jackson Foundation Professor in Environment, Gresham College;* b. 30 May 1955; ed Univ. Coll. of North Wales, Univ. of Guelph, Canada, Univ. of Cambridge, UK; early career as Sr Research Scientist, Dept of Fisheries and Oceans, Canada; fmr academic positions include Prof. of Biological Sciences, Univ. of Warwick, England, Dir of Theoretical Ecology, Forschungszentrum Jülich, Germany, Prof., Aachen Univ., Germany, Adrian Fellow, Darwin Coll., Univ. of Cambridge, UK, Assoc. Prof., Int. Ecotechnology Research Centre, Cranfield Univ., UK; Dir NERC Centre for Coastal and Marine Sciences –2000; NERC Professorial Fellow in Environmental Informatics, Univ. Coll. London 2000–03, Prof. of Math. Biology 2003–; Exec. Dir, European Environment Agency 2003–13; Chief Scientist and Dir Div. of Early Warning and Assessment, UNEP, Nairobi 2014–17; Frank Jackson Foundation Prof. in Environment, Gresham Coll. 2018–; fmr Chair. The Earth Centre; Bd mem. Environment Agency 1998–2003; Trustee, Natural History Museum; mem. UK-China Forum; Hon. DSc (Kent) 2004; Swedish Jubileum Award 1990, Minerva Prize 1993, Masaryk Gold Medal 2005, Brno Univ. Gold Medal. *Radio:* The Ocean Planet (BBC Radio 4) 2000, King John's Treasure (BBC Radio 4) 2001, Learning from Nature (BBC Radio 4) 2002. *Television:* The Next Big Thing (BBC 2) 2000. *Publications include:* Integrated Fisheries Management: Understanding the Limits to Marine Resource Exploitation 1989, Governance of Fisheries and Aquaculture 1993, Ecology, Thermodynamics and Odum's Conjectures (co-author) 1993, Advanced Ecological Theory (ed.) 1999, Gulf of Guinea Ecosystem (co-ed.) 2002, The European Environment: State and Outlook 2005, Millennium Ecosystem Assessment, Vol. 2: Scenarios (co-ed.) 2005; more than 150 publs. *Address:* Gresham College, Barnard's Inn Hall, Holborn, London, EC1N 2HH, England (office). *Telephone:* (207) 831-0575 (office). *E-mail:* enquiries@gresham.ac.uk (office). *Website:* www.gresham.ac.uk/professors-and-speakers/jacqueline-mcglade/ (office).

McGOUGH, Roger Joseph, CBE, MA, DLitt, FRSL; British poet and children's writer; *President, The Poetry Society;* b. 9 Nov. 1937, Liverpool, England; s. of Roger McGough and Mary McGarry; m. 1st Thelma Monaghan 1970 (divorced 1980); m. 2nd Hilary Clough 1986; three s. one d.; ed St Mary's Coll., Liverpool, Hull Univ.; Poetry Fellow, Univ. of Loughborough 1973–75; Writer-in-Residence, Western Australia Coll. of Educ., Perth 1986, Univ. of Hamburg 1994; Vice-Pres. The Poetry Soc. 1996–2011, Pres. 2012–, mem. Exec. Council 1989–93; Fellow, John Moores Univ. 1999; Trustee Chelsea Arts Club 1987–, (fmr Chair.); Fellow, Liverpool John Moores Univ.; Hon. Prof. Thames Valley Univ. 1993, Freeman City of Liverpool 2001; Hon. MA (Nene Coll.) 1998; Hon. DLitt (Hull Univ.) 2004, (Univ. of Surrey) 2006, (Hull), (Liverpool), (Nottingham); Signal Award 1984, 1998, BAFTA Awards 1984, 1992, Cholmondeley Award 1998, Centre for Literacy in Primary Educ. Award for Best Book of Poetry for Children 2004, 2005. *Music:* wrote and performed Top Twenty hits Lily the Pink and Thank U Very Much 1968–69. *Plays include:* The Sound Collector and My Dad's a Fire-eater (for children); wrote lyrics for Broadway production of The Wind in the Willows 1984; adaptations of Molière's Tartuffe 2008, The Hypochondriac 2009, The Misanthrope 2012. *Plays for radio include:* Summer with Monika, FX, Walking the Dog. *Television:* Kurt, Mungo, B. P. and Me (Thames Television) 1985, The Elements (Channel 4) (Royal Television Soc. Award) 1993. *Publications:* The Mersey Sound (with Brian Patten and Adrian Henri) 1967, Watchwords 1969, After the Merrymaking 1971, Out of Sequence 1972, Gig 1972, Sporting Relations 1974, In the Glassroom 1976, Summer with Monika 1978, Holiday on Death Row 1979, Unlucky for Some 1981, Waving at Trains 1982, Melting into the Foreground 1986, Blazing Fruit: Selected Poems 1967–1987 1989, You at the Back 1991, Defying Gravity 1992, The Spotted Unicorn 1998, The Way Things Are 1999, Everyday Eclipses 2002, Collected Poems of Roger McGough 2003, Said and Done (memoir) 2005, Selected Poems 2006, That Awkward Age 2009, As Far As I Know 2012, It Never Rains 2014; for children: Mr Noselighter 1977, The Great Smile Robbery 1982, Sky in the Pie 1983, The Stowaways 1986, Noah's Ark 1986, Nailing the Shadow 1987, An Imaginary Menagerie 1988, Helen Highwater 1989, Counting by Numbers 1989, Pillow Talk 1990, The Lighthouse That Ran Away 1991, My Dad's a Fire-eater 1992, Another Custard Pie 1993, Lucky 1993, Stinkers Ahoy! 1995, The Magic Fountain 1995, The Kite and Caitlin 1996, Bad Bad Cats 1997, Until I Met Dudley 1998, Good Enough to Eat 2002, Moonthief 2002, The Bees' Knees 2002, Dotty Inventions 2002, What On Earth Can It Be? 2003, If Only We Had a Helicopter 2015, I Never Liked Wednesdays 2015, Poetry Pie 2015; editor: Strictly Private 1981, The Kingfisher Book of Comic Verse 1986, The Kingfisher Book of Poems About Love 1997, The Ring of Words (anthology) 1998, Wicked Poems 2002, All the Best 2002, Sensational (anthology) 2004. *Address:* United Agents, 12–26 Lexington Street, London, W1F 0LE, England (office). *Telephone:* (20) 3214-0800 (office). *Fax:* (20) 3214-0801 (office). *E-mail:* info@unitedagents.co.uk (office); personal@rogermcgough.org.uk (office). *Website:* unitedagents.co.uk (office); www.rogermcgough.org.uk.

McGOWAN, Kieran, BComm; Irish business executive; joined IDA Ireland (industrial devt agency f. as the Industrial Devt Authority) 1966, CEO 1990–98; mem. Bd of Dirs CRH plc 1998–2012, Chair. 2007–12 (retd); mem. Bd of Dirs Elan Corpn plc, Enterprise Ireland 1998–, Irish Life & Permanent plc, United Drug plc, Charles Schwab Worldwide Funds plc, UDG Healthcare PLC 1999–2010, Malin Corpn PLC 2016–; Chair. Governing Authority, Univ. Coll. Dublin 2004–09; Founder-mem. Inter Trade Ireland; fmr Pres. Irish Man. Inst., Dublin Molecular Medicine Centre. *Address:* c/o Malin Corporation PLC, 2 Harbour Square, Dun Laoghaire Co, Dublin, Ireland.

McGRATH, Glenn Donald, AM; Australian professional cricketer (retd); *President, McGrath Foundation;* b. 9 Feb. 1970, Dubbo, NSW; m. 1st Jane Louise (died 2008); two c.; m. 2nd Sara Leonardi; one d.; ed Narromine High School, NSW; right-handed batsman, right-arm fast-medium bowler; teams: NSW 1992–2008, Australia 1993–2007 (retd), Worcs. 2000, Middx 2003, Delhi Daredevils 2008–10; First-class debut: 1992/93; Test debut: Australia v NZ, Perth Nov. 1993; One-Day Int. (ODI) debut: Australia v S Africa, Melbourne Dec. 1993; T20I debut: NZ v Australia, Auckland Feb. 2005; played in 124 Tests, scored 641 runs and took 563 wickets (average 21.64) with 29 five-wicket and three 10-wicket performances, best bowling 8/24 against Pakistan at the WACA 2004; ODIs: played in 250 matches, took 381 wickets (average 22.02), best bowling 7/15; First-class: scored 977 runs and took 835 wickets (average 20.85) with 42 five-wicket and seven 10-wicket performances; test hat-trick against West Indies at Perth 2001; 32 wickets in 2001 series against England; first Australian fast bowler to play in 100 Test matches; retd from Test cricket 23 Dec. 2006, from all int. cricket following World Cup 2007; f. McGrath Foundation 2002, currently Pres.; Wisden Cricketer of the Year 1998, Wisden Australian Cricketer of the Year 1999, 2005–06, Allan Border Medal 2000, Test Player of the Year 2000, One-Day Int. Player of the Year 2001, World Cup Player of the Series 2007, inducted into ICC Hall of Fame 2013. *Publication:* World Cup Diary: Glenn McGrath. *Leisure interests:* time with family, golf. *Address:* McGrath Foundation, PO Box 471, Saint Leonards, NSW 1590, Australia (office). *Telephone:* (2) 8962-6100 (office). *Fax:* (2) 9958-0140 (office). *Website:* www.mcgrathfoundation.com.au (office).

McGRATH, John Brian, BSc, FRSA; British business executive; *Chairman, Cicely Saunders International;* b. 20 June 1938, Ruislip, Middlesex; m. Sandy Watson 1964; one s. one d.; ed Brunel Univ.; worked at UKAEA 1962–65; with NCB 1965–67; with Ford Motor Co. 1967–71; with Jaguar Cars 1971–75; with Stone-Platt 1976–82; Man. Dir Construction and Mining Div. and Chief Exec. Compair 1982–83; joined Grand Metropolitan PLC 1985, Group Dir Watney Mann & Truman Brewers Ltd 1985, Chair. and Man. Dir Grand Metropolitan Brewing 1986–88, Jt Man. Dir Int. Distillers & Vintners 1988–91, Man. Dir and COO 1991–92, Chief Exec. 1992–93, Chair. and Chief Exec. 1993–96, Group Chief Exec. Grand Metropolitan PLC 1996–97; Dir (non-exec.) Cookson Group 1993–; Chair. Scotch Whisky Assen 1995–2000; CEO Guinness Ltd (now Diageo plc) 1997–2000; Chair. Boots Co. PLC 2000–03 (Dir 1998–2003); Dir Carlton Communications PLC 2003, ITV PLC (formed by merger of Carlton Communications and Granada) 2004–07; Chair. Cicely Saunders Int. 2002–; Gov. Brunel Univ. 2004–12; Fellow,

King's Coll. London; Dr hc (Brunel). *Telephone:* (18) 5385-0367 (office). *E-mail:* jbmcgrath99@gmail.com (home).

McGREGOR, Ewan Gordon, OBE; British actor; b. 31 March 1971, Perth, Scotland; s. of James McGregor and Carol McGregor; m. Eve Mavrakis 1995; three d. and one adopted d.; ed Guildhall School of Music and Drama, London; began career with Perth Repertory Theatre; has acted in mainstream, indie and art house films; Hon. DLitt (Univ. of Ulster). *Theatre includes:* What the Butler Saw, Little Malcolm and his Struggle against the Eunuchs (Hampstead Theatre Club) 1999 and Comedy Theatre, London, Guys and Dolls (Piccadilly Theatre, London) 2005, Othello (Donmar Warehouse, London) 2007–08. *Films include:* Being Human, Family Style, Shallow Grave (Best Actor Dinard Film Festival 1994), Blue Juice, The Pillow Book, Trainspotting, Emma, Brassed Off, Nightwatch, The Serpent's Kiss, A Life Less Ordinary, Velvet Goldmine, Star Wars Episode I: The Phantom Menace, Little Voice, Rogue Trader, Eye of the Beholder, Nora, Moulin Rouge (Best Actor, Berlin Film Festival, Empire Award, Variety Club Awards, Film Critics' Awards) 2001, Black Hawk Down 2002, Star Wars Episode II: Attack of the Clones 2002, Down with Love 2003, Young Adam (Scottish BAFTA Award for Best Actor 2004) 2003, Big Fish 2004, Stay 2004, Star Wars Episode III: Revenge of the Sith 2005, The Island 2005, Stay 2005, Stormbreaker 2006, Scenes of a Sexual Nature 2006, Miss Potter 2006, Cassandra's Dream 2007, Deception 2008, Incendiary 2008, I Love You Phillip Morris 2009, Angels and Demons 2009, The Men Who Stare At Goats 2009, Amelia 2009, The Ghost (European Film Award for Best Actor) 2010, Nanny McPhee and the Big Bang 2010, Jackboots on Whitehal (voice) 2010, Beginners 2010, Perfect Sense 2011, Salmon Fishing in the Yemen 2011, Haywire 2011, The Impossible 2012, Jack the Giant Slayer 2013, August: Osage County 2013. *Television includes:* Lipstick on Your Collar 1993, Scarlet and Black 1993, Kavanagh QC 1995, Doggin' Around, Tales From the Crypt 1996, ER 1997, Long Way Round 2004, Long Way Down 2007, The Corrections (film) 2012, Fargo (Golden Globe Award for Best Performance By An Actor In A Limited Series Or Motion Picture Made For Television 2018) 2014. *Publications:* Long Way Round (with Charley Boorman) 2005, Long Way Down (with Charley Boorman) 2007. *Leisure interest:* motor bikes. *Address:* c/o United Agents, 12–26 Lexington Street, London W1F 0LE, England (office); c/o Creative Artists Agency, 2000 Avenue of the Stars, Los Angeles, CA 90067, USA (office). *Website:* unitedagents.co.uk (office); www.caa.com (office). *Telephone:* (424) 288-2000 (office). *Fax:* (424) 288-2900 (office).

MacGREGOR, Joanna Clare, OBE, MA; British pianist, conductor, curator and academic; *Head of Piano, Royal Academy of Music;* b. 16 July 1959, London; d. of Alfred MacGregor and Angela Hughes; m. 1st Richard Williams 1986 (divorced 2002), remarried 2012; one d. (deceased); ed South Hampstead High School for Girls, New Hall, Cambridge, Royal Acad. of Music, London; Young Concert Artists Trust 1985–88; performances of classical, jazz and contemporary music in more than 80 countries at venues including Royal Albert Hall, Royal Festival Hall, Wigmore Hall, Lincoln Center and Carnegie Hall, New York, Sydney Opera House, Leipzig Gewandhaus, Opéra Bastille, Paris, Concertgebouw, Amsterdam; has performed with Rotterdam, Oslo and Netherlands Radio and Royal Philharmonic Orchestras, Sydney, Berlin, Chicago, BBC, RTÉ and London Symphony Orchestras, MDR Sinfonieorchester and Salzburg Camerata, New York and Hong Kong Philharmonics, Philharmonia, London Mozart Players, Manchester Camerata, Royal Scottish, Royal Liverpool, Hallé, English and Irish Chamber Orchestras; has worked with John Adams, Sir Harrison Birtwistle, Pierre Boulez, Sir Colin Davis, Sir Simon Rattle, Valery Gergiev, Lou Harrison, Arvo Pärt and numerous jazz artists, including Jason Yarde, Seb Rochford and Andy Sheppard; electronica artists and world music artists including Dhafer Youssef, Kuljit Bhamra, Brian Eno, Scanner, Bishi, Moses Molelekwa and Sibongile Khumalo; numerous radio and TV appearances, including Last Night of the Proms 1997, South Bank Show 2002, Messiaen's Turangalila (BBC 4) 2012, Mozart/Gershwin (BBC 2) 2012; est. own record label SoundCircus 1998; Prof. of Music, Gresham Coll. 1998–2002; Prof. of Performance, Liverpool Hope Univ.; Head of Piano, RAM 2011–, also Prof. of the Univ. of London, RAM 2013–; Visiting Musician, Oriel Coll., Oxford 2015–16; mem. Arts Council of England 1998–2002; conducting debut on UK tour with Britten Sinfonia 2000, Assoc. Artistic Dir 2002–05; cr. Cross Border, multimedia work touring China with Jin Xing's Dance Theatre of Shanghai 2003; Artistic Dir Bath Int. Music Festival 2005–12; created On the Edge of Life examining social issues through music/multimedia 2006–12; performed complete Chopin Mazurkas 2010; curated Deloitte Ignite at Royal Opera House, Covent Garden 2011, Aventure at Luxembourg Philharmonique 2012–13; Artistic Dir Dartington Int. Summer School and Festival 2015–; Hon. FRAM, Hon. Fellow, Trinity Coll. of Music, RSA, New Hall, Cambridge; Dr hc (Open Univ.) 2005, (Bath Univ.) 2008, (Bath Spa Univ.) 2011, (Univ. of Cambridge) 2016; European Encouragement Prize for Music 1995, NFMS Sir Charles Grove Award 1998, South Bank Show Award for Classical Music 2000, Royal Philharmonic Soc. Audience Development Award 2003. *Play:* Memoirs of an Amnesiac (radio play about Erik Satie). *Compositions include:* Lute Songs (orchestra), Lullaby for M (percussion), arrangements of Piazzolla tangos, Lost Highway: Gospel and Spirituals of the Deep South (orchestral), new arrangement of The Magic Flute (ensemble), settings of Angela Carter poems (voice and ensemble), Sidewalk Dances and Art of Fugue (Bach and Moondog, orchestral). *Recordings include:* American contemporary music (Ives, Monk, Nancarrow, Copland, Barber, Cage, Lou Harrison), Britten Concerto, Satie, Gershwin recordings with LSO, and music by Bach (The Art of Fugue, French Suites, Goldberg Variations), Scarlatti, Bartók, Debussy, Ravel and Messaien (Vingt Regards, Harawi, Quartet for the End of Time), Deep River (music of the Deep South, with Andy Sheppard) 2006, orchestral arrangements of Moondog: Sidewalk Dances 2007, commissions and recordings of Harrison Birtwistle, Nitin Sawhney, Talvin Singh, Moses Molelekwa, Django Bates, Live in Buenos Aires (Piazzolla, Bach, Gismonti). *Publications:* wrote series of children's books for Faber Music 2001, Piano World (five vols) 2001, Art Not Chance 2001, Unbeaten Tracks 2006, Lowside Blues 2009. *Address:* Department of Piano, Royal Academy of Music, Marylebone Road, London, NW1 5HT, England (office). *Website:* www.ram.ac.uk/departments/piano (office); soundcircus.com.

MacGREGOR, Baron (Life Peer), cr. 2001, of Pulham Market in the County of Norfolk; **John Roddick Russell MacGregor,** OBE, PC, MA, LLB; British politician and business executive; b. 14 Feb. 1937, Glasgow; s. of Dr. N. S. R. MacGregor; m. Jean Mary Elizabeth Dungey 1962; one s. two d.; ed Merchiston Castle School, Edin., St Andrews Univ., King's Coll., London; Univ. Admin. 1961–62; Editorial Staff, New Society 1962–63; Special Asst to Prime Minister, Sir Alec Douglas-Home 1963–64; Conservative Research Dept 1964–65; Head of Pvt. Office of Rt Hon. Edward Heath (Leader of Opposition) 1965–68; Conservative MP for South Norfolk 1974–2001; an Opposition Whip 1977–79; a Lord Commr of HM Treasury 1979–81, Parl. Under-Sec. of State, Dept of Industry 1981–83; Minister of State, Minister of Agric., Fisheries and Food 1983–85, 1987–89; Chief Sec. to HM Treasury 1985–87; Sec. of State for Educ. and Science 1989–90; Lord Pres. of the Council and Leader of the House of Commons 1990–92; Sec. of State for Transport 1992–94; mem. House of Lords 2001–, Chair. Select Cttee on Econ. Affairs 2010–15, Asscn of Conservative Peers 2012–16; with Hill Samuel & Co. Ltd 1968–79, Dir 1973–79, Deputy Chair. Hill Samuel Bank 1994–96, also Dir; Dir Slough Estates 1995–2006, Associated British Foods 1994–2007, Unigate (now Uniq) 1996–2005, London and Manchester Group 1997–98, Friends Provident 1998–2007, Supervisory Bd Daf Trucks NV 2000–08; Jt Chair. UK Food and Agriculture Advisory Bd, Rabobank International 1995–2011; Vice-Pres. Local Govt Asscn 1997–99; mem. Cttee on Standards in Public Life 1998–2003; Chair. Fed. of Univ. Conservative and Unionist Asscns 1959, Bow Group 1963–64; Chair. Pension Fund Trustees, SEGRO 2006–09, British Energy (now EDF) 2007–, Anglian Water Group 2009–12, Eggborough Power Ltd 2010–; First Pres. Conservative and Christian Democratic Youth Community 1963–65; mem. Magic Circle 1989, Inner Magic Circle 1999; mem. Council King's Coll. London 1996–2002, Inst. of Dirs 1996–2007, Norwich Cathedral Council 2002–, High Steward and Chair. of Council 2007–; Deputy Chair., Asscn of Governing Bodies of Ind. Schools 2001–06; Trustee Royal Norfolk Agricultural Asscn 2006–09; Hon. Fellow, King's Coll. London 1990; Hon. LLD (Westminster) 1995. *Leisure interests:* music, reading, travelling, gardening, conjuring. *Address:* House of Lords, London, SW1A 0PW, England. *Telephone:* (20) 7219-4439 (office).

MACGREGOR, Dame Judith Anne, DCMG, CMG, LVO, MA; British diplomatist; b. 17 June 1952, London, England; m. John Malcolm Macgregor CVO; three s. one d.; ed Univ. of Oxford; joined FCO 1976, First Sec., Belgrade 1978–81, Polish and Hungarian Desk Officer, FCO 1981–83, Head of Recruitment 1983–84, mem. Planning Staff 1985–86, First Sec., Prague 1989, Paris 1992, Deputy Head of Western European Dept 1993–95, Counsellor and Head of Security Strategy Unit 2001–03, FCO Chair. Civil Service Selection Bd 2003–04, Amb. to Slovakia 2004–07, Dir Migration, FCO 2007–09, Amb. to Mexico 2009–13, High Commr to South Africa (also accred to Lesotho and Swaziland) 2013–17. *Leisure interests:* walking, gardening, reading.

MacGREGOR, (Robert) Neil, OM, FSA; British museum director; *Founding Artistic Director, Humboldt Forum;* b. 16 June 1946; s. of Alexander MacGregor and Anna MacGregor (née Neil); ed Glasgow Acad., New Coll., Oxford, Univ. of Edinburgh, Courtauld Inst. of Art; Lecturer, Univ. of Reading 1976; Ed. The Burlington Magazine 1981–86; Dir Nat. Gallery 1987–2002; Dir British Museum 2002–15; Founding Artistic Dir, Humboldt Forum, Berlin 2016–; Trustee Pilgrim Trust 1990–, Raad van Toezicht, Rijksmuseum, Amsterdam; Chair. Conf. of UK Nat. Museum Dirs 1991–97; Curator Cen. Inst. for Art History, Munich 1992–; mem. Supervisory Bd Rijksmuseum 1995–; mem. Bd of Electors Ashmolean Museum, Fitzwilliam Museum; mem. UNESCO; mem. Advisory Bd of the Hermitage, St Petersburg 1997–; mem. Visiting Cttee J. Paul Getty Museum, Malibu, Calif., USA; fmr Chair. Nat. Museums Dirs' Conf.; mem. Courtauld Inst. of Art 2002–; mem. Faculty of Advocates, Edin. 1972; Fellow, New Coll. Oxford, Birkbeck Coll. London 2004; Hon. Officer, Order of Australia 2013; Hon. mem. Royal Scottish Acad. 1995; Hon. Fellow, Ecole Normale Supérieure, Paris, British Acad.; Dr hc (York) 1992, (Edinburgh) 1994, (Reading) 1997, (Leicester) 1997, (Glasgow) 1998, (Strathclyde) 1998, (Oxford) 1998, (Exeter) 1998, (London) 1999; Friedrich-Gundolf-Preis 2015, Nayef Al-Rodhan Prize 2015. *Radio:* contributor to numerous BBC radio programmes including A History of the World in 100 Objects 2010, Germany: Memories of a Nation 2014, Living with the Gods 2017, As Others See Us 2019. *Television:* has presented two major series on art. *Video:* Making Masterpieces (three-video set; writer and presenter). *Publications:* A Victim of Anonymity 1994, Seeing Salvation 2000, Britain's Paintings: the story of art through masterpieces in British Collections 2003, A History of the World in 100 Objects 2010, Shakespeare's Restless World 2012, Germany: Memories of a Nation 2014; numerous articles in Apollo, The Burlington Magazine, Connoisseur, etc. *Address:* Berlin Palace–Humboldtforum Foundation, Unter den Linden 3, 10117 Berlin, Germany (office). *Telephone:* (30) 31805720 (office). *Website:* www.sbs-humboldtforum.de (office).

MacGREGOR, Susan (Sue) Katriona, CBE, OBE; British broadcaster and journalist; b. 30 Aug. 1941, Oxford; d. of Dr James MacGregor and Margaret MacGregor; ed Herschel School, Cape, SA; announcer/producer, South African Broadcasting Corpn 1962–67; BBC Radio reporter World at One, World This Weekend, PM 1967–72; Presenter, (BBC Radio 4) Woman's Hour 1972–87, Tuesday Call, Conversation Piece, Today 1984–2002, A Good Read 2003–10, The Reunion 2003–, (BBC TV) Around Westminster, Dateline London; Visiting Prof. of Journalism, Nottingham Trent Univ. 1995–2003; mem. Royal Coll. of Physicians Cttee on Ethical Issues in Medicine 1985–2000; mem. Bd Royal Nat. Theatre 1998–2003; Trustee, John Ellerman Foundation 2002–12, UNICEF UK 2004–13; Bd mem. Young Classical Artists' Trust 2003–12; Hon. MRCP 1995; Hon. DLitt (Nottingham) 1996; Hon. LLD (Dundee) 1997; Hon. DLitt (Nottingham Trent) 2000, (Staffordshire) 2001, (North London) 2002. *Publication:* Woman of Today 2002. *Leisure interests:* theatre, cinema, skiing. *Address:* c/o Knight Ayton Management, 29 Gloucester Place, London, W1U 8HX, England (office). *Telephone:* (20) 3795-1806 (office). *E-mail:* info@knightayton.co.uk (office). *Website:* www.knightayton.co.uk (office).

McGREGOR, Wayne, CBE; British choreographer and director; *Resident Choreographer, Royal Ballet;* b. 12 March 1970, Stockport, Greater Manchester; ed Univ. Coll. Bretton Hall and José Limon School, NY, USA; originally trained in contemporary dance; cr. works for The Royal Ballet, Skindex, Stuttgart Ballet, English Nat. Ballet, San Francisco Ballet and Rambert Dance Co.; other work includes choreography for film Harry Potter and The Goblet of Fire and for Channel 4 (UK), BBC TV, The Old Vic, Nat. Theatre, Royal Court Theatre, ENO and Peter Hall Co.; Founder Random Dance (now Studio Wayne McGregor) 1992–, became Resident Co. of Sadler's Wells Theatre 2001–; Resident Choreographer,

Royal Ballet 2006–; Choreographer of Big Dance (Olympic-funded project) 2012; Vice Pres. Elmhurst Ballet School 2019–; presented TED talk titled A Choreographer's Creative Process in Real Time 2012; Hon. DSc (Plymouth Univ.) 2013; Outstanding Achievement in Dance Award, Time Out Live Awards 2001, Outstanding Choreography Award, Time Out Live Awards 2002, IMZ Dance Screen Award 2002, Laurence Olivier Award 2004. *Dances include:* Chroma, Engram, Qualia, Symbiont(s), NDT1 for Royal Ballet, over 30 pieces for Random Dance, Outlier, cr. two new ballets in celebration of Les Ballet Russes – Dyad 1909, for Wayne McGregor/Random Dance, and Dyad 1929, for Australian Ballet, Borderlands for San Francisco Ballet 2013, Raven Girl, Royal Ballet 2013. *Address:* Royal Opera House, Bow Street, Covent Garden, London, WC2E 9DD (office); Studio Wayne McGregor, Broadcast Center, Here East, 10 East Bay Lane, Queen Elizabeth Olympic Park, London E15 2GW, England (office). *E-mail:* studio@waynemcgregor.com (office). *Website:* www.roh.org.uk/discover/artistdetail.aspx?id=535 (office); waynemcgregor.com.

McGUANE, Thomas Francis, III, BA, MFA; American writer; b. 11 Dec. 1939, Wyandotte, Mich.; m. 1st Portia Rebecca Crockett 1962 (divorced 1975); one s.; m. 2nd Margot Kidder 1976 (divorced 1977); one d.; m. 3rd Laurie Buffett 1977; one step-d. one d.; ed Univ. of Michigan, Olivet Coll., Michigan State Univ., Yale Univ., Stanford Univ.; Wallace Stegner Fellowship, Stanford Univ. 1966–67; mem. American Acad. of Arts and Letters; Dr hc (Montana State Univ.) 1993, (Rocky Mountain Coll.) 1995; Richard and Hinda Rosenthal Foundation Award, American Acad. of Arts and Letters 1971, Fly Rod and Reel Angler of the Year 2010, Trout Unlimited Land Conservation Award, Americans Rivers Award for River Conservation, Montana Governors Award, Wallace Stegner Award, Center for the American West, Lifetime Achievement Award, Western Literature Asscn, inducted into Fly Fishing Hall of Fame 2012, National Cutting Horse Hall of Fame. *Publications include:* The Sporting Club 1969, The Bushwacked Piano 1971, Ninety-Two in the Shade 1973, Panama 1977, An Outside Chance: Essays on Sports (revised edn as An Outside Chance: Classic and New Essays on Sports) 1980, Nobody's Angel 1982, In the Crazies: Book and Portfolio 1984, Something to Be Desired 1984, To Skin a Cat 1986, Silent Seasons: Twenty-One Fishing Stories 1988, Keep the Change 1989, Nothing but Blue Skies 1992, Some Horses 1999, Upstream: Fly Fishing in the American Northwest 1999, The Longest Silence 2000, The Cadence of Grass 2002, Horses 2005, Gallatin Canyon 2006, Driving on the Rim 2010, Crow Fair (short stories) 2015. *Address:* PO Box 25, McLeod, MT 59052-0025, USA (home). *Website:* tommcguane.com.

McGUFFIN, Peter, CBE, MB ChB, PhD, FRCP, FRCPsych, FMedSci; British/Irish psychiatrist and geneticist; *Professor Emeritus of Psychiatric Genetics, King's College London;* b. 4 Feb. 1949, Belfast, Northern Ireland; s. of Capt. William McGuffin and Melba M. Burnison; m. Prof. Anne Farmer 1972; one s. two d.; ed Univs of Leeds and London; MRC Fellow and Lecturer, Inst. of Psychiatry, London 1979–81; Visiting MRC Fellow, Washington Univ. Medical School, St Louis, Mo. 1981–82; MRC Sr Fellow, Hon. Consultant and Sr Lecturer, Inst. of Psychiatry, King's Coll. Hosp. London 1982–86; Prof. of Psychological Medicine, Univ. of Wales Coll. of Medicine 1987–98; Prof. of Psychiatric Genetics, MRC Social, Genetic and Developmental Psychiatry Centre, Inst. of Psychiatry, King's Coll. London 1998–2013, Dean and Head of School 2006–09, Dir MRC Social, Genetic and Developmental Psychiatry Centre 2010–12, Prof. Emer. 2013–; Hon. Consultant Psychiatrist, Affective Disorders Service, South London & Maudsley Trust –2013; Distinguished Fellow, Int. Soc. of Affective Disorders 2000; Fattorini Prize, Univ. of Leeds 1972, Foundation Fellow, Acad. of Medical Sciences (UK) 1998, Stromgren Medal, Danish Psychiatric Asscn 2004, Lifetime Achievement Award, Int. Soc. for Psychiatric Genetics 2007. *Publications include:* Scientific Principles of Psychopathology, The New Genetics of Mental Illness, Seminars on Psychiatric Genetics, Essentials of Postgraduate Psychiatry, Behavioural Genetics (4th edn), Measuring Psychopathology, Psychiatric Genetics and Genomics; many scientific papers and articles. *Leisure interests:* music (especially classical guitar), horse riding, running with my dogs. *Address:* MRC Social, Genetic and Developmental Psychiatry Centre, Institute of Psychiatry, Box P001, De Crespigny Park, London, SE5 8AF, England (office). *Telephone:* (20) 7848-0871 (office). *Fax:* (20) 7848-0866 (office). *E-mail:* p.mcguffin@iop.kcl.ac.uk (office). *Website:* www.kcl.ac.uk/ioppn/depts/mrc/about/history/McGuffinTribute.aspx (office).

McGUINNESS, Frank, BA, MPhil, DLit; Irish playwright and academic; *Professor, School of English, Drama and Film, University College Dublin;* b. 29 July 1953, Buncrana, Donegal; s. of Patrick McGuinness and Celine McGuinness; ed University Coll. Dublin; Lecturer in English, Univ. of Ulster, Coleraine 1977–79; Lecturer in English, Univ. Coll. Dublin 1979–80, Writer-in-Residence, School of English, Drama and Film 1997–, Prof. of Creative Writing 1997–; Lecturer in English, St Patrick's Coll., Maynooth 1984–97; Dir Abbey Theatre, Dublin 1992–96; Officier des Arts et Lettres; Hon. DLitt (Ulster) 2000; Harvey's Award, Evening Standard Drama Award, Ewart-Biggs Peace Prize, Cheltenham Literary Prize, Fringe First, Irish American Literary Prize 1992, Independent on Sunday Best Play 1992, New York Drama Critics' Award 1993, Writers' Guild Award 1993, Tony Award for Best Revival 1997, PEN Irish Writer Award 2014, London Theatre Offies Best Play Award 2014. *Publications include:* plays: The Factory Girls 1982, Observe the Sons of Ulster Marching towards the Somme 1985, Baglady 1985, Innocence 1986, Carthaginians 1988, Mary and Lizzie 1989, The Bread Man 1990, Someone Who'll Watch Over Me 1992, The Bird Sanctuary 1994, Mutabilitie 1997, Dolly West's Kitchen 1999, Gates of Gold 2002, Speaking Like Magpies 2005, There Came a Gypsy Riding 2007, Oedipus 2008, Greta Garbo Came to Donegal 2010, Ghosts 2011, The Match Box 2012, John Gabriel Borkman 2011, The Dead 2012, Damned by Despair 2012, The Hanging Gardens 2013, The Thebans: Libretto 2014, Electra 2014; poetry: Booterstown 1994, In Loving Memory 1989, The Sea with no Ships 1999, The Stone Jug 2003, Dulse 2007, In A Town of Five Thousand People 2012. *Leisure interests:* walking, painting, botany. *Address:* School of English, Drama and Film, University College Dublin, Belfield, Dublin 4, Ireland (office). *Telephone:* (1) 716-8420 (office). *Fax:* (1) 716-1174 (office). *E-mail:* pauline.slattery@ucd.ie (office). *Website:* www.ucd.ie/englishanddrama/staff/academicstaff/mcguinnessfrank (office).

McGUINTY, Hon. Dalton, JD; Canadian politician; b. 19 July 1955; s. of Dalton McGuinty, Sr and Elizabeth McGuinty; m. Terri McGuinty; three s. one d.; ed Univ. of Ottawa, McMaster Univ.; practised law Ottawa; mem. Ontario Legislature representing Ottawa South 1990–; Leader Ontario Liberal Party 1996–2013; Premier of Ont. 2003–13 (resgnd), also Minister of Intergovernmental Affairs 2003–13; currently Fellow, School of Public Policy & Admin. *Address:* School of Public Policy & Administration, 5224 Richcraft Hall, 1125 Colonel By Drive, Ottawa, ON K1S 5B6, Canada.

McGUIRE, William W., MD; American physician and business executive; *Owner, Minnesota United FC;* b. Troy, NY; ed Univ. of Texas, Austin, Univ. of Texas Medical Br., Galveston; grew up in League City, Tex.; worked in Calif. and Colo before moving to Minn.; practising physician specializing in cardiopulmonary medicine 1980–85; Pres. and CEO Peak Health Plan 1985–88; joined United HealthCare Corpn (renamed UnitedHealth Group) 1988, Pres. and COO 1989–91, CEO and Chair. 1991–2006 (resgnd); required by Securities and Exchange Comm. to repay $468 million as a partial settlement of a backdating prosecution, fined $7 million and agreed to not serve as an officer or dir of a public co. for ten years 2007; purchased Minnesota Stars FC Nov. 2012, rebranded as Minnesota United FC Jan. 2013; mem. Nat. Insts of Health Nat. Cancer Policy Bd; One of the 50 Best CEOs in America, Worth Magazine 2001. *Address:* Minnesota United FC, National Sports Center, 1700 105th Avenue NE, Blaine, MN 55449, USA (office). *Telephone:* (763) 476-2237 (office). *E-mail:* info@mnunitedfc.com (office). *Website:* www.mnunitedfc.com (office).

MACH, David Stefan, MA, RA; British sculptor; *Professor of Inspiration and Discovery, Dundee University;* b. 18 March 1956, Methil, Fife, Scotland; s. of Joseph Mach and Martha Cassidy; m. Lesley June White 1979; ed Buckhaven High School, Duncan of Jordanstone Coll. of Art, Dundee and Royal Coll. of Art; full-time sculptor 1982–; Prof. of Inspiration and Discovery, Univ. of Dundee 1994–; sculpture installation and collage exhibited at galleries and museums world-wide; Hon. Prof., Sculpture Dept, Edin. Coll. of Art 1999; Pat Holmes Memorial Prize 1975, Duncan of Drumfork Travelling Scholarship 1976, SED Minor Travelling Scholarship 1977, SED Major Travelling Scholarship 1978, RCA Drawing Prize 1982, City of Glasgow Lord Provost Prize 1992. *Publications:* David Mach 2002, David Mach – Precious Light 2011. *Leisure interests:* music (drumming), writing, travelling, driving, films, skiing. *Address:* 8 Havelock Walk, Forest Hill, London, SE23 3HG, England (office). *Telephone:* (20) 8699-5659 (office). *E-mail:* davidmach@davidmach.com (office). *Website:* www.davidmach.com (office).

MACHADO VENTURA, José Ramón; Cuban physician and politician; *Member, Council of State;* b. 26 Oct. 1930, San Antonio de las Vueltas, Las Villas; ed Universidad de La Habana; served as guerrilla in Sierra Maestra mountains and cared for mems of rebel army during Cuban Revolution against Batista govt; Asst to the Pres. and Chief of Medical Services, City of Havana 1959; Minister of Health 1960–67; Politburo Del. to Matanzas Prov. 1968–71; First Sec. Havana Provincial Cttee, Partido Comunista de Cuba 1971–75, mem. Secr. of Cen. Cttee 1975–2008, mem. Politburo 1975–; Deputy, Asamblea Nacional del Poder Popular (Parl.) for Guantánamo 1976–2008; Vice-Pres. and Secr. Political Bureau 1976–2008, mem. Council of State 2008–, First Vice-Pres. 2008–13. *Address:* Oficina del Consejo de Estado, Havana, Cuba (office).

MACHAR TENY, Riek; South Sudanese politician and fmr resistance fighter; b. 1952; m. 1st Angelina Jany Teny; m. 2nd Emma McCune (died 1993); m. 3rd Becky Hagmann; ed Univ. of Bradford, UK; fmr mem. Sudan People's Liberation Army (SPLA), f. breakaway group SPLA-Nasir 1991–93, later SPLA-United 1993–94, Leader, South Sudan Defence Forces 1997–2002; Asst to Pres. of Repub. of Sudan 1997–2000; Pres. South Sudan Coordinating Council 1997–2000; Vice-Pres. of Southern Sudan (autonomous region) 2005–11; First Vice-Pres. of South Sudan following independence 2011–13 (dismissed), April–July 2016 (dismissed); led opposition forces during conflict Dec. 2013; in exile in South Africa.

MACHEL, Graça, DBE BA; Mozambican international organization official; *President, SOAS, University of London;* b. 1945, southern Gaza Prov.; m. 1st Samora Machel 1975 (died 1986); two c.; m. 2nd Nelson Mandela 1998; ed Univ. of Lisbon, Portugal; worked underground for Front for Liberation of Mozambique (Frelimo) movt during country's war of independence from Portugal, Deputy Dir Frelimo Secondary School in Tanzania 1974; Minister for Educ. 1975–86; mem. Int. Steering Cttee, World Conf. on Educ. for All 1990; f. Foundation for Community Devt 1990, Graça Machel Trust, New Faces New Voices; Co-founder Mandela Inst. for Development Studies; Chancellor Univ. of Cape Town 1999–; Pres. SOAS, Univ. of London, UK 2012–; Chair. UNICEF study 1994, currently UNICEF Goodwill Amb., Pres. UNESCO Mozambique Nat. Comm.; Chair. Leadership Council for the Campaign to End Paediatric HIV/AIDS, African Centre for the Constructive Resolution of Disputes (ACCORD), Nat. Org. of Children of Mozambique; mem. Sec.-Gen.'s High-Level Advisory Bd on Mediation, UN 2017–; Founding mem. The Elders; mem. Africa Progress Panel, High Level Task Force on Innovative Int. Finance for Health Systems, UN Millennium Development Goals Advocates Panel; Eminent Person of GAVI Alliance and UN Foundation; Hon. DBE (UK) 2007; Dr hc (Univ. of the Western Cape) 1992, (Univ. of Évora) 2008; Laureate of Africa Prize for Leadership for the Sustainable End of Hunger, Hunger Project 1992, Nansen Medal (for outstanding contrib. on behalf of refugee children) 1995, InterAction Humanitarian Award 1997, CARE Award, North-South Prize 1998. *Address:* Office of the President, SOAS, University of London, Thornhaugh Street, Russell Square, London, WC1H 0XG, England (office); Graça Machel Trust, 7 Eton Road, Block A, Sandhurst, 2196, South Africa. *E-mail:* info@gracamachel.org. *Website:* www.soas.ac.uk/president (office); gracamacheltrust.org; awes.nfnv.org.

MACHEN, J. Bernard (Bernie), DDS, MS, PhD; American dental surgeon, educational psychologist and university administrator; *President, University of Florida;* b. Greenwood, Miss.; m. Chris Machen; two s. one d.; ed Vanderbilt Univ., St Louis Univ., Univ. of Iowa; Diplomate, American Bd of Pediatric Dentistry; veteran US Army Maj.; Prof. and Assoc. Dean, Univ. of North Carolina School of Dentistry 1983–89; Dean School of Dentistry, Univ. of Michigan 1989–95, Provost and Exec. Vice-Pres. for Academic Affairs, Univ. of Michigan 1995–97; Pres. Univ. of Utah 1997–2003; Pres. Univ. of Florida 2004–; mem. NAS Inst. of Medicine Cttee on Educating Dentists for the Future 1992–95; fmr Chief of Dept of Extension Services at US Army Inst. of Dental Research; Pres. American Asscn of Dental Schools 1987; mem. Bd of Trustees, Salt Lake Olympic Organizing Cttee for the 2002 Winter Olympics; Pres. Exec. Cttee Southeastern Conf. 2010–, Chair. Southeastern Conf. Academic Consortium 2010–; mem. Econ. Devt Transition Team of Gov.-elect Rick Scott 2010. *Address:* Office of the President, University of Florida, 226 Tigert Hall, PO Box 113150, Gainesville, FL 32611, USA (office). *Telephone:* (352) 392-1311 (office). *Fax:* (352) 392-9506 (office). *E-mail:* president@ufl.edu (office). *Website:* president.ufl.edu (office).

McHENRY, Donald F., MSc; American diplomatist and academic; b. 13 Oct. 1936, St Louis, Mo.; m. Mary Williamson (divorced 1978); one s. two d.; ed Illinois State Univ., Southern Illinois and Georgetown Univs; taught at Howard Univ., Washington 1959–62; joined Dept of State 1963, Head Dependent Areas Section, Office of UN Political Affairs 1965–68; Asst to US Sec. of State 1969; Special Asst to Dept Counselor 1969–71; Lecturer, School of Foreign Service, Georgetown Univ., Guest Scholar, The Brookings Inst. and Int. Affairs Fellow, Council on Foreign Relations (on leave from State Dept) 1971–73; resgnd from State Dept 1973; Project Dir Humanitarian Policy Studies, Carnegie Endowment for Int. Peace, Washington 1973–76; served Pres. Carter's transition team 1976–77; Amb. and Deputy Perm. Rep. to UN 1977–79, Perm. Rep. 1979–81; Distinguished Prof. in the Practice of Diplomacy, School of Foreign Service, Georgetown Univ. 1981–2014 (retd); Founder and Pres. IRC Group (consultancy) 1981–2007; mem. Council on Foreign Relations (fmr Dir, now Hon. Dir); fmr mem. Editorial Bd Foreign Policy Magazine; Chair. Ford Foundation Int. Fellows Program; fmr Chair. Bd Africare, now Chair. Emer.; fmr Gov. American Stock Exchange; fmr mem. Bd of Dirs Coca Cola Co., GlaxoSmithKline PLC, Fleet Boston Financial, Fleet Boston Bank, AT&T, Int. Paper Co., Inst. for Int. Econs, The American Ditchley Foundation; Trustee Emer. Columbia Univ., Mayo Foundation; fmr Trustee, The Brookings Inst., Johnson Foundation; Fellow, American Acad. of Arts and Sciences; mem. American Acad. of Diplomacy, Asscn of Black American Ambassadors, Global Leadership Forum; Superior Honor Award, Dept of State 1966. *Publication:* Micronesia: Trust Betrayed 1975. *Address:* c/o School of Foreign Service, Georgetown University, Washington, DC 20057, USA.

MACHETE, Rui, LLB; Portuguese lawyer and politician; b. 7 April 1940, Setúbal; ed Univ. of Lisbon; practised as lawyer 1964–; Head of Legal Services, Companhia Portuguesa de Eletricidade 1969–76; fmr adviser to Man. Bd, Energias de Portugal; fmr Prof., Inst. of Social Studies and Higher Inst. of Labour and Enterprise; fmr Visiting Prof., Univ. Católica Portuguesa; Sec. of State for Immigration 1975, Minister of Social Affairs 1976–79, of Justice 1983–85, Deputy Prime Minister and Minister of Nat. Defence 1985, Minister of State and of Foreign Affairs 2013–15; Chair. Inst. for Financial Man. of Public Enterprises 1983; Dir Bank of Portugal 1981–89, Luso-American Devt Foundation 1985– (Chair. Exec. Bd 1988–2010); mem. Supreme Council, Portuguese Bar Asscn 2005–06; mem. Nat. Inst. of Dirs 1981–83; mem. Partido Social Democrata (PSD), Sec.-Gen. 1974–75, Vice-Pres. PSD Parl. Group 1979; Hon. DHumLitt (Univ. of Massachusetts, Dartmouth) 1997, Hon. LLD (Univ. Católica Portuguesa) 2007. *Address:* c/o Ministry of Foreign Affairs, Palácio das Necessidades, Largo do Rilvas, 1399-030 Lisbon, Portugal (office).

MACHIDA, Katsuhiko; Japanese electronics industry executive; ed Kyoto Univ.; joined Sharp Corpn 1969, various positions in audio-visual and household appliance depts, with Dept of Int. Business 1992–97, Pres. and Chair. Man. Bd, Sharp Corpn 1998–2007, Chair. and CEO 2007–12, Dir and Corp. Advisor 2012–15; apptd Outside Dir, Sekisui House Ltd 2008, Shionogi & Co. Ltd 2012–.

MACHINEA, José Luis, PhD; Argentine economist; b. 5 Oct. 1946, Buenos Aires; s. of José Martin and Beatriz A. Rey; ed Univ. of Minnesota, USA; fmr Prof. of Macroeconomics, Catholic Univ. of Argentina; fmr Chief of Public Finance Dept and Chief of Research Dept at Argentine Cen. Bank, later Pres. Argentine Cen. Bank; Under-Sec. of Political Economy and Under-Sec. of Planning 1980s; consultant to World Bank and Inter-American Devt Bank 1990s; Dir of Research, Industrial Devt Inst. of the Argentine Industrial Union 1992–97; Pres. consultancy firm 1995–99; Pres. Argentine Foundation for Devt with Equity 1998–99; Minister of Economy 1999–2001; Exec. Sec. ECLAC 2003–08; Prebisch Chair, Univ. of Alcalá 2008–09; currently Prof. of Macroeconomics and Econ. Devt, Univ. Torcuato Di Tella, also Dean, School of Govt 2010–11. *Publications:* La Crisis de la Deuda, El Financiamiento Internacional y la Participacion del Sector Privado 2002, Economic Growth with Equity: Challenges for Latin America (co-author) 2007; numerous articles in books and journals on macroeconomics, monetary and financial issues. *Address:* Universidad Torcuato Di Tella, Miñones 2177, Buenos Aires, Argentina (office).

MACHT, Michael; German engineer and business executive; b. 28 Aug. 1960, Stuttgart; ed Univ. of Stuttgart; worked at Fraunhofer Inst. for Industrial Eng IAO –1990; specialist in engine planning, Porsche AG 1990–91, Head of Labour Org. Dept 1991–92, Personal Asst to CEO 1992–98, Man. Dir Porsche Consulting GmbH 1994–98, Head of Production and Logistics and mem. Bd of Man. 1998–2009, oversaw construction and start of operation of Porsche's Leipzig factory, involved in devt of Cayenne SUV and four-door Panamera models, Chair. Bd of Man. (CEO) Porsche AG 2009–10, mem. Bd of Man. Porsche SE in charge of tech. and products 2009–10; Chief of Group Production Volkswagen AG 2010–14, mem. Bd of Man. 2010–14; Dr hc (Univ. of Stuttgart) 2010.

MACHULSKI, Juliusz; Polish film director, screenwriter, producer and actor; *CEO, Studio Filmowe Zebra;* b. 10 March 1955, Olsztyn; s. of Jan Machulski and Halina Machulski; m. 1995; two c.; ed State Acad. of Film Television and Theatre, Łódź, California Inst. of Arts, Valencia, USA; CEO Studio Filmowe Zebra 1988–; acted in Personnel (Personel) by Krzysztof Kieslowski, The Index (Indeks) by Janusz Kijowski, and Kill Me, Cop (Zabij mnie, glino) by Jacek Bromski; lectured on film directing at Hunter Coll., New York 1993; producer of more than 30 films; Wyspianski Award 1985, Chair. of the Cttee of Cinematography Award 1990, Ministry of Culture and Art Award 1998. *Films directed include:* Vabank (Dir's Best Debut, Gdynia Film Festival) 1981, Sexmission (Golden Dollar, Gdańsk Film Festival) 1984, Vabank II czyli riposta 1985, King Size 1988, Déjà vu 1989, V.I.P. 1991, Szwadron 1992, Girl Guide 1995, Kiler (Golden Duck 1998) 1997, Kilerów 2-óch 1999, Money Is Not Everything 2001, Superprodukcja 2003, Vinci (Prize for Best Screenplay, Polish Film Festival, Gdynia 2004, Golden Lion 2004) 2004, Solidarnosc, Solidarnosc... (segment 'Sushi') 2005, How Much Does the Trojan Horse Weigh? 2008, Kolysanka 2010, Ambassada 2013. *Films produced include:* Kochankowie roku tygrysa 2005, Palimpsest 2006, The World Is Waiting for Us (co-producer) 2006, Saviour Square 2006, Hania 2007, All Will Be Well 2007, Twists of Fate 2007, The Last Action 2009, Projekt dziecko, czyli ojciec potrzebny od zaraz 2010, Uwiklanie 2011, In Darkness 2011, Bilet na ksiezyc (co-producer) 2013. *Television includes:* Goraczka mleka (short) 1977, Bezposrednie polaczenie (film) 1979, Matki, zony i kochanki (mini-series) 1996, Matki, zony i kochanki II (mini-series) 1998; plays: The Jury 1995, Meridian 19 2003. *Publications:* Vabank 1 and 2 (scripts) 1986, V.I.P. (script) 1990, Kiler (script) 1998, Kiler 2 1999, Sexmission 2001. *Leisure interest:* reading. *Address:* Studio Filmowe Zebra, ul. Puławska 61, 02-595 Warsaw, Poland (office). *Telephone:* (22) 8455484 (office).

MACHUNGO, Mário Fernandes da Graça; Mozambican politician; *President, Seguradora Internacional de Moçambique;* b. 1 Dec. 1940, Chicuque-Maxixe, Inhambane Prov.; m. Maria Eugénia Paiva Cruz; two d.; ed Inst. for Higher Learning in Econ. and Financial Sciences (ISCEF), Portugal; became underground mem. Mozambique Liberation Front (FRELIMO) 1962; Pres. Students' Union, ISCEF 1964–65; subsequently expelled from ISCEF; completed studies 1969; returned to Mozambique, worked as economist with Nat. Devt Bank; apptd. Minister for Econ. Co-operation in transitional Govt 1974; Minister for Trade and Industry 1975–76, for Industry and Energy 1976–78, for Agric. 1978–80, for Agric. and Planning 1980–83, for Planning 1983–94, Prime Minister of Mozambique 1986–94; elected to Cen. Cttee and Political Bureau of FRELIMO Party 1977, re-elected 1983, elected to Secr. and fmr Sec. for Econ. Policy 1986; Chair. Banco Internacional de Moçambique 1995; currently Pres. Seguradora Internacional de Moçambique (insurance co.). *Address:* Seguradora Internacional de Moçambique, Av 25 Setembro 1800, Maputo, Mozambique (office). *Telephone:* 21430959 (office). *Fax:* 21430241 (office). *E-mail:* simseg@zebra.uem.mz (office).

MACIEREWICZ, Antoni; Polish historian, academic, human rights activist and politician; b. 3 Aug. 1948, Warsaw; s. of Zdzisław Macierewicz and Maria Macierewicz; m. Hanna Macierewicz; ed Univ. of Warsaw, Polish Acad. of Sciences; a leader of the anti-communist resistance in Poland using non-violent civil disobedience; f. Komitet Obrony Robotników (Workers' Defence Cttee, forerunner of Solidarność—Solidarity) 1976; directed Centre for Social Research of Solidarność and was one of the trade union's key advisers 1980s; fmr political prisoner, escaped from incarceration and was in hiding directing work and issuing underground publs –1984; Minister of Internal Affairs 1991–92; mem. Zjednoczenie Chrześcijańsko-Narodowe (Christian Nat. Union) 1992–95, Akcja Polska (Polish Action) 1993–95, Ruch Odbudowy Polski (Movt for Reconstruction of Poland) 1993–97, Ruch Katolicko-Narodowy (Catholic-Nat. Movt) 1997–2012, Ruch Patriotyczny (Patriotic Movt) 2005–12, Prawo i Sprawiedliwość (PiS—Law and Justice) party 2012– (Deputy Leader 2013–); mem. (PiS), Sejm (Parl.) for 10 Piotrków Trybunalski Dist 1991–93, 1997–2005, 2007–, Chair. Parl. Cttee for Investigation of Causes of 2010 Polish Air Force Tu-154 crash (Macierewicz Comm.) 2010–; mem. European Parl. 2003–04; Head of Mil. Counterintelligence Service 2006–07; Sec. of State, Ministry of Nat. Defence 2006–07; Chair. Verification Comm. 2006–07; Minister of Nat. Defence 2015–18; mem. Faculty, Univ. of Warsaw and Jagiellonian Univ., Kraków; Order of Polonia Restituta 1990; named by Gazeta Polska magazine as Man of the Year 2010, Przemysla Medal 2013. *Address:* Sejm, 00-902 Warsaw, ul. Wiejska 4/6/8, Poland (office). *Website:* macierewicz.com.

McILROY, Rory, MBE; British professional golfer; b. 4 May 1989, Holywood, Co. Down, Northern Ireland; s. of Gerry McIlroy and Rosie McIlroy; ed Sullivan Upper School; introduced to golf by his father who coached him from the age of 18 months; became youngest-ever mem. of Holywood Golf Club aged seven; played in his first professional European Tour event at The Forest of Arden aged 16; second person to top World Amateur Rankings 2007; represented Europe in winning Junior Ryder Cup team 2004; became youngest winner of West of Ireland and Irish Close Championships 2005, retained both Irish amateur titles 2006; won European Amateur Championship 2006; turned professional 2007; won the Silver Medal as leading amateur at British Open 2007; first professional event at Quinn Direct British Masters; finished third in his second professional event, the Alfred Dunhill Links Championship; entered the top 100 in the Official World Golf Rankings after making it to the Volvo Masters at Valderrama 2008; runner-up at UBS Hong Kong Open title 2009; maiden victory came in Dubai Desert Classic 2009; finished in second place in inaugural European Tour Race To Dubai; winner: Quail Hollow Championship 2010, UBS Hong Kong Open 2011, Lake Malaren Shanghai Masters 2011, The Honda Classic 2012, Deutsche Bank Championship 2012, DP World Tour Championship, Dubai 2012, BMW Championship 2012, Emirates Australian Open 2013, BMW PGA Championship 2014, WGC Bridgestone Invitational 2014, Wells Fargo Championship 2015, Deutsche Bank Championship 2016, Tour Championship (FedEx Cup playoff event) 2016; European Tour wins: Omega Dubai Desert Classic 2015, DP World Tour Championship, Dubai 2015, Dubai Duty Free Irish Open 2016; won his first major, US Open at Congressional Country Club, Md 2011; other results in major championships: tied for tenth at US Open 2009, won US Open 2011, tied for third at PGA Championship 2009, 2010, tied for third at the Open Championship 2010, tied for 15th at US Masters 2011, won PGA Championship 2012, tied for eighth at US Masters 2014, won the Open Championship 2014, PGA Championship 2014; mem. Seve Trophy team representing GB & Ireland 2009 (winners), World Cup team representing Ireland 2009, Ryder Cup team representing Europe 2010 (winners), 2012 (winners), 2014 (winners); first became No. 1 in World Rankings 4 March 2012; Amb. for UNICEF Ireland 2011–; RTÉ Sports Person of the Year 2011, 2014, Mark H. McCormack Award 2012, Laureus World Breakthrough of the Year 2012, PGA Tour leading money winner 2012, PGA Player of the Year 2012, PGA Tour Player of the Year 2012, 2014, Vardon Trophy 2012, Byron Nelson Award 2012, European Tour Order of Merit winner 2012, European Tour Golfer of the Year 2012. *Achievements include:* first European to win three different majors, joined Jack Nicklaus and Tiger Woods to win three majors by the age of 25. *Leisure interests:* Manchester United Football Club, cars, tennis, movies, music. *Address:* c/o Holywood Golf Club, Nuns Walk, Demesne Road, Holywood, Co. Down, BT18 9LE, Northern Ireland. *E-mail:* mail@holywoodgolfclub.co.uk. *Website:* www.holywoodgolfclub.co.uk; www.rorymcilroy.com.

MACINA, Stefano; San Marino politician; b. 23 Jan. 1956; m.; one d.; Sec. Fed. Industry, San Marino Labour Confed. –1980, Adjunct Gen. Sec. 1981–84, Gen. Sec.

1984–91; Sec. Partito Progressista Democratico Sammarinese (PPDS) 1992–96, mem. Grand and Gen. Council 1993, Pres. Group to advise PPDS-IM 1996; Sec. of State for Econ. Planning, Foreign Trade, Social Security, Labour and Co-operation 2000–01; Pres. Comm. on Foreign Policy, Emigration and Immigration, Information, Transport and Telecommunications, Security and Public Order 2002–03; Dir Centro Commerciale 'Azzurro' 2003–06; Sec. of State for Finance, the Budget, Post and Relations with the Azienda Autonoma di Stato Filatelica e Numismatica (AASFN) 2006–08; mem. several orgs and institutional comms, including Interparl. Group and Council of the XII; mem. Secr. Partito dei Socialisti e dei Democratici; Pres. San Marino Baseball Club. *Address:* c/o Secretariat of State for Finance, the Budget, Post and Relations with the Azienda Autonoma di Stato Filatelica e Numismatica (AASFN), Palazzo Begni, Contrada Omerelli, 47890 San Marino.

McINERNEY, Jay; American writer; b. 13 Jan. 1955; m. 1st Linda Rossiter; m. 2nd Merry Raymond; m. 3rd Helen Bransford 1991; m. 4th Anne Hearst; one s. one d.; ed Williams Univ.; fmr wine columnist, House & Garden Magazine; wine columnist, The Wall Street Journal. *Publications include:* Bright Lights, Big City 1984, Ransom 1986, Story of My Life 1988, Brightness Falls 1992, The Last of the Savages 1996, Model Behavior 1998, How It Ended 2000, The Good Life (novel) 2006, A Hedonist in the Cellar: Adventures in Wine 2006, The Last Bachelor 2009, How it Ended: New and Collected Stories 2009, The Juice: Vinous Veritas 2012, Bright, Precious Days 2016. *Website:* www.jaymcinerney.com.

MacINNIS, Joseph Beverly, CM, MD; Canadian physician, marine research scientist and author; b. 2 March 1937, Barrie, Ont.; s. of Allistair MacInnis and Beverly Saunders; m. Deborah J. Ferris 1971; one s. three d.; ed Univs of Toronto and Pennsylvania; Pres. Undersea Research Ltd and has held consulting contracts for the USN, Smithsonian Inst., IBM, Canadian Ministry of State for Science and Tech. and Canadian Dept of Environment; est. SUBLIMNOS, Canada's first underwater manned station programme 1969; led 14 scientific expeditions into Arctic 1970–79 and during third expedition, SUB-IGLOO, world's first polar dive station established under ice; co-ordinated diving programme for ICE Station LOREX 1979; led team which discovered remains of English barque Breadalbane, sunk in 1853, 700 miles north of Arctic Circle in 340 feet of water; host, The New Wave (CBC television series) 1975–76, The Newfoundlanders: Voices from the Sea 1978; scientific consultant, Mysteries of the Sea (ABC) 1979; co-ordinator, Shot Point 260 (Texaco Canada film), Breakthrough (Dome Petroleum film) 1979; consultant Titanic Project 1985; first Canadian to dive to the Titanic 1987; Co-leader IMAX-Titanic Expedition 1991; has lectured and shown his films in all parts of world including Israel, Germany, Australia, the Philippines, USSR and Singapore; Pres. Undersea Research Ltd; mem. Canadian Environmental Advisory Council, Canadian Council of Fitness and Health, Pierre Elliott Trudeau Foundation; Fellow, Royal Canadian Geographical Soc.; Hon. FRCP; Queen's Anniversary Medal, The Admiral's Medal; Hon. LLD; Dr hc (Queen's) 1990; Hon. DSc (Lakehead Univ.) 2008, and three other hon. degrees. *Publications:* Underwater Images 1971, Underwater Man 1974, Coastline Canada 1982, Shipwreck Shores 1982, The Land that Devours Ships 1984, Titanic: In a New Light 1992, Saving the Oceans (gen. ed.) 1992, Fitzgerald's Storm: The Wreck of the Edmund Fitzgerald 1997, Surviving Terrorism: How to Protect Your Health, Wealth and Safety 2002, Titanic Dreams: Reflections on the Discovery, Exploration and Salvage of the World's Most Famous Shipwreck 2007, Breathing Underwater 2004, James Cameron's Aliens of the Deep 2004, Deep Leadership: Essential Insights from High-Risk Environments 2012; more than 30 scientific papers and articles in Scientific American, National Geographic Magazine etc. *Leisure interest:* jazz. *Address:* Undersea Research Ltd, 14 Dale Avenue, Toronto, ON M4W 1K4, Canada. *Telephone:* (416) 962-8258. *E-mail:* drjoemacinnis@sympatico .ca. *Website:* www.drjmacinnis.com.

McINTOSH, Toga Gayewea, BSc, MA, PhD; Liberian economist and politician; m.; five c. (one d. deceased); ed Univ. of Ghana, Univ. of Colorado, USA, Univ. of Tennessee, Williams Coll., Williamstown, Mass, Univ. of Ife, Nigeria; Statistician, Bureau of Statistics, Ministry of Planning and Econ. Affairs 1969–74, becoming successively Dir for Manpower Planning, Sr Economist, Asst Minister, Deputy Minister, Minister of Planning and Econ. Affairs 1975–81; Sr Econ. Affairs Officer, UN Econ. Comm. for Africa, Ethiopia 1982–91; Sr Nat. Policy Adviser to Pres. of Liberia 1991–93; Man. Dir and Devt Consultant, Devt Man. Assocs, Gaborone, Botswana 1993–2004; Exec. Dir Governance Reform Comm., Monrovia 2004–05; Minister for Planning and Econ. Affairs 2006–08; Exec. Dir for Africa Constituency Group 1 2008–10; Minister of Foreign Affairs 2010–12; apptd Vice-Pres. Econ. Community of West African States (ECOWAS) 2012; fmr consultant to several African govts and int. agencies including World Bank Group, UNDP, African Devt Bank, African Union, USAID. *Publications include:* around 20 technical and professional articles on development issues. *Leisure interest:* football. *Address:* ECOWAS Executive Secretariat, 101 Yakubu Gowon Crescent, PMB 401, Asokoro, Abuja, Nigeria (office). *Telephone:* (9) 3147647 (office); (9) 3147646 (office). *E-mail:* info@ecowas.int (office). *Website:* www.ecowas.int (office).

McINTOSH OF HUDNALL, Baroness (Life Peer), cr. 1999, of Hampstead in the London Borough of Camden; **Genista Mary McIntosh,** BA, FRSA; British arts consultant; b. 23 Sept. 1946, London, England; d. of Geoffrey Tandy and Maire Tandy; m. Neil Scott Wishart McIntosh 1971 (divorced 1990); one s. one d.; ed Hemel Hempstead Grammar School, Univ. of York; Casting Dir, RSC 1972–77, Planning Controller 1977–84, Sr Admin. 1986–90, Assoc. Producer 1990; Dir Marmont Man. Ltd 1984–86; Exec. Dir Royal Nat. Theatre 1990–96, 1997–2002; Chief Exec. Royal Opera House Jan.–May 1997; mem. (Labour), House of Lords 1999–; Prin. The Guildhall School of Music and Drama 2002–03; mem. Bd RSC, The Roundhouse Trust, Southbank Sinfonia, Nat. Opera Studio; Patron, Helena Kennedy Bursary Scheme; Hon. Fellow, Goldsmiths Coll. 2003; Hon. DUniv. (York) 1998, (Middx) 2002, (City) 2002. *Leisure interests:* music, gardening, reading. *Address:* House of Lords, Westminster, London, SW1A 0PW, England (office). *E-mail:* mcintoshg@parliament.uk (office).

MACK, Connie, III, BA; American banker and fmr politician; *Partner, Senior Policy Advisor and Chairman Emeritus, Liberty Partners Group, LLC;* b. (Cornelius McGillicuddy, III), 29 Oct. 1940, Philadelphia, Pa; s. of Cornelius M. McGillicuddy and Susan McGillicuddy (née Sheppard); m. Ludie Priscilla 1960; one s. one d.; ed Univ. of Fla; Vice-Pres. Business Devt First Nat. Bank, Ft Myers, Fla 1968–71; Sr Vice-Pres., Dir Sun Bank, Cape Coral, Fla 1971–75; Pres., Dir Fla Nat. Bank, Cape Coral 1972–82; mem. US House of Reps 1983–89, Senator from Fla 1989–2000; Republican Conf. Chair. 105th Congress 1996–2001; Sr Policy Advisor, Shaw Pittman 2001; fmr Sr Policy Advisor, Govt Advocacy and Public Policy Practice Group, King and Spalding LLP, Washington, DC; Partner and Sr Policy Advisor, Liberty Partners Group, LLC 2007–, also, Chair. Emer.; Vice-Chair. M2Gen; mem. Bd of Dirs H. Lee Moffitt Cancer Center and Research Inst., Darden Restaurants, Exact Sciences Corpn, Genzyme Corpn, Moody's Corpn, Mutual of America Life Insurance Co., American Momentum Bank, Spirit Aerosystems; Trustee Emer. American Cancer Soc. Foundation (fmr Pres.); mem. Pres's Advisory Panel for Fed. Tax Reform 2005; Republican; Hon. DJur (Tampa Univ.); Hon. DHumLitt (St Thomas Univ.); Hon. Dr of Public Service (Miami Univ.); American Cancer Soc. Courage Award 1992, Nat. Coalition for Cancer Research Lifetime Achievement Award 1999, Susan G. Komen Breast Cancer Foundation Betty Ford Award. *Address:* Liberty Partners Group, LLC, 1050 K Street, NW, Suite 315, Washington, DC 20001, USA (office). *Telephone:* (202) 442-3710 (office). *Fax:* (202) 638-0604 (office). *E-mail:* cmack@ libertypartnersgroup.com (office). *Website:* www.libertypartnersgroup.com (office).

MACK, James F., BA; American diplomatist and international organization executive; *Executive Secretary, Inter-American Drug Abuse Control Commission (Comisión Interamericana para el Control del Abuso de Drogas—CICAD);* b. 1941, Norwalk, Conn.; m. Sheila Marvin; four c.; ed Cornell Univ., Ithaca, NY; raised in Rye, NY; served as Peace Corps volunteer in Honduras; joined US Foreign Service 1966, first diplomatic postings were as political officer in Saigon and Nha Trang, S Viet Nam, and as Political Advisor to US Commdr of I Corps in Danang, served as S Viet Nam analyst in Bureau of Intelligence and Research, Dept of State 1969, as Political/Labor Officer, San José, Costa Rica, as Labor Officer, São Paulo, Brazil, as Prin. Officer, Ponta Delgada, Azores, Portugal, subsequent positions included Guatemala/Belize Desk Officer, Chief of Office of Labor/Man. Relations, Dept of State, Political Counselor at Embassy in San Salvador, Deputy Chief of Mission, Embassy in Asuncion, Dir Office of Andean Affairs, Dept of State 1990, Deputy Chief of Mission, Embassy in Quito, where also served as Chargé d'affaires for two years, Deputy Chief of Mission, Embassy in Lima 1994–97, additionally, while posted to US Embassies in Ecuador, Paraguay and Peru, coordinated US anti-narcotics assistance to those countries, Amb. to Guyana 1997–2000, now retd career mem. Sr Foreign Service, US Dept of State, served as Prin. Deputy Asst Sec. in Bureau of Int. Narcotics and Law Enforcement Affairs; Co-ordinator Inter-American Observatory on Drugs, Inter-American Drug Abuse Control Comm. (Comisión Interamericana para el Control del Abuso de Drogas—CICAD), OAS 2002, Exec. Sec. CICAD 2004–; numerous State Dept awards for superior service. *Address:* Inter-American Drug Abuse Control Commission (CICAD), 1889 F Street, NW, Washington, DC 20006, USA (office). *Telephone:* (202) 458-3178 (office). *Fax:* (202) 458-3658 (office). *E-mail:* oidcicad@oas.org (office). *Website:* www.cicad.oas.org (office).

MACK, John J., BA; American financial services industry executive; *Senior Advisor, Morgan Stanley;* b. 17 Nov. 1944, Mooresville, NC; m. Christy King; two s. one d.; ed Duke Univ.; joined Morgan Stanley 1972, positions in bond dept 1972–76, Vice-Pres. 1976–77, Prin. 1977–79, Man. Dir 1979–85, Head Worldwide Taxable Fixed Income Div. 1985–92, apptd Dir 1987, Chair. Operating Cttee 1992–93, Pres. Morgan Stanley 1993–97; Pres., COO and Dir Morgan Stanley Dean Witter & Co. (later Morgan Stanley) 1997–2001, Chair. and CEO Morgan Stanley 2005–10, Chair. 2010–11, Sr Advisor 2012–; CEO Credit Suisse First Boston 2001–04, Co-CEO Credit Suisse Group 2003–04; Sr Advisor, KKR & Co. LP 2012–; Sr Advisor and Strategic Investor, Star Mountain Capital LLC 2015–; fmr Chair. Pequot Capital Man.; mem. Bd of Dirs IMG, Catalyst Inc., Lending Club 2012–, Bloomberg Family Foundation; fmr Dir CICC (first investment bank in China), India Business School; mem. Int. Advisory Panel, Monetary Authority of Singapore, Chair.'s Advisory Cttee Nat. Asscn of Securities Dealers (NASD); Vice-Chair. NYC 2012 (New York City bid for Olympic Games); mem. Business Council, Business Roundtable, Advisory Bd China Investment Corpn, Int. Business Leaders Advisory Council for the Mayor of Beijing, Int. Advisory Panel of The Monetary Authority of Singapore, Exec. Cttee of the Partnership for New York City, Financial Services Forum, Bd Bloomberg Family Foundation, Int. Business Council of World Econ. Forum, NYC Financial Services Advisory Cttee, Shanghai Int. Financial Advisory Council; Dir Business Cttee for the Arts; mem. Advisory Bd bkm Capital Partners; Int. Advisory Council China Investment Corpn; Chair. Bd of Trustees NY Presbyterian Hosp., Columbia and Cornell Univ. Hosps; fmr mem. Bd of Trustees Duke Univ., now Trustee Emer.; mem. Bd of Trustees New York-Presbyterian Hospital, Doris Duke Charitable Foundation. *Address:* Morgan Stanley, 1585 Broadway, New York, NY 10036, USA (office). *Telephone:* (212) 761-4000 (home). *Fax:* (212) 762-0575 (office). *E-mail:* mediainquiries@morganstanley .com (office). *Website:* www.morganstanley.com (office).

MACKAY, Charles Dorsey, CBE, MA, MBA; British business executive; *Chairman, Historic Royal Palaces;* b. 14 April 1940, Congleton, Cheshire, England; s. of Brig. Kenneth Mackay CBE, DSO and Evelyn Mackay (née Ingram); m. Annmarie Joder-Pfeiffer 1964; two s. (one deceased) one d.; ed Cheltenham Coll., Queens' Coll. Cambridge, Institut Européen d'Admin des Affaires (INSEAD), Fontainebleau; with BP Co. 1957–69, McKinsey & Co. 1969–76, Pakhoed Holding NV, Rotterdam 1976–81 (Exec. Chair. Paktrans Div.); Dir Chloride Group PLC 1981–86, Chair. Overseas Div. 1981–85, Power Electronics Div. 1985–86; Dir Inchcape PLC 1986–96, Chair. and Chief Exec. Inchcape Pacific Ltd 1986–91, Chief Exec. 1991–96, Deputy Chair. 1995–96; mem. Bd of Dirs (non-exec.) Hongkong and Shanghai Banking Corpn Ltd 1986–92, HSBC Holdings 1992–98, Midland Bank 1992–93, British Airways 1993–96, Gucci Group NV 1997–2001, Johnson Matthey PLC (Sr Ind. Dir) 1999–2008, Eurotunnel Group 1997–2004 (Deputy Chair. 1999–2001, Chair. 2001–04); Deputy Chair. Thistle Hotels PLC 1996–2003; Chair. DSL Group Ltd 1996–97; Chair. TDG PLC 2000–08; Chair. Historic Royal Palaces 2006–; Chair. Production Services Network Ltd 2009–11; mem. Bd INSEAD 2000–11, mem. Advisory Council 2011–; mem. of Business Bd, House of Habib 2007–; Trustee, Development Trust (for the mentally handicapped) 1993–. *Leisure interests:* restoring old buildings, travel, fly fishing, tennis, skiing, classical music, opera. *Address:* Historic Royal Palaces, Kensington Palace, Kensington Gardens, London, W8 4PX, England (office). *Telephone:* (20) 3166-6130 (office). *Fax:* (20) 3166-6132 (office). *E-mail:* charles.mackay@hrp.org.uk (office). *Website:* www.hrp.org.uk (office).

MACKAY, David, BBA; Australian business executive; *President and CEO, Kellogg Company;* b. 16 Aug. 1955, Hamilton, New Zealand; m. Michelle Mackay; two c.; ed Charles Sturt Univ., NSW; joined Kellogg Australia as Group Product Man. 1985–87, Category Dir for ready-to-eat cereals, Kellogg HQ, USA 1987–91, Marketing and Sales Dir, Australia 1991–92, Man. Dir Sara Lee Bakery, Australia 1992–98, Man. Dir Australia 1998, UK and Ireland 1998–2000, Sr Vice-Pres. Kellogg Co. and Pres. Kellogg USA 2000, Exec. Vice-Pres. Kellogg Co. 2000–03, Pres. and COO 2003–06, Pres. and CEO 2006–; mem. Bd of Dirs Fortune Brands, Inc., Kalamazoo Inst. of Arts. *Address:* Kellogg Company, 1 Kellogg Square, Battle Creek, MI 49016-3599, USA (office). *Telephone:* (269) 961-2000 (office). *Fax:* (269) 961-6598 (office). *Website:* www.kelloggcompany.com (office).

McKAY, David I., BMath, MBA; Canadian banking executive; *President and CEO, Royal Bank of Canada;* b. Montreal; m. Karen McKay; two c.; ed Univ. of Waterloo, Richard Ivey School of Business at Univ. of Western Ontario; joined Royal Bank of Canada (RBC) 1988, held progressively sr roles in Canada and Japan in retail and business banking, group risk management and corp. banking, including Group Head of Canadian Banking 2008–12, Exec. Vice-Pres. of Personal Financial Services, Sr Vice-Pres. of Financing Products, Group Head of Personal and Commercial Banking world-wide 2012–14, Pres. RBC Feb. 2014–, also CEO and mem. Bd of Dirs Aug. 2014–; Vice-Chair. Bd of Govs, Univ. of Waterloo; mem. Bd of Trustees, Hosp. for Sick Children (SickKids), Toronto; Retail Banker Int. Retail Banker of the Year Award 2012. *Address:* Royal Bank of Canada, 200 Bay Street, 9th Floor, South Tower, Toronto, ON M5J 2J5, Canada (office). *Telephone:* (514) 974-5151 (office). *Fax:* (514) 974-7800 (office). *E-mail:* banks@rbc.com (office). *Website:* www.rbc.com (office).

MacKAY, Donald James, BL; New Zealand diplomatist and lawyer; b. 1948; m.; two c.; ed Victoria Univ. of Wellington; solicitor and law clerk to Judges of Court of Appeal and High Court 1971–75; with Ministry of Foreign Affairs 1975–2001, positions include Head of Special Arbitration Unit, Dir of Disarmament and Int. Security Div., Amb. to Fiji and High Commr to Naura and Tuvalu 1991–95; Dir of Legal Div. 1995–96, Deputy Sec. Ministry of Foreign Affairs and Trade 1997–2001; Amb. and Perm. Rep. to UN, New York 2001–05, to UN Office, Geneva and Amb. for Disarmament 2006–09.

MACKAY, Sir Francis H., Kt; British business executive; *Owner, Graysons Restaurants Limited;* b. 24 Oct. 1944, London, England; m. Christine Mackay; one s., two d.; ed Bonaventure Grammar School; qualified as accountant, Appleby and Wood 1967; began career in financial positions with LCS Ltd, SGT PLC; fmr Finance Dir Global Ltd; Finance Dir Compass Group PLC 1986–91, CEO 1991–99, Chair. 1999–2006; Chair. (non-exec.) Kingfisher PLC 2001–06; Chair. Carlton Partners LLP 2006–09; Chair. ISS (Denmark) 2006–08; Founder and Owner Graysons Restaurants Ltd 2007–; Hon. DUniv (Oxford Brookes) 2002. *Leisure interests:* flying, opera, golf, family. *Address:* Graysons Restaurants Ltd, Devon House, Anchor Street, Chelmsford, CM2 0GD, England (office). *Telephone:* (1245) 200100 (office). *E-mail:* simona.oproiu@graysonsrestaurants.com. *Website:* www.graysonsrestaurants.com (office).

MacKAY, The Hon. Peter Gordon, PC, QC; Canadian lawyer and politician; *Partner, Baker & McKenzie LLP;* b. 27 Sept. 1965, New Glasgow, Nova Scotia; m. Nazanin Afshin-Jam; one s.; ed Acadia and Dalhousie Univs; called to the Bar, Nova Scotia 1991; Crown Attorney for Cen. Region, Nova Scotia 1993; mem. Parl. for Pictou-Antigonish-Guysborough 1997–2004, for Central Nova 2004–15; Leader Progressive Conservative Party of Canada 2003–04, Deputy Leader Conservative Party of Canada 2004; fmr Critic for the Prime Minister, for the Solicitor Gen., for Public Security, for the Leader of the Govt in the House of Commons, for Justice, for Public Safety and Emergency Preparedness; fmr mem. Interim Cttee on Nat. Security and Intelligence; Minister of Foreign Affairs 2006–07, of Nat. Defence 2007–13, Minister of Justice and Attorney-Gen. of Canada 2013–15; Partner, Baker & McKenzie LLP (law firm), Toronto 2016–. *Leisure interests:* rugby, baseball, football, hockey. *Address:* Baker & McKenzie LLP, Brookfield Place, Bay/Wellington Tower, 181 Bay Street, Suite 2100, Toronto, ON M5J 2T3, Canada (office). *Telephone:* (416) 863-1221 (office). *E-mail:* peter.mackay@bakermckenzie.com (office). *Website:* www.bakermckenzie.com (office).

MACKAY, Trudy Frances Charlene, BSc, MSc, PhD, FRS; Canadian/American geneticist and academic; *William Neal Reynolds Distinguished University Professor of Biological Sciences, North Carolina State University;* b. 10 Sept. 1952, Moncton, NB; d. of Charles Edward Mackay and Jean McGregor Somerville; m. Robert Rene Henri Anholt 1990; ed Dalhousie Univ., NS, Univ. Edinburgh, UK; Postdoctoral work at Dalhousie Univ.; Lecturer, Univ. Edinburgh 1980–87; Asst Prof. of Genetics, North Carolina State Univ., Raleigh, NC 1987–93, Prof. of Genetics 1993–96, William Neal Reynolds Prof. of Genetics 1996–, Distinguished Univ. Prof. of Genetics 2006–13, Assoc. Mem. of Entomology 2008–, William Neal Reynolds Distinguished Univ. Prof. of Biological Sciences 2013–, Goodnight Distinguished Chair. of Biological Sciences 2017–; mem. NAS 2010; Fellow, AAAS 2003, American Acad. of Arts and Sciences 2005, Royal Soc. 2006; North Carolina Award, Genetics Soc. of America Medal 2004, Wolf Prize in Agric. 2016. *Achievements include:* cr. publicly available Drosophila Genetic Reference Guide. *Publications:* numerous papers in professional journals. *Address:* 3550 Thomas Hall, Program in Genetics, Department of Biological Sciences, Box 7614, North Carolina State University, Raleigh, NC 27695-7614, USA (office). *Telephone:* (919) 515-5810 (office). *Fax:* (919) 515-5833 (office). *E-mail:* trudy_mackay@ncsu.edu (office). *Website:* genetics.sciences.ncsu.edu (office).

MACKAY OF CLASHFERN, Baron (Life Peer), cr. 1979, of Eddrachillis in the District of Sutherland; **James Peter Hymers Mackay,** Kt, KT, PC, QC, LLB, MA, FRSE; British advocate and judge (retd); b. 2 July 1927, Scotland; s. of James Mackay and Janet Hymers; m. Elizabeth Gunn Hymers 1958; one s. two d.; ed George Heriot's School, Edin., Univ. of Edin., Trinity Coll., Cambridge; Lecturer in Math., Univ. of St Andrews 1948–50; Major Scholar, Trinity Coll., Cambridge 1947, Sr Scholar 1951; admitted to Faculty of Advocates 1955; QC 1965; Vice-Dean Faculty of Advocates 1973–76, Dean 1976–79, Lord Advocate 1979–84; Sheriff Prin., Renfrew and Argyll 1972–74; Commr Northern Lighthouses 1972–84; Dir Stenhouse Holdings Ltd 1976–78; mem. (Conservative) House of Lords 1979–;

Senator of Coll. of Justice in Scotland 1984–85; Lord of Appeal in Ordinary 1985–87; Lord Chancellor 1987–97; Chancellor Heriot-Watt Univ. 1991–2005; Ed.-in-Chief Halsbury's Laws of England 1998–2014; Part-time mem. Scottish Law Comm. 1976–79; mem. Insurance Brokers' Registration Council 1978–79; Pres. Soc. of Conservative Lawyers, Scottish Bible Soc.; Vice-Pres. Family Mediators' Asscn, Carers Trust, Highlanders' Museum Appeal Fund; Founding mem. World Prevention Alliance (eliminating disease in low-resource countries); mem. Int. Ethics Cttee, Int. Prevention Research Inst. (iPRI); Commissary, Univ. of Cambridge; Non-Voting Elder Brother of Trinity House; Lord Clerk Register (unremunerated post in Scottish system of govt); Fellow, Inst. of Taxation, American Coll. of Trial Lawyers, Int. Acad. of Trial Lawyers; Hon. FICE; Hon. FRCPE; Hon. FRCSE; Hon. FRCOG; Hon. Fellow Trinity Coll., Cambridge, Girton Coll., Cambridge; Hon. LLD (Edin., Dundee, Strathclyde, Aberdeen, St Andrews, Birmingham, Newcastle, Bath, Leicester, De Montfort, Glasgow, Cambridge, Robert Gordon Nat. Law School of India); Hon. DCL (Newcastle), (Oxford) 1998. *Publication:* Armour on Valuation for Rating (Sr Ed.) 1961, 1971. *Leisure interests:* walking, travel. *Address:* House of Lords, Westminster, London, SW1A 0PW, England (office). *E-mail:* mackayjp@parliament.uk (office).

McKEE, J(ohn) Angus; Canadian business executive; b. 31 Aug. 1935, Toronto, Ont.; s. of John W. McKee and Margaret E. Phippen; m. Susan E. Harley 1970; one s. one d.; ed Trinity Coll. School, Port Hope, Ont. and Univ. of Toronto; joined Patiño Mining Corpn 1962, Asst to Pres. 1963, Vice-Pres. (Corp. Devt) 1966; Man. Dir Consolidated Tin Smelters Ltd 1968–71; Owner J. A. McKee and Assocs Ltd 1971–83; Pres. and CEO Canadian Occidental Petroleum Ltd 1983–93; Chair., Pres. and CEO Gulfstream Resources Canada 1993–2001; Dir, Stone & Webster Canada Ltd, Stone & Webster Inc. (USA) (both acquired by The Shaw Group 2000, then by Technip 2012); Teradyne Canada Ltd, CVI Ltd, Hardy Oil and Gas PLC 2000–01, Gulfstream Qatar Ltd 2001; mem. Bd of Govs, Trinity Coll. School, Port Hope. *Leisure interests:* skiing, shooting. *Address:* Stone & Webster, Inc., 100 Technology Center Drive, Stoughton, MA 02072-4705, USA. *Telephone:* (617) 589-5111. *Fax:* (617) 589-2156.

McKELLEN, Sir Ian Murray, Kt, CH, CBE, BA; British actor; b. 25 May 1939, Burnley, Lancs., England; s. of Denis Murray McKellen and Margery McKellen (née Sutcliffe); partner Brian Taylor 1964–72, Sean Mathias 1978–88; ed Bolton School, St Catharine's Coll., Cambridge; Council mem. British Actors' Equity 1970–71; Cameron Mackintosh Prof. of Contemporary Theatre, Univ. of Oxford 1991; Freedom of the City of London 2014; Hon. DLitt (Nottingham) 1989, (Oxford) 1991; Clarence Derwent Award 1964, Variety and Plays and Players awards 1966, Actor of the Year (Plays and Players) 1976, Soc. of West End Theatres Award for Best Actor in Revival 1977, for Best Comedy Performance 1978, for Best Actor in a New Play 1979, Tony Award 1981, Drama Desk 1981, Outer Critics Circle Award 1981, Royal TV Soc. Performer of the Year 1983, Laurence Olivier Award 1984, 1991, Evening Standard Best Actor Award 1984, 1989, Screen Actor's Guild Award for best supporting Actor 2000, British Ind. Film Awards, Variety UK Personality Award 2003, Lifetime Achievement Award, San Sebastián Film Festival 2009. *Stage appearances include:* first stage appearance as Roper (A Man for All Seasons), Belgrade Theatre, Coventry 1961; numerous other parts include title-roles in Henry V, Luther, Ipswich 1962–63; Aufidius (Coriolanus), Arthur Seaton (Saturday Night and Sunday Morning), title-role in Sir Thomas More, Nottingham Playhouse 1963–64; London début as Godfrey (A Scent of Flowers), Duke of York's Theatre 1964; Claudio (Much Ado About Nothing), Capt. de Foenix (Trelawny of the Wells), Nat. Theatre Co. 1965; Alvin (A Lily in Little India), Hampstead and St Martin's 1965–66; Andrew Cobham (Their Very Own and Golden City), Royal Court 1966; title-part in O'Flaherty, VC and Bonaparte (The Man of Destiny), Mermaid 1966; Leonidik (The Promise), Oxford Playhouse, Fortune and Henry Miller (Broadway début) 1966–67; Tom (The White Liars), Harold Gorringe (Black Comedy), Lyric 1968; Richard II (Edin. Festival 1969), Edward II, Hamlet, Prospect Theatre Co. 1968–71; British tour, Mermaid and Piccadilly Theatres; Darkly (Billy's Last Stand), Theatre Upstairs 1970; Capt. Plume (The Recruiting Officer), Corporal Hill (Chips With Everything), Cambridge Theatre Co. 1970; Svetlovidov (Swan Song), Crucible, Sheffield 1971; founder-mem. Actors' Co., Edin. Festival 1972 and touring as Giovanni ('Tis Pity She's A Whore), Prince Yoremitsu (The Three Arrows), title-role in Michael, the Wood Demon, Footman (The Way of The World), then Knots, Shaw Theatre, Edgar (King Lear), Brooklyn Acad. and Giovanni, Wimbledon 1973–74; début with RSC as Dr Faustus (Edin. Festival) 1974; title-role in The Marquis of Keith, Philip the Bastard (King John), Aldwych 1974–75; Colin (Ashes), Young Vic. 1975; Aubrey Bagot (Too True to Be Good), also at Globe, Romeo, Macbeth, Bernick (Pillars of the Community), Face (The Alchemist) Stratford season 1976; Langevin (Days of the Commune) 1976–78; organized RSC British tour of Twelfth Night (Toby Belch) and Three Sisters (Andrei); Max (Bent), Royal Court and Criterion 1979, Amadeus (New York) 1980, Short List (Hampstead Theatre Club), Cowardice (Ambassadors) 1983; int. tour of one-man show Acting Shakespeare (LA and Ritz Theatre, New York) 1984, (London) 1987; Assoc. Dir Nat. Theatre of Great Britain (also actor) 1984–86; Venice Preserv'd (Pierre), Coriolanus; Wild Honey (Platonov); McKellen/Petherbridge Nat. Theatre Group: Duchess of Malfi (Bosola), Real Inspector Hound (Hound), The Critic (Mr Puff), The Cherry Orchard (Lopakhin); Wild Honey (Va Theatre, New York), USA Shakespeare tour 1987; Henceforward (Vaudeville Theatre) 1988–89; Othello (Iago) RSC 1989; Royal Nat. Theatre: Bent (Max), King Lear (Kent), Richard III 1990–92 (World Tour then US Tour), Napoli Milionaria 1991, Uncle Vanya 1992, An Enemy of the People 1997, Peter Pan 1997; Present Laughter, The Tempest (W Yorks. Playhouse) 1998–99, Dance of Death (Broadhurst Theatre, NY) 2001, (Wyndham's Theatre, London) 2003, (Sydney Festival) 2004, The Seagull (RSC) 2007, King Lear (RSC) 2007, Waiting for Godot 2009–10, The Syndicate by Eduardo De Filippo, Chichester Festival 2011, No Man's Land and Waiting for Godot (double bill), Broadway 2013–14. *Films include:* Alfred the Great 1969, The Promise 1969, A Touch of Love 1969, Priest of Love 1981, The Keep 1982, Plenty, Zina 1985, Scandal 1988, The Ballad of Little Jo 1992, I'll Do Anything 1992, Last Action Hero 1993, Six Degrees of Separation 1993, The Shadow 1994, Jack and Sarah 1994, Restoration 1994, Richard III 1995, Bent 1996, Swept from the Sea 1996, Apt Pupil 1997, Gods and Monsters 1998, X-Men 1999, Lord of the Rings: The Fellowship of the Ring 2001, Lord of the Rings: The Two Towers 2002, X-Men 2 2003, Emile 2003, Lord of the Rings: The Return of the King 2003, Asylum 2005, Neverwas 2005, Doogal (voice) 2006, The Da Vinci Code

2006, Flushed Away (voice) 2006, For the Love of God 2007, Stardust (voice) 2007, The Golden Compass (voice) 2007, The Academy (short) 2009, The Academy Part 2: First Impressions 2009, Small-Time Revolutionary (Short) (voice) 2010, A Lost and Found Box of Human Sensation (Short) (voice) 2010, E'gad, Zombies! (Short) 2010, Lady Grey London (Short) 2010, Claude et Claudette (short, voice) 2011, The Hobbit: An Unexpected Journey 2012, The Egg Trick (short) 2013, The Wolverine (uncredited) 2013, The Hobbit: The Desolation of Smaug 2013, Miss in Her Teens 2014, X-Men: Days of Future Past 2014, The Hobbit: The Battle of the Five Armies 2014, Mr. Holmes 2015. *Television includes:* David Copperfield 1965, Ross 1969, Richard II, Edward II and Hamlet 1970, Hedda Gabler 1974, Macbeth, Every Good Boy Deserves Favour, Dying Day 1979, Acting Shakespeare 1981, Walter, The Scarlet Pimpernel 1982, Walter and June 1983, Countdown to War 1989, Othello 1990, Tales of the City 1993, Cold Comfort Farm 1995, Rasputin 1996, Coronation Street 2005, Great Performances (series) – King Lear 2008, King Lear (film) 2008, The Prisoner (mini-series) 2009, London 2012 Paralympic Opening Ceremony: Enlightenment – The Tempest (film) 2012, The Academy: Special (film) 2012, Doctor Who (series, voice) 2012, The Five(ish) Doctors Reboot (film) 2013, Vicious (series) 2013, The Dresser 2015. *Publication:* William Shakespeare's Richard III (co-author) 1996. *Address:* c/o ICM, 3rd Floor, Marlborough House, 10 Earlham Street, London, WC2H 9LN, England (office). *Telephone:* (20) 7836-8564 (office). *Website:* www.icmtalent.com (office); www.mckellen.com.

McKENNA, Andrew J., Sr, BBA, DJur; American business executive; *Chairman Emeritus, McDonald's Corporation;* b. 17 Sept. 1930; m. Mary Joan Pickett 1953; two s. five d.; ed Univ. of Notre Dame, DePaul Univ. Coll. of Law; Chair. Chicago White Sox professional baseball team 1975–81, Chicago Cubs 1981–84; currently Chair. Schwarz Supply Source; mem. Bd of Dirs McDonald's Corpn 1991–, Chair. (non-exec.) 2004–16 (retd), Chair. Emer. 2016–; Founding Chair. Chicago Metropolis 2020 1999; fmr Chair. Econ. Club of Chicago, The Commercial Club of Chicago; Dir The American Ireland Fund, Children's Memorial Hosp. of Chicago, Lyric Opera, United Way of Metropolitan Chicago; Vice-Chair. Bd of Trustees, Univ. of Notre Dame 1986–92, Chair. 1992–2000, Chair. Emer. 2000–; Trustee and Chair. Emer., Museum of Science and Industry; mem. Bd of Dirs Dean Foods 1982–2000, Tribune Co. 1982–2002, Aon Corpn 1982–, Bank One 1991–99, Ryan Specialty Group LLC 2012–, Chicago Bears Football Club Inc., Click Commerce Inc., Skyline Corpn. *Address:* McDonald's Corporation, 110 North Carpenter Street, Chicago, IL 60607-2101, USA (office). *Telephone:* (630) 623-3000 (office). *Fax:* (630) 623-5004 (office). *Website:* www.mcdonalds.com (office).

McKENNA, Catherine, BA, LLB, MSc, PC; Canadian lawyer and politician; *Minister of Environment and Climate Change;* b. 5 Aug. 1971, Hamilton, Ont.; d. of John McKenna and Pat McKenna; m. Scott Gilmore; one s. two d.; ed Univ. of Toronto, McGill Univ., London School of Econs, UK; Assoc., Soewito Suhardiman Eddymurthy Kardono 1999–2001; summer student, Stikeman Elliott LLP May–Aug. 2000, Assoc. 2002–05; Legal Counsel, UN Mission in East Timor (UNTAET) 2001–02; Competition Counsel, Canadian Real Estate Asscn 2005–10; Co-Pres., Banff Forum 2011–12, Exec. Dir 2013–14; Lecturer in Global Civil Soc., Masters of Global Affairs Program, Univ. of Toronto Munk School of Global Affairs 2012–; mem. House of Commons (Parl.) for Ottawa Centre 2015–; Minister of Environment and Climate Change 2015–; Co-founder Canadian Lawyers Abroad 2005–; mem. Bd Elizabeth Fry Soc. of Ottawa 2003–04, Good Morning Preschool and Creative Arts 2009–12, Trudeau Centre for Peace and Conflict Studies 2010 –; mem. Bd and Co-Vice-Pres., Glebe Community Asscn 2012–14; mem. Liberal Party of Canada. *Address:* Environment Canada, Les Inquiry Centre, 23rd Floor, 10 Wellington Street, Gatineau, PQ K1A 0H3, Canada (office). *Telephone:* (819) 997-2800 (office). *Fax:* (819) 994-1412 (office). *E-mail:* enviroinfo@ec.gc.ca (office). *Website:* www.ec.gc.ca (office); catherinemckenna.liberal.ca.

McKENNA, Hon. Frank Joseph, PC, OC, LLB, QC; Canadian diplomatist, politician, lawyer and business executive; *Deputy Chairman, Toronto-Dominion Bank;* b. 19 Jan. 1948, Apohaqui, Kings Co., NB; s. of Joseph McKenna and Olive Moody; m. Julie Friel 1972; two s. one d.; ed St Francis Xavier Univ., Queen's Univ. and Univ. of NB; Special Asst to Pres., Privy Council 1971; Research Asst Constitutional Law Unit, PMO 1973; Partner, Martin, Lordon, McKenna, Martin & Bowes; Counsel, McInnes, Cooper 1998–; mem. NB Bar Asscn, Canadian Bar Asscn; mem. Legis. Ass. 1982–97; Leader, NB Liberal Party 1985–97; Premier, Prov. of NB 1987–97; Amb. to USA 2005–06; Deputy Chair. Toronto-Dominion Bank 2006–; Chair. Bd of Dirs CanWest Global Communications Corpn –2005, mem. Bd of Dirs Gen. Motors of Canada Ltd –2005, Bank of Montreal –2005; Hon. LLD (Univ. of NB) 1988, (Mount Allison) 1991, (St Francis Xavier) 1994, (St Thomas) 1996, (Ryerson Polytechnic) 1999, (Royal Mil. Coll.) 2000; Vanier Award 1988, Econ. Developer of the Year, Econ. Developers' Asscn of Canada 1993, Distinction Award, Canadian Advanced Tech. Asscn 1996. *Leisure interests:* reading, sports, current affairs. *Address:* Toronto-Dominion Bank, Toronto-Dominion Centre, King Street West and Bay Street, Toronto, ON M5K 1A2, Canada. *Telephone:* (416) 982-8222. *Fax:* (416) 982-5671. *Website:* www.td.com.

McKENNA, Virginia, OBE; British actress and conservationist; *Co-Founder and Trustee, Born Free Foundation;* b. 7 June 1931, London; d. of Terence McKenna and Anne Marie Dennis; m. Bill Travers (died 1994); three s. one d.; ed Herons Ghyll, Horsham, Herschel, South Africa, Cen. School of Speech and Drama; co-f. Zoo Check Charitable Trust (now the Born Free Foundation) 1984; film debut in The Second Mrs Tanqueray 1951; speaker at numerous events; patron to numerous orgs; Belgian Prix Femina Award 1957, British Animal Honours Outstanding Contribution award 2013, Lifetime Achievement Award, New York Wildlife Conservation Film Festival 2013, Lifetime Achievement Award, Royal Soc. for the Prevention of Cruelty to Animals/Daily Mirror Animal Hero Awards 2017. *Stage appearances include:* The King and I 1979 (Soc. of West End Producers Award for Best Actress in a musical), Hamlet (RSC) 1985, Winnie 1988, A Little Night Music, The Devils (RSC), The Beggar's Opera (RSC), A Winter's Tale, As You Like It, The River Line, Penny for a Song, I Capture the Castle, A Personal Affair, The Bad Samaritan. *Films include:* Father's Doing Fine, The Cruel Sea 1953, Simba 1955, The Ship that Died of Shame, A Town Like Alice (BAFTA Best Actress Award) 1956, The Smallest Show on Earth 1957, The Barretts of Wimpole Street 1957, Carve Her Name With Pride (Prix Fémina Award, Belgium) 1957, Passionate Summer 1958, The Wreck of the Mary Deare 1959, Two Living, One Dead 1961, Born Free (Best Actress Award, Variety Club) 1966, Ring of Bright Water 1969, An Elephant Called Slowly 1969, Waterloo 1970, Swallows and Amazons 1974, The Disappearance 1977, Holocaust 2000 1977, Staggered 1994, Sliding Doors 1998, What Do You See? 2005, Golden Years 2016, Ethel and Ernest (voice) 2016. *Radio:* The Devils, The Flame Trees of Thika, A Town Like Alice, The Tempest. *Television includes:* Romeo and Juliet 1955 (BBC TV Best Actress Award, Guild of TV Producers and Dirs Award), Play of the Month: A Passage to India 1965, Play of the Month: Girls in Uniform 1967, The Lion at World's End (documentary) 1971, Play of the Month: The Deep Blue Sea 1974, The Gathering Storm 1974, Shades of Greene (episode Cheap in August) 1975, Peter Pan 1976, Waters of the Moon 1983, Puccini 1984, Lovejoy 1991, The Camomile Lawn (mini-series) 1992, Ruth Rendell Mysteries (episode The Speaker of Mandarin: Part One) 1992, September (mini-series) 1996, The Scold's Bridle 1998, Kavanagh QC (episode Time of Need) 1999, The Whistleblower 2001, Marple: A Murder is Announced 2005. *Publications include:* On Playing with Lions (with Bill Travers), Some Of My Friends Have Tails, Into the Blue 1992, Journey to Freedom 1997; Co-Ed. and Contrib.: Beyond the Bars, Headlines from the Jungle (verse) 1990, Back to the Blue 1997, The Life in My Years 2009, Tonight the Moon is Red (poetry) 2014. *Leisure interests:* classical music, poetry, walking in the countryside, gardening. *Address:* Stanton Davidson Associates (office); Born Free Foundation, Broadlands Business Campus, Langhurstwood Road, Horsham, West Sussex, RH12 4QP, England (office). *Telephone:* (20) 7581-3388 (office); (1403) 240-170 (office). *E-mail:* contact@stantondavidson.co.uk (office); virginia@bornfree.org.uk (office). *Website:* www.bornfree.org.uk (office).

MACKENZIE, Andrew, BSc, PhD; Australian business executive; *Executive Director and CEO, BHP Billiton;* experienced in oil and gas, petrochemicals and minerals since 1980s; held several sr roles at BP, including Group Vice-Pres. for Tech. and Eng and Group Vice-Pres. for Chemicals; Chief Exec. of Diamonds and Minerals, Rio Tinto –2008; joined BHP Billiton as Chief Exec. of Non-Ferrous 2008, Dir, BHP Billiton Ltd and BHP Billiton Plc and CEO BHP Billiton 2013–; Dir (non-exec.), Centrica plc 2005–13. *Address:* BHP Billiton Ltd, BHP Billiton Centre, 180 Lonsdale Street, Melbourne, Vic. 3000, Australia (office). *Telephone:* 1300-55-4757 (office). *Fax:* (3) 9609-3015 (office). *Website:* www.bhpbilliton.com (office).

McKENZIE, Dan Peter, CH, MA, PhD, FRS; British geologist and academic; *Emeritus Royal Society Professor, Department of Earth Sciences, University of Cambridge;* b. 21 Feb. 1942, Cheltenham, Glos.; s. of W. S. McKenzie and N. M. McKenzie (née Fairbrother); m. Indira M. Misra 1971; one s.; ed Westminster School and King's Coll., Cambridge; Fellow, King's Coll. 1965–73, 1977–, Sr Asst in Research, Dept of Earth Sciences, Univ. of Cambridge 1969–73, Asst Dir of Research 1973–79, Reader in Tectonics 1979–85, Prof. of Earth Sciences 1985–96, Royal Soc. Research Prof. 1996–2006, BP Prof. 2010–12, Emer. Royal Soc. Prof. 2012–; Foreign Assoc. NAS; Hon. DSc (Bristol) 2000; Balzan Prize 1981, Wollaston Medal, Geological Soc. of London 1983, Rutherford Memorial Lecturer 1988, Japan Prize (co-recipient) 1990, William Bowie Medal 2001, Crafoord Prize, Royal Swedish Acad. of Sciences 2002, Copley Medal, Royal Soc. 2011. *Publications:* numerous papers in professional journals. *Leisure interest:* gardening. *Address:* Bullard Laboratories, Madingley Rise, Madingley Road, Cambridge, CB3 0EZ, England (office). *Telephone:* (1223) 337177 (office). *Website:* www.esc.cam.ac.uk/people/academic-staff/dan-mckenzie (office).

MACKENZIE, Gen. Sir Jeremy John George, Kt, GCB, OBE, DL; British army officer; b. 11 Feb. 1941, Nairobi, Kenya; s. of Lt-Col John William Elliot Mackenzie and Valerie Mackenzie (née Dawes); m. Elizabeth Lyon (née Wertenbaker) 1969; one s. one d.; ed Duke of York School, Nairobi, Kenya, Staff Coll., Camberley; commissioned Queen's Own Highlanders 1961; Canadian Forces Staff Coll. 1974; Brigade Maj. 24 Airportable Brigade 1975–76; CO 1 Queen's Own Highlanders, NI and Hong Kong 1979–82; Instructor Staff Coll. 1982–83; Col Army Staff Duties 2 1983–84; Commdr 12th Armoured Brigade 1984–86; Service Fellowship King's Coll., Univ. of London 1987; Deputy Commdt 1987–89; Commdt 1989, Staff Coll.; GOC 4th Armoured Div. BAOR 1989–91; Col Commdt WRAC 1990–92, AG Corps 1992–98, APTC 1997; Col Highlanders 1994–2001; Commdr 1st (British) Corps 1991–92, NATO's ACE Rapid Reaction Corps (ARRC) 1992–94, Deputy Supreme Allied Commdr, Europe 1994–98, now consultant to NATO aspirant cos; ADC (Gen.) 1997–99; Gov. Royal Hosp. Chelsea 1999–2006; Sr Mil. Adviser, Fabbrica d'Armi Pietro Beretta SpA 2006; Ensign Brig. Queen's Bodyguard of Scotland (RCA); mem. Bd of Dirs, Sirva plc 2003–08, Selex Communications 2003–, UK Gear 2012–; mem. Advisory Bd, Blue Hackle Security 2006– (also Chair.); Commdr, US Legion of Merit 1997 (second award 1999), Hungarian Presidential Order of Merit (1st Class) 1998, Czech Defence Minister's Order of Merit (1st Class) 1998, Bulgarian Order of the Madara Horseman (1st Class) 1999, Slovenian Gold Medal of the Armed Forces 2003; Officer, Order of St John. *Publication:* The British Army and the Operational Level of War 1989. *Leisure interests:* shooting, fishing, painting.

MacKENZIE, Kelvin; British media executive; b. 22 Oct. 1946; m. 1st Jacqueline M. Holland 1969 (divorced 2006); m. 2nd Sarah McLean 2008; two s. one d.; joined The Sun newspaper, London, as sub-editor 1972, subsequently Night Ed. 1980, rejoined as Ed. 1981–94, columnist 2006–11, 2015–17; apptd Man. Ed. New York Post 1978; Night Ed. Daily Express Feb. 1981 Man. Dir BSkyB Jan.–Oct. 1994 (resgnd); Dir Mirror Group PLC 1994–98, Deputy Chief Exec. and Group Man. Dir 1997–98; Chair. and CEO Talk Radio UK 1998–2000; Chair. and CEO The Wireless Group –2005; Exec. Chair. Highbury House Communications PLC Sept.–Dec. 2005 (resgnd); columnist, Daily Mail 2011–12. *Address:* Christophers, 4 Lockestone Close, Weybridge, KT13 8EF, England.

McKENZIE, Kevin; American ballet dancer, choreographer and director; *Artistic Director, American Ballet Theater;* b. 29 April 1954, Burlington, Vt; s. of Raymond James McKenzie and Ruth Davison; ed Acad. of Washington School of Ballet; soloist with Nat. Ballet of Washington 1972–74; Prin. Dancer, Joffrey Ballet 1974–78; Prin. Dancer, American Ballet Theater (ABT) 1979–91, Artistic Dir 1992–; Perm. Guest Artist, Washington Ballet 1990–91, Artistic Assoc. 1991–92; Assoc. Dir New Amsterdam Ballet 1984–; Panel mem., Dutch Nat. Opera & Ballet; Hon. PhD (St Michael's Coll.); Silver Medal, Sixth Int. Ballet Competition, Varna 1972. *Principal roles include:* leading roles in all the major full-length classics, including Solor in La Bayadère, Don Jose in Carmen, the Prince in Cinderella, Franz in Coppélia, Gentleman With Her in Dim Lustre, Basil and Espada in Don Quixote (Kitri's Wedding), Albrecht in Giselle, a leading role in The Garden of

Villandry, Her Lover in Jardin aux Lilas, leading role in The Leaves Are Fading, the Friend in Pillar of Fire, leading role in Raymonda (Grand Pas Hongrois), featured role in Requiem, Champion Roper in Rodeo, Romeo and Mercutio in Romeo and Juliet, Prince Desire in The Sleeping Beauty, Prince Siegfried in Swan Lake, James in La Sylphide and leading roles in Other Dances, Paquita, Les Sylphides, Sylvia Pas de Deux and Theme and Variations; cr. role of Amnon in Martine van Hamel's Amnon V'Tamar and a leading role in Clark Tippet's S.P.E.B.S.Q.S.A. *Directed:* Groupo Zamboria (New Amsterdam Ballet—NAB) 1984, Liszt Études (now called Transcendental Études) (NAB) 1991, Lucy and the Count (The Washington Ballet) 1992, The Nutcracker 1993; (with Susan Jones): Don Quixote (ABT) 1995, Swan Lake (ABT) 2000; (with Anne-Marie Holmes): Raymonda (ABT) 2004; The Sleeping Beauty (ABT) 2007. *Address:* American Ballet Theater, 890 Broadway, New York, NY 10003, USA (office). *Telephone:* (212) 477-3030 (office). *Fax:* (212) 254-5938 (office). *Website:* www.abt.org (office).

McKENZIE SMITH, Ian, CBE, PRSA, PPRSW, RGI, FMA, FRSA, FRSE, FSA (Scot), FSS, HRA, HRHA, HRUA, HRWA; British artist; b. 3 Aug. 1935, Montrose, Angus, Scotland; s. of James McKenzie Smith and Mary Benzie; m. Mary Rodge Fotheringham 1963; two s. one d.; ed Robert Gordon's Coll., Aberdeen, Gray's School of Art, Aberdeen, Hospitalfield Coll. of Art, Arbroath, Aberdeen Coll. of Educ.; teacher of art, Fife 1960–63; educ. officer, Council of Industrial Design, Scottish Cttee 1963–68; Dir Aberdeen Art Gallery and Museums 1968–89; City Arts and Recreation Officer, Aberdeen 1989–96; Sec. Aberdeen Highland Games 1989–96; Deputy Pres. and Treas. RSA 1990–91, Sec. 1991–98, Pres. 1998–2007; Trustee Nat. Galleries of Scotland 1999; mem. Scottish Arts Council 1970–77 (Chair. Art Cttee 1975–77), Scottish Museums Council 1980–87 (Chair. Industrial Cttee 1985–87); Chair. Marguerite McBey Trust; mem. Advisory Council on Export of Works of Art 1991–, Museums and Galleries Comm. 1997–2000; mem. Bd, Friends of RSA 1972–, RSA Enterprises 1972–; mem. MacDonald Art Centre, City of Aberdeen, Robert Gordon Univ. Art and Heritage Forum, RSA William Littlejohn Panel, Royal Glasgow Inst. of the Fine Arts; trustee of numerous funds; Hon. RA 1999; Hon. LLD (Aberdeen) 1991; Hon. DArt (The Robert Gordon Univ., Aberdeen) 2000; RSA Guthrie Award 1971, RSA Gillies Award 1980, May Marshall Brown Award, Royal Scottish Soc. of Painters in Watercolours 1980.

McKERNAN, James, BA, PhD, FRS; American mathematician and academic; *Professor, Above Scale, and Charles Lee Powell Endowed Chair in Mathematics II, University of California, San Diego;* ed Trinity Coll., Cambridge, UK, Harvard Univ.; apptd instructor at Univ. of Utah 1991, later at Univ. of Texas –1995; Visiting Asst Prof., Oklahoma State Univ. 1994–95; Prof., Univ. of California, Santa Barbara 1995–2007; Prof. of Math., MIT 2007–13, Norbert Weiner Prof., 2009–13; currently Prof., Above Scale, and Charles Lee Powell Endowed Chair in Math. II, Univ. of California, San Diego; External Sr Fellow, Freiburg Inst. for Advanced Studies, Univ. of Freiburg 2014; Clay Research Award, Clay Math. Inst. 2007, Frank Nelson Cole Prize in Algebra (jt recipient) 2009, Breakthrough Prize for Mathematics 2018. *Publications:* numerous papers in professional journals on algebraic geometry. *Address:* Department of Mathematics, University of California, San Diego, 9500 Gilman Drive, # 0112, La Jolla, CA 02139-4307, USA (office). *Telephone:* (858) 534-6347 (office). *Fax:* (858) 534-5273 (office). *E-mail:* jmckernan@math.ucsd.edu (office). *Website:* www.math.ucsd.edu (office).

MACKEY, James Patrick, BA, LPh, BD, STL, DD, PhD; Irish philosopher, theologian and academic; *Thomas Chalmers Professor Emeritus of Theology, University of Edinburgh;* b. 9 Feb. 1934, Waterford; s. of Peter Mackey and Esther Morrissey; m. Noelle Quinlan 1973; one s. one d.; ed Mount St Joseph Coll., Nat. Univ. of Ireland, Pontifical Univ., Maynooth and Queen's Univ., Belfast, doctoral Research at Univ. of Oxford, UK and Univ. of Strasbourg, France; ordained priest 1958; Lecturer in Hebrew and Old Testament, Pontifical Univ., Maynooth 1959; Lecturer in Philosophy, Queen's Univ., Belfast 1960–66; Lecturer in Philosophy and Theology, St John's Coll., Waterford 1966–69; Assoc. Prof. of Philosophical and Systematic Theology, Univ. of San Francisco, USA 1969–73, Prof. 1973–79; Visiting Prof., Univ. of California, Berkeley, USA 1974–75; Thomas Chalmers Prof. of Theology, Univ. of Edin., UK 1979–99, Dean of Faculty of Divinity 1984–88, Dir Grad. School and Assoc. Dean 1995–98, Prof. Emer. 1999–, Fellow, Faculty of Divinity 1999–2002; Visiting Prof., Univ. of Dublin Trinity Coll. 2000–10; curricular consultant, Univ. Coll., Cork 2000–04; Visiting Prof., Dartmouth Coll., NH, USA 1989, Univ. of San Francisco 1990; mem. Ind. Assessment Panel and jt author of Report on NI Policing Bd 2005; Dir Derry City Int. Conf. on the Cultures of Europe 1992; mem. Consultative Group on the Past of N Ireland 2007–09; Assoc. Ed. Herder Correspondence 1966–69, Concilium 1965–73, Horizons 1973–79, Monograph Series: Biblical Foundations of Theology 1985–91; Founding Ed. Studies in World Christianity: the Edinburgh Review of Theology and Religion 1995–2001; British Acad. Research Scholarship, Univs of Oxford and Strasbourg 1964–65, Lifetime Achievement Award, The Gerard Manley Hopkins Int. Soc. 2012. *Television:* scripted and presented two eight-part series on world religions for Channel 4, The Hall of Mirrors 1984, The Gods of War 1986, two six-part series for the BBC, Perspectives (on Northern Ireland) 1986, Perspectives II 1987, numerous other contribs to TV and radio. *Publications include:* The Modern Theology of Tradition 1962, Life and Grace 1966 (American edn, The Grace of God, the Response of Man 1967, Spanish trans., Vida y Gracia 1969), Tradition and Change in the Church 1968 (French trans., Tradition et Evolution de la Foi 1969, Polish trans., Tradycja i Zmiana w Kosciele 1974), Morals, Law and Authority (ed.) 1969 (Italian trans., Il Magistero Morale; Compiti e Limite 1973), The Church: Its Credibility Today 1970, The Problems of Religious Faith 1972, Jesus, The Man and the Myth 1979 (German trans., Jesus der Mensch und der Mythos 1981, 1991), The Christian Experience of God as Trinity 1983, Religious Imagination (ed.) 1986, New Testament Theology in Dialogue (with J. D. G. Dunn) 1987, Modern Theology 1987, An Introduction to Celtic Christianity (ed.) 1989, Power and Christian Ethics 1994, The Cultures of Europe (ed.) 1994, The Critique of Theological Reason 2000, Religion and Politics in Ireland at the Turn of the Millennium (ed.) 2003, Christianity and Creation 2006, The Scientist and the Theologian 2007, Jesus of Nazareth 2008. *Leisure interest:* sailing. *Address:* 15 Glenville Park, Dunmore Road, Waterford, Ireland. *Telephone:* (51) 844624. *E-mail:* jpmackey_ie@yahoo.co.uk.

MACKI, Ahmad bin Abd an-Nabi; Omani government official; fmr Minister of Civil Service; Minister of Nat. Economy, Supervisor of Finance Ministry and Deputy Chair. Financial Affairs and Energy Resources Council –2011.

MACKIE, Robert (Bob) Gordon; American costume and fashion designer; b. 24 March 1940, Monterey Park, Calif.; s. of Charles Robert Smith and Mildred Agnes Mackie (née Smith); m. LuLu Porter (née Marianne Wolford) 1960 (divorced 1963); one s.; ed Pasadena City Coll. and Chouinard Art Inst.; mem. staff Edith Head 1962–63; designed costumes for film Divorce, American Style 1966; Co-designer for films Divorce American Style 1967, Lady Sings the Blues 1972, Funny Lady 1975, The Villain 1979, Smokey and the Bandit II 1980, Encore! 1980,...All the Marbles 1981, Pennies from Heaven 1981, Fake-Out 1982, Butterfly 1982, Max Dugan Returns 1983, Staying Alive 1983, Brenda Starr 1989; designer for numerous TV shows, including: Brigadoon 1966, Alice Through the Looking Glass 1966, Carousel 1967, Kismet 1967, Fred Astaire Show 1968, Diana Ross and The Supremes 1969, The Carol Burnett Show 1967–77, Sonny and Cher Comedy Hour 1971, Cher 1975, Donny and Marie 1976, Mitzi... Roarin' in the 20's 1976, The 48th Annual Academy Awards 1976, Diahann Carroll Summer Show 1976, Sonny and Cher Show 1976–77, An Evening with Diana Ross 1977, Mitzi... Zings Into Spring 1978, Mitzi... What's Hot, What's Not 1978, The Goldie Hawn Special 1978, The Grass Is Always Greener Over the Septic Tank 1978, The Star Wars Holiday Special 1978, The Captain & Tennille Songbook 1979, Goldie and Liza Together 1980, Ann-Margret: Hollywood Movie Girls 1980, Celebration 1981, The 54th Annual Academy Awards 1982, Fresno (mini-series) 1986, Plaza Suite 1987, Cher... at the Mirage 1990, The Carol Burnett Show (series) 1991, The Carol Burnett Show: A Reunion 1993, Gypsy 1993, Men, Movies & Carol 1994, Golden Anniversary 1995, Mrs. Santa Claus 1996, Blue Suede Shoes: Ballet Rocks! 1997, Bernadette Peters in Concert 1998, Cher: Live in Concert from Las Vegas 1999, Putting It Together 2000, Cher: The Farewell Tour 2003, Once Upon a Mattress 2005, Terror Toons 2 2007, Diahann Carroll: The Lady. The Music. The Legend 2010; Co-designer of theatrical productions On The Town 1971, Lorelei 1972, The Best Little Whorehouse Goes Public 1994; outfits worn by numerous stars, including Julie Andrews, Lucille Ball, Barbie, Ann-Margret, Mikhail Baryshnikov, Beyoncé, David Bowie, Carol Burnett, Carol Channing, Cyd Charisse, Cher, Petula Clark, Rosemary Clooney, Natalie Cole, Joan Collins, Marlene Dietrich, Phyllis Diller, Sally Field, Ella Fitzgerald, Peggy Fleming, Judy Garland, Mitzi Gaynor, Whoopi Goldberg, Betty Grable, Teri Hatcher, Goldie Hawn, Rita Hayworth, Whitney Houston, Anjelica Huston, The Jackson 5, Elton John, Grace Jones, Chaka Khan, Cheryl Ladd, Angela Lansbury, Janet Leigh, Annie Lennox, Liberace, Eva Longoria, Jennifer Lopez, Shirley MacLaine, Madonna, Jayne Mansfield, Steve Martin, Ethel Merman, Bette Midler, Liza Minnelli, Kylie Minogue, Mary Tyler Moore, Marie Osmond, Jack Palance, Dolly Parton, Katy Perry, Helen Reddy, Debbie Reynolds, Joan Rivers, Diana Ross, RuPaul, Brooke Shields, Dinah Shore, Jean Simmons, Maggie Smith, Britney Spears, Sharon Stone, Barbra Streisand, Donna Summer, The Supremes, John Travolta, Tina Turner, Raquel Welch, Mae West, Oprah Winfrey; launched first ready-to-wear collection in 1982, line grew rapidly to include fragrances, eyewear, furs and various fashion accessories, added a line of knitwear, eveningwear, suits, a new fragrance, men's ties, handbags, scarves, watches, jewellery and stationery 1990s, launched made-to-order couture collection 1999; teamed up with Cher for her three year run at The Colosseum, Caesar's Palace, Las Vegas 2008; collaborated with P!nk to design her costumes for worldwide Funhouse Tour 2009; designed 50th Anniversary Golden Legacy Barbie® doll 2009, Brazilian Banana Bonanza Barbie® 2012; Bob Mackie Design Group partnered with KAS Rugs 2013; often called "the sultan of sequins, the rajah of rhinestones"; Dr hc (Otis Coll. of Art and Design) 2005; Emmy Award 1967 (co-recipient), 1969, 1976, 1983, Costume Designers' Guild Award 1968, inducted into Television Acad. Hall of Fame 2002, tdf/Irene Sharaff Lifetime Achievement Award 2007, Charlie Award for Fashion Arts, The Hollywood Arts Council 2008, Design Legend Award, Otis Coll. of Art and Design 2011. *Television:* The Hanna-Barbera Happy Hour (series) (dir) 1978, Armistead Maupin's Tales of the City (mini-series) (actor) 1993. *Publication:* Dressing for Glamour 1969. *Address:* Bob Mackie Design Group Ltd, 230 Park Avenue, Suite 303, New York, NY 10169, USA (office). *Telephone:* (212) 370-0721 (office). *E-mail:* info@bobmackie.com (office). *Website:* bobmackie.com (office).

McKIERNAN, Gen. (retd) David D., MPA; American army officer (retd); ed Coll. of William & Mary, Shippensburg Univ.; received ROTC comm., entered US Army 1972, gained experience in the Balkans as a staff officer 1990s, joined Allied Command Europe Rapid Reaction Corps (ARRC) serving as Deputy Chief of Staff G-2/G-3 forward deployed in both Sarajevo, Bosnia-Herzegovina and Rheindahlen (Mönchengladbach), Germany 1996–98, Deputy Chief of Staff, Operations, HQ, US Army, Europe and Seventh Army during period of simultaneous operations in Bosnia, Albania and Kosovo 1998–99, assigned as G-3 (Operations), HQ, Dept of the Army 2001–02, assumed command of Third US Army and US Army Forces Cen. Command (ARCENT) 2002, became Coalition Forces Land Component Commdr for US Cen. Command in preparation for Operation Iraqi Freedom, led all coalition and US conventional ground forces that attacked Iraq March 2003, assigned as Deputy Commdg Gen./Chief of Staff for US Army Forces Command (largest major command in US Army), assumed command of 7th Army/US Army Europe, commands have included: 1st Bn, 35th Armor (Iron Knights), 1st Armored Div. 1988–90, 1st Brigade (Iron Horse), 1st Cavalry Div. 1993–95, 1st Cavalry Div. 1999–2001, 3rd US Army/Combined Forces Land Component Command 2002–04, Commdr CFLCC 2002–04, 7th US Army/US Army Europe 2005–, Commdg Gen. US Army, Europe 2004–08, Commdr Int. Security Assistance Force (ISAF), NATO 2008–09; mem. Faculty, Thayer Leader Development Group; awards and decorations include Ranger Tab, Parachutist Badge, Army Achievement Medal (with Oak Leaf Cluster), Army Commendation Medal (with 3 Oak Leaf Clusters), Meritorious Service Medal (with 3 Oak Leaf Clusters), Defense Meritorious Service Medal, Bronze Star, Legion of Merit (with 2 Oak Leaf Clusters), Defense Superior Service Medal, Army Distinguished Service Medal (with Oak Leaf Cluster), Defense Distinguished Service Medal; hon. doctorate in Public Service (The Coll. of William & Mary). *Address:* Thayer Leader Development Group, The Thayer Hotel, 674 Thayer Road, West Point, NY 10996, USA. *Website:* www.thayerleaderdevelopment.com.

McKILLOP, Sir Thomas (Tom) Fulton Wilson, Kt, BSc, PhD, FRSE, FMedSci; British business executive and chemist; *Chairman, Elova Holdings SA;* b. 19

March 1943, Dreghorn, nr Irvine, Ayrshire, Scotland; s. of Hugh McKillop and Annie McKillop (née Wilson); m. Elizabeth Kettle 1966; one s. two d.; ed Irvine Royal Acad., Univ. of Glasgow, Centre de Mécanique Ondulatoire Appliquée, Paris; research scientist, ICI Corp. Lab. 1969–75; Head of Natural Products Research, ICI Pharmaceuticals Ltd 1975–78, Dir of Research, France 1978–80, Chem. Man. 1980–84, Gen. Man. of Research 1984–85, Gen. Man. Devt 1985–89, Tech. Dir 1989–94; CEO AstraZeneca (fmrly Zeneca) 1994–2005, Dir 1996–2005; Deputy Chair. Royal Bank of Scotland Group 2005, Chair. 2006–08 (retd); Dir (non-exec.) Amersham Int. PLC 1992–97, Nycomed Amersham PLC 1997–2000, Lloyds TSB PLC 1999–, BP 2004–09; Dir Almirall 2007–; Pres. European Fed. of Pharmaceutical Industries and Asscns (EFPIA) 2002–05; Science Council 2007–11; Pro-Chancellor Univ. of Leicester 1998–2008; Chair. Elova Holdings SA 2012– (also Dir (non-exec.) 2010–); mem. Soc. for Drug Research, ACS, Royal Inst.; mem. Bd of Dirs, UCB SA, Alere Inc. 2013–; Trustee, Darwin Trust of Edin. 1995–, Council for Industry & Higher Educ.; Fellow, Royal Soc. of London; Hon. Fellow, Univ. of Lancashire 2004, ICHEME 2006; Hon. LLD (Manchester) 1999, (Dundee) 2003; Hon. DSc (Glasgow) 2000, (Leicester) 2000, (Huddersfield) 2000, (Nottingham) 2001, (St Andrews) 2004, (Salford) 2004, (Manchester) 2005, (Lancaster) 2007; Dr hc (Middlesex) 2000, (Paisley) 2006; Hon. DLit (Heriot-Watt) 2006. *Leisure interests:* carpentry, music, reading, walking. *Address:* Evolva Basel SA, Duggingerstrasse 23, 4153 Reinach, Switzerland (office). *Telephone:* (61) 485-2000 (office). *Website:* www.evolva.com (office).

MACKIN, Martin, MA; Irish politician; *Director, Q4 Public Relations Ltd.;* b. 23 Dec. 1963, Drogheda, Co. Louth; s. of Thomas Mackin and Josephine Mackin; ed Univ. Coll. Dublin, Coll. of Commerce, Dublin, Nat. Univ. of Ireland; press officer, Fianna Fáil 1992–95, Dir Fianna Fáil European Office 1995–98, Gen. Sec. Fianna Fáil 1998–2003; fmr mem. Bd of Culture Ireland, Seanad Eireann; Dir Q4 Public Relations Ltd 2003–; mem. Bd of Dirs British Irish Chamber of Commerce, Temple Bar Gallery and Studios; Fellow Institute of Politics, Kennedy School of Government, Harvard 2003. *Leisure interests:* music, current affairs, reading. *Address:* Q4PR, 88 St Stephens Green, Dublin 2, Ireland (office). *Telephone:* (1) 475-1444 (office). *Fax:* (1) 475-1444 (office). *E-mail:* info@q4pr.ie (office). *Website:* www.q4pr.ie (office).

McKINLEY, Brunson, BA, MA; American diplomatist and international organization official; *Co-Chairman, Association for International Mobility;* b. 8 Feb. 1943, Fla; s. of Kenneth William McKinley and Lois Rebecca McKinley; m. Nancy Padlon (deceased); one s. one d.; ed Univ. of Chicago, Harvard Univ.; served in US Army 1965–70, with service in Viet Nam; joined diplomatic service, overseas postings include Italy, China, Viet Nam, UK, Germany, Amb. to Haiti 1986–89, specialized in refugee and migration issues 1990–94, helped defuse Haitian–Cuban boat crisis 1994, developed transatlantic dialogue on migration, directed US participation in comprehensive action plan for Indo-Chinese refugees, US Bosnia Humanitarian Co-ordinator 1995–98, prin. compiler of refugee annex of Dayton Accords; Dir Gen. Int. Org. for Migration, Geneva 1998–2008; Co-Chair. Asscn for Int. Mobility 2008–; several foreign decorations; Bronze Star, Air Medal, Award for Valor. *Publications:* numerous studies on migration subjects. *Address:* AIM, World Trade Center II, 29 route de Pré-Bois, PO Box 885, 1215 Geneva 15 (office); 15 Grand Rue, 1260 Nyon, Switzerland (home). *E-mail:* brunsonmick@gmail.com (office).

McKINNELL, Henry A. (Hank), Jr, BS, MS, MBA, PhD; American business executive; *Chairman, Moody's Corporation;* b. 23 Feb. 1943, Victoria, BC, Canada; ed Univ. of British Columbia, Canada, Stanford Univ. Grad. School of Business; joined Pfizer Inc., Tokyo 1971, served in various exec. positions, including Pres. Pfizer Asia, Hong Kong, Pres. Medical Tech. Group, Chief Financial Officer, Pres. Pharmaceutical Group 1997, Pres. and COO Pfizer Inc. 1999–2000, Pres. 1999–2001, Chair. and CEO 2001–06 (resgnd); CEO Optimer Pharmaceuticals, Inc. Feb.–Oct. 2013; currently Chair. Moody's Corpn (mem. Bd 1997–); Co-founder and Chair. Accordia Global Health Foundation (mem. Bd 2003–); Dir Chamber of Commerce, Business Council, Royal Shakespeare Co. America, Medal of Honor Foundation; mem. Bd of Dirs John Wiley & Sons –2005, ExxonMobil Corpn –2007, Emmaus Life Sciences, Inc. 2010– (currently Chair.), Angiotech Pharmaceuticals, Inc. –2011; fmr Chair. Advisory Council, Stanford Univ. Grad. School of Business; Chair. Emer. Connecticut Science Center, Business Roundtable, Pharmaceutical Research Mfrs Asscn, Food and Drug Law Inst., Medical Device Mfrs Asscn; fmr Vice-Chair. World Econ. Forum, fmr mem. WEF Foundation Bd of Trustees; mem. Presidential Advisory Council on HIV/AIDS (PACHA), Academic Alliance for AIDS Care and Prevention in Africa; Trustee, Memorial-Sloan Kettering Cancer Center, New York City Public Library, New York City Police Foundation; Life Trustee, Japan Soc.; Fellow, New York City Public Library, New York City Police Foundation, Channel Thirteen/WNET, J.F. Kennedy Center for the Performing Arts; Grand Cordon, Order of the Rising Sun (Japan); Dr hc (Polytechnic Univ.); Sitara-i-Eisaar Award (Pakistan), Presidential Distinguished Service Award for contributions to health services in Uganda, Global Leadership Award, UNA of the USA, Corp. Service Award, Woodrow Wilson Inst., Cleveland E. Dodge Medal for Distinguished Service to Educ., Columbia Univ. Teachers Coll., Excellence in Leadership Award, Stanford Univ. Grad. School of Business. *Address:* Moody's Corporation, 250 Greenwich Street, Floor 19, New York, NY 10007, USA (office). *Telephone:* (212) 553-4195 (office). *E-mail:* info@moodys.com (office). *Website:* www.moodys.com (office).

McKINNON, Rt Hon. Sir Donald (Don) Charles, Kt, PC, ONZ, GCVO; New Zealand politician and international organization official; *Chairman and Executive Director, New Zealand China Council;* b. 27 Feb. 1939; s. of Maj.-Gen. Walter McKinnon and Anna McKinnon (née Plimmer); m. 1st Patricia Maude Moore 1964 (divorced 1995); three s. one d.; m. 2nd Clare de Lore 1995; one s.; fmr estate agent and farm man. consultant; Nat. Party MP for Albany 1978–2000, fmr Jr and Sr Govt Whip, Opposition Spokesperson for Defence and Health, Sr Opposition Whip 1984–87; Deputy Prime Minister 1990–96; Leader of the House 1993–96; Minister of Foreign Affairs and Trade, of Pacific Island Affairs, 1990–99, for Disarmament and Arms Control 1996–99; Sec.-Gen. of the Commonwealth 2000–08; interim Dir and CEO Auckland War Memorial Museum 2010–11; Chair. and Exec. Dir New Zealand China Council 2012–; Assoc., Aspen Atlantic Group; Chair. Regional Facilities Auckland; mem. Int. Advisory Bd, Tilray, Inc. 2018–; Trustee Asia Foundation, Patron New Zealand War Graves Trust; Hon. DComm (Lincoln, NZ),

Dr hc (four Univs of Manchester) 2002, (Heriot-Watt Univ., Edinburgh), Hon. DJur (Univ. of Swaziland), Hon. DLitt (Univ. of Buea); Foreign Minister of the Year, World Economic Forum 1998, Kea Supreme World Class New Zealander of the Year 2013. *Leisure interests:* rugby, cricket, jogging, tennis, reading, riding. *Address:* New Zealand China Council, Level 13, 51 Shortland Street, Auckland 1010 (office); 49 Dell Rd, Waiau Pa, RD4, Pukekohe, 2679, New Zealand (home). *Telephone:* (9) 379-4641 (office); (9) 232-0064. *Fax:* (9) 309-2677. *E-mail:* maria.miliner@RFA.com (office); deltamike41@hotmail.com. *Website:* nzchinacouncil.com (office).

McKINNON, Sir James, Kt, CA, FCMA; British public servant (retd); b. 1929; ed Camphill School; Co. Sec. Macfarlane Lang & Co. Ltd, Glasgow 1955–65; Business Consultant, McLintock, Moores & Murray, Glasgow 1965–67; Finance Dir Imperial Group PLC, London 1967–86; Dir-Gen. Office of Gas Supply 1986–93; Chair. Ionica 1993–98; Chair. (non-exec.) Cowie Group 1994–, Trafficmaster plc –2004, Discovery Trust PLC 2004–05; Deputy Chair. (non-exec.) United Business Media plc –2000; mem. Bd Dirs Martin Currie Capital Return Trust plc (renamed F&C Private Equity Trust plc) 2005; Pres. Inst. of Chartered Accountants of Scotland 1985–86; Dr hc (Paisley) 1995. *Publications:* articles in professional publs. *Leisure interest:* skiing.

MacKINNON, Roderick, BA, MD; American physician, biophysicist and academic; *John D. Rockefeller Jr Professor, Laboratory of Molecular Neurobiology and Biophysics, The Rockefeller University;* b. 19 Feb. 1956, Burlington, Mass; ed Univ. of Massachusetts, Brandeis Univ., Tufts Univ. School of Medicine, Harvard Medical School; medical residency at Beth Israel Hosp., Harvard Medical School; postdoctoral work at Brandeis Univ. 1986–89; Asst Prof. of Physiology, Harvard Medical School 1989–92, Assoc. Prof. of Neurobiology 1992–95, Prof. of Neurobiology 1995–96; Prof. and Head of Lab. of Molecular Neurobiology and Biophysics, The Rockefeller Univ. 1996–, now John D. Rockefeller Jr Prof.; Investigator, Howard Hughes Medical Inst. 1997–; Visiting Researcher, Brookhaven Nat. Lab.; mem. NAS 2000; Hon. DSc (Tufts) 2002; Newcomb Cleveland Prize 1997, W. Alden Spencer Award 1998, Albert Lasker Basic Medical Research Award 1999, Lewis S. Rosenstiel Award for Distinguished Work in Basic Medical Science 2000, Gairdner Foundation Int. Award 2001, Perl-UNC Neuroscience Prize 2001, Louisa Gross Horwitz Prize, Columbia Univ. 2003, Nobel Prize in Chem. (with Peter Agre) 2003. *Publications:* numerous papers in scientific journals on ion channels. *Address:* Laboratory of Molecular Neurobiology and Biophysics, The Rockefeller University, 1230 York Avenue, New York, NY 10021, USA (office). *Telephone:* (212) 327-7288 (office). *Fax:* (212) 327-7289 (office). *E-mail:* roderick.mackinnon@rockefeller.edu (office); mackinnon_admin@rockefeller.edu (office). *Website:* www.rockefeller.edu (office).

McKINSTRY, Nancy, BA, MBA; American publishing industry executive; *Chairman of the Executive Board and CEO, Wolters Kluwer NV;* b. 4 Jan. 1959, Conn.; ed Univ. of Rhode Island, Columbia Univ.; held man. positions with Booz Allen Hamilton (int. man. consulting firm) 1980s; held a succession of man. positions with Wolters Kluwer cos in North America 1991–99, including Vice-Pres. Product Man. and Sr Officer for CCH Inc. and Asst Vice-Pres. Electronic Products Div. for CCH –1996, Pres. and CEO CCH Legal Information Services 1996, CEO Wolters Kluwer's operations in North America –2001, mem. Exec. Bd Wolters Kluwer NV 2001–, Chair. Exec. Bd Wolters Kluwer NV, responsible for Wolters Kluwer's Divs, Business Devt, Strategy and Tech. 2001–03, Chair. Exec. Bd and CEO 2003–; CEO SCP Communications (medical information co.) 1999; mem. Bd of Dirs Abbott, Russell Reynolds Associates; mem. Advisory Council of Amsterdam Inst. of Finance, Dutch Advisory Council of Institut Européen d'Admin des Affaires (INSEAD); mem. Advisory Bd Univ. of Rhode Island, Harrington School of Communication and Media; mem. Bd of Overseers, Columbia Business School, University Club of New York City; mem. Foreign Consultant Committee, Chinese State Council Information Office 2011–; Hon. LLD (Univ. of Rhode Island) 2005. *Address:* Wolters Kluwer NV, Zuidpoolsingel 2, PO Box 1030, 2400 BA Alphen aan den Rijn, The Netherlands (office). *Telephone:* (172) 641400 (office). *Fax:* (172) 474889 (office). *E-mail:* info@wolterskluwer.com (office). *Website:* www.wolterskluwer.com (office).

MACKINTOSH, Sir Cameron Anthony, Kt; British theatre producer; *Chairman, Cameron Mackintosh;* b. 17 Oct. 1946, Enfield; s. of Ian Mackintosh and Diana Mackintosh; ed Prior Park Coll. Bath; stage hand then Asst Stage Man. Theatre Royal, Drury Lane; worked with Emile Littler 1966, with Robin Alexander 1967; producer 1969–; Chair. Cameron Mackintosh 1981–; Dir Delfont Mackintosh 1991; owns seven theatres in London's West End (Prince of Wales, Prince Edward, Novello, Wyndham's, Noël Coward, Queen's and Gielgud); Pres. Royal Scottish Acad. of Music and Drama 2004; Co-Owner, Music Theatre International; Hon. Fellow, St Catherine's Coll., Oxford 1990; Observer Award for Outstanding Achievement, Laurence Olivier Award 1991, Richard Rodgers Award 2002, Oscar Hammerstein Award 2002, Nat. Enjoy England Award for Excellence for Outstanding Contribution to Tourism 2006, inducted into American Theater Hall of Fame 2014. *Productions:* Little Women 1967, Anything Goes 1969, Trelawny 1972, The Card 1973, Winnie the Pooh 1974, Owl and the Pussycat Went to See 1975, Godspell 1975, Side by Side by Sondheim 1976, Oliver! 1977, Diary of a Madam 1977, After Shave 1977, Gingerbread Man 1978, Out on a Limb 1978, My Fair Lady 1979, Oklahoma! 1980, Tomfoolery 1980, Jeeves Takes Charge 1981, Cats 1981, Song and Dance 1982, Blondel 1983, Little Shop of Horrors 1983, Abbacadabra 1983, The Boyfriend 1984, Les Misérables 1985, Café Puccini 1985, Phantom of the Opera 1986, Follies 1987, Miss Saigon 1989, Just So 1990, Five Guys Named Moe 1990, Moby Dick 1992, Putting it Together 1992, The Card 1992, Carousel 1993, Oliver! 1994, Martin Guerre 1996, The Fix 1997, Oklahoma! 1999, The Witches of Eastwick 2000, My Fair Lady 2001, Mary Poppins 2004, Avenue Q 2006. *Leisure interests:* cooking, taking holidays. *Address:* Cameron Mackintosh Ltd, 1 Bedford Square, London, WC1B 3RB, England. *Telephone:* (20) 7637-8866. *Fax:* (20) 7436-2683.

McKNIGHT, Hon. William (Bill) Hunter, PC; Canadian fmr politician; *Principal, McKnight & Associates;* b. 12 July 1940, Elrose, Sask.; m. Beverley Ogden; two s.; ed Wartime and Elrose, Sask.; fmr farmer and business exec.; MP for Kindersley-Lloydminster (Sask.) 1979–93, fmr Chair. House Standing Cttee on Agric., fmr mem. Transport Cttee, Man. and Mem.'s Services Cttee, Finance, Trade and Econ. Affairs Cttee, fmr Progressive Conservative Party spokesperson on Canadian Wheat Bd, on Int. Trade, fmr Deputy Opposition House Leader; Progressive Conservative Party Minister of Labour 1984–86, of Indian Affairs and Northern Devt 1986–89, of Defence 1989–91, of Agric. 1991–93, of Energy, Mines and Resources 1993; Chair. NAFTA Trade Consultants Inc. 1993; Founder, Dir and Chair. Anvil Range Mining Corpn 1994; Prin., McKnight & Assocs (int. trade and financial consultancy), Saskatchewan 1993–; Dir Gamblers Restaurant Inc. 1995–, Marvas Developments Ltd 1995–, Mid-North Resources Ltd 1995–, R.E.S. Int. Inc. 1995, Sci-Tec Instruments Inc. 1995–, Diadem Resources Ltd 2002–; mem. Saskatchewan Order of Merit; Hon. Consul, Ecuador 1995, Chief, Muskeg Lake Cree Nation.

MacLACHLAN, Kyle, BFA; American actor; b. 22 Feb. 1959, Yakima, Wash.; m. Desiree Gruber; ed Univ. of Washington, Seattle; stage appearances in regional Shakespeare productions and off-Broadway in Palace of Amateurs. *Films include:* Dune 1984, Blue Velvet 1986, The Hidden 1988, Don't Tell Her It's Me 1990, The Doors 1991, Where the Day Takes You 1992, The Trial 1993, Twin Peaks: Fire Walk With Me 1992, Rich in Love 1993, Against the Wall 1994, The Flintstones 1994, Showgirls 1995, Trigger Effect 1996, Mad Dog Time 1996, One Night Stand 1997, X-Change 2000, Hamlet 2000, Timecode 2000, Perfume 2001, Me Without You 2001, Miranda 2002, Northfork 2003, Touch of Pink 2004, Free Jimmy (voice) 2006, Mao's Last Dancer 2009, The Smell of Success 2009, Peace, Love, & Misunderstanding 2011, Breathe In 2013, Twin Peaks: The Missing Pieces 2014, Inside Out (voice) 2015, Giant Little Ones 2018. *Plays include:* Palace of Amateurs, Minetta Lane Theatre (off Broadway), New York, On An Average Day, Comedy Theatre, London 2002. *Television includes:* Twin Peaks (series) 1990–91, Roswell 1994, Moonshine Highway 1996, Windsor Protocol 1996, The Invisible Man 1998, Thunder Point 1998, Route 9 1998, The Spring 2000, Sex and the City 2000–02, Jo 2002, The Librarian: Quest for the Spear 2004, Mysterious Island 2005, In Justice (series) 2006, Justice League: The New Frontier 2008, Desperate Housewives (series) 2006–12, How I Met Your Mother (series) 2010–14, Portlandia (series) 2011–16, Made in Jersey (series) 2012, The Good Wife (series) 2013–14, Believe (series) 2014, Agents of S.H.I.E.L.D. (series) 2014–15, Twin Peaks 2017. *Website:* www.kylemaclachlan.com.

McLACHLIN, Hon. Beverley, MPh, PC, CC, CStJ; Canadian lawyer, judge and author; b. 7 Sept. 1943, Pincher Creek, Alberta; d. of Ernest Gietz and Eleanora Kruschell; m. 1st Roderick McLachlin (died 1988); one s.; m. 2nd Frank McArdle 1992; ed Univ. of Alberta; practised law with Wood, Moir, Hyde & Ross, Edmonton 1968–71; called to the Bar of BC; practised law with Bull, Housser and Tupper, Vancouver 1972–75; Assoc. Prof., Univ. of British Columbia 1974–81; named to Co. Court of Vancouver 1981, Supreme Court of BC 1981–85, BC Court of Appeal 1985–88; Chief Justice of the Supreme Court of BC 1988; Justice, Supreme Court of Canada 1989–2000, Chief Justice of Canada (first woman) 2000–17; Non-Perm. Judge, Hong Kong Court of Final Appeal 2018–; Chair. Canadian Judicial Council, Advisory Council of the Order of Canada, Bd of Govs of Nat. Judicial Inst.; mem. Privy Council of Canada; Hon. Patron, Inst. of Parl. and Political Law; Hon. LLD (Toronto) 1995, (York) 1999, (Law Soc. Upper Canada) 2000, (Ottawa) 2000, (Calgary) 2000, (Brock Univ.) 2000, (Simon Fraser Univ.) 2000, (Victoria) 2000, (Alberta) 2000, (Lethbridge) 2001, (Bridgewater State Coll.) 2001, (Mount St Vincent Univ.) 2002, (PEI) 2002, (Montreal) 2003, (Manitoba) 2004, (Queen's Univ. Belfast) 2004, (Dalhousie) 2004, (Carleton) 2004, (Maine at Fort Kent) 2005, (Manila) 2006, (Windsor) 2010, (Ryerson) 2010, (Cape Breton) 2010, (Queen's Univ.) 2011, (Concordia Univ.) 2011, (Western Ontario) 2012, (Lakehead Univ.) 2012, (Edinburgh) 2014, (Bishop's Univ.) 2015, (Laurentian Univ.) 2016, (McGill) 2016, (Memorial Univ. of Newfoundland) 2017. *Publication:* Full Disclosure 2015. *Leisure interests:* hiking, swimming, cross-country skiing. *Address:* Hong Kong Court of Final Appeal, 8 Jackson Road, Central, Hong Kong Special Administrative Region, People's Republic of China (office). *Telephone:* 21230123 (office). *Fax:* 21210300 (office). *E-mail:* cfaenquiries@hkcfa.hk (office). *Website:* www.hkcfa.hk (office).

MacLAINE, Shirley; American film actress, writer and film director; b. 24 April 1934, Richmond, Va; d. of Ira Beaty and Kathlyn MacLean; sister of Warren Bull Beatty (q.v.); m. Steve Parker 1954 (divorced 1982); one d.; ed grammar school and Lee High School, Washington; fmr chorus girl and ballet dancer; Theater Owners of America Star of the Year Award 1967, Berlin Film Festival Lifetime Achievement Award 1999, Malibu Film Festival Life Achievement Award 2001. *Films include:* The Trouble With Harry (Golden Globe Award for New Star of the Year) 1955, Artists and Models 1955, Around The World in 80 Days 1956, Hot Spell 1958, The Matchmaker 1958, Career 1959, Can-Can 1960, The Apartment 1960, The Children's Hour 1961, Two For The Seesaw 1962, Irma La Douce 1963, What A Way To Go 1964, The Yellow Rolls-Royce 1964, Gambit 1966, Woman Times Seven 1967, The Bliss of Mrs Blossom 1968, Sweet Charity 1969, Two Mules For Sister Sara 1970, Desperate Characters (Best Actress Award, Berlin Film Festival) 1971, The Possessions of Joel Delaney 1972, The Turning Point 1977, Being There 1979, Loving Couples 1980, The Change of Seasons 1981, Slapstick 1981, Terms of Endearment (Acad. Award for Best Actress) 1984, Out on a Limb 1987, Madame Sousatzka (Golden Globe Award for Best Actress) 1989, Steel Magnolias 1989, Waiting for the Light 1990, Postcards from the Edge 1990, Used People 1993, Wrestling Ernest Hemingway 1994, Guarding Tess 1994, Mrs Westbourne 1995, Mrs Winterbourne 1996, The Celluloid Closet, The Evening Star 1996, Looking for Lulu, Bet Bruce, Bruno (also dir), Joan of Arc 1999, The Dress Code 2000, Rumor Has It… 2005, In Her Shoes 2005, Bewitched 2005, Ant Bully 2006, Closing the Ring 2007, Valentine's Day 2010, Bernie 2011, The Secret Life of Walter Mitty 2013, Elsa & Fred 2014, Wild Oats 2016, The Last Word 2017, The Little Mermaid 2018. *Revues:* If My Friends Could See Me Now 1974, To London With Love 1976, London 1982, Out There Tonight 1990. *Television includes:* The West Side Waltz 1994, Joan of Arc, These Old Broads 2001, Downton Abbey (series) 2012–13, A Heavenly Christmas (film) 2016. *Video:* Shirley MacLaine's Inner Workout 1989. *Produced and co-directed:* The Other Half of the Sky – A China Memoir 1973. *Publications include:* Don't Fall Off the Mountain 1971, The New Celebrity Cookbook 1973, You Can Get There From Here 1975 (Vols 1 and 2 of autobiog.), Out on a Limb (Vol. 3) 1983, Dancing in the Light 1985 (Vol. 4), It's All in the Playing (Vol. 5) 1987, Going Within (Vol. 6) 1989, Dance While You Can (Vol. 7) 1991, My Lucky Stars (Vol. 8) 1995, The Camino 2000, Out on a Leash 2003, Sageing While Age-ing 2007, I'm Over All That: And Other Confessions 2011. *Address:* MacLaine Enterprises Inc., 25200 Malibu Road, Suite 101, Santa Monica, CA

90265, USA (office). *Telephone:* (310) 317-8500. *Fax:* (310) 317-8504. *E-mail:* info@shirleymaclaine.com. *Website:* shirleymaclaine.com.

MacLAREN, Hon. Roy, PC, MA, MDiv; Canadian fmr diplomatist, politician and business executive; b. 26 Oct. 1934, Vancouver; s. of Wilbur MacLaren and Anne Bailey MacLaren; m. Alethea Mitchell 1959; two s. one d.; ed Univ. of British Columbia, Univ. of Cambridge, UK, Harvard Univ., USA, Univ. of Toronto; joined Dept of External Affairs 1957; served in Hanoi, Prague, Geneva, Ottawa, New York; Dir Public Affairs, Massey Ferguson Ltd 1969–73; Pres. Ogilvy and Mather (Canada) Ltd 1974–76; Chair. CB Media Ltd 1977–83, 1984–93; Dir Deutsche Bank (Canada), Royal LePage Ltd, London Insurance Group Inc.; elected Liberal MP for Etobicoke North 1979–96; Parl. Sec. to Minister of Energy, Mines & Resources 1980–82; Minister of State (Finance) 1983, Minister of Nat. Revenue 1984, for Int. Trade 1993–96; High Commr in UK 1996–2000; Commr Trilateral Comm.; Dir (non-exec.) Standard Life, Brascan, Patheon, Broadview Press, Pacific Safety Products, Amec N American Advisory Bd 2001–; Dir Canadian Opera Co.; Chair. Canada-India Business Council, Canadian Inst. of Int. Affairs, Canada-Europe Round Table; currently Sr Fellow, Massey Coll., Univ. of Toronto; Hon. Col 7th Toronto Regt Royal Canadian Artillery 1997–2007; Hon. Dr Sacred Letters (Toronto); Hon. Dr Civil Letters (Univ. of N Alabama); Hon. LLD (Univ. of New Brunswick, Univ. of Prince Edward Island). *Publications:* Canadians in Russia, 1918–1919 1976, Canadians on the Nile, 1882–1898 1978, Canadians Behind Enemy Lines, 1939–1945 1981, Honourable Mentions 1986, African Exploits: The Diaries of William Grant Stairs 1997, Commissions High 2006, The Fundamental Things Apply 2011. *Leisure interests:* skiing, cross-country walking. *Address:* 425 Russell Hill Road, Toronto, Ont. M5P 2S4, Canada (home). *Telephone:* (416) 932-9255 (home). *Fax:* (416) 932-3571 (home).

McLARTY, Thomas F. (Mack), III; American business executive and fmr politician; *Chairman, McLarty Associates;* b. 1946, Hope, Ark.; m. Donna K. Cochran 1969; two s.; ed Univ. of Arkansas; worked in family automobile and transport business; elected to Ark. House of Reps 1969; Chair. Ark. State Democratic Party 1974–76; apptd mem. Bd Arkla Inc., La, subsequently joined staff, apptd Chair. 1983; Chief of Staff to Pres. Bill Clinton 1993–94, Presidential Counselor 1994–2001, Special Envoy for Americas 1997; Chair. Kissinger McLarty Assocs, Washington DC and New York City and Chair. McLarty Cos, Little Rock, Ark. 1998– (Kissinger McLarty Assocs separated to form Kissinger Assocs and McLarty Assocs 2008); Dir Acxiom Corpn 1999–2010, Union Pacific Railroad; mem. Advisory Bd Leeds Equity Partners, Cato Inst./Inter-American Dialogue, Diligence Llc, New Democrat Network; Sr Advisor, The Carlyle Group 2003–; Vice-Chair. Asbury Automotive Arkansas LLC 2002–06, non-Exec. Chair. and Dir 2005–06; mem. Bd Council of Americas, Inter-American Dialogue, US-Mexico Binational Council, Council on Foreign Relations 2001; Trustee, Center for the Study of the Presidency; mem. Int. Council of Trustees, Religions for Peace; Democratic; Hon. LLD (Univ. of Arkansas) 2000; Sec. of State's Distinguished Service Medal, Center for the Study of the Presidency Distinguished Service Award, Order of Aztec Eagle (Mexico) and numerous other awards and honours. *Address:* McLarty Associates, 900 Seventeenth Street NW, Suite 800, Washington, DC 20006, USA. *Telephone:* (202) 419-1420. *E-mail:* info@maglobal.com. *Website:* www.maglobal.com.

MacLAUCHLAN, H. Wade, CM, LLB, LLM; Canadian politician and fmr university administrator; *Premier, Prince Edward Island;* b. 1954, Stanhope, PEI; s. of Harry MacLauchlan and Marjorie MacLauchlan; partner Duncan McIntosh; ed Univ. of Prince Edward Island, Univ. of New Brunswick, Yale Univ., USA; worked as Law Prof., Dalhousie Univ.; fmr Dean of Law School, Univ. of New Brunswick; Pres. Univ. of Prince Edward Island 1999–2011; Leader, Prince Edward Island Liberal Party 2015–; Premier, Prince Edward Island 2015–, also Pres. of Exec. Council, Minister of Finance and Energy, Minister Responsible for Intergovernmental Affairs, for Aboriginal Affairs, and for Acadian and Francophone Affairs; Chair. Palmer Conf. on Public Sector Leadership 2012; Co-Chair. Georgetown Conf.: Redefining Rural 2013; Order of Prince Edward Island 2014; Inst. of Public Admin of Canada IPAC Award for Excellence in Public Service 2010. *Publication:* Alex B. Campbell: The Prince Edward Island Premier Who Rocked the Cradle. *Address:* Office of the Premier, Fifth Floor, South Shaw Building, 95 Rochford Street, PO Box 2000, Charlottetown, PEI C1A 7N8, Canada (office). *Telephone:* (902) 368-4400 (office). *Fax:* (902) 368-4416 (office). *E-mail:* premier@gov.pe.ca (office). *Website:* www.gov.pe.ca/premier (office).

McLAUGHLIN, Alden M., LLB, MBE, JP; Cayman Islands lawyer and politician; *Premier;* b. 6 Sept. 1961, George Town; m. Kim McLaughlin; two s.; ed Univ. of Liverpool, UK; joined Civil Service as Asst Labour Officer 1981, transferred to Judicial Dept, Deputy Clerk of the Court 1982–84; Articled Clerk, Charles Adams and Co. (law firm, now Charles Adams, Ritchie and Duckworth) 1984, Assoc. Attorney 1988, Partner 1993–2005; Founding mem. People's Progressive Movt, Gen. Sec. 2002–06, Leader 2011–; mem. Legis. Assembly for George Town 2000–; Minister of Educ., Training, Employment, Youth, Sports and Culture 2005–09; Leader of the Opposition 2011–13; Premier 2013–; fmr Pres. Cayman Islands Bar Asscn. *Address:* Office of the Premier, Government Administration Bldg, Elgin Avenue, George Town, Grand Cayman, Cayman Islands (office).

MacLAURIN OF KNEBWORTH, Baron (Life Peer), cr. 1996, of Knebworth in the County of Hertfordshire; **Ian Charter MacLaurin,** Kt, DL, FRSA; British business executive; b. 30 March 1937, Blackheath; s. of Arthur MacLaurin and Evelina MacLaurin; m. 1st Ann Margaret Collar 1962 (died 1999); one s. two d.; m. 2nd Paula Elizabeth Brooke 2001; ed Malvern Coll., Worcs.; joined Tesco as a Trainee Man. 1959; Dir Tesco Stores (Holdings) Ltd 1970, Man. Dir 1974–83, Deputy Chair. 1983–85, Chair. 1985–97; Chair. Vodafone 1998–99, Deputy Chair. 1999–2000, Chair. 2000–06, Adviser 2006–, Chair. Vodafone Group Foundation 2006–09; Chancellor, Univ. of Herts. 1996–; Chair. England and Wales Cricket Bd 1996–2002; Dir (non-exec.) Enterprise Oil 1984–91, Gleneagles Hotels PLC 1992–, Guinness PLC 1986–95, Nat. Westminster Bank PLC 1990–97, Whitbread PLC 1997–2001 (Deputy Chair. 1999–), Health Clinic 2001–02, Evolution 2004–10; Pres. Inst. of Grocery Distribution 1989–92; Fellow Inst. of Marketing 1987; Freeman of City of London 1981; Chair. Malvern Coll. Council 2003–; mem. MCC; mem. Lords Taverners and Worshipful Co. of Carmen; Hon. Fellow (Wales Cardiff) 1996; Hon. DUniv (Stirling) 1986, Dr hc (Hertfordshire). *Publication:* Tiger by the

Tail (memoirs) 1999. *Leisure interests:* cricket, golf. *Address:* House of Lords, London, SW1A 0PW, England (office). *E-mail:* maclaurini@gmail.com (home).

MacLAVERTY, Bernard, BA, DipEd; Irish writer; b. 14 Sept. 1942, Belfast, Northern Ireland; s. of John MacLaverty and Mary MacLaverty; m. Madeline McGuckin 1967; one s. three d.; ed Queen's Univ., Belfast; fmrly medical lab. technician, English teacher; fmr Writer-in-Residence, Univ. of Aberdeen, Augsburg, Liverpool John Moore's, Iowa State Univ., St Michael's Coll., Univ. of Toronto; mem. Aosdána; Dr hc (Univ. of Strathclyde) 2014; NI and Scottish Arts Councils Awards, Irish Sunday Independent Award 1983, Scottish Writer of the Year (co-recipient) 1988, Soc. of Authors Travelling Scholarship 1994, Stakis Scottish Writer of the Year, Creative Scotland Award 2003, Lord Provost of Glasgow's Award for Literature 2005, Sunday Herald's Writer of the Year 2018 inducted into Hennessy Hall of Fame 2018. *Stage includes:* opera libretti: The King's Conjecture 2008, The Letter 2010, The Elephant Angel 2012, Grace Notes 2018. *Screenplays include:* Cal (London Evening Standard Award for Screenplay 1984) 1984, Lamb 1985, Bye-Child (short film, also Dir) (Best First Dir, BAFTA Scotland 2004) 2003. *Radio plays include:* My Dear Palestrina 1980, Secrets 1981, No Joke 1983, The Break 1988, Some Surrender 1988, Lamb 1992, Grace Notes 2003, The Woman from the North 2007, Winter Storm 2009. *Television includes:* plays: My Dear Palestrina 1980, Phonefun Limited 1982, The Daily Woman 1986, Sometime in August 1989; drama documentary: Hostages 1992; adaptation: The Real Charlotte, by Somerville and Ross 1989. *Publications include:* novels: Lamb 1980, Cal 1983, Grace Notes (Saltire Scottish Book of the Year Award) 1997, The Anatomy School 2001, Midwinter Break (Novel of the Year 2017) 2017; short story collections: Secrets and Other Stories 1977, A Time to Dance and Other Stories 1982, The Great Profundo and Other Stories 1987, Walking the Dog and Other Stories 1994, Matters of Life & Death and Other Stories 2006, Collected Stories 2013; juvenile fiction: A Man in Search of a Pet 1978, Andrew McAndrew 1988. *Address:* c/o Gill Coleridge, Rogers, Coleridge & White, 20 Powis Mews, London, W11 1JN, England (office). *Telephone:* (20) 7221-3717 (office). *Fax:* (20) 7229-9084 (office). *E-mail:* info@rcwlitagency.co.uk (office). *Website:* www.rcwlitagency.co.uk (office); www.bernardmaclaverty.com.

McLAY, James (Jim) Kenneth, CNZM, QSO, LLB; New Zealand diplomatist, politician, lawyer and business consultant; b. 21 Feb. 1945, Devonport, Auckland; s. of Robert McLay and Joyce Evelyn Dee; m. Marcy Farden 1983; one s.; ed King's Coll., Auckland, Univ. of Auckland; officer, Territorial Force 1967–70; barrister 1968–; Man. Ed. Recent Law 1969–70; MP for Birkenhead 1975–87; Attorney-Gen. and Minister of Justice 1978–84; Deputy Prime Minister 1984; Leader of Opposition 1984–86; Man. Dir J.K. McLay Ltd 1987–2009; Amb. and Perm. Rep. to UN, New York 2009–15; apptd Rep. to Palestinian Authority 2015; Consul-Gen. in Honolulu 2016–17; Deputy Chair. TrustBank Auckland Ltd 1988–93; Chair. Macquarie New Zealand Ltd (Subsidiary of Macquarie Bank, Australia) 1994, Unichem Chemist Ltd 1999; Chair. (non-exec.) and Dir Healthphone Ltd 2007; mem. 1990 Comm. 1988–91; mem. Ministerial Working Party on Accident Compensation 1991; Chair. Review of Defence Funding and Man. 1991, Wholesale Electricity Market Study 1991–92, Wholesale Electricity Market Devt Group 1993–94; NZ Commr to Int. Whaling Comm. 1994–2002; Chair. Roading Advisory Group 1997, Project Marukav Audit Group 1998, Council for Infrastructure Devt 2005–06; mem. Bd Evergreen Forests Ltd 1995–, MotorRace NZ Ltd 1996–99, Neurouz Ltd 2001–, Generator Bonds Ltd 2003–, Metlifecare Ltd 2005–; mem. Advisory Bd Westfield New Zealand Ltd 1998–; Adviser to Building Industry Authority on revision to earthquake codes 1997; Trustee, Auckland Medical School Foundation 1993–99; Nat. Party; Companion, NZ Order of Merit; NZ Suffrage Centennial Medal. *Publications:* numerous papers, articles, etc. on political, commercial and environmental issues. *Leisure interest:* trout fishing.

McLEAN, Alistair Murray, AO, BA; Australian diplomatist; b. 1947, Melbourne, Vic.; s. of Rev John Alistair Kenneth McLean; m.; two c.; ed Geelong Coll., Univs of Melbourne and Hong Kong; joined Dept of Foreign Affairs 1970, Asst Sec. E Asia Br. 1992–96, First Asst Sec. N Asia Div. 2001–04, Deputy Sec. 2004; overseas posts in Hong Kong 1971–73, Beijing 1973–76, Counsellor, Embassy in Beijing 1979–83, in Washington, DC 1983–86, Consul-Gen. in Shanghai 1987–92, High Commr to Singapore 1997–2001, Amb. to Japan 2004–11; Non-Resident Fellow, Lowy Inst. 2014–16, East Asia Program, 2018–; Order of Australia Medal 1991. *Leisure interests:* golf, tennis, classical music, Asian arts.

McLEAN, Dame Angela, DBE, MA, PhD, FRS; British mathematician, biologist and academic; *Professor of Mathematical Biology and Senior Research Fellow in Theoretical Life Sciences, All Souls College, University of Oxford;* ed Somerville Coll., Oxford, Univ. of California, Berkeley, USA, Imperial Coll., London; brief period working in City of London; joined Math. Biology Group at Nat. Inst. for Medical Research, Mill Hill, London; Royal Soc. Research Fellow, Univ. of Oxford 1990–98, secondment at Pasteur Inst., Paris 1994–98, Head of Math. Biology, Biotechnology and Biological Sciences Research Council's Inst. for Animal Health 1998–2000, Prof. of Math. Biology 2000–, Fellow of St Catherine's Coll., Oxford 2000–05, Dir Inst. for Emerging Infections of Humans, James Martin 21st Century School 2005–08, Co-Dir 2008–13, Sr Research Fellow in Theoretical Life Sciences, All Souls Coll., Oxford 2008–; mem. Science Advisory Council, Dept for Environment, Food and Rural Affairs, Nat. Expert Panel for New and Emerging Infections, Dept of Health; Prix Franco-britannique, Acad. des sciences 1996, Gabor Medal, Royal Soc. 2011. *Publications:* numerous papers in professional journals on the use of mathematical models to aid our understanding of the evolution and spread of infectious agents. *Address:* Institute for Emerging Infections, Department of Zoology, University of Oxford, South Parks Road, Oxford, OX1 3PS, England (office). *Telephone:* (1865) 271210 (office); (1865) 279379 (All Soul's College) (office). *Fax:* (1865) 310447 (office). *E-mail:* angela.mclean@zoo.ox.ac.uk (office). *Website:* www.zoo.ox.ac.uk (office); www.emdis.ox.ac.uk (office).

MacLEAN, Brian W., BA, MA; American business executive; *President and Chief Operating Officer, The Travelers Companies Inc.;* m. Kathy MacLean; six c.; ed Fordham Univ., Univ. of South Carolina; Audit Man., Peat Marwick (now KPMG LLP) –1988; joined Travelers 1988, served in several sr financial roles, Pres. of Select Accounts for Travelers Insurance Group Holdings, Inc. 1999–2002, Exec. Vice-Pres., Claim Services, The Travelers Companies Inc. 2002–05, Exec. Vice-Pres. and COO 2005–08, Pres. and COO 2008–; fmr Adjunct Prof., Gabelli School of Business, Fordham Univ.; Chair. Hartford Healthcare; mem. Bd of Trustees Fordham Univ., also Chair. Pres.'s Council. *Address:* The Travelers Companies Inc., 385 Washington Street, St Paul, MN 55102, USA (office). *Telephone:* (651) 310-7911 (office). *Fax:* (651) 310-3386 (office). *E-mail:* info@travelers.com (office). *Website:* www.travelers.com (office).

McLEAN, Don; American singer, instrumentalist and composer; b. 2 Oct. 1945, New Rochelle, NY; s. of Donald McLean and Elizabeth Bucci; m. Patrisha Shnier 1987 (divorced 2016); one s. one d.; ed Iona Coll.; Pres. Benny Bird Publishing Corpn, Inc., Don McLean Music, Starry Night Music; mem. Hudson River Sloop Singers 1969; solo concert tours throughout USA, Canada, Australia, Europe, Far East etc.; numerous TV appearances; composer of film scores for Fraternity Row, Flight of Dragons; composer of over 200 songs including Prime Time, American Pie, Tapestry, Vincent (Starry, Starry Night), And I Love You So, Castles In the Air, etc.; mem. American Soc. of Composers, Authors and Publrs, BMI Broadcast Music, Inc. (BMI), Nat. Acad. of Recording Arts and Sciences, American Fed. of Television and Radio Artists, Lotos Club, Coffee House NYC, Groucho Club, London; Dr hc (Iona Coll.) 2001; recipient of numerous gold discs in USA, Australia, UK and Ireland; Israel Cultural Award 1981, American Pie inducted into Grammy Hall of Fame 2002, inaugurated into Songwriters Hall of Fame 2004, lifetime Achievement Award for Folk Music, BBC Radio 2 2012. *Recordings include:* albums: Tapestry 1970, American Pie 1971, Don McLean 1972, Playin' Favorites 1973, Homeless Brother 1974, Solo 1976, Prime Time 1977, Chain Lightning 1979, Believers 1982, Dominion 1983, Love Tracks 1988, Headroom 1991, Don McLean Christmas 1992, Favorites and Rarities (Box Set) 1993, The River of Love 1995, For the Memories Vols I and II 1996, Christmas Dreams 1997, Starry Starry Night 2000, Don McLean Sings Marty Robbins 2001, The Western Album 2003, You've Got to Share 2003, Christmastime! 2004, Rearview Mirror 2005, Addicted to Black 2009, American Troubadour 2012, Live in Manchester 2014; singles include: The Mountains of Mourne 1973, Wonderful Baby 1975, Crying 1980, Since I Don't Have You 1981; hit cover versions: And I Love You So (Perry Como) 1973, American Pie (Madonna) 2000; compilation albums: The Very Best of Don McLean 1980, Don McLean's Greatest Hits – Then & Now 1987, The Best of Don McLean 1991, Favorites and Rarities 1992, Legendary Songs of Don McLean 2003, The Legendary Don McLean 2007, American Pie & Other Hits 2008. *Publications:* Songs of Don McLean 1972, The Songs of Don McLean (Vol. II) 1974. *Leisure interests:* antique furniture, film history, western horsemanship (trail riding). *Address:* c/o Guy Richard, 1880 Century Park East, Suite 711, Los Angeles, CA 90067, USA (office). *Telephone:* (310) 385-2800 (office). *Fax:* (310) 385-1220 (office). *E-mail:* guyrichard@theagencygroup.com (office). *Website:* www.theagencygroup.com (office); www.don-mclean.com.

McLEAN, (William Henry) Irwin, BSc, PhD, DSc, FRS, FRSE, FMedSci; British geneticist and academic; *Professor of Human Genetics, Head of Division of Molecular Medicine and Scientific Director, Centre for Dermatology and Genetic Medicine, University of Dundee;* b. 9 Jan. 1963, Ballymoney, Co. Antrim, Northern Ireland; ed Queen's Univ. of Belfast; Postdoctoral Research Fellow, Univ. of Dundee 1992–96; Assoc. Prof. in Dermatology and Cutaneous Biology, Thomas Jefferson Univ., Philadelphia, USA 1996–98; Prof. of Human Genetics, Head of Div. of Molecular Medicine and Scientific Dir Centre for Dermatology and Genetic Medicine, Univ. of Dundee 2002–; CERIES Dermatology Research Award 2006, Times Higher Research Project of the Year 2006, Paul Gerson Unna Dermatology Research Award 2007, Research Merit Award, Royal Soc. 2007, Achievement Award, American Skin Assn 2009, Buchanan Medal (hygienic science or practice), Royal Soc. 2015. *Publications:* numerous papers in professional journals on the genetic basis of heritable skin diseases. *Address:* College of Life Sciences, University of Dundee, Dow Street, Dundee, DD1 5EH, Scotland (office). *Telephone:* (1382) 381047 (office). *E-mail:* w.h.i.mclean@dundee.ac.uk (office). *Website:* www.lifesci.dundee.ac.uk (office).

McLEAN, Hon. Rev. Walter Franklin, PC, BA, LLD, MDiv, DD; Canadian politician, clergyman and business consultant; *Honorary Consul for Namibia in Canada;* b. 26 April 1936, Leamington, Ont.; s. of J. Lewis W. McLean and Frances Blair McLean; m. Barbara Scott 1961; four s.; ed Victoria Coll., Univ. of Victoria, Univ. of British Columbia, Knox Coll., Univ. of Toronto, Univ. of Edinburgh; Pres. Students' Admin. Council, Univ. of Toronto 1959-60; Pres. Nat. Fed. of Canadian Univ. Students 1961–62; Presbyterian mission staff, Nigeria 1962–67; Chaplain Univ. of Nigeria; Minister St Andrew's Presbyterian Church, Enugu; Co-ordinator CUSO 1963–67; Exec. Dir Man. Centennial Corpn 1969–71; Minister of Knox Presbyterian Church, Waterloo 1971–79; Alderman for City of Waterloo 1976–79; MP 1979–93; fmr mem. Standing Cttee on Communications and Culture, on External Affairs, on Nat. Defence; fmr mem. Special Sub-Cttee on Latin America and Caribbean; sworn to Privy Council 1984, Sec. of State of Canada 1984–85, Minister of State (Immigration) and Minister Responsible for the Status of Women 1984–86; mem. Canadian Del. to UN 1986–93; Prime Minister's Special Rep. on Southern Africa and Commonwealth Affairs 1989–93; Canadian Rep. at Southern Africa Devt Co-ordination Conf. (SADCC) 1987–93, at Commonwealth Foreign Ministers' Confs 1987, 1988, 1989, 1991; Chair. Parl. Sub-cttee on Devt and Human Rights 1990–93; Hon. Consul for Namibia in Canada 1993–; Pres. Franklin Consulting Services Ltd 1994–; Convenor Millennium Celebration, Presbyterian Church in Canada 2000; Prin. Osborne Group 2000–11; Pres. McLean and Associates 2004–; fmr Pres. Int. Council of Parliamentarians for Global Action; Chair. Canadian UNA Human Rights Cttee, Criminal Compensation Bd of Ontario 2000–03; Dir TAB/Ambit International, Calgary 2005–10; mem. Advisory Bd Royal Reads Univ., Victoria, BC 1995–2011, Bd Toronto School of Theology, Univ. of Toronto 2005–07; Hon. LLD (Wilfrid Laurier) 1995, Hon. DD (Knox Coll. Toronto) 2002; Paul Harris Fellow, Rotary International 1984, Canada's 125th Anniversary Medal 1992, Canadian Bureau for Int. Educ. Award of Merit 1994, Queen's 50th Anniversary Medal 2002, Distinguished Alumni Award (Univ. of Victoria) 2002. *Publication:* Parliamentary Report: Canada's Relations With Southern Africa 1992. *Leisure interests:* golf, curling, music. *Address:* 424-139 Father David Bauer Dr., Waterloo, Ont. N2L 6L1, Canada (office). *Telephone:* (519) 578-5932 (office). *Fax:* (519) 578-7799 (office). *E-mail:* walter@mcleanandassociates.ca (office). *Website:* www.namibiaembassyusa.org (office); www.mcleanandassociates.ca (office).

MACLEAN OF PENNYCROSS, Nicolas Wolfers Lorne, CMG, MA; British economist and strategic analyst; *Chief Executive, MWM (Strategy);* b. (Nicolas

Lorne Maclean Wolfers), 3 Jan. 1946, London, England; s. of Marcel Wolfers and Audrey Wolfers (née Maclean of Pennycross); m. Qamar Sultan Aziz 22 Aug. 1978; two s.; ed Eton Coll., Oriel Coll., Oxford; fmrly with Schroders, Kemp-Gee, Samuel Montagu, Midland Bank Group; fmr Group Adviser, Prudential Corpn, and Exec. Dir Prudential Corpn Asia Ltd; Sr Fellow for Int. Affairs, IISS 2000–07; Chief Exec. MWM (Strategy) 2007–; mem. Chatham House Council, Chair. of Membership 1988–94; fmr mem. Jt Exec., currently Advisory Bd, British-American Project; fmr mem. Bd, UK-Korea Forum for the Future; mem. Council, Canada-UK Colloquia, UK Adviser for colloquia 2009, 2011, 2012; Founder-mem. UK-Japan 21st Century Group; fmr Chair. Business-Europe (UNICE) Asia Cttee, Brussels; Jt Chair. Japan400 2012–; fmr Chair. Japan Festival Educ. Trust; Founder British English Teaching Programme, prototype for Japan Exchange and Teaching (JET) Programme; Coordinator for the Sponsors, 'The Great Japan Exhibition: Art of the Edo Period 1600–1868', Royal Acad. of Arts, London 1981–82; Special Adviser, 'Treasures from Korea: Two Thousand Years of Korean Civilization', British Museum 1983–84 (innovated with first ever Public Pvt. Partnership); Organiser, 'Visions from Vietnam', Royal Coll. of Art 1998; Gov., Sadler's Wells Theatre 1988–99; Pres. Clan Maclean Asscn of England and Wales 2009–; Fellow Emer., British Asscn of Japanese Studies 2003; Special Millennium Award, Japan Soc. 2000. *Publications:* Trading with China: A Practical Guide (co-author) 1979, Journey into Japan 1600–1868 (co-author) 1981, The Eurobond and Eurocurrency Markets (co-author) 1984, Mongolia Today (co-author) 1988; several articles. *Leisure interests:* reading, cinema, theatre, exhbns, listening to music, travel, rowing, Scotland, Isle of Mull. *Address:* MWM (Strategy), 30 Malwood Road, London, SW12 8EN, England (office). *Telephone:* (20) 8675-6886 (office). *E-mail:* nmatmwm@hotmail.com (office).

McLEISH, Rt Hon Henry, PC; British politician and academic; b. 15 June 1948, Methil, Fife, Scotland; m. 1st (died 1995); one s. one d.; m. 2nd Julie McLeish 1998; ed Buckhaven High School, Methil, Heriot-Watt Univ.; fmr professional football for East Fife FC and Leeds United FC; began career as local govt research officer and planning officer; lecturer in Social Sciences, Heriot-Watt Univ. 1973–87; mem. Kirkcaldy Dist Council 1974–77; mem. Fife Regional Council 1978–87, Leader 1982–87; MSP for Fife Cen. 1999–2001, Opposition Spokesman on Social Security 1996–97; Minister for Enterprise and Lifelong Learning 1997–2000; First Minister of Scotland 2000–01; Consultant on Govt and Political Relations, Halogen Communications 2005; mem. Scottish Broadcasting Comm. 2007–; Visiting Prof., Univ. of Arkansas, USA, Fulbright Coll. of Arts and Sciences, Grad. School of Int. Studies, Univ. of Denver; Visiting Lecturer, US Air Force Acad.; Hon. Fellow, Coll. of Humanities and Social Science, Univ. of Edinburgh, Cambridge Land Inst., Fitzwilliam Coll., Cambridge. *Publications:* Scotland First: Truth and Consequences 2004, Global Scots: Voices from Afar (with Kenny MacAskill) 2006, Wherever the Saltire Flies (with Kenny MacAskill) 2006, Scotland: The Road Divides (with Tom Brown) 2007. *Leisure interests:* reading, history, life and work of Robert Burns. *Address:* Old College, South Bridge, University of Edinburgh, Edinburgh, EH8 9YL, Scotland (office). *Telephone:* (13) 1650-1000 (office). *Fax:* (13) 1650-2147 (office). *E-mail:* communications.office@ed.ac.uk (office). *Website:* www.ed.ac.uk (office).

McLELLAN, Rt Hon. Anne, OC, PC, BA, LLB, LLM; Canadian lawyer, academic and fmr politician; *Chancellor, Dalhousie University;* b. 31 Aug. 1950, Hants. Co., Nova Scotia; d. of Howard Gilmore McLellan and Joan Mary Pullan; ed Dalhousie Univ. and King's Coll. London, UK; Asst Prof. of Law, Univ. of New Brunswick 1976–80; Acting Assoc. Dean and Assoc. Prof. of Law, Univ. of Alberta 1980–89, Assoc. Dean 1985–87, Prof. 1989–93, Acting Dean 1991–92; MP for Edmonton W. 1993–2006; Minister of Natural Resources and Fed. Interlocutor for Métis and Non-Status Indians 1993–97; Minister of Justice and Attorney-Gen. 1997–2002; Minister of Health 2002–03; Deputy Prime Minister and Minister of Public Safety and Emergency Preparedness 2003–06; Counsel, Bennett Jones LLP, Edmonton 2006–; Distinguished Scholar-in-Residence, Inst. for American Studies, Univ. of Alberta 2006–13; Chancellor, Dalhousie Univ. 2015–; Chair. Social Union Cttee 1997; Vice-Chair. Special Cttee of Council 1997; fmr Vice-Pres. Univ. of Alberta Faculty Asscn; mem. Econ. Union Cttee 1997, Treasury Bd 1997, Premier's Council for Econ. Strategy; mem. Bd Agrium Inc., Cameco Corpn, Edmonton Regional Airport Authority; fmr mem. Bd of Dirs Canadian Civil Liberties Asscn, Alberta Legal Aid; mem. Advisory Panel, Health Quality Council of Alberta 2011; Alberta Order of Excellence 2013; Hon. DrIur (Univ. of Alberta) 2007, (Cape Breton Univ.). *Address:* Bennett Jones LLP, 10020 100 Street NW, Edmonton, AB T5J 0N3, Canada (office). *Telephone:* (780) 421-8133 (office). *Website:* www.bennettjones.com (office); www.annemclellan.ca; www.dal.ca/dept/senior-administration/chancellor.html.

MacLENNAN, Murdoch; British newspaper executive; began career as graduate trainee, The Scotsman newspaper; Production Dir Scottish Daily Record and Sunday Mail 1982–84; Dir of Production, Mirror Group 1984–85; Production and Tech. Dir, Express Newspapers 1985–89; Man. Dir 1989–92; Group Operations Dir, Mirror Group Newspapers and Man. Dir Scottish Daily Record and Sunday Mail 1992–94; Group Man. Dir, Associated Newspapers 1994–2004; CEO Telegraph Media Group Ltd 2004–17; fmr Pres. IFRA (newspaper publrs' asscn); Chair. Press Asscn Remuneration Cttee; Vice-Pres. and Appeals Chair. Newspaper Press Fund; Chair. (non-exec.) PA Group 2010–; Vice-Chair. World Asscn of Newspapers; mem. Comm. on Scottish Devolution; Chancellor's Assessor, Univ. of Glasgow; Companion Inst. of Man.; Freeman of the City of London; Dr hc (Paisley); MacMillan Memorial Lecturer, Inst. of Engineers and Shipbuilders in Scotland 1998. *Address:* 111 Buckingham Palace Road, London, SW1W 0DT, England.

MACLENNAN OF ROGART, Baron (Life peer), cr. 2001, of Rogart Sutherland; **Rt Hon. Robert Adam Ross Maclennan,** PC, MA, LLB; British politician and barrister; b. 26 June 1936, Glasgow, Scotland; s. of Sir Hector Maclennan and Lady Maclennan; m. Helen Cutter Noyes 1968; one s. one d. one step-s.; ed Glasgow Acad., Balliol Coll., Oxford, Trinity Coll., Cambridge, Columbia Univ., New York; MP for Caithness and Sutherland 1966–97, Caithness, Sutherland and Easter Ross 1997–2001; Parl. Pvt. Sec. to Sec. of State for Commonwealth Affairs and Minister without portfolio 1967–70, Parl. Under-Sec. of State for Prices and Consumer Protection 1974–79; Opposition Spokesman on Scottish Affairs 1970–71, on Defence 1971–72, on Foreign Affairs 1980–81; resgnd from Labour Party 1981; Founder mem. SDP 1981; SDP Spokesman on Agriculture 1981–87, on

Home and Legal Affairs 1983–87, on Econ. Affairs 1987; Leader SDP 1987–88; Jt Leader SLD 1988; Liberal Democrat convenor on Home Affairs 1988–94, Legal Affairs 1988–94, Nat. Heritage 1992–94; mem. Public Accounts Cttee 1979–2001; Liberal Democrat 1994–98, Spokesperson on Constitutional Affairs, Culture and Media 1994–2001; mem. Convention on Future of Europe 2002–03; Liberal Democrats Lords Spokesman on Europe 2001–04, European Constitution 2004–05, Scotland 2004–09, Cabinet Office 2005–10, Constitutional Affairs 2007–, Select Cttee on Europe 2010–, Sub-cttee on External Policy of EU 2010–; Chevalier, Légion d'honneur 2004. *Opera libretti:* The Lie 1992 and Friend of the People 1999. *Leisure interests:* music, theatre and visual arts. *Address:* House of Lords, London, SW1A 0PW, England (office). *Telephone:* (20) 7219-5353 (office). *Fax:* (20) 7219-5979 (office). *E-mail:* maclennanr@parliament.uk (office).

MACLEOD, Hugh Angus MacIntosh, BSc, DTech; American (b. British) professor of optical sciences and business executive; *President, Thin Film Center Inc.;* b. 20 June 1933, Glasgow, Scotland; s. of Dr John Macleod and Agnes Donaldson Macleod; m. Ann Turner 1957; four s. one d.; ed Lenzie Acad., Univ. of Glasgow; engineer, Sperry Gyroscope Co. Ltd 1954–60; Chief Engineer, Williamson Mfg Co. Ltd 1960–62; Sr Physicist, Mervyn Instruments Ltd 1963; Tech. Man. Sir Howard Grubb, Parsons and Co. Ltd 1963–70; Reader in Thin Film Physics, Newcastle upon Tyne Polytechnic 1971–79; Assoc. Prof., Univ. of Aix-Marseille III 1976, 1979; Prof. of Optical Sciences, Univ. of Arizona, USA 1979–95, Prof. Emer. of Optical Sciences 1995–; Dir-at-Large, Optical Soc. of America 1987–89; Pres. Thin Film Center Inc. 1992–; Dir OptoSigma Corpn 1995–98, Precision Optics Corpn 1997–2002; Dir Soc. of Vacuum Coaters 1998–2004, Vice-Pres. 2006–08, Pres. 2008–10; Fellow, Int. Soc. for Optical Eng (SPIE), Optical Soc. of America, Inst. of Physics (London); Dr hc (Aix-Marseille); Gold Medal SPIE 1987, Esther Hoffman Beller Medal, Optical Soc. of America 1997, John Matteuci Award 2000, Nathaniel H. Sugerman Award 2002, Life for Thin Film Award, Workshop of European Vacuum Coaters, Anzio 2004, Senator Award, Workshop of European Vacuum Coaters, Anzio 2008. *Publications:* Thin-Film Optical Filters 1969 (4th edn 2010); more than 200 articles, papers and book chapters on optics of thin films. *Leisure interests:* piano, computing. *Address:* Thin Film Center, Inc., 2745 East Via Rotonda, Tucson, AZ 85716-5227, USA (office). *Telephone:* (520) 322-6171 (office); (520) 795-5019 (home). *Fax:* (520) 325-8721 (office). *E-mail:* angus@thinfilmcenter.com (office). *Website:* www.thinfilmcenter.com (office).

McLEOD, James Graham, AO, MD, DPhil, DSc, FRACP, FRCP, FAA, FTSE; Australian professor of neurology and medicine; *Professor Emeritus of Neurology, University of Sydney;* b. 18 Jan. 1932, Sydney, NSW; s. of Hector R. McLeod and Dorothy S. McLeod (née Craig); m. Robyn E. Rule 1962; two s. two d.; ed Univ. of Sydney, Univs of Oxford and London, UK, Harvard Univ., USA; Sr Lecturer, Univ. of Sydney 1967–69, Assoc. Prof. 1970–72, Bosch Prof. of Medicine 1972–97, Bushell Prof. of Neurology 1978–97, Prof. Emer. 1997–; Visiting Medical Officer, Royal Prince Alfred Hosp., Sydney 1965–97, Head, Dept of Neurology 1978–94, Hon. Consultant Physician 1997–; mem. Bd Dirs Royal North Shore Hosp., Sydney (Vice-Chair.) 1978–86; Pres. Australian Asscn of Neurologists 1980–83; Rhodes Scholar 1953–56; Nuffield Travelling Fellow 1964–65; Sir Arthur Sims Travelling Prof. 1983–84; Commonwealth Sr Medical Fellowship 1989; mem. Australian Science and Tech. Council 1987–93; Fellow, Australian Acad. of Tech., Science and Eng, Australian Acad. of Science (Vice-Pres. 1987–88, Treas. 1993–97); Dr hc (Aix-Marseille) 1992; Rhodes Scholar 1953. *Publications include:* A Physiological Approach to Clinical Neurology (with J. W. Lance), Introductory Neurology (with J. W. Lance) 1989, Peripheral Neuropathy in Childhood (with R. A. Ouvrier and J. D. Pollard) 1999, Inflammatory Neuropathies (ed.) 1994. *Leisure interests:* swimming, boating, music, literature. *Address:* 2 James Street, Woollahra, NSW 2025, Australia (home). *Telephone:* (2) 9362-8362 (home). *Fax:* (2) 9362-8348 (home). *E-mail:* james.mcleod@sydney.edu.au (home).

MACLEOD, Sir (Nathaniel William) Hamish, Kt, KBE, MA; British civil servant (retd); b. 6 Jan. 1940; s. of George Henry Torquil Macleod and Ruth Natalie Wade; m. Fionna Mary Campbell 1970; one s. one d.; ed Strathallan School, Perthshire, St Andrews Univ., Univ. of Bristol; commercial trainee Stewarts and Lloyds, Birmingham 1958–62; Admin. Officer Hong Kong Govt 1966, Dir of Trade and Chief Trade Negotiator 1983–87, Sec. for Trade and Industry 1987–89, Sec. for the Treasury 1989–91, Financial Sec. 1991–95; JP (Hong Kong) 1979–95; mem. Bd Scottish Oriental Smaller Cos Trust 1995–2011, Morgan Fleming Asian Investment Trust 1997–2003. *Leisure interests:* walking, golf. *Address:* 20 York Road, Edinburgh, EH5 3EH, Scotland (home). *Telephone:* (131) 552-5058 (home). *E-mail:* macleodhamish@hotmail.com (home).

McLOUGHLIN, Rt Hon. Sir Patrick Allen, Kt; British politician; b. 30 Nov. 1957, Stafford, Staffs.; m. Lynn Newman 1984; one s. one d.; ed Cardinal Griffin Roman Catholic School, Cannock, Staffordshire Coll. of Agric. at Rodbaston Coll.; farm worker 1974–79; miner at Littleton Colliery, Cannock from 1979; mem. Nat. Union of Mineworkers, becoming an industrial rep. for Nat. Coal Bd's Western Area Marketing Dept; Councillor, Cannock Chase Dist Council 1980–87, Staffordshire Co. Council 1981–87; contested Wolverhampton SE constituency 1983; MP for W Derbyshire (by-election) 1986–2010, for Derbyshire Dales 2010–, mem. (Select Cttees), Broadcasting 1994–95, Selection 1997–2001, Finance and Services 1998–2005, Accommodation and Works 2001–05, Modernization of the House of Commons 2004–05, Selection 2005, Admin 2005, Parl. and Political Service Honours 2012; Parl. Pvt. Sec. to Angela Rumbold as Minister of State, Dept of Educ. 1987–88, to Lord Young of Graffham as Sec. of State for Trade and Industry 1988–89; Parl. Under-Sec. of State, Dept of Transport (Minister for Aviation and Shipping) 1989–92; Jt Parl. Under-Sec. of State, Dept of Employment 1992–93; Parl. Under-Sec., Dept of Trade and Industry (Trade and Tech.) 1993–94; Asst Govt Whip 1995–96, Govt Whip 1996–97; Opposition: Pairing Whip 1997–98, Deputy Chief Whip 1998–2005, Chief Whip 2005–10; Parl. Sec. to the Treasury 2010–12; Chief Whip 2010–12; Sec. of State for Transport 2012–16; Chancellor of the Duchy of Lancaster 2016–18; Nat. Vice-Chair. Young Conservatives 1982–84; Chair. Conservative Party 2016–18; Conservative. *Leisure interests:* walking, gardening. *Address:* House of Commons, Westminster, London, SW1A 0AA, England (office). *Telephone:* (20) 7219-3511 (office). *E-mail:* psleaderofthelords@cabinetoffice.gov.uk (office); patrick.mcloughlin.mp@parliament.uk (office).

McMAHON, Linda Marie, BA; American government official and fmr sports administrator; b. 4 Oct. 1948, New Bern, N Carolina; d. of Henry Edwards and

Evelyn Edwards; m. Vincent McMahon 1966; one s. one d.; ed East Carolina Univ.; Co-founder World Wrestling Entertainment, Inc. (WWE, professional wrestling franchise) 1980, becoming Pres. 1993 and CEO 1997–2009; unsuccessful cand. for Senator from Connecticut 2010, 2012; Admin., US Small Business Admin 2017–19; mem. Conn. State Bd of Educ. 2009–10; Republican. *Address:* c/o US Small Business Administration, 409 3rd Street, SW, Washington, DC 20416, USA.

McMANUS, Sean J., BA; American broadcasting executive; *Chairman, CBS Sports;* b. 16 Feb. 1955; s. of Jim McKay; ed Fairfield Coll. Preparatory School, Conn., Duke Univ.; with ABC (American Broadcasting Corpn) Sports 1977–79, positions including Production Asst, Assoc. Producer; Assoc. Producer NBC Sports 1979, Vice-Pres. Program Planning and Devt 1982–87; joined Trans World International 1987, Sr Vice-Pres. US TV Sales and Programming –1996; Pres. CBS Sports 1996–2011, Chair. 2011–, Exec. Producer Nat. Football League (NFL) on CBS, Pres. CBS News 2005–11; ten-time Emmy Award-winner, inducted into the Broadcasting & Cable Hall of Fame 2010. *Address:* CBS Sports, 1401 West Cypress Creek Road, Fort Lauderdale, FL 33309, USA (office). *E-mail:* pr@cbssports.com (office). *Website:* www.cbssports.com/cbssports/team/smcmanus (office).

McMASTER, Sir Brian John, Kt, CBE, LLB; British arts administrator; b. 9 May 1943, Hitchin, Herts.; ed Wellington Coll., Univ. of Bristol; with Int. Artists' Dept, EMI Ltd 1968–73; Controller of Opera Planning, ENO 1973–76; Gen. Admin., subsequently Man. Dir Welsh Nat. Opera 1976–91; Artistic Dir Vancouver Opera 1984–89; Festival Dir and CEO Edin. Int. Festival 1991–2006; mem. Bd Barbican Centre 2009–, Manchester International Festival; Artistic Adviser, Cultural Olympiad 2012.

McMASTER, Henry Dargan, BA, JD; American lawyer and politician; *Governor of South Carolina;* b. 27 May 1947; s. of William Appleby McMaster and Linda Ann McMaster (née Beljambe); m. Peggy McMaster 1978; two c.; ed Univ. of South Carolina; served in US Army Reserves 1969–75; admitted to Richland County Bar Asscn (South Carolina Bar) 1973; Legis. Asst to Senator Strom Thurmond 1973–74; entered private practice with Tompkins & McMaster (family law business) 1974; US Attorney for Dist of South Carolina 1981–85, Head, SC Law Enforcement Coordinating Cttee 1981–85; mem. SC Comm. on Higher Educ. 1991–; mem. Bd of Dirs SC Policy Council 1991–2003 (Chair. 1992–93); Attorney-Gen. of South Carolina 2003–11; Lt Gov. of South Carolina 2015–17; Gov. of South Carolina 2017–; Republican, mem. Republican Nat. Cttee 1993–2002, Chair. SC Republican Party 1994–2001; Order of the Palmetto 1996. *Address:* Office of the Governor, State House, POB 12267, Columbia, SC 29211, USA (office). *Telephone:* (803) 734-2100 (office). *Fax:* (803) 734-5167 (office). *Website:* www.governor.sc.gov (office); www.henrymcmaster.com (office).

McMASTER, Lt-Gen. H(erbert) R(aymond), MA, PhD; American army officer and fmr government official; b. 24 July 1962; m. Kathleen Trotter; three d.; ed Valley Forge Mil. Acad., US Mil. Acad., West Point, Univ. of North Carolina at Chapel Hill, Stanford Univ. Hoover Inst. (Army War Coll. research fellowship); commissioned as officer in US Army 1984; several platoon and company level leadership assignments with 1st Bn 66th Armor Regt, 2nd Armored Div., Fort Hood; assigned to 2nd Armored Cavalry Regt 1989–92 (including deployment to Iraq during Operation Desert Storm); Squadron Exec. Officer and Regimental Operations Officer, 11th Armored Cavalry Regt 1997–99; Commdr, 1st Squadron, 4th Cavalry Regt 1999–2002; Dir, Commdr's Advisory Group, US Central Command 2003–04; Commdr, 3rd Armored Cavalry Regt 2004–06 (commanded regt during second tour in Iraq); Sr Research Assoc., Int. Inst. for Strategic Studies, London 2006; Advisor to Gen. David Petraeus, Commdr, Multinational Force-Iraq 2007–08; rank of Brig. Gen. 2008, Maj. Gen. 2012, Lt Gen. 2014; Dir, Concept Devt and Experimentation, Army Capabilities Integration Center 2008–10; Deputy to Commdr for Planning, Int. Security Assistance Forces HQ, Kabul, Afghanistan 2010; Commdr, Army Maneuver Center of Excellence, Fort Benning 2012–14; Deputy Commdr, Training and Doctrine Command and Dir, Army Capabilities Integration Center 2014–17; Nat. Security Advisor 2017–18; Asst Prof. of History, US Mil. Acad. 1994–96; Contributing Ed. Survival magazine; mem. Council on Foreign Relations; Order of the Spur Cavalry Hat and Spurs (Gold); numerous mil. awards including Army Distinguished Service Medal, Silver Star Defense Superior Service Medal, Legion of Merit, Bronze Star, Purple Heart, Defense Meritorious Service Medal, Army Meritorious Service Medal, Jt Service Commendation Medal. *Publications:* Dereliction of Duty: Lyndon Johnson, Robert McNamara, The Joint Chiefs of Staff, and the Lies that Led to Vietnam 1997; numerous articles on historical and national security affairs in various newspapers, magazines and professional journals.

McMILLAN, C. Steven, MBA; American business executive; b. Troy, Ala; twice divorced; two d.; ed Auburn Univ., Ala, Harvard Business School (Baker Scholar); supply officer, USN 1970–73; man. consultant, McKinsey & Co., Chicago 1973–78; joined Sara Lee Corpn 1978, Pres. and CEO Aqualux Water Processing Co. 1978–79, Pres. and CEO Electrolux Canada 1979–82, Pres. and CEO Electrolux Corpn 1982–86, Sr Vice-Pres., Strategy Devt, Sara Lee Corpn 1986–90, Head of Packaged Meats, Bakery and Foodservices Businesses 1990–93, and Coffee & Grocery and Household & Bodycare Businesses 1993–97, Pres. and COO Sara Lee Corpn 1997–2000, Pres. and CEO 2000–01, Chair., Pres. and CEO 2001–04, Chair. and CEO 2004–05; mem. Bd of Dirs Monsanto 2000–18; fmr Dir, Bank of America; mem. Advisory Bd J.L. Kellogg Grad. School of Man., Northwestern Univ.; mem. Bd Grocery Mfrs Asscn, Econ. Club of Chicago, Chicago Council on Foreign Relations, Catalyst; mem. Business Council, The Business Roundtable, G-100, Exec. Club of Chicago, Civic Cttee of Commercial Club of Chicago; serves on Bd of Steppenwolf Theatre Co.; Trustee, Chicago Symphony Orchestra; Dir Sara Lee Foundation, Charlie Trotter's Culinary Educ. Foundation.

McMILLAN, David Loch, MA; British civil servant and international organization executive; *Chairman, Board of Governors, Flight Safety Foundation;* b. 16 Sept. 1954, Edinburgh, Scotland; ed Univ. of Edinburgh; began his career in FCO 1976, served in Morocco and Zimbabwe, also worked as Transport Sec.-Gen. at British Embassy in Washington, DC; held several posts in Dept of Transport (DfT), including Head of Information, Leader Div. responsible for air traffic control policy 1998–2001, DfT Dir of Rail Restructuring 2001–02, Dir of Strategy and Delivery, responsible for DfT's delivery agenda and for relations with the EU 2002–04, Dir-Gen. of Civil Aviation 2004–07; Dir Gen. EUROCONTROL (European Org. for the Safety of Air Navigation) 2008–12; Chair. Bd of Govs Flight Safety Foundation 2012–; mem. Bd of Dirs Gatwick Airport Limited 2013–; First Vice-Pres. European Civil Aviation Conf. and spokesman for Europe on aviation and environment at Int. Civil Aviation Org. 2005–07; participated in EU's High Level Group on the future of aviation regulation in Europe 2006, 2007. *Address:* Flight Safety Foundation, 801 North Fairfax Street, Suite 400, Alexandria, VA 22314-1774, USA (office). *Telephone:* (703) 739-6700 (office). *Website:* flightsafety.org (office).

MacMILLAN, David W. C., BSc, PhD, FRS; British chemist and academic; *James S. McDonnell Distinguished University Professor, Princeton University;* b. Bellshill, Scotland; ed Univ. of Glasgow, Univ. of California, Irvine, USA; Postdoctoral Research Fellow, Harvard Univ., USA 1996–98; ind. research at Univ. of California, Berkeley, USA 1998–2000; mem. Faculty, California Inst. of Tech., USA 2000–06, Earle C. Anthony Chair of Organic Chem. 2004–06; A. Barton Hepburn Prof. of Chem., Princeton Univ., USA 2006–11, Dir Merck Center for Catalysis 2006–, Chair. Dept of Chem. 2010–, James S. McDonnell Distinguished Univ. Prof. 2011–; Ed.-in-Chief Chemical Science 2010–; mem. Editorial Advisory Bd, Tetrahedron 2001–, Tetrahedron Letters 2001–, Chemical Communications 2004–, Chemistry, An Asian Journal 2005–, Advanced Synthesis & Catalysis 2009–; Co-founder Chiromics, mem. Scientific Advisory Bd 2010–; mem. American Acad. of Arts and Sciences 2012; Boehringer-Ingelheim New Investigator Award 2000, Woodward Scholarship Award, Harvard Univ. 2001, Cottrell Scholar Award 2001, Astra-Zeneca Excellence in Chem. Award 2001, Eli-Lilly New Investigator Award 2001, Glaxo Smithkline Chem. Scholar Award 2001, Eli-Lilly Grantee Award 2001, Pfizer Award for Excellence in Synthesis 2002, Bristol-Meyers Squibb Award for Organic Synthesis 2002, Sloan Fellowship 2002, Camille and Henry Dreyfus Teacher-Scholar Award 2003, Corday-Morgan Medal, Royal Inst. of Chem. 2005, Tetrahedron Young Investigator Award 2005, Elias J. Corey Award for Outstanding Contrib. in Organic Synthesis by a Young Investigator 2005, Thieme-IUPAC Prize in Organic Synthesis 2006, ACS Cope Scholar Award 2007, ISHC Award in Heterocyclic Chem. 2007, Mukaiyama Award 2007, ACS Award for Creative Work in Synthetic Organic Chem. 2011, Harrison Howe Award 2014, Ernst Schering Prize 2015. *Publications:* numerous papers in professional journals on asymmetric organocatalysis and the synthesis of complex natural products. *Address:* Frick Laboratory, Washington Road, Princeton, NJ 08544, USA (office). *Telephone:* (609) 258-2254 (Asst) (office); (626) 354-7502 (mobile) (office). *E-mail:* dmacmill@princeton.edu (office). *Website:* www.princeton.edu/chemistry (office).

MacMILLAN, Margaret Olwen, CH, CC, BA, BPhil, DPhil, FRSL; Canadian university administrator, historian and writer; *Professor of History, University of Toronto;* b. 23 Dec. 1943, Toronto, Ont.; d. of Robert Laidlaw MacMillan and Eluned Carey Evans; ed Univ. of Toronto, St Hilda's Coll., St Antony's Coll., Oxford, UK; Prof. of History, Ryerson Univ., Toronto 1975–2002; Provost and Vice Chancellor, Trinity Coll., Univ. of Toronto 2002–07; Warden St Antony's Coll., Oxford 2007–17; currently Prof. of History, Univ. of Toronto; Ed. International Journal 1995–2003; delivered BBC Reith Lectures 2018; Sr Fellow, Massey Coll., Univ. of Toronto; Hon. Fellow, St Hilda's Coll., Oxford, Massey Coll., Toronto, Lady Margaret Hall, St Antony's Coll. *Publications include:* Women of the Raj 1988, Canada and NATO: Uneasy Past, Uncertain Future 1990, Peacemakers: the Paris Conference of 1919 and Its Attempt to Make Peace 2001, Paris 1919: Six Months that Changed the World (Samuel Johnson Prize for Non-Fiction, Duff Cooper Award, Hessell-Tiltman Prize for History, Gov.-Gen.'s Literary Award 2003) 2002, Parties Long Estranged: Canada and Australia in the 20th Century (co-ed.) 2003, Canada's House: Rideau Hall and the Invention of a Canadian Home (with Marjorie Harris and Anne L. Desjardins) 2004, Seize the Hour: When Nixon Met Mao 2006, Nixon and Mao 2007, Dangerous Games: The Uses and Abuses of History 2009, The War that Ended Peace: How Europe Abandoned Peace for the First World War 2013, History's People 2016. *Leisure interests:* opera, film, ski-ing, hiking. *Address:* c/o Caroline Dawnay, United Agents, 12–26 Lexington Avenue, London, W1F 0LE, England (office). *Telephone:* (20) 3214-0882 (office). *Fax:* (20) 3214-0802 (office). *E-mail:* sscard@unitedagents.co.uk (office); margaret.macmillan@sant.ox.ac.uk (office). *Website:* www.unitedagents.co.uk (office); www.margaretmacmillan.com.

McMILLON, (Carl Douglas) Doug, BS, MBA; American business executive; *President and CEO, Wal-Mart Stores, Inc.;* b. 17 Oct. 1966, Memphis, Tenn.; s. of Morris McMillon and Laura McMillon; m. Shelley McMillon; two s.; ed Univ. of Arkansas, Univ. of Tulsa; began as an hourly summer assoc. in a Walmart distribution centre 1984, rejoined co. as an Asst Man. in a Tulsa Walmart store 1990, moved to merchandising as a buyer trainee, subsequently served in several exec. positions, Sr Vice-Pres. and Gen. Merchandise Man. 1999–2002, Exec. Vice-Pres. Sam's Club (operating segment of Walmart) 2002–05, Pres. and CEO Sam's Club 2005–09, Pres. and CEO Walmart International 2009–14, mem. Bd of Dirs 2013–, Pres. and CEO Wal-Mart Stores, Inc. (Walmart) 2014–; mem. Pres.'s Strategic and Policy Forum Jan.–Aug. 2017; mem. Bd of Dirs Consumer Goods Forum, Enactus, Crystal Bridges Museum of American Art; fmr Dir, Walmart Mexico, US China Business Council; mem. Exec. Cttee Business Roundtable, Dean's Advisory Bd for Walton Coll. of Business at Univ. of Arkansas. *Address:* Walmart, 702 SW 8th Street, Bentonville, AR 72716-8611, USA (office). *Telephone:* (479) 273-4000 (office). *Fax:* (479) 277-1830 (office); (479) 277-4053 (office). *Website:* www.walmart.com (office); corporate.walmart.com (office).

McMULLEN, (William) Rodney, BA, BBA, MA; American business executive; *Chairman and CEO, The Kroger Company;* m. Kathy McMullen; ed Univ. of Kentucky; joined The Kroger Co. as a part-time stock clerk in Lexington, Ky 1978, has served in numerous positions, including Financial Analyst 1985–88, Asst Treas. 1988–90, Vice-Pres. of Planning and Capital Man. 1990–93, Vice-Pres. Financial services and Control 1993–95, Group Vice-Pres. and Chief Financial Officer 1995–97, Sr Vice-Pres. and Chief Financial Officer 1997–2000, Exec. Vice-Pres. of Strategy, Planning and Finance 2000–03, Vice-Chair. 2003–09, mem. Bd of Dirs 2003, Pres. and COO The Kroger Co. 2009–14, CEO 2014–, Chair. 2015–; Chair. Bd of Govs GS1 US 2010–; mem. Bd of Dirs, Cincinnati Financial Corpn; mem. Bd of Trustees Xavier Univ., Business Partnership Foundation, Gatton Coll. of Business and Econs at Univ. of Kentucky. *Leisure interests:* travelling, hiking. *Address:* The Kroger Company, 1014 Vine Street, Cincinnati, OH 45202-1100, USA (office). *Telephone:* (513) 762-4000 (office). *Fax:* (513) 762-1160 (office).

E-mail: info@kroger.com (office); kroger.investors@kroger.com (office). *Website:* www.kroger.com (office); www.thekrogerco.com (office).

McMURTRY, Larry Jeff, BA, MA; American writer; b. 3 June 1936, Wichita Falls, Tex.; s. of William Jefferson McMurtry and Hazel McIver; m. Josephine Ballard 1959 (divorced 1966); one s.; m. Norma Faye Kesey 2011; ed Univ. of North Texas, Rice Univ.; Nat. Humanities Medal 2015. *Television includes:* co-writer and co-producer with Diana Ossana of CBS mini-series Streets of Laredo and ABC mini-series Dead Man's Walk 1996. *Publications include:* Horseman Pass By (aka Hud) 1961, Leaving Cheyenne 1963, The Last Picture Show 1966, In a Narrow Grave (essays) 1968, Moving On 1970, All My Friends Are Going to be Strangers 1972, It's Always We Rambled (essay) 1974, Terms of Endearment 1975, Somebody's Darling 1978, Cadillac Jack 1982, The Desert Rose 1983, Lonesome Dove 1985, Texasville 1987, Film Flam: Essay on Hollywood 1987, Anything for Billy 1988, Some Can Whistle 1989, Buffalo Girls 1990, The Evening Star 1992, Streets of Laredo 1993, Pretty Boy Floyd (with Diana Ossana) 1993, The Late Child 1995, Dead Man's Walk 1995, Zeke and Ned (novel, with Diana Ossana) 1996, Comanche Moon 1997, Duane's Depressed 1998, Walter Benjamin at the Dairy Queen 1999, Boone's Lick 2000, Sin Killer: The Berrybender Narratives, Book One 2002, The Wandering Hill: The Berrybender Narratives, Book Two 2003, Folly and Glory: The Berrybender Narratives, Book Three 2004, Loop Group 2004, When the Light Goes 2007, Books: A Memoir 2008, Rhino Ranch 2009, Literary Life: A Second Memoir 2010, Hollywood: A Third Memoir 2011, Custer 2012, The Last Kind Words Saloon 2014. *Leisure interest:* antiquarian bookselling. *Address:* c/o Adam Shulman, Anonymous Content, 3532 Hayden Avenue, Culver City, CA 90232, USA (office); Saria Co. Inc., PO Box 552, Archer City, AZ 76351, USA (office). *Telephone:* (310) 558-6537 (office). *E-mail:* ashulman@anonymouscontent.com (office). *Website:* www.flashandfiligree.com (office).

McNALLY, Alan G., BSc, MSc, MBA; Canadian business executive; b. 1945, Quebec City; m. Ruth McNally; two c.; ed Cornell Univ., York Univ. (including studies at Harvard Grad. School of Business, Oxford University Centre for Man. Studies and Institut Européen d'Admin des Affaires (INSEAD), France); spent six years with Aluminum Co. of Canada, in finance and other functions in Arvida, Quebec and Montreal head office 1984–90; Vice-Chair. Bank of Montreal 1990–2002; CEO Harris Trust and Savings Bank and Harris Bankcorp, Inc. 1993–2002, Chair. 1995–2004; Chair. Harris Financial Corpn (fmrly Bankmont Financial Corpn) 1998–2006, mem. Bd of Dirs May–Dec. 2006, Special Advisor 2007–; mem. Bd of Dirs Walgreen Co. 1999–, Chair. (non-exec.) 2009–12, Lead Dir Jan.–Oct. 2008, Acting CEO Oct. 2008–Feb. 2009; fmr Chair. MasterCard International Inc., New York; fmr Rep. of Fed. Reserve Bank of Chicago on Fed. Advisory Council to Bd Govs of Fed. Reserve, Washington, DC; Sr Advisor, TeleTech North America 2003–06; mem. Bd Chicago Clearing House Asscn, Econ. Club of Chicago, Commercial Club of Chicago; fmr mem. Bd of Evanston Northwestern Healthcare, Advisory Bd Northwestern Univ.'s Kellogg Grad. School of Man., Civic Cttee and Dir Chicago Club, Bd of Govs York Univ.; fmr Campaign Chair. for the Chicago United Way; fmr Dir Chicago Youth Centers, Kids' Help Phone, Canadian Council for Aboriginal Business; fmr Treas. Commercial Club of Chicago, Queen Elizabeth Hosp. Foundation; fmr Trustee, DePaul Univ., Kenyon Coll., Ohio; Hon. LLD (York Univ., Toronto); Daniel H. Burnham Award for outstanding efforts and involvement in Chicago's business, cultural, educational and philanthropic communities, Americanism Award, Anti-Defamation League, Community Builder Award, Christian Industrial League, Prime Movers Award honouring individuals and orgs that have created opportunities for minority and women-owned businesses in Chicago, Outstanding Exec. Leadership Award, York's Schulich School of Business.

McNALLY, Derek, PhD; British astronomer (retd); *Emeritus Fellow in Astronomy, University of Hertfordshire;* b. 28 Oct. 1934, Belfast, Northern Ireland; s. of David McNally and Sarah McNally (née Long); m. Shirley Allen 1959 (deceased); one s. one d.; ed Royal Belfast Acad. Inst., Queen's Univ., Belfast and Royal Holloway Coll., London; Sec. Royal Astronomical Soc. 1966–72, Vice-Pres. 1972–73, Treas. 1996–2001; Asst Dir Univ. of London Observatory 1966–88, Dir 1988–97; Sr Lecturer in Astronomy, Univ. Coll. London 1970–99; Asst Gen. Sec. of Exec. Cttee, Int. Astronomical Union 1985–88, Gen. Sec. 1988–91, Chair. Resolutions Cttee 1997–2000, Finance Sub-cttee 1988–91, 2000–03, Advisor of Sec. of Exec. 1991–94, mem. Div. VI Interstellar Matter –2012, Div. XII Union-Wide Activities –2012, Div. B Facilities, Technologies and Data Science, Div. C Educ., Outreach and Heritage, Div. H Interstellar Matter and Local Universe, Div. B Comm. 5 Documentation & Astronomical Data, Div. H Comm. 34 Interstellar Matter, Div. C Comm. 46 Astronomy Educ. & Devt, Div. B Comm. 50 Protection of Existing & Potential Observatory Sites; Chair. ICSU Working Group on Adverse Environmental Impacts on Astronomy 1993–96; Emer. Fellow in Astronomy, Univ. of Hertfordshire 2017–; Hon. Research Fellow, Univ. of Hertfordshire 1999–2018. *Achievement:* brought awareness that light pollution and radio noise are serious threats to ground-based astronomy, and not helped by possible climate change. *Publications:* Positional Astronomy 1974, The Vanishing Universe (ed.) 1994, New Trends in Astronomy Teaching (ed.) 1998; numerous articles in astronomical journals. *Leisure interests:* natural history, music, travel. *Address:* 17 Greenfield, Hatfield, Herts., AL9 5HW, England (home). *Telephone:* (1707) 267145 (home). *E-mail:* d.mcnally@herts.ac.uk (office); dmn@star.herts.ac.uk (office). *Website:* www.iau.org/administration/membership/individual/2081.

McNAMARA, Michael (Mike) M., BS, MBA; American electronics industry executive; *CEO, Flex Ltd;* ed Univ. of Cincinnati, Santa Clara Univ.; held several leadership positions at Intel Corpn; Prin., Pittiglio, Rabin, Todd & McGrath (consulting firm) 1987–92; Vice-Pres., Mfg Operations, Anthem Electronics 1992–93; Pres. and CEO Relevant Industries 1993–94, Vice-Pres. N America Operations, Flextronics Int. Ltd (after Flextronics acquisition of Relevant Industries, later renamed to Flex Ltd) 1994–97, Pres. N America Operations 1997–2001, COO, Singapore 2002–05, mem. Bd of Dirs 2005–, CEO 2006–; fmr Lecturer, MIT Sloan School of Man., Tsinghua Univ. *Address:* Flex Ltd, 2 Changi South Lane, 486123, Singapore (office). *Telephone:* 68769899 (office). *E-mail:* board@flex.com (office). *Website:* www.flex.com (office).

MacNAUGHTON, David, BA; Canadian consultant and diplomatist; *Ambassador to USA;* m. Leslie Noble; four d.; ed Univ. of New Brunswick; Exec. Asst to Liberal MP Don Jamieson 1971–77; Pres. KinMac Consultants, Ottawa 1977–81; Campaign Chair., Ont. Liberal Party 1987; Pres., Public Affairs Resource Group 1981–89; Pres. and CEO, Hill+Knowlton Strategies (consulting firm), Toronto 1989–94; Pres., Strathshore Financial Inc. 1996–2000; Sr Adviser, CIBC Capital Markets 2000–03; Prin. Sec. to Dalton McGuinty, Premier of Ont. 2003–05; Bd Chair., Comcare Ltd 2007–10; Chair., StrategyCorp Inc. 2005–16; Bd Chair., Aereus Technologies Inc. 2015–; Ont. Co-Chair., Liberal Party election campaign 2015; Amb. to USA 2016–; has served on numerous bds of dirs, including TV Ontario, Stratford Festival, North York Gen. Hosp., Toronto Int. Film Festival, Toronto French School, National Ski Acad., Alpine Ontario. *Address:* Canadian Embassy, 501 Pennsylvania Avenue NW, Washington, DC 20001-2111, USA (office). *Telephone:* (202) 682-1740 (office). *Fax:* (202) 682-7726 (office). *Website:* can-am.gc.ca/washington (office).

McNEALY, Scott Glenn, BA, MBA; American computer industry executive; *Chairman, Wayin;* b. 13 Nov. 1954, Columbus, Ind.; s. of Raymond William McNealy and Marmaline McNealy; m. Susan McNealy (née Ingemanson) 1994; four s.; ed Cranbrook School, Bloomfield Hills, Mich., Harvard and Stanford Univs; sales engineer, Rockwell International Corpn, Troy, Mich. 1976–78; staff engineer, FMC Corpn, Chicago 1980–81; Dir Operations, Onyx Systems, San José, Calif. 1981–82; Co-founder Sun Microsystems Inc., Mountain View, Calif. 1982, Vice-Pres. of Operations 1982–84, Pres. and COO 1984, Chair., Pres. and CEO 1984–99, Chair. and CEO 1999–2002, Chair., Pres. and CEO 2002–04, Chair. and CEO 2004–06, Chair. 2006–10, also Chair. Sun Federal, Inc. (subsidiary); Chair. Wayin, Denver, Colo 2011–; Founder Curriki; outspoken libertarian and proponent of laissez-faire capitalism, regularly appears on Fox Business channel; Strategic Advisor and Equity Partner, 18Birdies; Distinguished Fellowship Award, British Computer Soc. 2007. *Leisure interests:* ice hockey, golf. *Address:* Wayin, 1623 Blake Street, #350, Denver, CO 80202, USA (office). *Telephone:* (303) 997-1722 (office). *E-mail:* info@wayin.com (office). *Website:* wayin.com (office).

McNEE, Sir David Blackstock, Kt, QPM, FBIM, FRSA; British fmr police officer; b. 23 March 1925, Glasgow, Scotland; s. of John McNee and Mary McNee (née Blackstock); m. 1st Isabella Clayton Hopkins 1952 (died 1997); one d.; m. 2nd Lillian Bissland Campbell Bogie 2002; ed Woodside Senior Secondary School, Glasgow; Deputy Chief Constable, Dunbartonshire Constabulary 1968–71; Chief Constable, City of Glasgow Police 1971–75; Chief Constable, Strathclyde Police 1975–77; Commr Metropolitan Police 1977–82; Dir Fleet Holdings 1983–86; Chair. (non-exec.) Scottish Express Newspapers 1983; Adviser Bd British Airways 1982–87; fmr Dir Orr Pollock & Co. Ltd (Greenock Telegraph), Craig M. Jeffrey Ltd (Helensburgh Advertiser), Integrated Security Services Ltd, Clydesdale Bank PLC, among other cos; Pres. Royal Life Saving Soc. 1982–90, Nat. Bible Soc. of Scotland 1983–96, Glasgow City Cttee, Cancer Relief 1987–93; CBIM 1980; Freeman, City of London 1977; Hon. Col 32 (Scottish) Signal Regt (Volunteers) 1988–92; KStJ 1974, Commdr 1977. *Publication:* McNee's Law: The Memoirs of Sir David McNee 1983. *Leisure interests:* fishing, golf, music.

McNEE, John, BA, MA; Canadian diplomatist; *Secretary-General, Global Centre for Pluralism;* m. Susan McNee; two c.; ed York Univ., Univ. of Cambridge, UK; joined Dept of External Affairs 1978, positions in Embassies in Madrid, London, Tel-Aviv, Amb. to Syria 1993–97 (also accred to Lebanon 1993–95); positions with Policy Devt Secr., Canada–US Transboundary Div., Ottawa, fmr Dir Personnel Div., Dir Gen. Middle East, North Africa and Gulf States Bureau; fmr mem. Prime Minister Trudeau's Task Force on Int. Peace and Security, Privy Council Office; Asst Deputy Minister, Africa and Middle East, Foreign Affairs, Ottawa 2001, Amb. to Belgium (also accred to Luxembourg) 2004–06, Amb. and Perm. Rep. to UN, New York 2006–11; inaugural Sec.-Gen. Global Centre for Pluralism, Ottawa 2011–. *Address:* Global Centre for Pluralism, c/o Delegation of the Ismaili Imamat, 199 Sussex Drive, Ottawa, ON K1N 1K6, Canada (office). *Telephone:* (613) 241-2532 (office). *Fax:* (613) 241-2533 (office). *E-mail:* info@pluralism.ca (office). *Website:* www.pluralism.ca (office).

McNEIL, General (retd) Dan K., BS; American military officer (retd) and business executive; *President, The Logistics Company;* ed North Carolina State Univ., US Army Command and Gen. Staff Coll., Fort Leavenworth, Kan.; began mil. career 1968, command positions have included E Company, 2nd Bn (Airborne), 505th Infantry, 82nd Airborne Div. 1977–78, 1st Bn, 325th Infantry, 82nd Airborne Div. 1986–88, 3rd Brigade, 82nd Airborne Div. 1991–93, Asst Div. Commdr, 2nd Infantry Div., Eighth US Army, Korea 1995–96, Deputy Commanding Gen., I Corps and Fort Lewis 1997–98, Commanding Gen., 82nd Airborne Div. 1998–2000, Commanding Gen., XVIII Airborne Corps and Fort Bragg 2000–03, including duty as Commanding Gen., Combined Jt Task Force-180, Afghanistan, Deputy Commanding Gen./Chief of Staff, US Army Forces Command 2003–07, Commanding Gen., Int. Security Assistance Force, Afghanistan 2007–08 (retd); Pres. The Logistics Co. Inc. 2011–; Founder Dan K McNeill Associates (consultancy); Chair. NC Military Foundation; mem. Bd of Dirs New Century Bancorp 2011–; mem. First Command Military Advisory Bd; Defense Distinguished Service Medal, Defense Superior Service Medal, Legion of Merit, Bronze Star Medal, Expert Infantryman Badge, Master Parachutist Badge (with Bronze Service Star), Army Aviator Badge, Special Forces Tab. *Address:* The Logistics Company, 3400 Walsh Parkway, Fayetteville, NC 28311, USA (office). *Telephone:* (910) 482-8084 (office). *Website:* www.tlc-inc.net (office).

MacNEILL, Brian F., BCom, CPA, CM; Canadian accountant and business executive; b. 1939, Calgary; m.; four c.; ed Montana State Univ.; began career as accounts clerk at oil and gas co., Calgary 1960; Accountant, Haskins & Sells, San Francisco 1967; Vice-Pres. and Treas. Hiram Walker Resources Ltd 1980–82; fmr Exec. Vice-Pres. and COO Enbridge Inc., CEO 1990–2001; mem. Bd of Dirs Petro-Canada 1995, Chair. 2000–09; mem. Bd of Dirs Toronto Dominion Bank 1994–2009, Telus Corpn 2001–11, ArcelorMittal Dofasco, Inc. 2001–06, West-Fraser Timber Co. Ltd, Oilsands Quest Inc. 2009–12, Suncor Energy Inc. 2009–12; fmr mem. Bd of Dirs Dofasco Inc., Veritas DGC Inc., Legacy Hotels REIT, Sears Canada Inc., Western Oil Sands Inc., Capital Power Corpn, Marathon Oil Canada Corpn, Veritas DGC I Inc., Enbridge Inc.; Chair. Bd of Govs Univ. of Calgary; fmr Chair. United Way of Calgary; mem. Canadian Inst. of Chartered Accountants, Financial Execs Inst.; Trustee, Legacy Hotels Real Estate Investment Trust 2001–05; Fellow, Alberta Inst. of Chartered Accountants, Inst of Corp. Dirs.

McNERNEY, Walter James (Jim), Jr, BA, MBA; American business executive; b. 22 Aug. 1949, Providence, RI; m.; five c.; ed Yale and Harvard Univs; began career in brand man., Procter & Gamble; Sr Man. McKinsey & Co. –1982; Gen. Man. General Electric (GE) Mobile Communications 1982–86, Pres. GE Information Services 1988–89, Exec. Vice-Pres. GE Financial Services and GE Capital 1989–91, Pres. and CEO GE Electrical Distribution and Control 1991–92, Pres. GE Asia-Pacific, Hong Kong 1993–95, Pres. and CEO GE Lighting 1995–97, Pres. and CEO GE Aircraft Engines 1997–2000, Chair. and CEO 3M 2000–05; Chair., Pres. and CEO The Boeing Co. 2005–13, Chair. and CEO 2013–15, Chair. 2015–16; mem. Bd Dirs, Procter & Gamble, IBM; mem. The Field Museum Bd of Trustees, Chicago; Trustee, Northwestern Univ.; mem. Northwestern Memorial HealthCare Bd; mem. Exec. Cttee The Business Roundtable; mem. Pres.'s Strategic and Policy Forum Jan.–Aug. 2017; fmr Chair. The Business Council, US-China Business Council, American Soc. of Corp. Execs; Fellow, American Acad. of Arts and Sciences; Hon. FRAeS; Hon. DSc (Cranfield Univ., UK) 2009; Exec. of the Year, Nat. Man. Asscn 2008, John W. Dixon Award, Asscn of the US Army 2011, Semper Fidelis Award, Marine Corps Scholarship Foundation 2012, inaugural Turning Point Award, US Army War Coll. Foundation 2012, Juran Medal, American Soc. for Quality, Woodrow Wilson Award for Corp. Citizenship, Wilson Center, named CEO of the Year by Chief Executive magazine 2015. *Leisure interests:* skiing, golf, hiking, hockey. *Address:* c/o The Boeing Company, 100 North Riverside Plaza, Chicago, IL 60606-1596, USA. *E-mail:* info@boeing.com.

McNICOL, Donald, PhD; Australian psychologist, academic and fmr university vice-chancellor; b. 18 April 1939, Adelaide, S Australia; s. of Ian Robertson McNicol and Sadie Isabelle Williams; m. Kathleen Margaret Wells 1963; one s. two d.; ed Unley High School, Univ. of Adelaide, Cambridge Univ.; Lecturer in Psychology, Univ. of Adelaide 1967–71; Sr Lecturer in Psychology, Univ. of NSW 1971–74, Assoc. Prof. 1975–81; Prof. of Psychology, Univ. of Tasmania 1981–86; Commr for Univs and Chair. Univs Advisory Council of Commonwealth Tertiary Educ. Comm. 1986–88; Vice-Chancellor Univ. of New England 1988–90, Univ. of Sydney 1990–96, Univ. of Tasmania 1996–2003; Deputy Pres. Australian Vice-Chancellors' Cttee 1993–94, Pres. 1994–96; Pres. Asscn of Univs of S Asia and the Pacific (AUAP) 1998–99; Pres. Australian Higher Educ. Industrial Asscn 2000–01; Fellow, Australian Psychological Soc. *Publication includes:* A Primer of Signal Detection Theory 1972, 2005. *Leisure interests:* walking, music, reading. *Address:* PO Box 1155, Sandy Bay, Tasmania 7006, Australia (home). *E-mail:* don.mcnicol@mcnicol.info (home).

McNUTT, Marcia K., BA, PhD; American geophysicist, academic, government official and editor; *President, National Academy of Sciences;* b. 1 Feb. 1952, Minneapolis, Minn.; m. 2nd Ian Young 1996; three d. from previous marriage; ed Northrop Collegiate School, Minneapolis, Colorado Coll., Scripps Inst. of Oceanography; Visiting Asst Prof., Univ. of Minnesota 1978–79; Geophysicist, Br. of Tectonophysics, Office of Earthquake Studies, US Geological Survey (USGS), Menlo Park, Calif. 1979–82; Asst Prof. of Geophysics, Dept of Earth, Atmospheric and Planetary Sciences, MIT, Cambridge, Mass 1982–86, Assoc. Prof. of Geophysics 1986, Prof. of Geophysics 1989–98, Griswold Prof. of Geophysics 1991–97, Assoc. Dir MIT SeaGrant Coll. Program 1993–95, Dir MIT/Woods Hole Oceanography Inst. Jt Program in Oceanography and Applied Ocean Science and Eng 1995–97; Pres. and CEO Monterey Bay Aquarium Research Inst. 1997–2009; apptd Prof., Dept of Earth Science, Univ. of California, Santa Cruz 1998 and Prof. of Geophysics, Stanford Univ. 1998; Dir US Geological Survey and Science Advisor to Sec. of the Interior 2009–13; Ed.-in-Chief Science magazine 2013–16; mem. NAS 2005–, Pres. NAS 2016–; Pres. American Geophysical Union 2000–02; Chair. Univ.-Nat. Oceanographic Lab. System 2006, Bd of Govs Jt Oceanographic Insts 2006; fmr Chair. Pres.'s Panel on Ocean Exploration; fmr Pres. and CEO Monterey Bay Aquarium Research Inst.; mem. Advisory Cttee, Div. on Earth and Life Studies, Forum on Open Science, has also served as mem. of numerous other evaluation and advisory bds, including Schlumberger Tech. Advisory Cttee, Whale Conservation Fund Advisory Council, Ocean Council, Advisory Bd Winchell School of Earth Sciences, Univ. of Minnesota; apptd Chair. Visiting Cttee, Dept of Earth and Planetary Science, Harvard Univ. 2002; mem. Visiting Cttee, School of Earth Sciences, Stanford Univ. 1999–, Dept of Mechanical Eng, MIT 2005–; mem. American Acad. of Arts and Sciences 1999–, American Philosophical Soc. 2002–; Fellow, American Geophysical Union 1988– (Pres. 2000–02), Geological Soc. of America 1998–, AAAS 1998–Int. Asscn of Geodesy; Trustee, Consortium for Ocean Leadership; Dr hc (Colorado Coll.) 1988, (Univ. of Minnesota) 2004; Univ. of California Dissertation Fellowship 1977–78, Ed.'s Citation for Excellence in Refereeing, Journal of Geophysical Research 1984, 1993, Grad. Student Council Award for Teaching 1985, Mary Ingraham Bunting Fellow, Radcliffe Coll. 1985–86, Macelwane Award, American Geophysical Union 1988, NSF Visiting Professorship for Women, Lamont-Doherty Geological Observatory, Columbia Univ. 1989–90, Outstanding Alumni Award, The Blake Schools, Minneapolis 1993, Capital Science Lecturer, Carnegie Inst. 1995, MIT School of Science Grad. Teaching Prize 1996, Science and Tech. Fellow, CSU Monterey Bay 1997, Sanctuary Reflections Award, Special Recognition Category, Monterey Bay Nat. Marine Sanctuary 1998, ARCS Scientist of the Year 2003, Nat. Assoc., NAS 2004, Alumna of the Year, Univ. of California, San Diego 2004, Maurice Ewing Medal, American Geophysical Union 2007. *Publications include:* more than 100 peer-reviewed scientific articles on studies of ocean island volcanism in French Polynesia, continental break-up in Western USA and uplift of the Tibet Plateau. *Address:* National Academy of Sciences, 500 Fifth Street, NW, Washington, DC 20001, USA (office). *Telephone:* (202) 334-2000 (office). *Website:* www.nasonline.org (office).

McPEAK, Gen. Merrill Anthony, BA, MS; American air force officer (retd), investor and company director; *Chairman, American Battle Monuments Commission;* b. 9 Jan. 1936, Santa Rosa, Calif.; s. of Merrill Addison McPeak and Winifred Alice McPeak Bendall (née Stewart); m. Elynor Fay Moskowitz 1956; two s.; ed San Diego State Coll., Calif., George Washington Univ., Washington, DC; commissioned officer, USAF 1957, progressed through ranks to Gen. 1988; C-in-C Pacific Air Forces, Hickam, HI 1988–90; Chief of Staff USAF 1990–94; Chair. ECC Int. Corpn 1997–2002, Ethicspoint, Inc. 2003–12, Coast Plating, Inc. 2012–13; Chair. American Battle Monuments Comm. 2011–; DSM, Silver Star, Legion of Merit, DFC (two awards), Air Medal (13 awards); Thomas White Space Award, Oregon Aviation Hall of Honor, Lifetime Achievement Award, San Diego State Univ., 'George' Award, George Washington Univ. *Achievements include:* flew 269 combat missions in Viet Nam, some while in command of the Misty squadron of high speed forward air controllers; performed as demonstration pilot in 199 official air shows as mem. of Air Force aerobatic team the Thunderbirds 1967–68. *Publications:* Hangar Flying 2012, Below the Zone 2013, Roles and Missions 2017; op-eds in New York Times, Washington Post, Wall Street Journal. *Address:* 123 Furnace Street, Lake Oswego, OR 97034, USA (office). *Telephone:* (503) 699-2931 (office). *E-mail:* mamcpeak@comcast.net (office). *Website:* generalmcpeak.com.

McPHEE, John Angus, AB; American writer and academic; *Ferris Professor of Journalism, Princeton University;* b. 8 March 1931, Princeton, NJ; m. 1st Pryde Brown 1957; four d.; m. 2nd Yolanda Whitman 1972; two step-s. two step-d.; ed Princeton Univ., Univ. of Cambridge; dramatist, Robert Montgomery Presents television programme 1955–57; Assoc. Ed., Time magazine, New York 1957–64; staff writer, The New Yorker magazine 1965–; Ferris Prof. of Journalism, Princeton Univ. 1975–; Fellow, Geological Soc. of America; mem. American Acad. of Arts and Letters; various hon. doctorates; American Acad. and Inst. of Arts and Letters Award 1977, Princeton Univ. Woodrow Wilson Award 1982, American Asscn of Petroleum Geologists Journalism Award 1982, 1986, United States Geological Survey John Wesley Powell Award 1988, American Geophysical Union Walter Sullivan Award 1993, Pulitzer Prize for Non-Fiction 1999, Geological Soc. of America Public Service Award 2002, Acad. of Natural Sciences Gold Medal for Distinction in Natural History Art 2005, George Polk Career Award 2008, Sandrof Award for Lifetime Achievement, Nat. Books Critic Circle 2018. *Publications:* A Sense of Where You Are 1965, The Headmaster 1966, Oranges 1967, The Pine Barrens 1968, A Roomful of Hovings 1969, The Crofter and the Laird 1969, Levels of the Game 1970, Encounters with the Archdruid 1972, Wimbledon: A Celebration 1972, The Deltoid Pumpkin Seed 1973, The Curve of Binding Energy 1974, Pieces of the Frame 1975, The Survival of the Bark Canoe 1975, The John McPhee Reader 1977, Coming into the Country 1977, Giving Good Weight 1979, Alaska: Images of the Country (with Galen Rowell) 1981, Basin and Range 1981, In Suspect Terrain 1983, La Place de la Concorde Suisse 1984, Table of Contents 1985, Rising from the Plains 1986, Outcroppings 1988, The Control of Nature 1989, Looking for a Ship 1990, Assembling California 1993, The Ransom of Russian Art 1994, The Second John McPhee Reader 1996, Irons in the Fire 1997, Annals of the Former World 1998, The Founding Fish 2002, Uncommon Carriers 2006, Silk Parachute 2010, The Princeton reader: contemporary essays by writers and journalists at Princeton University 2011, Draft No. 4: On the Writing Process 2017. *Address:* Joseph Henry House, Princeton University, Princeton, NJ 08544 (office); 475 Drake's Corner Road, Princeton, NJ 08540, USA (home).

McPHEE, Jonathan, LRAM, BM, MM; American music director and conductor; *Music Director and Principal Conductor, Boston Ballet;* b. Philadelphia, Pa; ed Royal Acad. of Music, London and Juilliard School of Music, New York, studied with Leonard Brain, David Diamond, Thomas Stacy, Rudolf Kempe, Sixten Ehrling, and participated in masterclasses with Sir Georg Solti and James Levine; affiliate, Martha Graham Dance Co., New York 1979–89, Joffrey Ballet, Chicago 1980–86, Dance Theater of Harlem 1980–86; now Music Dir and Prin. Conductor Boston Ballet; Music Dir Longwood Symphony Orchestra 2005–11, Lexington Symphony, Symphony New Hampshire; has conducted for numerous dance cos, including American Ballet Theater and New York City Ballet, Royal Ballet (UK), Martha Graham Dance Company, The Joffrey Ballet, Nat. Ballet of Canada, Australian Ballet, Den Norske Ballett (Norway), Royal Danish Ballet; has conducted Royal Philharmonic Orchestra, London, Nat. Arts Centre Orchestra, Ottawa, in guest engagements with Boston Ballet and Houston Ballet, Hamburg Philharmonic, Orquesta Sinfonica de Tenerife, Lithuanian Nat. Orchestra; invited to conduct Nashville Symphony as one of the conductors featured in Bruno Walter National Conductor Preview by the League of American Orchestras 2009; has also conducted dance music, musical theatre, operetta and grand opera (with Opera Boston, American Opera Center, New York, Boston Univ. Opera Inst.); works as arranger and composer are part of repertoires of orchestras and ballet companies world-wide, his edn of Stravinsky's Rite of Spring is the only reduced orchestration of this work authorized by the Stravinsky Trust; Naumburg Scholarship in Conducting and English Horn, Juilliard School of Music, Met-Life Award for Community Engagement, League of American Orchestras 2007, Commonwealth Award, State of Mass 2011. *Orchestral compositions:* Overture, Summer Day 1988, Trinity 1990, The Seduction 1992, Nightingale 1996, The Dream Whisperer 1997, Re:Marks 1998, Fantasy for two pianos and orchestra 2001, Images 2004. *Radio:* Kids Classical Hour (WCRB radio station) (Gabriel Award 1998). *Recordings include:* The Nutcracker, The Sleeping Beauty, Romeo & Juliet (all three with Boston Ballet Orchestra), Holiday in Boston, Michael Gandolfi's Caution to the Wind; conducted Danish Radio Symphony Orchestra and Aarhus Orchestra for the films of Martha Graham's works telecast by Dance In America that included Samuel Barber's Cave of the Heart, Gian Carlo Menotti's Errand into the Maze, and Edgard Varese' Integrales, Offrandes, and Octandre 2006. *Publications:* arrangements and compositions, including the reduced orchestration of Stravinsky's Rite of Spring and the complete Firebird. *Leisure interests:* skiing, scuba diving. *Address:* Boston Ballet, 19 Clarendon Street, Boston, MA 02116-6100, USA (office). *Telephone:* (617) 695-6950 (office). *E-mail:* jmcphee@bostonballet.org (office). *Website:* www.bostonballet.org (office); jonathanmcphee.com.

MacPHERSON, Elle; Australian model, actress and business executive; b. (Eleanor Nancy Gow), 29 March 1963, Cronulla, New South Wales; d. of Peter Gow and Frances Macpherson; m. 1st Gilles Bensimon 1986 (divorced 1989); two s. with Arpad Busson; m. 2nd Jeffrey Soffer 2013; Founder and Chief Exec. Elle Macpherson Inc.; f. Elle Macpherson sportswear, Elle Macpherson Intimates, The Body (beauty product line); Co-Owner Fashion Cafe, New York; appeared in Sports Illustrated Swimsuit magazine edition 1986, 1987, 1988, 1989, 1990, 1991, 1992, 1993, 1994, 2004, 2006; modelled for major fashion houses including Louis Vuitton, Ralph Lauren, Christian Dior, Michael Kors, Calvin Klein, Valentino; appeared in ad campaigns including H&M, Victoria's Secret, Diet Coke, KFC; Co-Founder, WelleCo 2014; European Amb. RED; Amb. UNICEF, Smile Foundation; Patron Nat. Asscn for the Children of Alcoholics (NACOA); fmr mem. Bd of Dirs Hot Tuna Clothing; Style Icon Award, Elle Style Awards 2006, Everywoman Amb. Award 2007, World Career Award, Women's World Awards 2009. *Films include:* Alice 1990, Sirens 1994, Jane Eyre 1996, If Lucy Fell 1996, The Mirror Has Two Faces 1996, Batman and Robin 1997, The Edge 1997, Beautopia 1998, With

Friends Like These 1998, South Kensington 2001; video: Stretch and Strengthen, The Body Workout 1995. *Television includes:* H3O (series) 1995, Friends 1999–2000, 2004, A Girl Thing (mini-series) 2001, The Beautiful Life: TBL (series) 2009. *Address:* c/o Donna Rooney, Donna Management (office). *Telephone:* (78) 2558-2987 (office). *E-mail:* donna@donna.management (office). *Website:* www.welleco.com.

McPHERSON, James Munro, PhD; American historian, academic and writer; *George Henry Davis '86 Professor Emeritus of History, Princeton University;* b. 11 Oct. 1936, Valley City, ND; s. of James M. McPherson and Miriam O. McPherson; m. Patricia Rasche 1957; one d.; ed Gustavus Adolphus Coll. and Johns Hopkins Univ.; Instructor Princeton Univ. 1962–65, Asst Prof. 1965–66, Assoc. Prof. 1966–72, Prof. of History 1972–82, Edwards Prof. of American History 1982–91, George Henry Davis '86 Prof. of American History 1991, now Prof. Emer.; Pres. Soc. of American Historians 2000–01; Woodrow Wilson Fellow and Danforth Fellow 1958–62; Guggenheim Fellow 1967–68; Huntingdon Library-Nat. Endowment for the Humanities Fellowship 1977–78; Center for Advanced Study in the Behavioural Sciences Fellowship 1982–83; Huntington Seaver Fellow 1987–88; Pres. American Historical Asscn 2003; mem. American Philosophical Soc. 1991; Fellow, American Acad. of Arts and Sciences 2009; 10 hon. degrees from American colls and univs; Anisfield-Wolf Prize in Race Relations 1965, Pulitzer Prize in History 1989, Christopher Award 1989, Best Book Award, American Military Inst. 1989, Lincoln Prize 1998, Theodore and Franklin D. Roosevelt Prize in Naval History 1998, Jefferson Lecturer 2000, Pritzker Mil. Library Literature Award for lifetime achievement in mil. writing 2007, Lincoln Prize 2009. *Publications include:* The Struggle for Equality: Abolitionists and the Negro in the Civil War and Reconstruction 1964, The Negro's Civil War 1965, Marching Toward Freedom 1968, The Anti-Slavery Crusade in America (co-ed, 59 vols) 1969, Blacks in America (essays) 1971, The Abolitionist Legacy 1975, Ordeal by Fire: The Civil War and Reconstruction 1982, Religion, Race and Reconstruction (essays, co-ed) 1982, Battle Cry of Freedom: The Civil War Era 1988, Battle Chronicles of the Civil War (ed, six vols) 1989, Abraham Lincoln and the Second American Revolution 1991, Images of the Civil War 1992, Gettysburg 1993, What They Fought For 1861–1865 1994, The Atlas of the Civil War 1994, Drawn With the Sword: Reflections on the American Civil War 1996, The American Heritage New History of the Civil War (ed) 1996, For Cause and Comrades: Why Men Fought in the Civil War 1997, Lamson of the Gettysburg: The Civil War Letters of Lt Roswell H. Lamson, US Navy 1997, Is Blood Thicker Than Water? Crises of Nationalism in the Modern World 1998, The Encyclopedia of Civil War Biographies (ed, three vols) 1999, To the Best of My Ability: The American Presidents (ed) 2000, Crossroads of Freedom: Antietam, The Battle That Changed the Course of the Civil War 2002, Hallowed Ground: A Walk at Gettysburg 2003, The Illustrated Battle Cry of Freedom 2003, Into the West (juvenile) 2006, Tried by War: Abraham Lincoln as Commander in Chief (Lincoln Prize, Gettysburg Coll. 2009) 2008, This Mighty Scourge: Perspectives on the Civil War 2009, Abraham Lincoln 2009; contrib. to reference works, scholarly books and professional journals. *Leisure interests:* tennis, bicycling, sailing. *Address:* c/o 41 William Street, Princeton, NJ 08540, USA (office); Department of History, 130 Dickinson Hall, Princeton University, Princeton, NJ 08544 (office); 15 Randall Road, Princeton, NJ 08540, USA (home). *Telephone:* (609) 258-4173 (office); (609) 924-9226 (home). *Fax:* (609) 258-5326 (office). *E-mail:* jmcphers@princeton.edu (office). *Website:* his.princeton.edu (office).

McPHERSON, Melville Peter, BA, MBA, JD; American lawyer, academic administrator and fmr government official; *President, Association of Public and Land-grant Universities;* b. 27 Oct. 1940, Lowell, Mich.; s. of Donald McPherson and Ellura E. McPherson (née Frost); m. Joanne Paddock 1989; four c.; ed Michigan State Univ., Western Michigan Univ., American Univ.; Peace Corps volunteer, Peru 1964–65; with Internal Revenue Service, Washington, DC 1969–75; Special Asst to the Pres. and Deputy Dir Presidential Personnel, White House, Washington, DC 1975–77; Partner, Vorys, Sater, Seymour & Pease, Washington, DC 1977–80; Special Counsel to Pres. Gerald Ford 1980–81; Admin., USAID, Washington, DC 1981–87; Deputy Sec., Dept of Treasury 1987–89; Exec. Vice-Pres. Bank of America 1989–93; Pres. Michigan State Univ. 1993–2004, Pres. Emer. 2004–; Financial Co-ordinator, Office of Reconstruction and Humanitarian Assistance, Iraq 2003; Founding Co-Chair. Partnership to Cut Hunger and Poverty in Africa 2005–, now Chair.; Pres. Nat. Asscn of State Univs and Land-Grant Colls (now the Asscn of Public and Land-grant Univs) 2006–; Co-founder and Chair. Harvest Plus (org. working to breed crops for better nutrition); Chair. Dow Jones & Co. 2007; fmr Chair. Int. Fertilizer Devt Center, Abraham Lincoln Study Abroad Comm.; fmr Dir of Econ. Policy for the Coalition Provisional Authority of Iraq (took five-month leave from MSU to work with Iraqi Ministry of Finance, Cen. Bank of Iraq and country's banks); mem. Bd of Trustees, Gerald R. Ford Foundation; Dr hc (Michigan State Univ., Virginia State Univ., Mount St Mary's Coll.); UNICEF Award for Outstanding Contribution to Child Survival, Humanitarian of the Year Award, American Lebanese League 1983, Jewish Nat. Fund Tree of Life Award 1998, Alexander Hamilton Award, Dept of Treasury, US Presidential Certificate of Outstanding Achievement, Sec. of State's Distinguished Service Award 2004, Banker of the Year Award for Lifetime Achievement, US Bankers Asscn for Finance and Trade 2005. *Address:* Association of Public and Land-grant Universities, 1307 New York Avenue, NW, Suite 400, Washington, DC 20005-4722, USA (office). *Telephone:* (202) 478-6060 (office). *Fax:* (202) 478-6046 (office). *E-mail:* pmcpherson@aplu.org (office). *Website:* www.aplu.org (office).

McQUEEN, Steve Rodney, CBE; British artist, film director and producer; b. 9 Oct. 1969, London, England; ed Drayton Manor High School, Chelsea School of Art, Goldsmith's Coll., Tisch School of the Arts, New York Univ.; has exhibited widely in Europe and USA; major solo exhbn Inst. of Contemporary Art (ICA), London; works primarily in corp. film, photography and sculpture, apptd Official War Artist in response to the Iraq conflict, Imperial War Museum, London 2003; represented GB at Venice Biennale 2009; lives and works in London and Amsterdam; ICA Futures Award 1996, DAAD artist's scholarship 1998, Turner Prize 1999, London Critics Circle Film Award for Breakthrough British Film-maker 2008, BAFTA Carl Foreman Award for Most Promising Newcomer 2009. *Films include:* Bear (silent) 1993, Deadpan (silent) 1997, Drumroll (short) 1998, Prey (short) 1999, Cold Breath (short) 2000, Illuminer (short) 2001, Girls, Tricky (short) 2001, 7th Nov. (short) 2001, Western Deep (short) 2002, Carib's Leap (short) 2002, Charlotte (short) 2004, Pursuit (short) 2005, Unexploded (short) 2007, Running Thunder (short) 2007, Gravesend (short) 2007, Hunger (writer and dir) (Caméra d'Or (first-time dir) Award, Cannes 2008, inaugural Sydney Film Festival Prize 2008, Diesel Discovery Award, Toronto Int. Film Festival 2008, Los Angeles Film Critics Asscn Award for a New Generation Film 2008, BAFTA Carl Foreman Award for Special Achievement by a British Dir 2009, Best Film Prize, London Evening Standard Film Awards 2009) 2008, Rayners Lane (short) 2008, Static (short) 2009, Giardini (short) 2009, Shame (writer and dir) 2011, 12 Years a Slave (writer and dir) (People's Choice Award, Toronto Int. Film Festival 2013, BAFTA Award for Best Picture, Golden Globe Award for Best Motion Picture, Drama, Academy Award for Best Picture 2014) 2013, Widows 2018. *Address:* c/o Casarotto Marsh Ltd, Waverley House, 7–12 Noel Street, London, W1F 8GQ, England (office); c/o Thomas Dane Associates, First Floor, 11 Duke Street, St James's, London, SW1Y 6BN, England; c/o Marian Goodman Gallery, 24 West 57th Street, New York, NY 10019, USA. *E-mail:* jenne@casarotto.co.uk (office).

McRAE, Donald Malcolm, CC, LLB, LLM, FRSC; Canadian professor of law; *Hyman Soloway Professor of Law, University of Ottawa;* b. 1944, Ottawa; ed Univ. of Otago, New Zealand; fmr Prof. and Assoc. Dean, Faculty of Law, Univ. of British Columbia; Dean, Common Law Section, Faculty of Law, Univ. of Ottawa 1987–94, currently Hyman Soloway Prof. of Law; also Adjunct Prof., Norman Paterson School of Int. Affairs, Carleton Univ.; fmr Prof., Visiting Lecturer and Assoc. Dean at several univs including Univs of Otago, Western Ontario, British Columbia, Cambridge, Hebei, Houston Law School; fmr Adviser to Govt of Canada Dept of External Affairs and Counsel for Canada in several int. fisheries and boundary arbitrations, including as Chief Negotiator for Canada for Pacific Salmon Treaty 1998–99; consultant to numerous int. bodies and foreign govts in the field of int. law, law of the sea and maritime boundaries; elected to Int. Law Comm. 2006; Ed.-in-Chief Canadian Yearbook of International Law; Pres. Canadian Council on Int. Law 1990–92; John E. Read Medal, Canadian Council on Int. Law 2003. *Publications:* numerous publications in the field of int. law, fisheries and oceans. *Address:* University of Ottawa Law Faculty, 57 Louis Pasteur Street, Room 340, Ottawa, ON K1N 6N5, Canada (office). *Telephone:* (613) 562-5800 (office). *E-mail:* Donald.McRae@uOttawa.ca (office). *Website:* www.commonlaw.uottawa.ca (office).

McREYNOLDS, John W.; American lawyer and business executive; *President, Chief Financial Officer and Director of the General Partner, Energy Transfer Equity, LP;* Partner, Hunton & Williams LLP int. law firm for over 20 years; mem. Bd of Dirs, Energy Transfer Partners 2004–, Pres. Energy Transfer Equity, LP (ETE) 2005–, Dir and Chief Financial Officer ETE 2005–; mem. Bd of Dirs, Regency GP LLC 2010–, Sunoco, Inc. 2012–. *Address:* Energy Transfer Equity, LP, Dallas Office, 3738 Oak Lawn Avenue, Dallas, TX 75219, USA (office). *Telephone:* (214) 981-0700 (office). *Fax:* (214) 981-0703 (office). *E-mail:* info@energytransfer.com (office). *Website:* www.energytransfer.com (office).

MACRI, Mauricio; Argentine politician and head of state; *President;* b. 8 Feb. 1959, Tandil, Buenos Aires; m. 3rd Juliana Awada; four c.; ed Catholic Univ. of Argentina, Universidad del CEMA, Columbia Business School, Wharton Business School, USA; joined family business 1985 and served in various man. positions in cos including Sideco, SOCMA and Sevel; Pres. Boca Juniors football club 1995–; defeated in second round of election for Head of Govt of the Autonomous City of Buenos Aires 2003; serves as deputy representing city of Buenos Aires in Lower House of Congress 2005–; with Ricardo López Murphy created Propuesta Republicana (PRO) electoral front 2005–; Mayor of Buenos Aires 2007–; Pres. of Argentina Dec. 2015–; Founder mem. Compromiso para el Cambio (Commitment to Change). *Address:* General Secretariat to the Presidency, Balcarce 50, C1064AAB, Buenos Aires (office); Compromiso para el Cambio, Edif. Anexo de la Cámara de Diputados, Riobamba 25, C 1025 ABA, Buenos Aires, Argentina (office). *Telephone:* (11) 4344-3674 (presidency) (office); (11) 6310-7710 (office). *Fax:* (11) 4344-2647 (presidency) (office). *E-mail:* dgi@presidencia.gov.ar (office); ccambio@hcdn.gov.ar (office). *Website:* cpcambio.org.ar (office); www.ciudadpro.com; www.secretariageneral.gov.ar (office).

McROBBIE, Michael A., BSc, MSc; Australian computer scientist, academic and university administrator; *President, Indiana University;* b. 11 Oct. 1950; m. Laurie Burns; three c., three step-c.; ed Univ. of Queensland, Australian Nat. Univ.; Prof. of Information Tech., Inst. of Advanced Study, ANU, also CEO Co-operative Research Centre for Advanced Computational Systems; Vice-Pres. for Information Tech., Indiana Univ., Bloomington, USA 1997–2006, also Vice-Pres. for Research 2003–06, Interim Provost and Vice-Pres. for Academic Affairs 2006–07, Pres. 2007–; Co-Chair. Nat. Acads. of Science, Eng and Medicine's Cttee on the Future of Voting: Accessible, Reliable, Verifiable Tech.; fmr Chair. Bd of Trustees, Internet2, Bd of Dirs Digital Preservation Network; mem. Council on Foreign Relations, Big Ten Council of Presidents and Chancellors, Nat. Security Higher Educ. Advisory Bd, Univ. Research Assocs.; fmr mem. Bd ChaCha; Fellow, American Acad. of Arts and Sciences; Hon. mem. Alliance of Distinguished and Titled Profs, Hon. Fellow Australian Acad. of Humanities; Sagamore of the Wabash 2007, Officer of the Order of Australia 2010; Dr hc (Queensland) 2007, (Sungkyunkwan Univ., Korea) 2008, (Australian Nat. Univ.) 2010, (S E European Univ., Macedonia) 2011, (Griffith Univ., Australia) 2014, Man of Achievement Award, Anti-Defamation League 2014, Int. Citizen of the Year Award, Int. Center 2016. *Publications:* several books, papers, and technical reports. *Leisure interests:* travel, reading, collecting art, theatre, opera. *Address:* Office of the President, Indiana University, Bryan Hall 200, 107 South Indiana Avenue, Bloomington, IN 47405, USA (office). *Telephone:* (812) 855-4613 (office). *E-mail:* iupres@indiana.edu (office). *Website:* www.indiana.edu/~pres (office).

MACRON, Emmanuel; French government official, politician, fmr investment banker and head of state; *President;* b. 21 Dec. 1977, Amiens (Somme); s. of Prof. Jean-Michel Macron, MD and Françoise Macron-Nogues; m. Brigitte Trogneux 2007; ed Lycée La Providence, Lycée Henri-IV, Univ. of Paris-Nanterre, Institut d'études politiques de Paris (Sciences Po), École nationale d'admin, Strasbourg; studied piano at Conservatory of Amiens for ten years; asst to philosopher Paul Ricoeur in the writing of his book La Mémoire, l'histoire, l'oubli (Memory, History, Forgetting) 1999–2001; with Inspection générale des Finances 2004–08; rapporteur, Comm. pour la libération de la croissance française (Comm. for the Liberation of French Growth) 2007; investment banker, Rothschild 2008–12; rapporteur on globalization, Jean Jaures Foundation 2010; Deputy Sec.-Gen., Presidency of the Repub. 2012–14; Minister of the Economy, Industry and Information Tech. 2014–16 (resgnd); Pres. of France 2017–, Co-Prince of Andorra 2017–; mem. 2012 Class of 'Young Leaders' of the French-American Foundation; mem. Parti Socialiste (Socialist Party) 2006–09; f. En Marche! (cross-party political movement), Leader 2016–; Laureate, Concours général de français 1994, Charlemagne Prize 2018, UN Champions of the Earth Award 2018. *Publication:* Revolution 2016. *Leisure interests:* piano, literature, classical music, tennis, boxing, football, skiing. *Address:* Office of the President, Palais de l'Elysée, 55–57 rue du Faubourg Saint Honoré, 75008 Paris, France (office). *Telephone:* 1-42-92-81-00 (office). *Fax:* 1-47-42-24-65 (office). *Website:* www.elysee.fr (office).

MacSHANE, Denis, MA, PhD; British politician; b. (Josef Denis Matyjaszek), 21 May 1948, Glasgow, Scotland; s. of Jan Matyjaszec and Isobel MacShane; one d. with Carol Barnes; m. 1st Liliana Kłaptoć 1983 (divorced 1986); m. 2nd Nathalie Pham 1987 (divorced 2003); one s. three d.; ed Merton Coll., Oxford, Birkbeck Coll., London; reporter, BBC 1969–77; Pres. Nat. Union of Journalists 1978–79; Policy Dir Int. Metalworkers Fed. 1980–92; Dir European Policy Inst. 1992–94; MP for Rotherham (Labour Party) 1994–2012 (resgnd); Parl. Pvt. Sec. to Ministers of Foreign Affairs 1997–2001; Parl. Under-Sec. of State, FCO 2001–02; Minister of State for Europe 2002–05; Visiting Fellow, St Antony's Coll., Oxford 1998–99; mem. Council, Royal Inst. of Int. Affairs from 1999, Council of Europe Parl. Ass. 2005, NATO Parl. Ass. 2005; sentenced to six months imprisonment for false accounting Dec. 2013, removed from Privy Council 2013. *Publications include:* Solidarity: Poland's Independent Trade Union 1981, François Mitterrand: A Political Odyssey 1982, Black Workers, Unions and the Struggle for Democracy in South Africa 1984, International Labour and the Origins of the Cold War 1992, Britain's Steel Industry in the 21st Century 1996, Globalising Hatred: The New Anti-Semitism 2008. *Leisure interests:* skiing, running.

MacSHARRY, Ray; Irish fmr politician; b. 29 April 1938, Sligo; s. of Patrick McSharry and Annie Clarke; m. Elaine Neilan 1960; three s. three d.; ed Summerhill Coll., Sligo; fmr haulier, auctioneer, farm-owner; joined Sligo Jr Chamber of Commerce 1966 (past Pres.); mem. Sligo County Council, Sligo Borough Council and Sligo Town Vocational Educ. Cttee 1967–78; mem. Dáil 1969–89; Minister of State, Dept of Finance and Public Service 1977–79; Minister for Agriculture 1979–81; Tanaiste and Minister for Finance March–Nov. 1982; MEP for Connaught/Ulster 1984–87; Minister for Finance 1987–88; EC Commr with responsibility for Agric. and Rural Devt 1989–93; pvt. business 1993–; Chair. London City Airport, Irish Equine Centre 1995; Dir Ryanair, Bank of Ireland Group 1993–2005; Gov. E.I.B. 1982; Fianna Fáil; Freeman Borough of Sligo 1993; Grand-Croix, Order of Leopold II 1993; Hon. DEconSci (Limerick) 1994; Hon. LLD (Nat. Univ. of Ireland) 1994; Business and Finance Man. of the Year 1988, Marcora Prize, Italy 1991, European of the Year 1992. *Leisure interest:* sport. *Address:* Alcantara, Pearse Road, Sligo, Ireland. *Telephone:* (71) 69902. *Fax:* (71) 69902.

McTAGGART, Roy Michael, JP; Cayman Islands business executive and politician; *Minister of Finance and Economic Development;* s. of William McTaggart, Sr and Carlene McTaggart; m.; three d.; joined KPMG, Cayman Islands 1985, transferred to KPMG, Orlando office 1986, returned to Cayman Islands 1988, admitted to partnership 1991, Jt Man. Partner 2003–07, Man. Partner 2007, Man. Dir, KMPG, British Virgin Islands 2007–12; mem. Legis. Ass. for George Town East 2017–; fmr Councillor, Ministry of Health, interim Minister of Health 2013–17; Minister of Finance and Econ. Devt 2017–; fmr Chair. Cayman Airways; fmr mem. Bd of Dirs Cayman Islands Stock Exchange; mem. Comm. for Standards in Public Life; Chair. Young Caymanian Leadership Foundation; mem. People's Progressive Movement (PPM). *Address:* Minister of Finance and Economic Development, 5th Floor, Government Administration Building, POB 106, 133 Elgin Ave, George Town, Grand Cayman, Cayman Islands (office). *Telephone:* 244-2224 (office). *Website:* www.mof.gov.ky (office).

McTEER, Janet, OBE; British actress; b. 8 May 1961, Newcastle upon Tyne, England; d. of Alan McTeer and Jean McTeer; ed Royal Acad. of Dramatic Arts, London; Bancroft Gold Medal 1983. *Theatre includes:* Much Ado About Nothing, Uncle Vanya, Simpatico, Vivat! Vivat Regina, London 1995, A Doll's House, London (Tony Award 1997, Laurence Olivier Theatre Award for Best Actress 1997, London Critics' Circle Theatre Award for Best Actress 1997), New York 1996–97. *Films include:* Half Moon Street 1986, Hawks 1988, Sweet Nothing 1990, I Dreamt I Woke Up 1991, Prince 1991, Wuthering Heights 1992, Carrington 1995, Velvet Goldmine (voice) 1998, Populous: The Beginning (video game; voice) 1998, Tumbleweeds 1999, Waking the Dead 2000, Songcatcher 2000, The King is Alive 2000, The Intended (also co-writer) 2002, Romeo and Me 2004, Tideland 2005, As You Like It 2006, Cat Run 2011, Island 2011, Albert Nobbs 2011, The Woman in Black 2012, Hannah Arendt 2012, Angelica 2015, Insurgent 2015. *Television appearances include:* Les Girls (series) 1988, Precious Bane 1989, Yellowbacks 1990, Portrait of a Marriage 1990, 102 Boulevard Haussmann 1990, The Black Velvet Gown 1991, A Masculine Ending 1992, Dead Romantic 1992, Don't Leave Me This Way 1993, The Governor (series) 1995, Marple: The Murder at the Vicarage 2004, Daphne 2007, Into the Storm 2009, Weekends at Bellevue 2011, Parade's End (mini-series) 2012, The White Queen (mini-series) 2013, The Honourable Woman (mini-series) 2014, Battle Creek (series) 2015. *Leisure interests:* cooking, gardens. *Address:* c/o International Creative Management, 40 West 57th Street, Floor 16, New York, NY 10019-4098, USA (office); c/o Michael Foster, ARG, 46 Maddox Street, London, W1S 1QA, England (office). *Telephone:* (20) 7436-6400 (London) (office). *E-mail:* argtalent@argtalent.com (office).

McTIERNAN, John; American film director; b. 8 Jan. 1951, Albany, NY; m. 2nd Donna Dubrow 1988 (divorced 1997); m. 3rd Kate Harrington 2003; ed Juilliard School of Drama, State Univ. of New York, Old Westbury Filmmaking Coll.; pleaded guilty to making false statements to FBI during investigations into pvt. detective Anthony Pellicano in 2010, fined $100,000 and sentenced to one year in prison, released 2014; Franklin J. Schaffner Award, American Film Inst. 1997. *Films include:* Nomads (also screenplay) 1986, Predator 1987, Die Hard 1988, The Hunt for Red October 1990, Medicine Man 1992, Last Action Hero (also exec. producer) 1993, Die Hard: With a Vengeance (also producer) 1995, Amanda (1996) (producer) 1996, The 13th Warrior (also producer) 1999, The Thomas Crown Affair 1999, Rollerball (also producer) 2002, Basic 2003. *Television includes:* Robin Hood (exec. producer) 1991, The Right to Remain Silent (producer) 1996, Quicksilver Highway (exec. producer) 1997.

McVEIGH, Elliot R., BS, PhD; Canadian medical scientist and academic; *Massey Professor and Director, Department of Biomedical Engineering, School of Medicine, Johns Hopkins University;* ed Univ. of Toronto; joined Faculty of Radiology, Johns Hopkins Univ. School of Medicine 1988, Founder and Dir Medical Imaging Lab., Dept of Biomedical Eng 1991, Massey Prof. and Dir Dept of Biomedical Eng 2007–; apptd Sr Investigator, Lab. of Cardiac Energetics, NIH, Bethesda, Md 1999, later Prin. Investigator; Whitaker Development Award 1991. *Publications:* more than 150 peer-reviewed research papers in professional journals on cardiovascular MRI, image guided therapy and novel MRI methods. *Address:* Medical Imaging Laboratory, Whitaker Biomedical Engineering Institute, Johns Hopkins University School of Medicine, 720 Rutland Avenue, Ross 720, Baltimore, MD 21205, USA (office). *Telephone:* (410) 502-7145 (office). *Fax:* (410) 502-9814 (office). *E-mail:* emcveigh@bme.jhu.edu (office). *Website:* www.bme.jhu.edu (office).

McVEY, Esther, PC, LLB, MA, MSc; British politician, business executive and fmr television presenter; b. 24 Oct. 1967, Liverpool; ed Queen Mary Univ. of London, City Univ. London, Liverpool John Moores Univ.; began career as TV presenter for GMTV and BBC North West 1990s; Dir J. G. McVey & Co. (family construction business), Liverpool 2000–06; Founder and Man. Dir Making It (UK) Ltd; Founder Winning Women (business network); mem. House of Commons (Conservative) for Wirral West 2010–15, for Tatton 2017–; Minister of State, Dept for Work and Pensions 2013–15, Sec. of State for Work and Pensions Jan.–Nov. 2018; Conservative. *Address:* House of Commons Information Office, Norman Shaw North, London, SW1A 2TT, England (office).

McVIE, John Gordon, BSc, MB, ChB, MD, PhD, DSc, FRCP, FRCPS, FRCPE, FRCSE, FMedSci; British doctor and cancer specialist; *Senior Consultant, Istituto Europea Oncologica, Milan;* b. 13 Jan. 1945, Glasgow, Scotland; s. of John McVie and Lindsaye Mair; m. 1st Evelyn Strang 1966 (divorced 1996); three s.; m. 2nd Claudia Joan Burke; one step-s. one step-d.; ed Royal High School, Edin. and Univ. of Edinburgh; House Officer, Royal Hosp. for Sick Children and Royal Infirmary, Edinburgh 1969–70; MRC Fellow, Univ. of Edinburgh 1970–71, Lecturer in Therapeutics 1971–76; Sr Lecturer in Clinical Oncology, Univ. of Glasgow 1976–80; Head, Clinical Research Unit, Netherlands Cancer Inst. Amsterdam 1980–84, Clinical Research Dir 1984–89; Scientific Dir, Cancer Research Campaign 1989–96; Dir Gen. Cancer Research UK 1996–2002; Sr Consultant, Istituto Europea Oncologica, Milan 2004–; Visiting Prof., Univ. of Sydney, Australia 1983, British Postgraduate Medical Fed., Univ. of London 1990–96, Univ. of Glasgow 1996–, Univ. of Wales 2004–; Pres. European Org. for Research and Treatment of Cancer 1994; European Ed., Journal of the National Cancer Institute 1995–2001; Founding Ed. ecancermedicalscience.com 2007; Dir, Beatson Inst. for Cancer Research 1989–96, Cancer Research Technology Ltd 1991–2002, Photo Therapeutics Group Ltd 1999–2001, 2001–02, Cancer Intelligence Ltd 2002–; mem. numerous advisory cttees etc.; Hon. DSc (Univ. of Abertay, Dundee) 1996, (Univ. of Nottingham) 1997, (Univ. of Portsmouth) 1999, (Edinburgh Napier Univ.) 2002, (Univ. of Ghent, Belgium) 2005; Gunning Victoria Jubilee Prize in Pathology, Univ. of Edinburgh, Honeyman Gillespie Lecturer in Oncology 1977. *Publications include:* Cancer Assessment and Monitoring 1979, Autologous Bone Marrow Transplantation and Solid Tumours 1984, Microspheres and Drug Therapy 1984, Clinical and Experimental Pathology and Biology of Lung Cancer 1985; 35 chapters in books; 230 articles in books and journals. *Leisure interests:* opera, music in general, theatre, walking, rugby, cooking, Italian wine-tasting, family. *Address:* Istituto Europea Oncologica, Via Ripamonti 435, 20141 Milan, Italy (office). *Telephone:* (02574) 89946 (office). *Fax:* (02574) 89922 (office). *E-mail:* gordonmcvie@doctors.org.uk (home). *Website:* www.ieo.it (office); www.cancerintelligence.com (office).

McWHA, James Alexander, AO, BSc, BAgr (Hons), PhD; British/New Zealand university administrator (retd) and academic; b. 28 May 1947, Co. Down, Northern Ireland; s. of David McWha and Sarah Isabel Caughey; m. Jean Lindsay Farries 1970; one s. two d.; ed Queen's Univ., Belfast, Univ. of Glasgow; Lecturer in Plant Physiology, Univ. of Canterbury, NZ 1973–79, Head of Dept of Plant and Microbial Sciences 1980–85; Prof. of Agricultural Botany, Queen's Univ. Belfast 1985–89; Deputy Chief Scientific Officer, Dept of Agric. for NI 1985–89, Council Nat. Inst. of Agricultural Botany 1985–89; Dir Dept of Scientific and Industrial Research Fruit Trees (NZ) 1989–92; CEO Horticulture and Food Research Inst. (NZ) 1992–95; Vice-Chancellor and Pres. Massey Univ. 1996–2002; Vice-Chancellor and Pres. Univ. of Adelaide 2002–12; Vice-Chancellor Univ. of Rwanda 2013–15; Patron Children's Univ. of Australia; Hon. Treas. Asscn of Commonwealth Univs 2007–, Exec. Cttee of Int. Asscn of Univ. Presidents; PhD (ad eundem gradum) (Adelaide) 2002; Hon. DSc (Massey Univ.) 2004; Centenary Medal for services to educ. 2003. *Leisure interests:* classic and vintage cars, rugby union. *Telephone:* (8) 8344-2524 (Australia). *E-mail:* james@mcwha.org.

McWILLIAMS, Sir Francis, GBE, BSc, FREng, FCGI; British fmr lawyer, arbitrator and civil engineer; b. 8 Feb. 1926, Edin.; s. of John McWilliams and Mary McWilliams; m. Winifred Segger 1950; two s.; ed Holy Cross Acad., Edin., Univ. of Edin.; engineer with various local authorities and contractors in UK 1945–53; Town Engineer, Petaling Jaya Devt Corpn, Malaysia 1954–64; Consulting Civil and Structural Engineer, F. McWilliams & Assocs, Kuala Lumpur 1964–76; full-time student 1976–78; called to English bar at Lincoln's Inn 1978; pupil barrister 1978–79; Int. Arbitrator 1979–; magistrate, City of London Bench 1980–96; Chair. Centre for Econs and Business Research 1992–2002; Vice-Pres. and Chair. British/Malaysian Soc. 1994–2001; mem. Panel of Arbitrators of Inst. of Civil Engineers and other bodies; Sheriff City of London 1988–89, Lord Mayor of London 1992–93; Bencher of Lincoln's Inn 1993; fmr mem. Court of Aldermen, City of London; Master Worshipful Co. of Engineers 1990–91, Worshipful Co. of Loriners 1995; Hon. FICE; KStJ, Kt of St Gregory, Kt, Dato Sri Selera (Malaysia) 1973; Hon. DCL (City Univ.) 1992; Hon. DEng (Kingston); Dr hc (Edin.); several other awards and hons. *Publication:* Urban Regeneration and Environmental Challenge, Pray Silence for 'Jock' Whittington (From Building Sewers to Suing Builders). *Leisure interests:* golf, skiing. *Address:* Flat 7, Whittingehame House, Whittingehame, East Lothian, EH41 4QA, Scotland (home). *Telephone:* (1368) 850619 (home). *Fax:* (1368) 850619 (home).

MACY, William H.; American actor; b. 13 March 1950, Miami, Fla; m. Felicity Huffman; ed Goddard Coll.; co-f. St Nicholas Theater Co., Atlantic Theater Co. *Stage appearances include:* The Man in 605 1980, Twelfth Night, Bureaucrat, A Call From the East, The Dining Room, Speakeasy, Wild Life, Flirtations, Baby With the Bathwater, The Nice and the Nasty, Bodies Rest and Motion, Oh Hell!, Prairie du Chien, The Shawl, An Evening With Dorothy Parker, The Dining Room, A Call From the Sea, The Beaver Coat, Life During Wartime, Mr Gogol and Mr Preen, Oleanna, Our Town. *Play directed:* Boy's Life. *Films include:* Without a Trace, The Last Dragon, Radio Days, Somewhere in Time, Hello Again, House of Games, Things Change, Homicide, Shadows and Fog, Benny and Joon, Searching for Bobby Fischer, The Client, Oleanna, The Silence of the Lambs, Murder in the First, Mr Holland's Opus, Down Periscope, Fargo, Ghosts of Mississippi, Air Force One, Wag the Dog, Pleasantville 1998, A Civil Action, Psycho 1998, Magnolia 1999, State and Maine 2000, Panic 2000, Focus 2001, Jurassic Park III 2001, Welcome to Collinwood 2002, The Cooler 2003, Stealing Sinatra 2003, Out of Order (TV mini series) 2003, Seabiscuit 2004, Spartan 2004, Cellular 2004, Sahara 2005, Edmond 2005, Thank You for Smoking 2005, Doogal (voice) 2006, Bobby 2006, Inland Empire 2006, Everyone's Hero (voice) 2006, Wild Hogs 2007, He was a Quiet Man 2007, The Sessions 2012, A Single Shot 2013, Trust Me 2013, Rudderless 2014, Two-Bit Waltz 2014, Walter 2015. *Film directed:* Lip Service (TV) 1988. *Television appearances include:* The Murder of Mary Phagan (mini-series) 1988, The Lionharts (series) 1998, Sports Night (series) 1999–2000, Out of Order (mini-series) 2003, Family Man (film) 2008, ER (series) 1994–2009, Shameless (Outstanding Performance by a Male Actor in a Comedy Series, Screen Actors Guild 2015, SAG Award for Outstanding Performance by a Male Actor in a Comedy Series 2017) 2011–16. *Address:* c/o Creative Artists Agency, 9830 Wilshire Blvd, Beverly Hills, CA 90212-1825, USA. *Website:* www.caa.com.

MĄDALSKI, Wojciech, MSc, MEng; Polish business executive; b. 2 May 1956, Wrocław; s. of Jozef Mądalski and Hanna Mądalska (née Machowska); m. Kasia Swiatek 1980; one d.; ed Tech. Univ. Wrocław, McMaster Univ., Hamilton, Ont., Canada; Teaching/Research Asst, McMaster Univ., Hamilton, Ont., Canada 1980–82; Research Engineer, Tech. Devt Div., Polysar Ltd, Sarnia, Ont. 1982–84; Marketing/Business Planning Analyst, Styrenics Div. 1984–86, Business Man., Adhesives and Sealants Div. 1986–88; Gen. Man., Silicone Business, Novacor Chemicals Inc., Akron, OH, USA 1988–91; Pres. and CEO, Shincor Silicones Inc. 1991–93; CEO, E. Wedel SA and Pres., PepsiCo Foods International (PFI), Poland 1993–95; Vice-Pres., PFI Europe Group, UK 1996–97; ECR Dir, Walkers Snack Foods Ltd 1998; CEO and Pres., Hortex Holding SA 1998–2001; Man. Dir, Carlsberg Breweries A/S, Poland 2002; CEO and Pres. of the Man. Bd, Netia Holdings SA 2002–06. *Address:* c/o Netia Holdings SA, ul. Poleczki 13, 02-822 Warsaw, Poland. *E-mail:* info@netia.pl.

MADANI, Iyad bin Amin; Saudi Arabian media executive and international organization official; b. 26 April 1946, Mecca; ed Arizona State Univ., USA; Gen. Dir of admin. office, Saudi Airlines 1970; Gen. Dir Okaz Org. for Press and Publication –1993; Ed.-in-Chief Saudi Gazette (newspaper) –1999; mem. Shura Council –1999; Minister of Hajj 1999–2005, Minister of Information and Culture 2005–09; Head, Islamic Int. News Agency and Org. of Islamic Broadcasting 2007–09; Chair. Knowledge Econ. City, Madina 2012; Sec.-Gen., Organization of Islamic Cooperation 2014–16; mem. Bd of Dirs Dept of Water and Sanitation; mem. King Abdulaziz and His Companions Foundation for Giftedness and Creativity; mem. Advisory Bd of Supreme Council, Gulf Cooperation Council; mem. Bd of Trustees, Gulf Univ., Bahrain; editorial consultant for Ahlan Wa Sahlan magazine; fmr Vice-Pres. King Abdullah bin Abdulaziz Foundation for Housing Devt; Darjah Kebesaran Panglima Setia Mahkota (Malaysia) 2009, Order from Sultanate of Oman, 2nd Class; Dr hc (Int. Islamic Univ. of Malaysia); Medal of Honor (China).

MAĎARIČ, Marek; Slovak politician; b. 23 March 1966, Bratislava; m. Zuzana Madarič; ed Acad. of Musical and Dramatic Arts; Script Ed., Office of Literary and Dramatic Broadcasting, Slovak TV 1990–93, Ed.-in-Chief 1996–97, Script Ed., Slovak TV 1997–99; Deputy Pres. of the Council 2002–04; freelance scriptwriter 1993–96; copywriter, Istropolitana D'Arcy (advertising agency) 1999–2000; Head of Media and Press Dept, Social Democracy Party 2000–02, 2004–06; Minister of Culture 2006–10, 2012–18; mem. Národná rada (Parl.) 2006– (Social Democracy Party –2018, Ind. 2018–. *Leisure interests:* literature, film, dog, garden. *E-mail:* marek_madaric@nrsr.sk. *Website:* madaric.blog.sme.sk.

MADBOULY, Moustafa, PhD; Egyptian politician and architect; *Prime Minister;* b. 28 April 1966; ed Cairo Univ., Inst. for Housing and Urban Devt Studies; Chair. General Authority for Urban Planning, Ministry of Housing, Utilities and Urban Devt 2009–11, also UnderSec.; Regional Dir UNCHS 2012–14; Minister of Housing, Utilities and Urban Devt 2014–; Acting Prime Minister June 2018, Prime Minister 2018–; fmr Exec. Dir Training and Urban Studies Inst., Ministry of Housing. *Address:* Office of the Prime Minister, 2 Sharia Majlis al-Sha'ab, Cairo 11582, Egypt (office). *Telephone:* (2) 27935000 (office). *Fax:* (2) 27958048 (office). *E-mail:* questions@cabinet.gov.eg (office). *Website:* www.cabinet.gov.eg (office).

MADDEN, Sir David, Kt, KCMG, MA; British fmr diplomatist; b. 1946; m. Lady Penelope Anthea Madden; ed Univ. of Oxford, Courtauld Inst., London; joined British Diplomatic Service 1970; overseas assignments in Berlin, Moscow, Athens and Belgrade; various positions in FCO including Head of S European Dept –1994; High Commr to Cyprus 1994–99; Amb. to Greece 1999–2004 (retd); Political Adviser, EU Force in Bosnia and Herzegovina (EUFOR) 2004–05; Chair. SEESOX Devt Cttee, mem. SEESOX Steering Cttee; Sr mem. St Anthony's Coll., Oxford; Trustee, The Brooke (equine welfare charity) 2008–, mem. Finance and Governance Cttees. *Leisure interests:* music (especially opera), sport (especially tennis, cricket and rowing), reading, animal welfare. *Address:* The Brooke, 30 Farringdon Street, London, EC4A 4HH, England (office). *Telephone:* (20) 3012-3456 (office). *Fax:* (20) 3012-0156 (office). *Website:* www.thebrooke.org (office).

MADDEN, John; British film director; b. 8 April 1949, Portsmouth, Hants., England. *Films include:* Golden Gate 1994, Mrs. Brown 1997, Shakespeare in Love (Acad. Award for Best Film, BAFTA Award for Best Film) 1998, Captain Corelli's Mandolin 2001, Proof 2004, Killshot 2006, The Debt 2011, The Best Exotic Marigold Hotel 2011, The Second Best Exotic Marigold Hotel 2015, Miss Sloane 2016. *Television includes:* Grown-Ups 1985, The Return of Sherlock Holmes

(series; episode The Priory School) 1986, A Wreath of Roses 1987, Inspector Morse (series; episodes Dead on Time, The Infernal Serpent, Promised Land, The Way Through the Woods) 1987, After the War (mini-series) 1989, The Widowmaker 1990, The Storyteller: Greek Myths (mini-series; episode Theseus and the Minotaur) 1990, The Casebook of Sherlock Holmes (series; episode The Disappearance of Lady Frances Carfax) 1990, Ethan Frome 1993, Meat 1994, Prime Suspect 4: The Lost Child 1995, Truth or Dare 1996, Masters of Sex 2013.

MADDEN, Paul Damian, CMG, MA, MBA; British diplomatist; *Ambassador to Japan;* b. 25 April 1959, Devon, England; m. Sarah Pauline Madden; two s. one d.; ed School of Oriental and African Studies, Univ. of London, Univ. of Cambridge, Durham Univ.; began career at Dept for Trade and Industry 1980, Pvt. Sec. to Minister for Small Business 1984–85, to Minister for Corp. Affairs 1985–86, Head Japan Desk 1986–87; First Sec., Embassy in Tokyo 1988–92, Desk Officer, Environment, Science and Energy Dept, FCO 1992–94, EU Dept 1994–96, First Sec., Embassy in Washington, DC 1996–2000, Deputy High Commr 2000–03, Head of Public Diplomacy Policy Dept, FCO 2003–04; Man. Dir UK Trade and Investment 2004–06; High Commr to Singapore 2007–11, to Australia 2011–15, Additional Dir, Asia Pacific, FCO 2015, Japanese language training 2015–17, Amb. to Japan 2017–. *Publications include:* Raffles: Lessons in Business Leadership 2003. *Address:* British Embassy, 1 Ichiban-cho, Chiyoda-ku, Tokyo 102-8381, Japan (office). *Telephone:* (3) 5211-1100 (office). *Fax:* (3) 5275-3164 (office). *E-mail:* consular.tokyo@fco.gov.uk (office); public-enquiries.tokyo@fco.gov.uk (office). *Website:* www.gov.uk/government/world/organisations/british-embassy-tokyo (office); www.gov.uk/government/world/japan (office).

MADDISON, Vice-Adm. (retd) Paul, CMM, MSM, CD, BA; Canadian naval officer (retd) and diplomatist; *High Commissioner to Australia;* m. Fay Maddison; ed Royal Mil. Coll., Saint-Jean; joined Royal Canadian Navy 1975, served on various vessels and in appointments with both Atlantic and Pacific fleets, deployed to Persian Gulf with Canadian Task Group 1991, Exec. Officer for frigate HMCS Winnipeg 1994–96, Commdr HMCS Calgary 1997–99, posted to NORAD HQ 1999–2002, Capt. of destroyer HMCS Iroquois 2002–04, also deployed to Persian Gulf and Arabian Sea as part of Combined Task Force 151, Dir Gen. Maritime Force Devt, Nat. Defence HQ, Ottawa 2005–06, Commdr Standing Contingency Task Force 2006–07, Asst Chief of Mil. Personnel 2007–08, Commdr Maritime Forces Atlantic as well as Jt Task Force Atlantic (mil. org. responsible for domestic operations in Atlantic Canada) 2007–10, Asst Chief of Maritime Staff under Vice-Adm. Dean McFadden, Commdr Royal Canadian Navy 2011–13; High Commr to Australia 2015–; Commdr, Order of Mil. Merit, Meritorious Service Medal (MSM), Gulf and Kuwait Medal with Clasp, South-West Asia Service Medal with Clasp, Special Service Medal, Queen Elizabeth II Diamond Jubilee Medal 2012, Canadian Forces Decoration (CD) with two Clasps, Commdr, Legion of Merit (USA) 2013, Officier, Légion d'honneur 2013. *Address:* Canadian High Commission, Commonwealth Avenue, Canberra ACT 2600, Australia (office). *Telephone:* (2) 6270-4000 (office). *Fax:* (2) 6270-4081 (office). *E-mail:* cnbra@international.gc.ca (office). *Website:* www.australia.gc.ca (office).

MADDOW, Rachel Anne, DPhil; American television presenter and political commentator; b. 1 April 1973, Castro Valley, Calif.; d. of Robert B. (Bob) Maddow and Elaine Maddow (née Gosse); pnr Susan Mikula 1999–; ed Castro Valley High School, Stanford Univ., Lincoln Coll., Oxford, UK (Rhodes Scholar); first radio hosting job at WRNX, Holyoke, Mass after winning contest to find new on-air personality; hired to co-host WRNX's morning show, The Dave in the Morning Show (first openly gay anchor to be hired to host a prime-time news programme in USA); went on to host Big Breakfast on WRSI, Northampton, Mass 2002–04; joined Air America 2004, hosted Unfiltered along with Chuck D (of the hip hop group Public Enemy) and Lizz Winstead (co-creator of The Daily Show) 2004–05, then The Rachel Maddow Show 2005–10; given position of MSNBC Political Analyst 2008, regular panellist on MSNBC's Race for the White House with David Gregory and MSNBC's election coverage, as well as frequent contrib. on Countdown with Keith Olbermann; substitute host for Countdown with Keith Olbermann April 2008 (first time hosting a programme on MSNBC); began hosting own nightly MSNBC TV show 2008–; Hon. LLD (Smith Coll., Northampton, Mass) 2010; John Gardner Fellowship, Stanford Univ., Gracie Award, American Women in Radio and Television 2009, Proclamation of Honor from Calif. State Senate 2009, 21st Annual GLAAD Media Awards in category, Outstanding TV Journalism-Newsmagazine for her segment, Uganda Be Kidding Me 2010, Commencement Speaker, Smith Coll. 2010, Maggie Award for ongoing reporting of health-care reform, the murder of Dr George Tiller, and the anti-abortion movement 2010, Walter Cronkite Faith & Freedom Award, The Interfaith Alliance 2010. *Television includes:* host of The Rachel Maddow Show (TV series) on MSNBC 2008– (highest rated show on MSNBC on several occasions). *Publication:* Drift: the Unmooring of American Military Power 2012. *Address:* The Rachel Maddow Show, c/o MSNBC Interactive News LLC, 30 Rockefeller Plaza, New York, NY 10112, USA (office). *Telephone:* (212) 664-4444 (office). *Fax:* (212) 664-4085 (office). *Website:* www .msnbc.msn.com/id/26315908/ns/msnbc_tv-rachel_maddow_show (office); maddowblog.msnbc.msn.com (office).

MADDY, Penelope, BA, PhD; American academic; *Distinguished Professor of Logic and Philosophy of Science, and of Mathematics and of Philosophy, University of California, Irvine;* b. 4 July 1950, Tulsa, Okla; d. of Richard Parsons and Suzanne Parsons; ed Univ. of California, Berkeley, Princeton Univ.; Lecturer then Asst Prof. of Philosophy, Univ. of Notre Dame 1978–83; Assoc. Prof. of Philosophy, Univ. of Illinois, Chicago 1983–87; Assoc. Prof. of Philosophy and Math., Univ., of California, Irvine 1987–89, Prof. 1989–98, Chair. Philosophy Dept 1991–95, Prof. of Logic and Philosophy of Science and of Math. 1998–2007, Distinguished Prof. of Logic and Philosophy of Science and of Math. 2007–, and of Philosophy 2014–; Founding Chair. Logic and Philosophy of Science 1998–2001; mem. American Acad. of Arts and Sciences 1998; Phi Beta Kappa/Romanell Prof. 2014–15; Westinghouse Science Scholarship 1968–72, Marshall Fellowship 1972–73, American Asscn of Univ. Women Fellowship 1982–83, NSF Fellowships 1986, 1988–89, 1990–91, 1994–95, Romanell Lecturer 2001, Gauss Lecturer 2006, Ambrose/Tymoczko Lecturer 2007. *Publications including:* Realism in Mathematics 1990, Naturalism in Mathematics (Lakatos Prize 2002) 1997, Second Philosophy 2007, Defending the Axioms 2011, The Logical Must 2014, What Do Philosophers Do? 2017. *Address:* Department of Logic and Philosophy of Science,

Office SST 759, School of Social Sciences, University of California, Irvine, CA 92697-5100, USA (office). *Telephone:* (949) 824-4133 (office). *E-mail:* pjmaddy@uci .edu (office). *Website:* faculty.sites.uci.edu/pjmaddy (office).

MADE, Joseph; Zimbabwean politician; *Minister of Agriculture, Mechanisation and Irrigation Development;* b. 21 Nov. 1954; mem. Zimbabwe African Nat. Union-Patriotic Front (ZANU-PF); Minister for Lands, Agric. and Rural Devt 2000–07, of Agric., Mechanisation and Irrigation Devt 2007–17; mem. fmr Pres. Robert Mugabe's 'Gang of Four' politicians.

MADELIN, Alain, LenD; French lawyer and politician; b. 26 March 1946, Paris; three c.; lawyer, Paris office, Fed. nat. des Républicains indépendants (FNRI) 1968–; mem. Nat. Secr. FNRI 1977; Deputy to Nat. Ass. (Union pour la démocratie française—UDF) 1978–86, 1988–93, 1995–2002, 2002–07 (UMP); co-organizer UDF 1989–93; Vice-Pres. UDF 1991–96; Minister of Industry, Posts and Telecommunications and Tourism 1986–88, of Enterprise and Econ. Devt 1993–95, of Econ. and Finance May–Aug. 1995; Sec.-Gen. Republican Party 1988–89, Vice-Pres. 1989–96; Pres. France-Corée Asscn 1991–93; Vice-Pres. Regional Council of Brittany 1992–98; Mayor of Redon 1995–2000; mem. European Parl. 1989–2002; Pres. Inst. Euro 92 1988–97, Founder and Pres. Idées Action 1993–97; Leader Démocratie libérale 1997–2002; unsuccessful presidential cand. 2002; Pres. Cercles libéraux (think-tank), Paris 2002–; Pres. Fonds mondial de solidarité numérique (Global Digital Solidarity Fund), Geneva 2008–10. *Publications:* Pour libérer l'école 1984, Chers compatriotes 1994, Quand les autruches relèveront la tête 1995, Aux Sources du modèle libéral français 1997, Le Droit du plus faible 1999, Quand les autruches prendront leur retraite 2003, Faut-il supprimer la carte scolaire? 2009. *Website:* www.alainmadelin.fr.

MADFAI, Husham H. Fahmi al-, BSc; Iraqi engineering consultant and government official; b. 28 Oct. 1928, Baghdad; s. of Hassan Fahmi al-Madfai and Wajiha Nouri al-Madfai; m. 1st Suad A. Mohloom (died 1984); one s. one d.; m. 2nd Suha M. A. Bakri 1993; ed Cen. High School, Baghdad, Eng Coll., Univ. of Baghdad, Hammersmith School of Art & Design, London and Inst. of Structural Engineers, London, UK; civil engineer, Basrah Petroleum Co. 1953–55; with Dept of Housing and Tourism Design and Policies, Devt Bd 1957–63; Head. Tech. Dept, Municipality of Baghdad 1963–68; own consulting firm (architects, planners and designers) 1968–80; Deputy Mayor (responsible for planning and man.), City of Baghdad 1980–88; own consulting firm (studies and eng) 1988–; Regional Consultant (feasibility, studies and design), Amman, Jordan 1994–; currently heading Dar Al Imara (DAI) for the Reconstruction Program of Iraq; mem. Iraqi Asscn of Philosophers and Scientists 1994. *Publications include:* Health Aspects in Town Planning 1968, Low-cost Prefabricated Housing 1975, Housing Programme for Iraq until the year 2000 1976, Environmental Problems in Arab Cities 1995. *Leisure interests:* archaeology, studying ancient cities, music, paintings, reading biographies, swimming, long walks. *Address:* PO Box 941021, Shmesan 1, Amman 11194, Jordan; Maghrib Street, Adhamiya 22/14/302, Baghdad, Iraq; MGTC LLC, ICON Tower, Unit 904, Tecom, Dubai UAE. *Telephone:* (6) 5688470 (Amman); (1) 4225021/2 (Baghdad); (4) 4437330 (Dubai). *Fax:* (6) 5688498 (Amman); (4) 4431937 (Dubai).

MADFAI, Kahtan al, BArch, PhD; Iraqi architect, town planner and author; b. 15 April 1926, Baghdad; s. of Hassan Fahmi al Madfai and Wajiha Shaikh Noori Shirwai; m. Lily Vassiliki Vorré 1957; one d.; ed Central High School, Baghdad, Univ. of Wales Inst. of Science and Tech., Cardiff, UK; practised as architect in public housing sector 1957, planning and design 1961; co-f. Architectural School of Baghdad 1961; lecturer on theory of design 1955–69; f. architectural firm Dar al Imara 1954–79; Asst Man. Gen. Housing Iraq Project 1973–2000; designer and consultant architect; Chair. Pan-Arab Jury for awarding prizes for Arab Town Projects 1985–87; delivered papers and seminars Istanbul 1985, Oxford 1986, Tunis 1987, 1989, Bahrain 1994, Baghdad 1994, Univ. of South Georgia, USA 1996, AIA, Atlanta, USA 1996, Amman 1996; co-f. Soc. of Iraqi Artists; mem. S.P. Group of Artists, Baghdad; works in Baghdad include Ministry of Finance 1968, Bunniyd Mosque 1972, Museum of Natural History 1973, Burj Rubaya apartment building Abu Dhabi 1990, Fatiha Halls project 2003; mem. Baghdad Union and Soc. of Engineers; several first prizes in architectural competitions, including Rohoon Bank Bldg, Baghdad 1955, Baghdad Cen. Commercial Zone 1970, Cen. PO 1975, Mohammedia Touristic Project, Basra 1977, Great Mosque Competition 1984, Tamayouz Lifetime Achievement Award for Architecture 2016. *Publications:* several books on architecture and town planning including Development of the Iraqi House 1956, Criteria for Baghdad's New Master Plan 1965, A Manifesto for Arabic Architecture 1986, Architecture and Language 1987, Allah and the Architect 1997; poetry: Fulool 1965, Zem Zem Zeman 1972, Reconstruction of the Sumerian God Abu 1990. *Leisure interests:* modern art, modern poetry, modern philosophy. *Address:* 11 Aristoxenov, Pangrati, Athens; 22 Vassileos Constantinou, 11635 Athens, Greece. *Telephone:* (210) 721-7189 (Athens) (home); (210) 751-4120 (Athens) (home); (1) 4225021 (Baghdad) (office); (210) 723-2836 (Athens) (office); (1) 4220680 (Baghdad) (home). *Fax:* (210) 724-9920 (Athens) (office).

MADKOUR, Nazli, MA; Egyptian artist and painter; b. 25 Feb. 1949, Cairo; d. of Mokhtar Madkour and Malak Salem; m. Mohamed Salmawy 1970; one s. one d.; ed Cairo Univ., American Univ., Cairo; fmrly econ. expert for Industrial Devt Centre for Arab States; professional artist 1981–; numerous solo and collective exhbns; represented in public and pvt. collections in Egypt and internationally. *Publication:* Egyptian Women and Artistic Creativity 1989. *Leisure interests:* travel, reading, music. *Address:* #40 Street 13, Maadi, Cairo 11431, Egypt. *Telephone:* (2) 3804446.

MADONNA; American singer, actress and fashion designer; b. (Madonna Louise Veronica Ciccone), 16 Aug. 1958, Bay City, Mich.; d. of Sylvio Ciccone and Madonna Ciccone; m. 1st Sean Penn 1985 (divorced 1989); one d. by Carlos Leon; m. 2nd Guy Ritchie 2000 (divorced 2008); two s. (one adopted); ed Rochester Adams High School, Mich., Univ. of Michigan, Alvin Ailey Dance School; moved to New York 1979, dancer 1979–, actress 1980–, solo singer 1983–; numerous worldwide concerts, tours, TV appearances; f. Maverick record label 1992 (sold to Warner Music Group 2004); Vice-Pres. ICA, London, UK; est. children's clothing line, Sweet Hearts 2004; launched Material Girl clothing line with daughter Lourdes 2010; numerous MTV Video Awards, including Vanguard Award 1986, American Music Awards for Favorite Female Video Artist 1987, Favorite Dance Single 1991,

Academy Award for Best Song 1991, Juno Award for Int. Song of the Year 1991, Grammy Award for Best Longform Music Video 1992, BRIT Award for Best Int. Female 2001, 2006, numerous awards from Billboard, Vogue and Rolling Stone magazines, Echo Award for Best Int. Female Artist, Germany 2006, Ivor Novello Award for Int. Hit of the Year (for Sorry) 2007, Billboard Music Awards for Top Dance Artist 2013, for Top Touring Artist 2013, Woman of the Year, Billboard magazine 2016. *Tours:* The Virgin Tour 1985, Who's That Girl World Tour 1987, Blond Ambition World Tour 1990, The Girlie Show World Tour 1993, Drowned World Tour 2001, Re-Invention World Tour 2004, Confessions Tour 2006, Sticky & Sweet Tour 2008–09, M.D.N.A. Tour 2012, Rebel Heart Tour 2015. *Plays:* Speed-the-Plow (Broadway) 1988, Up for Grabs (Wyndhams Theatre, London) 2002. *Films include:* A Certain Sacrifice 1979, Vision Quest 1985, Desperately Seeking Susan 1985, Shanghai Surprise 1986, Who's That Girl? 1987, Bloodhounds on Broadway 1989, Dick Tracy 1990, Shadows and Fog 1991, Madonna: Truth or Dare (aka In Bed with Madonna) (documentary) 1991, A League of Their Own 1992, Body of Evidence 1993, Dangerous Game (aka Snake Eyes) 1993, Blue in the Face (aka Brooklyn Boogie) 1995, Four Rooms 1995, Girl 6 1996, Evita 1996, The Next Best Thing 2000, Swept Away 2002, I'm Going to Tell You a Secret 2005, Arthur and the Minimoys (aka Arthur and the Invisibles) (voice) 2006, Filth and Wisdom (writer and dir) 2008, I Am Because We Are (documentary, writer) 2008, W.E. (co-writer and dir) (Golden Globe Award for Best Original Song, 'Masterpiece' 2012) 2011. *Television includes:* Will & Grace (series) 2003. *Recordings include:* albums: Madonna 1983, Like A Virgin 1984, True Blue 1986, Who's That Girl? (film soundtrack) 1987, Like A Prayer 1989, I'm Breathless (soundtrack to film Dick Tracy) 1990, The Immaculate Collection 1990, Erotica 1992, Bedtime Stories 1994, Something To Remember 1995, Evita (film soundtrack) 1997, Ray Of Light (Grammy Award for Best Pop Album) 1998, Next Best Thing (film soundtrack) 2000, Music 2000, GHV2 2001, American Life 2003, Remixed and Revisited (EP) 2004, Confessions On A Dance Floor (Grammy Award for Best Electronic/Dance Album 2007) 2005, I'm Going to Tell You a Secret 2006, Hard Candy 2008, M.D.N.A. (Billboard Music Award for Top Dance Album 2013) 2012, Rebel Heart 2015. *Publications:* Sex 1992, The English Roses (juvenile) 2003, Mr Peabody's Apples (juvenile) 2003, Yakov and the Seven Thieves (juvenile) 2004, The Adventures of Abdi (juvenile) 2004, Lotsa de Casha (juvenile) 2005. *Website:* www.madonna.com.

MADRAZO PINTADO, Roberto, LLB; Mexican politician and lawyer; b. 30 July 1952; s. of Carlos Madrazo Becerra y la Profra and Graciela Pintado Jiménez; m. Isabel de la Parra Trillo; two s. three d.; ed Universidad Nacional Autónoma, Mexico; entered civil service 1971; legal asst to Alvaro Obregón 1971–72; worked in office of Chief Justice 1972, adviser on social affairs 1979–81; Deputy Sec.-Gen. for Youth, Partido Revolucionario Institucional (PRI) 1975, Sec.-Gen. Nat. Movt of Revolutionary Youth 1977, Sec. of Public Relations and Man. 1984–87, Sec. of Org. 1988–, Pres. PRI 2002–06; elected Fed. Deputy, State of Tabasco 1976, State Gov. 1988–91, Governor 1994–2000; mem. 55th legislature, Fed. Govt 1991–93; Founder and Pres. Escuela Nacional de Cuadros; apptd Sec. of the Great Comm., Palace of San Lazaro; unsuccessful Cand. for Pres. of Mexico 2006. *Publications:* Urbanism, Services and Public Security; numerous articles on social affairs, int. relations and devt. *Address:* c/o Partido Revolucionario Institucional, Insurgentes Norte 59, Edif. 2, subsótano, Col Buenavista, 06359 México, DF, Mexico (office).

MADSEN, Ib, PhD; Danish mathematician and academic; *Professor Emeritus of Mathematics, Copenhagen University;* b. 12 April 1942, Copenhagen; s. of Hennig Madsen and Gudrun Madsen (née Davids-Thomsen); m. 1st Benedicte Rechnitzer 1963 (divorced 1982); m. 2nd Ulla Lykke Jorgensen 1984; two s.; ed Univ. of Copenhagen, Univ. of Chicago, USA; Research Stipend, Århus Univ. 1965–70; Research Instructor, Univ. of Chicago 1971–72; Assoc. Prof., Århus Univ. 1971–83, Prof. of Math. 1983–2009; Prof. of Math., Copenhagen Univ. 2009–16, then Prof. Emer.; Ed Acta Mathematica 1988–; Asst Ed. Journal of the European Mathematical Soc. 2002–; mem. Royal Danish Acad. of Sciences 1978, Inst. for Advanced Study, Princeton 1986–87, Royal Swedish Acad. of Sciences 1998, Royal Norwegian Acad. 2002; Rigmor and Carl Holst-Knudsen Science Prize 1982, Humboldt Research Award 1992, Plenary Lecturer, Int. Congress of Mathematicians, Madrid 2006, ERC advanced grant 2009–13, Ostrowski Prize 2011. *Publications include:* The Classifying Spaces for Surgery and Cobordism of Manifolds (with R. J. Milgram) 1979, From Calculus to Cohomology (with J. Tornehave) 1997; approx. 90 journal articles. *Telephone:* 22-59-46-99 (office); 22-59-46-99 (office). *Address:* Department of Mathematics, Copenhagen University, Universitetsparken 5, DK- 2100 Copenhagen Ø (office); Saabyesvej 10-2, 2100 Copenhagen Ø, Denmark (home). *E-mail:* imadsen@math.ku.dk (office). *Website:* www.math.ku.dk (office).

MADSEN, Michael Søren; American actor, poet and photographer; b. 25 Sept. 1958, Chicago, Ill.; s. of Calvin Madsen and Elaine Madsen (née Melson); brother of Virginia Madsen; m. 1st Georganne LaPiere; m. 2nd Jeannine Bisignano; two s.; m. 3rd Deanna Morgan 1996; three s.; began acting career at Steppenwolf Theatre, Chicago where he served an apprenticeship under actor John Malkovich, appeared in plays including Of Mice and Men, A Streetcar Named Desire; appeared in Broadway production of A Streetcar Named Desire 1992; has appeared in more than 150 films; invited and appeared in Norway for the Norwegian trans. and release of Burning In Paradise 2008; guest of honour for his poetry at Crossing Border Festival, The Hague 2010; 9th Annual Malibu Int. Film Festival Award 2008. *Films include:* Against All Hope 1982, WarGames 1983, Racing with the Moon 1984, The Natural 1984, The Killing Time 1987, Shadows in the Storm 1988, Iguana 1988, Kill Me Again 1989, Blood Red 1989, The End of Innocence 1990, Fatal Instinct 1991, The Doors 1991, Thelma and Louise 1991, Beyond the Law 1992, Almost Blue 1992, Reservoir Dogs 1992, Straight Talk 1992, Inside Edge 1993, A House in the Hills 1993, Trouble Bound 1993, Free Willy 1993, Money for Nothing 1993, Dead Connection 1994, Season of Change 1994, The Getaway 1994, Wyatt Earp 1994, Species 1995, Free Willy 2: The Adventure Home 1995, Man with a Gun 1995, Mulholland Falls 1996, The Winner 1996, Red Line 1996, Papertrail 1997, Surface to Air 1997, The Last Days of Frankie the Fly 1997, Donnie Brasco 1997, The Girl Gets Moe 1997, The Maker 1997, Catherine's Grove 1997, Executive Target 1997, Flat Out 1998, The Thief and the Stripper 1998, Ballad of the Nightingale 1998, Rough Draft 1998, Species II 1998, The Sender 1998, Fait Accompli 1998, The Florentine 1999, Detour 1999, Fall 2000, Bad Guys

2000, Ides of March 2000, The Stray 2000, Luck of the Draw 2000, The Alternate 2000, The Price of Air 2000, Outlaw 2001, Pressure Point 2001, The Ghost 2001, Choke 2001, L.A.P.D.: To Protect and to Serve 2001, Extreme Honor 2001, Welcome to America 2002, Love.com 2002, Die Another Day 2002, The Real Deal 2002, Where's Angelo? 2003, My Boss's Daughter 2003, Kill Bill: Vol. 1 2003, Vampires Anonymous 2003, Blueberry 2004, Kill Bill: Vol. 2 2004, Jacked$ 2004, Hoboken Hollow 2005, Firedog (voice) 2005, Sin City 2005, Chasing Ghosts 2005, The Last Drop 2005, L.A. Dicks 2005, Muzhskoy sezon. Barkhatnaya revolutsiya 2005, BloodRayne 2005, Living and Dying 2006, All In 2006, Last Hour 2006, Scary Movie 4 2006, Canes 2006, UKM: The Ultimate Killing Machine 2006, Strength and Honour (Best Actor Award, 23rd Annual Boston Film Festival) 2007, Hell Ride 2008, Vice 2008, Green Lantern: First Flight (voice) 2009, Outrage 2009, The Bleeding 2009, Corruption.Gov 2010, Federal 2010, Terror Trap 2010, The 5th Execution 2010, The Killing Jar 2010, The Brazen Bull 2011, Eldorado 2012, Refuge From The Storm 2012, Piranhaconda 2012, Magic Boys 2012, As Pik – Losa Sudbina 2012, Upside Down 2013, Sins Expiation 2013, Along the Roadside (Best Supporting Actor, IFS Film Festival, Beverly Hills) 2013, Ashley 2013, Terrible Angels 2013, I'm in Love with a Church Girl 2013, The Whole World at Our Feet 2014, Skoryy 'Moskva-Rossiya' 2014, The Ninth Cloud 2014, Hope Lost 2014, Water Wars 2014, 2047 – Sights 2014, Turn Around Jake 2014, Skin Traffik 2014, Lumberjack Man 2015, Two Cranes 2014, The Lost Tree 2015, The Hateful Eight 2015, Sacred Blood 2015, Magi 2015. *Television includes:* War and Remembrance (mini-series) 1988, Vengeance Unlimited (series) 1998, Big Apple (series) 2001, 44 Minutes: The North Hollywood Shoot-Out 2003, Frankenstein 2004, Tilt (series) 2005, CSI: Miami (series) 2010, 24 (series) 2010, Celebrity Big Brother 2012 (UK) 2012, The Mob Doctor (series) 2012–13, Axe Cop (series) 2013, Paulie (film) 2013, Hawaii Five-0 (series) 2014. *Publications:* poetry: Beer, Blood and Ashes 1995, Eat the Worm 1995, Burning in Paradise (Ind. Firecracker Award) 1998, A Blessing of the Hounds 2002, 46 Down: A Book of Dreams and Other Ramblings 2004, When Pets Kill 2005, The Complete Poetic Works of Michael Madsen, Vol. I: 1995–2005 (Lifetime Achievement Award, Red Hen Press) 2006, American Badass 2009, Expecting Rain 2013; photography: Signs of Life 2006. *Address:* c/o Michael Manchal, Creative Artists Agency, 2000 Avenue of the Stars, Los Angeles, CA 90067, USA; c/o Celebrity Talent International, 1250 Newland Court, Carlsbad, CA 92008, USA (office). *Telephone:* (424) 288-2000; (760) 729-2000 (office). *Fax:* (424) 288-2900. *Website:* www.caa.com; www.celebritytalent.net (office); www.facebook.com/ActorMichaelMadsen. *E-mail:* info@celebritytalent.net (office).

MADUNA, Penuell Mpapa, LLD; South African lawyer and politician; b. 29 Dec. 1952; m. Nompumelelo Cheryl Maduna; three c.; ed Univ. of Zimbabwe, Univ. of Witwatersrand; worked in underground structures of ANC in 1970s, twice incarcerated and prosecuted; left SA 1980; fmr Regional Admin. Sec. Tanzania, Office of Treasurer-Gen. of ANC; fmr staff mem. and Legal Adviser, ANC HQ Lusaka, est. Dept of Legal and Constitutional Affairs 1985, Founder mem. Constitutional Cttee, participated in meetings with South African Govt and officials in 1980s and early 1990s leading to establishment of Convention for a Democratic South Africa, mem. Negotiating Comm., now mem. Nat. Exec. Cttee; fmr MP Nat. Ass.; Minister of Mineral and Energy Affairs 1996–99, of Justice and Constitutional Devt 1999–2004; Pnr, Bowman Gilfillan (law firm), Johannesburg; Bd mem. Faculty of Law, Univ. of Witwatersrand 1996. *Publication:* Fundamental Rights in the New Constitution 1994 (co-author). *Leisure interests:* soccer, reading, debating. *Address:* c/o Bowman Gilfillan, 165 West Street, Sandton, Johannesburg, South Africa (office).

MADURO JOEST, Ricardo, BA; Honduran fmr central banker and fmr head of state; b. 20 April 1946, Panamá, Panama; m. 1st Miriam Andreu; one s. (deceased) three d.; m. 2nd Aguas Santas Ocaña Navarro 2002 (divorced 2006); m. 3rd Melissa Callejas 2009; ed Stanford Univ., USA; mem. Partido Nacional (Nationalist Party), Chair. Cen. Cttee; Dir Rafael Callejas's election campaigns 1985, 1989; apptd Chair. Banco Cen. de Honduras 1990; fmr Co-ordinator of the Econ. Office; Pres. of Honduras 2002–05. *Address:* c/o Partido Nacional (PN), Paseo el Obelisco, Comayagüela, Tegucigalpa, Honduras (office).

MADURO MOROS, Nicolás; Venezuelan politician and head of state; *President;* b. 23 Nov. 1961, Caracas; m. Cilia Flores; two c.; worker on Caracas metro and founder of trade union for Caracas metro workers in 1980s; also mem. Movimiento Bolivariano Revolucionario 200 in 1980s, mem. Nat. Directorate 1994–97; Founding mem. Movimiento Quinta Republica 200 (MVR) 1997, elected to Asamblea Nacional 1998, Pres. Citizens' Participation Cttee 1999, Co-ordinator of MVR parl. team 2000–01, Co-ordinator of majority bloc parl. team 2001–05, Pres. Asamblea Nacional 2005–06; Minister of Foreign Affairs 2006–12; Vice-Pres. 2012–13, Pres. 2013–; Pres. pro tempore of the Union of South American Nations 2016–17; Sec.-Gen. Non-Aligned Movement 2016–. *Address:* Central Information Office of the Presidency, Torre Oeste 18°, Parque Central, Caracas, 1010, Venezuela (office). *Telephone:* (2) 572-7110. *Fax:* (2) 572-2675. *Website:* www.presidencia.gob.ve (office); www.nicolasmaduro.org.ve.

MADY, Mohamed H. al-, BS, MS; Saudi Arabian business executive and chemical engineer; *President, Military Industries Corporation (MIC);* ed Univs of Colorado and Wyoming, USA; joined Saudi Basic Industries Corpn (SABIC) 1976, Dir-Gen. for Projects –1998, Vice-Chair. and CEO 1998–2015, Chair. R&T Exec. Cttee, SABIC EuroPetrochemicals Exec. Bd; Chair. and Man. Dir Saudi Arabian Fertilizer Co. (SAFCO); Pres. Military Industries Corpn (MIC) 2015–; Chair. Gulf Petrochemicals & Chemicals Asscn; Co-Chair. US-Saudi Arabia Business Council; mem. Int. Business Council, World Econ. Forum, mem. Bd Boao Forum for Asia, World Sustainability Council, Int. Advisory Council King Abdullah Univ. of Science & Tech., Int. Advisory Bd, King Fahd Univ. of Petroleum and Minerals; mem. Bd of Trustees, Prince Mohammad bin Fahd Univ.; Chair. and Man. Dir Saudi Arabian Fertilizer Co.; Hon. Fellow, London Business School 2007; Hon. mem. Advisory Council for Meteorology and Environment Protection; Hon. DS (Eng of Colorado) 2012; named Industry CEO of the Year, Middle East CEO of the Year Awards 2005, Int. Petrochemical Heritage Award 2009, elected by Colorado Eng and Applied Sciences Coll. amongst the gifted students with global scientific and industrial contribs 2010, Distinguished Eng Alumni Award, Eng of Colorado 2012. *Address:* Military Industries Corporation, PO Box 3637, Riyadh 11481, Saudi Arabia (office). *Telephone:* (1) 4056990 (office). *Fax:* (1) 4058296 (office).

MAE, Vanessa; British violinist; b. (Vanessa-Mae Vanakorn Nicholson), 27 Oct. 1978, Singapore; ed Cen. Conservatoire, Beijing, People's Repub. of China, Royal Coll. of Music, UK, studied with Lin Yao Ji and Felix Andrievsky; concerto debut aged ten, Philharmonic Orchestra 1989; first nat. tour of UK with Tchaikovsky Concerto 1990; first int. tour with London Mozart Players 1990; released three classical recordings with orchestra (youngest artist to record both Tchaikovsky and Beethoven Violin Concertos) 1990–92; over 800 live performances in the Middle East, South Africa, China, SE Asia, Russia, Europe, Baltic States, Cen. Asia, USA, Cen. and S America; The Classical Tour 1997, Int. Red Hot Tour 1995, Storm on World Tour 1998, Subject to Change Tour 2002; performed at Hong Kong to China Reunification Ceremony 1996, exclusively for HM The Queen, Buckingham Palace 1998, at 50th Anniversary of Geneva Conventions 1999; opened Classical Brit Awards, Royal Albert Hall 2000; live and recorded collaborations with Prince, Janet Jackson, Jose Carreras, the Backstreet Boys, the Scorpions, George Martin; collaborated on soundtrack for Walt Disney film Mulan; catwalk debut with Jean-Paul Gaultier; frequent TV appearances and participant in crossover concerts; involved in work with ICRC, participated in TV Campaign Even Wars Have Limits; Global Amb. Cruelty Free Int; BAMBI Top Int. Classical Artist Award, Echo Klassik Award for Bestselling Album of the Year 1995, World Music Award for Best Selling Classical Artist 1996. *Recordings include:* Tchaikovsky and Beethoven Concertos 1990, The Violin Player (quadruple platinum) 1994, The Classical Album I 1996, China Girl: The Classical Album II 1997, Storm 1997, The Original Four Seasons 2000, Vanessa Mae: The Classical Collection Part I 2000, Subject to Change 2001, Choreography 2004. *Film:* Arabian Nights 2000. *Achievements include:* competed for Thailand in Giant Slalom at 2014 Sochi Winter Olympics. *Leisure interests:* snow skiing, dining out, academic studies, waterskiing, reading, animal welfare. *Address:* c/o Ad Lib Management, Medius House, 2 Sheraton Street, London, W1F 8BH, England (office). *Telephone:* (7944) 578342 (office). *E-mail:* info@adlibmanagement.co.uk (office); vanessamaeoffice@gmail.com. *Website:* www.adlibmanagement.co.uk (office).

MAEDA, Terunobu, LLB; Japanese business executive; b. 2 Jan. 1945; ed Univ. of Tokyo; joined Fuji Bank Ltd 1968, Dir and Gen. Man. Credit Planning Div. 1995–96, Dir and Gen. Man. Corp. Planning Div. 1996–97, Man. Dir 1997–98, Man. Dir and Head of Public and Financial Insts Group 1998–99, Man. Dir and Chief Financial Officer (CFO) 1999–2001, Deputy Pres. and CFO 2001–02; mem. Bd Dirs Mizuho Holdings, Inc. (present Mizuho Financial Strategy Co. Ltd, subsidiary of Mizuho Asset Trust & Banking Co. Ltd (fmrly Mizuho Trust & Banking Co. Ltd)) 2002–07, Pres. and CEO Mizuho Financial Group 2002–07, Pres. and CEO Mizuho Financial Group, Inc. 2003–09, Chair. 2009–10, Sr Adviser 2010; Vice-Chair. Nippon Keidanren.

MAEENA, Khaled al-; Saudi Arabian journalist and public relations consultant; ed St Patrick's Coll., Univ. of Karachi; served as diplomat in China and Russia; Ed.-in-Chief, Arab News 1982–93, 1998–2011, Saudi Gazette 2012–14; Pres. and CEO Saudi Public Relations Co. (SPRC) 1993–2000; sr columnist for Gulf News, Urdu News, Asharq Al-Awsat, Al-Iqtisadiah, Times of Oman, China Post; joined Saudi Arabian Airlines (Saudia) 1982, held a variety of posts including public relations advisor and Editor-in-Chief of Saudia World (magazine); has hosted news and talk shows on Saudi TV; has represented Saudi Arabian media at several important Arab summit meetings including in Baghdad and Morocco.

MAEHARA, Seiji; Japanese politician; *President, Democratic Party;* b. 30 April 1962, Kyoto; m. Airi Maehara; ed Matsushita Inst. of Govt and Man., Chigasaki; mem. Kyoto Prefectural Ass. 1991–93; mem. House of Reps 1993–, Chair. Special Cttee on Okinawa and N Problems, mem. Cttee on Fundamental Nat. Policies; mem. Sakigake Party 1994–98, Japan New Party 1993–94; mem. Democratic Party of Japan 1998–2016, Pres. (youngest ever) 2005–06, Chair. Public Works Reform Project Team, Road-Related Special Corpn Working Team, New Public Works Research Cttee, Expressways Project Team; fmr Shadow Cabinet Dir-Gen., Defence Agency, fmr Shadow Cabinet Minister of State for Social Capital Devt; Minister of Land, Infrastructure, Transport and Tourism 2009–10, also Minister of State for Okinawa and N Territories and Disaster Man. 2009–10, Minister of Foreign Affairs 2010–11 (resgnd); Minister for Nat. Strategy and Econ. Policy Oct.–Dec. 2012; mem. Democratic Party 2016–, Pres. 2017–; Leader of the Opposition 2017–; mem. Cttee on Financial Affairs, Cttee on Budget. *Leisure interest:* photography. *Address:* Headquarters of Democratic Party, #809, 1st Members' Office Building, Tokyo 100-0014, Japan (office). *Telephone:* (3) 3508-7171 (office). *Fax:* (3) 3592-6696 (office). *Website:* www.minshin.or.jp (office).

MAEHLER, Herwig Gustav Theodor, PhD, FBA; German papyrologist and academic; *Professor Emeritus, University College London;* b. 29 April 1935, Berlin; s. of Ludwig Maehler and Lisa Maehler; m. Margaret Anderson 1963; two d.; ed Katharineum, Lübeck and Univs of Hamburg, Tübingen and Basle; British Council Scholarship, Oxford 1961–62; Research Asst, Dept of Classics, Univ. of Hamburg 1962–63, Dept of Manuscripts, Hamburg Univ. Library 1963–64; Keeper of Greek Papyri, Egyptian Museum, West Berlin 1964–79; Lecturer in Classics, Freie Universität Berlin 1975–79; Reader in Papyrology, Univ. Coll. London 1979–81, Prof. 1981–2000, Prof. Emer. 2000–; Visiting Fellow, Inst. for Advanced Studies in the Humanities, Edin. 1977; Visiting Prof., Univs of Urbino 1984, Bologna 1986, Bari 1988, Basle 1990, Budapest 1998, 2001, 2004, Rome 1999, Venice 2004, Florence 2005, Graz 2011–12; Corresp. mem. German Archaeological Inst.; Fellow, Accad. Nazionale dei Lincei, Rome, Hungarian Acad. of Sciences, Budapest; Dr hc (Helsinki) 2000, (Budapest) 2001, (Rome II Tor Vergata) 2003. *Publications include:* Die Auffassung des Dichterberufs im frühen Griechentum bis zur Zeit Pindars 1963, Die Handschriften der S. Jacobi-Kirche Hamburg 1967, Urkunden römischer Zeit 1968, Papyri aus Hermoupolis 1974, Die Lieder des Bakchylides (two vols) 1982, 1997, Greek Bookhands of the Early Byzantine Period (with G. Cavallo) 1987, Bacchylides: A Selection 2004, Urkunden aus Hermupolis 2005, Hellenistic Bookhands (with G. Cavallo) 2008; editions of Bacchylides and Pindar. *Leisure interests:* chamber music (viola), horse riding (dressage). *Address:* Zeltgasse 6/12, 1080 Vienna, Austria. *Telephone:* (1) 408-3499. *E-mail:* hgt.maehler@virgin.net.

MAEMA, Lebohang Fine, KC, BA, LLB, LLM; Lesotho diplomatist and lawyer; *Clerk to the National Assembly;* b. 22 July 1957, Masery; three d.; ed Nat. Univ. of Lesotho, Univ. of Cambridge, UK; fmr mem. of Bd Cen. Bank of Lesotho; fmr Pres. Matlama Football Club; worked at Nat. Univ. of Lesotho; Crown Counsel,

Attorney-Gen.'s Chambers 1982–83; Lecturer-in-Law, Nat. Univ. of Lesotho 1984–87; Deputy Pvt. Sec. to King of Lesotho, Royal Palace 1987–89, Pvt. Sec. 1989–90; Prin. Sec., Ministry of Justice and Prisons 1990–93; Attorney-Gen. 1993–2005; Amb. and Perm. Rep. to UN, New York 2005–09; Amb. to Ethiopia 2009–11, also Perm. Rep. African Union and High Commr to Kenya and Uganda; Clerk to the Nat. Ass. 2013–; Commdr of the Most Meritorious Order of Mohlomi; Cambridge Livingstone Scholar 1983. *Leisure interests:* listening to music, watching TV, soccer and movies. *Address:* Office of the Clerk to the National Assembly, POB 190, Maseru, Lesotho (office). *Telephone:* 22323035 (office). *Website:* www.parliament.ls (office).

MAFAEL, Rolf; German lawyer and diplomatist; *Ambassador and Permanent Representative, Council of Europe;* b. 1955, Bruchsal/Baden; m.; five c.; ed Univs of Heidelberg and Berlin; began career as prosecutor, Mannheim; joined Foreign Office 1985, Del. to Conf. on Disarmament, Geneva 1989–93, served in Embassy in Tehran 1993–95, with Perm. Mission to European Comm. 1995–98, Brussels, Perm. Mission to NATO 1998–99, Deputy Head, Political Dept, Ministry of Foreign Affairs 1989–2002, Embassy in Tokyo 2002–05, Head, European Political Co-ordination Unit, Ministry of Foreign Affairs, later Deputy Dir-Gen. for EU External Issues and Relations with EU Mem. States 2005, Amb. to South Korea 2012–16, Amb. to Kazakhstan 2016–18, Amb. and Perm. Rep. to Council of Europe and Consul-Gen., Strasbourg 2018–. *Address:* Council of Europe, 6, Quai Mullenheim, 6700 Strasbourg, France (office). *Telephone:*)(3) 88-24-67-30 (office). *Fax:* (3) 88-25-50-41 (office). *E-mail:* info@strassburg-io.diplo.de (office). *Website:* strassburg-europarat.diplo.de (office).

MAFI, HE Cardinal Soane Patita Paini; Tongan ecclesiastic; *Bishop of Tonga, Pacific (Oceania);* b. 19 Dec. 1961, Nuku'alofa; ed Pacific Regional Seminary, Fiji, Loyola Univ., Baltimore, USA; joined youth group in Parish of Kolofo'ou, nr Nuku'alofa; ordained priest, Diocese of Tonga, Pacific (Oceania) 1991; carried out parish work on island of Ha'apai 1991–95; apptd Vicar-Gen. of Diocese 1995–97; stationed in Suva training of local priests 2000–06; Coadjutor Bishop of Tonga, Pacific (Oceania) 2007–08, consecrated 2007, Bishop of Tonga, Pacific (Oceania) 2008–; cr. Cardinal (Cardinal-Priest of Santa Paola Romana) 2015. *Address:* Toutaimana Catholic Centre, PO Box 1, Nuku'alofa, Tonga (office). *Telephone:* 23822 (office). *Fax:* 23854 (office).

MAGAN OF CASTLETOWN, Baron (Life Peer), cr. 2011, of Kensington in the Royal Borough of Kensington and Chelsea; **George Morgan Magan,** FCA; British merchant banker and politician; b. 14 Nov. 1945; with Peat Marwick Mitchell 1964–70, Kleinwort Benson Ltd 1971–74; Dir Morgan Grenfell & Co. Ltd 1974–88; Co-founder and Chair. J.O. Hambro Magan 1988–96, Chair. NatWest Markets Corp. Finance (upon sale of firm to NatWest 1996, assisted in creation and separation of firm to create Hawkpoint Partners, where he was Chair. 1997–2001); Chair. Mallett plc 2001–08, Morgan Shipley Ltd, Dubai 2001, emuse, Dublin 2004, Strategic Asset Management Solutions 2008, Carlton Capital Partners (Deputy Chair. Carlton Corporate Finance); Dir Edmiston & Co. 2001, Bank of Ireland 2003–09 (Deputy Gov. 2006–09), Allied Investment Partners, Abu Dhabi 2007, St James's Company Ltd, Edmiston & Co Ltd, Fitzwilliam Trust Corporation Ltd, SJA Services Ltd; Partner, Rhone Group LLC; Deputy Treas. Conservative Party 2002–03, Party Treas. and mem. Bd Conservative Party 2003, Dir Conservative Party Foundation 2003–13, Deputy Chair. 2009–13; Chair. St George's Chapel Windsor Castle Devt Appeal 2007; mem. Advisory Bd AXA Private Equity, Abdul Latif Jameel Group, Banque Heritage; Trustee, Foundation of The Coll. of St George, Windsor Castle 2008, London Philharmonic Orchestra 1992–2006 (Chair. 1997–2006), Royal Opera House, Covent Garden 1995–2001, British Museum Devt Trust 1999–2003; mem. (Conservative), House of Lords 2011–. *Address:* House of Lords, Westminster, London, SW1A 0PW, England (office). *Telephone:* (20) 7219-5353 (office). *Fax:* (20) 7219-5979 (office).

MAGANDE, Ng'andu Peter, BA, MSc; Zambian diplomatist, business executive and farmer; b. 5 July 1947, Namaila, Mazabuka; m.; two s. three d.; ed Univ. of Zambia, Makerere Univ., Uganda; joined Civil Service 1971; apptd Dir of Budget, Ministry of Finance 1981; Perm. Sec. in various govt depts 1983–94; Man. Dir Zambia Nat. Commercial Bank, Lima Bank; Exec. Dir Industrial Devt Corpn, Zambia Industrial and Mining Corpn 1986–94; technical assistance consultant to Govt 1994; Sec.-Gen. African, Caribbean and Pacific Secr. 1996; Minister of Finance and Nat. Planning 2003–08; mem. of Parl. for Chilanga 2006–10; mem. Movt for Multi-party Democracy; Commdr of the Order of the Repub. of Benin; Best Commercial Tobacco Farmer 1989.

MAGARIÑOS, Carlos Alfredo, MBA; Argentine government official, UN official, business executive, academic and diplomatist; *Ambassador to Brazil;* b. 16 Aug. 1962, Buenos Aires; ed Nat. Univ. of Buenos Aires, Int. Devt Law Inst., Italy, Wharton School, Univ. of Pennsylvania, USA; Nat. Dir for Foreign Trade 1991–92; joined Ministry of Economy 1992, Under-Sec. of State for Industry 1992–93, Sec. of State for Industry 1993–95, for Mining and Industry 1995–96; Econ. and Trade Rep. of Argentina, Washington, DC, USA 1996–97; attained rank of Amb. 1996; Dir Gen. UNIDO 1997–2005; Sr Assoc. mem. St Antony's Coll., Oxford, UK 2006; Dir Gen. Econ. and Social Foresight Observatory, Universidad San Ignacio de Loyola 2012–16, Visiting Prof. 2015–16; Non-Resident Sr Fellow, Chongyang Inst. for Financial Studies, Renmin Univ. of China 2013–; Chair. Global Business Devt Network LLC (investment co.), Washington, DC 2010–16; Dir Gen. Prospectiva/Foresight 2020 (consultancy), Buenos Aires, Lima, Vienna, Mumbai; Vice-Pres. Foro PAIS (think tank on agri-business) 2011–14; Chair. Global Alliance of SMEs (China-US) Chair. –2016, Emer. 2016–; Amb. to Brazil 2016–; mem. Bd of Dirs, Universidad San Ignacio of Loyola, Lima, Peru; mem. Bd, Banco de la Provincia de Buenos Aires 2007–11, Universidad San Ignacio de Loyola 2010–16, San Ignacio Coll. 2012–16; Dir, Macrovision Consulting 2012–16; mem. Advisory Bd, Manav Sadhan Vikas Sanstha 2012–16; mem. Int. Advisory Bd, Council on Energy, Environment and Water 2012–16; Order of San Carlos, Colombia 2000, Order of Quetzal, Guatemala 2001, Order of Merit, Gov. of Italy 2003, Order of Industrial Merit, Gov. of Colombia 2004, Nat. Order of Merit, Grand Cross, Gov. of Ecuador 2005, Friendship Medal, Gov. of Cuba 2006, Grand Decoration of Honour, Gov. of Austria 2006; Dr hc (Lomonosov, Moscow) 1999, (Econ. Sciences and Public Admin., Budapest) 2000, (Univ. of Social and Business Sciences of Argentina) 2001, (Nat. Tech. Univ. of Ukraine) 2002; Trophée des performances de l'année 2000, Inst. Supérieur de Gestion, Paris 2000, Peter the Great Int. Award, Russian Fed. 2002, Prix de la Fondation 2002, Crans Montana Forum, Monte Carlo 2002, Kennedy Cross, John F. Kennedy Univ. Argentina 2004, Priyadarshni Acad. Award, India 2004. *Publications:* El Rol del Estado en la Política Industrial de los 90 1995, China in the WTO: The Birth of a New Catching-Up Strategy 2002; articles on econ. and industrial issues: Gearing Up for a New Development Agenda 2000, Reforming the UN System: UNIDO's Need-Driven Model 2001, Updating and Fleshing Out the Development Agenda 2003, Economic Development and UN Reform: Towards a Common Agenda for Action 2005. *Address:* Embassy of Argentina, SES Avenida das Nações, Quadra 803, Lote 12, 70200-0300 Brasília, DF, Brazil (office). *Telephone:* (61) 3212-7600 (office). *Fax:* (61) 3364-7666 (office). *E-mail:* carlos@carlosmagarinos.com (home); ebras@cancilleria.gob.ar (office); ebras@mrecic.gov.ar (office). *Website:* www.carlosmagarinos.com.

MAGD, Wael Ahmed Kamal Aboul, LLB, MA; Egyptian lawyer and diplomatist; b. 17 April 1964; m.; ed Cairo Univ., Univ. of London, UK; Prof. of Public Law, Cairo Univ. 1958–; fmr Minister of Youth, fmr Minister of Information; fmr Arab League Commr responsible for dialogue between civilizations; Vice-Pres. Nat. Council for Human Rights –2010; Deputy Asst Minister for Human Rights Affairs –2010; apptd Amb. to Canada 2010; fmr Legal and Constitutional Adviser to the Crown Prince and Prime Minister of Kuwait; fmr Judge, Vice-Pres. and Pres. World Bank Admin. Tribunal; mem. Supreme Council of Research, Univ. of El-Azhar, Cairo; mem. Maghreb Acad., Egyptian Soc. of Human Rights, Egyptian Supreme Council for Women's Affairs and Rights. *Publications:* numerous articles in English and Arabic on constitutional and administrative law, including A Contemporary Islamic Point of View (pamphlet), Dialogue, Not Confrontation (book).

MAGEE, Bryan, MA, DLitt; British author; b. 12 April 1930, London; s. of Frederick Magee and Sheila Lynch; m. Ingrid Söderlund 1954 (died 1986); one d.; ed Christ's Hosp., UK, Lycée Hôche, Versailles, France, Keble Coll. Oxford, UK, Yale Univ., USA; served with Army Intelligence Corps 1948–49; fmr TV reporter, This Week; music and theatre critic, Musical Times and The Listener; Lecturer in Philosophy, Balliol Coll., Oxford 1970–71; Visiting Fellow, All Souls Coll. Oxford 1973–74; MP for Leyton 1974–83; Pres. Critics Circle of GB 1983–84, Hon. mem. 2012–; Hon. Sr Research Fellow, King's Coll. London 1984–94, Visiting Prof. 1994–2000; Fellow, Queen Mary and Westfield Coll. London 1989–; Visiting Fellow, Wolfson Coll., Oxford 1991–94, New Coll. Oxford 1995, Merton Coll., Oxford 1998, St Catherine's Coll., Oxford 2000, Peterhouse, Cambridge 2001, Clare Hall, Cambridge (Life Mem.) 2004; Visiting Prof., Univ. of Otago, Dunedin, New Zealand 2006, 2009, 2012, also fmr Visiting Fellow at Yale Univ., Harvard Univ., Univ. of Sydney, LSE; newspaper columnist; mem. Arts Council of GB and Chair. Music Panel 1993–94; mem. Soc. of Authors; Hon. Fellow, Queen Mary Coll. London 1988–, Keble Coll. Oxford 1994–; Hon. DLitt (Univ. of Leicester) 2005; Silver Medal, Royal TV Soc. 1978. *Television:* Men of Ideas 1978, The Great Philosophers 1987. *Publications:* Crucifixion and Other Poems 1951, Go West Young Man 1958, The New Radicalism 1962, The Democratic Revolution 1964, Towards 2000 1965, One in Twenty 1966, The Television Interviewer 1966, Aspects of Wagner 1968 (revised edn 1988), Modern British Philosophy 1971, Popper 1973, Facing Death 1977, Men of Ideas 1978, The Philosophy of Schopenhauer 1983, 1997, The Great Philosophers 1987, On Blindness 1995 (re-issued as Sight Unseen 1998), Confessions of a Philosopher 1997, The Story of Philosophy 1998, Wagner and Philosophy 2000, Talking Philosophy 2001, Clouds of Glory: A Hoxton Childhood (J. R. Ackerley Prize for autobiog. 2004) 2003, Growing Up In a War 2007, Ultimate Questions 2016. *Leisure interests:* music, theatre. *Address:* c/o Norah Perkins, Curtis Brown, Haymarket House, 28–29 Haymarket, London, SW1Y 4SP, England (office); Wolfson College, Oxford, OX2 6UD, England (office). *Telephone:* (20) 7393-4262 (office). *E-mail:* norah.perkins@curtisbrown.co.uk (office). *Website:* www.curtisbrown.co.uk (office).

MAGEE, Jeff, MSc, PhD, CE, FREng; British computer scientist and academic; *Principal, Faculty of Engineering, Imperial College London;* fmr Prof. of Computing and Head of Computing Dept, Imperial Coll., London, fmr Dean, Faculty of Eng; Chair. Steering Cttee, Int. Conf. on Software Eng 2002–04; fmr Co-Ed. IEE Proceedings on Software Engineering; adviser or consultant to numerous cos, including BP, BT, NATS, Fujitsu, Barclays Capital, QinetiQ, Kodak, Philips; Chartered Fellow, British Computer Soc.; Fellow, Royal Acad. of Eng; IEE Informatics Premium Prize 1999, British Computer Soc. Brendan Murphy Memorial Prize 1999, Asscn for Computing Machinery Outstanding Research Award 2005. *Publications:* Concurrency-State Models and Java Programs (co-author) 2006; over 100 refereed publs. *Address:* Faculty of Engineering, Imperial College London, South Kensington Campus, London, SW7 2AZ, England (office). *Telephone:* (20) 7594-8601 (office). *E-mail:* j.magee@imperial.ac.uk (office). *Website:* www.imperial.ac.uk/people/j.magee (office).

MAGERS, Philomene Korinna Kornelia; German gallery owner; b. 18 March 1965, Bonn; d. of Wolfgang Magers and Philomene Magers; m. Jan Schmidt-Garré; two s.; ed studies of art history, philosophy, Christian archaeology and German philology, Rheinische Friedrich-Wilhelms Univ. Bonn, Ludwig-Maximilians Univ. Munich; Direction and Dramaturgy Trainee, Asst in Opera and Theatre, Städtische Bühnen, Bonn 1984–86; Curatorial Asst, German Pavilion, 43rd Venice Biennale 1988, Städtische Galerie Lehnbachhaus, Munich 1988, Siemens Arts Program, Munich 1988–90; f. Philomene Magers Gallery, Bonn 1990, relocated to Cologne 1991, merged with Galerie Monika Sprüth as Sprüth Magers, Cologne 1998, opened in Munich 2000, opened new galleries in London 2003, Berlin 2008, Los Angeles 2016, Hong Kong 2016. *Address:* Sprüth Magers Berlin, Oranienburger Straße 18, 10178 Berlin, Germany (office); Sprüth Magers London, 7A Grafton Street, London, W1S 4EJ, England (office); Sprüth Magers Los Angeles, 5900 Wilshire Blvd, Los Angeles, CA 90036, USA (home). *Telephone:* (30) 28884030 (Berlin) (office); (20) 7408-1613 (London) (office); (323) 634-0600 (LA) (office). *Fax:* (30) 288840352 (Berlin) (office); (20) 7499-4531 (London) (office); (323) 634-0602 (LA) (office). *E-mail:* info@spruethmagers.com (office). *Website:* www.spruethmagers.com (office).

MAGGI, Blairo; Brazilian farmer, business executive and politician; b. 29 May 1956, São Miguel do Iguaçu, Paraná; Owner of André Maggi Group (harvests, processes and exports soybeans, world's largest soyabean producer), group also involved in infrastructure projects to sustain soy industry, notably soy terminals, highways and waterways; Gov. Mato Grosso state 2003–10, Senator 2011–16;

apptd Pres. Cttee on Environment, Surveillance and Control of Federal Senate 2013; joined Progressive Party (Partido Progressista—PP) 2016; Minister of Agric. Livestock and Food Supply 2016–19; Greenpeace Golden Chainsaw Award for being the Brazilian who most contributed to destruction of Amazon rainforest 2006, ranked 62nd by Forbes magazine amongst The World's Most Powerful People 2009. *Address:* c/o Ministry of Agriculture, Livestock and Food Supply, Esplanada dos Ministérios, Bloco D, Anexo B, 70043-900 Brasília, DF, Brazil (office).

MAGIDOR, Menachem, BSc, MSc, PhD; Israeli mathematician, fmr university administrator and academic; *Professor of Mathematics and President Emeritus, Hebrew University of Jerusalem;* b. 24 Jan. 1946, Petah Tikva; m.; four d.; ed Hebrew Univ. of Jerusalem; served in Israeli Navy and reached rank of Lt Commdr; has conducted research in math. logic (mainly set theory), also in computer science, dealing with artificial intelligence and semantics of programming languages; Prof. of Math., Hebrew Univ. of Jerusalem 1982–, Dean Faculty of Science 1992–96, Pres. Hebrew Univ. of Jerusalem 1997–2009, Pres. Emer. 2009–; Pres. Asscn of Symbolic Logic 1996–98, Div. of Logic, Methodology and Philosophy of Science 2016–19; Hon. Foreign Fellow, American Acad. of Arts and Sciences; Commdr, Ordre des Palmes académiques. *Publications include:* about 80 papers on set theory, model theory and computer science. *Address:* Institute of Mathematics, Hebrew University of Jerusalem, 91904 Jerusalem, Israel (office). *Telephone:* (2) 658-4143 (office). *Fax:* (2) 658-4784 (office). *E-mail:* mensara@savion.huji.ac.il (office).

MAGLIANO, Giandomenico, MBA, MPA; Italian diplomatist; b. 12 Feb. 1955, Naples; m.; three c.; ed Lycée 'Leonardo da Vinci' and Institut d'etudes politiques, Paris, Univ. 'La Sapienza', Rome, Institut Européen d'Admin des Affaires (INSEAD), Kennedy School of Govt, Harvard Univ., USA; joined diplomatic service 1978, mem. Italian Del. to Madrid Meeting of CSCE 1982, First Sec., Embassy to the Holy See (Vatican City) 1983–85, First Sec. (Commercial), subsequently Commercial Dir, Embassy in Budapest 1986–88, Office of UN and Human Rights, Directorate of Political Affairs 1989–91, Diplomatic Advisor to Minister of Agric. and Forests 1991–92, Diplomatic Advisor to Minister of Finance 1992–93, Cabinet of Minister of Foreign Affairs 1994, Chief of Cabinet of Sec. of State for Foreign Affairs delegated to European Affairs 1995–97, Deputy Dir Gen., Directorate Gen. of Cultural Relations (renamed Directorate Gen. for Cultural Promotion and Co-operation 2000) 1997–2000, rank of Minister Plenipotentiary 2000, Dir Gen. for Devt Co-operation 2000–03, chaired Task Force of G-8 on Educ. for Devt 2001; Italian Rep. to Global Fund Board to Fight AIDS, Tuberculosis and Malaria, Dir Gen. for Multilateral Econ. and Financial Co-operation 2003–10, rank of Amb. 2010, Dir Gen. for Globalization and Global Issues 2010–12, Amb. to France 2013–18; lecturer at several Italian univs; fmr mem. Inst. of Dirs, European Univ. Inst., Florence; Kt Grand Cross, Order of Merit of the Italian Repub. *Publications:* essays in Italian and English on the theory and practice of int. relations, int. econs, devt policies, cultural policies, UN issues, G8 and EU matters.

MAGLOIRE, Paul Gustave; Haitian government official; b. 2 Dec. 1953; ed Ecole Normale Supérieure d'Haïti; fmr adviser to Prime Minister Gerard Latortue; Minister of the Interior and Nat. Security 2005–06; played a key role in the organization of legis. and presidential elections 2006; Founder and Pres. Foresight Company System International (PROSINT); influential amongst Haitian communities in USA for 18 years; worked at Information Agency of the US (USIA), Washington, DC for seven years, represented Haitian Govt in Oslo, Norway during UN Conf. on Integrated Missions May 2005; fmr CEO Soc. Agricole et de Production Agro-industrielle; fmr mem. Bd of Dirs Soc. Haïtienne de Filature (SAFICO); Co-founder Asscn Nationale des Artistes Haïtiens; fmr Special Advisor to industrialist Thomas Désulmé; mem. Parti Nat. du Travail (Nat. Labour Party).

MAGNAGNA, Christian; Gabonese engineer and politician; b. 31 Aug. 1961, Mounana; nine c.; ed École des Hautes Études d'Ingénieur, Lille, Inst. supérieur de Gestion de Paris, France; Financial Man., Groupe Société auxiliaire d'entreprises (SAE), Paris Region 1988–90, Chief Works Engineer 1991–92; Man. MEGE BETON SA, France 1992–95; Deputy Dir CARMO (SME), Mounana 1995–99; Sales and Marketing Dir, Société Nationale des Bois du Gabon 1999–2003; Dir-Gen., Fond d'entretien Routier (road maintenance fund) 2004–06, Man. Dir 2007–09; mem. Parti Démocratique Gabonais, mem. Central Cttee 1993–2002, mem. Nat. Council 2003–05, 2008–10, Dir of Campaign Cttee (for both legislative and presidential elections), mem. Political Bureau 2006–08; Minister-Del. to Minister of Budget, Public Accounts and Civil Service 2009, Minister of Water and Forests 2011, of Budget, Public Accounts and the Civil Service 2014–16, of Water and Energy –2019. *Leisure interests:* reading, tourism, golf, running, tennis. *Address:* c/o Ministry of Water and Energy, blvd Triomphal Omar Bongo Ondimba, BP 1172, Libreville, Gabon (office).

MAGNER, Marjorie (Marge), BS, MSIA; American banker and business executive; *Managing Partner, Brysam Global Partners;* b. 1949, Brooklyn, New York; one s.; ed Brooklyn Coll., Krannert School of Man., Purdue Univ.; joined Chemical Bank 1973, Man. Dir Chemical Technologies Div. –1983, actuarial analyst, Equitable Life Insurance Co. 1983–87; with Commercial Credit (predecessor of Citigroup) 1987, COO Global Consumer Group, Citigroup Inc., New York 2002–03, Chair. and CEO 2003–05, mem. Man. Cttee and Global Consumer Planning Group, Citigroup 2003–05; Founding Mem. and Man. Pnr, Brysam Global Partners 2007–; mem. Bd of Dirs Accenture Ltd 2006–, Gannett Co., Inc. 2006–, Ally Financial, Inc. 2010–; Brooklyn Coll. Foundation; mem. Dean's Advisory Council, Krannert School of Man., Purdue Univ.; Hon. DMan (Purdue) 2004; Distinguished Alumni Medal, Brooklyn Coll. 2005, The Marjorie Magner Lifetime Achievement Award named in her honour 2005. *Address:* Brysam Global Partners, 515 Madison Avenue, New York, NY 10022, USA (office). *Telephone:* (212) 297-2777 (office). *E-mail:* bgp@brysam.com (office). *Website:* www.brysam.com (office).

MAGNIEN, Agnès; French archivist and librarian; *Executive Director, Archives nationales;* trained archivist-palaeographer; Dir of Departmental Archives 1994–2000, Deputy Dir Gen. of Services, Gen. Council of Seine-Saint-Denis 2000–08; has worked at Archives nationales since 2006, Exec. Dir Archives nationales 2011–, also directs activities at Paris and Fontainebleau sites, responsible for Maison de l'Histoire de France from 2015. *Address:* Archives nationales, 59 rue Guynemer, 90001, 93383 Pierrefitte-sur-Seine Cedex, France (office). *Telephone:* 1-75-47-21-32 (office). *Fax:* 1-75-47-29-10 (office). *E-mail:* amagnien@ina.fr (office). *Website:* www.archivesnationales.culture.gouv.fr (office).

MAGNO, Adaljíza Albertina Xavier Reis, (Ajiza Magno); Timor-Leste politician; b. 7 Jan. 1975; d. of Alberto dos Reis Magno and Ana Xavier G. Magno; m. Rosantino Amado Hei dos Anjos 2003; one d.; ed Sebelas Maret National Univ., Indonesia, Victoria Univ. of Wellington, New Zealand; Co-founder Sahe Inst. for Liberation, Dili 1999–2001; and remained with SIL until 2001 when represented FRETILIN in Constituent Ass. 2001–02; mem. Parl. 2002–05, mem. Cttee of Economics and Finance; Vice-Minister of Foreign Affairs and Cooperation 2005–07, Acting Minister of Foreign Affairs May–Aug. 2007; left to attend univ. in New Zealand 2011–13 then returned to Timor-Leste; mem. Comissão de Preparacao da Cimeria da CPLP (Commission for Preparation of Community of Portuguese Speaking Countries Summit) 2014–.

MAGNUSSEN, James; Australian swimmer; b. 11 April 1991, Port Macquarie, NSW; s. of Robert Magnussen and Donna Magnussen; ed Australian Coll. of Physical Educ.; mem. Australian Trans-Tasman team vs New Zealand 2008; Telstra Australian Swimming Championships 2010: bronze medal, 100m freestyle (qualified for nat. team), gold medal, 100m freestyle 2011; Australian Short course championships 2011: gold medal, 100m freestyle, 200m freestyle; Commonwealth Games: Delhi 2010: gold medal, 4×100m freestyle; Glasgow 2014: gold medal, 100m freestyle, 4×100m freestyle, silver medal, 4×100m medley, bronze medal, 50m freestyle; Gold Coast 2018: gold medal, 4×100m freestyle; Pan Pacific Championships: California 2010: silver medal, 4×100m freestyle; Queensland 2014: gold medal, 4×100m freestyle, bronze medal, 50m freestyle; World Championships (long course): Shanghai 2011: gold medal, 100m freestyle, 4×100m freestyle, silver medal, 4×100m medley relay; Barcelona 2013: gold medal, 100m freestyle, silver medal, 4×100m medley relay; Olympic Games, London 2012: silver medal, 100m freestyle, bronze medal, 4×100m medley relay; Rio de Janeiro 2016: bronze medal, 4×100m freestyle relay; swam for Sydney Olympic Park Aquatic Centre Swim Club; coach: Brant Best; Swimmer of the Year 2011, Swimmers' Swimmer of the Year 2011, People's Choice Award 2011. *Leisure interests:* Rugby League, surfing. *Telephone:* (2) 8968-2858. *E-mail:* info@jamesmagnussen.com.

MAGNUSSON, Thor Eyfeld, BA; Icelandic state antiquary (retd); b. 18 Nov. 1937, Hvammstangi; s. of Magnus Richardson and Sigridur Thordardóttir; m. Maria Vilhjalmsdottir 1964; two s. one d.; ed Univ. of Iceland, Univ. of Uppsala, Sweden; Asst Curator, Nat. Museum 1964, Dir 1968, State Antiquary 1968–2001; travel abroad includes numerous trips to Scandinavia and UK, group tour to Egypt, Lebanon, Jordan, Soviet Union, Bulgaria, Turkey, Greece and Italy 1965; visit to USA for pvt. programme at Carnegie Museum, Pittsburgh 1967. *Publications:* articles on archeology and ethnology in the Journal of the Icelandic Archaeological Society. *Address:* c/o National Museum, Suðurgata 41, 101 Reykjavik; Bauganes 26, 101 Reykjavik, Iceland (home). *Telephone:* 530-2200.

MAGOMEDOV, Magomedali Magomedovich; Russian/Dagestan politician; b. 15 June 1930, Levashi, Dagestan Autonomous Repub.; m. Zulgizhat Magomedova; six c.; ed Dagestan State Pedagogical Inst., Dagestan Inst. of Agric.; teacher, Dir Levashi secondary school, then Head Levashi Dept of Nat. Educ. 1949–57; mem. Communist Party of the Soviet Union (KPSS) 1954–91; Chair. Levashi Kolkhoz 1957–66; Head Agric. Production unit Levashi Dist 1966–69; Chair. Levashi Dist Exec. Cttee 1969–70; First Sec. Levashi Dist CP Cttee 1970–75; Head Div. of Agric. Dagestan Regional CP Cttee 1975–79; Deputy Chair., Chair. Council of Ministers Dagestan Autonomous Repub. 1979–87; Chair. Presidium Supreme Soviet Dagestan Autonomous Repub. 1987–94; Chair. State Council (Head Repub. of Dagestan) 1994–2006 (resgnd); mem. Russian Council of Fed. 1993–2001; Order of Honour 1995, Order of Merit for the Fatherland 1995, 2000, 2005, Order of Oct. Revolution, Order of the Red Banner of Labour, Order of the Badge of Honour. *Address:* c/o House of Government, Lenina pl., 167005 Makhachkala, Dagestan, Russia (office).

MAGRIS, Claudio; Italian journalist, writer and academic; *Professor Emeritus of German Language and Literature, University of Trieste;* b. 10 April 1939, Trieste; s. of Duilio Magris and Pia de Grisogono Magris; m. Marisa Madieri 1964; two s.; ed Univ. of Turin; Lecturer in German Language and Literature, Univ. of Trieste 1968–70, Turin 1970–78, Trieste 1978–, now Prof. Emer.; mem. Deutsche Akad. für Sprache und Dichtung (Darmstadt), Österreichische Akad. der Wissenschaften, Accad. delle Scienze di Torino, Ateneo Veneto, Akad. der Wissenschaften (Göttingen); Österreichisches Ehrenzeichen für Wissenschaft und Kunst 2012, Cross of the Order of Merit (Germany) 2012; Debenedetti 1972, Val di Comino 1978, Goethe Medaille 1980, Aquileia 1983, Premiolino 1983, San Giusto d'Oro 1984, Musil Medaille der Stadt Klagenfurt 1984, Bagutta 1987, Accad. dei Lincei 1987, Marotta 1987, Città di Modena 1987, Antico Fattore 1988, Juan Carlos I 1989, Premio Strega 1997, Premio Chiara alla Carriera 1999, Premio Würth per la Cultura Europea 1999, Premio Grinzane Piemonte 1999, Medaglia d'Oro della Cultura della Scuola e dell'Arte 1999, Premio Sikken 2000, Premio Nietsche 2000, Premium Erasmianum 2001, Leipziger Buchpreis zur Europäischen Verständigung 2001, Osterreichisches Ehrenkreuz für Wissenschaft und Kunst (First Class), Premio Principe de Asturias for Literature 2004, Österreichischem Staatpreis für Europäische literatur 2006, Friedenspreis des Deutschen Buchhandels 2009, Prix Européen de l'Essai Charles Veillon 2009, FIL Literary Award in Romance Languages 2014. *Plays:* Stadelmann 1988, Le Voci 1999, La Mostra 2001. *Publications include:* Il Mito absburgico nella letteratura austriaca moderna 1963, 1988, Wilhelm Heinse 1968, Tre studi su Hoffman 1969, Lontano da dove 1971, Joseph Roth e la tradizione ebraico-orientale 1971, L'altra ragione. Tre saggi su Hoffman 1978, Dietro le parole 1978, Itaca e oltre 1982, Trieste. Un'identità di frontiera 1982, 1987, L'anello di Clarisse 1984, Illazioni su una sciabola 1984, Danubio 1986 (trans. in numerous languages), Stadelmann 1988, Un altro mare 1991, Microcosmi 1997, Utopia e disincanto 1999, Telling Tales (contrib. to charity anthology) 2004, Alla cieca 2005, L'infinito viaggiare 2005, Lei dunque capirà 2006, La storia non è finita 2006, Davanti alla legge. Due Saggi 2006, Alfabeti 2008; numerous essays and book reviews in Corriere della Sera and other European newspapers and periodicals; trans. Ibsen, Kleist, Schnitzler, Büchner.

Address: The Wylie Agency, 17 Bedford Square, London, WC1B 3JA, England (office).

MAGSI, Nawab Zulfikar Ali; Pakistani politician and government official; b. 14 Feb. 1954, Jhal Magsi, Balochistan; m. Shama Parveen Magsi; ed Aitchison Coll., Lahore; current Nawab (Chief) of Magsi Tribe; first came to politics in 1977, won seat in prov. ass. as ind. cand.; served in numerous prov. ministries, also worked in Home Ministry 1990s; mem. Pakistan People's Party; Chief Minister of Balochistan Prov. in Govt of Benazir Bhutto May–July 1993, Oct. 1993–96; stood as ind. cand. from his native PB-32 Jhal Magsi constituency and won without opposition Feb. 2008; Gov. of Balochistan 2008–13 (resgnd). *Address:* Pakistan Peoples Party, 8, Street 19, F-8/2, Islamabad, Pakistan (office). *Telephone:* (51) 2255264 (office). *Fax:* (51) 2282741 (office). *E-mail:* ppp@comsats.net.pk (office). *Website:* www.ppp.org.pk (office).

MAGUFULI, John Pombe Joseph, BSc, MSc, PhD; Tanzanian industrial chemist, politician and head of state; *President;* b. 29 Oct. 1959, Chato Dist, Kagera Region; m. Janet Magufuli; five c.; ed Mkwawa Coll. of Educ., Univ. of Dar es Salaam, Univ. of Salford, UK; began career as chemistry and mathematics teacher, Sengerema Secondary School; industrial chemist, Nyanza Cooperative Union Ltd (cotton producer), Mwanza –1995; mem. Nat. Ass. (Parl.) for Chato constituency 1995–2015; Deputy Minister of Works 1995–2000, Minister for Lands, Housing and Human Settlements 2006–08, Minister for Livestock Devt and Fisheries 2008–10, Minister for Public Works 2010–15; Pres. of Tanzania 2015–; mem. Chama Cha Mapinduzi (CCM) 1977–. *Address:* Office of the President, State House, POB 2483, Dar es Salaam, Tanzania (office). *Telephone:* (22) 2116538 (office). *Fax:* (22) 2113425 (office). *E-mail:* permsec@estabs.go.tz (office). *Website:* www.tanzania.go.tz (office).

MAGUIRE, Adrian Edward, BPhil, MA, FSA; Irish fmr professional jockey; b. 29 April 1971; s. of Joseph Maguire and Philomena Maguire; m. Sabrina Maguire 1995; one d.; ed Kilmessan Nat. School, Trim Vocational School; champion pony race rider 1986, champion point-to-point rider 1990–91, champion conditional jockey 1991–92; wins include Cheltenham Gold Cup, Irish Grand Nat. (youngest ever winning jockey), Galway Plate, Imperial Cup, Greenalls Gold Cup, Queen Mother Champion Chase, King George VI Chase, Triumph Hurdle, Cathcart Chase 1994, Scottish National 1998, 2000, Whitbread Gold Cup 1998; holds records for most point-to-point winners in a season, most winners in a season for a conditional jockey (71) 1991–92; retd 2002 following neck injury, having won over 1,000 races. *Leisure interests:* squash, watching television. *Address:* 17 Willes Close, Faringdon, Oxon. SN7 7DU, England (home).

MAGUIRE, Joanne M., BEng, MEng; American aerospace industry executive; *Executive Vice-President, Lockheed Martin Space Systems Company;* d. of Mike Maguire; ed Michigan State Univ., Univ. of California, Los Angeles, Exec. Program in Man. at UCLA's Anderson School of Man., Harvard Program for Sr Execs in Nat. and Int. Security; joined TRW Space & Electronics (S&E) (now Northrop Grumman Space Tech.) 1975, held succession of increasingly responsible tech. and man. positions, later Program Man. for Defense Support Program, later Deputy Gen. Man. Defense Systems Div., later Vice-Pres. and Gen. Man. Space & Tech. Div., later Vice-Pres. and Gen. Man. Space & Laser Programs Div., later Deputy and Vice-Pres. Business Devt –2003; Vice-Pres. Special Programs, Lockheed Martin Space Systems Co. 2003, Vice-Pres. and Deputy of Lockheed Martin Space Systems Co. 2003–06, mem. Bd of Dirs 2004–, Exec. Vice-Pres. Lockheed Martin Space Systems Co. 2006–, officer of Lockheed Martin Corpn, also Chair. United Launch Alliance (Lockheed Martin jt venture); mem. Bd of Dirs Space Foundation, INROADS, Inc.; mem. AIAA, Soc. of Women Engineers; Outstanding Leadership Award, Women in Aerospace 1999. *Address:* Lockheed Martin Space Systems Company, 12257 South Wadsworth Blvd, Littleton, CO 80125-8500, USA (office). *Telephone:* (303) 977-3000 (office). *E-mail:* martha.a.hirschfield@lmco.com (office). *Website:* www.lockheedmartin.com (office).

MAGUIRE, Robert Francis, III, BA; American real estate executive; b. 18 April 1935, Portland, Ore.; s. of Robert Francis Maguire, Jr and Jean Maguire (née Shepard); ed Univ. of California, Los Angeles; Vice-Pres. Security Pacific Nat. Bank, Los Angeles 1960–64; Chair. Maguire Thomas Partners 1965, Chair. Maguire Properties Inc. (renamed MPG Office Trust 2010 Inc.) 2002–08, Chair. Emer. 2008–10, Co-CEO 2002–05, CEO June–Nov. 2002, 2006–08; mem. Exec. Bd Medical Sciences, UCLA; mem. Bd Dirs LA County Museum of Art, St John's Hosp., Santa Monica, Calif.; mem. Bd of Govs LA Music Center; Trustee, UCLA Foundation, Bard Coll., St John's Hosp., Santa Monica; mem. Bd Los Angeles County Museum of Art, Los Angeles Music Center. *Address:* c/o MPG Office Trust Inc., 333 South Grand Avenue, Suite 400, Los Angeles, CA 90071, USA.

MAGUIRE, Tobey; American actor; b. 27 June 1975, Santa Monica, Calif.; s. of Vincent Maguire and Wendy Maguire; m. Jennifer Meyer 2007 (divorced 2017); one d., one s.; began career acting in commercials; debuted in feature film The Wizard 1989; participated in poker tournaments and championships 2004–07; f. production company Material Pictures 2012; produced and acted in numerous films. *Television includes:* sitcoms: Blossom 1991, Roseanne 1991, Jake and the Fatman, Great Scott! 1992, This Boy's Life 1993, The Spoils of Babylon 2014; films: Spoils of War 1994, A Child's Cry for Help 1994, Seduced by Madness 1996, Duke of Groove 1996, The Spoils of Babylon 2014. *Films include:* S.F.W. 1994, Revenge of the Red Baron 1994, Duke of Groove 1995, Joyride 1996, Deconstructing Harry 1997, The Ice Storm 1997, Pleasantville (Saturn Award for Best Performance by a Younger Actor/Actress 1999) 1998, Fear and Loathing in Las Vegas 1998, Don's Plum 1998, Ride With the Devil 1999, The Cider House Rules 1999, Wonderboys (Toronto Film Critics Asscn Award for Best Supporting Performance, Male 2000) 2000, Spider-Man 2002, Seabiscuit 2003, Spider-Man 2 (Saturn Award for Best Actor 2005) 2004, The Good German 2006, Spider-Man 3 2007, Tropic Thunder 2008, Brothers 2009, The Great Gatsby 2013, Labour Day 2013, Good People (producer) 2014, Pawn Sacrifice (also producer) 2014, Z for Zachairah (producer) 2015, The 5th Wave (producer) 2015, Brittany Runs a Marathon (producer) 2018. *Leisure interests:* boardgames, basketball, backgammon, yoga.

MAGWOOD, William Donald, IV, BS, BA, MFA; American government official and international organization official; *Director-General, Nuclear Energy Agency, Organisation for Economic Co-operation and Development;* b. 1961; ed Carnegie-Mellon Univ., Univ. of Pittsburgh; held technology man. positions at Edison Electric Inst. and Westinghouse Electric Corpn, Pittsburgh, Pa 1984–94; Exec. Sec., Highly Enriched Uranium Oversight Cttee, Office of Nuclear Energy, Science and Tech., US Dept of Energy, then Assoc. Dir Tech. and Program Planning 1994–95, Acting Dir Office of Nuclear Energy, Science and Tech. 1996–98, Dir Office of Nuclear Energy, Science and Tech. 1998–2005; Commr US Nuclear Regulatory Comm. (NRC) 2010–14; Dir-Gen. Nuclear Energy Agency, OECD Sept. 2014–; James N. Landis Medal, American Soc. of Mechanical Engineers International 2004. *Address:* Office of the Director-General, OECD Nuclear Energy Agency, Le Seine Saint-Germain, 12, Blvd des Îles, 92130 Paris, France (office). *Telephone:* 1-45-24-82-00 (office). *E-mail:* nea@oecd-nea.org (office). *Website:* www.oecd-nea.org (office).

MAGYAR, Bálint; Hungarian sociologist and politician; b. 1952, Budapest; m. Róza Hodosán; one d.; ed Eötvös Loránd Univ.; Research Fellow, Inst. of World Econ., Hungarian Acad. of Sciences 1977–81, Inst. of Co-operation 1982–88; Financial Research Ltd 1988–90; involved in dissident political activities from 1979; Founding mem. Alliance of Free Democrats (SZDSZ), Pres. 1998–2000, mem. Exec. Bd 2001; mem. Parl. 1990–2010; Minister of Culture and Educ. 1996–98, of Educ. 2002–06; Vice-Pres. Nat. Devt Council under the direction of the Prime Minister 2006–08, State Sec. for Devt Policy, Prime Minister's Office 2007–08; currently Sr Researcher, Financial Research Ltd, Budapest; mem. Bd of Dirs and Treas. Empower European Universities; mem. Governing Bd European Inst. of Innovation and Technology 2008–12; János Neumann Prize 1998. *Film:* Dir Hungarian Stories (documentary) (Special Prize, Critics' Prize, Budapest Film Festival 1988). *Publication:* Dunaapáti 1944–1958 (sociography of a Hungarian village, three vols) (Ferenc Erdei Prize 1986). *Address:* c/o Empower European Universities, Kloosterweg 54, 6241 GB Bunde, Netherland.

MAH, Bow Tan, MSc; Singaporean politician; b. 12 Sept. 1948; m. Sheryn Kaye Von Senden; two s. two d.; ed St Joseph's Inst., Univ. of New South Wales, Australia; joined Singapore Bus Services 1974, Gen. Man. –1983; CEO Singapore Monitor, Singapore News and Publs Ltd (SNPL), later Group Gen. Man. SNPL, Group Gen. Man. (Co-ordination) Singapore Press Holdings Ltd 1985–88; Chair. Bd of Dirs NTUC Comfort 1983–86, Bd of Trustees 1988–93; Chair. Nat. Productivity Bd, Nat. Productivity Council, Skills Redevelopment Fund Advisory Council 1986–91; mem. Parl. for Tampines GRC (Tampines East) 1988–2015; Minister of State for Trade and Industry and Minister of State for Communications and Information 1988, Minister of State for Trade and Industry and Minister of State for Communications 1990, Minister for Communications 1991–99, concurrently Minister for the Environment 1993–95, Minister for Nat. Devt 1999–2011; Chair. Service Improvement Unit, Political Supervisory Cttee 1991; Chair. Bd of Govs, Singapore Inst. of Labour Studies 1990–2002; Chair. Nat. Youth Achievement Award Advisory Bd 1994–, Singapore Labour Foundation 2001–; Adviser Football Asscn of Singapore (FAS) Council 1991–99, Pres. FAS 1999–2004, Adviser 2004–; Hon. DSc (Univ. of New South Wales) 2001; Nat. Trades Union Congress Medal of Honour 1991, Univ. of New South Wales Alumni Award for Achievement 1996. *Leisure interests:* golf, travelling, reading, football.

MAHA VAJIRALONGKORN, HM King of Thailand (King Rama X), BA, LLB; b. 28 July 1952, Dusit Palace, Dusit, Bangkok; s. of HM King Bhumibol Adulyadej and Queen Sirikit; m. 1st Mom Luang Soamsawali Kitiyakara 1977 (divorced 1991); one d.; m. 2nd Yuvadhida Polpraserth 1994 (divorced 1996); four s. one d.; m. 3rd Mom Srirasmi Mahidol na Ayudhya (HRH Princess Srirasmi Suwadee, The Royal Consort) 2001 (divorced 2014); one s.; m. 4th Suthida Tidjai 2019; ed Royal Mil. Coll. Duntroon and Univ. of New South Wales, Australia, Royal Thai Army Command and Gen. Staff Coll., Sukhothai Thammatirat Univ., Bangkok, Royal Coll. of Defence Studies, UK; conferred with title Somdech Phra Boroma Orasadhiraj Chao Fah Maha Vajiralongkorn Sayam Makutrajakuman (heir to the throne) 28 Dec. 1972; Staff Officer Directorate of Army Intelligence 1975–78, Exec. Officer, King's Own Bodyguard 1978–80, Commdr 1980–84, CO 1984–88, Commdg Gen. 1988–92, Commdg Gen., Royalty Security Command, Office of the Supreme Commdr 1992–, Instructor Pilot, F-5 E/F fighter 1994, holds ranks of Gen. in Royal Thai Army, Adm. in Royal Thai Navy, Air Chief Marshal in Royal Thai Air Force; succeeded to the throne following the death of his father, King Bhumibol Adulyadej 13 Oct. 2016; formal coronation 4–6 May 2019. *Address:* The Government Public Relations Department, Rama VI Road, Bangkok, Thailand (office). *Telephone:* 618-2373 (office). *Fax:* 618-2358 (office).

MAHAFALY, Solonandrasana Olivier; Malagasy public servant and politician; b. 21 June 1964, Nosy Be; m.; three c.; ed École nat. d'admin de Madagascar, Univ. de Toliary; Lecturer, Coll. Sacré-Coeur, Toliary 1989–94; Head Teacher, Alliance Française, Toliary 1989–96; Communications Dir, Aide et Action (French non-govt org.), Toliary 1992–96; Deputy Prefect, Nosy Be 1999–2002; Dir, Chamber of Commerce, Industry, Agric. and Handicraft, Nosy Be 1999–2002; Commr-Gen. of Territorial Admin, Antsiranana territorial govt 2001–02; Electoral Supervisor, Antsiranana Dist 2002–03; Deputy Prefect, Befandriana Nord 2003–04; Prefect, Boeny Region May–Sept. 2004, Sec.-Gen., Boeny Region 2004–05; Electoral Supervisor, Ministry of the Interior Jan.–April 2006; Sec.-Gen., Toliary Dist 2006–08; Pres., Toliary ad hoc Comm. 2008–09; Dir of Territorial Admin, Ministry of Interior 2009–14, also Nat. Dir 'Ezaka Kopia Ho an'ny Ankizy' (birth registration programme) 2009–14; Minister of the Interior and Decentralization 2014–16; Prime Minister 2016–18; mem. Hery Vaovao ho an'i Madagasikara (HVM).

MAHAJAN, Sumitra, MA, LLB; Indian politician; *Speaker of Lok Sabha;* b. 12 April 1943, Chiplun, Maharashtra; d. of Purushotam Neelkanth Sathe and Usha Sathe; m. Jayant Mahajan 1965 (deceased); two s.; ed Devi Ahilya Univ. (Indore Univ.); Corporator, Municipal Corpn, Indore 1982–85, Deputy Mayor 1984–85; elected to Lok Sabha 1989, 1991, 1996, 1998, 1999, 2004, 2009, 2014; MP 1990–; Pres. Mahila Morcha, Bharatiya Janata Party (BJP) 1990–91, Vice-Pres. 1992–94, Sec., BJP Parl. Bd, later Chair. Parliamentary Bd 1995–96, Sec., BJP 1996–98, apptd Gen. Sec. 1998; Union Minister of State, Ministry of Human Resource Devt 1999–2002, Union Minister of State, Ministry of Communication and Information Tech. 2002–03, Union Minister of State, Ministry of Petroleum and Natural Gas 2003–04; Prabhari, Mahilla Morcha, BJP 2005; Chair. Standing Cttee on Social Justice and Empowerment 2007–09; Chair., Standing Cttee on Rural Devt 2009; Speaker of Lok Sabha (Parl.) 2014–; mem. Consultative Cttee, Ministry of Health and Family Welfare 1990–91, Jt Cttee for 73rd Constitution Amendment Bill

1991–92, Jt Cttee for Pre-Natal Diagnostic Techniques (Regulation and Prevention of Misuse) Bill, 1991 1991–93, Consultative Cttee, Ministry of Communications 1991–96, Cttee on Public Accounts 1997, Consultative Cttee on Civil Aviation 2005, Cttee on Empowerment of Women 2009–14, Panel of Chairmen 2004–09; Dr hc (Hankuk Univ. of Foreign Studies, Seoul) 2016. *Publication:* Matoshree 2017. *Leisure interests:* reading, music, drama and cinema. *Address:* Office of the Speaker, Lok Sabha, 16 Parliament House, New Delhi 110 001, India (office). *Telephone:* (11) 23017795 (office); (11) 23017914 (office). *Fax:* (11) 23792927 (office). *E-mail:* speakerloksabha@sansad.nic.in (office). *Website:* speakerloksabha.nic.in (office).

MAHAMA, John Dramani; Ghanaian politician and fmr head of state; b. 29 Nov. 1958, Damongo, Northern Region; s. of Emmanuel Adama Mahama; m. Lordina Mahama; seven c.; ed Univ. of Ghana, Legon, Moscow Inst. of Social Sciences, USSR; Information, Culture and Research Officer, Embassy of Japan, Accra 1991–96; Int. Relations, Sponsorship Communications and Grants Man., PLAN International (non-govt org.) Ghana Country Office 1996; MP for Bole/Bamboi Constituency 1997–2009; Deputy Minister of Communications 1997–98, Minister of Communications 1998–2001; mem. Pan-African Parl., S Africa 2004–11, Chair. West African Caucus; Vice-Pres. of Ghana 2009–12, Pres. and C-in-C of the Armed Forces 2012–17; Chair. Econ. Community of West African States (ECOWAS) 2014–15; apptd Co-Chair. Sustainable Development Goals Advocates 2016; mem. Nat. Democratic Congress, Dir of Communications 2002; Visiting Scholar, Johns Hopkins Univ., Baltimore, USA; Bill Gates Fellow; Great Cross, Nat. Order of Benin; Dr hc (Ekiti State Univ. of Nigeria, fmrly affiliated to Obafemi Awolowo Univ.); Daniel Award, Gen. Council of Assemblies of God, African Servant Leadership Award, Grad. School of Governance and Leadership, Prize of the Inst. of Public Relations, Friendship Medal (Cuba), Africa Award for Excellence in Food Security and Poverty Reduction, Forum for Agricultural Research in Africa 2013. *Publication:* My First Coup d'État and Other True Stories From the Lost Decades of Africa 2012. *Address:* c/o Office of the President, Flagstaff House, Liberation Crescent, Accra, Ghana (office).

MAHAMADOU, Karidjo; Niger politician; fmr teacher; Mayor, urban district of Tillabéri 1992; mem. Nat. Ass. (Parl.) (PNDS) 1993–; Prefect, Maradi Region 1995; Minister of Nat. Defence 2011–16; Founding mem. Parti Nigérien pour la Démocratie et le Socialisme—Tarayya (PNDS—Tarayya), fmr First Deputy, Nat. Exec. Cttee, fmr Regional Man. for Tillabéri region, First Deputy Sec. for Org. 1990, Fourth Deputy Sec.-Gen. 2004.

MAHANTA, Prafulla Kumar, BSc, LLB; Indian politician; b. 23 Dec. 1952, Rupnarayan Satra; s. of Deva Kanta Mahanta and Lakshmi Prava Mahanta; m. Joyasree Goswami; one s. one d.; leader of Assam Movt 1979–85; f. Asom Gana Parishad (AGP) (regional political party) 1985, expelled 2005, f. AGP (Progressive) 2005, reinducted into AGP (after merger of AGP and AGP Progressive) 2008, Pres. 2012–14; Chief Minister of Assam 1985–90, 1996–2001; apptd Chief Advisor North-East Regional Political Front 2013; fmr Pres. All Assam Students Union. *Address:* Rupnarayan Satra, Kaliabor, Nagaon District (home); Asom Gana Parishad, Ambari, Guwahati 781 001, India (office). *Telephone:* (361) 562222 (office); (361) 561291. *Fax:* (361) 562069 (office). *Website:* www.asomganaparishad.in (office).

MAHAR, Sardar Ali Mohammad Khan; Pakistani politician; b. Khan Garh Mahar, Ghotki Dist, Sindh; s. of Haji Ali Anwar Khan Mahar; m.; Chief of Mahar tribe; Chief Minister of Sindh 2002–04 (resgnd); fmr mem. Nat. Security Council; mem. (Pakistan Peoples Party Parliamentarians) Nat. Ass. of Pakistan for NA-201(Ghotki-II) constituency 2013–. *Address:* Village Khangarh Sharif, Taluka Khangarh District, Ghotki; H. # E-27, Gizri Blueward Defence, Phase-IV, Karachi; H-212, Parliament Lodges, Islamabad, Pakistan. *Telephone:* (300) 2220222. *E-mail:* assembly@na.gov.pk. *Website:* www.na.gov.pk/en/profile.php?uid=17.

MAHARA, Krishna Bahadur, BEd; Nepalese politician and fmr teacher; *President, House of Representatives;* b. 29 June 1958, Liwang Rolpa Dist; s. of Rabi Chandra Mahara and Samudra Devi; m.; two s. two d.; ed Tribhuvan Univ.; schoolteacher, Rolpa 1979–91; Minister of Information and Communications April–Sept. 2007, Deputy Prime Minister 2016–18, Minister of Finance 2016–17, Minister of Foreign Affairs 2017–18; mem. Constituent Ass. from Dang-3 constituency 2008– (parl. renamed Legis. Parl. 2015), currently MP for Rolpa-1 constituency; mem. House of Reps 2017–, Pres. 2018–; mem. Communist Party of Nepal (Unity Centre) 1991–94, Communist Party of Nepal—Unified Marxist-Leninist (UML) 1994–, fmr mem. Politburo and Standing Cttee, Party Spokesperson 2003–08. *Address:* House of Representatives, Singerbar, Kathmandu, Nepal (office). *Website:* hr.parliament.gov.np (office).

MAHARAJ, Mac (Sathyandranath Ragunanan), BA, MBA; South African politician and business executive; *Spokesperson for President of South Africa;* b. 27 April 1935, Newcastle, Natal (now KwaZulu-Natal); s. of N. R. Maharaj; m. Zarina Maharaj; two c.; ed St Oswald's High School and Univ. of Natal, Durban; Ed. New Age 1956; lived in UK where he worked as a teacher, rubbish collector and a canning factory and building site worker 1957–61, Founding mem. British Anti-Apartheid Movement; mem. Umkhonto Wesizwe (African Nat. Congress—ANC's armed wing) 1961, underwent mil. training in GDR 1961–62; returned to SA 1962; sentenced to 12 years' imprisonment Dec. 1964, served prison sentence on Robben Island 1965–76; left SA 1976; with ANC HQ, Lusaka, Zambia, Sec. Underground Section 1977; mem. Revolutionary Council 1978, Politico-Mil. Council 1985; mem. ANC Negotiation Cttee, Political Cttee 1984, Nat. Exec. Council 1985–90, 1991–, Nat. Working Cttee; Commdr Operation Vula, SA 1988–90; mem. Political Bureau and Cen. Cttee 1990; with Codesa Secr.; Jt Sec. Transitional Exec. Council 1994; Minister of Transport, Govt of Nat. Unity 1994–99; active in business 1999–; Dir (non-exec.), FirstRand Bank 1999–2003 (resgnd); Spokesperson, Pres. of South Africa, Jacob Zuma 2011–; mem. Faculty, Bennington Coll., Vt, USA 2005–. *Address:* Office of the Presidency, Private Bag X1000, Union Buildings, West Wing, Government Avenue, Pretoria 0001, South Africa. *Telephone:* (12) 3005200. *Fax:* (12) 3238246. *E-mail:* president@po.gov.za. *Website:* www.thepresidency.gov.za.

MAHARAJ, Pandit Birju; Indian dancer and choreographer; *Director, Kalashram;* b. (Brijmohan Mishra), 4 Feb. 1938, Lucknow; s. of Acchan Maharaj; m.; two s. three d.; Kathak teacher, Sangeet Bharti, Bharatiya Kala Kendra, Delhi; Head of Faculty and Dir Kathak Kendra, New Delhi –1998; Founder-Dir Kalashram (school for Kathak and associated disciplines) 1998–; Dr hc (Banaras Hindu Univ.), (Khairagarh Univ.); Padma Vibhushan 1986, Sangeet Natak Akademi Award, Kalidas Samman, Nritya Choodamani, Andhra Ratna, Nritya Vilas, Adharshila Shikhar Samman, Soviet Land Nehru Award, Shiromani Samman, Rajiv Gandhi Peace Award, Lata Mangeshkar Puraskaar 2002, Filmfare Award for Best Choreography (Mohe Rang Do Laal, Bajirao Mastani) 2016. *Films:* Shatranj Ke Khiladi 1977, Dil To Pagal Hai 1997, Gadar: Ek Prem Katha 2001, Devdas 2002, Umrao Jaan 2006, Vishwaroopam (Nat. Award for Best Choreography, Tamil Nadu State Film Award for Best Choreographer 2017) 2013, Dedh Ishqiya 2014, Bajirao Mastani 2015. *Leisure interests:* painting, poetry. *Address:* Kalashram, D-II/33, Shahjahan Road, New Delhi 110 011, India (office). *Telephone:* (11) 26277367 (office). *Fax:* (11) 23782889 (office). *Website:* contact@birjumaharaj-kalashram.com (office); www.birjumaharaj-kalashram.com (office).

MAHAREY, Hon. Steve, CNZM, BA, MA (Hons); New Zealand academic, university administrator and fmr politician; *Vice-Chancellor, Massey University;* b. 3 Feb. 1953, Palmerston North; s. of William Maharey and Irene Maharey; m. Liz Mackay; two step-s.; ed Freyberg High School, Massey Univ.; taught sociology and business admin. at Massey Univ. from 1978, Sr Lecturer in Sociology; mem. Palmerston North City Council 1986–89, Chair. Palmerston North Labour Electorate Cttee, mem. Policy Council; Labour MP for Palmerston North 1990–2008; Opposition Spokesperson on Social Welfare and Employment, Broadcasting and Communications and Labour Relations 1994–97; Assoc. Spokesperson on Educ. with specific responsibility for Tertiary Educ., Educ. and Employment 1990–93, served on the Social Services, Educ. and Science, Commerce, Justice and Law Reform and Broadcasting Parl. Select Cttees; Minister for Social Devt and Employment 1999–2005, Assoc. Minister of Educ. (Tertiary Educ.) 1999–2004, Minister responsible for Community and Voluntary Sector 1999–2002, Minister of Broadcasting 2002–07, of Housing 2003–04, of Youth Affairs 2004, of Research, Science and Tech. 2004–07, Minister for Crown Research Insts. 2004–07, Minister of Educ. 2005–07, Minister responsible for the Educ. Review Office –2007; Vice-Chancellor Massey Univ. 2008–; fmr Chair. Cabinet Social Devt Cttee; fmr mem. Cttees for Cabinet Policy, Appointments and Honours, Econ. Devt and Legislation; retd from politics 2008; mem. Bd Wellington Employers Chamber of Commerce, Cttee for Auckland, Territorial Force Employers Support Council, Bd of the Manawatu Cancer Soc.; Patron Australasian Tertiary Educ. Managers Asscn, Manawatu Squash Asscn; Companion, NZ Order of Merit 2008. *Publications:* numerous articles on media and cultural studies and social change. *Leisure interests:* mountain biking, swimming, music, social and political theory, travel, spectator sports. *Address:* Vice-Chancellor's Office, University House, Private Bag 11 222, Palmerston North, New Zealand (office). *Telephone:* (6) 350-5096 (office). *Fax:* (6) 350-5603 (office). *E-mail:* s.maharey@massey.ac.nz (office). *Website:* www.massey.ac.nz/massey/about-massey/university-management/vice-chancellor (office).

MAHASHER, Nasser al-, BS, MS; Saudi Arabian oil company executive; *Representative Director and CEO, S-Oil Corporation;* ed King Fahd Univ. of Petroleum and Minerals, Eastern Michigan Univ. and Wayne State Univ., USA; worked for Saudi Aramco (state-owned oil co.) for 22 years, including as Global Refining Co-ordinator, also Sr Vice-Pres.; fmr Pres. and CEO Saudi Petroleum International, Inc.; Pres. Saudi Petroleum Ltd, Tokyo 2008–12; Rep. Dir and CEO S-Oil Corpn 2012–. *Address:* S-Oil Corporation, 471 Gongduk-dong, Mapo-gu, Seoul 121-805, Republic of Korea (office). *Telephone:* (2) 3772-5151 (office). *E-mail:* info@s-oil.com (office). *Website:* www.s-oil.com (office).

MAHAT, Prakash Sharan, MEcon, MSc, PhD; Nepalese politician; b. 5 Nov. 1959, Nuwakot Dist; m. Bina Mahat; two c.; ed Tribhuvan Univ., Univ. of Illinois at Urbana–Champaign and Southern Illinois Univ., USA; Gen. Sec., Nepal Students' Union 1983–97; mem. Nepali Congress Action Cttee during People's Movement 1990; Mem. Sec., Nepal Govt High-Level Cttee for Resolution of Maoist Insurgency 1999; Adviser to Prime Minister 2001–02; mem. Nat. Planning Comm. April–Oct. 2002; State Minister for Foreign Affairs 2004–05; mem. Nat. Peace Cttee 2006–07; mem. Interim Legis. Parl. 2006–08; mem. Govt Dialogue Team in negotiations with various insurgent groups in Nepal 2007–08; mem. first Constituent Ass. 2008–12, second Constituent Ass. 2013–, mem. Constitution Drafting Cttee, State Affairs Cttee, Special Parl. Hearing Cttee; Minister for Energy 2010–11, for Foreign Affairs 2016–17; mem. Nepali Congress, mem. Central Econ. Policy Cttee 1998–99, Central Exec. Cttee 2007–. *Publications:* numerous policy papers, research analyses and newspaper articles on econ. devt, peace process and contemporary political devt.

MAHAT, Ram Sharan, MA, PhD; Nepalese economist and politician; b. 1 Jan. 1951, Nuwakot; s. of Tol Kumari Mahat; m. Roshana Mahat; one s. one d.; ed Tribhuban Univ., Gokhale Inst. of Politics and Econs, Pune, India, School of Int. Service, American Univ.; Hubert Humphrey Fellowship 1987–88; Asst Resident Rep., UNDP, Islamabad 1989–90; econ. adviser to Prime Minister of Nepal 1991–92; Vice-Chair. Nat. Planning Comm. 1991–94; mem. Constituent Assembly (Parl.) from Nuwakot Dist 1994–2017; Minister of Finance 1995–99, Minister of Foreign Affairs 1999–2000, Minister of Finance 2001, 2006–07, 2014–15; Sr Leader, Nepali Congress, also Central Cttee mem.; fmr Chair. Univ. Grants Comm.; mem. Bd of Trustees Asian Inst. of Technology, Bangkok 1993–94; Hon. Fellow, Univ. of Connecticut; Francis Humbert Humphrey Award for Leadership Role in Public Service, USIA and Inst. of Int. Educ., Finance Minister of the Year, Banker Magazine 2016. *Publications include:* Industrial Financing in Nepal, In Defense of Democracy: Dynamics and Faultlines of Nepal's Political Economy 2005; numerous articles on nat. and int. econ. issues. *Leisure interests:* social service, reading books. *Address:* Bansbari, Kathmandu, Nepal (home). *E-mail:* ramsmahat@gmail.com. *Website:* www.ramsmahat.com.np.

MAHATHIR, Seri Dato Mukhriz Bin; Malaysian business executive and politician; *Chief Minister of Kedah;* b. 25 Nov. 1964; s. of Mahathir bin Mohamad (Prime Minister of Malaysia) and Siti Hasmah Mohamad Ali; m. Norzieta Zakaria; four c.; ed Sophia Univ., Tokyo, Boston Univ.; worked with several companies including Opcom Holdings, Kosmo Tech, Malaysian Franchise Asscn; mem. Youth Exec. Council, United Malays Nat. Org. (UMNO) 2004–16; Deputy Minister of Int. Trade and Industry 2008–13; mem. Parl. (UMNO) for Jerlun 2008–13, (PPBM) 2018–; mem. Kedah State Legis. Ass. (UMNO) for Ayer Hitam 2013–18, (PPBM) for Jitra 2018–; Chief Minister of Kedah 2018–; currently Chair. Bd of Dirs Bioven (pharmaceutical co.); Exec. Dir Prime Peace Global Foundation; mem. UMNO 2004–16; mem. Parti Pribumi Bersatu Malaysia (PPBM, Malaysian United Indigenous Party) 2016–, currently Deputy Pres.; Exalted Order of the Crown of Kedah, Illustrious Order of Loyalty to Sultan 'Abdu'l Halim Mu'azzam Shah, Illustrious Order of Loyalty to the Royal House of Kedah. *Address:* Parliament of Malaysia, Parliament Building, 50680 Kuala Lumpur, Malaysia (office). *Telephone:* (3) 20721955 (office); (3) 26017222 (office). *Fax:* (3) 20727436 (office). *Website:* www.parlimen.gov.my.

MAHATHIR BIN MOHAMAD, Tun; Malaysian politician; *Prime Minister;* b. 20 Dec. 1925, Alur Setar, Kedah; m. Dr Siti Hasmah binti Haji Mohd Ali 1956; seven c.; ed Sultan Abdul Hamid Coll. and Univ. of Malaya in Singapore; Medical Officer, Kedah, Langkawi and Perlis 1953–57; private practice 1957–64; mem. UMNO-Barisan Nasional 1946–2016, mem. UMNO (now Umno Baru) Supreme Council 1965–69, 1972–2008 (Pres. 1981), mem. Supreme Council 1972–2008; mem. Dewan Rakyat (House of Reps.) for Kota Setar Selatan 1964–69, for Kubang Pasu 1974–2004; mem. Dewan Negara 1972–74; mem. Senate 1973; Chair. Food Industries of Malaysia Sdn. Bhd. 1973; Minister of Educ. 1974–77, of Trade and Industry 1977–81, of Defence 1981–86, of Home Affairs 1986–99, of Justice 1987, of Natural and Rural Devt; Deputy Prime Minister 1976–81, Prime Minister of Malaysia 1981–2003, 2018– (retd from politics 2003, came out of retirement to stand as Pakatan Harapan prime ministerial candidate 2018); Sec.-Gen. Non-Aligned Movt 2003; fmr Adviser, Petronas, Proton; Chancellor, Univ. Teknologi Petronas 2004–16; mem. PPBM-Pakatan Harapan (opposition alliance) 2016–; Hon. Pres. Perdana Leadership Foundation; Dr hc (Meiji Univ., Japan) 2001, (Univ. Teknologi Malaysia) 2003, (Univ. Islam Antarabangsa) 2003. *Publications:* The Malay Dilemma 1969, The Way Forward 1998. *Address:* Prime Minister's Office, Federal Government Administration Center, Bangunan Perdana Putra, 62502 Putrajaya, Malaysia (office). *Telephone:* (3) 88888000 (office). *Fax:* (3) 88883444 (office). *E-mail:* ppm@pmo.gov.my (office). *Website:* www.pmo.gov.my (office).

MAHATO, Rajendra; Nepalese politician; *Chairman, Sadbhavana Party;* b. 19 Nov. 1958, Sarlahi; s. of Khobhari Mahato; m. Sahil Devi Mahato; Nepal Sadbhavana Party (NSP) cand. for Sarlahi-2 constituency in parl. election 1994, won seat 1999; broke away from NSP and formed own party, Sadbhavana Party 2007, Chair. 2007–; Minister for Industry, Commerce and Supply 2007–08; resgnd from interim Parl. Jan. 2008; won Sarlahi-4 seat in Constituent Ass. election April 2008; Minister of Health and Population 2011–13. *Address:* Sadbhavana Party, Kathmandu, Nepal (office).

MAHAYNI, Mohammad Khaled al-, PhD; Syrian economist and politician; b. 30 May 1943, Damascus; s. of Salim al-Mahayni and Weedad Araman; m. Falak Sakkal 1966; two s. two d.; ed Damascus Univ.; various public financial and econ. appointments 1961–70; auditor 1970–77; Dir of Debt Fund and Information, Ministry of Finance 1979–80, of Public Enterprises 1981–84; Deputy Minister of Finance 1984–87, Minister 1987–2001; Gov. IBRD 1987–2001, Arab Bank for Econ. Devt in Africa 1989; Dir Nat. Inst. of Admin, Damascus; Prof., Damascus Univ. 1992. *Publications:* Methodology of the General Budget of the State in the Syrian Arab Republic 1984, Supplementary Policies for Financial Planning 1995, Government Accounting 1996, Public Finance and Tax Legislation 1999. *Leisure interests:* reading and computing.

MAHDI, Adil Abd al-, PhD; Iraqi economist and politician; *Prime Minister;* b. 1942, Baghhad; m.; four c.; ed Coll. of Trade and Econs, Baghdad; moved to France 1969, worked for several think-tanks; has also lived in Lebanon and Iran; Supreme Council for the Islamic Revolution in Iraq (SCIRI) rep. in Kurdistan 1992–96; returned to Iraq; interim Minister of Finance 2004–05, Vice-Pres. of Iraq 2005–11 (resgnd); Minister of Oil 2014–16; Prime Minister 2018–; mem. Supreme Islamic Iraqi Council. *Address:* Office of the Prime Minister, Baghdad, Iraq (office). *Website:* www.almejlis.org.

MAHDI, Sadiq al-, (since 1978 known as Sadiq Abdul Rahman), BSc, MSc; Sudanese politician; *President, Umma National Party;* b. 25 Dec. 1935, Al-Abasya, Omdurman; s. of Imam Al-Siddik Abdel-Rahman al-Mahdi and Sayeda Rahma Abdallah Jad-Allah; great grandson of Imam Abdul-Rahman El Mahdi; m. 1st Sayeda Hafya Mamoun Sharief 1960; m. 2nd Sayeda Sarrah al-Fadil Mahmoud 1962; ten c.; ed Comboni School, Victoria Coll., Gordon Memorial Coll., Khartoum, Univ. of Khartoum, St John's Coll., Oxford, UK; Pres. Unified Nat. Front 1961–64, Umma Mahdist (now Umma Nat. Party—Hizb al-Umma) from 1964, 1986–89, Pres. 2003–, Pres. Nat. Front 1972–77; Prime Minister 1966–67, 1986–89; arrested on a charge of high treason 1969; exiled April 1970; returned to Sudan and arrested Feb. 1972, released April 1974; exiled 1974–77; led unsuccessful coup against fmr Pres. Nimeri July 1976, returned to Sudan Sept. 1977; reconciliation with Pres. Nimeri 1977; led mediation mission over US hostages in Iran Crisis Jan. 1980; returned to prison Sept. 1983, released Dec. 1984; mem. Nat. Ass. 1986–89; Minister of Defence 1986–89; overthrown in coup June 1989, arrested July 1989, released and put under house arrest Nov. 1989; granted amnesty May 1991; arrested on charges of conspiring against mil. govt June 1994; re-arrested May 1995; escaped from house arrest Dec. 1996; in Eritrea 1996–2000, returned to Sudan Nov. 2000; unsuccessful cand. in presidential elections 2010; mem. Cttee, Sudanese Socialist Union 1978–79; mem. Club of Madrid, Arab Water Council (also mem. Bd of Trustees), Nat. Islamic Conf., Beirut; mem. Bd Arab Democracy Foundation; mem. Bd of Trustees, Org. for Democracy in the Arab World (Qatar); Visiting Fellow, St Antony's Coll., Oxford 1983; Imam of the Ansar (Sufi sect that pledges allegiance to Muhammad Ahmad) 2002–; selected by Inst. of Objective Studies, New Delhi as one of the great Muslim Leaders of the 20th Century in the realm of Leaders and Rulers 2006. *Publications include:* The Southern Question 1964, Speeches in Exile 1976, Questions on Mahadism 1979, Legitimate Penalties and Their Position in the Islamic Social System 1987, Democracy in Sudan: Will Return and Triumph 1990, Challenges of the Nineties 1991. *Leisure interests:* breeding and rearing horses, horse riding, polo, tennis, reading. *E-mail:* ralsadig@hotmail.com; zakioffice@yahoo.com. *Website:* www.umma.org.

MAHENDRA, Ranbir Singh, BA, LLB; Indian politician, sports organization administrator and lawyer; b. 7 Jan. 1944, Golagarh, Haryana; s. of Chaudhary Bansi Lal; m. Nirmal Kanta; one s. one d.; trained as lawyer; elected Jt Sec., Bd of Control for Cricket in India (BCCI), Kolkata 1980–85, Sec. 1985–89, mem. Finance Cttee, Pres. 2004–05; conducted first cricket World Cup outside of England 1987; fmr Sec. Haryana Cricket Asscn; Man. of Indian Cricket Team, World Cup, Australia 1992; fmr Vice-Pres. Nat. Cricket Acad.; mem. Indian Nat. Congress; MLA Haryana Vidhan Sabha 2005; Hon. mem. Cricket Club of India, Karnataka State Cricket Club House and Delhi, Dist Cricket Asscn, Punjab Haryana High Court Bar Asscn Ltd. *Address:* 95, Sector 10 A, Chandigarh 160 011, India (home). *Telephone:* (172) 2742885.

MAHENDRA, Yusron Ihza, LLM, PhD; Indonesian lawyer, politician and diplomatist; b. 5 Feb. 1958, Lalang, Manggar, Bangka Belitung; s. of Idris Haji Zainal Abidin and Nursiha Sandon; m. Margaretha Suryanti; four c.; ed Univ. of Indonesia, Univ. of Tsukuba, Japan; began career as a researcher at Tsukuba Advanced Research Alliance, Japan, also served as Corresp. and Chief Rep. of Kompas newspaper and as East Asian econ. analyst at NHK TV station; later Political Consultant, Ministry of Justice, Japan; returned to Indonesia and est. Ihza & Ihza law firm; apptd by Govt as Special Adviser to Minister of Industry and Trade 2002; joined Partai Bulan Bintang (Crescent Star Party), DPP Chair. 2005–10, Vice-Chair. 2009–14; elected mem. Parl. for Bangka-Belitung constituency 2004; Vice-Chair. Comm. I of House of Reps (Defence) 2004–09; Chair. Indonesia–Japan Parl. League 2004–09; Amb. to Japan (also accred to Federated States of Micronesia) 2013–17; Chair. Indonesian Student Asscn-Japan 1993–94.

MAHENDRAN, Arjuna, BA, MA; Sri Lankan (b. Singaporean) financial services industry executive and central banker; b. 16 July 1959; ed Balliol Coll., Oxford, UK; has worked in numerous financial services orgs in Hong Kong, Singapore and Sri Lanka, including s positions with Central Bank of Sri Lanka and Sri Lanka Ministry of Finance; fmr Dir and Head of Econ. Research (ASEAN and South Asia), Société Générale Cross Asset Research; Chair. and Dir-Gen., Bd of Investment of Sri Lanka 2001–04; Chief Economist and Strategist-Asia Pacific, Credit Suisse Group AG 2004–08, also Head of Research for Asia Pacific 2006–08; Man. Dir and Chief Investment Strategist-Asia, HSBC Private Bank 2008–13; Chief Investment Officer, Wealth Man. Div., Emirates NBD, Dubai 2013–15; Gov. and Chair. of Monetary Bd, Central Bank of Sri Lanka 2015–16; Investment Advisor to Prime Minister 2016–.

MAHER, Terence Anthony, FCCA; British bookseller and publisher; b. 5 Dec. 1935, Manchester; s. of Herbert Maher and Lillian Maher; m. Barbara Grunbaum 1960; three s.; ed Xaverian Coll., Manchester; Controller, Carborundum Co. Ltd 1961–69; Dir Corp. Finance, First Nat. Finance Corpn 1969–72; f. Pentos PLC 1972, Chair. and CEO –1993; Chair. and CEO Dillons Bookstores 1977–93; Athena Int. 1980–93, Ryman 1987–93; Chair. The Chalford Publishing Co. Ltd 1994–98, Maher Booksellers Ltd 1995–2008, Race Dynamics Ltd 1998–2007; Founder Trustee, Liberal Democrats 1988–2001; mem. Advisory Council on Libraries 1997–98; Fellow, Chartered Asscn of Certified Accountants. *Achievements include:* led successful campaign to abolish price control on books in UK. *Publications:* Counterblast (co-author) 1965, Effective Politics (co-author) 1966, Against My Better Judgement (autobiog.) 1994, Unfinished Business (fiction) 2003, Grumpy Old Liberal – A Political Rant 2005, What would a Liberal Do? – A Polemic 2010, One of Lowry's Children – A Personal Memoir 2015. *Leisure interests:* skiing, tennis, walking, reading, bridge. *Address:* 33 Montagu Square, London, W1H 2LJ, England (home). *Telephone:* (20) 7723-4254 (London).

MAHER ALI, Abdel Moneim, PhD; Egyptian biologist and business executive; *President, ARADIS Company SAE;* b. 9 March 1922, Dammanhour; s. of Ali Elsayed Shehata and Nagia M. Manaã; m. Fardous Abbas Abdelal 1948; two s.; ed Cairo Univ., Univ. Coll. London, UK and Ein Shams Univ.; Founder, Gen. Sec. Egyptian Youth Hostel Assoc. 1955–70; Dir Cen. Agric. Pesticide Lab. UNDP Project 1963–69; Demonstrator, Dept of Plant Protection, Faculty of Agric., Assiut Univ. 1948–69, Assoc. Prof. 1969, Prof. 1969–82, Head, Dept of Plant Protection 1970, Prof. Emer. 1982–; Gen. Sec. Egyptian Zoological Soc., Egyptian Asscn for Conservation of Nature and Natural Resources, Egyptian Asscn for Environment Care, Egyptian Asscn for Medicinal Plants 1975–; Founder then Consultant, Wady Elassiuty Protected Area 1980–94; Pres. ARADIS Co. SAE, Arab Co. Environment Disinfection SAE Co. 1983–; now Chief Ed. Egyptian Journal for Natural Resources and Wildlife; Conservation Merit Award, World Wildlife Fund, Science and Arts 1st Class, Order of the Repub. 5th, 3rd and 2nd and other awards. *Publications include:* textbook on pest control, articles in scientific periodicals. *Leisure interests:* travel, sightseeing, archaeological tours. *Address:* 45 Jule Gamal Street, Agouza, Gizah (office); 50 Wizaret El Ziraã Street, 12th Floor, Dokki, Gizah (home); PO Box 318, Dokki Gizah, Egypt. *Telephone:* (2) 346-2029 (office); (2) 337-3988 (office); (2) 336-0846 (home). *Fax:* (2) 346-2029 (office). *E-mail:* medplantus@yahoo.com (office).

MAHIGA, Augustine Philip, BA, MA, PhD; Tanzanian diplomatist, politician and fmr UN official; b. 28 Aug. 1945; m.; ed Univ. of East Africa, Dar-es-Salaam, Univ. of Toronto, Canada; Sr Lecturer in Int. Affairs and Regional Co-operation, Univ. of Dar-es-Salaam 1975–77; Dir of Research and Training, Office of the Pres. of Tanzania 1977–80, Acting Dir Gen. Office of the Pres. 1980–83; High Commr to Canada 1983–89; Amb. and Perm. Rep. to UN, Geneva 1989–92; on secondment to UNHCR 1993, UNHCR Chief of Mission, Monrovia, Liberia 1992–94, Deputy Dir and Co-ordinator Great Lakes Region of Africa Refugee Emergency Operation, Geneva 1994–98, UNHCR Chief of Mission, New Delhi 1998–2002, UNHCR Rep. to Italy (also accred to Malta and San Marino) 2002–03; Amb. and Perm. Rep. to UN, New York 2003–10, Head of del. to UN Security Council 2005, also Asst Sec.-Gen. for Peacebuilding Support for UN Peacebuilding Comm., Special Rep. for Somalia and Head of UN Political Office for Somalia (UNPOS) 2010–13; Minister of Foreign Affairs and East African Co-operation 2015–19; Lifetime Achievement Award, Miracle Corners of the World 2007.

MAHINDRA, Anand G., MBA; Indian business executive; *Chairman and Managing Director, Mahindra and Mahindra Limited;* b. 1 May 1955, Bombay (now Mumbai); m. Anuradha Mahindra; two d.; ed Harvard Coll., Harvard Business School, USA; Exec. Asst to Finance Dir, Mahindra Ugine Steel Co. Ltd 1981–89, Pres. and Deputy Man. Dir 1989–91; Deputy Man. Dir Mahindra and Mahindra Ltd 1991–97, apptd Man. Dir 1997, Vice-Chair. 2003–2012, Chair. and Man. Dir 2012–; Co-founder Harvard Business School Asscn of India; fmr Chair. Nat. Inst. of Industrial Eng., Mumbai; fmr Pres. Automotive Research Asscn of

India; Co-promoter Kotak Mahindra Bank (fmrly Kotak Mahindra Finance Ltd); mem. Confed. of Indian Industry (Pres. 2003–04); mem. Advisory Cttee, Harvard Univ. Asia Centre, Exec. Cttee, The Nehru Centre, Mumbai, Advisory Council, Initiative on Corp. Governance, Harvard Business School, Harvard Global Advisory Council, Nat. Council of Applied Econ. Research, India Council for Sustainable Devt, Nehru Centre, Nat. Sports Devt Fund, Econ. Devt Bd of Rajasthan, Int. Advisory Council of Singapore's Econ. Devt Bd, Global Bd of Advisors of Council on Foreign Relations, New York; mem. Bd of Govs, Mahindra United World Coll. of India; Trustee, K. C. Mahindra Educ. Trust; Hon. Amb. of Foreign Investment Promotion for Repub. of Korea; Chevalier, l'Ordre du Mérite; Rajiv Gandhi Award 2004, Leadership Award, American India Foundation 2005, Harvard Business School Alumni Achievement Award 2008, Nat. Statesman for Excellence in Business Practices–Qimpro Platinum Standard Award 2008, Leadership Award (co-winner), US India Business Council 2012, Business Courage Award, Asia Business Leadership Forum 2012, Best Transformational Leader Award, Asian Centre for Corp. Governance and Sustainability 2012, Sustainability Devt Leadership Award, The Energy and Resources Inst. 2014. *Leisure interests:* playing tennis, sailing, photography. *Address:* Mahindra and Mahindra Ltd, Gateway Building, Apollo Bunder, Mumbai 400 001, India (office). *Telephone:* (22) 22895500 (office). *Fax:* (22) 22028980 (office). *Website:* www.mahindra.com (office).

MAHINDRA, Keshub, BSc; Indian business executive (retd); *Chairman Emeritus, Mahindra and Mahindra Ltd.;* b. 9 Oct. 1923, Simla; s. of Kailash Chandra Mahindra and Savitri Mahindra; m. Sudha Y. Varde 1956; three d.; ed Wharton Business School, Univ. of Pennsylvania, USA; joined Mahindra and Mahindra Ltd 1947, Chair. 1963–2012, Chair. Emer. 2012–; Chair. Housing and Urban Devt Corpn Ltd 1971–75, Indian Inst. of Man., Ahmedabad 1975–85, India Nominating Cttee "Single Nation Programme", Eisenhower Exchange Fellowships, USA 1998–2005; Pres. Asscn of Indian Automobile Mfrs 1964–65, Bombay Chamber of Commerce and Industry 1966–67, Assoc. Chamber of Commerce and Industry 1969–70, MVIRDC, World Trade Center 1978–95, Employers' Fed. of India 1985–97, Indo-American Soc. 1991–92; Dir Bombay Dyeing and Mfg Co. Ltd, Bombay Burmah Trading Corpn Ltd, Housing Devt Finance Corpn Ltd, United World Coll. International Ltd, UK, Mahindra Ugine Steel Co. Ltd etc.; Dir Pratham India Educ. Initiative 2003–08; Pres. Centre for Research in Rural and Industrial Devt, Chandigarh, Governing Council, Univ. of Pennsylvania Inst. for Advanced Study of India, New Delhi; Chair. Mahindra Foundation, Health and Environment Cttee, Bd Trustees, Population First; Chair. and Trustee, K.C. Mahindra Educ. Trust; Pres. Emer. Employers' Fed. of India; mem. Apex Advisory Council of Assoc. Chambers of Commerce and Industry of India, International Council Asia Soc. New York, USA 1983–97; Founding mem., Indo-Hellenic Friendship League, Governing Council, Integrated Research and Action for Devt (IRADe), New Delhi; mem. Foundation Bd, International Man. Inst., Geneva 1984–89, Prime Minister's Council on Trade and Industry; mem. Bd of Govs Mahindra United World Coll. of India; mem. Governing Body of HelpAge India 2000–04, Governing Body/Bd Govs of Bharat Shiksha Kosh 2002–05, Governing Bd United Way of Mumbai, Bombay First, International Advisory Bd Univ. of Pennsylvania Center for Advanced Study of India, Philadelphia; Hon. Fellow, All India Man. Asscn 1990, Hon. mem. Business Advisory Council, IFC, Washington, DC 1986–96, Rotary Club of Bombay 1984; Chevalier, Légion d'honneur 1987; numerous awards including Giants Int. Business Leadership Award 1972–82, Madras Man. Asscn Business Leadership Award 1983, Business India Indian Businessman of the Year 1989, Rotary Award for Vocational Excellence 1992, Shiromani Award 1992, Vikas Jyoti Award 1993, Sir Jengahir Ghandy Medal for Industrial Peace, XLRI, Jamshedpur 1994, Rotary Vocational Excellence Award in the Field of Industry 1996, IMC Diamond Jubilee Endowment Trust Award 1998, Motorindia Automan Award 2000, Dadabhai Naoroji Int. Award for Excellence and Lifetime Achievement 2000, All India Man. Asscn Lifetime Achievement Award for Man. 2003, Inst. of Co. Secs of India Lifetime Achievement Award for Excellence in Corp. Governance 2004, Qimpro Platinum Standard 'Statesman for Quality' Business Award 2005, Lakshya Business Visionary Award, NITIE 2006, Indian Business School Kolkata Lifetime Achievement Award 2007, Ernst and Young Entrepreneur of the Year Lifetime Achievement Award 2007, Soc. of Indian Automobile Manufacturers Award for Lifetime Contrib. to the Automotive Industry 2008, CNBC TV18 India Business Leaders Lifetime Achievement Award 2008. *Leisure interests:* golf, tennis, photography, reading. *Address:* Mahindra and Mahindra Ltd, Mahindra Towers, G M Bhosale Marg, Mumbai 400 018 (office); St Helen's Court, Pedder Road, Mumbai 400 026, India (home). *Telephone:* (22) 23514206 (home). *E-mail:* mahindra.keshub@mahindra.com (office). *Website:* www.mahindra.com (office).

MAHJOUB, Abdelmajid, BSc, MSc, PhD; Tunisian microbiologist, academic and international organization official; *Director General, Arab Atomic Energy Agency;* b. 5 Feb. 1950, Béni Hassen-Monastir; m.; four c.; ed High School of Radès & Tunis, Univ. of Tunis, Tulane Univ. and Univ. of Nebraska-Lincoln, USA; high school teacher (biology), La Marsa 1974–75; Asst Prof. and Head of Nutrition Educ. Section, Teaching and Man., Nat. Inst. of Nutrition, Tunis 1977–80, Assoc. Prof., Research and Teaching, Food Tech. and Microbiology, School of Food Industry, Univ. Tunis II 1985–92, Head of Dept of Food Tech. 1992–97; Dir Gen. Nat. Centre for Nuclear Sciences and Technologies 1997–2001; Programme Man. Officer, Africa Div., IAEA Dept of Tech. Co-operation 2001–08; Dir Gen. Arab Atomic Energy Agency 2009–. *Address:* Arab Atomic Energy Agency, PO Box 402, 7 Rue de l'assistance, Cité el Khadhra, 1003 Tunis, Tunisia (office). *Telephone:* (71) 808400 (office); 98-460711 (mobile). *Fax:* (71) 808450 (office). *E-mail:* amahjoub@aaea.org.tn (office); am.mahjoub@yahoo.fr. *Website:* www.aaea.org.tn (office).

MAHLAB, Ibrahim, BEng; Egyptian engineer and politician; b. 1949; ed Cairo Univ.; several years with Arab Contracting Co., including as Dir of Bridges 1994, Vice-Chair. 1997, later Chair.; fmr mem. Shura Council (upper house of fmr Parl., abolished 2014); Minister of Housing 2013–14; Prime Minister 2014–15; mem. Bd of Govs Arab Water Council; mem. Egyptian-French Business Asscn, American Chamber of Commerce in Egypt; mem. National Democratic Party, mem. Policy Cttee.

MAHLANGU, Mninwa Johannes; South African politician and diplomatist; *Ambassador to USA;* m. Nomaswazi Mahlangu; three s. two d.; began political career when elected Pres. of Student Christian Movt, Eastern Transvaal late 1960s; Asst Sec., Transvaal United African Teachers Asscn 1973–76; negotiator at Congress for Democratic South Africa (CODESA) and Multiparty Negotiation Forum 1991–94, Co-Chair. of these bodies 1993; mem. Transitional Exec. Council 1993–94; elected to Nat. Ass. as rep. of African Nat. Congress (ANC) 1994, mem. Constitutional Ass. that drafted South African Constitution, chaired Core Group of Theme Cttee on Chapter 4 dealing with Parl., also chaired several House cttees, Perm. Deputy Chair. Nat. Council of Provs (NCOP) in Parl. 2002–04, Chair. NCOP 2005–14; represented South Africa on numerous int. platforms, including UN and G20 Speakers Confs; led South African Parl.'s del. to Pan-African Parl. and served in Cttee on Rules, Privileges and Discipline; fmr Chair. Commonwealth Parl. Asscn (Africa Region); fmr Pres. Commonwealth Parl. Asscn (Int.); Amb. to USA 2015–. *Address:* Embassy of South Africa, 3051 Massachusetts Avenue, NW, Washington, DC 20008, USA (office). *Telephone:* (202) 232-4400 (office). *Fax:* (202) 265-1607 (office). *E-mail:* amb.washington@dirco.gov.za (office). *Website:* www.saembassy.org (office).

MAHMOOD, Gen. (retd) Rashad; Pakistani fmr army officer; m.; one s. one d.; ed Canadian Army Command and Staff Coll., Canada, Nat. Defence Univ.; commissioned into Baloch Regt 1975, served as Platoon Commdr, Pakistan Mil. Acad., Brigade Major Infantry Brigade, Instructor, Command and Staff Coll., Nat. Defence Univ., Chief, Staff Bahawalpur Corps, Mil. Sec. to Pres.; has commanded two Infantry Bns, two Infantry Brigades and UN contingent, Congo, Infantry Div., Jhelum, Dir-Gen., Inter-Service Intelligence Directorate, Commdr, Lahore IV Corps, Chief of Gen. Staff Jan.–Nov. 2013, Chair., Joint Chiefs of Staff Cttee Nov. 2013–16 (retd); Hilal-i-Imtiaz, Nishan-e-Imtiaz.

MAHMOUD, Lt-Gen. Ali Muhammad Habib; Syrian army officer and government official; b. 1 Jan. 1939, Safita, Tartus; s. of Ahmed Habib Mahmud; ed Military Acad., Damascus; joined Syrian Army 1959, regiment commdr 1971–75, Chief of Staff of mechanised infantry div. 1975–78, commdr of infantry brigade 1978–84, Commdr of mechanised infantry div. 1984–94, apptd Commdr of Special Forces 1994–2002, Deputy Chief of Staff 2002–04, Chief of Gen. Staff of Army and Armed Forces 2004–09; Minister of Defence 2009–11 (resgnd with rest of cabinet at Pres.'s request following popular protests), April–Aug. 2011; led Syrian forces in Lebanon 1982; mem. Baath Party; received several military medals, and promotions for participation in Oct. 1973 War.

MAHMOUD ABBAS, Badr al-Din, BA; Sudanese government official and fmr central banker; ed Khartoum Univ.; fmr Deputy Gov., Central Bank of Sudan; Minister of Finance and Nat. Economy 2013–17; fmr Gov. Eastern and Southern African Trade and Devt Bank, IMF, Islamic Devt Bank, African Devt Bank; mem. Bd of Dirs The Arab Investment Co.; Chair. Sudan Mems Panel, Asscn of Chartered Certified Accountants; over 20 years' experience in both internal and external consulting roles with several int. orgs. *Address:* Arab Investment Company, POB 26630, Safat 13127, Kuwait (office). *Telephone:* 22249999 (office). *Fax:* 22246887 (office). *E-mail:* (office). *Website:* www.arabinv.com (office).

MAHMUD, Aksa; Indonesian business executive; *Founder, Bosowa Group;* b. 16 July 1945, Barru; m. H. Siti Ramlah Aksa; five c.; ed Hasanuddin Univ.; f. CV Moneter 1973, PT Bosowa Berlian Motor 1978, later renamed Bosowa Group (conglomerate), associated cos include PT Asuransi Bosowa Periskop, Bosowa Taxis, PT Semen Bosowa Maros, PT Tuju Waliwali, PT Bosowa Cocoa Industries, PT Bumi Sawit Permai, PT Celebes Minahasa Suraya Adira; fmr mem. Regional Reps Council (Dewan Perwakilan Daerah, DPD) for S Sulawesi. *Address:* Bosowa Group, Menara Karya Lt 16, JL HR Rasuna Said (Kuningan), Blok X-5 Kav 1-2, Jakarta 12950, Indonesia (office). *Telephone:* (21) 57944344 (office). *Fax:* (21) 57944544 (office). *Website:* www.bosowa.co.id (office).

MAHMUD ALI, Abul Hasan, BA, MA; Bangladeshi politician and fmr diplomatist; b. 2 June 1943, Dinajpur; two s.; ed Dhaka Univ.; Lecturer in Econs, Dhaka Univ. 1964–66; joined Pakistan Foreign Service 1966, Vice-Consul of Pakistan, New York 1968; joined Bangladesh Liberation Movt 1971, worked for independence of Bangladesh in USA as US Rep. of Provisional Govt of Bangladesh (in exile in Mujibnagar) 1971; Exec. Asst to Justice Abu Sayeed Chowdhury (Chief Overseas Rep. of Mujibnagar Govt and Leader, Bangladesh Del. to UN) 1971; following independence of Bangladesh 1971 served in various roles with Ministry of Foreign Affairs, including as First Sec. and Deputy High Commr, then High Comm. in Delhi 1977–79, Dir-Gen. for Admin, Int. Orgs, UN and Econ. Affairs 1979–82, Deputy Chief of Mission with rank of Amb., Embassy in Beijing 1983–86, Amb. to Bhutan 1986–90, to Germany 1992–95, to Nepal Feb.–Oct. 1996, High Commr to UK 1996–2001; mem. Jatiya Sangsad (Parl.) for Dinajpur constituency 2009–13; Minister of Disaster Man. and Relief 2012–13, Minister of Foreign Affairs 2013–19; mem. Bangladesh Awami League 2001–, mem. Party Cen. Election Comm. 2001.

MAHMUDI, Al-Baghdadi Ali al-; Libyan politician; b. 1945, Az Zawiyah Dist of northwestern Libya; trained as a physician, has a medical degree specializing in obstetrics and gynaecology; Sec. of the Gen. People's Cttee for Health and Social Security 1992–97; Minister for the People's Cttees' Affairs 1997–2000; Deputy Prime Minister for Services Affairs March–Sept. 2000; Minister of Human Resources Affairs 2000–01, for Infrastructure, Urban Planning and Environment Affairs 2001; Deputy Prime Minister for Production Affairs 2001–06; Asst Sec. of the Gen. People's Cttee (Deputy Prime Minister) 2004–06, Sec. (Prime Minister) 2006–11; Chair. High Council for Oil and Gas 2006, Libyan Investment Authority 2007; subject of a travel ban issued by UN Security Council (Resolution 1970) 26 Feb. 2011; fled to Tunisia Aug. 2011, extradited back to Libya for trial 2012.

MAHONEY, Rev. John Aloysius (Jack), SJ, MA, STD; British ecclesiastic and academic; b. 14 Jan. 1931, Coatbridge, Scotland; s. of Patrick Mahoney and Margaret Doris; ed Our Lady's High School, Motherwell, St Aloysius Coll., Glasgow, Univ. of Glasgow and Gregorian Univ., Rome; Lecturer in Moral and Pastoral Theology, Heythrop Coll., Oxon. 1967–70; Lecturer in Moral and Pastoral Theology, Heythrop Coll., Univ. of London 1970–86, Prin. 1976–81; F.D. Maurice Prof. of Moral and Social Theology, King's Coll. London 1986–93, Prof. Emer. 1999–; Founding Dir King's Coll. Business Ethics Research Centre 1987–93; Mercers' School Memorial Prof. of Commerce, Gresham Coll. City of London 1987–93, Prof. Emer. 1993–; Dixons Prof. of Business Ethics and Social Responsibility, London Business School 1993–98; Founder and Dir Lauriston Centre for

Contemporary Belief and Action, Edin. 1998–2005; Lecturer in Theology, St Andrews Univ. 2004; Distinguished Prof., Dept of Theology, Georgetown Univ. 2008; Companion, Chartered Man. Asscn 1996; mem. Mount Street Jesuit Centre, London 2005–08, Mount Street Jesuit Community 2009–12, Lauriston Centre, Edinburgh 2012–; Hon. Fellow, Faculty of Divinity, Univ. of Edinburgh 1998–2003, Gresham Coll., London 1999–, St Mary's Univ. Coll. 1999–, Heythrop Coll., Univ. of London 2000–, Hon. Lecturer in Business Ethics, Glasgow Business School 2003–04; Hon. DD (Univ. of London) 2004; Pres.'s Medal, Georgetown Univ., Washington, DC 2003. *Publications:* Seeking the Spirit: Essays in Moral and Pastoral Theology 1981, Bioethics and Belief: Religion and Medicine in Dialogue 1984, The Making of Moral Theology: A Study of the Roman Catholic Tradition 1987, Teaching Business Ethics in the UK, Europe and the USA 1990, Business Ethics in a New Europe (ed.) 1992, The Challenge of Human Rights: Origin, Development and Significance 2007, Christianity in Evolution: An Exploration 2011. *Address:* 28 Lauriston Street, Edinburgh, EH3 9DJ, Scotland (home). *Telephone:* (131) 447-5700 (office). *E-mail:* jmlaur@aol.com (office).

MAHONY, HE Cardinal Roger Michael, STB, BA; American ecclesiastic; *Archbishop Emeritus of Los Angeles;* b. 27 Feb. 1936, Hollywood, Calif.; s. of Victor James Mahony and Loretta Marie Baron; ed St John's Seminary Coll., St John's Theologate, Calif., Catholic Univ. of America, Washington, DC; ordained RC Priest, Fresno, Calif. 1962; Bishop, Fresno, Calif. 1975; Bishop of Stockton, Calif. 1980; Archbishop of Los Angeles 1985–2011, Archbishop Emer. 2011–; cr. Cardinal (Cardinal-Priest of Santi Quattro Coronati) 1991; participated in Papal Conclave 2005, 2013; mem. numerous cttees of Nat. Confs of Catholic Bishops, USA 1976–; several Pontifical Councils, Vatican 1984–; Dr hc (Loyola Marymount, LA) 1986, (Portland, Ore.) 1988, (Notre Dame, Ind.) 1989, (St Patrick's Coll., Ireland) 1991, (Southern California) 2002. *Address:* 3424 Wilshire Boulevard, Los Angeles, CA 90010, USA (office). *Telephone:* (213) 637-7288 (office). *Fax:* (213) 637-6510 (office).

MAHUAD WITT, Jamil, PhD; Ecuadorean lawyer, politician and fmr head of state; b. 29 July 1949, Loja; s. of Jorge Antonio Mahuad Chalela and Rosa Witt García; m. Tatiana Calderón (divorced); one d.; ed Pontificia Universidad Católica del Ecuador, John F. Kennedy School of Govt, Harvard Univ., USA; legal assessor and dir of pvt. credit banks 1973–78; Pres. Federación de Estudiantes Universitarios Católicos del Ecuador 1974–75; Regional Sec. Federación de Estudiantes de las Universidades Católicas de América Latina 1975–81; mem. Democracia Popular 1981; Dir Empresa Nacional de Productos Vitales 1981–83; Minister of Labour 1981–83; Minister-Sec. of State for Labor and Human Resources 1983–84; deputy in the Nat. Congress representing the province of Pichincha 1986–88, 1990–92; Pres. Democracia Popular 1987–88, 1991–93; Vice-Pres. Demócrata Cristiano de América (ODCA), Andina Region 1991–97; Mayor of Quito 1992–98; Pres. of Ecuador 1998–2000 (deposed by armed forces); Academic fellow, Center for Public Leadership, Kennedy School of Govt, Harvard Univ. 2000–; Great Collar of the National Order of San Lorenzo; hc Nat. Univ. of San Marcos. *Address:* c/o Democracia Popular, Calle Luis Saá 153 y Hnos Pazmiño, Casilla 17-01-2300, Quito, Ecuador.

MAIA, Rodrigo; Brazilian politician; *President, Chamber of Deputies;* b. (Rodrigo Felinto Ibarra Epitacio Maia), 12 June 1970, Santiago, Chile; s. of Cesar Maia and Mariângeles Maia; m. Patrícia Vasconcelos; one s. three d.; ed Candido Mendes Univ.; worked with Banco BMG and Banco Icatu 1993–97; Municipal Sec. Rio de Janeiro City Hall 1997–98; Federal Deputy (Partido da Frente Liberal, renamed Democratas 2007) for Rio de Janeiro 1998–, fmr Chair. Cttee on Labour, Admin and Public Service; apptd Chair. Comm. of Transport and Transportation 2013, Pres. Chamber of Deputies 2017–. *Address:* Chamber of Deputies, Palácio do Congresso Nacional, Edif. Principal, Praça dos Três Poderes, 70160-900 Brasília, DF, Brazil (office). *Telephone:* (61) 3216-0000 (office). *E-mail:* presidencia@camara .gov.br (office). *Website:* www.camara.gov.br (office).

MAIDA, HE Cardinal Adam Joseph, JD; American ecclesiastic; *Archbishop Emeritus of Detroit;* b. 18 March 1930, East Vandergrift, Pa; s. of Adam Maida and Sophie Maida (née Cieslak); ed Scott Township High School, St Mary's High School, Orchard Lake, Mich., St Vincent's Coll., Latrobe, Pa, St Mary's Univ., Baltimore, Md, Pontifical Lateran Univ., Rome, Italy, Duquesne Univ., Pittsburgh; admitted to practice law in Pa and before US Supreme Court; ordained priest 1956; further studies in Rome 1956–60; pastoral work in Diocese of Pittsburgh and as Asst Chancellor, Vice-Chancellor, Diocesan Gen. Consultor in the diocesan tribunal 1960–83; fmr Asst Prof. of Theology, La Roche Coll.; fmr Chaplain St Thomas More's Soc.; faculty mem. Duquesne Univ. 1971–83; consecrated Bishop of Green Bay, Wis. 1984; Archbishop of Detroit 1990–2008, currently Archbishop Emer.; cr. Cardinal (Cardinal Priest of SS Vitale, Valeria, Gervasio e Protasio) 1994; mem. Roman Curia Congregation for Catholic Educ., Congregation for the Clergy, Pontifical Council for the Interpretation of Legislative Texts, Pontifical Council for the Pastoral Care of Migrants and Itinerant Peoples, Cardinal Comm. for the Supervision of the Inst. for Works of Religion; served as Chair. US Conf. of Catholic Bishops Canonical Affairs Cttee, Washington, DC 1992, mem. Ad Hoc Cttee for Aid to the Church in Cen. and Eastern Europe, Bishops' Cttee on Evangelization, ex-officio mem. Int. Policy Cttee, Consultant to Cttee on Migration, Cttee on Pro-Life Activities, Episcopal Liaison Cttee for the Polish Apostolate; Chairman Bd of Trustees Mich. Catholic Conf., Sacred Heart Major Seminary, Detroit, SS Cyril and Methodius Seminary, Orchard Lake; Ecclesiastical Protector Int. Order of Alhambra; mem. Bd of Govs Ave Maria School of Law, Ann Arbor, Mich.; Episcopal Moderator and Pres. John Paul II Cultural Foundation, USA; Pres. Pope John Paul II Cultural Center, Washington, DC; mem. Bd of Trustees Catholic Univ. of America, Washington, DC, Basilica of the Nat. Shrine of the Immaculate Conception, Washington, DC, The Papal Foundation, Phila, Pa, John Paul II Cultural Foundation, Rome; mem. Bd of Dirs Nat. Catholic Bioethics Center, Phila; Ecclesial Advisor, Nat. Fellowship of Catholic Men, Gaithersburg, Md; Papal Legate to 19th Int. Marian Congress, Czestochowa, Poland 1996; attended Special Ass. for America of World Synod of Bishops, Vatican City 1997, Special Ass. for Europe of World Synod of Bishops, Vatican City 1999; Superior of Mission sui iuris of Cayman Islands 2000. *Publications:* The Tribunal Reporter: A Casebook and Commentary on the Grounds for Annulment in the Catholic Church, Vol. 1 (ed.) 1970, Ownership, Control and Sponsorship of Catholic Institutions 1975, Issues in the Labor-Management Dialogue: Church Perspectives (ed.) 1982, Church Property, Church Finances and Church-Related Corporations, a Canon Law Handbook 1983. *Address:* c/o Archdiocese of Detroit, 305 Michigan Avenue, Detroit, MI 48226-2605, USA.

MAIDEN, Sir Colin James, Kt, MEng, DPhil; New Zealand fmr university vice-chancellor and company director; b. 5 May 1933, Auckland; s. of Henry A. Maiden and Lorna Richardson; m. Jenefor Mary Rowe 1957; one s. three d.; ed Univs of New Zealand and Oxford, UK; Head, Hypersonic Physics Section, Canadian Armament Research and Devt Establishment, Québec City, Canada 1958–60; Sr lecturer in Mechanical Eng Univ. of Auckland 1960–61; Head, Material Sciences Lab. Gen. Motors Corpn Defence Research Labs Santa Barbara, Calif. 1961–66; Man. of Process Eng Gen. Motors Corpn Tech. Centre, Warren, Mich. 1966–70; Vice-Chancellor, Univ. of Auckland 1971–94; Chair. New Zealand Energy Research and Devt Cttee 1974–81, New Zealand Vice-Chancellor's Cttee 1977–78, 1991, Liquid Fuels Trust Bd 1978–86, New Zealand Synthetic Fuels Corpn Ltd 1980–90, Tower Insurance Co. Ltd 1988–2002, Fisher & Paykel Ltd 1978–2001, Independent Newspapers Ltd 1989–2003; Dir Mason Industries Ltd 1971–78, Farmers Trading Co. Ltd 1973–86, Winstone Ltd 1978–88, Wilkins & Davies Ltd 1986–89, New Zealand Steel Ltd 1988–92, ANZ Banking Group (NZ) Ltd 1990–93, New Zealand Refining Co. Ltd 1991–2007, Progressive Enterprises Ltd 1992–2000, DB Breweries Ltd 1994–2008, Sedgwick (New Zealand) Ltd 1994–98, Transpower New Zealand Ltd 1994–2004, Tower Ltd 1995–2003, Foodland Associated Ltd 2000–05, Fisher and Paykel Healthcare Corpn Ltd 2001–11; Hon. LLD (Auckland); Queen Elizabeth Silver Jubilee Medal 1977, Medal of Univ. of Bonn 1983, Thomson Medal, Royal Soc. of New Zealand 1986, Symons Award, Asscn of Commonwealth Univs 1999. *Publications include:* numerous scientific and tech. papers. *Leisure interest:* tennis. *Address:* Apartment 503, Oakridge, 10 Middleton Road, Remuera, Auckland, New Zealand. *Telephone:* (9) 524-7412. *E-mail:* colinmaiden@xtra.co.nz.

MAÏGA, Abdoulaye Idrissa; Malian engineer and politician; b. 11 March 1958, Gao; five c.; ed Institut polytechnique rural, Katibougou; began career as Head of Gao Regional Office, Ministry of Livestock and Fisheries 1982; Dir Gen., Mali Livestock Project, NE Gao 1988–89; Livestock Project Coordinator, Mopti Region 1999–2001; Researcher, Ministry of Rural Devt 2001–03; Head of Environmental Monitoring Dept, Agence du Bassin du Fleuve Niger, Bamako 2003–08; Head of election campaign for presidential cand. Ibrahim Boubacar Keita 2013; fmr Minister of Environment, Water and Sanitation, fmr Minister of Territorial Admin; Minister of Defence and War Veterans 2016–17, Prime Minister April–Dec. 2017; Deputy Sec.-Gen., Association malienne des Droits de l'Homme (human rights org.) 1990–99; Pres. Ministerial Council, Org. pur la Mise en Valeur du Fleuve Senegal (Senegal River Devt Org.). *Publications:* several technical publs; Mali: entre doutes et espoirs (co-ed.) 2013. *Address:* 868 Rue Faladié Sema, Porte 66, Bamako, Mali (home). *Telephone:* 220-12-60 (home). *E-mail:* mokesn@ yahoo.fr (home).

MAÏGA, Ousmane Issoufi; Malian politician; b. 1946, Gao; m.; four c.; ed Univ. of Kiev, Ukraine, American Univ., Washington, DC, USA; early internships at World Bank and French Ministry of Finance; fmr Deputy Dir Gen. Caisse Autonome d'Amortissement; Minister of Finance 2002–03; Minister of Equipment and Transport 2003–04; Prime Minister of Mali 2004–07.

MAÏGA, Soumeylou Boubèye; Malian journalist and politician; b. 8 June 1954, Gao; ed Centre d'études des sciences et techniques de l'information, Univ. Cheikh Anta Diop, Dakar, Senegal, Univ. Paris-Sud, France; began career as journalist with L'Essor (state-owned daily newspaper); Special Adviser to cabinet of Pres. Amadou Toumani Touré 1991–92; fmr mem. Parti malien du travail; Founder-mem. and Vice-Pres. Alliance pour la démocratie au Mali—Parti pan-africain pour la liberté, la solidarité et la justice (ADEMA) 1990; Chef de cabinet to Pres. Alpha Oumar Konaré 1992; Dir-Gen. Direction Générale de la Sécurité Extérieure (intelligence agency) 1993; unsuccessful cand. in presidential election 2002 (for ADEMA), 2007 (for Convergence); Minister of Foreign Affairs and Int. Co-operation 2011–12, of Defence and Veterans 2013–14; Prime Minister 2017–19. *Address:* c/o Office of the Prime Minister, Quartier du Fleuve, BP 790, Bamako, Mali (office).

MAILLOT, Jacques; French director and writer; b. 12 April 1962, Besançon; ed Institut d'Etudes Politiques de Lyon; worked as a graphic designer; hired at Cinémathèque Française as a conscientious objector; began his film career by directing four short films 1990; acted in Mille bornes (Milestones) 1999. *Films:* Des fleurs coupées (Cut Flowers) 1993, Corps inflammables (Flammable Material) (Prix Tournage, Avignon Film Festival 1995) 1995, 75 centilitres de prière (aka A Bottle of Wishes, USA) (Special Jury Award, Nat. Competition, Clermont-Ferrand Int. Short Film Festival 1994, Prix Jean Vigo for Short Film 1994) 1995, Entre ciel et terre (Between Heaven and Earth) 1996, Nos vies heureuses (Our Happy Lives) (Prix Tournage, Avignon Film Festival 1999) 1999, Froid comme l'été (Cold as Summer) (Prix Italia 2003) 2002, Les liens du sang (Rivals) 2008, Un singe sur le dos (Monkey on My Back) 2009, La mer à boire 2011, Blood Ties 2013. *Television:* Les prédateurs (screenplay) 2007. *Address:* c/o Delphine Gamory, Artmedia, 20 avenue Rapp, 75007 Paris, France. *Telephone:* 1-43-17-33-63. *E-mail:* d.gamory@ artmedia.fr. *Website:* www.artemedia.fr.

MAINALI, Chandra Prakash; Nepalese politician; *Deputy Prime Minister and Minister for Women, Children and Social Welfare;* b. 22 Aug. 1951, Chokpur; s. of Dhanpati Mainali and Chandrakumari Mainali; m.; one s. two d.; joined Communist Party of Nepal 1970, currently Gen. Sec., Communist Party of Nepal (Marxist-Leninist) (CPN-ML); fmr Minister for Local Devt and Supply; fmr Leader United Left Front; joined interim Parl. 2007, mem. of Constituent Ass. 2008–; Deputy Prime Minister and Minister for Women, Children and Social Welfare 2015–. *Address:* Office of the Prime Minister and Council of Ministers, Singha Durbar, POB 23312, Kathmandu, Nepal (office). *Telephone:* (1) 4211000 (office). *E-mail:* info@opmcm.gov.np (office). *Website:* www.opmcm.gov.np (office).

MAINI, Sir Ravinder Nath, Kt, BA, MB, BChir, FRCP, FRCPE, FMedSci, FRS; British rheumatologist and academic; *Professor Emeritus of Rheumatology, Imperial College London;* b. 17 Nov. 1937, Ludhiana, Punjab, India; s. of Sir Amar (Nath) Maini and Saheli Maini (née Mehra); m. 1st Marianne Gorm 1963 (divorced 1986); one s. one d. (and one s. deceased); m. 2nd Geraldine Room 1987; two s.; ed Sidney Sussex Coll., Cambridge; jr medical appointments at Guy's,

Brompton and Charing Cross Hosps 1962–70; Consultant Physician, St Stephen's Hosp., London 1970–79, Rheumatology Dept, Charing Cross Hosp. 1970; Prof. of Immunology of Rheumatic Diseases, Charing Cross and Westminster Medical School 1981–89, Dir Kennedy Inst. of Rheumatology 1990–2000 (Head Clinical Immunology Div. 1979); Prof. of Rheumatology, Imperial Coll. School of Medicine at Charing Cross Hosp. Campus (fmrly Charing Cross and Westminster Medical School), Univ. of London 1989–2002, Prof. Emer. of Rheumatology 2002–, Head of Kennedy Inst. of Rheumatology Div. 2000–02; Visiting Prof., Univ. of Oxford 2011–; Pres. British Soc. for Rheumatology 1989–90 (Heberden Orator 1988), British League Against Rheumatism 1985–89; Chair. Research Sub-Cttee 1980–85 and mem. Scientific Coordinating Cttee, Arthritis and Rheumatism Council 1985–95; Chair. Standing Cttee for Investigative Rheumatology, European League Against Rheumatism 1990–97; mem. Exec. Cttee, Asscn of Physicians of GB and Ireland 1989–91; Chair. Rheumatology Cttee, Royal Coll. of Physicians 1992–96 (Croonian Lecturer 1995, Lumleian Lecturer 1999); mem. European Union of Medical Specialists 1994– (Pres. Section of Rheumatology 1996–99, Chair. European Bd of Rheumatology 1996–99); Samuel Hyde Lecturer, Royal Soc. of Medicine 1998; mem. Scientific Advisory Bd Nicholas Piramal India Ltd 2003–, Arana Therapeutics Ltd, Australia (previously known as Peptech) 2003–09; mem. Bd of Dirs Piramal Life Sciences, India 2008–11, Domantis, Cambridge 2003–07; mem. Council Medical Protection Soc. 2001–09; mem. Advisory Bd F-Star Biotechnologische Forschungs und Entwicklungsgesellschaft 2007–; mem. Bd of Trustees, Kennedy Inst. of Rheumatology Trust, Beit Memorial Fellowship, Sir Jules Thorn Trust, Graham Dixon Trust; Assoc. mem. NAS 2011; Hon. Consultant, Charing Cross Hosp., Hammersmith Hosps NHS Trust; Hon. mem. Australian Rheumatism Asscn 1977, Norwegian Soc. for Rheumatology 1988, American Coll. of Rheumatology 1988, Hellenic Rheumatology Soc. 1989, Hungarian Rheumatology Soc. 1990, Scandinavian Soc. for Immunology 1996, Mexican Soc. for Rheumatology 1996, Hon. Fellowship, Sidney Sussex Coll., Univ. of Cambridge 2004, Hon. Fellowship, Royal Soc. of Medicine 2004, Master, American Coll. of Rheumatology 2004; Dr hc (Univ. René Descartes, Paris) 1994; Hon. DSc (Glasgow) 2004; Carol Nachman Prize for Rheumatology (jtly), City of Wiesbaden 1999, Distinguished Investigator Award, American Coll. of Rheumatology 1999, Crafoord Prize (jtly), Royal Swedish Acad. of Sciences 2000, Courtin-Clarins Prize (jtly), Asscn de Recherche sur la Polyarthrite 2000, Albert Lasker Award for Clinical Medical Research 2003, Fothergillian Medal, Medical Soc. of London 2004, Cameron Prize (jtly), Univ. of Edin. 2004, Ambuj Nath Bose Prize, Royal Coll. of Physicians 2005, EULAR Meritorious Service Award in Rheumatology (jtly) 2005, Langdon Brown Lecture, Royal Coll. of Physicians 2005, Galen Medal, The Worshipful Soc. of Apothcaries of London 2006, Japan Rheumatism Foundation Int. RA Award (jtly) 2007, Dr Paul Janssen Award for Biomedical Research (jtly) 2008, Ernst Schering Prize (jtly) 2010, Canada Gairdner Int. Award (jtly) 2014. *Publications include:* Immunology of Rheumatic Diseases 1977, Modulation of Autoimmune Disease (ed.) 1981, Textbook of the Rheumatic Diseases, 6th edn (contrib.) 1986, T-Cell Activation in Health and Disease (ed.) 1989, Rheumatoid Arthritis (ed.) 1992, Oxford Textbook of Rheumatology (contrib.) 1993, Rheumatology (section ed.) 1993, Manual of Biological Markers of Disease (co-ed.: Section A, Methods of Autoantibody Detection 1993, Section B, Autoantigens 1994, Section C, Clinical Significance of Autoantibodies 1996), Oxford Textbook of Medicine (contrib.) 2001; 480 articles in scientific journals. *Leisure interests:* music appreciation, walking. *Address:* Kennedy Institute of Rheumatology, 65 Aspenlea Road, London, W6 8LH, England (office). *Telephone:* (20) 8383-4403 (office). *Fax:* (20) 8563-1585 (office). *E-mail:* r.maini@imperial.ac.uk (office). *Website:* wwwfom.sk.med.ic.ac.uk/medicine (office); www.kennedy.ox.ac.uk (office).

MAISKY, Mischa (Michael); Belgian/Israeli cellist; b. 10 Jan. 1948, Riga, Latvia (frmly USSR); m. 2nd Evelyn De Silva 2003; four s. two d.; ed Moscow Conservatory, studied with Mstislav Rostropovich and Gregor Piatigorsky, Univ. of Southern California, USA; debut with Leningrad Philharmonic Orchestra 1965; imprisoned in labour camp near Gorky for 18 months 1970; emigrated from USSR to Israel 1972; debut with Pittsburgh Symphony Orchestra at Carnegie Hall 1973; London concerto debut with Royal Philharmonic Orchestra 1976, London recital debut with pianist Radu Lupu 1977; debut at Berlin Philharmonic Hall 1978; returned to Moscow for the first time in 23 years to give a concert and to record works by Prokofiev and Miaskovsky with Mikhail Pletnev and Russian Nat. Orchestra 1995; All-Soviet prizewinner 1965, Int. Tchaikovsky Competition 1966, winner, Cassada Competition, Florence 1973, Grand Prix du Disque, Paris 1985, Record Acad. Prize, Tokyo (five times), ECHO award, Germany (three times). *Recordings include:* Six Suites for Solo Cello (Bach), Three Sonatas for Cello and Piano (Bach), Concerto in A minor Op. 102 for Violin, Cello and Orchestra (Brahms), Concerto for Cello and Orchestra in A Minor (Schumann), Morgen 2009, ¡España! Songs and Dances from Spain (with Lily Maisky) 2011. *Leisure interests:* music, chess, computing. *Address:* Weinstadt Artists Management, Populierenlaan 3, bus 26, 2020 Antwerp, Belgium (office). *E-mail:* info@concerts-weinstadt.be (office); MM@MischaMaisky.com. *Website:* www.mischamaisky.com.

MAITLIS, Peter M., PhD, FRS, FRSC, FCIC; British chemist and academic; *Research Professor Emeritus, Department of Chemistry, University of Sheffield;* b. 15 Jan. 1933, Berlin, Germany; s. of Jacob Maitlis and Judith Maitlis; m. Marion Basco 1959; three d.; ed Univ. of Birmingham and Univ. of London; Asst Lecturer, Univ. of London 1956–60; Fulbright Fellow and Research Assoc., Harvard and Cornell Univs, USA, 1960–62; Asst Prof., Assoc. Prof. and Prof., McMaster Univ., Canada 1962–72; Prof. of Inorganic Chem., Sheffield Univ. 1972–94, Research Prof. 1994–2002, Research Prof. Emer. 2003–; Fellow, Alfred P. Sloan Foundation 1967–69; Chair. Chem. Cttee Science and Eng Research Council 1985–88; Pres. Dalton Div., RSC 1985–87; mem. Council Royal Soc. 1991–93; Foreign mem. Accad. dei Lincei (Italy) 1999; Steacie Prize in Natural Sciences 1970, RSC Medal 1981, Kurnakov Medal, Russian Acad. of Sciences 1998. *Lectures:* Sir Edward Frankland Lecturer, RSC 1985, Tilden Lecturer 1979, Ludwig Mond Lecturer 1999, David Craig Lecturer, ANU 2000, Stone Lecturer, Univ. of Bristol 2001, Paolo Chini Lecturer, Italian Chemical Soc. 2001, Glenn T. Seaborg Memorial Lecturer, Univ. of California, Berkeley 2004–05. *Publications:* The Organic Chemistry of Palladium (two vols) 1971, Metal-catalysis in Industrial Organic Processes (with G P Chiusoli) 2006; numerous research publs in scientific journals. *Leisure interests:* music, travel, reading, discussing politics, finance. *Address:* Department of Chemistry, Room C52, University of Sheffield, Sheffield, Yorks., S3

7HF, England (office). *Telephone:* (114) 222-9320 (office). *Fax:* (114) 222-9346 (office). *E-mail:* p.maitlis@sheffield.ac.uk (office).

MAÏWENN; French actress and film director; b. (Maïwenn Le Besco), 17 April 1976, Les Lilas, Seine-Saint-Denis, Île-de-France; d. of Catherine Belkhodja; one d. with Luc Besson; m. Jean-Yves Le Fur; one s.; performed as stand-up comedian in Le Pois Chiche and I'm an Actress. *Theatre writing:* Café de la Gare 2003. *Films include:* L'Année prochaine… si tout va bien 1981, L'été meurtrier 1983, L'état de grâce 1986, L'autre nuit 1988, Lacenaire 1990, La Gamine 1992, Leon 1994, The Professional 1994, The Fifth Element (dir Luc Besson) 1997, Coquillettes (short) 1998, Keskidi? (short) 1998, Le marquis (short) 2000, The Mechanics of Women 2000, 8 rue Charlot 2001, Haute Tension 2003, Osmose 2003, Switchblade Romance 2003, Les Parisiens 2004, Le genre humain – 1ère partie: Les Parisiens 2004, Le courage d'aimer 2005, Pardonnez-moi (also screenwriter, dir and producer) 2006, Le bal des actrices (also screenwriter and dir) 2009, Polisse (also screenwriter and dir) (Jury Prize, Cannes Film Festival 2011) 2011, Pirate TV 2012, Love Is the Perfect Crime 2013; dir: Mon roi (also screenwriter) 2015. *Music video:* played The Scarecrow in The Cranberries: The Best Videos 1992–2002 2002. *Television includes:* Cinéma 16 (series) 1983, Les enquêtes du commissaire Maigret (series) 1983, Double face (film) 1987, La famille Ramdam (series) 1990, L'oiseau rare (film) 2001, Nestor Burma (series) 2002, Caméra café (series) 2002.

MAJALIWA, Kassim; Tanzanian politician; *Prime Minister;* b. 22 Dec. 1960; m. Mary Majaliwa; ed Univ. of Dar es Salaam, Univ. of Stockholm, Sweden; Teacher, Lindi 1984–86; Instructor, Ministry of Educ. 1988–2000; Urambo Dist Commr 2006–10; mem. Nat. Ass. (Parl.) for Ruangwa 2010–15; Deputy Minister of State for Regional Admin and Local Govt 2010–15; Prime Minister 2015–; mem. Chama Cha Mapinduzi (CCM, Revolutionary Party of Tanzania). *Address:* Office of the Prime Minister, PO Box 3021, Dar es Salaam, Tanzania (office). *Telephone:* (22) 2111249 (office). *E-mail:* ps@pmo.go.tz (office). *Website:* www.pmo.go.tz (office).

MAJBRI, Ahmed; Libyan oil industry executive; fmrly with Finance Dept, Arabian Gulf Oil Co. (Agoco), Benghazi, apptd Chair. Agoco Feb. 2011. *Address:* Arabian Gulf Oil Co. (Agoco), POB 2134, Benghazi, Libya (office). *Telephone:* (61) 222-8931 (office). *Website:* www.agoco.com.ly (office).

MAJEED, Gen. Tariq, MA; Pakistani army officer (retd); b. 23 Aug. 1950, Lahore; ed Command and Staff Coll., Quetta, Malaysian Armed Forces Staff Coll., Kuala Lumpur, Asia-Pacific Center for Security Studies, Honolulu, Hawaii, Nat. Defence Coll., Islamabad; commissioned in Pakistan Army (Infantry, Baloch Regt) 1971, has commanded Light Anti-Tank Unit and an Infantry Bn, two Infantry Brigades, Infantry Div., participated in Indo-Pakistan War 1971, took part, as GOC Lahore in absence of Corps Commdr, in counter-coup launched by army high command against then govt of Mian Nawaz Sharif Oct. 1999, also led mil. operation on Jamia Hafsa, Dir Gen. Mil. Intelligence 2001–03, promoted to Lt-Gen. Dec. 2003, Chief of Gen. Staff 2003–06, Commdr 10 Corps, Rawalpindi 2006–07, in charge of armed forces who took down armed militias stationed inside mosque at Lal Masjid Siege 2007, promoted to four-star Gen. Oct. 2007, Chair. Jt Chiefs of Staff Cttee Oct. 2007–10; Hilal-e-Imtiaz (Mil.), Nishan-e-Imtiaz (Mil.).

MAJEWSKI, Tomasz; Polish athlete; b. 30 Aug. 1981, Nasielsk; m. Ani Majewski; one s.; ed Uniwersytet Kardynała Stefana Wyszyńskiego; winner Shot Put, Nat. Championships 2003, 2004, 2005, Nat. Indoor Championships 2004, 2005, 2006; fourth place, Shot Put, World Indoor Championships, Budapest 2004; gold medal, Shot Put, 23rd Summer Universiade, İzmir 2005; bronze medal, Shot Put, European Winter Throwing Cup, Tel-Aviv 2006, World Indoor Championships, Valencia 2008 (threw 20.93m); gold medal, Shot Put, Olympic Games, Beijing 2008 (achieved personal best throw of 21.51m during Olympic final on 15 Aug., Poland's first Olympic medal in shot put since 1972); gold medal, IAAF World Athletics Final, Stuttgart 2008; silver medal, IAAF World Athletics Final, Thessaloniki 2009; silver medal, Shot Put, World Championships, Berlin 2009, European Championships, Barcelona 2010; bronze medal, Shot Put, World Indoor Championships, Valencia 2008, Istanbul 2012; gold medal, Shot Put, European Indoor Championships, Torino 2009; silver medal, Continental Cup, Split 2010; gold medal, Shot Put, Olympic Games, London 2012, gold medal, Jeux de la Francophonie 2013, bronze medal, European Athletics Championship 2014; coach Henryk Olszewski 2001–; Pres. Warsaw-Mazovian Regional Athlete's Athletics Asscn 2016–; mem. Bd Polish Athletics Asscn 2016–; Knight's Cross of the Order of Polonia Restituta (5th Class) 2008, Officer's Cross, Order of Polonia Restituta (4th Class) 2009. *Leisure interest:* basketball. *Address:* Polish Athletics Federation (Polski Związek Lekkiej Atletyki), 01-612 Warsaw, ul. Mysłowicka 4, Poland. *E-mail:* pzla@pzla.pl. *Website:* www.pzla.pl.

MAJID, Chaudhry Abdul, BA, LLB; Pakistani politician; b. 14 Feb. 1946, Tangdev, Mirpur; ed Karachi Muslim Law School; mem. Azad Jammu and Kashmir (AJK) Legis. Ass., Speaker 1998–2001, Leader of the Opposition Feb.–July 2011; AJK Minister for Revenue, Agric. and Northern Resource Man. Project 1996; mem. Pakistan People's Party (PPP), mem. PPP Overseas Cttee, Chair. Social Action Programme, apptd mem. Cen. Exec. Cttee 2006, Vice-Pres. AJK PPP 1993, Sr Vice-Pres. 2005, currently Pres.; Prime Minister of Azad Jammu and Kashmir 2011–16. *Address:* House No 167-G, Sector F/2, Mirpur, Azad Kashmir (home). *Website:* www.ajk.gov.pk (office).

MAJKO, Pandeli Sotir, LLB; Albanian politician; b. 15 Nov. 1967; s. of Sotir and Janulla; m. Enkeleida Majko; one s., one d.; ed Univ. of Tirana; Rep. Dec. 1990 Movt; co-f. Democratic Party 1990, left party 1991; Jt Socialist Party of Albania 1991, Sec.-Gen. of Public Relations 1996–97, Sec. 1997–99, also leader of Parl. Group, Head of Del. to OSCE; Prime Minister of Albania 1998–99, Feb.–July 2002; Minister of Defence 2002–05; fmr Sec.-Gen., Socialist Party of Albania; f. Forum of Euro-Socialist Youth 1991; Chair. Euro-Socialist Forum 1992–95; mem. Parl. 1992–, Parliamentary Cttee on Legal Issues, Public Admin and Human Rights 1992–2012; Chair. Albanian Delegation to Parliamentary Ass., NATO 2013–17 (mem. 2005–07); Torch of Democracy Award 1993. *Leisure interest:* reading. *Address:* Kuvendi Popullor (People's Assembly), Bulevardi Dëshmorët e Kombit 4, Tirana, Albania (office). *Telephone:* (4) 2264887 (office); (42) 251299 (home). *Fax:* (4) 2221764 (office). *E-mail:* marlind@parlament.al (office); pandelimajko@hotmail.com (home). *Website:* www.parlament.al (office).

MAJOR, Clarence, BS, PhD; American poet, painter, novelist and academic; *Professor Emeritus of English, University of California, Davis;* b. 31 Dec. 1936, Atlanta, Ga; s. of Clarence Major and Inez Huff; m. Pamela Ritter 1980; ed Union Inst. and Univ., Yellow Springs and Cincinnati, Ohio, State Univ. of New York, Albany; Prof. of English, Univ. of California, Davis 1989–2010, Prof. Emer. 2010–; various appointments at Sara Lawrence Coll., Brooklyn Coll., Queens Coll., New York Univ., Temple Univ., Washington Univ., Univ. of California, San Diego, State Univ. of NY, Binghamton; has given lectures in USA, Europe and in N and W Africa; Fulbright Fellowship, Pushcart Prize, Nat. Council on the Arts Award, Int. Writers' Hall of Fame, Gwendolyn Brooks Foundation Award, Chicago State Univ., Western States Book Award, Sister Circle Book Award, Stephen Henderson Poetry Award for Outstanding Achievement, Bronze Medal as Finalist for Nat. Book Award, Lifetime Achievement Award in the Fine Arts, Congressional Black Caucus Foundation 2015, PEN Oakland Lifetime Achievement Award 2016. *Publications include:* novels: All-Night Visitors 1969, NO 1973, Reflex and Bone Structure 1975, Emergency Exit 1979, My Amputations (Western States Book Award for Fiction) 1986, Such Was the Season 1987, Painted Turtle: Woman with Guitar 1988; short stories: Fun and Games 1990, Calling the Wind: Twentieth Century African-American Short Stories 1993, Dirty Bird Blues 1996, All-Night Visitors (new version) 1998, Chicago Heat and Other Stories 2016; poetry: Swallow the Lake 1970, Symptoms and Madness 1971, Private Line 1971, The Cotton Club 1972, The Syncopated Cakewalk 1974, Inside Diameter: The France Poems 1985, Surfaces and Masks 1987, Some Observations of a Stranger at Zuni in the Latter Part of the Century 1989, The Garden Thrives, Twentieth Century African-American Poetry 1995, Configurations: New and Selected Poems 1958–98 1998, Waiting for Sweet Baby 2002, Down and Up: Poems 2013, From Now On: New and Selected Poems 1970–2015 2016; non-fiction: Dictionary of Afro-American Slang 1970, The Dark and Feeling: Black American Writers and their Work 1974, Juba to Jive: A Dictionary of African-American Slang 1994, Necessary Distance: Essays and Criticism 2001, Come by Here: My Mother's Life 2002, Conversations with Clarence Major, Clarence Major and His Art; numerous works in anthologies and periodicals. *Address:* Department of English, Voorhies Hall, University of California, Davis, CA 95616, USA (office). *E-mail:* clmajor@ucdavis.edu (office). *Website:* english.ucdavis.edu/people/cmajor (office); www.clarencemajor.com.

MAJOR, Air Chief Marshal Fali Homi; Indian air force officer (retd); b. 29 May 1947, Secunderabad; m. Zareen Major; one s. one d.; ed Wesley High School, Secunderabad, Nat. Defence Coll., Army War Coll.; commissioned in Indian Air Force (IAF) 1967, has flown over 7,000 hours on Sentinel, T-6G, Mi-4, Mi-8 and Mi-17 helicopters, as Wing Commdr, commanded IAF's first Mi-17 Squadron, which operated at Siachen Glacier (world's highest battlefield), as Group Capt., commanded another Mi-17 Squadron, leading it during operations of Indian Peace Keeping Force in Sri Lanka, as Station Commdr of Air Force Station Sarsawa, led rescue of 11 passengers from stranded cable car at resort in Himachal Pradesh, has held several important staff and field appointments, including Jt Dir (Helicopter Operations) and Dir Operations (Transport & Helicopter), Air Officer Commdg Leh (Ladakh) following Kargil conflict 1999, promoted to rank of Air Vice-Marshal 2002, Asst Chief of the Air Staff (Personnel Airmen & Civilians) at Air HQ 2002–04, promoted to rank of Air Marshal 2004, Deputy Chief of Integrated Defence Staff (Operations), HQ Integrated Defence Staff 2004–05, directed relief, rescue and rehabilitation operations of Indian Armed Forces in India and abroad in aftermath of tsunami of Dec. 2004, Air Officer C-in-C Eastern Air Command 2005–07, Chief of the Air Staff 2007–09; Ind. Dir Air India 2010–; mem. Bd of Dirs Reliance Defence and Eng Ltd 2016–; mem. Nat. Security Advisory Bd, Govt of India; Vayu Sena Medal (Gallantry), Shaurya Chakra for gallantry, Ati Vishist Seva Medal 2002, Param Vishisht Seva Medal 2006. *Leisure interests:* avid golfer and cricket fan. *Address:* Reliance Defence and Engineering Limited, Devidas Lane, Off SVP Road, Borivali (W), Mumbai, 400103, Maharashtra, India (office). *E-mail:* rdel.secretary@relianceada.com (office). *Website:* www.reliancedefence.co (office).

MAJOR, Jean-Louis, CM, LPh, MA, PhD, FRSC, OC; Canadian author and academic; *Professor Emeritus, University of Ottawa;* b. 16 July 1937, Cornwall, Ont.; s. of Joseph Major and Noella Daoust; m. Bibiane Landry 1960; one d.; ed Univ. of Ottawa, Ecole Pratique des Hautes Etudes, Paris, France; Lecturer, Dept of Philosophy, Univ. of Ottawa 1961–65, Prof. Dept des Lettres Françaises 1965, Titular Prof. 1971–99, Assoc. Dean (Research), Faculty of Arts 1991–97, Prof. Emer. 1999–; Visiting Prof., Dept of French, Univ. of Toronto 1970–71; Dir Corpus d'éditions critiques and Bibliothèque du nouveau monde 1981–; Chair. Academic Advisory Cttee of Ont. Council on Univ. Affairs 1991–93; Excellence in Research Award 1990, Lorne Pierce Medal, RSC 2000. *Publications include:* Saint-Exupéry, l'écriture et la pensée 1968, Anne Hébert et le miracle de la parole 1976, Le jeu en étoile 1978, Entre l'écriture et la parole 1984, a critical edn of Cocteau's Léone, Journal d'Henriette Dessaules 1989, Trente arpents de Ringuet 1991, Mailles à l'envers 1999, Québec Literature: From Collective Identity to Modernity and Back 1999, Contes par-ci par-là 2001, Antifables 2002, Appartenances 2010, Contes inactuels 2015. *Address:* Département des Lettres Françaises, University of Ottawa, Ottawa, ON K1N 6N5, Canada (office).

MAJOR, Rt Hon., Sir John, KG, CH, AIB, FIB; British banker and fmr prime minister; b. 29 March 1943, Merton, London, England; s. of Thomas Major and Gwendolyn Minnie Coates; m. Norma Christina Elizabeth Johnson 1970; one s. one d.; ed Rutlish Grammar School, Merton; mem. Lambeth Borough Council 1968–71, Chair. Housing Cttee 1970–71; Sr Exec. Standard Chartered Bank PLC, various exec. posts in UK and overseas 1965–79; MP for Huntingdon 1983–2001 (Huntingdonshire 1979–83); Jt Sec., Conservative Parl. Party Environment Cttee 1979–81; Parl. Pvt. Sec. to Home Office Minister 1981–83; Asst Govt Whip 1983–84; Lord Commr of HM Treasury 1984–85; Parl. Under-Sec. of State for Social Security 1985–86; Minister for Social Security and the Disabled 1986–87; Chief Sec. to Treasury 1987–89; Sec. of State for Foreign and Commonwealth Affairs July–Oct. 1989; Chancellor of the Exchequer 1989–90; Prime Minister, First Lord of the Treasury and Minister for the Civil Service 1990–97; Leader of the Conservative Party 1990–97; Pres. Eastern Area Young Conservatives 1983–85, mem. Int. Bd of Govs., Peres Centre for Peace, Israel 1997–; Chair. Emerson Electric Co. 1999–2015; mem. Baker Inst. 1998–2005, InterAction Council, Tokyo 1998–2008; Adviser to Carlyle Group 1998–2001, Chair. (European Bd) 2001–05; Pres. Surrey Co. Cricket Club 2000–02; Chair. Ditchley Council of Man. 2000–09, Advisory Bd Global Infrastructure Partners 2007–, Int. Advisory Bd Nat. Bank of Kuwait 2007–14, AECOM Global Advisory Bd 2011–16; Dir (non-exec.) Mayflower Corpn 2000–03; Sr Adviser Credit Suisse 2001–; mem. European Bd, Siebel Systems Inc. 2001–03, Club de Madrid 2002–06; mem. Main Cttee Marylebone Cricket Club (MCC) 2001–04, 2005–08, 2009–11, Norfolk Cricket Umpires and Scorers Asscn 2002–; Pres. Asthma UK 1998–, Research Action Fund, Prostate Cancer UK 2009–, The Bow Group 2012–14; Vice-Pres. Macmillan Cancer Relief, Inst. of Sports Sponsorship 2001–, Greater London Fund for the Blind 2005–; Chair. Queen Elizabeth Diamond Jubilee Trust 2011–; mem. British and Commonwealth Cricket Charitable Trust 2002–; Amb. Chance to Shine 2005–, Vision 2020; Patron of Mercy Ships, Support for Africa 2000, Atlantic Partnership 2001–, Foreign and Commonwealth Office Asscn 2001–, Professional Cricketers' Asscn 2001–, Deafblind UK 2002–, Consortium for Street Children 2002–, 21st Century Trust 2002–, Goodman Fund, Chicago 2002–, DEMAND 2002–, Wavemakers 2004–07, Foundation for Peace 2004–, Future Ireland 2004–, Dickie Bird Foundation 2004–, SeeAbility's Sight Pioneers 2006–, Margaret Thatcher Scholarship Trust 2012–, British Music Hall Soc. 2012–, Hoxton Hall 2012–; Vice-Patron, The Atlantic Council of the UK; Hon. Master of the Bench of the Middle Temple 1992, Hon. Bencher 1993–, Hon. Freeman, Merchant Taylors' Co. 2002–, Hon. Life Vice-Pres. Surrey Co. Cricket Club, Hon. Pres. Sight Savers Appeal 2001–, Hon. FCIB, Hon. Commr, Sir John A. Macdonald Bicentennial Comm. 2012–, Distinguished Elder Brother of the Court of Trinity House 2012, Hon. Patron, British Gymnastics 2013–; Grand Cordon, Order of the Rising Sun (Japan) 2012. *Publications include:* John Major: The Autobiography 1999, More Than A Game: The Story of Cricket's Early Years 2007, My Old Man: A Personal History of Music Hall 2012. *Leisure interests:* reading, travel, theatre, music, opera, football, cricket and other sports. *Address:* PO Box 38506, London, SW1P 1ZW, England.

MAJOR, Kendal, DDS; Bahamian dentist and politician; b. 9 Aug. 1961, Nassau; m. Monique Major (née Smith); three c.; ed Tuskegee Univ., Howard Univ. Coll. of Dentistry, Washington DC, Univ. of Medicine and Dentistry of New Jersey, USA; began professional dental career as Sr Dental Officer, Princess Margaret Hosp., Nassau, becoming Dir of Dental Services; mem. House of Ass. (PLP) for Garden Hills 2012–, Speaker 2012–17; fmr Chair. Dental Council of The Bahamas; Founder and Dir Bahamas' First Study Club, Nassau; Dir Teen Challenge Bahamas; fmr mem. Nat. Comm. on Prison Reform; mem. Progressive Liberal Party (PLP), Vice-Chair. 2008–10. *Leisure interests:* reading, traveling. *Address:* House of Assembly, POB N 3003, Nassau, Bahamas (office). *Telephone:* (1242) 322 2041 (office). *Fax:* (1242) 322 1118 (office). *E-mail:* houseofassembly@bahamas.gov.bs (office). *Website:* www.bahamas.gov.bs (office).

MAJOR, Dame Malvina Lorraine, ONZ, GNZM, DBE; New Zealand operatic soprano; *Senior Fellow, Conservatorium of Music Faculty of Arts and Social Sciences, University of Waikato;* b. 28 Jan. 1943, Hamilton; d. of Vincent Major and Eva Major; m. Winston William Richard Fleming 1965 (died 1990); one s. two d.; ed Hamilton Tech. Coll. and London Opera Centre; debut as Rosina in The Barber of Seville, Salzburg Festival 1968; performances in Europe, UK, USA, Australia, Japan, Jordan, Egypt and NZ; concerts, opera and recording with NZ Symphony Orchestra, Auckland Philharmonia and Southern Symphony Orchestra; Founder Dame Malvina Major Foundation (for excellence in the performing arts) 1991; Amb. for NZ Year of the Family 1994; fmr Prof. of Vocal Studies, Univ. of Canterbury; currently Sr Fellow, Conservatorium of Music Faculty of Arts and Social Sciences, Univ. of Waikato; fmr Chair. Diana, Princess of Wales Trust; Patron, Christchurch City Choir, Canterbury Opera, Nelson School of Music, Waikato Multiple Sclerosis; Hon. Life mem. NZ Horticultural Soc.; Dame Grand Companion, NZ Order of Merit 2007; Hon. DLitt (Massey Univ.); Dr hc (Waikato); NZ Winner, Mobil Song Quest 1963, Kathleen Ferrier Competition winner 1966, Outstanding Achievements in Music Award 1988, NZ Medal 1990, Entertainer and Int. Performer of the Year 1992, NZ Music Award—Classical Disc 1993, 1994, Benny Award, Variety Club of NZ 1998, Lifetime Achievement Award, Women of Influence Awards 2014, and numerous other awards for services to music. *Recordings:* numerous recordings, including Ovation: The Very Best Of Dame Malvina Major 2015. *Leisure interests:* family, golf, sewing, gardening. *E-mail:* info@dmmfoundation.org.nz. *Website:* www.dmmfoundation.org.nz.

MAJORO, Moeketsi, PhD; Lesotho economist and politician; *Minister of Finance;* ed Nat. Univ. of Lesotho, Washington State Univ.; Lecturer in Econs, Nat. Univ. of Lesotho 1991–2000; Prin. Sec., responsible for public finance, Ministry of Finance and Devt Planning 2003–08; Alt. Exec. Dir, IMF 2008–10, Exec. Dir 2010–12; Minister for Devt Planning 2013–15, Minister of Finance 2017–; mem. Nat. Ass. (Parl.) (ABC) for Thetsane constituency no. 33 2017–; policy consultant in the areas of business and econs, Quality Economics (QE) 2015–; fmr mem. bd of dirs of several cos; mem. All Basotho Convention (ABC). *Address:* Ministry of Finance, Finance House, 3rd Floor, High Court Road, POB 395, Maseru 100, Lesotho (office). *Telephone:* 22310826 (office). *Fax:* 22310411 (office). *Website:* www.finance.gov.ls (office).

MAK, Tak Wah, OC, BSc, MSc, PhD, FRSC; Canadian (b. Chinese) immunologist, molecular biologist and academic; *Professor, Department of Medical Biophysics and Department of Immunology and Director, Campbell Family Institute for Breast Cancer Research, University of Toronto;* b. 4 Oct. 1946, People's Repub. of China; s. of Kent Mak and Shu-tak Chan; m. Shirley Suet-Wan Lau (died 1998); two c.; ed Univ. of Wisconsin, Univ. of Alberta; Sr Scientist, Div. of Stem Cell and Developmental Biology, Advanced Medical Discovery Inst., Ont. Cancer Inst. 1974–, Head of Div. of Cellular and Molecular Biology 1991–93, currently Dir Advanced Medical Discovery Inst.; mem. Inst. of Medical Science, of Toronto 1979–, Assoc. Prof., Dept of Medical Biophysics 1979–84, Prof., Dept of Medical Biophysics and Dept of Immunology 1984–, Univ. Prof. 1997–, Grad. Sec., Dept of Medical Biophysics 1995–2001, Dir Advanced Medical Discovery Inst., Univ. Health Network, Toronto 2002–, Dir Campbell Family Inst. for Breast Cancer Research, Princess Margaret Hosp., Toronto 2004–; Founding Dir Amgen Inst. 1993–2002; mem. Bd Cancer Research Inc., New York 1989–; Ed. or Assoc. Ed. The International Journal of Immunology 1987–, The Immunologist 1994–, Current Opinion in Immunology 2001–, Cancer Cell 2002–, Proceedings of the National Academy of Sciences, USA 2003–; mem. numerous advisory bds of scientific journals and medical centres; Foreign Assoc., NAS 2002; mem. American Acad. of Arts and Sciences 2005; Hon. Prof., Cancer Inst., Chinese Acad. of Medical

Sciences 1986, Beijing Union Medical Univ. 1986, Dept of Pathology, Univ. of Hong Kong 2004–07, Dept of Medicine Faculty, Univ. of Rome 'Tor Vergata', Italy 2007, Dept of Biology and Chem., City Univ. of Hong Kong 2007; Hon. mem. Scandinavian Soc. of Immunology 1995; Order of Ont. 2008; Hon. DSc (Carleton Univ.) 1989, (Laurentian Univ.) 1992, (York Univ., Ont.) 2004, (Ryerson Univ., Ont.) 2004, (Univ. of Hong Kong) 2008; Hon. MD (Univ. of Zurich) 2001; Hon. MD in Surgery (Univ. of Rome) 2008; hon. degree (Georg August Univ., Germany) 2008; The Outstanding Award of the Year, Chinese Cultural Asscn of Canada 1984, E.W.R. Steacie Award, Nat. Sciences and Eng Research Council 1984, Ayerst Award, Canadian Biochemical Soc. 1985, Merit Award, Fed. of Chinese Professionals of Canada 1985, Stacie Prize, Stacie Trust Foundation 1986, Canadian Asscn of Mfrs of Medical Devices Award 1988, Emil von Behring Prize, Phillips-Universität Marburg (FRG) 1988, Univ. of Alberta 75th Anniversary Distinguished Scientist Award 1989, Gairdner Int. Award, Gairdner Foundation 1989, RSC McLaughlin Medal 1990, Canadian Foundation for AIDS Research Award 1991, Cinader Award 1994, Royal Soc. of London 1994, Sloan Prize, General Motors Cancer Foundation 1994, King Faisal Int. Prize for Medicine 1995, Sloan Prize, General Motors Cancer Research Foundation 1996, McLeans Magazine's Honour Roll 1996, Robert Noble Prize, Nat. Cancer Inst. of Canada 1997, Alumni of the Year, Univ. of Alberta 1997, McLaughlin Medal, University of Texas, Galveston, Texas 1997, Novartis Immunology Prizes, Novartis, Inc. Basel, Switzerland 1998, Killam Prize, Canada Council 2003, Paul Ehrlich and Ludwig Darmstaedter Prize 2004, Premier's Summit Awards in Medical Research, Ont. 2007, Alumni Recognition Award, Univ. of Alberta 2008, inducted into Canadian Medical Hall of Fame 2009. *Achievements include:* recognized world-wide for his discovery of T cell receptor (TCR), a key component of the immune system. *Publications:* more than 640 scientific papers in professional journals; more than 26 patents. *Leisure interests:* music, tennis, golf. *Address:* Department of Medical Biophysics, University of Toronto, Toronto Medical Discovery Tower, MaRS Centre, 101 College Street, Room 15-701, Toronto, ON M5G 1L7, Canada (office). *Telephone:* (416) 946-4501 (ext. 2234) (office). *E-mail:* tmak@uhnres.utoronto.ca (office). *Website:* medbio.utoronto.ca/faculty/mak.html (office).

MAKARCZYK, Jerzy, LLD; Polish professor of law and judge; *Professor of Legal Sciences, Polish Academy of Sciences;* b. 24 July 1938; s. of Zbigniew Makarczyk and Hanna Olszowska; ed Warsaw Univ. and Inst. of Legal Sciences, Polish Acad. of Sciences; Assoc. Prof. of Int. Public Law 1975, Prof. 1988; Deputy Dir Inst. of Legal Sciences, Polish Acad. of Sciences 1981–88, Prof. 1992–; Deputy Minister of Foreign Affairs 1989–90; Sec. of State, Ministry of Foreign Affairs 1990–92; in charge of negotiations with USSR and then Russia on withdrawal of troops from Polish territory 1990–2002; Judge, European Court of Human Rights 1992–2002; mem. ILO High Level Team to Myanmar 2001–; Adviser to Pres. of Repub. of Poland from 2002; Pres. Int. Law Asscn 1988–90; mem. Inst de Droit Int. 1993, Pres. from 2003; Judge, Court of Justice of the EU 2004–09; Commdr, Légion d'honneur; Officer's Cross, Order of Polonia Restituta 2011; Manfred Lachs Foundation Award 1998. *Publications:* Financing of Economic Development in the United Nations System 1974, Principles of a New International Economic Order 1988; ed. Collection of Essays in Honour of Judge Manfred Lachs 1984, Theory of International Law at the Threshold of the XXIst Century (ed.) 1996. *Leisure interests:* tennis, sailing. *Address:* Al. Przyjaciol 3 m. 14, 00-565 Warsaw, Poland. *Telephone:* (22) 6769135. *Fax:* (22) 6429540. *E-mail:* jmakarczyk@prezydent.pl.

MAKAREVICH, Andrey Vadimovich; Russian composer, singer and artist; b. 11 Dec. 1953, Moscow; one s. two d.; ed Moscow Inst. of Architecture; Founder, Artistic Dir, soloist, Mashina Vremeni (Time Machine, first professional rock group in Russia) 1969–; creator, presenter Smak (TV programme); Leader, Creol Tango Orchestra; drawings have been exhibited in Moscow, St Petersburg, Riga, Caserta (Italy), London, New York; Merited Artist of RSFSR, Order of Honour, Order of Contrib. to the Motherland. *Television:* presenter, Smak, Underwater World of Andrei Makarevich. *Recordings:* 26 albums, including music for nine films, YO 5 2018. *Publications:* nine books of poetry and prose. *Leisure interest:* spear hunting. *Website:* www.mashina.ru (office); www.makar.info.

MAKAROV, Andrey Mikhailovich, CJur; Russian barrister; b. 22 July 1954, Moscow; ed Moscow State Univ.; worked in Research Inst., USSR Ministry of Internal Affairs 1976–83; mem. Moscow City Bd of Lawyers 1983–, acted as the defence lawyer in numerous major trials, including trial of fmr Deputy Minister of Internal Affairs V. Churbanov; Chief of Dept supervising activities of Comm. of Security Council in struggle against crime and corruption July–Oct. 1993; mem. State Duma (Parl.) 1993–99, 2003–, Vice-Chair. Budget and Taxation Cttee; Exec. Dir Russian br. of SOROS Foundation; Pres. Chess Fed. of Russia 1994–97; mem. Exec. Cttee Int. Chess Fed. (FIDE); Head, Barristers co. A. Makarov and A. Tobak 1998–; Chair. Council of Experts on Improving Tax System, State Duma 2000, Cttee on Budget and Taxes 2011–; Order of Honour 2014. *Address:* Andrey Makarov and Aleksandr Tobak Barristers Bureau, 125167 Moscow, Leningradsky Prospect 39A, Russia (office). *Telephone:* (495) 213-86-94 (office).

MAKAROV, Gen. Nikolai Yegorovich; Russian army officer; b. 7 Oct. 1949, Glebovo, Ryazan Oblast; m.; one s.; ed Moscow Combined Arms Command School, Frunze Mil. Acad., Gen. Staff Acad., Moscow; began career as Commdr, Soviet Platoon, German Democratic Repub., becoming Commdr of Co. and Bn; Deputy Regt Commdr, Baikal Mil. Dist (later Transbaikal Mil. Dist) 1979; Deputy Div. Commdr, Russian Jt Force, Tajikistan, becoming Commdr, Motorized Rifle Div., Chief of Staff 1993; Chief of Staff, Volga Mil. Dist –1998; Commdr of Ground and Shore Troops and Deputy Commdr of Baltic Fleet 1998–99; Chief of Staff and First Deputy Commdr, Moscow Mil. Dist 1999–2002; Commdr, Siberian Mil. Dist 2002; attained rank of Gen. 2005; Chief of Armaments for Russian Armed Forces and Deputy Minister of Defence 2007–08, Chief of Gen. Staff and First Deputy Minister of Defence 2008–12; mem. Historical Truth Comm. 2009–12; apptd aide to Minister of Defence Sergei Shoigu 2013; Order for Service in USSR Armed Forces (Third Class), Order for Distinguished Mil. Service, Order of St George (Second Class); 12 medals; Honoured Mil. Specialist of Russian Fed.

MAKAROV, Valery Leonidovich, PhD; Russian economist, academic and university administrator; *Director, Graduate School of Public Administration, Lomonosov Moscow State University;* b. 25 May 1937, Novosibirsk; s. of Leonid Makarov and Dina Yershov; m. Irena Nikolaev 1961; one s. one d.; ed Moscow Econ. Inst.; scientific worker, Inst. of Math., Siberian Div. USSR Acad. of Sciences

1961–67, Lab. Chief 1967–73, Deputy Dir 1973–80, Gen. Sec. Siberian Div. 1980–83; Prof. of Mathematical Econs Novosibirsk Univ. 1970–83; Dir Nat. Inst. of Industrial Man., Moscow 1983–85; Dir Central Econs and Math. Inst. 1985; Prof. at Moscow Univ.; Founder and Rector, New Econ. School, Moscow 1992; currently Dir Graduate School of Public Admin, Lomonosov Moscow State Univ.; Ed.-in-Chief, Journal of Math. and Econ. Methods.; mem. Ed. Bd Econs of Planning, Econs of Transition, Econ. Systems Research; mem. Exec. Cttee, Int. Econ. Asscn 1995–; mem. several govt comms; Corresp. mem. USSR (now Russian) Acad. of Science 1979, mem. 1990; Fellow, Econometric Soc.; Kantorovich Award (for contrib. to econ. theory) 1995. *Publications:* Mathematical Theory of Economic Dynamics and Equilibria (with A. Rubinov) 1977, Models and Computers in Economics 1979, Computer Simulation in Analysis of Regional Problems 1987, Mathematical Economic Theory: Pure and Mixed Types of Economic Mechanisms (with A. Rubinov and M. Levin) 1994. *Leisure interests:* tennis, skiing. *Address:* Graduate School of Public Administration, Lomonosov Moscow State University, Moscow 119991, GSP-1, 1-61 Leninskie Gory, Russia (office). *Telephone:* (495) 510-52-05 (office), (495) 229-01-50 (home). *E-mail:* info@anspa.ru (office). *Website:* en .anspa.ru (office).

MAKAROVA, Inna Vladimirovna; Russian actress; b. 28 July 1926, Taiga, Kemerovo Dist; d. of Vladimir Makarov and Anna German; m. 1st S. Bondarchuk 1947; m. 2nd M. Perelman; one d.; ed All-Union Film Inst.; Order of Red Banner of Labour, Order of Merit RSFSR 1967; USSR State Prize 1949, People's Artist of USSR 1985. *Films include:* Molodaya gvardiya (The Young Guard) 1948, Selskiy vrach (The Village Doctor) 1951, Vozvrashcheniye Vasiliya Bortnikova (The Return of Vasili Bortnikov) 1952, Dimitrovgradtsy (People of Dimitrovgrad) 1956, Vysota (Height) 1957, Dorogoy moy chelovek (My Dear Fellow!) 1958, Nash korespondent 1959, Devchata (Girls) 1961, Bratya Komarovy 1961, Zhenitba Balzaminova (The Marriage of Balzaminov) 1964, Bolshaya ruda (The Big Ore) 1964, Zhenshchiny 1966, Malenkiy beglets (The Little Runaway) 1966, Urok literatury (A Literature Lesson) 1968, Novenkaya (The Rookie) 1968, Prestupleniye i nakazaniye (Crime and Punishment) 1969, Lyubov Yarovaya 1970, Russkoye pole (Russian Field) 1971, Neispravimyy lgun (Incorrigible Liar) 1973, Bezotvetnaya lyubov (Unanswered Love) 1979, Kontrolnaya po spetsialnosti 1981, Zhivaya raduga (Living Rainbow) 1982, Detstvo Bambi (Bambi's Childhood) 1985, Yunost Bambi (Bambi's Youth) 1986, Lermontov 1986, Ssuda na brak (Loan for a Marriage) 1987, Bolshaya lyubov 2006. *Television includes:* Vas vyzyvaet Taymyr (Taimyr Calls You) 1970, Harsnatsun hyusisits (A Bride from the North) 1975, Pechniki (Stove Builders) 1982, Myortvye dushi (Dead Souls) (mini-series) 1984, Maritsa 1985. *Leisure interest:* gardening.

MAKAROVA, Natalia Romanovna; Russian ballerina; b. 21 Nov. 1940, Leningrad; m. 3rd Edward Karkar 1976 (died 2013); one s.; ed Vagonova Ballet School, Leningrad; mem. Kirov Ballet 1959–70; sought political asylum, London 1970; Prin. Dancer, American Ballet Theater 1970–92; appeared with Kirov Co. in London 1988, USSR 1989; f. Makarova and Co. 1980; Guest Artist, Royal Ballet 1972; Guest Artist, London Festival Ballet 1984; retd from dancing 1992; Dir Sleeping Beauty, Royal Ballet 2003; currently Dir Dutch Nat. Opera; Honoured Artist of RSFSR 1969, School of American Ballet Artistic Achievement Award 2004, Carina Ari Medal 2006, Kennedy Center Honor 2012. *Television:* In a Class of Her Own, Assoluta, Natasha 1985, Makarova Returns 1989, Great Railway Journeys: St Petersburg to Tashkent 1994. *Plays:* On Your Toes (musical), Broadway, New York (Tony Award for Best Actress in a Musical), West End, London (Laurence Olivier Award) 1984, Tovarich, Chichester Festival then West End, London 1991, Two for the Seesaw, Moscow 1992. *Films include:* Black Swan Pas de Deux 1970, Giselle 1977, Other Dances 1978, Assoluta 1979, La Bayadère 1980, The President's Command Performance 1981, Stars Salute the President 1983, Gala of the Stars 1984, Natasha 1985, In a Class of Her Own 1985, Reunion With the Kirov Ballet 1988, Makarova Returns 1989, BBC Great Railway Journeys 1994, Natalia Makarova Two Lives 2011. *Publications:* A Dance Autobiography 1979, On Your Toes 1984. *Address:* Dutch National Opera, PO Box 16822, 1001 RH Amsterdam, Netherlands (office). *Telephone:* (20) 5518117 (office). *Fax:* (20) 5518068 (office). *E-mail:* info@operaballet.nl (office). *Website:* www.operaballet.nl (office).

MAKEI, Uladzimir Uladzimiravich; Belarusian politician; *Minister of Foreign Affairs;* b. 5 Aug. 1958, Nekrashevichi, Korelichskiy Dist, Grodno (Horadnia) Oblast, Belarusian SSR, USSR; m.; three c.; ed Minsk State Teachers' Training Inst. of Foreign Languages, Diplomatic Acad., Austrian Ministry of Foreign Affairs; served in Soviet Army 1980–92, Col in Reserve; Third Sec., Information and Humanitarian Co-operation Dept, later Second Sec., Analysis and Forecasting Dept, later Second Sec., Secr. of the Ministry of Foreign Affairs 1993–95, Deputy Head of State Protocol Service 1995–96, Belarusian Rep. to Council of Europe, Counsellor, Embassy in Paris 1996–99, Head of All-European Co-operation Dept, Ministry of Foreign Affairs 1999–2000; Aide to the Pres. of Belarus 2000–08, Head of Presidential Exec. Office 2008–12; Minister of Foreign Affairs 2012–. *Address:* Ministry of Foreign Affairs, 220030 Minsk, vul. Lenina 19, Belarus (office). *Telephone:* (17) 327-29-22 (office). *Fax:* (17) 327-45-21 (office). *E-mail:* mail@mfa .gov.by (office). *Website:* mfa.gov.by (office).

MAKEN, Ajay, BA, BSc; Indian trade unionist and politician; b. 12 Jan. 1964, Delhi; s. of C. P. Maken and Santosh Maken; m. Radhika Maken; one s. two d.; ed St Xavier's School, Delhi, Univ. of Delhi; fmr leader, trade union movts of Delhi Transport Corpn and Delhi Electric Supply Undertaking; mem. Delhi Legis. Ass. 1993–2004, Speaker 2003–04; mem. Lok Sabha (lower house of Parl.) for New Delhi constituency 2004–14; Gen. Sec. Delhi Pradesh Congress Cttee 1993–97, Indian Youth Congress 1997–98, Indian Nat. Congress 2013–15 (also Head of Communication, Publicity and Publication); Chief, Delhi Congress 2015–18; Parl. Sec. to Chief Minister, Govt of Delhi 1998–2001; Minister of Transport, Power and Tourism, Govt of Delhi 2001–03; Union Cabinet Minister of State for Urban Devt 2006–09, for Home Affairs 2009–11, for Youth Affairs and Sports 2011–12, Union Cabinet Minister of Housing and Urban Poverty Alleviation 2012–13. *Leisure interests:* cricket and golf, surfing the net, watching science fiction movies, listening to old movie songs, ghazals (poetry) and reading non-fiction books. *Address:* c/o Indian National Congress, 24 Akbar Road, New Delhi 110 011, India (office). *Telephone:* (11) 23019080. *Fax:* (11) 23017047. *E-mail:* aicc@congress.org .in. *Website:* www.aicc.org.in.

MAKGOBA, Archbishop Thabo Cecil, BSc, MA, PhD; South African ecclesiastic; *Anglican Archbishop of Cape Town;* b. 15 Dec. 1960, Johannesburg; m. Lungelwa Manona; ed Orlando High, Soweto, Univ. of the Witwatersrand, St Paul's Coll., Grahamstown, Univ. of Cape Town; ordained priest in Anglican Diocese of Johannesburg 1990, first as a curate at Cathedral, then as Chaplain of Univ. of the Witwatersrand; part-time Lecturer, Univ. of the Witwatersrand 1993–96; put in charge of St Alban's Church and later of Christ the King, Sophiatown, Archdeacon of Sophiatown 1999; consecrated Bishop of Queenstown (Suffragan Bishop of Grahamstown) 2002–04, Bishop of Grahamstown 2004–07; Archbishop of Cape Town and Metropolitan of the Anglican Church of Southern Africa 2007–; Procter Fellow, Episcopal Divinity School (USA) 2008; Chancellor Univ. of the Western Cape 2012–; Chair. Nat. Church Leaders' Consultation; Prior of the Order of St John in South Africa 2018; Hon. DD (Gen. Theological Seminary) 2009, (Huron Univ. Coll.) 2013; Ernest Oppenheimer Memorial Trust Scholarship for PhD. *Address:* Anglican Diocese of Cape Town, PO Box 1932, Zonnebloem Estate, Woodstock, Cape Town 8000, South Africa (office). *Telephone:* (21) 469-3760 (office). *Fax:* (21) 465-1571 (office). *E-mail:* goodhopeads@ctdiocese.org.za (office). *Website:* www.capetown.anglican.org (office).

MAKGOTHI, Lesego Casayel; Lesotho politician; *Minister of Foreign Affairs and International Relations;* mem. Nat. Ass. (Parl.) (ABC) for Maseru constituency no. 32 2015–; Minister of Foreign Affairs and Int. Relations 2017–; mem. All Basotho Convention (ABC). *Address:* Ministry of Foreign Affairs and International Relations, Qhobosheaneng Govt Complex, Griffith Hill Road, POB 1387, Maseru 100, Lesotho (office). *Telephone:* 22311150 (office). *Fax:* 22310178 (office). *E-mail:* moeketsim@foreign.gov.ls (office). *Website:* www.foreign.gov.ls (office).

MAKHALINA, Yulia Victorovna; Russian ballet dancer; b. 23 June 1968, St Petersburg; ed Vaganova Acad. of Russian Ballet under Prof. Marina Vasilyeva; joined Mariinsky Theatre 1985, Prin. Dancer 1989–; Gold Medal and Grand Prix, Fourth Int. Ballet Competition in Paris 1990, Prix de Lumière (Italy), Merited Artist of Russia 1995, Benois de la Dance Prize 1998, People's Artist of Russia 2008. *Roles include:* Aurora and Lilac Fairy (Sleeping Beauty), Giselle and Myrtha (Giselle), Kitri (Don Quixote), Medora (Le Corsaire), Odette/Odile (Swan Lake), Nikiya and Gamzatti (La Bayadère), Mekhmene and Banu (Legend of Love), Raymonda (Raymonda), Sylphide (La Sylphide), Maria (Fountain of Bakhchisarai), Juliet (Romeo and Juliet), Zobeide (Sheherezade), Fire Bird (Firebird), Maria Taglioni (Pas de Quatre), (Dying Swan), Anna (Anna Karenina), Fairy (Cinderella), Carmen (Carmen), Duchess of Alba (Goya Divertissement), Terpsichore (Apollo), Second Movt (Symphony in C), Third Movt (In the Night), Manon (Manon), (Youth and Death), Soloist ("Paquita" Grand Pas), Soloist (Theme and Variations). *Address:* Mariinsky Theatre, St Petersburg, 190000, Teatralnaya pl. 1, Russia (office). *Telephone:* (812) 326-41-41 (office). *Website:* www.mariinsky.ru (office).

MAKHMALBAF, Mohsen; Iranian film director and novelist; b. 29 May 1957, Tehran; raised by his single mother; m. Marzieh Makhmalbaf; one s. two d.; 13 different jobs, including bellboy and plains worker aged 8–17; mem. of an underground Islamic militia group, shot and arrested while attempting to disarm a policeman aged 17; formed the Makhmalbaf Film House to teach film 1996; retrospective at Kerala Int. Film Festival, India; left Iran in 2005, then lived in Paris; mem. Jury, Venice Film Festival 2006; now lives in Kabul, Afghanistan with his family; Hon. Dr of Cinema (Univ. of Nanterre, France) 2010; Hon. DLitt (St Andrews Univ., UK) 2011; selected as the best filmmaker after the revolution by readers of cinema publs 1988, Federico Fellini Honour, UNESCO, Paris 2001, Sergei Parajanov Award, Yerevan Film Festival 2006, Freedom to Create Prize for his human right activity and promoting social justice through his art, Art Action (UK) 2009. *Films:* Towjeeh 1981, Hesar dar Hesar 1982, Marg Deegari 1982, Tobeh Nosuh (also writer) 1983, Do Cheshman Beesu (also actor) 1984, Este'aze 1984, Boycott 1985, Zangha 1985, The Cyclist (also production designer) 1987, The Pedlar (also writer) 1987, Arousi-ye Khouban (also writer) 1989, Rajayi School 1989, A Time for Love 1990, Farmandar 1990, The Nights of Zayandeh-Rood 1991, Nassereddin Shah, Actor-e Cinema 1992, The Unfinished Man 1992, The Actor (also writer) 1993, Images from the Ghajar Dynasty (short, also writer) 1993, Stone and Glass 1994, Salaam Cinema (documentary) 1995, Gabbeh 1996, A Moment of Innocence (also actor) (Among the Top Ten Films of the Decade, Int. Festival Dirs and Critics 1999) 1996, The Apple (also writer) 1998, The Silence (also writer and set designer) 1998, Madresei keh baad bord (short, also writer) 1998, Ghessé hayé kish (segment 'The Door') 1999, Blackboards (also producer) 2000, The Day I Became a Woman (also producer) 2000, Tales of an Island (segment 'Testing Democracy') (also actor and cinematographer) 2000, Kandahar (also producer) (Ecumenical Jury Prize, Cannes Int. Film Festival 2001, The Afghan Alphabet (documentary) 2002, At Five in the Afternoon (novel) (also producer) 2003, Joy of Madness (documentary, also producer) 2003, Sex & Philosophy (also producer) 2005, Poet of the Wastes 2005, The Chair (short) 2005, Scream of the Ants (also producer) 2006, Two-Legged Horse (also writer and producer) 2008, The Man Who Came with the Snow (also screenplay) 2009, Mother's Paradise (also screenplay) 2011, The Gardener (documentary, also writer and producer) 2012, Ongoing Smile (documentary) 2013; Osama (exec. producer) 2003. *Publications:* Disgrace, Two Blind Eyes, The Sultan's Lake, The Crystal Graden, Death of Another, Divine Arrow, The Martyred Sheikh, The Dumb Man's Dream First Volume, The Dumb Man's Dream Second Volume, The Dumb Man's Dream Third Volume, Life is Color, Introduction on Islamic Art, Notes about Storywriting and Playwriting, The Budhha Was Not Demolished in Afghanistan, It Collapsed Out of Shame, The Bells, Mother, Legitimate Parliament, Rajayi's School, Birth of an Old Woman, The Cyclist, Marriage of the Blessed, Time of Love, Hail the Sun, Bread and the Vase, The Apple, Travel To Kandehar, To See and Not to See (some translated into 12 different languages). *Address:* Green Film House, 98 Mirdamad Boulevard, PO Box 19395/4866, Tehran, Iran (office); c/o MK2 Diffusion, 55 rue Traversière, 75012 Paris, France (office). *Telephone:* (21) 2225960 (Tehran) (office); 1-43-07-92-74 (Paris) (office). *Fax:* (21) 2270970 (Tehran) (office); 1-43-41-32-30 (Paris) (office). *Website:* www.makhmalbaf.com (office).

MAKHMUDOV, Lt-Gen. Eldar Akhmed oğlu; Azerbaijani government official and politician; b. 1956, Baku; m.; three c.; ed D. Bunyatzade Inst. of Economy, Baku State Univ.; career in mil. service; served Organized Crime and Criminal Investigation Divs, Ministry of Interior 1980–2004, positions included Chief of Br., Drugs Suppression Unit 1993, Chief, Economic Crimes Dept, Chief of Branch, Drugs Suppression Dept 2004; Minister of Nat. Security 2004–15; promoted to Maj.-Gen. 2004, to Lt-Gen. 2005, Col-Gen. 2014.

MAKHULU, Most Rev. Walter Paul Khotso, CMG; British ecclesiastic; *Archbishop Emeritus of Central Africa;* b. 2 July 1935, Johannesburg, SA; s. of Paul Makhulu; m. Rosemary Makhulu 1966; one s. one d.; ed Pimville Govt School, Johannesburg, Khaiso Secondary School, Coll. of the Resurrection and St Peter, SA, St Andrew's Coll., Birmingham; Area Sec. for Eastern Africa and African Refugees, Comm. on Inter-Church Aid Refugee and World Service, World Council of Churches 1975–79; Bishop of Botswana 1979–2000; Archbishop of Cen. Africa 1980–2000, Archbishop Emer. 2000–; Pres. All Africa Conf. of Churches 1981–86; Pres. World Council of Churches 1983–91; Hon. Curate Holy Trinity, Geneva; Presidential Order of Honour (Botswana) 2002, Officier, Ordre des Palmes académiques 1981; Hon. DD (Kent) 1988, (Gen. Theological Seminary, New York) 1990. *Leisure interests:* music, int. affairs. *Address:* 16 Downside, 8 St John's Avenue, London, SW15 2AE, England (home). *Telephone:* (20) 8704-1220 (home). *E-mail:* makhulu@btinternet.com (home).

MAKI, Fumihiko, MArch; Japanese architect; *Principal Partner, Maki and Associates;* b. 6 Sept. 1928, Tokyo; m.; two c.; ed Univ. of Tokyo, Cranbrook Acad. of Art, Harvard Univ. Grad. School of Design, USA; Assoc. Prof., Washington Univ. 1956–62, Harvard Univ. 1962–66; Lecturer, Dept of Urban Eng, Univ. of Tokyo 1964–79, Prof. of Architecture 1979–89; Prin. Pnr, Maki and Assocs 1964–; Hon. FAIA 1980, FRIBA; Hon. Fellow, German Inst. of Architects, French Acad. of Architecture, Czech Inst. of Architects, Mexican Inst. of Architects, Bund Deutscher Architekten, American Acad. of Arts & Sciences, Academia Scientiarum et Artium Europaea, Royal Australian Inst. of Architects, Royal Incorporation of Architects in Scotland, Taiwan Inst. of Architects; Officier, Ordre des Arts et Lettres 1998; Hon. Dr of Art and Architecture (Washington, USA), (Nagoya Univ.); Wolf Foundation Prize in Arts 1988, Thomas Jefferson Medal for Architecture 1990, Int. Union of Architects (UIA) Gold Medal 1993, Pritzker Architecture Prize 1993, Prince of Wales Prize in Urban Design 1993, Arnold Brunner Memorial Prize in Architecture 1994, Praemium Imperiale 1999, AIA Gold Medal 2011, Japan Art Acad. Award 2013, Person of Cultural Merit 2013. *Major works include:* Toyoda Memorial Hall, Nagoya Univ. 1960, Nat. Aquarium, Okinawa 1975, Hillside Terrace Housing Complex 1978–98, Iwasaki Art Museum 1979, Keio Univ. Library, Mita Campus 1981, Spiral 1985 (Reynolds Memorial Award 1987), Nat. Museum of Modern Art, Kyoto 1985, Tepia 1989, Nippon Convention Centre (Makuhari Messe) Stage 1 1989, Stage 2 1998, Tokyo Metropolitan Gymnasium 1990, Keio Univ. Fujisawa Campus 1992, YKK Research and Devt Centre 1993, Center for Arts Yerba Buena Gardens 1993, Isar Buropark 1995, Kaze-No-Oka Crematorium 1996, TV Asahi HQ 2003, Toki Messe 2003, Nat. Inst. for Japanese Language Tachikawa, Tokyo 2004, Sam Fox School of Design and Visual Arts, Washington Univ. 2006, Shimane Museum of Ancient Izumo 2007, Mihara Performing Arts Center 2007, Repub. Polytechnic Singapore 2007, Toyoda Memorial Hall Renovation, Nagoya, Aichi 2007, Univ. of Pennsylvania Annenberg Public Policy Center 2008, Novartis Campus, Basel, Switzerland 2009, MIT Media Lab., Massachusetts, USA 2009, WTC New York 2013, Aga Khan Museum, Toronto 2014, Skyline @ Orchard Boulevard, Singapore 2015, Sea World Culture and Arts Center 2017. *Publications include:* Investigations in Collective Form 1964, Movement Systems in the City 1965, Metabolism 1960, Structure in Art and Science (contrib.) 1965, Miegakuresuru Toshi: A Morphological Analysis of the City of Edo-Tokyo 1979, Kioku no Keisho: A Collection of Essays 1992, Selected Passages on the City and Architecture 2000, Nurturing Dreams: Collected Essays on Architecture and the City 2008. *Address:* 13-4, Hachiyama-cho, Shibuya-ku, Tokyo 150-0035 (office); 16-22, 5-chome Higashi-Gotanda, Shinagawa-ku, Tokyo 141-0022, Japan (home). *Telephone:* (3) 3780-3880 (office). *Fax:* (3) 3780-3881 (office). *E-mail:* fmaki@maki-and-associates.co.jp (office). *Website:* www.maki-and-associates.co.jp (office).

MAKIHARA, Minoru, BA; Japanese business executive; *Senior Corporate Advisor, Mitsubishi Corporation;* b. 12 Jan. 1930, Hampstead, London, England; m. Kikuko Makihara; ed in UK, Japan, Harvard Univ.; joined Mitsubishi Corpn Marine Products Dept 1956–59, London Br. 1959–70, Rep. Mitsubishi Int. Seattle and Washington 1970–80, Gen. Man. Marine Products Dept, Tokyo 1980–87, Pres. Mitsubishi International, New York 1987–90, Sr Man. Dir Mitsubishi Corpn, also Chair. Mitsubishi International 1990–92, apptd Pres. Mitsubishi Corpn 1992, Chair. 1998–2004, now Sr Corp. Advisor; mem. Chair.'s Council, DaimlerChrysler AG (Daimler AG from 2007) 2001–07; mem. Bd of Dirs IBM Corpn 1997–2003, 2004–08, Ayala Corpn 1999–, Shinsei Bank Ltd 2000–, Tokio Marine Holdings Inc. 2002–; mem. Int. Advisory Council, Coca-Cola Co., J.P. Morgan Chase & Co., Inc.; Hon. KBE 2014. *Address:* Mitsubishi Corporation, 6-3, Marunouchi 2-chome, Chiyoda-ku, Tokyo 100-8086, Japan (office).

MAKINE, Andreï, (Gabriel Osmonde); French/Russian writer; b. 10 Sept. 1957, Siberia; s. of Maria Stepanovna Dolina; worked as journalist in Nijni-Novgorod; emigrated from USSR to France 1987, writes in French; Priz de la Fondation Prince Pierre de Monaco 2005, Prix Mondial de la Fondation Simone & Cino del Duca-Institut de France 2014. *Play:* Le Monde selon Gabriel 2007. *Publications include:* fiction: La Fille d'un Héros (trans. as A Hero's Daughter) 1990, Confession d'un Porte-Drapeau Déchu (trans. as Confessions of a Fallen Standard-Bearer) 1992, Au Temps du Fleuve Amour (trans. as Once Upon the River Love) 1994, Le Testament Français (trans. as Dreams of My Russian Summers) (Prix Goncourt, Prix Médicis Étranger, Prix Goncourt des Lycéens, Eeva Joenpelto Prize, Finland) 1995, Le Crime d'Olga Arbelina (trans. as The Crime of Olga Arbelina) 1998, Requiem pour l'Est (trans. as Requiem for a Lost Empire) 2001, La Musique d'un Vie (trans. as A Life's Music) (Prix RTL-Lire) 2001, La Terre et le ciel de Jacques Dorme (trans. as The Earth and Sky of Jacques Dorme) 2003, La Femme qui Attendait (trans. as The Woman Who Waited) (Prix Lanterna Magica 2005) 2004, L'Amour Humain (trans. as Human Love) 2006, La Vie d'un Homme Inconnu (trans. as The Life of an Unknown Man) 2009, Le Livre des brèves amours éternelles (trans. as Brief Loves that Live Forever) 2011, Une Femme Aimée (Prix Casanova 2013) 2012, Le pays du lieutenant Schreiber (Prix Wartburg de Littérature) 2014; non-fiction: St Pétersbourg (with Ferrante Ferranti) 2002, Cette France qu'on oublie d'aimer 2006. *Address:* c/o Editions du Seuil, 25 boulevard Romain Rolland, 75014 Paris, France. *Website:* www.andreimakine .com.

MÄKINEN, Tommi; Finnish entrepreneur and fmr rally driver; b. 26 June 1964, Puuppola, Jyväskylä; s. of Jukka Mäkinen; partner Eliisa Järvelä; two s.; first competed on farm tractors, won jr Finnish nat. ploughing title 1982, 1985, sr title 1992; began rally car racing career in Finnish Championships 1985; Group N Finnish Champion 1988; won Arctic Rally 1989; with Nissan Motorsports Europe Team 1992; with Mitsubishi Ralliart Europe Team 1995–2001 (World Rally Champion 1996, 1997, 1998, 1999), set record for most world championship rally race wins (24 victories 1994–2002); record four consecutive wins at the Monte Carlo Rally –2002; with Subaru World Rally Team 2002–03; five time Rally Finland winner; est. Tommi Mäkinen Racing Oy Ltd 2004. *Leisure interests:* skiing, cycling, trial biking, hunting. *Address:* Tommi Mäkinen Racing Oy Ltd, Tervamaantie 9, 41120 Puuppola, Finland. *Telephone:* (20) 722-9750. *Fax:* (20) 722-9751. *E-mail:* info@tommimakinenracing.fi. *Website:* www.tommimakinen .net.

MAKKAWI, Khalil, PhD; Lebanese diplomatist; *President of the Circle of Lebanese Ambassadors;* b. 15 Jan. 1930, Beirut; s. of Abdel Basset Makkawi and Rosa Makkawi; m. Zahira Sibaei 1958; one s. one d.; ed American Univ. of Beirut, Cairo Univ., Egypt, Columbia Univ., New York, USA; joined Foreign Ministry 1957, served in UN Section 1957–59, Deputy Perm. Rep. to UN, New York 1961–64, First Sec., Embassy in Washington, DC 1964–67, Chief of Int. Relations Dept, Foreign Ministry, Beirut 1967–70, Counsellor, Embassy in London 1970–71, Minister Plenipotentiary, London 1971–73, Amb. to GDR 1973–78, to UK and Repub. of Ireland 1978–83; Dir Political Dept, Foreign Ministry, Beirut, Chair. Preparatory Cttee of Lebanese Nat. Dialogue, mem. Lebanese Security Arrangement Cttee for South of Lebanon 1983–85, Amb. to Italy and Perm. Rep. to FAO 1985–90, Perm. Rep. to UN, New York 1990–94; Vice-Chair. Exec. Bd UNICEF 1993–95, Pres. 1995; Co-Chair. Int. Support Group for mine clearance in Lebanon (representing Ministry of Nat. Defence) 2002–05; fmr Pres. Lebanese-Palestinian Dialogue Cttee, Presidency of the Council of Ministers; Pres. Worldwide Alumni Asscn of American Univ. of Beirut 2005–09, President of the Circle of Lebanese Ambassadors; Chevalier, Nat. Order of the Cedar (Lebanon), Great Cross of Merit (Italy); Pres.'s Medal for Outstanding Voluntary Service, American Univ. of Beirut 2011. *Leisure interests:* music, swimming, reading, walking. *Address:* Bldg Al-Nada, 9th Floor, John Kennedy Street, Ain Mreisseh, Beirut, Lebanon. *Telephone:* (1) 362662; 3-774656 (mobile). *Fax:* (1) 372550. *E-mail:* khalil30@inco.com.lb.

MAKOGON, Yuri Fedorovich, PhD, DSc; Ukrainian physicist and engineer; *Visiting Professor/Research Associate, Texas A&M University;* b. 15 May 1930, Kherson; s. of Feodor Ivanovich Makogon and Efrosinia Dmitrievna Shevchenko; m. Inna Aleksandrovna Makogon 1961; one s. one d.; ed Krasnodar Tech. School, Gubkin Petroleum Inst., Moscow; worked at Shebelinskoe Gas-condensate Field, Ukraine 1956–58; Asst then Asst Prof., Gubkin Oil and Gas, Moscow Inst. 1961–74; Prof., Indian School of Mines, Dhanbad 1965–67, Freiberg Mining Acad., FRG 1967–68; Head, Gas-hydrate Lab., Cen. Gas Research Inst. of the USSR 1974–87; Dir Gas-hydrate Lab., Oil and Gas Research Inst., Russian Acad. of Sciences 1990–95, Hydrocarbon and Environment Inst., Russian Acad. of Natural Sciences 1987–93; Co-founder Russian Acad. of Natural Sciences 1990, first Chair. Oil-Gas Consulate, Chair. Cttee on Data for Science and Tech. and Regional Sec. US Section; Co-founder and first Chair. Russian Section Int. Soc. of Petroleum Engineers (SPE) 1991–93; invited to join Texas A&M Univ., USA 1992, currently Visiting Prof./Research Assoc. and Head of Gas-hydrate Lab., Petroleum Eng Dept; recorded as scientific discoverer of gas hydrates in nature, State Register of USSR 1969; mem. Acad. of Sciences of Ukraine 2010; Hon. Diploma (Mendeleev Union Soc. of Russia) 1982; Dr hc (Nikolayev Inst. of Inorganic Chem., Russian Acad. of Sciences) 2005; Winner's Diploma, Ukraine Republican Inventors' Competition 1958, First Prize, Young Petroleum Scientist Conf. of Russia 1965, First Prize, Chess Tournament of Indian School of Mines 1967, Diploma of the Scientific Discovery Natural Gas Hydrates 1969, Golden Jubilee Medal of Russia 1970, Honour Diploma of Mendeleev Union Soc. Russia 1982, Gubkin State Prize 1989, Golden L. Kapitca Medal for Scientific Discovery 1997, V. Vernadsky Medal of Honour 2000, Albert Einstein Medal of Honour, Russian Acad. of Natural Sciences (US Section) 2002, Distinguished Lecturer Merit of SPE 2002–03, Golden Peter the Great Medal 2004, Hon. Merit in Science and Econs, Russian Acad. of Natural Sciences 2005, Certificate of Lifetime Achievement Awards of Honor, Sixth Int. Gas Hydrate Conf. 2008. *Publications:* eight monographs, 270 papers and 29 patents on gas hydrates. *Leisure interests:* painting, travelling, photography. *Address:* Harold Vance Department of Petroleum Engineering, 3116 TAMU - 721 Richardson Building, Texas A&M University, College Station, TX 77843-3116 (office); 1720 Purple Martin Cove, College Station, TX 77845, USA (home). *Telephone:* (979) 845-4066 (office); (979) 690-8871 (home). *E-mail:* makogon@tamu .edu (office). *Website:* www.pe.tamu.edu (office).

MAKONE, Theresa, BSc; Zimbabwean chemist, business executive and politician; b. 6 Oct. 1952, Mbare; d. of Titus Chigariro; m. Ian Makone; two d. (one deceased); ed Univ. of Rhodesia, Univ. of Nottingham, UK; in exile in UK 1973–78; Devt Chemist, Chibuku Breweries 1978–81; Quality Assurance Dir Sterling Winthrop Pharmaceuticals 1981; fmr Chief Technologist, Cairns Foods, later Research and Devt Man.; est. own beauty clinic and runs several businesses in Harare; mem. Movt for Democratic Change (MDC) 2000–, MDC Br. Treas. in Zviyambe West 2000, Prov. Chair. 2005–07, Chair. MDC Nat. Women's Ass. 2007; MP for Harare North 2009–; Minister of Public Works 2009–10, Co-Minister of Home Affairs 2010–13.

MAKONI, Simba Herbert Stanley, BSc, PhD; Zimbabwean politician; b. 22 March 1950, Makoni; s. of Basil Kamunda and Clara Kamunda (née Matimba); m. Chipo Makoni (née Ususu) 1975; three s.; ed Univ. of Leeds and Leicester Polytechnic, UK; joined Zimbabwe African Nat. Union-Patriotic Front (ZANU-PF); ZANU Chief Rep. to W Europe 1977–80; mem. Nat. Ass. of Zimbabwe 1980–84; Deputy Minister of Agric. 1980; Minister of Industry and Energy Devt 1981–83, of Youth, Sport and Culture 1984, of Finance and Econ. Devt 2000–02; Exec. Sec., Southern African Devt Community 1984–93; Chief Exec. and Man. Dir Zimbabwe Newspapers Ltd, Zimpapers 1994–; Man. Pnr Makonsult Ltd; mem. UN Panel of Advisers on African Devt 1992–94, Inst. of Dirs, Zimbabwe 1994–, Zimbabwe Inst. of Man. 1994–, Council of Reps., South Centre 1994–, Nat. Blood Transfusion

Service 1995–; mem. Nat. Council, Conf. of Zimbabwe Industries (CZI) 1996–, Chair. Econ. Affairs Cttee 1996–; mem. Nat. Econ. Consultative Forum 1998; Patron Nat. Council of Disabled Persons of Zimbabwe 1982–, Zimbabwe Inst. of Motor Industry 1995–; resgnd from ZANU-PF party 2008, ind. cand. for Pres. of Zimbabwe 2008. *Leisure interests:* gardening, reading, squash, health and fitness.

MAKOVETSKY, Sergey Vasilievich; Russian actor; b. 13 June 1958, Kiev, Ukrainian SSR, USSR; ed Moscow Shchukin Theatre School; with Moscow Vakhtangov Theatre 1980–; with Roman Viktyuk Theatre 1990–; Golden Aries Prize for Actor of the Year 1993, Nika Acad. of Cinema Award 1993. *Plays include:* The Master's Lessons, Madame Butterfly, Loika's Flat, Zoya's Apartment (Moscow Theatre Spring Prize 1989). *Films include:* Ekipazh mashiny boevoy (Battle Vehicle Crew) 1983, Polosa prepyatstviy (aka Stripe of Obstacles) 1984, Zaveshchaniye (Testament) 1986, Topinambury (American Artichokes) 1988, Posvyashchyonnyy (Initiated) 1989, Sukiny deti (Sons of Bitches) 1990, Chernov/ Chernov 1990, Rebyonok k noyabryu (A Child by November) 1992, Patrioticheskaya komediya (Patriotic Comedy) 1992, Nash amerikanskiy Borya (Our American Borya) 1992, Prorva (Moscow Parade) 1992, Trotsky 1993, Malenkie chelovechki Bolshevistskogo pereulka, ili Khochu piva (Little People of the Bolshevik Lane, or I Want Beer) 1993, Makarov 1993, Khorovod (Round Dance) 1994, Pyesa dlya passazhira (A Play for a Passenger) 1995, Pribytiye poyezda (The Arrival of a Train) 1995, Letnie lyudi (Country Visitors) 1995, Chyornaya vual (The Black Veil) 1995, Le violon de Rothschild (Rothschild's Violin) 1996, Tri istorii (Three Stories) 1997, Sochineniye ko dnyu pobedy (Composition for Victory Day) 1998, Retro vtroyem 1998, Pro urodov i lyudey (Of Freaks and Men) 1998, Russkiy bunt (The Captain's Daughter) 2000, Brat 1 (The Brother 1) 2000, Brat 2 (The Brother 2) 2000, Mekhanicheskaya syuita 2001, Klyuch ot spalni 2003, Tretiy variant 2003, 72 metra (72 Meters) 2004, Alesha Popovich i Tugarin Zmey (voice) 2004, Zhmurki 2005, Blind Man's Bluff 2005, It Doesn't Hurt Me 2006, Karnavalnaya noch 2, ili 50 let spystya 2007, Nevalyashka 2007, Iskushenie 2007, 12 2007, The Russian Game 2007, Duska 2007, Ilya and the Robber (voice) 2007, Live and Remember 2008, The Priest 2009, The Miracle 2009, Utomlyonnye solntsem 2: Predstoyanie 2010, How Not to Rescue a Princess (voice) 2010, Samyy luchshiy film 3-DE 2011, Utomlennye solntsem 2 2011, The Girl and Death 2012, Eternal Homecoming 2012, Three Heroes on Distant Shores (voice) 2012. *Television includes:* Zhizn Klima Samgina (The Life of Klim Samgin) (series) 1986, Teatr imeni menya (voice) 1994, Operatsiya 'S novym godom' (Operation Happy New Year) 1996, Neudacha Poirot 2002, Gibel imperii (mini-series) 2005, S dnyom rozhdeniya, koroleva! (film) 2006, Nevernost (film) 2006, Liquidation (series) 2007, Isaev (series) 2009, Na solnechnoy storone ulitsy (film) 2011, Petr Pervyy. Zaveshchanie (mini-series) 2011, Delo Gastronoma No. 1 (mini-series) 2011, Utomlennye solntsem 2 (mini-series) 2011, Zhizn i sudba (series) 2012. *Address:* Vakhtangov Theatre, Arbat str. 26, 121007 Moscow, Russia. *Telephone:* (495) 241-01-28.

MAKRAM-EBEID, Mona, PhD; Egyptian professor of political science, international organization official and fmr politician; b. Cairo; grand-d. of Makram Ebeid Pasha; m.; one s.; ed Univ. of Cairo and American Univ. in Cairo, Harvard Univ., USA; Prof. of Political Science and Political Sociology, American Univ. in Cairo 1983–2005, Distinguished Lecturer, Dept of Political Science 2005–; mem. People's Ass. (Parl.) 1990–95, mem. Foreign Affairs and Educ. Cttees; Pres. Parliamentarians for Global Action 1990–95; Founder-mem. Arab Org. for Human Rights; Adviser to World Bank for the Middle East and North Africa Region 1992–96; Founder and Chair. Asscn for the Advancement of Educ., Cairo 1995; apptd Expert to UN Cttee for Policy Devt 2000–03; mem. Shura Council 2012–13 (resgnd); Head of Cttee of Social Rights, Nat. Council on Human Rights; mem. Bd of Dirs British Univ. In Egypt, Jordan German Univ., Amman, Center for Political and Futuristic Studies, Cairo, Citadel Investment, Talal Abu Ghazalah Org.; Consultant to Search for Common Ground, Initiative for Peace and Co-operation in the Middle East, Washington, DC; Exec. mem. Club of Rome, Ibn Khaldum Centre for Developmental Studies, Nat. Centre for Middle Eastern Studies; mem. Int. Consultative Group for the Middle East Center for Strategic and Int. Studies, Washington, DC 1991, UNICEF Women for Devt Cttee, Women for Foreign Policy Group, Washington, DC, The Arab Thought Forum, Amman; Fulbright Scholar 1981, 1983; Fellowship MIT Center for Int. Studies 2016; Chevalier de la Légion d'Honneur 1994, Commdr de la Pléiade, AIPLF (Int. Asscn for French-speaking Parliamentarians) 1995, Officier de la Legion d'Honneur 2008; Woman of the Year, Civil Soc. Review 1994, Distinguished Annual Award for Women, AMADEUS Inst. 2013. *Publications:* many contributions and articles on politics in books, journals and magazines published in English, Arabic and French. *Leisure interests:* tennis, theatre, ballet, swimming. *Address:* Department of Political Science, The American University in Cairo, PO Box 74, New Cairo 11835 (office); Apt 16, 4th Floor, 14 Guezira Street, Zamalek, Cairo, Egypt (home). *Telephone:* (2) 3407603. *Fax:* (2) 2608288. *Website:* www.aucegypt.edu/huss/pols/Pages/default.aspx (office).

MAKTOUM, Sheikh Ahmed bin Saeed al-, BA, FRAeS; United Arab Emirates government official and business executive; *Chairman and CEO, Emirates Airline and Group;* b. 22 Dec. 1958, Abu Dhabi; s. of fmr Ruler of Dubai Sheikh Saeed bin Maktoum al-Maktoum; brother of fmr Ruler of Dubai Sheikh Rashid bin Saeed al-Maktoum and uncle of current Ruler of Dubai Sheikh Muhammad bin Rashid al-Maktoum; ed Univ. of Denver, Colo, USA; Pres. Dubai Civil Aviation Authority 1985–; Chair. Emirates Airline and Group 1985–, later also CEO; also holds several other portfolios with Govt of Dubai, including Second Vice-Chair. Dubai Exec. Council; Chair. Dubai Airports, flydubai, Dubai Supreme Fiscal Cttee, Dept of Oil Affairs, Supreme Council for Energy, Dubai World DW, Econ. Devt Cttee, Dubai Power & Energy Cttee, Dubai Airport Free Zone Authority, Emirates Nat. Bank of Dubai, Noor Investment Group, Noor Takaful, Alliance Insurance Co., The British Univ. in Dubai, Dubai Air Wing, Dubai Aerospace Enterprises, Supreme Cttee– Dubai Events & Promotions Establishment (consisting of Dubai Shopping Festival and Dubai Summer Surprises), Exec. Authority for Expo 2020, Wasl Hospitality; Vice-Chair. Dubai World Trade Centre; mem. Bd of Dirs Investment Corpn of Dubai; mem. Bd Gen. Civil Aviation Authority of UAE, Dubai Council for Econ. Affairs; Patron, Emirates Foundation, Dubai Duty Free Foundation, Rotary Club of Dubai, Dubai Terry Fox Run, Rashid Therapy Centre; Int. Life Vice-Pres. Chelsea Football Club; Commdr, Légion d'honneur, Verfassungsportugaleser (Germany) for outstanding services to the City of Hamburg 2008. *Address:* Emirates, PO Box 686, Dubai, United Arab Emirates (office). *E-mail:* media

.relations@emirates.com (office). *Website:* www.theemiratesgroup.com (office); www.emirates.com (office).

MAKTOUM, HH Hamdan bin Muhammad bin Rashid al-, Crown Prince of Dubai; United Arab Emirates royal and politician; b. 14 Nov. 1982; s. of Sheikh Muhammad bin Rashid al-Maktoum and Sheikha Hind bint Maktoum bin Juma al-Maktoum; ed Rashid Private School, Sandhurst Mil. Acad. and London School of Econs, UK, Dubai School of Govt; Chair. Dubai Exec. Council 2006–; named Crown Prince of Dubai 2008–; Head of Sheikh Muhammad bin Rashid Establishment for Young Business Leaders; Pres. Dubai Sports Council; known for his poems, published under the name Faz'za. *Achievements include:* won gold medal in equestrian event, Asian Games, Doha 2006. *Leisure interests:* horse riding, diving, skydiving, poetry. *Address:* Dubai Executive Council, Emirates Towers Building, 37th Floor, Sheikh Zayed Road, POB 73311, Dubai, United Arab Emirates (office). *Telephone:* (4) 330-2111 (office). *Fax:* (4) 330-3636 (office). *Website:* fazza.ae/en.

MAKTOUM, Sheikh Hamdan bin Rashid al-; United Arab Emirates politician; *Joint Deputy Ruler of Dubai and Minister of Finance and Industry;* b. 25 Dec. 1945; s. of Rashid bin Said al-Maktoum; brother of Sheikh Maktoum Bin Rashid Al Maktoum; Deputy Prime Minister UAE 1971–73, Minister of Finance and Industry 1971–, also Jt Deputy Ruler of Dubai 1995–; Pres. Dubai Municipal Council. *Address:* Ministry of Finance and Industry, PO Box 433, Abu Dhabi, United Arab Emirates. *Telephone:* (2) 6726000 (office). *Fax:* (2) 66663088 (office). *E-mail:* mofi@uae.gov.ae (office).

MAKTOUM, Maktoum bin Muhammad al-, BSc; United Arab Emirates government official; *Joint Deputy Ruler of Dubai;* b. 24 Nov. 1983; s. of Sheikh Muhammad bin Rashid al-Maktoum; ed Rashid School, American Univ. of Dubai; Chair. Dubai Tech. and Media Free Zone Authority (TECOM Investments); Chair. Dubai Media Inc.; Jt Deputy Ruler of Dubai 2008–; Pres. Financial audit Authority 2018–; Vice-Pres. Al-Ahli Club (football club). *Leisure interest:* horse riding. *Address:* Office of the Chairman, Dubai Media Inc., POB 835, Dubai, United Arab Emirates (office). *Telephone:* (4) 336-9999 (office). *E-mail:* info@dmi.ae (office). *Website:* www.dmi.ae (office).

MAKTOUM, Sheikh Muhammad bin Rashid al-; United Arab Emirates politician and race horse owner; *Ruler of Dubai; Vice-President, Prime Minister and Minister of Defence of UAE;* b. 15 July 1948; s. of Rashid bin Said al-Maktoum; m. 1st Sheikha Hind bint Maktoum bin Juma al-Maktoum 1979; 12 c. (one s. deceased); m. 2nd Princess Haya bint al-Hussein 2004; one s. one d.; ed Mons Officer Cadet Training Coll., Sandhurst Coll., Univ. of Cambridge, UK; trained in British army and RAF; Dir of Police and Public Security 1971; Minister of Defence 1972; Crown Prince of Dubai 1990–2006, succeeded his brother, Sheikh Maktoum bin Rashid al-Maktoum, as 6th Sheikh 2006, Vice-Pres. of Dubai 2006–, Prime Minister 2006–, currently also Minister of Defence; with brothers the late Sheikh Maktoum al-Maktoum, Sheikh Hamdan al-Maktoum and Sheikh Ahmed al-Maktoum, has had racing interests in UK 1976–; first winner, Hatta, Goodwood 1977; with brothers owns studs, stables, country houses and sporting estates in Newmarket and elsewhere in UK; worldwide racing interests based at Dalham Hall Stud, Newmarket; horses trained in England, Ireland and France; founder and Dir Godolphin Racing, Dubai 1994; f. Racing Post (daily) 1986; Owner, Balanchine, winner of Irish Derby 1994; winner, numerous classic races; leading owner 1985–89, 1991–93. *Publications:* My Vision: Challenges in the Race for Excellence 2006, 40 Poems from the Desert 2009, Flashes of Thought: Inspired by a dialogue at the Government Summit 2013, Flashes of Thought: Lessons in Life and Leadership from the Man Behind Dubai 2015, Reflections on Happiness & Positivity 2017, My Story 2019. *Address:* Ruler's Palace, Dubai (office); Office of the Prime Minister, POB 12848, Dubai, United Arab Emirates (office); c/o Warren Towers, Newmarket, Suffolk, England (office). *Telephone:* (4) 3534550 (office). *Fax:* (4) 3530111 (office). *Website:* www.sheikhmohammed.co.ae.

MAKUBUYA, (Edward) Khiddu, JSD; Ugandan lawyer, academic and politician; b. 30 July 1949, Bulemezi; m.; ed Makerere Univ., Yale Univ. Law School, USA; advocate, Uganda High Court 1985; Lecturer, Faculty of Law, Makerere Univ. 1979–82, Sr Lecturer 1982–84, Assoc. Prof. 1985–95; mem. Uganda Constitutional Comm., participated in drawing up 1995 draft of Constitution of Repub. of Uganda; mem. Comm. of Inquiry into Violations of Human Rights; Pnr, Kasolo & Khiddu Advocates; MP for Katikamu South, Luwero Dist 1996–; State Minister for Foreign Affairs (Int. Cooperation) 1998–99, Minister of Educ. and Sports 1999–2005, of Justice and Constitutional Affairs and Attorney-Gen. 2005–11, Minister in charge of General Duties, Office of the Prime Minister 2011–12 (resgnd); Ed.-in-Chief, Uganda Law Soc. Review 1984–87; Fellow, Inst. for the Study of Politics, New York, USA.

MAKÚCH, Jozef; Slovak economist, academic and fmr central banker; b. 26 Aug. 1953, Podhájska; m.; three c.; ed Faculty of Nat. Economy, Univ. of Econs, Bratislava; Loan Inspector, Bratislava Br., Czechoslovak State Bank 1976–78; Asst Prof., Dept of Finance, Faculty of Nat. Economy, Univ. of Econs, Bratislava 1978–89, Assoc. Prof. 1989–94, Dean 1991–94; mem. Bd Národná banka Slovenska (Nat. Bank of Slovakia—NBS) 1993–96, 2006–, Exec. Dir Research Section 1994–2000, Exec. Dir NBS 2007–10, Gov. 2010–19; Chair. Financial Market Authority (FMA) 2000–02, Chair. Bd of Dirs FMA 2002–05; Rep. of Slovakia in Cttee of European Securities Regulators; Rep. in Int. Asscn of Insurance Supervisors; mem. Governing Council of European Cen. Bank 2010–; Gov. IMF 2010–; Alt. Gov. EBRD 2010–; mem. Academic Council of Faculty of Nat. Economy, Univ. of Econs, Bratislava; mem. Editorial Bd BIATEC, Účtovníctvo, audítorstvo, danovníctvo (Accounting, Auditing, Taxation), scientific periodical of Faculty of Finance, Matej Bel Univ. *Publications include:* numerous textbooks, monographs, research papers and articles, published in Slovakia and abroad. *Address:* c/o Národná banka Slovenska, Imricha Karvaša 1, 813 25 Bratislava, Slovakia (office).

MAKUZA, Bernard, LLB; Rwandan politician and fmr diplomatist; *President of the Senate;* b. 30 Sept. 1961, Butare; m.; fmr mem. Mouvement démocratique républicain (dissolved); fmr Amb. to Burundi, Amb. to Germany –2000; Prime Minister of Rwanda 2000–11; mem. Senate for Southern Prov. 2011–, Vice-Pres. of Senate 2011–14, Pres. 2014–; Ind. *Address:* Office of the President of the Senate, PO Box 6729, Kigali, Rwanda (office). *Telephone:* 252594506 (office); 0788-302311 (mobile). *Fax:* 252594583 (office). *E-mail:* bernard.makuza@parliament.gov.rw (office). *Website:* www.parliament.gov.rw/senate (office).

MALAJ, Arben; Albanian economist and politician; b. 19 Sept. 1961; m. Raimonda Malaj; one c.; ed Univ. of Tirana; began career with Nat. Commercial Bank of Albania, Vlora; Dir Foundation of SME-s, Tirana –1997; apptd Assoc. Prof. of Econ. Sciences, Univ. of Tirana 1997; mem. Kuvendi Popullor (Parl.) for Kelmendi Dist (Socialist Party) 1997–; Minister of Finance and Gov. of Albania to the World Bank 1997–98; Chief of Parl. Comm. for the Economy and Econ. Table of the Stability Pact 1998–2000; Chief of Parl. Group of the Socialist Party 2000–02; Minister of Economy 2002–04, of Finance 2004–05; lecturer in numerous academic insts including Univ. of Bocconi, Italy, Univ. of Tetova, Macedonia, Univ. of Pristina, Kosova; mem. Int. Acad. of Emerging Markets, New York, USA. *Publications:* author or co-author of several publications and scientific articles. *Address:* Kuvendi Popullor (People's Assembly), Bulevardi Dëshmorët e Kombit 4, Tirana, Albania (office). *Telephone:* (4) 2264887 (office). *Fax:* (4) 2221764 (office). *E-mail:* kontakto@arben-malaj.com.

MALAN, Pedro, PhD; Brazilian economist; *Chairman, Unibanco SA;* b. 19 Feb. 1943, Rio de Janeiro; s. of Elysio S. Malan and Regina S. Malan; m. 1st Ana María Toledo Piza Rudge; m. 2nd Catarina Gontijo Souza Lima 1980; two s. one d.; ed St Ignatius School, Rio de Janeiro, Polytechnic School of Catholic Univ. of Rio de Janeiro, School of Econs and Univ. of California, Berkeley; with Inst. of Applied Research, Brazilian Ministry of Planning 1966–69, 1973–83; Faculty of Econs, Catholic Univ. of Rio de Janeiro Jan.–Dec. 1979; Head Int. Trade and Finance Section, Inst. of Applied Econ. Research 1980–83; Dir Policy Analysis and Research Div. Centre of Transnat. Corpns, UN, New York 1983–84, Dept of Int. Econs and Social Affairs 1985–86; Exec. Dir World Bank, Washington, DC 1986–90; Exec. Dir Inter-American Devt Bank 1990–92; Pres. Cen. Bank of Brazil 1993–94; Minister of Finance 1994–2002; Vice-Chair. Bd of Dirs, Unibanco SA 2003–04, Chair. 2004–; Fed. of São Paulo Industries Prize for book External Economic Policy and Industrialization in Brazil 1980, Légion d'honneur 1996, Order of Mil. Merit 1998, Order of Naval Merit 1998. *Publications:* The Structure of Protection in Brazil (with J. Bergsman) 1971, The Brazilian Economy in the 1970s: Old and New Developments (with R. Bonelli) 1977, Brazilian External Debt and its Implications 1978, Financial Integration with the World Economy, The Brazilian Case 1983, Structural Models of Inflation and Balance of Payments Disequilibria in Semi-Industrialized Economies (with John R. Wells) 1984, Relações Econômicas Internacionais do Brasil no Período 1945–64 1984, Debt, Trade and Development: The Crucial Years Ahead 1985. *Leisure interests:* literature, classical music, diplomatic and financial history, swimming, tennis. *Address:* Unibanco Holdings SA, Avenida Eusébio Matoso 891, 22nd Floor, 05423-901 São Paolo, Brazil (office). *Telephone:* (11) 3047-1313 (office). *Fax:* (11) 3813-6182 (office). *Website:* www.unibanco.com.br (office).

MALAN, Wynand Charl, BA, LLB; South African politician, attorney, consultant and business executive; b. 25 May 1943, Port Elizabeth; s. of Dawid Johannes Malan and Annie Malan (née de Swardt); m. Judith Rousseau 1967 (died 2011); two s. one d.; ed Linden Hoërskool, Johannesburg and Univ. of Pretoria; grew up in Johannesburg; attorney and Partner, van Wyk de Vries, Malan & Steyn, Johannesburg 1966–67, Leader Nat. Jeugbond, Transvaal 1972–74; mem. Rapportraad 1971–73, Nat. Chair. 1974–76; Randburg Town Councillor and Chair. Man. Cttee 1977; Nat. Party MP for Randburg 1977–87, Ind. MP for Randburg 1987–88, Democratic Party MP for Randburg 1989–90; fmr Leader Nat. Democratic Movt; fmr Co-Leader Democratic Party; mem. The Truth and Reconciliation Comm. 1994–2002, Vice-Chair. 1994; CEO Thebe Securities Ltd 2002–05; strategy consultant, pvt. practice 2006–; Eisenhower Fellowship 1980; ASPU Newsmaker of the Year Award 1987. *Leisure interests:* golf, chess, numismatics, clivia propagation. *Address:* PO Box 2075, Randburg 2125, South Africa (office). *Telephone:* (11) 7820119 (office). *Fax:* (11) 7820119 (office). *E-mail:* wcmalan@mweb.co.za (office).

MALANJI, Joseph; Zambian business executive and politician; *Minister of Foreign Affairs;* b. 28 Aug. 1965; m.; Chair. Nat. Exec. Cttee for Land and Natural Resources 2011; mem. Nat. Ass. (parl.) for Kwacha (PF) 2016–; Minister of Foreign Affairs 2018–; fmr Chair. MMD Copperbelt Taskforce; Pres. African Golf Confed. 2013–; fmr mem. Movt for Multiparty Democracy (MMD); mem. Patriotic Front (PF). *Leisure interest:* golf. *Address:* Ministry of Foreign Affairs, POB RW50069, Lusaka, Zambia (office). *Telephone:* (21) 1252718 (office). *Fax:* (21) 1222440 (office). *E-mail:* foreignlsk@zamnet.zm (office). *Website:* www.foreignaffairs.gov.zm (office).

MALASHENKO, Igor Yevgenyevich, PhD; Russian journalist; b. 2 Oct. 1954, Moscow; m. Yelena Pivovarova; two d.; ed Moscow State Univ.; jr, sr researcher, Inst. for US and Canadian Studies, USSR Acad. of Sciences 1980–89, research in problems of the concept of nuclear deterrence and public opinion; staff-mem. Int. Div. Cen. Cttee CPSU, admin. of Pres. Gorbachev March–Dec. 1991; Political Dir TV & Radio Co. Ostankino 1992–93; Co-founder, Pres. and Dir-Gen. Ind. TV Co. NTV 1993, Pres. NTV-Telemost Holding 1998; First Deputy Chair. Bd of Dirs Media-Most Co. 1998–2001; Adviser to Pres. of Russia on public relations problems, mem. election campaign staff of Boris Yeltsin 1996; Russian Union of Journalists Prize 1994. *Leisure interests:* golf, photography.

MALAURIE, Jean, PhD; French anthropogeographer and writer; *Director Emeritus, Centre d'études arctiques (EHESS-CNRS);* b. 22 Dec. 1922, Mainz, Germany; s. of Albert Malaurie and Isabelle (Regnault) Malaurie; m. Monique Laporte 1951; one s. one d.; ed Lycée Condorcet, Faculté des Lettres de Paris, Inst. of Geography Univ. of Paris; Attaché then Research Fellow, CNRS 1948–56; mem. Nat. Comm. on Geography 1955–67, 1980–82; Prof. of Arctic Geomorphology and Anthropogeography, Ecole des Hautes Etudes en Sciences Sociales (EHESS), Paris 1957–, Founder and Dir Centre for Arctic Studies, EHESS-CNRS 1957, Dir Arctic Research, CNRS 1979–91, Dir Emer. EHESS–CNRS 1992–; Pres. Fondation Française d'études nordiques 1964–75, Soc. Arctique Française 1981–90; Founder and Dir Terre Humaine anthropological book series 1955–; Founder, Dir Inter-Nord int. journal of Arctic studies 1961 (21 vols); Chair. and organizer 14 int. Arctic confs and seminars; made 9 documentary films on the Inuit; led 31 Arctic scientific expeditions; first explorer to reach North geomagnetic pole by dog-sledge 29 May 1951; Chair. Cttee for the Defence of Arctic Minorities in Russia, Foundation for Culture, Moscow 1990–; Dir Acad. of Human Sciences of Russia 1997–; UNESCO Goodwill Amb. in charge of Arctic Polar issues 2007–; Pres. Uummannaq Polar Inst. (Greenland) 2009–; Hon. Pres. Fonds Polaire Jean Malaurie, Bibliothèque centrale, Nat. Museum of Natural History, Paris 1992–, State Polar Acad., St Petersburg 1994–; Hon. Dean Northern People's State Univ. Herzen, St Petersburg 1992 (and Gold Medal); Hon. Prof., Hautes études commerciales de Paris 2005; Commdr, Légion d'honneur, Ordre nat. du mérite, Ordre des Arts et Lettres, Order of the Dannebrog (Denmark) 2007; Hon. PhD (State Univ., St Petersburg) 2001; Dr hc (State Univ. of NY) 2007; Award of Acad. française 1968, Polar Medal, Soc. de Géographie, Paris 1953, 1961, Acad. des sciences Award 1967, Gold Medal, Soc. arctique française 1990, CNRS Medal 1992, Gold Medal, Soc. de Géographie Paris 1996, Grand Prix de la Ville de Paris 1999 Grand Prix Jules Verne 2000, Gold Medal of St Petersburg 2003, Patron's Gold Medal, Royal Geographical Soc., London 2005, Mungo Park Medal, Royal Scottish Geographical Soc. 2005, Gold Medal of Greenland 'Nersornaat' 2009, Gold Medal of Strasbourg 2013. *Films:* Les Derniers Rois de Thulé 1969, 2002, Inuit from Greenland to Siberia (seven films) 1980, Haïnak Inuit 1993, La Saga des Inuit (four films) 2007. *Music:* Chants et tambours inuit. De Thulé au Détroit de Béring 1987, Jean Malaurie. De la pierre à l'homme 2004. *Publications include:* Hoggar 1954, Les Derniers Rois de Thulé (translated into 22 languages) 1955, Thèmes de recherche géomorphologique dans le nord-ouest du Groenland 1968 (second edn 2012), Ultima Thulé (second edn) 1990, Hummocks (second edn) 1999, L'appel du nord 2001, L'allée des baleines (second edn) 2003, Ot Kaminya K Tcheloveky 2003, Uummaa 2013. *Address:* Centre d'études arctiques (EHESS-CNRS), 27 rue Damesme, bureau 511, 75013 Paris, France (office). *E-mail:* jean.malaurie@ehess.fr (office). *Website:* www.jean-malaurie.fr.

MALCHÁREK, Jirko; Slovak politician and fmr racing driver; b. 28 June 1966, Jeseník, Czechoslovakia (now part of Czech Repub.); widowed; one s.; ed Secondary School of Mechanical Eng, Bratislava, Slovak Tech. Univ., Bratislava; raced for 11 years, including occasional forays into int. racing, including FIA GT Championship, test driver for Minardi 2002; Co-founder BECEP (safety org.); Asst Dir Bratislava Transport Co. 1989–91; Office of Govt Commr for Automotive Industry and Conversion of Special Production 1991; Man. Dir VSŽ Selecta Praha, Slovak br. 1993–98; Founder and Head of operational leasing co., Slovakia 1995–98; mem. (Strana občianskeho porozumenia—Party of Civic Understanding 1998–2002, for Alliance of the New Citizen 2002–05) Nat. Council of Slovak Repub. (Parl.) 1998–2005; left Alliance of the New Citizen and joined Nádej (Hope) 2005; Deputy Prime Minister and Minister of the Economy 2005–06.

MALCOLM, James Ian (Jim), OBE; British diplomatist (retd); b. 29 March 1946; s. of William Kenneth Malcolm and Jennie Malcolm; m. Sheila Nicholson Moore 1967; one s. one d.; ed Royal High School, Edinburgh; entered British Diplomatic Service in 1966, Attaché, UK Del. to NATO, Brussels 1969–72, Attaché, Embassy in Rangoon, Burma (Union of Myanmar) 1972–74, Third Sec., FCO, London 1974–77, Commercial Attaché, British High Comm., Nairobi, Kenya 1977–80, Consul, British Embassy, Damascus, Syria 1980–83, Second Sec. (Commercial), Embassy in Angola 1983–85, First Sec., FCO (dealing with Counter-Terrorism issues) 1985–87, First Sec. (Political/Econ.), Embassy in Jakarta, Indonesia 1987–94, First Sec., FCO (Head of BBC World Service Section) 1994–97, Deputy High Commr in Kingston, Jamaica and British Trade Commr to Cayman Islands 1997–2001, Amb. to Panama 2002–06 (retd). *Leisure interests:* reading and researching British history in Indonesia, Jamaica and Panama, playing golf, riding motorcycles, photography.

MALCOLM, Steven J., BCE; American energy industry executive; b. Sept. 1948, St Louis, Mo.; m. Gwen Malcolm; one d.; ed Univ. of Missouri-Rolla, Northwestern Univ.; began career in refining, marketing and transportation depts, Cities Gas Co.; joined Williams Cos Inc. 1984, Dir of Business Devt, Williams Natural Gas Co. 1984–86, Dir of Gas Man. 1986–89, Vice-Pres. of Gas Man. and Supply 1989–93, Sr Vice-Pres. and Gen. Man. Mid-Continent Region, Williams Field Services 1993–94, Sr Vice-Pres. and Gen. Man. Gathering and Processing 1994–96, Sr Vice-Pres. and Gen. Man. Midstream Gas and Liquids, Williams Energy Services 1996–98, Pres. and CEO Williams Energy Services 1998–2001, apptd Dir The Williams Cos Inc. 2001, Pres. and COO 2001–02, Pres. and CEO 2002–03, Chair., Pres. and CEO 2002–10; mem. Bd Tusla Area United Way, Tusla Community Foundation, YMCA, St John Medical Center, Boy Scouts of America Indian Nations Council; mem. Univ. of Tusla Advancement and Athletics Cttees, YMCA Exec. Cttee; mem. Business Roundtable, Cttee to Encourage Corp. Philanthropy, Nat. Petroleum Council; fmr mem. Nat. Energy Services Asscn.

MALCOMSON, James Martin, MA, PhD, FBA; British economist and academic; b. 23 June 1946, Staunton-on-Wye, Herefords., England; s. of E. Watlock Malcomson and Madeline Malcomson (née Stuart); m. Sally Claire Richards 1979; one d. (deceased); ed Gonville and Caius Coll., Univ. of Cambridge, Harvard Univ., USA; Research Fellow, Lecturer, Sr Lecturer, Univ. of York 1971–85; Prof. of Econs, Univ. of Southampton 1985–98; Prof. of Econs, Univ. of Oxford 1999–2013, Fellow, All Souls Coll. 1999–2013, Fellow Emer. 2013–; Fellow, Econometric Soc. 2005. *Publications:* numerous articles in scientific journals. *Leisure interests:* walking, music, film, theatre. *Address:* All Souls College, Oxford, OX1 4AL, England (office). *Telephone:* (1865) 618106 (office). *Fax:* (1865) 279299 (office). *E-mail:* james.malcomson@economics.ox.ac.uk (office).

MALCORRA, Susana Mabel; Argentine engineer, politician and fmr UN official; b. 1954; m.; one s.; ed Univ. of Rosario; grad. trainee with IBM, eventually becoming Dir of Public Sector, later assigned to IBM's corp. HQ in USA resp. for relations between HQ and Mexico and the Andean region of Latin America –1993; various admin. positions with Telecom Argentina 1993–2003, COO and Exec. Dir 1995–2001, CEO 2001–02; co-f. Vectis Management 2002; Deputy Exec. Dir (Admin) WFP 2004–07 (led initial phase of operational response to tsunami emergency Dec. 2004), Deputy Exec. Dir and COO Jan.–March 2008, Under-Sec.-Gen. and Head of Dept of Field Support, UN 2008–12, Chef de Cabinet to Sec.-Gen. 2012–15; Minister of Foreign Affairs 2015–17; Founding mem. Argentine chapter, Int. Women's Forum; mem. Advisory Bd of Business School of Univ. of San Andres, Buenos Aires, Advisory Bd of Equidad.

MALDONADO AGUIRRE, Alejandro Baltazar; Guatemalan judge, politician, acting head of state and fmr diplomatist; b. 6 Jan. 1936, Guatemala City; m. Ana Fagianni de Maldonado; one s.; ed San Carlos Univ.; mem. Council, Guatemala City 1956; mem. Congreso de la República (Parl., Nat. Liberation Movt) 1966–70; Minister of Educ. 1970–74; Amb. and Perm. Rep. to UN, New York 1974–76, to UN, Geneva 1978–80; Deputy, Nat. Constituent Ass. 1984–86; Judge, Constitutional Court 1986–91, 1996–2001, 2006–11 (Pres. 1989–91, 1997–98, 2006–07); Amb. to Mexico 1991–95; Minister of of Foreign Affairs 1995–96; mem. Congreso de la República (Partido Unionista) 2004–06; Vice-Pres. of Guatemala May–Sept. 2015, Acting Pres. Sept. 2015–Jan. 2016; mem. Democracia Cristiana Guatemalteca 1980–2001, Partido Unionista 2001–08; Ind. 2008–.

MALECELA, Cigwiyemisi John Samwel, BCom; Tanzanian politician and diplomatist; b. 1934, Dodoma; m. Ezerina Mwaipopo; one s. three d.; ed Minaki Secondary School, Bombay Univ., India and Univ. of Cambridge, UK; Admin. Officer, Civil Service 1960–61; Consul in USA and Third Sec. to the UN 1962; Regional Commr, Mwanza Region 1963; Amb. and Perm. Rep. to the UN, New York 1964–68; Amb. to Ethiopia 1968; E African Minister for Communications, Research and Social Services, E African Community 1969–72; Minister of Foreign Affairs 1972–75, of Agric. 1975–80, of Mines 1980–81, of Transport and Communications 1982–85; Regional Commr, Iringa 1987–89; High Commr to UK 1989–90; MP for Mtera 1990–2010; Prime Minister and First Vice-Pres. of Tanzania 1990–94; Minister without Portfolio 1995; Vice-Chair. Chama Cha Mapinduzi Party 1995–2007; Vice-Chair. Desert Locust Control Org. for East Africa; mem. Group of Eminent Persons of the Commonwealth on the South African situation 1985; Order of Merit of First Degree (Egypt), First Order of Independence (Equatorial Guinea); Hon. PhD (Univ. of Texas) 1977. *Leisure interests:* reading, sports.

MALEENONT, Vichai; Thai business executive; *Chairman and CEO, BEC World Public Co. Ltd;* b. 1918; m.; seven c.; co-f. BEC World Public Co. Ltd (media group) 1970, currently Chair. and CEO. *Address:* BEC World Public Co. Ltd, 3199 Maleenont Tower, Rama 4 Rd, Klongton, Klongtoey, Bangkok 10110, Thailand (office). *Telephone:* (2) 204-3333 (office). *Fax:* (2) 204-1384 (office). *E-mail:* ir@becworld.com (office). *Website:* www.becworld.com (office).

MALEIANE, Adriano Afonso, BSc, MSc, Dip.Acc; Mozambican politician and fmr banking executive; *Minister of the Economy and Finance;* ed Univ. Eduardo Mondlane, Instituto Comercial de Maputo, SOAS, Univ. of London, UK; fmr Nat. Dir for Agrarian Economy in Ministry of Agric.; Vice-Gov. Banco de Moçambique (central bank) 1990–91, Gov. 1991–2006; fmr CEO Banco Nacional de Investimento (BNI); fmr CEO MaleFinanceiro, MaleSeguros; Minister of Economy and Finance 2015–; fmr lecturer, Univ. Eduardo Mondlane; fmr Chair. (non-exec.) Visabeira; Dir (non-exec.) Tongaat Hulett Ltd 2009. *Address:* Ministry of the Economy and Finance, Praça da Marinha Popular, CP 272, Maputo, Mozambique (office). *Telephone:* 21315000 (office). *Fax:* 21306261 (office). *Website:* www.mf.gov.mz (office).

MALEK, Rami Said, BFA; American actor; b. 21 May 1981, Los Angeles; ed Univ. of Evansville; started acting career with supporting roles in films and TV; achieved critical acclaim for portraying Freddie Mercury in the biopic Bohemian Rhapsody; voice acting for TV and video games; Young Alumnus Award, Univ. of Evansville 2017. *Films include:* Night at the Museum 2006, Night at the Museum: Battle of the Smithsonian 2009, Larry Crowne 2011, Battleship 2012, Ain't Them Bodies Saints 2013, Short Term 12 2013, Oldboy 2013, Need for Speed 2014, Da Sweet Blood of Jesus 2014, Night at the Museum: Secret of the Tomb 2014, Buster's Mal Heart 2016, Papillon 2017, Bohemian Rhapsody (numerous leading actor awards including Academy Award, Golden Globe Award, BAFTA Film Award, Screen Actors Guild Award—all 2019) 2018. *Television includes:* series: The War at Home 2005–07, The Pacific (mini series) 2010, Mr. Robot (Primetime Emmy Award for Outstanding Lead Actor in a Drama Series 2016, Critics Choice TV Award for Best Actor in a Drama Series 2016) 2015–19, BoJack Horseman 2017–18.

MALENCHENKO, Col Yuri Ivanovich; Russian/Ukrainian cosmonaut; b. 22 Dec. 1961, Svetlovodsk, Kirovograd Oblast, Ukrainian SSR, USSR; m.; one s.; ed Kharkov Higher Mil. Aviation School, Zukovsky Mil. Aviation Eng Acad.; army service 1979–; Col, Russian Air Force; mil. pilot of 3rd class, flew more than 800 hours in fighters; served as a pilot, sr pilot and multi-ship flight lead in Odessa Region 1983–87, selected as a cosmonaut at Yu. A. Gagarin Research and Test Cosmonaut Training Centre 1987, underwent general space training 1987–89, qualified as a test-cosmonaut; took advanced training courses in preparation for spaceflight 1989–93; trained as Commdr of Mir-14 reserve crew Jan.–July 1993, completed training as a backup Commdr of Mir-15 crew 1993–94; trained for Mir-16 mission Feb.–June 1994; participant in flight to space station Mir Aug.–Sept. 1994; cosmonaut-explorer 1995–; missions include Soyuz TM-19, Mir EO-16, STS-106, Soyuz TMA-2, Expedition 7, Soyuz TMA-11, Expedition 16, Soyuz TMA-05M, Expedition 32, Expedition 33; carried out first and second career spacewalks during Mir-16 mission 9 and 14 Sept. 1994, third spacewalk during STS-106 mission to Int. Space Station (ISS) 11 Sept. 2000, fourth spacewalk 9 Nov. 2007, fifth spacewalk 20 Aug. 2012; became first person to marry in space when he married Ekaterina Dmitrieva, who was in Texas, while he was 240 miles over NZ on ISS 10 Aug. 2003; retired as cosmonaut 27 July 2009, return to the cosmonaut corps Feb. 2010; Hero of the Russian Fed., Nat. Hero of Kazakhstan Medal, Mil. Award of Excellence, Commendation Medal, Achievement Medal, Jubilee Medal '70 Years of the Armed Forces of the USSR', Meritorious Service Medals 1st, 2nd and 3rd Class. *Leisure interests:* sports and games, music, hunting. *Address:* Yu. A. Gagarin Research and Test Cosmonaut Training Centre, Star City, Moscow Region 141160, Russia. *Telephone:* (495) 526-34-07. *Fax:* (495) 526-26-12. *E-mail:* info@gctc.ru (home). *Website:* www.gctc.su.

MÄLER, Karl-Göran, PhD; Swedish economist and academic; b. 3 March 1939, Sollefteå; s. of Karl Markus Mäler and Henny Kristina Mäler; m. Sara Aniyar; two d.; ed Stockholm Univ.; Prof. of Econs, Stockholm School of Econs 1975–2002, then Prof. Emer.; Dir Beijer Int. Inst. of Ecological Econs, Royal Swedish Acad. of Sciences 1991–2006; Founding mem. European Asscn of Environmental and Resource Economists (EAERE); Co-organizer Ecological and Environmental Econs Research and Training Activity at Int. Centre for Theoretical Physics, Trieste, Italy; Dr hc (Haifa); Volvo Environment Prize 2002, EAERE European Lifetime Achievement Award in Environmental Econs (co-recipient) 2005, Older Linné Medal in Gold, Royal Swedish Acad. of Science. *Publications:* Environmental Economics: A Theoretical Inquiry 1974, Priskompensation Och Planeringsosakerhet I Forsvaret: Utredning Utford Pa Uppdrag Av 1978 ars Forsvarskommitte (co-author) 1981, Environmental Decision Making (co-author) 1984, Environment and Development: An Economic Approach (co-author) 1992, Economic Science, 1981–1990: The Sveriges Riksband (ed.) 1992, Poverty, Institutions, and the Environmental-Resource Base (co-author) 1994, Current Issues in Environmental Economics (co-ed.) 1995, Rights to Nature: Ecological, Economic, Cultural, and Political Principles of Institutions for the Environment (co-ed.) 1996, Biodiversity Loss: Economic and Ecological Issues (co-ed.) 1997, The Economics of Transnational Commons (co-ed.) 1997, The Environment and Emerging Development Issues (co-ed.) 2001, The Economics of Non-Convex Ecosystems (co-ed.) 2004. *Leisure interest:* bird watching.

MALER, Leopoldo Mario, LLB, JD; Argentine artist and art foundation executive; b. 2 April 1937, Buenos Aires; s. of Abraham Maler and Esther Kraiselburd; m. 1st Silvia Oclander 1967; m. 2nd Joyce Pieck 1973 (divorced 1979); m. 3rd María Rosa Baquero 1988 (divorced 2003); one s.; ed New School for Social Research, New York, Univ. of Buenos Aires, Univ. Coll., London, UK, Int. Faculty of Comparative Law, Strasbourg, France (scholarship); worked for BBC World Service in the production of art and educ. programmes 1961–64; conducted a series of radio programmes on the theatre, Municipal Radio, Buenos Aires 1964–67; made TV programmes for Cen. Office of Information and radio programmes on arts and music for BBC World Service and BBC Radio 1 and 2, London 1967–74; conducted a four-hour daily radio show on current affairs and the arts, Radio Belgrano Network (23 radio stations), Buenos Aires 1974–75; consultant and producer for Latin American Radio Service of UN Dept of Public Information 1980–83; Co-founder Centre for Research and Studies of Latin American Art (CIEDAL), Santo Domingo, Dominican Repub. 1986; Co-founder and Admin. Dir, Design Center for Global Needs, San Francisco State Univ.; Ed. NACA Journal, Dept of Industry and Design 1988–93; Co-ordinator, Domus Acad. courses, Centro Cultural Borges, Buenos Aires 1997–99; Guest Lecturer, Architectural Asscn, London 1975; Lecturer, Leeds Polytechnic 1975, Hornsey Coll. of Art, London 1975; External Examiner Prof., Middlesex Polytechnic, London 1979–81; Guest Lecturer, Art Dept, Univ. of Iowa 1982, Univ. of Sydney 1982; Prof., Art Psychology, Parsons School of Design, Dominican Repub. 1983–85, First Dean, Parsons School of Design (Altos de Chavón/La Escuela de Diseño) 1983–85; Guest Lecturer, Universidad del Este, Dominican Repub. 1984, Miami Dade Community Coll., Miami, Fla 1985, Art Dept, Sonoma State Univ., Calif. 1991, San Francisco Art Inst., Calif. 1992, Dept of Arts Practice, Univ. of California, Berkeley 1993, School of Fine Arts, Lamentin, Guadeloupe 1995, Univ. of Puerto Rico 1996, Santa Fe Art Inst., NM 1998, School of Fine Arts of Puerto Rico 2004; Dir Milan's Domus Acad. programme at Centro Cultural Borges, Buenos Aires 1997, 1999; Condecoracion Orden al Merito Artistico (Spain) 1992; Special Jury Prize, Leipzig Film Festival 1964, First Grand Prize, Int. Biennale of Art, São Paulo, Brazil 1977, Guggenheim Fellowship 1977, Special Jury Mention, Argentina 78, Buenos Aires 1978, General Motors Prize, First Biennale of Sports in the Arts, Montevideo, Argentina 1980, Premio Konex, Buenos Aires 1982, Gandhi Award for Social Communications, Buenos Aires 1983, Arawak Prize for the Best Foreign Art Show, Santo Domingo 1986, Medal from Mayor of Lamentin, Guadaloupe 1994, Gran Premio, competition for a monument at Universidad de San Juan, Puerto Rico 1996. *Works include:* monumental sculpture commissioned by IOC for the Olympic Park, Seoul, South Korea 1988; monumental sculpture commissioned by the City of Madrid to celebrate its designation as Cultural Capital of Europe, Parque Juan Carlos I 1992; Madona and Child, monumental sculpture entitled commissioned by the local French authorities of the island of Guadeloupe 1994; La Conciencia Empirica, monumental sculpture for the Botanical Gardens commissioned by the Universidad de San Juan 1996; monumental sculpture commissioned for Suwon (Folk Village), South Korea, celebrating the Football World Cup 2002; monumental sculpture commissioned for the city of Santo Tirso, Porto, Portugal 2003. *Works in public collections:* BEST Collection, Camara Municipal de Santo Tirso, Portugal, Hara Museum, Tokyo, Hess Collection, Napa, Calif., Jaragua Hotel Collection, Santo Domingo, Museum of Contemporary Art, Puerto Rico, Parque Ferial Juan Carlos I, Madrid, Seoul Olympic Park Collection, Seoul, Tamayo Museum, Mexico, Univ. of Puerto Rico, Victoria & Albert Museum, London, Watari Collection, Tokyo. *Ballets:* Ultrazoom (multimedia ballet, visual co-ordinator), Instituto Torcuato di Tella, Buenos Aires 1965, Wrote and directed Caperucita Rota, a scripted happening for a narrator and 14 Dancers, Centro de Experimentacion Audiovisual, Instituto Torcuato Di Tella, Buenos Aires 1966, X-IT (programme of six choreographic works with 14 dancers, fork-lift trucks and inflatable objects), The Place, London 1969. *Performance art:* Outrage, in commemoration of The Sharpville massacre, The Round House, London 1969, X-IT 2, a programme of choreographic works at The Place, London 1969, Playback 625, a play co-written with N. F. Simpson and directed at the Royal Court Theatre, London 1970, Crane Ballet, a ballet for three cranes and three acrobats, Camden Festival of Music, London 1971, Popol Vuh, a choreographic work, The Place, London 1972, Carnem et Cyclum (a medium rare event), Great Georges, Liverpool, UK 1972, Son et Lumière, Cathedral of Cuernavaca, Mexico 1978, Jurisdiction, Palazzo Grassi, Venice 1979, Three Easy Pieces, performance and video installations, Center Georges Pompidou, Paris 1979, 25HP, Trinity College, Dublin 1980, Fuoco-Forma-Forno, Vennice Biennale, Piazza San Marco and Furnace Segusso, Murano 1980, Pre-Esenciia, performance-installation, Palazzo Reale, Milan 1980, Dance Performance, Goldsmith Coll., London, from a workshop conducted by Merce Cunningham and John Cage 1980, From Amaru to Barthes, co-created with Marta Minujin at the bullfight ring of La Macarena, Medellin, Colombia 1981, You See I Eat, Gallery Watari, Tokyo 1982, Shadows and Exhumations, Hara Museum, Tokyo 1982, H2Ombre, Center for Inter-American Relations, New York 1982, Echoes and Reflection, installation, The Center for Inter-American Relations, New York 1982, Bookabulary, choreographic work and a monumental sculpture commissioned for Miami's International Book Fair 1985, Visiones del Bilinguismo, Center for Latin-American Arts and Studies, Miami 1985, Fifteen Weightless Answers, Voluntariado de las Casas Reales, Santo Domingo 1986, BA BE BI. . .linguism. . ., American-Dominican Cultural Center, Santo Domingo 1988, We bring food, in collaboration with Marta Minujin, Museum of Contemporary Art, Los Angeles 1998, Metrobolism, in celebration of the first centenary of the Univ. of Puerto Rico 2004. *Film:* Men in Silence (Best Short Film, London Film Festival) 1964. *Leisure interests:* scuba-diving, psychology, sailing, horseback riding, music. *Address:* c/o Nohra Haime Gallery, 730 Fifth Avenue, Suite 701, New York, NY 10019, USA; Apdo Postal 25320, Santo Domingo, Dominican Republic. *Telephone:* (212) 888-3550 (New York); (809) 696-0072 (Santo Domingo). *E-mail:* gallery@nohrahaimegallery.com; nohrahaime@aol.com. *Website:* www.nohrahaimegallery.com.

MALESKI, Denko, PhD; Macedonian diplomatist and professor of law; *Professor of Law, University of Saints Cyril and Methodius;* b. 14 Nov. 1946, Skopje; s. of Vlado Maleski and Maria Alivantova; m. Miriana Ivanskova 1970; three d.; ed Univs of London, Skopje and Ljubljana; Prof. of Int. Politics, Univ. of Sts Cyril and Methodius, Skopje 1981–91, currently Prof. of Law; Visiting Prof. (Fulbright Scholar), Bowling Green State Univ., Ohio, USA 1990; Minister of Foreign Affairs 1991–93; Amb. and Perm. Rep. to UN, New York 1993–97; Borjan Tanevski Foundation Award 2005. *Publications:* Contemporary Political Systems 1986, International Politics 2000, The Worlds of Thucydidies and Machiavelli 2001; numerous articles on democracy, political systems and int. relations. *Leisure interests:* reading, jogging. *Address:* University of Cyril & Methodius, PO Box 576, Bulevar Krste Misirkov b.b., 1000 Skopje, North Macedonia.

MALEWEZI, Rt Hon. Justin Chimera, BA; Malawi teacher, educational administrator and politician; b. 23 Dec. 1944, Ntchisi; s. of Canon John Julius Malewezi and Bartlet Rachel Malewezi; m. Felicity Rozina Chizalema 1970; two s. two d.; ed Columbia Univ., New York, USA; secondary school teacher 1967–69, headmaster 1969–74, educ. admin. 1974–78; mem. Nat. Ass., for Ntchisi North East; Deputy Sec., Ministry of Finance and Prin. Sec. in various ministries 1978–89; Head of Civil Service 1989–91; Vice-Pres. of Malawi 1994–99, 1999–2003; unsuccessful cand. during presidential election 2004; fmr mem. United Democratic Front (UDF), currently mem. People's Progressive Movement (PPM). *Leisure interests:* tennis, football. *Address:* PO Box 30086, Lilongwe 3, Malawi (home). *Telephone:* 1773566 (office).

MALHAS, Omar Zuhair Abdelfattah, BBA, MBA; Jordanian banking executive and politician; b. 30 March 1960, Al Salt; m.; three s.; ed Univ. of Louisiana, USA, Univ. of Birmingham, UK; with Audit Dept, Housing Bank for Trade & Finance 1984–85, Foreign Relations Dept 1985–86, Head of Foreign Relations and Investment Dept 1987–88, Head of Investment Dept 1988–90, Dir, Treasury Dept 1995–97, Dir, Int. Investment Centre 1997–98, Exec. Dir, Dept of Foreign Affairs and Investment 2002–04, Gen. Man., Housing Bank 2010–15; Sr Man., Alliance Capital Corpn, USA/Bahrain office 2000–02; Minister of Finance 2015–18; mem. Bd of Dirs Electricity Distribution Co. 2011–15, CEO 2015; Vice-Chair. Bd of Dirs Kingdom Investment Group 2013–15; mem. Jordanian Inst. of Banking Studies, Asscn of Banks in Jordan.

MALHOTRA, Manish; Indian fashion designer; b. 5 Dec. 1966, Mumbai (then Bombay); ed Elphinstone Coll., Mumbai; early career as a model; joined Equinox (boutique) 1989; designer, Reverie 1998–; designed team gear for Indian Premier League's Kolkata Knightriders; host The Manish Malhotra Show (TV talk show) 2005–; German Public Bollywood Award, Stylish Designer Of the Year, Elle Style Awards 1999, Indira Priyadarshini Memorial Award, Int. Indian Film Acad. (IIFA) Award 2000, IIFA Award and Designer of the Year Award 2002, Rajiv Gandhi Award, IIFA Award for Best Costume Designing 2017. *Films as costume designer include:* Dilwale Dulhaniya Le Jayenge 1995, Rangeela (Filmfare Award 1996) 1995, Khamoshi: The Musical 1996, Raja Hindustani (Showtime Opinion Poll Award 1998) 1997, Dil To Pagal Hai (Siemen's Viewer's Choice Award 1998) 1997, Kuch Kuch Hota Hai 1998, Dil Kya Kare 1999, Mohabbatein 2000, Kabhi Khushi Kabhie Gham 2001, Kal Ho Naa Ho 2003, Main Hoon Na 2004, Maine Pyaar Kyun Kiya 2005, Fanaa 2006, Kabhi Alvida Naa Kehna 2006, Sivaji: The Boss 2007, Om Shanti Om 2007, U Me Aur Hum 2008, Blue 2009, 3 Idiots 2009, My Name is Khan 2010, Robot 2010, Anjaana Anjaani 2010, Bodyguard 2011, Agneepath 2012, Student Of The Year 2012, Chennai Express 2013, 2 States 2014, Ae Dil Hai Mushkil 2016, Mom 2017, Judwaa 2 2017. *Leisure interests:* music, movies. *Address:* Shop 4/5 Vishnudham CHS, Corner of 14th Road, Linking Road, Khar (W), Mumbai 400 052, Maharashtra, India (office). *Telephone:* (22) 26050723 (office); 9987719978 (mobile) (office). *Fax:* (22) 26050724 (office). *Website:* www.manishmalhotra.in.

MALHOUTRA, Manmohan (Moni), MA; Indian international official and consultant; *Trustee, Indira Gandhi Memorial Trust and Jawaharlal Nehru Memorial Fund;* b. 15 Sept. 1937, Izatnagar; s. of Col Gopal Das Malhoutra and Shukla Malhoutra; m. Leela Nath 1963; two d.; ed Delhi Univ., Balliol Coll., Oxford, UK; entered Indian Admin. Service 1961; mem. Prime Minister's Secr. 1966–73; joined Commonwealth Secr. 1974; Dir Sec.-Gen.'s Office and Int. Affairs Div. 1977–82, Asst Commonwealth Sec.-Gen. 1982–93; Conf. Sec. to Commonwealth Heads of Govt Meetings, London 1977, Lusaka 1979, Melbourne 1981, also at Asia-Pacific Regional Heads of Govt Meetings; led Commonwealth Secr. team in Observer Group at pre-independence elections in Zimbabwe 1980; elections in Uganda 1980; Sec. Commonwealth Southern Africa Cttee; Head of Secr. of Commonwealth Group of Eminent Persons on South Africa 1986; Chef de Cabinet, Commonwealth Sec.-Gen.'s Office 1982–90, Head, Commonwealth Secr. Human Resource Devt Group 1983–93; mem. Bd of Dirs Int. Inst. for Democracy and Electoral Assistance, Stockholm 1996–2003; Sec.-Gen. Rajiv Gandhi Foundation, New Delhi 2001–07; mem. UK-India Round Table 2004–13; Trustee, Indira Gandhi Memorial Trust, Jawaharlal Nehru Memorial Fund, Ambuja Cement Foundation, Unltd. India Trust; Al Merito Civil, Spain 2007; Rhodes Scholar 1958. *Publications:* New Century: Whose Century (ed.) 2000, First Proof (contrib.) 2004, India: The Next Decade (ed.) 2006, Social Democracy in India 2011. *Leisure interests:* reading, music, theatre, travel. *Address:* 118 Golf Links, New Delhi 110 003, India. *Telephone:* (11) 24643630; 98688 50075 (mobile). *E-mail:* monimalhoutra@googlemail.com.

MALI, Siniša, MA, MBA, PhD; Serbian economist and politician; *Minister of Finance;* b. 25 Aug. 1972, Belgrade, SFR Yugoslavia; two s. one d.; ed Univ. of Belgrade Faculty of Econs, of Organizational Sciences, Washington Univ., St Louis; worked at Deloitte & Touche, Belgrade 1995–97, in Prague 1999–2001; Asst Minister of Privatization 2001; Dir Tender Privatization Centre, Privatization Agency of Repub. of Serbia 2001–03; apptd Adviser for Economy to First Deputy Prime Minister Aleksandar Vučić 2012; Pres. Temporary Council of Belgrade 2013; Mayor of Belgrade 2014–18; mem. Presidency, Serbian Progressive Party 2017; Minister of Finance 2018–; fmr Chair., Fiat Automobili Srbija, Komercijalna banka, Air Serbia; mem., CFA Inst., Serbian Business Angels Network, Fulbright Alumni Asscn of Serbia, British-Serbian Business Club. *Address:* Ministry of

Finance, 11000 Belgrade, Kneza Miloša 20, Serbia (office). *Telephone:* (11) 3642656 (office). *Fax:* (11) 3642828 (office). *E-mail:* kabinet@mfin.gov.rs (office). *Website:* www.mfin.gov.rs (office).

MALICK, Terrence; American film director, writer and film producer; b. 30 Nov. 1943, Ottawa, Ill.; s. of Emil Malick and Irene Malick (née Thompson); ed Harvard Univ., Magdalen Coll., Oxford, UK (Rhodes Scholar), Center for Advanced Film Studies, American Film Inst.; taught philosophy at MIT; worked as journalist for Newsweek, Life, The New Yorker; f. Sycamore Pictures LLC (production co.); Prof. of Film, European Graduate School, Switzerland. *Films directed and written include:* Badlands (also producer) 1973, Days of Heaven 1978 (New York Film Critics Award, Nat. Soc. of Film Critics Award, Cannes Film Festival Award), The Thin Red Line (Golden Berlin Bear Award 1999, Chicago Film Critics Asscn Award 1999, Golden Satellite Award 1999) 1998, The New World (also producer) 2005, The Unforeseen (exec. producer) 2007, Tree of Life (Palme D'Or, Cannes Film Festival 2011), To the Wonder 2012, Red Wing (exec. producer) 2013, The Better Angels (producer) 2014, Knight of Cups 2015, Crocodile Gennadiy (exec. producer) 2015. *Address:* Sycamore Pictures LLC, 6010 Wilshire Blvd, Suite 402, Los Angeles, CA 90036, USA (office). *Telephone:* (323) 938-1785 (office). *E-mail:* info@sycamorepictures.com (office). *Website:* www.sycamorepictures.com (office).

MALIELEGAOI, Tuila'epa Sailele, BCom, MCom; Samoan economist and politician; *Prime Minister and Minister of Foreign Affairs and Trade;* b. 14 April 1945, Lepa; m. Gillian Muriel Malielegaoi; eight c.; ed Univ. of Auckland; early career working for European Economic Community and Coopers & Lybrand; mem. Legis. Ass. (Parl.) for Lepa Dist 1980–; Leader Human Rights Protection Party 1998–; Prime Minister of Samoa 1998–, also Minister of Foreign Affairs and Trade 2014–, of Finance 2014–16; fmr Deputy Prime Minister and Minister of Finance, Trade, Industry and Commerce and Tourism; f. Apia West Rugby; currently Chair. Samoa Rugby Union. *Address:* Prime Minister's Department, PO Box L 1861, Apia, Samoa (office). *Telephone:* 63222 (office). *Fax:* 26322 (office). *E-mail:* presssecretariat@samoa.ws (office). *Website:* www.samoagovt.ws (office).

MALIK, Art; British (b. Pakistani) actor; b. (Athar-Ul-Haque Malik), 13 Nov. 1952, Bahawalpur, Pakistan; m. Gina Rowe; two d.; ed Guildhall School of Music and Drama, London. *Television:* The Jewel in the Crown, Chessgame, The Far Pavilions, The Black Tower, Death is Part of the Process, After the War, Shadow of the Cobra, Stolen, Cleopatra 1999, In the Beginning 2000, The Seventh Scroll 2001, Holby City (series) 2003–05, The English Harem 2005, The Path to 9/11 2006, The Nativity (mini-series) 2010, Upstairs Downstairs (series) 2010–12, Borgia (series) 2011–14, Homeland (series) 2014, Indian Summers (mini-series) 2016. *Films:* Richard's Things, A Passage to India, Underworld, Living Daylights, Side Streets, City of Joy 1992, Wimbledon Poisoner 1994, True Lies 1994, A Kid in King Arthur's Court 1995, Path to Paradise 1997, Booty Call 1997, Side Streets 1998, Tabloid 2001, Out Done 2002, Tempo 2003, Fakers 2004, Nina's Heavenly Delights 2006, Dean Spanley 2008, Franklyn 2008, Hotel 2009, The Wolfman 2010, Ghosted 2011, John Carter 2012, Diana 2013, Bhaag Milkha Bhaag 2013. *Theatre:* Othello (RSC), Cymbeline and Great Expectations (Royal Exchange, Manchester). *Address:* c/o United Agents, 12-26 Lexington Street, London, W1F 0LE, England (office).

MALIK, Gunwantsingh Jaswantsingh, BSc, MA; Indian diplomatist; b. 29 May 1921, Karachi; s. of Jaswant Singh Malik and Balwant Kaur Malik (née Bhagat); m. Gurkirat Kaur 1948 (divorced 1982); two s.; ed Downing Coll., Cambridge, UK, Gujrat Coll., Ahmedabad; RAF 1943–46; Indian Foreign Service 1947–79, Second Sec., Indian Embassy, Brussels 1948–50, Addis Ababa 1950; Under-Sec. Ministry of External Affairs 1950–52; First Sec. and Chargé d'affaires Argentina 1952–56; in Japan 1956–59; Counsellor (Commercial) and Asst Commr Singapore 1959–63; Dir Ministry of Commerce 1963–64; Jt-Sec. Ministry of External Affairs 1964–65; Amb. to Philippines 1965–68, to Senegal, concurrently to Côte d'Ivoire, Mauritania, The Gambia and Upper Volta 1968–70, to Chile (also Accred to Peru, Ecuador and Colombia) 1970–74, to Thailand 1974–77, to Spain 1977–79; Leader trade del. to S. America 1964; mem. del. to ECAFE 1965, to Group of 77 in Lima 1971, to Gov. Body of UNDP 1971, to UNCTAD III 1972, to ESCAP 1975; Chair. Tech. and Drafting Cttee, ESCAP 1976; Deputy Chair. Cttee of the Whole 1977; Dir Indian Shaving Products 1986–88; Sec. Asscn Indian Diplomats 1983–84, 1989–91, Vice-Pres. 1985–86, Pres. 1986–87; Vice-Chair. Delhi Chapter Soc. for Int. Devt 1985–89; Chair. Ahluwalia Baradi Trusts 1988–93; Vice-Pres. Alliance Française de Delhi 1990–98, Pres. 2000–02; Chair. Maharani Voyages Pvt. Ltd 1995–2004. *Publications:* books: A Sikh Diplomat 2008, Susan's Tiger 2010; numerous literary, political and economic articles. *Leisure interests:* photography, writing, touring. *Address:* C224 Defence Colony, New Delhi 110 024, India (home). *Telephone:* (11) 40793410 (home). *Fax:* (11) 41550379 (home).

MALIK, Iftikhar Ali, BA; Pakistani business executive; *CEO, Guard Group of Companies;* b. 30 Dec. 1944, Lahore; s. of Muhammad Shafi Malik and Mumtaz Begum; m.; two s.; ed FC Coll., Lahore; currently Owner and CEO Guard Group of Companies (autofilter, brake lining and brake oil mfrs); Chair. Pakistan Automobile Spare Parts Importers and Dealers Asscn 1985–86; mem. Exec. Cttee Lahore Chamber of Commerce and Industry 1980, Pres. 1990; Vice-Pres. and Zonal Chair. Fed. of Pakistan Chambers of Commerce and Industry 1994–97, Pres. and Life Mem. 2001–02; Life mem. SAARC Chamber of Commerce and Industry (currently Vice-Chair.), Indo-Pak Chamber of Commerce and Industry; mem. Man. Cttee, ECO Chamber of Commerce and Industry; Chair. Punjab Olympic Asscn; Vice-Chair. Mumtaz Bakhtawar Trust Hosps, Pakistan Olympic Asscn; Special Lifetime mem. Confed. of Asia Pacific Chambers of Commerce and Industry; Hon. mem. Islamic Chamber of Commerce and Industry. *Address:* Guard Group of Companies, 80 Badami Bagh, PO Box 465, Lahore (office); 57-FCC, Gulberg III, Lahore, Pakistan (home). *Telephone:* (42) 7725616 (office); (42) 5757996 (home). *Fax:* (42) 7722627 (office). *E-mail:* guard@brain.net.pk (office).

MALIK, Moazzam, BA, MPhil; British accountant, civil servant and diplomatist; *Ambassador to Indonesia;* b. London, England; m.; three c.; ed London School of Econs, Univ. of Oxford, Chartered Diploma in Accounting and Finance from ACCA; has worked as a consultant economist advising large UK corp. clients and the World Bank, amongst others; fmr researcher at LSE and Overseas Devt Inst.; adviser on monetary and foreign exchange policy to Cen. Bank of Uganda; ran a production eng business and an urban regeneration non-governmental org. based in London; Prin. Pvt. Sec. to Baroness Valerie Amos and then to Rt Hon. Hilary Benn MP, Sec. of State for Int. Devt, Dept for Int. Devt (DFID), also managed DFID programmes in Pakistan, Iraq and on trade policy 2003–05, led work on UK White Paper on int. devt 'Making Governance Work for the Poor' 2006, DFID Dir for UN, Conflict and Humanitarian Issues 2006–10, DFID Dir for Western Asia and Stabilization 2010–13, Acting Dir Gen., DFID –2014, Amb. to Indonesia (also accred to Timor Leste and to ASEAN, Jakarta) 2014–; fmr mem. Advisory Bd to UK All Party Parl. Group on Conflict, UN Sec.-Gen.'s Advisory Group on Cen. Emergency Revolving Fund; served as an OECD DAC Peer Reviewer for Sweden; Trustee, Goodweave UK. *Leisure interests:* reading novels, watching films and theatre, following football (Liverpool Football Club) and cricket, cooking South Asian food, playing golf (badly). *Address:* British Embassy, Jalan Patra Kuningan Raya, Blok L5-6, Jakarta 12950, Indonesia (office). *Telephone:* (21) 23565200 (office). *Fax:* (21) 23565351 (office). *E-mail:* jakarta.mcs@fco.gov.uk (office). *Website:* www.gov.uk/government/world/organisations/british-embassy-jakarta (office); www.gov.uk/government/world/indonesia (office).

MALIK, Muneer A., BS, JD, CPA; Pakistani laywer and fmr government official; *Senior Partner, MCA Law Associates;* b. 8 April 1950, Karachi; m.; one s. one d.; ed San Jose State Univ. and Santa Clara Univ., USA; passed the California Bar exam 1974; CPA, State of Calif., USA 1975; Pres., Karachi Bar Asscn 1986, Sindh High Court Bar Asscn 2002–03, Supreme Court Bar Asscn 2006–07; mem. Pakistan Bar Council 1990–95; Leader of Lawyers' Movt in Pakistan; mem. of legal defence team of Chief Justice Iftikhar Muhammad Chaudhry when the latter was dismissed by Gen. Pervez Musharraf; arrested following declaration of a state of emergency by Musharraf and kept in confinement at Attock jail 2007; Attorney-Gen. of Pakistan 2013–14; currently Sr Partner, MCA Law Associates; mem. Law and Justice Comm. of Pakistan 2012–14; Dorab Patel Rule of Law Award, Human Rights Comm. of Pakistan, Human Rights Defender Award, Asian Human Rights Comm. (co-recipient), Gwangju Prize for Human Rights 2008. *Publication:* The Pakistan Lawyers Movement – An Unfinished Agenda 2011. *Address:* MCA Law Associates, 14-C, 21st Street, Off Kh-e-Seher, Phase 6, DHA, Karachi 75600, Pakistan (office). *Telephone:* (21) 35171183 (office). *Fax:* (21) 5873223 (office). *E-mail:* muneermalik@hotmail.com (home); muneermalik@mcalaw.com.pk (office). *Website:* www.paklaw.com (office); mcalaw.com.pk (office).

MALIK, Satya Pal, BSc, LLB; Indian agriculturalist and politician; *Governor of Jammu and Kashmir;* b. 25 Dec. 1946, Baghpat Dist, Uttar Pradesh; m. Iqbal Malik; ed Meerut Univ.; fmr mem. Uttar Pradesh Legis. Ass.; mem. Rajya Sabha (upper house of parl.) for Uttar Pradesh 1980–89; mem. Lok Sabha (lower house of parl.) for Aligarh (Janata Dal) 1989–91; Union Minister of State for Parl. Affairs and Tourism April–Nov. 1990; Gov. of Bihar Sept. 2017–Aug. 2018, also of Odisha March–May 2018, of Jammu and Kashmir Aug. 2018–; mem. Bharatiya Janata Party (BJP). *Address:* Raj Bhawan, Srinagar, Kashmir 190001, India (office). *Telephone:* (191) 2544989 (office). *E-mail:* rakesh.jamwal@nic.in (office). *Website:* jkrajbhawan.nic.in (office).

MALIK, Shoaib; Pakistani professional cricketer; b. 1 Feb. 1982, Sialkot, Punjab; m. 1st Ayesha Siddiqui 2008 (divorced 2010); m. 2nd Sania Mirza 2010; all-rounder; right-handed batsman; right-arm off-break bowler; played for Gujranwala Cricket Asscn 1997–99, Pakistan Int. Airlines 1998–, Pakistan Reserves 1999–2000, Pakistan 1999– (Capt. 2007–09), Sialkot Cricket Asscn 2001–07, Glos. 2003–04, Sialkot Stallions 2004–07, Delhi Daredevils 2008, Barbados Tridents 2013–17, Hobart Hurricanes 2013–14, Karachi Kings 2016–17, Multan Sultans 2018–, Guyana Amazon Warriors 2018–, Asia XI; First-class debut: 1997/98; Test debut: Pakistan v Bangladesh, Multan 29–31 Aug. 2001; One-Day Int. (ODI) debut: Pakistan v West Indies, Sharjah 14 Oct. 1999; T20I debut: England v Pakistan, Bristol 28 Aug. 2006; played 35 Tests (till Nov. 2015), scored 1,898 runs (average 35.14) and took 32 wickets (average 47.46) with 1 double hundred, 3 hundreds and 8 fifties, highest score 245 against England, Abu Dhabi 2015, best bowling 4/33 against England, Sharjah 2015; played 271 ODIs (till Sept. 2018), scored 7,226 runs (average 35.59) and took 156 wickets (average 39.11) with 9 hundreds and 43 fifties, highest score 143 against India, Colombo 2004, best bowling 4/19 against Hong Kong, Colombo 2004; played 103 T20Is (till July 2018), scored 2,121 runs (average 32.13) and took 28 wickets (average 22.57) with 7 fifties, highest score 75 against England, Sharjah 2015, best bowling 2/7 against Bangladesh, Dhaka 2011; played 126 First-class matches (till Sept. 2017), scored 6,559 runs (average 37.26) and took 260 wickets (average 28.61) with 17 hundreds and 30 fifties, and 9 five-wickets haul, highest score 245, best bowling 7/81; fined Rs2m (£15,900) and banned for 12 months by Pakistan Cricket Bd from int. cricket following tour of Australia March 2010, ban overturned two months later; retd from Test cricket Nov. 2015; ranked second in ICC (Int. Cricket Council) ODI all-rounder rankings June 2008. *Address:* c/o Pakistan Cricket Board, Gaddafi Stadium, Lahore 54600, Pakistan. *Telephone:* (42) 571-7231. *Fax:* (42) 571-1860. *E-mail:* info@pcboard.com.pk. *Website:* www.pcboard.com.pk/home.html.

MALIKI, Nuri Kamal (Jawad) al-; Iraqi politician; b. (Nouri Kamel al-Maliki), 20 June 1950, Hindiya; m.; four c.; ed Baghdad Univ.; official of Dawa party, fled Iraq to Syria 1980; returned to Iraq as one of Dawa leaders serving as spokesman and adviser to Dawa leader and Iraq interim Prime Minister Ibrahim al-Jaafari 2003; helped draft new constitution; mem. cttee tasked to purge Iraq Baathist legacy; Prime Minister of Iraq 2006–14, also acting Minister of Defence and of the Interior 2010–14; Vice-Pres. of Iraq 2014–15.

MALIKI, Riyad Najib al-, PhD; Palestinian politician; *Minister of Foreign Affairs and Expatriates;* b. 31 May 1955, Bethlehem; ed American Univ.; Prof., Coll. of Eng, Bir Zeit Univ. 1981–96; Founder and Dir-Gen. Panorama, the Palestinian Centre for the Dissemination of Democracy & Community Devt 1991–2007; Minister of of Information 2007–09, of Foreign Affairs and Expatriates 2007–12, 2012–; Coordinator Arab Program to Support and Develop Democracy; Chair. Bd of Dirs, Palestinian Int. Cooperation Agency (PICA) 2016–; mem. Exec. Bd Pugwash (Conf. on Int. Affairs, Science and Nobel Peace Prize) 1995–, World Movt for Democracy 1997–; columnist, Al-Ayyam (weekly newspaper); European Peace Prize 2000, Democracy Courage Award, South Africa 2004, Italian Peace Prize 2005. *Address:* Ministry of Foreign Affairs, POB 1336, Ramallah, Palestinian Territories (office). *Telephone:* (2) 2943140 (office). *Fax:* (2) 2943165 (office). *E-mail:* media@mofa.pna.ps (office). *Website:* www.mofa.pna.ps (office).

MALINGA, Separamadu Lasith, (Separamadu Lasith Malinga Swarnajith); Sri Lankan professional cricketer; b. 28 Aug. 1983, Galle; ed Devapathiraja Coll., Mahinda Coll., Galle; right-arm fast pace bowler; right-handed batsman; specialist fast bowler with a rare round-arm action, plays for Galle Cricket Club 2001–04, Nondescripts Cricket Club 2004–, Sri Lanka (Vice-Capt. T20I team) 2004–, Kent 2007, Mumbai Indians 2008–17, Tasmania 2009–11, Ruhuna Royals 2012, Melbourne Stars 2012–14, Dhaka Gladiators 2013, Rangpur Riders 2017–, BCCSL Acad. XI, Ruhuna; First-class debut: 2001/02; Test debut: Australia v Sri Lanka, Darwin 1–3 July 2004; One-Day Int. (ODI) debut: Sri Lanka v UAE, Dambulla 17 July 2004; T20I debut: England v Sri Lanka, Southampton 15 June 2006; played in 30 Tests (to Aug. 2018), scored 275 runs and took 101 wickets (average 33.15) with three five-wicket performances, best bowling of 5/50 against India in Galle 2010; played in 210 ODIs (to Oct. 2018), scored 506 runs and took 311 wickets (average 28.71) with eight five-wicket performances, best bowling of 6/38 against Kenya in Colombo 2011; played 68 T20Is (to Sept. 2017), scored 73 runs and took 90 wickets (average 19.77), with one five-wicket performance, best bowling of 5/31 against England in Pallekele 2012; played 84 First-class matches (to Dec. 2017), scored 585 runs and took 257 wickets (average 30.28) with seven five-wicket performances, best bowling of 6/17; retd from Test cricket April 2011. *Achievements include:* became first ever player in int. cricket history to take four wickets in four consecutive balls, against S Africa during Cricket World Cup (also only the fifth hat-trick in World Cup history, the third ODI hat-trick for Sri Lanka and the 24th in all ODI history) 28 March 2007; only bowler with two Cricket World Cup hat tricks, against S Africa 2007, against Kenya 2011; with Angelo Mathews, holds highest run partnership for the 9th wicket in an ODI (132 runs), against Australia in Melbourne 2010. *Address:* Sri Lanka Cricket, 35, Maitland Place, Colombo 07000, Sri Lanka (office). *Telephone:* (11) 26816014. *Fax:* (11) 4722236 (office). *E-mail:* info@srilankacricket.lk (office).

MALINI, Hema; Indian actress, film director, dancer and politician; b. (Hema Malini Chakravarty), 16 Oct. 1948, Ammankudi, Tiruchirappalli district, Tamil Nadu; d. of V.S. Ramanujam Chakravarthy and Jaya Chakravarthy; m. Dharmendra 1980; two c.; ed Andhra Mahila Sabha, Chennai; trained as Bharatanatyam dance artist; film actress 1965–; mem. Bharatiya Janata Party (BJP) 2003–09, Gen. Sec. 2010–; MP (BJP) for Karnataka, Rajya Sabha 2011–; Owner, Natya Vihar Kalakendra dance school; Chair., Nat. Film Devt Corpn 2000–03; Padma Shri 2000; Filmfare Lifetime Achievement Award 2000, SaMapa Vitasta Award 2006. *Television:* Jai Mata Ki 2003, Noopur. *Films include:* as actress: Pandava Vanavasam 1965, Sapno Ka Saudagar 1968, Waris 1969, Jahan Pyar Mile 1969, Tum Haseen Main Jawaan 1970, Sharafat 1970, Abhinetri 1970, Aansoo Aur Muskan 1970, Johny Mera Naam 1970, Sri Krishna Vijayam 1971, Paraya Dhan 1971, Naya Zamana 1971, Lal Patthar 1971, Andaz 1971, Tere Mere Sapne 1971, Seeta Aur Geeta (Filmfare Award for Best Actress 1972) 1972, Raja Jani 1972, Gora Aur Kala 1972, Garam Masala 1972, Bhai Ho To Aisa 1972, Babul Ki Galiyaan 1972, Shareef Budmaash 1973, Prem Parvat 1973, Chhupa Rustam 1973, Gehri Chaal 1973, Jugnu 1973, Joshila 1973, Dulhan 1974, Amir Garib 1974, Dost 1974, Prem Nagar 1974, Kasauti 1974, Patthar Aur Payal 1974, Haath Ki Safai 1974, Sunehra Sansar 1975, Sanyasi 1975, Kahte Hain Mujhko Raja 1975, Do Thug 1975, Dharmatma 1975, Khushboo 1975, Pratigya 1975, Sholay 1975, Sharafat Chod Di Maine 1976, Naach Uthe Sansaar 1976, Maa 1976, Charas 1976, Aap Beati 1976, Dus Numbri 1976, Mehbooba 1976, Jaaneman 1976, Shirdi Ke Sai Baba 1977, Kinara 1977, Khel Khilari Ka 1977, Dream Girl 1977, Dhoop Chhaon 1977, Chacha Bhatija 1977, Palkon Ki Chhaon Mein 1977, Dillagi 1978, Azaad 1978, Apna Khoon 1978, Trishul 1978, Ratnadeep 1979, Janta Hawaldar 1979, Dil Kaa Heera 1979, Meera 1979, Hum Tere Aashiq Hain 1979, The Burning Train 1980, Bandish 1980, Do Aur Do Paanch 1980, Alibaba Aur 40 Chor 1980, Maan Gaye Ustad 1981, Jyothi 1981, Dard 1981, Aas Paas 1981, Krodhi 1981, Kranti 1981, Naseeb 1981, Kudrat 1981, Meri Aawaz Suno 1981, Samraat 1982, Farz Aur Kanoon 1982, Do Dishayen 1982, Bhagawat 1982, Satte Pe Satta 1982, Suraag 1982, Rajput 1982, Desh Premee 1982, Meharbaani 1982, Taqdeer 1983, Razia Sultan 1983, Andha Kanoon 1983, Nastik 1983, Justice Chaudhury 1983, Sharara 1984, Ram Tera Desh 1984, Raaj Tilak 1984, Qaidi 1984, Ek Naya Itihas 1984, Ek Nai Paheli 1984, Phaansi Ke Baad 1985, Durga 1985, Aandhi-Toofan 1985, Ramkali 1985, Yudh 1985, Hum Dono 1985, Babu 1985, Ek Chadar Maili Si 1986, Sitapur Ki Geeta 1987, Hirasat 1987, Apne Apne 1987, Anjaam 1987, Jaan Hatheli Pe 1987, Kudrat Ka Kanoon 1987, Vijay 1988, Mulzim 1988, Mohabbat Ke Dushman 1988, Rihaee 1988, Galiyon Ka Badshah 1989, Deshwasi 1989, Sachche Ka Bol-Bala 1989, Santosh 1989, Desh Ke Dushman 1989, Paap Ka Ant 1989, Lekin... 1990, Jamai Raja 1991, Hai Meri Jaan 1991, Vivekananda 1994, Param Vir Chakra 1995, Aatank 1996, Maahir 1996, Himalay Putra 1997, Hey Ram 2000, Censor 2001, Aman Ke Farishtey 2003, Baghban 2003, Veer-Zaara 2004, Bhagmati 2005, Ganga 2006, Baabul 2006, Laaga Chunari Mein Daag 2007, Gangotri 2007, Sadiyaan 2010, Bbuddah... Hoga Terra Baap 2011, Aarakshan 2011; as dir: Dil Aashna Hai 1992, Tell Me O Khuda 2011. *Address:* 17th Jai Hind Society, 12th Road, JBPD Scheme, Mumbai 49 (office); C-302, Swarna Jayanti Sadan, New Delhi 110 001, India. *Telephone:* (22) 28402716 (Mumbai); (22) 28493319 (Mumbai); (11) 23739900 (New Delhi). *Fax:* (22) 28493320 (Mumbai). *E-mail:* hhemammalini@gmail.com.

MALJERS, Floris Anton; Dutch business executive; b. 12 Aug. 1933, Middelburg; m. J. H. de Jongh 1958; two s. one d. (deceased); ed Univ. of Amsterdam; joined Unilever 1959, Man. Dir Unilever, Colombia 1964, Unilever, Turkey 1966, Man. Dir Vdberg & Jurgens, Netherlands 1970, mem. Parent Bd of Unilever and Head of Man. Edible Fats Group 1974, Chair. Unilever NV 1984–94, Vice-Chair. Unilever PLC 1984; Chair. Supervisory Bd Philips, Electronics NV 1994; mem. Bd of Dirs Amoco 1994–98, ABN/Amro Bank, KLM, Royal Dutch Airlines, Philips Electronics, Guinness 1994–98; Gov. European Policy Forum 1993; Chair. Bd of Trustees, Utrecht Univ. Hosp. 1994, Rotterdam School of Man., Erasmus Univ. 1999 (now Prof. Emer.); Chair. Turkije Instituut (Turkey Inst.); Hon. KBE 1992. *Address:* Turkije Instituut (Turkey Institute), Doelensteeg 16, 2311 VL Leiden, Netherlands. *Telephone:* (71) 527-2541. *E-mail:* sprangerslily@gmail.com; info@turkije-instituut.nl. *Website:* www.turkije-instituut.nl.

MÄLK, Raul; Estonian diplomatist, economist and fmr journalist; *Special Diplomatic Representative for the Baltic Sea Region;* b. 14 May 1952, Parnu; ed Tartu Univ., Leningrad Inst. of Political Studies; economist and researcher, Inst. of Econs, Estonian Acad. of Sciences 1975–77; Sr Ed., Deputy Ed.-in-Chief, Ed.-in-Chief Estonian Radio 1977–90; Deputy Head Office of Chair. Supreme Soviet of Estonia 1990–92; Adviser to Minister of Foreign Affairs 1992–93; Head Office of Minister of Foreign Affairs 1993–94; Deputy Perm. Under-Sec. Ministry of Foreign Affairs 1994–96; Amb. to UK 1996–2001, also accred to Ireland 1996–2003 and to Portugal 2000–03; Minister of Foreign Affairs 1998–99; Head Estonian dels for negotiations with Russia, Finland, Latvia 1994–96; Dir-Gen. Policy Planning Dept, Ministry of Foreign Affairs 2001–07; Perm. Rep. of Estonia to EU 2007–11, Special Diplomatic Rep. for the Baltic Sea Region, Ministry of Foreign Affairs 2011–; Order of the White Star, Third Class (Estonia), also decorations from Portugal, Latvia, Malta and Poland; Estonian Journalists' Union Award 1990, Baltic Assembly Medal. *Leisure interests:* theatre, music, attending sports events. *Address:* Ministry of Foreign Affairs, Islandi Square 1, 15049 Tallinn, Estonia (office). *Telephone:* 637-7000 (office). *Fax:* 637-7099 (office). *E-mail:* vminfo@mfa.ee (office). *Website:* www.mfa.ee (office).

MALKIN, Evgeni Vladimirovich; Russian professional ice hockey player; b. 31 July 1986, Magnitogorsk, Chelyabinsk Oblast; s. of Vladimir Malkin and Natalia Malkin; partner Anna Kasterova; one s.; Russian Super League debut at age 17, 2003–04 season; first int. appearance with Russia at Int. Ice Hockey Fed. (IIHF) World Under-18 Championships, Yaroslavl 2003; played with Metallurg Magnitogorsk (Russian Super League) 2003–06, signed again for 2012–13 season; with Nat. Hockey League's Pittsburgh Penguins 2006–; mem. Team Russia, Winter Olympic Games, Turin 2006, Vancouver 2010; represented Russia at IIHF World Championships 2005, 2006, 2007, 2010, 2012, 2014, 2015; Nat. Hockey League awards include Calder Memorial Trophy (awarded to best rookie) 2006/07, Conn Smythe Trophy 2009, Art Ross Trophy 2009/10, 2011/12, Hart Memorial Trophy 2012, Kharlamov Trophy 2012; IIHF awards include Best Forward 2012, Most Valuable Player 2012, Ted Lindsay Award 2012, Kharlamov Trophy 2012. *Address:* c/o Pittsburgh Penguins, CONSOL Energy Center, 1001 Fifth Avenue, Pittsburgh, PA 15219, USA. *Website:* penguins.nhl.com.

MALKOVICH, John; American actor and producer; b. 9 Dec. 1953, Christopher, Ill.; s. of Dan Malkovich and Joe Anne Malkovich; m. Glenne Headley 1982 (divorced 1988); m. 2nd Nicoletta Peyran; one s. one d.; ed Eastern Illinois and Illinois State Univs; co-f. Steppenwolf Theatre, Chicago 1976; mem. Creative Bd of Dirs Artists Ind. Network; Co-founder Mr. Mudd (production co.) 1998; has directed three fashion shorts (Strap Hangings, Lady Behave, Hideous Man) for London-based designer Bella Freud; co-f. Mrs Mudd (clothing co.) 2002. *Theatre appearances include:* True West 1982, Death of a Salesman 1984, Burn This 1987; Dir Balm in Gilead 1984–85, Arms and the Man 1985, Coyote Ugly 1985, The Caretaker 1986, Burn This 1990, A Slip of the Tongue 1992, Libra 1994, Steppenwolf 1994. *Films include:* Places in the Heart 1984, The Killing Fields 1984, Eleni 1985, Making Mr. Right 1987, The Glass Menagerie 1987, Empire of the Sun 1987, Miles from Home 1988, The Accidental Tourist (exec. producer) 1988, Dangerous Liaisons 1989, Jane, La Putaine du roi 1989, Queen's Logic 1989, The Sheltering Sky 1989, The Object of Beauty 1991, Shadows and Fog 1992, Of Mice and Men 1992, Jennifer Eight, Alive, In the Line of Fire, Mary Reilly 1994, The Ogre 1995, Mulholland Falls 1996, Portrait of a Lady 1996, Con Air 1997, The Man in the Iron Mask 1997, Rounders 1998, Time Regained 1998, Being John Malkovich 1999, The Libertine 1999 (also dir), Ladies Room 1999, Joan of Arc 1999, Shadow of the Vampire 2000, Les Âmes fortes 2001, Je Rentre à la Maison 2001, Hotel 2001, Knockaround Guys 2001, The Dancer Upstairs (dir and producer) 2002, Ripley's Game 2003, Johnny English 2003, Um Filme Falado 2003, The Libertine (also producer) 2004, The Hitchhiker's Guide to the Galaxy 2005, Colour Me Kubrick: A True...ish Story 2005, Art School Confidential (also producer) 2006, Klimt 2006, The Call 2006, Eragon 2006, Drunkboat 2007, In Tranzit 2008, Beowulf 2007, Gardens of the Night 2007, The Great Buck Howard 2008, Changeling 2008, The Mutant Chronicles 2008, Burn After Reading 2008, Disgrace 2008, Afterwards 2008, Jonah Hex 2010, Red 2010, Transformers: Dark of the Moon 2011, Lines of Wellington 2012, Warm Bodies 2013, Deadly Code 2013, RED 2 2013, Cesar Chavez 2014, Cesar Chavez 2014, Casanova Variations 2014, Penguins of Madagascar (voice) 2014, 100 Years 2015, Zoolander 2 2016. *Television includes:* Death of a Salesman 1985, RKO 281 1999, Les Misérables 2000, Napoleon (miniseries) 2002, As Linhas de Torres Vedras (mini-series) 2012, Crossbones (series) 2014. *Address:* Principato-Young Entertainment, 9465 Wilshire Blvd, Suite 900, Beverly Hills, CA 90212, USA (office). *Website:* www.principatoyoung.com (office).

MALLABY, Sir Christopher Leslie George, Kt, GCMG, GCVO, BA; British diplomatist and business executive; b. 7 July 1936, Camberley, Surrey, England; s. of Brig. A. W. S. Mallaby and M. C. Mallaby (née Jones); m. Pascale Thierry-Mieg 1961; one s. three d.; ed Eton Coll., King's Coll., Cambridge; diplomatic postings in Moscow 1961–63, Berlin 1966–69, New York 1970–74, Moscow 1974–77, Bonn 1982–85; Head of Arms Control, Soviet and E European and Planning Depts, FCO 1977–82; Deputy Sec. to Cabinet 1985–88; Amb. to FRG (now Germany) 1988–92, to France 1993–96; Man. Dir UBS Warburg (later UBS Investment Bank) 1996–2006; Chair. Primary Immunodeficiency Asscn 1996–2002, Advisory Bd Great Britain Centre, Humboldt Univ. Berlin 1998–2005, Advisory Bd German Studies Inst., Birmingham Univ. 1999–2006, European Org. for Research and Treatment of Cancer 2000–14; Dir Charter European Investment Trust 1996–2007, Sun Life and Provincial Holdings PLC 1996–2000, EDF Trading 1999–2003, Vodafone Germany 2000–; Adviser to RMC 1996–2000, Herbert Smith 1997–2001; Trustee, Tate Gallery 1996–2002, Reuters (now Thomson-Reuters) 1998–2011; Founder Trustee, Entente Cordiale Scholarships 1996–2008 (Chair. 2001–08); Chair. Somerset House Trustees 2002–06; Hon. Fellow, GB Centre, Humboldt Univ. 2005; Grand Cross, Order of Merit (Germany), Grand Officier, Légion d'honneur, Commdr, Ordre des Palmes académiques; Dr hc (Univ. of Birmingham) 2004. *Leisure interests:* grandchildren. *E-mail:* christopher.mallaby@tiscali.co.uk (home).

MALLINCKRODT, Georg Wilhelm von; German banker; b. 19 Aug. 1930, Eichholz; s. of Arnold von Mallinckrodt and Valentine von Mallinckrodt (née von Joest); m. Charmaine Brenda Schroder 1958; two s. two d.; ed Schule Schloss Salem; with AGFA, Munich 1948–51; with Munchmeyer & Co., 1951–53; with Kleinwort & Co., London 1953–54; with J. Henry Schroder Bank Corp., NY 1954–55, 1957–, with J. Henry Schroder & Co. Ltd 1960, Dir Schroders PLC 1977, Chair. 1985–95, apptd Pres. 1995; Chair. J. Henry Schroder Bank AG, Zurich

1984–2003, Schroder Inc., NY 1984–; Dir Schroders Australia Holdings Ltd, Sydney 1984–2001, Schroder & Co. Inc., NY 1986–2000, Schroder Int. Merchant Bankers Ltd, Singapore 1988–2000, Siemens PLC 1989–2001; with Union Bank of Switzerland, Geneva 1956–57; Adviser, McGraw Hill 1986–89, Bain & Co.; Chair., Council of World Econ. Forum; Vice-Pres., German-British Chamber of Commerce, Trustee, Christian Responsibility in Public Affairs, Inst. of Business Ethics; Hon. DCL (Bishop's Univ., Québec) 1994, Hon. KBE 1997, Freeman of the City of London 2004; Cross of the Order of Merit 1990, Commdr's Cross, Order of Merit 2001, Kt Commdr, Order of St Gregory the Great 2012; Annual Sternberg Interfaith Award 2005. *Leisure interests:* opera, shooting.

MALLOCH-BROWN, Baron (Life Peer), cr. 2007, of St Leonard's Forest in the County of West Sussex; **(George) Mark Malloch-Brown,** KCMG, MA, PC; British government minister, international organization official and fmr business executive; *Special Adviser, FTI Consulting;* b. 16 Sept. 1953, London; m.; four c.; ed Magdalene Coll., Cambridge, Univ. of Michigan, USA; Political Corresp., Economist 1977–79; worked for UNHCR first in Thailand in charge of field operations for Cambodian refugees 1979–81, then in Geneva as Deputy Chief of Emergency Unit 1981–83; Founder Economist Devt Report 1983–86; lead int. partner, Sawyer Miller Group (communications management firm), advising govts political leaders and corpns 1986–94; mem. Soros Advisory Cttee on Bosnia and Herzegovina 1993–94; Dir of External Affairs, IBRD 1994–96, Vice-Pres. for External Affairs 1996–99, for UN Affairs 1996–99, Admin. UNDP 1999–2005, Chief of Staff in Exec. Office of UN Sec.-Gen. 2005–06, Deputy Sec.-Gen. April–Dec. 2006; Distinguished Visiting Fellow, Yale Center for the Study of Globalization 2007; Vice-Chair. Quantum Group of Funds (hedge fund group) 2007; Vice-Chair. Open Soc. Inst. 2007; Minister for Africa, Asia and UN 2007–09 (resgnd), also attended Cabinet; Chair. of Europe, Middle East and Africa, FTI Consulting, London, 2010–14, Special Adviser 2014–; fmr Vice-Chair. World Econ. Forum, Davos, Switzerland; Adviser, SouthWest Energy (Ethiopia) 2010–; Chair. Royal Africa Soc.; mem. Advisory Bd International Crisis Group, Open Society Foundation; fmr Vice-Chair. Bd of Refugees Int., Washington, DC, USA; Hon. mem. Philosophical Soc., Trinity Coll., Dublin; Hon. Fellow, Magdalene Coll., Cambridge; Dr hc (Michigan State) 2003, (Catholic Univ., Lima) 2004, (Pace Law School) 2005, (Walden Univ.) 2008; numerous awards including one of Time Magazine's 100 Most Influential People in the World 2005. *Publication:* The Unfinished Global Revolution. *Address:* FTI Consulting, 200 Aldersgate, London, EC1A 4HD, England (office). *Telephone:* (20) 3727-1128 (office). *Fax:* (20) 3727-1007 (office). *E-mail:* mark.malloch-brown@fticonsulting.com (office). *Website:* www.fticonsulting.com (office).

MALLON, Séamus; Northern Irish politician, teacher and playwright; b. 17 Aug. 1936, Markethill, Co. Armagh, Northern Ireland; m. Gertrude Cush (deceased 2016); one d.; ed Christian Bros; Grammar School, Newry, St Joseph's Coll. of Educ., Belfast; Chair. Social Democratic and Labour Party (SDLP) 1973–74, Deputy Leader 1979–2001; mem. Nat. Ass. 1973–74, Armagh Dist Councillor 1973–86; mem. Nat. Convention 1974–75; elected to Nat. Ass. 1982 but disqualified; mem. Irish Senate 1982, New Ireland Forum 1983–84, Forum for Peace and Reconciliation 1994–95, Nat. Forum and Talks 1996–98, British-Irish Inter-Parl. Body; MP, House of Commons for Newry and Armagh 1986–2005; mem. NI Ass. for Newry and Armagh 1998–2000; (Ass. suspended 11 Feb. 2000); Deputy First Minister (desig.) 1998–99, Deputy First Minister 1999–2000; Hon. LLD (Queen's Belfast) 1999, (NCEA) 2000, (Nat. Univ. Ireland) 2002. *Leisure interests:* golf, fishing, literature. *Address:* 5 Castleview, Markethill, Armagh, BT60 1QP, Northern Ireland (home). *Telephone:* (28) 3755-1411 (home).

MALLOY, Dannel Patrick (Dan), BA, LLB; American lawyer, politician and fmr state governor; b. 21 July 1955, Stamford, CT; s. of William F. Malloy and Agnes Malloy (née Egan); m. Cathy Malloy 1982; three s.; ed Boston Coll. and Boston Coll. Law School; Asst Dist Attorney, Brooklyn, NY 1980–84; Partner, Abate & Fox law firm, Stamford 1984–95; mem. Stamford Bd of Finance 1983–94; Mayor of Stamford 1995–2009; Gov. of Connecticut 2011–19 (retd); Chair. Democratic Governors Asscn 2015–, mem. Council of Govs 2012–, co-Chair. 2014–; fmr Trustee and Vice-Chair. for Educ., Jobs, Educ. and Workforce Cttee, US Conf. of Mayors, Co-Chair. Small Business/Partner America Task Force; fmr mem. Mayors Against Illegal Guns Coalition; fmr mem. Exec. Cttee Democratic Nat. Cttee; fmr Pres. Conn. Conf. of Municipalities; Adjunct Prof., Univ. of Connecticut; mem. Bd of Trustees, Mitchell Coll., New London, Conn.; mem. ABA, Asscn of Trial Lawyers of America, Connecticut Trial Lawyers Asscn, Connecticut Bar Asscn, Nat. Trial Lawyers Asscn; Democrat; hon. degrees from several institutions, including Univ. of New Haven, Univ. of Saint Joseph, Univ. of Bridgeport, Nichols Coll.; John F. Kennedy Profile in Courage Award, John F. Kennedy Library Foundation 2016.

MALLY, Komlan; Togolese politician; b. 12 Dec. 1960, Adiva; one s.; ed Ecole Nationale d'Administration, Univ. of Benin, Lomé; Prefect, Wawa Pref. 1996–99, Golfe Pref. 2002–06; mem. Parl. 2007–; Minister of Towns and Town Planning 2006–07; Prime Minister 2007–08 (resgnd); Minister of State and Minister of Health 2008–11; mem. Rassemblement du peuple togolais (RPT). *Address:* Rassemblement du peuple togolais, place de l'Indépendance, BP 1208, Lomé, Togo (office).

MALLYA, Vijay, BCom; Indian business executive and fmr politician; *Chairman, United Breweries Group;* b. 18 Dec. 1955, Calcutta (now Kolkata); s. of Vittal Mallya and Lalitha Ramaiah; m. 1st Samira Mallya; m. 2nd Rekha Mallya; one s. two d.; ed La Martiniere Boys Coll., St. Xavier's Coll., Univ. of Kolkata; fmrly with American Hoechst Corpn (now Aventis) USA, UK; Man. Brewing and Spirits Divs, United Breweries (UB) Group (mfr of Kingfisher Beer) 1980, Chair. 1983–; Founder and Chair. Kingfisher Airlines 2005–12; Man. Dir Force India F1 Team 2007–18; Chair. Hoechst Marion Roussel India (Aventis), Aventis CropScience, Royal Challengers Bangalore, East Bengal FC, Inst. of Econ. Studies of India, Fed. of Indian Chamber of Commerce and Industries, Motorsports Asscn of India; f. UBICS Inc. (software co.) 1993; f. Mallya Hospital, Bangalore; mem. Rajya Sabha (Parl.) for Karnataka 2002–08, 2010–16; Nat. Working Pres. Janata Party; Officier, Légion d'honneur 2008; Dr hc (California Southern Univ.); Entrepreneur of the Year, Asian Awards 2010. *Leisure interests:* sports, yachting. *Address:* UB Group, UB Anchorage, 5th Floor, 100/1, Richmond Road, Bangalore 560 025, India (office). *E-mail:* cmo@ubmail.com (office). *Website:* www.theubgroup.com (office).

MALMSTRÖM, Cecilia, BA, PhD; Swedish academic, politician and EU official; *Commissioner for Trade, European Commission;* b. 15 May 1968, Stockholm; m.; two c.; ed Gothenburg Univ., Univ. of Paris (Sorbonne), France; tech. asst and translator, SKF, Paris, Stuttgart, Barcelona 1986–89; psychiatric nurse, Lillhagen Hosp., Gothenburg 1989–92; social studies teacher, Lindholmen 1991–92; lay assessor, Gothenburg City Court 1991–94; Vice-Chair. Gothenburg Municipal Immigration Cttee 1994–98; Research Asst, Dept of Political Science, Gothenburg Univ. 1994–98, Sr Lecturer 1998–99; mem. Västra Götaland Regional Council 1998–2001; MEP 1999–2006, Vice-Chair. Dels to Hungary and Croatia Jt Parl. Cttees, served on Constitutional and Foreign Affairs cttees, Sub-cttee on Human Rights, substitute mem. Sub-cttee on Security and Defence 2004–06, Cttee on Internal Market and Consumer Protection 2004–06; Minister for EU Affairs 2006–10; Commr for Home Affairs, EC, Brussels 2010–14, for Trade 2014–; mem. Liberal Party, mem. Bd 1997–, mem. Exec. 2001–. *Publications:* books and articles on European regionalism and politics, Spanish politics, terrorism and immigration. *Address:* European Commission, 200 Rue de la Loi/Wetstraat 200, 1049 Brussels, Belgium (office). *Website:* ec.europa.eu/trade (office); ec.europa.eu/commission/2014-2019/malmstrom_en (office).

MALOFEYEV, Anatoly Aleksandrovich; Belarusian politician; b. 14 May 1933, Gomel; one d.; ed Gomel Railway Coll., Belarus State Inst. of Nat. Econ., Higher Party School; worked as locksmith, Minsk, then Gomel and Minsk carriage repair plants 1949–62; mil. service; mem. CPSU 1954–91; various posts on CP cttees Gomel, at Dept of Chemical and Light Industries of Cen. Cttee of CP of Belarus, Chair. Gomel Regional Exec. Cttee of CP of Belarus, mem. Cen. CPSU Cttee 1986–91, Politburo 1990–91; USSR People's Deputy 1989–91; Deputy Supreme Soviet of Belorussia 1982–92; First Sec. Cen. Cttee of CP of Belorussia 1990–93; mem. Chamber of Reps 1996–2000, 2000–, Chair. 1997–2000; Chair. Parl. Comm. for Econ. Policies and Reforms 1996, Cttee on Int. Affairs and Ties with the CIS 2000–, Standing Cttee for Regional Policy and Local Self-Govt 2007; Order Red Banner of Labour (twice), Award of the Fatherland (3rd degree) 1999, Hon. Charter of Council of Ministers, Hon. Charter of Nat. Ass. *Address:* Sovetskaya Str. 11, 220010 Minsk, Belarus (office). *Telephone:* (17) 222-63-98 (office); (17) 222-62-37 (office). *Fax:* (17) 222-6461 (office). *E-mail:* mizhn@house.gov.by (office).

MALONE, David M., PhD; Canadian diplomatist, writer, academic and university administrator; *Rector, United Nations University for Peace;* ed l'École des Hautes Études Commerçiales, Montreal, American Univ., Cairo, Harvard Univ., Oxford Univ.; joined Dept of External Affairs in 1975, overseas postings include Cairo, Amman, New York, Perm. Rep. to UN 1993; Pres. International Peace Inst., New York 1998–2004; High Commr to India (also accred to Nepal and Bhutan) 2006–08; Pres. International Devt Research Centre, Ottawa 2008–13; Rector, UNU, Tokyo 2013–, Chair. Global Migration Group 2017–; has taught at Univ. of Toronto, Columbia Univ., New York Univ. School of Law, Institut d'Etudes Politiques, Paris. *Publications include* Decision-Making in the UN Security Council: The Case of Haiti 1999, Greed and Grievance: Economic Agendas in Civil Wars (co-ed.) 2000, From Reaction to Conflict Prevention (co-ed.) 2002, Unilateralism and US Foreign Policy (co-ed.) 2002, The UN Security Council from Cold War to Twenty-First Century 2004, The International Struggle Over Iraq: Politics in the UN Security Council, 1980–2005 2006, Preventing a Future Generation of Conflict in Iraq (co-ed.) 2007, The Law and Practice of the United Nations (co-author) 2008, Does the Elephant Dance? Contemporary Indian Foreign Policy 2011, Nepal in Transition: From Civil War to Fragile Peace (co-ed.) 2012, International Development: Ideas, Experience, and Prospects (co-ed.) 2014, The UN Security Council in the 21st Century 2015, The Oxford Handbook of Indian Foreign Policy 2015, The Law and Practice of the United Nations 2016. *Address:* United Nations University, Centre 5–53–70 Jingumae, Shibuya-ku, Tokyo 150-8925, Japan (office). *Telephone:* (3) 5467-1212 (office). *Fax:* (3) 3499-2828 (office). *Website:* www.unu.edu (office).

MALONE, John C., BS, MS, PhD; American telecommunications industry executive; *Chairman, Liberty Media Corporation;* b. 7 March 1941, Milford, Conn.; m. Leslie Malone; two c.; ed Yale Univ, Johns Hopkins Univ; worked at Bell Telephone Laboratories/AT&T 1963; joined McKinsey & Co. 1968; Group Vice-Pres. General Instrument Corpn 1970, later Pres. Jerrold Electronics (subsidiary of General Instrument Corpn); fmr Pres. Jerrold Electronics Corpn; Pres. and CEO Tele-Communications Inc. (TCI), Denver 1973–96, Chair. and CEO (until merger with AT&T) 1996–99; mem. Bd of Dirs and Chair. Liberty Media Corpn, Denver 1999–, CEO Liberty Media International (formed by spinoff of Liberty Media's non-North American operations) 2004–, Chair. Liberty Global, Inc. 2005–, also Chair. Liberty Broadband; Chair. and CEO Discovery Holding Co.; Chair. The DIRECTV Group, Inc. 2008–; Chair. Emer. Cable Television Laboratories, Inc. mem. Bd of Dirs Bank of New York, IAC/InterActiveCorp, Expedia, Inc., Nat. Cable TV Asscn 1974–77, 1980–93, Charter Communications, Inc., Lions Gate Entertainment Corpn; Hon. DHumLitt (Univ. of Denver) 1992, (Johns Hopkins Univ) 2012; Vanguard Award, Nat. Cable TV Asscn 1983, Wall Street's Transcript Silver Award 1984, 1989, Women In Cable's Betsy Magness Fellowship Honoree, Univ. of Pennsylvania Wharton School Sol C. Snider Entrepreneurial Center Award of Merit for Distinguished Entrepreneurship, American Jewish Cttee Sherrill C. Corwin Human Relations Award, Hopkins Distinguished Alumnus Award 1994, Hopkins Medal 2004. *Address:* Liberty Media Corpn, 12300 Liberty Blvd, Englewood, CO 80112, USA (office). *Telephone:* (720) 875-5400 (office). *Fax:* (720) 875-7469 (office). *E-mail:* info@libertymedia.com (office); info@directv.com (office). *Website:* www.libertymedia.com (office); www.directv.com (office).

MALOSSE, Henri, DEA; French international organization official; *President, European Economic and Social Committee;* b. 6 Oct. 1954, Montpellier (Hérault); m.; one c.; ed Institut d'études politiques de Paris (Sciences Po), Diplomas from Univ of Munich, Germany and Univ of Warsaw, Poland; led French Chambers of Commerce and Industry Del. to EU 1979; cr. European Network of Euro Information Centres 1987; Founder and Pres. French Perm. Dels Circle (CDPF) bringing together 140 orgs represented in Brussels 1995–2003, Hon. mem. 2003–; mem. European Econ. and Social Cttee (EESC) Bureau 1995–, responsible for EESC's activities with cand. countries in connection with Convention on the Future of Europe 2001–03, Pres. ECO Section (Econ. and Monetary Union and Econ. and Social Cohesion) 2002–04, Pres. SOC Section (Employment, Social

Affairs and Citizenship) 2004–06, Pres. Employers Group (Group I) 2006–13, Co-Pres. EU-Bulgaria Jt Cttee, Pres. EESC 2013–; Prof., Kaunas Univ, Lituania, Wrocław Univ, Poland, Diplomatic Inst., Moscow, Russia; est. Masters/DESS course on European Public Policies at Robert Schuman Univ, Strasbourg 1993; mem. Policy Bd Centre for European Studies, Strasbourg (CEES), École nat. d'admin, Strasbourg; mem. Steering Cttee Jean Monnet Asscn; Hon. Pres. Europe Defence Circle; Chevalier, Ordre nat. du Mérite. *Publications include:* Europe at Your Doorstep (l'Europe à votre porte), A Guide to EU Funding Mechanisms 1990, 1992, 1994, 1995, The European Institutions (Les institutions européennes) (with Pascal Fontaine) 1991, 1993, Towards a Greater Europe (Vers la Grande Europe 1996, Unifying the Greater Europe (Unifier la Grande Europe) (with Bernard Huchet) 2001, Europe from A to Z (with Pascal Fontaine) 2006, We Must Save the European Citizen! – A 'C plan' to a Citizen's Europe (Il faut sauver le citoyen européen! – Un 'plan C' pour rendre l'Europe aux citoyens) (with Bruno Vever) 2008, Building Europe: The History and Future of a Europe of the People 2012. *Address:* European Economic and Social Committee, Rue Belliard 99, 1040 Brussels, Belgium (office). *Telephone:* (2) 546-8912 (Dir of Pres.'s Office) (office). *Fax:* (2) 513-48-93 (office). *E-mail:* PressEESC@eesc.europa.eu (office). *Website:* www.eesc.europa.eu/president (office).

MALOUF, David George Joseph, AO, BA; Australian writer and poet; b. 20 March 1934, Brisbane, Qld; s. of G. Malouf; ed Brisbane Grammar School and Univ. of Queensland; Hon. Fellow, Australian Acad. of the Humanities; Gold Medal, Australian Literature Soc. 1974, 1982, 2009, Age Book of the Year, NSW Premier's Award for Fiction, Vance Palmer Award, Pascal Prize, Commonwealth Writers' Prize and Prix Fémina Etranger, for The Great World 1991, inaugural IMPAC Dublin Literary Award 1993, Neustadt Int. Prize for Literature 2000, Criticos Prize 2010, many other awards. *Publications include:* poetry: Bicycle and other poems 1970, Neighbours in a Thicket 1974, First Things Last 1981, Selected Poems 1991, Poems 1959–89 1992, Typewriter Music 2007, Revolving Days: selected poems 2008, Earth Hour 2014; novels: Johnno 1975, An Imaginary Life 1978, Child's Play 1982, Fly Away Peter 1982, Harland's Half Acre 1984, 12 Edmondstone Street 1985, The Great World 1990, Remembering Babylon 1993, The Conversations at Curlow Creek 1996, Ransom 2009; short stories: Antipodes 1983, Dream Stuff 2000, Every Move You Make 2006, The Complete Stories 2007; play: Blood Relations 1987; opera librettos: Voss 1986, Mer de Glace 1991, Baa Baa Black Sheep 1993, Jane Eyre 2000; miscellaneous prose: A First Place 2014, The Writing Life 2014, Being There 2015. *Address:* c/o Rogers, Coleridge & White, 20 Powis Mews, London, W11 1JN, England (office); c/o Barbara Mobbs, 35A Sutherland Crescent, Darling Point, Sydney, NSW 2027, Australia (office). *Telephone:* (20) 7221-3717 (office). *Fax:* (20) 7229-9084 (office).

MALPAS, Sir Robert, Kt, CBE, BSc, FIMechE, FIChemE, FRSA; British business executive (retd); b. 9 Aug. 1927, Birkenhead, Merseyside, England; s. of Cheshyre Malpas and Louise Marie Marcelle Boni; m. Joan Holloway; ed Taunton School, St George's Coll., Buenos Aires, Argentina, Univ. of Durham; joined ICI Ltd 1948, with ICI Europa, Brussels 1966–75, CEO ICI Europa Ltd 1973–75, Dir ICI 1975–78; Pres. Halcon Int. Inc., New York 1978–82; Man. Dir BP PLC 1983–89; Chair. Power Gen PLC 1989–90, Cookson Group PLC 1991–98; Dir (non-exec.) Bd BOC Group 1981–96, Eurotunnel 1987–2000 (Chair. 1996–98), Barings PLC 1989–95, Repsol SA (Spain) 1989–2002; mem. Advisory Bd SpecialChem Paris 1996–2000; Chair. Ferghana Pnrs 1998–2003, Evolution PLC 2000–05; Exec. Dir ENAGAS Spain 2002–06; fmr Chair. RL Capital; Pres. SCI 1988–89; Sr Vice-Pres. Royal Acad. of Eng 1989–92; Chair. LINK 1986–93, Natural Environment Research Council 1993–96; Hon. FRSC; Order of Civil Merit, Spain 1968; Hon. degrees from Loughborough, Newcastle, Surrey, Bath, Durham, Sheffield Hallam, Westminster Univs. *Leisure interests:* theatre, opera, reading, music, sports. *Address:* 2 Spencer Park, London, SW18 2SX, England (home). *Telephone:* (20) 8877-1147 (home). *Fax:* (20) 8877-1197 (office). *E-mail:* bobmalpas@aol.com (home).

MALPASS, David Robert, BA, MBA; American economist and international banking executive; *President, World Bank Group;* b. 8 March 1956; m. Adele Malpass; four c.; ed Colorado Coll., Univ. of Denver; Fellow, Georgetown Univ. Walsh School of Foreign Service 1983; Sr Analyst for Taxes and Trade, Senate Budget Cttee 1984–86; Legis. Man., US Dept of the Treasury 1986–88, Deputy Asst Sec. of the Treasury for Developing Nations 1988–89; Staff Dir, Congress Jt Econ. Cttee 1989–90; Deputy Asst Sec. of State for Latin American Econ. Affairs, Dept of State 1990–93; Chief Int. Economist, Bear Stearns & Co. 1993–2002, Chief Economist 2002–08; Sr Economist, JP Morgan March–June 2008; Founder and Pres. Encima Global LLC 2008–17; UnderSec. of the Treasury for Int. Affairs 2017–19; Pres., World Bank Group 2019–; fmr mem. Bd of Dirs Council of the Americas, Economic Club of New York, Nat. Cttee on US–China Relations, Manhattan Inst., Gary Klinsky Children's Centers. *Publications:* numerous articles on economic development. *Address:* The World Bank, 1818 H Street, NW, Washington, DC 20433, USA (office). *Telephone:* (202) 473-1000 (office). *Website:* www.worldbank.org/en/about/people/d/david-malpass (office).

MALTSEV, Col Gen. Leonid Semenovich, Cand. Sci., DrPolSci; Belarusian army general and government official; *Pro-Rector, International University "MITSO";* b. 29 Aug. 1949, Slonim Dist, Grodno Region; s. of Semen Danilovich Maltsev and Anna Vasilyevna Maltseva; m.; two s.; ed Minsk Suvorov Mil. High School, Belarus, Kiev Higher Combined Arms Command School, Ukraine, Frunze Mil. Acad., Moscow, Mil. Acad. of Gen. Staff of Russian Fed. Armed Forces, Moscow; commdr of platoon, co. and battalions in Grouping of Soviet Forces, Germany 1970s; Motorized Rifle Regt Deputy Commdr, Commdr, Chief of Staff, then Commdr of Motorized Rifle Div. in Far East Dist 1979–90; First Deputy Army Commdr in Belarus Armed Forces, 28th Arms Corps Commdr, Chief of Gen. Staff, First Deputy Minister of Defence then Minister of Defence of Repub. of Belarus 1992–96; First Deputy Chief, CIS Mil. Cooperation Coordination Staff 1997–2000; Deputy State Sec., Security Council of Belarus 2000–01, State Sec. 2009–13; Minister of Defence 2001–09; Chair. State Border Cttee 2014; Pro-Rector Int. Univ. "MITSO" 2017–; Hon. Specialist of Belarus Mil. Force 2002, Order of Mil. Glory 2008, Order for Serving Motherland in USSR Armed Forces (Third Class) 1982, (Second Class) 1990, Order for Serving Motherland (First Class) 2003; 20 medals from USSR and Repub. of Belarus. *Publications:* four monographs, 25 scientific articles. *Address:* International University "MITSO", 220099 Minsk, Kazintsa Street 21/3, Belarus (office). *Telephone:* (17) 279-98-60 (office). *Fax:* (17) 279-98-10 (office). *E-mail:* international@mitso.by (office). *Website:* www.mitso.by (office).

MALU, Jorge; Guinea-Bissau politician; Pres. Assembleia Nacional Popular 1999–2003; presidential cand. 2014; Minister for Foreign Affairs, Int. Co-operation and Communities 2016–18; mem. Parti de la Rénovation Sociale.

MALWAL, Akuei Bona, MA; South Sudanese diplomatist; *Permanent Representative to United Nations;* b. 10 Sept. 1959; m.; one c.; ed Univ. of California, Santa Barbara, Univ. of Wisconsin; Amb. and Deputy Dir African Affairs Dept 2006–07; Amb. and Deputy Head of Mission Embassy of Sudan 2007–11; Dir of Protocol, South Sudan Ministry of Foreign Affairs and Int. Cooperation 2012–12, Dir-Gen. of Protocol 2012–14; Amb. to Ethiopia and Djibouti 2014–16, concurrently Perm. Rep. to African Union, IGAD, UN ECA; Perm. Rep. to UN 2016–. *Address:* Permanent Mission of South Sudan, 336 E 45th Street, 5th Floor, New York, NY 10017, USA (office). *Telephone:* (212) 937-7977 (office). *Fax:* (212) 867-9242 (office). *E-mail:* info@rssun-nyc.org (office).

MALYSHEV, Andrey Borisovich, CandSocSci, CandEngSci; Russian nuclear engineer; b. 26 Sept. 1959, Moscow; m.; one d.; ed Moscow Power Eng Inst.; began career as engineer, Atomenergoproekt State Research and Devt Design Inst. 1982, apptd Dir-Gen. 1997; Deputy Minister, Ministry of Atomic Energy 2002–03; Head of Gosatomnadzor (State Atomic Inspection) of Russia (transformed into Fed. Nuclear Supervision Service 2004) 2003–06; Deputy Head, Fed. Agency for Nuclear Power 2006–07; mem. Man. Bd and Deputy Gen. Dir Russian State Corpn of Nanotechnologies (Rosnanotech) 2007–11, Deputy Chair. Man. Bd, JSC Rosnano (fmrly SC Rosnanotech) 2011–12; mem. Bd of Dirs, JSC Ruspolymet; Ind. Dir JSC RusHydro 2010–; Order of Honour 2005; Hon. Builder of Russia Award. *Publications:* reports, articles and conf. papers. *Leisure interest:* tennis. *Address:* RusHydro, 7 Malaya Dmitrovka Str., 127006 Moscow, Russia (office). *Telephone:* (495) 333-80-00 (office). *E-mail:* contact@rushydro.ru (office). *Website:* www.rushydro.ru (office).

MAŁYSZ, Adam Henryk; Polish rally driver and fmr professional ski jumper; b. 3 Dec. 1977, Wisła; s. of Jan Małysz and Ewa Małysz; m. Izabela Polok 1997; one d.; ed Vocational School, Ustroń; coached by Heinz Kuttin (nat. coach) and by his uncle, Jan Szturc, Austria; debut for Poland in Czech Repub. 1994; World Champion, Normal Hill, Lahti, Finland 2001, runner-up, Large Hill 2001; Winner, World Cup in ski jumping 2001, 2002, 2003 (first ski jumper to win three consecutive overall World Cup titles); Four Ski-Jumps competition 2001; Winner, Polish Championships 2002; Silver and Bronze Medals, Olympic Games, Salt Lake City 2002; World Champion, Val di Fiemme, Italy 2003; Winner, Large Hill, World Cup: Lahti, 2003, Oslo, Norway 2003, Zakopane, Poland 2005, Harrachov, Czech Repub. 2005; Winner, Ski Flying, World Cup, Tauplitz, Austria 2005; Second Place, Large Hill, World Cup: Zakopane 2004, Titisee-Neustadt, Germany 2005, Innsbruck, Austria 2005; Third Place, Large Hill, Kuopio, Finland 2005; World Champion, Sapporo, Japan 2007; two Silver Medals, Olympic Games, Vancouver 2010; Bronze Medal, World Championships, Oslo 2011; announced retirement from competition 26 March 2011; mem. KS Wisla Ustronianka Ski Club, Wisla; Dir/Coordinator, Nat. Ski Team (jumping and nordic), Polish Ski Asscn 2016–; new career as rally driver; competed in Dakar Rally 2012, 2013, 2014; Order of Polonia Restituta: Officer's Cross (4th Class) 2002, Commdr's Cross (3rd Class) 2007, Commdr's Cross with Star (2nd Class) 2010; Polish Sports Personality of the Year 2001, 2002, 2003, 2007. *Leisure interests:* football, cars. *Address:* 43-374 Wisła ul. Kopydło 59 (office); c/o Polski Zwiazek Narciarski, 30-313 Kraków, ul. Mieszczanska 18/3, Poland. *Telephone:* (12) 260-99-70. *Fax:* (12) 269-71-12. *E-mail:* office@pzn.pl. *Website:* www.pzn.pl.

MALYUTIN, Alexander; Russian journalist; b. 4 Feb. 1964, Novocherkassk, Rostov Oblast; ed AA Zhdanov State Univ., Leningrad, Mil. Acad. of Logistics and Transport; mil. service 1988–92; joined Kommersant publishing house 1992, initially as freelance, later joined staff, becoming Corresp., Special Corresp., Columnist; joined Russian edn of Forbes magazine 2003, Deputy Ed. 2011; First Deputy Chief Ed. Smart Money (business magazine) 2005–09; Ed.-in-Chief, Izvestiya (leading daily newspaper) 2011–12, Aug.–Dec. 2013; Co-founder Market.ru (internet portal). *Address:* c/o Izvestiya, 127994 Moscow, ul. Tverskaya 18/1, POB 4, Russia (office).

MAMABOLO, Jeremiah Nyamane Kingsley, MPA; South African diplomatist; *Joint Special Representative for Darfur and Head of the African Union-UN Hybrid Operation in Darfur, United Nations;* b. 13 Aug. 1955, Johannesburg; m. Alenore Cecilia Mamabolo; four c.; ed Moscow School of Social Sciences, USSR, Harare Polytechnic, Zimbabwe, Univ. of Pretoria; Deputy Head of Mission of African Nat. Congress (ANC) to Tanzania 1978, held various leadership positions in ANC in exile, including Head of Information and Publicity of ANC Mission in Harare, Zimbabwe 1984, ANC Deputy Head of Mission in Harare 1985, ANC Head of Mission in Maputo, Mozambique 1987–89, Cuba 1989–93, ANC Head of Mission in Harare 1993–94; returned to South Africa and joined Ministry of Foreign Affairs 1994, High Commr to Zimbabwe 1994–99, Perm. Rep. to OAU and to UN ECA in Addis Ababa (also accred to as Amb. to Ethiopia, Sudan and Djibouti) 1999–2002, Special Envoy of OAU Sec.-Gen. Salim Ahmed Salim to Sierra Leone and MANU River Basin 2002–04, Deputy Dir-Gen. for African Affairs, Ministry of Foreign Affairs and Resident Expert on Africa 2002–06, Special Envoy to Great Lakes Region 2006–09, apptd Deputy Facilitator in Burundi peace process, High Commr to Nigeria 2009–13, Amb. and Perm. Rep. to UN, New York 2013–16, Deputy Jt Special Rep. for African Union-UN Hybrid Operation in Darfur (UNAMID) 2016–17, Jt Special Rep. for Darfur and Head UNAMID 2017–. *Address:* UNAMID, PO Box 5041, Grand Central Station, New York, NY 10163, USA (office). *Telephone:* (212) 963-8077 (office). *Fax:* (212) 963-9222 (office). *E-mail:* unamid-publicinformation@un.org. *Website:* unamid.unmissions.org (office).

MAMATGELDIYEV, Maj.-Gen. Agageldy, MD; Turkmenistani army officer and politician; trained as physician; career in Turkmenistan Armed Forces, rank of Maj.-Gen.; fmr Head of Turkmen Border Guard Service; Minister of Defence 2003–09.

MAMBERTI, HE Cardinal Dominique François Joseph; French (b. Moroccan) ecclesiastic and diplomatist; *Prefect of the Supreme Tribunal, Apostolic*

Signatura, Roman Curia; b. 7 March 1952, Marrakesh, Morocco; ed degrees in civil and canon law; ordained priest, Diocese of Ajaccio 1981; travelled to Rome to study diplomacy at Pontifical Ecclesial Acad. 1984, joined Vatican diplomatic service 1986, has held posts in Algeria, Chile, UN, New York, Lebanon; consecrated Titular Archbishop of Sagone 2002; Secr. of State Section for Foreign Affairs, Apostolic Del. to Somalia 2002–04, Apostolic Nuncio (Amb.) to Sudan 2002–06, to Eritrea 2004–06, Sec. for Relations with States, Roman Curia 2006–14; Prefect of the Supreme Tribunal, Apostolic Signatura 2014–; cr. Cardinal (Cardinal-Deacon of Santo Spirito in Sassia) 2015. *Address:* Supremo Tribunale della Segnatura Apostolica, Palazzo della Cancelleria, Piazza della Cancelleria 1, 00186 Rome, Italy (office). *Telephone:* (06) 69887520 (office). *Fax:* (06) 69887553 (office). *Website:* www.vatican.va/roman_curia/tribunals/apost_signat (office).

MAMBERTI, HE Cardinal Dominique François Joseph; French (b. Moroccan) ecclesiastic and diplomatist; *Prefect of the Apostolic Signatura;* b. 7 March 1952, Marrakesh, Morocco; ed degrees in civil and canon law; ordained priest, Diocese of Ajaccio 1981; consecrated Titular Archbishop of Sagone 2002; Apostolic Nuncio to Sudan 2002–06, Apostolic Del. to Somalia 2002–04, Apostolic Nuncio to Eritrea 2004–06; Sec. (Relations with States), Secr. of State 2006–14; Prefect of Apostolic Signatura 2014–; cr. Cardinal (Cardinal-Deacon of Santo Spirito in Sassia) 2015. *Address:* Supremo Tribunale della Segnatura Apostolica, Palazzo della Cancelleria, Piazza della Cancelleria 1, 00186 Rome, Italy (office). *Telephone:* (06) 69887520 (office). *Fax:* (06) 69887553 (office). *Website:* www.vatican.va/roman_curia/tribunals/apost_signat (office).

MAMET, David Alan, BA; American playwright, screenwriter and director; b. 30 Nov. 1947, Chicago, Ill.; s. of Bernard Morris Mamet and Lenore June Mamet (née Silver); m. 1st Lindsay Crouse 1977 (divorced); m. 2nd Rebecca Pidgeon 1991; ed Goddard Coll.; Artist-in-Residence, Goddard Coll. 1971–73; Artistic Dir St Nicholas Theatre Co., Chicago 1973–75; Guest Lecturer, Univ. of Chicago 1975, 1979, New York Univ. 1981; Assoc. Artistic Dir Goodman Theatre, Chicago 1978; Assoc. Prof. of Film, Columbia Univ. 1988; Hon. DLitt (Dartmouth Coll.) 1996; Outer Critics Circle Award for contrib. to American theatre 1978, PEN/Laura Pels Foundation Award for Drama 2010. *Films directed include:* House of Games 1986, Things Change 1987, Homicide 1991, Oleanna 1994, The Spanish Prisoner 1997, The Winslow Boy 1999, Catastrophe 2000, State and Main 2000, Heist 2001, Spartan 2004, Redbelt 2008. *Films written include:* The Postman Always Rings Twice 1981, The Verdict 1982, About Last Night 1986, The Untouchables 1987, House of Games 1987, Things Change 1988, We're No Angels 1989, Homicide 1991, Glengarry Glen Ross 1992, Hoffa 1992, Oleanna 1994, American Buffalo 1996, The Edge 1997, The Spanish Prisoner 1997, Wag the Dog 1997, Ronin 1998, State and Main 2000, Hannibal 2001, Heist 2001, Spartan 2004, Edmond 2005, Redbelt 2008. *Works include:* The Duck Variations 1971, Sexual Perversity in Chicago 1973 (Village Voice Obie Award 1976), The Reunion 1973, Squirrels 1974, American Buffalo (Village Voice Obie Award 1976, New York Drama Critics Circle Award 1977) 1976, A Life in the Theatre 1976, The Water Engine 1976, The Woods 1977, Lone Canoe 1978, Prairie du Chien 1978, Lakeboat 1980, Donny March 1981, Edmond 1982 (Village Voice Obie Award 1983), The Disappearance of the Jews 1983, The Shawl 1985, Glengarry Glen Ross (Pulitzer Prize for Drama, New York Drama Critics Circle Award) 1984, Speed-the-Plow 1987, Bobby, Gould in Hell 1989, The Old Neighborhood 1991, Oleanna 1992, Ricky Jay and his 52 Assistants 1994, The Village (novel) 1994, Death Defying Acts 1996, Boston Marriage 1999, The Wicked Son 2006, Race 2009; screenplays: The Postman Always Rings Twice 1979, The Verdict 1980, The Untouchables 1986, House of Games 1986, Things Change (with Shel Silverstein) 1987, We're No Angels 1987, A Life in the Theatre (also dir) 1989, Oh Hell! 1991, Homicide 1991, Hoffa 1991, Glengarry Glen Ross 1992, The Rising Sun 1992, Oleanna 1994, The Edge 1996, The Spanish Prisoner 1996, Wag the Dog 1997, State and Main 2000, The Winslow Boy 1999, Boston Marriage 2001, Heist 2001, Hannibal 2001, Spartan 2004; children's books: Mr Warm and Cold 1985, The Owl (with Lindsay Crouse) 1987, The Winslow Boy 1999; essays: Writing in Restaurants 1986, Some Freaks 1989, On Directing Film 1990, The Hero Pony 1990, The Cabin 1992, A Whore's Profession (also screenplay adaptation) 1993, The Cryptogram 1994, Passover 1995, Make-Believe Town: Essays and Remembrances 1996, Plays 1996, Plays 2 1996, The Duck and the Goat 1996, The Old Religion 1996, True and False 1996, The Old Neighborhood 1998, Jafsie and John Henry 2000, Bambi vs Godzilla (non-fiction) 2007, The Secret Knowledge: On the Dismantling of American Culture 2012; Three Stories (fiction) 2013. *Address:* c/o ICM Partners, 10250 Constellation Blvd, Los Angeles, CA 90067 (office); Abrams Artists Agency, 275 Seventh Avenue, 25th Floor, New York, NY 10001, USA (office). *E-mail:* vincent.devito@abramsart.com (office). *Website:* www.abramsartists.com (office).

MAMET, Noah Bryson, BA; American political campaign organizer and diplomatist; b. 1971, Manhattan Beach, Calif.; ed Univ. of California, Los Angeles; worked for Democratic Party as driver and bodyguard during primary election campaign of Senate cand. Mel Levine; went on to work for Calif. Democratic Party and helped run the 1992 Bill Clinton campaign in Santa Barbara Co.; campaign manager for Peter Mathews' unsuccessful Congressional candidacy in Long Beach 1994; Sr Advisor and Nat. Finance Dir for US House Minority Leader Richard Gephardt 1995–2003, continued working for Gephardt's unsuccessful presidential bid 2004; f. Noah Mamet & Assocs, Los Angeles (political consulting firm) 2004; worked for Hillary Clinton's unsuccessful presidential campaign 2008, involved in Pres. Obama's re-election campaign 2012; Amb. to Argentina 2014–17; mem. Pacific Council on Int. Policy, American Council of Young Political Leaders; mem. Bd Green Dot Public Schools, Los Angeles, NatureBridge; mem. int. del. for Nat. Democratic Inst. monitoring first elections in Sierra Leone following civil war 2007; fmr adviser to Wasserman Family Foundation, Los Angeles.

MAMI, Kayrat Abdrazakovich; Kazakhstani lawyer and politician; *Chairman of the Supreme Court;* b. 9 May 1954, Zhambyl dist, Alma-Ata Region; m.; three c.; ed Law Faculty of Kazakh State Univ.; held posts of Deputy Justice Minister and Deputy Head of the Presidential Admin; Prosecutor Gen. of Kazakhstan 2009–11; Chair. of the Senate 2011–13; Chair. of the Supreme Court 2013–. *Address:* Supreme Court of the Republic of Kazakhstan, 010000 Nur-Sultan, Orynbor kosh. 8, Kazakhstan (office). *Telephone:* (7172) 71-24-07 (office). *E-mail:* gp-rk@mail.online.kz (office). *Website:* www.sud.kz (office).

MAMIN, Asqar Uzaqbaiulı; Kazakhstani engineer and politician; *Prime Minister;* b. 23 Oct. 1965, Tselinograd (now Astana), Kazakh SSR, USSR; m. Altynai Mamina; one s. one d.; ed Tselinograd Civil Eng Inst. and Plekhanov Russian Univ. of Econs, Moscow, Russian Fed.; began career as an installer at Tselintyazhstroi (Tselinograd Heavy Construction) Corpn; served as Deputy Dir Gen. of Innovative Enterprises Union of Kazakhstan; First Deputy Mayor of Astana from 1996; mem. Bd of Dirs, Qazaqstan Temir Jolı (Kazakhstan Railways) 2008–16, later Pres.; Chair. Kazakhstan Engineering (defence industry group industrial group) 2017–; mem. Nur Otan Partiyası (Light of the Fatherland Party); Minister of Transport and Communication 2005–06; Mayor of Astana 2006–08; First Deputy Prime Minister 2016–19, Prime Minister 2019–; Pres. Kazakhstan Ice Hockey Fed. 2008–; Hon. Citizen of Astana 2011; Hon. Railwayman 2012; Hon. Builder of Kazakhstan 2013; Medal 'Eren enbegi ushin' (For Distinguished Labour) 1998; Order 'Qurmet' (Honour) 2006; Order of 'Barys' (Second Degree) 2011; Order of the Holy Prince Daniel of Moscow (Third Degree) 2010; Chevalier, Légion d'honneur 2013; Order of the Cross of Recognition (Second Degree) (Latvia) 2013; Order 'For Civil Merit' (First Degree) (Spain) 2014. *Address:* Office of the Prime Minister, 010000 Nur-Sultan, Orynbor kösh. 6, Kazakhstan (office). *Telephone:* (7172) 74-52-61 (office). *Fax:* (7172) 32-40-89 (office). *Website:* primeminister.kz (office); www.government.kz (office).

MÄMMÄDOV, Etibar, BA, PhD; Azerbaijani academic and politician; *Chairman, Azärbaycan Milli İstiqlal Partiyası (Azerbaijan National Independence Party);* b. 2 April 1955, Baku; m.; three c.; ed Baku State Univ.; Prof., Baku State Univ. from 1981; led opposition movt against Popular Front of Azerbaijan (PFA); led protest movt 1989; Co-founder Interim Initiative Centre of Popular Front of Azerbaijan 1988; travelled to Moscow for a press conf. following the Black January events in Baku 1990, arrested by KGB and imprisoned at Lefortovo prison for nine months, pardoned after a public petition with 1.5 million signatures; elected to Supreme Soviet of Azerbaijan SSR 1991; split with Popular Front 1991; Founding Chair. Azerbaycan Milli İstiqlal Partiyası (Azerbaijan Nat. Independence Party) 1992–; elected to Parl. 1995; cand. in presidential elections 1998, 2003; formed new political alliance between İstiqlal and Democratic Party of Azerbaijan to oppose Govt 2000; co-f. new opposition bloc Yeni Siyaset (YeS—New Politics) 2005; Vice-Chair. Int. Democrat Union. *Address:* Azärbaycan Milli İstiqlal Partiyası (Azerbaijan National Independence Party), 1000 Baku, Näsimi rayonu, Mirqasımov küç. 4, Azerbaijan (office). *Telephone:* (12) 444-55-66 (office). *E-mail:* info@amip.az (office).

MÄMMÄDOV, Novruz İsmayıl oğlu, PhD; Azerbaijani translator and politician; *Prime Minister;* b. 1947, Şıxmahmud village, Babäk Dist, Naxçıvan ASSR, Azerbaijan SSR, USSR; m.; three c.; ed Azerbaijani Pedagogical Foreign Languages Inst. (APFLI); worked as translator and interpreter in Algeria 1967–68, 1978–81, in Guinea 1971–73; Dean, Preparatory Faculty, APFLI 1992–93, Dean, French Language Dept 1993–97, Chair of French Language Lexicology and Methodology Dept 2003–18; French language translator for the Pres. 1995–97; Head, Foreign Relations Dept of Presidential Admin 1997, Deputy Head of Presidential Admin 2012; rank of Amb. extraordinary and plenipotentiary 2002; Asst to the Pres. for Foreign Policy Issues and Head, Foreign Policy Dept 2017–18; Prime Minister 2018–; Chair. Supervisory Bd State Oil Fund of Repub. of Azerbaijan (SOFAZ) 2018–; mem. Azerbaijan Nat. UNESCO Comm. 2005–; Ordre, Légion d'honneur (France) 1998, Shohrat Order (Order of Glory) 2005, Polish Legion of Honour 2009, Sharaf Order (Order of Honour) 2017. *Publications:* more than 150 articles on scientific, social and political issues; several books including French Language Practical Phonetics 1997, Diplomacy: Encyclopaedic Dictionary (Ed.) 2005, Introduction to Geopolitics (two volumes) 2011, Azerbaijan Foreign Policy Model 2012, Global Politics: Threats, Challenges, Hopes (Ed.) 2013, Foreign Policy: Realities and Perspectives for the Future 2015, Behind the Curtain of Today's Geopolitical Processes (Ed.) 2015, 25 Years of Independent Azerbaijan 2016; translated several books including (into French) Erich Feigl's A Myth of Terror 2001; (into Azerbaijani) Pierre Gamarra's L'Assassin a le prix Goncourt 2010, Philippe Braillard's Les relations internationales 2010. *Address:* Office of the Prime Minister, 1066 Baku, Lermontov küç. 68, Azerbaijan (office). *Telephone:* (12) 492-41-61 (office). *Fax:* (12) 498-97-86 (office). *E-mail:* nk@cabmin.gov.az (office). *Website:* www.cabmin.gov.az (office).

MÄMMÄDYAROV, Elmar Mähärräm oğlu, PhD; Azerbaijani diplomatist; *Minister of Foreign Affairs;* b. 2 July 1960, Baku, Azerbaijan SSR, USSR; m.; two s.; ed Kyiv State Univ. School of Int. Relations and Int. Law, Ukrainian SSR, USSR Diplomatic Acad., Exchange Scholar at Center for Foreign Policy Devt, Brown Univ., USA; Second Sec. then First Sec., Ministry of Foreign Affairs 1982–88; Dir Div. of State Protocol 1991–92; First Sec. Perm. Mission to UN, New York 1992–95; Deputy Dir Dept of Int. Orgs, Ministry of Foreign Affairs 1995–98; Counsellor, Embassy in Washington, DC 1998–2003; Amb. to Italy 2003–04; Minister of Foreign Affairs 2004–; currently Chair. Nat. Comm., UNESCO. *Address:* Ministry of Foreign Affairs, 1009 Baku, S. Qurbanov küç. 50, Azerbaijan (office). *Telephone:* (12) 596-90-00 (office). *Fax:* (12) 498-84-80 (office); (12) 596-90-01 (office). *E-mail:* katiblik@mfa.gov.az (office); press-service@mfa.gov.az (office). *Website:* www.mfa.gov.az (office).

MÄMMEDOWA, Gülşat; Turkmenistani politician; *Chairman, Majlis (Parliament);* b. 1964, Aşgabat, Turkmen SSR, USSR; ed Turkmen State Univ.; Head, Aşgabat City Dept of Educ. 2005–07; First Deputy Minister of Educ. 2007–09, Minister of Educ. 2009–15; Deputy Chair., Cabinet of Ministers for Culture and Media 2016; Deputy Chair. Majlis (Parl.) 2017–18, Chair. (Speaker) 2018–; Magtymguly Pyragy Medal, Medal In Honour of 25th Anniversary of Independence of Turkmenistan, Gayrat Medal. *Address:* Office of the Chairman, Majlis, 744000 Aşgabat, Garaşyslyk Şaýoly 110, Turkmenistan (office). *Telephone:* (12) 35-31-25 (office). *Fax:* (12) 35-31-47 (office).

MAMUT, Alexander Leonidovich, LLB; Russian lawyer and business executive; b. 29 Jan. 1960, Moscow; s. of Leonid Mamut; widowed; three c.; ed Moscow State Univ.; lawyer 1985–; Founder and Head, ALM Consulting Co. 1990–; business activities 1989–; Founder and mem. Bd of Dirs Bank Imperial 1990–; Founder and Chair. Exec. Bd Co. on Project Financing 1993–, later Jt Stock Interbanking Credit Org. Co. for Project Financing (COPF) 1996–2000; Chair. Troika-Dialog; mem. Council on Industrial Policy and Business of Russian Govt from 1994; adviser to Head of Admin. Russian Presidency from 1998; mem. Bd of

Dirs Sobinbank 1999; mem. Observation Council Bank Moskovsky Delovoy Mir MDM-Bank from 1999, Chair. 1999–2001; bought LiveJournal (Russia's most popular blogging platform) 2007; bought UK bookshop chain Waterstone's 2011; sold stake in mobile phone chain Evroset to Alisher Usmanov and cellular operator Megafon 2012, gained stake in Internet co. SUP Media; merged SUP with another Internet co., Afisha-Rambler, owned by Vladimir Potanin to form Afisha-Rambler-SUP 2013, also owns Russian news sites Lenta.ru and Gazeta.ru; holds substantial stake in precious metals co. Polymetal; sold half his stake in fertilizer giant Uralkali 2013, and his stake in industrial warehouse real estate co. Multinational Logistic Partnership (MLP) 2013; bought stake in homebuilder PIK Group 2013; Co-founder Strelka Inst. for Media, Architecture and Design. *Address:* LiveJournal Inc., 28 2nd Street, Third Floor, San Francisco, CA 94104, USA (office). *E-mail:* press@livejournalinc.com (office). *Website:* www.livejournal.com (office).

MANABE, Syukuro (Suki), BA, MA, DSc; American meteorologist and academic; *Senior Meteorologist, Atmospheric and Oceanic Science Program, Princeton University;* b. 21 Sept. 1931, Shingu, Shikoku-Chuo-Shi, Ehime Pref., Japan; s. of Seiichi Manabe and Sueko Manabe (née Akashi); m. Nobuko Nakamura 1962; two d.; ed Tokyo Univ., Japan; entered USA 1958, naturalized 1975; Research Meteorologist, Gen. Circulation Research Section, US Weather Bureau, Washington, DC 1958–63; Sr Research Meteorologist, Geophysical Fluid Dynamics Lab., Environmental Science Services Admin., Washington, DC 1963–68, Nat. Oceanic and Atmospheric Admin., Princeton, NJ 1968–97, mem. Sr Exec. Service, USA 1979–96, Sr Scientist 1996–97; Dir Global Warming Research Program, Frontier Research System for Global Change 1997–2001; Lecturer with rank of Prof., Atmospheric and Oceanic Sciences Program, Princeton Univ. 1968–97; Visiting Research Collaborator, Atmospheric and Oceanic Science Program, Princeton Univ. 2002–03, Sr Meteorologist 2005–; Consultant, Japan Marine-Earth Science Tech. Org., Japan 2002–09; mem. NAS 1990; Foreign mem. Academia Europaea 1994, RSC 1995, Japan Acad. 2009; Fellow, American Geophysical Union 1967, AAAS 1997; Hon. mem. American Meteorological Soc. 1997, Japan Meteorological Soc. 2000, Royal Meteorological Soc. 2006; Hon. DS (McGill Univ.) 2004; Fujiwara Award, Japan Meteorological Soc. 1966, Meisinger Award, American Meteorological Soc. 1967 (2nd Half Century Award 1977, Rossby Research Medal 1992), Blue Planet Prize, Asahi Glass Foundation 1992, Revelle Medal, American Geophysical Union 1993 (Bowie Medal 2010), Asahi Prize (Asahi Shimbun Cultural Foundation) 1995, Volvo Environmental Prize, Volvo Environmental Foundation 1997, Milankovitch Medal, European Geophysical Soc. 1998, inducted into Earth Hall of Fame, Kyoto 2009, Benjamin Franklin Medal, Franklin Inst. 2015, and numerous other awards. *Achievement:* pioneered prediction of global warming using computer simulations. *Publications:* more than 140 papers in scientific journals. *Leisure interests:* swimming, yoga. *Address:* Program in Atmospheric and Oceanic Sciences, Princeton University, 107 Sayre Hall, 300 Forrestal Road, Princeton, NJ 08540 (office); 6 Governors Lane, Princeton, NJ 08540-3666, USA (home). *Telephone:* (609) 258-2790 (office); (609) 924-0734 (home). *Fax:* (609) 258-2850 (office). *E-mail:* manabe@princeton.edu (office). *Website:* www.aos.princeton.edu (office).

MANAEV, Oleg T., MA, PhD; Belarusian research institute director and professor of media and communications studies; b. 3 Feb. 1952, Vladivostok, USSR; ed Belarusian State Univ.; Jr Research Fellow, Scientific Centre for Sociological Research, Belarusian State Univ. 1976–78, Sr Research Fellow 1978–84, Head of Div. 1984–88, Prof., Dept of Sociology 1992–99, Founder and Prof., Dept of Social Communication 1999–2012; Founding Dir Ind. Inst. of Socio-Econ. and Political Studies 1992–2006; Founding Chair. Belarusian Asscn of Think-Tanks (BTT), also Ed. BTT Analytical Bulletin; Chair. Belarusian Soros Foundation 1993–95; Fullbright Visiting Prof., Univ. of Southern California 2001; Prof., Dept of Media and Communication, European Humanities Univ., Vilnius, Lithuania 2012–16; Visiting Lecturer and Fellow at univs and insts in USA, Canada, Brazil, UK, France, Sweden and Germany; dir several nat. and int. projects for UNESCO, OSCE, MacArthur Foundation, Westminster Foundation; Corresp. Ed. European Journal of Communication, London, Political Communication, Durham, NC; Visiting Prof. Dept of Political Science, Univ. of Tennessee Knoxville; Visiting Prof., Slavic Research Centre, Hokkaido Univ., Japan June–Oct. 2013; mem. International Asscn for Media and Communications Research 1990–2000, World Asscn for Public Opinion Research 2007–10, American Political Science Asscn 2009–, Asscn for Slavic, East European and Eurasian Studies 2015–, American Asscn for Public Opinion Research 2017–; Scholar Rescue Fund Award, Inst. of Int. Educ., USA 2007. *Publications:* 20 authored and edited books, including: Effectiveness of Mass Media (co-ed.) 1981, Youth and the Democratization of Soviet Society (co-ed.) 1990, Interaction of Media, Public and Power in the Democratization Process (co-ed.) 1991, Media in Transition: From Totalitarianism to Democracy (co-ed.) 1993, Emerging Civil Society in Independent Belarus. Sociological Experience: 1991–2000 2000, Belarus on the Way to the Third Millennium (co-ed.) 2001, Mass Media in Belarus 2003, Independent Research in Independent Belarus: Fighting for Reality (ed.) 2004, Emerging Civil Society in Independent Belarus. Sociological Experience: 2001–2005 2005, Presidential Elections in Belarus: From Limited Democracy to Unlimited Authoritarianism (1994–2006) (ed.) 2006, Belarus and 'Wider Europe': Quest for Geopolitical Self-Identification (ed.) 2007, Emerging Civil Society in Independent Belarus. Sociological Experience: 2006–2010 2011, Youth and Civil Society in Belarus: New Generation 2011, Future of Belarus. Views of Independent Experts (ed) 2012; more than 200 scholarly articles and chapters in books. *Leisure interests:* sea travels, fishing. *Address:* Department of Political Science, University of Tennessee, McClung Tower 1014, Knoxville, TN 37996 (office); 11130 Hatteras Drive, Knoxville, TN 37934, USA (home). *Telephone:* (865) 974-7045 (office); (865) 235-2232 (home). *E-mail:* omanaev@utk.edu (office); manaev.oleg@gmail.com (home). *Website:* www.utk.academia.edu (office).

MANAGADZE, Irakli; Georgian economist and fmr central banker; b. 27 Oct. 1967, Tbilisi; s. of Nodar Managadze and Manana Janelidze; m. Nino Simonia; one d.; ed State Univ., Tbilisi; Attaché, Ministry of Foreign Affairs 1991–92, Sr Specialist, State Cttee of External Econ. Relations 1992–93; Chief State Adviser, Econ. and Political Reform Comms, Georgian Cabinet of Ministers 1993–94; Asst Exec. Dir World Bank 1994–96, Institutional Specialist, Municipal and Social Infrastructure Div., European Dept IV 1996–98, Consultant, World Bank 2017–; Pres. and Chair. Bd, Nat. Bank of Georgia 1998–2005; Sr Policy Adviser, Financial Institutions Group, EBRD 2005–15.

MANANDHAR, Krishna Bahadur, MA; Nepalese fmr central banker; ed Tribhuvan Univ., Univ. of Manchester, UK; Research Officer, Centre for Econ. Devt and Admin, Kathmandu 1973; Section Officer, Planning Comm. 1973–74; served as Asst Research Officer, Nepal Rastra Bank (cen. bank), fmr Asst Controller, later Deputy Chief Controller, Exec. Dir Foreign Exchange Dept c. 2003, Deputy Gov. –2007, 2009–10, Chair., Acting Gov. and Chair. Man. Cttee 2007–09; mem. Bd of Dirs Rastriya Banijya Bank 1998–99, Nepal Arab Bank (now Nabil Bank Ltd) 1999–; Trustee and mem. Senate, Kathmandu Univ. *Address:* c/o Board of Directors, Nabil Bank Limited, Beena Marga, Durbar Marg, Kathmandu, Nepal.

MANASIEVSKI, Jovan; Macedonian politician; b. 21 May 1968, Gostivar; ed Skopje Univ., St Cyril and Methodius; Counsellor to Mayor of Skopje, responsible for Communications and Co-ordination of Int. Co-operation 1997–2002; mem. Parl. 2002–; Minister of Labour and Social Policy 2004; Deputy Prime Minister and Minister of Defence –2006; mem. Liberalno-Demokratska Partija (Liberal-Democratic Party), Chair. 2006–12. *Address:* Liberalno-Demokratska Partija (Liberal-Democratic Party), 1000 Skopje, 11 Oktombri 8, North Macedonia (office). *Telephone:* (2) 6091268 (office). *E-mail:* liberaldemocraticparty@gmail.com (office). *Website:* www.ldp.org.mk (office).

MANAWI, Fazal Ahmad, MA; Afghan civil servant; ed Islam Abad Int. Univ.; positions held include Deputy of Islamic Educ., Ministry of Educ., Instructor in Alberoni Univ., Deputy of Educ. in interlude of Resistance, Deputy Minister, Ministry of Educ., Deputy of Supreme Court, Deputy for Afghanistan's Scholars Council; has taken part in Jt Peace Jirga; Chair. Ind. Election Comm. 2010–13; has participated in numerous nat. and int. seminars.

MANCEL, Jean-François; French politician; b. 1 March 1948, Beauvais (Oise); s. of Michel Mancel and Renée Baque; six c.; ed Faculté de droit et Inst d'études politiques, École nationale d'admin, Paris; Deputy to Nat. Ass. 1978– (RPR 1978–2002, Union pour un mouvement populaire 2002–), mem. Finance Cttee; mem. Conseil Municipal of Beauvais 1977–89, of Novillers 1995–2001; Conseiller Général de l'Oise 1979–2004, Pres. Oise Departmental Ass. 1985–2004; Sec.-Gen. RPR 1995–97; mem. European Parl. 1984–86. *Leisure interests:* skiing, tennis. *Address:* Conseil Général de l'Oise, 1 rue Cambry, CS 80941, 60024 Beauvais Cedex (office); Assemblée nationale, 126 rue de l'Université, 75355 Paris 07 SP, France (office). *Telephone:* (3) 44-06-60-67 (Beauvais) (office). *Fax:* (3) 44-06-63-01 (Beauvais) (office). *E-mail:* jfmancel@assemblee-nationale.fr (office). *Website:* www.assemblee-nationale.fr/14/tribun/fiches_id/2048.asp (office).

MANCHIN, Joseph (Joe), III, BS; American business executive and politician; *Senator from West Virginia;* b. 24 Aug. 1947, Farmington, Marion Co., W Va; s. of John Manchin and Mary Manchin (née Gouzd); m. Gayle Conelly 1967; one s. two d.; ed Farmington High School, West Virginia Univ.; Operator Manchin's Carpet Center, Marion Co. (chain of family-owned retail stores) 1970; Dir Enersystems –2004; elected to State House of Dels 1982, 1984, to State Senate 1986, 1988, 1992; unsuccessful cand. for Democratic gubernatorial nomination 1996; Sec. of State for W Va 2001–05; energy. of W Va 2005–10; Senator from West Virginia 2010–, mem. Armed Services Cttee, Energy and Natural Resources Cttee, Commerce, Science and Transportation Cttee, Cttee on Veterans Affairs; Chair. Nat. Govs Asscn 2010; mem. Nat. Rifle Asscn; Democrat; Dr hc (Wheeling Jesuit Univ.) 2006, (Davis & Elkins Coll.) 2010. *Leisure interests:* licensed pilot, the outdoors, hunting, angling, motorcycling. *Address:* 306 Hart Senate Office Building, Washington, DC 20510, USA (office). *Telephone:* (202) 224-3954 (office). *Fax:* (202) 228-0002 (office). *Website:* manchin.senate.gov (office).

MANCINI, Ange; French government official; *Prefect of Martinique;* b. 15 June 1944, Beausoleil (Alpes-Maritimes); began career in Police nationale (Nat. Police) 1963; Head of Service Régional de Police Judiciaire of Ajaccio 1983–85; Founder and Head of Recherche Assistance Intervention Dissuasion (RAID) 1985–90, helped arrest members of Action directe in the Loiret 1987; Head of SRPJ of Versailles 1990–95; Deputy Head of Direction Centrale de la Police Judiciaire 1995–96; Deputy Prefect for Security of Corse-du-Sud and Haute-Corse 1999–2002; Prefect of French Guiana 2002–06, of Landes 2006–07, of Martinique 2007–. *Leisure interests:* golf, cross-country cycling, hunting. *Address:* Préfecture, 82 rue Victor Sévère, BP 647–648, 97262 Fort-de-France Cedex, Martinique (office). *Telephone:* (5) 96-39-36-00 (office). *Fax:* (5) 96-71-40-29 (office). *E-mail:* contact.prefecture@martinique.pref.gouv.fr (office). *Website:* www.martinique.pref.gouv.fr (office).

MANCINO, Nicola; Italian lawyer and politician; b. 15 Oct. 1931, Montefalcione, Avellino; mem. Christian Democracy (DC) 1976–94; fmr communal, prov. and regional councillor, Chair. Campania Regional Exec. Council (twice), DC Prov. Sec., Avellino, Regional Sec. Campania; elected Senator from Avellino 1976, 1979, 1983, 1987; Chair. DC Parl. Group 1984; Minister of the Interior 1992–94, mem. Italian People's Party (PPI) 1994–2002; Pres. of the Senate 1996–2001; Acting Pres. of Italy 1999; mem. Democrazia è Libertà – La Margherita (Democracy is Freedom – The Daisy) 2002–07; Vice-Pres. Consiglio Superiore della Magistratura (Magistrates' Governing Body) 2006–10; mem. Partito Democratico (Democratic Party) 2007–; ordered by prosecutors to stand trial for withholding evidence on talks between Italian state and Mafia during its bombing campaign in 1992 July 2012. *Address:* c/o Partito Democratico, Via Sant'Andrea delle Fratte 16, 00187 Rome, Italy. *Telephone:* (06) 695321. *E-mail:* redazione@partitodemocratico.it. *Website:* www.partitodemocratico.it.

MANCUSO, Frank G.; American film industry executive; b. 25 July 1933, Buffalo, NY; m. Fay Mancuso; one s. one d.; ed State Univ. of New York; joined Paramount Pictures Corpn, Buffalo, NY 1962, Vice-Pres. and Gen. Sales Man. Paramount Pictures Corpn of Canada Ltd, Toronto 1970–72, Pres. and subsequently head of Paramount's Western Div., Los Angeles 1972–76, Vice-Pres., Gen. Sales Man., Paramount's Motion Picture Div., New York 1976–78, Sr Vice-Pres. 1978–79, Exec. Vice-Pres. in charge of Distribution and Marketing 1979–80, Pres. Paramount Distribution 1980–83, Pres. Motion Picture Group of Paramount Pictures Corpn 1983–84, Chair. and CEO Paramount Pictures Corpn 1984–91; Chair. and CEO MGM 1993–99; consultant, Santa Monica, Calif. 1999–; Chair.

Motion Picture and Television Fund Corp. 2003–10; Vice-Pres. Variety Clubs International and of Motion Picture Pioneers; Chair. Will Rogers Memorial Fund; Dir New York-Cornell Medical Center, Burke Rehabilitation Center, UCLA Medical Center, Museum of Broadcasting, Acad. of Motion Picture Arts and Sciences, Motion Picture Asscn and other orgs; Sherrill G. Corwin Human Relations Award, American Jewish Cttee 1985, received a star on the Italian Walk of Fame in Toronto, Canada 2010.

MANDAL, Badri Prasad; Nepalese politician; Deputy Prime Minister, Minister of Home Affairs, of Agric. and of Co-operatives and Local Devt 2002–03; Ministry of Forests and Soil Conservation Feb.–July 2005, of Agric. and Co-operatives July 2005–06; mem. Nepali Sadbhavana Party (NSP), Acting Pres. 2002, fmr leader of Mandal faction, expelled from party 2007.

MANDELSON, Baron (Life Peer), cr. 2008, of Foy in the County of Herefordshire and Hartlepool in the County of Durham; **Rt Hon. Peter Benjamin Mandelson,** PC; British politician; *Chairman, Global Counsel LLP;* b. 21 Oct. 1953, London, England; s. of George Mandelson and Mary Mandelson (née Morrison); ed Hendon County Grammar School, St Catherine's Coll., Oxford; joined TUC Econ. Dept 1977–78; Chair. British Youth Council 1978–80; mem. Council, London Borough of Lambeth 1979–82; Producer, London Weekend TV 1982–85; Dir of Campaigns and Communications, Labour Party 1985–90; MP for Hartlepool 1992–2004; an Opposition Whip 1994–97, Shadow Frontbench Spokesman on Civil Service 1995–96, Dir Tony Blair's election campaign 1997; Minister without Portfolio 1997–98; Sec. of State for Trade and Industry July–Dec. 1998, for NI 1999–2001, for Business, Enterprise and Regulatory Reform 2008–10, First Sec. of State and Lord Pres. of the Council 2009–10; EU Commr for Trade 2004–08; Chair. Global Counsel LLP (consultancy) 2010–; Sr Adviser then Chair., Lazard International Ltd (int. financial advisory firm) 2011–; Chair. UK-Japan 21st Century Group 2001–04; mem. Bd of Dirs Willbury Ltd, Sistema; industrial consultant, SRU Group 1990–92; mem. Int. Advisory Cttee Centre for European Policy Studies 1993; mem. Advisory Bd Sapinda; Pres. Hartlepool United Football Club –2016; Trustee, Alfred Herrhausen Soc.; High Steward of Kingston upon Hull. *Publications:* Youth Unemployment: Causes and Cures 1977, Broadcasting and Youth 1980, The Blair Revolution: Can New Labour Deliver? 1996, Pro-Europe, Pro-Reform: A Progressive Vision of the EU 2001, The European Union in the Global Age 2007, The Third Man (memoirs) 2010. *Leisure interests:* country walking, swimming, reading. *Address:* House of Lords, Westminster, London, SW1A 0PW (office); Global Counsel LLP, 5 Welbeck Street, London, W1G 9YQ, England. *Telephone:* (20) 7219-4893 (office); (20) 3667-6500. *E-mail:* info@global-counsel.co.uk. *Website:* www.global-counsel.co.uk.

MANDIĆ, Andrija; Montenegrin metallurgical engineer, business executive and politician; *President, Nova Srpska Demokratija (NOVA—New Serbian Democracy);* b. 19 Jan. 1965, Šavnik, Socialist Repub. of Montenegro, Socialist Fed. Repub. of Yugoslavia; m.; two c.; ed Faculty of Tech. and Metallurgy, Veljko Vlahović Univ., Titograd (now Podgorica); owned a night club in Podgorica called The Scene; co-owner of smelting plant that produced aluminium alloys in Montenegro; mem. Savez Reformskih Snaga Jugoslavije (Union of Reform Forces of Yugoslavia) 1990–91, abandoned political life following dissolution of party after outbreak of civil wars in Yugoslavia; returned to pvt. business; joined Narodna Stranka (People's Party) mid-1990s; Co-founder Srpska Narodna Stranka Crne Gore (SNS—Serb People's Party of Montenegro) 1997, held numerous posts, originally as a Vice-Pres. of Municipal Bd for Podgorica and mem. Supreme Bd Board of the party, as well as mem. Exec. Bd, also served one term as Dir of the Party, Pres. 2002–09, Pres. Nova Srpska Demokratija (NOVA—New Serbian Democracy, formed from merger of SNS and Narodna Socijalistička Stranka Crne Gore—People's Socialist Party of Montenegro) 2009–; mem. Parl. of Montenegro, Head of NOVA Parl. faction; fmr Deputy Minister for Industry. *Address:* Nova Srpska Demokratija (NOVA—New Serbian Democracy), 81000 Podgorica, Vojislava Grujića 4, Montenegro (office). *Telephone:* (20) 651903 (office). *Fax:* (20) 652147 (office). *E-mail:* centar@nova.org.me (office); pobjeda@andrijamandic.com. *Website:* www.nova.org.me (office); www.andrijamandic.com.

MANDIL, Claude; French administrative official, engineer and business executive; b. 9 Jan. 1942, Lyon; s. of Léon Mandil and Renée Mandil (née Mizraki); m. Annick Goubelle 1966; four s. one d.; ed Lycée Pasteur de Neuilly and Ecole Polytechnique; mining engineer, Metz 1967–71, Rennes 1971–74; Délégation à l'Aménagement du Territoire et à l'Action régionale (DATAR) 1974–77; Inter-Dept Dir and Regional Del. Agence nat. de Valorisation de la Recherche, Anvar 1978–81; Tech. Adviser to Prime Minister 1981–82; Dir-Gen. Inst. of Industrial Devt (IDI) 1983, Pres. 1984–88; Dir-Gen. Bureau des recherches géologiques et minières 1988; Dir-Gen. Energies et Matières Premières, Ministry of Industry and Land Devt 1990–98; Deputy Man. Dir Gaz de France 1998–2000; Pres. Institut français du pétrole 2000–03; Exec. Dir IEA 2003–07 (retd); mem. Bd of Dirs Total SA 2008–14; mem. Bd SBC Energy Inst. 2011; Commdr, Ordre nat. du Mérite, Officier, Légion d'honneur, decorations from Germany, Norway, Japan and UK; Dr hc (Catholic Univ. of Louvain) 2008. *Leisure interest:* music. *Address:* 28 rue Sainte-Anne, 78000 Versailles, France. *E-mail:* claude.mandil@orange.fr.

MANDINGA, Vítor Fernando; Guinea-Bissau politician; fmr Leader, Democratic Convergence Party; Minister of Finance 2005–07, also mem. IMF Bd of Govs; Leader, Aliança Democrática 2008.

MANDOKI, Luis; Mexican film director, writer and producer; b. 1954, Mexico City; m. Olivia Mandoki; one s. two d.; ed studied fine arts in Mexico and at San Francisco Art Inst., London Coll. of Printing, London Int. Film School; directed first short film Silent Music which won an award at Int. Amateur Film Festival of Cannes Film Festival 1976; directed short films and documentaries for Instituto Nacional Indigenista (Nat. Inst. for the Indigenous), Conacine (Nat. Comm. of Film) and Centro de Produccion de Cortometraje (Center for the Production of Short Films); film Motel selected to represent Mexico in film festivals world-wide 1984; film Voces inocentes selected to represent Mexico at Academy Awards for Best Foreign Film 2005. *Films directed:* Mundo mágico 1980, Campeche, un estado de animo (also producer) 1980, El secreto (Ariel Award, Mexican Acad. of Film 1980) 1980, Papaloapan 1982, Mundo mágico (segment La venganza de Carlos Mango) 1983, Motel (aka Murderer in the Hotel) 1984, Gaby: A True Story (also developer and co-producer) 1987, Noche de Califas (producer) 1987, White Palace 1990, Born Yesterday 1993, When a Man Loves a Woman (aka To Have and to Hold) 1994, Message in a Bottle 1999, Meeting Genevieve 2000, Amazing Grace 2000, Angel Eyes (Ojos de ángel) 2001, Trapped (aka 24 Stunden Angst) (also producer) 2002, Voces inocentes (Innocent Voices) (also screenplay and producer) (Glass Bear, 14plus: Best Feature Film, Berlin Int. Film Festival 2005, Jury Prize for Best Feature Film, RiverRun Int. Film Festival 2006) 2004, Fraude: México 2006 (aka Stolen) (documentary) (also producer) 2007, The Translator 2009, La Vida precoz y breve de Sabina Rivas 2012. *Television:* The Edge 1989, Utopia (series) (exec. producer) 2003, ¿Quien es el Señor Lopez? (series) (also producer) 2006.

MANDUCA, Paul; British business executive; *Chairman, Prudential plc;* Founding CEO Threadneedle Asset Management Ltd 1994–99; Global CEO Rothschild Asset Management 1999–2002; European CEO Deutsche Asset Management 2002–05; Chair. Bridgewell Group plc –2007; Dir (non-exec.) Wm Morrison Supermarkets Plc (Morrisons) 2005–11, chaired Audit Remuneration, later Sr Ind. Dir, mem. Nomination Cttee and Chair. Remuneration Cttee; Ind. Dir (non-exec.), Prudential 2010–, Sr Ind. Dir and mem. Nomination Cttee 2011–12, mem. Audit Cttee, Remuneration Cttee 2010–12, Chair. Prudential plc 2012–, also Chair. Nomination Cttee; Chair. Aon Ltd –2012; Dir (non-exec.) and Chair. Audit Cttee KazmunaiGas Exploration & Production Plc –2012; Chair. Henderson Diversified Income Ltd, JPM European Smaller Companies Investment Trust Plc –2012; Chair. TheCityUK's Advisory Council 2015–, Templeton Emerging Markets Investment Trust 2015–; Sr Ind. Dir and Chair. Audit Cttee, Development Securities plc –2010; Dir, Eagle Star 1994–99, Allied Dunbar 1994–99, Henderson Smaller Companies Investment Trust plc –2006; mem. Securities Inst. *Address:* Prudential plc, Laurence Pountney Hill, London, EC4R 0HH, England (office). *Telephone:* (20) 7548-3901 (office); (20) 7220-7588 (switchboard) (office). *Fax:* (20) 7548-3631 (office). *E-mail:* info@prudential.co.uk (office). *Website:* www.prudential.co.uk (office).

MANDUR, László, BSc; Hungarian politician; b. 12 Feb. 1958, Csömör; m.; three c.; ed Coll. of Transport and Communication, Győr, Univ. of Econs, Budapest; clerk of works at Ferihegy II Airport; worked at Betonútépítő Construction Co. 1979–81; mem. of Hungarian Socialist Workers' Party 1979–89; mem. of staff, Young Communist League of Budapest Cttee, then Dist Sec. and later Budapest Sec. 1981–89; founding mem., Hungarian Socialist Party (MSZP) 1989, mem. of party exec. and faction leader, Budapest Dist III Ass. 1994–97, Co-Chair. MSZP Nat. Econs Section 1998–2000, mem. Budapest Party Council 1999–2000, MSZP Budapest Pres. 2000–04, mem. Nat. Exec. 2004–09; Man. Dir Budapest Radio Kft. 1989–97; mem. Bd, then Chair., Hortobágy Fishery Rt. 1995–97; Chair. Antenna Hungaria Rt. 1996–98; mem. Supervisory Bd, Hajógyári Sziget Asset Man. Rt. 1996–99; Man. Dir Antel Invest Kft. 1997–98; Man. Dir Honline Kft. 1999; mem. Bd Budapest Waterworks Rt. 1999–2000; Man. Dir Trangon Bt. 2000–02; mem. Hungarian Nat. Ass. 2002–14, Deputy Speaker 2002–10; Commdr, Ordre Nat. du Mérite 2004. *Publications:* Mr. Producer (co-author) 1993. *Website:* www.mandur.hu.

MANDVIWALLA, Saleem; Pakistani politician; *Deputy Chairman of Senate;* b. 25 Jan. 1959; s. of Hakim Mandviwalla; ed Fort Worth School of Aviation, Texas, USA; Chair. Bd of Investment 2008–13; Minister of State for Finance Div. 2008–13, Fed. Minister of Finance, Revenue, Planning and Devt, Econ. Affairs and Statistics Feb.–March 2013; Pres. Lasbela Chamber of Commerce and Industry, Balochistan; mem. Man. Cttee Fed. of Chambers of Commerce and Industries (FPCCI); mem. Senate for Sindh (Pakistan People's Party) 2012–, Deputy Chair. of Senate 2018–. *Address:* Parliament House, Islamabad, Pakistan (office). *Telephone:* (51) 9022022 (office). *Website:* www.senate.gov.pk.

MANENIARU, John, BCom; Solomon Islands politician; b. 20 June 1965, Uhu Village, Malaita Prov.; ed Papua New Guinea Univ. of Tech.; Bank Officer, Nat. Bank of Solomon Islands 1986–91; Public Servant 1992–2002; Gen. Man., Investment Corpn of Solomon Islands 2002–10; mem. Nat. Parl. for West 'Are'are, Malaita Prov. 2010–; leader, ind. mems in parl. 2011–14; Minister for Fisheries and Marine Resources 2014–17, Minister for Finance and Treasury Oct.–Nov. 2017; mem. Kadere Party of Solomon Islands. *Address:* Kadere Party of Solomon Islands (KPSI), Honiara, Solomon Islands (office).

MANFREDI, Valerio Massimo; Italian archaeologist, academic and writer; *Professor of Archaeology, Bocconi University;* b. 8 March 1943; specialist in topography of ancient world; has taken part in many archaeological excavations in Italy and abroad; has taught at Università Cattolica, Milan, Venice Univ., Loyola Univ., Chicago and Ecole Pratique des Hautes Etudes, Paris, currently Prof. of Archaeology, Bocconi Univ., Milan; corresp. on antiquities for publs Panorama and Il Messaggero; Commendatore della Repubblica; Corrado Alvaro Rhegium Julii Prize 2003, Booksellers of the City of Padua Prize, Hemingway Prize for fiction 2004, Bancarella Prize 2008, Scanno Prize 2010. *Television:* Stargate (LA7–TV). *Publications include:* Xenophon's Anabasis (translator), Lo Scudo di Talos, Palladion, Il Faraone delle Sabbie, L'Oracolo, Le Paludi di Hesperia, La Torre della Solitudine, Alexandros: Child of a Dream, Alexander: The Sands of Amon, Alexander: The Ends of the Earth, Chimaira Akropolis 2001, L'ultima legione (The Last Legion: Spartan) 2002, Il tiranno (trans. as Tyrant) 2003, L'impero del draghi 2005, Zeus e altro racconti 2006, L'armata perduta 2007, Idi di Marzo 2008, L'antica maledizione 2010, Otel Bruni 2011, Odysseus: The Oath 2013, Odysseus: The Return 2014. *Leisure interest:* motorcycling. *Address:* c/o Laura Grandi (Agent), Via Degli Olivetani 12, 20123, Milan, Italy (office). *E-mail:* agenzia@grandieassociati.it (office). *Website:* www.valeriomassimomanfredi.it/en.

MANGAL, Mohammad Gulab; Afghan politician; b. Laja Mangal, Paktika Prov.; ed Kabul Univ.; fmr mem. People's Democratic Party of Afghanistan; served as a Col in the Afghan Army; worked in Ministries of Interior and of Defence late 1970s; later joined the insurrection fighting the Soviet invasion of Afghanistan; fmr UN worker; apptd a Regional Co-ordinator of the Constitutional Loya Jirga (Grand Council) in Paktia Prov. 2001; Gov. of Paktika Prov. 2004–06, of Laghman Prov. 2006–08, of Helmand Prov. 2008–12, of Nangarhar Prov. 2016–18; Minister of Border and Tribal Affairs 2015–16.

MANGALAZA, Eugène; Malagasy professor of anthropology and politician; b. 13 July 1950; three c.; ed Univ. Bordeaux III, France; Inspector of Higher Educ. in 1970s and 1980s; Deputy, Nat. People's Ass. 1975–91; Dir of Human Resources,

Port of Toamasina 1989; Prof. of Philosophy and Anthropology, Univ. of Toamasina, Rector 1989–2002; Visiting Prof., Toliara Univ., Univ. Bordeaux III, France; mem. Asscn pour la renaissance de Madagascar; resident in La Reunion –Oct. 2009; Prime Minister Oct.–Dec. 2009. *Publications include:* several publications in the field of anthropology.

MANGANYI, Noel Chabani, MA, DLitt et Phil; South African psychologist, academic and fmr civil servant; *Council Professor, University of Pretoria;* b. 13 March 1940, Louis Trichardt dist; s. of Frans Manganyi and Sophie Manganyi; m. 1st Esmé Kakana (divorced); m. 2nd Dr Peggy Sekele 1990; two d.; ed Douglas Laing Smit Secondary School, Univ. of South Africa (UNISA); internship in clinical psychology, Baragwanath Hosp., Clinical Psychologist 1970–73; Postdoctoral Fellow, School of Medicine, Yale Univ., USA 1973–75; Prof. of Psychology Univ. of Transkei 1976–80; Prof., Sr Research Fellow, Univ. of the Witwatersrand 1981–90; in active forensic practice of psychology as expert witness for defence of anti-apartheid activists at Supreme Court, SA –1991; Vice-Chancellor Univ. of the North, Pietersburg 1991–92; Exec. Dir PSI Jt Educ. Trust 1993–94; Dir-Gen. of Nat. Educ. 1994–99; Advisor to Vice-Chancellor and Prin. of Univ. of Pretoria 1999–2003, Vice-Prin. Univ. of Pretoria 2003–06, Council Prof. 2006–; Founder, Violence and Health Resources Project, Univ. of the Witwatersrand 1986, mem. Bd Wits University Press; mem. several psychology orgs; Hon. DLitt (Witwatersrand); Hon. DLitt et Phil (UNISA). *Publications:* published a series of monographs, including Being Black in the World 1973, Alienation and the Body in Racist Society 1977, Looking through the Keyhole 1981; Exiles and Homecomings: A Biography of Es'kia Mphahlele 1983, Bury Me at the Marketplace: Selected Letters of Es'kia Mphahlele, 1943–1980 1984, Political Violence and the Struggle in South Africa (co-ed.) 1990, Treachery and Innocence: Psychology and Racial Difference in South Africa 1991, A Black Man Called Sekoto 1996, Gerard Sekoto: I Am an African 2004, On Becoming a Democracy: Transition and the Transformation of South African Society (ed.) 2004; several articles in scientific and professional journals. *Address:* Unit for Advanced Scholarship, University of Pretoria, PO Box 471, Wendywood, Johannesburg 2144, South Africa (office). *E-mail:* chabani@iafrica.com (office). *Website:* web.up.ac.za (office).

MANGESHKAR, Lata; Indian singer, actress and songwriter; b. (Hema Hardikar), 28 Sept. 1929, Indore; d. of actor and singer Dinanath Mangeshkar and Shudhhamati Mangeshkar; sister of Asha Bhosle; Indian film playback singer; first sang in Kiti Hasaal 1942; has recorded thousands of songs in 20 Indian languages; Hon. Citizenship of Republic of Suriname 1980, Hon. Citizenship of Houston, Texas, USA 1987; Hon. DLitt (Pune Univ.) 1990; Filmfare Awards 1958, 1962, 1965, 1969 (refused to be considered for this award after 1969 to encourage new talent), Filmfare Lifetime Achievement Award 1993, Filmfare Special Award 1994, National Awards, Best Female Playback Singer 1972, 1975, 1990, Maharashtra State Award, Best Playback Singer 1966, 1967, Bengal Film Journalist's Award, Padma Bhushan 1969, Best Female Playback Singer 1964, 1967, 1968, 1969, 1970, 1971, 1973, 1975, 1981, 1985, Key of the City of Georgetown, Guyana 1980, Dada Saheb Phalke Award 1989, Videocon Screen Lifetime Achievement Award 1996, Rajiv Gandhi Award 1997, Lux Zee Cine Lifetime Achievement Award 1998, Padma Vibhushan 1999, IIFA London, Lifetime Achievement Award 2000, Noorjehan Award 2001, Maharashtra Ratna 2001, Bharat Ratna 2001, Noorjehan Award 2001, Maharashtra Ratna 2001, Hakim Khan Sur Award 2002, Asha Bhosle Award 2002, Swar Bharati Award, One Time Award for Lifetime Achievement 2008, Brand Laureate Legendary Award 2017. *Films include:* Pahill Mangala Gaur 1942, Chimukla Sansaar 1943, Maakhe Baal 1943, Gajabhau 1944, Badi Maa 1945, Jeevan Yaatra 1946, Subhadra 1946, Mandir 1948, Chattapati Shivaji 1953, Pukar 2000. *Recordings include:* albums: soundtracks: Sargam 1979, Darr 1993, Hum Aapke Hain Koun...! 1994, Dilwale Dulhania Le Jayeng 1995, Dil To Pagal Hai 1997, Lagaan 2001; solo: Lata In Concert – An Era In An Evening 1997, Saadgi 2007. *Leisure interests:* photography, cooking. *Address:* Prabhu Kunj, 101 Peddar Road, Mumbai 400 026, India.

MANGLA, P. B., MA, MLibSc, MSLS, MInfSc, DLSc; Indian professor of library and information science; *Professor Emeritus, University of Delhi;* b. 5 July 1936, India; s. of Radha Krishan; m. Raj Mangla 1961; one s. one d.; ed Univ. of Punjab, Univ. of Delhi, Columbia Univ., New York and in London; Prof. and Head of Dept of Library Sciences, Univ. of Tabriz, Iran 1970–72, Visiting Prof. 1974–75; UNESCO expert, Guyana 1978–79; Prof. and Head of Dept of Library and Information Sciences, Univ. of Delhi 1972–2001, Dean Faculty of Arts 1976–78, 1984–88, Chair. Bd of Research Studies 1979–85; Library Consultant, Reserve Bank of India, Bombay 1992–93; apptd Library Adviser, YMCA New Delhi 1992; various other admin. posts in Delhi and numerous other univs 1972; Chair. Manpower Devt Cttee of Nat. Information System in Science and Tech. 1977; Sr Vice-Pres. and Founder-mem. Indian Asscn of Academic Librarians 1981–83; mem. Bd Int. Fed. of Library Asscns and Insts 1983 (Vice-Pres. 1987–89, 1989–91), Inst. of Information Scientists; Nat. Prof., UGC 1984–86; Chair. Bd of Eds Univ. of Delhi Annual Reports 1989–96; mem. Editorial Bd Third World Libraries (USA) 1989, Journal of Library and Information Science, Education for Information, Amsterdam 1982–, Review in Library and Information Science, USA, LIBRI (Copenhagen), Third World Libraries (Chicago), Int. Journal of Information and Library Research (UK) 1989; Special Adviser, IFLA Regional Section for Asia and Oceania 1991; Chair. Programme Implementation Cttee, Nat. Service Scheme, Delhi Univ. 1989–, Governing Body Deshbandhu Coll., Delhi Univ. 1990–95, Dyal Singh Coll., Delhi Univ. 2001–04, Univ. Grants Cttee (UGC) Panel of Library and Information Science 1992; Prof., Mangla Research Foundation 2001, Dyal Singh Coll., Delhi Univ. 2001–04 (Prof. Emer. 2004–); mem. Steering Cttee Inflibnet (UGC) 1990–99; mem. Planning Comm. (Govt of India) Working Group on Modernization of Libraries and Informatics for 7th, 8th and 9th Five-Year Plans; mem. Research Cttee INSDOC New Delhi 2000–02, Nat. Inst. of Science Communication and Information Resources 2002; mem. Nat. Advisory Cttee Nat. Library 2002, Expert Cttee Asiatic Soc. 2002–, Working Group on Libraries, Nat. Knowledge Comm. 2006, Search Cttee for Chair., Inflibnet (UGC) 2006; mem. Bd of Man., Nat. Library of India (Kolkata) 2004; Fellow, Indian Library Asscn, Tagore Nat., Govt of India Ministry of Culture, New Delhi 2010–12; Hon. Fellow, Indian Library Asscn; Rockefeller Foundation (New York) Merit Scholarship 1961–62, British Council sponsorship 1979, 1980, 1987, 1989, IDRC (Canada) sponsorship 1983, 1991, Int. Library Movt Award (India) 1984, Shiromani Award for Human Excellence 1991, IFLA Gold Medal 1991, Distinguished Services Award and Citation, Punjab Library Asscn 1997, Library and Information Science: Parameters and Perspectives (two-vol. Festchrift) 1997, Certificate of Honour, IASLIC 2006; several memorial lectures. *Publications:* author/ed. of numerous books and specialist reviews in India and overseas. *Leisure interests:* travel, reading. *Address:* EB-210 Maya Enclave, New Delhi 110 064, India. *Telephone:* (11) 2512-0458; (11) 2512-0331 (home). *E-mail:* manglapb@yahoo.co.in (home).

MANGOAELA, Percy Metsing, BSc, BEd, LLB; Lesotho diplomatist and international civil servant; b. 26 Aug. 1942, Berea; m.; two d.; ed Memorial Univ. of Newfoundland and Dalhousie Univ., Canada, Makerere Univ., Kampala, Uganda, Harvard Univ., USA; radio news reporter, Dept of Information and Broadcasting 1966–68; joined Lesotho civil service 1968, Asst Sec., Ministry of Foreign Affairs, then Desk Officer, Int. Orgs and N America –1970; Dir of Civil Aviation 1973–76, Prin. Sec., Ministry of Transport and Communications 1976–79, 1990; Deputy Co-ordinator, UN Transport and Communications Decade for Africa, UN ECA 1979–89; Prin. Sec., Depts of Trade and Industry and Consumer Affairs 1991–92; Dir Southern Africa Transport and Communications Comm., Maputo 1992–95; Amb. and Perm. Rep. to UN, New York 1995–2001, Vice-Pres. High Level UN Conf. on South–South Co-operation 2001, Amb. and Perm. Rep. to Comprehensive Nuclear-Test-Ban Treaty Org., New York; Chair. Lesotho Communications Authority *c.* –2013. *Address:* 30 Princess Margaret Road, Old Europa, Maseru, Lesotho (home). *Telephone:* 22224300 (office). *E-mail:* (office).

MANGOLD, Klaus, DrIur; German business executive; *Chairman of the Supervisory Board, Knorr-Bremse AG;* b. 6 June 1943, Pforzheim; m.; two s.; ed Univs of Munich, Heidelberg and Mainz, Univ. of Geneva, Switzerland, Univ. of Paris, France, Univ. of London, UK; Asst Man. German-Mexican Chamber of Commerce, Mexico City 1972–73; Section Jr Barrister Thyssen 1973–75; Man. Union of German Textile Industry, Stuttgart 1976; mem. Bd of Dirs Rhodia AG (Rhone Poulenc Group) 1983–90, Chair. 1985–90; Chair. Quelle-Schickedanz AG, Fürth 1991–94; mem. Bd of Dirs DaimlerChrysler AG and CEO DaimlerChrysler Services AG 1995–2003, Exec. Adviser to Chair. DaimlerChrysler AG for Cen. and Eastern Europe and Cen. Asia 2003–07; Exec. Adviser to Chair. DaimlerChrysler AG for Cen. and Eastern Europe and Cen. Asia 2003–07; apptd Vice-Chair. Rothschild Europe 2004, now Chair. Supervisory Bd Rothschild GmbH; Chair. Supervisory Bd,, TUI AG 2011–18, Knorr-Bremse AG 2018–; Chair. Cttee on Eastern European Econ. Relations 2000–10; mem. of numerous supervisory and advisory bds including Rothschild & Cie, France and Germany, Chubb Corpn, USA, Rhodia, SA, Continental AG, Metro AG, Jenoptik AG, Magna International Inc., Canada, Daimler AG; mem. Bd Alstom SA, Leipziger Messe GmbH, Universitätsklinikum Freiburg; Hon. Consul, Russian Federation in Baden-Württemberg 2005; Chevalier, Légion d'honneur 2000, Order of Merit of Baden-Württemberg 2004, Order of Merit of the Fed. Repub. of Germany (1st Class) 2007; Prize for Understanding and Tolerance, Jewish Museum Berlin 2012. *Publications:* Die Zukunft der Dienstleistung (ed.) 1997, Die Welt der Dienstleistung (ed.) 1998. *Address:* Knorr-Bremse AG, Moosacher Str. 80, 80809 München, Germany (office). *Telephone:* (89) 35470 (office). *E-mail:* info@knorr-bremse.com (office). *Website:* www.knorr-bremse.com (office).

MANGOLD, Robert Peter, BFA, MFA; American artist; b. 12 Oct. 1937, N Tonawanda, New York; s. of Aloysius Mangold and Blanche Mangold; m. Sylvia Plimack 1961; ed Cleveland Inst. of Art and Yale Univ.; minimalist artist; Instructor, School of Visual Arts, New York 1963–, Hunter Coll. 1964–65, Cornell Univ. Skowhegan Summer Art School 1968; work represented in numerous public collections in USA, UK and Europe, including Museum of Modern Art, Solomon R. Guggenheim Museum and Whitney Museum of American Art, New York, San Francisco Museum of Modern Art, Tate Collection, London, Art Inst. of Chicago, Fundacío La Caixa, Barcelona, Hirshhorn Museum and Sculpture Garden, Washington, DC, J. Paul Getty Trust, Los Angeles, Kunstmuseum Basel, Switzerland, Los Angeles County Museum of Art, Museo Nacional de Arte Reina Sofia, Madrid, Tokyo Metropolitan Art Museum, Hallen für Neue Kunst, Schaffhausen, Switzerland; represented by The Pace Gallery, New York 1991–; Fellow, American Acad. of Arts and Letters; lives and works in upstate New York; Nat. Council on Arts Award 1966, Nat. Endowment for the Arts grant 1967, Guggenheim Fellowship 1969. *Address:* c/o The Pace Gallery, 32 East 57th Street, New York, NY 10022, USA. *Telephone:* (212) 421-3292. *Fax:* (212) 421-0835. *E-mail:* info@pacegallery.com. *Website:* www.pacegallery.com.

MANGUDYA, John Panonetsa, BSc, MSc; Zimbabwean economist, banking executive and central banker; *Governor, Reserve Bank of Zimbabwe;* b. 5 Oct. 1963, Mutambara, Chimanimani; m. Tapiwa Mangudya; three c.; ed Univ. of Zimbabwe; Economist, Reserve Bank of Zimbabwe 1986–96; Regional Man. in charge of Southern Africa, African Export-Import Bank (Afreximbank) 1996–99; Gen. Man. (int. banking), CBZ Bank Ltd 2000–04, Exec. Dir (corporate and merchant banking) 2004–06, Man. Dir 2006–09, CEO 2009–12, Group CEO CBZ Holdings Ltd 2012–14; Gov. Reserve Bank of Zimbabwe 2014–; Chair. of Bd Industrial Devt Corpn of Zimbabwe, Agricultural Marketing Authority of Zimbabwe; fmr Pres. Bankers Asscn of Zimbabwe; mem. Bd of Dirs Africa Univ., Willowvale Mazda Motor Industries Pvt. Ltd; mem. Men's Fellowship of United Methodist Church. *Address:* Reserve Bank of Zimbabwe, 80 Samora Machel Avenue, POB 1283, Harare, Zimbabwe (office). *Telephone:* (4) 703000 (office). *Fax:* (4) 707800 (office). *E-mail:* rbzmail@rbz.co.zw (office). *Website:* www.rbz.co.zw (office).

MANGUEL, Alberto; Canadian (b. Argentine) writer, editor and translator; b. 13 March 1948, Buenos Aires, Argentina; Fellow, Simon Guggenheim Foundation, S. Fischer Stiftung; Officier, Ordre des Arts et des Lettres; Dr hc (Univ. of Liège, Anglia Ruskin Univ., Cambridge); Premio La Nacion 1971, Harbourfront Festival Prize 1992, Canadian Authors' Asscn Prize 1992, Prix France-Culture 2000, Premio German Sánchez Ruiperez 2002, Prix Poitou-Charentes 2004, Prix Roger Caillois 2004, Premio Grinzane Cavour 2004. *Publications include:* (in English) novels: News from a Foreign Country Came (McKitterick Prize 1992) 1991, Stevenson Under the Palm Trees 2002, The Return 2006, The Overdiscriminating Lover 2006, At the Mad Hatter's Table 2006, The Library at Night 2008, All Men Are Liars 2010; collections: In Another Part of the Forest: The Flamingo Anthology of Gay Literature (with Craig Stephenson) 1968, The Gates of Paradise: The Flamingo Anthology of Erotic Literature 1969, Black Water: The Flamingo Anthology of Fantastic Literature 1990; non-fiction: The Dictionary of Imaginary

Places 1980, Into the Looking-Glass Wood: Essays on Books, Reading and the World 1985, A History of Reading (TLS Int. Book of the Year, Prix Médicis 1998) 1996, Reading Pictures 2001, A Reading Diary 2005, With Borges 2006, Homer's The Iliad and The Odyssey: A Biography 2007, The City of Words 2008, A Reader on Reading 2010, The Traveler, the Tower, and the Worm: the Reader as Metaphor 2013, Curiosity 2015, Packing My Library 2018; ed. of numerous anthologies, many trans. *Address:* c/o Guillermo Schavelzon Agency, Calle Muntaner 339 5, 08021 Barcelona, Spain (office). *Telephone:* (93) 2011310 (office). *Fax:* (93) 2006886 (office). *E-mail:* info@schavelzon.com (office). *Website:* www.schavelzon.com (office); www.alberto.manguel.com.

MANHIRE, William (Bill), BA, MLitt, MPhil, FRSNZ; New Zealand poet, writer and academic; b. 27 Dec. 1946, Invercargill; s. of Jack Manhire and Madeline Mary Manhire; m. Barbara Marion McLeod 1970; one s. one d.; ed South Otago Dist High School, Otago Boys' High School, Univ. of Otago at Dunedin, Univ. Coll., London, UK; Lecturer in English, Vic. Univ., Wellington 1973, f. creative writing programme 1976, Prof. of Creative Writing and English Literature 1997–2013; Dir Int. Inst. of Modern Letters 2001–13; UNESCO Visiting Prof. of Creative Writing, Univ. of East Anglia 2015; Fiction Ed. Victoria Univ. Press 1976–96; Fulbright Visiting Prof. in NZ Studies, Georgetown Univ., USA Jan.–June 1999; inaugural Te Mata Estate New Zealand Poet Laureate 1997–99; Companion NZ Order of Merit; Hon. DLitt (Otago); NZ Book Award 1977, 1984, 1992, 1996, Nuffield Fellowship 1981, Montana Book Award 1994, Katherine Mansfield Fellowship 2004, NZAF Arts Laureate 2005, Montana NZ Book Award 2006, Prime Minister's Award for Literary Achievement (Poetry) 2007, Icon Award, Arts Foundation 2018. *Compositions:* Buddhist Rain, Making Baby Float. *Publications include:* Malady 1970, The Elaboration 1972, Song Cycle 1975, How to Take Your Clothes Off at the Picnic 1977, Dawn/Water 1980, Good Looks 1982, Locating the Beloved and Other Stories 1983, Zoetropes: Poems 1972–82 1984, Maurice Gee 1986, The Brain of Katherine Mansfield 1988, The New Land: A Picture Book 1990, The Old Man's Example 1990, Milky Way Bar 1991, An Amazing Week in New Zealand 1993, Fault 1994, South Pacific 1994, Hoosh 1995, My Sunshine 1996, Songs of My Life 1996, Sheet Music: Poems 1967–1982 1996, Mutes and Earthquakes 1997, What to Call Your Child 1999, Doubtful Sounds: Essays and Interviews 2000, Collected Poems 2001, Under the Influence (memoir) 2003, Lifted (poems) 2005, Pine 2005, The Victims of Lightning 2010, Selected Poems 2012, These Rough Notes 2012, Falseweed 2015, The Stories of Bill Manhire 2015, Tell Me My Name 2017, Some Things to Place in a Coffin 2017; editor: New Zealand Listener Short Stories Vol. 1 1977, Vol. 2 1978, Some Other Country: New Zealand's Best Short Stories (with Marion McLeod) 1984, Six by Six 1989, Soho Square 1991, 100 New Zealand Poems 1994, Denis Glover: Selected Poems 1995, Spectacular Babies (with Karen Anderson) 2001, The Wide White Page: Writers Imagine Antarctica 2004, 121 New Zealand Poems 2006, The Goose Bath 2006, Are Angels OK? (with Paul Callaghan) 2006, Still Shines When You Think of It (with Peter Whiteford) 2007, The Best of Best New Zealand Poems (with Damien Wilkins) 2011, The Exercise Book 2011, Ein Anderes Land 2012. *Leisure interest:* swimming. *E-mail:* bill.manhire@vuw.ac.nz (office). *Website:* www.thearts.co.nz/artists/professor-bill-manhire (office).

MANIATOPOULOS, Constantinos S.; Greek EU official and business executive; b. 1941; m. Theodora Hiou; one s.; ed Athens and Paris; fmrly employed in energy and industry sectors; Chair. and Man. Dir EKO Petroleum Co., Greece 1983–86; mem. Bd various nat. advisory bodies; Gen. Sec. Tech. Chamber of Greece 1975–82; Advisor to Minister of Energy 1981–84, Public Power Corporation of Greece 1995–98, Public Gas Corpn of Greece 1997–98, Greek Energy Regulator 2003–04; Dir-Gen. for Energy, EC (now EU) Comm. 1986–95; Chair. Bd of Dirs Greek Organization for School Buildings 1982–84, M.O.U. (Community Support Framework for Greece) 1995–99, Piraeus Port Authority 1998–2002; Chair. European Energy Charter WG1 1992–94, Inst. of Energy for SE Europe 2007–09; mem. Oxford Energy (Oil) Club 1986–96, Governing Bd, IEA 1986–95, Bd of Dirs Athens Int. Airport 1995–2004; fmr Chair. Hellenic Republic Asset Devt Fund. *Address:* 13 Makedonias Street, Kifissia, Athens, Greece.

MANIBE NGAI, Kosti; South Sudanese politician; b. W Equatoria; Minister of Cabinet Affairs in caretaker govt (between independence 9 July 2011 and appointment of new cabinet 26 August 2011); Minister of Finance and Econ. Planning Aug. 2011–13 (suspended June 2013).

MANIGLIA FERREIRA, Adm. Ramón Orlando; Venezuelan government official and naval officer; commissioned into Venezuelan Navy, fmr Navy Commdr, C-in-C 2003, rank of Vice-Adm., then Three-Sun Adm. 2005; Inspector Gen. Nat. Armed Forces 2004–05; Minister of Nat. Defence 2005–06.

MANIK, Moosa (Reeko); Maldivian actor, politician and business executive; *Deputy Speaker of Parliament;* currently mem. People's Special Majlis (Hulhu-Henveiru), Deputy Speaker 2014–; Owner, Heavy Load Pvt. Ltd; Chair. Maldivian Democratic Party 2012–14; mem. Progressive Party of Maldives 2017–. *Address:* People's Majlis Secretariat, Medhuziyaaraiy Magu, Malé 20-080, Maldives (office). *Telephone:* 3322617 (office). *Fax:* 3324104 (office). *E-mail:* admin@majlis.gov.mv (office). *Website:* www.majlis.gov.mv (office).

MANIKU, K. D. Ahmed; Maldivian government official; Deputy Minister of Environment and Construction –2005; Commr of Elections and Registrar of Political Parties 2005–08; Minister of State, Controller of Immigration and Emigration 2008.

MANIKU, M(oamed) U(mar); Maldivian business executive; Founder-Chair. Universal Enterprises Pvt. Ltd; fmr Special Econ. Adviser to the Pres.; Chair. Mahaweli Reach Hotels PLC 2012–; Chair. Maldives Asscn of Tourism Industry. *Address:* Universal Enterprises Pvt Ltd, 39, Orchid Magu, Malé, Maldives (office). *Telephone:* 3323080 (office). *E-mail:* iyaz.waheed@universalenterprises.com (office). *Website:* www.universalresorts.com (office); matimaldives.com; www.mahaweli.com.

MANILOV, Col-Gen. Valery Leonidovich, PhD; Russian civil servant and army officer; b. 10 Jan. 1939, Tulchin, Ukraine; m.; one d.; ed Odessa Higher Infantry School, Mil.-Political Acad., Gen. Staff Mil. Acad.; service in Odessa, Baikal mil. commands, S Group of armed forces, service in Afghanistan; apptd on staff Ministry of Defence 1988; Head Information Service of Jt Armed Forces of

CIS 1992–93; Asst to Sec. Russian Security Council July–Oct. 1993, Deputy Sec. 1993–96; First Deputy Head of Gen. Staff. 1998–2000; mem. Acad. of Mil. Sciences, Russian Acad. of Natural Sciences, Int. Acad. of Informatization; mem. Council of Fed., Rep. Primorsky Territory 2001.

MANILOW, Barry; American singer, musician (piano) and songwriter; b. (Barry Alan Pincus), 17 June 1946, New York; s. of Harold Manilow and Edna Manilow; m. Garry Kief 2014; ed New York Coll. Music, Juilliard School of Music; worked in mailroom at CBS; film ed. WCBS-TV; Dir Music Ed Sullivan's Pilots; Music Dir, conductor and producer for Bette Midler; Amb. for Prince's Trust 1996; solo artist 1974–; resident shows in Las Vegas, including at Paris Las Vegas, Las Vegas Hilton; f. Manilow Health and Hope Fund (nonprofit includes Manilow Music Project); Producer of the Year 1975, After Dark magazine Ruby Award 1976, Photoplay Gold Medal 1976, Grammy Award for Song of the Year (for I Write The Songs) 1977, Emmy Award (for The Barry Manilow Special) 1977, American Music Awards for Favorite Male Artist 1978–80, Grammy Award for Best Male Pop Vocal Performance (for At The Copa from Copacabana) 1979, Songwriters Hall of Fame Hitmaker Award 1991, Starlight Foundation Humanitarian of the Year 1991, Soc. of Singers Ella Award 2003. *Theatre:* Barry Manilow on Broadway (jt recipient Tony Award 1977) 1976, Barry Manilow at the Gershwin (Broadway) 1989, Copacabana (West End, London) 1994. *Television appearance:* Copacabana (film) 1985. *Recordings include:* albums: Barry Manilow I 1973, Barry Manilow II 1974, Tryin' To Get The Feelin' 1975, This One's For You 1976, Live 1977, Even Now 1978, One Voice 1979, Barry 1980, A Nice Boy Like Me 1980, If I Should Love Again 1981, Live In Britain 1982, I Wanna Do It With You 1982, Here Comes The Night 1982, Oh, Julie! 1982, 2.00 AM Paradise Café 1984, Manilow 1985, Live On Broadway 1987, Swing Street 1987, Barry Manilow 1989, Songs To Make The Whole World Sing 1989, Because It's Christmas 1990, Showstoppers 1991, Hidden Treasures 1993, Singin' With The Big Bands 1994, Another Life 1995, Summer of '78 1996, Manilow Sings Sinatra 1998, Here At The Mayflower 2001, A Christmas Gift Of Love 2002, Two Nights Live 2004, Scores: Songs From Copacabana and Harmony 2004, The Greatest Songs of the Fifties 2006, The Greatest Songs of the Sixties 2006, The Greatest Songs of the Seventies 2007, In the Swing of Christmas 2007, Beautiful Ballads and Love Songs 2008, The Greatest Songs of the Eighties 2008, Happy Holiday! 2008, In the Swing of Christmas 2009, The Greatest Love Songs of All Time 2010, 15 Minutes 2011, My Dream Duets 2014. *Publication:* Sweet Life: Adventures on the Way to Paradise 1987. *Address:* William Morris Endeavor Entertainment, 9601 Wilshire Blvd, Suite 300, Beverly Hills, CA 90210, USA (office). *Website:* www.barrymanilow.com.

MANIN, Yuri Ivanovich, BSc, PhD, DPhysMathSci (Habil.); Russian/German mathematician and academic; *Professor Emeritus, Max Planck Institute for Mathematics;* b. 16 Feb. 1937, Simferopol, Crimea, Ukrainian SSR, USSR; s. of Ivan Manin and Rebecca Miller; m. Xenia Semenova; one s.; ed Moscow State Univ.; Researcher, Steklov Math. Inst. Moscow 1960–, now Prin. Researcher; Prof. of Math., Moscow State Univ. 1965–91; Visiting Prof., several univs including Harvard Univ. and Columbia Univ., USA 1991–93; Prof., MIT, USA 1992–93; Scientific mem. Max Planck Inst. for Math., Bonn 1993–, Dir, Man. Dir 1995, now Prof. Emer.; Bd of Trustees Prof., Northwestern Univ., USA 2002–11, Bd of Trustees Prof. Emer. 2011–; mem. Academia Europaea, Pontifical Acad. of Science, Vatican, Acad. Leopoldina Germany, American Acad. of Arts and Sciences; Corresp. mem. Russian Acad. of Sciences, Göttingen Acad. of Sciences; Foreign mem. Royal Netherlands Acad. of Arts and Sciences, French Acad. des Sciences; Hon. mem. London Math. Soc. 2011; Order 'pour le Mérite' for Arts and Sciences (Germany) 2007, Grosses Verdienstkreuz mit Stern (Germany) 2008; Dr hc (Sorbonne, Univ. Pierre et Marie Curie, Paris VI) 1999, (Warwick) 2006; Abel Bicentennial DPhil hc (Oslo) 2002; Lenin Prize 1967, Brouwer Gold Medal 1987, Frederic Esser Nemmers Prize 1994, Rolf Schock Math. Prize (Royal Swedish Acad. of Sciences) 1999, King Faisal Prize for Science 2002, Georg Cantor Medal of German Math. Soc. 2002, Bolyai Int. Prize, Hungarian Acad. of Science 2010. *Publications:* Frobenius Manifolds, Quantum Cohomology and Moduli Spaces 1999; author, co-author of 11 monographs and more than 260 scientific papers. *Leisure interests:* literary criticism, linguistics, cultural studies. *Address:* Max Planck Institute for Mathematics, Vivatsgasse 7, 53111 Bonn, Germany (office). *Telephone:* (228) 402271 (office). *Fax:* (228) 402277 (office). *E-mail:* manin@mpim-bonn.mpg.de (office). *Website:* www.mpim-bonn.mpg.de (office).

MANITAKIS, Antonis, LLM, PhD; Greek lawyer, academic and politician; *Dean of Faculty of Law and Social Sciences, Neapolis University, Cyprus;* b. 19 April 1944, Thessaloniki; m. Kleopatra Theodorou; two s.; ed Aristotle Univ. of Thessaloniki, Université Libre de Bruxelles, Belgium; Prof. of Constitutional Law, Aristotle Univ. of Thessaloniki 1982–2011, taught Constitutional Law, Gen. Theory of the State, Human Rights and Judicial Review of Constitutionality for 35 years, later Dean of Faculty of Law and Econs and Head of Dept of Public Law and Political Science, as well as Dir of Postgraduate Studies Programme, Faculty of Law, Prof. Emer. 2012–; currently Dean, Faculty of Law and Social Sciences, Neapolis Univ., Cyprus; Visiting Prof., Univ. of Montpellier, Univ. of Paris X, Univ. of Rome 'La Sapienza', Univ. of Nantes; Visiting Research Fellow, Princeton Univ.; Alt. Chair. Nat. Council for Radio & Television 1997–99; fmr Pres. Nat. Comm. for Human Rights; active in the European Social Forum; served in caretaker govt between two elections under Prime Minister Panayiotis Pikrammenos May–June 2012; Minister of Admin. Reform and e-Governance following formation of coalition govt between New Democracy (Nea Demokratia), Panhellenic Socialist Movt (PASOK) and Democratic Left (Dimokratiki Aristera) 2012–13; Minister of the Interior and Admin. Reconstruction Aug.–Sept. 2015; honoured for his contrib. to academia by the Pres. of Greece 2007. *Publications include:* (in Greek): Constitutional Law, The Relation between Nation-State and Church, The Constitution of Europe Facing National and People's Sovereignty; Ti to kirion tis politias esti; three handbooks: What a State Is, What a Constitution Is, What a Political System Is; 16 monographs and 125 original research papers. *Address:* Office of the Dean, Faculty of Law and Social Sciences, Neapolis University, 2 Danais Avenue, 8042 Paphos, Cyprus (office). *Telephone:* 2684-3503 (office). *E-mail:* antonis.manitakis@nup.ac.cy (office); antouanmanitakis@gmail.com (home); amanitas@otenet.gr (home). *Website:* www.nup.ac.cy/prof-antonis-manitakis (office).

MANJHI, Jitan Ram; Indian politician; b. 6 Oct. 1944, Mahkar village, Gaya Dist, Bihar; s. of Ramjit Ram Manjhi and Sukri Devi; m. Shanti Devi; two s. five d.; ed Gaya Coll.; clerk, Gaya Telephone Exchange 1968–80; entered politics 1980 as mem. Bihar Legis. Ass. (state Parl.) from Fatehpur constituency (Congress) 1980, elected to five subsequent assemblies, most recently as mem. Bihar Legis. Ass. for Makhdoompur constituency, Jehanabad Dist 2010–; served as minister in several Bihar state govts, including as Human Resources Devt Minister 1990, Minister of Educ. mid-1990s; Chief Minister of Bihar 2014–15; mem. Indian Nat. Congress 1980–90, Janata Dal 1990–96, Rashtriya Janata Dal 1996–2005, Janata Dal (United) 2005–15 (expelled); f. Hindustani Awam Morcha (now Hindustani Awam Morcha (Secular)) 2015. *Website:* www.facebook.com/pages/Hindustani-Awam -Morcha-HAM.

MAŃKO, Dariusz, PhD; Polish business executive; *President of the Management Board and CEO, Grupa Kęty SA;* b. 1968; ed Agricultural Univ., Poznań, Acad. of Econs, Katowice; sales rep. and later Head of Marketing and Devt, SAPA POLAND 1993–96; joined Grupa Kęty SA 1996, Man., ZML Kęty SA 1996–99, CEO and Gen. Dir, Metalplast-Bielsko SA 1999–2000, mem. Man. Bd Grupa Kęty SA 2000–, Pres. and CEO 2005–; Chair. Supervisory Bd ZRE Metalplast 1999–; mem. Supervisory Bd, Elektrobudowa SA 2002–03 (Chair. 2004–), Alupol Sp. Ltd (Chair. 2005–, Chair. Supervisory Bd Alupol Packaging SA 2010–). *Address:* Grupa Kęty SA, 32-650 Kęty, z siedzibą w Kętach, ul. Kościuszki 111, Poland (office). *Telephone:* (33) 8446000 (office). *Fax:* (33) 8446100 (office). *E-mail:* kety@grupakety.com (office). *Website:* www.grupakety.com (office).

MANLEY, Hon. John, PC, OC, BA, LLB; Canadian business executive, lawyer and fmr politician; *President and CEO, Canadian Council of Chief Executives;* b. 5 Jan. 1950, Ottawa; s. of John Joseph Manley and Mildred Charlotte Scharf; m. Judith Manley; one s. two d.; ed Carleton Univ., Univ. of Ottawa; fmrly practitioner in business and income tax law, Ottawa; law clerk to Chief Justice of Canada 1976–77; Chair. Ottawa-Carleton Bd of Trade 1985–86; mem. of Parl. 1988–2004; Minister of Industry 1993–2000, also Minister responsible for Atlantic Canada Opportunities Agency, Canada Econ. Devt and Western Econ. Diversification 1996–97; Minister of Foreign Affairs 2000–02; Chair. Ad Hoc Cabinet Cttee on Public Security and Anti-terrorism; Deputy Prime Minister of Canada and Minister of Infastructure and Crown Corpn 2002–03; Minister of Finance 2002–03; Political Minister for Ont. 2002–03; Chair. Cabinet Cttees on Econ. Union and on Social Union 2002–03; retd from politics 2003; Sr Counsel, McCarthy Tétrault LLP, Ottawa 2003–; mem. Bd of Dirs Nortel Networks 2004–, CIBC 2005–; Chair. Ind. Task Force on the Future of North America, Council on Foreign Relations 2005; named Chair. of govt panel on future of Canada's presence in Afghanistan 2007; Pres. and CEO, Canadian Council of Chief Executives 2010–; Dr hc (Ottawa Univ.) 1998, (Carleton Univ.), (Toronto Univ.), (Western Ontario Univ.); Internet Person of the Year 2000, Newsmaker of the Year, Time Canada 2001. *Leisure interest:* marathon runner. *Address:* Canadian Council of Chief Executives, 99 Bank Street, Suite 1001, Ottawa, ON K1P 6B9, Canada (office). *Telephone:* (613) 238-3727 (office). *Fax:* (613) 238-3247 (office). *E-mail:* info@thebusinesscouncil.ca (office). *Website:* thebusinesscouncil.ca (office).

MANN, Emily Betsy, BA, MFA; American writer, theatre director and playwright; *Artistic Director, McCarter Theatre;* b. 12 April 1952, Boston, Mass; d. of Arthur Mann and Sylvia Mann (née Blut); m. Gary Mailman; one s. from previous m.; ed Harvard Univ., Univ. of Minnesota; Resident Dir Guthrie Theater, Minneapolis 1976–79; Dir Brooklyn Acad. of Music Theater Co., Brooklyn, NY 1980–81; freelance writer and dir, New York 1981–90; Artistic Dir McCarter Theatre, Princeton, NJ 1990–; mem. Soc. of Stage Dirs and Choreographers, Theater Communications Group, New Dramatists, PEN, Writer's Guild; mem. Exec. Bd Dramatists' Guild; Dr hc (Princeton Univ.) 2002; BUSH Fellowship 1975–76, Obie Awards for Directing 1981, 2002, Obie Award for Playwriting 1981, New Drama Forum Asscn Rosamond Gilder Award 1983, Nat. Endowment for the Arts (NEA) Asscns Grant 1984, Tony Award for Outstanding Regional Theater 1984, Guggenheim Fellowship 1985, McKnight Fellowship 1985, CAPS Award 1985, NEA Playwrights Fellowship 1986, Brandeis Univ. Women of Achievement Award 1995, Douglass Coll. of NJ Woman of Achievement Award 1996, Rosamond Gilder Award for Outstanding Achievement in the Theater 1999, Harvard Univ. Alumnae Recognition Award 1999, Nat. Conf. for Community and Justice Award 2004, Leader of the Year Award, Princeton Regional Chamber of Commerce 2005, Person of the Year, Nat. Theatre Conf. 2011. *Publications include:* plays: Annulla Allen: The Autobiography of a Survivor 1977, Still Life (six Obie Awards 1981, Fringe First Award 1985) 1982, Execution of Justice (Helen Hayes Award, Bay Area Theater Critics Circle Award, HBO/USA Award, Playwriting Award Women's Cttee Dramatists Guild for Dramatizing Issues of Conscience) 1986, Having Our Say: The Delaney Sisters' First 100 Years (LA NAACP Award for Best Play) 1994, Greensboro: A Requiem 1996, Gloria: A Life 2018; musicals: Betsey Brown: A Rhythm and Blues Musical (co-author with Ntozake Shange); screenplays: Fanny Kelly (unproduced) 1981, You Strike a Woman, Greensboro: A Requiem 1996, Having Our Say (Christopher Award, Peabody Award) 1999, Political Stages (co-ed.) 2002, A Seagull in the Hamptons (adaptation) 2008. *Address:* McCarter Theatre, 91 University Place, Princeton, NJ 08540-5121, USA (office). *Telephone:* (609) 258-6502 (office). *Fax:* (609) 497-0369 (office). *E-mail:* emann@mccarter.org (office). *Website:* www.mccarter.org (office).

MANN, Matthias, BA, MA, PhD; German chemist, biochemist and academic; *Director, Department of Proteomics and Signal Transduction, Max Planck Institute of Biochemistry;* b. 10 Oct. 1959; ed Univ. of Göttingen, Yale Univ.; Postdoctoral Fellow, later Sr Scientist, Dept of Molecular Biology, Univ. of Southern Denmark 1989–92, Prof. of Bioinformatics, Dept of Biochemistry and Molecular Biology and Dir Centre for Experimental BioInformatics 1998–2007; Group Leader, Protein and Peptide Group, European Molecular Biology Lab., Heidelberg 1992–98; Dir Max Planck Inst. of Biochemistry, Martinsried 2005–; also Dir Dept of Proteomics, Novo Nordisk Foundation Centre for Protein Research, Faculty of Heath Sciences, Univ. of Copenhagen, Denmark 2007–, affiliated with NNF Centre for Protein Research; Visiting Prof., Harvard Medical School, USA 1999; mem. Editorial Bd, Journal of Proteome Research, Molecular and Cellular Proteomics, Cell, Carcinogenesis, Cell Systems, Clinical Mass Spectrometry; mem. European Molecular Biology Org. (EMBO) 1999, Leopoldina German Nat. Acad. of Sciences 2013; Hon. Prof., Novo Nordisk Foundation Centre for Protein Research, Faculty of Health Sciences, Univ. of Copenhagen 2007; Order of Dannebrog Knights Cross (Denmark) 2015; Dr hc (Utrecht) 2004; Malcom Award, Journal of Organic Mass Spectrometry 1991, Mattauch Herzog Prize in Mass Spectrometry 1996, Hewlett-Packard Prize for Strategic Research in Automation of Sample Preparation 1997, Edman Prize, Methods in Protein Structure Analysis Soc. 1998, Bieman Medal for Outstanding Achievement in Mass Spectrometry, American Soc. for Mass Spectrometry 1999, Bernhard and Matha Rasmussen's Memorial Award in Cancer Research 2001, Meyenburg Cancer Research Award 2001, Fesenius Prize for Analytical Chem., German Chemical Soc. 2001, Lundbeck Nordic Research Prize 2004, Novo-Nordisk Prize (co-recipient) 2004, Anfinsen Award, Protein Soc. 2005, Biochemical Analysis Prize, German Soc. for Clinical Chem. and Lab. Medicine 2006, HUPO Distinguished Achievement Award in Proteomic Sciences (co-recipient) 2008, Friedrich Wilhelm Joseph von Schelling Prize, Bavarian Acad. of Sciences 2010, Fyodor Lynen Lecture Medal, German Soc. of Biochemistry and Molecular Biology 2011, Leibniz Prize, German Research Soc. 2012, Ernst Schering Prize 2012, Louis-Jeantet Foundation Prize for Medicine 2012, Körber European Science Award 2012, Barry L. Karger Medal in Bioanalysis 2015, Theodor Bücher Medal 2015, Lennart Philipson Award 2017. *Publications:* more than 500 papers in professional journals. *Address:* Max Planck Institute of Biochemistry, Am Klopferspitz 18, 82152 Martinsried, Germany (office). *Telephone:* (89) 85782557 (office). *Fax:* (89) 85782219 (office). *E-mail:* mmann@biochem.mpg.de (office). *Website:* www .biochem.mpg.de/mann (office).

MANN, Michael K.; American film producer, director and writer; b. 5 Feb. 1943, Chicago, Ill.; ed Univ. of Wisconsin, London Film School; Exec. Producer (TV) Miami Vice, Crime Story, Drug Wars: Camarena Story, Drug Wars: Cocaine Cartel, Police Story, Starsky and Hutch; mem. Writers Guild, Directors Guild; two Emmy Awards. *Films include:* The Jericho Mile (TV film, dir, scriptwriter) (Best Dir Award, Directors Guild) 1979, Thief (dir, exec. producer, scriptwriter) 1981, The Keep (dir, scriptwriter) 1981, Manhunter (dir, scriptwriter) 1986, Last of the Mohicans (dir, co-producer, scriptwriter) 1992, Heat (dir, co-producer, scriptwriter) 1995, The Insider (dir, producer) 1999, Ali 2001, Collateral (dir, producer) (Best Dir, Nat. Bd of Review) 2004, The Aviator (producer) (Best Film, BAFTA Awards 2005), Miami Vice 2006, The Kingdom 2007, Hancock 2008, Public Enemies 2009. *Address:* c/o Creative Artists Agency, 9830 Wilshire Boulevard, Beverly Hills, CA 90212, USA.

MANN, Stephen, BSc, MSc, DPhil, FRS, FRSC; British chemist and academic; *Professor of Chemistry, University of Bristol;* b. 1 April 1955; m.; ed Univ. of Manchester Inst. of Science and Tech. and Univ. of Manchester, Univ. of Oxford; Prof. of Chem., Univ. of Bath 1990–98; Prof. of Chem., Univ. of Bristol 1998–, Dir Centre for Organized Matter Chem., Centre for Protolife Research, Prin. Bristol Centre for Functional Nanomaterials, mem. Scientific Steering Cttee, Bristol Synthetic Biology 2014–, Univ. of Bristol Governing Body (Council) 2014–; Visiting Prof., Weizmann Inst. of Science 1988, Univ. of California, Santa Barbara 1993–94, Collège de France 2009, Harvard Univ. 2011–12; Chair. Scientific Advisory Bd for the Frontier Eng Centre for Nature Inspired Eng, Univ. Coll., London; mem. editorial advisory bds of several journals, including Advanced Materials, Angewandte Chemie, Chemical Science, Small; mem. Alexander von Humboldt Foundation 1998; EPA Jr Research Fellowship, L.G. Knafel Fellow; Royal Soc. of Arts Silver Medal Award, UMIST 1976, Keble Coll., Oxford 1981–84, RSC Corday-Morgan Medal 1993, Vinci of Excellence Trophy, Science for Art Prize, Paris 1996, Max-Planck Soc./Alexander von Humboldt Foundation Research Award 1998–2003, RSC Interdisciplinary Award 1999, Royal Soc. Sr Fellowship: Wolfson Research Merit Award 2006–11, RSC Joseph Chatt Lecturer and Medal 2007–08, French-British Prize, Chemical Soc. of France (SCF) 2011, RSC de Gennes Prize and Medal 2011, Radcliffe Inst. for Advanced Study, Harvard Univ., USA 2011–12, Advanced Grant, European Research Council 2011–16, Davy Medal, Royal Soc. 2016. *Achievements include:* a founder of biomimetic materials chemistry. *Publications:* more than 480 papers in professional journals on biomineralization and the synthesis and self-assembly of functional nanostructures and hybrid nanoscale objects. *Address:* Office E207, School of Chemistry, University of Bristol, Cantock's Close, Clifton, Bristol, BS8 1TS, England (office). *Telephone:* (117) 928-9935 (office). *E-mail:* s.mann@bristol.ac.uk (office). *Website:* www.bris.ac.uk/chemistry (office); www.bristolcomc.co.uk (office); www.bcfn.bris .ac.uk (office); www.stephenmann.co.uk; www.bristolprotolife.co.uk (office).

MANN, Yuri Vladimirovich; Russian literary scholar and historian; *Professor, Russian State Humanitarian University;* b. 9 June 1929, Moscow; s. of Vladimir Mann and Sonja Mann; m. Galina Mann 1956 (died 2007); two s.; ed Moscow Univ.; school teacher, Moscow 1952–56; Prof. of Russian Literature, Gorky Inst. of World Literature –1992; Prof., Russian State Humanitarian Univ. 1992–; Visiting Prof., Chicago Univ., USA 1991; Chief Ed. Complete Academic Works of N. V. Gogol (23 vols); mem. CPSU 1952–90, Russian PEN Centre 1995, Acad. of Natural Sciences 1996. *Publications include:* The Grotesque in Literature 1966, Russian Philosophical Aesthetics 1820's–1830's 1969, The Poetics of Russian Romanticism 1976, The Poetics of Gogol 1978, In Search of a Live Soul –Gogol's Dead Souls 1984, The Dialectics of Image 1987, The Aksakov Family 1992, Beyond the Mask of Laughter: The Life of Nikolai Gogol 1994, The Dynamics of Russian Romanticism 1995, The Poetics of Gogol: Variations on the Theme 1996, Russian Literature XIX Century. Romanticism 2001, Gogol: The Life and the Creation 1809–1845 2004, Exploring Gogol 2005, 19th Century Russian Literature (Romanticism) 2007, Creations of Gogol: Meaning and Form 2007, Turgenev and the Others 2008, Gogol: The End of the Road, 1845–1852 2009, Gogol: Fate and Creation 2009, Memory as Happiness as well as Memory as Pain 2011. *Address:* Moscow 125267, Russian State Humanitarian University, Ul. Chayanov 15 (office); Moscow 125047, 3 Tverskaya-Yamskaya 44, Apt 5, Russian Federation (home). *Telephone:* (499) 250-66-92 (office); (499) 250-52-97 (home). *E-mail:* ymann@si.ru.

MANNAI, Jassim Abdullah al-, PhD; Bahraini business executive and international organization official; b. 1948; ed Univ. of Paris (Sorbonne), France, Harvard Business School, USA; Exec. Vice-Pres. Gulf Investment Corpn, Kuwait 1987–94; Chair. and CEO Arab Trade Financing Program, Abu Dhabi 1994–2014; Dir-Gen. and Chair. Arab Monetary Fund, Abu Dhabi 1994–2014; Chair. Inter Arab Rating Co. EC (mem. Fitch IBCA Group) 1995–2001. *Publications include:* numerous articles on economic and financial issues in various publs.

MANNHARDT, Thilo, MSc, MBA, PhD; German business executive; ed Technische Universität Berlin; fmr Pres. IMIFARMA (pharmaceutical company); Sr Partner and Dir, McKinsey & Co. 1985–2012; Advisor and mem. Bd of Dirs Ultrapar Holdings 2011–12, CEO 2013–17; mem. Bd of Dirs Algar Telecom 2017–. *Address:* c/o Algar Telecom SA, Rua Jose Alves Garcia 415, Uberlandia, Minas Gerais 38400-668, Brazil. *Telephone:* (80) 0942-2009. *Fax:* (34) 3256-2954. *E-mail:* comprovante@algartelecom.com.br. *Website:* www.algartelecom.com.br.

MANNING, Sir David Geoffrey, Kt, GCMG, KCVO, BA; British diplomatist (retd); *Co-founder and Director, Gatehouse Advisory Partners Ltd;* b. 5 Dec. 1949, Portsmouth, Hants.; s. of John Robert Manning and Joan Barbara Manning; m. Catherine Marjory Parkinson 1973; ed Ardingly Coll., Oriel Coll., Oxford, Johns Hopkins Univ., USA; Third Sec., Mexico, Cen. America Dept, FCO 1972, Third, later Second Sec., Embassy in Warsaw 1974–76, Second, later First Sec., Embassy in New Delhi 1977–80, E European and Soviet Dept, FCO 1980–82, Policy Planning Staff, FCO 1982–84, First Sec. (Political Internal), Embassy in Paris 1984–88, Counsellor on loan to Cabinet Office 1988–90, Counsellor, Head of Political Section, Moscow 1990–93, Head, Eastern Dept (fmrly Soviet Dept), FCO 1993–94, British mem. of ICFY Contact Group on Bosnia April–Nov. 1994, Head of Planning Staff 1994–95, Amb. to Israel 1995–98, Deputy Under-Sec. of State, FCO 1998–2000, Perm. Rep. to NATO, Brussels Jan.–Aug. 2001, Foreign Policy Adviser to Prime Minister 2001–03, Head of Cabinet Office Defence and Overseas Secr. 2001–03, Amb. to USA 2003–07; apptd to part-time advisory role to Household of Duke and Duchess of Cambridge and Household of Prince Harry; Co-founder and Dir Gatehouse Advisory Partners 2010–; Sr Adviser, Chatham House; Chair. IDEAS, LSE; mem. Bd of Dirs Lloyds Banking Group plc 2008–09, BG Group plc (fmrly British Gas plc) 2008–, Lockheed Martin UK Holdings Ltd 2008–; mem. Advisory Bd Hakluyt & Co.; Trustee, Turner Contemporary; Patron, Afghan Connection, World Wide Volunteering. *Address:* Gatehouse Advisory Partners Ltd, 1 Tudor Street, London, EC4Y 0AH, England (office). *Telephone:* (20) 7099-5553 (office). *Fax:* (20) 7990-9779 (office). *E-mail:* info@gatehouseadvisorypartners.com (office). *Website:* www.gatehouseadvisorypartners.com (office).

MANNING, Jane Marian, OBE, LRAM, FRAM, ARCM, FRCM, GRSM; British singer (soprano), lecturer and writer; *Visiting Professor, Royal College of Music;* b. 20 Sept. 1938, Norwich, Norfolk, England; d. of Gerald Manning and Lily Thompson; m. Anthony Payne 1966; ed Norwich High School for Girls, Royal Acad. of Music, Scuola di Canto, Switzerland; London debut concert 1964; since then active world-wide as freelance soprano soloist with special expertise in contemporary music; more than 350 BBC broadcasts; regular tours of USA since 1981 and of Australia since 1978; appearances at most leading European festivals and concert halls; New York debut 1983; more than 300 world premiers including several operas; Founder/Artistic Dir Jane's Minstrels (ensemble) 1988; Vice-Pres. Soc. for Promotion of New Music 1996–2008; Visiting Prof., Mills Coll., Oakland, Calif. 1981, 1982, 1983, 1986, Royal Coll. of Music, London 1995–; Arts and Humanities Research Council Creative Arts Research Fellow, Kingston Univ. 2003–07, Visiting Prof. 2007–10; Fellow in Research Dept Guildhall School of Music and Drama 2012–16; Vocal Studies Teacher, Guildhall School of Music and Drama, London; frequent visiting lecturer at univs in UK, USA, Canada, Australia, NZ and Scandinavia; Chair. Eye Music Trust; fmr Trustee, Help-Musicians UK; Hon. Prof., Keele Univ. 1996–2002; Hon. DUniv (York) 1988; Hon. DMus (Keele) 2004, (Dunelm) 2007; Hon. DArts (Kingston) 2013; Special Award for Services to British Music, Composers' Guild of GB 1973, Gold Badge of Merit, British Asscn of Songwriters and Composers 2013. *Recordings:* numerous recordings, including complete vocal works of Messiaen and Satie. *Publications include:* New Vocal Repertory (Vol. I) 1986, (Vol. II) 1998; contrib. to A Messiaen Companion 1995, Voicing Pierrot (A Practical Guide) 2011; contrib. to History of Musical Performance 2014, Vocal Repertoire for the 21st Century (two vols) 2018; numerous articles in Tempo, etc. *Leisure interests:* ornithology, cinema, history, philosophy, theatre, reading. *Address:* 2 Wilton Square, London, N1 3DL, England (home). *Telephone:* (20) 7359-1593 (home). *E-mail:* janetone@gmail.com (home). *Website:* www.classical-artists/janemanning.com.

MANNING, Peyton Williams, BA; American professional football player (retd); b. 24 March 1976, New Orleans, La; s. of Archie Manning and Olivia Manning; m. Ashley Thompson 2001; ed Isidore Newman High School, New Orleans, Univ. of Tennessee; quarterback; holds 42 Nat. Collegiate Athletic Asscn (NCAA), South Eastern Conf. (SEC) and Univ. of Tennessee records, including 33 Univ. of Tennessee single game, season and career records; first pick in 1998 Nat. Football League (NFL) draft by Indianapolis Colts 1998, holds numerous NFL passing records including most seasons (nine) with at least 4,000 passing yards 1999–2004, 2006–08 (Colts won Super Bowl championship 2007), released by Colts 2012; signed with Denver Broncos 2012– (Broncos won Super Bowl championship 2016); f. Peyback Foundation 1999; Gatorade Circle of Champions Nat. Player of the Year in high school, voted third-best quarterback in SEC history, named in SEC All-Decade Team, Maxwell Trophy (for coll. football's best player) 1997, Sullivan Award Winner 1997, named to Pro Bowl team 1999–2000, 2002–10, 2012–14, AFC Player of the Year 1999, 2003, 2004, 2005, 2008, 2009, Henry P. Iba Citizen Athlete Award 2002, USA Weekend's Most Caring Athlete Award 2002, First-team All-Pro 2003, 2004, 2005, 2008, 2009, 2012, 2013, Associated Press (AP) Most Valuable Player of the NFL 2003 (jtly with Steve McNair) 2004, 2008, 2009, 2013, Bert Bell Award 2003, 2004, AP NFL Offensive Player of the Year 2004, John Wooden Trophy 2004, Walter Payton Man of the Year Award 2005, Pro Bowl Most Valuable Player 2005, Byron 'Whizzer' White Humanitarian Award 2005, AFC champion 2006, 2009, Super Bowl XLI Most Valuable Player 2007, Best Championship Performance ESPY Award 2007, Youthlinks Indiana Nat. Pathfinder Award 2010, NFL 2000s All-Decade Team, NFL Comeback Player of the Year 2012, Sports Illustrated Sportsman of the Year 2013. *Achievements include:* fastest player ever to reach 50,000 yards passing, fastest to 4,000 completions. *Publications:* Manning: A Father, His Sons and a Football Legacy (with Archie Manning) 2000. *Address:* c/o Brian Bishoff, IMG, 1360 East 9th Street, Suite 100, Cleveland, OH 44114, USA (office). *Telephone:* (216) 436-3571 (office). *Website:* www.imgfootball.com (office); www.peytonmanning.com.

MANNINGHAM-BULLER, Baroness Eliza(beth) Lydia, DCB; British fmr government official; b. 14 July 1948; d. of Sir Reginald Manningham-Buller (later Viscount Dilhorne) and Lady Mary Lilian Lindsay; m. 1991; ed Northampton High School, Benenden School, Kent and Lady Margaret Hall, Univ. of Oxford; fmr English teacher; joined MI5 Security Service 1974, worked on case of KGB defector Oleg Gordievsky and on Lockerbie disaster, served as MI5 liaison officer at Embassy in Washington, DC, Dir for Surveillance and Tech. Operations 1993, Dir of Irish Counter-terrorism, Dir of Finance and Information Tech., Deputy Dir-Gen. 1997–2002, Dir-Gen. 2002–07 (retd); mem. House of Lords 2008–; Vice-Chair. Pollen Estate; mem. Bd of Dirs Ark Continuity Ltd, Genome Research Ltd; Sr Adviser to Inter Mediate Ltd; mem. Council, Imperial Coll. 2008–, Chair. 2011–15; Gov. Wellcome Trust 2009–, Chair. 2015–; Hon. Fellow, Lady Margaret Hall, Oxford 2003, Northampton Univ. 2008; Order of the Garter 2014; Dr hc (Cranfield) 2003, (Open) 2005. *Address:* House of Lords, London, SW1A 0PW, England (office). *Telephone:* (20) 7219-5353 (office). *Fax:* (20) 7219-5979 (office).

MANOLI, Mihail, PhD; Moldovan economist, diplomatist and politician; b. 20 Sept. 1954, Valea Mare; m.; one c.; ed Polytechnic Inst. of Chisinau, M. Lomonosov Moscow State Univ.; Lecturer, Academy of Economic Studies, State Univ. of Moldova 1978–79, 1983–95; with Price Waterhouse 1993–95; Deputy Minister of Finance 1995–99, Minister of Finance 1999–2002; Amb. to USA (also accred to Canada) 2002–06; Deputy Pres. of Council of Experts, National Securities Comm. 2006–07; Adviser to Pres. of CB Universalbank 2007–08; Pres. Union of Insurers of Moldova 2008–10; Deputy Chair. Partidul Democrat din Moldova (PDM, Democratic Party of Moldova) 2010; Exec. Dir Nat. Green Card Bureau Jan.–Sept. 2015. *Address:* Partidul Democrat din Moldova, 2011 Chișinău, str. Armenească 44, Moldova (office). *Telephone:* (22) 54-17-22 (office). *Fax:* (22) 27-70-08 (office). *E-mail:* pdm@mtc.md (office). *Website:* www.pdm.md (office).

MANOLIČ, Josip, (Joža); Croatian politician and lawyer; b. 22 March 1920, Kalinovac; m. Marija Manolić (née Eker); three d.; ed Zagreb Univ.; mem. youth orgs and trade union activist 1938–; mem. anti-fascist movt; Sec., Dist Cttee League of Communist Youth of Croatia; Chief, Dept of Nat. Security in Bjelovar 1945–46 (dismissed); worked in Ministry of Internal Affairs of Croatia 1948–60; Interior Affairs Secr. in Zagreb 1960–65; mem. of Parl. Repub. of Croatia, Pres. Legis. Body of Constitutional Comm. 1965–71; mandate suspended because of nationalist activities; Co-founder Croatian Democratic Union (HDZ), first Chair. Exec. Cttee 1989, elected Vice-Pres. 1990; mem. of Croatian Parl. 1990–; Pres. Croatian Govt 1990–91, Vice-Pres. Presidency of Repub. of Croatia –1999; Pres. House of Counties of Croatian Parl. 1992–94; Pres. Emergency Bd of Croatia; Dir Bureau for the Protection of Constitutional Order 1991–93; Founder Croatian Ind. Democrats (HND), Pres. of HND; certificate for participation in anti-Fascist struggle 1941–45, certificate for participation in the defence of the homeland 1991–92. *Publication:* Manolić 1989–95 (collection of interviews). *Leisure interest:* chess. *Address:* 41000 Zagreb, Nazorova Str. 57, Croatia (office). *Telephone:* (1) 4848476 (office).

MANOOGIAN, Richard Alexander, BA; American business executive; *Chairman Emeritus, Masco Corporation;* b. 1936, Detroit, Mich.; s. of Alex Manoogian and Marie Manoogian; ed Yale Univ.; joined Masco Corpn 1958, apptd Dir 1964, Vice-Pres. 1964–68, Pres. 1968–85, Chair. and CEO 1985–2007, Exec. Chair. 2007–09, Chair. 2009–12, Chair. Emer. 2012–; CEO Metaldyne Corpn –1998; Chair. TriMas 1989–98; mem. Bd of Dirs JPMorgan Chase 1978–, Bank One Corpn 1978–, First Chicago NBD Corpn 1978–, Ford Motor Co. 2001–, Metaldyne Corpn 1984–2005, MSX International Inc. 1997–2004, Detroit Renaisssance, The American Business Conf., MSX Int.; Life Pres. Armenian Gen. Benevolent Union; Chair. Detroit Inst. of Arts, Alex and Marie Manoogian Foundation; Dir, Yale Univ. Art Gallery, Center for Creative Studies, The Fine Arts Cttee of the State Dept, Council of the Nat. Gallery of Art, Armenian Gen. Benevolent Union, Henry Ford Museum, Greenfield Village; mem. Henry Ford Museum, Michigan Business Roundtable, Mackinac Island State Park Comm., American Fed. of Arts, American Asscn of Museums, Museum Trustees Asscn, Chief Execs Org. (YPO); Trustee, Community Foundation of Southeastern Michigan, Archives of American Art (Smithsonian Inst.). *Address:* Masco Corporation, 21001 Van Born Road, Taylor, MI 48180-1300, USA (office). *Telephone:* (313) 274-7400 (office). *Fax:* (313) 792-4177 (office). *E-mail:* info@masco.com (office). *Website:* www.masco.com (office).

MANOROHANTA, Cécile; Malagasy politician, academic and university administrator; *President, Université Nord Madagascar;* mem. Faculty, Université Nord Madagascar, Antsiranana 2000–02, then Acting Rector and Pres., Pres. 2013–; Nat. Vice-Pres. ruling Tiako i Madagasikara (I Love Madagascar—TIM) party; Minister of Defence (first woman) 2007–09 (resgnd), Deputy Prime Minister, responsible for the Interior Sept.–Dec. 2009, apptd acting Prime Minister for two days 18–20 Dec. 2009; Pres. Scientific Council of the Francophonie Summit; mem. AUF Scientific Council; Commdr, Légion d'Honneur 2007. *Publications:* A Quantitative Study of Voice in Malagasy (UCLA Working Papers in Linguistics 6: Papers in African Linguistics 1) 2001; numerous papers on linguistics in professional journals. *Address:* Office of the President, Université Nord Madagascar, BP 0, 201 Antsiranana, Madagascar (office). *Telephone:* (20) 82-29-409 (office). *Fax:* (20) 82-29-409 (office). *E-mail:* presidence@univ-antsiranana.org (office). *Website:* www.univ-antsiranana.org (office).

MANSARAY, Binta, BA, MA; Sierra Leonean lawyer and UN official; *Registrar, Residual Special Court for Sierra Leone;* ed Fourah Bay Coll., Univ. of Sierra Leone, Freetown, Fordham Univ., New York and American Univ., Washington DC, USA; fmr human rights advocate with several orgs for victims and ex-combatants from Sierra Leone's civil conflict; held post of Country Rep. for Women's Comm. for Refugee Women and Children in Sierra Leone, worked with Campaign for Good Governance, and served as consultant with UN Mission in Sierra Leone (UNAMSIL) and several civil society orgs; Outreach Co-ordinator, UN Special Court for Sierra Leone, Freetown 2003–07, designed Court's grassroots programme to keep the people of Sierra Leone, and later Liberia, informed about the Court and the trials, Deputy Registrar, Special Court for Sierra Leone 2007–09, Acting Registrar 2009–10, Registrar 2010–13, Acting Registrar, Residual Special Court for Sierra Leone Jan.–Sept. 2014, Registrar Sept. 2014–; Hon. Mem., Pi Alpha Alpha Global Honor Soc. for Public Affairs and Public Admin.; Commdr, Order of the Rokel 2014. *Address:* The Residual Special Court for Sierra Leone, PO Box 19536, 2500 CM The Hague, The Netherlands (office). *Telephone:* (70) 525-8481 (office). *Fax:* (70) 322-2711 (office). *E-mail:* info@rscsl.org (office); binta.scsl@gmail.com (office). *Website:* www.rscsl.org (office).

MANSBRIDGE, Peter, OC; Canadian (b. British) broadcaster and journalist; b. 6 July 1948, London, England, UK; s. of Stanley Harry Mansbridge and Brena Louise Mansbridge; m. 1st Parm Dhillon (divorced 1975); m. 2nd Wendy Mesley 1989 (divorced 1992); m. Cynthia Dale 1998; ed Glebe Collegiate Inst., Trinity Coll. School, Port Hope, Ont.; raised in Ottawa, Ont.; served in Royal Canadian Navy 1966–67; fmr airline freight man.; disc jockey and newscaster, CBC Radio, Churchill 1968, reporter, CBC Radio, Winnipeg 1971, reporter, CBC TV News 1972–85, reporter, The National, Saskatchewan 1975, with Parl. Bureau, Ottawa 1976–80, Co-Anchor, Quarterly Report, Anchor Sunday Report 1985, Anchor, The National 1988–92, Anchor of news segment on The National 1992, Anchor, Prime Time News 1992, Chief Corresp. for CBC News; launched a new programme, Mansbridge One on One 1999; Chancellor Mount Allison Univ., NB 2009–17; Queen Elizabeth II Diamond Jubilee Medal 2012; Hon. LLD (Mount Allison Univ.) 1999, (Univ. of Manitoba, Winnipeg) 2001, (Univ. of Western Ontario) 2008, (Univ. of Windsor, Ont.) 2010; Hon. Dr of Journalism (Ryerson Univ., Toronto) 2005; 12 Gemini Awards for excellence in broadcast journalism.

MANSELL, Kevin B.; American retail executive; *Chairman, President and CEO, Kohl's Corporation;* b. St Louis, Mo.; ed Univ. of Missouri; various buying and merchandising roles, Venture Stores Div., May Dept Stores 1975; Div. Merchandise Man. Kohl's Corpn 1982–87, Gen. Merchandise Man. 1987–96, Sr Exec. Vice-Pres. of Merchandising and Marketing 1998–99, Dir 1999–, Pres. 1999–, CEO 2008–, Chair. 2009–. *Address:* Kohl's Corporation, N56 W17000 Ridgewood Drive, Menomonee Falls, WI 53051, USA (office). *Telephone:* (262) 703-7000 (office). *Fax:* (262) 703-6143 (office). *E-mail:* info@kohls.com (office). *Website:* www .kohlscorporation.com (office).

MANSELL, Nigel Ernest James, CBE, OBE; British racing driver; b. 8 Aug. 1953, Upton-on-Severn, Worcs., England; s. of Eric Mansell and Joyce Mansell; m. Rosanne Perry; two s. one d.; ed Matthew Boulton Polytechnic, Solihull Tech. Coll.; began racing in karts; won 11 regional Championships 1969–76; Formula Ford and Formula Three 1976–79; Formula Two, later Formula One 1980; Lotus team 1981–84; Williams-Honda team 1985–87; Williams-Judd team 1988; Ferrari team 1989–90; Williams-Renault team 1991–92 and 1994 (part-time); McLaren team 1995; first competed in a Grand Prix, Austria 1980; won 31 Grand Prix races 1980–94 (record since beaten by Michael Schumacher); Formula One World Drivers Champion 1992; American Newman-Haas Indy Car Team 1993; CART Indy Car World Series Champion 1993; Special Constable, Isle of Man –1995, Devon and Cornwall Constabulary; Owner Woodbury Park Golf and Country Club 1993–; Pres., UK Youth (charity), Inst. of Advanced Motorists (IAM); Hon. DEng (Birmingham) 1993; BBC Sports Personality of the Year 1986, 1992, CART Rookie of the Year 1993, inducted into Int. Motorsports Hall of Fame 2005. *Publications:* Mansell and Williams (with Derick Allsop) 1992, Nigel Mansell's IndyCar Racing (with Jeremy Shaw) 1993, My Autobiography (with James Allen) 1995, Driven to Win (with Derick Allsop). *Leisure interests:* golf, fishing, flying. *Website:* www .nigelmansell.co.uk.

MANSFIELD, Michael, QC, BA, FRSA; British barrister; *Professor of Law, City University;* b. 12 Oct. 1941, London; s. of Frank Mansfield and Marjorie Sayers; m. 1st Melian Mansfield 1967 (divorced 1992); three s. two d.; m. 2nd Yvette Mansfield 1992; one s.; ed Highgate School and Keele Univ.; called to the Bar 1967; est. Tooks Chambers 1984; apptd Prof. of Law, Westminster Univ. 1997; currently Prof. of Law, City Univ., London; est. Mansfield Chambers, London 2013; Pres. Haldane Soc. of Socialist Lawyers, Amicus, Nat. Civil Rights Movement; Founder Interights; Visiting Prof., School of Law, Birkbeck, Univ. of London 2014–; Patron, Acre Lane Neighbourhood Chambers, Brixton, Vegetarians Int. Voice for Animals (Viva!); Bencher, Gray's Inn 2008; Hon. Fellow, Kent Univ.; Hon. LLD (South Bank Univ.) 1994, (Univ. of Herts.) 1995, (Keele Univ.) 1995, (Westminster Univ.) 2005, (Ulster Univ.); Lifetime Achievement Award, Asscn of Muslim Lawyers 2007, Lifetime Achievement Award, Chambers & Partners 2008, Lifetime Achievement Award, The Monitoring Group 2009. *Radio:* Moral Maze, BBC Radio 4 1995–98, Today, BBC Radio 4. *Television:* Inside Story 1991, Presumed Guilty; contribution to Newsnight, BBC 2. *Publications:* Presumed Guilty 1994, Home Lawyer 2004, Memoirs of a Radical Lawyer 2010. *Leisure interests:* my children, drumming. *Address:* Mansfield Chambers, 16 High Holborn, London, WC1V 6BX, England (office). *Telephone:* (20) 7406-7550 (office). *Website:* www .mansfieldchambers.co.uk (office); www.city.ac.uk/law (office).

MANSFIELD, Terence Arthur, PhD, FRS, FSB; British biologist and academic; *Professor Emeritus and Honorary Fellow, Lancaster University;* b. 18 Jan. 1937, Ashby-de-la-Zouch, Leics.; s. of Sydney W. Mansfield and Rose Mansfield (née Sinfield); m. Margaret M. James 1963; two s.; ed Univs of Nottingham and Reading; Research Fellow, Univ. of Reading 1961–65; Lecturer and Prof., Lancaster Univ. 1965–87, Dir Inst. of Environmental and Biological Sciences 1987–94, Provost of Science and Eng 1994–97, Research Prof. 1996–2001, Prof. Emer. and Hon. Fellow 2001–; mem. Agric. and Food Research Council 1989–93; Fellow, Soc. of Biology. *Publications include:* Physiology of Stomata (co-author) 1968, Stomatal Physiology (co-ed.) 1981, Plant Adaptation to Environmental Stress (co-ed.) 1993, Disturbance of the Nitrogen Cycle (co-ed.) 1998, Glimpses of the Victorians at Church 2004; numerous chapters and journal articles on aspects of botanical science. *Leisure interests:* cricket, hill-walking, church history. *Address:* 25 Wallace Lane, Forton, Preston, Lancs., PR3 0BA, England (home). *Telephone:* (1524) 791338 (home).

MANSHA, Mian Muhammad; Pakistani industrialist; *Chairman and CEO, Nishat Group;* b. 1 Dec. 1947, Lahore; s. of Mian Muhammad Yahya; m. Naz Saigol; three c.; ed studies in London, UK, Univ. of the Punjab; grew up in Faisalabad; joined family business after completing studies in London; Chair. and CEO Nishat Group (conglomerate with interests in banking, insurance, textiles and cement, including MCB Ltd, Nishat Mills, D.G. Khan Cement); Owner Pakistan Aviators & Aviation Ltd (domestic charter plane service), St James's Hotel and Club, Mayfair, London; mem. Bd of 46 cos in Pakistan; Sitara-e-Imtiaz 2004, selected for a special Lunch with the Financial Times 2012. *Address:* Office of the Chairman, MCB Ltd, 10th Floor, MCB Building, 15 Main Gulberg, Jail Road, Lahore (office); Nishat Chunian Group, 31-Q, Gulberg II, Lahore 54660, Pakistan (office). *Telephone:* (42) 36041998 (MCB Ltd) (office); (42) 35761730 (Nishat Chunian) (office). *Fax:* (42) 35878696 (Nishat Chunian) (office). *E-mail:* info@mcb

.com.pk (office); info@nishat.net (office). *Website:* www.nishatpak.com (office); www.nishat.net (office); www.mcb.com.pk (office).

MANSHARD, Walther, Dr rer. nat; German geographer, academic and international civil servant; *Professor, Geographisches Institut, University of Freiburg;* b. 17 Nov. 1923, Hamburg; s. of Otto and Ida Manshard; m. Helga Koch 1951; one d.; ed Univ. of Hamburg; Asst lecturer, Univ. of Southampton, UK 1950–52; lecturer, Univ. of Ghana 1952–60; Dozent, Univ. of Cologne 1960–63; Prof. Univ. of Giessen 1963–70; Prin. Dir UNESCO Dept of Environmental Sciences 1970–73; Prof., Head of Dept Univ. of Freiburg 1973–77, 1980–; Vice-Rector, UN Univ., Tokyo 1977–80; Sec.-Gen. and Treas. Int. Geographical Union 1976–84; Sr Adviser UN Univ. 1990–93; Hon. DLitt 1991. *Publications:* Die geographischen Grundlagen der Wirtschaft Ghanas 1961, Tropisches Afrika 1963, Agrargeographie der Tropen 1968, Afrika–Südlich der Sahara 1970, Tropical Agriculture 1974, Die Städte des tropischen Afrika 1977, Renewable Natural Resources and the Environment 1981, Entwicklungsprobleme in Agrarräumen Tropen-Afrikas 1988, Umwelt v. Entwicklung in den Tropen 1995. *Address:* Geographisches Institut, University of Freiburg, Werderring 4, 79085 Freiburg i. Br.; Schwarzwaldstrasse 24, 79189 Bad Krozingen, Germany. *Telephone:* (761) 2033565 (office); (7633) 9888941 (home). *Fax:* (761) 2033575 (office); (7633) 3488 (home). *E-mail:* walther .manshard@geographie.uni-freiburg.de (office). *Website:* www.geographie.uni -freiburg.de (office).

MANSILLA FERNÁNDEZ, Brig.-Gen. Williams Agberto; Guatemalan military commander and government official; b. 24 April 1964, Guatemala City; m.; two c.; ed Gloriosa y Centenaria Escuela Politécnica Mil. Acad.; long career in Guatemalan Armed Forces; Commdr, Presidential Guard 2013–15; Minister of Nat. Defence 2015–17; Medalla de Constancia en el Servicio 1ra. Clase, Medalla de Constancia en el Servicio 2da. Clase, Distintivo de Tiempo de Servicio de 30 años, Medalla de Constancia en el Servicio de Tercera Clase, Medalla de Conducta de Primera Clase, and numerous other mil. awards.

MANSINGH, Lalit, BA (Hons), MA; Indian diplomatist (retd); b. 29 April 1941, Cuttack; s. of Mayadhar Mansingh and Hemalata Mansingh (née Behura); m. Indira Mansingh 1976; one s. one d.; ed Utkal Univ., Orissa, Indian School of Int. Studies, Univ. of Delhi, Jawaharlal Nehru Univ.; lecturer in political science 1961–63; joined diplomatic service 1963, Third Sec. to Geneva 1964–67, Deputy Chief of Mission to Kabul 1971–74, to Brussels 1976–79, to Washington, DC 1989–92, Amb. to UAE 1980–83; High Commr to Nigeria, Benin, Chad and Cameroon 1993–95, to UK 1998–99; Jt Sec. Dept of Econ. Affairs, Ministry of Finance 1984–85; Dir-Gen. Indian Council for Cultural Relations 1985–89; Dean, Foreign Services Inst., New Delhi 1995–96, now Prof. Emer.; Foreign Sec. (West), Ministry of External Affairs 1997–98; Amb. to USA 2001–04; Chair. World Cultural Forum India, Political Science Asscn, Ravenshaw Univ., Cuttack, The Kalinga Indonesia Dialogue; Founder-Pres. Kalinga Lanka Foundation; Global Envoy, Int. Buddhist Confed., New Delhi; mem. Exec. Bd, Forum for Strategic Initiatives; mem. Governing Body of Devt Alternatives, New Delhi; mem. Ambassadors Forum, Washington DC; mem. Track II dialogue between India, Pakistan, Afghanistan and other South Asian countries; mem. Bd of Trustees, Asia Pacific Leadership Network, Canberra; Hon. LLD (Univ. of North Odisha) 2013; Univ. Gold Medals for top-ranking graduate in History and Political Science, Kharavela Award, Govt of Orissa 2009. *Publications include:* Indian Foreign Policy: Agenda for the 21st Century (Ed.-in-Chief) 1998, Purbasa: East meets East (ed.) 2018. *Leisure interests:* classical music, dance, fine arts, theatre. *Address:* N-38 Panchsheel Park, New Delhi 110 017, India (home). *E-mail:* lalitmansingh@ yahoo.com (office).

MANSON, Marilyn; American singer and songwriter; b. (Brian Warner), 5 Jan. 1969, Canton, Ohio; m. Dita Von Teese 2005 (divorced 2007); fmr music journalist; Founder-mem. Marilyn Manson & the Spooky Kids 1989–, later Marilyn Manson; numerous TV appearances, tours; Kerrang! Icon Award 2005. *Recordings include:* albums: Portrait of an American Family 1994, Smells Like Children 1995, Antichrist Superstar 1996, Mechanical Animals 1998, The Last Tour on Earth 1999, Holy Wood (In the Shadow of the Valley of Death) 2000, Genesis of the Devil 2001, Live 2002, The Word According to Manson 2002, The Golden Age of Grotesque 2003, White Trash 2003, From Obscurity 2 Purgatory 2004, Eat Me, Drink Me 2007, The High End of Low 2009, Born Villain 2012, The Pale Emperor 2015. *Publication:* The Long Hard Road Out of Hell (autobiography) 1997. *Address:* c/o CAA, 162 Fifth Avenue, 6th Floor, New York, NY 10010, USA (office). *Telephone:* (212) 277-9000 (office). *Fax:* (212) 277-9099 (office). *Website:* www.caa .com (office); www.marilynmanson.com.

MANSOORI, Mubarak Rashed Khamis al-, MBA; United Arab Emirates investment manager and central banker; *Governor, Central Bank of the United Arab Emirates;* ed Univ. of West Florida, USA; Deputy Dir Abu Dhabi Investment Authority 1991–2000; Dir Gen. Abu Dhabi Pension Fund 2000–08; CEO Emirates Investment Authority 2008–14; Gov. Cen. Bank of UAE 2014–, mem. Bd of Dirs 2014–; Co-Chair. Regional Consultative Group for Middle East and North Africa, Financial Stability Bd; mem. Governing Bd, Int. Islamic Liquidity Man. Corpn; mem. Bd of Dirs Abu Dhabi Securities Exchange 2010–, Etisalat Misr, Egypt, Etihad Etisalat Co., Mobily, Nat. Co. for Building Materials (BILDCO); fmr mem. Bd of Dirs Arab Banking Corpn, Egypt –2006, of Jordan –2008, Securities & Commodities Authority of UAE, Arab Int. Bank, Egypt, Banco Atlantico, Spain, Tabreed, Abu Dhabi Holding Co. *Address:* Central Bank of the United Arab Emirates, POB 854, Abu Dhabi, United Arab Emirates (office). *Telephone:* (2) 6652220 (office). *Fax:* (2) 6652504 (office). *E-mail:* admin@cbuae.gov.ae (office). *Website:* www.centralbank.ae (office).

MANSOUR, Adly, LLB; Egyptian lawyer, judge and fmr head of state; b. 23 Dec. 1945, Cairo; m.; one s. two d.; ed Cairo Univ.; graduated from Faculty of Law 1967; joined State Council 1970, rose through the ranks to become Deputy Pres. of Supreme Constitutional Court (SCC) 1992–1 July 2013, Pres. SCC 2013–16; Acting Pres. of Egypt following ousting of Muhammad Mursi 4 July 2013–8 June 2014.

MANSOUR, Adnan; Lebanese diplomatist and government official; b. 1946, Bourj al-Barajneh; ed Saint Joseph Univ. Beirut; joined foreign service 1974, served as Consul in numerous countries, including Egypt, Athens, Australia, Oman, fmr mem. Del. to UN, New York, Amb. to Democratic Repub. of Congo

1990–94, to Iran 1999–2007, Perm. Rep. European Comm., Brussels 2008–11, Minister of Foreign Affairs and Emigrants 2011–14.

MANSOUR, Mohamed, MBA; Egyptian business executive and fmr government official; *Chairman, Man Capital LLP;* b. 23 Jan. 1948, Sharkia; s. of Loutfy Mansour; brother of Yasseen Mansour and Youssef Mansour; m.; two s.; ed North Carolina State Univ., Auburn Univ., USA; taught at Auburn Univ., USA –1973; Minister of Transport 2005–08; fmr Chair. Mansour Automotive Co., mem. Bd of Dirs Mansour Group; Chair. Man Capital LLP 2010–, Mantrac Group; Pres. Mansour Foundation for Development, Lead Foundation; fmr Chair. Unatrac, Crédit Agricole Bank Egypt, Egypt-US Business Council; fmr Pres. American Chamber of Commerce in Egypt; Bd mem. Centre for Contemporary Arab Studies, Georgetown Univ., USA; mem. Advisory Bd, George Washington School of Business, USA; fmr mem. Special Olympics of Egypt, Cairo, Alexandria Stock Exchanges, Social Fund for Development, Int. Advisory Bd, Coca Cola Co.; fmr Sec.-Gen. Egyptian Centre for Economic Studies. *Address:* Man Capital LLP, 1 Knightsbridge, London, SW1X 7LX, England (office). *Telephone:* (20) 78387300 (office). *E-mail:* enquiry@mancapllp.com (office). *Website:* www.man-capital.com (office).

MANSOUR, Yasseen, BSc; Egyptian business executive; *Chairman, Palm Hills Developments;* b. 1961; s. of Loutfy Mansour; brother of Mohamed Mansour and Youssef Mansour; m.; four c.; ed George Washington Univ., USA; started career at Mansour Automotive Co. 1986, Founder Manfoods (owner, operator of McDonald's franchise in Egypt), currently Chair. Palm Hills Developments (retail estate developer), mem. Bd of Dirs Mansour Group; mem. Bd of Dirs Nat. Cancer Inst.; Co-founder Lead Foundation; Gen. Sec. Mansour Foundation for Development; Sec.-Gen. Future Foundation. *Address:* Palm Hills Developments, Smart Village, A4 - B83, KM28, Cairo-Alexandria Desert Road, Abou Rawash, Egypt (office). *Telephone:* (2) 35351200 (office). *Fax:* (2) 35351208 (office). *Website:* www .palmhillsdevelopments.com (office); www.yassenmansour.com.

MANSOUR, Youssef L., BSc, MBA; Egyptian business executive; *Chairman, Al Mansour Holding Company for Financial Investments;* b. 1945; s. of Loutfy Mansour; brother of Yasseen Mansour and Mohamed Mansour; m.; five c.; ed North Carolina State Univ., Auburn Univ., USA; CEO Loutfy Mansour Trading Co. 1976–81, Chair. Al Mansour Holding Co. for Financial Investments 1992–, Mansour Automotive Co. 2006–09, mem. Bd of Dirs Mansour Group; Chair. and CEO Mantrac –1992; launched Metro (first domestic supermarket chain) 1998, Kheir Zaman chain 2006; Vice-Pres. Mansour Foundation for Development; Founding mem. American Chamber of Commerce, Egypt; fmr mem. Bd of Dirs Credit Agricole Egypt. *Address:* Al Mansour Holding Company for Financial Investments, Zahraa El Maadi Industrial Zone, PO Box 97, New Maadi, Cairo, Egypt (office). *Telephone:* (2) 27548360 (office). *Fax:* (2) 27548385 (office). *E-mail:* info@mansourgroup.com (office). *Website:* www.mmd.mansourgroup.com (office).

MANSOUR ZEMAM, Mohammed, PhD; Yemeni politician; *Governor, Central Bank of Yemen;* b. 29 Sept. 1964, San'a; ed Univs. of New Mexico and Kingsburg, USA; Gen. Man., Yemen Port Cities Devt Program 2007; Chair. Yemen Customs Authority –2014; Minister of Finance 2014–15; Gov. Arab Monetary Fund –2016; Gov. Cen. Bank of Yemen 2018–; mem. Council, Union of Arab Cen. Banks. *Address:* Central Bank of Yemen, POB 59, San'a, Yemen (office). *Telephone:* (1) 274311 (office). *Fax:* (1) 274360 (office). *E-mail:* cbyemcn@cbycmen.com (office). *Website:* www.centralbank.gov.ye (office).

MANSUROV, Tair Aimukhametovich, PhD; Kazakhstani construction engineer, politologist, diplomatist and regional governor; b. 1 Jan. 1948, Sarkand, Taldykorgan Region, Kazakhstan; s. of Aimukhamet Mansurov and Maken Tursynbekova; m. Saule Bakirova 1973; one s. two d.; ed Kazakh Politechnical Inst., Almaty, Higher Party School at Cen. Cttee of CP, Moscow; worked in construction orgs Alma-Ata, Chief Engineer Almaatacentrestroy 1965–79; Chief, Dept of Construction, Alma-Ata Regional CP Cttee 1979–87; First Sec. Leninskiy Dist CP Cttee, Alma-Ata 1979–87; Instructor, Dept of Construction, Cen. CP Cttee, Moscow 1988–91; Second Sec. Karaganda Region CP Cttee 1989–91; Chief of Section, Dept of Econs, Cen. CP Cttee, Moscow 1988–91; Deputy to Supreme Soviet of USSR 1988–91; Pres. Kazakhstan Devt Fund, Moscow 1991–93; Amb. to Russian Fed. 1994–2002 (also accred to Finland); Amb. at Large and Advisor to Pres. of Kazakhstan 2002–03; Gov. N Kazakhstan Region 2003–07; Sec.-Gen. Eurasian Econ. Community, Moscow 2007–14, mem. Bd Energy and Infrastructure, Eurasian Econ. Comm. 2014–15; mem. Acad. of Creativity, Int. Acad. of High School, Acad. of Social Sciences; Kurmet Order 1996, Order of Dostyk 2001, Order of St Prince Daniel Moskovski (Russia) 2002, Order of Friendship (Russia) 2002, Order of St Segey Radonezhski (Russia) 2005, Order of Kazakhstan's First President Narsultan Nazarbeyev 2006; several medals. *Publications include:* Faces of Sovereignty: Sovereignty in the Prism of Social History 1994, Kazakhstan and Russia: Sovereignization, Integration, Experience of Strategic Partnership 1997, Kazakh–Russian Relations in the Epoch of Changes 2001, scientific and feature books about diplomatist N. Turiakulov 2004, Regulation of External Economic Activity of the Customs Union in Framework of EurAsEC (co-author) 2011, Eurasian Project of Nursultan Nazarbayev 2011, EurAsEC: From Economic Co-operation to Single Economic Space 2011. *Leisure interests:* political, historical and economic literature, sport.

MANTASHE, Gwede, MA; South African trade union official and politician; *Minister of Mineral Resources;* b. 21 June 1955, Transkei; m. Nolwandle Mantashe; ed Univ. of South Africa; Br. Chair. Matla Coal, Nat. Union of Mineworkers 1982–84, Regional Sec. Witbank 1985–88, Nat. Organizer 1988–93, Regional Co-ordinator 1993–94, Asst Gen. Sec. 1994–98, Gen. Sec. 1998–2006; Govt Councillor, Ekurhuleni 1995–99; mem. Cen. Cttee and Politburo SA Communist Party, Chair. 2007–12; fmr mem. Exec. Cttee Congress of South African Trade Unions (COSATU); Sec.-Gen. African Nat. Congress 2007–17, Chair. 2017–; Minister of Mineral Resources 2018–; Dir Samancor 1995–; Exec. Dir Devt Bank of Southern Africa 2006–; Chair. Tech. Task Team, Jt Initiative for Priority Skills Acquisition. *Address:* Ministry of Mineral Resources, Trevenna Campus, Bldg 2c, Meintje and Francis Baard St, Sunnyside, Pretoria, South Africa (office). *Telephone:* (12) 4443000 (office). *Fax:* (86) 6245509 (office). *E-mail:* mediaenquiries@dmr.gov.za (office). *Website:* www.dmr.gov.za (office).

MANTEGA, Guido, MA, PhD; Brazilian economist, academic and government official; b. 7 April 1949, Genoa, Italy; s. of Giuseppe Mantega and Anna Costa Mantega; m. Eliana Berger Mantega; ed Coll. of Econs and Business Admin, Univ. of São Paulo, Inst. of Devt Studies, Univ. of Sussex, UK; Prof. of Econs, School of Business Admin, Fundação Getúlio Vargas 1981–; Budget Dir and Head, Office of Municipal Dept of Planning, São Paulo 1982–92; Prof. of Econs, Pontifícia Universidade Católica de São Paulo-PUC-SP 1984–87; mem. Coordination of Econ. Program for Brazilian Labor Party (PT) in presidential elections 1984, 1989, 1998; Econ. Advisor to President Luiz Inácio Lula da Silva 1993–2002; coordinator PT's Econ. Program 2002; Minister of Planning, Budget, and Admin 2003–04; Pres. Banco Nacional de Desenvolvimento Econômico e Social (BNDES) 2004–06; Minister of Finance 2006–14; mem. Bd of Dirs Petróleo Brasileiro SA (Petrobras) and Petrobras Distribuidora SA (BR) 2007–, currently Chair. *Publications include:* numerous articles and books, including Acumulação Monopolista e Crises no Brasil 1981, A Economia Política Brasileira 1984, Custo Brasil: Mito ou Realidade 1997, Conversas com Economistas Brasileiros II 1999. *Address:* Workers' Party (PT), SCS, Block 2, Block C, Ed. Toufic, Room 256, 70302-000 São Paulo -SP, Brazil (office). *Telephone:* (11) 3213-1313 (office). *Fax:* (11) 3213-1360 (office). *E-mail:* presidencia@pt.org.br (office). *Website:* www.pt.org.br (office).

MANTEGAZZA, Sergio, Dipl. Bus. Admin; Swiss travel industry executive; *Owner, Globus brands;* b. 31 Oct. 1927, Mendrisio; s. of Antonio Mantegazza; m.; two s. (one deceased) one d.; ed Instituto Elvetico, Lugano, Gademann Handelsschule, Zurich; Man. Globus Gateway Tours, Lugano, Switzerland 1945–48, Gen. Man. 1948–52, Dir 1952–56, Man. Dir 1956–60, Pres. 1960–2008, CEO 2009–; Order of San Gregorio Magno 1992. *Address:* Globus Travel Services SA, Via alla Roggia, 6916 Grancia, Switzerland (office). *Telephone:* (91) 985-71-11 (office). *Fax:* (91) 985-73-78 (office). *E-mail:* smante@globuscosmos.ch (office). *Website:* www.globusandcosmos.com (office).

MANTEL, Dame Hilary Mary, DBE, CBE, FRSL; British writer; b. 6 July 1952, Hadfield, Derbyshire; d. of Henry Thompson and Margaret Mary Thompson; m. Gerald McEwen 1973; ed London School of Econs, Univ. of Sheffield; Fellowship, Kings Coll. London 2011; Hon. DLitt (Sheffield) 2003, (Sheffield Hallam) 2004, (RHUL) 2008, (Exeter) 2011, (Cambridge) 2013, (Bath Spa) 2013, (Derby) 2014, (Univ. of London) 2013, (Queens Belfast) 2013, (Oxford Brookes) 2015, (Oxford) 2015; Shiva Naipaul Memorial Prize 1987, David Cohen Prize 2013, President's Medal, British Acad. 2016, Kenyon Review Award for Literary Achievement 2016. *Plays:* Wolf Hall, Bring Up The Bodies. *Radio:* The Giant, O'Brien (drama) 2002, Learning to Talk (5 plays) 2003, The Price of Light (drama) 2005. *Publications include:* Every Day is Mother's Day 1985, Vacant Possession 1986, Eight Months on Ghazzah Street 1988, Fludd (Southern Arts Literature Prize 1990, Winifred Holtby Memorial Award 1990, Southern Arts Literature Prize 1990, Cheltenham Festival Prize 1990) 1989, A Place of Greater Safety (Sunday Express Book of the Year Award 1993) 1992, A Change of Climate 1994, An Experiment in Love (Hawthornden Prize 1996) 1995, The Giant, O'Brien 1998, Giving up the Ghost (MIND Book of the Year 2004) 2003, Learning to Talk 2003, Beyond Black (Yorkshire Post Fiction Award) 2005, Wolf Hall (Man Booker Prize 2009, Nat. Book Critics' Circle Award for Fiction 2009, Walter Scott Prize for Historical Fiction 2009, Galaxy Nat. Book Awards UK Author of the Year 2010, Ind. Booksellers' Book of the Year 2010) 2009, Bring Up the Bodies (Man Booker Prize 2012, Costa Book Award 2012, Author of the Year, Specsavers Nat. Book Awards 2012, South Bank Sky Arts Award 2013) 2012, The Assassination of Margaret Thatcher (short stories) 2014. *Address:* c/o A. M. Heath & Co., 6 Warwick Court, Holborn, London, WC1R 5DJ, England (office). *Telephone:* (20) 7242-2811 (office). *Fax:* (20) 7242-2711 (office). *Website:* www.amheath.com (office); hilary-mantel.com.

MANTUROV, Denis, PhD; Russian business executive and government official; *Minister of Industry and Trade;* b. 23 Feb. 1969, Murmansk; m.; one s. one d.; ed Lomonosov Moscow State Univ., Presidential Acad. of Public Admin; Deputy Dir Gen. Ulan-Ude Aviation Plant 1998–2000; Business Dir Mil Moscow Helicopter Plant 2000–01; Deputy Chair. State Investment Corpn 2001–03; Dir Gen. Oboronprom (aerospace holding co.) 2003–07; Deputy Minister of Industry and Energy 2007–12, Minister of Industry and Trade 2012–; Chair. Bd of Dirs United Aircraft Corpn (PJSC UAC) 2015–; Order of Friendship 2008, Order of Honor 2009; Medal of the Order of Merit to the Motherland, 2nd Class 2007, 4th Class 2013. *Address:* Ministry of Industry and Trade, 109074 Moscow, Kitaigorodskii proyezd 7, Russia (office). *Telephone:* (495) 539-21-87 (office). *Fax:* (495) 539-21-72 (office). *E-mail:* info_admin@minprom.gov.ru (office). *Website:* www.minpromtorg.gov.ru (office).

MANUEL, Armando; Angolan politician; Dir of Treasury and Head of Research Dept and Treasury, Ministry of Finance –2012, Minister of Finance 2013–16; Chair. Fundo Soberano de Angola (sovereign wealth fund) 2012–13; Econ. Adviser to Pres. José Eduardo dos Santos –2013.

MANUEL, Trevor Andrew; South African politician; *Minister in the Presidency for National Planning and Chair of the National Planning Commission;* b. 31 Jan. 1956, Cape Town; s. of Abraham J. Manuel and Philma van Söhnen; m. Lynn Matthews; three s.; ed Harold Cressy High School, Peninsula Technikon; mem. Labour Party Youth 1969–71, Policy Man. on Devt 1989–; construction technician 1974–81; Sec. Kensington Civic Asscn 1977–82; Founding mem. Western Cape United Democratic Front (UDF) 1980s, Sec. Regional Exec. UDF 1983–90, mem. UDF Nat. Exec. Cttee 1983–86, 1989–90; Organizer CAHAC 1981–82; field worker Educational Resource and Information Centre 1982–84; in detention 1985, 1987–88, 1989, restricted 1985–86, 1986–90 (when not in detention); Publicity Sec. ANC Western Cape; mem. ANC Nat. Exec. Cttee 1991–; Minister of Trade and Industry, Govt of Nat. Unity 1994–96; Minister of Finance 1996–2009, Minister in the Presidency for National Planning and Chair. Nat. Planning Comm. 2009–; also currently Gov. World Bank, African Development Bank, Development Bank of Southern Africa; Chair. Devt Cttee of World Bank 2001–05, Commr on Comm. for Africa 2004–05, on Comm. for Growth and Devt 2006–08; apptd Special Envoy for Devt Finance by UN Sec.-Gen. 2008; Chancellor Cape Peninsula Univ. of Technology; Woodrow Wilson Public Service Award 2008. *Address:* National Planning Commission, Office of the Presidency, Union Buildings, West Wing, Government Avenue, Pretoria 0001, South Africa (office). *Website:* www .thepresidency.gov.za (office).

MANUELLA, Sir Tulaga, GCMG, MBE; Tuvaluan accountant and fmr Governor-General; b. 26 Aug. 1936; s. of Teuhu Manuella and Malesa Moevasa; m. Milikini Uinifaleti; two s. three d.; sub-accountant and ledger keeper 1953–55; clerical officer 1955–57; Sr Asst, then Asst Accountant, Treasury 1957–75; Asst Accountant, Tuvalu Govt; Accountant, then Acting Financial Sec., Ministry of Finance 1976–84; Financial Sec. Financial Div. Church of Tuvalu 1984–86; Pacific Conf. of Churches, Suva, Fiji 1987–91; Co-ordinator of Finance and Admin. Ekalesia Kelisiano 1992–94; Gov.-Gen. of Tuvalu 1994–98; Chancellor Univ. of the S Pacific 1997–2000; Patron Pacific Islands Soc. in Britain and Ireland 1995.

MANUKYAN, Vazgen, PhD; Armenian mathematician, academic and politician; *President, Public Council of Armenia;* b. 13 Feb. 1946, Leninakan (now Gyumri); s. of Mikael Manukyan and Astkhik Manukyan; m. Varduhi Ishkhanyan; three d.; ed Yerevan State Univ., Siberian Dept of USSR Acad. of Sciences; Prof., Yerevan State Univ. 1972–95; political activities since 1960s, one of the founders and leaders of Club of Armenian Culture 1967, mem. and co-ordinator Cttee Karabakh 1988; elected Head of the Bd Armenian Nat. Movt 1989; Prime Minister of Armenia 1990–91; Leader, Nat. Democratic Union 1991–; Deputy, Armenian Supreme Soviet 1990–91; Minister of Defence 1992–93; mem. Council of Nat. Security, Pres. 1992–93; Pres. Center for Strategic Studies 1993, Public Council of Armenia, currently Pres.; Chair. Cttee on Econ. Reform, State Cttee on Land Reform and Privatization. *Publications include:* It is Time to Jump Off the Train 1990, Armenian Dream of a Deadlock of Survival 2002. *Address:* 0010 Yerevan, Public Council of Armenia, 26/1 Vazgen Sargsyan Street, 'Erebuni Plaza' Business Centre, Armenia (office). *Telephone:* (10) 523405 (office); (91) 428977 (home). *Fax:* (10) 523766 (home). *E-mail:* v_manukyan@publiccouncil.am (office); vazgenmanukian@gmail.com (home). *Website:* www.publiccouncil.am/en (office).

MANWANI, Harish, BA, MBA; Indian business executive; b. 1954; m.; two d.; ed Mumbai Univ., Jamnalal Bajaj Inst. of Man. Studies, Advanced Man. Program, Harvard Business School, USA; joined Hindustan Lever Ltd (HLL) in 1976, Div. Vice-Pres. Marketing, Detergents 1995, mem. Bd as Dir for Personal Products 1995, also held regional responsibility for Cen. Asia and Middle East Business Group, moved to UK as Sr Vice-Pres. (Global Hair Care and Oral Care) and Exec. Vice-Pres. Latin America Business Group 2000–01, Pres. (Home and Personal Care), Latin America Business Group 2001–04, also served as Chair. Unilever's Latin America Advisory Council, Pres. and CEO (Home and Personal Care), N America Business Group 2004–05, joined Unilever Exec. as Pres. Asia and Africa 2005, also Chair. (non-exec.) Hindustan Unilever Ltd 2005–18 (retd), COO –2014; mem. Exec. Bd Indian School of Business; India Business Leader Award CNBC-TV18 2007, Asia Business Leader of the Year Award, CNBC Asia 2008, Public Service Medal, Singapore Govt 2012. *Leisure interests:* spending time with family, playing golf and bridge.

MANYANG JUUK, Kuol; South Sudanese politician; *Minister of Defence and Veteran Affairs;* m. Priscilla Nyankot Kuot; one s. two d.; fmr rebel commdr; fmr lecturer in Juba; Minister of Roads and Transport in govt of Nat. Unity of Sudan (prior to creation of South Sudan 2011); Gov. Jonglei State 2007–13; Minister of Defence and Veteran Affairs 2013–; mem. Sudan People's Liberation Movt (SPLM), Chair. Jonglei Br., mem. SPLM Higher Exec. Council. *Address:* Ministry of Defence, Juba, South Sudan (office). *Telephone:* (249) 915485232 (mobile) (office). *E-mail:* kdeimkuol@yahoo.com (office).

MANZONI, Giacomo, MusM; Italian composer; b. 26 Sept. 1932, Milan; m. Eugenia Tretti 1960; one s.; ed Bocconi Univ., Univ. of Tübingen, Germany, Conservatorio Verdi; Ed. Il Diapason (music review) 1956; music critic, l'Unità 1958–66; music ed. Prisma 1968; mem. editorial staff, Musica/Realtà 1980–; Prof., Conservatorio Verdi 1962–64, 1974–91, Conservatorio Martini, Bologna 1965–68, 1969–74, Scuola di Musica Fiesole 1988–2004, Accad. Musicale Pescarese 1993–96; mem. Accad. Nazionale di Santa Cecilia, Rome 1994–; has given master-classes in composition in Buenos Aires, Granada, Tokyo, Santiago, Córdoba, Beijing, etc.; Dr hc (Udine) and others; Premio Abbiati 1989, Golden Lion for musical career, Biennale Musica, Venice 2007, Premio Principe Gesualdo 2012. *Compositions include:* music theatre: La Legge 1955, La Sentenza 1960, Atomtod 1965, Per M. Robespierre 1975, Dr. Faustus—Scene dal romanzo di T. Mann 1989; with orchestra: Insiemi 1967, Ombre (alla memoria di Che Guevara) for chorus and orchestra 1968, Parole da Beckett 1971 for 2 choruses, tape and orchestra, Masse: omaggio a E. Varèse, for piano and orch. 1977, Ode 1982, Scene Sinfoniche per il Dr Faustus 1984, Dedica (text by B. Maderna) 1985, 10 versi di E. Dickinson 1989, Malinamusik 1991, Finale e aria (I. Bachmann) 1991, Il deserto cresce (F. Nietzsche) 1992, Moi, Antonin A. (Artaud) 1997, Trame d'Ombre (da Zeami) 1998, O Europa! (A. József) 1999; Sul passaggio del tempo (R. Sanesi) 2001, Sembianti 2003, Studio da concerto for violin, winds and percussion 2005, Mercurio transita davanti al sole 2006, KOKIN b for two voices and orchestra 2008, Progetto Eliogabalo for narrator and orchestra 2009, Studio 2012, Più mosso for 2 pianos and strings 2014 etc., Schuld (A.Haushofer) for tenor and orchestra 2016; chamber music: Musica notturna 1966, Percorso C2 for bassoon and 11 strings, Omaggio a Josquin 1976, Nymphes des bois... (Déploration d'Ockeghem) for soprano and 5 instruments 1985, Una voce chiama, for voice, viola and live electronics (F. Fortini) 1994, Quanto oscura selva trovai (Dante), for trombone, chorus and live electronics 1995, Oltre la soglia, for soprano and string quartet 2000, Pensiero XX di G. Leopardi for narrator and string quartet 2001, Vergers for choir 2006, 6 Canti dal Kokin shū 2007, Il rumore del tempo for soprano and instruments 2010, 4° Rivolto for string sextet 2012, Per questo, for soprano and trumpet 2012, Percorso C3 for piano and 12 strings 2013, Thanatopsis (W.C. Bryant) for baritone and ensemble 2014, Dedica for guitar 2015; film and incidental music. *Publications include:* A. Schoenberg 1975, Scritti 1991, Tradizione e Utopia 1994, Parole per musica 2007, Écrits 2007, Musica e progetto civile 2009, Pensare attraverso il suono (co-author) 2016; trans of Adorno and Schönberg. *Address:* Viale Papiniano 31, 20123 Milan, Italy. *Telephone:* (02) 4817955. *E-mail:* gmanz-@libero.it.

MAO, Chi-kuo, BEng, MEng, PhD; Taiwanese politician; b. Oct. 1948; ed Nat. Cheng Kung Univ., Asian Inst. of Tech., Bangkok, Thailand, Massachusetts Inst. of Tech., USA; Engineer and Div. Chief, Transportation Planning Bd, Ministry of Transportation and Communications (MOTC) 1976–78, Chief Sec., MOTC Secr. 1987–89, Dir-Gen., Tourism Bureau 1989–91, Dir-Gen., Provisional Eng Office of High Speed Rail 1991–93, Admin. Deputy Minister 1993–2000, also Dir-Gen., Civil Aeronautics Admin 1994, Minister of Transportation and Communications 2008–13; Chair. Chunghwa Telecom Co. Ltd 2000–03; Assoc. Prof., Nat. Cheng Kung Univ. 2003–06, Dean and Prof., Coll. of Man. 2006–08; Adviser to Exec. Yuan (Cabinet) 2003, Vice-Premier 2013–14, Premier 2014–16 (resgnd). *Address:* c/o Executive Yuan, No.1, Sec. 1, Zhongxiao East Road, Zhongzheng District, Taipei 10058, Taiwan (office).

MAO, Rubai; Chinese politician; b. 1938, Yangzhou City, Jiangsu Prov.; ed Nanjing Univ.; joined CCP 1959; Deputy Dir then Dir Meteorological Office of Tibet (Deputy Sec. CCP Party Cttee); Deputy Sec. CCP Tibet Autonomous Regional Cttee 1984, Vice-Chair. Tibet Autonomous Region 1986–93; Vice-Minister of State Construction Ministry 1993–97; Sec. CCP Ningxia Hui Autonomous Regional Cttee 1997–2002; Chair. People's Congress of Ningxia Hui Autonomous Region 1998–2002; mem. 15th CCP Cen. Cttee 1997–2002; Vice-Chair. Environment Protection and Resources Conservation Cttee of 10th Nat. People's Congress 2002, Chair. 2003; mem. Standing Cttee 10th Nat. People's Congress; Pres. Meteorology Soc.

MAOR, Galia, BA, MBA; Israeli economist and banker; b. 1943; m.; three c.; ed Hebrew Univ. of Jerusalem; joined Bank of Israel 1963, held numerous supervisory positions including Head of Open Market Operations, Supervisor of Banks 1982–89, Sr Dir Banking Systems, currently mem. Advisory Cttee; pvt. consultancy 1989–91; joined Bank Leumi as Deputy Gen. Man. 1991, Pres. and CEO 1995–2012; mem. Bd of Dirs Equity One, Inc. 2012–, Teva Pharmaceutical Industries Ltd 2012–, Strauss Group Ltd 2013–; mem. Bd of Govs Hebrew Univ. of Jerusalem; Chair. Friends of Yeladim (Council for the Child in Placement), Friends of Acad. of the Hebrew Language, Israeli Cttee of INSEAD; Dr hc (Technion-Israel Inst. of Technology), (Ben Gurion Univ.), (Bar Ilan Univ.), (Open Univ.), (Netanya Coll.); Recannati Award for Women's Excellence in Man. 2001, Women's Excellence Award, Hadassah 2001, Woman of the Year, Globes magazine 2008.

MAPFUMO, Thomas Tafirenyika 'Mukanya'; Zimbabwean musician (mbira, guitar), singer and songwriter; b. 2 July 1945, Marondera; important figure in local Shona music 1970s–; singer in local bands, including The Cosmic Dots, the Springfields; f. Hallelujah Chicken Run Band 1973, Black Spirits 1976; performed with The Pied Pipers 1977; f. Acid Band 1977–, later banned from the radio, renamed Blacks Unlimited 1978; Mapfumo imprisoned for subversion 1977; currently lives in exile in Eugene, Ore., USA; researcher in traditional Zimbabwean folk music; Dr hc (Univ. of Zimbabwe) 1999, (Ohio Univ.) 2001; National Arts Award for Zimbabwe's Person of the Century 2000. *Recordings include:* albums: Hokoya! 1977, Mbira Music of Zimba 1980, Gwindingwe 1980, Mabesa 1983, Congress 1983, The Chimurenga Singles 1983, Ndangariro 1984, Corruption 1984, Mr Music 1985, Chimurenga For Justice 1986, Zimbabwe-Mozambique 1987, Corruption 1989, Nyamaropa Nhimutimu 1989, Shumba 1990, The Spirit of the Eagle 1991, Chimurenga Masterpis 1991, Hondo 1993, Chimurenga Int'l 1993, Vanhu Vatema 1994, Chimurenga: African Spirit Music 1997, Rise Up 2006, Exile 2009, Danger Zone 2015, Lion Songs 2015. *Website:* www.thomas-mapfumo.com.

MAPISA-NQAKULA, Nosiviwe; South African politician; *Minister of Defence and Military Veterans;* b. 13 Nov. 1956, Cape Town; m. Charles Nqakula; one s.; ed Newport Univ.; Head African National Congress (ANC) Taskforce to relaunch Women's League 1990, Nat. Organizer 1991, Pres. 2003–08, Deputy Chair. ANC Parl. Political Cttee 2001, mem. ANC Nat. Exec. Cttee 2007–; mem. SA Communist Party (SACP); MP, Chair. Intelligence Portfolio Cttee (Nat. Ass) 2004–; apptd mem. Judicial Services Comm. 2001; Deputy Minister of Home Affairs 2002–04, Minister 2004–09, Minister of Correctional Services 2009–12, of Defence and Military Veterans 2012–. *Address:* Ministry of Defence and Military Veterans, Armscor Building, Block 5, Level 4, Nossob Street, Erasmusrand 0001 (office); Private Bag X427, Pretoria 0001, South Africa (office). *Telephone:* (12) 3556101 (office). *Fax:* (12) 3470118 (office). *E-mail:* mil@mil.za (office). *Website:* www.dod.mil.za (office).

MAPLE, M(errill) Brian, AB, MS, PhD; American physicist and academic; *Bernd T. Matthias Endowed Chair in Physics, University of California, San Diego;* b. 20 Nov. 1939, Chula Vista, Calif.; ed San Diego State Univ., Univ. of California, San Diego; Asst Research Physicist, Univ. of California, San Diego 1969–75, Asst Adjunct Prof. of Physics 1973–75, Assoc. Research Physicist 1975–79, Acting Assoc. Prof. of Physics 1975–77, Assoc. Prof. 1977–81, Prof. 1981–90, Bernd T. Matthias Endowed Chair in Physics 1990–, Dir Center for Interface and Materials Science 1990–2009, Dir Inst. for Pure and Applied Physical Sciences 1995–2009, Chair. Dept of Physics 2009–10; Visiting Scientist, Univ. of Chile, Santiago 1971, 1973; Visiting Prof., Instituto de Fisica José Balseiro, Argentina 1974; Assoc. Research Physicist, Inst. for Theoretical Physics, Univ. of California, Santa Barbara 1980; Chair. Div. of Condensed Matter Physics, American Physical Soc. 1987–88; Bernd T. Matthias Scholar, Center for Materials Science, Los Alamos Nat. Lab. 1993; Chair. Gordon Conf. on Superconductivity 1990, 2000; mem. Advisory Bd, Superconductivity Review 1989–, CONNECT 1990–, Journal of Physics: Condensed Matter 1997–; mem. numerous int. advisory cttees; mem. American Physical Soc. 1977 (Fellow 1985), California Catalysis Soc. 1977, American Vacuum Soc. 1977, Materials Research Soc. 1977, NAS 2004; Fellow, AAAS 1997; Trzebiatowski Institute for Low Temperature and Structure Research, Poland 2006; Guggenheim Fellowship 1984, David Adler Lectureship Award 1996, Humboldt Research Award 1998, Frank H. Spedding Award 1999, American Physical Soc. James C. McGroddy Prize for New Materials 2000, Berndt T. Matthias Prize 2000, Science Lectureship Award, Chiba Univ., Tokyo 2010. *Publications:* Valence Fluctuations in Solids (co-ed.) 1982, Superconductivity in Ternary Compounds (co-ed.) 1982, Handbook on the Physics and Chemistry of Rare Earths (co-ed.) 2000; numerous papers on solid state physics and surface physics. *Address:* Department of Physics, University of California, San Diego, MH 1230, 9500 Gilman Drive, MC 0319, La Jolla, CA 92093-0319, USA (office). *Telephone:* (858) 534-3968 (office); (858) 534-6832 (office). *Fax:* (858) 534-1241 (office). *E-mail:* bmaple@physics.ucsd.edu (office); mbmaple@ucsd.edu (office). *Website:* physics.ucsd.edu (office); mbmlab.ucsd.edu (office).

MAPONYA, Richard John Pelwana, GCOB; South African entrepreneur and property developer; *CEO, Maponya Group;* b. 24 Dec. 1926, Lenyenye, Northern Transvaal (now Limpopo Prov.); s. of Godfrey Kgabane Maponya and Mary

Machichane Maponya (née Mogashoa); m. Marina Nompinti Sondlo (died 1992); eight c.; ed Kagiso Teacher's Training Coll., Pietersburg; worked as an admin clerk after qualifying as a teacher; Propr Maponya's Supply Stores 1952, now CEO Maponya Group; Dir Maponya's Bus Services 1965, Maponya's Funeral Parlour (Pty) Ltd 1976, Afro Shopping Construction Enterprises (Pty) Ltd, Maponya's Discount Supermarket 1983–, Maponya's Bottle Store, Maponya's Motors (Pty) Ltd, Maponya Motors Property Holdings (Pty) Ltd, Maponya's Orlando Restaurant (Pty) Ltd, Maponya's Stud Farm, Lebowa Devt Corpn, numerous other cos; Man. Dir MA Africa (Pty) Ltd, Mountain Motors, Soweto 1978–; Propr BMW Agency, Soweto; opened Maponya Mall in Soweto 2007; Chair. Kilimanjaro Investments (East London-based bottler); racehorse owner; Founder and Pres. Nat. African Federated Chamber of Commerce and Industry 1965–; Chair. Trade and Transport Cttee, Soweto Council; mem. Urban Bantu Council 1965–77; Pres. Black Proprietors Garage Owners' Asscn; Founder and Trustee, The Nelson Mandela Children's Fund; Trustee, Baragwanath Hospital, SA Foundation, Urban Foundation; Grand Counsellor, Order of the Baobab in Gold 2007; Lifetime Achievement Award, Africa Awards for Entrepreneurship 2012. *Leisure interests:* racing, music. *Address:* PO Box 3302, Cramerview 2060; Maponya Developments, First Floor, Entrance 2, 32 Fricker Road, Illovo 2196, South Africa. *Telephone:* (861) 333264. *Fax:* (866) 852112. *E-mail:* info@mapdev.co.za. *Website:* www.mapdev.co.za.

MAPP, Kenneth E., MPA; American politician; b. Brooklyn, New York; s. of Alfred Mapp and Vashti Hewitt Mapp; ed Univ. of the Virgin Islands, John F. Kennedy School of Govt, Harvard Univ.; worked as police trainee in New York City; fmr police officer, US Virgin Islands; Senator, US Virgin Islands Senate 1982–84, 1988–90, 1992–94, fmr Chair. Cttee on Public Safety and Judicial Affairs, Standing Mem. Cttee on Finance; Lt-Gov., US Virgin Islands 1995–99, Gov. US Virgin Islands 2015–19; Dir of Finance and Admin, US Virgin Islands Public Finance Authority 2002.

MAPP, Wayne, LLB, LLM, PhD; New Zealand lawyer and politician; b. 12 March 1952, Te Kopuru; m. Denise Henare; one c.; ed Auckland Univ., Univ. of Cambridge, UK; lawyer in pvt. practice 1978–82; Lecturer in Commercial Law, Auckland Univ. 1984–94, Assoc. Prof. 1994–96; mem. New Zealand Nat. Party 1982–, Divisional Policy Chair., Auckland 1993–96; MP for North Shore 1996–2011, mem. Select Cttees on Foreign Affairs, Defence and Trade 1997–99, on Justice and Law Reform 1997–2002, on Māori Affairs 1999–2001, 2003–04, on Social Services 2002, on Educ. and Science 2003–04, Transport and Industrial Relations 2005–06, on Privileges 2005–08; Spokesman for Defence 1999–2002, for Justice 1999–2002, for Disarmament and Arms Control 2002–03, for Foreign Affairs 2002–03, for Housing 2002–03, for Constitutional and Treaty of Waitangi Issues 2003–04, for Immigration 2003–04, for Labour and Industrial Relations 2004–06; Assoc. Spokesman for Treaty of Waitangi 1999–2002, for Constitutional and Treaty of Waitangi Issues 2004–05; Minister of Defence, of Research, Science and Tech., Assoc. Minister for Econ. Devt and for Tertiary Educ. 2008–11; Commr New Zealand Law Comm. 2012–; Companion of the Queen's Service Order 2013. *Address:* New Zealand Law Commission, Level 19, 171 Featherston Street, Wellington 6011, New Zealand (office). *Telephone:* (4) 473-3453 (office). *Fax:* (4) 471-0959 (office). *E-mail:* com@lawcom.govt.nz (office). *Website:* www.lawcom.govt.nz (office).

MAQBOOL VOHRA, Lt-Gen. Khalid, MSc; Pakistani army officer (retd) and government administrator; b. 1948, Faisalabad; ed Staff Coll., Quetta, Nat. Defence Coll., Rawalpindi, Naval Postgraduate Inst., Monterey, USA; commissioned in Pakistan Army 1966, saw action with infantry regt in Kashmir Sector 1971, Commdr of Corps, Infantry Div./Brigade, Chief Instructor, Nat. Defence Coll. and Command and Staff Coll., Quetta, Defence and Mil. Attaché to USA for two and half years; Chair. Nat. Accountability Bureau 2000–01; Gov. of Punjab Prov. 2001–08 (resgnd); fmr Chancellor Univ. of Sargodha; Hilal-e-Imtiaz (Mil.), Hilal-e-Imtiaz.

MAQUEDA, Juan Carlos; Argentine politician, lawyer and university teacher; *Minister, Supreme Court of Justice;* b. 29 Dec. 1949, Río Tercero; m. María Belén Ferrer; ed La Salle Coll. and Catholic Univ. of Córdoba; Prof. of Law, Catholic Univ. of Córdoba 1977–80, Adjunct Prof. of Natural Law 1980, Prof. of History of Political Insts of Argentina 1981, Asst Prof. of Natural Law 1981–82, 1983–84, Prof. 1984–85, Adjunct Prof. of Constitutional Law 1985, Prof. of Political Theory 1986; Tech. Sec., Faculty of Law and Social Sciences, Univ. of Córdoba 1980–86; mem. Justicialista party; Prov. Deputy, Córdoba 1986–91; Deputy to Nat. Ass. 1991–99; Minister of Educ., Prov. of Córdoba 1999–2001; Pres. Constitutional Convention of Prov. of Córdoba Aug. 2001; Senator from Córdoba 2001–03, Vice-Pres. Nat. Senate 2001, Pres. 2002; Minister, Supreme Court Justice 2002–, Pres. Academic Council of the School of Justice 2005–; mem. Fed Council of Nat. Culture and Educ. 1999–2001; Vice-Pres. Argentine Group, Parliamentarians for Global Action. *Publications include:* El Pensamiento Político Español del Siglo XVI 1980, Los Partidos Políticos: Ordenamiento Legal 1985, Sistemas Electorales y los Sistemas de Partidos 1985, La Nueva Constitución de Córdoba: Labor Constituyente y Debates 1987, Labor Parlamentaria en la Cámera de Diputados de la Provincia de Córdoba y Debates 1988, 1989. *Address:* Corte Suprema de Justicia de la Nación, Talcahuano 550, Ciudad Autónoma de Buenos Aires, Argentina (office). *Telephone:* (11) 4370-4600. *E-mail:* jurisprudencia@csjn.gov.ar (office). *Website:* www.csjn.gov.ar (office).

MARA, Moussa; Malian accountant and politician; b. 2 March 1975, Bamako; s. of Joseph Mara and Kadiatou Ly; m.; two c.; ed Intel de Paris; trained as accountant, mem. Asscn of Chartered Accountants 2000, Certified Public Accountant 2000; trainee accountant, Société d'Expertise Comptable Diarra (SECD), Bamako 1997, later becoming Assoc. Dir for Africa; Mayor, Dist IV, Bamako 2009–10, 2011; Founding Pres. Yéléma (political party) 2010–, cand. in presidential election 2013; Minister of Planning and Policy, Bamako City Council 2013–14; Prime Minister 2014–Jan. 2015 (resgnd); fmr Sec.-Gen. Mali Asscn of Chartered Accountants; fmr Vice-Pres. West African Accounting Council; mem. Bd West African Accounting Diploma. *Address:* Yéléma, Hamdallaye, BP E 2546, Bamako, Mali (office). *Telephone:* 75444534 (mobile) (office). *E-mail:* yelema@yelema.net (office). *Website:* www.yelema.net (office); www.moussamara.com.

MARADONA, Diego Armando; Argentine football manager and fmr professional footballer; b. 30 Oct. 1960, Lanús, Buenos Aires; s. of Diego Maradona and Dalma Salvadora Franco; m. Claudia Villafañe 1989 (divorced 2004); two d.; one s. with Cristina Sinagra; attacking midfielder/second striker; youth player, Argentinos Juniors 1969–76; sr career with Argentinos Juniors 1976–81, Boca Juniors 1981–82 (won Primera División 1981), FC Barcelona, Spain 1982–84 (won Copa del Rey 1983, Copa de la Liga 1983, Spanish Super Cup 1983), Napoli, Italy 1984–91 (won Serie A 1987, 1990, Coppa Italia 1987, UEFA Cup 1989, Italian Super Cup 1990), Sevilla, Spain 1992–93, Newell's Old Boys 1993, Boca Juniors 1995–97, Badajoz 1998; mem. Argentina nat. team 1977–94 (91 appearances, 34 goals, won Youth World Cup 1979, 75th anniversary FIFA Cup 1979, World Cup 1986 (Capt.), Artemio Franchi Trophy 1993), Head Coach 2008–10; Head Coach Al-Wasl, UAE 2011–12; f. Maradona Producciones; fmr Amb. for UNICEF; banned from football for 15 months after drugs test; convicted by Naples Court on charges of possession of cocaine, 14-month suspended sentence and fine of 4 million lire, Sept. 1991; Fed. Court in Buenos Aires ruled he had complied with the treatment; suspended for 15 months for taking performance-enhancing drug, ephedrine, in World Cup Finals June 1994; indicted for shooting an air rifle at journalists Aug. 1994; resgnd as coach of Deporto Mandiyu 1994; Man. Racing Club 1995; retd from playing 1997; host La Noche del Diez (talk show) 2005; Dir of Football Boca Juniors football club 2005–06; appointed Goodwill Amb. of Intergovernmental Inst. for use of Micro-algae Spirulina Against Malnutrition, IIMSAM 2006; Tech. Dir Al-Fujairah S.C 2017–; South American Player of the Year 1979, World Footballer of the Year 1986, Footballer of the Century Award, Féd. Int. de Football Asscn (France) 2000. *Achievements include:* Golden Ball for Best Player of FIFA U-20 World Cup 1979, Argentine league Top Scorer 1979, 1980, 1981, Argentine Football Writers' Footballer of the Year 1979, 1980, 1981, 1986, South American Footballer of the Year, El Mundo, Caracas 1979, 1986, 1989, 1990, 1992, Italian Guerin d'Oro 1985, Argentine Sports Writers' Sportsman of the Year 1986, Golden Ball for Best Player of FIFA World Cup 1986, Best Footballer in the World Onze d'Or 1986, 1987, World Player of the Year, World Soccer Magazine 1986, United Press International Athlete of the Year 1986, Olimpia de Oro 1986, Capocannoniere (Serie A top scorer) 1987–88, Golden Ball for services to football, France Football 1996, Argentine Sports Writers' Sportsman of the Century 1999, 'FIFA Best Football Player of the Century', people's choice 2000, 'FIFA Goal of the Century' (1986 (2–1) vs England; second goal) 2002, Argentine Senate 'Domingo Faustino Sarmiento' recognition for lifetime achievement 2005. *Publication:* El Diego (autobiography) 2005. *Address:* c/o Asociación del Fútbol Argentino, Viamonte 1366, C1053ACB Buenos Aires, Argentina. *Website:* www.diegomaradona.com.

MARAFINO, Vincent Norman, MBA; American business executive; b. 8 June 1930, Boston, Mass; m. Doris M. Vernall 1958; three d.; ed San Jose State Coll. and Santa Clara Univ.; served with USAF 1953–55; Chief Accountant, American Standard Advance Tech. Lab., Mountain View, Calif. 1956–59; with Lockheed Missiles & Space Co., Sunnyvale, Calif. 1959–70, Asst Controller, Lockheed Corpn Burbank, Calif. 1970–71, Vice Pres., Controller 1971–77, Sr Vice-Pres. Finance 1977–83, Exec. Vice-Pres., Chief Financial and Admin. Officer 1983–88, Vice-Chair. and Chief Financial and Admin. Officer 1988–95, mem. Bd of Dirs Lockheed Missiles and Space Co., Inc., Chair. Lockheed Finance Corpn; mem. Bd of Dirs Airport Group International, Inc., Rohr Inc., Holy Cross Health System; mem. Financial Execs Inst., American Inst. of CPAS. *Address:* c/o Lockheed Martin Corporation, 6801 Rockledge Drive, Bethesda, MD 20817, USA.

MARAGALL, Pasqual, PhD; Spanish civil servant and academic; b. 13 Jan. 1941, Barcelona; m. Diana Garrigosa; three c.; ed Barcelona Univ., New School for Social Research, New York; lecturer in Econs Barcelona Univ.; Mayor of Barcelona 1982–97, organizer of 1992 Olympic Games in Barcelona; mem. Partit dels Socialistes de Catalunya, Pres. 2000–07; Pres. Council of Municipalities and Regions of Europe 1991–97, Cttee of the Regions of EU 1996–98; Pres. Govt of Catalonia 2003–06; apptd Pres. Fundació Catalunya Europa 2007; Insignia Order of the Légion d'honneur 1993, Hon. OBE; Hon. DLitt (Winchester Art School, UK), Dr hc (Johns Hopkins USA) 1997, Laurea hc (Reggio Calabria Italy) 1998; Medal of the Council of Europe 1984, Olympic Golden Award 1992, Golden Medal Award Spanish Inst. New York 1993.

MARAH, Kaifala, PhD; Sierra Leonean accountant, government official and central banker; b. Koidu Town, Kono Dist; m.; four c.; ed Fourah Bay Coll., Rockefeller Coll. and State Univ. of New York, Albany USA, Univ. of Hull, UK; fmr Deputy Town Clerk, Koidu-New Sembehun City Council; fmr Legis. Aide, conducting budget analysis, New York State Senate, USA; fmr Public Finance Adviser, Commonwealth Secr., London; Chief of Staff to Pres. Ernest Bai Koroma 2010–12, Sr Econ. Advisor 2010–12; Minister of Finance and Econ. Devt 2012–16; Gov. and Chair. Bank of Sierra Leone 2016–17; Minister of Foreign Affairs and Int. Co-operation 2017–18; served as mem. Bd of Govs ADB, Islamic Devt Bank, IMF; fmr Chair. G7+ group of fragile states; Co-Chair. Int. Dialogue on Peacebuilding and State Building; mem. Advisory Council on Gender, World Bank 2013–15; Excellence in International Student Leadership Award, Rockefeller Coll. of Public Affairs and Policy 2003, Nat. Excellence and Role Model for Youth Award 2011, Africa Young Leadership Award 2012.

MARAINI, Dacia; Italian writer and poet; b. 13 Nov. 1936, Fiesole; d. of Fosco Maraini and Alliata Topazia; m. 1st Lucio Pozzi; ed Collegio S.S. Annunziata, Florence and Rome. *Films:* as actress: Io sono nata viaggiando 2013. *Plays include:* La famiglia normale 1967, Centocelle gli anni del fascismo 1971, Dialogo di una prostituta con un solo cliente 1973, Da Roma a Milano 1975, Don Juan 1976, Due Donne di Provincia 1978, Erzbeth Bartory 1980, Donna Lionora giacubina 1981, I Sogni di Clitennestra 1981, Dramma d'amore al circo Bagno Balò 1981, Lezioni d'Amore 1982, Bianca Garofani 1982, Delitto 1987, Charlotte Corday 1989, Celia Carli 1990, Commedia Femminile 1994, Camille 1995. *Publications include:* La Vacanza 1962, L'Età del Malessere (The Age of Discontent, Prix Formentor) 1962, Crudeltà All'Aria Aperta 1966, A Memoria 1967, Mio Marito 1968, Memoirs of a Female Thief 1973, Donne mie 1974, Donna in Guerra 1975, Mangiami Pure 1978, Lettere a Marina 1981, Dimenticato di Dimenticare 1983, Il treno per Helsinki 1984, Isolina (Premio Fregene 1985) 1985, Devour me too 1987, La Bionda, la bruna e l'asino 1987, La Lunga Vita di Marianna Ucria (Premio Campiello 1990) 1990, L'Uomo tatuato 1990, Viaggiando con passo de volpe (Premio Mediterraneo

1991, Premio Citta di Penne 1991) 1991, Bagheria 1993, Voci (Premio Napoli 1994, Sibilla Aleramo Prize 1994) 1994, La ragazza con la treccia 1994, Mutino, Orlov e il gatto che si crede pantera 1995, Dolce per sé 1997, Se amando troppo 1998, Buio (Premio Strega 1999) 1999, La nave per Kobe 2001, Colomba 2004, Il gioco dell'universo 2007, Il treno dell'ultima notte 2008, La Ragazza di via Maqueda 2009, La grande festa 2011, L'amore rubato 2012, Chiara d'Assisi: Elogio della disobbedienza 2013, La bambina e il sognatore 2015, La mia vita, le mie battaglie 2015. *Address:* c/o Rizzoli, RCS Libri, Via Bianca di Savoia, 12, 20122 Milan; Via Beccaria 18, 00196 Rome, Italy (home). *Telephone:* 3611795 (home). *Website:* www.rcslibri.it; www.daciamaraini.com.

MARAJ, Rashid Muhammad al-, BS; Bahraini central banker and fmr government official; *Governor, Central Bank of Bahrain;* ed Univ. of Houston, USA, Strathclyde Univ., UK; Engineer, Ministry of Industry and Devt 1979–80; Asst Under-Sec. for Econ. Affairs, Ministry of Finance and Nat. Economy 1981–95; Under-Sec., Ministry of Transport 1995–99; Gen. Man. and CEO, Arab Petroleum Investments Corpn, Saudi Arabia 1999–2005; Gov. Cen. Bank of Bahrain 2005–; Chair. Islamic Financial Services Bd 2012; mem. Bahrain Econ. Devt Bd, Natural Oil and Gas Authority, Telecommunications Regulatory Authority. *Address:* Central Bank of Bahrain, POB 27, Building 96, Block 317, Road 1702, Manama, Bahrain (office). *Telephone:* 17547777 (office); 17547500 (office). *Fax:* 17530399 (office); 17537799 (office). *E-mail:* governor@cbb.gov.bh (office); info@cbb.gov.bh. *Website:* www.cbb.gov.bh (office).

MARAPANA, Hon. Tilak Janaka, BSc, LLB; Sri Lankan lawyer and politician; *Minister of Foreign Affairs and Development Assignments;* b. Aug. 1942, Ratnapura, Sabaragamuwa; s. of P. Marapana; m. Stella Marapana; two s.; ed St Thomas's Coll., Mount Lavinia; joined Attorney Gen.'s Dept as a Crown Counsel 1968, Solicitor Gen. of Sri Lanka 1990–92, Attorney-Gen. 1992–95; apptd mem. Pres.'s Counsel 1988; elected mem. Parl. 2000, 2015; Minister of Defence and of Transport, Highways and Aviation 2001–04, of Law and Order Sept.–Nov. 2015, of Foreign Affairs and Devt Assignments 2017–. *Address:* Ministry of Foreign Affairs, Republic Bldg, Colombo 1, Sri Lanka (office). *Telephone:* (11) 2325371 (office). *Fax:* (11) 2446091 (office). *E-mail:* cypher@mea.gov.lk (office). *Website:* www.mfa.gov.lk (office).

MARAPE, James, BA MBA; Papua New Guinea politician; b. 24 April 1971; m. Rachael Marape; three s.; ed Univ. of Papua New Guinea; Asst Sec., Policy Devt, Dept of Personnel Man. 2001–06; mem. Nat. Parl. for Tari-Pori Open constituency 2007–, Parl. Sec. for Works and Transport 2007, Deputy Chair., Privileges Cttee 2007, mem. Parl. Referral Cttee on Inter-Govt Relations 2007, Minister for Educ. 2008–11, Minister of Finance –2019, also Leader of Govt Business, also responsible for Fisheries, Works, Police and Attorney-Gen. and Justice in caretaker Govt Aug. 2017; mem. Nat. Alliance Party –2012; mem. People's Nat. Congress 2012–. *Address:* c/o Department of Finance, POB 710, Waigani, Vulupindi Haus, NCD1, Papua New Guinea (office).

MARAT, Allan, CBE, DPhil; Papua New Guinea politician; b. 28 Sept. 1954; ed Univ. of Oxford; Leader People's Progress Party; Deputy Prime Minister, Minister for Trade and Industry 2002–03; Leader Melanesian Liberal Party 2007, now mem.; Attorney-Gen. and Minister of Justice 2007–10, 2011; mem. of Parl. (Rabaul Open) 2012. *Leisure interests:* reading books on law, economics, business, politics. *Address:* POB 7431, Boroko, NCD, Papua New Guinea (home).

MARBER, Patrick; British writer and director; b. 19 Sept. 1964, London; s. of Brian Marber and Angela Benjamin; m. Debra Gillett 2002; three c.; ed Wadham Coll., Oxford; Cameron Mackintosh Prof. of Contemporary Theatre, Univ. of Oxford 2004. *Films:* screenplays: Old Street 2004, Asylum (co-screenwriter) 2005, Notes on a Scandal (sole screenwriter) 2006, Saturday 2008, Late One Night 2008. *Television:* The Day Today 1994, Paul Calf Video Diary 1994, Knowing Me Knowing You 1994–95, 3 Fights 2 Weddings and a Funeral 1994, The Curator 1995, After Miss Julie 1995. *Plays:* Dealer's Choice (Evening Standard Award for Best Comedy, Writers' Guild Award for Best West End Play) 1995, After Miss Julie 1996, Closer (Evening Standard Award for Best Comedy, Critics' Circle Theatre Award, Laurence Olivier Award for Best New Play) 1997, Howard Katz 2001, The Musicians 2004, Don Juan in Soho 2006, The Red Lion 2015. *Radio:* On the Hour 1991–92, Knowing You Knowing Me 1992–93, Bunk Bed 2014–. *Address:* c/o Judy Daish Associates Ltd, 2 St Charles Place, London, W10 6EG, England (office). *Telephone:* (20) 8964-8811 (office). *Fax:* (20) 8964-8966 (office). *E-mail:* judy@judydaish.com (office); tracey@judydaish.com (office). *Website:* www.judydaish.com (office).

MARCEAU, Sophie; French actress; b. (Sophie Danièle Sylvie Maupu), 17 Nov. 1966, Paris; d. of Benoît Maupu and Simone Morisset; one s.; one d.; Meilleur Espoir Féminin (for César) 1982, (for Molière) 1991, Grand Prix Special des Amériques 2007 and several foreign prizes. *Films include:* La Boum 1980, La Boum 2 (César Award) 1982, Fort Saganne 1984, Joyeuses Pâques 1985, L'Amour Braque 1985, Police 1985, 'Round Midnight (uncredited) 1986, Descente aux Enfers (Jupiter Award for Best International Actress 1988) 1986, Chouans! (Best Actress, Cabourg Romantic Film Festival 1988) 1987, L'etudiante 1988, Mes nuits sont plus belles que vos jours 1989, Pacific Palisades 1989, Pour Sacha 1991, La note bleue 1991, Fanfan 1993, La fille de D'Artagnan 1994, Braveheart 1995, L'Aube à l'envers (dir) 1995, Al di là delle nuvole (Beyond the Clouds) 1995, Firelight 1995, Anna Karenina 1997, Marquise 1997, The World is Not Enough 1998, Lost & Found 1999, A Midsummer Night's Dream 1999, La fidelité (Best Actrress, Cabourg Romantic Film Festival Award 2000) 2000, Belphégor – Le fantôme du Louvre (Belphecor: Curse of the Mummy) 2001, Parlez-moi d'amour (dir) (Best Director, Montréal World Film Festival 2002) 2002, Alex and Emma 2003, Je reste! 2003, Les clefs de bagnole (The Car Keys) 2003, À ce soir (aka Nelly) 2004, Anthony Zimmer 2005, Lezioni di volo 2006, La Disparue de Deauville 2007, Les Femmes de l'ombre 2008, LOL (Laughing Out Loud) (Jury Prize for Best Actress, Monte-Carlo Comedy Film Festival) 2008, De l'autre côté du lit 2008, Ne te retourne pas (Don't Look Back) 2009, L'homme de chevet 2009, With Love from the Age of Reason 2010, Happiness Never Comes Alone 2012, Arrêtez-moi 2013, Quantum Love 2014, The Missionaries 2014, Jailbirds 2015, Madame Mills, une voisine si parfaite (also dir and screenwriter) 2018. *Stage appearances include:* Eurydice 1991, Pygmalion 1993. *Publication:* Menteuse 1996. *Leisure interests:* countryside, music, reading, travel. *Address:* c/o Dominique Besnehard, Artmédia, 8 rue Danielle Casanova, 75002 Paris, France (office). *Telephone:* 1-72-33-25-00 (office). *E-mail:* info@artmedia.fr (office). *Website:* www.artmedia.fr (office).

MARCEGAGLIA, Emma, MBA; Italian business executive; *Chairman, Eni SpA;* b. 24 Dec. 1965, Mantua; d. of Steno Marcegaglia and Palmira Bazzani; m. Roberto Vancini; one d.; ed Bocconi Univ., Milan, New York Univ., USA; Deputy Chair. and CEO Marcegaglia SpA, Mantua (f. by her father); Pres. Young Entrepreneurs for Europe (YES) 1996–2000; Nat. Vice-Pres. Young Italian Employers of Confindustria 1994–96, Pres. 1996–2000, Vice-Pres. Confindustria for Europe 2000–02, Deputy Vice-Pres. for infrastructures, energy, transport and environment 2004–08, Pres. Confindustria 2008–12; Deputy Chair. and CEO Marcegaglia SpA; Chair. Eni SpA 2014–; mem. Bd of Dirs, Bracco SpA, Italcementi SpA, Gabetti Property Solutions SpA; fmr mem. Man. Bd Banco Popolare, FinecoBank SpA; Pres. Businesseurope, Luiss Guido Carli Univ.; Pres. Areté Onlus Foundation to support activities of Vita-Salute San Raffaele; Perm. mem. Enterprise Policy Group – Professional Chamber, Exec. Cttee of Aspen Italia Inst.; Chevalier, Légion d'honneur 2011; Premio Guido Carli 2015. *Leisure interests:* collecting antique watches, spending time with her family. *Address:* Marcegaglia SpA, via Bresciani 16, 46040 Gazoldo Ippoliti, Mantua (office); Eni SpA, Piazzale Enrico Mattei 1, 00144 Rome, Italy (office). *Telephone:* (0376) 6851 (Gazoldo Ippoliti) (office); (06) 59821 (Rome) (office). *Fax:* (0376) 685600 (Gazoldo Ippoliti) (office); (06) 59822141 (Rome) (office). *E-mail:* info@marcegaglia.com (office); segreteriasocietaria.azionisti@eni.it (office); ufficio.stampa@eni.it (office). *Website:* www.marcegaglia.com (office); www.eni.com (office).

MARCHANT, Ian D.; British business executive; *Chairman, Wood Group;* b. 9 Feb. 1961; worked for Coopers & Lybrand including a two-year secondment to Dept of Energy working on electricity privatization; joined Southern Electric 1992, Finance Dir and mem. Bd of Dirs 1996–98, Finance Dir Scottish and Southern Energy plc (after merger of Southern Electric and Scottish Hydro Electric) 1998–2002, apptd mem. Bd Dirs 1998, Chief Exec. 2002–13; Chair. Wood Group 2014–; UK Business Council for Sustainable Energy, Scottish Climate Change Business Delivery Group, 2020 Delivery Group, Eng Construction Forum 2009–15; Chair. Infinis Energy plc 2013–15; Dir (non-exec.) Maggie's Cancer Centres (currently Chair.), Linknode 2013–, Cyberhawk Innovations 2013–, Aggreko 2013–; mem. Ofgem's Environmental Advisory Group, Energy Research Partnership. *Address:* Wood Group, 15 Justice Mill Lane, Aberdeen, AB11 6EQ, Scotland (office). *Telephone:* (1224) 851000 (office). *Fax:* (1224) 851474 (office). *Website:* www.woodgroup.com (office).

MARCHENKO, Grigori Alexandrovich; Kazakhstani government official and central banker; b. 26 Dec. 1959, Almaty; m.; ed Moscow State Inst. of Int. Relations, Georgetown Univ., USA; served in army 1979–81; engineer and acting Deputy Head, Dept of Sr Mans Ministry of Non-Ferrous Metals, Kazakh SSR 1984–85; Trans., Ed. and Leader Marketing Information Group, Kazakh Scientific Research Inst. 1986–88; acting head, Design Bureau of Semiconductor Machine Building, Chair. Scientific Production Co-operative Centre 1988–90; Asst to Vice-Pres. of Kazakhstan 1992–93; Deputy Gov. Nat. Bank of Kazakhstan 1994–96, Gov. 1999–2004, 2009–13 (resgnd); Pres. Deutsche Bank-Securities (Kazakhstan) 1998–99; First Deputy Prime Minister of Kazakhstan 2004–06, Adviser to Pres. of Kazakhstan 2004–09; Chair. Halyk Bank 2005–09; Chair. Nat. Securities Comm. of Kazakhstan 1996–98; Pres. DB Securities of Kazakhstan 1998–99; Pew Fellow, Georgetown Univ. 1994.

MARCHUK, Gen. Yevgen Kirilovich, CJur; Ukrainian politician; b. 28 Jan. 1941, Dolinivka, Kirovograd Region; m.; two s.; ed Kirovograd Pedagogical Inst.; fmr school teacher of Ukrainian and German languages; with Ukrainian KGB (State Security Cttee) 1963–91, Deputy Chair. 1990–91; Chair. Nat. Security Service of Ukraine 1991; State Minister of Defence, Nat. Security and Emergencies 1991–94; Deputy Prime Minister July 1994, First Deputy Prime Minister 1994–95; Prime Minister of Ukraine 1995–96; mem. Verkhovna Rada (United Social Democratic Party faction) 1996–; Head of Cttee of Social Policy and Labour 1998–; Sec., Ukrainian Nat. Security and Defence Council 2000–03; Minister of Defence 2003–04; apptd Advisor of Pres. Viktor Yushchenko 2008; Pres. Ukrainian Transport Union 1998; unsuccessful presidential cand. 1999.

MARCINKIEWICZ, Kazimierz; Polish politician; b. 20 Dec. 1959, Gorzów Wielkopolski; m. 1st Maria Marcinkiewicz 1981 (divorced 2009); m. 2nd Izabela Olchowicz 2009 (divorced 2016); ed Wrocław Univ., Adam Mickiewicz Univ., Poznan; worked as teacher; mem. Solidarity Ind. Self-Governing Trade Union 1983–90; Founding mem. Christian-Nat. Union party (ZChN) 1989; Supt Bd of Educ. in Gorzów Wielkopolski 1990–92; Deputy Minister of Nat. Educ. 1992–93; consultant and Deputy Dir Voivodship Methodological Centre in Gorzów 1993–95; mem. main Bd of ZChN and head of bd in Gorzów Wielkopolski 1994; Deputy third Sejm representing Electoral Action Solidarity-ZChN, later Deputy Chair. and Chair., Sejm Educ., Science and Youth Comm., also Deputy Chief, Special Comm. on Admin. Reform; Head of Cabinet 1999–2000; left ZChN and f. Right Wing Alliance 2001, then head Parliamentary Club of Law and Justice party; Deputy fourth Sejm and Chair. of State Treasury Comm.; Prime Minister of Poland 2005–06; ed and publr ind. educational periodical Pokolenie; Co-founder, Ed. and Publr of Aspekty (Catholic weekly); Cyberpolitician 2003. *Publications:* numerous articles on economics. *Address:* c/o Law and Justice (Prawo i Sprawiedliwość—PiS), 02-018 Warsaw, ul. Nowogrodzka 84/86, Poland. *Telephone:* (22) 6215035. *Fax:* (22) 6216767. *E-mail:* biuro@pis.org.pl. *Website:* www.pis.org.pl.

MARCKER, Kjeld Adrian, PhD; Danish molecular biologist and academic (retd); b. 27 Dec. 1932, Nyborg; s. of Kjeld A. C. Marcker and Minna C. Callesen; m. Anne Birgit Hansen 1964; three d.; ed Nyborg Gymnasium and Univ. of Copenhagen; Dept of Physical Chem., Univ. of Copenhagen 1958; Carlsberg-Wellcome Fellow, MRC Lab. of Molecular Biology, Cambridge, UK 1962, mem. staff 1964, Fellow, King's Coll., Cambridge 1968; Prof. in Molecular Biology, Århus Univ. 1970–2002; mem. Royal Danish Acad., Danish Acad. of Tech. Science, Academia Europaea, European Molecular Biology Org.; Novo Medical Prize 1971, Anders Jahre Medical Prize 1973. *Publications include:* articles in scientific journals. *Leisure interests:* soccer, bird-watching, history. *Address:* Tjoernehegnet 32, 8541 Skoedstrup, Denmark. *Telephone:* 86-22-01-18 (office); 51-92-71-23 (home). *E-mail:* KM@mb.au.dk.

MARCÓ DEL PONT, Mercedes; Argentine economist, politician and fmr central banker; *President, Fundación de Investigaciones para el Desarrollo;* b. 28 Aug. 1959, Buenos Aires; m. Jorge Cafferata; one s. two d.; ed Univ. of Buenos Aires, Yale Univ., USA; Sr Researcher, Fundación de Investigaciones para el Desarrollo (think-tank) 1982–87, Dir 1991–, Pres. 2015–; teaching asst, Univ. of Buenos Aires School of Econs 1984–85; Chief Adviser on petrochemical industry policy for Ministry of Economy Planning Secr. 1989–91; consultant on econ. statistics, City of Buenos Aires Statistical Dept 1999–2000; teacher, Center for Advanced Studies, Nat. Univ. of Lomas de Zamora 1999–2002; cabinet adviser to Minister of Production 2002; mem. Cámara de Diputados (parl.) for Buenos Aires (Front for Victory, FPV) 2005–08, also Pres. Comm. for Small and Medium Enterprises; Pres. Banco de la Nación Argentina 2008–10; Pres. Banco Central de la República Argentina (central bank) 2010–13; Coordinator, Productive Innovation and Devt Program, Univ. of San Martin 2014–; mem. Plan Fénix (econ. think-tank), Univ. of Buenos Aires 2001–; mem. Movimiento de Integración y Desarrollo. *Publication:* Crisis y Reforma Económica 2004. *Address:* Fundación de Investigaciones para el Desarrollo, Reconquista 962, 2nd Floor, 1003, Buenos Aires, Argentina (office). *Telephone:* (11) 4313–9494 (office). *E-mail:* info@fide.com.ar (office). *Website:* www.fide.com.ar (office).

MARCO TORRES, Gen. Rodolfo Clemente; Venezuelan politician and fmr army officer; *Governor of Aragua State;* b. 10 Sept. 1966; ed Academia militar de Venezuela; took part in attempted coup against Pres. Carlos Andres Perez Feb. 1992; has served in various capacities in govt insts including as Pres. Agricultural Supply and Services Corpn 2008, Exec. Sec. Fondo Nacional para el Desarrollo Nacional (FONDEN, nat. devt fund), sr position in Nat. Treasury Office, Pres. Banco de Venezuela SA, Banco Bicentenario and Banco del Tesoro (state-owned banks) 2005; Minister of State for Public Banking 2011–14, Minister of Finance and of Public Banking 2014–16, Vice-Pres. of Economy and Finance 2014–16, also Alt. Gov., World Bank, Sr Gov., Inter-American Devt Bank, Sr mem. Bd for Venezuela, Devt Bank of Latin America; Gov. Aragua State 2017–; Mil. Order of Gen.-in-Chief Eleazar López Contreras.

MARCOS, Imelda Romualdez; Philippine politician and social leader; b. (Imelda Remedios Visitacion Romualdez), 2 July 1929, Manila; d. of Vicente Orestes Romualdez and Remedios Trinidad; m. Ferdinand E. Marcos 1954 (died 1989); one s. two d.; First Lady of The Philippines 1965–86; Gov. of Metro Manila 1975–86; visited Beijing 1976; took part in negotiations in Libya over self-govt for southern provs 1977; Leader, Kilusan Bagong Lipunan (New Society Movt) 1978–81; mem. Batasang Pambansa (Interim Legis. Ass.) 1978–83; Minister of Human Settlements 1978–79, 1984–86, of Human Settlements and Ecology 1979–83; apptd Amb. Plenipotentiary and Extraordinary 1978; mem. Cabinet Exec. Cttee 1982–84; Chair. Southern Philippines Devt Authority 1980–86; indicted for embezzlement 1988, acquitted 1990; returned to Philippines Nov. 1991; sentenced to 18–24 years' imprisonment for criminal graft Sept. 1993; convicted of two charges of corruption, sentenced to 9–12 years on each Sept. 1993; sentenced on appeal to Supreme Court; faced four charges of graft Sept. 1995; presidential cand. 1992, 1998; mem. Philippine House of Reps from first dist of Leyte 1995–2001, from Ilocos Norte's 2nd district 2010–; opened Marikina City Footwear Museum in Manila in which most of the exhibits are her own footwear 2001; arrested on charges of corruption and extortion committed during her husband's presidency 2001; acquitted of 32 counts of graft 2008; voted 'Muse of Manila' 1950. *Records include:* Imelda Papin featuring songs with Mrs Imelda Romualdez Marcos 1989. *E-mail:* congw.imeldamarcos@gmail.com.

MARCUS, Claude, DrEcon; French fmr advertising executive; b. 28 Aug. 1924, Paris; s. of Jack Marcus and Louise Bleustein; m. Claudine Pohl 1948; one s. three d.; ed Faculté des Lettres, Aix and Faculté de Droit, Paris; fmr Vice-Chair. Supervisory Bd, Man. Dir Publicis, Chair. Publicis Int.; fmr Chair. Perm. Comm. Advertising Profession/Consumer Unions; Chevalier, Légion d'honneur, Officier, Ordre nat. du Mérite, Médaille des Evadés, Chevalier, Ordre des Palmes académiques et de l'Economie nationale. *Leisure interests:* antiques, tennis. *Address:* 12 rue Félicien David, 75016 Paris, France. *Telephone:* 1-45-20-16-01. *Fax:* 1-45-20-18-01. *E-mail:* claudius6@wanadoo.fr (home).

MARCUS, Gill, BCom; South African academic, politician and fmr central banker; b. 10 Aug. 1949, Johannesburg; d. of Nathan Marcus and Molly Marcus; ed Univ. of South Africa; mem. Nat. Exec. Cttee African Nat. Congress (ANC) 1991–99; MP 1994–99, Chair. Jt Standing Cttee on Finance 1994–96, Deputy Minister of Finance 1996–99; Deputy Gov. S African Reserve Bank 1999–2004, Gov. 2009–14; Prof., Policy, Leadership and Gender Studies, Gordon Inst. of Business Science 2004, then Extraordinary Prof.; Chair. ABSA Group 2007; Exec. Chair. Western Areas Ltd (gold mine) 2005–07; mem. Bd Bidvest (BVT) 2005–, Gold Fields Ltd, Int. Marketing Council; mem. Advisory Bd Auditor Gen. and Ind. Regulatory Bd for Auditors; Patron, Pretoria Sungardens Hospice, Working on Fire Programme. *Leisure interests:* reading, debating.

MARCUS, Rudolph Arthur, BSc, PhD; American chemist and academic; *John G. Kirkwood and Arthur A. Noyes Professor of Chemistry, California Institute of Technology;* b. 21 July 1923, Montreal, Canada; s. of Myer Marcus and Esther Marcus; m. Laura Hearne 1949 (died 2003); three s.; ed McGill Univ., Montreal; worked for Nat. Research Council of Canada 1946–49; Univ. of N Carolina 1949–51; Asst Prof., Polytech. Inst. of Brooklyn 1951–54, Assoc. Prof. 1954–58, Prof. 1958–64; Prof., Univ. of Ill. 1964–68; John G. Kirkwood and Arthur A. Noyes Prof. of Chem., Calif. Inst. of Tech. 1978–; Visiting Prof. of Theoretical Chem., Univ. of Oxford, UK 1975–76; Visiting Linnett Prof. of Chem., Univ. of Cambridge, UK 1996; mem. Courant Inst. of Math. Sciences, New York Univ. 1960–61, Council, Gordon Research Confs 1965–68, Chair. Bd of Trustees and mem. Bd 1966–69; Chair. Div. of Physical Chem., ACS 1964–65; mem. Exec. Cttee American Physical Soc. Div. of Chemical Physics 1970–72, Advisory Bd ACS Petroleum Research Fund 1970–72, Review Cttee Argonne Nat. Lab. Chem. Dept 1966–72 (Chair. 1968–69), Brookhaven Nat. Lab. 1971–73, Radiation Lab., Univ. of Notre Dame 1976–78, External Advisory Bd, NSF Center for Photoinduced Charge Transfer 1990–, Nat. Research Council/NAS, Cttee on Climatic Impact; Chair. numerous cttees including Cttee on Chemical Sciences 1977–79, Advisory Cttee for Chem., NSF 1977–80, Review Cttee, Chem. Depts, Princeton Univ. 1972–78, Polytech. Inst. of New York 1977–80, Calif. Inst. of Tech. 1977–78; Adviser, State Key Lab. for Structural Chem. of Unstable and Stable Species, Beijing 1995,

Center for Molecular Sciences, Chinese Acad. of Sciences, Beijing 1995–; mem. Editorial Bds numerous publs including Laser Chem. 1982–, Advances in Chemical Physics 1984–, International Reviews in Physical Chemistry 1988–, Progress in Physics, Chemistry and Mechanics (China) 1989–, Chemical Physics Research (India) 1992–, Trends in Chemical Physical Research (India) 1992–; Hon. Ed. International Journal of Quantum Chemistry 1996–; mem. NAS, American Philosophical Soc., Int. Acad. of Quantum Molecular Science; Foreign mem. Royal Society, London, Chinese Acad. of Sciences; Assoc. mem. Center for Advanced Studies, Univ. of Ill. 1968–69; Fellow, American Acad. of Arts and Sciences; NSF Sr Post-Doctoral Fellowship 1960–61; Alfred P. Sloan Fellowship 1960–63; Fulbright-Hays Sr Scholar 1971–72; numerous lectureships; Hon. FRSC, Hon. Fellow, Univ. Coll., Oxford 1995–, Hon. Prof., Fudan Univ., Shanghai 1994–, Inst. of Chem., Chinese Acad. of Sciences, Beijing 1995–, Hon. Visitor, Nat. Science Council, Taiwan 1999, Hon. mem. American Philosophical Soc. 1990, Int. Soc. of Electrochemistry, Korean Chemical Soc. 1996, Int. Soc. for Theoretical Chemical Physics, Literary and Historical Soc., Univ. Coll., Dublin 2004, European Acad. of Science 2004; Hon. DSc (Chicago) 1983, (Polytechnic Univ.) 1986, (Gothenburg) 1987, (McGill) 1988, (New Brunswick) 1993, (Queen's) 1993, (Oxford) 1995, (Yokohama Nat. Univ.) 1996, (Univ. of NC) 1996, (Univ. of Ill.) 1997, (Technion–Israel Inst. of Tech.) 1998, (Univ. Politécnica de Valencia, Spain) 1999, (North-western Univ.) 2000, (Univ. of Waterloo, Canada) 2002, (Hyderabad, India) 2012, (Tumkur Univ., India) 2012, (Univ. of Santiago, Chile) 2017, Hon. LLD (Univ. of Calgary, Canada) 2013; many awards including Anne Molson Prize for Chem. 1943, Alexander von Humboldt Foundation Sr US Scientist Award 1976, R.A. Robinson Medal, Faraday Div., Royal Soc. of Chem. (RSC) 1982, C.F. Chandler Medal (Univ. of Columbia) 1983, Wolf Prize 1985, ACS Peter Debye Award in Physical Chem. 1988, Centenary Medal, Faraday Div., RSC 1988, Nat. Medal of Science 1989, ACS Theodore William Richards Medal 1990, ACS Edgar Fahs Smith Award, ACS Remsen Award, ACS Pauling Medal 1991, Nobel Prize in Chem. 1992, Hirschfelder Prize in Theoretical Chem. (Univ. of Wisconsin) 1993, American Acad. of Achievement Golden Plate Award 1993, Lavoisier Medal (Soc. Française de Chimie) 1994, ACS Auburn-Kosolapoff Award 1996, ACS Award in Theoretical Chem., ACS Oesper Award 1997, Top 75 Award, Chemical and Eng News, ACS 1998. *Achievements include:* devt of the Marcus Theory of electron transfer reactions in chemical systems and RRKM Theory of unimolecular reactions. *Publications:* numerous articles in scientific journals, especially Journal of Chemical Physics and Journal of Physical Chem. *Leisure interests:* music, history. *Address:* Noyes Laboratory, Caltech Chemistry 127-72, California Institute of Technology, Pasadena, CA 91125 (office); 331 South Hill Avenue, Pasadena, CA 91106, USA (home). *Telephone:* (626) 395-6566 (office). *Fax:* (626) 792-8485 (office). *E-mail:* ram@caltech.edu (office). *Website:* www.cce.caltech.edu/people/rudolph-a-rudy-marcus (office).

MARCY, Geoffrey W., BA, PhD; American astronomer and academic; b. 29 Sept. 1954, Los Angeles, Calif.; s. of Robert Misrahi and Gloria Isaacs; m. Dr Susan Kegley 1994; ed Granada Hills High School, Los Angeles, Univ. of California, Los Angeles, Univ. of California, Santa Cruz; Carnegie Fellow, Carnegie Inst. of Washington 1982–84; Prof. of Physics and Astronomy, San Francisco State Univ. 1984–96, Distinguished Univ. Prof. 1997–99, Adjunct Prof. of Physics and Astronomy 1999–2015; Prof. of Astronomy, Univ. of California, Berkeley 1999–2015 (resgnd), apptd Dir Center for Integrative Planetary Science 2000; a Prin. Invesigator for NASA's Space Interferometry Mission 2001; mem. Cttee on the Status of Women in Astronomy (American Astronomical Soc.—AAS) 1994–97, Publs Bd, Publs of the Astronomical Soc. of the Pacific 1997–2002, Bd of Dirs, Astronomical Soc. of the Pacific 1997–99, Bd of Councillors, American Astronomical Soc. 1998–2000, NASA Working Group: Origins of Solar Systems 1998–2000, NASA Working Group: Terrestrial Planet Finder 1998–2001; mem. NAS 2002; Fellow, Calif. Acad. of Sciences 1996; ABC News Hour Person of the Week 26 Jan. 1996, Manne Siegbahn Award, Physics Cttee of Swedish Acad. 1996, Bunyan Lecturer, Stanford Univ. 1997, Alumnus of the Year, Univ. of California, Santa Cruz 1997, first Int. Astronomical Union Comm. 51 Bioastronomy Medal of Honor 1997, first Certificate of Recognition, Extrasolar Planetary Foundation 1999, UCLA Alumni Professional Achievement Award 1999, Invited Lecture and Exhibit, Centennial Meeting of American Physical Soc. 1999, G. Darwin Lecturer, Royal Astronomical Soc. 2000, California Scientist of the Year 2000, NSF Distinguished Lecturer 2000, NAS Henry Draper Medal 2001, Sackler Lecturer, Univ. of Leiden 2001, AAS Beatrice Tinsley Prize 2002, Carl Sagan Award, American Astronautical Soc. and Planetary Soc. 2002, NASA Medal for Exceptional Scientific Achievement 2003 Discover Magazine: Space Scientist of the Year 2003, Shaw Prize in Astronomy (Lecture) 2005, Niels Bohr Lecturer, Niels Bohr Inst. 2005, George Gamow Lecturer, Univ. of Colorado 2006, NASA Astrobiology Inst. 'Getting to the Core of Exoplanets: From Gas Giants to Ice Giants' 2007, Lecture: Nat. Air and Space Museum: New Worlds, Yellowstone, and Life in the Universe 2007. *Achievements include:* discovered 70 of first 100 known extrasolar planets; discovered first system of planets around a Sun-like star (Upsilon And), discovered first transiting planet around another star (HD209458), discovered first cand. Saturn-mass planets (HD46375, HD16141), discovered first extrasolar planet orbiting beyond 5 AU (55 Cancri d, co-discovered first Neptune-sized planets: Gliese 436b and 55 Cancri e. *Publications:* numerous scientific papers in professional journals.

MARDEN, Brice, BFA, MFA; American artist; b. (Nicholas Brice Marden, Jr), 15 Oct. 1938, Bronxville, New York; m. Pauline Baez 1960 (divorced); m. Helen Marden 1968; one s. two d.; ed Boston Univ., Yale School of Art and Architecture; moved to New York and worked as a guard at Jewish Museum 1963; travelled to France, Greece and Asia in the 1970s; regarded as one of the most important contemporary abstract painters; currently lives and works in Manhattan, New York; mem. American Acad. of Arts and Letters 1988–; Hon. DFA (Brown Univ.) 2000. *Address:* c/o Gagosian Gallery, 980 Madison Avenue, New York, NY 10075, USA. *Telephone:* (212) 744-2313. *Fax:* (212) 772-7962. *E-mail:* newyork@gagosian.com. *Website:* www.gagosian.com.

MÅRDH, Per-Anders, MD, PhD; Swedish university professor and physician; *Professor Emeritus of Obstetrics and Gynaecology, Lund University;* b. 9 April 1941, Stockholm; s. of Gustav-Adolf Mårdh and Inga-Greta Mårdh (née Bodin); ed Univ. of Lund; Assoc. Prof., Univ. of Lund 1973, Dir WHO Collaboration Centre for Sexually Transmitted Diseases 1980–85, currently Emer. Prof. of Obstetrics and

Gynaecology; apptd Prof. of Clinical Bacteriology, Univ. of Uppsala 1984; Founder Scandinavian Asscn for Travel Medicine and Health 1990; Chair. Healthy Travel and Tourism Centre, Simrishamn; mem. Bd Int. Tourist Health Org., Osterlen Acad.; Assoc., Inst. of Clinical Sciences; Fernström's Award for young prominent research workers 1982. *Publications:* as ed.: Genital Infections and Their Complications 1975, Chlamydia trachomatis in Genital and Related Infections 1982, Chlamydial Infections 1982, International Perspectives on Neglected Sexually Transmitted Diseases 1983, Gas Chromatography/Mass Spectrometry in Applications in Microbiology 1984, Sexually Transmitted Diseases 1984, Bacterial Vaginosis 1984, Coagulase-negative Staphylococci 1986, Infections in Primary Health Care 1986, Genital Candida-infection 1990, Vaginitis/Vaginosis 1991, Travel and Migration Medicine 1997; Author: Chlamydia 1988, Swedish Red Houses 1991, Travel Well Travel Healthy 1992, Travel Medicine 1994, Women's Health 2013. *Leisure interests:* art, skiing. *Address:* Department of Obstetrics and Gynaecology, Faculty of Medicine, Lund University, 221 00 Lund, Sweden (office). *Telephone:* (46) 17-25-07 (office); (46) 15-78-68 (office); 73-611119 (mobile) (home). *E-mail:* per-anders.mardh@med.lu.se (office). *Website:* www.med.lu.se (office).

MARGA, Andrei, BA, PhD; Romanian philosopher, academic, writer and politician; b. 22 May 1946, Bucharest; m. Prof. Felicia-Delia Marga; Asst Lecturer, Babeş-Bolyai Univ., Cluj 1971–79, Lecturer 1979–90, Prof. of Contemporary Philosophy and Logic 1990–, Dean, Faculty of History and Philosophy 1990–92, Vice-Rector Babeş-Bolyai Univ. 1992–93, Rector 1993–2004, 2008–12, Pres. Academic Council 2004–08; Erich Voegelin Guest Prof., Ludwig Maximilians Univ., Munich, Germany 2004; Guest Prof., Univ. of Vienna, Austria 2004–05; Visiting Prof., Paul Valery Univ., Montpellier, France 2005, Prof., Hebrew Univ. of Jerusalem, Israel 2012; Minister of Nat. Educ. 1997–2000; mem. Christian-Democratic Nat. Peasants' Party (PNŢCD) 1999–2001, Chair. Jan.–July 2001; formed the Popular Christian Party 2001; currently mem. Nat. Liberal Party (PNL); Minister of Foreign Affairs May–Aug. 2012; Vice-Chair. UNESCO-CEPES (European Centre for Higher Educ./Centre Européen pour l'Enseignement Supérieur) Bd 1998–; mem. Kuratorium of Institut für Kulturgeschichte Sud-Ost Europa, Munich 2001–, Collegium of the Journal of Law, Univ. of São Paulo, Brazil 2011–, Collegium of the Journal of Society and Economy, Corvinus Univ., Budapest, Hungary 2011–; Expert of the Agenzia per la Valutazione e la Promozione della Qualità delle Facoltà Ecclesiastiche (Vatican) 2011–, Hochschulrektorenkonferenz (HRK) (Germany) 2011–; Sr Consultant, Int. Network of Confucius Insts (HANBAN Foundation, Beijing, China) 2011–; mem. Academia Europaea (Jena) 2004–, Academia Europaea (Salzburg) 2005–, Uniunea Scriitorilor din România 2010–; Hon. Citizen, City of Bistriţa 1999; Hon. Pres. Danubian Rectors Conf. 2006–10; Hon. Dignitary of Carmel City (Israel) 2008; numerous decorations including Grand Officier, Ordre nat. du Mérite 1999, Gra-Cruz da Ordem Nat. do Merito (Portugal) 2000, Ordinul Crucea Sfântului Apostol Andrei – Galaţi 2000, Ordinul Naţional Pentru Merit, rangul Mare Cruce 2000, Chevalier des Palmes académiques 2002, Das Grosse Verdienstkreuz 2003, Medaglia Pontificia. Anno XXVI. Joannes Paulus II (Vatican) 2005, Medaglia Pontificia. Anno I. Benedictus XVI (Vatican) 2006, Ordine della Stella della Solidarietà Italiana in grado di Cavaliere (Italy) 2009, Crucea Patriarhala – Patriarhia Româna 2011; Dr hc ('Alexandru Ioan Cuza' Univ., Iaşi) 1999; Insigne Aureum (Univ. of Maribor, Slovenia) 2000; Dr hc (Univ. of Baia Mare) 2000, ('Ion Creangă' Univ. of Chişinău, Moldova) 2000, (Debrecen Univ., Hungary) 2003, (Paul Valery Univ.) 2008, ('Petru Maior' Univ. of Târgu-Mures) 2008, (Univ. of Oradea) 2009, (Corvinus Univ. of Budapest) 2010, ('Alecu Russo' Bălţi State Univ., Moldova) 2010, ('1 Decembrie 1918' Univ. of Alba Iulia) 2010, (Baku Pedagogical State Univ., Azerbaijan) 2011, (Ştefan cel Mare Univ. of Suceava) 2011, (Constantin Brâncusi Univ. pf Târgu Jiu) 2011; Hon. DHumLitt (Plymouth State Univ., NH) 2006; Simion Bărnuţiu Award, Romanian Acad. 1985, România – Israel Award and The Medal of Jerusalem (Israel) 2002, Premiul Naţional 'Brătianu' 2003, Gold Medal, Univ. of Tübingen (Germany) 2003, Herder Prize (Austria/Germany) 2005, A Commendation of the Gov. of the State of NH (USA) 2006, Prize of Sara and Haim Ianculovici Foundation, Haifa (Israel) 2008, Medalia 'Prieten al Comunitatilor Evreiesti din România' – Federatia Comunitatilor Evreiesti din România (Fed. of Jewish Communities from Romania) 2009. *Publications include:* Herbert Marcuse. Studiu critic (Herbert Marcuse. A Critical Study) 1980, Cunoaştere şi sens. Perspective critice asupra pozitivismului (Cognition and Sense. A Critical Approach of Positivism) 1984, Acţiune şi raţiune în concepţia lui Jürgen Habermas (Action and Reason with Jürgen Habermas) 1985, Raţionalitate, comunicare, argumentare (Rationality, Communication, Argumentation) 1991, Introducere în metodologia şi argumentarea filosofică (Introduction to Philosophical Methodology and Argumentation) 1992, Explorări în actualitate (Explorations into the Present Time) 1995, Filosofia unificării europene (The Philosophy of the European Unification) 1995 (second edn 1997), Academic Reform. A Case Study 1997, Reconstrucţia pragmatică a filosofiei (The Pragmatic Reconstruction of Philosophy) 1998, Educaţia în tranziţie (Education in Transition) 1999, Relativismul şi consecinţele sale (Relativism and Its Consequences) 1999, Anii reformei: 1997–2000 (The Years of Reform: 1997–2000) 2001, Bildung und Modernisierung (Education and Modernization) 2001, Introducere în filosofia contemporană (Introduction to Contemporary Philosophy) 2002, Ieşirea din trecut (documente şi reflecţii) (Path out of the Past. Documents and Reflections) 2002, Filosofia lui Habermas (The Philosophy of Habermas) 2006, Philosophia et Theologia Hodie 2008, La Sortie du Relativisme 2008, Fraţii mai mari. Intâlniri cu iudaismul (The Older brothers. Encounters with Judaism) 2009, Absolutul astăzi. Teologia and filosofia lui Joseph Ratzinger (Absolute today. Joseph Ratzinger's theology and philosophy) 2010, Criza and după criză (Crisis and after the crisis) 2010, Argumentarea (Argumentation) 2010, Challenges, Values and Vision 2011, Riflessioni italiane 2011, După cincisprezece ani. Fifteen Years after (1998–2004 şi 2008–2012) 2011, România actuală (Diagnoză) 2011, The Destiny of Europe 2011, The Pragmatic Reconstruction of Philosophy 2012, Crizele Modernităţii Târzii 2012; numerous articles in learned journals. *Address:* Faculty of History and Philosophy, Babeş-Bolyai University, 400084 Cluj-Napoca, Str. Mihail Kogălniceanu 1, Romania (office). *Telephone:* (264) 405300 (office). *Fax:* (264) 405326 (office). *E-mail:* hiphi@hiphi.ubbcluj.ro (office). *Website:* hiphi.ubbcluj.ro (office).

MARGARYAN, Taron, MEng, CandEconSci; Armenian politician and government official; b. 17 April 1978, Yerevan, Armenian SSR, USSR; s. of fmr Prime Minister Andranik Margaryan; m.; five s. one d.; ed School No. 177, Avan, Armenian Acad. of Agric., Yerevan State Univ. of Econs; leading specialist, later Head of Div., Nor Nork territorial div. of State Cttee of Real Estate Cadastre attached to Govt 2001–03; Deputy Head of Bio-resources Man. Agency, Ministry of Nature Protection 2003–05; Leader of Avan Community, Yerevan 2005–09; mem. Council of Elders of Yerevan 2009, First Deputy Mayor of Yerevan 2009–11, Mayor of Yerevan 2011–18; Chair. Bd of Trustees, Khut charitable fund 2005–; mem. Hayastani Hanrapetakan Kusaktsutyun (HHK—Republican Party of Armenia) 1996–, Head of HHK Territorial Council of Avan 1998–2011, mem. HHK Council 2006–, mem. HHK Exec. Body 2012–, mem. HHK Bd 2016–, Head of HHK Yerevan territorial org. 2017–; mem. Volunteer Homeland Defenders Union 2010–; Chair. Nat. Univ. of Architecture and Construction of Armenia (fmrly YSUAC) 2012; Anania Shirakatsi Medal Pres. of Armenia 2008, Gold Medal, Mayor of Yerevan 2008, Medal of Honour, Nat. Ass. of Armenia 2011, 'Garegin Nzhde' and 'Andranik Ozanyan' Medals, Ministry of Defence 2011, Second Rank Medal 'For the Services Rendered to the Homeland', Pres. of Armenia 2013, Gold Medal, Agrarian Univ. of Armenia, Gold Service Medal, Frityof Nansen, Gold Service Medal 'Mountainous Armenian Eagle', 'Sparapet Vazgen Sargsyan' Order, Volunteer Homeland Defenders Union, Golden Service Medal, Union Communities of Armenia, Medal 'For Co-operation', Police Medal 'Honorary Collaborator', Ministry of Emergency Situations 2014, Medal 'Shahamir Shahamiryan', Ministery of Justice 2014, Medal of Int. Council of Museums 2014, Khachatur Abovyan Gold Medal, Rector of Armenian State Pedagogical Univ. 2015, 'Mecenate of Arts' Medal, Yerevan State Inst. of Theatre and Cinema 2015, Gold Medal of Armenian Gen. Benevolent Union 2015, Medal 'For Collaboration', Investigative Cttee 2015, Gold Medal, Chamber of Trade and Industry 2015, Gold Medal 'For Achievements in Agriculture', Ministry of Agric. 2015, Avetik Isahakyan Medal, Cen. Library 2015, First Rank Medal 'For Services Rendered to the Homeland' 2016, Mesrop Mashtot Order 2016, Medal 'Glory Cross Noy' 2017. *Address:* c/o Hayastani Hanrapetakan Kusaktsutyun (HHK) (Republican Party of Armenia), 0010 Yerevan, M. Adamyan poghots 2, Armenia.

MARGELISCH, Claude-Alain; Swiss lawyer and banking executive; *CEO, Swiss Bankers Association;* b. 1963; ed Univ. of Berne; qualified as an attorney-at-law and notary and worked in a law firm until 1993; joined Swiss Bankers Asscn 1993, Deputy CEO responsible for Int. Financial Markets –2010, CEO and Del. of Bd of Dirs 2010–. *Address:* Swiss Bankers Association, Aeschenplatz 7, PO Box 4182, 4002 Basel, Switzerland (office). *Telephone:* (61) 2959393 (office). *Fax:* (61) 2725382 (office). *E-mail:* office@sba.ch (office). *Website:* www.swissbanking.org (office).

MARGELOV, Mikhail Vitalyevich; Russian politician; *Vice-President, Transneft, JSC;* b. 22 Dec. 1964, Moscow; m.; one s.; trans., Int. Dept, CPSU Cen. Cttee 1984–86; Arabic teacher, Higher KGB School 1986–89; Chief Ed. Arab Dept, ITAR-TASS 1989–90; with consulting cos World Resources, Boston Consulting Group, Ban & Co. 1990–95; with Video Int. 1995–; co-ordinator Boris Yeltsin Presidential election campaign; First Deputy Head Dept of Man., Russian Presidium 1996–97, Head of Dept of Public Relations 1997–98; Head of Advisory Group to the Chair., State Customs Cttee 1998; Head of Political Advisory Group, Novosti Information Agency 1999; Head of Russian Information Centre 1999–2000; Rep. for Pskov region, Russian Fed. Ass. 2000, mem. Council of the Fed., Chair. Int. Affairs Cttee 2001–14; Vice-Pres. Parliamentary Ass. of the Council of Europe 2003–08; Special Rep. of the Pres. of Russian Fed. on Sudan 2008–11, on Cooperation with African Countries 2011; Vice-Pres. Transneft, JSC 2014–; mem. Council for Foreign and Defense Policy (CFDP), Russian Council for Int. Affairs (RCIA); Order of Honour 2007; Pushkin Medal 2003, Pro Merito Medal 2010, Medal of Merit, Woodrow Wilson Award. *Address:* Transneft, JSC, 57 Bolshaya Polyanka, 119180 Moscow, Russia (office). *Telephone:* (495) 950-81-78 (office). *E-mail:* transneft@ak.transneft.ru (office). *Website:* www.en.transneft.ru (office).

MARGETTS, Sir Robert John, Kt, CBE, FREng, FIChemE; British insurance industry executive; *Deputy Chairman, Uralkali;* b. 10 Nov. 1946; ed Univ. of Cambridge; trained as chemical engineer; joined ICI PLC as process design 1969, Dir Agricultural Div. 1982–85, Petrochemicals & Plastics Div. 1985–87, Research & Operations Chemicals & Polymers Group 1987, ICI Eng 1987–89, Gen. Man. Personnel 1989–90, Chair. and Chief Exec. Tioxide Group 1991–92, Exec. Dir 1992–97, Vice-Chair. 1998–2000, Chair. ICI Pension Fund Trustee Ltd 1994–2000; Sr Ind. Dir and Deputy Chair. Uralkali (produces potash fertilisers) 2011–; Chair. Huntsman Corpn (Europe) 2000–10, Ensus PLC 2007–, Energy Technologies Inst. LLP 2007–, Ordnance Survey 2008–, Energy Technologies Institute; Vice-Pres. Royal Acad. of Eng 1994–97; Chair. Action for Engineering 1995–97, UK Natural Environment Research Council (NERC) 2001–06, Govt Industry Forum Non-Food Uses of Crops 2001–04; Dir Anglo American plc 1998–2010, Wellstream plc 2010–11, English China Clays plc 1992–99, Legal & General Group plc 1996–2010 (Vice-Chair. 1998–2000, Chair. 2000–10), BOC Group plc 2001–06 (Deputy Chair. 2001–02, Chair. 2002–06), Falck Renewables plc 2007–10, Neochimiki SA 2008–10, Huntsman Corpn 2010–, Foundation for Science and Tech.; Trustee, Council for Industry and Higher Educ. 2001–10 (mem. 1992–), Brain Research Trust 2002–; mem. CIA Council 1992–96, 2001–, Bd CEFIC 1993–95, 1998–2000, Council for Science and Tech. 1998–2007, Advisory Cttee on Business and the Environment 1999–2001, Technology Foresight Steering Group, Economy and Science and Tech. Honours Cttees 2005–, Advisory Bd Teijin Ltd (Japan) 2004–06; Gov. ICSTM 1991–2004; mem. Court Univ. of Surrey; Fellow, City & Guilds 2001; Hon. Fellow, Imperial Coll. 1999, Univ. of Cardiff 2007, Inst. of Energy 2008, Council for Industry and Higher Educ. 2011; Hon. Freeman, City of London 2004, Salters' Co. 2004; Hon. DEng (Sheffield) 1997, Hon. DSc (Cranfield) 2003. *Leisure interests:* sailing, skiing, tennis, watersports. *Address:* Uralkali Moscow Office, 123317 Moscow, 6 Presnenskaya embankment, Building 2, 34th floor, Russia (office). *Telephone:* (495) 730-23-71 (office). *Fax:* (495) 730-23-93 (office). *E-mail:* msc@msc.uralkali.com (office). *Website:* www.uralkali.com (office).

MARGRETHE II, HM, Queen of Denmark; b. 16 April 1940; d. of King Frederik IX and Queen Ingrid; m. Count Henri de Laborde de Monpezat (Prince Consort Henrik of Denmark 2005–16, Henrik, Prince of Denmark from 2016) 1967 (died 2018); two s., HRH Crown Prince Frederik and HRH Prince Joachim; ed Univs of Copenhagen, Århus and Cambridge, Sorbonne, Paris and London School of Econs, UK; succeeded to the throne 14 Jan. 1972; has undertaken many official visits abroad with her husband, travelling extensively in Europe, the Far East, N and S America; Hon. KG 1979; Hon. Freedom of City of London 2000; Hon. Bencher of the Middle Temple 1992; Hon. Fellow, Lucy Cavendish Coll. Cambridge 1989, Girton Coll. Cambridge 1992; Sovereign Kt Grand Cross with Collar, Order of the Elephant, Sovereign Kt Grand Commdr with Collar, Order of the Dannebrog, Sovereign Dame, Royal Family Order of King Christian X, Sovereign Dame, Royal Family Order of King Frederik IX, Sovereign Recipient of the Cross of Honour of the Order of the Dannebrog, Sovereign Recipient of the Nersornaat Medal for Meritorious Service, First Class (Greenland); Grand Cross with Collar, Order of the Cross of Terra Mariana (Estonia), Grand Croix, Légion d'honneur, Grand Cross, Order of the Redeemer (Greece) and numerous others; Hon. LLD (Cambridge) 1975; Dr hc (London) 1980, (Univ. of Iceland) 1986, (Oxford) 1992, (Edin.) 2000; Mother-Tongue Soc.'s Prize 1987, Medal of the Headmastership, Univ. of Paris 1987, Adeil Order 1990. *Achievements (miscellaneous):* illustrated J. R. R. Tolkien's Lord of the Rings 1977, Historierne om Regnar Lodbrog, Norse Legends as told by Jorgen Stegelmann 1979, Bjarkemaal 1982, Poul Oerum's Comedy in Florens 1990 and Cantabile poems by HRH the Prince Consort 2000, designed costumes for TV Theatre's The Shepherdess and the Chimney-sweep 1987, scenography and costumes for the ballet A Folk Tale, Royal Theatre 1991, découpages for TV film about the Hans Christian Andersen fairy tale Snedronningen 1999–2000, scenography and costumes for Tivoli pantomime ballet Kaerlighed i Skarnkassen 2001, illustrations for Karen Blixen's Seven Gothic Tales 2002. *Publications include:* (trans.) All Men are Mortal (with HRH the Prince Consort) 1981, The Valley 1988, The Fields 1989, The Forest (trans.) 1989. *Address:* Amalienborg, 1257 Copenhagen K; PO Box 2143, 1015 Copenhagen K, Denmark. *E-mail:* hofmarskallatet@kongehuset.dk (office). *Website:* www.kongehuset.dk (office).

MARGULIS, Grigoriy, DSc; American (b. Russian) researcher, academic and educator; *Professor of Mathematics, Yale University;* b. 24 Feb. 1946, Moscow, Russia; m. Raisa Margulis; one s.; ed Moscow High School and Moscow Univ.; Jr Scientific Fellow, Inst. for Problems in Information Transmission, Moscow 1970–74, Sr Research Fellow 1974–86, Leading Research Fellow 1986–91; Prof. of Math., Yale Univ. 1991–; Foreign Hon. mem. American Acad. of Arts and Science 1991, NAS 2001; Hon. Fellow, Tata Inst. of Fundamental Research 1996; Dr hc (Univ. of Bielefeld, Germany) 2000, (École Normale Supérieure, Paris) 2010, (Univ. of York, UK) 2011, (Univ. of Lyon, France) 2013, (Univ. of Chicago) 2014; Young Mathematicians' Prize, Moscow Math. Soc. 1968, Fields Medal, Int. Congress of Mathematicians, Helsinki 1978 (prevented by Soviet Govt from travelling to Helsinki to receive medal), Medal of Collège de France 1991, Humboldt Prize 1995, Lobachevski Prize 1996, Wolf Foundation Prize in Math. 2005, Dobrushin Int. Award 2011. *Publications include:* numerous articles in math. journals on ergodic theory, dynamical systems, discrete subgroups of Lie groups, geometry, number theory, combinatorics. *Address:* Yale University, Department of Mathematics, 438 DL, PO Box 208283, New Haven, CT 06520-208283, USA (office). *Telephone:* (203) 432-4687 (office). *E-mail:* margulis@math.yale.edu (office). *Website:* www.math.yale.edu (office).

MARGVELASHVILI, Giorgi, PhD; Georgian philosopher, academic, politician and head of state; b. 4 Sept. 1969, Tbilisi, Georgian SSR, USSR; one d. from 1st m.; m. 2nd Maka Chichua 2014; one s.; ed Tbilisi State Univ., Central European Univ., Hungary, Inst. of Philosophy, Georgian Acad. of Sciences; Mountain Guide and Group Leader, Caucasus Travel Ltd 1992–94; Jr Scientist, Psychological Lab. of Marginal Conditions 1993; Jr Scientist, Lab. of Georgian Culture 1993; Head, Dept of Advertising, Business Diary Ltd 1994–95; Lecturer in Philosophy and Cultural Studies, Tbilisi Independent Univ. 1996–97; Local Government Specialist/Program Consultant, Nat. Democratic Inst. for Int. Affairs, Tbilisi 1995–2000; Rector Georgian Inst. of Public Affairs (jt Georgian–USA establishment) 2000–06, 2010–12, Head of Research Dept 2006–10; became involved in politics 2003; Minister of Educ. and Science 2012–13; First Deputy Prime Minister 2013; named as Qartuli Ocneba (Georgian Dream) coalition presidential cand. for Oct. 2013 presidential election May 2013; Pres. of Georgia 2013–18; Ind. *Publications include:* The Problem of Finality in Mythology 1993, Legislative Amendments to Local Government Training Manual #2 (ed.) 1998, Local Government Manual (co-author and ed.) 1998, Election Campaign and Training Manual (co-author) 1998, Philosophy of Individual Substance 1998, Legislative Amendments to Local Government Training Manual #1 (ed.) 1999, Our Generation's Privilege by Z. Zhvania (ed.) 2005; numerous articles and editorials on political, public, int. relations, culture and philosophy issues in newspapers and journals. *Leisure interest:* knitting.

MARHELY, Daniel; French business executive; *Founder and Chief Technology Officer, Deezer;* b. 19 Aug. 1984, Paris; left school aged 16; headed web dept of Agrafe communications agency 2001; focused exclusively on web devt from 2002; co-f. dating website Lovelee.com 2004; co-f. Aliza Medias 2006; started Blogmusik streaming music site which was not approved by SACEM (Soc. des auteurs, compositeurs et éditeurs de musique) music rights asscn, abandoned Blogmusik and dealt directly with rights owners; Blogmusik renamed Deezer.com as first legal music-on-demand website streaming service 2007, Chief Tech. Officer, now expanded globally into more than 160 countries with 20 million licensed music tracks, 32,000 radio channels, 26 million users and two million paid subscribers; mem. Conseil Nat. du Numérique 2011–12. *E-mail:* pr@deezer.com (office). *Website:* www.deezer.com (office).

MARIAL BENJAMIN, Barnaba; South Sudanese politician; fmr Minister of Regional Cooperation, Govt and Minister of Information and Broadcasting –2013, Minister of Foreign Affairs and Int. Co-operation 2013–16; mem. Sudan People's Liberation Movt.

MARIAM, Lt-Col Mengistu Haile; Ethiopian fmr head of state and army officer; b. 26 May 1937, Addis Ababa; m. Wubanchi Bishaw 1968; one s. two d.; ed Holeta Mil. Acad.; served in Army's Third Div., attaining rank of Maj.; mem. Armed Forces Co-ordinating Cttee (Derg) June 1974–; took leading part in overthrow of Emperor Haile Selassie Sept. 1974, Head of Derg Exec. Cttee Nov. 1974; First Vice-Chair. Provisional Mil. Admin. Council (PMAC) 1974–77, Chair. (Head of State) 1977–91; Pres. of Democratic Repub. of Ethiopia 1987–91 (overthrown in coup); Chair. PMAC Standing Cttee; Chair. Council of Ministers 1976–91, OAU 1983–84; Sec.-Gen. Workers' Party of Ethiopia 1984–91; accused of genocide in absentia; now living in Zimbabwe as political refugee; convicted of genocide 2006. *Publication:* Tiglatchin (Our Struggle) 2012. *Leisure interests:* swimming, tennis, chess, reading, watching films. *Address:* PO Box 1536, Gunhill Enclave, Harare, Zimbabwe. *Telephone:* 745254.

MARIANI, Carlo Maria; Italian artist; b. 25 July 1935, Rome; s. of Anastasio Mariani and Anita de Angelis; m. 1st B. Brantsen 1959 (divorced 1983); m. 2nd Carol Lane 1990; one s. one d.; ed Accad. di Belle Arti, Rome; lives and works in Rome and New York; participated in Documenta 7, Kassel 1982, Venice Biennale 1982, 1984, 1990, Sydney Biennial 1986, Centre George Pompidou, Paris, Hirshorn Museum, Washington, DC, Museum of Modern Art, New York, Guggenheim Museum, New York, Centro Italian Arte Contemporanea di Foligno, San Francisco Museum of Modern Art, Mathildenhohe Darmstadt, Germany, Frankfurt Kunstverein, Germany, Museum of Modern Art, Rome, Palais des Beaux Art, Charleroi, France, Venice Bienniale, Italy, California Center for the Arts, Frye Museum, Seattle, Philadelphia Museum of Art, Museum of Palazzo Te Mantova, Italy, Smithsonian Nat. Portrait Gallery, Washington, DC and numerous other group exhbns in USA, Canada, UK, USSR, Europe and S America; Feltrinelli Prize, Accad. dei Lincei 1998. *Website:* info@carlomariamariani.com; www.carlomariamariani.com.

MARIANI, Pierre; French business executive and fmr government official; b. 6 April 1957; ed Ecole des hautes études commerciales, Ecole nationale d'admin; occupied various functions in Ministry of Economy and Finance 1982–92; Dir Cabinet of Budget Minister, Govt Spokesman and Head of Communication 1993–95; Man. Dir Soc. française d'investissements immobiliers et de gestion (real estate co. in Fimalac Group) 1995–96; Man. Dir and mem. Man. Bd Banque pour l'expansion industrielle (Banexi; commercial arm of BNP) 1996–97, Chair. Man. Bd 1997–99; Head of Int. Retail Banking, BNP Paribas Group 1999–2003, Head of Financial Services and Int. Retail Banking 2003–08, Deputy Man. Dir jtly responsible for Retail Banking activities and for Int. Retail Services of BNP Paribas 2008; Chair. Man. Bd and CEO Dexia SA 2008–11; Chair. Denizbank Anonim Şirketi 2011–12; mem. Bd of Dirs Dexia Bank Belgium, Dexia Crédit Local, Dexia Banque Internationale à Luxembourg; mem. Exec. Cttee FBF; Vice-Chair. AFB; Dir and Chair. Audit Cttee, EDF SA 2009–14.

MARIANI-DUCRAY, Francine, LenD; French state counsellor; b. 7 Oct. 1954, Paris; m. Pierre Mariani; three c.; ed Ecole nationale d'administration (ENA) Paris, Inst. d'études politiques de Paris; joined Ministry of Culture 1979, Tech. Adviser to François Léotard, Minister of Culture and Communication 1986–88, a Dir Musée du Louvre 1988–91, Dir of Gen. Admin, Ministry of Culture 1993–98, Head of Gen. Inspections of Admin of Cultural Affairs, Ministry of Culture and Communication 1998–2001, Pres. Réunion des musées nationaux (RMN) 2001–03, Dir Musées de France 2001–08; Conseiller d'Etat 2008–; Chair. Bd of Mans, Académie de France à Rome 2008–11; Chair. Conseil des ventes volontaires de meubles aux enchères publiques 2009–11; mem. Conseil Supérieur de l'Audiovisuel 2011–; Chevalier, Légion d'honneur 2005, Commdr, Ordre des Arts et des Lettres, Officier du mérite. *Address:* 19 rue des Hauts Closeaux, 92310 Paris, France (home). *Telephone:* 1-45-34-04-32 (home). *E-mail:* francine.mariani-ducray@cda.fr (office). *Website:* www.cda.fr (office).

MARÍAS FRANCO, Javier; Spanish writer and translator; b. 20 Sept. 1951, Madrid; s. of Julián Marías Aguilera and Dolores Franco Manera; ed Institución Libre de Enseñanza, Colegio Estudio, Universidad Complutense de Madrid; trans. and writer of film screenplays 1969–; Ed. Alfaguara 1974; lecturer at various univs worldwide; mem. Int. Parliament of Writers (exec. council 2001–); Chevalier, Ordre des Arts et des Lettres, Premio Comunidad de Madrid 1998; Premio Nacional de Traducción (for translation of Tristram Shandy) 1979, Alberto Moravia Int. Prize, Rome 2000, Grinzane Cavour prize, Turin 2000. *Publications include:* novels: Los dominios del lobo 1971, Travesía del horizonte 1972, El Monarca del tiempo 1978, El Siglo 1982, El hombre sentimental (Premio Herralde de Novela, Premio Ennio Flaiano 2000) 1986, Todas las almas (Premio Ciudad de Barcelona) 1989, Corazón tan blanco (Premio de la Crítica 1993, Prix L'Oeil et la Lettre 1993, Int. IMPAC Prize 1997) 1992, Mañana en la batalla piensa en mí (Premio Fastenrath de la Real Academia Española de la Lengua 1995, Premio Internacional de Novela Rómulo Gallegos 1995, Prix Fémina Étranger, France 1996, Premio Arzobispo Juan de San Clemente 1995, Premio Letterario Internazionale Mondello-Città di Palermo 1998) 1994, Negra espalda del tiempo 1998, Tu rostro mañana 1. Fiebre y lanza (Premio Salambó 2003) 2002, Tu rostro mañana 2: Baile y sueño 2006, Tu rostro mañana 3. Veneno y sombra y adiós 2007, Los enamoramientos 2011, Así empieza lo malo 2014; other fiction: Gospel (screenplay) 1969, Mientras ellas duermen (short stories) 1990, Cuando fui mortal (short stories) 1996, Mala índole (short story) 1998; non-fiction: Pasiones pasadas (articles and essays) 1991, Vidas escritas (articles) 1992, Literatura y fantasma (articles and essays) 1993, Vida del fantasma (articles) 1995, Si yo amaneciera otra vez (articles and poems) 1997, Miramientos (articles) 1997, Mano de sombra (articles) 1997, Desde que te vi morir (articles and poems) 1999, Seré amado cuando falte (articles) 1999, Salvajes y sentimentales (articles) 2000, A veces un caballero (articles) 2001, While the Women Are Sleeping (in trans., short stories) 2010; numerous translations; contrib. to anthologies, including Cuentos únicos 1989, El hombre que parecia no querer nada 1996; contrib. to journals and newspapers, including El País, El Diario de Barcelona, Hiperión, Revista de Occidente. *Address:* Mercedes Casanovas Agencia Literaria, Iradier 24, 08017 Barcelona, Spain. *E-mail:* webmaster@javiermarias.es. *Website:* www.javiermarias.es.

MARIĆ, Ljerka, BSc; Bosnia and Herzegovina economist and government official; *Director, Directorate for Economic Planning;* Minister of Finance, Canton of Fojnica 1998; Asst Minister of Finance and the Economy, Bosnian Fed. 2000; fmr Adviser to the Prime Minister; Minister of Finance and the Treasury of the Insts of Bosnia and Herzegovina 2003–07; currently Dir Directorate for Econ. Planning, Council of Ministers, also mem. Admin. Council, Council of Europe Development Bank. *Address:* Directorate for Economic Planning, Ministry of Finance, 71000 Sarajevo, trg Bosne i Hercegovine 1, Bosnia and Herzegovina (office). *Telephone:* (33) 205345 (office). *Fax:* (33) 471822 (office). *E-mail:* trezorbih@trezorbih.gov.ba (office).

MARIC, Zdravko, PhD; Croatian politician; *Minister of Finance;* b. 3 Feb. 1977, Slavonski Brod; m.; two c.; ed Univ. of Zagreb, John F. Kennedy School of Govt, Harvard Univ., USA; Asst, Inst. of Econs, Zagreb 2001–06; Asst Minister for Macroeconomic Analysis and Planning, Ministry of Finance 2006–08, Sec. of State 2008–12, Minister of Finance 2016–; Exec. Dir for Strategy and Capital Markets, Agrokor dd (pvt. co.) 2012–16; regular lecturer, Zagreb Univ. School of Econs and Man., Int. Graduate Business School, Zagreb; mem. (ex-officio) Bd of Govs., EBRD 1993–, EIB 2016–, Multilateral Investment Guarantee Agency, World Bank. *Publications:* several scientific papers. *Leisure interests:* tennis, jogging, basketball, cinema. *Address:* Ministry of Finance, 10000 Zagreb, ul. Katančićeva 5, Croatia (office). *Telephone:* (1) 4591333 (office). *Fax:* (1) 4922583 (office). *E-mail:* kabinet@mfin.hr (office). *Website:* www.mfin.hr (office).

MARICAN, Tan Sri Dato' Mohamed (Mohd) Hassan, FCA; Malaysian petroleum industry executive; *Chairman, Sembcorp Industries Ltd.;* b. 18 Oct. 1952, Sungai Petani; m. Puan Sri Datin Sri Noraini Mohd Yusoff; ed Malay Coll., Kuala Kangsar; with Touche Ross & Co. 1972–80; Partner, Hanafiah Raslan and Mohamed 1980–89; Sr Vice-Pres. of Finance, Petroliam Nasional Berhad (PETRONAS) 1989–95, Pres. and CEO 1995–2010, Acting Chair. 2004–10, also mem. Bd of Dirs and Chair. PETRONAS subsidiaries PETRONAS Dagangan Berhad, PETRONAS Gas Berhad, Malaysia Int. Shipping Corpn Berhad, Engen Ltd SA; Chair., Perusahaan Otomobil Nasional Berhad (Proton) 2000–03; Dir, Int. Centre for Leadership in Finance; Ind. Dir, Sembcorp Industries Ltd 2010–, Chair. 2014–; currently Chair., Singapore Power, Pavilion Gas, Pavilion Gas and Lang Ting Holdings; Sr Advisor Linhart Group, Temasek Int. Advisors; mem. Bd of Dirs, Regional Econ. Devt Authority of Sarawak, Sarawak Energy Berhad, Lambert Energy Advisory, MH Marican Advisory; mem. Malaysian Inst. of Accountants, Malaysian Asscn of CPAs, Commonwealth Business Council; Dato' Setia Sultan Mahmud Terengganu, with title of Dato' 1992, Seri Paduka Mahkota Terengganu, with title of Dato' 1996, Panglima Setia Mahkota, with title Tan Sri 1997, Commdr, Légion d'honneur 2000, Friendship Medal (Viet Nam) 2001, Panglima Negara Bintang Sarawak, with title of Datuk Seri 2003; Dr hc (Univ. of Malaya). *Address:* Sembcorp Industries Ltd, 30 Hill Street, #05-04, Singapore 179360, Singapore (office). *Telephone:* 6723-3113 (office). *Fax:* 6822-3254 (office). *E-mail:* gcr@sembcorp.com (office). *Website:* www.sembcorp.com (office).

MARIN, Angel; Bulgarian army officer (retd) and politician; b. 8 Jan. 1942, Batak; m.; two c.; ed secondary school in Devin, Higher Mil. Artillery School, Shoumen, civilian degree in Radio Electronics Eng, Mil. Artillery Acad., Leningrad (now St Petersburg), USSR, univ. degree in mil. educ.; began mil. career as Lt-Engineer, held various positions in Missile Force, including Commdr Missile Launcher Unit, Commdr Start Platoon and Commdr Start Battery 1965–74, Commdr Separate Missile Div., Stara Zagora 1978–80, Commdr Artillery Regt, Stara Zagora 1980–82, Chief of Missile Force and Artillery, Second Div., Stara Zagora 1982–87, Chief of Missile Force and Artillery, Third Army, Sliven 1987–90, Commdr Missile Force and Artillery of the Ground Force of Bulgarian Armed Forces 1990–98, promoted to Maj.-Gen. 1991, dismissed from Army due to disagreement with the manner of army reform, retd 1998; Vice-Pres. of Bulgaria 2002–12; graduated with distinction and a gold medal in 'Command of Chief of Staff HQ and Operative-Tactical', Mil. Artillery Acad., Leningrad. *Publication:* The Last War.

MARIN, Vice-Adm. Gheorghe, PhD; Romanian naval officer; b. 1 Jan. 1952, Negru-Vodă, Constanţa dist; m. Elena Marin; one d.; ed Mircea cel Bătrân Naval Acad., Constanţa, Faculty of Econ. Planning and Cybernetics, Econ. Studies Acad., Bucharest; Navigation and Communication Officer FPB (M) Squadron 1974–78; CO, Fast Patrol Boat 1980–81; Staff Officer, N3 1981–85; Chief Software Programming Section, Naval Informatics Centre 1985–89; Chief Naval Informatics Center 1989–95; CO Electronic Warfare Brigade within Naval Forces 1995–99; Supt, Mircea cel Bătrân Naval Acad. 1999–2003; Dir of Gen. Staff 2003–04, Chief of Naval Forces Staff 2004–06, Chief of Gen. Staff 2006–10; Knight, Ordinul Naţional Steaua României, Grande Ufficiale, Ordine al Merito della Repubblica Italiana; Dr hc (Dunarea de Jos Univ.). *Publications:* more than 20 books and 70 articles.

MARIN, Jean-Claude; French lawyer and judge; *Public Prosecutor, Court of Cassation;* First Advocate Gen., Court of Cassation, Dir of Criminal Affairs and Pardons 2002–04, apptd Solicitor and Chief Public Prosecutor of Repub. of Paris 2004, Public Prosecutor, Court of Cassation 2011. *Address:* Cour de cassation, 5 quai de l'Horloge, 75055 Paris Cedex 1, France (office). *Website:* www.courdecassation.fr (office).

MARIN, Maguy; French choreographer and artistic director; b. 2 June 1951, Toulouse; s. of Antonio Marin and Luisa Calle; ed Conservatoire de Toulouse; active since 1973; joined Maurice Béjart's Ballet du XXème siècle; joined Ballet Théâtre de l'Arche (subsequently Compagnie Maguy Marin) 1979; began long collaboration with musician-composer Denis Mariotte 1987; Dir Nat. Choreographic Centre in Créteil and Val-de-Marne from 1985 and Nat. Choreographic Centre of Rillieux-la-Pape 1998–2011; settled in Toulouse to carry out artistic research 2012; Chevalier, Ordre des Arts et des Lettres; Grand Prix of Int. Choreographic Competition Bagnolet 1978, Grand Prix Nat. de la chorégraphie 1983, American Dance Festival Award 2003. *Choreographic works include:* May B 1981, Babel Babel 1982, Jaleo 1983, Hymen 1984, Calambre 1985, Cinderella 1985, Eden 1986, Leçons de Ténèbres 1987, Coups d'états 1988, Groosland 1989, Cortex 1991, Made in France 1992, Ay Dios 1993, Waterzooï 1993, Ramdam 1995, Aujourd'hui peut-être 1996, Pour ainsi dire 1999, Quoi qu'il en soit 1999, Points de fuite 2001, Les applaudissements ne se mangent pas (One Can't Eat Applause) 2002, Ça, quand même 2004, Umwelt (Bessie Award 2008) 2005, Ha! Ha! 2006. *Dance:* Ku Yu Ri (Brussels) 1976, Nieblas Niño (est. int. dance contest Bagnolet) 1978, Zoo (Villeneuve-lès-Avignon) 1979, May B. (Angers) 1981, Babel Babel (Angers) 1982, Hymen (Avignon) 1984, Calambre (Paris) 1985, Cinderella (for the Ballet de l'Opéra de Lyon) 1985, Eden (Angers) 1986, Otello (Nancy) 1987, The Seven Deadly Sins (Lyon) 1987, Coups (Montpellier) 1988, Well what does it's making me? (Avignon) 1989, Groosland (Amsterdam) 1989, Cortex (Créteil) 1991, Made in France (The Hague) 1992, Coppelia (for the Ballet de l'Opéra de Lyon) 1993, Waterzooï (Italy) 1993, Ram Ram Dam (Cannes) 1995, Soliloquy (Paris) 1995, Perhaps Today 1996, So to Speak, and Somehow Anyway (Mulhouse) 1999, Vanishing Points (Cannes) 2001, The Applause Did Not Eat (Villeurbanne) (Grand Prix de la danse du Syndicat de la critique 2003) 2002, That Still (duet with Denis Mariotte, Le Mans) 2004, Umwelt (Décines) (Prix spécial du jury du Syndicat de la critique 2006, Bessie Award 2008) 2004, Ha! Ha! (Rillieux-la-Pape) 2006, Turba (with Denis Mariotte, Cannes) (Grand Prix de la danse du Syndicat de la critique 2008) 2007, Description of a Struggle (Festival d'Avignon, Gym Aubanel) 2009, Salves (Dance Biennial in Lyon) (Prix Danza and Danza for Best Contemporary Dance 2011) 2010, Faces (for the Ballet de l'Opéra de Lyon) 2011, Nocturnes (with Denis Mariotte, Dance Biennial in Lyon) 2012. *Address:* Compagnie Maguy Marin, Centre Chorégraphique National de Rillieux-la-Pape, 30 Ter, avenue Général Leclerc, BP 106, 69143 Rillieux-la-Pape Cedex, France (office). *Telephone:* (4) 72-01-12-30 (office). *Fax:* (4) 72-01-12-31 (office). *E-mail:* info@compagnie-maguy-marin.fr (office). *Website:* www.compagnie-maguy-marin.fr (office).

MARÍN ROMANO, José Javier; Spanish banking executive; b. 1966, Madrid; ed graduate in law and holds a degree in business admin; joined Santander Group in 1991, CEO Banif at Banco Santander SA (fmrly Banco Santander Central Hispano SA), also served as Deputy Sec. of Bd and Deputy Gen. Sec. of Banco Santander SA, Exec. Vice-Pres. of Global Pvt. Banking, Banco Santander SA 2007–10, Sr Exec. Vice-Pres. and Head of the Global Insurance, Asset Man. and Pvt. Banking Div. 2010–13, mem. Bd of Dirs 2013–14, CEO Banco Santander SA 2013–14; Dir, Sam Investment Holdings Limited 2014 (resgnd).

MARINAC, Darko, BEng, PhD; Croatian business executive; b. 1950, Zagreb; ed Zagreb Univ., Croatian Chamber of the Economy, Cologne Business School, Germany; joined Pliva (pharmaceutical group) 1975, Project Man. 1978, later Dir-Gen., penicillin plant, Dir, Veterinary and Agro-Chemical Div. 1984, Dir, Research and Devt Div. 1990–92, also Vice-Pres., Man. Bd 1996–99; Integration Dir, Polfa Krakow and Lachema Brno 1999–2000; Pres., Man. Bd, Podravka d.d. 2000–09; Pres., Man. Bd, Croatian Employers' Asscn 2004–05; mem. Nacionalnog vijeća za konkurentnost 2001–, Chair. 2005–.

MARINHO, Roberto Irineu; Brazilian media executive; *Chairman of Board, Grupo Globo;* b. 13 Oct. 1947, Rio de Janeiro; s. of Roberto Pisani Marinho; m. 1st Aparecida Marinho; one s.; m. 2nd Karen Marinho; ed Getúlio Vargas Foundation; joined O Globo newspaper 1963; reporter ABC TV, New York 1969–70; Dir Rio Gráfica 1971–77; Vice-Pres. TV Globo 1978–98, Vice-Pres. Grupo Globo (media conglomerate) 1998–2003, CEO 2002–03, Pres. 2003–17, Chair. of Bd 2017–. *Leisure interests:* coffee production. *Website:* globoir.globo.com (office); www.globo.com (office).

MARINI, Franco, LLB; Italian politician; b. 9 April 1933, S. Pio; Sec.-Gen. Confed. of Workers' Trade Unions (CISL, trade union) 1985–91; Minister of Labour 1991–92; mem. Chamber of Deputies (lower house of parl.) 1992–2006, mem. Senato della Repubblica (upper house of parl.) 2006–13, Pres. 2006–08; mem. European Parl. (Italian Popular Party) 1999–2004; unsuccessful cand. in presidential election 2013; Sec. Partito Popolare Italiano 1997–99; mem. Partito Democratico 2007–. *Address:* Partito Democratico, Via Sant'Andrea delle Fratte 16, 00187 Rome, Italy (office). *Telephone:* (06) 675471 (office). *E-mail:* redazione@partitodemocratico.it (office). *Website:* www.partitodemocratico.it (office).

MARININA, Col. Aleksandra Borisovna, PhD; Russian writer and fmr criminologist; b. (Marina Anatolyevna Alekseyeva), 16 June 1957, Lviv, Ukraine; m. Col Sergey Zatochny; ed Moscow State Univ.; fmr mem. of staff, Acad. of Internal Affairs; began writing detective stories 1991–; mem. of staff, Moscow Inst. of Justice, Ministry of Internal Affairs 1994–97. *Films for television:* Kamenskaya (48 episodes). *Publications include:* Death and Some Love, Ghost of Music, Stolen Dream, I Died Yesterday, Men's Game, Forced Murderer, Black List, Requiem, When Gods Laugh, He Who Knows (vols 1–2), and numerous others. *Leisure interests:* collecting hand bells, reading, Verdi operas, computer solitaire. *Address:* COP Literary Agency, Zhukovskogo str. 4, Apt 29, 103062 Moscow (office); Verhnaya Krasnoselskaya str. 9, Apt 44, 107140 Moscow, Russia (home). *Telephone:* (495) 628-84-56 (office); (495) 628-84-56 (home). *Fax:* (495) 628-84-56 (office). *E-mail:* alexandra@marinina.ru (office). *Website:* www.marinina.ru (home).

MARINO, Daniel Constantine (Dan), Jr; American sports commentator and fmr professional football player; b. 15 Sept. 1961, Pittsburgh, Pa; s. of Daniel Marino and Veronica Marino; m. Claire Marino; three s. two d. (one adopted); ed Cen. Catholic High School, Univ. of Pittsburgh; quarterback; played coll. football at Univ. of Pittsburgh 1979–82; played for Miami Dolphins (Nat. Football League—NFL) 1983–99, retd 2000, returned to org. in Jan. 2004 as Sr Vice-Pres. of Football Operations but resgnd three weeks later; holds or held 25 NFL records and tied for five others, including most attempts (8,358), most passing yards (61,361), most completions (4,967), most passing touchdowns (420), most passing yards in a season (5,084 in 1984), most games, 400 or more yards passing (13); co-f. with his wife The Dan Marino Foundation 1992, The Dan Marino Center 1995; Dir Business Devt, Dreams Inc. 2000–; fmr studio analyst on HBO's weekly football programme 'Inside the NFL'; commentator, CBS's The NFL Today; Advisory Bd mem. 3Cinteractive, Fla; opened two restaurants in S Florida called Dan Marino's Town Tavern (later Dan Marino's Fine Food and Spirits) 2005, since closed, restaurant opened in other locations, in Miami, St Petersburg, Las Vegas, Nev. 2007; Dr hc in broadcast journalism (Univ. of Pittsburgh) 2008; 16-time winner of American Football Conf. (AFC) Offensive Player of the Week, AP NFL Most Valuable Player 1984, NFL Comeback Player of the Year Award 1994, NFL Man of the Year Award 1998, Walter Payton Man of the Year Award 1998, College Football Hall of Fame 2002, Pro Football Hall of Fame 2005. *Films include:* Ace Ventura: Pet Detective (as himself) 1994; cameo appearances in Holy Man 1998, Little Nicky 2000, Bad Boys II 2003; Any Given Sunday (project consultant) 1999, featured in video by Hootie & the Blowfish. *Television includes:* guest-starred as himself in The Simpsons episode Sunday, Cruddy Sunday 1999. *Publications include:* Marino – On the Record 1999, Dan Marino: My Life in Football 2005. *Address:* Dan Marino Foundation, 400 North Andrews Avenue, Fort Lauderdale, FL 33301, USA (office). *Telephone:* (954) 368-6000 (office). *Website:* www.danmarinofoundation.org (office); www.fanatics.com.

MARINOS, Ioannis, (Kritovoulos, Popolaros, W.), BA; Greek journalist; b. 20 July 1930, Hermoupolis; s. of Paul and Elisabeth Marinos; ed School of Law, Univ. of Athens; journalist, To Vima (daily political journal) 1953–65, apptd columnist 1992; journalist, Economicos Tachydromos, Ed.-in-Chief 1956, Ed. and Dir

1964–96, consultant/columnist 1996–; political commentator in Ta Nea (daily) 1972–75; commentator for many radio and TV stations in Greece; mem. European Parl., European Popular Party 1999–2004; Chair., Structural Reforms Cttee, Ministry of Economy and Finance 2004–09; mem. Bd Music Hall of Athens, Red Cross, Amnesty Int.; fmr mem. Exec. Cttee European Financial Press Union; Hon. PhD (Aristotelian Univ. Salonika) 1999; more than 30 awards, including Best European Journalist of 1989 (EC Comm. and Asscn of European Journalists) and awards from UN and Athens Acad. *Publications include:* The Palestinian Problem and Cyprus 1975, For a Change Towards Better 1983, Greece in Crisis 1987, Common Sense 1993, Constitutional Reform: Ideas & Proposals (co-author) 2007, The Disincentives to Invest in Greece 2012, We Should Have Known Better 2013. *Leisure interests:* literature, history, classical music, fishing. *Address:* 2 Kontziadon Street, Piraeus 185 37, Greece (home). *Telephone:* (210) 452-6823 (home). *Fax:* (210) 452-6723 (home).

MARINUȚA, Vitalie, BSc, MA; Moldovan politician and fmr army officer; b. 16 June 1970, Holercani, Dubasari dist; m.; two c.; ed Airborne Command Mil. Acad., Reazani, Russia, US Army Command and Gen. Staff Coll., Fort Leavenworth, USA, Naval Postgraduate School, Monterey, USA, Int. Relations and Political Sciences Inst., Chisinau; held numerous positions in Moldovan Army including Platoon Leader, Company CO, Special Forces Officer 1992–99, CO 22nd Peacekeeping Bn 2000–02, Sr Staff Officer, Operations Directorate, Main Staff 2004–05; Mil. Policy Planning Staff Officer, US CENTCOM, Tampa, Fla USA 2005–06; Chief of Int. Cooperation and Euro-Atlantic Integration Section, Moldovan Ministry of Defence 2006–07; retd from active mil. service with rank of Lt Col July 2007; Minister of Defence 2009–14 (resgnd); apptd Admin. Mari-Group SRL 2015; Cherch 'Stefan cel Mare' Medal, 'Fraternity in Arms' Medal.

MARIO, Ernest, BS, MS, PhD; American pharmacist and business executive; *Chairman, Capnia, Inc.;* b. 12 June 1938, Clifton, NJ; s. of Jerry Mario and Edith Mario; m. Mildred Martha Daume 1961; three s.; ed Rutgers Coll. of Pharmacy, New Brunswick, New Jersey, Univ. of Rhode Island; Vice-Pres. Mfg Operations, Smith Kline 1974–77; joined E.R. Squibb & Sons 1977, Vice Pres. Mfg for US Pharmaceuticals Div. 1977–79, Vice-Pres. Gen. Man., Chemical Div. 1979–81, Pres. Chemical Eng Div. and Sr Vice-Pres. 1981–83, Pres. and CEO Squibb Medical Products 1983–86, mem. Bd 1984–85; Pres. Glaxo Inc. 1986–89, Chair. 1989–91, apptd to Bd of Glaxo Holdings PLC 1988, Chief Exec. 1989–93, Deputy Chair. 1992–93; Co-Chair. CEO ALZA Corpn 1993–97, Chair., CEO 1997–2001; Chair. and CEO Apothogen, Inc. 2002; Chair. IntraBiotics Pharmaceuticals, Inc. 2002–03; Chair. and CEO Reliant Pharmaceuticals Inc. 2003–07; Chair. and CEO Capnia Inc. 2007–14, Chair. 2014–; Chair. Audit Cttee and mem. Compensation Cttee Kindred Biosciences, Inc.; mem. Bd of Dirs, Boston Scientific Corpn, Maxygen, Inc., Pharmaceutical Product Devt Inc., Vivus Pharmaceuticals 2010–, Delpor Inc. 2012–, XenoPort Inc. 2012–, Gladstone Foundation, Celgene Corpn, TONIX Pharmaceuticals Holdings Corpn; Chair. American Foundation for Pharmaceutical Educ., Chimerix, Inc. 2013–; Trustee, Duke Univ. 1989–2007, Rockefeller Univ., Univ. of Rhode Island Foundation; Dr hc (Rutgers Coll. of Pharmacy, Univ. of Rhode Island); Rutgers Univ. Coll. of Pharmacy renamed the Ernest Mario School of Pharmacy in his honour 2001, Remington Medal (American Pharmacists Asscn) 2007. *Leisure interests:* golf, swimming. *Address:* Capnia Inc., 1235 Radio Road, Suite 110, Redwood City, CA 94065, USA (office). *Telephone:* (650) 213-8444 (office). *Fax:* (650) 213-8383 (office). *E-mail:* info@capnia.com (office). *Website:* www.capnia.com (office).

MARION, Jean-Luc, LèsL, PhD; French professor of philosophy; *Professor, University of Paris, Sorbonne;* b. 3 July 1946, Meudon; s. of Jean E. Marion and Suzanne Roussey; m. Corinne Nicolas 1970; two s.; ed Lycée Int. de Sèvres, Ecole Normale Supérieure (Ulm), and Univ. of Paris, Sorbonne; Asst Prof., Univ. of Paris, Sorbonne 1973–81, Prof. 1995–, Dir Centre d'Etudes Cartésiennes 1995–; Dir Ecole Doctorale V 1998–95; Prof., Univ. of Poitiers 1981–88; Prof., Univ. of Paris X (Nanterre) 1988–95; John Nuveen Prof., Univ. of Chicago 1992–2010, Andrew Thomas Greeley Prof. 2010–; Visiting Prof., Washington Univ. 1990, Villanova Univ. 2000, Boston Coll. 2001–03; Assoc. Prof., Laval Univ., Canada 1993–96; Dir serie Epiméthée, Presses Universitaires de France, Paris 1981–; Co-Dir Les Études Philosophiques (journal); mem. Faculty Steering Cttee, Chicago Centre in Paris 2001–04; mem. Acad. Française 2008–, Accademia dei Lincei 2009–, Pontifical Council on Culture 2011, Academia Chilena de Ciencias Sociales, Politicas y Morales 2015; Chevalier des Palmes académiques, Chevalier de la Légion d'honneur, Chevalier du Tastevin, Clos-Vougeot, Burgundy 2015; Dr hc (Utrecht Univ.), (Univ. San Martin, Buenos Aires), (Haverford Coll., PA), (Australian Catholic Univ.), Melbourne 2015; Prix Charles Lambert, Acad. des Sciences Morales et Politiques 1978, Grand Prix de Philosophie, Acad. Française 1992, Karl-Jaspers Preis, Univ. of Heidelberg, Germany 2008. *Publications:* Sur l'ontologie grise de Descartes 1975, L'idole et la distance 1977, Sur la théologie blanche de Descartes 1981, Dieu sans l'être 1982, Sur le prisme métaphysique de Descartes 1986, Prolégomènes à la charité 1986, Réduction et Donation 1989, La croisée du visible 1991, Questions cartésiennes 1991, Questions cartésiennes II 1996, Hergé. Tintin le terrible 1996, Etant donné 1997, De surcroît 2001, Le phénomène érotique 2003, Le visible et le révélé 2005, Au lieu de soi, l'approche de saint Augustin 2007, Certitudes négatives, Le croire pour le voir 2010, Givenness and Revelation 2016, Believing in Order to See: On the Rationality of Revelation and the Irrationality of Some Believers 2017, Descartes' Grey Ontology: Cartesian Science and Aristotelian Thought in the Regulae 2017. *Leisure interest:* running. *Address:* Université de Paris Sorbonne, 1 rue Victor Cousin, 75005 Paris, France (office); University of Chicago, Swift Hall 300A, 1025 East 58th Street, Chicago, IL 60637, USA (office); 80 rue Michel-Ange, 75016 Paris, France (home); 28 rue Serpente, #311, 75006 Paris. *Telephone:* (1) 53-10-58-58 (office); (773) 702-8244 (office); (1) 42-83-76-30 (home). *E-mail:* Jean-Luc.Marion@ens.fr (office); jmarion@uchicago.edu (office).

MARK, Sir Alan F., KNZM, CBE, PhD, FRSNZ; New Zealand botanist, ecologist and academic; *Professor Emeritus of Botany, University of Otago;* b. 19 June 1932, Dunedin, South Island; s. of Cyril L. Mark and Frances E. Marshall; m. Patricia K. Davie 1957; two s. two d.; ed Mosgiel District High School, Univ. of Otago, Duke Univ., USA; Otago Catchment Bd, Dunedin 1959–61; Sr Research Fellow, Hellaby Indigenous Grasslands Research Trust 1961–65, Adviser in Research 1965–2000, Chair. Bd Govs 2000–09; Lecturer, Univ. of Otago 1960, Sr Lecturer 1966, Assoc. Prof. 1969, Prof. of Botany 1975–98, Prof. Emer. 1998–; Visiting Asst Prof., Duke Univ. 1966; Hon. mem. NZ Alpine Club 2002; Hon. DSc (Otago) 2014; Fulbright Travel Award 1955, James B. Duke Fellowship 1957, Loder Cup 1975, NZ 1990 Commemoration Medal, The Inaugural Awards of NZ (Conservation/Environment) 1994, Hutton Medal (Botanical/Conservation Research), Royal Soc. of NZ 1997, The Fleming Environmental Award, Royal Soc. of NZ 2010. *Publications include:* New Zealand Alpine Plants (with N. M. Adams) 1973, Above the Treeline: A Nature Guide to Alpine New Zealand 2012, Standing my ground: A voice for nature conservation 2015; more than 190 scientific papers. *Leisure interests:* nature conservation, enjoying the outdoors. *Address:* Department of Botany, University of Otago, Box 56, Dunedin (office); 205 Wakari Road, Helensburgh, Dunedin, New Zealand (home). *Telephone:* (3) 479-75-73 (office); (3) 476-32-29 (home). *Fax:* (3) 479-75-83 (office). *E-mail:* alan.mark@otago.ac.nz (office). *Website:* www.otago.ac.nz/botany (office).

MARK, Ron Stanley; New Zealand politician and former army officer; *Minister of Defence, and for Veterans;* b. 29 Jan. 1954, Carterton; m. Gail Berry (divorced); five c.; ed Tararua Coll.; served in New Zealand Army 1971–85; served in Sultan of Oman's Armed Forces and Sultan of Oman's Special Forces 1985–90; retd from army (rank of major) 1990; worked as business consultant, Christchurch; MP (New Zealand First) 1996–2008, 2014–, Sr Govt Whip 1996–98; Dir Pouakani Trust Farms 1999, Mangakino Township Incorporation 1999, Wairarapa Moana Trust 1999; Deputy Chair. Wairarapa Moana Incorporation; worked as radio talkshow host, Radio Live and Newstalk ZB 2008–14, also regular political commentator for TV1 and TV3; Trustee, Ngati Kahungunu ki Wairarapa Tamaki Nui a Rua (Maori Treaty Settlement) Trust 2010, Lead Negotiator 2012–14; Mayor of Carterton Dist 2010–14; Minister of Defence, and for Veterans 2017–; Patron, Te Awa Ora (Maori mental health service provider); mem. Wairarapa and Hutt Valley Dist Health Boards 2013; mem. New Zealand First Party, Deputy Leader 2015–18; Royal Order of Oman, Oman Peace Medal, NZ Operational Service Medal, NZ Gen. Service Medal (Sinai), Multinational Force and Observers Medal with bar. *Address:* Ministry of Defence, Freyberg House, Level 4, 20 Aitken Street, POB 12-703, Wellington 6144, New Zealand (office). *Telephone:* (4) 496-0999 (office). *Fax:* (4) 496-0859 (office). *E-mail:* r.mark@ministers.govt.nz (office). *Website:* www.beehive.govt.nz (office).

MARKELL, Jack, BA, MBA; American business executive and politician; b. 26 Nov. 1960, Newark, Del.; s. of William Markell and Elaine 'Leni' Markell; m. Carla Markell; two c.; ed Brown Univ., Univ. of Chicago; fmr Sr Vice-Pres. for Corp. Devt, Nextel; fmr Consultant for McKinsey and Co. Inc.; fmr banker, First Chicago Corp.; Founder Del. Money School; State Treas. of Delaware 1999–2009; Gov. of Delaware 2009–17; Chair. Information Services Task Force 2001, Del. Coll. Investment Plan Bd; Co-Chair. Gov.'s Task Force for Financial Independence 2002, Deferred Compensation Council, Common Core Standards Initiative; Chair. Democratic Govs Asscn 2010–11, Nat. Govs Asscn (NGA) 2012–13; fmr Chair. Nat. Bd of Dirs for Jobs for America's Graduates, Metropolitan Wilmington Urban League; fmr Chair. Educ., Early Childhood and Workforce Cttee, NGA July–Dec. 2010; fmr Vice-Chair. NGA Econ. Devt and Commerce Cttee Jan.–July 2010; mem. Bd of Pardons, Cash Man. Policy Bd, Del. Econ. Financial Advisory Cttee, Employee Benefits Cttee, Strategic Econ. Devt Council; Henry Crown Fellow, Rodel Fellow; Democrat.

MARKER, Laurie; American zoologist and academic; *Executive Director, Cheetah Conservation Fund;* Co-owner, Jonicole Vineyards and Winery, Ore. 1973–88; Veterinary Clinic Asst, Wildlife Safari, Winston, Ore. 1974–76, Veterinary Clinic Supervisor 1976–80, Cheetah Curator 1977–88, Dir, Marketing and Educ. 1980–88; Exec. Dir Centre for New Opportunities in Animal Health Sciences Center, Nat. Zoo, Smithsonian Inst., Washington, DC 1988–91, Research Fellow 1991–; Founder and Exec. Dir Cheetah Conservation Fund, Namibia 1990–, Cheetah Conservation Fund; developed the Int. Cheetah Studbook 1988, currently Int. Studbook Keeper; Vice-Chair. World Conservation Union's (IUCN) Species Survival Comm.'s Cat Specialist Group 1988, mem. core management group; Andrew D. White Prof.-at-Large, Cornell Univ. 2013; Dr hc (Oxford) 2002; Conservationist of the Year, African Safari Club 1992, Burrows Conservation Award, Cincinnati Zoo 2000, Paul Harris Fellowship, Rotary Club International, Windhoek, Namibia 2001, Humanitarian of the Year, Marin Co. Humane Soc. 2001, Sandveld Conservancy's Certificate of Honour, Namibia 2002, Chevron-Texaco Conservationist of the Year 2003, Living Desert's Track's in the Sand – Conservationist of the Year 2005, Gold Medal, Soc. of Women Geographers 2008, Lifetime Achievement Award, San Diego Zoo 2008, Intel Environmental Award, Tech Museum 2008, Lifetime Achievement Award, Int. Wildlife Film Festival 2009, Tyler Prize for Environmental Achievement Recipient (co-recipient) 2010, Rainer Arnhold Fellow 2011–12, Distinguished Alumni, Eastern Oregon State Univ. 2011. *Publications:* numerous papers in professional journals. *Address:* Cheetah Conservation Fund, PO Box 2496, 2210 Mount Vernon Avenue, 2nd Floor, Alexandria, VA 22301-0496, USA (office). *Telephone:* (866) 909-3399 (office). *Fax:* (206) 338-2161 (office). *E-mail:* info@cheetah.org (office). *Website:* www.cheetah.org (office).

MARKHAM, Kenneth Ronald, PhD, FRSNZ, FNZIC; New Zealand research chemist (retd); b. 19 June 1937, Christchurch; s. of Harold W. Markham and Alicia B. Markham; m. E. P. Eddy 1966; two d.; ed Victoria Univ. of Wellington, Melbourne Univ.; Tech. Trainee, Dominion Lab., Wellington 1955–62; Scientist, Chem. Div., Distinguished Scientist Industrial Research (DSIR) Ltd, Lower Hutt 1962–65, Scientist, Organic Chem. Section, Chem. Div., DSIR 1968–75, Section Leader, Natural Products Section 1976–92, Group Leader Chem. Div. 1980–87, Sr Research Fellow 1987, Plant Chem., Team Man. 1992–2004, Research Assoc. 2004; Post-Doctoral Fellow, Botany Dept, Univ. of Texas 1965–66, Asst Prof. 1967; Monsanto Chemicals Research Fellow 1960; Hon. Research Assoc., Biological Sciences, Vic. Univ. of Wellington 1998–; mem. Ed. Advisory Bd int. journal Phytochemical Analysis 1990, Int. Journal of Flavonoid Research 1998; Int. Corresp., Groupe Polyphenols 1992; Easterfield Award, Royal Inst. of Chem. 1971, NZ Govt Ministerial Award for Excellence in Science 1990, Science and Tech. Medal, Royal Soc. of NZ 1997, Pergamon Phytochemistry Prize 1999. *Publications:* The Systematic Identification of Flavonoids (with Mabry and Thomas) 1970, Techniques of Flavonoid Chemistry 1982, Flavonoids: Chemistry, Biochemistry and Applications (co-ed. with O. M. Andersen) 2006; 18 invited chapters on flavonoids, spectroscopy and Hebe, 255 scientific papers on phytochemistry and its interpretation in int. journals 1960–; one patent on UV screens. *Leisure interests:* philately, swimming, stock market, photography, world news, petanque, palms, genealogy. *Address:* 160 Raumati Road, Paraparaumu, New Zealand (home). *Telephone:* (4) 905-5285 (home). *E-mail:* kpmarkham@paradise.net.nz (home).

MARKHAM, Richard J. (Dick), BS; American business executive; *Partner, Care Capital LLC;* b. 26 Sept. 1950, Hornell, NY; ed Purdue Univ. School of Pharmacy; Dist Man. Merck Sharp & Dohme Div., Merck & Co. Inc., served successively as Product Man., Sr Product Man., Dir of Market Planning 1973–86, Exec. Dir of Marketing Planning 1986–87, Vice-Pres. of Marketing 1987–89, Vice-Pres. Merck Sharp & Dohme Int. 1989–91, Sr Vice-Pres. Merck & Co. 1993; mem. Bd of Dirs Marion Merrell Dow Inc. 1993, Pres. and COO 1993–95; COO Hoechst Marion Roussel 1995–97, CEO 1997–99; CEO Aventis Pharma 1999–2002, Chair. Man. Bd Aventis Pharma AG 1999–2002, Vice-Chair. 2002–04, COO 2002–05; Partner Care Capital LLC 2004–; Chair. Acura Pharmaceuticals Inc. 2006–08, Chair. (non-exec.) 2008–13; mem. Bd of Dirs Pharmaceutical Research and Mfrs Asscn 1991–93, Anacor Pharmaceuticals, Inc. 2005–12, NephroGenex, Inc. 2007– (Chair. 2013–), CoLucid Pharmaceuticals, Inc. 2008–, Aventis Behring LLC, Vaxart, Inc.; mem. Bd of Trustees, Health Care Inst., NJ; Hon. ScD (Purdue Univ.). *Address:* Care Capital LLC, 47 Hulfish Street, Suite 310, Princeton, NJ 08542, USA (office). *Telephone:* (609) 683-8300 (office). *Fax:* (609) 683-5787 (office). *E-mail:* info@carecapital.com (office). *Website:* www.carecapital.com (office).

MARKHAM, Rudolph (Rudy) Harold Peter, MA, FCMA; British accountant and business executive; b. 1946, Alresford, Hants.; ed Christ's Coll., Cambridge; joined Unilever Plc 1968, numerous roles, including Group Treas. Nippon Lever Japan 1986–89, Chair. 1992–96, Financial Dir, Unilever Plc 2000–07, Chief Financial Officer, Dir of Strategy and Tech. and Treas. 2005–07, fmr Chair. and CEO Unilever Japan, fmr Chair. Unilever Australia; fmr Chair. Moorfields Eye Hosp. Foundation Trust; mem. Bd of Dirs, Legal & General 2006–, Sr Ind. Dir and Vice-Chair. 2013–16, Interim Chair. June–Oct. 2016, currently Dir (non-exec.); Chair. Supervisory Bd, Corbion NV 2012–15, Vice-Chair. 2015–; mem. Bd of Dirs (non-exec.) AstraZeneca Plc 2008–15 (Sr Ind. Dir 2015–16), United Parcel Service Inc., Standard Chartered Plc; Fellow, Asscn of Corp. Treasurers; CIMA Lifetime Contrib. to Man. Accounting Award 2005. *Address:* c/o Legal & General Group Plc, One Coleman Street, London, EC2R 5AA, England (office). *Telephone:* (20) 3124-2000 (office). *Fax:* (20) 7528-6222 (office). *E-mail:* info@legalandgeneralgroup.com (office). *Website:* www.legalandgeneralgroup.com (office).

MARKÓ, Béla; Romanian/Hungarian politician and poet; b. 8 Sept. 1951, Târgul Secuiesc; m.; three c.; ed Faculty of Philology, Univ. of Babeş-Bolyai, Cluj-Napoca; poetry teacher, Santana de Mures Elementary School 1974–76; Ed. Igaz Szo Literary Magazine 1976–89; Ed.-in-Chief Lato Literary Magazine 1989; Sr mem. Democratic Alliance of Hungarians in Romania (Romániai Magyar Demokrata Szövetség—RMDSz) 1989, Vice-Pres. 1989–93, mem. Standing Cttee 1990–91, Pres. in Senate 1991–92, Pres. RMDSz 1993–2011 (re-elected 1995, 1999, 2003), Pres. Parl. Group 2010–; Senator for Mures 1990–, mem. Culture and Educ. Comms 1992, Foreign Policy and Culture Comms 1992–96; State Minister in charge of coordinating activities in fields of culture, educ. and European integration 2004–07; Deputy Prime Minister 2009–12; f. Kós Károly Acad. 2010; advocated autonomy for parts of Transylvania where ethnic Hungarians (Magyar) in a majority; signed cooperation agreement with Pres. Ion Iliescu's Social Democratic Party, leading to schism in RMDSz 2000; mem. Writers' Union in Romania 1978–, Writers' Union in Hungary 1990–; Sec.-Gen. PEN Group of Hungarian Writers in Romania 1990–; Sec. Writers' Union Subsidiary in Târgu Mureş 1990–96. *Publications:* poetry: 18 vols –1974, Notes on a Happy Pear Tree 1999, Comme un échiquier fermé 2001, Despre natura metaforelor, Timp canibal 1997; one vol. of Hungarian literature for 11th grade 1980–83, 1990–2002, two vols of essays and literary analysis, three vols of studies and political discourses, trans. into Hungarian of some plays by Lucian Blaga and Radu Stanca. *Address:* Democratic Alliance of Hungarians in Romania, 400489 Kolozsvár, Str. Majális 60, Romania (office). *Telephone:* (264) 590758 (office). *E-mail:* office@rmdsz.ro (office). *Website:* www.rmdsz.ro (office).

MARKOV, Sergey Aleksandrovich, DPolSci; Russian political scientist, academic and politician; *Director, Institute of Political Studies;* b. 18 April 1958, Dubna, Moscow Region; s. of Aleksander Nikolayevich Markov and Anna Dmitriyevna Markova; m. Nina Leonidovna Markova; one d.; ed Moscow State Univ.; teacher, Moscow Inst. of Radio Electronics and Automatics, Moscow Inst. of Political Sciences; consultant, Security Council, Russian Fed.; Asst Prof., Public Policy Dept, Faculty of Philosophy, Moscow State Univ.; Prof., Faculty of Political Science, Moscow State Inst. of Int. Relations (MGIMO); Dir Inst. of Political Studies 1997–; Prof., Higher School of Econs 2000–; Visiting Scholar, Univ. of Wisconsin-Madison; Sr Consultant, Nat. Democratic Inst. of Int. Relations 1997–; mem. Public Chamber of Russia 2006–08; elected to State Duma, representing United Russia 2007; consulting expert, numerous nat. and int. orgs, including Security Council at Russian Presidium, State Duma, Nat. Democratic Inst. of Int. Relations, Chase Manhattan Bank, ING Baring, Renaissance Capital 1990–; Exec. Dir Asscn of Consulting Centres, Russian Asscn of Political Sciences 1991–; Ed.-in-Chief, internet publr for strana.ru; Co-Chair. Moscow Carnegie Centre 1994–97; Chair. Organizing Cttee Civil Forum 2001; Co-ordinator Nat. Civil Council on Foreign Policy 2002–; declared persona non grata in Estonia 2007; expelled from Ukraine 2008; has criticized historians from states formerly under Soviet occupation for distorting the historical record with the documentation of events. *Publications:* numerous articles in nat. and int. publs. *Leisure interests:* tennis, swimming, cycling. *Address:* Institute of Political Studies, Ostankino 1st House 41/9, 129515 Moscow Russia (office). *Telephone:* (495) 202-82-70 (office).

MARKOVIĆ, Duško; Montenegrin politician; *Chairman of the Government (Prime Minister);* b. 6 July 1958, Mojkovac; m.; three c.; ed Faculty of Law in Kragujevac, Serbia; Legal Dept, Brskovo Mine, Mojkovac 1983–86; Sec. of Municipal Ass., Mojkovac 1986–89, Pres. 1989–91; Sec.-Gen. of the Govt 1991–98; mem. Parl. 1997–98; Deputy Minister of Internal Affairs and Head of State Security Service 1998–2005; Dir Nat. Security Agency 2005–10; Minister without Portfolio 2010, Deputy Chair. of the Govt, responsible for the Political System, Internal and Foreign Affairs 2010–16, also Minister of Justice 2011–16, Chair. of the Govt (Prime Minister) 2016–. *Address:* Office of the Chairman of the Government, 81000 Podgorica, Karađorđeva bb, Montenegro (office). *Telephone:* (20) 242530 (office). *Fax:* (20) 242329 (office). *E-mail:* kabinet@mfa.gov.me (office). *Website:* www.gov.me (office).

MARKOVIĆ, Predrag; Serbian politician and publisher; b. 7 Dec. 1955, Cepure; ed Univ. of Belgrade; Ed. Student, Vreme (newspapers), Vidici (magazine); Owner Stubovi kulture (publishing house) 1993–; Pres. G17 PLUS Man. Bd 2000–01, Pres. Political Council, mem. Exec. Bd 2001–02, Vice-Pres. G17 PLUS party 2003–; Pres. Nat. Ass. of Serbia 2004–06; Acting Pres. of Serbia March–July 2004; Minister of Culture, Media and Information Soc. 2011–12; fmr Pres. Asscn of Publrs of Serbia and Montenegro; mem. PEN, Serbian Literary Soc. *Publications include:* Morali su doći nasmejani lavovi 1983, Otemenost duše 1989. *Address:* G17 PLUS, Trg Republike 5, 11000 Belgrade, Serbia (office). *Telephone:* (11) 3210355 (office). *Fax:* (11) 3284054 (office). *E-mail:* office@ujedinjeniregionisrbije.rs (office). *Website:* www.ujedinjeniregionisrbije.rs (office).

MARKOWITZ, Harry M., PhD; American economist, business executive and fmr professor of finance; *President, Harry Markowitz Company;* b. 24 Aug. 1927, Chicago, Ill.; s. of Morris Markowitz and Mildred Gruber; m. Barbara Gay; research staff, Rand Corpn, Santa Monica, Calif. 1952–60, 1961–63; Tech. Dir, Consolidated Analysis Centers, Ltd, Santa Monica 1963–68; Prof. of Finance, UCLA 1968–69; Pres. Arbitrage Man. Co., New York 1969–72; in pvt. practice as consultant, New York 1972–74; research staff, T. J. Watson Research Center, IBM, Yorktown Hills, NY 1974–83; Speiser Prof. of Finance, Baruch Coll., City Univ. of New York 1982–90, Vice-Pres. Inst. of Man. Science 1960–62; Pres. Harry Markowitz Co. 1984–; Dir Research Daiwa Securities Trust Co. 1990–2000; Fellow, Econometric Soc., American Acad. of Arts and Sciences; Pres. American Finance Asscn 1982; Von Neumann Prize in Operations Research Theory 1989, Nobel Prize in Econs (with W. F. Sharpe and M. H. Miller) 1990. *Publications:* Portfolio Selection: Efficient Diversification of Investments 1959, Mean-Variance Analysis in Portfolio Choice 1987; co-author, SIMSCRIPT Simulation Programming Language 1963; co-ed. Process Analysis of Economic Capabilities 1963. *Address:* 1010 Turquoise Street, Suite 245, San Diego, CA 92109, USA (office). *Telephone:* (858) 488-7212 (office). *E-mail:* HarryHMM@aol.com (office).

MARKS, Matthew Stuart, BA; American art dealer and gallery owner; *Owner, Matthew Marks Gallery;* b. 14 Nov. 1962, New York, NY; s. of Dr Paul Marks; ed Bennington Coll.; consultant, Pace Editions Inc., New York 1982–86, Assoc., Pace Gallery 1985–87; Dir Anthony D'Offay Gallery, London 1987–89; opened first gallery 1989; moved to garage-door warehouse on 22nd Street in 1994. *Address:* Matthew Marks Gallery, 523 West 24th Street, New York, NY 10011, USA (office). *Telephone:* (212) 243-0200 (office). *E-mail:* info@matthewmarks.com (office). *Website:* www.matthewmarks.com (office).

MARKS, Michael, CBE; British business executive; b. 28 Dec. 1941, London; one s. two d.; ed St Paul's School, London; joined Smith Bros 1958, Dir 1975, Chief Exec. 1987, Chief Exec. and Exec. Chair. Smith New Court 1995; Co-Head Global Equities Group, Merrill Lynch 1995–98, Exec. Chair. Merrill Lynch Europe, Middle East & Africa 1997–2003, Exec. Vice-Pres. Merrill Lynch & Co. 2001–03, Chair. Merrill Lynch Investment Managers 2001–03; mem. Exec. Man. Cttee Merrill Lynch; mem. Int. Markets Advisory Bd, Nat. Asscn of Securities Dealers 1991–, Bd London Stock Exchange 1994–2004; Chair. London Investment Banking Asscn 1998–2002; Vice-Pres. British Bankers Asscn from 1998; Founding Partner, NewSmith Capital Partners LLP 2003–14 (later NewSmith LLP); Dir (non-exec.) Old Mutual plc 2004–, RIT Capital Partners plc 2004–.

MARKS, Michael E., MA, MBA; American business executive; *Founding Partner, Riverwood Capital, LLC;* b. 5 Nov. 1960; ed Oberlin Coll., Harvard Business School; fmr Pres. and CEO Metcal, Inc. (precision heating instrument co.); mem. Bd of Dirs, Flextronics Corpn (electronics mfg services provider) 1991–, Chair. 1993–2003, 2006–08, CEO 1994–2006, Pres. 2003; Founding Partner, Riverwood Capital, LLC (fmrly Bigwood Capital, LLC) (pvt. equity firm), Menlo Park, Calif. 2007–; Partner and Sr Advisor, Kohlberg Kravis Roberts & Co. (pvt. equity firm), Menlo Park, Calif. 2006–07, Sr Advisor 2007–08; mem. Bd of Dirs, SanDisk Corpn, Milpitas, Calif. 2003–, Chair. 2011–; mem. Bd of Dirs Sun Microsystems, Inc., Santa Clara, Calif., iFLYSchlumberger Ltd 2005–, Houston, Tex., Avago Technologies Ltd 2006–, Oracle America, Inc. 2007–, Virtual Instruments Corpn 2009–, Calix Inc. 2009–10, GoPro, Inc. 2011–, Globant SA 2012–, Berkeley Lights, Inc. 2015–; Trustee, Juilliard School. *Address:* Riverwood Capital LLC, 70 Willow Road, Suite 100, Menlo Park, CA 94025, USA (office). *Telephone:* (650) 618-7399 (office). *E-mail:* marks@rwcm.com (office). *Website:* www.riverwoodcapital.com (office).

MARKS, Paul Alan, AB, MD; American oncologist, cell biologist, academic and research institute director; b. 16 Aug. 1926, New York, NY; s. of Robert R. Marks and Sarah Marks (née Bohorad); m. Joan Harriet Rosen 1953; two s. one d.; ed Columbia Coll. and Columbia Univ.; Fellow, Columbia Coll. of Physicians and Surgeons 1952–53, Assoc. 1955–56, mem. of Faculty 1956–82, Dir Haematology Training 1961–74, Prof. of Medicine 1967–82, Dean Faculty of Medicine and Vice-Pres. Medical Affairs 1970–73, Dir Comprehensive Cancer Center 1972–80, Vice-Pres. Health Sciences 1973–80, Prof. of Human Genetics and Devt 1969–82, Frode Jensen Prof. of Medicine 1974–80; Prof. of Medicine and Genetics, Cornell Univ. Coll. of Medicine, New York 1982–, Prof., Cornell Univ. Grad. School in Medical Sciences 1983–; Attending Physician, Presbyterian Hosp., New York 1967–83; Pres. and CEO Memorial Sloan-Kettering Cancer Center 1980–99, Pres. Emer. 2000, mem. Sloan-Kettering Inst. for Cancer Research 1980–; Attending Physician, Memorial Hosp. for Cancer and Allied Diseases 1980–; Adjunct Prof., The Rockefeller Univ. 1980–, Visiting Physician, The Rockefeller Univ. Hosp. 1980–; Trustee, Hadassah Medical Centre, Jerusalem 1996–2000; mem. Advisory Cttee to Dir, NIH 1993–96, NIH External Advisory Cttee-Intramural Research Program Review 1993–94; mem. editorial bds of several scientific journals; Gov., Weizmann Inst. 1976–96; Dir Revson Foundation 1976–91; Master American Coll. of Physicians; mem. Inst. of Medicine, NAS; Fellow, American Acad. of Arts and Sciences, American Philosophical Soc., Royal Soc. of Medicine, London; Dr hc (Urbino) 1982, (Tel-Aviv) 1992, (Columbia Univ.) 2000; Hon. PhD (Hebrew Univ. of Jerusalem) 1987; Recognition for Acad. Accomplishments, Chinese Acad. of Medical Sciences 1982, Centenary Medal, Institut Pasteur 1987, Pres.'s Nat. Medal of Science 1991, Gold Medal for Distinguished Academic Accomplishments,

Coll. of Physicians and Surgeons of Columbia Univ., New York, Japan Foundation for Cancer Research Award 1995, John Jay Award for Distinguished Professional Achievement, Columbia Coll. 1996, Lifetime Achievement Award, Greater NY Hosp. Asscn 1997, Humanitarian Award, Breast Cancer Foundation 2000, The John Stearns Award for Lifetime Achievement in Medicine, New York Acad. of Medicine 2002 and other awards; The Paul Marks Prize for Cancer Research cr. by Memorial Sloan Kettering Cancer Center's Bds of Overseers and Managers in his honour 2001. *Publications:* over 350 articles in scientific journals on histone deacetylase inhibitors, mechanism of action and potential as anti-cancer agents. *Leisure interest:* tennis. *Address:* Memorial Sloan-Kettering Cancer Center, 1275 York Avenue, New York, NY 10065 (office); PO Box 1485, Washington, CT 06793, USA (home). *Telephone:* (212) 639-6568 (office). *Fax:* (212) 639-2861 (office). *E-mail:* marksp@mskcc.org (office). *Website:* www.mskcc.org/research/lab/paul-marks (office).

MARKS, Peter Vincent, CBE; British retail executive; b. 27 Oct. 1949, Bradford, Yorks., England; m. Julia Law 1971; two d.; ed St Bede's Grammar School, Bradford High School, Heaton; left school aged 17 to stack shelves in what became Yorkshire Co-operatives (mem.-owned retailer) in Bradford, man. trainee in Food Div. 1967, Asst Personnel Man. 1974–76, Personnel Man. 1976–91, apptd Non-Food Trades Officer, responsible for Dept Stores, Funeral and Travel divs 1991, Food Div. 1996, Chief Gen. Man. (Retail) 1996–99, Deputy Chief Exec. 1999–2000, Chief Exec. 2000–02, Chief Exec. United Co-operatives (following merger of Yorkshire and United Norwest Co-operatives) 2002–07, Group Chief Exec. The Co-operative Group (following merger of United Co-operatives with The Co-operative Group to create world's largest consumer co-operative) 2007–13. *Leisure interests:* drumming (plays in Bradford band, Last Orders), working out, playing racquetball, supporting Bradford City Football Club, music, reading biographies.

MARKS, Tobin Jay, BS, PhD, FRSC; American chemist and academic; *Vladimir N. Ipatieff Professor of Catalytic Chemistry, Northwestern University;* b. 25 Nov. 1944, Washington, DC; ed Univ. of Maryland, Massachusetts Inst. of Tech.; Asst Prof. of Chem., Northwestern Univ., Evanston, Ill. 1970–74, Assoc. Prof. 1974–78, Prof. 1978, Charles E. & Emma H. Morrison Prof. of Chem. 1986–, Prof. of Materials Science and Eng 1987–, Vladimir N. Ipatieff Prof. of Catalytic Chem. 1999–; mem. or fmr mem. Editorial Bd, Journal of Inorganic and Nuclear Chemistry, Inorganic Syntheses, Organometallics, Inorganica Chimica Acta, Polyhedron, Polymer, Progress in Inorganic Chemistry, Chemical Communications, Accounts of Chemical Research, Journal of Molecular Catalysis, Topics in Organometallic Chemistry, Catalysis Letters, Actinide and Lanthanide Reviewer for Annual Surveys of Organometallic Chemistry, Topics in Catalysis, Nouveau Journal de Chimie/New Journal of Chemistry, Chemistry of Materials, Advanced Materials, CVD, Oxford Monographs on the Physics and Chemistry of Materials, Crystal Engineering Communications, Proceedings of the National Academy of Sciences, MRS Communications, Organic Photonics and Photovoltaics; mem. Corp. Tech. Advisory Bd, Dow Corning Corpn 1994–, Dow Chemical Co. 1995–; mem. AAAS, American Acad. of Arts and Sciences, NAS, ACS (Councillor, Inorganic Chem. Div. 1980–85), Indian Nat. Acad. of Sciences, Int. Soc. for Magnetic Resonance, Materials Research Soc., German Acad. of Sciences Leopoldina 2005, Soc. for Applied Spectroscopy, US Nat. Acad. of Eng 2012; Fellow, Materials Research Soc. 2009; Hon. Fellow, Chemical Research Soc. of India 2008; Hon. mem. Israel Chemical Soc. 2012; Hon. DSc (Univ. of South Carolina) 2011, (Hong Kong Univ. of Science and Tech.) 2011, (Ohio State Univ.) 2012; ACS Award in Organometallic Chem. 1989, ACS Award in Organic Chem. 1994, Royal Soc. of Chem. Centenary Medal 1997, Univ. of Pittsburgh Francis Clifford Phillips Award 1998, Italian Chemical Soc. Paolo Chini Award 1999, ACS Cotton Medal 2000, ACS Linus Pauling Medal 2001, ACS Willard Gibbs Medal 2001, Royal Soc. of Chem. Frankland Medal 2003, German Chemical Soc. Karl Ziegler Medal 2003, RSC Sir Edward Frankland Prize 2004, US Medal of Science 2005, Príncipe de Asturias Prize for Technical and Scientific Research (Spain) 2008, Alan G. MacDiarmid Medal 2013, Sir Geoffrey Wilkinson Medal 2014, Materials for Industry-Derek Birchall Award 2015, Luigi Sacconi Medal, Italian Chemical Soc. 2015, Harvey Prize, Technion-Israel Inst. of Tech. 2017; numerous distinguished named lectureships. *Address:* WCAS Chemistry, Northwestern University, 2220 Campus Drive, Cook Hall 2036, Evanston, IL 60208, USA (office). *Telephone:* (847) 491-5658 (office). *Fax:* (847) 491-7713 (office). *E-mail:* t-marks@northwestern.edu (office). *Website:* www.chemistry.northwestern.edu/people/core-faculty/profiles/tobin-marks.html (office); chemgroups.northwestern.edu/marks (office).

MARKS OF HENLEY-ON-THAMES, Baron (Life Peer), cr. 2011, of Henley-on-Thames in the County of Oxfordshire; **Jonathan Marks,** QC, BA; British barrister; b. 19 Oct. 1952; ed Univ. of Oxford; called to the Bar 1975; QC 1995; TECBAR approved Adjudicator; trained mediator; Barrister, 4 Pump Court chambers; mem. Federal Policy Cttee 2004–10, Lord's Rep. 2011–; Leader, Liberal Democrat Justice Team 2012–15; Liberal Democrat Lords Prin. Spokesperson for Justice 2015–. *Address:* 4 Pump Court, Temple, London, EC4Y 7AN (office); House of Lords, Westminster, London, SW1A 0PW, England. *Telephone:* (20) 7842-5555 (office); (20) 7219-5353. *Fax:* (20) 7583-2036 (office); (20) 7219-5979. *E-mail:* clerks@4pumpcourt.com (office). *Website:* www.4pumpcourt.com (office).

MARKUS, Alim; Indonesian business executive; *President Director, Maspion Group;* b. 24 Sept. 1951, Surabaya; s. of Alim Husin; m.; six c.; ed Nat. Univ. of Singapore; joined family co. Maspion (housewares and appliances mfr), becoming Pres. Dir PT Maspion and Maspion Group 1971–; Chair. Indonesia–China Asscn; Vice-Chair. East Java Indonesia Chamber of Commerce; Bintang Jasa Nararya 2013. *Address:* Maspion Group, Kembang Jepun 38–40, Surabaya 60162, Indonesia (office). *Telephone:* (31) 3530333 (office). *Fax:* (31) 3533055 (office). *E-mail:* info.hq@maspion.com (office). *Website:* www.maspion.com (office).

MARKWALDER, Christa; Swiss lawyer and politician; *President, National Council;* b. 27 July 1975, Burgdorf; m. Walter Bär (divorced); ed Univ. of Berne, Nijmegen Univ., Netherlands; Asst Inst. for European and Econ. Int. Law, Univ. of Berne; lawyer Zurich Insurance Co. 2008–; worked at Municipal Council of Burgdorf 1999–2002, Grand Council, Canton of Berne 2002–03; mem. Nat. Council 2003–, Second Vice Pres. 2013–14, First Vice Pres. 2014–15, Pres. 2015–; fmr Pres. New European Movement, Switzerland; mem. Bd FDP.The Liberals. *Address:* Parlamentsgebäude, 3003 Bern, Switzerland (office). *Telephone:* 313228790 (office). *E-mail:* information@pd.admin.ch (office).

MARKWORT, Helmut; German journalist, publisher, editor and presenter; *Editor, FOCUS Magazine;* b. 8 Dec. 1936, Darmstadt; began career as journalist 1956, various posts in local media –1964; Man. Ed. STERN in Düsseldorf 1964–66; Founder and Ed.-in-Chief of several magazines and radio stations; Dir Hubert Burda Media Holding KG 1991–2010; Publr and Ed.-in-Chief FOCUS Magazine 1993–2010, Ed. 2010–, Man. FOCUS TV 1996–2010, Publr FOCUS Money 2000–, mem. Bd Tomorrow FOCUS AG 2001–11, Head of Bd Playboy Publishing Deutschland AG 2002–10, Publr FOCUS Schule 2004–13; Nat. Merit Cross (First Class) 1999; 'Horizont Mann der Medien' Award 1983, 1993, Advertising Age 'Marketing Superstar' 1994, Hildegard von Bingen Award for Journalism, BDS Mittelstandspreis, Bavarian Merit Medal 1996, Premio Capo Circeo 2004, Reinhold Maier Medal 2007, Karl Carstens Award 2007, Lifetime Achievement Award, Medium Magazine 2010, Wirtschaftspreis der Wirtschafts- und Mittelstandsunion 2010, Saumagen Medal 2011, Hessian Award for Journalism 2011, Medienmann Award 2011, Radio Regenbogen 2012, Thomas Dehler Award 2012. *Television:* presenter, Bookmark 2004–07, Der Sonntags Stammtisch panel show 2007–. *Leisure interests:* football, theatre. *Address:* FOCUS Magazine, Arabellastr. 23, 81925 Munich, Germany (office). *Website:* www.focus.de (office).

MARLEY, Rita; Jamaican singer, songwriter and philanthropist; b. (Alpharita Constantia Anderson), 25 July 1946, Santiago de Cuba, Cuba; d. of Leroy Anderson and Cynthia 'Beda' Jarrett; m. Bob Marley 1966 (died 1981); two s. one d. and three d. from various relationships; grew up in upper level of Beachwood, Kingston, Jamaica; was singing with female ska trio named The Soulettes (later became the I-Threes), recording for Studio One, when she met her future husband mid-1960s; became involved in Rastafari Movt 1966, remains active mem. Ethiopian Orthodox Church; following her husband's death, recorded albums under her own name and looked after his estate; f. Rita Marley Foundation 2000; currently lives in Konkonuru, nr Aburi, Ghana. *Films include:* The Mighty Quinn (actress and reggae music consultant) 1989, The Reggae Movie (special thanks) 1995, How High (writer and performer, One Draw) 2001, Africa Unite (exec. producer) 2008. *Albums include:* Pied Piper (single, on Club Ska '67) 1967, Rita Marley 1980, Who Feels It Knows It 1981, Harambe (Working Together for Freedom) 1988, We Must Carry on 1988, Beauty of God's 1990, Good Girls Cult 1990, One Draw 1990, Sings Bob Marley ... and Friends 2003, Play Play 2004, Sunshine After Rain 2005, Gifted Fourteen Carnation 2006. *Publication:* No Woman No Cry (autobiography) 2004. *Address:* c/o Rita Marley Foundation, PO Box 34, Aburi-Akwapim, Ghana. *Website:* www.ritamarleyfoundation.org.

MARLIN, William V.; St Maarten politician; *Leader, National Alliance;* b. 21 Oct. 1950, Curaçao; m. Gabrielle U. Brill; ed Curaçao Teacher Training Coll.; started career as teacher, Margriet School, Curaçao; apptd Prin., Leonard Conner School, St Maarten 1976; fmr teaching coach, St Maarten Teacher Training School; mem. Coordinated Tests Cttee and Admittance Cttee for examination and admission of pupils, Dept of Educ. 1979–86; fmr mem. Island Council and Commr, Island Territory of St Maarten; mem. Parl. of Netherlands Antilles (dissolved 2010); mem. St Maarten Political Steering Group; leader, St Maarten Del. to Round Table Conf. of Countries and Island Territories within the Kingdom of the Netherlands 2010; mem. Latin American Parl. (Parlatino), Vice-Pres. Cttee for Environment and Tourism; fmr Minister of Public Works, Deputy Prime Minister and Minister of Public Housing, Spatial Planning, Environment and Infrastructure 2012–15, Prime Minister and Minister of Gen. Affairs 2015–17 (resgnd); fmr Pres. Windward Islands Teachers Union; co-founder St Maarten Patriotic Movement 1978; mem. Nat. Alliance, Leader 2010–. *Leisure interests:* volleyball, boxing, cooking.

MARLIN-ROMEO, Leona, BA, MA; St Maarten civil servant and politician; *Prime Minister and Minister of General Affairs;* b. 3 July 1973; d. of Marius Romeo and Marilyn Thomas; m. Richard Marlin 1997; two c.; ed Adelphi Univ., Univ. of Amsterdam; fmr Man., Sint Maarten Student Support Services (S4), Netherlands; Head, Civil Registry Dept, Philipsburg 2004–14; mem. States (parl.) 2014–16, Vice-Chair. of parl. 2014–15; Prime Minister and Minister of Gen. Affairs 2018–; mem. Community Police Officer Bd; fmr mem. Upper Princess Quarter Community Council; f. Sint Maarten Sickle Cell Disease Foundation; mem. United People's Party 2016–17, United Democrats 2018–. *Address:* Office of the Prime Minister, Clem Labega Sq., POB 943, Philipsburg, Sint Maarten (office). *Telephone:* 542-2233 (office). *Fax:* 542-4300 (office). *Website:* www.sintmaartengov.org (office).

MARLOWE, Hugh (see PATTERSON, Harry).

MARMEI, Eerik, BA, MA; Estonian diplomatist; *Director-General, Policy Planning Department, Ministry of Foreign Affairs;* b. 6 May 1970, Tartu; m. Birgit Volmer; two s. one d.; ed Univ. of Tartu, Univ. of Notre Dame, USA; US Desk Officer, Ministry of Foreign Affairs (MFA) 1993–95, Dir Security Policy and Int. Orgs 1996–98, Deputy Head of Mission, Perm. Mission to NATO, Brussels 1998–99, Deputy Head of Mission, Embassy in Washington, DC 2000–03, with Political Dept, MFA 2003–05, Deputy Head of Mission, Embassy in London 2005–08, Dir NATO and EU Dept, Ministry of Defence 2008–10, Security Policy Dir Political Dept, MFA 2010–13, Amb. to Poland and Romania 2013–14, Amb. to USA 2014–17; apptd foreign policy adviser to Pres. 2017, currently Dir-Gen. Policy Planning Dept, MFA. *Address:* Ministry of Foreign Affairs, Islandi väljak 1, Tallinn 15049, Estonia (office). *Telephone:* 637-7000 (office). *Fax:* 637-7400 (office). *E-mail:* Eerik.Marmei@mfa.ee (office). *Website:* vm.ee (office).

MARMOT, Sir Michael Gideon, PhD, FFPHM, FRCP; British academic and director of health research; *Director, Institute of Health Equity and Professor of Epidemiology and Public Health, University College London;* b. 26 Jan. 1945; s. of Nathan Marmot and Alice Marmot (née Weiner); m. Alexandra Naomi Ferster 1971; two s. one d.; ed Univ. of Sydney, Australia, Univ. of California, Berkeley, USA; Resident Medical Officer, Royal Prince Alfred Hosp. 1969–70; Fellowship in Thoracic Medicine 1970–71; Resident Fellow and Lecturer Univ. of California, Berkeley 1971–76 (fellowships from Berkeley and American Heart Asscn); Lecturer then Sr Lecturer in Epidemiology, London School of Hygiene and Tropical Medicine, Univ. Coll. London 1976–85, Prof. of Epidemiology and Public Health Medicine 1985–; Bernard Lown Visiting Prof. of Social & Behavioral

Sciences, Harvard 2015; Dir International Centre for Health and Soc., Univ. Coll. London 1994–; Visiting Prof., Royal Soc. of Medicine 1987; Pres. British Medical Asscn 2010–11, World Medical Asscn 2015–16; MRC Research Professorship 1995; Chair. Comm. on Social Determinants of Health, WHO 2005–08; est. Inst. of Health Equity, Univ. Coll. London 2011; mem. Faculty of Community Medicine; Foreign Assoc. mem. Inst. of Medicine (Nat. Acads of Sciences); Hon. Consultant in Public Health Medicine, Bloomsbury and Islington Dist Health Authority 1985–; Hon. MD (Sydney) 2006, Dr hc (Université Libre de Bruxelles) 2008, (Universidad Peruana Cayetano Heredia) 2011, (Malmo) 2012, (Leuven) 2014, (Lund) 2015, (Norwegian Univ. of Science and Tech.) 2016, (Ghent) 2016, Hon. DSc (Northumbria) 2012; numerous awards including Balzan Prize for Epidemiology 2004, Harveian Oration 2006, William B. Graham Prize for Health Services Research 2008, Royal Coll. of Physicians Ambuj Nath Bose Prize 2011, Irish Cancer Soc. Charles Cully Lecture & Memorial Award 2013, Yale School of Public Health Centennial Winslow Medal 2015, WHO İhsan Dogramacı Family Health Prize 2016, Gold Medal of the Royal Soc. of Medicine 2017. *Publications include:* Mortality of Immigrants to England and Wales 1984, Coronary Heart Disease Epidemiology 1992, Stress and the Heart (with S. Stansfeld) 2002, Social Determinants of Health (with R. Wilkinson) 1999, Status Syndrome 2004, Calling Time: The Nation's Drinking as a Major Health Issue 2004, Coronary Heart Disease Epidemiology (co-author) 2005, The Status Syndrome: How Social Standing Affects Our Health and Longevity 2015, The Health Gap: The Challenge of an Unequal World 2015. *Leisure interests:* viola, tennis. *Address:* Department of Epidemiology and Public Health, University College London, 1–19 Torrington Place, London, WC1E 6BT (office); Wildwood Cottage, 17 North End, London, NW3 7HK, England (home). *Telephone:* (20) 7679-1694 (office). *Fax:* (20) 7419-6732 (office). *E-mail:* m.marmot@ucl.ac.uk (office). *Website:* www.ucl.ac.uk (office).

MAROIS, Pauline, MBA; Canadian politician; b. 29 March 1949; m. Claude Blanchet; four c.; ed Univ. of Laval, HEC Montréal; Dir-Gen., Centre local de services communautaires, Île-de-Hull 1973–74; press attaché to Minister of Finance, Québec 1978–79; Prof., Univ. du Québec en Outaouais 1988; mem. Nat. Assembly of Quebec for La Peltrie 1981–85, for Taillon 1989–2006, for Charlevoix 2007–14, Leader of the Official Opposition 2008–12; Minister for the Status of Women (Govt of Québec) 1981–83, Minister of Finance 1995–96, of Educ. 1996–98, of Health and Social Services 1998–2001, of Finance 2001–03; Deputy Premier of Québec 2001–03, Premier 2012–14; Leader Parti Québécois 2007–14.

MARONI, Roberto; Italian politician; b. 15 March 1955, Varese; m.; two s.; graduated in law; worked in banks for 10 years, then head of legal office of a US multinational for eight years; entered politics 1979; co-f. Lega Lombarda party (subsequently Lega Nord), mem. Nat. Council, Political Sec. 2012–; mem. Chamber of Deputies 1992–94, 2006–08; elected Councillor, Varese; Minister of Internal Affairs 1994–95, 2008–11, of Labour and Social Affairs 2001–06; Pres. of Lombardy 2013–18. *Leisure interests:* football, playing saxophone.

MAROONE, Michael E., BS; American automobile retail executive; b. 1953; ed Univ. of Colorado, Boulder; fmr CEO and Pres. Maroone Auto Group 1977–97, Pres. New Vehicle Dealer Div., AutoNation Inc. (after acquisition of Maroone Group by AutoNation) 1997–98, Group Pres. 1998–2015, COO 1999–2015, mem. Bd of Dirs 2005–12; mem. Bd of Dirs, TrueCar 2011–12; Partner, Florida Panthers ice hockey team; recognized as Entrepreneur of the Year by Florida Atlantic Univ., inducted into Nova Southeastern Univ. Entrepreneur Hall of Fame 2007, Ford Motor Co. Chairman's Award, Time magazine Quality Dealer, named by Automotive News as one of the "fifty industry's Visionary Dealers" 2009, Lifetime Achievement Award, Boca Raton Concours D'Elegance 2014. *Address:* c/o AutoNation Inc., 200 SW 1st Avenue, Fort Lauderdale, FL 33301, USA.

MAROSI, Ernő, PhD; Hungarian art historian and academic; *Professor Emeritus of Art History, Eötvös Loránd University;* b. 18 April 1940, Miskolc; s. of Ferenc Marosi and Magdolna Kecskés; m. 1st Julia Szabó (died 2004); two d.; m. 2nd Anna Gabriella Nagy 2013; ed Eötvös Loránd Univ.; Lecturer, Dept of Art History, Eötvös Loránd Univ. 1963, later Asst Prof., Deputy Head of Institute for Art History Research Group 1974, later Hon. Assoc. Prof., Prof. 1991–2000, now Prof. Emer.; mem. Research Group, Hungarian Acad. of Sciences, then Deputy Dir of Research Inst. 1974–91, Head of Dept 1974–91, Dir 1991–2000, Sr Fellow; mem. Int. Cttee of UNESCO on the History of Art 1991–; Sec. of TMB (Nat. Postgrad. Degree Granting Board), Special Cttee on the History of Art, Architecture and Archaeology; Ed. Acta Historiae Artium; Corresp. mem. of Hungarian Acad. of Sciences 1993–2001, mem. 2001–, Vice-Pres. 2002–08; mem. UNESCO Cttee for Art History 1991–96, Comm. Kossuth-Széchenyi Prize –1997, 2003–10; Order of Merit Cross with the Star 2009; Shepherd Fellow, Univ. of Vienna 1968–69, Joseph Fitz Award 1991, Jeno Szucs Award 1995, Széchenyi Award 1997, Arnold Ipolyi Science Devt Award 2001, Deák Ferenc Research Award (Pro Cultura Renovanda Hungariae) 2007, Bonum ut pulchrum – Essays in Art History in Honour of Ernő Marosi on His Seventieth Birthday (Festschrift) presented to him 2010. *Publications:* A középkori müvészet világa (The World of Arts of the Middle Ages) 1969, A román kor müvészete (The Arts of the Romanesque Age) 1972, Bevezetés a müvészettörténetbe (Introduction to the History of Arts) 1973, Magyar falusi templomok (Village Churches in Hungary) 1975, Emlék márványból vagy homokköböl (Relics from Marble or Sandstone) 1976, Die Anfänge der Gotik in Ungarn 1984, Magyarországi müvészet 1300–1470 körül (Arts in Hungary 1300–1470) 1984, A budavári szoborlelet (co-author) 1989, Kép és hasonmás 1996, A középkor művészete I–II 1996–97, A középkori művészet történetének olvasókönyve (ed.) 1997, Az Árpád-kor művészeti emlékei 1997, A magyar művészettörténet-írás programjai 1999, Templomok Magyarországon 2002, A gótika Magyarországon 2008. *Address:* 1088 Budapest, Room 109, Institute of Art History, Faculty of Arts, Eötvös Loránd University, Múzeum körút 6–8 (office); 1245 Budapest, Hungarian Academy of Sciences, PO Box 1000, Hungary. *Telephone:* (1) 4116500 (office). *E-mail:* emarosi@btk.mta.hu (office).

MAROVIĆ, Svetozar; Montenegrin lawyer, politician and fmr head of state; b. 31 March 1955, Kotor; s. of Jovo Marović and Ivana Marović; m. Đurdina 'Đina' Prelević; one s. one d.; ed Faculty of Law, Veljko Vlahović Univ., Titograd, Univ. of Montenegro; Dir Municipal Public Accounting Dept in Budva; mem. Presidency of Cen. Cttee of League of Communists of Montenegro; Sec.-Gen. Democratic Party of Socialists of Montenegro (Demokratska Partija Socijalista Crne Gore), then Deputy Chair.; mem. Parl. of Montenegro, Speaker 1998–2002; mem. Chamber of Citizens Parl. of Yugoslavia 1997; Pres. of Serbia and Montenegro 2003–06; Deputy Prime Minister, responsible for the Political System and Domestic and Foreign Policy 2009–10; November's Award, Budva. *Leisure interest:* volleyball.

MARQUAND, David Ian, FBA, FRHistS, FRSA; British academic, author and fmr politician; *Visiting Fellow, Department of Politics, University of Oxford;* b. 20 Sept. 1934, Cardiff, Wales; s. of Rt Hon. Hilary Marquand and Rachel Marquand; m. Judith M. Reed 1959; one s. one d.; ed Emanuel School, Magdalen Coll., Oxford, St Antony's Coll., Oxford, Univ. of California, Berkeley, USA; Sr Scholar, St Antony's Coll. Oxford 1957–58; Teaching Asst, Univ. of California 1958–59; editorial writer, The Guardian 1959–61; Research Fellow, St Antony's Coll. Oxford 1962–64, Hon. Fellow 2003–; Lecturer in Politics, Univ. of Sussex 1964–66; MP (Labour) for Ashfield, Notts. 1966–77; del. to Council of Europe and WEU assemblies 1970–73; Opposition Spokesman on Treasury Affairs 1971–72; Chief Adviser, Sec.-Gen. EC 1977–78; Prof. of Contemporary History and Politics, Univ. of Salford 1978–91; Prof. of Politics, Univ. of Sheffield 1991–96, Dir Political Economy Research Centre 1993–96, Hon. Prof. 1997–; Prin. Mansfield Coll. Oxford 1996–2002, Hon. Fellow, also Hon. Fellow, St Antony's Coll., Visiting Fellow, Dept of Politics, Univ. of Oxford 2002–; Jt Ed. The Political Quarterly 1987–96; Chair. Advisory Council, Demos (think-tank); Hon. DLitt (Salford, Sheffield), Hon. Dr of Political Science (Bologna); George Orwell Memorial Prize 1979, Isaiah Berlin Prize for Lifetime Achievement in Political Studies. *Publications include:* Ramsay Macdonald 1973, Parliament for Europe 1979, The Unprincipled Society 1988, The Progressive Dilemma 1991, The New Reckoning 1997, Religion and Democracy 2000, Decline of the Public 2004, Britain Since 1918 2008, The End of the West: The Once and Future Europe 2011. *Leisure interest:* walking. *Address:* Department of Politics and International Relations, Manor Road, University of Oxford, Oxford, OX1 3UQ (office); Mansfield College, Oxford, OX1 3TF, England (office). *Telephone:* (1865) 751026 (office). *Fax:* (1865) 278725 (office). *E-mail:* david.marquand@politics.ox.ac.uk (office); david.marquand@mansfield.ox.ac.uk (office). *Website:* www.politics.ox.ac.uk (office); davidmarquand.com.

MARQUES AMADO, Luís Filipe; Portuguese economist, politician and banker; *Chairman, Banif (Banco Internacional do Funchal, SA);* b. 17 Sept. 1953; m.; two c.; ed Universidade Técnica de Lisboa, Inst. of Nat. Defense, Simon Fraser Univ., Canada; fmr Auditor, Court of Auditors; fmr mem. Regional Legis. Ass. of Madeira; mem. Assembléia da República (Ass. of the Repub.); Sec. of State for Internal Admin 1995–97, for Foreign Affairs and Co-operation 1997–99, 1999–2002; Minister of Nat. Defence and Maritime Affairs 2005–06, of Foreign Affairs 2006–11; currently Chair. Banif (Banco Internacional do Funchal, SA,); mem. Bd of Dirs Sociedade de Desenvolvimento da Madeira; Guest Prof., Instituto Superior de Ciências Sociais e Políticas, Universidade de Lisboa Business School; fmr Visiting Prof., Georgetown Univ., USA. *Address:* Office of the Chairman, Banif, Avenida José Malhoa, 22, 1099-012, Lisbon, Portugal (office). *E-mail:* info@banif.pt (office). *Website:* www.banif.pt (office).

MARR, Andrew William Stevenson, BA; British journalist; b. 31 July 1959, Glasgow, Scotland; s. of Donald Marr and Valerie Marr; m. Jackie Ashley 1987; one s. two d.; ed Dundee High School, Craigflower School, Loretto School, Trinity Hall, Cambridge; gen. reporter, business reporter The Scotsman 1982–84, Parl. Corresp. 1984–86, Political Ed. 1988; Political Ed. The Economist 1988–92; Political Corresp. The Independent 1986–88, Chief Commentator 1992–96, Ed. 1996–98, Ed.-in-Chief 1998; columnist The Express and The Observer 1998; Political Ed. BBC 2000–05; presenter Start the Week, BBC Radio 4 2002–; presenter morning interview programme, Sunday AM (BBC One) 2005–07, The Andrew Marr Show (BBC One) 2007–; Chair. Jury Bd Samuel Johnson Prize for Non-Fiction 2001; What The Papers Say Award for Columnist of the Year 1995, British Press Award for Columnist of the Year 1995, Creative Freedom Award for Journalist of the Year 2000, Channel 4 Political Awards Journalist Award 2001, Royal TV Soc. TV Journalism Award for specialist journalism 2001, Voice of the Listener and Viewer Award for Best Individual Contrib. on TV 2002, BAFTA Richard Dimbleby Award 2004. *Publications include:* The Battle for Scotland 1992, Ruling Britannia 1996, The Day Britain Died 2000, My Trade: A Short History of British Journalism 2004, A History of Modern Britain (also TV series; winner, British Documentary Award for Best Series 2008) 2007, The Making of Modern Britain (Galaxy Nat. Book Awards Non-Fiction Book of the Year 2010) 2009. *Leisure interests:* reading, wining and dining, painting. *Address:* BBC Television, Broadcasting House, London, W1A 1AA, England (office). *Website:* www.bbc.co.uk (office).

MARRA, Thomas M., BS, FSA; American business executive; *Executive Chairman, Symetra Financial Corporation;* b. 1959; ed St Bonaventure Univ.; joined Hartford Life Inc. as Assoc. Actuary 1980, Vice-Pres. and Dir, Individual Annuity Div. 1990–94, Sr Vice-Pres. and Dir 1994–96, Exec. Vice-Pres. 1996–2000, COO 2000–07, Pres. Hartford Life, Inc. 2002–07, Exec. Vice-Pres. Hartford Financial Services Group Inc. (The Hartford) 1990–2007, Dir Investment Products Div. 1998–2000, mem. Bd of Dirs 2002–09, Pres. and COO 2007–09; Sr Advisor, North America Financial Services Div., Boston Consulting Group 2009–10; mem. Bd of Dirs, Pres. and CEO Symetra Financial Corpn 2010–18, Exec. Chair. 2018–; fmr Chair. American Council of Life Insurers, Nat. Asscn of Variable Annuities; mem. Bd of Trustees, St Bonaventure Univ., Bushnell Performing Arts Center, Hartford, Conn.; mem. American Acad. of Actuaries;. *Address:* Symetra Financial Corpn, 777 108th Avenue NE, Suite 1200, Bellevue, WA 98004, USA (office). *Telephone:* (425) 256-5351 (office). *E-mail:* karin.vanvleet@symetra.com (office). *Website:* www.symetra.com (office).

MARRACK, Philippa C., PhD, FRS; British/American immunologist and academic; *Professor of Immunology, Biochemistry and Molecular Biology and Medicine, School of Medicine, University of Colorado;* b. 28 June 1945, Ewell, Surrey, England; m. John W. Kappler; ed Univ. of Cambridge and Univ. of California, San Diego; Postdoctoral Fellow, MRC Lab. for Molecular Biology, Cambridge 1970–71; Research Bye Fellow, Girton Coll., Cambridge 1970–71; Postdoctoral Fellow, Damon Runyon Soc. for Cancer Research, Dept of Biology, Univ. of California, San Diego, La Jolla 1971–73; Postdoctoral Fellow, Dept of Microbiology, Univ. of Rochester, NY 1973–74, Assoc. 1974–75, Asst Prof. 1975–76, Asst Prof. of Oncology, Dept of Microbiology and James P. Wilmot Cancer Center, Univ. of Rochester School of Medicine and Dentistry 1976–79, Assoc. Prof. of Oncology 1979–82; Established Investigator, American Heart Asscn, Dallas, Tex. 1976–81; mem. Dept of Medicine, Nat. Jewish Hosp. and Research Center, Denver,

Colo 1979–; Assoc. Prof., Depts of Biophysics, Biochemistry and Genetics and Dept of Medicine, Univ. of Colorado Health Sciences Center 1980–85, Prof., Dept of Biochemistry and Molecular Genetics and Dept of Medicine 1985–, Prof., Dept of Microbiology and Immunology 1988–94, Prof., Dept of Immunology 1994–; Investigator, Howard Hughes Medical Inst., Denver 1986–; Head, Nat. Jewish Center for Immunology and Respiratory Medicine Denver 1988–90, Head, Div. of Basic Immunology, Nat. Jewish Medical and Research Center (now Nat. Jewish Health) 1998–99, currently Sr Faculty mem., Integrated Dept of Immunology; Distinguished Prof., Univ. of Colorado; mem. Laskar Award Selection Cttee 1993–; mem. Advisory Bd Cancer Research Inst. 1986–; mem. Council American Asscn of Immunologists 1995–, Vice-Pres. 1999–2000, Pres. 2000–01; Charter Bd mem. Molecular Medicine Soc. 1995–; Sec.-Gen. Tri-Annual Meeting, Int. Union of Immunologists 1995–; Vice-Pres. Int. Union of Immunological Socs 1998–; mem. Trudeau Inst. 1997–, Scientific Advisory Bd Sandler Foundation 1999–; Advisory Ed. Journal of Experimental Medicine 1985–, Therapetic Immunology 1992–; Assoc. Ed. Cell 1987–; Contributing Ed. Molecular Medicine 1995–; mem. Editorial Bd Cellular Immunology 1983–, Proceedings of the National Academy of Science 1997–, Journal of Autoimmunity 1997–; mem. NAS 1989–, British Soc. for Immunology, American Asscn of Immunologists, American Heart Asscn (Basic Science Council); Fellow, American Acad. of Arts and Sciences 1991–; Hon. mem. Scandinavian Soc. for Immunology 1990–; Hon. DSc (Univ. of Rochester) 1991, (Macalester Coll.) 1996; Arthur B. Lorber Award for Distinguished Service, Nat. Jewish Center for Immunology and Respiratory Medicine 1990, Prize Winner and Lecturer, Royal Soc. Wellcome Foundation 1990, Feodor Lynen Medal for Special Achievement and Distinguished Service Award 1990, Ernst W. Bertner Memorial Award, M.D. Anderson Cancer Center 1992, Christopher Columbus Discovery Award for Biomedical Research 1992, Paul Ehrlich and Ludwig Darmstädter Prize (Germany) 1993, William B. Coley Award for Distinguished Research in Fundamental Immunology, Cancer Research Inst. 1993, Dickson Prize in Medicine, Univ. of Pittsburgh 1995, Behring-Heidelberger Lecture Award 1995, FASEB Excellence in Science Award 1995, Louisa Gross Horwitz Prize, Columbia Univ. 1995, Rabbi Shai Schacknai Memorial Prize, Hadassah Univ. 1998, Howard Taylor Ricketts Prize, Univ. of Chicago 1999, Interscience Conf. on Antimicrobial Agents and Chemotherapy Award 1999, Irvington Inst. Scientific Leadership Award in Immunology 2001, Lifetime Achievement Award, American Asscn of Immunologists 2003, L'Oréal-UNESCO For Women in Science Award 2004, Pearl Meister Greengard Prize, Rockefeller Univ. 2005, Rabbi Shai Shackner Prize, Univ. of Jerusalem, Wolf Prize in Medicine (co-recipient) 2015. *Publications:* more than 250 articles in scientific journals on devt, specificity, activation and life history of T cells. *Address:* Kappler/Marrack Laboratory, Howard Hughes Medical Institute, National Jewish Health, 1400 Jackson Street, 5th Floor, Goodman Building, Denver, CO 80206, USA (office). *Telephone:* (303) 398-1322 (office). *Fax:* (303) 398-1396 (office). *E-mail:* marrackp@njhealth.org (office). *Website:* www.nationaljewish.org/professionals/research/programs-depts/immunology/labs/kmlab (office); www.hhmi.org/scientists/philippa-marrack (office).

MARRAKCHI, Ahmad, MSc, PhD; Tunisian university administrator; b. 9 Feb. 1935, Sfax; m.; four c.; ed Toulouse Univ., France; Assoc. Prof., then Prof., Univ. of Tunis; Scientific Advisor and Dir Tunis Nat. School of Eng (ENIT) 1975–85; est. Faculty of Tech. at Univ. of Qatar, Dean of Faculty and adviser to Pres. of Univ. 1990–99; mem. French Soc. of Electricians, European Soc. for Engineers Training; Founding mem. and Pres. Tunisian Soc. of Electronics Specialists; Founding Fellow, Islamic Acad. of Sciences 1986; elected Beit Al Hikma of the Tunisian Acad. 2012. *Address:* c/o Islamic World Academy of Sciences, PO Box 830036, Zahran, Amman 11183, Jordan. *Telephone:* 5522104. *Fax:* 5511803. *E-mail:* ias@go.com.jo. *Website:* www.iasworld.org/prof-ahmad-marrakchi.

MARRI, Helal Saeed Khalfan al-, BA, MBA, ACA; United Arab Emirates business executive; *Director General, Dubai World Trade Centre;* b. 1976; m.; three s.; ed Univ. of Kent and London Business School, UK; previously worked with KPMG, London; Strategy Consultant, McKinsey & Co. –2004; Dir Gen. Dubai World Trade Centre 2004–; Ind. Dir (non-exec.) Aramex, Depa United Group, Depa Ltd 2008–; Chair. Emirates NBD Asset Management, Emirates Financial Services, Hamdan bin Mohammed bin Rashid Sports Complex; mem. Bd Dubai Chamber of Commerce, Zabeel Investments, Taaleem PJSC; mem. Inst. of Chartered Accountants in England and Wales. *Leisure interests:* fishing, volleyball, football. *Address:* Dubai World Trade Centre, PO Box 9292, Dubai, United Arab Emirates (office). *Telephone:* (4) 3321000 (office). *Fax:* (4) 3312173 (office). *E-mail:* info@dwtc.com (office). *Website:* www.dwtc.com (office).

MARRI, Maj.-Gen. Mohammed Ahmed al-; United Arab Emirates government official; *Director, General Directorate of Residency and Foreigners Affairs, Dubai;* ed Dubai Police Acad.; joined Dubai Police 1980, becoming Deputy Dir Dept of Criminal Evidence 2001–04, Deputy Dir Gen. of Inquiries and Criminal Investigation Dept 2004–06; Dir, Gen. Directorate of Residency and Foreigners Affairs, Dubai (fmrly Dubai Naturalisation and Residency Dept) 2007–; Chair. Labour Welfare Cttee; Head of Perm. Cttee of Labour Affairs; Bd Deputy, Community Devt Authority; mem. Higher Cttee for Crisis Man.; mem. Organizing Cttee Dubai Shopping Festival. *Address:* General Directorate of Residency and Foreigners Affairs-Dubai, Al Jaffliya area next to Bur Dubai Police Station, PO Box 4333, Dubai, United Arab Emirates (office). *Telephone:* (4) 313-9999 (office). *Fax:* (4) 501-1111 (office). *E-mail:* amer@dnrd.ae (office). *Website:* dnrd.ae (office).

MARRI, Mona Ghanem al-, BBA; United Arab Emirates public relations executive; *Chairman, Dubai Press Club;* b. 1979; m. Mohammad al-Gergawi; two c.; ed Dubai Higher Coll. of Tech.; Media and Public Relations Man., First Dubai Shopping Festival 1997; Project Man. Dubai Summer Surprises 1998; Founder and Chair. Dubai Press Club 1999–; currently Dir-Gen. Govt of Dubai Media Office; fmr CEO Jiwin (public relations co.); CEO Brand Dubai 2009–; Vice-Pres. Dubai Ladies' Club; Exec. Dir Arab Media Forum; Sec.-Gen. Int. Asscn of Press Clubs, Arab Journalism Award; Dir Dubai Media Inc., Young Arab Leaders; Outstanding Contribution to Community Outreach, Middle East Women's Achievement Awards 2008, named Outstanding Business Leader of the Middle East by World BPO Forum, New York, Most Influential Arab Media Personality, Arab Union of Electronic Media 2014. *Address:* Dubai Government of Media Office, Convention Tower, 1st floor, PO Box 3933, Dubai, United Arab Emirates (office). *E-mail:* dubaipressclub@dpc.org.ae (office). *Website:* www.dpc.org.ae (office).

MARRIOTT, J(ohn) W(illard) (Bill), Jr, BS; American business executive; *Executive Chairman and Chairman of the Board, Marriott International, Inc.;* b. 25 March 1932, Washington, DC; s. of J. Willard Marriott and Alice Sheets Marriott; m. Donna Garff; three s. one d.; ed St Albans School, Washington, DC, Univ. of Utah; ship's service supply officer, USS Randolph 1954–56; joined The Hot Shoppes (family-owned restaurant chain, later renamed Marriott Corpn) 1956, various positions including Head of Hotels Div., Exec. Vice-Pres. and mem. Bd of Dirs Jan. 1964, Pres. Marriott Corpn Nov. 1964, elected CEO 1972, Chair. 1985, Chair. and CEO Marriott International, Inc. 1997–2012, Exec. Chair. and Chair. of the Bd 2012–; mem. Bd The J. Willard & Alice S. Marriott Foundation; mem. Exec. Cttee World Travel & Tourism Council; fmr mem. Bd of Trustees Nat. Geographic Soc., Naval Acad. Endowment Trust, Nat. Urban League; Hon. DH (Weber State Univ.) 2006; Distinguished Eagle Scout Award, CEO of the Year Award, Chief Executive Magazine 1988. *Publications include:* The Spirit to Serve: Marriott's Way (with Kathi Ann Brown) 1997. *Address:* Marriott International, Inc., Corporate Headquarters, 10400 Fernwood Road, Bethesda, MD 20817, USA (office). *Telephone:* (301) 380-3000 (office). *Fax:* (301) 380-3969 (office). *E-mail:* info@marriott.com (office). *Website:* www.marriott.com (office); news.marriott.com (office).

MARRON, Donald Baird; American banker and art collector; *Chairman, Lightyear Capital;* b. 21 July 1934, Goshen, NY; m. Catherine D. Calligar; ed Bronx High School of Science, The City Univ. of New York, New York and Baruch School of Business; investment analyst, New York Trust Co. 1951–56, Lionel D. Edie Co. 1956–58; Man. Research Dept, George O'Neill & Co. 1958–59; Pres. D.B. Marron & Co. Inc. 1959–65, Mitchell Hutchins & Co. Inc. (merger with D.B. Marron & Co. Inc.) 1965–69, Pres., CEO 1969–77; Co-founder and Chair. Data Resources Inc. 1969–79; Pres. PaineWebber Inc. (merger with Mitchell Hutchins & Co. Inc.) 1977–88, Chair. and CEO 1980–2000, merged with UBS AG 2000, Chair. UBS America 2000–03; Founder and Chair. Lightyear Capital 2000–, Chair. Lightyear portfolio co. RidgeWorth Holdings LLC, mem. Bd of Dirs portfolio cos Clarion Partners Holdings LLC, Cooper Gay Swett & Crawford Ltd; Co-founder and fmr Chair. Data Resources Inc.; Dir, New York Stock Exchange 1974–81; mem. Bd Fannie Mae 2001–06; mem. Advisory Bd Carlyle Group from 2005; Vice-Pres. Bd of Trustees, Museum of Modern Art, later Pres., now Pres. Emer.; mem. Council on Foreign Relations Inc., Pres.'s Cttee on the Arts and the Humanities Inc.; Trustee, Center for Strategic and Int. Studies, George Bush Presidential Library; fmr Gov. and Vice-Chair. Securities Industry Asscn; fmr Gov. Nat. Asscn of Securities Dealers; Chair. Emer. Center for the Study of the Presidency; mem. Council on Foreign Relations, Memorial Sloan-Kettering Cancer Center's Bd of Overseers; Trustee, Center for Strategic and Int. Studies, New York Univ. *Address:* Lightyear Capital LLC, 9 West 57th Street, New York, NY 10019, USA (office). *Telephone:* (212) 328-0555 (office). *Fax:* (212) 328-0516 (office). *E-mail:* info@lycap.com (office). *Website:* www.lycap.com (office).

MARS, John Franklyn; American business executive; *Chairman, Mars Inc.;* b. 15 Oct. 1935; s. of Forrest Mars, Sr; brother of Forrest Edward Mars, Jr; m. Adrienne Bevis 1958; three c.; ed Yale Univ.; Chair. Kal Kan Foods, Inc.; Co-Pres. Mars, Inc. 1973–, CEO 2000, now Chair. *Address:* Mars, Inc., 6885 Elm Street, McLean, VA 22101-3810, USA (office). *Telephone:* (703) 821-4900 (office). *Fax:* (703) 448-9678 (office). *Website:* www.mars.com (office).

MARS-JONES, Adam, FRSL; British novelist, critic and teacher; *Research Professor in Creative Writing, Goldsmiths, University of London;* b. 26 Oct. 1954, London; s. of Sir William Mars-Jones; partner Keith King; one d.; ed Westminster School, Trinity Hall, Cambridge, Univ. of Virginia, USA; film critic, The Independent 1989–97, The Times 1999–2001; regular contrib. since 1980 to Times Literary Supplement, Guardian, Observer and currently to London Review of Books; Research Prof. in Creative Writing, Goldsmiths, Univ. of London 2016–; Hatchet Job of the Year Award 2012. *Publications:* Lantern Lecture (short stories) (Somerset Maugham Award 1982) 1981, Mae West is Dead 1983, The Darker Proof: Stories from a Crisis (with Edmund White) 1987, Monopolies of Loss 1992, The Waters of Thirst (novel) 1993, Blind Bitter Happiness (essays) 1997, Pilcrow (novel) 2008, Cedilla (novel) 2011, Noriko Smiling (film study) 2011, Kid Gloves (memoir) 2015, Second Sight (selected writing on film) 2019. *Address:* 38 Oakbank Grove, Herne Hill, London, SE24 0AJ, England (home). *E-mail:* amarsj@btinternet.com.

MARSALIS, Wynton; American musician (trumpet), music administrator and composer; b. 18 Oct. 1961, New Orleans, La; s. of Ellis Marsalis and Dolores Marsalis; three c.; ed Berkshire Music Center, Tanglewood, Juilliard School; played with New Orleans Philharmonic age 14; joined Art Blakey and the Jazz Messengers 1980; toured with Herbie Hancock 1981; formed own group with brother Branford Marsalis 1982; leader Wynton Marsalis Septet; in addition to regular appearances in many countries with his own jazz quintet, follows a classical career and has performed with the world's top orchestras; regularly conducts master-classes in schools and holds private tuition; Artistic Dir Lincoln Center Jazz Dept, New York 1990–; Cultural Corresp., CBS News 2012–14; A. D. White Prof., Cornell Univ. 2015–; apptd UN Messenger of Peace 2001; Hon. RAM 1996; Chevalier, Légion d'honneur 2009; numerous hon. doctorates; Edison Award, Netherlands, Grand Prix du Disque, numerous Grammy Awards in both jazz and classical categories, Algur H. Meadows Award, Southern Methodist Univ. 1997, National Medal of Arts 2005, Ronnie Scott Award for Int. Trumpeter 2007, Gold Medal (Vitoria, Spain) 2009, Nat. Endowment of the Arts Jazz Masters Award 2011, Nat. Humanities Medal 2015, Global Citizen Award, Atlantic Council 2016. *Compositions include:* Soul Gestures in Southern Blues 1988, Citi Movement 1992, Blood on the Fields (oratorio) (Pulitzer Prize for Music 1997) 1994, Jazz/Syncopated Movements 1997, Abyssinian 200: A Celebration 2008. *Recordings include:* All American Hero 1980, Wynton 1980, Wynton Marsalis 1981, Think of One 1983, Trumpet Concertos: Haydn, Hummel, Mozart 1983, English Chamber Orchestra 1984, Hot House Flowers 1984, Baroque Music: Wynton Marsalis, Edita Gruberova, Raymond Leppard and the English Chamber 1985, Black Codes (From the Underground) 1985, J Mood 1985, Live at Blues Alley 1986, Tomasi/Jolivet: Trumpet Concertos 1986, Carnaval 1987, Baroque Music for Trumpets 1988, The Majesty of the Blues 1989, Crescent City Christmas Card 1989, Tune in Tomorrow (soundtrack) 1991, Quiet City 1989, 24 1990, Trumpet Concertos 1990, Blue Interlude 1992, Citi Movement 1992, In This House, On This Morning 1992, Hot

Licks: Gypsy 1993, On the Twentieth Century 1993, Joe Cool's Blues 1994, Live in Swing Town 1994, In Gabriel's Garden 1996, Jump Start and Jazz 1996, Live at Bubba's 1996, One By One 1998, The Marcial Suite 1998, At the Octoroon Ball: String Quartet No. 1 1999, Big Train 1999, Fiddler's Tale 1999, Reeltime 1999, Sweet Release and Ghost Story 1999, Listen To The Storyteller 1999, Goin' Down Home 2000, Immortal Concerts: Jody 2000, The London Concert 2000, All Rise 2002, Angel Eyes 2002, The Magic Hour 2004, Two Men with the Blues (with Willie Nelson) 2008, He and She 2009. *Television includes:* consultant on documentary series Jazz 1999. *Publications include:* Sweet Swing Blues on the Road 1994, Marsalis on Music 1995, Requiem 1999, Jazz In the Bittersweet Blues of Life (co-author) 2002, To a Young Jazz Musician: Letters From The Road (co-author) 2004, Jazz ABZ: An A to Z Collection of Jazz Portraits 2007, Moving to Higher Ground: How Jazz Can Change Your Life (co-author) 2008, Squeak, Rumble, Whomp! Whomp! Whomp!: A Sonic Adventure (co-author) 2012. *Address:* c/o James Ziefert, Kurland Agency, 173 Brighton Avenue, Boston, MA 02134-2003, USA (office). *Website:* www.thekurlandagency.com/artists/wynton-marsalis (office); www.wyntonmarsalis.org; www.jazz.org. *E-mail:* info@wyntonmarsalis.org.

MARSH, Henry Thomas, CBE, FRCS; British neurosurgeon and author; *Senior Consultant Neurosurgeon, Atkinson Morley Wing, St George's Hospital, London;* b. 5 March 1950; m. 2nd Kate Fox; one s. two d.; ed Westminster School, London, Univ. Coll., Oxford, Royal Free Medical School; currently Sr Consultant Neurosurgeon, Atkinson Morley Wing, St George's Hospital, London; also operates at Lipska Street Hospital, Kyiv, Ukraine 1992–. *Films:* The English Surgeon (documentary) (Emmy Award for Outstanding Science and Technology 2009, Dupont-Columbia Silver Baton Award 2011) 2007. *Publication:* Do No Harm: Stories of Life, Death and Brain Surgery (J. R. Ackerley Prize for Autobiography 2015) 2014. *Leisure interest:* bee-keeping, classic cars. *Address:* Academic Neurosurgery Unit, St George's Hospital, University of London, Cranmer Terrace, London, SW17 0RE, England (office). *E-mail:* henry.marsh@stgeorges.nhs.uk (office). *Website:* stgeorges.nhs.uk (office).

MARSH, Rodney William, MBE; Australian professional cricket coach and fmr professional cricketer; b. 4 Nov. 1947, Armadale, WA; m.; three s.; ed Univ. of Western Australia; wicket-keeper; left-handed batsman; right-arm off-break bowler; played for Western Australia 1969–84, Australia 1970–84; played in 96 Test matches, scoring 3,633 runs (average 26.51, highest score 132) including three hundreds; played in 92 One-Day Ints, scoring 1,225 runs (average 20.08, highest score 66); scored 11,067 First-class runs (average 31.17, highest score 236) including 12 hundreds; Head Coach Commonwealth Bank Cricket Acad. 1990–2001; Dir England and Wales Cricket Bd Nat. Acad. 2002–05; England selector 2003–05; worked with Global Cricket Acad., Dubai; apptd consultant, South Australian Cricket Asscn to undertake review of cricket throughout S Australia 2006; Chair. of Selectors, Cricket Australia 2014–16; Wisden Cricketer of the Year 1982, inducted into Australian Cricket Hall of Fame 2005. *Publication:* (with Jack Pollard) The Glovemen 1994. *Leisure interests:* golf, watching Aussie rules football. *Address:* 4 Briar Avenue, Medindie, South Australia 5081, Australia (home). *E-mail:* rmarsh@bettanet.net.au (home).

MARSHALL, Barry James, AC, MB BS, FRACP, FAA, FRS; Australian gastroenterologist and academic; *Director, Marshall Centre for Infectious Diseases Research and Training, University of Western Australia;* b. 30 Sept. 1951, Kalgoorlie, WA; m. Adrienne Joyce Feldman 1972; four c.; ed Univ. of Western Australia; physician, Royal Perth Hosp. 1974–83; Prof. of Medicine, Univ. of Virginia, USA 1986–96; currently Sr Prin. Research Fellow, Helicobacter pylori Research Lab. and Dir Marshall Centre for Infectious Diseases Research and Training, Univ. of Western Australia School of Biomedical and Chemical Sciences, Sir Charles Gairdner Hosp., Perth, Burnet Fellowship 1998–2003, Sir McFarlane Burnett Fellowship, Nat. Health and Medical Research (NHMR) 2013–15, now Hon. Clinical Prof.; Companion of the Order of Australia 2007; Dr hc (Oxford) 2009; Albert Lasker Award 1995, Dr A.H. Heineken Prize for Medicine 1998, Australian Achiever Award 1998, Florey Medal 1998, Buchanan Medal, Royal Soc. of Medicine, London 1998, Benjamin Franklin Award for Life Sciences 1999, Poppy Award, Australian Inst. of Political Sciences 2000, Nobel Prize for Medicine 2005, Western Australian of the Year 2007, Galen Medal, Soc. of Apothecaries 2009. *Research:* collaborated with Robin Warren on research leading to culture of Helicobacter pylori 1982 and recognition of asscn between H.pylori, gastritis, peptic ulcer and gastric cancer. *Leisure interests:* computers, electronics, photography. *Address:* University of Western Australia, Marshall Centre M504, 35 Stirling Highway, Crawley, WA 6009, Australia (office). *Telephone:* (8) 9346-4815 (office); (8) 6457-4815 (home). *Fax:* (8) 6457-4816 (office). *E-mail:* admin@hpylori.com.au (office); barry.marshall@uwa.edu.au (home). *Website:* www.hpylori.com.au (office).

MARSHALL, Hon. (Cedric) Russell, CNZM, BA, Dip Tchg; New Zealand politician and diplomatist (retd); b. 15 Feb. 1936, Nelson; s. of Cedric Thomas Marshall and Gladys Margaret Marshall (née Hopley); m. Barbara May Watson 1961; two s. one d.; ed Nelson Coll., Christchurch Teachers' Coll., Trinity Theological Coll., Auckland, Victoria Univ.; teacher at various schools 1955–56; Methodist Minister in Christchurch 1960–66, Masterton 1967–71; MP for Wanganui (Labour) 1972–90; Minister of Environment 1984–86, of Educ. 1984–87, of Conservation 1986–87, of Disarmament and Arms Control 1987–89, of Foreign Affairs 1987–90, of Pacific Island Affairs 1989–90; Sr Opposition Whip 1978–79; Chair. NZ Comm. for UNESCO 1990–99, NZ Rep., UNESCO Exec. Bd 1995–99; Chancellor, Victoria Univ. of Wellington 2000–01; High Commr to UK and Nigeria and Amb. to Ireland 2002–05; Chair. Africa Information Centre Trustees 1991–95, Commonwealth Observer Group, Seychelles 1993, Commonwealth Observer Mission to S Africa 1994, Cambodia Trust (Aotearoa-NZ) 1994–2001, Polytechnics Int. NZ 1994–2001, Educ. NZ 1998–2001, Tertiary Educ. Advisory Comm. 2000–01, Cambodia Trust (UK) 2002–05, Tertiary Educ. Comm. 2005–07; Pres. NZ Inst. of Int. Affairs 2007–11; Chair. Robson Hanan Trust – Rethinking Crime and Punishment 2010–11; Hunter Fellow, Victoria Univ. of Wellington 2009; mem. Commonwealth Observer Group, Lesotho 1993, Victoria Univ. of Wellington Council 1994–2002, Nelson Mandela Trustees 1995–2008; Labour. *Leisure interests:* classical music, genealogy. *Address:* 5 Whitianga View, Paremata, Porirua 5024, New Zealand. *Telephone:* (4) 233-6608. *E-mail:* russellmarshall@clear.net.nz.

MARSHALL, Ray, PhD; American economist, academic and fmr government official; *Professor Emeritus and Audre and Bernard Rapoport Centennial Chair in Economics and Public Affairs, Lyndon B. Johnson School of Public Affairs, University of Texas;* b. 22 Aug. 1928, Oak Grove, La.; m. Patricia Williams 1946; one s. three d.; ed Millsaps Coll., Miss., Louisiana State Univ., Univ. of Calif. at Berkeley; Fulbright Research Scholar, Finland; post-doctoral research, Harvard Univ.; Instructor San Francisco State Coll.; Assoc. Prof. and Prof. Univs of Miss., Ky, La.; Prof. of Econs, Univ. of Texas 1962–67, Prof. of Econs 1969, Chair. Dept 1970–72, Prof. of Econs and Public Affairs, Lyndon B. Johnson School of Public Affairs 1981, Rapoport Prof. Econs and Public Affairs, Prof. Emer. 1998–, fmrly Dir Center for Study of Human Resources; US Sec. of Labor 1977–81; Co-Chair. Comm. on the Skills of the American Workforce; Trustee German Marshall Fund and Carnegie Corpn of NY 1982–90; mem. Comm. on Future of Labor/Man. Relations; Dr hc (Maryland, Cleveland State, Millaaps Coll., Bates Coll., Rutgers, Ind., Tulane, Utah State, St Edward's); Lifetime Achievement Award, Industrial Relations Research Asscn 2001. *Publications:* The Negro Worker 1967, The Negro and Apprenticeship 1967, Cooperatives and Rural Poverty in the South 1971, Human Resources and Labor Markets 1972, Anthology of Labor Economics 1972, Human Resources and Labor Markets 1975, Labor Economics: Wages, Employment and Trade Unionism 1976, The Role of Unions in the American Economy 1976, An Economic Strategy for the 1980s 1981, Work and Women in the Eighties 1983, Unheard Voices: Labor and Economic Policy in a Competitive World 1987, Economics of Education 1988, Losing Direction: Families, Human Resource Development and Economic Performance 1991, Thinking for a Living (with Marc Tucker) 1992, Back to Shared Prosperity (ed.) 2000. *Address:* c/o University of Texas, L.B.J. School of Public Affairs, Drawer Y, University Station, Austin, TX 78713, USA. *Telephone:* (512) 471-6242 (office); (512) 345-1828 (home). *Fax:* (512) 345-8491 (home). *E-mail:* ray.marshall@mail.utexas.edu (office). *Website:* www.utexas.edu/lbj (office).

MARSHALL, Robin, BSc, PhD, FRS, FRAS, FInstP; British physicist and academic; *Professor Of Physics and Biology, University of Manchester;* b. 5 Jan. 1940, Skipton, Yorks.; s. of Robert Marshall and Grace Eileen Marshall; m. 1963 (divorced 2002); two s. one d.; ed Ermysted's Grammar School, Skipton, Univ. of Manchester; Research Scientist, DESY, MIT, Daresbury Lab., Rutherford Appleton Lab. 1965–92; Sr Prin. Scientific Officer (Individual Merit) Rutherford Appleton Lab. 1985–92; Prof. of Experimental Physics and Head, Particle Physics Group, Univ. of Manchester 1992–2005, apptd Research Prof. of Particle Physics and Life Sciences 2005, now Prof. of Physics and Biology; Dir and Co. Sec. Frontiers Science and TV Ltd; mem. Council Royal Soc., Royal Soc. Rep. on Univ. of Manchester Ass., Chair. Royal Soc. Univ. Fellowship Cttee; Trustee, Museum of Science and Industry, Manchester; Max Born Medal and Prize, German Physical Soc. 1997. *Publications:* more than 200 scientific papers. *Leisure interests:* painting and drawing, movies. *Address:* School of Physics and Astronomy, Schuster Building-5.01, University of Manchester, Manchester, M13 9PL, England (office). *Telephone:* (161) 275-4170 (office); (161) 275-4175 (office). *Fax:* (161) 275-4246 (office). *E-mail:* Robin.Marshall@manchester.ac.uk (office). *Website:* www.physics.manchester.ac.uk (office); www.robinmarshall.eu.

MARSHALL, Ruth Ann, BBA, MBA; American business executive; ed Southern Methodist Univ.; began career at IBM, held numerous managerial and exec. positions over 18-year period; served as Group Exec. Vice-Pres. two Electronic Payment Service cos, MAC Regional Network and Buypass Corpn, Sr Exec. Vice-Pres. combined cos following acquisition by Concord EFS; Pres. MasterCard N America 1999, Pres., Americas, MasterCard Int. –2006 (retd); mem. Bd of Dirs Global Payments Inc. 2006–, American Standard Corpn, Pella Corpn, ConAgra Foods, Inc. 2007–, Regions Financial Corpn 2011–; mem. Bd several civic and academic orgs, including Citymeals-on-Wheels, The PGA First Tee, Cox School of Business at Southern Methodist Univ. *Leisure interest:* competitive sports (especially golf), piano, travel. *Address:* 4923 Fisher Island Drive, Fisher Island, FL 33109, USA.

MARSHALL, Thomas (Tom) Wendell, BCom, LLB, QC; Canadian lawyer and politician; b. 26 Oct. 1946, Glace Bay, Nova Scotia; s. of Jack Marshall and Sylvia Marshall; ed Memorial Univ. of Newfoundland, Dalhousie Univ.; began career as Assoc., Barry, Wells & Monaghan (law firm), Corner Brook 1972, Partner, Barry, Wells, Monaghan, Seaborn & Marshall 1975, Sr Partner, Monaghan, Marshall, Murphy & Watton –2003; mem. Newfoundland and Labrador House of Ass. for Humber East Dist 2003–; numerous portfolios in Newfoundland and Labrador Govt including Minister of Justice 2003–06, 2008–09, Jan.–Oct. 2013, also Attorney-Gen. 2003–05, 2008–09, 2012–, Minister of Finance and Pres. Treasury Bd 2006–08, 2009–13, 2013–14; Premier of Newfoundland and Labrador Jan.–Sept. 2014; mem. Progressive Conservative Party of Canada. *Address:* Newfoundland and Labrador House of Assembly, East Block, Confederation Building, PO Box 8700, St John's, NL A1B 4J6, Canada (office). *Telephone:* (709) 729-3570 (office). *Fax:* (709) 729-5875 (office). *E-mail:* tommarshall@gov.nl.ca (office). *Website:* www.assembly.nl.ca/members/cms/TomMarshall.htm (office).

MARSHALL, Thurgood, Jr, BA, JD; American lawyer and business executive; *Partner, Bingham McCutchen LLP;* b. 1956; s. of Supreme Court Justice Thurgood Marshall, Sr; m. Teddi Levy; two s.; ed Univ. of Virginia; began legal career as law clerk to US Dist Judge Barrington D. Parker, US Dist Court for the Dist of Columbia; Partner, Bingham McCutchen LLP, Prin. with Bingham Consulting LLC; Dir of Legis. Affairs and Deputy Counsel for Vice-Pres. Al Gore and mem. congressional leadership staff –1997; Asst to Pres. Clinton and Cabinet Sec. 1997–2001, mem. President's Man. Council, served as sr mem. Continuity in Govt team and directed White House response to natural disasters and transportation emergencies, also Vice-Chair. White House Olympic Task Force for Winter Olympic and Paralympic Games, Salt Lake City 2002; Gov. US Postal Service (USPS) 2006–12, Vice-Chair. Bd of Govs 2010–11, Chair. 2011–12; mem. Bd Ford Foundation; Sec. of Transportation's Award for Outstanding Public Service, US Coast Guard Distinguished Public Service Award, Fed. Govt Meritorious Service Medal, named by Washingtonian as one of Washington's top lawyers (Campaigns & Elections), named by Newsweek as one of the 100 people to watch in the new century, named by The Washington Post Magazine on its Best Lawyers List 2007, Leading Lawyer in Govt Affairs Law, The Best Lawyers in America 2008–09, 2011–14. *Address:* Bingham McCutchen LLP, 2020 K Street NW, Washington, DC

20006-1806, USA (office). *Telephone:* (202) 373-6598 (office). *Fax:* (202) 373-6001 (office). *E-mail:* tmarshall.jr@bingham.com (office). *Website:* www.bingham.com/People/Marshall-Thurgood (office).

MARSTERS, Tom John; Cook Islands politician; *Queen's Representative;* b. 4 Aug. 1945, Palmerston Island; m. Tuaine Tumupu; ed Avele Agric. Coll., Samoa, Grimsby Inst. of Tech., UK; began career as Agric. Officer; worked on Tuna Longline Feasibility Study, Island Foods Ltd; fmrly with Office of Sec. to Govt; fmr Clerk, House of Ariki (Parl.); fmr Dir of Fisheries, becoming Chief Admin Officer, Ministry of Agric. and Fisheries, later Deputy Sec. of Agric.; MP for Murienua 1991–2013; Deputy Prime Minister and Minister of Foreign Affairs, Immigration, Transport and Natural Resources 2010–13; Queen's Rep. 2013–; mem. Cook Islands Party, Sec.-Gen. 1968–99. *Achievements include:* has represented Cook Islands in boxing, rugby and golf. *Leisure interest:* golf. *Address:* Office of the Queen's Representative, Titikaveka, POB 134, Rarotonga, Cook Islands (office). *Telephone:* 29311 (office). *Fax:* 29311 (office). *E-mail:* queenrep@oyster.net.ck (office).

MARSUDI, Retno Lestari Priansari, MA; Indonesian diplomatist and politician; *Minister of Foreign Affairs;* b. 27 Nov. 1962, Semarang, Central Java; m. Agus Marsudi; two s.; ed Gadjah Mada Univ., The Hague Univ. of Applied Science, Netherlands; joined Ministry of Foreign Affairs (MFA) 1986, starting in Bureau of Analysis and Evaluation for ASEAN Partnerships, later posted to Embassy in Canberra, becoming First Sec. (Econs), later Head, Dept of Econs, served at Embassy in The Hague 1997–2001, Dir for Europe and America, MFA 2001–03, Dir for W Europe 2003, Amb. to Norway 2005–08, Gen. Dir for America and Europe, MFA 2008, Amb. to Netherlands 2012–14, Minister of Foreign Affairs 2014–; Royal Norwegian Order of Merit 2011, Kt, Grand Cross Ordre van Oranje-Nassau (Netherlands) 2015, El Sol del Peru 2018; Agent of Change Award for Gender Equality and Empowerment of Women, UN 2017, Migrant Worker Protection Award, Serikat Buruh Migran Indonesia 2017, Anugerah Perhumas Indonesia Tahun 2018, Special Award for Humanitarian Diplomacy Leaders, PKPU Human Initiative 2018. *Publications include:* numerous articles on issues related to Foreign Affairs. *Address:* Ministry of Foreign Affairs, 10th Floor, Jalan Taman Pejambon 6, Jakarta Pusat 10110, Indonesia (office). *Telephone:* (21) 3441508 (office). *Fax:* (21) 3857316 (office). *E-mail:* dipten@deplu.go.id (office). *Website:* www.deplu.go.id (office).

MARTA; Brazilian professional footballer; b. (Marta Vieira da Silva), 19 Feb. 1986, Dois Riachos, Alagoas; d. of Aldário da Silva and Tereza da Silva; forward; discovered by Brazilian female coach, Helena Pacheco, aged 14; player with Centro Sportivo Alagoano youth team 1999, Vasco da Gama club, Rio sr team 2000–02, Santa Cruz 2002–04, Umeå IK, Sweden 2004–08 (won Damallsvenskan 2005, 2006, 2007, 2008, Svenska Cupen 2007, UEFA Women's Cup 2004), Los Angeles Sol, USA 2009 (Women's Professional Soccer Regular Season Champion 2009), on loan to Santos of Copa do Brasil 2009–10 (won Copa Libertadores de Fútbol Femenino 2009, Copa do Brasil de Futebol Feminino 2009), FC Gold Pride 2010, Santos 2011, Western New York Flash 2011, Tyresö FF 2012–14, FC Rosengard 2014–; mem. Brazilian Nat. Women's Team 2002–, won Sudamericano Femenino 2003, 2010, gold medal, Pan American Games 2003, 2007, silver medal at Olympic Games, Athens 2004, Beijing 2008, silver medal, FIFA Women's World Cup 2007; also competed in World Cup in 2003, 2011, 2015 and Olympic Games in London 2012; top scorer in Damallsvenskan league (Sweden) 2004, 2005, 2006, 2008, Sudamericano Femenino 2010; became all-time top scorer in Women's World Cup 2015; UN Goodwill Amb. 2010–; U-20 World Cup Golden Ball 2004, Golden Ball (MVP) FIFA Under-19s Women's World Championship 2004, U-20 World Cup Golden Ball 2004, FIFA Women's World Player of the Year 2006, 2007, 2008, 2009, 2010 (runner-up 2005, 2011, 2012, 2014), FIFA Women's World Cup Golden Ball 2007, FIFA Women's World Cup Golden Shoe 2007, Damallsvenskan Best Forward of the Year 2007, 2008, Women's Professional Soccer MVP 2009, 2010, Women's Professional Soccer Golden Boot 2009, 2010, Copa Libertadores de Fútbol Femenino Golden Ball 2009, Women's Professional Soccer Championship MVP 2010, Inaugural Winner of FIFA Ballon d'Or 2010, Best Female Player, Best FIFA Football Awards 2018. *Website:* www.fcrosengard.se.

MARTEL, Yann, BA; Canadian writer; b. 25 June 1963, Salamanca, Spain; s. of Emile Martel and Nicole Perron; partner Alice Kuipers; three s. one d.; ed Trent Univ.; grew up in Alaska, BC, Costa Rica, France, Ont. and Mexico; fmr tree planter, dishwasher, security guard; became professional writer 1990. *Publications:* The Facts Behind the Helsinki Roccamatios (short stories) (Journey Prize) 1993, Self (novel) 1996, Life of Pi (novel) (Hugh MacLennan Prize for Fiction 2001, Man Booker Prize 2002, Boeke Prize 2003) 2001, Beatrice and Virgil (novel) 2010, 101 Letters to a Prime Minister 2012, The High Mountains of Portugal 2016. *Leisure interests:* visual arts, theatre, keeping fit. *Address:* c/o Knopf Canada, Penguin Random House Canada, 320 Front Street West, Suite 1400, Toronto, ON M5V 3B6, Canada. *Telephone:* (416) 364-4449. *Fax:* (416)-598-7764. *Website:* www.penguinrandomhouse.ca.

MARTELLI, Claudio; Italian politician; b. 24 Sept. 1943, Milan; m. Camilla Apollonj Ghetti 2000 (separated 2007); four c.; mem. Italian Socialist Party (PSI) 1967–93, mem. Secr. 1973–75, Leader PSI Group, Milan Municipal Council 1975–79; elected Deputy 1979, 1983, 1987, 1992; Deputy Prime Minister 1989–92, Minister of Justice 1991–93; MEP for Italian Democratic Socialists (SDI) 1999–2004, mem. Cttee on Foreign Affairs, Human Rights, Common Security and Defence Policy, mem. Interparliamentary Del. for Relations with South-East Europe; Spokesman League of Socialists 2000–2005; TV Presenter 2005–; Ed.-in-Chief La Sinistra Sociale socialist review. *Television:* Claudo Martelli racconta, L'incudine, Flash back, Il libro della Repubblica. *Radio:* Alle 8 della sera, Quell'estate del '92.

MARTELLY, Michel Joseph, (Sweet Mickey); Haitian musician, politician and fmr head of state; b. 12 Feb. 1961, Port-au-Prince; m. Sophia Martelly; four c.; ed Saint-Louis de Gonzague High School; spent several years in Miami, Fla, USA employed as construction worker; successful career in Haiti as performing and recording artist, known as pioneer of 'kompas' Haitian dance music; politically active for several years but held no political positions; Pres. of Haiti 2011–16; co-f. (with wife) Rose et Blanc Foundation. *Recordings include:* singles include: Ooo La La 1988, Konpas Foret des Pins, Magouyè, 2008, Bal Bannann Nan 2016; 14 studio albums including Woule Woule 1989, Pa Manyen (Don't Touch) 1997, Dènye Okazyon 1999, SiSiSi 2001.

MÅRTENSON, Jan; Swedish diplomatist; b. 14 Feb. 1933, Uppsala; m.; two s. two d.; ed Univ. of Uppsala; held various Foreign Ministry and diplomatic posts –1966; Head of Section, UN Dept Ministry for Foreign Affairs, Stockholm 1966–67, Head Information Dept 1973–75; Deputy Dir Stockholm Int. Peace Research Inst. 1968–69; Sec.-Gen. Swedish Prep. Cttee for UN Conf. on Human Environment 1970–72; Chef de Cabinet for King of Sweden 1975–79; Asst Sec.-Gen. Centre for Disarmament, UN Dept of Political and Security Council Affairs 1979–82, Under-Sec.-Gen. for Disarmament Affairs 1983–87; Chair. UN Appointments and Promotions Bd 1984–86; Sec.-Gen. Int. Conf. on Relationship between Disarmament and Devt 1987; Dir-Gen. UN Office, Geneva 1987–92, Under-Sec.-Gen. and Head UN Centre for Human Rights, Geneva 1987–92, Co-ordinator UN Second Decade Against Racism 1987; Amb. to Switzerland and Liechtenstein 1993–95; Amb.-at-Large, Ministry of Foreign Affairs 1996–98; Marshal of the Diplomatic Corps 1999–2004; Chair. Int. Club, Stockholm, Travellers' Club, Stockholm. *Publications include:* some 50 books; articles on disarmament and human rights. *Leisure interests:* gardening, fishing. *Address:* Karlaplan 14, 115 20 Stockholm, Sweden (home). *Telephone:* (8) 660-98-39 (home). *E-mail:* jm@swedishvision.se (office).

MÅRTENSSON, Arne, MBA; Swedish banker (retd); b. 10 Oct. 1951, Vänersborg; s. of Aldo Mårtensson and Ingrid Mårtensson; m. 2nd Heléne Melin-Mårtensson 1996; ed Stockholm School of Econs, Harvard Business School, USA; Industrial Devt Dept, Svenska Handelsbanken 1972–75, Vice-Pres. and Head Credit Dept, Regional Unit, Western Sweden 1975–77, Sr Vice-Pres. Admin., Cen. Sweden 1977–80, Sr Vice-Pres. and Area Man. Stockholm City 1980–84, Exec. Vice-Pres. and Gen. Man., Western Sweden, 1984–89, Pres. Stockholm 1989–91, Group Chief Exec. 1991–2001, Chair. 2001–06, Hon. Chair. 2006–; Deputy Chair. Telefonaktiebolaget LM Ericsson 2003–06; Dir (non-exec.) Holmen AB, Industrivärden AB, Sandvik AB, Skanska AB, V & S Vin & Spirit AB, Stockholm School of Econs Advisory Bd (Chair.), mem. Int. Business Council of World Econ. Forum –2006; following retirement, sailed round the world with his wife 2006; Hon. DEcon; Serafim Medal 2004. *Publications:* Back at the Helm 2010, In the Wake of Cook 2011. *Leisure interests:* sailing, jogging, skiing.

MARTÍ PETIT, Antoni; Andorran architect and politician; *Cap de Govern (Head of Government);* b. 10 Nov. 1963, Escaldes-Engordany; m.; three c.; ed École Nationale Supérieur d'Architecture de Toulouse, France; mem. Consell Gen. (Parl.) 1994–2003; Mayor of Andorra la Vella 2004–11; Cap de Govern (Head of Govt) 2011–, also Acting Minister of Culture; Leader, Demòcrates per Andorra (Democracy for Andorra). *Address:* Office of the Head of Government, Govern d'Andorra, Carrer Prat de la Creu 62–64, Edif. Administratiu, AD500 Andorra la Vella, Andorra (office). *Telephone:* 875700 (office). *E-mail:* portal@govern.ad (office). *Website:* www.govern.ad (office).

MARTIN, Carolyn (Biddy), PhD; American academic and university administrator; *President, Amherst College;* b. Lynchburg, Va; ed Coll. of William and Mary, Middlebury Coll., Univ. of Wisconsin; Asst Prof., Dept of German Studies, Cornell Univ. 1985–91, Assoc. Prof. 1991–97, Prof. 1997–2008, Chair Dept of German Studies 1994–97, Sr Assoc. Dean, Coll. of Arts and Sciences 1996; Provost Cornell Univ. 2000–08; Chancellor Univ. of Wisconsin, Madison 2008–11; Pres. Amherst Coll. 2011–. *Address:* Amherst College, 103 Converse Hall, 100 Boltwood Avenue, Amherst, MA 01002, USA (office). *Telephone:* (413) 542-2234 (office). *E-mail:* president@amherst.edu (office). *Website:* www.amherst.edu (office).

MARTIN, Christopher (Chris) Anthony John; British singer, musician (guitar, piano) and songwriter; b. 2 March 1977, Devon, England; m. Gwyneth Paltrow 2003 (separated 2014); one s. one d.; ed University Coll., London; mem. Coldplay 1998–; BRIT Awards for Best British Group 2001, 2003, 2012, 2016, for Best British Single (for Speed of Sound) 2006, for Best Live Act 2014, MTV Europe Music Awards for Best UK and Ireland Act 2002, for Best Song (for Speed of Sound) 2005, for Best Rock Act 2015, 2016, 2017, Billboard Music Awards for Group of the Year 2002, for Top Rock Artist 2012, for Top Alternative Artist 2012, for Top Rock Tour 2017, Ivor Novello Awards for Songwriters of the Year 2003, for Best Selling British Song (for Viva la Vida) 2009, for PRS Most Performed Work (for Hymn for the Weekend) 2017, Grammy Awards for Record of the Year (for Clocks) 2004, for Best Rock Vocal Performance by a Duo or Group (for In My Place) 2004, for Song of the Year 2009, for Best Pop Performance by a Duo or Group (both for Viva la Vida) 2009, Q Awards for Best Act in the World 2005, 2011, Digital Music People's Choice Award for best official site, for Best Digital Music Community (for Coldplay.com) 2005, American Music Award for Favorite Alternative Music Artist 2005, Echo Award for Best Int. Group, Germany 2006, ASCAP Award for Song of the Year (for Speed of Sound) 2006, World Music Award for Best Rock Act 2008. *Recordings include:* albums: Parachutes (BRIT Award for Best Album 2001, Grammy Award for Best Alternative Album 2002) 2000, A Rush Of Blood To The Head (BRIT Award for Best British Album 2003, NME Award for Best Album 2003) 2002, X&Y (MasterCard British Album, BRIT Awards 2006, Juno Award for Int. Album of the Year 2006) 2005, Viva la Vida (Grammy Award for Best Rock Album 2009) 2008, Mylo Xyloto (Billboard Music Awards for Top Rock Album and Top Alternative Album 2012) 2011, Ghost Stories (Billboard Music Award for Top Rock Album 2015) 2014, A Head Full of Dreams 2015. *Address:* c/o Dave Holmes, 3-D Management, 1901 Main Street, #3000, Los Angeles, CA 90405, USA (office). *Telephone:* (310) 314-1390 (office). *Website:* www.coldplay.com.

MARTIN, Hon. Clare, BA; Australian organization official, academic and fmr politician; *Professorial Fellow, Northern Institute, Charles Darwin University;* b. 15 June 1952, Sydney; d. of Prof. Noel Desmond Martin and Bernice Martin (née Downey); m. David Alderman; one s. one d.; ed Loreto Convent, Normanhurst, Sydney Univ.; Sr Political Journalist and Broadcaster ABC (TV and Radio) 1978–95; elected MLA (Australian Labour Party—ALP) for Fannie Bay NT 1995; Shadow Minister for Statehood, then Shadow Minister for the Arts 1995–96, Ethnic Affairs 1995–96, Correctional Services 1995–97, Lands, Planning and Environment 1995–97, Arts and Museums 1995–2001, Urban Devt 1996–97, Housing 1996–99, Asian Relations, Trade and Industry 1997–99, Racing and Gaming 1997–99, Young Territorians 1997–99; Leader ALP 1999–2007; Minister for Communications Science and Advanced Tech. 2001–02; Northern Territory

Chief Minister 2001–07; Minister for Arts and Museums 2001–07, Young Territorians 2001–07, Women's Policy 2001–07, Sr Territorians 2001–07, Territory Devt 2002–07, Indigenous Affairs 2002–07; Treasurer 2001–07; CEO Australian Council of Social Service 2008–10; Professorial Fellow, Northern Inst., Charles Darwin Univ. 2010–; fmr Bd mem. YWCA NT; mem. Jt Ethics Cttee Menzies School Health Research, Royal Darwin Hosp. *Leisure interests:* being fit, reading, music, sport, family. *Address:* Northern Institute, Charles Darwin University, Darwin, NT 0909, Australia (office). *Telephone:* (8) 8946-7468 (office). *Fax:* (8) 8946-7175 (office). *E-mail:* thenortherninstitute@cdu.edu.au (office). *Website:* www.cdu.edu.au/the-northern-institute (office).

MARTIN, Claude Pierre Marcel; French diplomatist; b. 14 April 1944, Saint-Germain-en-Laye; m.; ed Lycée de Saint-Germain-en-Laye, Institut d'Etudes Politiques de Paris, Ecole Nationale des Langues Orientales; joined Ministry of Foreign Affairs 1968, Adviser to Cabinet on European Affairs 1974–78, Minister at Embassy in Beijing 1979–84, Perm. Rep. to EC 1984–86, Dir Asia/Oceania Div., Ministry of Foreign Affairs 1986–90, Amb. to China 1990–93, Assoc. Sec.-Gen. to Dir-Gen. European and Economic Affairs 1993–98, Amb. to Germany 1999–2007, Presidential Conseil des Affaires Etrangères, Ministry of Foreign Affairs; fmr Judge, Cour des comptes (audit court), Paris.

MARTIN, Sir Clive Haydn, Kt, OBE, TD, DL, FCMA, FCIS; British business executive; b. 20 March 1935; s. of Thomas Stanley Martin and Dorothy Gladys Martin; m. Linda Constance Basil Penn 1959; one s. three d.; ed St Alban's School, Haileybury and Imperial Service Coll., London School of Printing and Graphic Arts; nat. service in Germany 1956–58; Man. Dir Staples Printers Ltd (now MPG Ltd) 1972–85, Chair. 1972–; ADC to The Queen 1982–86; Alderman, City of London 1985–2005, Sheriff 1996–97, Lord Mayor of London 1999–2000; Master, Stationers' and Newspaper Makers' Co. 1997–98; CO, Hon. Artillery Co. 1978–80, Regimental Col 1981–83, Master Gunner, Tower of London 1981–83; Master, Chartered Secretaries and Admins' Co. 2004–05; Fellow, Inst. of Paper, Printing and Publishing; Hon. DCL (City Univ.); Dr hc (London Inst.) 2001, (Univ. of the Arts London) 2009 Hon. Col, 135 Ind. Geographic Squadron, Royal Engineers 1999–2004; Hon. Col, The London Regiment 2001–. *Leisure interests:* ocean racing (owner and skipper, British Sardinia Cup Team 1984), walking, cycling. *Address:* MPG Contracts Ltd, Building 3, Oakleigh Road South, New Southgate, London, N11 1GN, England (office). *Telephone:* (20) 3668-1522 (office). *E-mail:* info@mpgcontracts.co.uk (office). *Website:* www.mpgcontracts.co.uk (office).

MARTIN, Dominic David William, CVO, BA (Hons); British diplomatist (retd); *Vice-President, Communication, Global Strategy and Business Development, Statoil Ltd;* b. 25 Nov. 1964, London, England; m. Emily Walter; three d.; ed Dulwich Coll., Westminster School, Oriel Coll., Oxford; joined FCO 1987, Asst Desk Officer, Falkland Islands Dept 1987, Third, later Second Sec. (Political), Embassy in New Delhi 1989–92, First Sec., European Communities Dept (External), FCO 1992–93, First Sec., Policy Planning Staff 1994, First Sec. (Political and Econ.), Embassy in Buenos Aires 1995–99, Deputy Head, EU Dept (External), FCO 1999–2001, Counsellor (Political), Embassy in New Delhi 2001–04, Counsellor (Political, Econ. and Public Affairs), Embassy in Washington, DC 2004–08, Amb. and Perm. Rep. to OECD, Paris 2008–11, Dir, Prosperity, FCO 2011–12; Dir, G8 Presidency Team, Europe and Global Issues Secr., Cabinet Office 2012–14; Vice-Pres., Communication, Global Strategy and Business Devt, Stateoil Ltd 2014–. *Address:* Statoil Ltd, One Kingdom Street, London, W2 6BD, England (office). *Telephone:* (203) 204-3200 (office). *Website:* www.statoil.com (office).

MARTIN, G. Steven, PhD, FRS; American/British biochemist, biologist and academic; *Professor Emeritus of Cell and Developmental Biology, University of California, Berkeley;* b. 19 Sept. 1943, Oxford, England; s. of Kurt Martin and Hanna Martin; m. Gail Zuckman 1969; one s.; ed Manchester Grammar School, Univ. of Cambridge; Postdoctoral Fellow, Virus Lab., Univ. of California, Berkeley 1968–71; mem. of staff, Imperial Cancer Research Fund, London 1971–75; Asst Prof. Dept of Zoology, Univ. of Calif., Berkeley 1975–79, Assoc. Prof. 1979–83, Prof. 1983–89, also Asst Research Virologist Cancer Research Lab. 1975–79, Assoc. Research Virologist 1979–83, Research Virologist 1983–2016, Prof., Dept of Molecular and Cell Biology 1989–2016, Richard and Rhoda Goldman Prof. of Cell and Developmental Biology 2002–07, Judy C. Webb Prof. of Cell and Developmental Biology 2007–12, Head, Div. of Cell and Developmental Biology 1999–2004, Chair. Dept of Molecular and Cell Biology 2007–11, Dean of Biological Sciences 2011–16, Prof. Emer. of Cell and Developmental Biology 2016–; NIH Merit Award 1989–97, 2002–11, John Simon Guggenheim Memorial Foundation Fellowship 1991–92, American Cancer Soc. Scholar Award in Cancer Research 1991–92. *Publications:* articles in various learned journals including Nature, Science, Cell. *Leisure interests:* hiking, travel, reading. *Address:* Department of Molecular and Cell Biology, University of California, Berkeley, 450 Li Ka Shing Center #3370, Berkeley, CA 94720-3370, USA (office). *Telephone:* (510) 642-1508 (office). *E-mail:* gsm@berkeley.edu (office). *Website:* mcb.berkeley.edu/faculty/CDB/martins.html (office).

MARTIN, George R. R., BS; American novelist and screenwriter; b. 20 Sept. 1948, Bayonne, New Jersey; s. of Raymond Collins Martin and Margaret Martin (née Brady); m. 1st Gale Burnick 1975 (divorced 1979); m. 2nd Parris McBride 2011; ed Medill School of Journalism, Northwestern Univ., Evanston, Ill.; journalism intern, Medill News Service, Washington, DC 1971; sportswriter and public relations officer, New Jersey Dept of Parks, Bayonne 1971; Communications & Educ. Coordinator, Cook County Legal Assistance Foundation, Chicago 1972–74; Founder and Chair. Windy City Science Fiction Writers' Workshop, Chicago 1972–76; Instructor in journalism, Clarke Coll. 1976–78, Writer-in-Residence 1978–79; mem. Writers Guild of America West, Science Fiction & Fantasy Writers of America (Vice-Pres. 1996–98); World Fantasy Award for Life Achievement 2012, Medill Hall of Achievement Award, Northwestern Univ. 2015. *Television includes:* The Twilight Zone (writer) 1986, Beauty and the Beast 1987–90, Game of Thrones (TV adaptation of A Song of Ice and Fire books) (Hugo Award for Best Dramatic Presentation Long Form 2012, Primetime Emmy Award for Outstanding Drama Series (as co-Exec. Producer) 2015, 2016, 2018) 2011–. *Publications include:* Dying of the Light 1977, Sandkings (Nebula Award for Best Novelette 1979, Hugo Award for Best Novelette 1980) 1979, The Ice Dragon 1980, Windhaven 1981, Fevre Dream 1982, The Armageddon Rag (Balrog Award for Fantasy Novel 1983) 1983, The Pear-Shaped Man (Bram Stoker Award) 1987, The Skin Trade (World Fantasy Award) 1988, Jokers Wild 1987, Ace in the Hole 1990, Dead Man's Hand 1990, Dealer's Choice 1992, Blood of the Dragon (Hugo Award) 1997; A Song of Ice and Fire series: A Game of Thrones (Locus Fantasy award 1997, Ignotus Award for Best Foreign Novel 2002) 1996, A Clash of Kings (Locus Fantasy Award 1999) 1998, A Storm of Swords (Locus Fantasy Award 2001, Ignotus Award for Best Foreign Novel 2006) 2000, A Feast for Crows 2005, A Dance with Dragons (Locus Award for Best Fantasy Novel 2012) 2011, Fire and Blood 2018; A Song of Ice and Fire series prequels: The Princess and the Queen 2013, The Rogue Prince 2014, The Sons of the Dragon 2017; The Tale of Dunk And Egg Series: The Hedge Knight 1998, The Sworn Sword 2003, The Mystery Knight 2010; Hunter's Run (with Daniel Abraham, Gardner Dozois) 2008; collections and companions: A Song for Lya 1976, Songs of Stars and Shadows 1977, Songs the Dead Men Sing 1983, Nightflyers 1985, Tuf Voyaging 1987, Portraits of His Children 1985, Quartet 2001, The World of Ice & Fire 2014. *Website:* www.georgerrmartin.com.

MARTIN, Harold; New Caledonian politician; b. 6 April 1954, Nouméa; m. Hélène Messud; Pres. Council on the Regulation and Establishment of Agricultural Prices 1991, 1993, 1994–95; Pres. Congress of New Caledonia 1997–98, 2004–07, 2009–11; Pres. of the Govt 2007–10, 2011–14; Pres. L'Avenir Ensemble (Future Together Party) 2007–08, 2010–; Mayor of Paita 1995–. *Address:* c/o Congrès de la Nouvelle-Calédonie, 1 boulevard Vauban, BP. P3 98 851, Nouméa Cedex, New Caledonia (office).

MARTIN, Ian; British UN official; *Member, High-Level Independent Panel on Peace Operations, United Nations;* b. 10 Aug. 1946; s. of Collin Martin and Betty Martin; Community Relations Officer, Redbridge Community Relations Council 1973–75, Councillor, London Borough of Redbridge 1978–82; Head of Asia Research Dept, Amnesty International 1985–86, Sec.-Gen. 1986–92; Sr Assoc., Carnegie Endowment for International Peace, Washington, DC 1993; Dir of Human Rights and Deputy Exec. Dir UN Mission to Haiti 1993–95, Chief of UN Human Rights Field Operation, Rwanda 1995–96, also served in Office of High Rep. in Bosnia, Deputy High Rep. Human Rights Field Operation in Bosnia and Herzegovina 1998–99, Dir Human Rights, International Civilian Mission in Haiti, Special Rep. for East Timor Popular Consultation 1999; Deputy Special Rep. of Sec.-Gen. UN Mission in Ethiopia and Eritrea 2000–01; Vice-Pres. International Centre for Transitional Justice 2002–05; UN human rights adviser during Sri Lankan peace process 2003–05, Rep. to UN High Commr for Human Rights, Nepal 2005–06, Special Envoy for Timor-Leste 2006, Special Rep. of Sec.-Gen. in Nepal 2006–09, Head of HQ Bd of Inquiry, Gaza Strip 2009, Special Adviser to Sec.-Gen. on Post-Conflict Planning for Libya –2011, Special Rep. of the Sec.-Gen. for Libya and Head, UN Support Mission in Libya (UNSMIL) 2011–12; mem. UN High Level Independent Panel on Peace Operations 2014–; UNA-UK Sir Brian Urquhart Award for Distinguished Service to the UN 2013. *Publications include:* Immigration Law and Practice (co-author) 1982, Self-Determination in East Timor: the United Nations, the Ballot, and International Intervention 2001. *Address:* United Nations, New York, NY 10017, USA (office). *Telephone:* (212) 963-1234 (office). *Fax:* (212) 963-4879 (office). *Website:* www.un.org/sg (office).

MARTIN, James (Jim) Grubbs, PhD; American chemist, chemist and fmr politician; *Senior Advisor, McGuireWoods Consulting;* b. 11 Dec. 1935, Savannah, Ga; s. of Arthur M. and Mary J. Grubbs Martin; m. Dorothy A. McAulay 1957; two s. one d.; ed Davidson Coll., Princeton Univ.; Assoc. Prof. of Chem., Davidson Coll. 1960–72; mem. US House of Reps from NC 9th Dist, Washington, DC 1973–85; Gov. of North Carolina 1985–93; Corp. Vice-Pres. Research, Carolinas HealthCare System 1993–2000, Vice-Pres. Gov. Relations, 2000–08; Sr Advisor, McGuire-Woods Consulting 2008–; Chair. Inst. for Defense and Business, Global TransPark Foundation Inc; fmr mem. Bd of Dirs, J.A. Jones Construction, Duke Energy Co., Palomar Medical Technologies, Inc., aaiPharma Inc., Family Dollar Stores, Inc.; mem. Bd of Dirs John W. Pope Center for Higher Educ. Policy 2013–; mem. Bd of Visitors, McColl . Grad. School of Business, Queens Univ. of Charlotte; Trustee, Davidson Coll. 1998–; apptd to lead investigation into academic improprieties at Univ. of North Carolina, Chapel Hill 2012; Dr hc (Queens Univ. of Charlotte) 1997; ACS Charles Lathrop Parsons Award 1983. *Publications:* holds four patents in chemistry of butyl rubber vulcanization. *Leisure interests:* golf, sailing, music. *Address:* McGuireWoods Consulting, 100 Peachtree Street NW, Suite 2200, Atlanta, GA 30303, USA (office). *Telephone:* (404) 443-5800 (office). *Fax:* (404) 443-5839 (office). *Website:* www.mwcllc.com (office).

MARTIN, Kevin Jeffrey, MA, JD; American business executive and fmr government official; *Vice-President, Mobile and Global Access Policy, Facebook;* b. 14 Dec. 1966, Charlotte, NC; m. Catherine Jurgensmeyer; two s.; ed Univ. of North Carolina, Chapel Hill, Duke Univ., Harvard Law School; fmr law clerk for US Court Dist Judge William M. Hoeveler; fmrly with Wiley, Rein & Fielding; later with US Office of the Ind. Counsel; Legal Advisor to Fed. Communications Comm. (FCC) Commr 1997–99; Deputy Gen. Counsel to Bush campaign, Austin, Tex. 1999–2000; fmr Prin. Tech. and Telecommunications Advisor, Bush-Cheney Transition team, later Special Asst to the Pres. for Econ. Policy; fmr mem. staff, Nat. Econ. Council; Commr FCC 2001–09, Chair. 2005–09; Chair. Fed.-State Jt Bd on Separations, Fed.-State Jt Conf. on Advanced Telecommunications Services, mem. Fed.-State Jt Bd on Universal Service; fmr Partner and Co-Chair. Squire Patton Boggs LLP; Vice-Pres. Mobile and Global Access Policy, Facebook 2015–; Co-founder and Man. Partner, Carmichael Partners; fmr Sr Fellow, Aspen Inst.; mem. Bd of Dirs, Xtera Communications 2009–, UbeeAirWalk, Inc. 2011–, Electronic Recyclers International, Inc. 2013–, Corning, Inc. 2013–; mem. Florida Bar, Dist of Columbia Bar, Fed. Communications Bar Assn. *Address:* Facebook, 1 Hacker Way, Menlo Park, CA 94025, USA (office). *Telephone:* (650) 543-4800 (office). *Website:* www.facebook.com (office).

MARTIN, Sir Laurence Woodward, Kt, MA, PhD, DL; British academic; *Professor Emeritus, Newcastle University;* b. 30 July 1928, St Austell, Cornwall; s. of Leonard Martin and Florence Mary Woodward; m. Betty Parnall 1951; one s. one d.; ed St Austell Grammar School, Christ's Coll., Cambridge, Yale Univ., USA; RAF Flying Officer 1948–51; Asst Prof., MIT, USA 1956–61; Assoc. Prof., Johns Hopkins Univ., USA 1961–64; Prof., Univ. of Wales 1964–68, King's Coll. London 1968–78, Fellow, London 1984; Vice-Chancellor Newcastle Univ. 1978–90, Prof. Emer. 1991–; Arleigh Burke Chair in Strategy, Center for Strategic and Int. Studies, Washington, DC 1998–2000; Visiting Prof., Univ. of Wales 1985–90; Dir Royal Inst. of Int. Affairs 1991–96; Bodichon Fellow, Girton Coll. Cambridge 2010;

Hon. DCL (Newcastle) 1991; Lees Knowles Lecturer, Cambridge. *Radio:* Reith Lecturer (BBC) 1981. *Publications:* Peace Without Victory 1958, The Sea in Modern Strategy 1967, Arms and Strategy 1973, The Two Edged Sword 1982, The Changing Face of Nuclear War 1987, British Foreign Policy (co-author) 1997. *Leisure interests:* travel, walking, fishing. *Address:* 35 Witley Court, Coram Street, London, WC1N 1HP, England (home). *E-mail:* lw.martin@hirundo.co.uk (office).

MARTIN, Lynn Morley, BA; American academic, consultant and fmr politician; *President, Martin Hall Group LLC;* b. 26 Dec. 1939, Chicago, Ill.; m. Harry Leinenweber; two d.; ed Univ. of Illinois-Urbana-Champaign; mem. Winnebago Co. Bd 1972–76; mem. Ill. House of Reps 1977–79, Ill. Senate 1979–81; mem. US House of Reps 1981–91, mem. House Administration Cttee, House Budget Cttee, Cttee on Public Works and Transportation, House Rules Cttee, Armed Services Cttee, Vice-Chair. House Repub. Conf. 1984–88; Vice- Co-Chair. Bi-partisan Ethics Task Force; US Sec. of Labor 1991–93; Prof., J.L. Kellogg Graduate School of Man., Northwestern Univ. 1993–99, Davee Chair. 1993–; Chair. Deloitte & Touche (now Deloitte LLP) Council on Advancement of Women 1993–2005; Pres. Martin Hall Group, LLC, Chicago 2005–; mem. Council on Foreign Relations, Chicago Council on Global Affairs; mem. Bd of Dirs Ameritech Corpn 1993–99, Ryder System, Inc. 1993–2012, Harcourt General, Inc. 1993–, AT&T 1999–2012, Proctor & Gamble Co. 1994–2010, Constellation Energy Group Inc. 2003–09, Dreyfus Funds; fmr mem. Int. Advisory Council, Coco-Cola Co.; mem., Client Advisory Bd Deutsche Bank Trust Company Americas 2007–; Advisor, Ameritech Corpn 2011–; Fellow, Kennedy School of Govt, Harvard Univ.; Order of Lincoln 2000; inducted as a Laureate of The Lincoln Acad. of Ill., International ATHENA Award 2002. *Address:* Martin Hall Group, LLC, 3750 N Lake Shore Drive 10A, Chicago, IL 60613-4238, USA.

MARTIN, Micheál, MA; Irish politician; *Leader, Fianna Fáil;* b. 16 Aug. 1960, Cork; s. of Paddy Martin; m. Mary O'Shea; one s.; ed Colaiste Chríost Rí, Univ. Coll., Cork; fmr secondary school teacher; elected to Cork Corpn 1985, Alderman 1991; Lord Mayor of Cork 1992–93; mem. Dáil Éireann 1989–; fmr Chair. Oireachtas All Party Cttee on the Irish Language; fmr mem. Dail Cttee on Crime, Dail Cttee on Finance and Gen. Affairs; Minister for Educ. 1997–2000, for Health and Children 2000, for Enterprise, Trade and Employment –2008, of Foreign Affairs 2008–11 (resgnd); Nat. Chair. Fianna Fáil Nat. Exec. 1988–, Leader Fianna Fáil 2011–; Nat. Chair. Ogra Fianna Fáil; mem. Bd Cork Opera House, Graffiti Theatre Co., Nat. Sculpture Factory, Everyman Palace Theatre, Crawford Gallery, College of Commerce and several school bds; fmr mem. Governing Body Univ. Coll., Cork; won Cork Examiner Political Speaker of the Year Award 1987. *Address:* Fianna Fáil, 65–66 Lower Mount St, Dublin 2, Ireland (home). *Telephone:* (1) 6761551 (office). *Fax:* (1) 6785690 (office). *E-mail:* info@fiannafail.ie (office). *Website:* www.fiannafail.ie (office).

MARTIN, Rt Hon Paul, CC, PC, BA, LLB; Canadian politician; b. 1938, Windsor, Ont.; s. of Paul Martin and Eleanor Martin; m. Sheila Ann Cowan 1965; three s.; ed Univs of Ottawa and Toronto; worked in legal branch of ECSC; called to Bar, Ont. 1966; with Power Corpn of Canada, Montreal; Chair. and CEO Canada Steamship Lines; Dir of seven major Canadian cos; MP for LaSalle-Émard, Montreal 1988–; cand. for leadership of Liberal Party 1990, Leader 2003–06; Co-Chair. Nat. Platform Cttee, Liberal Party of Canada 1993; Minister of Finance 1993–2002, also Minister Responsible for Fed. Office of Regional Devt 1993–95; Prime Minister of Canada 2003–06; Chair. G-20 (int. group) 1999–2002; Samuel Cunard Prize for Vision, Courage and Creativity 2017. *Publications:* Creating Opportunity: The Liberal Plan for Canada (jtly), Making History: The Politics of Achievement, Hell or High Water: My Life In and Out of Politics (auto-biog.) 2008. *Address:* Room 418-N Centre Block, House of Commons, Ottawa, ON K1H 7R3, Canada (office). *Telephone:* (613) 992-4284 (office). *Fax:* (613) 992-4291 (office). *E-mail:* martip@parl.gc.ca (office). *Website:* www.paulmartin.ca.

MARTIN, Ricky; Puerto Rican singer and actor; b. (Enrique Martin Morales), 24 Dec. 1971, San José, PR; two s.; mem. Latin pop band, Menudo 1984–89; solo artist 1989–; worked as actor and singer in Mexico; f. Ricky Martin Foundation 2000; American Music Award for Favorite Latin Artist 2000, Int. Humanitarian Award 2005. *Television:* Alcanzar una Estrella II (Mexican soap opera), played Miguel in General Hospital (US series). *Theatre:* Marius in Les Misérables (Broadway), Che in Evita (Broadway). *Film:* Hercules (voice in Spanish-language version). *Recordings include:* albums: Ricky Martin 1991, Me Amarás 1993, A Medio Vivir 1995, Vuelve (Grammy Award for Best Latin Pop Album) 1998, Ricky Martin 1999, Sound Loaded 2000, La Historia 2001, Almas de Silencio 2003, Life 2005, MTV Unplugged (Latin Grammy Awards for Best Male Pop Vocal Album and Best Long Form Music Video 2007) 2006, A Quien Quiera Escuchar (Grammy Award for Best Latin Pop Album 2016) 2015. *Publication:* Me (autobiog.) 2010. *Address:* Columbia Records, Sony BMG Music Entertainment, 550 Madison Avenue, New York, NY 10022-3211, USA (office). *Telephone:* (212) 833-7100 (office). *Fax:* (212) 833-7416 (office). *Website:* www.sonybmg.com (office); www.rickymartin.com; www.rickymartinfoundation.org.

MARTIN, Simon; British diplomatist; *Ambassador to Bahrain;* partner Sophie Pike; one s. one d.; joined FCO 1984, South Africa Sanctions Desk Officer, Southern African Dept 1985–86, Second Sec. and Vice-Consul, Embassy in Rangoon 1986–90, with Gulf War Emergency Unit 1990–91, Head of Multilateral Section, Drugs and Int. Crime Dept 1991–93, Head of Middle East Terrorism and Lockerbie Section, Security Coordination Dept 1993–95, Head of Commercial Section, Embassy in Budapest 1995–2001, Deputy Head, Southern European Dept 2001–03, Corp. Relations Adviser, Unilever PLC Africa Business Group 2003–05, Deputy Head of Mission, Embassy in Prague 2005–09, Dir Protocol and Vice-Marshal of the Diplomatic Corps, Protocol Directorate 2009–12, Deputy Pvt. Sec. to TRH The Prince of Wales and the Duchess of Cornwall, Clarence House 2012–15, Amb. to Bahrain 2015–. *Address:* British Embassy, POB 11421, Government Avenue, Manama 306, Bahrain (office). *Telephone:* 17574100 (office). *Fax:* 17574161 (office). *E-mail:* BahrainConsularEnquires@fco.gov.uk (office). *Website:* www.gov.uk/government/world/organisations/british-embassy-manama (office); www.gov.uk/government/world/bahrain (office).

MARTIN, Steve; American actor, comedian, writer and musician (banjo); b. 14 Aug. 1945, Waco, Tex.; s. of Glenn Martin and Mary Lee Martin; m. 1st Victoria Tennant 1986 (divorced 1994); m. 2nd Anne Stringfield 2007; ed Long Beach State Coll., Univ. of California, Los Angeles; TV writer for several shows; nightclub comedian; TV special Steve Martin: A Wild and Crazy Guy 1978; Georgie Award, American Guild of Variety Artists 1977, 1978, American Cinematheque Career Achievement Honour 2004, John F. Kennedy Center for Performing Arts Mark Twain Prize for American Humor 2005, Kennedy Center Honor 2007, Academy Honorary Award 2013, Grammy Award for Best Roots Song (for Love Has Come for You, with Edie Brickell) 2014. *Recordings include:* Let's Get Small 1977 (Grammy Award), A Wild and Crazy Guy 1978 (Grammy Award), Comedy is Not Pretty 1979, The Steve Martin Bros, The Crow: New Songs for the Five-String Banjo (Grammy Award for Best Bluegrass Album 2010) 2009, Rare Bird Alert (with Steep Canyon Rangers) 2011, Love Has Come for You (with Edie Brickell) 2013, So Familiar (with Edie Brickell) 2015, The Long Awaited Album 2017. *Films include:* The Absent Minded Waiter 1977, Sgt Pepper's Lonely Hearts Club Band 1978, The Muppet Movie 1979, The Jerk 1979 (also screenwriter), Pennies from Heaven 1981, Dead Men Don't Wear Plaid (also writer) 1982, The Man With Two Brains (also writer) 1983, The Lonely Guy 1984, All of Me 1984 (Nat. Soc. of Film Critics Actor's Award), Three Amigos (also writer and exec. producer) 1986, Little Shop of Horrors 1986, Roxanne (also screenwriter and exec. producer) 1987, Planes, Trains and Automobiles 1987, Dirty Rotten Scoundrels 1988, Parenthood 1989, My Blue Heaven 1990, LA Story (also writer and exec. producer) 1991, Grand Canyon 1991, Father of the Bride 1991, Housesitter 1992, Leap of Faith 1992, A Simple Twist of Fate (also writer and exec. producer) 1994, Mixed Nuts 1994, Father of the Bride 2 1995, Sgt Bilko 1996, The Spanish Prisoner 1997, The Out of Towners 1999, Bowfinger (also writer) 1999, Joe Gould's Secret 2000, Novocaine 2001, Bringing Down the House 2003, Looney Tunes: Back in Action 2003, Cheaper by the Dozen 2003, Jiminy Glick in La La Wood 2004, Shopgirl (also screenplay and producer) 2005, Cheaper by the Dozen 2 2005, Pink Panther (also screenplay) 2006, It's Complicated 2009, Tangled (voice) 2010, The Big Year 2011. *Publications include:* The Pleasure of My Company 2003, Born Standing Up (autobiog.) 2007, An Object of Beauty 2010. *Website:* www.stevemartin.com.

MARTIN, Todd Christopher; American fmr professional tennis player; b. 8 July 1970, Hinsdale, Ill.; s. of Dale Martin and Lynn Martin; m. Amy Martin; one s.; ed Northwestern Univ.; winner, New Haven Challenger 1989; turned professional 1990; winner, Coral Springs 1993, Memphis 1994, 1995, Sydney 1996, 1999, Barcelona 1998, Scania Stockholm Open 1998; semifinalist Stella Artois Grass Court Championships, London 1993, Champion 1994, Champion (doubles with Pete Sampras q.v.) 1995; finalist, Australian Open 1994, Grand Slam Cup, Munich 1995; semifinalist, US Open 1994, Wimbledon 1994, 1996, Paris Open 1998; winner of 8 singles and 5 doubles titles; mem. US Davis Cup Team 1994–99; Pres. ATP Players' Council 1995–97, 1998–99; est. Todd Martin Devt Fund, Lansing, Mich. 1994; Special Adviser, USA Tennis High Performance Program 2003–; announced retirement 2004; contrib. to ESPN.com; mem. Bd of Dirs Tim and Tom Gullickson Foundation; coached by Robert Van't Hof 1994–96, by Dean Goldfine 1997–2002; briefly coached Mardy Fish; part of coaching team of Novak Djokovic 2009–12; Adidas/ATP Tour Sportsmanship Award 1993, 1994, ATP Tour Most Improved Player 1993. *Address:* c/o Todd Martin Development Fund, Foster Community Center, 200 North Foster, Lansing, MI 48912, USA. *Telephone:* (517) 483-4021. *Fax:* (517) 377-0180. *E-mail:* danhof.nancy@toddmartinkids.org. *Website:* www.toddmartinkids.org.

MARTIN, Tony; German professional road bicycle racer; b. 23 April 1985, Cottbus, East Germany; turned professional 2008, for Team High Road; rode for Köstritzer 2004, Gerolsteiner (stagiaire) 2005, Thüringer Energie Team 2006–07, Team High Road 2008–11, UCI ProTeam Omega Pharma-Quick Step 2012–; time trial specialist, three-time world champion 2011, 2012, 2013; part of two world championship-winning team time trial squads with Omega Pharma-Quick Step 2012, 2013; also won three Grand Tour individual time trial stages, two at the Tour de France 2011, 2013, one at Vuelta a España 2011; has also won several stage races, including the Eneco Tour 2010, Volta ao Algarve 2011, 2013, Paris–Nice 2011, Tour of Beijing 2011, 2012, Tour of Belgium 2012, 2013; silver medal, Summer Olympics, London 2012. *Address:* c/o Bund Deutscher Radfahrer e.V., Otto-Fleck-Schneise 4, 60528 Frankfurt am Main, Germany. *E-mail:* info@bdr-online.org. *Website:* www.rad-net.de.

MARTIN, Valerie; American writer and academic; *Professor of English, Mount Holyoke College;* b. 1948, Missouri; partner John Cullen; one d.; taught at Univ. of New Mexico, Univ. of Alabama Univ. of New Orleans, Univ. of Massachusetts, Sarah Lawrence Coll.; currently Prof. of English, Mount Holyoke Coll. *Publications include:* Love: Short Stories 1976, Set in Motion (novel) 1978, Alexandra (novel) 1980, A Recent Martyr (novel) 1987, The Consolation of Nature and Other Stories 1988, Mary Reilly (novel) 1990, The Great Divorce (novel) 1994, Italian Fever (novel) 1999, Salvation: Scenes from the Life of St Francis (biog.) 2001, Property (novel) (Orange Prize for Fiction) 2003, The Unfinished Novel and Other Stories 2006, Trespass 2007, The Confessions of Edward Day 2009, The Ghost of the Mary Celeste 2014. *Address:* The Friedrich Agency, 19 West 21st Street, Suite 201, New York, NY 10010, USA (office); Mount Holyoke College, 50 College Street, South Hadley, MA, 01075, USA (office). *E-mail:* mfriedrich@friedrichagency.com (office); valerie@valeriemartinonline.com. *Telephone:* (413) 538-2000 (office). *Website:* www.valeriemartinonline.com.

MARTÍN DELGADO, José María, DenD; Spanish university rector; b. 26 June 1947, Málaga; s. of Rafael Martín Delgado and María Jesús Martín Delgado; m. Irene Martín Delgado 1973; one s. two d.; ed Univs of Granada and Bologna; Prof. of Fiscal and Tax Law, Univ. of Granada, Univ. Autónoma de Madrid, Univ. Autónoma de Barcelona, Univ. La Laguna and Univ. of Málaga (fmr Dean Faculty of Law) 1969 (apptd); Rector Univ. of Málaga 1984–94; Minister of Culture, Junta de Andalucía 1994–96; Rector Universidad Internacional de Andalucía 1996–; mem. Spanish Asscn of Fiscal Law, Int. Fiscal Asscn; Dr hc (Dickinson Coll., Pa). *Publications:* Análisis Jurídico del Fondo de Previsiones para Inversiones, Ordenamiento Tributario Español 1977, Sistema Democrático y Derecho Tributario. *Leisure interests:* reading, music, fishing, tennis. *Address:* Universidad Internacional de Andalucía, Monasterio de Santa María de las Cuevas, Américo Vespucio nº2, Isla de la Cartuja, 41092 Seville, Spain (office). *Telephone:* (95) 446-2299 (office). *Fax:* (95) 446-2288 (office). *E-mail:* unia@uia.es (office). *Website:* www.unia.es (office).

MARTÍN FERNÁNDEZ, Miguel; Spanish banker; *President, Asociación Española de Banca;* b. 9 Nov. 1943, Jerez de la Frontera; m. Anne Catherine Cleary 1972; one s. two d.; ed Univ. Complutense, Madrid; Head Budget and Finance Sections, Ministry of Finance 1969–72, Deputy Dir 1972–76; Economist, World Bank, Latin American Region 1976–77, Alt. Exec. Dir for Spain, Italy and Portugal, World Bank 1977–78; Dir-Gen. Treasury, Ministry of Finance 1978–79; Under-Sec. for Budget and Public Expenditure 1979–81; Pres. Inst. for Official Credit 1982; Head Annual Accounts Centre, Banco de España 1983–84; Under-Sec. Economy and Finance 1984–86; Dir-Gen. Banco de España 1986–92, Deputy Gov. 1992–2000, Head Internal Audit Office 2000; Pres. Asociación Española de Banca 2006–; mem. SEPI Foundation 2017–; Gran Placa de la Orden del Mérito Postal, Encomienda del Mérito Agrícola. *Address:* Asociación Española de Banca, Velázquez 64–66, 28001 Madrid, Spain (office). *Telephone:* (91) 7891311 (office). *Fax:* (91) 7891310 (office). *Website:* www.aebanca.es (office).

MARTIN-LÖF, Per Erik Rutger, PhD; Swedish mathematician, philosopher and academic; *Professor Emeritus of Logic, Department of Mathematics, Stockholm University;* b. 8 May 1942, Stockholm; s. of Sverker Emil Bernhard Martin-Löf and Gertrud Cecilia Benedicks; m. Kerstin Maria Birgitta Forsell (died 2009); one s. two d.; ed Stockholm Univ.; Asst, Math. Statistics, Stockholm Univ. 1961–64, Doctoral Scholar, Faculty of Science 1965–66, 1967–68, Docent, Math. Statistics 1969–70, Prof. of Logic 1994–2009, Prof. Emer. 2009–; State Scholar of Swedish Inst., Moscow Univ. 1964–65; Amanuensis, Math. Inst., Århus Univ., Denmark 1966–67; Asst Prof., Dept of Math., Univ. of Ill., Chicago, USA 1968–69; Researcher in Math. Logic, Swedish Natural Science Research Council 1970–81, in Logic 1981–83, Prof. of Logic 1983–94; mem. Academia Europaea, Royal Swedish Acad. of Sciences; Dr hc (Leiden) 2004, (Marseilles) 2004. *Publications:* Notes on Constructive Mathematics 1970, Intuitionistic Type Theory 1984. *Leisure interest:* ornithology. *Address:* Department of Mathematics, Stockholm University, 106 91 Stockholm (office); Barnhusgatan 4, 111 23 Stockholm, Sweden (home). *Telephone:* (8) 20-05-83 (home). *Fax:* (8) 612-67-17 (office). *E-mail:* pml@math.su.se (office). *Website:* www.matematik.su.se (office).

MARTIN-LÖF, Sverker, MSc (Eng), DTech; Swedish construction industry executive; *Chairman, Skanska AB;* b. 1943, Stockholm; ed Royal Inst. of Tech., Stockholm; worked at Swedish Pulp and Paper Research Inst.; fmr Pres. MoDo Chemetics; fmr Tech. Dir Mo och Domsjö AB; fmr Pres. Sunds Defibrator AB; Pres. Svenska Cellulosa Aktiebolaget SCA 1988–2002, Chair. 2002–; Chair. Skanska AB 2001–, SSAB Svenskt Stål AB 2003–15; Vice-Chair. AB Industrivärden 2002–10, (Chair. 2010–15), Telefonaktiebolaget LM Ericsson 2006–15, Svenskt Näringsliv, Confed. of Swedish Enterprise; mem. Bd of Dirs LM Ericsson, Boliden 2002–03, Svenska Handelsbanken AB, Research Inst. of Industrial Econs; Hon. PhD (Mid-Sweden Univ., Sundsvall). *Address:* Skanska AB, Klarabergsviadukten 90, 111 91 Stockholm, Sweden (office). *Telephone:* (8) 753-88-00 (office). *Fax:* (8) 755-12-56 (office). *E-mail:* info@skanska.com (office). *Website:* www.skanska.com (office).

MARTÍN VILLA, Rodolfo; Spanish politician and business executive; b. 3 Oct. 1934, Santa María del Páramo, León; m. María Pilar Pena Medina; two c.; ed Escuela Superior de Ingenieros Industriales, Madrid; Leader of Madrid Section, Sindicato Español Universitario, Nat. Leader 1962–64; Sec.-Gen. Syndical Org. 1969–74; mem. Council of the Realm; Nat. Econ. Adviser, Nat. Inst. of Industry; Nat. Econ. Adviser, Banco de Crédito Industrial, later Pres.; Civil Gov. of Barcelona and Prov. Head of Falangist Movement 1974–75; Minister for Relations with Trade Unions 1975–76, of the Interior 1976–79, of Territorial Admin. 1980–82; mem. Parl. (for Unión de Centro Democrático) 1977–83; First Deputy Prime Minister 1981–82; mem. Parl. (for Partido Popular) 1989–97 (resgnd); mem. Exec. Cttee, Partido Popular 1989–; apptd Chair. Sociedad Estatal de Participaciones Industriales 1997; Chair. Endesa (govt-controlled electricity group) 1997–2002, Hon. Chair. 2002–; Govt Commr for the Prestige oil-tanker disaster 2003; Chair. Sogecable (pay-TV provider) 2003–10; Dir, Sociedad de Gestión de Activos procedentes de la Reestructuración Bancaria (Sareb) 2012–; mem. Sr Corps of Inspectors of State Finance, Advisory Cttee FRIDE (think tank); fmr mem. special group of industrial engineers assisting Treasury, Bd Caja de Madrid. *Address:* Sareb, Paseo de la Castellana, 89-8A Planta, 28046 Madrid, Spain. *Telephone:* (91) 5563700. *E-mail:* info@sareb.es; atencion2@pp.es. *Website:* www.sareb.es/es-es/Paginas/web-Sareb.aspx.

MARTINA, Dominico (Don) F.; Curaçao politician; b. 1 May 1935; m.; two s.; fmr finance officer, Govt of Curaçao; head, Govt social affairs Dept; f. Movimentu Antiyas Nobo 1979; MP 1979; Prime Minister of Netherlands Antilles 1979–84, 1985–88.

MARTINDALE, Ken; American business executive; *CEO, GNC Holdings Inc.;* began retail career with Smith's Food and Drug Centers 1975, rose from dist man. in store operations to Sr Vice-Pres. of Marketing and Sr Vice-Pres. of Sales and Merchandising; joined Fred Meyer, Inc. 1998, Exec. Vice-Pres., Sales and Procurement (following merger with Kroger Co.) 1998–99; f. and operated Orchard Street, Inc., Salt Lake City; consulted for nat. and regional food retailers on category management, marketing and strategic planning; fmr Chair., Pres. and CEO Intesource, Inc. (software co.); Co-Pres., Chief Merchandising and Marketing Officer, Pathmark Stores, Inc. (until co. sold to Great Atlantic & Pacific Tea Co.) –2007; Sr Exec. Vice-Pres. of Merchandising, Marketing and Logistics 2008–13, Sr Exec. Vice-Pres. and COO Rite Aid Corpn –2013, Pres. and COO Rite Aid Corpn 2013–15, Pres. Rite Aid Corpn and CEO Rite Aid Stores 2015–17; CEO GNC Holdings Inc. 2017–; Pres. The Rite Aid Foundation; mem. Bd of Dirs Nat. Asscn of Chain Drug Stores. *Address:* GNC Holdings Inc., Pittsburgh, PA, USA (office). *Website:* www.gnc.com (office).

MARTINELLI BERROCAL, Ricardo Alberto, MA, MBA; Panamanian business executive, politician and fmr head of state; b. 11 March 1952, Panamá City; s. of Ricardo Martinelli Pardini and Gloria Berrocal de Martinelli; m. Marta Linares de Martinelli; two s. one d.; ed Staunton Mil. Acad., USA, Univ. of Arkansas, INCAE Business School, Costa Rica; Dir Social Security Fund 1994–96; Chair. Panama Canal Authority and Minister for Canal Affairs 1999–2003; Pres. Cambio Democrático Party 1998–; Pres. of Panama 2009–14; Chair. Importadora Ricamar SA, Supermercados 99; Chair. Central Azucarera La Victoria, Plastigol SA; Dir, Gold Mills de Panamá, Global Bank, Panasal SA, Televisora Nacional de Panamá, Direct TV, Desarrollo Norte SA, Molino de Oro, AVIPAC, Calox Panameña; Ricardo A. Martinelli Berrocal Scholarship est. by Univ. of Arkansas 2010, also awarded Citation of Distinguished Alumnus Award and made an official Amb. of the State of Ark. 2010, acknowledged by FAO, Rome for helping to reduce child malnutrition in Panama 2013. *Address:* Cambio Democrático, Parque Lefevre, Plaza Carolina, arriba de la Juguetería del Super 99, Panamá, Panama (office). *Telephone:* 227-4062 (office); 217-2643 (office). *Fax:* 227-0076 (office); 217-2645 (office). *E-mail:* cambio.democratico@hotmail.com (office). *Website:* www.cambiodemocratico.org.pa (office).

MARTINEZ, Arthur C., BSc, MBA; American business executive; *Chairman, Abercrombie & Fitch Co.;* b. 25 Sept. 1939, New York; s. of Arthur F. Martinez and Agnes Martinez (née Caulfield); m. Elizabeth Rusch 1966; two c.; ed Polytechnic Univ., Harvard Univ.; joined Exxon Chemical Co. 1960; Int. Paper Co. 1967–69; Talley Industries 1969–70; exec. positions in int. finance, RCA Corpn New York 1970–80; Sr Vice-Pres. and Chief Financial Officer, Saks 1980–84, Exec. Vice-Pres. for Admin. 1984-87, Sr Vice-Pres. and Group Chief Exec. Retail Div. BATUS Inc. 1987–90, Vice-Chair. Saks Fifth Avenue 1990–92; Chair. and CEO Sears Merchandise Group, Sears, Roebuck & Co. 1992–95, Chair., CEO Sears, Roebuck & Co. 1995–2000, now Chair. and CEO Emer.; Chair. HSN, Inc. 2008–; Chair. Abercrombie & Fitch Co. 2014–; Chair. Supervisory Bd ABN AMRO Holding NV (now Royal Bank of Scotland) 2006; fmr Chair. Nat. Retail Fed.; mem. Bd of Dirs American International Group, Inc., IAC/InterActive Corpn, Kate Spade & Co., International Flavors & Fragrances, Inc. 2000– (Lead Dir 2006–), Northwestern Univ., Greenwich Hospital, Art Inst. of Chicago, Chicago Symphony Orchestra Asscn, Polytechnic Univ., Maine Coast Heritage Trust; fmr mem. Bd of Dirs Amoco Corpn, Ameritech Corpn, Fed. Reserve Bank of Chicago, PepsiCo, Inc. 1999–2012; Hon. JD (Notre Dame) 1997. *Leisure interests:* gardening, golf, tennis. *Address:* Office of the Chairman, Abercrombie & Fitch Company, 6301 Fitch Path, New Albany, OH 43054, USA (office). *Website:* www.abercrombie.com (office).

MARTÍNEZ, Chus, MA; Spanish curator and writer; *Director, Institute of Art, FHNW Academy of Art and Design;* b. 1972, Ponteceso (La Coruña); ed Bard School, USA; worked at Fundación La Caixa 2001–02; Artistic Dir Sala Rekalde, Bilbao 2002–05; Dir Frankfurter Kunstverein 2005–08; Chief Curator, Museo de Arte Contemporanea Barcelona 2008–10; Head of Dept, Artistic Direction, dOCUMENTA (13) (quinquennial exhibition), Kassel, Germany 2009–12; Head Curator, Museo del Barrio, New York 2012–14; Guest Prof., FHNW Acad. of Art and Design, Basel, Switzerland 2013–, Dir Inst. of Art, FHNW Acad. of Art and Design 2014–; Founder German Börse Residency Program for int. artists, art writers and curators; Curator, Cypriot Pavilion at 50th Venice Biennale 2005, Curatorial Adviser, 29th Bienal de São Paulo 2010; Fulbright Scholarship. *Publications:* regular contrib. to Artforum among other international art journals. *Address:* FHNW Academy of Art and Design, Freilager-Platz 1, 4123 Basel, Switzerland (office). *Telephone:* 612284411 (office). *E-mail:* direktion.hgk@fhnw.ch (office). *Website:* www.fhnw.ch/hgk (office).

MARTINEZ, Conchita; Spanish fmr professional tennis player; b. 16 April 1972, Monzón; d. of Cecilio Martínez and Conchita Martínez; turned professional 1988; reached last 16 French Open 1988; Singles: quarter-finals French Open 1989, 1990, 1991, 1992, 1993, 1999, 2003, WTA Championships 1990, 1992, 1993, 1994, 1995, 1996, 2000, US Opens 2001, Olympic Games 1992, Australian Open 1994, 1996, Wimbledon 2001; semi-finals Italian Open 1991, French Open 1994, 1995, 1996, Australian Opens 1995, US Opens 1995, 1996, French Opens 1995, 1996, Wimbledon 1995; finals Australian Open 1998, French Open 2000; winner, Wimbledon 1994 (first Spanish woman to win title); Doubles: quarter-finals Australian Open 1993, 1997, 2003, French Open 1993, 1997, 1998, 2000, 2004, Wimbledon 1995, 2003, US Opens 1995, 1997, 2000, 2003, 2004, WTA Championships 1995, 1997, 1998, 1999; semi-finals Australian Open 1998, 2002, US Opens 2005; finals French Open 1992, 2001; won Olympic Doubles silver medal 1992, 2004, and bronze medal 1996; has won 43 WTA tour titles; Spanish Fed. Cup Team 1988–96, 1998, 2000–01; retd April 2006; currently commentator for Eurosport Spain, Canal+ and DirecTV in USA 2006–; Tournament Dir Andalucía Tennis Experience 2009–11; f. Conchita Martinez Sports Consultancy; Capt. Spain Fed Cup Team 2013–17; Capt. Spain Davis Cup Team 2015–17; fmr Coach Garbine Muguruza team; WTA Tour Most Impressive Newcomer 1989, Most Improved Player, Tennis Magazine 1994, ITF Award of Excellence 2001, Int. Tennis Hall of Fame 2001. *Leisure interests:* golf, horse riding, music, soccer, cinema, beach volleyball, skiing. *Website:* www.conchitamartinez.com.

MARTÍNEZ, Diógenes, DJur; Paraguayan lawyer and politician; b. 9 April 1947, Villarrica, Guairá; m. Celeste Franco Galeano; three c.; ed Univ. Nacional de Asunción, Colegio Nacional de Guerra; Clerk, Criminal Court of First Instance, Asunción 1970–73, Judge, Criminal Court of First Instance 1973–77; practice as lawyer 1977–88; State Solicitor-Gen. 1989–90; mem. Senate (upper house of parl.) 1993–98; Minister of Foreign Affairs 1993, of the Interior 1996; Adviser on int. policy to Ministry of Foreign Affairs 1996–98; Minister of Nat. Defence 2015–18; several roles with nat. football asscns including Sec. of the Bd, Liga Paraguaya de Fútbol 1973–76, mem. Int. Relations Dept, Asociación Paraguaya de Fútbol 2004; del. to several sessions of UN Gen. Ass.; mem. Int. Asscn of Lawyers; mem. Partido Colorado; Grand Cross, Orden del Cóndor de los Andes (Bolivia) 1993; Juan León Mallorquín Medal of Honour 1987, Medalla del Honor al Mérito del Fútbol Sudamericano 1998.

MARTINEZ, Jean-Luc; French archaeologist and museum director; *President and Director, Musée du Louvre;* b. 22 March 1964, Paris; m.; one s. one d.; ed École du Louvre; secondary school teacher, Paris 1990–92; joined École française d'Athènes (archaeological inst.) 1993, carried out excavations at Delos and Delphi, also worked on renovation of Delphi Archaeological Museum; taught history of art and archaeology, Inst. français de restauration des objets d'art, Univ. catholique de Paris and Univ. Paris X Nanterre –1997; Chief Curator of Greek Sculpture, Musée du Louvre 1997–2007, Dir, Dept of Greek, Etruscan and Roman Antiquities 2007–13, Pres. and Dir, Musée du Louvre 2013–; Chevalier, Légion d'honneur 2015. *Publications:* several exhibition guides and works on Greek and Roman sculpture. *Address:* Musée du Louvre, Rue de Rivoli, 75058 Paris, France (office). *Telephone:* (1) 40-20-53-17 (office). *Website:* www.louvre.fr (office).

MARTÍNEZ, Julio César; Argentine agronomist and politician; b. 23 March 1962, Chilecito, La Rioja Prov.; m. Laura Rebeca Waidatt; three c.; ed Nat. Univ. of

Cordoba; worked in family-owned agricultural business in production of olive oil; mem. La Rioja Provincial Legislature 1999–2003; mem. Cámara de Diputados (Parl.) for La Rioja Prov. 2003–07, 2009–13, 2013–, mem. Defence Cttee (fmr Pres. and later Vice-Pres.); Minister of Defence 2015–17; fmr Prof., State Univ. of La Rioja, Nat. Univ. of Chilecito, Nat. Univ. of La Rioja; mem. Unión Cívica Radical.

MARTINEZ, Mel; American (b. Cuban) lawyer, politician and business executive; *Chairman, Southeast and Latin America, JPMorgan Chase & Company;* b. (Melquíades Rafael Martínez Ruiz), 23 Oct. 1946, Sagua La Grande, Cuba; m. Kitty Martinez; two s. one d.; ed Florida State Univ. Coll. of Law; lawyer, Orlando, Fla 1973–98; Chair. Orange Co., Fla 1998–2001, providing urban services to residents; US Sec. of Housing and Urban Devt 2001–03; Senator from Florida 2005–09; Chair. Republican Party 2006–07; lobbyist and Partner, DLA Piper 2009–10; Chair. Chase Bank Florida and its operations in Mexico, Central America and the Caribbean 2010–13, Chair., Southeast and Latin America, JPMorgan Chase & Co. 2013–; Co-Chair. Housing Comm., Bipartisan Policy Center; fmr Chair. of Gov. Jeb Bush's Growth Man. Study Comm., of Bd Greater Orlando Aviation Authority, of Bd Orlando/Orange Co. Expressway Authority; Republican. *Publication:* A Sense of Belonging: From Castro's Cuba to the U.S. Senate, One Man's Pursuit of the American Dream (autobiog., with Ed Breslin) 2008. *Address:* JPMorgan Chase & Co., 270 Park Avenue, New York, NY 10017-2070, USA (office). *Telephone:* (212) 270-6000 (office). *E-mail:* info@jpmchase.com (office). *Website:* www.jpmorganchase.com (office).

MARTINEZ, Susana, BA, JD; American lawyer and politician; b. 14 July 1959, El Paso, Tex.; d. of Jacobo 'Jake' Martinez and Paula Martinez (née Aguirre); m. Chuck Franco 1991; one step-s.; ed Riverside High School, El Paso, Univ. of Texas, El Paso, Univ. of Oklahoma Coll. of Law; moved to Las Cruces, NM mid-1980s; Asst Dist Attorney, Doña Ana Co. Dist Attorney's Office, Dist Attorney, Third Judicial Dist of NM 1997–2011 (re-elected three times); Special Prosecutor, New Mexico Children, Youth and Families Dept; Gov. of New Mexico 2011–18 (first female gov. and first Latina/Hispanic gov. in USA); Republican; named Woman of the Year by Heart Magazine 2008, Prosecutor of the Year, Prosecutors Section of State Bar of NM 2010. *Address:* c/o Office of the Governor, 490 Old Santa Fe Trail, Room 400, Santa Fe, NM 87501, USA (office).

MARTÍNEZ ALVARADO, Richard, MBA; Ecuadorean economist, academic and politician; b. 1981, Loja; m.; four c.; ed Catholic Univ. of Ecuador, IDE Business School, Univ. of Barcelona, Spain, Miguel de Cervantes Univ., Chile; Project Coordinator, Office of Agricultural Studies 2003–05; Technical Dir Chamber of Industries and Production 2009–12, Exec. Vice-Pres. 2012–14, Exec. Pres. 2014–18; Pres. Ecuadorian Business Cttee 2015–18, Nat. Fed. of Chambers of Industries, Ecuador 2015; Minister of Economy and Finance 2018–18; fmr Prof. of Econs Catholic Univ., Quito; mem. Exec. Cttee Consultative, Productive and Tax Council, Govt of Ecuador 2017; José Corsino Cárdenas.

MARTÍNEZ BONILLA, Hugo Roger; Salvadorean agronomist, politician and international organization official; b. 2 Jan. 1968, Concepción de Oriente; m.; ed Univ. of El Salvador, Univ. of Toulouse, France, Cen. American Univ., Nicaragua, Latin American Univ. of Science and Tech., Costa Rica; Sec.-Gen., Soc. of Salvadorean Students of Agricultural Sciences 1988; fmr Asst to Sec.-Gen., Univ. Superior Council of Cen. America; Dir of External Co-operation, Univ. of El Salvador 2000–09; joined Frente Farabundo Martí para la Liberación Nacional (FMLN), Nat. Youth Co-ordinator 1993–95, Substitute Deputy to FMLN Group in Parl. 1994–97, mem. FMLN Political Comm. 1999–2001, MP for San Salvador 2003–, Assoc. Co-ordinator, FMLN Parl. Group 2008–09, Pres., Foreign Affairs, Cen. American Integration and Salvadoreans Overseas Parl. Comm., mem. Consultative Comm., Ministry of Foreign Relations 2000–09, Minister of Foreign Affairs 2009–13, 2014–18; Sec.-Gen., Cen. American Integration System (Sistema de la Integración Centroamericana—SICA) 2013–14; cand. in presidential election 2019. *Address:* c/o Frente Farabundo Martí para la Liberación Nacional (FMLN), 27 Calle Poniente, Col. Layco 1316, San Salvador, El Salvador (office). *Telephone:* 2226-0899 (office). *Website:* www.fmln.org.sv (office).

MARTÍNEZ DE PERÓN, María Estela (Isabelita); Argentine politician and fmr dancer; b. 6 Feb. 1931, La Rioja Prov.; m. Gen. Juan Domingo Perón (Pres. of Argentina 1946–55, 1973–74) 1961 (died 1974); joined troupe of travelling folk dancers; danced in cabaret in several S American countries; met her future husband during his exile in Panama, lived in Spain 1960–73, returned to Argentina with Juan Perón, became Vice-Pres. of Argentina 1973–74, Pres. 1974–76 (deposed by mil. coup); Chair. Peronist Party 1974–85; detained under house arrest 1976–81; settled in Madrid, Spain 1985; arrested 2007 on Argentine warrant to testify about forced disappearances during her presidency, extradition denied by Spanish courts 2008.

MARTÍNEZ MARTÍNEZ, José Manuel; Spanish business executive; b. 15 July 1947, Murcia; ed Madrid Univ.; graduated as public works engineer, economist and actuary; began career at MAPFRE in 1972, first assigned to newly created dept of eng and construction risk insurance, acquired his first man. experience as Chief Exec. of re-insurance subsidiary, co. merged into holding co. Corporación MAPFRE 1985, Chief Exec. MAPFRE's listed holding co., Chair. MAPFRE VIDA 1996–2001, Chair. and CEO MAPFRE SA 2001–12, currently Hon. Chair., Chair. Fundación MAPFRE; mem. Bd of Dirs Consorcio Espafrol de Seguros, Consorcio de Compensacion de Seguros Fundación Carolina (Govt-sponsored foundation for Latin American scholarships), Banco de Sabadell 2013–; Hon. mem. Fundación Carlos III 2002, Alumni Asscn of ENAE Business School, Madrid 2006; Distinguished Service Award, Int. Insurance Soc. 1995, Los Mejores de 1997, La Verdad newspaper, Murcia 1997, Award International Character 2001, Academia Nacional de Seguros e Previdencia (Brazil) 2001, Dirigentes Award, Dirigentes Magazine 2002, Management Award, Confederación Española de Directivos y Ejecutivos 2006, Insurance Hall of Fame Award, Int. Insurance Soc. 2007, Gold Medal, Latin American Commerce Chambers (AICO) 2007, Tiepolo Award, Italian Chamber in Spain and Chamber of Commerce of Madrid 2007. *Address:* c/o MAPFRE SA, Carretera de Pozuelo-Majadahonda 52, 28220 Majadahonda, Madrid, Spain. *E-mail:* info@mapfre.com.

MARTÍNEZ SISTACH, HE Cardinal Lluís, DCL; Spanish ecclesiastic; *Archbishop Emeritus of Barcelona;* b. 29 April 1937, Barcelona; s. of Joan Martínez Puig and Maria Sistach Masllorens; ed Pontifical Lateran Univ., Rome; ordained priest

in Barcelona 1961; worked with Catholic Action and was notary on Barcelona's archdiocesan tribunal; Sec., then Judge of the Ecclesiastical Tribunal of Barcelona; apptd Vice-Gen. Archdiocese of Barcelona 1979; elected pres. of Spain's asscn of canonists in 1983, and taught canon law for several years; Auxiliary Bishop of Barcelona and Titular Bishop of Aliezira 1987–91; Bishop of Tortosa 1991–97; Archbishop of Tarragona 1997–2004, of Barcelona 2004–15, Archbishop Emer. 2015–; cr. Cardinal (Cardinal-Priest of San Sebastiano alle Catacombe) 2007; participated in Papal Conclave 2013; mem. Apostolic Signature (a Vatican court), Pontifical Council for Legis. Texts, Pontifical Council for the Laity, Prefecture for Econ. Affairs of the Holy See; apptd a Synod Father for the 13th Ordinary Gen. Ass. of the Synod of Bishops on the New Evangelization Oct. 2012; Gold Medal, Universitat Ramon Llull 2011, Lawyer of the Roman Rota, Granted by Pope Francis 2017. *Address:* Arzobispado, Carrer del Bisbe 5, 08002 Barcelona, Spain (office). *Telephone:* (93) 270-1012 (office). *Fax:* (93) 270-1303 (office). *E-mail:* webpalau@arqbcn.cat (office). *Website:* www.arqbcn.org (office).

MARTÍNEZ SOMALO, HE Cardinal Eduardo, DCL; Spanish ecclesiastic; *Chamberlain Emeritus of the Apostolic Chamber;* b. 31 March 1927, Baños de Río Tobía, La Rioja; ed diocesan seminary of Logroño, Pontifical Spanish Coll., Pontifical Gregorian Univ., Pontifical Ecclesiastical Acad., Pontifical Lateran Univ.; ordained 1950, pastoral and curial work in Calahorra; Prof., Pontifical Ecclesiastical Acad.; entered the Roman Curia, in the Secr. of State, later Head of Spanish section; elevated to rank of Mgr 1970; apptd Apostolic Nuncio to Colombia 1975; consecrated Archbishop of Thagora 1975; Substitute for Gen. Affairs 1979–88; cr. Cardinal (Cardinal-Deacon of Santissimo Nome di Gesù) 1988, Cardinal Protodeacon 1996–99, Cardinal-Priest of Santissimo Nome di Gesù 1999; Prefect Congregation for Divine Worship and the Discipline of the Sacraments 1988–92, Congregation for Insts of Consecrated Life and for Socs of Apostolic Life 1992–2004; Chamberlain (Camerlengo) of the Apostolic Chamber 1993–2007; mem. Pontifical Comm. for Latin America, Congregations for Evangelization of Peoples, for the Clergy, for Catholic Educ.; participated as a Cardinal-elector in the Papal Conclave 2005. *Address:* c/o Palazzo delle Congregazioni, Piazza Pio XII 3, 00193 Rome, Italy.

MARTÍNEZ VINUEZA, Diego Alfredo, BSc, MA; Ecuadorean economist and central banker; *General Manager, Banco Central del Ecuador;* b. 31 Aug. 1978; ed Colegio San Gabriel, Pontificia Universidad Católica del Ecuador, Inst. of Social Studies, The Hague, Netherlands; Planning and Projects Man., Inst. for Regional Eco-Devt, Quito 2004; Research Asst, Econ. Devt Programme, Inst. of Social Studies, The Hague 2004–05; Researcher, Latin American School of Social Sciences, Quito 2006–07; Under-Sec. for Planning, Public Policy and Investment, Nat. Secr. for Planning and Devt, Quito 2007–08, Under-Sec. for Public Investment 2008–09, Under-Sec.-Gen. for Planning and Devt 2009–10, Under-Sec.-Gen. for Planning and Sec., Nat. Planning Bd 2011; Adviser to Nat. Sec. for Higher Educ., Science, Tech. and Innovation 2011–12, Under-Sec.-Gen. for Science, Tech. and Innovation 2012–13; Pres. Banco Central del Ecuador 2013, Gen. Man. 2015–. *Address:* Banco Central del Ecuador, Avda 10 de Agosto N11-409 y Briceño, Casilla 339, Quito, Ecuador (office). *Telephone:* (2) 257-2522 (office). *Fax:* (2) 258-3059 (office). *E-mail:* info@bce.ec (office). *Website:* www.bce.fin.ec (office).

MARTINO, Antonio; Italian politician and university lecturer; b. 22 Dec. 1944, Messina, Sicily; s. of Gaetano Martino; Lecturer in Monetary History and Politics, Libera Università Internazionale degli Studi Sociali (LUISS), Rome, Chair. Faculty of Political Science and mem. Bd of Dirs; mem. Italian Liberal Party (PLI) –1994; mem. Forza Italia party 1994–2008, 2013–; Parl. Deputy 1994–; mem. The People of Freedom 2009–13; Minister for Foreign Affairs 1994–95, of Defence 2001–06; Pres. Mont Pelerin Soc. 1988–90. *Publication:* Stato Padrone. *Address:* Forza Italia, Via dell'Umiltà 36, 00187 Rome, Italy (office). *Telephone:* (06) 6731381 (office). *E-mail:* lettere@forzaitalia.it (office). *Website:* www.forzaitalia.it (office); www.antoniomartino.org.

MARTINO, HE Cardinal Renato Raffaele, JCD; Italian ecclesiastic; *President Emeritus, Pontifical Council for Justice and Peace;* b. 23 Nov. 1932, Salerno; ordained priest 1957; entered Diplomatic Service of the Holy See, serving in Nicaragua, the Philippines, Lebanon and Brazil 1962–80; Titular Archbishop of Segermes 1980; Apostolic Pro-Nuncio to Thailand and Singapore and Apostolic Del. to Laos and Malaysia 1980, Apostolic Del. to Brunei Darussalam 1983; Perm. Observer of the Holy See to the UN 1986–2002, participated in Conf. of Sustainable Devt, Rio de Janeiro, Brazil 1992, Conf. on Population Devt, Cairo, Egypt 1994, Summit on Women, Beijing, China 1995, Conf. on Sustainable Devt, Johannesburg, SA 2002; Pres. Pontifical Council for Justice and Peace 2002–09 (now Pres. Emer.), Pontifical Council for Pastoral Care of Migrants and Itinerant Peoples 2006–09 (now Pres. Emer.); cr. Cardinal (Cardinal-Deacon of S. Francesco di Paola ai Monti) 2003; participated in Papal Conclave April 2005; Cardinal Protodeacon 2014; Grand Prior, Sacred Mil. Constantinian Order of St George 2010–; decorations from govts of Italy, Portugal, Thailand, Argentina, Venezuela, Lebanon; eight hon. doctorates.

MARTINON, David, DEA; French civil servant and diplomatist; *Ambassador to Afghanistan;* b. 13 May 1971, Leiden, Netherlands; ed Institut d'études politiques, École nationale d'administration; began career as communications officer, États généraux de l'opposition 1990; communications adviser, Acte Public Communication 1991–94, Ministry of Defence 1995–98; Deputy Spokesman, Ministry of Foreign Affairs 1998–2001; Diplomatic Adviser to Minister of the Interior, Nicolas Sarkozy 2002–04, 2005–07; served as Dir of Int. Relations, Union pour un Mouvement Populaire (UMP); Chief of Staff, presidential campaign of Nicolas Sarkozy 2006–07; Spokesman for the Pres. 2007–08; apptd Special Rep. to int. negotiations on the information society and digital economy, Ministry of Foreign Affairs and Int. Devt 2013, Amb. to Afghanistan 2018–. *Address:* Embassy of France, Cherpour Ave, Shar-i-Nau, POB 62, Kabul, Afghanistan (office). *Telephone:* (20) 2105293. *E-mail:* consul@ambafrance-af.org. *Website:* af.ambafrance .org (office).

MARTINS, Geraldo João; Guinea-Bissau economist and politician; ed Univ. of London; fmr Assoc. Researcher, Nat. Inst. of Studies and Research of Guinea-Bissau (INEP); fmrly worked as Task Team Project Leader with World Bank, specialising in educ. issues; Minister of Educ. 2001–03; Minister of the Economy and Finance 2014–16. *Address:* c/o Ministry of the Economy and Finance, Avenida dos Combatentes da Liberdade da Pátria, CP 67, Bissau, Guinea-Bissau (office).

MARTINS, Peter; Danish ballet director (retd), choreographer and fmr dancer; b. 27 Oct. 1946, Copenhagen; m. 1st Lise la Cour (divorced 1973); one s.; m. 2nd Darci Kistler 1991; one d.; ed pupil of Vera Volkova and Stanley Williams with Royal Danish Ballet; mem. Royal Danish Ballet 1965–67, Prin. Dancer (including Bournonville repertory) 1967; Guest Artist, New York City Ballet 1967–70, Prin. Dancer 1970–83; Guest Artist, Regional Ballet Cos, USA, also Nat. Ballet, Canada, Royal Ballet, London, Grand Theatre, Geneva, Paris Opera, Vienna State Opera, Munich State Opera, London Festival Ballet, Ballet Int., Royal Danish Ballet; teacher, School of American Ballet 1975; teacher, New York City Ballet 1975–81, Ballet Master 1981–83, Co-Ballet Master-in-Chief 1983–89, Ballet Master-in-Chief 1990–2018 (retd); Artistic Adviser, Philadelphia Ballet 1982–; Knight of The First Order of Dannebrog 1983; Dance magazine Award 1977, Cue's Golden Apple Award 1977, Man of the Year, Danish American Soc. 1980, Award of Merit, Phila Art Alliance 1985, inducted into Nat. Museum of Dance's Mr & Mrs Cornelius Vanderbilt Whitney Hall of Fame 2008. *Choreographed works include:* Calcium Light Night 1977, Tricolore (Pas de Basque Section) 1978, Rossini Pas de Deux 1978, Tango-Tango (ice ballet) 1978, Dido and Aeneas 1979, Sonate di Scarlatti 1979, Eight Easy Pieces 1980, Lille Suite 1980, Suite from L'Histoire du Soldat 1981, Capriccio Italien 1981, The Magic Flute 1981, Symphony No. 1 1981, Délibes Divertissement 1982, Piano-Rag-Music 1982, Concerto for Two Solo Pianos 1982, Waltzes 1983, Rossini Quartets 1983, Tango 1983, A Schubertiad 1984, Mozart Violin Concerto 1984, Poulenc Sonata 1985, La Sylphide 1985, Valse Triste 1985, Eight More 1985, We Are the World 1985, Eight Miniatures 1985, Ecstatic Orange, Tanzspiel 1988, Jazz 1993, Symphonic Dances 1994, Barber Violin Concerto 1994, Mozart Piano Concerto (No. 17) 1994, X-Ray 1995. *Choreographed Broadway musicals include:* Dream of the Twins (co-choreographer) 1982, On your Toes 1982, Song and Dance 1985. *Publications:* Far From Denmark (autobiog.) 1982, NYCB Workout 1997. *Address:* c/o New York City Ballet, David H. Koch Theater, 20 Lincoln Center, New York, NY 10023, USA (office).

MARTINSON, Ida Marie, PhD; American nurse; *Professor Emerita, School of Nursing, University of California, San Francisco;* b. 8 Nov. 1936, Mentor, Minn.; m. Paul Martinson 1962; one s. one d.; ed St Luke's Hosp. School of Nursing, Duluth, Minn. and Univs of Minnesota and Illinois; Instructor in Tuberculosis Nursing, St Luke's Hosp., Duluth 1957–58; Instructor in Nursing, Thornton Jr Coll., Harvey, Ill. 1967–69; Asst Prof. and Chair. of Research, Univ. of Minn. School of Nursing 1972–74, Assoc. Prof. and Dir of Research 1974–77, Prof. and Dir of Research 1977–82; Prof. Dept of Family Health Care Nursing, Univ. of Calif., San Francisco 1982–2003, now Prof. Emer., Chair. 1982–89; Carl Walter and Margaret Davis Walter Visiting Prof. at Payne Bolton School of Nursing, Case Western Reserve Univ., Cleveland, Ohio 1994–96; Chair. and Prof., Dept of Health Sciences, Hong Kong Polytechnic Univ. 1996–2000, now Advisor, Hong Kong Polytechnic Univ. Honor Soc. of Nursing; Fellow, American Acad. of Nursing; mem. Inst. of Medicine, NAS 1981–, mem. Governing Council 1984–86; Pres. Children's Hospice Int. 1986–88; Co-founder of Children's Cancer Foundation, Taiwan; f. East Asia Forum of Nursing Schools (EAFONS); Sigma Theta Tau Int. Soc. of Nursing 1999. *Publications:* Home Care: A manual for implementation of home care for children dying of cancer 1978, Home Care: A manual for parents (with D. Moldow) 1979, Family Nursing 1989, Home Care Health Nursing 1989; more than 100 articles in journals, 56 book chapters (1994) and one film; ed. of several books on home and family nursing. *Leisure interests:* skiing, walking, reading. *Address:* Department of Family Health Care Nursing, Box 0606, 521 Parnassus Ave, Nursing 431Y, University of California, San Francisco, San Francisco, CA 94143-0606, USA (office). *Telephone:* (415) 476-4668 (office). *Fax:* (415) 753-2161 (office). *E-mail:* ida.martinson@nursing.ucsf.edu (office). *Website:* nurseweb.ucsf.edu/www/ix-fd.shtml (office).

MARTIROSSIAN, Radick Martirosovich, PhD, DeS; Armenian scientist, fmr university rector and academic; *Head of Chair, Department of Microwave Radiophysics and Telecommunications, Yerevan State University;* b. 1 May 1936, Madagis, Nagorno Karabakh; s. of Martiros A. Martirossian and Astkhik G. Harutunian; m. Rena A. Kasparova 1965, two s.; ed Yerevan State Univ. and Lebedev Physics Inst. of Acad. of Sciences, Moscow; Assoc. Prof., Yerevan State Univ. 1966–82, Prof. 1982–, Rector 1993–2006; Corresp. mem. Nat. Acad. of Sciences of Armenia 1986, Academician 1990, Pres. 2006–, fmr Dir Inst. of Radiophysics and Electronics, Adviser to the Dir 2006–; Order of the St Mesrop Mashtots, several orders and medals of Armenia and USSR; Armenian State Prize in Science and Eng 1988, Ukrainian State Prize 1989, Gagarin Medal for Space Research, Laureate of Armenian and Ukrainian State Prizes. *Publications:* numerous papers on quantum electronics, applied problems of superconductivity, space research, radio astronomy, radio physics research methods of remote sensing of Earth. *Leisure interest:* chess. *Address:* Faculty of Radiophysics, Yerevan State University, 1 Alex Manoogian Street, 0025 Yerevan, Armenia. *Telephone:* (10) 55-52-40. *Fax:* (10) 55-46-41. *E-mail:* radiophys@ysu.am. *Website:* www.ysu.am/faculties/en/Radiophysics/section/staff/person/280.

MARTIROSYAN, Grigori, BA, MA; Armenian economist and politician; *Minister of State, 'Republic of Nagornyi Karabakh (Artsakh)';* b. 14 Nov. 1978, Stepanakert, Nagornyi Karabakh Autonomous Oblast, Azerbaijan SSR, USSR; m.; three c.; ed Artsakh State Univ., Yerevan State Univ.; Economist, Dept of Statistics, State Register and Analysis, 'Repub. of Nagornyi Karabakh' 1998–99; Leading Specialist, State Procurement Agency 2000–05, Deputy Head 2007–08; Chief Specialist, Ministry of Finance and Economy, 'Repub. of Nagornyi Karabakh' 2005–07, Deputy Minister of Finance 2008–15, First Deputy Minister of Finance 2015–17, Minister of Finance 2017–18; Minister of State, Repub. of Nagornyi Karabakh (Artsakh)' 2018–; Lecturer, Artsakh State Univ. 2010–; Anania Shirakatsi Medal. *Address:* Office of the Minister of State, 75000 Stepanakert, Petrvari 20 poghots 1, 'Republic of Nagornyi Karabakh (Artsakh)', Azerbaijan (office). *Telephone:* (47) 94-32-14 (office). *E-mail:* info@gov.nkr.am (office). *Website:* gov.nkr.am (office).

MARTO, Michel Issa, BSc, MA, PhD; Jordanian economist, banker and fmr government official; b. 21 Aug. 1940, Jerusalem; s. of Issa Marto; m. Lucy Peridakis 1970; one s. two d.; ed Middle East Tech. Univ., Turkey, Univ. of Southern California, Stanford Univ., USA; Dir Econ. Research, Central Bank of Jordan 1969–70, Deputy Gov. 1989–97; Dir Econ. Research, Royal Scientific Soc. 1970–75; economist, World Bank, Washington, DC 1975–77; Deputy Gen. Man. Jordan Fertilizer Industry 1977–79; Deputy Gen. Man. Bank of Jordan 1979–86, Man. Dir 1986–89; Chair. Jordanian Securities Comm. 1997–98; Minister of Finance 1998–2003; Chair. Housing Bank for Trade and Finance, Amman 2004–16; Chevalier, Ordre nat. du Mérite, Commdr, Légion d'honneur; Al-Hussein Distinguished Service Medal, Jordanian Star Medal (First Class), Jordanian Independence Medal (First Class), Jordan Star Medal (Second Order), Jordan Star Medal (First Order), Omicron Delta Epsilon (Honor Soc. in Econs), USA, Phi Kappa Phi (Top Univ. Grad.), USA. *Publications include:* various articles on economic topics in specialist journals. *Leisure interests:* reading, music, theatre. *Address:* PO Box 2927, Amman 11118, Jordan. *Telephone:* (6) 5926745 (home). *Fax:* (6) 5930718 (home). *E-mail:* michelmarto1@yahoo.com (home).

MARTONYI, János, PhD; Hungarian lawyer and politician; b. 5 April 1944, Kolozsvár (now Cluj-Napoca, Romania); m.; one s. one d.; ed József Attila Univ., Szeged, City of London Coll., Hague Acad. of Int. Law, The Netherlands, Hungarian Acad. of Sciences; corp. lawyer 1969–79; Trade Sec., Brussels 1979–84; Head of Dept then Sr Head of Dept, Ministries of Foreign Trade and Trade 1984–89; Commr for Privatization 1989–90; State Sec., Ministry of Int. Econ. Relations 1990–91, Ministry of Foreign Affairs 1991–94, Minister of Foreign Affairs 1998–2002, 2010–14; Pres. Council of the EU Jan.–June 2011; Lecturer, Faculty of Law and Public Admin, Eötvös Loránd Univ., Budapest 1987–90, Prof. 1990–97; Head of Inst. for Int. Trade Law and Head of Dept, József Attila Univ., Szeged 1997–2002; Visiting Prof., Coll. of Europe, Bruges, Belgium and Natolin, Poland 1995–98, Cen. European Univ., Budapest 1996; full-time Prof. and Man. Partner, Martonyi és Kajtár, Baker & McKenzie (law firm), Budapest office 2002–09; Chair. Nézőpont Inst., Budapest; Pres. Free Europe Centre for European Integration of the Fidesz Hungarian Civic Union; Perm. Guest of Fidesz Presidium; mem. Bd Perm. Arbitration Court of Hungarian Chamber of Commerce and Industry Exec. Bd Centre for European Studies (foundation of European People's Party based in Brussels), Batthyány Soc. of Profs, Advisory Bd Heti Válasz (weekly), Budapest Chamber of Attorneys, Hungarian Lawyers' Soc., European Acad. of Sciences and Arts; Commdr, Légion d'honneur, Grosses Goldenes Ehrenzeichen (Austria) 2000. *Publications include:* numerous articles and essays in various languages in the fields of int. trade law, competition policy and competition law, European integration and community (European) law, global regulations, co-operation in Cen. Europe and int. politics.

MARTORE, Gracia, BA, MBA; American business executive; *President and CEO, Gannett Company;* ed Wellesley Coll.; worked in banking industry 1973–85; joined Gannett as Asst Treas. 1985, Vice-Pres. in Treasury group 1993–98, added Investor Relations duties 1995–98, Treas. 1998–2003, Vice-Pres., Investor Relations 1998–2001, Sr Vice-Pres. of Finance 2001–03, Sr Vice-Pres. and Chief Financial Officer (CFO) 2003–05, mem. Man. Cttee 2003–, Exec. Vice-Pres. and CFO 2005–10, Pres. and COO 2010–11, mem. Bd of Dirs, Pres. and CEO Gannett Co., Inc. 2011–; mem. Bd of Dirs FM Global, MeadWestvaco Corpn 2012–. *Address:* Gannett Co., 7950 Jones Branch Drive, McLean, VA 22107-0150, USA (office). *Telephone:* (703) 854-6000 (office). *Fax:* (703) 854-2053 (office). *E-mail:* info@gannett.com (office). *Website:* www.gannett.com (office).

MARTOWARDOJO, Agus, BA; Indonesian central banker and government official; b. 24 Jan. 1956, Amsterdam, Netherlands; m.; two c.; ed Univ. of Indonesia; Int. Loan Officer, Bank of America, Jakarta 1984–86; Vice-Pres., Corp. Banking Group, Bank Niaga, Jakarta 1986–94; Deputy CEO Empress Holding 1994; Pres. Dir Bank Bumiputera 1995–98; Pres. Dir Export Import Bank of Indonesia 1998–2002; Man. Dir of Risk Man. and Credit Restructuring, Bank Mandiri 1999–2000, Man. Dir of Retail Banking and Operations Coordinator 2000–01, Man. Dir of Human Resources and Support Services 2001–02, Pres. Dir 2005–10; Pres. Dir Bank Permata 2002–05; Minister of Finance and State Enterprises Devt 2010–13; also worked with Indonesian Bank Restructuring Agency 2002–05; Gov. Bank Indonesia (central bank) 2013–18; Chair. Asscn of Nat. Commercial Banks Pvt. 2003–06; Pres. Bankers Club Indonesia 2000–03, Indonesia Bankers Asscn 2005; Best Indonesian Exec., Asiamoney 2006, Leadership Achievement Award, Asia Banker 2006, Top Banker, Majalah Investor 2007, Best CEO Warta Ekonomi magazine 2008, Top Banking Exec., Majalah Investor 2008.

MARTY, Martin E., MDiv, PhD, STM; American ecclesiastic and academic; *Fairfax M. Cone Distinguished Service Professor Emeritus of the History of Modern Christianity, Divinity School, University of Chicago;* b. 5 Feb. 1928, West Point, Neb.; s. of Emil A. Marty and Anne Louise Wuerdemann Marty; m. 1st Elsa Schumacher 1952 (died 1981); seven c.; m. 2nd Harriet Lindemann 1982; ed Concordia Seminary, St Louis, Lutheran School of Theology, Chicago and Univ. of Chicago; Lutheran Minister 1952–63; Prof. of History of Modern Christianity, Univ. of Chicago 1963–98, Fairfax M. Cone Distinguished Service Prof. 1978–98, now Prof. Emer., mem. Advisory Bd Martin Marty Center; Assoc. Ed. The Christian Century 1956–85, Sr Ed. 1985–98; Sr Scholar-in-Residence, Park Ridge Center 1985, Pres. 1985–89; Pres. American Soc. of Church History 1971, American Catholic History Asscn 1981, American Acad. of Religion 1988; Dir Fundamentalism project, American Acad. of Arts and Sciences 1988–94, The Public Religion Project 1996–99; Fellow, AAAS, Soc. of American Historians; more than 70 hon. degrees; Nat. Book Award for Righteous Empire 1972, Nat. Medal Humanities 1997, Medal of AAAS, Univ. of Chicago Alumni Medal, Distinguished Service Medal, Order of Lincoln Medallion. *Publications include:* Modern American Religion 1997, The One and the Many: America's Search for the Common Good 1998, The Mystery of the Child 2007, The Christian World: A Global History 2007, Building Cultures of Trust 2010, Dietrich Bonhoeffer's Letters and Papers from Prison: A Biography 2011; collaborated with photographer Micah Marty in producing Places Along the Way 1994, Our Hope for Years to Come 1995, The Promise of Winter 1997, When True Simplicity Is Gained 1998. *Leisure interests:* good eating, baroque music, calligraphy. *Address:* 175 East Delaware, #85081, Chicago, IL 60611, USA (home). *E-mail:* memarty@aol.com (home). *Website:* www.illuminos.com; divinity.uchicago.edu/martin-marty-center.

MARTYNAU, Syarhey Mikalayevich; Belarusian politician and diplomatist; b. 22 Feb. 1953, Leninakan (Gyumri), Armenian SSR, USSR; m.; two s.; ed Moscow State Inst. of Int. Econ. Relations, USSR; with Dept of Int. Econ. Orgs, Ministry of Foreign Affairs, USSR 1975–80, Asst to Minister of Foreign Affairs 1980–88, Deputy Head Dept of Int. Orgs 1988–91; Deputy Perm. Rep. of Repub. of Belarus to

UN, New York, 1991–92; Chargé d'Affaires, Washington, DC, 1992–93; Amb. to USA 1993–97; First Deputy Minister of Foreign Affairs 1997–2001; Amb. to Belgium, Head of Mission to EC and Head of Mission to NATO 2001–03; Minister of Foreign Affairs 2003–12; Vice-Chair. First Cttee (Int. Security and Disarmament) of UN Gen. Ass. 1988–97; fmr Vice-Pres. Amendment Conf. of the State Parties to the (1963) Treaty Banning Nuclear Tests in the Atmosphere in Outer Space and Under Water; three-times Chair. Nuclear Disarmament Group of UN Disarmament Comm., several-times Vice-Chair. and Rapporteur UN Disarmament Comm., Chair. 1998; Pres. Conf. on Disarmament, Geneva 2000; mem. UN Cttee on Econ., Cultural and Social Rights, Geneva 2001–; mem. Minsk Int. Educational Centre.

MARTYNOV, Aleksandr Vladimirovich; Moldovan accountant and government official; *Chairman of the Government, 'Transnistrian Moldovan Republic';* b. 12 Jan. 1981, Tiraspol, Moldovan SSR, USSR; m.; two d.; ed Tiraspol Coll. of Informatics and Law, Acad. of Econ. Knowledge, Chişinău, Russian Acad. of Nat. Economy and Public Admin under the Pres. of Russian Fed., Moscow, training courses with Ernst & Young, Kyiv and PricewaterhouseCoopers, Moscow; worked as Head of Econ. Dept of Sheriff sports club, Finance Dir of CJSC Tiraspol Bakery, Head of State Service of Tax Policy and Methodology of Accounting of Ministry of Finance, adviser to Chair. of Supreme Council of 'Transnistrian Moldovan Republic'; expert of Russian journal Korporativnaya Finansovaya Otchetnost (Corporate Financial Reporting); mem. Cen. Expert Council, IFRS Professional, Moscow; Chair. of the Govt, 'Transnistrian Moldovan Republic' 2016–. *Publications:* author and teacher of special courses for professional economists and accountants. *Address:* Office of the Chairman of the Government, 3300 Tiraspol, ul. 25 Oktyabrya 45, Moldova (office). *Telephone:* (533) 6-24-43 (office). *E-mail:* office@gov-pmr.org (office). *Website:* gov-pmr.org (office).

MARUKYAN, Edmon, LLB, LLM, LLM; Armenian lawyer and politician; *Leader, Lusavor Hayastan (LH—Bright Armenia);* b. 13 Jan. 1981, Kirovakan (now Vanadzor, Lori Marz), Armenian SSR, USSR; m.; two s.; ed School 6, Vanadzor, Moscow Inst. of Commerce and Law, Russian Fed., Public Admin Acad. of the Repub. of Armenia, Univ. of Minnesota Law School (Hubert H. Humphrey Fellow), USA, numerous specialized advocacy and human rights training courses in Armenia, Poland, Hungary, USA, Switzerland, Denmark, France, Germany and Russia; served in Armenian Army; actively involved in human rights activism 2001–, head of several non-govt human rights orgs; Head of Legal Dept, Media Group non-governmental org. (NGO) 2002–04; mem. Public Monitoring Group, Police Detention Centre 2005–, Group Leader and Co-ordinator of activities of the group 2006–; mem. monitoring group in penitentiary insts and bodies of Ministry of Justice 2005–; qualified as a Specialist for the Protection of Human Rights and Interests, Helsinki Foundation for Human Rights 2006; Founding mem. Int. Org. for Human Rights Educ. 2006–; Lecturer in Philosophy and Political Science, Vanadzor State Univ. 2007–08; Partner, Populex Ltd law firm 2007–12; mem. Chamber of Advocates of Armenia 2008–; Sr Lawyer, Advocacy and Assistance Centre of Lori Marz 2009; Co-founder Centre for Strategic Trials 2010; mem. Azgayin Zhoghov (Nat. Ass.) for 30th Electoral Dist 2012–17, on proportional list of Yeql dashniq (Exit Alliance) 2017–; Leader, Lusavor Hayastan (LH—Bright Armenia) party 2015–; Chair. 'Center for Strategic Litigations' Human Rights NGO 2008–. *Publications:* articles and reports on human rights in Armenia. *Address:* 0028 Yerevan, Lusavor Hayastan (Bright Armenia), Marshal Baghramyan poghota 1, Armenia (office). *Telephone:* (10) 52-39-01 (office). *E-mail:* brightarmenia@gmail.com (office). *Website:* brightarmenia.am (office); edmonmarukyan.com.

MARURAI, Jim; Cook Islands politician; b. 9 July 1947; m. Tuainekore Au Tamariki Marurai (died 2005); ed Tereora Coll., Rarotonga, Otago Univ., NZ; Prime Minister 2004–10, also Minister of Educ. 1999, Human Resources and Police, Head of State Telecommunications and Information Broadcasting 2004, Minister of Foreign Affairs and Finance 2009–10, of Educ., Police Dept, Public Service Comm. and Nat. Environment Service 2010; MP for Ivirua; mem. Democratic Party. *Address:* Democratic Party, PO Box 73, Rarotonga, Cook Islands (office). *Telephone:* 21224 (office). *E-mail:* demo1@oyster.net.ck (office).

MARUSIN, Yury Mikhailovich; Russian singer (tenor); b. 8 Dec. 1945, Kizel, Perm Region; ed Leningrad State Conservatory; soloist, Maly Opera and Ballet Theatre, Leningrad 1972–80; soloist, Mariinsky Theatre 1980–90; guest soloist, Wiener Staatsoper 1986–91; toured to Italy, France, Spain, the USA, Japan, China, Canada, Belgium, The Netherlands, Sweden, Finland, Switzerland, Austria, Luxemburg and Israel; Order of Honour 2008; Best Foreign Singer Diploma (Italy) 1982, People's Artist of USSR 1983, USSR State Prize 1985. *Repertoire includes:* over 50 parts in operas. *Recordings include:* The Queen of Spades, Ruslan and Lyudmila, Khovanshchina, Gianni Schicchi, La forza del destino, War and Peace, Iolanta, All about You, My Russia and Georgy Sviridov. *Address:* IMC Artists Management Inc., 51 MacDougal Street, Suite 300, New York, NY 10012, USA. *Telephone:* (212) 560-2221 (office). *E-mail:* imcartist@onebox.com (office).

MARUSTE, Rait, PhD; Estonian judge and politician; b. 27 Sept. 1953, Pärnu; s. of Albert Maruste and Mare Maruste; m. 1st Mare Maruste (née Nurk) 1976; one s. one d.; m. 2nd Elisabet Fura'ga; ed Pärnu Jaagupi Secondary School, Tartu Univ., University of Leningrad; Lecturer, Faculty of Law, Tartu Univ. 1977–85, Docent 1985–92, Head of Dept of Criminal Law and Procedure 1991; cand. for doctorate 1991–93; studies abroad at HEUNI, Finland, 1991, Åbo Akademi Univ., Finland 1991, Max Planck-Inst., Freiburg, Germany 1991, Univ. of Cambridge, UK 1992, Max Planck Inst., Heidelberg, Germany 1995, Centre For Advanced Studies, Oslo, Norway 2001; Chief Justice of Supreme Court 1992–98, Chair. (ex-officio) Constitutional Review Chamber 1998–; Judge (Section IV), European Court of Human Rights (ECHR) 1998–2010; mem. Estonian Reform Party 2010–; Chair. and Founding mem. Estonian Academic Law Soc., Bd of Estonian Law Centre Foundation, 1995–98; mem. Int. Soc. for the Reform of Criminal Law, Estonian Working Group for Accession to ECHR, Editorial Bd of law journal Juridica 1993–98, Comm. of Europe Drafting Cttee on Status of Judges in Europe 1998, Int. Justice in the World Prize Jury 2001–; Order of the White Star (Second Class) 1999. *Publications include:* (in Estonian): Human Rights and Principles of Fair Trial 1993, Constitution and Its Review 1997, Psychology (with Talis Bachmanniga) 2003, Constitutionalism and the Protection of Fundamental Rights and Freedoms 2004; more than 100 articles in journals. *Leisure interests:* sailing, skiing. *Address:* Estonian Reform Party, Tõnismägi 9, Tallinn 10119 (office); Pikk Str. 94, Apt. 27, 2400 Tartu, Estonia (home). *Telephone:* 680-80-80 (office). *E-mail:* info@raitmaruste.ee; info@reform.ee. *Website:* www.reform.ee/search/gss/Rait%20Maruste (office); www.raitmaruste.ee.

MARX, Anthony W., BS, MA, PhD; American political scientist, academic and university administrator; *President and CEO, New York Public Library;* b. 28 Feb. 1959, New York; m. Karen Barkey 1992; one s. one d.; ed Wesleyan, Yale and Princeton Univs; co-founder Khanya Coll., SA 1984; Asst to Pres. of Univ. of Pennsylvania 1981–84; Prof. of Political Science, Columbia Univ., New York 1990–2003, Co-Dir Center for Historical Social Studies, Faculty Dir Masters of Int. Affairs, Dir Undergraduate Studies and of Dept's Honors Program, Co-founder Columbia Urban Educators Program 2001, Dir Mellon Foundation's Sawyer Seminar on Democracy and Inequality 2001–02; Pres. Amherst Coll. 2003–11; Pres. and CEO, New York Public Library 2011–; consultant to UNDP 1991; Fellow, US Inst. of Peace 1992–93, Nat. Humanities Center 1997–98, Howard Foundation, Harry Frank Guggenheim Foundation 1994, John Simon Guggenheim Fellow 1997; Ralph Bunche Award, American Political Science Asscn 1999, Barrington Moore Award, American Sociological Asscn 2000. *Publications include:* Lessons of Struggle: South African Internal Opposition 1960–1990 1992, Making Race and Nation: A Comparison of the United States, South Africa and Brazil 1998, Faith in Nation: Exclusionary Origins in Nationalism 2002; numerous articles. *Address:* The New York Public Library, Stephen A. Schwarzman Building, Fifth Ave & 42nd Street, New York, NY 01018, USA (office). *Telephone:* (212) 930-0698 (office). *E-mail:* president@nypl.org (office). *Website:* www.nypl.org (office).

MARX, HE Cardinal Reinhard, DTh; German ecclesiastic; *Archbishop of Munich and Freising;* b. 21 Sept. 1953, Geseke, North Rhine-Westphalia; ordained priest, Diocese of Paderborn 1979; Auxiliary Bishop of Paderborn 1996–2001; Titular Bishop of Petina 1996–2001; Bishop of Trier 2001–07; Archbishop of Munich and Freising 2007–; Chair. Cttee for Social Issues at German Bishops' Conf. 2004–14; cr. Cardinal (Cardinal-Priest of San Corbiniano) 2010; participated in Papal Conclave 2013; Co-ordinator of the Secr. for the Economy 2014–. *Publication:* Das Kapital: A Plea for Man 2008. *Address:* Archdiocese of Munich and Freising, Postfach 330360, Rochusstrasse 5–7, 80063 Munich, Germany (office). *Telephone:* (89) 21370 (office). *Fax:* (89) 21371585 (office). *E-mail:* info@erzbistum-muenchen.de (office). *Website:* www.erzbistum-muenchen.de (office).

MARY, Sister Avelin, PhD, FIBR, FLS; Indian RC nun and marine biologist; *Director, Sacred Heart Marine Research Centre;* b. 5 May 1942, Sawyerpuram, Tuticorin dist, Tamil Nadu; d. of M. P. Raj and Annapooranam; ed Marathwada Univ., Aurangabad, postdoctoral research at New York Aquarium and Osborn Laboratories of Marine Science, USA; Asst Prof. in Zoology 1977; post-doctoral position, New York Aquarium 1985; involved in bioactive marine natural products research 1986–; Reader, Zoology, St Mary's Coll., Tuticorin 1993–97, Prin. 1997–2000; research collaboration with Poseidon Ocean Sciences, New York 1994–; Visiting Scientist working on research projects in biofouling (biological coating acquired on ships during years at sea) at Duke Univ. Marine Lab., Univ. of Delaware, Fu Jen Univ., Taiwan, Tulane Univ., Univ. of Hawaii; Founder, Sacred Heart Marine Research Centre, Tuticorin, India 1991, Dir of Research 2000–; RC nun belonging to Congregation of Mother of Sorrows, Servants of Mary; Scientist of the Year, Nat. Environmental Science Acad. (NESA) 2002, Netaji Subhash Chandra Bose Nat. Award for Excellence, Jagruthi Kiran Foundation 2003, Best Citizen of India Award, International Publishing House, New Delhi 2009. *Achievements include:* has isolated 12 active compounds from Indian Ocean soft coral as non-toxic antifoulants. *Publications:* numerous scientific papers on marine biology. *Leisure interests:* reading, computer art design. *Address:* Office of the Director, Sacred Heart Marine Research Centre, St Mary's College Campus, Tuticorin 628 001, Tamil Nadu, India (office). *Telephone:* (461) 2325400 (office); 94-43323491 (mobile) (office); (461) 2321896 (home). *E-mail:* info@poseidonsciences.com (office); avelinmary@yahoo.com (home). *Website:* www.poseidonsciences.com/shmrc.html (office).

MARZOUKI, Moncef, PhD; Tunisian physician, academic, human rights activist and politician; b. 7 July 1945, Grombalia; s. of Mohammed al-Badawi and Aziza Marzouki bin Karim; divorced; two d.; m. 2nd Beatrix Rhein 2011; ed Univ. of Strasbourg, France; f. Centre for Community Medicine, Sousse 1979; Prof. of Community Medicine, Sousse Univ. 1981–2000; mem. Ligue tunisienne des droits de l'homme (human rights org.) 1980, Vice-Pres. 1987, Pres. 1989–92 (org. banned); Founding mem. Nat. Cttee for the Defence of Prisoners of Conscience 1993 (resgnd), jailed for four months 1994, went into exile in France; Pres. Arab Comm. for Human Rights, Cairo 1996–2000; Lecturer, Univ. of Paris 2001; Leader, Congress for the Republic (opposition group) 2001–11 (banned 2002, legalized 2011); returned from exile after fall of Zine al-Abidine Ben Ali 2011; Interim Pres. of Tunisia Dec. 2011–Dec. 2014. *Publications include:* Dictateurs en sursis: Une voie démocratique pour le monde arabe 2009.

MAS-COLELL, Andreu, PhD; Spanish economist and academic; *Professor of Economics, Pompeu Fabra University;* b. 29 June 1944, Barcelona; m.; three c.; ed Univs of Barcelona and Valladolid, Univ. of Minnesota, USA; Profesor Ayudante, Univ. of Madrid 1966–68; Asst Research Economist, Univ. of California, Berkeley, USA 1972–75, Asst Prof. of Econs and Math. 1975–77, Assoc. Prof. 1975–78, Prof. 1979–81, Research Fellow, Math. Sciences Research Inst. and Ford Visiting Prof. 1985–86; Visiting Scholar, Univ. of Bonn, Germany 1976–77; Visiting Prof., Autonomous Univ. of Barcelona 1981–82; Visiting Prof., Pompeu Fabra Univ. 1993, Prof. of Econs 1995–, apptd Head of Dept of Econs and Business 1997; Prof. of Econs, Harvard Univ. 1981–95 (first Louis Berkman Prof. of Econs 1988); Commr for Univs and Research, Generalitat de Catalunya 1999–2000; Minister of Univs, Research and the Information Society, Generalitat de Catalunya 2000–03; Sec.-Gen. European Research Council 2009–10; Minister of Economy and Knowledge, Govt of Catalonia 2010–16; mem. Council Econometric Soc. 1982–89, Exec. Cttee 1986–94, Second Vice-Pres. 1991, First Vice-Pres. 1992, Pres. 1993; Ed. Journal of Mathematical Economics 1985–89 (mem. Advisory Bd 1989–), Econometrica 1988–92; Assoc. Ed. Journal of Economic Theory 1975–80, SIAM Journal of Applied Mathematics 1977–80, Journal of Mathematical Economics 1977–85, Econometrica 1978–84, Revista Española de Economía 1984–90, Economic Theory 1990–94, Mathematics of Social Sciences 1990–97, Games and Economic Behavior

1993–95, Theoretical Economics 2006–08; mem. Advisory Council, Economic Notes 1990–94; mem. Advisory Bd, International Journal of Game Theory 1999–2003, Mathematics and Financial Economics 2006–09; mem. or chair. of numerous advisory panels and cttees; mem. Institut d'Estudis Catalans 2005, Real Academia de Ciencias Morales y Políticas 2007, Academia Europaea 2009; Foreign Assoc. NAS 1997; Fellow, American Acad. of Arts and Sciences 1985, Econometric Soc. 1978, Soc. for the Advancement of Econ. Theory 2011; Foreign Hon. mem. American Econ. Asscn 1997; Creu de Sant Jordi of the Generalitat de Catalunya, 2006; Dr hc (Alicante) 1992, (Toulouse) 2002, (HEC, Paris) 2005, (Universidad Nacional del Sur, Argentina) 2007 Sloan Fellow 1978–80, Guggenheim Fellow 1985–86, recipient of NSF grants 1978–79, 1981–84, 1985–87, 1992–95 and grants from Spanish Educ. Sec. 1996–99, Fisher-Schultz Lecturer, Cambridge World Meeting of the Econometric Soc. 1985, King Juan Carlos Prize in Econs 1988, Narcís Monturiol Medal for Scientific Merit, Generalitat de Catlayuna 1990, Fundació Catalana per a la Recerca Science Prize (co-recipient) 1994, Walras-Bowley Lecturer, North American Summer Meeting of the Econometric Soc. 1997, Spanish Nat. Research Prize in Social Sciences Pascual Madoz 2006, Co-ordinator of Consolider Award, Ministry of Educ. and Science 2006, Cercle d'Economia Prize 2008, Reconeixement CECOT al Progrés Empresarial 2008, Prof. Luigi Tartufari Int. Prize for Econ. Sciences, Accad. Nazionale dei Lincei (co-recipient) 2009, Prize of Fundación BBVA Fronteras del Conocimiento en Economía, Finanzas y Gestión de Empresas (co-recipient) 2009. *Publications include:* trans. into Spanish of G. Debreu's Theory of Value (with J. Oliu) 1974, Non-cooperative Approaches to the Theory of Perfect Competition (ed.) 1982, The Theory of General Economic Equilibrium: A Differentiable Approach 1985, Contributions to Mathematical Economics, in Honor of Gérard Depardieu (co-ed.) 1986, Equilibrium Theory and Applications (co-ed.) 1991, Microeconomic Theory (with M. Whinston and J. Green) 1995, Cooperation: Game Theoretic Approaches (co-ed.) 1997, Nuevas Fronteras de la Política Económica (co-ed.) 1998, Higher Aspirations: An Agenda for Reforming European Universities (co-author) 2008; 128 articles in learned journals. *Address:* Department of Economics and Business, Pompeu Fabra University, Ramon Trias Fargas 25–27, 08005 Barcelona, Spain (office). *Telephone:* (93) 5422498 (office). *Fax:* (93) 5421223 (office). *E-mail:* andreu.mas-colell@upf.edu (office). *Website:* www.econ.upf.edu/~mcolell/en (office).

MAS I GAVARRÓ, Artur; Spanish politician; b. 1956, Barcelona; m.; three c.; ed Liceu Francès de Barcelona, L'Escola Aula, Faculties of Law and Econs, Univ. of Barcelona (degree in Econs and Business Science); Councillor, Barcelona City Council 1987–95, acted as Econ. Affairs Spokesman and Spokesman and Pres. Municipal Group of CiU; mem. Parl. of Catalonia 1995–; fmr Minister for Public Works, then Minister for Economy and Finance, then Chief Minister; Pres. Govt of Catalonia 2010–16; Pres. Convergència Democràtica de Catalunya 1997–, Convergència i Unió 2000–. *Leisure interest:* French literature. *Address:* Convergència Democràtica de Catalunya (CDC), Còrsega 331–333, 08037 Barcelona, Spain. *Telephone:* (93) 2363100. *Fax:* (93) 2363105. *E-mail:* cdc@convergencia.org. *Website:* www.convergencia.org.

MASANGU MULONGO, Jean-Claude, BSc, MBA; Democratic Republic of the Congo economist and fmr central banker; b. 8 Aug. 1953, Jadotville, Likasi, Katanga Prov.; s. of Jacques Masangu Mwanza and Antoinette Mwamba Monga; m. Irène Kayembe Maloba; ed Ecole Internationale, Geneva, Switzerland, Worcester Polytechnic Inst., USA, Louisiana State Univ.; began career as mechanical engineer with Consolidated Aluminum Corpn, USA; 17 years with Citibank, Kinshasa, positions include Sec.-Gen. responsible for Financial Man., Human Resources, Credit Admin and Legal Services 1988–91, Commercial Dir responsible for Man. of Multinationals, Deputy Gen. Man. 1992–93, Man. Dir 1993–97; Gov. Banque Centrale du Congo 1997–2013; Pres. Social Cttee, Asscn Congolaise des Banques (ACB) 1990, ACB Vice-Pres. 1993; Pres. Club Service Fifty-One Int. (non-profit org.). *Publications include:* Pourquoi je crois au progrès de l'Afrique 2009, Parole de Gouvernour 2015. *Website:* jcmasangu.com.

MASÁR, Vladimír, Ing.; Slovak fmr central banker; *Chairman, Deloitte Slovakia;* b. 2 May 1958, Partizánske; s. of Vladimír Masár and Jolana Masárová; m. Dagmar Glasová 1983; one s. two d.; ed Univ. of Econs Bratislava; State Bank of Czechoslovakia 1981–90; Deputy Dir City Br., Gen. Credit Bank 1990–91; Dir Credit Dept Tatra Bank-Slovakia 1992; State Sec. Ministry of Finance of Slovakia 1992; Gov. Nat. Bank of Slovakia 1993–99; Chair. Deloitte Slovakia 2000–; Crystal Wing Award for Economy. *Leisure interests:* swimming, tennis. *Address:* Deloitte Slovakia, Apolla BC, Prievozská 2/B, 821 09 Bratislava, Slovakia (office). *Telephone:* (2) 5824-9130 (office). *Fax:* (2) 5824-9222 (office). *E-mail:* vmasar@deloittece.com (office). *Website:* www.deloitte.sk (office).

MASARSKY, Mark Veniaminovich, CandPhilSc; Russian business executive and journalist; b. 19 June 1940, Muryinskoye, Novgorod Region; m. Olga Yevgen'yevna Fedosova; one s. one d.; ed Rostov Univ., Moscow State Univ.; teacher, Taganrog Radio-Tech. Inst. 1965–67, Rostov Univ. 1967–70, Khabarovsk Polytechnical Inst. 1970–75; Corresp. Young Communist 1977–82; f. and mem. Gold-diggers of Petchora co-operative 1982–87; f. and Chair. Volkhov Jt-stock co. 1987–, Russian Gold co.; one of founders of Moscow Commodity Exchange; Pres. Int. Asscn of Factory Leaders 1992–2001; apptd Chair. Entrepreneurs Council, Moscow Govt 1996; mem. Bd Dirs Russian Bank of Reconstruction and Devt, Novobank Volkhov-Presnaya Investment Co., ITAR-TASS Co.; mem. Expert-Analytical Council to Pres. Yeltsin; mem. Conciliatory Comm. on Public Accord Agreement; mem. Bd Public Chamber, Pres.'s Admin. *Publications:* The Convincing, Time of Orders and Times of Troubles. *Leisure interests:* literature, history, painting.

MASEEH MOHAMED, Abdulla; Maldivian politician; b. Fuvahmulah; m.; one s.; ed Univ. of Plymouth; MP for Fuvahmulah-South, People's Majlis (Parl.), Speaker 2014–18 (resgnd), fmr Chair. Social Affairs Cttee; mem. Judicial Service Comm. 2014–; mem. Progressive Party of Maldives (PPM). *Address:* Progressive Party of Maldives, H. Sakeena Manzil, Medhuziyaaraiy Magu, Malé 20-007, The Maldives (office). *Telephone:* 3303838 (office). *E-mail:* admin@ppm.mv (office). *Website:* www.ppm.mv (office).

MASEFIELD, (John) Thorold, KStJ, CMG, MA; British diplomatist; b. 1 Oct. 1939, Kampala, Uganda; s. of Dr Geoffrey Bussell Masefield and Mildred Joy Thorold Rogers; m. Jennifer Mary Trowell MBE 1962; two s. one d. (and one d. deceased); ed Repton School, Derbyshire, St John's Coll. Cambridge; joined Commonwealth Relations Office 1962, Pvt. Sec. to Perm. Under-Sec. 1963–64, Second Sec., Kuala Lumpur 1964–65, Warsaw 1966–67, FCO 1967–69, First Sec., UK Del. to Disarmament Conf., Geneva 1970–74, Deputy Head of Planning Staff, FCO 1974–77, Far Eastern Dept 1977–79, Counsellor, Head of Chancery, Consul-Gen. Islamabad 1979–82, Head Personnel Services Dept FCO 1982–85, Head Far Eastern Dept 1985–87, Fellow Center for Int. Affairs, Harvard Univ. 1987–88, Resident Chair. Civil Service Selection Bd 1988–89; High Commr in Tanzania 1989–92; Asst Under-Sec. of State for S and SE Asia and the Pacific, FCO 1992–94; High Commr in Nigeria 1994–97 (also Accred to Benin and Chad); Gov. and C-in-C of Bermuda 1997–2001; Chair. Brockenhurst Parish Council 2007–10. *Leisure interest:* fruit and vegetables.

MASEKO, Zola; South African film director; b. 1967; ed Nat. Film and TV School, Beaconsfield, England; born and raised in exile, Tanzania and Swaziland; joined Umkhonto We Sizwe (armed wing of African Nat. Congress) 1987; made first documentary Dear Sunshine 1992; returned to S Africa 1994; joined Pistoleros Films 2005. *Films include:* The Foreigner (also writer) 1997, The Life and Times of Sarah Baartman (documentary) 1998, The Return of Sarah Baartman 2002, Children of the Revolution 2002, A Drink in the Passage (Special Jury Award, Fespaco) 2002, Drum (also writer) (Etalon d'Or de Yennenga Award Fespaco 2005) 2004, The Manuscripts of Timbuktu (documentary) 2009. *Television:* Homecoming (series writer) 2005. *Address:* Pistoleros Films, 12 Ottawa Avenue, Camps Bay, Cape Town 8001, South Africa (office). *Telephone:* 83-3016333 (mobile) (office). *E-mail:* producer@pistoleros.co.za (office). *Website:* www.pistoleros.co.za (office).

MASERA, Rainer Stefano, DPhil; Italian economist, academic and banker; *Dean of Economics Faculty and Professor of Political Economy, Università degli Studi Guglielmo Marconi;* b. 6 May 1944, Como; s. of Francesco Masera; m. Giovanna Aveta; two c.; ed Univ. 'La Sapienza', Rome, Univ. of Oxford, UK; Exec. Officer, BIS, Basle 1971–75, mem. Bd 1975–88; mem. staff, then Head of Int. Dept, Research Dept, Bank of Italy 1975–77, Head of Research Dept 1982–84, Cen. Dir for Econs Research 1985–88; Alt. mem. EEC Monetary Cttee 1977–81; Man. Dir Istituto Mobiliare Italiano (IMI) SpA 1988–98; Minister for the Budget and Econ. Planning 1995–96; CEO Grupo SanPaolo IMI SpA, Turin 1998–2001, Chair. 2001–04; Chair. Banca Fideuram, Rome 2003–04; Chair. Rete Ferroviaria Italiana SpA 2004–07; Strategic Int. Advisor and Sr Dir, Mercer Oliver Wyman 2004–07; Chair. Advisory Cttee, SACE, Rome 2004–07; Man. Dir and Chair. Financial Inst. Group, Lehman Brothers (Italy), Rome 2007–08; Chief of Italian Del. of Frano-Italian Govt Cttee for the new Turin-Lyon railway link 2005–12; Expert mem. Bd, European Investment Bank 2001–13; Chair. Banca delle Marche SpA; mem. Bd of Dirs Colacem SpA; Chair. Advisory Cttee, Financial Man. of Fondazione Roma; Dean of Econs Faculty and Prof. of Political Economy, Università degli Studi Guglielmo Marconi, Rome; apptd one of the five 'wise men' for the review of the Lamfalussy process (IIMG) 2007; mem. de Larosière Group 2009; Cavaliere di Gran Croce of the Italian Repub. 1996, Cavaliere del Lavoro 2002, Officier, Légion d'honneur 2003; Dr hc (Turin) 2001. *Publications:* L'Unificazione Monetaria e lo SME 1980, A European Central Bank 1989, International Monetary and Financial Integration 1988, Prospects for the European Monetary System 1990, Intermediari, Mercati e Finanza d'Impresa 1991. *Leisure interests:* tennis, skiing. *Address:* Department of Economic and Business Sciences, Università degli Studi Guglielmo Marconi, Via Plinio 44, 00193 Rome, Italy (office). *Telephone:* (06) 377251 (office). *Fax:* (06) 37725214 (office). *E-mail:* info@marconiuniversity.org (office). *Website:* www.marconiuniversity.org (office).

MASERI, Attilio, MD, FRCP; Italian cardiologist; *President, Heart Care Foundation;* b. 12 Nov. 1935, Udine; s. of Adriano Maseri and Antonietta Albini; m. Countess Francesca Maseri Florio di Santo Stefano Filippo 1960 (died 2000); one s.; ed Classical Lycée Cividale, Padua Univ. Medical School; Research Fellow Univ. of Pisa 1960–65, Columbia Univ., New York, USA 1965–66, Johns Hopkins Univ., Baltimore, USA 1966–67; Asst Prof., Univ. of Pisa 1967–70, Prof. of Internal Medicine 1970, Prof. of Cardiovascular Pathophysiology, Prof. of Medicine (Locum) 1972–79, Sir John McMichael Prof. of Cardiovascular Medicine, Royal Postgraduate Medical School, Hammersmith Hosp., Univ. of London 1979–91; Prof. of Cardiology and Dir Inst. of Cardiology, Catholic Univ. of Rome 1991–; Prof. of Cardiology, Università Vita-Salute, San Raffaele Hospital 2001–08, also Dir Dept of Cardio-Thoraco-Vascular, Istituto Scientifico S. Raffaele; Pres. Italian Fed of Cardiology 2004–07; Pres. Heart Care Foundation 2008–; Life mem. Johns Hopkins Soc. of Scholars; Fellow, American Coll. of Cardiology; Kt of Malta; Gold Medal Culture and Science from Pres. of the Italian Repub. 2004; Gold Medal of Merit for Public Health Service 2010; King Faisal Int. Prize 1992, Distinguished Scientist Award, American Coll. of Cardiology 1996, Invernizzi Prize for Medicine 1998, European Soc. of Cardiology Gold Medal Award 2002, Grand Prix Scientifique Fondation Lefoulon-Delalande, Institut de France 2004. *Publications:* Myocardial Blood Flow in Man 1972, Primary and Secondary Angina 1977, Perspectives on Coronary Care 1979, Ischaemic Heart Disease 1995; articles in major int. cardiological and medical journals. *Leisure interests:* skiing, tennis, sailing, wine. *Address:* Via Zandonai 9–11, 00194 Rome (home); Heart Care Foundation, Via La Marmora 36, 50121 Florence, Italy (office). *Telephone:* (055) 5101367 (office). *Fax:* (055) 5101360 (office). *E-mail:* amaseri@heartcarefound.org (office); heartcarefound@heartcarefound.org (office). *Website:* www.anmco.it/PerllTuoCuore/ (office).

MASHAT, Mahdi al-; Yemeni politician; *President, Supreme Political Council;* b. 1980, Haydan Dist, Saada Governorate; mem. Ansar Allah (al-Houthi movt), fmr Dir, office of Abd al-Malik al-Houthi (Houthi leader); mem. Supreme Political Council (exec. body, not internationally recognised) 2017–, Pres. 2018–.

MASHEKE, Gen. Malimba Nathaniel; Zambian politician and army officer; b. 17 June 1941; fmr Army Commdr; Minister of Defence 1985–88, of Home Affairs 1988–89; Prime Minister of Zambia 1989–91; fmr Chair. United Nat. Independence Party (UNIP); Chair. Interreligious and Int. Fed. for World Peace (IIFWP), Zambia chapter; apptd Chair. Alliance of Opposition Political Parties in Zambia (comprises Movt for Multiparty Democracy, Alliance for Better Zambia, People's Party, Zambians for Empowerment and Devt) 2014; mem. Forum for Democracy and Devt; Order of Eagle of Zambia.

MASHELKAR, Raghunath Anant, PhD, FRS; Indian research scientist and academic; *National Research Professor, National Chemical Laboratory;* b. 1 Jan. 1943, Mashel, Goa; m. Vaishali R. Mashelkar; one s. two d.; ed Univ. of Bombay; Dir Gen. Council of Scientific and Industrial Research 1995–2006; currently Nat. Research Prof., Nat. Chemical Lab.; Pres. Global Research Alliance; mem. Bd of Dirs, Reliance Industries Ltd, GeneMedix Life Sciences Ltd, Piramal Enterprises Ltd, KPIT Technologies Ltd, Tata Motors Ltd 2007–; Chair. Nat. Innovation Foundation, Reliance Innovation Council, Thermax Innovation Council, KPIT Innovation Council, Marico Innovation Foundation; Chair. Standing Cttee on Information Tech., WIPO; mem. Int. Intellectual Property Rights Comm. of UK Govt; Vice-Chair. WHO Comm. in Intellectual Property Rights, Innovation and Public Health (CIPIH); fmr mem. Scientific Advisory Council to the Prime Minister, Scientific Advisory Cttee to the Cabinet; has chaired 12 high-powered cttees set up to look into issues of higher educ., nat. auto fuel policy, overhauling the Indian drug regulatory system, dealing with the menace of spurious drugs, reforming Indian agriculture research system, etc.; consultant for restructuring publicly funded R&D insts world-wide, especially in S Africa, Indonesia and Croatia; fmr Pres. Indian Nat. Science Acad., Inst. of Chemical Engineers (UK); Foreign Assoc., NAS 2005; Assoc. Foreign mem. American Acad. of Arts and Sciences 2011; only the third Indian engineer to have been elected Fellow of the Royal Soc., London in 20th century 1998; Fellow, Royal Acad. of Eng (UK) 1996, World Acad. of Art and Science (USA) 2000; Foreign Fellow, US Nat. Acad. of Eng 2003, Australian Technological Science and Eng Acad. 2008; hon. doctorates from 35 univs, including Hon. DSc (Salford, UK) 1993, (Kanpur) 1995, (Indian School of Mines) 1997, (Bundelkhand Univ.) 2000, (Guwahati Univ.) 2000, (Anna Univ.) 2000, (Univ. of London) 2001, (Univ. of Wisconsin) 2002, (Banaras Hindu Univ.) 2002, (Allahabad Univ.) 2002, (MS Univ. of Baroda) 2003, (Kalyani Univ.) 2004, (Pretoria), (Delhi); more than 50 honours, awards and medals, including Shanti Swarup Bhatnagar Prize 1982, 2001, UDCT Outstanding Alumni Medal 1985, Fed. of Indian Chambers of Commerce and Industry Award 1987, Pandit Jawaharlal Nehru Tech. Award 1991, Padma Shri 1991, G.D. Birla Scientific Research Award 1993, Goyal Prize 1996, JRD Tata Corp. Leadership Award (first scientist) 1998, appeared on cover of Business India as CEO of CSIR Inc. 1999, Padma Bhushan from Pres. of India 2000, Material Scientist of Year Award 2000, IMC Juran Quality Medal 2002, HRD Excellence Award 2002, Lal Bahadur Shastri Nat. Award for Excellence in Public Admin and Man. Sciences 2002, Medal of Eng Excellence, World Fed. of Eng Orgs, Paris 2003, Lifetime Achievement Award, Indian Science Congress 2004, Science Medal, Acad. of Science for the Developing World 2005, Ashutosh Mookherjee Memorial Award, Indian Science Congress 2005, Business Week (USA) Award of 'Stars of Asia' from George Bush, Sr (first Asian Scientist) 2005, Padma Vibhushan 2014. *Publications include:* books: Intellectual Property and Competitive Strategies in the 21st Century (with S.A. Khan) 2003, Advances in Transport Processes Vol. 1 1980, Vol. 2 1982, Vol. 3 1983, Vol. 4 1986, Transport Phenomena in Polymeric Systems Vol. 1 (ATP Vol. 5) 1987, Vol. 2 (ATP Vol. 6) 1989, Advances in Transport Phenomena in Fluidizing Systems (ATP Vol. 7) 1987, Vol. 8 1992, Vol. 9 1993, Frontiers in Chemical Reaction Engineering Vol. 1 1984, Vol. 2 1984, Recent Trends in Chemical Reaction Engineering Vol. 1 1987, Vol. 2 1987, Reactions and Reaction Engineering 1987, Heat Transfer Equipment Design 1988, Reading in Solid State Chemistry 1994, Dynamics of Complex Fluids 1998, Structure and Dynamics in the Mesophasic Domain 1999; author or co-author of 236 research papers on macromolecules in books and scientific journals since 1968; co-authored 28 patents 1988–2003. *Address:* National Chemical Laboratory, Dr Homi Bhabha Road, Pune 411 008 (office); 'Raghunath', D-4, Varsha Park, Baner, Pune 411 045, India (home). *Telephone:* (20) 25902605 (home); (20) 25902197 (home); (20) 27291268 (office). *Fax:* (20) 25902607 (office). *E-mail:* ram@ncl.res.in (office). *Website:* www.ncl-india.org (office).

MASHKOV, Vladimir Lvovich; Russian actor; b. 27 Nov. 1963, Tula; s. of Lev Petrovich Mashkov and Natalya Ivanovna Nikiforova; m. 1st Tatyana Lvovna Mashkova; one d.; 2nd Ksenia Borisovna Mashkova; ed Moscow Art Theatre School; actor and Stage Dir, Oleg Tabakov Theatre-Studio 1988–; main roles in most productions; staged five productions; various film roles; numerous awards, including K. Stanislavsky Prize for Best Direction 1994, Crystal Turandot Prize for Best Play 1995, Baltic Pearl for fast career growth 1997; various awards for best actor in film and theatre. *Plays (as stage director):* Star House by Local Time, Passions for Bumbarash, The Death-Defying Act, The Threepenny Opera, Number 13 2001. *Films include:* Zelyonyy ogon kozy (The Goat's Green Fire) 1989, Ha-bi-assy 1990, Delay – raz! (aka Do It – One!) 1990, Lyubov na ostrove smerti (Love at the Death Island) 1991, Alyaska, ser! (Alaska, Sir!) 1992, Moi Ivan, toi Abraham (Me Ivan, You Abraham) 1993, Moscow Nights, Limita (San Raphael Russian Cinema Festival Blue Sail Award 1994, Sochi Open Russian Film Festival Best Actor Award 1994, Geneva Film Festival Int. Jury Prize 1995, Geneva Film Festival Youth Jury Award 1995) 1994, Katya Ismailova 1994, American Daughter 1995, Koroli i kapusta (Cabbages and Kings; voice) 1996, Noch pered Rozhdestvom (voice) 1997, Vor (The Thief) (Open CIS and Baltic Film Festival Best Actor Award 1997, Sozvezdie Best Actor Award 1997, Nika Awards Best Actor Award 1998) 1997, Sirota kazanskaya (Sympathy Seeker) (also dir) 1997, Sochineniye ko dnyu pobedy (Composition for Victory Day) 1998, Dve luny, tri solntsa (Two Moons, Three Suns) 1998, Mama (Mummy) 1999, Russkiy bunt (The Captain's Daughter) 2000, Dancing at the Blue Iguana 2000, 15 Minutes 2001, An American Rhapsody 2001, The Quickie (Moscow Int. Film Festival Silver St George Best Actor Award) 2001, Behind Enemy Lines 2001, Oligarkh 2002, Papa (also writer, dir and producer) (Moscow Int. Film Festival Audience Award) 2004, Statski sovetnik 2005, The Good Shepherd 2006, Piranha 2006, Piter FM 2006, The Ghost 2008, Kandagar 2010, The Edge 2010, Mission: Impossible - Ghost Protocol 2011, Rasputin 2013, About Love 2015, Flight Crew 2016, Three Seconds 2017, Billion 2019. *Television includes:* Casus Improvisus 1991, Dvadtsat minut s angelom 1996, Idiot (mini-series) 2003, Alias (series) 2005, Likvidatsya (Liquidation) (series) 2007, Raspoutine (film) 2011, Pepel (series) 2013, Grigoriy R. (mini-series) 2014, Nalyot (series) 2017. *Address:* Oleg Tabakov Theatre-Studio, Chaplygina str. 12A, Moscow, Russia. *Telephone:* (495) 916-21-21 (Theatre); (495) 925-73-44 (Yelena Chukhrai Art Agency). *E-mail:* grtagent@mtu-net.ru (office); v_mashkoff@mtu-net.ru (home).

MÄSIMOV, Kärım Qajimqanuli, DSc (Econ); Kazakhstani economist and politician; *Chairman, National Security Committee;* b. 15 June 1965, Tselinograd (now Astana), Kazakh SSR, USSR; ed Beijing Language and Culture Univ., Inst. of Int. Law, Wuhan Univ., China, Kazakh State Acad. of Man., Columbia Univ., USA; Chief Economist and Head of Dept, Ministry of Labour 1991–92; Sr Specialist, Rep. Office of Ministry of Foreign Econ. Relations in Urumqi, China 1992–93; Exec. Dir Trade House of Kazakhstan, Hong Kong 1994; Chair. Almaty Trade and Finance Bank 1995–97; Chair. People's Saving Bank of Kazakhstan 1997–2000; Minister of Transport and Communications 2000; Deputy Prime Minister 2001–03; Asst to the Pres. 2003–06; Deputy Prime Minister and Minister of Economy and Budget Planning April–Oct. 2006; Prime Minister of Kazakhstan 2007–12, 2014–16; Head, Exec. Office of the Pres. 2012–14; Chair. Nat. Security Cttee 2016–; Dr hc (Peoples' Friendship Univ., Russia) 2007. *Address:* National Security Committee, 010000 Nur-Sultan, Turkestan street, 8/1, Kazakhstan (office). *Telephone:* (7172) 76-11-36 (office). *Website:* www.knb.kz (office).

MASIRE-MWAMBA, Gabaipone Mmasekgoa, BSc, MBA, LLB; Botswana business executive and international organization official; ed Univ. of London, UK, Univ. of Pittsburgh, USA; fmr Chief Exec. Investment Promotion Agency (BEDIA); fmr Group Man. of Corp. Business and Regulatory Affairs, Botswana Telecommunications Corpn; fmr UK Business Devt Man., Commonwealth Telecommunications Org.; Deputy Sec.-Gen. Commonwealth Secr. 2008–14.

MASISI, Mokgweetsi Eric Keabetswe, BEd, MEd; Botswana politician, teacher and head of state; *President;* b. 21 July 1962; s. of Edison Setlhomo K. Masisi and Precious Masego Masisi; m. Neo Masisi; one d.; ed Univ. of Botswana, Florida State Univ.; teacher, Mmanaana Secondary School 1984; Curriculum Specialist Dept of Curriculum Devt and Evaluation 1987; Nat. Coordinator for Social Studies Educ. 1990; Rep. African Social and Environmental Studies Programme 1990; mem. of Bd, Environmental Educ. Asscn of Southern Africa 1990–95; Educ. Project Officer UNICEF 1995–2003; Deputy Sec. Moshupa Branch Cttee 2003; Epidemiologist Community Information and Epidemiological Tech. 2004; mem. Botswana Democratic Party, Chair. 2017–; MP for Moshupa-Manyana Constituency 2009–18; Asst Minister for Presidential Affairs and Public Admin 2009–11, Minister for Presidential Affairs and Public Admin 2011–14, Acting Minister of Educ. and Skills Devt April–Oct. 2014, Minister of Educ. and Skills Devt 2014; Vice-Pres. 2014–18, Pres. 2018–. *Address:* Office of the President, Private Bag 001, Gaborone, Botswana (office). *Telephone:* 3950800 (office). *Fax:* 3904017 (office). *E-mail:* op.registry@gov.bw (office). *Website:* www.gov.bw (office).

MASISI, Motlhware Kgori James; Botswana diplomatist; m. Naledi T. Masisi; ed Ball State University, USA; accountant, Botswana Power Corpn 1976–79; joined Ministry of Commerce and Industry 1979, held various positions including Acting Dir Commerce and Consumer Affairs 1983–84; Dir Dept of Tourism 1987–90; Marketing Man. Shell Oil Botswana 1990–93; joined Foreign Service 1996, has held numerous posts including Charges d'affairs, Embassy in Tokyo, Minister-Counsellor, Embassy in Brussels, High Commr to South Africa 2004–06; Chief Trade Negotiator in Econ. Partnership Agreement 2006–08; Chair. Citizen Entrepreneurial Devt Agency (CEDA) 2008–09.

MASIULIS, Eligijus; Lithuanian political scientist and politician; *Leader, Lietuvos Respublikos liberalų sąjūdis (Liberal Movement of the Republic of Lithuania);* b. 15 Oct. 1974, Klaipėda; partner Ieva Masiulienė; one s. one d.; ed high school, Klaipeda Smeltė, Univ. of Klaipėda; mem. Klaipeda City Council 1997–98, 2000–02, mem. Educ., Culture and Sports Cttee; adviser to Mayor Eugene Gentvilas, Klaipeda Municipality 1998–2000; mem. Seimas (Parl.) 2000–, Chair. Youth and Sports Comm. 2008–12; Leader Lietuvos Respublikos liberalų sąjūdis (Liberal Movt of the Repub. of Lithuania) 2008–; Minister of Transport and Communications 2008–12. *Address:* Lietuvos Respublikos liberalų sąjūdis (Liberal Movement of the Republic of Lithuania), Vašingtono aikštė 1, Vilnius 01108, Lithuania (office). *Telephone:* (5) 249-6959 (office). *Fax:* (5) 212-1083 (office). *E-mail:* eligijus.masiulis@lrs.lt (office). *Website:* www.liberalai.lt (office).

MASIYIWA, Strive, BEng; Zimbabwean business executive and philanthropist; *Founder and Executive Chairman, Econet Wireless Group;* b. 29 Jan. 1961; m. Tsitsi Masiyiwa; six c.; ed Univ. of Wales, UK; worked briefly as telecoms engineer for Posts and Telecommunications Corpn of Zimbabwe (state-owned telephone co.) 1984; f. Econet Wireless, currently Exec. Chair. Econet Wireless Group (global telecommunications co. operating in more than 20 countries), subsidiaries include Econet Wireless International, Econet Wireless Africa, Econet Solar International, Econet Wireless, Liquid Telecom; left Zimbabwe 2000, now based in London; Co-Chair. Grow Africa (African Union/World Econ. Forum platform for investment in African agric.); co-f. (with Sir Richard Branson) Carbon War Room (global environmental think-tank); Chair. Alliance for a Green Revolution in Africa; mem. numerous int. bds including Rockefeller Foundation, Council on Foreign Relations Global Advisory Bd, Africa Progress Panel, UN Sec.-Gen.'s Advisory Bd for Sustainable Energy, Morehouse Coll., Hilton Foundation's Humanitarian Prize Jury; f. Capernaum Trust, 1996, Higher Life Foundation; Founding mem. Global Business Coalition on Educ.; mem. The Giving Pledge (philanthropy commitment est. by Bill Gates and Warren Buffett); several awards including Zimbabwean Businessman of the Year Award 1990, Builder of the Modern Africa Award 2010. *Address:* Econet Wireless Group, 200 Strand, London, WC2R 1DJ, England (office). *Telephone:* (20) 7101-6100 (office). *Fax:* (20) 7101-6102 (office). *Website:* www.econetwireless.com (office).

MASKAWA, Toshihide, PhD; Japanese physicist and academic; *Director, Kobayashi Maskawa Institute for the Origin of Particles and the Universe, Nagoya University;* b. 7 Feb. 1940; ed Nagoya Univ.; Research Assoc., Nagoya Univ. 1967, Dir Kobayashi-Maskawa Inst. for the Origin of Particles and the Universe 2009–; Research Assoc., Kyoto Univ. 1970–76, Prof. 1980–2003, Prof. Emer. 2003–, Dir Yukawa Inst. for Theoretical Physics 1997–99; Assoc. Prof., Univ. of Tokyo 1976–80; Prof. of Physics, Kyoto Sangyo Univ. 2007; mem. Japanese Science Council 1997–2000, Japan Acad. 2010–; Nishina Memorial Award 1979, JJ Sakurai Prize (American Inst. of Physics) 1985, Japan Acad. Award 1985, Asahi Award 1994, Sino-Japanese Cultural Award 1995, Nagoya Univ. Grad. School of Science Lecture Award 2002, European Physical Soc. High-energy Elementary Particle Physics Prize 2007, Nobel Prize for Physics (jtly) 2008. *Address:* Nagoya

University, Furo-cho, Chikusa-ku, Nagoya 464-8601, Japan (office). *Telephone:* (5) 2789-5111 (office). *Website:* www.en.nagoya-u.ac.jp (office).

MASKELL, Duncan, MA, PhD, FMedSci; British biochemist and academic; *Senior Pro-Vice-Chancellor, University of Cambridge;* b. 30 May 1961; ed Gonville and Caius Coll., Cambridge; co-founder Arrow Therapeutics Ltd 1998; worked at Univ. of Oxford and Imperial Coll., London; Marks and Spencer Prof. of Farm Animal Health, Food Science and Food Safety, Univ. of Cambridge 1996–, Head, Dept of Veterinary Medicine 2004–13, Head, School of Biological Sciences 2013–15, Senior Pro-Vice-Chancellor 2015–; mem. Cambridge Enterprise Seed Fund Investment Cttee, Bd mem. Genus, PLC, Cambridge Innovation Capital. *Publications:* published more than 250 research papers. *Leisure interests:* music, sport, food, wine. *Address:* University of Cambridge, Department of Veterinary Medicine, Madingley Road, Cambridge, CB3 0ES, England (office). *E-mail:* duncan .maskell@admin.cam.ac.uk (office); djm47@cam.ac.uk (office). *Website:* www.v-c .admin.cam.ac.uk (office).

MASKIN, Eric Stark, AB, AM, PhD; American economist and academic; *Adams University Professor, Harvard University;* b. 12 Dec. 1950, New York City, NY; s. of Meyer Maskin and Bernice Rabkin Maskin; partner Leslie Griffith; one s. one d.; ed Harvard Univ.; Research Fellow, Jesus Coll., Cambridge, UK 1976–77, Visiting Overseas Fellow, St John's Coll., Cambridge 1987–88; Asst Prof. of Econs, MIT 1977–80, Assoc. Prof. 1980–81, Prof. 1981–84, Visiting Prof. 1999–2000; Overseas Fellow, Churchill Coll., Cambridge 1980–82; Prof. of Econs, Harvard Univ. 1985–2000, Louis Berkman Prof. of Econs 1997–2000, Adams Univ. Prof. 2012–; Albert O. Hirschman Prof. of Social Science, Inst. for Advanced Study, Princeton, NJ 2000–11; Dir Jerusalem Summer School in Econ. Theory, Hebrew Univ. of Jerusalem 2008–; Visiting Prof. Hong Kong Univ. of Science and Tech. 2010–; research areas have included game theory and mechanism design theory; mem. Educ. Advisory Bd, J.S. Guggenheim Foundation 2007–, Scientific Council, Toulouse School of Econs, Solvay School of Econs, Brussels, Higher School of Econs (Russia), Santa Fe Inst.; Ed. Quarterly Journal of Economics 1984–90, Economics Letters 1992–2011; mem. Advisory Bd Cryptic Labs LLC 2018–; mem. American Econ. Asscn, NAS, Econometric Soc. (Pres. 2003), Game Theory Soc. (Pres. 2010–12), European Econ. Asscn; Fellow, Econometric Soc. 1981, American Acad. of Arts and Sciences 1994, European Econ. Asscn 2004, Royal Spanish Acad. of Econ. Science and Finance 2008, Soc. for Advances of Econ. Theory 2010; Corresp. Fellow, British Acad. 2003; Hon. Prof., Wuhan Univ. 2004, Tsinghua Univ. 2007, Shenzhen Univ. 2008, Higher School of Econs, Russia 2008, Eurasian Nat. Univ. 2012, Saint Petersburg Univ. of Man. and Econs 2012, Tumkur Univ. 2013; Hon. Fellow, (St John's Coll. Cambridge) 2004, (Jesus Coll. Cambridge) 2009; Hon. MA, Univ. of Cambridge 1977; Hon. DHumLitt (Bard Coll.) 2008; Dr hc (Corvinus Univ., Budapest) 2008, (Univ. of Cambodia) 2010, (Université Libre de Bruxelle) 2010, (Universidad del Norte, Paraguay) 2011, (Azerbaijan State Univ. of Econs) 2011, (Tech. Univ. of Lisbon) 2012, (Tumkur Univ., India) 2013, (Nat. Univ. of San Marcos, Peru) 2014; Erik Kempe Award in Environmental Econs 2007, Nobel Prize in Econs (co-recipient with Leo Hurwicz and Roger B. Myerson) 2007, Centennial Medal, Harvard Univ. 2010, Cristobal Gabarron Foundation Int. Econs Award 2011, Memorial Medal, Comenius Univ., Bratislava 2013, James Joyce Award, Trinity Coll., Dublin 2014 and numerous other awards. *Leisure interest:* music. *Address:* Harvard University, Littauer Center 312, 1805 Cambridge Street, Cambridge, MA 02138, USA (office). *Telephone:* (617) 495-1746 (office). *Fax:* (617) 495-7730 (office); (617) 495-7730 (office). *E-mail:* emaskin@fas .harvard.edu (office). *Website:* scholar.harvard.edu/maskin (office).

MASMANIDIS, Costas, BSc, PhD; Greek chemist, business executive and international organization executive; b. 1946, Thessaloniki; ed Aristotelian Univ., Thessaloniki, Univ. of Cincinnati, USA; Post-doctoral Research Fellow, Rensselaer Polytechnic Inst., Troy, NY; 18-year career as Gen. Man. with Dow Chemical Co. in int. positions in USA, Switzerland, SA and Balkan countries and as Man. Dir of Greek subsidiary, and with int. positions as Country Man., Corp., sales and market Man.; fmr Sec.-Gen. Black Sea Econ. Cooperation (BSEC) Business Council, Istanbul; Founding mem. and twice-elected Pres. Hellenic Asscn of Chemical Industries; mem. CEFIC; fmr Sec.-Gen. Athens-Piraeus Industry Asscn, Hellenic-Chinese Chamber of Commerce and Industry; fmr mem. Bd of Dirs Hellenic-American Chamber of Commerce and Industry; fmr mem. Gen. Council Fed. of Greek Industries. *Publications include:* Globalisation, Dematerialisation and the New Economy: The Transformation of Business and the Workplace at the Dawn of the 21st Century 2000, SME Innovation and Competitiveness (training manual), The Prospects of Business Cooperation in the Countries of the Mediterranean (study).

MASON, Dame Monica, DBE, OBE; British (b. South African) fmr ballet dancer and ballet company artistic director; b. 6 Sept. 1941, Johannesburg, SA; d. of Richard Mason and E. Fabian; m. Austin Bennett 1968; ed Johannesburg, Nesta Brooking School of Ballet, UK and Royal Ballet School, London; joined Royal Ballet in Corps de Ballet 1958, Soloist 1963, Prin. 1968, Sr Prin. –1989; selected by Kenneth MacMillan to create role of Chosen Maiden in Rite of Spring 1962; other roles created for her include: Diversions, Calliope Rag in Elite Syncopations, Electra, Mistress in Manon, Romeo and Juliet, Midwife in Rituals, Adieu 1980, Nursey in Isadora, Summer in The Four Seasons, The Ropes of Time; appeared in mime roles including Carabosse in The Sleeping Beauty and Lady Capulet in MacMillan's Romeo and Juliet; created role of Mrs Grose in William Tuckett's The Turn of the Screw; Répétiteur and Asst to Prin. Choreographer, Royal Ballet 1980–84, Prin. Répétiteur 1984–91, Asst Dir Royal Ballet 1991–2002, Dir 2002–12; Hon. DUniv (Surrey) 1996; Olivier Special Award 2012; Achievement in Dance Award 2003, Queen Elizabeth II Coronation Award 2011. *Repertory includes:* Odette/Odile in Swan Lake, Princess Aurora in The Sleeping Beauty, title role in Giselle, Prelude and Mazurka in Les Sylphides, leading role in Raymonda Act III, dramatic parts including Hostess in Les Biches and the Black Queen in Checkmate; other major roles performed include: leading role in MacMillan's Song of the Earth, Nijinska's Les Noces and Nureyev's Kingdom of the Shades scene from La Bayadère; appeared in first performances by Royal Ballet of Hans van Manen's Adagio Hammerklavier, Jerome Robbins' Dances at a Gathering and In the Night, Balanchine's Liebeslieder Walzer and Tudor's Dark Elegies; other roles include: the Lilac Fairy in The Sleeping Beauty, Empress Elisabeth and Mitzi Caspar in MacMillan's Mayerling, title role in The Firebird, Variations in Frederick Ashton's Birthday Offering, the Fairy Godmother and Winter Fairy in Cinderella, Lady Elgar in Enigma Variations, Queen of Denmark in Helpmann's Hamlet.

MASON, Paul James, CB, PhD, FRS; British meteorologist (retd); *Professor Emeritus, University of Reading;* b. 16 March 1946, Southampton, Hants.; s. of Charles Ernest Edward Mason and Phyllis Mary Mason (née Swan); m. Elizabeth Mary Slaney 1968; one s. one d.; ed Univs of Nottingham and Reading; Scientific Officer, then Prin. Scientific Officer, Meteorological Office 1967–79, Head Meteorological Research Unit, Cardington 1979–85, Asst Dir Boundary Layer Br., Meteorological Office 1985–89, Deputy Dir Physical Research, Meteorological Office 1989–91, Chief Scientist 1991–2003; Dir Univs Weather Research Network (UWERN), Univ. of Reading 2003–06, Prof. Emer. 2006–; mem. Council Royal Meteorological Soc. 1989–90, Pres. 1992–94; Chair. Steering Cttee Global Climate Observing System 2002–06; mem. Editorial Bd Boundary Layer Meteorology 1988–98; L.G. Groves Prize for Meteorology 1980, Buchan Prize, Royal Meteorological Soc. 1986, Mason Medal, Royal Meteorological Soc. 2006. *Publications:* scientific papers in meteorology and fluid dynamics journals. *Leisure interests:* walking, travel. *Address:* Department of Meteorology, University of Reading, PO Box 243, Earley Gate, Reading, Berks., RG66 6BB, England (office). *E-mail:* p.j .mason@reading.ac.uk (office).

MASON, Peter, AM, BCom (Hons), MBA, FAICD; Australian investment banker; Dir Mayne Group Ltd 1992–2005; fmr Deputy Chair. Children's Hosp. Sydney; fmr Chair. and CEO Schroders Australia Ltd, Group Man. Dir Schroders Asia Pacific; Chair. JP Morgan Chase Bank Australia 2000–05, Ord Minnett Holdings Pty 2004–05; mem. Bd AMP Ltd 2003–14, Chair. 2005–14; Chair. UBS Australia Foundation Pty Ltd, Centre for Int. Finance and Regulation; mem. Bd of Dirs, David Jones Ltd 2007–14 (Chair. 2013–14), Singapore Telecommunications Ltd 2010–, Taylors Wines Pty Ltd; fmr Chair. Children's Hosp. Fund; Dir, Australian Research Alliance for Children and Youth; fmr Dir Lloyds Bank Australia, UK, Univ. of New South Wales Foundation; Sr Adviser, UBS Investment Bank Australasia; Govt Appointee, Univ. of New South Wales Council; Trustee, Sydney Opera House Trust; Fellow, Australian Inst. of Co. Dirs; Hon. DBus (Univ. of New South Wales).

MASON, Sir Ronald, Kt, KCB, DSc, FRS, CChem, FRSC, CEng, FIM; British professor of chemical physics (retd) and civil servant; b. 22 July 1930, Wales; s. of David John Mason and Olwen Mason (née James); m. 1st E. Pauline Pattinson 1953; m. 2nd E. Rosemary Grey-Edwards 1979; three d.; ed Quaker's Yard Grammar School and Univs of Wales and London; Research Assoc., Univ. Coll. London (UCL) 1953–60, Fellow 1995–; Lecturer, Imperial Coll. London 1960–63; Prof., Univ. of Sheffield 1963–70; Prof., Univ. of Sussex 1970–88; Chief Scientific Adviser, Ministry of Defence 1977–83; Pro-Vice-Chancellor, Univ. of Sussex 1977–78; Chair. Hunting Ltd 1986–87, British Ceramics Research Ltd 1990–98, UCL Hosps Nat. Health Service Trust 1993–2001, Science Applications Int. Corpn (UK) Ltd 1993–96; Pres. British Hydromechanics Research Asscn 1986–95, Inst. of Materials 1995–96; Chair. Council for Arms Control, London 1986–91; mem. UN Disarmament Studies Comm. 1983–91; Chair. UCL Hosps Charities 2004–08, Global Haps Communications Network 2009; Hon. Fellow, Univ. of Glamorgan 1987; Hon. FIMechE 1993; Hon. DSc (Wales) 1986, (Keele) 1993; medals of various learned socs. *Publications:* many scientific research publs on structural chem. and chemical physics of surfaces, author/ed. of 10 monographs, papers on defence policies and tech. *Leisure interests:* gardening, travelling, music, opera. *E-mail:* mason.r@virgin.net (home).

MASON, Dame Sandra Prunella, GCMG, DA, QC, LLB; Barbadian lawyer, judge and fmr diplomatist; *Governor-General;* b. 17 Jan. 1949, St Philip, Bridgetown; one s.; ed Univ. of the West Indies (UWI); teacher, Princess Margaret Secondary School, St Philip 1968–69; clerk, Barclay's Bank 1969; admitted to the bar 1975 (first female mem. Barbados Bar Asscn); worked in Trust Administration Dept, Barclay's Bank 1975–78; taught family law, UWI 1978–83; Magistrate, Juvenile and Family Court 1978–92; Amb. to Venezuela 1992–94; Chief Magistrate for Barbados 1994–97; Registrar of the Supreme Court 1997–2005; Queen's Counsel to the Inner Bar of Barbados 2005–08; Appeals Judge (first woman to serve on Barbados Court of Appeals) 2008–17; Gov.-Gen. of Barbados 2018–; mem. UN Cttee on the Rights of the Child 1991–99 (Vice Chair. 1993–95, Chair. 1997–99). *Address:* Government House, Government Hill, Bridgetown, Barbados (office). *Telephone:* 429-2646 (office). *Fax:* 436-5910 (office).

MASOUD, Ahmad Wali, MA; Afghan diplomatist and politician; *Leader, Nizat-i Melli-i Afghanistan (National Movement of Afghanistan);* b. 1 Nov. 1964, Kabul; brother of Ahmed Shah Masoud, leader of Northern Alliance mil. forces in Afghanistan, and Ahmad Zia Masoud; m. Beheshta Masoud; three d.; ed Muslim Public School, Peshawar, Pakistan, Mid-Cornwall Coll. of Further Educ., Polytechnic of Cen. London and Westminster Univ., UK; Foreign News Reporter, Times Newspaper 1989; Ed. Ariana News Bulletin 1989–92; Rep. Jamiat-i Islami (Islamic Soc.), main political faction in Afghanistan, fighting Russian occupation 1989–92; Second Sec., Embassy of Afghanistan, London 1992, First Sec. and Chargé d'affaires a.i. 1993, Minister Counsellor and Chargé d'affaires a.i. 1993–2003, Amb. to UK 2003–07; currently Leader, Nizat-i Melli-i Afghanistan (Nat. Movt of Afghanistan), Kabul. *Address:* Nizat-i Melli-i Afghanistan, Taimani, St 1, Kabul, Afghanistan (office).

MASOUD, Ahmad Zia; Afghan diplomatist and politician; b. 1 May 1956, brother of Ahmad Shah Masoud and Ahmad Wali Masoud; m.; one s. three d.; ed Lycée Esteqlal and Kabul Polytechnic Inst.; mem. Shora-e-Nizar Movt; Amb. to Russian Fed. (non-resident Envoy to Moldova, Armenia, Azerbaijan, Georgia and Belarus), Moscow 2002–04; First Vice-Pres. 2004–09.

MASOUM, (Muhammad) Fouad, PhD; Iraqi politician and fmr head of state; b. 1938, Koya; m.; one s. (deceased) five d.; ed Univ. of Baghdad, Al-Azhar Univ., Egypt; Prof. of Literature, Univ. of Basra 1968, also Asst Prof., Faculties of Law and Educ.; veteran Kurdish politician; mem. Iraqi Communist Party 1962–64; mem. Kurdistan Democratic Party 1964–75; co-f. Patriotic Union of Kurdistan (PUK) 1976–; first Prime Minister of Kurdistan 1992–93; mem. del. representing Kurdistan, Baghdad (following invasion of Iraq) 2003; mem. cttee drafting new Iraqi constitution 2005; first Speaker, Council of Reps June–Nov. 2010; Pres. of Iraq 2014–18.

MASRANI, Bharat Bhagwanji, MBA; Canadian banking executive; *CEO, Toronto-Dominion Bank;* b. May 1956, Uganda; m. Shabnam Nasrani; two c.; ed York Univ.; joined Toronto-Dominion Bank as Commercial Lending Trainee 1987, becoming Account Man., Commercial Accounts 1988, Vice-Pres. and Country Head for India 1996–97, Sr Vice-Pres., Corp. Finance and Co-Head in Europe 1997–99, Sr Vice-Pres. and CEO, Waterhouse Investor Services Europe 1999, Pres. and CEO, TD Waterhouse International 2002, Vice-Chair., Credit Asset Management TD Securities LLC 2002–03, Exec. Vice-Pres., Toronto-Dominion Bank 2002–03, Exec. Vice-Pres., Risk Management 2003–05, Vice-Chair. and Chief Risk Officer 2005–06, Dir, TD Banknorth, Inc. 2005–06, Pres. and CEO, TD Banknorth, Inc. 2007, CEO and Pres., TD Bank US Holding Co. 2007, Group Head, US Personal and Commercial Banking, TD Bank Group –2014, CEO Toronto-Dominion Bank 2014–; Pres. and CEO e.Bank 2002. *Address:* Toronto-Dominion Bank, Toronto-Dominion Centre, 55 King Stret West and Bay Street, POB 1, Toronto, ON M5K 1A2, Canada (office). *Telephone:* (416) 982-8222 (office). *Fax:* (416) 982-5671 (office). *E-mail:* customer.service@td.com (office). *Website:* www.td.com (office).

MASRI, Munib Rashid al-, MA; Palestinian business executive; *Chairman, Palestinian Development and Investment Company;* b. 1934, Nablus, British Mandate for Palestine; m. Angela Masri; four s. two d.; ed an-Najah School, Nablus, an-Najah Nat. Univ., Univ. of Texas, Austin, USA; fmr Jordanian cabinet minister; f. Edgo (eng services co.), London, UK; served as emissary of King Hussein of Jordan to Palestinian leader Yasser Arafat's HQ during fighting between Jordanian troops and Palestinian fighters 1970; acted as mediator between Israeli Prime Minister Benjamin Netanyahu and Yasser Arafat mid-1990s; first Palestinian businessman to return to Palestinian territories following Oslo agreements 1994; launched a political movement to rival Fatah and Hamas, called the Palestine Forum 2007; turned down an offer to become Prime Minister on three separate occasions; Founder and Chair. Palestine Devt and Investment Co. (Padico) 1994; f. Paltel phone co.; Deputy Chair. Palestine Investment Fund; mem. Palestinian Cen. Council; involved in education through the establishment of the Al Quds Univ. Investment Fund; Chair. Bd of Trustees, Sakakini Cultural Centre, Ramallah; helped set up the Eng and Tech. Coll. at an-Najah Univ. (named after him); mem. Bd of Trustees, American Univ. of Beirut. *Address:* Padico Holding, PO Box 316, Nablus, Palestinian Autonomous Areas (office). *Telephone:* (9) 2384480 (office). *Fax:* (9) 2384355 (office). *E-mail:* padico@padico.com (office). *Website:* www.padico.com (office).

MASRI, Sabih Taher Darwish al-, BSc; Jordanian banking executive; *Chairman, Arab Bank;* b. 2 Dec. 1937; ed Univ. of Texas, Austin, USA; Founder Asra Group 1966–; Founder Palestine Securities Exchange, Chair. –2004; Chair. Sikon for Building Materials Co. (UAE) 1968–, Arab Supply & Trading Co. (Saudi Arabia) 1979–, Palestine Telecommunication Corpn (Palestine) 1998–, ZARA Holding Co. (Jordan) 1999–, ASTRA Industrial Group (Saudi Arabia) 2007–; Vice-Chair. Palestine Investment Fund 2002–; mem. Bd of Dirs Arab Bank 1998–, Deputy Chair.–Aug. 2012, Acting Chair. Aug.–Sept. 2012, Chair. Sept. 2012–; mem. Bd of Dirs Palestine Development & Investment Co. (Padico) 1994–, Cairo Amman Bank, VTEL Holdings Ltd, Al Masira Investment Co., Ayla Oasis Development Co., Rum Agricultural Co., Palestine Investment and Development Co. *Address:* Arab Bank Plc, PO Box 950545, Amman 11195, Jordan (office). *Telephone:* (6) 560-0000 (office). *Fax:* (6) 560-6793 (office). *E-mail:* info@arabbank .com (office). *Website:* www.arabbank.com (office).

MASRI, Taher Nashat, BBA; Jordanian politician and diplomatist; b. 5 March 1942, Nablus; s. of Nashat Masri and Hadiyah Solh; m. Samar Bitar 1968; one s. one d.; ed Al-Najah Nat. Coll., Nablus and North Texas State Univ., USA; with Cen. Bank of Jordan 1965–73; mem. Parl. (Lower House) 1973–74, 1984–88, 1989–97; Minister of State for Occupied Territories Affairs 1973–74; Amb. to Spain 1975–78, to France 1978–83, also accred to Belgium 1979–80, Rep. to EEC 1978–80; Perm. Del. to UNESCO 1978–83; Amb. to UK 1983–84; Minister of Foreign Affairs 1984–88, Jan.–June 1991; Deputy Prime Minister and Minister of State for Econ. Affairs April–Sept. 1989; Chair. Foreign Relations Cttee 1989–91, 1992–93; Prime Minister and Minister of Defence June–Nov. 1991; Speaker, Nat. Ass. 1993–94; Senator 1998–2001, 2005, Deputy Speaker 2005–09, Speaker 2009–13; fmr Rep. to Arab League; mem. and Rapporteur, Royal Comm. for Drafting the Nat. Charter 1990; Chair. Bd Princess Haya Cultural Centre for Children 1992–2006; Pres. Nat. Soc. for the Enhancement of Freedom and Democracy (JUND) 1993–97, Jordanian-Spanish Friendship Asscn 1998–, Bd of Trustees Jordan Univ. for Science and Tech., Irbid 1998–2010, Jordan British Soc. 2006–12, Exec. Cttee Arab Thought Forum 2009–; Commr for Civic Socs with Arab League, Cairo (stationed in Amman) 2002; mem. and Head, Political Cttee of the Royal Comm. for Drafting the Nat. Agenda 2005; mem. Alkuods Al-Sharif Defending Asscns 1996–2001, 2003–07, Advisory Cttee Anna Lindh Euro-Mediterranean Foundation for the Dialogue between Cultures 2004, 2006; Grand Cordon, Jewelled Al-Nahda (Order of the Renaissance) (Jordan), Order of Al-Nahda (1st Degree) (Jordan), Order of Al-Kawkab (Jordan) 1974, Gran Cruz de Mérito Civil (Spain) 1977, Order of Isabel la Católica (Spain) 1978, Commdr, Légion d'honneur 1981, Grand Officier, Ordre Nat. du Mérite, Order of Merit (Grand Cross, First Class, FRG), Kt Grand Cross (Italy); Hon. GBE; Grand Cordon, Ordre Nat. de Cedre (Lebanon), Grand Decoration of Honour in Gold with Sash for Services (Austria), Order of Diplomatic Service Merit and Gwanghawa Medal (Repub. of Korea); numerous awards. *Address:* PO Box 5550, Amman 11183, Jordan. *Telephone:* (6) 4642227 (office); (6) 5920600 (home). *Fax:* (6) 4642226 (office). *E-mail:* t.n.masri@index.com.jo (office). *Website:* www.tahermasri .com.

MASSA, Sergio Tomás; Argentine politician and government official; b. 28 April 1972, Buenos Aires; m. Malena Galmarini; two c.; ed Belgrano Univ.; joined Unión del Centro Democrático 1989, then joined Partido Justicialista; Social Devt Adviser in Vice-Presidential campaign of Ramon Ortega 1999; Exec. Dir Nat. Agency for Social Security Admin (ANSES) 2002–07; elected mem. Chamber of Deputies 2005 (relinquished seat to stay at ANSES), 2013–17; Mayor of Tigre 2007–08, 2009–13; Cabinet Chief 2008–09; cand. in presidential election 2015; mem. Frente Renovador; Lifetime mem. Club Atlético Tigre 2007–09.

MASSAD ABUD, (Alberto) Carlos, MA, PhD; Chilean banker, economist and academic; b. 29 Aug. 1932, Santiago; m.; five c.; ed Univ. of Chile, Univ. of Chicago, USA; Dir Dept of Econs, Univ. of Chile 1959–64; Vice-Gov. Cen. Bank of Chile

1964–67, Gov. 1967–70, 1996–2003 (resgnd); Exec. Dir IMF, Washington, DC 1970–74; mem. Advisory Cttee, World Bank 1978–81; held various posts in Econ. Comm. for Latin America (CEPAL) 1970–92; Exec. Pres. Eduardo Frei Montalva Foundation 1993–94; Minister of Health 1994–96; Prof., Econs Faculty, Univ. of Santiago 1982–90; Visiting Prof., UCLA 1988; Dir, CorpBanca 2004–09, Saieh group 2004–09; Euromoney Best Cen. Banker of Latin America 1997, The Banker Cen. Bank Gov. For the Americas Region of the Year 2001. *Publications include:* Macroeconomics 1979, Rudiments of Economics 1980, Adjustment with Growth 1984; Economic Analysis: An Introduction to Microeconomics 1986, Internal Debt and Financial Stability (Vol. 1) 1987, (Vol. 2) 1988, The Financial System and Resource Distribution: Study Based on Latin America and the Caribbean 1990, Elements of Economics: An Introduction to Economic Analysis 1993, On Public Health and Other Topics 1995, Macroeconomía en un mundo interdependiente (with Guillermo Patillo) 2000; numerous articles.

MASSAOUDOU, Hassoumi; Niger politician; Minister of Communication, Culture, Youth and Sports 1993–94; mem. Nat. Ass. (Parl.) 1999–, Pres. PNDS Parl. Group 1999–2004; headed electoral campaign for Mahamadou Issoufou during presidential election 2011; Dir Cabinet of the Pres. 2011–13; Minister of the Interior 2013–16, of Nat. Defence April–Oct. 2016, of Finance Oct. 2016–Feb. 2019; Founder mem. Parti Nigérien pour la Démocratie et le Socialisme (PNDS—Tarayya) 1990, First Deputy Sec.-Gen. 2004.

MASSARD KABINDA MAKAGA, Etienne; Gabonese biologist and politician; b. 1963; several years as Researcher with CENAREST (scientific research centre); Special Adviser to Pres. on Environment –2014; Head, Secr.-Gen. of the Presidency 2014; Minister, Sec.-Gen. to the Presidency, responsible for Nat. Defence 2016–19; fmr Pres. Man. Council, Agence nat. des parcs nationaux (ANPN), Conseil nat. des Affaires climatiques (Climate Council); fmr Pres., Tech. Cttee, Agence nat. des bourses du Gabon (ANBG); Dir, Agence gabonaise d'études et d'observations spatiales (AGEOS).

MASSENGALE, Martin Andrew, BS, MS, PhD; American university administrator, agronomist and academic; *Director, Center for Grassland Studies, Foundation Distinguished Professor and President Emeritus, University of Nebraska;* b. 25 Oct. 1933, Monticello, Ky; s. of Elbert G. Massengale and Orpha Conn Massengale; m. Ruth A. Klingelhofer 1959; one s. one d.; ed W Kentucky Univ. and Univ. of Wis.; Asst Agronomist and Asst Prof., Univ. of Ariz., Tucson 1958–62, Assoc. Agronomist and Assoc. Prof. 1962–65, Agronomist and Prof. 1965–66, Agronomist, Prof. and Head of Dept 1966–74, Assoc. Dean, Coll. of Agric. and Assoc. Dir Agricultural Experiment Station 1974–76; Vice-Chancellor for Agric. and Natural Resources, Univ. of Nebraska, Lincoln 1976–81, Chancellor Univ. of Nebraska 1981–91, Interim Pres. 1989–91, Pres. 1991–94, Pres. Emer. 1994–, Dir Center for Grassland Studies and Foundation Distinguished Prof. 1994–; Pres. Crop Science Soc. of America 1973–74, Grazing Lands Forum 1997–98; Chair. Agronomic Science Foundation; mem. numerous cttees, nat. panels, advisory bds etc. including Chair., Exec. Comm. and Advisory Bd to US Sec. of Agric., US Senate and House of Reps Agric. and Appropriations Cttees; Fellow, AAAS, American Soc. of Agronomy, Crop Science Soc. of America and other professional socs; Hon. Lifetime Trustee, Neb. Council on Econ. Educ. 1999; Dr hc (Neb. Wesleyan Univ., Senshu Univ., Tokyo), Distinguished Alumni (Western Kentucky) 2002; numerous honours and awards, including Triumph of Agri Award 1999, Nebraska Agriculture Relations Co. Honoree 2000, Nebraska LEAD Alumni Asscn 'Friend of LEAD' Award 2001, Outstanding Pres.'s Award, All-American Football Foundation 2001, Alpha Gamma Rho Brothers of the Century Award 2004, US Dept of Agric. Charter Hall of Fame 2004, Nebraskaland Foundation Wagonmaster Award 2006, Gamma Sigma Delta Distinguished Achievement in Agric. Award 2008, Univ. of Nebraska Coll. of Agricultural Sciences and Natural Resources Alumni Asscn Service Award 2009. *Publications:* Renewable Resource Management for Forestry and Agriculture (co-ed.) 1978; numerous peer-reviewed articles in scientific journals. *Leisure interests:* reading, travel, golf, photography. *Address:* 203 Keim Hall, University of Nebraska, Lincoln, NE 68583-0953 (office); 3436 West Cape Charles Road, Lincoln, NE 68516, USA (home). *Telephone:* (402) 472-4101 (office); (402) 420-5350 (home). *Fax:* (402) 472-4104 (office). *E-mail:* mmassengale1@unl .edu (office). *Website:* www.grassland.unl.edu (office).

MASSERET, Jean-Pierre; French politician; b. 23 Aug. 1944, Cusset (Alliers); s. of Lucien Masseret and Claudia Rollet; m. Marie-Hélène Roddier 1967; three c.; ed Institut des Hautes Etudes de Défense Nationale; fmr Chief Insp., Inland Revenue; Gen. Councilor, Moselle 1979–85; mem. staff of Minister for War Veterans 1981–86; Senator for Moselle 1983–2011, Vice-Chair. Senate Finance Cttee; mem. groupe socialiste et apparentés (SOC) 1983–2017; Minister of State attached to Minister of Defence, with responsibility for War Veterans 1997–2001; Mayor of Havange (Moselle) 1995–97; Pres., Lorraine Regional Council 2004–15, mem. Parti Socialiste Political Cttee; mem. Parl. Ass. of WEU, of Council of Europe, Socialist Party Nat. Office; fmr Chair. Lorraine Athletics League 1986–92; fmr regional champion runner; mem. groupe La République en marche (LREM) 2017–.

MASSEY, Walter Eugene, BS, PhD; American physicist, academic and business executive; *President, School of the Art Institute of Chicago;* b. 5 April 1938, Hattiesburg, Miss.; m. Shirley Massey (née Anne); two s.; ed Morehouse Coll., Washington Univ. in St Louis, Mo.; served as Vice-Pres. for Research and Prof. of Physics, Univ. of Chicago 1979–91; Dir Argonne Nat. Lab. 1979–84; fmr Dean of the Coll. and Prof. of Physics, Brown Univ.; fmr Asst Prof. of Physics, Univ. of Illinois; Dir NSF 1991–93; fmr Sr Provost of Univ. of California System; Pres. Morehouse Coll. 1995–2007, now Pres. Emer.; Pres. School of the Art Inst. of Chicago 2010–; mem. Bd of Dirs, Bank of America Corpn, Chair. 2009–10; mem. or fmr mem. Bd of Dirs, BP Oil, Motorola, McDonalds 1998–; mem. Bd, Salzburg Global Seminar, Salzburg, Austria (with offices in Washington, DC) 1995–, Chair. 2007–; Chair. Bd of Trustees, Asscn of Ind. Coll. of Art and Design 2014–; Trustee, The Andrew W. Mellon Foundation; Trustee Emer., Univ. of Chicago, Brown Univ.; Fellow, AAAS (also fmr Pres.), American Physical Soc. (also fmr Vice-Pres.); fmr Trustee Illinois Math. and Science Acad.; mem. American Acad. of Arts and Sciences, American Philosophical Soc., Council of Foreign Relations; more than 30 hon. degrees from Yale, Columbia, Brown, Northwestern, Tufts, Morehouse, Howard, Washington Univ. in St Louis, Ohio State, Amherst, and Williams, amongst others; Distinguished Service Citation of the American Association of

Physics Teachers, Enrico Fermi Award, Chicago Historical Soc. 2012. *Address:* School of the Art Institute of Chicago, 36 S Wabash Avenue, Chicago, IL 60603, USA (office). *Telephone:* (312) 899-5136 (office). *Fax:* (312) 263-5629 (office). *E-mail:* wmassey@saic.edu (office). *Website:* www.saic.edu (office).

MASSOTE DE GODOY, Tarcísio José, BEng, MEcons; Brazilian business executive; *Chairman, Banco do Brasil;* b. 5 April 1964, Campo Belo, Minas Gerais; m.; ed Univ. of Brasília, Wharton School, Univ. of Pennsylvania and Minerva Inst., George Washington Univ., USA; began career as Navigable Ports and Roads Engineer, Bahia Dock Co. 1986; held various positions in federal public sector from 1992, including Co-ordinator-Gen. and Deputy Sec. of Complementary Welfare, Ministry of Welfare and Social Assistance; Co-ordinator Gen. and Restructuring Liabilities and Admin of Gen. Co-ordinator of Public Debt and Deputy Sec. of the Fiscal Policy Area, Nat. Treasury 2002–06, Acting Sec. 2006–07; CEO Brasilprev 2007–10; Dir Bradesco Seguros 2010–; Chair. Banco do Brasil 2015–. *Address:* Banco do Brasil SA, SBS Qd. 01 Bloco C, Edificio Sede III, 24º Andar, 70073-901 Brasília, DF, Brazil (office). *Telephone:* (61) 3310-3400 (office); (61) 3310-5920 (office). *Fax:* (61) 3310-3735 (office). *E-mail:* presidencia@bb.com.br (office). *Website:* www.bb.com.br (office).

MASTELLA, Clemente; Italian journalist and politician; *Mayor of Benevento;* b. 5 Feb. 1947, Ceppaloni, Benevento; m. Sandra Lonardo 1975; three c.; early career as journalist, RAI Naples; mem. Parl. 1976–; Mayor of San Giovanni di Ceppaloni 1987–1992, 2003–08; Co-founder Centro Cristiano Democratico party (after dissolution of Christian Democracy party) 1994; Minister of Labour 1994–95; Co-founder Cristiano Democratici per la Repubblica, then Unione Democratici per la Repubblica 1998; Sec. Popolari—UDEUR (Alleanza Popolare—Unione Democratici per l'Europa) (Union of Democrats for Europe) 1999–; Deputy Speaker of the House 2001–06; Minister of Justice 2006–08 (resgnd); Mayor of Benevento 2016–. *Address:* Via Aldo Moro, 5B 82100 Benevento, Italy (office). *Telephone:* 347 2548758 (mobile) (office); 345 7033871 (mobile) (office). *E-mail:* segreteria@mastellasindaco.it. *Website:* www.mastellasindaco.it; www.comune.benevento.it (office).

MASTERSON, Patrick, PhD, MRIA; Irish university professor; b. 19 Oct. 1936, Dublin; s. of Laurence Masterson and Violet Masterson; m. Frances Lenehan; one s. three d.; ed Belvedere Coll., Castlenock Coll., Univ. Coll., Dublin, Univ. of Louvain; mem. staff Dept of Metaphysics, Univ. Coll., Dublin 1963–72, Prof. Faculties of Arts, Philosophy and Sociology 1972–80, Dean of the Faculty of Philosophy and Sociology 1980–83, Registrar 1983–86, Pres. 1986–93, currently Prof. Emer.; Pres. European Univ. Inst., Florence 1994–2002; Vice-Chancellor Nat. Univ. of Ireland 1987, 1988, 1993; Grande Oficial, Ordem do Mérito da República Portuguesa, Grande Ufficiale della Repubblica Italiana; Dr hc (Caen, Trinity Coll. Dublin, New York). *Publications:* Atheism and Alienation: A Study of the Philosophical Sources of Contemporary Atheism 1971, Images of Man in Ancient and Medieval Thought: (Studia Gerardo Verbeke ab amicis et collegis dictata) 1976, The Sense of Creation: Experience and the God Beyond 2008, Articulations: poetry, philosophy, and the shaping of culture 2008, Approaching God: Between Phenomenology and Theology 2013, Quality Time at St Chinian 2017. *Leisure interests:* modern art, reading, theatre, fishing.

MASTERSON, (Margaret) Valerie, CBE; British singer (soprano); b. Birkenhead; d. of Edward Masterson and Rita McGrath; m. Andrew March; one s. one d.; Prof. of Singing, RAM, London 1992–97; Pres. British Youth Opera 1994–99, Vice-Pres. 2000–; has sung with D'Oyly Carte Opera, Glyndebourne, Royal Opera House, Covent Garden and English Nat. Opera and on TV and radio; also in major opera houses abroad including Paris, Aix-en-Provence, Toulouse, Munich, Geneva, Milan, San Francisco and Chicago; Hon. FRCM 1992; Hon. FRAM 1993; Hon. DLitt (South Bank Univ.) 1999; Award for Outstanding Individual Performance of the Year in a New Opera, Soc. of West End Theatre 1983. *Opera roles include:* La Traviata, Manon, Semele, Merry Widow, Louise, Lucia di Lammermoor, Mireille; other leading roles in Faust, Alcina, Die Entführung aus dem Serail, Le Nozze di Figaro, Così fan Tutte, La Bohème, Magic Flute, Julius Caesar, Rigoletto, Orlando, Der Rosenkavalier, Xerxes, The Pearl Fishers, Die Fledermaus. *Recordings include:* Julius Caesar, La Traviata, Elisabetta Regina d'Inghilterra, Bitter Sweet, Ring Cycle, recitals and various Gilbert and Sullivan discs. *Leisure interests:* enjoying life. *Address:* c/o Music International, 13 Ardilaun Road, London, N5 2QR, England (office). *Telephone:* (20) 7359-5183 (office). *Fax:* (20) 7226-9792 (office). *E-mail:* music@musicint.co.uk (office). *Website:* www.musicint.co.uk (office).

MASTIAUX, Frank, BSc, PhD; German business executive; *Chairman of the Board of Management and CEO, Energie Baden-Württemberg AG (EnBW);* b. 24 March 1964, Essen; m.; four c.; management functions in areas of R&D and Supply & Trading, Asst to the CEO, Veba Oel AG, Gelsenkirchen 1993–99; Business Devt Man., CITGO Petroleum, Tulsa, Okla, USA 1998–99; Div. Head of Procurement and Sales, Veba Oel 1999–2000, Gen. Man. ARAL Mineralöl-Vertrieb GmbH (following merger with ARAL) 2000–01, Gen. Man. for Marketing Strategy and Planning as well as Market Research for entire BP group in London (following takeover of Veba Oel/ARAL by BP) 2001–05, Head of Global Liquefied Petroleum Gas (LPG) business as CEO at BP 2005–07; CEO, Devt and Man. of Renewable Energies business, E.ON Climate & Renewables, Düsseldorf 2007–10, CEO E.ON International Energy 2010–12; Chair. Bd of Man. and CEO Energie Baden-Württemberg AG (EnBW) 2012–; Deputy Chair. Supervisory Bd and mem. Exec. Cttee, EWE AG 2012–17; mem. Advisory Bd Baden-Württembergische Bank AG 2014–. *Address:* Energie Baden-Württemberg AG, Durlacher Allee 93, 76131 Karlsruhe, Germany (office). *Telephone:* (721) 6300 (office). *Fax:* (721) 6313143 (office). *E-mail:* info@enbw.com (office). *Website:* www.enbw.com (office).

MASUDA, Hiroya; Japanese politician; b. 20 Dec. 1951; ed Univ. of Tokyo; began career at Ministry of Construction 1977; Dir Traffic Enforcement Div., Traffic Dept, Chiba Pref. Police HQ 1982–86; Dir Railway Traffic Div., Dept of Planning, Ibaraki Pref. 1986–93; Dir River Admin Policy Planning, Gen. Affairs Div., River Bureau, Ministry of Construction 1993–94, Dir Construction Disputes Settlement, Construction Industry Div., Econ. Affairs Bureau 1994–95; Gov. of Iwate Pref. 1995–2007; Minister for Internal Affairs and Communications, Minister of State for Decentralization Reform, Correcting Regional Disparities, Regional Govt (doshu-sei) and Privatization of the Postal Services 2007–08 (resgnd); apptd Deputy Chair. Decentralization Reform Cttee 2007; Visiting Prof., Graduate School of Public Policy, Univ. of Tokyo. *Publications:* Local Extinctions 2014.

MASUI, Yoshio, PhD, FRS, OC, FRSC; Canadian (b. Japanese) biologist and academic; *Professor Emeritus, Department of Cell and System Biology, University of Toronto;* b. 6 Oct. 1931, Kyoto; s. of Fusa-Jiro Masui and Toyoko Masui; m. Yuriko Masui 1959; one s. one d.; ed Kyoto Univ.; teacher of biology, Konan High School, Kobe; Research Asst, Biology Dept, Konan Univ. 1955–61, Lecturer 1961–65, Asst Prof. 1965–68, Prof. Emer. 1997–; Lecturer, Biology Dept, Yale Univ. 1969; Assoc. Prof., Zoology Dept, Univ. of Toronto 1969–78, Prof., Dept of Cell and System Biology 1978–97, Prof. Emer. 1997–; Visiting Prof. Tokyo Univ. 1999, Hiroshima Univ. 2000, Konan Univ. 2002–04; discovered Maturation Promoting Factor (MPF), cytostatic factor (CSF) proteins in the cytoplasm of cells that controls cell div.; Manning Award 1991, Gairdner Int. Award 1992, Albert Lasker Medical Research Award 1998. *Publications include:* numerous scientific papers. *Address:* Department of Cell and System Biology, University of Toronto, 25 Harbord Street, Toronto, ON M5S 3G5 (office); 401-640 Sheppard Avenue East, North York, Toronto, ON M2K 1B8, Canada (home). *Telephone:* (416) 978-3493 (office); (647) 343-0497 (home). *Fax:* (416) 978-8532 (office). *E-mail:* yoshio.masui@utoronto.ca (office); masui@rogers.com. *Website:* www.csb.utoronto.ca (office).

MASUKO, Osamu; Japanese automotive industry executive; *Acting Chairman and CEO, Mitsubishi Motors Corporation;* ed Waseda Univ.; joined Mitsubishi Corpn 1972, Man. Korea Team, Motor Vehicle Dept 1990–91, Man. Indonesia Team 1991–95, Asst Gen. Man. Motor Vehicle Dept 1995–97, Chief Adviser, P.T. Krama Yudhi Tiga Berlian Motors, Jakarta 1997–2002, Gen. Man. Motor Vehicle Unit 2002–03, Sr Vice Pres. and Div. COO Motor Vehicle Business Div. 2003–04, Man. Dir and Head Overseas Operations 2004–05, Pres., COO, Chief Business Ethics Officer Mitsubishi Motors Corpn Jan.–April 2005, Rep. Dir, Pres. and Chief Business Ethics Officer April 2005–11, Rep. Dir and Pres. 2011–, Rep. Dir, Chair. 2014–16 (Acting Chair. 2018–), CEO 2014–. *Address:* Mitsubishi Motors Corpn, 33-8, Shiba 5-chome, Minato-ku, Tokyo 108-8410, Japan (office). *Telephone:* (3) 6719-2111 (office). *Fax:* (3) 6719-0059 (office). *E-mail:* info@mitsubishi-motors.com (office). *Website:* www.mitsubishi-motors.com (office).

MASUKU, Melusi Martin, MA; Swazi lawyer and diplomatist; *Permanent Representative to United Nations;* m.; two c.; ed St John's Univ., New York, Univ. of Swaziland (now Univ. of Eswatini); Asst Protocol Officer, Ministry of Foreign Affairs (MFA) 1993–94; First Sec. of Legal Affairs, Perm. Mission to UN 1994–2004, Counsellor, Embassy of Swaziland (now Eswatini), Kenya 2004–05, Legal Officer, MFA 2005–06, Legal Adviser 2006–13, Under-Sec. (Political) 2013–14, Chief of Protocol 2014–17, Perm. Rep. to UN 2017–. *Address:* Permanent Mission of Eswatini, 408 E 50th Street, New York, NY 10022, USA (office). *Telephone:* (212) 371-8910 (office). *Fax:* (212) 754-2755 (office). *E-mail:* swazinymission@yahoo.com (office).

MASUREL, Jean-Louis Antoine Nicolas, MBA; French industrialist and vintner; b. 18 Sept. 1940, Cannes; s. of Antoine and Anne-Marie Masurel (née Gallant); m. 1st 1964; two d.; m. 2nd Martine Fabrega 1987; ed Hautes Etudes Commerciales, Graduate School of Business Admin., Harvard Univ.; with Morgan Guaranty Trust Co., New York, last position Sr Vice-Pres. New York 1964–80; Sr Exec. Vice-Pres. Banque de Paris & des Pays Bas 1980–82; Deputy Pres. Banque Paribas 1982–83; Legal Man. Société des Vins de Fontfroide 1983–89, now Managing Partner; Man. Dir Moët-Hennessy 1983–89, Vice-Chair. 1987; Man. Dir LVMH Moët-Hennessy Louis Vuitton 1987–89; Pres. Arcos Investissement SA 1989–, Hediard SA 1991–95; Hon. Pres. Harvard Business School Club de France 1993–96; mem. Supervisory Bd Peugeot SA 1987–, 21 Centrale Partners SA, Oudart SA; Dir Soc. des Bains de Mer (SBM), Monaco 1994–15; Sr Int. Adviser, BBL Investment Banking 1997–99, ING Barings 1999–2001; Dir Banque du Gothard SAM, Monaco 1998–, Oudart SA 1999–; Gov. American Hosp. in Paris; wine producer in Néoules (Domaine de Trians-Var); Chevalier des Arts et des Lettres 1996; Chevalier Légion d'honneur 2001. *Leisure interests:* hunting, skiing, windsurfing. *Address:* Arcos Investissement, 10a rue de la Paix, 75002 Paris; Domaine de Trians, 83136 Néoules, France (home). *Telephone:* 1-42-96-01-96. *Fax:* 1-42-96-01-70. *E-mail:* jlmasurel@wanadoo.fr (office). *Website:* www.trians.com (home).

MASUZOE, Yoichi, LLB; Japanese academic, politician and television commentator; b. 29 Nov. 1948, Fukuoka Pref.; ed Univ. of Tokyo; Research Fellow, Univ. of Tokyo 1971–73, Institut d'Histoire des Relations Internationales Contemporaines, Univ. of Paris, France 1973–75, Institut d'Hautes Etudes Internationales, Univ. of Geneva, Switzerland 1976–78; Assoc. Prof. of Political Science and History, Univ. of Tokyo 1979–89; Dir Masuzoe Inst. of Political Economy 1989–; mem. House of Councillors (Senator) 2001–13, fmr Dir Budget Cttee, Research Comm. on Constitution, Pres. Cttee on Foreign Affairs and Defence 2005–07; Minister of Health, Labour and Welfare 2007–09; Gov. of Tokyo 2014–16 (resgnd); mem. Liberal Democratic Party (LDP) –2010, Chair. Senate Policy Bd 2006–07; Ed.-in-Chief Cahiers Du Japon 1998–2001; Pres. The New Renaissance Party 2010–13. *Publications include:* Akai bara wa saitaka (Politics in France) 1983, Sengyo to siteno seijika (Political Leadership) 1989, Sengo Nihon no Gen'ei (Dangerous Cult) 1995, 20 Seiki Energi Kakumei no Jidai (The Meaning of the 20th Century) 1998, Years of Trial: Japan in the 1990s 2000, Haha ni Mutsuki wo Aterutoki (Care for My Mother) 1998, Naikaku Soridaijin (Prime Minister) 2002, Nagata-cho vs. Kasumigaseki 2007, Watashi no Genten soshite Chikai (My History) 2008, Masuzoe Memo 2010, Nihon Shinsei Keikaku 2010.

MATA FIGUEROA, Gen.-in-Chief Carlos José; Venezuelan army officer and government official; b. 30 Oct. 1957, Pedregal, Nueva Esparta; s. of Naphtali Mata and Hilda Figueroa Mata; ed Universidad Santa María, Mil. Acad. of Venezuela; Head of Mil. Affairs of the Pres. 2009, Chief of Operational Strategic Command 2009–; Minister of Defence 2010–12; Gov. of Nueva Esparta 2012–; mem. United Socialist Party of Venezuela. *Address:* c/o Ministry of Defence, Edif. 17 de Diciembre, planta baja, Base Aérea Francisco de Miranda, La Carlota, Caracas, Venezuela. *E-mail:* info@carlosmatafigueroa.org; noiralith.gil@mindefensa.gov.ve. *Website:* carlosmatafigueroa.org.

MATACZYŃSKI, Maciej, LLD; Polish lawyer, business executive and academic; *Managing Partner, SMM Legal;* ed Faculty of Law, Adam Mickiewicz Univ. (Fulbright Scholar), Poznań, T.M.C. Assera Inst., The Hague, Netherlands; tutor,

European Law Professorship, Faculty of Law, Adam Mickiewicz Univ., Poznań 2003–; legal adviser on civil law contracts 2004–; Sec. and Ind. mem., subsequently Chair. Supervisory Bd PKN Orlen Jan.–Nov. 2006, Chair. Supervisory Bd 2008–13, Chair. Nomination and Remuneration Cttee, mem. Corp. Governance Cttee; Partner, Sowisło and Topolewski audit office, Poznań 2008–13; Managing PnrMataczyński Dybiński Krzemień (now SMM Legal) 2013–; Sec. Supervisory Bd TC Dębica SA and mem. Audit Cttee 2008–. *Publications:* numerous law publs in Poland and abroad. *Address:* SMM Legal, 00-872 Warsaw, ul. Chłodna 52, Poland (office). *Telephone:* (22) 1010430 (office). *Fax:* (22) 1010437 (office). *E-mail:* maciej.mataczynski@smmlegal.pl (office). *Website:* smmlegal.pl (office).

MATAKA, Elizabeth; Botswana social worker and UN official; b. 1946, Francistown; m.; four c.; ed Univ. of Zambia; several years' experience in the field of HIV/AIDS with govt insts, private sector and non-govt orgs in Zambia; Founder and Exec. Dir Family Health Trust, Lusaka 1990–2003; fmr Vice-Chair. Global Fund to Fight AIDS, Tuberculosis and Malaria; Exec. Dir Zambia Nat. AIDS Network 2003–07; Special Envoy of Sec.-Gen. for HIV/AIDS in Africa, UN 2007–12; mem. Advisory Bd UNESCO, North Star Foundation; mem. Reference Group, Swedish/Norwegian HIV/AIDS Team for Africa; Dir Centre for Infectious Disease Research, Zambia; Dir and Chair. Children Int. Zambia; Founder-mem. Southern African Network of AIDS Service Orgs; mem. Compact Working Group on Gender, Global Task Force on Women, Girls Gender Equality and HIV 2009–. *Address:* c/o UNAIDS Secretariat 20, Avenue Appia, 1211 Geneva 27, Switzerland.

MATAKI, Tateo; Japanese advertising industry executive; b. 2 March 1939; joined Dentsu 1962, held several positions until mem. Bd of Dirs 1995, first as Man. Dir Newspaper and Magazines Divs, then as Sr Man. Dir in charge of Account Services, Exec. Vice-Pres. Dentsu Inc. 1999–2002, Pres. and COO 2002–03, Pres. and CEO 2004–07, Chair. and CEO 2007–08, Sr Corp. Advisor 2008; Dir Japan Productivity Centre for Socio-Econ. Devt (JPC-SED) 2003; Corp. Advisor, Japan Advertising Industry Assen 2017–18; mem. Supervisory Bd, Publicis Groupe SA (fmrly Saatchi & Saatchi Plc) from 2004; Order of the Rising Sun, Gold and Silver Star 2015; named to Asian Fed. of Advertising Asscns' (AFAA) Hall of Fame at AdAsia Vietnam 2013.

MATAMBO, Ontefetse Kenneth, MA; Botswana economist and politician; *Minister of Finance and Development Planning;* b. 1 Dec. 1947, Tonota; ed Univs of Botswana, Lesotho and Swaziland, Univs of Bradford and Sussex, UK, Williams Coll., USA; various roles within Ministry of Finance and Devt Planning including Economist 1972–74, Sr Economist 1974–76, Prin. Economist 1976–78, Sec. of Econ. Affairs 1978–90, Perm. Sec. 1995–98, Minister of Finance and Devt Planning 2014–; mem. Nat. Ass. (parl.) (Specially Elected Mem.) 2009–; Alt. Exec. Dir World Bank, Washington DC 1990–92, Exec. Dir 1992–94; Vice-Chair. Botswana Inst. of Devt Policy Analysis 1995–98; Chair. Lobatse Clay Works (Pty) Ltd 1998; fmr Man. Dir Botswana Development Corpn Ltd; fmr mem. Bd of Dirs Bank of Botswana, Debswana, De Beers Consolidated Mines, De Beers Centenary AG, Botswana Diamond Valuing Co. (Pty) Ltd. *Address:* Ministry of Finance and Development Planning, Government Enclave, Khama Crescent, Blk 25, State Drive, PMB 008, Gaborone, Botswana (office). *Telephone:* 3950100 (office). *Fax:* 3905742 (office). *E-mail:* kmutasa@gov.bw (office). *Website:* www.finance.gov.bw (office).

MATANE, Sir Paulias Nguna, Kt, CMG, OBE, GCMG; Papua New Guinea diplomatist; b. 21 Sept. 1931, Viviran, Rabaul; s. of Ilias Matane and Elta Matane (née Toto); m. Kaludia Peril 1957; two s. two d.; worked in Dept of Educ. 1957–69; mem. Public Service Bd 1969; Head, Dept of Lands, Surveys and Mines 1969, of Business Devt 1970–75; Amb. to USA and Mexico 1975–80, Perm. Rep. to UN 1975–81, High Commr in Canada 1977–81; Sec., Dept of Foreign Affairs and Trade 1980–85; Chair. Cttee on the Philosophy of Educ. for Papua New Guinea 1986–88, Cocoa Industry Investigating Cttee of Cocoa Quality in Papua New Guinea 1986–88, Ocean Trading Co. Pty Ltd 1989–91, Newton Pacific (PNG) Pty Ltd 1989; Censorship Bd of PNG 1990–93; Dir Treid Pacific (PNG) Pty Ltd 1987–96 (Chair. 1987–91); apptd Presenter weekly radio programme Insait Long Komuniti 1998, weekly programme on EMTV 1990; columnist, The Time Traveller, in The National Newspaper 1999; Dir Nat. Museum and Art Gallery (Bd of Trustees) 1995–99, Pres. 1999–; Dir Nat. Library and Archives 1996; Chair. Community Consultative Cttee on East New Britain Provincial Govt of Autonomy –2004; Gov.-Gen. of Papua New Guinea 2004–11; mem. Nat. Investment and Devt Authority, Nat. Tourism Authority, Nat. Citizenship Advisory Cttee, Univ. of Papua New Guinea Council; Hon. DTech (Papua New Guinea) 1985, Hon. DPhil (Papua New Guinea) 1985; 10th Independence Anniversary Medal 1985, UN 40th Anniversary Medal, Silver Jubilee Medal 2001. *Publications include:* My Childhood in New Guinea, A New Guinean Travels through Africa, Two New Guineans Travel through South East Asia, What Good is Business?, Aimbe the Magician, Aimbe the Challenger, Aimbe the School Dropout, Aimbe the Pastor, Kum Tumun of Minj, Two Papua New Guineans Discover the Bible Lands (later retitled Travels Through the Bible Lands) 1987, To Serve with Love 1989, Chit-Chats 1991, East to West–The Longest Train Trip in the World 1991, Let's Do It PNG, Trekking through the New Worlds, Voyage to Antarctica 1996, Laughter Made in PNG 1996, Amazing Discoveries in 40 Years of Marriage 1996, The Word Power 1998, The Other Side of Port Moresby . . . In Pictures 1998, A Trip of a Lifetime 1998, Waliling Community United Church Then and Now 1998, Coach Adventures Down Under 1999, Some Answers to our Management Problems in the Public and Private Sectors 1999, More Answers to Our Management Problems 1999, Chit-Chats (vol. 3) 2000, Management for Excellence 2001, Exploring the Holy Lands 2001, Travels Through South-East Asia (vols 1 and 2) 2001, Humour: The Papua New Guinean Way, Ripples in the South Pacific Ocean, India: a Splendour in Cultural Diversity, Papua New Guinea: The Land of Natural Beauty, Diversity: The Time Traveller. *Leisure interests:* reading, squash, writing, travel, gardening, swimming. *Address:* Paulias Matane Foundation Inc., Government House, PO Box 79, Port Moresby, NCD (office); Newton Pacific and Associates Ltd, PO Box 3405, Kokopo, ENBP, Papua New Guinea. *Telephone:* 9829152 (office). *Fax:* 9829151 (office). *E-mail:* ggeneral@global.net.pg (office); pnggg9@gmail.com (office).

MATASKELEKELE, Kalkot; Ni-Vanuatu lawyer, judge and fmr head of state; b. 24 April 1949; m. Heather Lini (2014); ed Univ. of Papua New Guinea; fmr Judge, Supreme Court; fmr Solicitor-Gen.; mem. Nat. United Party; Pres. of Vanuatu 2004–09; Ombudsman of Vanuatu.

MATATA PONYO, Augustin, BEcons; Democratic Republic of the Congo economist and politician; b. 5 June 1964, Kindu, Maniema Prov.; Hortense Kachoko Mbonda; five c.; ed Univ. of Lubumbashi, Univ. of Kinshasa; began career as Asst, Econs Faculty, Univ. of Kinshasa; Econ. Researcher, Banque centrale du Congo 1988–2000; joined Ministry of Finance, becoming Econ. and Monetary Adviser, Macro-Econ. Adviser, responsible for Relations with IMF, World Bank and Int. Co-operation 2000–03, later Pres. Planning Dept, Bureau central de coordination internationale (BCECO) (procurement office under Ministry of Finance), Dir-Gen. BCECO 2003–10, Minister of Finance 2010–12; Prime Minister 2012–16 (resgnd); mem. People's Party for Reconstruction and Democracy (Parti du Peuple pour la Reconstruction et la Démocratie).

MATCHAVARIANI, Ivane; Georgian business executive and politician; *Minister of Finance;* b. 11 Feb. 1974, Tbilisi; ed Ivane Javakhishvili Tbilisi State Univ.; Specialist, Financial Dept, Geocell Ltd 1997–2000, Sr Specialist July–Dec. 2000, Man., Financial Services and Int. Accounts Dept 2001–06, Financial Dir 2006–13, Commercial Dir 2013–18; Team mem., Eurasian Operations, TeliaSonera 2010–11; participated in commercial and technological studies with various consulting cos (McKinsey, Accenture, Informa Telecoms, Delta Partners) 2012–15; Minister of Finance 2018–. *Address:* Ministry of Finance, 0114 Tbilisi, V. Gorgasali 16, Georgia (office). *Telephone:* (32) 226-14-44 (office). *E-mail:* minister@mof.ge (office). *Website:* mof.ge (office).

MATE, Dragutin; Slovenian politician, defence expert and fmr government official; b. 2 May 1963, Čakovec; ed Univ. of Ljubljana; teacher, Polanje Gymnasium, Ljubljana 1989–90; Deputy Sector Chief for Civil Defence and mem. Repub. Civil Defence Staff, Ministry of Defence 1990–91, worked in Counter-intelligence Dept 1991–92; Int. Co-operation Adviser, Office of Defence Minister 1992–96; Mil. and Air Force Attaché and Doyen, Mil. Diplomatic Corps, Bosnia and Herzegovina 1996; Deputy Dir Mil. Affairs Admin, Ministry of Defence, Dir Personnel Service then Dir Defence Admin 2000–04; Minister of Internal Affairs 2004–08; mem. Parl. 2011–; mem. City Council of Ljubljana; mem. Slovenian Democratic Party 2008–16.

MATEPARAE, Lt-Gen. Rt Hon. Sir Jeremiah (Jerry), GNZM, QSO, KStJ, MA (Hons); New Zealand army officer, government official and diplomatist; *High Commissioner to UK;* b. 14 Nov. 1954, Whanganui; m. Janine Mateparae; five c.; ed Officer Cadet School, Portsea, Australia, Univ. of Waikato; enlisted in Regular Force of NZ Army 1972; mem. Royal NZ Infantry Regt (RNZIR) 1976; appointments included command at platoon, co. and battalion level in NZ Infantry Bns, also served with NZ Special Air Service, commanded First Bn, RNZIR; other appointments included Chief Instructor NZ Army's Tactical School, Staff Officer Operations, NZ Army Training Group, Army Gen. Staff and Dir of Force Devt, HQ NZ Defence Force; apptd NZ Army's Land Commdr 1999; jt command of NZ forces in East Timor 1999–2001; re-apptd Land Component Commdr in HQ of Jt Forces NZ 2001; Chief of Army 2002–06; Chief NZ Defence Force (first Maori) 2006–11; Dir Govt Communication Security Bureau Feb.–July 2011; Gov.-Gen. of NZ 2011–16; High Commr to UK 2017–; Fellow, NZ Inst. of Man.; Kt Grand Companion, NZ Order of Merit, Companion of the Queen's Service Order, Kt of Justice of the Order of St John, NZ Operational Service Medal, UNIFIL Medal, NZ General Service Medal (Non-Warlike) 1992, East Timor Medal, NZ Armed Forces Award with Clasp, Darjah Utama Bakti Cemerlang (Tentera); Hon. DLitt (Massey Univ.); Distinguished Alumni Award, Univ. of Waikato. *Address:* New Zealand High Commission, New Zealand House, 80 Haymarket, London, SW1Y 4TQ, England (office). *Telephone:* (20) 7930-8422 (office). *Fax:* (20) 7839-4580 (office). *E-mail:* aboutnz@newzealandhc.org.uk (office); email@newzealandhc.org.uk (office). *Website:* www.nzembassy.com/united-kingdom (office).

MATER, Ahmed, MBBS; Saudi Arabian artist; b. 25 July 1979, Abha; s. of Mater Ahmed al-Ziad and Fatimah Hassan Abdullah Aseeri; m. Arwa Yahya al-Neimy; ed King Khalid Univ. Abha Coll. of Medicine; early career as physician at Aseer central hospital, before becoming artist; joined al-Miftaha Arts Village (part of King Fahd Culture Centre) 1999; works include painting, photography, installations, video and calligraphy; Founder Edge of Arabia (independent arts initiative), co-curator Edge of Arabia's first show, SOAS Brunei Gallery, London 2008; invited to participate in 53rd Venice Biennale 2009. *E-mail:* info@ahmedmater.com (office). *Website:* ahmedmater.com (office).

MATEŠA, Zlatko, DrSc; Croatian politician, judge, academic and organization executive; *Assistant Dean, Zagreb School of Economics and Management;* b. 17 June 1949, Zagreb; divorced; two c.; ed Zagreb Univ., Henley Man. College, UK, J.F. Kennedy School of Govt, Harvard, USA, Beijing Sport Univ., People's Repub. of China; Asst Judge, Judge Zagreb Municipal Court 1978; Asst Man., Man. Legal Dept INA-Trade (Industrija Nafte Asscn) 1978–82, Dir Legal and Personnel Dept 1982–85, Dir Joint Admin. Services 1985–89, mem. Man. Bd, Vice-Pres. 1989–90; Asst to Gen.-Man. INA-HQ 1990–92; mem. Croatian Democratic Union (HDZ); Dir Agency for Reconstruction and Devt of Govt of Croatia 1992–93; Minister without Portfolio 1993–95; Minister of Economy Sept.–Nov. 1995; Prime Minister of Croatia 1995–2000; currently Asst Dean, Zagreb School of Econs and Man.; Pres. Croatian Olympic Cttee 2002–. *Publications:* numerous books and articles, including Strategic Management, Sport Management, An Introduction to Sport Law. *Leisure interests* flying, water polo. *Address:* Zagreb School of Economics and Management, Jordanovac 110, 10000 Zagreb, Croatia (office). *Telephone:* (1) 2354242 (office). *Fax:* (1) 2354243 (office). *E-mail:* zlatko.matesa@zsem.hr (office). *Website:* www.zsem.hr (office).

MATEU PI, Meritxell; Andorran diplomatist and politician; b. 19 Jan. 1966, Escaldes Engordany; three s. one d.; ed Paul Valéry Univ., Montpellier and Inst. of Int. Relations, Paris, France; Amb. to France 1995–99, also Perm. Rep. to Council of Europe and UNESCO, Amb. to EU, Belgium and Luxembourg 1997–98, to Netherlands 1998–99, to Denmark 1999, to Germany 1999–2004, to Slovenia 2001; Minister of Housing, Higher Educ. and Research 2001–07, of Foreign Affairs, Culture and Co-operation 2007–09; mem. Consell General (Parl.); mem. Parl. Ass., Council of Europe 2011–; mem. Demòcrates per Andorra; mem. Alliance des démocrates et des libéraux pour l'Europe 2011–, Vice-Chair. 2013–; Officier, Ordre nat. du Mérite 1999. *Address:* Consell General del Principat d'Andorra, Carrer de la Vall s/n, 500 Andorra la Vella, Andorra (office). *Telephone:* 877877 (office). *E-mail:* meritxellmateupi@gmail.com (home). *Website:* www.parlament.ad (office).

MATHAS, Theodore (Ted) A., AB, JD; American insurance executive; *Chairman and CEO, New York Life Insurance Company;* b. 1967, Norfolk, Va; m. Keryn Mathas; three c.; ed Stanford Univ., Univ. of Virginia; attorney, Debevoise & Plimpton –1995; joined Asset Man. Div., New York Life Insurance Co. 1995, Pres. Eagle Strategies Corpn (subsidiary co.) 1996–99, also Pres. NYLIFE Securities Inc. 1997–99, COO for career agency distribution system 1999–2001, COO Life & Annuity 2001–04, mem. Exec. Man. Cttee 2002–, mem. Bd Dirs and Vice-Chair. 2006–07, COO 2006–08, Pres. 2007–15, CEO 2008–, Chair. 2009–; Dir, Haier New York Life Insurance Ltd, Shanghai, Max New York Life Insurance Co. Ltd, New Delhi; mem. Bd, American Council of Life Insurers. *Address:* New York Life Insurance Co., 51 Madison Avenue, Suite 3200, New York, NY 10010, USA (office). *Telephone:* (212) 576-7000 (office). *Fax:* (212) 576-8145 (office). *E-mail:* info@newyorklife.com (office). *Website:* www.newyorklife.com (office).

MATHER, Graham Christopher Spencer, CBE, MA; British politician, solicitor and administrator; *President, European Policy Forum;* b. 23 Oct. 1954, Preston, Lancs.; s. of Thomas Mather and Doreen Mather; m. 1st Fiona Marion McMillan Bell 1981 (divorced 1995); two s.; m. 2nd Geneviève Elizabeth Fairhurst 1997; ed Hutton Grammar School, New Coll., Oxford (Burnet Law Scholar); Asst to Dir-Gen. Inst. of Dirs 1980, est. Policy Unit 1983, Head of Policy Unit 1983–86; Deputy Dir Inst. of Econ. Affairs 1987, Gen. Dir 1987–92; Pres. European Policy Forum 1992–, European Media Forum 1997–2015, European Financial Forum 1999–, The Infrastructure Forum 2009–; MEP for Hampshire North and Oxford 1994–99; Visiting Fellow, Nuffield Coll. Oxford 1992–99; mem. Competition Appeals Tribunal 2000–11; mem. Monopolies and Mergers Comm. 1989–94, Westminster City Council 1982–86; Conservative parl. cand. for Blackburn 1983; Vice-Pres. Asscn of Dist Councils 1994–97; Consultant, Tudor Investment Corpn 1992–2012; Adviser, Elliott Assocs 2006–; Chair. World Free Zone Convention 2000–; Dir (non-exec.), Ofcom 2015–, Office of Road & Rail 2016–. *Publications:* Striking out Strikes (with C. G. Hanson) 1988; Europe's Constitutional Future (contrib.) 1990, Making Decisions in Britain 2000; papers and contribs to journals. *Address:* European Policy Forum, 49 Whitehall, London, SW1A 2BX, England (office). *Telephone:* (20) 7839-7565 (office). *Fax:* (20) 3137-2040 (office). *E-mail:* graham.mather@epfltd.org (office). *Website:* www.epfltd.org (office).

MATHER, John C., BA, PhD; American astrophysicist; *Senior Project Scientist, James Webb Space Telescope, Goddard Space Flight Center, National Aeronautics and Space Administration (NASA);* b. 7 Aug. 1946, Roanoke, Va; s. of Robert Eugene Mather and Martha Belle Cromwell Mather; m. Jane Anne Hauser; ed Swarthmore Coll., Pa, Univ. of California, Berkeley; began career as NAS Research Assoc., Goddard Inst. for Space Studies, NASA, becoming Study Scientist for Cosmic Background Explorer satellite (COBE), Goddard Space Flight Center 1976–88, then Project Scientist 1988–94, Head of Infrared Astrophysics Br. 1988–89, 1990–93, Study Scientist, James Webb Space Telescope (JWST) 1995–99, Sr Project Scientist 1999–; Chief Scientist, NASA HQ Science Mission Directorate 2007–08; mem. NAS 1997, American Acad. of Arts and Sciences 1998; Fellow, American Physical Soc. 1996, Int. Soc. for Optical Eng (SPIE) 2007, Optical Soc. of America 2009, AAAS, AIAA; Hon. DSc (Swarthmore Coll.) 1994, (Maryland) 2008, (Notre Dame) 2011, (Muhlenberg Coll.) 2017; Goddard Sr Fellow, holder of numerous awards, including John C. Lindsay Memorial Award 1990, NASA Exceptional Scientific Achievement Award 1991, Nat. Air and Space Museum Trophy 1991, American Inst. of Aeronautics and Astronautics Space Science Award 1993, American Acad. of Arts and Sciences Rumford Prize 1996, Univ. of Ariz. Marc Aaronson Memorial Prize 1998, George W. Goddard Award, Soc. of Photo-Optical Instrumentation Engineers 2005, Franklin Inst. Benjamin Franklin Medal 1999, Gruber Cosmology Prize 2006, Nobel Prize in Physics (with George F. Smoot) 2006, Antoinette de Vaucouleurs Medal, Univ. of Texas 2007, Robinson Prize in Cosmology, Univ. of Newcastle upon Tyne, UK 2008, Gold Medal from Prime Minister of India 2009, Chalonge Medal, Observatoire de Paris 2011. *Publication:* The Very First Light (with John Boslough) 1996, 2008. *Address:* Astrophysics Science Division, NASA/GSFC, Mail Code 443, Observational Cosmology, Greenbelt, MD 20771, USA (office). *Telephone:* (301) 286-6885 (office). *Fax:* (301) 286-5558 (office). *E-mail:* john.c.mather@nasa.gov (office). *Website:* science.gsfc.nasa.gov/sed/bio/john.c.mather (office).

MATHEWS, (Forrest) David, AB, PhD; American educationalist and foundation executive; *President, CEO and Trustee, Charles F. Kettering Foundation;* b. 6 Dec. 1935, Grove Hill, Ala; s. of Forrest Lee and Doris Mathews; m. Mary Chapman 1960; two d.; ed Univ. of Alabama and Columbia Univ.; Infantry Officer, US Army Reserves 1959–67; Lecturer and Prof. of History, Univ. of Alabama 1965–80, Pres. 1969–80; Sec. of Health, Educ. and Welfare 1975–77; Chair. Nat. Council for Public Policy Educ. 1980–; Dir Acad. Educ. Devt 1975–2003; mem. Bd of Trustees, Charles F. Kettering Foundation 1972–, Pres. and CEO 1981–; mem. Bd Dirs, Nat. Civic League 1996–2005; mem. numerous advisory and other bds including Acad. for Educ. Devt, Nat. Civic League, Exec. Cttee of Public Agenda; Trustee, Nat. March of Dimes 1977–85, John F. Kennedy Center for Performing Arts 1975–77, Woodrow Wilson Int. Center for Scholars 1975–77, Miles Coll. 1978–, Teachers Coll., Columbia Univ. 1977–95, Gerald R. Ford Foundation 1988–; 16 hon. degrees; numerous awards. *Publications:* works on history of Southern USA, higher educ. in public policy, including The Changing Agenda for American Higher Education, The Promise of Democracy, Is There a Public for Public Schools? 1996, Politics for People: Finding a Responsible Voice 1999, Why Public Schools? Whose Public Schools? 2003, Reclaiming Public Education by Reclaiming Our Democracy 2006, The Ecology of Democracy: Finding Ways to Have a Stronger Hand in Shaping Our Future 2014. *Leisure interest:* gardening. *Address:* The Charles F. Kettering Foundation, 200 Commons Road, Dayton, OH 45459 (office); 6050 Mad River Road, Dayton, OH 45459, USA. *Telephone:* (937) 434-7300 (office). *Fax:* (937) 428-5353 (office). *E-mail:* info@kettering.org (office). *Website:* www.kettering.org/people/david-mathews-president-and-ceo (office).

MATHEWSON, Sir George (Ross), Kt, CBE, MBA, PhD, FRSE, CEng, MIEE, CIMgt; British banking executive; b. 14 May 1940, Dunfermline, Fife, Scotland; s. of George Mathewson and Charlotte Gordon (née Ross); m. Sheila Alexandra Graham (née Bennett) 1966; two s.; ed Perth Acad., Univ. of St Andrews, Canisius Coll., Buffalo, NY, USA; Asst Lecturer, St Andrews Univ. 1964–67; various posts in Research and Devt, Avionics Engineer, Bell Aerospace, Buffalo, NY 1967–72; joined Industrial & Commercial Finance Corpn, Edinburgh 1972, Area Man., Aberdeen 1974, Asst Gen. Man. and Dir 1979; Chief Exec. and mem. Scottish Devt Agency 1981–87; Dir of Strategic Planning and Devt, Royal Bank of Scotland Group 1987–90, Deputy Group Chief Exec. 1990–92, Group Chief Exec. 1992–2000, Exec. Deputy Chair. 2000–01, Chair. 2001–06 (retd); Chair. Campaign Bd, Royal Botanic Gardens, Edinburgh 2006–; Chair. (non-exec.) Tosca (hedge fund); Dir (non-exec.), Scottish Investment Trust PLC (Chair. Nominations Cttee and Chair.'s Advisory Group) 1981–, Inst. of Int. Finance Inc. 2001–, Santander Central Hispano, SA 2001–, Cheviot Asset Management, Stagecoach Group; Pres. British Bankers' Asscn 2002–05, Int. Monetary Conf.; Convener of Scotland's Council of Econ. Advisers; Fellow, Chartered Inst. of Bankers in Scotland 1994; Hon. LLD (Dundee) 1983, (St Andrews) 2000; Hon. DUniv (Glasgow) 2001. *Publications include:* several articles on eng and finance. *Leisure interests:* rugby, golf, tennis and water sports.

MATHIES, Richard A., BS, MS, PhD, FRSC; American chemist and academic; *Professor of Chemistry, Graduate School, University of California, Berkeley;* b. 1946, Seattle, Wash.; m. JoAnne Mathies; two c.; ed Univ. of Washington, Cornell Univ.; Helen Hay Whitney Fellow, Yale Univ. 1974–76; Asst Prof., Coll. of Chem., Univ. of California, Berkeley 1976–82, Alfred P. Sloan Fellow 1979–81, Assoc. Prof. 1982–86, Prof. of Chem. 1986–, Dir Center for Analytical Biotechnology 2003–08, Gilbert Newton Lewis Prof. 2008–13, Dean, Coll. of Chem. 2008–13, Prof. of Chem., Grad. School 2013–; mem. Scientific Advisory Bd, IntegenX, Singule, NanoString, Inc., C8 Medisensors, Affymetrix; mem. Editorial Bd, Biomedical Microdevices: BioMEMS and Biomedical Nanotechnology 1998–; mem. American Optical Soc., American Soc. for Photobiology, AAAS; Fellow, Optical Soc. of America 2004, Soc. for Applied Spectroscopy 2008, Nat. Acad. of Inventors 2015; Harold Lamport Award, New York Acad. of Sciences 1983, Research Award, American Soc. for Photobiology 1989, Frederick Conf. on Capillary Electrophoresis Award 1998, Research Award, Asscn for Lab. Automation 2001, Ellis R. Lippincott Award, Optical Soc. of America 2004, Instrumentation Award, Analytical Chem. Div., ACS 2010. *Achievements include:* development of energy transfer fluorescent labels that were critical to the early completion of the Human Genome Sequence. *Publications:* more than 380 publs and 35 patents on photochemistry, photobiology, bioanalytical chemistry and genome analysis tech. *Address:* Office of the Dean, College of Chemistry, 307 Lewis, 420 Latimer Hall, University of California, Berkeley, CA 94720-1460, USA (office). *Telephone:* (510) 642-4192 (office). *Fax:* (510) 642-3599 (office). *E-mail:* ramathies@berkeley.edu (office). *Website:* chemistry.berkeley.edu/faculty/chem/mathies (office).

MATHIESEN, Árni M., MSc; Icelandic politician and UN official; *Assistant Director-General, Fisheries and Aquaculture Department, United Nations Food and Agriculture Organization;* b. 2 Oct. 1958, Reykjavík; s. of Matthías Á. Mathiesen and Sigrún Þorgilsdóttir Mathiesen; m. Steinnun Kristín Fridjónsdóttir 1991; three d.; ed Flensborgarskóli, Hafnarfjödur, Univs of Edin. and Stirling, Scotland, UK; qualified as veterinarian 1983, worked as veterinary officer for fish diseases 1985–95; Man. Dir of Acquaculture, Faxalax hf. 1988–89; Chair. Flensborgarskóli Student Asscn 1977–78; Vice-Pres. Icelandic Asscn of Young Conservatives (SUS) 1985–87; Pres. Asscn of Young Conservatives (Stefnir), Hafnarfjödur 1986–88; elected mem. of Parl.; mem. Independence Party; Rep. of Iceland to Nordic Council 1991–95; mem. Parl. Cttee on EFTA and EEC 1995–99; Minister of Fisheries 1999–2005, of Finance 2005–09 (resgnd); currently Asst Dir-Gen., Fisheries and Aquaculture Dept, FAO; fmr Chair. Prevention of Cruelty to Animals; mem. Bd Guarantee Div., Acquaculture Loans 1990–94, Bd Icelandic Veterinary Asscn 1986–87, Bd of Búnadarbanki Islands; mem. Salary Council, Confed. of Univ. Grads 1985–87; mem. Flensborgarskóli School Bd 1990–99; fmr mem. Bd of Búnadarbanki Islands, Agricultural Loan Fund. *Address:* Fisheries and Aquaculture Department, UN Food and Agriculture Organization, Viale delle Terme di Caracalla, 00100 Rome, Italy (office). *Telephone:* (06) 5705-1 (office). *Fax:* (06) 5705-3152 (office). *E-mail:* fao-hq@fao.org (office). *Website:* www.fao.org/fishery/en (office).

MATHIESON, Peter William, MB BS (Hons), PhD, FRCP, FRCPE, FMedSci; British medical scientist, academic and university administrator; *Principal and Vice-Chancellor, The University of Edinburgh;* b. 18 April 1959, Colchester; s. of William Archibald Mathieson and Elizabeth Alice Mathieson; m. Christina Mathieson; one s. one d.; ed London Hosp. Medical Coll., Univ. of Cambridge; held junior posts in and around West London; MRC Training Fellow, Univ. of Cambridge; held MRC-funded Fellowship in Lab. of Profs Peter Lachmann and Doug Fearon on complement/immunology; Foundation Prof. of Renal Medicine, Univ. of Bristol and Hon. Consultant Nephrologist, North Bristol NHS Trust 1995–2013, Head of Univ. Dept of Clinical Science at North Bristol and Dir of Research and Devt for North Bristol NHS Trust 2007, Dean of Faculty of Medicine and Dentistry 2008–13, now Hon. Prof. of Medicine; Pres. and Vice-Chancellor The Univ. of Hong Kong 2014–18; Prin. and Vice-Chancellor Univ. of Edinburgh 2018–; mem. Renal Asscn Clinical Trials Cttee 1996–2007, Chair. 2000–03, Pres. Renal Asscn 2007–10; Chair. Research Grants Cttee, Kidney Research UK (fmrly Nat. Kidney Research Fund) 2003–07; mem. Advisory Panel, Cyberport, Hong Kong; mem. Univs. UK; mem. Bd Russell Group; mem. Exec. Cttee, Universitas21; mem. Main Cttee, Universities Scotland; mem. Univ. Council for the All-Party Parliamentary Univ. Group; mem. Governing Council, Chinese Government's Confucius Inst. Headquarters; Hon. Life mem. Australian & New Zealand Soc. of Nephrology 2011; Hon. Fellow, Hughes Hall, Cambridge 2015, Hong Kong Coll. of Physicians 2016; Hon. Pres. Coimbra Group. *Publications:* numerous papers in professional journals on human glomerular cell biology and regulation of glomerular permeability. *Leisure interests:* hill walking, travelling, spending time with family. *Address:* Principal's Office, University of Edinburgh, South Bridge, Edinburgh, EH8 9YL UK (office). *Telephone:* (13) 1650-2150 (office). *E-mail:* principal@ed.ac.uk (office). *Website:* www.ed.ac.uk (office).

MATHIS-EDDY, Darlene, PhD; American poet and academic; *Professor Emerita, Ball State University;* b. 19 March 1937, Elkhart, Ind.; d. of William Eugene Mathis and Fern Roose Paulmer Mathis; m. Spencer Livingston Eddy, Jr 1964 (died 1971); ed Goshen Coll. and Rutgers Univ.; Instructor in English, Douglass Coll. 1962–64; Instructor in English, Rutgers Univ. 1964, 1965, Rutgers Univ. Coll. (Adult Educ.) 1967; Asst Prof. in English, Ball State Univ. 1967–71, Assoc. Prof. 1971–75, Prof. 1975–99, Poet-in-Residence 1989–93, Prof. Emer., English and Humanities 1999–, Ralph S. Whitinger Lecturer, Ball State Univ.

Honors Coll. 1998–99; Adjunct Prof., Core Program and Coll. Seminar Program, Univ. of Notre Dame, South Bend, Ind. 2001–06; Consulting Ed. Blue Unicorn 1995–; Founding Ed. The Hedge Row Press 1995–; Docent, Midwest Museum of American Art 2010–; mem. Comm. on Women for the Nat. Council of Teachers of English 1976–79; Poetry Ed. BSU Forum; Vice-Pres. of Programs, American Asscn of Univ. Women, Elkhart Br.; Pres. American Asscn of Univ. Women 2008–10, Bd mem. 2010–; Bd mem., Friends of the Elkhart Public Library 2016–; Woodrow Wilson Nat. Fellow 1959–62, Rutgers Univ. Grad. Honors and Honors Dissertation Fellow 1964–65, 1966–67, Notable Woodrow Wilson Nat. Fellow 1991; numerous creative arts, creative teaching, research grants and awards. *Publications:* Leaf Threads, Wind Rhymes 1986, The Worlds of King Lear 1971, Weathering 1992, Reflections: Studies in Light 1993; Contributing Ed. Snowy Egret 1988–90; numerous poems in literary reviews; book reviews and essays in numerous journals; articles in American Literature, English Language Notes, etc. *Leisure interests:* gardening, music, antiques, reading, sketching, photography, bird watching, cooking. *Address:* 1840 West Cobblestone Boulevard, Elkhart, IN 46514-4961, USA (home). *Telephone:* (574) 266-4394 (home).

MATHUR, Murari Lal, PhD; Indian mechanical engineer and academic; *Professor Emeritus, Faculty of Engineering, University of Jodhpur;* b. 10 July 1931, Masuda; s. of Dr S. D. Mathur and Lalti Devi; m. Vimla Mathur 1961; one s. three d.; ed Govt Coll., Ajmer, Birla Engineering Coll., Pilani, Glasgow Univ., UK; Asst Prof., MBM Eng Coll., Govt of Rajasthan 1952–57; Deputy Dir of Tech. Educ. and Sec. Bd of Tech. Educ., Govt of Rajasthan 1957–58; Prof. and Head Mechanical Eng Dept, Univ. of Jodhpur 1963–85, Prof., Dean Faculty of Eng 1966–68, 1974, 1977–80, Vice-Chancellor 1985–90, Prof. Emer. 1991–; Chair. Automotive Prime-Movers Sectional Cttee, Indian Bureau of Standards; Co-ordinator Solar Passive House Project; design consultant heat exchanger and heat recovery equipment; consultant Cen. Silk Bd and other industries; Fellow, Inst. of Engineers (India); Sri Chandra Prakash Memorial Gold Medal, Pres. of India's Prize, Inst. of Engineers Award. *Films:* has produced two educational films. *Publications:* books on thermal eng, internal combustion engines, gas turbines and jet propulsion, thermodynamics, fluid mechanics and machines, machine drawing and heat transfer; over 80 research papers. *Leisure interests:* reading, writing, lecturing on educational topics and topics concerning energy and environment, social service. *Address:* Alok Villa, 17-A, Shastri Nagar, Jodhpur 342 003, India (home). *Telephone:* 2433207 (home); (98) 29253207 (mobile) (home).

MATHYS, Adidjatou; Benin economist and government official; b. 1956, Porto-Novo; m.; three c.; ed Nat. Univ. of Benin; held several posts at Directorate Gen. of Treasury and Public Accounting, including work with Chief of Financial Affairs 1982, Asst Receiver, Recovery Center 1984–85, Deputy Head of Service for Expenditure 1985–86, Chief of Expenditure 1986–94, Receiver of Finance for Ouémé 1994–98, Deputy Gen. Man. 1998–99, Gen. Man. 1999–2003; Asst to Minister of Economy and Finance 2004–06, apptd Chief of Staff to Minister for Budget 2007, Chief of Staff to Minister of Economy and Finance 2007–11, Minister of Economy and Finance 2011–12; campaign co-ordinator in presidential elections for Bruno Amoussou 2006, for Boni Yayi 2011; fmr mem. Bd of Dirs Banque Centrale des Etats de l'Afrique de l'Ouest, Continental Bank Benin; fmr mem. Parti Social-Démocrate; Hon. Pres. Front pour la Restauration de l'Unite Democratique (FRUD); Knight of the Order of Merit of Benin.

MATIN, Abdul, MA, PhD; Pakistani economist; b. 1 March 1932, Sawabi; s. of Dur Jamil Khan; m. Azra Matin 1959; three s.; ed Univ. of Peshawar and Univ. of Bonn, FRG; Chair. Dept of Econs, Univ. of Peshawar and Dir Bd of Econs, North-West Frontier Prov. (NWFP, Khyber Pakhtunkhwa since 2010) 1959–70; Chief Economist, Govt of NWFP 1970–72; Minister and Deputy Perm. Rep., Mission to UN, New York 1973–76; Exec. Dir ADBP, Islamabad 1977–85; Vice-Chancellor Univ. of Peshawar 1987–89; Vice-Pres. and mem. of Cen. Cttee, Pakistan Tehrik-i-Insaaf (Movt for Justice) 1996–; Chair. of Task Forces to Regulate Pvt. Educational Insts in NWFP 1999–, to Reform Higher Secondary Govt Schools in NWFP 2000–; mem. Nat. Comm. on Manpower, Govt of Pakistan, Educ. Inquiry Cttee, NWFP, Prov. Finance Comm., NWFP 2002–, Health Regulatory Authority, NWFP 2003–, Higher Educ. Comm. of Pakistan 2003–, Econ. Reform Comm., NWFP 2004, Search Cttee for Vice-Chancellors, NWFP; Chair. Govt Working Group on Transport Policy 1991–92, Univs Services Reforms and Man. Cttee, Govt of NWFP 1998; mem. Bd of Man. Quaid-e-Azam Mazar 2000–, Pakistan Bait-ul-Mal; engaged in research project 'Revival and Reconstruction of Muslim World'; prepared policy draft for Nat. Centre for Rehabilitation of Child Labour 2001; Chair. Think Tank, Hamdard Shura, NWFP 1994–; Hamdard Foundation Award for Outstanding Services 1992, Khawaja Farid Sang, Lahore 2004. *Publications:* Industrialization of NWFP 1970; 95 articles on the problems, policies and pattern of econ. devt in professional journals. *Leisure interests:* extension lectures, public speeches, involvement in discourses on rectification of West-Ummah relations. *Address:* House No. 27, Street No. 9, Sector D-3, Phase I, Hayatabad, Peshawar, Khyber Pakhtunkhwa, Pakistan (home). *Telephone:* 5817144 (home). *Fax:* 5817144 (home).

MATLANYANE, Retšelisitsoe Adelaide, BA, MEconSc, PhD; Lesotho economist and central banker; *Governor, Central Bank of Lesotho;* ed Nat. Univ. of Lesotho, Univ. of Botswana, Univ. of Pretoria, South Africa; joined Central Bank of Lesotho 2006, spent a year of attachment at IMF and participated in a country mission to Malawi, Second Deputy Gov. 2006–07, First Deputy Gov. 2007–11, Acting Gov. 2011–12, Gov. 2012–. *Address:* Office of the Governor, Central Bank of Lesotho, cnr Airport and Moshoeshoe Roads, POB 1184, Maseru 100, Lesotho (office). *Telephone:* 22314281 (office). *Fax:* 22310051 (office). *E-mail:* cbl@centralbank.org.ls (office). *Website:* www.centralbank.org.ls (office).

MATLYUBOV, Lt Gen. Bahodir Ahmedovich; Uzbekistani government official; b. 10 March 1952, Samarqand, Uzbek SSR, USSR; ed Samarqand State Univ.; held various positions at Samarqand Regional Internal Affairs Directorate 1978–94; Head, Buxoro Regional Internal Affairs Directorate 1994–97; held several sr positions in Ministry of Internal Affairs, including First Deputy Minister of Internal Affairs 1997–2004, Chair. State Cttee on Demonopolization and Competition and Business Support, Chair. State Customs Cttee 2004–06, Minister of Internal Affairs 2006–13; rank of Lt-Gen. 2001; mem. Security Council under the Pres. of Uzbekistan 2004–13; Shon-Saraf (Glory) Order (First and Second Degrees).

MATOLCSY, György; Hungarian economist, central banker and politician; *Governor, Hungarian National Bank (Magyar Nemzeti Bank);* b. 18 July 1955, Budapest; m.; two s.; ed Budapest Univ. of Economic Sciences; jr official, Industrial Org. Inst. 1977–78; mem. staff Ministry of Finance 1978–81, mem. Secr. 1981–85; Fellow, Finance Research Inst. 1985–90; Political State Sec., Prime Minister's Office 1990–91; Dir Privatization Research Inst. 1991; Dir EBRD, London 1991–94; Dir Property Foundation, Inst. for Privatization Studies 1995–99; Minister of Econ. Affairs 1999–2002, of Nat. Economy 2010–13; mem. Országgyülés (Nat. Ass.) 2006–; EIB Gov. for Hungary 2010–; Gov. Hungarian Nat. Bank (Magyar Nemzeti Bank) 2013–; mem. and econ. strategist, Fidesz—Hungarian Civic Union. *Address:* Magyar Nemzeti Bank, 1850 Budapest, Szabadság tér 8–9, Hungary (office). *Telephone:* (1) 428-2600 (office). *Fax:* (1) 429-8000 (office). *E-mail:* info@mnb.hu (office). *Website:* www.mnb.hu (office).

MATOMÄKI, Tauno Antero, MSc (Eng); Finnish business executive; *Chairman and CEO, Rosenlew RKW Finland Ltd;* b. 14 April 1937, Nakkila; s. of Niilo Matomäki and Martta Matomäki; m. Leena Matomäki (née Nilsson) 1963; one s. three d.; ed Tech. Univ., Helsinki; joined Rauma-Repola 1967, various positions, Pres. and CEO 1987–90, Pres. and CEO Repola Ltd 1991–96; Chair. and CEO Rosenlew RKW Finland Ltd; Chair. Rauma Ltd, United Paper Mills Ltd, Pohjolan Voima Ltd, Finnyards Ltd, UPM-Kymmene 1999–2001, Confed. of Finnish Industries, Finnish Employers' Confed.; mem. Bd of Dirs Effjohn AB; mem. Supervisory Bd Teollisuuden Voima Oy (Chair.), Kansallis-Osake-Pankki, Pohjola Insurance Co., Ilmarinen Pension Insurance Co., Polar Rakennusosakeyhtiö, Uusi Suomi Oy; Kt, Order of the White Rose of Finland (First Class). *Address:* Rosenlew RKW Finland Ltd, PL 22, Ulasoorintie 185, 28601 Pori, Finland. *Telephone:* (2) 517-8899. *Fax:* (2) 517-8890. *E-mail:* info@rosenlewrkw.com. *Website:* www.rosenlewrkw.com.

MATORIN, Vladimir Anatolievich; Russian singer (bass); b. 2 May 1948, Moscow; s. of Anatoly Ivanovich Matorin and Maria Tarasovna Matorina; m. Svetlana Sergeyevna Matorina; one s.; ed Gnessin Pedagogical Inst. (now Acad.) of Music; soloist, Moscow Stanislavsky and Nemirovich-Danchenko Music Theatre 1974–91, Bolshoi Theatre 1991–; teacher at Russian Acad. of Theatre Art 1991–, Prof. and Head of Faculty of Solo Singing 1994–; numerous int. tours; winner, All-Union Glinka Competition of vocalists and Int. Competition of Singers in Geneva, Merited Artist of Russia, People's Artist of Russia. *Opera roles include:* Boris Godunov, Ivan Susanin, King René (Iolanthe), Gremin (Eugene Onegin), Dosifei (Khovanshchina), Count Galitsky (Prince Igor), Don Basilio (Barber of Seville), Count (Invisible City of Kitezh) and more than 65 others. *Recordings include:* Modest Mussorgsky's Sorochintsy Fair 1983, Sergei Rachmaninov's Ale 1990, Rachmaninov's Francesca da Rimini 1992, Nikolai Rimsky-Korsakov's May Night 1997, Rimsky-Korsakov's Kashchey the Immortal, Vissarion Shebalin's The Taming of the Shrew. *Leisure interests:* poetry, sacred music, travelling by car. *Address:* Robert Gilder & Co., N102, Westminster Business Square, 1–45 Durham Street, London, SE11 5JH, England (office); Bolshoi Theatre of Russia, 103009 Moscow, Teatralnaya pl. 1 (office); 129090 Moscow, Periy Koptelskiy Pereulok 9/29; 103045 Moscow, Ulansky per. 21, korp. 1 Apt. 53, Russia (home). *E-mail:* rgilder@robert-gilder.com (office). *Website:* robertgilder.co/vladimir-matorin (office); www.bolshoi.ru (office). *Telephone:* (495) 692-38-86 (office); (495) 680-44-17 (home). *Fax:* (495) 680-44-17 (home).

MATOTO, Lord Matoto of Tu'anekivale 'Otenifi Afu'alo, BA, MA; Tongan civil servant and politician; m. Lavinia Matoto; two d.; ed Univ. of Auckland, New Zealand, Univ. of Durham, UK; Asst Teacher, Tonga High School 1968; joined Ministry of Finance as an Asst Sec. in 1971, twice acted as Devt Officer 1971–77, Sec. of Finance 1977–83; Man., Devt and Planning, Bank of Tonga 1983, held various managerial positions 1983–99; Man. Dir Tonga Devt Bank 1999–2006; Minister for Public Enterprises 2006–07, for Public Enterprises and Information 2007, for Finance and Information 2008–10; Treas. Tonga Rugby Football Union (TRFU) 1975–82; Chair. TRFU Referees' Asscn early 1980s–early 1990s; mem. Nuku'alofa Rotary Club 1974–, served as Pres. for several years; ordained Minister of the Constitutional Free Church of Tonga. *Leisure interest:* sports, especially rugby.

MATOVIČ, Igor; Slovak politician; *Leader, Obyčajní Ľudia a Nezávislé Osobnosti (Ordinary People and Independent Personalities);* b. 11 May 1973, Trnava, Slovak Socialist Repub., Czechoslovak Socialist Repub.; m. Pavlina Matovičová; ed Comenius Univ., Bratislava; worked as a freelancer from 1997; f. regionPRESS publishing co. 2002, currently publishes 36 regional weeklies in Slovakia; elected to Nat. Council of the Slovak Repub. on the Sloboda a Solidarita (Freedom and Solidarity) list 2010; Leader, Obyčajní Ľudia a Nezávislé Osobnosti (Ordinary People and Ind. Personalities) party 2011–. *Address:* Obyčajní Ľudia a Nezávislé Osobnosti, Študentská 2, 91701 Trnava, Slovakia (office). *Telephone:* 90-7750558 (mobile). *E-mail:* igor.matovic@obycajniludia.sk (office); kontakt@obycajniludia.sk (office). *Website:* www.obycajniludia.sk (office); matovic.blog.sme.sk.

MATSUDA, Iwao; Japanese politician; b. 19 May 1937; ed Univ. of Tokyo; elected mem. House of Reps 1986, 1990, 1993; Parl. Vice-Minister, Ministry of Educ., Science, Culture and Sports 1991–92; mem. House of Councillors 1998–2014; Sr State Sec. for Int. Trade and Industry 2000–01; Sr Vice-Minister of Economy, Trade and Industry 2001; Chief Dir Cttee on Economy and Industry 2002–04; Chair. Research Cttee on Int. Affairs 2004–05; Minister of State for Science and Tech. Policy, for Food Safety and for Information Tech. 2005–06.

MATSUDA, Masatake; Japanese transport industry executive; b. 1936, Hokkaido; ed Hokkaido Univ.; began career with Japan Nat. Railway (JNR) 1961, held positions successively as Planning Man. Office of Planning Man., Planning Man. Hokkaido HQ, Dir-Gen. Reconstruction Promotion HQ, Man.-Dir and Gen. Man. Corp. Planning HQ E Japan Railway Co. (JR East–co. created following privatisation of JNR 1987), Vice-Pres., Pres. 1993, Chair. JR East –2006, apptd Dir and Adviser 2006; Dir Mizuho Holdings Inc.; Pres. World Exec. Council, Int. Union of Railways (UIC), Vice-Pres. UIC 2003–04; apptd mem. Prime Ministerial Advisory Panel tasked with overseeing Privatisation of Semigovernmental Expressway Corpns 2003, resgnd from panel in protest of privatisation scheme.

MATSUDA, Seiko; Japanese singer and actress; b. (Noriko Kamachi), 10 March 1962, Fukuoka; m. 1st Masaki Kanda 1985 (divorced 1998); one c.; m. 2nd Hiroyuki Hatano 1998 (divorced 2000); Best Vocal Performance, Japan Record Awards 2015.

Films include: Nogiku no haka 1981, Yume De Aetera 1982, Natsufuku no Ibu 1984, Karibu: Ai no shinfoni 1985, Final Vendetta 1996, Armageddon 1998, Drop Dead Gorgeous 1999, Partners 2000, Gedo 2000, Sennen no koi – Hikaru Genji monogatari 2002, Shanghai Baby 2007, Hotaru no Haka 2008, Yazima Beauty Salon The Movie 2010. *Television includes:* The Big Easy (series) 1996, Tattahitotsuno takaramono (film) 2004, Yo nimo kimyo na monogatari: Aki no tokubetsu hen 2005. *Recordings include:* albums: Squall 1980, North Wind 1980, Silhouette 1981, Kaze Tachi Nu 1981, Pineapple 1982, Candy 1982, Utopia 1983, Canary 1983, Tinkerbell 1984, Windy Shadow 1984, The Ninth Wave 1985, Sound of My Heart 1985, Supreme 1986, Strawberry Time 1987, Citron 1988, Precious Moment 1989, Seiko 1990, We Are Love 1990, Eternal 1991, Nouvelle Vague 1992, Sweet Memories 1992, A Time For Love 1993, Diamond Expression 1993, Glorious Revolution 1994, It's Style 1995, Was It The Future 1996, Guardian Angel 1996, Vanity Fair 1996, Sweetest Time 1997, My Story 1997, Forever 1998, Seiko Matsuda Remixes 1999, 20th Party 2000, Love & Emotion Vol. 1 2001, Love & Emotion Vol. 2 2001, Area 62 2002, Sunshine 2004, Fairy 2006, Baby's Breath 2007, My Pure Melody 2008, My Prelude 2010, Cherish 2011, Very Very 2012, A Girl in the Wonder Land 2013, Dream and Fantasy 2014. *Publication:* Yume de Aetara 1982. *E-mail:* office@seikomatsuda.jp. *Website:* www.seikomatsuda.co.jp/english/index.html.

MATSUEV, Denis Leonidovich; Russian musician (piano); b. 11 June 1975, Irkutsk, Siberia; s. of Leonid Matsuev and Irina Gomelskaya; ed Central Music School, Moscow, studied with Aleksey Nasedkin and Sergei Dorensky; moved to Moscow 1991, concerts 1993–; regular engagements with Russian orchestras such as St Petersburg Philharmonic, Mariinsky Orchestra and Russian Nat. Orchestra; performs world-wide with orchestras such as New York Philharmonic, Chicago Symphony Orchestra, Philadelphia Orchestra, Los Angeles Philharmonic Orchestra, Pittsburgh Symphony Orchestra, Berlin Philharmonic Orchestra, Leipzig Gewandhaus Orchestra, Bavarian Radio Symphony Orchestra, London Symphony, London Philharmonic, Royal Philharmonic Orchestra, Royal Concertgebouw Orchestra, Rotterdam Philharmonic, Orchestra Filarmonica della Scala, Orchestre de Paris, Orchestre Nat. du Capitole de Toulouse, European Chamber Orchestra, Helsinki Philharmonic, among numerous others; has appeared with conductors including Valery Gergiev, Yuri Temirkanov, Yevgeny Svetlanov, Mariss Jansons, Lorin Maazel, Zubin Mehta, Kurt Masur, Paavo Jarvi, Antonio Pappano, Charles Dutoit, Alain Gilbert, Leonard Slatkin, Myung-Whun Chung, Semyon Bychkov, Iván Fischer, Adam Fisher, Gianandrea Noseda, Jukka-Pekka Saraste, James Conlon, Vladimir Spivakov, Mikhail Pletnev, Vladimir Fedoseyev, Yury Bashmet, Claudio Abbado; recitals at Carnegie Hall, New York, Lincoln Center, Washington, DC, Salle Gaveau and Théâtre des Champs-Elysées, Paris, Concertgebouw, Amsterdam, Mozarteum Salzburg, Musikverein Vienna, Royal Festival Hall, London, Great Hall of Philharmonie, St Petersburg, La Scala, Milan, Suntory Hall, Tokyo, Mariinsky Theatre Concert Hall; has performed at numerous festivals including BBC Proms, Edinburgh, Ravinia, Chicago, Schleswig-Holstein, Chopin Festival, Poland, Maggio Musicale Fiorentino, La Roque d'Anthéron, France, Montreux, Budapest Spring, Russian Winter in Moscow, Stars of the White Nights in St Petersburg, Shanghai; soloist at New York Philharmonic's 15,000th concert in Avery Fisher Hall conducted by Valery Gergiev; torchbearer Winter Olympics, Sochi 2014, performed at opening and closing ceremonies; Founder and Artistic Dir Crescendo music festival (classical and jazz), held annually in cities such as Moscow, St Petersburg, Yekaterinburg, Tel-Aviv, Kaliningrad, Paris and New York 2005–; Artistic Dir Annecy Music Festival, France 2010–, Int. Astana Piano Passion Festival and Competition 2012–, Int. Sberbank Debut Festival and Competition, Kiev 2013–; organiser, Stars on Baikal, Irkutsk, Siberia 2004–; Pres. New Names charity discovering and supporting talented children and developing music education in regions of Russia 2008–; has collaborated for many years with Sergei Rachmaninov Foundation, and was chosen to perform and record Rachmaninov's unknown pieces on the composer's own piano at Rachmaninov's house Villa Senar in Lucerne, later Artistic Dir; mem. Presidential Council for Culture and Arts 2006–; UNESCO Goodwill Amb. 2014–; apptd 2018 FIFA World Cup Russia Amb.; Hon. Citizen of Irkutsk 2009, Hon. Prof., Moscow State Univ.; winner, 11th Int. Tchaikovsky Competition 1998, Shostakovich Music Prize, State Prize in Literature and Arts, People's Artist of Russia, Honoured Artist of Russia, State Order of Honour 2017. *Recordings include:* Unknown Rachmaninov 2007, Denis Matsuev: Concert at Carnegie Hall 2009, Rachmaninov Concerto No. 3 2009, Shostakovich Concertos No. 1, No. 2 and Schedrin's Fifth (Mariinsky Orchestra/Gergiev) 2011, Rachmaninov Piano Concerto No. 2 and Gershwin Rhapsody in Blue (New York Philharmonic/Gilbert) 2013, Szymanowski Symphonia Concertante (LSO/Gergiev) 2013, Tchaikovsky Concerti Nos. 1 & 2 2014, Encores 2016. *Address:* c/o Douglas Sheldon, Columbia Artists Management, 5 Columbus Circle at 1790 Broadway, New York, NY 10019-1412, USA (office). *Telephone:* (212) 841-9500 (office). *Fax:* (212) 841-9744 (office). *E-mail:* info@cami.com (office); alexeypilyugin@gmail.com. *Website:* www.cami.com (office); matsuev.com.

MATSUHISA, Nobuyuki (Nobu); Japanese chef and restaurateur; b. 10 March 1949, Saitama; m.; two d.; served apprenticeship in sushi bars in Tokyo, including Matsue Sushi, Shinjuku; opened sushi bar in Peru 1973, later moved to Argentina, Japan and Alaska, USA; opened Matsuhisa restaurant in Beverly Hills, Calif. 1987, Aspen, Colo 1999; opened Nobu restaurant in New York 1994, London 1997, Tokyo 1999, Milan, Greece, Dallas, Honolulu, Moscow, Dubai, Budapest, Hong Kong, Mumbai 2012, now manages 33 restaurants; Nobu Hotel Las Vegas opened 2013; Award from Japan Soc. 2009, Michelin One Star each for Nobu, New York, Nobu, London, Nobu Berkeley Street, London. *Film roles:* Casino 1995, Austin Powers in Goldmember 2002, Memoirs of a Geisha 2005, The Girl from Nagasaki 2013. *Publications:* Nobu: The Cookbook 2001, Nobu Now 2005, Nobu West 2007, Nobu Miami: The Party Cookbook 2008. *Address:* Matsuhisa Restaurant, 129 North La Cienega Blvd, Beverly Hills, CA 90211, USA (office). *Telephone:* (310) 659-9639 (office). *Fax:* (310) 659-0492 (office). *Website:* www.noburestaurants.com (office); www.nobumatsuhisa.com.

MATSUI, Hideki; Japanese professional baseball player (retd); b. 12 June 1974, Kanazawa; ed Seiryo High School, Kanazawa; left fielder; drafted out of high school by Yomiuri Giants of Japanese Cen. League 1993 (number one selection), played 1993–2003, won three Japanese Series titles, hit Japan career 332 home runs with overall batting average of .308; left Japan to sign with NY Yankees 2003–09, Los Angeles Angels of Anaheim 2010, Oakland Athletics 2011, Tampa Bay Rays 2012; special advisor to Gen. Man., New York Yankees 2015–; operates Hideki Matsui House of Baseball, Neagari; nine times Japanese League All-Star; three Japanese League Most Valuable Player awards; American League All-Star Team 2003; runner-up American League Rookie of the Year 2003, Most Valuable Player, 2009 World Series, People's Honour Award (Japan) 2013. *Address:* Office of the General Manager, New York Yankees, Yankee Stadium, 161st Street and River Avenue, Bronx, NY 10452, USA (office). *Website:* newyork.yankees.mlb.com (office).

MATSUMOTO, Hiroshi, BEng, MEng, PhD; Japanese engineer, academic and university administrator; *President, Kyoto University;* b. 17 Nov. 1942; ed Kyoto Univ.; Research Assoc., Dept of Electronics, Kyoto Univ. 1967–69, Research Assoc., Dept of Electrical Eng 1969–74, Assoc. Prof., Ionosphere Research Lab., Kyoto Univ. 1974–81, Assoc. Prof., Radio Atmospheric Science Centre 1981–87, Prof. 1987–2000, Centre Dir 1992–98, Prof., Radio Science Centre for Space and Atmosphere 2000–02, Prof. and Dir 2002–04, Prof. and Dir Research Inst. for Sustainable Humanosphere 2004–05, Exec. Vice-Pres. (Research, Finance), Kyoto Univ. 2005–08, Pres. Kyoto Univ. 2008–; Visiting Prof., Inst. for Space and Astronomical Sciences (JAXA/ISAS), Inst. for Fusion Sciences (NIFS) of Japan & Wuhan Univ., People's Repub. of China; Fellow, Japan Geoscience Union 2014; Hon. DEng (Univ. of Bristol) 2014; AGU Fellow Award for Space Plasma Physics 1999, IEEE Fellow Award 2002, Assoc. Award, Royal Astronomical Soc., Science and Tech. Award, Ministry of Educ., Culture and Sports 2006, Russian Fed. of Cosmonautics Gagarin Medal 2006, Medal with Purple Ribbon 2007, Gold Booker Medal, Union Radio-Scientifique Internationale 2008, Hasegawa Nagata Award, Soc. of Geomagnetism and Earth, Planetary and Space Sciences (Japan) 2008. *Publications:* has authored and contributed to several books; approx. 300 scientific papers in English in int. journals and 133 scientific papers in Japanese. *Address:* Office of the President, Kyoto University, Yoshida-Honmachi, Sakyo-ku, Kyoto 606-8501, Japan (office). *Telephone:* (75) 753-7531 (office). *Fax:* (75) 753-2091 (office). *Website:* www.kyoto-u.ac.jp/en/profile/25president (office).

MATSUMOTO, Masayoshi; Japanese business executive; *President and CEO, Sumitomo Electric Industries;* mem. Bd of Dirs Sumitomo Electric Industries 1999–, fmr Sr Man. Dir, fmr Pres. and COO, Pres. and CEO 2004–17, Chair. 2017–; Vice-Chair. Optoelectronic Industry and Tech. Devt Asscn. *Address:* Sumitomo Electric Industries Ltd, 5-33 Kitahama 4-chome, Chuo-ku, Osaka 541-0041, Japan (office). *Telephone:* (6) 6220-4141 (office). *E-mail:* info@sei.co.jp (office). *Website:* global-sei.com (office); www.sei.co.jp (office).

MATSUMOTO, Masayuki; Japanese engineer and transport industry executive; joined Japanese Nat. Railways (now Japan Railways–JR) 1972, Tech. Dir East Japan Railway Co. 2000, sr positions with Transport & Rolling Stock Dept 2001–02, Vice-Pres. Central Japan Railway Co. (JR Tokai) –2004, Pres. and Rep. Dir 2004–10, Vice-Chair. and Rep. Dir 2010–11; mem. Inst. of Electrical Engineers of Japan, Inst. of Electronics, Information and Communication Engineers, Information Processing Soc. of Japan. *Address:* c/o Central Japan Railway Company, 1-1-4 Meieki, Nakamura-ku, Nagoya 450-6101, Japan.

MATSUO, Kenji; Japanese insurance industry executive; *Senior Advisor, Meiji Yasuda Life Insurance Company;* Dir Meiji Life Insurance Co. –2003, mem. Bd of Dirs Meiji Yasuda Life Insurance Co. 2004– (after merger of Meiji Life Insurance Co. and Tasuda Mutual Life Insurance Co.), Man. Dir and Gen. Man. Real Estate Dept –2005, Pres. and Rep. Exec. Officer 2005–13, Rep. Exec. Officer 2–19 July 2013, Sr Advisor July 2013–, mem. Nominating Cttee, Compensation Cttee; Outside Corp. Auditor, Bank of Tokyo-Mitsubishi UFJ, Ltd 2009–16, Dir 2016–; Statutory Auditor, Mitsubishi Estate Co. Ltd 2014–16; Auditor, Mitsubishi Research Inst., Inc. 2015–; currently Chair. The Dia Foundation for Research on Ageing Societies; mem. Bd of Dirs Life Insurance Asscn of Japan, Nikon Corpn 2006–16; Dir (non-voting) Société Generale Group 2006–. *Address:* Meiji Yasuda Life Insurance Co., 1-1, Marunouchi 2-chome, Chiyoda-ku, Tokyo 100-0005, Japan (office). *Telephone:* (3) 3283-8293 (office). *Fax:* (3) 3215-8123 (office). *E-mail:* info@meijiyasuda.co.jp (office). *Website:* www.meijiyasuda.co.jp (office).

MATSUO, Minoru, DEng; Japanese university administrator and professor of engineering; b. 4 July 1936, Kyoto; ed Kyoto Univ.; Asst Prof. School of Eng, Kyoto Univ. 1964–65, Assoc. Prof. 1965–72; Assoc. Prof. School of Eng, Nagoya Univ. 1972–78, Prof. 1978–98, Univ. Senator 1987–89, Dean 1989–92, Dir Center for Integrated Research in Science and Eng 1995–97, Pres. of Nagoya Univ. 1998–2004, currently Advisor, Nagoya Univ. Alumni Asscn; with Nagoya Urban Devt Public Corpn, Supreme Advisor, Nagoya Urban Inst. *Publications include:* Reliability in Geotechnical Design 1984. *Address:* c/o Nagoya University Alumni Association Bureau, Nagoya University, Furo-cho, Chikusa-ku, Nagoya, 464–8601 (office); Nagoya Urban Development Public Corporation, 8 Iidamachi, Higashi-Ku Nagoya, Aichi 461-0013, Japan. *Telephone:* (52) 783-1920 (office). *E-mail:* nual-jimu@adm.nagoya-u.ac.jp (office). *Website:* www.nual.nagoya-u.ac.jp (office).

MATSUSHIMA, Midori; Japanese politician and fmr journalist; b. 15 July 1956, Osaka; ed Univ. of Tokyo; reporter, Asahi Shimbun, mainly covering economic and political news 1980–95; mem. House of Reps (lower house of Parl.) for Tokyo No. 14 constituency 2000–; Parl. Vice-Minister for Foreign Affairs 2006–07; Sr Vice-Minister for Land, Infrastructure, Transport and Tourism 2007, for Economy, Trade and Industry 2013; served as Minister of Justice 2014; mem. Liberal Democratic Party. *Leisure interests:* swimming, running.

MATSUSHITA, Isao; Japanese business executive; ed Univ. of Tokyo; joined Nippon Mining Co. 1970; fmr Exec. Vice-Pres. and Man. Exec. Officer, Japan Energy Corpn, Pres. and Dir 2006–12; Exec. Vice-Pres. JX Nippon Oil & Energy Corpn 2010–12; Pres. and Rep. Dir JX Holdings, Inc. 2012–14; Rep. Dir, Japan Energy Devt from 2007; Dir, United Petroleum Devt Co. Ltd, JX Nippon Oil & Energy Corpn, JX Holdings, Inc. 2010–14, Nippon Mining Holdings Inc.

MATTARELLA, Sergio; Italian lawyer, politician, judge and head of state; *President;* b. 23 July 1941, Palermo; s. of Bernardo Mattarella; m. Marisa Chiazzese (died 2012); three c.; ed Palermo Univ.; fmr mem. Nat. Council and Cen. Leadership Christian Democrat Party, Deputy Political Sec. 1990–92; Deputy for Palermo-Trapani-Agrigento-Caltanissetta 1983–87, for Sicilia 1 1994–2008; Minister for Relations with Parl. 1987–89, Minister for Educ. 1989–90, Deputy Prime

Minister 1998–2001, Minister for Defence 1999–2001; fmr Vice-Pres. Parl. Cttee on Terrorism; fmr mem. Parl. Inquiry Cttee on Mafia; mem. Third Standing Comm. on Foreign and EC Affairs; Political Ed. Il Popolo 1992–94; Pres. of Italy 2015–; Prof. of Parl. Law, Univ. of Palermo; mem. Italian People's Party 1994–2002, Democracy is Freedom – The Daisy 2002–07, Democratic Party 2007–; Cavaliere di gran croce dell'Ordine al merito della Repubblica italiana 2011. *Address:* Office of the President, Palazzo del Quirinale, 00187 Rome, Italy (office). *Telephone:* (06) 46991 (office). *Fax:* (06) 46993125 (office). *Website:* www.quirinale .it (office).

MATTHÄUS, Lothar Herbert (Loddar); German professional football manager and fmr professional footballer; b. 21 March 1961, Erlangen, Bavaria; m. 1st Silvia Matthäus 1981 (divorced 1992); two d.; m. 2nd Lolita Morena 1994 (divorced 1999); one s.; m. 3rd Marijana Kostić 2003 (divorced 2009); m. 4th Liliana Chudinova 2008; midfielder/defender/sweeper; youth player, FC Herzogenaurach; professional debut with Borussia Mönchengladbach 1979–84; played for Bayern Munich 1984–88, 1992–2000 (won Bundesliga 1984/85, 1985/86, 1986/87, 1993/94, 1996/97, 1998/99, 1999/2000, DFB-Pokal 1986, 1998, DFB-Ligapokal 1997, 1998, 1999, 2000, DFB-Supercup 1987, UEFA Cup 1996, Fuji-Cup 1987, 1988, 1994, 1995), Inter Milan 1988–92 (won Italian Championship (Serie A) 1989, Supercoppa Italiana 1989, UEFA Cup 1991), New York MetroStars March–Nov. 2000; mem. West German U-21 team 1979–83, West German B team 1979–81, West German/German nat. team 1980–96, 1998–2000 (won Euro 1980, Capt. 1988–94, won World Cup 1990, US Cup 1993), played in 25 World Cup matches, 150 appearances for nat. team, scored 23 goals; Sports Dir Rapid Vienna 2001–02; Man. Partizan Belgrade, Serbia and Montenegro 2002–03; Coach, Hungarian Nat. Team 2003–05, Atlético Paranaense, Brazil 2006, Red Bull Salzburg (fmrly Austria Salzburg) 2006–07, Maccabi Netanya, Israel 2008–09, Bulgarian Nat. Team 2010–11; Ballon d'Or 1990, Onze d'Or 1990, FIFA World Player of the Year 1991, World Soccer Awards Player of the Year 1990, German Footballer of the Year 1990, 1999, named to FIFA 100. *Address:* Wim Vogel, c/o die sportmanufaktur, Brühlerstraße 29, 50968 Cologne, Germany. *Website:* www.lothar-matthaeus.com.

MATTHÄUS-MAIER, Ingrid; German banking executive and fmr politician; b. 9 Sept. 1945, Werlte, Aschendorf Co.; d. of Heinz-Günther Matthäus and Helmtraud Matthäus (née von Hagen); m. Robert Maier 1974; one s. one d.; ed studied law in Giessen and Münster; Research Asst, Münster Higher Admin. Court, then Admin. Court Judge in Münster; joined Free Democratic Party (Freie Demokratische Partei—FDP) 1969, mem. North Rhine-Westphalian Exec. Cttee and of Fed. Exec. Cttee FDP; Fed. Chair. Young Democrats 1972; mem. Bundestag 1976, Chair. Finance Cttee 1979–82, resgnd all posts, left FDP and resgnd seat in Bundestag in protest at coalition change of FDP 1982; joined SPD 1982; re-elected to Bundestag 1983, Deputy Chair. SPD Parl. Group (in charge of fiscal, budgetary/borrowing, banking, stock exchange and monetary affairs) 1988, mem. Exec. Cttee SPD 1995–99, Titular mem. Mediation Cttee 1995, resgnd seat in Bundestag 1999; mem. Bd of Man. Dirs KfW Bankengruppe 1999–2006, Spokeswoman of Bd of Man. Dirs 2006–08, responsible for Secr. of Man. Affairs/Legal Affairs, Secr. of Domestic Credit Affairs, Communications and Internal Auditing, also responsible for Berlin Br.; Chair. mem. Supervisory Bd Deutsche Telekom AG, Deutsche Post AG, Bonn Deutsche Steinkohle AG, Herne 2007–, EVONIK Industries AG (fmrly, Essen –2009, RAG Aktiengesellschaft, Essen, Salzgitter Mannesmann Handel GmbH, Dusseldorf.

MATTHEI FORNET, Evelyn Rose, BA; Chilean economist and politician; *Mayor of Providencia;* b. 11 Nov. 1953, Santiago; d. of Fernando Matthei and Elda Fornet; m. Jorge Desormeaux Jiménez; three c.; ed Colegio Alemán de Santiago, Pontificia Universidad Católica de Chile; began career with Research Dept, Forestry SA; Financial Analyst, later Head of Research Dept, Administradoras de Fondos de Pensiones (pension fund); fmr Deputy Dir Bancard SA; Deputy for Santiago Dist 23, Cámara de Diputados 1989–93, for San Antonio Dist 15 1993–97; mem. Senate for Coquimbo 1998–2011; mem. Finance and the Budget Cttees in both Chambers, also mem. Cttees on Health, Labour and Social Security, Senate Audit Cttee; Minister of Labour and Social Security 2011–13; cand. in presidential election Dec. 2013; Mayor of Providencia 2016–; mem. Unión Demócrata Independiente. *Address:* Municipality of Providencia, Av. Pedro de Valdivia 963, Santiago, Chile (office). *Telephone:* (2) 6543200 (office). *E-mail:* municipalidad@ providencia.cl (office). *Website:* www.providencia.cl (office).

MATTHES, Ulrich; German actor; b. 9 May 1959, Berlin; s. of Günter Matthes and Else Matthes; with Düsseldorfer Schauspielhaus 1986–87, Bayerisches Staatstheater, Munich 1987–89, Kammerspiele, Munich 1989–92, Schaubühne, Berlin 1992–98, Deutsches Theater, Berlin; Förderpreis, Kunstpreis Berlin 1991, O.E. Hasse-Preis 1992, Bayerischer Filmpreis 1999. *Films:* Herr Ober! 1992, Ein falscher Schritt 1995, Winter Sleepers 1997, Feuerreiter 1998, Aimee & Jaguar 1999, Framed (short) 1999, The Farewell 2000, Traffic Affairs 2004, The Ninth Day 2004, Downfall 2004, Who Was Kafka? (voice) 2006, Vineta 2006, Novemberkind 2008, Die Unsichtbare 2011, Calm at Sea 2011, A Little Suicide (short, voice) 2012, Kunduz: The Incident at Hadji Ghafur 2012, The Notebook 2013. *Television:* An einem Tag im September (short) 1969, Die Wesenacks (film) (as Ulli Matthes) 1970, Artur, Peter und der Eskimo (film) 1973, Derrick (series) 1987–97, Wolff's Turf (series) 1995, Der Mörder und sein Kind (film) 1995, Nikolaikirche (film) 1995, The Old Fox (series) 1997, Todesspiel (film documentary) 1997, Polizeiruf 110 (series) 1997–99, Abgehauen (film) 1998, Der Hahn ist tot (film) 2000, A Case for Two (series) 2000, Mörderherz (film) 2002, The Bill (series) 2008, SOKO Leipzig (series) 2009, Neue Vahr Süd (film) 2010, Tatort (series) 2011–14, Bornholmer Straße (film) 2014.

MATTHEW, Norman; Marshall Islands politician; b. 14 Jan. 1941; m. Rosalind Bien Matthew; seven c.; Co–Man., Ajidrik Wholesale 1961–86; Owner/Manager, RN Trading Co. 1986–95; apptd mem. Nitijela (Parl.) for Aur Atoll 1995; Minister of Internal Affairs 2008–12; fmr mem. United People's Party (UPP), then mem. Aelon Kein Ad (Our Islands) party; Del. to Asia Pacific Parl. Forum. *Leisure interests:* fishing, sport, gardening.

MATTHEWS, Peter Hugoe, LittD, FBA; British professor of linguistics; *Professor Emeritus, Department of Theoretical and Applied Linguistics, University of Cambridge;* b. 10 March 1934, Oswestry, Shropshire, England; s. of John Hugo Matthews and Cecily Eileen Elmsley Hagarty; m. Lucienne Marie Jeanne Schleich

1984; one step-s. one step-d.; ed Montpellier School, Paignton, Clifton Coll., St John's Coll., Cambridge; Lecturer, Univ. Coll. of North Wales, Bangor 1960–65, at Indiana Univ., Bloomington 1963–64; Lecturer, Reader and Prof., Univ. of Reading 1965–80; Visiting Prof., Deccan Coll., Pune 1969–70; Sr Research Fellow, King's Coll., Cambridge 1970–71; Fellow, Nias Wassenaar, the Netherlands 1977–78; Prof. and Head of Dept of Linguistics, Univ. of Cambridge 1980–2001, Fellow, St John's Coll. 1980–, Praelector 1987–2001, Prof. Emer. 2001–; Pres. Philological Soc. 1992–96, Vice-Pres. 1996–; Hon. mem. Linguistics Soc. of America 1994. *Publications:* Inflectional Morphology: A Theoretical Study Based on Aspects of Latin Verb Conjugation 1972, Morphology 1974, Generative Grammar and Linguistic Competence 1979, Syntax 1981, Grammatical Theory in the United States from Bloomfield to Chomsky 1993, The Concise Oxford Dictionary of Linguistics 1997, 2005, 2014, A Short History of Structural Linguistics 2001, Linguistics: A Very Short Introduction 2003, Syntactic Relations: A Critical Survey 2007, The Positions of Adjectives in English 2014. *Leisure interests:* cycling, gardening. *Address:* St John's College, Cambridge, CB2 1TP (office); 10 Fendon Close, Cambridge, CB1 7RU, England (home); 22 Rue Nina et Julien Lefevre, 1952 Luxembourg. *Telephone:* (1223) 338768 (office); (1223) 247553 (home). *Website:* www.mml.cam.ac.uk/dtal/staff/phm1000/index.html (office).

MATTHEWS, Sir Terence Hedley (Terry), Kt, KBE, OBE, BSc, FREng, FIEE; British/Canadian telecommunications industry executive; *Chairman, Mitel Networks Corporation;* b. 6 June 1943, Newport, South Wales; m. Ann Matthews; four c.; ed Univ. of Wales, Swansea; emigrated to Ottawa, Canada 1969; co-f. Mitel Corpn (with Michael Cowpland) 1972, Chair. 1972–85, Chair. Mitel Networks Corpn (communications system div.) 2001–; f. Newbridge Networks Corpn 1986, Chair. and CEO 1986–2000; f. March Networks Corpn 2000, Chair. and CEO 2000–; Co-founder Celtic House International Corpn; Founding Chair. Celtic Manor Resort (host of Ryder Cup 2010), Wesley Clover (investment group); Owner Brookstreet Hotel, Ottawa; Chair. Bridgewater Systems, Convedia Corpn (acquired by RadiSys 2006), Kanata Research Park, March Networks, nTerop Corpn, Tundra Semiconductor Corpn, Ubiquity Software; mem. Bd of Dirs DragonWave, Solace Systems, CounterPath Corpn; Patron Cancer Stem Cell Research Inst., Cardiff Univ. 2011–; Fellow, Royal Acad. of Eng; Hon. PhD (Univs of Wales, Glamorgan and Swansea), (Carleton Univ., Ottawa); Hon. DEng (Bath) 2006. *Address:* Mitel Networks Corporation, 350 Legget Drive, PO Box 13089, Ottawa, ON K2K 2W7, Canada (office). *Telephone:* (613) 592-2122 (office). *Fax:* (613) 592-4784 (office). *E-mail:* info@mitel.com (office). *Website:* www.mitel.com (office); www.wesleyclover.com (office).

MATTHIAS, Stefanos; Greek judge (retd); b. 27 May 1935, Athens; m.; one d.; ed Univ. of Athens, Univ. of Poitiers, France; judge 1961–2002; Pres. Supreme Civil and Penal Court 1996–2002; Dir Nat. School for Judges 1994–96; First Class Honour Cross. *Publications:* more than 40 studies and articles on pvt. law and on European Convention on Human Rights. *Leisure interest:* painting. *Address:* 26 Niriidon Str., 17561 Paleon Faliron, Greece (home). *Telephone:* (210) 9882632 (home); (210) 9827466 (home). *E-mail:* stefmatt@otenet.gr (home).

MATTHIESSEN, Poul Christian, MA, DSc (Econ); Danish demographer and academic; *Professor Emeritus of Demography, University of Copenhagen;* b. 1 Feb. 1933, Odense; s. of Jens P. E. Matthiessen and Laura C. Nielsen; m. Ulla Bay 1986; two d.; Research Asst, Copenhagen Telephone Co. 1958–63; Lecturer in Statistics and Demography, Univ. of Copenhagen 1963–70, Prof. of Demography 1971–95, Prof. Emer. 1995–; Pres. Carlsberg Foundation 1993–2002; Chair. Carlsberg's Bequest in Memory of Brewer J.C. Jacobsen 1993–2003; mem. Bd of Dirs Museum of Nat. History at Frederiksborg Castle 1993–2002, Den Berlingske Fond 1999–2008; mem. European Population Cttee 1972–2000; mem. Supervisory Bd Carlsberg A/S 1989–2003 (Chair. 1993–2003), Royal Scandinavia 1993–2001, Fredericia Bryggeri 1993–97, Falcon Bryggerier AB 1998–2001; mem. Royal Danish Acad. of Science and Letters 1982, Academia Europaea 1988; Chevalier, Ordre nat. du Mérite. *Publications:* Infant Mortality in Denmark 1931–60 1964, Growth of Population: Causes and Implications 1965, Demographic Methods (Vols I–III) 1970, Some Aspects of the Demographic Transition in Denmark 1970, The Limitation of Family Size in Denmark (Vols I–II) 1985, Immigration to Denmark 2009, Population and Society 2012, Følg med tiden, ikke med strømmen (memoir) 2018. *Leisure interests:* literature, history, architecture. *Address:* Collstrups Foundation, Ny Kongensgade 20, 1553 Copenhagen, Denmark (office). *Telephone:* 21-65-50-78 (office). *E-mail:* pcm@post.tele.dk (office).

MATTHUS, Siegfried; German composer; b. 13 April 1934, Mallenuppen, E Prussia; s. of Franz Matthus and Luise Perrey; m. Helga Spitzer 1958; one s.; ed Hochschule für Musik, Berlin, Acad. of Arts and Music, Berlin, master-class with Hanns Eisler; composer and consultant, Komische Oper, Berlin 1964–2002; Prof. 1985–; Artistic Dir Chamber Opera Festival, Rheinsberg 1991; mem. Acad. of Arts of GDR, Acad. of Arts of W Berlin, Acad. of Arts, Munich; Bundesverdienstkreuz (First Class) 2000; Nat. Prize 1972, 1984. *Compositions include:* Te Deum, 10 operas, one oratorio, concertos, orchestral and chamber music, etc. *Leisure interests:* swimming, jogging, carpentry. *Address:* Elisabethweg 10, 13187 Berlin (home); Seepromenade 15, 16348 Stolzenhagen, Germany (home). *Telephone:* (30) 4857362 (Berlin) (home); (33397) 21736 (Stolzenhagen) (home). *Fax:* (30) 48096604 (Berlin) (home); (33397) 71400 (Stolzenhagen) (home). *E-mail:* smatthus@t-online .de (home). *Website:* www.siegfried-matthus.de.

MATTILA, Karita Marjatta; Finnish singer (soprano); b. Somero; d. of Arja Mattila and Erkki Mattila (née Somerikko); m. Tapio Kuneinen; ed Sibelius Acad., and studied with Liisa Linko-Malmio, and Vera Rozsa in London; performs in all major opera houses and festivals world-wide and regularly with conductors including Levine, Abbado, Davis, Dohnanyi, Haitink, Pappano, Rattle, Salonen and Sawallisch; operatic repertoire encompasses works by Beethoven, Strauss, Tchaikovsky, Verdi, Puccini, Wagner and Janáček; has worked with prominent stage dirs, including Luc Bondy in his Don Carlos at Paris, London and Edinburgh Festival; collaborations with Lev Dodin in productions of Elektra for Salzburg Easter Festival and Pique Dame and Salome at Opéra Bastille, Peter Stein's productions of Simon Boccanegra in Salzburg and Don Giovanni in Chicago, and Jürgen Flimm's Fidelio in New York; regularly collaborates with contemporary composers in debut performances of modern works, including world premiere of Mirage by Kaija Saariaho with Orchestre de Paris led by Christoph Eschenbach in Paris; Chevalier des Arts et des Lettres 2003; First Prize, Finnish Nat. Singing

Competition 1981, First Prize, BBC Singer of the World, Cardiff 1983, François Reichenbach Prize Orphée du Lyrique, Acad. du Disque Lyrique, Paris, Evening Standard Ballet, Opera and Classical Music Award for Outstanding Performance of the Year 1997, Acad. du Disque Lyrique Award 1997, Grammy Award for Best Opera 1998, chosen by the New York Times as the Best Singer of the Year for her performance in Fidelio at the Metropolitan Opera 2001, Pro Finlandia 2001, Musical America Musician of the Year 2005, Opera News Award for invaluable contrib. to opera 2011. *Recordings include:* numerous solo and opera recordings, including 40th birthday concert, Helsinki (CD); other recordings include Strauss's Four Last Songs with Claudio Abbado, Arias & Scenes from the operas of Puccini, Verdi, Janacek, Tchaikovsky, Wagner and R. Strauss, German Romantic Arias by Beethoven, Mendelssohn and Weber with Sir Colin Davis, Grieg and Sibelius Songs with Sakari Oramo; complete recordings of Die Meistersinger von Nürnberg with the late Sir Georg Solti (Grammy Award for Opera 1998), Jenufa with Bernard Haitink (Grammy Award for Opera 2004), Schoenberg's Gurrelieder, Shostakovich's Symphony No. 14 with Sir Simon Rattle. *Leisure interests:* sport, yoga, golf, sailing. *Address:* c/o Bill Palant, IMG Artists, 7 West 54th Street, New York, NY 10019, USA (office). *Telephone:* (212) 994-3527 (office). *E-mail:* bpalant@imgartists.com (office). *Website:* imgartists.com/artist/karita_mattila (office).

MATTINGLY, Mack Francis, BS; American business executive, diplomatist and fmr politician; b. 7 Jan. 1931, Anderson, Ind.; s. of Joseph Hilbert Mattingly and Beatrice Wayts Mattingly; m. 1st Carolyn Longcamp 1957 (deceased); two d.; m. 2nd Leslie Ann Davisson 1998; ed Indiana Univ.; served in USAF 1951–55; Account Supervisor, Arvin Industries, Ind. 1957–59; Marketing, IBM Corpn 1959–79; Owner, M's Inc. 1975–80; Senator from Georgia 1981–87; Asst Sec.-Gen. for Defence Support, NATO, Brussels 1987–90; Amb. to Seychelles 1992–93; fmr Chair. Southeastern Legal Foundation, Georgia Ports Authority (now adviser); mem. Cumberland Island Asscn; mem. Bd of Dirs Novecon Tech., Atlanticus Corpn; US Trustee to Puerto Rico Conservation Trust; Trustee Emer., Kennesaw Univ.; Republican; Sec. of Defense Distinguished Service Medal for Outstanding Public Service 1988 and other awards for public service; also medals from USAF 1951–55, Good Conduct Medal, National Defense Medal. *Publications include:* numerous articles, speeches and book chapters. *Address:* 4315 10th Street, East Beach, St Simons Island, GA 31522, USA (home). *Telephone:* (912) 638-5430 (home). *E-mail:* mlmattingly@comcast.net (home).

MATTIOLO, Luigi; Italian diplomatist; *Ambassador to Germany;* b. 1957, Rome; ed Univ. of Rome; joined diplomatic service 1981, first assignment in Directorate Gen. for Emigration and Social Affairs, Ministry of Foreign Affairs (MFA) 1981–82, Second Sec., Embassy in Moscow 1982–86, First Sec., Embassy in Berne 1986–88, First Sec., Embassy in Belgrade 1988–91, Legation Counsellor, Belgrade 1991, Counsellor, Belgrade 1992, Gen. Directorate of Personnel, MFA 1992–93, Office of Diplomatic Advisor to Presidency of Council of Ministers 1993–95, Secr. of Council of EU, Brussels 1995–97, Adviser to Perm. Mission to EU, Brussels 1997–98, Embassy Counsellor 1998, First Counsellor 1999–2001, First Counsellor, Perm. Mission to UN, New York 2001–04, rank of Minister Plenipotentiary 2004, European Corresp. and Co-ordinator of Activities Related to Common Foreign and Security Policy, Gen. Directorate for European Integration, MFA 2004–05, Minister, Perm. Mission to North Atlantic Council and NATO, Brussels 2005–08, Amb. to Israel 2008–12, Dir Gen. for the EU, MFA 2012–15, Amb. to Turkey 2015–18, apptd Amb. to Germany 2018. *Address:* Embassy of Italy, Hiroshimastr. 1, 10785 Berlin, Germany (office). *Telephone:* (30) 25440101 (office). *Fax:* (30) 25440116 (office). *E-mail:* segreteria.berlino@esteri.it (office). *Website:* www.ambberlino.esteri.it (office).

MATTIS, Gen. (retd) James N.; American army officer (retd); ed Cen. Washington State Univ., Amphibious Warfare School, Marine Corps Command and Staff Coll., Nat. War Coll.; entered US Marine Corps and commissioned as Second Lt 1972; as a Lt, served as rifle and weapons platoon commdr in 3rd Marine Div., as a Capt., commanded rifle co. and weapons co. in 1st Marine Brigade; as Maj., commanded Recruiting Station Portland; as Lt-Col, commanded 1st Bn, 7th Marines, one of Task Force Ripper's assault bns in Operation Desert Shield and Desert Storm; as Col, commanded 7th Marines (Reinforced); as Brig.-Gen., commanded 1st Marine Expeditionary Brigade and then Task Force 58, during Operation Enduring Freedom in southern Afghanistan; as Maj.-Gen., commanded 1st Marine Div. during initial attack (2003) and subsequent stability operations in Iraq during Operation Iraqi Freedom; in first tour as Lt-Gen., commanded Marine Corps Combat Devt Command and served as Deputy Commdt for combat Devt; commanded I Marine Expeditionary Force, Camp Pendleton, Calif. 2006–07; served as Commdr of US Marine Forces Cen. Command; rank of Gen. 2007; Supreme Allied Commdr Transformation, NATO 2007–09; Commdr US Jt Forces Command (USJFCOM), Norfolk, Va 2007–10; Commdr US Cen. Command 2010–13 (retd); US Sec. of Defense 2017–18 (resgnd); Kuwait Liberation Medal (Kuwait), Kuwait Liberation Medal (Saudi Arabia), Marine Corps Recruiting Service Ribbon (with Bronze Service Star), Sea Service Deployment Ribbon (with one Silver and two Bronze Service Stars), Humanitarian Service Medal, Global War on Terrorism Service Medal, Global War on Terrorism Expeditionary Medal, Iraq Campaign Medal, Afghanistan Campaign Medal, Southwest Asia Service Medal (with two Bronze Service Stars), Nat. Defense Service Medal (with two Bronze Service Stars), Marine Corps Expeditionary Medal, Navy and Marine Corps Meritorous Unit Commendation, Navy Unit Commendation, Jt Meritorious Unit Award, Presidential Unit Citation, Combat Action Ribbon, Navy and Marine Corps Achievement Medal, Meritorious Service Medal (with two Gold Award Stars), Bronze Star (with Combat Valor Device), Legion of Merit, Defense Superior Service Medal, Navy Distinguished Service Medal, Defense Distinguished Service Medal (with Oak Leaf Cluster).

MATTSON, Mark Paul, BS, MS, PhD; American neuroscientist and academic; *Chief, Laboratory of Neurosciences and Chief, Cellular and Molecular Neurosciences Section, Intramural Research Program, National Institute on Aging, Baltimore;* b. 1 April 1957, Rochester, Minn.; s. of DeWayne Paul Mattson and Martha Eileen Mattson (née Arvidson); m. Joanne Mattson (née Youngblood) 1983; one s. one d.; ed Iowa State Univ., North Texas State Univ., Univ. of Iowa; Postdoctoral Researcher in Developmental Neuroscience, Colorado State Univ. 1986–87; Asst Prof. of Anatomy and Neurobiology, Univ. of Kentucky 1989–93, joined faculty Sanders-Brown Research Center on Aging, Univ. of Kentucky Medical Center 1989, Assoc. Prof. 1993–97, Prof. 1997–2000; Chief, Lab. of Neurosciences, Nat. Inst. on Aging, Baltimore, Md, also Chief, Cellular and Molecular Neurosciences Section, Intramural Research Program 2000–; Prof. of Neuroscience, Johns Hopkins Univ. 2000–; Ed.-in-Chief Neuromolecular Medicine, Ageing Research Reviews; Assoc. Ed. Journal of Neuroscience, Neurobiology of Aging, Journal of Neurochemistry, Journal of Neuroscience Research; mem. Soc. for Neuroscience, New York Acad. of Sciences; Fellow, AAAS; numerous awards including Metropolitan Life Foundation Medical Research Award, Alzheimer's Asscn Zenith Award, Jordi Folch Pi Award, Santiago Grisolia Chair Prize, Tovi Comet-Wallerstein Award, Glenn Award, Alumni Fellow Award, Univ. of Iowa, several Grass Lectureships. *Publications include:* ed. of 12 books on topics in neuroscience, aging, neurological disorders, diet and adaptive stress responses; more than 500 original research articles and more than 100 review articles in peer-reviewed journals. *Leisure interests:* running, dirt bike riding, gardening, animal husbandry. *Address:* Laboratory of Neurosciences, Biomedical Research Center, 05C214, 251 Bayview Boulevard, Suite 100, Baltimore, MD 21224-6825, USA (office). *Telephone:* (410) 558-8463 (office). *Fax:* (410) 558-8465 (office). *E-mail:* mark.mattson@nih.gov (office). *Website:* www.grc.nia.nih.gov/branches/irp/mmattson.htm (office).

MATUBRAIMOV, Almambet Matubraimovich; Kyrgyzstani politician; b. 1952, Osh Oblast; ed Tashkent Inst. of Light and Textile Industry; worker in sovkhoz Kursheb Osh Oblast; master, sr master, textile factory KKSK 1977–80; army service 1980–82; head of workshop, head of production textile factory KKSK now Bishkek) 1982–84, Dir 1984–90; Chair. Exec. Cttee Sverdlov Region, Frunze (now Bishkek) 1990–91; First Deputy Minister of Industry Repub. of Kyrgyzstan 1991–93; First Deputy Prime Minister 1991–93; Chair. People's Council of Repub. of Kyrgyzstan (Uluk Kenesh) 1995–99; in opposition to Pres. Akayev 1999; worked in Mining Br. 1999–2005; Plenipotentiary of the Pres. for Southern Region 2005–06, Plenipotentiary on Econ. Cooperation with Eurasian Countries 2006; Deputy in Zhogorku Kenesh (Parl.) 2006–. *Address:* Supreme Council (Jogorku Kenesh), 720053 Bishkek, Abdymomunov 207, Kyrgyzstan (office). *Telephone:* (312) 61-16-04 (office). *Fax:* (312) 62-50-12 (office). *E-mail:* zs@kenesh.gov.kg (office). *Website:* www.kenesh.kg (office).

MATUSCHKA, Mario, Graf von, DJur; German fmr diplomatist; b. 27 Feb. 1931, Oppeln, Silesia; s. of Michael, Graf von Matuschka and Pia, Gräfin Stillfried-Rattonitz; m. Eleonore Gräfin von Waldburg-Wolfegg 1962 (died 2017); two s. two d.; ed St Matthias Gymnasium, Breslau, Domgymnasium, Fulda and Univs of Fribourg, Paris and Munich; entered foreign service 1961; Attaché, German Observer's Mission at UN, New York 1961–62; Vice-Consul, Consul, Salzburg 1963–66; Second Sec., Islamabad 1966–68; First Sec., Tokyo 1968–71; Foreign Office, Bonn 1971–75, 1978–80, 1982–88, 1990–93; Economic Counsellor, London 1975–78; Deputy Chief of Protocol, UN, New York 1980–82; State Sec., Chief of Protocol, Land Berlin 1988–90; Amb. and Perm. Rep. of Germany to OECD 1993–96; Diplomatic Adviser to Commr Gen., Expo 2000, Hanover 1996–97, Dir Holy See's Pavilion June–Oct. 2000; Sec.-Gen. Internationaler Club La Redoute e.V. 1997–2000, mem. Bd 2000–02; Grand Officer's Cross of Merit, Sovereign Mil. Order of Malta 1961, Kt Grand Cross of Honour and Devotion in Obedience 2013; Order of Merit (Germany) 1990; decorations from Japan 1972, Portugal 1989, Holy See 2002. *Publication:* 'Manuale' Prayer Book for German Asscn SMRO (co-ed.) 2005 (second edn 2011). *Address:* Godesberger Hof 14, 53173 Bonn, Germany (home). *Telephone:* (228) 71025578 (home). *Fax:* (228) 71022579 (home). *E-mail:* mario.matuschka@gmx.de (home).

MATUTES JUAN, Abel; Spanish international organization official and politician; b. 31 Oct. 1941, Ibiza; s. of Antonio and Carmen Matutes; m. Nieves Prats; one s. three d.; ed Univ. of Barcelona; studies in law and econs; fmr entrepreneur in tourism and property in island of Ibiza; fmr Lecturer in Econs and Public Finance, Univ. of Barcelona; Deputy Chair. Ibiza & Formentera Tourist Bd 1964–69; Mayor of Ibiza 1970–71; Senator for Ibiza and Formentera 1977–82; Deputy Alianza Popular 1982–85; Deputy Nat. Chair. Alianza Popular; mem. Community Comm. 1986–94; EC Commr for Credits and Investments, Small and Medium-Sized Enterprises and Financial Eng 1986–89, for American Policy, Latin American Relations 1989–93, for Energy and Euratom Supply Agency, Transport 1993–95; Nat. Vice-Pres., then mem. Exec. Cttee, political party Partido Popular (fmrly Alianza Popular) 1979–; mem. European Parl. 1994–96, Cttee on Foreign Affairs, Security and Defence Policy 1994 (Chair. 1994–96), Del. for relations with the countries of Central America and Mexico 1994–96, Pres. Comm. for External Relations and Security of European Parl. 1994–96; Minister of Foreign Affairs 1996–2000; Pres. and Founder Matutes Group of Companies; Pres. Foundation Empresa y Crecimiento; Exec. Vice-Pres. EXCELTUR (Hoteliers Asscn); mem. Eurogroup, Spanish Group of the Trilateral Comm.; mem. Bd of Dirs, BSCH, FCC, Insecc, Balearia, Assecurationi Internationali di Previdenza; mem. Royal Spanish Acad. of Econs and Financial Sciences; Hon. Cttee Mem., Royal Inst. for European Studies; more than 40 nat. and foreign decorations and hons including Grand Cross of the Order of Merit (FRG), Grand Official Legion of Honor Order (France), Grand Gold Cross of Austrian Repub., Grand Cross Order of Merit (Italy), Grand Cross Order of Carlos III (Spain); Dr hc (Complutense Univ., Madrid), (Univ. of Santiago, Chile). *Leisure interests:* tennis, sailing.

MATVEEV, Victor A., DrPhysMathSci; Russian physicist; *Director, Joint Institute for Nuclear Research (JINR);* b. 11 Dec. 1941, Taiga, Krasnojarsk region; m.; two c.; ed Leningrad State Univ.; Postgraduate Researcher, Jr then Sr Researcher, Acting Head of Sector, Lab. of Theoretical Physics of the Joint Inst. of Nuclear Research, Russian Acad. of Sciences 1965–78, Deputy Dir 1978–87, Dir 1987–2012, Dir Joint Institute for Nuclear Research (JINR), Dubna 2012–; Leader, JINR Physicists' Group at Fermi Nat. Accelerator Lab. (USA) 1976–77; mem. Editorial Bd Yadernaya Fyzika (journal); Corresp. mem. Russian Acad. of Sciences 1991–94, Full mem. and mem. Presidium 1994–, Sec. Physics Div. 2008–12; Foreign mem. Bulgarian Acad. of Science, Tajikistan Acad. of Science; Lenin Prize 1988, several Russian Fed. State Prizes in Science and Tech., Order of Honour 1999, Order 'For Service to the Fatherland', IV degree 2007. *Publications include:* Gravitation and Elementary Particle Physics 1980, Nonconservation of Barrion Numbers in Extreme Conditions 1988; numerous scientific papers on relativistic quark models of elementary particles, quantum field theory. *Address:* JINR, Joliot-Curie 6, 141980 Dubna, Russia (office). *Telephone:* (49621) 65-059 (office); (495)

334-00-71 (office). *E-mail:* matveev@inr.ac.ru (office); post@jinr.ru (office). *Website:* www.jinr.ru (office).

MATVEYENKO, Valery Pavlovich, DrTech; Russian physicist; *Chairman, Institute of Continuous Media Mechanics, Russian Academy of Sciences;* b. 9 Feb. 1948, Kizel, Perm region; m.; one d.; ed Perm State Polytechnic Inst.; Engineer, later Jr, then Sr Researcher, Urals Scientific Centre, Russian Acad. of Sciences 1972–79; Head of Lab., Scientific Sec., Deputy Dir, Inst. of Continuous Media Mechanics, Urals br. of Russian Acad. of Sciences 1979–93, Dir 1993–; currently mem. Presidium of Russian Acad. of Sciences, Presidium of Urals branch, Russian Acad. of Sciences, Presidium of Russian Nat. Cttee on Theoretical and Applied Mechanics, Joint Scientific Council on Mathematics, Mechanics and Computer Science of Urals branch of Russian Acad. of Sciences, Russian Acad. of Sciences Scientific Councils on Mechanics of Solids and Mechanics of Composite Structures; Chair. Perm Scientific Center of Urals branch of Russian Acad. of Sciences; Chair. Dept Department of Applied Mechanics and Computational Engineering at the Perm State Univ.; mem. Russian Acad. of Sciences (corresp. mem. 1997–2003), academician 2003–; State Prize of Russian Fed. 1998; For Labour Valour Medal 1986, Order of Honour 1998, Order of Merit for the Motherland (fourth degree) 2008. *Publications include:* over 290 scientific works, five monographs. *Leisure interests:* fishing. *Address:* Institute of Continuous Media Mechanics, Urals branch of the Russian Academy of Sciences, Koroleva str. 1, Perm 614013, Russia (office). *Telephone:* 3422-37-84-61 (office). *Fax:* 3422-37-84-87 (office). *E-mail:* mvp@icmm .ru (office). *Website:* www.icmm.ru (office).

MATVIYENKO, Valentina Ivanovna; Russian politician; *Chairman, Federation Council (Sovet Federatsii);* b. (Valentina Tyutina), 7 April 1949, Shepetivka, Kamyanets-Podilsky Oblast (now Khmelnytsky Oblast), Ukrainian SSR, USSR; m. Vladimir Vasilyevich Matviyenko (died 2018); one s.; ed Leningrad Inst. of Chem. and Pharmaceuticals, Acad. of Social Sciences at CPSU Cen. Cttee, Acad. of Diplomacy USSR Ministry of Foreign Affairs; Komsomol work 1972–84; First Sec. Krasnogvardeisk CP Cttee, Leningrad 1984–86; Deputy Chair. Exec. Cttee Leningrad City Council 1986–89; USSR Peoples' Deputy, mem. Supreme Soviet 1989–92; mem. of Presidium, Chair. Cttee on Family, Motherhood and Childhood Protection Affairs 1989–91; Russian Amb. to Malta 1991–94, to Greece 1997–98; rank of Amb. Extraordinary and Plenipotentiary; Dir Dept on Relations with Federal Subjects, Parl. and Public Orgs Ministry of Foreign Affairs 1995–97, Deputy Prime Minister responsible for social issues 1998–2003, Chair. Comm. on Int. Humanitarian Aid and Religious Orgs; Presidential Rep. in the North-Western Fed. Okrug March–Oct. 2003; Gov. of St Petersburg 2003–11; Deputy, St Petersburg City Authority 2011–; Chair. Fed. Council of the Russian Fed. 2011–; mem. Security Council of the Russian Fed. 2011–; placed under exec. sanction by US Pres. Barack Obama following the Crimean status referendums, freezing her assets in the USA and banning her from entering the USA March 2014; Hon. mem. Russian Acad. of Arts; Order of the Badge of Honour 1976, Order of the Red Banner of Labour 1981, Order of Honour 1996, Order of Merit for the Fatherland (Fourth Class) 1999, (Third Class) 2003, (Second Class) 2009; Decoration of Honour for Services to the Repub. of Austria 2001, Order Martyr Tryphon (Second Class) (Russian Orthodox Church) 2001, Order of St Princess Olga (Second Class) (Russian Orthodox Church) 2001, (First Class) 2006, Medal 'In Commemoration of the 300th Anniversary of St Petersburg' 2003, Grand Cross of the Order of Honour (Greece) 2007, Medal 'For outstanding contributions to the National Year of China and Russia' (China) 2008, Order of People's Friendship 2009, Grand Cross of Order of Lion (Finland) 2009, Order 'For the great love of independent Turkmenistan' (Turkmenistan) 2009, Order of Friendship of Peoples (Belarus) 2009, Kt's Cross, Order of the Lion of Finland 2009, Order of St Sergius (Second Class) (Russian Orthodox Church), (First Class) 2010; Gratitude of Pres. of Russian Fed. 1995, 2008, Pushkin Medal (MAPRYAL) 2003, Diploma of Pres. of Russian Fed. 2010, Prize of Russian Fed. in Science and Tech. 2010, Badge of Honour 'For services to St Petersburg' 2011. *Address:* Office of the Chairman, Federation Council, 103426 Moscow, ul. B. Dmitrovka 26, Russia (office). *Telephone:* (495) 629-70-09 (office). *Fax:* (495) 629-67-43 (office). *E-mail:* post_sf@gov.ru (office). *Website:* www.council .gov.ru (office).

MATYJASZEWSKI, Krzysztof, PhD; Polish/American chemist and academic; *University Professor, Carnegie Mellon University;* b. 8 April 1950, Poland; s. of Henryk Matyjaszewski and Antonina Matyjaszewski; m. Malgorzata Matyjaszewska; one s. one d.; ed Technical Univ. of Moscow, USSR, Polish Acad. of Sciences, Polytechnical Univ. of Łódź; Post-doctoral Fellow, Univ. of Florida 1977–78; Research Assoc., Polish Acad. of Sciences 1978–84; Research Assoc., CNRS, France 1984–85; Invited Prof., Univ. of Paris, France 1985; Asst Prof., later Assoc. Prof., later Prof., Carnegie Mellon Univ., Pittsburg, Pa 1985–98, Head, Chem. Dept 1994–98, J.C. Warner Prof. of Natural Sciences 1998–, Univ. Prof. 2004–; Elf Chair, Acad. des sciences, Paris 1998; Adjunct Prof., Dept of Chemical and Petroleum Eng, Univ. of Pittsburgh 2000–, Polish Acad. of Sciences, Łódź 2000–; Visiting Prof., Univ. of Paris 1985, 1990, 1997, 1998, Univ. of Freiburg, Germany 1988, Univ. of Bayreuth, Germany 1991, Univ. of Strasbourg, France 1992, Univ. of Bordeaux, France 1996, Univ. of Ulm, Germany 1999, Univ. of Pisa, Italy 2000, Mich. Molecular Inst. 2004, Univ. of Paris, France 2005, École supérieure de physique et de chimie industrielles, Paris 2009, 2011, Pusan Nat. Univ., S Korea 2010; Ed. Progress in Polymer Science; present or past mem. editorial bds of numerous journals, including Macromolecules, Macromolecular Chemistry and Physics, Marcromolecular Rapid Communications, Journal of Polymer Science, Journal of Inorganic and Organometallic Polymers, Journal of Macromolecular Science, Pure and Applied Chemistry, International Journal of Polymeric Materials, Chinese Journal of Polymer Science, International Journal of Applied Chemistry, Chemistry Central Journal, Polymer, Polimery; ACS Polymeric Materials Science and Eng Fellow 2001; IUPAC Fellow 2002–, Corresp. mem. IUPAC Comm. on Polymer Nomenclature; Chair. ACS Polymer Curriculum Devt Award Cttee ACS, mem. Program Cttee, Polymer Chem. Div., Chair. Int. Cttee, Polymer Chem. Div.; mem. US Nat. Acad. of Eng, Polish Acad. of Sciences, Russian Acad. of Sciences, Pacific Polymer Fed. (Pres. 2013–15); Fellow, US Nat. Acad. of Inventors; Hon. Fellow, Chinese Chemical Soc. 2012; Commdr's Cross, Order of Merit 2011; Dr hc (Ghent) 2002, (Russian Acad. of Sciences) 2006, (Tech. Univ. of Łódź) 2007, (Athens) 2009, (Institut Polytechnique, Toulouse) 2010, (Pusan Nat. Univ.) 2013, (Université Pierre et Marie Curie, Paris) 2013, (Technion, Israel) 2015, (Poznań Univ., Poland) 2016; Award of Scientific Sec. of

Polish Acad. of Sciences 1974, Award of Polish Chemical Soc. 1980, Award of Polish Acad. of Sciences 1981, Award of Presidential Young Investigator, NSF 1989, ACS Carl S. Marvel-Creative Polymer Chem. Award 1995, Reed Lecturer, Rensellaer Polytechnic Inst. 1998, Milkovitch Lecturer, Univ. of Akron 1998, Humboldt Award for Sr US Scientists 1999, ACS Pittsburgh Award 2001, ACS Polymer Chem. Award 2002, ACS Cooperative Research Award in Polymer Science and Eng 2004, Award of Foundation for Polish Science 2004, Macro Group Medal (UK) 2005, ACS Hermann F. Mark Sr Scholar Award 2007, Presidential Green Chem. Challenge Award (USA) 2009, Gutenberg Award, Mainz (Germany) 2010, Wolf Prize in Chem. 2011, ACS Applied Polymer Science Award 2011, Carnegie Science Award in Advanced Materials 2011, Japanese Soc. Polymer Science Award 2011, ACS Hermann F. Mark Award 2011, Maria Sklodowska-Curie Medal, Polish Chemical Soc. 2012, Dannie-Heineman Prize, Göttingen Acad. of Sciences 2012, Soc. Chimique de France Prize 2012, inaugural ACS AkzoNobel North America Science Award 2013, ACS Madison Marshall Award 2013, Nat. Inst. of Materials Science (Japan) Award 2014, ACS Charles G. Overberger Prize 2015, The Dreyfus Prize in the Chemical Sciences 2015, Casimir Funk Award, Polish Inst. of Arts and Sciences (USA) 2016, Medema Award, The Netherlands 2017, Benjamin Franklin Medal in Chem. 2017. *Publications:* co-author/ed. 20 books, 90 book chapters, more than 950 scientific papers, 56 US and 140 int. patents. *Address:* Department of Chemistry, Carnegie Mellon University, 4400 Fifth Avenue, Pittsburgh, PA 15213, USA (office). *Telephone:* (412) 268-3209 (office). *Fax:* (412) 268-6897 (office). *E-mail:* km3b@andrew.cmu.edu (office). *Website:* www.cmu.edu/maty (office).

MATYUKHIN, Gen. Vladimir Georgyevich, DTechSci; Russian business executive and government official; b. 4 Feb. 1945, Moscow; ed Moscow Inst. of Energy, Moscow State Univ.; mem. staff Moscow Pedagogical Inst. 1962–64; engineer Construction Bureau, Moscow Inst. of Energy 1964–73; service in state security organs 1969–; Deputy Dir-Gen. Fed. Agency of Govt Telecommunications and Information 1993–99, Dir-Gen. 1999–2003; First Deputy Minister of Defence –2004, Head of State Defence Procurements Cttee –2004; rank of Gen. (Army) 2004; Head, Fed. Information Tech. Agency 2004; mem. Acad. of Cryptography, Acad. of Int. Communication; several medals including For Labour Valour 1986, For Services to the Motherland 1999, For Military Merit 2000, St Daniil of Moscow Second degree 2000, First degree 2007. *Publications:* numerous journal articles. *Leisure interests:* photography, floriculture.

MATYUSHEUSKI, Vasil Stanislavovich, PhD; Belarusian economist, banking executive, government official and fmr diplomatist; b. 26 March 1969, Orsha, Vitebsk (Viciebsk) Oblast, Belarusian SSR, USSR; ed V.I. Lenin Belarusian State Univ., Minsk, Inst. of Econs, Acad. of Sciences of Belarus, London Business School, UK; Head of Dept, Research and Manufacturing Enterprise, Research Assoc., Research Econ. Inst. under auspices of State Econ. Planning Cttee 1991–92; Attaché, Third Sec., Ministry of Foreign Affairs 1992–94; Chief Economist, Div. Head, Deputy Head of Directorate, Nat. Bank of the Repub. of Belarus 1994–97, Dept Dir and Deputy Chair. 1998–2010; Econ. Adviser to Minister of Finance 1997–98; Dir-Gen. and Chair. BPS-Bank Open Jt Stock Co. 2010–11, Chair. 2011–14; First Deputy Prime Minister 2014–18.

MAU, Vladimir Alexandrovich, DrEcon, PhD; Russian politician and economist; *Rector, Academy of National Economy;* b. 29 Dec. 1959, Moscow; m. Victoria Ashrafian; one s. one d.; ed Moscow Plekhanov Inst. of Nat. Econs, Inst. of Econs USSR Acad. of Sciences, Acad. de Grenoble, Université Pierre Mendès, France; with Inst. of Econs, USSR (now Russian) Acad. of Sciences 1981–91, Inst. for the Economy in Transition; Sr Lecturer, Faculty of Econ. Dept, Moscow State Univ. 1988–92; Head of Dept, Inst. of Econ. Policy 1991; Adviser to Chair., Govt of Russian Fed. 1992; mem. Bd Dirs and Head of Dept, Inst. for the Economy in Transition 1993; Adviser to Deputy Mayor of Moscow 1993, to First Deputy Chair., Govt of Russian Fed. 1993–94; Prof., High School of Econs 1993–2002; Adviser to Leader of the Faction in the State Duma of Russia 1994–95; Deputy Dir, Inst. for the Economy in Transition and Head of Dept for Political Studies of Econ. Reforms 1994–97; Dir Working Centre for Econ. Reform, Govt of Russian Fed. 1997–2002; Lecturer, Stanford Univ. Overseas Dept 1997–; Rector Acad. of Nat. Economy (under Govt of Russian Fed.) 2002–10, Russian Presidential Acad. of Nat. Economy and Public Admin 2010–; Hon. Economist of Russian Fed. 2000; Order for Merit to the Fatherland (3rd class) 2017. *Publications:* 700 articles in books, scientific journals, magazines and newspapers in Russian, English, French, German, Italian on history of econ. thought, political economy, social and political issues of market reforms, econ. policy; 29 books including In The Quest of Planification 1990, The Laws of Revolution: Experience of Perestroika and Our Future (with Irina Starodubrovskaia) 1991, History of Economic Studies in the USSR: Outlines for Conception 1992, Reforms and Dogma: 1861–1929 1993, Economy and Power 1995, Political History of Economic Reform in Russia 1985–1994 1996, Economy and Law (Constitutional Problems of Economic Reforms in Russia) 1998, Economic Reform: Through the Prism of Constitution and Politics 1999, Russian Economic Reforms as Seen by an Insider: Success or Failure? 2000, Challenge of Revolution (with Irina Starodubrovskaia) 2001, Great Revolutions from Cromwell to Putin 2001, Constitutional Economics (with Peter Barenboimand and Vladimir Lafitsky) 2002, From Crisis to Growth 2005, Crises and Lessons 2015. *Leisure interest:* history, reading. *Address:* Russian Presidential Academy of National Economy and Public Administration, 119571 Moscow, Vernadskogo Prospekt 82-84, Russia (office). *Telephone:* (495) 434-83-89 (office); (495) 633-60-84 (office). *Fax:* (495) 433-24-85 (office). *E-mail:* rector@ranepe.ru (office); decp@ranepa.ru (office). *Website:* www.ranepa.ru (office).

MAUDE OF HORSHAM, Baron (Life Peer), cr. 2015, of Horsham, of Shipley in the County of West Sussex; **Rt Hon. Francis Anthony Aylmer Maude,** PC, MA; British politician and business executive; b. 4 July 1953, Abingdon, Oxon.; s. of Baron Maude of Stratford-upon-Avon; m. Christina Jane Hadfield 1984; two s. three d.; ed Abingdon School, Corpus Christi Coll., Cambridge, Coll. of Law; called to Bar, Inner Temple 1977 (Forster Boulton Prize); Councillor, Westminster City Council 1978–84; MP for Warwicks. N 1983–92, for Horsham 1997–2015; Parl. Pvt. Sec. to Minister of State for Employment 1984–85; an Asst Govt Whip 1985–87; Parl. Under-Sec. of State Dept of Trade and Industry 1987–89; Minister of State, FCO 1989–90; Financial Sec. to HM Treasury 1990–92; Chair. Govt's Deregulation Task Force 1994–97; Shadow Chancellor 1998–2000, Shadow Foreign Sec. 2000–01; Minister for the Cabinet Office 2010–15; Paymaster Gen. 2010–15;

Minister of State for Trade and Investment 2015–16; Chair. Prestbury Holdings, Jubilee Investment Trust, Incepta Group plc 2004–05; Chair., Conservative Party 2005–07; Dir Salomon Brothers 1992–93, Asda Group 1992–99, Utek 2006–; Man. Dir Morgan Stanley and Co. 1993–97; Deputy Chair. Benfield Group Ltd 2003–; Deputy Chair. Huntsworth plc. *Leisure interests:* skiing, cricket, reading, music.

MAUMOON, Dunya, BA, MPhil; Maldivian UN official and politician; b. 1970; d. of Maumoon Abdul Gayoom (fmr Pres. of Maldives) and Nasreena Ibrahim; m. Shuaib Shah; two s. one d.; ed Univ. of Cambridge, London School of Econs, UK; Asst Rep. Head, UN Population Fund (UNFPA), Maldives 1998–2007; Deputy Minister of Foreign Affairs 2007–08, Head of Multilateral Dept, later Minister of State, Ministry of Foreign Affairs 2012, Minister of Foreign Affairs 2013–16 (resgnd), Minister of State for Health 2017–18; fmr mem. Dhivehi Raiyyithunge Party (DRP); mem. Progressive Party of Maldives (PPM), Pres. of Women's Wing 2013–.

MAUNG, Deputy Sr Gen. Aye, BSc; Myanma military officer; b. 25 Dec. 1937, Kon Balu; m.; ed Defence Services Acad.; joined Myanma Army 1959; Deputy C-in-C Defence Services 1993–2011; Vice-Chair. State Law and Order Restoration Council (SLORC) 1994–97, State Peace and Devt Council 1997–2011 (council dissolved).

MAUNG, Cynthia, MD; Myanma physician; *Director, Mae Tao Clinic;* b. 6 Dec. 1959, Rangoon; m. Kyaw Hein; two d.; ed Univ. of Rangoon; trained at North Okkalapa Gen. Hosp.; worked in rural clinic in Karen State; participated in nationwide anti-govt protests in 1988, fled to Thailand several months later; f. Mae Tao Clinic in Thailand to treat refugees fleeing from Myanmar; John Humphries Freedom Award 1999, American Women's Medical Asscn Pres.'s Award 1999, Jonathan Mann Award 1999, Van Hueven Goedhart Award, Foundation for Human Rights in Asia Special Award 2001, Ramon Magsaysay Award 2002, Global Concern for Human Life Award, Chou-Ta Kuan Foundation 2005, Unsung Heroes of Compassion Award 2005, World's Children's Hon. Award 2007, Asia Democracy and Human Rights Award 2007, Catalonia Int. Prize (jtly) 2008, Democracy Award, Nat. Endowment for Democracy (US) 2012, Sydney Peace Prize 2013, Toux Prize 2018. *Address:* Mae Tao Clinic, PO Box 67, Mae Sot, Tak 63110, Thailand (office). *Telephone:* (55) 563-644 (office). *Fax:* (55) 544-655 (office). *E-mail:* win7@loxinfo.co.th (office). *Website:* www.maetaoclinic.org (office).

MAURA, Carmen, BA; Spanish actress; b. 15 Sept. 1945, Madrid; d. of Antonio Maura; worked as a cabaret singer and translator; has appeared in numerous films including many of Pedro Almodóvar's works; European Film Academy Lifetime Achievement Award 2018. *Other films include:* El espíritu 1969, Mantis 1971, El hombre oculto (The Man In Hiding) 1971, El asesino está entre los trece 1973, Un casto varón español 1973, Tanata 1974, Don Juan 1974, Vida íntima de un seductor cínico 1975, La encadenada (A Diary of a Murderess) 1975, El love feroz 1975, Leonor 1975, Pomporrutas imperiales 1976, La petición (The Request) 1976, Una pareja como las demás 1976, Ir por lana 1976, La mujer es cosa de hombres 1976, El libro del buen amor II (The Book of Good Love 2) 1976, Tigres de papel (Paper Tigers) 1977, ¿Qué hace una chica como tú en un sitio como éste? (What's a Girl Like You Doing in a Place Like This?) 1978, Mi blanca Varsovia 1978, Menos mi madre y mi hermana 1978, Folle… folle… fólleme Tim! 1978, De fresa, limón y menta (Strawberry, Lemon and Mint) 1978, Los ojos vendados (Blindfolded Eyes) 1978, Tal vez mañana… 1979, Café, amor y estereofonía 1979, La mano negra (The Black Hand) 1980, Aquella casa en las afueras (That House in the Outskirts) 1980, Pepi, Luci, Bom y otras chicas del montón (Pepi, Luci, Bom and Other Girls Like Mom) 1980, El hombre de moda (Man of Fashion) 1980, Gary Cooper, que estás en los cielos (Gary Cooper, Who Art in Heaven) 1980, Femenino singular 1982, Entre tinieblas (Dark Habits) 1983, El Cid cabreador 1983, ¿Qué he hecho yo para merecer esto!! (What Have I Done to Deserve This?) 1984, Extramuros (Beyond the Walls) 1985, Sé infiel y no mires con quién (Be Wanton and Tread No Shame) 1985, Matador 1986, Delirios de amor 1986, Tata mía (Dear Nanny) 1986, La ley del deseo (Law of Desire) 1987, 2.30 A.M. 1988, Mujeres al borde de un ataque de nervios (Women on the Verge of a Nervous Breakdown) (Best Actress, European Film Awards 1989) 1988, Bâton rouge 1988, ¡Ay, Carmela! (Best Actress, European Film Awards 1991) 1990, Cómo ser mujer y no morir en el intento (How to Be a Woman and Not Die Trying) 1991, Chatarra 1991, Sur la terre comme au ciel (In Heaven as on Earth) 1992, La reina anónima (The Anonymous Queen) 1992, Louis, enfant roi (Louis, the Child King) 1993, Sombras en una batalla (Shadows in a Conflict) 1993, Cómo ser infeliz y disfrutarlo (How to Be Miserable and Enjoy It) 1994, El rey del río 1995, Parella de tres 1995, El palomo cojo (The Lame Pigeon) 1995, Le bonheur est dans le pré (Happiness is in the Field) 1995, Amores que matan 1996, Vivir después 1997, Tortilla y cinema 1997, Alliance cherche doigt 1997, Elles 1997, Alice et Martin 1998, El entusiasmo (Enthusiasm) 1998, El cometa (The Comet) 1999, Lisboa 1999, Superlove 1999, Carretera y manta (To the End of the Road) 2000, Le harem de Mme Osmane 2000, La comunidad 2000, El apagón 2001, El palo (The Hold-Up) 2001, Arregui, la noticia del día 2001, Clara y Elena 2001, Assassini dei giorni di festa (Killers on Holiday) 2002, Valentín 2002, 800 balas (800 Bullets) 2002, Le ventre de Juliette 2003, Le pacte du silence 2003, 25 degrés en hiver (25 Degrees in Winter) 2004, La promesa 2004, Al otro lado 2004, Entre vivir y soñar 2004, Reinas 2005, Free Zone 2005, Volver (Best Actress, Cannes Film Festival 2006, Goya Award for Best Supporting Actress 2007) 2006, El Menor de los males 2007, La Virgen negra 2008, The Garden of Eden 2008, Que parezca un accidente 2008, Tetro 2009, Le mac 2010, Chicas 2010, The Women on the 6th Floor (César Award for Best Supporting Actress 2012) 2010, Escalade 2011, Let My People Go! 2011, Sofía y el Terco 2012, Paulette 2012, Las brujas de Zugarramurdi 2013. *Television includes:* Juan y Manuela (series) 1974, Suspiros de España (series) 1974, El coleccionismo y los coleccionistas (series) 1979, Cervantes (mini-series) 1980, La huella del crimen: El crimen de la calle Fuencarral 1984, Sal gorda (Coarse Salt) 1984, La mujer de tu vida: La mujer feliz 1988, Mieux vaut courir 1989, A las once en casa (series) 1998, Famosos y familia (series) 1999, Une mère en colère 2000, Arroz y tartana 2003, Mentir un peu 2004, Mentir un peu 2006, Círculo rojo (series) 2007, The War of the Saints 2009, Las chicas de oro (series) 2010, Carta a Eva (mini-series) 2012, Stamos okupa2 (series) 2012. *Address:* c/o Françoise Salimov, Artmedia, 8 rue Danielle Casanova, 75002 Paris, France. *Telephone:* 1-72-33-25-00. *E-mail:* f.salimov@artmedia.fr. *Website:* www.artmedia.fr.

MAURER, Peter, PhD; Swiss diplomatist; *President, International Committee of the Red Cross;* b. 20 Nov. 1956, Thun; m. Doris Maurer-Scheidegger; two d.; ed Univ. of Bern, Univ. of Perugia, Italy; joined Fed. Dept of Foreign Affairs 1987, served as Diplomatic Adviser, Political Secr. 1989–91, Pvt. Sec. to State Sec. for Foreign Affairs 1991–96; Deputy Perm. Observer to Observer Mission to UN, New York 1996–2000; Head, Political Affairs Div. IV (Human Security), Political Affairs Govt Directorate 2000–04; Amb. and Perm. Rep. to UN, New York 2004–10, Head of Fifth Comm. (overseeing budget and admin. matters); Sec. of State, Fed. Dept of Foreign Affairs 2010–12; Pres. International Cttee of the Red Cross 2012–; mem. Foundation Bd, World Economic Forum 2014–. *Address:* International Committee of the Red Cross (ICRC), 19 ave de la Paix, 1202 Geneva, Switzerland (office). *E-mail:* press.gva@icrc.org (office). *Website:* www.icrc.org (office).

MAURER, Ueli; Swiss communications consultant and politician; *President and Head of Federal Department of Finance;* b. 1 Dec. 1950, Wetzikon; m.; six c.; Dir Zürich Farmers Asscn 1994–2008; mem. Zürich Cantonal Parl. 1978–86 (Pres. 1991); mem. House of Reps 1991; mem. Schweizerischen Volkspartei (Swiss People's Party), Pres. 1996–2008, Pres. Zürich Div. 2008; mem. Swiss Federal Council 2009–, Head of Fed. Dept of Defence, Civil Protection and Sports 2009–16, of Finance 2016–, Vice-Pres. 2012, 2018, Pres. 2013, 2019; fmr Pres. Swiss Vegetable Farmers Asscn, Farmers Machinery Asscn (Maschinenring). *Address:* Federal Department of Finance, Bernerhof, Bundesgasse 3, 3003 Bern, Switzerland (office). *Telephone:* 584622111 (office). *E-mail:* info@gs-efd.admin.ch (office). *Website:* www.efd.admin.ch (office).

MAURESMO, Amélie; French professional tennis player (retd) and tennis coach; b. 5 July 1979, Saint-Germain-en-Laye; began playing tennis aged four; turned professional 1994; won both Jr French Open and Wimbledon titles 1996; finalist, Australian Open 1999; semifinalist, US Open singles 2002, 2006; quarterfinalist, French Open singles 2003, 2004; silver medal, Olympic Games, Athens 2004; winner of two Grand Slam singles titles, Australian Open 2006, Wimbledon 2006; ranked World No. 1 Sept.–Oct. 2004; doubles finalist with Svetlana Kuznetsova, Wimbledon 2005; lives in Geneva, Switzerland; retd 2009; currently tennis commentator, EuroSport; Capt. l'Equipe de France de Fed-Cup; coach, Michaël Llodra 2010, Victoria Azarenka 2012, Marion Bartoli 2013, Andy Murray 2014–16; Int. Tennis Fed. Jr World Champion 1996. *E-mail:* agence@interactive-one.fr. *Website:* www.ameliemauresmo.fr.

MAURSTAD, Toralv; Norwegian actor and theatre director; b. 24 Nov. 1926, Oslo; s. of Alfred and Tordis Maurstad; m. 1st Anne-Ma Burum (divorced); m. 2nd Eva Henning 1954 (divorced 1970); m. 3rd Beate Eriksen 2000; one s.; ed Universitet i Uppsala and Royal Acad. of Dramatic Art, London; debut in Trondheim 1947; Oslo Nye Teater 1951; Oslo Nat. Theatre 1954; Man. Dir Oslo Nye Teater (Oslo Municipal Theatre) 1967–78; Man. Dir Nat. Theatre 1978–86, actor/Dir Nat. Theatre 1987–; Norwegian Sr Golf Champion 1992; Kt First Class, Order of St Olav (Norway), Commdr of St Olav 2006, Order of Oranian (Netherlands); Oslo Critics' Award, Ibsen Prize, Amanda, Aamot Statuette. *Plays acted in or directed include:* Young Woodley 1949, Pal Joey 1952, Peer Gynt 1954, 2018–19, Long Day's Journey 1962, Teenage Love 1963, Hamlet 1964, Arturo Ui (in Bremen, Germany) 1965, Brand (Ibsen) 1966, Of Love Remembered (New York) 1967, Cabaret 1968, Scapino 1975, Two Gentlemen of Verona 1976, The Moon of the Misbegotten 1976, Same Time Next Year 1977, Twigs 1977 (also TV production), Sly Fox 1978, Whose Life is it Anyway? 1979, Masquerade 1980, Amadeus 1980, Much Ado about Nothing 1981, Kennen Sie die Milchstrasse? 1982, Duet for One 1982, Hamlet 1983, Private Lives (with Liv Ullman) 1993, Dear Liar 1996, The Pretenders 1998, Copenhagen 2000, Enigma Variation 2001, Waiting for Godot 2005, Rigoletto (opera) 2005, Twelfth Night 2005, Moon for the Misbegotten 2008, The Dresser 2012, Sokrates Defence Speech 2012. *Films:* Fant 1937, Trysil-Knut 1942, Kranes konditori 1951, Andrine og Kjell 1952, Cirkus Fandango 1954, Hjem går vi ikke 1955, Line 1961, Kalde Spor 1962, Om Tilla (About Tilla) 1963, Svarta palmkronor (Black Palm Trees) 1968, Hennes meget kongelige høyhet 1968, Song of Norway 1970, Flåklypa Grand Prix (voice) 1975, Glade vrinsk (writer) 1975, Etter Rubicon (After Rubicon) 1987, Det var en gang (voice) 1994, Jakten på nyresteinen (Chasing the Kidney Stone; voice) 1996, Solan, Ludvig og Gurin med reverompa (Gurin with the Foxtail; voice) 1998, Olsenbanden Junior på rocker'n 2004, Blåfjell 2 2011, Solan og Ludvig - Jul i Flåklypa 2013. *Radio plays:* Doll's House, Peer Gynt, Masquerade. *Television:* Gengangere 1962, Frydenberg 1965, Ett köpmanshus i skärgården (mini-series) 1972, Spyship (mini-series) 1983, The Last Place on Earth (mini-series) 1985, Konsultasjon eller helbredelsens kunst (dir) 1988, Olsenbandens første kupp (mini-series) 2001, Enigmavariasjoner (film) 2002, Hotel Cesar (series) 2004, Waiting for Godot 2006, Størst av alt (mini-series) 2007, Stjernene På Slottet 2013. *Publication:* Du Store Min (autobiog.), For et liv 2012. *Leisure interests:* skiing, hunting, fishing, golf, tennis. *Address:* Nationaltheatret, Stortingsgt. 15, Oslo 1 (office); Box 58, Holmenkollen, 0712, Norway (home); Thorleif, Hangsvei 20, Voksenkollen 0791, Oslo, Norway (home). *Telephone:* 22-14-18-84 (home); 91370972 (mobile). *E-mail:* toral-ma@online.no (home).

MAÚRTUA DE ROMAÑA, Óscar José Ricardo, BA, BL; Peruvian government minister, politician and diplomatist; *President, Society Peruana de Derecho Internacional;* b. 7 Feb. 1947, Lima; m. Lourdes María del Carmen Briseño-Meiggs García; three c.; ed Univ. Católica y San Marcos, Univ. of Oxford, Johns Hopkins Univ.; Second, then First Sec., Embassy in Washington, DC; Counsellor, Embassy in Brussels and at EU; Head, Dept of Int. Political Econs; Sec.-Gen. Presidency of the Repub.; Amb. to Canada (also accred to Bolivia); Dir-Gen. of Planning, of Judicial Affairs; Amb. to Thailand (also accred to Viet Nam and Laos); Perm. Rep., ESCAP; Amb. to Ecuador; Dir Acad. of Diplomacy; Sub-Sec. for American Affairs, later Sec. for Foreign Affairs; Minister of Foreign Affairs 2005–06; OAS Rep. in Mexico 2007–11; Gen. Dir School of Int. Relations and Govt, Technological Univ. of Peru 2011–13; Gen. Dir of Int. Affairs, CENTRUM PUCP; Del. to Confs of APEC, Asia Pacific Parl. Forum, Pacific Basin ECO Council, Pacific ECO Cooperation Council; Prof. of Int. Law, Univ. Nacional de San Marcos y de Derecho; mem. Colegio de Abogados de Lima, Soc. Peruana de Derecho Int. (Pres. 2017–), Oxford Soc., Centre of Int. Understanding; Hon. mem. Soc. Boliviana de Historia, Soc. de la Academia Boliviana de Estudios Int., Siam Soc., Sociedad Fundadores de la Independencia; Hon. Prof., Univ. Andina Simon Bolivar, Quito; Dr. hc (Univ. of Winnipeg, Canada) 1988, (Univ. of Assumption, Thailand) 1999,

(Domingo Savio Univ., Bolivia) 2005, (National Nat. Univ. of Piura) 2012; Band of the Order of the Aztec Eagle 2012; Grand Cross, Order of Merit for Distinguished Service; Grand Cross, Order of the Sun; Grand Officer, Order of Naval Merit; Commdr, Order of May (Argentina); Grand Officer, Order of the Southern Cross (Brazil); Grand Officer, Order of Leopold (Belgium); First Class of Order of Francisco de Miranda (Venezuela); Grand Officer, Order of Isabella the Catholic (Spain); Commdr, Order of San Carlos (Colombia); Commdr, Order of Merit of Lower Austria; Grand Cross, Order of Merit (Korea); Grand Officer, Order of the Condor of the Andes (Bolivia); Grand Cross, Order of the White Elephant (Thailand); Grand Cross, Order of Merit (Chile); Grand Cross, Order of Rio Branco (Brazil); Grand Cross, Order of the Crown (Belgium); Nat. Award of Culture, Nat. Award Journalism (Mexico) 2009. *Publications:* El Mariscal Andres de Santa Cruz y el encuentro de dos mundos 1992, Derecho Internacional y Política Exterior 1995, Una Visión Latinoamericana del Asia Pacifico 1999, Las Nuevas Relaciones Bilaterales Perú-Ecuador 2000, Perú y Ecuador: Socios en el siglo XXI 2001, Apuntes sobre la Agenda Interamericana México 2010, Bitácora Interamericana 2012, Chaumette des Fossés y el inicio de las Relaciones Franco-Peruanas (1826–1827) 2014, Impacto de las Migraciones Internacionales en el Desarrollo del Perú 2017. *Address:* Jr. Miró Quesada 247, of. 508, Lima 1, Peru (office). *Telephone:* (1) 2043531 (office). *E-mail:* osjomar@hotmail.com; spdi@spdi.org.pe (office). *Website:* www.spdi.org.pe (office).

MAURYA, Baby Rani, BEd, MA; Indian politician and activist; *Governor of Uttarakhand;* b. 15 Aug. 1956; m. Pradeep Kumar Maurya; Mayor of Agra 1995–2000; mem. Uttar Pradesh State Social Welfare Bd 2002; mem. Nat. Comm. for Women 2002–05; mem. Bharatiya Janata Party; Rajiv Gandhi Samaj Ratna Award 1996, Uttar Pradesh Ratna Award 1997, Nari Ratna Award 1998. *Address:* Rajbhawan, New Cantt. Road, Dehradun 248003, Uttarakhand; 4/A, Cariappa Road, Agra, Uttar Pradesh, India (home). *Telephone:* (135) 2757403; (135) 2757400. *E-mail:* adcahe-ua@nic.in. *Website:* www.governoruk.gov.in.

MAVRIKOS, George; Greek trade union official and international organization executive; *General Secretary, World Federation of Trade Unions;* b. 1950, Skyros; ed Faculty of Political and Social Sciences, Moscow, USSR; moved to Athens aged 15; work in textile factories during the dictatorship 1967–74, participated in students' uprising Nov. 1973; worked in agricultural machinery factory for 14 years, elected chair. of workers' union; elected organizational sec. of Athens Labour Centre 1982; fmr mem. European Social Fund in EU; Gen. Sec. Gen. Confed. of Greek Workers 1993–98; Sec. All Workers Militant Front (PAME) (a CP of Greece-affiliated trade union) 1999–2007; Vice-Pres. WFTU and Co-ordinator of its Regional European Office 2000–05, Gen. Sec. WFTU 2005–; mem. Parl. (Kommunistiko Komma Elladas) 2007–12. *Address:* World Federation of Trade Unions, 40 Zan Moreas str., 117 45 Athens, Greece (office). *Telephone:* (210) 9214417 (office); (210) 9236700 (office). *Fax:* (210) 9214517 (office). *E-mail:* gensec@wftucentral.org (office). *Website:* www.wftucentral.org/general-secretary (office).

MAVRONICOLAS, Kyriakos, FRCS; Cypriot ophthalmologist and politician; b. 1955, Paphos; m. Irene (Roula) Kokkinidou; two c.; ed First Gymnasium, Paphos, Nat. and Kapodistrian Univ. of Athens Medical School, Athens Law School; began career as ophthalmologist, Nicosia 1960, practised in UK 1981–87; fmr Gen. Sec. Democratic Students' Movement (AGONAS); Sec. Athens Br., Socialist Party (EDEK), becoming EDEK Dist Sec., Nicosia 1989–93, later Party First Vice-Pres.; Deputy Pres. Social Democrat Movement (KISOS); Minister of Defence 2003–06; Rep. of Cyprus in European Parl. 2006–12.

MAVROYIANNIS, Andreas D., DipLaw; Cypriot diplomatist and politician; *Permanent Secretary, Ministry of Foreign Affairs;* b. 20 July 1956, Agros; m. Calliopi Efthyvoulou (deceased); one s. one d.; ed Univ. of Thessalonica, Greece, Université de Droit et de Sciences Economique, Paris, Université de Paris X, Nanterre; joined Ministry of Foreign Affairs (MFA) 1987; served at Embassy in Paris 1989–93, also in Political Div., Cyprus Question Div., EU Div., and as Assoc. European Correspondent; Dir, Office of Minister of Foreign Affairs 1995–97, 2002–03; Amb. to Ireland 1997–99, to France (also accred to Andorra, Tunisia and Morocco) 1999–2002; Acting Perm. Sec., MFA 2003; Amb. and Perm. Rep. to UN, New York 2003–, also accred as High Commr to St Lucia 2003–08 and Amb. to Brazil 2007–08; Chair. UN Cttee on Relations with Host Country 2003–; Amb. and Perm. Rep. to EU, Brussels 2008–11; Deputy Minister for European Affairs 2011–13, Perm. Sec., MFA 2013–, also Negotiator for Greek-Cypriot side in inter-communal talks on the Cyprus problem 2013–; Rep. at Cttee of Legal Advisers on Public Int. Law (CAHDI), Council of Europe 1988–92; Rep. Prep. Comm. for High Authority, Law of the Sea 1989; mem. Greek Cypriot negotiating team in bi-communal talks for solution of Cyprus issue 2002–03; Lecturer, Cyprus Mediterranean Inst. of Man., Cyprus Acad. for Public Admin, Law School of Univ. of Athens; Diploma of The Hague Acad. of Int. Law 1984. *Publications:* articles and reviews in scholarly journals and newspapers. *Address:* Ministry of Foreign Affairs, Presidential Palace Ave, 1447 Nicosia, Cyprus (office). *Telephone:* 22651000 (office). *Fax:* 22661881 (office). *E-mail:* minforeign1@mfa.gov.cy (office). *Website:* www.mfa.gov.cy (office).

MAWER, Sir Philip John Courtney, Kt, MA, DPA; British parliamentary official and church official; *Chairman, All Churches Trust Ltd;* b. 30 July 1947; s. of Eric Douglas Mawer and Thora Constance Mawer; m. Mary Ann Moxon 1972; one s. two d.; ed Hull Grammar School, Univ. of Edinburgh, Univ. of London; Sr Pres. EU Student Rep. Council 1969–70; joined Home Office 1971; Pvt. Sec. to Minister of State 1974–76; Nuffield and Leverhulme Travelling Fellowship 1978–79; Sec. Lord Scarman Inquiry into Brixton Riots 1981; Asst Sec. Head of Industrial Relations, Prison Dept 1984–87; Prin. Pvt. Sec. to Home Sec. Douglas Hurd 1987–89; Under-Sec. Cabinet Office 1989–90; Sec.-Gen. Church of England Synod 1990–2002; Sec.-Gen. Archbishops' Council 1999–2002; Parl. Commr for Standards 2002–08, then ind. adviser to Prime Minister 2008–11; Chair. Professional Regulation Exec. Cttee of the Actuarial Profession 2009–13; Dir (non-exec.) Ecclesiastical Insurance Group 1996–2002, 2008–13 (Deputy Chair. 2009–13); Trustee, All Churches Trust 1992– (Dir 2010–, Chair. 2013–); mem. Governing Body SPCK 1994–2002; Patron, Church Housing Trust 1996–; Hon. Lay Canon of St Alban's Cathedral 2003–12; Hon. DLitt (Hull) 2006, Hon. LLD (Herts.) 2007. *Leisure interests:* family, friends. *Address:* All Churches Trust, Beaufort House, Brunswick Road, Gloucester, GL1 1JZ, England (office). *Telephone:* (1452) 423557 (office). *Website:* www.allchurches.uk (office).

MAWHINNEY, Baron (Life Peer), cr. 2005; **Brian Stanley Mawhinney,** Kt, PC, PhD; British politician and company director; b. 26 July 1940; s. of Frederick Stanley Arnot Mawhinney and Coralie Jean Mawhinney; m. Betty Louise Oja 1965; two s. one d.; ed Royal Belfast Academical Inst., Queen's Univ. Belfast, Univ. of Michigan, USA, Univ. of London; Asst Prof. of Radiation Research, Univ. of Iowa, USA 1968–70; Lecturer, subsequently Sr Lecturer, Royal Free Hosp. School of Medicine 1970–84; mem. MRC 1980–83; MP for Peterborough 1979–97, for Cambridgeshire NW 1997–2005; Parl. Under-Sec. of State for Northern Ireland 1986–90; Minister of State, Northern Ireland Office 1990–92, Dept of Health 1992–94; Sec. of State for Transport 1994–95; Chair. Conservative Party 1995–97; Opposition Front Bench Spokesman on Home Affairs 1997–98; Pres. Conservative Trade Unionists 1987–90; mem. Gen. Synod of Church of England 1985–90; Chair. Football League 2003–10; Jt Deputy Chair. England 2018 World Cup Bid Co. 2008–10; Freedom of the City of Peterborough 2008; Hon. Pres. Football League 2010–13; Hon. LLD (Queen's, Belfast) 2008. *Publications include:* Conflict and Christianity in Northern Ireland (co-author) 1976, In the Firing Line – Faith, Power, Politics, Forgiveness 1999. *Leisure interests:* sport, reading, business. *Address:* House of Lords, Westminster, London, SW1A 0PW, England (office). *Telephone:* (1733) 261868 (office). *Fax:* (1733) 266887 (office). *E-mail:* judith5@waitrose.com (office).

MAXSTED, Lindsay, DipBus, FCA; Australian business executive; *Chairman, Westpac Banking Corporation;* b. 21 May 1954, Geelong; ed Robert Gordon Univ., Deakin Univ.; Partner, KPMG 1984–2008, CEO 2001–07; mem. Bd Public Transport Corpn 1995–2001, Chair. 1997–2001; mem. Bd of Dirs Westpac Westpac Banking Corpn 2008–, Chair. 2011–; Chair. Transurban Group; Man. Dir Align Capital Pty Ltd; Dir (non-Exec.) Transurban Infrastructure Man., Ltd 2008–, BHP Billiton plc 2011–; mem. Bd of Dirs Baker IDI Heart & Diabetes Inst. Holdings Ltd; Fellow, Australian Inst. of Co. Dirs. *Address:* Westpac Banking Corporation, Level 20, Westpac Place, 275 Kent Street, Sydney, NSW 2000, Australia (office). *Telephone:* (2) 9293-9270 (office). *Fax:* (2) 8253-4128 (office). *E-mail:* online@westpac.com.au (office). *Website:* www.westpac.com.au (office).

MAY, Elaine; American actress, film director and screenwriter; b. 21 April 1932, Philadelphia; d. of Jack Berlin; m. 1st Marvin May (divorced); one d.; m. 2nd Sheldon Harnick 1962 (divorced 1963); appeared on radio and stage as child; performed Playwright's Theater, Chicago; appeared in student production Miss Julie, Univ. of Chicago; with Mike Nichols and others in improvisatory theatre group, The Compass (nightclub), Chicago 1954–57; improvised nightclub double-act with Mike Nichols, appeared New York Town Hall 1959; An Evening with Mike Nichols and Elaine May, Golden Theater, New York 1960–61; numerous TV and radio appearances; weekly appearance NBC radio show Nightline; Nat. Medal of Arts 2012. *Films:* Luv 1967, A New Leaf (also Dir) 1972, The Heartbreak Kid (Dir) 1973, Mikey and Nicky (Dir) 1976 (writer, Dir remake 1985), California Suite 1978, Heaven Can Wait (co-author screenplay) 1978, Ishtar (writer and Dir) 1987, In The Spirit 1990, The Birdcage 1996 (co-author screenplay), Primary Colors (co-author screenplay) 1998, The John Cassavetes Collection (director) 1999, Small Time Crooks 2000. *Publications:* Better Part of Valour (play) 1983, Hotline 1983, Mr. Gogol and Mr. Preen 1991, Death Defying Acts 1995.

MAY, Rt Hon. Theresa Mary, MA; British politician; *Prime Minister;* b. 1 Oct. 1956; d. of Rev. Hubert Brasier and Zaidee Brasier (née Barnes); m. Philip John May 1980; ed St Hugh's Coll., Oxford; worked for Bank of England 1977–83; with Inter-Bank Research Org. 1983–85; with Asscn for Payment Clearing Services 1985–97 (Head of European Affairs Unit 1989–96); mem. (Conservative Party) Merton London Borough Council 1986–94; contested (Conservative Party) Durham NW 1992, Barking June 1994; MP (Conservative) for Maidenhead 1997–, Opposition Frontbench Spokeswoman on Educ. and Employment 1998–99, Shadow Sec. of State for Educ. and Employment 1999–2001, Shadow Sec. for Transport, Local Govt and the Regions 2001–02; Shadow Sec. of State for Environment and Transport 2003–04, for the Family 2004–05, for the Family and Culture, Media and Sport 2005, Shadow Leader, House of Commons 2005–09, Shadow Minister for Women 2007–10, Shadow Sec. of State for Work and Pensions 2009–10, Sec. of State for the Home Dept 2010–16, also Minister for Women and Equality 2010–12, Prime Minister 2016–, also Minister for the Civil Service and First Lord of the Treasury; Chair. Conservative Party 2002–03, Leader 2016–. *Publications include:* articles: Women in the House: The Continuing Challenge, in Parliamentary Affairs Vol. 57, No. 4 2004. *Leisure interests:* walking, cooking. *Address:* Office of the Prime Minister, 10 Downing Street, London, SW1A 2AA (office); Constituency Office, c/o Maidenhead Conservative Association, 2 Castle End Farm, Ruscombe, RG10 9XQ, England (office). *Telephone:* (20) 7270-3000 (Downing Street) (office); (20) 7930-4433 (office); (118) 934-5433 (Ruscombe) (office); (20) 7219-5206 (Westminster) (office). *Fax:* (20) 7219-1145 (Westminster) (office). *E-mail:* mayt@parliament.uk (office). *Website:* www.number10.gov.uk (office).

MAY, Thomas; German university administrator; *General Secretary, German Council of Science and Humanities;* b. 1958, Hildesheim; ed Univ. of Hamburg, Ludwig-Maximilians Univ. Munich; Adviser, Deutsche Forschungsgemeinschaft (DFG, German Research Foundation) 1987–95; Deputy Sec.-Gen. German Council of Science and Humanities (Wissenschaftsrat) 1995–2003, Sec.-Gen. 2008–; Chancellor Ludwig-Maximilians Univ. Munich 2003–08. *Address:* German Council of Science and Humanities, Brohler Strasse 11, 50968 Cologne, Germany (office). *Website:* www.wissenschaftsrat.de (office).

MAY OF OXFORD, Baron (Life Peer), cr. 2001, of Oxford in the County of Oxfordshire; **Robert McCredie May,** Kt, OM, AC, PhD, PRS, FAAS; Australian/British biologist and academic; *Professor, University of Oxford;* b. 1 Aug. 1936, Sydney, NSW, Australia; s. of Henry W. May and Kathleen M. McCredie; m. Judith Feiner 1962; one d.; ed Sydney Boys' High School, Univ. of Sydney; Gordon MacKay Lecturer in Applied Math., Harvard Univ., USA 1959–61; at Univ. of Sydney 1962–73, Sr Lecturer in Theoretical Physics 1962–64, Reader 1964–69, Personal Chair 1969–73; Class of 1877 Prof. of Biology, Princeton Univ., USA 1973–88, Chair. Univ. Research Bd 1977–88; Royal Soc. Research Prof., Dept of Zoology, Univ. of Oxford and Imperial Coll., London, UK 1988–95, currently Prof. and Fellow, Merton Coll., Oxford 1988–; Chief Scientific Adviser to UK Govt and Head, Office of Science and Tech. 1995–2000; Pres. Royal Soc. 2000–05, British Ecological Soc. 2000–05; Crossbench Peer in House of Lords 2001–, mem. Science and Tech. Select Cttee 2006–, Science and Cttee Sub-cttees: I (Scientific Aspects of Ageing) 2005, I (Allergy/Waste Reduction) 2007–08, Systematics and Taxonomy Enquiry 2008, Draft Climate Change Bill Jt Cttee 2007; fmr Ind. mem. Jt Nature Conservancy Councils; Overseas mem. Australian Acad. of Sciences 1991–; Foreign mem. USA NAS 1992–; mem. Academia Europaea 1994–; fmr Chair. Bd of Trustees, Natural History Museum, London; Trustee, British Museum 1989–, Royal Botanic Gardens, Kew 1991–95, WWF (UK) 1990–94, Nuffield Foundation (Exec. Trustee) 1993–, BAAS (now the British Science Asscn) 2006– (also Hon. Fellow, Pres.-Elect 2010); hon. degrees from univs including (Uppsala) 1990, (Yale) 1993, (Sydney) 1995, (Princeton) 1996, (ETH) 2003; Croonian Lecturer, Hitchcock Lecturer, John M. Prather Lecturer, Weldon Memorial Prize, Univ. of Oxford 1980, Medal of Linnean Soc. of London 1991, Marsh Christian Prize 1992, Frink Medal, Zoological Soc. of London 1995, Crafoord Prize 1996, Balzan Prize 1998, Blue Planet Prize 2001, Copley Medal, Royal Soc. 2007. *Publications include:* Stability and Complexity in Model Ecosystems 1973, Exploitation of Marine Communities (ed.) 1974, Theoretical Ecology: Principles and Applications (ed.) 1976, Population Biology of Infectious Diseases (ed.) 1982, Exploitation of Marine Ecosystems (ed.) 1984, Perspectives in Ecological Theory (ed.) 1989, Population Regulation and Dynamics (ed.) 1990, Infectious Diseases of Humans: Transmission and Control (with R. M. Anderson) 1991, Large Scale Ecology and Conservation Biology 1994, Extinction Rates 1995, Evolution of Biological Diversity 1999, Virus Dynamics: the Mathematical Foundations of Immunology and Virology (with Martin Nowak) 2000. *Leisure interests:* tennis, running, hiking. *Address:* Department of Zoology, University of Oxford, The Tinbergen Building, South Parks Road, Oxford, OX1 3PS (office); House of Lords, Westminster, London, SW1A 0PW, England. *Telephone:* (1865) 271276 (office). *E-mail:* robert.may@zoo.ox.ac.uk (office). *Website:* www.zoo.ox.ac.uk (office).

MAYAKI, Ibrahim Assane, PhD; Niger politician; *CEO, New Partnership for Africa's Development (NEPAD);* b. 24 Sept. 1951, Niamey; s. of Assane Adamou Mayaki and Marie Mosconi; m. Marly Perez Marin 1976; one s. one d.; ed Ecole nationale d'admin de Québec, Canada, Univ. of Paris II, France; fmr Prof. of Public Admin in Niger and Venezuela; worked in uranium sector in Niger at Soc. des mines de l'air (SOMAIR), subsidiary of COGEMA Group; Minister of Foreign Affairs and Co-operation 1996–97; Prime Minister of Niger 1997–2000; Guest Prof. of Int. Relations, Univ. of Paris XI 2000–04, researcher at Research Centre on Europe and the Contemporary World (CREMOC) 2000–04; Exec. Dir The Hub (initiative to coordinate agricultural devt in Western and Cen. Africa) 2004–09; CEO New Partnership for Africa's Devt (NEPAD) 2009–; Chair. Devt Assistance Cttee 2016–; mem. Lead Group of the Scaling Up Nutrition Movement, UN 2016; Grand Officier, Ordre Nat. Niger; Commdr du Mérite agricole, Officer in the National Order of Agricultural Merit 2011. *Publications:* several books on public affairs, planning and local devt; Quand la caravane passe… (autobiog.). *Leisure interest:* taekwondo (5th dan). *Address:* NEPAD Secretariat, Block B, Gateway Park Corner Challenger & Columbia Avenues Midridge Office Park, Midrand 1685, South Africa (office). *Telephone:* (11) 256-3600 (office). *E-mail:* ibrahimassanem@nepad.org (office). *Website:* www.nepad.org (office).

MAYALEH, Adib, (André Mayard), PhD; Syrian/French academic and fmr central banker; b. 15 May 1955, Bassir; ed Univ. of Aix-en-Provence, France; fmr Prof. of Econs, Damascus Univ.; fmr Dean, Nat. Inst. of Public Admin; Gov. Cen. Bank of Syria 2005–16, Pres. Monetary and Credit Bd.

MAYANJA, Rachel N., BL, LLM; Ugandan UN official; *Special Adviser to the Secretary-General on Gender Issues and Advancement of Women, United Nations;* three c.; ed Makarere Univ., Harvard Univ. Law School, USA; early career in UN Div. for Equal Rights for Women, Centre for Social Devt and Humanitarian Affairs; served in UN peacekeeping missions in Namibia (UNTAG) 1989–90 and Iraq/Kuwait (UNIKOM) 1992–94; sr positions in UN Office of Human Resources Man. including Chief of Common System, Specialist Services, Sec. to Sec.-Gen.'s Task Force on reform of Human Resources Man. 1999, Dir of Human Resources Man. Div., UN FAO 2000–04; Special Adviser to Sec.-Gen. on Gender Issues and Advancement of Women 2004–. *Address:* Office of the Special Adviser on Gender Issues and Advancement of Women (OSAGI), Department of Economic and Social Affairs, Two United Nations Plaza, 12th Floor, New York, NY 10017, USA (office). *Telephone:* (212) 963-5086 (office). *Fax:* (212) 963-1802 (office). *E-mail:* osagi@un.org (office). *Website:* www.un.org/womenwatch/osaginew (office).

MAYARD-PAUL, Thierry; Haitian lawyer and politician; s. of Constantin Mayard-Paul; ed St Louis De Gonzague High School, Port-au-Prince; pvt. practice as criminal lawyer with brother, Cabinet Constantin Mayard-Paul (family law firm); Chief of Staff for Pres. Michel Martelly 2011; Minister of the Interior and Territorial Collectivities 2011–12, also of Nat. Defence 2011–12; Special Advisor to Pres. 2012–.

MAYAWATI, BA, BEd, LLB; Indian lawyer and politician; *President, Bahujan Samaj Party;* b. (Mayawati Naina Kumari), 15 Jan. 1956, Badalpur, Gautam Budh Nagar Dist, UP; d. of Prabhu Das and Ram Rati; ed Univ. of Delhi, Meerut Univ.; mem. Lok Sabha (lower house of parl.) 1989–91, 1998–2004; Chief Minister of UP (first Dalit Chief Minister of an Indian state) June–Oct. 1995, March–Sept. 1997, 2002–03, 2007–12; mem. Rajya Sabha (upper house of parl.) 1994–96, 2004–07, 2012–17; mem. UP Legis. Ass. 1996–98, 2002–03; Pres. Bahujan Samaj Party 2003–; mem. UP Legis. Council 2007–. *Publications include:* Bahujan Samaj Aur Uski Rajniti (Hindi version) 2000 (English version) 2001, Mere Sangarshmai Jeevan Evam Bahujan Movement Ka Safarnama (four vols) (Hindi version) 2006 (English version) 2008. *Leisure interest:* Indian cuisine. *Address:* C-57, Indrapuri, New Delhi 110 012 (home); 13A Mall Avenue, Lucknow 226 001, India (home). *Telephone:* (11) 2621122 (New Delhi) (home).

MAYBERRY, John T., CM, BA; Canadian business executive; *Honorary Director, Bank of Nova Scotia (Scotiabank);* b. 1945; ed Univ. of Western Ontario, McMaster Univ.; fmr Chair. and CEO Dofasco Inc.; mem. Bd of Dirs Bank of Nova Scotia (Scotiabank) 1994–, Chair. 2009–14, Hon. Dir 2014–, mem. Exec. and Risk Cttee, Corp. Governance and Pension Cttee, ex-officio mem. Audit and Conduct Review Cttee, Human Resources Cttee; Lead Dir Fort Reliance Ltd (parent co. of Irving Oil Ltd); Dir or fmr Dir CFM Corpn, Decoma International Inc., Inco Ltd 2006–10, MDS Inc. (also Chair. (non-exec.)) 2006–10; Hon. LLD (McMaster Univ.). *Address:* Bank of Nova Scotia (Scotiabank), 44 King Street West, Toronto, ON M5H 1H1, Canada. *Telephone:* (416) 866-6161 (office). *Fax:* (416) 866-3750 (office). *E-mail:* info@scotiabank.ca (office). *Website:* www.scotiabank.ca (office).

MAYER, Colin Peter, CBE, BA, BPhil, DPhil, FBA, FRSA; British academic; *Peter Moores Professor of Management Studies, Saïd Business School, University of Oxford;* b. 12 May 1953, London, England; s. of Harold Charles Mayer and Anne Louise Mayer; m. Annette Patricia Haynes 1979; two d.; ed St Paul's School, London, Oriel Coll., Oxford, Wolfson Coll., Oxford, Harvard Univ., USA; HM Treasury, London 1976–78; Harkness Fellow, Harvard Univ. 1979–80; Fellow in Econs, St Anne's Coll. Oxford 1980–86, Price Waterhouse Prof. of Corp. Finance, City Univ. Business School 1987–92; Prof. of Econs and Finance, Univ. of Warwick 1992–94; Peter Moores Prof. of Man. Studies, Saïd Business School, Oxford 1994–, Peter Moores Dean 2006–11, Dir Oxford Financial Research Centre 1998–2006; del., Oxford University Press 1996–2006; Chair. OXERA Ltd 1987–2010; Assoc. Ed. Annals of Finance, European Financial Management Journal, Scottish Journal of Political Economy; mem. Exec. Cttee Royal Econ. Soc. 2002–06; Professorial Fellow, Wadham Coll. Oxford 1994–2006, 2011–, St Edmund Hall 2006–11; Gov. St Paul's School London 2002–11; Fellow, European Corp. Governance Inst.; Hon. Fellow, St Anne's Coll. Oxford, Oriel Coll. Oxford. *Publications:* Economic Analysis of Accounting Profitability (co-author) 1986, Risk, Regulation and Investor Protection (co-author) 1989, European Financial Integration (co-author) 1991, Capital Markets and Financial Intermediation (co-author) 1993, Hostile Takeovers (co-author) 1994, Asset Management and Investor Protection (co-author) 2002, Handbook of European Financial Markets and Institutions (co-author) 2008, Firm Commitment: Why the Corporation is Failing Us and How to Restore Trust in It 2013; contribs to academic journals and books. *Leisure interests:* piano, jogging, reading philosophy and science. *Address:* Saïd Business School, University of Oxford, Park End Street, Oxford, OX1 1HP (office); Wadham College, Oxford, OX1 3PN, England (office). *Telephone:* (1865) 288111 (office). *E-mail:* colin.mayer@sbs.ox.ac.uk (office). *Website:* www.sbs.ox.ac.uk (office).

MAYER, Marissa Ann, MS; American computer scientist and business executive; b. 30 May 1975, Wausau, Wis.; m. Zachary Bogue 2009; one s.; ed Wausau West High School, Nat. Youth Science Camp, W Va, Stanford Univ., Calif.; fmrly with UBS Research Lab. (Ubilab), Zürich, Switzerland and SRI Int., Menlo Park, Calif.; joined Google Inc. as software engineer 1999, Vice-Pres. Search Products and User Experience –2010, Vice-Pres. Local, Maps and Location Services 2010–12; Pres. and CEO Yahoo! Inc., Sunnyvale, Calif. 2012–17; Lecturer in Computer Science, Stanford Univ.; mem. Bd of Dirs Walmart 2012–; Hon. DEng (Illinois Inst. of Tech.) 2009; Centennial Teaching Award, Stanford Univ., Forsythe Award, Stanford Univ.

MAYETTE, Muriel; French actress and theatre director; b. 2 May 1964, Paris; m. Gérard Holtz 2013; ed Nat. School of Arts and Theatre Technique, Lyon, Conservatoire nat. Supérieur d'art dramatique; joined the Comédie-Française 1985, became a sociétaire 1988, worked with Antoine Vitez, Jacques Lassalle and Alain Françon, Administrateur Général (first woman) 2006–14; teacher at Conservatoire nat. Supérieur d'art dramatique, also directed eight productions, including Le Retour au désert by Bernard-Marie Koltès; mem. comm. led by Hugues Gall of the Ministry of Culture to fill the post of Dir of Villa Medicis, Rome 2008; Officier des Arts et des Lettres; Prix Femme de l'art, Trophée des Femmes en Or 2013. *Stage roles include:* The Return (Harold Pinter), Comédie-Française 2000, Les Grelots du fou (Luigi Pirandello), théâtre du Vieux-Colombier 2005, and théâtre des Célestins 2006, La Leçon de Mr. Pantalon, Le Grand Bleu Lille 2006. *Plays directed include:* Mistero Buffo (Dario Fo), salle Richelieu 2010, Andromaque (Racine), salle Richelieu 2010, Bérénice (Racine), Comédie-Française on tour to Espace Malraux de Joué-lès-Tours, Opéra royal de Versailles, Théâtre Millandy de Luçon etc., salle Richelieu 2011, Une histoire de la Comédie-Française (Christophe Barbier), théâtre Ephémère 2012, A Midsummer Night's Dream (Shakespeare), salle Richelieu 2014. *Films include:* Petits arrangements avec les morts 1994, Dis-moi que je rêve 1998, Le conservatoire, corps et âme (documentary) 2005. *Television includes:* Madame Sans-Gêne (film) 1981, Paroles d'acteurs de la Comédie-Française (film documentary) 1993, Dossier: disparus (series) 2000, L'avare (film) 2000,La nuit des Molières (series documentary) 2007, L'heure de Molière (film documentary) 2009, Vivement dimanche (series) 2009–11, The Screen Illusion (film) 2010, We Can't Go on Like This! (film) 2012, Avant-premières (series) 2012, On n'est pas couché (series) 2012–13, La troupe d'un soir (film, uncredited) 2013, La dernière échappée (film) 2014, Thé ou café (series) 2014.

MAYFIELD, Rt Rev. Christopher John, MA, MSc; British ecclesiastic (retd); b. 18 Dec. 1935, Plymouth, Devon; s. of Roger Mayfield and Muriel Mayfield; m. Caroline Roberts 1962; two s. one d.; ed Sedbergh School, Gonville & Caius Coll. Cambridge, Linacre House, Oxford, Cranfield Univ.; ordained deacon 1963, priest 1964; curate, St Martin-in-the-Bull Ring, Birmingham 1963–67; Lecturer, St Martin's, Birmingham 1967–71; Vicar of Luton 1971–80; Archdeacon of Bedford 1979–85; Bishop Suffragan of Wolverhampton 1985–93; Bishop of Manchester 1993–2002; Lord Bishop of Manchester, House of Lords 1998–2002; Hon. Asst Bishop, Worcester; Dr hc (Manchester) 2002. *Leisure interests:* marriage, evangelism, walking, watching cricket and rugby. *Address:* Harewood House, 54 Primrose Crescent, St Peter's, Worcester, WR5 3HT, England (home). *Telephone:* (1905) 764822 (office); (1905) 764822 (home). *E-mail:* christopher@mayfield54.orangehome.co.uk.

MAYHEW JONAS, Dame Judith, DBE, LLM; New Zealand politician, lawyer and academic; *Chancellor, Bishop Grosseteste University;* b. 18 Oct. 1948, Dunedin; m. 1976 (divorced 1986); m. 2nd Christopher Jonas 2003; ed Otago Girls' High School, Univ. of Otago; barrister and solicitor, NZ 1973, solicitor, England and Wales 1993; Lecturer in Law, Univ. of Otago 1970–73; Lecturer in Law and Sub-Dean, Univ. of Southampton, UK 1973–76, King's Coll., London 1976–89; Dir Anglo-French law degree, Sorbonne, Paris 1976–79; Dir of Training and Employment Law, Titmuss Sainer Dechert 1989–94; mem. Bd London Guildhall Univ. 1992–2002; mem. Court and Council Imperial Coll., London 2001–03; Dir of Educ. and Training, Wilde Sapte 1994–99; City and Business Adviser to Mayor of London 2000; mem. Court of Common Council Corpn of London 1986–2004, Chair. Policy and Resources Cttee 1997–2003; Special Adviser to Chair. of Clifford Chance 2000–03; Chair. Bd of Govs 1999–2003; Chair. Royal Opera House, London 2003–08, Ind. Schools' Council 2008–11, New West End Co.

2008–, London and Partners 2011–; Provost, King's Coll., Cambridge 2003–05; apptd Provost, Bishop Grosseteste Univ. 2008, currently Chancellor; Dir Gresham Coll. 1990, London First Centre 1996, Int. Financial Services London (fmrly British Invisibles) 1996, London First 1997, 4Ps 1997, London Devt Agency 2000 (Chair. Business and Skills Cttee –2004, Vice-Chair. 2003), Cross River Partnership; Trustee Natural History Museum 1998; Dir (non-exec.) Merrill Lynch 2006–; Sr Advisor, Tishman Speyer 2013–; Gov. Birkbeck Coll. London 1993–; Trustee, Natural History Museum, Imperial War Museum (also Chair. re-development Cttee) 2008–, Urban Land Inst. 2013–; Hon. LLD (Otago) 1998, (City Univ. London) 1999; named New Zealander of the Year in the UK 2004. *Leisure interests:* opera, theatre, old English roses, tennis. *Address:* Bishop Grosseteste University, Longdales Road, Lincolnshire LN1 3DY, England (office). *Telephone:* (15) 2252-7347 (office). *E-mail:* enquiries@bishopg.ac.uk (office). *Website:* www.bishopg.ac.uk (office).

MAYIIK, Kornelio Koryom, BSc; South Sudanese economist and central banker; b. Warrap State; ed Khartoum Univ.; Minister for Coordination, High Exec. Council for S Sudan (govt of autonomous region) 1983; Minister of Finance for Greater Bahr el Ghazal State, S Sudan 1983–86; est. Ivory Bank, Khartoum 1991, Gen. Man. 1994–2000; Gen. Man. Central Bank of Sudan 2000–11; Deputy Gov. Bank of South Sudan (following establishment of separate S Sudan state) July–Aug. 2011, Gov. Aug. 2011–17.

MAYNE, David Quinn, PhD, DSc, FRS, FREng, FIEEE, FIET; British engineer and academic; *Professor Emeritus and Senior Research Investigator, Imperial College London;* b. 23 April 1930, Germiston, S Africa; s. of Leslie Harper Mayne and Jane Quin; m. Josephine Mary Hess 1954; three d.; ed Christian Brothers' Coll., Boksburg and Univ. of the Witwatersrand, S Africa; Lecturer, Univ. of the Witwatersrand 1951–59; Research Engineer, British Thomson Houston Co. 1955–56; Lecturer, Imperial Coll. of Science, Tech. and Medicine 1959–66, Reader 1967–70, Prof. 1970–89, Prof. Emer. 1989–, Sr Research Investigator, Dept of Electrical and Electronic Eng 1996–, Fellow 2000–; Prof. of Electrical and Computer Eng, Univ. of California, Davis 1989–96, Prof. Emer. 1997–, Head Dept of Electrical Eng 1984–88, Sr Research Investigator Science Research Council 1979; Visiting Research Fellow, Harvard Univ., USA 1970; Visiting Prof., Univ. of California, Berkeley, Univ. of Newcastle, Australia, IIT, Delhi, Academia Sinica, Beijing, Univ. of California, Santa Barbara, Univ. of Wisconsin, Madison; Hon. Prof., Beihang Univ., Beijing 2008; Hon. DTech (Lund) 1995; Heaviside Premium 1979, 1984, Sir Harold Hartley Medal 1986, IEEE Control Systems Award 2009, IFAC High Impact Award 2011, IFAC Quazza Medal 2014. *Publications:* Differential Dynamic Programming 1970, Model Predictive Control: Theory and Design (with J. B. Rawlings) 2009, Model Predictive Control: Theory Computation and Design (with J.B. Rawlings and M. Diehl); 300 papers in professional journals on optimization, optimal control, adaptive control and optimization-based design. *Leisure interests:* walking, cross-country skiing, music. *Address:* Department of Electrical and Electronic Engineering, Imperial College London, London, SW7 2BT (office); 11 St Olaves Court, St Petersburgh Place, London, W2 4JY, England (home). *Telephone:* (20) 7594-6287 (office); (20) 7792-0972 (home). *Fax:* (20) 7594-6282 (office). *E-mail:* d.mayne@imperial.ac.uk (office). *Website:* www.imperial.ac.uk/electrical-engineering (office).

MAYOPOULOS, Timothy J.; American lawyer and business executive; *President and CEO, Fannie Mae (Federal National Mortgage Association);* ed Cornell Univ., New York Univ. School of Law; fmrly in private practice; served in sr man. roles at Deutsche Bank AG, Credit Suisse First Boston, Donaldson, Lufkin & Jenrette, Inc.; Exec. Vice-Pres. and Gen. Counsel, Bank of America Corpn –2009; Exec. Vice-Pres., Gen. Counsel and Corp. Sec., Fannie Mae (Fed. Nat. Mortgage Asscn) 2009–10, Chief Admin. Officer 2010–12, Pres. and CEO 2012–. *Address:* Fannie Mae, 3900 Wisconsin Avenue NW, Washington, DC 20016-2892, USA (office). *Telephone:* (202) 752-7000 (office). *E-mail:* headquarters@fanniemae.com (office). *Website:* www.fanniemae.com (office).

MAYOR, Michel G. E., MPhys, PhD, DrAstron; Swiss astronomer and academic; *Professor Emeritus of Astrophysics, University of Geneva;* b. 12 Jan. 1942, Lausanne; m. Francoise Mayor-Pirolet; one s. two d.; ed Univs of Lausanne and Geneva; Researcher, Cambridge Observatory 1971; Research Assoc., Univ. of Geneva 1971–84, Assoc. Prof. 1984–88, Prof. of Astrophysics 1988–2007, Prof. Emer. 2007–; Researcher, Univ. of Hawaii, USA 1994–95; Pres. Int. Astronomical Union (IAU) Comm. on Galactic Structure 1988–91, Swiss Soc. for Astrophysics and Astronomy 1990–93, IAU Comm. on Extra-Solar Planets 2006–09; Chair. Scientific Tech. Cttee, European Southern Observatory 1990–92; Dir Geneva Observatory 1998–2004; Swiss del. to European Southern Observatory Council 2003–07; Foreign Assoc., Acad. des sciences 2003; mem. European Acad. of Sciences 2004; Foreign mem. NAS 2010, American Acad. of Arts and Sciences 2010; Hon. Fellow FRAS 2008; Chevalier, Légion d'honneur 2004; Dr hc (Catholic Univ. of Louvain, Belgium) 2001, (Swiss Inst. of Tech., Lausanne) 2002, (Fed. Univ. of Rio Grande del Norte, Brazil) 2006, (Uppsala Univ., Sweden) 2007, (Paris Observatory, France) 2008, (Université Libre de Bruxelles, Belgium) 2009, (Univ. of Provençe, France) 2011, (Université Joseph Fourier, Grenoble, France) 2014; Charles Louis de Saulces de Freycinet Prize, Acad. Française des Sciences 1983, IAU Comm. of Bioastronomy Medal 1997, Prix Marcel Benoist 1998, Janssen Prize, Astronomical Soc. of France 1998, Adion Medal, Observatory of the Côte d'Azur 1998, Balzan Prize for Physics, Natural Sciences and Medicine (co-recipient) 2000, Einstein Medal 2004, Shaw Prize for Astronomy 2005, Karl Schwarzschild Medal 2010, Viktor Ambartsumian Prize 2010, BBVA Foundation Frontiers of Knowledge Award of Basic Sciences (co-recipient) 2011, Gold Medal, Royal Astronomical Soc. 2015, Kyoto Prize, Inamori Foundation (co-recipient) 2015. *Achievements include:* discovered first extrasolar planet, 51 Pegasi b 1995. *Publications:* New Worlds in the Cosmos: The Discovery of Exoplanets (with Pierre-Yves Frei) 2003; more than 300 scientific papers. *Address:* Observatoire de Genève, 51 chemin des Maillettes, 1290 Sauverny, Switzerland (office). *Telephone:* (22) 379-2460 (office). *Fax:* (22) 379-2205 (office). *E-mail:* Michel.Mayor@obs.unige.ch (office). *Website:* www.unige.ch/sciences/astro (office).

MAYOR ZARAGOZA, Federico, DrPhar; Spanish politician, biologist and university official; *President, Fundación Cultura de Paz;* b. 27 Jan. 1934, Barcelona; s. of Federico Mayor and Juana Zaragoza; m. María Angeles Menéndez 1956; two s. one d.; ed Univ. Complutense of Madrid; Prof. of Biochemistry, Faculty

of Pharmacy, Granada Univ. 1963–73; Rector, Granada Univ. 1968–72; Prof. of Biochemistry, Autonomous Univ., Madrid 1973, Chair. Severo Ochoa Molecular Biology Centre (Higher Council of Scientific Research) 1974–78; Under-Sec. Ministry of Educ. and Science 1974–75; mem. Cortes (Parl.) for Granada 1977–78; Chair. Advisory Cttee for Scientific and Tech. Research 1974–78; Deputy Dir-Gen. UNESCO 1978–81, Dir-Gen. 1987–99; Minister for Educ. and Science 1981–82; Dir Inst. of the Sciences of Man, Madrid 1983–87; mem. European Parl. 1987; Pres. Scientific Council, Ramón Areces Foundation, Madrid 1989–, European Research Council Expert Group 2002–05; Founder and Pres. Fundación Cultura de Paz 1999–; Co-Chair. Alliance of Civilizations, UN 2005–06; Pres. Initiative for Science in Europe (ISE) 2007–11, Int. Comm. Against Death Penalty 2010–; mem. Club of Rome 1981–; Academician, Royal Acad. of Pharmacy, Royal Acad. of Medicine; mem. European Acad. of Arts, Sciences and Humanities, Int. Cell Research Org. (ICRO), AAAS, The Biochemical Soc. (UK), French Soc. of Biological Chem., ACS, Academia de Bellas Artes, and numerous other orgs; Grand Cross, Alfonso X El Sabio, Orden Civil de la Sanidad Carlos III, Caro y Cuervo (Colombia), Commdr Placa del Libertador (Venezuela), Grand Officier, Ordre Nat. du Mérite (France); Dr hc (Westminster) 1995; Press Freedom Prize, Int. Fed. of Newspaper Publrs. *Publications:* A contraviento (poems) 1987, Mañana siempre es tarde 1987 (English version: Tomorrow Is Always Too Late 1992), Aguafuertes (poems) 1991 (English version: Patterns 1994), La nueva página 1994, Memoria del futuro 1994, La paix demain? 1995, Science and Power 1995, UNESCO: Un idéal en action 1996, El fuego y la esperanza (poems) 1996, Terral (poems) 1998 (English version: Land Wind 1998), Un mundo nuevo (English version: The World Ahead: Our Future in the Making) 1999, Los nudos gordianos 1999, La fuerza de la palabra 2005, Un diálogo ibérico enel marco europeo y mundial 2006, Alzaré mi voz (poems) 2007, Voz de vida, voz debida 2007, Tiempo de acción 2008, En pie de paz (poems) 2008, Donde no habite el miedo 2011; numerous specialized works, trans., articles. *Leisure interests:* reading, writing, music. *Address:* Fundación Cultura de Paz, Ciudad Universitaria de Cantoblanco, C/Einstein, 13, Bajo, 28049 Madrid (office); Mar Caribe 15, Majadahonda, 28220 Madrid, Spain (home). *Telephone:* (91) 4973701 (office). *Fax:* (91) 4973706 (office). *E-mail:* f.mayor@fmayor.e.telefonica.net (office); info@fund-culturadepaz.org (office). *Website:* www.fund-culturadepaz.org (office).

MAYR-HARTING, Thomas; Austrian diplomatist; *Managing Director for Europe and Central Asia, European External Action Service;* b. 22 May 1954, Epsom, Surrey, England; m.; three c.; ed Univ. of Vienna, Coll. of Europe, Bruges, Belgium, The Hague Acad. of International Law, Netherlands; joined Diplomatic Service 1979, served with Austrian Mission to the European Communities, Brussels 1982–86, Embassy in Moscow 1986–90, Pvt. Office of Minister of Foreign Affairs 1991–95, as Deputy Political Dir and Dir for Security Policy and Policy Planning 1995–99, Amb. to Belgium and Head of Perm. Mission to NATO 1999–2003, Special Rep. of the Minister of Foreign Affairs for the Western Balkans 2002–04, Political Dir (Dir-Gen. for Political Affairs), Ministry of Foreign Affairs 2003–08, Chair. Supervisory Bd Austrian Devt Agency 2008, Perm. Rep. of Austria to UN, New York 2008–11, represented Austria on Security Council 2009, 2010, Pres. Security Council Nov. 2009, Amb. and Head of Del. of the EU to the UN, New York 2011–15, Man. Dir for Europe and Cen. Asia, European External Action Service 2015–. *Address:* European External Action Service, 1046 Brussels, Belgium (office). *Telephone:* (2) 584-11-11 (office). *Website:* eeas.europa.eu (office).

MAYRHUBER, Wolfgang; Austrian business executive; b. 22 March 1947, Waizenkirchen; ed Tech. Coll. of Steyr, Bloor Inst., Canada, Massachusetts Inst. of Tech., USA; joined Deutsche Lufthansa AG 1970, various positions including engineer, Engine Overhaul Facility, Hamburg, man. posts in Maintenance, Repair and Overhaul (MRO) Operation, Exec. Vice-Pres. and COO of Tech. Operations 1992–94, Chair. of Exec. Bd Lufthansa Technik AG 1994–2000, apptd to Exec. Bd Deutsche Lufthansa AG 2001–02, Deputy Chair. 2002–03, Chair. Exec. Bd and CEO 2003–10, Chair. Supervisory Bd 2013–17, Chair. Supervisory Bd Lufthansa CityLine; Chair. Supervisory Bd Infineon Technologies AG 2011–; Vice-Chair. AMECO Corpn, Beijing, People's Repub. of China; mem. Supervisory Bd Fraport AG, Munich Re Group (Münchener Rückversicherungs-Gesellschaft AG), BMW Group, Austrian Airlines AG, Lufthansa Technik AG; mem. Bd of Dirs SN Airholding SA/NV (Belgium), HEICO Corpn, Fla, USA, UBS AG (Switzerland); mem. Steering Cttee Asscn of European Airlines, Chair. 2006; Chair. Strategy and Policy Cttee IATA, mem. Bd Govs IATA.

MAYS, Willie Howard, Jr; American fmr baseball player; b. 6 May 1931, Westfield, Ala; s. of William Howard Mays and Annie Mays (née Satterwhite); m. 1st Margherite Wendell Chapman 1956 (divorced 1962 or 1963, died 2010); one adopted s.; m. 2nd Mae Louise Allen 1971 (died 2013); ed Fairfield Industrial High School; played for the New York Giants 1951–57, San Francisco Giants (after team relocation) 1958–72, New York Mets 1972–73; career statistics include 3,283 hits and 660 home runs; hit 4 home runs in one game 30 April 1961; hit over 50 home runs in 1955 and 1965, representing the longest time span between 50-plus home run seasons for any player in Major League Baseball (MLB) history; played in a record-tying 24 All-Star games between 1954 and 1973; participated in four World Series, World Series champion 1954; retd, signed ten-year contract as Goodwill Amb. and part-time coach for the New York Mets; Special Asst to Team Pres., San Francisco Giants 1986–; nicknamed The Say Hey Kid; Hon. DHumLitt (Yale) 2004, (San Francisco State Univ.) 2009; Dr hc (Dartmouth Coll.) 2007; Nat. League Rookie of the Year 1951, Most Valuable Player 1954, 1965, Associated Press Athlete of the Year Award 1954, Gold Glove Award 1957, 1958, 1959, 1960, 1961, 1962, 1963, 1964, 1965, 1966, 1967, 1968, MLB All-Star Game MVP 1963, 1968, Roberto Clemente Award 1971, elected to Baseball Hall of Fame 1979, 100 Greatest World Athletes, ranked second on The Sporting News's List of the 100 Greatest Baseball Players 1999, elected to MLB All-Century Team 1999, MLB All-Time Team 1999, inducted into Caribbean Baseball Hall of Fame 2005, Lifetime Achievement Award, Bobby Bragan Youth Foundation 2005, Tee Ball Commr, White House Tee Ball Initiative 2006, inducted into California Hall of Fame 2007, service road in Harlem named Willie Mays Drive 2008, inducted into African-American Ethnic Sports Hall of Fame 2010, MLB Beacon of Life Award 2010, Presidential Medal of Freedom 2015. *Television:* appeared in several sitcoms, always as himself; performed Say Hey: The Willie Mays Song on episode 4.46 of The Colgate Comedy Hour 1954; appeared as the mystery guest in game show What's My Line?; appeared in three episodes of ABC's The Donna Reed Show 1964,

1966, Bewitched 1966, My Two Dads 1989. *Address:* c/o San Francisco Giants, AT&T Park, 24 Willie Mays Plaza, San Francisco, CA 94107, USA. *Telephone:* (415) 972-2000. *Website:* sanfrancisco.giants.mlb.com; baseballhall.org/hof/mays-willie.

MAYWEATHER, Floyd, Jr; American professional boxer; b. (Floyd Joy Sinclair), 24 Feb. 1977, Grand Rapids, Mich.; s. of Floyd Mayweather, Sr and Deborah Sinclair; amateur record of 84 wins, 6 losses; won nat. Golden Gloves championships 1993, 1994, 1996, Mich. State Golden Gloves Champion 1994, 1996; US Nat. Amateur Featherweight Champion 1995; bronze medal, Featherweight (57 kg) Div., Summer Olympics, Atlanta 1996; first professional bout against Roberto Apodaca Oct. 1996; trained by his uncle, Roger Mayweather; major world titles: WBC Super Featherweight Champion 1998–2002 (vacated), WBC Lightweight Champion 2002–04 (vacated), WBC Light Welterweight Champion 2005–06 (vacated), IBF Welterweight Champion April–June 2006 (vacated), WBC Welterweight Champion 2006–08 (vacated), WBC Light Middleweight Champion May–July 2007, (second) WBC Welterweight Champion 2011–, WBA Light Middleweight Champion 2012–, WBA (Super) Light Middleweight Champion 2014–; minor world titles: IBO Welterweight Champion, IBA Welterweight Champion; The Ring/Lineal Championship titles: Lineal Super Featherweight Champion 1998–2002, The Ring Lightweight Champion 2002–04, The Ring Welterweight Champion 2006–08, 2013–, The Ring Jr Middleweight Champion 2013–, Lineal Welterweight Champion 2015–; World Boxing Org. (WBO) Welterweight Champion May–July 2015 (stripped of title for noncompliance with regulations 6 July 2015); special titles: WBC All Africa Light Welterweight Champion, WBC Emer. Light Middleweight Champion, WBC Diamond Welterweight Champion, WBC 24K Gold Light Middleweight Champion, WBC Supreme Light Middleweight Champion; defeated eight-div. world champion Manny Pacquiao by unanimous points decision 2 May 2015; currently undefeated as a professional boxer and a five-div. world champion, having won 11 world titles and the lineal championship in four different weight classes; professional boxing record: 48 fights, 48 wins (26 by knockout), no defeats; recipient of WBC Diamond Belt; appeared at World Wrestling Entertainment (WWE)'s No Way Out pay-per-view in Las Vegas, Nev. 2008; sentenced to serve a three-month jail term for domestic abuse Dec. 2011, released from prison after two months Aug. 2012; Int. Boxing Award Fighter of the Year 1998, 2007, The Ring 'Fighter of the Year' 1998, 2007, Nat. Golden Gloves Champion Outstanding Boxer Award 1994, Nat. PAL Champion Outstanding Boxer Award 1995, Yahoo! Sports, Best of the Decade 2000–09, World Boxing Hall of Fame Fighter of the Year 2002, World Boxing Council Boxer of the Year 2005, 2007, The Ring No. 1 pound for pound 2005–08, 2013, Boxing Writers Asscn of America Fighter of the Year 2007, 2013, ESPN Fighter of the Year 2007, New York Daily News Fighter of the Year 2007, World Boxing Council Event of the Year (The World Awaits) 2007, World Boxing Council Knockout of the Year (against Ricky Hatton) 2007, Best Fighter ESPY Award 2007, 2008, 2010, 2012, 2013, 2014, The Ring Magazine Event of the Year 2007, 2008, 2010, The Ring Magazine Comeback of the Year 2009, BoxRec, BBC Sport and Yahoo! Sports No. 1 pound for pound 2009–10, The Best Ever Award 2015. *Television includes:* Dancing With the Stars 2007, guest host for WWE Raw in Las Vegas 2009; numerous documentary appearances 2005–15. *Address:* c/o Mayweather Promotions, 4616 West Sahara Avenue #290, Las Vegas, NV 89102, USA (office). *E-mail:* contact@mayweatherpromotions.com (office). *Website:* www.mayweatherpromotions.com (office); floydmayweather.com.

MAZAHERI, Tahmasb, MS; Iranian civil engineer, government official and banking official; b. 12 Feb. 1953, Tehran; ed Univ. of Tehran; fmr Univ. lecturer; Head, Bonyad Mostazafan and Janbazan Foundation 1985–91; Sec.-Gen. Bank Markazi Jomhouri Islami Iran (Cen. Bank) 1991–94, Gov. 2007–08; Minister of Econ. Affairs and Finance 2001–04, Deputy Minister of Econ. Affairs and Finance 2005–06; Man.-Dir Export Devt Bank of Iran (EDBI) 2007–08.

MAZANKOWSKI, Rt Hon. Donald Frank, PC, CC; Canadian politician and business consultant; b. 27 July 1935, Viking, Alberta; s. of Frank Mazankowski and Dora Lonowski; m. Lorraine E. Poleschuk 1958; three s.; ed high school; MP 1968–93; Minister of Transport and Minister responsible for Canadian Wheat Board 1979; Minister of Transport 1984–86; Pres. Treasury Bd 1987–88; Minister responsible for Privatization, Regulatory Affairs and Operations 1988, of Agric. 1989–91, of Finance 1991–93; Deputy Prime Minister 1986–93, Pres. of the Queen's Privy Council for Canada 1989–91; business consultant 1993–; fmr Chair. Inst. of Health Econs, Canadian Genetics Diseases Network, Alberta Premier's Advisory Council on Health; Gov. Univ. of Alberta; dir numerous cos; Progressive Conservative Party; Queen's Golden Jubilee Medal 2002, Diamond Jubilee Medal 2012, Alberta Order of Excellence 2003; Hon. DEng (Tech. Univ. of Nova Scotia) 1987, Hon. LLD (Univ. of Alberta) 1993, Hon. BA (Grant McEwan Univ.) 2009, Hon. BSc (Lakeland Coll.) 2013; Paul Harris Fellow, Rotary Int., Alberta Centennial Medal 2005, Canadian Asscn of Former Parliamentarians Lfetime Achievement Award 2010. *Leisure interests:* fishing, golf. *Address:* 80 Nottingham Inlet, Sherwood Park, AB T8A 6N2, Canada. *Telephone:* (780) 410-0728. *Fax:* (780) 410-0748. *E-mail:* donmaz@shaw.ca.

MAZEAUD, Pierre, Docteur en droit; French politician; *President, Fondation Charles de Gaulle;* b. 24 Aug. 1929, Lyon; s. of Jean Mazeaud and Paulette Duirat; m. 1st Marie Prohom 1953 (divorced 1960); two d.; m. 2nd Sophie Hamel 1967; one s. one d.; ed Lycée Louis-le-Grand et Faculté de droit de Paris; Judge of Tribunal of Instance, Lamentin, Martinique 1961; in charge of conf., Faculty of Law, Paris 1955; Tech. Adviser to Prime Minister 1961; Judge of Tribunal of Great Instance, Versailles 1962; Tech. Adviser to Minister of Justice 1962; Tech. Adviser to Jean Foyer's Cabinet 1962–67; Tech. Adviser to Minister of Youth and Sports 1967–68; Deputy for Hauts-de-Seine 1968–73, for Haute-Savoie 1988–98, Vice. Pres. Assemblée Nationale 1992–93, 1997–98, Vice-Pres. Groupe des députés sportifs 1968; Minister responsible for Youth and Sport 1973–76; Councillor of State 1976; Pres. Law Comm. of Assemblée Nationale 1987–88, 1993–98; Vice-Pres. l'Assemblée Nationale 1992–93, 1997–98; Titular Judge, High Court 1987–97; Mayor, Saint-Julien-en-Genevois 1979–89; regional councillor, Rhône-Alpes 1992–98, Pres. Commission des finances de Rhône-Alpes; mem. Constitutional Council 1998, Pres. 2004–07; Pres. Fondation Charles de Gaulle 2007–; Vice-Pres. Cttee de réflexion sur la modernisation et le rééquilibrage des institutions 2007–; in charge of courses IEP (l'Institut d'études politiques) d'Aix-en-Provence; Professeur, IEP Paris 1999–; mem. Acad. des Sciences Morales et Politiques 2005–, Acad. des Sports; Officier, Légion d'honneur, Commdr de la Légion d'honneur, Officier du Mérite sportif. *Achievements include:* climbed Mount Everest 1978 (oldest man to do so). *Publications:* Montagne pour un homme nu 1971, Everest 78 1978, Sport et Liberté 1980, Nanga Parbat – montagne cruelle 1982, Des cailloux et des mouches ou l'échec à l'Himalaya 1985, Rappel au Règlement 1995. *Leisure interests:* mountaineering, skiing, swimming. *Address:* Fondation et Institut Charles de Gaulle, 5 rue de Solférino, 75007 Paris, France (office). *Telephone:* 1-44-18-66-77 (office). *Fax:* 1-44-18-66-99 (office). *E-mail:* contact@charles-de-gaulle.org (office). *Website:* www.charles-de-gaulle.org (office); r (office).

MAZROUEI, HE Suhail Mohamed Faraj al-; United Arab Emirates business executive and government official; *Minister of Energy;* b. 1 July 1973, Dubai, UAE; m.; three c.; ed Univ. of Tulsa, USA; worked at Abu Dhabi Nat. Oil Co. (ADNOC) 1984–94, specialized in reservoir eng and production operations, CEO ADNOC –1994, currently mem. Audit Cttee; also worked at Royal Dutch Shell for a year; various roles in int. oil and gas projects in Nigeria, the North Sea, Brunei and the Netherlands; apptd Vice-Chair. Sorouh Real Estate Co. 2009; Deputy Chief Exec. Mubadala Oil and Gas (state-owned co.) –2013, Chair. 2013–; Chair. Emirates Liquified Gas Co.; mem. Higher Advisory Cttee, Supreme Petroleum Council of Abu Dhabi; mem. Bd of Dirs, Petroleum Development Co., Dolphin Energy Co.; Minister of Energy 2013–, also Chair. Fed. Electricity and Water Authority; Man. Dir Int. Petroleum Investment Co. (IPIC) 2015–. *Leisure interests:* poetry, letters, history. *Address:* Ministry of Energy, PO Box 59, Abu Dhabi (office); International Petroleum Investment Co., PO Box 7528, Sheikh Zayed the 1st Street, Al Muhairy Centre, Office Tower, 10th Floor, Abu Dhabi, United Arab Emirates (office). *Telephone:* (2) 6126500 (Ministry) (office); (2) 6336555 (IPIC) (office). *Fax:* (2) 2929629 (Ministry) (office); (2) 6330111 (IPIC) (office). *E-mail:* moenr@moenr.ae (office); info@ipic.ae (office). *Website:* www.moenr.gov.ae (office); www.ipic.ae (office).

MAZUKA, Michiyoshi; Japanese business executive; *Senior Executive Advisor and Director, Fujitsu Limited;* ed Gakushuin Univ.; joined Fujitsu Ltd 1971, has held several sr exec. positions including Chief Dir of Higashi Nihon Sales, Man. Exec. Officer, Sr Man. Dir and Vice-Pres., with fujitsureseller.com 2005, with Fujitsu America Inc. 2006–08, later Corp. Sr Vice-Pres. Fujitsu Ltd –2008, Chair. and Rep. Dir 2008–14, Sr Exec. Advisor and Dir 2014–. *Address:* Fujitsu Headquarters, Shiodome City Centre, 1-5-2 Higashi-Shimbashi, Minato-ku, Tokyo 105-7123, Japan (office). *Telephone:* (3) 6252-2220 (office). *Fax:* (3) 6252-2783 (office). *E-mail:* info@fujitsu.com (office). *Website:* www.fujitsu.com (office).

MAZUMDAR-SHAW, Kiran, BSc; Indian business executive; *Chairman and Managing Director, Biocon India Ltd;* b. 23 March 1953, Bangalore; m. John Shaw 1997; ed Bishop Cotton Girls School, Mount Carmel Coll., Bangalore, Bangalore Univ., Ballarat Coll., Melbourne Univ., Australia; trainee Brewer, Carlton & United Breweries, Melbourne and trainee Maltster, Barrett Bros & Burston, Australia 1975–77; Brewery Consultant, Jupiter Breweries Ltd, Calcutta (now Kolkata) 1975–76; Tech. Man. Standard Malting Corpn, Baroda 1976; Trainee Man. Biocon Ltd, Cork, Repub. of Ireland 1978; Chair. and Man. Dir Biocon India Ltd 1978–; Dir Pharmacia United Ltd, Bangalore 1987–94; Chair. Syngene Int., Bangalore 1994–; Chair. Clinigene Int., Bangalore 2000–; mem. Bd Bio-Ventures for Global Health; Chair. and Mission Leader Confed. of Indian Industries Nat. Task Force on Biotechnology; Council mem. Basic Chemicals, Pharmaceuticals and Cosmetics Export Promotion Council 1983–; Vice-Pres. Asscn of Women Entrepreneurs of Karnataka (AWAKE) 1983–89, Indo-American Chamber of Commerce, Bangalore 1986–87; Chair. (non-Exec.) Asscn of Biotechnology Led Enterprises; Founder mem. Vision Group on Biotechnology, Karnataka (also Chair.), Soc. for the Inst. for Stem Cell Biology and Regenerative Medicine, Bangalore; mem. Prime Minister's Council on Trade and Industry in India, Confed. of Indian Industries, Greater Mysore Chamber of Industries, Advisory Cttee, Dept of Biotechnology, Young Presidents' Org., Research Council, CFTRI, Bangalore Agenda Task Force, Bd of Science Foundation, Ireland, Governing body, Indian Pharmacopoeia Comm., Bd Infosys Ltd; mem. Bd Govs Indian Inst. of Man. Bangalore; mem. Governing Council, National Inst. of Immunology; fmr mem. Bd Trustee, US Pharmacopeia Convention, Trustee, Karnataka Chitrakala Parishat; Chair. All India Art Exhbn; Global Alumni Amb. for Australia, Department of Foreign Affairs and Trade, Australia Chevalier, Légion d'honneur; Hon. DSc (Ballarat) 2004; Dr hc (Manipal Acad. of Higher Educ.) 2005, (Univ. of Abertay) 2007, (Univ. of Glasgow) 2008, (Heriot-Watt Univ.) 2008, (National Univ. of Ireland) 2012, (Trinity Coll. Dublin) (2012); numerous awards including Padma Shri 1989, Sir M. Visveswaraya Memorial Award, Fed. of Karnataka Chambers of Commerce and Industry 2002, Rajyotsava Award 2002, Australian Alumni High Achiever Award, IDP Australian Alumni Asscn 2003, Padma Bhushan 2005, Indian Chamber of Commerce Lifetime Achievement Award 2005, Nikkei Asia Prize 2009, Othmer Gold Medal, Chemical Heritage Foundation (USA) 2014, Global Economy Prize for Business, Kiel Inst. for the World Economy (Germany) 2014, Global Leadership in Eng Award, USC Viterbi School of Eng 2016, Advancing Women in Science and Medicine Award for Excellence, Feinstein Inst. for Medical Research 2017. *Publication:* Ale and Arty. *Leisure interests:* trekking, art collecting. *Address:* Biocon India Ltd, 20th K.M. Hosur Road, Electronic City, Bangalore 560 100, India (office). *Telephone:* (80) 28082808 (office). *Fax:* (80) 28523423 (office). *E-mail:* contact.us@biocon.com (office). *Website:* www.biocon.com (office).

MAZZONI DELLA STELLA, Vittorio; Italian banker; b. 21 May 1941, Siena; ed Univ. of Florence; joined Monte dei Paschi di Siena bank, Naples 1966, worked in Rome, then Siena brs, then in Market and Econ. Research Dept, apptd Man. 1976, mem. Bd of Dirs 1990, Deputy Chair. 1991–, Deputy Chair. Monte dei Paschi Banque, Paris 1991; mem. Bd of Dirs Sindibank, Barcelona 1991; Chair. ICLE (MPS banking group), Rome 1991; apptd mem. Bd Dirs Centro Finanziaria SpA, Rome 1987; mem. Bd Dirs and Exec. Cttee Deposit Protection Fund, Rome 1991; mem. Bd Asscn of Italian Bankers (ABI) 1991; elected Prov. Councillor, Siena 1980, Deputy Chair. Prov. Council 1980–82, Mayor 1983–90; Chair. Chigiana Foundation (music acad.), Siena 1991.

MBA, Paul Biyoghé; Gabonese politician; b. 18 April 1953, Donguila; ed Univ. of Rennes, France; Deputy Dir Banque Gabonaise de Développement 1977–83; apptd First Deputy Prime Minister for Health 1980, 2015–; Chargé des Affaires to Pres.

of the Repub. 1980–83, Political Adviser to Pres. 1983–84, Jt Chief of Staff in Pres.'s Office 1984–89, Minister of Trade, Consumer Affairs and Technology Transfer 1989–90, Minister of State Control, Parastatal Reform and Privatization 1992–94, Minister of Small and Medium Enterprises 1999–2003, Minister of Trade and Industrial Devt, in charge of NEPAD 2003–08, Minister of Agric., Animal Husbandry and Rural Devt 2008–09, Prime Minister 2009–12 (resgnd); Deputy, Assemblée Nationale 1990–92, 1994–96, mem. Sénat 1997–99; Man. Dir Gabon Br., Banque Internationale pour l'Afrique Occidentale 1986–92; Dir Société Nat. des Bois du Gabon 1987–90; Pres. Econ. and Social Council 2012–14; mem. Parti démocratique gabonais (PDG); Hon. Pres. Gabonese Boxing Fed.; Grand Officier, Ordre Nat. de l'Etoile Equatoriale, Commdr, Ordre Nat. du Mérite, Commdr, Ordre du Mérite Maritime, Commdr, Ordre Nat. du Portugal, Chevalier, Légion d'Honneur.

MBA-ABESSOLE, Paul, PhD, DTheol; Gabonese ecclesiastic and government official; b. 9 Oct. 1939, Ngnung-Ako, Kango; ed Univ. de Paris, Inst. Catholique de Paris, France; teacher of French 1964–65; religious instructor 1965–73; curate 1973–76; political refugee in France 1983–89; typesetter 1984, 1986–87; returned to Gabon 1989; Founder and Leader Morena-bûcheron 1990, renamed Rassemblement nat. des bûcherons 1991, then Rassemblement pour le Gabon 2000; presidential cand. 1993, 1998; Mayor of Libreville 1996; Pres. of World Conf. of Mayors 1999; Minister of State for Human Rights and Missions 2002–03, later Deputy Prime Minister, also Minister of Agric., Livestock and Rural Devt, in charge of Human Rights 2003–07, of State in the Office of Pres. 2007, of Reform, Human Rights, the Fight against Poverty and Illicit Enrichment 2007, of Culture, the Arts, Educating the Population, Reconstruction Projects and Human Rights 2007–09; mem. Nat. Ass. 2011, Fifth Vice-Pres. 2012. *Leisure interest:* reading.

MBA ABOGO, César-Augusto; Equatorial Guinean economist, politician and writer; *Minister of Finance, the Economy and Planning;* b. 1979, Bata; m.; c.; ed Univ. of the Balearic Islands, Univ. Pompeu Fabra, Univ. Autonoma de Madrid; Political and Econ. Adviser, US Embassy in Malabo 2006–08; Assoc. Prof. of Econs, Univ. Nacional de Equatorial Guinea 2008–09; Chief Economist, Office of the Minister of Mines, Industry and Energy 2008–09; Govt Adviser on oil econs 2009–12; Dir-Gen. of Petroleum Econs, Ministry of Mines, Industry and Energy 2011–13; Sec. of State for Horizon 2020 (nat. econ. devt plan) 2013; Minister of Finance, the Economy and Planning 2019–. *Publications:* novels: El Portador de Marlow (Marlow's Porter) 2007, Malabo Blues 2011. *Address:* Ministry of Finance, the Economy and Planning, Zona Nuevo Ministerios, Malabo II, Equatorial Guinea (office).

MBA MOKUY, Agapito, MA; Equatorial Guinean politician; b. 10 March 1965; m.; ed Instituto Nacional 'Carlos Lwanga' de Bata, South Carolina State Univ., USA, Man., Training and Devt Inst., San Diego, Calif., USA, Louisiana State Univ., USA, Bangkok Univ., Thailand; with Protocol Dept, Presidency of the Repub. 1980–85; Admin. Sec., Nat. Univ. of Distance Educ. (UNED) Bata 1981–85; Consultant on Econs, UNDP, Malabo 1991; Chief Admin., Financial Electricity Co. of Equatorial Guinea (SEGESA) 1992–93; Consultant, Walter International, Malabo 1992–93; Asst Budget Officer, Budget Dept, UNESCO, Paris 1993–94, Asst Admin. Officer, Sector of Communication and Information 1995–96, Chief of Admin. and Financial Services, UNESCO Regional Office for Asia and the Pacific (PROAP), Bangkok, Thailand 1996–2001, mem. Cttee on Training and Human Resource Devt 2004–10, Sec. Cttee on Admin and Finance Exec. Bd 2006–10, Chief of Admin. Services, Financial and Human Resources, Social Sciences Sector 2002–10; Counsellor-Consultant of the Pres. of the Repub. 2010–12; Nat. Co-ordinator, Pan-African Project Creation, African Observatory of Science, Tech. and Innovation; Nat. Project Co-ordinator, Tech. Information and Communication Technologies in Rural Areas of the Repub. of Equatorial Guinea (TICGE) 2010–12; Minister of Foreign Affairs and Co-operation 2012–18; UNESCO Int. Award 2010. *Leisure interests:* reading, swimming, jogging.

MBA NGUEMA, Gen. Antonio; Equatorial Guinean military officer and politician; *Minister of National Defence;* brother of Pres. Obiang Nguema Mbasogo; fmr Dir Gen. of Nat. Security; Minister of Nat. Defence 2004–. *Address:* Ministry of National Defence, Malabo, Equatorial Guinea. *Telephone:* (09) 27-94.

MBABAZI, John Patrick Amama, LLB; Ugandan lawyer and politician; b. 16 Jan. 1949, Mparo village, Rukiga Co.; m. Jacquleine Susan Mbabazi; three s. three d.; ed Makerere Univ., Law Devt Centre, Kampala; State Attorney in Attorney-Gen.'s Chambers 1976–78; Sec., Uganda Law Council 1977–79; Prin. Asst to Yoweri Museveni 1978–79; Pnr Kategaya Mbabazi & Tumwesigye Advocates, Kampala 1981; in exile in Kenya and Sweden 1981–85; Dir-Gen. External Security Org. 1986–92; Minister of State for Defence 1992–98, for Foreign Affairs and Regional Co-operation 1998–2001, Minister of Defence 2001–09, also Attorney-Gen. 2004–06, Minister for Security 2009–11, Prime Minister 2011–14; del. to Constitutional Ass. (responsible for drafting new Ugandan constitution) 1994–95; MP for Kanungu District 2003–16; mem. Nat. Resistance Movt (Sec.-Gen. 2005–15); fmr head of Bd of Dirs of several state and pvt. cos; mem. Ugandan Law Soc. 1977–; cand. in presidential election 2016; Nalubaale Medal of Honour.

MBANEFO, Arthur Christopher Izuegbunam, FCA; Nigerian financial consultant and fmr diplomatist; b. 11 June 1930; m.; one s.; ed St Patrick's Coll., Calabar; Minister for Commerce and Industries, Eastern Region of Nigeria (Repub. of Biafra) 1968–70; staff mem. Price Waterhouse & Co., London 1970–71; fmr Partner, Akintola Williams & Co., Chartered Accountants; f. Arthur Mbanefo and Assocs. (Corp. and financial consulting Co.) 1986; Pro-Chancellor and Chair. of Council, Univ. of Lagos 1984–86, Obafemi Awolowo Univ. 1986–90, Ahmadu Bello Univ. 1990–93; Perm. Rep. to UN, New York 1999–2003, Chair. G77 2000, Chair. Bd of Trustees UNITAR 2000–04; Dir Orient Petroleum Resources Ltd; Fellow, Inst. of Chartered Accountants in England and Wales, Inst. of Chartered Accountants of Nigeria, Nigerian Inst. of Man. (mem. Council 1979–87); Pro-Chancellor and Chair. of Council Ahmadu Bello Univ. 1990–93, Obafemi Awolowo Univ. 1986–90, Univ. of Lagos 1984–86; f. Asscn of Accountancy Bodies of W Africa 1982, Pres. 1987; mem. Bd UAC of Nigeria PLC, Mobil Oil Nigeria PLC, Glassforce Ltd, Shebah Exploration and Production Co. Ltd CITIBANK Nigeria Ltd; mem. Business Advisory Bd LaGray Chemical Co.; Hon. Yoruba Chieftaincy, Distinguished Order of Fed. Repub. of Nigeria 1981, Odu of Onitsha 1994, Commdr

Order of the Niger 2002; several Nat. and Int. awards and medals, including from Govts of Italy and Brazil.

M'BAREK, Sghair Ould; Mauritanian politician; *President, Constitutional Council;* b. 1954, Néma; m.; four c.; ed Univ. of Nouakchott; Minister of Nat. Educ. 1992–93, 1997–98, 2000, of Rural Devt and the Environment 1994–95, of Health and Social Affairs 1995, of Commerce and Tourism 1998–99, of Equipment and Transport 1999, of Justice 2001–03; Prime Minister of Mauritania 2003–05; Mediator of the Repub. –2010; Pres. Constitutional Council 2010–. *Address:* Office of the President of the Constitutional Council, Nouakchott, Mauritania (office).

MBEKI, Thabo Mvuyelwa, MA, KStJ, GCB; South African politician and fmr head of state; b. 18 June 1942, Idutywa; s. of Govan Mbeki and Epainette Mbeki; m. Zanele Dlamini 1974; one c.; ed Lovedale, Alice, St John's Umtata, Univs of London and Sussex; Leader African Students Org. 1961; Youth Organizer for African Nat. Congress (ANC), Johannesburg 1961–62; six weeks' detention, Byo 1962; left SA 1962; official, ANC offices, London, England 1967–70; mil. training, USSR 1970; Asst Sec. ANC Revolutionary Council 1971–72; Acting ANC Rep., Swaziland 1975–76; ANC Rep., Nigeria 1976–78, mem. ANC, Nat. Exec. Cttee 1975, re-elected 1985; Dir Information and Publicity, ANC 1984–89, Head of Dept of Int. Affairs 1989–93, Del. on Talks about Talks, with SA Govt 1990, Chair. ANC 1993; First Deputy Pres. of South Africa 1994–99; Pres. ANC 1997–2007; Pres. of South Africa 1999–2008 (resgnd); mem. Bd IOC 1993; Pres. African Union 2002–03; f. Thabo Mbeki Foundation 2010; Hon. KCMG; Hon. DBA (Arthur D Little Inst.) 1994, Dr. hc (Univ. of South Africa) 1995, (Rand Afrikaans Univ.) 1999, Hon. DIur, (Sussex Univ.) 1995, (Glasgow Caledonian Univ.) 2000, Hon. DCS (Univ. of Stellenbosch) 2004; Good Governance Award, Corp. Council on Africa 1997, Pretoria News Press Asscn 2000, 2008, Oliver Tambo/Johnny Makatini Freedom Award 2000, Peace and Reconciliation Award, Gandhi Awards for Reconciliation, Durban 2003, Good Brother Award, Nat. Congress of Black Women 2004, Medal of Honour, Athens 2005, Champion of the Earth Award, UN(O) 2005, Presidential Award 2006. *Address:* Thabo Mbeki Foundation, Private Bag X 444, Houghton 2041, South Africa (office). *Website:* www.mbeki.org (office).

MBELLA MBELLA, Lejeune; Cameroonian diplomatist and government official; *Minister of External Relations;* b. 9 July 1949, Ebone, Nkongsamba; Dir, Nat. Presidential Archives 1976–79; joined Ministry of External Relations 1979, roles include Dir, UN Div., Ministry of External Relations, Second Sec., later First Sec., Embassy in Ottawa, Political Counsellor and chargé d'affaires, Embassy in Paris, Consul in Marseilles, Head of Francophonie Div., Ministry of External Relations 1997, also Cameroon Del. to Agence intergouvernementale de la Francophonie, Amb. to Japan 2002–06, Amb. to France 2007–15, also Perm. Rep. to UNESCO; Minister of External Relations 2015–. *Address:* Ministry of External Relations, Yaoundé, Cameroon (office). *Telephone:* 2220-3850 (office). *Fax:* 2220-1133 (office). *E-mail:* minrex@diplocam.cm (office). *Website:* www .diplocam.cm (office).

MBETE, Baleka; South African politician; *Speaker, National Assembly;* b. 24 Sept. 1949, Durban; ed Inanda Seminary, Durban, Lovedale Teachers Coll., King William's Town, East Cape; teacher, Isibonelo High School, KwaMashu, Durban 1975; went into exile, then teacher, Matter Dolorosa High School, Mbabane, Swaziland (renamed Eswatini 2018) 1976–77; joined African Nat. Congress (ANC) 1976, worked in ANC Dept of Information and Publicity (Radio Freedom) and Women's Section, Dar es Salaam, Tanzania 1977–81, Public Relations work for ANC, Nairobi, Kenya 1981–83, worked in ANC underground political structures, Gaborone, Botswana 1983–86, mem. ANC Regional Women's Cttee and Regional Political Cttee, Harare, Zimbabwe 1986–87, Admin. Sec., Exec. Cttee, Lusaka, Zambia 1987–90, Sec.-Gen. ANC Women's League 1991–93, mem. ANC Nat. Exec. Cttee 1991, Chair. ANC Parl. Caucus 1995–, Nat. Chair. ANC 2007–; Deputy Speaker, Nat. Ass. 1996–2004, Speaker 2004–08, 2014–; Deputy Pres. of South Africa 2008–09; apptd mem. Presidential Panel, Truth and Reconciliation Comm. 1995, African Peer Review Mechanism (APRM) Panel of Eminent Persons 2012–. *Address:* Office of the Speaker, National Assembly, Parliament Building, Room E118, Parliament Street, POB 15, Cape Town 8000, South Africa (office). *Telephone:* (21) 4032595 (office). *Fax:* (21) 4619462 (office). *E-mail:* info@ parliament.gov.za (office). *Website:* www.parliament.gov.za (office).

MBOWENI, Tito, MA, PhD; South African politician, fmr central banker and business executive; *Minister of Finance;* b. 16 March 1959, Tzaneem, Northern Prov.; ed Nat. Univ. of Lesotho, Univ. of E Anglia, UK, Univ. of KwaZulu-Natal; mem. African Nat. Congress—ANC 1980 (ANC, Zambia 1988), fmr Deputy Head Dept of Econ. Planning, Co-ordinator for Trade and Industry, elected to Nat. Executive Council, later became mem. Nat. Working Cttee, Head, Policy Dept 1997–98; Minister of Labour, Govt of Nat. Unity 1994–98; Advisor to Gov. 1998–99, SA Reserve Bank, Gov. 1999–2009; Chair. AngloGold Ashanti Ltd 2010–14; Int. Adviser Goldman Sachs Int. 2010–; founder mem. Mboweni Brothers Investment Holdings; Gov. Prof. Extraordinary in Econs, Univ. of Stellenbosch 2002–03; Chancellor Univ. of North-West 2002–05; Chair. Nampak Ltd 2010–18, Efora Energy Ltd (fmrly SacOil Holdings Ltd) 2013–17; Dir for South Africa, New Devt Bank (BRICS Devt Bank) 2015–17, Chair. of Bd of Govs; Minister of Finance 2018–; mem. Bd of Dirs, PPC Ltd 2015–17; mem. Bd of Govs, Asia School of Business 2015–; Hon. Prof. of Econs (Univ. of S Africa) 2002–03; Hon. DComm (Univ. of Natal) 2001; became one of the Global Leaders of Tomorrow, World Econ. Forum 1995. *Leisure interests:* fly-fishing, soccer. *Address:* Ministry of Finance, 40 Church Square, Old Reserve Bank Builiding, 2nd Floor, Pretoria 0002, South Africa (office). *Telephone:* (12) 323 8911 (office). *Fax:* (12) 323 3262 (office). *Website:* www.treasury.gov.za/ministry.

MDLALOSE, Frank Themba, BSc, UED, MB, CH.B.; South African politician and fmr diplomatist; b. 29 Nov. 1931, Nqutu Dist KwaZulu; s. of Jaconiah Zwelabo Mdlalose and Thabitha Mthembu; m. Eunice Nokuthula 1956; three s. two d.; ed Univ. of Fort Hare, Rhodes Univ. and Univ. of Natal; Intern, King Edward VII Hosp., Durban 1959; pvt. medical practice, Pretoria 1960–62, Steadville, Lady-smith, Natal, Atteridgeville 1962–70; medical practitioner, Madadeni 1970–78; mem. Inkatha (Later Inkatha Freedom Party) 1975–, Nat. Chair. 1978–97; Minister of Health, KwaZulu 1983–90, Acting Minister of Educ. 1990, Minister without Portfolio 1991–94; Premier, KwaZulu-Natal 1994–97; Amb. to Egypt –2002 (retd); Hon. DrIur (Zululand) 1998. *Publication:* My Life (autobiog.) 2006.

MEAD, Carver Andress, BS, MS, PhD; American engineer, physicist, computer scientist and academic; *Gordon and Betty Moore Professor Emeritus of Engineering and Applied Science, California Institute of Technology;* b. 1 May 1934, Bakersfield, Calif.; ed California Inst. of Tech.; began teaching at Caltech 1957, Instructor in Electrical Eng 1958–59, Asst Prof. 1959–62, Assoc. Prof. 1962–67, Prof. 1967–77, Prof. of Computer Science and Electrical Eng 1977–80, Gordon and Betty Moore Prof. of Computer Science 1980–92, Gordon and Betty Moore Prof. of Eng and Applied Science 1992–99, Emer. 1999–, est. Dept of Applied Physics, Dept of Computer Science, Dept of Computation and Neural Systems; pioneer of very-large-scale integrated (VSLI) circuit technology; developed first techniques for designing complex microchips, Collective Electrodynamics, G4v gravitation; cr. gallium-arsenide (GaAs) MESFET transistor and first software compilation of a silicon chip; f. Lexitron, Silicon Compilers, Silerity, Actel, Synaptics, Sonic Innovations, Foveon, Impinj; mem. Nat. Acad. of Eng (NAE), NAS; Fellow, IEEE, American Physical Soc., Computer History Museum, American Acad. of Arts and Sciences, Nat. Acad. of Inventors; Hon. DSc (Univ. of Lund); Dr hc (Univ. of Southern California); Callinan Award, Electrochemical Soc. 1971, Achievement Award, Electronics Magazine 1981, Harold Pender Award 1984, Harry Goode Memorial Award 1985, Walter B. Wriston Public Policy Award 1987, IEEE John Von Neumann Medal 1996, Phil Kaufman Award 1996, Allen Newell Award, Asscn for Computing Machinery 1997, Lemelson-MIT Prize 1999, Medal of Tech. 2002, NAE Founders Award 2003, BBVA Frontiers of Knowledge Award of Information and Communication Technologies 2011. *Publications include:* Introduction to VLSI Systems (co-author with Lynn Conway) 1980, Analog VLSI and Neural Systems 1989; over 100 articles in scientific journals and more than 50 patents. *Address:* California Institute of Technology, 1200 East California Boulevard, MC 136-93, Pasadena, CA 91125, USA (office). *Telephone:* (626) 395-2812 (office). *E-mail:* carver@caltech.edu (office). *Website:* carvermead.caltech.edu (office).

MEAD, Matthew Hansen (Matt), JD; American lawyer, politician and fmr state governor; b. 11 March 1962, Jackson, Teton Co., Wyo.; s. of Peter Bradford Mead and Mary Elisabeth Mead (née Hansen); grand-s. of Gov. and US Senator Clifford P. Hansen; m. Carol L. Mintzer; one s. one d.; ed Trinity Univ., Univ. of Wyoming Coll. of Law; Deputy Co. Attorney, Cambell Co. Attorney's Office, Wyo. 1987–90; Asst US Attorney, US Dept of Justice 1991–95; pvt. law practice, Cheyenne 1995–97; Partner, Mead & Phillips 1997–2001; fmr Special Asst, Attorney-Gen., State of Wyo.; US Attorney for Dist of Wyoming, Cheyenne 2001–07; unsuccessful cand. in special election for Senate seat vacated by death of Craig L. Thomas; rancher, Albany/Goshen Co.; Owner Mead Land & Livestock, LLC; Gov. of Wyoming 2011–19; mem. Bd of Dirs Wyoming Bank & Trust, Wyoming Business Council; Lifetime mem. Nat. Rifle Asscn; Republican.

MEADE, Hon. Reuben Theodore; Montserratian economist and politician; b. 7 March 1954; m. Joan DelSol Meade; five c.; ed Univ. of the West Indies; fmr Dir and Project Man., L&M Construction Inc.; fmr Dir of Devt, Govt of Montserrat; mem. Legis. Council, Leader of the Opposition 1997–2006; fmr Minister of Agric., Land, Housing and Environment, Chief Minister of Montserrat 1991–96, 2009–10, also Minister of Finance and Econ. Devt, Tourism and Sport 2009, Premier 2010–14, also Minister of Finance and Econ. Man. with responsibility for Local Govt, Immigration, Information Communication, Regional and Int. Affairs, and Tourism; fmr Leader, Nat. Progressive Party (now defunct); mem. Movt for Change and Prosperity; Pres. Montserrat Cricket Asscn; Montserrat Certificate and Medal of Honour.

MEADE KURIBREÑA, José Antonio, PhD; Mexican economist, lawyer and government official; b. 27 Feb. 1969, Mexico City; ed Instituto Tecnológico Autónomo de México (ITAM), Faculty of Law of Universidad Nacional Autónoma de Mexico, Yale Univ., USA; began career in Nat. Insurance and Finance; has served as Gen. Man. of Financial Planning of Nat. System of Savings for Retirement, Asst Sec. of Savings Protection Inst. of Bank Savings Protection, Gen. Dir Bank and Savings of the Ministry of Finance, Dir Gen. of Nat. Rural Credit Bank, Dir Financiera Rural; fmr Prof. of Econs, ITAM; Under-Sec. of Dependence 2010–11; Sec. of Energy Jan.–Sept. 2011, Sec. of Finance and Public Credit 2011–12; Chair. Petróleos Mexicanos (PEMEX) 2011; Sec. of Foreign Affairs 2012–15, of Finance and Public Credit 2016–17. *Publications:* several articles on microeconomics and economic analysis of law. *Address:* c/o Partido Revolucionario Institucional (PRI), Edif. 2, Insurgentes Norte 59, Col. Buenavista, Del. Cuauhtémoc, 06000 México, DF, Mexico.

MEADOWS, Dennis L., BA, PhD; American scientist and academic; *Professor Emeritus of Systems Policy and Social Science Research, University of New Hampshire;* b. 7 June 1942; m. Donella Meadows (died 2001); ed Carleton Coll., Sloan School of Man., Massachusetts Inst. of Tech.; mem. Faculty, MIT during late 1960s, Dir Club of Rome Project on the Predicament of Mankind 1970–72, later Prof. in Faculties of Man., Eng and Social Sciences, fmr Dir Grad. Program in business and engineering; fmr Dir of Research Inst. at Dartmouth Coll.; Prof. Emer. of Systems Policy and Social Science Research Univ. of New Hampshire 1988– and fmr Dir Inst. for Policy and Social Science Research; Pres. Lab for Interactive Learning; Past Pres. Int. System Dynamics Soc., Int. Simulation and Games Asscn; co-f. Balaton Group (int. network of more than 300 professionals in more than 30 countries involved in systems science, public policy and sustainable devt); Hon. DHumLitt (Univ. of New Hampshire) 2009; UNESCO Berlin Peace Clock Prize 2007, Japan Prize (co-recipient) 2009, inducted into The Earth Hall of Fame KYOTO 2018. *Publications:* Dynamics of Commodity Production Cycles 1970, The Limits to Growth (co-author) 1972, Toward Global Equilibrium: Collected Papers (co-ed.) 1973, Dynamics of Growth in a Finite World 1974, Beyond Growth: Essays on Alternative Futures (co-ed.) 1975, Alternatives to Growth-I: A Search for Sustainable Futures: papers adapted from entries to the 1975 George and Cynthia Mitchell Prize and from presentations before the 1975 Alternatives to Growth Conference, held at the Woodlands 1977, Beyond the Limits: Confronting Global Collapse, Envisioning a Sustainable Future 1992, The Systems Thinking Playbook 1995, Limits to Growth: The 30-Year Update (co-author) 2004, Les Limites à la croissance (dans un monde fini) (co author) 2012; numerous papers in scientific journals. *Address:* PO Box 844, Durham, NH 03824-0844, USA (home). *Telephone:* (603) 397-7442 (home). *E-mail:* dmeadows@cisunix.unh.edu (office).

MEAKINS, Ian K.; British business executive; *Group Chief Executive, Wolseley PLC;* b. 31 Aug. 1956; fmrly with Bain & Co., Procter & Gamble; Founding Partner, Kalchas Group; joined United Distillers 1991, several int. man. positions with Diageo plc, including Pres. European Major Markets and Global Supply 2000–04; mem. Bd of Dirs and CEO Alliance UniChem plc (until merger with Boots PLC 2006) 2004–06; Chief Exec. Travelex Holdings Ltd 2006–09; Group Chief Exec. Wolseley PLC 2009–; Dir mem. Bd of Dirs Centrica PLC, Impetus Trust. *Address:* Wolseley PLC, Parkview 1220, Arlington Business Park, Theale, West Berks., RG7 4GA, England (office). *Telephone:* (118) 929-8700 (office). *Fax:* (118) 929-8701 (office). *E-mail:* info@wolseley.com (office). *Website:* www.wolseley.com (office).

MEARSHEIMER, John J., BS, MA, MA, PhD; American academic; *R. Wendell Harrison Distinguished Service Professor of Political Science, University of Chicago;* ed West Point Mil. Acad., Univ. of Southern California, Cornell Univ.; served as officer in USAF 1970–75; Research Fellow, Brookings Institution 1979–80; Research Assoc., Center for Int. Affairs, Harvard Univ. 1980–82; Asst Prof., Political Science Dept, Univ. of Chicago 1982–84, Assoc. Prof. 1984–87, Prof. 1987–96, R. Wendell Harrison Distinguished Service Prof. 1996–, also Co-Dir Program on Int. Security Policy; Visiting Scholar, Olin Inst. for Strategic Studies, Harvard Univ. 1992–93; mem. or fmr mem. editorial bds International Security, Security Studies, International History Review, JFQ: Joint Forces Quarterly, Journal of Transatlantic Studies, Asian Security, China Security; mem. American Acad. of Arts and Sciences, IISS, Chicago Council on Global Affairs, Council on Foreign Relations; Hon. Prof., Renmin Univ. of China 2012, Beijing Foreign Studies Univ. 2012; Hon. Patron, Philosophical Soc., Trinity Coll., Dublin 2012; Dr hc (Panteion Univ., Athens) 2011; Clark Award for Distinguished Teaching, Cornell Univ., Quantrell Award for Distinguished Teaching, Univ. of Chicago 1985, George Kistiakowsky Scholar, American Acad. of Arts and Sciences 1986–87, Distinguished Scholar Award, Int. Studies Asscn 2004, Graduation Speaker, Univ. of Chicago 2004, E.H. Carr Memorial Lecturer, Univ. of Aberystwyth, UK 2004, Hisham B. Sharabi Memorial Lecturer, Palestine Centre 2010, Michael Hintze Lecturer in Int. Security, Univ. of Sydney 2010, Robert G. Bone Distinguished Lecturer, Illinois State Univ. 2011, Dr Jerzy Hauptmann Distinguished Guest Lecturer, Park Univ., Kansas City 2011, Hall of Distinguished Grads, Croton-Harmon High School 2012. *Publications:* Conventional Deterrence (Edgar S. Furniss, Jr Book Award) 1983, Nuclear Deterrence: Ethics and Strategy (co-ed.) 1985, Liddell Hart and the Weight of History 1988, The Tragedy of Great Power Politics (Joseph Lepgold Book Prize) 2001, The Israel Lobby and US Foreign Policy (with Stephen M. Walt) 2007, Why Leaders Lie: The Truth about Lying in International Politics 2011; contribs to Perspectives on International Relations, London Review of Books, Middle East Policy, Foreign Policy, International Relations, New Republic, International Security, New York Times, Chicago Tribune and numerous chapters in books. *Address:* Political Science Department, University of Chicago, 5828 South University Avenue, Chicago, IL 60637, USA (office). *Telephone:* (773) 702-8667 (office). *Fax:* (773) 702-1689 (office). *E-mail:* j-mearsheimer@uchicago.edu (office). *Website:* mearsheimer.uchicago.edu (office).

MEBE N'GO, Edgar Alain; Cameroonian government official and politician; b. 22 Jan. 1957, Sangmélima; ed Ecole Nat. d'Admin et de Magistrature, Yaoundé; mem. Rassemblement démocratique du peuple camerounais (RDPC); Econ. Affairs Adviser to Gov. of E Prov. 1985–88; Sec.-Gen. N Prov. 1988–91; Préfet, Ocean Département 1991–95, Mefou and Afamba Département 1995–96, Mfoundi Département 1996–97; Dir Civil Cabinet of the Presidency 1997–2004; Del.-Gen. for Nat. Security (head of nat. police) 2004–09; Minister-Del. at the Presidency in charge of Defence (Minister of Defence) 2009–15; Minister of Transport 2015–18.

MEBOUTOU, Michel Meva'a; Cameroonian politician; b. 4 June 1939, Prov. du Sud. Francophone; ed Univ. of Yaounde, Univ. of Poitiers; apptd Head of the Dept of Economic Affairs 1968, promoted to Deputy Dir of Legislation 1969; fmr Dir Studies, Resources and Techniques, Perm. Secr. of Nat. Defense; Principal Civil Admin. 1972; apptd Sec.-Gen., Ministry of Social Affairs 1975, Ministry of Transport 1979; Sec.-Gen. Ministry of the Armed Forces (now Ministry of Defence) 1982–85; Deputy Minister, Presidency of the Repub. in charge of Defence 1986–90; Sec.-Gen., Nat. Ass. 1992–2001; Minister of the Economy and Finance 2001–02; Minister of Finance and the Budget 2002–04; mem. Bd of Govs Govs. IMF; mem. Bulu tribe.

MECHANIC, David, BA, MA, PhD; American sociologist and academic; *Rene Dubos University Professor of Behavioral Sciences, Rutgers University;* b. 21 Feb. 1936, New York; s. of Louis Mechanic and Tillie Mechanic (née Penn); m. Kate Mechanic; two s.; ed City Coll. of New York and Stanford Univ.; mem. Faculty, Univ. of Wisconsin 1960–79, Prof. of Sociology 1965–73, John Bascom Prof. 1973–79, Dir Center for Medical Sociology and Health Services Research 1971–79, Chair. Dept of Sociology 1968–70; Prof. of Social Work and Sociology, Rutgers Univ. 1979–, Univ. Prof. and Dean Faculty of Arts and Sciences 1981–84, Rene Dubos Univ. Prof. of Behavioral Sciences 1984–, Dir Inst. for Health, Health Care Policy and Aging Research 1985–2013; mem. various advisory panels etc.; mem. NAS, Inst. of Medicine of NAS, American Acad. of Arts and Sciences; Guggenheim Fellowship 1977–78; numerous awards. *Publications include:* author of 12 books and about 400 papers and chapters and ed. of 11 books on sociological and health care subjects. *Address:* Institute for Health Policy, 112 Paterson Street, New Brunswick, NJ 08901, USA (office). *Telephone:* (848) 932-8415 (office). *E-mail:* mechanic@rci.rutgers.edu (office). *Website:* www.rutgers.edu (office).

MECHANIC, William M. (Bill), PhD; American film industry executive; *Chairman and CEO, Pandemonium LLC;* b. 1950, Detroit, Mich.; ed Michigan State Univ., Univ. of Southern California; Dir of Programming SelecTV 1978–80, Vice-Pres. Programming 1980–82; Vice-Pres. Pay TV, Paramount Pictures Corpn 1982–84; Vice-Pres. Pay TV Sales, Walt Disney Pictures and TV 1984–85, Sr Vice-Pres. Video 1985–87, Pres. Int. Theatrical Distribution and Worldwide Video 1987–93; Pres. and COO 20th Century Fox Film Entertainment 1993–96, Chair. and CEO 1996–2000; Founder, Chair. and CEO Pandemonium LLC (ind. production co.) 2000; mem. Bd of Councilors, School of Cinema Arts, Univ. of Southern California; mem. Bd of Govs, Acad. of Motion Picture Arts and Sciences (Execs Br.) 2002–05, 2016–18, Bd of Nat. Film Theatre American Friends; Pres. of the Jury, Berlin Int. Film Festival 2001; Chair. Int. Jury, Venice Int. Film Festival 2007; Showman of the Year Award, Producers Guild of America, Crystal Award, Women in Film. *Films include:* Dark Water (producer) 2005, The New World (exec.

producer) 2005, Coraline 2009, The Moon and the Sun (producer) 2016, Hacksaw Ridge (producer) 2016, 2:22 (exec. producer) 2016. *Television includes:* The 82nd Annual Academy Awards (TV Special) (producer) 2010. *Address:* Pandemonium LLC, 9777 Wilshire Boulevard, #700, Beverly Hills, CA 90212-1907, USA (office). *Telephone:* (310) 550-9900 (office).

MEČIAR, Vladimír, DrIur; Slovak politician; b. 26 July 1942, Zvolen; s. of Jozef Mečiar and Anna (née Tomková) Mečiarová; m. Margita Mečiarová (née Bencková); two s. two d.; ed Comenius Univ., Bratislava; clerk 1959–69; various posts in Czechoslovak Union of Youth 1967–68; expelled from all posts and CP; employed as manual worker because of his attitude to Soviet occupation of Czechoslovakia at Heavy Engineering Works in Dubnica nad Váhom 1970–73; clerk, later commercial lawyer for Skloobal Nemšová 1973–90; politically active again after collapse of communist system 1989; Minister of Interior and Environment, Govt of Slovak (Fed.) Repub. 1990, Deputy to House of Nations, Fed. Ass. 1990–92; Chair. People's Party—Movement for a Democratic Slovakia (Ľudová strana—Hnutie za Demokratické Slovensko—ĽS-HZDS) 1991–2014; Prime Minister of Slovakia 1990–91, 1992, 1994–98; Acting Pres. of Slovakia (served alongside Ivan Gašparovič) March–Oct. 1998; Opposition mem. Parl. 2002–10; presidential cand. 2004 elections; Order of Maltese Cross 1995; Dr hc (Lomonosov Univ., Moscow) 1995, (Braća Karić Univ., Yugoslavia) 1996; Peutinger Award (Germany) 1995. *Publications:* Slovakia, Be Self-Confident!, Slovak Taboo. *Leisure interests:* sport, music, literature, hiking.

MECKSEPER, Friedrich; German painter and printmaker; b. 8 June 1936, Bremen; s. of Gustav Meckseper and Lily Ringel-Debatin; m. 1st Barbara Müller 1962; one s. two d.; m. 2nd Sibylle Lewitscharoff; ed State Art Acad., Stuttgart, State Univ. for the Visual Arts, Berlin; apprentice mechanic, Robert Bosch GmbH, Stuttgart 1952–55; more than 100 solo and group exhbns of his prints, collages and paintings in Europe, USA, Australia and Japan; represented in many major museums of contemporary art and at print biennials world-wide; Prof. of Art, Int. Summer Acad., Salzburg 1977–79; Guest Lecturer, London 1968; German-Rome Prize 1963, Prize of the 7th Bienniale, Tokyo 1970, of the 6th Bienniale, Fredrikstad 1982, of the 1st Kochi Int. Print Triennial, Japan 1990. *Publications include:* Friedrich Meckseper, Etchings 1956–1994; catalogue raisonné of the graphic work 1994, Pong redivivus (with Sibylle Lewitscharoff) 2013. *Leisure interests:* locomotives, steamboats, ballooning, paintings, etchings, books. *Address:* Landhausstrasse 13, 10717 Berlin, Germany.

MEDAK, Peter; British/Hungarian/American film, theatre, opera and television director; b. 23 Dec. 1937, Budapest, Hungary; m. 1st Katherine La Kermance; m. 2nd Carolyn Seymour; m. 3rd Julia Migenes 1989; two s. four d.; worked with AB-Pathe, London 1956–59; Second and First Asst Film Dir 1959–63; Dir Universal Pictures 1963–, Paramount Pictures 1967–; has directed several operas, plays and series for US TV; Evening Standard Award for Best Director and Film: The Krays 1990. *Plays directed include:* Miss Julie. *Operas directed include:* Salome (Richard Strauss), La Voix Humaine (Poulenc), Schubert. *Films directed include:* Negatives (Festival dei Popoli Firenze 1970) 1968, A Day in the Death of Joe Egg 1970, The Ruling Class 1973, Third Girl From the Left 1973, Ghost in the Noonday Sun 1975, The Odd Job 1978, The Changeling 1979, Zorro, The Gay Blade 1981, Breaking Through 1984, The Men's Club 1986, The Krays (London Evening Standard Award for Best Dir and Film 1990) 1990, La Voix Humaine 1991, Let Him Have It 1991, Romeo is Bleeding 1994, Pontiac Moon 1994, Hunchback of Notre Dame 1996, Species II 1997, David Copperfield 1998, Peter Gabriel: Play (video) 2004. *Television includes:* Court Marshall 1965, The Third Girl from the Left 1973, Space 1999 (two episodes) 1976–77, Alfred Nobel, The Babysitter 1980, Mistress of Paradise 1981, Hart to Hart (two episodes) 1982, Cry for the Strangers 1982, Remington Steele 1983, Faerie Tale Theatre (five episodes) 1984–87, Magnum, P.I. 1985, The Twilight Zone (seven episodes) 1985–87, Crime Story 1987, Beauty and the Beast 1987, China Beach 1989, Nabokov 1989, Tales from the Crypt 1992, Homicide: Life on the Street (six episodes) 1994–98, Falls Road, Kindred 1996, The Hunchback 1997, Law & Order: Special Victims Unit 1999, David Copperfield 2000, Feasts of All Saints 2001, The Guardian 2001, The Wire 2002, South Beach 2002, Carnivale 2003, 7th Heaven 2004, House M.D. 2004, Marple: By The Pricking of My Thumbs 2006, In Justice 2006, Masters of Horror 2007, Sex and Lies in Sin City 2008, Breaking Bad 2009, Cold Case 2009, Hannibal 2013–14, The Assets 2014. *Address:* c/o Sean Gascoine, United Agents Ltd, 12–26 Lexington Street, London, W1F 0LE, England (office); c/o Michael Lewis Associates, 2505 5th Street, Santa Monica, CA 90405, USA (office); c/o George Hayum, Hirsch Wallerstein Hayum Matlof & Fishman – Attorneys at Law, 10100 Santa Monica Blvd, Suite 1700, Los Angeles, CA 90067, USA (office). *Telephone:* (20) 3214-0800 (office); (310) 399-1999 (office); (310) 703-1777 (office); (323) 650-9770. *Fax:* (20) 3214-0801 (office); (310) 703-1799 (office). *E-mail:* info@unitedagents.co.uk (office); ghayum@hwhmf.com (office); petermedak@mac.com. *Website:* unitedagents.co.uk (office); www.hwhmf.com (office).

MEDGYESSY, Péter, PhD; Hungarian politician, economist and diplomatist; b. 19 Oct. 1942, Budapest; m. 2nd Katalin Csaplár; one s. one d. (from previous marriage); ed Budapest Univ. of Econs (then Karl Marx Univ.); held several positions in Ministry of Finance, Dept of Finance, Dept of Prices, Dept of Int. Finances; fmr Dir-Gen. Dept of State Budget; Deputy Minister of Finance 1982–87; Minister of Finance 1987–88; Deputy Prime Minister in interim Govt of Miklós Németh (q.v.) 1988–89; Pres., Chief Exec. Magyar Paribas 1990–94; Pres. and CEO Hungarian Bank for Investment and Devt Ltd 1994–96; Minister of Finance 1996–98; Chair. Bd Dirs Inter-Europa Bank 1998–2001; Vice-Pres. Atlasz Insurance Co. 1998–2001; Prime Minister of Hungary 2002–04 (resgnd), Man. Prime Minister Aug.–Sept. 2004; Amb. at Large 2004–08; Prof., Coll. of Finance and Accounting, Budapest; Pres. Hungarian Econ. Soc.; Dir Int. Inst. of Public Finance, Saarbrücken; mem. Presidium Hungarian Bank Asscn 1996–, Council of World Econ. Forum; Commdr's Cross with Star, Order of Merit of Hungarian Repub. 1998, Chevalier de la Légion d'honneur 2000, Officer's Cross 2004, Order of Crown of Belgium 2002, Order of the Rising Sun – Gold and Silver Star (Japan) 2002, Grand Cross, Order of Merit (Chile) 2003, Grand Cross, Order of Merit (Norway) 2003, Grand Cross, Order of Merit (Germany) 2004; Medal of Irish Hungarian Econ. Asscn 2005. *Publications:* several articles on budgetary and exchange rate policies and monetary system in financial and econ. publs. *Leisure interests:* nature, music.

MEDINA DEL RÍO, Rodolfo; Venezuelan economist and politician; b. 4 Jan. 1976, Caracas; ed Univ. Central de Venezuela; Prof. of Econs, Univ. Central de Venezuela 2009–; Deputy Dir, Nat. Securities Comm., also Head, Directorate of Fiscal Revenues and Expenditures, Nat. Treasury Office 2007; Dir of Admin, Office of the Pres. 2013; Head, Nat. Budget Office (ONAPRE) 2014–16; Minister of Finance and Public Banking 2016–17; Deputy Dir, Banco del Tesoro 2014–16; Dir, Bicentennial Public Securities Exchange 2014; Alt. mem., Cttee on Disposal of Public Assets 2014.

MEDINA ESTÉVEZ, HE Cardinal Jorge Arturo, DTheol, DCL; Chilean ecclesiastic; *Prefect Emeritus of Divine Worship and the Discipline of the Sacraments;* b. 23 Dec. 1926, Santiago de Chile; ed Major Seminary of Santiago; ordained priest 1954; mem. Major Seminary of Santiago, Theological Faculty of Santiago; attended Second Vatican Council early 1960s; Auxiliary Bishop of Rancagua and Titular Bishop of Tibili 1984–87, consecrated 1985, Bishop of Rancagua 1987–93, of Valparaíso 1993–96; Pro-Prefect Congregation for Divine Worship and the Discipline of the Sacraments 1996–98, Prefect 1998–2002, Prefect Emer. 2002–; cr. Cardinal (Cardinal-Deacon of San Saba) 1998, Cardinal Proto-Deacon –2007, Cardinal-Priest of San Saba 2008–; participated in Papal Conclave 2005, announced to the world the election of Pope Benedict XVI. *Address:* c/o Congregation for Divine Worship and the Discipline of the Sacraments, Palazzo delle Congregazioni, Piazza Pio XII 10, 00193 Rome, Italy. *Telephone:* (06) 69884005. *Website:* www.vatican.va/roman_curia/congregations/ccdds.

MEDINA GONZÁLEZ, Cuauhtémoc, BA, PhD; Mexican art critic, historian and curator; *Chief Curator, Museo Universitario Arte Contemporáneo;* b. (Cuauhtémoc Medina González), 5 Dec. 1965, Mexico City; s. of José Humberto Medina Ortiz and Gladys González Alarcón; m. Danna Levin Rojo (divorced); one d.; partner Cristina Paoli Charles; ed Univ. Nacional Autónoma de Mexico, Mexico City, Univ. of Essex, England; Researcher, Instituto de Investigaciones Estéticas, Univ. Nacional Autónoma de Mexico 1992–, Chief Curator, Museo Universitario Arte Contemporáneo (MUAC), Mexico City 2013–; mem. Curare (Espacio Crítico para las Artes) 1992–97; columnist, Reforma newspaper 2000–13; First Curator, Latin American Art Collections, Tate London 2002–08; co-f. Teratoma, group of curators, critics and anthropologists, Mexico City 2003–09; Dir 7th Int. Symposium on Contemporary Art Theory, Mexico City 2009; has taught at Center for Curatorial Studies, Bard Coll., USA; Walter Hopps Award for Curatorial Achievement 2013. *Publications include:* Graciela Iturbide 55 2001, Francis Alÿs: Cuando la fe mueve montañas/When Faith Moves Mountains 2005, Francis Alÿs 2007, Manifesta 9: The Deep of the Modern (co-ed.) 2012; essays and articles in numerous publs. *Address:* Museo Universitario Arte Contemporáneo (MUAC), Universidad Nacional Autónoma de Mexico, Insurgentes Sur 3000, Ciudad Universitaria, Coyoacán, DF 04510 Mexico (office). *Telephone:* (55) 5622-6911 (office). *E-mail:* cuauhtemoc.medina@muac.unam.mx (office). *Website:* muac.unam.mx (office).

MEDINA-MORA ICAZA, Eduardo Tomás, LLB; Mexican lawyer, judge, politician and diplomatist; *Associate Justice of the Supreme Court of Justice of the Nation;* b. 30 Jan. 1957, Mexico City; s. of Raúl Medina Mora Martin del Campo and Luisa Icaza Conrey; m. Laura Perez de Medina-Mora; three c.; ed Nat. Univ. of Mexico; fmr Asst Dir DESC, Corp. Strategic Planning Dir 1991–2000; fmr Co-ordinator of Advisers to Under-Secr. of Fisheries; fmr Head of Dept of Promotion and Market Research, Conasupo; fmr adviser to NAFTA Negotiating Team for Agric., Norms, Unfair Trading Practices, Investment and Rules of Origin; fmr legal adviser to Nat. Agric. and Fisheries Bd; fmr nat. adviser to Business Co-ordination Bd; fmr Dir Tech. Secr. Alliance for the Mexico-US Border; Gen. Dir Center for Research and Nat. Security (CISEN, civil intelligence agency) 2000–05; Sec. of State for Public Security 2005–06; Attorney-Gen. 2006–09 (resgnd); Amb. to UK 2009–12, to USA 2013–15; Assoc. Justice of the Supreme Court of Justice of the Nation 2015–; mem. and Tech. Sec., Nat. Security Cabinet; mem. Nat. Security Council; mem. Mexican Coll. of Lawyers, ABA; Orden del Mérito Civil, Reino de España; Medalla Blanca CNP España, Medalla de Honor Policía Nacional de Colombia. *Publications:* Las Pesquerías en la Zona Económica Exclusiva 1979, Uso Legítimo de la Fuerza 2008. *Address:* Suprema Corte de Justicia de la Nación, Pino Suárez No. 2, Colonia Centro, Delegación Cuauhtémoc, 06065 Mexico City, CP Mexico (office). *Telephone:* (55) 4113-1000 (office). *E-mail:* info@scjn.gob.mx (office). *Website:* www.scjn.gob.mx (office).

MEDINA QUIROGA, Cecilia, Licenciada en Ciencias Jurídicas y Sociale, DIur; Chilean jurist and academic; b. 17 Nov. 1935, Concepción; ed Univ. of Chile, Santiago, Univ. of Utrecht, Netherlands; Prof. of Int. Law of Human Rights, Faculty of Law, Univ. of Chile, Founder and Co-Dir Human Rights Centre; Visiting Prof., Harvard Law School, USA; has also taught at Lund Univ., Int. Inst. of Human Rights, Univ. of Toronto, UN Univ. for Peace, Univ. of Utrecht and in Sweden; mem. UN Human Rights Cttee 1995–2002, Chair. 1999–2000, author of General Comment 28 on the rights of men and women as set out in Article 3 of the Int. Covenant on Civil and Political Rights; Judge, Inter-American Court of Human Rights (Corte Interamericana de Derechos Humanos) 2004–09, Vice-Pres. 2007–08, Pres. 2008–09; mem. Int. Comm. of Jurists 2004–; selected by UN Human Rights Council for group of ind. experts assigned to investigate Nov. 2006 Beit Hanoun incident Dec. 2006; Commdr, Order of Orange Nassau (Netherlands); Gruber Prize for Women's Rights, Peter Gruber Foundation Int. Awards 2006. *Publications:* Nomenclature and Hierarchy: Basic Latin American Sources (co-author) 1979, Chile: La Nueva Constitución, Democracia y Derechos Humanos, Cuadernos ESIN, No. 18 1981, The Battle of Human Rights: Gross, Systematic Violations and the Inter-American System 1988, Derecho Internacional de los Derechos Humanos. Manual de Enseñanza (ed.) 1990, SIM Special No. 13, Training Course on International Human Rights Law: Selected Lectures, Peace Palace, The Hague, 16 Sept.–4 Oct. 1991 (ed.) 1992, Special Issue on The Americas, NQHR, Vol. 10, No. 2 (ed.) 1992, Constitución, Tratados y Derechos Esenciales Introducción y Selección de textos, Corporación Nacional de Reparación y Reconciliación 1994, Sistema Jurídico y Derechos Humanos. El derecho nacional y las obligaciones internacionales de Chile en materia de Derechos Humanos (co-ed.) 1996; numerous book chapters and articles in professional journals. *Address:* Centro de Derechos Humanos, Facultad de Derecho, Pio Nono 1, Santiago, Chile (office). *Telephone:* (2) 9785271 (office). *Fax:* (2) 9785366 (office). *E-mail:* diredch@derecho.uchile.cl (office). *Website:* www.derecho.uchile.cl/cdh (office).

MEDINA SÁNCHEZ, Danilo; Dominican Republic politician and head of state; *President;* b. 10 Nov. 1951, Arroyo Cano, San Juan de la Maguana; s. of Juan Pablo Medina and Amelia Sánchez; m. Cándida Montilla; three d.; ed Universidad Autónoma de Santo Domingo (UASD), INTEC; f. San Juan de la Maguana br., Frente Revolucionario Estudiantil Nacionalista, UASD; joined Partido de la Liberación Dominicana 1973, mem. Cen. Cttee 1983; elected Deputy, Nat. Congress 1986, Pres. Chamber of Deputies 1990–94; Sec. of State to the Presidency 1996–2006; unsuccessful cand. in presidential election 2000, 2006; Pres. of the Dominican Repub. 2012–. *Address:* Office of the President, Palacio Nacional, Avenida México, esq. Dr Delgado, Gazcue, Santo Domingo, Dominican Republic (office). *Telephone:* 695-8107 (office). *Fax:* 682-4558 (office). *E-mail:* info@ presidencia.gob.do (office). *Website:* www.presidencia.gob.do (office); danilomedina .do.

MEDINA VILLAVEIRÁN, Ernesto; Cuban economist and central banker; has worked in Cuban banking sector since 1977; worked on int. mission in Angola; Pres. Banco Financiero Internacional SA –2009; Pres. Banco Central de Cuba 2009–17.

MEDIU, Fatmir; Albanian politician; *President, Republican Party of Albania;* b. 21 Jan. 1967, Durrës; m. Xhuljeta Mediu; two c.; ed Faculty of Geology and Mines, Tirana Univ.; engineer Albpetrol Enterprise, Fier 1990–91; joined Republican Party 1990, Chair. Fier Dist Br. 1991–92, Deputy Chair. Albanian Republican Party 1992–97, Chair. 1997–; elected mem. Parl. 2001, Chair. Republican Parl. Group 2001–05, Chair. Parl. Comm. on Stability Pact and European Integration 2001–05, mem. Comm. for Legislation and Foreign Affairs 2001–05, mem. Del. to European Parl. 2001–05; Minister of Defence 2005–08 (resgnd), of the Environment, Forestry and Water Admin 2009–13; Pres. Building Democracy Foundation, Tirana 1998; mem. Int. Foundation, Washington DC, USA 1999, Exec. Cttee East-West Parliamentarian Practice, Amsterdam, Netherlands 2001, Parliamentarians for Global Action, New York 2002; Pres. Republican Party of Albania 1997–. *Address:* Republican Party of Albania, Abdi Toptani, Tirana, Albania (office). *E-mail:* info@prsh.al (office).

MEDOJEVIĆ, Nebojša; Montenegrin politician; *President, Movement for Changes (Pokret za Promjene—PZP);* b. 13 June 1966, Pljevlja; m.; one s. one d.; ed Faculty of Electrical Eng, Univ. of Montenegro; Founder and Pres. Students Forum-Movt for Peace 1989; Founder Montenegrin Movt against Fascism 1992; Co-founder Social-Democratic Party 1989, mem. of Presidency 1992–99; worked as Privatisation Man, Agency for Econ. Restructuring and Foreign Investments 1991–99; Leader Centre for Transition, Podgorica 1999–2002; Exec. Dir Group for Change 2002–06; Pres. and Leader Movt for Changes (Pokret za Promjene—PZP); mem. Parl. 2006–; Cand. for Pres. of Montenegro 2008. *Publications include:* Montenegrin Economy in Transition, Mass Voucher Privatisation, Public Procurements, Privatisation and Corruption, Conflict of Interests; has published more than 100 articles on problems of post-Communism transition. *Address:* Movement for Changes (Pokret za Promjene—PZP), 81000 Podgorica, bul. Ivana Crnojevica 107/1, Montenegro (office). *Telephone:* (81) 667010 (office). *E-mail:* gzpkotor@cg.yu (office); nm@nebojsamedojevic.org. *Website:* www.promjene.org (office); www.nebojsamedojevic.com.

MEDVEDCHUK, Viktor Volodymyrovich, DIur; Ukrainian politician, lawyer and business executive; *Chairman, Ukrainian Choice;* b. 7 Aug. 1954, Pochet Village, Aban Rayon, Krasnoyarsk Krai, Russian SFSR; s. of Volodymyr Nesterovych Medvedchuk and Faina Hryhorivna Hulko; m. Oksana Marchenko 1973; two d.; ed Nat. Taras Shevchenko Univ. of Kiev; lawyer, Kiev City Bar Asscn 1978–89; Head, Legal Advice Office, Shevchenko Dist, Kiev 1989–91; Pres. Union of Lawyers of Ukraine; fmr Head of the Supreme Board of Experts of the Ukrainian Bar; Pres. Int. Law Co. B.I.M. 1991–; mem. Social Democratic Party of Ukraine (SDPU) (later Social Democratic Party of Ukraine (United)—SDPU(U)) 1994–, SDPU(U) Cen. Council 1995–98, Head, SDPU Comm. on Legal Reform 1995–96, mem. SDPU(U) Politburo 1995–, Deputy Chair. SDPU(U) 1996–98, Chair. 1998–2006, mem. SDPU(U) Parl. faction 2001–; Adviser to Pres. of Ukraine on Tax Policy Issues 1996–2000; Nat. Deputy of Ukraine to 2nd Verkhovna Rada 1997, mem. Cttee on Law and Order 1997–98, Co-ordinating Council on Legal Reforms affiliated to Pres. of Ukraine 1997–2000, Supreme Econ. Council affiliated to Pres. of Ukraine, State Comm. on Admin. Reforms in Ukraine, Nat. Deputy to 3rd Verkhovna Rada 1998, Deputy Chair. Verkhovna Rada 1998–2000, mem. Supreme Legal Council, Coordinating Council on Local Self-Govt, Deputy Chair. Co-ordinating Council on Internal Affairs, First Deputy Chair. Verkhovna Rada of Ukraine 2000–01, Nat. Deputy to 4th Verkhovna Rada, Head, SDPU(U) Parl. faction May–June 2002; Head, Admin of Pres. of Ukraine 2002–04; mem. Supreme Council of Justice from 2008; currently Chair. pro-Russian Ukrainian Choice which opposes Euromaidan protests supporting closer ties between Ukraine and the EU; Head, Nat. Council on Youth Policies affiliated to Pres. of Ukraine 1999–; Head, Comm. on State Awards and Heraldry 2002–, Organizing Cttee on Conduct of the Year of Ukraine in the Russian Fed. 2002–03, Working Group for putting forward suggestions on ensuring publicity and openness in work of public authorities 2002–; Chair. Comm. for guaranteeing smooth work of int. experts checking export of Kolchuga reconnaissance radio-electronic stations 2002–, Ukraina Nat. Palace Supervisory Bd 2002–, Organizing Cttee for carrying out the Year of the Russian Fed. in Ukraine 2002–, Public Service Coordinating Cttee under Pres. of Ukraine 2003–, Organizing Cttee for commemorating the Eastern (Crimean) War of 1853–1856 2003–, Coordinating Comm. for the reconstruction of the Zhashkiv-Chervonoznamyanka section of the Kiev-Odesa motorway 2003–, Organizing Cttee for celebrating the 150th anniversary of Ivan Franko's birthday 2003–, Supervisory Bd of Nat. Acad. of Public Admin under Pres. of Ukraine 2004–; Deputy Chair. Information Policy Council under Pres. of Ukraine 2002–; Co-Chair. Coordinating Cttee for charting and publishing the Nat. Atlas of Ukraine 2002–; mem. Bd USSR Union of Lawyers from Ukraine 1990–91, Coordinating Cttee on Struggle against Corruption and Organised Crime affiliated to Pres. of Ukraine 1994–99, Council of Employers and Producers affiliated to Pres. of Ukraine 1995–2000, Nat. Council for Security and Defence of Ukraine 2002–; mem. Ukrainian Acad. of Law, Int. Slavic Acad., Acad. of Econs; Honoured Lawyer of Ukraine 1992; Hon. Award of Ukrainian Pres.– Order 'For Merit' (3rd Class) 1996, (2nd Class) 1998, Order 'For Merit' 2000, Hon. Award of Ukrainian Pres.– Order of Prince Yaroslav the Wise (5th Class) 2004, Slovak Order of the White

Cross (2nd Class) 2004. *E-mail:* info@medvedchuk.org.ua. *Website:* medvedchuk .org.ua.

MEDVEDEV, Armen Nikolayevich, Cand. of Arts; Russian film critic, film producer, journalist and civil servant; b. 28 May 1938, Moscow; m.; one d.; ed All-Union Inst. of Cinematography; mem. staff, Bureau of Propaganda of Soviet Cinema, USSR (now Russian) State Cttee on Cinematography 1959–, mem. Bd of Dirs 1984–87, First Deputy Chair. 1987–89, Chair. 1992–99; Prof., All-Union Inst. of Cinematography; Ed.-in-Chief Soviet Film magazine 1966–72; Deputy Ed.-in-Chief Iskusstvo Kino magazine 1972–75, 1976–82, Ed.-in-Chief 1982–84; Ed.-in-Chief All-Union Co. Soyuzinformkino 1975–76; Head Dept of Culture and Public Educ., USSR Council of Ministers 1989–91; fmr consultant, Govt of USSR 1991; Pres. Rolan Bykov Int. Fund of Devt of Cinema and TV for Children and Youth 1999–; Pres. 18th Int. Film Festival for Children and Young People 2001; Chair. Jury, Open Russian Film Festival, Sochi 2004; mem. Jury, XXVIth Moscow Int. Film Festival 2004; Hon. Worker of Arts; several decorations, including Order for Service to Motherland; numerous awards, including Prize "For outstanding contribution to the development of Russian cinema", Kinotaur Festival, Sochi 2008. *Film role:* Letniy dozhd 2002. *Films produced:* Velikiy polkovodets Georgiy Zhukov 1995, Brigands-Chapter VII 1996, Sreda (documentary, co-producer) 1997, Khrustalyov, mashinu! Khrustalyov, My Car!) 1998, Troe i snezhinka 2007, Vzroslaya doch, ili Test na... (co-producer) 2010. *Television role:* Krasnaya ploschad (Red Square) (mini-series) 2004. *Publications:* several books on cinema; articles and essays. *Address:* 117454 Moscow, Koshtoyanz str. 6, Apt 225, Russia. *Telephone:* (495) 133-12-19.

MEDVEDEV, Dmitrii Anatolyevich, PhD; Russian business executive, government official and fmr head of state; *Chairman of the Government;* b. 14 Sept. 1965, Leningrad (now St Petersburg), Russian SFSR, USSR; s. of Anatoly Afanasevich Medvedev and Yulia Veniaminovna Medvedeva (née Shaposhnikova); m. Svetlana Vladimirovna Linnik 1993; one s.; ed Leningrad State Univ.; Asst Prof., Leningrad State Univ. 1990–99; Adviser to Chair. Leningrad City Council and Expert Consultant, Cttee for External Relations, St Petersburg Mayor's Office 1990–95, mem. Exec. Cttee on Int. Relations 1991–95; Deputy Chief of Staff, Govt of Russian Fed. 1999–2000; Deputy Head, then First Deputy Head of Presidential Admin 2000–03, Head 2003–05; First Deputy Chair. of the Govt 2005–08; Pres. of Russian Fed. 2008–12; Chair. of the Govt 2012–; Chair. Yedinaya Rossiya (United Russia) 2012–; mem. Bd of Dirs, OAO Gazprom 2000–08, Chair. 2000–01, 2002–08, Deputy Chair. 2001–02; Order in the Name of Russia 2004. *Publications include:* two short articles on the subject of his doctoral dissertation in Russian law journals, co-author of a textbook on civil law for univs first published 1991, Questions of Russia's National Development (textbook for univs) 2007, A Commentary on the Federal Law 'On the State Civil Service of the Russian Federation' (lead co-author) 2008. *Leisure interests:* British hard rock, including Deep Purple, Black Sabbath, Pink Floyd and Led Zeppelin, swimming, jogging, chess, yoga, reading the works of Mikhail Bulgakov and the Harry Potter books of J. K. Rowling, football (follows FC Zenit St Petersburg). *Address:* Office of the Chairman of the Government, 103274 Moscow, Krasnopresnenskaya nab. 2, Russia (office). *Telephone:* (495) 205-57-35 (office). *Fax:* (495) 205-42-19 (office). *E-mail:* duty_press@aprf.gov.ru (office). *Website:* premier.gov.ru/en/events (office); er.ru (office).

MEDVEDEV, Nikolai Yakovlevich, DrSc; Russian business executive; *Managing Director, CJSC Sberbank CIB;* b. 1943; ed Moscow State Inst. of Int. Relations, Univ. of the Witwatersrand, South Africa; began career with Brunswick, Moscow 1994; Chief Geologist, Neftyanaya Kompaniya Surgutneftegas 2000–03, Chief Geologist and Deputy Dir-Gen. OJSC Surgutneftegas 2000–06, Dir 2001–06, 2008–, Chair. March–May 2006; with UBS, New York 1996–2007, Head of Int. Sales, UBS, Moscow 2007–08; Global Head of Equity Sales, JSC VTB Bank (fmrly VTB Bank) 2008–13; Man. Dir CJSC Sberbank CIB (fmrly Troika Dialog) 2013–. *Address:* CJSC Sberbank CIB, Moscow 125009, 4 Romanov per., Russia Federation (office). *Telephone:* (495) 258-05-00 (office). *Fax:* (495) 258-05-47 (office). *Website:* www.sberbank.ru (office).

MEDVEDEV, Roy Aleksandrovich, PhD; Russian historian and sociologist; b. 14 Nov. 1925, Tbilisi (now Georgia); s. of Aleksandr Romanovich Medvedev and Yulia Medvedeva (née Reiman); twin brother of Zhores Medvedev; m. Galina A. Gaidina 1956; one s.; ed Leningrad State Univ., Acad. of Pedagogical Sciences of USSR; mem. CPSU –1969, 1989–91; worker at mil. factory 1943–46; teacher of history, Ural Secondary School 1951–53; Dir of Secondary School in Leningrad region 1954–56; Deputy to Ed.-in-Chief of Publishing House of Pedagogical Literature, Moscow 1957–59; Head of Dept, Research Inst. of Vocational Educ., Acad. of Pedagogical Sciences of USSR 1960–70, Senior Scientist 1970–71; freelance author 1972–; People's Deputy of USSR, mem. Supreme Soviet of USSR 1989–91; mem. Cen. Cttee CPSU 1990–91; Co-Chair. Socialist Party of Labour 1991–2003. *Publications include:* Vocational Education in Secondary School 1960, Faut-il réhabiliter Staline? 1969, A Question of Madness (with Zhores Medvedev) 1971, Let History Judge 1972, On Socialist Democracy 1975, Qui a écrit le 'Don Paisible'? 1975, La Révolution d'octobre était-elle inéluctable? 1975, Solschenizyn und die Sowjetische Linke 1976, Khrushchev–The Years in Power (with Zhores Medvedev) 1976, Political Essays 1976, Problems in the Literary Biography of Mikhail Sholokhov 1977, Samizdat Register 1978, Philip Mironov and the Russian Civil War (with S. Starikov) 1978, The October Revolution 1979, On Stalin and Stalinism 1979, On Soviet Dissent 1980, Nikolai Bukharin–The Last Years 1980, Leninism and Western Socialism 1981, An End to Silence 1982, Khrushchev 1983, All Stalin's Men 1984, China and Superpowers 1986, L'URSS che cambia (with G. Chiesa) 1987, Time of Change (with G. Chiesa) 1990, Brezhnev: A Political Biography 1991, Gensek s Lybianki: A Political Portrait of Andropov 1993, 1917. The Russian Revolution 1997, Capitalism in Russia? 1998, The Unknown Andropov 1998, Post-Soviet Russia 2000, The Unknown Stalin (with Zhores Medvedev) 2004, Putin 2004, Solzhenitsyn and Sakharov (with Zhores Medvedev) 2004, Moscow Model of Yuri Luzhkov 2005, Putin 2007, Divided Ukraine 2007, Nursaltan Nazarbayev 2008, The Soviet Union. The Last Years 2009, Boris Yeltsyn 2010, Putin's Time 2012; and over 400 professional and general articles. *Leisure interest:* allotment gardening. *Address:* c/o Z. A. Medvedev, 4 Osborn Gardens, London, NW7 1DY, England (home); 143025

Moscow, Pos.Novo-Ivanovskoye 129, Post Box 16, P/O Nemchinovka, Odintsovky district, Russia (home). *Telephone:* (495) 597-6120 (Moscow) (home).

MEDZHITOV, Ruslan M., BSc, PhD; Uzbekistani immunologist, biochemist and academic; *Sterling Professor of Immunobiology, School of Medicine, Yale University;* b. 1996, Tashkent; m. Akiko Iwasaki 2007; two d.; ed Tashkent State Univ., Moscow Univ.; postdoctoral studies at Yale Univ. Medical School, David W. Wallace Prof. of Immunobiology 1999, Investigator, Howard Hughes Medical Inst. 2000–, currently Sterling Prof. of Immunobiology, School of Medicine; mem. NAS 2010; Dr hc (Munich); MA Privatum (Yale Univ.); selected as Searle Scholar 2000, William B. Coley Award for Distinguished Research in Basic and Tumor Immunology, Cancer Research Inst., Emil von Behring Award, AAI -BD Biosciences Investigator Award, Blavatnik Award for Young Scientists, New York Acad. of Arts and Sciences, Howard Taylor Ricketts Award, Univ. of Chicago, Lewis S. Rosenstiel Award for Distinguished Work in Basic Medical Science, Brandeis Univ. 2010, Shaw Prize in Life Science and Medicine (co-recipient) 2012, Vilcek Prize in Biomedical Science 2013. *Publications:* numerous papers in professional journals. *Address:* Department of Immunobiology, Anlyan Center for Medical Research and Education, 300 Cedar Street, PO Box 208011, New Haven, CT 06520-8011, USA (office). *Telephone:* (203) 785-7541 (office). *E-mail:* ruslan.medzhitov@yale.edu (office). *Website:* medicine.yale.edu/immuno/people/ruslan_medzhitov.profile (office).

MEECE, Roger A., BS; American diplomatist and UN official; b. 1949, Indianapolis, Ind.; ed Michigan State Univ., Nat. Defence Coll. of Canada, US Foreign Service Inst.; Peace Corps volunteer in Sierra Leone 1971, several Peace Corps staff assignments, including Assoc. Dir for Peace Corps in Niger and Cameroon, Deputy Dir for Peace Corps, Brazzaville, Repub. of the Congo, Dir Peace Corps in Gabon; joined Foreign Service 1979, served in Embassies in Cameroon and Malawi, worked in Bureau of Int. Narcotics Matters, Washington, DC, assigned to Office of Vice-Pres. of the USA 1986–88, Deputy Chief of Mission, Brazzaville, Consul-Gen., Halifax, Canada, Deputy Chief of Mission, Kinshasa 1995–98, Dir for Cen. African Affairs, State Dept 1998–2000, Amb. to Malawi 2000–03, Diplomat-in-Residence, Florida Int. Univ. 2003, served as Chargé d'affaires a.i., Embassy in Nigeria 2003, Amb. to Democratic Repub. of the Congo 2004–07, Chargé d'affaires a.i., Embassy in Ethiopia 2010 (retd); Special Rep. of the Sec.-Gen. and Head, UN Org. Stabilization Mission in the Democratic Repub. of the Congo (MONUSCO) 2010–13.

MEEKER, Mary, BA, MBA; American technical and investment analyst and author; *General Partner, Kleiner Perkins Caufield & Byers;* ed DePauw Univ., Cornell Univ.; began career as a securities analyst 1986; worked at Morgan Stanley 1991–2010, served as Man. Dir and Research Analyst; Gen. Partner, Kleiner Perkins Caufield & Byers 2011–; mem. Bd of Dirs Square, Lending Club, DocuSign, Quirky; Hon. DLitt (DePauw Univ.). *Publications include:* co-author: The Internet Report 1995, The Internet Advertising Report 1996, The Internet Retailing Report 1997, The Online Classified Advertising Report: It's About Search/Find/Obtain (SFO) 2002, The China Internet Report 2004, The Mobile Internet Report 2009, Internet Trend Report 2012, The Technology IPO Yearbooks; cr., with Liang Wu, USA, Inc. (award winning report/video about US Govt financial transactions) 2011. *Address:* Kleiner Perkins Caufield & Byers, 2750 Sand Hill Road, Menlo Park, CA 94025, USA (office). *Telephone:* (650) 233-2750 (office). *Fax:* (650) 233-0300 (office). *E-mail:* plans@kpcb.com (office). *Website:* www.kpcb.com (office).

MEESE, Edwin, III, BA, JD; American academic, lawyer and fmr government official; *Ronald Reagan Distinguished Fellow and Chairman, Center for Legal and Judicial Studies, The Heritage Foundation;* b. 1931; s. of Edwin Meese, Jr and Leone Meese; m. Ursula Meese; one s. one d.; ed Yale Univ. and Univ. of California, Berkeley; taught law at Univ. of San Diego Law School, Dir Center for Criminal Justice Policy and Man.; sr position under Gov. Reagan, State Capitol, Sacramento, Calif.; Reagan's Campaign Chief of Staff, presidential elections 1980, Dir Transition Org. 1980–81; Counsellor to Pres. Reagan and mem. Nat. Security Council, Domestic Policy Council and Cabinet 1981–85; US Attorney-Gen. 1985–88; Ronald Reagan Distinguished Fellow and Chair. Center for Legal and Judicial Studies, The Heritage Foundation, Washington 1988–; Distinguished Visiting Fellow, Hoover Inst., Stanford Univ., Calif. 1988–; mem. Iraq Study Group, US Inst. of Peace 2006; Distinguished Sr Fellow, Inst. for United States Studies, Univ. of London 1996–2003; mem. Bd of Dirs Capital Research Center, Landmark Legal Foundation, Center for the Study of the Presidency, American Prosecutors Research Inst.; retd Col US Army Reserve; Harvard Univ. John F. Kennedy School of Govt Medal 1986. *Publications:* With Reagan: The Inside Story 1992, Making America Safer (co-ed.) 1997, Leadership, Ethics and Policing (co-author) 2004. *Leisure interest:* collecting models of police patrol cars. *Address:* The Heritage Foundation, 214 Massachusetts Avenue, NE, Washington, DC 20002, USA. *Telephone:* (202) 608-6180. *Fax:* (202) 547-0641. *E-mail:* staff@heritage.org. *Website:* www.heritage.org.

MEGAWATI, Sukarnoputri; Indonesian politician and fmr head of state; *Chairman, Partai Demokrasi Indonesia Perjuangan (Indonesian Democratic Struggle Party);* b. 23 Jan. 1947, Jogjakarta; d. of Achmed Sukarno (fmr Pres. of Indonesia) and Fatmawati; m. 1st Surendro (deceased); m. 2nd Hassan Gamal Ahmad Hassan; m. 3rd Taufik Kiemas; three c.; mem. House of Reps (Partai Demokrasi Indonesia–PDI) 1987; Leader PDI 1993–96 (deposed); Chair. Partai Demokrasi Indonesia Perjuangan (PDI-P) 1996–; Vice-Pres. of Indonesia 1999–2001, Pres. 2001–04; ranked by Forbes magazine amongst 100 Most Powerful Women (eighth) 2004. *Address:* Partai Demokrasi Indonesia Perjuangan (Indonesian Democratic Struggle Party), Jalan Lenteng Agung 99, Jakarta Selatan, Indonesia (office). *Telephone:* (21) 7806028 (office). *Fax:* (21) 7814472 (office). *Website:* www.pdiperjuangan.or.id (office).

MEGHJI, Hon. Zakia Hamdan; Tanzanian teacher and politician; b. 31 Dec. 1946; ed Univ. of Dar es Salaam; secondary school teacher 1971–72; tutor at women's training cooperative and at Moshi Cooperative Coll. 1972–78; tutor, World Cooperative Coll. 1978–86; mem. Nat. Ass. 1985–; Dist Commr 1988–90; Regional Commr 1990; Exec. Sec., Dept of Econs and Social Welfare 1991; Minister of Health 1992–95, of Natural Resources and Tourism 1996–2005, of Finance 2006–08; mem. Chama Cha Mapinduzi party. *Address:* National Assembly, POB 9133, Dar es Salaam, Tanzania (office). *Telephone:* (22) 2112065 (office). *E-mail:* zmeghji@parliament.go.tz (office). *Website:* www.parliament.go.tz (office).

MÉGRET, Bruno André Alexandre, MSc; French politician and engineer; *Leader, Mouvement national républicain;* b. 4 April 1949, Paris; s. of Jacques Mégret and Colette Constantinides; m. Catherine Rascovsky 1992; two c.; ed Lycée Louis-le-Grand, Paris, Univ. of California, Berkeley, École Polytechnique, École nationale des Ponts et Chaussées; Head of Dept Nat. Devt Programme 1975–76; Dist Engineer, Eng Dept, Essonne Département 1977–79; tech. adviser, Office of Minister for Overseas Service 1979–81; Deputy Dir Infrastructure and Transport Ile-de-France Region 1981–86; Deputy, Front nat. d'Isère 1986–88, Vice-Pres. Front nat. Parl. Group 1987–98, left party Dec. 1998; Founder and Leader Mouvement nat. républicain (MNR) 1999–; mem. European Parl. 1989–99; Regional Councillor Provence-Côte d'Azur 1992–2004, Special Adviser to Mayor of Vitrolles 1997–2004; mem. and Hon. Pres. Comités d'action républicaine. *Publications include:* Demain le chêne 1982, L'Impératif du renouveau 1986, La Flamme 1990, L'Alternative nationale 1996, La Troisième voie 1997, La Nouvelle Europe 1998, Le Chagrin et l'espérance 1999, Pour que vive la France 2000, La France à l'endroit 2001, L'autre scénario 2006, Le temps du phénix 2016. *Address:* Mouvement national républicain, 78 rue de Malnoue, 93160 Noisy le Grand, France (office). *Telephone:* 9-51-45-84-93 (office). *E-mail:* presse@m-n-r.fr (office). *Website:* www.m-n-r.fr (office); www.bruno-megret.com.

MEGUID, Nagwa Abdel, PhD; Egyptian geneticist and academic; *Professor of Human Genetics, National Research Centre;* Clinical Researcher and Geneticist, Nat. Research Centre, Cairo, now Prof. of Human Genetics, also Head of Dept of Research on Children with Special Needs 2002–; Fellow, Genetics Inst., Pasadena, Calif., USA, Uppsala Univ., Sweden; mem. Regional Bio-Ethics Soc. of UNESCO, Int. Child Neurology Asscn, TWAS, Neuroinsight Foundation for Brain Research, Gender Research in Africa into ICT for Empowerment (GRACE); L'Oreal-UNESCO For Women in Science Award 2002, Prize for Scientific Excellence in Advanced Technology 2008. *Publications:* more than 100 articles and papers in scientific journals. *Address:* National Research Centre, El Buhoth Street, Dokki, Giza, 12311 Cairo, Egypt (office). *Telephone:* (2) 7617590 (office). *Fax:* (2) 3370597 (office). *E-mail:* meguid@nrc.org.eg (office). *Website:* www.nrc.sci.eg (office).

MÉHAIGNERIE, Pierre; French politician and engineer; *Mayor of Vitré;* b. 4 May 1939, Balazé, Ille-et-Vilaine; s. of Alexis Méhaignerie and Pauline Méhaignerie (née Boursier); m. Julie Harding 1965; one s. one d.; ed Lycée Saint-Louis, Paris, Ecole nationale supérieure agronomique, Rennes, Ecole nationale supérieure de sciences agronomiques appliquées, Paris; engineer, Génie Rural des Eaux et Forêts, Dept of Agric. 1965–67; tech. counsellor, Ministry of Agric. 1969–71, Ministry of Cultural Affairs 1971–73; mem. Nat. Ass. for Ille-et-Vilaine 1973–76, 1981–86, 1988–93, 1995–2012; Co. Councillor for Vitré-Est 1976–2001, elected Mayor of Vitré April 1977–; Sec. of State to Minister of Agric. 1976–77; Minister of Agric. 1977–81, of Housing, Transport and Urban Affairs 1986–88, of Justice 1993–95; Pres. Finance Comm., Nat. Ass. 1995–97, 2002–07; mem. European Parl. 1979; Vice-Pres. Union pour la démocratie française 1988–2002; Pres. Conseil Gen. d'Ille-et-Vilaine 1982–2001, Pres. Centre des démocrates sociaux 1982–94; Secrétaire général Union pour une Majorité Populaire 2004–; mem. Centre des démocrates sociaux 1968–95, Force démocrate 1995–98, Union pour la démocratie française 1998–2002, Union pour un mouvement populaire 2002–12, Union des démocrates et indépendant 2012–; Commdr du Mérite agricole. *Publications:* Aux Français qui ne veulent plus être gouvernés de haut 1995, Bretagne: désir d'avenir 1998. *Address:* Mairie de Vitré, 5 Place du Château, 35500 Vitré (office); Assemblée Nationale, 75355 Paris; 76 rue du Rachapt, 35500 Vitré, France (home). *Telephone:* (2) 99-75-07-21 (office); 1-40-63-66-17 (office). *E-mail:* pmehaign@club-internet.fr (office). *Website:* pierre-mehaignerie.fr (office).

MEHDORN, Hartmut; German transport industry executive (retd); b. 31 July 1942, Berlin; m. Hélène Mehdorn (née Vuillequez); two s. one d.; ed studied mechanical eng in Berlin; began career as operating asst, Focke Wulf Bremen (renamed Fokker GmbH) 1966, led design and production of Airbus A 300 1974, Head of Production 1978–80; mem. Exec. Cttee and Head of Production, Planning and Purchase, Airbus Industrie AG 1980–84; Man. Dir Mfg, MBB (Messerschmidt Bölkow Blohm) 1984–86, mem. Man. Bd 1986–89; Pres. German Airbus GmbH, Hamburg 1989–92; mem. Bd and Exec. Cttee Deutsche Aerospace AG (Daimler Benz Aerospace AG—DASA) 1992–95; CEO Heidelberger Druckmaschinen AG 1997–98; Chair. Man. Bd Deutsche Bahn (DB) AG 1999–2003, Chair. Man. Bd and CEO 2003–09 (resgnd); CEO Flughafen Berlin Brandenburg GmbH 2013–15; Chair. Supervisory Bd Vattenfalls Europe AG, DB Cargo AG, DB Wetz AG, DB Regio AG, DB Reise & Touristik AG; mem. Exec. Cttee SAP AG 2002; mem. Bd of Dirs RWE AG 1998–99; Dir (non-exec.) Air Berlin PLC & Co. Luftverkehrs KG 2009–13 (Head 2011–13); mem. Advisory Bd Baden-Württemberg Commerzbank AG 2000; mem. Supervisory Bd DEVK (Deutsche Eisenbahn Versicherung Lebensversicherung) AG, Lufthansa Technik AG, West LB AG; Hon. Senator, Ruprecht Karl Univ., Heidelberg 1999; Cross of Order of Merit of FRG, Commdr, Légion d'honneur; Dr hc (Moscow State Univ. of Printing Arts) 1996, (Tech. Univ. of Hamburg-Harburg) 2000.

MEHEID, Minwer al-, BS, MA, PhD; Saudi Arabian civil engineer, architect and academic; *Professor, General Manager and Fellow, Royal Al-Albeit Institute for Islamic Thought;* b. 1 May 1957, Treif; ed California State Univ., USA, Prince's Foundation for the Built Environment, Wales and Univ. of London, UK; Founder Inst. of Traditional Islamic Arts and Architecture, World Islamic Sciences & Educ. (WISE) Univ.; currently Prof., Gen. Man. and Fellow, Royal Al-Albeit Inst. for Islamic Thought; winner of int. competition to restore fire-damaged Minbar (pulpit) of Saladin 1994, managed team of 20 craftsmen from Egypt, Jordan, Indonesia and Turkey during successful restoration; numerous exhbns locally and internationally; numerous TV interviews at home and abroad; First Prize in six local and int. competitions. *Film:* assisted in the making Stairway to Heaven (documentary about reconstruction of the Minbar of Saladin in the Al-Aqsa Mosque) 2008. *Publication:* book of translated articles on sacred art. *Address:* Institute of Traditional Islamic Arts and Architecture, World Islamic Sciences & Education University (WISE), PO Box 3644, 11953 Amman, Jordan (office). *Telephone:* (6) 5539496 (office). *Fax:* (6) 5539484 (office). *E-mail:* minwer1@gmail.com (home). *Website:* www.itiaa.edu.jo (office).

MEHMET, Alper (Alp), MVO; British diplomatist (retd); *Vice-Chairman, Migration Watch UK;* b. 28 Aug. 1948, Cyprus; s. of Bekir Mehmet and Leman Mehmet (née Yussuf); m. Elaine Mehmet; two d.; Immigration Officer 1970–79, seconded to British High Comm. from the Home Office, Lagos 1979–83, transferred to FCO 1983, Asst Pvt. Sec. to Parl. Under-Sec. of State 1983–85, Second Sec., Chancery/Information, Bucharest 1986–89, Deputy Head of Mission and Consul, Reykjavík 1989–93, Parl. Clerk, FCO 1993–95, FCO Spokesman for Asia, Press Office 1995–98, First Sec. and Head of Press and Public Affairs, Bonn Jan.–Sept. 1999, First Sec. and Head of Press and Public Affairs, Berlin 1999–2003, Amb. to Iceland 2004–08 (retd); Sr Special Adviser, Iceland for Fipra International 2009–; Chair. Old Parmiterians' Soc. 2014–16; Vice-Chair. Migration Watch UK 2010–; mem. Bd of Dirs, FCO Asscn 2013–; UK Dir Aqua Omnis water co.; interviewer for Stabilisation Unit 2009–13; Chair. of Govs and Foundation Trustee, Parmiter's School; Bd mem. and Treas., City and Hackney Alcohol Service 2010–13; regular commentator in print and broadcast media on UK and non-UK radio and TV; public speaking coach and media adviser; Kt, Order of the Falcon (Iceland). *Plays and musicals:* numerous roles, including Mosca in Volpone and Captain Cat in Under Milk Wood, Fagin and Bill Sykes in Oliver and Todd in Sweeney Todd. *Achievements include:* first first-generation immigrant, mem. of HM Diplomatic Service and first Muslim to be appointed a UK Amb. *Publications:* articles for various newspapers and magazines. *Leisure interests:* football and cricket (played both, now watch), mem. Chingford Amateur Dramatic and Operatic Soc. *Address:* Tenter House, 45 Moorfields, London, EC2Y 9AE, England (office). *Telephone:* 7983-384734 (mobile) (office). *E-mail:* alp.mehmet@fipra.com (office); alp.mehmet@migrationwatchuk.com (office). *Website:* www.fipra.com (office); www.migrationwatchuk.com (office).

MEHRA, K. S.; Indian civil servant (retd); m. Vimal Mehra 1978 (divorced 2008); various positions in Admin of Andaman and Nicobar Islands, Govt of Arunachal Pradesh, Govt of Delhi; Jt Sec. Ministry of Textiles –1999; Additional Commr Municipal Corpn of Delhi 1998–2000, Commr 2008–12; Admin. Union Territory of Lakshadweep 2001–04; Prin. Sec. (Urban Devt), Delhi –2008; Chair. Lakshadweep Devt Corpn; ex-officio Insp.-Gen. of Police; Patron, Lakshadweep Sahitya Kala Acad.; mem. New Delhi Municipal Council, Commr 2008–12; Commr for Disabled People, Delhi City Govt 2012–15. *Telephone:* (11) 23312652 (home).

MEHRETU, Julie, BA, MFA; American (b. Ethiopian) artist; b. 1970, Addis Ababa; pnr Jessica Rankin; two s.; ed Kalamazoo Coll., The Rhode Island School of Design; Core Resident, Glassell School of Art, Museum of Fine Arts, Houston 1997–98; Artist-in-Residence, Studio Museum in Harlem 2001, Walker Art Center 2003; MacArthur Fellowship 2005; American Acad. in Berlin Fellowship 2007; Penny McCall Award 2001, Whitney Museum's American Art Award 2005, RISD's Alumni Award for Artistic Achievement 2006, Barnett and Annalee Newman Award 2013, Medal of Arts, US State Dept 2015. *Address:* c/o Marian Goodman Gallery, 24 West 57th Street, New York, NY 10019, USA. *Telephone:* (212) 977-7160. *Fax:* (212) 581-5187. *E-mail:* newyork@mariangoodman.com. *Website:* www.mariangoodman.com.

MEHTA, Ajai Singh (Sonny); American (b. Indian) publishing executive; *Chairman and Editor-in-Chief, Knopf Publishing Group;* b. 1942, India; m. Gita Mehta; one s.; ed Lawrence School, Sanawar, and St Catherine's Coll., Univ. of Cambridge; fmrly with Paladin, Pan and Picador Publs, UK; Pres. Alfred A. Knopf Div. of Random House (now Knopf Publishing Group), New York 1987–, Chair. and Ed.-in-Chief 2005–, mem. Exec. Bd Random House; Dr hc (Bard Coll.); Lifetime Achievement Award, Asian American Writers Workshop 2009, London Book Fair Lifetime Achievement Award in Int. Publishing 2011. *Leisure interest:* music. *Address:* Alfred A. Knopf Inc., 1745 Broadway, New York, NY 10019, USA (office). *E-mail:* knopfpublicity@randomhouse.com (office). *Website:* www.randomhouse.com/knopf (office).

MEHTA, Aman M., BA; Indian banker (retd) and business executive; *General Manager of Medical, Tata Power Co. Ltd;* b. 1946, India; m.; two c.; ed Univ. of Delhi; with Mercantile Bank Ltd 1967–69; joined Hongkong and Shanghai Banking Corpn Ltd (HSBC) 1969, roles in various depts including Operations, Credit, Br. and Area Man., Merchant Banking, Man. Corp. Planning 1985, Chair. and Chief Exec. HSBC USA Inc. 1993–95, Deputy Chair. HSBC Bank Middle East 1995–98, Gen. Man. Int. and later Exec. Dir Int. HSBC 1998, CEO 1999–2003; Gen. Man. of Medical, Tata Power Co. Ltd 1976–; Chair. HSBC Bank Malaysia Berhad 1999–2004, Dir HSBC Bank Australia, HSBC Investment Bank Asia Holdings Ltd, HSBC Holdings BV Netherlands; Man. Dir The Saudi British Bank 1988–91, Group Gen. Man. 1991–92; mem. Bd of Dirs Vedanta Resources PLC 2004–14 (Sr Ind. Dir 2013–14), Tata Consultancy Services 2004–, Jet Airways Ltd 2004–, Raffles Holdings Ltd 2004–, PCCW Ltd 2004–, Godrej Consumer Products Ltd 2006–, Cairn India Ltd 2006–, Emaar MGF Land Ltd 2007–, Max Healthcare Inst. Ltd; Dir (non-exec.), Wockhardt Ltd 2004–; mem. Bd of Govs Indian School of Business; mem. Supervisory Bd ING Group 2008–12; mem. Int. Advisory Council of INSEAD. *Address:* Tata Power Co. Ltd, Corporate Centre, Mumbai 400 009, Maharashtra, India (office). *Telephone:* (22) 66658282 (office). *Fax:* (22) 66658801 (office).

MEHTA, Goverdhan, BSc, MSc, PhD, FRS; Indian organic chemist, academic and international organization official; *National Research Professor and Eli Lilie Chair Professor, School of Chemistry, University of Hyderabad;* b. 26 June 1943, Jodhpur; ed Univ. of Poona; Hon. Prof., Jawaharlal Nehru Centre for Advanced Scientific Research, Bangalore 1990–; Vice-Chancellor Univ. of Hyderabad 1994–98, currently Nat. Research Prof. and Eli Lilie Chair Prof., School of Chem.; Prof. of Organic Chemistry and fmr Dir Indian Inst. of Science, Bangalore, CSIR Bhatnagar Fellow 2005–10; Pres. Indian Nat. Science Acad. 1999–2001; mem. Exec. Bd Int. Council for Science (ICSU) 1999–2002, Pres. 2005–08, fmr Chair. ICSU Nat. Cttee; Co-Chair. Inter-Acad. Council 2001–05; Fellow, Int. Union of Pure and Applied Chem., fmr Chair. Int. Cttee; currently mem. Bd of Dirs Piramal Group; mem. Research Advisory Panel, Inst. of Life Sciences; Foreign mem. Russian Acad. of Sciences; Fellow, Third World Acad. of Science, World Innovation Foundation; Hon. FRSC; Officier dans l'Ordre Palmes Academiques, Chevalier de la Legion d'Honneur 2004; DSc hc (Univ. of Marseilles); Humboldt Research Prize, Germany, Third World Acad. of Sciences Medal, Padma Shri 2000, Shanti Swarup Bhatnagar Prize, Trieste Prize. *Publications:* more than 370 papers in int. journals. *Address:* School of Chemistry, University of Hyderabad, Hyderabad 500 046, India (office). *Fax:* (40) 23012460 (office). *E-mail:* gmsc@uohyd.ac.in (office). *Website:* www.chemistry.uohyd.ac.in (office).

MEHTA, Adm. (retd) Sureesh; Indian naval officer (retd) and diplomatist; b. 18 Aug. 1947; m. Maria Teresa Mehta; two c.; ed Nat. Defence Acad., Defence Services Staff Coll., Wellington, Nat. Defence Coll., New Delhi; commissioned in Indian Navy 1967, joined Fleet Air Arm and flew Sea Hawk jet fighters from carrier INS Vikrant 1967, carried out instructional duties as Directing Staff in Defence Services Staff Coll., earlier appointments included command of frigate INS Beas and guided missile frigate INS Godavari, also commanded Naval Air Stations, INS Garuda, C-in-C Eastern Naval Command 2005–06, other operational Flag appointments have included Flag Officer Naval Aviation, Fleet Commdr Western Fleet during Kargil Crisis 1999, has held various staff appointments in Flag rank at New Delhi, including Asst Controller Carrier Projects, Asst Chief of Personnel (Human Resources Devt), Controller of Personnel Services, Chief of Personnel, Dir-Gen. Coast Guard, Deputy Chief of Naval Staff, Chief of Naval Staff 2006–09, Chair. Chiefs of Staff Cttee 2007–09; High Commr to New Zealand 2009–11; apptd Chair. Nat. Maritime Foundation 2012; mem. Bd of Dirs Advani Hotels and Resorts (India) Ltd 2014–; Ati Vishist Seva Medal 1997, Param Vishist Seva Medal 2005.

MEHTA, Tasneem Zakaria, BA, MA; Indian art historian, writer and art critic; *Director and Managing Trustee, Dr Bhau Daji Lad Mumbai City Museum;* d. of Rafique Zakaria and Fatma Zakaria; ed J. J. School of Art, Mumbai, Columbia Univ., USA, Univ. of Delhi; Dir and Man. Trustee, Dr Bhau Daji Lad Mumbai City Museum 2003–; Convenor (Mumbai chapter) Indian Nat. Trust for Art and Cultural Heritage, mem. Governing Council 1996–, currently Vice-Chair.; mem. Advisory Bd Nat. Gallery of Modern Art; mem. Governing Council, Salar Jung Museum, Hyderabad, Nat. Inst. of Design, Ahmedabad; mem. Cen. Advisory Bd for Museums; fmr Sr Expert Adviser to UNESCO; Gov. Mumbai Metropolitan Regional Devt Authority, Heritage Soc. 1998–2009; Chair. The Škoda Prize. *Publication:* The Artful Pose (co-author). *Address:* Dr Bhau Daji Lad Mumbai City Museum, 91 A, Rani Baug, Veer Mata Jijbai Bhonsle Udyan, Dr Baba Saheb Ambedkar Marg, Byculla East, Mumbai 400 027, India (office). *Telephone:* (22) 23731234 (office); (22) 65560394 (office). *Website:* www.bdlmuseum.org (office).

MEHTA, Ved (Parkash), MA, FRSL; American (naturalized) writer and academic; b. 21 March 1934, Lahore, British India; s. of Dr Amolak Ram and Shanti Mehta (née Mehra); m. Linn Cary 1983; two d.; ed Arkansas School for the Blind, Pomona Coll., USA, Balliol Coll., Oxford, UK, Harvard Univ., USA; staff writer, New Yorker magazine 1961–94; Visiting Scholar, Case Western Reserve 1974; Visiting Prof. of Literature, Bard Coll. 1985, 1986; Noble Foundation Visiting Coll. of Art and Cultural History, Sarah Lawrence Coll. 1988; Fellow, New York Inst. for the Humanities 1988–92; Visiting Fellow (Literature), Balliol Coll., Oxford 1988–89; Visiting Prof. of English, New York Univ. 1989–90; Rosenkranz Chair in Writing, Yale Univ. 1990–93, Lecturer in History 1990, 1991, 1992, Lecturer in English 1991–93; Assoc. Fellow, Berkeley Coll. (a constituent of Yale Coll.) 1988–89, Residential Fellow 1990–93; Arnold Bernhard Visiting Prof. of English and History, Williams Coll. 1994; Randolph Visiting Distinguished Prof. of English and History, Vassar Coll., New York 1994–96; Sr Fellow, Freedom Forum, Media Studies Center and Visiting Scholar, Columbia Univ., New York 1996–97; Fellow, Center for Advanced Study in Behavioral Sciences 1997–98; mem. Council on Foreign Relations, Usage Panel of American Heritage Dictionary 1982; Hon. Fellow, Balliol Coll. Oxford 1999–; Hon. DLtrs (Pomona Coll.) 1972, (Williams Coll.) 1986; Hon. DLitt (Bard Coll.) 1982; Hon. DUniv (Stirling, Scotland) 1988; Hon. LHD (Bowdoin) 1995; Hazen Fellow 1956–59, Harvard Prize Fellow 1959–60, Residential Fellow, Eliot House 1959–61, Guggenheim Fellow 1971–72, 1977–78, Ford Foundation Travel and Study Grantee 1971–76, and Public Policy Grantee 1979–82, MacArthur Prize Fellow 1982–87, Asscn of Indians in America Award 1978, Signet Medal, Harvard Univ. 1983, Distinguished Service Award, Asian/Pacific American Library Asscn 1986, New York City Mayor's Liberty Medal 1986, Centenary Barrows Award, Pomona Coll. 1987, New York Public Library Literary Lion Medal 1990, and Literary Lion Centennial Medal 1996, New York State Asian-American Heritage Month Award 1991, South Asian Literary Asscn Lifetime Achievement Award 2004. *Television:* writer and narrator of documentary film, Chachaji: My Poor Relation (DuPont Columbia Award for Excellence in Broadcast Journalism 1977–78) (PBS) 1978, (BBC) 1980. *Publications include:* Face to Face (Secondary Educ. Annual Book Award 1958, serial reading on BBC Light Programme 1958, dramatization on BBC Home Programme 1959) 1957, Walking the Indian Streets 1960, Fly and the Fly Bottle 1963, The New Theologian 1966, Delinquent Chacha (novel) 1967, Portrait of India 1970, John Is Easy to Please 1971, Mahatma Gandhi and His Apostles 1977, The New India 1978, Photographs of Chachaji 1980, A Family Affair: India Under Three Prime Ministers 1982, Three Stories of the Raj (fiction) 1986, Rajiv Gandhi and Rama's Kingdom 1995, A Ved Mehta Reader: The Craft of the Essay 1998; Continents of Exile (autobiography): Daddyji 1972, Mamaji 1979, Vedi 1982 (serial reading on BBC Book at Bedtime 1990), The Ledge Between the Streams 1984, Sound-Shadows of the New World 1986, The Stolen Light 1989, Up at Oxford 1993, Remembering Mr. Shawn's New Yorker 1998, All For Love 2001, Dark Harbor 2003, The Red Letters 2004, Veritas (concluding vol.) 2012, The Essential Ved Mehta 2013. *Leisure interest:* daydreaming. *Address:* 139 East 79th Street, New York, NY 10075, USA (home). *Fax:* (212) 472-7220 (home). *E-mail:* mehta.ved@gmail.com (home). *Website:* www.vedmehta.com.

MEHTA, Zubin; Indian conductor; b. 29 April 1936, Bombay; s. of Mehli Mehta and Tehmina Daruvala Mehta; m. 1st Carmen Lasky 1958 (divorced 1964); one s. one d.; m. 2nd Nancy Diane Kovack 1969; ed St Xavier's Coll., Mumbai, Vienna Acad. of Music, Austria, studied under Hans Swarowsky; first professional conducting in Belgium, Yugoslavia and UK (Liverpool); Music Dir Montreal Symphony 1961–67, Los Angeles Philharmonic Orchestra 1962–78, Conductor Emer. 2019–, New York Philharmonic Orchestra 1978–91; Music Dir Israel Philharmonic 1969–, apptd Dir for Life 1981; Music Dir Maggio Musicale, Florence 1969, 1986–, Chief Conductor 1985–; Gen. Music Dir Bavarian State Opera 1998–2006; conductor at festivals of Holland, Prague, Vienna, Salzburg and Spoleto; debut at La Scala, Milan 1969; conducts regularly with Vienna and Berlin Orchestras; conducted Vienna New Year's Concert 1990, 1995, 1998, 2007 and 2015; conducted Daniel Barenboim and Vienna Philharmonic in all-Beethoven concert, Vienna Musikverein April 2016; Pres. Annual Festival del Mediterrani in Valencia 2006–; co-f. Mehli Mehta Music Foundation, Mumbai; Hon. mem. Vienna State Opera 1997, Hon. Conductor, Vienna Philharmonic Orchestra 2001, Hon. Conductor, Munich Philharmonic Orchestra 2004, Hon. Conductor, Los Angeles Philharmonic 2006, Hon. Conductor, Teatro del Maggio Musicale Fiorentino 2006, Hon. Conductor, Bavarian State Opera 2006, Hon. mem. Bavarian State Opera 2006, Hon. mem., Gesellschaft der Musikfreunde Wien 2007, Hon. citizenship Florence and Tel-Aviv; Commendatore (Italy), Médaille d'Or Vermeil (City of Paris), Commdr, Ordre des Arts et des Lettres, Great Silver Medal of Service (Austria) 1997, Commander's Cross of Order of Merit (Germany) 2012; Dr hc (Tel-Aviv Univ., Weizmann Inst. of Science, The Hebrew Univ. of Jerusalem, Jewish Theological Seminary, Westminster Choir Coll., Princeton, Brooklyn Coll., Colgate Univ.); winner of Liverpool Int. Conducting Competition 1958, Padma Bhushan 1966, co-winner Wolf Prize 1996, Lifetime Achievement Peace and Tolerance Award, UN 1999, Padma Vibhushan 2001, Kennedy Center Honor 2006, Bridge-builder Award 2007, Dan David Prize 2007, Praemium Imperiale Award for Music, Tokyo 2008, Int. Classical Music Award for DVD Performance 2011, Tagore Award for cultural harmony 2013. *Publication:* Zubin Mehta: The Score of My Life 2009. *Leisure interest:* cricket. *Address:* c/o Natalia Ritzkowsky, Assistant to Zubin Mehta, Traubingerstr. 10 D, 82327 Tutzing, Germany (office). *Telephone:* (49) 8158906791 (office). *Fax:* (49) 8158906794 (office). *E-mail:* info@zubinmehta.net. *Website:* www.zubinmehta.net.

MEIDANI, Rexhep Qemal, DèsSc; Albanian academic and fmr head of state; *Professor, University of New York Tirana;* b. 17 Aug. 1944, Tirana; m.; two c.; ed Univs of Caen and Paris XI, France, Univ. of Tirana; scientific collaborator, C.E.N., Saclay, France 1974–96; Asst, then Lecturer, then Docent, Univ. of Tirana and Univ. of Pristina, Kosova 1966–96, Prof. of Theoretical Physics 1987–, Dean of Faculty of Natural Sciences 1988–92; Visiting Scientist and Visiting Prof., Italy, France, Germany, UK, USA, Greece etc.; mem. Socialist Party of Albania 1996–97, 2002–, Gen. Sec. 1996–97; mem. Parl. 1997; Pres. of Albania 1997–2002; currently Prof., Univ. of New York Tirana, Univ. of Marlin Barleti; Chair. Bd Albanian Centre for Human Rights 1994–96, Ed.-in-Chief Human Rights quarterly 1994–96; Co-founder Citizens of Helsinki, Democratic Albania; mem. Albanian Cttee for Understanding and Cooperation in the Balkans 1986–90; Co-Ed. Bulletin of Natural Sciences 1978–89, Ed.-in-Chief 1989–94; Co-Ed. Balkan Physics Letters 1992–96; mem. Acad. of Sciences 2003, Club of Madrid, Int. Cttee for Democracy in Cuba, Int. Raoul Wallenberg Foundation, Editorial Advisory Bd World Leaders Magazine, European Asscn of Law Students (Elsa), Albania, War Invalids' Asscn against Nazism; Hon. Amb. of Millennium Goals, Amb. for Peace, Int. Hon. Citizen, New Orleans, USA 2002; Order 'Naim Frasheri', Third Class 1981, Nat. Order Golden Star of Romania 1999, Order of King Tomislav (Croatia) 2001, Nat. Order of Merit (Grade of Companion of Honour) (Malta) 2002; Hon. PhD (Istanbul Tech. Univ.) 1998, Dr hc (Aristotle Univ. of Thessaloniki) 1998, (Sofia Univ.) 1998, Hon. DHumLitt (American Univ., Rome) 1999, (Univ. of Bridgeport, Conn.) 2001, Preside d'Onore (Università Mediterranea René Cassin, Bari) 1999, Hon. DSc (Portsmouth, UK) 2002; Prize of the Repub., Second Class 1988, Gold Medal of Merit of the City of Athens 1998, Great Cross of Salvation (Greece) 1998, Médaille du Mérite (U.P. Universelle) 1998, Honorary Medal of the Centre Democritos (Greece) 1998, F. Lux Award, Clark Univ., Worcester, Mass, USA 2000, Golden Key of the City of Worcester 2000, Golden Key of the City of Prague, Czech Repub. 2001, Jan Masaryk Medal, Univ. of Economics, Prague 2001, Medal of the Robert Schumann Foundation, Paris 2001, Chancellor's Int. Medallion of Distinction, New Orleans Univ. 2002, Golden Key of the City of New Orleans 2002, Golden Medal of Freedom (Kosovo) 2010. *Publications:* President Meidani and Kosovo 2000, The Balkans – A General Outlook. Montenegro, Bosnia, Kosovo, FYR of Macedonia, Serbia: Near-Term Challenges 2001, Dall'Indipendenza verso L'Interdipendenza dell'Integrazione 2002, Globalization, Integration and the Albanian Nation 2002, Jus Gentium 2003, Politics, Moral and State 2003, Agreement with Myself 2004, The Traps of Nation-State 2005, Politics in Vivo-in Vitro 2006, Las trampas del Estado-nacion 2007, Is It Deterministic the Quantum Theory? 2007, On Space-Time 2008, Constitution: Bilan and Perspective 2009, On the Government (I) 2009, On the Government (II, III) 2010, Battle on the Voting Right 2010; numerous scientific monographs and books and hundreds of scientific and political articles published in Albania; many articles in int. scientific publs and numerous others on political and social problems. *Address:* IDM, Rr. Shenasi Dishnica, Nr 37, PO Box 8177, Tirana (office); Bulevardi Zogu I, Pallati 57, Shkalla 1, Apt 12, Tirana, Albania (home). *Telephone:* (4) 2400241 (office); (4) 2271887 (home); (4) 2271844 (home). *Fax:* (4) 2400640 (office). *E-mail:* rmeidani@hotmail.com (home); rmeidani@gmail.com (home); info@idmalbania.org (office); rmeidani@rmeidani .info (home). *Website:* www.idmalbania.org (office).

MEIER, Beat H., PhD; Swiss chemist and academic; *Head, Department of Chemistry and Applied Sciences, Eidgenössische Technische Hochschule Zürich (ETH Zürich);* b. 1954, Solothurn; ed Eidgenössische Technische Hochschule Zürich; Post-Doctoral Researcher, Los Alamos Nat. Labs, USA 1985–87; Staff Scientist, Eidgenössische Technische Hochschule Zürich (ETH Zürich) 1987, Prof. 1998–, also Head, Dept of Chem. and Applied Sciences; Prof. of Physical Chem., Nijmegen Univ., Netherlands 1994–98; mem. Nat. Acad. of Sciences Leopoldina. *Address:* Laboratorium fur Physikalische Chemie, HCI D 225, Wolfgang-Pauli-Str. 10, 8093 Zürich, Switzerland (office). *Telephone:* (44) 632-44-01 (office). *Fax:* (1) 632-1621 (office). *E-mail:* beat.meier@nmr.phys.chem.ethz.ch (office). *Website:* www.ethz.ch (office); www.nmr.ethz.ch/~beme (office).

MEIER, Richard Alan, BArch, FAIA; American architect; b. 12 Oct. 1934, Newark, NJ; s. of Jerome Meier and Carolyn Meier (née Kaltenbacher); m. Katherine Gormley 1978 (divorced); one s. one d.; ed Cornell Univ.; with Frank Grad & Sons, NJ 1957, Davis, Brody & Wisniewski, New York 1958–59, Skidmore, Owings & Merrill 1959–60, Marcel Breuer & Assocs 1961–63; Prof. Architectural Design Cooper Union 1962–73; Prin. Architect, Richard Meier & Assocs, New York 1963–80, Richard Meier & Partners 1980–; Visiting Critic, Pratt Inst. 1960–62, 1965, Princeton 1963, Syracuse Univ. 1964; Architect American Acad. in Rome 1973–74; Visiting Prof. of Architecture, Yale Univ. 1975, 1977, Harvard 1977; Eliot Noyes Visiting Critic in Architecture 1980–81; Visiting Prof., UCLA 1987, 1988, 1990, 2000; Univ. Professorship, Cornell Univ. 2000–04, mem. Advisory Council; mem. Jerusalem Comm.; mem. Bd of Dirs American Acad. and Inst. of Arts and Sciences; mem. Bd of Trustees, Cooper-Hewitt Museum; mem. Acad. Royale des

Sciences, des lettres et des Beaux-Arts 1991; Fellow, American Acad. of Arts and Sciences; Hon. FRIBA; Dr hc (NJ Inst. of Tech.) 1987, (Universita di Napoli) 1991, (Parsons School of Deisgn) 1996, 1998, (Pratt School of Fine Arts) 1999, (Univ. of Bucharest) 2001, (NC State Univ.) 2004, (Mercy Coll.) 2004; Nat. AIA Awards: 1969, 1971, 1974, 1976, 1977, 1983–85, 1987, 1990, 1993, 2000, 2002, 2003, 2005, 2006, Regional AIA Awards: 1968, 1971, 1972, 1974, 1976, 1982, 1984–87, 1989, 1990–93, 1996–2001, 2003–05, Progressive Architecture Award 1979, 1989–91, 1996, Architectural Record Award of Excellence for House Design 1964, 1968, 1969, 1977, Nat. Inst. of Arts and Letters Award in Architecture 1972, Pritzker Architecture Prize 1984, RIBA Gold Medal 1987, Progressive Architecture Gold Medal 1997, AIA Gold Medal 1998, Praemium Imperiale 1997; Commdr des Arts et Lettres (France) 1992, Deutscher Architektur Preis 1993, 1995, AIA Twenty-Five Year Award 2000, World Architecture Award 2001, Pratt Legend Award 2004, American Acad. of Arts and Letters Gold Medal 2008, AIANY Pres.'s Award 2011, Sidney Strauss Award, New York Soc. of Architects 2011, Ellis Island Family Heritage Award 2012. *Major works include:* Smith House, Darien, Conn. 1965–67, Westbeth Artists' Housing, New York 1967–70, Saltzman House, East Hampton, New York 1967–69, House in Old Westbury, Old Westbury, New York 1969–71, Bronx Devt Center 1970–77, Douglas House, Harbor Springs, Mich. 1971–76, Shamberg House, Chappaqua, New York 1972–77, The Atheneum, New Harmony, Ind. 1975–79, Hartford Seminary, Conn. 1978–81, Museum for Decorative Art, Frankfurt am Main, Germany 1979–85, High Museum of Art, Atlanta, Ga 1980–83, Renault HQ, France 1981, Museum für Kunsthandwerk, Germany 1984, Grotta House NJ 1984–89, The Getty Center, Los Angeles, Calif. 1985–97, Museum of Contemporary Art, Barcelona, Spain 1987–95, Canal+ Headquarters, Paris, France 1988–92, Rachofsky House, Dallas, Tex. 1991–96, US Courthouse, Islip, New York 1993–2000, Sandra Day O'Connor US Courthouse, Phoenix, Ariz. 1994–2000, City Hall and Cen. Library, The Hague 1995, Neugebauer House, Naples, Fla 1995–98, Int. Center for Possibility Thinking, Garden Grove, Calif. 1996–2003, Jubilee Church, Rome, Italy 1996–2003, J. Paul Getty Center 1997, San Jose Civic Center, San Jose, Calif. 1998–2005, 173/176 Perry Street Condominiums, New York 1999–2002, 66 Restaurant, New York 2002–03, Burda Collection Museum, Baden-Baden, Germany 2001–04, Charles Street Apartments, New York 2003–06, Italcementi i.lab, Bergamo 2005–12, New York Historical Society, New York 2006, Oxfordshire Residence Oxfordshire, England 2007–17, OCT Shenzhen Clubhouse, Shenzhen 2008–12, Harumi Residential Towers Tokyo, Japan 2009–16, Gardone Residence Gardone Riviera, Italy 2010–17, Montagnola Residence Lugano, Switzerland 2011–18, CDC Xin-Yi Residential Tower Taipei, Taiwan 2012–18, Vitrvm Bogota, Colombia 2013–18, 1 Waterline Square, New York 2014–19. *Publications include:* Richard Meier Museums, Building the Getty, Richard Meier, Richard Meier Architect 1–4, American Dream: The Houses at Sagaponac, Architecture in Detail: The Getty Center, Between Nature and Culture, Building the Getty/Richard Meier, Dives in Misericordia Church Rome: Project by Richard Meier Vols 1–3, Five Architects, Getty Center Design Process, Meier/Stella – Art and Architecture, Richard Meier, Richard Meier Architect (Monacelli Press), Richard Meier in Europe, Richard Meier Sculpture: 1992–1994, Richard Meier: The Architect as Designer and Artist, Richard Meier: Barcelona Museum of Contemporary Art, Richard Meier: Building for Art, Richard Meier: Collages, Richard Meier Details, Weishaupt Forum. *Address:* Richard Meier & Partners, 475 10th Avenue, Floor 6, New York, NY 10018, USA (office). *Telephone:* (212) 967-6060 (office). *Fax:* (212) 967-3207 (office). *E-mail:* mail@richardmeier .com (office). *Website:* www.richardmeier.com (office).

MEIMARAKIS, Evangelos-Vasileios (Vangelis); Greek lawyer and politician; b. 14 Dec. 1953, Athens; m. Ioanna Kolokota; two d.; ed Athens Univ. Law School, Panteion Univ.; Founding mem. New Democracy youth group ONNED, fmr Pres.; mem. Nea Demokratia (New Democracy) 1974–; mem. Parl. (New Democracy) for Athens B 1989–, New Democracy Political Planning and Programme Sec. 2000–01, Cen. Cttee Sec. 2001–06; Deputy Minister for Culture, responsible for sports 1992–93; Minister of Nat. Defence 2006–09; Speaker of the Vouli (Parl.) 2012–14. *Address:* Vouli, Parliament Building, Leoforos Vassilissis Sofias 2, 100 21 Athens (office); Solonos 113, 106 81 Athens (office); Nea Demokratia (New Democracy), Leoforos Syngrou 340, 176 73 Kallithea, Athens, Greece; Alkaiou 57, 157 71 Athens (home). *Telephone:* (210) 3822024 (office); (210) 3822024; (210) 7798804 (home). *Fax:* (210) 3845609. *E-mail:* meimarakis@parliament.gr (office); info@ meimarakis.gr. *Website:* www.hellenicparliament.gr (office); www.meimarakis.gr.

MEIRELLES, Fernando; Brazilian film director; *Owner / Director, 02 Filmes;* b. (Fernando Ferreira Meirelles), 11 Sept. 1955, São Paulo; m. Ciça Meirelles; one s. one d.; ed Universidade de São Paulo; trained as architect; created experimental video productions at univ.; producer of TV programmes including Crig Rá, O Mundo no Ar, Ernesto Varella, TV Mix, Comédia da Vida Privada, Cidade dos Homens; Dir Rá-Tim-Bum (children's series, TV Cultura) 1989–90; Co-founder 02 Filmes Co. (largest commercial production co. in Brazil); debut as feature film dir (City of Men 1997); several awards for Rá-Tim-Bum including New York Film and TV Festival Gold Medal, Cannes Film Festival Lion and Clio Awards; over 20 other prizes. *Films include:* O Menino Maluquinho (Crazy Kid) 1997, E no Meio Passa um Trem (short film) 1998, Domesticas (Maids) 2000, Cidade de Deus (City of God) 2001, Palace II (short film) 2001, The Constant Gardener 2005, Blindness 2008, '360' 2012. *Address:* Rua Baumann 930, Vila Hamburguesa, São Paulo, SP 05318-000, Brazil (office). *Telephone:* (11) 38399410 (office). *E-mail:* liane@o2filmes .com (office). *Website:* www.o2filmes.com (office).

MEIRELLES, Henrique de Campos, BCE, MBA; Brazilian banker and politician; b. 31 Aug. 1945; m. Eva Missini; ed Univ. of São Paulo, Fed. Univ. of Rio de Janeiro and Harvard Business School, USA; Man. Dir BankBoston Leasing 1974, Vice-Pres., São Paulo 1978, Head Commercial Bank in Brazil 1980, Deputy Country Man. 1981, Pres. and Regional Man. in Brazil 1984, Pres. and COO BankBoston Corpn 1996, Pres. FleetBoston's Global and Wholesale Bank and mem. Bd of Dirs, also Office of the Chair. FleetBoston Financial 1999–2002; Fed. Dep. for Goías state 2002; Gov. Cen. Bank of Brazil 2003–10; Minister of Finance 2016–18; mem. Bd of Dirs Raytheon Corpn, New York, New England Conservatory, Inst. of Contemporary Art, Acción Int.; mem. Advisory Council Sloan School of Man., MIT, Harvard Business School Initiative on Global Corp. Governance, Boston Coll. Carroll School of Man., Center for Latin American Issues of the George Washington Univ., Brazilian-American Chamber of Commerce, New York, Adolfo Ibañez Univ., Santiago, Chile; Founding Pres. Latin American Leasing

Fed.; Chair. Emer. Brazilian Asscn of Int. Banks; Chair. Soc. for the Revitalization of the City of São Paulo, Travessia Foundation; mem. Exec. Cttee US-Brazilian Business Council, American Chamber of Commerce, São Paulo; joined Partido do Movimento Democrático Brasileiro 2009.

MEIRING, Gen. Georg Lodewyk, MSc; South African army officer; b. 18 Oct. 1939, Ladybrand; m. Anna Maria G. Brink; three s. two d.; ed Univ. of the Orange Free State; joined S African Army as a signals officer 1963, later Dir of Signals; Officer Commdg Witswatersrand Command, Johannesburg 1981–82; Chief of Army Staff, Logistics, S African Defence Force (SADF), Pretoria 1982–83; Gen. Officer Commdg SW Africa Territory Defence Forces, Windhoek 1987–89; Gen. Officer Commdg Far North, Pietersburg 1989–90; Deputy Chief, S African Army, SADF, Pretoria 1983–87, 1990–93, Chief 1993–94; Chief S African Nat. Defence Force (SANDF) 1994–98; several mil. decorations, including Order of the Star of South Africa (Gold) 1998, Order of the Cloud and Banner, Fourth Class (Taiwan), Southern Cross Decoration, Southern Cross Medal, Mil. Merit Medal. *Leisure interests:* hunting, gardening, reading, walking. *Address:* Private Bag X414, Pretoria 0001, South Africa.

MEISEL, Steven; American fashion photographer; *Principal Photographer, Vogue*; b. 1955, New York City; ed High School of Art and Design, Parsons The New School for Design; began career as Lecturer at Parsons School of Design; work for fashion designer Halston as an illustrator; worked as illustrator for Women's Wear Daily; professional photographer 1980–; currently prin. photographer for American and Italian versions of Vogue magazine and for W magazine; photographer for advertising campaigns of designers Versace, Yves Saint Laurent, Prada, Dolce & Gabbana, Valentino, Louis Vuitton, Balenciaga and Calvin Klein; credited with discovering or promoting the careers of numerous successful models, including Linda Evangelista, Naomi Campbell, Nadège du Bospertus, Christy Turlington, Kristen McMenamy, Amber Valletta, Snejana Onopka, Iris Strubegger, Lara Stone, Coco Rocha, Caroline Trentini, Liya Kebede, Karen Elson, Doutzen Kroes and Raquel Zimmerman; exhbn of photography at White Cube2 Gallery, London 2001; has contributed photos for covers of albums including two RIAA Diamond-certified albums, Madonna's Like a Virgin 1984, Mariah Carey's Daydream 1995. *Publications include:* Sex. Erotic Fantasies. Madonna (with Madonna) 1992, Stern Portfolio No. 32: Steven Meisel 2003. *Address:* c/o Jim Moffat, Art+Commerce, 531 West 25th Street, 4th Floor New York, NY 10001, USA (office); c/o Vogue, Condé Nast Publications, 4 Times Square, New York, NY 10036, USA (office). *Telephone:* (212) 206-0737 (office); (212) 286-2860 (office). *Fax:* (212) 463-7267 (office). *E-mail:* artists@artandcommerce.com (office). *Website:* www.artandcommerce.com/artists/photographers/steven-meisel (office); www .vogue.com/magazine (office).

MEJÍA DOMÍNGUEZ, Rafael Hipólito; Dominican Republic politician; b. 22 Feb. 1941; m. Rosa Gómez 1964: four c.; worked as agricultural researcher with TInstituto del Tabaco, apptd Chief Dir 1965; fmr Pres. Asociación Nacional de Profesionales Agrícolas; Minister of Agriculture 1978–82; worked with Pvt. Cos. including Rohm and Haas, Industrias Linda; Pres. of the Dominican Repub. 2000–04; mem. Revolutionary Party.

MEKASSA, Motuma, BSc, MSc; Ethiopian public servant and politician; *Minister of Defence*; b. 30 July 1965, Gendeberet; m.; ed Addis Ababa Univ., Patiala Univ., India; served in different capacities, from Jr Planning and Budgeting Expert to Sr Planning and Budgeting Expert with various public agencies in Oromia Regional State 1988–99; Head of Oromia Regional Procurement and Property Admin 2000–05; Head of Planning and Budgeting Dept, Oromia Regional State Water Resource Bureau 2005–06; Mayor, Burayu Town, Oromia Regional State 2006–08; Head of Addis Ababa City Govt Mayor's Office, also Head of Cabinet Affairs Office of City Admin 2009–12; mem. House of Reps (lower house of parl.) 2010–; Head of Oromia Regional State Water, Mining and Energy Bureau 2012–16; Minister of Water, Irrigation and Electricity 2016, Minister of Mines, Petroleum and Natural Gas 2016–18, Minister of Defence 2018–; mem. Oromo Peoples' Democratic Org. (OPDO), mem. OPDO Cen. Cttee; mem. Ethiopian People's Revolutionary Democratic Front, mem. EPRDF Council. *Address:* Ministry of Defence, PO Box 1373, Addis Ababa, Ethiopia (office). *Telephone:* (11) 5511777 (office). *Fax:* (11) 5516053 (office). *E-mail:* info@fdremod .gov.et (office). *Website:* www.fdremod.gov.et (office).

MEKSI, Aleksandër Gabriel; Albanian politician and engineer; *Leader, Pole of Freedom (Polit të Lirisë)*; b. 8 March 1939; fmr construction engineer and restorer of medieval architecture; mem. Democratic Party of Albania; Prime Minister of Albania 1992–97 (first following end of communist rule); Leader of Pole of Freedom (Polit të Lirisë—right-wing coalition between Christian Democratic Party, Movt for Nat. Devt and several asscns of landowners expropriated by the communist regime and victims of communist prosecution) 2009–. *E-mail:* info@ aleksandermeksi.com. *Website:* aleksandermeksi.com.

MEKSI, Ermelinda, DEcon, PhD; Albanian economist, academic and politician; *Deputy Co-ordinator of Economic and Environmental Activities, OSCE*; b. 1957, Tirana; ed European Univ. of Tirana, Univ. La Sapienza, Italy; mem. of Faculty, Faculty of Econs, Univ. of Tirana 1975–80; Asst Prof. of Econs, Tirana Univ. 1981–87; co-f. Socialist Party 1991; mem. Parl. (Socialist Party) 1992–2011; Minister of State for Devt and Econ. Cooperation 1997–98; Minister of Econ. Cooperation and Trade 1998–2000; Head of Albanian Parl. Del. to European Parl. 2002–03; Deputy Prime Minister and State Minister of European Integration 2003, Minister of European Integration 2003–05; chief negotiator for Albanian WTO Accession 2000, Stability Pact and Stabilization and Asscn Agreement negotiations with EC 2004–06; mem. Parl. Cttee on Economy, Finances and Privatization; Visiting Prof., La Sapienza Univ., Rome 1992–93, Univ. of Bari, Univ. of Dublin, Kosovo Univ., Univ. La Signora del Buon Consiglio, Tirana, Marin Barleti Univ., Tirana, European Univ., Tirana; del. to several int. orgs including EC, World Bank, IMF, EBRD, UNDP, WTO, European Investment Bank; Deputy Co-ordinator/Head, OSCE Econ. and Environmental Activities; mem. Supervisory Council, Bank of Albania 2011; mem. Bd of Trustees, Marin Barleti Univ. *Publications:* author of several publications and co-author of several reference books and school texts. *Address:* OSCE Secretariat, Wallnerstrasse 6, 1010 Vienna, Austria (office). *Telephone:* (1) 514-360 (office). *Fax:* (1) 514-36-6996 (office). *E-mail:* quest@osce.org (office). *Website:* www.osce.org (office).

MELAMED, Leonid A., CandSci, PhD; Russian business executive; *Deputy Chairman, AFK Sistema*; b. 1967, Moscow; ed Sechenov Moscow Medical Acad.; worked at ROSNO 1991–2006, Dir-Gen. and Chair. Man. Bd 2003–06; Chair. Expert Council on Insurance Legislation (part of Russian State Duma Cttee on Credit Orgs and Financial Markets) 2004–06; mem. Bd of Dirs Mobile TeleSystems OJSC 2006–, Pres. and CEO 2006–08; Pres. and CEO AFK Sistema 2008–11, Deputy Chair. 2011–; Chair. Russneft 2010–; mem. Bd of Dirs MTS Inc. 2006–, GSM Asscn 2008–, OJSC Rosno –2011, Bashneft Jt Stock Oil Co.; Exec. Dir Mobile Telesystems OJSC 2006–08; Chair. Expert Council in Insurance Legislation (part of Russian State Duma Cttee on Credit Orgs and Financial Markets) 2004–06; numerous awards in Russia, including being named Person of the Year in annual People of the Year project by internet holding co. Rambler 2004, Golden Salamander Russian Public Award in the insurance sector in the category of The Manager of Insurance Company. *Address:* AFK Sistema, 125009 Moscow, 13 Mokhovaya Street, Russia (office). *Telephone:* (495) 228-15-01 (office). *Fax:* (495) 629-12-52 (office). *E-mail:* chairman@sistema.ru (office). *Website:* www.sistema.ru (office); www.sistema.com (office).

MELAMID, Aleksandr; Russian artist; b. 14 July 1945, Moscow; ed Stroganov School and Acad. of Art, Vilnius; initial artistic training at Moscow Art School; originator (with Vitaliy Komar) of 'Sots-art'; mem. USSR Union of Artists, expelled for "distortion of Soviet reality and non-conformity with the principles of Socialist realism" 1972; moved to Israel 1977, to USA 1978. *Principal works include:* Young Marx 1976, Colour Writing 1972, Quotation 1972, Post Art 1973, Onward to the Victory of Communism! 1974, Factory for Producing Blue Smoke 1975, Poster Series 1980, The Bear 1982, Red Flag 1983, Composition with Missiles in Rothko 1985. *Publications include:* Turkey (Around the world program) 1957, Painting by Numbers: Komar and Melamid's Scientific Guide to Art (co-ed.) 1999, When Elephants Paint: The Quest of Two Russian Artists to Save the Elephants of Thailand 2000.

MELANDRI, Giovanna, BEcons; Italian politician and foundation executive; b. 28 Jan. 1962, New York, USA; m.; one d.; ed Univ. of Rome; mem. Camera dei Deputati (Chamber of Deputies) 1994–2012; Minister of Culture 1998–2001, for Youth and Sports 2006–08; Shadow Minister for Communication 2008–09; Head of Culture Dept, Democratic Party 2009–; mem. Nat. Secr. of Environment 1989–94, Nat. Direction of Partito Democratico della Sinistra 1991–2007 (mem. Exec. Cttee, in charge of Communication Policy 1996–98), Partito Democratico 2007; responsible for Italian edition of World Watch Magazine, WorldWatch Inst. 1986–91; Head of Int. Legambiente 1988–94; mem. Young Progressive Networks of Policy Network 2005; Pres. Fondazione MAXXI 2012–; Founder and Pres. Human Foundation 2013–; mem. Women for Expo 2014–, Cttee of Strategic Reflection 2015–; Officier, Légion d'honneur 2003; Hon. PhD (John Cabot Univ.) 2000; Architetto ad honorem, Nat. Council of Architects 2014. *Publications include:* (ed.): Ambiente Italia (annual environmental report of Legambiente) 1989–94, Italian World Watch Magazine 1986–91, Digitalia, l'ultima rivoluzione 1998, Cultura, paesaggio e turismo 2006, Come un chiodo: la moda, le ragazze, l'alimentazione 2007. *Address:* MAXXI National Museum of XXI Century Arts, Via Guido Reni, 4/A, 00196 Rome, Italy (office). *Telephone:* (06) 3225178 (office). *E-mail:* segreteria@ fondazionemaxxi.it (office). *Website:* www.fondazionemaxxi.it (office).

MELCHIOR, Torben, LLM; Danish judge; b. 19 Aug. 1940; ed Univ. of Copenhagen, Harvard Law School, USA; Sec., Ministry of Justice 1966–81, Head, Directorate of Family Law 1982–86; High Court Judge 1986–90; Justice of Supreme Court 1991, Pres. Supreme Court 2004–10; Chair. Advokatævnet 1995–2002.

MELE, Eugene J., PhD; American physicist and academic; *Christopher H. Browne Distinguished Professor of Physics, University of Pennsylvania*; ed St Joseph's Univ., Pa, Massachusetts Inst. of Tech.; Grad. Research Asst, Dept of Physics, MIT 1975–78, Postdoctoral Assoc. 1978; Assoc. Scientist, Xerox Webster Research Center, Webster, NY 1978–81; Asst Prof. of Physics, Univ. of Pennsylvania 1981–85, Assoc. Prof. of Physics 1985–89, Prof. of Physics 1989–, Assoc. Chair for Undergraduate Affairs, Dept of Physics 1998–2002, Christopher H. Browne Distinguished Prof. of Physics 2017–, mem. Cttee on Undergraduate Academic Standing 2011–; Leverhulme Distinguished Visiting Prof., Loughborough Univ., UK 2014–15; Organizer, Symposium on Weyl and Dirac Semimetals, March Meeting of the American Physical Soc., Denver, Colo 2014; Fellow, American Physical Soc. 2001; NSF Grad. Fellow 1972–75, Alfred P. Sloan Fellow 1983–87, Ira Abrams Award for Distinguished Teaching, School of Arts and Sciences, Univ. of Pennsylvania 1998, Christian R. and Mary F. Lindback Award for Distinguished Teaching, Univ. of Pennsylvania 2010, Europhysics Prize, European Physical Soc. 2010, Benjamin Franklin Medal, Franklin Inst. (co-recipient) 2015, Breakthrough Prize in Fundamental Physics (co-recipient) 2019, Frontiers of Knowledge Award in Basic Sciences, BBVA Foundation (co-recipient) 2019. *Publications:* numerous papers in professional journals on quantum electronic phenomena in condensed matter. *Address:* DRL 2N17A, David Rittenhouse Laboratory, University of Pennsylvania, 209 South 33rd Street, Philadelphia, PA 19104-6396, USA (office). *Telephone:* (215) 898-3135 (office). *Fax:* (215) 898-2010 (office). *E-mail:* mele@physics.upenn.edu (office). *Website:* www.physics .upenn.edu (office).

MÉLENCHON, Jean-Luc Antoine Pierre; French politician; *President, La France Insoumise*; b. 19 Aug. 1951, Tangiers, Morocco; ed Univ. of Franche-Comté; mem. Parti Socialiste (PS) 1976–2008; Municipal Councillor, Massy, Essonne département 1983–2001, Deputy Mayor of Massy 1983–95; Gen. Councillor, Essonne 1985–92, 1998–2004, 1998–, Vice-Pres., General Council of Essonne 1998–2001; Senator from Essonne 1986–2000, 2004–10; Minister-Del. of Vocational Educ. 2000–02; Co-f. Parti de Gauche (PG) 2008, co-Pres. 2008–14; mem. of European Parl. 2009–; co-f. La France Insoumise (Unsubmissive France) 2016; cand. in presidential election 2017; Grand officier, Argentinian Nat. Order of Merit. *Publications include:* À la conquête du chaos 1991, En quête de gauche 2007, L'ère du peuple 2014, Le hareng de Bismarck: Le poison allemand 2016, L'avenir en commun: Le programme de la France insoumise et son candidat 2016, De la vertu 2017. *Address:* La France Insoumise, BP 10031, 75462 Paris Cedex 10, France (office). *Telephone:* 1-42-81-02-92 (office). *E-mail:* contact@jlm2017.fr (office). *Website:* www.jlm2017.fr (office).

MELÉNDEZ, Florentín, MA, PhD; Salvadorean academic, international organization official and judge; *Judge, Supreme Court of Justice;* ed Nat. Univ. of El Salvador, Complutense Univ. of Madrid, Spain; worked at UN and in public and pvt. insts in El Salvador on issues related to human rights; joined Inter-American Comm. on Human Rights (IACHR—Comisión Interamericana de Derechos Humanos), OAS 2004, Pres. 2004; currently Judge, Supreme Court of Justice; Special Rapporteur for rights of persons deprived of liberty in Americas; prepared Draft Declaration of Principles on Protection of Persons Deprived of Freedom; has also been Rapporteur for Argentina, Bolivia, Mexico and Dominican Repub.; del. on several occasions to Inter-American Court of Human Rights; visiting lecturer on human rights at several univs; Freedom Award, Marcelino Pan Y Vino/MAPAVI Foundation 2007. *Publications:* numerous books and compilations on human rights. *Address:* Supreme Court of Justice, Frente a Plaza José Simeón Cañas, Centro de Gobierno, San Salvador, El Salvador (office). *Telephone:* 2271-8888 (office). *Fax:* 2271-3767 (office). *Website:* www.csj.gob.sv (home).

MELÉNDEZ RIVAS, Adm.-in-Chief Carmen Teresa; Venezuelan naval officer and government official; *Governor of Lara;* b. 3 Nov. 1961; m. Orlando Maniglia; three c.; ed Catia La Mar Naval Acad., Vargas, Escuela Naval de Venezuela, Univ. José María Vargas; Cand. Platoon Commdr, Naval School of Venezuela 1984–85, Head of Payment Man. Dept, Finance Div. of Fuerza Armada Bolivariana (Navy) 1986–87, Women's Platoon Commdr, Naval School of Venezuela 1987–88, Head of Customs Dept of Chief of Navy Supply 1988–90, Head, Office of Planning and Budget Control Supply, Navy HQ 1990–92, Dir of Admin and Services, Planning and Budget Div., Ministry of Defence 1992–95, Head of Navy Financial Control Materials Div. 1995–96, Head of Control Div. (Navy Materials) 1996–97, Chief of Procurement Div. of Gen Admin Sector, Ministry of Defence 1997–99, Chief, Expenditure Control Div., Navy Finance Div. 1999–2000, Dir-Gen, Ministry of Admin. 2000–02; Internal Man. Dir of Office of Pres. 2002–03, Nat. Treasurer 2003–07; Dir Naval Budget and Financial Programming April–Sept. 2007, Dir of Naval Org. and Human Resource Devt 2010; Minister of Office of Presidency and Govt Man. 2012–13, Minister of Defence 2013–14, of Interior Relations Justice and Peace 2014–15, apptd Minister of the Office of Presidency 2015, Deputy for State of Lara, Nat. Ass. of Venenzuela Jan.–Oct. 2016, Gov. of Lara 2017–; rank of Vice-Adm. 2007, Adm. 2012, Adm.-in-Chief 2013.

MELEŞCANU, Teodor-Viorel, PhD; Romanian jurist and politician; *Minister of Foreign Affairs;* b. 10 March 1941, Brad, Hunedoara Co.; m. Felicia Meleşcanu (died 2004); one d.; ed Moise Nicoara High School, Arad, Bucharest Univ., Univ. Inst. for Higher Int. Studies, Geneva; joined Ministry of Foreign Affairs 1966, mem. numerous dels to UN confs; Second Sec. UN, Geneva 1978–85; Sec., Ministry of Foreign Affairs, Minister of Foreign Affairs 1992–96, 10–18 Nov. 2014, 2017–, Dir, Foreign Intelligence Service 2012–14; Deputy Prime Minister; Senator (for Prahova constituency) 1996–2000; Minister of Defence 2007–08; Assoc. Prof. of Int. Law, Univ. of Bucharest 1996–; researcher, Romanian Inst. for Int. Studies 1996–; Founder and Pres. Alianţa pentru România (Alliance for Romania) 1997–2001, merged into Partidul Naţional Liberal (Nat. Liberal Party) 2001, First Vice-Pres. 2001–12 (expelled); presidential cand. 2000; mem. Asscn of Int. Law and Int. Relations (ADIRI), Int. Law Comm. (UN) (First Vice-Chair. 55th Session, Chair. 56th Session); Commdr's Cross with Star, Order of Merit of the Repub. of Poland 2013. *Publications:* Responsibility of States for the Peaceful Use of Nuclear Energy 1973, International Labour Organization Functioning and Activity, numerous studies and articles. *Leisure interests:* sports (tennis and ski), hunting and fishing. *Address:* Ministry of Foreign Affairs, 011822 Bucharest, Al. Alexandru 31, Romania (office). *Telephone:* (21) 3192108 (office). *Fax:* (21) 3196862 (office). *E-mail:* opinia_ta@mae.ro (office). *Website:* www.mae.ro (office).

MELGAR, Oscar Cabrera, BEcons, PhD; Salvadorean academic, economist and central banker; *President, Banco Central de Reserva de El Salvador;* ed Univ. of Seville, Spain, Univ. of El Salvador; fmr Prof., Univ. of Seville; Economist, Banco Central de Reserva de El Salvador (cen. bank) 1992–93, Chief Econ. Statistics Section 1998–99, Head Dept for Econ. and Financial Research 1999–2014, Pres. 2014–; Prof. of Macroeconomics, Univ. of Zulia 2012–13; Economist of the Year, Asscn of Professionals in Econ. Sciences 2015. *Address:* Banco Central de Reserva de El Salvador, Alameda Juan Pablo II, entre 15 y 17 Avda Norte, Apdo 01-106, San Salvador, El Salvador (office). *Telephone:* 2281-8000 (office). *Fax:* 2281-8011 (office). *E-mail:* info@bcr.gob.sv (office). *Website:* www.bcr.gob.sv (office); www.oscarcabreramelgar.com.

MELIANAS, Artūras, MA (Econ); Lithuanian politician; *Chairman, Liberal and Centre Union;* b. 25 June 1964, Panevėžys; s. of Joana Melianas and Teodor Melianas; m. Lina Melianas; three s.; ed Panevėžys Secondary School No. 3, Vilnius Coll., Vilnius Univ.; engineer at Vilnius Drill Plant 1985–90; Deputy Head of Social Security Div., Vilnius City Municipality 1990–97; mem. Vilnius City Municipality Council, Chair. Social Affairs Cttee 1997–2000; mem. Lithuanian Liberal Union from 1990, mem. Bd Liberal and Centre Union after consolidation of the Lithuanian Liberal, Lithuanian Centre and Modern Christian Democrats unions from 2003, Vice-Chair. Liberal and Centre Union 2009–; mem. Seimas (Parl.) 2000–04, elected in a multi-mandate electoral dist in accordance with the list of the Lithuanian Liberal and Centre Union, mem. Social Affairs and Labour Cttee (Chair. 2000–01) 2000–04; Adviser to the Mayor of Vilnius 2005; Head of Social Security Div. of Vilnius City Municipality 2005–06; Deputy Gov. Vilnius Co. 2006–08; mem. Seimas for Naujoji Vilnia electoral dist (No. 10), nominated by the Liberal and Centre Union 2008–12, mem. Social Affairs and Labour Cttee (Vice-Chair. 2008–12), mem. Comm. for Parl. Scrutiny of Operational Activities 2008–12; Minister of the Interior 2012; est. in co-operation with Vilnius foundation 'Children and World' free leasure club Debesėlis (Cloudlet) for young people in Naujininkai 1996; est. Naujininkų bendruomenė (Naujininkai Community) 2001, Day Centre in Pavilnys 2007; Co-founder and mem. Bd Dvarčionys Community 2008–; Vice-Chair. Lithuanian Red Cross 2003–04, Lithuanian Social Workers Asscn; Pres. Vilnius Capital LIONS club 2013–; mem. Viltis (Hope) Soc. *Leisure interests:* travelling, music, communication, socializing. *Address:* LiCS, Vilniaus g. 22/1, 01402 Vilnius (office); Raitininkų 8b-12, Vilnius 09232, Lithuania (home). *E-mail:* arturas.melianas@lics.lt (office). *Website:* www.lics.lt (office); www.melianas.lt.

MELINESCU, Gabriela; Romanian poet, editor, essayist and translator; b. 16 Aug. 1942, Bucharest; m. René Coeckelberghs (died 1989); ed Univ. of Philology, Bucharest; began career as Ed. Femeia and Luceafarul magazines; based in Sweden 1975–; trans. of works by Swedenborg, Strindberg, Brigitta Trotzig, Goran Sonevi; Albert Bonniers Prize 2002, Nichita Stanescu Prize 2002, Inst. of Romanian Culture Prize 2004. *Publications include:* poetry: Ceremonie de iarna 1965, Fiintele abstracte 1967, Interiorul legii 1968, Boala de origine divina 1970, Juramantul de saracie, castitate si supunere (Writers' Union Prize) 1972, Inginarea lumiir 1972, Impotriva celui drag 1975, Zeul fecunditatii 1977, Oglinda femeii 1986, Lumina spre lumina 1993; prose: Jurnal suedez Vols I–III, Bobinocarii 1969, Catargul cu doua corabii (juvenile) 1969, Viata cere viata (jtly) (non-fiction) 1975, Copiii rabdarii 1979, Lupii urca in cer 1981, Vrajitorul din Gallipoli 1986, Regina strazii 1988, Omul pasare (Swedish Acad. De Nio Prize) 1991, Hemma utomlands (novel) 2003, Mamma som Gud (novel) (Albert Bonniers Stipendiefond 2011) 2010; contrib. to Crossing Boundaries: An International Anthology of Women's Experiences in Sport 1999.

MELKERT, Adrianus (Ad) Petrus Wilhelmus, MA; Dutch politician, banker, independent adviser and UN official; *Extraordinary Councillor, Council of State, Netherlands;* b. 1956, Gouda; ed Univ. of Amsterdam; Pres., Council of European Nat. Youth Cttees 1979–81; Sec.-Gen. Youth Forum of the EC 1981–84; Pres. Nat. Cttee, UN Int. Youth Year 1984–85; Asst to Gen. Sec., Dir Internal Affairs, Netherlands Org. for Int. Devt Co-operation 1984–86; mem. Parl. 1986–94, 1998–2002; Minister of Social Affairs and Employment 1994–98; Parl. Leader Partij van de Arbeid (PvdA – Labour Party) 1998–2002, Party Leader 2001–02; Exec. Dir for the Netherlands and 11 other mem. states, World Bank (IBRD) 2002–06; Under-Sec.-Gen. and Assoc. Admin., UNDP 2006–09; UN Sec.-Gen.'s Special Rep. for Iraq and Head, UN Assistance Mission for Iraq (UNAMI) 2009–11; Special Rapporteur, Global Child Labour Conf., The Netherlands 2010; currently Extraordinary Councillor, Council of State, Netherlands; independent adviser of governments, companies and civil soc. orgs; Order of Oranje-Nassau 1998, Gran Cruz en la Orden de Bernardo O'Higgins (Chile) 1998, Das Grosse Verdienstkreuzmit Stern des Verdienstordens der Bundesrepublik Deutschland 2001. *E-mail:* adrianusmelkert@gmail.com.

MELLO, Craig Cameron, BS, PhD; American geneticist and academic; *Professor, Program in Molecular Medicine, University of Massachusetts Medical School;* b. 18 Oct. 1960, New Haven, Conn.; ed Fairfax High School, Va, Brown Univ., Harvard Univ.; Postdoctoral Fellow, Fred Hutchinson Cancer Research Center; joined faculty, Univ. of Massachusetts Medical School 1994, currently Prof. in Program in Molecular Medicine, Howard Hughes Medical Investigator 2000–; affiliated with Center for AIDS Research, Interdisciplinary Grad. Program, Cell Biology, Cancer Center, Program in Cell Dynamics; Co-founder and mem. Scientific Advisory Bd, RXi Pharmaceuticals (now Galena Biopharma); mem. Tech. Advisory Bd, Beeologics (acquired by Monsanto 2011); mem. NAS 2005; Dr hc (Brown Univ.) 2007, (Simmons Coll.) 2008; Warren Triennial Prize, Massachusetts Gen. Hosp., Wiley Prize in Biomedical Sciences (co-recipient), Rockefeller Univ. 2003, NAS Award in Molecular Biology (co-recipient) 2003, Lewis S. Rosenstiel Award for Distinguished Work in Medical Research (co-recipient), Brandeis Univ. 2005, Gairdner Foundation Int. Award 2005, Massry Prize (co-recipient) 2005, Paul Ehrlich and Ludwig Darmstaedter Prize (co-recipient) 2006, inaugural recipient Dr Paul Janssen Award for Biomedical Research, Johnson & Johnson 2006, Nobel Prize in Physiology or Medicine (co-recipient with Andrew Fire) for the discovery of RNA interference 2006, gave keynote Baccalaureate Address at Commencement Ceremonies, Brown Univ. 2007, Hope Funds Award of Excellence in Basic Research 2008. *Publications:* numerous scientific papers in professional journals. *Address:* Office ASC5-2049, Program in Molecular Medicine, University of Massachusetts, 373 Plantation Street, Worcester, MA 01605, USA (office). *Telephone:* (508) 856-1602 (office). *E-mail:* craig.mello@umassmed.edu (office). *Website:* www.umassmed.edu/pmm (office); www.hhmi.org/node/14409 (office).

MELLOR, Rt Hon. David, PC, QC, FZS; British lawyer, journalist, fmr politician and broadcaster; b. 12 March 1949, Wareham, Dorset; s. of Douglas H. Mellor; m. Judith Hall 1974 (divorced 1996); two s.; ed Swanage Grammar School, Christ's Coll., Cambridge, Inns of Court School of Law; called to the Bar (Inner Temple) 1972; apptd QC 1987; Chair. Cambridge Univ. Conservative Asscn 1970; fmr Vice-Chair. Chelsea Conservative Asscn; MP for Putney 1979–97; Parl. Under-Sec. of State, Dept of Energy 1981–83, Home Office 1983–86, Minister of State, Home Office 1986–87, FCO 1987–88; Minister for Health 1988–89; Minister of State, Home Office 1989–90; Minister for the Arts July–Nov. 1990; Chief Sec. to Treasury 1990–92; Sec. of State for Nat. Heritage April–Sept. 1992; Consultant Middle East Broadcasting Centre, Middle East Economic Digest, Abela Holdings, RACAL Tacticom, British Aerospace, Ernst & Young, G.K.N.; mem. Bd Amor Holdings, ENO 1993–95; Chair. Sports Aid Foundation 1993–97, Football Task Force 1997–99; Deputy Chair. Trustees London Philharmonic Orchestra 1989–90; presenter Six-O-Six BBC Radio 5 1993–99, The Midnight Hour, BBC 2 1997–99, Classic FM 1998–; sports columnist, Evening Standard 1997–2008; Exec. Dir Three Delta LLP 2006–; music critic, Mail on Sunday 2000–; Co-Presenter (with Ken Livingstone) Ken and David radio show, LBC 2008–16; fmr mem. Council Nat. Youth Orchestra; Special Trustee, Westminster Hosp. 1979–86; Hon. Assoc. British Veterinary Asscn (for work for animal welfare) 1986; Variety Club Award for BBC Radio Personality of the Year 1994. *Leisure interests:* classical music, football, reading. *Address:* c/o Classic FM, 30 Leicester Square, London, WC2H 7LA, England. *Website:* www.classicfm.com.

MELLOR, David Hugh, MA, MEng, MS, PhD, ScD; British philosopher and academic; *Professor Emeritus of Philosophy, University of Cambridge;* b. 10 July 1938, London; s. of S. D. Mellor and E. N. Mellor (née Hughes); ed Newcastle Royal Grammar School, Manchester Grammar School and Pembroke Coll., Cambridge; Harkness Fellowship in Chem. Eng, Univ. of Minnesota, USA 1960–62, MIT School of Chem. Eng Practice 1962; Tech. Officer, ICI 1962–63; research student in philosophy 1963–68; Fellow, Pembroke Coll., Cambridge 1964–70; Fellow, Darwin Coll., Cambridge 1971–2005, Vice-Master 1983–87; Asst Lecturer in Philosophy, Univ. of Cambridge 1965–70, Lecturer 1970–83, Reader in Metaphysics 1983–86, Prof. of Philosophy 1986–99, Prof. Emer. 1999–, Pro-Vice-Chancellor 2000–01; Visiting Fellow in Philosophy, ANU 1975; Radcliffe Fellow in Philosophy 1978–80; Visiting Prof., Auckland Univ., NZ 1985; Pres. British Soc. for the Philosophy of Science 1985–87, Aristotelian Soc. 1992–93; Fellow, British Acad. 1983–2008; Hon.

Prof. of Philosophy, Univ. of Keele 1989–92; Hon. PhD (Lund) 1997. *Publications include:* The Matter of Chance 1971, Real Time 1981, Matters of Metaphysics 1991, The Facts of Causation 1995, Real Time II 1998, Probability: A Philosophical Introduction 2005, Mind, Meaning and Reality 2012; numerous articles on philosophy of science, metaphysics and philosophy of mind. *Leisure interest:* theatre. *Address:* 25 Orchard Street, Cambridge, CB1 1JS, England (home). *Telephone:* 7815-687505 (mobile) (home). *E-mail:* dhm11@cam.ac.uk (home). *Website:* people.ds.cam.ac.uk/dhm11 (office).

MELLOR, James R., BEE, MS; American business executive and electrical engineer; *Chairman, USEC Inc.;* b. 1931; m. Suzanne Mellor; three c.; ed Univ. of Michigan; Research Engineer, then Section Man. in charge of Electronics Systems Design, Hughes Aircraft Co. 1955–58; various eng and man. positions Litton Industries, including Corpn Vice-Pres., Pres. Data Systems Div., Vice-Pres. of Business Devt, Vice-Pres. of Eng, Dir of Advanced Devt, Sr Vice-Pres. Communications and Electronics Data Systems Group 1970–73, Exec. Vice-Pres. Defense Systems Group 1973–77; Dir AM Int. Inc. 1977–81, also Pres. and COO; joined Gen. Dynamics 1981, Exec. Vice-Pres. Marine, Land Systems and Int. 1986–91, Pres. and COO 1991–93, Pres. and CEO 1993–94, Chair. and CEO 1994–97, Consultant and mem. Bd of Dirs 1997; Chair. USEC Inc. 1998–; Chair. AmerisourceBergen Corpn 2004–06 (retd); Consultant to Dept of Defense 1972–75; fmr Chair. Shipbuilders Council of America, Computer and Business Equipment Mfrs Asscn; currently mem. Nat. Advisory Cttee, Univ. of Michigan, United States–Egypt Pres.'s Council; Officer, Order of the Crown (Belgium) 1987; Business Leader Recipient, Ellis Island Medals of Honour 1998. *Achievements include:* granted three patents relating to large screen display and digital computing tech. *Address:* Office of the Chairman, USEC Inc., 6903 Rockledge Drive, Bethesda, MD 20817, USA (office). *Website:* www.usec.com (office).

MELNIZKY, Walter, DJur; Austrian judge; b. 1 Nov. 1928, Vienna; s. of Ernst Melnizky and Maria Melnizky; m. Gertrude Melnizky 1953; one s.; ed Univ. of Vienna; judge 1954–57, 1962–69; Public Prosecutor 1957–62; Gen. Prosecutor 1969–86; Pres. Supreme Court 1987–93; Chair. Court of Arbitration Gen. Medical Council of Vienna from 1995; Pres. Austrian Automobile and Motorcycle Touring Club (ÖAMTC) 1981–2001; consultant, Syndicus Asscn of Public Experts 1988–; Komturkreuz des Landes Niederösterreich und Burgenlandes, Grosses Goldenes Ehrenzeichen am Bande (Austria), Grosses Verdienstkreuz mit Stern und Schulterband (Germany); received 'Der große Verein. Festschrift Walter Melnizky zum 85. Geburtstag' publ. on the occasion of his 85th birthday 2013. *Publications:* Österreichischer Juristentag (7.): Referate und Diskussionsbeiträge zu Zipf, Allgemeine Grundsätze des Strafgesetzbuches und die Rechtsprechung: TEILBD II/2 (co-author) 1980, Strafrecht, Strafprozessrecht und Kriminologie: Festschrift für Franz Pallin Zum 80. Geburtstag (co-author) 1989; numerous juridical essays, especially on traffic law and criminal law. *Leisure interests:* classical music, opera. *Address:* c/o ÖAMTC, Schubertring 1–3, 1010 Vienna; Hannplatz 4/14, 1190 Vienna, Austria (home). *Telephone:* (1) 711-99-702; (1) 368-73-74 (home). *Fax:* (1) 368-73-74 (home).

MELROSE, Donald Blair, DPhil, FAA; Australian physicist and academic; *Professor Emeritus, University of Sydney;* b. 13 Sept. 1940, Hobart, Tasmania; s. of Andrew B. Melrose and Isla L. Luff; m. Sara C. Knabe 1969; one s. one d.; ed N Sydney Boys' High School, John Curtin High School, Fremantle, Univs of Western Australia and Tasmania, Univ. of Oxford, UK; Research Fellow, Univ. of Sussex, UK 1965–66; Research Assoc., Belfer Grad. School of Science, Yeshiva Univ., New York, USA 1966–68; Research Fellow, Center for Theoretical Physics, Univ. of Maryland, USA 1968–69; Sr Lecturer in Theoretical Physics, ANU 1969–72, Reader 1972–79; Prof. of Theoretical Physics, Univ. of Sydney 1979–15, Prof. Emer. 2015–, Dir Research Centre for Theoretical Astrophysics 1991–99, Head of School 2001–02, Prof. of the Univ. 2000–; Australian Research Council Professorial Research Fellow 2003–07; Rhodes Scholar for Tasmania 1962, Pawsey Medal, Australian Acad. of Science 1974, Walter Boas Medal, Australian Inst. of Physics 1986, Thomas Ranken Lyle Medal, Australian Acad. of Science 1987, Harrie Massey Medal and Prize, Inst. of Physics 1998. *Publications:* Plasma Physics (two vols) 1980, Instabilities in Space and Laboratory Plasmas 1986, Electromagnetic Processes in Dispersive Media (with R. C. McPhedran) 1991, Plasma Astrophysics (with J. G. Kirk and E. R. Priest) 1994, Quantum Plasmadynamics 2008; more than 300 papers in scientific journals. *Leisure interests:* jogging, surfing, walking. *Address:* School of Physics, University of Sydney, Sydney, NSW 2006 (office); 8/84 Milray Avenue, Wollstonecraft, NSW 2065, Australia (home). *Telephone:* (2) 9351-4234 (office); (2) 9438-3635 (home). *Fax:* (2) 9351-7726 (office); (2) 9351-7726 (office). *E-mail:* donald.melrose@sydney.edu.au (office). *Website:* www.physics .usyd.edu.au/~melrose (office).

MELROY, Col (retd) Pamela Ann, MSc; American astronaut and air force officer (retd); *Deputy Director, Tactical Technology Office, Defense Advanced Research Projects Agency (DARPA);* b. 17 Sept. 1961, Palo Alto, Calif.; d. of David Melroy and Helen Melroy; m. Douglas W. Hollett; ed Wellesley Coll., Massachusetts Inst. of Tech.; participated in US Air Force ROTC program 1983; Undergraduate Pilot Training, Reese Air Force Base, Tex. 1985; flew KC-10 as Copilot, Aircraft Commdr and Instructor Pilot, Barksdale Air Force Base, La 1985–91; attended Air Force Test Pilot School, Edwards Air Force Base, Calif. 1991; Test Pilot, C-17 Combined Test Force 1991–94; logged over 5,000 hours in flight time in over 45 different aircraft; Astronaut Cand., NASA 1994; Shuttle Pilot training, Johnson Space Center 1995–96, has since served on Columbia Reconstruction Team, CAPCOM duties at mission control, as Pilot on STS-92 Discovery 2000, STS-112 Atlantis 2002, as Commdr STS-120 2007; logged over 38 days in space; Deputy Dir Orion Space Exploration Initiatives, Lockheed Martin Corpn 2009–11; Technical Advisor to the Assoc. Admin. and Dir of Field Operations, Office of Commercial Space Transportation, Federal Aviation Admin 2011–13, acting Deputy Assoc. Admin. 2013; Deputy Dir Tactical Technology Office, Defense Advanced Research Projects Agency (DARPA) 2013–; mem. Soc. of Experimental Test Pilots, Order of Daedalians, 99s (Int. Org. of Women Pilots); Air Force Meritorious Service Medal, First Oak Leaf Cluster; Air Medal, First Oak Leaf Cluster; Aerial Achievement Medal, First Oak Leaf Cluster; Expeditionary Medal, First Oak Leaf Cluster. *Address:* Defense Advanced Research Projects Agency, 675 North Randolph Street, Arlington, VA 22203-2114, USA (office). *Telephone:* (703)

526-6630 (office). *E-mail:* pamela.melroy@darpa.mil (office). *Website:* www.darpa .mil/Our_Work/TTO (office).

MELVILLE-ROSS, Sir Timothy David, Kt, CBE, FCIS, FIOB, FRSA, CIMgt; British business executive; b. 3 Oct. 1944, Westward Ho, Devon; s. of Antony Melville-Ross and Anne Fane; m. Camilla Probert 1967; two s. one d.; ed Uppingham School and Portsmouth Coll. of Tech.; BP 1963–73; Rowe Swann & Co. (stockbrokers) 1973–74; Nationwide Bldg Soc. 1974–94, Dir and Chief Exec. 1985–94; Dir Monument Oil & Gas PLC 1992–99; Dir-Gen. Inst. of Dirs 1994–99; Deputy Chair. Monument Oil and Gas PLC 1997–99; Dir Bovis Homes Ltd 1997–2008 (Chair. 2005–08), DTZ Holdings PLC (Chair. 2000–11), Equity Trust SARL 2003–05; Chair. Investors in People UK 1999–2006; Chair. Supervisory Bd Bank Insinger de Beaufort NV 2000–05; Deputy Chair. Royal London Mutual Insurance 2003–05, Chair. 2006–13; Chair. Manganese Bronze PLC 2003–13; Chair. Higher Educ. Funding Council 2008–; mem. Bd of Dirs, Equity Trust SARL, Octopus Ventures Ltd. *Leisure interests:* reading, music, bridge, sport, the countryside. *Address:* Little Bevills, Bures, Suffolk, CO8 5JN, England (home). *Telephone:* (1787) 227424 (home). *Fax:* (20) 7643-6062 (home).

MEMBE, Bernard Kamillius, MA; Tanzanian politician; b. 9 Nov. 1953; ed Univ. of Dar es Salaam and The John Hopkins Univ., USA; Nat. Security Analyst, Office of the Pres. 1977–90; Ambassadorial Adviser, Ministry of Foreign Affairs 1992–2000; mem. Parl. (Chama Cha Mapinduzi Party—CCM) for Mtama 2000–; Deputy Minister of Home Affairs Jan.–Oct. 2006, of Energy and Minerals 2006–07; Minister of Foreign Affairs and Int. Co-operation 2007–15.

MEMMI, Albert; French writer; b. 15 Dec. 1920, Tunis; s. of François Memmi and Marguerite née Sarfati; m. Germaine Dubach 1946; three c.; ed Lycée Carnot, Tunis, Univ. of Algiers and Univ. de Paris à la Sorbonne; Teacher, Lycée Carnot, Tunis 1953, Teacher of Philosophy, Tunis 1955; Dir Psychological Centre, Tunis 1953–57; moved to France 1956; attached to Centre Nat. de la Recherche Scientifique (CNRS) 1957, Researcher, CNRS, Paris 1959–; Chargé de conférences, Ecole pratique des hautes études 1958, Asst Prof. 1959–66, Prof. 1966–70; Prof., Inst. de Psychanalyse, Paris 1968–; Prof., Univ. of Paris 1970–, Dir, Social Sciences Dept 1973–76, Dir, Anthropological Lab.; mem. Acad. des Sciences d'Outre-mer; Vice-Pres., Pen-Club 1976–79; Managing Agent, Syndicat des Écrivains de Langue Française (SELF) 1981; Vice-Pres., Comité Nat. Laïcité-République 1991; mem. Comité de patronage du MRAP; mem. Ligue Internationale Contre le Racisme et l'Anti-sémitisme (LICRA); Scientific Cttee mem. Cahiers Francophones d'Europe Centre-Orientale 1996; Cttee mem. sponsoring Asscn des Anciens Elèves du Lycée Carnot de Tunis 1996; Advisory mem., Institut des Études Transrégionales du Centre d'Études, Int. Study Centre, Princeton Univ. 1995; mem. Acad. des Sciences d'Outremer, Accad. Internazionale, Acad. de la Méditerranée; Hon. Prof., Walker Aims Univ., Washington Univ., École des Hautes Études Commerciales, Hon. Cttee mem. l'Union Rationaliste, Comité Culturel Tunisien en France 1995, Hon. mem. Asscn des Etudes Françaises en Afrique Australe 1996; Officier, Légion d'honneur, Commdr, Ordre de Nichan Iftikhar, Officier des Palmes académiques, des Arts et des Lettres, Ordre de la République Tunisienne, Chevalier des affaires culturelles du Burkina Faso; Dr hc (Ben Gurion) 1999, (Beer Schéba); Prix de Carthage 1953, Prix Fénéon 1953, Prix Simba 1978, Prix de l'Union Rationaliste 1994, Grand Prix Littéraire de l'Afrique du Nord, Grand Prix Littéraire du Maghreb 1995, Prix littéraire Tunisie-France 1999, Chalom du Crif 2000, Grand Prix de la ville de Bari 2000, Prix de l'Afrique méditeranéenne 2002, Prix de la Fondation Ignacio Silone 2003, Grand Prix de la Francophonie décerné par l'Acad. française 2004. *Publications include:* novels: Le Statue de Sel (trans. as The Pillar of Salt) 1953, Strangers 1955, Agar 1955, Le Scorpion 1969, Le Désert 1977, Le Pharaon 1988; poems: Le Mirliton du ciel 1990; short stories: Le nomade immobile 2000, Térésa et autre femmes 2004; non-fiction: Portrait du colonisé 1957, Portrait d'un Juif 1962, Anthologie des écrivains Maghrebins 1964, 1969, Anthologie des écrivains nord-africains 1965, Les français et le racisme 1965, The Liberation of the Jew 1966, Dominated Man 1968, Decolonisation 1970, Juifs et Arabes 1974, Entretien 1975, La terre intérieure 1976, La dependance 1979, Le racisme 1982, Ce que je crois 1984, Les écrivains francophones du Maghreb 1985, L'Écriture colorée 1986, Testament insolent 1990, Bonheurs 1992, A contre-courants 1993, Ah, quel bonheur 1995, Le Juif et l'autre 1995, L'Exercice du bonheur 1996, Le Buveur et l'amoureux 1996, Feu sur 40 idées recues 1999, Dictionnaire à l'usage des incrédules 2002, Portrait du décolonisé, arabo-musulman et de quelques autres 2004; contrib. to Le onde 1989–94, Le Figaro 1995, New York Times, L'Action. *Leisure interest:* writing. *Address:* 5 rue Saint Merri, 75004 Paris, France. *Telephone:* 1-40-29-08-31. *Fax:* 1-42-74-25-22. *E-mail:* albert.memmi@ yahoo.fr.

MEN, Mikhail Aleksandrovich, CandSci; Russian politician; *Auditor, Accounts Chamber of the Russian Federation;* b. 12 Nov. 1960, Semkhoz, Moscow Region; s. of Aleksander Men; m.; six c.; ed Moscow Gubkin Inst. of Gas and Oil, Moscow State Inst. of Culture; Russian Acad. of State Service; fmr stage dir, amateur theatre and clubs of Moscow 1983–91; bass guitarist and singer for rock band Most 1986; mem. Moscow Region Duma 1993–95; mem. State Duma (Parl.) 1995–99; Deputy Chair. Cttee on Culture 1995–2005; Chair. All-Union Christian Union 1996–; Chair. Aleksander Men Foundation; Vice-Gov. Moscow Region 2000–02 (resgnd); Deputy Mayor of Moscow 2002–05; Gov. of Ivanovo Oblast 2005–13; Minister of Construction Industry, Housing and Utilities 2013–18; Auditor, Accounts Chamber of the Russian Fed. 2018–; Order of Honour, Order of Friendship, Order of Holy Prince Daniel of Moscow, Third Grade, Order of St Sergius of Radonezh, Second and Third Grade. *Publication:* Culture and Religion 2001. *Leisure interests:* music, sport. *Address:* Accounts Chamber of the Russian Federation, 119991 Moscow, Zubovskaya street, 2, Russia (office). *Website:* www .ach.gov.ru (office).

MENA KEYMER, Carlos Eduardo; Chilean lawyer, academic and fmr diplomatist; m.; two c.; fmr Under-Sec. of Navy; Amb. to Brazil 2000–03; apptd Vice-Pres. Ejecutivo del Comité de Inversiones Extranjeras (Exec. Cttee on Foreign Investments) 2006; Pres. Empresa Portuaria Arica (cargo handling co.).

MENAGARISHVILI, Irakli; Georgian politician; *Director, Strategic Research Centre, Tbilisi;* b. 18 May 1951, Tbilisi; s. of Afinogen Menagarishvili and Ekaterine Jorbenadze; m. Manana Mikaberidze 1975; two s.; ed Tbilisi State Inst. of Medicine; leader Comsomol Orgs 1976–80; head of City Public Health Dept

1980–82; First Deputy Minister of Public Health 1982–86, Minister 1986–91, 1992–93; Dir Georgian Cen. of Strategic Studies; Co-ordinator of Humanitarian Aid of State Council of Georgia 1991–92; Deputy Prime Minister 1993–95; Minister of Foreign Affairs 1995–2003; Dir Strategic Research Centre, Tbilisi 2004–; Presidential Order of Excellence. *Address:* Strategic Research Center, 6 V. Beridze Street, 380008 Tbilisi, Georgia (office). *Telephone:* (32) 223-09-65 (office). *E-mail:* i.menagari@yahoo.com (office).

MENARD, John R., Jr, BA; American entrepreneur and retail executive; *President and CEO, Menards Inc.;* b. 22 Jan. 1940, Eau Claire, Wis.; m. 1st (divorced); six c.; m. 2nd Paula Menard (divorced); m. 3rd Fay Obiad 2008; ed Eau Claire Regis High School, Univ. of Wisconsin-Eau Claire; opened his first home-improvement store in 1972; Founder, Pres. and CEO Menards Inc. 1972–, owns over 280 stores in the Mid-West; mem. Bd of Dirs Polaris Industries Partners LP 2001–; fmr IndyCar racing team owner; sponsors Menards Racing team, won Indy Racing League championships 1997, 1999; partner with NASCAR owner and driver Robby Gordon in Robby Gordon Motorsports; also owns an engine shop in UK that produced engines for Team Menard and Robby Gordon Motorsports; also owns thoroughbred horses. *Address:* Menards Inc., 4777 Menard Drive, Eau Claire, WI 54703-9604, USA (office). *Telephone:* (715) 876-5911 (office). *Fax:* (715) 876-2868 (office). *Website:* www.menards.com (office); www.menardsracing.com.

MENCHÚ TUM, Rigoberta; Guatemalan human rights activist; b. 9 Jan. 1959, Laj Chimel, El Quiché Prov.; d. of Vicente Menchu and Juana Menchu; m. Angél Canil 1995; one c.; belongs to K'iche' ethnic group; began campaigning for rights of Indians as a teenager; fled to Mexico after parents and brother were killed by security forces 1980; co-ordinated protests in San Marcos against 500th anniversary of arrival of Columbus in Americas 1992; f. Rigoberta Menchú Tum Foundation, Guatemala City; UNESCO Goodwill Amb. 1996–; Founding mem. Nobel Women's Initiative 2006; unsuccessful cand. in presidential election 2007, 2011; Pres. UN Indigenous Initiative for Peace 1999; Commdr, Légion d'honneur 1996; numerous hon. degrees; Nobel Peace Prize 1992. *Publications:* I, Rigoberta (trans. into 12 languages) 1983, Rigoberta: Grandchild of the Mayas (co-author) 1998. *Address:* Fundacion Rigoberta Menchú Tum, Avenida Simeón Cañas 4-04 Zona 2, Ciudad de Guatemala, Guatemala (office). *Telephone:* 2230-2431 (office). *Fax:* 2221-3999 (office). *E-mail:* guatemala@frmt.org (office). *Website:* www.frmt.org (office).

MENDES, Gino; Guinea-Bissau politician; Sec. of Treasury and Fiscal Affairs –2013, Minister of Finance 2013–15.

MENDES, Jorge Paulo Agostinho; Portuguese football agent; *Principal, GestiFute;* b. 7 Jan. 1966, Lisbon; m. Sandra Barbosa; one s. two d.; began career as football player, but gave up after being turned down by several professional clubs; fmr nightclub owner; f. GestiFute (football management co.) 1996, clients include Diego Costa, Yacine Brahimi, José Mourinho, Luiz Felipe Scolari, Carlos Queiroz, Simão Sabrosa, Anderson, Fábio Coentrão, Pepe, Ángel Di María, Cristiano Ronaldo, Radamel Falcao, Ricardo Carvalho, Nani, Ricardo Quaresma, Burak Yılmaz, João Moutinho, James Rodríguez, David de Gea and Víctor Valdés; adviser to Quality Sports Investment (sports fund); collaborates with American agency Creative Artists Agency; Colar de Honra ao Mérito Desportivo (Govt of Portugal) 2012; named Best Agent in Globe Soccer Awards 2010, 2011, 2012, 2013, 2014, 2015. *Address:* GestiFute, Alameda dos Oceanos, Espace Building, Lot 1.06.1.4, Office 3:18, 1990–207 Lisbon, Portugal (office). *Telephone:* (21) 898-7070 (office). *Fax:* (21) 898-7079 (office). *E-mail:* gestifute@gestifute.com (office). *Website:* gestifute.com (office).

MENDES, Sam, CBE; British theatre director and film director; b. 1 Aug. 1965; s. of Valerie Mendes and Peter Mendes; m. 1st Kate Winslet (q.v.) 2003 (divorced 2011); one s.; m. 2nd Alison Balsom 2017; one c.; ed Magdalen Coll. School, Oxford and Peterhouse, Cambridge; fmr artistic Dir Minerva Studio Theatre, Chichester; Artistic Dir Donmar Warehouse 1992–2002; Co-Dir The Bridge Project (theatre Co. est. with Kevin Spacey at Old Vic Theatre, London and Brooklyn Acad. of Music, NY) 2007–; Critics' Circle Award 1989, 1993, 1996, Olivier Award for Best Dir 1996, Tony Award 1998, LA Critics' Award, Broadcast Critcs' Award, Toronto People's Choice Award, Golden Globe Award (all 1999), Shakespeare Prize, Directors' Guild of Great Britain lifetime achievement award 2005. *Films include:* American Beauty (Acad. Award for Best Dir, Best Film 2000, Golden Globe Award for Best Dir, Dirs Guild of America Award for Best Dir) 1999, Road to Perdition 2002, Jarhead 2005, Revolutionary Road 2008, Away We Go 2009, Skyfall (Jupiter Award for Best Int. Film 2012, Empire Award for Best Dir 2012) 2012, Penny Dreadful 2014 (exec. producer), Spectre 2015. *Plays directed include:* London Assurance (Chichester), The Cherry Orchard (London), Kean (Old Vic, London), The Plough and the Stars (Young Vic, London) 1991, Troilus and Cressida (RSC) 1991, The Alchemist (RSC) 1991, Richard III (RSC) 1992, (Old Vic) 2011, (Brooklyn Acad. of Music) 2012, The Tempest (RSC) 1993, (Brooklyn Acad. of Music) 2010; Nat. Theatre debut with The Sea 1991, The Rise and Fall of Little Voice (Nat. and Aldwych) 1992, The Birthday Party 1994, Othello (also world tour); Assassins, Translations, Cabaret, Glengarry Glen Ross, The Glass Menagerie, Company, Habeas Corpus, The Front Page, The Blue Room, To the Green Fields Beyond (all at Donmar Warehouse) 1992–2000; Uncle Vanya and Twelfth Night (Donmar Warehouse, Olivier Award for Best Dir 2003, Olivier Special Award 2003) 2002, Oliver! (London Palladium), Cabaret, The Blue Room (Broadway, NY), The Vertical Hour (Broadway) 2006, As You Like It (Brooklyn Acad. of Music) 2010, Charlie and the Chocolate Factory (Theatre Royal, Drury Lane) 2013, King Lear (Royal Nat. Theatre) 2014, The Ferryman (Royal Court Theatre) 2017. *Leisure interest:* cricket. *Address:* Creative Artists Agency, 2000 Avenue of the Stars, Los Angeles, CA 90067, USA (office). *Telephone:* (424) 288-2000 (office). *Fax:* (424) 288-2900 (office). *Website:* www.caa.com (office).

MENDES, Sérgio; Brazilian singer and songwriter; b. 11 Feb. 1941, Niterói; s. of Benedicto Mendes; m. Gracinha Leporace; ed Music Conservatory of Niterói; pioneered Bossa Nova movt in Brazil with Antonio Carlos Jobim, João Gilberto and Moacyr Santos; f. Bossa Rio Sextet in 1958, toured Brazil, Europe, Middle East and Japan; Bossa Nova Festival, New York 1962; moved to Calif., USA 1964; f. Brasil 64 band, toured USA, tour with Frank Sinatra 1967, tour of Japan 1968, Europe 1980; recorded albums with Black Eyed Peas 2006, 2008; continues to tour around the world. *Recordings include:* over 40 albums including Brasileiro (Grammy Award for Best World Music Album 1992) 1992, Timeless (Latin Grammy Award for Best Brazilian Pop Album 2006) 2006, Encanto 2008, Bom Tempo (Latin Grammy Award for Best Brazilian Contemporary Pop Album) 2010, Magic 2014. *Address:* c/o Concord Music Group, Inc., 23307 Commerce Park Road, Cleveland, OH 44122 USA (office). *E-mail:* press@concordmusicgroup.com (office). *Website:* www.concordmusicgroup.com (office); www.sergiomendesmusic.com.

MENDES CABEÇADAS, Adm. José Manuel; Portuguese naval officer; b. 1943, Lisbon; m. Sibylle Ninette; two s. one d.; ed Naval Acad., Portuguese Naval War Coll.; began career in Portuguese Navy 1961; several sea duty tours with various ships, Commdr NRP Quanza and NRP Oliveira e Carmo; held positions successively as Dir Communication Centre, Lake Niassa and Ministry of Defence, Dir Naval Radio Station, Metangula, Mozambique, Staff Officer Personnel and Org. Div., Staff Officer Intelligence Div., Naval Command, Head of 1st Section Directorate of Personnel, Teacher of Man. Portuguese Naval War Coll.; assigned to Mil. Rep. to NATO, Brussels 1984, later Exec. Asst Iberian Atlantic Area, NATO HQ; Exec. Asst to Chief of Naval Command 1996–2000; Dir of Portuguese Naval War Coll. 2000–02; Chief of Naval Staff May–Nov. 2000; Chief of Defence 2002–06; apptd Vice Adm. 2000, Adm. 2002; Grand Officier Ordem Militar de Avis; Distinguished Service Gold Medal, 2 Distinguished Service Silver Medals, Mil. Merit Medals 1st, 2nd and 3rd Class, 2 Navy Cross Medals 2nd Class.

MENDES DA ROCHA, Paulo; Brazilian architect; b. 25 Oct. 1928, Vitória; ed Faculty of Architecture and Urban Planning, Mackenzie Univ., São Paulo; started pvt. practice 1955; Prof. Faculty of Architecture and Urban Planning, Univ. of São Paulo 1959–98; won nat. competition to design part of Paulistano Athletic Club in Sao Paulo; fmr Pres. Brazilian Inst. of Architects; Mies van der Rohe Award for Latin American Architecture, Barcelona, 2000, Pritzker Prize 2006. *Major works include:* Club Atletico Paulistano, Pinacoteca of São Paulo restoration project, Museu Brasileiro de Escultura (MuBE) project, Cultural Center FIESP, Pinacoteca de São Paulo, Poupatempo Itaquera, Urban Bus Terminal Parque D. Pedro II. *Publications include:* Paulo Mendes da Rocha: Projects 1967/2006 (with Rosa Artigas) 2007.

MENDEZ, Nestor Enrique, MA; Belizean diplomatist; *Assistant Secretary-General, Organization of American States;* m. Elvira R. Mendez; ed Eliot School of Int. Affairs at George Washington Univ., USA; Counsellor, High Comm. in London 1997–99, Minister Counsellor/Deputy Chief of Mission, Embassy in Washington, DC –2007, Chargé d'affaires a.i. 2007–08, Amb. to USA and Perm. Rep. to OAS, Washington, DC 2008–15, Asst Sec.-Gen., OAS 2015–. *Address:* Organization of American States, 17th Street and Constitution Avenue, NW, Washington, DC 20006-4499, USA (office). *Telephone:* (202) 370-5000 (office). *Fax:* (202) 458-3967 (office). *Website:* www.oas.org (office).

MÉNDEZ GUTIÉRREZ, Gonzalo; Bolivian government official and academic; b. Cochabamba; ed Universidad Mayor de San Simón, Univ. of Amberes, Catholic Univ. of Louvain, Belgium; fmr Nat. Dir of Academic Planning, Universidad Católica Boliviana; fmr Prof. Universidad Andina Simón Bolívar; fmr Dir of Finance and Planning, Municipality of Cochabamba; Minister of Nat. Defence 2005–06 (resgnd); charged with corruption Oct. 2018.

MÉNDEZ ROMERO, Brig.-Gen. (retd) Arévalo Enrique; Venezuelan diplomatist, business executive and fmr army officer; ed Mil. Acad. of Venezuela, Inst. of Higher Defense Studies; Pvt. Sec. to Pres. and Vice Minister of Foreign Affairs 2000–05; Amb. to Spain 2005–07, to Argentina 2007–11; apptd Chair. Carbones del Zulia Sociedad Mercantil, SA (nat. coal co.) 2011; fmr Dir Banco de Desarrollo Económico y Social de Venezuela.

MENDILLO, Jane, BA, MBA; American investment manager and business executive; *President and CEO, Harvard Management Company, Inc.;* ed Yale Univ.; man. consultant with Bain & Co., Boston, Mass –1987; joined Harvard Management Co. (Harvard Univ.'s endowment arm) 1987, mem. Internal Equities Man. Team 1987–89, Vice-Pres. for Pvt. Equity 1989–91, Vice-Pres. for Trusts 1992–96, Vice-Pres. of External Investments 1997–2002, Pres. and CEO 2008–; Chief Investment Officer, Wellesley Coll. 2002–08; mem. Yale Univ. Investment Cttee 2002–08, Partners HealthCare System Investment Cttee (includes Massachusetts Gen. Hosp. and Brigham and Women's Hosp.), Harvard-Yenching Inst. Investment Cttee, Dimock Community Health Center Bd of Visitors, Roxbury; mem. Boston Security Analysts Soc., Inc., Boston Cttee on Foreign Relations, Boston Econ. Club; 100 Women in Hedge Funds Industry Leadership Award 2007. *Address:* Harvard Management Company, Inc., 600 Atlantic Avenue, Suite 15, Boston, MA 02210-2211, USA (office). *Telephone:* (617) 523-4400 (office). *E-mail:* general@hmc.harvard.edu (office). *Website:* www.hmc.harvard.edu (office).

MENDIS, Sunil; Sri Lankan business executive and central banker; ed Royal Coll., Colombo; joined Hayleys Ltd 1962, mem. Bd of Dirs 1977–2004, Chair. and CEO 1993–2004; Gov. Central Bank of Sri Lanka 2004–06, Chair. Monetary Bd 2004–06; mem. Nat. Council for Econ. Devt 2004–06; mem. Bd of Govs South East Asian Central Banks (SEACEN) Research and Training Centre 2004–; fmr mem. Bd of Dirs Bank of Ceylon, US Educational Foundation in Sri Lanka, Private Sector Infrastructure Devt Co. Ltd, Export Devt Bd, Bd Investment, Presidential Salaries Comm., and more than 100 cos and several state insts in Sri Lanka and overseas; mem. Asscn of Chartered Certified Accountants.

MENDONÇA BATISTA, Joesley; Brazilian business executive; *Chairman, JBS SA;* Partner, J&F Participações SA; has served in various capacities at JBS SA since 1988, including as Pres. Inalca JBS SpA, CEO JBS SA 2006–11, mem. Bd of Dirs 2009–, Chair. 2011–, mem. Bd of Dirs JBS USA Holdings, Inc. (also known as Swift & Co.), Pilgrim's Pride Corpn. *Address:* JBS SA, Avenida Marginal Direita do Tietê, 500 Vila Jaguará, 05118-100 São Paulo, Brazil (office). *Telephone:* (11) 3144-4000 (office). *Fax:* (11) 3144-4279 (office). *E-mail:* info@jbs.com.br (office). *Website:* www.jbs.com.br (office).

MENDONÇA BATISTA, Wesley; Brazilian business executive; *President and CEO, JBS SA;* mem. JBS founding family and has served in various capacities at JBS since 1987, Pres. and CEO JBS USA 2007–11, Pres. and CEO JBS SA 2011–, Vice-Pres. Bd of Dirs 2011–, Pres. and CEO JBS USA Holdings Inc. (also known as Swift & Co.) 2007–; Chair. Pilgrim's Pride Corpn 2009–. *Address:* JBS SA, Avenida Marginal Direita do Tietê, 500 Vila Jaguará, 05118-100 São Paulo, Brazil (office).

Telephone: (11) 3144-4000 (office). *Fax:* (11) 3144-4279 (office). *E-mail:* info@jbs.com.br (office). *Website:* www.jbs.com.br (office).

MENDONÇA E MOURA, Álvaro; Portuguese politician and diplomatist; *Secretary-General of Ministry Foreign Affairs;* b. 17 March 1951, Oporto; m. Maria Cristina Mendonça e Moura; four c.; ed Univ. of Colmbra; Embassy Attaché 1975–78, Third Sec. 1978, Second Sec. 1978–82, First Sec. 1982–90, Counsellor 1990–93, Minister 1993–2002, Amb. 2002–, posted to Perm. Del. to EFTA, GATT, Geneva 1979, posted to Embassy, Pretoria, S Africa 1985, Chargé d'affaires a.i. 1988–89, Dir for African Affairs, Ministry of Foreign Affairs 1990–91, Chef de Cabinet, Sec. of State for Foreign Affairs and Co-operation 1991–92, Chef de Cabinet, Minister for Foreign Affairs 1992–95, Amb. to Austria and Perm. Rep. to UN Office in Vienna 1995 (also accred to as Amb. to Slovenia and Slovakia 1996), Amb. and Perm. Rep. to UN Office and other Int. Orgs, Geneva 1999–2002, to EU, Brussels 2002–08, Amb. to Spain 2008–13, Amb. and Perm. Rep. to UN, New York 2013–17, Sec.-Gen. of Ministry of Foreign Affairs 2017–; Head of Portuguese Del. to UN Comm. on Crime Prevention and Criminal Justice 1996, 1997, 1998, 1999; Chair. Preparatory Cttee, Cttee of Whole of UN Gen. Ass.'s Special Session on Narcotic Drugs 1997–98; Vice-Chair. UN Human Rights Comm. 2001–02; Chair. Gen. Ass., World Intellectual Property Org. 2001–02; Prof., Dept of Int. Relations, Lusiada Univ., Lisbon; mem. High-Level Group of Experts appointed by UN Sec.-Gen. to review Int. Drug Control Programme, to strengthen UN machinery for Int. Drug Control, Vienna, New York 1998. *Address:* Ministry of Foreign Affairs, Palácio das Necessidades, Largo do Rilvas, 1399-030 Lisbon, Portugal (office). *Telephone:* (21) 3946000 (office). *Fax:* (21) 3946322 (office). *E-mail:* secgeral@mne.pt (office). *Website:* www.portaldiplomatico.mne.gov.pt (office).

MENDONÇA PREVIATO, Lucia, BS, PhD; Brazilian biophysicist, parasitologist and academic; *Professor of Biophysics and Parasitology, Biophysics Institute, Federal University of Rio de Janeiro;* b. 17 Feb. 1949, Maceió, Alagoas; m. Jose Osvaldo Previato; one s. one d.; ed St Ursula Univ., Fed. Univ. of Rio de Janeiro; Biologist, Universidade Santa Ursula 1971–72; Specialist (Microbiology), Fed. Univ. of Rio de Janeiro 1972–80, Founder and Dir Surface Structure of Microorganisms Lab., Inst. of Microbiology 1980–2001, Assoc. Prof. (Microbiology) 1980–92, Prof. 1992–, currently Prof. of Biophysics and Parasitology, Biophysics Inst. and Dir Carlos Chagas Filho Lab. of Glycobiology; Research Assoc., Nat. Council of Canada Research 1977; post-doctorate work in Dept of Biochemistry, Univ. of California, Berkeley 1978–79; Int. Scholar, Howard Hughes Medical Inst. 1997–2001; Chief Ed. Annals of the Brazilian Academy of Sciences 2003–08; mem. Brazilian Acad. of Sciences 1992–, TWAS 2008–; Commdr, Nat. Order of Scientific Merit 2002; Petrobras Award, Nat. Invention Prize, in 1987, Nat. Medal of Science (Ordem Nacional do Mérito Cientifico) 2001, L'Oréal-UNESCO for Women in Science Award 2004, Mizutani Foundation for Glycosciences Award 2006, TWAS Prize (Biology) 2007. *Publications:* numerous articles in scientific journals on the study of *Trypanosoma cruzi*, the protozoan parasite responsible for Chagas disease. *Address:* Biophysics Institute, Federal University of Rio de Janeiro, Rio de Janeiro 21944–170, Brazil (office). *E-mail:* luciamp@biof.ufrj.br (office). *Website:* www.biof.ufrj.br (office).

MENDOZA, Heidi Lloce, CPA; Philippine accountant and UN official; *Under-Secretary-General, Office of Internal Oversight, United Nations;* b. 3 Nov. 1962, Tayabas, Quezon; d. of Agapito Lloce, Sr and Silveria Macaraan; m. Meynardo Mendoza; three c.; ed Univ. of the Philippines-Dilima, Nat. Defense Coll. of the Philippines; Auditing Aide II, Performance Audit Office, Philippines Comm. on Audit 1984, State Auditor 1996–2006, later State Auditor IV and Head, Value for Money Audit Div. –2000, Commr and Officer-in-Charge 2011–15; Consultant to Presidential Anti-Graft Comm. and Transparency Group, Office of Presidential Chief of Staff 2003–04; Local Govt Procurement Specialist for World Bank, Manila 2006; Governance and Anti-Corruption Consultant, Asian Devt Bank 2008–10; Under-Sec.-Gen., UN Office of Internal Oversight, New York 2015–; fmr Accounting and Internal Audit Expert, European Comm. ALTAIR project; external auditor to various orgs including FAO, WHO, ILO; fmr Project Chair., Audit Steering Cttees of various programs funded by Australian Assistance for Int. Devt Aid (AusAid); several awards including Medalya Ng Karangalan, Ateneo de Zamboanga Univ. Pro Deo et Patria Award. *Publication:* A Guide to Investigation of Common Procurement Fraud and Irregularities 2005. *Leisure interest:* writing poetry. *Address:* Office of Internal Oversight Services, United Nations, New York, NY 10017, USA (office). *Telephone:* (212) 963-1111 (office). *Fax:* (212) 963-7774 (office). *Website:* oios.un.org (office).

MENDOZA, June, AO, OBE, RP, ROI; British portrait painter; b. Melbourne, Australia; d. of John Morton and Dot Mendoza; m. Keith Mackrell; one s. three d.; ed Lauriston School for Girls, Melbourne, Australia, St Martin's School of Art; portraits include HM Queen Elizabeth II, HM Queen Elizabeth, the Queen Mother, HRH The Prince of Wales, Diana, Princess of Wales, Baroness Thatcher, Prime Ministers of Fiji, Australia, Philippines, Singapore, Pres. of Iceland, Philippines and many other govt, academic, industrial, regimental, theatrical and sporting personalities, series of internationally known musicians, large boardroom and family groups; large canvas for the House of Commons (440 portraits) of the House in session, for Australian House of Reps (170 portraits) for Parl., Canberra; has made numerous TV appearances and lectures regularly in UK and overseas; mem. Royal Soc. of Portrait Painters, Royal Inst. of Oil Painters; Freeman of City of London 1997; Hon. mem. Soc. of Women Artists; Hon. DLitt (Bath, Loughborough); Dr hc (Open Univ.). *Leisure interests:* classical and jazz music, theatre. *Address:* 34 Inner Park Road, London, SW19 6DD, England (home). *Telephone:* (20) 8788-7826 (home). *Fax:* (20) 8780-0728 (home). *E-mail:* contact@junemendoza.co.uk. *Website:* www.junemendoza.co.uk.

MENEAR, Craig, BA; American business executive; *Chairman, President and CEO, Home Depot, Inc.;* ed Eli Broad Coll. of Business, Michigan State Univ.; held various merchandising positions within retail industry with cos including IKEA, Builders Emporium, Grace Home Centers, Montgomery Ward, as well as operating an ind. retail business; joined Home Depot 1997, held increasingly responsible positions in Merchandising Dept, including Merchandising Vice-Pres. of Hardware, Merchandising Vice-Pres. of SW Div. and Div. Merchandise Man. of SW Div. 1997–2003, Sr Vice-Pres., Merchandising 2003–07, Exec. Vice-Pres., Merchandising 2007–14, Pres., US Retail Feb.–Oct. 2014, mem. Bd of Dirs, Pres. and CEO Home Depot, Inc. 2014–, Chair. 2015–, Chair. The Home Depot Foundation. *Address:* The Home Depot Inc., 2455 Paces Ferry Road NW, Atlanta, GA 30339, USA (office). *Telephone:* (770) 433-8211 (office). *Fax:* (770) 384-2805 (office). *E-mail:* info@homedepot.com (office). *Website:* www.homedepot.com (office).

MENEGAUX, Florent, BA; French business executive; *General Managing Partner, Michelin;* ed Université Paris-Dauphine; consultant, Pricewaterhouse-Coopers 1986, then Man.; Finance Dir Exel Logistics, France 1991–95, then Gen. Man.; Gen. Man., General Cargo Transport Division, Norbert Dentressangle Group 1995–96; Commercial Dir, Truck Tyres, Michelin, UK 1997–2000, Sales Dir, Truck Tyres Original Equipment and Replacement markets, N America 2000, Head of Truck Tyres, S America 2003, Africa–Middle East Zone 2005, Passenger Car and Light Truck Tyre Replacement Business Unit, Europe 2006, Exec. Vice-Pres., Passenger Car and Light Truck 2008, CEO 2014, Sr Exec. Vice-Pres. 2017, also mem. Exec. Cttee, Gen. Man. Partner 2018–19. *Address:* 23 Place des Carmes Dechaux, 63000 Clermont-Ferrand, France (office). *Telephone:* 4-73-32-20-00 (office). *Website:* www.michelin.com (office).

MENEM, Carlos Saul, DJur; Argentine politician; *President, Partido Justicialista, La Rioja Province;* b. 2 July 1935, Anillaco, La Rioja; s. of Saul Menem and Muhibe Akil; m. 1st Zulema Fátima Yoma 1966 (divorced); one s. (deceased) one d.; m. 2nd Cecilia Bolocco 2001; one s.; ed Córdoba Univ.; f. Juventud Peronista (Peron Youth Group), La Rioja Prov. 1955; defended political prisoners following Sept. 1955 coup; Legal Adviser, Confederación General del Trabajo, La Rioja Prov. 1955–70; cand. Prov. Deputy 1958; Pres. Partido Justicialista, La Rioja Prov. 1963–; elected Gov. La Rioja 1973, re-elected 1983, 1987; imprisoned following mil. coup 1976–81; cand. for Pres. Argentine Repub. for Partido Justicialista 1989; Pres. of Argentina 1989–99; Vice-Pres. Conf. of Latin American Popular Parties (COPPAL) 1990–; arrested for alleged involvement in illegal arms sales during his presidency June 2001, charged July 2001, placed under house arrest for five months; Presidential Cand. 2003. *Publications:* Argentine, Now or Never, Argentina Year 2000, The Productive Revolution (with Eduardo Duhalde). *Leisure interests:* flying, tennis. *Address:* Partido Justicialista, Buenos Aires, Argentina.

MENÉNDEZ, Ana Maria; Spanish diplomatist and UN official; *Senior Adviser on Policy, United Nations;* b. 1 Sept. 1960, Madrid; one s.; ed Complutense Univ., Madrid; joined Spanish Diplomatic Service 1985, worked in European Div., Ministry of Foreign Affairs 1985–88, First Sec. Embassy of Spain in Japan 1988–90, Counsellor Perm. Representation to UN 1990–96, 1998–2003, Head of Bilateral Affairs Section, North American Affairs, Ministry of Foreign Affairs 1996–98, Amb. and Deputy Perm. Rep. to UN 2003–05, Head of Latin America–EU Relations, Ministry of Foreign Affairs 2005–06, Deputy Head of Mission, Embassy of Spain in Ireland 2006–08, in Tunisia 2009–12, Deputy Dir-Gen. UN Div., Ministry of Foreign Affairs 2008–09, Amb. and Perm. Rep. to UN and other Int. Orgs in Geneva 2012–17, UN Sec.-Gen.'s Sr Adviser on Policy 2017–. *Address:* United Nations Headquarters, 405 E 42nd Street, New York, NY 10017, USA (office). *Telephone:* (212) 963-1234 (office). *Fax:* (212) 963-4879 (office). *Website:* www.un.org (office).

MENENDEZ, Robert (Bob), BA, JD; American politician; *Senator from New Jersey;* b. 1 Jan. 1954, New York, NY; m. Jane Jacobsen 1976 (divorced 2005); one s. one d.; ed St Peter's Coll., Jersey City, Rutgers Univ., Newark; entered public service when he launched a successful petition drive to reform his local school bd 1973, elected to Union City Bd of Educ. 1974–78; admitted to NJ Bar 1980; Mayor of Union City 1986–92, simultaneously served in New Jersey Gen. Ass. 1987–91 and New Jersey Senate 1991–93; mem. US House of Reps for NJ 13th Congressional Dist 1993–2006, fmr Vice-Chair. House Democratic Caucus 1999–2003, Chair. 2003–06, Chair. Democratic Task Force on Educ. 2001–03, Democratic Task Force on Homeland Security 2001–03, Democratic Senatorial Campaign Cttee 2008–11; Chair. Credentials Cttee, Democratic Nat. Convention 2004; highest-ranking Hispanic in Congressional history; Senator from New Jersey 2006–, mem. Finance Cttee, Banking, Housing and Urban Affairs Cttee, Foreign Relations Cttee (Chair. 2013–15); Democrat. *Publication:* Growing American Roots. *Address:* 528 Hart Senate Office Building, Washington, DC 20510, USA (office). *Telephone:* (202) 224-4744 (office). *Fax:* (202) 228-2197 (office). *Website:* menendez.senate.gov (office).

MENÉNDEZ CORTE, Jorge Edgardo; Uruguyan dentist and politician; b. 13 Aug. 1951, Villa del Carmen, Duranzo; m. Gloria Otegui; three d.; ed Univ. of the Republic; Mayor, Durazno Dept 1985–99, elected Nat. Rep. of Dept 2004, Deputy for Dept 2005–10; Undersecretary of Defence, Ministry of Nat. Defence 2008–09, 2011–15, Minister of Nat. Defence 2016–19; fmr Rep. of Uruguay to Union of South American Nations; Acting Sec., Conferencia de Ministros de las Américas 2010; Founding mem. Centre for Strategic Studies on Defence.

MENG, Fengchao; Chinese engineer and business executive; *Chairman and General Manager, China Railway Construction Corporation Limited;* ed Southwest Jiaotong Univ.; served in various positions at Ministry of Railways and its eng affiliates; Chair. China Zhongtie Major Bridge Eng Group Co. Ltd 1982–98; Vice-Pres. China Railway Eng Co. 2000–04; Pres. China Harbour Eng Co. (Group) 2005, mem. Bd of Dirs and Pres. China Communications Construction Group 2005–06, Exec. Vice-Chair. and Pres. China Communications Construction Co. Ltd 2006–10; Chair., Gen. Man. and Sec., CCP Cttee, China Railway Construction Corpn Ltd 2010–. *Address:* China Railway Construction Corporation Ltd, 40 Fuxing Road, Beijing 100855, People's Republic of China (office). *Telephone:* (10) 51888114 (office). *Fax:* (10) 52688302 (office). *E-mail:* ir@crcc.cn (office). *Website:* www.crcc.cn (office).

MENG, Hongwei, LLB; Chinese politician and international organization official; b. 1953, Harbin City; ed Peking Univ.; several positions with Ministry of Public Security including Dir, Patrol Police Div., Dir-Gen., Traffic Control Dept, Asst Minister of Public Security, Vice Minister of Public Security 2004, Vice Chair., Nat. Narcotics Control Comm., Dir Nat. Counter-Terrorism Office, mem. Chinese Council of the Shanghai Cooperation Org. Regional Counter-Terrorism Structure, Dir-Gen. China Coast Guard 2013–17, Deputy Dir, State Oceanic Admin of China 2013–17; Head, Interpol Nat. Central Bureau of China, Pres., Interpol 2016–18.

MENG, Jianzhu; Chinese politician; *Secretary, CCP Central Committee Politics and Law Commission;* b. July 1947, Wuxian Co., Jiangsu Prov.; joined CCP 1968; Deputy Political Instructor and Deputy Leader of Boat Fleet, Supply Marketing and Transport Station, Qianwei Farm (also Sec. CCP Shanghai Communist Youth League) 1968–73, Sec. CCP Party Br. 1973–76, mem. CCP Qianwei Farm Party Cttee 1976–77 (also Leader, Publicity Dept), Sec. Cork Gen. Plant, Qianwei Farm, CCP Party Br. 1977–81, Dir Political Dept, Qianwei Farm 1977–81, Deputy Sec., later Dir CCP Party Cttee 1981–86; Sec. CCP Chuansha Co. Cttee, Shanghai 1986–90, Jiading Co. Cttee, Shanghai 1990–91; Sec. Rural Work Cttee, CCP Shanghai Municipal Cttee 1991–92; Deputy Sec.-Gen. Shanghai Municipal Govt 1992–93; Vice-Mayor and Chair. Shanghai Econ. Restructuring Comm. 1993–96; Deputy Sec. Shanghai Municipal Cttee 1996; Sec. Jiangxi Prov. Cttee 2001–07, Chair. Standing Cttee Jiangxi People's Congress 2001; Alt. mem. 15th CCP Cen. Cttee 1997–2002, mem. 16th CCP Cen. Cttee 2002–07, mem. 17th CCP Cen. Cttee 2007–12; mem. 18th CCP Cen. Cttee 2012–17, mem. CCP Politburo 2012–17; Minister of Public Security 2007–12; State Councillor 2008–13; Sec. CCP Cen. Cttee Politics and Law Comm. 2012–. *Address:* CCP Central Committee Politics and Law Commission, Beijing, People's Republic of China (office).

MENG, Weilin; Chinese business executive; *President, Zhejiang Materials Industry Group Corporation;* Chair. Logistics Cttee, Zhejiang Fed. of Logistics and Purchasing; currently Pres. Zhejiang Materials Industry Group Corpn. *Address:* Zhejiang Materials Industry Group Corporation, 56 West Huancheng Road, Hangzhou 310006, Zhejiang Prov., People's Republic of China (office). *Telephone:* (571) 87054509 (office). *Fax:* (571) 87054509 (office). *E-mail:* office@zjmi.com (office). *Website:* www.zjmi.com (office).

MENG, Xuenong, MSc, MBA; Chinese politician; b. 8 Aug. 1949, Penglai, Shandong Prov.; ed Beijing Normal Univ., Chinese Univ. of Science and Tech., Anhui Prov.; joined CCP 1972; worked in No. 2 Motor Vehicle Plant, Beijing 1969–71 (also Sec. CCP Communist Youth League 1971–74); Office Sec., Beijing Automobile Industry Co. 1971–74 (also Deputy Sec., later Sec. CCP Communist Youth League); Office Sec. Org. Dept CCP Zhejiang Prov. Cttee 1977–80, later Sec. of Gen. Office of Prov. Cttee; fmr Deputy Sec. CCP Communist Youth League Beijing Municipal Cttee; Gen. Man. Beijing Hotel Allied Co. 1986–87 (also Deputy Sec., later Sec. CCP Communist Youth League); Dir Admin for Industry and Commerce, Beijing 1987–93 (also Sec. CCP Leading Party Group); worked under Hu Jintao, Pres. of People's Repub. of China; Vice-Mayor of Beijing 1993–98, Exec. Vice-Mayor 1998–2002, Mayor 2003–04, mem. CCP Standing Cttee, Beijing Municipal Cttee; Deputy Dir Construction Comm. for Project for Diverting Water from the South to the North 2003–07 (mem. CCP Leading Party Group 2004–07); mem. 16th CCP Cen. Cttee 2002–07, 17th CCP Cen. Cttee 2007–12, 18th CCP Cen. Cttee 2012–17; Acting Gov. Shanxi Prov. 2007–08, Gov. 2008 (resgnd).

MENGES, Chris; British cinematographer and film director; b. 15 Sept. 1940, Kington, Herefordshire; s. of Herbert Menges; m. 2nd Judy Freeman 1978; five c. from 1st marriage; TV cameraman on documentaries filmed in Africa, Asia and S America; mem. American Soc. of Cinematographers, British Soc. of Cinematographers. *Films include:* camera operator: Poor Cow 1967, If…. 1968; cinematographer: Abel Gance: The Charm of Dynamite 1968, Loving Memory 1969, Kes 1969, Black Beauty (dir of photography) 1971, Gumshoe 1971, A Sense of Freedom 1979, Black Jack 1979, Bloody Kids 1979, Star Wars: Episode V – The Empire Strikes Back (dir of photography: studio second unit) 1980, The Gamekeeper 1980, Babylon 1980, East 103rd Street 1981, Looks and Smiles 1981, Warlords of the 21st Century 1982, Couples and Robbers 1982, Angel 1982, Local Hero 1983, Winter Flight 1984, Which Side Are You On? 1984, Comfort and Joy 1984, The Killing Fields (Acad. Award) 1984, Marie 1985, Fatherland 1986, The Mission (Acad. Award) 1986, Singing the Blues in Red, Shy People 1987, High Season 1987, Michael Collins (LA Film Critics Award 1997) 1996, The Boxer (dir of photography) 1997, The Pledge 2001, Dirty Pretty Things 2002, The Good Thief 2002, Criminal (dir of photography) 2004, Tickets 2005, The Three Burials of Melquiades Estrada 2005, North Country 2005; Dir: East 103rd Street (also producer) 1981, A World Apart 1988, Criss-Cross 1992, The Life and Death of Chico Mendes, Second Best 1994, The Lost Son 1999, North Country 2005, Notes on a Scandal 2006, The Reader (dir of photography) 2008, Stop-Loss (dir of photography) 2008, The Yellow Handkerchief (dir of photography) 2008, Route Irish 2010, Extremely Loud and Incredibly Close (dir of photography) 2011, Redemption 2013; Dir: A World Apart 1988, CrissCross 1992, Second Best 1994, The Lost Son 1999. *Television includes:* Auditions 1980, A Question of Leadership 1981, Tales Out of School: Made in Britain 1982, Walter 1982, Walter and June 1983, The Red and the Blue: Impressions of Two Political Conferences – Autumn 1982 1983, Concert for George 2003.

MENGISTU HAILE MARIAM (see MARIAM, Mengistu Haile).

MENKEN, Alan Irwin; American composer; b. 22 July 1949, New York, NY; ed New York Univ.; began composing and performing Lehman Engel Musical Theater Workshop, BMI; Richard Kirk Career Achievement Award 1998, Disney Legends 2002, Grammy Award for Best Song Written for Visual Media (for I See The Light) 2012, Freddie G. Award for Musical Excellence 2013, The Oscar Hammerstein Award 2013. *Theatre music includes:* God Bless You Mr Rosewater 1979 (Off-Broadway debut), Little Shop of Horrors (with Howard Ashman), Kicks, The Apprenticeship of Duddy Kravitz, Diamonds, Personals, Let Freedom Sing, Weird Romance, Beauty and the Beast, A Christmas Carol. *Film music includes:* A Dancer's Life 1972, Little Shop of Horrors 1986, The Little Mermaid 1988 (two Acad. Awards 1989, two Grammy Awards 1990), Beauty and the Beast 1990 (two Acad. Awards 1991, three Grammy Awards 1992), Lincoln 1992, Newsies 1992 (Tony Award 2012), Aladdin 1992 (two Acad. Awards 1993, four Grammy Awards 1993), Life with Mikey 1993, Pocahontas (with Stephen Schwartz) (Golden Globe Award 1996, two Acad. Awards 1996, Grammy Award 1995) 1995, The Hunchback of Notre Dame 1996, Hercules 1997, Home on the Range 2004, Noel 2004, A Christmas Carol 2004, The Shaggy Dog 2006, Enchanted 2007, Tangled (Grammy Award 2011) 2010, Mirror Mirror: The Untold Adventures of Snow White 2012, Sausage Party 2016, Beauty and the Beast 2017. *Television includes:* The Neighbors (series) 2013, Galavant (series) 2015–16. *Address:* The Shukat Company, 340 West 55th Street, Apartment 1A, New York, NY 10019, USA. *Telephone:* (212) 582-7614. *Website:* www.alanmenken.com.

MENKERIOS, Haile, MA; South African (b. Eritrean) economist, diplomatist and UN official; b. 1 Oct. 1946, Adi Felesti; s. of Drar Menkerios and Negusse Giorgis; m. Hebret Berhe 1979 (divorced); two s. one d.; ed Addis Ababa Univ., Brandeis and Harvard Univs, USA; Teaching Fellow, Harvard Univ. 1971–73; guerrilla fighter in Eritrean People's Liberation Army (EPLA) 1973–74; Head of Tigrigna Section, Dept of Information and Propaganda, Eritrean People's Liberation Front (EPLF) 1974–75, mem. Foreign Relations Cttee 1976–77, mem. Cen. Council 1977–2001, Deputy Head of Dept of Foreign Relations 1977–79, Head of Research Div., Political, Educ. and Culture Dept 1979–86; Dir Research and Information Centre of Eritrea 1986–87; Head, Research and Policy Div., Dept of Foreign Relations 1987–90; Gov. of East and South Zone of Eritrea 1990–91; mem. Eritrean Nat. Council 1991–2001; Rep. of Provisional Govt of Eritrea to Ethiopia 1991–93; Special Envoy of Pres. to Somalia 1991–96, to the Greater Lakes Region 1996–97; mem. High Level Horn of Africa Cttee on Somalia 1993–95; Amb. of Eritrea to Ethiopia and OAU 1993–96; Perm. Rep. of Eritrea to UN 1997–2001; Chair. UN Cttee of Experts re Sanctions on arms and terrorist camps, Afghanistan 2001; Sr Adviser to Special Envoy of UN Sec.-Gen. to the Inter-Congolese Dialogue 2002–03; Dir Africa Div., UN Dept of Political Affairs 2003–05; Deputy Special Rep. of the Sec.-Gen. for UN Mission in the Democratic Repub. of the Congo (MONUC) 2005–07; Asst Sec.-Gen. for Political Affairs, UN 2007–10; Special Rep. of the Sec.-Gen. for Sudan and Head of UN Mission in Sudan (UNMIS) 2010–11; Special Envoy of the Sec.-Gen. for Sudan and South Sudan, UN 2011–16, also Special Rep. of the Sec.-Gen. and Head, UN Office to the African Union (UNOAU) 2013–18; mem. Advisory Bd, Conflict Prevention and Peace Forum; Fellow, Rift Valley Inst.; Medal of Honour for the fight against Genocide (Pres. of Rwanda), Medal of Recognition for support to the Liberation of Rwanda (Pres. of Rwanda). *Publications include:* various articles on African politics. *Leisure interests:* reading, sports, travel.

MENON, Anjolie Ela; Indian artist and muralist; b. 17 July 1940, Burnpur, West Bengal; m. Raja Menon; ed Sir J.J. Inst. of Applied Art, Mumbai, Univ. of Delhi, École des Beaux-Arts, Paris; mem. Advisory Cttee and Art Purchase Cttee, Nat. Gallery of Modern Art, New Delhi; mem. Bd of Trustees, Indira Gandhi Nat. Centre for Arts; represented India at Algeirs Biennale and Sao Paulo, Brazil; participated in several Int. shows; Padma Shri 2000, Limca Book of Records, Lifetime Achievement Award, Govt of NCT of Delhi 2013. *E-mail:* anjolieelamenon@indianartcircle.com; a_menon@indianartcircle.com.

MENON, Maj.-Gen. Jai Shanker, BA, MA; Indian military commander and UN official; b. 1959; m.; two d.; ed Jawaharlal Nehru Univ., Nat. Defence Acad., Khadakvasla, Army War Coll., Mhow, Defence Services Staff Coll., Wellington, Tamil Nadu, Coll. of Defence Management, Secunderabad, Osmania Univ., Hyderabad, Madras Univ., Chennai; long career in Indian Army, roles include fmr Brigade Commdr and Battalion Commdr, fmr Commandant of Regimental Training Centre, Gen. Officer Commanding, Infantry Div. 2012–13, Additional Dir-Gen. of Equipment Man. –2016; Mil. Observer with UN Operation in Mozambique 1993 and UN Interim Force in Lebanon 2007–09, Head of Mission and Force Commdr, UN Disengagement Observer Force (UNDOF) 2016–17.

MENON, Raghu; Indian civil servant, government official and airline executive; officer of Indian Admin. Service of Assam-Nagaland cadre 1974, served in Ministry of Information and Broadcasting, apptd Jt Sec., Ministry of Civil Aviation 2002, Special Sec. and Financial Advisor –2008, Chair. and Man. Dir Air-India Ltd (state-owned airline merged with Indian airline under Nat. Aviation Co. of India Ltd) 2008–09; Sec. Ministry of Information and Broadcasting 2009; Chair. Inter-Governmental Council of the Int. Programme for Devt of Communication 2010–12.

MENON, Ravi, BS, MPA; Singaporean government official and banking executive; *Managing Director, Monetary Authority of Singapore;* ed National Univ. of Singapore, Harvard Univ., USA; joined Monetary Authority of Singapore 1987, served in several sr positions including one year at BIS, Basel, Switzerland, as mem. of Secr. to Financial Stability Forum, Asst Man. Dir Monetary Authority of Singapore 2002–03, seconded to Ministry of Finance, Deputy Sec. (Policy), Ministry of Finance 2003–07, Permanent Sec., Ministry of Trade and Industry 2007–11, Man. Dir Monetary Authority of Singapore 2011–; Chair. Asia-Pacific Econ. Cooperation Sr Officials Meetings 2009; Chair. Standing Cttee on Standards Implementation, Financial Stability Bd, mem. Steering Cttee; mem. Bd of Govs Raffles Inst.; mem. Bd of Trustees Singapore Indian Development Asscn; Prime Minister's Book Prize (twice), Public Administration Medal. *Address:* Monetary Authority of Singapore, 10 Shenton Way, MAS Building, 079117, Singapore (office). *Telephone:* 62255577 (office). *Fax:* 62299229 (office). *E-mail:* webmaster@mas.gov.sg (office). *Website:* www.mas.gov.sg (office).

MENON, Shivshankar, MA; Indian diplomatist; *Chairman, Advisory Board, Institute of Chinese Studies;* b. 5 July 1949, Palakkad, Kerala; m. Mohini Sathe; one s. one d.; ed Univ. of Delhi; joined Indian Foreign Service 1972, Second Sec., Embassy in Beijing 1974–77; Under-Sec. in charge of Africa and then China 1977–79; First Sec., Embassy in Vienna 1979–83, also Alt. Gov. IAEA Bd and Deputy Perm. Rep. to UN Orgs; Dir Dept of Atomic Energy, Mumbai 1983–86; Counsellor and Deputy Chief of Mission, Embassy in Beijing 1986–89; Deputy Chief of Mission, Embassy in Tokyo 1989–92; Jt Sec. in charge of NE Div. 1992–95; Amb. to Israel 1995–97; High Commr to Sri Lanka 1997–2000; Amb. to China 2000–03; High Commr to Pakistan 2003–06; Foreign Sec. 2006–09; Nat. Security Adviser to the Prime Minister 2010–14; currently Chair. Advisory Bd Inst. of Chinese Studies; Distinguished Visiting Fellow, Inst. of South Asian Studies, Nat. Univ. of Singapore; Distinguished Fellow, Brookings Inst., Washington DC, Asia Soc. Policy Inst., New York; mem. Bd of Trustees, Int. Crisis Group; Madhav Award, Scindia School Gwalior 2000. *Leisure interest:* classical music. *Address:* Institute of Chinese Studies, Sri Ram Road, Civil Lines, Delhi 110 045, India. *Telephone:* (11) 23938202. *E-mail:* shivshankar.menon@gmail.com (office). *Website:* www.icsin.org/chairman/faculty/shivshankar-menon.

MENSHIKOV, Oleg Yevgenyevich; Russian actor, singer and director; b. 8 Nov. 1960, Serpukhov, Moscow Region; ed Shchepkin Higher School of Theatre Art, Maly Theatre; began film career playing in the comedy Pokrovskie vorota and in Nikita Mikhalkov's Rodnya early 1980s; collaborated again with Mikhalkov in their most famous film, Burnt by the Sun 1993–94; Pres. of the Jury, Moscow Int. Film Festival 1997; Laurence Olivier Prize for Yesenin 1991, Film Critics' Prize for Best Actor of 1994, prizes for best men's role at Festivals Kinotaurus 1996, Baltic Pearl 1996, other awards. *Theatre includes:* Ganya Ivolgin (Idiot after Dostoyevsky) 1981, Sergey (Sports Scenes of 1981) 1986, Caligula (Caligula) 1989,

Yesenin (When She Danced) London 1991, Ikharev (Gamblers) London 1992, Nizhinsky (N. Nizhinsky) 1993. *Films include:* Rodnya (Kinfolk) 1983, Polyoty vo sne i nayavu (Flights in Dreams and in Reality) 1983, Kiss, Polosa prepyatstviy (Stripe of Obstacles) 1984, Mikhailo Lomonosov 1984, Po glavnoy ulitse s orkestrom (Through Main Street with an Orchestra) 1986, Moy lyubimyy kloun (My Favourite Clown) 1986, Moonzund (also singer) 1987, Po glavnoy ulitse s orkestrom 1987, Bryzgi shampanskogo (Splashes of Champagne) 1988, Zhizn po limitu (Limited Life) 1989, Lestnitsa (The Stairway) 1989, Yama (The Pit) 1990, Dyuba-Dyuba 1992, Utomlyonnye solntsem (Burnt by the Sun) (Grand Prize, Cannes Film Festival, Academy Award for Best Foreign Language Film) 1994, Kavkazskiy plennik (Prisoner of the Caucasus) 1996, Sibirskiy tsiryulnik (The Barber of Siberia) 1998, Mama (Mummy) 1999, Est-Ouest (East-West) 1999, Statski sovetnik (The State Counsellor) 2005, Utomlyonnye solntsem 2: Predstoyanie (Burnt by the Sun 2: Anticipation) 2010, Utomlennye solntsem 2 (Burnt by the Sun 2) 2011, Legenda No. 17 2013; appeared in films of dirs N. Mikhalkov, A. Proshkin, A. Muratov, D. Khvan, S. Bodrov, R. Balayan, V. Kozakov, A. Sakharov. *Television includes:* Zhdu i nadeyus (film) 1980, Pokrovskiye vorota (Pokrov Gates) (film) 1982, Potseluy (The Kiss) (film) 1983, Kapitan Fracasse (mini-series) 1984, Volodya bolshoy, Volodya malenkiy (Big and Small Volodya) (film) 1985, Mikhaylo Lomonosov (mini-series) 1986, Prime Suspect 6: The Last Witness (series) 2003, Zolotoy telenok (mini-series) 2005, Doctor Zhivago (mini-series) 2006, Utomlennye solntsem 2 (Burnt by the Sun 2) (mini-series) 2011. *Address:* Maly Kozykhinsky per. 8/18, Apt 3, Moscow, Russia. *Telephone:* (495) 299-02-17.

MENSHOV, Vladimir Valentinovich; Russian film director, actor, screenwriter and producer; b. 17 Sept. 1939, Baku; m. Vera Alentova 1963; one d.; ed Moscow Arts Theatre Studio School, All-Union State Inst. of Cinema (VGIK) 1970; RSFSR State Prize 1978, Acad. Award for Moscow Does Not Believe in Tears 1980, USSR State Prize 1981, RSFSR Artist of Merit 1984, Prize of American Guild of Cinema Owners. *Leading roles in:* A Man in His Place 1973, Last Meeting 1974, Personal Opinions 1977, Time for Reflection 1983, The Intercept 1986, Where is Nofelet? 1987, The Town Zero 1988, Red Mob 1993, Russian Ragtime 1993, Chtoby vyzhit 1993, Shirli-myrli 1995, Tsarevich Aleksei 1996, Sochineniye ko dnyu pobedy 1998, 8 ½ $ 1999, Kitayskiy serviz 1999, Spartak i Kalashnikov 2002, Nochnoy dozor (Night Watch) 2004, Vremya sobirat' kamni (also producer) 2005, Dnevnoy dozor (Day Watch) 2006, The Apocalypse Code 2007, 07-y menyaet kurs 2007, Generation P 2011, Vysotskiy. Spasibo, chto zhivoy 2011, O chyom eshchyo govoryat muzhchiny 2011, Möbius 2013, Legenda No. 17 2013, Dialogi 2013. *Films directed:* Practical Joke 1976, Loss (Rozygrysh) 1977, Moscow Does Not Believe in Tears 1980, Love and Doves 1984, Das Duell des Alexander Puschkin 1988, Schatten über Moskau 1990, Shirli-myrli 1995, The Envy of Gods (also producer) 2000. *Films produced:* Kadril 1999, Lyubov zla 1999, Sosed 2004, Partia v bridge (TV film) (supervising producer) 2010, Kitayskaya babushka 2010, Doktor 2012. *Television includes:* Vremya dlya razmyshleniy (film) 1982, Snegurochku vyzyvali? (film) 1985, Dorogoy Edison (film) 1986, Ubiystvo na monastyrskikh prudakh (film) 1990, Dose detektiva Dubrovskogo (series) 1999, Lednikovyy period (mini-series) 2002, Moskva. Tsentralnyy okrug (series) 2003, Vremya zhestokikh (mini-series) 2004, Diversant (mini-series) 2004, Balzakovskiy vozrast, ili Vse muzhiki svo... (series) 2004, Moskva. Tsentralnyy okrug – 2 (mini-series) 2004, 32 dekabrya (film) 2004, Brezhnev (film) 2005, Zakoldovannyy uchastok (series) 2006, Liquidation (mini-series) 2007, Diversant 2: Konets voyny (mini-series) 2007, Shag za shagom (series) 2008, Sudebnaya kolonka (series) 2008, Techet reka Volga (film) 2009, Balzakovskiy vozrast, ili Vse muzhiki svo... 5 let spustya (mini-series) 2013, Tretya mirovaya (series) 2013, Vystrel (series) 2014. *Address:* 125047 Moscow, 3-d Tverskaya-Yamskaya 52, Apt 29, Russia. *Telephone:* (495) 250-85-43.

MENTRÉ, Paul; French civil servant and diplomatist; b. 28 June 1935, Nancy; s. of Paul Mentré and Cécile de Loye; m. 1st Sabine Brundsaux 1958 (divorced 1975); two d.; m. 2nd Gaëlle Bretillot 1975; two s.; m. 3rd Jehanne Collard 1992; ed Ecole Polytechnique, Ecole Nat. d'Admin; Insp. of Finance 1960; Special Asst, French Treas. 1965–70; Deputy Dir of the Cabinet of the Minister of Finance (V. Giscard d'Estaing) 1971–73; Under-Sec. Ministry of Economy and Finance 1971–72; Dir Crédit National 1973–75, Crédit Lyonnais 1973–75; Gen. Del. for Energy 1975–78; Financial Minister, French Embassy in Washington, DC 1978–82; Exec. Dir IMF and World Bank 1978–81; apptd Insp.-Gen. of Finances 1981; Man. Dir Banque Nationale de Paris 1986–87, Dir-Gen. 1987–90; Pres. Dir-Gen. Crédit Nat. 1987–90; Pres. Crédit sucrier 1990, technopole de Caen Synergia 1991–94, Valréal 1992–, Trouville-Deauville Dist 1995– (Communauté de communes Cœur Côte Fleurie from 2002); Exec. Sec. Cttee for the Monetary Union of Europe; Dir European Investment Bank 1987–91; Prof., Ecole des Hautes Etudes Commerciales; mem. Supervisory Council Crédit local de France 1987–90, Franco-German Council of Econ. Analysis 2004–; Dir, Affine; Founder Victimes et Citoyens (support group for victims of road traffic accidents) 2001, Pres. 2004–; Chevalier, Ordre nat. du Mérite, des Arts et des Lettres; Saudi Royal Order. *Publications:* Imaginer l'avenir, Gulliver enchaîné 1982, The Fund, Commercial Banks, and Member Countries 1984, L'Amerique et nous: L'insoutenable légèreté du fort 1989, Crise financière: Les fondements de l'analyse franco-allemande 2009, L'Allemagne et la France face a la crise financière 2009; articles on economic issues in Le Figaro, Le Monde and Les Echos. *Leisure interests:* tennis, skiing. *Address:* Communauté de Communes Coeur Côte Fleurie, 12 Rue Robert Fossorier BP 30086, 14803 Deauville Cedex (office); 18 rue de Bourgogne, 75007 Paris, France (home). *Telephone:* 2-31-88-54-49 (office). *Fax:* 2-31-88-19-76 (office). *E-mail:* info@coeurcotefleurie.org (office). *Website:* www.coeurcotefleurie.org (office).

MENYAYLO, Sergei Ivanovich; Russian naval officer and government official; *Presidential Representative to the Siberian Federal Okrug;* b. 22 Aug. 1960, Alagir, North Osetiyan ASSR (now Repub. of North Osetiya—Alaniya), Russian SFSR, USSR; ed S.M. Kirov Caspian Higher Naval School, Baku, Azerbaijan SSR, Adm. N.G. Kuznetsov Mil. Acad., St Petersburg, Mil. Acad. of Gen. Staff of Armed Forces of the Russian Fed.; trawler commdr 1986–90; Deputy, Murmansk Oblast Soviet from 1990; commdr of sea trawler 'Rear Admiral Vlasov' from 1991; apptd Commdr in the Caspian Flotilla 1998; Capt. of the First Rank 2004; Commdr Novorossiisk Naval Base 2005–09; rank of Vice-Adm. 2007; led naval amphibious campaign in Abkhazian territorial waters during war in South Ossetia 2008, led peacekeeping contingent in area of combat operations; Deputy Commdr, Black Sea Fleet 2009–10; nominated as one of three cands of Yedinaya Rosiya (United Russia) for post of Head of Rep. of North Osetiya-Alaniya 2010; Head of Crimean Maritime Ports –2014; Gov. and Chair. Govt of Sevastopol City 2014–16; Presidential Rep. to the Siberian Fed. Okrug 2016–. *Address:* Office of the Presidential Representative to the Siberian Federal Okrug, 630091 Novosibirsk, ul. Derzhavina 18, Russian Federation (office). *Telephone:* (3832) 20-17-56 (office). *Fax:* (3832) 20-13-90 (office). *E-mail:* info@sibfo.ru (office); orgdep@sfo.rsnet.ru (office). *Website:* sfo.gov.ru (office).

MENZEL, Jiří; Czech film and theatre director and actor; b. 23 Feb. 1938; s. of Josef Menzel and Božena Jindřichová; ed Film Acad. of Performing Arts, specialized in film directing, 1957–61; film Dir and actor 1962–89; Head of Dept of Film Directing, Film Acad. of Performing Arts, Prague 1990–92; Producer of Studio 89 1991–; Dir Vinohradské divadlo (theatre) 1997, 1998–, Artistic Dir 2000; mem. Supervisory Bd OPS, Prague, European City of Culture 2000 1999; Officier des Arts et des Lettres 1990, Medal of Merit 1996; Oscar Prize, Santa Monica 1968 for Closely Observed Trains, Akira Kurosawa Prize for Lifelong Merits in Cinematography, San Francisco 1990, Ennio Flaiano, Prize for Lifetime Achievement in Cinematography, Pescara, Italy 1996; Czech Lion Prize, Czech Film and TV Acad. (for lifetime career) 1997, Golden Seal Prize (Yugoslavia) 1997. *Plays directed:* Pré by J. Suchyś, Prague 1999, A Midsummer Night's Dream, Český Krumlov 2000. *Opera directed:* Dalibor by Smetana Cagliari 1999. *Recent film roles:* Jak si zaslouzit princeznu (How to Deserve a Princess) 1995, Ma je pomsta (Revenge is Mine) 1995, Truck Stop 1996, Une trop bruyante solitude (Too Loud a Solitude) 1996, Franciska vasárnapjai (Every Sunday) 1997, Vsichni moji blízcí (All My Loved Ones, USA) 1999, Ab ins Paradies (When Grandpa Loved Rita Hayworth) 2000, Potonulo groblje (The Sunken Cemetery) 2002, Útek do Budína 2002, Világszám! 2004, Rokonok 2006, Medvídek 2007, Operation Dunaj 2009, Signál 2012, The Door 2012. *Films directed include:* Ostre sledované vlaky (Closely Observed Trains) 1966, Vesnicko má strediskovа́ (My Sweet Little Village) 1985, Konec starych casu (The End of the Good Old Days) (Grand Prize of the Int. Film Producers' Meeting, Cannes 1990) 1989, Skriváncі na niti (Skylarks on the String) 1990, The Beggar's Opera 1991, The Life and Extraordinary Adventures of Private Ivan Chonkin 1994, Ten Minutes Older: The Cello 2002, Obsluhoval jsem anglického krále (I Served the King of England) 2006, Jirí Menzel: 7 Questions (video documentary short) 2011, The Don Juans 2013. *Television includes:* Drákuluv svagr (mini-series) 1996, Hospoda (series) 1996–97, Zimni vila (film) 1999, A bárány utolsó megkísértése (film) 2007, Setkání v Praze, s vrazdou (film) 2009, Vyprávej (series) 2009. *Publication:* Tak nevím (novel) 1998. *Leisure interest:* literature. *Address:* Studio 89, Krátký film Praha a.s., Jindřišská 34, 112 07 Prague 1 (office); Divadlo na Vinchradech, Náměstí míru 7, 120 00 Prague 2, Czech Republic (home). *Telephone:* (2) 22520452 (office). *Fax:* (2) 22520452. *E-mail:* dnv@anet.cz.

MER, Francis Paul, LèsL (Econs); French business executive; b. 25 May 1939, Pau, Basses Pyrénées; s. of René Mer and Yvonne Casalta; m. Catherine Bonfils 1964; three d.; ed Lycée Montesquieu, Bordeaux, Ecole Nationale Supérieure des Mines, Paris and Ecole Polytechnique; mining engineer, Ministry of Industry 1966; tech. adviser, Abidjan 1967–68; Chair. Inter-ministerial Cttee on European Econ. Co-operation 1969–70; Head of Planning, Saint-Gobain Industries 1971; Dir of Planning, Compagnie Saint-Gobain-Pont-à-Mousson 1973; Dir of Planning, later Dir-Gen. Saint-Gobain Industries 1973; Dir Société des Maisons Phénix 1976–78; Asst Dir-Gen. Saint-Gobain-Pont-à-Mousson 1978–82, Pres.-Dir-Gen. de Pont-à-Mousson SA 1982–86; Pres.-Dir-Gen. Usinor-Sacilor 1986–2002, Chair. Usinor Group 2001–02; Pres. Chambre syndicale de la sidérurgie française 1988–, Conservatoire Nat. des Arts et Métiers 1989–, Eurofer 1990–97, Asscn nat. de Recherche Technique 1991–, Centre d'études prospectives et d'informations internationales 1995–2000; Pres. Int. Iron and Steel Inst. (INSI) 1997–98; Dir Crédit Lyonnais 1997–, Electricité de France 1997–, Air France 1997–; Minister of the Economy, Finance and Industry 2002–04; Chair. Fondation pour L'Innovation Politique 2004; mem. Bd of Dirs Inco 2005–; Chair. Supervisory Bd Group Safran 2006–13; Commdr, Légion d'honneur, Ordre nat. du Mérite. *Address:* 9 rue Bobierre-de-Vallière, 92340 Bourg-la-Reine, France (home).

MERABISHVILI, Ivane (Vano); Georgian politician; b. 15 April 1968, Ude, Adigen Dist (now in Samtskhe-Javakheti Mkhare), Georgian SSR, USSR; m. Tamar (Tako) Salaqaia; two s.; ed Tech. Univ. of Georgia; began career as Lab. Asst, Tech. Univ. of Georgia and Agrarian Univ., becoming Chief Lab. Asst, Asst, Jr Researcher 1992–95; Pres. Asscn for the Protection of Landowners' Rights 1995–; mem. Sakartvelos Parlamenti (Parl.) 1999–, Chair. Parl. Cttee for Econ. Policy and Reforms 2000–; Sec., Nat. Security Council Jan.–June 2004; Minister of State Security June–Dec. 2004, of Internal Affairs 2004–12; Prime Minister of Georgia July–Oct. 2012; mem. Union of Citizens of Georgia –2002, Ertiani Natsionaluri Modzraoba (ENM—United Nat. Movt) 2002– (Sec.-Gen. 2012–15); arrested along with Zurab Tchiaberashvili over alleged misspending of public funds by party activists during the 2012 election campaign May 2013, found guilty by Kutaisi City Court of abuse of office, bribery of voters and inefficient use of budget funds and sentenced to five years' imprisonment Feb. 2014, appealing the sentence, European Court of Human Rights declared his pre-trial detention to have been ordered on political grounds June 2016. *Address:* c/o Ertiani Natsionaluri Modzraoba (United National Movement), 0118 Tbilisi, Kakheti 45A, Georgia (office). *Telephone:* (32) 292-30-84 (office). *Fax:* (32) 292-30-91 (office). *E-mail:* info@unm.ge (office). *Website:* www.unm.ge (office).

MERAIKHI, Ahmed al-, PhD, MSc; Qatari diplomatist and UN official; *Secretary-General's Humanitarian Envoy, UN;* ed Sheffield Hallam Univ., UK; Vice-Chair., Qatar Coordination Cttee for Charity Asscns 2008; Dir, Int. Devt Dept, Ministry of Foreign Affairs 2010–16, also Dir-Gen., Qatar Devt Fund 2010–16; mem. UN Central Emergency Response Fund (CERF) Advisory Group 2013, Vice-Chair. 2015; UN Sec.-Gen.'s Humanitarian Envoy 2017–; Vice-Pres., Qatar Regulatory Authority for Charitable Activity 2014–; mem. Exec. Cttee, Education Above All Foundation 2011–. *Address:* Office of the Secretary-General, United Nations, New York, NY 10017, USA (office). *Telephone:* (212) 963-1234 (office). *Fax:* (212) 963-4879 (office). *Website:* www.un.org/sg (office).

MERALI, Naushad Noorali; Kenyan business executive; *Chairman and CEO, Sameer Group of Companies;* b. 1 Feb. 1951, Nairobi; m. Zarin Merali; launched first ind. Pan-African mobile phone network, Kencell Communications (with Vivendi Telecom) 2000 (later sold to Celtel and Bharti Airtel); currently Chair. and

CEO Sameer Group of Cos; est. first Kenya Export Processing Zone 1991; Dir, Sasini Ltd, Ryce East Africa Ltd; Co-founder Zarina and Naushad Merali Foundation; mem. Conf. Bd, New York; Chief of the Order of the Burning Spears; Hon. Dr of Business Leadership (Kabarak Univ.) 2016. *Address:* Sameer Group of Companies, 49 Riverside Drive, PO Box 55358, Nairobi 00200, Kenya (office). *Telephone:* (20) 4204000 (office). *E-mail:* info@sameer-group.co.ke (office). *Website:* www.sameer-group.com (office).

MERCADO RAMOS, Fernando, BA, JD; Puerto Rican politician, lawyer and poet; b. 18 June 1957, Lares; s. of Tomas Mercado-Estremere and Luz M. Ramos-Valez; m. Michelle Waters; two s.; ed Univ. of Puerto Rico, Univ. of Madrid, Spain; teacher of psychology and sociology, Colegio Nuestra Señora del Carmen Rió Piedras 1979–1981; legal counsel, Culture Comm., House of Reps 1982–84; Exec. Dir Comm. of the Govt 1985–88, Sec.-Gen. 1989–92; judge, Court of the First Instance 1992, Sec.-Gen. 1999; Sec.-Gen. Partido Popular Democrático 1999–2000; Sec. of State 2001–03; prominent political analyst for the Notiuno radio network in Puerto Rico; mem. American Acad. of Judicial Educ. 1996, American Judicature Soc., ABA Judicial Admin. Div., American Judges' Asscn, Colegio de Abogados de Puerto Rico 1981. *Publications include:* Grito a la Intimidad 1976, Un Pensamiento en Viaje 1990, Un Nuevo Lider: Esperanza de una Nueva Generacıón 1991. *Leisure interests:* reading, swimming, writing.

MERCIER, Gen. Denis; French air force officer and international organization official; *Supreme Allied Commander Transformation, NATO;* b. 4 Oct. 1959, Barcelonnette; m. Agnès Mercier; three c.; ed Air Force Acad.; long career in French Air Force, beginning as fighter pilot, air force bases in Orange 1983–87 and Dijon 1987–88, Commdr, Ile de France Fighter Squadron, Orange 1988–91, Commdr, Cambrésis Fighter Squadron, Cambrai 1991–94, at aerial combat command centre, Metz 1994–97, Jt Operational Planning HQ, Creil 1997–99; Deputy Head, Allied Jt Force Command, Brunssum, Netherlands 1999–2002; Commdr, Marin-la-Meslée air force base, Reims 2002–04; assigned to Air Force HQ, Paris, first in planning div. 2004–07, becoming Deputy Head of budget and performance div. 2007–08; Commdr, Air Force Acad., Salon de Provence 2008–10; Sr Mil. Adviser, Ministry of Defence 2010–12; Chief of Staff, Air Force 2012–15; Supreme Allied Commdr Transformation, NATO, Brussels 2015–; Officier, Légion d'honneur, Officier, Ordre national du Mérite; several medals including Médaille de l'Aéronautique, Médaille de Reconnaissance de la Nation, Médaille commémorative française. *Leisure interests:* drawing and painting, skiing. *Address:* North Atlantic Treaty Organization, blvd Léopold III, 1110 Brussels, Belgium (office). *Telephone:* (2) 707-41-11 (office). *Fax:* (2) 707-45-79 (office). *E-mail:* natodoc@hq.nato.int (office). *Website:* www.nato.int (office).

MERCIER, Michel; French lawyer and politician; *Deputy Mayor of Thizy;* b. 7 March 1947, Bourg-de-Thizy (Rhône); ed Institut d'études politiques, Lyon; began career as Lecturer, Dept of Law, Univ. Lyon III; Municipal Councillor, Thizy 1971–, Mayor of Thizy 1977–2001, Deputy Mayor 2006–; Gen. Councillor, Rhône 1978–, Pres. Rhône Gen. Council 1990–; Vice-Pres. Rhône-Alpes Regional Council 1992–93 (resgnd), Regional Councillor 1992–93 (resgnd); mem. Assemblée nationale (Parl.) for Rhône 1993–95; mem. Court of Justice of the Repub. 1994–2009; Senator for Rhône 1995–2009, 2012–14, 2014–; Pres. Senate Union Centriste Group 2002–09; Minister of Rural Areas and Spatial Planning 2009–10, of Justice and Freedoms and Keeper of the Seals 2010–12; Treas. Mouvement Démocrate 2007–09, Union pour la démocratie française 1998–2007; mem. Union pour un Mouvement Populaire (UMP) 2009; mem. Union des démocrates et indépendants (UDI); Kt, Holy Order of Saint-Sépulcre. *Address:* Mairie de Thizy, Parc Charles Moncorgé, 69240 Thizy, France (office). *Telephone:* (4) 74-64-05-29 (office). *Fax:* (4) 74-64-30-22 (office). *E-mail:* info@thizy.fr (office). *Website:* www.thizy.fr (office).

MERCKX, Eddy; Belgian fmr cyclist; b. 17 June 1945, Meen, Brussels sel-Kiezegem; m. Claudine Merckx; one s. one d.; world amateur champion 1963, first professional race 1964, winner World Road Championships 1967, 1971, 1974, Tours of Italy 1968, 1970, 1972, 1973, 1974, Tours de France 1969, 1970, 1971, 1972, 1974, 2016 (shares record for most wins, holds record (34) for most stage wins), Tours of Belgium 1970, 1971, Tour of Spain 1973, Tour of Switzerland 1974, 32 major classics; broke the then world hour record, Mexico City 1972; retd 1978 with 525 wins in 1,800 races; involved with manufacture of bicycles which bear his name 1980–; Co-Owner, Tour of Qatar, Tour of Oman; Belgian Sportsman of the Year 1969–74 (record), Belgian Athlete of the Century.

MEREDOV, Myratgeldy; Turkmenistani oil industry executive and government official; b. 1977; ed Turkmen Polytechnic Inst.; began career as a research asst at Turkmen Polytechnic Inst. 1994–95; worked at Oil and Gas Inst. of state gas holding Turkmengas 2000–13; transferred to Office of Pres.'s Chief of Staff 2013–14; Deputy Minister in charge of oil and gas production 2014–15, Minister of Petroleum and Gas Industry and Mineral Resources (renamed Ministry of Oil and Gas 2016) 2015–16.

MEREDOV, Rashid; Turkmenistani politician; *Deputy Chairman of the Government and Minister of Foreign Affairs;* b. 1960, Aşgabat, Turkmen SSR, USSR; ed Faculty of Law, Moscow Lomonosov State Univ.; teacher, Dept of Civil Law, Turkmen State Univ. 1982; Lecturer, then Sr Lecturer 1987–90; Chief Consultant and Head of Section, Head of Dept, Ministry of Justice, Turkmen SSR 1990–91; Head of law enforcement agencies under Pres. of Turkmenistan 1991–; Head of Law Dept, Office of the Pres. 1993–; Deputy Dir, Nat. Inst. for Democracy and Human Rights 1996–99, Dir 2001–05; First Deputy Minister of Foreign Affairs 1999–2001, Minister of Foreign Affairs 2001–; First Deputy Chair. of Majlis (Nat. Ass.) 1999–2001, Chair. 2001–; Deputy Chair. of the Govt 2003–05; Deputy Chair. of the Govt, responsible for the police and army 2007–; For the Love of Fatherland Medal, Gayrat Medal, Galkynyş Order, 20 Years of Independence of Turkmenistan Medal. *Address:* Ministry of Foreign Affairs, 744000 Aşgabat, Arşabil şaýoly 108, Turkmenistan (office). *Telephone:* (12) 44-56-92 (office). *Fax:* (12) 44-58-12 (office). *E-mail:* info@mfa.gov.tm (office). *Website:* www.mfa.gov.tm/en (office).

MERENTES DÍAZ, Nelson José, PhD; Venezuelan politician and central banker; ed Central Univ. of Venezuela and Univ. of Budapest, Hungary; Minister of Science and Tech. Feb.–Nov. 2002, of State for Devt and Econs 2002–04, of State for Financial Devt Sept.–Dec. 2004, of Finance 2004–07, 2013–14; Pres. Nat. Bank for Econ. and Social Devt 2002–04; fmr Gov. for Venezuela World Bank, IMF, Caribbean Devt Bank; Head of Public Finance Office 2004–07; mem. Bd of Dirs Banco Central de Venezuela 2007–, Pres. 2009–13, 2014–17. *Address:* Banco Central de Venezuela, Avda Urdaneta, esq. de Carmelitas, Caracas 1010, Venezuela (office). *Telephone:* (212) 801-5111 (office). *Fax:* (212) 861-0048 (office). *E-mail:* info@bcv.org.ve (office). *Website:* www.bcv.org.ve (office).

MEREZHKO, Viktor Ivanovich; Russian scriptwriter; b. 28 July 1937, Olginfeld, Rostov-on-Don Region; widowed; one s. one d.; ed Ukrainian Inst. of Polygraphy, Lvov, All-Union Inst. of Cinematography; engineer Molot Publrs, Rostov-on-Don 1961–64; freelance 1968–; TV broadcaster and Head of History Programming; Vice-Pres. TV-6 Ind. TV; Chair. Kinoshock Festival, Nika Prize Cttee; State Prize 1986. *Plays include:* I'm a Woman, Cry, Caucasian Roulette. *Film scripts:* Slepoy dozhd (short) 1968, Tigry na ldu 1971, Zdravstvuy i proshchay (Hello and Goodbye) 1972, Odinozhdy odin (One Once) 1974, Tryn-trava 1976, Vasilisa Prekrasnaya (short) 1977, Zhuravl v nebe (Crane in the Sky) 1977, Vas ozhidayet grazhdanka Nikanorova (Citizen Nikanorova Waits for You) 1978, Ukhodya – ukhodi 1978, Tryasina (Quagmire) 1978, Ukhodya – ukhodi 1978, Premudryy peskar (short) 1979, Kholostyaki (short) 1980, Otstavnoy kozy barabanshchik 1981, Rodnya (Kinfolk) 1983, Polyoty vo sne i nayavu (Flights in Dreams and in Reality) 1983, Polosa vezeniya (Goldfishes) 1983, Osobyy sluchay 1983, Yesli mozhesh, prosti… (If You Can, Forgive…) 1984, Aplodismenty, aplodismenty… (Applause, Applause…) 1984, Scamper the Penguin (as V. Merezhko) 1986, Odinokaya zhenshchina zhelayet poznakomitsya (Lonely Woman Seeks Lifetime Companion) 1986, Prosti (Forgive Me) (also actor) 1986, Zabavy molodykh (Joys of Youth) 1987, 9 maya (short) 1987, Under the Blue Sky (Fipressi Prize, Venice Festival) 1989, Avtoportret neizvestnogo (Selfportrait of an Unknown Man) 1989, Martokhela monadire (Lonely Hunter) 1989, Shag (aka Message from the Future) 1990, Sobachiy pir (Dogs' Feast) 1990, Nochnye zabavy (Night Fun) 1991, Yesli by znat… (If We'd Only Known…) 1993, Kurochka Ryaba (Ryaba My Chicken) 1994, Greshnye apostoly lyubvi 1995, Ligne de vie (Line of Life) 1996, The Two from Big Road 1996, Kavkazskaya ruletka (Caucasus Roulette) 2002, Lisa Alisa (video) 2003, Zhuliki 2006. *Film roles:* Yesli yest parusa 1969, Pod nebom golubym 1989, Dikiy plyazh 1990, Russkiy roman (Russian Romance) 1993. *Television includes:* scriptwriter: Lisa Patrikeevna (short) 1982, Medved lipovaya noga (film) 1984, Krot (series) 2001, Saga o kriminale (series) 2001, Provintsialy (series) (also actor) 2002, Sonka zolotaya ruchka (series) 2007, Sonka. Prodolzheniye legendy (series) 2010, Khutoryanin (series) 2013. *Leisure interest:* collecting side-arms. *Address:* 125319 Moscow, Usiyevicha str. 8, Apt 133, Russia. *Telephone:* (495) 217-57-58; (495) 155-74-59.

MERIDOR, Dan, LLB; Israeli lawyer and politician; b. 23 April 1947, Jerusalem; m. Liora Meridor; four c.; ed Hebrew Univ. of Jerusalem; served in Israel Defence Forces (IDF) as tank commander in 1967 Six Day War, continued to serve as captain in IDF reserves; practised law Jerusalem 1973–82; Cabinet Sec. of Govt 1982–84; mem. Knesset 1984–2003, 2009–13; Minister of Justice 1988–92, of Finance 1996–97; Chair. Foreign Affairs and Defense Cttee 1997–2001; Minister without Portfolio responsible for Nat. Defence and Diplomatic Strategy 2001–03; Leader Centre Party 2001; fmr Deputy Prime Minister and Minister of Intelligence and Atomic Energy; mem. Likud Party 1984–99, 2009–13; Lamont Lecturer, Harvard Kennedy School 2013; Chair. Bezalel Acad. of Art and Design, Jerusalem; fmr Chair. Israel Museum, Int. Chair Jerusalem Foundation, Sr Fellow, Israel Democracy Inst. *Address:* c/o Bezalel Academy of Arts and Design, Mount Scopus, PO Box 24046, 9124001, Jerusalem, Israel (office).

MERIMÉE, Jean-Bernard, LenD; French diplomatist (retd); b. 4 Dec. 1936, Toulouse (Haute-Garonne); s. of Jacques Merimée and Germaine Merimée (née Larrieu); m. Anna Mirams 1965; one s. two d.; ed Lycées Pasteur, Neuilly-sur-Seine and Louis-le-Grand, Paris, Institut d'Etudes Politiques de Paris, Ecole Nat. d'Admin, Paris; with Cen. Admin, Ministry of Foreign Affairs 1965, with Sec.-Gen. 1972–75; Second then First Sec. to UK 1966–72; Chief of Mission of Co-operation, Côte d'Ivoire 1975–78, Chief of Protocol 1978–81; Amb. to Australia 1982–85, to India 1985–87, to Morocco, Rabat 1987–91; Amb. and Perm. Rep. to Security Council and Chief of Perm. Mission to UN, New York 1991–95; Amb. to Italy, Rome 1995–98, to Repub. of San Marino (resident in Rome) 1997–98, to Cen. Admin 1998–99; Perm. Rep. to UN 1999, Special Adviser to Sec.-Gen. on European Affairs with rank of Under-Sec.-Gen. 1999–2001; Dir Groupe Benjelloun (mobile telephone, banking and insurance cos), Morocco; mem. Advisory Bd BMCE Bank, France; Officier, Légion d'honneur, Officier, Ordre nat. du Mérite, Commdr of the Order of Christ (Portugal), Grand Officer of the Order of the Phoenix (Greece), Kt of the Dannebrog (Denmark), Officer of the Oak Crown (Luxembourg), Merit Commdr of the Supreme Order of Malta. *Address:* 21 bis rue Molière, 75001 Paris, France.

MÉRINDOL, Nicolas, BA, MBA; French certified public accountant and banking executive; *President, Carmin Group;* b. 20 Feb. 1961; ed Institut Supérieur de Gestion, Institut Nat. des Techniques Economiques et Comptables; began career with Renault in Argentina and France; later worked at Caisse des Dépôts; joined Exec. Cttee of Groupe Caisse d'Epargne 1988, moved to Caisse d'Epargne de Picardie 1991, served as Finance and Risk Man. Dir before joining Man. Bd of regional savings bank, apptd Dir for Org. 1996, later Dir of Financial Planning at Caisse Nationale des Caisses d'Epargne, mem. Man. Bd Caisse Nationale des Caisses d'Epargne with responsibility for banking operations and finance 2002–03, responsible for Commercial Banking Div. and Corp. Strategy 2003–06, CEO Caisse Nationale des Caisses d'Epargne 2006–08; Vice-Pres. Banca Leonardo 2009–; Chair. Crédit Foncier, Gce Fidelisation; apptd Pres. Amilton Finance 2012; Pres. Carmin Group 2014–; Chair. Supervisory Bd Banque Palatine, Compagnie 1818, Gestrim, Ecureil Gestion, Ixis Pvt. Capital Management, Banquiers Prives, Sa Cemm, Ecureuil-vie F; Chair. European Banking Industry Cttee 2006, Vice-Chair. 2007–; mem. Nat. Council for Sustainable Devt; mem. Bd Dirs Nat. Agency for Personal Care Services 2006–; mem. Bd Fund for Social Cohesion, Steering Cttee France Investissement; mem. Supervisory Bd Ixis Asset Management, Ecufoncier-SCA, Natixis Corporate & Investment Bank (fmr Vice-Chair.), CNP Assurances, Gce - Newtec SAS F, BPCE International et Outre-Mer SA; Chevalier de la Légion d'honneur 2015, l'ordre du Ouissam El Alaouite, Morocco. *Address:* Carmin Group, 153 Blvd Haussman, 75008 Paris, France (office). *Telephone:* 1-85-08-74-26 (office). *E-mail:* contact@carmin-group.com (office). *Website:* www.groupe-carmin.com (office).

MERINO LUCERO, Beatriz, MA; Peruvian lawyer, politician and government official; *President, Sociedad Peruana de Hidrocarburos;* b. 1949, Lima; ed Universidad Nacional Mayor de San Marcos, London School of Econs, UK, Harvard Univ. Law School, USA; lawyer, fmrly specializing in tax and int. trade; elected Senator (Movimiento Libertad) 1990–92; mem. Congreso (Frente Independiente Moralizador) 1995–2000; Dir Master Tax and Fiscal Policy, Univ. of Lima 2000–01; elected Head of Sunat (tax agency) 2001–03; Pres. Council of Ministers (Prime Minister) June–Dec. 2003; mem. Inter-American Dialogue, Washington, DC –2005; Defensora del Pueblo (Ombudsman) 2005–11; Pres. Asociación de Administradoras de Fondos de Pensiones 2011–12; Pres. Sociedad Peruana de Hidrocarburos (Peruvian Soc. of Hydrocarbons) 2013–; Orden de la Cruz del Sur en el grado de Gran Cruz 2003, Orden 'El Sol del Perú' en el Grado de Gran Cruz 2006, Orden al Mérito de la Mujer 2010; Dr hc (Universidad Nacional Federico Villarreal) 2003, (Universidad Particular de Chiclayo) 2003, (Universidad Nacional San Agustín de Arequipa) 2007; María Elena Moyano Prize, Ministry of Women and Social Devt, Vaso de Leche Award of the Women of Peru, Woman of the Year, OWIT Peru, Robert G. Storey Int. Award for Leadership, Center for American and Int. Law 2004, Lifetime Achievement Award, Harvard Univ. 2015. *Address:* Sociedad Peruana de Hidrocarburos, Av. César Vallejo 627, Lima 14, Peru (office). *Telephone:* (1) 4211556 (office). *Website:* www.sphidrocarburos.com (office).

MÉRITON, Vincent, MA; Seychelles politician; *Vice-President;* b. 28 Dec. 1960, Victoria; m.; one s. two d.; ed Lomonosov Moscow State Univ., Russia; mem. Nat. Ass. (Parl.) 1998–2002; various ministerial portfolios since 2004, including Minister for Employment, Health, Culture, Designated Minister 2010–16, also Minister for Community Devt, Social Affairs and Sports 2015–16; Vice-Pres. 2016–, with additional responsibility for Industry and Entrepreneurship Devt, Foreign Affairs, Information, ICT and the Blue Economy 2018–. *Address:* Office of the Vice-President, State House, POB 55, Victoria, Seychelles (office). *Telephone:* 4295600 (office). *Fax:* 4225152 (office).

MERKEL, Angela Dorothea, Dr rer. nat; German politician; *Chancellor;* b. 17 July 1954, Hamburg; d. of Horst Kasner and Herlind Kasner; m. 1st Ulrich Merkel (divorced 1982); m. 2nd Joachim Sauer 1998; ed Univ. of Leipzig; Research Assoc. in quantum chem., Zentralinstitut für physikalische Chemie, East Berlin 1978–90; joined Demokratischer Aufbruch (DA) 1989, Press Spokesperson 1990; Deputy Spokesman for Govt of Lothar de la Maizière, March–Oct. 1990; joined CDU (Christian Democratic Union) 1990, mem. Bundestag for Stralsund – Nordvorpommern – Rügen constituency 1990–2013, for Vorpommern-Rügen and Vorpommern-Greifswald I 2013–, Deputy Fed. Chair. 1991–98, CDU Chair. Fed. State of Mecklenburg-Vorpommern 1993–2000, Gen. Sec. CDU 1998–2000, Chair. 2000–18, also Parl. Leader 2002–05; Fed. Minister for Women and Young People 1991–94, for Environment, Nature Conservation and Nuclear Safety 1994–98; Chancellor 2005–; Pres. European Council and Chair. G8 2007; Chair. G7 2015; mem. Council of Women World Leaders; Bundesverdienstkreuz 2008, Order Stara Planina (Bulgaria) 2010, Grosses Goldenes Ehrenzeichen am Bande für Verdienste um die Republik Österreich 2015; Dr hc (Hebrew Univ. of Jerusalem) 2007, (Univ. of Leipzig) 2008, (Univ. of Tech., Wrocław) 2008, (Univ. of Bern) 2009, (Babeş-Bolyai Univ., Cluj Napoca) 2010, (Womens Univ. EWHA, Seoul) 2010, (Univ. of Tel-Aviv) 2011, (Radboud Univ., Nijmegen) 2013, (Comenius Univ., Bratislava) 2014, (Szeged Univ., Budapest) 2015, (Nanjing) 2016, (Catholic Univ. of Leuven) 2017, (Univ. of Ghent) 2017, (Univ. of Haifa) 2018; named a Hero of the Environment 2007, Charlemagne Prize for distinguished services to European unity 2008; Presidential Medal of Freedom (USA) 2011, Jawaharlal Nehru Award 2011, Indira Ghandi Prize for Peace 2013, Presidential Award of Distinction (Israel) 2014, Four Freedoms Awards Freedom Medal 2016, Eugen Bolz Prize 2017, Elie Wiesel Award 2017, Lamp of Peace 2018, J. William Fulbright Prize for Int. Understanding 2018. *Publications include:* Der Preis des Überlebens: Gedanken und Gespräche über zukünftige Aufgaben der Umweltpolitik (The Price of Survival: Ideas and Conversations about Future Tasks for Environmental Policy) 1997, I believe in that: Christian points of view 2013. *Leisure interests:* reading, hiking, gardening. *Address:* Office of the Federal Chancellery, Willy-Brandt-str. 1, 10557 Berlin, Germany (office). *Telephone:* (30) 182722720 (office). *E-mail:* internetpost@bpa.bund.de (office). *Website:* www.bundeskanzlerin.de (office); www.angela-merkel.de.

MERKIN, J(acob) Ezra; American business executive; b. 19 April 1953; s. of Hermann Merkin and Ursula Sara Merkin (née Breuer); ed Columbia Coll., New York, Harvard Univ. Law School, Cambridge, Mass; Man. Partner, Gabriel Capital Group (and its predecessor) 1985–2008; Chair. GMAC Financial Services 2008–09 (resgnd); fmr Trustee and Chair. Investment Cttees, Yeshiva Univ. and of UJA/Fed. of New York; Trustee, Carnegie Hall, New York, Beyeler Foundation and Museum, Basel, Switzerland, Gruss Foundation; mem. Bd of Visitors, Columbia Coll.; Gov. Levy Econs Inst. of Bard Coll., Annandale-on-Hudson, NY; Pres. Fifth Avenue Synagogue, New York; fmr Vice-Chair. Ramaz School, New York.

MERKLEY, Jeffery (Jeff) Alan, BA, MA; American politician; *Senator from Oregon;* b. 24 Oct. 1956, Myrtle Creek, Ore.; m. Mary Sorteberg 1992; one s. one d.; ed Stanford Univ., Princeton Univ.; Presidential Man. Fellow, Office of the US Sec. of Defense, Washington, DC 1982–91; Man. Partner, Computer Medics 1989–91; Exec. Dir Portland Habitat for Humanity 1991–94; Dir of Housing Devt at Human Solutions 1995–96; Pres. World Affairs Council of Oregon 1996–2003, mem. Bd of Trustees 1991–; mem. Oregon State House of Reps 1998–2009, Speaker 2007–09; Senator from Oregon 2009–, mem. Health, Educ., Labor and Pensions Cttee, Banking, Housing and Urban Affairs Cttee, Environment and Public Works Cttee, Budget Cttee; Founder People's Investment Opportunity Program, Walk for Humanity; Democrat. *Address:* 313 Hart Senate Office Building, Washington, DC 20510 (office); PO Box 14172, Portland, OR 97293, USA. *Telephone:* (202) 224-3753 (Washington, DC) (office). *Fax:* (202) 228-3997 (Washington, DC) (office); 503-295-0670 (Portland). *Website:* merkley.senate.gov (office); www.jeffmerkley.com.

MERLINI, Cesare; Italian international affairs scholar and fmr professor of nuclear technologies; *Chairman, Board of Trustees, Istituto Affari Internazionali;* b. 29 April 1933, Rome; m.; two s. two d.; ed Classical Licée, Turin, Turin Polytechnic; Lecturer in Nuclear Technologies 1967–76; Prof. of Nuclear Technologies, Turin Polytechnic 1976–85; Dir Istituto Affari Internazionali, Rome 1970–79, Pres. 1979–2000, currently Chair. Bd of Trustees; Vice-Pres. Exec. Cttee Consiglio per le Relazioni fra Italia e Stati Uniti (Council for USA and Italy) 1983–2009; mem. Bd of Dirs and Exec. Cttee, Unione Tipografico-Editrice Torinese Publrs SpA, Turin, Chair. 1999–2002; mem. Trilateral Comm. 1973–2001, Council, IISS, London 1993–99; Non-resident Sr Fellow, Center on the United States and Europe, Brookings Inst., Washington DC 2010–. *Publications:* Fine dell'atomo? Passato e futuro delle applicazioni civili e militari dell'energia nucleare 1987, L'Europa degli Anni Novanta: Scenari per un futuro imprevisto (co-author and ed.) 1991, Arab Society in Revolt: The West's Mediterranean Challenge (co-ed.) 2012; co-author and ed. of numerous books on nuclear energy and int. strategy, author of numerous articles on European and int. affairs and of scientific publs on nuclear reactors and related technological and eng problems. *Leisure interest:* horse riding. *Address:* Istituto Affari Internazionali, Via Angelo Brunetti 9, 00186 Rome, Italy (office). *Telephone:* (06) 3224360 (office). *Fax:* (06) 3224363 (office). *E-mail:* iai@iai.it (office). *Website:* www.iai.it (office); www.brookings.edu/experts/merlinic.

MERLO, Larry J.; American business executive; *President and CEO, CVS Health;* Exec. Vice-Pres.– Stores of CVS Pharmacy, Inc. 1998–2007, Exec. Vice-Pres.– Stores of CVS Corpn 2000–07, Exec. Vice-Pres. CVS Caremark Corpn 2007–10, Pres. CVS/pharmacy – Retail 2007–11, Pres. and COO 2010–11, Pres. and CEO CVS Caremark Corpn (now called CVS Health) 2011–; mem. Bd of Dirs, Nat. Asscn of Chain Drug Stores, Chair. 2010–11. *Address:* CVS Health, 1 CVS Drive, Woonsocket, RI 02895, USA (office). *Telephone:* (401) 765-1500 (office). *Fax:* (401) 766-2917 (office). *E-mail:* info@cvshealth.com (office). *Website:* www.cvshealth.com (office); www.cvs.com (office).

MERLONI, Andrea; Italian business executive; b. 1967, Rome; s. of Vittorio Merloni and Franca Carloni; Chair. Aermarche SpA 1992–96; bought Benelli SpA brand 1996, relaunched it in scooter and large motorbike industry, Chair. and CEO 1996–2005; Chair. and CEO WRAP SpA (part of Indesit group) 2000–07, Dir Indesit Co. SpA (fmrly Merloni Elettrodomestici SpA) 2006–, Deputy Chair. 2008–10, Chair. 2010–13; mem. Bd of Dirs Fineldo SpA (family holding co.), fmr Chair.; Chair. ISTAO – Adriano Olivetti Institute for the Study of Company Management; Chair. and CEO Alpha67 Srl. *Address:* c/o ISTAO – Adriano Olivetti Institute for the Study of Company Management, Villa Favorita, Via Zuccarini, 15, Ancona, Italy (office). *E-mail:* presidenza@istao.it (office). *Website:* istao.it (office).

MERMAZ, Louis, Agrégé d'histoire; French politician and professor of history; b. 20 Aug. 1931, Paris; m. Annie d'Arbigny; three c.; teacher Lycée le Mans, Lycée Lakanal, Sceaux; Jr Lecturer in Contemporary History, Univ. of Clermont-Ferrand; Sec.-Gen. Convention des institutions républicaines 1965–69; mem. Socialist Party Nat. Secr. 1974–79, 1987–; mem. Nat. Ass. for Isère 1967–68, 1973–90, 1997–2001; Mayor of Vienne 1971–2001; Conseiller Gén. Canton of Vienne-Nord 1973–79, Vienne-Sud 1979–88; Pres. Conseil gén. of Isère 1976–85; Chair. Socialist Party Exec. Cttee 1979; Minister of Transport May–June 1981, of Equipment and Transport May–June 1988, of Agric. and Forests 1990–92, for Relations with Parl. and Govt Spokesman 1992–93; Pres. Nat. Ass. 1981–86, Socialist Group in Nat. Ass. 1988–90, Asscn Mer du Nord-Méditerranée 1989–94; mem. Senate for Isère 2001–11; Chevalier Légion d'honneur, Officier de la Légion d'honneur. *Publications:* Madame Sabatier, Les Hohenzollern, L'autre volonté 1984, Madame de Maintenon 1985, Les Geôles de la République 2001, Il faut que je vous dise 2013. *Address:* Sénat, Palais du Luxembourg, 15 rue du Vaugirard, 75005 Paris, France (office). *Telephone:* 1-42-34-38-81 (office). *E-mail:* louismermaz@hotmail.com (office).

MERO, Modest Jonathan, BSc, MSc; Tanzanian Govt official and diplomatist; *Permanent Representative to United Nations;* b. 28 Sept. 1959; ed Univ. of Dar es Salaam, Univ. of Strathclyde, Glasgow; Sr Economist, Ministry of Industry and Trade 1987–2005; Trade Policy Adviser to Exec. Sec., SADC; Head of Policy, Ministry of Foreign Affairs and Int. Cooperation 2005–06; Minister Plenipotentiary, Econ. Adviser and Head of Chancery, Perm. Mission to UN 2007–13; Perm. Rep. to UN and int. orgs in Geneva 2013–16, Perm. Rep. to UN, New York 2016–; Vice-Pres. Int. Labour Conference 2015. *Address:* Permanent Mission of Tanzania, 307 E 53rd Street, 5th Floor, New York, NY 10022, USA (office). *Telephone:* (212) 697-3612 (office). *Fax:* (212) 697-3618 (office). *E-mail:* newyork@nje.go.tz (office). *Website:* www.un.int/tanzania (office).

MERO, Muhammad Mustafa, PhD; Syrian politician (retd); b. 1941, Tal-Mineen, Damascus; m.; two s. three d.; ed Damascus Univ.; joined Arab Teachers' Union, becoming its Sec.-Gen. for Cultural Affairs and Publs; Mayor of Daraa 1980–86, of Al-Hasaka 1986–93; Gov. of Aleppo Governorate 1993–2000; Prime Minister of Syria 2000–03 (resgnd), headed a ministerial and commercial del. to Iraq Aug. 2001 (first Syrian prime minister to visit Iraq since the Gulf War, also first Syrian prime minister to visit Turkey in 17 years 2003).

MERON, Theodor, LLM, MJ, JSD; American judge and academic; b. 28 April 1930, Kalisz, Poland; ed Univ. of Jerusalem, Harvard Univ. Law School, Univ. of Cambridge, UK; fmr Legal Adviser, Israeli Foreign Ministry, fmr Amb. of Israel to Canada, later to UN in Geneva, resgnd 1977; US citizen 1984–; Visiting Prof. of Law, New York Univ. School of Law 1975, Prof. of Law 1977, Charles L. Denison Prof. of Int. Law 1994–2003, Charles L. Denison Prof. of Law Emer. and Judicial Fellow 2006–; Prof. of Int. Law, Grad. Inst. of Int. Studies, Geneva, Switzerland 1991–95; Ed.-in-Chief American Journal of Int. Law 1993–98; Judge UN Criminal Tribunal for the Fmr Yugoslavia (ICTY) 2001–, Pres. 2003–05, 2011–13, also mem. Appeals Chamber (ICTY) and UN Criminal Tribunal for Rwanda (ICTR) 2001–; apptd Pres. Mechanism for Int. Criminal Tribunals 2012; fmr Counsellor on Int. Law US Dept of State; mem. Council on Foreign Relations; Public mem. US Del. to CSCE Conf. on Human Dimension, Copenhagen; numerous visiting lectureships in univs in Europe and USA; mem. Inst. of Int. Law; Fellow, American Acad. of Arts and Sciences 2009–; Officier, Légion d'Honneur (France) 2007, Grand Officier, Ordre nat. du mérite 2014; Int. Bar Asscn Rule of Law Award, American Soc. of Int. Law Hudson Medal 2006, American Council of Learned Soc. Haskins Prize 2008. *Publications include:* Investment Insurance in International Law, Henry's Wars and Shakespeare's Laws 1994, Bloody Constraint: War and Chivalry in Shakespeare 1998, War Crimes Law Comes of Age: Essays 1999, International Law in the Age of Human Rights 2003, The Humanization of International Law 2006, The Making of International Justice: A View from the Bench 2011; numerous articles and publs on int. law and human rights. *Address:* UN Criminal Tribunal for the Former Yugoslavia, Public Information Unit, PO Box 13888, 2501 The

Hague, Netherlands (office); New York University School of Law, Vanderbilt Hall, 40 Washington Square South, Room 304, New York, NY 10012-1099, USA. *Telephone:* (70) 512-8840 (office); (212) 998-6191 (NY). *Fax:* (70) 512-5252 (office). *E-mail:* meront@juris.law.nyu.edu. *Website:* www.un.org/icty (office); its.law.nyu.edu/facultyprofiles/profile.cfm?personID=20122 (office).

MÉRORÈS, Léo, LLB, MA, PhD; Haitian diplomatist and UN official; b. 21 April 1943; ed State Univ. of Haiti, Ecole de Commerce Maurice Laroche, Port-au-Prince, New York Univ., USA; early career as salesman, Enterprises Gerard Theard, Port-au-Prince 1961; worked part-time as accountant and Asst to Head of Credit Dept, Shapiro & Sons Textile Corpn, New York, USA 1969–73; UNDP Deputy Resident Rep. in Togo and Madagascar 1978–84, worked in UNDP office in Rwanda 1974–78, UNDP Deputy Resident Rep. for Liberia, Mali and Cameroon 1984–92, responsible for UNDP offices in Gabon and Burundi 1989–92, Prin. Counsellor for UNDP working with Econ. Community of West African States (ECOWAS) countries 1992–2001, consultant on man. and econ. co-operation issues for several UN entities, including Dept of Econ. and Social Affairs, UN Office for Project Services (UNOPS) and UNDP 2001–04; Chargé d'affaires a.i., Perm. Mission to UN, New York 2004–05, Amb. and Perm. Rep. to UN 2005–12; Vice-Pres. ECOSOC, representing Group of Latin America and Caribbean 2006–08, Pres. ECOSOC 2008–09.

MERRILL, Susan L., JD; American lawyer and securities industry executive; *Partner, Sidley & Austin LLP;* b. 1957; m.; two c.; ed Univ. of Maryland, Brooklyn Law School; moved to New York to pursue acting career; judicial clerk for Hon. Francis Van Dusen, US Court of Appeals of the Third Circuit 1986–87; Assoc. Davis Polk & Wardell (law firm), New York 1987, Partner 1994–2004; Chief Enforcement Officer, NYSE Group Inc. (fmrly New York Stock Exchange) 2004–07, Exec. Vice Pres., Enforcement, Financial Industry Regulatory Authority, Inc. (formed after consolidation of NYSE Mem. Regulation with Nat. Asscn of Securities Dealers) 2007–10; Partner, Broker-Dealer Group, Bingham McCutchen LLP 2010–13; Partner, Sidley & Austin LLP 2013–; mem. Faculty, Practising Law Inst. *Address:* Sidley & Austin LLP, 787 Seventh Avenue, New York, NY 10019, USA (office). *Telephone:* (212) 839-8558 (office). *E-mail:* smerrill@sidley.com (office). *Website:* www.sidley.com/people/susan-merrill (office).

MERSCH, Yves; Luxembourg fmr central banker; b. 1 Oct. 1949, Luxembourg Ville; ed Univ. of Paris; called to the Bar, Luxembourg 1974; Public Law Asst, Univ. Paris XI 1974; Budget Asst, Ministry of Finance 1975; mem. staff IMF, Washington, DC, USA 1976–77; Ministry of Finance, Fiscal Affairs and Structural Policies 1977–80; Adviser, Ministry of Finance, Monetary Affairs and Int. Financial Relations 1981; Govt Commr Luxembourg Stock Exchange 1985; Dir Treasury 1989–98; Pres. Luxembourg Cen. Bank 1998–2012, Alt. Gov. for Luxembourg, IMF Bd Govs 1998–2012; apptd mem. Governing Council and Gen. Council, European Cen. Bank 1998, mem. Exec. Bd 2012–; Deputy Chair. Governing Bd, Int. Islamic Liquidity Management Corpn 2010–12; Co-Chair. Regional Consultative Group for Europe, Financial Stability Bd 2011–12; Pres. The Bridge Forum Dialogue a.s.b.l 2000–12, Fondation de la Banque centrale du Luxembourg 2011–12; mem. Bd Luxembourg School of Finance 2006–; Voting mem. Gen. Bd, European Systemic Risk Bd 2011–; mem. Systemic Risk Centre Scientific Advisory Board, LSE 2013–, Central Bank Governance Group, BIS 2015–; Hon. Prof., Univ. of Luxembourg 2014; Officer, Légion d'honneur; Grand Officer, Cross of Recognition (Latvia); Dr hc (Miami Univ.) 2013; Lámfalussy Award, Magyar Nemzeti Bank 2019. *Address:* European Central Bank, Eurotower, Kaiserstrasse 29, Postfach 160319, 60311 Frankfurt am Main, Germany (office). *Telephone:* (69) 13441300 (office). *E-mail:* info@ecb.europa.eu (office). *Website:* www.ecb.europa.eu (office).

MERSON, Michael H., BA, MD; American physician and academic; *Founding Director, Duke Global Health Institute and Wolfgang Joklik Professor of Global Health, Duke University;* b. 7 June 1945, New York, NY; ed Amherst Coll., State Univ. of New York Downstate Medical Center, Johns Hopkins Univ., Baltimore, Md; Asst Medical Resident, Johns Hopkins Hosp., Baltimore 1971–72, Fellow, Infectious Diseases, Baltimore City Hosp. 1976–77; supervised medical ward aboard hosp. ship, USS Hope, northeast Brazil May–June 1972; joined Centers for Disease Control, Atlanta 1972, Commissioned Officer, US Public Health Service, assigned to Enteric Diseases Br., Bacterial Diseases Div., Epidemic Intelligence Service 1972–74, Chief, Enteric Diseases Br. 1974–75, Chief Medical Epidemiologist, Cholera Research Lab., Dhaka, Bangladesh 1977–78; Fellow, Infectious Diseases, Beth-Israel Children's Hosp. Programme, Harvard Medical School, Boston 1975–76; joined WHO 1978, Medical Officer Dir WHO Diarrhoeal Diseases Control Programme 1978–80, Programme Man. 1980–81, Dir 1984–90, Dir Acute Respiratory Infections Control Programme 1987–90, Dir Global Programme on AIDS 1990–93, Exec. Dir 1993–95; Prof., Dept of Epidemiology and Public Health, Yale Univ. School of Medicine, New Haven, Conn. 1995–2006, Dean and Chair. Dept of Epidemiology and Public Health 1995–2004, Jt Appointment, Inst. for Social and Policy Studies 1997–2006, Dir Center for Interdisciplinary Research on AIDS (CIRA) 1997–2006, Lecturer, Dept of Political Science, Yale Coll., July–Dec. 2005; Prin. Investigator Yale's AIDS Int. Training and Research Program (AITRP), St Petersburg, Russia and extension activities in China and South Africa, Prin. Investigator Int. Clinical, Operational and Health Services Research and Training Award (ICOHRTA) Programme, Pretoria, South Africa; Co-investigator, Bill and Melinda Gates Foundation, Global Health Programme; Founding Dir Duke Global Health Inst., Duke Univ., Durham, NC 2006–, Wolfgang Joklik Prof. of Global Health 2008–, Prof., Dept of Medicine, Duke Univ. Medical Center 2007–, Prof., Dept of Community and Family Medicine 2007–, Prof., Dept of Public Policy Studies 2007–, Vice-Chancellor Duke-Nat. Univ. of Singapore School of Medicine 2010–, Vice-Pres. and Vice-Provost, Duke Univ. Office of Global Strategy and Programs 2011–; mem. Center for Strategic and Int. Studies Comm. on Smart Global Health Policy 2009–; Founding mem. Consortium of Univs for Global Health Bd of Dirs 2007–; mem. Tech. Steering Cttee, Dept of Maternal, Newborn, Child and Adolescent Health, WHO 2011–, London School of Hygiene and Tropical Medicine Visiting Cttee 2011–, John E. Fogarty Int. Center Advisory Bd 2012–, External Advisory Bd of Mount Sinai Global Health 2013–, Nat. Cancer Inst. Working Group on Global Cancer Research (NIH/NCI) 2013–; mem. Editorial Bd, AIDS Journal 1993–96, Global Public Health Journal 2005–, Epidemiologic Reviews 2009–; mem. American Epidemiology Soc., Int. AIDS Soc., Royal Soc. of Tropical Medicine and Hygiene, Soc. of Scholars, Johns Hopkins Univ., Connecticut Acad. of Science and Eng, Inst. of Medicine of NAS, Paul G. Rogers Soc. for Global Health Research (Amb.); Hon. Prof., London School of Hygiene and Tropical Medicine, UK 2006–; Hon. DSc (Amherst Coll.) 1996; Hon. DHumLitt (State Univ. of NY Health Sciences Center, Brooklyn, New York) 1997; Commendation Medal, US Public Health Service 1975, 1986, Arthur S. Flemming Award for Outstanding Federal Service 1983, Surgeon Gen.'s Exemplary Service Medal 1993, Frank Bobbott Alumni Award 1995, Connecticut Health Commr's AIDS Leadership Award 1997, 1998, Outstanding Contrib. to the Campaign Against HIV/AIDS, Russian Asscn Against AIDS 2000, Master Teacher Award in Preventive Medicine, Downstate Medical Center 2010. *Publications:* International Health: Diseases, Programs, Systems and Policies (co-ed.) 2000 (second edn 2005, third edn as: Global Health: Diseases, Programs, Systems and Policies 2011); more than 150 articles on subjects from food-borne diseases to effectiveness of HIV interventions and numerous book chapters (co-author). *Address:* Box 90519, Duke University, Durham, NC 27708, USA (office). *Telephone:* (919) 681-7760 (office). *E-mail:* michael.merson@duke.edu (office). *Website:* globalhealth.duke.edu/people/faculty/merson-michael (office).

MERTLÍK, Pavel, PhD, Hab. Dozent; Czech economist and fmr politician; b. 7 May 1961, Havlíčkův Brod; s. of Rudolfa Mertlíka; m. Dana Mertlík; two s.; ed School of Econs, Prague, Charles Univ., Prague; Prof. of Econs, Prague School of Econs 1983–88; Research Fellow, Inst. of Forecasting of the Czech Repub. 1989–91; Prof. of Econs, Charles Univ. 1991–98, 2001–; Research Fellow, Czech Nat. Bank 1995–98; mem. Czech Social Democratic Party 1995–; Minister of Finance and Deputy Prime Minister 1998–2001; Chief Economist, Raiffeisen Bank, Prague 2001–12; mem. Czech Econ. Soc., Pres. 2004–06; Visiting Prof. of Econs, Staffordshire Univ., UK 2008–; Rector, Banking Inst. of Coll. 2012–15; Consultant to Prime Minister for Industry, Finance, Transport and Trade 2014; Rector, Škoda Auto Univ. 2015–; mem. Czech Acad. of Sciences, mem. Academic Ass. 2010–. *Publications:* numerous articles on price theory, monopolies, econ. transformation and privatization. *Leisure interests:* cycling, fishing, skiing.

MERTON, Robert C., BS, MS, PhD; American economist and academic; *School of Management Distinguished Professor of Finance, A.P. Sloan School of Management, Massachusetts Institute of Technology;* b. 31 July 1944, New York, NY; s. of Robert K. Merton and Suzanne Merton; m. June Rose 1966 (separated 1996); two s. one d.; ed Columbia Univ., New York, California Inst. of Tech., Massachusetts Inst. of Tech.; Instructor in Econs, MIT 1969–70, Asst Prof. of Finance, Alfred P. Sloan School of Man. 1970–73, Assoc. Prof. 1973–74, Prof. 1974–80, J.C. Penney Prof. of Man. 1980–88, School of Man. Distinguished Prof. of Finance 2010–; Visiting Prof. of Finance, Harvard Univ. Business School 1987–88, George Fisher Baker Prof. of Business Admin. 1988–98, John and Natty McArthur Univ. Prof. 1998–2010, Univ. Prof. Emer. 2010–; Research Assoc. Nat. Bureau of Econ. Research 1979–; Sr Adviser, Office of Chair., Salomon Inc. 1988–93; Prin., Co-Founder Long-Term Capital Man. Greenwich, Conn. 1993–99; Sr Adviser, JP Morgan & Co. 1999–2001; Co-founder and Dir, Integrated Finance Ltd (IFL) 2002–07, Chief Science Officer and Dir, Trinsum Group (after merger of IFL and Marakon) 2007–08; Resident Scientist, Dimensional Holdings, Inc., Austin, Tex. 2010–; mem. numerous editorial bds; mem. NAS, American Finance Asscn (Dir 1982–84, Pres. 1986, Fellow 2000); Sr Fellow, Int. Asscn of Financial Engineers; Fellow, Econometric Soc., American Acad. of Arts and Sciences, Financial Man. Asscn 2000; Hon. Prof., HEC School of Man. (École des Hautes Études Commerciales), Paris 1995–, St Petersburg Univ. of Man. and Econs, Russian Fed. 2011–; Hon. MA (Harvard) 1989; Hon. LLD (Chicago) 1991; Hon. DEconSc (Lausanne) 1996; Dr hc (Paris-Dauphiné) 1997, (Universidad Nacional Mayor de San Marcos, Lima, Peru) 2004, (Universidad Catolica de Chile, Santiago) 2014; Hon. DrManSc (Nat. Sun Yat-sen Univ., Taiwan) 1998; Hon. DSc (Athens Univ. of Econs and Business) 2003, (Claremont Grad. Univ.) 2008, (Chinese Univ. of Hong Kong) 2014; Hon. DBA (Univ. of Macao) 2014; Hon. PhD (Universidad Nacional Federico Villarreal, Lima, Peru) 2004; Leo Melamed Prize, Univ. of Chicago Business School 1983, Financial Engineer of the Year Award, Int. Asscn of Financial Engineers 1993, shared Nobel Prize for Econs 1997 for a new method for determining the value of derivatives, Michael Pupin Medal for Service to the Nation, Columbia Univ. 1998, Distinguished Alumni Award, Calif. Inst. of Tech. 1999, Distinguished Finance Educator Award, Financial Educ. Asscn 2008, Robert A. Muh Award in the Humanities, Arts, and Social Sciences, MIT 2009, Tjailing C. Koopmans Asset Award, Tilburg Univ. 2009, Kolmogorov Medal, Univ. of London 2010, Hamilton Medal, Royal Irish Acad. 2010, CME Group Fred Arditti Innovation Award 2011, numerous other awards. *Publications:* The Collected Scientific Papers of Paul A. Samuelson, Vol. III (Ed.) 1972, Continuous-Time Finance 1990, Casebook in Financial Engineering: Applied Studies in Financial Innovation (co-author) 1995, The Global Financial System: A Functional Perspective (co-author) 1995, Finance (co-author) 2000, numerous articles in professional journals. *Address:* Massachusetts Institute of Technology, E62-634, 77 Massachusetts Avenue, Cambridge, MA 02139, USA (office). *Telephone:* (617) 715-4866 (office). *Fax:* (617) 258-6855 (office). *E-mail:* rmerton@mit.edu (office). *Website:* mitsloan.mit.edu (office); robertcmerton.com.

MERZ, Friedrich; German politician and lawyer; *Senior Council, Mayer Brown LLP;* b. 11 Nov. 1955, Brilon; m. Charlotte Gass; one s. two d.; judge, Saarbrücken Dist Court 1985–86; lawyer 1986–, Asscn of Chemical Industry 1986–89, Regional Court of Appeal, Cologne 1992–; Partner Mayer Brown LLP 2004–14, Sr Council 2014–; mem. European Parl. 1989–94; mem. Bundestag 1994–2009, Parl. Leader CDU 2000–02; mem. International Advisory Cttee, Robert Bosch GmbH 2011–; mem. Supervisory Bd Deutsche Börse Aktiengesellschaft 2005–15, HSBC Trinkaus & Burkhardt AG (also mem. Advisory Bd) 2010–; Dolf Sternberger Award 2006, Lucius D. Clay Medal 2016. *Address:* Mayer Brown LLP, Königsallee 61, 40215 Düsseldorf, Germany (office). *Telephone:* (211) 86224110 (office). *Fax:* (211) 86224100. *Website:* www.mayerbrown.com (home).

MERZ, Hans-Rudolf, Dr rer. pol; Swiss management consultant and politician; b. 10 Nov. 1942, Herisau; m.; three s.; ed Univ. of St Gallen; Asst Lecturer, Univ. of St Gallen 1967–69; Sec., FDP St Gallen; Man. Appenzell Ausserhoden Industrial Asscn 1969–74; Deputy Dir UBS Wolfsberg training centre 1974–77; worked in pvt. practice as ind. consultant 1977–2003; Chair. Helvetia Patria Insurance Co., AG Cilander Textile Finishing, Anova Holding 1977–2003; elected Rep. Council of

States 1997, served as Chair. Finance Cttee, mem. Foreign Affairs and Security Cttee; Vice-Pres. OCSE del.; mem. Fed. Council 2004–10, Head of Fed. Dept of Finance 2004–10, Vice-Pres. Fed. Council 2008, Pres. Swiss Confed. 2009.

MERZENICH, Michael M., SB, PhD; American neuroscientist and academic; *Professor Emeritus, University of California, San Francisco;* b. 15 May 1942, Lebanon, Ore.; m. Diane Merzenich; ed Univ. of Portland, Johns Hopkins Medical School, Univ. of Wisconsin; Neurophysiology Fellowship, Univ. of Wisconsin 1968–71; Asst Prof., then Assoc. Prof., Univ. of California, San Francisco 1971–80, Francis A. Sooy Prof. 1981–2008, Prof. Emer. 2007–, fmr Co-Dir Coleman Memorial Lab.; Founder, Pres. and CEO Scientific Learning Corpn 1995–96, Chief Scientific Officer 1996–2003; Chief Scientific Officer, Posit Science Corpn 2004–; Pres. and CEO Brain Plasticity Inst. 2008–; Founder Neuroscience Solutions Corpn 2003; mem. NAS 1999, Inst. of Medicine 2008; IPSEN Prize 1997, Zotterman Prize 1998, Craik Prize 1998, Lashley Award, American Philosophical Soc. 1999, Thomas Edison Prize 2000, American Psychological Soc. Distinguished Scientific Contrib. Award 2001, Zülch Prize, Max-Planck Soc. 2002, Genius Award, Cure Autism Now 2002, Purkinje Medal, Czech Acad. 2003, Neurotechnologist of the Year 2006, Russ Prize, Nat. Acad. of Eng (co-recipient) 2015. *Publications include:* Plasticity and Signal Representation in the Auditory System (co-ed.) 2003, A Childhood in the Sticks (self-published memoir) 2007, Soft-Wired: How the New Science of Brain Plasticity Can Change Your Life 2013; approx. 220 papers in professional journals on neurological illness, learning processes and the neurological processes of the cerebral cortex; approx. 100 US patents. *Address:* Department of Otolaryngology, UCSF School of Medicine, Core Campus, HSE, San Francisco, CA 94143, USA (office). *Telephone:* (415) 476-0490 (office). *E-mail:* merz@phy.ucsf.edu (office). *Website:* profiles.ucsf.edu/michael .merzenich (office); www.brainhq.com.

MESA GISBERT, Carlos Diego; Bolivian politician; b. 12 Aug. 1953, La Paz; s. of Jose de Mesa and Teresa Gisbert; ed Universidad Mayor de San Andrés; fmr historian and journalist; Vice-Pres. of Bolivia 2002–03, Pres. 2003–05 (resgnd); mem. Bolivian History Acad.

MESELSON, Matthew Stanley, PhB, PhD; American biologist and academic; *Thomas Dudley Cabot Professor of the Natural Sciences and Principle Investigator, Meselson Laboratory, Harvard University;* b. 24 May 1930, Denver, Colo; s. of Hymen Avram and Ann Swedlow Meselson; m. 1st Katherine Kaynis 1960; m. 2nd Sarah Leah Page 1969; two d.; m. 3rd Jeanne Guillemin 1986; ed Univ. of Chicago, Univ. of Calif. (Berkeley) and Calif. Inst. of Tech.; Research Fellow, Calif. Inst. of Tech. 1957–58, Asst Prof. of Physical Chem. 1958–59, Sr Research Fellow in Chemical Biology 1959–60; Assoc. Prof. of Biology, Harvard Univ. 1960–64, Prof. of Biology 1964–76, Thomas Dudley Cabot Prof. of Nat. Sciences 1976–; Chair. Fed. of American Scientists 1986–88; mem. NAS, Inst. of Medicine, American Acad. of Arts and Sciences, Acad. Santa Chiara, American Philosophical Soc., Council on Foreign Relations; Life Mem. New York Acad. of Sciences; Foreign mem. Royal Soc., Acad. des Sciences, Russian Acad. of Sciences; Fellow, AAAS; Hon. DSc (Oakland Coll.) 1966, (Columbia) 1971, (Chicago) 1975; Hon. ScD (Yale) 1987, (Northwestern) 2003; Dr hc (Princeton) 1988; Prize for Molecular Biology, NAS 1963, Eli Lilly Award in Microbiology and Immunology 1964, Public Service Award, Fed. of American Scientists 1972 Alumni Medal, Univ. of Chicago Alumni Asscn 1971, Alumni Distinguished Service Award, Calif. Inst. of Tech. 1975, Lehman Award of New York Acad. of Sciences 1975, Leo Szilard Award, American Physical Soc. 1978, Presidential Award of New York Acad. of Sciences 1983, MacArthur Fellow 1984–89, Scientific Freedom and Responsibility Award, AAAS 1990, Thomas Hunt Morgan Medal, Genetics Soc. of America 1995, Public Service Award, American Soc. for Cell Biology 2002, Linus Pauling Award 2004, Lasker Award for Special Achievement in Medical Science 2004, Mendel Medal, British Genetics Soc. 2008. *Publications:* numerous papers on the biochemistry and molecular biology of nucleic acids and on arms control of biological and chemical weapons, in various numbers of Proceedings of NAS and of Scientific American etc. *Address:* Biological Laboratories, Harvard University, 16 Divinity Avenue, Cambridge, MA 02138, USA (office). *Telephone:* (617) 495-5099 (office); (617) 495-2264 (office). *Fax:* (617) 496-2444 (office). *Website:* mcb.harvard.edu/meselson (office).

MESFIN, Seyoum; Ethiopian politician and diplomatist; *Ambassador to China;* b. 25 Jan. 1949, Tigray; m. four c.; ed Bahir Dar Polytechnic Inst., Addis Ababa Univ.; exec. mem. Tigray People's Liberation Front (TPLF); Chair. Foreign Affairs Cttee Ethiopian People's Revolutionary Democratic Front (EPRDF); Minister of Foreign Affairs 1991–2010; Amb. to China 2010–. *Address:* Ethiopian Embassy, 3 Xiu Shui Nan Jie, Jian Guo Men Wa, Beijing, 100600, People's Republic of China (office). *Telephone:* (10) 65325258 (office). *Fax:* (10) 65325591 (office). *E-mail:* eth .beijing@mfa.gov.et (office). *Website:* (office).

MESGUICH, Daniel Elie Emile; French actor and theatre and opera director; b. 15 July 1952, Algiers; s. of William Mesguich and Jacqueline Boukabza; m. Danielle Barthélémy 1971; one s. three d.; ed Lycée Thiers, Marseille, Sorbonne, Paris and Conservatoire Nat. Supérieur d'Art Dramatique; actor 1969–; stage dir 1972–; f. Théâtre du Miroir 1974; Prof. Conservatoire Nat. Supérieur d'Art Dramatique 1983–; Dir Théâtre Gérard Philippe, Saint-Denis 1986–88, Théâtre de la Métaphore, Lille 1991–98; numerous appearances on stage, film and TV and dir of numerous stage plays and operas; Chevalier, Ordre Nat. du Mérite; Commdr des Arts et des Lettres, Officier, Légion d'Honneur. *Films:* La Fille de Prague avec un sac très lourd 1978, Dossier 51 1978, L'Amour en fuite 1978, Molière 1978, Clair de femme 1979, La Banquière 1980, Allon-z'enfants 1981, La Chanson du mal-aimé 1981, Quartet 1981, Les Iles 1982, La Belle captive 1982, Contes clandestins 1983, Les Mots pour le dire 1983, Bon Plaisir 1983, Paris vu par... vingt ans après 1984, Mon inconnue 1984, L'Araignée de satin 1986, L'Autrichienne 1989, La Femme fardée 1990, Jefferson in Paris 1995, Tiré à part 1997, Le Radeau de la Méduse 1998, D'Artagnan 2001, Nuit d'argent 2002, Le Tango des Rasherski 2003, Le divorce 2003, Le Capital 2012. *Plays directed:* Shakespeare: Hamlet 1977, 1996, 2011, 2014, Le Roi Lear 1981, Romeo et Juliet 1985, Titus Andronicus 1989,1993, La Tempête 1998, Antoine et Cleopâtre 2003; Racine: Andromaque 1975, 1992, Britannicus 1975, Bérénice 1994, Mithridate 1996, Esther 2001; Molière: Don Juan; Chekhov: Platonov 1982, Actes 2005; Marivaux: Le Prince Travesti 1972, 2015, La Seconde Surprise de l'Amour 1991; Jean-Bernard Moraly: Les Catcheuses 1973; Jean-Claude Brisville: Le Souper 2018; Harold Pinter: Trahisons 2014; Roland Dubillard: Le Bain de Vapeur 2016; Marguerite Duras: Agatha 2010; Jean Cocteau: Le Bel Indifférent 2010; Jacques Attali: Du Cristal la Fume 2008; Charlotte Escamez: La Légende du Pirate 2008; Clarisse Nicodski: Le Désespoir tout Blanc 2007; Daniel Mesguich: Remembrances d'Amour 1976, Boulevard du boulevard du boulevard 2006. *Operas directed include:* Le Grand Macabre (Ligeti) 1981, 1986, Catherine Ribeiro 1982, La Passion de Gilles (Michel Boesmans and Pierre Mertens) 1983, L'Amour des trois oranges (Prokofiev) 1983, Le Crépuscule des Dieux (Wagner) 1988, Un Bal Masqué (Verdi) 1994, Wozzeck (Berg) 1998, Des Saisons en Enfer (Marius Constant) 1999, Le Manège, comédie musicale (Manon Landowski) 2000, Le fou (Landowski) 2000, Elephant Man (Laurent Petit Guard) 2002, Damnation de Faust (Berlioz) 2002, Les Contes d'Hoffmann (Jacques Offenbach) 2005, La Flute Enchantée (Mozart) 2012, La Ettre des Sables (Christian Lauba) 2014. *TV roles include:* Kafka: la lettre au père 1975, Le Cardinal de Retz 1975, Lazare Carnot ou Le glaive de la révolution 1978, Joséphine ou la comédie des ambitions 1979, Aéroport: Charter 2020 1980, Médecins de nuit 1980, Dans quelques instants 1981, La Sorcière 1982, Napoleón, La Vie de Berlioz 1983, Le disparu du 7 octobre 1983, Le Château 1984, Grand hôtel 1986, La Garçonne 1988, Döende dandyn, Den 1989, Les Nuits révolutionnaires 1989, Mon dernier rêve sera pour vous 1989, La Garonne 1987, Une partie de trop 1992, L'Affaire Dreyfus 1995, L'Allée du roi 1996, Un rêve 1999, Un pique-nique chez Osiris 2001, L'affaire Salengro 2008, Chateaubriand 2009, Pompidou 2010, Meurtre d'état 2012, Crime d'état 2013. *Publications:* L'Eternel éphémère 1991, Le Passant composé 2004, Vie d'artiste (with Jocelyne Sauvard) 2012, Je n'ai jamais quitté l'école... (interviews with Rodolphe Fouano) 2009, L'Effacée 2009, Vie d'artiste (with Jocelyne Sauvard) 2012, Je n'ai jamais quitté l'école... (interviews with Rodolphe Fouano) 2009, L'Effacée 2009, Que sais-je: Le Théâtre (with Alain Viala) 2011, Estuaires (with Albin Michel) 2017. *Telephone:* 6-12-22-02-62 (office). *E-mail:* pjrobin2@gmail.com (office); damesguich@gmail.com (home). *Address:* Agence A, Monita Derrieux, 28 rue du Faubourg Poissonnière, 75010 Paris, France.

MESHAAL, Khalid, BSc; Palestinian politician; b. 28 May 1956, Silwad, West Bank; m.; four s. three d.; ed Kuwait Univ.; joined Muslim Brotherhood 1971; f. List of the Islamic Right (student org.), Kuwait Univ.; Physics Teacher, Kuwait 1978–84; Founding mem. Islamic Resistance Movt (Hamas—Harakat al-Muqawama al-Islamiyya) 1987, mem. Political Bureau, Chair. 1996–2017, Political Leader (in exile), Hamas 2004–.

MESHKOV, Alexey Yuryevich; Russian diplomatist and politician; *Ambassador to France;* b. 22 Aug. 1959, Moscow; m. Galina Ivanovna Meshkova; two s. two d.; ed Moscow State Inst. of Int. Relations; with diplomatic service 1981–; referent, Attaché then Third Sec., USSR Embassy, Spain 1981–86, First Sec., Counsellor then Sr Counsellor (Russian Embassy) 1992–97; Third, Second, First Sec. then Head of Div., Dept of Co-operation in Science and Tech., Ministry of Foreign Affairs 1986–92, Deputy Head, Dept of European Co-operation 1997–98, Head, Dept of Foreign Policy Planning 1998–2001, Deputy Minister of Foreign Affairs 2001–04, Amb. to Italy (also accred to San Marino) 2004–12, to France (also accred to Principality of Monaco) 2017–, Perm. Rep. to UN FAO, Rome and to WFP 2006–12, Deputy Minister of Foreign Affairs 2012–17; Order of Honour, Order of Friendship, Order of Alexandr Nevsky, Grand Cross of the Order of Merit of the Italian Repub., Order of Holy Prince Daniel of Moscow (1st class), Order of Saint-Charles, Monaco; Certificate of Gratitude of Pres. of Russian Fed., Diploma the Govt of Russian Fed. *Address:* Embassy of the Russian Federation, 40–50 boulevard Lannes, 75116 Paris, France (office). *Telephone:* 1-45-04-05-50 (office). *Fax:* 1-45-04-17-65 (office). *E-mail:* ambrusfrance@mid.ru (office). *Website:* www .ambassade-de-russie.fr (office).

MESI, Senida; Albanian accountant and politician; b. 16 Dec. 1977, Shkodër; m. Artan Mesi; three c.; ed Univ. of Tirana; Regional Man., Procredit Bank (PCB) Albania 2009–10, mem. Exec. Man. Bd 2009–14, Man., Private Individuals and Business Div. 2011–14; Lecturer, Eastern European Regional PCB Acad. 2010–12; freelance ind. financial consultant 2014–17; Man. Pnr, SM Consulting Financial Services 2015–17; mem. Shkodër City Council 2015–17; external lecturer, Faculty of Econs, Luigj Gurakuqi Univ., Shkodër, Admin. –2017; mem. Kuvendi Popullor (People's Ass., parl.) for Shkodër constituency 2017–; Deputy Prime Minister 2017–18; mem. Partia Socialiste e Shqipërisë (Albanian Socialist Party).

MESIĆ, Stjepan (Stipe); Croatian lawyer, politician and fmr head of state; b. 24 Dec. 1934, Orahovica; m. Milka Mesić (née Dudunić); two d.; ed gymnasium in Požega and Univ. of Zagreb; active in student politics; lawyer in Orahovica and Našice; compulsory mil. service; became a municipal judge after passing judicial exams; ind. cand. in municipal council elections 1966; Mayor of Orahovica 1967; mem. Parl. of Socialist Repub. of Croatia 1967; indicted for "acts of enemy propaganda", served one-year prison sentence in Stara Gradiška prison for participation in Croatian Spring Movt 1975; Sec. Croatian Democratic Union (Hrvatska demokratska zajednica—HDZ), later Chair. Exec. Council; Prime Minister first govt of Repub. of Croatia 1990; mem. Presidency of Socialist Fed. Repub. of Yugoslavia, subsequently Pres. until resgnd 1991; Speaker Croatian Parl. 1992–94; left HDZ and f. Croatian Ind. Democrats (Hrvatski Nezavisni Demokrati—HND) 1994, merged with Croatian People's Party (Hrvatska narodna stranka—HNS) 1997, later Exec. Vice-Pres.; Pres. Repub. of Croatia 2000–10; Hon. mem. Int. Foundation of Raoul Wallenberg 2002; Hon. Citizen of Podgorica, Montenegro 2007; State Order of the Star of Romania 2000, Grand Star of the Decoration of Honour for Merit (Austria) 2001, Golden Order Gjergj Kastrioti Skënderbeu (Albania) 2001, Grand Cross of the Order of Saviour (Greece) 2001, Order of St Michael and St George (UK), Kt of the Grand Cross with Grand Sash (Italy) 2001, Grand Order of the Crown of Malaysia 2002, Order of the Grand Cross with Chain (Hungary) 2002, Dostyk Medal of the First Degree (Kazakhstan) 2002, Medal for Merit (Chile) 2004, Grand Order of King Tomislav with Sash and Grand Star (Croatia) 2005; Charles Univ. Medal (Czech Repub.) 2001, Crans Montana Forum Award 2002, ABA Award 2002, Gold Medal of the Presidency of the Italian Repub. 2004, Raoul Wallenberg Award 2006, Int. League of Humanists Award 2007. *Publications:* The Break-up of Yugoslavia: Political Memoirs 1992, 1994. *Leisure interests:* nanbudo (martial art), swimming, golf.

MESSAGER, Annette; French artist; b. 30 Nov. 1943, Berck-sur-Mer; d. of André Messager and Marie L. Messager (née Chalessin); ed Ecole Nationale Supérieure des Arts Décoratifs; Chevalier des Arts et des Lettres, Légion d'honneur 2004;

Officier, Ordre nat. du Mérite 2008; Prix Nat. de Sculpture 1996, Lion d'Or de la Biennale de Venice 2005. *Address:* c/o Marian Goodman, 79 rue du Temple, 75003 Paris; 146 blvd Camelinat, 92240 Malakoff, France (home). *Telephone:* 1-42-53-45-77.

MESSAHEL, Abdelkader; Algerian diplomatist and politician; b. 11 July 1949, Tlemcen; long career with Ministry of Foreign Affairs (MFA), including as Head, Liberation Movements Section 1971, Dir Gen., Africa Div. 1986–88, 1996–97, Amb. to Burkina Faso 1987, Amb. to Minister of Foreign Affairs, in charge of African Affairs, posted to Perm. Mission to UN, New York (responsible for African Issues), Amb. to the Netherlands, Special Envoy of the Pres. in charge of follow-up to peace process in Democratic Repub. of the Congo and the Great Lakes Region (during Algerian OAU Presidency) 1999–2000, Deputy Minister to Minister of State, in charge of African Affairs, MFA 2000, Minister Del. to Minister of Foreign Affairs, in charge of Maghreb and African Affairs 2012, 2014–15; Minister of Communications 2013; Minister of Maghreb and African Affairs and of the Arab League 2015–17, Minister of Foreign Affairs 2017–19.

MESSI, Lionel Andrés (Leo); Argentine professional football player; b. 24 June 1987, Santa Fe; s. of Jorge Horacio Messi and Celia María Messi (née Cuccitini); winger/striker; played football for Grandoli (local club coached by his father) aged five; as youth, played for Newell's Old Boys, Rosario 1995–2000, Barcelona, Spain 2000–04; sr career, played for Barcelona B 2004–05 (22 appearances, 6 goals), Barcelona 2004– (296 appearances, 262 goals (club record)), Argentina U20 2004–05 (18 appearances, 14 goals), Argentina U23 2007–08 (5 appearances, 2 goals), Argentina 2005– (96 appearances, 45 goals); winner, La Liga 2004–05, 2005–06, 2008–09, 2009–10, 2010–11, 2012–13, Copa del Rey 2008–09, 2011–12, Supercopa de España 2005, 2006, 2009, 2010, 2011, 2013, UEFA (Union of European Football Asscns) Champions League 2005–06, 2008–09, 2010–11, UEFA Super Cup 2009, 2011, FIFA Club World Cup 2009, 2011; FIFA U-20 World Cup 2005, Olympic Gold Medal, Beijing 2008; Runner-up, FIFA World Cup 2014; UNICEF Goodwill Amb. 2010–; retd from int. football June 2016; found guilty by a Spanish court of tax fraud, fined 1.7 million euros and given a suspended 21 month jail sentence July 2016, launched appeal against the sentence; Tuttosport Golden Boy 2005, Olimpia de Plata 2005, 2007, 2008, 2009, 2010, 2011, 2012, 2013, FIFA U-20 World Cup Top Scorer 2005, FIFA U-20 World Cup Player of the Tournament 2005, U-21 European Footballer of the Year 2007, Copa América Young Player of the Tournament 2007, Player of the Year of Argentina 2005, 2007, FIFPro Special Young Player of the Year 2007, 2008, FIFPro World Young Player of the Year 2006, 2007, 2008, World Soccer Young Player of the Year 2006, 2007, 2008, Premio Don Balón (Best Foreign Player in La Liga) 2007, 2009, 2010, EFE Trophy (Best Ibero-American Player in La Liga) 2007, 2009, 2010, 2011, 2012, FIFA/FIFPro World XI 2007, 2008, 2009, 2010, 2011, 2012, 2013, 2014, Bravo Award 2007, UEFA Team of the Year 2008, 2009, 2010, 2011, 2012, 2014, FIFA Team of the Year 2008, UEFA Club Forward of the Year 2008–09, FIFPro World Player of the Year 2008–09, Trofeo Alfredo Di Stéfano 2009, Toyota Award 2009, Marca Leyenda 2009, UEFA Club Footballer of the Year 2009, UEFA Champions League Top Goalscorer 2009, 2010, 2011, 2012, UEFA Champions League Forward of the Year 2009, World Soccer Player of the Year 2009, 2011, 2012, LFP Best Player 2009, 2010, 2011, 2012, 2013, LFP Best Forward 2009, 2010, 2011, 2012, 2013, Onze d'Or 2009, 2010, 2012, La Liga Player of the Year 2009, 2010, 2011, FIFA Club World Cup Golden Ball 2009, 2011, Goal.com Player of the Year 2009, 2011, 2013, FIFA Ballon d'Or 2010, 2011, 2012, 2013, 2015, FIFA World Player of the Year 2009, 2010, 2011, UEFA Champions League Final Fans' Man of the Match 2009, 2011, European Golden Shoe 2010, 2012, 2013, 2018, Pichichi Trophy 2010, 2012, 2013, Copa del Rey top goalscorer 2010–11, 2013–14, UEFA Champions League Final Man of the Match 2011, UEFA Best Player in Europe Award 2011, Olimpia de Oro 2011, Male Best Athlete in Latin America 2011, L'Équipe Champion of Champions 2011, ESPY Best Int. Athlete 2012, World Soccer Greatest XI of All Time 2013, FIFA World Cup Golden Ball for Best Player 2014, FIFA Top Scorer 2014, FIFA World Cup: Dream Team 2014, amongst others. *Achievements include:* broke La Liga record for youngest footballer to play a league game; youngest to score a league goal; youngest Argentine to play in FIFA World Cup, Germany 2006. *Address:* FC Barcelona (Communication Department), Avenida Arístides Maillol s/n, 08028 Barcelona, Spain. *Telephone:* (93) 496-36-00. *Fax:* (93) 496-37-67 (Press). *E-mail:* premsa@fcbarcelona.cat. *Website:* arxiu.fcbarcelona.cat/web/english/futbol/temporada_09-10/plantilla/jugadors/messi.html; www.leomessi.com.

MESSIER, Jean-Marie Raymond Pierre; French business executive; b. 13 Dec. 1956, Grenoble; s. of Pierre Messier and Janine Delapierre; m. Antoinette Fleisch 1983; three s. two d.; ed Lycée Champollion, Grenoble, Ecole Polytechnique, Ecole Nat. d'Admin; Inspecteur des Finances 1982; Dir Office of Minister in charge of privatization at Ministry of Econ., Finance and Privatization, then Tech. Adviser to Minister 1986–88; Man. Pnr, Lazard Frères et Cie 1989–94; Chair. Fonds Partenaires 1989–94; Dir, Gen. Man. and Chair. Exec. Comité Général des Eaux group (now Vivendi) 1994, Chair. and Man. Dir 1996–2002; Chair. and Man. Dir Cégétel 1996–2000, Cie Immobilière Phénix 1994–95, Cie Générale d'Immobilier et de Services (CGIS) 1995–96, SGE 1996–97; Dir Canal Plus 1995 (merged with Universal and Vivendi 2000 to form Vivendi Universal), Chair. and CEO 2000–02; fmr Dir LVMH, Strafor-Facom, Saint-Gobain, UGC, Daimler-Benz, New York Stock Exchange 2001–02; Founder and CEO Messier Partners LLC, New York 2002–; mem. Bd of Dirs Rentabiliweb 2007–; given a suspended three-year jail sentence on charges of providing financial misinformation relating to his time at Vivendi, later given a suspended ten-month sentence and a fine by a Paris court of appeal on charges relating to his severance pay, reversing the earlier ruling May 2014. *Publication:* j6m.com: faut-il avoir peur de la nouvelle économie? 2000, My True Diary 2002. *Leisure interests:* flying, skiing, tennis. *Address:* Messier Partners LLC, One Rockerfeller Plaza, 15th Floor, Suite 1502, New York, NY 10020, USA (office). *Telephone:* (212) 332-6050 (office).

MESSINA, Carlo; Italian economist, academic and business executive; *Managing Director and CEO, Intesa Sanpaolo SpA;* b. 1962, Rome; ed Libera Università Internazionale degli Studi Sociali 'Guido Carli' (LUISS Univ.); began career in Finance Dept of Banca Nazionale del Lavoro 1987, rose to position of Man. in charge of Corp. Finance 1990; Prof. of Econs of Financial Intermediaries, Business Admin Master, LUISS School of Man.; Prof. of Corp. Finance, Faculty of Econs and Business of Ancona; joined Banco Ambrosiano Veneto as Man. in charge of Planning Dept 1995, successively Head of Planning and Research, Head of Control Dept within Intesa BCI, Head of Planning and Control Dept, Head of Risk Man. Dept within Banca Intesa, Head of Value Creation Governance –2008, Chief Financial Officer and Gen. Man.–May 2013, Gen. Man. Deputy to the CEO and responsible for the Chief Financial Officer Governance Area within Intesa Sanpaolo May–Sept. 2013, Head of Retail Div. May 2013–16, Man. Dir and CEO Intesa Sanpaolo Sept. 2013–; mem. Exec. Cttee, Italian Bankers' Asscn (ABI), Bd of Bocconi Univ. 2014–. *Address:* Intesa Sanpaolo SpA, Piazza San Carlo 156, 10121 Turin, Italy (office). *Telephone:* (011) 5551 (office). *Fax:* (011) 5557007 (office). *E-mail:* info@intesasanpaolo.com (office). *Website:* www.group.intesasanpaolo.com (office).

MESSING, Joachim W., BSc, MSc, Dr rer. nat; German/American molecular biologist and academic; *University Professor of Molecular Biology, Selman A. Waksman Chair in Molecular Genetics and Director of the Waksman Institute of Microbiology, Rutgers University;* b. 1946; ed Univ. of Düsseldorf, Free Univ. of Berlin, Ludwig Maximilians Univ., Munich; Research Fellow, Max Planck Inst. of Biochemistry, Munich 1975–78; Research Assoc. in Bacteriology, Univ. of California, Davis, USA 1978–80; Asst Prof. of Biochemistry, Univ. of Minnesota, St Paul 1980–82, Assoc. Prof. of Biochemistry 1982–84, Prof. of Biochemistry 1984–85; Univ. Prof. of Molecular Biology, Rutgers Univ. 1985–, Founding Chair. Dept of Molecular Biology and Biochemistry and Dept of Genetics, first Selman A. Waksman Chair in Molecular Genetics 2009–, Dir Waksman Inst. of Microbiology 1988–; mem. German Acad. of Sciences Leopoldina 2007, NAS 2015, AAAS 2016; Fellow, AAAS 2002, American Acad. of Microbiology 2015, Nat. Acad. of Inventors 2018; Honor Award, Sec. of US Dept of Agric. (US Rice Genome) 2004, Wolf Prize in Agric. (Israel) (co-recipient) 2013. *Achievements include:* co-developed the shotgun DNA sequencing method 1970s–1980s. *Publications:* numerous papers in professional journals. *Address:* Waksman Institute of Microbiology, Rutgers, The State University of New Jersey, 190 Frelinghuysen Road, Piscataway, NJ 08854, USA (office). *Telephone:* (848) 445-4256 (office). *E-mail:* messing@waksman.rutgers.edu (office). *Website:* www.waksman.rutgers.edu/messing (office).

MESSNER, Hon. Anthony, AM, FCA; Australian government official and chartered accountant; b. 24 Sept. 1939, East Melbourne, Vic.; s. of Colin Thomas Messner and Thelma Luxford Messner; ed South Australia Inst. of Tech., Adelaide; practised as chartered accountant 1965–75, 1990–97; mem. Fed. Senate for S Australia 1975–90; Minister for Veterans' Affairs, Asst Treas. 1980–83; Shadow Minister for Social Security 1983–85, for Finance and Taxation 1985–87, for Communications 1987–88, for Public Admin 1988–89; Admin. Norfolk Island 1997–2003; consultant 2003–; Dir Health Services Australia 2004–06, Chair. 2006–09; Centennial Medal 2001. *Leisure interests:* rugby, reading biographies and history, music, cricket. *Address:* 59 Bride Road, Nowra, NSW 2541 (office); 100 Kanearoo Road, Berry, NSW 2535, Australia (home). *Telephone:* (2) 4422-1611 (office); (2) 4464-2768 (home). *Fax:* (2) 4464-2768 (home). *E-mail:* messnert@optusnet.com.au (office).

MESSNER, Reinhold; Italian mountaineer, lecturer and author; b. 17 Sept. 1944, Bressanone, South Tyrol; one s. three d.; ed Univ. of Padua; began climbing aged four with his father; joined expedition to Nanga Parbat (8,125m), Pakistan 1970; with partner, Peter Habeler, became first person to climb Mount Everest without supplementary oxygen; later climbed Everest alone by North Col route without oxygen; the first person to climb all the world's 8,000m peaks in Himalayas and adjoining ranges; made first crossing of Antarctica on foot (2,800km) since Shackleton 1989–90; collaborated with Dir Werner Herzog in filming his story Schrei aus Stein 1991; f. Messner Mountain Museum—MMM Juval (collections of Asiatica), MMM Dolomites/Monte Rite 2002, MMM Ortles/Sulden 2004, MMM Firmian/Bozen 2006, MMM Ripa/Bruneck 2011, MMM Corones 2015; mem. European Parl. (Green Party) 1999–2004; ITAS 1975, Primi Monti 1968, DAV 1976, 1979, Sachbuchpreis for Donauland 1995, Coni 1998, Bambi Lifetime Award 2000, Royal Geographical Soc.'s Gold Medal 2001, Piolet d'Or carrière 2010, Diners Club Magazine Award 2011. *Publications:* The Crystal Horizon 1989, Free Spirit: A Climber's Life 1991, Antarctica 1991, To the Top of the World 1992, Moving Mountains 2001, The Second Death of George Mallory 2001, The Naked Mountain 2003, Free Spirit 2014, My Life at the Limit 2014. *Address:* MMM Firmian, Sigmundskronerstr. 53, 39100 Bozen (office); Castle Juval, 39020 Kastelbell, Italy (home). *Telephone:* (0471) 631265 (office). *Fax:* (0471) 633890 (office). *E-mail:* info@reinholdmessner.it (office). *Website:* www.reinhold-messner.de (office).

MESTAN, Lyutvi Ahmed; Bulgarian politician and lecturer; b. 24 Dec. 1960, Chorbadzhyisko; m.; mem. Narodno Sobranie (Nat. Ass.) for Kardzhali 2001–, Deputy Chair. Parl. Group 2009–13, Chair. 2013–, mem. Culture, Civil Society and Media Cttee 2009–13, Educ., Science, Children, Youths and Sports Cttee 2009–13, Substitute mem. Del. to Parl. Ass. of OSCE 2012–13, mem. Friendship groups Bulgaria-India, Bulgaria-Kazakhstan, Bulgaria-Canada, Bulgaria-South Korea, Bulgaria-Norway, Bulgaria-Portugal, Bulgaria-Finland, Bulgaria-Croatia, Bulgaria-Japan 2009–13; Chair. Dvizhenie za Prava i Svobodi (Movement for Rights and Freedoms) 2013–15 (expelled). *Address:* Narodno Sobranie (National Assembly), 1169 Sofia, pl. Narodno Sobranie 2, Bulgaria (office). *E-mail:* lyutvi.mestan@parliament.bg (office). *Website:* www.parliament.bg/en/MP/2473 (office).

MESTERHÁZY, Attila, PhD; Hungarian politician; b. 30 Jan. 1974, Pécs; m.; two c.; ed Lovassy László Gimnázium, Veszprém, Corvinus Univ. and Semmelweis Univ., Budapest; Fellow, Univ. of Valladolid, Spain 1995–96, Diplomatic Acad., Vienna 1996–98, Univ. of Groningen, the Netherlands 1997; worked in Prime Minister's Office as a specialist on econ. and European integration 1998; Man. Hill & Knowlton Strategies dealing with public relations 1999–2000; adviser to Prime Minister Péter Medgyessy 2000; State Sec. for Children, Youth and Sports, Office of the Prime Minister 2002–04; mem. Nat. Ass. 2004–; State Sec., Ministry of Youth, Family, Social Affairs and Equal Opportunities 2004–06; mem. Nat. Exec., Hungarian Socialist Party (Magyar Szocialista Párt—MSzP) 2003–, Chair. MSzP 2010–14, Vice-Pres. and apptd Chair. Parl. Caucus 2009; Socialist cand. for post of Prime Minister in parl. elections 2010, 2014; Hungarian Socialist Party entered into alliance with four other parties to put forward a joint list for the parl. elections Jan. 2014; Pres. Budgetary Cttee, Parl. Ass. 2016–18, Head of Socialist group, NATO 2018. *Address:* c/o Magyar Szocialista Párt (Hungarian Socialist Party), 1073 Budapest, Erzsébet körút 40-42. fsz. I-1., Hungary. *E-mail:* info@mszp.hu.

MESTRALLET, Gérard; French business executive; *Chairman, Engie;* b. 1 April 1949, Paris; s. of Georges Mestrallet and Paule Mestrallet-Besnard; m. Joëlle Emillienne Renée Arcens 1974; three c.; ed École Polytechnique, École Nationale d'Admin; joined Cie de Suez (provider of electricity, natural gas, water and waste man. services) 1984, Special Asst 1984–86, Deputy Chief Exec. for Industrial Affairs 1986–91, Chair. and CEO Suez 1995–97, Chair. Exec. Bd Suez Lyonnaise des Eaux (water treatment subsidiary co.) 1997–2001, Chair. and CEO Cie de Suez 2001–08, Chair. and CEO GDF Suez SA (formed by merger of Gaz de France and Suez SA) (renamed Engie 2015) 2008–16, Chair. 2016–, Chair. Engie E.S, Suez Environnement Co. (France), Electrabel, GDF Suez E.M.T (Belgium); Exec. Dir and Chair. Man. Cttee Société Générale de Belgique 1991–95; Vice-Chair. Aguas de Barcelona (Spain); mem. Bd of Dirs, Société Générale, International Power (UK); mem. Supervisory Bd, Siemens AG; Chair. Paris EUROPLACE Asscn; Rep. of Govt of France in negotiations with Walt Disney Co. to est. Euro Disney Theme Park 1995; mem. Advisory Bd, CECIA (Council of Int. Advisers) 2000–08, Shanghai and Beijing Mayors' Int. Econ. Advisory Councils; Dir, Tongji Univ., Shanghai; mem. Institut Français des Administrateurs (French Inst. of Corp. Dirs); Hon. Chair. Chongqing Mayor's Int. Econ. Advisory Council; Commdr, Légion d'honneur, Chevalier, Ordre nat. du Mérite; Dr hc (Cranfield Univ., UK); Person of the Year Award, French-American Chamber of Commerce, NY Chapter 2001. *Leisure interest:* cycling. *Address:* Engie SA, 1 place Samuel de Champlain, 92400 Courbevoie, France (office). *Telephone:* 1-44-22-00-00 (office). *E-mail:* info@engie.com (office). *Website:* www.engie.com (office).

MESYATS, Gennady Andreyevich, DSc; Russian physicist and academic; *Vice-President, Russian Academy of Sciences;* b. 29 Feb. 1936, Kemerovo; s. of Andrei Mesyats and Anna Mesyats; m. Nina Alexandrovna (née Mashukova) Mesyats 1959; one s.; ed Tomsk Polytechnical Inst.; Sr Research Physicist, Research Inst. for Nuclear Physics, Tomsk Polytechnical Inst. 1961–64, Head of Lab. 1966–71; Deputy Dir Inst. of Atmospheric Optics, Tomsk 1971–76; Dir and Prof., Inst. of High Current Electronics, Tomsk 1976–86; Dir and Prof., Inst. of Electrophysics 1987–; Corresp. mem. USSR (now Russian) Acad. of Sciences 1979, mem. 1984, Pres. Ural Div. 1986–99, Vice-Pres. of Acad. 1987–; Int. Chair. Supreme Attestation Comm. 1999–; Dir Lebedev Physical Inst. 2004–; Pres. Demidov Foundation; Vice-Pres. Int. Unit of Science and Eng Fellowships; mem. Russian Electrical Eng Acad.; Hon. Prof., Tomsk Polytechnic Univ. 1996, Russian Technological Univ. 2000; Hon. Citizen of Tomsk Oblast, of Yekaterinburg; Dr hc (Urals State Technical Univ.) 1996; Honour of the Komsomol 1960, Jubilee Medal "For Valiant Labour. To commemorate the 100th anniversary of Lenin" 1970, Order of Red Banner of Labour 1971, Badge of Honour 1976, Order of Lenin 1986, Order for Services to the Motherland, Fourth Class 1996, Third Class 1999, Second Class 2006, Chevalier, Légion d'honneur 2008, Order of Honour 2011; State Prize of USSR 1978, Lenin Komsomol Prize 1968, Dyke Award 1990, Walter Dine Int. Prize 1990, Ervin Marx Award in Pulsed Power 1991, USSR Council of Ministers Prize 1990, A.G. Stoletov Prize 1996, State Prize of Russian Fed. for Science and Tech. 1998, Gold Medal of Academician N.N. Moiseev 2000s, Demidov Prize 2002, Global Energy Prize 2003, IEE Marie Sklodowska-Curie Award 2012. *Publications:* Techniques for the Production of High-Voltage Nanosecond Pulses 1963, Generation of High-Power Nanosecond Pulses 1974, Field Emission and Explosive Processes in Gas Discharges 1982, High-Power Nanosecond X-Ray Pulses 1983, Pulsed Electrical Discharge in Vacuum 1989, Ectons 1994, About Our Science 1995, Pulsed Gas Lasers 1995, Explosive Electron Emission 1998, Physics of Pulsed Breakdown in Gases 1998, Ectons in a Vacuum Discharge: Breakdown, the Spark and the Arc 2000. *Leisure interests:* reading fiction, studying Russian history, writing articles. *Address:* Russian Academy of Sciences, Moscow 119991, 14 Leninsky Prospekt (office); Moscow 117900, Apt 29, 3 Akademika Petrovskogo, Russia (home). *Telephone:* (495) 237-53-12 (office); (495) 954-33-20. *E-mail:* mesyats@pran.ru (office); mesyts@sci.lebedev.ru (office). *Website:* www.ras.ru/win/db/show_per.asp?P=.id-5.ln-en (office).

MÉSZÁROS, Márta; Hungarian film director and screenwriter; b. 19 Sept. 1931, Budapest; d. of László Mészáros; m. 2nd Jan Nowicki; ed Moscow Film School; emigrated with family to USSR 1936; now lives in Hungary; Béla Balázs Prize 1977, Artist of Merit 1989, Berlinale Camera 2007. *Films include:* End of September 1973, Free Breath 1973, Adoption (Golden Bear, Berlin Int. Film Festival 1975) 1975, Nine Months 1976, The Two of Them 1977, En Route 1979, Heritage 1980, Diary for My Children (Grand Prize of the Jury, Cannes Film Festival 1984) 1982, Fata Morgana Land 1983, Diary for My Lovers (Silver Bear for Outstanding Single Achievement, Berlin Int. Film Festival 1987) 1987, Diary III 1989, Bye bye chaperon rouge 1989, Napló apámnak, anyámnak (Diary for My Father and Mother) 1990, A Magzat 1993, Siódmy pokój 1995, A Szerencse lányai 1999, Kisvilma: Az utolsó napló (Little Vilna: The Last Diary) 2000, Csodálatos mandarin (The Miraculous Mandarin) 2001, A Temetetlen halott 2004, The Last Report on Anna (Gold Plaque, Chicago Int. Film Festival 2010) 2009, Magyarország 2011 2012, Aurora Borealis: Északi fény 2017.

META, Ilir Rexhep; Albanian politician and economist; *President;* b. 24 March 1969, Skrapar; m. Monika Kryemadhi; one s. two d.; ed Tirana Univ.; apptd Deputy, People's Ass. (Kuvendi Popullor) 1992, Speaker 2013–17; Co-founder Forumi Rinor Eurosocialist Shqiptar (FRESSH—Euro-Socialist Youth Forum of Albania) (Deputy Chair. 1992–95, Chair. 1995–2001); Deputy Chair. Parl. Comm. for Foreign Relations 1996–97; fmr Deputy Prime Minister 1998–99, Sec. of State for European Integration (Ministry of Foreign Affairs) and Minister of Govt Co-ordination March–Oct. 1998; Prime Minister of Albania 1999–2002; Deputy Prime Minister and Minister of Foreign Affairs 2002–03, 2009–10, Deputy Prime Minister and Minister of Economy, Trade and Energy 2010–11; mem. Steering Council of Partia Socialiste e Shqipërisë (Socialist Party of Albania) 1992–2004, Deputy Chair. and Int. Sec. 1993–96, left party 2004; Pres. 2017–; Co-founder and Chair. Lëvizja Socialiste për Integrim (LSI—Socialist Movt for Integration) 2004–17; mem. Socialist Youth International (Vice-Chair. 1993–96), Int. Comm. on the Balkans; Visiting Lecturer, Faculty of Econs, Tirana Univ.; Most Positive Personality of 2010 in Foreign Policy Award, Int. Inst. IFIMES, Ljubljana 2012. *Leisure interest:* sports. *Address:* Office of the President, Bulevardi Dëshmorët e Kombit, Tirana, Albania (office). *Telephone:* (4) 2389813 (office). *E-mail:* info@president.al (office); imeta@ilirmeta.com (home). *Website:* www.president.al (office); www.lsi.al.

METCALF, John Wesley, BA, CM; Canadian author and editor; *Editor, Canadian Notes and Queries;* b. 12 Nov. 1938, Carlisle, UK; s. of Thomas Metcalf and Gladys Moore; m. Myrna Teitelbaum 1975; three s. three d.; ed Beckenham and Penge Grammar School and Univ. of Bristol; emigrated to Canada 1962; Writer-in-Residence, Univs of NB 1972–73, Loyola of Montreal 1976, Ottawa 1977, Concordia Univ. Montreal 1980–81, Univ. of Bologna 1985; Sr Ed. Porcupine's Quill Press 1989–, Ed. Canadian Notes and Queries (literary magazine) 1997–; Sr Ed. Biblioasis Press 2005–. *Publications:* The Lady Who Sold Furniture 1970, The Teeth of My Father 1975, Girl in Gingham 1978, Selected Stories 1982, Kicking Against the Pricks 1982, Adult Entertainment 1986, What is a Canadian Literature? 1988, Volleys 1990, How Stories Mean 1992, Shooting the Stars 1992, Freedom from Culture: Selected Essays 1982–1992 1994, Acts of Kindness and of Love (jtly) 1995, Forde Abroad 2003, An Aesthetic Underground 2003, Standing Stones: The Best Stories of John Metcalf 2004, Shut Up He Explained 2007, The Museum at the End of the World 2016. *Leisure interest:* collecting modern first editions. *Address:* 253 Botanica Private, Suite 5, Ottawa, ON K1Y 4P8, Canada. *Telephone:* (613) 761-6031 (office); (613) 761-6031 (home). *Website:* www.biblioasis.com.

METHENY, Patrick (Pat) Bruce; American jazz musician (guitar); b. 12 Aug. 1954, Lee's Summit, Mo.; ed Univ. of Miami; taught guitar at Univ. of Miami and Berklee Coll. of Music; fmrly guitarist with Gary Burton Quintet; has performed and recorded with musicians and composers, including Ornette Coleman, Herbie Hancock and Steve Reich; formed Pat Metheny Group 1978–; Boston Music Awards for Outstanding Jazz Album, Outstanding Guitarist, Outstanding Jazz Fusion Group 1986, Grammy Award for Best Instrumental Composition 1990, 1993, Best Contemporary Jazz Performance 1995, Best Rock Instrumental Performance 1996, Orville H. Gibson Award for Best Jazz Guitarist 1996, Best Guitarist (Jazz Times Magazine) 2000. *Recordings include:* albums: Bright Size Life 1976, Watercolours 1977, Pat Metheny Group 1978, New Chautauqua 1979, An Hour With Pat Metheny 1979, American Garage 1980, As Falls Wichita, So Falls Wichita Falls 1981, Offramp 1981, 80/81 1981, Travels 1983, Rejoicing 1983, Works 1984, First Circle 1984, Song X (with Ornette Coleman) 1985, Still Life (Talking) 1987, Works II 1988, Letter From Home 1989, Question And Answer (with Roy Haynes and Dave Holland) 1990, Secret Story 1992, Under Fire (film-score) 1992, Zero Tolerance For Silence 1992, I Can See Your House From Here 1993, The Road To You: Recorded Live In Europe 1993, Dream Teams 1994, Zero Tolerance for Silence 1994, We Live Here 1995, This World 1996, Quartet 1996, The Sign Of Four 1996, Imaginary Day 1997, Beyond the Missouri Sky 1997, Passaggio Per Il Paradiso (film-score) 1998, Like Minds 1998, All The Things You Are 1999, A Map Of The World (film-score) 1999, Last Train Home 1999, Jim Hall and Pat Metheny 1999, Trio 99>00 2000, Trio Live 2000, Move To The Groove 2001, Parallel Universe 2001, Sassy Samba 2001, Speaking Of Now 2002, One Quiet Night 2003, The Way Up (Grammy Award for Best Contemporary Jazz Album 2006) 2005, Metheny Mehldau 2006, Day Trip 2008, Orchestrion 2010, What's It All About (Grammy Award for Best New Age Album 2011) 2012, Unity Band (Grammy Award for Best Jazz Instrumental Album 2013) 2012, KIN 2014, The Unity Sessions 2016, Cuong Vu Meets Pat Metheny 2016. *Address:* The Kurland Agency, 173 Brighton Avenue, Boston, MA 02134-2003, USA (office). *Telephone:* (617) 254-0007 (office). *Fax:* (617) 782-3524 (office). *E-mail:* agents@thekurlandagency.com (office). *Website:* www.thekurlandagency.com (office); www.patmetheny.com.

METNAR, Lubomír; Czech politician and fmr police officer; *Minister of Defence;* b. 6 Oct. 1967, Olomouc, Czechoslovak Socialist Repub. (now Czech Repub.); ed Ostrava Univ., Ministry of the Interior Higher Police School; began career in Criminal Investigation Dept, Moravia-Silesia regional police force, becoming Head, Dept of Violence, Gen. Crime Dept, Regional Police Directorate, Moravia-Silesia 1988–2011; Security Dir, Vítkovice a.s. (eng co.) 2011–13, 2014–17; Deputy Minister of the Interior for Internal Security 2013–14, Minister of the Interior 2017–18, of Defence 2018–; mem. Supervisory Bd, Vítkovice Heavy Machinery 2016–. *Address:* Ministry of Defence, Tychonova 221/1, 160 00 Prague 6, Czech Republic (office). *Telephone:* 973201111 (office). *E-mail:* e-podatelnamo@army.cz (office). *Website:* www.army.cz (office).

METTLER, Ann, MA; German/Swedish research institute director and political scientist; *Head of the European Political Strategy Centre, European Commission;* ed Univ. of New Mexico, USA, Centre for European Integration Studies, Bonn, Germany; American Coll. of Greece, Athens; fmrly with Governmental Affairs Cttee, US Senate; fmrly with strategic communications firm, Washington DC; with Foreign Policy Div., EC, Brussels; Assoc. Dir, responsible for relations with the USA, Canada and EU insts, World Econ. Forum 2001–02, Dir for Europe 2000–03; Co-founder and Exec. Dir Lisbon Council 2003–14; Head of European Political Strategy Centre, EC, Brussels 2014–. *Publications include:* contribs to Wall Street Journal Europe, Financial Times, Newsweek, Handelsblatt, FT Deutschland, European Voice, USA and Europe in Business. *Address:* European Commission, CHARL 9/234, Rue de la loi, 200, 1049 Brussels, Belgium (office). *Telephone:* (2) 296-23-28 (office). *E-mail:* ann.mettler@ec.europa.eu (office). *Website:* www.ec.europa.eu/epsc (office).

METZ, Johann Baptist, DPhil, DTheol; German professor of theology; *Professor Emeritus of Theology, University of Münster;* b. 5 Aug. 1928, Auerbach; s. of Karl M. Metz and Sibylle Müller; ed Univs of Bamberg, Innsbrück and Munich; Prof. of Fundamental Theology, Univ. of Münster 1963–, currently Prof. Emer.; Prof. of Philosophy of Religion, Univ. of Vienna, Austria 1993–; mem. Founding Comm. of Univ. of Bielefeld 1966; consultant to Papal Secr. Pro Non Credendibus 1968–73; Adviser to German Diocesan Synod 1971–75; mem. Advisory Council, Inst. für die Wissenschaften vom Menschen (Vienna) 1982–; mem. Advisory Council Wissenschaftszentrum Nordrhein-Westfalen/Kulturwissenschaftliches Inst. 1989–2000; numerous guest professorships; Dr hc (Univ. of Vienna), (Jesuit School of Theology, Berkeley) 2009; awards from Univ. of Innsbrück and Boston Coll., Mass.; Buber-Rosenzweig-Medaille 2002, Preis de Salzburger Hochschulwochen 2007. *Publications:* books on theological and political themes in several languages, published in Europe, Russia, Repub. of China, Japan, N and S America. *Address:* Katholisch-Theologische Fakultät, Seminar für Fundamentaltheologie, Johannisstrasse 8–10, 4400 Münster (office); Kapitelstrasse 14, 48145 Münster,

Germany. *Telephone:* (251) 83-2631 (office); (251) 36662 (home). *Fax:* (251) 36662 (home). *E-mail:* j.metz@uni-muenster.de.

MEWA, Commins Aston, BA; Solomon Islands politician; *Minister for Home Affairs;* b. 11 April 1965, Uta, Santa Cruz, Temotu Prov.; ed Univ. of the South Pacific; fmr Chief Educ. Officer, Temotu Prov.; mem. Nat. Parl. for Temotu Nende Constituency 2010–; Minister for Justice and Legal Affairs 2010–14, for Communication and Aviation 2014–15, for Police, Nat. Security and Correctional Services Sept.–Oct. 2015, of Home Affairs 2017–. *Address:* Ministry of Home Affairs, POB G11, Honiara, Solomon Islands (office). *Telephone:* 28602 (office). *Fax:* 24837 (office). *E-mail:* psaffairs@pmc.gov.sb (office).

MEXIA, António Luís Guerra Nunes; Portuguese economist, politician and business executive; *CEO, EDP - Energias de Portugal;* b. 12 July 1957, Lisbon; ed Univ. of Geneva, Switzerland; fmr Prof. in Econs, Univ. of Geneva, Universidade Católica Portuguesa, Lisbon, Universidade Nova de Lisboa; Asst to Sec. of State for Foreign Trade 1986–88; Vice-Chair. ICEP (Portuguese bd of external trade and foreign investment) 1988–90; joined Banco ESSI (investment bank of Espírito Santo group) 1990, served as mem. Exec. Bd of Dirs in charge of equity capital markets and project finance divs 1990–98; Chair. and CEO GDP (Gas de Portugal) and of Transgás 1998–2001; CEO GALP Energia 2001–04; mem. Partido Social Democrata; Minister of Public Works, Transport and Communications 2004–05; CEO EDP - Energias de Portugal SA 2006–, Chair. EDP Renováveis, SA (Spain); mem. Bd of Dirs EDP–Energias do Brasil SA; Chair. Eureletric 2015–, Fundação EDP; Vice-Pres. Portuguese Industrial Asscn; mem. Bd of Dirs Banco Comercial Português, SA 2015–; Grand Cross of the Order of Industrial Merit Business Class 2014. *Address:* EDP - Energias de Portugal, Praça Marquês de Pombal 12, 1250-162 Lisbon, Portugal (office). *Telephone:* (21) 001-2500 (office). *Fax:* (21) 002-1403 (office). *E-mail:* info@edp.pt (office). *Website:* www.edp.pt (office).

MEY, Alamine Ousmane; Cameroonian engineer, banker and politician; *Minister of the Economy, Planning and Regional Development;* b. 1966; s. of Ousmane Mey; ed Rheinisch-Westfaelische Technische Hochschule Aachen, Germany, studies in Belgium and Tunisia; trained as electronic engineer; two years as Asst Engineer with Asea Brown Boveri, Mannheim; Credit Analyst, CCEI Bank, Yaoundé 1994, Head, Industrial and Tourist Projects Div. 1996, Dir of Research and Devt 1999, Dir Gen. Cenainvest, Dir Gen. Afriland First Bank 2004–11; Minister of Finance 2011–18, of the Economy, Planning and Regional Devt 2018–; Chair. Vetagri (veterinary co.); fmr Dir Safar, Chad, Ccic (soap mfr), Saconets (telecommunications co.), Soil and Water (geotechnical research co.). *Address:* Ministry of the Economy, Planning and Regional Development, Yaoundé, Cameroon (office). *E-mail:* lecinfosminepat@gmail.com (office). *Website:* www .minepat.info (office).

MEYER, Sir Christopher John Rome, Kt, KCMG, MA; British diplomatist, broadcaster, commentator, author and academic and company director; *Chairman of the Advisory Board, Pagefield Communications;* b. 22 Feb. 1944, Beaconsfield, Bucks.; s. of Flight Lt R. H. R. Meyer and Mrs E. P. L. Landells; m. 1st Françoise Hedges 1976; two s. one step-s.; m. 2nd Catherine Laylle 1997; two step-s.; ed Lancing Coll., Lycée Henri IV, Paris, Peterhouse, Cambridge, Johns Hopkins School of Advanced Int. Studies, Bologna, Italy; Foreign Office 1966–67; Army School of Educ. 1967–68; Third Sec., later Second Sec. Moscow 1968–70; Second Sec. Madrid 1970–73; FCO 1973–78; First Sec. Perm. Representation of UK at EC 1978–82; Counsellor and Head of Chancery, Moscow 1982–84; Head of News Dept, FCO 1984–88; Visiting Fellow, Center for Int. Affairs, Harvard 1988–89; Minister (Commercial), Washington, DC 1989–92, Minister and Deputy Head of Mission 1992–93; Press Sec. to Prime Minister 1994–96; Amb. to Germany 1997, to USA 1997–2003; Chair. Press Complaints Comm. 2003–09; Morehead-Cain Visiting Prof., Univ. of North Carolina 2010; currently Dir (non-exec.) Arbuthnot Banking Group Plc; Chair. Advisory Bd, Pagefield Communications; mem. Int. Advisory Bd, British-American Business Inc.; Sr Assoc. Fellow, Royal United Services Inst.; Hon. Fellow, Peterhouse, Cambridge 2001; mem. Worshipful Co. of Stationers and Newspaper Makers 2009; Freeman of the City of London 2009. *Radio:* BBC Radio 4: presenter and scriptwriter of How to Succeed at Summits, Corridors of Power 2006, Lying Abroad 2007, The Watchdog and the Feral Beast 2009. *Television:* Mortgaged to the Yanks (BBC 2/4) (presenter, co-writer) 2006, Getting Our Way (BBC 4) (presenter, co-writer) 2010, Networks of Power (Sky Atlantic) (co-writer and presenter) 2012, World War Three: Inside The War Room (BBC2) 2016. *Publications:* DC Confidential 2005, Getting Our Way 2010, Only Child 2013. *Leisure interests:* jazz, history, football. *Address:* JLA, 14 Berners Street, London, W1T 3LJ, England (office); Pagefield, 18 Marshall Street, London, W1F 7BE (office); Arbuthnot Banking Group, 7 Wilson Street, London, EC2M 2SN, England (office). *Telephone:* (20) 7907-2800 (office); 7789-462199 (mobile) (office). *E-mail:* talk@jla.co.uk (office); chrismeyer@btinternet.com (office). *Website:* www.jla.co.uk (office).

MEYER, (Donatus) Laurenz (Karl); German politician; b. 2 Feb. 1948, Salzkotten; m.; four d.; ed Univ. of Münster; fmr mem. staff VEW AG, Dortmund; mem. Hamm City Council 1975–95; Parl. Group Chair. Christian Democratic Union (CDU), Hamm 1989–95; mem. Land Parl. of N Rhine-Westphalia (NRW) 1990–2002, Econ. Policy Spokesman of Land Parl. of NRW 1990–99, Vice-Chair. CDU Parl. Group of Land Parl. of NRW 1997–99, Chair. 1999–2000, Vice-Pres. Land Parl. of NRW 2000, Treas. CDU of NRW 1997–2001; mem. Fed. Party Exec., Sec.-Gen. CDU Germany 2000–04, currently Chair. Economy and Tech. Group; mem. Bundestag 2002–09; Order of Merit (FRG). *Leisure interests:* tennis, golf. *Address:* Christlich-Demokratische Union, Konrad-Adenauer-Haus, Klingelhöferstrasse 8, 10785 Berlin, Germany (office). *Telephone:* (30) 220700 (office). *Fax:* (30) 22070111 (office). *E-mail:* laurenz.meyer@cdu.de (office). *Website:* www.laurenz -meyer.de; www.cdu.de (office).

MEYER, Edgar, BMus; American composer and double bassist; b. 24 Nov. 1960, Tulsa, Okla.; s. of Edgar A. Meyer and Anna Mary Metzel; m. Cornelia (Connie) Heard 1988; one s.; ed Georgia Inst. of Tech., Indiana Univ. School of Music; began playing bass aged five under tutelage of father; began composing pop songs and classical pieces as a child; studied with Stuart Stanley at univ.; formed bluegrass band Strength in Numbers, Nashville, Tenn. 1984; regular bass player, Santa Fe Chamber Music Festival 1985–93; appeared with concert artists Emanuel Ax (piano) and Yo-Yo Ma (cello), Joshua Bell (violin); joined Chamber Music Soc.,

Lincoln Center, New York 1994; formed band Quintet for Bass and String Quartet, soloist debut performance 1995; frequent collaborations with Chris Thile, Amy Dorfman, Bela Fleck, Mike Marshall; performed at Aspen, Caramoor and Marlboro Festivals; debuted with Boston Symphony Orchestra, Tanglewood, Mass 2000; Visiting Prof. of Double Bass, Curtis Inst. of Music 2003–; Visiting Prof., RAM, UK; winner, Zimmerman-Mingus Competition, Int. Soc. of Bassists 1981, Avery Fisher Prize 2000, Grammy Award for the Best Crossover Album 2001, MacArthur Award 2002. *Compositions include:* three concertos for double bass and orchestra, triple concerto for double bass, banjo, and tabla, Double Concerto for Bass and Cello 1995, Violin Concerto 2000, Double Concerto for Double Bass and Violin 2012, Overture for Violin and Orchestra 2017. *Recordings include:* albums: Unfolding 1986, The Telluride Sessions (Strength in Numbers) 1989, Dreams of Flight 1987, Love of a Lifetime 1988, Appalachia Waltz (with Yo-Yo Ma and Mark O'Connor) 1996, Uncommon Ritual 1997, Short Trip Record 1999, Bach Unaccompanied Cello Suites Performed on a Double Bass 1999, Appalachian Journey (with Yo-Yo Ma and Mark O'Connor) (Grammy Award 2001) 2000, Perpetual Motion 2000, Edgar Meyer 2006, The Melody of Rhythm 2009, The Goat Rodeo Sessions (with Yo-Yo Ma, Chris Thile, and Stuart Duncan) (Grammy Award for Best Folk Album 2012) 2011, Bass and Mandolin (with Chris Thile) (Grammy Award for Best Contemporary Instrumental Album 2015) 2014, Bach Trios (with Chris Thile, Yo-Yo Ma) 2017; collaborated with Katty Mattea on album Where Have You Been (Grammy Award, Country Music Award, Acad. of Country Music Asscn Award) 1990. *Address:* c/o Dean Shultz, IMG Artists, 7 West 54th Street, New York, NY 10019, USA (office). *Telephone:* (212) 994-3533 (office). *E-mail:* dshultz@imgartists.com (office). *Website:* edgarmeyer.com.

MEYER, Lynn (see SLAVITT, David Rytman).

MEYER, Robert; Norwegian art photographer, photohistorian, academic and writer; b. 2 Oct. 1945, Oslo; s. of Robert Castberg Meyer and Edel Nielsen; m. Ingebjørg Ydstie 1985; one s. one. d.; ed Fotoskolan, Univ. of Stockholm; photographer, Norwegian State Police 1963–64; advertising photographer 1964–; freelance photographer 1964–71; debut exhbn LYS, Oslo 1970; photojournalist, Norwegian Broadcasting, Oslo 1971–77; Ed. and Publr Ikaros 1976–80; full-time photohistorian engaged in research work 1977–; Prof., Nat. Coll. of Art, Bergen, f. Inst. of Photography (SHDK) 1990–; returned to Oslo 1998, est. a private coll. for photography; est. Forbundet Frie Fotografer (Asscn of Ind. Photographers) 1974, Norsk Fotohistorisk Forening (Norwegian Photohistorical Soc.) 1976; Chair. Fotogalleriet (Norwegian Photo Gallery Foundation) 1979; curator for several galleries and museums; Munch stipend 1981; art stipend 1988–90; two book prizes. *Publications:* Norsk fotohistorisk Journal 1976–78, Jim Bengston i Photographs 1981, Slow Motion 1985, Simulo 1987, Norsk Landskapsfotografi 1988, Den glemte tradisjonen 1989, Splint 1991. *Address:* c/o Fotogalleriet, Møllergata 34, 0179 Oslo; Professor Hansteens gate 68, 5006 Bergen, Norway (home). *Telephone:* 22-20-05-59; 22-20-21-20; 55-31-07-93 (home). *E-mail:* post@fotogalleriet.no; post@ fffotografer.no.

MEYER, Robert B., BA PhD; American physicist and academic; *Professor, Department of Physics, Brandeis University;* ed Harvard Univ.; Sloan Foundation Research Fellow 1971–75; Researcher, Asst Prof., Assoc. Prof., Dept of Physics, Harvard Univ. 1970–78; fmr Nordita Visiting Prof., Chalmers Inst. of Tech., Göteborg, Sweden, Ecole Supérieure de Physique et de Chimie Industrielles de la Ville de Paris, France; joined Dept of Physics, Brandeis Univ. 1978, Prof. of Physics 1985–, Dir Materials Research Science and Eng Center 2008–; Fellow, American Physical Soc. 1992; Joliot Curie Medal of City of Paris 1978, Special Recognition Award, Soc. for Information Display 1989, Second Prize, LVMH Science for Art Prize Vinci of Excellence 1993, Benjamin Franklin Medal in Physics 2004, Oliver Buckley Prize, American Physical Soc. 2006, George Gray Medal, British Liquid Crystal Soc. 2007. *Address:* Brandeis University, Department of Physics, MS 057, PO Box 549110, Waltham, MA 02454-9110, USA (office). *Telephone:* (781) 736-2870 (office). *Fax:* (781) 736-2915 (office). *E-mail:* meyer@brandeis.edu (office). *Website:* www.brandeis.edu/departments/physics (office).

MEYER, Roelof (Roelf) Petrus, BComm, LLB; South African fmr politician; b. 16 July 1947, Port Elizabeth; s. of Hudson Meyer and Hannah Meyer; m. 1st Carené Lubbe 1971; two s. two d.; m. 2nd Michèle de la Rey 2002; ed Fickburg High School, Univ. of the Free State; practised as attorney, Pretoria and Johannesburg –1980; MP for Johannesburg West 1979–97; Deputy Minister of Law and Order 1986–88, of Constitutional Devt 1988–91 and of Information Services 1990–91; Minister of Defence and of Communication 1991–92, of Constitutional Devt and of Communication 1992–94, of Provincial Affairs and Constitutional Devt 1994–96; Sec.-Gen. Nat. Party 1996–97; Co-Founder United Democratic Movt 1997, Deputy Pres. 1998–2000; MP 1998–2000; Tip O'Neill Chair. in Peace Studies, Univ. of Ulster 2000–01; Chair. Civil Soc. Initiative 2000–; Chief Govt Negotiator at Multi-Party Negotiating Forum for new SA Constitution; Nat. Party, fmr Chair. Standing Cttee on Nat. Educ., fmr Chair. Standing Cttee on Constitutional Devt, fmr Parl. Whip; apptd Dir TILCA Infrastructure Corpn 2001, later Deputy Exec. Chair.; Chair Defence Review Cttee 2012–14; mem. Bd of Dirs Armscor. *Leisure interests:* reading, outdoor life, jogging. *Address:* PO Box 2271, Brooklyn Square, Pretoria 0075 (office); 732 Skukuza Street, Faerie Glen, 0043 Pretoria, South Africa (home). *Telephone:* (12) 3341826 (office); (82) 9900004. *Fax:* (12) 3341867 (office). *E-mail:* roelf.meyer@tilca.com (office); rmeyer@lantic.net (home). *Website:* www.tilca.com (office).

MEYER, Ron; American business executive; *Vice-Chairman, NBC Universal;* b. 1944; m. Kelly Chapman; one s. three d.; served in US Marine Corps; messenger, Paul Kohner Agency 1964–70; TV agent, William Morris Agency 1970–75; Co-founder and Pres. Creative Artists Agency 1975–95; Pres., COO, Universal Studios 1995–13, Vice-Chair. NBC Universal 2013–. *Address:* NBC Universal, 5750 Wilshire Blvd, Los Angeles, CA 90036, USA (office). *Website:* www.nbcuni.com (office).

MEYER, Stephenie, BA; American author; b. 24 Dec. 1973, Hartford, Conn.; d. of Stephen Morgan and Candy Morgan; m. Christian Meyer 1994; three s.; ed Chaparral High School, Scottsdale, Ariz., Brigham Young Univ.; grew up in Phoenix, Ariz.; early job as receptionist in an Ariz. property co. *Publications include:* Twilight series: Twilight (Publishers Weekly Best Book of the Year, American Library Asscn Top Ten Best Book for Young Adults) 2005, New Moon

2006, Eclipse (British Book Award) 2007, Breaking Dawn 2008; other books: Prom Nights from Hell (section) 2007, The Host (science-fiction novel) 2008, The Short Second Life of Bree Tanner (novella) 2010, The Chemist 2016. *Address:* c/o Jodi Reamer, Writers House LLC, 21 West 26th Street, New York, NY 10010, USA (office). *Telephone:* (212) 685-2400 (office). *Fax:* (212) 685-1781 (office). *Website:* www.writershouse.com (office); www.stepheniemeyer.com; www.thetwilightsaga.com.

MEYER, Thomas J., BS, PhD; American chemist and academic; *Arey Distinguished Professor of Chemistry, University of North Carolina;* ed Ohio Univ., Stanford Univ.; Woodrow Wilson Grad. Fellow, Stanford Univ. 1963–64, NSF Grad. Fellow 1965–66; NATO Postdoctoral Research Fellow, Univ. Coll., London, UK 1967; Asst Prof. of Chem., Univ. of North Carolina at Chapell Hill 1968–72, Assoc. Prof. 1972–75, Prof. 1975–82, M.A. Smith Prof. of Chem. 1982–87, Chair. Dept of Chem. 1985–90, Kenan Prof. of Chem. 1987–99, Chair. Applied Sciences Curriculum 1992–94, Adjunct Prof., Curriculum in Applied Science 1994–99, Dean, Grad. School 1994–96, Vice-Provost for Grad. Studies and Research 1994–99, Arey Distinguished Prof. of Chem., Univ. of North Carolina at Chapel Hill 2005–; Adjunct Prof., Dept of Chem., Univ. of Utah 2000–05; Assoc. Lab. Dir, Los Alamos Nat. Lab., NM 2000–01, Assoc. Dir Strategic Research 2002–04; Visiting Prof., Sydney Univ., Australia 1976; Visiting Scientist, Xerox Webster Research Center, Webster, NY 1978; Visiting Scientist, Sandia Nat. Lab. 1981; Visiting Prof., Univ. Louis Pasteur, Strasbourg, France 1983; Visiting Scientist, Centre d'Etudes Nucleaires, Grenoble, France 1983; Visiting Prof., Univ. de Rennes, France 1986, Univ. di Ferrara, Italy 1992, Univ. of Buenos Aires, Argentina 1993; Dir Triangle Univs Licensing Consortium 1989–95, Triangle Univs Center for Advanced Studies Inc. 1994–99, NC Biotechnology Center 1994–99, Associated Universities Inc. 1995–97, NC Bd of Science and Tech. 1995–99, Research Triangle Inst. 1995–99, UNC Energy Frontier Research Center 2009–; mem. Editorial Bd, Inorganic Chemistry 1983–87, 2005–, Journal of the American Chemical Soc. 1983–87, Accounts of Chemical Research 1991–96, Structure and Bonding 1997–2011, Journal of Photochemistry and Photobiology A 1998–; mem. numerous socs, including ACS, American Asscn of Univ. Profs, AAAS (Fellow 1981), American Acad. of Arts and Sciences 1994; Fellow, World Tech. Network 2013; Dr hc (Ohio Univ.) 2013; ACS Charles H. Stone Award 1982, ACS Award in Inorganic Chem. 1990, ACS Southern Chemist of the Year Award 1992, Nyholm Award, Royal Australian Chemical Inst. 1996, Inter-American Photochemical Soc. Award 1997, ACS Remsen Award 1999, ACS Award for Distinguished Service to Inorganic Chem. 2002, Welch Lecturer 2003, Pres.'s Award, Research Triangle Inst. 2008, Porter Medal, European Photochemical Asscn, Inter-American Photochemical Soc. and the Asian and Oceanian Photochemical Asscn 2012, Kosolapoff Award, Auburn Univ. 2012, Honda-Fujishima Lectureship Award, Japan Photochemical Asscn 2013, Samson Prime Minister's Prize for Innovation in Alternative Fuels for Transportation 2014; numerous hon. lectures in USA and abroad. *Publications:* more than 710 publs and five patents; one of the most highly cited chemists in the world. *Address:* Department of Chemistry, Murray Hall 2202F, University of North Carolina, Campus Box 3290, Chapel Hill, NC 27599-3290, USA (office). *Telephone:* (919) 843-8313 (office). *Fax:* (919) 962-2388 (office). *E-mail:* tjmeyer@email.unc.edu (office). *Website:* www.chem.unc.edu/people/faculty/meyer (office).

MEYER, Tobias; German art dealer; m. Mark Fletcher 2011; ed Univ. of Vienna; joined Sotheby's 1992, Worldwide Head of Contemporary Art 1997–2013, apptd Prin. Auctioneer for Sotheby's sales of Contemporary Art and Impressionist and Modern Art in New York as well as for co.'s Contemporary Art sales in London 2000, then Chair. Worldwide Contemporary Art and Exec. Vice-Pres. Contemporary Art; has produced three of the four highest auction prices ever paid for post-war art, including Mark Rothko's White Center (Yellow, Pink and Lavender on Rose) for $72.8 million May 2007, Francis Bacon's Triptych 1976, which sold for $86.3 million May 2008, auction record for any work by a living artist at the time of the sale with Jeff Koons' Hanging Heart ($23.6 million) November 2007, was also auctioneer for Sotheby's sales of Pablo Picasso's Garçon à la pipe ($104.2 million) and Dora Maar au chat ($95.2 million), currently Chair. Worldwide Contemporary Art and Exec. Vice-Pres. Contemporary Art; Movers and makers: Most Powerful People in the art world, Guardian 2014.

MEYER-LANDRUT, Andreas, PhD; German diplomatist and business executive; b. 31 May 1929, Tallinn, Estonia; s. of Bruno Meyer-Landrut and Käthe Meyer-Landrut (née Winter); grandfather of Lena Meyer-Landrut who won Eurovision Song Contest in 2010 and uncle of Amb. Nikolaus Meyer-Landrut; m. Hanna Karatsony von Hodos 1960; one s. one d.; m. 2nd Natali Somers (née Seferov); ed Univs of Göttingen and Zagreb; entered foreign service 1955, served in Moscow, Brussels and Tokyo 1956–68, Amb. to Congo (Brazzaville) 1969, in Foreign Office, Bonn 1971–80, Head of Sub-Dept for Policy towards Eastern Europe and GDR 1974–78, Dir Dept of Relations to Asia, Near and Middle East, Africa and Latin America 1978–80, Amb. to USSR 1980–83, 1987–89, State Sec. to Foreign Office 1983–87; Head of Fed. Pres.'s Office and State Sec. 1989–94; Man. Daimler Chrysler AG, Moscow 1994–2002, then adviser to German cos in Russia and CIS countries; Hon. Pres. German-Russian Forum Berlin; Hon. mem. German Equestrian Fed.; Grand Commdr, Order of Merit; Order of the Cross of Terra Mariana (Estonia). *Publications include:* Mit Gott und langen Unterhosen: Erlebnisse eines Diplomaten in der Zeit des Kalten Krieges 2003.

MEYER-LANDRUT, Nikolaus; German diplomatist; *Ambassador to France;* b. 7 Sept. 1960, Düsseldorf; m.; four c.; mil. service 1979–81; history and German literature studies 1981–87; preparatory service for Higher Foreign Service 1987–89, promoted 1987, Fed. Foreign Office 1989–90, German Del. at negotiations on Conventional Armed Forces in Europe, Vienna 1990–93, Perm. Mission to EU, Brussels 1993–95, Fed. Foreign Office 1995–99, Perm. Mission to EU, Brussels 1999–2002, Head of Press Unit of EU, Constitutional Convention, Int. Orgs, Brussels 2002–03, Head of Unit, Dept of State 2003–06, Deputy Dir, German Chancellery 2006–11, Dept Head, Federal Chancellery 2011–15, Amb. to France 2015–. *Address:* Embassy of Germany, 13–15 avenue Franklin D. Roosevelt, 75008 Paris, France (office). *Telephone:* 1-53-83-45-00 (office). *Fax:* 1-43-59-74-18 (office). *E-mail:* ambassade@amb-allemagne.fr (office). *Website:* www.paris.diplo.de (office).

MEYEROWITZ, Elliot Martin, AB, MPhil, PhD, FAAS; American biologist and academic; *George W. Beadle Professor of Biology, California Institute of Technology;* b. 22 May 1951, Washington, DC; m. Joan Agnes Kobori; two c.; ed Columbia Univ., New York, Yale Univ., New Haven, Conn.; Jane Coffin Childs Memorial Fund Postdoctoral Fellow, Dept of Biochemistry, Stanford Univ. School of Medicine, Calif. 1977–79; Asst Prof. of Biology, California Inst. of Tech., Pasadena 1980–85, Assoc. Prof. 1985–89, Prof. of Biology 1989–2002, Exec. Officer for Biology 1995–2000, Chair. Div. of Biology 2000–10, George W. Beadle Prof. of Biology 2002–; currently Investigator, Howard Hughes Medical Inst.; Visiting A.F. Wood Prof., Univ. of Florida, Gainesville 2000; European Flying Fellowship in Plant Molecular Biology, Grad. School of Experimental Plant Sciences, Univ. of Ghent, Belgium, Institut des Sciences Vegetales, France, Max-Planck-Institut für Zuchtungsforschung, Germany 2001; Inaugural Dir Sainsbury Lab., Univ. of Cambridge 2011–12; mem. Editorial Bd, Current Biology 1993–, Current Opinion in Plant Biology 1997–, BMC Biology 2001–; mem. Man. Bd, Sainsbury Lab., Univ. of Cambridge 2011–, Int. Bd, Weizmann Inst. 2011–; mem. Scientific Advisory Cttee, Weizmann Inst. 2012–, Supporters of Agricultural Research Foundation 2015–; mem. American Acad. of Arts and Sciences 1991, NAS 1995, American Philosophical Soc. 1998; Foreign Assoc. Acad. des sciences, France 2002–; Foreign mem. Royal Soc. (UK) 2004; Assoc. mem. European Molecular Biology Org. 2008; Dr hc (École Normale Supérieure, Lyon) 2007; Hon. DSc (Yale Univ.) 2014; Huebschman Prize in Biology, Columbia Univ. 1972, John S. Nicholas Award for Outstanding Biology Dissertation, Yale Univ. 1977, Sloan Foundation Research Fellowship, California Inst. of Tech. 1981, Pelton Award, Botanical Soc. of America and Conservation and Research Foundation 1994, Gibbs Medal, American Soc. of Plant Physiologists 1995, Genetics Soc. of America Medal 1996, Science pour l'Art Science Prize, LVMH Moët-Hennessy-Louis Vuitton 1996, Mendel Medal and Mendel Lecturer, Genetical Soc. of GB 1997, Int. Prize for Biology, Japan Soc. for the Promotion of Science 1997, Richard Lounsbery Award, NAS 1999, Wilbur Cross Medal, Yale Univ. 2001, Ross Harrison Prize, Int. Soc. of Developmental Biologists 2005, Balzan Prize 2006, Prix la Recherche 2009, Sibthorp Medal 2011, Dawson Prize in Genetics, Trinity Coll. Dublin 2013, Gruber Genetics Prize 2018. *Publications:* more than 250 articles in scientific journals. *Address:* Division of Biology and Biological Engineering, California Institute of Technology, Mail Code 156-29, 1200 East California Boulevard, Pasadena, CA 91125, USA (office). *Telephone:* (626) 395-6889 (office). *E-mail:* meyerow@caltech.edu (office). *Website:* plantlab.caltech.edu (office).

MEYEROWITZ, Joel; American photographer; b. 6 March 1938, Bronx, New York; s. of Hy Meyerowitz; one s.; fmr art dir in an advertising firm; began photography career 1962; early advocate of colour photography mid-1960s; gave lessons in colour photography at Cooper Union, New York 1971; commissioned by St Louis Art Museum, Missouri to photograph Eero Saarinen's Gateway Arch 1977; photographed Empire State Bldg 1978; produced and directed his first film, POP, an intimate diary of a three-week road trip made with his son and father 1998; cr. The World Trade Center Archive of more than 8,000 images, documenting destruction and recovery at Ground Zero and immediate neighbourhood following attacks on World Trade Center 2001; works in collections of Albertina Museum, Vienna, Amon Carter Museum, ATT Collection, Boston Museum of Fine Art, Carnegie Inst. Museum of Art, Chicago Art Inst., George Eastman House, IBM Collection, Int. Center of Photography, New York, Merrill Lynch Collection, Metropolitan Museum of Art, Museum of Modern Art, New York, Miami Art Museum, Museum of Photographic Art, Philadelphia Museum of Art, San Francisco Museum of Modern Art, San Jose Museum of Art, Seagram Collection, St Louis Museum, Stedelijk Museum, Toledo Museum of Art, Virginia Museum, Whitney Museum of American Art, US Trust Company, Gund Collection, Hallmark Cards Collection; Hon. FRPS 2002; Guggenheim Fellow 1971, 1978, C.A.P.S. New York State Arts Fellowship 1974, Nat. Endowment for the Arts Fellowship 1978, Nat. Endowment for the Humanities Award 1980, Photographer of the Year, Friends of Photography 1981, Photography Book of the Year, American Soc. of Media Photographers 1986, Photographer of the Year (Japan) 1990, Century Award for Lifetime Achievement, Museum of Photographic Arts, San Diego 2001, Centenary Medal, Royal Photographic Soc. 2002, Professional Photographer Leadership Award, Int. Photographic Council 2003, Award for Service and Dedication as CultureConnect Amb., Bureau of Educational and Cultural Affairs, Dept of State 2004, Aperture honouree 2009. *Film:* POP (feature-length documentary) (Best of Festival, Windy City Film Festival 1999, Best Documentary in Humanitarian Tradition, Athens Film Festival 1999) 1998. *Television:* Hy's Gift (ABC/Nightline segment) Nov. 1996. *Publications:* Cape Light 1978 (revised edn 2002), St. Louis and the Arch 1981, Wild Flowers 1983, A Summer's Day 1986, The Arch 1988, Redheads 1990, Creating Sense of Place 1990, Bay/Sky 1993, The Nutcracker 1993, La natura delle città (The Nature of Cities) 1994, Bystander: A History of Street Photography 1994, At the Water's Edge 1996, Joel Meyerowitz, 55 2001, Tuscany: Inside the Light 2003, Aftermath (Deutscher Fotobuchpreis) 2006, Out of the Ordinary 1970–1980 2006, Aftermath: World Trade Center Archive 2011, Legacy: The Preservation of Wilderness in New York City Parks 2009, Between the Dog and the Wolf 2013. *Address:* Joel Meyerowitz Photography, LLC, 817 West End Avenue, New York, NY 10025, USA. *Telephone:* (212) 666-6505. *Fax:* (212) 666-9102. *E-mail:* joel@joelmeyerowitz.com. *Website:* www.joelmeyerowitz.com.

MEYROWITZ, Carol M.; American business executive; *CEO, The TJX Companies, Inc.;* joined Hit or Miss div., The TJX Companies, Inc. 1983, later held sr man. positions with Hit or Miss and Chadwick's of Boston, Sr Exec. Vice-Pres. and Pres. The Marmaxx Group (co.'s largest div.) 2001–05, Pres. The TJX Companies, Inc. 2005–07, mem. Bd of Dirs and CEO 2007–, mem. Cttee of Exec. Man. 2007–; advisory consultant, Berkshire Partners LLC, Boston 2005–. *Address:* The TJX Companies, Inc., 770 Cochituate Road, Framingham, MA 01701, USA (office). *Telephone:* (508) 390-1000 (office). *Fax:* (508) 390-2828 (office). *E-mail:* info@tjx.com (office). *Website:* www.tjx.com (office).

MÉZARD, Marc, PhD; French physicist, academic and university administrator; *Director, École Normale Supérieure;* b. 29 Aug. 1957, Aurillac; m. Annie Cohen-Solal; ed École Normale Supérieure, Paris; joined CNRS 1981, Chargé de Recherche Lab. of Theoretical Physics, École Normale Supérieure 1981–89 Research Dir 1989–98, Research Dir CNRS Université Paris-Sud 1999–2010; Dir Laboratoire de Physique Théorique et Modèles Statistiques, Université Paris-Sud

2010–12; Lecturer, École Polytechnique 1987–2012; conducted research at La Sapienza Univ., Rome 1984–86; Research Scientist Kavli Inst., Univ. of California, Santa Barbara 1998–99; Visiting Scientist, Oldenburg Univ. 2009–10; Dir École Normale Supérieure 2012–; mem. European Acad. of Sciences 2012–; Chevalier de la Légion d'Honneur 2013; CNRS Bronze Medal 1985, CNRS Silver Medal 1990, Prix Ampère de l'Électricité de France, Acad. des sciences 1996, Humboldt Prize 2009, Onsager Prize of American Physics Soc. 2016. *Publications:* Spin Glass Theory and Beyond (co-author) 1987, Information, Physics, and Computation (co-author) 2009, Contrib. to numerous papers in professional journals on statistical physics, applied in particular to disordered systems. *Address:* Office of the Director, École normale supérieure, 45 rue d'Ulm, 75005 Paris Cedex 05 France (office); Laboratory of Physics, École normale supérieure, 24 rue Lhomond, 75231 Paris Cedex 05 France (office). *Telephone:* 1-44-32-30-01 (office). *Fax:* 1-44-32-20-99 (office). *E-mail:* marc.mezard@ens.fr (office). *Website:* www.ens.fr (office); lptms .u-psud.fr/membres/mezard (office).

MEZOUAR, Salaheddine, MSc(Econ); Moroccan politician and business executive; b. 11 Dec. 1953, Meknès; m.; two c.; ed Institut européen d'admin des affaires (INSEAD), Fontainebleau, France, Institut supérieur de commerce et d'admin des entreprises (ISCAE), Casablanca, Université des sciences sociales, Grenoble, France; held admin. and financial posts with Régies d'Eau et d'Électricité de Rabat et de Tanger early 1980s; Chief Financial Officer Franco-Tunisian electrical, plumbing, refrigeration and maintenance co. based in Tunis –1986; Chief of Div. and in charge of mission, Office d'exploitation des Ports (ODEP) 1986–91; joined Spanish co. specializing in manufacture of tissue where he served as Gen. Man. of subsidiary Settat and Commercial Dir of group for Morocco, Africa and Middle East 1991; Pres. Moroccan Asscn of Textile Industries and Clothing (AMITH) 2002; also served as Pres. Textile and Leather Fed. in Gen. Confed. of Moroccan Enterprises (CGEM); Minister of Industry, Trade and Upgrading of the Economy 2004–07, of the Economy and Finance 2007–11, of Foreign Affairs 2013–17; Pres. Conference of the Parties (COP 22, UN climate change convention), Marrakech 2016; mem. Cen. Cttee Rassemblement nat. des Indépendants, Sec.-Gen. –2016; fmr Vice-Pres. Raja athletic club; fmr capt. nat. basketball team.

MEZZOGIORNO, Giovanna; Italian actress; b. 9 Nov. 1974, Rome; d. of Vittorio Mezzogiorno and Cecilia Sacchi; m. Alessio Federico Fugolo 2009; studied dancing for 13 years; moved to Paris aged 19 and attended the stages by Arianne Mnouchkine, worked for two years at the Peter Brook Workshop (Le Centre Int. de Créations Théatrales); stage debut with role of Ofelia in Qui est là, toured several European cities; film debut in Il viaggio della sposa 1997; Premio Coppola-Prati 1996, Targa d'Argento as the New Talent in Italian Cinema, Premio Flaiano as Best Actress 1997–98. *Theatre includes:* 4.48 Psicosi (by Sarah Kane, directed by Piero Maccarinelli). *Films include:* Il viaggio della sposa (The Bride's Journey) 1997, Del perduto amore (Nastro d'Argento, Ciak d'Oro and Premio Pasinetti as Best Actress in a starring role) 1998, Asini 1999, Un uomo perbene 1999, Afrodita, el sabor del amor 2001, State zitti per favore 2001, L'ultimo bacio (Premio Flaiano) 2001, Malefemmene 2001, Nobel 2001, Tutta la conoscenza del mondo 2001, Ilaria Alpi – Il più crudele dei giorni 2002, La finestra di fronte (Facing Windows) (David di Donatello, Ciak d'Oro, Nastro d'Argento, Grolle d'Oro and Globo d'Oro, Foreign Press Asscn, Flaiano Award, Karlovy Vary Award as Best Actress in a Leading Role) 2003, L'amore ritorna 2004, Stai con me 2004, Last Chance Saloon 2004, Il club delle promesse (Au secours, j'ai trente ans!) 2004, La bestia nel cuore (The Beast in the Heart) 2005, Don't Tell 2005, Lezioni di volo 2006, AD Project (video) 2006, Flying Lessons 2007, Night Bus 2007, Love in the Time of Cholera 2007, Les murs porteurs 2007, L'amore non basta 2008, Palermo Shooting 2008, Sono viva 2008, Vincere 2009, La Prima Linea 2009, Basilicata Coast to Coast 2010, Vinodentro 2013, The Dinner 2014; producer: In the Eyes (documentary) 2009. *Television includes:* Più leggero non basta (film for Italian Nat. TV Network, RaiDue) 1999, Les Misérables (mini-series) 2000, Entrusted (film) 2003, Virginia, la monaca di Monza (film) 2004.

MGALOBLISHVILI, Grigol, BA, MA; Georgian diplomatist and politician; *Assistant to Commandant of Academic Affairs, National Defence College of United Arab Emirates;* b. 7 Oct. 1973; m.; two c.; ed Tbilisi State Univ., Istanbul Univ., Univ. of Oxford, UK; interpreter, Georgian Trade Mission in Turkey 1995–96, Attaché, Dept of Western European Countries, Ministry of Foreign Affairs 1996–98, First Sec., Embassy in Ankara 1998–2000, Political Counsellor 1998–2002, Deputy Dir Dept of US, Canada and Latin American Countries, Ministry of Foreign Affairs 2003–04, Dir Dept of European and Euro-integration 2004, rank of Envoy Extraordinary and Plenipotentiary 2005, rank of Amb. 2006, Amb. to Turkey 2006–08; Prime Minister of Georgia Nov. 2008–Feb. 2009; apptd Amb. and Perm. Rep. to NATO, Brussels 2009; joined as Assoc. Prof., Nat. Defence Coll. of UAE, currently Asst to Commdt for Academic Affairs; fmr Visiting Distinguished Faculty mem., Coll. of Int. Security Affairs, Nat. Defence Univ. *Address:* National Defence College of United Arab Emirates, Sheikh Rashid bin Saeed Street, POB 28881, Abu Dhabi, UAE (office). *Telephone:* (2) 4961221 (office). *Fax:* (2) 6157038 (office). *E-mail:* administration@ndc.ac.ae (office). *Website:* administration@ndc.ac.ae (office).

MGEBRISHVILI, Giorgi; Georgian lawyer and government official; b. 9 May 1970, Tbilisi, Georgian SSR, USSR; m.; two c.; ed Ivane Javakhishvili Tbilisi State Univ.; Intern, Investigation Dept, Ministry of Internal Affairs 1997, Investigator 1998–2004; Investigator of Finance Police, Ministry of Finance 2004–07, Head of Customs Control Dept, Tbilisi Int. Airport, LEPL Revenue Service 2007–08, Head of Dept of Customs Transactions Processing, Rustavi Regional Centre (Tax Inspectorate) 2007–08, Deputy Head of Rustavi Regional Centre (Tax Inspectorate) 2008–10, Deputy Head of Poty Regional Centre (Tax Inspectorate) 2010–11, Main Div. Head of Western Portal, Econ. Border Protection Dept Jan.–May 2011, Deputy Head of Tax Prevention Dept 2011–12, Deputy Head of Tax Monitoring Dept July–Nov. 2012, Head of Customs Dept 2012–13, Sr Advisor, Customs Dept Nov.–Dec. 2013; Deputy Head of Dept of Internal Audit, State Audit Service April–Sept. 2013; Deputy Head of Main Div., State Security Agency, Ministry of Internal Affairs Sept.–Nov. 2013; Gov. Lower Kartli State Plenipotentiary Rep. 2013–14; Minister of Prisons and Probation 2014–15, of Internal Affairs 2015–17.

M'HENNI, Hedi; Tunisian physician and politician; b. 24 Dec. 1942, Sayada; m.; two c.; began career as physician specializing in preventive medicine; Dir Office national de la famille et de la population 1986; Minister of Public Health

1992–2001; Minister of Interior and Local Devt 2003–04, of Nat. Defence 2004–05; Sec.-Gen. Rassemblement constitutionnel démocratique 2005–08.

MIA, Mohammed Sidik; Malawi politician; b. 1965; s. of Abdul Sidik Mia; m.; three c.; MP for Chikwawa Nkombezi 2004–; Deputy Minister of Agric., Irrigation and Food Security 2004–05, of Mines, Natural Resources and Environment 2005, of Transport and Public Works 2005, Minister for Irrigation and Water Devt 2005–09, Minister of Nat. Defence 2009–11, of Transport and Public Infrastructure 2011–14 (resgnd).

MIAO, Wei; Chinese politician; *Minister of Industry and Information Technology;* b. May 1955, Beijing; ed Hefei Univ. of Tech., CCP Cen. Cttee Central Party School; joined CCP 1984; Deputy Man., Sales Dept, China Nat. Automotive Industry Corpn 1985–89, Deputy Dir-Gen., Production Dept 1989–93; Deputy Dir, Automobile Dept, First Ministry of Machine-Building Industry 1993–95; Deputy Chief Engineer, Dongfeng Automobile Corpn 1995–97, Gen. Man. 1999–2005, also Sec., CCP Party Cttee 1997–2001; mem., CCP Provincial Cttee, Hubei Prov. 2003–05, mem. Standing Cttee 2005–08; Chair., City People's Congress, Wuhan City, Hubei Prov. 2007–08; Vice-Minister of Industry and Information Tech. 2008–10, Minister 2010–; Deputy, 10th NPC 2003–08, 11th NPC 2008–13; alt. mem. 17th CCP Cen. Cttee 2007–12, mem. 18th CCP Cen. Cttee 2012–17, mem. 19th CCP Cen. Cttee 2017–. *Address:* Ministry of Industry and Information Technology, 13 Xichangan Dajie, Beijing 100804, People's Republic of China (office). *Telephone:* (10) 68208025 (office). *E-mail:* mail@miit.gov.cn (office). *Website:* www.miit.gov.cn (office).

MICALI, Silvio, PhD; American/Italian electrical engineer and academic; *Associate Head, Electrical Engineering and Computer Science Department, Massachusetts Institute of Technology;* b. 13 Oct. 1954, Palermo, Italy; ed Univ. of Rome, Univ. of California, Berkeley; Post-Doctoral Fellow, Univ. of Toronto, Canada 1982–83; Asst Prof., MIT 1983–86, Assoc. Prof. 1986–88, Tenured Assoc. Prof. 1988–91, Full Prof. 1991–, Assoc. Head Electrical Eng and Computer Science Dept 2015–, currently Ford Prof. of Eng, Electrical Eng and Computer Science Dept, also mem. Computer Science and Artificial Intelligence Lab.; mem. NAS 2007, Nat. Acad. of Eng, American Acad. of Arts and Sciencesm, Accademia dei Lincei; Fellow, Int. Asscn for Cryptologic Research 2007; Dr hc (Univ. of Salerno) 2015; Gödel Prize 1993, RSA Prize in Cryptography, A.M. Turing Award, Asscn for Computing Machinery 2012, Thomas M. Menino Award. *Publications:* Randomness and Computation (ed.), 5th vol. of the series Advances in Computing Research 1989; more than 100 papers in scientific journals; 47 patents. *Address:* Room G644, The Stata Center, Massachusetts Institute of Technology, 32 Vassar Street, 32-G866, Cambridge, MA 02139, USA (office). *Telephone:* (617) 253-5949 (office); (617) 253-6090 (office). *Fax:* (617) 253-6652 (office). *E-mail:* silvio@csail.mit.edu (office). *Website:* people.csail.mit.edu/silvio (office).

MICHAEL, Rt Hon. Alun Edward, BA, JP; British politician; *Police and Crime Commissioner for South Wales;* b. 22 Aug. 1943, Bryngwran, Anglesey, Wales; s. of Leslie Charles Michael and Elizabeth (Betty) Michael; m. Mary Sophia Crawley; two s. three d.; ed Keele Univ.; journalist South Wales Echo 1966–71; Youth and Community Worker, Cardiff 1972–84; Area Community Education Officer, Grangetown and Butetown 1984–87; mem. Cardiff City Council 1973–89 (fmr Chair. Finance, Planning, Performance Review and Econ. Devt, Chief Whip, Labour Group); MP (Labour and Co-operative) for Cardiff S and Penarth 1987–2012, Opposition Whip 1987–88, Opposition Frontbench Spokesman on Welsh Affairs 1988–92, on Home Affairs and the Voluntary Sector 1992–97; Minister of State, Home Office 1997–98; Sec. of State for Wales 1998–99; First Sec. of Nat. Ass. for Wales 1999–2000; Minister of State for Rural Affairs and Local Environmental Quality, Dept for the Environment, Food and Rural Affairs 2001–05, Minister of State for Industry and Regions 2005–06; Police and Crime Commr for South Wales 2012–; mem. Nat. Ass. for Wales for Mid and W Wales 1999–2000; Leader of Welsh Labour 1999–2000; Vice-Pres. Youth Hostel Asscn. *Publications:* Building the Future Together 1997, Labour in Action: Tough on Crime, Tough on the Causes of Crime – A Collection of Essays (ed.) 1997, Dragon on Our Doorstep: New Politics for a New Millennium in Wales 2000. *Leisure interests:* opera, reading, long-distance running, mountain-walking, National Parks, classical music. *Address:* South Wales Police HQ, Ty Morgannwg, Cowbridge Road, Bridgend, South Wales, CF31 3SU, Wales (office). *Telephone:* (1656) 869366 (office). *Fax:* (1656) 869407 (office). *E-mail:* commissioner@south -wales.pnn.police.uk (office). *Website:* www.southwalescommissioner.org.uk (office); www.alunmichael.com.

MICHAEL, Ib; Danish novelist and poet; b. (Ib Michael Rasmussen), 17 Jan. 1945, Roskilde; ed Univ. of Copenhagen; Dannebrogordenen 2010; Otto Gelsted Prize 1978, De Gyldne Laurbær 1989, Booksellers Club Golden Laurel for Author of the Year 1990, Kritikerprisen 1991, Søren Gyldendal Prize 1993, Danish Acad. Prize 1994, Drachmannlegate 2017. *Publications include:* novels: En hidtil uset drøm om skibe (A Previously Unseen Dream of Ships) 1970, Den flyvende kalkundræber (The Flying Turkey Hunter) 1971, Hjortefod (Stag's Hoof) 1974, Rejsen tilbage (The Journey Back) 1977, Kejserfortællingen (The Tiger's Tale) 1981, Troubadurens læring (The Minstrel's Apprentice) 1984, Kilroy, Kilroy 1989, Vanillepigen (The Vanilla Girl) 1991, Den tolvte rytter (The Midnight Soldier) 1993, Brev til månen (Letter to the Moon) 1995, Prins (Prince) 1997, Kejserens atlas (The Emperor's Atlas) 2001, Paven af Indien (The Pope of India) 2003, Grill 2005, Orbit 2010, Så var verdens deres 2010, Hjertets hemmeligheder (The Heart's Secrets) 2012, Himlen brændte 2013, En anden sol 2015; travelogues: Mayalandet (The Land of the Maya) 1973, Rejse i koralhavet-optegnelser fra en truet verden (Travel in the Coral Sea: Records From a Threatened World) 2016; poetry: Himmelbegravelse: Digte fra Tibet (Sky Burial: Poems from Tibet) 1986, Vinden i metroen (The Wind in the Metro) 1990; short stories: Atkinson's biograf (Atkinson's Cinema) 1998. *Address:* c/o Gyldendal Publishing, Klareboderne 3, 1001 Copenhagen, Denmark (office). *Website:* www.gyldendal.dk/forfattere/ib -michael (office).

MICHAELIS, Peter; Austrian business executive; b. 18 March 1946; ed Univ. of Salzburg, Univ. of Kiel, Germany; with Mannesmann Group 1975–2001; Speaker of the Bd, Österreichische Industrieholding AG (OIAG—govt holding co.) 2001–11, Chair. Man. Bd and Man. Dir –2011; Chair. or fmr Chair. Supervisory Bd Austrian Airlines (Österreichische Luftverkehrs) AG, Österreichische Post AG, Telekom

Austria AG, APK Pensionskasse AG; mem. Supervisory Bd OMV (originally ÖMV for Österreichische Mineralölverwaltung meaning Austrian mineral oil authority) Group 2001–11, then Deputy Chair., Chair. –2011.

MICHAELS, Lorne, CM; Canadian/American television and film producer; *Executive Producer, Saturday Night Live;* b. 17 Nov. 1944, Toronto, Ont.; m. 1st Rosie Schuster 1973 (divorced 1980); m. 2nd Susan Forristal 1981 (divorced 1987); m. 3rd Alice Barry 1991; three c.; ed Forest Hill Collegiate Inst., Toronto, Univ. of Toronto; began career as a writer and broadcaster for CBC 1966; moved to Los Angeles to work as a writer for Rowan & Martin's Laugh-In (TV show) and The Beautiful Phyllis Diller Show 1968; creator and Exec. Producer, Saturday Night Live, NBC 1975–80, 1985–, Exec. Producer, Late Night with Conan O'Brien, The Tonight Show (moved to New York as The Tonight Show Starring Jimmy Fallon 2014); f. Broadway Video Inc. (production co.) 1979; US citizenship 1987; Order of Canada 2002; inducted into the Television Acad. Hall of Fame 1999, ten Emmy Awards, including Emmy Award for Best Writing in a Variety/Comedy Series 2002, awarded a star on the Hollywood Walk of Fame 2002, on Canada's Walk of Fame 2003, Mark Twain Prize for American Humor, John F. Kennedy Center for the Performing Arts 2004, Gov. Gen.'s Award for Lifetime Artistic Achievement 2006, Webby for Film & Video Lifetime Achievement 2008, Personal Peabody Award 2013, Presidential Medal of Freedom 2016. *Films produced include:* Gilda Live (also writer) 1980, Coneheads 1983, Three Amigos (also co-writer) 1986, Wayne's World 1992, Wayne's World II 1993, Lassie 1994, Tommy Boy 1995, Kids in the Hall: Brain Candy 1996, A Night at the Roxbury 1998, Superstar 1999, The Ladies Man 2000, Enigma 2001, Mean Girls 2004, Hot Rod 2007, Baby Mama 2008, MacGruber 2010, The Guilt Trip 2012, Brothers in Law 2015, The Taliban Shuffle 2015, Loomis Fargo 2015. *Television includes:* Things We Did Last Summer (film) 1977, Frosty Returns (short) 1992, Man Seeking Woman (film) 2014. *Television shows produced:* The Hart and Lorne Terrific Hour (also co-star and writer) 1970–71, Saturday Night Live (exec. producer, creator) 1975–80, (Primetime Emmy Award for Outstanding Variety Special 2015) 1985–, The Paul Simon Special (also writer) 1977, All You Need Is Cash (aka The Rutles) 1978, Mr. Mike's Mondo Video 1979, Steve Martin's Best Show Ever (also writer) 1981, The New Show 1984, Sunday Night 1988–90, The Kids in the Hall 1989, Late Night with Conan O'Brien 1993–2009, Where in Time Is Carmen Sandiego 1996–98, The Rutles 2: Can't Buy Me Lunch 2002, The Colin Quinn Show 2002, Sons and Daughters 2006, 30 Rock 2006–10, Late Night with Jimmy Fallon 2009–14, Portlandia 2011–, Up All Night 2011–13, The Tonight Show Starring Jimmy Fallon 2014–, Late Night with Seth Meyers 2014–, Mulaney 2014–, The Maya Rudolph Show 2014–, Man Seeking Woman 2015, Documentary Now! 2015–. *Address:* c/o Saturday Night Live, NBC Television Network, 30 Rockefeller Plaza, New York, NY 10112, USA (office). *Telephone:* (212) 664-4444 (office). *Fax:* (212) 664-4085 (office). *Website:* www.nbc.com/saturday-night-live (office); www.lornemichaels.com.

MICHAELS-MOORE, Anthony, BA; British singer (baritone); b. (Anthony Michael Frederick Moore), 8 April 1957, Grays, Essex, England; s. of John Frederick Moore and Isabel Shephard; m. 1st Ewa Bozena Migocki 1980; one d.; m. 2nd Emily Doyle Schluter 2010; one s. one d.; ed Gravesend School for Boys, Univ. of Newcastle, Royal Scottish Acad. of Music and Drama, Fenham Teacher Training Coll.; Prin. Baritone, Royal Opera House, Covent Garden 1987–97; roles in all British opera cos; debut La Scala, Milan (Licinius in La Vestale) 1993, Paris Bastille (Sharpless in Madama Butterfly) 1995, New York Metropolitan Opera (Marcello in La Bohème) 1996, Teatro Colón Buenos Aires (Andrea Chénier) 1996, Vienna Staatsoper (Lescaut in Manon) 1997, San Francisco Opera (Eugene Onegin) 1997, Santa Fe Opera (title role in Simon Boccanegra) 2004, Paris Théâtre des Champs-Elysées (title role in Falstaff) 2010, Opéra de Montréal (title role in Rigoletto) 2010, Opernhaus Zurich (title role in Falstaff) 2011, Seoul, Korea (Scarpia in Tosca) 2012, Oper Köln (Scarpia in Tosca) 2012; specialises in 19th-century baritone repertoire and English song; winner, Luciano Pavarotti/Opera Co. of Philadelphia Prize 1985, Royal Philharmonic Soc. Award Winner 1997. *Radio:* regular BBC Radio 3 broadcasts, Verdi operas from Royal Opera House, Met Opera relays from New York. *Television includes:* BBC Proms (Beethoven's Missa Solemnis, Mahler's Symphony No. 8), Carmina Burana recorded at La Scala, Milan 1996. *Recordings include:* Carmina Burana, Lucia di Lammermoor, La Vestale, La Favorite, Falstaff and Il Tabarro, Aroldo. *Leisure interests:* distance running, dog training, Indian cuisine, road biking. *Address:* c/o Alex Fletcher, Fletcher Artist Management, 14 Murray Street, #124, New York, NY 10007, USA (office). *Telephone:* (347) 875-7146 (office). *Website:* www.fletcherartists.com/artists/anthony-michaels-moore (office); www.anthonymichaelsmoore.com.

MICHAL, Jiři, BSc; Czech business executive; ed Univ. of Chem. and Tech., Prague; joined Zentiva a.s. 1974, various man. roles, including Operational Dir, Chief Financial Officer, CEO and Chair. 1993–2010 (co. acquired by Sanofi-Aventis 2009); Vice-Pres. Czech Chemical Industry Asscn; Chair. Prague Chemical Univ. 2011–; mem. Bd of Dirs Moser (Czech Repub.), Actavis plc. *Address:* Moser, Na Prikope 12, 110 00 Prague 1, Czech Republic (office). *Telephone:* (2) 24211293 (office). *Fax:* (2) 24228686 (office). *E-mail:* pha-prikopy@moser-glass.com (office). *Website:* www.moser-glass.com (office).

MICHALCZEWSKI, Dariusz, (The Tiger); Polish/German fmr professional boxer; b. 5 May 1968, Gdańsk; m.; two s.; amateur boxer 1982–91, European Junior semifinalist in middleweight div. 1986, German Nat. Champion in light heavyweight div. 1990, European Champion in light heavyweight div. 1991; 133 wins in 150 amateur fights; defected from Polish amateur nat. team while competing in Germany 1988, gained citizenship and turned professional 1991; professional boxer 1991–2003, 2004–05; 48 wins (38 by knockout) in 50 professional fights; European champion, Göteborg 1991; became World Boxing Org. (WBO) light-heavyweight champion 1994 and defended the title 23 times; won WBO cruiserweight title in 1994 (abandoned 1995); won World Boxing Asscn (WBA), Int. Boxing Fed. (IBF) light-heavyweight titles in 1997; defeated by Julio César González Oct. 2003 (retd); came out of retirement to box Fabrice Tiozzo for WBA light heavyweight title in Hamburg Feb. 2005, stopped in six rounds, announced retirement May 2005. *Address:* Waldeweg 134B, 22393 Hamburg, Germany (office). *Telephone:* (40) 68912656 (office). *Website:* www.dariusz-tiger.de.

MICHALIK, Archbishop Józef, DTheol; Polish ecclesiastic; b. 20 April 1941, Zambrów; ed Acad. of Catholic Theology, Warsaw, Angelicum, St Thomas Pontifical Univ., Rome; ordained priest, Łomża 1964; Vice-Chancellor Bishops' Curia, Łomża 1973–78; fmr lecturer Higher Theological Seminary, Łomża, Rector Pontifical Polish Coll., Rome 1978–86; staff mem. Pontifical Laity Council 1978–86; Bishop of Gorzów 1986–92; Chair. Episcopate Cttee for Academic Ministry 1986–95; Bishop Zielona Góra and Gorzów 1992–93; Archbishop of Przemyśl 1993–2016; Chair. Episcopate's Council for Poles Abroad, Councils of Episcopates of Europe Cttee for Laity; Vice-Chair. Consilium Conferentiarum Episcoporum Europea 2011–; mem. Main Council of Conf. of Polish Episcopate, (Chair. 2004–14), Vatican Congregation for Bishops; Polonia Mater Nostra Est 2002. *Publications:* My Talks with God 1976, La Chiesa e il suo rinnovamento secondo Andrea Frycz Modrzewski 1973, Brothers Look at Your Vocation 1991, Bóg i Ojczyzna, Wiara i Naród 1998, Mocą Twoją Panie 1998, Pan was potrzebuje 2000, Szukającym Prawdy 2002, Raport o stanie wiary w Polsce 2011.

MICHALOLIAKOS, Nikolaos G.; Greek politician; *General Secretary, Chrysi Avgi (Golden Dawn);* b. 16 Dec. 1957, Athens; m. Eleni Zaroulia; one d.; ed Faculty of Math., Nat. and Kapodistrian Univ. of Athens; joined nationalist 4th of August Party aged 16; participated in Athens local org. of EOKA-B; joined the Army's special forces, arrested after becoming mem. of a far-right extremist group July 1978, sentenced to one year's imprisonment for illegally carrying guns and explosives Jan. 1979, subsequently dismissed from the army; launched Chrysi Avgi (Golden Dawn) magazine 1980 (ceased publication April 1984); joined Nat. Political Union and became leader of youth section 1984; broke away from party and f. Popular Nat. Movt– Chrysi Avgi (Golden Dawn) 1985, remained as leader until its disbandment 2005; continued political activity through the Patriotic Alliance 2005–07; Chrysi Avgi reformed under his leadership 2007, currently Gen. Sec.; mem. Athens Council 2011–12; mem. Parl. 2012–; arrested along with four other Chrysi Avgi MPs and 15 others, charged with belonging to a criminal organization Sept. 2013, released July 2015, trial is ongoing. *Publications:* Enemies of the State 2000, For a Greater Greece in a Free Europe 2000, Against All 2001, The Last Loyals 2002, Pericles Giannopoulos: The Apollonian Speech 2006, The Confession of a Nationalist (reprinted) 2008, From the Ashes of Berlin to Globalisation 2008, Defending National Memory 2009. *Address:* Chrysi Avgi (Golden Dawn), Diligiannis 50, 104 39 Athens, Greece (office). *Telephone:* (210) 6985121 (office). *Fax:* (210) 3706579 (office). *E-mail:* info@xryshaygh.com (office). *Website:* xryshaygh.com (office).

MICHAUD, Jean-Claude Georges; French broadcasting executive; b. 28 Oct. 1933; s. of Maurice Michaud and Suzanne Michaud; m. Annette Chasserot 1957; one s. one d. (from fmr marriage); ed Lycée Louis-le-Grand, Paris and Ecole Normale Supérieure, Paris; Counsellor, Ministry of Educ. 1961–62, Ministry of Information 1962–64; Asst Dir Television ORTF 1964–68, Counsellor to Dir-Gen. 1968–70; man. position, Librairie Hachette 1970–73; Deputy Dir for External Affairs and Co-operation, ORTF 1973–74; Dir of Int. Affairs and Co-operation, Télédiffusion France 1975–80, Dir of Commercial Affairs 1982–83, Overseas Dir 1983–85; Pres.-Dir-Gen. Soc. Française Radio-Télévision d'Outre-Mer (RFO) 1986–89; Pres. Dir-Gen. Sofratev 1989–98. *Publications:* Teoria e Storia nel Capitale di Marx 1960, Alain Peyrefitte 2002. *Leisure interests:* walking, skiing, reading. *Address:* 66 rue de la République, 69002 Lyon, France (home). *Telephone:* 4-78-68-20-32 (home). *E-mail:* michaud.jeanclaude@free.fr (home).

MICHAUD, Yves, DèsL; French philosopher, art critic and academic; b. 11 July 1944, Lyon; ed Ecole normale supérieure and Univ. of Paris I (Sorbonne); taught successively at Univs of Montpellier, Rouen and Paris I (Sorbonne); holds various positions as Visiting Prof. at Univ. of California, Berkeley, and Univs of Tunis, São Paulo and Edinburgh; Dir Ecole nationale supérieure des Beaux-Arts 1989–97; returned to academic life and concentrated on philosophy of art and of culture while continuing to write on violence 1997; launched Université de tous les savoirs (Univ. of All Knowledge) 2000, a free univ. that popularizes the most recent results of scientific research; mem. Institut universitaire de France; Chevalier, Légion d'honneur; Officier des Arts et des Lettres. *Publications include:* Violence et politique 1978, Hume et la fin de la philosophie 1983, La Violence 1986, Locke 1986, Enseigner l'art?: Analyses et réflexions sur les écoles d'art 1993, La Crise de l'art contemporain 1997, Critères esthétiques et jugement de goût 1999, Humain, inhumain, trop humain 2001, Jan Voss, oeuvres 1986–2001 2001, Changements dans la violence: Essai sur la bienveillance et sur la peur 2002, L'Art à l'état gazeux: Essai sur le triomphe de l'esthétique 2003, Université de tous les savoirs: Le renouvellement de l'observation dans les sciences 2004, Chirac dans le texte, la parole et l'impuissance 2004, Précis de recomposition politique: Des incivismes à la française et de quelques manières d'y remédier 2006, Humain, inhumain, trop humain: Réflexions philosophiques sur les biotechnologies, la vie et la conservation de soi à partir de l'œuvre de Peter Sloterdijk 2006, L'artiste et les commissaires: Quatre essais non pas sur l'art contemporain mais sur ceux qui s'en occupent 2007, Qu'est-ce que le mérite? (ed.) 2009, La crise de l'art contemporain: Utopie, démocratie et comédie 2011, Ibiza mon amour: Enquête sur l'industrialisation du plaisir 2012, Emmanuelle Pérat: In vivo 2012, Le nouveau luxe: Expériences, arrogance, authenticité 2013, Narcisse et ses avatar 2014. *Address:* c/o Éditions Grasset, 61 rue des Saints-Pères, 75006 Paris, France. *E-mail:* info@grasset.fr. *Website:* grasset.fr/yves-michaud.

MICHEL, Charles, LenD; Belgian lawyer and politician; *Caretaker Prime Minister;* b. 21 Dec. 1975, Namur; s. of Louis Michel; partner Amélie Derbaudrenghien; ed Free Univ. of Brussels, Univ. of Amsterdam, The Netherlands; lawyer, Brussels Bar 1998–; joined Jeunes Réformateurs Libéraux de Jodoigne (Young Liberals of Jodoigne); Prov. Councillor in Walloon Brabant 1994–99, Vice-Pres. Prov. Council 1995–99; mem. Fed. Chamber of Reps for Walloon Brabant 1999–; Minister of Home Affairs in Walloon Govt 2000–04, Alderman in Utilities and Urban Devt 2004–06; City Councillor, Wavre 2000–07, Mayor of Wavre 2006–; Chair. Mouvement Réformateur (MR) 2011–; Minister of Devt Co-operation 2007–11; Prime Minister of Belgium 2014–18 (resigned following no-confidence motion), Caretaker Prime Minister Dec. 2018–. *Address:* Cabinet of the Prime Minister, 16 Rue de la Loi, 1000 Brussels, Belgium (office). *Telephone:* (2) 501-02-11 (office). *Fax:* (2) 512-69-52 (office). *E-mail:* info@premier.fed.be (office). *Website:* www.premier.be (office); www.charlesmichel.be.

MICHEL, James Alix; Seychelles politician and fmr head of state; b. 16 Aug. 1944; m. Natalie Michel; two s. (one deceased) one d.; ed Teacher Training Coll., Seychelles; teacher 1960–61; with Cable & Wireless Telecommunications 1962–71;

Accountant, Asst Man., then Man. Hotel des Seychelles 1971–74; mem. Exec. Cttee Seychelles People's United Party and Co-ordinator of Party Brs, also Ed. of The People 1974–77; Minister of State, Admin and Information 1977–79; mem. Cen. Exec. Cttee Seychelles People's Progressive Front 1978–, also Sec.; Chief of Staff, Seychelles People's Defence Forces 1979–93; Minister of Educ., Information, Culture and Telecommunications 1979–86, of Educ., Information, Culture and Sports 1986–89, of Finance 1989–91, of Finance and Information 1991–93, of Finance, Information, Communications and Defence, also First Desig. Minister to discharge the functions of Pres. 1993–96; Vice-Pres. (retaining portfolios for Finance, Information and Communications) 1996, Vice-Pres. (with portfolios of Econ. Planning and Environment and Transport) 1998–2000, Vice-Pres. and Minister of Finance, Econ. Planning, Information Tech. and Communications 2001–04; Pres. of the Seychelles, with additional responsibility for Defence, Police, Information and Public Relations, Legal Affairs and Risk and Disaster Man. 2004–16, also Minister of Finance 2005–06; Co-Chair. Global Island Partnership (GLISPA); Chancellor, Univ. of Seychelles; Patron, Seychelles Football Fed., Seychelles Islands Foundation, Seychelles Scouts Asscn, Jj Spirit Foundation; Foreign mem. Russian Acad. of Natural Sciences; Grand Cross of the Order Pro Merito Melitensi (Malta) 2001, Grand Cross of the Knightly Order, Special Class 2010; Outstanding Civilian Service Medal, US Army 1995, UNESCO Gold Medal of the Five Continents 2009, Special Award for Eco-Safety, World Eco-Safety Ass. of the International Eco-Safety Cooperative Org. 2010, Sustainable Development Leadership Award, Delhi Sustainable Development Summit 2013.

MICHEL, Louis; Belgian politician; b. 2 Sept. 1947, Tirlemont; one s.; fmr lecturer at Inst. Supérieur de Commerce Saint-Louis; Prof. of Dutch, English and German Literature, Ecole Normale provinciale de Jodoigne 1968–78; Alderman of Jodoigne 1977–83, Mayor 1983–2004; Sec.-Gen. Parti Réformateur Libéral (PRL) 1980–82, Pres. 1982–90; Pres. Fed. of Local and Provincial PRL Office Holders 1990–92; Pres. parl. group in Council of Walloon Region 1991–92, in House of Reps 1992–95; MP 1978–99; Pres. PRL 1995–2001; Deputy Pres. of Liberal Int.; Deputy Prime Minister and Minister of Foreign Affairs 1999–2004; apptd Rep. of Belgium to EU Special Convention on a European Constitution 2001; Commr for Devt and Humanitarian Aid, EC 2004–09 (resgnd); MEP 2009–; mem. Parl. Comms on Finance, Budget, Institutional Reforms and Comm. charged with supervising electoral expenditures; mem. Benelux Inter parl. Consultative Council; Commdr Order of Leopold. *Address:* Mouvement Réformateur (MR), 84–86 ave de la Toison d'Or, 1060 Brussels, Belgium (office). *Telephone:* (2) 500-35-11 (office). *E-mail:* contact@mr.be (office). *Website:* www.mr.be (office).

MICHEL, Mohamedou Ould, BSc, MSc; Mauritanian government official and fmr diplomatist; b. 1954, Akjoujt; m.; two c.; ed Montreal Univ. of Canberra; Chief of Service, In-Charge of Financing and Foreign Aid, Ministry of Planning 1976–79, Sr Advisor 1983–89, Minister of Planning 1991–93; Dir of Devt Mauritanian Bank for Devt and Commerce 1979–89; CEO Nat. Bank of Mauritania 1983–89; Deputy Gov. Central Bank of Mauritania 1989–90, Gov. 1993–97; Minister of Finances 1990–91; Econ. Advisor to Pres. of Mauritania 2000–01; fmr Amb. to Australia, fmr Amb. to USA.

MICHELAKIS, Ioannis; Greek journalist and politician; b. 10 April 1960, Kalymnos; m.; ed Grad. School of Industrial Studies, Univ. of Piraeus; worked as a journalist from 1979 before becoming New Democracy Rep.; fmr Chief Ed. MEGA Channel, fmr Dir MEGA Channel Cyprus; fmr Dir ANT1 TV; fmr Dir Eleftheros Typos newspaper; Spokesperson for New Democracy 2011–13; mem. Parl. 2012–, mem. Standing Cttee on Nat. Defence and Foreign Affairs, Cttee on Armament Programmes and Contracts, Special Perm. Cttee on Greeks Abroad; Minister of the Interior 2013–14; Pres. Inst. for Democracy 'Konstantinos Karamanlis' 2013–. *Address:* Amerikis 10, 106 71 Athens, Greece. *Telephone:* (210) 3388700. *Fax:* (210) 3388704. *E-mail:* johnmichelakis@parliament.gr (office).

MICHELE, Alessandro; Italian fashion designer; *Creative Director, Gucci SpA;* b. 1972, Rome; ed Accademia di Costume e di Moda, Rome; began career, three years as Designer with knitwear brand Les Copains, Bologna; Sr Accessories Designer, Fendi 1998–2002; joined Gucci SpA 2002, worked in design studio, London, becoming Leather Goods Design Dir 2006, Assoc. to Creative Dir Frida Giannini 2011–15, also Creative Dir of Richard Ginori (Florentine porcelain brand) 2014–15, Creative Dir, Gucci SpA 2015–; British Fashion Awards Int. Fashion Designer of the Year awards 2015, 2016, Council of Fashion Designers of America Int. Award 2016. *Address:* Gucci SpA, Via Tornabuoni 73/r, 50123 Florence, Italy (office). *Telephone:* (55) 75921 (office). *Fax:* (55)-75922305 (office). *Website:* www.gucci.com (office).

MICHELETTI BAÍN, Roberto; Honduran business executive, politician and fmr head of state; b. 13 Aug. 1943, El Progreso, Yoro; s. of Umberto Micheletti and Donatella Baín; m. Xiomara Girón 1993; three c.; mem. Honour Guard of Pres. Ramón Villeda Morales 1963; in exile in USA 1973–76; fmr Pres. Empresa de Transporte TUTSA, El Progreso; mem. Congreso Nacional (Parl.) 1982–2006, Pres. 2006–09, Pres. 2006–09; Dir-Gen. Hondutel 1982–2002; mem. Partido Liberal de Honduras (PL), Pres. Yoro Regional PL Council, later Sec. PL Cen. Exec. Council, unsuccessful PL cand. for Pres. of Honduras 2008; Pres. of Honduras (following dismissal of Manuel Zelaya) 2009–10.

MICHELIN, Nicolas; French architect and town planner; b. 25 Jan. 1955, Paris; associate of Finn Geipel at Labfac (Laboratory for Architecture) 1990s; co-f., with Michel Delplace and Cyril Trétout, ANMA (Agence Nicolas Michelin & Associés), Paris 2000; Dir Ecole Nationale Superieure d'Architecture de Versailles 2000–09, est. Art Center 'La Maréchalerie'; Ed.-in-Chief Agora (biennial publ. on structure, town planning and design in Bordeaux) 2008; Grand Prix de l'Urbanisme 2007. *Film:* Nouveaux Paris: la ville et ses possibles (dir) 2005. *Publications include:* Finn Geipel, Nicolas Michelin: LABFAC/Laboratory for Architecture 1998, Cinq sur cinq 2008, Attitudes 2010. *Address:* ANMA Agence Nicolas Michelin & Associés, 9 cour des Petites Écuries, 75010 Paris, France (office). *Telephone:* 1-53-34-00-01 (office). *Fax:* 1-53-34-09-99 (office). *E-mail:* agence@anma.fr (office); communication@anma.fr (office). *Website:* anma.fr (office).

MICHELL, Robert H. (Bob), PhD, FRSB, FMedSci, FRS; British biochemist and academic (retd); *Professor Emeritus of Biochemistry, University of Birmingham;* b. 16 April 1941, Yeovil, Somerset; s. of Rowland C. Michell and Elsie L. Michell (née Hall); m. 1st June Evans 1967 (divorced 1971); m. 2nd Esther Margaret Oppenheim 1992; two s. one d.; ed Crewkerne School, Univ. of Birmingham; Research Fellow, Univ. of Birmingham 1965–66, 1969–70, Harvard Medical School 1966–68; Lecturer, Univ. of Birmingham 1970–81, Sr Lecturer 1981–84, Reader 1984–86, Prof. of Biochemistry 1986–2006, Royal Soc. Research Prof. 1987–2006, Prof. Emer. 2006–; mem. European Molecular Biology Org. 1991, Council, Royal Soc. 1996–97; Hon. mem. Biochemical Soc. 2010; CIBA Medal, Biochemical Soc. 1988, Royal Soc. UK-Canada Rutherford Lecturer 1994, Biochemical Soc. Morton Lecturer 2002. *Publications include:* Membranes and their Cellular Functions (with J. B. Finean and R. Coleman) 1974, 1978, 1984, Membrane Structure (co-ed.) 1981, Inositol Lipids and Transmembrane Signalling (co-ed.) 1988, Inositol Lipids in Cell Signalling (co-ed.) 1989, Lipids: Biochemistry, Biotechnology and Health 2016. *Leisure interests:* bird watching, photography, modern literature, wilderness, pottery. *Address:* School of Biosciences, University of Birmingham, Edgbaston, Birmingham, B12 2TT, England (office). *Telephone:* 7411-792640 (mobile) (home). *E-mail:* r.h.michell@bham.ac.uk (office). *Website:* www.birmingham.ac.uk/schools/biosciences (office).

MICHELS, Sir David Michael Charles, Kt; British leisure industry executive; *Chairman, Michels & Taylor (London) Ltd;* b. 1943; ed London Hotel School; various sales and marketing positions including Man. Dir, Grand Metropolitan 1966–81; joined Ladbroke Group PLC 1981, Sales and Marketing Dir Ladbroke Hotels 1981–83, Man. Dir Leisure Div. 1983–95, Man. Dir Ladbroke Hotels 1985–97; Sr Vice-Pres. of Sales and Marketing, Hilton Int. (following acquisition of Ladbroke Group by Hilton Group PLC 1987) 1987–89, Deputy Chair. Michels & Taylor Hilton UK and Exec. Vice-Pres. Hilton Int. 1989–91, CEO Stakis PLC 1991–99, apptd mem. Bd Hilton Group PLC 1999 (after acquisition of Stakis by Hilton Group), CEO 1999–2000, Group CEO 2000–06 (after reunification of Hilton International with Hilton Hotel Corpn); currently Chair. Michels & Taylor (London) Ltd; Pres. The Tourism Alliance, Inst. of Hospitality; mem. Bd of Dirs Strategic Hotels and Resorts 2006–, Jumeirah Hotels, The Savoy, Miroma; Sr Ind. Dir Marks and Spencer Group plc 2006–08, Deputy Chair. 2008; fmr Pres. British Hospitality Asscn; fmr Dir Arcadia Group PLC; fmr Pres. Hilton in the Community Foundation; Trustee Anne Frank Trust; Hon. Fellow, Acad. of Food & Wine Service 2003. *Address:* Michels & Taylor (London) Ltd, Suite 3, Caspian House, The Waterfront, Elstree Road, Elstree, WD6 3BS, England (office). *Telephone:* (20) 8905-2500 (office). *E-mail:* info@michelsandtaylor.com (office). *Website:* www.michelsandtaylor.com (office).

MICHELSEN, Axel, DPhil; Danish biologist and academic; *Professor Emeritus, University of Southern Denmark;* b. 1 March 1940, Haderslev; s. of Erik Michelsen and Vibeke Michelsen; m. Ulla West-Nielsen 1980 (died 2008); two s. one d.; ed Univ. of Copenhagen; Asst Prof. of Zoophysiology and Zoology, Univ. of Copenhagen 1963–72; Prof. of Biology, Odense Univ. 1973–2005; Prof. Emer., Univ. of Southern Denmark; Chair. Danish Science Research Council 1975–78, Max-Planck Gesellschaft Fachbeirat 1977–81, Danish Nat. Cttee for Biophysics 1980–90, Danish Nat. Cttee for ICSU 1986–2000, 2004–06, Centre for Sound Communication 1994–2003, Carlsberg Lab. 2003–09; Dir Carlsberg Foundation 1986–2009; mem. Royal Danish Acad. of Sciences and Letters, Akad. der Naturforscher Leopoldina, Academia Europaea; Corresp. mem. Akad. der Wissenschaften und der Literatur (Mainz), Bayerische Akad. der Wissenschaften, Akad. der Wissenschaften zu Göttingen; Kt, Order of the Dannebrog (First Class) 1990; Alexander von Humboldt Prize 1990. *Publications:* The Physiology of the Locust Ear 1971, Sound and Life 1975, Time Resolution in Auditory Systems 1985, The Dance Language of Honeybees 1992. *Leisure interests:* wines, beekeeping, gardening. *Address:* Rosenvænget 74, 5250 Odense SV, Denmark (home). *Telephone:* 61-26-35-82 (home). *E-mail:* a.michelsen@biology.sdu.dk (office). *Website:* findresearcher.sdu.dk/portal/da/person/a-michelsen (office).

MICHELSON, Poul Johan Sundberg; Faroese business executive and politician; *Minister of Industry, Trade and Foreign Affairs;* b. 22 July 1944, Tórshavn; s. of Johan Michelsen and Paula Michelsen; m. Sólrún Midjord; three c.; f. P/F Poul Michelsen (food supply co.) 1974; Mayor of Tórshavn 1981–92; mem. Løgting (parl.) for Suðurstreymoy constituency 1984–90; Minister of Industry, Trade and Foreign Affairs 2015–; Finnish Consul-Gen. in the Faroe Islands; mem. People's Party (Fólkaflokkurin) –2010; Co-founder and Leader, Progress (Framsókn) 2011–. *Address:* Ministry of Trade and Industry, Tinganes, POB 377, 110 Tórshavn, Faroe Islands (office). *Telephone:* 306600 (office). *Fax:* 306665 (office). *E-mail:* vmr@vmr.fo (office). *Website:* www.vmr.fo (office); www.pm.fo.

MICHNIK, Adam; Polish journalist and historian; *Editor-in-Chief, Gazeta Wyborcza;* b. 17 Oct. 1946, Warsaw; s. of Ozjasz Szechter and Helena Michnik; m.; one s.; ed Adam Mickiewicz Univ., Poznań; active in anti-communist movt 1965–80, spent six years in prison; Co-Founder and mem. Cttee for the Defence of Workers (KOR) 1976–80; Biuletyn Informacyjny, Krytyka, Zapis (ind. periodicals); activist Solidarity Self-governing Ind. Trade Union in the 1980s; imprisoned 1985–86; participant Round Table plenary debates 1989; Deputy to Sejm (Parl.) 1989–91; Ed.-in-Chief Gazeta Wyborcza (daily) 1989–; mem. Int. Advisory Bd, Council on Foreign Relations; Officer's Cross of Merit (Hungary) 1998, Bernardo O'Higgins Commdr's Order (Chile) 1999, Order for Contrib. to Polish-German Reconciliation, European Univ. Viadriana, Frankfurt 2000, Grand Prince Gedymin Order (Lithuania) 2001, Grand Cross of Merit (Germany) 2001; Dr hc (New School for Social Research, New York, Univ. of Minnesota, Univ. of Michigan, Connecticut Coll., Klaipėda Univ. 2012); French Pen Club Freedom Award 1982, Robert F. Kennedy Human Rights Award 1986, Alfred Jurzykowski Foundation Award, La Vie Man of the Year 1989, Shofar Award 1991, Brucke-Preis (Germany) 1995, Award of the European Journalists Asscn 1995, Medal of Imre Nagy 1995, OSCE Prize in Journalism and Democracy 1996, The Golden Pen (Bauer Verlag) 1998, The Francisco Cerecedo Journalist Prize 1999, Int. Press Inst. Freedom Hero 2000, Carl Bertelsmann Prize 2001, Erasmus Prize 2001, Dan David Prize 2006, Goethe Medal 2011. *Publications:* Cienie zapomnianych przodków (The Shadows of the Forgotten Ancestors) 1975, Kościół, Lewica, Dialog (Church, The Left, Dialogue) 1977, Penser la Pologne 1983, Szanse polskiej Demokracji (Chances for Polish Democracy) 1984, Z dziejów honoru w Polsce. Wypisy więzienne (From the History of Honour in Poland. Prison Notes) 1985, Takie czasy: Rzecz o kompromisie (Such Other Times: Concerning Compromise) 1985, Listy z Białołęki (Letters from Białołęka), Polskie pytania (Polish Questions) 1987, Druga faza rewolucji 1990, Między Panem a Plebanem 1995, Diabeł naszego czasu 1995, Letters From Freedom 1998, Confessions of a Converted Dissident – Essay for the Erasmus Prize 2001; many articles in Gazeta Wyborcza, Der Spiegel, Le Monde, Libération, El País, Lettre Internationale, New York Review of Books, The Washington Post and others. *Address:* 00-732 Warsaw, Gazeta Wyborcza, ul. Czerska 8/10, Poland (office). *Telephone:* (22) 5504000 (office); (22) 5554002 (office). *Fax:* (22) 8416920 (office). *E-mail:* contact@agora.pl (office).

MICHON, John Albertus, MSc, PhD; Dutch psychologist and academic; *Professor Emeritus of Psychonomics, Leiden University;* b. 29 Oct. 1935, Utrecht; s. of J. J. Michon and S. Ch. A. de Ruijter; m. Hetty Sommer 1960; one s. one d. (deceased); ed Utrecht Mun. Gymnasium and Univs of Utrecht and Leiden; Research Assoc., Inst. for Perception, Soesterberg 1960–73, Head, Dept of Road User Studies 1969–73; Co-founder Netherlands Psychonomics Foundation 1968, Sec. 1968–72, Pres. 1975–80; Prof. of Experimental Psychology and Traffic Science, Univ. of Groningen 1971–92, Dir Inst. for Experimental Psychology 1971–92, Chair. Traffic Research Center 1977–92, Chair. Dept of Psychology 1978, 1983–86, Assoc. Dean, Faculty of Social Sciences 1983–86; mem. Bd Center for Behavioral, Cognitive and Neurosciences 1990–92, co-f. Dept of Cognitive Science 1990; Dir Netherlands Inst. for the Study of Criminality and Law Enforcement 1992–98; Prof. of Criminality Research, Leiden Univ. 1992–98, Sr Research Prof. of Psychonomics 1998–2002, Prof. Emer. 2002–; Pres. Int. Soc. for the Study of Time 1983–86, Hon. mem. 2004–; Co-founder and mem. Bd European Soc. for Cognitive Psychology 1984–90; Vice-Chair. Nat. Council for Road Safety 1977–86; Ed.-in-Chief, Acta Psychologica 1971–74; Visiting Prof. Carnegie Mellon Univ., Pittsburgh, Pa 1986–87; Co-ordinator EEC DRIVE Project Generic Intelligent Driver Support 1988–92; Chair. Advisory Cttee for Cognitive Science 1995–97, Accreditation Cttee Research Schools 2000–07, Steering Cttee for the Cognitive Sciences, Netherlands Org. for Scientific Research (NWO) 2002–12; mem. Social Sciences Council (SWR) 1994–2003, Supervisory Cttee, Artificial Intelligence, Univ. of Groningen 2013–16; mem. and Hon. Sec. Jury, Heineken Prize for Cognitive Science 2004–10; mem. Royal Netherlands Acad. of Arts and Sciences (KNAW) 1981 (Chair. Behavioral and Social Sciences Section 1988–98), Academia Europaea 1989, European Acad. of Sciences and Arts 1995–2010; Kt, Order of the Netherlands Lion 2002; Dr hc (Liège) 1995; NATO Science Fellowship 1965, NIAS Fellowship 1976, Honda Foundation Lecturing Award 1977, Medal of Honour, Netherlands Psychonomics Soc. 2005. *Publications:* Timing in Temporal Tracking 1967, Sociale Verkeerskunde 1976, Handboek der Psychonomie 1976, 1979, Beïnvloeding van Mobiliteit 1981, Time, Mind and Behavior 1985, Guyau and the Idea of Time 1988, Handboek der Sociale Verkeerskunde 1989, Soar: A Cognitive Architecture in Perspective 1992, Generic Intelligent Driver Support 1993, Nederlanders over Criminaliteit en Rechtshandhaving 1997, Kritisch maar Loyaal 2016; more than 270 articles and chapters in scientific journals and books. *Leisure interests:* visual arts (painting, drawing, cartoons), music. *Address:* Brigantijnwal 7, 2317 GL Leiden, The Netherlands (home). *E-mail:* michonja@xs4all.nl (home). *Website:* www.jamichon.nl.

MICHOT, Yves Raoul; French aviation executive; b. 4 Nov. 1941, Nantes; s. of Raoul Michot and Lucienne Ruffel; m. Michèle Gouth 1964; two s. one d.; ed Ecole Polytechnique and Ecole Nationale Supérieure d'Aeronautique; Brétigny Flight Test Centre 1965–73; Govt Concorde Project Man. 1973–75; Tech. Adviser to Nat. Armament Dir 1975–78, to Minister of Defence 1978–80; Mirage 2000 Program Man., Ministry of Defence 1980–84; Mil. Programs Gen. Man. Aérospatiale 1984, Programs Gen. Man. 1985; Exec. Vice-Pres. Aérospatiale 1987, Exec. Vice-Pres. and COO 1989, Sr Exec. Vice-Pres. and COO and Pres. Aérospatiale 1995–99, Pres., Dir-Gen. 1996–99, Pres. Bd Dirs 1999; fmr Pres. European Asscn of Aerospace Industries (AECMA); apptd Pres. Club d'affaires franco-singapourien 1998; Chair. Défense Conseil Int. –2007; Pres. Descartes Prize Grand Jury 2001, 2002; Officier, Légion d'Honneur, Commdr, Ordre Nat. du Mérite, Médaille de l'Aéronautique.

MICKELSON, Philip (Phil) Alfred, BS; American professional golfer; b. 16 June 1970, San Diego, Calif.; s. of Philip Mickelson and Mary Mickelson; m. Amy McBride 1996; one s. two d.; ed Arizona State Univ.; jr career won 34 San Diego County titles, three Nat. Collegiate Athletics Asscn (NCAA) Championships, three Jack Nicklaus Awards as Nat. Coll. Player of the Year, mem. Walker Cup team 1989, 1991, US Amateur Championships 1990, played in World Amateur Team Championship 1990, Tucson Chrysler Classic 1991; turned professional 1992; Professional Golf Asscn (PGA) titles Northern Telecom Open 1991 (last amateur player to win PGA event and first since 1985), 1995, 1996, Buick Invitational Calif. 1993, 2000, 2001, The International 1993, Mercedes Championships 1994, 1998, Phoenix Open 1996, GTE Byron Nelson Golf Classic 1996, NEC World Series of Golf 1996, Bay Hill Invitational 1997, Sprint International 1997, Pebble Beach Nat. Pro-Am, 1998, BellSouth Classic 2000, MasterCard Colonial 2000, The Tour Championship 2000, Canon Greater Hartford Open 2001, 2002, Bob Hope Chrysler Classic 2002, 2004, US Masters 2004, 2006, 2010, US PGA Championship 2005, Players Championship 2007, World Golf Championship–Calif. 2009, Shell Houston Open 2011, AT&T Pebble Beach Nat. Pro-Am 2012, The Open Championship, Muirfield 2013; mem. Presidents Cup team 1994 (winners), 1996 (winners), 1998, 2000 (winners), 2003 (tied), 2005 (winners), 2007 (winners), 2009 (winners), 2011 (winners), Alfred Dunhill Cup team 1996, Ryder Cup team 1995, 1997, 1999 (winners), 2002 (postponed from 2001), 2004, 2008 (winners), 2010, 2012, 2014; scored 59, lowest score in professional strokeplay history, at Grand Slam of Golf in Hawaii 2004 (only achieved on three other occasions on PGA tour); sponsored the Special Operations Warrior Project 2004 to support US troops; Co-Chair. American Jr Golf Asscn; involved in golf course design; Golf World Amateur of the Year 1991, Haskins Award 1990, 1991, 1992, ESPY Award Best Championship Performance 2004, ESPY Award Best Male Golfer 2004, elected into World Golf Hall of Fame 2011, inducted 2012. *Leisure interests:* football, flying. *Address:* c/o Steve Loy, Gaylord Sports Management, 13845 North Northsight Blvd, Suite 200, Scottsdale, AZ 85260, USA (office). *Telephone:* (480) 483-9500 (office). *E-mail:* sloy@gaylordsports.com (office). *Website:* www.gaylordsports.com (office); www.philmickelson.com.

MICKLETHWAIT, John, CBE; British journalist and writer; *Editor-in-Chief, Bloomberg News;* ed Magdalen Coll., Oxford; fmrly with Chase Manhattan Bank; joined The Economist as Media Corresp. 1987, then est. Los Angeles office 1990–93, Ed., business section 1993–97, New York Bureau Chief 1997–99, US Ed.

1999–2006, Ed.-in-Chief 2006–15; Ed.-in-Chief, Bloomberg News 2015–; Trustee, British Museum; Harold Wincott Press Award for Young Financial Journalist 1989, named Ed.'s Ed. by British Soc. of Magazine Eds 2010. *Publications include:* The Witch Doctors (with Adrian Wooldridge) (Financial Times/Booz Allen Global Business Book Award 1997) 1996, A Future Perfect: The Challenge and Hidden Promise of Globalisation (with Adrian Wooldridge) 2000, The Company: A Short History of a Revolutionary Idea (with Adrian Wooldridge) 2003, The Right Nation (with Adrian Wooldridge) 2004, God is Back (with Adrian Wooldridge) 2009, The Fourth Revolution: The Global Race to Reinvent the State (with Adrian Wooldridge) 2014; contrib. of articles to the New York Times, Los Angeles Times, Wall Street Journal, Guardian, Spectator and the New Statesman, Boston Globe. *Address:* Bloomberg News, 731 Lexington Avenue, New York, NY 10022, USA (office). *Telephone:* (800) 955-4003 (office). *Fax:* (212) 617-5999 (office). *Website:* www.bloomberg.com/news (office).

MICKOSKI, Hristijan; Macedonian mechanical engineer and politician; *President, Vnatrešno-Makedonska Revolucionerna Organizacija-Demokratska Partija za Makedonsko Nacionalno Edinstvo (Internal Macedonian Revolutionary Organization-Democratic Party for Macedonian National Unity);* b. 29 Sept. 1977, Skopje, Socialist Repub. of Macedonia, Socialist Fed. Repub. of Yugoslavia; m.; two c.; ed SS Cyril and Methodius Univ.; Project Engineer, FONKO Group 2001–02; Teaching Asst, Faculty of Mechanical Eng, St Cyril and Methodius Univ. 2002–09, Asst Prof. 2009–14, Assoc. Prof. 2014; Adviser on energy to Prime Minister 2015–17; Pres. Bd of Dirs and Gen. Dir, Elektrani na Makedonija (ELEM) (Macedonian Power Plants, state-owned electricity production co.) 2016–17; mem. Vnatrešno-Makedonska Revolucionerna Organizacija-Demokratska Partija za Makedonsko Nacionalno Edinstvo (Internal Macedonian Revolutionary Org.-Democratic Party for Macedonian Nat. Unity), Pres. 2017–. *Address:* Vnatrešno-Makedonska Revolucionerna Organizacija-Demokratska Partija za Makedonsko Nacionalno Edinstvo, 1000 Skopje, Ploshtad VMRO 1, North Macedonia (office). *Telephone:* (2) 3215550 (office). *Fax:* (2) 3215551 (office). *E-mail:* contact@vmro-dpmne.org.mk (office). *Website:* vmro-dpmne.org.mk (office).

MICOSSI, Stefano, MA, MPhil; Italian economist and academic; *Director General, Assonime;* b. 27 Oct. 1946, Bologna; m. Daniela Zanotto; one s. one d.; ed Università Statale di Milano, Yale Univ., USA; economist, Bank of Italy Research Dept 1974–78, Head 1980–84, Asst Dir 1984–86, Dir Int. Div. 1986–88; seconded to IMF as Asst to Italy's Exec. Dir 1978–80; Dir of Econ. Research Confindustria (Confed. of Italian Industries) 1988–94; Prof. of Macroeconomic Policy Int. Free Univ. of Social Sciences 1989–94, Prof. of Monetary Theory and Policy 1993–94; Prof. of Int. Monetary Econs, Coll. of Europe, Bruges 1990–94, Prof. of European Integration 1999–2016, Hon. Prof. 2016–; Dir-Gen. for Industry, EC 1994–99; Dir-Gen. Assonime (business asscn association and think tank), Rome 1999–; Chair. Scientific Council School of European Political Economy, LUISS 2013–; mem. Bd of Dirs, Int. Yehudi Menuhin Foundation in Brussels 2003– (also Treasurer), Centre for European Policy Studies, Brussels 2005, BNL – BNP Paribas 2006–, CIR Group 2009– (Chair. 2009–13). *Publications:* Jt Ed. Adjustment and Integration in the World Economy 1992, The Italian Economy 1993, Inflation in Europe 1997 and books on the European Monetary System 1988, Europe in the XXI Century: Perspectives on the Treaty of Lisbon (co-ed with Gian Luigi Tosato) 2009, numerous articles in professional journals. *Address:* Assonime, Piazza Venezia 11, 00187 Rome, Italy (office). *Telephone:* (06) 69529214 (office). *Fax:* (06) 69529219 (office). *E-mail:* eleonora.riccardi@assonime.it (office). *Website:* www.assonime.it (office).

MIĆUNOVIĆ, Branislav; Montenegrin theatre director and politician; Prof. of Acting, Faculty of Dramatic Arts, Belgrade and Faculty of Dramatic Arts, Cetinje; fmr Theatre Dir at Yugoslav Drama Theatre, Belgrade, Serbian Nat. Theatre, Croatian Nat. Theatre, Nat. Theatre, Tuzla, Nat. Theatre, Nis, Zvezdara Theatre, Belgrade; directed works by Aleksandra Popovic, Velimir Lukic, Ljubomir Simovic, Veljko Radovic, Jordan Plevneša, Goran Stefanovskog, Iva Bresan, Gordan Mihic; Dir Montenegrin Nat. Theatre 2003–07; apptd Minister of Culture, Sports and Media 2008; mem. Cttee for the Arts Theatre, Montenegrin Acad. of Sciences and Arts.

MIDDELHOEK, André, PhD; Dutch civil servant; b. 13 Dec. 1931, Voorburg; s. of J. Middelhoek; m. Trudy van den Broek 1982; two d.; ed Univ. of Amsterdam; Cen. Planning Office, Govt of Netherlands 1958–69, Deputy Dir 1966–69; Lecturer, Int. Inst. for Social Studies, The Hague 1960–69; Dir-Gen. of the Budget, Ministry of Finance 1969–77; mem. Court of Auditors of European Communities 1977–93; Pres. European Court of Auditors 1993–96; Pres. Cttee of Wise Men 1999; Commdr, Order of Netherlands Lion; Grand Croix, Couronne de Chêne (Luxembourg). *Publications include:* publs on econs, econ. planning, public finance, policy analysis, EU finance and audit. *Leisure interests:* swimming, tennis, genealogy, hiking. *Address:* Val des Seigneurs 32, #47, 1150 Brussels, Belgium (home). *Telephone:* (2) 687-55-53 (home). *E-mail:* andre.middelhoek@skynet.be (home).

MIDDELHOFF, Thomas, MBA, PhD; German business executive; b. 11 May 1953, Düsseldorf; m.; five c.; ed Univ. of Münster, Univ. des Saarlandes; fmr Lecturer in Marketing, Univ. of Münster; Head of Sales and Marketing, Middelhoff GmbH (family-owned textile co.) 1983; Man. Asst to CEO, Mohndruck Graphische Betriebe GmbH 1986–87, Man. Dir 1989–90, Chair. of Man. Bd 1990; Man. Dir Elsnerdruck GmbH, Berlin 1987–88; mem. Bd responsible for multi-media, Bertelsmann publishing 1990–94, Head of Corp. Devt and Coordinator for Multimedia 1994–97, Chair. and CEO Bertelsmann AG 1998–2004; Head of Europe Investcorp International Ltd 2003–05; Chair. Supervisory Bd Karstadt-Quelle AG 2004–05, of Bd of Man. 2005–09, also Chair. Supervisory Bd Arcandor AG (new name for holding group 2007) 2004–09, CEO 2005–09; Chair. Thomas Cook Group PLC 2005–09, Polestar Group Ltd 2004–06, 2007–, Moneybookers.com, London 2007–, Senator Entertainment AG 2006–14; Founding Partner and Chair., Berger Lahnstein Middelhoff & Partners (BLM Partners) 2009; mem. Bd of Dirs New York Times Co. 2003–14; mem. Supervisory Bd Apcoa Parking 2003; Vernon A. Walters Award 1998.

MIDDENDORF, J(ohn) William, II, BS, MBA; American diplomatist, business executive and fmr government official; b. 22 Sept. 1924, Baltimore, Md; s. of Henry Stump and Sarah Boone Middendorf; m. Isabelle J. Paine 1953; two s. two d.; ed

Holy Cross Coll., Harvard Univ. and New York Grad. School of Business Admin; USN service during World War II; in Credit Dept of Bank of Manhattan Co. (now Chase Manhattan Bank) 1947–52; Analyst, Wood Struthers and Co. Inc. (brokerage firm), New York 1952–58, Pnr 1958–62; Sr Pnr Middendorf, Colgate and Co. (investment firm), New York 1962–69; Amb. to Netherlands 1969–73; Under-Sec. of the Navy 1973–74, Sec. 1974–76; Pres. and CEO First American Bankshares, Washington, DC 1977–81; Pres. and CEO Middendorf & Co., Inc., Washington, DC 1989–, Chair. Middendorf SA 1989–; Amb. to OAS 1981–85, to EC 1985–87; Chair. Presidential Task Force on Project Econ. Justice 1985–86; mem. Bd of Dirs and Sec.-Treasurer, Int. Republican Inst.; Trustee Heritage Foundation 1989–; numerous hon. degrees; State Dept Superior Honor Award 1974, Dept of Defense Distinguished Public Service Award 1975, 1976, USN Public Service Award 1976, Ludwig Von Mises Inst. Free Market Award 1985, Arleigh Burke Award 1998; numerous other awards; Grand Master of Order of Naval Merit (Brazil) 1974, Distinguished Service Medal (Brazil) 1976, Order of Arab Repub. of Egypt (Class A) 1979, Grand Officer of the Order of Orange Nassau, Netherlands 1985. *Athletic achievements:* US Nat. Sculling Champion in Masters Div. 1979, won a world masters championship in rowing at the 1985 Toronto Masters Games. *Compositions:* has composed seven symphonies, an opera and numerous marches and concertos. *Publications:* Investment Policies of Fire and Casualty Insurance Companies. *Address:* 565 West Main Road, Little Compton, RI 02837, USA.

MIDDLETON, Sir Peter Edward, Kt, GCB, BA; British business executive and fmr civil servant; *Chairman, Burford Capital Ltd;* b. 2 April 1934, Sheffield; s. of Thomas Edward Middleton; m. 1st Valerie Ann Lindup 1964 (died 1987); one s. (deceased) one d.; m. 2nd Connie Owen 1990; ed Sheffield City Grammar School, Univs of Sheffield and Bristol; Sr Information Officer, HM Treasury 1962, Prin. 1964, Asst Dir, Centre for Admin. Studies 1967–69, Pvt. Sec. to Chancellor of Exchequer 1969–72, Treasury Press Sec. 1972–75, Head, Monetary Policy Div. 1975, Under-Sec. 1976, Deputy Sec. 1980–83, Perm. Sec. 1983–91; Deputy Chair., Barclays Group 1991–98, Chair. 1999–2004, Chair., BZW Div. 1991–98; Chair., Sheffield Urban Regeneration Co. Ltd 2001–06; mem. Council Univ. of Sheffield 1991–2015, Pro-Chancellor 1997–99, Chancellor 1999–2015; mem. Bd of Dirs United Utilities Group PLC 1994–2007, Vice-Chair. 1998–99, Chair. 1999–2000, Deputy Chair. 2000–07; Chair., Marsh & McLennan Companies UK 2005–14, Burford Advisors LLP 2008–09, Bridge Int. Trust 2008–09, Burford Capital Ltd 2009–, Hamilton Ventures 2009–, ST Telemedia, Singapore 2010–12, Burford Capital Holdings, UK 2012–, The Resort Group 2015–, Directa Plus UK 2015–, Chair. Centre for Effective Dispute Resolution 2004–11, Creative Sheffield 2006–11; Pres. British Bankers' Asscn 2004–06; Vice-Chair. Bankers Benevolent Fund 2005; Chair. European Asscn for Banking & Financial History 2008–; Sr Adviser, Fenchurch Advisory Pnrs 2005–; mem. Council Manchester Business School 1985–92; Gov. London Business School 1984–90, Ditchley Foundation 1985–; mem. Nat. Econ. Research Asscn 1991–2008; Chair. Inst. of Contemporary History 1993–2001, Dir 2001–; mem. Bd of Dirs, General Accident (later CGU) 1992–95; mem. Financial Reporting Council 1997–98; Dir Int. Monetary Conf. 2001–02; Visiting Fellow, Nuffield Coll., Oxford 1981–89; Trustee Philharmonia Trust Ltd 2013–; Hon. LittD (Sheffield) 1984. *Leisure interests:* music, walking, outdoor sports. *Address:* Burford Capital Ltd, 24 Cornhill, London, EC3V 3ND, England (office). *Telephone:* (20) 7357-2673 (office). *E-mail:* pmiddleton@burfordcapital.com (office). *Website:* www.burfordcapital.com (office).

MIDLER, Bette; American singer and actress; b. 1 Dec. 1945, Honolulu, Hawaii; m. Martin von Haselberg 1984; one d.; ed Univ. of Hawaii; début as actress in film Hawaii 1965; mem. of cast, Fiddler on the Roof, New York 1966–69, Salvation, New York 1970, Tommy, Seattle Opera Co. 1971; night-club concert performer 1972–; After Dark Ruby Award 1973, Grammy Awards for Best New Artist 1973, for Best Female Pop Vocal Performance 1981, for Record of the Year 1990, Special Tony Award 1973, Emmy Award 1978, Sammy Cahn Lifetime Achievement Award, Songwriters Hall of Fame 2012. *Film appearances include:* The Rose (two Golden Globe Awards) 1979, Jinxed 1982, Down and Out in Beverly Hills 1986, Ruthless People 1986, Outrageous Fortune 1987, Big Business 1988, Beaches 1989, Stella 1990, For The Boys (Golden Globe Award) 1991, Hocus Pocus 1993, Gypsy (TV), The First Wives Club 1996, That Old Feeling 1997, Get Bruce 1999, Isn't She Great? 1999, Drowning Mona 2000, What Women Want 2001, Stepford Wives 2004, Then She Found Me 2007, The Women 2008, Parental Guidance 2012, Freak Show 2017. *Stage:* I'll Eat You Last: A Chat with Sue Mengers 2013, New York 2016, Hello, Dolly! (Tony Award 2017) 2017. *Recordings include:* The Divine Miss M. 1973, Bette Midler 1973, Broken Blossom 1977, Live at Last 1977, Thighs and Whispers 1979, New Depression 1979, Divine Madness 1980, No Frills 1984, Some People's Lives 1991, Best Of 1993, Bette of Roses 1995, Experience the Divine 1997, Bathhouse Betty 1998, From a Distance 1998, Bette 2000, Bette Midler Sings the Rosemary Clooney Songbook 2003, Bette Midler Sings the Peggy Lee Songbook 2005, Cool Yule 2006, Memories of You 2010, It's the Girls! 2014, A Gift Of Love 2015. *Television includes:* The Tonight Show (Emmy Award) 1992, Gypsy 1993, Seinfeld 1996, Diva Las Vegas 1997, Murphy Brown 1998, Bette (series) 2000–01. *Publications include:* A View From A Broad 1980, The Saga of Baby Divine 1983. *Address:* c/o Peter Levine, Creative Artists Agency, 2000 Avenue of the Stars, Los Angeles, CA 90067, USA (office). *Website:* www.bettemidler.com.

MIDORI, MSc; Japanese violinist; b. (Midori Goto), 25 Oct. 1971, Osaka; d. of Setsu Goto; ed Professional Children's School, Juilliard School of Music, New York Univ.; began violin studies with mother aged four; moved to USA 1982; debut with New York Philharmonic 1982; recording debut 1986 aged 14; now makes worldwide concert appearances; Founder and Pres. Midori and Friends (foundation) 1992–; mem. Faculty, Manhattan School of Music 2001–06; Jascha Heifetz Chair in Violin, Thornton School of Music, Univ. of Southern California 2006–18, also Distinguished Prof. and Chair. Strings Dept, currently Visiting Artist; mem. Faculty, Curtis Inst., Phila 2018–; Dorothy B. Chandler Performing Arts Award, New York State Asian-American Heritage Month Award, Crystal Award (Japan), Suntory Award 1994, Kennedy Center Gold Medal in the Arts 2010, Award of Merit for Achievement in Performing Arts, Association of Performing Arts Presenters 2015. *Recordings include:* Paganini: Caprices, Op.1 1989, Bach & Vivaldi - Double & Violin Concertos 1990, Encore 1992, Tchaikovsky and Shostakovich: Violin Concertos 1999, Mendelssohn & Bruch: Violin Concertos 2003, Partitas for Solo Violin I-III 2011, J.S. Bach: Partitas & Sonatas for Violin Solo 2015, The Art of Midori 2016. *Leisure interests:* cooking, reading, listening to music, art. *Address:* c/o Intermusica Artists Management Ltd, Crystal Wharf, 36 Graham Street, London, N1 8GJ, England (office); c/o Midori and Friends, 352 Seventh Avenue, Suite 301, New York, NY 10009, USA (office). *Website:* www.intermusica.co.uk/artists/violin-viola/midori/biography (office); www.midoriandfriends.org; www.gotomidori.com; music.usc.edu/midori-goto. *E-mail:* mgoto@usc.edu; violin@gotomidori.com (office).

MIDWINTER, John Edwin, OBE, BSc (Hons), PhD, DSc, FRS, FREng, FIET, FIEEE, FInstP; British professor of optoelectronics (retd); *Pender Professor Emeritus, University College London;* b. 8 March 1938, Newbury, Berks.; s. of H. C. Midwinter and V. J. Midwinter (née Rawlinson); m. Maureen A. Holt 1961; two s. two d.; ed King's Coll., London; Sr Scientific Officer, Royal Radar Establishment 1967–68; Sr Research Physicist, Perkin-Elmer Corpn, USA 1968–70; Head, Fibre Optic Devt, British Telecom Research Labs 1971–77, Head Optical Communications Technology 1977–84; British Telecom Prof. of Optoelectronics, Univ. Coll. London 1984–91, Head, Dept of Electronic and Electrical Eng 1988–98, Pender Prof. of Electronic Eng 1991–2004, Prof. Emer. 2004–, Vice-Provost 1994–99, Dir Univ. Coll. London Adastral Park Campus 2000–03; Vice-Pres. IEE 1994, Deputy Pres. 1998–2000, Pres. 2000–01; Dir Young Engineers 2004–05; Fellow, Inst. of Eng and Tech.; Hon. DSc (Nottingham) 2000, (Loughborough) 2001, (Queen's Univ. Belfast) 2004; IEE J.J. Thompson Medal 1987, Faraday Medal 1997, IEEE Eric Sumner Award and Medal 2002. *Publications:* Applied Non-Linear Optics 1972, Optical Fibers for Transmission 1977; more than 200 papers on lasers, non-linear optics and optical communications. *Leisure interests:* walking, skiing, writing, climate change, renewable energy.

MIELI, Paolo; Italian journalist; *President, RCS Libri;* b. 25 Feb. 1949, Milan; two s.; ed classical lycée, La Sapienza Univ., Rome; Asst to Chair of History of Political Parties, Univ. of Rome; Corresp., Political Commentator at Home, Head of Cultural Desk and then Cen. Man. Ed., Espresso (weekly) 1967–85; worked for La Repubblica 1985–86; Leader Writer, La Stampa 1986–90, Ed.-in-Chief 1990–92; Ed. Corriere della Sera 1992–97, Dir 2004–09; Pres. RCS Libri 2009–; apptd Pres. RAI (Radiotelevisione Italiana) March 2003 (resgnd after five days); Prof. of Contemporary History, Univ. of Milan; mem. Bd Govs Storia Illustrata, Pagina and has collaborated with Tempi Moderni, Questi Istituzioni, Mondo operaio; Premio Spoleto 1990, Premio Mediterraneo 1991, Premio Alfio Russo 1995. *Publications include:* Litigo a Sinistra, Il Socialismo Diviso, Storia del Partito Socialista Negli Anni della Repubblica, Le Storie – La Storia 1999, Storia e Politica: Risorgimento, fascismo e comunismo 2001, La goccia cinese 2002. *Leisure interests:* ancient history, skiing. *Address:* RCS Libri, RCS MediaGroup, Via Angelo Rizzoli 8, 20132 Milan (office); Via Medaglie d'Oro 391, 00136 Rome, Italy (home). *Website:* www.rcslibri.it (office).

MIERS, Sir David, Kt, KBE, CMG, MA; British diplomatist (retd); b. 10 Jan. 1937, Liverpool, England; s. of Col R. Miers, DSO and Honor Bucknill; m. Imelda Wouters 1966; two s. one d.; ed Winchester Coll. and Univ. Coll., Oxford; joined diplomatic service 1961, served in Tokyo 1963, Vientiane 1966, Paris 1972, Tehran 1977, Amb. to Lebanon 1983–85, Asst Under-Sec. FCO 1986, Amb. to Greece 1989–93, to Netherlands 1993–96; Chair. Soc. of Pension Consultants 1998–2007, British Lebanese Asscn 1999–2011, The Anglo-Hellenic League 1999–; British Lebanese Asscn Lecturer, The Royal Thames Yacht Club 2012. *Leisure interest:* open air. *Address:* The Anglo-Hellenic League, The Hellenic Centre, 16–18 Paddington Street, London, W1U 5AS, England. *Telephone:* (20) 7486-9410 (voicemail). *E-mail:* info@anglohellenicleague.org. *Website:* www.anglohellenicleague.org.

MIFSUD BONNICI, Carmelo (Carm), LLD; Maltese lawyer, politician and academic; b. 17 Feb. 1960, Floriana; s. of fmr Pres. Ugo Mifsud Bonnici; m. Sandra Gatt; three s.; ed St Aloysius' Coll., Birkirkara, De La Salle Coll., Cottonera, Univ. of Malta; practised in criminal, civil and commercial fields; Sr Lecturer in Roman Law, Univ. of Malta; Pres. MKSU as univ. student; active in Partit Nazzjonalista (Nationalist Party) Youth Movt (MZPN) 1982–, held several posts in Exec.; mem. Parl. 1998–2013, perm. mem. several cttees, including Privileges and Laws; mem. Malta Environment and Planning Authority 2001–03; Parl. Sec., Ministry for Justice and Home Affairs 2003–08; apptd Minister for Justice and Home Affairs 2008; Minister for Home and Parliamentary Affairs Jan.–May 2012. *Publications:* Zewg Minuti Flimkien 1998, Il-Principji Hemm Jibqghu 2003, Sens u Sustanza 2008, Il-Politika tas-Sewwa 2013. *Address:* Partit Nazzjonalista, Herbert Ganado Street, Pietà 1541, Malta (office). *Telephone:* 21243641 (office). *Fax:* 21243640 (office). *E-mail:* admin@pn.org.mt (office). *Website:* www.pn.org.mt (office).

MIFSUD BONNICI, Ugo Enrico, BA, LLD; Maltese politician, lawyer and fmr head of state; b. 8 Nov. 1932, Cospicua; s. of Carmelo Mifsud Bonnici and Maria Mifsud Bonnici (née Ross); m. Gemma Bianco; two s. one d.; ed Royal Univ. of Malta; practising lawyer 1955–87; mem. Parl. 1966–94; Opposition Spokesman for Educ. 1972–87; Pres. Gen. Council and Admin. Council of Nationalist Party 1977–87; Minister of Educ. 1987, of Educ. and Interior 1990–92, of Educ. and Human Resources 1992–94; Pres. of Malta 1994–99; currently Lecturer on History of Law and Human Rights, Univ. of Malta, also Lecturer on Comparative Law, International Maritime Law Inst.; fmr Chair. Cttee of Guarantee under the Law for the Protection of the Cultural Heritage; mem. Council of Europe Comm. for Democracy Through Law (Venice Comm.) 2002; Hon. DLitt (Univ. of Malta) 1995, (Univ. of Paris IV) 1998. *Publications include:* Biex il-futur jerga' jibda 1976, Il-linja t-tajba 1981, Biex il-futur rega beda 1992, Il-Manwal tal-President 1997, Kif Sirna Republika 1999, Introduction to Comparative Law 2004, An Introduction to Cultural Heritage Law 2008, Il-Gross: Il-Kontribut Letterarju (ed) 2012, An Introduction to Law of Education 2014, Diritto civile: lezioni del Professore Giovanni Caruana (1866–1923), trascritte da Carmelo Mifsud Bonnici (1897–1948) 2014, Konvinzjoni u Esperjenza (autobiography) 2015, Leggi di Procedura Civile, Lezioni del Prof G. Caruana (1866–1923), trascritte da Giovanni Calleja (1893–1958) 2015; numerous newspaper articles. *Address:* 18 Erin Serracino Inglott Road, Cospicua, Malta (home). *Telephone:* 826975 (home). *E-mail:* ugomb@maltanet.net.

MIGAŠ, Jozef, DPhil, CSc; Slovak diplomatist and politician (retd); b. 7 Jan. 1954, Pušovce; m. Alena Migašová; one s. one d.; ed Univ. of Kiev; fmrly with Acad. of Sciences, Košice, Political Univ., Bratislava; diplomatic service from 1993, including as Adviser at Embassy in Kiev, Amb. to Ukraine 1995–96, to Russian

Fed. 2009–14; f. Party of the Democratic Left, Chair. 1996–2001; Chair. Nat. Council of the Slovak Repub. (parl.) 1998–2002; Acting Pres. of Slovakia 1998–99; Order of Friendship (Russia) 2014.

MIGIRO, Asha-Rose Mtengeti, LLB, LLM, PhD; Tanzanian lawyer, politician, academic and UN official; *High Commissioner to the United Kingdom;* b. 9 July 1956, Songea; m. Cleophas Migiro; two d.; ed Univ. of Dar-es-Salaam, Univ. of Konstanz, Germany; Head, Dept of Constitutional and Admin. Law, Univ. of Dar-es-Salaam 1992–94, fmr Sr Lecturer, Faculty of Law; mem. Parl. (Chama Cha Mapinduzi—CCM party) 1994–2000; Sec. for Politics and Foreign Relations, CCM 2012–13; mem. Regional Exec. Council 2000–05; Minister of Community Devt, Gender and Children's Affairs 2000–06, of Foreign Affairs and Int. Co-operation 2006–07; Minister of Justice and Constitutional Affairs 2014–15; High Commr to UK 2016–; Deputy Sec.-Gen. UN 2007–12, mem. Sec.-Gen.'s High-Level Advisory Bd on Mediation 2017–; Special Envoy of the Sec.-Gen. for HIV/AIDS in Africa, UN 2012–13; mem. Advisory Bd UN Fund for Int. Partnerships; mem. UN Cttee on Elimination of Discrimination against Women. *Address:* High Commission of Tanzania, 3 Stratford Place, London, W1C 1AS, London, England (office). *Telephone:* (20) 7569-1470 (office). *Fax:* (20) 7491-3710 (office). *E-mail:* Ubalozi@tzhc.uk (office). *Website:* www.tzhc.uk (office).

MIGNON, Emmanuelle; French lawyer and civil servant; *Partner, August & Debouzy;* b. 26 April 1968; ed École supérieure des sciences économiques et commerciales, Institut d'études politiques de Paris, École nationale d'administration; OSCE electoral observer, Bosnia and Herzegovina 1997; with Conseil d'État 1998–2002, 2009–10, 2012–15, apptd conseiller d'Etat 2013; adviser to Minister of Interior, Nicolas Sarkozy 2002–04; Educ. Dir, Union pour un Mouvement Populaire (UMP) 2004–06; Chief of Staff, Office of Pres. 2007–08; French Rep. to Andorra 2007–08; adviser to Pres. 2008–09; Gen. Sec. Strategy, Devt, Legal and Human Resources, EuropaCorp 2010–12; Partner, August & Debouzy, Paris 2015–; Pres., Chambord Admin. Council 2007; Nat. Commr, Scouts Unitaires de France 1990; teaches French and European public law and public governance at Institut d'Etudes Politiques, Paris. *Address:* August & Debouzy, 8, avenue de Messine, 75008 Paris, France (office). *Telephone:* 1-45-61-79-73 (office). *E-mail:* emignon@augdeb.com (office). *Website:* www.august-debouzy.com (office).

MIGRANYAN, Andranik Movsesovich, MA, PhD; Russian/Armenian academic; *Director, Institute for Democracy and Cooperation;* b. 10 Feb. 1949, Yerevan; m.; one d.; ed Moscow State Inst. of Int. Relations, Inst. of Int. Workers' Movt USSR Acad. of Sciences; Prof., Moscow Inst. of Automobile Construction 1976–85; leading researcher, Inst. of Econ. and Political Studies Acad. of Sciences 1985–88; Head Cen. for Studies of Social-Political Problems and Interstate Relations of CIS 1992–93; mem. Pres.'s Council 1993–2000; Chief Expert Cttee on CIS countries of State Duma 1993–96; Chair. Bd Scientific Council on CIS Countries; Prof., Moscow State Inst. of Int. Relations (MGIMO) 1991–; Dir Inst. for Democracy and Cooperation, New York 2008–; co-f. Politika Fund; Vice-Pres. Reforma Fund 1994–2003; First Vice-Pres., Soglasie Fund 2004–; mem. Public Chamber of Russian Fed. 2005–. *Publications include:* Democracy and Morality 1989, Russia in Search for Identity 1997, Russia: From Chaos to Order? 2001; numerous book chapters and articles in newspapers and journals. *Address:* Institute for Democracy and Cooperation, 655 Third Avenue, Suite 2010, New York, NY 10017, USA (office). *Telephone:* (212) 922-0030 (office). *Fax:* (212) 922-1555 (office). *E-mail:* info@indemco.org (office). *Website:* www.indemco.org (office).

MIGUEL, Elritha; Saint Vincent and the Grenadines banking executive; currently Country Dir Eastern Caribbean Cen. Bank—Saint Vincent and the Grenadines Office. *Address:* Eastern Caribbean Central Bank, Saint Vincent and the Grenadines Office, Frenches House, POB 839, Frenches, Saint Vincent and the Grenadines (office). *Telephone:* 456-1413 (office). *Fax:* 456-1412 (office). *E-mail:* info@eccb-centralbank.org (office); eccbnetwork@vincysurf.com (office).

MIHAJLOVIĆ, Svetozar; Bosnia and Herzegovina politician; fmr Vice-Pres. of Serb Repub. of Bosnia and Herzegovina; Co-Prime Minister of Bosnia and Herzegovina 1999–2000; Minister for Civil Affairs and Communications 2001–03.

MIHÓCZA, Brig.-Gen. Zoltán, BA, MA; Hungarian military officer and diplomatist; b. 18 March 1963, Budapest; m. Erzsébet Bencze; one d.; ed Military Univ., Minsk, Byelorussian SSR, USSR, ADA Officers Advanced Course, El Paso, Texas and War Coll., Montgomery, Ala, USA; radio tech. engineer 1980–86; Deputy Commdr 11/7th Air Defence Bn (SA-2) 1986–89; Commdr Maintenance Co., 11th Air Defence Brigade 1989–92, Chief of Maintenance Service 1992–94, Chief of Missile Service 1995–96, Chief of Mil. Tech. 1997; Sr Officer, Meteorological Office, Hungarian Defence Force 1998; Sr Officer, Modernization Man. Office, J5 Defence Staff, Ministry of Defence 1999, 2002–03; Sr Officer, Logistics Br., J1/4 NATO HQ, JCS, Verona, Italy 1999–2002; MA Chief for Integration Defence Staff, Ministry of Defence 2003–04, MA Dir of Defence Staff 2005, Chief of NATO and Doctrines Br., Mil. Planning Directorate, Defence Staff 2005–06, Deputy Head of Operations and Training Dept 2006, Head of Force Planning Dept 2010–11; Deputy Chief-of-Staff, Joint Force Command, Hungarian Defence Force 2013–15, Chief-of-Staff 2016–; Chief-of-Staff European Union Force Althea (EUFOR) 2015–16; Mil. Rep. to NATO and EU, Brussels 2011–13; rank of 2nd Lt-Gen. 1986, 1st Lt-Gen. 1988, Capt. 1993, Maj. 1996, Lt-Col 2002, Col 2005, Brig.-Gen. 2010; Meritorious Service Medals Bronze and Gold, Distinguished Service Medals Third (10 years), 2nd (20 years) and 1st (30 years), NATO Meritorious Service Medal, NATO Kosovo Medal, Medal for Peacekeeping. *Address:* c/o Ministry of Foreign Affairs, 1027 Budapest, Bem rakpart 47, Hungary (office).

MIHÓK, Peter, PhD; Slovak business administrator and fmr diplomatist; *President, Slovak Chamber of Commerce and Industry (CCI);* b. 18 Jan. 1948, Topoľčianky; s. of Augustin Mihók and Johanna Mihoková; m. Elena Škulová 1971; two d.; ed Econ. Univ., Bratislava; with Czechoslovak Chamber of Commerce 1971–78; Commercial Counsellor, Embassy, Morocco 1978–82; Dir Foreign Relations Dept; Incheba (Foreign Trade Co.) 1982–90; Dir Foreign Dept, Office of Govt of Slovakia 1990–91; Vice-Pres. Czechoslovak Chamber of Commerce and Industry (CCI) 1991–92; Dir Int. Politics Dept, Ministry of Foreign Affairs of Slovakia 1991; Plenipotentiary of Govt of Slovakia in EU, Head Negotiator in Brussels 1991–94; Pres. Slovak CCI 1992–; Vice-Chair. Supervisory Bd Heineken Slovakia 1998–, Globtel Orange Bratislava 2001–; Vice-Chair. World Chamber Fed. Paris 2001–; Pres. Ecosoc Slovakia 2000–; Deputy Pres. Eurochambers 2001–; mem. Supervisory Bd Incheba a.s. Bratislava 1999–, Chair. 2004–; mem. Presidency, European Econ. and Social Cttee, Brussels 2004–; mem. Advisory Body to Pres. of Slovakia; mem. Econ. Council of Govt of Slovakia, Chair. Govt Pricing Cttee; mem. Council Slovak Electricity Works; Vice-Chair. Omnia Group, Kooperativa; mem. Scientific Council, Econ. Univ. Bratislava; Gold Medal of Hungarian CCI 1999, Officer, Order of Léopold II, Belgium 1995, Officier Ordre du Mérite, France 1996, Prominent of Economy, Slovakia 1997, Great Silver Order, Austria 1998, Commendatore Ordine, Stella della Solidarita Italiana 2003, Gold Medal, House of Europe 2003. *Publication:* Advertising in the Market Economy. *Leisure interests:* literature, philately, swimming. *Address:* Slovak Chamber of Commerce and Industry, Gorkého 9, 816 03 Bratislava, Slovakia (office). *Telephone:* (2) 5443-3291 (office). *Fax:* (2) 5413-1159 (office). *E-mail:* predseda@scci.sk (office). *Website:* www.scci.sk (office).

MIHOV, Gen. Miho, MA; Bulgarian air force officer (retd) and fmr diplomatist; b. 1 Feb. 1949, Sennik; s. of Dimitar Mihov and Stanka Mihov; m. 1973; one s. one d.; ed Benkovski Air Force Acad., Dolna Mitropolia, Rakovski Nat. War Coll., Sofia, Gen. Staff Coll., Moscow, USAF Special Operations School; Training Flight Air Unit Deputy Commdr/Instructor; Air Squadron Deputy Commdr, Commdr, Air Regt, Deputy Commdr, Commdr; Air Corps Deputy Commdr; Air Defence Div. Commdr, Air Force Commdr; Chief of Gen. Staff of Bulgarian Armed Forces 1997–2002; Adviser to Pres. of Bulgaria 2002; Amb. to Macedonia 2005–09; Order of Merit and Valour, Medal for Service to the Bulgarian Armed Forces, Medal for the 40th Anniversary of the Victory over Hitler and Fascism, Medals and Orders of Distinguished Service, Order of Merit of Aviation (presented by King of Spain), Order presented by King of Sweden, Order presented by Pres. of Repub. of Bulgaria, Legion of Merit (USA). *Leisure interests:* hunting, skiing. *Address:* 18 T. Teznovski str., Sofia, Bulgaria (home). *Telephone:* (2) 963-01-81 (home).

MIHYCHUK, MaryAnn, PC, BSc, MGeol; Canadian geoscientist and politician; b. 27 Feb. 1955, Vita, Manitoba; m. Kenneth Marshal; one s. two d.; ed Univ. of Winnipeg, Brock Univ.; mem. Legis. Ass. of Manitoba 1995–2004; Dir of Regulatory Affairs, Prospectors and Developers Asscn of Canada (PDAC) 2005–07, mem. Securities Cttee 2007–14; Partner, North of 60 2005–10; Dir of Corp. Relations, Hudbay Minerals Inc. 2007–09; Owner, Corporate Relations Services 2008–; Coordinator, Manitoba Mineral Resources Training Program 2009–12; apptd Dir and Professional Geoscientist, Gossan Resources 2009, Vice-Pres. Manitoba BacTech Environmental Corpn 2010; mem. House of Commons (Parl.) for Kildonan-St Paul 2015–, Chair. Standing Cttee on Indigenous and Northern Affairs (INAN) 2017–; Minister of Employment, Workforce Devt and Labour 2015–17; Jack Gallagher Visiting Geoscientist, Univ. of Manitoba 2010; Founder, Women in Mining Canada, Women in Mining Manitoba (fmr Pres.); mem. Liberal Party of Canada; Women in Mining Canada Trailblazer Award 2012. *Address:* House of Commons Ottawa, Ontario, K1A 0A6 (office); 1575 Main Street, Winnipeg, Manitoba R2W 3W5, Canada (office). *Telephone:* (613) 992-7148 (office); (204) 984-6322 (office). *Fax:* (613) 996-9125 (office); (204) 984-6415 (office). *E-mail:* maryann.mihychuk@parl.gc.ca (office). *Website:* mmihychuk.liberal.ca (office).

MIIKE, Takashi; Japanese film director and actor; b. 24 Aug. 1960, Yao, Osaka; ed Yokohama Film School; worked in TV for a decade before becoming Asst Dir to Shohei Imamura; directed first theatrically distributed film Shinjuku Triad Society 1995; int. debut with Audition 2000. *Films:* Toppuu! Minipato tai – Aikyacchi Jankushon (video) 1991, Red Hunter: Prelude to Kill (video) 1991, Ningen kyôki: Ai to ikari no ringu (video) 1992, Bodyguard Kiba (video) 1993, Oretachi wa tenshi ja nai (video) 1993, Oretachi wa tenshi ja nai 2 (video) 1993, Shinjuku autoroo (video) 1994, Bodyguard Kiba: Combat Apocolypse (video) 1994, The Third Gangster (video) 1995, Bodyguard Kiba: Combat Apocolypse 2 (video) 1995, Naniwa yuukyôden (video) 1995, Shinjuku kuroshakai: Chaina mafia sensô 1995, Shin daisan no gokudô – boppatsu Kansai gokudô sensô (video) 1996, Shin daisan no gokudô II (video) 1996, Jingi naki yabô (video) 1996, Rakkasei: Piinattsu (video) 1996, Kenka no hanamichi: Oosaka saikyô densetsu (video) 1996, Fudoh: The New Generation 1996, Young Thugs: Innocent Blood 1997, Jingi naki yabô 2 (video) 1997, Rainy Dog 1997, Full Metal gokudô (video) 1997, The Bird People in China 1998, Andromedia 1998, Blues Harp 1998, Kishiwada shônen gurentai: Bôkyô 1998, Nihon kuroshakai 1999, Silver – shirubaa (video) 1999, Audition 1999, Dead or Alive 1999, Sarariiman Kintarô 1999, The City of Lost Souls 2000, The Guys from Paradise 2000, Dead or Alive 2: Tôbôsha 2000, Tsukamoto Shin'ya ga Ranpo suru (video short documentary) 2000, Family 2001, Visitor Q (video) 2001, Ichi the Killer 2001, Agitator (also actor) 2001, The Happiness of the Katakuris 2001, Kikuchi-jô monogatari – sakimori-tachi no uta 2001, Zuiketsu gensô – Tonkararin yume densetsu 2001, Dead or Alive: Final 2002, Onna kunishuu ikki 2002, Shin Jingi no Hakaba (also actor) 2002, Shangri-La 2002, Pandoora (video) 2002, Deadly Outlaw: Rekka 2002, The Man in White 2003, Gozu 2003, Kikoku (video) 2003, One Missed Call 2003, The Man in White Part 2: Requiem for the Lion 2003, Zebraman 2004, Three… Extremes (segment 'Box') 2004, Izo 2004, Demon Pond (video) 2005, The Great Yokai War 2005, Big Bang Love, Juvenile A 2006, Waru 2006, Waru: kanketsu-hen (video) 2006, Sun Scarred 2006, Like a Dragon 2007, Sukiyaki Western Django 2007, Detective Story 2007, Crows Zero 2007, God's Puzzle 2008, Yatterman 2009, Crows Zero II 2009, Zebraman 2: Attack on Zebra City 2010, 13 Assassins 2010, Hara-Kiri: Death of a Samurai 2011, Ninja Kids!!! 2011, Ace Attorney 2012, For Love's Sake 2012, Lesson of the Evil 2012, Shield of Straw 2013, The Mole Song: Undercover Agent Reiji 2013, Kuime 2014. *Television:* Last Run: 100 Million Ten's Worth of Love & Betrayal (film) 1992, Tennen shôjo Man (mini-series) 1999, Tennen shôjo Man Next: Yokohama hyaku-ya hen (film) 1999, Multiple Personality Detective Psycho – Kazuhiko Amamiya Returns (mini-series) 2000, Sabu (film) 2002, Paato-taimu tantei (film) 2002, Negotiator (film) 2003, Paato-taimu tantei 2 (film) 2004, Ultraman Max (series) (multiple episodes) 2005, Masters of Horror (series, one episode) – Imprint (2006), Kêtai sôsakan 7 (series, one episode) – Ketai aruku!?/ Tsunagaru kizuna 2008, Q.P. (series, one episode) – Episode 1.1 2011.

MIKATI, Najib Azmi, MBA; Lebanese business executive and politician; b. 24 Nov. 1955, Tripoli; m.; three c.; ed American Univ. of Beirut, Harvard Univ., USA, Institut Européen d'Admin des Affaires (INSEAD), France; co-f. Investcom (telecommunications co.) with brother 1982; Minister of Public Works and Transport 1998–2004; mem. Majlis al-Nuab (Nat. Ass.) for Tripoli 2000–; Prime Minister April–July 2005, 2011–13 (resgnd); mem. Bd of Trustees American Univ.

of Beirut; mem. Advisory Bd Harris School, Univ. of Chicago. *E-mail:* info@najib-mikati.net. *Website:* www.najib-mikati.net.

MIKEREVIĆ, Dragan, PhD, DSc; Bosnia and Herzegovina politician; b. 12 Feb. 1955, Doboj; m.; two c.; ed Univ. of Novi Sad; fmr Chief of Finance Dept, Municipality of Doboj, later Pres. Municipality Ass.; fmr Financial Dir Health Assurance Bureau, Republika Srpska; fmr Prof. of Econs, Univ. of Banja Luka, later Man. and mem. of research teams, Inst. for Economy, Univ. of Banja Luka; mem. Party of Democratic Progress 1999–, fmr Vice-Pres.; Chair. Council of Ministers (Prime Minister) of Bosnia and Herzegovina 2002, Minister for European Integration 2001–02; Prime Minister of Serb Repub. (Republika Srpska) of Bosnia and Herzegovina 2003–04 (resgnd). *Address:* c/o Party of Democratic Progress of Republika Srpska (Partija Demokratskog Progresa Republike Srpske), 78000 Banja Luka, ul. Prvog Krajiškog Korpusa 130, Bosnia and Herzegovina.

MIKHAILOV, Nikolai Vasilyevich, DPhil; Russian politician; b. 14 May 1937, Sevsk, Bryansk Region; son of Vasiliy Mikhailov, Lyubov Mikhailova; m.; one s.; ed Moscow Bauman Higher School of Tech.; with defence industry enterprises 1961–96; Dir-Gen., Vympel Co. 1986–96; Deputy Sec. Security Council of Russian Fed. 1996–97; State Sec., First Deputy Minister of Defence of Russian Fed. 1997–2000; Co-Chair. Russian-American Comm. on Econ. and Tech. Co-operation 1998; Adviser to Chair. Bd of Dirs AFC Systema Co. 2001–13; adviser to Dir Gen. of Innovation Devt, Radiotechnical Inst. 2013–; USSR State Prize, State Prize of Russian Fed. 1997. *Publications:* (titles in trans.) Global World and Global Problems: Science and Labour in a Modern World; Military Defence Complex: Analyses and Challenges; Science and Knowledge: From Modern Times to the Future. *Leisure interests:* sports, music, classic literature. *Address:* 123060 Moscow, Raspletina str. 39, bied 14 (home); 127083 Moscow, 10, bild1, 8 Marta str. (office); Systema Financial Corporation, 103009 Moscow, Leont'yevsky per. 10, Russian Federation (office). *Telephone:* (495) 614-03-41 (office); (495) 598-04-34 (home); (495) 105-44-21 (home). *Fax:* (495) 614-38-22 (office). *E-mail:* nmikhailov@sistema.ru (office); nmikhailov@mtu-net.ru (home). *Website:* www.sistema.ru (office); www.oaorti.ru (office).

MIKHAILOV, Vyacheslav Aleksandrovich, DrHist; Russian politician; b. 13 April 1938, Dubovka, Volgograd Region; m.; two d.; ed Lvov State Univ.; teacher, secondary school, Lecturer, Lvov State Univ.; Head of Sector, Inst. of Marxism-Leninism at CPSU Cen. Cttee 1987–90; Head, Div. of Nat. Policy, CPSU Cen. Cttee 1990–91; scientific consultant, I and World (magazine), Head, Centre on Int. Problems and Protection of Human Rights 1991–93; Prof., Moscow Inst. of Int. Relations (MGIMO) 1992–93, 1999–; Deputy Chair. State Cttee on Problems of Fed. and Nationality 1993–95; First Deputy Minister on Problems of Nationality and Regional Policy Jan.–July 1995, Minister 1995–98, 1999–2000; First Deputy Sec. Security Council 1998–99; Chair. Expert Council on Nat., Migration Policy and Interaction with Religious Asscns under the Plenipotentiary Rep. of the Russian Pres. in the Cen. Fed. Dist 2003. *Publications:* three monographs on nat. problems and numerous articles. *Address:* MGIMO, Vernadskogo Prosp. 76, 117454 Moscow, Russia (office). *Telephone:* (495) 206-43-26 (office). *E-mail:* va.mikhaylov@migsu.ranepa.ru. *Website:* igsu.ranepa.ru/person/p6285.

MIKHALKOV, Nikita Sergeyevich; Russian film director; b. 21 Oct. 1945, Moscow; s. of Sergey Vladimirovich Mikhalkov and Natalia Petrovna Konchalovskaya; m. 1st Anastasya Vertinskaya 1966; m. 2nd Tatyana Mikhalkova 1973; two s. two d.; ed Shchukin Theatre School, State Film Inst. under Mikhail Romm; mem. State Duma 1995 (resgnd); First Sec. Russian Union of Cinematographers 1997–98, Chair. 1998–; Artistic Dir TRITE Studio; first worked as actor in films: Strolling Around Moscow, A Nest of Gentlefolk, The Red Tent; mem. Bd of Dirs Pervyi Kanal; Hon. mem. Russian Acad. of Arts; Chevalier, Légion d'honneur 1994, Kt Grand Cross of the Order of Merit of the Italian Republic 2004, Order of Merit for the Fatherland, 3rd Class 1995, 2nd Class 2005, 4th Class 2010, 1st Class 2015; RSFSR People's Artist 1984, Felix Prize for Best European Film 1993, State Prize of Russian Fed., Honoured Artist of Russia, Special Lion for Overall Work, Venice Film Festival 2007 and several other awards. *Films directed:* A Quiet Day at the End of the War, At Home Among Strangers, A Stranger at Home 1975, The Slave of Love 1976, An Unfinished Piece for Mechanical Piano 1977, Five Evenings 1978, Several Days in the Life of I. I. Oblomov 1979, Kinsfolk 1982, Without Witnesses 1983, Dark Eyes 1987, Urga 1990 (Prize at Venice Biennale 1991), Anna from 6 to 18 1994, Burned by the Sun (Acad. Award for Best Foreign Film) 1994, The Barber of Siberia 1998, 12 2007, Burnt by the Sun 2: Exodus 2010, Burnt by the Sun 2: Citadel 2011, Sunstroke 2014. *Film appearance:* Persona non grata 2005. *Play:* An Unfinished Piece for Mechanical Piano, Rome 1987. *Leisure interests:* sport, hunting. *Address:* Maly Kozikhinsky per. 4, Apt. 16–17, 103001 Moscow, Russia.

MIKHALKOV-KONCHALOVSKY, Andrey Sergeyevich; Russian film director and scriptwriter; b. 20 Aug. 1937, Moscow; s. of Sergey Mikhalkov and Natalia Konchalovskaya; m. 1st Irina Kandat; m. 2nd Natalia Arinbasarova; one s.; m. 3rd Viviane Godet; one d.; m. 4th Irina Ivanova; two d.; m. 5th Yulia Vysotskaya; one s. one d.; ed USSR State Inst. of Cinema, Moscow 1961–65; worked in Hollywood 1979–93; frequent collaborator of Andrei Tarkovsky earlier in his career; RSFSR People's Artist 1980, Special Silver St George, Moscow Int. Film Festival 1997, Silver Lion, Venice Festival 2014, 2016. *Films include:* Roller and Violin (with A. Tarkovsky) 1959, Malchik i golub (The Boy and the Pigeon) 1961, Ivanovo detstvo (Ivan's Childhood) (actor) 1962, Mne dvadtsat let (I am Twenty) (actor) 1964, Pervyy uchitel (The First Teacher) 1965, Istoriya Asi Klyachinoy, kotoraya lyubila, da ne vyshla zamuzh (The Story of Asya Klyachina, Who Loved but Did Not Marry) 1966, Dvoryanskoe gnezdo (A Nest of Gentlefolk) 1969, Dyadya Vanya (Uncle Vanya) 1971, Romans o vlyublyonnykh (Romance of Lovers) 1974, Siberiada 1979, Split Cherry Tree 1982, Maria's Lovers (also composer of song Maria's Eyes) 1984, Runaway Train 1985, Duet for One 1986, Shy People 1987, Homer and Eddie 1988, Tango and Cash 1989, The Inner Circle 1991, Kurochka Ryaba (Ryaba My Chicken) (also producer) 1994, Lumière et compagnie (Lumière and Company) 1996, Dom durakov (House of Fools) (also producer) 2002, Moscow Chill (producer) 2005, Gloss 2007, In the Dark (Dans le noir) in the collective film To Each His Own Cinema 2007, The Nutcracker in 3D 2010, Belye nochi pochtalona Alekseya Tryapitsyna (also writer) 2014, Paradise (also writer) 2016; scriptwriter (with Tarkovsky) Andrei Rublev 1969; also opera dir and theatre dir (productions at La Scala, Bastille, Mariinski Theatre). *Television includes:* The Odyssey (mini-series) 1997, The Lion in Winter 2003; 'Geniuses' documentary series: Sergei Prokofiev 2003, Sergei Rachmaninoff 2003, Alexander Scriabin 2006, Igor Stravinsky 2006, Dmitri Shostakovich 2007, Vladimir Sofronitsky 2007; 'The Burden of Power' documentary series: Yuri Andropov 2004, Heydar Aliyev 2004; documentaries: Culture is Destiny 2005, Bitva za Ukrainu 2012. *Address:* Andrei Konchalovsky Production Centre, 125124 Moscow, ul. Pravda House 21, str. 1, Russia (office). *Telephone:* (495) 255-16-17 (office). *E-mail:* inna@konchalovsky.ru. *Website:* www.pc.konchalovsky.ru (office); konchalovsky.ru.

MIKHEEV, Vladimir Andreyevich, DrPhysSc, FInstP, FIMechE; Ukrainian physicist and engineer; b. 5 Aug. 1942; m. Tatiana Mikheeva 1969; one s. one d.; ed Kharkov Polytechnic; researcher 1964–86; discovery of quantum diffusion 1972–77; Head of Lab. of Ultralow Temperatures, Inst. for Low Temperature Physics and Eng, Ukrainian Acad. of Science 1986; Visiting Prof., Royal Holloway and Bedford New Coll. 1992; Consultant Engineer, Tech. Devt, Oxford Instruments NanoScience Ltd 1994–2010; Ed. Research Matters –2004; Lenin Prize for Science and Tech. *Publications:* more than 120 articles published worldwide. *Address:* 35 Browning Drive, Bicester, Oxon., OX26 2XN, England (home).

MIKHELSON, Leonid Viktorovich; Russian engineer, business executive and art collector; *Chairman of Executive Management Board and CEO, OAO Novatek;* b. 11 Aug. 1955, Kaspiysk, Repub. of Dagestan, Russian SFSR, USSR; m.; one d.; ed Kuibyshev Inst. of Civil Eng; began career as foreman at construction and assembling co. in Surgut, Tyumen region, promoted to Chief Engineer; Chief Engineer, Ryazantruborovodstroy trust 1985–87; replaced his father as Head of Kuybyshevtruboprovodstroy 1987, co. privatized 1991, then turned into jt stock co. Samara nat. enterprise, Nova, head of it until 1994; CEO and Gen. Dir OJSC Novafininvest man. co. 1994–2000, Chair. 2000–02; Chair. OJSC Pur-Land Oil & Gas Co. 1998–2001, Gen. Dir 2001–; CEO OJSC Nordpayps 1998–2001; Chair. OJSC Tarkosaleneftegaz 1998, OJSC Yurharovneftegaz 2001, NGK Itera 2002, PJSC Stroytransgaz –2010; Chair. Exec. Man. Bd and CEO OAO Novatek 2003–; mem. Bd of Dirs OJSC CB Solidarity 1995, OJSC Rosneftegazstroy 1997–2001, OJSC Selkup Oil Co. 1998–2001, OJSC Polar Star 1998–2001, OJSC Mangazeya 1998, OJSC Truboizolyatsiya 1998, ZAO NOVA Bank 2000, OJSC Minley 2001, PJSC Stroytransgaz 2008–10; mem. Supervisory Bd OJSC Novokuibyshevsk Television 1999–2001; Stock and Exchange Bd mem. Interregional Oil-and-Gas Exchange (non-profit partnership) 2004; supporter of the arts in Russia through his co. OAO Novatek; Founder and Pres. Victoria the Art of Being Contemporary foundation 2009–; mem. Supervisory Bd Russian Regional Devt Bank 2011–13; Znak Pochyota Order (Order of Honour). *Leisure interests:* volleyball, sponsor of Wings of Soviets soccer team. *Address:* OAO Novatek, 22A Pobedy Street, 629850 Tarko-Sale, Yamalo-Nenets Autonomous, Tyumenskaya Oblast (office); Victoria — The Art of Being Contemporary, Olsufievsky pereulok 8, Bld 2, Moscow, Russia. *Telephone:* (34997) 24951 (office); (495) 6431976. *Fax:* (34997) 24479 (office). *E-mail:* novatek@novatek.ru (office); v-a-c@v-a-c.ru. *Website:* www.novatek.ru (office); www.v-a-c.ru.

MIKI, Shigemitsu; Japanese financial executive; *Senior Advisor, Bank of Tokyo-Mitsubishi UFJ Limited;* b. 1935; joined Mitsubishi Bank Ltd 1958, Pres. and Co-CEO Mitsubishi Tokyo Financial Group Inc. (later became Mitsubishi UFJ Trust and Banking Corpn) 2001–02, Pres. and CEO 2002–04, Man. Dir Bank of Tokyo-Mitsubishi 1989–94, Sr Man. Dir 1994–97, Rep. Dir 1996–, Deputy Pres. Bank of Tokyo-Mitsubishi UFJ Ltd 1997–2000, Pres. 2001–04, Chair. 2004–08, Sr Advisor 2008–; Standing Corp. Auditor, Tokio Marine Holdings Inc. 2000–02; Chair. Japanese Bankers Asscn –2003; Counsellor, Policy Bd, Bank of Japan; Vice-Chair. Exec. Bd Nippon-Keidanren 2003–; mem. Bd of Dirs Mitsubishi Motors Corpn 2002–, Outside Statutory Auditor 2004–; Dir, UnionBanCal Corpn 2004–08, Japan Int. Medical Tech. Foundation; Trustee, Financial Accounting Standards Foundation, Accounting Standards Bd of Japan. *Address:* Bank of Tokyo-Mitsubishi UFJ Ltd, 2-7-1, Marunouchi, Chiyoda-ku, Tokyo 100-8388, Japan (office). *Telephone:* (3) 3240-8111 (office). *Fax:* (3) 3240-8203 (office). *E-mail:* info@bk.mufg.jp (office). *Website:* www.bk.mufg.jp/global (office).

MIKITA, Kunio; Japanese business executive; *Chairman, Mediceo Paltac Holdings Company Ltd;* b. 23 Oct. 1943; ed Kinki Univ.; joined Daisho Co. Ltd (named changed to Paltac 1976) 1966, mem. Bd of Dirs 1990–, Man. Dir 1995–96, Exec. Vice-Pres. 1996–98, Pres. 1998–2004, Rep. Dir and CEO 2004–, apptd Exec. Vice-Pres. Mediceo Paltac Holdings Co. Ltd (following acquisition of Paltac) 2005, later Vice-Pres. and Rep. Dir, Chair. 2008–. *Address:* Mediceo Paltac Holdings Co. Ltd, 7-15, Yaesu 2-chome, Chuo-ku, Tokyo 104-8464, Japan (office). *Telephone:* (3) 3517-5800 (office). *Fax:* (3) 3517-5011 (office). *E-mail:* info@mediceo-paltac.co.jp (office). *Website:* www.mediceo-paltac.co.jp (office).

MIKITANI, Hiroshi, BCom, MBA; Japanese business executive; *Chairman and CEO, Rakuten Inc.;* b. 11 March 1965, Kobe; m.; one c.; ed Hitotsubashi Univ., Harvard Business School, USA; began career as investment banker, Industrial Bank of Japan 1988–96; Founder and CEO Crimson Group (merger and acquisition consulting co.) 1995; f. MDM (Magical Digital Market) (online retail mall) 1997, renamed Rakuten Inc. 1999, Chair. and CEO 1997–; Chair. Japan Asscn of New Economy. *Publication:* Marketplace 3.0: Rewriting the Rules of Borderless Business 2013. *Leisure interest:* golf. *Address:* Rakuten Inc, Roppongi Hills, Mori Tower 6-10-1, Roppongi, Minato-ku, Tokyo 106-6138, Japan (office). *Telephone:* (3) 6387-0555 (office). *Website:* corp.rakuten.co.jp (office).

MIKKELSEN, Brian, MSc; Danish politician; b. 31 Jan. 1966, Copenhagen; m. Eliane Wexøe Mikkelsen; four c.; ed Univ. of Copenhagen; Business Man. Conservative Secondary School Students 1985–86, Nat. and Scandinavian Chair. 1986–87; mem. Nat. Exec. Cttee, Conservative Youth 1987–89, Nat. Chair. 1989–90; mem. Exec. Cttee Christian Democratic Youth Org. 1989–90; mem. Nat. Exec. Conservative People's Party 1989–91, 1998–, Deputy Chair., Conservative People's Party Parl. Group 1999–2001, 2011–12, 2015–18, Chair. 2012–15; mem. Parl. (West Zealand Co. Constituency) 1994–2007, of Zealand Greater Constituency 2007–18; Minister for Culture 2001–08, of Justice 2008–10, of Econ. and Business Affairs 2010–11, of Business 2016–18; Ed. The Conservative Season 2004; Exec. mem. Ledøje-Smørum FC 1983–84, FOF 1987–89, Tech. Council 1997–2001; Chair. Olympisk Idrætsforum 2013; mem. Danish Youth Council 1989–91, Holbæk Coll. of Educ. Council 1994–2001, Railway Council 1996–2001,

Council for the Danish Centre for Human Rights 1998–2001, Danish Cultural Inst. Council 1998–2001, Danish Road Safety Council 2000–01, VL Group 7 2000–01, ARTE Council 2000–01; mem. World Anti-Doping Agency Foundation Bd 2002–03, Vice-Pres. 2004–06, mem. Exec. Cttee 2007–08; Gold member, Gardernetværk.dk 2009. *Publications include:* Nicaragua 1986, Namibia on the Road to Democracy 1988, The Conservative Breakthrough 1991, Land and Small Businesses 1994. *Address:* c/o Det Konservative Folkeparti, Christiansborg, 1240 Copenhagen K, Denmark.

MIKKELSEN, Mads Dittmann; Danish actor; b. 22 Nov. 1965, Østerbro, Copenhagen; s. of Henning Mikkelsen and Bente Christiansen; ed Ballet Acad., Gothenburg, Sweden, Århus Theatre School; originally gymnast and dancer, began acting career 1996. *Films include:* Pusher 1996, Wildside 1998, Nattens engel 1998, Bleeder 1999, Flickering Lights 2000, Monas verden 2001, Shake It 2001, I Am Dina 2002, Open Hearts 2002, Wilbur Wants to Kill Himself 2002, The Green Butchers 2003, Torremolinos 73 2003, King Arthur 2004, With Blood on My Hands: Pusher II 2004, Adam's Apples 2005, After the Wedding 2006, Prague 2006, Exit 2006, Casino Royale 2006, Flame and Citron 2008, Coco Chanel & Igor Stravinsky 2009, Valhalla Rising 2009, The Door 2009, Clash of the Titans 2010, Moomins and the Comet Chase (English version, voice) 2010, The Three Musketeers 2011, A Royal Affair 2012, The Hunt (Best Actor Award, Cannes Film Festival) 2012, Move On 2012, The Necessary Death of Charlie Countryman 2013, Age of Uprising: The Legend of Michael Kohlhaas 2013, The Salvation 2014, Men & Chicken 2015, Kung Fu Panda 3 (voice) 2016. *Television includes:* Rejseholdet (Unit One) (series) 2000–04, Bertelsen – de uaktuelle nyheder (series) 2002, Julie (series) 2005, Hannibal (series) 2013–. *Address:* c/o Ulrich Møller-Jørgensen, Art Management ApS, Kronprinsensgade 9A, 2, 1114 Copenhagen C, Denmark (office). *Telephone:* 35-37-42-32 (office); 26-80-26-79 (mobile) (office). *E-mail:* umj@artmanagement.dk (office). *Website:* www.artmanagement.dk (office); madsmikkelsen.com.

MIKL-LEITNER, Johanna, Mag. rer. soc. oec.; Austrian politician; *Governor, Lower Austria (Landtag Niederösterreich);* b. (Johanna Leitner), 9 Feb. 1964, Hollabrunn; m.; two d.; ed Vienna Univ. of Economics and Business; teacher, Commercial Coll. of Laa an der Thaya 1989–90; business consultant 1989–90; trainee, Fed. of Austrian Industries 1990–93; Deputy Head, Signum Publishing House 1993–95; Marketing Dir Austrian People's Party (Lower Austrian br.) 1995–98, Exec. Dir 1998–2003, mem. Nat. Council 1999–2003; mem. Parl. (Austrian People's Party) 1999–2003; mem. Govt of Lower Austria with responsibility for Social Affairs, Labour and Family 2003–11; Vice-Pres. Ass. of European Regions 2008–11; Fed. Minister of the Interior 2011–16; Gov. Lower Austria (Landtag Niederösterreich) 2017–. *Address:* Landtag Niederösterreich, Landhauspl. 1, 3109 Saint Pölten, Austria (office). *Telephone:* (2742) 900-51-24-31 (office). *Fax:* (2742) 900-51-34-30 (office). *E-mail:* post.landtagsdirektion@noel.gv.at (office). *Website:* www.landtag-noe.at (office).

MIKLAIFI, Abd al-Malek al-; Yemeni politician; *Deputy Prime Minister;* b. 19 Aug. 1959, Taiz; ed San'a Univ.; journalist, Al-Jumhuriya (The Republic, daily newspaper) 1979–81; joined Nasserite Unionist Popular Org. 1974, various party positions including Sec.-Gen. 1982; Founder mem. Arab Nat. Conf. 1990, Sec.-Gen. 2012; Founder mem. Islamic Nat. Conf. 1994, also mem. Coordinating Cttee; mem. Shura Council (upper house of parl.) 2001; Deputy Prime Minister 2015–, also Minister of Foreign Affairs 2015–18. *Address:* Office of the Deputy Prime Minister, San'aa, Yemen (office).

MIKLOŠ, Ivan, DipEngEcon; Slovak politician and economist; b. 2 June 1960, Svídník; m. Jarmila Miklošová; two c.; ed Univ. of Econs, Bratislava, London School of Econs, UK; Asst, Univ. of Econs, Bratislava 1983–87, Chief Asst 1987–90; Adviser to Deputy Prime Minister responsible for Econ. Reform 1990; Dir Govt Dept of Econ. and Social Policy 1990–91; Minister of Privatization 1991–92; Exec. Dir and Pres. MESA 10 Org. 1992–98; Deputy Prime Minister for Econ. Affairs 1998–2002; Deputy Prime Minister and Minister of Finance 2002–06, 2010–12; mem. Parl. 2006–; First Deputy Chair. Civil Democratic Union 1992–93; Chair. Democratic Party 1993–2000; mem. Slovak Democratic and Christian Union-Democratic Party (SDKÚ-DS) 2001–, Vice-Chair. 2002–; First Vice-Pres. East-West Inst., New York 1998; apptd mem. Windsor Group 1993, Int. Advisory Bd, New Atlantic Initiative 1995, World Econ. Forum – Global Leaders of Tomorrow 1999, Int. Advisory Bd, BELA Foundation 2007; Consultant of Ukrainian Finance and Economy Ministers 2015; Hon. PhD (Alma Coll., Mich., USA) 2000; named by Euromoney magazine Minister of Finance of the Year 2004, Crystal Wing Award for Economy. *Publications include:* numerous articles in specialized and popular press. *Leisure interests:* tennis, windsurfing, skiing, biking.

MIKLOŠKO, Jozef, Doz., RNDr, DrSc; Slovak politician, mathematician, diplomatist, journalist and writer; b. 31 March 1939, Nitra; s. of Ondrej Mikloško and Marta Mikloško (née Kutliková); m. Mária Bitterová 1964; two s. two d.; ed Pedagogical Univ., Bratislava, Komenský Univ., Bratislava; teacher, Nové Zámky 1961–62; scientific worker, Inst. of Tech. Cybernetics, Slovak Acad. of Sciences, Bratislava 1963–90; Lecturer, Faculty of Mathematics and Physics, Komenský Univ., Bratislava 1969–89; Head of Int. Base Lab. for Artificial Intelligence 1985–90; Vice-Chair. Christian-Democratic Movt 1990; Deputy to Slovak Nat. Council 1990–91; Fed. Deputy Premier for Human Rights in Czechoslovak Fed. Repub. 1990–92; Deputy to House of the People, Fed. Ass. June–Dec. 1992; Adviser to Pres. of Slovakia 1993–95; Deputy to Town Council, Bratislava V 1994–2000; Deputy to the Nat. Council (Parl.) 2012–; Head of DACO publishing house 1995–2000, 2005; Sec. Justice and Peace Comm. 1995–2000; Lecturer and Vice-Rector Trnava Univ. 1996–2000; Amb. to Italy, Malta and San Marino 2000–05; Chair. Solidarity Foundation 1993–97, Schiller Foundation for Protection of Life and Human Rights 1995–2000, Asscn of Slovak Catholic Publrs 2006–08, Asscn of Christian Seniors of Slovakia 2007–; mem. Govt Council for Seniors 2008; mem. World Ecological Acad., Moscow 1994, Int. Informatization Acad., Moscow 1995, Slovak Asscn of Writers 1995– (mem. Presidium 2007–09), Slovak Asscn of Journalists 1997–2000; apptd moderator, World Apostolate of Fatima 2011; Grande Ufficiale d'Italia 2006; Laudis et Honoris Signum (Italy) 2001, Gold Star for European Culture 2005. *Publications:* Strong Secret: When We Were Young 1995, Farewell 1996, Very Top Secret: When We Were Free 1999, Top Secret: When We Were Italian 2006, Whom Maria Took To Heaven 2006, When We Were Young: After 60 Years 2007, Two Years Blogger 2010; five scientific books, 65 scientific publs, 250 newspaper articles, numerous blog posts. *Leisure interests:* literature, blogging, music, sport, history, church, politics. *Address:* Malokarpatská 22, 90021 Svätý Jur, Slovakia (home). *Telephone:* (2) 4497-0689 (home). *E-mail:* mikloskojozef@gmail.com (home); jozef.miklosko@nrsr.sk (office). *Website:* www.jozefmiklosko.sk; www.jozefmiklosko.blog.sme.sk.

MIKOLAJ, Ján, CSc; Slovak engineer, academic and politician; b. 19 Oct. 1953; ed Žilina Transport Univ.; Asst Prof., later Assoc. Prof., Road Construction Dept, Žilina Transport Univ. 1983–, mem. Scientific Council, Civil Eng Faculty 1992, Prof. and Head of Construction Implementation Dept, now the Dept of Construction Techs and Man. 1999–; Gen. Dir Slovak Road Admin 1995–98; elected to Nat. Council of Slovak Repub. (Slovak Nat. Party—Slovenská národná strana) 2002, 2006; Deputy Prime Minister and Minister of Educ. 2008–10.

MIKOSZ, Andrzej; Polish lawyer and politician; b. 17 Oct. 1965, Poznań; ed Adam Mickiewicz Univ., Poznań; Pnr Ziemski i Partnerzy (law firm), Poznań 1993–96; co-f. Głowacki, Grynhoff, Hałaziński, Mikosz (law firm) 1996–97; mem. Polish Securities and Exchanges Comm. and advisor to Minister of Agric. and Rural Devt 1998–2000; lawyer Weil, Gotshal and Manges, Warsaw 2000–02; Dir of Capital Markets practice, Lovells (law firm), Warsaw 2002–05; Minister of the Treasury 2005–06. *Publications:* numerous papers on company law, capital markets and corporate governance.

MIKOV, Mihail Raikov; Bulgarian politician, academic and jurist; *Chairman, Balgarska Sotsialisticheska Partiya (Bulgarian Socialist Party);* b. 16 June 1960, Kula; m.; two c.; ed St Clement of Ohrid Univ. of Sofia; Assoc. Prof. of Criminal Law, St Clement of Ohrid Univ. of Sofia; mem. Narodno Sobraniye (Nat. Ass.) for 5-Vidin 1997–, Chair. Parl. Group of leftist Coalition for Bulgaria 2005–08, mem. Legal Matters Cttee, European Integration Cttee, Chair. Nat. Ass. 2013–14; Minister of the Interior 2008–09; Chair. Balgarska Sotsialisticheska Partiya (BSP—Bulgarian Socialist Party) 2014–. *Address:* Balgarska Sotsialisticheska Partiya (Bulgarian Socialist Party), 1000 Sofia, ul. Positano 20, Bulgaria (office). *Telephone:* (2) 810-72-00 (office). *Fax:* (2) 981-21-85 (office). *E-mail:* bsp@bsp.bg (office). *Website:* www.bsp.bg (office).

MIKSER, Sven; Estonian politician; b. 8 Nov. 1973, Tartu, Estonian SSR, USSR; one d.; ed Univ. of Tartu; Div. Asst, Dept of Romance-Germanic Philology, Univ. of Tartu 1996–99; mem. Eesti Keskerakond (Estonian Centre Party) 1995–2004, Political Sec. 1998–99; mem. Riigikogu (Parl.) for Tartu City constituency 1999–2002, 2003–14; Minister of Defence 2002–03, 2014–15, of Foreign Affairs 2016–19; mem. Sotsiaaldemokraatlik Erakond (Estonian Social Democratic Party) 2005–, Pres. 2010–15; Chair. Sub-cttee, NATO Parl. Ass. of the Trans-Atlantic Defence and Security Cooperation; mem. Bd of Trustees, Univ. of Tartu. *Publications:* articles in nat. publs. *Address:* c/o Ministry of Foreign Affairs, Islandi Väljak 1, Tallinn 15049, Estonia (office).

MIKULSKI, Barbara Ann, BA, MSW; American politician and fmr teacher; b. 20 July 1936, Baltimore, Md; d. of William Mikulski and Christina Eleanor Kutz; ed Mount St Agnes Coll. and Univ. of Maryland; Baltimore Dept Social Services 1961–63, 1966–70; York Family Agency 1964; VISTA Teaching Center 1965–70; teacher, Mount St Agnes Coll. 1969; teacher, Community Coll., Baltimore 1970–71; Adjunct Prof., Loyola Coll. 1972–76; mem. US House of Reps from 3rd Md Dist 1977–87; Senator from Maryland 1987–2017, first woman Democrat elected to US Senate in her own right, became longest serving woman in history of US Congress 17 March 2012, Dean of the Women; mem. Democratic Nat. Strategy Council; mem. Nat. Bd of Dirs Urban Coalition; mem. Nat. Asscn of Social Workers; Democrat; Hon. Fellow, American Acad. of Nursing 2007; Polish Order of Merit 2001, Commdr's Cross and Star (Poland) 2001; Hon. LLD (Goucher Coll.) 1973, (Hood Coll.) 1978, (Bowie State Univ.) 1989, (Morgan State Univ.) 1990, (Massachusetts) 1991; Hon. DHL (Pratt Inst.) 1974; Presidential Medal of Freedom 2015. *Address:* 503 Hart Office Building, Washington, DC 20510, USA (office). *Telephone:* (202) 224-4654 (office). *Fax:* (202) 224-8858 (office). *Website:* mikulski.senate.gov (office).

MIKVABIA, Artur; Georgian (Abkhaz) economist and politician; b. 22 May 1949, Sukhumi, Abkhaz ASSR, Georgian SSR, USSR; m.; two c.; ed secondary school in Sukhumi, All-Union Inst. of Food Production, Moscow, Russian SFSR (by correspondence), Higher Party School (by correspondence); played for Dinamo Sukhumi football club; worked in mill factory in Sukhumi; served in Soviet Army 1974–76; joined CP of Soviet Union (CPSU), Instructor, then Deputy Head, Econs Dept of Abkhaz br. of CPSU 1979–88, Second Sec., Sukhumi City Cttee of CPSU 1988–92; Regional Man. YUKOS Oil Co. –2001; mem. United Abkhazia, Leader 2004–09; Prime Minister of the 'Republic of Abkhazia' 2015–16.

MÍL, Jaroslav, MA, MBA; Czech business executive; b. 10 Aug. 1958, Prague; ed Electrotechnology Faculty, Czech Tech. Univ., Prague, Sheffield Business School, UK; various tech. positions, then Dir responsible for Procurement and Fuel Cycles, Czech Power Co. (ČEZ) 1985–2000, Chair. and CEO 2000–03; Chair. and CEO Elektrárny Opatovice (EOP) 2000; mem. Bd of Dirs Škoda-ÚJP Praha 1994–2000, Siberian Coal Energy Co. 2013–; apptd Pres. Confed. of Industry of the Czech Repub. 2003; Chair. Radioactive Waste Repository Authority 1997–2000, European Nuclear Council 2003–; mem. Bd of Govs World Nuclear Fuel Market, Atlanta, USA 1993–99; mem. Supervisory Bd Severočeské doly 1998–99, Bd Czech Asscn of Employers in Energy Sector 2000–; fmr Vice-Pres. BUSINESSEUROPE; fmr mem. ICC, Bd of Dirs EURELECTRIC, Slovenske elektrarne – ENEL SpA, Int. Advisory Cttee of Soc. for Strategic Man.; mem. Bd of Dirs Czech Tech. Univ. *Leisure interests:* family, skiing, golf, squash, cycling, hiking. *Address:* Siberian Coal Energy Co., 115054 Moscow, 53/7 Dubininskaya str., Russia. *Telephone:* (495) 795-2538. *Fax:* (495) 795-2542. *E-mail:* info@suek.ru. *Website:* www.suek.ru.

MILAKNIS, Valentinas Pranas; Lithuanian business executive and politician; b. 4 Oct. 1947, Rokiskis; m. Sofija Milakniene; one s. one d.; ed Kaunas Polytech. Inst.; fmr engineer, then Head of Group, Head of Sector, Deputy Chief Engineer Control System Planning and Design Construction Bureau, Municipal Econ. Planning Inst. 1970–89; apptd Man. Dir, then Dir-Gen. Alna AB Co. 1989, Chair. –2001; Minister of Nat. Economy 1999–2000; Dir-Gen. LRT (Lithuanian public TV and radio broadcaster) 2001–03; apptd Chair. Nat. Radio and TV Council of Lithuania 2008; Business Glory Gallery 1999. *Leisure interest:* shooting.

MILANI, Cesare (Chez) Andrea, BA, LLB; South African trade union official and lawyer; b. 27 Nov. 1966, Cape Town; m.; one d.; ed Stellenbosch Univ., Univ. of South Africa School of Business Leadership; Nat. Legal Adviserm, Hospersa 1994–97; Gen. Sec. Fed. of Unions of SA (FEDUSA) 1997–2007; mem. Pres. Mbeki's Working Group, NEDLAC Exec. Cttee and Man. Cttee, CCMA Governing Body. *Leisure interests:* antiques, sailing. *Address:* c/o FEDUSA, PO Box 7779, Westgate 1734, South Africa. *E-mail:* info@fedusa.org.za.

MILANOVIĆ, Zoran; Croatian politician; b. 30 Oct. 1966, Zagreb; s. of Stipe Milanović and Gina Milanović; m. Sanja Musić-Milanović 1994; two s.; ed Centre for Man. and Judiciary, Univ. of Zagreb; became an intern at Croatian Trade Court; joined Croatian Foreign Ministry 1993, went to Nagornyi Karabakh as part of UN peace mission 1994, adviser at Croatian Mission to EU and NATO, Brussels 1996–99, returned to Foreign Ministry 1999; enrolled in Socijaldemokratska Partija Hrvatske (SDP—Social Democratic Party of Croatia) 1999, given responsibility for liaison with NATO 2000–03, elected to Chief Cttee of SDP 2004, Party Spokesman 2006, elected Co-ordinator for IVth election area for 2007 elections, Chair. SDP 2007–16; Asst to Minister of Foreign Affairs 2003; Leader of the Opposition 2007–11, Jan.–Nov. 2016; Prime Minister of Croatia 2011–16. *Address:* Socijaldemokratska Partija Hrvatske (Social Democratic Party of Croatia), 10000 Zagreb, Iblerov trg 9, Croatia (office). *Telephone:* (1) 4552055 (office). *Fax:* 1) 4552842 (office). *E-mail:* info@sdp.hr (office). *Website:* www.sdp.hr (office).

MILBERG, Joachim, Dr-Ing; German automotive industry executive and engineer; *Chairman of the Supervisory Board, BMW AG;* b. 10 April 1943, Verl, Westphalia; ed Technische Universität Berlin; Research Asst, Inst. of Machine Tools and Production Tech., Berlin Tech. Univ. 1970–72; exec. employee, Werkzeugmaschinenfabrik Gildemeister AG (machine tools factory) 1972–78, Head of Automatic Tuning Machines division 1978–81; Prof. of Machine Tools and Man. Science, Munich Tech. Univ. 1981–93; mem. Bd of Man. Bayerische Motoren Werke (BMW) AG (Production) 1993–98, (Eng and Production) 1998–99, Chair. Bd of Man. 1999–2002, mem. Supervisory Bd 2002–04, Chair. 2004–; mem. Bd of Dirs Bertelsmann AG, Allianz SE, Munich, Festo AG, Esslingen, Leipziger Messe GmbH, Leipzig, MAN AG, Munich, SAP AG 2007–, Walldorf, ZF Friedrichshafen AG, John Deere & Co., USA 2003–; mem. Partner Cttee TÜV Süddeutschland, Munich; Pres. acatech – Deutsche Akad. der Technikwissenschaften 2003–09; Hon. Prof., Dept of Machine Tools and Industrial Eng, Tech. Univ. of Munich 1998, Univ. of Duisburg-Essen 2010; Verdienstkreuz am Bande des Verdienstordens der Bundesrepublik Deutschland 1994, Bayerischer Verdienstorden 2001, Bayerischer Maximiliansorden für Wissenschaft und Kunst 2010; Hon. Dr-Ing, Dr hc (Ljubljana, Slovenia) 1994, (Hanover) 1996, (Cranfield, UK) 2002, (Tech. Univ. of Berlin) 2004; Gottfried Wilhelm Leibniz Prize, German Research Foundation (DFG) 1989, Fritz Winter Prize 1991, Herwart Opitz Hon. Medal, VDI-Gesellschaft Produktionstechnik 1992, State Medal for outstanding service to the Bavarian economy 1999, Grashof Medal, Asscn of German Engineers (VDI) 2000, Gen. Pierre Nicolau Award, Collège Int. pour la Recherche en Productique Int. 2001, Hon. Award 'Golden Steering Wheel', Axel Springer Verlag 2001, Bavarian Environmental Medal for outstanding contribs to environmental protection and land devt 2002, Ernst Blickle Prize, SEW Euro Drive Foundation, Bruchsal 2003, Carl Friedrich Gauss Medal, Brunswick Scientific Soc. 2004, Arthur Burkhardt Prize 2005, Hanns Martin Schleyer Prize 2009. *Address:* BMW AG, Petuelring 130, 80788, Munich, Germany (office). *Telephone:* (89) 382-0 (office). *Fax:* (89) 382-244-18 (office). *E-mail:* info@bmwgroup.com (office). *Website:* www.bmwgroup.com (office); www.bmw.com (office).

MILBRADT, Georg, Dr rer pol; German politician and academic; b. 23 Feb. 1945, Eslohe, Sauerland; m. Angelika Meeth; two s.; ed Univ. of Münster; Asst, Inst. of Finance, Univ. of Münster 1970–80, Guest Prof. 1985–; Deputy Prof. of Finance and Econs, Univ. of Mainz 1980–83; Head, Dept of Finance, Münster 1983–90, later responsible for econ. devt and property man.; mem. CDU 1991–, Fed. Admin 2000–; Minister of Finance, Saxony State 1990–2001; mem. Bundesrates (Upper House of Parl.) Cttee on Mediation; mem. Saxony State Parl. 1994–; Minister-Pres. of Saxony April 2002–08 (resgnd); Regional Deputy Chair. Sächsischen Union 1999; Chair. Bd Sächsischen Aufbaubank, Dresden Airport, Sächsischen Landesbank; Deputy Chair. Bd Leipzig-Halle Airport; Chair. Tariff Community of German Länder (TdL); currently Research Prof. IFO Inst.; Chair. Economics, ESP Public Economics, Technische Universität Dresden; Bundesvierdienstkreuz 2005. *Leisure interests:* literature, computers. *Address:* CDU, Konrad-Adenauer-Haus, Klingelhöferstrasse 8, 10785 Berlin, Germany (office); Center for Public Finance and Political Economy, IFO Inst., Stiller Winkel 4, 01328 Dresden, Germany. *Telephone:* (30) 220700 (office). *Fax:* (30) 22070111 (office). *E-mail:* info@cdu.de (office); milbradt@t-online.de. *Website:* www.cdu.de (office); www.georg-milbradt.de (office); tu-dresden.de (office); www.cesifo-group.de (office).

MILBURN, Rt Hon. Alan, PC, BA; British politician; *Chairman of the European Advisory Board, Bridgepoint Capital;* b. 27 Jan. 1958; m. Mo O'Toole 1982 (divorced 1992); m. Ruth Briel; two s.; ed Stokesley Comprehensive School, Lancaster Univ.; co-ordinator Trade Union Studies Information Unit, Newcastle 1984–90; Sr Business Devt Officer N Tyneside Municipal Borough Council 1990–92; MP for Darlington 1992–2010; Opposition Front Bench Spokesman on Health 1995–96, on Treasury and Econ. Affairs 1996–97; Minister of State, Dept of Health 1997–98; Chief Sec. to Treasury 1998–99, Sec. of State for Health 1999–2003; Chancellor of the Duchy of Lancaster 2004–05; Chair. Parl. Labour Party Treasury Cttee 1992–95; mem. Public Accounts Cttee 1994–95; Chair. Charities Scrutiny Cttee 2004; Adviser, Bridgepoint Capital 2007–, currently Chair., European Advisory Cttee; Chair. Social Mobility and Child Poverty Comm. 2012–, PricewaterhouseCoopers UK Health Industry Oversight Bd 2013–; mem. Bd of Dirs, Diaverum AB, Apos Therapy; Chancellor, Lancaster Univ. 2015–; mem. Nutritional Advisory Bd, PepsiCo UK 2007–; mem. Advisory Bd Mars Inc. *Address:* Bridgepoint Capital, 30 Warwick Street, London, W1B 5AL, England (office). *Telephone:* (20) 7034-3500 (office). *E-mail:* advisoryboard@bridgepoint.eu (office). *Website:* www.bridgepoint.eu (office).

MILCHAN, Arnon; American film producer; b. 6 Dec. 1944, Tel-Aviv, Israel. *Plays produced:* Tomb, It's So Nice To Be Civilized, Amadeus (Paris production). *Films include:* Black Joy 1977, The Medusa Touch (exec. producer) 1978, Dizengoff 99 1979, The King of Comedy 1983, Can She Bake a Cherry Pie? (actor) 1983, Once Upon a Time in America (also actor) 1984, Brazil 1985, Legend 1985, Stripper (exec. producer) 1986, Man on Fire 1987, Big Man on Campus 1989, The Adventures of Baron Munchausen 1989, Who's Harry Crumb 1989, The War of the Roses 1989, Pretty Woman 1990, Q&A 1990, Guilty by Suspicion 1991, Switch (exec. producer) 1991, JFK (exec. producer) 1991, Memoirs of an Invisible Man (exec. producer) 1992, The Mambo Kings 1992, The Power of One 1992, Under Siege 1992, That Night 1992, Heaven and Earth 1993, Sommersby 1993, Falling Down (exec. producer) 1993, Made in America 1993, Free Willy (exec. producer) 1993, Striking Distance 1993, The Nutcracker (exec. producer) 1993, Six Degrees of Separation 1993, The Client 1994, Natural Born Killers (exec. producer) 1994, Second Best 1994, The New Age 1994, Cobb (exec. producer) 1994, Boys on the Side 1995, Under Siege 2 1995, Free Willy 2: The Adventure Home 1995, Empire Records 1995, Copycat 1995, Heat (exec. producer) 1995, The Sunchaser 1996, A Time to Kill 1996, Tin Cup (exec. producer) 1996, Bogus 1996, The Mirror Has Two Faces 1996, Murder at 1600 1997, L.A. Confidential 1997, Free Willy 3: The Rescue (exec. producer) 1997, The Devil's Advocate 1997, Breaking Up (exec. producer) 1997, The Man Who Knew Too Little 1997, Dangerous Beauty 1998, City of Angels (exec. producer) 1998, Goodbye Lover (exec. producer) 1998, The Negotiator 1998, Simply Irresistible (exec. producer) 1999, A Midsummer Night's Dream (exec. producer) 1999, Entrapment (exec. producer) 1999, Fight Club (exec. producer) 1999, Up at the Villa (exec. producer) 2000, Big Momma's House (exec. producer) 2000, Tigerland 2000, Freddy Got Fingered (exec. producer) 2001, Joy Ride (exec. producer) 2001, Don't Say a Word 2001, Black Knight 2001, Joe Somebody (exec. producer) 2001, High Crimes 2002, Life or Something Like It 2002, Unfaithful (exec. producer) 2002, Daredevil 2003, Down with Love (exec. producer) 2003, Runaway Jury 2003, The Girl Next Door (exec. producer) 2004, Man on Fire 2004, First Daughter (exec. producer) 2004, Elektra 2005, Mr. & Mrs. Smith 2005, Bee Season (exec. producer) 2005, Stay (exec. producer) 2005, Just My Luck 2006, The Sentinel 2006, Meet the Spartans (exec. producer) 2008, What Happens in Vegas (exec. producer) 2008, Bride Wars (exec. producer) 2009, Knight and Day (exec. producer) 2010, Monte Carlo (producer) 2011, Broken City 2013, 12 Years a Slave (BAFTA Award for Best Picture, Golden Globe Award for Best Motion Picture, Drama 2014) 2013. *Television includes:* Masada (mini-series) (supervising producer) 1981, Free Willy (series; exec. producer), The Client (series; exec. producer) 1995, Michael Hayes (series; exec. producer) 1997, The Hunt for the Unicorn Killer 1999, Noriega: God's Favorite (exec. producer) 2000. *Address:* New Regency Enterprises, 10201 West Pico Boulevard, Building 12, Los Angeles, CA 90035, USA (office). *Telephone:* (310) 369-8300 (office). *E-mail:* info@newregency.com (office). *Website:* www.newregency.com (office).

MILES, (Henry) Michael (Pearson), OBE; British business executive; *Non-Executive Chairman, London Mining Plc;* b. 19 April 1936; s. of Brig. H. G. P. Miles and Margaret Miles; m. Carol Jane Berg 1967; two s. one d.; ed Wellington Coll., Nat. Service, Duke of Wellington's Regt; joined John Swire & Sons 1958, Dir John Swire & Sons (HK) Ltd 1970–99, Chair. 1984–88; Man. Dir John Swire & Sons (Japan) Ltd 1973–76; Man. Dir Cathay Pacific Airways Ltd 1978–84, Chair. 1984–88; Chair. Swire Pacific 1984–88; Exec. Dir John Swire & Sons Ltd 1988–99, Adviser to Bd 1999–; Dir Johnson Matthey PLC 1990–2006, Chair. (non-exec.) 1998–2006; Chair. (non-exec.) Schroders 2003–12; Dir (non-exec.) London Mining Plc 2012–, Chair. (non-exec.) 2013–; Dir (non-exec.) Baring PLC 1989–95 (Jt Deputy Chair. 1994–95), Portals Holdings 1990–95, BICC 1996–2002, HSBC Holdings 1984–88, ING Baring Holdings Ltd 1989–2002, BP PLC 1994–2006, Balfour Beatty 1996–2002, Pacific Assets Trust PLC 1997–2003, Thomas Cook Group, Fleming Far Eastern Investment Trust, Sedgwick Lloyd's Underwriting Agents; Chair. Hong Kong Tourist Asscn 1984–88, Korea-Europe Fund Ltd; Vice-Pres. China-Britain Business Council 1992–2002; Gov. Wellington Coll. 1990–2005. *Leisure interests:* golf, tennis, shooting, family. *Address:* London Mining Plc, Nations House, 103 Wigmore Street, London, W1U 1QS (office); Shalbourne House, Shalbourne, nr Marlborough, Wilts., SN8 3QH, England (home). *Telephone:* (20) 7408-7500 (office). *Fax:* (20) 7647-4440 (office). *Website:* www.londonmining.com (office).

MILES, Michael A. (Mike), Jr, BA, MBA; American business executive; *Advisory Director, Berkshire Partners;* ed Yale and Harvard Univs; began career at Bain & Co.; joined PepsiCo Inc. as Dir of Strategic Planning, Restaurants 1993, Div. Vice-Pres., Pizza Hut 1994, then Sr Vice-Pres., Concept Devt and Franchise, Pizza Hut (after Yum Brands Inc. spinoff from PepsiCo that included Pizza Hut) 1996–99, COO Pizza Hut Inc. 2000–03; COO Staples Inc. 2003–13, Pres. 2006–13; Advisory Dir, Berkshire Partners 2013–. *Address:* Berkshire Partners, 200 Clarendon Street, 35th Floor, Boston, MA 02116, USA (office). *Telephone:* (617) 227-0050 (office). *Fax:* (617) 227-6105 (office). *E-mail:* info@berkshirepartners.com (office). *Website:* www.berkshirepartners.com (office).

MILES, Sarah; British actress; b. 31 Dec. 1941, Ingatestone, Essex; m. Robert Bolt 1967 (divorced 1976), remarried 1988 (died 1995); one c.; ed Royal Acad. of Dramatic Art; with Nat. Theatre Co. 1964–65; Shakespeare stage season 1982–83; Assoc. mem. Royal Acad. of Dramatic Art. *Theatre appearances include:* Vivat! Vivat Regina!, Asylum 1988. *Films include:* Term of Trial 1962, The Servant 1963, The Ceremony 1963, Those Magnificent Men in Their Flying Machines 1965, I Was Happy Here 1965, Blowup 1966, Ryan's Daughter 1970, Lady Caroline Lamb 1972, The Hireling 1973, The Man Who Loved Cat Dancing 1973, Pepita Jiménez 1975, The Sailor Who Fell From Grace With the Sea 1976, The Big Sleep 1978, Priest of Love 1981, Venom 1982, Ordeal by Innocence 1984, Steaming 1985, Hope and Glory 1987, White Mischief 1987, Hope and glory 1987, Dotkniecie reki (The Silent Touch) 1992, Jurij 2001, I giorni dell'amore e dell'odio (Days of Grace) 2001, The Accidental Detective 2003. *Television includes:* Great Expectations 1974, James A. Michener's Dynasty 1976, Walter and June 1983, Harem 1986, Queenie 1987, A Ghost in Monte Carlo 1990, Dandelion Dead (mini-series) 1994, Ring Around the Moon, The Rehearsal, Poirot: The Hollow 2004. *Publications:* Charlemagne (play) 1992, A Right Royal Bastard (memoirs) 1993, Serves Me Right (memoirs) 1994, Bolt from the Blue (memoirs) 1996.

MILHAUD, Charles; French banking executive; b. 20 Feb. 1943; s. of Georges and Fernande; m. 1st 1964 (divorced 1967); Gisèle 1969; two c.; ed Univ. of Montpellier; science grad.; has spent entire career with Groupe Caisse d'Epargne, joined Caisse d'Epargne de Sète 1964, CEO 1967–80, CEO, then Chair. Man. Bd Caisse d'Epargne des Bouches du Rhône et de la Corse 1980–99, Chair. Man. Bd Centre Nat. des Caisses d'Epargne (thereafter Caisse Nationale des Caisses d'Epargne when it was cr. in Sept. 1999) 1999–2008 (resgnd), Chair. Caisses d'Epargne Foundation for Social Solidarity; Chair. Supervisory Bd Natixis, Financière OCEOR; Chair. French Banking Fed. 2006–07; Vice-Pres. Nexity; mem. Municipal Council of Marseille 2008–; Officier, Ordre nat. du Mérite 2001, Légion d'honneur 2005.

MILIBAND, Rt Hon. David Wright, PC, BA (Hons), SM; British politician and international organization official; *President and CEO, International Rescue Committee;* b. 15 July 1965, London, England; s. of Ralph Miliband and Marion Miliband (née Kozak); brother of Ed Miliband; m. Louise Shackelton 1998; two adopted s.; ed Haverstock Comprehensive School, North London, Corpus Christi Coll., Oxford, Massachusetts Inst. of Tech., USA (Kennedy Scholar); Research Fellow, Inst. for Public Policy Research 1989–94; Sec. Comm. on Social Justice 1992–94; Head of Policy, Office of Leader of Opposition 1994–97; Head, Prime Minister's Policy Unit 1997–2001; MP (Labour) for South Shields 2001–13; Minister of State, Dept for Educ. and Skills 2002–04; Minister for the Cabinet Office 2004–05; Minister of Communities and Local Govt 2005–06; Sec. of State for the Environment, Food and Rural Affairs 2006–07, for Foreign and Common-wealth Affairs 2007–10; unsuccessful cand. in Labour Party leadership election Sept. 2010; Pres. and CEO Int. Rescue Cttee, New York 2013–; mem. Bd of Dirs, The Office of David Miliband Ltd 2010–; Vice-Chair. Sunderland AFC 2011–13 (resgnd). *Publications:* Publish and Still Not be Damned: A Guide for Voluntary Groups on the Provisions of the 1986 and 1988 Local Government Acts Regarding Political Publicity and the Promotion of Homosexuality, National Council for Voluntary Organisation (with Richard Gutch and Richard Percival) 1989, Beyond Economics: European Government after Maastricht. Discussion Paper, No. 12, Fabian Society (with Stephen Tindale) 1991, A More Perfect Union? Britain and the New Europe 1992, Reinventing the Left (ed.) 1994, Paying for Inequality: The Economic Cost of Social Injustice (co-ed.) 1994, Empowerment and the Deal for Devolution 2006. *Leisure interests:* supporting Arsenal Football Club, hoping for South Shields Football Club. *Address:* International Rescue Committee, 263 West 38th Street, 6th Floor, New York, NY 10018, USA (office). *Telephone:* (212) 377-4728 (office). *E-mail:* newyork@rescue.org (office). *Website:* www.rescue.org (office).

MILIBAND, Rt Hon. Edward (Ed) Samuel, PC, BA, MSc; British politician; b. 24 Dec. 1969, London, England; s. of Ralph Miliband and Marion Kozak; brother of David Miliband; m. Justine Thornton 2011; two s.; ed London School of Econs, Corpus Christi Coll., Oxford; Special Adviser to Chancellor of Exchequer 1997, becoming Chair. Treasury Council of Econ. Advisers; MP (Labour) for Doncaster N 2005–; Parl. Sec. to Cabinet Office 2006, Chair. All-Party Group on Young People, Minister for Third Sector 2006–07, Minister for Cabinet Office and Chancellor, Duchy of Lancaster 2007–08; Sec. of State for Energy and Climate Change 2008–10; Leader of the Labour Party and Leader of the Opposition Sept. 2010–15; Visiting Lecturer, Dept of Govt, Harvard Univ., USA 2003, also Visiting Scholar, Center for European Studies. *Address:* House of Commons, Westminster, London, SW1A 0AA (office); Hutton Business Centre, Bridge Works, Bentley, Doncaster, S Yorks., DN5 9QP, England (office). *Telephone:* (20) 7276-1234 (Westminster) (office); (20) 7219-4778 (Westminster) (office); (1302) 875462 (Doncaster) (office). *E-mail:* ed.miliband.mp@parliament.uk (office).

MILIĆ, Jelena; Serbian political activist; *Director and Chair, Center for Euro-Atlantic Studies;* b. 15 Jan. 1965, Belgrade; studied nuclear physics at univ.; worked as political analyst and researcher for Int. Crisis Group and Helsinki Cttee for Human Rights in Serbia; currently Dir and Chair., Governing Bd, Center for Euro-Atlantic Studies, Belgrade; mem. Forum for Int. Relations (think tank); frequent speaker at int. confs dealing with South-East Europe, Western Balkans and transitional justice. *Address:* Center for Euro-Atlantic Studies, 11000 Belgrade, Dr Dragoslava Popovića 15, Serbia (office). *Telephone:* (11) 3239579 (office). *E-mail:* jelena.milic@ceas-serbia.org (office). *Website:* www.ceas-serbia .org/sr (office).

MILIĆ, Srđan; Montenegrin (ethnic Serb) politician; b. 17 Sept. 1965, Bar; m.; one s. two d.; ed Faculty for Foreign Trade and Tourism, Univ. of Dubrovnik, Croatia; moved to Budva following graduation; worked in tourism 1983–90; Asst, Faculty for Tourism, Kotor 1991–92; in pvt. commerce 1992–2002; joined reformed Socijalistička Narodna Partija Crne Gore (SNP—Socialist People's Party of Montenegro) 2002, researcher on EU and European integration of outside countries, mem. Main Bd and Main Bd's Exec. Cttee, Pres. SNP's Comm. for European and Euro-Atlantic integration, Pres. SNP 2006–17; mem. Parl. (SNP) 2006–10, Leader of SNP Parl. Group 2006–10, mem. Parl. Comm. for European Integration; cand. in presidential election 2008; Pres. Nat. Council for European Integration 2008–09. *E-mail:* matigor@t-com.me (office); snp@t-com.me (office). *Address:* Socijalistička Narodna Partija Crne Gore (Socialist People's Party of Montenegro), 81000 Podgorica, Vaka Đurovića 5, Montenegro (office). *Telephone:* (20) 272421 (office). *Fax:* (20) 272420 (office). *Website:* www.snp.co.me (office).

MILINGO, Most Rev. Archbishop Emmanuel, DipEd; Zambian ecclesiastic; *Archbishop Emeritus of Lusaka;* b. 13 June 1930; s. of Yakobe Milingo and Tomaida Lumbiwe; m. Maria Sung 2001 (divorced); ed St Mary's Presbyterial School, Fort Jameson and Kasina Junior Seminary and Kachebere Major Seminary, Nyasaland (now Malawi); studied Pastoral Sociology (Diploma), Rome, Univ. Coll. Dublin, Ireland; curate, Minga Mission 1958–61; Parish Priest, St Ann's Mission, Chipata 1963–66; Sec. for Mass Media, Zambia Episcopal Conf. 1966–69; Archbishop of Lusaka 1969–83, Archbishop Emer. 1983–; Special Del. to Pontifical Comm. for Pastoral Care of Migrants, Refugees and Pilgrims 1983–; drew worldwide headlines in 2001 when he married a Korean woman in a large ceremony in New York organised by the Unification Church ('Moonies'), later expressed regret and contrition to Pope John Paul II, subsequently spent a year in seclusion, returning to Rome in 2002; f. Married Priests Now! 2006. *Publications:* Make Joni, Demarcations, The World in Between, The Flower Garden of Jesus the Redeemer, My Prayers are Not Heard, Precautions in the Ministry of Deliverance, Against Satan, The World in Between: Christian Healing and the Struggle for Spiritual Survival, Confessions of an Excommunicated Catholic (auto-biog.); has produced his own CD. *Leisure interests:* writing and preaching to make Jesus Christ known and loved. *E-mail:* emmanuelmilingo@hotmail.com (home).

MILINKEVICH, Alyaksandr Uladzimeravich, PhD; Belarusian politician; b. 25 July 1947, Grodno, Byelorussian SSR, USSR; m. 2nd Inna Kuley; two c. from first m.; ed Grodno Teacher Inst., USSR Acad. of Sciences, European Centre for Security Research, Garmisch-Partenkirchen, FRG; early career as teacher, Grodno 1969–72; Jr Researcher, USSR Acad. of Sciences (Belarus) 1972–78; Assoc. Prof., Grodno State Univ. 1978–80, 1984–90; Head, Dept of Physics, Univ. of Setif, Algeria 1980–84; Deputy Chair. Grodno Admin Exec. Cttee 1990–96; Leader, Ratusha (Town Hall) Org. 1996–2003; Pres. Grodno-93 football team; Founder and Head, Ratusha Resource Centre 1997 (closed by authorities 2003); headed presidential campaign of Syamyon Domash 2001; contested presidential election as cand. for coalition of United Democratic Forces 2006; Founder and Leader, For Freedom Movt (Rukh 'Za Svabodu') (human rights group) 2008 (apptd); jailed by Govt for 15 days for taking part in an unsanctioned rally April 2006; Sakharov Prize, European Parl. 2006; Hanno R. Ellenbogen Citizenship Award, Prague Soc. for Int. Cooperation. *E-mail:* info@milinkevich.org. *Website:* www.milinkevich.org.

MILIUS, John Frederick; American screenwriter, director and actor; b. 11 April 1944, St Louis, Mo.; s. of William Styx Milius and Elizabeth Milius (née Roe); m. 1st Renée Fabri 1967; two s.; m. 2nd Celia K. Burkholder 1978; ed Univ. of Southern California. *Films include:* The Devil's 8 1969, Evel Knievel 1971, Jeremiah Johnson 1972, The Life and Times of Judge Roy Bean 1973, Magnum Force 1973, Purvis FBI (for TV) 1974, The Wind and the Lion (also dir) 1975, Big Wednesday ((also dir), 1978, Apocalypse Now (Acad. Award for Best Screenplay 1980) 1979, 1941 (with Francis Ford Coppola q.v.) 1979, Conan the Barbarian (also dir) 1982, Red Dawn (also dir) 1984, Extreme Prejudice 1987, Farewell to the King (also dir) 1989, Flight of the Intruder (dir) 1991 Geronimo: An American Legend 1993, Clear and Present Danger 1994. *Television includes:* Rough Riders (film, writer) 1997, Rome (series, creator and writer) 2005–07.

MILLAR, Sir Fergus Graham Burtholme, Kt, MA, DPhil, DLitt, FBA, FSA; British historian and academic (retd); *Camden Professor of Ancient History Emeritus, University of Oxford;* b. 5 July 1935, Edinburgh, Scotland; s. of J. S. L. Millar and J. B. Taylor; m. Susanna Friedmann 1959; two s. one d.; ed Edinburgh Acad., Loretto School, Trinity Coll., Oxford; Fellow, All Souls Coll., Oxford 1958–64; Fellow and Tutor in Ancient History, The Queen's Coll., Oxford 1964–76; Prof. of Ancient History, Univ. Coll., London 1976–84; Camden Prof. of Ancient History, Univ. of Oxford 1984–2002, currently Emer. Prof. of Ancient History; Fellow, Brasenose Coll. Oxford 1984–2002; Pres. Soc. for the Promotion of Roman Studies 1989–92 (Vice-Pres. 1977–89, 1992–2001, Hon. Vice-Pres. 2001–; Pres. Classical Asscn 1992–93; Publications Sec. British Acad. 1997–2002; Corresp. mem. German Archaeological Inst. 1977, Bavarian Acad. 1987, Finnish Acad. 1989, Russian Acad. 1999, American Acad. 2003; Hon. DPhil (Helsinki) 1994, Hon. DLitt (St Andrews Univ.) 2004; Premio Cultori di Roma 2005, Kenyon Medal for Classical Studies, British Acad. 2005. *Publications:* several historical studies, The Roman Near East 1993, The Crowd in Rome in the Late Republic 1998, The Roman Republic in Political Thought 2002. *Address:* Oriental Institute, Pusey Lane, Oxford, OX1 2LE (office); 80 Harpes Road, Oxford, OX2 7QL, England (home). *Telephone:* (1865) 288093 (office); (1865) 515782 (home). *Fax:* (1865) 278190 (office). *E-mail:* fergus.millar@bnc.ox.ac.uk (office).

MILLER, Aleksei Borisovich, PhD; Russian business executive; *Deputy Chairman of the Board of Directors and Chairman of the Management Committee (CEO), OAO Gazprom;* b. 31 Jan. 1962, Leningrad (now St Petersburg), Russian SFSR, USSR; m.; one s.; ed N.A. Voznesenskii Leningrad Inst. of Finance and Econs; engineer-economist, Gen. Planning Div., LenNIIProekt – Leningrad Civil Construction Research and Design Inst.; researcher, Leningrad Inst. of Finance and Econs 1990–91; mem. Cttee on Foreign Econ. Relations, Office of the Mayor of St Petersburg 1991–96; Dir of Devt and Investments, Morskoy Port of St Petersburg Open Jt Stock Co. 1996–99; Dir-Gen. Balttiiskaya Truboprovodnaya Sistema (Baltic Pipeline System) 1999–2000; Deputy Minister of Energy 2000–01; Chair. Man. Cttee (CEO) OAO Gazprom 2001–, Deputy Chair. Bd of Dirs 2002–; Order for the Services to the Fatherland, IV Class, Medal of Order for Services to the Fatherland, II Class, Order of Hungarian Repub. Cross, II Class, St Mesrop Mashtots Order (Armenia), Dostyk (Friendship) Order, II Class (Kazakhstan), Order of Honour (South Ossetia), Order of Merit of Italian Repub., Sergiy Radonezhsky Order of Russian Orthodox Church, II Class, Patriarchal Merit Certificate; named by Ekspert magazine (Russian business weekly) Person of the Year (jtly) 2005. *Address:* OAO Gazprom, 117997 Moscow, ul. Nametkina 16, V-420, GSP-7, Russia (office). *Telephone:* (495) 719-30-01 (office). *Fax:* (495) 719-83-33 (office). *E-mail:* gazprom@gazprom.com (office). *Website:* www.gazprom.com (office).

MILLER, Andrew; British publishing executive; Audit Man., Price Waterhouse 1991–94, also held various finance roles at Procter and Gamble; Group Finance Man., Bass plc 1994–95; Financial Planning Man., PepsiCo—Frito Lay 1995–98, then various finance roles with Pepsico Europe 1995–2000; Group Financial Controller, Trader Media Group (jtly owned by Guardian Media Group and Apax Partners pvt. equity group) 2001–04, Chief Financial Officer (CFO), Trader Media Group 2004–09, CFO Guardian Media Group 2009–10, Interim CEO Guardian Media Group April–July 2010, CEO July 2010–15; mem. Bd of Dirs Decoded Ltd 2014–15, The AA 2014–, Top Right Group 2015, mem. Inst. of Chartered Accountants; Gov. Benjamin Franklin House 2013–.

MILLER, Andrew, CBE, MA, PhD, FRSE; British academic; b. 15 Feb. 1936, Kelty, Fife; s. of William Hamilton Miller and Susan Anderson Miller (née Auld); m. Rosemary Singleton Hannah Fyvie 1962; one s. one d.; ed Beath High School, Univ. of Edinburgh; Asst Lecturer in Chem., Univ. of Edinburgh 1960–62; Post-Doctoral Fellow, CSIRO Div. of Protein Chem., Melbourne 1962–65; Staff Scientist, MRC Lab. of Molecular Biology, Cambridge 1965–66; Lecturer in Molecular Biophysics, Univ. of Oxford 1966–83; First Head, European Molecular Biology Lab., Grenoble Antenne, France 1975–80; Prof. of Biochemistry, Univ. of Edinburgh 1984–94, Vice-Dean of Medicine 1991–93, Vice-Provost, Medicine and Veterinary Medicine 1992–93, Vice-Prin. 1993–94, Visiting Prof. 2001–03; Prin. and Vice-Chancellor, Univ. of Stirling 1994–2001, Prof. Emer. 2001–; Interim Chief Exec. Cancer Research, UK 2001–02; mem. Science and Eng Research Council Biological Sciences Cttee 1982–85; mem. Council Inst. Laue-Langevin, France 1981–85; mem. Univ. Grants Cttee, Biological Sciences Cttee 1985–88; Dir of Research, European Synchrotron Radiation Facility, Grenoble 1986–91; Fellow,

Wolfson Coll., Oxford 1967–83, Hon. Fellow 1995–; mem. Univ. Funding Council-Biological Science Advisory Panel, Medical Advisory Panel 1989; mem. Council, Grenoble Univ. 1990–91, Royal Soc. of Edinburgh 1986 (Gen. Sec. 2001–05), Council Open Univ. 2001–05; mem. Minister of Educ.'s Action Group on Standards in Scottish Schools 1997–99, Scottish Exec. Science Strategy Group 1999–2000, UNESCO UK Science Cttee 2000–02; Adviser to Wellcome Trust on UK-French Synchrotron 1999–2000; Chair. Int. Centre for Math. Sciences, Edinburgh 2001–05; Leverhulme Emer. Fellow 2001–03; Bd mem. Food Standards Agency; Deputy Chair. Scottish Food Advisory Cttee 2003–05; Sec. and Treas., Carnegie Trust for the Univs of Scotland 2004–13; Hon. DUniv (Stirling) 2002, (Open) 2006. *Publications:* Minerals in Biology (co-ed.) 1984; 180 research papers. *Leisure interests:* reading, walking, music.

MILLER, Axel, LenD; Belgian banking executive; b. 20 Feb. 1965, Uccle; m. Catherine Duhen; one s. three d.; ed Université Libre de Bruxelles; fmr Partner, Clifford Chance (law firm) for 14 years specializing in finance, mergers and acquisitions, int. commercial law; Gen. Counsel, Dexia Group 2001–02, mem. Man. Bd 2002–08, Man. Dir and Chair. Man. Bd 2003–08, CEO Dexia SA 2006–08, Group Head, Personal Financial Services 2003–08, mem. Strategy and Appointments Cttees, mem. Man. Bd Dexia Bank 2002–08, Dexia BIL, mem. Bd of Dirs Dexia Crédit Local; Vice-Pres. Financial Security Assurance Holdings; apptd CEO D'Ieteren 2013; mem. Man. Bd Fédération des entreprises de Belgique; mem. Bd of Dirs Ethias, Crédit du Nord, LVI Holding (Carmeuse group).

MILLER, Bennett; American film director; b. 30 Dec. 1966, New York; ed New York Univ.; early experience as filmmaker's asst and as dir of fundraising videos. *Films include:* The Cruise (documentary) 1998, Capote 2005, Moneyball 2011, Foxcatcher (Cannes Film Festival Best Dir Award 2014, Gotham Independent Film Dir Award 2014) 2014. *Address:* Creative Artists Agency, 2000 Avenue of the Stars, Los Angeles, CA 90067, USA (office). *Telephone:* (424) 288-2000 (office). *Fax:* (424) 288-2900 (office). *Website:* www.caa.com (office).

MILLER, Hon. Dame Billie Antoinette; Barbadian politician and lawyer; b. 8 Jan. 1944; d. of Frederick Edward Miller; ed Queen's Coll., Barbados, King's Coll., Durham, UK; worked as lawyer and barrister 1969–76, 1987–94; mem. Int. Fed. of Women Lawyers 1975–76; elected mem. Parl. for City of Bridgetown 1976, Mininster of Health and Nat. Insurance 1976–81, of Educ. 1981–85, of Educ. and Culture 1985–86; mem. Council Univ. of the West Indies 1981–86; apptd to Senate, Leader of Opposition Business 1986–91; re-elected mem. Parl. 1991, Deputy Leader of Opposition 1993–94; Sr Minister and Minister of Foreign Affairs and Foreign Trade 1994–2008; Deputy Prime Minister- 1994–2003; Chair. Exec. Cttee Commonwealth Parl. Asscn 1991–99, NGO Planning Cttee for Int. Conf. on Population and Devt, Cairo, Egypt 1994, IDB's Advisory Council on Women in Devt, Washington, DC 1996–2002, Caribbean Tourism Org. 1997–98, Asscn of Caribbean States' Ministerial Council 2000–01; Pres. Int. Planned Parenthood Fed., Western Hemisphere Region 1991–97, African, Caribbean and Pacific States Council of Ministers 1998, 32nd Regular Session of the Gen. Ass. of OAS 2002; Pres. Bd of Dirs Interamerican Parl. Group on Population and Devt for the Caribbean and Latin America, New York; Co-ordinator of Caribbean Community (CARICOM) Ministerial Spokespersons with Responsibility for External Negotiations in Bilateral, African Caribbean and Pacific States-European Union (ACP-EU), WTO and Free Trade Area of the Americas (FTAA) Matters 2002; Vice-Chair. Commonwealth Ministerial Action Group 2000–02, 6th WTO Ministerial Conf. 2005; currently Vice-Pres. Barbados Asscn of Retired Persons; mem. Bd of Dirs Women Deliver 2010–; mem. Int. Planned Parenthood Fed. Cen. Council, Planned Parenthood Fed. of America Inc., UN Population Fund's Advisory Panel for Activities Concerning Women, Inter-American Dialogue; Hon. Fellow, Honors Coll., Florida International Univ. 2001; Grand Officer, Nat. Order of Benin 2000, Nat. Order of Juan Mora Fernandez (Costa Rica) 2001, Dame of St Andrew 2003, Order Bernardo O'Higgins (Chile) 2006 Dr hc (Univ. of the West Indies) 2015; Queen's Silver Jubilee Medal 1977, Barbados Centennial Award 2000, Grantley Adams Award, Barbados Labour Party 2001, Woman of Great Esteem Award, Kingdom Ministries, USA 2002, Dame Elsie Payne Award of Excellence, Queen's Coll. Asscn 2002, The Dame Billie Miller Lecture Series on Women in Govt in association with Medgar Evers Coll., CUNY 2004, Lifetime Achievement Award, Caribbean Tourism Org. 2006, United Nations Population Award 2008. *Publications:* numerous papers and articles on population and women's issues. *Leisure interests:* reading, interior design, Ikebana. *Address:* Barbados Association of Retired Persons, Collymore Rock, St Michael, BB14004, Barbados. *Website:* www.barpbb.com.

MILLER, Bode; American professional skier (retd); b. (Samuel Bode Miller), 12 Oct. 1977, Easton, New Hampshire; s. of Jo Miller and Woody Miller; m. Morgan Beck 2012; four c. (one deceased); ed Carrabassett Valley Acad., Me; World Cup debut: Park City, UT, USA 1996; mem. US Nat. Team 1996–; Gold Medals, Combined and Giant Slalom events, World Championships, St Moritz, Switzerland 2003, Silver Medal, Super-G; Silver Medals, Combined and Giant Slalom events, Winter Olympic Games, Salt Lake City, USA 2002, Bronze Medal, Winter Olympic Games, Vancouver, Canada 2010, Bronze Medal, Winter Olympic Games, Sochi, Russia 2014; 12 World Cup wins (six Giant Slalom, four Slalom, two Combined); won Alpine Skiing World Cup 2005, 2008; won Super G World Cup 2007; left US Ski Team 2007; f. Team America (ind. race team) 2007–09, rejoined US Ski Team 2009; f. SkiSpace.com (social networking and information site for skiers and snowboarders). *Leisure interest:* reggae and rap music, horse racing. *Address:* c/o Lowell Taub, CAA Sports, 162 Fifth Avenue, 8th Floor, New York, NY 10010, USA. *Website:* alpine.usskiteam.com/athletes/bode-miller.

MILLER, Bruce, BA (Hons), LLB; Australian diplomatist; b. 1961, Sydney, NSW; ed Univ. of Sydney; joined Dept of Foreign Affairs and Trade 1986, has had several positions including three years with Legal Br., Third Sec., Embassy in Tehran 1987–88, First Sec., later Counsellor, Embassy in Tokyo 1992–96; seconded to Dept of the Prime Minister and Cabinet 1997–98; Asst Sec., Strategic Policy and Intelligence, Dept of Foreign Affairs and Trade 2000–02, Asst Sec., NE Asia Br. 2003–04, Minister (Political), Embassy in Tokyo 2004–09, Deputy Dir-Gen., Office of Nat. Assessments 2009–11, Acting Dir-Gen. 2017; Amb. to Japan 2011–17. *Leisure interests:* art, literature, hiking.

MILLER, David, LLB, MA; Canadian/American lawyer and politician; *President and CEO, WWF-Canada;* b. USA; m. Jill Arthur; two c.; ed Faculty of Law, Univ. of Toronto, Harvard Univ., USA; trained in employment and immigration law; fmr Partner, Aird & Berlis law firm, Toronto, Counsel –2013; cand. for New Democratic Party (NDP) in fed. elections, Parkdale-High Park constituency 1993, by-election in York S-Weston 1996; elected to Municipality of Metropolitan Toronto Council 1994–97, City of Toronto Council 1997–2003; Mayor of Toronto 2003–10; Pres. and CEO World Wildlife Fund-Canada 2013–; Future of Cities Global Fellow, New York Univ. Poly 2010–13; Adjunct Prof., York Univ. 2014–; mem. Bd of Govs, Centennial Coll.; mem. Toronto Transit Comm.; mem. Law Soc. of Upper Canada; mem. of numerous cttees, bds and orgs; Founder Mrs Joan Miller Scholarship Fund. *Address:* WWF-Canada, 245 Eglinton Avenue, East Suite 410, Toronto, ON M4P 3J1, Canada (office). *Telephone:* (416) 489-8800 (office). *Fax:* (416) 489-0819 (office). *E-mail:* drmiller@wwfcanada.org (office). *Website:* www.wwf.ca (office).

MILLER, David A. B., BSc, PhD, FRS, FRSE; British physicist, academic and engineer; *W.M. Keck Foundation Professor of Electrical Engineering, Stanford University;* b. 19 Feb. 1954, Hamilton, South Lanarkshire, Scotland; ed Heriot-Watt Univ., St Andrews Univ.; Research Assoc., Heriot-Watt Univ. Dept of Physics 1979–80, Lecturer 1980–81; mem. Tech. Staff, AT&T Bell Laboratories, Holmdel, NJ, USA 1981–87, Head Photonics Switching Device Research Dept 1987–92, Head of Advanced Photonics Research Dept 1992–96; Prof. of Electrical Eng, Stanford Univ. 1996, W.M. Keck Foundation Prof. of Electrical Eng 1997–, Prof. by Courtesy of Applied Physics 1997–, Dir Stanford Univ. Solid State and Photonics Lab. 1997–2011, Dir E.L. Ginzton Lab. 1997–2006, Co-Dir Stanford Photonics Research Center; Pres. IEEE Lasers and Electro-Optics Soc. 1995–96; Vice-Pres. Int. Comm. for Optics 1999–2002; Dir Optical Soc. of America 2000–03; mem. Editorial Bd Semiconductor Science and Technology 1987–90, Optical and Quantum Electronics 1988–2017, Applied Physics Reviews 1991–97; mem. NAS 2008, Nat. Acad. of Eng 2010; Fellow, Optical Soc. of America 1988, American Physical Soc. 1988, IEEE 1995; Dr hc (Vrije Universiteit) 1997; Hon. DEng (Heriot-Watt) 2003; Adolph Lomb Medal, Optical Soc. of America 1986, R.W. Wood Prize, Optical Soc. of America 1986, Int. Comm. for Optics Prize 1991, IEEE Third Millennium Medal 2000. *Achievement:* holder of 74 patents. *Publications:* Quantum Mechanics for Scientists and Engineers 2008; over 270 papers on optics and optoelectronics. *Address:* Room 203, E.L. Ginzton Laboratory, Stanford University, Spilker Building, 348 Via Pueblo Mall, Stanford, CA 94305-4088, USA (office). *Telephone:* (650) 723-0111 (office). *E-mail:* dabm@ee.stanford.edu (office). *Website:* profiles.stanford.edu/david-miller (office); www-ee.stanford.edu/~dabm (office).

MILLER, David W., MS; American professor of aeronautics and space scientist; *Vice President and Chief Technology Officer, Aerospace Corporation;* ed Massachusetts Inst. of Tech.; Research Assoc., MIT 1988–91, Prin. Research Scientist 1991–97, Asst Prof. 1997–2000, Assoc. Prof. 2000–06, Jerome C. Hunsaker Prof. of Aeronautics and Astronautics, Dir Space Systems Lab. –2014; held various positions on NASA projects, including Prin. Investigator for Regolith X-ray Imaging Spectrometer and for 2016 OSIRIS-REx asteroid sample return mission, Prin. Investigator for Synchronized Position, Hold, Engage and Reorient Experimental Satellites (SPHERES) project on Int. Space Station, apptd Chief Technologist, NASA 2014; Vice Pres. and Chief Tech. Officer (CTO), Aerospace Corporation 2019–; fmr Vice-Chair. Air Force Scientific Advisory Bd; Sr Mem. American Inst. of Aeronautics and Astronautics; mem. American Soc. of Mechanical Engineers, American Astronautical Soc., Int. Soc. for Optical Eng. *Address:* 2310 E. El Segundo Blvd, El Segundo, CA 90245, USA (office). *Telephone:* (310) 336-5000 (office). *Website:* aerospace.org (office).

MILLER, Edward D., Jr, AB, MD, FRCP, FRCA; American anaesthesiologist, academic and fmr university administrator; b. 1 Feb. 1943, Rochester, NY; m. Lynne R. Miller; ed Ohio Wesleyan Univ., Univ. of Rochester School of Medicine and Dentistry; surgical intern, Univ. Hosp., Boston 1968–69; Chief Resident in Anaesthesiology, Peter Bent Brigham Hosp., Boston 1969–71; Research Fellow in Physiology, Harvard Medical School 1971–73; Dir of Anaesthesia Research, Brooke Army Medical Center, Fort Sam Houston, Tex. 1973–75; Asst Prof. of Anaesthesiology, Univ. of Virginia 1975–79, Assoc. Prof. 1979–82, Prof. of Anaesthesiology 1982–83, Prof. of Anaesthesiology and Surgery 1983–86; E.M. Papper Prof. of Anaesthesiology and Chair., Dept of Anaesthesiology, Coll. of Physicians and Surgeons, Columbia Univ. 1986–94; Mark C. Rogers Prof. and Dir Dept of Anaesthesiology and Critical Care Medicine, Johns Hopkins Univ. 1994–96, Interim Dean 1996–97, CEO 1997–2012, Vice-Pres. School of Medicine 1997–2012, Dean of Medical Faculty, Johns Hopkins Univ. School of Medicine 1997–2012, est. Center for Innovation in Quality Patient Care; mem. Asscn of Univ. Anaesthesiologists (Pres. 1990–92); Ed. Anesthesia and Analgesia 1982–92; fmr Chair. Food and Drug Asscn Advisory Cttee on Anaesthesia and Life Support Drugs; fmr Ed. Critical Care Medicine; Bd mem. Greater Baltimore Cttee, Mercantile Safe Deposit and Trust Fund, PNC Mutual Funds, CareFusion; Trustee Emer., Int. Anesthesia Research Soc. (mem. 1988–98); mem. Inst. of Medicine, NAS, Maryland's Health Care Access and Cost Comm.; Career Research Devt Award, NIH. *Publications:* book chapters and more than 150 scientific papers in professional journals. *Address:* International Anesthesia Research Society, 44 Montgomery Street, Suite 1605, San Francisco, CA 94104-4703, USA (office). *Telephone:* (415) 296-6900 (office). *Fax:* (415) 296-6901 (office). *E-mail:* info@iars.org (office). *Website:* www.iars.org (office).

MILLER, George 'Kennedy', AO, MB, BS; Australian film director, producer, writer and physician; b. 3 March 1945, Chinchilla, Queensland; s. of James Miller and Angela Miller (née Balson); m. Sandy Gore 1985; one d.; ed Sydney Boys' High School, Univ. of New South Wales Medical School; Resident Medical Officer, St Vincent's Hosp., Sydney 1971–72; f. Kennedy Miller film co. with the late Byron Kennedy 1977, Chair. 1977–; Pres. Jury Avoriaz Film Festival 1984; mem. Jury Cannes Film Festival 1988; Chair. Byron Kennedy Memorial Trust 1984–; mem. Bd Dirs Museum of Contemporary Art, Sydney 1987–; Hon. mem. Visual Effects Soc. (first non-US filmmaker) 2010; Chevalier des Arts et des Lettres 2009; Hon. LLD (Univ. of New South Wales) 1999; Hon. MA (Australian Film Television and Radio School) 2007; Dr hc (Griffith Univ.) 2008; Best Dir, Australian Film Inst. 1982, Best Dir TV Drama, Penguin Awards 1983, Grand Prix Avoriaz 1983, Best Foreign Film, LA Film Critics 1983, The Queensland – United States Personal Achievement Award, Queensland Expatriate Awards 2007, FIAPF Award for

Outstanding Achievement in Film, Asia Pacific Screen Awards 2007, AFI Global Achievement Award 2007, and numerous other prizes and awards. *Films include:* dir: Violence In the Cinema, Part 1 (also writer) 1971, Mad Max (also writer) 1979, Mad Max 2 (also writer) 1981, Twilight Zone: The Movie (segment 4) 1983, Mad Max Beyond Thunderdome (also writer and producer) 1985, The Witches of Eastwick 1987, Lorenzo's Oil (also producer and writer) 1992, 40,000 Years of Dreaming (also producer and writer) 1997, Babe: Pig in the City (also producer and writer) 1998, Happy Feet (also producer and writer) (BAFTA Award for Best Animated Film 2007) 2006, Happy Feet Two 2011, Mad Max: Fury Road (also writer and producer) 2015; producer: The Chain Reaction (assoc. producer) 1980, The Year My Voice Broke 1987, Dead Calm 1989, Flirting 1991, Video Fool for Love 1995, Babe (also writer) (Golden Globe Award for Best Picture 1996) 1995, 40,000 Years of Dreaming 1997, Babe: Pig in the City 1998, Happy Feet (Acad. Award for Best Animated Feature Film 2007) 2006, Happy Feet Two 2011, Forgotten Wars, Forgotten Victims (video documentary short) (exec. producer) 2012, Mad Max: Fury Road 2015. *Television includes:* Ryan (series) (dir) 1973, Bellamy (series; episode 1.02 The Carver Gang) (dir) 1981, The Dismissal (mini-series) (writer, dir and exec. producer) 1983, The Last Bastion (mini-series) (co-dir) 1984, Cowra Breakout (mini-series) 1984, Bodyline: It's Not Just Cricket (mini-series) 1984, The Riddle of the Stinson 1987, Vietnam (mini-series) 1987, The Dirtwater Dynasty (mini-series) 1988, The Clean Machine 1988, Fragments of War: The Story of Damien Parer 1988, Bangkok Hilton (mini-series) 1989, 40,000 Years of Dreaming producer) (film documentary) 1997, Mad Max Motion Comic (mini-series) (characters, uncredited) 2013. *Leisure interests:* art, music, sport. *Address:* 30 Orwell Street, King's Cross, NSW 2011, Australia. *Telephone:* (2) 357-2322.

MILLER, George H., BS, MS, PhD; American physicist and academic; *Director Emeritus, Lawrence Livermore National Laboratory;* ed Coll. of William and Mary; Physicist, Lawrence Livermore Nat. Lab., Univ. of California 1972–80, A-Div. Leader and Program Leader, Thermonuclear Design and Computational Physics Devt 1980–85, Assoc. Dir for Nuclear Design 1985–89, apptd Assoc. Dir for Defense and Nuclear Techs 1990, Assoc. Dir for Nat. Security 1996–2000, Assoc. Dir for Nat. Ignition Facility programs 2000–05, Interim Dir 2005–06, Lab. Dir and Pres. Lawrence Livermore Nat. Security LLC 2007–11, now Dir Emer. Lawrence Livermore Nat. Lab.; Special Scientific Adviser on Weapon Activities, US Dept of Energy, Washington, DC 1989–90; mem. Sr Man. Group, Univ. of California; mem. American Physical Soc., Strategic Advisory Group, United States Strategic Command (also Chair. Science and Tech. Panel); Fellowship Awards from NSF, Gulf Gen. Atomics. *Address:* Lawrence Livermore National Laboratory, 7000 East Avenue, Livermore, CA 94550, USA (office). *Telephone:* (925) 422-1100 (office). *Fax:* (925) 422-1370 (office). *Website:* www.llnsllc.com (office).

MILLER, Heidi G., PhD; American investment banker; b. 1953; m. Brian Miller; two c.; ed Princeton Univ., Yale Univ.; began career at Chemical Bank in 1979, Man. Dir and Group Head, Emerging Markets 1987–92; Vice-Pres. and Asst to Pres. Travelers Group Inc. 1992–98, later Chief Risk Officer of its Salomon Smith Barney unit, Chief Financial Officer Travelers Group Inc. 1995–98; Chief Financial Officer Citigroup Inc. 1998–2000; Sr Exec. Vice-Pres. Strategic Planning and Admin and mem. Bd of Dirs Priceline.com 2000–01; Vice-Chair. Marsh & McLennan Co. Inc. 2001–; Exec. Vice-Pres., Chief Financial Officer and mem. Bd Dirs Bank One, Chicago 2002–04, Exec. Vice-Pres. and CEO Treasury and Security Services, JPMorgan Chase & Co. (following merger with Bank One) 2004–10, Pres. of International 2010–12; mem. Bd of Dirs General Mills Inc., Mead Corpn, Merck & Co. Inc., Local Initiatives Support Corpn 2004–, Progressive Corpn 2011–, First Data Corpn 2014–; Trustee, Princeton Univ.; topped Crain's list of the 50 Most Powerful Women in New York 2008.

MILLER, Jacques Francis, AC, BA, MD, PhD, DSc, FAA, FRS; Australian (b. French) medical research scientist and academic; *Professor Emeritus, University of Melbourne and Walter and Eliza Hall Institute of Medical Research;* b. (Jacques Francis Meunier), 2 April 1931, Nice, France; s. of Maurice Miller and Fernande Debarnot; m. Margaret D. Houen 1956 (died 2012); ed Univs of Sydney and Melbourne, Univ. of London, UK; received Australian citizenship 1955; Jr Resident Medical Officer, Royal Prince Alfred Hosp., Sydney 1956; pathological research, Univ. of Sydney 1957; cancer research, Chester Beatty Research Inst., London 1958–65; Head, Experimental Pathology and Thymus Biology Unit, Walter and Eliza Hall Inst. (WEHI), Melbourne 1966–, Prof. and Chair of Experimental Immunology, Univ. of Melbourne and WEHI 1990–97, Prof. Emer. 1997–; various other professional appointments; Foreign Assoc., NAS; Laureate Prof.; numerous awards and honours, including Esther Langer-Bertha Teplitz Memorial Prize 1965, Paul Ehrlich-Ludwig Darmstaedter Prize 1974, Inaugural Sandoz Prize for Immunology 1990, Florey-Faulding Medal and Prize 2000, Copley Medal, Royal Soc. 2001, Prime Minister's Prize for Science 2003, Japan Prize for Medicine and Medicinal Science 2018. *Achievements:* discovered the immunological function of the thymus gland and identified the two major lymphocyte cells, T and B cells. *Publications:* more than 400 papers in scientific journals, mostly on immunology and cancer research. *Leisure interests:* art, photography, music, literature. *Address:* Walter and Eliza Hall Institute of Medical Research, 1G Royal Parade, Parkville, Vic. 3050 (office); 5 Charteris Drive, East Ivanhoe, Vic. 3079, Australia (home). *Telephone:* (3) 9345-2555 (office); (3) 9499-3481 (home). *Fax:* (3) 9347-0852 (office). *E-mail:* miller@wehi.edu.au (office). *Website:* www.wehi.edu.au/about-history/notable-scientists/professor-jacques-miller (office).

MILLER, James Clifford, III, BBA, PhD; American business executive, academic and government official; *Senior Advisor, Husch Blackwell, LLP;* b. 25 June 1942, Atlanta, Ga; s. of James Clifford Miller, Jr and Annie Miller (née Moseley); m. Demaris Humphries 1961; one s. two d.; ed Univs of Georgia and Virginia; Asst Prof., Georgia State Univ., Atlanta 1968–69; Economist, US Dept of Transport 1969–72; Assoc. Prof. of Econs, Texas A&M Univ. 1972–74; Economist, US Council of Econ. Advisers, Washington, DC 1974–75; Asst Dir US Council of Wage and Price Stability 1975–77; Resident Scholar, American Enterprise Inst. 1977–81; Admin., Office of Information and Regulatory Affairs, Office of Man. and Budget and Exec. Dir Presidential Task Force on Regulatory Relief 1981; Chair. Fed. Trade Comm., Washington, DC 1981–85; Dir Office of Man. and Budget 1985–89; Adjunct Scholar, Center for Study of Public Choice, George Mason Univ. 1988–, Chair. Citizens for a Sound Econ. 1988–2003; Founder and Chair. The Cap Analysis Group (div. of int. law firm Howrey LLP) 2003–06; mem. Bd of Govs US Postal Service 2003–11, Chair. 2005–08; currently Sr Advisor to int. law firm Husch Blackwell LLP; chaired The Miller Comm. (ind. comm. apptd to address the fiscal and econ. health of the Cayman Islands) 2009; Thomas Jefferson Fellow 1965–66; DuPont Fellow 1966–67, Ford Foundation Fellow 1967–68; Distinguished Fellow, Center for Study of Public Choice, George Mason Univ. 1988–, Mercatus Center, George Mason Univ. 1997–; Sr Fellow (by courtesy), Hoover Inst., Stanford Univ. 1988–; mem. Bd of Dirs Washington Mutual Investors Fund 1992–, Independence Air 1995–99, Tax-Exempt Fund of Maryland 2000–, Tax-Exempt Fund of Virginia 2000–, Americans for Prosperity 2004–, Clean Energy Fuels Corpn 2006–; Chair. Exec. Cttee, Int. Tax and Investment Center; mem. American Econ. Asscn, Federalist Soc., Public Choice Soc., Southern Econ. Asscn. *Publications:* Why the Draft? The Case for a Volunteer Army 1968, Economic Regulation of Domestic Air Transport; Theory and Policy 1974, Perspectives on Federal Transportation Policy 1975, Benefit – Cost Analyses of Social Regulation 1979, Reforming Regulation 1980, The Federal Trade Commission: The Political Economy of Regulation 1987, The Economist as Reformer 1989, Fix the U.S. Budget! 1994, Monopoly Politics 1999; more than 100 articles in professional journals. *Leisure interests:* politics, econs. *Address:* Husch Blackwell LLP, 750 17th Street NW, Suite 1000, Washington, DC 20006, USA (office). *Telephone:* (202) 378-2302 (office). *Fax:* (202) 378-2319 (office). *E-mail:* jim.miller@huschblackwell.com (office). *Website:* www.huschblackwell.com (office).

MILLER, Jerzy; Polish politician and civil servant; b. 7 June 1952, Kraków; m.; ed Faculty of Electrical Eng, Electronics and Automatics, AGH Univ. of Science and Tech., Kraków; began career in public admin 1990, Dir Org. and Supervision Div. 1990–91, Dir Małopolskie Voivodship Office, Kraków 1991–92; Vice-Gov. fmr Krakow Voivodship 1993–98; Under-Sec. of State 1998–2000, Sec. of State, Ministry of Finance 2000–01; Govt Plenipotentiary for Decentralization of Public Finance under Prime Minister Jerzy Buzek 2001; Adviser to Pres. Nat. Bank of Poland 2001–03; Pres. Agency for Restructuring and Modernization of Agric. 2003; Dir Dept for Social Communication, Nat. Bank of Poland 2003–04, mem. Man. Bd 2004; Pres. Nat. Health Fund 2004–06; Deputy Mayor of Warsaw 2006–07; Gov. Małopolskie Voivodship 2007–09, 2011–15; Minister of Internal Affairs and Admin 2009–11; Hon. mem. of Nat. Order of Merit, Malta 2009; Grand Officer of Order of Merit 2008, Kt of Royal Norwegian Royal Order of Merit 2012, Officer of Order of St Charles, Monaco 2012; Medal for Local Self-Government 2015.

MILLER, Jonathan (Jon); American media executive; *Partner, Advancit Capital, LLC;* b. 1957; ed Harvard Univ.; early career as Vice-Pres. of Programming and NBA Entertainment with Nat. Basketball Asscn; CEO and Man. Dir Nickelodeon UK, then Man. Dir Int.; Pres. and CEO USA Broadcasting 1997–1999; Pres. and CEO USA Electronic Commerce Solutions 1999–2000; Pres. and CEO USA Information and Services (USAIS) 2000–02; Chair. and CEO America Online Inc. (later AOL LLC) 2002–06; Founding Partner, Velocity Investment Group/Velocity Interactive Group 2007–09; Chief Digital Officer, News Corpn 2009–12; Partner, Advancit Capital, LLC 2013–; mem. Bd of Dirs TripAdvisor Inc.,YP Intellectual Property, LLC 2012–, Shutterstock, Inc 2012–, Houghton Mifflin Harcourt Company 2013–, RTL Group SA 2014–, True[X] Media, Inc. 2014–, j2 Global, Inc 2015–; Dir/Trustee American Film Inst., BBC Global News, International Emmy Asscn, Independent Film Project, Paley Center for Media; Advisor, MESA Ventures; Inaugural Pioneer Prize, Producers Guild of America 2005, Inaugural Vanguard Award, International Emmy Asscn 2006, Power Player of the Year, Hollywood Reporter 2009, Interactive Pioneer Award, Monaco Media Festival 2010. *Address:* Advancit Capital, LLC, 846 University Avenue, Norwood, MA 02062, USA (office). *E-mail:* info@advancitcap.com (office). *Website:* www.advancitcapital.com (office).

MILLER, Sir Jonathan Wolfe, Kt, CBE, MB, BCh, FRCP; British stage director, film director, physician and writer; b. 21 July 1934, London; s. of Emanuel Miller; m. Helen Rachel Collet 1956; two s. one d.; ed St Paul's School, St John's Coll., Cambridge and Univ. Coll. Hosp. Medical School, London; co-author of and appeared in Beyond the Fringe 1961–64; Dir John Osborne's Under Plain Cover, Royal Court Theatre 1962, Robert Lowell's The Old Glory, New York 1964 and Prometheus Bound, Yale Drama School 1967; Dir at Nottingham Playhouse 1968–69; Dir Oxford and Cambridge Shakespeare Co. production of Twelfth Night on tour in USA 1969; Research Fellow in the History of Medicine, Univ. Coll., London 1970–73; Assoc. Dir Nat. Theatre 1973–75; mem. Arts Council 1975–76; Visiting Prof. in Drama, Westfield Coll., Univ. of London 1977–; Exec. Producer Shakespeare TV series 1979–81; Artistic Dir Old Vic 1988–90; Research Fellow in Neuropsychology, Univ. of Sussex; Pres. Rationalist Soc. 2006–; Fellow, Univ. Coll. London 1981–, Royal Coll. of Physicians; mem. American Acad. of Arts and Sciences; Hon. Fellow, St John's Coll. Cambridge, Royal Coll. of Physicians (Edin.) 1998; Hon. Assoc., British Humanist Asscn, Nat. Secular Soc.; Dr hc (Open Univ.) 1983, Hon. DLitt (Leicester) 1981, (Kent) 1985, (Leeds) 1996, (Cambridge) 1996, (London) 2015; Royal Television Soc. Silver Medal 1981, Royal Soc. of Arts Albert Medal 1992. *Productions include:* for Nat. Theatre, London: The Merchant of Venice 1970, Danton's Death 1971, The School for Scandal 1972, The Marriage of Figaro 1974; other productions The Tempest, London 1970, Prometheus Bound, London 1971, The Taming of the Shrew, Chichester 1972, The Seagull, Chichester 1973, The Malcontent, Nottingham 1973, Arden Must Die (opera) 1973, The Family in Love, Greenwich Season 1974, The Importance of Being Earnest 1975, The Cunning Little Vixen (opera) 1975, All's Well That Ends Well, Measure For Measure, Greenwich Season 1975, Three Sisters 1977, The Marriage of Figaro (ENO) 1978, Arabella (opera) 1980, Falstaff (opera) 1980, 1981, Otello (opera) 1982, Rigoletto (opera) 1982, 1984, Fidelio (opera) 1982, 1983, Don Giovanni (opera) 1985, The Mikado (opera) 1986, Tosca (opera) 1986, Long Day's Journey into Night 1986, Taming of the Shrew 1987, The Tempest 1988, Turn of the Screw 1989, King Lear 1989, The Liar 1989, La Fanciulla del West (opera) 1991, Marriage of Figaro (opera), Manon Lescaut (opera), Die Gezeichneten (opera) 1992, Maria Stuarda (opera), Capriccio (opera), Fedora (opera), Bach's St Matthew Passion 1993, Der Rosenkavalier (opera), Anna Bolena (opera), Falstaff (opera), L'Incoronazione di Poppea (opera), La Bohème (opera) 1994, Così fan tutte (opera) 1995, Carmen (opera) 1995, Pelléas et Mélisande (opera) 1995, She Stoops to Conquer, London 1995, A Midsummer Night's Dream, London 1996, The Rake's Progress, New York 1997, Ariadne auf Naxos, Maggio Musicale, Florence 1997, Falstaff, Berlin State Opera 1998, The Beggar's Opera 1999, Tamerlano, Sadler's Wells, Paris and Halle 2001, Jenůfa, Glimmerglass Opera 2006, The Cherry

Orchard, Sheffield Crucible 2007, La Bohème, ENO, London 2009, La Traviata, Vancouver 2011, Cosi fan tutter, Washington 2012. *Films include:* Alice in Wonderland 1966, Take a Girl Like You 1969 and several films for television including Whistle and I'll Come to You 1967, The Body in Question (series) 1978, States of Mind (series) 1983, The Emperor 1987, Jonathan Miller's Opera Works (series) 1997, Brief History of Disbelief (series) 2005. *Publications include:* McLuhan 1971, Freud: The Man, his World, his Influence (ed.) 1972, The Body in Question 1978, Subsequent Performances 1986, The Don Giovanni Book: Myths of Seduction and Betrayal (ed.) 1990, On Reflection 1998, Nowhere in Particular 2001. *Leisure interest:* deep sleep.

MILLER, Leslie O.; Bahamian politician; mem. Parl. for Tall Pines 1987–2017; Chair. Bahamas Electricity Corpn 1989–91, 2012–15; fmr Minister of Trade and Industry; mem Progressive Liberal Party (PLP).

MILLER, Leszek Cezary, MPolSci; Polish politician; *Chairman, Sojusz Lewicy Demokratycznej (SLD—Democratic Left Alliance);* b. 3 July 1946, Żyrardów; m. Aleksandra Borowiec; one s.; ed Higher School of Social Sciences; electrician Enterprise of Linen Industry, Żyrardów 1963–70; mem. Polska Zjednoczona Partia Robotnicza (PZPR—Polish United Workers' Party) 1966–90, Staff mem. Cen. Cttee 1977–86; First Sec. Skierniewice Voivodeship Cttee 1986–89, mem. Cen. Cttee 1989–90, mem. Politburo Cen. Cttee 1989–90; participant in Round Table Talks 1989; Deputy to Sejm (Parl.) 1991–2005 (Chair. Left Alliance Caucus 1997–2001); Minister of Labour and Social Policy 1993–96, of Interior and Admin. Jan.–Oct. 1997; Minister, Head Council of Ministers Office 1996; mem. and Co-founder Social Democracy of Repub. of Poland 1990–99 (Gen. Sec. 1990–93, Vice-Chair. 1993–97, Chair. 1997–99); Chair. Sojusz Lewicy Demokratycznej (SLD—Democratic Left Alliance) 1999–2007, 2011–; Chair. Polish Left 2007–10; Prime Minister of Poland 2001–04 (resgnd); Kt's Cross of Polonia Restituta Order 1984, Golden Cross of Merit 1979, Chevalier of the Order of the Smile; Goodwill Amb., Polish Cttee of UNICEF 2000. *Leisure interests:* angling, literature. *Address:* Sojusz Lewicy Demokratycznej (Democratic Left Alliance), 00-419 Warsaw, ul. Rozbrat 44A, Poland (office). *Telephone:* (22) 6210341 (office). *Fax:* (22) 6216069 (office). *E-mail:* rk@sld.org.pl (office). *Website:* www.sld.org.pl (office).

MILLER, Rt Hon. Maria Frances Lewis, PC, BSc; British politician and marketing consultant; b. 24 March 1964, Wolverhampton, West Midlands, England; m. Iain Miller; two s. one d.; ed Brynteg Comprehensive School, Bridgend, London School of Econs; Advertising Exec., Greys Advertising Ltd 1985–90, Dir 1994–99; Marketing Man. with Texaco 1990–94; Dir, Rowland Group 1999–2003; joined Conservative Party 1983; contested Wolverhampton North East constituency in Gen. Election 2001; MP for Basingstoke 2005–10, for Basingstoke (revised boundary) 2010–, mem. Trade and Industry Cttee 2005–06, Children, Schools and Families Select Cttee 2007; Shadow Minister for Educ. 2005–06, for Family Welfare, including Child Support Agency 2006–07, for Families 2007–10; Parl. Under-Sec. of State (Minister for Disabled People), Dept for Work and Pensions 2010–12; Sec. of State for Culture, Media and Sport 2012–14, also Minister for Women and Equalities 2012–14; Pres. Wolverhampton North East Conservative Asscn 2001–07; Chair. Wimbledon Conservative Asscn 2002–03, Women and Equalities Select Cttee 2015–; Conservative. *Address:* House of Commons, Westminster, London, SW1A 0AA, England (office). *Telephone:* (20) 7219-5749 (office). *Fax:* (20) 7219-5722 (office). *E-mail:* maria.miller.mp@ parliament.uk (office). *Website:* www.parliament.uk/biographies/commons/mrs -maria-miller/1480 (office); www.maria4basingstoke.co.uk (office).

MILLER, Robert; Canadian electronics industry executive; m. Margaret Antonier 1967 (divorced 2006); two s.; co-f. Future Electronics (electronics distributor) 1968. *Address:* Future Electronics, 237 Hymus Boulevard, Pointe-Claire, PQ H9R 5C7, Canada (office). *Telephone:* (514) 694-7710 (office). *Fax:* (514) 695-3707 (office). *Website:* www.futureelectronics.com (office).

MILLER, Robert (Bob) G., BA, MBA; American business executive; *Chairman and CEO, Albertsons, LLC;* ed Univ. of Missouri, Kansas City, Iowa State Univ.; joined Albertsons Inc. 1961, Sr Vice-Pres. and Regional Man. 1985–89, Exec. Vice-Pres. Retail Operations 1989–91, CEO Albertsons, LLC 2006–, Chair. 2015–; CEO Fred Meyer Stores Inc. 1991–99; Vice-Chair. and COO The Kroger Co. (following acquisition of Fred Meyer Stores Inc. by Kroger) 1999; Chair. and CEO Rite Aid Corpn 1999–2003, Chair. 1999–2007, Dir and mem. Exec. Cttee 1999–2011; Chair. Wild Oats Markets, Inc. 2004–06; mem. Bd of Dirs, Harrah's Entertainment Inc. 1999–2008, Caesars Entertainment Corpn 1999–2008, Nordstrom, Inc. 2005–, The Jim Pattison Group, Inc., Food Marketing Inst. 2008–, Safeway, Inc. 2015–. *Address:* Albertsons LLC, 250 East Parkcenter Blvd, Boise, ID 83706, USA (office). *Telephone:* (208) 395-6200 (office). *E-mail:* info@albertsons.com (office). *Website:* www.albertsons.com (office).

MILLER, Robert Joseph (Bob), BA, JD; American lawyer and politician; *Principal, Robert J. Miller Consulting;* b. 30 March 1945, Evanston, Ill.; s. of Ross Wendell Miller and Coletta Jane Doyle; m. Sandra Ann Searles; one s. two d.; ed Santa Clara Univ., Loyola Law School; First Legal Advisor, Las Vegas Metropolitan Police Dept 1973–75; JP 1975–78; Deputy Dist Attorney, Clark Co., Las Vegas 1971–73, Dist Attorney 1979–86; Lt Gov. of Nevada 1987–89, 1989–90, Gov. 1989–99; Chair. Nev. Comm. on Econ. Devt, Nev. Comm. on Tourism 1987–89; mem. Nat. Govs Asscn (Vice-Chair. Exec. Cttee 1995–96, Chair. 1996–97, fmr Chair. Cttee on Justice and Public Safety, Chair. Legal Affairs Cttee 1992–94, Lead Gov. on Transport 1992–); Sr Partner, Jones Vargas, Las Vegas 1999–2005; Prin., Dutko Worldwide (now Grayling) 2005–15, Sr Adviser 2009–; currently Prin., Robert J. Miller Consulting; Co-Chair. of Hillary Clinton's Govs Council 2008; mem. Bd of Dirs Wynn Resorts 2002–, Int. Game Technology 1999–2015; Prin., Robert J. Miller Consulting, Nat. Center for Missing and Exploited Children, K12 Inc.; Co-Chair. Russian Heritage Highway Foundation; mem. Int. Asscn of Gaming Advisers, Pres. 2009; Democrat; Hon. Consul Officer of Repub. of Bulgaria; Dr hc (Santa Clara Univ.); Distinguished Nevadan, Nev. Univ. Regents. *Publication:* Son of a Gambling Man (autobiog.) 2013. *Leisure interests:* basketball, golf. *Address:* Robert J. Miller Consulting, 900 South Pavilion Center Drive, Las Vegas, NV 89144, USA (office). *Telephone:* (702) 240-0831 (office). *Fax:* (702) 240-0331 (office). *E-mail:* contact@rjmillerconsulting.com (office). *Website:* www .rjmillerconsulting.com (home).

MILLER, Stephen; American government official; *Senior Advisor to the President;* b. Santa Monica, Calif.; ed Duke Univ.; began career as Press Sec. for Republican mems of Congress Michele Bachmann and John Shadegg; worked for Alabama Senator Jeff Sessions from 2009, becoming Communications Dir; Sr Policy Advisor to Donald Trump's presidential campaign 2016, becoming Head of econ. policy team Aug. 2016, Nat. Policy Dir, Trump transition team 2016–17; Sr Advisor to the Pres. Jan. 2017–; regular speechwriter for Pres. Donald Trump (including inauguration speech). *Address:* The White House, 1600 Pennsylvania Avenue, NW, Washington, DC 20500, USA (office). *Telephone:* (202) 456-1414 (office). *Fax:* (202) 456-2461 (office). *E-mail:* vice_president@whitehouse.gov (office). *Website:* www.whitehouse.gov (office).

MILLER, (Robert) Steven (Steve), Jr, LLB, MBA; American business executive; b. 4 Nov. 1941, Portland, Ore.; s. of Robert Stevens Miller and Barbara Weston Miller; m. 1st Margaret (Maggie) Miller 1966 (died 2006); three s.; m. 2nd Jill Jablonski 2007; ed Harvard Law School, Stanford Grad. School of Business; mem. financial staff, Ford Motor Co. 1968–71, Investment Man., Ford Motor de Mexico 1971–73, Dir of Finance, Ford Asia Pacific, Melbourne, Australia 1974–77, Vice-Pres. (Finance), Ford Motor de Venezuela, Caracas 1977–79; Vice-Pres.—Treas. Chrysler Corpn, Detroit 1980–81, Exec. Vice-Pres. (Finance) 1981–88, Exec. Vice-Pres. 1988–92; Sr Partner, James D. Wolfensohn Inc. 1992–93; Chair. Morrison Knudson Corpn 1995–96; Chair. Waste Management Inc. 1998–99, Pres. and CEO 1999, now Dir; Chair. and CEO Federal-Mogul Corpn 2000–05; Chair. and CEO Delphi Corpn 2005–07, Exec. Chair. 2007–09; mem. Bd of Dirs, American International Group (AIG), Inc. 2009–, Chair. (non-exec.) 2010–15; CEO Hawker Beechcraft, Inc. 2012–13; Chair. MidOcean Partners (pvt. equity firm) 2009–; mem. Bd of Dirs, Symantec Corpn, UAL Corpn, Soc. of Automotive Engineers (Detroit Section). *Address:* American International Group, Inc., 70 Pine Street, New York, NY 10270, USA (office); MidOcean Partners, 320 Park Avenue, Suite 1600, New York, NY 10022, USA. *Telephone:* (212) 770-7000 (AIG) (office). *Fax:* (212) 509-9705 (AIG) (office). *E-mail:* rsmiller@midoceanpartners.com (office). *Website:* www.aigcorporate.com (office); www.midoceanpartners.com.

MILLER, Stuart A., BS, JD; American real estate executive; *Executive Chairman, Lennar Corporation;* b. 1957; s. of Leonard Miller and Susan Miller; m. Vicki Miller; four c.; ed Harvard Univ., Univ. of Miami; joined Lennar Corpn 1981, Dir 1990–, Vice-Pres. 1992–97, Pres. and CEO 1997–2010, CEO 2010–18, Chair. LNR Property Corpn 1997–, Exec. Chair. 2018–; Chair. Riley Property Holdings LLC 1997–2005; Dir, Union Bank of Florida, Builder Homesite Inc.; mem. Jt Center for Housing Studies Policy Advisory Bd, Harvard Univ.; America's Most Powerful People, Forbes 2000. *Address:* Lennar Corporation, 700 NW 107th Avenue, Suite 400, Miami, FL 33172, USA (office). *Telephone:* (305) 559-4000 (office). *Fax:* (305) 229-6453 (office). *E-mail:* allison.bober@lennar.com (office). *Website:* www.lennar .com (office).

MILLER, Thomas J., MA, PhD; American diplomatist; *Chairman, International Commission on Missing Persons (ICMP);* b. 9 Dec. 1948, Chicago, Ill.; ed Univ. of Michigan; mem. Sr Foreign Service at rank of Minister-Counselor; joined State Dept 1976; analyst for Vietnam, Laos and Cambodia 1976–77; Special Asst to Under-Sec. for Political Affairs 1977–79; Deputy Prin. Officer, US Consulate, Chiang Mai, Thailand 1979–81; served twice on Israeli Desk (once as Dir); Head Office of Maghreb Affairs; Acting Dir of an office on counter-terrorism; political section, Athens Embassy 1985–87, Deputy Chief of Mission, Athens 1994–97; Special Coordinator for Cyprus (with rank of Amb.) 1997–99; Amb. to Bosnia and Herzegovina 1999–2001, to Greece 2001–04; retd from US State Dept 2005; CEO Plan Int. (non-profit) 2005–08; CEO and Pres. United Nations Asscn 2009–10; apptd Dir Washington, DC office, Independent Diplomat (advisory org.) 2010; Pres. and CEO Int. Exec. Service Corps (IESC) 2010–18; Chair. Int. Comm. on Missing Persons (ICMP) 2011–; fmr Prof. of Diplomacy and Int. Relations, George Mason Univ.; mem. Bd of Dirs Lampsa Hellenic Hotels SA, Partnership for a Secure America (non-profit); mem. Int. Advisory Bd Hellenic-American Heritage Council; Dr hc (Univ. of Michigan) 2003; Equal Opportunity Award, Dept of State, Superior Honor Award, Dept of State (five times), Meritorious Award, Dept of State among others. *Address:* ICMP Headquarters, Koninginnegracht 12, 2514 AA The Hague, The Netherlands (office). *Telephone:* (70) 8506700 (office). *E-mail:* icmp@icmp.int (office). *Website:* www.icmp.int.

MILLER, Walter Geoffrey Thomas, AO; Australian diplomatist (retd); b. 25 Oct. 1934, Tasmania; s. of Walter T. Miller and Gertrude S. Galloway; m. Rachel C. Webb 1960; three s. one d.; ed Launceston High School, Univs of Tasmania and Oxford; served in Australian missions in Kuala Lumpur, Djakarta and at UN, New York; Deputy High Commr, India 1973–75; Amb. to Repub. of Korea 1978–80; Head, Int. Div. Dept of the Prime Minister and Cabinet, Canberra 1982; Deputy Sec. Dept of Foreign Affairs 1985–86; Amb. to Japan 1986–89; Dir-Gen. Office of Nat. Assessments Canberra 1989–95; High Commr to NZ 1996–2000; Vice-Pres. Australian Inst. of Int. Affairs 2005; Rhodes Scholar 1956. *Leisure interests:* international relations, literature, ballet, tennis, reading, golf. *Address:* 124 Kent Street, Sydney, NSW 2000 (office); Australian Institute of International Affairs, Stephen House, 32 Thesiger Court, Deakin ACT 2600; 85 Union Street, McMahons Point, NSW 2060, Australia (home). *Telephone:* (2) 9247-2709 (office). *Website:* www.aiia.asn.au.

MILLER, William Hughes, BS, AM, PhD; American chemist and academic; *Kenneth S. Pitzer Distinguished Professor Emeritus of Chemistry, University of California, Berkeley;* b. 16 March 1941, Kosciusko, MS; s. of Weldon Howard Miller and Jewell Irene Miller (née Hughes); m. Margaret Westbrook (died 2010); two d.; ed Georgia Inst. of Tech., Harvard Univ.; NATO Postdoctoral Fellow, Univ. of Freiburg, Germany 1967–68; Jr Fellow, Harvard Univ. 1967–69; Asst Prof., Dept of Chem., Univ. of Calif., Berkeley 1969–72, Assoc. Prof. 1972–74, Prof. 1974–, Miller Research Prof. 1978–79, 1998–99, Vice-Chair. Dept of Chem. 1984–88, Chair. 1989–93, Chancellor's Research Prof. 1998–2001, Kenneth S. Pitzer Distinguished Prof. 1999–2015, Emer. 2015–; Sr Staff Scientist, Chemical Sciences Div., Lawrence Berkeley Nat. Lab. 1969–; mem. Editorial Bd Chemical Physics 1973–96, Nouveau Journal de Chimie 1977–87, International Journal of Quantum Chemistry 1979–89, Journal of Physical Chemistry 1983–89, Advances in Quantum Chemistry 1987–, Theoretical Chemistry Accounts 1997–; mem. ACS 1980, Int. Acad. of Quantum Molecular Science 1985, NAS 1987, Deutsche Akad. der Naturforscher Leopoldina 2011; Foreign mem. Royal Soc. (UK) 2015; Fellow

AAAS 1983, American Physical Soc. 1984 (Vice-Chair. and later Chair., Div. of Chemical Physics 1997–2000), American Acad. of Arts and Sciences 1993; Hon. Prof., Univ. of Shandong 1994; Int. Acad. of Quantum Molecular Science Annual Prize 1974, Humboldt Foundation Sr Scientist Award 1981, E.O. Lawrence Award 1985, ACS Irving Langmuir Award in Chemical Physics 1990, ACS Award in Theoretical Chem. 1994, J.O. Hirschfelder Prize in Theoretical Chem. 1996, ACS Ira Remsen Award 1997, Royal Soc. of Chem. Faraday Div. Spiers Medal 1998, ACS Peter Debye Award Award in Physical Chem. 2003, Welch Award in Chem. 2007, Herschbach Award in Chemical Dynamics 2007, Ahmed Zewail Award in Molecular Sciences 2011. *Publications:* more than 400 articles in scientific journals. *Leisure interest:* playing 'old time' banjo. *Address:* Department of Chemistry, University of California, 213 Gilman Hall, Berkeley, CA 94707-1460, USA (office). *Telephone:* (510) 642-0653 (office). *Fax:* (510) 642-6262 (office). *E-mail:* millerwh@berkeley.edu (office). *Website:* chemistry.berkeley.edu/faculty/chem/miller (office); www.cchem.berkeley.edu/millergrp (office).

MILLER SMITH, Charles, MA, CIMgt; British business executive; b. 7 Nov. 1939, Glasgow, Scotland; s. of William Smith and Margaret Wardrope; m. Dorothy Adams 1964 (died 1999); one s. two d.; m. 2nd Debjani Miller 2004 (divorced 2009); ed Glasgow Acad. and St Andrews Univ.; Financial Dir Vinyl Products, Unilever 1970–73, Head of Planning 1974; Finance Dir Walls Meat Co. 1976; Vice-Chair. Industan Lever 1979–81; Speciality Chemicals Group 1981; Chief Exec. PPF Int. 1983; Chief Exec. Quest Int. 1986; Financial Dir Unilever Bd 1989; Exec. Unilever Foods 1993–94; Exec. Dir ICI PLC 1994–95, Chief Exec. 1995–99, Chair. 1999–2001; Deputy Chair. (non-exec.) Scottish Power PLC (now ScottishPower Ltd) 1999–2000, Chair. (non-exec.) 2000–07; Dir HSBC Holdings PLC 1996; Dir (non-exec.) Premier Foods 2009–, Royal Scottish Nat. Orchestra; Int. Adviser, Goldman Sachs 2001–05; fmr European Adviser, Warburg Pincus LLC; currently Ind. Dir (non-exec.) Firstsource Solutions Ltd and Chair. Firstsource Solutions UK Ltd; Deputy Chair. Premier Foods Plc 2009–; mem. Defence Man. Bd, Ministry of Defence; mem. Court of Govs, Henley Management Coll.; Hon. LLD (St Andrews) 1995; Hon. Gov., Glasgow Acad. *Leisure interests:* reading, walking. *Address:* Firstsource Solutions UK Ltd, Space One, 1 Beadon Road, London, W6 0EA, England (office). *Telephone:* (20) 8237-4500 (office). *Fax:* (20) 8237-4501 (office). *E-mail:* marketing@firstsource.com (office). *Website:* www.firstsource.com (office).

MILLETT, Baron (Life Peer), cr. 1998, of St Marylebone in the City of Westminster; **Peter Julian Millett,** MA (Cantab.); British judge (retd); b. 23 June 1932; s. of Dennis Millett and Adele Millett; m. Ann Harris 1958; three s. (one deceased); ed Harrow School and Univ. of Cambridge; called to Bar, Middle Temple 1955, Lincoln's Inn 1959, Singapore 1976, Hong Kong 1979; at Chancery Bar 1958–86; Lecturer in Practical Conveyancing and Examiner Council of Legal Educ. 1962–76; mem. Gen. Council of the Bar 1971–75; Judge, High Court of Justice, Chancery Div. 1986–94, Lord Justice of Appeal 1994–98, Lord of Appeal in Ordinary 1998–2004; mem. House of Lords 1998–; Non-Perm. Judge of the Court of Final Appeal, Hong Kong 2000–; Hon. Fellow, Trinity Hall, Cambridge; Hon. LLD (Queen Mary Coll. and Westfield Coll., London). *Address:* House of Lords, Westminster, London, SW1A 0PQ (office); Essex Court Chambers, 24 Lincoln's Inn Fields, London, WC2A 3EG, England (office). *Telephone:* (20) 7219-3202 (office); (20) 7813-8000 (office). *Fax:* (20) 7219-5979 (office); (20) 7813-8080 (office).

MILLIKEN, Hon. Peter Andrew Stewart, OC, BA, LLB, MA, FRSC; Canadian politician and lawyer; b. 12 Nov. 1946, Kingston, Ont.; s. of John Andrew Milliken and Catherine Margaret Milliken; ed Queen's Univ., Kingston, Wadham Coll., Oxford, UK, Dalhousie Univ., Halifax; Lecturer in Business Law, School of Business, Queen's Univ. 1973–81; called to Bar of Ont., Solicitor of Supreme Court of Ont. 1973; solicitor, Cunningham, Little, Kingston (law firm) 1973–78, PNR, Cunningham, Little, Bonham and Milliken 1978–89; MP for Kingston and the Islands 1988–2011; served as Asst to House Leader, Vice-Chair. Standing Cttee on Privileges and Elections; Parl. Sec. to Leader of Govt in House of Commons 1993–96; Deputy Chair. Cttees of Whole House 1996, Deputy Speaker and Chair. Cttees of Whole House 1997, elected Speaker of House of Commons 2001–11; Special Advisor, Cunningham, Swan 2011–16; Chair. Bd of Internal Economy 2001–11; Fellow, School of Policy Studies, Queen's Univ. 2011–; Hon. Patron Genealogical Soc. of Ont., Hon. Lt-Col, The Princess of Wales' Own Regiment 2016; Hon. LLD (State Univ. of New York) 2001, (Queen's Univ.) 2012, (McGill Univ.) 2012. *Publications include:* Question Period: Developments from 1960 to 1967 1968. *Address:* School of Policy Studies, Robert Sutherland Hall, 138 Union Street, Queen's University, Kingston, ON K7L 3N6 (office); 2626 Leeman Road, Elginburg, ON K0H 1M0, Canada (home). *Telephone:* (613) 548-7889 (home). *E-mail:* pasm@rogers.com (home). *Website:* www.queensu.ca/sps (office).

MILLON, Charles, LèsScEcon; French politician and international organization official; b. 12 Nov. 1945, Belley, Ain; s. of Gabriel Millon and Suzanne Gunet; m. Chantal Delsol 1970; three s. two d.; ed Ecole Sainte-Marie, Lyon, Faculté de Droit et de Sciences Economiques de Lyon; univ. tutor 1969; legal and taxation adviser 1970–; Mayor of Belley 1977–2001; Deputy 1981–86, 1988–93, First Vice-Pres. Ass. Nat. 1986–88, Leader Union pour la Démocratie Française in Nat. Ass. 1989; Minister of Defence 1995–97; Local Councillor, Ain 1985–88; Vice-Pres. Regional Council, Rhône-Alpes 1981–88, Pres. 1988–99, Pres. 1988–98; Founder and Pres. la Droite Movt 1998–99; Leader Droite Libérale Chrétienne 1999–2003; Municipal Councillor and Urban Community Councillor, Lyon 2001–08; Pres. Unir Pour Lyon 2001–08; Amb. to FAO 2003–07. *Publications:* L'Extravagante histoire des nationalisations 1984, L'Alternance-vérité 1986, La Tentation du Conservatisme 1995, La Paix civile 1998, Lettre d'un ami impertinent 2002. *Leisure interests:* reading, walking, mountaineering.

MILLS, Hayley Cathrine Rose Vivien; British actress; b. 18 April 1946, London; d. of Sir John Mills and Lady Mills (Mary Hayley Bell); m. Roy Boulting 1971 (divorced 1977); two s.; partner Firdous Bamji 1997–; ed Elmhurst Ballet School, Inst. Alpine Videmanette; first film appearance in Tiger Bay 1959; on contract to Walt Disney; first stage appearance as Peter Pan 1969; Silver Bear Award, Berlin Film Festival 1958, British Acad. Award; Special Oscar (USA), TV Best Actress Award 1982. *Stage appearances include:* The Wild Duck 1970, Trelawny 1972, The Three Sisters 1973, A Touch of Spring 1975, Rebecca 1977, My Fat Friend 1978, Hush and Hide 1979, The Importance of Being Earnest (Royal Festival Theatre, Chichester), The Summer Party 1980, Tally's Folly 1982, The Secretary Bird 1983, Dial M for Murder 1984, Toys in the Attic 1986, The Kidnap Game 1991, The King and I (Australian and NZ tour) 1991–92, The Card 1994, Fallen Angels 1994, Dead Guilty 1995–96, Brief Encounter 1997–98, The King and I (US tour) 1997–98, Suite in Two Keys (New York) 2001, A Little Night Music (USA) 2001, The Vagina Monologues (New York) 2001, Humble Boy (UK) 2004. *Films include:* Pollyanna 1960, The Parent Trap 1961, Whistle Down the Wind 1961, Summer Magic 1962, In Search of the Castaways 1963, The Chalk Garden 1964, The Moonspinners 1965, The Truth about Spring 1965, Sky West and Crooked 1966, The Trouble with Angels 1966, The Family Way 1966, Pretty Polly 1967, Twisted Nerve 1968, Take a Girl Like You 1970, Forbush and the Penguins 1971, Endless Night 1972, Deadly Strangers 1975, The Diamond Hunters 1975, What Changed Charley Farthing? 1975, The Kingfisher Caper 1975, Appointment with Death 1987, After Midnight 1990, 2BPerfectlyHonest 2004, Stricken 2005. *Television includes:* The Flame Trees of Thika 1981, Parent Trap II 1986, Good Morning Miss Bliss, Murder She Wrote, Back Home, Tales of the Unexpected, Walk of Life 1990, Parent Trap III, IV, Wild at Heart (series) 2007–09. *Publication:* My God (with Marcus Maclaine) 1988. *Leisure interests:* riding, reading, children, cooking, travel. *Address:* c/o Chatto and Linnit, 123A Kings Road, London, SW3 4PL, England. *Telephone:* (20) 7352-7722 (office). *Website:* www.hayleymills.com.

MILLS, Ian Mark, OBE, BSc, DPhil, FRS; British chemist and academic; *Professor Emeritus of Chemical Spectroscopy, University of Reading;* b. 9 June 1930, Sonning, Berks., England; s. of John Mills and Marghuerita Alice Gertrude Mills (née Gooding); m. Margaret Maynard 1957; one s. one d.; ed Leighton Park School, Univ. of Reading, St John's Coll. Oxford; Research Fellow, Univ. of Minn. 1954–56; Research Fellow in Theoretical Chem., Corpus Christi Coll., Cambridge 1956–57; Lecturer in Chem. Univ. of Reading 1957–64, Reader 1964–66, Prof. of Chemical Spectroscopy 1966–95, Prof. Emer. 1995–, Leverhulme Emer. Research Fellow 1996–98; Ed. Molecular Physics 1972–77, 1995–2004; mem. and Chair. of various cttees of IUPAC; Pres. Int. Bureau of Weights and Measures, Sèvres; Pres. Emer. Comité Consultatif des Unites; Vice-Pres. Faraday Div. of RSC 1984–86; mem. British Nat. Cttee for IUPAC of RSC 1992–2000, Chair. 1998–2000; Pres., Consultative Cttee on Units of the Bureau Int. des Poids et Mesures 1995–2014; Chair. British Standards Inst. Cttee on Symbols and Units 1996–2004; mem. Council, Royal Inst. 2000–03; Hon. DSc (Reading) 2015; Lomb Medal 1960, Fellow 1974, Lippincott Medal of Optical Soc. of America 1982, RSC Spectroscopy Award 1990. *Publications:* Quantities, Units and Symbols in Physical Chemistry (co-author) 1988; various papers in learned journals on quantum mechanics and molecular spectroscopy. *Leisure interests:* sailing, walking, cooking, keeping fit. *Address:* Department of Chemistry, University of Reading, Reading, RG6 6AD (office); 57 Christchurch Road, Reading, RG2 7BD, England (home). *Telephone:* (118) 931-8456 (office); (118) 987-2335 (home). *Fax:* (118) 931-6331 (office). *E-mail:* i.m.mills@reading.ac.uk (office). *Website:* www.reading.ac.uk/chemistry/about/staff/i-m-mills.aspx (office).

MILLS, Janet T., BA, JD; American lawyer and politician; *Governor of Maine;* b. 30 Dec. 1947, Farmington, Me; d. of Sumner Peter Mills, Jr. and Katherine Louise Mills (née Coffin); m. Stanley Kuklinski 1985 (died 2014); five step-d.; ed Univ. of Massachusetts, Univ. of Maine School of Law; Asst Attorney-Gen., Me 1976–80; Dist Attorney for Androscoggin, Franklin and Oxford Counties 1980–95; Attorney, Wright and Mills 1995–; Attorney-Gen. for Me 2009–11, 2013–19; mem. House of Reps, Me 2002–08, mem. Criminal Justice and Public Safety Cttee, Judiciary Cttee; Vice-Chair. Democratic Party 2011–13; Gov. of Me 2019–; co-founder Maine Women's Lobby 1978, mem. Bd of Dirs 1998; fmr Pres., Me Prosecutors Asscn; mem. Bd, Margaret Chase Smith Foundation. *Address:* Office of the Governor, 1 State House Station, Augusta, ME 04333, USA (office). *Telephone:* (207) 287-3531 (office). *Website:* www.maine.gov (office).

MILLS, Kyle David; New Zealand professional cricketer (retd); b. 15 March 1979, Auckland; right-arm fast-medium pace bowler; right-handed batsman; plays for Auckland 1998–2015, New Zealand 2001–15, Kings XI Punjab, Lincs. 2001, Kings XI Punjab 2008, Mumbai Indians 2009–10, Middx 2013; First-class debut: 1998/99; Test debut: England v NZ, Nottingham 10–13 June 2004; One-Day Int. (ODI) debut: NZ v Pakistan, Sharjah 15 April 2001; T20I debut: NZ v Australia, Auckland 17 Feb. 2005; announced retirement in 2015; ranked first on Reliance Mobile ICC (Int. Cricket Council) ODI Bowling Rankings Oct. 2009.

MILLS JONES, Joseph; Liberian economist and fmr central banker; s. of Joseph Humphrey Jones and Catherine Cooper Jones; m. Esther Buxton Jones; ed Cuttington Univ., American Univ., Washington, DC; began career as Asst Minister of State for Presidential Affairs; fmr Chief Economist and Special Asst to Minister of Planning and Econ. Affairs; Exec. Gov., Central Bank of Liberia 2006–16; Chair., Cttee of Govs, West African Monetary Zone 2012. *Publications include:* A Macroeconometric Study of the Liberian Economy: A Short-run Analysis 1976.

MILNES, Sherrill, MMusEd; American singer (baritone); b. 10 Jan. 1935, Hinsdale, Ill.; s. of James Knowlton Milnes and Thelma Roe Milnes; m. 2nd Nancy Stokes 1969; one s.; one s. one d. by first marriage; m. 3rd Maria Zouves 1996; ed Drake Univ., Northwestern Univ., studied with Boris Goldovsky, Rosa Ponselle, Andrew White, Hermanes Baer; with Goldovsky Opera Co. 1960–65, New York City Opera Co. 1964–67, debut with Metropolitan Opera Co., New York 1965, leading baritone 1965–; has performed with all American city opera cos and major American orchestras 1962–73; performed in Don Giovanni, Vespri Siciliani and all standard Italian repertory baritone roles, Metropolitan Opera and at San Francisco Opera, Hamburg Opera, Frankfurt Opera, La Scala, Milan, Covent Garden, London, Teatro Colón, Buenos Aires, Vienna State Opera, Paris Opera and Chicago Lyric Opera; Co-founder (with Maria Zouves) and Artistic Dir VOICE (Vocal and Operatic Intensive Creative Experience) 2001–, f. Savannah VOICE Festival 2013; Chair. of Bd Affiliate Artists Inc.; Order of Merit (Italy) 1984, Chevalier, Ordre des Arts et des Lettres 1996; three hon. degrees; three Grammy Awards, Sanford Medal, named mem. Lincoln Acad. 2003, Yale Univ., Opera News Award for Distinguished Achievement 2008. *Recordings:* over 60 albums. *Publication:* American Aria: From Farm Boy to Opera Star 2000. *Leisure interests:* table tennis, swimming, horse riding. *Address:* Barrett Vantage Artists, 505 8th Avenue, Suite 12A00 New York, NY 10018, USA (office); The VOICExperience Foundation, PO Box 1576, Plain Harbor, FL 34682-1576, USA (office). *E-mail:* abacon@barrettvantage.com (office); voicexp@aol.com (office). *Website:* www.voiceexperiencefoundation.com (office); sherrillmilnes.com.

MILNOR, John Willard, AB, PhD; American mathematician and academic; *Distinguished Professor of Mathematics and Co-Director, Institute for Mathematical Sciences, State University of New York, Stony Brook;* b. 20 Feb. 1931, Orange, NJ; m. Prof. Dusa McDuff; ed Princeton Univ.; faculty, Princeton Univ. 1953–55, Alfred P. Sloan Fellow 1955–59, Prof. of Math. 1960–62, Henry Putman Prof. of Math. 1962; on staff, State Univ. of New York, Stony Brook 1988–, currently Distinguished Prof. of Math. and Co-Dir Inst. for Math. Sciences; Ed. Annals of Mathematics 1962–; mem. NAS 1963, American Acad. of Arts and Sciences, American Philosophy Soc.; Fellow, American Math. Soc. 2013; Hon. DSc (Syracuse Univ.) 1965, (Univ. of Chicago) 1967; Putnam Fellow, Princeton Univ. 1949–50, Fields Medal, Int. Congress of Mathematicians, Stockholm 1962, Nat. Medal of Science 1967, Leroy P. Steele Prize, American Math. Soc. 1982, 2004, 2011, Wolf Prize (Israel) 1989, Abel Prize 2011, Norwegian Acad. of Science and Letters 2011. *Publications:* Morse Theory 1963, Lectures on the h-Cobordism Theorem 1965, Singular Points of Complex Hypersurfaces 1968, Introduction to Algebraic K-theory 1971, Symmetric Bilinear Forms (co-author), Characteristic Classes (co-author) 1974, Topology from the Differentiable Viewpoint 1997, Dynamics in One Complex Variable 1999; numerous articles in math. journals on differential topology, differential geometry and algebraic topology. *Address:* Institute for Mathematical Sciences, State University of New York, 5D-148 Math Tower, Stony Brook, NY 11794-3660, USA (office). *Telephone:* (516) 642-7307 (office); (516) 642-7318 (Sec.) (office). *Fax:* (516) 632-4774 (office). *E-mail:* jack@math.stonybrook.edu (office). *Website:* www.math.stonybrook.edu (office).

MILO, Paskal, PhD; Albanian politician; *Chairman, Social Democracy Party;* b. 22 Feb. 1949, Vlorë; s. of Koço Petromilo and Parashqevi Petromilo; m. Liliana Balla-Milo 1976; one s. two d.; ed Univ. of Tirana; journalist 1971–74; high school teacher 1975–80; Lecturer in History, Univ. of Tirana 1981–91, Dean Faculty of History and Philology 1991–92, Prof. 1996; Sec. of State for Educ. 1991; mem. Parl. (Social Democratic Party—SDP) 1992–96, 1997–, Chair. Parl. Comm. for Educ. and Science 1992–96, Minister of Foreign Affairs 1997–2001, for European Integration 2001–02; left SDP to form Social Democracy Party (Partia Demokracia Sociale—PDS) 2003, Chair. 2003–; Chair. SE European Co-operation Process (SEECP); mem. Parl., Council of Europe 2006–. *Publications:* The End of an Injustice 1984, Albania and Yugoslavia 1918–27 1992, A Good Understanding and Cooperation in the Balkans, From Utopia to Necessity 1997, Albania and the Balkan Entente 1997, Constitutional Rights and Minorities in the Balkans: A Comparative Analysis 1997, The Soviet Union and Albania's Foreign Policy 1944–46 1997, Albania in East-West Relations 1944–45 1998, European Union: Identity, Integration, Future 2002, Diary of a Foreign Minister: Kosova Conflict 1997-2001 2009, Kosova from Rambouillet to Independence 2009. *Leisure interests:* football, music. *Address:* Partia Demokracia Sociale, Bulevardi 'Zogu i I', ish klinika dentare, Tirana, Albania (office). *Telephone:* (4) 274487 (office); (4) 250973 (home). *Fax:* (4) 274487 (office). *E-mail:* paskalmilo@yahoo.it (home).

MILOŠOSKI, Antonio, MA; Macedonian lawyer, politician, diplomatist and researcher; b. 29 Jan. 1976, Tetovo; m.; ed SS. Cyril and Methodius Univ., Skopje, Friedrich Wilhelm Univ., Bonn, Germany, Gerhard Merkator Univ. of Duisburg, Germany; mem. Exec. Cttee Youth Force Union of Internal Macedonian Revolutionary Org.—Democratic Party for Macedonian Nat. Unity 1995–97, Vice-Pres. 1997–98; Chair. Office of the Deputy Prime Minister of Fmr Yugoslav Repub. of Macedonia 1999–2000; Govt Spokesman 2000–01; Counsellor to the Prime Minister Jan.–May 2001; Research Fellow, Inst. for Political Science, Gerhard Merkator Univ., Duisburg 2005–06; Minister of Foreign Affairs 2006–11; Founder Youth Euro-Atlantic Forum (MEAF); columnist, Dnevnik newspaper 2000.

MILOW, Keith Arnold; British artist; b. 29 Dec. 1945, London; s. of Geoffrey Keith Milow and Joan Ada Gear; ed Camberwell School of Art and Royal Coll. of Art, London; experimental work at Royal Court Theatre, London 1968; teacher, Ealing School of Art 1968–70; Artist-in-Residence, Univ. of Leeds (Gregory Fellowship) 1970; worked in New York (Harkness Fellowship) 1972–74; teacher, Chelsea School of Art 1975, School of Visual Arts, New York City 1981–85; works in public collections in six countries, including Tate Modern and Victoria and Albert Museum, London, Guggenheim Museum and Museum of Modern Art, New York; Harkness Fellowship 1971, Calouste Gulbenkian Foundation Visual Arts Award 1976, equal First Prize, Tolly Cobbold/Eastern Arts 2nd Nation Exhbn 1979, Pollock-Krasner Foundation Award 2017, Arts Council of GB Major Award. *Address:* 58B Eglinton Hill, London, SE18 3NR, England (home). *Telephone:* (20) 7207-2175 (home). *E-mail:* keithmilow@dds.nl (office). *Website:* www.keithmilow.com.

MILUTINOVIĆ, Milan, LLM; Serbian lawyer, politician, diplomatist and fmr head of state; b. 19 Dec. 1942, Belgrade; s. of Aleksandar Milan Milutinović and Ljubica Vladimir Jokić; m. Olga Branko Spasojević; one s.; ed Univ. of Belgrade; mem. Presidency of Socialist Youth Union of Yugoslavia 1969–71; MP 1969–74; Sec. Communal Cttee of League of Communists 1972–74; Sec. for Ideology, City Cttee of League of Communists 1974–77; Minister of Science and Educ. of Serbian Repub. 1977–82; Dir Serbian Nat. Library 1983–87; Head of Sector for Press, Information and Culture, Sec. for Foreign Affairs 1987–89; Amb. to Greece 1989–95; Minister of Foreign Affairs, Fed. Repub. of Yugoslavia 1995–98; Pres. of Serbia 1997–2002; accused of crimes against humanity and violations of the customs of war by UN War Crimes Tribunal 2001, charged with crimes against humanity and war crimes by Int. Court of Justice 2003, found not guilty 2009; Order of Merit with Silver Star 1974, Medal for work with Gold Coronet 1980. *Publications include:* University – Eppur si muove! 1985. *Leisure interest:* philately.

MILYUKOV, Yuri Aleksandrovich, CandPhysMathSc; Russian banker; *Chairman, Managing Company Number One;* b. 29 April 1957; m.; two s.; ed Moscow Inst. of Physics Eng; researcher, Lebedev Inst. of Physics USSR (now Russian) Acad. of Sciences 1984–87; Chair. Council of Altair 1989–91; f. Moscow Commodity Exchange (MTB) 1990, Pres. 1993–97; mem. Council on Business, Govt of Russian Fed. 1992–; mem. Bd Dirs, Russian Industrialists and Entrepreneurs Union 1992–; mem. Presidium, All-Russian Movt Businessmen for New Russia 1993–94; mem. Co-ordination Council, Round Table of Russian Business 1994; mem. Beer Lovers Party; mem. Cen. Cttee 1995; mem. Political Consultative Council of Russian Presidency 1996; Chair. Rosmed; Chair. Russian Union of Stock Exchanges 1991; Chair. Managing Company Number One; Chair. Stock Cttee,

Moscow Stock Exchange 1996; First Deputy Chair. Bd MDM Bank 1997. *Leisure interest:* theatre. *Address:* Managing Company Number One, Romanov pereulok 3 building 1, office 68, 125009 Moscow, Russia (office). *Telephone:* (495) 234-0815 (office). *E-mail:* milyukov@yk1.ru (office); info@yk1.ru (office).

MIMICA, Neven; Croatian politician, diplomatist and EU official; *Commissioner for International Co-operation and Development, European Commission;* b. 12 Oct. 1953, Split, Socialist Repub. of Croatia, Socialist Fed. Repub. of Yugoslavia; m.; two c.; ed Univ. of Zagreb; held positions in various governmental bodies related to foreign relations and foreign trade policies, including several counselling positions at embassies in Cairo, Egypt and Ankara, Turkey 1979–97; apptd Asst to Minister of Economy 1997, served as Chief Negotiator during Croatia's accession to WTO and EU Asscn Agreement; Minister of European Integration 2001–03; mem. Socijaldemokratska Partija Hrvatske (SDP—Social Democratic Party of Croatia); mem. (SDP) Parl. 2003–, Deputy Speaker 2008–11, Chair. Cttee for European Integration; Deputy Prime Minister, responsible for Interior, Foreign and European Affairs 2011–13; Commr for Consumer Policy, EC, Brussels 2013–14, for Int. Co-operation and Devt 2014–; apptd by UN Sec.-Gen. as mem. of Lead Group of the Scaling Up Nutrition Movt 2016–. *Address:* European Commission, 200 Rue de la Loi/Wetstraat 200, 1049 Brussels, Belgium (office). *Telephone:* (2) 299-11-11 (switchboard) (office). *E-mail:* cab-mimica-webpage@ec.europa.eu (office). *Website:* ec.europa.eu/commission/2014-2019/mimica_en (office).

MIMURA, Akio, BS; Japanese business executive; *Senior Advisor and Honorary Chairman, Nippon Steel & Sumitomo Metal Corporation;* b. 2 Nov. 1940; ed Tokyo Univ.; with Fuji Iron & Steel 1963–70 (remained with co. following merger with Yawata Steel to form Nippon Steel Corpn 1970), Man. Dir 1998–2000, Vice-Pres. 2000–03, Pres. and Rep. Dir 2003–08, Chair. and Rep. Dir 2008–12, currently Senior Advisor and Hon. Chair.; Vice-Chair. (fmrly Chair.) Japan Iron and Steel Fed. Industry Asscn (JISF); Vice-Chair. Int. Iron and Steel Inst. (ISII) 2006–07; fmr Vice-Chair. World Steel Asscn (currently Dir); fmr Corp. Auditor, Nisshin Seifun Group, Inc., Dir 2009–; mem. Int. Advisory Bd, Rolls-Royce PLC, Global Advisory Bd Mitsubishi UFJ Financial Group, Inc.; Dir Tokio Marine Holdings Inc. 2010–, Japan Post Holdings Co., Ltd 2013, Devt Bank of Japan 2016– (also mem. Advisory Bd). *Address:* Nippon Steel & Sumitomo Metal Corpn, Marunouchi Park Building, 6-1, Marunouchi 2-chome, Chiyoda-ku, Tokyo 100-8071, Japan. *E-mail:* info@nssmc.com.

MIN, Keh-sik, MS; South Korean business executive; b. 1941; ed Univ. of California, Berkeley, USA; fmr Man. Dir Daewoo Shipbuilding; fmr Pres. and COO, Research and Devt Centre, Hyundai Heavy Industries Co. Ltd, becoming Pres. 2001, Dir, Vice-Chair., Co-CEO and Chief Tech. Officer 2007–09, Chair. and Co-CEO 2009–11; Pres., S Korea Br., Int. Conf. on Control, Automation and Systems (ICCAS), also mem. Advisory Council.

MINANI, Thomas; Burundian politician; fmr Dir-Gen. Coffee Office; Minister of Commerce and Industry 2003–05; mem. FRODEBU.

MINAYEV, Valery Vladimirovich, DrEcon, CandHist; Russian economist, historian, academic and university administrator; *Provost, Russian State University for the Humanities;* b. 1949, Moscow region; ed Moscow State Inst. of Archives and History; teacher, Prof., Chair. Russian State Univ. for the Humanities 1973–2002, Provost 2002–; Deputy Chair. Scientific Council; mem. Editorial Bd, Novy Istorichesky Vestnik, Yurisprudentsya, Popular Economic Encyclopaedia; mem. Russian Acad. of Nat. Sciences; medal of 850th anniversary of Moscow. *Publications include:* more than 70 scientific papers and monographs, including On Periodization of Demographic History 1995, The Formation of the Labour Market in Modern Russia: Population and Crises 2001, Problems of the Labour Market in Classical Theoretical Schools 2001, Tolerance and Polycultural Society 2002. *Address:* Russian State University for the Humanities, Moscow 125993, Miusskaya pl. 6, GSP-3, Russian Federation. *Telephone:* (495) 250-61-31. *Fax:* (495) 250-62-11. *Website:* rggu.com.

MIÑBAEV, Sawat Mukhametbayuly, CandEcon; Kazakhstani politician; *Chairman and CEO, KazMunayGas;* b. 19 Nov. 1962, Taldy-Kurgan; s. of Mukhametbai Miñbaev and Oralbaeva Rakhima; m. Kaliyeva Janar Miñbaeva; one s. one d.; ed Moscow State Univ.; teacher, Almaty Inst. of Nat. Economy, later Assoc. Prof. 1989–91; Pres. Kazakhstan Construction Exchange 1991–92; First Deputy Chair. and Dir Kazkommerts Bank 1992–95; Deputy Minister of Finance and Dir of Treasury 1995–98, Minister of Finance 1998–99; Deputy Head of Pres.'s Admin. 1999; Minister of Agric. 1999–2001; Pres. Devt Bank of Kazakhstan 2001–02; head, Caspian Industrial Financial Group (man. consulting venture) 2002–03; Deputy Prime Minister of Kazakhstan 2003–06; Minister of Industry and Trade 2004–06, of Energy and Mineral Resources 2007–10, of Oil and Gas 2010–13; Chair. Samruk (state holding co.) 2006–07, Chair. and CEO KazMunayGas 2013–. *Address:* KazMunayGas, 010000 Nur-Sultan, Kabanbai batyr kosh. 19, Kazakhstan. *E-mail:* Astana@kmg.kz. *Website:* www.kmg.kz.

MINC BAUMFELD, Carlos, MSc, PhD; Brazilian geographer, academic and politician; b. 12 July 1951, Rio de Janeiro; m.; two c.; ed Fed. Univ. of Rio de Janeiro, Tech. Univ. of Lisbon, Univ. of Paris I (Sorbonne); Co-founder Partido Verde 1986; now mem. Partido dos Trabalhadores; State Deputy for Rio de Janeiro 1986–; Asst Prof., Dept of Geography, Fed. Univ. of Rio de Janeiro; Sec. for the Environment, State Govt of Rio de Janeiro 2006–08, 2011; Minister of the Environment 2008–10; UNEP Global Award 500·1989. *Publications:* Como Fazer Movimento Ecológico 1985, A Reconquista da Terra 1986, Ecologia e Política no Brasil 1987, Despoluindo a Política 1994, Ecologia e Cidadania 1997. *Website:* www.minc.com.br.

MINCATO, Vittorio; Italian business executive; b. 14 May 1936, Torrebelvicino, Vicenza; joined Ente Nazionale Idrocarburi (Eni) Group SpA (oil and gas co.) 1957, various positions including Admin. and Finance Man. Lanerossi (textile co.) 1957–77, Admin. Man. Eni SpA 1977–84, Asst to Chair. 1984–88, Man. Human Resources and Org. 1988–92, Chair. Savio (textile machinery) and Head of Fertilizers Section, EniChem 1990–92, Deputy Chair. and Man. Dir EniChem 1993–95, Chair. EniChem 1996–98, Man. Dir Eni SpA 1998–2005, CEO 2002–05, fmr Dir numerous other Eni cos including Agip, Lanerossi, Immobiliare Metanopoli, Sofid and Polimeri Europa; Chair. Poste Italiane SpA 2005–08, Fondazione CUOA (Centro Universitario Organizzazione Aziendale) 2007–13;

Pres. Camera di Commercio di Vicenza 2008–10; mem. Bd of Dirs Il Sole 24 Ore SpA 2000–, Fondazione Eni Enrico Mattei, Exec. Bd Assonime (Asscn of Italian Ltd Liability Cos) 2001–, Bd Dirs Fondazione Teatro alla Scala, Man. Bd Assolombarda (industrialists' asscn); mem. Bd of Dirs Finmeccanica SpA 2013; Cavaliere del Lavoro 2002; Dr hc (Politecnico di Milano) 2003, (Univ. of Turin) 2004. *Leisure interests:* classical music (especially Wagner), reading.

MINCHIN, Hon. Nicholas (Nick), BEcons, LLB; Australian lawyer, politician and diplomatist; *Consul-General in New York;* b. 15 April 1953, Sydney, NSW; m. Kerry Minchin; two s. one d.; ed Hawken School (AFS Scholar), Australian Nat. Univ.; various positions with Liberal Party Fed. Secr., including Deputy Fed. Dir 1977–83; State Dir S Australian Liberal Party 1985–93; elected to Commonwealth Parl. as Liberal Senator for S Australia 1993–2011, Deputy Leader of the Govt in the Senate 2001–07, Leader of the Opposition 2007–10; Parl. Sec. to Leader of the Opposition 1994–96, to the Prime Minister (upon election win) 1996–97; Special Minister of State and Minister Assisting the Prime Minister 1997–98; Minister for Industry, Science and Resources 1998–2001, for Finance and Admin 2001–07; Vice-Pres. Exec. Council 2004–07; Australian Consul-Gen. in New York 2014–. *Address:* Australian Consulate-General, 150 East 42nd Street, Floor 34, New York, NY 10017-5612, USA (office). *Telephone:* (212) 351-6500 (office). *Fax:* (212) 351-6501 (office). *Website:* www.newyork.usa.embassy.gov.au/nycg/ConsulGeneralMinchin.html (office).

MINCKWITZ, Bernhard von; German business executive; b. 11 Aug. 1944, Göttingen; m. Cornelia Böhning; mem. Man. Bd Bertelsmann AG 1971–98; mem. Bd and Man. Dir Süddeutscher Verlag 1998–2003, Man. Dir Süddeutscher Verlag Hüthig Fachinformationen –2002; Chair. Supervisory Bd Softline AG 2006–13; mem. Sponsorship Foundation for Chinese Excellent Students from Poor Families from 2005.

MINDADZE, Aleksandr Anatol'yevich; Russian scriptwriter; b. 28 April 1949, Moscow; s. of Anatoly Grebnyev; m. Galina Petrovna Orlova; two d.; ed All-Union State Inst. of Cinematography; screenplays since 1972; has worked with dir Vadim Abdrashitov since 2003; Merited Worker of Art of Russia, State Prize of Russia 1984, Silver Pegas Prize of Cultural Asscn Ennio Flaiano 1985, USSR State Prize 1991, co-recipient of Golden Ram Award with Vadim Abdrashitov for their contribution to Russian cinema 1994. *Film scripts include:* Vesenniy prizyv (Spring Selection) 1976, Slovo dlia zashchity (Speech for the Defence) (Prize of All-Union Film Festival, Prize of Lenin's Komsomol) 1976, Spring Mobilization (A. Dovzhenko Silver Medal) 1977, Povorot (The Turning Point) 1978, Okhota na lis (A Fox Hunt) 1980, Predel zhelaniy 1982, Ostanovilsya poyezd (The Train Has Stopped) 1982, Parad planet (Parade of the Planets) 1984, Plyumbum, ili opasnaya igra (Plumbum, or The Dangerous Game) 1986, Sluga (The Servant) 1988, Armavir 1991, Pyesa dlya passazhira (Play for a Passenger) (Silver Bear, Berlin Int. Film Festival) 1995, Vremya tantsora (Time of the Dancer) (Grand Prix, Kinotavr Film Festival, Sochi 1997 and several int. awards) 1998, Magnitnye buri (Magnetic Storms) 2003, Trio 2003, Kosmos kak predchuvstvie (Golden Eagle Award) 2005, Otryv (The Soar) (White Elephant Award, Munich Film Festival) 2007, Minnesota 2009, Innocent Saturday 2011, Break Loose 2013, My Good Hans 2015. *Address:* 125319 Moscow, Usiyevicha str. 8, Apt 89, Russia (office). *Telephone:* (499) 155-75-34 (home). *E-mail:* mindadze@mail.ru (home).

MINDAOUDOU SOULEYMANE, Aïchatou, BA, MA, PhD; Niger politician, lawyer, academic and UN official; *Special Representative of the Secretary-General and Head, United Nations Operation in Côte d'Ivoire (UNOCI);* b. 1959; ed Univ. of Abidjan, Côte d'Ivoire, Univ. of the Sorbonne, Paris, France; Minister of Social Devt, Population and Women 1996–99, of Foreign Affairs 1999–2000, of Foreign Affairs, Co-operation and African Integration 2001–10; Deputy Jt Special Rep. for Political Affairs, African Union-UN Hybrid Operation, Darfur (UNAMID) 2011–12, Acting Jt Special Rep. 2012–13 and Acting Jt African Union-UN Chief Mediator for Darfur 2012–13; Special Rep. of the Sec.-Gen. and Head, UN Operation in Côte d'Ivoire (UNOCI) 2013–; fmr Sr Lecturer in Int. Law. *Address:* United Nations Operation in Côte d'Ivoire (UNOCI), Department of Peacekeeping Operations, United Nations, New York, NY 10017, USA (office); PO Box 11529, Niamey, Niger (home). *Telephone:* (212) 963-1234 (office); 72-35-15 (home). *Fax:* (212) 963-4879 (office). *E-mail:* indo-ai@ifrance.com. *Website:* www.un.org (office).

MINETA, Hon. Norman (Norm) Yoshio, BS; American politician, transport industry executive, communications consultant and fmr government official; b. 12 Nov. 1931, San Jose, Calif.; s. of Kay Kunisaku Mineta and Kane Mineta (née Watanabe); m. Danealia Mineta; two s. two step-s.; ed Univ. of California, Berkeley; agent/broker, Mineta Insurance Agency 1956–89; mem. Advisory Bd, Bank of Tokyo in Calif. 1961–75; mem. San Jose City Council 1967–71; Vice-Mayor, City of San Jose 1969–71, Mayor 1971–75; mem. House of Reps from 13th (now 15th) Calif. Dist 1975–95, Sub cttee on Surface Transportation 1989–92; Sr Vice-Pres. and Man. Dir Transportation Systems and Services, Lockheed Martin 1995–2001; US Sec. of Transportation, Washington, DC 2001–06 (resgnd); Vice-Chair. Hill & Knowlton Strategies, Washington, DC 2006–13; Vice-Chair. L&L Energy, Inc 2011–12; f. Mineta and Associates, LLC 2013; Co-Chair. Joint Ocean Commission Initiative 2010–; mem. Bd of Regents, Santa Clara Univ., Smithsonian Nat. Bd 1996–; Sr Advisor, Credit Suisse AG 2008–; mem. Bd of Councilors, US–Japan Council; Hon. PhD (Embry Riddle Aeronautical Univ.) 1991, (Univ. of Calif. at Berkeley) 2004, (UCLA) 2006, (Univ. of Wash.) 2008, Hon. DH (Rust Coll.) 1993; Hon Directorate (San Jose State Univ.) 2005; Presidential Medal of Freedom 2006, Asian Hall of Fame Award 2014. *Address:* Mineta & Associates, 1631 Cliff Drive, Edgewater, MD 21037, USA (office).

MINFORD, (Anthony) Patrick (Leslie), CBE, PhD; British economist and academic; *Professor of Applied Economics, Cardiff Business School;* b. 17 May 1943; s. of Leslie Mackay Minford and Patricia Mary Sale; m. Rosemary Irene Allcorn 1970; two s. one d.; ed Horris Hill, Winchester Coll., Univ. of Oxford, London School of Econs; Econ. Asst, Ministry of Overseas Devt 1966; Economist, Ministry of Finance, Malawi 1967–69; Econ. Adviser Courtaulds Ltd 1970–71; HM Treasury 1971–73; HM Treasury Del. Washington, DC 1973–74; Visiting Hallsworth Fellow, Univ. of Manchester 1974–75; Edward Gonner Prof. of Applied Econs, Univ. of Liverpool 1976–97; Visiting Prof., Cardiff Business School 1993–97, Prof. of Applied Econs 1997–; Dir Merseyside Devt Corpn 1988–89; mem. Monopolies and Mergers Comm. 1990–96, Treasury Panel of Independent Econ. Forecasters 1993–96; Ed. Nat. Inst. for Econ. and Social Research Review 1975–76, Liverpool Quarterly Econ. Bulletin 1980–; Hon. DSc (Buckingham) 2002. *Publications:* Substitution Effects, Speculation and Exchange Rate Stability 1978, Unemployment – Cause and Cure 1983 (second edn 1985), Rational Expectations and the New Macroeconomics (with David Peel) 1983, The Housing Morass 1987, The Supply-Side Revolution in Britain 1991, The Cost of Europe (ed.) 1992, Rational Expectations Macroeconomics 1992, Markets not Stakes 1998, Britain and Europe: Choices for Change (with Bill Jamieson) 1999, Advanced Macroeconomics: A Primer (with David Peel) 2002, Money Matters: Essays in honour of Alan Walters 2004, Should Britain Leave the EU? – An Economic Analysis of a Troubled Relationship (co-author) 2005 (second edn 2015), An Agenda for Tax Reform 2006; articles in journals. *Address:* Cardiff Business School, Cardiff University, Colum Drive, Cardiff, CF10 3EU, Wales (office). *Telephone:* (29) 2087-5728 (office). *Fax:* (29) 2087-4419 (office). *E-mail:* minfordp@cardiff.ac.uk (office). *Website:* www.patrickminford.net.

MINGOS, (David) Michael Patrick, BSc, DPhil, FRS, FRSC; British scientist and academic; *Professor of Inorganic Chemistry, University of Oxford;* b. 6 Aug. 1944, Basra, Iraq; s. of Vasso Mingos and Rose Enid Billie Griffiths; m. Stacey Mary Hosken 1967; one s. one d.; ed Harvey Grammar School, Folkestone, King Edward VII School, Lytham, Univ. of Manchester, Univ. of Sussex; Fulbright Fellow, Northwestern Univ. Ill., USA 1968–70; ICI Fellow, Univ. of Sussex 1970–71; Lecturer, Queen Mary Coll. London 1971–76; Lecturer in Inorganic Chem., Univ. of Oxford 1976–90, Reader 1990–92, Prof. of Inorganic Chem. 2000–; Fellow, Keble Coll. Oxford 1976–92; Univ. Assessor 1991–92; Sir Edward Frankland BP Prof. of Inorganic Chem., Imperial Coll. London 1992–99, Visiting Prof. 1999–2002; Dean, Royal Coll. of Science 1996–99; Prin. St Edmund Hall, Oxford 1999–2009; visiting professorships in USA, Canada, France, Germany, Switzerland and consultant for various UK and US chemical cos; Gov. Harrow School; mem. numerous editorial bds; Hon. Fellow, Keble Coll., Oxford 2001, St Edmund Hall 2009, Univ. of Sussex 50th Anniversary Fellow 2011; Hon. DSc (UMIST) 2000, (Sussex) 2001; Corday Morgan Medal, Noble Metal Prize, Tilden Medal of RSC, Manchott Prize 1995, Michael Collins Award for Innovation in Microwave Chemistry 1996, Alexander von Humboldt Forschungs Prize 1999, Blaise Pascal Medal for Chemistry 2017. *Publications include:* An Introduction to Cluster Chemistry 1989, Essentials of Inorganic Chemistry 1 1996, Essential Trends in Inorganic Chemistry 1998, Essentials of Inorganic Chemistry 2 1998, Regional Ed. Journal of Organometallic Chemistry 1997–2007, Series Ed. Structure and Bonding 2000. *Leisure interests:* cricket, tennis, walking, gardening, travel. *Address:* Inorganic Chemistry Laboratory, South Parks Road, Oxford, OX1 3QR, England (office). *Telephone:* (1865) 272600 (office). *Fax:* (1865) 279030 (office). *E-mail:* michael.mingos@seh.ox.ac.uk (office). *Website:* www.seh.ox.ac.uk (office).

MINKIN, Vladimir Isaakovich, CandSci, DSc, CChem, FRSC; Russian chemist and academic; *Research Adviser, Southern Federal University;* b. 4 March 1935; m.; one d.; ed Rostov State Univ.; tech. asst, Novocherkassk Tech. Univ. following graduation; Asst Prof., Dept of Organic Chem., Rostov State Univ. 1958–61, Assoc. Prof. 1961–67, Prof. 1967–, Distinguished Prof. 1995, Head of Inst. of Physical and Organic Chem. 1981–2012, Research Adviser, Southern Federal Univ. 2012–; Visiting Prof., Univ. of Havana 1973, Queens Univ. (Canada) 1980, Regensburg Univ. 1990, Univ. of Strathclyde 1993, Cornell Univ. 1993, Univ. of Marseille 1998, 2000, Humboldt Univ., Berlin 1999, Univ. of Florida 2006; Corresp. mem. USSR (now Russian) Acad. of Sciences 1990, Academician 1994, Deputy to Pres. of Southern Research Centre 2003–; Chair. IUPAC Working Party on Terminology in Theoretical Organic Chem. 1991–98; Titular mem. IUPAC Comm. on Physical Organic Chem. 1992–2003; mem. Editorial Bd, Journal of Molecular Structure (THEOCHEM) 1992–95, Journal of Physical Organic Chemistry 1996–2001, Isotopes in Organic Chemistry 1983–86, Advances in Heterocyclic Chemistry 1995–, Mendeleev Communications, Russian Chemical Reviews, Journal of General Chemistry (Russian), Journal of Organic Chemistry (Russian), Bulletin of Russian Academy of Sciences (Chemistry), Journal of Heterocyclic Chemistry (Latvia); P. Kapitsa Fellow, Royal Soc. 1993; Fellow, D. Mendeleev Russian Chemical Soc. 1965, Italian Acad. of Sciences 'Gioennia' 2006; Distinguished Prof., Taganrog Univ. 2005; Dr hc (Mediterranean Univ. of Aix-Marseille) 1995, (St Petersburg Technological Univ.) 2011; Award for the Excellence in Teaching, Ministry of Higher Educ. 1986, USSR State Prize 1989, Fulbright Research Scholar 1993, Alexander von Humboldt Sr Research Award 1999, A.M. Butlerov Prize, Russian Acad. of Sciences 2000, L.A. Chugaev Prize, Russian Acad. of Sciences 2003, Prize of Foundation for Support of Russian Science for "Outstanding Scientists of the Russian Acad. of Sciences" 2003, 2004, A.N. Necneyanov Prize, Russian Acad. of Sciences 2010. *Publications:* Dipole Moments in Organic Chemistry 1968, Quantum Chemistry of Organic Compounds 1986; 18 monographs and more than 900 papers in professional journals on applied quantum chemistry, tautomerism and molecular rearrangements, stereodynamics of metal coordination compounds, photochromism, nonclassical organic and organoelement structures and organotellurium chemistry; 95 Russian and int. patents. *Leisure interests:* chess, literature. *Address:* Institute of Physical and Organic Chemistry, Southern Federal University, 344090 Rostov on Don, Stachka Avenue 194/2, Russian Federation (office). *Telephone:* (863) 243-47-00 (office). *Fax:* (863) 243-47-00 (office). *E-mail:* minkin@ipoc.rsu.ru (office); ipoc@ipoc.sfedu.ru (office). *Website:* www.ipoc.rsu.ru/index.php?lang=en (office).

MINNELLI, Liza; American singer and actress; b. 12 March 1946, Los Angeles, Calif.; d. of Vincente Minnelli and Judy Garland; m. 1st Peter Allen 1967 (divorced 1972); m. 2nd Jack Haley, Jr 1974 (divorced 1979); m. 3rd Mark Gero 1979 (divorced 1992); m. 4th David Gest 2002 (divorced 2007, died 2016). *Films include:* Charlie Bubbles 1968, The Sterile Cuckoo 1969, Tell Me That You Love Me, Junie Moon 1971, Cabaret (played Sally Bowles) 1972 (Acad. Award for Best Actress, The Hollywood Foreign Press Golden Globe Award, the British Acad. Award and David di Donatello Award, Italy), Lucky Lady 1976, A Matter of Time 1976, New York, New York 1977, Arthur 1981, Rent-a-Cop 1988, Arthur 2: On the Rocks 1988, Sam Found Out 1988, Stepping Out 1991, Parallel Lives 1994, Sex and the City 2 2010. *Television includes:* Liza, Liza with a Z (Emmy Award) 1972, Goldie and Liza Together 1980, Baryshnikov on Broadway 1980 (Golden Globe Award), A Time to Live 1985 (Golden Globe Award), My Favourite Broadway: The Leading Ladies 1999, Arrested Development (series) 2013. *Theatre includes:* Best Foot Forward

1963, Flora, the Red Menace 1965 (Tony Award), Chicago 1975, The Act 1977–78 (Tony Award), Liza at the Winter Garden 1973 (Special Tony Award), The Rink 1984, Victor-Victoria 1997, Liza's at the Palace 2008. *Recordings include:* Liza! Liza! 1964, It Amazes Me 1965, There is a Time 1966, Liza Minnelli 1967, Come Saturday Morning 1968, New Feelin' 1970, Liza with a Z 1972, Liza Minnelli: The Singer 1973, Tropical Nights 1977, The Act 1977, The Rink 1984, Results 1989, Maybe This Time 1996, Minnelli on Minnelli 2000, Liza's Back 2002, The Very Best of Liza Minnelli: Life is a Cabaret! 2002, Confessions 2010.

MINNICK, Mary E., BS, MBA; American business executive and fmr beverage industry executive; *Partner, Lion Capital LLP;* b. 27 Nov. 1959, Evanston, Ill.; ed Bowling Green State Univ., Duke Univ.; joined The Coca-Cola Co. in 1983, later Pres. S Pacific Div., The Coca-Cola Co., later Pres. Coca-Cola Japan, Exec. Vice-Pres. The Coca-Cola Co. and Pres. and COO Coca-Cola Asia 2001–05, Exec. Vice-Pres. and Pres. Marketing, Strategy, and Innovation, Coca-Cola Co. 2005–07 (resgnd); Partner, Lion Capital LLP, London 2007–; mem. Bd of Dirs Target Corpn, Heineken; mem. Dean's Council, John F. Kennedy School of Govt, Harvard Univ.; mem. Bd Visitors, Fuqua School of Business, Duke Univ.; Alumni Wf360 (Womenfuture). *Address:* Lion Capital LLP, 21 Grosvenor Place, London, SW1X 7HF, England (office). *Telephone:* (20) 7201-2200 (office). *Fax:* (20) 7201-2222 (office). *Website:* www.lioncapital.com (office).

MINNIKHANOV, Rustam Nurgaliyevich; Russian mechanical engineer and politician; *Acting President of Tatarstan;* b. 1 March 1957, Yaña Arış, Rybno-Slobodsky Dist; m.; two s.; ed Kazan Agricultural Inst., Correspondence Inst. of Soviet Trade; began career as engineer with Selkhoztekhnika (machinery mfrs), Sabinsky Dist Asscn 1978; fmr Sr Engineer and Chief Power Engineer with state timber enterprise; fmr Chair. Dist Consumer Soc., also Chair. Exec. Cttee of People's Deputies Dist Council and First Deputy Head of Dist Admin, Arsky Dist 1985–93; Head of Vysokogorsky Dist Admin 1993–96; Minister of Finance, Repub. of Tatarstan 1996–98, Prime Minister of Tatarstan 1998–2010, Pres. of Tatarstan 2010–15, Acting Pres. 2015–; Chair. Tatneft (oil co.) 2005–06. *Leisure interest:* rally driving. *Address:* Office of the President, Kazan, Tatarstan, Russia (office). *Telephone:* (843) 567-89-01 (office). *Fax:* (843) 292-70-88 (office). *Website:* www .tatarstan.ru (office).

MINNIS, Hubert Alexander, MD, MRCOG; Bahamian physician and politician; *Prime Minister;* b. 17 April 1954, Bain Town; s. of Randolph Minnis and Rosalie North; m. Patricia Beneby; three s.; ed Univ. of the West Indies, Univ. of Minnesota; began career as physician, Princess Margaret Hosp., Nassau, becoming Consultant and Head, Dept of Obstetrics and Gynaecology; fmr Assoc. Lecturer in Obstetrics and Gynaecology, Univ. of the West Indies; mem. House of Ass. (lower house of parl.) for Killarney, New Providence 2007–; Leader of the Opposition 2012–16; Minister of Health 2007–12; Prime Minister 2017–; fmr Pres. Medical Asscn of the Bahamas; fmr Chair. Hotel Corpn of the Bahamas; mem. Free Nat. Movt, Leader 2012–16, 2017–. *Address:* Office of the Prime Minister, Sir Cecil Wallace-Whitfield Centre, West Bay St, POB CB-10980, Nassau, Bahamas (office). *Telephone:* 327-5826 (office). *Fax:* 327-5806 (office). *E-mail:* primeminister@ bahamas.gov.bs (office). *Website:* www.bahamas.gov.bs (office).

MINOGUE, Kylie Ann, OBE; Australian singer, actress, producer, fashion designer and entrepreneur and philanthropist; b. 28 May 1968, Melbourne, Vic.; started acting in Skyways 1980, The Sullivans 1981, The Henderson Kids 1984–85, then Neighbours 1986–88 (all TV series); solo artist 1988–, first female vocalist to have her first (released) five singles obtain silver discs in UK; numerous tours, concerts, TV and radio performances world-wide; launched own range of lingerie 2003; labels: PWL, Mushroom, Deconstruction, Parlophone, Warner Music Australia; Ordre des Arts et des Lettres 2008; Hon. Dr of Health Sciences (Anglia Ruskin Univ.) 2011; Woman of the Decade award 1989, nine Logies (Australian TV Industry awards), six Music Week Awards (UK), three Australian Record Industry Asscn Awards, three Japanese Music Awards, Irish Record Industry Award, Canadian Record Industry Award, World Music Award, Australian Variety Club Award, MO Award (Australia), Amplex Golden Reel Award, Diamond Award (Belgium), MTV Video of the Year (for Did it Again) 1998, MTV Awards for Best Pop Act, Best Dance Act 2002, BRIT Award for Best Int. Female Solo Artist 2002, 2008, Grammy Award for Best Dance Recording (for Come into my World) 2004, Music Industry Trusts' Award 2007, Q Idol Award 2007, inducted into Australian Recording Industry Asscn (ARIA) Awards Hall of Fame 2011. *Tours:* Disco in Dream 1989, Enjoy Yourself Tour 1990, Rhythm of Love Tour 1991, Let's Get to It Tour 1991, Intimate and Live 1998, On a Night Like This 2001, KylieFever2002 2002, Showgirl: The Greatest Hits Tour 2005, Showgirl: The Homecoming Tour 2006–07, KylieX2008 2008–09, For You, For Me 2009, Aphrodite World Tour 2011, Anti Tour 2012, Kiss Me Once Tour 2014. *Play:* The Tempest 1999. *Films:* The Delinquents 1989, Streetfighter 1994, Biodome 1996, Sample People 1999, Cut 1999, Sample People 2000, Moulin Rouge 2001, Holy Motors 2012. *Television:* judge and mentor, The Voice UK (BBC 1) 2014. *Recordings include:* albums: Kylie 1988, Enjoy Yourself 1989, Rhythm of Love 1990, Let's Get To It 1991, Kylie – Greatest Hits 1992, Kylie Minogue 1994, Kylie Minogue (Impossible Princess) 1997, Intimate And Live 1998, Light Years 2000, Hits + 2000, Fever (BRIT Award for Best Int. Album 2002) 2001, Confide In Me (compilation) 2002, Body Language 2003, X 2007, Aphrodite 2010, Kiss Me Once 2014, Golden 2018. *Publications:* Kylie 1999, Kylie La La La (with William Baker) 2003, The Showgirl Princess (juvenile) 2006. *Address:* Terry Blamey Management Pty Ltd, 329 Montague Street, Albert Park, Vic. 3206, Australia (office); Terry Blamey Management, PO Box 13196, London, SW6 4WF, England (office). *Telephone:* (20) 7371-7627 (London) (office). *Fax:* (20) 7731-7578 (London) (office). *E-mail:* info@terryblamey.com (office). *Website:* www.kylie.com (office).

MINOSKI, Kiril, MA, PhD; Macedonian economist and politician; b. 20 Oct. 1971, Skopje; ed St Kiril and Methodius Univ., Skopje, Univ. of Antwerp, Belgium, Staffordshire Univ., UK, Univ. degli studi di Bari, Italy; Man., Export-Import Dept, ORKA TRADE DOOEL 1997–99; Consultant and Deputy Project Man. and Acting Chief of Party, Booz Allen & Hamilton, Inc. (man. consulting firm), projects included Macedonian Banking Project/USAID 2000–02, Financial and Human Resourses Man., Macedonia Business Environment Activity/USAID 2002–06, Team Leader, Labour Market and Pension Reforms Component 2006–10, Man. of Export Component 2010–13; Business Devt Consultant, BS Co. Serbia 2005–07; Sr Consultant, World Bank Jan.–March 2007; Consultant, European Training Foundation 2007–08; Head of Project Implementation Unit, Reconstruction and Rehabilitation of Macedonian Health Provider Institutions Project (Council of Europe Devt Bank/Ministry of Health) 2013–14; Dir-Gen., State Market Inspectorate, Ministry of Economy 2014–15, Dir-Gen., Public Revenue Office 2015–16; Minister of Finance 2016–17; Manager, ETC Consulting 2017–. *Address:* c/o Ministry of Finance, 1000 Skopje, ul. Dame Gruev 12, North Macedonia.

MINOVES TRIQUELL, Juli F., Lic. rel. pol., MA, MPhil, PhD; Andorran political scientist, economist, academic, politician and international organization official and fmr diplomatist; *President, Liberal International;* b. 15 Aug. 1969, Andorra la Vella; ed Lycée Comte de Foix, Andorra, Fribourg Univ., Switzerland, Yale Univ., USA; Teaching Asst, Constitutional Law and Political Economy, Dept of Political Science, Yale Univ. 1993; Counsellor, Perm. Mission of Andorra to the UN, New York 1993–94, Deputy Perm. Rep. and Chargé d'affaires a.i. 1994–95, Amb. and Perm. Rep. 1995–2001; Alt. Head of Andorran Del. to World Summit on Social Devt, Copenhagen; Special Plenipotentiary Rep. of Andorran Govt in negotiations to establish diplomatic relations with various govts 1994–98; Amb. to USA and Canada 1996; Vice-Pres. UN Gen. Ass. 1997; Head of Andorran del. to UN Special Ass. Rio+5 1997; Chief of Cabinet a.i. of the Minister of Foreign Affairs 1997–99; mem. special group of UN diplomats for inspections in Iraq 1998; Head of Andorran del. for the establishment of an Int. Criminal Court, Rome, 1998; Amb. to Spain 1998, to Finland and Switzerland 1999, to UK 2000; Minister of Foreign Affairs, Culture and Co-operation 2001–07, of Econ. Devt, Tourism, Culture, Univs, and Govt Spokesman 2007–09; Vice-Pres. and mem. of the Bureau, Liberal International, London 2005–09, Deputy Pres. Liberal International 2009–12, Pres. 2014–; Council mem. CIDOB, Barcelona 2013; Asst Prof., Univ. of La Verne, Calif. 2012; Visiting Prof., Écoles des Affaires internationales, Institut d'Études Politiques de Paris (Sciences Po) 2012; Grand Cross, Order of Merit (Portugal) 1997, Grand Officer, First Class, Order of the Star of Italian Solidarity (Italy) 2009; Tristaina de periodisme journalism award 1986, Nat. Literature Award Fiter-i-Rosell 1988, El futur de les Valls Research Award 1989, Grad. Fellowship, Foundation Crèdit Andorrà 1991, Scholarship, Yale Univ. 1993, Departmental Distinction on Yale PhD dissertation. *Publications:* articles in Andorra 7 weekly magazine 1986–88, Segles de Memòria (novel) (Fiter i Rossell Award) 1989, Les Pedres del Diable (short stories) (Sant Carles Borromeu Award 1992). *Leisure interest:* running. *Address:* Liberal International, 1 Whitehall Place, London, SW1A 2HD, England (office). *Telephone:* (20) 7839-5905 (office). *Fax:* (20) 7925-2685 (office). *E-mail:* jminoves@aya.yale.edu (office). *Website:* www.liberal -international.org (office).

MINOW, Newton N., JD; American lawyer; *Senior Counsel, Sidley Austin LLP;* b. 17 Jan. 1926, Milwaukee, Wis.; s. of Jay A. Minow and Doris Minow (née Stein); m. Josephine Baskin 1949; three d.; ed Northwestern Univ.; Law Clerk to Supreme Court Chief Justice Vinson 1951; Admin. Asst to Gov. of Illinois Adlai E. Stevenson 1952–53; served Stevenson's law firm 1955–57, Partner 1957–61; Chair. Fed. Communications Comm. 1961–63; Exec. Vice-Pres. Gen. Counsel Encyclopaedia Britannica, Chicago 1963–65; Chair. Arthur Andersen & Co. Public Review Bd 1974–83, Public Broadcasting Service 1978–80; mem. Bd of Trustees, Rand Corpn 1965–75, 1976–86, 1987, Chair. 1970–72; Partner, Sidley Austin LLP (fmrly Leibman, Williams, Bennett, Baird & Minow and fmrly Sidley & Austin) 1965–91, Counsel 1991, now Sr Counsel; mem. Bd Trustees, Carnegie Corpn of New York 1987–97, Chair. 1993–97; Chair. Advisory Cttee to Sec. of Defense on protecting civil liberties in fight against terrorism; Walter Annenberg Univ. Prof., Northwestern Univ. 1987, now Walter Annenberg Prof. Emer.; Dir The Annenberg Washington Program 1987–96; Life Trustee, Univ. of Notre Dame, Mayo Clinic, Northwestern Univ.; Democrat; Hon. Chair. and Dir Chicago Educational TV Asscn; Hon. LLD (Wisconsin) 1963, (Brandeis) 1963, (Northwestern Univ.) 1965, (Columbia Coll.) 1972, (Notre Dame) 1994, (Santa Clara) 1998, (Catholic Theological Union) 2001, (John Marshall Law School) 2011, (Dominican Univ.) 2012; Silver Gavel Award, ABA, John Paul Stevens Award, Chicago Bar Asscn, Federal Communications Bar Asscn Lifetime Achievement Award, American Lawyer Lifetime Achievement Award, Presidential Medal of Freedom 2016. *Publications include:* Equal Time: The Private Broadcaster and the Public Interest 1964, Presidential Television (co-author) 1973, Electronics and the Future (co-author) 1977, For Great Debates (co-author) 1987, Abandoned in the Wasteland: Children, Television and the First Amendment 1995, Inside the Presidential Debates: Their Improbable Past and Promising Future (co-author) 2008. *Leisure interest:* reading. *Address:* Sidley Austin LLP, 1 South Dearborn Street, Chicago, IL 60603 (office); 179 East Lake Shore Drive, Chicago, IL 60611, USA (home). *Telephone:* (312) 853-7555 (office). *Fax:* (312) 853-7036 (office). *E-mail:* nminow@ sidley.com (office). *Website:* www.sidley.com (office).

MINT SOUEINAE, Fatma Vall; Mauritanian politician; fmr Minister of Culture and Handicrafts; Minister of Foreign Affairs and Co-operation Jan.–Sept. 2015, also Chair., Exec. Council.

MINTER, Alan; British fmr professional boxer; b. 17 Aug. 1951, Penge, London, England; s. of Sidney Minter and Anne Minter; m. Lorraine Bidwell 1974; one s. one d.; ed Sarah Robinson School, Ifield; middleweight, southpaw; amateur boxer 1965–72; Amateur Boxing Asscn of England Middleweight Champion 1971; bronze medal, Olympic Games, Munich 1972; 145 amateur fights, 125 wins; professional boxer 1972–82; British Middleweight Champion 1975; won Lonsdale Belt outright 1976; won European Championship from Germano Valsecchi Feb. 1977, lost it to Gratien Tonna Sept. 1977; forfeited British title Feb. 1977, regained it Nov. 1977; won vacant European title v. Angelo Jacopucci July 1978, retained it v. Tonna Nov. 1978; relinquished British title Nov. 1978; WBA Middleweight Champion and WBC Middleweight Champion v. Vito Antuofermo, Las Vegas March 1980 (first British boxer to win a world championship in USA for 63 years); retained titles v. Antuofermo June 1980, lost them to Marvin Hagler Sept. 1980; lost European title to Tony Sibson Sept. 1981; retd from boxing Feb. 1982, 39 wins (KO 23), 9 losses (KO 8), 1 no contest; nickname Boom Boom; lives in Littlehampton, West Sussex and tours UK in autograph and lecture shows, alongside fmr world boxing champion Jim Watt. *Publication:* Minter: An Autobiography 1980. *Leisure interest:* golf.

MINTON, Mark C., BA, MA; American diplomatist and academic; *Professor of Practice and Distinguished Scholar, School of Global and International Studies, Indiana University;* ed Columbia Univ., Yale Univ.; served for three years in US

Army; career mem. Foreign Service, began career as Political Officer, Embassy in Tokyo 1977, served on Policy Planning Staff, Washington, DC, followed by assignment with Office of Soviet Union Affairs, Consul-Gen. in Sapporo, Japan 1984, subsequent assignments with Dept of State's Exec. Secr., as Pearson Fellow with US Senate and as Deputy Dir (Japanese Affairs), Minister-Counselor for Political Affairs, Embassy in Seoul 1992, returned to Washington, DC as Dir of Korean Affairs, Minister-Counselor for Political Affairs, Perm. Mission to UN, New York 1998, Deputy Chief of Mission, Embassy in Seoul –2006, served as Chargé d'affaires a.i., then Amb. to Mongolia 2006–09, fmr Diplomat-in-Residence, CUNY; Pres. Korea Soc. 2010–15; Prof. of Practice and Distinguished Scholar, Indiana Univ. 2015–. *Address:* Hamilton Lugar School of Global and International Studies, Global and International Studies Building, 355 North Jordan Avenue, Bloomington, IN 47405-1105, USA (office). *E-mail:* mcminton@indiana.edu (office); mintonmc@gmail.com (office). *Website:* www.sgis.indiana.edu (office).

MINTON BEDDOES, Zanny, BA; British economist and journalist; *Editor-in-Chief, The Economist;* b. 1968; m. Sebastian Mallaby; four c.; ed Univ. of Oxford, Harvard Univ., USA; began career as adviser to Minister of Finance in Poland; Economist with IMF 1992–94; joined The Economist 1994, Emerging Markets Corresp., London 1994–96, Econs Ed., Washington, DC 1996–2014, Business Affairs Ed., London 2014–15, Ed.-in-Chief (first female), The Economist 2015–; Trustee, Carnegie Endowment for Int. Peace; mem. Research Advisory Bd, Cttee for Econ. Devt; regular TV and radio commentator; Gerald Loeb Award for Commentary 2012, for Breaking News 2017, Wincott Foundation Financial Journalist of the Year 2012. *Publications include:* numerous articles on int. finance including the IMF and EU, economic reform in emerging markets; regular contribs to Foreign Affairs and Foreign Policy. *Address:* The Economist, The Adelphi, 1–11 John Adam Street, London, WC2N 6HT, England (office). *Telephone:* (20) 7830-7000 (office). *Fax:* (20) 7839-2968 (office). *E-mail:* letters@economist.com (office). *Website:* www.economist.com (office).

MINTZ, Shlomo; Israeli/American violinist, conductor and academic; b. 30 Oct. 1957, Moscow, USSR; s. of Abraham Mintz and Eve Mintz (née Labko); m. Corina Ciacci; two s.; ed Juilliard School of Music, USA, studied with Dorothy DeLay, also studied with Ilona Fehér; moved to Israel aged two; Premio Accad. Musicale Chigiana, Siena, Italy 1984; Music Dir, Conductor and Soloist, Israel Chamber Orchestra 1989–93; Artistic Adviser, Limburg Symphony Orchestra, The Netherlands 1994; Artistic Adviser and Prin. Guest Conductor, Maastricht Symphony Orchestra 1994–98; Prin. Guest Conductor, Arena di Verona 1999–2000, Zagreb Philharmonic Orchestra 2008–10; Artistic Dir, Int. Music Festival, Sion Valais 2002–12; Artistic Dir, Crans Montana Classics (masterclass), Switzerland 2012–; Mentor and Pres. of the Jury, Int. Violin Competition, Buenos Aires, HKIVS Shlomo Mintz Int. Violin Competition, Beijing; presides over Munetsugu Angel Violin Competition, Japan; Pres. of the Jury, Sion Valais Int. Violin Competition, Switzerland 2002–11; Co-founder and Patron, Keshet Eilon Int. Violin Mastercourse, Israel 1992–2010; guest conductor and soloist for numerous orchestras world-wide; Dr hc (Ben-Gurion Univ.) 2006; Diapason d'Or 1981, Premio Accademia Musicale Chigiana 1984, Edison Award 1985, 2001, 2007, Grand Prix du Disque 1992, 1997, 1998, Gramophone Award 1994, Cremona Music Award 2016. *Recordings include:* Violin Concertos by Mendelssohn and Bruch (Grand Prix du Disque, Diapason d'Or) 1981, J.S. Bach Complete Sonatas and Partitas for Solo Violin, The Miraculous Mandarin by Bartok (with Chicago Symphony Orchestra, conducted by Abbado), Compositions and Arrangements by Kreisler (with Clifford Benson, piano), Twenty-four Caprices by Paganini, Two Violin Concertos by Prokofiev (with London Symphony Orchestra, conducted by Abbado), The Four Seasons by Vivaldi (with Stern, Perlman, Mehta). *Telephone:* 6-07249734 (Spain, mobile) (office). *E-mail:* b.alonsomonedero@gmail.com (office). *Website:* belenalonsomanagement.com (office); www.shlomomintzviolin.com.

MINUTO-RIZZO, Alessandro, LLD; Italian diplomatist, international organization official and academic; *Member of Faculty, School of Government, Libera Università Internazionale degli Studi Sociali 'Guido Carli';* b. 10 Sept. 1940, Rome; m.; two s.; mem. staff, Directorate of Cultural Affairs, Ministry of Foreign Affairs, Rome 1969–72; First Sec. Washington, DC 1972–75; Counsellor, Prague 1975–80; Head of Eastern Europe Desk, Directorate for Econ. Affairs 1980–81, Head of EEC External Relations Desk 1981–86; Minister-Counsellor, OECD, Paris 1986–92; Minister Plenipotentiary Jan. 1992; Diplomatic Counsellor of Minister for Budget and Econ. Planning 1992–96, of Minister for Co-ordination of European Policies (a.i.) 1995–96; Deputy Chief of Cabinet, Ministry of Foreign Affairs Jan.–Oct. 1996, Co-ordinator for EU Affairs 1996–97; Diplomatic Counsellor of Minister of Defence 1997–2000; Amb. to Cttee for Policy and Security of EU 2000–01; Deputy Sec.-Gen. NATO 2001–07, Acting Sec.-Gen. 2003–04; currently mem. Faculty, School of Govt, Libera Università Internazionale degli Studi Sociali 'Guido Carli'; Del. to Council, ESA 1986–92; Chair. Admin. and Financial Cttee 1993–96; Chair. Ass. of Parties of Eutelsat 1989; mem. Man. Bd, Italian Space Agency 1994–95; Chair. EU Cttee for Territorial Devt 1996. *Address:* School of Government, Libera Università Internazionale degli Studi Sociali 'Guido Carli', Via di Villa Emiliani 14, 00197 Rome, Italy (office). *Telephone:* (06) 85225053 (office). *Fax:* (06) 85225056 (office). *E-mail:* sog@luiss.it (office). *Website:* sog.luiss.it (office).

MIOU-MIOU; French actress; b. (Sylvette Héry), 22 Feb. 1950, Paris; one d. by Patrick Dewaere; one d. by Julien Clerc; worked as child in Les Halles wholesale market; apprenticed in upholstery workshop; with comedian Coluche helped create Montparnasse café-theatre 1968; stage appearance in Marguerite Duras' La Musica 1985. *Films:* La cavale 1971, Themroc 1972, Quelques missions trop tranquilles 1972, Elle court la banlieue 1972, Les granges brûlées 1972, Les aventures de Rabbi Jacob 1972, Les valseuses 1973, La grande Vadrouille 1974, Lily aime-moi 1974, Pas de Problème 1974, Un génie, deux associés, une cloche 1975, La marche triomphale 1975, F. comme Fairbanks 1976, On aura tout vu 1976, Jonas qui aura vingt ans en l'an 2000 1976, Portrait de province en rouge 1977, Dites-lui que je l'aime 1977, Les routes du Sud 1978, Au revoir à lundi 1978, Le grand embouteillage 1978, La Dérobade 1978, La femme flic 1980, Est-ce bien raisonnable? 1980, La gueule du loup 1981, Josépha 1981, Guy de Maupassant 1982, Coup de foudre 1983, Attention, une femme peut en cacher une autre! 1983, Canicule 1983, Blanche et Marie 1984, Tenue de soirée 1986, Ménage, Les portes tournantes 1988, La lectrice 1988, Milou en mai 1990, Netchaiev est de retour 1991 La Totale! 1991, Le Bal des Casse-Pieds 1992, Tango 1993, Germinal 1993, Montparnasse–Pondichéry 1994, Un indien dans la ville 1994, Ma femme me quitte 1996, Le Huitiéme jour 1996, Nettoyage à sec 1997, Elles 1997, Hors jeu 1998, Tout va bien, on s'en va 2000, Mariages! 2004, L'Après-midi de monsieur Andesmas 2004, L'Un reste, l'autre part 2005, Riviera 2005, The Science of Sleep 2006, Avril 2006, Family Hero 2006, Les Murs porteurs 2007, Affaire de famille 2008, Le Grand alibi 2008, Mia et le Migou (voice) 2008, Pour un fils 2009, Quand je serai petit 2012, Landes 2013, Family Business 2018.

MIQDAD, Faisal al-; Syrian diplomatist; *Deputy Foreign Minister;* ed Damascus Univ., Charles Univ., Prague; fmr Deputy, then Acting Amb. to UN, New York, Perm. Rep. 2002–05; Deputy Foreign Minister 2006–. *Address:* Ministry of Foreign Affairs, ave Shora, Muhajireen, Damascus, Syria (office). *Telephone:* (11) 3331200 (office). *Fax:* (11) 3320686 (office).

MIRABAUD, Pierre G.; Swiss banker and national organization official; b. 1948; ed Univ. of Geneva; past positions with Banque Rivaud SA, Morgan Guaranty Trust, Blunt Ellis & Loewi, Swiss Bank Corpn; joined Mirabaud & Cie 1976, Pnr 1979, Sr Pnr 1995–; Chair. Swiss Pvt. Bankers Asscn 1990–93, Swiss Bankers Asscn 2003–09; Vice-Chair. Avenir Suisse –2003; currently Man. Partner, Mirabaud & Cie Banquiers Privés; Founder and Chair. Pro Democratia Foundation; Chair. Quantum Endowment Fund NV; Vice-Pres. Aéroport International De Genève; mem. Bd of Dirs ACH Management SA; Trustee Central European Univ. *Address:* Mirabaud & Cie Banquiers Privés, 29, boulevard Georges-Favon, Geneva 1204, Switzerland (office).

MIRAKHOR, Abbas, PhD; Iranian international banking executive, economist and academic; *Chair of Islamic Finance, International Centre for Education in Islamic Finance;* b. 1 July 1941, Tehran; m. Loretta Thomas 1965; two s.; ed Kansas State Univ., USA; Asst and Assoc. Prof. and Chair. Dept of Econs, Univ. of Alabama 1968–77, Prof. and Chair. Dept 1977–79, Vice-Chancellor 1979–80; fmr Prof., Az-Zahra Univ., Tehran; Prof. and Chair. Grad. Study Dept, Alabama A&M Univ. 1980–83; Prof. of Econs Fla Inst. of Tech. 1983–84; Economist, IMF 1984–87, Sr Economist 1987–90, Exec. Dir 1990–2008 (retd); Chair of Islamic Finance, Int. Centre for Educ. in Islamic Finance, Kuala Lumpur 2010–; Quaid-e-Azam Star for Service to Pakistan 1999, Order of Companion of Volta for Service to Ghana 2005; IEEE Eng Man. Soc. First Paper Prize 1972, Islamic Devt Bank Prize for Research in Islamic Econs (jtly) 2003. *Publications:* numerous articles on econs. *Address:* International Centre for Education in Islamic Finance, Second Floor, Annexe Block, Menara Tun Razak (Menara Tradewinds), Jalan Raja Laut, 50350 Kuala Lumpur, Malaysia (office). *Telephone:* (3) 27814010 (office). *Fax:* (3) 26924094 (office). *E-mail:* abbasmirakhor@inceif.org (office). *Website:* www.inceif.org (office).

MIRANDA, Lin-Manuel; American composer, lyricist and actor; b. 16 Jan. 1980, New York; m. Vanessa Adriana Nadal 2010; two s.; ed Wesleyan Univ.; wrote and directed several musicals and acted in numerous stage productions whilst at Wesleyan Univ.; worked as English teacher, Hunter Coll. High School 2002; wrote music and lyrics for musical In the Heights (opened on Broadway 2008); Co-founder and mem. Freestyle Love Supreme (hip-hop improv group); mem. Theater Subdistrict Council, New York City 2015–; Council mem., The Dramatists Guild; mem. Bd Young Playwrights, Inc.; Hon. DHumLitt (Yeshiva) 2009; Dr hc (Wesleyan) 2015, (Pennsylvania) 2016; Nat. Arts Club Medal of Honor 2008, John D. and Catherine T. MacArthur Foundation Genius Award 2015, Kennedy Center Award 2018; Grammy Award for Best Song Written for Visual Media (for How Far I'll Go) 2018. *Theatre includes:* In the Heights (actor and writer) (Tony Award for Best Original Score 2008, Grammy Award for Best Musical Theater Album 2009, Theater World Award for Outstanding Debut Performance 2007, Clarence Derwent Award for Most Promising Male Performance 2007) 2008–11, The Electric Company (composer and actor) 2009, Bring It On: The Musical (co-wrote music and lyrics) 2011, 21 Chump Street (narrator) 2014, Hamilton (wrote book and score, starred as title role) (numerous awards including History Makers Award 2015, Grammy Award for Best Musical Theater Album 2016, Edward M. Kennedy Prize for Drama 2016, Pulitzer Prize for Drama 2016, Tony Award Best Book of a Musical 2016) 2015–. *Television appearances include:* The Sopranos 2007, House 2009, Modern Family 2011, How I Met Your Mother 2013, Do No Harm 2013, Sesame Street 2014, This American Life 2014, Curb Your Enthusiasm 2017, Bartlett 2018. *Films include:* Clayton's Friends (writer, dir and actor) 1996, Looking for Maria Sanchez (actor) 2013, Star Wars: The Force Awakens (actor and music) 2015, Speech & Debate 2017, Mary Poppins Returns 2018. *Website:* www.linmanuel.com (office).

MIRANDA FLAMENCO, Jaime, MA, MBA; Salvadorean politician; b. 1955; ed Universidad Centroamericana José Simeón Cañas, Instituto Centroamericano de Administración de Empresas; fmr Programme Coordinator, Friedrich-Ebert-Stiftung, El Salvador; fmr Political Affairs Officer for UN Verification Mission in Guatemala; fmr Dir-Gen., Salvadorean Asscn for Integral Devt; fmr Deputy Minister of Devt Cooperation and Econ. Relations; Minister of Foreign Affairs 2013–14; Pres. Community of Democracies 2013–.

MIRANI, Aftab Shahban; Pakistani politician; b. Shikarpur; s. of Ghulam Kadir Shahban Mirani and Begum Sharfunisa Shahban Mirani; m. Safia Aftab Mirani (died 2007); one s. three d.; ed studies in farm man. and agric. in USA; fmr Pres. Shikarpur Municipality; mem. Sindh Prov. Ass. (Pakistan People's Party) 1977–90; Chief Minister of Sindh Feb.–Aug. 1990; mem. Nat. Ass. 1990–, for NA-202 constituency 2008–, mem. Public Accounts Cttee; Minister of Defence 1993–96; Vice-Chair. and Treas., Shaheed Zulfikar Ali Bhutto Inst. of Science and Tech.; pioneer mem. Parl. Comm. for Judicial Appointments 2010. *Leisure interests:* walking, swimming. *Address:* National Assembly Secretariat, Parliament House, Islamabad (office); R/o Mirani Muhalla, Shikarpur, Pakistan (home). *Telephone:* 3-442481454 (mobile); (21) 5855930 (office); (21) 5850554 (office). *E-mail:* assembly@na.gov.pk (office). *Website:* www.na.gov.pk/en/profile.php?uid=19 (office).

MIRAPEIX LUCAS, Ferran, LenD, MBA; Andorran politician; b. 7 Sept. 1957; ed Univ. of Barcelona, Spain, London School of Econs, UK, Northwestern Univ., USA; Finance Counsellor, Comú de Sant Julià de Lòria 2000–03, Chief Finance Counsellor 2004–05; Minister of Finance 2006–09; Vice-Pres. Liberal Party of Andorra; Dir Meridien Group, SA 2014–. *Address:* Meridien Group, SA, Andorra la Vella, Andorra (office). *Telephone:* 741175 (office). *E-mail:* info@meriden-ipm.com (office).

MIRICIOIU, Nelly, Diploma of Bacalaureat (Piano) and Degree (Voice); Romanian/British singer (soprano); b. 31 March 1952, Adjud; d. of Voicu Miricioiu and Maria Miricioiu; m. Barry J Kirk; one s.; ed Octav Bancila Music School, Iasi, George Enescu Conservatoire; professional debut as Queen of the Night in The Magic Flute in Romania 1970; West European debut as Violetta in Scottish Opera production of La Traviata 1981; debut at Covent Garden as Nedda in I Pagliacci 1982, at La Scala as Lucia in Lucia di Lammermoor 1983; has since appeared at all major opera houses of the world and in int. recitals and concerts (Salzburg Festival, Concertgebouw, Royal Festival Hall); repertoire includes Mimi (La Bohème), Julietta (I Capuleti e I Montecchi), Gilda (Rigoletto), Elvira (Ernani), Marguerite and Elena (Mefistofele), Michaela (Carmen), Marguerite (Faust), Violetta (La Traviata), Roberto Devereux, Lucrezia Borgia and Maria Stuarda (Donizetti), Tancredi (Rossini), Elisabeth (Don Carlos), Il Pirata and Norma (Bellini), Emma d'Antiochia (Mercadante), Helena in I Vespri Siciliani (Verdi), Jerusalem (Verdi), Semiramide (Rossini), Desdemona in Othello, title roles in Giovanna d'Arco, Tosca, Luisa Miller, Manon Lescaut, Anna Bolena, Lucia di Lammermoor and many more; has worked with many leading conductors and dirs, singing leading roles such as Tosca with José Carreras, José Cura, Neil Schicoff, Mimi in La Bohème with Plácido Domingo, Violetta in La Traviata with Franco Bonisolli, with Roberto Alagna, Renato Bruson, Alfredo Kraus, and many other leading artists; began 20-year series of Vara Matinee Concerts at Amsterdam Concertgebouw 1986; first recording, recital at Wigmore Hall, London 1986; master-classes at numerous venues; jury mem. Maria Callas Grand Prix 2003, London Int. Music Festival 2003, Athens 2003, Dutch IVC 2004, 2010, 2012; Guest Prof., Acad. of Music, Maastricht 2010–; Cross Royal House of Romania, Comandor Meritul Cultural; winner of 10 int. competitions, including Second Prize, Francisco Viñas (First Prize not awarded) 1974, First Prize, Maria Callas Competition, Athens 1974, Second Prize, Paris 1975, Second Prize, Geneva 1976, Gold Medal, Katia Popova Competition 1977, First Prize, 's-Hertogenbosch Competition 1978, First Prize, Ostende 1980, American Biographical Insts Award 1994, Romanian Medal of Cultural Merit 2004. *Recordings include:* Puccini's Tosca, Mercadante's Orazi e Curiazi, Donizetti's Rosamunda d'Inghilterra (with Renée Fleming and Bruce Ford) and Maria de Rudenz (Maria), Rossini's Riccardo e Zoraide, Pacini's Maria Regina d'Inghilterra (Maria) 1998, Mascagni's Cavalleria Rusticana (Santuzza), a live recording in Rome of Respighi's La Fiamma (Silvana) and Nelly Miricioiu Live at the Concertgebouw, Nelly Miricioiu – A Rossini Gala 2000, Nelly Miricioiu – Bel Canto Portrait 2001, Roberto Devereux (Elisabetta) at Covent Garden 2003, Mercadante's Emma d'Antiochia 2005, Donizetti's Maria Padilla 2012. *Leisure interests:* literature, TV, cooking, socializing, movies. *Address:* c/o Zemsky/Green Artists Management, 104 West 73rd Street, New York, NY 10023, USA (office). *Telephone:* (212) 579-6700 (office). *Fax:* (212) 579-4723 (office). *E-mail:* agreen@zemskygreen.com (office); bzemsky@zemskygreen.com (office). *Website:* www.zemskygreen.com (office); www.nellymiricioiu.com.

MIRISIM, Solan; Papua New Guinea politician; ed Lae Business Coll., Papua New Guinea Univ. of Tech.; mem. Nat. Parl. for Telefomin Open constituency 2012–; Minister of Defence 2017–19; Chair. Citizenship Advisory Council; mem. People's Nat. Congress (PNC). *Address:* c/o Department of Defence, CDC House, MacGregor Street, Port Moresby, NCD, Papua New Guinea (office).

MIRKAZEMI, Masoud Seyed, BS, MS, PhD; Iranian industrial engineer and politician; b. 1960, Tehran; ed Elm va San'at Univ.; joined Revolutionary Cttees after 1979 revolution; fmr Lecturer, Imam Hossein Univ., Elm va San'at (Science and Industry) Univ.; Head, Centre for Promotion of Productivity and System Evaluation 1989–2000; Head, Centre for Research and Logistic Studies, Ministry of Defence 2000, Adviser to Minister of Defence 2001–03; Dir Islamic Revolutionary Guard Corps Centre for Foundational Studies 2002–04; Pres. Shahed Univ. 2004–; Minister of Commerce 2005–09, Minister of Petroleum 2009–11; Man. Dir Etka Org., Tehran; Ed.-in-Chief Faramad (journal); f. Iran Logistics Assen; Head, Comm. on Energy, Parl. 2012–14; MP 2012–16; mem. Univ. Scientific Bd.

MIRONOV, Oleg Orestovich, LLD; Russian lawyer; b. 5 June 1939, Pyatigorsk; m.; one s.; ed Saratov Inst. of Law; local investigator Pyatigorsk 1964; teacher, Prof. Constitutional Law Dept Saratov Inst. of Law; State Duma Deputy with CP of Russian Fed. 1993–95; mem. State Duma for Saratov Region 1995–98; mem. Cttee on Law and Legal Reform; mem. Central Cttee of CP of Russian Fed. –1998; Commr on Human Rights (Ombudsman) in Russian Fed. 1998–2003; mem. Interparl. Ass. of CIS, Acad. of Social Sciences, Russian Acad. of Lawyers; Honoured Jurist of Russian Fed. *Publications:* about 200 articles including monographs on problems of constitutional law, theory of state and law, politology. *Leisure interests:* mountain tourism, sports. *Address:* c/o Office of the Commissioner on Human Rights in the Russian Federation, Myasnitskaya str. 47, Moscow, Russia. *Telephone:* (495) 207-76-30 (office).

MIRONOV, Sergey Mikhailovich, CandJur; Russian engineer and politician; *Chairman, Spravedlivaya Rossiya (A Just Russia);* b. 14 Feb. 1953, Pushkin, Leningrad Oblast; m. 4th Olga Ivanovna Mironova; ed Leningrad (now St Petersburg) Plekhanov Mining Inst., St Petersburg State Tech. Univ., Russian Acad. of State Service at the Pres. of the Russian Fed., Faculties of Law and Philosophy, St Petersburg State Univ.; served in Soviet Army Airborn Forces (VDV) 1971–73, now senior sergeant in the reserve; senior geophysical engineer, SPO RusGeoPhysica (production co.) 1978–86; later Sr Geophysicist, Zelenogorsk expedition, USSR Ministry of Geology; senior geophysicist of air reconnaissance mission under authority of USSR Ministry of Geology in Mongolian People's Republic 1986–91; received certificate of Russian Ministry of Finance for the right to engage in securities market 1993; Exec. Dir JSC Construction Corpn Vozrozhdenie, St Peterburg 1994–95; mem. Legis. Ass. of St Petersburg 1995–2000, First Deputy Chair. 1998–2000, Vice-Pres. 2000; Head, Political Council, The Will of Petersburg (Volya Peterburga) regional political movt 2000–01; Rep. of St Petersburg Ass. to Sovet Federatsii (Fed. Council) June 2001, Chair. Fed. Council Dec. 2001–11; Founder and Chair. Russian Party of Life 2003, Chair. Spravedlivaya Rossiya (A Just Russia) (merger of Motherland, Russian Party of Life and Russian Pensioners' Party) 2006–; Chair. Council of the House of A Just Russia Party Deputies 2011–; unsuccessful presidential cand. 2004, 2012; Prof. Emer., North West Acad. of Public Admin 2004, Perm State Tech. Univ., Bryansk State Univ.; Hon. Firearm 2000, 2003 and 2005; Hon. Prof., South Ural State Univ. 2003, Moscow State Pedagogical Univ.; Hon. Citizen of Makhachkala 2006; Order of St Sergius Radonezh, Second Class (Russian Orthodox Church) 2003, First Class 2008; Medal 'In Commemoration of the 300th Anniversary of St Petersburg' 2003; Collar of the Order of Merit of Peru 2005; Medal 'In Commemoration of the 1000th Anniversary of Kazan' 2005; Order of Merit for the Motherland (Third Degree) 2008; Medal of Honour (South Ossetia) 2009; Jubilee Medal '300 Years of the Russian Navy'; Dr hc (Nizhny Novgorod State Univ.), (Nat. Acad. of Sciences of Armenia), (Russian State Social Univ.), (Mongolian Univ. of Science and Tech.), (Far Eastern State Univ. of Communications), (Moscow State Forest Univ.), (Khakassia State Univ.), (NF Katanova and Russian-Tajik Slavonic Univ.), (Bashkir State Univ.) 2006, (Slavonic Univ., Moldova) 2007. *Address:* Spravedlivaya Rossiya, 123104 Moscow, ul. M. Dmitrovka 12/1, Russia (office). *Telephone:* (495) 787-85-15 (office). *Fax:* (495) 787-85-20 (office). *E-mail:* reception@mironov.ru (home); info@spravedlivo.ru (office). *Website:* www.spravedlivo.ru (office); mironov.ru; sergey-mironov.livejournal.com/profile.

MIRONOV, Yevgeniy Vitalyevich; Russian actor; *Artistic Director, State Theatre of Nations;* b. 29 Nov. 1966, Saratov; s. of Vitaly Sergeyevich Mironov and Tamara Petrovna Mironova; ed Slonov Theatre School of Saratov, Studio School of Moscow Art Theatre; actor, Oleg Tabakov Theatre-Studio 1990–; Artistic Dir State Theatre of Nations 2006–; Co-founder Artist Support Foundation; Artistic Dir TERRITORIA Int. Theatre Festival; mem. Arts and Culture Council, Office of the Pres. of the Russian Fed.; Merited Artist of Russia 1996, State Prize of the Russian Federation 1996, 2010, People's Artist of Russia 2004. *Theatre includes:* Gotcha (dir Oleg Tabakov, The Oleg Tabakov Theatre) 1987, Biloxi Blues (dir Oleg Tabakov, The Oleg Tabakov Theatre) 1987, A Common Story (dir Oleg Tabakov, The Oleg Tabakov Theatre) 1990, My Big Land (Silent Sailor Street) (dir Oleg Tabakov, The Oleg Tabakov Theatre) 1990, The Inspector General (dir Sergei Gazarov, The Oleg Tabakov Theatre) 1991, The Don Juan Myth (dir Aleksandr Marin, The Oleg Tabakov Theatre) 1992, Hour of Triumph, Local Time (dir Vladimir Mashkov, The Oleg Tabakov Theatre) 1992, The Passions of Bumbarash (dir Vladimir Mashkov, The Oleg Tabakov Theatre)) 1993, The Oresteia (dir Peter Stein, Int. Confed. of Theatre Asscns) 1994, The Karamazovs and Hell (dir Valery Fokin, The Sovremennik Theatre) 1996, Anecdotes (dir Vladimir Mashkov, The Oleg Tabakov Theatre) 1996, The Last Night of the Last Czar (dir Valery Fokin, The BOGIS Entrepreneurial Theatre Agency) 1996, Another Van Gogh... (dir Valery Fokin, a joint project of the Oleg Tabakov Theatre and the Meyerhold Creative Centre) 1998, Hamlet (dir Peter Stein, Int. Confed. of Theatre Asscns) 1998, Boris Godunov (dir Declan Donnellan, a joint project of the Cheek by Jowl Theatre Co. and Moscow Int. Chekhov Festival) 2000, The Seagull (dir Oleg Yefremov, The Moscow Art Theatre (new cast)) 2001, No. 13 (Out of Order) (dir Vladimir Mashkov, The Moscow Art Theatre) 2001, The Cherry Orchard (dir Eimuntas Nekrošius, The Stanislavsky Foundation) 2003, The Golovlyovs (dir Kirill Serebrennikov, The Moscow Art Theatre) 2005, Figaro. The Events of One Day (dir Kirill Serebrennikov, The Y. Mironov Theatre Co.) 2006, Shukshin's Stories (dir Alvis Hermanis, State Theatre of Nations) 2008, Caligula (dir Eimuntas Nekrošius, State Theatre of Nations) 2011, Miss Julie (dir Thomas Ostermeier, State Theatre of Nations) 2011. *Films include:* roles in films by A. Kaidanovsky, A. Mitta, V. Todorovsky, Khotinenko, D. Yevstigneyev, N. Mikhalkov, S. Gazarov, including The Kerosene Seller's Wife 1988, The Women That Were Lucky 1989, Before the Dawn 1989, Beast Triumphant 1989, Ready... One! 1990, Lost in Siberia 1991, The Gold of Carpathia 1991, Love (Prize for Best Kinotaurus Festival, Constellation-92, Young Stars of Europe, Geneva 1992, Cinema Critics Prize-Best Actor of the Year 1992) 1991, Encore Again! (Prize of Cinema Critics, Best Actor of the Year 1993) 1992, What's Up, Poor Fish? 1992, The Last Saturday 1993, Limita (The Provincials) (Nika Prize 1995) 1994, Utomlyonnye solntsem (Burnt by the Sun) (Prize for Supporting Actor, Constellation-95) 1994, Moslem 1994, A Tram in Moscow 1995, The Inspector General (Prize for Best Actor Role, Ural Festival 1996) 1996, Snake Spring 1997, Mama 1999, His Wife's Diary 2000, August of '44 2000, House of Fools 2001, The Metamorphosis 2001, A Game In The Modern Style 2002, I Got An Idea... 2003, The Evening Chime 2004, On Upper Maslovka 2005, Dreaming of Space 2005, Escape 2005, Piranha 2006, In Tranzit 2008, Khranit vechno 2008, Space Dogs 3D (voice) 2010, Burnt by the Sun 2. Exodus 2010, Moscow, I Love You! 2010, The Diamondchasers 2011, Belka i Strelka: Lunnye priklyucheniya (voice) 2014, Vychislitel 2014. *Television includes:* Dvadtsat minut s angelom 1996, Idiot (mini-series) 2003, The First Circle/To Treasure Forever (mini-series) 2006, The Apostle (mini-series) 2008, Utomlennye solntsem 2 (mini-series) 2011, Dostoevskiy (mini-series) 2011–13, Pepel (series) 2013. *Address:* State Theatre of Nations, 107031 Moscow, 3 Petrovsky Lane, Russian Federation (office). *Telephone:* (495) 629-37-39 (box office) (office). *E-mail:* studio@emironov.ru; info@tofnations.ru (office). *Website:* theatreofnations.ru (office); emironov.com.

MIRONYUK, Svetlana, MBA; Russian media executive; b. 3 Jan. 1968, Moscow; m. S. A. Zverev; three c.; ed Lomonosov Moscow State Univ., Eötvös Loránd Univ.; began career as Deputy Man. for Information Analysis and Public Relations, Media Post 1992–2000; Vice-Pres. Kros (public relations co.) 2000–03; joined RIA Novosti news agency 2003–14, Chair. 2003–06, Dir-Gen. 2004–06, Ed.-in-Chief 2006–14; Sr Vice-Pres. and Dir of Marketing, Sberbank 2016–17; mem. World Econ. Forum, Valdai Discussion Club, Russian Geographic Society, WWF; Media Manager of the Year 2007, Editor of the Year, Russian Fed. of Journalists 2011, C4F - Communiction for Future Award, World Econ. Forum 2011.

MIROVIĆ, Igor; Serbian economist and politician; *President, Government of Vojvodina ;* b. 12 July 1968, Kruševac, Socialist Repub. of Serbia, Socialist Fed. Repub. of Yugoslavia; m. Vera Mirović; two s.; ed Univ. of Novi Sad; Vice-Pres. City Ass. of Novi Sad 1992–94, Councillor 2012; mem. Narodna skupština Republike Srbije (Nat. Ass., Repub. of Serbia) 1992–96, 1996–98, 2003–07; Deputy, Ass. of Autonomous Prov. of Vojvodina 1996–2000, 2004–08, 2012–13, Vice-Pres. 2008–12, Pres. Govt of Vojvodina 2016–; Deputy, Fed. Ass. of FR Yugoslavia 2000–03, Deputy Minister of Finance 1998–2000, Minister of Regional Devt and Local Self-Govt 2013–14, Acting Minister of the Economy 2014; Chair. Managing Bd, Novi Popovac (cement factory), Paraćin 1998–2001; Dir PE Novi Sad City Devt Inst. 2004–08; Pres. Vojvodina Volleyball Club 2004–08; mem. Srpska Napredna Stranka (Serbian Progressive Party), Pres. 2012–16. *Address:* Office of the Provincial Government of Vojvodina, 21000 Novi Sad, bul. Mihajla Pupina 16,

Vojvodina, Serbia (office). *Telephone:* (21) 4874000 (office). *E-mail:* presbiro@vojvodina.gov.rs (office). *Website:* www.vojvodina.gov.rs (office).

MIROW, Thomas; German economist and banking executive; b. 6 Jan. 1953, Paris, France; s. of Eduard Mirow; m. Barbara Mirow; two d.; ed Univ. of Bonn; Asst and later Chef de Cabinet to fmr Chancellor Willy Brandt 1975–83; Dir Hamburg Press Office 1983–87; Political and Man. Consultant 1988–91; State Minister and Head of Chancellery, Hamburg State Admin 1991–93, State Minister for Urban Devt and Head of Chancellery 1993–97, State Minister for Econs 1997–2001; mem. EC High-Level Group on Lisbon Strategy 2004, Personal Rep. of Fed. Chancellor for Lisbon Strategy and Dir-Gen. for Econ. Policy, Fed. Chancellery 2005, State Sec. Fed. Finance Ministry 2005–08; Pres. EBRD 2008–12; Chair. Supervisory Bd Hamburger Hafen- und Lagerhaus AG (Hamburg Port) 1997–2001, Flughafen Hamburg GmbH 1997–2001; mem. Supervisory Bd Daimler Chrysler Luft- und Raumfahrtholding (Daimler Chrysler Aerospace Holding) 1997–2001; Man. Dir Alstertor Schienenlogistik Beteiligung GmbH 2002–05; mem. Admin. Council Hamburgische Landesbank 1997–2001; mem. Bd of Supervisory Dirs Kreditanstalt für Wiederaufbau 1997–2001; Sr Adviser Ernst & Young AG 2002–05; Adviser MM Warburg Bank 2002–05; Sr Fellow, Hertie School of Governance 2012–.

MIRREN, Dame Helen Lydia, DBE; British actress; b. 26 July 1945, Chiswick, London; m. Taylor Hackford 1997; first experience with Nat. Youth Theatre culminating in appearance as Cleopatra in Antony and Cleopatra, Old Vic 1965; joined RSC 1967 to play Castiza in The Revenger's Tragedy and Diana in All's Well that Ends Well; Dr hc (St Andrews) 1999; Lifetime Achievement Award for her 'outstanding and lasting' contrib. to film and TV, Women In Film And TV Awards, London 2009. *Plays include:* Cressida in Troilus and Cressida, Hero in Much Ado About Nothing, RSC, Stratford 1968; Win-the-Fight Littlewit in Bartholomew Fair, Aldwych 1969, Lady Anne in Richard III, Stratford, Ophelia in Hamlet, Julia in The Two Gentlemen of Verona, Stratford 1970 (the last part also at Aldwych), Tatyana in Enemies, Aldwych 1971; title role in Miss Julie, Elyane in The Balcony, The Place 1971; with Peter Brook's Centre Int. de Recherches Théâtrales, Africa and USA 1972–73; Lady Macbeth, RSC, Stratford 1974 and Aldwych 1975; Maggie in Teeth 'n' Smiles, Royal Court 1975; Nina in The Seagull and Ella in The Bed Before Yesterday, Lyric for Lyric Theatre Co. 1975; Margaret in Henry VI (Parts 1, 2 and 3), RSC 1977–78; Isabella in Measure for Measure, Riverside 1979; The Duchess of Malfi, Manchester Royal Exchange 1980 and Roundhouse 1981; The Faith Healer, Royal Court 1981; Antony and Cleopatra 1983, 1998, The Roaring Girl, RSC, Barbican 1983, Extremities (Evening Standard Award) 1984, Madame Bovary 1987, Two Way Mirror 1989; Sex Please, We're Italian, Young Vic 1991; The Writing Game, New Haven, Conn. 1993, The Gift of the Gorgon (New York) 1994; A Month in the Country 1994, Orpheus Descending 2001, Dance of Death (New York) 2001, Phèdre (London) 2009, The Audience (London) (Olivier Award for Best Actress 2013, WhatsOnStage Award for Best Actress in a Play 2014) 2013. *Films include:* Age of Consent 1969, Savage Messiah, O Lucky Man! 1973, Caligula 1977, The Long Good Friday 1979, Excalibur 1981, Cal (Best Actress, Cannes) 1984, 2010 1985, White Nights 1986, Heavenly Pursuits 1986, The Mosquito Coast 1987, Pascali's Island 1988, When the Whales Came 1988, Bethune: The Making of a Hero 1989, The Cook, the Thief, His Wife and Her Lover 1989, The Comfort of Strangers 1989, Where Angels Fear to Tread 1990, The Hawk, The Prince of Jutland 1994, The Madness of King George 1995, Some Mother's Son 1996, Teaching Mrs Tingle 1998, The Pledge 2000, No Such Thing 2001, Greenfingery 2001, Gosford Park (Screen Actors' Guild Award for Best Supporting Actress) 2002, Calendar Girls 2003, The Clearing 2004, Raising Helen 2004, The Hitchhiker's Guide to the Galaxy (voice) 2005, Shadowboxer 2005, The Queen (Best Actress, Venice Film Festival, Nat. Bd of Review, Los Angeles Film Critics Asscn, Toronto Film Critics Asscn, Nat. Soc. of Film Critics 2006, Golden Globe for Best Actress (drama) 2006, Screen Actors' Guild Award for Outstanding Performance by a Female Actor in a Leading Role 2007, Best British Actress, London Film Critics' Circle Awards 2007, Best Int. Actress, Irish Film and TV Awards 2007, BAFTA Award for Best Actress 2007, Acad. Award for Best Actress 2007) 2006, National Treasure Book of Secrets 2007, Inkheart 2008, State of Play 2009, The Last Station 2009, Love Ranch 2009, The Debt 2010, The Tempest 2010, Brighton Rock 2010, Legend of the Guardians: The Owls of Ga'Hoole 2010, Red 2010, Arthur 2011, The Door 2012, Hitchcock 2012, Monsters University (voice) 2013, Red 2 2013, The Hundred-Foot Journey 2014, Woman in Gold 2015. *Television includes:* Miss Julie, The Apple Cart, The Little Minister, As You Like It, Mrs. Reinhardt, Soft Targets 1982, Blue Remembered Hills, Coming Through, Cause Celebre, Red King White Knight, Prime Suspect (BAFTA Award) 1991, Prime Suspect II 1992, Prime Suspect III 1993, Prime Suspect IV: Scent of Darkness 1995 (Emmy Award 1996), Prime Suspect V: Errors of Judgement 1996, Painted Lady 1997, The Passion of Ayn Rand 1998, Prime Suspect VI 2004, Elizabeth I (Golden Globe Award for Best Actress in a mini-series or film made for TV 2007, Screen Actors' Guild Award for Outstanding Performance by a Female Actor in a TV Movie or Mini-series 2007) 2005, Prime Suspect VII (Emmy Award for Best Actress in a Mini-series 2007) 2006, Nat. Theatre Live (series) – Phèdre 2009, Phil Spector (Screen Actors Guild Award for Outstanding Performance by a Female Actor in a TV Movie or Mini-Series 2014) 2013. *Publication includes:* In the Frame (autobiog.) 2007. *Address:* c/o Raj Raghavan, CAA, 4th Floor, Space One, 1 Beadon Road, London, W6 0EA, England (office). *Telephone:* (20) 8846-300 (office). *Fax:* (20) 8846-3090 (office). *Website:* www.caa.com (office); www.helenmirren.com; www.helenmirrenofficial.com.

MIRVIS, Chief Rabbi Ephraim, BA; South African/British rabbi and Talmudic scholar; *Chief Rabbi, United Hebrew Congregations of the Commonwealth;* b. 7 Sept. 1956, Johannesburg; s. of Rabbi Dr Lionel Mirvis and Freida Mirvis and Freida Mirvis; m. Valerie Kaplan; four s. one d. (deceased); ed Herzlia High School, Cape Town, Yeshivat Kerem B'Yavneh, Yeshivat Har Etzion, Machon Ariel, Jerusalem, Univ. of South Africa, Yaakov Herzog Teachers' Coll.; moved to Israel to study 1973; received his rabbinic ordination in Jeruslaem; certified by Yaakov Herzog Teachers' Coll. as high school teacher in Israel; Rabbi of Adelaide Road Synagogue, Dublin, later Chief Rabbi of Ireland 1984–92; Rabbi of Western Marble Arch Synagogue, London 1992–96; Sr Rabbi at Finchley United Synagogue, also known as Kinloss, London 1996–2013; Founder Rabbi and Hon. Prin. of Morasha Jewish Primary School and Founder and Pres. Kinloss Community Kollel; Chief Rabbi of United Hebrew Congregations of Commonwealth 2013–; Chair. Bd Govs Stratford Jewish Schools, Dublin 1984–92; mem. Steering Cttee of Conf. of European Rabbis; Religious Advisor to Jewish Marriage Council 1997–; has served on Council of London School of Jewish Studies, on Steering Cttee of Encounter Conf., Singer's Prayer Book Publs Cttee; mem. Chief Rabbi's Cabinet 1996–; Chair. Rabbinical Council of United Synagogue 1999–2002; Pres. Irish Council of Christians and Jews 1985–92; Jerusalem Prize for Education in Diaspora, on behalf of Stratford Jewish Schools, from Pres. Chaim Herzog 1990. *Leisure interest:* supports Tottenham Hotspur Football Club. *Address:* Office of the Chief Rabbi, 305 Ballards Lane, London, N12 8GB, England (office). *Telephone:* (20) 8343-6301 (office). *E-mail:* info@chiefrabbi.org (office). *Website:* chiefrabbi.org (office).

MIRVISH, David, CM; Canadian theatrical producer, art collector and art dealer; b. 29 Aug. 1944; s. of Edwin Mirvish, CBE and Anne Lazar Macklin; producer and owner of The Old Vic Theatre, London and The Royal Alexandra and The Princess of Wales Theatres, Toronto; Dir Williamstown Theatre Festival, USA –1992, Nat. Gallery of Canada, Nat. Theatre School of Canada 1989–91, Toronto French School; mem. Canadian Cultural Property Export Review Bd 1983–86; announced a partnership with architect Frank Gehry 2012; Chancellor Univ. of Guelph 2012–; Order of Ontario 2001; hon. degree from Univ. of Toronto 2004; Rayne Award, Royal Nat. Theatre, Toronto Theatre Alliance (Dora) Humanitarian Award, Toronto Arts Award 1994. *Productions and co-productions include:* Candide and Too Clever by Half (London), Into the Woods (London), Les Misérables (Canada) 1989–90, The Good Times Are Killing Me (New York), Miss Saigon 1993–95, Crazy for You 1994–95, Tommy (Toronto) 1995, Rent 1997–98, Jane Eyre 1996–97, The Lion King 2000–04, The Producers 2003–04, Hairspray 2004, The Lord of the Rings 2006, We Will Rock You and The Sound of Music opened 2008. *Address:* Mirvish Productions, 284 King Street West, Suite 400, Toronto, ON M5V 1J2, Canada (office); The Old Vic, Waterloo Road, London, SE1 8NB, England (office). *Telephone:* (20) 7928-2651 (London) (office); (416) 593-0351 (Toronto) (office). *Fax:* (416) 593-9221 (office). *E-mail:* webmaster@mirvishproductions.com (office). *Website:* www.mirvishproductions.com (office); www.mirvish.com (office).

MIRZA, Fehmida, BS, MD; Pakistani politician, physician and business executive; *Federal Minister for Inter Provincial Coordination;* b. 20 Dec. 1956, Sialkot; d. of Qazi Abdul Majeed Abid; m. Zulfikar Ali Mirza; two s. two d.; ed Liaquat Medical Coll., Jamshoro; physician at MCH Centre, then School Health Centre 1983–89; Dir Mirza Sugar Mills 1989–99, CEO 1999–; mem. Nat. Ass. representing Badin 1997–, Speaker 2008–13; mem. Grand Democratic Alliance 2018–; Federal Minister for Inter Provincial Coordination 2018–; fmr mem. Pakistan People's Party. *Address:* Ministry of Inter-provincial Co-ordination, 2nd Floor, Cabinet Block, Constitution Avenue, Islamabad, Pakistan (office); Deh Jakheji, Golarchi, Taluka S.F. Rahu, District Badin, Pakistan (home). *Telephone:* (51) 9103600 (office); (51) 9103193 (office). *Fax:* (51) 9103600 (office). *E-mail:* info@ipc.gov.pk (office). *Website:* www.ipc.gov.pk (office).

MIRZA, Hamid Ali, BSc, LLB; Pakistani fmr judge; b. 14 Sept. 1940, Jacobabad, Sindh; ed Univ. of Sindh, Jamshoro, Nat. Inst. of Public Admin, Lahore; practised as an advocate 1961–73; Sr Civil Judge and Asst Sessions Judge, Prov. Judicial Service 1973–76; Additional Dist and Sessions Judge 1976–83, served at Karachi, Sukkur, Nawabshah and numerous other places of Prov. of Sindh, also served as OSD Law reforms, High Court of Sindh, Karachi for two years; Dist and Session Judge 1983–95, posted at Nawabshah July–Sept. 1985, at Karachi South 1990–91, 1992–94, also served as Judge, Small Causes Court, Karachi Jan.–March 1983, 1984–85; Registrar, High Court of Sindh 1983–84, 1994–95; Solicitor, Govt of Sindh 1985–90; Chair. Appellate Tribunal for Local Councils of Sindh 1991–92; Judge, High Court of Sindh 1995–2000; Judge, Supreme Court of Pakistan 2000–05 (retd); mem. Syndicate, Univ. of Sindh, Jamshoro 1995–97, 1998–2000; mem. Election Comm. of Pakistan, Chief Election Commr 2009–12 (retd); Trustee, Agha Khan Medical Univ.

MIRZA, Sania; Indian professional tennis player; b. 15 Nov. 1986, Mumbai; d. of Imran Aziz Mirza and Nasima Mirza; m. Shoaib Malik 2010; ed Nasr School, St Mary's Coll.; winner, India Fed. Cup 2003, Wimbledon Championships (girls' doubles) 2003, Women's Tennis Asscn Title (doubles) 2005, 2014, Hyderabad Open 2005, Doha Asian Games (silver medal) (women's singles), (gold medal) (mixed doubles) 2006, Bank of the West Classic (women's doubles) 2007, Australian Open (mixed doubles) 2009, Commonwealth Games (silver medal) (women's singles), (bronze medal) (women's doubles), French Open (mixed doubles) 2012, US Open (mixed doubles) 2014, BNP Paribas Open, Indian Wells (women' doubles) 2015; Hon. DLit (MGR Educational and Research Inst. Univ., Chennai) 2008; Arjuna Award 2004. *Leisure interests:* cricket, music. *Website:* www.facebook.com/sania.mirza.

MIRZIYOYEV, Shavkat; Uzbekistani politician and head of state; *President;* b. 24 June 1957, Zomin Dist, Samarqand Viloyat (now in Jizzax Viloyat), Uzbek SSR, USSR; m. Ziroatkhon Hoshimova; ed Tashkent Inst. of Irrigation, Eng and Agric. Mechanization; worked in irrigation centres and establishments 1974–91; Sec. of Komsomol section, then lecturer, party organizer, Pro-Rector, Tashkent Inst. of Irrigation and Mechanization of Agric. –1996; Head of Admin, Mirzo-Ulugbeg Dist, Tashkent 1992; Hokim (Gov.) Jizzax Viloyat 1996–2001, Samarqand Viloyat 2001–03; elected mem. Oly Majlis (Parl.) 1990; mem. Fidokorlar Milliy Demokratik Partiyasi (Fidokorlar—Self-Sacrificers' People's Democratic Party) –2008, O'zbekiston Milliy Tiklanish Demokratik Partiyasi (MT—People's Revival Democratic Party of Uzbekistan) 2008–16, Tadbirkorlar va Ishbilarmonlar Harakati—O'zbekiston Liberal Demokratik Partiyasi (O'zlidep—Movement of Entrepreneurs and Businessmen—Liberal Democratic Party of Uzbekistan) 2016–; Prime Minister of Uzbekistan 2003–16; Head of the Agro-Industrial Complex 2005, responsible for Agric. and Water Resources, Agricultural Processing and Consumer Goods 2014; Acting Pres. of Uzbekistan Sept.–Dec. 2016, Pres. 14 Dec. 2016–; Order of Danaker (Kyrgyzstan) 2017. *Address:* Office of the President, 100163 Tashkent, O'zbekiston shoh ko'ch. 43, Uzbekistan (office). *Telephone:* (71) 239-54-04 (office). *Fax:* (71) 239-53-25 (office). *E-mail:* presidents_office@press-service.uz (office). *Website:* www.press-service.uz (office).

MIRZO, Maj.-Gen. Sherali; Tajikistani army officer and government official; *Minister of Defence;* b. 24 May 1967, Maskav Dist, Kulob Viloyat (now Hamadoni Dist, Khatlon Viloyat), Tajik SSR, USSR; m.; three c.; ed Perm Marshall V.I.

Chykov Missile Forces Higher Mil. Command Acad., Russia, V.I. Frunze Mil. Acad., Moscow, Russia; joined armed forces of Tajikistan 1994, commanded troops from Vose during te Tajikistani civil war, fought against opposition forces in Tavildara Dist and Khovaling Dist; commdr of infantry brigade of Land Forces of Repub. of Tajikistan 1995–97; commdr of rapid reaction forces, infantry brigade of Armed Forces of Repub. of Tajikistan 1997–2002; Deputy Minister of Defence and Commdr of Land Forces of Repub. of Tajikistan 2005–06; First Deputy Chair. State Cttee of Nat. Security, Head of Chief Directorate of the Border Forces and Commdr of the Border Troops 2006–13; Minister of Defence 2013–. *Address:* Ministry of Defence, 734025 Dushanbe, Kuchai Bokhtar 59, Tajikistan (office). *Telephone:* (372) 21-69-83 (office). *Fax:* (372) 21-32-47 (office).

MIRZOEFF, Edward, CVO, CBE, MA; British television producer, director and executive producer; b. 11 April 1936, London; s. of Eliachar Mirzoeff and Penina Asherov; m. Judith Topper 1961; three s.; ed Hasmonean Grammar School, London, The Queen's Coll., Oxford; market researcher, Social Surveys (Gallup Poll) Ltd 1958–59, Public Relations Exec., Duncan McLeish & Assocs 1960–61; Asst Ed., Shoppers' Guide 1961–63; with BBC TV 1963–2000, Exec. Producer, Documentaries 1983–2000; Dir and producer of many film documentaries including: (with Sir John Betjeman) Metro-land 1973, A Passion for Churches 1973, The Queen's Realm 1977; Police – Harrow Road 1975, The Regiment 1977, The Front Garden 1979, The Ritz 1981, The Englishwoman and The Horse 1981, Elizabeth R (marking the Queen's 40th anniversary) 1992, Facing the Music: The Return of Torvill and Dean 1994, Treasures in Trust 1995, John Betjeman: The Last Laugh 2001; Ed. Bird's-Eye View 1969–72, 40 Minutes 1985–89; Exec. Producer, many documentary series including Real Lives 1985, Pandora's Box 1992, The Ark 1993, True Brits 1994, Situation Vacant 1995, The House 1995, Full Circle with Michael Palin 1997, The Fifty Years War: Israel and the Arabs 1998; Producer, Richard Dimbleby Lectures 1972–82, A.J.P. Taylor Lectures (three series); Exec. Producer, The Lord's Tale (Channel 4) 2002, A Very English Village 2005, The Lie of the Land (Channel 4) 2007; Chair. BAFTA 1995–97 (Vice-Chair., TV 1991–95); Trustee, BAFTA 1999–2011, Grierson Trust 1999–2009 (Vice-Chair. 2000–02, Chair. 2002–06, Patron 2010–15); Vice-Pres. The Betjeman Soc. 2006–; mem. Bd of Dirs' and Producers' Rights Soc. 1999–2007, Salisbury Cathedral Council 2002–10; BAFTA Awards: Best Documentary 1981, Best Factual Series 1985, 1989, Alan Clarke Award for outstanding creative contribution to TV 1995; Samuelson Award, Birmingham Festival 1988, BFI TV Award 1988, British Video Award 1992, Broadcasting Press Guild Award 1996, Royal Philharmonic Soc. Music Award 1996, Int. Emmy 1996. *Publications:* articles, principally for The Oldie. *Leisure interests:* lunching with friends, opera. *Address:* 9 Westmoreland Road, London, SW13 9RZ, England (home).

MIRZOYAN, Ararat, Cand.Hist.Sci, PhD; Armenian historian and politician; *First Deputy Premier;* b. 23 Nov. 1979, Yerevan, Armenian SSR, USSR; m.; two c.; ed Yerevan State Univ., Armenian Genocide Museum Inst. of Postgraduate Studies; Jr Researcher, Armenian Genocide Museum Inst. of Postgraduate Studies 2003–05; Chief Archivist, Dept of Socio-Political Documents, Nat. Archives of Armenia 2005–07; Specialist, HSBC Bank Armenia CJSC 2007–10; Analyst, Regnum (int. news agency) 2011–12; Coordinator, Int. Foundation for Electoral Systems (IFES) 2012–13; Lecturer, Yerevan State Univ. 2012–13; Head of Research Group, Aurora and 100 Lives initiative, IDeA Foundation Armenia 2013–15; Expert on political parties and strategic planning, Netherlands Inst. for Multi-Party Democracy (NIMD) 2014–17; mem. Nat. Ass. (Yelq dashinq—Exit Alliance) for electoral dist No. 3 2017–18, mem. Standing Cttee on Science, Educ., Culture, Youth and Sport 2017–18; First Deputy Premier 2018–; Founding mem. Kaghakatsiakan Paymanagir (KP—Civil Contract); Ministry of Defence Certificate of Honour 2016. *Address:* Office of the Prime Minister, 0077 Yerevan, Marshal Baghramyan poghota 26, Armenia (office). *Telephone:* (10) 52-53-94 (office). *Website:* www.gov.am (office).

MIRZOYEV, Gasan Borisovich, DJur; Russian lawyer and politician; *President, Guild of Russian Lawyers;* b. 11 Dec. 1947, Baku, Azerbaijan; ed Azerbaijan State Univ., Moscow Inst. of Man.; State Arbiter of Moscow 1987–; Founder and Chair. Moscow State Centre on Legal Assistance, later Moscow Legal Centre 1993–, leading to creation of Russian Lawyers Guild; Rector and mem. Russian Bar Acad.; Vice-Pres. Russian Acad. of Natural Sciences; Pres. Human Rights Bd Int. Informatization Acad.; mem. Political Council, Union of Right Forces; Pres. Guild of Russian Lawyers 1994–; Deputy, State Duma of Russian Fed. 1999–, First Deputy of Chair. of Expert Council of Cttee of State Duma of Fed. Council on labour, social policy and veterans' affairs; mem. Council of Rectors of Insts of Higher Educ.; Chair. Editorial Bd Rossiyskiy Advokat; Academician, Russian Acad. of Advocacy and Notary, Head of Chair of Advocacy and Law Enforcement Activity; Merited Lawyer of the Russian Fed.; Honoured Worker of Justice of Russia; Hon. Lawyer of Russia; Order 'For Fidelity to Lawyer's Duty'; F.N. Plevako Bronze Bust Award. *Publications:* more than 300 scientific works, articles and published works, including more than 20 monographs and several literary works. *Leisure interest:* chess. *Address:* Guild of Russian Lawyers, 105120 Moscow, Maly Poluyaroslavsky per. 3/5, Building 1, Russia (office). *Telephone:* (495) 916-12-48 (office). *Fax:* (495) 916-30-67 (office). *E-mail:* advokat@gra.ru (office); mirzoev@hotmail.ru. *Website:* www.gra.ru (office).

MIRZOYEV, Ramason Zarifovich; Tajikistani diplomatist and government official; *Director of the Resettlement Unit, Directorate of the Flooding Area of Rogun Hydro Power Project;* b. 15 Feb. 1945, Kulyab Region; m. Akobirova Sarvarbi; four s. one d.; ed Tadjik Inst. of Agric.; worked with construction teams Kulyab Region; in Afghanistan 1975–78; worked in CP bodies and orgs 1983–; USSR People's Deputy 1989–92; Deputy Chair. USSR Supreme Soviet 1989–91; Man. Council of Ministers Repub. of Tajikistan 1992–95; Amb. to Russian Fed. 1995–2001, to Iran 2001–11; Dir Resettlement Unit, Directorate of the Flooding Area, Rogun Hydro Power Project 2011–.

MIRZOYEV, Vladimir V.; Russian stage director; b. 21 Oct. 1957; m.; one s. two d.; ed Moscow State Lunacharsky Inst. of Theatre Art (now the Russian Acad. of Theatre Art), studied in faculty of circus directing and Mark Mestechkin workshop; Artistic Dir, Studio Domino of the Union of Theatre Workers 1987–89; lived and worked in Canada from 1989, Founder and Artistic Dir, Horizontal Eight theatre co., Toronto 1989–93; Stage Dir, Moscow Stanislavsky Drama Theatre 1994–; stage dir for productions at Moscow Vakhtangov Theatre, Lenkom Theatre, Vilnius Theatre of Russian Drama, Maryinsky Theatre and for TV; staged Harold Pinter's The Homecoming at Mayakovsky Theatre, in which the main character resembles Stalin 2014; planning on staging a play based on Mikhail Khodorkovskii's (q.v.) biography. *Plays include:* Possibilities, Feast Day (Studio Domino), Proposal, Bear, Caligula (studio Horizontal Eight, Toronto), Cyrano de Bergerac, Amphitrion (Moscow Vakhtangov Theatre), Two Women (Lenkom Theatre), Twelfth Night, Marriage, Khlestakov (Moscow Stanislavsky Drama Theatre), Tartuffe (Vilnius Theatre of Russian Drama). *Television includes:* Russian People's Post (based on the play by Oleg Bogaev to mark 75th birthday of M. Ulyanov) 2002, Passionate and Considerate Contemplation (after the play by Maxim Kurochkin, Kultura channel) 2002. *Publications include:* contrib. to Sovietski Teatr journal 1981–87. *Address:* c/o Mariinsky Theatre, 1 Theatre Square, Moscow, Russian Federation. *E-mail:* info@mariinsky.ru. *Website:* www.mariinsky.ru/en/company/common_opera/mirzoev.

MIŞA, Ionuţ; Romanian economist and politician; b. 7 Jan. 1975; m.; three c.; ed Ovidius Univ., Constanta; Economist, SC Agroservice, Constanta 1998–99; Inspector, Gen. Public Finance Dept, Constanta city council 1999–2001, Head, Fiscal Agency No. 1, Financial Dept Jan.–April 2001; Expert, Budget Dept, Authority for the Privatization of State Assets (APAPS), Constanta Br. April–Dec. 2001; Econ. Dir, Public Tax Service, Gen. Taxes and Local Taxes Directorate, Constanta 2001–03, Deputy Exec. Dir 2003–04; Chief of Public Finance Admin, City of Eforie 2005–09; Head of Public Finance Admin, Constanta 2009–13; Gen. Dir, Nat. Agency of Fiscal Admin (ANAF) 2013–17; Sec. of State, Ministry of Public Finance Jan.–June 2017, Minister of Public Finance June 2017–18; mem. Partidul Social Democrat (PSD).

MISHIMA, Yoshinao, BEng, MEng, PhD, DEng; Japanese engineer, academic and university administrator; *President, Tokyo Institute of Technology;* ed Tokyo Inst. of Tech., Univ. of California, Berkeley, USA; Asst Research Engineer, Univ. of California, Berkeley 1979–81; Asst Prof., Precision and Intelligence Lab., Tokyo Inst. of Tech. 1981–89, Assoc. Prof., Precision and Intelligence Lab. 1989–97, Prof., Dept of Materials Science and Eng, Interdisciplinary Grad. School of Science and Eng 1997–, Dean, Interdisciplinary Grad. School of Science and Eng 2006–10, Dir Frontier Research Centre 2010–11, Dir Solutions Research Lab. 2011, Exec. Vice-Pres. for Educ. and Int. Affairs 2011–12, Pres. Tokyo Inst. of Tech. 2012–. *Publications:* numerous papers in professional journals. *Address:* Office of the President, Tokyo Institute of Technology, 4259 Nagatsuta-cho, Midori-ku, Yokohama, Kanagawa Prefecture, 226-0026, Japan (office). *Telephone:* (45) 924-5902 (office). *E-mail:* pr@jim.titech.ac.jp (office). *Website:* www.titech.ac.jp (office).

MISHRA, Brig. (retd); **B. D.,** MA, MSc, PhD; Indian state governor and fmr army officer; *Governor of Arunachal Pradesh;* b. 20 July 1939, Gopiganj, Sant Ravidas Nagar Dist, Uttar Pradesh; s. of Jagannath Mishra and Dhirajee Devi; m. Neelam Mishra; one s. one d.; ed Allahabad Univ., Madras Univ., Jiwaji Univ.; served in Indian Army 1961–95, served in Sino-Indian War 1962, Indo-Pakistani War 1965, Bangladesh War of Independence 1971; Commdr, Infantry Bn, Poonch Sector, Jammu and Kashmir 1979–81; fmr Commdr, Infantry Brigade as part of Indian Peacekeeping Force in Sri Lanka; fmr Commdr, Nat. Security Guard (NSG) Counter Hijack Force; fmr Instructor, Coll. of Combat, Mhow Cantonment, Madhya Pradesh and Defence Services Staff Coll., Wellington Cantonment, Tamil Nadu; retd from army 1995 (rank of Brig.); Gov. of Arunachal Pradesh 2017–; mem. Bharatiya Janata Party. *Address:* Raj Bhavan, P-Sector, Papum Pare District, Itanagar 791 111, Arunachal Pradesh, India (office). *Telephone:* (360) 2212457 (office). *Fax:* (360) 2212508 (office). *Website:* arunachalgovernor.gov.in (office).

MISIŪNAS, Eimutis, DScS (Law); Lithuanian lawyer, academic and politician; *Ministry of the Interior;* b. 1 April 1973, Vilnius, Lithuanian SSR, USSR; m.; one s. one d.; ed Lithuanian Police Acad. (now Mykolas Romeris Univ.); Asst of Police Law and Professional Tactics Dept, Lithuanian Police Acad. 1996–98; lawyer, PI Legal Assistance Centre 1997–2004; Lecturer, Dept of Police Law, Faculty of Police, Univ. of Law of Lithuania 1998–2005; Lecturer, Dept of Police Law and Activity, Faculty of Law Enforcement, Mykolas Romeris Univ. 2005–06, Dean, Int. School of Law and Business, Faculty of Law 2005–08, Lecturer, Inst. of Constitutional and Admin. Law 2006–14; Chief Specialist, Corruption Prevention Bd, Special Investigation Service of the Repub. of Lithuania 2008–15; judge, Vilnius Dist Çourt 2015–16; Minister of the Interior 2016–. *Address:* Ministry of the Interior, Šventaragio 2, Vilnius 01510, Lithuania (office). *Telephone:* (5) 271-7130 (office). *Fax:* (5) 271-8551 (office). *E-mail:* bendrasisd@vrm.lt (office); korespondencija@vrm.lt (office). *Website:* www.vrm.lt (office).

MIŠKOV, Juraj; Slovak politician and fmr advertising executive; b. 15 April 1973, Bratislava; divorced; two c.; ed Comenius Univ., Bratislava; Ed. Slovak Radio, Bratislava 1991; Ed. SME (daily newspaper) 1992; Exec., Randolph, Young & Moore (advertising agency), Bratislava 1992–93; Exec., Burian, Miškov & Partners, Bratislava 1993–99; co-f. Miškov-Uličný-Weber (MUW, advertising agency) 1999, Gen. Dir MUW Saatchi & Saatchi, Bratislava 2000–09; apptd mem. Nat. Council of the Slovak Repub. (Parl.) 2010; Minister of the Economy and Construction 2010–12; mem. Freedom and Solidarity Party, Deputy Chair. 2010–13; Founder, Slovenská občianska koalícia.

MISRA, Dipak; Indian lawyer and judge; b. 3 Oct. 1953; joined bar in 1977, practised at Orissa High Court, Additional Judge 1996; apptd Perm. Judge Madhya Pradesh High Court 1997; Chief Justice Patna High Court Dec. 2009–May 2010; Chief Justice Delhi High Court 2010–11; Judge Supreme Court 2011–17, Chief Justice 2017–18; Exec. Chair. Nat. Legal Services Authority.

MISSONI, Angela; Italian fashion designer; *Creative Director, Missoni SpA;* b. 1958; d. of Ottavio (Tai) Missoni and Rosita Missoni; m. Marco Maccapani 1982 (divorced 1989); two s. one d.; partner Bruno Ragazzi; Missoni SpA founded by her parents 1953, notable for knitwear designs, Creative Dir 1996–, developed more than 25 sub-lines including M Missoni (lower-priced line owned by the Valentino Fashion Group), Missoni Home, Missoni menswear, fragrances (first launched 1980), and at one time, Missoni Sport (now discontinued); launched Hotel Missoni (Rezidor Hotel Group project) in Kuwait 2009, with others following in Paris, Miami and Dubai; other product lines include beauty, eyewear, fragrances, home, handbags, jeans, lingerie, shoes, sneakers, underwear; collaborations with Margherita Missoni for ProKeds to benefit Orphan Aid Africa 2008, Estee Lauder

2005, Converse Spring 2010, Missoni for Target 2011; Dr hc (School of Fashion, Acad. of Art Univ., San Francisco) 2014; Rodeo Drive Walk of Style Award 2011. *Address:* Missoni SpA, Via Solferino 9, 20121 Milan, Italy (office). *Telephone:* (02) 8545821 (office). *E-mail:* press.info@missoni.it (office). *Website:* www.missoni.com (office); www.missonihome.it (office); www.m-missoni.com (office).

MISTRETTA, Charles A., BS, MS, PhD; American biomedical engineer, physicist and academic; *John R. Cameron Professor, Department of Biomedical Engineering, University of Wisconsin;* ed Univ. of Illinois and Harvard Univ.; James Picker Advanced Fellow in Academic Radiology 1972–74; apptd Prof., Depts of Medical Physics and Radiology, Univ. of Wisconsin, Madison, currently John R. Cameron Prof., Dept of Biomedical Eng, Coll. of Eng; mem. Nat. Acad. of Eng 2014; Fellow, American Asscn of Physicists in Medicine 1999, American Inst. for Medical and Biologic Eng 2003, Int. Soc. for Magnetic Resonance in Medicine 2006; Laufman-Greatbatch Prize, Asscn for the Advancement of Medical Instrumentation 1983, J. Allyn Taylor Int. Prize in Medicine, Robarts Research Inst. and Univ. of Western Ontario (co-recipient) 1998, Special Physics Award, Univ. of Wisconsin-Madison 2005, Tech. Achievement Award, MIT (Boston) Club of Wisconsin 2010, Outstanding Researcher, Radiological Soc. of North America 2010, Edith H. Quimby Lifetime Achievement Award 2012, Hilldale Award in Biosciences 2012, Marie Curie Skłodowska Award, Int. Org. for Medical Physics 2012. *Publications:* more than 120 articles in medical journals on investigations of non-invasive techniques for magnetic resonance imaging of cardiovascular system; 33 US patents with 13 additional patents pending. *Leisure interests:* fishing, golfing, music. *Address:* Clinical Science Center, University of Wisconsin, Box 3252, Module E3 E1/398, 600 Highland Avenue, Madison, WI 53792, USA (office). *Telephone:* (608) 263-8313 (office); (608) 265-9685 (office). *Fax:* (608) 263-0876 (office). *E-mail:* camistre@wisc.edu (office); camistre@facstaff.wisc.edu (office). *Website:* www.engr.wisc.edu/bme (office).

MISTRY, Cyrus Pallonji, BE, MSc, FICE; Irish business executive; b. 4 July 1968; s. of Pallonji Mistry and Patsy Perin Dubash; m. Rohiqa Chagla; two s.; ed Cathedral and John Connon School, Mumbai, Imperial Coll., London, London Business School; Dir Tata Elxsi Ltd 1990–2009; Dir Shapoorji Pallonji and Co. 1991–94, Man. Dir Shapoorji Pallonji Group 1994, currently mem. Bd of Dirs; Dir Tata Power Co. Ltd –2006, Dir Tata Sons 2006–16, Deputy Chair. and Chair.-Designate, Tata Group 2011–12, Chair. 2012–16; mem. Bd of Dirs, Forbes Gokak, Afcons Infrastructure, United Motors (India).

MISTRY, Dhruva, CBE, MA, RA, FRBS; Indian sculptor; b. 1 Jan. 1957, Kanjari, Gujarat; s. of Pramodray Mistry and Kantaben Mistry; m. Trupti Patel; one s.; ed Maharaja Sayajirao Univ. of Baroda, Royal Coll. of Art, London; British Council Scholar, RCA 1981–83; Artist in Residence in association with Arts Council of Britain at Kettle's Yard Gallery with Fellowship at Churchill Coll., Cambridge 1984–85; freelance Sculptor-Agent, Nigel Greenwood Gallery, London 1983–97; Sculptor in Residence, Victoria and Albert Museum, London 1988; Rep. GB for the Grand Rodin Prize Exhbn, Japan 1990; Prof., Head of Sculpture and Dean, Faculty of Fine Arts, Maharaja Sayajirao Univ. of Baroda 1999–2002; youngest Royal Academician since J.M.W. Turner when elected 1991; mem. Royal Acad. of Arts 1991; Fellow (first Indian), Royal Soc. of British Sculptors 1993; Prof., Head of Sculpture and Dean, Faculty of Fine Arts, Maharaja Sayajirao Univ. of Baroda 1998–2002; works in Vadodara; Hon. CBE 2001; Hon. DUniv (Univ. of Central England) 2007; Madame Tussaud's Award for Art, RCA 1983, Jack Goldhill Award, Royal Acad. of Arts 1991, Award for the Design of Humanities Prize Medal, London 1994, Design and Pres.'s Award for Victoria Square Sculptures 1995, The Landscape Inst. and Marsh Fountain of the Year Award 1995, Award of Excellence, Gujarat Gaurav Samiti 2006. *Major commissions include:* Mitchell Beazley 1982, Peter Moores Foundation, Liverpool 1983, Merseyside Devt Corpn, Liverpool 1984, Churchill Coll., Cambridge 1985, Nitchiman Corpn, Japan 1987, Glasgow Garden Festival 1988, British Art Medal Soc., London 1988, Nat. Museum of Wales, Cardiff 1989, Hunterian Art Gallery, Glasgow 1990, Victoria Square, The City Council, Birmingham 1992, Quaglino's, London 1993, Int. Classical Music Awards, London 1993, Tamano City Project, Uno, Japan 2002, Petronet LNG Ltd, Dahej 2004, Delhi Devt Authority, New Delhi for Delhi Univ. 2005, RMZ Foundation, Bangaluru 2017. *Public collections include:* Arts Council, London, Birmingham Museum and Art Gallery, Birmingham Contemporary Art Soc., London, Churchill Coll., Cambridge, Cartwright Hall, Bradford, City Art Gallery, Manchester, City of Stoke-on-Trent, Dept of Fine Arts, Punjab Univ., Chandigarh, Fukuoka Art Museum and Asian Art Gallery, Fukuoka, Glynn Vivian Art Gallery, Swansea, Govt Museum and Art Gallery, Chandigarh, Hunterian Art Gallery, Glasgow, Harris Museum and Art Gallery, Preston, Jigyo-Chuo-Koen Park, Fukuoka, Lalit Kala Akademi, New Delhi, Leicestershire Educ. Authority, Laing Art Gallery, Newcastle-upon-Tyne, LNG Petronet Ltd, Dahej, Milton Keynes Devt Corpn, Merseyside Devt Corpn, Liverpool, Nat. Museum of Wales, Cardiff, Oriana, P&O Cruises, Osians Archive, New Delhi, Peter Moores Foundation, Liverpool, Roopankar Museum of Fine Art, Bhopal, RCA, London, Southampton Art Gallery, Sculpture at Goodwood, Tate Gallery, London, British Council, London, British Museum, London, British Library, London, Hakone Open Air Museum, Japan, Ulster Museum, Belfast, Victoria & Albert Museum, London, Walker Art Gallery, Liverpool, West Zone Culture Centre, Udaipur, Yorkshire Sculpture Park, West Bretton, Tamano City Council, Uno, Japan. *Publications include:* exhbn catalogues: Art Heritage, New Delhi, 1981, Sculpture and Drawings, Kettle's Yard Gallery, Univ. of Cambridge 1985, Cross-Sections, Sculpture and Drawings 1982–88, Collins Gallery, Univ. of Strathclyde, Glasgow 1988–89, Bronzes 1985–1990, Nigel Greenwood Gallery, London 1990, Asian Artist Today: Fukuoka Annual VII, Asian Art Museum, Fukuoka, Japan 1994, Work 1990–1995, Royal Acad., Friends Room in Association with Anthony Wilkinson Fine Art, London 1995, Prints 1988–1998, Gallery Espace, New Delhi 1989, Work 1997–2001, Sakshi Gallery, Mumbai 2001, Table Pieces 2003–2004, Sakshi Gallery, Mumbai 2005, Steel, Stainless Still, New Work 2004–2006, Coimbatore Palace, Bodhi Art, New Delhi 2007, Ink Jet, Canvas & Sculpture, Art Pilgrim, New Delhi 2007, Artist in Focus, Contemporary Works: India 2008, Harmony Show, Harmony Art Foundation, Mumbai 2008, Prisms 366°: Sounds & Echoes 1997–2007, Meru 2008, Bronzes 1987–1990, Grosvenor Vadehra, London 2011, Something Else, 2010–2014, Sakshi Gallery, Mumbai (e-book) 2014. *Leisure interests:* photography, reading, walking. *Address:* 76 Anushakti Nagar, Sama,

Vadodara 390 024, India (office). *Telephone:* (265) 2712949 (office). *E-mail:* dhruva@dhruvamistry.com (home). *Website:* www.dhruvamistry.com.

MISTRY, Pallonji Shapoorji; Irish (b. Indian) construction industry executive; *Chairman, Shapoorji Pallonji Group;* b. 1 June 1929; m. Pat (Patsy) Perin Dubash 2003; two s. two d.; joined family business, Shapoorji Pallonji & Co. Ltd aged 18; mem. Bd of Dirs Union Bank of India, Bombay Dyeing & Manufacturing Co. Ltd, W. H. Brady Group of Cos, The Associated Cement Cos Ltd (Chair. 1977–79, 1997–2000); Chair. Forbes Gokak –2003; currently Chair. Shapoorji Pallonji Group, owns Shapoorji Pallonji Construction Ltd, Forbes Textiles and Eureka Forbes Ltd; largest individual shareholder in Tata Sons (holding co. of Tata Group which owns Corus Steel in UK and brands including Jaguar, Land Rover and Tetley tea); family owns a 200 acre (0.81 square km) stud farm in Pune; gave up Indian citizenship in order to obtain Irish citizenship as dual citizenship currently not allowed by Indian Govt 2003; Hon. mem. World Zarathushti Chamber of Commerce 2004; Padma Bhushan 2016. *Address:* Shapoorji Pallonji & Co. Ltd, Shapoorji Pallonji Centre, 41/44 Minoo Desai Marg, Colaba, Mumbai 400 005 (office); Deendayal Upadhyay Research Institute, 5th Floor, 7E, Jhandelwala Extension, New Delhi 110 035, India (office). *Telephone:* (22) 67490263 (Mumbai) (office). *Fax:* (22) 66338176 (Mumbai) (office). *Website:* www.sp-group.co.in/keypersonnel.php (office); www.shapoorji.in (office).

MISTRY, Pranav, MS; Indian research scientist; b. 1981, Palanpur, Gujarat; ed Nirma Inst. of Tech., Ahmedabad, Indian Inst. of Tech., Bombay, Massachusetts Inst. of Tech., USA; Project Man. Microsoft India Devt Centre 2004, UX Researcher 2005–06; Research Intern with Global Connection Project (Carnegie Mellon Univ., NASA, Google and UNESCO); Teaching Asst Media Arts and Sciences, MIT 2007; Research Asst Ambient Intelligence, MIT Media Lab 2006–08, Researcher Microsoft Research, Visiting Researcher Japan Science and Tech. Agency; Research Asst Fluid Interfaces, MIT Media Lab 2008–; Inventor of SixthSense (interface using gestures) and Mouseless (invisible computer mouse); Pres. Zombie.labs, (research group); Lead Coordinator, HCI India; f. Sorotics (social robotics) group at Indian Inst. of Tech., Bombay; fmr Pres. Young Scientist Club, Palanpur; fmr coordinator Asscn of Computer Eng Students; Young Indian Innovator Award, Digit Magazine 2009, Invention of the Year Award 2009, TR35 2009 Award, Tech. Review, Netexplorateurs of the Year Award 2010, Netexplorateurs Grand Prix 2010, France, listed among the 50 Most Creative People of the Year 2010. *Achievements include:* patents for digital user interface for inputting Indic scripts, radio frequency control of computing system, start menu display model, multi-mode multimedia device and computing system, task-oriented start menu, hardware control initiated task switching, single hardware control initiated switching between application and utilities. *Address:* Massachusetts Institute of Technology Media Lab, E14-548G75, Amherst Street, Cambridge, MA 02139, USA (office); Post Box 10, Palanpur 385 001, India (home). *Telephone:* (617) 835-4030 (office); (27) 42253536 (home). *E-mail:* pranav@mit.edu (office); pranavmistry@gmail.com. *Website:* www.media.mit.edu (office); www.pranavmistry.com.

MISTRY, Rohinton, CM, BA, BSc, FRSL; Canadian author; b. 3 July 1952, Bombay (now Mumbai), India; m. Freny Elavia 1975; ed St Xavier's High School, Bombay, Univ. of Bombay, Univ. of Toronto and York Univ., Canada; moved to Canada 1975, worked as bank clerk, Toronto 1975–85; began writing short stories 1982; writings have been translated into more than 30 languages; Hon. PhD (Ottawa) 1996, (Toronto) 1999, (York) 2003, (Ryerson Univ., Toronto) 2012; Trudeau Fellows Prize 2004, Guggenheim Fellowship 2005, Neustadt Int. Prize for Literature 2012. *Publications include:* Tales from Firozsha Baag (short stories) 1987, Such a Long Journey (novel) (W.H. Smith/Books in Canada First Novel Award 1991, Gov.-Gen.'s Award for Fiction 1991, Trillium Book Award 1991, Commonwealth Writers Prize for Best Book 1992) 1991, A Fine Balance (novel) (Los Angeles Times Book Prize for Fiction 1995, Giller Prize 1995, Commonwealth Writers Prize for Best Book 1996, Winifred Holtby Award 1996, ALOA Prize for Fiction (Denmark) 1997) 1995, Family Matters (novel) (Kiriyama Pacific Rim Book Prize for Fiction 2002, Canadian Authors Asscn Fiction Award 2002) 2002, The Scream 2008; essays and articles in various languages and periodicals. *Address:* c/o Bruce Westwood, Westwood Creative Artists Ltd, 94 Harbord Street, Toronto, ON M5S 1G6, Canada (office). *Telephone:* (416) 964-3302 (office). *Fax:* (406) 975-9209 (office). *E-mail:* wca_office@wcaltd.com (office). *Website:* www.wcaltd.com (office); www.facebook.com/RohintonMistryAuthor.

MITA, Katsushige, BEE; Japanese business executive; *Chairman Emeritus, Hitachi Ltd;* b. 6 April 1924, Tokyo; s. of Yoshitaro Mita and Fuji Mita; m. Toriko Miyata 1957 (died 1989); two d.; ed Univ. of Tokyo; joined Hitachi Ltd 1949, Gen. Man. Omika Works Aug.–Nov. 1971, Kanagawa Works 1971–75, Dir 1975, Man. Computer Group 1976–78, Exec. Man. Dir 1977–79, Sr Exec. Man. Dir 1979–80, Exec. Vice-Pres. 1980–81, Pres. and Rep. Dir, Hitachi Ltd 1981–91, Chair. and Rep. Dir 1991–2000, Chair. Emer. 2000–, Hon. Chair. Advisory Bd The Hitachi Center for Tech. and Int. Affairs, Founder The Hitachi Foundation; Vice-Chair. Keidanren (Japan Fed. of Econ. Orgs) 1992–; mem. Int. Business Program Advisory Council, The Fletcher School, Tufts Univ., USA; Dr hc (Tufts Univ.) 1991; Blue Ribbon Medal (Japan) 1985, Officier, Légion d'honneur 1993, DSPN Dato (Malaysia) 1993; Will Rogers Award (USA) 1994. *Leisure interests:* golf, gardening. *Address:* c/o Hitachi Ltd, 6-6, Marunouchi, 1-Chome, Tokyo, Japan.

MITA, Toshio; Japanese energy industry executive; *Advisor, Chubu Electric Power Company, Inc.;* b. 12 Nov. 1946, Aichi Pref.; ed Seikei Univ.; joined Chubu Electric Power Co., Inc. 1969, served in various man. positions including Dir Hekinan Thermal Power Station 1995–97, Atsumi Thermal Power Station 1997–99, Kawagoe Thermal Power Station 1999–2001, Thermal Power Centre 2001–03, Tokyo Br. 2003–05, Man. Dir and Gen. Man. Sales Dept 2005–06, Pres. and Dir 2006–07, Pres. and Dir (Exec. Officer) 2007–10, Chair. 2010–15, currently Advisor, Chair. Chubu Econ. Fed. 2011–, Chair. Chubu Industrial and Regional Advancement Centre 2011–; Corp. Auditor, Toyota Industries Corpn 2010–16; Dir Japan Atomic Power Co. 2011–. *Address:* Chubu Electric Power Co., Inc., 1 Higashi-shincho, Higashi-ku, Nagoya 461-8680, Japan (office). *Telephone:* (52) 951-8211 (office). *Fax:* (52) 962-4624 (office). *E-mail:* info@chuden.co.jp (office). *Website:* www.chuden.co.jp (office).

MITARAI, Fujio, BA; Japanese business executive; *Chairman and CEO, Canon Inc.;* b. 23 Sept. 1935, Kamae, Oita (Kyushu); m. Chizuko Mitarai (died 2002);

several c.; ed Chuo Univ.; joined Canon Camera Co. Inc. 1961, transferred to newly est. Canon USA 1966, Pres. and CEO Canon USA Inc. 1979–89, Vice-Pres. Canon Inc. –1995, Pres. and CEO 1995–2006, Chair. and CEO 2006–; Corp. Auditor Dai-ichi Mutual Life Insurance Co.; Vice-Chair. Nippon Keidanren (Japan Business Fed.) 2002–06, Chair. 2006–10, Chair. Emer. 2010–, Chair. Cttee on Corp. Governance 2000–; Person of the Year Award, Photographic Mfrs and Distributors Asscn 1999, recipient Business Reformer Commendation from govt of Japan 2002. *Leisure interest:* golf. *Address:* Canon Corporate Headquarters, 30-2 Shimomaruko 3-chome, Ohta-ku, Tokyo 146-8501, Japan (office). *Telephone:* (3) 3758-2111 (office). *Fax:* (3) 5482-5135 (office). *E-mail:* info@canon.com (office). *Website:* www .canon.com (office).

MITCHELL, Rt Hon. Andrew John Bower, PC, BA; British politician; b. 23 March 1956, Hampstead, London, England; s. of David Mitchell, MP; m. Dr Sharon Bennett; two d.; ed Rugby School, Warwicks., Jesus Coll., Cambridge; Chair. Cambridge Univ. Conservative Asscn Michaelmas 1977, Pres. Cambridge Union 1978; served as UN peacekeeper in Cyprus 1970s, went on to work and travel extensively in Africa and Asia; served in Royal Tank Regt of British Army; joined Lazard and worked with British cos seeking overseas contracts; fmr Sr Strategy Adviser for Accenture (man. consultancy firm); mem. (Conservative) Islington Health Authority, North London 1980s; contested Sunderland South constituency 1983; MP for Gedling 1987–97; contested Gedling 1997; MP for Sutton Coldfield 2001–10, for Sutton Coldfield (revised boundary) 2010–; Parl. Pvt. Sec. to William Waldegrave as Minister of State, FCO 1988–90, to John Wakeham as Sec. of State for Energy 1990–92; Asst Govt Whip 1992–93, Govt Whip 1993–95; Parl. Under-Sec. of State, Dept of Social Security 1995–97; Shadow Minister for Econ. Affairs 2003–04, Home Affairs 2004–05; Campaign Man. for David Davis in Conservative leadership contest 2005; Shadow Sec. of State for Int. Devt 2005–10; Sec. of State for Int. Devt 2010–12; Chief Whip in the House of Commons and Parl. Sec. to the Treasury Sept.–Oct. 2012 (resgnd), mem. Parl. and Political Service Honours Cttee Sept.–Oct. 2012; Sec. One Nation Group of Conservative MPs 1989–92, 2005–; Vice-Chair. Conservative Party (cands) 1992–93; mem. Work and Pensions Select Cttee 2001–03, Modernization of House of Commons Select Cttee 2002–04; Founder of Project Umubano (Conservative Party social action project in Rwanda and Sierra Leone) 2007; Trustee, International Inspiration; fmr Trustee, E.M. Radiation Research Trust (Radiation Research Trust); Freeman of the City of London; Liveryman of the Vintners' Company. *Achievements include:* Winner, Westminster Dog of the Year Award for his Welsh Springer Spaniel Molly 2009. *Address:* House of Commons, Westminster, London, SW1A 0AA (office); Constituency Office, Sutton Coldfield Conservative Association, 36 High Street, Sutton Coldfield, B72 1UP, England. *Telephone:* (20) 7219-8516 (London) (office); (121) 354-2229 (Sutton Coldfield). *Fax:* (20) 7219-1981 (London) (office); (121) 321-1762 (Sutton Coldfield). *E-mail:* andrew.mitchell.mp@parliament.uk (office); info@ sutton-coldfield-tories.org.uk. *Website:* www.andrew-mitchell-mp.co.uk.

MITCHELL, Andrew Jonathan, CMG, BA; British diplomatist (retd) and business executive; b. 7 Feb. 1967, Lancs., England; m. Helen Mitchell; two s. one d.; ed Univ. of Oxford; Desk Officer, Southern European Dept, FCO 1991–93, Second Sec., Embassy in Bonn 1993–96, Head of Section, Human Rights Policy Dept, FCO 1996–99, Deputy Head of Mission, Embassy in Kathmandu 1999–2002, Dir Future Firecrest IT Programme 2002–07; Amb. to Sweden 2007–11; Dir for 2012 Olympic and Paralympic Games, London, FCO 2011–12, Dir, Prosperity, FCO 2012–14; Dir, Insight, M-is Plc 2015–. *Address:* M-is Plc, Home House, 10 Church Street, Isleworth, Greater London, TW7 6DA, England (office). *Website:* www.m-is.com (office).

MITCHELL, David, MA; British writer; b. 12 Jan. 1969, Southport; m. Keiko Mitchell; one s. one d.; ed Univ. of Kent; worked in Waterstone's, Canterbury 1990–91; taught English in Japan 1994–2002; named one of Granta's Best of Young British Novelists 2003. *Publications include:* Ghostwritten (Mail on Sunday/John Llewellyn Rhys Prize, James Tait Black Memorial Prize) 1999, Number9Dream 2001, Cloud Atlas (British Book Awards for Richard & Judy Best Read of the Year 2005, South Bank Show Literary Fiction Award, Geoffrey Faber Memorial Prize 2005) 2004, Black Swan Green 2006, The Thousand Autumns of Jacob de Zoet 2010, The Bone Clocks 2014, Slade House 2015. *Address:* c/o Jynne Martin, Random House, 20 Vauxhall Bridge Road, London, SW1V 2SA, England (office). *E-mail:* jymartin@randomhouse.com (office). *Website:* www.randomhouse .com (office); www.thousandautumns.com.

MITCHELL, Duncan, MSc, PhD, FRSSAf; South African professor of physiology; *Professor Emeritus, Brain Function Research Group, School of Physiology, University of Witwatersrand;* b. 10 May 1941, Germiston; s. of Thomas Mitchell and Maud K. Mitchell (née Abercrombie); m. Lily May Austin 1966; one s. one d.; ed St John's Coll., Johannesburg, Univ. of Witwatersrand; mem. scientific staff, Research Org. of Chamber of Mines of SA 1964–72, Nat. Inst. for Medical Research, London 1973–75; Hon. Lecturer, Dept of Mechanical Eng, Univ. of Witwatersrand 1969–72, Sr Lecturer, Dept Physiolog 1975–76, Head, Prof. of Physiology, Medical School 1976–2006, Asst Dean, Faculty of Health Sciences 1989–96, Dept of Physiology 1987–90, Prof. Emer. 2007–; Gold Medal, Zoological Soc. of SA 2000. *Publications:* more than 200 papers in thermal, pain and sleep physiology. *Leisure interests:* nature conservation, ballet. *Address:* School of Physiology, University of the Witwatersrand, 1 Jan Smuts Avenue Braamfontein, 2000 Johannesburg (office); 73A Fourth Street, Linden, Johannesburg 2195, South Africa (home). *Telephone:* (11) 717-2359 (office); (11) 888-2671 (home); (83) 260-7205 (home). *Fax:* (11) 643-2765 (office). *E-mail:* Duncan.Mitchell@wits.ac.za (office); duncanmitch@gmail.com (home). *Website:* www.wits.ac.za (office).

MITCHELL, Hon. Frederick Audley, JR, MPA, BA, LLB; Bahamian lawyer and politician; b. 5 Oct. 1953, Nassau; s. of Fredrick A. Mitchell, Sr. and Lilla Angelina Mitchell (née Forde); ed St Augustine's Coll., Antioch Univ., OH and John F. Kennedy School of Govt, Harvard Univ., USA, Univ. of Buckingham, UK; mem. Senate 1992–2002, fmr Chair. Senate Select Cttee on Culture; Public Relations Consultant, Al Dillette & Assocs; mem. House of Assembly (Parl.) for Fox Hill, fmr Opposition Spokesman on Foreign Affairs, Labour and Immigration; Minister of Foreign Affairs and Public Service 2002–07, of Foreign Affairs and Immigration 2012–17; Founding mem. Bahamas Cttee on S Africa; mem. Progressive Liberal Party 1975–; mem. New Providence Human Rights Asscn.

Address: c/o Ministry of Foreign Affairs, Goodman's Bay Corporate Centre, West Bay Street, PO Box N-3746, Nassau, Bahamas (office).

MITCHELL, George John, BA, LLB; American business executive, lawyer, diplomatist and fmr politician; *Chairman Emeritus, DLA Piper LLP;* b. 20 Aug. 1933, Waterville, Me; s. of George J. Mitchell and Mary Mitchell; m. Heather M. Mitchell; ed Bowdoin Coll., Brunswick, Me, Georgetown Univ., Washington, DC; served in US Army 1954–56; called to Bar 1960; trial attorney, US Dept of Justice, Washington, DC 1960–62; Exec. Asst to Senator Edmund Muskie 1962–65; Partner, Jensen & Baird, Portland 1965–77; Chair. Maine Democratic Cttee 1966–68; mem. Nat. Cttee Maine 1968–77; US Attorney for Maine 1977–79; US Dist Judge 1979–80; US Senator from Maine (Democrat) 1980–95, Majority Leader, US Senate 1988–95; Special Adviser to Pres. Clinton for Econ. Initiatives in Ireland 1995–2000; Chair. Cttee on NI 1995; Chancellor Queen's Univ., Belfast 1999–2009; Adviser Thames Water 1999; mem. Bd of Dirs The Walt Disney Co. 1994–2006, Chair. 2004–06; with Verner, Liipfert, Bernhard McPherson & Hand (law firm) 1995–2002; Partner, DLA Piper LLP, Washington, DC 2002–04, Chair. Global Bd, Co-Chair. Govt Controversies Practice Group 2005, now Chair. Emer.; Special US Envoy to the Middle East 2009–11; Co-chair Housing Comm., Bipartisan Policy Center; mem. Bd of Dirs Staples Inc., Boston Red Sox (professional baseball team); headed investigation into alleged steroid use by major league baseball players 2007; Hon. KBE 1999, Freedom of City of Belfast 2018; Hon. LLD (Queen's, Belfast) 1997; Philadelphia Liberty Medal 1998, Presidential Medal of Freedom 1999, Houphouët-Boigny Peace Prize (co-recipient) 1999, Tipperary Int. Peace Award 2000, Truman Inst. Peace Prize, German Peace Prize, UN Educational Peace Prize, Harry Hopkins Medal, Harry S. Truman Good Neighbor Award 2007. *Publications include:* Men of Zeal (with William S. Cohen), World on Fire, Not for America Alone: The Triumph of Democracy and the Fall of Communism, Making Peace, The Negotiator 2015, A Path To Peace 2016. *Address:* DLA Piper, 1251 Avenue of the Americas, New York, NY 10020-1104, USA (office). *Telephone:* (212) 335-4600 (office). *Fax:* (212) 335-4605 (office). *E-mail:* george .mitchell@dlapiper.com (office). *Website:* www.dlapiper.com (office); bipartisanpolicy.org (home).

MITCHELL, Rt Hon. Sir James Fitz-Allen, Kt, KCMG, PC, BSc, CBiol; Saint Vincent and the Grenadines politician, agronomist, biologist and hotelier; b. 15 May 1931, Bequia, Grenadines; s. of Reginald Mitchell and Lois Mitchell (née Baynes); m. Patricia Parker 1965 (divorced); four d.; ed St Vincent Grammar School, Imperial Coll. of Tropical Agric., Trinidad and Univ. of British Columbia; Agricultural Officer, Saint Vincent 1958–61; Ed. Pest Control Articles and News Summaries, Ministry of Overseas Devt, London 1964–65; MP for the Grenadines 1966–2001; Minister of Trade, Agric., Labour and Tourism 1967–72; MP (as an ind.) for the Grenadines 1972–79, re-elected in by-election 1979–2001; Premier of St Vincent 1972–74; Prime Minister of Saint Vincent and the Grenadines 1984–2000, also Minister of Finance and Planning and fmr Minister of Foreign Affairs; Founder New Democratic Party 1975, Leader 1975–2000; Chair. Caribbean Democrat Union 1991; Vice-Chair. Int. Democrat Union 1992; Chair. Hotel Frangipani, Gingerbread, and several other cos; mem. Inst. of Biologists, London 1965–; Order of the Liberator (Venezuela) 1972, Grand Cross, Kts of Malta 1998, Order of Propitious Clouds, Grand Cross Don Infanta (Portugal), Chevalier d'honneur, Chaine de Rotisseur 1995, and other awards. *Publications include:* World Fungicide Usage 1965, Caribbean Crusade 1989, Guiding Change in the Islands 1996, A Season of Light 2001, Beyond the Islands (autobiog.) 2005. *Leisure interests:* sailing, farming. *Address:* Hotel Frangipani, Box One, Bequia, Saint Vincent (office). *Telephone:* (458) 3255 (office). *Fax:* (458) 3824 (office). *E-mail:* frangi@vincysurf.com (office).

MITCHELL, John; New Zealand professional rugby coach, fmr professional rugby union player and business executive; b. 23 March 1964, Hawera; made 134 appearances for Waikato Chiefs rugby team (86 as Capt.) and set record for most tries scored in a NZ season (21); made six mid-week appearances for NZ; Asst Coach England rugby team 1997–2000; returned to coach Waikato Chiefs 2001 season; All Blacks Coach 2001–03, team finished 3rd in World Cup 2003; Coach Waikato Nat. Provincial Championship Team 2003–04; Head Coach, Emirates Western Force, WA 2005–10, Golden Lions 2010–12, Lions (Super Rugby) 2011–12; UKZN Head of Rugby 2013–14; commentator, Super Sport 2012–; CEO Egli (engineering firm) 2014–. *Publication:* Mitch: The Real Story 2014. *Address:* Egli, PO Box 14000, Cascades 3202, South Africa (office). *E-mail:* mitchj@egli.co.za (office). *Website:* egli.co.za (office).

MITCHELL, Joni, CC; Canadian singer, songwriter, visual artist and poet; b. (Roberta Joan Anderson), 7 Nov. 1943, Fort Macleod, Alberta; d. of William A. Anderson and Myrtle Anderson (née McKee); m. 1st Chuck Mitchell 1965 (divorced); m. 2nd Larry Klein 1982; one d. by Brad McGrath; ed Alberta Coll.; Jazz Album of Year and Rock-Blues Album of Year for Mingus, Downbeat Magazine 1979, Juno Award 1981, Century Award, Billboard Magazine 1996, Polar Music Prize (Sweden) 1996, Gov. Gen.'s Performing Arts Award 1996, Nat. Acad. of Songwriters Lifetime Achievement Award 1996; inducted into Rock & Roll Hall of Fame 1997, into Nat. Acad. of Popular Music–Songwriters Hall of Fame 1997, into Canadian Songwriters Hall of Fame 2007, Grammy Award for Best Pop Instrumental Performance (for One Week Last Summer) 2008, Jack Richardson Producer of the Year 2008, Grammy Award for Best Album Notes (for Love Has Many Faces: A Quartet, A Ballet, Waiting To Be Danced) 2014. *Recordings include:* albums: Song to a Seagull 1968, Clouds 1969, Ladies of the Canyon 1970, Blue 1971, For the Roses 1972, Court and Spark 1974, Miles of Aisles 1974, The Hissing of Summer Lawns 1975, Hejira 1976, Don Juan's Reckless Daughter 1977, Mingus 1979, Shadows and Light 1980, Wild Things Run Fast 1982, Dog Eat Dog 1985, Chalk Mark in a Rain Storm 1988, Night Ride Home 1991, Turbulent Indigo (Grammy Awards for Best Pop Album, Best Art Direction 1996) 1994, Hits 1996, Misses 1996, Taming the Tiger 1998, Both Sides Now (Grammy Award for Best Traditional Pop Vocal Album 2001) 2000, Travelog 2002, Songs of a Prairie Girl 2005, Shine 2007, Love Has Many Faces: A Quartet, A Ballet, Waiting To Be Danced 2014. *Dance:* The Fiddle and the Drum (score for ballet with the Alberta Ballet) 2007. *Songs include:* Both Sides Now, Michael from Mountains, Urge for Going, Circle Game. *Television includes:* Joni Mitchell: Intimate and Interactive (Gemini Award 1996). *Publication:* Joni Mitchell: The Complete Poems and Lyrics.

Telephone: (310) 288-6262 (office). *Fax:* (310) 288-6362 (office). *E-mail:* jtani@gtba.com (office). *Website:* www.jonimitchell.com.

MITCHELL, Julian, BA, MA, FRSL, FSA; British writer; b. (Charles Julian Humphrey Mitchell), 1 May 1935, Epping, Essex; s. of William Moncur Mitchell and Christine Mitchell (née Browne); partner Richard Rowson (deceased); ed Winchester and Wadham Coll., Oxford; mem. Literature Panel, Arts Council 1966–69, Welsh Arts Council 1988–92; John Llewellyn Rhys Prize 1965, Somerset Maugham Award 1966, BAFTA Award (Inspector Morse). *Films:* Arabesque (with Stanley Price) 1965, Another Country 1982, Vincent and Theo 1990, August 1996, Wilde 1997. *Plays:* Half-Life 1977, Another Country (SWET Play of the Year 1982, BAFTA Award for Best Adapted Screenplay 1984) 1981, Francis 1983, After Aida (or Verdi's Messiah) 1986, August 1994 (adapted from Uncle Vanya), Falling Over England 1994, The Good Soldier (adapted from Ford Madox Ford) 2010, Family Business 2011, The Welsh Boy 2012. *Television:* more than 50 TV plays and adaptations. *Publications include:* novels: Imaginary Toys 1961, A Disturbing Influence 1962, As Far As You Can Go 1963, The White Father 1964, A Circle of Friends 1966, The Undiscovered Country 1968; biography: Jennie: Lady Randolph Churchill (with Peregrine Churchill), A Disgraceful Anomaly 2003. *Leisure interests:* fishing, local history. *Address:* c/o Anthony Jones, United Agents, 12–26 Lexington Street, London, W1F 0LE, England (office); 35 Abingdon Court, London, W8 6BT, England (home). *Telephone:* (20) 3214-0800 (office); 7973-500164 (mobile) (home). *Fax:* (20) 3214-0801 (office). *E-mail:* info@unitedagents.co.uk (office); julian.mitchell606@btinternet.com (home). *Website:* unitedagents.co.uk (office).

MITCHELL, Katie, OBE; British theatre director; b. 23 Sept. 1964; d. of Michael Mitchell and Sally Mitchell; m.; one d.; Pres. Oxford Univ. Dramatic Soc. 1984; awarded a Winston Churchill Memorial Trust Award to research Eastern European theatre in Russia, Lithuania, Georgia, Poland and Germany 1989; f. Classics on a Shoestring Theatre Co. 1990; Assoc. Dir, RSC 1997–98, Royal Court Theatre, London 2001–03, Abbey Theatre, Dublin 2000–02, Royal Nat. Theatre 2003–; Evening Standard Award for Best Dir 1996, Pres.'s Medal of the British Acad. 2017. *Plays directed include:* Arden of Faversham, Vassa Zheleznova and Women of Troy (with Classics on a Shoestring) 1990–91, A Woman Killed with Kindness 1991, The Dybbuk 1992, Ghosts 1993, Henry VI 1994, Rutherford and Son 1994, The Machine Wreckers 1995, Easter 1995, The Phoenician Women 1996, Endgame (Donmar Warehouse) 1996, Don Giovanni 1996, The Last Ones 1996, The Mysteries 1997, The Beckett Shorts 1997, Uncle Vanya (RSC) 1998, Jenůfa 1998, The Oresteia 1999, Attempts on Her Life (Piccolo Theatre, Milan) 1999, The Maids (Young Vic, London) 1999, The Country 2000, Mountain Language Ashes to Ashes 2001, Katya Kabanova 2001, Iphigenia in Aulis (Abbey Theatre, Dublin) 2001, Nightsongs 2002, Ivanov 2002, Three Sisters 2003, Jephtha 2003, Iphigenia at Aulis 2004, Forty Winks (Royal Court) 2004, The Seagull 2006, The Waves 2006, Attempts on her Life 2006, The Sacrifice (Welsh Nat. Opera) 2007, The Jewish Wife/A Respectable Wedding (Young Vic) 2007, St Matthew Passion (Glyndebourne) 2007, The Idiot (Royal Nat. Theatre) 2008, The City 2008, The Maids (Sweden) 2008, Pains of Youth (Nat. Theatre) 2009, Royal Opera House (ROH): Parthenogenesis 2009, Clemency 2011, Die Wellen (Cologne, Germany) 2011, Wastewater (Royal Court Theatre, London) 2011, Written on Skin (ROH) (Gramophone Award for Best Contemporary Recording 2014) 2013, Pelléas et Mélisande (Festival d'Aix-en-Provence) 2016, Anatomy of a Suicide (Royal Court Theatre, London) 2017. *TV work includes:* The Widowing of Mrs Holroyd 1995, The Stepdaughter 2000 (BBC), Turn of the Screw 2004. *Address:* c/o Leah Schmidt, The Agency, 24 Pottery Lane, London, W11 4LZ, England (office).

MITCHELL, Keith Claudius, MS, PhD; Grenadian politician; *Prime Minister;* b. 12 Nov. 1946, St George's; m. Marietta Mitchell; one s.; ed Presentation Coll., Grenada, Univ. of West Indies, Barbados, Howard Univ. and American Univ., Washington, DC; cand. for Grenada Nat. Party in 1972 elections; Gen. Sec. New Nat. Party 1984–89, Leader 1989–; Minister of Communication, Works, Public Utilities, Transportation, of Civil Aviation and Energy 1984–87, of Communications, Works, Public Utilities, Co-operatives, Community Devt, Women's Affairs and Civil Aviation 1988–89; Prime Minister and Minister of Finance, External Affairs, Mobilization, Trade and Industry, Information and Nat. Security 1995–99; Prime Minister and Minister of Nat. Security and Information 1999–2008, re-elected 2003, also Minister of Finance 2007–08; Prime Minister 2013–, also Minister of Finance, Energy, Nat. Security, Disaster Preparedness, Home Affairs, Public Affairs, Public Admin, Implementation and Information; Capt. Grenada Nat. Cricket Team 1971–74; Order of the Brilliant Star (Taiwan) 1995. *Leisure interest:* playing cricket. *Address:* Office of the Prime Minister, Ministerial Complex, 6th Floor Botanical Gardens, Tanteen, St. George's (office); New National Party (NNP), Upper Lucas Street, St. George's, Grenada (office). *Telephone:* 440-2255; 440-1875 (office). *Fax:* 440-4116; 440-1876 (office). *E-mail:* pmsec@gov.gd; nnpadmin@nnpnews.com (office). *Website:* www.gov.gd; www.nnpnews.com (office).

MITCHELL, Mark Patrick; New Zealand politician; b. 22 May 1968, Auckland; m. 3rd Peggy Bourne; ed The Wharton School, Univ. of Pennsylvania; served in New Zealand Police 1989–2002, including as mem. Dog Section and Armed Offenders Squad; f. int. private security firm based in Kuwait 2002, worked in Iraq providing security to Coalition Provisional Authority and training Iraqi security forces; mem. House of Reps for Rodney 2011–, Chair. Foreign Affairs, Defence and Trade Cttee 2014–16; Minister of Statistics 2016–17, Minister for Land Information 2016–17, also Minister of Defence May–Oct. 2017; mem. National Party. *Address:* New Zealand National Party, 41 Pipitea St, Thorndon, Wellington 6011, New Zealand (office). *Telephone:* (4) 894-7016 (office). *Fax:* (4) 894-7031 (office). *E-mail:* hq@national.org.nz (office). *Website:* markmitchell.national.org.nz; www.national.org.nz (office).

MITCHELL, Pat, MA; American broadcasting executive and television producer; *President and CEO, Paley Center for Media;* m. Scott Seydel; six c.; ed Univ. of Georgia; fmr news anchor and producer WBZ-TV Boston; first woman to host and produce her own nat. talk show, Woman to Woman 1980s; Co-Founder, developer of series, specials, documentaries, VU Productions –1992; has worked for NBC, CBS and ABC; Head CNN Productions, Time Inc. TV –2000; Pres. and CEO Public Broadcasting Service (PBS) 2000–06; Pres. and CEO Paley Center for Media (fmrly Museum of TV and Radio), New York 2006–; mem. Council on Foreign Relations, Women's Advisory Council of the Kennedy School of Govt, US–Afghan Women's Council; mem. Bd of Dirs Bank of America 2001–09, Participant Productions, Sun Microsystems 2005–10, Human Rights Watch; mem. Bd of Trustees Sundance Inst. (currently Vice-Chair.), Mayo Clinic; Founding mem. American chapter, Global Green USA; Dr hc (Emerson Coll., Hollins Univ., Bloomsburg Univ., Converse Coll.); Cable and Telecommunications Woman of the Year Award, CINE Golden Eagle for Lifetime Achievement, PROMAX Century Award, Sandra Day O'Connor Award for Leadership, Business Hall of Fame, Georgia State Univ. 2008, NATPE Brandon Tartikoff Legacy Award. *Television includes:* Woman to Woman (Emmy Award for Best Daytime Talk Program 1984), CNN Perspectives, Cold War (Peabody Award), Millennium: A Thousand Years of History. *Address:* Paley Center for Media, 25 West 52nd Street, New York, NY 10019, USA (office). *Telephone:* (212) 621-6800 (office). *Website:* www.paleycenter.org (office).

MITCHELL, Thomas Noel, PhD, LittD, MRIA; Irish classicist and academic; b. 7 Dec. 1939, Castlebar, Co. Mayo; s. of Patrick Mitchell and Margaret Mitchell; m. Lynn S. Hunter 1965; three s. one d.; ed Univ. Coll. Galway, Trinity Dublin and Cornell Univ., USA; Instructor, Cornell Univ. 1965–66; Asst Prof., Swarthmore Coll. 1966–73, Assoc. Prof. 1973–78, Prof. of Classics 1978–79, Cornell Visiting Prof. 1986; Prof. of Latin, Trinity Coll. Dublin 1979–91, Fellow 1980–, Sr Dean 1985–87, Sr Lecturer 1987–90, Provost 1991–2001; Distinguished Visiting Prof. Victoria Univ., Melbourne 2001–; Visiting Fellow, The Hoover Inst., Stanford Univ., USA 2002; Chair. Press Council of Ireland from 2007; fmr Chair. St James Hosp., Dublin, Ireland Nat. Children's Trust, The Irish Council for Science, Eng and Tech.; fmr Dir, Trinity Foundation, Community Foundation for Ireland, The Ireland Funds; mem. Bd The Atlantic Philanthropies 2002–, currently Deputy Chair.; Vice-Pres. Royal Irish Acad. 1989; mem. American Philosophical Soc. 1996–; Fellow, Oriel Coll., Oxford, St John's Coll., Cambridge; Hon. Fellow, RCPI 1992, Royal Coll. of Surgeons in Ireland 1993; Hon. LLD (Queen's Univ. Belfast) 1992, (Nat. Univ. of Ireland) 1992; Hon. DHumLitt (Swarthmore) 1992, (Lynn Univ., USA) 1998, (State Univ. of NY) 1998; Hon. PhD (Charles Univ., Prague) 1998, (Dublin Inst. of Tech.) 1999; Hon. DLitt (Victoria Univ. of Tech.) 2000. *Publications:* Cicero, The Ascending Years 1979, Cicero, Verrines II.1. 1986, Cicero the Senior Statesman 1990; numerous articles and reviews on Cicero and Roman History. *Leisure interest:* gardening. *Address:* The Rubrics, Trinity College, Dublin 2 (office); Dodona, Blackwood Lane, Malahide, Co. Dublin, Ireland (home). *Telephone:* (1) 6081843 (office).

MITCHISON, (Nicholas) Avrion, DPhil, FRS; British professor of zoology and comparative anatomy; b. 5 May 1928, London; s. of Baron Mitchison and Naomi Mitchison; m. Lorna Margaret Martin 1957; two s. three d.; ed Leighton Park School and Univ. of Oxford; Lecturer, later Reader in Zoology, Univ. of Edin. 1956–62; Head, Div. of Experimental Biology, Nat. Inst. for Medical Research, Mill Hill 1962–71; Jodrell Prof. of Zoology and Comparative Anatomy, Univ. Coll. London 1970–89; Scientific Dir Deutsches Rheuma-Forschungszentrum, Berlin 1990–96; Sr Fellow, Dept of Immunology, Univ. Coll. London 1996–; Hon. Dir Imperial Cancer Research Fund, Tumour Immunology Unit, Univ. Coll. London; Hon. MD (Edin.); Paul Ehrlich Prize, Mitchison Prize for Rheumatology est. in his honour. *Address:* Department of Immunology, University College London, Windeyer Building, 46 Cleveland Street, London, W1P 6DB (office); 14 Belitha Villas, London, N1 1PD, England (home). *Telephone:* (20) 7380-9349. *Fax:* (20) 7380-9357. *E-mail:* n.mitchison@ucl.ac.uk (office).

MITHI, Mukut, BSc; Indian government official and politician; b. 1 Jan. 1952, Roing, Arunachal Pradesh; s. of Kumso Mithi and Anachi Mega; m. Pomaya Mithi; three s.; ed J.N. Coll., Pasighat; mem. Indian Nat. Congress (INC), later of Arunachal Congress, broke from latter to form Arunachal Congress (Mithi)—AC(M) 1998, AC(M) later merged with INC 1999; Chief Minister of Arunachal Pradesh 1999–2003; Lt-Gov. Puducherry (fmrly Pondicherry) 2006–08 (resgnd); mem. Rajya Sabha (Parl.) 2008–; mem. Cen. Advisory Cttee for Nat. Cadet Corps, Governing Council, North-Eastern Indira Gandhi Regional Inst. of Health and Medical Sciences, Shillong 2008–. *Leisure interests:* basketball, jogging, singing, dancing, reading. *Address:* AB-8, Pandara Road, New Delhi 110 065; Ezengo, P.O./P.S. Roing, Lower Dibang Valley District, Arunachal Pradesh, India. *Telephone:* (3803) 222960; 9868181088. *E-mail:* mukut.mithi@sansad.nic.in.

MITOV, Daniel Pavlov; Bulgarian politician; b. 4 Dec. 1977, Sofia; ed St Clement of Ohrid Univ. of Sofia; CEO Democracy Foundation, Sofia 2006–09; fmr Deputy Chair. Democrats for Strong Bulgaria; Program Man., Nat. Democratic Inst. for Int. Affairs (NDI) 2010–14, worked on devt programmes in Iraq, Libya, Democratic Repub. of Congo, Ukraine, Yemen and Tunisia, becoming Resident NDI Rep. in Brussels 2013–14; Minister of Foreign Affairs 2014–17; co-f. Balgariya na Grazhdanite (BG—Bulgaria of Citizens) party. *Address:* c/o Ministry of Foreign Affairs, 1040 Sofia, ul. Al. Zhendov 2, Bulgaria. *E-mail:* info@mfa.bg.

MITRI, Tarek; Lebanese politician, academic and fmr UN official; *Director, Issam Fares Institute for Public Policy and International Affairs, American University of Beirut;* b. 1950, Tripoli; ed American Univ. of Beirut, Univ. de Nanterre Paris X; Dir Faith and Unity Bureau, WCC, Geneva mid-1980s, later Co-ordinator Islamic-Christian Dialogue; Programme Dir for Christian-Muslim Dialogue, Middle East Council of Churches 1984–91; Minister of Environment and Admin. Devt 2005–06, Minister of Culture 2006–08, Acting Minister of Foreign Affairs and Emigrants 2006–08, Minister of Information 2008–11; Co-founder Centre of Christian-Muslim Studies; Special Rep. of Sec.-Gen. and Head of Support Mission in Libya (UNSMIL), UN 2012–14; Dir, Issam Fares Inst. for Public Policy and Int. Affairs, American Univ. of Beirut 2014–; fmr Prof., Harvard Univ., Amsterdam Free Univ., Univ. of Geneva, Univ. of Balamand; active mem. several groups and orgs concerning Muslim-Christian dialogue in Middle East and world-wide; fmr UNESCO Chair on Dialogue, St Joseph Univ., Beirut. *Address:* Issam Fares Institute for Public Policy and International Affairs, American University of Beirut, PO Box 11-0236, Riad El-Solh, Beirut 1107 2020, Lebanon (office). *Telephone:* (1) 340460 (office). *Website:* www.aub.edu.lb (office).

MITROFANOV, Aleksey Valentinovich; Russian politician and writer; b. 16 March 1962, Moscow; s. of Zoya Mitrofanova; m. Marina Lillevyali; ed Moscow Inst. of Int. Relations; with Ministry of Foreign Affairs 1985–88; researcher, Inst. of USA and Canada 1988–91; TV producer, Leisure Centre Sokol; mem. Higher

Council, Liberal Democratic Party of Russia 1991–93; Minister of Foreign Affairs, Shadow Cabinet of Liberal Democratic Party 1992–96; mem. State Duma 1993–2008, 2011–, Deputy Chair. Cttee on Int. Relations 1993–96, Chair. Cttee on Geopolitics 1996–99, Chair. Parliamentary Cttee on Media 2012; mem. Spravedlivaya Rossiya (A Just Russia) 2007–, mem. Cen. Council; Pres. Nat. Center of Geopolitics 2008. *Films:* scriptwriter: Pchiojka (A Little Bee), Yuliya 2006; numerous documentaries including Yury Andropov 1993, Andrey Gromyko 1993. *Publications include:* Steps of New Geopolitics, Secret Visit of Professor Voland, t.A.T.u Come Back 2006. *Leisure interest:* chess, volleyball. *Address:* State Duma, 103265 Moscow, Okhotnyi ryad 1, Russia (office). *Telephone:* (495) 692-62-66 (office). *Fax:* (495) 697-42-58 (office). *E-mail:* stateduma@duma.gov.ru (office). *Website:* www.duma.gov.ru (office).

MITROFANOV, Alexandr; Czech political columnist; b. 27 June 1957, Rostov, Russia; m.; one s. one d.; ed Rostov State Univ., Russia; Ed. Škodovák, Škoda Plzeň 1980–88, Právo Lidu 1991–92; contrib. to Právo 1992–2018, Political Commentator; personal column on novinky.cz 2014–; undertook sabbatical study in UK 1994, 1997; Křepelky Prize, Czech Literary Fund 1994, Ferdinand Peroutka Prize for Journalism 2001, Karel Havlíček Borovský Prize for Journalism 2015, Jiří Ješ Prize for Journalism 2016. *Publications:* Behind the Façade of Lidový dům, Czech Social Democracy, People and Events 1992–1998 1998, Politics Under Lid (with Markéta Maláčova) 2002, three chapters in Erratic Paths of Social Democracy 2005. *Leisure interests:* reading, Twitter activities (@alexandrmitrofa). *Address:* Právo, Slezská 13, 121 50 Prague 2, Czech Republic (office). *E-mail:* alexandr.mitrofanov@pravo.cz (office). *Website:* www.novinky.cz/komentare (office).

MITROPOULOS, Efthimios E.; Greek academic and international organization official; b. 30 May 1939, Piraeus; m. Chantal Mitropoulos (née Byvoet); one s. one d.; ed Aspropyrgos Merchant Marine Acad., Hellenic Coast Guard Acad.; with Greek Merchant Navy 1959–62; Coast Guard Officer, Corfu and Piraeus 1964–65; mem. Greek Del. to IMO 1966–77, becoming Head; Harbour Master, Corfu 1977–79; joined IMO Secr. 1979, Head of Navigation Section 1985–89, Sr Deputy Dir for Navigation and Related Matters 1989–92, Dir Maritime Safety Div. 1992–2003, Asst Sec.-Gen. 2000–03, Sec.-Gen. 2004–11, Chair. Int. Maritime Law Inst. 2004–11; Chancellor, World Maritime Univ., Malmo, Sweden 2004–12; mem. Bd of Dirs Tsakos Energy Navigation Ltd 2012–, now Ind. Dir; Gov. Royal Nat. Lifeboat Inst.; Fellow, Royal Inst. of Navigation; mem. Hellenic Inst. of Marine Tech., Shipmasters' Union of Greece, Royal Automobile Club; Hon. Citizen of Galaxidi, Greece, Hon. mem. Int. Asscn of Marine Aids to Navigation and Lighthouse Authorities, Int. Fed. of Shipmasters' Asscns, Propeller Club, Hon. Fellow, Nautical Inst., Inst. of Marine Eng, Science and Tech., Royal Inst. of Naval Architects, Hon. Life mem. Baltic Exchange; Officier, Orde du Mérite Maritime, Mil. Valour Medal and Phoenix Order (Hellenic Repub.), Commendatore, Order of Merit (Italy), St Marcus Cross, Patriarchate of Alexandria and All Africa, Grand Commdr, Order of the Phoenix (Hellenic Repub.), Medal for Valour & Honour (Hellenic Coast Guard), Grand'Ufficiale, Order of Merit (Italy), Medalla Blanca de Primera Clase (Guatemala), Medal of the Order of Naval Merit (Brazil), Order of Sikatuna, Rank of Datu (The Philippines), Grand Cross of Merit with Star and Sash Cross (Germany) 2012; Dr hc (Nicola Vaptsarov Naval Acad., Bulgaria, Maritime Univ., Constanza, Romania, Schiller Int. Univ., Dalian Maritime Univ., China, Chung-Ang Univ., Seoul, Repub. of Korea, Univ. of Messina, Italy, City Univ., London, Univ. of the Aegean, Greece, Odessa Nat. Maritime Acad., Korea Maritime Univ., Busan, Univ. of Malta, World Maritime Univ.); numerous awards, including Coastguard Award (Grand Cross), Argentina, 15 November Medal, Uruguay, Medal of Naval Merit, Brazil, US Coast Guard Distinguished Public Service Award, Colombian Navy Medal for 'Servicios Distinguidos a la Dirección General Marítima', Danish Shipowners' Asscn Maritime Award, Union of Greek Shipowners Environment Award 2006, Seatrade Personality of the Year 2008, Turkish Shipping Golden Anchor Lifetime Achievement Award 2008, Greek Personality of the Year, Lloyd's List 2008, Niki Award 2010. *Publications include:* Tankers: Evolution and Technical Issues 1969, Studies in Shipping Economics 1970, Safety of Navigation 1971, Categories and Types of Merchant Ships 1973, Collision Avoidance at Sea 1975, Separation of Traffic at Sea 1976, Shipping Economics and Policy 1981. *Leisure interests:* swimming, diving, fishing, football, classical music, naval history. *Address:* c/o Board of Directors, Tsakos Energy Navigation Ltd, 367 Syngrou Avenue, Athens 17564, Greece.

MITSOTAKIS, Kyriakos, BA, MA, MBA; Greek business executive and politician; *President, Nea Demokratia (New Democracy);* b. 4 March 1968, Athens; s. of Konstantinos Mitsotakis and Marika Mitsotakis; younger brother of Dora Bakoyannis; m. Mareva Grabowski; one s. two d.; ed Harvard Univ., USA, Athens Coll., Stanford Univ., USA, Harvard School of Business, USA; left Greece for Paris with his family 1968, returned when democracy was restored 1974; Econ. Analyst, Chase Manhattan Bank, London 1990–91; later returned to Greece and fulfilled mil. duty with Hellenic Air Force with 111th Combat Wing, Nea Anchialos; returned to USA to continue his studies; consultant, McKinsey & Co., London 1995–97; later returned to Greece to work at Alpha Ventures (pvt. equity subsidiary of Alpha Bank); fmr Man. Dir NBG Venture Capital, Nat. Bank of Greece group; worked at Int. Council, Nat. Enterprise Council 2000–03; mem. Nea Demokratia (ND—New Democracy), Pres. 2016–; mem. (ND), Vouli (Parl.) for Athens B 2004–, Chair. Environment Cttee, 2007–09, Parl. Spokesman for ND 2015; Shadow Minister for Environment and Climate Change –2012; Minister of Admin. Reform and e-Governance 2013–15; Leader of the Opposition 2016–; Hon. Pres. Konstantinos K. Mitsotakis Foundation; Hoopes Prize, Harvard Univ., Tocqueville Prize, Harvard Univ. *Address:* Nea Demokratia (New Democracy), Leoforos Peiraios 62, 183 46 Moschato, Athens, Greece (office). *Telephone:* (210) 9444000 (office). *Fax:* (210) 7251491 (office). *E-mail:* ndpress@nd.gr (office). *Website:* www.nd.gr (office).

MITTA, Aleksander Naumovich; Russian film director; b. 29 March 1933, Moscow; ed Moscow Inst. of Construction Eng, All-Union Inst. of Cinematography; with Mosfilm studio 1961; Prof., Hamburg Univ. 1995–; Merited Worker of Arts of Russia 1974. *Films include:* The Fearless Ataman 1961, Drug moy Kolka (My Friend Kolka) 1961, Bez strakha i upryoka (No Fear, No Blame) 1962, Bolshoy fitil 1963, Zvonyat, otkroyte dver (Someone is Ringing, Open the Door) (Grand Prix Int. Festival in Venice) 1965, Gori, gori, moya zvezda (Twinkle, Twinkle, My Star) 1969, Tochka, tochka, zapyataya... (Period, Period, Comma...) 1972, Moskva, lyubov moya (Moscow, My Love) 1974, Skaz pro to, kak tsar Pyotr arapa zhenil (How Czar Peter the Great Married Off His Moor) 1976, Klouny i deti 1976, Ekipazh (The Crew) (Prize of All-Union Film Festival) 1980, Skazka stranstviy (The Story of the Voyages) 1982, Safety Margin 1988, Shag (A Step) 1988, Zateryannyy v Sibiri (Lost in Siberia) 1991, Raskalyonnaya subbota 2002, Chagall - Malevich 2013. *Television includes:* Alfred Schnittke and His Friends 1994, Border of the State (series) 1999–2000, Granitsa. Tayozhnyy roman (mini-series) 2000, Red-Hot Weekend 2003, Swan Paradise 2005. *Publication:* Cinema Between Hell and Paradise. *Leisure interest:* watching films on DVD. *Address:* Malaya Gruzinskaya str. 28, Apt 105, 123557 Moscow, Russia (home). *Telephone:* (495) 253-51-57 (Moscow) (home). *Fax:* (495) 253-73-20 (home).

MITTAL, Lakshmi Niwas, BCom; Indian steel industry executive; *Chairman and CEO, ArcelorMittal Steel Company NV;* b. 15 June 1950, Sadulpur, Rajasthan; s. of Mohan Lal Mittal and Geeta Mittal; m. Usha Mittal; one s. one d.; ed St Xavier's Coll., Calcutta; began career in family's steel-making business; Founder, Chair. and CEO LNM Group (later Mittal Steel Co.) 1976; f. Caribbean Ispat 1989; acquired Ispat Mexicana 1992, Ispat Sidbec, Canada 1994, Ispat Hamburger Stahlwerke, Germany 1995, Karmet, Kazakhstan 1995, Irish Ispat 1996, Thyssen's Long Product Div., Germany 1997, Ispat Unimetal Group 1999; Chair. and CEO of all mem. cos of LNM Group Inc., Ispat Int. NV, Ispat Karmet, Ispat Indo, Ispat Coal; Chair. and CEO Mittal Steel Co. NV (after merger with Int. Steel Group) 2004–06; Chair. and CEO ArcelorMittal Steel Co. NV (after merger with Arcelor) 2006–; Dir (non-exec.) ArcelorMittal South Africa; mem. Bd Dirs ICICI Bank Ltd, Goldman Sachs; mem. Exec. Cttee Int. Iron and Steel Inst., Foreign Investment Council in Kazakhstan, Int. Investment Council in South Africa, Investors' Council to Cabinet of Ministers, Ukraine, World Steel Asscn (fmr Chair.), Presidential Int. Advisory Bd, Mozambique, Int. Business Council, World Econ. Forum, Advisory Bd Kellogg School of Man., USA; Hon. Fellow, King's Coll., London 2007; Grand Cross of Civil Merit, Spain; Dr hc (AGH Univ. of Science and Tech., Kraków, Poland); Steelmaker of the Year Award 1996, Eighth Hon. Willy Korf Steel Vision Award 1998, Fortune European Businessman of the Year 2004, Wall Street Journal Entrepreneur of the Year 2004, Sunday Times Business Person of 2006, Financial Times Man of the Year 2006, Die Welt Gewinner 2006, Time magazine Int. Newsmaker of the Year 2006, Dwight D. Eisenhower Global Leadership Award 2007, Padma Vibhushan 2008, Forbes Lifetime Achievement Award 2008, World Steel Asscn Medal 2010. *Leisure interests:* swimming, yoga, golf. *Address:* ArcelorMittal, Hofplein 20, 3032 Rotterdam, Netherlands (office); ArcelorMittal, 7th Floor, Berkeley Square House, Berkeley Square, London, W1J 6DA, England (office); ArcelorMittal, 24–26 Boulevard d'Avranches, 1160 Luxembourg Ville, Luxembourg (office). *Telephone:* (10) 217-88-00 (Rotterdam) (office); (20) 7629-7988 (London) (office); 4792-1 (Luxembourg) (office). *Fax:* (10) 217-88-50 (Rotterdam) (office); (20) 7629-7993 (London) (office); 4792-2675 (Luxembourg) (office). *E-mail:* contact@arcelormittal.com (office). *Website:* corporate.arcelormittal.com (office).

MITTAL, Som, BEng, MBA; Indian engineer and computer industry executive; b. 7 Feb. 1952; ed Indian Inst. of Tech., Kanpur, Indian Inst. of Man., Ahmedabad; has worked for Larsen & Toubro, Escorts; fmr Managing Dir Compaq India Ltd; est. SRF Ltd (jt venture); worked for Wipro Infotech, CEO Business Solutions Div. 1993–94; fmr Pres. and CEO Digital Equipment (India) Ltd, Bangalore; Head of Services Business for Asia-Pacific and Japan region, Hewlett-Packard –2007; Chair. Nat. Asscn of Software and Services Cos (NASSCOM) 2003–04, Pres. 2008–14; fmr Chair. Confed. of Indian Industry; mem. Bd of Dirs EXL 2013–; mem. Exec. Council and fmr Pres. (South) Mfrs Asscn of Information Tech.; mem. Chief Minister's Task Force (Govt of Karnataka), Governing Council, Indian Inst. of Information Tech.; Founder-mem. Bd of Educ. Standards; Distinguished Alumnus Award, Indian Inst. of Tech., Kanpur 2000.

MITTAL, Sunil Bharti; Indian telecommunications executive; *Chairman and Group CEO, Bharti Enterprises;* s. of Sat Paul Mittal; m.; two s. one d.; ed Punjab Univ., Harvard Univ., USA; Founder Bharti Enterprises 1976–, Dir 1995–, Chair. and Group CEO 2001–; Chair. Indo-US Jt Business Council; mem. Nat. Council of Confed. of Indian Industry (Pres. 2007–08); Chair. ICC 2016–18; mem. Fed. of Indian Chambers of Commerce and Industry; Co-Chair. World Econ. Forum 2007; Chair. GSM Asscn 2017–; mem. Int. Business Council, World Econ. Forum; mem. Indo-US CEOs Forum, Exec. Bd, Indian School of Business, Acad. of Distinguished Entrepreneurs, Babson Coll., Mass; mem. Leadership Council, Climate Group; mem. Bd of Trustees Carnegie Endowment for Int. Peace; mem. Int. Advisory Cttee, New York Stock Exchange Euronext Bd of Dirs; mem. Int. Business Advisory Council of London; mem. Advisory Bd, Global Econ. Symposium; mem. Telecom Bd of Int. Telecommunication Union; Hon. Consul of Seychelles, Hon. Fellow, Inst. of Electronics and Telecommunication Engineers of India; Hon. DSc (Govind Ballabh Pant Univ. of Agric. and Tech.), Hon. LLD (Univ. of Leeds); Padma Bhushan 2007, GSM Asscn Chair.'s Award 2008, Global Economy Prize, Kiel Inst. (Germany) 2009, Global Vision Award, US-India Business Council 2008, Lal Bahadur Shastri Nat. Award 2009. *Address:* Bharti Enterprises Ltd, Aravali Crescent 1, Nelson Mandela Road, Vasant Kunj, Phase II, New Delhi 110 070 (office); Bharti Tele-Ventures Ltd, Qutab Ambience (at Qutab Minar), Mehrauli Road, New Delhi 110 030, India (office). *Telephone:* (11) 41666000 (office); (11) 46666100 (office). *Fax:* (11) 41666011 (office); (11) 42666500 (office). *E-mail:* corpcomm@bharti.com (office). *Website:* www.airtel.in (office); www.bharti.com (office).

MITTERLEHNER, Reinhold; Austrian politician; b. 10 Dec. 1955, Helfenberg, Upper Austria; m. Anna Maria Mitterlehner; three d.; ed Johannes Kepler Univ.; worked at Upper Austrian Econ. Chamber, including as Head of Marketing Dept 1980–92; mem. Ahorn Municipal Council 1991–97; Sec.-Gen. Austrian Econ. League (Wirtschaftsbund), Vienna 1992–2000; Deputy Sec.-Gen. Wirtschaftskammer Österreich (Austrian Fed. Econ. Chamber) 2000–08; mem. Nationalrat (Parl.) 2000–, Chair. Econ. and Industrial Affairs Cttee 2001–08; Vice-Pres. Austrian Energy Agency 2008; Fed. Minister of Economy 2008–17, also of Science and Research 2013–17; Fed. Vice-Chancellor 2014–17, Acting Fed. Chancellor following resignation of Werner Faymann 9–17 May 2016; mem. Österreichische Volkspartei (ÖVP—Austrian People's Party), Chair. 2014–17; Grosses Goldenes Ehrenzeichen am Bande für Verdienste um die Republik Österreich.

MITTERRAND, Frédéric; French/Tunisian writer, film and television producer and fmr government official; b. 21 Aug. 1947, Paris; s. of Robert Mitterrand and Edith Cahier; nephew of François Mitterrand; ed Univ. of Nanterre, Inst. d'études politiques, Paris; Dir Cinéma d'Art et Essai, Olympic Palace, Entrepôt and Olympic-Entrepôt 1971–86; Dir Comm. d'avances sur recettes du cinéma français (cinema funding comm.) 2000–03; Dir-Gen. for Programming, Channel TV5 2003; Dir Acad. de France à Rome, Villa Médici 2008–09; Minister of Culture and Communication 2009–12; Chevalier, Légion d'honneur, Officier, Ordre nat. du Mérite, Commdr, Ordre des Arts et des Lettres, Officer, Order of Cultural Merit (Monaco) 2007. *Films:* as actor: Lettres d'amour en Somalie 1981, Madame Butterfly 1995, Mon copain Rachid 1997, Le Fabuleux Destin d'Amélie Poulain 2001, Folle de Rachid en transit sur Mars 2001, Bécassine - Le trésor viking 2001, The Car Keys (voice) 2003. *Television:* producer: Ne (assoc. producer) 1975, Les écrans déchirés (short) 1976, Étoiles et toiles 1981–86, Acteur Studio 1986–87, Ciné-Fêtes 1984, Permission de minuit 1987–88, Etoiles 1987–92, Destins 1987–88, Étoile Palace 1990, Du Côté de chez Fred 1988–91, C'est votre vie 1993, Les Amants du siècle 1993, Caravane de nuit 1994, Fairouz 1998, Je suis la Folle de Brejnev 2001; actor: Ça s'est passé comme ça (series, host) 2005. *Publications include:* Tous désirs confondus 1988 (new edn) 2009, Mémoires d'exill 1990, Destins d'étoiles, Vols 1, 2, 3, 4 1991–92, Monte Carlo: la légende 1993, Une saison tunisienne (under the direction of Frédéric Mitterrand and Soraya Elyes-Ferchichi) 1995, L'Ange bleu: un film de Joseph von Sternberg 1995, Madame Butterfly 1995, Les Aigles foudroyés – la fin des Romanov des Habsbourg et des Hohenzollern 1998, Un jour dans le siècle 2000, La Mauvaise Vie 2005, Lettres d'amour en Somalie 2006, Maroc, 1900–1960 Un certain regard (with Abdellah Taïa) 2007, Le Festival de Cannes 2007, Le désir et la chance 2012, La récréation 2013. *Address:* 104 rue de l'Université, 75007 Paris, France.

MITYUKOV, Mikhail Alekseyevich, Cand.Jur.Sc., Jur.Sc.; Russian politician, lawyer and academic; b. 7 Jan. 1942, Ust-Uda, Irkutsk Region; m. Ludmila Aleksandrovna Mityukova; two s. (one deceased) one d.; ed Irkutsk State Univ.; worked in Khakassia Autonomous Region (now Repub.), Deputy Chair. regional court 1968–87; Sr Teacher, Head of Chair of History and Law Abakan State Pedagogical Inst. 1987–90; Russian Fed. People's Deputy and mem. Supreme Soviet, Deputy Chair. then Chair. Cttee on Law 1990–93; First Deputy Minister of Justice 1993–94; mem. State Duma (Parl.) 1993–95, First Deputy Chair. 1994–95; participated in drafting new Russian Constitution; First Deputy Sec., Security Council of Russia 1996–98; Plenipotentiary Rep. of Russian Pres. in Constitutional Court 1998–2005; Prof., State Univ. (MSLA) 2000–; Chair. Presidential Comm. for Rehabilitation of the Victims of Political Repression 2007–; Merited Jurist of the Russian Fed. Award, several medals, Order for Merit to the Fatherland (3rd and 4th degrees) 2005, 2017, Order of Honor, numerous medals. *Publications include:* The Speech on the 50th Anniversary of United Nations session 1995, Constitutional Courts in Post-Soviet Territory 1999, The History of Constitutional Justice in Russia 2002, Constitutional Court's Supervision 1924-1933 2005, Threshold of Constitutional Justice 2006, Bibliography of Constitutional justice 2008–11, Federal Constitutional Law of Constitutional Court 2012, In State Duma 2013, The Stages of History of Constitutional Court of Russia 2014, Birth and Adoption of Constitution of Russia: Constitutional Conference 2014–17, Constitution of Russia, Birth of the Russian Constitution: The Constitutional Meeting of 1993 2018, Constitution of Russia and the Federal Treaty: Problems of Correlations (Diploma of Laureate for Best Scientific Publication) 2019. *Address:* 103132 Moscow, Ilinka str. 8/4, Russia (office). *Telephone:* (495) 606-24-94 (office). *Fax:* (495) 606-34-53 (office). *E-mail:* mma070142@mail.ru (home); rehabilitation@gov .ru (office). *Website:* rehabilitation@gov.ru.

MITZNA, Amram, MA; Israeli politician and army general (retd); b. 20 Feb. 1945, Kibbutz Dovrat; m.; three c.; ed Haifa Univ., Harvard Univ.; joined Israeli Armed Forces 1963; served as Brig. in Six-Day War 1967, Yom Kippur War 1973; resgnd in protest at Israeli treatment of Palestinians in Sabra and Shatila, Lebanon 1982; re-apptd Defence Force Commdr in West Bank during Palestinian uprising 1987–93, later Gen. of the Cen. Region Command, retd from army 1993, rank of Maj.-Gen.; Mayor of Haifa 1993–2003, Yeruham 2005–10; Chair. Israel Labour Party (Mifleget HaAvoda HaYisraelit) 2002–03; mem. Knesset 2003–05, 2013–15; mem. Hatnua (The Movement) 2013–15; advocates removal of West Bank and Gaza settlements and direct negotiations with Palestinian leadership.

MIURA, Satoshi; Japanese telecommunications executive; *Chairman, Nippon Telegraph and Telephone Corporation (NTT);* b. 3 April 1944; joined Nippon Telegraph and Telephone Corpn 1967, held several exec. positions including Sr Vice-Pres. and Exec. Man., Personnel Dept 1996–97, Sr Vice-Pres. and Exec. Man. Personnel and Industrial Relations Dept 1997–98, Exec. Vice-Pres. and Exec. Man. Personnel and Industrial Relations 1998–99, Exec. Vice-Pres. and Deputy Sr Exec. Man. NTT East Provisional HQ 1999–2002, Sr Exec. Vice-Pres. NTT East 1999–2002, Pres. 2002–07, Sr Exec. Vice-Pres. NTT 2005–07, Pres. and CEO 2007–12, Chair. 2012–; External Dir, Hiroshima Bank Ltd 2016–. *Address:* Nippon Telegraph and Telephone Corporation, Otemachi First Square, East Tower, 5-1, Otemachi 1-Chome, Chiyoda-ku, Tokyo 100-8116 Japan (office). *Telephone:* (3) 6838-5111 (office). *Fax:* (3) 5205-5589 (office). *E-mail:* info@ntt.co.jp (office). *Website:* www.ntt.co.jp (office).

MIURA, Zenji; Japanese business executive; *Representative Director, President and CEO, Ricoh Company Limited;* joined Ricoh Co. Ltd 1976, Pres. Ricoh France SA Jan.–Aug. 1993, Chair. Aug. 1993, Deputy Gen. Man. Finance and Accounting Div., Ricoh Co. Ltd 1998–2000, Gen. Man. 2000–03, Exec. Vice-Pres. 2003–05, mem. Bd of Mans, Ricoh Production Print Solutions, LLC, Man. Dir Investor Relations and Man. Control, Internal Control, Finance and Accounting 2004–06, Corp. Exec. Vice-Pres., Ricoh Co. Ltd 2005–06, Rep. Dir, Ricoh Co. Ltd 2005–, Chief Financial Officer 2005–06, Gen. Man. Corp. Planning Div. and Chief Information Officer 2006–09, Chief Strategy Officer 2009–11, Gen. Man. Global Marketing Support Div. and Gen. Man. Trade Affairs and Export/Import Admin Div. 2009–11, Deputy Pres. 2011–13, Rep. Dir, Pres. and CEO Ricoh Co. Ltd 2013–, Pres. and CEO Ricoh Ireland Ltd –2017; Audit and Supervisory Bd mem. Coca-Cola West Co. Ltd, Outside Audit & Supervisory Bd, Coca-Cola Bottlers Japan, Inc.; Dir Nippon Venture Capital Co. Ltd. *Address:* Ricoh Company Ltd, 8-13-1 Ginza, Chuo-ku, Tokyo 104-8222, Japan (office). *Telephone:* (3) 6278-2111 (office).

Fax: (3) 3543-9329 (office). *E-mail:* www-admin@ricoh.co.jp (office). *Website:* www .ricoh.com (office).

MIYAHARA, Hideo, ME, DE; Japanese computer scientist, academic and fmr university administrator; *Professor Emeritus, Osaka University;* ed Osaka Univ.; Asst Prof., Dept of Applied Math. and Physics, Faculty of Eng, Kyoto Univ. 1973–80; Assoc. Prof., Dept of Information and Computer Sciences, Faculty of Eng Science, Osaka Univ. 1980–86, Prof., Computation Centre 1986–89, apptd Prof., Dept of Infomatics and Math. Science, Grad. School of Information Science and Tech. 1989, Dir Computation Centre 1995–98, Dean Faculty of Eng Science 1998–2000, Dean Grad. School of Information Science and Tech. 2000–03, Pres. Osaka Univ. 2003–07, now Prof. Emer.; Visiting Scientist, IBM Thomas J. Watson Research Center, USA 1983–84; Pres. Nat. Inst. of Information and Communications Tech., Japan; Chair. Japan Cttee of Univs for Int. Exchange (JACUIE); Fellow, Information Processing Soc. of Japan, IEEE. *Publications:* numerous scientific papers in professional journals on performance evaluation of computer communication networks, broadband ISDN and multimedia systems. *Address:* Graduate School of Information Science and Technology, Osaka University, 1-1 Yamadaoka, Suita, Osaka 565-0871, Japan (office). *Telephone:* (6) 6850-6585 (office). *Fax:* (6) 6850-6589 (office). *E-mail:* miyahara@ist.osaka-u.ac.jp (office). *Website:* www.osaka-u.ac.jp (office).

MIYAHARA, Kenji, BA; Japanese business executive; ed Kyoto Univ.; joined Sumitomo Shoji Kaisha 1958, Pres. and CEO Sumitomo Corpn of America 1990–96, Pres. and CEO Sumitomo Corpn 1996–2001, Chair. 2001–07, Sr Adviser 2007, now Hon. Adviser; Chair. Japan Foreign Trade Council Inc. 2000–04, Japan-Viet Nam Econ. Cttee 2003, Japan Fed. of Trading Cos (JFTC) 2004; Vice-Chair. Japan Fed. of Econ. Orgs (KEIDANREN) 2004; Counsellor, Bank of Japan 2004–; mem. Panel of Conciliators and Arbitrators, Int. Centre for the Settlement of Investment Disputes (ICSID); mem. US-Japan Pvt. Sector/Govt Comm. 2002–03; mem. Bd of Dirs NEC Corpn 2007–; Hon. Chair. Japan Foreign Trade Council Inc. 2004–. *Address:* c/o Sumitomo Corporation, 1-8-11 Harumi, Chuo-ku, Tokyo 104-8610, Japan (office).

MIYAHARA, Koji; Japanese shipping industry executive; Sr Man. Dir Nippon Yusen Kaisha (NYK Line) –2004, Pres. 2004–09, Chair. Nippon Cargo Airlines 2007–15, Chair. 2009–15, Chief Exec. CSR Man. HQ, Chair. Bulk/Energy Resources Transportation Strategy Cttee, Dir-Gen. NYK Cool Earth Project, Chair. Corp. Officer 2011–15; Chair. Japanese Ship-owners Asscn 2009–11; Vice-Chair. Japan Business Fed. 2011–15; fmr Chair. Japan Fed. of Freight Industries; fmr Exec. Man. Officer, Toho Gas Co., Ltd, also Dir; Dir Mitsubishi Logistics Corpn; mem. Bd of Advisors Autoridad del Canal de Panamá; Commdr, Ordre de la Couronne (Belgium) 2010, Order "Manuel Amador Guerrero", Panama 2012; Minister of Land, Infrastructure, Transport and Tourism Award, Int. Shipping Industry of Japan 2012.

MIYAKE, Issei 'Issey'; Japanese fashion designer; b. (Kazunaru Miyake), 22 April 1938, Hiroshima; ed Tama Art Univ. Tokyo and La Chambre Syndicale de la Couture Parisienne, Paris; Asst Designer to Guy Laroche, Paris 1966–68, to Hubert de Givenchy, Paris 1968–69; Designer, Geoffrey Beene (ready-to-wear firm), New York 1969–70; est. Miyake Design Studio, Tokyo 1970; Dir Issey Miyake International, Issey Miyake & Assocs, Issey Miyake Europe, Issey Miyake USA and Issey Miyake On Limits (Tokyo); Exec. Adviser and Planner, First Japan Culture Conf., Yokohama 1980; developed Pleats Please universal form of contemporary clothing combining technology, functionality and beauty 1993, exhibited at Pompidou Centre, Paris; embarked upon A-POC (A Piece of Cloth) project with Dai Fujiwara and team of young designers 1998; est. Miyake Issey Foundation 2004; opened own brand 2007; work has been exhibited in Paris, Tokyo and at MIT and appears in collections of Metropolitan Museum of Art, New York and Victoria & Albert Museum, London; Co-Dir 21 21 DESIGN SIGHT (Japan's first design museum) 2012–; Order of Culture 2010; Dr hc (RCA) 1993; Japan Fashion Editors' Club Awards, 1974, 1976, Mainichi Design Prize 1977, Pratt Inst. New York Award for Creative Design 1980, International Award, Council of America Fashion Designers 1984, Neiman-Marcus Award 1984, Award of Les Oscars 1985 de la Mode, Paris for Best Collection Presented by a Foreign Designer 1985, Award of the Japanese magazine for the textile industry Senken Shimbun 1986, Mainichi Newspaper Fashion Awards 1977, 1984, 1996, Praemium Imperiale for Sculpture 2005, Kyoto Prize for Arts and Philosophy 2006, XXIII Premio Compasso d'Oro ADI 2014. *Address:* Tokyo Headquarters, Miyake Design Studio, 1-23, Ohyama-cho, Shibuya-ku, Tokyo 151, Japan (office). *Telephone:* (3) 3481-6411 (office). *Website:* www.isseymiyake.com (office).

MIYAKE, Senji, BS; Japanese brewery executive; *Representative Director, President and CEO, Kirin Holdings Company Ltd;* b. 26 Jan. 1948; ed Keio Univ.; joined Kirin Brewery Co. Ltd 1970, Sales Man., Osaka Br. 1988–93, Pres. Kirin Brewery Co. Ltd (separated from Kirin Holdings Co. Ltd) 2007–09, Exec. Vice-Pres. Kirin Holdings Co. Ltd 2009–10, Rep. Dir, Pres. and CEO 2010–15, Chair. 2015–16; Exec. Vice-Pres. Heineken Japan 1993–97, Sales Devt Man., Marketing Div. 1997–98, Sales Man., Sales and Marketing Div. 1998–2000, Nat. Chain Sales Man. Shutoken Regional Head Office 2000–01, Gen. Man. Tokai Regional Head Office 2001–02, Dir and Gen. Man. Tokai Regional Head Office 2002–03, Exec. Officer and Gen. Man. Tokai Regional Head Office 2003–04, Man. Exec. Officer and Gen. Man. Shutoken Regional Head Office 2004–06, Man. Exec. Officer and Pres. Beer, Wine and Spirits Div. 2006–07; Dir Lion Nathan Pty Ltd, Mercian Corpn. *Address:* Kirin Holdings Co. Ltd, 10-1 Shinkawa 2-chome, Chuo-ku, Tokyo 104-8288, Japan (office). *Telephone:* (3) 5541-5321 (office). *Fax:* (3) 5540-3547 (office). *E-mail:* info@kirin.co.jp (office). *Website:* www.kirinholdings.co.jp (office).

MIYAKO, Harumi; Japanese singer; b. 22 Feb. 1948, Kyoto City; d. of Shoji Matsuda (Yi Jong Tack) and Matsuyo Kitamura; m. Hiroomi Asatsuki 1978 (divorced 1982); partner Ikko Nakamura; ed pvt. music schools; began traditional Japanese dancing lessons aged 6, ballet lessons aged 9, joined a theatrical co. aged 11; winner Colombia Nationwide Popular Song Contest aged 15 1963; recording debut with release of Komaru kotoyo (You Upset Me) 1964; began career singing traditional enka (ethnic) music; appeared on annual New Year's Eve Contest Kohaku uta gassen, NHK 1965–85; retd as singer 1984; worked as music producer and news commentator; special performance on music programme Kohaku uta gassen, NHK 1989; re-launched music career singing modern pop music 1990; annual concerts in Budo-Kan; regular appearances on TV music programmes; Rookie of the Year Award 1964, Nihon Kayo Taisho (Japan Annual Pop Grand Prize) 1976, Nihon Record Taisho (Japan Record Annual Grand Prize) 1976. *Singles include:* Komaru kotoyo 1964, Anko tsubaki wa koi no hana (New Artist Award, Japanese Recording Industry) 1964, Namida no renraku fune 1965, Bakattcho debune 1965, Sukini natta hito 1968, Kita no shuka kara (Record of the Year, Japan Popular Music Award) 1976, I Want to Become an Everyday Woman 1984, Sennen No Koto 1990, Sakure Shigure 1993, Nana no ran 1994, Ajia Densetsu 1996, Jashu mon 1998, Ohara zessho 2000.

MIYAMOTO, Mikihiko; Japanese insurance executive; Pres. Yasuda Mutual Life Insurance Co. Ltd –2004; Chair. Meiji Yasuda Life Insurance Co. (cr. through merger of Yasuda Mutual and Meiji Life Insurance Cos 2004) Jan. 2004–06 (resgnd).

MIYAMOTO, Yoichi; Japanese business executive; *Representative Director and Chairman, Shimizu Corporation;* joined Shimizu Corpn (contractor in eng and construction projects) 1971, positions held include Man. of Hokuriku Office, Exec. Officer, Man. of Kyushu Office, Man. Exec. Officer and Sr Man. Exec. Officer, Pres. 2007–16, Rep. Dir 2007–, Chair. 2016–; mem. Overseas Construction Asscn of Japan, Inc. *Address:* Shimizu Corpn, 2-16-1 Kyobashi, Chuo-Ku, Tokyo 104-8370, Japan (office). *Telephone:* (3) 3561-1111 (office). *Fax:* (3) 5441-0349 (office). *E-mail:* info@shimz.co.jp (office). *Website:* www.shimz.co.jp (office).

MIYANAGA, Shunichi; Japanese business executive; *President and CEO, Mitsubishi Heavy Industries;* b. 27 April 1948; joined Mitsubishi Heavy Industries Ltd 1972, Sr Vice-Pres. and Deputy Head of Machinery HQ April–May 2006, Sr Vice-Pres. and Deputy Head of Machinery and Steel Structures HQ May 2006–08, Exec. Vice-Pres. and Head of Machinery and Steel Structures HQ April–June 2008, mem. Bd of Dirs 2008–, fmr Gen. Man., Asst to Pres., Rep. Dir 2008–, Exec. Vice-Pres. and Head of Machinery and Steel Structures HQ 2008–11, Sr Exec. Vice-Pres. and Head of Presidential Admin Office 2011–13, Pres. and CEO Mitsubishi Heavy Industries 2013–, Dir Mitsubishi Motors Corpn 2014–. *Address:* Mitsubishi Heavy Industries, 16-5, Konan 2-chome, Minato-ku, Tokyo 108-8215, Japan (office). *Telephone:* (3) 6716-3111 (office). *Fax:* (3) 6716-5800 (office). *E-mail:* info@mhi.co.jp (office). *Website:* www.mhi.co.jp (office).

MIYATA, Koichi; Japanese business executive; *President and Representative Director, Sumitomo Mitsui Financial Group, Inc.;* joined The Mitsui Bank Ltd 1976, mem. Bd of Dirs Sumitomo Mitsui Banking Corpn (subsidiary of Sumitomo Mitsui Financial Group, Inc.) 2003, 2009, 2011–, Man. Dir Sumitomo Mitsui Banking Corpn 2006–09, Sr Man. Dir 2009–10, mem. Bd of Dirs Sumitomo Mitsui Financial Group, Inc. 2010–, Gen. Man. Planning Dept and Treasury Unit, later Deputy Head of Treasury Unit and Sr Man. Dir 2010–11, Pres. and Rep. Dir Sumitomo Mitsui Financial Group, Inc. 2011–; Auditor, Japan Securities Depository Centre. *Address:* Sumitomo Mitsui Financial Group, Inc., 1-1-2, Marunouchi, Chiyoda-ku, Tokyo 100-0005, Japan (office). *Telephone:* (3) 3282-8111 (office). *Fax:* (3) 5512-4429 (office). *E-mail:* info@smfg.co.gp (office). *Website:* www.smfg.co.jp (office).

MIYATO, Naoteru, BA; Japanese insurance industry executive; *Chairman and Representative Director, T&D Holdings, Inc.;* b. 20 May 1943; ed Keio Univ.; joined Daido Life 1967, positions included Pres. Daido Int., New York and Gen. Man. Research Dept, Gen. Man. Gen. Marketing Dept 1994–99, mem. Bd of Dirs Daido Life 1994–, Man. Dir 1996–99, Sr Man. Dir March–July 1999, Pres. and Rep. Dir 1999–2004, Pres. and Rep. Dir T&D Holdings, Inc. (holding co.) 2004–11, Chair. and Rep. Dir 2011–, mem. Bd of Dirs Taiyo Life 2008–; Dir Mitsubishi UFJ Securities Holdings Co. 2010–, Morgan Stanley Securities Co., Ltd 2010–. *Address:* T&D Holdings Inc., 2-7-9 Nihonbashi, Chuo-Ku, Tokyo 103-0027, Japan (office). *Telephone:* (3) 3231-8685 (office). *Fax:* (3) 3231-8893 (office). *E-mail:* info@td-holdings.co.jp (office). *Website:* www.td-holdings.co.jp (office).

MIYAUCHI, Ken; Japanese business executive; *Representative Director, President and COO, SoftBank Group Corporation;* b. 1 Nov. 1949; joined SoftBank Corpn Japan (currently SoftBank Group Corpn) 1984, Dir 1988, Exec. Vice-Pres., Dir and COO Vodafone KK (currently SoftBank Corpn) 2006–07, Rep. Dir and COO SoftBank Mobile Corpn 2007–13, Dir, Yahoo Japan Corpn 2012–, Rep. Dir and Exec. Vice-Pres., SoftBank Corpn April–June 2013, Rep. Dir and Sr Exec. Vice-Pres. 2013–15, Dir, Brightstar Global Group Inc. 2014–15, Pres. and CEO SoftBank Mobile Corpn 2015–, Dir, SoftBank Group Corpn 2015–, Rep., SoftBank Group Japan GK 2016–, Rep. Dir, Pres. and COO SoftBank Group Corpn 2016–; mem. Japan Man. Asscn 1977. *Address:* SoftBank Group Corporation, 1-9-1 Higashi-shimbashi, Minato-ku, Tokyo 105-7303, Japan (office). *Telephone:* (3) 6889-2000 (office). *E-mail:* info@softbank.jp (office). *Website:* www.softbank.jp (office).

MIYAZAKI, Hayao; Japanese film producer, film director and animator; b. 5 Jan. 1941, Tokyo; s. Katsuji Miyazaki; m. Akemi Ōta 1965; two s.; ed Gakushuin Univ.; started career as animator Toei Douga Studios 1963; joined A Pro 1971, moved to Nippon Animation 1973; directed first TV series Mirai Shonen Conan 1978; moved to Tokyo Movie Shinsha 1979, directed first film Rupan Sansei: Kariosutoro no shiro 1979; Co-f. Ghibli Studios with Isao Takahata 1981–; Mononoke Hime and Sen to Chihiro no Kamikakushi both set Japanese box office records; Venice Film Festival lifetime achievement award 2005. *Television includes:* Okami shônen Ken (series) 1963, Fujimaru of the Wind 1964, Hustle Punch 1965, Mahô tsukai Sarî 1968, Akko's Secret (series) 1969–70, Isamu the Wilderness Boy (series) 1973, A Dog of Flanders (series) 1975, Anne of Green Gables (series) 1979. *Films include:* as writer/dir: Rupan Sansei: Kariosutoro no Shiro (Lupin III: The Castle of Cagliostro) (Ōfuji Noburō Award) 1979, Kaze no tani no Nausicaa (Nausicaa of the Valley of the Wind) (Ōfuji Noburō Award) 1984, Tenku no Shiro no Laputa (Floating Island of Laputa) 1986, Tonari no Totoro (My Neighbour's Totoro) (Ōfuji Noburō Award) 1988, Majo no Takkyubin (Kiki's Delivery Service) (Mainichi Film Award for Best Animation Film) 1989, Kurenai no Buta (The Red Pig) 1992, On Your Mark 1995, Mononoke Hime (Princess Mononoke) (Mainichi Film Award for Best Animation Film) 1997, Tonari no Yamada-kun (My Neighbour Yamada) 1999, Sen to Chihiro no Kamikakushi (Spirited Away) (Japanese Acad. Award for Best Film 2002, Hong Kong Film Award for Best Asian Film 2002, Berlin Int. Film Festival Golden Bear Award 2002, Best Animation Acad. Award 2003, Mainichi Film Award for Best Animation Film) 2001, Kujira Tori 2001, Hauru no ugoku Shiro (Howl's Moving Castle) (Venice Film Festival Golden Osella, Nebula Award 2007) 2004, Yadosagashi 2006, Mizugumo monmon 2006, Hoshi wo katta hi 2006; as producer: Yanagawa horiwari monogatarai (The Story of Yanagawa's Canals) 1987, Omohide poro poro (Memories of Yesterday) 1991, Heisei tanuki gassen pompoko (The Raccoon War) 1994, Mimi wo Sumaseba (Whisper of the Heart) 1995, Neko no ongaeshi (The Cat Returns) 2002, Akage no An: Gurîn Gêburuzu e no michi 2010. *Website:* www.studioghiblidvd.co.uk; www.ghibli.jp.

MIYAZAWA, Yoichi, MPA; Japanese politician; *Minister of Economy, Trade and Industry;* b. 21 April 1950, Fukuyama; s. of Hiroshi Miyazawa; ed Univ. of Tokyo, Harvard Univ., USA; joined Ministry of Finance 1974, served in various positions including District Dir, Kishiwada Tax Office, Osaka Regional Taxation Office 1980, Research and Planning Dir, Minister's Secr. 1989, Exec. Sec. to Prime Minister 1992; mem. House of Reps (lower house of Parl.) for Hiroshima 7th Dist 2000–10; mem. House of Councilors (upper house of Parl.) for Hiroshima Pref. 2010–; Sr Vice-Minister in Cabinet Office, in charge of Econ. and Fiscal Policy and Decentralization 2008; Minister of Economy, Trade and Industry 2014–, also Minister in charge of Response to Econ. Impact caused by Nuclear Accident and of Industrial Competitiveness, and Minister of State for Nuclear Damage Compensation and Decommissioning Facilitation Corpn; mem. Liberal Democratic Party. *Address:* Ministry of Economy, Trade and Industry, 1-3-1, Kasumigaseki, Chiyoda-ku, Tokyo 100-8901, Japan (office). *Telephone:* (3) 3501-1511 (office). *Fax:* (3) 3501-6942 (office). *E-mail:* webmail@meti.go.jp (office). *Website:* www.meti.go.jpy (office).

MIYOSHI, Toru, LLB; Japanese judge (retd); b. 31 Oct. 1927; ed Univ. of Tokyo; Asst Judge, Tokyo Dist Court and Tokyo Family Court 1955; Judge, Hakodate Dist Court and Hakodate Family Court 1965; Judge, Tokyo Dist Court (Presiding Judge of Div.) 1975; Pres. Research and Training Inst. for Court Clerks 1982; Pres. Oita Dist Court and Oita Family Court 1985; Pres. Nagano Dist Court and Nagano Family Court 1986; Chief Judicial Research Official of Supreme Court 1987; Pres. Sapporo High Court 1991, Tokyo High Court 1992; Justice of Supreme Court 1992; Chief Justice of Supreme Court 1995–97; mem. Advisory Council to Consider the Direct Election of the Prime Minister 2001; Head of Japan Conference (conservative pressure group) *c.* 2007.

MIZOTE, Kensei; Japanese politician; b. 13 Sept. 1942; ed Faculty of Law, Univ. of Tokyo; with Fuji Steel Co. (now Nippon Steel Corpn) 1966–71; Vice-Pres. Koyo Dockyard Co. Ltd 1971–79, Pres. 1979–87; Mayor of Mihara City, Hiroshima Pref. 1987–93; mem. House of Councillors for Hiroshima Pref. 1993–, Chair. Cttee on Gen. Affairs 2001, Cttee on Rules and Admin 2004, Cttee on Budget 2008, Cttee on Fundamental Nat. Policies 2008, mem. Cttee on Budget and Finance 2001; Parl. Vice-Minister of Int. Trade and Industry 1997; Chair. Finance Sub-cttee, New Constitution Drafting Cttee, LDP 2005, Coastal Shipping Activation Sub-cttee, Special Cttee on Marine Transportation and Shipbuilding 2006, Chair. Jt Plenary Meeting of Party Members of Both Houses of the Diet; Minister of State, Chair. Nat. Public Safety Comm. and Minister of State for Disaster Man. 2006–07; Deputy Chair. Research Comm. on the Tax System. *Publication:* Seinen yo Kokyo ni Kaette Shicho ni Naro (co-author). *Telephone:* (848) 640025. *E-mail:* senkyo@mizote.info. *Website:* www.sangiin.go.jp/japanese/joho1/kousei/eng/members/profile/5993006.htm; mizote.info.

MIZRAHI, Isaac; American fashion designer, set and costume designer, television presenter and stage director; b. 14 Oct. 1961, Brooklyn, NY; s. of Zeke Mizrahi and Sarah Mizrahi; m. Arnold Germer 2011; ed Yeshiva of Flatbush, High School of Performing Arts, Manhattan, Parsons School of Design; apprenticed to Perry Ellis 1982, full-time post 1982–84; worked with Jeffrey Banks 1984–85, Calvin Klein 1985–87, Mark Morris, Twyla Tharp, Bill T. Jones and Mikhail Baryshnikov; started own design firm in partnership with Sarah Hadad Cheney 1987, first formal show 1988, first spring collection Nov. 1988, first menswear line launched April 1990, announced closure of firm Oct. 1998; partnered with Target Stores to launch a collection of women's sportswear and accessories 2002, cr. home collection for Target 2005; appeared off-Broadway in one-man show Les Mizrahi 1999; hosted The Isaac Mizrahi Show on Oxygen Network 1999; wrote and directed Supermodelhero, which first appeared online in 2005; designed for Claiborne 2009; launched label IsaacMizrahiLIVE! exclusively on QVC shopping channel 2010, sold to Xcel Brands, Inc. 2011, remains a shareholder, Creative Dir and media personality for his namesake brand under Xcel; costume designer for three Broadway revivals, including two plays, The Women (Drama Desk Award for Outstanding Costume Design 2002) 2001, Barefoot in the Park 2006, and one operetta, Threepenny Opera 2006, for Metropolitan Opera's production of Orfeo ed Euridice 2008; designed pro bono the Smithsonian American Art Museum and Nat. Portrait Gallery's conservators' denim work aprons 2006; designed sets and costumes and directed Stephen Sondheim's A Little Night Music for Opera Theatre of St Louis 2010; designed and directed Mozart's The Magic Flute for Opera Theatre of St Louis 2014; has appearances in numerous TV shows and films since the 1990s; narrated Peter and the Wolf at Guggenheim Museum's Works & Process performing arts series 2007, 2010; began co-hosting first season of The Fashion Show on Bravo TV with singer Kelly Rowland 2009, returned as co-host opposite supermodel Iman 2010; Womenswear Designer of the Year 1989, 1991, Drama Desk Award for Outstanding Costume Design 2002. *Film appearances:* Celebrity 1998, Small Time Crooks 2000, Hollywood Ending 2002. *Radio:* appeared on public radio game show Wait, Wait, Don't Tell Me 2006. *Television includes:* appearances on Sex and the City, Spin City, Ugly Betty, The Apprentice, Jeopardy! Million Dollar Celebrity Invitational, The Red Carpet Show for the Golden Globes (interviewer) 2006, Project Runway: All Stars (head judge) 2012, Live! With Kelly (red carpet corresp. during 84th Annual Academy Awards) 2012, The Big C 2013; co-wrote historical documentary Kingdom of David: The Saga of the Israelites for PBS. *Publications:* series of comic books called Isaac Mizrahi Presents the Adventures of Sandee the Supermodel. *Address:* c/o Xcel Brands, Inc., 475 10th Avenue #4, New York, NY 10018, USA. *Telephone:* (347) 727-2474. *E-mail:* info@xcelbrands.com. *Website:* www.xcelbrands.com/isaac_mizrahi.html; www.isaacmizrahiny.com.

MIZRAHI, Valerie, PhD; Zimbabwean biologist and academic; *Director, Institute of Infectious Disease and Molecular Medicine, University of Cape Town;* b. 1958; ed Univ. of Cape Town, South Africa; postdoctoral work at Pennsylvania State Univ.,

USA 1983–86; held positions with South African Council for Scientific and Industrial Research, Smith Kline & French Research & Devt; fmr Head of Molecular Biology Unit, South African Inst. for Medical Research –2000; Prin. Investigator and Dir Molecular Mycobacteriology Research Unit, South African Medical Research Council, Univ. of the Witwatersrand (fmrly South African Inst. for Medical Research) 2000–10; Prof. and Dir Inst. of Infectious Disease and Molecular Medicine, Univ. of Cape Town 2011–, also Dir Molecular Mycobacteriology Research Unit; Int. Research Scholar, Howard Hughes Medical Inst., Chevy Chase, Md 2000, 2005; Fellow, Royal Soc. of South Africa, American Acad. of Microbiology 2009; Assoc. Fellow, Acad. of Sciences of the Developing World; mem. Acad. of Science of South Africa; Order of the Mapungubwe in Silver 2007; L'Oréal-UNESCO For Women in Science Award 2000, DST Distinguished Woman Scientist Award 2006, Gold Medal of the South African Soc. for Biochemistry and Molecular Biology 2006, Christophe Mérieux Prize 2013. *Publications:* numerous articles in medical journals. *Address:* Institute of Infectious Disease and Molecular Medicine, Faculty of Health Sciences, University of Cape Town, Anzio Road, Observatory 7925, Cape Town 2050, South Africa (office). *Telephone:* (21) 4066098 (office). *Fax:* (21) 4066068 (office). *E-mail:* valerie.mizrahi@uct.ac.za (office). *Website:* www.iidmm.uct.ac.za (office).

MIZUKOSHI, Koshi; Japanese metal industry executive; b. 1 Sept. 1938, Seoul, S Korea; m.; two s.; ed Univ. of Tokyo; joined Planning and Business Admin Dept, Kobe Steel Ltd (KOBELCO) 1961, Inspection Section, Devt Dept 1965–73, Man. Corp. Planning Dept 1973–78, Asst to Pres. 1978–81, Gen. Man. Planning and Admin Dept, Iron and Steel Div.'s Production Group 1983–91, Man. Dir 1991–93, Sr Man. Dir 1993–96, mem. Bd of Dirs 1989, Rep. Dir 1996, Exec. Vice-Pres. 1996–99, CEO and Pres. 1999–2004, Chair. 2004–09 (resgnd), Advisor 2009; Vice-Chair. Kansai Econ. Fed.; mem. Bd of Dirs Foundation for Biomedical Research and Innovation, Kansai Int. Public Relations Promotion Office.

MIZUNO, Akihisa, MCivilEng; Japanese business executive; *Chairman, Chubu Electric Power Company, Inc.;* ed Univ. of Tokyo; joined Chubu Electric Power Co., Inc. 1978, Man., Washington Office, Gen. Man. Int. Business Dept, Dir and Sr Man. Exec. Officer, Gen. Man. Corp. Planning and Strategy Div. 2008–09, Dir and Exec. Vice-Pres., Gen. Man. Corp. Planning and Strategy Div. and Affiliated Business Planning and Devt Dept 2009–10, Pres. and Dir Chubu Electric Power Co., Inc. 2010–15, Chair. 2015–, mem. Strategic Cttee, Chubu Energy Trading, Inc.; fmr Consultant, World Bank; mem. Outside Audit & Supervisory Bd, Toyota Industries Corpn. *Address:* Chubu Electric Power Co., Inc., 1 Higashi-shincho, Higashi-ku, Nagoya 461-8680, Japan (office). *Telephone:* (52) 951-8211 (office). *Fax:* (52) 962-4624 (office). *E-mail:* info@chuden.co.jp (office). *Website:* www .chuden.co.jp (office).

MIZUTORI, Mami; Japanese diplomatist; *Assistant Secretary-General and Special Representative for Disaster Risk Reduction, United Nations Office for Disaster Risk Reduction (UNISDR);* b. 1960; m.; ed Hitotsubashi Univ., Tokyo, Diplomatic School of Spain; worked for 27 years in Japanese Ministry of Foreign Affairs in various positions including Budget Dir, Dir, Japan Information and Culture Centre, Embassy of Japan in London, Nat. Security Policy Div., UN Policy Div., Dir of Status US Forces Agreement Div., Deputy Dir Personnel Div.; Exec. Dir Sainsbury Inst. for the Study of Japanese Arts and Cultures 2011–18; Asst Sec.-Gen. and Special Rep. for Disaster Risk Reduction, UN Office for Disaster Risk Reduction (UNISDR) 2018–; Lecturer, Ritsumeikan Asia Pacific Univ., Waseda Univ., Tokyo. *Address:* United Nations Office for Disaster Risk Reduction (UNISDR), 9–11 rue de Varembé, 1201 Châtelaine, Geneva 10, Switzerland (office). *Telephone:* 229178908 (office). *Fax:* 227339531 (office). *E-mail:* isdr@un.org (office). *Website:* www.unisdr.org (office).

MKAPA, Benjamin William, BA; Tanzanian politician, journalist and diplomatist; b. 12 Nov. 1938, Masasi; s. of William Matwani and Stephania Nambanga; m. Anna Joseph Maro 1966; two s.; ed Makerere Univ. Coll.; Admin. Officer, Dist Officer 1962; Foreign Service Officer 1962; Man. Ed. Tanzania Nationalist and Uhuru 1966, The Daily News and The Sunday News 1972; Press Sec. to Pres. 1974; Founding Dir Tanzania News Agency 1976; High Commr in Nigeria 1976; Minister for Foreign Affairs 1977–80, for Information and Culture 1980–82; High Commr to Canada 1982–83; Amb. to USA 1983–84; Minister for Foreign Affairs 1984–90; MP for Nanyumbu 1985–95; Minister for Information and Broadcasting 1990–92, for Science, Tech. and Higher Educ. 1992–95; Pres. of Tanzania and C-in-C of Armed Forces 1995–2005; Chair. Chama Cha Mapinduzi (CCM) party 1996–2005; Chair. Southern African Devt Community 2003–04; Trustee, Aga Khan Univ., Karachi, Pakistan 2007–12; Dr hc (Soka Univ., Tokyo) 1998, (Open Univ. of Tanzania) 2003, (Nat. Univ. of Lesotho) 2005, Kenyatta Univ.) 2005, (Univ. of Dar Es Salaam, Tanzania) 2006, (Newcastle Univ.) 2007, (Univ. of Cape Coast, Ghana) 2008, Hon. DHumLitt (Morehouse Coll., Atlanta, USA) 1999; Global Leadership Award 2007. *Leisure interest:* reading.

MKHATSHWA, Father Smangaliso, ThM, PhD; South African ecclesiastic and local government official; b. 26 June 1939, Barberton, Mpumalanga; s. of Elias Mkhatshwa and Maria Mkhatshwa (née Nkosi); ed Pax Coll., Pietersburg, St Peter's Seminary, KwaZulu Natal, Univ. of Leuven, Belgium; ordained RC priest 1965, worked as a pastor in Witbank until 1970, seconded to Church's Gen. Secr., Pretoria; detained for four months under Internal Security Act following Soweto uprising 1976, restricted by five-year banning order to Pretoria magisterial dist 1977–83, apptd Parish Priest of St Charles Lwanga, Soshanguve; Sec.-Gen. Southern African Catholic Bishops' Conf. 1981–88; Patron, United Democratic Front 1983; detained in Ciskei Oct. 1983 and charged with subversion, incitement to public violence and addressing an unlawful meeting, found not guilty and released March 1984; detained under emergency regulations 1986, released and successfully sued the state for torture and assault; Sec.-Gen. Inst. for Contextual Theology 1988–94; mem. Parl. (African Nat. Congress—ANC) 1994–99, mem. Reconstruction and Devt Standing Cttee and Educ. Standing Cttee; Deputy Minister of Educ. 1996–99; mem. ANC Nat. Exec. Cttee 1997–99; Trustee, Kagiso Trust, Matla Trust; Pres. Cen. Transvaal Civics Asscn (later renamed SANCO Pretoria); Exec. Mayor of City of Tshwane 2000–06; Dr hc (Tübingen, Germany), (Georgetown Univ., USA), (Univ. Coll. of New Rochelle, USA); Steve Biko Human Rights Award, Indicator Newspaper Award. *Publications:* articles on theology and politics. *Leisure interests:* tennis, music, reading, theatre. *Address:* c/o Father Smangaliso Mkhatshwa Child and Youth Care Centre, Private Bag X73,

Soshanguve 0164, South Africa. *Telephone:* (12) 7978300. *E-mail:* yaya@gauteng .gov.za.

MKRTUMYAN, Yuri Israelovich, CandHisSc; Armenian ethnographer; b. 1 Jan. 1939, Tbilisi; ed Moscow State Univ.; lab. asst, jr researcher Inst. of Archaeology and Ethnography, Armenian Acad. of Sciences 1962–71, Prof. 1996–; Sr Lecturer Yerevan State Univ. 1971–89; Head Chair of Ethnography, Yerevan State Univ. 1989–94; Sec. CP Cttee Yerevan State Univ.; mem. Cen. CPSU Cttee, mem. Bureau Cen. Cttee Armenian CP 1990–91; counsellor to Minister of Foreign Affairs, Repub. of Armenia April–June 1994; Amb. to Russia 1994–96; apptd Dir Inst. of Ethnography and Archaeology 1997. *Publications:* over 40 scientific works on theoretical and regional ethnography in Russian, Armenian and English.

MKULO, Mustapha; Tanzanian politician; b. 26 Sept. 1946; Dir-Gen. Nat. Social Security Fund 1987–2000; mem. Chama Cha Mapinduzi Party: Mem. of Parl. for Kilosa Constituency 2005–15; Deputy Minister of Finance –2008, Minister of Finance, Planning, Economy and Empowerment 2008–12.

MKWEZALAMBA, Maxwell, MEcon, PhD; Malawi economist and politician; b. 2 Dec. 1959; m.; four c.; ed Chancellor Coll., Univ. of Malawi, Univ. of Manchester, UK, Univ. of Illinois at Urbana-Champaign, USA; Lecturer in Econs, Univ. of Malawi 1984–90, Lecturer and Head of Econs Dept, Chancellor Coll., Univ. of Malawi 1995–96; Research Fellow, Cornell Univ., USA 1995; Consultant Macroeconomist, Ministry of Econ. Planning and Devt 1996–97; Chief Economist and Coordinator for Advisory Services for Private Business Promotion, Malawi Chamber of Commerce and Industry 1997–98; Macroeconomist, World Bank, Malawi Country Office 1998–2000, 2003–04, Country Economist, World Bank, Washington, DC 1999; Commr for Econ Affairs, African Union Comm. 2004–13; Minister of Finance 2013–14; Ed.-in-Chief, Malawi Chamber of Commerce and Industry Business Review 1997–98; Pres., Econs Asscn of Malawi 1998–2000; mem. Monetary Policy Cttee, Reserve Bank of Malawi 2000–03; Sec. to Cabinet Cttees on Economy and Budgetary and Financial Matters 2000–03; mem. Bd of Dirs several orgs including Nat. Roads Authority, Shire Bus Lines, David Whitehead and Sons, PFG Wright Insurance Brokers, Malawi Inst. of Man. 1997–2003; consultant on devt, financial and econ. man. issues for Malawi Govt, UNDP, UNICEF, German Agency for Tech. Cooperation. *Publications:* numerous papers and publications on macro-economic theory and policy, monetary econs, public finance, int. trade and finance and econs of devt.

MLABA, Obed Thembinkosi; South African politician and diplomatist; b. 1943, Estcourt, Natal; m.; several d.; ed St Augustine's Coll.; fmr mem. Umlazi Resident Asscn, later joined United Democratic Front; joined African National Congress 1990, participated actively in its KZN br.; Mayor of Durban 1996–2011; also held titles of Chair. Kwa-Zulu Natal Local Govt Asscn and South African Local Govt Asscn; High Commr to UK 2014–17.

MLADENOV, Nikolay Evtimov, BA, MA; Bulgarian politician and UN official; *Special Coordinator for the Middle East Peace Process, Secretary-General's Personal Representative to the Palestine Liberation Organization and the Palestinian Authority, and Secretary-General's Envoy to the Quartet, United Nations;* b. 5 May 1972, Sofia; m.; one c.; ed Univ. of Nat. and World Economy, Sofia, King's Coll. London, UK; worked for Open Soc. Inst., Sofia 1996–98; Programme Coordinator, Social Dept for Bulgaria, World Bank 1998; Founder and Dir European Inst., Sofia 1999–2001; mem. Narodno Sobranie (Parl.) 2001–02; mem. Union of Democratic Forces (UDF), mem. Nat. Exec. Council 2002, Deputy Chair. European Integration Cttee, Vice-Pres. UDF 2004–05; Consultant to World Bank, Int. Republican Inst. and Nat. Democratic Inst. in Bulgaria, Afghanistan, Yemen and other Middle East countries 2005–07; Adviser to Defence and Foreign Policy Comms, Iraqi Parl. 2006; mem. European Parl. (Citizens for European Devt of Bulgaria—GERB—party, aligned with Group of the European People's Party—European Democrats) 2007–09, Chair. del. for relations with Iraq, mem. dels for Afghanistan and Israel; Minister of Defence 2009–10, of Foreign Affairs 2010–13; Special Rep. of the Sec.-Gen. for Iraq and Head, Assistance Mission for Iraq (UNAMI), UN 2013–15, UN Special Coordinator for Middle East Peace Process, Sec.-Gen.'s Personal Rep. to Palestine Liberation Org. and Palestinian Authority, and Sec.-Gen.'s Envoy to Quartet 2015–; signatory of the Prague Declaration on European Conscience and Communism. *Address:* Office of the Secretary-General, UN Headquarters, First Avenue at 46th Street, New York, NY 10017, USA (office). *E-mail:* info@un.org (office). *Website:* www.un.org (office).

MLADIĆ, Gen. Ratko; Bosnia and Herzegovina fmr military leader; b. 12 March 1943, Kalinovik; m. Bosiljka 'Bosa' Mladić; one s. one d. (deceased); Serb nationalist; began mil. career as tank officer, Yugoslav People's Army (JNA), Bosnia and Herzegovina; gained popularity among Serb population for supporting their claim to enclave of Krajina during civil war in Croatia 1991; apptd CO JNA 1992; commanded siege of Sarajevo 1992–94; supported creation of a 'Greater Serbia' and opposed any peace settlement of Bosnian civil war, including Gen. Framework Agreement for Peace in Bosnia and Herzegovina 1995; indicted as war criminal 1995; given protection by Slobodan Milošević until his arrest by Yugoslav authorities and extradition to Int. Criminal Tribunal for the Fmr Yugoslavia (ICTY), The Hague 2001; went into hiding 2001; report issued by Netherlands Inst. for War Documentation held Mladić to be principally responsible for massacre of up to 8,000 Muslim men and boys in Srebrenica in 1995; arrested in Lazarevo, northern Serbia 26 May 2011, extradited to The Hague to stand trial for alleged war crimes and genocide, trial began 3 June 2011; found guilty by ICTY and sentenced to life imprisonment 22 Nov. 2017.

MLAMBO-NGCUKA, Phumzile, BA, MPhil; South African politician and UN official; *Under-Secretary-General and Executive Director, UN Women;* b. 3 Nov. 1955, KwaZulu Natal, Clermont Township; m. Bulelani Ngcuka; one s.; ed Nat. Univ. of Lesotho; teacher in KwaZulu Natal 1981–83; founder and Dir Young Women's Int. Programme, YWCA World Office, Geneva, Switzerland 1984–87; Dir TEAM (non-governmental org.), Cape Town 1987–89; Dir World Univ. Services 1990–92; est. Phumelela Services 1993–94; MP 1994–2008, Chair., Public Service Portfolio Cttee 1994–; Deputy Minister, Dept of Trade and Industry (DTI) 1996–99; Minister of Minerals and Energy 1999–2005; Deputy Pres. 2005–08 (resgnd); Under-Sec.-Gen. and Exec. Dir UN Women 2013–; Chancellor, Tshwane Univ. of Tech. 2007–; Founding mem., Guguletu Community Devt Corpn; mem. Nat. Exec. Cttee, African Nat. Congress 1997–. *Address:* UN Women, 405 East

42nd Street, New York, NY 10017, USA (office). *Telephone:* (646) 781-4400 (office). *Fax:* (646) 781-4444 (office). *Website:* www.unwomen.org (office).

MLECHIN, Leonid M.; Russian journalist and writer; b. 12 June 1957, Moscow; m.; one s.; ed Moscow State Univ.; staff, head of division, Deputy Ed.-in-Chief weekly Novoye Vremya 1979–93; Deputy Ed.-in-Chief newspaper Izvestia 1993–96; political reviewer, All-Russian State Cttee on Radio and Television 1996–97; writer and narrator, Particular Dossier (TV-Tsentr) 1997–; mem. Union of Writers 1986–; Order of Friendship 2011; Honored Worker of Culture of Russian Federation 2004, Medal of Order For Services to the Fatherland 2007, Taffy Award 2007, 2009. *Publications include:* numerous books, including detective stories, novels, historical non-fiction, and biographies of Yevgeny Primakov and chairmen of KGB. *Address:* TV-Tsentr, Moscow 113184, ul. B. Tatarskaya 33/1, Russia (office). *Telephone:* (495) 215-18-12 (office); (495) 217-75-50 (office). *Website:* www .mlechin.com.

MLECZKO, Andrzej; Polish graphic designer and illustrator; b. 5 Jan. 1949, Tarnobrzeg; one d.; ed Faculty of Architecture, Kraków Tech. Univ.; illustrator of books, paintings, drawings; contrib. to magazines in Poland and abroad 1971–; worked as theatre consultant for Kochanowski 1975–80, for Slowacki 1980–92; Andrzej Mleczko Author's Gallery, Kraków 1983–, Warsaw 2002–; has designed over 20,000 graphics, drawings and posters; mem. Polish Artists Soc. 1974–. *Film appearances:* Chłopaki nie płaczą (Boys Don't Cry) 2000, 'E=mc²' 2002. *Radio:* co-hosted (with Paweł Pawlik) Galeria Andrzeja Mleczki on RMF FM 2001, took part in Moja szkoła w Unii Europejskiej (My School in the European Union) 2003. *Publications:* Seks, mydło i powidło (Krakowska Książka Miesiąca (Cracovian Book of the Month Award) 2008); 46 books and albums. *Address:* Andrzej Mleczko Author's Gallery, ul. Św. Jana 14, 31-018 Kraków; ul. Marszatkowska 140, 00-061 Warsaw, Poland. *Telephone:* (12) 4217104 (Kraków); (22) 8295760 (Warsaw). *Fax:* (12) 4217104. *E-mail:* galeria@mleczko.pl. *Website:* mleczko.interia.pl.

MLINARIC, David, CBE; British interior designer; b. 12 March 1939; m. Martha Laycock 1969; one s. two d.; ed Bartlett School of Architecture, Univ. Coll., London; f. own co. David Mlinaric Ltd 1964, joined by Hugh Henry 1969, and by Tino Zervudachi 1983, now the int. interior design practice Mlinaric, Henry & Zervudachi Ltd 1989–, Tino Zervudachi moved to Paris to form Mlinaric, Henry & Zervudachi SA 1991, Mlinaric, Henry & Zervudachi, Inc., New York formed in 1998. *Publication:* Mlinaric on Decorating (illustrated) (with Mirabel Cecil) 2008. *Address:* Mlinaric, Henry & Zervudachi Ltd, 38 Bourne Street, London, SW1W 8JA, England (office). *Telephone:* (20) 7730-9072 (office). *Fax:* (20) 7823-4756 (office). *E-mail:* info@mhzlondon.com (office). *Website:* mhzlondon.com (office).

MMARI, Geoffrey Raphael Vehaeli, DipEd, PhD; Tanzanian university teacher and administrator; b. 24 June 1934, Moshi, Kilimanjaro region; s. of Vehaeli Mmari and Luisia Mmari; m. Salome Mmari 1959; one s. three d.; ed Univ. of E Africa, Univ. of N Iowa, USA, Univ. of Dar es Salaam; teacher and admin. 1966–69; univ. teacher 1969–73; Dir Inst. of Educ., Univ. of Dar es Salaam 1973–74, Head Dept of Educ. 1974–77, Dean, Faculty of Arts and Social Sciences 1977–82, Chief Academic Officer 1982–84, Vice-Chancellor 1988–91; Vice-Chancellor Sokoine Univ. of Agric. 1984–88; Co-ordinator Open Univ. Planning Office 1991–, Vice-Chancellor Open Univ. of Tanzania 1993–2005; Provost, Tumaini Univ., Dar es Salaam Coll. 2005–13; Chair. Higher Educ. Accreditation Council, Nat. Examinations Council, Media Council of Tanzania, Tanzania Family Planning Asscn, Media Council of Tanzania; mem. Council Mzumbe Univ., Sokoine Univ. of Agric., State Univ. of Zanzibar, Math. Asscn of Tanzania; Dr Martin Luther King Drum Major for Justice Award 2003. *Publications:* Mwalimu: The Influence of Julius Nyerere (ed. with Colin Legum) 1995; ed. secondary math. books series; articles in journals and chapters in books 1960–. *Leisure interests:* reading, travelling, walking. *Telephone:* (22) 260-2359 (home). *E-mail:* tudarco@ yahoo.com (office).

MNANGAGWA, Emmerson; Zimbabwean politician and head of state; *President;* b. 15 Sept. 1946, Zvishavane; m. 2nd Auxillia C. Mnangagwa; nine c.; ed Univ. of Zambia, Univ. of London; guerrilla fighter during Zimbabwe War of Liberation 1960s; worked as clerk in legal private practice with law firm in Lusaka; fmr Admin. Sec. Zimbabwe African Nat. Union-Patriotic Front (ZANU-PF); Head Cen. Intelligence Org. 1980s; Minister of State Security 1980–88; Minister of Justice, Legal and Parl. Affairs 1989–2000; Speaker, House of Assembly (Parl.) 2000–05, mem. House of Assembly for Chirumanzu-Zibagwe 2008–15; Minister of Rural Housing 2005–09, of Defence 2009–13, of Justice and Legal Affairs 2013–17; Vice-Pres. of Zimbabwe 2014–17, Pres. 2017–; mem. ZANU-PF; Hon. DrIur (Univ. of Zimbabwe) 2018. *Address:* Office of the President, cnr Samora Machel Avenue and Sam Nujoma Street, Private Bag 7700, Causeway, Harare, Zimbabwe (office). *Telephone:* (4) 707091 (office). *E-mail:* info@opc.gov.zw (office). *Website:* www .theopc.gov.zw (office).

MNATSAKANYAN, Zohrab; Armenian diplomatist and politician; *Minister of Foreign Affairs;* b. 20 March 1966, Yerevan, Armenian SSR, USSR; m.; two s.; ed Moscow State Inst. of Int. Relations, Univ. of Manchester; Third, later Second Sec., European Dept, Ministry of Foreign Affairs (MFA) 1991–2003; Second, later First Sec., Embassy in London 1993–97, also accred to Vatican 1995–97; Asst to Prime Minister 1997; Dir, First European Dept, MFA 1997–98, Head of European Dept 1998–99, Head of Foreign Relations Dept of the Presidential Staff 1999–2002; Perm. Rep. to UN and other int. orgs in Geneva 2002–08, concurrently Amb. to Switzerland 2002–08; Perm. Rep. to Council of Europe 2008–11; Deputy Foreign Minister and Chief Negotiator for Armenia—EU Asscn Agreement 2011–14; Perm. Rep. to UN 2014–18; Minister of Foreign Affairs 2018–; Mkhitar Gosh Medal 2011. *Address:* Ministry of Foreign Affairs, 0010 Yerevan, Hanrapetutyun Hraparak, Govt Bldg 2, Armenia (office). *Telephone:* (60) 62-00-00 (office). *Fax:* (60) 62-00-62 (office). *E-mail:* info@mfa.am (office). *Website:* www.mfa.am (office).

MNUCHIN, Robert; American art dealer, gallery curator and fmr investment banker; *Co-Director, Mnuchin Gallery;* b. 5 Sept. 1933, New York, NY; m. 1st Elaine Terner Cooper; two s.; m. 2nd Adriana Mnuchin; one d.; ed Yale Univ.; joined Goldman Sachs 1957, became Partner 1967, headed up trading and arbitrage div. during 1970s, served as mem. Man. Cttee 1980s, retd 1994; Co-founder (with Los Angeles dealer James Corcoran) C&M Arts, New York, later L&M when Corcoran left and merger with gallerist/art dealer Dominique Lévy 2005, renamed as Mnuchin Gallery 2013; artists exhibited include Willem de

Kooning, Julian Schnabel and Cy Twombley. *Address:* Mnuchin Gallery, 45 East 78th Street, New York, NY 10075, USA (office). *Telephone:* (212) 861-0020 (office). *Fax:* (212) 861-7858 (office), *E-mail:* robert@mnuchingallery.com (office). *Website:* www.mnuchingallery.com (office).

MNUCHIN, Steven (Steve) Terner, BA; American banker, business executive and government official; *Secretary of the Treasury;* b. 21 Dec. 1962, New York; s. of Robert E. Mnuchin and Elaine Terner Cooper; m. 2nd Heather Crosby (divorced); three c.; ed Yale Univ.; trainee, Salomon Brothers in early 1980s; with Goldman Sachs Group, Inc. (fmrly Goldman, Sachs & Co.) 1985–2002, held various man. positions including Chief Information Officer 1999, Exec. Vice-Pres. 2001; CEO, SFM Capital Management LP 2003–04; Co-founder, Chair. and CEO Dune Capital Management, LP (hedge fund) 2004–, Chair. and CEO OneWest Bank Group, LLC (fmrly IndyMac Federal Bank, acquired by Dune Capital) 2009–15, OneWest acquired by CIT Group 2015 and merged to form CIT/OneWest, Vice-Chair. CIT/ OneWest 2015–17; Founder and Partner, RatPac-Dune Entertainment (film production co.) 2006; Co-Chair. Relativity Media 2015; nat. finance dir, Donald Trump presidential campaign 2016; US Sec. of the Treasury 2017–; mem. Bd of Dirs Kmart Holding Corpn 2003–05, then Sears Holdings Corpn 2005–16; mem. Yale Development Bd; Trustee Whitney Museum of American Art, Hirshhorn Museum & Sculpture Garden, Riverdale Country School, New York Presbyterian Medical Center 2004–. *Address:* Department of the Treasury, 1500 Pennsylvania Ave, NW, Washington, DC 20220, USA (office). *Telephone:* (202) 622-2000 (office). *Fax:* (202) 622-6415 (office). *E-mail:* dcfo@do.treas.gov (office). *Website:* www .ustreas.gov (office).

MO, Chul-min, BA, MA, PhD; South Korean civil servant, diplomatist and academic; *Ambassador to France;* ed Univ. of Sungkyunkwan, Seoul Nat. Univ. Grad. School of Political Studies, Univ. of Oregon School of Tourism, USA; joined Ministry of Public Admin 1982, apptd Dir, Div. of Int. Tourism 1994, seconded to OECD, Paris, France 1994, joined Cabinet of Pres. 1999, Dir-Gen., Ministry of Culture and Tourism 2002–04, promoted to Minister, Embassy in Paris 2004–07, with Tourism Industry Div., Ministry of Culture 2007–08, Sr Sec. to Pres. for Educ. and Culture 2008–13, Deputy for Culture, Sports and Tourism 2010, Presidential Sec. 2013–15, Amb. to France (also accred to Monaco) 2015–; Pres. Seoul Arts Centre 2012–15; Prof., Dong-A Univ. 2012, Seoul Nat. Univ. 2014; Order of Arts and Culture (France) 2007. *Address:* Embassy of Republic of Korea, 125 rue de Grenelle, 75007 Paris, France (office). *Telephone:* 1-47-53-01-01 (office). *Fax:* 1-47-53-00-41 (office). *E-mail:* koremb-fr@mofat.go.kr (office). *Website:* fra.mofa.go.kr (office).

MO, Shaoping; Chinese lawyer; *Senior Partner, Beijing Mo Shaoping Law Firm;* b. 19 Feb. 1958, Beijing; m.; one d.; ed Beijing Coll. of Politics and Law, Chinese Acad. of Social Sciences; served in Chinese People's Liberation Army; China's leading advocate for political dissidents; in pvt. practice since 1992; f. Beijing Mo Shaoping Law Firm, Sr Partner 1995–; one of the initial signatories of Charter 08 manifesto calling for fundamental changes in China; Liberté, Egalité, Fraternité Human Rights Prize (France) 2007. *Address:* Beijing Mo Shaoping Law Firm, Waterside Pavilion, Inside Zhongshan Park, Dongcheng District, Beijing, People's Republic of China (office). *Telephone:* (10) 66055431 ext. 328-302 (office). *Fax:* (10) 66058311 (office). *E-mail:* shaoping@public.bta.net.cn (office).

MO, Yan; Chinese novelist and teacher; b. (Guan Moye), 17 Feb. 1955, Gaomi, Shandong Prov.; ed PLA Acad. of Arts, Beijing Normal Univ.; joined PLA 1976; Hon. Fellow, Modern Language Asscn 2010; Dr hc (Sofia Univ.) 2014; Fukuoka Asian Culture Prize XVII 2006, Nobel Prize in Literature 2012. *Publications include:* Red Sorghum (adapted for film) 1987, Thirteen Steps, The Herbivora Family, Jiuguo, The Republic of Wine 1992, Garlic Ballads 1995, Big Breasts and Wide Hips (Kiriyama Prize 2005) 1996, Shifu You'll Do Anything for a Laugh (adapted for film as Happy Times) 2001, Life and Death Are Wearing Me Out (Newman Prize for Chinese Literature 2009) 2008, Frog (Mao Dun Literature Prize) 2011; other: White Dog Swing (adapted for film as Nuan 2003), Man and Beast, Soaring, Iron Child, The Cure, Love Story, Shen Garden and Abandoned Child. *Address:* c/o Arcade Publishing, 307 West 36th Street, 11th Floor, New York, NY 10018, USA.

MOBERG, Anders C.; Swedish business executive; *Chairman, OBH Nordica AB;* b. 1950, Almhult; with IKEA 1970–98, Dir of Operations in Switzerland and Austria, Dir of IKEA in France 1982, CEO 1986–99; Chief of Int. Affairs, Home Depot (US home improvements co.) 1999–2002; Pres. and CEO Royal Ahold NV, Netherlands 2003–07; CEO Majid Al Futtaim, Dubai (retail and real estate conglomerate) 2007–08; Chair. OBH Nordica AB 2011–; Adjunct Prof., Copenhagen Business School 2009–; mem. Bd of Dirs Byggmax 2006–, Ahlstrom 2009–, Zeta Display AB 2009–, Hema B.V. 2009–, Amor GmbH 2010–, Rezidor AB 2010–, ITAB AB 2010–, Bergendahl & Son AB 2013–, Suomen Lähikauppa Oy 2013–; Sr Advisor, Triton & Partners. *Address:* OBH Nordica AB, Löfströms Allé 5, 172 66 Sundbyberg, Sweden (office). *Website:* www.obhnordica.com (office).

MOBY; American musician (guitar, drums, keyboards) and producer; b. (Richard Melville Hall), 11 Sept. 1965, Harlem, New York; s. of James Hall and Elizabeth Hall; ed Univ. of Connecticut; cr. first band 1979, new wave/punk rock band Vatican Commandos 1980, new wave band AWOL 1982; DJ The Beat, Port Chester, New York 1984, Mars, Palladium, Palace de Beauté, MK, New York 1989; production and remixes for Metallica, Smashing Pumpkins, Michael Jackson, Depeche Mode, Soundgarden, Blur, David Bowie, Orbital, Prodigy, Freddie Mercury, Brian Eno, B-52s, Ozzy Osbourne, John Lydon, Butthole Surfers, Erasure, Aerosmith, OMD, Pet Shop Boys, Jon Spencer Blues Explosion; numerous tours, festival appearances, TV and radio broadcasts; owner tea shop Teany, New York; mem. BMI, PMRS, AF of M, SAG, AFTRA; MTV Web Award 2002, Q Magazine Best Producer Award 2002, MTV Video Music Award for Best Cinematography in a Video (for We Are All Made Of Stars) 2002. *Compositions for film:* Double Tap (score) 1997, contrib. to numerous other film soundtracks. *Recordings include:* albums: Moby 1992, The Story So Far 1993, Ambient 1993, Early Underground 1993, Move (EP) 1994, Underwater 1995, Everything is Wrong (Spin Magazine Album of the Year) 1995, Voodoo Child: The End of Everything 1996, Animal Rights 1996, Rare: Collected B-Sides 1989–1993 1996, Everything is Wrong: Non-stop DJ Mix By Evil Ninja Moby 1996, I Like To Score 1997, Play 1999, Mobysongs 2000, 18 2002, Play: The B Sides 2004, Hotel 2005, Last Night

2008, Wait for Me 2009, Destroyed 2011, Innocents 2013, These Systems Are Failing 2016, More Fast Songs About the Apocalypse 2017, Everything Was Beautiful, and Nothing Hurt 2018. *Publications:* Porcelain (memoir) 2016. *Address:* c/o DEF, 51 Lonsdale Road, Queen's Park, London, NW6 6RA, England (office). *Telephone:* (20) 7328-2922 (office). *Fax:* (20) 7328-2322 (office). *E-mail:* info@d-e-f.com (office). *Website:* www.moby.com.

MOCO, Marcolino José Carlos, LLD, PhD; Angolan lawyer and politician; b. 19 July 1953, Chitue, Ekunha, Huamba Prov.; ed Univ. Agostinho Neto, Univ. of Lisbon; Prof. of Portuguese and Universal History in secondary education, Huambo Prov. 1974–78; high-ranking official, Movimento Popular de Libertação de Angola (MPLA), Huambo Prov. 1978–86; Gov. Bié Prov. 1986–87, Huambo Prov. 1987–89; Minister of Youth and Sports 1989–90; mem. Assembléia Nacional 1992–2008; mem. MPLA, Sec.-Gen. 1991–92; Prime Minister of Angola 1992–96; Exec. Sec. Community of Portuguese Language Countries 1996–2000; Assoc. Prof., Lusíada Univ. 2004–10, Dir Law Faculty 2009–10; Trainer, Nat. Inst. of Judicial Studies (INEJ), specializing in human rights 2009–; consultant and lawyer, Marcolino Moco International Consulting 2010–; lawyer, Marcolino Moco & Advogados 2010–. *Address:* Marcolino Moco International Consulting, Avenida de Portugal, Prédio Zimbo Tower, 7° andar, n° 704, Luanda, Angola (office). *Telephone:* 92-1428951 (mobile) (office); 92-3666196 (mobile) (office). *Fax:* 222322883 (office). *E-mail:* marcolinomoco@gmail.com (office). *Website:* marcolinomoco.com (office).

MOCUMBI, Pascoal Manuel, MD; Mozambican medical doctor and fmr politician; b. 10 April 1941, Maputo; s. of Manuel Mocumbi Malume and Leta Alson Cuhle; m. Adelina Isabel Bernardino Paindane 1970; two s. two d.; ed Univ. of Lausanne; Founding mem. Frente de Libertação de Moçambique (FRELIMO) 1962, Head, FRELIMO Information Dept, Dar-es-Salaam, Tanganyika 1963–65, Rep. FRELIMO Algeria 1965–67; Dir José Macamo Hosp., Maputo 1975–76; Prov. Health Dir, Chief Medical Officer, Clinical Doctor Beira Central Hosp., Sofala Prov. 1976–80; Clinical Doctor, Maputo Hosp. 1980–87; Asst Lecturer, Faculty of Medicine, Eduardo Mondlane Univ., Maputo 1984–87; mem. Nat. Ass., FRELIMO Political Cttee 1987–2005; Minister of Health 1980–87, of Foreign Affairs 1987–94; Prime Minister of Mozambique 1994–2004; High Rep., European and Developing Countries Clinical Trials Partnership 2004–13; mem. Medicines for Malaria Venture 2004–10, WHO Comm. on Social Determinants of Health 2005–08. *Leisure interests:* jogging, squash, reading. *Address:* 164 Av. Primeiro Dezembro, Matola, Maputo Province, Mozambique (home). *Telephone:* (21) 722918 (home). *E-mail:* pascoal.mocumbi@tvcabo.co.mz (home).

MOCZULSKI, Leszek Robert, LLM, DPolitSc, PhD; Polish historian, politician, lawyer, journalist and academic; *Professor of East European Studies, University of Warsaw;* b. 7 June 1930, Warsaw; s. of Stanisław Moczulski and Janina Moczulska (née Reimer); m. 1st Małgorzata Moczulska (née Smogorzewska) 1951 (deceased); m. 2nd Maria-Ludwika (née Różycka) Moczulska 1968; two d.; ed Acad. of Political Science, Warsaw, Law Faculty, Warsaw Univ.; reporter on Życie Warszawy (daily) 1950–53, on dailies and weeklies, including Dookoła Świata, Warsaw 1955–57; imprisoned on charges of slandering Poland in foreign press 1957–58, acquitted; assoc. (pseud. Leszek Karpatowicz) Więź (monthly) 1959–62; Head History Section Stolica (weekly) 1961–77; ed. of underground journals Opinia 1977–78, Droga 1978–80, Gazeta Polska 1979–80; arrested Aug. 1980 and sentenced to seven years on charge of attempting to overthrow regime, amnestied Aug. 1984; sentenced to four years on charge of heading illegal org. March 1985, amnestied Sept. 1986; victim of reprisals 1946–89, including repeated 48-hour custody (250 times 1976–80), forbidden to publish, refused passport, prevented from finishing PhD; mem. Polish Journalists' Asscn 1951–, Theatre Authors and Composers' Union 1960– (mem. Bd 1972–77), Polish Historical Soc.; active in Movt for Rights of Man and Citizen (ROPCiO) 1977–80; Deputy to Sejm (Parl.) 1991–97; Hon. Chair. Parl. Club of Confed. of Independence of Poland (KPN) 1993–97; Chair. Parl. Cttee for Polish Connection Abroad 1993–97; mem. Confed. for an Independent Poland (KPN) 1979– (one of founders, temporary chair. 1979–80, Chair. 1980–2005, Hon. Chair. 2005–); mem. Polish del. to Parl. Ass., Council of Europe 1992–93, 1994–96; Prof. of East European Studies, Univ. of Warsaw; Prof., Dean of Law Dept and Pres. Coll. of Man., Legnica 2011–13; co-f. and mem. Ukraine Solidarity Cttee 2014; Gold Badge of Honour, Officer's Cross of Polonia Restituta Order (London) 1987. *Publications:* numerous contribs on history, politics and int. affairs, more than 20 books including Wojna polska (War) 1939 1972, Rewolucja bez rewolucji (Revolution Without Revolution) 1979, Trzecia Rzeczpospolita – zarys ustroju politycznego (A Constitutional System for Independent Poland) 1984, U progu niepodległości (Gateway to Independence) 1990, Bez wahania (Without Hesitation) 1992, Trzy drogi (Three Ways) 1993, Demokracja bez demokracji (Democracy Without Democracy) 1995, Geopolityka (Geopolitics) 1999, Investigation 2001, Narodziny Miedzymorza 2007, Wojna polska 1939 2009, Przerwane powstanie 1914 2010, Meloch: Paristwo jaho proedsignbionstinu, Spuiczenistwe jaho via robocza (Moloch: State as Company, Society as Manpower) 2013. *Leisure interests:* horse riding, old automobiles, sailing, old maps. *Address:* ul. Jaracza 3 m. 4, 00-378 Warsaw, Poland (home). *Telephone:* (22) 6252639 (home). *E-mail:* lmski@poczta.onet.pl (home).

MODESTE-CURWEN, Clarice, MD; Grenadian politician and fmr ophthalmologist; *Minister of Tourism, Civil Aviation, Culture and Cooperatives;* ed St Lucia Teachers' Technical Training Coll., Univ. of Havana Medical School; began career as science teacher, Waltham Jr Secondary School 1972–79; intern, Gen. Hosp. 1987–89, House Officer 1989–96, Registrar, Ophthalmology Dept 1997–98; taught Clinical Skills/Behavioural Sciences, St George's Univ. School of Medicine 1996–97; mem. Parl. representing St Mark 1999–; Minister of Environment and Health 1998–2003, of Communication, Works and Transport 2003–07, of Tourism, Civil Aviation, Culture and the Performing Arts 2007–14, of Foreign Affairs 2014–16, of Tourism, Civil Aviation, Culture and Cooperatives 2016–; Pres. Directing Council, Pan-American Health Org. 2002; Chair. Org. of Eastern Caribbean States Council of Tourism Ministers; mem. New Nat. Party. *Address:* Ministry of Tourism, Ministerial Complex, 4th Floor, Botanical Gardens, Tanteen, St George's, Grenada (office). *Telephone:* 440-0366 (office). *Fax:* 440-0443 (office). *E-mail:* tourism@gov.gd (office); www.grenada.mot.gd (office).

MODI, Narendra Damodardas, MA; Indian politician; *Prime Minister;* b. 17 Sept. 1950, Vadnagar, Mehsana Dist; ed Gujarat Univ.; mem. Nava Nirman Andolan movt 1972–77; joined Bharatiya Janata Party 1986, Gen. Sec. for Gujarat 1988, elected to Ass. 1995, Nat. Sec., Delhi 1995, re-elected in Gujarat 1998, Gen. Sec. for Himachal Pradesh, the Punjab and Haryana 1998–2001, Nat. Gen. Sec. 1999–; Chief Minister of Gujarat 2001–03, 2003–14; Prime Minister 2014–, also in-charge of Ministry of Personnel, Public Grievances and Pensions, Dept of Atomic Energy and Dept of Space; King Abdulaziz Sash (Saudi Arabia) 2016; The Asian Winner, fDi Magazine Personality of the Year Award 2009, UN Champions of the Earth Award 2018, Seoul Peace Prize 2018, Philip Kotler Presidential Award for Outstanding Leadership for the Nation 2018. *Publications include:* Sangharsha ma Gujarat (Gujarat under Struggle), Setu Bandh, Patra Roop Guruji. *Address:* Prime Minister's Office, South Block, Raisina Hill, New Delhi, 110 011, India (office). *Telephone:* (11) 23012312 (office); (11) 23016857 (home). *Fax:* (79) 23222101 (office); (79) 23222020 (home). *E-mail:* pmindia@pmindia.nic.in (office). *Website:* www.pmindia.nic.in (office); www.narendramodi.in.

MODI, Vinay Kumar, BTechChemEng, PhD; Indian industrialist; *Chairman, Gujarat Guardian Ltd;* b. 31 May 1943, Modinagar; s. of Rai Bahadur Gujar Mal Modi and Dayawati Modi; m. Chander Bala 1965; one s. one d.; ed Scindia School, Gwalior, Indian Inst. of Tech., Kanpur; Dir Modi Industries Ltd 1965–; Vice-Chair. and Man. Dir Modi Rubber Ltd 1976–2002; currently Chair. Gujarat Guardian Ltd, Modi Mirrlees Blackstone Ltd, Shree Acids and Chemicals Ltd; currently Chair. MAN Diesel India Ltd, Lombard Street Pvt. Ltd, Gujarat Acrylics Pvt. Ltd; fmr Pres. Steel Furnace Asscn of India; fmr Chair. Automobile Tyre Manufacturers Asscn; fmr Vice Chair. Chemical Allied Export Promotion Council, Calcutta; fmr Pres. All India Float Glass Manufacturing Asscn; mem. Bd Scindia School, Jaipuria Inst. of Man. and Tech., Inst. of Man. and Tech. Gaziabad; mem. Senate of Indian Inst. of Tech., Rourkee; Madhav Award 2007, Scindia School, various awards from govt for export performance, prizes from several asscns. *Publications:* various articles on steel, tyres and cement production. *Leisure interests:* golf, tennis, billiards. *Address:* Modi Industries (FC) Pvt. Ltd, 203, Bakshi, House, 40–41 Nehru Place, New Delhi 110 019; DDA Shopping Centre, New Friends Colony, New Delhi 110 065 (office); 55A, Friends Colony (East), New Delhi 110 065 (home); Modi Bhavan, Civil Lines, Modinagar 201 204, India (office). *Telephone:* 2643275106 (office); (11) 6830703 (office); (11) 6833088 (home); (11) 6833633 (home). *Fax:* 2643275105 (office); (11) 6464228 (office). *E-mail:* modiguard@guardian.com (office); modypump@vsnl.net (office). *Website:* www.modiguard.co.in (office).

MODIANO, Patrick Jean; French novelist; b. 30 July 1945, Boulogne-Billancourt; s. of Albert Modiano and Luisa Colpyn; m. Dominique Zehrfuss 1970; two d.; ed schools in Biarritz, Chamonix, Deauville, Thônes, Barbizon, coll. in Paris; Chevalier, Légion d'honneur 1996, Officier, Légion d'honneur 2015; Prix Pierre de Monaco 1984, Grand Prix du Roman de la Ville de Paris 1994, Grand Prix de Littérature Paul Morand de l'Acad. française 2000, Prix Marguerite-Duras 2011, Prix de la Bibliothèque nationale de France 2011, Austrian State Prize for European Literature 2012, Nobel Prize in Literature 2014. *Screenplays:* Lacombe, Lucien (with Louis Malle) 1973, Bon Voyage (with Jean-Paul Rappeneau) 2003. *Publications include:* La place de l'étoile 1968 (Prix Roger-Nimier 1968, Prix Fénéon 1969), La ronde de nuit 1969, Les boulevards de ceinture 1972 (Grand Prix de l'Acad. française 1972), Lacombe Lucien (screenplay) 1973, La polka (play) 1974, Villa triste (novel) (made into film Le parfum d'Yvonne 1994) 1975, Interrogatoire d'Emmanuel Berl 1976, Livret de famille (novel) 1977, Rue des boutiques obscures 1978 (Prix Goncourt 1978), Une jeunesse (made into film 1983) 1981, Memory Lane 1981, De si braves garçons (novel) 1982, Poupée blonde 1983, Quartier perdu 1985, Dimanches d'août 1986, Une aventure de Choura 1986, La fiancée de Choura 1987, Remise de peine (novel) 1988, Catherine Certitude 1988, Vestiaire de l'enfance (novel) 1989, Voyage de noces 1990, Fleurs de ruine (novel) 1991, Un cirque passe (novel) 1992, Chien de printemps 1993, Du plus loin de l'oubli 1995, Dora Bruder 1997, Des inconnues 1999, La petite bijou 2001, Accident nocturne 2003, Un pedigree 2005, Dans le café de la jeunesse perdue 2007, L'Horizon 2010, L'Herbe de nuit 2012, Pour que tu ne te perdes pas dans le quartier 2014. *Address:* c/o Editions Gallimard, 5 rue Gaston-Gallimard, 75328 Paris Cedex 07, France.

MODINE, Matthew Avery; American actor, director and writer; b. 22 March 1959, Loma Linda, Calif.; s. of Mark Alexander Modine and Dolores Modine (née Warner); m. Caridad Rivera 1980; one s. one d.; ed Brigham Young Univ.; mem. Dramatic Jury, Sundance Film Festival 1994; Founder Bicycle For A Day; Golden Globe Award, Venice Film Festival Volpi Cup, Golden Lion. *Films include:* Private School 1983, Streamers 1983, Birdy 1984, The Hotel New Hampshire 1984, Mrs. Soffel 1984, Vision Quest 1985, Orphans 1987, Full Metal Jacket 1987, Married to the Mob 1988, The Gamble 1988, Gross Anatomy 1989, Memphis Belle 1990, Pacific Heights 1990, Wind 1992, Equinox 1992, Short Cuts 1993, And the Band Played On (HBO Cable) 1993, The Browning Version 1994, Jacob 1994, Cutthroat Island 1995, Bye Bye Love 1995, Fluke 1995, The Maker 1997, The Blackout 1997, The Real Blonde 1997, Any Given Sunday 1999, Notting Hill 1999, Bamboozled 2000, Very Mean Men 2000, In the Shadows 2001, Hitler: The Rise of Evil 2003, Le Divorce 2003, Funky Monkey 2004, Opa 2005, Transporter 2 2005, Kettle of Fish 2006, Mary 2006, Go Go Tales 2007, The Neighbor 2007, Have Dreams, Will Travel 2007, PoliWood 2009, The Trial 2010, Mia and the Migoo (English language version) 2011, Too Big to Fail (HBO) 2011, Jesus Was a Commie 2011, The Flying House 2011, Family Weekend 2012, Ansiedad (aka See If I Care) 2011, The Dark Knight Rises 2012, Girl in Progress 2012, Jobs 2013, Family Weekend 2013, Altar 2014, The Heyday of the Insensitive Bastards 2015, The Confirmation 2016, Army of One 2016, The Hippopotamus 2017, 47 Metres Down 2017, Sicario: Day of the Soldado 2018, Speed Kills 2018; dir: When I Was a Boy (short) 1993, Smoking (short) 1995, Ecce Pirate (short) 1997, I Think I Thought (short) 2008, To Kill an American (short) 2008, Jesus Was a Commie (short) (also writer, actor) (Oldenberg Film Festival German Independence Award for Best Short Film shared with Terence Ziegler 2011) 2011, As Tears Go By 2012, Stars in Shorts: No Ordinary Love 2016. *Television includes:* What the Deaf Man Heard (film) 1996, Flowers for Algernon (film) 2000, The American (film) 2001, Jack and the Beanstalk: The Real Story (film) 2001, Redeemer (film) 2002, The Winning Season (film) 2004, Into The West (film) 2005, The Bedford Diaries (film) 2006, Weeds (film) 2007, Little Fish, Strange Pond (aka Frenemy) (film) 2009, Jobs (film) 2013, Proof (series) 2015, Stranger Things (series) (Screen Actors Guild Award for Outstanding Performance by an Ensemble in a Drama Series 2017) 2016–17. *Leisure interests:* painting, horticulture, carpentry. *Address:* c/o Workhouse PR, 175 Varick Street, New York NY 10014, USA (office). *E-mail:* info@workhousepr.com (office). *Website:* www .workhousepr.com (office); www.matthewmodine.com.

MODRIĆ, Luca; Croatian professional footballer; b. 9 Sept. 1985, Zadar; midfielder; youth player, NK Zadar 1996–2001; played for Dinamo Zagreb 2002–08, HŠK Zrinjski Mostar (loan) (22 appearances, 8 goals) 2003–04, Inter Zaprešić (loan) (18 appearances, 4 goals) 2004–05, Tottenham Hotspur (159 appearances, 17 goals) 2008–12, Real Madrid 2012–, won UEFA Supercup 2015, 2017, 2018, Team of the Year Award 2016, 2017, 2018; joined Croatia Nat. Team 2006, Captain 2016– (120 appearances, 14 goals to Mar. 2019); first Croatian player to win UEFA Men's Player of the Year Award 2018; Hon. Citizen, City of Zadar 2018; Order of Duke Branimir 2018; BH Telecom Premier League of Bosnia and Herzegovina Player of the Year 2003, Croatian Footballer Hope of the Year 2004, Prva HNL Player of the Year 2007, Croatian Footballer of the Year 2007, 2008, 2011, 2014, 2016, 2017, 2018, La Liga Best Midfielder 2013/14, 2015/16, FIFA FIFPro World XI 2015, 2016, 2017, 2018, La Liga Team of the Season 2015/ 16, ESPN Midfielder of the Year 2016, Državna nagrada za šport "Franjo Bučar" 2018, Best FIFA Men's Player 2018, Ballon d'Or FIFA 2018, IFFHS World's Best Playmaker 2018. *Website:* www.realmadrid.com/en/football.

MODRICH, Paul L., BS, PhD; American biochemist and academic; *James B. Duke Professor of Biochemistry, Duke University;* b. 13 June 1946, Raton, NM; ed Massachusetts Inst. of Tech., Stanford Univ.; postgraduate, Harvard Univ. 1974; Asst Prof. of Chem., Univ. of California, Berkeley 1974–76; Asst Prof. of Biochemistry, Duke Univ. 1976–80, Assoc. Prof. of Biochemistry 1980–84, Prof. of Biochemistry 1984–, Dir Program in Genetics 1989–92, currently James B. Duke Prof. of Biochemistry, Investigator, Howard Hughes Medical Inst., Duke Univ. 1994–; Assoc. Ed. Biochemistry 1992–94, mem. Editorial Advisory Bd 1986–91, 1995–2003; mem. Editorial Bd, Nucleic Acids Research 1980–82, Journal of Biological Chemistry 1982–83, Proceedings of the National Academy of Sciences USA 2000–08; mem. NAS 1993, Inst. of Medicine of The Nat. Acads 2003, American Soc. of Biochemistry and Molecular Biology (Councillor 1989–92, 1997–), Inst. of Medicine; Fellow, American Acad. of Arts and Sciences 2004; Award in Enzyme Chem., Pfizer 1983, NIH Health NIGMS Merit Award 1986, Mott Prize in Cancer Research GM 1996, Medal of Honor for Basic Research, American Cancer Soc. 2005, Pasarow Foundation Award in Cancer Research, Nobel Prize in Chem. (co-recipient with Tomas Lindahl and Aziz Sancar) 2015. *Publications:* numerous papers in professional journals. *Address:* Department of Biochemistry, Duke University, 156A, Nanaline H. Duke, Durham, NC 27708, USA (office). *Telephone:* (919) 684-2775 (office). *E-mail:* modrich@biochem.duke.edu (office). *Website:* www .biochem.duke.edu (office).

MOE, Scott, BSc; Canadian politician; *Premier of Saskatchewan and President of the Executive Council;* b. Prince Albert, Saskatchewan; m. Krista Moe; two c.; ed Univ. of Saskatchewan; worked with Sask. Econ. Devt Corpn and Shellbrook and Dist Health Services Project; mem. Sask. Legis. Ass. for Rosthern-Shellbrook 2011–; Sask. Minister of Advanced Educ. 2014–16, Minister of the Environment 2016–17, also fmr Minister responsible for Sask. Water Corpn, and Minister responsible for Saskatchewan Water Security Agency; Premier of Saskatchewan and Pres. of the Exec. Council 2018–, also Minister of Intergovernmental Affairs; mem. Saskatchewan Party, Leader 2018–. *Address:* Office of the Premier, Room 226, 2405 Legislative Drive, Regina, SK S4S 0B3, Canada (office). *Telephone:* (306) 787-9433 (office). *Fax:* (306) 787-0885 (office). *E-mail:* premier@gov.sk.ca (office). *Website:* www.saskatchewan.ca (office).

MOEDAS, Carlos Manuel Félix, MBA; Portuguese engineer, economist, banker, politician and EU official; *Commissioner for Research, Science and Innovation, European Commission;* b. 10 Aug. 1970, Beja; ed Instituto Superior Técnico, Ecole des Ponts et Chaussées, Paris (Erasmus Student), Univ. of Lisbon, Harvard Business School, USA; project man. for Suez Group (France) 1993–98; worked in mergers and acquisitions at Goldman Sachs from 2000; also worked in Real Estate Investment Banking Div., Eurohypo Investment Bank; Man. Partner, Aguirre Newman Portugal real estate consulting co. 2004–08; est. own investment man. co. Crimson Investment Management 2008; Co-ordinator Econ. Research Unit, Partido Social Democrata (PSD—Social Democratic Party), mem. PSD team that negotiated approval of the 2011 State Budget with the Govt; mem. Parl. (PSD) for Beja constituency 2011–; Sec. of State to the Prime Minister 2011–14; Commr for Research, Science and Innovation, European Comm. (EC), Brussels Nov. 2014–. *Address:* European Commission, 200 Rue de la Loi/Wetstraat 200, 1049 Brussels, Belgium (office). *Telephone:* (2) 299-11-11 (office). *Website:* ec.europa.eu (office).

MOELLER, Bernd, DTheol; German academic; *Professor Emeritus of Church History, University of Göttingen;* b. 19 May 1931, Berlin; s. of Max Moeller and Carola Bielitz; m. Irene Müller 1957; three d.; ed Univs of Erlangen, Mainz, Basle, Munich and Heidelberg; Research Asst Univ. of Heidelberg 1956–58, Privatdozent 1958–64; Prof. of Church History, Univ. of Göttingen 1964, Chair Dept of Early Church History 1964–99, Rector 1971–72, now Prof. Emer.; Chair. Verein für Reformationsgeschichte, Heidelberg 1976–2001; mem. Akad. der Wissenschaften zu Göttingen, Academia Europaea; Dr hc (Zürich) 1998. *Publications:* Reichsstadt und Reformation 1962, Geschichte des Christentums in Grundzügen 1965, Spätmittelalter 1966, Oekumenische Kirchengeschichte (with R. Kottje) I-III 1970–74, Deutschland im Zeitalter der Reformation 1977, Die Reformation und das Mittelalter 1991, Kirchengeschichte. Deutsche Texte (1699–1927) 1994, Städtische Predigt in der Frühzeit der Reformation (with K. Stackmann) 1996, Luther – Rezeption 2001, Albrecht Dürers Vier Apostel (with K. Arndt) 2003, Deutsche Biographische Enzyklopädie der Theologie und der Kirchen I–II 2005. *Address:* University of Göttingen, Platz der Göttinger Sieben 2, 37073 Göttingen (office); Goßlerstraße 6A, 37073 Göttingen, Germany. *Telephone:* (551) 397139 (office); (551) 42850. *Fax:* (551) 397488 (office). *Website:* www.uni-goettingen.de (office).

MOERLAND, Piet Willem; Dutch banker, business executive and academic; b. 1949; ed Erasmus Univ., Rotterdam; Prof. for nearly 25 years at Univ. of Groningen (Business Admin), then Univ. of Tilburg (Corp. Finance); mem. Bd of Supervision, Rabobank Nederland 1984–87, mem. Bd of Dirs 1987–2000, mem. Advisory Bd 2000–03, mem. Exec. Bd 2003, Chair. Exec. Bd 2009–13 (resgnd); mem. Supervisory Bd, Essent 1999–2009; mem. Advisory Bd Netherlands Order of

Accountants and Admin Consultants; mem. Bd of Dirs Netherlands Bankers' Asscn (NVB), International Raiffeisen Union; Chair. European Asscn of Co-operative Banks (EACB/Groupement), Bd of Nat. Co-operative Council for Agric. and Horticulture of the Netherlands.

MOERNER, W. E. (William Esco), BS, AB, MS, PhD; American physical chemist and academic; *Harry S. Mosher Professor in Chemistry and Professor, by courtesy, of Applied Physics, Stanford University;* b. 1953; ed Washington and Cornell Univs; Research Asst, Dept of Physics, Washington Univ., St Louis, Mo. 1972–75; Grad. Research Asst and NSF Grad. Fellow, Lab. for Atomic and Solid State Physics, Cornell Univ., Ithaca, NY 1975–81; research staff mem., IBM Almaden Research Center, San Jose, Calif. 1981–95, Man. Laser-Materials Interactions 1988–89, Project Leader 1989–95; Guest Prof. of Physical Chem., Swiss Fed. Inst. of Tech. (ETH Zurich) 1993–94; Prof. and Distinguished Chair in Physical Chem., Univ. of California, San Diego 1995–98; Robert Burns Woodward Visiting Prof., Harvard Univ. 1997–98; Prof. of Chem., Stanford Univ. 1998–2002, Harry S. Mosher Prof. of Chem. 2002–, Prof., by courtesy, of Applied Physics 2005–, Chair. Chem. Dept 2011–; Advisory Ed. Chemical Physics Letters 1998–, Chem-PhysChem 2004–, Single Molecules 2000–02; Sr mem. IEEE 1988–; mem. NAS 2007–; Fellow, American Physical Soc. 1992, Optical Soc. of America 1992, American Acad. of Arts and Sciences 2001, AAAS 2004; Geoffrey Frew Fellow, Australian Acad. of Sciences 2003; Roger I. Wilkinson Nat. Outstanding Young Electrical Engineer 1984, IBM Outstanding Tech. Achievement Awards for photon-gated spectral hole burning 1988, for single-molecule detection and spectroscopy 1992, Earle K. Plyler Prize for Molecular Spectroscopy, American Physical Soc. 2001, Wolf Prize in Chem. (with Allen Bard) 2008, Irving Langmuir Prize in Chemical Physics, American Physical Soc. 2009, Pittsburgh Spectroscopy Award 2012, Outstanding Alumni Achievement Award, Washington Univ. 2013, Kirkwood Award Medal, Yale Univ., New Haven Section of the ACS 2013, Nobel Prize in Chem. (co-recipient with Eric Betzig and Stefan Hell for the development of super-resolved fluorescence microscopy) 2014. *Publications include:* numerous papers in professional journals on physical chemistry of single molecules, biophysics, nanoparticle trapping and nanophotonics; eight US patents, four patents pending. *Address:* Department of Chemistry, Mail Code 5080, Stanford University, Stanford, CA 94305-5080, USA (office). *Telephone:* (650) 723-1727 (office). *Fax:* (650) 725-0259 (office). *E-mail:* moerner@stanford.edu (office); wmoerner@stanford.edu (office). *Website:* web.stanford.edu/group/moerner (office).

MOESER, James, BMus, MMus, DMus; American concert organist, university administrator and academic; *Chancellor Emeritus, Professor of Music and Senior Consultant, University of North Carolina;* b. Colorado City, Tex.; m. Dr Susan Dickerson Moeser; one s. one d.; ed Univ. of Texas, Univ. of Michigan; Asst Prof. and Chair. Organ Dept, Univ. of Kansas 1966–75, Dean School of Fine Arts 1975–86, later Althaus Distinguished Prof. of Organ; Dean Coll. of Arts and Architecture and Exec. Dir Univ. Arts Services, Pennsylvania State Univ. 1986–92; Vice-Pres. for Academic Affairs and Provost Univ. of S Carolina 1992–96; Chancellor Univ. of Nebraska at Lincoln 1996–2000; Chancellor Univ. of North Carolina at Chapel Hill 2000–08, Prof. of Music 2009–, now Sr Consultant and Chancellor Emer.; apptd by FBI to Nat. Security Higher Educ. Advisory Bd 2005; serves on Coll. Bd's Nat. Comm. on Writing and two Asscn of American Univs cttees; selected by Nat. Collegiate Athletic Asscn for its Presidential Task Force on the Future of Div. I Intercollegiate Athletics and its fiscal responsibility sub-cttee; mem. CEO Group of Six (group of pres and chancellors from major athletic confs); fmr mem. Bd of Dirs Nat. Asscn of State Univs and Land Grant Colls, Chair. Tech-Transfer Coll. Comm.; fmr mem. Kellogg Comm. on the Future of State and Land-Grant Univs; Fulbright Scholar in Berlin and Paris, honoured by Grad. School at Texas with Outstanding Alumnus Award 2001, Hill Hall auditorium, Univ. of North Carolina at Chapel Hill renamed after James and Susan Moeser. *Address:* Department of Music, University of North Carolina, 213 Hyde Hall, Chapel Hill, NC 27599-3320, USA (office). *Telephone:* (919) 929-8453 (office). *E-mail:* james_moeser@unc.edu (office). *Website:* music.unc.edu (office).

MOFAZ, Lt-Gen. Shaul, BA, MBA; Israeli politician and fmr army officer; *Leader, Kadima Party;* b. 4 Nov. 1948, Tehran, Iran; m. Orit Mofaz; four c.; ed Bar-Ilan Univ., US Marine Corps Command and Staff Coll., USA; migrated to Israel 1957; paratrooper, Israel Defense Forces (IDF) 1966, served in Six-Day War 1967; command positions in Paratroop Brigade; Commdr Paratroop Reconnaissance Unit 1973; Deputy Commdr Paratroop Brigade; infantry brigade commdr 1982; Commdr IDF Officers' School 1984; Commdr Paratroop Brigade 1986–88; promoted Brig.-Gen. 1988; Commdr Reserve Armour Div. 1988–90; Commdr Galilee Div. 1990–92; Commdr IDF forces in Judea and Samaria 1993–94; promoted Maj.-Gen. 1994; GOC Southern Command 1994–96; Chief of Planning Directorate Gen. Staff 1996–97; Deputy Chief IDF Gen. Staff 1997; 16th Chief of Gen. Staff 1998–2002; Minister of Defence 2002–06; mem. Knesset 2006–; Deputy Prime Minister and Minister of Transport 2006–09; left Likud party to join newly formed Kadima party Dec. 2005, Leader 2012–; Leader of the Opposition in the Knesset 2012–13; served as Acting Prime Minister, Vice-Prime Minister and Minister without Portfolio May–July 2012. *Address:* Kadima Party, Petach Tikva, Tel-Aviv (office); Knesset, Jerusalem, Israel. *Telephone:* 3-9788000 (office); 2-6496116. *Fax:* 3-9788020 (office); 2-6496421. *E-mail:* shaulm@knesset.gov.il (office). *Website:* www.kadima.org.il (office); knesset.gov.il/mk/eng/mk_eng .asp?mk_individual_id_t=720.

MOFFAT, Sir Brian Scott, Kt, OBE, FCA; British business executive; *Non-Executive Director, Macsteel Holdings Luxembourg SARL and Macsteel Global SARL;* b. 6 Jan. 1939; s. of Festus Moffat and Agnes Moffat; m. Jacqueline Cunliffe 1964; one s. (and one s. deceased) one d.; ed Hulme Grammar School; with Peat Marwick Mitchell & Co. 1961–68; joined British Steel Corpn (later British Steel PLC, now Corus Group PLC) 1968, Man. Dir Finance 1986–91, Chief Exec. 1991–99, Chair. 1993–2003; Dir (non-exec.) HSBC Holdings PLC 1998–2008, Deputy Chair. and Sr Ind. Dir (non-exec.) 2001–08; Dir (non-exec.) Enterprise Oil PLC 1995–2002, Bank of England 2000–06, Macsteel Global BV (fmrly Nosmas Holdings BV) 2003–10, Macsteel Global SARL BV 2010–, Macsteel Holdings Luxembourg SARL 2010–; Hon. DSc (Warwick) 1998, (Sheffield) 2001. *Leisure interests:* farming, fishing, shooting. *Address:* Springfield Farm, Earlswood,

Chepstow, Monmouthshire, NP6 6AT, England (home). *Telephone:* (1291) 650959. *Fax:* (1291) 650747. *E-mail:* sirbmoffat@btinternet.com.

MOFFAT, Leslie Ernest Fraser, JP, BSc, MB, CH.B., MBA, FRCSE, FRCS (GLASG.), FRCPE; British urologist; b. 3 Nov. 1949; m.; three d.; ed Univs of Edinburgh and Stirling; Professorial House Officer posts City Hosp., Royal Infirmary, Edin. 1974–75; Sr House Officer Dept of Surgery, Royal Infirmary, Edin. 1976, Surgical Registrar 1977–79; Munro Prosector, Royal Coll. of Surgeons Edin. 1977–78; Research Registrar, Clinical Shock Study Group, Western Infirmary, Glasgow 1980–81; Urological Sr Registrar, Glasgow Teaching Hosps 1982–86; Clinical Sr Lecturer, Univ. of Aberdeen 1986; Pres. Grampian Div. BMA 1994; Trustee, Prostate Cancer charity, Hammersmith Hosp., London, Vice-Chair. –2010; Chair. Urological Cancer Working Party in Scotland; Founding Ed. UroOncology 1999; Chair. Urological Cancer Working Party in Scotland 1999–; Medical and Specialist Adviser to Cancer BACUP; Urological Consultant to British Antarctic Survey; Medical mem., Employment and Support Allowance Trubunals; mem. Rates Appeal Tribunal; Hon. Consultant Royal Marsden Hosp. London; Burgess of Aberdeen 1999. *Publications:* Prostate Cancer – The Facts (co-author), Urological Cancer: A Practical Guide to Management; over 105 publs including 6 book chapters. *Leisure interests:* country life, opera. *Address:* Tillery House, Udny, Ellon, Aberdeenshire, Scotland (home).

MOFFAT, Steven William, OBE; British television writer, screenwriter and producer; b. 18 Nov. 1961, Paisley, Scotland; m. Sue Vertue; two s.; lead writer and exec. producer Doctor Who; co-creator, writer and exec. producer Sherlock; also acted in The Five(ish) Doctors Reboot (TV film) 2013; Emmy Award, five BAFTA Awards, including BAFTA Special Award 2012, four Hugo Awards. *Television includes:* Press Gang (series) 1989–93, Stay Lucky (series) 1990, Joking Apart (series) 1991–95, Exam Conditions (film) 1992, Murder Most Horrid (series) 1994–99, The Office (film) 1996, Chalk (series) 1997, Privates (series) 1999, Coupling (series) 2000–04, Jekyll (mini-series) 2007, Doctor Who: Time Crash 2007, Coupling (series) (original scenario) 2007–08, Sherlock (series) 2010–, The Adventures of Tintin: The Secret of the Unicorn (screenplay) 2011, Vastra Investigates (film) 2012, BBC Proms (series) – Prom 2: Doctor Who at the Proms 2013, Doctor Who: The Last Day (short) 2013, Doctor Who (series) 2012–17. *Address:* c/o Fiona Williams, Berlin Associates, 7 Tyers Gate, London, SE1 3HX, England (office). *Telephone:* (20) 7632-5281 (office). *Fax:* (20) 7632-5296 (office). *E-mail:* fionaw@berlinassociates.com (office). *Website:* www.berlinassociates.com/clients/steven-moffat (office).

MOFFATT, Henry Keith, ScD, FRS; British mathematician and academic; *Professor Emeritus of Mathematical Physics, University of Cambridge;* b. 12 April 1935, Edinburgh, Scotland; s. of Frederick Henry Moffatt and Emmeline Marchant Fleming; m. Katharine (Linty) Stiven 1960; two s. (one deceased) two d.; ed Univs of Edinburgh and Cambridge; Asst Lecturer, then Lecturer, Univ. of Cambridge 1961–76, Prof. of Math. Physics 1980–2002, Prof. Emer. 2002–; Fellow, Trinity Coll., Cambridge 1961–76, 1980–, Tutor 1971–74, Sr Tutor 1975; Prof. of Applied Math., Bristol Univ. 1977–80; Dir Isaac Newton Inst. for Math. Sciences 1996–2001; Pres. Int. Union of Theoretical and Applied Mechanics 2000–04, Vice-Pres. 2004–08; part-time Prof. Ecole Polytechnique, Paris 1992–99; Chair. Int. de Recherche Blaise Pascal 2002–03; Leverhulme Emer. Fellow 2003–05; Ed. Journal of Fluid Mechanics 1966–83; mem. Academia Europaea 1994; Foreign mem. Royal Netherlands Acad. of Arts and Sciences 1991, Acad. des Sciences, Paris 1998, Accad. Scienzia Lincei 2001, NAS 2008; Officier des Palmes académiques 1998; Dr hc (INPG Grenoble) 1987, (State Univ. of New York) 1990, (Edin.) 2001, (Eindhoven Tech. Univ.) 2006, (Glasgow) 2007; Smiths Prize 1960, Panetti-Ferrari Prize and Gold Medal 2001, Euromech Fluid Mechanics Prize 2003, Sr Whitehead Prize, London Math. Soc. 2005, Hughes Medal, Royal Soc. 2005, David Crighton Medal 2009. *Publications:* Magnetic Field Generation in Electrically Conducting Fluids 1978, Topological Fluid Mechanics (co-ed. with A. Tsinober) 1990, Topological Aspects of the Dynamics of Fluids and Plasmas (co-ed.) 1992. *Leisure interests:* French country cooking, hill walking. *Address:* DAMTP, Centre for Mathematical Sciences, Wilberforce Road, Cambridge, CB3 0WA (office); Trinity College, Cambridge, CB2 1TQ, England (office). *Telephone:* (1223) 363338 (home). *E-mail:* hkm2@damtp.cam.ac.uk (office). *Website:* www.damtp.cam.ac.uk (office).

MOFFETT, David McKenzie, BA, MBA; American banking executive; b. 22 Feb. 1952, Daytona Beach, Fla; s. of James Denny Jr and Dorothy McCall; m. 1st Cynthia Ann Daugherty 1973 (divorced 1977); m. 2nd Katherine Anne Martin 1979; three c.; ed Univ. of Oklahoma, Southern Methodist Univ.; planning analyst, First Nat. Bank & Trust Co. 1975–76, financial analyst 1978, Vice-Pres. 1978–80, Sr Vice-Pres. 1981–86, Exec. Vice-Pres. 1987–93; Chief Financial Officer Star Banc Corpn (merged with Firstar Corpn) 1993–98, Chief Financial Officer and Vice-Chair. Firstar Corpn 1998–2001, Chief Financial Officer, Vice-Chair. and Dir US Bancorp 2001–07 (after Firstar merger with US Bancorp 2001); CEO Fed. Home Loan Mortgage Corpn (Freddie Mac) Sept. 2008–March 2009; Sr Adviser The Carlyle Group 2007–08; fmr Chair. Chief Financial Officers' Council, Financial Services Roundtable; Chair. Bd of Dirs Ebay Inc. 2007–, MBIA Insurance Corpn 2007–, E.W. Scripps Inc. 2007–, Building Materials Holding Corpn 2007–; mem. Chief Financial Officers' Roundtable, Bank Admin Inst.; mem. Advisory Bd Price Coll. of Business, Univ. of Oklahoma; mem. Nat. Asset/Liability Man. Asscn, Bank Admin Inst.; Chair.'s Award, First Nat. Bank 1980. *Leisure interests:* running, golf, skiing, scuba diving, cycling.

MOFFETT, James R., BS, MS; American geologist and mining executive; *Chairman Emeritus and Consultant, Freeport-McMoRan Inc.;* ed Univ. of Texas at Austin, Tulane Univ.; consulting geologist 1964–69; Co-f. McMoRan Oil & Gas Co. 1969, merged with Freeport Minerals Co. to form Freeport-McMoRan Inc., Chair. and CEO 1984–97, mem. Bd of Dirs 1992–2015, Chair. Freeport-McMoRan Inc. June–Dec. 2015, Chair. Emer. and Consultant 2015–, also Pres. Commr of PT Freeport Indonesia (mining unit), also Co-Chair. McMoRan Exploration Co. 1998–2013; serves on numerous boards; mem. Mining Foundation of the Southwest; Hon. DSc (Louisiana State Univ.); Hon. Dr of Financial Econs (Univ. of New Orleans); Horatio Alger Asscn of Distinguished Americans Award 1990, Norman Vincent Peale Award, Horatio Alger Asscn of Distinguished Americans 2000, mem. American Mining Hall of Fame. *Address:* Freeport-McMoRan Inc., 333 N Central

Avenue, Phoenix, AZ 85004, USA (office). *Telephone:* (602) 366-8100 (office). *E-mail:* fcx_communications@fmi.com (office). *Website:* www.fcx.com (office).

MOGAE, Festus Gontebanye, MA; Botswana politician, business executive and fmr head of state; *Group Chairman, Choppies Enterprises Ltd;* b. 21 Aug. 1939, Serowe; s. of Ditlhabano Mogae and Dithunya Mogae; m. Barbara Gemma Modise 1968; three d.; ed Moeng Secondary School, North West London Polytechnic, Univs of Oxford and Sussex, UK; Planning Officer, Ministry of Devt Planning 1968–69, Ministry of Finance and Devt Planning 1970, Sr Planning Officer 1971, Dir Econ Affairs 1972–74, Perm. Sec. 1975–76; Alt. Exec. Dir of IMF 1976–78, Exec. Dir 1978–80; Alt. Gov. for Botswana, IMF 1971–72, African Devt Bank 1971–76, IBRD 1973–76; Dir Botswana Devt Corpn 1971–74 (Chair. 1975–76), De Beers Botswana Mining Co. Ltd 1975–76, Bangwato Concessions Ltd 1975–76, BCL Sales Ltd 1975–76, Bank of Botswana 1975–76 (Gov. 1980–81); Gov. IMF 1981–82; Perm. Sec. to Pres. of Botswana 1982–89, Minister of Finance and Devt Planning 1989–98, Vice-Pres. 1992–98; Pres. of Botswana 1998–2008; UN Sec.-Gen.'s Special Envoy for Climate Change 2008–; currently Group Chair. Choppies Enterprises Ltd (supermarket co.); Pres. Botswana Soc., Botswana Soc. of the Deaf; fmr mem. Jt Devt Cttee of World Bank and IMF on the transfer of real resources to developing countries 1992, Kalahari Conservation Soc., Commonwealth Parl. Assoc., Parliamentarians for Global Action, Global Coalition for Africa; Rep., Commonwealth Fund for Tech. Co-operation 1971; est. Champions for an HIV-Free Generation; Hon. Fellowship, Botswana Inst. of Bankers 1999; Officier, Ordre Nat. Côte d'Ivoire 1979, Mali 1997, Presidential Order of Honour of Botswana 1989, Grand Cross, Légion d'honneur 2008; Hon. LLD (Botswana) 1998; Achievement Awards for AIDS Leadership (USA 2000, Gaborone 2001), Nat. Leadership Award, Africa-America Inst. 2002, Mo Ibrahim Prize 2008. *Leisure interests:* reading, tennis, music. *Address:* Choppies Enterprises Ltd, PO Box 406, Gaborone, Botswana (office). *Website:* www.choppies.co.bw (office).

MOGAHED, Dalia, BEng, MBA; American (b. Egyptian) social scientist; *Chairman and CEO, Mogahed Consulting, LLC;* b. 1974, Cairo; m.; two s.; ed Univ. of Wisconsin, Univ. of Pittsburgh; began career as marketing products researcher for Procter & Gamble; Sr Analyst, Gallup Org. and Exec. Dir Gallup Center for Muslim Studies, New York 2006–13; Chair. and CEO Mogahed Consulting, LLC 2013–; Dir of Research, Inst. for Social Policy and Understanding, Washington, DC 2014–; Sr Public Policy Scholar (nonresident), Issam Fares Inst. for Public Policy and Int. Affairs, American Univ. of Beirut; mem. Pres. Obama's Advisory Council on Faith-Based and Neighborhood Partnerships 2009–; fmr Dir Muslim–West Facts Initiative; mem. Women in Int. Security, Project on US Engagement with Global Muslim Community, Brookings Inst. Crisis in the Middle East Task Force; mem. Agenda Council on the Arab World, World Econ. Forum; serves as Global Expert, UN Alliance of Civilizations; Arab World's Social Innovator of the Year 2010. *Publications include:* Who Speaks for Islam? What a Billion Muslims Really Think (with John Esposito) 2008; articles in numerous journals and newspapers including The Wall Street Journal, Harvard International Review, Middle East Policy. *Address:* Mogahed Consulting, LLC, 1210 South Glebe Road, Suite 4400, Arlington, VA 22204, USA (office). *Telephone:* (202) 644-9393 (office). *E-mail:* info@mogahed.com (office). *Website:* mogahedconsulting.com (office); www.ispu.org (office).

MOGG, Baron (Life Peer), cr. 2008, of Queen's Park in the county of East Sussex; **John Frederick Mogg,** KCMG; British civil servant and fmr EU official; *Chairman, Ofgem;* b. 5 Oct. 1943, Brighton; s. of Thomas W. Mogg and Cora M. Mogg; m. Anne Smith 1967; one d. one s.; ed Univ. of Birmingham; fmrly with Rediffusion group; First Sec. UK Perm. Representation at EC, Brussels 1979–82; various appointments in UK civil service 1982–89; Deputy Head, European Secr. Cabinet Office 1989–90; Deputy Dir-Gen. Internal Market and Industrial Affairs, European Comm. 1990–93, Dir-Gen. Internal Market (fmrly DG XV) Directorate-Gen. 1993–2002; mem. Gas and Electricity Markets Authority 2003; Chair. (non-exec.) Ofgem 2003–; Chair. Int. Confed. of Energy Regulators 2010–, Bd of Regulators, Agency for Cooperation of Energy Regulators 2011–, Advisory Bd of European Union Observatory on Infringements of Intellectual Property Rights 2012–; Pres. Council of European Energy Regulators 2003–; Special Adviser, European Comm. on Cooperation Fund 2009–; mem. Advisory Bd of Electric Power Research Inst. 2012–; Chair. of Govs, Univ. of Brighton 2005–. *Address:* Ofgem, 9, Millbank, London, SW1P 3GE, England (office). *Telephone:* (20) 7901-7000 (office). *Fax:* (20) 7901-7066 (office). *E-mail:* enquiries@energywatch.org.uk (office). *Website:* www.ofgem.gov.uk (office).

MOGGACH, Deborah, BA, DipEd, FRSL, OBE; British writer; b. 28 June 1948, London, England; d. of Richard Hough and Helen Charlotte Hough; m. 1st Anthony Moggach 1971 (divorced); one s. one d.; partner Mel Calman 1984 (died 1994); partner Csaba Pasztor 1994–2001; m. 2nd Mark Williams 2014; ed Camden School for Girls, Queen's Coll., London, Univs of Bristol and London; has lived in Pakistan and USA; trained as a teacher before going to work at Oxford Univ. Press; has adapted many of her novels as TV dramas and has also written several film scripts; Chair. Soc. of Authors 1999–2001; mem. PEN; Hon. DLitt (Bristol) 2005. *Play:* Double Take. *Screenplay:* Pride and Prejudice 2005, Tulip Fever 2017. *Television:* dramas: To Have and To Hold (mini-series) 1986, Stolen 1990, Goggle-Eyes (adaptation) (Writers' Guild Award for Best Adapted TV Serial) 1993, Seesaw (adaptation) 1998, Close Relations (adaptation) 1998, Love in a Cold Climate (adaptation) 2001, Final Demand (adaptation) 2003, The Diary of Anne Frank 2008. *Publications:* novels: You Must Be Sisters 1978, Close to Home 1979, A Quiet Drink 1980, Hot Water Man 1982, Porky 1983, To Have and To Hold 1986, Driving in the Dark 1988, Stolen 1990, The Stand-in 1991, The Ex-Wives 1993, Seesaw 1996, Close Relations 1997, Tulip Fever 1999, Final Demand 2001, These Foolish Things (adapted into film The Best Exotic Marigold Hotel 2012) 2004, In the Dark 2007, Heartbreak Hotel 2012, Something to Hide 2015; short stories: Smile and Other Stories 1987, Ta for the Memories 1994, Changing Babies and Other Stories 1995. *Leisure interests:* swimming in rivers, walking round cities. *Address:* c/o Curtis Brown Group Ltd, Haymarket House, 28–29 Haymarket, London, SW1Y 4SP, England (office). *Telephone:* (20) 7393-4400 (office). *Fax:* (20) 7393-4401 (office). *E-mail:* cb@curtisbrown.co.uk (office). *Website:* www.curtisbrown.co.uk (office); www.deborahmoggach.com (office).

MOGGIE, Tan Sri Datuk Leo, MA, MBA; Malaysian politician and business exectuive; *Non-Executive Chairman, Tenaga Nasional Berhad;* b. 1 Oct. 1941,

Kanowit, Sarawak; ed Univ. of Otago, New Zealand, Pennsylvania State Univ., USA; Dist Officer, Kapit, Sarawak 1966–68; Dir Borneo Literature Bureau, Kuching, Sarawak 1968–69; attached to Office of Chief Minister, Kuching 1969–72; Deputy Gen. Man. Borneo Devt Corpn Kuching 1973–74; mem. Sarawak State Legis. Ass. 1974–78; mem. Parl. 1974–2004; Sec.-Gen. Sarawak Nat. Party (SNAP) 1976; Minister of Welfare Services, State Govt of Sarawak 1976–77, of Local Govt 1977–78; Minister of Energy, Telecommunications and Posts 1978–89, of Works and Public Utilities 1989–90, of Public Works 1990–95, of Energy, Telecommunications and Posts 1995–98, of Energy, Communications and Multimedia 1998–2004; Non-Ind. Chair. (non-exec.) Tenaga Nasional Bhd at Kapar Energy Ventures Sdn Bhd 2004–, Dir, Kapar Energy Ventures Sdn Bhd; Ind. Dir (non-exec.), Asian Plantations Ltd, Digi Telecommunications Sdn Bhd 2005– (now Sr Ind. Dir (non-exec.)), Digi.com Bhd 2005–13 (Sr Ind. Dir (non-exec.) –2013; Dir (non-exec.), New Straits Times Press Bhd 2008–; Pro-Chancellor Univ. Tenaga Nasional 2005–, Chair. of the Bd; Adjunct Prof., Faculty of Communications and Modern Languages, Univ. Utara Malaysia 2005–; Hon. LLD (Univ. of Otago) 2000; Hon. DSc (Multimedia Univ., Malaysia) 2003. *Address:* Tenaga Nasional Berhad, 129 Jalan Bangsar, 59200 Kuala Lumpur, Selangor, Malaysia (office). *Telephone:* (3) 2296-5566 (office). *Fax:* (3) 2283-3686 (office). *E-mail:* info@tnb.com.my (office). *Website:* www.tnb.com.my (office).

MOGHERINI, Federica; Italian politician and EU official; *High Representative of the Union for Foreign Affairs and Security Policy and Vice-President of the European Commission, European Union;* b. 1973, Rome; m.; two c.; ed Univ. La Sapienza, Rome, Institut d'études politiques d'Aix-en-Provence, France; worked in External Affairs Dept of Partito Democratico (PD—Democratic Party), mem. Nat. Council of PD 2001–, responsible for contacts with int. parties and movts, then Dept Co-ordinator, then Nat. Officer for Foreign and Int. Relations of Nat. Sec. Piero Fassini, PD Nat. Officer for Reform and Insts 2007, PD Nat. Officer for European Community and Int. Affairs 2009; mem. Chamber of Deputies (Parl.) for Veneto I 2008–13, for Emilio-Romagna 2013–, mem. Chamber of Deputies Defence Cttee, Foreign Affairs Cttee; mem. Italian Del. to Council of Europe; Pres. Italian Del. to NATO Parl. Ass. 2013; Minister of Foreign Affairs Feb.–Oct. 2014; High Rep. of the Union for Foreign Affairs and Security Policy, EU and Vice-Pres. EC Nov. 2014–; mem. Istituto Affari Internazionali, Consiglio per le relazioni fra Italia e Stati Uniti; fmr Dir European Youth Forum; fmr Vice-Pres. European Community Org. of Socialist Youth (Ecosy); mem. Federazione Giovanile Comunista Italiana (Italian Communist Youth Fed.) 1988–, Sinistra giovanile (Youth Left, youth br. of PD), Officer for Univs and Foreigners; Fellow, German Marshall Fund of the USA. *Address:* BERL 12, 200 Rue de la Loi/Wetstraat 200, 1049 Brussels, Belgium (office). *Telephone:* (2) 298-85-90 (office). *Fax:* (2) 298-86-57 (office). *E-mail:* federica.mogherini@ec.europa.eu (office). *Website:* ec.europa.eu/commission/2014-2019/mogherini_en (office).

MOGODI, Crispin Atama Tabe, LLB; Democratic Republic of Congo politician; b. 18 Aug. 1956, Aba, Oriental Prov.; ed Kinshasa Univ.; began career with Nat. Intelligence Agency; high-ranking official in territorial admin of various provs 1992–2009; Provincial Minister of Interior and of Public Order, Oriental Prov. 2009–11; Minister of Hydrocarbons 2012–15, Minister of Nat. Defence, War Veterans and Rehabilitation 2015–19.

MOHADI, Kembo Dugish Campbell; Zimbabwean politician; b. 15 Nov. 1949, Beitbridge, S Rhodesia; m. Tambudzani Muleya Budagi (divorced); four c.; fmr resistance fighter; joined Zimbabwe African People's Union (ZAPU) 1970s, trained in Zambia with Zimbabwe People's Revolutionary Army (ZIPRA, mil. wing of party) from 1972; imprisoned, Khami Prison, Bulawayo 1976–80; ZANU-PF Educ. Officer, Beitbridge Dist 1981–85; mem. House of Ass. for Beitbridge constituency 1985–2008, for Beitbridge East 2008–17; Deputy Minister of Sport, Recreation and Culture 1995; Minister of Home Affairs 2002–15; Minister of State for Nat. Security in the Pres.'s Office 2015–17; Minister of Defence, Security and War Veterans Nov.–Dec. 2017; Second Vice-Pres. and Minister of Nat. Peace and Reconciliation 2017–18; mem. Zimbabwe African Nat. Union-Patriotic Front (ZANU-PF), mem. Cen. Cttee and Politburo.

MOHAMAD, Goenawan; Indonesian poet, writer and journalist; b. 29 July 1941, Batang, Cen. Java; ed Coll. of Europe; Founder and Ed. of Tempo magazine in Indonesia, forcibly closed twice by Suharto New Order admin; est. Inst. for Studies in the Free Flow of Information; mem. Int. Advisory Bd ARTICLE 19 human rights group; several awards for journalism, including CPJ Int. Press Freedom Award 1998, Int. Ed. of the Year, World Press Review 1999, Dan David Prize 2006. *Publications include:* Potret Seorang Penyair Muda Sebagai Si Malin Kundang (The Portrait of A Young Poet as Malin Kundang) 1972, Seks, Sastra, Kita (Sex, Literature, Us) 1980, Pariksit dan Interlude 2001, Setelah Revolusi Tak Ada Lagi (Once the Revolution No Longer Exists) 2001, Kata, Waktu (Word, Time) 2001, Eksotopi (Exotopia) 2003, Tuhan dan Hal-hal Yang Tak Selesai (God and Other Unfinished Things) 2007, Marxisme, Seni, dan Pembebasan (Marxism, the Arts, Emancipation) 2011, Indonesia/Proses (Indonesia/Process) 2011, Puisi dan Antipuisi (Poetry and Antipoetry) 2011, Di Sekitar Sajak (On Poems) 2011, Tokoh + Pokok (Persons + Issues) 2011, Teks dan Iman (Texts and Faith) 2011, Debu, Duka, Dst: Sebuah Pertimabngan anti-theodise (Ash, Grief, Etc.: A Consideration Against Theodicy) 2011), Ruang dan Kekuasaan (On Space and Power), 2011, Rupa (Images) 2011, Pagi dan Hal-hal Yang dipungut Kembali (Morning and Things Retrieved) 2011, Don Quixote 2011, 70 Puisi (70 Poems) 2011; plays published in Tan Malaka dan Tiga Lakon lain. *Address:* Tempo Interaktif, Kebayoran Center Blok A11–A15, Jl. Kebayoran Baru – Mayestik, Jakarta 12440, Indonesia (office). *Telephone:* (21) 725-5625 (office). *Fax:* (21) 720-6995 (office). *E-mail:* iklannews@tempo.co.id (office). *Website:* www.tempo.co (office); en.tempo.co (office).

MOHAMED, Abdirashid Abdullahi; Somali politician; worked for Norwegian Refugee Council; fmr Gov., Bay Admin. Region; Minister of Defence March–Oct. 2017.

MOHAMED, Abdoulkader Kamil, MS; Djibouti water engineer, government official and politician; *Prime Minister;* b. 1 July 1951, Souali, Obock; ed Water Inst., Univ. of Limoges; Interim Dir Office National des Eaux de Djibouti (public water co.) 1978–79, Dir-Gen. 1983–2005; Minister of Agric., Livestock and Water Resources 2005–11, Minister of Defence 2011–13, Prime Minister 2013–; mem.

Assemblée Nationale 2008–; mem. Rassemblement populaire pour le progrès (in charge of party discipline). *Address:* Office of the Prime Minister, BP 2086, Djibouti (office). *Telephone:* 21351494 (office). *Fax:* 21355049 (office). *Website:* www.primature.dj (office).

MOHAMED, Abdoulkarim; Comoran politician; b. 3 Feb. 1975, Mdjankagnoi; fmr teacher and researcher, Univ. des Comores, also fmr Dir-Gen., School of Medicine and Public Health; mem. Ass. of the Union (Parl.) for Badjini-ouest 2015–; Minister of Nat. Educ., Research, Culture and the Arts, with responsibility for Youth and Sports –2015, Minister of External Relations and Co-operation, with responsibility for Diaspora, and for Francophone and Arab Relations 2015–16; mem. Convention pour le Renouveau des Comores (CRC).

MOHAMED, Ali Naseer, MA, PhD; Maldivian politician and diplomatist; *Permanent Representative to United Nations;* b. 2 Nov. 1969; m. Azeema Adam; one s. one d.; ed ANU, Univ. of Leicester; Attaché, High Comm. of Maldives, Colombo 1985–91, Admin. Officer, Dept of Foreign Relations 1991–94, Protocol Officer 1994–96, Desk Officer (Head of Research Div.) 1997–2001, Asst Dir 2001–03; Asst Dir, Dept of External Resources 2003–05, Asst Dir-Gen. 2005–07, Dir-Gen. Political Affairs Directorate 2007–08, Additional Sec., Policy Planning Div. 2012–13, Foreign Sec. 2013–17; Perm. Rep. to UN 2017–, Amb. to USA (also accred to Canada) 2017–. *Address:* Permanent Mission of Maldives, 801 Second Avenue, Suite 202E, New York, NY 10017 (office); Embassy of Maldives, 800 2nd Ave, Suite 400E, New York, NY 10017, USA (office). *Telephone:* (212) 599-6195 (office). *Fax:* (212) 661-6405 (office). *E-mail:* Midhfa@MaldivesMission.com (office). *Website:* www.maldivesmission.com (office).

MOHAMED, Amina C., LLM; Somali/Kenyan lawyer, diplomatist, international organization official and politician; *Secretary for Sports, Culture and Heritage;* b. 5 Oct. 1961, Kenya; m. Khalid Ahmed; seven c. (five adopted); ed Univ. of Kiev, Ukraine, Kenya School of Law, Univ. of Oxford, UK; began career as legal officer at Kenyan Ministry of Local Govt 1985; Legal Adviser, Ministry of Foreign Affairs 1986–90; Legal Adviser, Kenyan Mission to UN, Geneva 1990–93, Amb. and Perm. Rep. 2000–06; Chair., Int. Org. for Migration, London 2002–03; Chair., Gen. Council, WTO 2005–06; Dir Europe and Commonwealth Countries and Dir for Diaspora matters 2006–07, Chair. Task Force Sub-Cttee on Strengthening and Restructuring, Dept of Foreign Trade and Econ. Affairs; Perm. Sec., Kenyan Ministry of Justice, Nat. Cohesion and Constitutional Affairs 2008–11; Pres. UN Conf. on Transnational Crime, Vienna 2010–11; Asst Sec.-Gen. and Deputy Exec. Dir, UNEP 2011–13; Sec. (Minister) for Foreign Affairs 2013–18, for Education 2018–19, for Sports, Culture and Heritage 2019–; mem. Advisory Cttee to Pres., Gen. Ass., UN 2017–; mem. Advisory Council, Life and Peace Inst., Advisory Bd, Strathmore Law School; Int. mem. World Econ. Forum Global Agenda Council on the Arctic; Life mem. Red Cross Soc.; UNITAR Fellow, Chief of the Order of the Burning Spear (Kenya), Kt, Order of the Star of Italian Solidarity. *Address:* Ministry Of Sports, Culture and Heritage, Kencom House, PO Box 49849-00100, Nairobi, Kenya (office). *Telephone:* (20) 2251164 (office). *E-mail:* csoffice@sportsheritage.go.ke (office). *Website:* www.sportsheritage.go.ke (office); www.aminamohamed.com.

MOHAMED, Caabi El-Yachroutou; Comoran politician; Minister of Finance 1993–94; Prime Minister of Comoros April 1995–March 1996; Interim Pres. Oct. 1995–Jan. 1996; Vice-Pres. with responsibility for Finance, the Budget, the Economy, Foreign Trade, Investments and Privatizations 2002–06 (resgnd to participate in election for Union president (unsuccessful)); also served as Sec.-Gen. of Indian Ocean Comm.; mem. Rally for Democracy and Renewal; a supporter of Anjouan Pres. Mohamed Bacar, arrested following invasion of Anjouan March 2008.

MOHAMED, Mohamed Abdullahi, MA; Somali/American diplomatist, politician and head of state; *President;* b. 1962, Mogadishu; m. Zeinab Moallim; two s. two d.; ed State Univ. of New York at Buffalo, USA; worked at Ministry of Foreign Affairs, Mogadishu, First Sec., Embassy in Washington, DC 1985–88; Commr and Finance Chair. Buffalo Municipal Housing Authority 1994–97, also case man. for lead abatement program 1995–99; Minority Business Co-ordinator, Erie Co. Div., US Equal Employment Opportunity Admin 2000–02; Commr for Equal Employment, New York State Dept of Transportation, Buffalo 2002–10; Prime Minister of Somalia 2010–11 (resgnd); Pres. of Somalia 2017–; fmr Chair. Buffalo Immigrant and Refugee Empowerment Coalition; fmr Pres. American Diversity of Buffalo; fmr teacher, Erie Community Coll. *Address:* Office of the President, 1 Villa Baidao, 2525 Baydhabo, Somalia (office). *E-mail:* president@president.somaligov.net (office). *Website:* www.president.somaligov.net (office).

MOHAMED, Omer Dahab Fadl; Sudanese diplomatist; *Permanent Representative to United Nations;* ed People's Friendship Univ. of Russia, Int. Inst. of Islamic Thought and Civilization in Malaysia; joined Ministry of Foreign Affairs (MFA) 1982, served in Embassy of Sudan in UAE 1984–87, in fmr Fed. Repub. of Yugoslavia 1987–90, in Malaysia 1991–94; Perm. Rep. to UN, New York 1994–99, 2015–, in Geneva 2004–10; Head Int. Treaties Section, MFA 1999–2001, Dir Crisis Man. and Conflict Resolution Dept 2010; Amb. to Russian Fed. 2012–15; fmr Chair. Cttee on Justice, Reconciliation, Human Rights and Fundamental Freedoms, Govt's del. to Inter-Sudanese Peace Talks on Darfur. *Address:* Permanent Mission of Sudan, 305 E 47th Street, 3 Dag Hammarskjöld Plaza, 4th Floor, New York, NY 10017, USA (office). *Telephone:* (212) 573-6033 (office). *Fax:* (212) 573-6160 (office). *E-mail:* sudan@sudanmission.org (office).

MOHAMEDOU, Mohamed Mahmoud Ould, PhD; Mauritanian academic and politician; b. 3 April 1968; ed Univ. Panthéon-Sorbonne, Paris, City Univ. of New York; fmr Research Dir Int. Council on Human Rights, Geneva; fmr Prof. of Political Science, Harvard Univ., Assoc. Dir Program on Humanitarian Policy and Conflict Research, Harvard School of Public Health; Minister of Foreign Affairs and Co-operation 2008–09. *Publications:* Societal Transition to Democracy in Mauritania 1995, Iraq and the Second Gulf War, State-Building and Regime Security 1998, Contre-Croisade: Origines et Conséquences du 11 Septembre 2004.

MOHAMMAD, Haji Din; Afghan provincial governor and fmr rebel leader; s. of Amanullah Khan Jabbarkhail; m.; one s. (deceased); fmr mem. Yunus Khalis faction, Hizb-i Islami; fmr Mujahidin commdr; Minister of Nat. Security in Afghanistan's Interim Govt in Exile during the 1990s and as Minister of Educ. in the Mujahideen Govt est. after collapse of Communist govt; also served as Deputy Prime Minister in the same period, resgnd because of infighting among rival factions of Ahmad Shah Massoud and Gulbuddin Hekmatyar; during the Taliban era, lived in exile and later helped Abdul Haq in his efforts to establish a broad-based post-Taliban govt; Gov. Nangarhar Prov. 2002–04, Kabul Prov. 2005–09.

MOHAMMAD HUSSEINI, Khial; Afghan politician; *First Deputy CEO;* b. 1957, Ghazni Prov.; Deputy Gov. of Ghazni Prov. –2004, Gov. 2004–05; Hezb-i-Islami; lawmaker representing Ghazni Prov. in Wolesi Jirga (Afghan Parl.) 2005–, headed Committee on Dispatches and Communications; currently First Deputy CEO; mem. and Deputy Leader, Hizb-e-islami Afghanistan (Islamic Party of Afghanistan); mem. Nat. Security Council, Council of Ministers, Econ. Council, Pashtun ethnic group; ran unsuccessfully for Presidential election 2014. *Address:* Office of the Chief Executive, Kabul (office); Hizb-i Islami Afghanistan, Area A, Khushal Mena, 5th District, Kabul, Afghanistan (office). *Telephone:* (74) 4200000 (office of CEO) (office); 799421474 (mobile) (Hizb-i Islami) (office). *Website:* ceo.gov.af (office).

MOHAMMED, Abdulaziz; Ethiopian politician; ed Haramaya Univ.; fmr Deputy Administrator, East Hararghe Zone and Harari Regional State; Mayor of Dire Dawa 2006; fmr Head of Addis Ababa City Mayor's Office; Vice-Pres., Oromia Regional State 2008; Minister of Finance and Econ. Co-operation 2015–16; mem. Oromo People's Democratic Org. (OPDO), mem. OPDO Exec. Cttee.

MOHAMMED, Amina J.; Nigerian politician and UN official; *Deputy Secretary-General, United Nations;* b. 1961, Rosterman; d. of Djibril Mohammed; m.; six c.; ed Butere Girls High School; worked with Archcon Nigeria (architectural partnership) in association with Norman and Dawbarn UK 1981–91; Founder-Dir Afri-Projects Consortium 1991–2001; Coordinator of Task Force on Gender and Education, UN Millennium Project 2002–05; Sr Special Asst to Pres. of Nigeria on Millennium Devt Goals 2005–11; Special Adviser of the Sec.-Gen. on Post-2015 Devt Planning, UN 2012–15; Minister of the Environment 2015–16; apptd Chair. Water Supply and Sanitation Collaborative Council (WSSCC) 2016; Deputy Sec.-Gen., UN 2017–; Founder-CEO Centre for Devt Policy Solutions (think-tank); Chair. Advisory Bd, UNESCO Global Monitoring Report on Educ.; Adjunct Prof., Columbia Univ., New York; mem. Bd of Govs, International Devt Research Centre, Canada; mem. numerous int. advisory panels and bds, including those of Global Devt Program, Bill and Melinda Gates Foundation, UN Sec.-Gen.'s Global Sustainability Panel, African Population and Health Research Centre; Nat. Honours Award of the Order of the Fed. Repub. 2006; inducted into Nigerian Women's Hall of Fame 2007; Ford Family Notre Dame Award for Human Devt and Solidarity 2015. *Address:* Office of the Deputy Secretary-General, United Nations, New York, NY 10017, USA (office). *Telephone:* (212) 963-1234 (office). *Fax:* (212) 963-4879 (office). *Website:* www.un.org (office).

MOHAMMED, Bello Haliru; Nigerian veterinarian and politician; b. 9 Oct. 1945, Kebbi State; m.; six c.; ed Government Coll. (now Barewa Coll.), Zaria, Ahmadu Bello Univ.; fmr Lecturer, Ahmadu Bello Univ., Zaria; Commr for Agric., Sokoto State 1977, later Commr for Educ.; joined Great Nigeria People's Party (GNPP) 1979, GNPP Sec. for Sokoto State 1979–83; several years in private sector as Man. Dir Alpha & Beta Merchants Ltd (general merchandise co.); fmr Asst Gen. Man., later Gen. Man., Rima River Basin and Rural Devt Authority (govt agency); Comptroller Gen., Nigerian Customs Service 1988–94; Commr, Revenue Mobilization Allocation and Fiscal Comm. 1999; Minister of Communications 2001–03; Minister of Defence 2011–12; fmr Chair. Nigerian Railway Corpn; Founding mem. Democratic Party of Nigeria (DPN); Founding mem. People's Democratic Party (PDP), Nat. PDP Vice-Chair. for NW Zone 2004–08, Deputy Nat. Chair. 2008–11, Acting Nat. Chair. 2011, 2015; Fellow, Coll. of Veterinary Surgeons of Nigeria; Diamond Nigerian Telecoms Award 2008.

MOHAMMED MUSSA, Aisha; Ethiopian civil engineer and politician; *Minister of Urban Development and Construction;* b. 27 Feb. 1978, Afar Region; m. Awal Wagris; ed Addis Ababa Univ., Univ. of Greenwich, UK; started professional career as site engineer; worked as nat. UN volunteer on UNDP urban devt project for three years; fmr Sr Site Engineer, construction project under Deutsche Gesellschaft für Int. Zusammenarbeit (GIZ, German int. devt agency), becoming Deputy Head of Contract Admin, GIZ head office, Addis Ababa; Head, Afar Nat. Regional State Disaster Prevention and Food Security Coordination Office 2010–15; fmr Minister of Construction; Minister of Tourism and Culture 2015, Minister of Nat. Defence (first female) Oct. 2018–April 2019, of Urban Devt. and Construction April 2019–. *Address:* Ministry of Urban Development and Construction, opp. National Bank of Ethiopia, POB POB 24134/1000, Addis Ababa, Ethiopia (office). *Telephone:* (11) 5531688. *Fax:* (11) 5541268. *E-mail:* mekuria .2000@gmail.com. *Website:* www.mwud.gov.et.

MOHAMMED VI, HM The King of Morocco; b. 21 Aug. 1963, Rabat; s. of King Hassan II; m. Lalla Salma Bennani 2002; one s. (Crown Prince Moulay Hassan, b. 2003) one d. (b. 2007); ed Collège Royal, Université Mohammed V, Faculté des Sciences Juridiques, Economiques et Sociales de Rabat; Head of Moroccan del., 7th Summit of Non-Aligned Nations, New Delhi 1983, 10th Franco–African Conf., Vittel 1983; apptd Co-ordinator Admin. and Services, Armed Forces 1985; rank of Gén. de Div. 1994; Hon. Pres. Asscn Socio–Culturelle du Bassin Méditerranéen 1979–; Chair. Org. Cttee 9th Mediterranean Games, Casablanca 1982; succeeded to the throne on the death of his father 23 July 1999; Award for Special Recognition of Leadership in Promoting Tolerance and Intercultural Reconciliation, Global Coalition for Hope 2017. *Address:* Royal Palace, Rabat, Morocco.

MOHAQEQ, Haji Mohammad; Afghan politician and government official; *Deputy Chief Executive;* b. 1955, Charkent Dist, Balkh Prov.; ed Mazar-e-Sharif; Chair. Political Cttee and of Northern Region, Hizb-i-Wahdat-i Islami Afghanistan (Islamic Unity Party of Afghanistan); fmr Minister of the Interior; Vice-Pres. and Minister of Planning, Interim Admin; presidential cand. 2004; Founder and Leader Hizb-i Wahdat-i Islami Mardum-i Afghanistan (People's Islamic Unity Party of Afghanistan); Deputy Chief Exec., Islamic Republic of Afghanistan 2014–; mem. Wolesi Jirga (House of the People) (Parl.), Chair. Cultural and Educational Comm., Judicial Comm. *Address:* Hizb-i Wahdat-i Islami Mardum-i Afghanistan, House 3, Mohammadia Street, Tapa-i-Salaam, Karte Sakhi, Kabul, Afghanistan (office). *Telephone:* 70278276 (mobile) (office).

MOHIELDIN, Mahmoud, BS, MS, PhD; Egyptian economist, academic, government official and international organization official; *Senior Vice-President, 2030 Development Agenda, United Nations Relations and Partnerships, World Bank Group;* b. 15 Jan. 1965; ed Cairo Univ., Univs of Warwick, York, UK; Asst, Dept of Econs, Cairo Univ. 1986–91, Asst Lecturer 1991–95, Lecturer in Financial Econs 1995–2001, Assoc. Prof. in Financial Econs 2001–06, Prof. of Econs 2006–; held several positions in Egyptian govt, including Econ. Adviser to Minister of State for Econ. Affairs, Sr Econ. Adviser to Minister of Economy and Foreign Trade, Sr Adviser to Minister of Foreign Trade; Minister of Investment 2004–10, also served as Gov. of Egypt to World Bank, Alt. Gov. to ADB, Alt. Gov. Islamic Development Bank; Man. Dir World Bank Group, Washington, DC 2010–12, Special Envoy of the World Bank Pres. on Millennium Development Goals 2013–14, Corporate Sec. and Special Envoy of the World Bank Pres. 2014–15, Sr Vice-Pres. 2030 Devt Agenda, UN Relations and Partnerships 2016–; fmr mem. Bd of Dirs Central Bank of Egypt; mem. Bd of Trustees, British Univ. of Egypt; mem. Centre of European Studies, Arab Soc. for Econ. Research, Comm. on Growth and Devt. *Publications include:* Financial Development in Emerging Markets (co-ed). *Address:* World Bank Group, 1818 H Street, NW, Washington, DC 20433, USA (office). *Telephone:* (202) 473-1000 (office). *Fax:* (202) 477-6391 (office). *Website:* www.worldbank.org (office).

MOHILYOV, Maj.-Gen. Anatoliy Volodymyrovych; Ukrainian police officer and government official; b. 6 April 1955, Petropavlovsk-Kamchatskii, Kamchatka Oblast (now Kamchatka Krai), Russian SFSR, USSR; ed Slovyansk Pedagogical Inst., Donetsk, Ukrainian Acad. of Internal Affairs; mil. service in USSR 1979–81; physics teacher, Slovyansk secondary school No. 18, Donetsk 1981–82; joined Ministry of Internal Affairs as Dist Militia Officer for Minor Matters, Slovyansk Dist 1982, becoming Officer, Criminal Investigation Div., Head of Dist Militia Officers Unit, later Deputy Head of Operations, Slovyansk Dist; Sr Special Operative Authorized Officer, Inner Security Div. 1992–95, Artemivsk City Dept 1995–2000, Makiyivka City Dept 2000–05; Head of Internal Affairs Dept, Autonomous Repub. of Crimea 2007, later Deputy Minister and Head of Crimean Police, Chair. Council of Ministers (Prime Minister) 2011–14 (dismissed by Supreme Council amid ongoing protests in the region); Adviser to Minister of Internal Affairs of Ukraine 2007–10, Minister of Internal Affairs 2010–11. *Address:* c/o Council of Ministers, 95005 Crimea, Simferopol, ul. Kirova 13, Ukraine.

MOHL, Andrew, BEc (Hons); Australian financial services executive; *Chairman, Federal Government Export Finance and Insurance Corporation;* b. 1955; ed Monash Univ.; began career at Reserve Bank of Australia 1978, roles included Sr Economist and Deputy Head of Research, seconded to Fed. Reserve Bank of New York 1983–84; with ANZ Banking Group 1986–96, roles included Sr Economist, Group Chief Economist, Div. Chief Man. ANZ Retail Banking and Man. Dir ANZ Funds Man.; Gen. Man. of Retail Distribution, AMP Financial Services 1996–99, Man. Dir AMP Asset Man., AMP Australian Financial Services 1999–2002, CEO AMP Group Ltd 2002–07, undertook a major restructuring of the group including demerger of AMP into Australian and UK-based cos; Dir, AMP Foundation –2013, Commonwealth Bank of Australia 2008–; Chair. and Ind. non-exec. mem. Fed. Govt Export Finance and Insurance Corpn 2008–; mem. Advisory Council, Australian School of Business, Corp. Council, European Australian Business Council, Review Panel Selection Bd of the Banking Finance Oath; mem. Bd of Govs, Cttee for Econ. Devt of Australia; exec. coach to CEOs. *Address:* Federal Government Export Finance and Insurance Corporation, Level 10 Export House, 22 Pitt Street, Sydney, NSW 2000, Australia (office). *Telephone:* (2) 8273-5333 (office). *Fax:* (2) 9251-3851 (office). *E-mail:* info@efic.gov.au (office). *Website:* www .efic.gov.au (office).

MÖHLER, Hanns, BSc, MSc, PhD; German pharmacologist and academic; *Professor of Pharmacology, Eidgenössische Technische Hochschule Zürich and University of Zurich;* b. 8 March 1940, Ehingen; m.; two c.; ed Univs of Bonn, Tübingen and Freiburg; research work at Michigan State Univ., USA and MRC Labs, London, UK; joined Hoffmann-La Roche, Basel in 1973, apptd Vice-Dir (Science) Research Dept; qualified as Univ. Lecturer at Univ. of Freiburg, later promoted to Assoc. Prof.; Prof. of Pharmacology, Dept of Chem. and Applied Biosciences, ETH Zürich 1989–, Faculty of Medicine, Univ. of Zurich 1989–, Head of Inst. of Pharmacology, Head, Center of Competence in Experimental and Clinical Pharma-Sciences 2003–05; Dir Swiss Nat. Center of Neuroscience 2001–05, currently Vice-Dir; Co-ed. of numerous journals; mem. European Acad. of Sciences 1991–; Bd mem. Swiss Acad. of Medical Sciences 1996; Fellow, Collegium Helveticum 2004–; Neuroscience Award of the European College of Neuropsychopharmacology, Ott-Prize of the Swiss Academy of Medical Sciences, Golden Kraepelin Medal, German Inst. for Psychiatric Research 2003. *Publications:* a textbook on biochemistry, Pharmacology of GABA and Glycine Neurotransmission (Handbook of Experimental Pharmacology) 2000, The GABA Receptors (with by S. J. Enna) 2007; numerous scientific papers in professional journals on the neurobiology of the brain and molecular pharmacology of the action of drugs. *Address:* Institute of Pharmacology and Toxicology, Irchel Campus Y17, University of Zurich, Winterthurerstrasse 190, 8057 Zurich, Switzerland (office). *Telephone:* (44) 635-59-10 (office). *Fax:* (44) 635-59-55 (office). *E-mail:* mohler@ pharma.uzh.ch (office). *Website:* www.pharma.uzh.ch (office).

MOHN, Christoph; German media industry executive; *Chairman of the Supervisory Board, Bertelsmann SE & Co. KGaA;* b. 6 July 1965, Stuttgart; s. of Reinhard Mohn; great-great-grand s. of Carl Bertelsmann (f. Bertelsmann AG 1835); ed Westfälische Wilhelms-Universität; fmr intern, Bantam Doubleday Dell; with Bertelsmann Music Group (BMG), Hong Kong and New York, USA 1991–94; specialist in electronics and telecommunications, McKinsey & Co. Germany 1994–96; Vice-Pres. Telemedia (subsidiary of Bertelsmann AG) 1996–97; CEO Lycos Europe NV 1997–2009; mem. Supervisory Bd, Bertelsmann SE & Co. KGaA 2006–, Chair. 2013–; Chair. Exec. Bd Reinhard Mohn Foundation; Man. Dir Christoph Mohn Internet Holding GmbH. *Address:* Bertelsmann, Carl-Bertelsmann-Strasse 270, 33311 Gütersloh, Germany (office). *Telephone:* (5241) 80-0 (office). *Fax:* (5241) 80-62321 (office). *Website:* www.bertelsmann.com (office).

MOHN, Elisabeth (Liz); German media industry executive; *Chairwoman of the Board, Bertelsmann Verwaltungsgesellschaft mbH;* b. 21 June 1941, Wiedenbrück; m. Reinhard Mohn 1982 (deceased); three c.; joined Bertelsmann group's book club unit 1958, Chief Exec. Bertelsmann Admin Co. 2002–; Man. Dir and mem. Supervisory Bd Bertelsmann Trust 2002–, currently Chair. Bd Bertelsmann Verwaltungsgesellschaft mbH, Vice-Chair. Exec. Bd Bertelsmann Stiftung, Deputy Chair. Bertelsmann Foundation; Founder and Pres. Assistance for Stroke Victims Foundation 1993–; f. Liz Mohn Foundation for Culture and Music 2005; Pres. Neue Stimmen (singing competition) 1987–; mem. European Acad. of Sciences, Salzburg 1997–, Club of Rome 1999–; Hon. Citizen, Gütersloh City 2016–; Grand Cross, Order of Merit of the Fed. Repub. of Germany 1996, Officer, Légion d'Honneur (France) 2013, Commdr's Cross, Order of the Oak Crown 2016; Dr hc (Univ. of Tel-Aviv) 2006; Bambi Award 1996, Ehrenzeichen der Bundeswehr 2000, Vernon A. Walters Award, Atlantik-Brucke 2008, UNESCO Children in Need Prize 2008, Karl Winnacker Prize 2009, Global Economy Prize 2010, Euriade Badge of Honor (Gold) 2014. *Address:* Bertelsmann SE & Co. KGaA, Carl-Bertelsmann-Strasse 270, 33311, Gütersloh, Germany. *Telephone:* (5241) 80-80-0 (office). *Fax:* (5241) 80-62321 (office). *E-mail:* info@bertelsmann.de (office). *Website:* www.bertelsmann.com (office).

MOHOHLO, Linah Kelebogile, BEcons, MA; Botswana economist and fmr central banker; ed Univ. of Botswana, George Washington Univ., USA, Univ. of Exeter, UK; Programme Officer, Radio Botswana 1970–71; Registry Clerk 1971–72; Sec., Anglo American Corpn 1973–74; Sec., Norman & Dawbarn (architectrual firm) 1975–76; joined Bank of Botswana 1976, served in various positions including Personal Asst to Deputy Gov. and later Gov. 1976–82, Board Sec. 1982–85, Deputy Dir Human Resources Dept 1986–87, Deputy Dir of Research 1988–89, Dir Financial Markets Dept 1989–94, secondment to IMF 1994–96, Deputy Gov. 1997–99, Gov. 1999–2016; Co-Chair. World Econ. Forum for Africa 2011–12; Deputy Chair. Univ. of Botswana Foundation 2002–; mem. Bd of Dirs Debswana Diamond Company 1998–, Non-Bank Financial Institutions Regulatory Authority 2007–, Diamond Empowerment Fund 2008–, Diamond Trading Company Botswana 2008–; mem. Botswana Soc., Alliance for a Green Revolution in Africa 2012–; Trustee, Investment Climate Facility for Africa 2011–; Presidential Order of Honour 2004; Exec. Woman of the Year (Botswana) 1993, named Eminent Person by UN Sec.-Gen. 2001, Africa Leadership Award, African Times 2007, Lifetime Leadership Award, Official Monetary and Financial Insts 2011, Africa Banker Award 2014, Central Bank Gov. of the Year Award for Africa, African Development Bank 2014. *Publications include:* numerous papers and book chapters in economics, finance, investments, reserves management and governance. *Leisure activities:* tennis, reading, listening to choral/classical/opera music. *E-mail:* lmohohlo@gmail.com.

MOHORITA, Vasil; Czech politician and business executive; b. 19 Sept. 1952, Prague; s. of Vasil Mohorita and Ludmila Mohoritová; m. Vlasta Mohoritová 1976; one s. one d.; ed Komsomol Coll., Moscow and CP of Czechoslovakia (CPCZ) Political Coll., Prague; joined CP of Czechoslovakia (Komunistická strana Československa—KSČ) 1970, mem. Cen. Cttee 1988–90, First Sec. Cen. Cttee 1989–90; apptd Chair. Socialistický svaz mládeže (SSM) Central Cttee 1986, later Vice-Chair. Central Cttee; Chair. Youth Union's Czechoslovak Cen. Cttee 1987–89; mem. Czechoslovak Nat. Front Presidium 1987; Deputy, Czechoslovak Nat. Council 1986–90; mem. Presidium Fed. Ass. Jan.–Oct. 1990, Deputy to Fed. Ass. House of People 1990–92; Chair. Communist Deputies Club Jan.–Nov. 1990; agent for Valemo, Parfia, Jamiko, CIS Group; Chair. Bd of Supervisors E.R. Tradings; Head of Sales, Frut Ovo (pvt. co.); mem. Party of Democratic Left 1993–97; Chair. Party of Democratic Socialism 1997–98; apptd Head of External Relations, Zbrojovka, Brno 2000. *Publications:* numerous articles. *Leisure interests:* reading historical and political literature, playing the guitar, basketball, tennis.

MOHSENI, Saad; Afghan media executive; *Chairman and CEO, Moby Media Group;* b. 23 April 1966, London, UK; s. of Yassin Mohseni and Safia Mohseni; m. 1st (divorced), one d.; m. 2nd (divorced), two c.; m. 3rd Sarah Takesh; childhood in exile with family in Australia; began career with equities and corp. finance div. of Australian investment banking firm 1985; f. trading co. in Tashkent, Uzbekistan 1995; head of investment banking, Tricom Equities, Australia 1999; moved to Kabul following fall of Taliban, f. Moby Capital (now Moby Media Group) 2002, Chair. and CEO 2002–, ventures include Arman Radio (Afghanistan's first privately-owned ind. FM radio station) 2003, Tolo TV network 2004, also owns music-recording co., advertising agency, TV and film production co., Afghan Scene magazine and two internet cafés; co-f. Farsi 1 TV channel (with Rupert Murdoch) 2009. *Address:* Moby Media Group, House #3, Street #12, Wazir Akbar Khan, PO Box 225, Kabul 1, Afghanistan (office). *Telephone:* (799) 321010 (office). *Fax:* (866) 2070812 (office). *E-mail:* info@mobygroup.com (office). *Website:* mobygroup.com (office).

MOHTASHAMI, Ali Akbar, DTheol; Iranian politician; b. 30 Aug. 1946, Tehran; s. of Seyed Hossein and Fatemeh Mohtashami; m. Fatemeh Mohtashami 1968; two s. five d.; studied theology in Iran and Iraq; mil. training in Palestinian camps, Lebanon; went to Paris with Ayatollah Khomeini 1978; returned to Iran and took part in overthrow of monarchy 1979; mem. political advisory office of Ayatollah Khomeini; Dir of Ayatollah's representative delegation in Foundation of the Oppressed 1980; mem. IRIB Supervisory Council 1980–81; Amb. to Syria 1981–85; a founder of Hezbollah in Lebanon; Minister of the Interior 1985–89; mem. Parl. 1989–91; Chair. Parl. Cttee on Defence 1991; Sec.-Gen. IPU Group of Iran (Chair. 1989–91); apptd Leader, Asscn of Combatant Clerics 1988, Sec.-Gen. 2010–; mem. Cttee to Protect the Islamic Revolution of Palestine; Sec.-Gen. of Int. Conf. on Intifada; Deputy Chair. Bd of Trustees Qods Inst.; Social Adviser to Pres. Mohammad Khatami; Man. Bayan newspaper (banned June 2000). *Publications include:* Plurality, From Iran to Iran (Memoirs) 1965–79. *Leisure interests:* study, sport (especially mountaineering and swimming). *Address:* 11, Adib-ol-Mamalek Street, Ray Street, Tehran, Iran (home). *Telephone:* (21) 361892 (home). *Website:* rouhanioon.com

MOI, Daniel Arap; Kenyan politician; b. 2 Sept. 1924, Sacho, Baringo district; m. Lena Moi (died 2004); seven c.; ed African Mission School, Kabartonjo A.I.M. School and Govt African School, Kapsabet; teacher 1945–57; Head Teacher, Govt African School, Kabarnet 1946–48, 1955–57, teacher Tambach Teacher Training School, Kabarnet 1948–54; African Rep. mem., Legis. Council 1957–63; Chair. Kenya African Democratic Union (KADU) 1960–61; mem. House of Reps 1961–; Parl. Sec., Ministry of Educ. April–Dec. 1961; Minister of Educ. 1961–62, Local

Govt 1962–64, Home Affairs 1964–67; Pres. Kenya African Nat. Union (KANU) for Rift Valley Province 1966–67; Vice-Pres. of Kenya 1967–78, concurrently Minister of Home Affairs; Pres. of Kenya and C-in-C of the Armed Forces 1978–2002; Minister of Defence 1979–2002; Chair. KANU –2003; Chair. OAU 1981–82; mem. Rift Valley Educ. Bd, Kalenjin Language Cttee; Chair. Rift Valley Provincial Court; Kt of Grace, Order of St John 1980.

MOILY, Moodbidri Veerappa, BA, BL; Indian lawyer and politician; b. 12 Jan. 1940, Marpadi Village, Moodibidri, Dakshina Kannada Dist, Karnataka; m. Malathi Moily; four c.; ed Govt Coll., Univ. Law Coll.; elected to Karnataka State Legis. Ass. from Udupi Dist constituency; Minister for Small-Scale Industries, Govt of Karnataka 1974–77, for Finance and Planning 1980–82; Leader of Opposition, Karnataka Ass. 1983–85; Minister for Law, Youth Service, Culture, Information, Parl. Affairs and Educ., Govt of Karnataka 1989–92; Chief Minister of Karnataka 1992–94; Chair. Tax Reforms Comm. 2000–02, Revenue Reforms Comm. 2002–04; Chair. Oversight Cttee apptd by Govt of India for Implementation of Reservations for Other Backward Classes (OBC) in cen. educational insts 2006–09; mem. Lok Sabha (lower house of Parl.) for Chikballapur 2009–; Minister of Law and Justice 2009–11, of Corp. Affairs 2011–12, of Power July–Oct. 2012, of Petroleum and Natural Gas 2012–14; apptd to various cttees by Indira Gandhi, one of which led to setting up of Nat. Bank for Agric. and Rural Devt (NABARD); Partner, Moily Assocs law firm; practised law in courts of Karkala, Mangalore, High Court in Bangalore and at Supreme Court of India; regular columnist for print and electronic media, including The Hindu, Deccan Herald, Samyukta Karnataka; Dr hc (Mangalore Univ.) 2009, (Russian Acad.); Ameen Sadbhavana Award 2000, Devaraj Urs Prashasthi 2001, Aryabhatta Award 2001, Dr B.R Ambedkar Award 2002, Moortidevi Award 2010. *Publications include:* Sri Ramayana Mahanveshanam (epic poem) Vols I–IV 2001–04 (originally published in Kannada, now being translated into Hindi), Musings on India (collection of articles) 2001, Suligali, Sagardeepa, Kotta and Thembare (anthropological novels originally written in Kannada, now translated into Hindi, English and Tamil; Kotta has been telecast as a tele-film in Kannada and Hindi directed by M. S. Sathyu), Milana, Parajitha and Premavendare (dramas), Halu-Jenu Maththe, Nadeyali Samara and Yakshaprashne (poetry collection), Unleashing India: A Road Map for Agrarian Wealth Creation, Unleashing India: Water- Meeting our Nation's Needs. *Address:* Kaustubha Number 1, R.T. Nagar, Bengaluru 560 032, India (home). *Telephone:* (80) 23430491 (home). *Fax:* (80) 23334784 (home). *E-mail:* vmoily@kar.nic.in. *Website:* www.moily.org.

MOÏSE, Jovenel; Haitian business executive, politician and head of state; *President;* b. 26 June 1968, Trou du Nord; s. of Etienne Moïse and Lucia Bruno; m. Martine Marie Etienne Joseph 1996; one d.; ed Centre Culturel, Coll. Canado-Haïtien, Université Quisqueya, Port-au-Prince; f. first business venture JOMAR Auto Parts, Port-de-Paix 1996; est. banana plantation, Nord-Ouest Dept 1996; jt venture with Culligan on drinking water project, Port-au-Prince 2001; mem. Chambre de Commerce et de l'Industrie du Nord-Ouest 2004, later becoming Pres.; Sec.-Gen. Chambre de Commerce et de l'Industrie d'Haïti; f. Compagnie Haïtienne d'Energie SA 2008; f. AGRITRANS SA (banana plantation) 2012; Parti Haïtien Tèt Kale (PHTK) cand. in presidential election 2015; Pres. of Haiti 2017–. *Address:* Office of the President, Palais National, ave de la République, Champs de Mars, Port-au-Prince, Haiti (office). *E-mail:* webmestre@palaisnational.info (office). *Website:* www.lapresidence.ht; www.jovenelmoise.ht (office).

MOÏSI, Dominique; French political scientist and academic; *Senior Advisor, Institut français des relations internationales;* b. 21 Oct. 1946, Neuilly-sur-Seine; s. of Jules Moïsi and Charlotte Tabakman; m. Diana Pinto 1977; two s.; ed Lycée Buffon, Paris, Institut d'études politiques, Paris, Faculté de droit de Paris, Harvard Univ., USA; Visiting Lecturer, Hebrew Univ. of Jerusalem 1973–75; Asst Lecturer, Univ. of Paris X 1975–89; Deputy Dir Inst. français des relations internationales 1979–2006, Sr Advisor 2006–; Lecturer, École nationale d'admin 1980–85, École des hautes études en sciences sociales 1988–; Sec.-Gen. Groupe d'étude et de recherche des problèmes internationaux 1975–78; Assoc. Prof., Johns Hopkins Univ. European Centre, Bologna 1983–84; Prof., Inst. d'études politiques, Paris; Visiting Prof., Collège d'Europe, Warsaw, Poland; Pierre Keller Visiting Prof., Harvard Univ.; Chairholder for Geopolitics, Coll. of Europe; Visiting Research Prof., King's Coll., London; Ed. Politique étrangère 1983–; mem. Bd of Dirs Salzburg Seminar, Aspen Inst., Berlin; editorial writer for Financial Times, Foreign Affairs, Project Syndicate, Die Welt, Der Standard. *Publications include:* Crises et guerres au XXe siècle: analogies et différences 1981, Le nouveau continent: plaidoyer pour une Europe renaissante (co-author) 1991, Les cartes de la France à l'heure de la mondialisation (co-author) 2000, Politique étrangère (co-author) 2003, La géopolitique de l'émotion: Comment les cultures de peur, d'humiliation et d'espoir façonnent le monde 2008, Un Juif improbable 2011. *Leisure interests:* music, cinema, tennis, skiing. *Address:* Institut français des relations internationales (IFRI), 27 rue de la Procession, 75740 Paris Cedex 15 (office); 4 rue Saint-Florentin, 75001 Paris, France (home). *Telephone:* 1-40-61-60-00 (office). *Fax:* 1-40-61-60-60 (office). *E-mail:* dpintmoisi@gmail.com (office); moisi@ifri.org (office). *Website:* www.ifri.org (home).

MOISIU, Alfred, DMilSc; Albanian fmr head of state; *Founder and Co-ordinator, Moisiu Foundation;* b. 1 Dec. 1929, Shkodër; s. of Spiro Moisiu; m. (deceased); one s. (deceased) three d.; ed High School of Tirana, mil. eng school in Leningrad (now St Petersburg) and Acad. of Mil. Eng, Moscow, USSR, Defence Acad. of Gen. Staff, Tirana, NATO Mil. Coll. Rome, Italy; participant in Nat. Liberation War 1943–45; platoon commdr, Jt Officers' School, Tirana 1948–49; Instructor, Skanderbeg Mil. Acad., Tirana 1949–51; assigned to Eng Directory, Ministry of Defence 1958–66; Commdr, Pontoon Brigade, Kavaja 1966–71; Head of Eng and Fortification Directory, Ministry of Defence 1971–81; Deputy Minister of Defence (discharged for political reasons) 1981–82; Co. Commdr, Burrel 1982–85; retd 1985–91; Minister of Defence 1991–92, Adviser on Defence 1992–94, Vice-Minister of Defence for Defence Policy 1994–97; Pres. of Albania 2002–07; Pres. Albanian Atlantic Asscn (pro-NATO non-governmental org.) 1994–2002; Founder and Co-ordinator, Moisiu Foundation and Civil Forum 2010–; Freeman of Bajram Curri, of Bari (Italy), of Vlora, of Martanesh Commune, of Lipljan (Kosovo), of Kavaje and Shengjin (Albania), of Presheve (Kosovo); Order of the Red Star, Order for Mil. Services, Skanderbeg Order (Second and Third Class), Hon. mem. (First Class) Kt Grand Cross of the Most Distinguished Order of St Michael (UK) and Order of St

George (UK), Order of King Tomislav with Great Band (Croatia), Gold Medal of the League of Prizren (Kosovo), Great Cross of Merit (Poland), Great Order of King Vytautas the Great (Lithuania), Jubilee Medal for 50, 60 and 65 Years of the Victory in the Great Patriotic War 1941–45 (Russia); Hon. Dr of Mil. Sciences 1979; Dr hc (Marin Barleti Univ., Albania); Gold Medal, Acad. of Mil. Eng, Moscow, Medal for Mil. Services, Medal of Liberation, Medal of the 10th Army Anniversary. *Publications:* Kosovo Between War and Peace (memoirs, three vols); has published many articles and studies in Albania and abroad on mil. affairs, defence and regional security policy, and about events in Kosovo. *Leisure interests:* scientific, military, historic and art literature. *Address:* Rr. Elbasanit, Pall. Amerikan 2, Nr 207, Tirana (office); Rr. Xhorxh W. Bush, Nd. 17, Hyrja 3, Ap. 1, 1017 Tirana, Albania (home). *Telephone:* (4) 2227757 (home); (4) 2274834 (home). *Fax:* (4) 2227757 (home); (4) 2274834 (home). *E-mail:* alfredmoisiu@yahoo.com (home). *Website:* www.forumicivil2010.al (office).

MOITINHO DE ALMEIDA, José Carlos de Carvalho, LenD; Portuguese judge (retd); b. 17 March 1936, Lisbon; m. Maria de Lourdes Saraiva De Menezes 1959; one s. one d.; Asst to Public Prosecutor 1963–68; Public Prosecutor, Court of Appeal, Lisbon 1962–72; Chef du Cabinet to Minister of Justice 1972–73; Deputy Attorney-Gen. 1974–79; Dir Office of European Law 1980–86; fmr Judge, Court of Justice of European Union and Pres. Third and Sixth Chambers; Judge, Supreme Court of Portugal 2000–11; Croix de Guerre, Ordre du Mérite (Luxembourg), Ordem de Merito (Portugal). *Publications:* Le contrat d'assurance dans le droit portugais et comparé, La publicité mensongère, Droit communautaire, ordre juridique communautaire, Les libertés fondamentales dans la CEE, Contrato de Seguro, Estudos. *Leisure interests:* swimming, gardening. *Address:* Vivenda Panorama, Av. do Monaco, 2675 Estoril, Portugal (home). *Telephone:* (21) 3218900 (office); (21) 4682997 (home). *Fax:* (21) 4647999 (home). *E-mail:* jcmoitinho@mail.telepac.pt (home).

MOKHOSI, Tšeliso Seth; Lesotho business executive and politician; b. 4 July 1955, Linotšing, Leribe Dist; ed South African Inst. of Marketing Man., Business School in the Netherlands, Bradford Univ., UK; Nurse Asst, S African coal mines 1976–80; worked at Dept of Statistics for six months in 1981; fmr Marketing Man. and Publicity Officer, Basotho Hat Co.; fmr Deputy Dir, Business Advisory and Promotion Services, Maseru; fmr CEO, Deputy Dir and Officer, Basotho Enterprise and Devt Corpn; commercial farmer (propr of pig farm), Leribe, also propr of various food industry businesses; mem. Nat. Ass. (Parl.) (Lesotho Congress for Democracy); Minister of Communications, Science and Tech. 2012–13, Minister of Energy, Meteorology and Water Affairs 2013–15, Minister of Defence and Nat. Security 2015–17.

MOKHTAR, Gamal el-Din, BBA, BSc; Egyptian institute director and academic; *President, Arab Academy for Science, Technology and Maritime Transport;* b. 29 Oct. 1928; one s. one d.; ed Marine Acad., Alexandria, American Univ. of Cairo; apptd Gen. Marine Insp. 1969; fmr Dir Arab Maritime Transport Acad.; Guest Prof. Univ. of Alexandria 1978, mem. Bd 1987; fmr Chair. Egyptian Antiquities Org.; currently Pres. Arab Acad. for Science, Tech. and Maritime Transport, Alexandria; Chair., Int. Asscn Maritime Univs. 2003; mem. Bd PAN ARAB Shipping Co. 1973, Federal Arab Maritime Company 1976, Misr Shipping Company 1983; Visiting Prof., Alexandria Univ. 1978, mem. Bd of trustees 1987; mem. Royal Automobile Club. *Publications include:* Cairo: The Site and the History (co-author) 1988, Alexandria: The Site and the History (co-author) 1993, Sinai: The Site and the History (co-author) 1998. *Address:* Arab Academy for Science, Technology and Maritime Transport, PO Box 1029 (office); 66, El Horreya Street, Flat 907, Alexandria, Egypt (home). *Telephone:* (3) 5565429 (office). *Fax:* (3) 5622525 (office). *E-mail:* info@aast.edu (office). *Website:* www.aast.edu (office).

MOLCHANOV, Vladimir Kyrillovich; Russian journalist and TV presenter; b. 7 Oct. 1950, Moscow; s. of Kyrill Molchanov; m. Consuella Segura; one d.; ed Moscow State Univ.; with Press Agency Novosti 1973–86; observer, USSR State Cttee for TV and Radio 1987–91; Artistic Dir studio of independent co. REN-TV 1991–, Observer, Reuter-TV 1994–; regular appearances in his own TV programmes Before and After Midnight 1987–93, Before and After, Panorama, Longer than Age 2000; academician, Acad. of Russian TV; Corresp. mem. Acad. of Natural Sciences; Order of Honor 2011; Prize of Journalists Union as Best TV Journalist 1990 and other awards. *Publications include:* TV films: Remembrance, I, You, He and She, People and Years, Zone, I Still Have More Addresses, Tied with One Chain, August of 1991 (screenplays), Retribution Must Come (M. Gorky Prize 1982). *Leisure interest:* life in the country.

MOLDAZHANOVA, Gulzhan, MBA; Russian business executive; *CEO, Basic Element;* ed Kazakh State Univ., Lomonosov Moscow State Univ., Finance Acad. of Govt of Russian Fed., Antwerp Univ., Belgium; sr man. at Sibirsky Aluminium (Sibal, later renamed Basic Element—Basel) 1995–2000, Dir Sales and Marketing, Russian Aluminium Co. (RUSAL) 2000–02, Dir for Strategy and Corp. Devt 2002–04, mem. Bd of Dirs and Man. Dir Aluminium Business, Basic Element Co. (RUSAL's major shareholder) 2004–06, CEO Basic Element 2005–09, 2012–; CEO ESN Corpn 2009–11. *Address:* Basic Element, Moscow 123022, 30 ul. Rochdelskaya, Russia (office). *Telephone:* (495) 720-50-25 (office). *Fax:* (495) 720-53-95 (office). *E-mail:* info@basicelement.ru (office). *Website:* www.basicelement.ru (office).

MOLEFE, Popo Simon; South African politician; *Founder, Popo Molefe Foundation;* b. 26 April 1952, Sophiatown; m. 1st Olympia Molefe (divorced); three c.; m. 2nd Boitumelo Plaatje 1991 (divorced 2003); ed Naledi High School; microfilm machine operator, photographic printing machine operator 1976–78; mem. SASM 1973–76; mem. Black Peoples' Convention 1974, 1977; First Chair. Azanian People's Org. (AZAPO), Soweto Br. 1979–81; mem. Gen. and Allied Workers Union 1980–83; Sec. Transvaal Region, United Democratic Front 1983, Nat. Gen. Sec. 1983–91; mem. Nat. Exec. Cttee African Nat. Congress (ANC) 1991–; charged with treason and murder after detention in 1985, convicted at Delmas Treason Trial, sentenced to ten years' imprisonment after being held in custody for four years 1988, released 1989; Vice-Chair. ANC PWV Region 1990–94; Premier NW Prov. Govt 1994–2004; Chair. ANC Nat. Elections Comm. 1992–94, ANC Alexandra Br. 1990; Sec. Nat. Organizing Comm. of ANC; fmr Chancellor North-West Univ.; Chair. Morvest Group Ltd 2004–, Armscor Precision, Inc. 2004–, Infrasors Holdings Ltd –2011, Protea Technologies Ltd; currently Founder and Exec. Chair. Lereko Investments (Pty) Ltd; Chair. Passenger Rail Services of South Africa; Founder, Popo Molefe Foundation; mem. Bd of Dir eXtract Group Ltd. Petroleum 2008–10, Petroleum, Oil and Gas Corpn of South Africa (Pty) Ltd 2004–, Eqstra Holdings Ltd, Anooraq Resources Corpn (also Advisor 2004–, Co-Chair. 2005–) 2004–, Imperial Holdings Ltd 2005–08, SEF (Pty) Ltd, WCW Construction (Pty) Ltd, CEF Group of Companies (Pty) Ltd, Mbane Power (Pty) Ltd, Tedcor Group (Pty) Ltd. *Address:* Private Bag X2018, Mmabatho 8681, South Africa. *Telephone:* (11) 268-0755 (office). *E-mail:* info@popomolefefoundation.co.za (office). *Website:* www.popomolefefoundation.co.za (office).

MOLEKANE, Rapulane Sydney; South African politician and diplomatist; *Ambassador to France;* b. 7 May 1961, Soweto; s. of Moraole Molekane and Mabese Molekane; m. Brenda Molekane; ed Soweto Coll. of Educ., Foreign Inst.; served in first democratically elected Parl. 1994, Chair. Parl. Portfolio Cttee on Safety and Security; joined the then Dept of Foreign Affairs 1999, appointments as Consul-Gen. in Munich, Dept of Int. Relations and Co-operation 1999–2003, High Commr to Ghana 2004–08, Deputy Dir-Gen. in charge of Europe 2010–15, Amb. to France and Perm. Del. to UNESCO, Paris 2015–. *Address:* South African Embassy, 59 quai d'Orsay, 75343 Paris Cedex 07, France (office). *Telephone:* 1-53-59-23-23 (office). *Fax:* 1-45-50-23-68 (office). *E-mail:* molekaner@dirco.gov.za (office); info@afriquesud.net (office). *Website:* www.afriquesud.net (office).

MOLELEKI, Monyane, MA; Lesotho politician; *Deputy Prime Minister and Minister of Parliamentary Affairs;* b. 5 Jan. 1951, Mohlaka-oa-Tuka, Maseru Dist; m.; one s. two d.; ed Nazareth Primary School, Christ the King High School, Moscow State Univ.; Head Teacher, St Thomas Secondary School 1972–73; reporter and sub-ed., The Echo newspaper 1973–74; news reader, reporter and sub-ed., Radio Lesotho 1974–75; Extension Educator, Media Section, Inst. of Extra Mural Studies (IEMS), Nat. Univ. of Lesotho 1983–87, Admin. 1985–86; Public Relations Man. Lesotho Highlands Devt Authority (LHDA) 1988–91; Minister of Natural Resources 1993–94, 1998–2004, 2007–12, of Information and Broadcasting 1996–98, of Foreign Affairs 2004–07, of Police 2015–16, of Parl. Affairs 2017–, Deputy Prime Minister 2017–; mem. Parl. for Senqunyane Constituency 1993, later for Machache No. 38 Constituency 1998, 2007–; Leader of Opposition in National Assembly 2012–14; Co-founder and Pres. Matela Multi-Purpose Co-Operative 1973–75; mem. Maseru Beautification Cttee 1984–91, Matlama Football Club Cttee 1984–91 (fmr Sec.-Gen.); fmr mem. Lesotho Congress for Democracy (LCD); Deputy Leader Democratic Congress 2015–16; Leader Alliance of Democrats 2017–. *Leisure interests:* classical music, sports, reading. *Website:* www.gov.ls (office).

MOLERO BELLAVIA, Adm. Diego Alfredo, BA, MA; Venezuelan army officer and government official; b. 12 Jan. 1960, Coro; ed Naval School of Venezuela, Central Univ. of Venezuela; performed duties as Chief of Intelligence Div. of the Security Unit Command; served in Honour Guard Regt of the Mil. 1989; Commdr Coast Guard Station School, Los Roques 1993–99; Commdr HQ of the Navy 1999–2007; Dir Basic School of the Bolivarian Nat. Armed Forces from 2007; Commdr Strategic Region of Integral Defence –2012; Minister of Defence 2012–13; Amb. to Brazil 2013–14, to Peru 2014–17; Military Order of General-in-Chief Rafael Urdaneta, Third Class, Second Class, Order Francisco de Miranda, Third Class, Officer, Order of the Liberator; Medalla Naval Almirante Luis Brión, UN Medal.

MOLI, Kalvau; Ni-Vanuatu politician; fmr Vanuatu Corresp., Radio New Zealand Int.; fmr CEO Northern Islands Stevedoring Co. Ltd; elected MP for Luganville (Ind.) 2012–16; Minister of Agric., Livestock, Forestry, Fisheries and Biosecurity 2012, Minister of Foreign Affairs, Int. Co-operation and External Trade 2015; fmr Nat. Treas., Union of Moderate Parties; f. Hope Party.

MOLIGA, Lolo Letalu Matalasi, BA, MPA; American Samoan politician, state governor, business executive and fmr educator; *Governor of American Samoa;* b. Ta'u, American Samoa; s. of High Chief Moliga Sa'ena Auauna Moliga, and Soali'i Galea'i; ed Samoana High School, Manu'a High School, Chadron State Coll., Neb. and San Diego State Univ., Calif., USA; began career as teacher, later elementary school prin. before becoming Prin. of Manu'a High School in Manu'a Islands; later elementary and secondary educ. admin. within American Samoan Dept of Educ.; fmr Dir ASG Budget Office, as well as American Samoa's Chief Procurement Officer for two terms; Owner of construction firm; elected to American Samoa House of Reps for four terms; later Senator within American Samoa Senate, Senate Pres.; Pres. Devt Bank of American Samoa 2009–12; Gov. of American Samoa 2013–; Ind. *Address:* Office of the Governor, Executive Office Building, Third Floor, Utulei, Pago Pago, AS 96799, American Samoa (office). *Telephone:* (684) 633-4116 (office). *Fax:* (684) 633-2269 (office). *E-mail:* tupitosoliai@americansamoa.gov (office). *Website:* americansamoa.gov (office).

MOLIN, Yuri Nikolaevich; Russian chemist and physicist; *Advisor, Russian Academy of Sciences;* b. 3 Feb. 1934, USSR; s. of N. N. Molin and A. F. Kuramova; m. 1st N. G. Molina 1965; two d.; m. 2nd G. E. Iakovleva 2005; ed Moscow Inst. of Physics and Tech.; worked in USSR Acad. of Sciences Inst. of Chemical Physics 1957–59, various posts in USSR (now Russian) Acad. of Sciences Inst. of Chem. Kinetics and Combustion 1959–67, Dir 1971–93, Head of Lab. 1993–2004, Advisor 2004–; teacher in Univ. of Novosibirsk 1966–, Head of Dept 1973–95, Prof. 1974–; Ed.-in-Chief, Russian Journal of Structure Chemistry 1978–88; mem. USSR (now Russian) Acad. of Sciences 1986–97, Council Russian Foundation for Basic Research, Moscow 1996; Fellow, Int. Electron Paramagnetic Resonance Soc. 1998; Lenin Prize 1986, Mendeleev Lecturer 1992, N.N. Semenov Golden Medal, Russian Acad. of Sciences 2006. *Publications:* Spin Exchange 1980, Spin Polarization and Magnetic Effects in Radical Reactions 1984, Infrared Photochemistry 1985. *Leisure interest:* mountain walking. *Address:* Institute of Chemical Kinetics and Combustion, Novosibirsk 630090, Russia (office). *Telephone:* (383) 333-16-07 (office); (383) 330-25-21 (home). *Fax:* (383) 330-73-50 (office). *E-mail:* molin@kinetics.nsc.ru (office). *Website:* www.kinetics.nsc.ru (office).

MOLINA, Alfred; British actor; b. 24 May 1953, London; m. Jill Gascoigne; ed Guildhall School of Music and Drama; on stage has appeared with RSC and at Nat. Theatre, Royal Court Theatre, Donmar Warehouse, Minskoff Theater, Broadway. *Films include:* Indiana Jones and the Raiders of the Lost Ark 1981, Anyone for Denis 1982, Number One 1984, Eleni 1985, Ladyhawke 1985, A Letter to Brezhnev 1985, Prick Up Your Ears 1987, Manifesto 1988, Not Without My Daughter 1991,

American Friends 1991, Enchanted April 1991, When Pigs Fly 1993, The Trial 1993, American Friends 1993, White Fang 2: Myth of the White Wolf 1994, Maverick 1994, Hideaway 1995, The Perez Family 1995, A Night of Love 1995, The Steal, Species 1995, Before and After 1996, Dead Man 1996, Scorpion Spring 1996, Mojave Moon 1996, Anna Karenina 1997, The Odd Couple II 1997, Boogie Nights 1997, The Man Who Knew Too Little 1997, The Imposters 1998, Magnolia 1999, Dudley Do-Right 1999, The Trial 2000, Chocolat 2000, Texas Rangers 2001, Agatha Christie's Murder on the Orient Express 2001, Pete's Meteor 2002, Road to Perdition 2002, Frida 2003, My Life Without Me 2003, Coffee and Cigarettes 2003, Spider-Man II 2004, Steamboy 2004, Sian Ka'an (voice) 2005, The Da Vinci Code 2006, As You Like It 2006, The Hoax 2006, Orchids 2006, The Moon and the Stars 2007, Silk 2007, The Ten Commandments 2007, Nothing Like the Holidays 2008, The Lodger 2009, Prince of Persia: The Sands of Time 2010, The Tempest 2010, The Forger 2012, The Truth About Emanuel 2013, Love Is Strange 2014, Swelter 2014. *Television includes:* The Losers (series) 1978, El C.I.D. (series) 1990–91, Ladies Man (series) 1999–2001, Bram and Alice (series) 2002, The Company (mini-series) 2007, Law & Order: LA (series) 2010–11, Roger & Val Have Just Got In (series) 2010–12, Monday Mornings (series) 2013, Matador (series) 2014, Penn Zero: Part-Time Hero (series) 2014–15, The Normal Heart (film) 2014. *Website:* www.alfred-molina.com (office).

MOLINA, Mario J., PhD; American/Mexican chemist and academic; *Professor of Chemistry, University of California, San Diego;* b. (José Mario Molina), 19 March 1943, Mexico City, Mexico; s. of Roberto Molina-Pasquel and Leonor Henriquez; m. Guadalupe Alvarez; one c.; ed Acad. Hispano Mexicana, Univ. Nacional Autónoma de Mexico (UNAM), Univ. of Freiburg and Univ. of California, Berkeley; Asst Prof., UNAM 1967–68; Research Assoc., Univ. of California, Berkeley 1972–73; Research Assoc., Univ. of California, Irvine 1973–75, Asst Prof. 1975–79, Assoc. Prof. 1979–82; Sr Research Scientist, Jet Propulsion Lab., Calif. 1983–89; Prof., Dept of Earth, Atmospheric and Planetary Sciences and Dept of Chem., MIT 1989–97, Inst. Prof. 1997–2003; Prof., Dept of Chem. and Biochemistry, Univ. of California, San Diego 2003–; Pres. Centro Mario Molina; mem. NAS, Inst. of Medicine; 40 hon. degrees; Max Planck Research Award 1994–96, UNEP Ozone Award 1995, Nobel Prize in Chem. 1995, Volvo Environment Prize 2004; many other awards and distinctions. *Publications:* numerous book chapters and articles in scientific journals. *Leisure interests:* music, reading, tennis. *Address:* University of California, San Diego, UHA 3050E, 9500 Gilman Drive #0356, La Jolla, CA 92093-0356 (office); 3535 Lebon Drive, Apt 2210, San Diego, CA 92122, USA (home). *Telephone:* (858) 534-1696 (office). *Fax:* (858) 534-1697 (office). *E-mail:* mjmolina@ucsd.edu (office). *Website:* www-chem.ucsd.edu/faculty/profiles/molina_mario_j.html (office); www.centromariomolina.org (office).

MOLINA BARRAZA, Col Arturo Armando; Salvadorean army officer and fmr head of state; b. 6 Aug. 1927, San Salvador; s. of Mariano Molina and Matilde Barraza de Molina; m. María Elena Contreras de Molina; four s. one d.; ed Instituto Nacional Gen. Francisco Menéndez, Escuela Militar, El Salvador, Escuela Superior de Guerra, Mexico, Escuela de Infanteria, Spain; Section and Co. Commdr, Escuela Militar; Artillery Garrison, Asst Dir Escuela de Armas, Section and Dept Chief, Staff HQ; Del. 6th Conf. of American Armed Forces, Peru 1965, 7th Conf. Buenos Aires; Gen. Co-ordinator, 2nd and 3rd Confs of Defence Council of Cen. American States; Dir Exec. Comm. for Shipping; Dir Nat. Cttee of Caritas, El Salvador; Pres. of El Salvador 1972–77; went into self-imposed exile, returning to El Salvador 1992.

MOLINA CONTRERAS, Gen. Jorge Alberto; Salvadorean army officer and politician; Del. to UN Conf. to Review Progress made in Implementation of Programme of Action to Prevent, Combat and Eradicate the Illicit Trade in Small Arms and Light Weapons in All Its Aspects, New York 2006; fmr Jt Chief of Staff of the Armed Forces; Minister of Nat. Defence 2008–09; rank of Brig.-Gen. 2005, Maj.-Gen. 2006, Gen. 2007.

MOLINA SÁNCHEZ, César Antonio, LicenDer; Spanish writer and politician; b. 14 Sept. 1952, La Coruña; fmr Prof. of Literary Theory and Criticism, Complutense Univ., Prof. of Humanities and Journalism, Univ. Carlos III; worked for Cambio 16 (magazine) and Diario 16 (newspaper) 1985–96, becoming Deputy Dir; Man. Dir Círculo de Bellas Artes 1996–2004; Dir Cervantes Inst. 2004–07; Minister of Culture 2007–09; Deputy (Spanish Socialist Workers' Party–PSOE) for A Coruña 2008–09; Partner, Cremades & Calvo Sotelo 2017–; Grand Cross, Orden Española de Carlos III 2009, Orden de Bernardo O'Higgins (Chile) 2009; Ferrol el III Premio Letras de Bretaña 2008. *Publications include:* Épica 1974, Proyecto preliminar para una arqueología de campo (poetry) 1978, Últimas horas en Lisca Blanca 1979, La estancia saqueada (poetry) 1983, La revista Alfar y la prensa literaria de su época (1920–1930) 1984, Antología de la poesía Gallega contemporánea 1984, Gobierno de un jardín 1986, Derivas 1987, El fin de Finisterre 1988, Prensa literaria en Galicia (1809–1920) 1989, Prensa literaria en Galicia (1920–1960) 1989, Medio siglo de Prensa literaria española (1900–1950) 1990, Sobre el iberismo y otros escritos de literatura portuguesa 1990, Las ruinas del mundo 1991, El fin de Finisterre 1992, Para no ir a parte alguna 1994, Sobre la inutilidad de la poesía 1995, Nostalgia de la nada perdida; ensayo sobre narrativa contemporánea 1996, Vivir sin ser visto 2000, A fin de Fisterra (poetry) 2001, A Coruña, agua y luz 2001, Olas en la noche 2001, Regresar a donde no estuvimos 2003, Viaje a la Costa da morte 2003, En el mar de Ánforas 2005, En honor de Hermes 2005, Fuga del amor 2005, El rumor del tiempo 2006, Custode delle antiche forme (poetry) 2007, Eume 2007, Esperando a los años que no vuelven 2007, Lugares donde se calma el dolor 2009, Cielo azar 2011, Donde la eternidad envejece 2012, La caza de los intelectuales 2014, Zhivago 2015, La poesía es un error necesario 2014, Todo se arregla caminando 2016, Vieja cima 2017, Calmas de enero 2017.

MOLINAROLI, Alex, BS, MBA; American business executive; *Chairman, President and CEO, Johnson Controls Inc.;* ed Univ. of South Carolina, Kellogg School of Man., Northwestern Univ.; joined Johnson Controls Inc. 1983, Vice-Pres. and Gen. Man., North America Systems & Middle East Controls 2004–07, Pres. Power Solutions 2007–13, Pres. and CEO 2013–, Chair. 2015–; mem. Bd of Dirs, Interstate Batteries; mem. Bd of Regents, Milwaukee School of Eng, Bd of Dirs, Nat. Center for the Arts and Tech.; Founding mem. Electrification Coalition. *Address:* Johnson Controls Inc., 5757 North Green Bay Avenue, Milwaukee, WI 53209, USA (office). *Telephone:* (414) 524-1200 (office). *Fax:* (414) 524-2077 (office). *E-mail:* info@johnsoncontrols.com (office). *Website:* www.johnsoncontrols.com (office).

MOLISA, Sela; Ni-Vanuatu politician and diplomatist; b. 15 Dec. 1952, Santo; s. of Mandei Rongtuhun and Ruth Rongtuhun; two s. one d.; ed Onesua High School, Malaba Coll., Efate, Univ. of the S Pacific, Fiji, Fifi School of Medicine; banker 1974–77; Gen. Man. Co-operative Fed. 1977–81; elected mem. Parl. 1982; Minister of Internal Affairs 1983, of Foreign Affairs 1983–87, of Finance 1987–91, 2002–04 (resgnd), 2008–10, of Trade, Commerce and Industry 1996, of Finance and Econ. Man. 1998–99, of Lands and Natural Resources 2001–02; Amb. to People's Republic of China 2014–15; apptd Govt Special Rep. to negotiate with rebels during attempted secession of Santo from Vanuatu 1980; involved in design and implementation of Vanuatu Comprehensive Reform Programme 1997–; mem. Vanua'aku Pati. *Leisure interests:* reading, swimming, listening to music, watching sports.

MÖLK, Ulrich, DPhil; German academic; *Professor Emeritus of Romance Literature, Akademie der Wissenschaften, University of Göttingen;* b. 29 March 1937, Hamburg; s. of Heinrich Mölk and Berta Mölk; m. Renate Mölk 1962; ed Univs of Hamburg and Heidelberg; Prof. of Romance Literature, Univ. of Giessen 1967; apptd Prof. of Romance Literature, Akad. der Wissenschaften, Univ. of Göttingen 1974, currently Prof. Emer., Dir Inst. für Lateinische und Romanische Philologie des Mittelalters 1974–2005; mem. Acad. of Göttingen, Vice-Pres. 1990–92, Pres. 1992–94. *Publications:* Berol. Tristan und Isolde. Klassische texte des Romanischen Mittelalters in zweisprachigen ausgaben 1962, Guiraut Riquier, Las cansos 1962, Trobar clus 1968, Répertoire métrique de la poésie lyrique française 1972, Trotzki, Literaturkritik 1973, Trobadorlyrik: Eine Einführung (Artemis Einführungen) 1982, Flaubert, Une Nuit de Don Juan, Edition 1984, Vita und Kult des hl. Metro von Verona 1987, Lohier et Malart 1988, Romanische Frauenlieder 1989, Die europäische Bedeutungsgeschichte von 'Motiv' 1992, Julien Sorel vor dem Schwurgericht 1994, Impressionistischer Stil 1995, Literatur und Recht 1996, Europäische Jahrhundertwende 1999, Albéric: le poème d'Alexandre 2000, Das älteste französische Kreuzlied 2001, Prousts Venedig 2002, Estetismo e decadentismo 2004. *Address:* Akademie der Wissenschaften, Theaterstrasse 7, 37073 Göttingen (office); Seminar für Romanische Philologie der Universität Göttingen, Humboldtstr. 19 37073 Göttingen (office); Höltystr. 7, 37085 Göttingen, Germany (home). *Telephone:* (551) 395331 (office). *Fax:* (551) 395365 (office). *E-mail:* umoelk@gwdg.de (office). *Website:* www.uni-goettingen.de/de/60123.html (office).

MOLLER, Gordon Desmond, ONZM, DipArch, FNZIA, PPNZIA; New Zealand architect; *Director, Moller Architects;* b. 26 July 1940, Hastings; s. of Oscar Carl Moller and Winifred Daisy Moller; m. Sylvia Anne Liebezeit 1962; one s. two d.; ed Wellington Coll., Hutt Valley High School, Univ. of Auckland; Dir Craig Craig Moller architectural practice 1969–2002, Moller Architects 2003–; Ed. New Zealand Architect Magazine 1976–83; Chair. Arts Marketing Bd, Aotearoa 1994, 1995, Site Safe NZ 2002, 2003, Construction Information Ltd 2006; Pres. Wellington Architectural Centre 1972, 1973; Professorial Teaching Fellow, Victoria Univ. School of Architecture 1990, 1991; Pres. NZ Inst. of Architects 2003–06; Co-convenor Auckland City Urban Design Panel 2003–10; mem. Design Consortium Wellington Civic Centre 1992, 1998, NZ Registered Architects Bd 2006–08, Tech. Advisory Group, Waterfront, Auckland; Chair. Auckland Theatre Co. 2011–; Chair. Judging Panel NZ Govt Starter Home Design Competition 2008–09; Trustee, Wellington City Gallery Foundation 1998–2006; mem. NZ Architectural Publications Trust 2003–; Hon. mem. Royal Australian Inst. of Architects; Officer, NZ Order of Merit 2006; Hon. DLitt (Victoria Univ. of Wellington) 2006; NZ Inst. of Architects Gold Medal 2006, 60 design awards 1970–2007. *Designs include:* School of Architecture, Wellington 1994, Sky Tower, Auckland 1994–97, numerous houses 1969–, Macau Tower and Entertainment Centre, Macau 1999–2001, Point Apartments, Auckland 2000, New Galleries, Te Papa, Wellington 2001, Viaduct Point Apartments, Auckland 2002, Sky City Conf. Centre 2002, Sky City Grand Hotel 2003, 67-storey Elliott Tower Project, Auckland 2006, new Houses of Parl., Muscat, Oman 2008–12, Viaduct Events Centre, Auckland Waterfront 2009–11, 30-storey commercial office bldg, Shortland Street Project, Auckland 2009, Hihiaua Cultural Centre, Whangarei 2009–11, various projects for Sky City and Auckland Waterfront 2011–. *Leisure interests:* photography, music, motoring, landscape gardening, design, travel, visual and performing arts. *Address:* Suite 6.01 Ironbank 150 Karangahape Road, Auckland, New Zealand (office). *Telephone:* (9) 357-0686 (office); (9) 357-1140 (office); (21) 241-9237 (office). *Fax:* (9) 357-0689 (office). *E-mail:* gordon@mollerarchitects.com (office). *Website:* www.mollerarchitects.com (office).

MØLLER, Michael, BA, MA; Danish diplomatist and UN official; *Director-General, United Nations, Geneva;* b. 1952, Copenhagen; ed Univ. of Sussex, UK, Johns Hopkins Univ., USA; joined UN 1979, served as Programme Officer, Legal Officer, Asst to Dir Div. of Int. Protection, and Asst Regional Rep., Office of UNHCR 1979–84, Political Adviser to UN Mil. Inspection Team in Iran 1985, Inter-Agency Affairs Officer and Special Asst to Asst Sec.-Gen., Office for Secr. Services for Econ. and Social Matters 1985–87, Head of Sub-Office for Southern Mexico, Office of UNHCR 1987–88, Special Asst to Asst Sec.-Gen., Centre Against Apartheid, Dept for Political and Security Council Affairs 1988–92, Special Asst to Asst Sec.-Gen., Dept of Political Affairs (DPA) 1992, Deputy Dir Americas Div., DPA 1992–93, Head of UN Component in Jt UN/OAS Int. Civilian Mission to Haiti (MICIVIH) 1993, Head of Office of Special Adviser to Sec.-Gen. 1994–95, Sr Political Adviser to Dir-Gen. UN Office, Geneva (UNOG) 1995–97, Special Asst to Under-Sec.-Gen. for Political Affairs, UN Secr. 1997–2001, Dir for Political, Peacekeeping and Humanitarian Affairs, Exec. Office of Sec.-Gen. 2001–05, Acting Deputy Chef de Cabinet to Sec.-Gen. March 2005, Special Rep. for Cyprus and Head of UN Peacekeeping Operation in Cyprus (UNFICYP) 2005–08; Exec. Dir Kofi Annan Foundation 2008–11; Acting Dir-Gen. UN Office at Geneva (UNOG) 2013–15, Dir-Gen. 2015–; Acting Exec. Sec. of UN ECE 2014; Sec.-Gen. Conf. on Disarmament 2015–. *Address:* Office of the Director-General, United Nations Office at Geneva, Palais des Nations, Avenue de la Paix 8–14, 1211 Geneva 10, Switzerland (office). *Telephone:* 229172100 (office). *Fax:* 229170002 (office). *E-mail:* protocol@unog.ch (office). *Website:* www.unog.ch (office).

MØLLER, Per Stig, MA, PhD; Danish politician; b. 1942; s. of Poul Møller and Lis Møller; ed Univ. of Copenhagen; Lecturer, Sorbonne Univ., Paris 1974–76;

Cultural Ed. Radio Denmark 1973–74, Deputy Head, Culture and Soc. Dept 1976–79, Chief of Programmes 1979–84; Vice-Chair. Radio Council 1985–86, Chair. 1986–87; Commentator, Berlingske Tidende 1984–2001; Chair. Popular Educ. Asscn (FOF) 1983–89; mem. Parl. (Danish Conservative Party) 1984–, mem. Exec. Cttee 1985–89, 1993–98, Chair. 1997–98, Parl. Leader 1997–98, Foreign Policy Spokesman 1998–2001; mem. Council of Europe 1987–90, 1994–97, 1998–2001; Minister for the Environment 1990–93; Chair. Security Policy Cttee 1994–96, mem. Foreign Policy Cttee 1994–2001; Minister for Foreign Affairs 2001–10, of Culture 2010–11; Nat. Chair. Union of Conservative Gymnasium Students 1960–61, Vice-Chair. Conservative Students' Asscn 1961–62, Pres. Students' Union; Chevalier, Ordre Nat. du Lion 1975, Chevalier des Arts et des Lettres 1986, Grosskreuz des Verdienstordens der Bundesrepublik Deutschland 2002, Commdr (First Class), Order of the Dannebrog 2002, Commdr, Ordre Nat. du Benin 2003, Grand-Croix, Ordre de la Couronne de Chêne (Belgium) 2003, Order of Stara Planina (First Class) 2006, Commdr Grand Cross, Royal Order of the Polar Star (Sweden) 2007, Grand Cross, Order of the South Cross (Brazil) 2007, Grand Cross and Commdr, Order for Merits to Lithuania 2007, Grand Cross, Order of the Phoenix (Greece) 2009, Order of the Cross of Terra Mariana (1st Class) 2011; Sound and Environment Award 1993, Georg Brandes Award 1996, Einer Hansen Research Fund Award 1997, G-1930s Politician of the Year 1997, Cultural Award of the Popular Educ. Asscn 1998, Raoul Wallenberg Medal 1998, Kaj Munk Award 2001, Rosenkjaer Award 2001, Robert Schumann Medal 2003, Nersornaat Medal of Merit in Gold 2005. *Publications include:* La Critique dramatique et littéraire de Malte-Brun 1971, Erotismen 1973, København-Paris (trans.) 1973, På Sporet af det forsvundne Menneske 1976, Livet I Gøgereden 1978, Fra Tid til Anden 1979, Tro, Håb og Faellesskab 1980, Midt I Redeligheden 1981, Orwells Håb og Frygt 1983, Nat uden Daggry 1985, Mulighedernes Samfund 1985, Stemmer fra Øst 1987, Historien om Estland, Letland og Litauen 1990, Kurs mod Katastrofer? 1993, Miljøproblemer 1995, Den naturlige Orden: Tolv år der flyttede Verden 1996, Spor: Udvalgte Skrifter om det åbne Samfund og dets Vaerdier 1997, Magt og Afmagt 1999, Munk 2000, Mere Munk 2003. *Address:* Folketinget, Palace of Christiansborg, 1240 Copenhagen K, Denmark.

MØLLER, Stig, LLM; Danish fmr university administrator; b. 29 Aug. 1939; ed Univ. of Copenhagen; Capt. of the Reserve 1963; Sec. Ministry of the Interior 1966–71, Ministry of Pollution Reduction 1971–73; Tutor in Admin. Law, Univ. of Copenhagen 1968–71; Teacher of Public Law, School of Admin 1968–79; Acting Head of Office, Dept of the Environment 1974–76, Head of Office 1976–79; Dir of Admin, Univ. of Aarhus 1979–2007; mem. Man. Group for Co-operation of Nordic Univ. Dirs of Admin (Chair. 1982–88) 1979–2000; mem. Bd of Dirs Ejendomsselskab AS, Aarhus Univ. Research Foundation. *Address:* c/o University of Aarhus, Nordre Ringgade 1, 8000 Århus C, Denmark. *E-mail:* au@au.dk.

MOLLOY, Patrick J.; Irish business executive; b. 4 Jan. 1938; m. Ann Lynch; three s. two d.; ed Trinity Coll., Dublin, Harvard Business School, USA; Asst Gen. Man. Bank of Ireland 1975–78, Gen. Man. Area East 1978–83, Man. Dir 1983–91, Group CEO 1991–98; Dir (non-exec.) CRH plc 1997–2007, Chair. 2000–07; Chair. Blackrock Clinic, Enterprise Ireland –2009; mem. Bd of Dirs Waterford Wedgwood plc; Pro-Chancellor Trinity Coll. Dublin 2008–13; Chair. Trinity Foundation; Hon. LLD (Trinity Coll. Dublin) 1999. *Leisure interests:* fishing, shooting.

MÖLLRING, Hartmut; German politician and business executive; b. 31 Dec. 1951, Groß Ilsede, Kreis Peine; m.; three c.; ed Scharnhorstgymnasium, Hildesheim, studied law in Marburg and Göttingen; with Bundeswehr for two years; worked as trainee judge and prosecutor; mem. CDU and Junge Union 1972–, Chair. CDU Dist of Hildesheim; Councillor, City of Hildesheim 1974–2003, Chair. CDU Council Faction 1981–2003; budget officer and spokesperson, Ministry of Justice 1984–90; mem. Lower Saxony State Parl. 1990–, apptd Vice-Chair. CDU Parl. group, responsible for finance, economy, environment, leisure and tourism, spas, marinas and boat rides 1998; Minister of Finance, Lower Saxony 2003–13, Minister of Science and Economy 2013–16; Chair. Supervisory Bd Norddeutsche Landesbank (NORD/LB) 2005–13; mem. Bd Bremer Landesbank, Deutsche Messe AG, German Bundesrat, Kreditanstalt für Wiederaufbau; mem. Advisory Bd Deutsche Bundesbank; Chair. Tarifgemeinschaft deutscher Länder 2003; Pres. Eintracht Hildesheim sports club.

MOLNÁR, Gyula; Hungarian chemical engineer and politician; *Chairman, Magyar Szocialista Párt (Hungarian Socialist Party);* b. 17 Aug. 1961, Budapest; s. of Gyula Molnár and Elizabeth Horvath; m. Rose Bóta 1989; two s.; ed Than Károl Chemical High School, Univ. of Moscow, USSR; worked as a technician for a year; later worked as a product devt engineer for Hungarian Silk Industry Co., and then for TricoInvest Kft., where he became Dir; co-f. and organized Left Youth Asscn 1988; mem. Municipal Ass. 1992–2010; mem. Magyar Szocialista Párt (Hungarian Socialist Party), Chair. 2016–; mem. Parl. 1994–2010; Mayor of XI dist (Újbuda) of Budapest 2002–10. *Address:* 1066 Budapest, Jókai u. 6, Hungary (office). *Telephone:* (1) 459-7200 (office). *E-mail:* info@mszp.hu (office). *Website:* www.mszp.hu (office).

MOLNÁR, József; Hungarian business executive; *Group CEO, MOL Group;* held various man. positions at BorsodChem Plc 1978–2001, Head of Pricing Dept 1982–87, Head of Controlling Dept 1987–91, Chief Financial Officer and first Deputy to CEO 1991–2001; CEO TVK (part of MOL Group) 2001–03, Group Planning and Controlling Dir, MOL Group 2003–04, Group Chief Financial Officer 2004–11, Group CEO 2011–, mem. Bd of Dirs TVK 2001–11, Slovnaft a.s. 2004–08, mem. Supervisory Bd INA 2010–, FGSZ 2011–, mem. Sustainable Devt Cttee 2013–. *Address:* MOL Hungarian Oil and Gas Plc, 1117 Budapest, Október huszonharmadika u. 18, Hungary (office). *Telephone:* (1) 209-0000 (office). *E-mail:* info@mol.hu (office). *Website:* www.mol.hu (office).

MOLNÁR, Ľudovít, Dr rer. nat, DrSc; Slovak computer scientist and fmr university administrator; *Dean, Faculty of Informatics and Information Technologies, Slovak Technical University;* b. 11 Oct. 1940, Komjatice Dist; m.; three c.; ed Comenius Univ., Bratislava; various teaching positions, Slovak Tech. Univ., Bratislava 1962–, Assoc. Prof. 1978–91, Prof. 1991–, Rector 2000–03, Co-founder and first Dean, Faculty of Informatics and Information Technologies; research periods in UK 1969–70, 1991, USSR 1974, Italy 1978, Cyprus 1983; mem. Asscn for Computing Machinery, IEEE Computer Soc.; IT Personality of the Year 2012. *Publications include:* numerous computer tech. manuals and textbooks; about 100 scientific papers in journals and proceedings of conferences at home and abroad. *Leisure interest:* literature. *Address:* Room 4.32, Faculty of Informatics and Information Technologies, Slovak University of Technology, Vazovova 5, 812 43 Bratislava 16, Slovakia (office). *Telephone:* (2) 21022432 (office). *E-mail:* ludovit.molnar@stuba.sk (office); molnar@fiit.stuba.sk (office); molnar@is.stuba.sk (office). *Website:* www.fiit.stuba.sk (office).

MOLNAR, Peter, AB, PhD; American geologist and academic; *Professor of Geological Sciences, University of Colorado;* ed Oberlin Coll., Columbia Univ.; taught at and carried out research at Scripps Inst. of Oceanography, MIT and at Univ. of Oxford, UK (amongst other insts); Prof. of Geological Sciences, Univ. of Colorado 2001–, Fellow, Co-operative Inst. for Research in Environmental Sciences 2001; Crafoord Prize in Geosciences, Royal Swedish Acad. of Sciences 2014. *Publications:* numerous papers in professional journals on the interactions between geodynamics, geomorphology and long-term climate change. *Address:* Geological Sciences, University of Colorado Boulder, UCB 399, Boulder, CO 80309-0399 (office); Room ESCI 462C, Co-operative Institute for Research in Environmental Science, University of Colorado Boulder, 216 UCB, Boulder, CO 80309-0216, USA (office). *Telephone:* (303) 492-4936 (office). *Fax:* (303) 492-2606 (office). *E-mail:* peter.molnar@colorado.edu (office); molnar@cires.colorado.edu (office). *Website:* www.colorado.edu/GeolSci (office); cires.colorado.edu (office).

MOLONEY, Thomas Walter, BA, MA, MBA, MPH; American academic, organization official and consultant; *Managing Partner, Futures Inc.;* b. 8 Feb. 1946, New York, NY; s. of Thomas Walter Moloney and Anne Heney; ed Colgate Univ., Columbia Univ.; Program Dir Nat. Center for the Deaf-Blind, New York 1971–72; Special Asst to Dir and Dean, Cornell Univ. Medical Center 1973–74; Asst Vice-Pres. Robert Wood John Foundation 1975–80; Visiting Lecturer, Princeton Univ. 1975–80; Sr Vice-Pres., The Commonwealth Fund, New York 1980–92; Dir of Public Policy and Health Programmes, Inst. for the Future 1992–99; Man. Partner, Futures Inc. (consulting firm) 1997–; mem. Bd Dirs, New England Medical Center, Boston 1982–89; mem. Bd, Grantmakers in Health, New York 1984–, Chair. 1984–88; Policy Scholar Eisenhower Center, Columbia Univ., New York 1992–, Inst. of Health Policy Studies, Univ. of California, San Francisco 1992–; mem. Nat. Bd of Medical Examiners 1986–90, Health Advisory Cttee, Gen. Accounting Office, Washington, DC 1987–; Bd, Foundation Health Services Research, Washington, DC 1989 and other bds; Fellow, American Acad. of Arts and Sciences; mem. Inst. of Medicine, NAS. *Publications:* New Approaches to the Medicaid Crisis (ed.) 1983; numerous articles. *Address:* Futures Inc., 4819 Emperor Blvd, Suite 305, Durham, NC 27703 (office); 72 Norwood Avenue, Upper Montclair, NJ 07043, USA. *Telephone:* (919) 474-8500 (office). *E-mail:* info@futuresinc.com (office). *Website:* www.futuresinc.com (office).

MOLONEY, Tom; British publishing executive; *Director, Talent and Transformation, Informa PLC;* b. 1962; joined Emap PLC 1981, apptd Group Man. Dir Emap Metro and Elan 1989, Chief Exec. Consumer Magazines UK 1995–99, oversaw launch of magazines Heat, More, Q and Empire, mem. Exec. Bd 1995–2007, COO then Pres. and CEO Emap USA 1999–2001, Group COO 2001–03, CEO 2003–07; CEO Dr Foster Intelligence 2008–11; Pnr The Inzito Partnership 2013–14; Chair. Pharmaceutical Press Ltd 2013–; Dir Talent and Transformation, Informa PLC 2014–. *Address:* Informa PLC, 5 Howick Place, London, SW1P 1WG, England (office). *Telephone:* (20) 7017-5000 (office). *E-mail:* headoffice@informa.com (office). *Website:* www.informa.com (office).

MOLSON, Eric H., AB; Canadian brewing industry executive; b. 16 Sept. 1937, Montreal, PQ; s. of Thomas H. P. Molson and Celia F. Cantlie; m. Jane Mitchell 1966; three c.; ed Selwyn House School, Montreal, Bishop's Coll. School, Lennoxville, Le Rosey, Switzerland, Princeton and McGill Univs and US Brewers' Acad. New York; served as apprentice brewer with Molson Breweries of Canada Ltd, rising through various appointments to Pres., Chair. Molson Inc. (now Molson Coors Brewing Co.) 1988–2008, Vice-Chair. 2008–09 (retd). *Address:* Molson Coors Brewing Co., 1555 Notre Dame Street East, Montreal, PQ H2L 2R5, Canada (office). *Telephone:* (514) 521-1786 (office). *Fax:* (514) 598-6866 (office). *Website:* www.molsoncoors.com (office).

MOLTERER, Wilhelm, MSc; Austrian politician; b. 14 May 1955, Steyr; s. of Johann Kletzmayr and Anna Kletzmayr, Josef Molterer and Cäcilia Molterer (adoptive parents); m. Brigitte Molterer; two c.; ed Fed. Agricultural Coll., St Florian and Johannes Kepler Univ., Linz; Research Asst Dept of Agric. Policy, Univ. of Linz 1979–81; Head Econ. Policy Div., Austrian Farmers Fed. 1981–84, Dir 1989–93; Municipal Councillor, Sierning 1985–87; Sec. Office of Fed. Minister Dr. Josef Riegler 1987–89; mem. Nat. Council 1990–94; Sec.-Gen. Austria People's Party (ÖAP) 1993–94, Parl. Group Leader 2003–07, Chair. 2007–08; Fed. Minister of Agric. and Forestry 1994–2003 (and Environment and Water Man. 2000–03), of Finance 2007–08, Vice-Chancellor of Austria 2007–08. *Address:* Austrian People's Party, Lichtenfelsgasse 7, 1010 Vienna, Austria (office). *Telephone:* (1) 401-26-0 (office). *Fax:* (1) 401-26-10-9 (office). *E-mail:* email@oevp.at (office). *Website:* www.oevp.at (office).

MOLTMANN, Jürgen, DTheol; German theologian and academic; *Professor Emeritus of Systematic Theology, University of Tübingen;* b. 8 April 1926, Hamburg; m. Dr. Elisabeth Moltmann-Wendel 1952; four d.; POW during World War II 1945–48; pastor, Evangelical Church, Bremen-Wasserhorst 1952–57; Prof. and Rector Wuppertal Church Univ. 1958–63; mem. theological faculty, Univ. of Bonn 1963–67; Prof. of Systematic Theology, Univ. of Tübingen in 1967–94, now Prof. Emer.; Co-ed. Deutsch-Polnische Hefte 1959–68; Dir Evangelische Theologie 1971–89; Dir CONCILIUM 1979–94; Robert W. Woodruff Distinguished Visiting Professor of Systematic Theology, Candler School of Theology, Emory Univ., USA 1983–93; mem. WCC Faith and Order Cttee 1963–83; Dr hc (Duke Univ., Bethlehem Theological Seminary, Kalamazoo Coll., Raday Kolleg, Budapest, St Andrews Univ., Emory Univ., Univ. of Leuven, Univ. of Iasi, Nottingham Univ., Managua, Nicaragua, Chung Yuan Univ., Taiwan, Methodist Univ., São Paulo, Univ. Alba Iulia, Romania, Pretoria, South Africa); Italian Prize of Literature, Isle of Elba 1971, Gifford Lecturer, Univ. of Edinburgh 1984–85, Amos Comenius Medal, Bethlehem, Pa 1992, Ernst Bloch Prize of the City of Ludwigshafen 1995, Robert Boyle Medal 2011. *Publications include:* Christliche Petzel und das Calvinismus in Bremen 1958, Prädestination und Perseveranz 1961, Anfänge Dialektische Theologie 1963, Theologie der Hoffnung (Theology of Hope) (Isle of

Elba Literary Prize) 1964, Mensch 1971, Der gekreuzigte Gott (The Crucified God) 1972, Der Sprache der Befreiung 1972, Das Experiment Hoffnung 1974, Kirche in der Kraft des Geistes 1975, Zukunft der Schöpfung 1977, Trinität und Reich Gottes 1980, Gott in der Schöpfung (God in Creation) 1985, Das Weg Jesu Christi (The Way of Jesus Christ) 1989, Der Geist des Lebens (The Spirit of Life) 1991, Das Kommen Gottes (The Coming of God) (Grawemeyer Religion Award) 1995, The Source of Life 1997, Experiences in Theology 1999, Science and Wisdom 2002, In the End – the Beginning: The Life of Hope 2004, Sun of Righteousness, Arise! 2010, Ethics of Hope 2012, Jürgen Moltmann: Collected Readings 2014, The Living God and the Fullness of Life 2015. *Address:* Theologicum, Universität Tübingen, Liebermeister Strasse 12–18, 72076 Tübingen (office); Biesinger Strasse 25, 72070 Tübingen, Germany (home). *Telephone:* (7071) 41673 (home).

MOLYVIATIS, Petros; Greek diplomatist and politician; b. 12 June 1928, Lesvos; m. Niovi Christaki; one d. one s.; ed Univ. of Athens; Gen. Sec. Presidency of the Repub. 1980–85, 1990–95, fmr Diplomatic Adviser to the Pres.; mem. Parl. (Nea Demokratia—New Democracy) 1996–2004, fmr mem. Standing Cttees on Defence, Foreign Affairs, European Affairs; fmr mem. Greek dels to UN, NATO; fmr Amb.; Minister of Foreign Affairs 2004–06, May–June 2012, Aug.–Sept. 2015; Pres. Greek Fire Relief Fund 2007–; Chair., Bd of Trustees, Konstantinos G. Karamanlis Foundation. *Address:* Konstantinos G. Karamanlis Foundation, 6 Karaiskaki and Eleftheriou Venizelou Streets, Filothei, 152 37, Athens, Greece. *Website:* www.ikk .gr.

MOMEN, Abulkalam Abdul, BA (Hons), MA, LLB, MBA, MPA, PhD; Bangladeshi diplomatist, human rights activist, columnist and government official; *Minister of Foreign Affairs;* m. Selina Momen; two s. three d.; ed Univ. of Dhaka, Harvard Univ. (Ford Foundation and Mason Fellow), Northeastern Univ., Boston, USA; captured by Pakistani occupation army 1971; worked in Bangladesh govt service 1970s–80s, forcibly retired under Martial Order No. 9 (since declared null and void) for opposing mil. rule 1982; mem. Democratic Nat. Cttee late 1980s, worked as South Asia Adviser for Michael Dukakis US presidential campaign 1988, also worked for John Kerry US presidential campaign 2004; worked for MIT, Cambridge, Mass and the World Bank, Washington, DC for two years; fmr Chair. Business Admin and Econs Dept, Framingham State Coll., USA; Faculty mem., Merrimack Coll., USA, Salem State Coll., USA, Northeastern Univ., USA, Univ. of Massachusetts, USA, Cambridge Coll., USA, Kennedy School of Govt, USA; US Expert (Econ. Adviser) under Saudi Arabian Ministry of Finance and Nat. Economy, Riyadh –2003; Amb. and Perm. Rep. to UN, New York 2009–15; Pres. UNICEF Exec. Bd 2009–11; apptd Facilitator for the UN Counter-Terrorism Strategy Review 2010; apptd Chair. Least Developed Country 2009, Second Cttee of UN Gen. Ass. 2012, Peacebuilding Comm. 2012; Vice-Pres. UN Econ. and Social Council 2011–12; Chair. Sub-cttee Kennedy School of Govt New England Alumni Council; Ministry of Foreign Affairs 2019–; fmr Pres. Women and Children International, Inc., Boston, Foundation for Eye Hosp., Bangladesh, Bangladesh Asscn of New England, Boston; Dir, American Anti-Slavery Org.; mem. Amnesty International; Life mem. Bangladesh Econ. Asscn; Co-chair. Cttee for Democratic Bangladesh (USA) 1986–90; started movt to end trafficking of women and children early 1990s; launched campaign to have a SAARC Resolution and a SAARC Fund for the victims and to create public awareness of trafficking; testified before US Congress and US Labor Dept in 1993, 1994, 1995 and 1996 to end Asian slave trade, sexual exploitation, sexual mutilation of young girls, child labour; organized movt for restoration of multi-party democracy in Bangladesh; developed an admin. and political man. programme known as TGS to achieve accelerated devt of Bangladesh and developing countries; Home Town Hero, Eagle Tribune, Humanitarian Award, North America Bangladesh Medical Asscn, Friend of the Poor, Probani, Inc. of New York, Mukto-Gaaner Paki, Marupalash, Saudi Arabia, Our Pride citation, The Bangladesh-America Foundation, Inc., Washington, DC 2004, Gentleman of the Year Award, American Women Empowerment 2007. *Publications:* two books and more than 250 papers and articles in professional journals and elsewhere. *Address:* Ministry of Foreign Affairs, Segunbagicha, Dhaka 1000, Bangladesh (office). *Telephone:* (2) 9556020 (office). *Fax:* (2) 9562188 (office). *E-mail:* info@mofabd.org (office). *Website:* www.mofa.gov.bd (office).

MOMIS, John; Papua New Guinea politician; *President of Bougainville;* b. Salamaua; m. Elizabeth Momis; ed St Brendan's Coll., Queensland, Australia; ordained as Roman Catholic priest 1970, served as priest 1970–93; mem. Papua New Guinea (PNG) House of Ass. for N Solomons (now Bougainville) 1972–99, Deputy Leader of the Opposition 1985–87, 1987–88, 1994, Chair. Constitutional Planning Cttee 1972–75 (co-writer PNG Constitution); fmr Minister for Decentralization, Deputy Prime Minister and Minister for Public Service 1985, Minister for Provincial Affairs 1988–92, Shadow Minister for Bougainville Affairs 1992, Shadow Minister for Provincial Affairs 1993, Minister of Information and Communication 1994; Gov. of Bougainville 1999–2005; unsuccessful cand. in presidential election 2005; Amb. to People's Repub. of China –2010; co-f. Melanesian Alliance Party; mem. New Bougainville Party, Leader 2010–; Pres. of Bougainville 2010–. *Address:* Office of the President, Bougainville, Papua New Guinea (office).

MOMOTARO, Dennis P., BA; Marshall Islands business executive and politician; b. 26 Oct. 1954, Majuro; m. Daisy Momotaro; two s. two d.; ed Rockhurst Coll., Kansas City, Mo., USA; began career with Majuro Stevedoring and Terminal Co. 1969–73; teacher, Head Start Program, Majuro 1973; janitor, 9th Street Nursing Home, Kansas City 1977–78; worked in Mailing Dept, Federal Reserve Bank, Kansas City 1978–80; Asst Man., Momotaro Corpn, Majuro 1980–91, Gen. Man. 1991–2007; mem. Nitijela (Parl.) for Mejit 2007–; Minister of Transportation and Communication 2008, of Finance 2012–14 (resgnd); fmr mem. Bd of Dirs of various businesses and orgs including Nat. Telecommunication Authority 1996–97, Marshall Islands Devt Authority 1997–2003, Marshall Islands Devt Bank 1999–2007, Majuro Stevedoring and Terminal Co. 2003–07. *Leisure interests:* fishing, tennis, baseball, basketball, volleyball, music. *Address:* c/o Ministry of Finance, PO Box P, Majuro, MH 96960, Marshall Islands. *E-mail:* secfin@ntamar.net.

MOMPER, Walter; German politician; b. 21 Feb. 1945, Sulingen; mem. Berlin Chamber of Deputies 1975–95, 1999–; party whip, SPD, Berlin 1985–89, Chair. –1992; Gov. Mayor of Berlin 1989–91; Vice-Pres. Lower House, Berlin 1999–2001, Pres. 2001–11.

MONAGENG, Sanji Mmasenono, LLB; Botswana judge; *Judge, Appeals Division, International Criminal Court;* b. 9 Aug. 1950, Serowe; m.; one s. one d.; ed Univ. of Botswana, Court Adm. Course, RIPA International, London, UK, Int. Criminal Law Course, Grotius Centre for Int. Law Studies, Leiden Univ., The Hague, Netherlands, Int. Commercial Arbitration; magistrate 1987–97; CEO and Exec. Sec. Law Soc. of Botswana 1997–2006; Judge of High Court of Repub. of The Gambia, under Commonwealth Fund for Tech. Co-operation Programme 2006–08; Judge of High Court of Kingdom of Swaziland 2008–; mem. and Commr African Comm. on Human and Peoples' Rights 2003–, Chair. 2007–09; Judge, Appeals Div., Int. Criminal Court, The Hague, Netherlands 2009–, First Vice-Pres., ICC 2012–15; secondment as Deputy Chief Adjudication Officer to UN Observer Mission to S Africa, Johannesburg March–May 1994, to Law Soc. of Zimbabwe Feb.–March 1998, to Law Soc. of England and Wales, London, UK Jan.–March 2005; Residency at Brandies Univ., Boston, USA Sept. 2005; Chair. Ethics, Law and Human Rights sector of Nat. AIDS Council in Botswana; sat on numerous bds, including Nat. Broadcasting Bd of Botswana, Open Soc. Initiative of Southern Africa, Human Rights Trust of Southern Africa; Co-founder Transparency International (Botswana Chapter), Dirs Inst. of Botswana; Commr, Int. Comm. of Jurists; mem. Int. Bar Asscn, Int. Soc. for the Reform of Criminal Law, Int. Asscn of Women Judges, Emang Basadi Women's Org., Women in Law and Devt in Africa (WILDAF), Media Inst. of Southern Africa (Botswana Chapter), Commonwealth Magistrates and Judges Asscn; Trustee, Southern Africa Litigation Centre; African Human Rights Consortium Award, Gaborone. *Publications:* Purpose of Sentencing, Role of Women in Promoting Peace. *Leisure interests:* farming, reading, walking.

MONCADA, Sir Salvador Enrique, Kt, MD, PhD, DSc, FRS, FRCP, FMedSci; British academic, physician and scientist; *Academic Lead, Manchester Cancer Research Centre, University of Manchester;* b. 3 Dec. 1944, Tegucigalpa, Honduras; s. of Salvador Moncada and Jenny Seidner; m. 1st 1966; one s. (deceased) one d.; m. 2nd HRH Princess Esmeralda of Belgium 1998; one s. one d.; ed Univ. of El Salvador; Assoc. Prof. of Pharmacology and Physiology, Univ. of Honduras 1974–75; Section Leader, Wellcome Research Laboratories, Beckenham, Kent 1975–77, Head of Prostaglandin Research 1977–84, Dir of Therapeutic Research 1984–86, Dir of Research 1986–95; Dir Wolfson Inst. for Biomedical Research, Univ. Coll. London 1996–2011, Prof. Emer. 2013–; Founding Dir Centro Nacional de Investigaciones Cardiovasculares (CNIC) Madrid 1999–2004; Prof. of Experimental Biology and Therapeutics 2011–13; Prof. of Translational Medicine and Strategic Adviser, Inst. of Human Devt, Univ. of Manchester 2013–, Dir, Institute of Cancer Sciences 2014–, Academic Lead (Cancer Domain), Manchester Cancer Research Centre 2016–; Foreign mem. NAS 1994; Hon. mem. Asscn of Physicians of GB and Ireland 1997, American Soc. of Hematology 1999, Soc. for Endocrinology 2005, Finnish Pharmacological Soc. 2008, Physiological Soc., London 2010; Hon. DMed (Universidad Complutense de Madrid) 1986, (Antwerp) 1997, Academico de Honor de la Real Academia Nacional de Medicina 1993; Hon. DSc (Sussex) 1994, (Mount Sinai School of Medicine New York), (Nottingham) 1995, (Univ. Pierre and Marie Curie, Paris) 1997, (Edin.) 2000; Dr hc, (Salamanca) 2000, (Montréal) 2002, (Liège) 2006, (Charles Univ., Prague) 2008, (Aarhus) 2008, (Buenos Aires) 2013; Prince of Asturias Prize for Science and Tech. 1990, Amsterdam Prize for Medicine 1992, First Roussel Uclaf Prize, Royal Medal 1994, Louis and Artur Lucian Award 1997, Galen Medal in Therapeutics, Dale Medal, Gold Medal of the Spanish Soc. of Cardiology 1999, Gold Medal of the Royal Soc. of Medicine 2000, Le Grand Prix Annuel Lefoulon-Delalande, Institut de France 2002, Croonian Lecturer, Royal Soc., London 2005, Dohme Lecturer, The Johns Hopkins Univ. School of Medicine, Baltimore 2010, Ernst Jung Gold Medal 2013. *Publications:* Nitric Oxide from L-Arginine: A Bioregulatory System (co-ed.) 1990, The Biology of Nitric Oxide (Vols 1–7) 1992–2000; more than 500 peer-reviewed papers and highly-cited review. *Leisure interests:* theatre, literature, music, walking, diving. *Address:* Manchester Cancer Research Centre, University of Manchester, 555 Wilmslow Road, Manchester, M20 4GJ, England (office). *Telephone:* (161) 306-0800 (office). *E-mail:* crc@manchester.ac.uk (office). *Website:* www.mcrc.manchester.ac.uk (office).

MONCADA ACOSTA, Samuel, DPhil; Venezuelan academic, politician and diplomatist; b. 13 June 1959, Caracas; m. Nelci Marin de Moncada; ed Universidad Cen. de Venezuela, Caracas, Venezuelan Mil. Acad., Caracas, Boston Coll., USA, St Anthony's Coll., Oxford, UK; Prof., Faculty of Mil. History, Venezuelan Mil. Acad. 1982–84, Head of Faculty of Polemology 1984–87; Assoc. mem. St Anthony's Coll., Univ. of Oxford 1990; Prof. of MBA Programme in History of America, Faculty of Humanities and Educ., Post-grad. Section, Universidad Cen. de Venezuela 1996, Prof. of PhD Programme in Political Sciences, Faculty of Political and Admin. Sciences, Post-grad. Studies Section 1997, Head of Faculty of History of America, Faculty of Humanities and Educ., School of History 1994, Head of Dept of History Theory and Practice 1998, Dir School of History 1999–2004; Head of Div. of Int. Affairs for electoral campaign of Pres. Hugo Rafael Chavez for the Referendum 2004; Minister of Higher Educ. 2004–07; Amb. to UK (also accred to Ireland) 2007–13; Amb. and Perm. Rep. to UN 2013–15, 2017, Deputy Perm. Rep. 2016–17; Vice-Minister for Europe 2016–17, for North America Feb.–June 2017; Amb. to OAS March–June 2017; Minister of Foreign Affairs June–Aug. 2017; lecturer at several nat. and int. univs in Latin America, N America and Europe; mem. Commando Maisanta; Order of the First Class Gen. Francisco de Miranda 2007; Dr hc (Univ. of Yacambu) 2005; Magister Honoris (Inst. of Higher Studies of the Nat. Defence—IAEDEN) 2005. *Radio:* producer of programme Combates por la Historia (Battles for History), Station YVKE 2002–. *Publications:* Partidos Políticos y Sindicatos en Venezuela (1936–1950) (co-author) 1982, Los Huevos de la Serpiente (Fedecámaras por dentro) 1984, Organizaciones Empresariales. Diccionario Histórico de Venezuela 1988, Momentos Decisivos en la Historia de la Asamblea Nacional. Poder Legislativo: Pasado, Presente y Futuro 2000, Vigencia del Pensamiento Bolivariano 2003, Las Relaciones Internacionales de la Revolución Bolivariana 2004, Las inmigraciones en Venezuela durante el siglo XX y la Redefinición de la Identidad Nacional 2005, Historia del Racismo en Venezuela 2005, Los Problemas de la Democracia en el siglo XX Venezolano 2006; numerous articles in Venezuelan and Latin American newspapers and magazines. *Address:* Permanent Mission of Venezuela to United Nations, 335 East 46th Street, New York, NY 10017, USA (office). *Telephone:* (212) 557-2055 (office). *Fax:* (212) 557-3528 (office). *E-mail:* misionvenezuelaonu@gmail.com (office).

MONCAYO GALLEGOS, Gen. Paco Rosendo, MSc, PhD; Ecuadorean army officer (retd) and politician; b. 8 Oct. 1940; s. of Francisco Altamirano and Prof. Aida Gallegos Garcia; m. Martha Miño de Moncayo; four c.; ed Universidad Cen. del Ecuador, Colegio Militar 'Eloy Alfaro', Inter-American Defense Coll.; fmr Pres. of Rumiñahui Bank; mil. positions held include Mil., Naval and Air Attaché in Israel, Co-ordinator of Ministry of Agric., Exec. Dir Austro Reconstruction Centre (during mil. govt), Head of Cabinet of Ministry of Nat. Defence, Chief of Army Operations, Chief of Jt Command of the Armed Forces, Chief of Staff of the Army, Gen. Commdr of the Army, Chief of Jt Command of the Armed Forces, Army Gen. of the Army of Ecuador, C-in-C of the Armed Forces, involved in Alto Cenepa War between Ecuador and Peru; fmr Head of the Ministry of Agric.; Nat. Deputy 1998–2000, Rep. for Pichincha Prov. under Alianza Libertad 2009–13, mem. Nat. Security Council and its Consultative Ass. for Foreign Affairs; Mayor of Quito (Izquierda Democrática—Party of the Democratic Left) 2000–09; cand. in presidential election 2017; fmr Co-Pres. United Cities and Local Govts; mem. Acad. of Ecuadorian History; Lecturer in Geopolitics and Int. Law, Universidad Cen. del Ecuador; Decoration of Abdon Calderón, First Class (twice), Award Winners Tarqui in Degree of Commdr, Honour Mil. Cross, Grand Cross of Mil. Honour, Armed Forces Medal, Third Class, Armed Forces Medal, Second Class, Armed Forces Medal, First Class, Mil. Cross of Honour (Brazil), Mil. Cross (Argentina), Medal of Mil. Merit (Chile), Col Bologniesi Award (Peru), Order of Mil. Merit Carabobo (Venezuela), Legion of Merit, Degree of Commdr (USA), Grand Collar of the Navy (Ecuador), War Merit Cross in the Great Cross (by Ecuadorian victory in Upper Cenepa), award for professional excellence granted by Congress, Decoration of War Acad. of Ecuador, Grand Collar of Mil. Honour; Simón Bolívar Medal, UNESCO 2004. *Address:* c/o Alcaldía de Quito, Quito, Ecuador.

MONDALE, Walter Frederick, LLB; American lawyer, diplomatist and fmr politician; *Senior Counsel, Dorsey and Whitney LLP;* b. 5 Jan. 1928, Ceylon, Minn.; s. of Rev. and Mrs Theodore Sigvaard Mondale; m. Joan Adams 1955; two s. one d.; ed Minnesota public schools, Macalester Coll., Univ. of Minnesota and Univ. of Minnesota Law School; admitted to Minn. Bar 1956, pvt. practice 1956–60; Attorney-Gen. of Minn. 1960–64; Senator from Minnesota 1964–77; Vice-Pres. of the US 1977–81, mem. Nat. Security Council 1977–81; unsuccessful Democratic Party cand. for US President 1984; Counsel, Winston and Strawn (law firm) 1981–87; Pnr, Dorsey and Whitney LLP (law firm) 1987–93, now Sr Counsel and Pnr, Int./Corp. Practice Group; Amb. to Japan 1993–96; Norway's Hon. Consul-Gen. in Minneapolis 2008–; mem. Exec. Cttee Nobel Peace Prize Forum; fmr mem. Bd of Dirs Control Data, Columbia Pictures; fmr Regent, Smithsonian Inst.; mem. Democrat-Farm Labor Party. *Publications:* The Accountability of Power: Towards a Responsible Presidency 1975, The Good Fight: A Life in Liberal Politics 2010. *Leisure interest:* fishing. *Address:* Dorsey and Whitney LLP, Suite 1500, 50 South Sixth Street, Minneapolis, MN 55402-1498, USA (office). *Telephone:* (612) 340-6307 (office). *Fax:* (952) 516-5673 (office). *E-mail:* mondale.walter@dorsey.com (office). *Website:* www.dorsey.com (office).

MONDJO, Charles Richard; Republic of the Congo army officer and politician; *Minister at the Presidency, responsible for National Defence;* b. 28 Jan. 1954, Brazzaville; s. of Nicolas Mondjo and Marguerite Konongo; m.; four c.; ed Prora Mil. Training Base, GDR, military school in USSR; mem. Congolese Armed Forces, Head of Section, First Co., First Bn, Makola Training Centre 1979–80, Commdr 1980, Chief of Staff, 15th Bn, Mechanized Infantry, Pointe-Noire 1981–82, Chief of Staff, First Armoured Regt, Brazzaville 1986–87, Dir of Studies, Marien Ngouabi Mil. Acad., Brazzaville 1987–93, Commdr, Mil. Zone I 1997–2002, Chief of Staff of Congolese Armed Forces 2002–12; Minister at the Presidency for Defence 2012–. *Address:* Office of the Minister at the Presidency, Brazzaville, Republic of Congo (office). *Telephone:* 22-281-22-31 (office).

MONDLANE, Agostinho Salvador, BEcons; Mozambican economist and politician; *Minister of the Sea, Inland Waters and Fisheries;* b. 21 Nov. 1959, Maputo; s. of Salvador Mondlane and Beatriz Rieza Alberto Nhaca; three c.; ed Eduardo Mondlane Univ., Univ. of London, UK; Prof., Commercial Inst. of Maputo 1982–83; Lecturer, Faculty of Econs, Eduardo Mondlane Univ. 1984; joined Ministry of Construction and Water 1988, Dir Urban Rehabilitation Project Implementation Unit –1990, Deputy Minister of Construction and Water 1990–94, of Public Works 1994–2000, of Defence 2007–14, Minister of Defence 2014–15, Minister of the Sea, Inland Waters and Fisheries 2015–; mem. Frente de Libertação de Moçambique (Frelimo). *Address:* Ministry of the Sea, Inland Waters and Fisheries, Maputo, Mozambique (office).

MONDRAGÓN DE VILLAR, María Elena, MEconSc; Honduran economist and fmr central banker; ed Univ. Nacional Autónoma de Honduras, Memphis State Univ., USA; 22 years with Banco Central de Honduras, various positions in Econs Dept, becoming Asst to Presidency, Pres. 2002–06, 2010–14; Dir of Econs and Finance, Foundation for Promotion of Democracy and Social Welfare (FUNDEMOS) –2010; fmr Dir of Integration and Trade Policy, Ministry of Economy and Trade; Founding mem. National Identity Foundation; fmr Exec. Sec., later Pres., Foundation for Educ. Ricardo Ernesto Maduro Andreu; fmr Dir of Finance, Grupo Atlántida; fmr Project Man., Fundación Democracia y Desarrollo de Honduras. *Address:* c/o Banco Central de Honduras, Avda Juan Ramón Molina, 7a Avda y 1a Calle, Apdo 3165, Tegucigalpa, Honduras (office).

MONEO, José Rafael, DArch; Spanish architect and academic; *Josep Lluis Sert Professor in Architecture, Emeritus, Harvard University;* b. 9 May 1937, Tudela, Navarra; s. of Rafael Moneo and Teresa Vallés; m. Belén Feduchi 1963; three d.; ed Madrid Univ. School of Architecture; Fellow, Acad. in Rome, Italy 1963–65; Asst Prof. Madrid School of Architecture 1966–70; Prof., Barcelona School of Architecture 1970–80; Visiting Fellow, Inst. for Architecture and Urban Studies, Cooper Union School of Architecture, New York, USA 1976–77; Chair. Dept of Architecture Harvard Univ. Grad. School of Design, USA 1985–90, Josep Lluís Sert Prof. in Architecture 1992, now Emer.; mem. American Acad. of Arts and Sciences, Accad. di San Luca di Roma, Real Academia de Bellas Artes de San Fernando de España; Hon. FAIA, Hon. mem., American Acad. of Arts and Letters; Dr hc (Leuven) 1993; Premio di Roma 1962, Gold Medal for Achievement in Fine Arts, Govt of Spain 1992, Brunner Memorial Prize, American Acad. of Arts and Letters, Schock Prize in the Visual Arts 1993, Pritzker Award 1996, Int. Union of Architects Gold Medal 1996, Antonio Feltrinelli Prize 1998, RIBA Gold Medal 2003, Prince of Asturias Award 2012, Thomas Jefferson Foundation Medal in Architecture 2012, Nat. Spanish Architecture Prize 2015, Praemium Imperiale 2017. *Work includes:* Bankinter Bank, Madrid, Nat. Museum of Roman Art, Mérida, Thyssen Bornemisza Museum, San Pablo Airport, Seville, Manzana Diagonal, Barcelona, Davis Museum, Wellesley Coll., USA, City Hall Extension, Murcia 1998, Barcelona Concert Hall 1999, Kursaal Concert Hall, San Sebastian 1999, Audrey Jones Beck Building, Houston Museum of Fine Arts 2000, Cathedral of Our Lady of the Angels, Los Angeles, Calif., USA 2002, Chivite Winery, Arínzano, Navarra 2002, Arenberg Campus Library, Catholic Univ. of Louvain, Belgium 2002, Gen. and Royal Archive of Navarra, Pamplona 2003, Gregorio Marañón Mother's and Children's Hosp., Madrid 2003, Bank of Spain Extension, Madrid 2006, Contemporary Art Center of Aragon Beulas Foundation, Huesca 2004, Prado Museum Extension, Madrid 2007, Lab. for Integrated Science and Eng Bldg, Harvard Univ. 2007, Chace Center, Rhode Island School of Design 2008, Museum of the Roman Theater, Cartagena 2008, Library of Univ. of Deusto, Bilbao 2009, Lab. for Novartis Campus, Basel 2009, Commercial Center 'Aragoña', Zaragoza 2009. *Publications:* Theoretical Anxiety and Design Strategies in the Work of Eight Contemporary Architects 2004, Rafael Moneo: Remarks on 21 Works 2010. *Address:* Calle Cinca 5, 28002 Madrid, Spain (home). *Telephone:* (1) 564-2257 (office). *Fax:* (1) 563-5217 (office). *E-mail:* rmoneo@gsd.harvard.edu (office); contacto@rafaelmoneo.com. *Website:* www.gsd.harvard.edu (office); www.rafaelmoneo.com.

MONGELLA, Gertrude Ibengwé; Tanzanian international organization official; *Honorary Councillor, World Future Council;* b. 13 Sept. 1945, Ukerewe Island, Lake Victoria; m. Silvin Mongella; four c.; ed Univ. of Dar Es Salaam; fmr teacher; mem. Parl. 1980–93, 2000–10; Minister of State, Prime Minister's Office 1982–88, Minister of Lands, Tourism and Natural Resources 1985–87, Minister without Portfolio 1987–90; High Commr to India 1991–92; UN Asst Sec.-Gen. and Sec.-Gen., Fourth World Conf. on Women, Beijing 1993–95, UN Under-Sec. and Special Envoy to UN Sec.-Gen. on Women's Issues and Devt 1996–97; Sr Adviser to Exec. Sec. of Econ. Comm. for Africa (ECA) on Gender Issues 1997–; mem. Parl. for Ukerewe Constituency 2000–04; Pres. Pan African Parl. (consultative ass. of the African Union) 2004–08; Head of African Union's election monitoring team during Zimbabwe presidential election 2002; WHO Goodwill Amb. for Africa Region 2003–04; Chair. Int. Advisory Bd, African Press Org. 2008–; Hon. Councillor, World Future Council, Johannesburg; hon. degree from Ewha Womans Univ. 2005; Delta Prize for Global Understanding 2005, Guarini Inst. Global Leadership Award 2012. *Address:* World Future Council, The Court in Melville, 76 4th Avenue, Melville, Johannesburg 2109, South Africa (office). *Telephone:* (11) 7261113 (office). *Fax:* (11) 5455136 (office). *E-mail:* africa@worldfuturecouncil.org (office). *Website:* www.worldfuturecouncil.org (office).

MONGIN, Pierre; French government official; b. 9 Aug. 1954, Marseille; m. Danielle Charpin 1981; three c.; ed École Nationale d'Admin; Dir Office of the Prefect of Ain 1980; Sec.-Gen. Pref. of Ariège 1981; Chief of Staff, Prefect of Yvelines 1982–84; Insp., Nat. Police, in charge of Gen. Inspectorate of Admin 1984–86; Chief of Staff, Office of Yves Galland, Minister of Local Govt 1987–88; Deputy Dir of the Budget, Police HQ 1988–93; Chief of Staff to Prime Minister Edouard Balladur 1993–95; Prefect of Eure-et-Loir 1995–99, of Vaucluse 1999, of Auvergne region and of Puy de Dome dépt 2002–04; Chief of Staff of Minister of Interior 2004–05, of the Prime Minister 2005–06; CEO RATP (Paris transport authority) 2006–15; Chair. SYSTRA (eng firm specializing in urban and rail transport whose main shareholders are RATP and SNCF) 2010–; Deputy Gen. Man. Engie (fmrly GDF Suez) 2015.

MONI, Dipu, MBBS, MPH, LLB, LLM; Bangladeshi politician; d. of M. A. Wadud; m. Tawfique Nawaz; one s. one d.; ed Dhaka Medical Coll., Johns Hopkins Univ. School of Public Health, USA, Univ. of London, UK; mem. Bangladesh Awami League, Sec. for Women's Affairs –2009, mem. Sub-cttee on Foreign Affairs; mem. Jatiya Sangsad (Parl.) for Chadnpur-3 2008–13; Minister of Foreign Affairs 2009–13; one of two Master Trainers for Women Political Activists. *Address:* c/o Bangladesh Awami League, 23 Bangabandhu Avenue, Dhaka 1000, Bangladesh.

MONIÉ, Alain, MBA; French business executive; *CEO, Ingram Micro Inc.;* b. 1951; ed Ecole Nationale Supérieure d'Arts et Metiers, Institut Supérieur des Affaires, Jouy en Josas; began career in Mexico City as a civil construction engineer; held general man. positions with Sogitec Inc. (French aerospace simulation corpn); fmr controller for Renault; joined Allied Signals 1984, promoted from a regional sales man. to Head of Asia-Pacific operations, joined Honeywell through corpn's merger with Allied Signals Inc. 1999, Pres. Latin American Div. of Honeywell International 2001–03; Exec. Vice-Pres. Ingram Micro Inc. 2003–04, Pres. Asia-Pacific 2004–07, Pres. and COO Ingram Micro Inc. 2007–10, 2011–12, Pres. and CEO 2012–13, CEO 2013–; CEO APRIL Management Pte, Singapore 2010–11; mem. Bd of Dirs Amazon.com, Inc. *Address:* Ingram Micro Inc., 1600 East St Andrew Place, PO Box 25125, Santa Ana, CA 92799-5125, USA (office). *Telephone:* (714) 566-1000 (office). *E-mail:* info@ingrammicro.com (office). *Website:* www.ingrammicro.com (office).

MONIZ, Ernest Jeffrey, BS, PhD; American nuclear physicist, academic and government official; *Cecil and Ida Green Professor of Physics and Engineering Systems Emeritus and Special Advisor to the MIT President Massachusetts Institute of Technology;* b. 22 Dec. 1944, Fall River, Mass; s. of Ernest Perry Moniz and Georgina Moniz (née Pavao); m. Naomi Hoki; one d.; ed Boston Coll., Stanford Univ., Univ. of Pennsylvania; Prof. of Physics, MIT 1973–97, Dir, Bates Linear Accelerator Center 1983–91, Head of Dept of Physics 1991–95, 1997, Prof. of Physics and Eng Systems 2001–, also Cecil & Ida Green Distinguished Prof. and Dir MIT Energy Initiative, Dir Lab. for Energy and the Environment; Assoc. Dir for Science, Office of Science and Tech. Policy, Exec. Office of the Pres. 1995–97; Under-Sec., US Dept of Energy 1997–2001, Sec. of Energy 2013–17; Consultant, Los Alamos Nat. Lab. 1975–95; Dir American Science and Engineering, Inc. 1990–95, 2002–, ICF Int. Inc. 2011–; Sec. of Energy 2013–17; currently Cecil and Ida Green Professor of Physics and Engineering Systems Emer. and Special Advisor to the MIT President, MIT; mem. Pres.'s Council of Advisors on Science and Tech. 2009–13; Fellow, AAAS, American Physical Soc.; mem. Council on Foreign Relations. *Address:* Department of Physics, 4-304 Massachusetts Institute of Technology, 77 Massachusetts Avenue, Cambridge, MA 02139-4307 USA (office). *Telephone:* (617) 253-7515. *E-mail:* ejmoniz@mit.edu. *Website:* web.mit.edu.

MONJI, Kenjiro, LLB; Japanese diplomatist; b. 1952, Kitakyushu, Fukuoka Pref.; ed Tokyo Univ.; joined Ministry of Foreign Affairs (MFA) 1975, has worked overseas in France, Australia, Belgium, UK and in Perm. Mission to EU, Brussels, in charge of bilateral co-operation for nat. security 1990s and 2000s, Deputy Dir-Gen., Treaties Bureau and Dir-Gen. for Int. Affairs, Ministry of Defence –2007, Amb. to Iraq 2007–08, to Qatar 2010–13, to Canada (also accred to ICAO, Montreal) 2015–17, Dir-Gen. for Public Diplomacy, MFA 2008–10, Perm. Del. to UNESCO, Paris 2013–15; Sake Samurai, Japan Sake Brewers Asscn Junior Council 2008. *Leisure interests:* reading, listening to music, whistling, photography, visiting galleries and museums, eating, drinking.

MÖNKH-ORGIL, Tsendiin, LLB; Mongolian politician; b. 18 Oct. 1964, Sühbaatar prov.; ed Moscow Higher School of Int. Relations, Harvard Univ., USA; Attaché, Int. Orgs Dept, Ministry of Foreign Affairs 1988–91; Third, then Second Sec. for Political and Legal Affairs, Perm. Mission to UN, New York 1991–95; with int. law firm, Washington DC 1996; Dir-Gen. Mönh-Orgil, Idesh, Lynch 1997; Deputy Minister of Law and Internal Affairs 2000–04; Minister of Foreign Affairs 2004–06 (resgnd), 2016–17, of Justice and Home Affairs 2007–08; mem. Parl. (State Great Khural) 2008–12, 2016–17; Sec. People's Party of Mongolia 2012–13. *E-mail:* munkhorgil.tsend@gmail.com (home). *Website:* munkh-orgil.mn.

MONKS, Baron (Life Peer), cr. 2010, of Blackley in the County of Greater Manchester; **John Stephen Monks,** BA; British trade union official; b. 5 Aug. 1945, Manchester; s. of Charles Edward Monks and Bessie Evelyn Monks; m. Francine Jacqueline Schenk 1970; two s. one d.; ed Univ. of Nottingham; joined TUC Org. Dept 1969, Asst Sec. Employment and Manpower Section 1974, Head Org., Employment Law and Industrial Relations Dept 1977–87, Deputy Gen. Sec. 1987–93, Gen. Sec. 1993–2003; Sec.-Gen. European Trade Union Confed. (ETUC) 2003–11; mem. Council Advisory, Conciliation and Arbitration Service (ACAS) 1979–95; mem. British Govt and EU Competitiveness Councils 1997; Visiting Prof., School of Man., Manchester Business School 1996–; mem. (Labour), House of Lords 2010–; Trustee, People's History Museum 1988–2017, Chair. 2005–16; Chevalier, Légion d'honneur 2014; Dr hc (Nottingham, UMIST, Salford, Cranfield, Cardiff, Kingston, Southampton and Open Univs). *Leisure interests:* hiking, music, cycling. *Address:* House of Lords, Westminster, London, SW1A 0PW, England (office). *Telephone:* (20) 7219-6943 (office). *E-mail:* monksj@parliament.uk (office). *Website:* www.parliament.uk/biographies/lords/lord-monks/4186 (office).

MONSEF, Maryam, PC, BSc; Canadian community organizer and politician; *Minister of International Development;* b. 1985, Herat, Afghanistan; ed Trent Univ.; moved with family to Canada 1996; worked on community projects with several local orgs including Fleming Coll., Peterborough Econ. Devt, Community Foundation of Greater Peterborough; Admin. Asst, Trent Univ. 2007–10, Dir, Active Minds at Trent Univ. 2008–10; Immigration Portal Researcher, Welcome-Peterborough Jan.–April 2011; Outreach Coordinator, New Canadians Centre 2011–12; Outreach Coordinator, Community Foundation of Greater Peterborough 2012–13; unsuccessful cand. for Mayor of Peterborough 2014; mem. House of Commons (Parl.) for Peterborough–Kawartha 2015–; Minister of Democratic Insts 2015–17, of Status of Women 2017–, of Int. Devt 2019–; represented Peterborough at UN Comm. on the Status of Women, New York City 2013; mem. Liberal Party of Canada; co-recipient, YMCA Peace Medallion, Trent Univ. Young Leaders Award. *Address:* House of Commons, Ottawa, ON K1A 0A6 (office); PO Box 8097, Station T CSC Ottawa, ON K1G 3H6 Canada (office). *Telephone:* (613) 995-6411 (office); (613) 995-7835 (office). *Fax:* (613) 996-9800 (office); (819) 420-6906 (office). *E-mail:* Maryam.Monsef@parl.gc.ca (office); minister-ministre@swc-cfc.gc.ca (office). *Website:* www.canada.ca/en/government/ministers/maryam-monsef.html (office); maryammonsef.liberal.ca.

MONSENGWO PASINYA, HE Cardinal Laurent; Democratic Republic of the Congo ecclesiastic and academic; b. 7 Oct. 1939, Mongobele, Inongo; ed Seminary of Bokoro, Major Seminary of Kabwe, Pontifical Urbaniana Univ. and Pontifical Biblical Inst., Rome, Pontifical Biblical Inst., Jerusalem, Israel; ordained priest, Diocese of Inongo 1963; carried out pastoral work and served as faculty mem. at Theological Faculty of Kinshasa for several years; Sec.-Gen. Congolese Episcopal Conf. 1976–80, Pres. 1980, 1992; Auxiliary Bishop of Inongo 1980–81; Titular Bishop of Aquae Novae in Proconsulari 1980–; Auxiliary Bishop of Kisangani 1981–88, Metropolitan Archbishop of Kisangani 1988–2007; Archbishop of Kinshasa 2007–18, concurrently Primate, Democratic Repub. of Congo; cr. Cardinal (Cardinal-Priest of Santa Maria 'Regina Pacis' in Ostia mare) 2010; participated in Papal Conclave 2013; Co-Pres. Pax Christi International 2007–10; mem. Council of Cardinals 2013–18. *Address:* c/o Archeveche, Avenue de l'Universite, BP 8431, Kinshasa 1, Democratic Republic of the Congo (office).

MONSER, Edward L., BEng, BEduc; American business executive; *President, Emerson Electric Company;* ed Illinois Inst. of Tech., Eastern Michigan Univ., Exec. Educ. Program, Stanford Univ. Grad. School of Business; began career as sr engineer at Emerson's Rosemount div. 1981, served in several eng man. positions, Dir of Tech. 1987–89, apptd Dir of New Products and Tech. 1989, went on to hold Vice-Pres. positions before becoming Exec. Vice-Pres. and Gen. Man., Pres. Rosemount 1996–2001, COO Emerson Electric Co. 2001–15, Pres. 2010–; mem. Bd of Dirs, The Backstoppers, Inc., Air Products and Chemicals, Inc. 2013–; mem. Advisory Econ. Devt Bd for China's Guangdong Prov.; mem. Advisory Bd, South Ural State Univ., Chelyabinsk, Russia; Chair. Ranken Tech. Coll., Armour Coll. of Eng; Vice-Chair. Midwest Cargo Hub Comm.; mem. Bd of Trustees, Eisenhower Fellowships; Trustee, St Louis Science Center; mem. Bd of Overseers, Illinois Inst. of Tech.; mem. Bd and Vice-Chair. US-India Business Council; fmr mem. Bd and Vice-Chair. US-China Business Council. *Address:* Emerson Electric Co., 8000 West Florissant Avenue, PO Box 4100, St Louis, MO 63136, USA (office). *Telephone:* (314) 553-2000 (office). *E-mail:* info@emerson.com (office). *Website:* www.emerson.com (office).

MONSUR, Hussain, MSc, DSc; Bangladeshi geologist, academic and oil industry executive; b. 27 Jan. 1953, Kushabari, Sirajgonj; m. Rehana Akhtar; two d.; ed Rajshahi College, Moscow Geological Prospecting Institute, USSR, Free University of Brussels, Belgium, Kingston University, London; began career as lecturer, Dept of Geology, Univ. of Dhaka 1978, later becoming Prof., several other positions including Chair., Dept of Geology, Provost of Fazlul Haque Hall; Chair., Bangladesh Oil, Gas and Mineral Corpn (PETROBANGLA) (state-owned oil and gas exploration co.) 2001, 2009–14. *Publications:* An Introduction to the Quaternary Geology of Bangladesh, Quaternary ebong Bangladesher Bhutattik Kramabikash; 28 scientific papers published in various nat. and int. journals.

MONTAGNA, Gilberto Luis Humberto; Argentine civil engineer; b. 28 Jan. 1935; m.; four c.; ed Univ. of Buenos Aires; Sec. Chamber of Food Industrialists (CIPA) 1964–84, First Vice-Pres. 1984–94; Sec. Fed. of Food and Derivatives Industries (FIPAA) 1975–84, Pres. 1984–87; Sec. to Co-ordinator of Food and Derivates Industry (COPAL) 1975–79, Pres. 1979–88; Sec. Industrial Transitory Comm. (COTEI) of Unión Industrial Argentina (UIA) 1978–79, mem. Advising Exec. Comm. of UIA Comptrolling 1979–81, First Vice-Pres. UIA 1981–89, Third Vice-Pres. 1991–93; Tech. Adviser, ILO, Geneva 1978; Alt. Del. 1979–81; Founder, later Vice-Pres. Action for Pvt. Initiative; Vice-Pres. Establecimientos Modelo Terrabusi SAIC 1987–94; Dir Terra Garba Sacai y F, Atilena SCA; Commendatore della Repubblica Italiana 1992; Konex Business Leaders Award 1988. *Address:* c/o Unión Industrial Argentina, Avda Leandro N Arem 1067, 11°, 1001 Buenos Aires, Argentina.

MONTAGNIER, Luc Antoine, LèsL, DMed; French research scientist, academic and international organization official; *President, World Foundation for AIDS Research and Prevention;* b. 18 Aug. 1932, Chabris; s. of Antoine Montagnier and Marianne Rousselet; m. Dorothea Ackermann 1961; one s. two d.; ed Univs of Poitiers and Paris; Asst in Faculty of Science, Paris 1955–60, Attaché 1960, Head 1963, Head of Research 1967; Dir of Research, CNRS 1974–; Head of Lab., Inst. of Radium 1965–71; Head of Viral Oncology Unit, Pasteur Inst. 1972–, Prof., Pasteur Inst. 1985–; Univ. Chair Prof., Shanghai Jiaotong Univ. 2010–; Vice-Pres. Scientific Council AIDS Research Agency 1989–; Pres. World Foundation for AIDS Research and Prevention (WFARP) 1993–; Prof., Queens Coll., New York 1997–2001; mem. Acad. nat. de Médecine 1989, Acad. des Sciences 1996; Commdr, Légion d'honneur 1994, Grand Officier 2009; Commdr, Ordre nat. du Mérite; Lauréat du CNRS 1964, 1973, Prix Rosen de Cancérologie 1971, Prix Galien 1985, Prix de la Fondation Louis-Jeantet 1986, Prix Lasker 1986, Prix Gairdner 1987, Japan Prize 1988, King Faisal Prize 1993, Warren Alpert Foundation Prize 1998, Prince of Asturias Prize for Science 2000, Nobel Prize in Physiology or Medicine (co-recipient) 2008 and many other prizes. *Publications include:* Vaincre le SIDA 1986, SIDA: les faits, l'espoir 1987, SIDA et infection par VIH (co-author) 1989, Des virus et des hommes 1994, Oxidative Stress in Cancer, AIDS and Neurodegenerative Diseases (co-author) 1997, New Concepts in Aids Pathogenesis (co-author), Virus (co-author) 2000, Les Combats de la Vie: Mieux que Guérir 2008, Le Nobel et le Moine 2009; numerous scientific papers. *Leisure interests:* piano playing, swimming. *Address:* World Foundation for AIDS Research and Prevention, UNESCO, 1 rue Miollis, 75015 Paris, France (office); Fondation Luc Montagnier, Rue du Mont-Blanc 16, 1201 Geneva, Switzerland. *Telephone:* 1-45-68-10-00 (office). *Fax:* 1-42-73-37-45 (office). *E-mail:* lucmontagnier@gmail.com (office).

MONTAGUE, Sir Adrian Alastair, Kt, CBE, MA; British solicitor and business executive; *Non-Executive Chairman, Aviva plc;* b. 28 Feb. 1948; s. of Charles Edward Montague and Olive Montague (née Jones); m. 1st Pamela Evans 1970 (divorced 1982, died 2000); one s. two d.; m. 2nd Penelope Webb 1986; one s.; ed Trinity Hall, Cambridge; admitted solicitor 1973; with Linklater & Paines Solicitors, London 1971–94, Partner 1979; Dir Kleinwort Benson (subequently Dresdner Kleinwort Benson) where he was Co-Head merged Global Project Finance businesses of Kleinwort Benson and Dresdner Bank 1994–97; Chief Exec. Pvt. Finance Initiative Taskforce, HM Treasury 1997–2000; Deputy Chair. Partnerships UK PLC 2000–01; Deputy Chair. Network Rail 2001–04; fmr Chair. Anglian Water Group Ltd, Cross London Rail Links Ltd (Crossrail); Chair. British Energy Group PLC 2002–09, Friends Provident PLC 2005–09, 3i Group 2010–15; fmr Deputy Chair. Network Rail Ltd, Partnerships UK PLC, UK Green Investment Bank PLC; Dir (non-exec.), Aviva plc Jan. 2013–, Sr Ind. Dir (non-exec.) May 2013–, Chair. 2015–; Dir, Michael Page International PLC 2001–, Chair. (non-exec.) 2002–; Chair. (non-exec.) Partnerships for Health PLC; Chair. Infrastructure Investors Ltd 2005–; Chair. The Manchester Airport Group plc; Chair. The Point of Care Foundation (charity); Dir (non-exec.), CellMark Holdings AB, Gothenburg; Sr Int. Adviser to Société Générale, Paris 2001–04; mem. Strategic Rail Authority 2000–01; fmr Pvt. Finance Adviser to Deputy Prime Minister; fmr Trustee, Historic Royal Palaces. *Address:* Aviva plc, St Helen's, 1 Undershaft, London, EC3P 3DQ, England (office). *Telephone:* (20) 7283-2000 (office). *E-mail:* aviva.info@aviva.com (office). *Website:* www.aviva.com (office).

MONTANA, Claude; French fashion designer; b. (Claude Montamat), 1947, Paris; m. Wallis Franken 1993 (died 1996); stint at the Paris Opera; began career in London designing papier-mâché jewellery created out of baked toilet paper and rhinestones, then worked for leather and knitwear firms; first ready-to-wear show 1976; f. Claude Montana Co. 1979; opened boutiques in Paris 1983, 1986; f. Montana Fragrances Co. 1984; designer in charge of Haute Couture, House of Lanvin 1990–92; designed men's wear for Complice, Italy; House of Montana bankrupted 1997; retreated from the public until 2013; mem. Chambre Syndicale du Pret-a-Porter; lives in Spain; Best Women's Collection, Summer 1985, Paris 1985, Best European Designer, Fall/Winter 1987/88, Münchener Modewoche, Germany 1988, Balenciaga Prize for Best Designer 1989, Golden Thimble Award 1991, 1992. *Publication:* Claude Montana – Fashion Radical (with Marielle Cro) 2011. *Address:* 137 boulevard Malesherbes, 75017 Paris, France. *Telephone:* 1-56-21-16-00. *Fax:* 1-56-21-16-10. *E-mail:* contact@montana.fr. *Website:* www.montana.fr.

MONTANA, Joseph (Joe) Clifford, Jr, BBA; American fmr professional football player; b. 11 June 1956, New Eagle, Pa; s. of Joseph C. Montana, Sr and Theresa Montana; m. 1st Kim Moses 1974 (divorced 1977); m. 2nd Cass Castillo 1981 (divorced 1984); m. 3rd Jennifer Wallace 1985; two s. two d.; ed Univ. of Notre Dame; quarterback, San Francisco 49ers 1979–93, Kansas City Chiefs 1993–94, Nat. Football League (NFL); commentator, NBC TV 1995–; career statistics include 3,409 completions, 40,551 passing yards, 273 touchdowns, 92.3 passer rating; mem. NFL Super Bowl championship teams 1982, 1985, 1989; played in Pro Bowl 1982–85; Pnr, Target-Chip Ganassi Racing Team 1995–; New Business Devt Dept, Viking Components Inc. 1999; owns horses and produces wine under the label Montagia; Founder Montana Property Group (property devt firm), Los Angeles; voted Most Valuable Player in NFL Super Bowl 1982, 1985, 1990 (record),

NFL Comeback Player of the Year Award (jtly with Tommy Kramer) 1986, AP NFL Most Valuable Player 1989, 1990, Associated Press Male Athlete of the Year 1989, 1990, elected to Pro Football Hall of Fame 2000. *Publication:* Cool Under Fire (with Alan Steinberg) 1989. *Address:* c/o IMG, Century Plaza Towers, 2049 Century Park East, #2480, Los Angeles, CA 90067, USA.

MONTANER, Julio, OC, OBC, MD, DSc, FRSC; Argentine/Canadian physician and medical researcher; *Director, British Columbia Centre for Excellence in HIV/AIDS;* b. 1956, Buenos Aires, Argentina; s. of Julio Gonzalez Montaner; m. Dorothée Montaner; one s. three d.; ed Univ. of Buenos Aires; Chief Resident, Dept of Medicine, Univ. of British Columbia 1986–87, mem. Faculty, St Paul's Hosp./Univ. of British Columbia 1987–, Dir AIDS Research Program and Infectious Disease Clinic 1989, currently Chair. in AIDS Research and Head of Div. of AIDS, Faculty of Medicine; Nat. Health Research Scholar of Canada 1988–98; Founding Co-Dir (with Martin Schechter), Canadian HIV Trials Network 1990; co-f. (with Michael O'Shaughnessy) BC Centre for Excellence in HIV/AIDS 1992, currently Dir, also Dir Immunodeficiency Clinic and Physician Program Dir for HIV/AIDS, Providence Health Centre; Pres. Int. AIDS Soc. 2008–10; Fellow, Royal Coll. of Physicians of Canada; Grand Decoration of Honour for Services to Repub. of Austria 2012; Hon. DSc (Simon Fraser Univ.) 2010; Distinguished Researcher Award in HIV.1 2002, Albert Einstein World Award of Science 2010, Queen Elizabeth II Diamond Jubilee Medal 2012, Frederic Newton Gibson Star, Canadian Medical Asscn 2013, inducted into Canadian Medical Hall of Fame 2015. *Publications:* over 450 publications on HIV/AIDS. *Address:* BC Centre for Excellence in HIV/AIDS, St Paul's Hospital, 608–1081 Burrard Street, Vancouver, BC V6Z 1Y6, Canada (office). *Telephone:* (604) 806-8477 (office). *Fax:* (604) 806-9044 (office). *E-mail:* info@cfenet.ubc.ca (office). *Website:* www.cfenet.ubc.ca (office).

MONTAÑO Y MARTÍNEZ, Jorge Mario, MPA, PhD; Mexican diplomatist and academic; b. 16 Aug. 1945, Mexico City; s. of Jorge Montaño and Lucia Montaño; m. Luz Maria Valdes de Montaño; one s. one d.; ed Nat. Autonomous Univ. of Mexico, London School of Econs, UK; posts with Nat. Inst. of Fine Arts, Ministry of Public Educ., Nat. Autonomous Univ. of Mexico; Dir-Gen., Office for UN Specialized Agencies, then Dir-in-Chief for Multilateral Affairs, Ministry of Foreign Affairs 1979–82; fmr Int. Affairs Adviser to Pres. Salinas de Gortari; fmr univ. lecturer, Mexico and UK; Amb. and Perm. Rep. to UN, New York 1989–93, 2013–16, Amb. to USA 1993–95; Prof. and Research Assoc., Instituto Tecnológico Autónoma de México 1995–; Founder and Pres. Asesoria y Analisis (consulting firm) c. 1999, private consultant on the enforcement of N American Free Trade Agreement (NAFTA); Founder Foreign Affairs en Español y del Consejo Mexicano de Asuntos Internacionales (journal); mem. OAS Multilateral Evaluation Mechanism on Drugs 2001–03, Int. Narcotics Control Bd 2009–12. *Publication:* several books, including The United Nations and the World Order 1945–1992 1992; articles on sociological, political, human rights and foreign policy issues in Mexico; contrib. to La Jornada, Reforma, El Universal, El País.

MONTEALEGRE RIVAS, Eduardo, ScB, MBA; Nicaraguan economist, business executive and politician; b. 9 May 1955, Managua; m. Eliza McGregor Raskosky; ed Brown and Harvard Univs, USA; early career as business exec. and dir of several financial insts, positions included Man. BANIC Corpn and Asst Dir Cen. Bank of Nicaragua; lived in exile in USA during Sandanista rule 1979–90, serving as Vice-Pres. Banking Investment Group, Shearson Lehman Hutton before forming Montealegre & Co (pvt. financial advisory co.); Chief of Staff in the Presidency 1998, 2003; Minister of Foreign Affairs 1999–2000, of Finance and Public Credit 2002–03; mem. Constitutionalist Liberal Party (PLC) –2005; co-f. Alianza Liberal Nicaragüense (ALN) 2005, presidential cand. 2006; Deputy, Nat. Ass. (Alianza Partido Liberal Independiente) 2007–; cand. for Mayor of Managua 2008. *Address:* Alianza Liberal Nicaragüense, del Hotel Mansión Teodolinda, 3C abajo, Managua, Nicaragua. *E-mail:* emontealegre@asamblea.gob.ni (office); emontealegrer@gmail.com (office). *Website:* www.asamblea.gob.ni/diputados (office).

MONTEBOURG, Arnaud, Maîtrise en droit; French lawyer and politician; b. 30 Oct. 1962, Clamecy (Nièvre); s. of Michel Montebourg and Leïla Ould Cadi; ed Panthéon Sorbonne, Sciences Po, Paris; barrister, Appeal Court of Paris; Deputy (Parti Socialiste) for Fifth Dist of Saône-et-Loire to Nat. Ass. 1997–2012; co-f., with Prof. Bastien François, Convention pour la VIe République (C6R) calling for constitutional change and the founding of a 'Sixth Republic' 2001; Founding mem. Nouveau Parti Socialiste (New Socialist Party), left to create new movt within Socialist Party; apptd spokesman for Ségolène Royal's presidential campaign 2006; Gen. Councillor, Gen. Council of Saône-et-Loire 2008–, Pres. 2008–12; cand. in Socialist presidential primary 2011; Minister of Industrial Renewal 2012–14, of Economy and Industrial Renewal –Aug. 2014 (resgnd); Juge titulaire, Cour de justice de la République 2002–07. *Publications:* La machine à trahir 2001, Des idées et des rêves 2011, Votez pour la démondialisation 2011. *Address:* General Council of Saône-et-Loire, Space Duhesme, 18 rue de Flacé, 71026 Macon Cedex 09, France (office). *Telephone:* (3) 85-39-66-00 (office). *Website:* www .arnaudmontebourg.fr.

MONTEGRIFFO, Peter Cecil Patrick, QC, LLB; British barrister; *Partner, Hassans;* b. 28 Feb. 1960, Gibraltar; s. of Dr Cecil Montegriffo and Lily Zammitt; m. Josephine Perera 1985; two s.; ed Bayside Comprehensive School, Univ. of Leeds and Lincoln's Inn/Council of Legal Educ.; called to the Bar 1982; practitioner in J.A. Hassan & Partners law firm (now Hassans), Partner 1988–; mem. Exec. Gibraltar Labour Party/Asscn for Advancement of Civil Rights 1982–88, Deputy Leader 1988–89; Leader, Gibraltar Social Democrats 1989–91; Deputy Chief Minister and Minister for Trade and Industry 1996–2000; mem. Int. Masters of Gaming Law. *Publications:* contribs to International Trust Laws, Practical Guide to Offshore Trusts, Offshore Materials, Asset Protection, Jordans (Changes and Development of Corporate Tax System). *Leisure interests:* literature, economics, music, travel. *Address:* Hassans, 57/63 Line Wall Road, Gibraltar GX11 1AA (office); 14 Admiral's Place, Old Naval Hospital, Gibraltar (home). *Telephone:* 79000 (office); 79912 (home). *Fax:* 71966 (office); 42772 (home). *E-mail:* peter .montegriffo@hassans.gi (office); pcm@gibnet.gi (home). *Website:* www.hassans.gi (office).

MONTEIRO DE BARROS, Patrick; Portuguese business executive; Sr Vice-Pres. Philipp Brothers 1975–87; Pres. and CEO Sigmoil Resources 1987–88; Chair. and CEO Argus Resources Ltd (UK) 1988–2006; Vice-Chair. Petroplus Holdings 2006–11, apptd Chair. 2011; Chair. Monteiro de Barros Foundation, Lisbon, Protea Holdings, NY, USA; Dir (non-exec.) Espirito Santo Financial Group.

MONTEIRO DE CASTRO, HE Cardinal Manuel; Portuguese ecclesiastic and diplomatist; b. 29 March 1938, S. Eufemia; ordained priest, Archdiocese of Braga 1961; apptd Titular Archbishop of Beneventum 1985; Apostolic Pro-Nuncio to The Bahamas (also accred to Barbados, Belize, Dominca, Grenada, Jamaica, Saint Lucia, and Trinidad and Tobago) and Apostolic Del. to Turks and Caicos Islands and Netherlands Antilles 1985–90, also accred as Apostolic Pro-Nuncio to Antigua and Barbuda 1987–90; Apostolic Nuncio to El Salvador 1990–98, to S Africa (also accred to Namibia, Swaziland and Lesotho) 1998–2000, to Spain (also accred to Andorra) 2000–09; Sec. of Congregation for Bishops 2009–12; Major Penitentiary of Apostolic Penitentiary 2012–13; cr. Cardinal (Cardinal-Deacon of San Domenico di Guzman) 2012; participated in Papal Conclave 2013; Knight Grand Cross, Military Order of Christ 2003. *Address:* c/o Paenitentiaria Apostolica, Palazzo della Cancelleria, Piazza della Cancelleria 1, 00186 Rome, Italy.

MONTENEGRO, HE Cardinal Francesco; Italian ecclesiastic and academic; *Archbishop of Agrigento;* b. 22 May 1946, Messina; ed Archdiocesan Seminary Saint Pius X, Ignatianum of Messina; ordained priest, Archdiocese of Messina-Lipari-Santa Lucia del Mela 1969; carried out parish work in suburban area of Messina 1969–71; Sec. to Archbishops of Messina, Francesco Fasola and Ignazio Reedy 1971–78; Pastor of Parish of San Clemente, Messina 1978–88, then Dir diocesan br. of Caritas, regional del. of Caritas, and finally regional rep. of Italian Caritas; fmr Prof. of Religion, Diocesan Asst of Italian Sports Centre, Diocesan Dir of Apostleship of Prayer, Rector of Church Sanctuary of Santa Rita and Spiritual Adviser of Minor Seminary, and mem. Council of Priests; Pro-Vicar Gen., Archdiocese of Messina-Lipari-Santa Lucia del Mela 1997–2000; Proto-Metropolitano Canon, Chapter of Cathedral of Messina and Prelate of Honour to His Holiness 1998–2000; Auxiliary Bishop of Messina-Lipari-Santa Lucia del Mela and consecrated Titular Bishop of Aurusuliana 2000–08; Pres. Italian Caritas 2003–08; Archbishop of Agrigento 2008–; Pres. Comm. for Migration, Italian Episcopal Conf. 2013–; cr. Cardinal (Cardinal-Priest of Santi Andrea e Gregorio al Monte Celio) 2015. *Address:* Arcivescovado, Via Duomo 96, 92100 Agrigento, Italy (office). *Telephone:* (0922) 490011 (office). *Fax:* (0922) 490024 (office). *E-mail:* arcivescovado@diocesiag.it (office). *Website:* www.diocesiag.it (office).

MONTENEGRO RIZZARDINI, Gloria, PhD; Chilean ecologist, botanist and academic; *Professor and Director of Botany, Faculty of Agronomy and Forestry Sciences, Pontificia Universidad Catolica de Chile;* b. 16 July 1941, Santiago; m.; two c.; ed Pontifical Catholic Univ. of Chile and Univ. of Texas, USA; Dir of Botany and of Research and Graduate Studies, Prof. of Botany and Phytochemistry, Faculty of Agronomy and Forestry Sciences, Pontificia Universidad Catolica de Chile; Visiting Prof., Univ. of Texas, Univ. of Arizona, USA; Pres. Advisory Bd COPEC-PUC Foundation for Science and Natural Resources, Fundación para la Investigación en Ciencia y Tecnología en Recursos Naturales; fmr Pres. Botanical Soc. of Chile, Latin-American Botany Asscn, Int. Soc. for Mediterranean Ecosystems; mem. Scientific Advisory Bd TWAS-TWNSO-Global Environmental Facility projects; mem. Exec. Cttee and Regional Co-ordinator of the Latin America Plant Science Network; mem. Int. Cooperative Biodiversity Group; Exec. mem. UNESCO Group 'Women, Science & Technology in Latin America'; mem. Bd 'Comunidad-Mujer in Chile Group' (for improvement of women's rights); Fellow, Latin American Acad. of Sciences, Third World Acad. of Sciences; Gold Medal of Providencia Co., L'Oréal-UNESCO Women in Science Award 1998, Pontificia Univ. Catolica de Chile Monseñor Carlos Casanueva Prize for Distinguished Prof. 2008, named one of the 100 Leading Women in Chile 2008, Energía de Mujer Chilectra Award 2011, Mujer Innovadora Award in Agriculture 2011. *Publications:* Landscape Disturbance and Biodiversity in Mediterranean-Type Ecosystems (co-ed.) 1998, Fire and Climatic Change in Temperate Ecosystems of the Western Americas (co-ed.) 2003; several patents and scientific publs. *Telephone:* 238-5042 (office); 354-7216 (office). *Address:* Facultad de Agronomia e Ingenieria Forestal, Pontificia Universidad Católica de Chile, Av. Vicuña Mackenna 4860, Santiago, Chile (office). *Fax:* 354-4117 (office). *E-mail:* gmonten@uc.cl (office). *Website:* agronomia.uc.cl (office).

MONTERISI, HE Cardinal Francesco, DTheol, DCL; Italian ecclesiastic; *Archpriest Emeritus of the Basilica di San Paolo fuori le Mura;* b. 28 May 1934, Barletta; ed Pontifical Minor Seminary and Pontifical Major Seminary, Rome, Pontifical Lateran Univ., Rome, Pontifical Ecclesiastical Acad., Pontifical Lateran Univ.; ordained priest Trani e Barletta (e Nazareth e Bisceglie) 1957; Vice-Rector and Spiritual Dir Don Pasquale Uva, Bisceglie 1958–61; Prof., Pius XII, Molfetta 1960–61; entered diplomatic service in Holy See 1964, served in Nunciatures in Madagscar and Egypt; returned to Rome 1970, worked in Secr. of State; Titular Archbishop of Alba Maritima 1982–; Pro-Nuncio to Korea 1982–93; Official of the Roman Curia 1987–; Apostolic Nuncio to Bosnia and Herzegovina 1993–98; Sec. Congregation for Bishops 1998–2009, served as Sec. of Papal Conclave that elected Pope Benedict XVI April 2005; Archpriest of Basilica di San Paolo fuori le Mura 2009–12, Archpriest Emer. 2012–; cr. Cardinal (Cardinal-Deacon of San Paolo alla Regola) 2010; participated in Papal Conclave 2013. *Address:* Basilica di San Paolo fuori le Mura, 00120 Città del Vaticano, Rome, Italy (office). *Telephone:* (06) 69880800 (office). *Fax:* (06) 69880803 (office). *E-mail:* info@annopaolino.org (office); spbasilica@org.va (office). *Website:* www.vatican.va/various/basiliche/san_paolo/index_en.html (office).

MONTERO, Luis García, BA, MA, PhD; Spanish poet, literary critic and academic; b. 4 Dec. 1958, Granada; s. of Luis García López and Elisa Montero Peña; m. Almudena Grandes 1994; three c.; ed Univ. of Granada; Assoc. Prof., Univ. of Granada 1981, later Prof. of Spanish Literature; frequent political columnist for online newspaper Público; mem. United Left coalition (Izquierda Unida); helped establish Izquierda Abierta (political party) 2012; Premio Poetas del Mundo Latino 2010, Ramón López Velarde Prize 2017, Parallel Prize 2018. *Publications:* poetry: Y ahora ya eres dueño 1980, Tristia (co-author) 1982, El jardín extranjero (Premio Adonáis de Poesía 1982) 1983, Rimado de ciudad 1983, Égloga de dos rascacielos 1984, En pie de paz 1985, Seis poemas del mar 1985, Diario cómplice 1987, Anuncios por palabras 1988, Secreto de amistad 1990, Las flores del frío 1990, En otra edad 1992, Fotografías veladas de la lluvia 1993, Habitaciones separadas (Premio Loewe 1994, Premio Nacional de Poesía 1995) 1994, Además 1994, Quedarse sin ciudad 1994, Completamente viernes 1998, La intimidad de la serpiente (Premio Nacional de la Critica 2003) 2003, Infancia 2006, Vista cansada 2008, Un invierno propio 2011, Ropa de calle 2011; essays and articles: Manifesto albertista (co-author) 1982, La otra sentimentalidad (co-author) 1983, La norma y los estilos en la poesía de Rafael Alberti 1986, Poesía, cuartel de invierno 1988, Confesiones poéticas 1993, La palabra de Ícaro 1996, Lecciones de poesía para niños inquietos 1999, El sexto día: historia intima de la poesía española 2000, Gigante y extraño: las Rimas de Gustavo Adolfo Bécquer 2001, Los dueños del vacio: La conciencia poética, entre la identidad y los vinculos 2006, Inquietudes bárbaras 2008; memoir: Luna del sur 1992; novels: Impares, fila 13 (co-author) 1996, Mañana no sera lo que Dios quiera 2009, No me cuentes tu vida 2012; juvenile: La mudanza de Adán 2002. *Address:* University of Granada, Facultad de Filosofía y Letras, Campus de Cartuja, 18071 Granada, Spain (office). *E-mail:* lgarciam@ugr.es (office). *Website:* luisgarciamontero.com.

MONTERO CUADRADO, María Jesús; Spanish politician; *Minister of the Treasury;* b. 4 Feb. 1966, Seville; m. Rafael Ibáñez Reche; two c.; ed Univ. of Seville; various positions with Junta de Andalusia (regional govt) including Deputy Minister of Health 2002–04, Counsellor of Health 2004–12, Counsellor of Health and Social Welfare 2012–13, Minister of Finance and Public Admin 2013–18; mem. Parl. of Andalusia for Seville 2008–18; Minister of the Treasury (in nat. govt) 2018–; mem. Partido Socialista Obrero Español (PSOE, Spanish Socialist Workers' Party). *Address:* Ministry of the Treasury and Public Administration, Calle Alcalá 9, 28014 Madrid, Spain (office). *Telephone:* (91) 5958000 (office). *Fax:* (91) 5958486 (office). *E-mail:* secretaria.prensa@minhap.es (office). *Website:* www.minhafp.gob .es (office).

MONTGOMERIE, Colin Stuart, OBE; British professional golfer; b. 23 June 1963, Glasgow, Scotland; s. of James Montgomerie; m. 1st Eimear Wilson 1990 (divorced 2004); one s. two d.; m. 2nd Gaynor Knowles 2008 (divorced 2017); ed Strathallan School, Leeds Grammar School, Houston Baptist Univ., Texas, USA; won Scottish Stroke Play Championship 1985, Scottish Amateur Championship 1987; turned professional 1987; won Portuguese Open 1989, Scandinavian Masters 1991, 1999, 2001, Heineken Dutch Open, Volvo Masters 1993, Peugeot Open de España, Murphy's English Open, Volvo German Open 1994, Volvo German Open, Trophée Lancôme, Alfred Dunhill Cup 1995, Dubai Desert Classic, Murphy's Irish Open 1996, 1997, 2001, Canon European Masters, Million Dollar Challenge 1996, World Cup (Individual), Andersen Consulting World Champion 1997, PGA Championship 1998, 1999, 2000, German Masters 1998, Compaq European Grand Prix 1997, King Hassan II Trophy 1997, British Masters 1998, Benson and Hedges Int. Open 1999, BMW Int. Open 1999, Cisco World Matchplay 1999, Loch Lomond Invitational 1999, Skins Game (US) 2000, Novotel Perrier Open de France 2000, Ericsson Australian Masters 2001, Volvo Masters Andalucia, TCL Classic 2002, Macao Open 2003, Caltex Masters 2004, UBS Hong Kong Open 2005, Smurfit Kappa Europen Open 2007; joined European and PGA seniors tours 2013; mem. European Ryder Cup team from 1991–2004 (undefeated in Ryder Cup singles), apptd Capt. European Ryder Cup team 2009, captained winning European team, Celtic Manor, Wales Oct. 2010; columnist, Bunkered 2008–10; named Pres. Golf Foundation (English jr golf charity) 2011; Amb. for the Scottish jr golf programme, Clubgolf 2012; Hon. LLD (St Andrews); Sir Henry Cotton Rookie of the Year 1988, eight times winner of Volvo Order of Merit Trophy 1993–2005, European Tour Player of the Year 1995, 1996, 1997, 1999, BBC Sports Personality of the Year Coach Award 2010, inducted into World Golf Hall of Fame 2013, Colin Montgomerie Golf Acad., Turnberry, Scotland named after him. *Publications:* Real Monty: The Autobiography of Colin Montgomerie, The Thinking Man's Guide to Golf (co-author) 2002. *Leisure interests:* music, cars, DIY, films. *Website:* www.colinmontgomerie.com.

MONTGOMERY, David; American photographer; b. 8 Feb. 1937, Brooklyn, New York; m. 1st (divorced); two d.; m. 2nd Martine King 1983; one s. one d.; ed Midwood High School, Brooklyn Coll., Juilliard School of Music; toured USA as musician; British resident early 1960s–; freelance photographer/dir 1960–; regular contrib. to Sunday Times Colour Magazine, Vogue, Tatler, Rolling Stone, Esquire, Fortune, New York Sunday Times, House and Garden magazines; has contributed to many books on home style: four in association with Tricia Guild of Designers Guild, a definitive English flower book for Pulbrook & Gould and four books on New Age aromatherapy entitled 'Romance', 'Relaxation', 'Vitality' and 'Well Being'; did photography for Nicky Haslam's book 'Sheer Opulence'; commissioned by Royal Mail to do a special edition stamp for the Millennium issue; photographic commissions for several major retailers, including Harrods, John Lewis, The Body Shop; has also shot major advertising campaigns for Designers Guild, Colefax and Fowler, Jane Churchill, Sandersons; has worked on campaigns for brands including Rolex, Saab, Fiat; has photographed HM Queen Elizabeth II, HM Queen Elizabeth the Queen Mother, TRH Duke and Duchess of York, Rt Hon. Margaret Thatcher, Rt Hon Pierre Trudeau, Mick Jagger, Clint Eastwood, Lord Mountbatten, Lord Hume, HM King Hussein, HRH Queen Noor, Rt Hon Edward Heath, Rt Hon James Callaghan, Baron Thyssen-Bornemisza, Prince and Princess Thurn und Taxis, HE Cardinal Basil Hume, Jimi Hendrix, The Rolling Stones, Sir Paul McCartney, Chrissie Hynde, Pierce Brosnan, Barbra Streisand, S Club 7, Atomic Kitten; teacher and Prof., Univ. of East London 2006–08; Master Class courses at The Observer/Guardian 2011; gives private photography lessons; numerous awards for photography and advertising. *Publications:* contrib. to New York Times/Sunday Times, Vogue, Homes and Gardens, Rolling Stone. *Leisure interests:* flowers, photography, day-dreaming, jazz music. *Address:* c/o M+M Management, Studio B, 11 Edith Grove, London, SW10 0JZ, England (office). *Telephone:* (20) 7823-3723 (office). *E-mail:* photography@mmmanagement.com (office); davidmontgomeryphoto@gmail.com (home). *Website:* www .mmmanagement.com (office); davidmontgomery.net.

MONTGOMERY, R. Lawrence (Larry), BS; American retail executive; b. 1949; ed Ferris State Univ.; retail career began in 1972; Pres., Block's Div., Allied Stores Corpn 1985–87; Sr Vice-Pres., L. S. Ayres Div., May Department Stores 1987–88; Sr Vice-Pres. and Dir of Stores, Kohl's Department Stores 1988–93, Exec. Vice-Pres. 1993–96, Vice-Chair. 1996–2000, mem. Bd of Dirs 1994–2010, CEO 1999–2002, Chair. Kohl's Corpn 2003–09; mem. Advisory Bd, Ember Technologies, Inc. *Address:* c/o Kohl's Corporation, N56 W17000 Ridgewood Drive, Menomonee Falls, WI 53051-5660, USA.

MONTGOMERY, Timothy (Tim); American fmr athlete; b. 28 Jan. 1975, Gaffney, SC; s. of Eddie Montgomery; fmr partner Marion Jones; one s.; m. Jamalee 2009; three c.; ed Gaffney High School, Blinn Coll., Tex., Norfolk State Coll.; fmrly American football and baseball player; ran 100m in 9.96 seconds aged 19; world record holder (9.78 seconds 100m), Grand Prix Final 2002; ran fastest 60m (6.48 seconds), Dortmund 2002; coached by Trevor Graham; runner-up: JUCO Indoor 1994, USA Championships 100m 1997, USA Indoors 60m 1997, USATF Outdoor Championship 100m 2002, Golden Gala 100m 2002, Norwich Union Grand Prix 100m 2002; winner, Bislett Golden Gala 100m 2001, Zurich 100m 2001, Sparkassen 100m 2002, Engen Grand Prix 100m 2002, Prefontaine 100m 2002, DN Galan 100m 2002, Weltklasse 100m 2002, Memorial Van Damme 100m 2002, Grand Prix Final 100m 2002; Bronze Medal, World Championships 100m 1997; Silver Medal, 4×100m relay, Summer Olympics, Atlanta 1996, 100m, Goodwill Games 2001, 60m, World Indoors 2001, 100m, World Championships 2001; Gold Medal, 4×100m relay, World Championships 1999, Summer Olympics, Sydney 2000; arrested on heroin distribution charges and sentenced to five years in prison 2008, released 2012; f. NUMA Speed LLC with wife Jamalee. *Address:* NUMA Speed LLC, 3000 NW, 83rd Street, Gainesville, FL 32606, USA (office). *Telephone:* (757) 343-1116 (office). *Website:* www.numaspeed.com (office).

MONTI, Mario; Italian international organization official, economist, government official and university administrator; *President, Università Bocconi;* b. 19 March 1943, Varese; m. Elsa Antonioli; two c.; ed Università Commerciale Luigi Bocconi, Yale Univ., USA; Assoc. Prof., Univ. of Trento 1969–70; Prof., Univ. of Turin 1970–79; Prof. of Monetary Theory and Policy, Università Bocconi 1971–85, Prof. of Econs, Dir Inst. of Econs 1985–94, f. Paolo Baffi Centre for Monetary and Financial Econs 1985, f. Innocenzo Gasparini Inst. of Econ. Research 1989, Rector, Università Bocconi 1989–94, Pres. 2005–; Econ. Commentator, Corriere della Sera 1978–94; Rapporteur, Treasury Cttee on Savings Protection 1981, Chair. Treasury Cttee on Banking and Financial System 1981–82, mem. Competition Act Drafting Cttee 1987–88, mem. Treasury Cttee on Debt Man. 1988–89, on Banking Law Reform 1989–91; mem. working party preparing Italy for single market 1988–90; mem. Macroeconomic Policy Group, European Comm. and Centre for Econ. Policy Studies (CEPS) 1985–86; mem. EC responsible for Internal Market, Financial Services and Financial Integration, Customs, Taxation 1995–99, for Competition 1999–2004; Int. Adviser, Goldman Sachs Int. 2005–; Founding Chair. Breughel (think-tank) 2005, now Hon. Chair.; Chair. EU High Level Group on Own Resources 2014–; European Chair., Trilateral Comm., Council on the Future of Europe of Berggruen Inst.; mem. Bilderberg Group, Académie des Sciences morales et politiques 2014–; named Senator for Life by Pres. Giorgio Napolitano 2011; Prime Minister of Italy (asked to lead new govt following resignation of Silvio Berlusconi) 2011–12 (resgnd, caretaker Prime Minister until formation of new govt in April 2013), also Minister of Economy and Finance 2011–12; contested gen. election, Feb. 2013, as founder of centrist coalition Civic Choice; Pres. Civic Choice May–Oct. 2013; Senator for Life (highest Italian honour). *Publications include:* Report on the Future of the Single Market 2010. *Address:* Office of the President, Università Bocconi, Via Sarfatti 25, 20136 Milan (office); Senate, Piazza Madama, 00187 Rome, Italy (office). *Telephone:* (02) 58361 (Milan) (home); (06) 67061 (Rome) (office). *E-mail:* infopoint@senato.it (office). *Website:* www.unibocconi.eu (office); www.senato.it (office).

MONTIEL, Eduardo Luis, DBA MS; Nicaraguan politician; b. San Sebastián, Managua; Eduardo Montiel Argüello; m. 1st; two c.; m. 2nd Eugenia Argeñal; ed Harvard Business School, MIT, USA; early career as industrial engineer; Dean, Instituto Centroamericano de Administración de Empresas (INCAE); Pres. Del. Comisión de Promoción de Inversiones; Adviser, govt enterprises in Latin America, USA, Europe; Minister of Finance and Public Credit 2004–05; mem. Editorial Council. *Publications include:* more than 70 publications.

MONTILLA AGUILERA, José, LLB; Spanish politician; b. 15 Jan. 1955, Iznájar, Cordoba; m.; five c.; ed Univ. of Barcelona; mem. Partit dels Socialistes de Catalunya (PSC) 1978–, mem. Exec. Comm. 2000-08, Sec. 1994–2000, First Sec. 2000–11; mem. City Council, Sant Joan Despí 1979–83; mem. Council and Mayor, Cornellá de Llobregat 1983–2004; Second Vice-Pres., Barcelona Del. 1987–95, First Vice-Pres. 1999; Deputy for Barcelona, Congress of Deputies (Congreso de los Diputados) 2004–08; Minister of Industry, Tourism and Trade 2004–06; Pres. Govt of Catalonia 2006–10; mem. Senate (Partit dels Socialistes de Catalunya) 2013–. *Address:* Senate (Senado), Plaza de la Marina Española 8, 28071 Madrid, Spain (office). *Telephone:* (91) 5381000 (office). *Fax:* (91) 5381003 (office). *E-mail:* informacion@senado.es (office). *Website:* www.senado.es (office).

MONTKIEWICZ, Zdzislaw; Polish business executive; b. 28 June 1944, Sokolów Podlaski; ed Mil. Tech. Acad.; mem. staff Polish Acad. of Sciences 1972–74, Ministry of Foreign Affairs 1974–78, UN Security Council 1978–82; Dir-Gen. Dernan & Sental Manufacturing and Financial Group 1983–88; Dir-Gen. Poland office, IBM World Trade/Europe/Middle East/Africa Corpn 1988–91; Pres. Ciech SA 1994–97; Pres. Prudential/Prumerica Financial Poland 1997–2001; Pres. Man. Bd Powszechny Zaklad Ubezpieczen (PZU) SA (state-controlled insurer) 2002–03; Founder-mem. Polish Trade and Finance Union; mem. Zacheta Art Soc. *Leisure interest:* reading historical books.

MONTORO ROMERO, Cristóbal Ricardo, DEcon; Spanish economist, academic and politician; b. 28 July 1950, Jaén; m.; two c.; ed Universidad Autónoma de Madrid; Deputy Dir of Studies, Banco Atlántico 1975–81; Dir of Studies, Inst. for Econ. Studies 1981–93; mem. Congreso de los Diputados (Parl.) for Madrid 1993–2000, for Jaén 2000–08, for Seville 2011–, Econ. Affairs Spokesperson for Partido Popula Parl. Group 2008–11; Sec. of State for the Economy 1996–2000, Minister for the Treasury 2000–04, for the Treasury and Public Admin 2011–18; mem. European Parl. 2004–08; Full Prof. of Applied Econs, Univ. of Cantabria; mem. Partido Popular, mem. Nat. Exec. Cttee 1999–, Econ. and Labour Coordinator 2008–12; Grand Cross, Royal and Distinguished Order of Carlos III.

MONTY, Jean Claude, CM, MA, MBA; Canadian business executive; b. 26 June 1947, Montreal; m. Jocelyne Monty; two s.; ed Coll. Sainte-Marie, Univ. of Western Ontario, Univ. of Chicago, USA; Merrill Lynch, New York, Toronto and Montreal 1970–74; Bell Canada, Montreal 1974; Pres. Télébec Ltée. 1976; Nat. Defence Coll.

Kingston, Ont. 1979–80; Bell Canada 1980–92, Pres. 1989, Pres. and CEO 1991–92; Pres. and COO Northern Telecom Ltd 1992, Pres. and CEO 1993–98; Chair. and CEO Bell Canada Enterprises (BCE) Inc. 1998–2002 (resgnd), Chair. BCE Emergis Inc. 2004–10; Dir Bombardier Inc. 1998–, Centria Inc., Fiera Capital Inc., Contramax Inc., Alcatel-Lucent 2008–; mem. Supervisory Bd Lagardère Group, Paris; fmr Special Advisor, General Atlantic LLC; Canada's Outstanding CEO of the Year 1997. *Leisure interest:* golf.

MONYAKE, Lengolo Bureng, MSc, UED; Lesotho fmr government official; b. 1 April 1930, Lesotho; s. of Bureng L. Monyake and Leomile Monyake; m. Molulela Mapetla 1957; two s. one d.; ed Fort Hare Univ. Coll., Univ. of Toronto, Carleton Univ., London School of Econs; Headmaster, Jordan High School 1952–61; Dir of Statistics, Govt of Lesotho 1968–74, Perm. Sec. 1974–76, Deputy Sr Perm. Sec. 1976–78; Amb. 1979–83; Man. Dir Lesotho Nat. Devt Corpn 1984–86; Minister for Foreign Affairs 1986–88, for Works 1988; Alt. Exec. Dir IMF 1988–90, Exec. Dir 1990–92; Deputy Exec. Sec. Southern African Devt Community 1993–98; worked with African Peer Review Mechanism (APRM), Lesotho; fmr Pres. Emer. Eighteenth Episcopal Dist, Connectional Lay Org., African Methodist Episcopal Church, Lesotho. *Leisure interests:* tennis, table tennis, music, photography. *Address:* PO Box 526, Maseruloo 100, Lesotho. *Telephone:* 22315995. *E-mail:* lengolob@leo.co.ls (home).

MOOD, Lt-Gen. Robert; Norwegian army officer and UN official; *Military Representative, NATO;* b. 8 Dec. 1958, Telemark; m. Eva Tverberg; one s.; ed US Marine Corps Univ., NATO Defence Coll., Rome, Norwegian Army Staff Coll.; started mil. career 1977, Leader, Operations Officer, Norwegian Bn, UN Interim Force in Lebanon (UNIFIL) 1989–90, Lt Commdr, Telemark Bn 1993–94; achieved rank of Lt Colonel 1996; Operations Officer, 6th Div. –1998; Head of Telemark Bn 1999–2000, Chief of Planning Br., High Command 2000–02, Chief of Hærens Kampvåpen 2002–04 Chief, Army Transformation and Doctrine Command (TRADOK) 2004–05, Chief of Staff 2005–09; Chief, Jt Implementation Comm., KFOR Command Group; CO, Norwegian Army Transformation and Doctrine Command; Head of Mission and Chief of Staff, UN Truce Supervision Org. (UNTSO) 2009–11; Insp.-Gen. Veteran Affairs, Defence Veteran Services 2011–14; Chief Mil. Observer and Head of Mission, UN Supervision Mission in Syria (UNSMIS) March–Aug. 2012; Mil. Rep. to NATO, Brussels 2014–; rank of Lt-Gen. 2014; Badge of Honour, Norwegian Veteran Asscn of Int. Operations, Chevalier, Ordre nat. du Mérite; Defense Service Medal, Armed Forces Medal for Int. Operations, Army Nat. Service Medal, UN Medal for Truce Supervision Org., UN Medal for UN Interim Force in Lebanon, NATO Medal for Kosovo, Defence Forces' Equal Opportunities Award 2008, UN Veteran Asscn recognition medal in Gold, Voluntary Women's Asscn for Preparedness Award 2014. *Leisure interests:* biking, hiking and fishing, mountaineering, traveling. *Address:* Permanent Representation of Norway to NATO, Blvd Léopold III, 1110 Brussels, Belgium (office). *Telephone:* (2) 707-63-11 (office). *Fax:* (2) 726-56-30 (office). *E-mail:* delnato@mfa .no (office). *Website:* www.norway-nato.org (office).

MOODY, Robert Vaughn, OC, BA, MA, PhD, FRSC; Canadian (b. British) mathematician and academic; *Professor Emeritus of Mathematics, Department of Mathematical and Statistical Sciences, University of Alberta; Adjunct Professor of Mathematics, University of Victoria;* b. 28 Nov. 1941; ed Univ. of Sask., Univ. of Toronto; Asst Prof., Dept of Math., Univ. of Sask. 1966–70, Assoc. Prof. 1970–76, Prof. 1976–89; Asst Prof., New Mexico State Univ., Las Cruces 1967–68; with Mathematisches Institüt, Universität Bonn 1973–74, Centre de Recherche de Mathematiques Appliquées, Montreal 1983–84; Prof., Concordia Univ., Montreal 1984–86; apptd Prof., Dept of Math., Univ. of Alberta 1989, Chair. Review Cttee, Dept of Math. and Statistics 1990, now Prof. Emer. of Math., Dept of Math. and Statistical Sciences; Scientific Dir Banff Int. Research Station for Math. Innovation and Discovery 2001–03; Guest Prof., Gesamthochschule Wuppertal Jan.– June 1979, Université de Paris VI Jan.–June 1979, Tata Inst. for Math., Bombay, India 1987; mem. Bd Fields Inst. for Research in Math. Sciences 1988–91, Council, Acad. of Science, RSC 1990–93; mem. Scientific Advisory Bd, Centre de Recherches de Mathematique, Université de Montréal 1993–96, Scientific Advisory Panel, Fields Inst. for Research in Math. Sciences 1993–98; mem. Editorial Bd Nova Journal of Algebra and Geometry 1992–98, Canadian Journal of Mathematics, Canadian Mathematics Bulletin; mem. Publs Cttee, Canadian Math. Soc. 1982–85, 1988–90; mem. PIMS Scientific Review Panel 1997–; mem. Aspen Inst. for Physics 1982, 1983, 1984, 1986, 1987, 1990, 1997; co-discoverer of Kac-Moody algebra; Dr hc (Université de Montréal) 2000; Coxeter-James Lectureship, Canadian Math. Soc. 1978, Japan Soc. for the Promotion of Science Fellowship 1981, Eugene Wigner Medal (jtly with Victor Kac) for "work on affine Lie algebras that has influenced many areas of theoretical physics", Int. Cttee for Group Theoretical Methods in Math. and Physics 1994, Jeffrey-William Lectureship, Canadian Math. Soc. 1994, Ireland Lectureship, Univ. of New Brunswick 1995, Kaplan Award for Science, Univ. of Alberta 1995, Britten Lectureship, McMaster Univ. 1996, Alberta Science and Tech. Award for Outstanding Research 1996, Frontiers of Mathematics Lectureship, Texas A&M Univ. 1996, CRM/Fields Inst. Prize 1998, Killam Prize 2002, Lansdowne Professorship, Univ. of Victoria 2004, Golden Jubilee Professorship, Benares Hindu Univ., Varanasi 2004. *Publications:* six books and more than 70 articles. *Address:* Department of Mathematical and Statistical Sciences, 632 Central Academic Building, University of Alberta, Edmonton, Alberta T6G 2G1, Canada (office). *Telephone:* (780) 492-3396 (office). *Fax:* (780) 492-6826 (office). *E-mail:* mathsci@math.ualberta.ca (office). *Website:* www.math.ualberta.ca/~rvmoody/rvm (office).

MOODY-STUART, Sir Mark, Kt, KCMG, MA, PhD, FGS, FRGS; British company director and geologist; *Chairman, Global Compact Foundation;* b. 15 Sept. 1940, Antigua, West Indies; s. of Sir Alexander Moody-Stuart and Judith Moody-Stuart (née Henzell); m. Judith McLeavy 1964; three s. one d.; ed Shrewsbury School and St John's Coll., Cambridge; with Shell Internationale Petroleum Mij. 1966–67, Koninklijke Shell E & P Lab. 1967–68, worked with Shell cos in Spain, Oman, Brunei 1968–72, Chief Geologist, Australia 1972–76, Shell UK 1977–78, Brunei Shell Services Man. 1978–79, Gen. Man. Shell 1978–79, Man. Western Div. Shell Nigeria 1979–82, Gen. Man. Shell Turkey 1982–86, Chair. and CEO Shell Malaysia 1986–89, Exploration and Production Co-ordinator, Royal Dutch/Shell 1990, Dir Shell Transport & Trading Co. PLC 1990–2005, Chair. 1997–2001, Man. Dir Royal Dutch/Shell Group 1991–2001, Chair. Cttee of Man.

Dirs 1998–2001; Chair. (non-exec.), Anglo American plc 2002–09, mem. Remuneration, Safety and Sustainable Devt and Nomination Cttees; Jt Chair. G8 Task Force on Devt of Renewable Sources of Energy 2000; mem. Bd of Dirs, Accenture 2001–15, HSBC Holdings PLC 2001–10, Saudi Aramco 2007–; Chair. Business Action for Sustainable Devt 2001–02, Global Compact Foundation 2006– (Vice-Chair. Bd UN Global Compact –2018), Hermes Equity Ownership Services 2009–16; Chair. Bd of Trustees, Innovative Vector Control Consortium 2008–18; Pres. Liverpool School of Tropical Medicine 2001–08; Hon. Co-Chair. Int. Tax and Advisory Centre 2011–; mem. UN Sec.-Gen.'s Advisory Council for the Global Compact 2001–04, Bd Global Reporting Initiative 2001–07, Bd Int. Inst. for Sustainable Devt 2002–10; Gov. Nuffield Hosps 2001–08; Fellow, Geological Soc. of London (Pres. 2002–04); Hon. FIChemE 1997; Hon. Fellow, St John's Coll., Cambridge 2001; Hon. DBA (Robert Gordon) 2000; Hon. LLD (Aberdeen) 2001; Hon. DSc (Royal Holloway, London); Cadman Medal Inst. of Petroleum 2002. *Publications:* Responsible Leadership – Lessons from the Front Line of Sustainability and Ethics 2014; papers in scientific and other journals. *Leisure interests:* sailing, travel, reading. *Website:* www.ivcc.com (office); www.unglobalcompact.org.

MOON, Jae-in, LLB; South Korean human rights lawyer, politician and head of state; *President;* b. 24 Jan. 1953, Geoje; s. of Moon Yong-hyung and Kang Han-ok; m. Kim Jong-suk; one s. one d.; ed Kyunghee Univ., Judicial Research and Training Inst.; active in student politics; arrested and imprisoned for leading protests against Pres. Park Chung-hee 1970s; conscripted to Repub. of Korea army, served in Special Forces Div. 1975–77; co-f. law firm, Busan 1982; Founding mem. Hankyoreh (progressive newspaper) 1988; Campaign Man. for Pres. Roh Moo-hyun 2003; Sr Presidential Sec. for Civil Affairs 2003–04, 2005–06, for Civil Soc. 2004–05, Chief Sec. of the Pres. 2007–08; mem. Nat. Ass. (Parl.) for Sasang 2012–16; mem. Minjoo Party of Korea (Democratic Party of Korea), Leader 2015–16; mem. Minbyun (social org. of progressive lawyers); Chair. of Human Rights, Busan Bar Asscn; Democratic Party cand. in presidential election 2012; Pres., Repub. of Korea 2017–. *Publications include:* Moon Jae-in: The Destiny (memoir) 2011, The Beginning is the Beginning 2013, Korea Asks 2017. *Address:* Office of the President, Chong Wa Dae, 1, Sejong-no, Jongno-gu, Seoul, 03048, Republic of Korea (office). *Telephone:* (2) 730-5800 (office). *E-mail:* webmaster@president.go.kr (office). *Website:* www.president.go.kr (office).

MOON, Kil-choo, BS, MS, PhD; South Korean engineer and research institute director; *President, University of Science and Technology;* ed Univ. of Ottawa, Canada, Univ. of Minnesota, USA; Sr Project Man., Interpoll Inc., USA 1984–86, AeroVironment Inc., USA 1986–91; Man., Air Pollution Lab., Korea Inst. of Science and Tech. (KIST) 1991–92, Principal Researcher, Center for Environment, Health and Welfare Research 1991–2016, Dir Environment Research Centre 1992–97, Dir Global Environmental Research Centre 1997–2001, Dir Tech. Transfer Div. 2003–04, Dir-Gen. KIST, Gangneung 2004–06, Vice-Pres. KIST 2006–09, Pres. 2010–13; Exec. Vice-Pres. Int. Union of Air Pollution Prevention and Environmental Protection Asscns (IUAPPA) 2004–10, Pres. 2010–; Pres. Univ. of Science and Tech. 2016–; mem. Air and Waste Management Asscn, Chair. Korean Section 1997–2008; Pres. Korean Asscn for Aerosol and Particle Research (KAPAR) 1996–97, Korea Soc. for Atmospheric Environment (KOSAE) 2008–09, Soc. of Automotive Eng; Dir Directorate for Nat. Science and Eng Programs, Nat. Research Foundation of Korea Jan.–Nov. 2010; Advisor, Presidential Advisory Council on Science & Tech. 2013–14; mem. Nat. Acad. of Eng of Korea 2004–, Presidential Council on Intellectual Property 2013–; Ministry Citation, Ministry of Environment 1994, Certification of Honour, IUAPPA, UK 2001, Scientific Award, KOSAE 2004, Ungbi Medal, Order of Science and Tech. Merit 2006. *Publications include:* Charging Mechanism of Submicron Diesel Particles 1984, Environment Vision in Korea 2050 2002, Obstacles to technology transfer: What the Practitioners want from the Government, Asia Pacific Tech Monitor 2004. *Address:* University of Science and Technology, 217 Gajeong-ro Yuseong-gu, Daejeon 34113, Republic of Korea (office). *Telephone:* (2) 864-5551 (office). *Fax:* (2) 864-5554 (office). *Website:* www.ust.ac.kr (office).

MOONEY, Beth E., BA, MBA; American banking executive; *Chairman and CEO, KeyCorp;* b. Midland, Mich.; ed Univ. of Texas, Southern Methodist Univ.; completed line assignments of increasing responsibility at Bank One Corpn, Citicorp Real Estate, Inc., Hall Financial Group and Republic Bank of Texas/First Republic; fmr Regional Pres., Bank One Corpn, Akron and Dayton, then Pres. Bank One Ohio; Sr Exec. Vice-Pres. and Chief Financial Officer, AmSouth Bancorporation (now Regions Financial Corpn), Ala, ran banking operations in Tenn. and northern La –2006; joined KeyCorp 2006, Vice-Chair. Key Community Banking, includes Retail Banking, Business Banking, Commercial Middle Market Banking, Wealth Man., Private Banking, Key Investment Services and KeyBank Mortgage –2010, Pres. and COO KeyCorp 2010–11, mem. Bd of Dirs, Chair. and CEO 2011–; mem. The Financial Services Roundtable; Trustee and Treas., Musical Arts Asscn (The Cleveland Orchestra); Trustee, Cleveland Clinic Foundation, Neighborhood Progress, Inc., United Way of Greater Cleveland; Distinguished Alumnus, Cox School of Business, Southern Methodist Univ. 2007–08, YWCA Women of Achievement Award 2008, Most Powerful Woman in Banking in US, American Banker 2013, 2014. *Address:* KeyCorp, 127 Public Square, Cleveland, OH 44114, USA (office). *Telephone:* (216) 689-3000 (office). *E-mail:* keyexpress@ keybank.com (office). *Website:* www.keycorp.net (office).

MOONEY, Harold (Hal) Alfred, MA, PhD; American biologist and academic; *Paul S. and Billie Achilles Professor Emeritus in Environmental Biology and Senior Fellow Emeritus, Woods Institute for the Environment, Stanford University;* b. (Harold Alfred Stefany), 1 June 1932, Santa Rosa, Calif.; s. of Harold Walter Stefany and Sylvia A. Hart; m. Sherry L. Gulmon 1974; three d.; ed Univ. of California, Santa Barbara and Duke Univ.; Instructor to Assoc. Prof., UCLA 1960–68; Assoc. Prof., Stanford Univ. 1968–73, Prof. 1975–, Paul S. and Billie Achilles Prof. in Environmental Biology 1976–, now Emer., Sr Fellow Emer., Woods Inst. for the Environment; fmr Chair. DIVERSITAS; served as Lead Author of UN Global Biodiversity Assessment 1995 and Co-Chair. Millennium Ecosystem Assessment; fmr Pres. Ecological Soc. of America, American Inst. of Biological Sciences; fmr Sec.-Gen. Int. Council of Science; mem. NAS, American Philosophical Soc.; Foreign mem. Russian Acad. of Sciences; Fellow, American Acad. of Arts and Sciences; Mercer Award, Ecology Soc. of America 1961, Guggenheim Fellow 1974, Humboldt Award 1988, ECI Prize in Terrestrial Ecology, Inst. of Ecology

Prize (Germany) 1990, Max Planck Research Award in Biosciences 1992, Eminent Ecologist Award (co-recipient), Ecological Soc. of America 1996, Blue Planet Prize, Asahi Glass Foundation 2002, Ramon Margalef Prize in Ecology and Environmental Sciences 2007, BBVA Foundation Award for Scientific Research in Ecology and Conservation Biology 2007, Tyler Prize for Environmental Achievement 2008, Volvo Environmental Prize 2010. *Address:* Department of Biological Sciences, Room 477, Herrin Labs, Stanford University, Stanford, CA 94305-5020 (office); 2625 Ramona Street, Palo Alto, CA 94306, USA (home). *Telephone:* (650) 725-1857 (office). *E-mail:* hmooney@stanford.edu (office).

MOONVES, Leslie (Les); American television industry executive; b. 6 Oct. 1949, Valley Stream, Long Island, NY; s. of Herman Moonves and Josephine Moonves (née Schleifer); great-nephew of David Ben-Gurion, first Prime Minister of Israel; m. 1st Nancy Moonves 1978 (divorced 2004); two s. one d.; m. 2nd Julie Chen 2004; one s.; ed Bucknell Univ.; trained as actor at Neighbourhood Playhouse, NY; performed in numerous stage and tv productions; began to produce plays for Broadway and LA 1977; TV Exec., Twentieth Century Fox TV, Saul Ilson Productions and Catalina Productions 1978–85; Vice-Pres. Lorimar TV 1985–89, Pres. 1989–93; Pres. Warner Bros. TV 1993–95; Pres. CBS Entertainment and Group Exec. Vice-Pres., CBS TV 1995–98, Pres. and CEO CBS TV 1998–2003, elected to Corp. Bd of Dirs 1999, Chair. and CEO 2003–, oversees productions of UPN, CBS Enterprises, CBS News, CBS Sports, CBS Entertainment, King World Productions; Co-Pres. and Co-COO Viacom Inc. (after Viacom acquired CBS) 2000–05, Pres. and CEO CBS Corpn (after CBS split from Viacom) 2005–18, Chair. 2016–18; Dir, ZeniMax Media 1999–; Co-Chair. LA Bd of Govs, Museum of TV & Radio; mem. Nat. Collegiate Athletic Asscn (NCAA) Advisory Bd; mem. Bd of Dirs LA Free Clinic; mem. Bd of Trustees, Entertainment Industries Council; Trustee, American Film Inst., Nat. Council of Families and TV; Sherrill Corwin Award, American Jewish Committee, Gold Medal Award, Int. Radio and Television Soc. 2003, Milestone Award for Lifetime Achievement, Producers Guild of America 2012, inducted into Television Hall of Fame 2013.

MOORCOCK, Michael John, (Edward P. Bradbury, Desmond Read); British novelist; b. 18 Dec. 1939, London, England; s. of Arthur Moorcock and June Moorcock; m. 1st Hilary Bailey 1963 (divorced 1978); one s. two d.; m. 2nd Jill Riches 1978 (divorced 1983); m. 3rd Linda M. Steele 1983; ed Michael Hall School, Sussex; worked as musician and journalist; Ed. Outlaws Own 1951–53, Tarzan Adventures 1957–59, Sexton Blake Library 1959–61, Current Topics 1961–62; Ed. New Worlds 1964–71, 1976–96, Consulting Ed. 1996–; British Fantasy Award 1993, World Fantasy Lifetime Achievement Award 2000, Science Fiction Hall of Fame 2002, Prix Utopia 2004, Bram Stoker Lifetime Achievement Award 2004, named Damon Knight Grand Master, Science Fiction and Fantasy Writers of America 2008. *Films:* The Final Programme 1973, The Land that Time Forgot 1975. *Records:* Warrior on the Edge of Time (Hawkwind) 1975, The New World's Fair 1975, The Brothel in Rosenstrasse 1982, Roller Coaster Holiday 2004. *Publications include:* The Eternal Champion sequence 1963–98, Behold the Man (Nebula Award 1967) 1966, The Knight of the Swords (August Derleth Fantasy Award 1972, 1973) 1971, The Jade Man's Eyes (British Fantasy Award) 1974, The Sword and the Stallion (August Derleth Fantasy Award 1975) 1974, The Hollow Lands (August Derleth Fantasy Award 1976) 1974, Condition of Muzak (Guardian Fiction Prize 1977) 1976, Gloriana (World Fantasy Award 1979) 1977, Gloriana (John W. Campbell Memorial Award, World Fantasy Award 1979) 1978, Byzantium Endures 1981, The Laughter of Carthage 1984, Mother London 1988, Jerusalem Commands 1992, Blood 1994, The War Amongst Angels 1996, Tales from the Texas Woods 1997, King of the City 2000, Silverheart (co-author) 2000, London Bone 2001, The Dreamthief's Daughter 2001, Firing the Cathedral 2002, The Skrayling Tree 2003, The Lives and Times of Jerry Cornelius 2004, Wizardry and Wild Romance 2004, The White Wolf's Son 2005, The Vengeance of Rome 2006, The Metatemporal Detective 2007, The Best of Michael Moorcock 2009, The Coming of the Terraphiles 2010, Modem Times 2.0 2011, The Sunday Books 2011, London Peculiar and Other Nonfiction (co-ed.) 2012. *Leisure interests:* climbing, travelling, walking, cats, birds. *Address:* c/o Howard Morhaim Literary Agency, 30 Pierrepont Street, Brooklyn, NY 11201, USA (office); PO Box 1230, Bastrop, TX 78602, USA (home). *Telephone:* (718) 222-8400 (office). *Fax:* (718) 222-5056 (office). *E-mail:* howard@morhaimliterary.com (office). *Website:* www.multiverse.org.

MOORE, Carole Irene, MS; Canadian librarian; b. 15 Aug. 1944, Berkeley, Calif., USA; ed Stanford and Columbia Univs; Reference Librarian, Columbia Univ. Libraries 1967–68; Reference Librarian, Univ. of Toronto Library 1968–73, Asst Head, Reference Dept 1973–74, Head 1974–80, Head, Bibliographic Processing Dept 1980–86, Assoc. Librarian, Tech. Services 1986–87, Chief Librarian, Univ. of Toronto Library 1986–2011, Research Libraries Group Dir 1994–96; mem. Preservation of Research Library Materials Cttee, Asscn of Research Libraries 2004–06; mem. Bd of Dirs Univ. of Toronto Press 1994–2011; Columbia Univ. School of Library Service Centenary Distinguished Alumni Award 1987. *Publications:* Labour Relations and the Librarian (ed.) 1974, Canadian Essays and Collections Index 1972–73 1976. *Leisure interest:* gardening. *Address:* Chief Librarian's Office, University of Toronto Libraries, 130 St George Street, Room 2015, Toronto, ON M5S 1A5, Canada (office). *Telephone:* (416) 978-2292 (office). *Fax:* (416) 971-2099 (office). *E-mail:* carole.moore@utoronto.ca (office). *Website:* www.library.utoronto.ca (office).

MOORE, Charles Hilary, MA; British journalist and writer; b. 31 Oct. 1956, Hastings; s. of Richard Moore and Ann Moore; m. Caroline Baxter 1981; twin s. and d.; ed Eton Coll. and Trinity Coll., Cambridge; mem. editorial staff, Daily Telegraph 1979–81, leader writer 1981–83; Asst Ed. and Political Columnist, The Spectator 1983–84, Ed. 1984–90, fortnightly columnist ('Another Voice') 1990–95; weekly columnist, Daily Express 1987–90; Deputy Ed. Daily Telegraph 1990–92, Ed. Sunday Telegraph 1992–95, Ed. Daily Telegraph 1995–2003, Group Consulting Ed. and columnist, Daily Telegraph 2003–; mem. Bd of Dirs Policy Exchange (think-tank) 2004–11 (Chairman –2011); Trustee, T. E. Utley Memorial Fund, Benenden Council, ShareGift. *Publications:* 1936 (co-ed. with C. Hawtree) 1986, The Church in Crisis (with A. N. Wilson and G. Stamp) 1986, A Tory Seer: The Selected Journalism of T. E. Utley (co-ed. with S. Heffer) 1986, Margaret Thatcher: The Authorised Biography – Volume One: Not for Turning 2013, Margaret Thatcher: The Authorised Biography – Volume Two: Everything She Wants 2015. *Address:* c/o Daily Telegraph, 111 Buckingham Palace Road, London, SW1W 0DT, England (office).

MOORE, Demi; American actress; b. (Demi Gene Guynes), 11 Nov. 1962, Roswell, NM; d. of Charles Harmon and Virginia King (later Guynes); step-d. of Danny Guynes; m 1st Freddy Moore 1980 (divorced 1985); m. 2nd Bruce Willis 1987 (divorced 2000); three d.; m. 3rd Ashton Kutcher 2005 (divorced 2013); ed Fairfax High School, Hollywood; began acting with small part in TV series; worked as a model, Los Angeles; f. Moving Pictures (production co.); launched (with Ashton Kutcher) Demi and Ashton Foundation (charity directed towards fighting child sexual slavery) 2011. *Theatre:* The Early Girl (Theater World Award). *Films include:* Choices 1981, Parasite 1982, Blame It on Rio 1984, No Small Affair 1984, St Elmo's Fire 1985, One Crazy Summer 1986, About Last Night 1986, Wisdom 1986, The Seventh Sign 1988, We're No Angels 1989, Ghost 1990, Nothing But Trouble 1991, Mortal Thoughts (also co-producer) 1991, The Butcher's Wife 1991, A Few Good Men 1992, Indecent Proposal 1993, Disclosure 1994, The Scarlet Letter 1995, Now and Then 1995, Striptease 1996, The Juror 1996, The Hunchback of Notre Dame (voice) 1996, Deconstructing Harry 1997, G.I. Jane (also producer) 1997, Passion of Mind 2000, The Hunchback of Notre Dame II (voice) 2002, Charlie's Angels: Full Throttle 2003, Half Light 2006, Bobby 2006, Flawless 2007, Mr Brooks 2007, The Joneses 2009, Happy Tears 2009, Bunraku 2010, Margin Call 2011, Another Happy Day 2011, LOL: Laughing Out Loud 2012, Very Good Girls 2013, Wild Oats 2015; producer: Mortal Thoughts (co-producer) 1991, Now and Then 1995, Austin Powers: International Man of Mystery 1997, G.I. Jane 1997, Austin Powers: The Spy Who Shagged Me 1999, Austin Powers in Goldmember 2002. *Television includes:* General Hospital (series) 1982–83, The Master 1984, Bedroom 1984, Moonlighting 1989, Tales from the Crypt 1990, Master Ninja 1991, If These Walls Could Talk (also exec. producer) 1996, Ellen 1997, Will and Grace 2003, The Magic 7 (film) 2009; exec. producer: The Conversation (series) 2012. *Address:* c/o Moving Pictures, 1453 Third Street, Suite 420, Santa Monica, CA 90401, USA. *Telephone:* (310) 576-0577.

MOORE, Gordon Earle, PhD, FIEEE, FRSEng; American fmr semiconductor executive; *Chairman Emeritus, Intel Corporation;* b. 3 Jan. 1929, San Francisco; m.; two c.; ed Univ. of Calif., Berkeley, Calif. Inst. of Tech.; with Fairchild Semiconductor –1968; Co-founder and Exec. Vice-Pres. Integrated Electronics (Intel, world's largest manufacturer of microprocessors) 1968–75, Pres. and CEO 1975–79, Chair. and CEO 1979–87, Chair. 1987–97, Chair. Emer. 1997–; Dir Gilead Sciences Inc.; mem. Nat. Acad. of Eng; mem. Bd Trustees Calif. Inst. of Tech.; Nat. Medal of Tech. 1990, Dan David Prize 2010. *Address:* Intel Corpn, 2200 Mission College Boulevard, Santa Clara, CA 95052-8119, USA (office). *Telephone:* (408) 765-8080 (office). *Fax:* (408) 765-9904 (office). *Website:* www.intel.com (office).

MOORE, The Hon. James, PC; Canadian politician; b. 10 June 1976, New Westminster; m. Courtney Moore; mem. House of Commons for Port Moody–Coquitlam 2000–04, for Port Moody–Westwood 2004–15; Parl. Sec. to Minister Public Works and Govt Services 2006–07; Sec. of State for Official Languages, Pacific Gateway and the Vancouver-Whistler Olympics 2007–08; Minister of Canadian Heritage and Official Languages 2008–13, of Industry 2013–15; mem. Canadian Alliance Party 2000–03, Conservative Party of Canada 2003–. *Address:* Conservative Party of Canada, 130 Albert Street, Suite 1720, Ottawa, ON K1P 5G4, Canada (office). *Telephone:* (613) 755-2000 (office). *Fax:* (613) 755-2001 (office). *E-mail:* info@conservative.ca (office). *Website:* www.conservative.ca (office).

MOORE, Hon. John Colinton, AO, BCom, AASA; Australian fmr politician and company director; b. 16 Nov. 1936, Rockhampton; s. of T. R. Moore and D. S. Moore; m. 2nd Jacquelyn Moore; two s. one d. from previous m.; ed Armidale School, Queensland Univ.; stockbroker 1960; mem. Brisbane Stock Exchange 1962–74; Vice-Pres. and Treas. Queensland Liberal Party 1967–73, Pres. 1973–76, 1984–90; MP for Ryan 1975–2001; Minister for Business and Consumer Affairs 1980–82; Opposition Spokesman for Finance 1983–84, for Communications 1984–85, for Northern Devt and Local Govt 1985–87, for Transport and Aviation 1987, for Business and Consumer Affairs 1987–89, for Business Privatization and Consumer Affairs 1989–90; Shadow Minister for Privatization and Public Admin. 1994, for Privatization 1994–95, for Industry, Commerce and Public Admin. 1995–96; Minister for Industry, Science and Tourism 1996–97, of Industry, Science and Tech. 1997–98, for Defence 1998–2001; Vice-Pres. Exec. Council 1996–98; Dir William Brandt & Sons (Australia), Phillips, First City, Brandt Ltd, Merrill Lynch, Pierce, Fennell and Smith (Australia) Ltd, Citinat, Agricultural Investments Australia Ltd; mem. various int. dels, Council Order of Australia, Advisory Council General Motors, Australia. *Leisure interests:* tennis, cricket, reading, golf. *Address:* PO Box 2191, Toowong, Brisbane 4066; 47 Dennis Street, Indooroopilly, Brisbane, Australia (home). *Telephone:* 419 704764 (office); (7) 3217-7427 (home). *Fax:* (7) 3876-8088 (office). *E-mail:* john_moore1@bigpond.com.au (home).

MOORE, Julianne, BA; American/British actress; b. (Julie Anne Smith), 3 Dec. 1960, Fort Bragg, North Carolina; d. of Peter Moore Smith and Anne Smith (née Love); m. 1st John Gould Rubin 1986 (divorced 1995); m. 2nd Bart Freundlich 2003; one s. one d.; ed Boston Univ. School for Arts TV; with the Guthrie Theater 1988–89; UK citizenship 2011. *Stage appearances include:* Serious Money 1987, Ice Cream with Hot Fudge 1990, Uncle Vanya, The Road to Nirvana, Hamlet, The Father, The Vertical Hour 2006. *Films include:* Tales from the Darkside 1990, The Hand That Rocks the Cradle 1992, The Gun in Betty Lou's Handbag 1992, Body of Evidence 1993, Benny and Joon 1993, The Fugitive 1993, Short Cuts 1993, Vanya on 42nd Street 1994, Roommates 1995, Safe 1995, Nine Months 1995, Assassins 1995, Surviving Picasso 1996, Jurassic Park: The Lost World 1997, The Myth of Fingerprints 1997, Hellcab 1997, Boogie Nights 1997, The Big Lebowski 1998, Eyes Wide Shut, The End of the Affair 1999, Map of the World 1999, Magnolia 1999, Cookie's Fortune 1999, An Ideal Husband 1999, Hannibal 2000, The Shipping News 2002, Far From Heaven (Best Actress, Venice Film Festival) 2002, The Hours 2002, Marie and Bruce 2004, Laws of Attraction 2004, The Forgotten 2004, Trust the Man 2005, Freedomland 2005, Children of Men 2006, Next 2007, I'm Not There 2007, Savage Grace 2007, Blindness 2008, Shelter 2009, The Private Lives of Pippa Lee 2009, A Single Man 2009, Chloe 2010, The Kids Are All Right 2010, Crazy, Stupid, Love 2011, Being Flynn 2012, What Maisie Knew 2012, The English Teacher 2012, Don Jon's Addiction 2013, Carrie 2013, The Seventh Son 2014, The Hunger Games: Mockingjay – Part 1 2014, Still Alice (Golden Globe for

Best Actress in a Motion Picture 2015, Best Actress, Critics' Choice Movie Awards, Broadcast Film Critics Asscn 2015, Actress of the Year, London Critics' Circle 2015, Outstanding Performance by a Female Actor in a Motion Picture, Screen Actors Guild 2015, BAFTA Award for Best Actress in a Leading Role 2015, Academy Award for Best Actress 2015) 2014, Maps to the Stars (Award for Best Actress, Cannes Film Festival 2014) 2014, Freeheld 2015, The Hunger Games: Mockingjay – Part 2 2015. *Television includes:* The Edge of Night (series) 1984, As the World Turns (series) 1985–87, 2010, Money, Power Murder (film) 1989, B.L. Stryker (series) 1990, Lovecraft 1991, I'll Take Manhattan (mini-series) 1987, The Last to Go (film) 1991, Cast a Deadly Spell (film) 1991, 30 Rock (series) 2009–13, A Child's Garden of Poetry (film) (voice) 2011, Game Change (film) (Emmy Award for Best Lead Actress in a Miniseries or Movie 2012, Golden Globe Award for Best Performance by an Actress in a Mini-Series or Motion Picture Made for TV 2013) 2012. *Publications include:* for children: Freckleface Strawberry (illustrated by LeUyen Pham) 2007, Freckleface Strawberry and the Dodgeball Bully (illustrated by LeUyen Pham) 2009, Freckleface Strawberry Best Friends Forever (illustrated by LeUyen Pham) 2011, My Mom is a Foreigner, But Not to Me (illustrated by Meilo So) 2013, Backpacks! 2015, Lunch, or What's That? 2015, Loose Tooth! 2016, Freckleface Strawberry & the Really Big Voice 2017. *Address:* c/o Kevin Huvane, Creative Artists Agency, 2000 Avenue of the Stars, Los Angeles, CA 90067, USA (office). *Telephone:* (424) 288-2000 (office). *Fax:* (424) 288-2900 (office). *Website:* www.caa.com (office).

MOORE, Michael Francis; American writer and filmmaker; b. 23 April 1954, Davison, Mich.; m. Kathleen Glynn 1991 (divorced 2014); ed Davison High School; elected to Davison, Mich. school bd aged 18; active in student politics; began career as journalist with The Flint Voice, later Ed., expanded into The Mich. Voice; Ed. Mother Jones magazine, San Francisco 1986–88; Founder and mem. Bd of Dirs Traverse City (Mich.) Film Festival. *Television includes:* Pets or Meat: The Return to Flint 1992, TV Nation (NBC series) 1994–95, 1997, And Justice for All (dir) 1998, The Awful Truth (series) 1999. *Films:* Roger and Me (writer, dir, producer) 1989, Canadian Bacon (writer, producer, dir) 1994, The Big One (dir) 1997, Bowling for Columbine (screenwriter, dir, producer; Jury Award, Cannes Film Festival 2003, Acad. Award for Best Documentary 2003) 2002, Fahrenheit 9/11 (dir; Palme d'Or, Cannes Film Festival, US People's Choice Award for Best Film 2005) 2004, Sicko 2007, Capitalism: A Love Story 2009, Where to Invade Next 2015. *Film appearances:* Lucky Number 1999, EdTV 1999. *Publications:* Downsize This!: Random Threats from an Unarmed America 1996, Stupid White Men (Book of the Year, British Book Awards 2003) 2001, Adventures in a TV Nation (with Kathleen Glynn) 2002, Dude, Where's My Country? 2003, Will They Ever Trust Us Again?: Letters from the War Zone 2004, The Official Fahrenheit 9/11 Reader 2004, Mike's Election Guide 2008 2008, Here Comes Trouble: Stories from My Life 2011, I Am Moore 2011. *E-mail:* mike@michaelmoore.com. *Website:* www.michaelmoore.com.

MOORE, Rt Hon. Michael (Mike) Kenneth, ONZ, PC; New Zealand politician, international organization official and diplomatist; *Ambassador to USA;* b. 28 Jan. 1949, Whakatane; s. of Alan Moore and Audrey Moore; m. Yvonne Dereaney 1975; fmr social worker, printer; MP for Eden 1972–75, Papanui, Christchurch 1978–84, Christchurch N 1984–96, Waimakariri 1996–99; Minister of Overseas Trade and Marketing, also Minister of Tourism and Publicity and of Recreation and Sport 1984–87; Minister of Overseas Trade and Marketing and of Publicity 1987–88, 1989–90, of External Relations and Int. Trade 1988–90; Minister of Foreign Affairs Jan.–Oct. 1990; Prime Minister Sept.–Oct. 1990; Leader of the Opposition 1990–93; fmr Assoc. Minister of Finance; Dir-Gen. WTO 1999–2002; Amb. to USA 2010–; held numerous appointments and board memberships with global policy and commercial organisations, including UN Comm. on the Legal Empowerment of the Poor, Commr for UN Global Comm. on int. Migration, several pvt. sector bds; served on Econ. Devt Bd of South Australia; fmr adviser to other Govts; mem. Trilateral Comm.; fmr Adjunct Prof., Adelaide Univ., La Trobe Univ.; Founder School Aid (charity); Hon. Prof., Beijing Normal Univ., Zuhai, Chinese Univ. for Political Science and Int. Law, Beijing, Shanghai Customs Coll.; numerous honours from governments in Africa, Europe and South America; Dr hc (Lincoln Univ., People's Univ. of China, Beijing, Auckland Univ. of Tech., Canterbury Univ., La Trobe Univ.). *Publications include:* ten books, including A Pacific Parliament, Hard Labour, Fighting for New Zealand 1993, Children of the Poor 1996, A Brief History of the Future 1998, A World Without Walls 2007, Saving Globalisation 2009. *Address:* Embassy of New Zealand, 37 Observatory Circle NW, Washington, DC 20008, USA (office). *Telephone:* (202) 328-4800 (office). *Fax:* (202) 667-5227 (office). *E-mail:* wshinfo@mfat.govt.nz (office). *Website:* www.nzembassy.com/usa (office).

MOORE, Michael Kevin; British chartered accountant and politician; b. 3 June 1965, Dundonald, Co. Down, Northern Ireland; ed Jedburgh Grammar School, Univ. of Edinburgh; moved with family to Wishaw, Scotland 1970, then to Scottish Borders 1981; worked for a year as researcher for Liberal Democrat MP Archy Kirkwood before joining Edinburgh office of accountants Coopers & Lybrand, later Man. in office's corp. finance practice; worked as researcher for David Steel (Liberal Democrat politician); MP for Tweeddale, Ettrick and Lauderdale 1997–2005, for Berwickshire, Roxburgh and Selkirk 2005–15, mem. Scottish Affairs Select Cttee 1997–99, Armed Forces Bill Select Cttee 2005–06; Liberal Democrat Spokesperson for Scotland 1997–99, 2001, for Transport 1999–2001; Shadow Minister for Foreign Affairs 2001–05; Shadow Sec. of State for Defence 2005–06, for Foreign and Commonwealth Affairs 2006–07, for Int. Devt 2007–08, for NI and Scotland 2008–10; Sec. of State for Scotland 2010–13; Campaign Chair. Scottish Parl. elections 1999, 2003; Parl. Group Convener 2000–01; Scottish MP Rep., Liberal Democrat Policy Cttee 2001–02; Deputy Leader Scottish Liberal Democrats 2002–10, Acting Leader July–Aug. 2008; mem. UK del. to NATO Parl. Ass. 2007–10; Liberal Democrat.

MOORE, Michael Rodney Newton, CBE, MA, MBA; British lawyer and business executive; b. 15 March 1936; s. of Gen. Sir Rodney Moore and Olive Marion Robinson; m. Jan Moore; one s.; ed Eton Coll., Magdalen Coll., Oxford and Harvard Business School, USA; called to the Bar 1961; Chair. Tomkins PLC 1984–95, Quicks Group plc 1993–2002, Linx Printing Technologies plc 1993–2005, London Int. Group PLC 1994–, Status Holdings PLC 2000–; mem. Bd of Dirs, Clerical Medical & General Life Assurance Soc. 1993–, Deputy Chair. 1996–; Dir, Caledonian Stoneywood Ltd 1992–94, Gemvolk Ltd 1992–93, Brixton Estates plc

1997–2006, HBOS Insurance & Investment Group Ltd 1997–98, 2001–03, Warm Zones C.I.C. 2001–04, Which? Ltd 1993–2008 (Chair. 1997–2008); Chair. Nat. Soc. for Prevention of Cruelty to Children (NSPCC) 1992–95; Trustee, Public Concern at Work 1996–2003. *Leisure interests:* reading, music (especially opera), visiting ruins, tennis. *Address:* Peppering High Barn, Burpham, Arundel, BN18 9RN, England.

MOORE, Nicholas G., JD, BS; American business executive; m. Jo Anne Moore; four c.; ed St Mary's Coll., Calif., Hastings Coll. of Law, Univ. of Calif., Berkeley; joined Coopers & Lybrand 1968, Pnr 1974, Head of Tax Practice, San José office 1974–81, Man. Partner San José Office 1981, mem. firm council 1984, Exec. Cttee 1988, Vice-Chair. W Region 1991–92, Client Service Vice-Chair. 1992, Chair., CEO Coopers & Lybrand USA 1994, Chair. Coopers & Lybrand Int. 1997, Global Chair. and CEO PricewaterhouseCoopers LLP (formed from merger of Coopers & Lybrand Int. and Price Waterhouse) 1999–2001; mem. Bd of Dirs, Network Appliance Inc. 2002–, Bechtel Group, Inc., NetApp, Inc. 2002–, Brocade Communications Systems, Inc. 2003–05, Hudson Highland Group, Inc. 2003–06, Gilead Sciences, Inc. 2004–, E2open, Inc. 2004–, Wells Fargo & Co. 2006–13; Chair. Co-operation Ireland; Vice-Chair. Business Cttee, Metropolitan Museum of Art; mem. Bush-Cheney election campaign 2004, Friends of Giuliani Exploratory Cttee; mem. Calif. Bar Asscn, American Inst. of CPAs, California & New York Soc. of CPAs; Trustee, Financial Accounting Foundation from 1997, St Mary's Coll. of Calif. (Past Chair.), Cttee for Econ. Devt. *Address:* Bechtel Group, Inc., 50 Beale Street, San Francisco, CA 94105-1895, USA (office). *Telephone:* (415) 768-1234 (office). *Fax:* (415) 768-9038 (office). *Website:* www.bechtel.com (office).

MOORE, Richard Peter, CMG; British diplomatist; *Director General for Political Affairs, FCO;* m. Margaret (Maggie) Patricia Isabel Moore; one s. one d.; joined FCO 1987, Third Sec., Embassy in Hanoi 1988, Second Sec. (Political), Embassy in Ankara 1990, Consul (Political and Press), Istanbul 1991–92, Desk Officer, Iran, FCO 1992–95, First Sec., High Comm. in Islamabad 1995–98, Section Head, Security Policy Group, FCO 1998–2001, Counsellor, High Comm. in Kuala Lumpur 2001–05, Deputy Dir, Middle East, FCO 2005–08, Stanford Exec. Program 2007, Dir, Programmes and Change, FCO 2008–10, Dir, Europe, Latin America and Globalization 2010–13, Amb. to Turkey 2014–17, Dir-Gen. for Political Affairs, FCO 2018–. *Address:* Foreign and Commonwealth Office, King Charles Street, London SW1A 2AH, England (office). *Telephone:* (20) 7008-1500 (office). *E-mail:* fcocorrespondence@fco.gov.uk (office). *Website:* www.gov.uk/government/organisations/foreign-commonwealth-office (office).

MOORE OF LOWER MARSH, Baron (Life Peer), cr. 1992, of Lower Marsh in the London Borough of Lambeth; **John Edward Michael Moore;** British politician; b. 26 Nov. 1937; s. of Edward O. Moore; m. Sheila S. Tillotson 1962; two s. one d.; ed London School of Econs; with Royal Sussex Regt Korea 1955–57; Pres. Students' Union LSE 1959–60; banking and stockbroking, Chicago 1962–65; Dir Dean Witter Int. Ltd 1968–79, Chair. 1975–79; underwriting mem. Lloyds 1978–92; Exec. Chair. Crédit Suisse Asset Man. 1991–, Energy Saving Trust Ltd 1992–95 (Pres. 1995–); mem. Parl. for Croydon Cen. 1974–92; Parl. Under-Sec. of State, Dept of Energy 1979–83; Econ. Sec. to HM Treasury June–Oct. 1983, Financial Sec. to HM Treasury Oct. 1983–86; Sec. of State for Transport 1986–87, for Dept of Health and Social Security 1987–88, for Social Security 1988–89; Dir Monitor Inc. 1990– (Chair. Monitor Europe 1990–), Blue Circle Industries 1993–, Camelot PLC 1994–96, Rolls-Royce PLC (Deputy Chair. 1996–2003, Acting Chair. 2003–05), Crédit Suisse Investment Man. Australia 1995–, Cen. European Growth Fund PLC 1995–, BEA Assocs USA 1996–98, TIG Inc. 1997–, Pvt. Client Partners, Zurich 1999–; mem. Court of Govs LSE 1977–. *Address:* House of Lords, Westminster, London, SW1A 0PW; Crédit Suisse Asset Management Ltd, Beaufort House, 15 St. Botolph Street, London, EC3A 7JJ, England (office). *Telephone:* (20) 7426-2626 (office). *Fax:* (20) 7426-2618 (office).

MOORMAN VAN KAPPEN, Olav, LLD; Dutch legal historian and academic; *Professor Emeritus of Legal History, Nijmegen University;* b. 11 March 1937, The Hague; s. of Karel S. O. van Kappen and Johanna J. Moorman; m. Froukje A. Bosma 1963; one s. one d.; ed Huygens Lyceum and Utrecht Univ.; Research Asst Faculty of Law, Utrecht Univ. 1961–64, Jr Lecturer 1965–68; Sr Lecturer Faculty of Law, Amsterdam Univ. 1968–71; Asst Prof. Faculty of Law, Leyden Univ. 1971–72; Prof. of Legal History, Nijmegen Univ. 1971–2000, Co. Dir Gerard Noodt Inst. for Legal History 1972–2000, Emer. Prof. 2000–; Visiting Prof. Munster Univ. 1982–83, Poitiers Univ. 1986, 1991 Düsseldorf Univ. 1989–90, Univ. René Descartes (Paris V) 1992, 1995, 1999; mem. Bd of Govs Netherlands School for Archivists 1979–81, Chair. 1981–95; mem. Netherlands Council of Archives 1979–89, Vice-Pres. 1986–89, Pres. 1990–95; mem. Nat. Council of Cultural Heritage 1990–95; mem. editorial Bd, Legal History Review 1983–2007; mem. Dutch Soc. of Sciences at Haarlem 1982, Royal Netherlands Acad. of Sciences 1986; Corresp. mem. Acad. of Sciences, Göttingen 1996; Dr hc (Univ. René Descartes (Paris V)); Cross of Merit 1st Class (FRG), Officier, Ordre des Palmes Académiques (France), Officier, Orde van Oranje-Nassau (Netherlands). *Publications:* over 360 books and articles on various aspects of legal history. *Address:* Institute of Legal Science of Nijmegen University, PO Box 9049, 6500 KK Nijmegen, Netherlands. *Telephone:* (24) 3612186. *Fax:* (24) 3616145.

MOOSA, Mohammed Valli, BSc; South African politician and international organization executive; *Chairman, Anglo American Platinum Limited;* b. 9 Feb. 1957, Johannesburg; m. Elsabé Wessels; ed Lenasia State Indian High School, Univ. of Durban-Westville; active in South African Students' Org., Nat. Indian Congress and other political and trade-union activities; teacher 1979–82; involved in est. of Anti-South African Indian Council Cttee 1982, revival of Transvaal Indian Congress 1983; Founder mem. and fmr mem. Nat. Exec. Cttee United Democratic Front; fmr Leader Mass Democratic Movt; detained 1987, escaped 1988; planned Defiance Campaign; detained 1989; involved in Conf. for a Democratic Future 1989; mem. Nat. Reception Cttee for released African Nat. Congress (ANC) leaders 1989–90; with ANC 1990–, mem. Nat. Exec. Cttee 1991, fmr mem. Nat. Working Cttee, rep. of negotiating team Convention for a Democratic South Africa 1991–94; Deputy Minister of Prov. Affairs and Constitutional Devt 1994, Minister 1996–99, Minister of Environmental Affairs and Tourism 1999–2004; Pres. Int. Union for the Conservation of Nature 2004–08, Chair. Congress Steering Cttee; Chair., Sun Int. Ltd 2009–, World Wide Fund for Nature, South Africa 2011; Chair. Anglo American Platinum Ltd 2013– (mem. Bd of Dirs 2008–, Deputy Chair. 2010–13); mem. Bd of Dirs Sanlam Life Insurance Ltd 2004, Sappi Imperial Holdings, Lereko Investments Pty Ltd. *Address:* Anglo American Platinum Limited, 55 Marshall Street, Marshalltown 2107, Johannesburg 2001, South Africa (office). *Telephone:* (11) 3736111 (office). *Website:* www.angloamericanplatinum.com (office).

MOOSHAHARY, Ranjit Shekhar, BA, MDPA; Indian fmr government official and fmr police officer; b. 1 March 1946, Oldaguri, Kokrajhar Dist (now under Bodoland Territorial Area Dists of Assam); s. of Shikendra Mooshahary and Nandeswari Mooshahary; m. Rema Menon Mooshahary; one s. one d.; ed Union Christian Coll., Umiam, St Anthony's Coll., Shillong, Indian Inst. of Public Admin, New Delhi; joined Indian Police Service 1967, assigned to Kerala cadre, fmr Chief of Crime Br., Criminal Investigation Dept and Vigilance and Anti-Corruption Bureau, Kerala; Dir-Gen. Nat. Security Guards 2002–05, Border Security Force 2005–06; State Chief Information Commr, Assam 2006–08; Gov. of Meghalaya 2008–13; Hon. DLitt; Indian Police Medal for Meritorious Service, Pres.'s Police Medal for Distinguished Services, Man of the Year Award, Engkhong Trust Bijni 2008, Adivasi Ratna Award 2011. *E-mail:* mooshahary@gmail.com.

MOOTHA, Vamsi Krishna, BS, MD; American (b. Indian) medical scientist, physician and academic; *Professor of Systems Biology, Harvard Medical School;* b. 1971, Kakinada, AP, India; ed Kelly High School, Beaumont, Tex., Stanford Univ., Calif., Harvard-MIT Div. of Health Sciences and Tech., Harvard Medical School, Mass; Internship and Residency in Internal Medicine, Brigham and Women's Hosp., Boston, Mass 1998–2001; Postdoctoral Fellowship, Whitehead Inst. for Biomedical Research, Cambridge, Mass 2001–04; Prof. of Systems Biology, Harvard Medical School 2004–, Prof. of Medicine, Massachusetts Gen. Hosp.; Investigator, Howard Hughes Medical Inst. (HHMI); Sr Research Mem., Broad Inst. of Harvard and MIT, Cambridge, Mass; mem. Editorial Bd, Molecular Systems Biology, Cell Metabolism, European Molecular Biology Organization Journal; mem. Assoc. of American Physicians, NAS 2014; Grand Award Winner, 40th Int. Science and Eng Fair 1989, David Starr Jordan Scholarship, Stanford Univ. 1990, HHMI Postdoctoral Fellowship for Physicians 2001, John D. and Catherine T. MacArthur Genius Grant 2004, NIH Wednesday Lectureship 2006, Judson Daland Prize, American Philosophical Soc. 2008, MGH Martin Prize for Basic Research 2011, NIH Transformative Research Project Award 2011, Keilin Medal, Biochemical Soc. 2014, Padma Shri, Govt of India 2014. *Publications:* numerous papers in professional journals. *Address:* Mootha Laboratory, MGH Molecular Biology, 185 Cambridge Street, CPZN 7250, Boston, MA 02114, USA (office). *E-mail:* vamsi@hms.harvard.edu (office). *Website:* mootha.med.harvard.edu (office).

MOQBEL, Samir; Lebanese engineer and politician; b. 1939; m. Joyce James; five c.; ed American Univ. of Beirut; CEO Samir Moqbel & Co. (real estate co.) 1965–; Minister of the Environment 1992–95, Deputy Prime Minister 2011–16, also Minister of Defence 2014–16; Pres. Alumni Asscn of the American Univ. of Beirut (Mount Lebanon) 1990–92; mem. Bd of Dirs Univ. of Balamand 1990–; mem. Chamber of Commerce and Industry of Beirut 1992–96.

MOQBEL OSMANI, Zarar Ahmad; Afghan fmr diplomatist and politician; b. 1964, Parwan Prov.; m.; two s. two d.; ed Polytechnical Univ. of Kabul; Chief of Police, Parwan Prov. 1994; First Sec., later Amb. to Iran 1998–2002; Gov. Parwan Prov. 2004; Deputy Minister of Interior Affairs –Sept. 2005, Acting Minister of Interior Affairs Sept. 2005–March 2006, Minister of Interior Affairs 2006–08, of Refugees and Repatriation 2008, of Counter Narcotics 2009–13, of Foreign Affairs 2013–15; Wazir Akbar Khan Medal.

MORA, Maira; Latvian diplomatist and international organization official; *Director-General, Permanent International Secretariat, Council of the Baltic Sea States (CBSS);* ed Univ. of Latvia, Swiss Int. Relations Univ., Graduate Inst. of Int. Studies, Geneva, Int. Security Studies Coll., Germany; joined Ministry of Foreign Affairs (MFA) 1992, becoming Head, Policy Planning Unit, Deputy Head, Latvian Del. to Org. for Security and Co-operation in Europe (OSCE), Vienna, Counsellor, Bureau of the State Sec., MFA European Corresp.; Amb. to Belarus and Lithuania 2002–04; Head, EU Del., Belarus 2011–15; Dir-Gen., Perm. Int. Secr., Council of the Baltic Sea States (CBSS) 2016–; fmr mem. Crisis Control Expert Comm., Office of the Prime Minister; Orders of Merit from Lithuania and Austria. *Publications:* trans.: Diplomātija (Diplomacy) 2001, Eiropas vesture (Europe: A History) (with Janis Zīdersem) 2009. *Leisure interests:* classical music, opera, tennis, skiing. *Address:* Council of the Baltic Sea States, POB 2010, 103 11 Stockholm, Sweden (office). *Telephone:* (8) 440-19-21 (office). *E-mail:* maira.mora@cbss.org (office). *Website:* www.cbss.org (office).

MORA GRAMUNT, Gabriel; Spanish architect; *Partner, Mora-Sanvisens Arquitectes Associats;* b. 13 April 1941, Barcelona; s. of Evaristo Mora Gramunt and Josefa Mora Gramunt; m. Carmina Sanvisens Montón 1985; one s.; ed Tech. Univ. of Architecture, Barcelona (ETSAB); Assoc. Piñón-Viaplana 1967; tutor, ETSAB 1973; in partnership with Jaume Bach Nuñez, Bach/Mora Architects 1976, currently Mora-Sanvisens; Prof. of History of Modern Architecture, EINA School of Design 1978; Design Tutor, ETSAB 1978–; Visiting Prof., Univ. of Dublin 1993; has given numerous seminars and confs in Spain, Germany, France, Italy, the Netherlands, Austria, Slovenia, UK, Ireland, Finland and Latin America; various professional awards. *Works include:* Grass Hockey Olympic Stadium, Terrassa 1992, Edificio Central de Telefónica, Olympic Village, Barcelona 1992, Instituto IES Mollet del Vallès, Mollet del Vallès 1995, Escuela Ramon Fuster Cerdanyola del Vallès 1998–2002, Gimnasio y Sala de actos de la Escuela Tècnic Eulàlia, Barcelona, 2002, Estación de metro 'el Maresme Fòrum', Línia 4 de TMB, Barcelona 2004, Casa MPS, en la playa del Ros, Cadaqués 2004, Viviendas sociales Can Llong, Sabadell 2005, Casa VM en el Pasaje de S'Alqueria, Cadaqués 2007, Estación de Metro 'Alfons X', Línia L4 de TMB, Barcelona 2008, Escuela pública de Cadaqués 2008, Estación Metro 'La Sagrera', Línia 9 de TMB, Barcelona 2008–10, Biblioteca Municipal 'Esteve Paluzie', Barberà del Vallès 2009, Escuela pública 'CEIP de Palautordera', Palautordera 2010, Conjunto de viviendas sociales en la 'Mina', Sant Adrià del Besòs 2011, Estaciones Metro Hosp. Clínic -Hosp. Sant Pau, Línia 5 TMB, Barcelona 2011, Edificio Secundaria 'Ramón Fuster', Cerdanyola del Vallès 2012, apartment bldgs, agric. complex, health clinic etc. *Publications include:* Junge Architekten in Europa (co-author) 1983, Guía de arquitectura de Barcelona 1985, Young Spanish Architects (co-author) 1985, Arquitectura de Barcelona (co-author) 1990, Barcelona olímpica 1992, Bach Mora Arquitectos 1996. *Address:* Mora-Sanvisens Arquitectes Associats, C. Hercegovia 24, Pral. 1A, 08006 Barcelona, Spain. *Telephone:* (93) 4147720. *Fax:* (93) 4141627. *E-mail:* g.mora@coac.es. *Website:* www.morasanvisens.com.

MORA RODAS, Nelson Alcides, Dr en Derecho; Paraguayan lawyer, politician and academic; b. 23 July 1956; m. Yolanda Peralta Álvarez; three c.; ed Nat. Coll. of the Capital, Faculty of Social Sciences, Nat. Univ. of Asunción, Catholic Univ. of Colombia, Bogotá, Univ. of Salamanca, Spain, Colegio Mayor de Nuestra Sra. del Rosario, Bogotá, Nat. War Coll., Asunción; Titular Prof. of Criminal Procedural Law, Catholic Univ., Villarrica; taught classes, courses and held confs at Nat. Univ. of Asunción, Visiting Prof., Faculty of Law and Social Sciences; fmr civil employee, Ministry of Justice and Labour; fmr Sec. of Court; fmr solicitor for Prosecutor Gen.; fmr Judge of First Instance in Penal and Civil Law; mem. Court of Criminal Appeal; Amb. to Colombia 1995–2003; Solicitor Gen. 2003–04; Minister of the Interior 2004–05, of Nat. Defence 2007–08; mem. Asoc. Nacional Republicana-Partido Colorado (Nat. Republican Asscn-Colorado Party); Degree of Grand Cross 'Academic Excellence', the Hispano-American Acad. of Sciences and Letters and Univ. Piloto of Colombia, Bogotá 1997, Grand Cross of Boyacá (Colombia) 2003. *Publications:* Amarras fraternas, Colombia Paraguay 1999, Delincuencias Internacional Organizada. Drogas. Narcotráfico. Espacio Judicial Común 2000, Código Penal Paraguayo, Doctrina, Comentarios, Concordancias, Leyes Especiales 2000, Cerca del amanecer 2001. *Address:* Asociación Nacional Republicana–Partido Colorado, Casa de los Colorados, 25 de Mayo 842, Asunción, Paraguay (office). *Telephone:* (21) 452543 (office). *Fax:* (21) 454136 (office). *E-mail:* contacto@anr.gov.py (office). *Website:* www.anr.org.py (office).

MORA WITT, Galo, PhD; Ecuadorean writer, musician and politician; *Permanent Delegate to UNESCO;* b. 1957, Loja; ed Salesiana Univ.; guitarist and singer with Pueblo Nuevo 1978–; adviser to Casa de la Cultura Ecuatoriana 1996–2004; apptd Minister of Culture 2008; Pvt. Sec. to Pres. Rafael Correa 2009–10; Exec. Sec., Movimiento Alianza País 2010–14; Amb. Extraordinary and Plenipotentiary, Perm. Delegate to UNESCO 2015–. *Publications include:* Un pájaro redondo para jugar (Memoria y Fútbol) 2002, Memorial de una Lumbrera (biografía de Pío Jaramillo Alvarado); numerous essays and articles. *Address:* Permanent Delegation of Ecuador to UNESCO, Maison de l'UNESCO Bureau M5.23 1, rue Miollis, 75732 Paris Cedex 15, France (office). *Telephone:* (1) 45-68-33-03 (office). *Fax:* (1) 43-06-49-06 (office). *E-mail:* dl.ecuador@unesco-delegations.org (office). *Website:* www.ministeriodecultura.gov.ec (office); en.unesco.org (office).

MORA ZEVALLOS, Daniel Emiliano; Peruvian politician; b. 18 Feb. 1945, Callao; ed Chorrillos Mil. School, Univ. of Lima, Int. Inst. of Humanitarian Law, San Remo, Italy; Prof., Political Acad. of Chile 1976–80; Founding mem. Perú Posible (PP) party 2000; Sec.-Gen., Ministry of Transport and Communication 2002–03, Head of advisory staff and Chair. Nat. Intelligence Council 2003–04; Presidential Adviser in Govt Palace 2005–06; mem. Congreso (Parl.) for Callao constituency 2011–16; Minister of Defence July–Dec. 2011.

MORAGODA, (Asoka) Milinda, MBA; Sri Lankan politician; b. 4 June 1964, Colombo; s. of Christopher Walter Pinto and Yasodha Neiliya Jayawardena; m. Jennifer Moragoda; ed Royal Coll., Colombo, Int. Inst. for Man. Devt, Switzerland; Special Rep. for Sri Lankan Govt under Admin of Pres. Ranasinghe Premadasa early 1990s; fmr Special Advisor Ministry of Policy Planning and Implementation; fmr Special Advisor to Ministry of Industries, Science and Tech.; fmr Chair. Ceylon Inst. for Scientific and Industrial Research (now ITI); Founder-mem. Bd and Man. Cttee Janasaviya Trust Fund; Fellow, Centre for Int. Affairs, Harvard Univ., USA 1994–95; Founder-Chair. Mercantile Merchant Bank Ltd; also involved in creation of Colombo Stock Exchange, served as Alt. Dir on first Bd; mem. bd of dirs of several corp. bds; first entered Parl. as Nat. List MP 2000, contested from Colombo Dist as Organizer for Colombo East, elected 2001, re-elected (United Nat. Party—UNP) 2004; Minister for Econ. Reform, Science and Tech. and Deputy Minister of Policy Devt and Implementation 2002–04, played key role in establishing ceasefire and beginning peace talks between Govt and LTTE (Tamil Tigers), subsequently served as a prin. govt negotiator; apptd Chief UNP Organizer for Colombo West 2005; Minister of Tourism 2007–09, of Justice and Law Reforms 2009–10; Leader Sri Lanka Nat. Congress 2010–11 (disbanded); joined Sri Lanka Freedom Party 2011; Leader of the Opposition, Colombo Municipal Council 2010–15; writes regular column in both Sunday Lankadeepa and in Sunday Thinakkural; mem. High Level Comm. on Legal Empowerment of the Poor (under UN Millennium Challenge Goals); mem. Young Global Leaders, World Econ. Forum, Geneva 2005–; Chair. Dayaka Sabawa of Amarapura Nikaya (one of three main Buddhist sects in Sri Lanka); Trustee, Soma Sadaham Sevana Trust (formed by Amarapura Dharmarakshitha Nikaya) 2005; also f. several non-profit orgs to engage in projects in areas of educ., social reform, social welfare, publishing, humanitarian services (including de-mining), culture and religion; Order of Rio Branco (Brazil) for services rendered as Hon. Consul for Brazil 1990–2004 1999; Global Leader of Tomorrow, World Econ. Forum 2000, Young Global Leader, World Econ. Forum 2009, www.milinda.org honoured in categories of Political and Personal Websites, Webby Awards 2007. *Radio:* weekly Sunday radio show on Sirasa FM, Sanvada (discusses relevant contemporary issues). *Television:* cr. and hosted series of talk shows, including: In Black and White, Obey Wedikawa (Your Forum), Gamin Gamata (Village to Village), Urumayaka Ulpath (Sources of Our Heritage), Turning Point. *Publications:* has contributed articles internationally to publs including The Washington Post and The Asian Wall Street Journal. *Address:* 8/30, Siddhartha Road, Colombo 6, Sri Lanka (office). *Telephone:* (11) 4020635 (office). *Fax:* (11) 4527111 (office). *E-mail:* email@milinda.org (office). *Website:* www.milinda.org (office).

MORAIS, Marisa Helena do Nascimento; Cabo Verde lawyer and politician; *Minister of Internal Administration;* b. 29 Sept. 1964, Ilha de São Vicente; ed Univ. of Coimbra, Portugal; lawyer in pvt. practice, then legal adviser to Minister of Justice; Minister of Justice 2009–11, of Internal Admin 2011–. *Address:* Ministry of Internal Administration, Praia, Santiago, Cabo Verde (office). *E-mail:* samory.araujo@govcv.gov.cv (office). *Website:* www.mai.gov.cv (office).

MORALES, Gerardo Rubén; Argentine politician; *Governor of Jujury Province;* b. 18 July 1959, Jujuy Prov.; m.; three s.; ed Universidad Nacional de Jujuy; worked on Ferrocarril General Manuel Belgrano railway as a waiter aged 18, promoted to post of admin.; later worked at Instituto de Seguros, Dir Liquidation Dept 1980–89; Asst in Political Econs, Universidad Nacional de Jujuy 1985–92, Head of Macroeconomics 1992–93; Fed. Deputy for Jujuy state 1989–2000, Chair. Fed. Finance Cttee 1991–92, Leader Unión Cívica Radical (UCR) in Chamber of Deputies 1993; Minister for Social Devt 2000–01; Senator for Jujuy 2001–15, Leader of UCR Caucus 2009–11; Pres. Unión Cívica Radical (UCR) 2006–09, Pres. UCR in Jujuy Prov. 2013–; unsuccessful cand. in governorship elections for Jujuy 1995, 1999; unsuccessful cand. for Vice-Pres. of Argentina on Roberto Lavagna's UNA ticket 2007; Gov. Jujury 2015–. *Website:* www.jujuy.gov.ar.

MORALES AIMA, Juan Evo; Bolivian politician and head of state; *President;* b. 29 Oct. 1959, Orinoca, Oruru; s. of Dionisio Morales Choque and Maria Mamani; fmr llama herder and trumpet player; farmed piece of land in Chapare for coca production 1980s; Founder and Leader, Movimiento al Socialismo 1987; became leader of the 'cocaleros' (coca producers) following US attempts to eradicate cocaine production (Plan Dignity) 1998; expelled from govt after three policemen were killed in farmers' riots; mem. Congress; ran second in presidential elections 2002, succeeded in gaining resignation and exile of Pres. Gonzalo Sanchez de Lozada on issue of Bolivian gas exports 2003; Pres. of Bolivia 2006–; FAO Special Goodwill Amb. for Int. Year of Quinoa 2012; plays for Sport Boys football team 2014–. *Address:* Office of the President, Palacio de Gobierno, Plaza Murillo, La Paz (office); Movimiento al Socialismo, La Paz, Bolivia (office). *Telephone:* (2) 237-1082 (office). *Fax:* (2) 237-1388 (office). *E-mail:* despacho@presidencia.gov.bo (office). *Website:* www.presidencia.gov.bo (office); www.masbolivia.org (office).

MORALES ANAYA, Juan Antonio, BS, MS, PhD; Bolivian economist, social scientist, academic and fmr central banker; *Distinguished Professor, Department of Economics, Catholic University of Bolivia;* b. 31 Dec. 1943, Cochabamba; m.; ed Catholic Univ. of Louvain, Belgium; Research Asst, Centre for Operations Research and Econometrics, Catholic Univ. of Louvain, Belgium 1967–70; Prof. of Econs and Statistics, Universidad Mayor de San Andrés, La Paz 1971; Prof. of Statistics and Operations Research, Dept of Math., Universidad Mayor de San Andrés 1973–74; Dir Inst. of Socio-Econ. Research 1974–95; Prof., Dept of Econs, Catholic Univ. of Bolivia 1974–95, Prof. (part-time) 1995–2006, Distinguished Prof. 2006–; Prof., Annual Seminars on Econ. Policy in Latin America (Santiago, Lima, Asunción and Montevideo) 1991–95; Dir Cen. Bank of Bolivia May–Aug. 1989, 1993–95, Pres. 1995–2006; Visiting Prof., Dept of Econs, Pontificia Universidad Católica de Lima, Peru 1972, Faculty of Econs and Social Sciences, Collège Notre Dame de la Paix, Namur, Belgium 1977, Dept of Econs and Center for the Study of Devt in Latin America, Boston Univ., USA 1979, 1981–83, Instituto Torcuato Di Tella, Buenos Aires, Argentina 1989, 1991, Jt Master Program, Univ. of Ottawa, Carleton and Univ. of Havana, Cuba 1995; Visiting Prof. of Monetary Econs (short seminar), Facultés Universitaires Notre Dame de la Paix, Namur 2003, 2004, 2005, 2006. *Publications:* Bayesian Full Information Analysis. Vol. 43 Series 'Lecture Notes in Operations Research and Mathematical Systems' 1971, Le Développement des Pays Pauvres: Quelques Aspects d'un Problème Actuel (co-author) 1977, Prices, Wages and Economic Policy During the Bolivian High Inflation 1982 to 1985 1987, Inflation, Stabilization and Growth. The Experience: Bolivia from 1982 to 1993 (co-author) 1995, Economic Policy and the Transition to Democracy: The Latin American Experience (co-author) 1995, Written Report of a Bolivian Economist 2002; reports and numerous articles in professional journals. *Address:* Masters Development, Catholic University of Bolivia, Avenida Obrajes 14 September 4807, SM Casilla 12428 La Paz, Bolivia (office). *Telephone:* (2) 278-6719 (office). *Fax:* (2) 278-6729 (office). *E-mail:* jamorales@mpd.ucb.edu.bo (office). *Website:* www.mpd-ucb.edu.bo (office).

MORALES-BERMÚDEZ CERRUTI, Gen. Francisco; Peruvian politician and army officer; b. 4 Oct. 1921, Lima; grandson of Col Remigio Morales Bermúdez (fmr Pres. of Peru); m. Rosa Pedraglio de Morales Bermúdez; four s. one d.; ed Colegio de la Inmaculada (Jesuit), Chorillos Mil. School; Founder-mem. Dept of Research and Devt, Army Gen. Staff; taught at School of Eng and at Army Acad. of War; Chief of Staff of First Light Div., Tumbes; Asst Dir of Logistics, Dir of Econ., War Ministry; advanced courses at Superior Acad. of War, Argentina and Centre for Higher Mil. Studies, Peru; apptd to reorganize electoral registration system 1962; Minister of Econ. and Finance 1968–74; Chief of Army Gen. Staff 1974–75: Prime Minister, Minister of War and Commdr-Gen. of Army Feb.–Aug. 1975; Pres. of Peru 1975–80; unsuccessful cand. in presidential elections 1985.

MORALES CABRERA, James (Jimmy) Ernesto, PhD; Guatemalan politician, writer, head of state and fmr comic actor; *President;* b. 18 March 1969, Guatemala City; s. of José Everardo Morales Orellana and Celita Ernestina Cabrera Acevedo; m. Patricia Marroquín; four c.; ed Univ. of San Carlos de Guatemala, Univ. Mariano Galvez; began career as adviser to small businesses 1990s; fmr teacher, Faculty of Econs and School of Communication Sciences, Univ. of San Carlos de Guatemala; several film and TV appearances, especially in comic series Moralejas (Morals); produced, directed and acted in several films; stood as Acción de Desarrollo Nacional cand. for mayor of Mixco 2011; joined Frente de Convergencia Nacional (FCN Nación) 2013, Sec.-Gen. 2013–; FCN cand. in presidential election 2015; Pres. of Guatemala 2016–. *Television:* Moralejas (Morals) (comic series). *Films:* Manzana güena en noche buena, La misteriosa herencia, Detectives por error, Ve que vivos, una aventura en el más allá, Repechaje, Looking for Palladin 2008, Gerardi 2010, Un presidente de a sombrero, Viva la crisis, Fe 2011. *Address:* Office of the President, Palacio Nacional de la Cultura, Guatemala City, Guatemala (office). *Website:* www.guatemala.gob.gt (office); www.jimmymorales.gt (office).

MORALES CARAZO, Jaime René; Nicaraguan business executive and politician; b. 10 Sept. 1936, Granada; s. of Carlos A. Morales and Anita Carazo Arellano; m. Amparo Vázquez Rovelo; two c.; f. Nicaraguan Devt Investments SA (INDES) in 1960s; mem. Nicaraguan Democratic Force 1983–93, Constitutional Liberal Party 1993–2002, Chair. Honour, Ethics and Justice Cttee 1993–2002, mem. Nat. Cttee 1993–2002; personal adviser (with rank of Minister) to Pres. of Nicaragua 1997–2001, Chair. Nat. Council on Sustainable Devt 1997–2001; Deputy in Nat. Ass. 2001–06; Vice-Pres. of Nicaragua 2007–12; mem. Central American Parliament (PARLACEN) 2012–. *Address:* Central American Parliament (Parlamento Centroamericano), 12 Avda 33-04, Zona 5, 01005 Guatemala City, Guatemala (office). *Website:* www.parlacen.int (office).

MORALES ELVIRA, Érik Isaac; Mexican professional boxer (retd); b. Tijuana; s. of José Morales; brother of Diego Morales; m. Andrea Morales; three c.; began boxing aged five, had 114 amateur fights (108–6); trained by father in family boxing gym, Tijuana and by Fernando Fernandez; winner of 11 major amateur titles in Mexico; professional debut 1993; career record of 52 wins (36 by knockout), 9 losses (3 by knockout); known as Érik "El Terrible" Morales; winner Mexican Super Bantamweight (SB) Title against Enrique Jupiter, Tijuana 1995, N American Boxing Fed. (NABF) SB Title against Juan Torres, Las Vegas, Nev. 1995, 1st NABF SB Defence against Alberto Martinez, Las Vegas 1995, 2nd NABF SB Defence against Kenny Mitchell, Tijuana 1995, 3rd NABF SB Defence against Rudy Bradley, Las Vegas 1996, 4th NABF SB Defence against Hector Acero-Sanchez, Las Vegas 1996, World Boxing Council (WBC) SB Title against Daniel Zaragoza, El Paso 1997, 1st WBC SB Defence against John Lowey, Tijuana 1997, 2nd WBC SB Defence against Remigio Molina, Tijuana 1998, 3rd WBC SB Defence against Jose Luis Bueno, Indio, Calif. 1998, 4th WBC SB Defence against Junior Jones, Tijuana 1998, 6th WBC SB Defence against Juan Carlos Ramirez, Las Vegas 1999, 7th WBC SB Defence against Reynante Jamiloi, Tijuana 1999, 8th WBC SB Defence against Wayne McCullough, Detroit, Mich. 1999, 9th WBC SB Defence against Marco Antonio Barerra, Las Vegas 2000, WBC Interim Featherweight Title against Kevin Kellery, El Paso, Tex. 2000, WBC Featherweight Title against Guty Espadas, Las Vegas 2001, 1st WBC Featherweight Defence against Injin Chi, LA 2001, Defence of Title fights against Croft 2003, Velardez 2003, WBC Super Featherweight Title against Jesus Chavez 2004, Int. Boxing Assсn (IBA) Jr Lightweight Title against Carlos Hernandez 2004, IBA Super Featherweight Title and WBC Int. Super Featherweight Title against Manny Pacquiao, Las Vegas 2005; moved up to Lightweight div. Sept. 2005; WBC Light Welterweight Champion 2011–12 (stripped); boxing promoter and man.; Owner web boxing magazine box-latino.com; NABF Boxer of the Year 1996. *Leisure interests:* computer enthusiast.

MORALES MOSCOSO, Carlos Raúl, Lic en Cien Jur y Soc; Guatemalan diplomatist and government official; b. 7 Oct. 1970, Chiquimula; m. Lizzette Matus Castro; two c.; ed Universidad de San Carlos de Guatemala; began career in diplomatic service as Second Sec., UN Div., Directorate of Multilateral Political 1989–91, Second Sec. in charge of Officers of Belize and Honduras Directorate of Integration 1991–93, Consul, later First Sec., Embassy in Belmopan, Belize 1993–2000, Acting Consul-Gen. in Benque Viejo del Carmen, Belize 2000, Dir-Gen. Ministry of Foreign Affairs 2000–03, Chargé d'affaires a.i., Embassy in Honduras 2003–06, Amb. and Dir-Gen. of Int. Bilateral Relations 2006–10, Deputy Minister of Foreign Affairs 2010–11, 2012–14, Exec. Sec. Comm. of Belize 2011–12, Minister of Foreign Affairs 2014–17; Gen. Co-ordinator of the Presidency Pro-Tempore held by Guatemala, System Integration Centroamericana (SICA) 2000; mem. Jt Comm. Guatemala-Belize, formed under the Settlement sponsored by the OAS 2000–02; Co-ordinator for Guatemala Comudad of Latin American and Caribbean States (CELAC) 2009–, in Ibero-American Summit 2009–; Pres. Pro-Tempore, Cen. American Security Comm. of the Cen. American Integration System Jan.–June 2011.

MORAN, Gerald W. (Jerry), BS, JD; American lawyer, politician and academic; *Senator from Kansas;* b. 29 May 1954, Great Bend, Barton Co., Kan.; m. Robba A. Moran; two d.; ed Fort Hays State Univ., Kan., Univ. of Kansas at Lawrence; early career as banker; est. law practice in Hays; returned to Fort Hays State Univ. as Adjunct Prof. of Political Science; Kansas State Special Asst Attorney Gen. 1982–85; Deputy Attorney, Rooks Co., Kan. 1987–95; mem. Kansas Senate 1989–97, Vice-Pres. 1993–95, Majority Leader 1995–97; mem. US House of Reps for 1st Congressional Dist of Kan. 1997–2010, mem. Cttee on Agric., Cttee on Transportation and Infrastructure, Cttee on Veterans Affairs (Chair. Health Sub-Cttee), numerous sub-cttees, Co-Chair. House Hunger Caucus; Chair. Nat. Republican Senatorial Cttee 2012–14; Senator from Kan. 2011–, mem. Appropriations Cttee, Banking, Housing, and Urban Affairs Cttee, Small Business Cttee, Veterans' Affairs Cttee, Banking, Housing and Urban Affairs Cttee, Commerce, Science and Transportation Cttee, Special Cttee on Aging; mem. Bd of Govs Univ. of Kansas School of Law 1990, Vice-Pres. 1993–94, Pres. 1994–95; mem. Bd of Dirs Kansas Chamber of Commerce and Industry 1996–97; Trustee, Eisenhower Foundation; mem. Bd of Trustees, Fort Hays State Univ. Endowment Assсn; mem. Exec. Cttee Coronado Area Council of the Boy Scouts of America; Republican; Hon. Bd mem. Special Olympics Kansas; Hon. Chair. Kansas Law Enforcement Torch Run 2008; named a Guardian of Small Business, Nat. Fed. of Ind. Business 2008, 2010, named Home Care Hero of the Year, Kansas Home Care Assсn 1998, Legis. Award, Nat. Rural Health Assсn 1999, Jim Edwards Alumnus of the Year Award, Leadership Kansas 2003, Intergovernmental Leadership Award, League of Kansas Municipalities 2003, Small Business Advocate Award, Small Business Survival Cttee 2004, Wheat Leader of the Year Award, Nat. Assсn of Wheat Growers & US Wheat Assocs 2004, Distinguished Leadership Award, American Assсn for Marriage & Family Therapy 2007. *Address:* Room 521,Dirksen Senate Office Building, Washington, DC 20510 (office); PO Box 1151, Hays, KS 67601, USA. *Telephone:* (202) 224-6521 (Washington, DC) (office); (785) 656-4295 (Hays). *Fax:* (202) 228-6966 (Washington, DC) (office); (785) 628-3791 (Hays). *E-mail:* info@moranforkansas.com. *Website:* www.moran.senate.gov (office); www.moranforkansas.com.

MORÁN LÓPEZ, Fernando; Spanish politician, diplomatist and author; b. 25 March 1926, Avilés, Asturias; m. María Luz Calvo-Sotelo Bustelo; one s. two d.; ed Univ. of Madrid, Institut des Hautes Etudes Internationales, Paris, London School of Econs; began diplomatic career 1954, Asst Consul, Consulate-Gen. in Buenos Aires 1956, Sec., Embassy in Pretoria, transferred to Ministry of Foreign Affairs 1963, specialized in African affairs, Asst Dir-Gen. for Africa, Near and Middle East, Political Dir Dept of Foreign Policy, later in charge of Africa, Near and Middle East 1971, Dir-Gen. of African Affairs 1975–77, First Sec., Embassy in Lisbon, Consul-Gen., Embassy in London 1974; Partido Socialista Popular cand. for elections to Congress of Deputies 1977; Partido Socialista Obrero Español Senator for Asturias 1977–82, Socialist Spokesman for Foreign Affairs in Senate; Deputy, Parl. of Spain for Jaén 1982–86; Minister of Foreign Affairs 1982–85; Amb. and Perm. Rep. to UN, New York 1985–87; mem. European Parl. 1987–99, Pres. Spanish Socialist Del. 1987–94; Alderman, City of Madrid 1999–2000; mem. Club of Rome, Ateneo de Madrid; Chevalier, Légion d'honneur, Grand Cross of Carlos III, Grand Cross Order of Isabel la Católica 1985, Grand Cross of Christ

(Portugal). *Publications:* También se muere el Mar 1958, El profeta 1961, José Giménez, promotor de ideas 1963, Nación y alineación en la literatura negro-africana 1961, El nuevo Reino 1967, Revolución y tradición en África negra 1971, Novela y semidesarrollo 1971, Explicación de una limitación 1971, La destrucción del lenguaje y otros ensayos 1982, Una política exterior para España 1982, España en su sitio 1990, El día en que 1997, Luz al fondo del túnel 1999, Palimpsesto: a modo de memorias (autobiog.) 2002. *Leisure interests:* literature, theatre. *Address:* Alvárez de Baena 5, 28006 Madrid, Spain. *Telephone:* (91) 5643719.

MORARU, Victor, MSc, MA; Moldovan diplomatist; *Permanent Representative to United Nations;* b. 1 Dec. 1961; m.; two c.; ed Agricultural Inst., Chişinău, Nat. School for Political and Admin. Studies, Bucharest; Counsellor/Deputy Perm. Rep. to UN, Geneva 2006–09, Perm. Rep. 2011–16, also Amb. to Switzerland 2012–16, Perm. Rep. to UN, New York 2017–; Chief Adviser to Deputy Prime Minister 2009–10; Amb. at Large for Global Affairs 2010–11; Deputy Dir of Gen. Dept for Multilateral Cooperation, Ministry of Foreign Affairs and European Integration 2016–17. *Address:* Permanent Missions of Moldova, 35 E 29th Street, New York, NY 10016, USA (office). *Telephone:* (212) 447-1867 (office). *Fax:* (212) 447-4067 (office). *E-mail:* unmoldova@mfa.md (office). *Website:* www.onu.mfa.md (office).

MORAUTA, Sir Mekere, Kt, KCMG, BEcons; Papua New Guinea politician and banker; b. 12 June 1946; s. of Morauta Hasu and Morikoai Elavo; m. Roslyn Morauta; two s.; ed Univ. of Papua New Guinea, Flinders Univ. of South Australia; research officer, Dept of Labour 1971; economist, Office of the Econ. Adviser 1972; Sec. for Finance, Govt of Papua New Guinea 1973–82; Man. Dir Papua New Guinea Banking Corpn 1983–92; Chair. Nat. Airline Comm. 1992–94; Gov. Bank of Papua New Guinea 1993–94; Exec. Chair. Morauta Investments Ltd 1994–97; MP for Moresby NW 1997–2012, Leader of the Opposition 2007–12; Minister for Planning and Implementation 1997, for Fisheries 1998–99, for Public Enterprise 2011–12; Prime Minister and Treas. of Papua New Guinea 1999–2002; Leader, Papua New Guinea Party 2007–12; apptd Papua New Guinea Sustainable Devt Program Ltd 2012; fmr Chair. Nat. Capital Dist Comm.; mem. Bd of Dirs Angco; mem. of Privy Council 2001; Hon. DTech (Univ. of Tech., Lae) 1987, DEcon (Univ. of Papua New Guinea). *Publications:* numerous econs-related papers. *Website:* www.mekeremorauta.net.

MORAVČÍK, Jozef, LLD, CSc; Slovak politician; b. 19 March 1945, Očová Zvolen Dist; m.; two d.; ed Charles Univ., Komenský Univ.; clerk with Chemapol (trade co.) Bratislava; lecturer Law Faculty, Komenský Univ., Bratislava 1972–85, Head of Dept of Business Law 1985–90; Dean, Law Faculty 1990–91; Deputy to Slovak Nat. Council 1991–92; mem. Movt for Democratic Slovakia (MDS) 1991–94; Minister of Foreign Affairs of ČSFR July–Dec. 1992; Chair. Council of Ministers of CSCE July–Dec. 1992; Minister of Foreign Affairs, Slovak Repub. 1993–94; Prime Minister of Slovakia March–Dec. 1994; Chair. Democratic Union of Slovakia 1994–97; apptd Chair. Policy Planning Council 1997; Mayor of Bratislava 1998–2002.

MORAWIECKI, Mateusz Jakub, BA, BBA, MBA; Polish lawyer, banking executive, politician and historian; *Prime Minister;* b. 20 June 1968, Wrocław; s. of Kornel Morawiecki; m.; four c.; ed Univ. of Wrocław, Wrocław Univ. of Tech., Central Connecticut State Univ., USA, Wrocław Univ. of Econs, Univ. of Basel, Switzerland, Univ. of Hamburg, Germany, Kellogg School of Man., Northwestern Univ., USA; engaged in opposition activities while a student, following introduction of martial law, printed and distributed various magazines; published articles under pseudonyms in underground press, mainly in Biuletyna Dolnośląski from 1986; worked for Solidarność Walcząca (Fighting Solidarity) as well as Niezależnym Zrzeszeniu Studentów (Ind. Students' Asscn); took part in occupations and strikes at Univ. of Wroclaw 1988, 1989; co-organized Wolni i Solidarni (Freedom and Solidarity) political discussion club late 1980s; co-f. Reverentia publishing co. 1990; Ed. Dwa Dni (Two Days) newspaper 1991; man. responsible for marketing and finance cos in consulting and publishing 1992–95; internship at Deutsche Bundesbank 1995; conducted research projects in banking and macroeconomics at Univ. of Frankfurt am Main, Germany 1996–97; Deputy Dir, Dept of the Accession Negotiations, Office of the Cttee for European Integration 1998; mem. of ministerial cttee negotiating conditions of Polish accession to EU in several areas; mem. Supervisory Bd, Dept of Energy, Wałbrzych 1998–2001, Industrial Devt Agency 1998–2001; mem. Lower Silesian Regional Ass. 1998–2002; began working at West Bank 1998, adviser to the CEO 1998–2001, then Dir of the bank following merger of Bank Zachodni and Wielkopolski Bank Credit 2001; mem. Man. Bd, Bank Zachodni WBK, Chair. 2007–15; Deputy Prime Minister 2015–17, also Minister of Devt 2015–16, of Devt and Finance 2016–18, Prime Minister 2017–; mem. Prawo i Sprawiedliwość (Law and Justice) party 2016–; Hon. Consul of Ireland in Poland 2007–15; Hon. Pearl of the Polish Economy 2015; Cross of Freedom and Solidarity 2013, Kt's Cross, Order of Polonia Restituta 2015. *Publications include:* European Law (textbook, co-author) 1997. *Address:* Chancellery of the Prime Minister, 00-583 Warsaw, Al. Ujazdowskie 1/3, Poland (office). *Telephone:* (22) 2500115 (office). *Fax:* (22) 8403810 (office). *E-mail:* kontakt@kprm.gov.pl (office). *Website:* www.premier.gov.pl (office).

MORCELI, Noureddine; Algerian middle-distance runner; b. 28 Feb. 1970, Ténès; coached by his brother Abderrahmane Morceli; World Champion, 1,500m Tokyo 1991, Stuttgart 1993, Gothenburg 1995; fmr world record-holder at 1,500m, one mile, 2,000m, 3,000m; gold medal, Olympic Games, Atlanta 1996; announced intention to compete in 2003 over 5,000m and 10,000m but did not race 2003–04; IAAF Athlete of the Year 1994. *Address:* c/o Ministry of Youth and Sports, 3 rue Mohamed Belouizdad, Algiers, Algeria. *Website:* www.iaaf.org/athletes/biographies/athcode=1936/index.html.

MORCHIO, Giuseppe; Italian automobile industry executive; b. 20 Nov. 1947, Rapallo, Genoa; m.; two c.; ed Genoa Polytechnic Univ.; began career in cable sector of Manuli Group; Dir of Logistics, Pirelli Group 1980, then Vice-Pres. Mfg, Quality and Logistics, Pirelli Group Worldwide, then Corp. Exec. Vice-Pres., Pirelli SpA; Chair. and CEO Pirelli Neumáticos, Barcelona; Pres. and CEO Pirelli Tyre North America; CEO Pirelli Cavi SpA Holding 1993–95; Chair. and CEO Pirelli Cavi e Sistemi SpA 1995–2003, Dir 1999–2003; CEO Fiat SpA 2003–04 (resgnd), Chair. Fiat Auto, Iveco, Magneti Marelli, Coamu, Teksid (all with Fiat Group) 2003–04; mem. Bd CNH, Ferrari, Banco di Desio e della Brianza; mem. Exec. Cttee Bd Dirs Confindustria (business asscn). *Leisure interest:* sailing. *Address:* c/o Fiat SpA, Corporate Headquarters, Via Nizza 250, 10126 Turin, Italy.

MORDACQ, Patrick; French fmr government official and international consultant; b. 20 May 1934, Bordeaux; m. Marie Thérèse de Yturbe 1967; one s. one d.; ed Ecole Nat. d'Admin; Commissariat Gen. du Plan d'Equipement et de la Productivité 1963–67, Head, Finance Service 1977; Office of Minister of Equipment and Housing 1968; Head, Office of Foreign Investment, Treasury 1969; Deputy Chair. Comm. of Industry for VIth Plan 1970; Head, Office of Loans, Aid and Guarantees to Business, Treasury 1971–74; Finance Dir Groupe Jacques Borel Int. 1974–77; Financial Counsellor, French Embassy, Bonn 1979; Head, Regulation of Finance, Treasury 1984–86; Govt Commr Centre Nat. des Caisses d'Epargne et de Prévoyance 1984–86; CEO Comm. des Opérations de Bourse 1986–91; Dir for France, EBRD (London) and Financial Counsellor, French Embassies, Poland, Romania and Bulgaria 1991–96; Conseiller-Maître, Cour des Comptes 1996–2002; Chair. Bd of Auditors, OECD 2002–07; consultant, institutional building projects (public finance man.) 2002–; Chevalier, Légion d'honneur, Officier, Ordre nat. du Mérite, Commdr, Bundesverdienstkreuz (Germany). *Address:* 5 rue Pierre le Grand, 75008 Paris, France. *E-mail:* mordacqpatrick@gmail.com.

MORDASHOV, Alexey A., MBA; Russian business executive; *Chairman, Severstal OAO;* b. 26 Sept. 1965; ed Leningrad Inst. of Eng and Econs, Newcastle Business School, Northumbria Univ., Newcastle, UK; has worked for Severstal OAO since 1988, started career as sr shop economist, Chief Financial Officer 1992–96, CEO 1996–2002, 2006–14, Chair. and CEO 2002–06, Gen. Dir JSC Severstal Man. 2014–15, Chair. PJSC Severstal 2015–, mem. Remuneration Cttee, Human Resources Cttee; Pres. Russian Steel Consortium 2013–, mem. Supervisory Bd 2010–; Chair. World Steel Manufacturers Asscn 2012–13, Vice-Chair. 2013–; Chair. Silovye mashiny OAO, Severstal-Holding OOO, Alyans-1420 ZAO, SVEZA OAO; Gen. Dir (CEO) Terrsprof OOO, Laguna-Delta ZAO, Algoritm OOO; fmr Gen. Dir Finkom OOO, Prima-Invest OOO, Severstal Garant ZAO; Head of Russian Union of Industrialists and Entrepreneurs (RSPP) Cttee on Trade Policy; mem. Entrepreneurs Council, Govt of Russian Fed., EU-Russia Business Co-operation Council 2006–, Atlantic Council Pres.'s Int. Advisory Bd, Russian-German work group responsible for strategic econ. and finance issues; Dr hc (St Petersburg State Univ. of Eng and Econs) 2001, (Univ. of Northumbria) 2003. *Leisure interests:* poetry, art, winter sports. *Address:* Severstal OAO, 127299 Moscow, 2–3 Klara Tsetkin Street, Russia (office). *Telephone:* (495) 926-7766 (office). *Fax:* (495) 926-7766 (office). *E-mail:* antonova@severstal.com (office). *Website:* www.severstal.com (office).

MORDAUNT, Rt Hon Penelope (Penny), FRSA, BA; British politician; *Secretary of State for Defence;* b. 4 March 1973, Torquay, Devon; m. Paul Murray (divorced); ed Univ. of Reading; Dir of Communications, Kensington and Chelsea London Borough Council 2001–03; mem. House of Commons (Conservative) for Portsmouth North 2010–; Parl. Under-Sec. of State for Communities and Local Govt 2014–15; Minister of State for the Armed Forces 2015–16; Minister of State for Disabled People 2016–17; Sec. of State for Int. Devt 2017–19; Minister for Women and Equalities 2018–; Sec. of State for Defence 2019–; Royal Naval Reservist 2013– (rank of acting sub-lt); Conservative; Spectator magazine Parliamentarian of the Year 2014. *Address:* Ministry of Defence, Main Bldg, 5th Floor, Whitehall, London, SW1A 2HB, England (office). *Telephone:* (20) 7218-9000 (office). *E-mail:* parlibranch-treat-official@mod.uk (office). *Website:* www.gov.uk/government/organisations/ministry-of-defence (office).

MOREIRA SALLES, Pedro, BA; Brazilian banking executive; *Chairman, Itaú Unibanco Holding SA;* ed Univ. of California, Los Angeles, USA; Chair. Unibanco Seguros SA 1995–2009; Chair. E. Johnston Representação e Participações SA 2001–09; Vice-Chair. and CEO Unibanco Holdings SA 2004–08; Vice-Chair. Unibanco – União de Bancos Brasileiros SA 2004–08, CEO 2004–08; Chair. Itaú Unibanco Holding SA 2008–, Vice-Pres. 2008–09, mem. Strategy Cttee, Appointment and Corp. Governance Cttee, Personnel Cttee 2009–; Vice-Chair. Banco Itaú BBA SA 2009–; Chair. Companhia E. Johnston de Participações 2008–, IUPAR – Itaú Unibanco Participações SA 2008–; Vice-Chair. Porto Seguro SA 2009–; mem. Bd of Dirs, Totvs SA 2010–. *Address:* Itaú Unibanco Holding SA, Praça Alfredo Egydio de Souza Aranha 100, Torre Olavo Setubal, Parque Jabaquara, São Paulo 04344-902, Brazil (office). *Telephone:* (11) 5019-1677 (office). *Fax:* (11) 5019-1114 (office). *E-mail:* info@itau.com.br (office). *Website:* www.itau.com.br (office).

MOREL, Pierre Jean Louis Achille; French diplomatist; b. 27 June 1944, Romans (Drôme); s. of André Morel and Janine Vallernaud; m. Olga Bazanoff 1978; three c.; ed Lycée du Parc, Lyon, Paris, Ecole nat. d'admin; Europe Dept, Ministry of Foreign Affairs 1971–73, Policy Planning Centre 1973–76, First Sec. then Second Counsellor, Embassy, Moscow 1976–79, Ministerial Rep., Gen. Secr. Interministerial Cttee on European Econ. Co-operation 1979–81, Office of Pres. of Repub., Technical Adviser to Gen. Secr. 1981–85, Dir Political Affairs, Ministry of Foreign Affairs 1985–86, Amb. and France's Rep. to Disarmament Conf., Geneva 1989, Head of French Del. Preparatory Cttee to CSCE 1990, Diplomatic Adviser, Office of Pres. of Repub. 1991–92; Amb. to Georgia 1992–93, to Russia (also accred to Moldova, Turkmenistan, Mongolia, Tajikistan and Kyrgyzstan) 1992–96, to China 1996–2002, to The Holy See 2002–05; Adviser to Policy Planning Centre, Ministry of Foreign Affairs 2005–06; EU Special Rep. for Cen. Asia 2006–12, for the crisis in Georgia 2008–11; Pres. Centre culturel de la Chartreuse de Villeneuve lez Avignon 2010; Dir, Observatoire Pharos 2012; Officier, Légion d'honneur 2006; Commdr, Ordre nat. du Mérite; Grand Cross, Order of Pius IX. *Publications:* trans. Mantrana 1984, Sauts de Temps 1989, Serpentara 1998 by Ernst Jünger. *Address:* Ministry of Foreign Affairs, 37 quai d'Orsay, 75351 Paris Cedex 07, France (office). *Telephone:* 1-43-17-53-53 (office). *Fax:* 1-43-17-52-03 (office). *Website:* www.diplomatie.gouv.fr (office).

MORENÉS EULATE, Pedro, LLB; Spanish lawyer, business executive, politician and academic; *Ambassador to USA;* b. 17 Sept. 1948, Las Arenas, Vizcaya; s. of Don José María de Morenés y Carvajal, 4th Viscount of Alesón and Doña Ana Sofía Álvarez de Eulate y Mac-Mahón; m. Goretti Escauriaza Barreiro; three c.; ed Univ. of Navarre, INSIDE Inst., Deusto Commercial Univ., Bremen Inst. of Shipping Econs; began career as lawyer 1979; worked in pvt. law firms; Head of Legal Services br., Shipbuilding Div., Nat. Industry Inst. (INI) 1991–94, Man. Dir

Commercial br., Shipbuilding Div. and mem. Steering Cttee 1994–96; fmr Prof. of Vessel Chartering and Shipping Freight, Spanish Maritime Inst., Madrid and in European Inst. for Maritime Studies; Sec. of State for Defence, Ministry of Defence 1996–2000, Sec. of State for Security, Ministry of Home Affairs 2000–02, Sec. of State for Science and Tech. Policy, Ministry of Science and Tech. 2002–05, Minister of Defence 2011–16; Gen. Sec. Círculo de Empresarios Business Circle 2005–10; Chair. Construcciones Navales del Norte SL 2009–11, MBDA Spain (missile systems firm) 2010–11, Segur Iberica 2011; Amb. to USA 2017–; mem. Bd of Dirs Telefónica SA, Tabacalera SA 1996–98; Great Cross, Order of Isabella the Catholic, Silver Cross of the Civil Guard, Medal for Police Merit. *Address:* Embassy of Spain, 2375 Pennsylvania Ave, NW, Washington, DC 20037, USA (office). *Telephone:* (202) 452-0100 (office). *Fax:* (202) 833-5670 (office). *E-mail:* emb.washington@maec.es (office). *Website:* www.exteriores.gob.es/Embajadas/washington (office).

MORENO, Glen, BA, JD; American/British business executive; *Chairman, Virgin Money Holdings (UK) plc;* b. 1943, Calif., USA; ed Stanford Univ., Univ. of Delhi, India, Harvard Law School; sr positions at Citigroup in Europe and Asia 1969–87; CEO Fidelity International 1987–91, also mem. Bd of Dirs; Sr Ind. Dir, Man Group plc, Dir (non-exec.) 1994–2009; Chair. Pearson plc 2005–15; Chair. Virgin Money Holdings (UK) plc 2014–; Acting Chair. UK Financial Investments 2009; Sr Ind. Dir, Lloyds Banking Group 2010–12; Gov., Ditchley Foundation; Dir Royal Acad. of Dramatic Art. *Address:* Virgin Money plc, Jubilee House, Gosforth, Newcastle upon Tyne, NE3 4PL, England (office). *E-mail:* info@virginmoney.com (office). *Website:* uk.virginmoney.com (office).

MORENO BARBER, Javier, Licenciado en Ciencias Químicas, Master of Journalism; Spanish journalist and editor; b. 1963, Paris, France; ed Univ. of Valencia, Autonomous Univ. of Madrid; worked in Germany –1992; worked for econs section of El País 1992–94, Man. Ed. Mexican edn of newspaper 1994, returned to to Spain and co-ordinated Latin American edn, served as special envoy to several int. events, Head of Econs section 1999–2002, corresp. in Berlin 2002–03, Dir econ. daily Cinco Dias 2003–06, Dir El País 2006–14; apptd Editorial Dir PRISA 2003; apptd cttee to undertake extensive redesign of newspaper Feb. 2007, completed Oct. 2007.

MORENO BARBERA, Admiral Antonio; Spanish fmr naval officer; b. 17 April 1940, Madrid; m. Pepa Deckler Andreu; four c.; ed Naval War Coll.; began career in Spanish Navy 1956; apptd Lt JG 1961; served on board destroyer Alava, submarines Almirante García de los Reyes S-31, Delfín S-61, Marsopa S-63, Submarine Flotilla Staff; Commdr submarines Tonina S-62 and Galerna S-71 1975–83; Commdg Officer frigate Asturias F-74 1983–89; Commdr Submarine Flotilla 1988–92; shore assignments include Leading Lecturer on Logistics, Naval Warfare Coll., Lecturer on Tactics, Submarine School, Chief of Tactical Studies, Dept at Naval Staff, Exec. Asst to Chief of Naval Staff; Commdr of Fleet of Amphibious Force (Delta Group) 1992–94; Chief of Rota Naval Base 1994–95; Chief of the Jt Defence Staff 1995–97; Chief of Naval Staff 1997–99; Chief of Defence Staff 1999–2004; apptd Vice-Admiral 1994, Admiral 1997; Grand Cross of St Hermenegildo, Commdr US Legion of Merit; four Naval Merit Crosses, Sahara Medal (Combat Zone), Brazilian Naval Merit Medal, Naval Merit Grand Cross, Mil. Merit Grand Cross, Chilean Great Star Mil. Merit Cross, Brazilian Naval Merit Grand Cross.

MORENO CHARME, Alfredo, BEng, MBA; Chilean civil engineer, business executive and politician; b. 1957, Santiago; m. Ana María Echeverría; four c.; ed Univ. Católica de Chile, Univ. of Chicago, USA; fmr Prof., School of Admin, Univ. Católica de Chile; Minister of Foreign Affairs 2010–14; Chair. Teletón Chile Foundation, Telemercadoes Europa SA, Telemercados Europa, Editorial Santiago; fmr Chair. ICARE, Ladeco, Banco de Chile, Fondos Mutuos BanChile, Radio Minería, Editorial Ercilla, Provida; mem. Bd of Dirs SACI Falabella SA 2004–, CMR Falabella y Mall Plaza, Empresas Conosur SA, Sodimac SA, Penta SA, Derco SA; Vice Chair. Banco Penta, Empresas Dersa SA; Vice-Pres. Organización Internacional de Teletones; Dir Federación de Criadores de Caballos Chilenos; mem. Int. Cabinet, Dom Cabral Foundation, Brazil; mem. Global Advisory Bd, Grad. School of Business, Univ. of Chicago.

MORENO FERNÁNDEZ, Abelardo; Cuban diplomatist; m.; one d.; joined Ministry of Foreign Affairs 1961; Perm. Sec. to UN, Geneva 1964–68, Deputy Rep. to UN Security Council, New York 1990–91, Minister Counsellor to UN 1992–95; Deputy Dir for Political Affairs, Ministry of Foreign Affairs 1995, Dir for Multilateral Affairs 1995–2000, Deputy Minister for Foreign Affairs 2000–09; Perm. Rep. to UN, New York Jan.–Aug. 2009; Prof., Higher Inst. for Int. Relations, Cuba; Visiting Lecturer, Columbia Univ., New York, Higher Inst. for Int. Relations, Geneva, Indian Inst. for Non-Aligned Studies.

MORENO GARCÉS, Lenín, Licenció en Administración Pública; Ecuadorean politician, organization executive and head of state; *President;* b. 19 March 1953, Nuevo Rocafuerte; s. of Senator Prof. Servio Moreno; m. Rocio Gonzalez; three d.; ed Instituto Nacional Mejía, Colegio Nacional Sebastián Benalcázar, Universidad Cen. del Ecuador; Dir Centro de Formación Profesional Continental 1976–78; Sales Man., Satho 1982–84; Marketing Man., Zitro 1985–86; Dir OMC Publigerencia Andina 1986–92; Admin. Dir Ministry of Govt 1996–97; Exec. Dir Cámara de Turismo de Pichincha 1997–99, Exec. Dir Federación Nacional de Cámaras de Turismo 1997–99; Exec. Dir Cámara de Turismo de Pichincha 1997–99; Dir Nat. Council on Disabilities (CONADIS) 2001–04; Academic Dir Eventa Foundation 2004–06; Vice-Pres. of Ecuador 2007–13, Pres. 2017–; UN Special Envoy on Disability and Accessibility 2013–16. *Publications:* several books, including Filosofía para la vida y el trabajo, Teoría y Práctica del Humor, Ser Feliz es Fácil y Divertido, Los Mejores Chistes del Mundo, Humor de los Famosos, Trompabulario, Ríase no sea enfermo, Cuentos no Ecológicos. *Address:* Office of the President, Palacio Nacional, García Moreno 10-43, entre Chile y Espejo, Quito, Ecuador (office). *Telephone:* (2) 382-7000 (office). *E-mail:* prensa.externa@secom.gob.ec (office). *Website:* www.presidencia.gob.ec (office); www.leninmoreno.com.

MORENO-MEJÍA, Luis Alberto, BA, MBA; Colombian journalist, diplomatist and international organization official; *President, Inter-American Development Bank;* b. 3 May 1953, Philadelphia, Pa, USA; m. Gabriela Febres-Cordero 1970; one s. one d.; ed Florida Int. Univ., Thunderbird Univ. and Harvard Univ., USA; Div. Man. Praco 1977–82; exec. producer of nationwide nightly news programme and other entertainment and children's programmes 1982–90; Neiman Fellow, Harvard Univ. 1990–91; Pres. Inst. de Foment Industrial 1991–92; Minister of Econ. Devt 1992–94; telecommunications adviser and pvt. consultant, Luis Carlos Sarmiento Org., Bogotá 1994–97; Partner, Westsphere Andean Advisers 1997–98; Campaign Man. of Andrés Pastrana 1994; Amb. to USA 1998–2005; Pres. IDB, Washington, DC 2005–, Chair. Bd of Exec. Dirs, IDB Invest, Donor's Cttee, Multilateral Investment Fund (MIF); Neiman Fellowship, Harvard Univ. 1990; Orden al Mérito Civil Ciudad de Bogotá, en el Grado de Gran Cruz, awarded by Mayor of Bogotá 1990, Orden al Mérito Industrial – José Gutiérrez Gómez, Colombian Nat. Business Asscn 2002, Orden de Boyacá en el Grado de Gran Cruz awarded by the Pres. of Colombia 2002, Grand Cross of the Order of Rio Branco, Brazil, Grand Cross of the Order of Isabel La Catolica, Spain, The Order of Jaguar, Guatemala, Order of Jose Cecilio del Valle of the Grand Cross of Gold Plate, Honduras; Dr. hc (Georgetown Univ.), (Icesi Univ.), (Baruch Coll.); King of Spain Prize for journalistic excellence, Distinguished Leadership in the Americas Award for Social Equity, Inter-American Dialogue, Woodrow Wilson Award for Public Service, Eagle of the Americas award, Asscn American Chambers of Commerce, Latin America. *Publications include:* articles on Colombian and int. politics and econs for publs in Colombia and USA; writings have appeared in New York Times, Boston Globe, Miami Herald, El Tiempo, Foreign Affairs en Español and Semana. *Address:* Inter-American Development Bank, 1300 New York Avenue, NW, Washington, DC 20577, USA (office). *Telephone:* (202) 623-1000 (office). *Fax:* (202) 623-3096 (office). *E-mail:* pic@iadb.org (office). *Website:* www.iadb.org (office).

MORENO OCAMPO, Luis Gabriel; Argentine lawyer and academic; *Global Practice Counsel, Getnick & Getnick LLP;* b. 4 June 1952, Buenos Aires; ed Univ. of Buenos Aires; Deputy Public Prosecutor in trials against mil. junta 1985–87; Dist Attorney, Fed. Circuit, City of Buenos Aires 1987–92; in pvt. practice (specializing in corruption control programmes and ethical advice for large cos) 1992–; Chief Prosecutor (first in position), Int. Criminal Court, The Hague 2003–12; Global Practice Counsel, Getnick & Getnick LLP, New York 2012–; apptd by World Bank to lead an expert panel to examine an alleged corruption conspiracy related to a $3 billion project in Bangladesh 2012; Sub-Dir Research Centre, Univ. of Buenos Aires Law School 1984, also Adjunct Prof. of Penal Law; Visiting Prof. of Law, Harvard Univ., USA; co-f. Poder Ciudadano; mem. Advisory Cttee Transparency Int., Pres. for Latin America and the Caribbean; mem. Carnegie Council for Ethics in Int. Affairs 2014–; Sr Fellow, Jackson Inst. for Global Affairs, Yale Univ.; Inaugural Gruber Distinguished Lecturer in Global Justice, Yale Law School 2013. *Film appearance:* (as himself) The Devil Came on Horseback 2006. *Publications include:* In Self Defense: How to Avoid Corruption 1993, When Power Lost the Trial: How to Explain the Dictatorship to Our Children 1996. *Address:* Getnick & Getnick LLP, 521 Fifth Avenue, 33rd Floor, New York, NY 10175, USA (office). *Telephone:* (212) 376-5666 (office). *Fax:* (212) 292-3942 (office). *E-mail:* lmoreno-ocampo@getnicklaw.com (office). *Website:* www.getnicklaw.com (office).

MORENO-RAZO, Alma Rosa, MA, PhD; Mexican economist, financial officer and fmr diplomatist; *Partner, ITG Consultores;* ed Instituto Tecnológico Autónomo de México, El Colegio de México, New York Univ., USA; fmr Deputy Dir for Planning, Promotion and Tech. Assistance, Nat. Bank of Public Works and Services (Banobras); fmr Exec. Dir Reconstruction and Syndicated Loans Multibanco Comermex; held various positions at Ministry of Finance and Public Credit, Gen. Co-ordinator for Income and Tax Policies 1998–99, Pres. Nat. Service for Tax Admin (SAT) 1999–2000, Head of Liaison Unit with Mexican Congress, Special Adviser to Sec. of Finance on Income Policies and Federalism, Dir-Gen. for Income Policies; Visiting Researcher, Centre for Econ. Investigation and Educ. in Mexico 2000–01; Amb. to UK 2001–04; Chief Admin. Officer, Grupo Financiero Banorte SAB de CV 2004–08; Partner, ITG Consultores 2009–; Adviser to Dir-Gen. of PEMEX (petroleum co.), Mexico City; Fellow, Center on Emerging and Pacific Economies, Univ. of California, San Diego 2010.

MORETTI, Nanni; Italian actor and filmmaker; b. (Giovanni Moretti), 19 Aug. 1953, Brunico, Bolzano; s. of Luigi Moretti and Agata Apicella Moretti; m.; one c.; co-f. Sacher Film S.r.l. (film production co.) 1986; est. Cinema Nuovo Sacher 1991; founder and artistic Dir Sacher Film Festival 1996; co-f. Tandem (film distribution co.) 1997; jury mem., Cannes Int. Film Festival 1997; jury Pres., Venice Int. Film Festival 2001, Cannes Film Festival 2012. *Films include:* as actor, dir and writer: Io sono un autarchico (I am Self Sufficient, also producer) 1976, Ecce Bombo 1978, Sogni d'oro (Sweet Dreams, Special Prize Venice Int. Film Festival) 1981, Bianca 1983, La Messa è finita (The Mass is Ended, Silver Bear Berlin Int. Film Festival 1986) 1985, Palombella rossa (Red Wood-Pigeon, also producer) 1989, Aprile (also producer) 1998, La Stanza del figlio (The Son's Room, also producer, Palme d'Or Cannes Film Festival) 2001; as dir: La Cosa (the Thing, also producer, writer) 1990, Caro diario (Dear Diary, also producer, writer, three David di Donatello Awards, Best Dir Cannes Int. Film Festival) 1994, L'unico paese al mondo 1994, Il Giorno della prima di Close Up (Opening Day of Close Up) 1996, The Last Customer (also producer) 2003, Il caimano (David di Donatello Awards for Best Film, Best Dir, Best Producer 2006, Silver Ribbon Best Producer 2007) 2006, We Have a Pope (Habemus Papam) (also actor) (Globi d'Oro Best Film Award 2011, Ciak d'Oro Awards for Best Film and Screenplay 2011, Silver Ribbon awards for Best Film, Best Story and Best Producer 2011) 2011, My Mother (Ecumenical Prize, Cannes Film Festival 2015, Ciak d'oro Award for Best Director 2015) 2015; also actor in: Domani accadrà (It's Happening Tomorrow) 1988, Il Portaborse 1991, La Seconda Volta (The Second Time) 1996, Trois vies & une seule mort (Three Lives and Only One Death) 1996, Quiet Chaos 2008. *Address:* Sacher Film S.r.l., Via Piramide Cestia 1, 00153 Rome (office); Via Pindemonte 22, 00152 Rome, Italy (home). *Telephone:* (06) 5745353 (office). *Fax:* (06) 5740483 (office).

MORGAN, Most Rev. Dr Barry, PhD; British ecclesiastic; *Archbishop of Wales;* b. 31 Jan. 1947, Neath, Wales; m. Hilary Morgan 1969 (deceased); one s. one d.; ed Ystalyfera Grammar School, Swansea Valley, Univ. Coll., London, Selwyn Coll., Cambridge, Westcott House, Cambridge, Univ. of Wales; ordained deacon 1972, priest 1973; subsequently curate in parish of St Andrews Major, Michaelston-le-Pit, Glam.; Chaplain and Lecturer, St Michael's Coll. and Univ. of Wales, Cardiff; Warden of Church Hostel, Bangor; Chaplain and Lecturer in Theology, Univ. of Wales, Bangor; Dir of Ordinands and In-service Training Adviser, Diocese of Bangor; Rector of Wrexham; Archdeacon of Meironnydd and Rector of Criccieth with Treflys 1986; elected and consecrated Bishop of Bangor 1993–99; Bishop of Llandaff 1999–2003; Archbishop of Wales 2003–; led Clergy School, Diocese of Kerala, India 2002; rep. Church in Wales on WCC; has served on several comms and working parties; Pres. Welsh Centre for Int. Affairs 2004–10; Pro Chancellor Univ. of Wales 2006; mem. Anglican Communion Standing Cttee 2003–11; Fellow, Bangor Univ. 1994, Cardiff Metropolitan Univ. 2003, Cardiff Univ. 2004, Univ. of Wales, Lampeter 2004, Trinity Univ., Carmarthen 2009, Swansea Univ. 2009, Learned Soc. of Wales 2013; Hon. DLitt (Cardiff Metropolitan Univ.) 2015. *Publications include:* O Ddydd i Ddydd 1980, The History of the Church Hostel and Anglican Chaplaincy at the University College of North Wales, Bangor 1986, Concepts of Mission and Ministry in Anglican Chaplaincy Work 1988, Ministry in the Church in Wales – The Shape of Things to Come? 2002, Strangely Orthodox – R.S. Thomas and his Poetry of Faith 2006. *Leisure interest:* golf. *Address:* Llys Esgob, The Cathedral Green, Llandaff, Cardiff, CF5 2YE, Wales (office). *Telephone:* (29) 2056-2400 (office). *Fax:* (29) 2056-8410 (office). *E-mail:* archbishop@churchinwales.org.uk (office). *Website:* www.churchinwales.org.uk (office).

MORGAN, David Raymond, AO, BEcons, MSc, PhD; Australian banking executive; b. 14 March 1947, Melbourne, Vic.; s. of Raymond K. Morgan and Verna Morgan; m. Roslyn Joan Kelly; two c.; ed La Trobe Univ., Univ. of London, UK, Harvard Univ., USA; Sr Economist Dept of Fiscal Affairs, IMF, Washington, DC 1976–79; Asst Sec. Foreign Investment Br., Fed. Treasury 1980–81, Fiscal and Monetary Policy Br. 1982–83, mem. Taxation Policy Div., Treasury Dept Canberra 1983–85; First Asst Sec.-Gen. Financial and Econ. Policy, Commonwealth Treasury 1986–87; Deputy Sec. of Finance 1987, of Econs 1989; Deputy Man. Dir Westpac Financial Services Group 1990, Chief Gen. Man. Asia Pacific Div., Westpac, Sydney 1990, Man. Dir Westpac Financial Services Group 1990–91, Group Exec. Retail Banking, Westpac Banking Corpn 1992–94, Group Exec. Institutional and Int. Banking 1994–97, Exec. Dir Westpac Banking Corpn 1997–2008, Man. Dir and CEO 1999–2008 (retd); moved to London to head up J.C. Flowers (private equity group) 2009–; Dir BHP Billiton; Dir (non-exec.) Castle Trust; mem. Union Club. *Leisure interests:* wine, tennis, classical music. *Address:* J.C. Flowers & Co. UK LLP, 125 Old Broad Street, 24th Floor, London, EC2N 1AR, England (office). *Telephone:* (20) 7710-0500 (office). *Fax:* (20) 7710-0519 (office). *E-mail:* info@jcfco.com (office). *Website:* www.jcfco.com (office).

MORGAN, Gwyn, CM, BSc (MechEng), PEng; Canadian business executive; b. 4 Nov. 1945, Carstairs, Alberta; s. of Ian Morgan and Margaret Morgan; m. Patricia Trottier; ed Univ. of Alberta and Cornell Univ., USA; Petroleum Engineer, Alberta Energy Resources Conservation Bd –1970; Man. Operations and Eng, Consolidated Natural Gas Ltd, Consolidated Pipelines Ltd, Norlands Petroleums Ltd 1970–75; joined Alberta Energy Co. Ltd 1975, positions including Pres. and CEO, Founding Pres. and CEO EnCana Corpn (following merger of Alberta Energy Co. Ltd and Pan Canadian Energy Corpn) 2002–05, Exec. Vice-Chair. 2005–09; Chair. SNC-Lavalin Inc. 2007–13; Chair. British Columbia Industry Training Authority 2014–16; Founding mem. Canadian Asscn of Petroleum Producers Bd of Govs; mem. Advisory Bd Accenture Energy; Past Pres. Ind. Petroleum Asscn of Canada; fmr Vice-Chair. Canadian Council of Chief Execs (fmrly Business Council on Nat. Issues); fmr Dir Public Policy Forum; fmr mem. Bd of Man. Calgary Foothills Gen. Hosp.; Fellow, Canadian Acad. of Eng 2005; Trustee Fraser Inst., Manning Centre for Building Democracy, Dalai Lama Center for Peace and Educ.; columnist, The Globe and Mail; Hon. Col (retd) 410 Tactical Fighter Squadron, Canadian Air Force; Ivey Business Leader Award, Univ. of Western Ont. 2002, inducted into Alberta Business Hall of Fame, Canadian Business Leader Award, Univ. of Alberta 2002, Canadian CEO of the Year 2005. *Leisure interests:* hiking, skiing, cycling, ocean sailing, physical fitness. *Website:* www.theglobeandmail.com/authors/gwyn-morgan.

MORGAN, Howard James, MFA; British artist; b. 21 April 1949, N Wales; s. of Thomas James Morgan and Olive Victoria Morgan (née Oldnall); m. Susan Ann Sandilands 1977 (divorced 1998); two s. one d.; two s. one d. (with Sarah Milligan); ed Fairfax High School, Sutton Coldfield, Univ. of Newcastle-upon-Tyne; career artist; comms by HM The Queen, HM The Queen of The Netherlands, HRH Prince Michael of Kent, TRH The Prince & Princess of Hanover, Tom Stoppard, Philip Larkin, Francis Crick, Paul Maurice Dirac, Dame Antoinette Sibley (Nat. Portrait Gallery, London), Mr & Mrs Neil McConnell; perm. display of work at Nat. Portrait Gallery, London; mem. Royal Soc. of Portrait Painters 1986–; Royal Soc. of Portrait Painters Prize 2004. *Leisure interests:* riding, 1938 Citröen, books. *Address:* Studio 401½, Wandsworth Road, Battersea, London, SW8 6JP; 12 Rectory Grove, Clapham Old Town, London, SW4 0EA, England (home). *Telephone:* (7892) 773870 (mobile). *E-mail:* howard@howard-morgan.co.uk (office). *Website:* www.howard-morgan.co.uk (office).

MORGAN, Joël, MEng; Seychelles politician; ed Heriot-Watt Univ., UK; apptd Prin. Sec., Ministry of Land Use and Habitat 2003; Minister of Home Affairs, Environment and Transport 2004–15, of Foreign Affairs and Transport 2015–16, of Educ. and Human Resources Devt 2016–18; fmr Head, Seychelles High Level Cttee on Piracy; fmr Chair. African, Caribbean, and Pacific Group of States Council of Ministers.

MORGAN, Baron (Life Peer), cr. 2000, of Aberdyfi in the County of Gwynedd; **Kenneth Owen Morgan,** DPhil, DLitt (Oxon.), FBA, FRHistS; British historian and academic; *Professor Emeritus, University of Wales;* b. 16 May 1934, Wood Green, London, England; s. of David James Morgan and Margaret Morgan (née Owen); m. 1st Jane Keeler 1973 (died 1992); one s. one d.; m. 2nd Elizabeth Gibson 2009; ed Univ. Coll. School, London, Oriel Coll., Univ. of Oxford; Lecturer, History Dept, Univ. Coll., Swansea 1958–66, Sr Lecturer 1965–66; Fellow and Praelector, Modern History and Politics, The Queen's Coll., Univ. of Oxford 1966–89; Prin., Univ. Coll. of Wales, Aberystwyth 1989–95; Pro-Vice-Chancellor, Univ. of Wales 1989–93, Vice-Chancellor 1993–95, Prof. 1989–99, Emer. Prof. 1999–; mem. (Labour), House of Lords 2000–, mem. House of Lords Constitutional Cttee 2001–04, 2015–, Houses of Parl. Archive and History Cttee 2014; Election Commentator, BBC Wales 1964–79; Ed. Welsh History Review 1961–2003; Jt Ed. 20th Century British History 1994–99; Fellow, American Council of Learned Socs, Columbia Univ. 1962–63, Visiting Prof. 1965; Visiting Prof., Univ. of Witwatersrand 1997–2000, Univ. of Bristol 2000, Univ. of Rouen 2003, King's Coll., London 2011–; Hon. Fellow, Univ. Coll., Swansea 1985, Hon. Prof. 1995–; Hon. Fellow, The Queen's Coll., Oxford 1992, Univ. of Wales, Cardiff 1997, Trinity Coll., Carmarthen 1998, Oriel Coll. Oxford 2003; Supernumerary Fellow, Jesus Coll., Oxford 1991–92; Hon. DLitt (Wales), (Glamorgan) 1997, (Greenwich) 2004; Dr hc (Univ. of Tours) 2017; Druid, Nat. Eisteddfod of Wales 2008, Gold Medal for Lifetime Achievement, Hon. Soc. of Cymmrodorion 2009. *Radio:* regular commentator (also on TV) on politics and modern history 1964–. *Publications:* Wales in British Politics 1963, David Lloyd George 1963, Freedom or Sacrilege? 1966, Keir Hardie 1967, The Age of Lloyd George 1971, Lloyd George: Family Letters (ed.) 1973, Lloyd George 1974, Keir Hardie: Radical and Socialist 1975, Consensus and Disunity 1979, Portrait of a Progressive (with Jane Morgan) 1980, Rebirth of a Nation: Wales 1880–1980 1981, David Lloyd George 1981, Labour in Power 1945–51 1984, The Oxford Illustrated History of Britain (ed.) 1984, Labour People 1987, The Oxford History of Britain (ed.) 1988, The Red Dragon and The Red Flag 1989, Academic Leadership 1991, The People's Peace: British History 1945–90 1992, Modern Wales: Politics, Places and People 1995, Young Oxford History of Britain and Ireland (Gen. Ed.), 1996, Callaghan: A Life 1997, Crime, Protest and Police in Modern British Society (ed.) 1999, The Great Reform Act of 1832 2001, The Twentieth Century 2001, Universities and the State 2002, Michael Foot: A Life 2007, Ages of Reform 2010, David Lloyd George (ed.) 2013, Revolution to Devolution 2014, My Histories 2015. *Leisure interests:* music, sport, travel, architecture. *Address:* House of Lords, Westminster, London, SW1A 0PW (office); The Croft, 63 Millwood End, Long Hanborough, Witney, Oxon., OX29 8BP, England. *Telephone:* (20) 7219-8616 (office); (1993) 881341 (home). *E-mail:* kenneth.morgan@hotmail.co.uk (home). *Website:* www.parliament.uk/biographies/lords/lord-morgan/2555 (office).

MORGAN, Rt Hon Nicola (Nicky) Ann, PC; British lawyer and politician; b. 1 Oct. 1972; m. Jonathan Morgan; one s.; ed Surbiton High School, St Hugh's Coll., Oxford; began career as solicitor specializing in corp. law with several pvt. and public cos 1994–2010; MP for Loughborough 2010–, Chair. Treasury Select Cttee 2017–; Parl. Pvt. Sec. to the Cabinet Minister for Univs and Science 2010–12; Asst Govt Whip 2012–13; Econ. Sec. to the Treasury (City Minister) 2013–14; Minister for Women and Financial Sec. to the Treasury April–July 2014, Sec. of State for Educ. and Minister for Women and Equalities July 2014–16; Conservative. *Address:* House of Commons, Westminster, London, SW1A 0AA; Constituency Office, 3/3A Nottingham Road, Loughborough, LE11 1ER, England. *Telephone:* (20) 7219-7224 (Westminster); (1509) 262723 (Loughborough). *Fax:* (20) 7219-6414 (Westminster). *E-mail:* nicky.morgan.mp@parliament.uk. *Website:* www.nickymorgan.org.

MORGAN, Peter William Lloyd, MBE, MA; British business executive; b. 9 May 1936, Neath, Wales; s. of Matthew Morgan and Margaret Gwynneth Morgan (née Lloyd); m. Elisabeth Susanne Davis 1964; three d.; ed Llandovery Coll., Trinity Hall, Cambridge; served in Royal Signals 1954–56; joined IBM UK Ltd 1959, Data Processing Sales Dir 1971–74, Group Dir of Data Processing Marketing, IBM Europe, Paris 1975–90, Dir IBM UK Ltd 1980–87, IBM UK Holdings Ltd 1987–89; Dir-Gen. Inst. of Dirs 1989–94; Dir South Wales Electricity PLC 1989–95, Chair. 1996; Dir Nat. Provident Inst. 1990–95, Chair. 1996–99; Dir, Zergo Holdings PLC (now Baltimore Technologies PLC) 1994–2003 (Deputy Chair. 1998–2000, Chair. 2000–03), Firth Holdings PLC (now Hyder Consulting PLC) 1994–2009, Oxford Instruments PLC 1999–2009; Chair. Pace Micro Tech. PLC 1996–99, KSCL Ltd 1999–2000, Technetix PLC 2002–, IDP SA (Paris) 2000–02, Active Risk Group Plc 2005–12; Dir Asscn of Lloyds' Mems 1997–, Council mem. Lloyds of London 2000–09; mem. Econ. and Social Cttee, EU 1994–2002, 2006–, Advisory Cttee Business and the Environment 2001–; Public mem. Network Rail 2012–; Master, Co. of Information Technologists 2002; Radical of the Year, Radical Soc. 1990. *Leisure interests:* gardening, wine, history, overseas travel, watching Welsh rugby, dog walking. *Address:* Cleeves, Weydown Road, Haslemere, GU27 1DT, England (home). *Telephone:* (1428) 642757 (home). *Fax:* (1428) 643684 (home).

MORGAN, Piers Stefan; British broadcaster, writer and fmr journalist; b. (Piers Stefan O'Meara), 30 March 1965, Guildford; s. of Anthony Pughe-Morgan and Gabrielle Oliver; m. 1st Marion E. Shalloe 1991 (divorced); three s.; m. 2nd Celia Walden 2010; one d.; ed Cumnor House Preparatory School, Chailey School, Sussex, Lewes Priory Sixth Form Coll. and Harlow Journalism Coll.; reporter, Surrey and S London newspapers 1987–89; Showbusiness Ed. The Sun newspaper 1989–94; Ed. The News of the World newspaper 1994–95, Daily Mirror (later The Mirror) 1995–2004; with CNN 2011–14, Good Morning Britain (ITV) 2015–; Ed.-at-Large (US), Mail Online 2014–, also weekly columnist, Mail on Sunday; Co-founder Press Gazette Ltd, Owner, Press Gazette 2005–07; Editorial Dir First News (newspaper for children) 2006; Atex Award for Nat. Newspaper Ed. of Year 1994, What the Papers Say Newspaper of the Year Award 2001, GQ Ed. of the Year 2002, British Press Awards Newspaper of the Year 2002, Magazine Design and Journalism Awards Columnist of the Year Award (Live Magazine) 2007. *Television includes:* presenter: The Importance of Being Famous (Channel 4) 2004, Morgan & Platell (Channel 4) 2005–06, You Can't Fire Me, I'm Famous (BBC1) 2006–07, Piers Morgan on Sandbanks (ITV 1) 2008, Piers Morgan's Life Stories 2009–10; judge: America's Got Talent (NBC) 2006–08, Britain's Got Talent (ITV 1) 2007–09, Piers Morgan's Life Stories 2009–, Piers Morgan On 2010, Piers Morgan Tonight (CNN) 2011–14. *Publications include:* Private Lives of the Stars 1990, Secret Lives of the Stars 1991, Phillip Schofield, To Dream a Dream 1992, Take That, Our Story 1993, Take That: On the Road 1994, The Insider (memoir) 2005, Don't You Know Who I Am? 2007, God Bless America 2009, Shooting Straight 2013. *Leisure interests:* cricket, Arsenal Football Club. *Website:* www.dailymail.co.uk.

MORGAN OF ELY, Baroness (Life Peer), cr. 2011, of the City of Cardiff 2011; **(Mair) Eluned Morgan;** British political scientist, academic and fmr politician; *Minister for Welsh Language and Lifelong Learning;* b. 16 Feb. 1967, Cardiff; d. of Rev. Bob Morgan and Elaine Morgan; m. Dr Rhys Jenkins; one s. one d.; ed United World Coll. of the Atlantic, Univ. of Hull; worked as researcher for S4C and BBC; worked as a Stagiaire in European Parl. 1990; MEP (Labour) for Mid and West Wales 1994–99, for Wales 1999–2009, mem. Nat. Ass. of Wales 2016–, Labour European Spokesperson on Energy Industry and Science, mem. Budgetary Control Cttee 1999–2009, Substitute mem. 2004–07, mem. Mashreq and Gulf States Del. 2002–04, Substitute mem. Environment, Public Health and Consumer Policy Cttee 2002–04, mem. Industry, Research and Energy Cttee 2004–09, EU-Bulgaria Jt Parl. Cttee 2004–06, Euro-Mediterranean Parl. Ass. Del. 2004–07, Substitute mem. Regional Devt Cttee 2004–07, ACP-EU Jt Parl. Ass. Del. 2004–09, mem. People's Repub. of China Del. 2007–08, Substitute mem. Climate Change Temporary Cttee 2007–09, Environment, Public Health and Food Safety Cttee 2007–09, mem. Russia Del. 2008–09, Shadow Spokesperson for Wales 2013–16, Oct. 2016–Jan. 2017, for Foreign and Commonwealth Affairs 2014–16, Opposition Whip 2015–16, Minister for Welsh Language and Lifelong Learning 2017–, fmr mem. Nat. Ass. Advisory Group (est. Rules of Welsh Ass.), Yes For Wales cross-party group campaigning for Welsh Ass.; Dir Nat. Business Devt in Wales for SSE (SWALEC) 2009–13; fmr Chair. Cardiff Business Partnership; fmr mem. Bd Int. Baccalaureate Org.; Fellow, Univ. of Wales, Trinity Saint David, Carmarthen; Hon. Distinguished Prof., School of European Studies, Cardiff Univ. 2010. *Publication:* European Parliament Position on the Energy Green Paper and the Electricity Directive. *Address:* Cardiff School of European Studies, Cardiff University, 65–68 Park Place, Cardiff, CF10 3AS, Wales (office); House of Lords, Westminster, London, SW1A 0PW, England (office); The National Assembly for Wales, Cardiff Bay, Cardiff, CF99 1NA, Wales (office). *Telephone:* (29) 2087-4889 (office); (20) 7219-5353; (30) 0200-6565 (office). *Fax:* (29) 2087-4946 (office); (20) 7219-5979. *E-mail:* euros@cardiff.ac.uk (office). *Website:* www.cardiff.ac.uk (office); contact@assembly.wales; www.assembly.wales.

MORGAN OF HUYTON, Baroness (Life Peer), cr. 2001, of Huyton in the County of Merseyside; **Sally Morgan,** MA; British politician; b. 28 June 1959, Liverpool, England; d. of Albert Edward Morgan and Margaret Morgan; m. John Lyons 1984; two s.; ed Belvedere Girls' School, Univs of Liverpool, Durham and London; secondary school teacher 1981–85; Labour Party Student Organizer of key seats 1985–93, Dir of Campaigns and Elections 1993–95, Head of Party Liaison for Leader of Opposition 1995–97; Political Sec. to Prime Minister 1997–2001; Minister of State for Women June–Nov. 2001; Dir of Govt Relations, Number 10 2001–05; mem. (Labour), House of Lords 2001–; Chair. Ofsted 2011–14; mem. Bd of Dirs, Olympic Delivery Authority 2006–12; Dir (non-exec.), Carphone Warehouse PLC; adviser to Bd, ARK; mem. Advisory Cttee, Virgin Group Holdings Ltd, NED Copthorn Group; mem. Council King's Coll. London; Chair. Future Leaders (charity); mem. Bd, Teaching Leaders; Trustee, Mayor's Fund for London 2009–11, Frontline. *Leisure interests:* relaxing with friends, cooking, gardening, walking. *Address:* House of Lords, Westminster, London, SW1A 0PW, England (office). *Telephone:* (20) 7219-3000 (office). *E-mail:* morgan@parliament.uk (office).

MORGENTHAU, Robert Morris, BA, LLB; American lawyer and fmr government official; *Of Counsel, Wachtell, Lipton, Rosen & Katz;* b. 31 July 1919, New York; s. of Henry Morgenthau, Jr and Elinor Morgenthau (née Fatman); m. 1st Martha Pattridge (deceased); one s. four d.; m. 2nd Lucinda Franks 1977; one s. one d.; ed Deerfield Acad., Amherst Coll., Yale Univ.; barrister, New York 1949; Assoc., Patterson, Belknap & Webb, New York 1948–53, Pnr 1954–61; US Attorney for Southern Dist of New York 1961–62, 1962–70; Dist Attorney, New York Co. (Manhattan) 1975–2009 (retd); currently Of Counsel, Wachtell, Lipton, Rosen & Katz, New York; mem. New York Exec. Cttee State of Israel Bonds; Democratic cand. for Gov. of New York 1962; mem. Bd of Dirs P.R. Legal Defense and Educ. Fund; Trustee, Baron de Hirsch Fund, Fed. of Jewish Philanthropies; Co. Chair. New York Holocaust Memorial Comm.; Pres. Police Athletic League 1962; mem. Bar Asscn of City of New York; Democrat; Dr hc (New York Law School) 1968, (Syracuse Law School) 1976, (Union Univ., Albany Law School) 1982, (Colgate Univ.) 1988; Frank Hogan Award, NY State Dist Attorney's Asscn 2000, Lone Sailor Award, USN Memorial Foundation 2000, Award for Excellence in Public Service, NY State Bar Asscn 2001. *Address:* Wachtell, Lipton, Rosen & Katz, 51 West 52nd Street, New York, NY 10019, USA (office). *Telephone:* (212) 403-1223 (office). *E-mail:* RMMorgenthau@wlrk.com (office). *Website:* www.wlrk.com (office).

MORGRIDGE, John P., BA, MBA; American computer industry executive; *Chairman Emeritus, Cisco Systems Inc.;* b. 1933, Wauwatosa, Wis.; m. Tashia Frankwurth; two s. (one deceased) one d.; ed Wauwatosa East High School, Univ. of Wisconsin, Stanford Univ., Calif.; Capt. USAF 1957–60; Vice-Pres. Honeywell Inc. 1960–80; Vice-Pres. Stratus Computer 1980–86; Pres. and COO Grid Systems 1987–88; Pres. and CEO Cisco Systems Inc. 1988–95, Chair. 1995–2006, Chair. Emer. 2006–; Lecturer (part-time), Grad. School of Business, Stanford Univ. from 1997; mem. Bd of Dirs American Leadership Forum for Silicon Valley, The Nature Conservancy, Business Execs for Nat. Security, Wis. Alumni Research Foundation, Cisco Foundation, Cisco Learning Inst., CARE, Interplast; mem. Tech. Advisory Bd Milwaukee Public Schools, Advisory Council Stanford Business School; Hon. DSc (Univ. of Wisconsin) 1994; Hon. LHD (Lesley Coll.); Hon. PhD (Northern Illinois Univ., The American Int. Univ. in London, Carleton Univ.); Ernest C. Arbuckle Award, Stanford Univ. 1996. *Film:* featured in documentary film Something Ventured 2011. *Address:* Cisco Systems Inc., 170 West Tasman Drive, San Jose, CA 95134-1706, USA. *E-mail:* info@cisco.com. *Website:* www.cisco.com.

MORI, Akira; Japanese business executive; *President and CEO, Mori Trust Co. Ltd;* b. 1936, Tokyo; s. of Taikichiro Mori; m.; two s. one d.; began career as banker; joined Mori Building Co. (family real estate business) 1972, CEO Mori Building Development Co. Ltd 1993–99, Pres. and CEO Mori Trust Co. Ltd (following reorganization of business) 1999–. *Address:* Mori Trust Co. Ltd, Toranomon 2-chome, Tower 2-3-17, Toranomon, Minato-ku, Tokyo 105-0001, Japan (office). *E-mail:* koho@mori-trust.co.jp (office). *Website:* www.mori-trust.co.jp (office).

MORI, Hanae; Japanese fashion designer; b. 8 Jan. 1926, Shimane; m.; two s.; graduate in Japanese literature; began career as costume designer for films in 1950s and has designed for over 500 films; opened first shop in Shinjuku, Tokyo 1951; now has 67 Hanae Mori shops in Japan, a store in New York, three shops in Paris and one in Monaco; first overseas show New York 1965; designed costumes for flight attendants of Japan Air Lines 1966; couture business and ready-to-wear; designed costumes for La Scala, Milan and for Paris Opera Ballet 1986; mem. Chambre Syndicale de la Haute Couture, Paris (first Asian mem.) 1977–; retrospective exhbn at The Space, Hanae Mori Bldg Tokyo 1989; Co-Founder Asscn for 100 Japanese books; launched Hanae Mori perfume brand 1995; Order of Cultural Merit 'Bunka Koro Sho' (Japan), Chevalier Légion d'honneur, Ordre des Arts et Lettres; numerous awards and prizes, including Neiman Marcus Award 1973. *Address:* Hanae Mori Haute Couture, 5 place de l'Alma, 75008 Paris, France

(office). *Telephone:* 1-47-23-52-03 (office). *Fax:* 1-47-23-62-82 (office). *Website:* www.hanaemori.com (office); www.hanaemoriusa.com (office).

MORI, Hideo, BA; Japanese business executive; b. 1 April 1925, Osaka City; s. of Shigekazu Mori and Ikue Mori; m. Masako (née Okano) Mori; two s.; ed Kyoto Univ.; joined Sumitomo Chemical Co. Ltd 1947, Dir 1977, Man. Dir 1980, Sr Man. Dir 1982, Pres. 1985–93, Chair. 1993–2000, later Counsellor, also Chair. Sumitomo Pharmaceuticals Co. Ltd; fmr Chair. ICI-Pharma Ltd, Japan Upjohn Ltd, Nippon Wellcome KK; fmr Dir and Counsellor, Japan Petrochemical Ind. Asscn; fmr Exec. Dir Japan Fed. of Employers' Asscns; fmr Dir Japan Tariff Asscn, Nihon Singapore Polyolefin Co. Ltd; Pres. Japan Chemical Industry Asscn 1990; mem. Bd of Exec. Dirs Fed. of Econ. Orgs (Keidanren); Blue Ribbon Medal 1987. *Leisure interest:* golf.

MORI, Immanuel (Manny), BA; Micronesian politician and fmr head of state; b. 25 Dec. 1948, Fefan Island, Chuuk State; m. 1st Elina Ekiek (deceased); four d.; m. 2nd Emma Mori; ed Xavier High School, Chuuk and Univ. of Guam; began career at Citicorp Credit-Guam Bank 1973, Asst Man., Saipan Branch 1974–76; Asst Admin. Trust Territory Social Security Admin 1976–79; Nat. Revenue Officer, State of Chuuk 1979–81; Controller, Federated States of Micronesia Devt Bank 1981–84, Pres. and CEO 1984–97; Exec. Vice-Pres. Bank of Federated States of Micronesia 1997–99; mem. Micronesian Congress 1999–2003, 2004–07, Vice-Chair. Judiciary and Govt Operations Cttee 1999–2003, Health Educ. and Social Affairs Cttee 1999–2003, Chair. Ways and Means Cttee 2001–03, Vice-Chair. External Affairs Cttee 2004–05, Chair. Resources and Devt Cttee 2005–07; Gen.-Man. and CEO Chuuk Public Utility Corpn 2004–07; Pres. of Federated States of Micronesia 2007–15; Ind.

MORI, Kazutoshi, PhD; Japanese molecular biologist, biophysicist and academic; *Professor of Biophysics, Graduate School of Science, Kyoto University;* b. 1958, Kurashiki, Okayama Pref.; ed Faculty of Pharmaceutical Sciences, Kyoto Univ.; Asst Prof., Gifu Pharmaceutical Univ. 1985–89; Postdoctoral Fellow, Univ. of Texas, USA 1989–93; Researcher, Heat Shock Protein Research Inst., Kyoto 1993–99; mem. Faculty, Kyoto Univ. 1999–, currently Prof. of Biophysics, Grad. School of Science; Wiley Prize in Biomedical Sciences (co-recipient) 2005, Canada Gairdner International Award (co-recipient) 2009, Asahi Prize 2013, Shaw Prize in Life Science and Medicine (co-recipient) 2014, Albert Lasker Basic Medical Research Award (co-recipient) 2014, Breakthrough Prize in Life Sciences 2018. *Publications:* numerous papers in professional journals on unfolded protein response. *Address:* Room 322, Mori Laboratory, 3rd Floor, Building 1, Faculty of Science, Northern Campus, Yubinbango, Kitashirakawa-Oiwake, Sakyo-ku, Kyoto 606-8502, Japan (office). *Telephone:* (75) 753-4067 (office). *Fax:* (75) 753-3718 (office). *Website:* www.upr.biophys.kyoto-u.ac.jp/en (office).

MORI, Shigefumi, MA, DrSci; Japanese mathematician and academic; *Professor, Research Institute of Mathematical Sciences, Kyoto University;* b. 23 Feb. 1951, Nagoya; ed Kyoto Univ.; Asst, Kyoto Univ. 1975, Prof., Research Inst. of Math. Sciences 1990–, Dir 2011–14; Lecturer in Math., Univ. of Nagoya 1980, Asst Prof. 1982–88, Prof. 1988–90; Asst Prof., Harvard Univ. 1977–80, Inst. for Advanced Study, Princeton, NJ 1981–82, Columbia Univ., New York 1985–87, Univ. of Utah, USA 1991–92; mem. Japan Acad. 1999; Iyanaga Prize, Japan Math. Soc. 1983, Chunichi Culture Prize 1984, Japan Math. Soc. Autumn Prize (co-recipient) 1988, Inoue Science Prize 1989, Cole Prize in Algebra, American Math. Soc. 1990, Japan Acad. Prize (co-recipient) 1990, Fields Medal, Int. Congress of Mathematicians, Kyoto 1990, Japanese Govt Prize (Person of Cultural Merits) 1990, Fujiwara Award, Fujiwara Foundation of Science 2004. *Publications:* numerous articles in math. journals on algebraic geometry. *Address:* Research Institute of Mathematical Sciences, Kyoto University, Kyoto 606-8502, Japan (office). *Telephone:* (75) 753-7227 (office). *Fax:* (75) 753-7276 (office). *E-mail:* mori@kurims.kyoto-u.ac.jp (office). *Website:* www.kurims.kyoto-u.ac.jp (office).

MORI, Shosuke; Japanese energy industry executive; *Advisor, Kansai Electric Power Company Inc.;* ed Kyoto Univ.; joined Kansai Electric Power Co. Inc. 1963, Gen. Man., Systems Eng Div. 1989–94, Exec. Officer and Gen. Man., Corporate Planning Office 1994–97, mem. Bd of Dirs and Man., Power Systems Div. 1997–99, Man. Dir 1999–2001, Exec. Vice-Pres. 2001–05, Pres. and Dir 2005–10, Chair. and Rep. Dir 2010–16, Advisor 2016–; Dir, The Japan Atomic Power Co.; Chair. Fed. of Electric Power Companies 2008–10; apptd Chair. Kansai Economic Fed. 2011; External Dir, All Nippon Airways Co. Ltd 2006–, Hankyu Hanshin Holdings Inc. 2010–; Dir The Royal Hotel Ltd 2012–. *Address:* Kansai Electric Power Co. Inc., 6-16 Nakanoshima 3-chome, Kita-ku, Osaka 530-8270, Japan (office). *Telephone:* (6) 6441-8821 (office). *Fax:* (6) 6447-7174 (office). *E-mail:* info@kepco.co.jp (office). *Website:* www.kepco.co.jp (office).

MORI, Yoshiro; Japanese politician; b. 14 July 1937, Nomi, Ishikawa Prefecture; s. of Shigeki Mori and Kaoru Mori; m. Chieko Mori 1961; one s. one d.; ed Waseda Univ.; with Sankei Newspapers, Tokyo 1960–62; mem. House of Reps, for Ishikawa Pref. Dist 1 1969–96, Dist 2 1996–; Deputy Dir-Gen. Prime Minister's Office 1975–76; Deputy Chief Cabinet Sec. 1977–78; Dir Educ. Div., Policy Research Council, Liberal Democratic Party (LDP) 1978–81, Deputy Sec.-Gen. LDP 1978–79, 1984–85, Chair. Special Cttee on Educational Reform, Policy Research Council 1984–87, Acting Chair. Policy Research Council 1986, Acting Chair. Gen. Council 1986–87, Chair. Nat. Org. Cttee 1987–88, Chair. Research Comm. on Educational System, Policy Research Council 1989–91, Chair. Policy Research Council 1991–92, Sec.-Gen. LDP 1993–95, Chair. Gen. Council 1996–98, Sec.-Gen. LDP 1998–2001; Chair. Standing Cttee on Finance, House of Reps 1981–82, on Rules and Admin. 1991; Minister of Educ. 1983–84, of Int. Trade and Ind. 1992–93, of Construction 1995–96; Prime Minister of Japan 2000–01; apptd Head, Organizing Cttee, 2020 Summer Olympics in Tokyo 2014–; Golden Pheasant Award, Scout Asscn of Japan2003, Padma Bhushan 2004.

MORIKAWA, Keizo; Japanese oil company executive; *Chairman, Cosmo Energy Holdings Company;* joined Cosmo Oil Co. Ltd 1971, Pres. Singaporean subsidiary, Cosmo Oil International Pte Ltd 1994–97, Dir for the Corp. Planning Dept 1997–2002, Sr Exec. Officer and Dir 2002–08, Exec. Vice-Pres. and Rep. Dir Cosmo Oil Co. Ltd 2008–12, Dir 2008–15, Rep. Dir, Pres. and CEO 2012–15, President and CEO Cosmo Energy Holdings Co. 2015–17, Chair. 2017–. *Address:* Cosmo Oil Co. Ltd, 1-1-1, Shibaura, Minato-ku, Tokyo 105-8528, Japan (office). *Telephone:* (3)

3798-3211 (office). *Fax:* (3) 3798-3841 (office). *E-mail:* info@cosmo-oil.co.jp (office). *Website:* www.cosmo-oil.co.jp (office).

MORIKAWA, Kosuke, PhD; Japanese scientist and academic; b. 28 Sept. 1942, Tokyo; m. Keiko Tanaka 1966; ed Koyamadai High School, Tokyo Univ.; instructor Tokyo Univ. 1971–75, research assoc. Århus Univ., Denmark 1975–77, MRC Lab. of Molecular Biology, Cambridge, UK 1978–80; instructor Kyoto Univ. 1980–86, apptd Dir First Dept Protein Eng Research Inst. 1986, Research Dir Biomolecular Eng Research Inst. (BERI) 1996. *Leisure interest:* listening to classical music, particularly by Bach and Mozart.

MORIKAWA, Toshio, LLB; Japanese banker; *Honorary Advisor, Sumitomo Mitsui Banking Corporation;* b. 3 March 1933, Tokyo; m. Sawako Morikawa; two d.; ed Univ. of Tokyo; joined Sumitomo Banking Corpn (now Sumitomo Mitsui Banking Corpn) 1955, Dir 1980–84, Man. Dir 1984–85, Sr Man. Dir 1985–90, Deputy Pres. 1990–93, Pres. 1993–97, Chair. 1997–2001, Advisor 2001–02, Exec. Advisor and Special Counsel 2002–05, Hon. Advisor 2005–; External Dir, NEC Corpn 2000–, The Royal Hotel Ltd 2005–, Taisho Pharmaceutical Holdings Co. Ltd; Chair. Fed. of Bankers' Asscns 1994–95. *Leisure interests:* golf, driving. *Address:* Sumitomo Mitsui Financial Group Inc., 1-1-2, Marunouch, Chiyoda-ku, Tokyo 100-0006, Japan (office). *Telephone:* (3) 3282-8111 (office). *Website:* www.smbc.co.jp (office); www.smfg.co.jp (office).

MORILLON, Gen. Philippe; French army officer (retd) and politician; b. 24 Oct. 1935, Casablanca, Morocco; m. 1st Anne Appert 1958 (deceased); three d.; m. 2nd Christine Gaudry 1998; ed Ecole Militaire de Saint-Cyr, Ecole Supérieure, Army Staff Coll.; platoon leader, French Foreign Legion during Algerian war of independence; fmr Div. Commdr of French units stationed in Germany; mil. expert, Assemblée Nationale 1984–86; Deputy Under-Sec. for Int. Relations, Ministry of Defence 1988–90; Deputy Commdr, then Commdr UN Protection Force (UNPROFOR) in Bosnia-Herzegovina 1992–93; Adviser on Defence to Govt of France 1993; Commdr Force d'Action Rapide 1994–96; mem. European Parl. (Union pour la démocratie française, mem. Group of the Alliance of Liberals and Democrats for Europe) 1999–2009, Chair. Cttee on Fisheries 2004–09; EU Chief Observer to Constitutional Referendum of Congo 2005, Legis. and Presidential Elections in Congo 2006, Elections in Afghanistan 2009; Pres. Asscn L'envol pour les enfants européens; fmr Pres. French Inter-ministerial Coordinating Cttee for the 12th World Youth Day, Paris 1997; Commdr Ordre nat. du Mérit 1988, Grand Officier de la Légion d'honneur 1993; Servitor Pacis Award, Path to Peace Foundation 1999. *Publications:* Croire et Oser 1993, Paroles de Soldat 1996, Mon Credo 1999, Le Testament de Massoud 2005. *Leisure interest:* reading.

MORIN, Edgar, Lic. en Hist. et Géog., Lic. en Droit et Sciences écon.; French scientific researcher and philosopher; *Director Emeritus, Centre national de la recherche scientifique (CNRS);* b. 8 July 1921, Paris; s. of Vidal Nahoum and Luna Beressi; m. Edwige Lannegrace; two d.; resistance fighter 1942–44; Head of Propaganda Dept, French mil. govt, Germany 1945; Ed.-in-Chief Paris newspaper 1947–50; Researcher, CNRS 1950–, Dir of Research 1970–93, Dir Emer. 1993–; Dir Review Arguments 1957–62, Communications 1972–; Dir Centre d'études transdisciplinaires (sociologie, anthropologie, politique), Ecole des hautes études en sciences sociales 1977–93; Commdr, Légion d'honneur, des Arts et des Lettres, Grande Croix, Ordre de Santiago de l'Espada (Portugal), Officier, Ordre du mérite (Spain); Dr hc (Brussels, Perugia, Palermo, Geneva, Natal, João Pessoa, Odense, Porto-Alegre, Milan, Guadalajara); Prix européen de l'Essai Charles Veillon 1987, Prix média de l'Asscn des Journalistes Européens 1992, Prix Internacional Catalunya 1994, Prix int. Nonino 2004. *Publications include:* L'Homme et la mort 1951, Le Cinéma ou l'homme imaginaire 1956, Autocritique 1959, Le Vif du sujet 1969, Le Paradigme perdu: la nature humaine 1973, La méthode (six vols) 1977–2004, De la nature de l'URSS 1983, Penser l'Europe 1987, Vidal et les siens 1989, Terre-Patrie 1993, Mes démons 1994, Amour, poésie, sagesse 1998, Vers l'Abîme 2007, La Voie 2011; numerous other publs. *Leisure interests:* music, theatre, movies, literature. *Address:* 7 rue Saint-Claude, 75003 Paris, France (home). *Telephone:* 1-42-78-90-99 (home). *Fax:* 1-48-04-86-35 (home). *E-mail:* lafaye@ehess.fr (office).

MORIN, Hervé; French politician; b. 17 Aug. 1961, Pont-Audemer; m. Catherine Broussot; two s. one d.; ed Deauville Lycée, Ecole Jeanne d'Arc, Caen, Univ. of Caen, Univ. of Paris II, Inst. of Political Studies, Paris; Dir of Services, Nat. Ass. 1987–93, 1998; Lecturer, Univ. of Paris V 1989–95; Municipal Councillor 1989–95; mem. Gen. Council of Eure 1992–2004; Tech. Adviser on Nat. Affairs and the Environment, Office of the Minister of Defence 1993–95; Mayor of Epaignes 1995–; Pres. Cormeilles Town Community 1995–; mem. Union pour la Démocratie Française (UDF) 1998–2007, Leader Parl. Group 2002–07; mem. Nouveau Centre 2007–, Leader 2008–; Deputy for Eure 1998–; Spokesperson for François Bayrou during presidential campaign 2002; Regional Councillor for Haute-Normandie 2004–; Minister of Defence 2007–10; Pres. France-Niger Group, Nat. Ass.; Pres. Asscn for the Reunification of Normandy 1999–. *Website:* www.herve-morin.net.

MORIN, Roland Louis, LenD; French public servant; b. 6 Sept. 1932, Taza, Morocco; s. Fernand Morin and Emilienne Morin (née Carisio); m. Catherine Roussy 1961; one s. one d.; ed Lycée Gouraud, Rabat, Faculty of Law and Humanities, Bordeaux and Ecole Nat. d'Admin; auditor, Audit Office 1960; Asst to Prime Minister and Chargé de Mission, Algeria 1960–61; Pvt. Recorder Comm. for Verification of Public Accounts, Asst to Recorder-Gen. 1964; Tech. Counsellor Louis Joxe Cabinet (Minister of State for Admin. Reform) 1966–67, Edmond Michelet Cabinet (Minister of State for Public Office) 1967-68; Referendary Counsellor Audit Office 1967; Asst to Prime Minister, Departmental Head for Econ. and Financial Programmes and Affairs 1968; Dir of Financial Affairs, Gen. Del. for Scientific and Tech. Research 1969, Asst to Del.-Gen. 1970, Asst Del.-Gen. 1974, Dir 1978; rejoined Audit Office 1980; Prof. Inst. d'Etudes Politiques de Paris 1965–90; Chargé de Mission with Jean-Pierre Chevènement (Minister of State, Minister for Research and Tech.) 1981–82, Dir-Gen. Research and Tech., Ministry of Research and Industry 1982–86; Conseiller maître, Cour des comptes 1986, Pres. 1993–2000, Hon. Pres. 2000–; mem. Comité nat. d'évaluation de la recherche (CNER) 1989–94, Comm. nationale des comptes de campagne et des financements politiques (CNCCFP) 1997–2000, 2011– (Vice-Pres. from 2000); Officier, Légion d'honneur, Ordre nat. de Mérite, Chevalier des Palmes académiques, Mérite agricole. *Publications:* Les sociétés locales d'économie mixte et leur contrôle 1964, Théorie des grands problèmes économiques contemporains. *Leisure interest:* tennis. *Address:* 24 Résidence des Gros-Chênes, 91370 Verrières-le-Buisson; Villa Ej-Jemaïa, 903 rocade des Playes, 83140 Six-Fours-les-Plages, France.

MORISSETTE, Alanis Nadine; Canadian rock singer, songwriter and actor; b. 1 June 1974, Ottawa; m. Mario Treadway 2010; one s.; signed contract as songwriter with MCA Publishing aged 14, recorded two albums for MCA's recording div.; moved to Toronto, later to LA, USA; BRIT Award for Best Int. Newcomer 1996, Grammy Awards for Best Female Rock Vocal Performance 1996, 1999, for Best Rock Song 1996, 1999, MTV European Music Award for Best Female Artist 1996. *Recordings include:* albums: Alanis 1991, Now Is The Time 1992, Jagged Little Pill (Grammy Awards for Album of the Year 1996, for Best Rock Album 1996, Juno Awards for Album of the Year 1996, for Best Rock Album 1996) 1995, Space Cakes (live) 1998, Supposed Former Infatuation Junkie (Juno Award for Album of the Year 2000) 1998, Alanis Unplugged (live) 1999, Under Rug Swept 2002, Feast On Scraps: Inside Under Rug Swept 2002, So-called Chaos 2004, Jagged Little Pill Acoustic 2005, Flavors of Entanglement (Juno Award for Pop Album of the Year 2009) 2008, Havoc and Bright Lights 2012, Live At Montreux 2012 2013. *Film appearances:* Anything for Love 1993, Dogma 1999, Jay and Silent Bob Strike Back 2001, De-Lovely 2004, Radio Free Albemuth 2010, The Price of Desire 2015. *Television appearances:* as actor: You Can't Do That on Television 1986, Degrassi: the Next Generation 2005, Lovespring International 2006, Nip/Tuck 2006, Weeds 2009–10, Up All Night 2012; host of Music Works series 1994. *Website:* www.alanis.com.

MORITA, Tomijiro; Japanese insurance executive; b. 1941; m.; ed Univ. of Tokyo; joined Dai-ichi Mutual Life Insurance Co. Ltd 1960, Vice-Pres. 1996–97, Pres. 1997–2004, Chair. Dai-ichi Life Insurance Co. Ltd 2004–11; fmr Chair. Seiko Holdings Corpn, currently Corp. Auditor; Exec. Dir Hotel Okura Co. Ltd; mem. Rep. Bd Japan Finance Org. for Municipal Enterprises, Advisory Cttee Japan Tobacco Inc.; Chair. Japan's Life Insurance Asscn; mem. Bd of Dirs Japan Productivity Centre for Socio-Econ. Devt (JPC-SED), Odakyu Group; mem. Exec. Cttee Japan-US Business Council 2003–. *Address:* c/o Dai-ichi Life Insurance Co. Ltd, 13-1, Yurakucho 1-chome, Chiyoda-ku, Tokyo 100-8411, Japan. *E-mail:* info@dai-ichi-life.co.jp.

MORITS, Yunna Petrovna; Russian poet; b. 2 June 1937, Kiev, Ukraine; m. Yuri Grigor'yevich Vasil'yev; one s.; ed Gorky Literary Inst.; began publishing poetry 1954; has participated in int. poetry festivals London, Cambridge, Toronto, Rotterdam, among other locations; has made recordings of recitations of her poetry; mem. Russian PEN, Exec. Cttee, Russian Acad. of Natural Sciences; Golden Rose (Italy) 1996, Triumph Prize 2000, A. D. Sakharov Prize for Civil Courage of Writer 2004. *Publications include:* eleven collections of poetry (trans. in many languages), including The Vine 1970, With Unbleached Thread 1974, By Light of Life 1977, The Third Eye 1980, Selected Poems 1982, The Blue Flame 1985, On This High Shore 1987, In the Den of Vice 1990, The Face 2000, In This Way 2000, By the Law to the Postman Hello 2005, and six books for children including The Great Secret for a Small Company 1987, A Bunch of Cats 1997, Move Your Ears 2003, Po zakonu-privet pochtalonu 2005, Krysha ehala domoy 2012; poems appeared in journal Oktyabr 1993–97; also short stories, essays, scripts for animated cartoons. *Leisure interests:* painting and drawing (more than 300 works published). *Address:* 129010 Moscow, Astrakhansky per. 5, Apartment 76, Russia (home). *Telephone:* (495) 680-08-16 (home). *E-mail:* morits@owl.ru (home). *Website:* morits.ru.

MORITZ, Sir Michael Jonathan, Kt, KBE, MA, MBA; British/American investment industry executive; *Chairman, Sequoia Capital;* b. 1954, Cardiff, Wales; m.; two c.; ed Howardian High School, Cardiff, Christ Church, Oxford, Wharton School, Univ. of Pennsylvania; worked as a reporter for Time 1984–86; Co-founder Technologic Pnrs (tech. newsletter and conf. co.) 1984–86; joined Sequoia Capital, Menlo Park, California as Man. Dir Partner 1986–, Chair. 2012–; mem. Bd of Dirs Flextronics 1993–2005, Yahoo! 1995–2003, PayPal 1999–2002, Google Inc. 1999–2007, 24/7 Customer 2003–, Green Dot Corpn 2003–, Kayak.com 2005–, Sugar Inc. 2007–, Klarna AB 2010–, LinkedIn 2011–; internet co. investments include Google, Yahoo!, PayPal, eBay, Apple Computer, Cisco, Webvan, YouTube, eToys; Hon. Student, Christ Church, Oxford 2005. *Publications:* Going For Broke: The Chrysler Story (with Barry Seaman) 1981, The Little Kingdom: The Private Story of Apple Computer 1984. *Address:* Sequoia Capital, 3000 Sand Hill Road, Building 4, Suite 180, Menlo Park, CA 94025, USA (office). *Telephone:* (650) 854-3927 (office). *Fax:* (650) 854-2977 (office). *E-mail:* moritz@sequoiacap.com (office). *Website:* www.sequoiacap.com (office).

MORIYAMA, Hiroshi; Japanese politician; *Minister of Agriculture, Forestry and Fisheries;* b. 8 April 1945, Kanoya, Kagoshima Pref.; mem. Kagoshima City Ass. 1975–97, Chair. 1982–84, 1989, 1992–94, 1994–96, 1996–97; mem. House of Councillors (upper house of parl.) 1998–2004, House of Reps (lower house of parl.) 2004–, Chair. HR Cttee on Agric., Forestry and Fisheries 2012–13, Parl. Vice-Minister of Finance 2002–03, State Minister of Finance 2007–08, Minister of Agric., Forestry and Fisheries 2015–; mem. LDP. *Address:* Ministry of Agriculture, Forestry and Fisheries, 1-2-1, Kasumigaseki, Chiyoda-ku, Tokyo 100-8950, Japan (office). *Telephone:* (3) 3502-5517 (office). *Fax:* (3) 3592-7697 (office). *Website:* www.maff.go.jp (office).

MORIYAMA, Raymond, OC, MArch, FRAIC, RCA, FRSA, FAIA; Canadian architect and planner; *Principal, Moriyama and Teshima Architects;* b. 11 Oct. 1929, Vancouver; s. of John Michi Moriyama and Nobuko Moriyama; m. Sachiko Miyauchi 1954; three s. two d.; ed Univ. of Toronto, McGill Univ.; Raymond Moriyama Architects and Planners 1958–70; Partner, Moriyama and Teshima Architects 1970–, Prin. 1980–; Design Tutor, Univ. of Toronto 1961–63; Chair. Ecological Research Ltd 1970; Chair. Mid-Canada Conf., Task Force on Environmental and Ecological Factors 1969–70; mem. Bd and Life mem. Royal Canadian Inst.; Dir Canadian Guild of Crafts 1973–75; mem. of Council, Ont. Coll. of Arts 1972–73; mem. Advisory Cttee, MBA Programme in Arts Admin, York Univ. 1982; Founding mem. Asia Pacific Foundation of Canada 1982; mem. Bd, Multilingual TV; mem. Bd of Trustees, Royal Ont. Museum; mem. Council's Advisory Cttee, N York Gen. Hosp.; Chancellor Brock Univ. 2001–07; Fellow, Toronto Soc. of Architects 1998; Int. FRIBA; several exhbns of architectural work of office; numerous TV documentaries; Regeneration Suite dedicated to work of Raymond

Moriyama; Order of Ontario 1992, Order of Rising Sun Gold Rays with Rosette 2004; 10 hon. doctorates, including from Univ. of Toronto, McGill Univ., York Univ.; Civic Awards of Merit (Toronto and Scarborough), Gov.-Gen.'s Medal for Architecture (four times), P.A. Award 1989, Toronto Arts Award 1990, Winner, int. competition for Nat. Saudi Arabian Museum, Riyadh 1996–99, Gold Medal, Royal Architectural Inst. of Canada 1997, Best Architect in Toronto Award 1997, 1998, Governor General's Medal in Architecture 2009, Aga Khan Award of Excellence in Architecture 2010 and many other awards. *Works include:* Japanese Canadian Cultural Centre/Noor Cultural Centre, Toronto 1954–2005, Ontario Science Centre, Toronto 1964–69, Scarborough Civic Centre 1968–74, Niagara Falls and River 100 Year Plan, and Work with 16 univs 1968–, Toronto Reference Library 1973–77, Meewasin Valley 100 Year Plan, Saskatoon 1974–76, Science North, Sudbury 1980–84, Ottawa City Hall 1987–91, Canadian Embassy, Tokyo, Japan 1988–92, Canadian War Museum, Ottawa 2001–05, 124 km Wadi Hanifa Reclamation/Bioremediation, Riyadh, Saudi Arabia 2003. *Publications:* Great American Goose Egg Co. (Canada) Ltd, The Global Living System and Mid-Canada Task Force Committee on Ecological and Environmental Factors 1970, Can Your Life Become a Work of Art 1975, The Satisfactory City: The Survival of Urbanity 1975, Into God's Temple of Eternity, Drive a Nail of Gold, TANT – Time, Appropriateness, Nature and Transition 1982, Architect as Nature's Collaborator (lecture at McGill Univ.) 1996, In Search of a Soul (documentary on the concept and realization of the new Canadian War Museum in Ottawa). *Leisure interests:* fishing, sailing. *Address:* 32 Davenport Road, Toronto, ON M5R 1H3, Canada (home). *Telephone:* (416) 925-4484 (home). *Fax:* (416) 925-4736 (home). *E-mail:* rm@mtarch.com (office). *Website:* www.mtarch.com (office).

MORJANE, Kamel; Tunisian international organization official, diplomatist, government official and politician; *Minister of the Civil Service, Modernisation of Administration and Public Policy;* b. 9 May 1948, Hammam-Sousse; m. Dorra Ben Ali; two c.; ed Faculty of Law and Nat. School of Admin, Univ. of Tunis, Graduate Inst. of Int. and Devt Studies, Univ. of Geneva, Switzerland; worked as journalist; fmr Asst Prof. Univ. of Geneva; joined staff UNHCR 1977, Dir, Human Resources 1988–89, SW Asia, Middle East and N Africa Div. 1990–94, Africa Div. 1994–96, Asst High Commr 2001–05; apptd Perm. Rep. to UN, Geneva 1996, later UN Sec.-Gen.'s Special Rep. for Democratic Repub. of Congo 1999–2001; Minister of Defence 2005–10, of Foreign Affairs 2010–11; Founder and Leader, L'Initiative (al-Moubadara) party 2011–; Minister of the Civil Service, Modernisation of Admin and Public Policy 2018–; mem. Advisory Bd UN Trust Fund for Human Security 2014–; Grand Officier, Ordre Sept Novembre, Grand Officier, Ordre de la République, Médaille de la Jeunesse (Tunisia), Commandeur, Ordre Mano (Togo). *Address:* Office of the Prime Minister, pl. du Gouvernement, La Kasbah, 1030 Tunis, Tunisia (office). *Telephone:* (71) 565-400 (office). *E-mail:* webmaster@pm.gov.tn (office). *Website:* www.almoubadara.tn (office).

MØRK, Truls; Norwegian cellist; b. 25 April 1961, Bergen; s. of John Mørk and Turid Otterbech; two s. one d.; ed studied under his father, with Frans Helmerson at Swedish Radio Music School, in Austria with Heinrich Schiff and in Moscow with Natalia Shakovskaya; debut, BBC Promenade Concerts 1989; has since appeared with leading European, American and Australian orchestras, including the Berlin Philharmonic, New York Philharmonic, Philadelphia Symphony, Cincinnati Philharmonic, Rotterdam Philharmonic, London Philharmonic, Pittsburgh Symphony, City of Birmingham Symphony, Orchestre de Paris, NHK Symphony, Royal Concertgebouw and Cleveland, Los Angeles and Gewandhaus Symphony Orchestras; regular appearances at int. chamber music festivals; Founder Int. Chamber Music Festival in Stavanger, Artistic Dir –2003; Artist-in-Residence, Gothenburg Symphony 2016–17; prizewinner, Moscow Tchaikovsky Competititon 1982, First Prize, Cassado Cello Competition, Florence 1983, UNESCO Prize European Radio-Union Competition, Bratislava 1983, W. Naumburg Competition, New York 1986, Norwegian Critics Prize 2011, Sibelius Prize 2011. *Recordings include:* Schumann, Elgar and Saint-Saëns concertos, Tchaikovsky Rococo Variations, recitals of cello works by Grieg, Sibelius, Brahms, Rachmaninov and Myaskovksy, Dvořák and Shostakovich cello concertos, Haydn cello concertos with Norwegian Chamber Orchestra, Britten Cello Symphony and Elgar Cello Concerto with Sir Simon Rattle and the City of Birmingham Symphony Orchestra, Britten Cello Suites (Grammy Award 2002), Schumann Cello Concerto with Paavo Jürvi and Orchestre Philharmonique de Radio France 2005, C.P.E. Bach Cello Concerti with Bernard Labadie and Les Violons du Roy (ECHO Klassik Award) 2011, Rautavaara Percussion Concerto/Cello Concerto No. 2 (Gramophone Award for Best Contemporary Recording 2012, Int. Classical Music Award for Contemporary Music 2013) 2011. *Address:* Harrison Parrott, The Ark, 201 Talgarth Road, London, W6 8BJ, England (office). *Telephone:* (20) 7229-9166 (office). *Fax:* (20) 7221-5042 (office). *E-mail:* info@harrisonparrott.co.uk (office). *Website:* www.harrisonparrott.com (office).

MORNEAU, William (Bill) Francis, PC, MSc, MBA; Canadian business executive and politician; *Minister of Finance;* b. 7 Oct. 1962, Toronto; s. of William (Bill) Francis Morneau, Sr and Helen (Lynch) Morneau; m. Nancy McCain; two s. one d.; ed Univ. of Western Ontario, London School of Economics, UK, Inst. européen d'admin des affaires (INSEAD), France; joined Morneau Shepell 1987, Pres. 1992, Pres. and CEO 1998, Chair. and CEO 2008–15; Pension Investment Adviser to Ont. Minister of Finance Dwight Duncan 2012; mem. House of Commons for Toronto Centre 2015–; Minister of Finance 2015–; mem. Bd of Dirs St Michael's Hosp. 2003–13, Chair. 2009–13; Chair. Covenant House 1997–2000, C.D. Howe Inst. 2010–14; mem. Liberal Party of Canada. *Publication:* The Real Retirement (with Fred Vettese) 2013. *Address:* Department of Finance Canada, 90 Elgin Street, Ottawa, ON K1A 0G5, Canada (office). *Telephone:* (613) 369-3710 (office). *Fax:* (613) 369-4065 (office). *E-mail:* inpub@fin.gc.ca (office). *Website:* www.fin.gc.ca (office); bmorneau.liberal.ca (office).

MOROSS, Manfred David, BSc, MBA; British business executive (retd); b. 30 Aug. 1931; s. of Dr H. Moross and A. Moross; m. Edna Fay Jacobson 1956; three s. one d.; ed Univ. of Witwatersrand and Harvard Univ.; joined ICI in UK 1953 then returned to South Africa to join Anglo-Transvaal Consolidated Investments; joined Schlesinger Org., Johannesburg, Chair. Int. Group –1974; fmr mem. Bd of Dirs Rand Selection Trust, Whitehall Financial Group, New York, Whitehall Investment Corpn, New York, Siem Industries Inc., Bermuda; mem. Bd of Govs Weizmann Inst. of Science 1982, Chair. Int. Bd 2005; f. Manfred D. Moross Foundation; Dr hc Weizmann Inst. of Science. *Leisure interests:* tennis, reading. *Address:* 7 Princes Gate, London, SW7 1QL, England (home).

MOROZ, Oleksandr Oleksandrovych; Ukrainian politician; b. 29 Feb. 1944, Buda, Kyiv Oblast; m. Valentina Andriyivna Lavrinenko; two d.; ed Ukrainian Agric. Acad., Higher CP School; trained as engineer in Kyiv; engineer and mechanic in state farm professional school, dist and regional enterprises of Selkhoztekhnika 1965–76; sec. regional trade union, First Sec. Dist CP Cttee; Head of Agric. Div. Regional CP Cttee; Co-founder and Chair. Socialist Party of Ukraine 1991–2010, 2011–12; People's Deputy of Ukrainian SSR, then mem. Verkhovna Rada (Parl.) 1994–2007, Chair. 1994–98, 2006–07; presidential cand. 1994, 1999, 2004, 2010. *Publications:* author or co-author of a number of legal projects including Code on Land: Where Are We Going?, Choice, Subjects for Meditation; several articles. *Address:* Socialist Party of Ukraine, 02100 Kyiv, vul. Bazhova 12, Ukraine (office). *Telephone:* (44) 573-58-97 (office). *E-mail:* pr@spu.in.ua (office). *Website:* www.spu.in.ua (office).

MOROZOV, Oleg Viktorovich, CPhilSc, PhD; Russian politician; b. 5 Nov. 1953, Kazan; m.; one d.; ed Kazan State Univ.; docent, Kazan State Univ.; Head of Div. Tatar Regional CP Cttee 1987–89; instructor, Asst to Sec., CPSU Cen. Cttee 1989–91; consultant, Office of USSR Pres. 1991–92; Deputy Dir-Gen. Biotekhnologiya; mem. State Duma 1993– (re-elected as mem. Otechestvo—Vsya Russia Movt 1999), fmrly Head, Regions of Russia Deputy Group and Deputy Speaker State Duma –2012; Head of the Presidential Administration 2012–15; Rep. of Exec. Authority, Republic of Tatarstan 2015–; mem. Federation Council Cttee on Foreign Affairs; mem. Deputies' group New Regional Politics 1994–96; Chair. Deputies' Group Russian Regions 1997–; joined Yedinstvo Party 2001; mem. of United Russia, Communist Party (political parties); Order of Honour, Order for Merit to the Fatherland, III Class, IV Class; received medals in Commemoration of 300th Anniversary of St Petersburg, in Commemoration of 1000th Anniversary of Kazan, in Commemoration of 850th Anniversary of Moscow. *Leisure interests:* collecting toy hippopotamuses, serious classical music. *Address:* Federation Council of the Federal Assembly of Russian Federation, 103426 Moscow, 26, Bolshaya Dmitrovka street, Russia. *Fax:* (495) 629-67-43. *Website:* www.council.gov.ru/en/structure/persons/1245/.

MORPARIA, Kalpana, BSc, LLB; Indian banker; *CEO, J.P. Morgan, India;* b. 1949; ed Sophia Coll., Univ. of Mumbai; Sr Legal Officer, ICICI Bank Ltd 1975–96, Gen. Man. in charge of Legal, Planning, Treasury and Corp. Communications Depts 1996–98, Sr Gen. Man. in charge also of Human Resources Devt, Planning and Strategic Support Group and Special Projects Dept 1998–2001, apptd Exec. Dir 2001, later Head, Corp. Center and Official Spokesperson, ICICI Bank Ltd, Deputy Man. Dir 2004–06, Jt Man. Dir 2006–07, Chief Strategy and Communications Officer, ICICI Group 2007–08; CEO J.P. Morgan, India 2008–; mem. Bd of Dirs Dr Reddy's Laboratories Ltd 2007–, CMC Ltd 2008–, Bennett Coleman & Company Ltd, Phillip Morris Int. Inc. 2011–, Hindustan Unilever Ltd 2014–; Women Achievers Award in the Field of Finance and Banking, Indian Merchants' Chamber (Ladies Wing) 1999. *Address:* JPMorgan Asset Management India Private Ltd, Kalpataru Synergy, 3rd Floor, West Wing, Santacruz - East, Mumbai 400 055 (office); CMC Ltd, PTI Building, 5th Floor, 4 Sansad Marg, New Delhi 110 001, India (office). *Telephone:* (22) 67837000 (Mumbai) (office); (11) 23736151 (New Delhi) (office). *Fax:* (22) 26531167 (Mumbai) (office); (11) 23736159 (New Delhi) (office). *Website:* www.jpmorganmf.com (office); www.cmcltd.com (office).

MORPURGO, Sir Michael, Kt, OBE, FRSL; British writer; b. 5 Oct. 1943, St Albans, Herts.; m. Clare Morpurgo; ed Kings Coll., Univ. of London; co-f. Farms for City Children project; Children's Laureate 2003–05; Writer-in-Residence, The Savoy Hotel, London 2007; Pres. Booktrust 2013–; Fellow, Kings Coll., Univ. of London; Chancellor, The Children's Univ.; Patron, Family Arts Festival 2014; Dr hc (Suffolk), (Exeter), (Plymouth), (Hertfordshire), (Sheffield), (Birmingham City), (Northampton), (Grosse Teste), (Worcester); Whitbread Children's Book Award 1995, Smarties Book Prize 1996, Children's Book Awards 1996, 2000, 2002, Bronze Prize in 6–8 years group 2003, Booksellers Asscn Author of the Year 2005. *Publications include:* Beyond the Rainbow Warrior, Billy the Kid, Black Queen, Colly's Barn, Conker, Dear Olly, Escape from Shangri-La, Farm Boy, Friend or Foe, From Hearabout Hill, Grania O'Malley, Joan of Arc, Kensuke's Kingdom, King of the Cloud Forests, Long Way Home, Marble Crusher, Mr Nobody's Eyes, My Friend Walter, Out of the Ashes, Red Eyes at Night, Sam's Duck, Snakes and Ladders, The Butterfly Lion, The Nine Lives of Montezuma, The Rainbow Bear, The Sleeping Sword, The War of Jenkins' Ear, The White Horse of Zennor, The Wreck of the Zanzibar, Toro! Toro!, Twist of Gold, Waiting for Anya, War Horse, Wartman, Who's a Big Bully Then?, Why the Whales Came, Wombat Goes Walkabout, The Last Wolf 2002, Private Peaceful (Prix Sorcières for children's novel, France, Blue Peter Book Award 2005, California Young Reader Medal 2008) 2003, The Amazing Story of Adolphus Tips 2005, Alone on a Wide Wide Sea 2006, On Angel Wings 2006, Born to Run 2007, Kaspar Prince of Cats 2008, Running Wild 2009, Not Bad for a Bad Lad 2010, An Elephant in the Garden 2010, Shadow 2010, Little Manfred 2011, The Pied Piper of Hamelin 2011, Sparrow: The True Story of Joan of Arc 2012, Outlaw: The Story of Robin Hood 2012, Homecoming 2012, A Medal For Leroy 2012, Beauty And The Beast, Pinocchio By Pinocchio 2013, 2013, The Goose is Getting Fat 2013, Listen to the Moon 2014, All I Said Was 2014, Half a Man 2014, Mini Kid 2014, Only Remembered (ed.) 2014, Such Stuff: A Story-Maker's Inspiration 2016, The Fox and the Ghost King (The Timeless Tale Of An Impossible Dream) 2016. *Address:* c/o Laura West, David Higham Associates, 7th Floor, Waverley House, 7–12 Noel Street, London, W1F 8GQ, England (office). *E-mail:* laurawest@davidhigham.co.uk (office). *Website:* www.davidhigham.co.uk (office); www.michaelmorpurgo.com.

MORRICONE, Ennio; Italian composer; b. 10 Nov. 1928, Rome; s. of Mario Morricone and Libera Morricone; m. Maria Travia; three s. two d.; ed Accad. of Santa Cecilia; began career in field of classical composition and arrangement; has composed and arranged scores for more than 500 film and TV productions; best known film scores include The Good, the Bad and the Ugly, Once Upon a Time in the West, The Mission, Le Professionnel; Grand Official, Ordine al merito della Repubblica Italiana 2006, Chevalier, Légion d'honneur 2008; Dr hc (Cagliari) 2000, (Seconda Università, Rome) 2002, (New Bulgarian Univ.) 2013, (Milan) 2017; numerous awards including Hon. Acad. Award 2007, Polar Music Prize 2010, Special Award for Career Achievement, Online Film Critics Soc. 2013, Premio

Toson d'Oro di Vespasiano Gonzaga 2016, Pontifical Gold Medal of Pope Francis 2019. *Film scores include:* Il Federale 1961, La Voglia matta 1962, Diciottenni al sole 1962, La Cuccagna 1962, Il Successo 1963, Le Monachine 1963, I Basilischi 1963, Duello nel Texas (as Dan Savio) 1963, La Scoperta dell'America 1964, I Motorizzati 1964, ...e la donna creò l'uomo 1964, I Maniaci 1964, Prima della rivoluzione 1964, Per un pugno di dollari (For A Fistful of Dollars, as Leo Nichols) 1964, Le Pistole non discutono 1964, I Malamondo 1964, Thrilling 1965, Slalom 1965, Menage all'italiana 1965, Idoli controluce 1965, La Battaglia di Algeri 1965, Gli Amanti d'oltretomba 1965, Altissima pressione 1965, I Pugni in tasca 1965, Centomila dollari per Ringo 1965, Il Ritorno di Ringo 1965, Per qualche dollaro in più (For a Few Dollars More) 1965, La Ragazza del bersagliere 1966, Per Firenze 1966, Navajo Joe (as Leo Nichols) 1966, Mi vedrai tornare 1966, Matchless 1966, I Lunghi giorni della vendetta 1966, Un Fiume di dollari 1966, Uccellacci e uccellini 1966, El Greco 1966, Un Uomo a metà 1966, La Resa dei conti 1966, Il Buono, il brutto, il cattivo (The Good, the Bad and the Ugly) 1966, Sette donne per i MacGregor 1967, Pedro Páramo 1967, Il Giardino delle delizie 1967, Dalle Ardenne all'inferno 1967, L'Avventuriero 1967, Le Streghe 1967, OK Connery 1967, I Crudeli (as Leo Nichols) 1967, Per pochi dollari ancora (theme) 1967, Arabella 1967, Il Mercenario 1968, Italia vista dal cielo 1968, Grazie, zia 1968, Il Grande silenzio 1968, Ecce Homo 1968, Diabolik 1968, Da uomo a uomo 1968, La Bataille de San Sebastian 1968, Roma come Chicago 1968, C'era una volta il West (Once Upon a Time in the West) 1968, Vergogna schifosi 1969, Giotto 1969, La Donna invisibile 1969, L'Assoluto naturale 1969, Cuore di mamma 1969, L'Alibi 1969, Galileo 1969, Un Bellissimo novembre 1969, Ruba al prossimo tuo 1969, Un Tranquillo posto di campagna 1969, Una Breve stagione 1969, Le Clan des Siciliens 1969, Zenabel 1969, Uccidete il vitello grasso e arrostitelo 1970, Metello 1970, Giochi particolari 1970, La Califfa 1970, Two Mules for Sister Sara 1970, La Moglie più bella 1970, Indagine su un cittadino al di sopra di ogni sospetto 1970, Hornets' Nest 1970, Vamos a matar, compañeros 1970, Oceano 1971, Gli Occhi freddi della paura 1971, Incontro 1971, Forza 'G' 1971, Una Lucertola con la pelle di donna 1971, Veruschka 1971, Il Decameron 1971, La Tarantola dal ventre nero 1971, Giornata nera per l'ariete 1971, Il Giorno del giudizio 1971, Sacco e Vanzetti 1971, L'Istruttoria è chiusa: dimentichi 1971, Malastrana 1971, Giù la testa 1971, Maddalena 1971, ¡Viva la muerte... tua! 1971, La Violenza: Quinto potere 1972, Questa specie d'amore 1972, Quando la preda è l'uomo 1972, Perché? 1972, Il Maestro e Margherita 1972, Lui per lei 1972, Guttoso e il 'Marat morto' di David 1972, Les Deux saisons de la vie 1972, D'amore si muore 1972, Crescete e moltiplicatevi 1972, La Cosa buffa 1972, Chi l'ha vista morire? 1972, Bianchi bandinelli e la Colonna Traiana 1972, Anche se volessi lavorare, che faccio? 1972, Le Tueur 1972, Cosa avete fatto a Solange? 1972, Bluebeard 1972, J. and S. – storia criminale del far west 1972, L'Attentat 1972, Sbatti il mostro in prima pagina 1972, Un Uomo da rispettare 1972, Il Ritorno di Clint il solitario 1972, Quando le donne persero la coda 1972, La Vita, a volte, è molto dura, vero Provvidenza? 1972, Vaarwel 1973, Allonsanfan 1973, Le Serpent 1973, Le Moine 1973, La Proprietà non è più un furto 1973, Revolver 1973, Rappresaglia 1973, Il Mio nome è Nessuno 1973, Il Giro del mondo degli innamorati di Peynet 1974, Fatti di gente per bene 1974, La Cugina 1974, L'Anticristo 1974, Spasmo 1974, Mussolini: Ultimo atto 1974, Sesso in confessionale 1974, Le Trio infernal 1974, Le Secret 1974, Labbra di lurido blu 1975, Gente di rispetto 1975, Peur sur la ville 1975, Leonor 1975, Der Richter und sein Henker 1975, The Human Factor 1975, Una Vita venduta 1976, Todo modo 1976, René la canne 1976, Per amore 1976, Film 1976, Il Deserto dei Tartari 1976, L'Arriviste 1976, Ariel Limon 1976, L'Agnese va a morire 1976, Der Dritte Grad 1976, Divina creatura 1976, 1900 1976, L'Eredità Ferramonti 1976, Stato interessante 1977, Il Mostro 1977, The Dragon, the Odds 1977, Corleone 1977, Le Ricain 1977, Exorcist II: The Heretic 1977, Orca 1977, Holocaust 2000 1977, L'Immoralità 1978, Forza Italia! 1978, Il Gatto 1978, One, Two, Two: 122, rue de Provence 1978, Così come sei 1978, La Cage aux folles 1978, Ten to Survive 1979, Il Prato 1979, Il Ladrone 1979, Dedicato al mare Egeo 1979, L'Umanoide 1979, Bloodline 1979, La Luna 1979, I... comme Icare 1979, Uomini e no 1980, The Fantastic World of M.C. Escher 1980, Windows 1980, Un Sacco bello 1980, The Island 1980, L'Oeil 1980, La Banquière 1980, La Cage aux folles II 1980, La Dame aux camélias 1980, Il Pianeta azzurro 1981, Bianco, rosso e Verdone 1981, So Fine 1981, Le Professionnel 1981, La Tragedia di un uomo ridicolo 1981, Porca vacca 1982, Nana 1982, A Time to Die 1982, The Thing 1982, White Dog 1982, Blood Link 1982, Maja Plisetskaja 1982, Hundra 1983, Le Ruffian 1983, Le Marginal 1983, Sahara 1983, Pelota 1984, Once Upon a Time in America 1984, Les Voleurs de la nuit 1984, Code Name: Wild Geese 1984, Red Sonja 1985, Kommando Leopard 1985, Il Pentito 1985, La Cage aux folles 3 – 'Elles' se marient 1985, La Venexiana 1986, La Gabbia 1986, The Mission 1986, Quartiere 1987, Mosca addio 1987, Il Giorno prima 1987, The Untouchables 1987, Gli Occhiali d'oro 1987, Il Cuore di mamma 1988, Frantic 1988, A Time of Destiny 1988, Rampage 1988, Cinema Paradiso 1989, Casualties of War 1989, Fat Man and Little Boy 1989, Tre colonne in cronaca 1990, Tempo di uccidere 1990, ¡Átame! 1990, Stanno tutti bene 1990, The Big Man 1990, Tracce di vita amorosa 1990, State of Grace 1990, Hamlet 1990, Money 1991, La Domenica specialmente 1991, Bugsy 1991, A Csalás gyönyöre 1992, Beyond Justice 1992, City of Joy 1992, La Villa del venerdì 1992, Love Potion No. 9 1992, Roma imago urbis 1993, In the Line of Fire 1993, Il Lungo silenzio 1993, La Scorta 1993, Jona che visse nella balena 1994, Wolf 1994, Love Affair 1994, Disclosure 1994, The Night and the Moment 1995, Pasolini, un delitto italiano 1995, L'Uomo delle stelle 1995, I Magi randagi 1996, Vite strozzate 1996, La Lupa 1996, Cartoni animati 1997, Marianna Ucrìa 1997, U Turn 1997, Lolita 1997, Il Fantasma dell'opera 1998, Lucignolo 1999, In the Line of Fire: The Ultimate Sacrifice 2000, Canone inverso – making love 2000, Mission to Mars 2000, Malèna 2000, La Ragion pura 2001, Cowboys Don't Kiss in Public 2001, Threnody 2002, Senso '45 2002, Ripley's Game 2002, Il Diario di Matilde Manzoni 2002, L'Ultimo pistolero 2002, Arena Concerto 2003, La Luz prodigiosa 2003, The Wages of Sin 2003, 72 metra 2004, Kill Bill: Vol. 2 2004, Guardiani delle nuvole 2004, Sorstalanság 2005, Karol, un uomo diventato papa 2005, Libertas 2005, Fateless 2005, E ridendo l'uccise 2005, Adolfo Celi, un uomo per due culture 2006, A Crime 2006, La Sconosciuta 2006, The Weatherman 2007, Ultrasordine 2007, I demoni di San Pietroburgo 2008, Baaria – La porta del vento 2009, Spider Dance 2010, The Best Offer 2013, The Hateful Eight (Golden Globe Award for Best Original Score 2016, BAFTA for Best Original Music 2016) 2015, The Correspondence 2015, A Rose in Winter 2017, Leningrad 2017. *Television scores include:* The Virginian (series theme) 1962, Lo Squarciagola 1966, 1943: un incontro 1969, La Sciantosa 1970, Nessuno deve sapere (series) 1971, Correva l'anno di grazia 1870 1971, L'Uomo e la magia 1972, L'Automobile 1972, Moses the Lawgiver 1975, Drammi gotichi 1976, Noi lazzaroni (series) 1978, Le Mani sporche 1978, Invito allo sport (series) 1978, Orient-Express (series) 1979, The Life and Times of David Lloyd George (series) 1981, Marco Polo (series) 1982, The Scarlet and the Black 1983, Wer war Edgar Allan? 1984, Die Försterbuben 1984, Via Mala (series) 1985, C.A.T. Squad 1986, I Promessi sposi (series) 1988, Gli Indifferenti (series) 1988, Camillo Castiglioni oder die Moral der Haifische 1988, Gli Angeli del potere 1988, C.A.T. Squad: Python Wolf 1988, Il Principe del deserto (series) 1989, The Endless Game 1990, Cacciatori di navi 1990, Una Storia italiana 1992, Piazza di Spagna (series) 1993, Missus 1993, La Piovra series 1–10 1984–99, Genesi: La creazione e il diluvio 1994, Abraham 1994, Jacob 1994, Joseph 1995, Moses (title music) 1996, Il Barone (series) 1996, Samson and Delilah 1996, In fondo al cuore 1997, Nostromo (series) 1997, David (theme) 1997, Ultimo 1998, I Guardiani del cielo 1998, Il Quarto re 1998, La Casa bruciata 1998, Ultimo 2 – La sfida 1999, Nanà 1999, Esther 1999, Padre Pio – Tra cielo e terra 2000, Un Difetto di famiglia 2002, Il Papa buono 2003, Musashi (series) 2003, Charlie Chaplin – Les années suisses 2003, Il Cuore nel pozzo 2005, Cefalonia 2005, Karol, un umono divetato Papa 2005, Lucia 2005, La Provinciale 2006, Giovanni Falcone, l'uomo che sfido Cosa Nostra 2006, L'ultimo de Corleonesi 2007, Résolution 819 2008, Pane e libertà 2009, Quatraro mysteriet 2009, Mi ricordo Anna Frank 2009. *Classical compositions:* more than 15 piano concertos, 30 symphonic pieces, choral music and one opera. *Address:* c/o Gorfaine/Schwartz Agency Inc., 4111 West Alameda Avenue, Suite 509, Burbank, CA 91505, USA (office). *Telephone:* (818) 260-8500 (office).

MORRILL, Rev. John Stephen, DPhil, FBA; British historian and academic; *Professor of British and Irish History, University of Cambridge;* b. 12 June 1946, Manchester; s. of William Henry Morrill and Marjorie Morrill (née Ashton); m. Frances Mead 1968 (died 2007); four d.; ed Altrincham Grammar School, Trinity Coll., Oxford; Research Fellow, Trinity Coll. Oxford 1970–74, Hon. Fellow 2006–; Lecturer in History, Univ. of Stirling 1974–75; Fellow, Selwyn Coll. Cambridge 1975–, Sr Tutor 1989–92, Vice-Master 1994–2005; Lecturer in History, Cambridge Univ. 1975–92, Reader in Early Modern History 1992–98, Prof. of British and Irish History 1998–; mem. Council, Royal Historical Soc. 1988–92, Vice-Pres. 1992–96; Chair. Communications and Activities Cttee, British Acad. 1998–, mem. Council 1998–, Vice-Pres. 2000–02; mem. and Trustee Arts and Humanities Research Council 2000–04, Chair. Rescue Cttee 2001–04; ordained Perm. Deacon, RC Diocese of East Anglia 1996; mem. Acad. of Finland 2001; Hon. DLitt (Univ. of East Anglia) 2001; Hon. DUniv (Surrey) 2001. *Publications include:* Cheshire 1630–1660 1974, The Revolt of the Provinces 1976, Reactions to the English Civil War 1981, Oliver Cromwell and the English Revolution 1989, The Impact of the English Civil War 1991, Revolution and Restoration 1992, The Nature of the English Revolution 1992, The British Problem 1534–1707 1996, The Oxford Illustrated History of Tudor and Stuart Britain 1996, Revolt in the Provinces 1998, Soldiers and Statesmen of the English Revolution (co-author) 1998; 40 articles in learned journals. *Leisure interests:* music, theology, whisky, cricket. *Address:* Selwyn College, Cambridge, CB3 9DQ (office); 1 Bradford's Close, Bottisham, Cambridge, CB25 9DW, England (home). *Telephone:* (1223) 335895 (office); (1223) 811822 (home). *Fax:* (1223) 335837 (office). *E-mail:* jsm1000@cam.ac.uk (office).

MORRIS, Christopher, FCA; British chartered accountant; *Partner, Begbies Traynor;* b. 28 April 1942; s. of Richard Archibald Sutton Morris, MC and Josephine Fanny Mary Morris (née Galliano); m. Isabel Ramsden (divorced); two s.; qualified 1967; Pnr, Head of UK insolvency arm Touche Ross & Co. (later Deloitte) 1972–2000; Sr Partner Corp. Recovery; Pnr Begbies Traynor 2004–; cases have included liquidation of Laker Airways 1982, British Island Airways, British Air Ferries, Rush & Tompkins, London & County Securities, Polly Peck Int., Banco Ambrosiano, Bank of Credit and Commerce International (BCCI); Fellow Soc. of Practitioners of Insolvency. *Leisure interests:* racing, wine, the countryside. *Address:* Begbies Traynor, 32 Cornhill, London, EC3V 3BT, England (office). *Telephone:* (20) 7398-3800 (office). *Fax:* (20) 7398-3799 (office). *Website:* www.begbies-traynor.com (office).

MORRIS, Sir Derek James, Kt, MA, DPhil; British economist and academic; *Chairman, The Cheviot Trust;* b. 23 Dec. 1945, Harrow, Middx, England; s. of Denis William Morris and Olive Margaret Morris; m. Susan Mary Whittles 1975; two s.; ed Harrow Co. Grammar School, St Edmund Hall and Nuffield Coll., Oxford; Research Fellow, Univ. of Warwick 1969–70; Fellow and Tutor of Econs Oriel Coll., Oxford 1970–98, Provost 2003–13; Econ. Dir Nat. Econ. Devt Office 1981–84; Chair. Oxford Econ. Forecasting Ltd 1984–98; mem. Monopolies and Mergers Comm. 1991–95, Deputy Chair. 1995–98, Chair. Competition (fmrly Monopolies and Mergers) Comm. 1998–2004; Chair. Morris Review of Actuarial Profession 2004; mem. Bd of Dirs Lucida plc 2007–13, later Chair.; Chair. The Cheviot Trust 2017–; Chair. of Trustees, Oxford Univ. Pension Fund; fmr mem. Bd of Govs. Nat. Inst. of Econ. and Social Research; Hon. Fellow, St Edmund Hall, Oxford 2002, Trinity Coll., Dublin 2004; Dr hc (Univ. Coll., Dublin) 2004, (Univ. of East Anglia) 2006. *Publications include:* The Economic System in the UK (ed.) 1971, Industrial Economics and Organisation (with D. Hay) 1985, Chinese State-Owned Enterprises and Economic Reform 1994, Pawn's Gambit (novel) 2012; numerous journal articles on econs. *Leisure interests:* skiing, rugby, history. *Address:* The Cheviot Trust, Kingswood House, 58–64 Baxter Avenue, Southend on Sea, Essex, SS2 6BG, England (office). *Telephone:* (1702) 354024 (office). *E-mail:* people@cheviottrust.com (office). *Website:* www.cheviottrust.com (office).

MORRIS, Desmond John, BSc, DPhil; British zoologist, artist and writer; b. 24 Jan. 1928, Purton, Wilts., England; s. of Capt. Harry Howe Morris and Marjorie Morris (née Hunt); m. Ramona Joy Baulch 1952; one s.; ed Dauntsey's School, Wilts., Univs of Birmingham and Oxford; zoological research worker Univ. of Oxford 1954–56; Head of Granada TV/Film Unit Zoological Soc. of London 1956–59, Curator of Mammals 1959–67; Dir Inst. of Contemporary Arts, London 1967–68; Research Fellow, Wolfson Coll., Oxford 1973–81; privately engaged in writing books on animal and human behaviour 1968–73, 1981–2019 and making TV programmes; also active as an exhibiting artist 1948–2019; Hon. FZS; Hon. FLS; Hon. DSc (Reading) 1998, (Malta). *Television:* Zootime (Granada) 1956–67, Life in the Animal World (BBC) 1965–67, The Human Race (Thames TV) 1982, The Animals Roadshow (BBC) 1987–89, The Animal Contract 1989, Animal Country 1991–95, The Human Animal 1994, The Human Sexes 1997. *Publications include:* The Reproductive Behaviour of the Ten-spined Stickleback 1958, The Story of

Congo 1958, Curious Creatures 1961, The Biology of Art 1962, Apes and Monkeys 1964, The Mammals: A Guide to the Living Species 1965, The Big Cats 1965, Men and Snakes (with Ramona Morris) 1965, Zootime 1966, Men and Apes (with Ramona Morris) 1966, Men and Pandas (with Ramona Morris) 1966, Primate Ethology (Ed.) 1967, The Naked Ape 1967, The Human Zoo 1969, Intimate Behaviour 1971, Manwatching: A Field-Guide to Human Behaviour 1977, Gestures, Their Origins and Distribution 1979, Animal Days (autobiog.) 1979, The Giant Panda 1981, The Soccer Tribe 1981, Inrock (fiction) 1983, Bodywatching 1985, The Illustrated Naked Ape 1986, Dogwatching 1986, Catwatching 1986, The Secret Surrealist 1987, The Human Nestbuilders 1988, The Animals Roadshow 1988, Horsewatching 1988, The Animal Contract 1990, Animal-Watching 1990, Babywatching 1991, Christmas Watching 1992, The World of Animals 1993, The Naked Ape Trilogy 1994, The Human Animal 1994, Body Talk: A World Guide to Gestures 1994, The Illustrated Catwatching 1994, Illustrated Babywatching 1995, Catworld: A Feline Encyclopedia 1996, Illustrated Dogwatching 1996, The Human Sexes 1997, Illustrated Horsewatching 1998, Cool Cats: The 100 Cat Breeds of the World 1999, Cosmetic Behaviour and the Naked Ape 1999, The Naked Eye 2000, Dogs, a Dictionary of Dog Breeds 2001, People-Watching 2002, The Silent Language 2004, The Nature of Happiness 2004, The Naked Woman: A Study of the Female Body 2004, Watching: Encounters with Humans and Other Animals (autobiog.) 2006, The Naked Man 2008, Baby, The Story of a Baby's First Two Years 2008, Planet Ape (with Steve Parker) 2009. *Leisure interest:* archaeology. *Address:* c/o Jonathan Cape, 20 Vauxhall Bridge Road, London, SW1V 2SA, England. *E-mail:* dmorris@ukstudio.org (office). *Website:* www.desmond-morris .com (home).

MORRIS, Doug; American record company executive, producer and songwriter; b. 23 Nov. 1938; ed Columbia Univ.; fmr songwriter music publisher Robert Mellin Inc.; writer and producer, Laurie Records from 1965, later Vice-Pres. and Gen. Man.; f. Big Tree label (sold to Atlantic Records 1978); Pres. ATCO Records (part of Warner Music) 1978–80, Pres. Atlantic Records 1980–90, Co-Chair. and Co-CEO Atlantic Recording Group 1990–94, Pres. and COO, then Chair. Warner Music USA 1995; co-cr. Interscope Records; Chair. and CEO MCA Music Entertainment Group (now Universal Music Group) 1995–2011, f. Universal Records, apptd to Vivendi Universal Management Bd 2005; Founder VEVO premium music video and entertainment service 2009; CEO Sony Music Entertainment 2011–17, Chair. 2017–18 (retd); Co-f. (with Jimmy Iovine) Jimmy and Doug's Farm Club project, comprising a record label, website and cable TV show 1999; Co-producer and lead financier of Broadway musical Motown: The Musical 2013; Co-owner Pressplay subscription-based music download website; mem. Bd of Dirs CBS Corpn, The Robin Hood Foundation, The Cold Spring Harbor Laboratory, Rock and Roll Hall of Fame; Pres.'s Merit Award, Nat. Acad. of Recording Arts and Sciences (NARAS) 2003, City of Hope Spirit of Life Award 2008, NARAS Icons Award 2009, received a star on the Hollywood Walk of Fame 2009, Howie Richmond Hitmaker Award, Songwriters Hall of Fame 2014. *Compositions include:* Sweet Talkin' Guy, The Chiffons 1966.

MORRIS, Errol Mark, BA; American film director; b. 5 Feb. 1948, Hewlett, NY; m. Julia Sheehan 1984; one s.; ed Univ. of Wisconsin, Princeton Univ., Univ. of California, Berkeley; documentary film dir; mem. American Acad. of Arts and Sciences; MacArthur Fellowship, Guggenheim Fellowship. *Films include:* Gates of Heaven 1980, Vernon, Florida 1982, The Thin Blue Line 1988, The Dark Wind 1991, A Brief History of Time 1991, Fast, Cheap and Out of Control 1997, Mr. Death: The Rise and Fall of Fred A. Leuchter, Jr. 1999, The Fog of War: Eleven Lessons from the Life of Robert S. McNamara (Academy Award for Best Documentary 2004) 2003, Standard Operating Procedure (Grand Jury Silver Bear, Berlin Film Festival) 2008, Tabloid 2010, The Unknown Known 2013. *Television includes:* First Person (documentary series) 2000–01, The Subterranean Stadium 2015, The Streaker 2015, The Heist 2015, Most Valuable Whatever 2015, Being Mr. Met 2015. *Publications:* Standard Operating Procedure (with Philip Gourevitch) 2008, Believing is Seeing: Observations on the Mysteries of Photography 2011, A Wilderness of Error: The Trials of Jeffrey MacDonald 2012. *Address:* Fourth Floor Productions Inc., 650 Cambridge Street, Cambridge, MA 02141, USA (office). *Telephone:* (617) 225-0012 (office). *Fax:* (617) 225-0016 (office). *E-mail:* info@errolmorris.com (office). *Website:* www.errolmorris.com (office).

MORRIS, Hon. Floyd Emerson, MPhil; Jamaican politician and consultant; *Director, Centre for Disability Studies, University of West Indies;* b. 23 July 1969, Bailey's Vale, Port Maria; s. of Lloyd Morris and Jemita Pryce; m. Shelley-Ann Morris 2011; ed Univ. of the West Indies (UWI); began career as consultant, Nat. Youth Service; fmr Politics Lecturer, Dept of Govt, UWI, Co-ordinator, UWI Centre for Disability Studies; Founder and CEO F.E. Morris International Consultancy Services; Minister of State in Ministry of Labour and Social Security 2001–07; apptd to Senate 1998–2007, 2012–, Pres. 2013–16; currently Dir Centre for Disability Studies, Univ. of West Indies; host of radio programme 'Seeing from a Different Perspective' 2011–; mem. Nat. Advisory Bd for Persons with Disabilities 1995–. *Leisure interests:* sports, dominoes. *Address:* Center for Disability Studies, University of the West Indies, Mona, Kingston 7, Jamaica (office). *Telephone:* 977-9423 (office). *Fax:* 927-1165 (office). *E-mail:* info@cds.mona.uwi.edu (office). morrisfloyd@gmail.com (office). *Website:* cds.mona.uwi.edu (office).

MORRIS, Howard R., BSc, PhD, FRS, FRSA; British chemist, biochemist, academic and entrepreneur; *Professor Emeritus of Biological Chemistry and Senior Research Investigator, Imperial College London;* b. 4 Aug. 1946, Bolton, Lancs., England; ed Univ. of Leeds; postdoctoral research, Univ. of Cambridge Chemical Lab., then at MRC Lab. of Molecular Biology, Cambridge 1970–75; Lecturer, Imperial Coll., London 1975, later Head of Dept of Biochemistry and Jt Head of Life Sciences Div., f. Imperial Coll. Biomolecular Mass Spectrometry Group 1975, Prof. of Biological Chem. and Sr Research Investigator 1980–2001, Teaching Fellow 1991, Prof. Emer. 2001–; Founder M-SCAN Group 1980 (merged with SGS 2010), Biopharmaspec Group, NJ and PA, USA 2014; mem. Cttee Advising Council on Gen. and Hon. Candidates, Royal Soc. of Chemistry2019; mem. Audit Cttee, Inst. of Cancer Research, London; Hon. DSc (Univ. of Naples) 2005, (Univ. of Leeds) 2015; Rector's Award for Excellence in Teaching 1996, Blaise Pascal Medal and Prize for Life Sciences and Medicine, European Acad. of Sciences 2010, Franklin Medal, Inst. of Physics 2012, Royal Medal and Prize (Queen's Medal) for Interdisciplinary Sciences, Royal Soc. 2014. *Publications:*

more than 440 peer-reviewed papers in professional journals. *Address:* Department of Life Sciences, 103 Sir Ernst Chain Building, Imperial College London, South Kensington Campus, London, SW7 2AZ, England (office). *Telephone:* (20) 7594-5221 (office). *E-mail:* h.morris@imperial.ac.uk (office). *Website:* www3 .imperial.ac.uk/lifesciences (office).

MORRIS, James Humphry (see MORRIS, Jan).

MORRIS, James Peppler; American singer (bass-baritone); b. 10 Jan. 1947; s. of James Morris and Geraldine Peppler; m. 1st Joanne F. Vitali 1971; one d.; m. 2nd Susan Quittmeyer 1987; one s. one d. (twins); ed Univ. of Maryland, Peabody Conservatory with Rosa Ponselle, Philadelphia Acad. of Vocal Arts with basso Nicola Moscona; debut at Metropolitan Opera, New York 1970; opera and concert appearances throughout USA, Canada, South America, Europe, Japan and Australia; repertoire including works by Wagner, Verdi, Puccini, Offenbach, Stravinsky, Mussorgsky, Mozart, Gounod and Britten; has performed in most int. opera houses and has appeared with major orchestras of Europe and USA; noted for his interpretation of the role of Wotan in Wagner's Der Ring des Nibelungen; has appeared in this role at Metropolitan Opera, Vienna State Opera, Bavarian State Opera, Munich, Deutsche Oper Berlin, Lyric Opera of Chicago, San Francisco Opera and many others; also noted interpreter of title role in Wagner's Der fliegende Holländer; has appeared as Hans Sachs in Die Meistersinger von Nürnberg in major houses of Europe and USA; debuted role of Oroveso in Norma at Metropolitan Opera 2013–14, also appeared as Hans Sachs in Die Meistersinger von Nürnberg at Lyric Opera of Chicago and as the Four Villains in Les contes d'Hoffmann; concert performances of Die Meistersinger von Nürnberg at Tanglewood, Mahler's 8th Symphony with Michael Tilson Thomas and San Francisco Symphony and Orchestre National de France under Daniele Gatti, and Verdi's Simon Boccanegra with Boston Symphony Orchestra; sang Beethoven's Symphony No. 9 at Blossom Festival with Cleveland Orchestra under Franz Welser-Möst and appeared with Montreal Symphony under Kent Nagano in a programme of arias by Verdi and Wagner; concert performances of Berlioz's La Damnation de Faust in Madrid; other concert appearances have included performances with Berlin Philharmonic, London's BBC Proms, concerts with Zubin Mehta and New York Philharmonic, 'Pavarotti Plus' special at New York's Avery Fisher Hall, and several televised gala events at Metropolitan Opera; also appeared in La Damnation de Faust with Los Angeles Philharmonic at the Hollywood Bowl; concert of opera arias and Broadway songs with Chicago Symphony at Ravinia; Mendelssohn's Elijah with Boston Handel and Haydn Soc. under Christopher Hogwood as well as at Cincinnati May Festival under James Conlon; has also appeared frequently in recitals in cities including Minneapolis, Baltimore, Washington, DC and at Teatro Colon, Buenos Aires. *Recordings include:* two complete Ring cycles, one under James Levine and one under Bernard Haitink, and other operas of Wagner, Offenbach, Mozart, Massenet, Verdi and Gounod; operas by Donizetti, Puccini, Bellini and Thomas with Dame Joan Sutherland; orchestral recordings include Haydn's Creation, Beethoven's Symphony No. 9 'Choral' and Requiems by Mozart and Fauré, Thomas' Desire Under the Elms with George Manahan and London Symphony, Mahler's Symphony No. 8 with Michael Tilson Thomas and San Francisco Symphony (Grammy Award 2010), Arias by Verdi and Wagner. *Address:* c/o Damon Bristo, Columbia Artists Management Inc., 5 Columbus Circle at 1790 Broadway, New York, NY 10019-1412, USA (office). *Telephone:* (212) 841-9500 (office). *Fax:* (212) 841-9744 (office). *E-mail:* info@cami.com (office). *Website:* www.cami.com (office).

MORRIS, James (Jim) T., BA, MBA; American international organization official and business executive; *Vice-Chairman, Pacers Sports & Entertainment, LLC;* b. 18 April 1943, Terre Haute, Ind.; m. Jacqueline Harrell Morris; three c.; ed Indiana Univ., Butler Univ.; worked with American Fletcher Nat. Bank 1965; Chief of Staff to Mayor of Indianapolis 1967–73; Dir of Community Devt, Lilly Endowment 1973, Vice-Pres., Pres. 1984–88; Chair. and CEO IWC Resources Corpn, Ind. Water Co. 1989–2002; Exec. Dir UN WFP 2002–07, Special Envoy of Sec.-Gen. for humanitarian crisis in Southern Africa 2002–07; Special Consultant to Pres. of Pacers Sports & Entertainment, LLC 2007–08, Pres. 2008–14, Vice-Chair. 2014–; Chair. NCAA Foundation, Riley Children's Foundation; Chair. Bd of Trustees, Ind. Univ. 2013–, Indiana State Univ.; Treas. US Gymnastics Fed.; fmr Treas. US Olympic Cttee; mem. Nat. Advisory Bd Boy Scouts of America, Elanco, Indianapolis Power and Light; mem. Bd Govs, American Red Cross; Bd mem. One America, Old Nat. Bank, Hulman & Co., Indianapolis Motor Speedway; inducted into Ind. Acad.; 18 hon. doctorates, including Dr hc (Butler Univ.), (Indiana Univ.), (Vincennes Univ.), (Rose Hufman Inst. of Tech.), (Univ. of Southern Indiana), (Martin Univ.), (Franklin Coll.), (Marian Coll.), (Wabash Coll.), (Univ. of Notre Dame); Medal of Freedom, Ellis Island, New York, Whitney Young Award, Indianapolis Urban League, Charles L. Whistler Award, Int. Citizen of the Year, Int. Center of Indianapolis and numerous other awards. *Address:* Pacers Sports & Entertainment, LLC, Indiana Pacers, 125 S Pennsylvania Street, Indianapolis, IN 00148, USA (office). *Telephone:* (317) 917-2520 (office). *Fax:* (317) 917-2599 (office). *E-mail:* jmorris@pacers.com (office). *Website:* www.nba.com/pacers (office).

MORRIS, Jan, (James Humphry Morris), CBE, MA, FRSL; British writer; b. 2 Oct. 1926, Somerset, England; ed Christ Church Coll., Oxford; mem. editorial staff, The Times 1951–56, The Guardian 1957–62; Commonwealth Fellowship, USA 1954; mem. Yr Academi Gymreig, Gorsedd of Bards, Welsh Nat. Eisteddfod; Hon. Fellow, Univ. Coll. Wales, Univ. of Wales, Bangor; Hon. FRIBA; Hon. Student, Christ Church Oxon.; Dr hc (Univ. of Wales) 1993, (Univ. of Glamorgan) 1996. *Publications include:* as James Morris: Coast to Coast (aka I Saw the USA) 1956, Sultan in Oman 1957, The Market of Seleukia (aka Islam Inflamed: A Middle East Picture) 1957, Coronation Everest 1958, South African Winter 1958, The Hashemite Kings 1959, Venice 1960, South America 1961, The Upstairs Donkey (juvenile) 1962, The World Bank: A Prospect (aka The Road to Huddersfield: A Journey to Five Continents) 1963, Cities 1963, The Outriders: A Liberal View of Britain 1963, The Presence of Spain 1964, Oxford 1965, Pax Britannica: The Climax of an Empire 1968, The Great Port: A Passage through New York 1969, Places 1972, Heaven's Command: An Imperial Progress 1973, Farewell the Trumpets: An Imperial Retreat 1978; as Jan Morris: Conundrum 1974, Travels 1976, The Oxford Book of Oxford 1978, Destinations: Essays from 'Rolling Stone' 1980, The Venetian Empire: A Sea Voyage 1980, My Favourite Stories of Wales 1980, The Small Oxford Book of Wales, Wales The First Place, A Venetian Bestiary

1982, The Spectacle of Empire 1982, Stones of Empire: The Buildings of the Raj 1983, Journeys 1984, The Matter of Wales: Epic Views of a Small Country 1984, Among the Cities 1985, Last Letters from Hav: Notes from a Lost City 1985, Stones of Empire: The Buildings of the Raj 1986, Scotland, The Place of Visions 1986, Manhattan, '45 1987, Hong Kong: Xianggang 1988, Pleasures of a Tangled Life 1989, Ireland Your Only Place 1990, City to City 1990, O Canada 1992, Sydney 1992, Locations 1992, Travels with Virginia Woolf (ed.) 1993, A Machynlleth Triad 1994, Fisher's Face 1995, The Princeship of Wales 1995, The World of Venice 1995, 50 Years of Europe 1997, Hong Kong: Epilogue to an Empire 1997, Lincoln: A Foreigner's Quest 1999, Our First Leader 2000, A Writer's House in Wales 2001, Trieste and the Meaning of Nowhere 2001, A Writer's World: Travels 1950–2000 2003, Portmeirion (with others) 2006, Hav 2007, A Venetian Bestiary 2007, Contact! A Book of Glimpses 2010, Ciao, Carpaccio! 2014. *Address:* United Agents, 12–26 Lexington Street, London W1F 0LE (office); Trefan Morys, Llanystumdwy, Gwynedd, LL52 0LP, Wales (home). *Website:* unitedagents.co.uk/jan-morris (office). *Telephone:* (1766) 522222 (home).

MORRIS, Mark William; American choreographer and dancer; *Artistic Director, Mark Morris Dance Group;* b. 29 Aug. 1956, Seattle, Wash.; s. of William Morris and Maxine Crittenden Morris; Artistic Dir Mark Morris Dance Group 1980–, Founder and Artistic Dir Mark Morris Dance Center, Brooklyn, NY 2001–; Dir of Dance, Théâtre Royal de la Monnaie, Brussels 1988–91; Co-founder White Oak Dance Project (with Mikhail Baryshnikov q.v.) 1990; performed with various dance cos including Lar Lubovitch Dance Co., Hannah Kahn Dance Co., Laura Dean Dancers and Musicians, Eliot Feld Ballet, Koleda Balkan Dance Ensemble; cr. over 120 works for Mark Morris Dance Group, including Gloria 1981, Mythologies 1986, Falling Down Stairs 1987, L'Allegro, il Penseroso ed il Moderato 1988, Dido and Aeneas 1989, The Hard Nut 1991, Grand Duo 1993, Lucky Charms 1994, The Office 1994, I Don't Want to Love 1996, Peccadillos 2000, V 2001, All Fours 2004, Mozart Dances 2006, Festival Dance 2011; Music Dir Ojai Music Festival 2013; has cr. dances for many ballet cos, including eight for San Francisco Ballet, and for Paris Opera Ballet, American Ballet Theatre, Boston Ballet and others; cr. Platee (for Edinburgh Festival) 1996, King Arthur (for ENO) 2006, Orfeo ed Euridice (for Metropolitan Opera) 2007; mem. American Acad. of Arts and Sciences, American Philosophical Soc.; numerous tours abroad including performance at Guangzhou Opera House, People's Repub. of China 2012; 11 hon. doctorates; New York Dance and Performance Award 1984, 1990, Guggenheim Fellowship 1986, MacArthur Foundation 'Genius' Award 1991, Leonard Bernstein Lifetime Achievement Award for the Elevation of Music in Society 2010, Benjamin Franklin Creativity Laureate 2012, Orchestra of St Luke's Gift of Music Award 2014, Dorris Duke Performing Artist Award 2016, Samuel H. Scripps'American Dance Festival Award for Lifetime Achievement. *Films:* WNET presents Mark Morris Dance Group in The Hard Nut, Dido and Aeneas (A Rhombus Media Production). *Television:* Great Performances presents Dance in America: Mark Morris 1986, South Bank Show (UK): Hidden Soul of Harmony 1990, Four Saints in Three Acts 2000. *Address:* Mark Morris Dance Group, 3 Lafayette Avenue, Brooklyn, NY 11217, USA (office). *Telephone:* (718) 624-8400 (office). *Fax:* (718) 624-8900 (office). *E-mail:* info@mmdg.org (office). *Website:* markmorrisdancegroup.org (office).

MORRIS, Michael G., MSc, LLB; American energy industry executive; b. 11 Nov. 1946, Fremont, Ohio; m. Linda Morris; two s.; ed Detroit Coll. of Law, East Michigan Univ.; f. and fmr Pres. ANR Gathering Co.; fmr Pres. Colorado Interstate Gas; fmr Exec. Vice-Pres. ANR Pipeline Co.; fmr Pres. CMS Marketing, Services and Trading; Pres. and CEO Consumers Energy –1997; Chair., Pres. and CEO Northeast Utilities System 1997–2003; Chair., Pres. and CEO American Electric Power 2004–11, mem. Bd of Dirs 2004–; Dir, St Francis Care Inc., Nuclear Electric Insurance Ltd, American Gas Asscn, Spinnaker Exploration, Flink Ink Corpn, Webster Financial Corpn, Cincinnati Bell; Second Vice-Chair. Edison Electrical Inst.; mem. US Dept of Energy Electricity Advisory Bd, Nat. Govs Asscn Task Force on Electricity Infrastructure, CT Gov.'s Council on Econ. Competitiveness and Tech.; fmr Chair. Connnecticut Business and Industry Asscn; fmr mem. Bd Detroit Coll. of Law, Inst. of Gas Tech., East Michigan Univ. Foundation, Olivet Coll. Leadership Advisory Council, Library of Michigan Foundation; mem. Michigan Bar Asscn; Trustee, Bushnell Overseers. *Address:* American Electric Power Company Inc., 28th Floor, 1 Riverside Plaza, Columbus, OH 43215-2373, USA (office). *Telephone:* (614) 716-1000 (office). *Fax:* (614) 223-1823 (office). *E-mail:* info@aep.com (office). *Website:* www.aep.com (office).

MORRIS, Michael Jeremy, MBE, MA; British performing arts producer; *Co-Director, Artangel;* b. 30 March 1958, London, England; s. of Lawrence Morris and Monica Morris; m. Sarah Culshaw 1991; one s. one d.; ed Oundle School, Keble Coll. Oxford and City Univ., London; Assoc. Dir of Theatre, Inst. of Contemporary Arts 1981–84, Dir of Performing Arts 1984–87; mem. Drama and Dance Panel, British Council 1984–90; Founding Dir Cultural Industry Ltd (presenting and producing contemporary theatre, music and dance) 1987–; Co.-Dir Artangel (commissioning artists to create new work) 1991–, Artangel Media 2000–, has commissioned and produced projects by Robert Wilson, Michael Clark, William Forsythe, Brian Eno and Laurie Anderson, John Berger and Simon McBurney, amongst numerous others; Dir Cultural Industry Ltd. *Opera:* dir first production and co-author of libretto of Michael Nyman's opera The Man Who Mistook His Wife for a Hat 1986, dir first production and author of libretto of Mike Westbrook's opera Coming Through Slaughter 1994. *Publication includes:* The Oxford Handbook of Dance and Theater, European Journal of Ecopsychology, Choreographic Practices. *Leisure interests:* world music, fine wine, foreign food, popular art. *Address:* Artangel, 31 Eyre Street Hill, London, EC1R 5EW, England (office). *Telephone:* (20) 7713-1400 (office). *Fax:* (20) 7713-1401 (office). *E-mail:* info@artangel.org.uk (office). *Website:* www.artangel.org.uk (office).

MORRIS, Sir Peter John, Kt, AC, MB, BS, PhD, FRCS, FMedSci, FRS; Australian surgeon and academic; *Emeritus Nuffield Professor of Surgery, University of Oxford;* b. 17 April 1934, Horsham, Vic.; s. of Stanley Henry Morris and Mary Lois (née Hennessy) Morris; m. Jocelyn Mary Gorman 1960; three s. two d.; ed Univ. of Melbourne; Resident Surgical Officer, St Vincent's Hosp. 1958–61; Surgical Registrar, Southampton Gen. Hosp., UK 1963–64; Clinical Assoc. and Fellow, Mass. Gen. Hosp., Boston, USA 1964–66; Asst Prof. of Surgery, Medical Coll., Richmond, Va, USA 1967; Dir Tissue Transplantation Labs, Univ. of Melbourne, Australia 1968–74, Reader in Surgery 1971–74; Consultant Surgeon, Lymphona Clinic, Cancer Inst., Melbourne 1969–74; Nuffield Prof. of Surgery, Univ. of Oxford, UK 1974–2002 (now Prof. Emer.), Dir Oxford Transplant Centre; Pres. The Transplantation Soc. 1984–86, European Surgical Asscn 1996–98, Int. Surgical Soc. 2001–; Vice-Chair. Clinical Medicine Bd, Univ. of Oxford 1982–84; Vice-Pres. Royal Coll. of Surgeons of England 2000–01, then Pres.; Chair. Council, Inst. of Health Sciences, Univ. of Oxford 2000–; Council mem. MRC, London 1983–87; Ed. Transplantation 1979–; Fellow, Balliol Coll., Univ. of Oxford 1974–; mem. UFC 1989–92; Gov. Health Foundation 1998–2003; Pres. Royal Coll. of Surgeons of England 2001–04, Medical Protection Soc.; fmr Chair. British Heart Foundation, Dir Centre for Evidence in Transplantation; Hon. FRCSE, FACS 1986, FRACS 1996, FRCP, FRCPE; Hon. Fellow, American Coll. of Surgeons, American Surgical Asscn, Royal Australasian Coll. of Surgeons, Japan Surgical Soc., German Surgical Soc., Coll. of Physicians and Surgeons of Glasgow; Hon. Prof., Univ. of London; Companion of the Order of Australia 2004; Hon. DSc (Hong Kong) 2000, (Imperial Coll.) 2003; Selwyn Smith Prize (Australia), Lister Medal (UK) 1998, Hamilton Fairley Medal, Royal Coll. of Physicians 2005; Medawar Prize, TTS 2006. *Publications:* Kidney Transplantation 1978 (revised sixth edn) 2008, Tissue Transplantation 1982, Transient Ischaemic Attacks 1982, Progress in Transplantation 1984, Oxford Textbook of Surgery (with R. Malt) 1993, (second edn with W. Wood) 2001. *Leisure interests:* golf, tennis, cricket. *Address:* Nuffield Department of Surgical Sciences, Room 6607, Level 6, John Radcliffe Hospital, Univ. of Oxford, Headington, Oxford OX3 9DU (office); 19 Lucerne Road, Oxford, OX2 7QB, England (home). *Telephone:* (20) 7869-6627 (office). *Fax:* (0)1865 289287 (office). *E-mail:* pmorris@rcseng.ac.uk (office). *Website:* www.nds.ox.ac.uk (office).

MORRIS, Richard Graham Michael, CBE, MA, DPhil, FRS, FRSE, FMedSci; British neuroscientist and academic; *Royal Society/Wolfson Professor of Neuroscience, University of Edinburgh;* b. 27 June 1948, Worthing, Sussex; s. of Robert Morris and Edith Morris; m. 1st Hilary Ann Lewis 1985 (divorced); two d.; m. 2nd Monica Muñoz-Lopez; one s.; ed Univs of Cambridge and Sussex; Lecturer in Psychology, Univ. of St Andrews 1977–86, MRC Research Fellow 1983–86; Reader, then Prof. of Neuroscience, Univ. of Edin. 1986–, Dir Centre for Neuroscience 1993–97, Chair. Dept of Neuroscience 1998, Royal Soc./Wolfson Prof. of Neuroscience 2006–, fmr Dir Centre for Cognitive and Neural Systems, now Researcher Centre for Discovery Brain Sciences; Sec. Experimental Psychology Soc. 1983–87; Chair. UK Brain Research Asscn 1990–94; mem. MRC Neuroscience Research Grants Cttee 1983–87, Neuroscience and Mental Health Bd 1993–97, Innovation Bd 1998–2000, MRC Strategy Group 2000–02; Forum Fellow, World Econ. Forum 2000; Life Sciences Co-ordinate OST Foresight Project on Cognitive Systems 2002–04; Pres. Fed. of European Neuroscience Socs 2006–08; Head, Neuroscience and Mental Health, The Wellcome Trust, London 2007–10; mem. various editorial bds, including Bd of Reviewing Eds, Science magazine 2007–; Decade of the Brain Lecturer 1998, Zotterman Lecturer 1999, Yngve Zotterman Prize, Karolinska Inst. 1999, Henry Dryerre Prize, Royal Soc. of Edin. 2000, BNA Outstanding Contrib. to Neuroscience 2002, EJN European Neuroscience Award 2004, Feldberg Prize 2006, Santiago Grisola Award 2007, Presidential Lecturer, Soc. for Neuroscience 2009, Ipsen Neuronal Plasticity Prize 2013, Royal Soc. of Edinburgh Royal Medal 2014, Brain Prize (jt winner) 2016. *Publications:* Parallel Distributed Processing (ed.) 1988, Neuroscience: Science of the Brain, 1994, 2003, Long-Term Potentiation (co-ed. with T. V. P. Bliss and G. L. Collingridge) 2004, The Hippocampus Book (co-author and ed.) 2007; more than 200 scientific papers on neural mechanisms of memory. *Leisure interest:* sailing. *Address:* Centre for Discovery Brain Sciences, University of Edinburgh, 1 George Square, Edinburgh, EH8 9JZ, Scotland (office). *Telephone:* (131) 650-3520 (office); 7736-477190 (mobile) (office); (131) 441-5501 (home). *Fax:* (131) 651-1835 (office). *E-mail:* r.g.m.morris@ed.ac.uk (office); ccns@ed.ac.uk (office). *Website:* www.ed.ac.uk/discovery-brain-sciences/our-staff/research-groups/prof-richard-morris (office).

MORRIS, Richard Keith, OBE, BPhil, MA, FSA; British writer, archaeologist and composer; b. 8 Oct. 1947, Birmingham; s. of John Richard Morris and Elsie Myra Wearne; m. Jane Whiteley 1972; two s. one d.; ed Denstone Coll., Staffs., Pembroke Coll., Oxford and Univ. of York; musician, writer 1971–; Research Asst, York Minster Archaeology Office 1972–75; Churches Officer, Council for British Archaeology 1975–77, Research Officer 1978–88, Dir 1991–99; Hon. Lecturer, School of History, Univ. of Leeds 1986–88, Dir Inst. for Medieval Studies 2003–10; Lecturer, Dept of Archaeology, Univ. of York 1988–91; Prof. Univ. of Huddersfield 2010–14; Commr, English Heritage 1996–2005, fmr Chair. Advisory Cttee; Chair. Ancient Monuments Advisory Cttee for England 1996–2001, Historic Settlements and Landscapes Cttee 2001–03, Bede's World 2001–09, Blackden Trust 2004–; mem. North East Cttee, Heritage Lottery Fund Expert Panel 2005–11; Trustee, Nat. Coal Mining Museum for England 2003–08, York Archaeological Trust 2011, Nat. Heritage Memorial Fund 2011–18, Landscape Research Centre 2012–; Hon. Visiting Prof., Univ. of York 1995, Hon. Vice-Pres. Council for British Archaeology; Frend Medal, Soc. of Antiquaries 1992. *Opera:* Tempest songs. *Music:* Five Auden songs. *Publications include:* Cathedrals and Abbeys of England and Wales 1979, The Church in British Archaeology 1983, Churches in the Landscape 1989, Guy Gibson (jtly) 1994, Churches, Chapels and Cathedrals: A Teacher's Guide 1996, Cheshire: The Biography of Leonard Cheshire VC OM 2000, Time's Anvil: England, Archaeology and the Imagination 2013, Yorkshire 2018. *Leisure interests:* aviation history, natural history, 20th-century music and opera. *Address:* 13 Hollins Road, Harrogate, N Yorks., HG1 2JF, England (home). *Telephone:* (1423) 504219 (home). *E-mail:* r.morris@hud.ac.uk (office); r.k.morris@btinternet.com (home). *Website:* www.hud.ac.uk/ourstaff/profile/index.php?staffuid=entrrkm (office).

MORRIS, Sarah, BA; American (b. British) artist and film maker; b. 20 June 1967, London; ed Jesus Coll., Cambridge, Brown Univ.; works held in numerous int. collections including Victoria and Albert Museum, Saatchi Gallery, Tate Modern, London, Palm Springs Art Museum, Musée d'Art Moderne de la Ville de Paris, Dallas Museum of Art, Deste Foundation, Athens, Museum of Modern Art, New York, and others; American Acad. Philip Morris Award/Berlin Prize Fellow 1999, Joan Mitchell Foundation Painting Award 2001. *Films:* Midtown (New York) 1998, AM/PM (Las Vegas) 2000, Capital (Washington, DC) 2001, Miami 2002, Los Angeles 2004, Robert Towne 2006, 1972 2008, Beijing 2008, Points on a Line 2010, Chicago 2011, Rio 2012, Strange Magic 2014, Abu Dhabi 2016, Finite and Infinite Games 2017. *Publications:* Modern Worlds 1999, Capital 2001, Sarah Morris: Bar Nothing 2004, Los Angeles 2005, You Cannot Trust A Surface 2012, An Open

System Meets an Open System 2013, Sarah Morris: Capital Letters Rear Better for Initials 2015. *Address:* c/o Friedrich Petzel Gallery, 537 West 22nd Street, New York, NY 10011, USA (office).

MORRIS, Warwick; British consultant on Asia and fmr diplomatist; b. 10 Aug. 1948; m. Pamela Morris, MBE; one s. two d.; joined FCO 1969, Information Dept 1969–71, Third Sec. (Information), Embassy in Paris 1972–74, full-time language training, Seoul 1975–76, Second Sec. (Political), Embassy in Seoul 1977–79, Pvt. Sec. to Deputy Perm. Under-Sec., FCO 1979–80, Personnel Operations Dept 1980–82, Head of Section, Hong Kong Dept 1982–84, First Sec. (Commercial), Embassy in Mexico City 1984–87, First Sec., Head of Chancery, Seoul 1988–91, Deputy Head, Far Eastern Dept, FCO 1992–93, Counsellor, later Head of Perm. Under-Sec.'s Dept 1993–94, Counsellor (Econ. and Commercial), New Delhi 1995–98; at Royal Coll. of Defence Studies, London 1999; Amb. to Viet Nam 2000–03, to Repub. of Korea 2003–08 (retd); Chair. Anglo-Korean Soc. (UK) 2011–; consultant on Korean and Vietnamese affairs; Chair. Locate in Kent 2012–; Vice-Chair. Vietnam-UK Network 2013–; Hon. PhD (Soonchunyang Univ.) 2006; Hon. Fellow, Robinson Coll., Univ. of Cambridge 2011. *Address:* Rosewood, Stonewall Park Road, Langton Green, Kent, TN3 0HD, England (home).

MORRIS OF ABERAVON, Baron (life Peer), cr. 2001, of Aberavon in the County of West Glamorgan and of Ceredigion in the County of Dyfed; **John Morris,** KG, PC, QC, LLD; British politician (retd) and barrister; b. 5 Nov. 1931, Aberystwyth; s. of D.W. Morris and Mary Olwen Ann Morris; m. Margaret M. Lewis JP 1959; three d.; ed Ardwyn, Aberystwyth, Univ. Coll. of Wales, Aberystwyth, Gonville and Caius Coll., Cambridge and Acad. of Int. Law, The Hague; commissioned Royal Welch Fusiliers and Welch Regt; called to Bar, Gray's Inn 1954, Bencher 1985; Labour MP for Aberavon 1959–2001; Parl. Sec. Ministry of Power 1964–66; Jt Parl. Sec. Ministry of Transport 1966–68; Minister of Defence Equipment 1968–70; Sec. of State for Wales 1974–79; a Recorder, Crown Court 1982–97; Legal Affairs and Shadow Attorney-Gen. 1983–97; Attorney-Gen. 1997–99; Chancellor, Univ. of Glamorgan; fmr Deputy Gen. Sec. and Legal Adviser, Farmers' Union of Wales; mem. UK Del., Consultative Ass., Council of Europe and WEU 1963–64; mem. Cttee of Privileges 1994–97, Select Cttee on Implementation of the Nolan Report 1995–97; Chair. Nat. Pneumoconiosis Jt Cttee 1964–66, Nat. Road Safety Advisory Council 1967–68, Jt Review of Finances and Man. British Railways 1966–67; mem. N Atlantic Ass. 1970–74; HM Lord Lt for Dyfed; Pres. London Welsh Asscn; Hon. Fellow, Univ. Coll. of Wales, Aberystwyth and Swansea, Trinity Coll., Carmarthen, Gonville and Caius Coll. Cambridge; Hon. LLD (Wales).

MORRIS OF HANDSWORTH, Baron (Life Peer), cr. 2006, of Handsworth in the County of West Midlands; **William (Bill) Morris,** FRSA, OJ; British trade union official (retd); b. 19 Oct. 1938, Jamaica; s. of William Morris and Una Morris; m. Minetta Morris 1957 (died 1990); two s.; ed Mizpah School, Manchester, Jamaica; Dist Officer, Transport & Gen. Workers' Union (TGWU), Nottingham 1973, Dist Sec. Northampton 1977, Nat. Sec. Passenger Services 1979–85, Deputy Gen. Sec. TGWU 1986–92, Gen. Sec. 1992–2003; mem. TUC Gen. Council 1988–2003; mem. Comm. for Racial Equality 1977–87, IBA Gen. Advisory Council 1981–86, ITF Exec. Bd 1986–2003, Prince of Wales Youth Business Trust 1987–90, BBC Gen. Advisory Council 1987–88, Employment Appeals Tribunal 1988–2008, Royal Comm. on Lords Reform 1999, Bd of Govs South Bank Univ. 1997, Comm. for Integrated Transport 1999–2005; Dir (non-exec.) Court of the Bank of England 1998–2006; Dir Unity Trust Bank 1994–2003; Chancellor Univ. of Tech., Jamaica 2000–10, Staffordshire Univ. 2004–11; Chair. Morris Enquiry 2003–04; mem. (Labour) House of Lords 2006–; Chair. Midland Heart Housing Asscn 2007–, Bd of Trustees Performance Birmingham Ltd 2008–; Vice-Chair. Jamaica Nat. Money Services 2007–; mem. Cricket Bd for England and Wales 2005–, Mergers and Take Over Panel 2005–; Adviser to Voice newspaper 2006–; Hon. Fellow, City & Guilds 1992, Royal Soc. of Arts; Dr hc (South Bank Univ.) 1994, (Open Univ.) 1995; Hon. DLitt (Westminster) 1998 and several other hon. degrees; Public Figure of the Year, Ethnic Multicultural Media Awards (EMMA) 2002. *Leisure interests:* walking, gardening, watching sports, jazz concerts. *Address:* House of Lords, Westminster, London, SW1A 0PW, England (office). *E-mail:* morrisw@parliament.uk (office).

MORRIS OF YARDLEY, Baroness (Life Peer), cr. 2005, of Yardley in the County of West Midlands; **Estelle Morris,** PC, BEd; British politician; b. 17 June 1952; d. of Charles Richard Morris and Pauline Morris; ed Whalley Range High School, Manchester, Coventry Coll. of Educ., Univ. of Warwick; teacher 1974–92; Councillor, Warwick Dist Council 1979–91, Labour Group Leader 1981–89; MP for Birmingham, Yardley 1992–; Opposition Whip 1994–95, Opposition Front-bench Spokeswoman on Educ. 1995–97; Parl. Under-Sec. of State, Dept for Educ. and Employment (DfEE) 1997–98, Minister of State 1998–2001, Sec. of State for Educ. and Skills 2001–02; Minister of State for the Arts, Dept for Culture, Media and Sport 2003–05; Pro Vice-Chancellor Sunderland Univ. 2005–08; Chair. Strategy Bd Inst. of Effective Educ., Univ. of York; hon. degrees (Warwick) 2003, (Wolverhampton) 2004, (Leeds Metropolitan) 2004, (Bradford) 2005, (Birmingham) 2006, (Manchester Metropolitan, Cumbria) 2007, (Sunderland) 2008, (Goldsmith, London) 2018. *Address:* House of Lords, Westminster, London, SW1A 0PW, England (office). *Telephone:* (20) 7219-3000 (office). *E-mail:* morrise@parliament.uk (office). *Website:* www.parliament.uk/biographies/lords/baroness-morris-of-yardley/305 (office).

MORRISON, Denise M., BS; American business executive; m. Tom Morrison; two d.; ed Boston Coll.; began career in sales at Procter & Gamble, Boston, Mass; later joined Pepsi-Cola in Trade and Business Devt; spent most of 1980s at Nestlé USA, held sr marketing and sales positions, including Business Dir for Confections Marketing, Nat. Sales Man. Frozen/Chilled, and Vice-Pres. of Marketing and Sales for Nestlé Ice Cream Co.; moved to Nabisco Inc. 1995, served as Sr Vice-Pres. and led Nabisco Food Co.'s sales org. and was Gen. Man. for the Down the Street div.; Exec. Vice-Pres. and Gen. Man. Kraft Foods' Snacks and Confections divs –2003; Pres. Global Sales and Chief Customer Officer, Campbell Soup Co. 2003–05, Pres. Campbell USA 2005–07, Sr Vice-Pres. and Pres. North America Soup, Sauces and Beverages 2007–10, Exec. Vice-Pres., mem. Bd of Dirs and COO 2010–11, Pres. and CEO Campbell Soup Co. 2011–18; fmr Dir The Goodyear Tire & Rubber Co., Ballard Power Systems Inc.; Founding mem. and mem. Bd Healthy Weight Commitment Foundation; mem. GMA Industry Affairs Council, NJ Econ. Advisory Council for the Gov.; mem. Pres. Trump's American Manufacturing Council 2017 (resgnd); mem. Bd Students In Free Enterprise; fmr Chair. Catalyst's Advisory Bd; fmr Pres. NJ Women's Forum; fmr mem. Bd Food Industry Crusade Against Hunger and Leadership California; New York YWCA Acad. of Women Achievers 2001, New Jersey Woman of Influence, NJBIZ magazine 2003, Althea Gibson Beacon Award for Business Leadership 2003, Exec. of the Year, Snack Food & Bakery magazine 2003, Salute to Policy Makers Award, Exec. Women of New Jersey 2007, Garden State Woman of the Year for Corpns, Garden State Women magazine 2007, Aiming High Award, Legal Momentum 2007, Top Woman in Grocery, Progressive Grocer magazine 2008, 2009, 2010, Trailblazer Award, Philadelphia Magazine 2010, Woman of Distinction, American Heart Asscn of NJ 2010. *Address:* c/o Campbell Soup Company, 1 Campbell Place, Camden, NJ 08103-1701, USA (office).

MORRISON, Graham, OBE, MA, DipArch, RIBA; British architect; *Partner, Allies and Morrison;* b. 2 Feb. 1951, Kilmarnock, Scotland; s. of Robert Morrison and Robina S. Morrison; divorced; one s. one d.; ed Brighton Coll., Jesus Coll., Cambridge; in partnership with Bob Allies, formed Allies and Morrison Architects 1983, Partner 1983–; mem. RIBA Council 1992–95; Royal Fine Arts Commr 1998–99; mem. Architecture Advisory Cttee, Arts Council 1996–97, Design Review Cttee, Comm. on Architecture and the Built Environment (CABE) 2000–04, London Advisory Cttee of English Heritage 2001–13, English Heritage's CABE and Urban Panel 2009–12, English Heritage Advisory Cttee 2013–; Commr with English Heritage 2011–; External Examiner, Univ. of Cambridge 1994–97, Univ. of Portsmouth 2003–05, Bartlett School of Architecture 2010–11; Special Prof. of Architecture, Univ. of Nottingham 2004–05; apptd mem. South Downs Nat. Park Authority 2018; 32 RIBA Awards and 12 Civic Trust Awards. *Projects include:* restoration of the Royal Festival Hall, London, BBC Media Village at White City, London, master plans for King's Cross Station and the London 2012 Olympics and legacy, Wood Wharf, Canary Wharf, London 2016, 100 Bishopsgate, City of London 2017, Stratford Waterfront, London 2017, Girton Coll. Masterplan, Cambridge 2017. *Exhibitions include:* New British Architecture, Japan 1994, Allies and Morrison Retrospective, USA Schools of Architecture 1996–98; also exhbns in Helsinki, Delft, Strasbourg 1999. *Publications:* Allies and Morrison 1996, Allies and Morrison Vol. 1 2012, The Fabric of Place 2013. *Address:* Allies and Morrison, 85 Southwark Street, London, SE1 0HX, England (office). *Telephone:* (20) 7921-0100 (office). *Fax:* (20) 7921-0101 (office). *E-mail:* gmorrison@alliesandmorrison.com (office). *Website:* www.alliesandmorrison.com (office).

MORRISON, Robert S., BA, MBA; American business executive; *Operating Partner, Z Capital Management LLC;* b. 4 April 1942, Chicago, Ill.; s. of Forrest John Morrison and Grayce Morrison Scheck Hopkins; m. Susan E. Brennan 1988; five c.; ed Coll. of the Holy Cross, Univ. of Pennsylvania; served in the United States Marine Corps from 1963 to 1967, rising to the rank of captain; Asst Brand Man. Procter & Gamble 1969–72, Brand Man. 1972–75, Assoc. Advertising Man. 1975–81, Div. Man. 1981–83; Vice-Pres. Marketing Kraft Inc. 1983–85, Group Vice-Pres., Pres. Refrigerated Products Group 1985–89, Pres. Kraft Gen. Foods Canada 1989–91, Gen. Foods USA 1991–95, Chair. and CEO Kraft Foods Inc. 1994–97; Chair., CEO and Pres. Quaker Oats Co. 1997–2001; Vice-Chair. Pepsi Co. Inc. 2001–03; currently Operating Partner, Z Capital Management LLC; mem. Bd of Dirs Aon Corpn, Illinois Tool Works Inc., 3M Co. (Interim Chair. and CEO June–Dec. 2005), Mrs. Fields Famous Brands, Chicago Club, Lyric Opera, Rush-Presbyterian-St. Luke's Medical Center, Museum of Science and Industry (Chair.); Trustee, Holy Cross Coll.; Decorated Silver Star, Purple Heart, Semper Fidelis Award, Marine Corps Scholarship Foundation 1997. *Leisure interests:* golf, tennis, skiing. *Address:* Z Capital Management LLC, Two Conway Park, 150 Field Drive, Suite 300, Lake Forest, IL 60045, USA (office). *Website:* www.zcap.net (office).

MORRISON, Scott John; Australian politician; *Prime Minister;* b. 13 May 1968; m. Jenny Morrison; two d.; ed Univ. of New South Wales; Nat. Man., Policy and Research Property Council of Australia 1989–95; Deputy Chief Exec., Australian Tourism Task Force 1995–96; Gen. Man., Tourism Council 1996–98; Dir, NZ Office of Tourism and Sport 1998–2000; Man. Dir, Tourism Australia 2004–06; Prin., MSAS Pty Ltd 2006–07; mem. House of Reps (Liberal Party) for Cook 2007–; Minister for Immigration and Border Protection 2013–14, for Social Services 2014–15, Treasurer 2015–18, also Acting Minister for Home Affairs 2018, Prime Minister 2018–; mem. Cabinet Expenditure Review Cttee, Nat. Security Cttee; mem. Liberal Party, State Dir, Liberal Party (NSW) 2000–04, Leader, Liberal Party 2018–. *Address:* Office of the Prime Minister, Parliament House, Canberra, ACT 2600, Australia (office); PO Box 545, Edgecliff, NSW 2027, Australia (office). *Telephone:* (2) 6271-5111 (office). *Fax:* (2) 6271-5414 (office). *Website:* www.pm.gov.au (office); www.scottmorrison.com.au.

MORRISON, Toni, MA; American novelist and academic; *Dean of Faculty, Princeton University;* b. (Chloe Anthony Wofford), 18 Feb. 1931, Lorain, Ohio; d. of George Wofford and Ella Ramah Wofford (née Willis); m. Harold Morrison 1958 (divorced 1964); two c.; ed Lorain High School, Howard Univ., Cornell Univ.; taught English and Humanities, Tex. Southern Univ. 1955–57, Howard Univ. 1957–64; Ed., then Sr Ed. Random House, New York 1965–85; Assoc. Prof. of English, State Univ. of New York 1971–72, Schweitzer Prof. of the Humanities 1984–89; Robert F. Goheen Prof. of the Humanities, Princeton Univ. 1989–, now Emer., currently Dean of Faculty, also founding Dir Princeton Atelier; Visiting Lecturer Yale Univ. 1976–77, Bard Coll. 1986–88; Clark Lecturer, Trinity Cambridge 1990; Massey Lecturer, Harvard Univ. 1990; mem. Council, Authors Guild, American Acad. of Arts and Sciences, American Acad. of Arts and Letters, Authors League of America, Nat. Council on the Arts; Hon. DLit (Princeton Univ.) 2013; Commdr, Ordre des Arts et des Lettres; Ohioana Book Award 1975, American Acad. and Inst. of Arts and Letters Award 1977, Nat. Book Critics Circle Awards 1977, 1997, NY State Gov.'s Arts Award 1987, Nobel Prize for Literature 1993, Nat. Book Foundation Medal 1995, Nat. Humanities Medal 2000, Presidential Medal of Freedom 2012, Ivan Sandrof Lifetime Achievement Award, Nat. Book Critics Circle 2015, PEN/Saul Bellow Award for Achievement in American Fiction 2016, The Edward MacDowell Medal 2016. *Publications include:* The Bluest Eye 1970, Sula 1974, The Black Book (ed) 1974, Song of Solomon 1977, Tar Baby 1983, Dreaming Emmett (play) 1986, Beloved 1987 (Pulitzer Prize and Robert F. Kennedy Book Award 1988), Jazz 1992, Playing in the Dark: Whiteness and the Literary Imagination (lectures) 1992, Race-ing Justice, En-gendering Power (ed, essays) 1992, Honey and Rue (song cycle) 1993, Nobel Prize Speech 1994, Birth of a

Nation'hood: Gaze, Script and Spectacle in the O. J. Simpson Trial 1997, Paradise 1998, Collected Essays of James Baldwin (ed) 1998, Love 2003, A Mercy 2008, Home 2011, The Origin of Others 2017, The Source of Self-Regard: Selected Essays, Speeches, and Meditations 2019, Mouth Full of Blood 2019; co-author, for children: The Big Box (poems) 1999, The Book of Mean People 2002, The Ant or the Grasshopper, The Lion or the Mouse 2003, Beloved 2004, Sula 2004, Peeny Butter Fudge 2009, Little Cloud and Lady Wind 2010, Home 2012, God Help the Child: A Novel 2015. *Address:* Office of the Dean of the Faculty, Princeton University, 9 Nassau Hall, Princeton, NJ 08544-5264, USA (office). *Telephone:* (609) 258-3021 (office). *Fax:* (609) 258-2168 (office). *E-mail:* dof@princeton.edu (office). *Website:* www.princeton.edu (office).

MORRISON, Sir Van, Kt, OBE; British singer, songwriter and musician; b. (George Ivan Morrison), 31 Aug. 1945, Belfast, Northern Ireland; one d.; left school aged 15; joined The Monarchs, playing in Germany; Founder and lead singer, Them 1964–67; solo artist 1967–; Officier, Ordre des Arts et des Lettres 1996; Dr hc (Univ. of Ulster) 1992, (Queen's Univ. Belfast) 2001; inducted into Rock and Roll Hall of Fame 1993, BRIT Award for Outstanding Contribution to British Music 1994, Ivor Novello Lifetime Achievement Award 1995, Q Award for Best Songwriter 1995, Grammy Awards for Best Pop Collaboration with Vocals 1996, 1998, BMI Icon Award 2004, Ronnie Scott Award for Int. Male Singer 2007, Freedom of Belfast 2013, GQ Legend Award 2014. *Recordings include:* albums: Blowin' Your Mind 1967, Astral Weeks 1968, Moondance 1970, His Band and Street Choir 1970, Tupelo Honey 1971, Saint Dominic's Preview 1972, Hardnose the Highway 1973, It's Too Late To Stop Now 1974, Veedon Fleece 1974, This Is Where I Came In 1977, A Period of Transition 1977, Wavelength 1978, Into the Music 1979, Common One 1980, Beautiful Vision 1982, Inarticulate Speech of the Heart 1983, Live At The Royal Opera House, Belfast 1984, A Sense of Wonder 1984, No Guru, No Method, No Teacher 1986, Poetics Champion Compose 1987, Irish Heartbeat 1988, Avalon Sunset 1989, Enlightenment 1990, Bang Masters 1990, Hymns to the Silence 1991, The Best of Van Morrison 1993, Too Long in Exile 1993, A Night in San Francisco 1994, Days Like This 1995, Songs of the Mose Allison: Tell Me Something 1996, The Healing Game 1997, Brown Eyed Girl 1998, The Masters 1999, Super Hits 1999, Back On Top 1999, The Skiffle Sessions: Live in Belfast 1998 2000, You Win Again 2000, Down The Road 2002, What's Wrong With This Picture? 2003, Magic Time 2005, Pay the Devil 2006, Keep it Simple 2008, Born to Sing: No Plan B 2012, Duets: Re-working the Catalogue 2015, Keep Me Singing 2016. *Website:* www.vanmorrison.com.

MORRITT, Rt Hon. Sir (Robert) Andrew, Kt, PC, CVO, QC; British fmr judge; *Arbitrator, One Essex Court;* b. 5 Feb. 1938, London; s. of Robert Augustus Morritt and Margaret Mary Morritt (née Tyldesley Jones); m. Sarah Simonetta Merton 1962; two s.; ed Eton Coll., Magdalene Coll., Cambridge; 2nd Lt Scots Guards 1956–58; called to Bar, Lincoln's Inn 1962, QC 1977, Bencher 1984, Treas. 2005; Jr Counsel to Sec. of State for Trade in Chancery Matters 1970–77, to Attorney-Gen. in Charity Matters 1972–77; Attorney-Gen. to HRH The Prince of Wales 1978–88; a Judge of High Court of Justice, Chancery Div. 1988–94; a Lord Justice of Appeal 1994–2000; Vice-Chancellor, Co. Palatine of Lancaster 1991–94; Chancellor of The High Court 2000–13 (retd); currently Arbitrator, One Essex Court; Pres. Council of the Inns of Court 1997–2000; mem. Gen. Council of Bar 1969–73, Advisory Cttee on Legal Educ. 1972–76, Top Salaries Review Body 1982–87. *Leisure interests:* fishing, shooting. *Address:* One Essex Court, Temple, London, EC4Y 9AR, England (office). *Telephone:* (20) 7583-2000 (office). *Fax:* (20) 7583-0118 (office). *Website:* www.oeclaw.co.uk (office).

MORSCHAKOVA, Tamara Georgyevna, DJurSc; Russian judge; b. 28 March 1938, Moscow; m.; one d.; ed Moscow State Univ.; jr researcher, Inst. of State and Law, USSR Acad. of Sciences 1958–71; Sr Researcher, Chief, then Leading Researcher, All-Union Research Inst. of Soviet Construction and Law 1971–91; mem. Scientific-Consultative Council, Supreme Court of Russian Fed. 1985; Prof., Moscow State Juridical Acad. 1987–; Justice, Constitutional Court of Russian Fed. 1991–95, Deputy Chair. 1995–2002, Councillor 2002; Head of Chair, State Univ. Higher School of Economics 2001–; mem. Independent Legal Expert Council, Independent Human Rights Council 2012–; Honoured Jurist of Russian Fed.; Honoured Scientist of Russian Fed. *Publications:* books include Efficiency of Justice 1975, Reform of Justice 1990, Commentary to Legislation on Judiciary 2003, Criminal Procedure Law 2003. *Address:* Independent Human Rights Council, Moscow, Pokrovsky Boulevard 4/17, p. 1, office D, Russia (office). *Telephone:* (915) 437-64-87 (office). *E-mail:* info@nspch.ru (office). *Website:* nspch .ru/en (office).

MORSCHEL, John P.; Australian business executive; b. June 1943; ed Univ. of New South Wales; Chair. Leighton Holdings Ltd 2001–04, Rinker Group Ltd 2003–07; mem. Bd of Dirs CSR Ltd 1996–2003, Chair. 2001–03; Ind. Dir (non-exec.) Australia and New Zealand Banking Group Ltd (ANZ) 2004–14, Chair. 2010–14, Chair. Governance Cttee and ex-officio mem. all other Bd Cttees; mem. Bd of Dirs Lend Lease Corpn Ltd 1983–95, Westpac Banking Corpn 1993–2001, Rio Tinto Plc 1998–2005, Rio Tinto Ltd 1998–2005, Tenix Pty Ltd 1998–2008, Gifford Communications Pty Ltd 2000–, Capitaland Ltd 2010–18, Tenix Group Pty Ltd 2008–; mem. Bd of Dirs Singapore Telecommunications Ltd 2001–10, Advisory Cttee Optus (subsidiary of Singapore Telecommunications Ltd) 2014–; Fellow, Australian Inst. of Co. Dirs, Australian Inst. of Man.; Kt, Légion d'Honneur (France) 2007; Public Service Medal, Singapore Nat. Day Award 2011. *Address:* c/o Singtel Optus Pty Limited, Level 4, Building C 1 Lyonpark Road, Macquarie Park, NSW 2113, Australia (office). *Telephone:* (2) 2 8082-7800 (office). *Fax:* (2) 8082-7100 (office). *Website:* www.optus.com.au (office).

MORTAZA, Mashrafe Bin; Bangladeshi professional cricketer; *Captain, Bangladesh ODI Cricket Team;* b. 5 Oct. 1983, Norail Dist, Jessore; m. Sumona Haque Shumi 2008; one s. one d.; ed Victoria Coll.; right-arm fast-medium pace bowler; right-handed lower-middle order batsman; has played for Bangladesh 2001–; Vice-Capt. Test side 2007–09, Capt. 2009, ODI side 2009, 2010, 2015–), Asia XI, Khulna Div. 2002–, Kolkata Knight Riders 2009, Dhaka Gladiators 2012–; First-class debut: 2001/02; Test debut: Bangladesh v Zimbabwe, Dhaka 8–12 Nov. 2001; One-Day Int. (ODI) debut: Bangladesh v Zimbabwe, Chittagong (MAA) 23 Nov. 2001; T20I debut: Bangladesh v Zimbabwe, Khulna 28 Nov. 2006; played in 36 Tests, took 78 wickets (average 41.52) and scored 797 runs with three fifties, highest score 79 against India, Chittagong 2007, best bowling 4/60 against

England, Chittagong 2003; played in 198 ODIs (to Oct. 2014), scored 1,722 runs (average 31.43) and took 252 wickets, highest score 51 not out against Scotland, Dhaka 2006, with one five-wicket performance, best bowling 6/26 against Kenya, Nairobi 2006; played 54 T20Is, took 42 wickets (average 36.35) and scored 377 runs, highest score 36 against Zimbabwe, Khulna 2006, best bowling 4/19 against Ireland, Belfast 2012; played 57 First-class matches (to April 2018), took 135 wickets (average 35.05) and scored 1,458 runs with one century and six fifties, highest score 132 not out, best bowling 4/27; retd from Test cricket 2009, from T20I cricket 2017. *Leisure interest:* motorcycling. *Address:* c/o Bangladesh Cricket Board, Sher-e-Bangla National Cricket Stadium, Mirpur, Dhaka 1216, Bangladesh. *E-mail:* pd@tigercricket.com. *Website:* www.tigercricket.com.

MORTELL, Michael Philip, MSc, MS, PhD; Irish mathematician and fmr university administrator; b. 9 Feb. 1941, Cork; s. of Philip Mortell and Constance Mortell; m. Patricia Yule 1967; two d.; ed Charleville Christian Brothers School, Univ. Coll., Cork and California Inst. of Tech., USA; Asst Prof. and Assoc. Prof., Center for Application of Math., Lehigh Univ., USA 1967–72; Lecturer in Math. and Physics, Univ. Coll. Cork 1972–89, Registrar 1979–89, Pres. 1989–99, Prof. Applied Math. 1999–2006; Visiting Prof., Univ. of British Columbia, Canada 1976–77, Univ. of Queensland, Australia 1979; Visiting Assoc., California Inst. of Tech. and New York Univ. 1999–2000; Foundation Fellow, Univ. of Auckland, NZ 2003; Vice-Chancellor Nat. Univ. of Ireland; Chair. Conf. of Heads of Irish Univs; Hon. LLD (Univ. of Dublin, Queen's Univ. Belfast, Limerick Univ.); Hon. DSc (Lehigh Univ.). *Publications:* Singular Perturbations – Introduction to System Order Reduction Methods with Applications (co-author) 2014, Nonlinear Waves In Bounded Media: The Mathematics Of Resonance 2017; some 50 papers on nonlinear waves and perturbation methods. *Leisure interests:* reading, art, gardening, sport. *Address:* Department of Applied Mathematics, University College, Cork, Ireland (office). *Telephone:* (21) 4205827 (office); 85-7543219 (mobile). *Fax:* (21) 4270813 (office). *E-mail:* m.mortell@ucc.ie (office). *Website:* euclid.ucc.ie (office).

MORTENSEN, Viggo Peter, Jr, BA; American/Danish actor, poet, photographer, painter and jazz musician; b. 20 Oct. 1958, New York City; s. of Viggo P. Mortensen (Danish) and Grace Mortensen (American); m. Exene Cervenka 1987 (divorced 1998); one s.; ed St Lawrence Univ., Canton, NY; spent early childhood in Manhattan, family travelled widely and spent several years living in Venezuela, Argentina and Denmark (where he worked as a truck driver); worked as trans. for Swedish ice hockey team during Winter Olympics, Lake Placid 1980; began acting in New York, studying with Warren Robertson; appeared in several plays and movies, eventually moved to Los Angeles; Co-founder Perceval Press (publishing co.) 2002–; Kt Cross, Order of Dannebrog 2010; Dr hc (St Lawrence Univ.) 2006; Gold Medal, Province and the City of León 2006. *Stage appearances:* Tybalt in Romeo and Juliet, Indiana Repertory Theatre, Indianapolis 1985–86, Nazi capt. in Bent, Coast Playhouse, West Hollywood, Calif. 1987, Live at Beyond Baroque, Beyond Baroque, Venice, Calif. 1999, Beyond Baroque Live 2, Beyond Baroque 2004. *Films include:* Witness 1985, Salvation! 1987, Prison 1988, Fresh Horses 1988, The Reflecting Skin 1990, Tripwire 1990, Leatherface: Texas Chainsaw Massacre III 1990, Young Guns II 1990, The Indian Runner 1991, Boiling Point 1993, Deception 1993, Carlito's Way 1993, The Young Americans 1993, American Yakuza 1993, The Crew 1994, Floundering 1994, Ewangelia wedlug Harry'ego 1994, Gimlet 1995, Crimson Tide 1995, The Passion of Darkly Noon 1995, Black Velvet Pantsuit 1995, The Prophecy 1995, The Portrait of a Lady 1996, Albino Alligator 1996, Daylight 1996, G.I. Jane 1997, La Pistola de mi hermano 1997, A Perfect Murder 1998, Psycho 1998, A Walk on the Moon 1999, 28 Days 2000, The Lord of the Rings: The Fellowship of the Ring 2001, The Lord of the Rings: The Two Towers 2002, The Lord of the Rings: The Return of the King 2003, Hidalgo 2004, A History of Violence 2005, Alatriste 2006, Eastern Promises (British Independent Film Award for Best Actor, Sant Jordi Award for Best Foreign Actor, Satellite Award for Best Actor, Toronto Film Critics Asscn Award for Best Actor, Vancouver Film Critics Circle Award for Best Actor) 2007, Appaloosa 2008, Good 2008, The Road 2009, A Dangerous Method 2011, On the Road 2012, Everybody Has a Plan 2012, The Two Faces of January 2014, Jauja 2014, Far from Men 2014, Captain Fantastic 2016. *Television:* George Washington (mini-series) 1984, Search for Tomorrow (series) 1985, Once in a Blue Moon 1990, Vanishing Point 1997. *Achievements include:* painted the large murals in his artist's studio in film A Perfect Murder 1998. *Albums:* 1991 (poetry) 1991, Don't Tell Me What to Do (music and poetry) 1994, One Less Thing to Worry About (music and poetry; with others) 1997, Live at Beyond Baroque (with others) 1999, One Man's Meat 1999, The Other Parade (music and poetry; with others) 1999, Pandemoniumfromamerica (with Buckethead) 2003, Beyond Baroque Live 2 (with others) 2004, Please Tomorrow (with Buckethead) 2004, This That and the Other (with Buckethead) 2004, Intelligence Failure (with Buckethead) 2005, 3 Fools 4 April 2006, Time Waits for Everyone 2007, At All 2008, Canciones de Invierno 2010, Reunion 2011, Acá 2013. *Publications include:* Ten Last Night (poetry) 1993, Recent Forgeries (also illustrator, with accompanying CD) 1998, Coincidence of Memory (also illustrator) 2002, Sign Language (also photographer) 2002, Un hueco en el sol 2003; audiobooks: Myth: Dreams of the World 1996, The New Yorker Out Loud (contrib.) 1998; non-fiction: The Horse Is Good (also photographer) 2004, Twilight of Empire: Responses to Occupation (co-author) 2004, Strange Familiar: The Work of Georg Gudni (co-author) 2005; photography: Hole in the Sun 2002, 45301 2003, Miyelo (with Mike Davis, James Mooney, and Sonny Richards) 2004, Mo Te Upoko-o-te-ika/For Wellington 2004, Linger 2005, I Forget You For Ever 2006, Skovbo 2008, Sådanset 2008, Winter Songs 2010, That Turned Ugly Fast 2015. *Leisure interests:* horse riding, San Lorenzo football club (Buenos Aires), New York Mets professional baseball team, Montréal Canadiens professional ice hockey team. *Address:* c/o Jenny Rawlings, Creative Artists Agency, 9830 Wilshire Blvd, Beverly Hills, CA 90212-1825, USA (office). *Telephone:* (310) 288-4545 (office). *Fax:* (310) 288-4800 (office). *Website:* www.caa.com (office); www.percevalpress.com.

MORTON, Donald Charles, PhD, FAA; Canadian astronomer; *Researcher Emeritus, National Research Council of Canada;* b. 12 June 1933; s. of Charles O. Morton and Irene M. Wightman; m. Winifred Austin 1970; one s. one d.; ed Univ. of Toronto, Princeton Univ., USA; astronomer, US Naval Research Lab. 1959–61; from Research Assoc. to Sr Research Astronomer (with rank of Prof.), Princeton Univ. 1961–76; Dir Anglo-Australian Observatory (Epping and Coonabarabran, NSW) 1976–86; Dir-Gen. Herzberg Inst. of Astrophysics, Nat. Research Council of

Canada 1986–2000, Researcher Emer. 2001–; mem. Int. Astronomical Union, Royal Astronomical Soc. (Assoc. 1980), Astronomical Soc. of Australia (Pres. 1981–83, Hon. mem. 1986), Canadian Astronomical Soc., Canadian Asscn of Physicists; Fellow, Australian Acad. of Science 1984–. *Publications:* research papers in professional journals. *Leisure interests:* mountaineering, meccano models. *Address:* 1985 rue de la Regence, St Bruno, QC J3V 4B7, Canada (home).

MOSA, Markus; German business executive; *Chairman of the Management Board and CEO, Edeka Zentrale AG & Co. KG;* b. 22 Dec. 1967, Brühl bei Köln; m.; two d.; ed Univ. of Cologne; joined Spar Handels AG 1994, Schenefeld 1994, held several positions –1999, joined Netto Marken-Discount 1999, Man. Dir Netto Marken-Discount AG & Co. KG (fmrly Michael Schels & Sohn GmbH & Co. oHG) 2001–07, fmr Spokesman of Exec. Bd, Edeka AG (acquired Netto), Hamburg, Chief Financial Officer Edeka Zentrale AG & Co. KG –2008, Chair. Man. Bd and CEO 2008–, Deputy Chair. Supervisory Bd Edekabank AG 2017–. *Address:* Edeka Zentrale AG & Co. KG, New York Ring 6, 22297 Hamburg, Germany (office). *Telephone:* (40) 63772182 (office). *Fax:* (40) 63772971 (office). *E-mail:* info@edeka.de (office). *Website:* www.edeka.de (office).

MOSBAKK, Kurt; Norwegian politician; b. 21 Nov. 1934, Orkdal; s. of Henrik Mosbakk and Jenny Mosbakk; m. Grete Tidemandsen 1975; two s. one d.; ed Norwegian Coll. Econs and Business Admin; Pvt. Sec. to Minister of Defence 1964–65; Minister of Trade and Shipping 1986–88; County Exec. of Østford 1988–97, Special Adviser Østford County Council 1997–99; Deputy Chair. Norwegian Defence Comm. 1990–92; fmr Deputy Mayor Lørenskog; Chair. Akershus Co. Labour Party 1969–74; Chief Co. Exec. Finnmark Co. 1976; Chair. Bd Norwegian State Housing Bank 1978–86; Man. Dir Sparebank 1 Nord-Norge 989–2000; Chair. Norwegian Tourist Bd 1990–94; King's Medal of Honor 2006. *Leisure interest:* literature.

MOSCA, Bertrand; French television executive; began as public relations officer at Centre Georges Pompidou 1977; began career as journalist for Première 1987, for C'est pas juste 1988; held several asst positions within France Télévisions group, Dir Youth Programmes for France 3, responsible for buying fiction 1996, Program Dir, France 3 2000–05, cr. Plus belle la vie drama series, Exec. Head of Innovation, Diversity and New Cultures Feb.–Sept. 2011, other programmes include C'est mon choix and les Minikeums; Dir France 2 2011–12. *Film:* Manège (short) 1986. *Television:* Les histoires du Père Castor (series) (unit programmer) 1993, Molly (film) (exec. producer) 1999.

MOSCOSO DE GRUBER, Mireya Elisa; Panamanian politician and fmr head of state; b. 1 July 1946, Panama; d. of Plinio Antonio Moscoso and Elisa Rodríguez de Moscoso; m. 1st Arnulfo Arias 1969 (died 1988); one s.; m. 2nd Richard Gruber 1990 (divorced 1997); ed Colegio Comercial María Inmaculada, Miami Dade Community Coll., USA; fmr Exec. Sec. Social Security Agency; fmr Sales Man., Deputy Man. and Gen. Man. Arkapal SA (coffee co.); Govt rep. on numerous int. missions; spent ten years in exile in USA; Pres. Partido Arnulfista; Pres. of Panama 1999–2004; fmr Pres. Arias Foundation, Madrid; fmr mem. Asscn of Boquete Coffee Growers, Asscn of Milk Producers, Nat. Asscn of Ranchers; Grand Officer, Order of St-Charles (Monaco) 2002, Sacred Military Constantinian Order of St George (Italy). *Address:* c/o Partido Panameñista, Avda Perú y Calle 38e, No 37–41, al lado de Casa la Esperanza, Apdo 9610, Panamá 4, Panama (office).

MOSCOVICI, Pierre; French politician and EU official; *Commissioner for Economic and Financial Affairs, Taxation and Customs, European Commission;* b. 16 Sept. 1957; s. of Serge Moscovici and Marie Bromberg; ed Univ. of Paris X, I, IV, Institut d'études politiques, Paris, Ecole nat. d'admin, Strasbourg; official, Cour des Comptes 1984–88; Adviser, pvt. office of Minister of Nat. Educ., Youth and Sport 1988–89, Special Adviser to Minister 1989–90; Head. Gen. Planning Comm.'s Public Sector Modernization and Finance Dept 1990; mem. Parti Socialiste (PS) Nat. Council and Nat. Bureau 1990, Nat. Sec. responsible for policy research and devt 1990–92, 1995–97, Nat. Treas. 1992–94; mem. Doubs Gen. Council, Sochaux-Grand-Charmont canton 1994–2001; Municipal Councillor, Montbéliard 1995–2008, Pres. Agglomeration community of the Pays de Montbéliard 2008–; Gen. Councillor, Doubs 1994–2001; Regional Councillor, Franche-Comté 1998–2004; Municipal Councillor, Valentigney 2008–; mem. European Parl. 1994–97, 2004–07, Vice-Pres. 2004–07; Nat. Ass. Deputy for 4th Doubs constituency 1997, 2007–12; Minister Del. attached to Minister for Foreign Affairs, with responsibility for European Affairs 1997–2002; Minister of the Economy, Finances and Foreign Trade 2012–14; Commr for Econ. and Financial Affairs, Taxation and Customs, European Comm. (EC), Brussels Nov. 2014–; Rep. Convention on the Future of Europe 2002. *Publications include:* A la recherche de la gauche perdue 1994, L'urgence, plaidoyer pour une autre politique 1997, Au coeur de l'Europe 1999, L'Europe, une puissance dans la mondialisation 2001, Les 10 questions qui fâchent les Européens 2004, L'Europe est morte, vive l'Europe 2006. *Leisure interests:* tennis, skiing. *Address:* European Commission, 200 Rue de la Loi/Wetstraat 200, 1049 Brussels, Belgium (office); Assemblée Nationale, 126 rue de la Université, 75355 Paris 07 SP, France. *Telephone:* (2) 299-11-11 (Brussels, switchboard) (office). *E-mail:* pmoscovici@assemblee-national.fr (office). *Website:* ec.europa.eu/about/juncker-commission/structure/index_en.htm (office).

MØSE, Erik; Norwegian judge; b. 9 Oct. 1950; ed Univ. of Oslo, postgraduate studies in Geneva, Switzerland; Lecturer, Univ. of Oslo 1981–; Head of Div., Ministry of Justice –1986; fmr Deputy Judge; Supreme Court Advocate at Solicitor Gen.'s Office 1986–93; Judge, Court of Appeals, Oslo 1993–99; Vice-Pres. Int. Criminal Tribunal for Rwanda 1999–2003, Pres. 2003–07, apptd Judge 2007; Justice, Supreme Court 2008; Judge, European Court of Human Rights 2011; fmr Chair. Council of Europe's Steering Cttee for Human Rights, Cttee for drafting European Convention for the Prevention of Torture, and several other cttees; Fellow Univ. of Essex, UK; Commdr, Royal Norwegian Order of Merit; Dr hc (Essex). *Publications:* numerous books and publs on human rights.

MOSER, Edvard Ingjald, BSc, BSc, BSc, PhD; Norwegian psychologist, neuroscientist and academic; *Professor and Head of Department, Kavli Institute for Systems Neuroscience / Centre for Neural Computation, Norwegian University of Science and Technology;* b. 27 April 1962, Ålesund; m. May-Britt Moser; ed Univ. of Oslo; postdoctoral training at Centre for Neuroscience, Univ. of Edinburgh, UK 1994–96; Visiting Postdoctoral Fellow, lab. of John O'Keefe at Univ. Coll., London; Assoc. Prof. in Psychology and Neuroscience, Norwegian Univ. of Science and Tech. 1996–98, Full Prof. 1998–, Founding Dir Centre for the Biology of Memory 2003–12 (Centre Kavli Inst. for Systems Neuroscience 2007), 2012–, Co-Dir Centre for Neural Computation, Head of Department; Chair. Programme Cttee of the European Neuroscience meeting (FENS Forum) 2006; mem. Bd of Reviewing Eds, Science 2004–; Reviewing Ed., Journal of Neuroscience 2005–; mem. Royal Norwegian Soc. of Sciences and Letters, Norwegian Acad. of Science and Letters, Norwegian Acad. of Technological Sciences; Foreign Assoc. NAS 2014; Grand Cross of the Order of St Olav; Prize for Young Scientists, Royal Norwegian Soc. of Sciences and Letters 1999, W. Alden Spencer Award, Coll. of Physicians and Surgeons, Columbia Univ. 2005, Betty and David Koetser Award for Brain Research, Univ. of Zurich 2006, Prix Liliane Bettencourt pour les Sciences du Vivant, Fondation Bettencourt, Paris 2006, Eric K. Fernström's Great Nordic Prize, Fernström Foundation, Univ. of Lund 2008, Louis-Jeantet Prize for Medicine 2011, Anders Jahre Award (with May-Britt Moser) 2011, Perl-UNC Neuroscience Prize (with May-Britt Moser) 2012, Louisa Gross Horwitz Prize (with May-Britt Moser and John O'Keefe) 2013, Karl Spencer Lashley Award (with May-Britt Moser) 2014, Nobel Prize in Physiology or Medicine (co-recipient with May-Britt Moser and John O'Keefe) 2014. *Publications:* numerous papers in professional journals. *Address:* Kavli Institute for Systems Neuroscience/Centre for Neural Computation, Norwegian University of Science and Technology, Olav Kyrres gate 9, 7489 Trondheim, Norway (office). *Telephone:* 73-59-50-00 (office). *E-mail:* edvard.moser@ntnu.no (office). *Website:* www.ntnu.edu/employees/edvard.moser (office); www.kavlifoundation.org/norwegian-university-science-and-technology-ntnu (office).

MOSER, May-Britt, BSc, PhD; Norwegian psychologist, neuroscientist and academic; *Professor, Kavli Institute for Systems Neuroscience / Centre for Neural Computation, Norwegian University of Science and Technology;* b. 4 Jan. 1963, Fosnavåg; m. Edvard Ingjald Moser; ed Univ. of Oslo; postdoctoral training at Centre for Neuroscience, Univ. of Edinburgh, UK 1994–96; Visiting Postdoctoral Fellow, lab. of Prof. John O'Keefe, Univ. Coll., London; Assoc. Prof. in Psychology and Neuroscience, Norwegian Univ. of Science and Tech. 1996–2000, Full Prof. 2000–, Founding Dir Centre for the Biology of Memory 2003–12 (later Kavli Inst. for Systems Neuroscience 2007), 2012–, Co-Dir Centre for Neural Computation 2013–; mem. of an evaluation panel for European Research Council start-up grants 2007–09; mem. Royal Norwegian Soc. of Sciences and Letters, Norwegian Acad. of Science and Letters, Norwegian Acad. of Technological Sciences; Grand Cross of the Order of St Olav 2018; Prize for Young Scientists, Royal Norwegian Soc. of Sciences and Letters 1999, Annual W. Alden Spencer Award, Coll. of Physicians and Surgeons of Columbia Univ. 2005, Betty and David Koetser Award for Brain Research, Univ. of Zurich 2006, Prix Liliane Bettencourt pour les Sciences du Vivant, Fondation Bettencourt, Paris 2006, Eric K. Fernström's Great Nordic Prize, Fernström Foundation, Univ. of Lund 2008, Louis-Jeantet Prize for Medicine 2011, Anders Jahre Award (with Edvard Moser) 2011, Perl-UNC Neuroscience Prize (with Edvard Moser) 2012, Louisa Gross Horwitz Prize (with Edvard Moser and John O'Keefe) 2013, Madame Beyer Best Female Boss Award 2013, Karl Spencer Lashley Award (with Edvard Moser) 2014, Nobel Prize in Physiology or Medicine (co-recipient with Edvard Moser and John O'Keefe) 2014. *Publications:* numerous papers in professional journals. *Address:* Kavli Institute for Systems Neuroscience/Centre for Neural Computation, Norwegian University of Science and Technology, Olav Kyrres gate 9, MTFS*3.433, 7489 Trondheim, Norway (office). *Telephone:* 73-59-82-77 (office). *E-mail:* may-britt.moser@ntnu.no (office). *Website:* www.ntnu.edu/employees/edvard.moser (office); www.kavlifoundation.org/norwegian-university-science-and-technology-ntnu (office).

MOSES, Dennis, BSc, MSc; Trinidad and Tobago politician and fmr diplomatist; *Minister of Foreign and CARICOM Affairs;* m.; two c.; ed Univ. of the West Indies, Univ. de Costa Rica Centro Agronómico Tropical de Investigación y Enseñanza; with Ministry of Foreign Affairs 1980–90, roles at Ministry HQ and Embassy in Belgium; joined CAB International, UK 1990, later becoming Regional Rep. of CAB International for Caribbean and Latin America, based in Trinidad and Tobago; fmr Deputy Rep. of Inter-American Inst. for Cooperation on Agric., Barbados; served 11 years as Rep. of OAS Gen. Secr. in Guyana, later Rep. of OAS Gen. Secr. in Dominica 2014–15; Senator 2015–; Minister of Foreign and CARICOM Affairs 2015–. *Address:* Ministry of Foreign and CARICOM Affairs, Tower C, Levels 10–14, International Waterfront Centre, 1a Wrightson Road, Port of Spain, Trinidad and Tobago (office). *Telephone:* 623-6894 (office). *Fax:* 623-5029 (office). *Website:* www.foreign.gov.tt (office).

MOSES, Edwin Corley, BSc, MBA; American sports administrator and fmr athlete; b. 31 Aug. 1955, Dayton, Ohio; m. Myrella Bordt Moses 1982; one s.; ed Fairview High School and Morehouse Coll., Atlanta, Ga, Pepperdine Univ.; won gold medals for 400m hurdles, Olympic Games, Montreal 1976 (in world record time), Los Angeles 1984, bronze medal, Seoul 1988; one of only three men to break 48 seconds for 400m hurdles; holds record for greatest number of wins consecutively in any event; winner 122 consecutive races (107 finals) 1977–87, lost to Danny Harris June 1987; won three World Cup titles and two World Championships; set world record in his event four times; at one time held 13 fastest times ever recorded; retd 1989, comeback 1991, second comeback 2003; competed int. for USA in bobsleigh and two- and four-man sleds; US Rep. to Int. Amateur Athletic Fed. from 1984; mem. Jt Olympic Cttee Athletes Comm., Exec. Bd of US Olympic Cttee, Bd of Dirs Jesse Owens Foundation, IOC Ethics Comm. 2000–; Pres. Int. Amateur Athletics Asscn; Chair. Laureus World Sports Acad. 2000–16, also Chair. Laureus Sport For Good Foundation; Vice-Chair. US Olympic Foundation; fmr Chair. US Olympic Cttee Substance Abuse Cttee; Founding Partner Platinum Group (representing athletes' business interests); Dr hc (Univ. of Massachusetts, Boston) 2009; Track & Field News Athlete of the Year 1980, Jesse Owens Int. Award 1981, James E. Sullivan Award, Amateur Athletic Union 1983, ABC Wide World of Sports Athlete of the Year 1984, Sports Illustrated Sportsman of the Year (shared) 1984, Speaker of the Athletes' Oath at Olympic Games 1984, Miami Boulevard West and Sunrise Avenue in Dayton, Ohio renamed Edwin C. Moses Boulevard 1984, inducted into Nat. Track and Field Hall of Fame 1994. *Leisure interests:* aviation, scientific breakthroughs in athletics, scuba diving. *Telephone:* (678) 705-1985 (office). *Fax:* (678) 705-1985 (office). *E-mail:* contact@edwinmoses.com. *Website:* www.edwinmoses.com.

MOSES, Tallis Obed; Ni-Vanuatu clergyman and head of state; *President;* b. 24 Oct. 1954, West Ambrym, Malampa Prov.; m. Estella Moses; ed Sydney Missionary and Bible Coll., Australia; several years as pastor at Erromango, Ranon in North Ambrym, Luganville and Bamefaul; elected Moderator (leader), Presbyterian Church in Vanuatu 2009; elected Pres. of Vanuatu 2017–. *Address:* Office of the President, Private Mail Bag 100, Port Vila, Vanuatu (office). *Website:* www.gov.vu (office).

MOSHAHED, Ahmad; Afghan diplomatist and government official; *Chairman, Independent Administrative Reform and Civil Service Commission;* Amb. to Iran in Transitional Govt 2004; Minister of Educ. 2004; currently Chair. Ind. Admin. Reform and Civil Service Comm., Kabul. *Address:* Independent Administrative Reform and Civil Service Commission, Shah Mahmood Khan Ghazi Watt, Prime Minister's Compound Opposite the Vice President's Office, Kabul, Afghanistan (office). *Website:* iarcsc.gov.af/en.

MOSHER, Gregory Dean, BFA; American theatre producer, director and academic; *Professor, School of the Arts, Columbia University;* b. 15 Jan. 1949, New York; s. of Thomas Edward Mosher and Florence Christine Mosher; ed Oberlin Coll., Ithaca Coll., Juilliard School; Dir Stage 2 Goodman Theatre, Chicago 1974–77, Artistic Dir 1978–85; Artistic Dir Lincoln Center Theater 1985–92, Resident Dir 1992–2004; Dir Univ. Arts Initiatives and Adjunct Asst Prof. of Theatre Arts, Columbia Univ., New York 2004–10, Prof., School of the Arts 2010–; has lectured or guest-taught at Yale Univ., New York Univ., Univ. of Pennsylvania, Juilliard School; has directed or produced nearly 200 stage productions at Lincoln Center and Goodman Theatres, on and off Broadway, at Royal Nat. Theatre and in London's West End; has written three screenplays, including adaptation of Vladimir Nabokov's Laughter in the Dark; Chevalier des Arts et des Lettres; two Tony Awards (as producer of revivals: Anything Goes, Our Town), Obie Award, Margo Jefferson, Outer Critics. *Productions include:* new works by Tennessee Williams, Studs Terkel, David Mamet, John Guare, Michael Weller, Wole Soyinka, Elaine May, David Rabe, Mbongeni Ngema, Edward Albee, Spalding Gray, Arthur Miller, Leonard Bernstein, Stephen Sondheim, Richard Nelson, Jerome Robbins; producer: Samuel Beckett's first directing work in US, Krapp's Last Tape 1979, Bosoms and Neglect 1979, Endgame 1980, The Man Who Had Three Arms 1983, Hurly-Burly 1984, The Flying Karamazov Brothers "Juggling and Cheap Theatrics" 1986, The House of Blue Leaves 1986, The Front Page 1987, Death and the King's Horseman 1987, The Regard of Flight 1987, The Comedy of Errors 1987, Anything Goes 1987, Sarafina! 1988, Speed-the-Plow (Broadway and RNT) 1988, Our Town 1988, The Tenth Man 1989, Some Americans Abroad 1990, Six Degrees of Separation 1990, Monster in a Box 1991, Mule Bone 1991, Two Shakespearean Actors 1992, A Streetcar Named Desire 1992, Freak 1998, James Joyce's The Dead 2000, A View from the Bridge 2009. *Plays directed:* Glengarry Glen Ross (David Mamet), Broadway 1984–85, American Buffalo 1975, A Life in the Theater 1977, Edmond 1982, Glengarry Glen Ross 1984, Speed-the-Plow (David Mamet), Danger: Memory (Miller premiere) 1987, Broadway 1988, London 1989, Our Town (50th anniversary production, Thornton Wilder), Broadway 1988, Oh Hell, Lincoln Center Theater 1989, Uncle Vanya 1990, Mr Gogol and Mr Preen 1991, A Streetcar Named Desire 1992, Stanley (producing dir) 1997. *Films:* American Buffalo (producer) 1996, The Prime Gig (dir) 2000. *Television includes:* Great Performances (series) – King Lear (actor) 1974, The Comedy of Errors (dir) 1987, American Playhouse (series) – The House of Blue Leaves (exec. producer) 1987, Uncle Vanya (dir, for BBC) 1991, Performance (series) 1991, A Life in the Theatre (film, dir) (CableACE Award for Best Drama) 1993, Freak (film) 1998. *Address:* School of the Arts, Columbia University, 601 Dodge Hall, MC 1807, 2960 Broadway, New York, NY 10027, USA (office). *Telephone:* (212) 851-1872 (office). *E-mail:* gm2127@columbia.edu (office). *Website:* arts.columbia.edu/node/2132 (office).

MOSIMANN, Anton, OBE, DL; Swiss chef and restaurateur; *Chairman, Mosimann's Limited;* b. 23 Feb. 1947, Solothun; s. of Otto Mosimann and Olga Mosimann; m. Kathrin Roth 1973; two s.; ed pvt. school in Switzerland; apprentice, Hotel Baeren, Twann; worked in Canada, France, Italy, Sweden, Japan, Belgium, Switzerland 1962–; cuisinier at Villa Lorraine, Brussels, Les Prés d'Eugénie, Eugénie-les-Bains, Les Frères Troisgros, Roanne, Paul Bocuse, Collonges au Mont d'Or, Moulin de Mougins; joined Dorchester Hotel, London 1975, Maître Chef des Cuisines 1975–88; Owner Mosimann's (fmr Belfry Club) 1988–, Mosimann's Party Service 1990–, The Mosimann Acad. 1995–, Creative Chefs 1996–; World Pres. Les Toques Blanches Internationales 1989–93; Visiting Prof., Univ. of Strathclyde 2003; Pres. Royal Warrant Holders' Asscn 2006–07; DL Greater London 2011; Hon. mem. Chefs' Asscns of Canada, Japan, Switzerland, SA, World Asscn of Chefs Socs 2008; Freedom of the City of London 1999; Royal Warrant of Appointment to HRH The Prince of Wales 2000; Hon. Prof., Thames Valley Univ. 2004; Croix de Chevalier du Mérite agricole, Ordre du Mérite agricole 2006; Hon. Dr of Culinary Arts (Johnson and Wales Univ., USA); Hon. DSc (Bournemouth) 1998; Personalité de l'Année Award 1986, Swiss Culinary Amb. of the Year 1995, Restauranteur of the Year, Int. Food and Beverage Forum, Rhode Island 2000, Lifetime Achievement Award (Hotel & Caterer) 2004, Lifetime Achievement Award, Davos Tourism for World Econ. Forum 2010, Carl-Freidrich von Rumohr Prize, Gastronomic Acad. Deutschlands for lifetime achievement 2013, numerous awards in int. cookery competitions. *Television includes:* Anton Goes to Sheffield (Glenfiddich Award 1986) 1986, Cooking with Mosimann (series) 1990, Anton Mosimann Naturally (series) 1991–92, Natürlich, Leichtes Kochen (Swiss TV) 1997, Mosimann's Culinary Switzerland (Swiss TV) 1998. *Publications:* Cuisine à la Carte 1981, A New Style of Cooking: The Art of Anton Mosimann 1983, Cuisine Naturelle 1985, Anton Mosimann's Fish Cuisine 1988, The Art of Mosimann 1989, Cooking with Mosimann 1989, Anton Mosimann – Naturally 1991, The Essential Mosimann 1993, Mosimann's World 1996, Mosimann's Fresh 2006, 25 Years of Mosimann's 2013. *Leisure interests:* classic cars and int. car rallies, collecting antiquarian cookery books, enjoying fine wine, passionate about food and travelling, especially to food markets of the Far East. *Address:* Mosimann's, 11B West Halkin Street, London, SW1X 8JL, England (office). *Telephone:* (20) 7235-9625 (office). *Fax:* (20) 7245-7847 (office). *E-mail:* amosimann@mosimann.com (office). *Website:* www.mosimann.com (office).

MOSISILI, Bethuel Pakalitha, BA; Lesotho politician; b. 14 March 1945, Waterfall; m.; two s. two d.; ed Univs of Botswana, Lesotho and Swaziland, Univ. of Wisconsin, USA, Univ. of South Africa, Simon Fraser Univ., Canada; joined Basutoland Congress Party 1967; Deputy Headmaster Bereng High School 1972–73; Asst Lecturer in African Languages, Univs of Botswana, Lesotho and Swaziland 1973–76; Lecturer in African Languages, Nat. Univ. of Lesotho 1976–83; Sr Lecturer, Univ. of Fort Hare, South Africa 1983–84, Univ. of Transkei 1985–88, Univ. of Zululand 1989–92; mem. Parl. 1993–; Minister of Educ. and Training, Sports, Culture and Youth Affairs 1993–95; apptd Deputy Prime Minister 1995; Minister of Home Affairs and Local Govt 1995–98; Prime Minister of Lesotho and Minister of Defence and Nat. Security 1998–2012; Prime Minister of Lesotho 2015–17; fmr Deputy Leader, Lesotho Congress for Democracy, apptd Leader 1998; mem. Lesotho Educational Research Asscn, African Languages Asscn of South Africa, South African Pedagogical Soc.

MOSKALKOVA, Tatyana Nikolaevna, LLD, DPhil; Russian lawyer and government official; *Human Rights Ombudsman;* b. 30 May 1955, Vitebsk, Byelorussian SSR; widow; one d.; ed All-Union Correspondence Inst. of Law (now Moscow State Law Acad.); joined Presidium of Supreme Soviet as clerk 1974, becoming Sr legal adviser and consultant –1984; 23 years in legal div. of Ministry of Internal Affairs 1984–2007, roles include Sr Asst to Legal Dept Man., becoming First Deputy Head of Legal Dept (retd 2007 with rank of Maj.-Gen.); mem. State Duma (parl.) (Spravedlivaya Rossiya, A Just Russia) 2007–16, Deputy Chair. Cttee on CIS Affairs, Eurasian Integration and Relations with Compatriots; Human Rights Ombudsman of the Russian Fed. 2016–; Order of Merit, Honoured Lawyer of Russia. *Address:* Office of the Human Rights Ombudsman, 101000 Moscow, ul. Myasnitskaya. 47, Russia (office). *Telephone:* (495) 607-19-22 (office). *Fax:* (495) 607-39-77 (office). *Website:* ombudsmanrf.org (office).

MOSLEY, Max Rufus; British fmr racing driver and lawyer; *Chairman, Towards Zero Foundation;* b. 13 April 1940, London; s. of Sir Oswald Mosley and Hon. Lady Diana Mosley (née Freeman-Mitford); m. Jean Marjorie Taylor 1960; two s.; ed Christ Church Oxford; called to Bar (Gray's Inn) 1964; fmr Dir March Cars Ltd, Legal Adviser to Formula One Constructors Asscn, fmr Formula Two racing driver, Co-founder March Grand Prix Team; Pres. Fed. Int. du Sport Automobile (FISA) 1991–93, Fed. Int. de l'Automobile (FIA) 1993–2009 (Hon. Pres. 2009–, mem. FIA Senate 2009–13); Chair. Mfrs Comm. 1986–91; Hon. Pres. European Parl. Automobile Users Group 1994–99; Chair. European New Car Assessment Programme 1997–2004; Chair. Global New Car Assessment Programme 2011–17; Vice-Chair. Supervisory Bd ERTICO Intelligence Transport Systems Europe 1999–2001, Chair. 2001–04, Pres. and Spokesperson 2004–06; currently Chair. Towards Zero Foundation; Founder-mem. Institut du Cerveau et de la Moelle Epiniere 2005, EC CARS 21 High Level Group 2005–09; Patron EU eSafety Aware Communications Platform 2006–09; Hon. Pres. Nat. Road Safety Council of Armenia 2006; Order of Merit (Italy) 1994, Order of Madarksi Kannik, First Degree (Bulgaria) 2000, Castrol/Inst. of the Motor Industry Gold Medal 2000, Quattroruote Premio Speciale per la Sicurezza Stradale (Italy) Gold Medal 2001, Goldene VdM-Dieselring (Germany) 2001, Order of Merit (Romania) 2004, Visitante Ilustre de la Ciudad de Asuncion (Ecuador) 2004, Chevalier, Légion d'honneur 2006, Commdr, Ordre de Saint Charles (Monaco) 2006; Hon. DCL (Northumbria) 2005. *Publication:* Formula One and Beyond: The Autobiography 2015. *Leisure interests:* walking, snowboarding. *Address:* 8 Blvd des Moulins, Monte Carlo 98000, Monaco (office). *E-mail:* callierflorence@gmail.com.

MOSLEY, Walter; American writer; b. 12 Jan. 1952, Los Angeles, Calif.; s. of Leroy Mosley and Ella Mosley (née Slatkin); m. Joy Kellman 1987 (divorced); ed Goddard Coll., Johnson State Coll., City Coll. CUNY; Artist-in-Residence, Africana Studies Inst., New York Univ. 1996; mem. Bd of Dirs Nat. Book Awards, Poetry Soc. of America –2007; Past Pres. Mystery Writers of America; Dr hc (City Coll. of New York); American Library Asscn Literary Award 1996, O. Henry Award 1996, Anisfield Wolf Award 1996, TransAfrica Int. Literary Prize 1998, PEN America Lifetime Achievement Award, Langston Hughes Medal 2014. *Plays:* The Fall of Heaven 2011, Lift 2014, Leading from the Affair. *Publications include:* Easy Rawlins Mystery Series: Devil in a Blue Dress (Shamus Award) 1990, A Red Death 1991, White Butterfly 1992, Black Betty 1994, A Little Yellow Dog 1996, Gone Fishin' 1997, Bad Boy Brawly Brown 2002, Fear Itself 2003, Six Easy Pieces (short stories) 2003, Little Scarlet 2004, Cinnamon Kiss 2005, Blonde Faith 2007, Little Green 2013, Rose Gold 2014, Charcoal Joe 2016; Socrates Fortlow Series Always Outnumbered, Always Outgunned 1997, Walkin' the Dog 1999, The Right Mistake 2008; fiction: RL's Dream 1995, Blue Light 1998, Fearless Jones 2001, Futureland: Nine Stories of an Imminent Future 2001, What Next: An African American Initiative Toward World Peace 2003, The Man in My Basement 2004, 47 (for young adults) (Carl Brandon Society Parallax Award 2006) 2006, Fortunate Son 2006, Killing Johnny Fry 2007, This Year You Write Your Novel 2007, Diablerie 2008, The Long Fall 2009, Known to Evil 2010, The Last Days of Ptolemy Grey 2010, Twelve Steps to Political Revelation 2011, When the Thrill Is Gone 2011, All I Did Was Shoot My Man 2012, Parishioner 2012, Debbie Doesn't Do It Anymore 2014, The Further Tales of Tempest Landry 2015, Inside a Silver Box 2015, John Woman 2018, Down the River Unto the Sea (Edgar Award for Best Novel 2019) 2018; nonfiction: Workin' on the Chain Gang: Shaking off the Dead Hand of History 2000, What Next: A Memoir Toward World Peace 2003, Life Out of Context 2005, This Year You Write Your Novel 2007, Twelve Steps Towards Political Revelation 2011; contribs to New York Times, Library of Contemporary Thought, New Yorker, GQ, Esquire, USA Weekend, Los Angeles Times Magazine, Savoy. *Address:* c/o Gloria Loomis Watkins/Loomis Literary Agency, PO Box 20925, New York, NY 10025, USA (office). *Telephone:* (212) 532-0080 (office). *Website:* www.waltermosley.com.

MOSMANN, Timothy R., BS, BSc, MD, FRSC; South African/Canadian microbiologist, immunologist and academic; *Professor, Department of Microbiology and Immunology, and Michael and Angela Pichichero Director in the David H. Smith Center for Vaccine Biology and Immunology, University of Rochester Medical Center, University of Rochester;* b. 7 March 1949; ed Univ. of Natal, Rhodes Univ., Univ. of British Columbia, Canada; emigrated to Canada; fmr Research Fellow, Univ. of Toronto, Canada, Univ. of Glasgow, UK; apptd Asst Prof., Univ. of Alberta, Canada, later Chair. Dept of Immunology; in between, spent eight years in industry, as a research scientist at DNAX Research Inst., Palo Alto, Calif., USA; recruited to Univ. of Rochester, NY, USA 1998, currently Prof., Dept of Microbiology and Immunology, and Michael and Angela Pichichero Dir in the

David H. Smith Center for Vaccine Biology and Immunology, Univ. of Rochester Medical Center; Int. Research Scholar, Howard Hughes Medical Inst. 1991–96, 1997–2001; numerous honours and awards, including Centennial Fellow, MRC of Canada 1975–77, Bernhard Cinader Lectureship, Canadian Soc. for Immunology 1993, Avery-Landsteiner Prize, German Soc. for Immunology 1994, NIH Fogarty Scholar-in-Residence 1996–99, William B. Coley Award, Cancer Research Inst. (USA) 1997, ASTECH Award for Outstanding Leadership in Alberta Science 1997, William S. Coley Award for Research in Immunology (jtly) 1997, Paul Ehrlich and Ludwig Darmstaedter Prize (Germany) 2008, Novartis Prize for Basic Immunology 2013. *Achievements include:* made fundamental discoveries about the regulation of immune responses in allergic and infectious diseases including, with Dr Robert L. Coffman of the Univ. of Rochester, the discovery of the TH1 and TH2 subsets of T-lymphocytes, the two major types of T-cells that control immune responses. *Publications:* numerous papers in professional journals. *Address:* University of Rochester School of Medicine and Dentistry, 601 Elmwood Avenue, Box 609, Rochester, NY 14642, USA (office). *Telephone:* (585) 275-8762 (office); (585) 273-1400 (office). *Fax:* (585) 273-2452 (office). *E-mail:* Joyce_Feltz@urmc.rochester.edu (office). *Website:* www.urmc.rochester.edu (office).

MOSS, Andrew, LLB, CA; British chartered accountant and insurance executive; b. March 1958; m. 1st Susan Moss; four c.; m. 2nd Deirdre Galvin 2012; ed Christ Church Coll., Oxford; accountancy training, Coopers & Lybrand; Vice-Pres. and Head of Fiduciary Compliance, Citibank NA 1988–89; Asst Dir Group Treasury, Midland Montagu/HSBC Markets 1989–95, Head of Group Asset and Liability Man. HSBC Group 1995–97, Chief Financial Officer, Investment Banking and Markets, HSBC Group 1997–2000; Dir Finance, Risk Man. and Operations, Lloyd's of London 2000–04; Group Finance Dir Aviva plc 2004–07, Group Chief Exec. 2007–12 (resgnd); Co-Chair. Insurance Industry Working Group with the Chancellor of the Exchequer 2009; mem. Bd and Appointments Cttee of the Asscn of British Insurers, Pan European Insurance Forum, European Financial Services Round Table; Treas. Geneva Asscn. *Leisure interests:* golf, rugby, gardening.

MOSS, Bernard K., MD, PhD, FAAS; American virologist and academic; *Genetic Engineering Section Chief and Chief, Laboratory of Viral Diseases, National Institute of Allergy and Infectious Diseases;* b. 26 July 1937, New York; ed New York Univ., New York Univ. School of Medicine and Massachusetts Inst. of Tech.; Intern, Children's Hosp. Medical Center, Boston, Mass 1961–62; Investigator, Lab. of Biology of Viruses, Nat. Inst. of Allergy and Infectious Diseases, NIH, Bethesda, Md 1966–70, Head, Macromolecular Biology Section 1971–84, Chief, Lab. of Viral Diseases 1984–, currently Chief, Genetic Eng Section; Foundation for Microbiology Lectureship 1980–81; Wellcome Visiting Prof. in Microbiology, American Soc. of Microbiology 1987; Adjunct Prof., George Washington Univ. Grad. Genetics Program, Washington, DC 1994–, Adjunct mem. Inst. for Biomedical Science 1996–; Adjunct Prof., Univ. of Maryland; Head, WHO Collaborating Center for Research on Viral Vectors for Vaccines 1988–2001; mem. Vaccinia Sub-cttee of Nat. Vaccine Program Interagency Group 1988–, Poxvirus Subgroup of Int. Cttee on Taxonomy of Viruses 1992–95, 1997–, WHO Advisory Cttee on Variola Virus 1999–, Fellowship Recruitment Cttee of AAAS 2000–; Ed. Virology 1992–; mem. Editorial Bd Journal of Virology 1972–, AIDS Research and Human Retroviruses 1989–, Current Opinion in Biotechnology 1990–; mem. Editorial Advisory Bd Advances in Virus Research 1984–, NIH Catalyst 1993–; mem. American Soc. for Microbiology, American Soc. of Biological Chemists, NAS 1987–, American Soc. for Virology 1994– (currently Pres.), American Acad. of Microbiology 1996–; NSF Research Fellowship 1958, US Public Health Service (PHS) Postdoctoral Fellowship 1963–66, PHS Commendation Medal 1979, PHS Meritorious Service Medal 1984, Science Digest magazine 100 Most Innovative Scientists of 1985, PHS Distinguished Service Medal 1986, Solomon A. Berson Medical Alumni Achievement Award, New York Univ. 1987, Dickson Prize for Medical Research, Univ. of Pittsburgh 1988, Invitrogen Eukaryotic Expression Award 1991, ICN Int. Prize in Virology, ICN Pharmaceuticals Research 1994, Sackler Scholarship, Univ. of Tel-Aviv 1996, J. Allyn Taylor Int. Prize in Medicine, Robarts Research Inst. 1997, Cancer Research Campaign Lecturer, Univ. of Glasgow, UK 1999, Bristol-Myers Squibb Award for Distinguished Achievement in Infectious Disease Research 2000. *Publications:* more than 560 articles in scientific journals. *Address:* Laboratory of Viral Diseases, National Institute of Allergy and Infectious Diseases, NIH, Building 33, Room 1E13C.1, 33 North Drive, Bethesda, MD 20892-3210, USA (office). *Telephone:* (301) 496-9869 (office). *Fax:* (301) 480-1535 (office). *E-mail:* bmoss@nih.gov (office); bmoss@niaid.nih.gov (office). *Website:* www.niaid.nih.gov/LabsAndResources/labs/aboutlabs/lvd/geneticEngineeringSection/Pages/moss.aspx (office).

MOSS, Kate; British model; b. 16 Jan. 1974, Addiscombe, Croydon, London, England; d. of Peter Edward Moss and Linda Rosina (Shepherd); one d. with fmr pnr Jefferson Hack; engaged to Pete Doherty 2007; m. Jamie Hince 2011; ed Riddlesdown High School, Purley; discovered at age 14 by Sarah Doukas, founder of Storm Model Management, at JFK Airport, New York 1988; has modelled for Face, Harpers and Queen, Vogue, Dolce & Gabbana, Katherine Hamnett, Versace, Yves Saint Laurent; exclusive contract world-wide with Calvin Klein 1992–; designed Kate Moss collection for Topshop 2007; named Female Model of the Year VH-1 Awards 1996. *Films:* Inferno (TV film) 1992, Unzipped 1996, Blackadder Back & Forth (short) 1999, The 4 Dreams of Miss X (video short) 2007. *Publication:* Kate 1994. *Address:* Storm Model Management, 1st Floor, 5 Jubilee Place, London, SW3 3TD, England (office). *Telephone:* (20) 7376-7764 (office). *Fax:* (20) 7376-5145 (office). *Website:* www.stormmanagement.com/models/kate-moss (office).

MOSS, Sir Stirling, Kt, OBE; British fmr racing driver and business executive; *Managing Director, Stirling Moss Limited;* b. 17 Sept. 1929, London, England; s. of Alfred Moss and Nora Aileen Moss; m. 1st Katherine Stuart Molson 1957 (divorced 1960); m. 2nd Elaine Barbarino 1964 (divorced 1968); one d.; m. 3rd Susie Paine 1980; one s.; ed Haileybury and Imperial Service Coll.; bought his first racing car, a Cooper 500, with prize money from show-jumping 1947; British Champion 1951; built his own car, the Cooper-Alta 1953; drove in H.W.M. Formula II Grand Prix team 1950, 1951, Jaguar team 1950, 1951; Leader of Maserati Grand Prix team 1954; mem. Mercedes team 1955; leader of Maserati Sports and Grand Prix teams 1956, Aston Martin team 1956; mem. Vanwall, Aston Martin, Maserati teams 1958; winner of Tourist Trophy (TT) race, UK 1950, 1951, 1953, 1955, 1958, 1959, 1960, 1961, Gold Coupe des Alpes (three rallies without loss of marks) 1954, Italian Mille Miglia 1955, Sicilian Targa Florio 1955, eight int. events including NZ, Monaco Grand Prix, Nurburgring 1,000 km (FRG) 1956, Argentine 1,000 km UK, Pescara (Italy), Moroccan Grand Prix 1957, 11 events including Argentine, Netherlands, Italian Grand Prix and Nurburgring 1,000 km 1958, 19 events including NZ, Portuguese, US Grand Prix 1959, 19 events including Cuban, Monaco, Austrian, S African Grand Prix 1960, 27 events including Monaco, German, Pacific Grand Prix, Nassau Tourist Trophy 1961; competed in 529 events, finishing in 387, winning 211, during motor racing career 1947–62; retd from racing after accident at Goodwood, UK April 1962, made comeback 1980, subsequently taking part in numerous vintage car races; many business ventures, consultancy work on vehicle evaluation, property conversion, design; Man. Dir Stirling Moss Ltd; Dir 28 cos; also journalism and lecturing; Pres. or Patron of 28 car clubs; Hon. FIE 1959; Gold Star, British Racing Drivers' Club 10 times 1950–61, Driver of the Year (Guild of Motoring Writers) (twice), Sir Malcolm Campbell Memorial Award 1957. *Publications include:* Stirling Moss 1953, In the Track of Speed 1957, Le Mans '59 1959, Design and Behaviour of the Racing Car 1963, All But My Life 1963, How to Watch Motor Racing 1975, Motor Racing and All That 1980, My Cars, My Career 1987, Stirling Moss: Great Drives in the Lakes and Dales 1993, Motor Racing Masterpieces 1995, Stirling Moss (a biog.) 2001, Stirling Moss Scrapbook 1955 2005, Stirling Moss Scrapbook 1956–1960 2009, Stirling Moss: All My Races 2009, Stirling Moss: My Racing Life 2015. *Leisure interests:* theatre and cinema, designing houses, model making, motor trials, historic racing, interior decorating, woodwork, cruising. *Address:* c/o Stirling Moss Ltd, 46 Shepherd Street, Mayfair, London, W1J 7JN (office); 44 Shepherd Street, London, W1J 7JN, England (home). *Telephone:* (20) 7499-3272. *E-mail:* stirlingmossltd@aol.com (office). *Website:* www.stirlingmoss.com.

MOSSUZ-LAVAU, Janine, PhD; French political scientist and academic; *Lecturer and CNRS Research Director, Centre for Political Research, Institut d'études politiques, Paris (Sciences Po);* ed Institut d'études politiques, Paris (Sciences Po); currently Lecturer and CNRS Research Dir, Centre for Political Research, Sciences Po (CEVIPOF), Paris, Educational Dir Copernicus Programme (Sciences Po/Ecole des Mines/Coll. of Engineers); Vice-Pres. Amitiés Internationales André Malraux; mem. Observatoire de la parité 1999–2005. *Publications include:* Les Professeurs du second degré: contribution à l'étude du corps enseignant (co-author) 1967, Les Cubs et la politique 1970, André Malraux et le gaullisme 1970 (second edn 1982), Les Jeunes et la gauche 1979, Enquête sur les femmes et la politique en France (co-author) 1983, André Malraux 1987, De Gaulle (co-author) 1988, Les Lois de l'amour: les politiques de la sexualité en France de 1950 à nos jours 1991, Les Fronts populaires (co-author) 1994, Les Français et la politique: enquête sur une crise 1994, La Politique, la culture: discours, articles, entretiens: 1925–1975 (by Aldré Malraux), presented by Janine Mossuz-Lavau 1996, Les Femmes ne sont pas des hommes comme les autres (co-author) 1997, Les Femmes et la politique (co-ed.) 1997, Que veut la gauche plurielle? 1998, Femmes/Hommes, pour la parité 1998, Les Lois de l'amour: les politiques de la sexualité en France: 1950–2002 2002, La Vie sexuelle en France: une enquête inédite: des hommes et des femmes racontent comment ils font l'amour aujourd'hui 2002 (translated into German and Korean 2005), Quand les femmes s'en mêlent: genre et pouvoir (co-ed.) 2004, La Vie sexuelle en France 2005, La Prostitution à Paris (co-ed.) 2005, L'Argent et nous 2007, Le Planning familial: histoire et mémoire, 1956–2006 (co-ed.) 2007, Pauvres parmi les pauvres? Des femmes 2008, Guerre des sexes: stop! 2009, Mes Années Malraux 2011, Dictionnaire André Malraux (co-ed.) 2011, Pour qui nous prend-on?: les 'sottises' de nos politiques 2012, Dictionnaire des sexualités (ed.) 2014; book chapters and numerous papers in professional journals. *Address:* CEVIPOF, 98 rue de l'Université, 75007 Paris, France (office). *Telephone:* 1-45-49-53-28 (office). *Fax:* 1-45-49-77-38 (office). *E-mail:* janine.mossuzlavau@sciencespo.fr (office). *Website:* www.cevipof.com (office).

MOSTAFAVI, Mohsen, Diploma in Architecture; Iranian architect and academic; *Dean, Graduate School of Design and Alexander and Victoria Wiley Professor of Design, Harvard University;* m. Homa Farjadi; ed Architectural Asscn School of Architecture, London, Univ. of Essex, Univ. of Cambridge, UK; fmr Design Critic, Univ. of Cambridge; fmr Visiting Prof., Frankfurt Acad. of Arts (Stadelschule); fmrly taught at Univ. of Pennsylvania School of Design; Assoc. Prof. of Architecture, Grad. School of Design, Harvard Univ. 1990–95, Dir MArch I Program 1992–95, Dean 2008–, Alexander and Victoria Wiley Prof. of Design; Chair. Architectural Asscn, School of Architecture, London 1995–2004; fmr Arthur L. and Isabel B. Wiesenberger Prof. in Architecture, Cornell Univ. –2007, Gale and Ira Drukier Dean, Coll. of Architecture, Art and Planning, Cornell Univ. 2004–07; mem. Steering Cttee Aga Khan Award for Architecture; jury mem. Holcim Foundation for Sustainable Construction; mem. Exec. Cttee, Mahindra Humanities Center, Harvard Innovation Lab; fmr mem. Design Cttee, London Devt Agency; winner of Pritzker Prize 2000. *Publications:* Architecture and Continuity (co-author) 1983, On Weathering: the Life of Buildings in Time (co-author, American Inst. of Architects Prize) 1993, Delayed Space (co-author) 1994 Approximations 2002, Surface Architecture 2002 (CICA Bruno Zevi Book Award), Logique Visuelle 2003, Landscape Urbanism: a Manual for the Machinic Landscape 2004, Structure as Space 2006; contribs to The Architectural Review, AAFiles, Arquitectura, Bauwelt, Casabella, Centre, Daidalos. *Address:* Office of the Dean, Graduate School of Design, Harvard University, 48 Quincy Street, Gund Hall, Cambridge, MA 02138, USA (office). *Telephone:* (617) 495-4364 (office). *Website:* www.gsd.harvard.edu (office).

MOTANYANE, Sephiri Enoch; Lesotho politician; b. 1935; began political career as youth cadre of Basutoland Congress Party (BCP) early 1960s; over 40 years as mem. Nat. Ass. for Malibamats'o constituency, Deputy Speaker Nat. Ass. –2012, Speaker 2012–15; held several govt portfolios including Minister of the Crown, Minister for Justice and Human Rights, Minister of Law, Constitutional Affairs and Rehabilitation, Minister in the Prime Minister's Office; mem. Lesotho Congress for Democracy, fmr Sec.-Gen. *Address:* National Assembly, PO Box 190, Maseru 100, Lesotho (office). *Telephone:* 22323035 (office). *Fax:* 22310438 (office). *Website:* www.parliament.ls (office).

MOTAZE, Louis Paul, DEA; Cameroonian politician; *Minister of Finance;* b. 31 Jan. 1959, Bengbis, Dja-et-Lobo Dist; s. of Arnold Motaze and Mary Monengono; m.; three c.; ed Univ. of Yaoundé, Nat. School of Admin and Judiciary (ENAM), Inst. Portuaire d'Enseignement et de Recherche, Le Havre, France; began career in Econ. Affairs Dept, Office of the Pres. 1983; Commercial Dir, CAMAIR (Cameroon Airlines) 1989–93, Dir of Audit and Man. Control 1993–98, Technical Adviser to Directorate-Gen. 1998–99; Dir Gen., Nat. Social Security Fund (CNPS) 1999–2008; Minister of the Economy, Planning and Spatial Planning 2007–11, 2015–18; Sec.-Gen., Office of the Prime Minister 2011–15; Minister of Finance 2018–; Chevalier, Officier, Commdr and Grand Officier, Ordre Nat. de la Valeur. *Address:* Ministry of Finance, BP 13750, Quartier Administratif, Yaoundé, Cameroon (office). *Telephone:* 677232099 (mobile) (office). *Website:* www.minfi.gov.cm (office).

MOTE, C(layton) Daniel (Dan), Jr, BS, MS, DSc; American university administrator and professor of mechanical engineering; *Regents Professor and Glenn L. Martin Institute Professor of Engineering, University of Maryland;* b. 5 Feb. 1937; m. Patricia Mote; one s. one d.; ed worked at Carnegie Institute of Technology, Pittsburgh; Univ. of Calif., Berkeley; mem. Faculty, Dept of Mechanical Eng, Univ. of Calif., Berkeley 1967–98, Chair in Mechanical Systems 1987–91, Vice-Chancellor and Pres. UC Berkeley Foundation 1991–98; Glenn L. Martin Inst. Prof. of Mechanical Eng 1998–, Pres. Univ. of Maryland, College Park 1998–2010, Regents Prof. 2011–; consultant to US Congress on educational issues; Pres. Atlantic Coast Conf. 2004–05; fmr Vice-Chair., Basic Research Cttee, US Dept of Defense; mem. Nat. Acads Cttee, Senate Energy Sub-Cttee, US Senate Energy and Natural Resources Cttee; mem. Leadership Council, Nat. Innovation Initiative, Council on Competitiveness; mem. Council, Nat. Acad. of Eng (Pres. 2013–) 1988; mem. Bd of Dirs and Audit Cttee, Nat. Academies Corpn 2010–; Int. Council of Confucius Inst., China 2009–; Fellow AAAS 2004, Int. Acad. of Wood Science, Acoustical Soc. of America; holds patents in USA, Norway, Finland and Sweden; two hon. professorships; Hon. mem. ASME International; four hon. doctorates; Humboldt Prize, FRG, Berkeley Citation 1998, UC Berkeley Distinguished Eng Alumnus 2001, J.P. Den Hartog Award, ASME Int. Tech. Cttee on Vibration and Sound 2005, Founders Award, Nat. Acad. of Eng 2005, Excellence in Achievement, Univ. of Calif. 2007, Champion of Diversity Award, Univ. of Maryland 2009, ASME Medal 2011. *Publications:* over 300 articles, books and chapters in books on dynamics of gyroscopic systems and biomechanics. *Address:* Department of Mechanical Engineering, University of Maryland, College Park, MD 20742, USA (office). *Telephone:* (202) 334-3201 (office). *Fax:* (301) 314-9477 (office). *E-mail:* dmote@umd.edu (office). *Website:* www.enme.umd.edu/faculty/mote (office); www.nae.edu/7222.aspx (home).

MOTEGI, Toshimitsu; Japanese politician; *Minister of State for Economic and Fiscal Policy;* b. 7 Oct. 1955; ed Faculty of Econs, Univ. of Tokyo, John F. Kennedy School of Govt, Harvard Univ., USA; joined Marubeni Corpn 1978; political journalist, Yomiuri Shimbun 1983–84; Man. Consultant, Mckinsey & Co. 1984–93; mem. House of Reps (Tochigi Pref. 5th Dist) 1993–, Dir Cttee on Foreign Affairs 1997, Cttee on the Budget 2004–07, Chair. Cttee on Health, Labour and Welfare 2007–; Vice-Minister for Int. Trade and Industry 1999–2002; Sr Vice-Minister for Foreign Affairs 2002–03; Minister of State for Okinawa and Northern Territories Affairs, Science and Tech. Policy, and Information Tech. 2003–08; apptd Minister of State for Financial Services and Admin. Reform 2008, Minister of Economy, Trade and Industry 2012–14, also Minister of State for Corpn in support of Compensation for Nuclear Damage, Minister in charge of Nuclear Incident Econ. Countermeasures, Minister in Charge of Industrial Competitiveness 2012–14, Minister of State for Economic and Fiscal Policy 2017–, Minister-in-charge of Total Reform of Social Security 2017–, Minister-in-charge of Human Resources Development 2017–, Minister-in-charge of Economic Revitalization 2017–; Deputy Sec.-Gen., LDP 1998–2006, Chief Deputy Sec.-Gen. 2006–. *Address:* Ministry of Economy, Trade and Industry 1-3-1, Kasumigaseki, Chiyoda-ku, Tokyo 100-8901, Japan (office). *Telephone:* (3) 3501-1511 (office). *Fax:* (3) 3501-6942 (office). *E-mail:* webmail@meti.go.jp (office). *Website:* www.meti.go.jp (office).

MOTION, Sir Andrew Peter, Kt, MLitt, FRSA; British biographer and poet; b. 26 Oct. 1952, London; s. of Andrew R. Motion and Catherine G. Motion; m. 1st Joanna J. Powell 1973 (divorced 1983); m. 2nd Janet Elisabeth Dalley 1985; two s. one d.; ed Radley Coll. and Univ. Coll., Oxford; Lecturer in English, Univ. of Hull 1977–81; Ed. Poetry Review 1981–83; Poetry Ed. Chatto & Windus 1983–89, Editorial Dir 1985–87; Prof. of Creative Writing Univ. of E Anglia, Norwich 1995–2003; Chair. Literature Advisory Panel Arts Council of England 1986–98; Poet Laureate 1999–2009; Prof. of Creative Writing, Royal Holloway Coll., Univ. Coll. London 2003–; Chair. Museums, Libraries and Archives Council 2008–; Pres. Campaign to Protect Rural England; Co-founder online The Poetry Archive; Chair. Man Booker Prize jury 2010; mem. Poetry Soc. (Vice-Pres.); Hon. DLitt (Hull) 1996, (Exeter) 1999, (Brunel) 2000, (A.P.U.) 2001, (Open Univ.) 2002; Arvon/Observer Prize 1982, Dylan Thomas Award 1987, Whitbread Biography Award 1993, Wilfred Owen Poetry Award 2014. *Radio:* Coming Home (Ted Hughes Award for New Work in Poetry) 2014. *Publications include:* poetry collections: The Pleasure Steamers 1978, Independence 1981, The Penguin Book of Contemporary British Poetry (ed., anthology) 1982, Secret Narratives 1983, Dangerous Play (Rhys Memorial Prize) 1984, Natural Causes 1987, Love in a Life 1991, The Price of Everything 1994, Salt Water 1997, Selected Poems 1996–97 1998, Public Property 2001, Here to Eternity: An Anthology of Poetry (ed.) 2001, The Cinder Path 2009, The Customs House 2012, Peace Talks 2015, Coming Home 2015; poems as Poet Laureate: Remember This: An Elegy on the Death of HM Queen Elizabeth The Queen Mother 2002, A Hymn for the Golden Jubilee 2002, On the Record (for Prince William's 21st birthday) 2003, Spring Wedding (for the wedding of Prince Charles and Camilla Parker Bowles) 2005, The Golden Rule (anthem for 80th birthday of HM Queen Elizabeth II, with music by Sir Peter Maxwell-Davies) 2006, Diamond Wedding (for the Diamond Wedding Anniversary of HM Queen Elizabeth II and HR Duke of Edinburgh) 2007; non-fiction: The Poetry of Edward Thomas 1981, Philip Larkin 1982, The Lamberts (Somerset Maugham Award 1987) 1986, Philip Larkin: A Writer's Life 1993, William Barnes Selected Poems (ed.) 1994, Keats 1997, Wainewright the Poisoner 2000, In the Blood: A Memoir of My Childhood 2006, Ways of Life: Selected Essays and Reviews, 1994–2006 2008; fiction: The Pale Companion 1989, Famous for the Creatures 1991, The Invention of Dr Cake 2003, Silver: Return to Treasure Island 2012; other: additional texts for a performance of Haydn's Seven Last Words of Our Saviour on the Cross 2003, Poetry at Heart anthology project 2014. *Leisure interest:* fishing. *Address:* c/o Faber & Faber, Bloomsbury House, 74–77 Great Russell Street, London, WC1B 3DA, England. *Website:* www.faber.co.uk/author/andrew-motion.

MOTLANTHE, Kgalema; South African trade union official, politician and fmr head of state; b. 19 July 1949, Johannesburg; m. 2nd Gugu Mtshali 2014; two c. from first marriage; mem. UmKhonto we Sizwe (ANC mil wing), detained during student protests 1976, arrested again 1977, spent 10 years in detention at Robben Island 1977–87; Educ. Officer Nat. Union of Mineworkers 1987–92, Sec.-Gen. 1992–97; Sec.-Gen. ANC 1997–2007, Deputy Pres. 2007–12; mem. Parl. 2008–14; Minister without Portfolio July–Sept. 2008; Acting Pres. of South Africa Sept. 2008–May 2009, Deputy Pres. 2009–14. *Address:* African National Congress, 54 Sauer Street, Johannesburg 2001, South Africa (office). *Telephone:* (11) 3761000 (office). *Fax:* (11) 3761134 (office). *E-mail:* nmtyelwa@anc.org.za (office). *Website:* www.anc.org.za (office).

MOTOC, Mihnea Ioan, LLM, JD; Romanian diplomatist and politician; b. 11 Nov. 1966; m. Iulia Motoc; one s.; ed Univ. of Bucharest, Univ. of Nice, France, George Washington Univ., USA; trainee prosecutor, Prosecutor's Bureau, Bolintin Vale and at Prosecutor's Bureau of Bucharest First Dist; joined Ministry of Foreign Affairs 1991, Attaché, Judicial and Treaties Directorate 1991–92, Third Sec., then Second Sec. and Deputy Dir Directorate for Human Rights 1992–97, First Sec. and Dir EU Dept 1996–97, Dir-Gen. Dept for European and Euro-Atlantic Orgs 1997–99, Amb. to The Netherlands and Perm. Rep. to OPCW 1999–2001, Sec. of State for European Integration and Multilateral Affairs 2001–03, Amb. and Perm. Rep. to UN, New York 2003–08, Romanian Rep. on UN Security Council 2004–05, Amb. and Perm. Rep. to EU, Brussels 2008–15, Amb. to UK Sept.–Nov. 2015; Minister of Nat. Defence 2015–17; Deputy Head of European Political Strategy Centre, EC 2017–; Pres. Nat. Security Authority, Inter-Departmental Comm. for accession to NATO 2001; Nat. Co-ordinator Stability Pact for Southeastern Europe; mem. Int. Humanitarian Fact Finding Comm.; Commdr, Nat. Order of Merit. *Address:* European Political Strategy Centre, European Commission, 200 Rue de la Loi, 1049 Brussels, Belgium (office). *Telephone:* (0) 229 63042 (office). *E-mail:* mihnea-loan.motoc@ec.europa.eu (office).

MOTSAMAI, Ntlhoi, BSc, MEd; Lesotho politician; b. 1963, Ha Pafoli, Mohale's Hoek Dist; ed Nat. Univ. of Lesotho; began career as teacher, St John's High School, Mafeteng; worked in Office of Dean of Student Affairs, Nat. Univ. of Lesotho; mem. Nat. Ass. (Parl.) 1995–, Deputy Speaker 1996–99, Speaker 1999–2012, 2015–17, Shadow Minister, Devt Planning 2012–14, Chair. SADC Parl. Forum 2002–04, Cttee on HIV and AIDS 2001–, Exec. Cttee 2015–; mem. Democratic Congress, Standing Cttee, Conference of Speakers and Presiding Officers of Commonwealth 2015–, Standing Cttee, Commonwealth Speaker's Conference Int. 2016–; Rep. of African Region, IPU Cttee on Middle East Question 2015–. *Address:* National Assembly, POB 190, Maseru 100, Lesotho (office). *Telephone:* 22323035 (office). *Fax:* 22310438 (office). *Website:* www.parliament.ls (office).

MOTSEPE, Patrice, BA, LLB; South African lawyer and business executive; *Chairman, African Rainbow Minerals Ltd;* b. 28 Jan. 1962, Soweto; s. of Augustine Motsepe; m. Precious Makgosi Moloi; three s.; ed Univ. of Swaziland, Univ. of Witwatersrand; Visiting Attorney, McGuire Woods Battle and Boothe 1991–92; Assoc. Partner, Bowman Gilfillan Attorneys, Johannesburg 1994–95, Partner 1995–96; Founder-Chair. Future Mining (Pty) Ltd 1995–; f. African Rainbow Minerals Ltd (ARMgold) 1997, mem. Bd of Dirs 2003–, Chair. 2004–; Chair. Naledi Mining 1997–, Teal Exploration and Mining Inc. 2005–, Ubuntu-Botho Investments; Chair. (non-exec.) Harmony Gold Mining Co. Ltd 2003–; Dir (non-exec.) Absa Group Ltd 2004–, Sanlam Ltd (also Deputy Chair.) 2004–, Sanlam Life Insurance Ltd (also Deputy Chair.) 2006–; Pres. Nat. African Federated Chamber of Commerce 2002, Business Unity South Africa 2004–08; Vice-Pres. South African Chamber of Mines; mem. Gauteng Law Soc.; mem. Bd of Dirs African Fashion International; Owner, Mamelodi Sundowns Football Club; South Africa's Business Leader of the Year, Ernst & Young 2002, South Africa's Best Entrepreneur Award 2002. *Achievements include:* first African to join Giving Pledge (campaign by Bill Gates and Warren Buffett to encourage wealthy people to give at least half of their wealth to philanthropic causes). *Address:* African Rainbow Minerals Ltd., PO Box 786136, Sandton 2146, South Africa (office). *Telephone:* (11) 7791300 (office). *Fax:* (11) 7791312 (office). *E-mail:* ir.admin@arm.co.za (office). *Website:* www.arm.co.za (office).

MOTSUENYANE, Samuel Mokgethi, BSc (Agric.); South African business executive and diplomatist; b. 11 Feb. 1927, Potchefstroom; s. of Solomon P. Motsuenyane and Christina D. Motsuenyane; m. Jocelyn Mashinini 1954; six s.; ed North Carolina State Univ., USA, Jan Hofmeyr School of Social Work; Nat. Organizing Sec. African Nat. Soil Conservation Assen 1952–59; NC State Univ., USA 1960–62; Pres. NAFCOC 1968–92; Chair. African Business Publications, African Business Holdings, NAFCOC Permanent, Venda Nat. Devt Corpn, New-Real African Investments; Dir African Devt and Construction Holdings, NAFCOC Nat. Trust, Barlow Rand, Blackchain Ltd, numerous other cos; Chancellor, Univ. of the North (SA) 1985–90; Pres. Motsuenyane Comm. to investigate torture and disappearances in ANC detention camps 1992–93; Amb. to Saudi Arabia (also accred to Yemen, Kuwait and Oman) 1996–2000; Leader South African Observer Mission to the Presidential Elections in Zimbabwe 2002; Pres. Boy Scouts of SA 1976–81; Leader of Senate 1994–96; Dr hc (Univ. of Witwatersrand) 1983; Hon. DEconSc (Cape Town) 1986; Harvard Business Award 1977. *Publications:* numerous articles. *Leisure interests:* gardening, reading.

MOTTAKI, Manouchehr, MA; Iranian diplomatist and politician; b. 12 May 1953, Bandar Gaz, Golestan; ed Bangalore Univ., India, Tehran Univ.; joined Islamic Revolutionary Guards Corps (IRGC) 1979, IRGC Liaison Officer to Ministry of Foreign Affairs (MFA) 1979–80; Deputy of Islamic Consultative Ass. (Majlis) 1980–84, 2004–; Head of Political Bureau, MFA 1984–85; Amb. to Turkey 1985–89, to Japan 1994–99; Dir-Gen. of W European Affairs, MFA 1989; Deputy Foreign Minister for Int. Affairs 1989–92, for Consular and Parl. Affairs 1992–94; Adviser to Minister of Foreign Affairs 1999–2001; Vice-Pres. Islamic Culture and Communications Org. 2001–04; Campaign Man. for presidential cand. Ali Larijani 2005; Minister of Foreign Affairs 2005–10. *Address:* c/o Ministry of Foreign Affairs, Imam Khomeini Square, Tehran, Iran. *E-mail:* matbuat@mfa.gov.ir.

MOTTLEY, Mia Amor, QC; Barbadian lawyer and politician; *Prime Minister and Minister of Finance;* b. 1 Oct. 1965; ed Merryvale Private School, UN Int. School, Queen's Coll., London School of Econs, UK; called to the Bar of England and Wales,

Inner Bar of Barbados 2002; Opposition Senator, Senate of Barbados and Shadow Minister of Culture and Community Devt 1991–94, served on several Jt Select Cttees including Praedial Larceny and Domestic Violence; MP for Saint Michael North East 1994–, Leader of the Opposition 2008–10; Minister of Educ., Youth Affairs and Culture 1994–2001, Attorney-Gen. and Minister of Home Affairs 2001–03, Deputy Prime Minister 2003–08, 2013–18, Minister of Econ. Affairs and Devt 2006–08, Prime Minister (first female) 2018–, also Minister of Finance 2018–; Gen. Sec. Barbados Labour Party 1996–2008, Leader 2008–; Chair. Caribbean Community (CARICOM) Standing Cttee of Ministers of Educ. 1996, 1997; mem. Nat. Security Council of Barbados, Barbados Defence Bd, Privy Council of Barbados 2002. *Address:* Office of the Prime Minister, Government HQ, Bay Street, St Michael (office); Barbados Labour Party, Grantley Adams House, 111 Roebuck Street, Bridgetown, Barbados (office). *Telephone:* 436-6435 (office); 429-1990 (office). *Fax:* 436-1970 (office); 427-8792 (office). *E-mail:* info@primeminister.gov.bb (office); will99@caribsurf.com (office). *Website:* www.primeminister.gov.bb (office); labourparty.wordpress.com (office); www.barbadosparliament.com (office).

MOTTRAM, Sir Richard Clive, Kt, GCB, KCB, BA; British civil servant and business executive; *Non-Executive Chairman, Amey plc;* b. 23 April 1946; s. of John Mottram and Florence Yates; m. Fiona Margaret Erskine 1971; three s. one d.; ed King Edward VI Camp Hill School, Birmingham, Keele Univ.; joined Civil Service and assigned to Ministry of Defence 1968, Asst Pvt. Sec. to Sec. of State for Defence 1971–72, Prin. Naval Programme and Budget 1973, Cabinet Office 1975–77, Pvt. Sec. to Perm. Under-Sec., Ministry of Defence 1979–81, Pvt. Sec. to Sec. of State for Defence 1982–86, Asst Under-Sec. of State (programmes) 1986–89, Deputy Under-Sec. of State (Policy) 1989–92, Perm. Sec., Office of Public Service and Science, Cabinet Office 1992–95, Ministry of Defence 1995–98, Dept of the Environment, Transport and the Regions 1998–2001, Dept for Transport, Local Govt and the Regions 2001–02, for Work and Pensions 2002–05, Perm. Sec., Intelligence, Security and Resilience and Chair. Jt Intelligence Cttee, Cabinet Office 2005–07 (retd); Vice-Pres. Commonwealth Asscn for Public Admin and Man. 1998– (Pres. 2000–02); Chair. (non-exec.), Amey plc 2008–, Defence Science and Tech. Lab. 2008–; mem. Int. Advisory Bd, GardaWorld 2008–, Ashridge Business School, Ditchley Foundation; Trustee, Royal Anniversary Trust 2010–; Visiting Prof., Dept of Govt, LSE 2008–; Gov., Ashridge Business School 1998–; Hon. DLitt (Keele) 1996. *Leisure interests:* cinema, theatre, tennis. *Address:* Amey plc, The Sherard Building, Edmund Halley Road, Oxford, OX4 4DQ, England (office). *Telephone:* (1865) 713100 (office). *E-mail:* communications@amey.co.uk (office). *Website:* www.amey.co.uk (office).

MOTZFELDT, Josef, (Tuusi), Higher Diploma (Teaching); Greenlandic politician; b. 24 Nov. 1941, Igaliko; ed Hjørring Coll. (Hjørring Statsseminarium); trained as a teacher; Minister for Trade, Traffic and Vocational Training 1984–88; mem. Inatsisartut (Parl.) 1987–, Pres. 2009–13; Chair. Inuit Ataqatigiit Party 1994–2007; Minister of Economy 1999–2001, Minister of Economy (Greenland Home Rule Govt) 2002–03; Minister of Finance and Foreign Affairs, Vice-Premier and Minister for Nordic Cooperation 2003–07; Chair. for the West-Nordic Council 2009–10, 2012–; Chair. Nat. Gallery of Arts of Greenland; Greenland Homerule Silver Award. *Film:* Tukuma (co-dir) 1984. *Leisure interests:* literature, the arts. *Address:* Inatsisartut, PO Box 1060, 3900 Nuuk, Greenland (office). *Telephone:* 346118 (office). *Fax:* 324606 (office). *E-mail:* tuusi@ina.gl (office). *Website:* www.inatsisartut.gl (office); ia.gl (office).

MOUALLEM, Walid, BA; Syrian diplomatist and politician; *Deputy Prime Minister and Minister of Foreign Affairs and Expatriates;* b. 17 July 1941, Damascus; m. Sawsan Khayat; three s.; ed Cairo Univ., Egypt; joined diplomatic corps 1964; held positions at missions in Tanzania, Saudi Arabia and Spain; fmr Chargé d'affaires a.i., London; Amb. to Romania 1975–80; Head, Foreign Ministry Bureau, Damascus 1984–90; Amb. to USA 1990–99; Deputy Minister of Foreign Affairs 2005–06, Minister of Foreign Affairs 2006–11 (resgnd with rest of cabinet at Pres.'s request following popular protests), Minister of Foreign Affairs and Expatriates April 2011–; Deputy Prime Minister 2012–. *Publications:* Palestine and Armed Peace 1970, Syria During the Mandate Period from 1917 until 1948, Syria from Independence to Unity from 1948 until 1958, The World and the Middle East in the American Perspective. *Address:* Ministry of Foreign Affairs and Expatriates, rue ar-Rashid, Damascus, Syria (office). *Telephone:* (11) 2181000 (office). *Fax:* (11) 2146252 (office). *E-mail:* info@mofaex.gov.sy (office). *Website:* www.mofa.gov.sy (office).

MOUALLIMI, Abdallah Yahya Al-, BS, MS; Saudi Arabian diplomatist and business executive; *Permanent Representative, United Nations;* b. 5 May 1952; m. Sahar Haider O. Hajjar; four c.; ed Oregon State Univ. and Stanford Univ., USA; Vice-Chair. Olayan Financing Co. 1991–98, now Adviser; Founder-Pres. Dar al-Mouallimi Consulting Co. 1995–; mem. of Shoura Council (Parl.) 1997–2001; Mayor of Jeddah 2001–05; Co-founder and Chair. HBG Holdings Ltd 2006–; Amb. and Perm. Rep. to EU, Brussels (also accred as Amb. to Luxembourg) 2007–11, Amb. and Perm. Rep. to UN, New York 2011–; Chair. (non-exec.) European Islamic Investment Bank PLC 2011–; Chair. Rasmala PLC 2011–; fmr Chair. Jeddah Chamber of Commerce, Egyptian Finance Co.; mem. Bd of Dirs Allujain Corpn –2008, Majid Bin Abdulaziz Soc. for Devt and Social Services, Sanad Insurance Co., Coca-Cola Bottling Co. Saudi Arabia, Jeddah Prov. Council, Alumni Soc. of Modern Capital Inst., Consulting Comm. to Supreme Council of Gulf Co-operation Council; mem. Bd Gen. Org. for Mil. Industries, Saudi Nat. Commercial Bank, Egypt Finance Co., Assir Establishment for Press, Saudi Telecom; mem. Consultative Council of Saudi Arabia 1997–2001; Grand Cross, Order of the Crown (Belgium) 2011. *Address:* Permanent Mission of Saudi Arabia to the United Nations, 809 United Nations Plaza, 10th Floor, New York, NY 10017, USA (office). *Telephone:* (212) 557-1525 (office). *Fax:* (212) 983-4895 (office). *E-mail:* saudi-mission@un.int (office). *Website:* www.saudimission.org (office).

MOUAMBA, Clément, DEcon; Republic of the Congo economist, banker and politician; *Prime Minister;* b. 1943, Lékoumou; 14 c.; ed Univ. of Paris (Sorbonne), France; joined Banque des Etats de l'Afrique Centrale (BEAC), Yaoundé 1973, becoming Deputy Dir 1980, also Pres., Office Monétaire d'Afrique Centrale (OMAC, banking authority), and Special Adviser to BEAC Gov.; fmr Dir, Banque internationale du Congo; Dir Banque commerciale du Congo (BCC) 1985–92; fmr Adviser on econ. affairs to Pres. of Repub. of the Congo; elected mem. Nat. Ass. (Parl.) for Sibiti 1992; Minister of Finance 1992–93; Prime Minister 2016–; mem. Union Panafricaine pour la Démocratie Sociale (UPADS) –2014 (expelled from party), fmr mem. Political Bureau, Vice-Pres. UPADS 2006–14. *Address:* Office of the Council of Ministers, Brazzaville, Republic of the Congo (office).

MOUBELET BOUBEYA, Pacôme, DEA, DESS; Gabonese government official; b. 12 March 1963, Bitam, Woleu-N'Tem Region; m.; three s.; ed Ealing Coll. and Salford Univ., UK, Institut des Hautes Etudes de Défense Nationale de Paris, France; began career as Research Officer, Gabonese Centre for Foreign Trade, Ministry of Commerce 1990, becoming Dir of Foreign Trade 1991; Chief of Staff to Sec.-Gen. of Govt 1993, Second Deputy Sec.-Gen. of Govt early 2000s, becoming First Deputy Sec.-Gen. of Govt, Sec.-Gen. of Govt 2009–14; Minister of Higher Educ. and Scientific Research 2014–15, Minister of the Interior, Decentralization and Public Security 2015–16; Minister of State, Minister of Foreign Affairs, the Francophonie and Regional Integration, responsible for Gabonese Nationals Abroad 2016–17; Gen. Coordinator, Coordination Office, Plan stratégique Gabon émergent (Strategic Emerging Gabon Plan); Chair. Bd of Dirs Agence nationale des infrastructures numériques et des fréquences (ANINF); mem. Parti Démocratique Gabonais, mem. Political Bureau 2008. *Leisure interests:* cookery, urban music. *Address:* c/o Ministry of Foreign Affairs, the Francophonie and Regional Integration, blvd du Bord de Mer, BP 2245, Libreville, Gabon (office).

MOUDENC, Jean-Luc, DESS, MA; French politician; *Mayor of Toulouse;* b. 19 July 1960, Toulouse; ed Toulouse Univ. of Social Sciences; worked as a journalist; Municipal Councillor, Toulouse 1987–92, Regional Councillor, Midi-Pyrénées 1992–94, Gen. Counsel, Haute-Garonne 1994–98; Vice-Pres. Syndicat mixte des transports en commune (became Tisséo) 1998–2001; Pres. Soc. de la mobilité de l'agglomération toulousaine 1998–2001; mem. Union pour un Mouvement Populaire; Mayor of Toulouse 2004–08, 2014–; Pres. Asscn des maires de grandes villes de France (Asscn of Mayors of the Cities of France) 2014–. *Address:* Mairie de Toulouse, 1 place du Capitole, 31000 Toulouse, France (office). *Telephone:* 5-61-22-29-22. *Website:* www.toulouse.fr/mairie (office); www.grandesvilles.org.

MOUFTAKIR, Mohammed; Moroccan film director and screenwriter; b. 1965, Casablanca; s. of Houcine Mouftakir; ed Univ. Hassan II, Aïn Chock; worked as asst dir on various int. productions for five years; achieved int. recognition with debut feature film Pegase. *Films include:* L'Ombre de la Mort (short) 2003, La Danse du Foetus (short) (Grand Jury Prize, Tangier Nat. Film Festival) 2005, Fin du Mois (short) (Grand Jury Prize, Tangier Nat. Film Festival) 2007, Chant Funèbre (short) 2008, Terminus des Anges 2009, Pegase (Golden Stallion, Pan African Film Festival, Burkina Faso 2011) 2009, L'orchestre des aveugles 2015.

MOUKNASS, Naha Mint Hamdi Ould; Mauritanian politician; b. 10 March 1969, Nouakchott; d. of Hamdi Ould Mouknass; ed Institut Supérieur de Gestion de Paris; following graduation, returned to Nouakchott to work for the Coca Cola Co. 1994–96; Pres. Union pour la Démocratie et le Progrès (Union for Democracy and Progress) 2000–; adviser to Pres. Ould Taya 2000–01, Minister-Advisor to the Presidency 2001–05; fmr mem. Parl. for City of Nouadhibou; fmr mem. Foreign Affairs Comm.; Minister of Foreign Affairs and Co-operation 2009–11, of Trade, Industry and Tourism 2014–18, of Social Affairs, Children and Family 2018, of Nat. Educ. and Vocational Training –2019; Deputy, Nat. Ass. 2013–.

MOUKOKO MBONJO, Pierre; Cameroonian political scientist, business executive and politician; b. 25 July 1954, Nkam; ed Institut d'Études Politiques, Paris; 25 years as Lecturer in Political Science, Institut des Relations internationales du Cameroun (Iric); Special Adviser to the Prime Minister and Govt Spokesman 1991–92, Chief of Cabinet in Prime Minister's Office 1996, Minister of Communications 2004–06, of External Relations 2011–15; CEO Cimenteries du Cameroun (Cimencam) –2011; Dir Soc. Nationale d'Investissement du Cameroun 1996. *Publications include:* The Political Thought of Kwame Nkrumah 1998. *Address:* c/o Ministry of External Relations, Yaoundé, Cameroon (office).

MOULAERT, Jacques, LLD, MPA; Belgian banker; *Vice-President and Executive Director, Viohalco SA;* b. 23 Oct. 1930, Ostend; s. of Albert Moulaert and Marie Magdeleine de Neckere; m. Christiane Laloux 1957; four d.; ed St Barbara Coll. Ghent, Univ. of Ghent, Catholic Univ. of Louvain, Harvard Univ., USA; Gen. Sec. Aleurope SA 1961; Asst Man. Compagnie Lambert 1967; Man., Compagnie Bruxelles Lambert (CBL) 1972, Man. Dir Groupe Bruxelles Lambert 1979, now Hon. Man. Dir; Chair. Bank Brussels Lambert (BBL) 1993–2001; Hon. Chair., ING Bank Belgium SA; Founder and Hon. Vice-Pres. Louvain Foundation; currently Vice-Pres. and Exec. Dir Viohalco SA, Brussels; fmr mem. Bd of Dirs Tractebel, Cockerill-Sambre, Royale Belge, Sabena; fmr Visiting Prof., Université Catholique de Louvain; Officier, Ordre de la Couronne; Commdr, Ordre de Léopold, Ordre de St-Sylvestre. *Address:* 2 Tailleur de Pierre, 1380 Lasne (home); Viohalco SA, 30 Marnix Avenue, 1000 Brussels, Belgium (office). *Telephone:* (2) 633-10-52 (home). *Fax:* (2) 633-64-15 (home). *E-mail:* jacques.moulaert@skynet.be (home). *Website:* www.viohalco.com (office).

MOULAYE, Mohamed, DSc; Mauritanian politician and public official; b. 1 Oct. 1936, Ouagadougou, Burkina Faso; s. of El Hassan Moulaye and Maimouna Dem; m. Ginette Marcin 1962; three s. five d.; Founder-mem. Asscn de la Jeunesse de Mauritanie 1956; Sec.-Gen. Section PRM Boutilimit 1960; mem. Nat. Ass. 1965–75; Directeur des finances 1966; Contrôleur financier 1967–75; Minister of Finance 1975–77, 1979; Parl. rapporteur to Comm. des Finances; fmr mem. IPU; Dir Office of Pres. of Mauritania 1979–80; Conseiller Econ. et Financier du Chef de l'Etat, Président de la Comm. Centrale des Marchés Publics; Pres. Parti du Centre démocratique mauritanien 1992, now Democratic Centre Party; First Vice-Pres. Action pour le Changement; mem. Conseil général, Banque Centrale de Mauritanie 1980; Dir Personnel Air Afrique, Financial Dir 1985; Chair. and Man. Dir Arrachad, Nouackchott 1990; Chevalier, Ordre nat. du Mérite. *Leisure interests:* reading, cinema.

MOULD, Jeremy R., PhD; Australian (b. British) astronomer and academic; *Professor, Centre for Astrophysics and Supercomputing, Swinburne University of Technology;* b. 31 July 1949, UK; ed Univ. of Melbourne, Australian Nat. Univ.; emigrated to Australia 1963; fmr Research Fellow, Kitt Peak Nat. Observatory; fmr Prof., California Inst. of Tech.; fmr Dir Research School of Astronomy and Astrophysics, ANU and American Nat. Optical Astronomy Observatory; currently Prof., Centre for Astrophysics and Supercomputing, Swinburne Univ. of Tech.; Asteroid 18240 Mould named in his honour, George Van Biesbroeck Prize (co-recipient) 1981, Newton Lacy Pierce Prize in Astronomy (co-recipient) 1984, Cosmology Prize, Gruber Foundation (co-recipient) 2009. *Publications include:* numerous papers in professional journals. *Address:* Room SA 117, Centre for Astrophysics and Supercomputing, Swinburne University of Technology, PO Box 218, Hawthorn, Vic. 3122, Australia (office). *Telephone:* (3) 9214-4921 (office). *Fax:* (3) 9214-8797 (office). *E-mail:* jmould@swin.edu.au (office). *Website:* astronomy.swin.edu.au/staff/jmould.html (office); astronomy.swin.edu.au/~jmould (office).

MOUNGAR, Fidèle; Chadian physician and politician; *Secretary-General, Chadian Action for Unity and Socialism (ACTUS);* b. Logone Region; fmr head of surgery, Peronne Hosp., Somme, France; Prime Minister of Chad 1993; Chair. Action tchadienne pour l'unité et le socialisme (ACTUS), Collectif des partis pour le changement (COPAC); Sec.-Gen. Chadian Action for Unity and Socialism (Action Tchadienne pour l'unité et le socialisme—ACTUS) 1981–. *Address:* Action Tchadienne pour l'Unité et le Socialisme (ACTUS), N'Djamena, Chad (office). *E-mail:* actus_pr@yahoo.com (office).

MOUNT, Sir (William Robert) Ferdinand, MA, FRSL, FSA; British writer and journalist; b. 2 July 1939, London; s. of Robert Mount and Julia Mount; m. Julia Margaret Lucas 1968; two s. (one deceased), one d.; ed Eton Coll., Christ Church, Oxford; Political Ed., The Spectator 1977–82, 1985, Literary Ed. 1984–85; Head, Prime Minister Margaret Thatcher's Policy Unit 1982–84; Dir, Centre for Policy Studies 1984–91; Political Columnist, The Standard 1980–82, The Times 1984–85, Daily Telegraph 1985–90; Ed., Times Literary Supplement 1991–2002; Sr Columnist, The Sunday Times 2002–04; Vice-Chair., Power Comm. 2004–05; mem. RSL (mem. of Council 2002–05); Hon. Fellow (Univ. of Wales, Lampeter) 2002. *Publications include:* Very Like a Whale 1967, The Theatre of Politics 1972, The Man Who Rode Ampersand 1975, The Clique 1978, The Subversive Family 1982, The Selkirk Strip 1987, Of Love and Asthma 1991 (Hawthornden Prize 1992), The British Constitution Now 1992, Communism 1992, Umbrella 1994, The Liquidator 1995, Jem (and Sam) 1998, Fairness 2001, Mind the Gap: The New Class Divide in Britain 2004, Heads You Win 2004, The Condor's Head 2007, Cold Cream: My Early Life and Other Mistakes 2008, Full Circle: How the Classical World Came Back to Us 2010, The New Few: A Very British Oligarchy 2012, The Tears of the Rajas: Mutiny, Money and the Marriage in India 1805–1905 2015. *Address:* 17 Ripplevale Grove, London, N1 1HS, England (home). *Telephone:* (20) 7607-5398 (home).

MOUNTAIN, Ross Stewart; New Zealand international organization official and UN official; b. 13 Nov. 1944, Christchurch; s. of Noel Stewart Mountain and Frida Thekla Monrad; m.; three d.; ed Victoria Univ., Wellington; Inter-Agency Youth Liaison Officer, Div. of Social Affairs, UN, Geneva 1973–75, Coordinator UN Non-Governmental Liaison Service 1975–83; Chief of Information Section, UNDP European Office 1976–85; Deputy Resident Rep. in S Pacific, Fiji 1985–88; UNDP Resident Rep. ad interim and Dir UN Information Centre, Kabul, Afghanistan 1988–91; UN Special Coordinator for Emergency Relief Operations, UNDP Resident Rep., World Food Programme and UN Population Fund (UNFPA) Rep. in Liberia 1991–93; UNDP Rep. and UN Humanitarian Affairs Coordinator, Haiti, on secondment from UN Resident Coordinator and UNDP Resident Coordinator for Eastern Caribbean, Barbados 1993–95; UN Resident Coordinator in Lebanon and Resident Rep. of UNDP and UNFPA 1995–98; Asst Emergency Relief Coordinator and Dir Geneva Office, Office for the Coordination of Humanitarian Affairs (OCHA) 1998–2003; Special Rep. of UN Sec.-Gen. for Iraq, also UN Humanitarian Coordinator and UNDP Resident Rep. 2003–04; Deputy Special Rep. of UN Sec.-Gen. in the Democratic Repub. of the Congo 2004–09; Dir Gen. DARA (int. aid and devt org.), Madrid 2010–12; Deputy Special Coordinator, Resident Coordinator, Humanitarian Coordinator, UNDP Resident Rep., Beirut 2014–15; fmr Humanitarian Coordinator ad interim for E Timor Crisis, Special Humanitarian Envoy for floods in Mozambique, Special Humanitarian Coordinator for Liberia, Head OCHA Crisis Task Team for Iraq.

MOUNTER, Julian D'Arcy, QM, MA; British journalist, television director, producer and broadcasting executive; *Chairman and CEO, Media Consultants and Investments;* b. 2 Nov. 1944, Cornwall, England; s. of Francis Mounter and Elizabeth Moore; m. Patricia A. Kelsall-Spurr 1983; two s.; ed Skinners Grammar School, Tunbridge Wells, Grenville Coll., Univ. of Leicester; reporter with various local newspapers 1961–65; journalist, The Times 1966–71; Weekend World, London Weekend TV 1971–73; Head of Current Affairs and Documentaries, Westward TV 1973–74; Reporter/Dir Panorama and Midweek, BBC TV 1974–78; Producer Inside Business, Thames TV 1978–79, Exec. Producer, Current Affairs 1979–81, Controller, Children's and Young Adults' Dept 1981–84; Dir Programmes and Production, Thorn-EMI Satellite and Cable 1984–86; Dir Cosgrove Hall Ltd 1981–84, JRA Ltd 1980–85, Cameralink Ltd 1980–85, Blackwell Videotec Ltd 1980–85; Dir-Gen. and CEO Television New Zealand 1986–91; Chair. South Pacific Pictures Ltd, Broadcast Communications Ltd 1988–91; Dir The Listener, Visnews (UK) Ltd 1987–89, Reuters TV Ltd 1989–91; Chief Exec. and Pres. Star TV Ltd Hutchvision Ltd, Media Assets Ltd, Asia News Ltd 1992–93; Chair. New Media Investments 1994–98, Majestic Films and TV Ltd 1993–95, Swoffers Ltd 1995–96, Renown Leisure Group Ltd 1995–2000; CEO and Man. Dir Seven Network Ltd, Australia 1998–2000; Dir, Deputy Chair. and Chair. Channel Television Ltd 1994–99; Chair. and CEO Media Consultants and Investments 2001–; Dir Int. Council of Nat. Acad. of Television Arts and Sciences, New York 1993–2005 (Assoc. Dir 2005–08), Diverse Productions Ltd, FBC Media and various others 2002–09; Chair. Steering Bd; mem. Advisory Bd Pax Mondial 2008–12; Trustee, Int. Inst. of Communications 1988–95; Hon. Visiting Fellow, Univ. of Leicester 2005; Queen's Medal for Services to NZ 1990; various press and TV awards. *Leisure interests:* ocean sailing, naval history, music, flying. *Address:* Media Consultants and Investments, 2 Clifton, St Peter Port, GY1 2PH, Guernsey, Channel Islands (office). *Telephone:* (709) 3206-5038 (office). *E-mail:* mediahelp@aol.com (office).

MOURÃO, Gen. (retd) Hamilton; Brazilian politician and fmr army officer; *Vice-President;* b. 15 Aug. 1953, Porto Alegre, Rio Grande do Sul; s. of Antônio Hamilton Mourão and Wanda Coronel Martins; m. Paula Mourão; ed Academia Militar das Agulhas Negras, Escola de Comando e Estado-Maior do Exército (ECEME); served in Brazilian army 1971–2018, including as Instructor, Academia Militar das Agulhas Negras, Mil. Attaché, Embassy in Caracas, fmr Commdr, 27th Campaign Artillery Group, Ijuí (Rio Grande do Sul), Second Jungle Infantry Brigade, São Gabriel da Cachoeira (Amazonas), Sixth Army Div., Porto Alegre; retd from army with rank of Gen. 2018; Vice-Pres. of Brazil 2019–; mem. Partido Renovador Trabalhista Brasileiro (PRTB) 2018–; Order of the Star of Carabobo (Venezuela), Grand Cross, Order of Mil. Merit; Amazon Service Medal, Marechal Osorio Medal, UN UNAVEM III Medal, Peacemaker Medal. *Address:* Office of the Vice-President, Palácio do Planalto, 3° andar, Praça dos Três Poderes, 70150-900 Brasília, DF, Brazil (office). *E-mail:* protocolo@planalto.gov.br (office). *Website:* www2.planalto.gov.br (office).

MOURINHO, José; Portuguese football manager; b. (José Mário Dos Santos Mourinho Félix), 26 Jan. 1963, Setubal; s. of José Mourinho Félix and Maria Júlia Dos Santos; m. Matilde 'Tami' Faria 1989; one s. one d.; ed Technical Univ. of Lisbon; completed UEFA coaching course after studying in Britain 1987; worked as fitness trainer at various clubs and coached jr team Vitoria Setubal then asst Estrela Amadora 1990–92; interpreter, Sporting Lisbon 1992–1993; interpreter and Asst Coach Porto 1993–1996; Asst Coach Barcelona, Spain 1996–2000; Coach Benfica 2000, Uniao de Leiria 2000–01, Porto 2002–04 (won UEFA Cup 2003, Portuguese Championship 2003, 2004, Taça de Portugal 2002/03, SuperCup Cândido de Oliveira 2003, Champions League 2004); Man. and First Team Coach, Chelsea Football Club, England 2004–07, 2013–15 (won FA Premier League 2004/05, 2005/06, FA Cup 2007, Football League Cup 2005, 2007, FA Community Shield 2005); Man. FC Internazionale Milano 2008–10 (won Supercoppa Italiana 2008, Serie A title 2008/09, 2009/10, Coppa Italia 2009/10, UEFA Champions League 2009/10); Man. Real Madrid Club de Fútbol 2010–13 (won Copa del Rey 2010/11, La Liga 2011/12, Supercopa de España 2012); Man. Manchester United Football Club 2016–18 (won FA Community Shield, League Cup, UEFA Europa League); Officer, Order of Infante Dom Henrique; Dr hc (Tech. Univ. of Lisbon) 2009; UEFA Champions League Man. of the Year 2002/03, 2003/04, Portuguese Liga Manager of the Year 2002/03, 2003/04, World Soccer Magazine Coach of the Year 2003/04, 2004/05, UEFA Team of the Year Coach of the Year 2003, 2004, 2005, FA Premier League Man. of the Year 2004/05, 2005/06, IFFHS World Man. of the Year 2004, 2005, FA Premier League Man. of the Month 11/2004, 01/2005, 03/2007, BBC Sports Personality of the Year Coach Award 2005, Onze d'Or European Coach 2005, selected as the New Statesman Man of the Year 2005, Serie A Man. of the Year 2009, Int. Sports Press Asscn Best Man. in the World 2010, Football Extravaganza's League of Legends 2011, Prémio Prestígio Fernando Soromenho 2012. *Address:* c/o Jorge Mendes, Gestifute SA, M. Alameda dos Oceanos, Edificio Espace Lote 1.06.1.4, Escritório 3.18, 1990-207 Lisbon, Portugal (office). *E-mail:* gestifute@gestifute.com (office). *Website:* gestifute.com (office).

MOUROU, Gérard A., BSc, MSc, PhD; French electrical engineer and academic; *A.D. Moore Distinguished Professor Emeritus, University of Michigan;* b. 22 June 1944; ed Univ. of Paris, Université d'Orsay, Univ. of Grenoble; Scientific cooperant, Université Laval, Québec, Canada 1970–73; Postdoctoral Fellow, San Diego State Univ., Calif., USA 1973–74; Scientist, Lab. for Laser Energetics, Univ. of Rochester, NY, USA 1979–88, Group Leader, Picosecond Research Group 1979–88, Sr Scientist 1981–88, Assoc. Prof., Inst. of Optics 1983–87, Div. Dir, Ultrafast Science Div. 1986–88, Prof., Inst. of Optics 1987–89; apptd Prof., Dept of Electrical Eng and Computer Science, Coll. of Eng, Univ. of Michigan 1988, Founding Dir Center for Ultrafast Optical Science, NSF and Tech. Center 1990, currently A.D. Moore Distinguished Prof. Emer., Univ. of Michigan, USA; Dir Laboratoire d'Optique Appliquée at ENSTA, Palaiseau, France –2009; Visiting Prof., Univ. of Tokyo, Japan 1994; Prof. of Physics, Municipal Chair, Université Joseph Fourier, Grenoble 1994; Prof., École Polytechnique, Palaiseau; mem. Editorial Bd, Laser Focus; mem. Nat. Acad. of Eng; Fellow, Optical Soc. of America, IEEE; R.W. Wood Prize, Optical Soc. of America 1995, SPIE Harold E. Edgerton Award 1997, IEEE David Sarnoff Award 1999, IEEE LEOS Quantum Electronics Award 2004, Willis E. Lamb Award for Laser Science and Quantum Optics 2005, Charles Hard Townes Award, Optical Soc. of America 2009, Berthold Leibinger Zukunftspreis 2016, Frederic Ives Medal/Quinn Prize, Optical Soc. of America 2016, Nobel Prize in Physics (jt winner) 2018. *Achievements include:* co-invented chirped pulse amplification technique later used to create ultrashort, very high-intensity (terawatt) laser pulses. *Publications:* numerous papers in professional journals; numerous patents. *Address:* ECE Division, Center for Ultrafast Optical Sciences, 6117 ERB I, 2200 Bonisteel Blvd, Ann Arbor, MI 48109-2099, USA (office). *Telephone:* (734) 763-4877 (office). *Fax:* (734) 763-4876 (office). *E-mail:* mourou@eecs.umich.edu (office). *Website:* cuos.engin.umich.edu/researchgroups/hfs/profiles/gerard-mourou (office); vhosts.eecs.umich.edu/OSL//Mourou (office).

MOURTADA, Hani; Syrian paediatrician, academic and fmr government official; b. 1939, Damascus; m.; three c.; ed Damascus Univ.; Head of Paediatrics Dept, Faculty of Medicine, Damascus Univ. 1987–92, Dean Faculty of Medicine 1991–2000, Pres. Damascus Univ. 2000–03; Minister of Higher Educ. 2003; currently Pres. Dar al-Shifa Hospital, Aleppo.

MOUSA, Ali bin Muhammad bin; Omani economist, central banker and fmr politician; fmr Minister of Health; apptd Chair. Oman Tender Bd 2010; Deputy Chair. Bd of Govs, Central Bank of Oman.

MOUSAWI, Faisal Radhi al-, MB, BCh, FRCSE; Bahraini government official and orthopaedic surgeon; b. 6 April 1944, Bahrain; one s. three d.; ed Univ. of Cairo, Egypt; fmr Rotary Intern, Cairo Univ. Hosp.; House Officer, Sr House Officer, Dept of Surgery, Govt Hosp., Bahrain; Sr House Officer, Accident and Orthopaedic Surgery, Cen. Middx Hosp., London; Orthopaedic Surgery, St Helier Hosp., Carshalton, Surrey; Gen. Surgery, Nelson Hosp., London, St Bartholomew's Hosp., London; Registrar, Orthopaedic Surgery, Whittington Hosp., London, Gen. and Traumatic Surgery, Wexford Co. Hosp., Ireland; locum consultant, Whittington Hosp. 1983–84; Consultant Orthopaedic Surgeon, Salmaniya Medical Centre, Bahrain 1976–, Chair. Dept of Surgery 1982–84, Chief of Medical Staff June–Aug. 1982, Chair. Dept of Orthopaedic Surgery; Asst Prof., Coll. of Medicine and Medical Sciences, Arabian Gulf Univ.; Asst Under-Sec., Ministry of Health 1982–85, Minister of Health 1995–2002; Chair. Shura Council 2002–06; mem. Scientific Council, Arab Bd for Surgery 1979; Chair. Arab Bd Cttee for Sub-specialities in Surgery, Arab Bd for Orthopaedic Surgery 1990, Chair. Training Cttee 1988; Chair. Nat. Arab Bd Cttee and Co-ordinator, Arab Bd Programme in Surgery, Bahrain; Examiner, Ministry of Health Qualification Examination 1982, Part B Fellowship Examination; apptd Pres. Royal Coll. of Surgeons, Ireland 2009, fmr Chair.; mem. Editorial Bd Bahrain Medical Bulletin; Founding mem. and

Pres. Gulf Orthopaedic Asscn; mem. European Soc. for Sport Medicine, Knee Surgery and Arthroscopy; Fellow, British Orthopaedic Asscn, Royal Coll. of Surgeons, Ireland. *Publications:* numerous papers and articles. *Leisure interest:* tennis.

MOUSKOURI, Ioanna (Nana); Greek singer and fmr politician; b. 13 Oct. 1934, Athens; d. of Constantin Mouskouri and Alice Mouskouri; m. 1st George Petsilas; one s. one d.; m. 2nd Andre Chapelle; ed Athens Nat. Conservatory; singer 1956–; living in Paris 1962–; has given concerts world-wide; has sold more than 300 million records world-wide; recorded more than 1,500 songs in Greek, French, English, German, Dutch, Italian and Spanish; numerous TV appearances, including Numéro 1 1979 and Nana Mouskouri à Athènes 1984; UNICEF Amb. 1993–, Special Rep. for Performing Arts and Hon. Spokesperson; mem. European Parl. 1994–99; Founder and Pres. Foundation 'Nana Mouskouri-Focus on Hope'; Gran Cruz Placa de Plata (Dominican Repub.) 2006, Officier, Légion d'honneur 2007, Grand Commdr, Order of Benefaction (Greece) 2007, Officier, Ordre Nat. du Québec 2013; Dr hc (McGill) 2013; Greek Broadcasting Festival Award 1959, Barcelona Festival Award, No. 1 French Female Singer 1979, No. 1 Female Singer World-wide, Canada 1980, IFPI Multiplatinum Music Award 1996, UNICEF World of Children Award 1997, Echo Music Prize for Outstanding Achievemenents 2015 and numerous other awards and prizes. *Songs include:* L'enfant au tambour, Les parapluies de Cherbourg, C'est bon la vie, Plaisir d'amour, Ave Maria, L'amour en héritage, Only Love, White Rose of Athens, Je chante avec toi Liberté. *Publications:* Chanter ma vie 1989, Memoirs 2007, My Name is Nana 2007, Itinéraire intime 2013. *Leisure interest:* collecting antique jewellery, antiques and paintings. *Address:* c/o Nema Productions SA, 12 Robert de Traz, 1206 Geneva, Switzerland (office). *Telephone:* (22) 3460130 (home). *Fax:* (22) 7522293 (home). *E-mail:* nemaprod@bluewin.ch (home); nemaprod@mac.com (office). *Website:* www.nanamouskouri.net.

MOUSSA, Abou; Chadian UN official; b. 1950; m.; three c.; ed Univ. of Lagos, Nigeria, Advanced School of Journalism, France, Univ. of Paris 1 Panthéon-Sorbonne, France; joined UNHCR 1980, served in several duty stations, including Democratic Repub. of Congo, Switzerland, Ethiopia, Zambia fmr Regional Dir for West Africa; Rep. of Sec.-Gen. and Head of UN Peacebuilding Support Office in Liberia (UNOL) 2002–03, Deputy Special Rep. of Sec.-Gen., Humanitarian Coordinator and UN Devt Programme Resident, Rep. for Liberia 2003–05, Prin. Deputy Rep. of Sec.-Gen. in Côte d'Ivoire 2005–11, Special Rep. of Sec.-Gen. and Head, UN Regional Office for Central Africa (UNOCA) 2011–14. *Address:* c/o United Nations Regional Office for Central Africa (UNOCA), 23773, Cité de la Démocratie, Villas 55–57, Libreville, Gabon.

MOUSSA, Amre Mahmoud, LLB; Egyptian politician, diplomatist and international organisation official; b. 3 Oct. 1936, Cairo; m. Laila Badawy 1968; two c.; ed Cairo Univ.; joined Ministry of Foreign Affairs 1958, served in several diplomatic posts, including Amb. to India 1983–86, Amb. and Perm. Rep. to UN, New York 1990–91, Minister of Foreign Affairs 1991–2001; Sec.-Gen. League of Arab States (Arab League) 2001–11; unsuccessful cand. for Pres. of Egypt 2011; apptd mem. Egyptian Constitutional Assembly drafting the country's new constitution 2012; Founder Egyptian National Alliance coalition; Grand Cordon of the Nile 2001, First Class Order of the Two Niles (Sudan) 2001; Dr hc (Lebanese American University of Beirut) 2010.

MOUSSA DAWALEH, Ilyas, BEcons; Djibouti business executive and politician; *Minister of the Economy and Finance;* b. 1966; ed Univ. Rabelais, Tours, Institut Portuaire du Havre, France, Washington State Inst. of Public Policy, USA, Int. Maritime Org. Inst., UK; Head, Private Sector Dept, Nat. Planning Directorate, attached to Presidency of the Repub. 1992–93; Head of Gen. Man.'s Office, Port Autonome Int. de Djibouti 1993–94, Project Man. 1994–96, Dir of Operations 1996–2004; Minister of the Economy and Finance, in charge of Industry and Planning 2011–; Chair. Tamamoul Motors; fmr Chair. Bureau Main d'œuvres des Dockers (trade union); Dir of electoral campaign of Pres. Ismaïl Omar Guelleh 2011; co-f. Club des jeunes Entrepreneurs, Djibouti; mem. COMESA Nat. Cttee, Djibouti-Ethiopia Jt Comm., Djibouti Chamber of Commerce Nat. Reform Comm.; mem. Rassemblement populaire pour le progrès. *Address:* Ministry of the Economy, Finance and Planning, BP 13, Djibouti (office). *Telephone:* 353331 (office). *Fax:* 356501 (office). *E-mail:* sg_mefpp@intnet.dj (office). *Website:* www.ministere-finances.dj (office).

MOUSSAVI, Farshid, OBE, BSc, DipArch, MArch II (Harvard); British (b. Iranian) architect and academic; *Professor in Practice of Architecture, Harvard University;* b. 17 Aug. 1965, Shiraz, Iran; d. of M. Mosavi and F. Kargozari-Moussavi; one d.; ed Univ. Coll., London, Bartlett School of Architecture, Harvard Univ., USA, Dundee Univ., RIBA; moved to London with family 1979; worked with Renzo Piano workshop, Genoa; with Office for Metropolitan Architecture, Rotterdam 1991–93; Co-founder and Owner (with ex-husband Alejandro Zaera-Polo) Foreign Office Architects Ltd, London 1995–2011; Founder Farshid Moussavi Architecture, London 2011–; Unit Master, Architectural Asscn School of Architecture 1993–2000; Visiting Prof., Princeton Univ., UCLA, Columbia Univ., Berlage Inst., Amsterdam, Hoger Architecture Inst., Belgium; Prof. and Head of Architecture Inst., Acad. of Fine Arts, Vienna 2002–05; Kenzo Tange Visiting Design Critic, Harvard Univ. Grad. Design School 2005, currently Prof. in Practice of Architecture; represented UK at Architecture Biennale, Venice, Italy 2002; mem. Int. Design Cttee, London 2003, Design and Architecture Advisory Group to British Council, Aga Khan Award for Architecture Steering Cttee 2005–15 (Chair. Jury 2004), Bd Strelka Inst. for Architecture, Media and Design, Moscow 2011–; mem. Jury, RIBA Gold Medal, RIBA Pres.'s Medal, Stirling Prize for Architecture, 11th Architecture Biennale; columnist, Architecture Review 2011–; Trustee, Whitechapel Art Gallery, Architecture Foundation; numerous awards, including RIBA Int. Awards 2005, 2006, 2011, Special Award for Topography, 9th Venice Architecture Biennale 2004, Enric Miralles Prize for Architecture 2004, Charles Jencks Award for Architecture 2005, Architect of the Year Award, Architectural Digest, Madrid 2007, ELLE Award for Architecture 2008, Condé Nast Traveller Innovation and Design Award 2009, Green Good Design Award 2011. *Architectural works include:* Yokohama Int. Ferry Terminal, Japan (Kanagawa Architecture Prize 2003, Eric Miralles Prize for Architecture 2004, RIBA Worldwide Award 2005) 1996–2002, Belgo Restaurant, Notting Hill Br., London 1998, Bristol 1999, New York 1999, Bluemoon Hotel, Groningen, Netherlands, Municipal Police HQ, La Villajoyosa, Spain 2000–04, Public Square and Theatre, nr Alicante 2001–06, Coastal Park, nr Barcelona 2002–04, T'Raboes Harbour Facilities, Amersfoort, Netherlands 2002–, Meydan retail complex and multiplex, Istanbul, Turkey (Building Design's Retail Architect of the Year Award 2008, European Business Award for the Environment, Urban Land Inst. Award for Excellence, Prime Property Award, ArkiPARC Award 2009) 2007, Carabanchel social housing complex, Madrid, Spain (RIBA European Award 2008, Int. Architecture Award 2010), John Lewis dept store and cineplex, Leicester (RIBA Award 2009, Civic Trust Award and Special Award 2010) 2008, Museum of Contemporary Art, Cleveland, Ohio, USA 2006–12, residential complex in La Défense dist of Paris, France 2011–, 13th Venice Architecture Biennale installation, 'Architecture and its Affects' 2012, l'Îlot 'Citroën' development, Nantes 2013–, Jardins de la Lironde residential complex, Montpellier 2013–; with Farshid Moussavi Architecture: La Défense Residential Complex, Paris 2011–, Museum of Contemporary Art, Cleveland, Ohio 2012, 130 Fenchurch Street Office Complex, London 2013–, Victoria Beckham Flagship Store, London 2014. *Publications include:* FOA Recent Projects 2001, The Yokohama Project 2002, El Croquis (monograph) 2003, Phylogenesis: FOA's Ark 2003, FOA's Ark Evolving Container for the Proliferating Singularities 2004, The Function of Ornament 2006, The Function of Form 2009, The Function of Style 2015. *Address:* Farshid Moussavi Architecture, 12F, 30 Fenchurch Street, London, ECM3 5DJ, England (office). *Telephone:* (20) 7033-6490 (home). *E-mail:* office@farshidmoussavi.com (office). *Website:* www.farshidmoussavi.com (office).

MOUSSAVI, Mir Hussein; Iranian politician; b. 29 Sept. 1941, Khameneh, Iran; m. Zahra Rahnavard; ed Nat. Univ., Tehran; trained as an architect; joined Islamic Soc. at univ. in Tehran and active in Islamic socs since; imprisoned briefly for opposition to the Shah 1973; a Founder-mem. Islamic Republican Party (IRP) 1979; apptd Chief Ed. Jomhouri-e Eslami (Islamic Republic) newspaper 1979; Foreign Minister Aug.–Oct. 1981; elected Prime Minister by Majlis (consultative ass.) 1981–89, Adviser to the Pres. 1997–2005; currently mem. Shura-ye Tashkhis-e Maslahat-e Nezam—Council to Determine the Expediency of the Islamic Order, High Council of Cultural Revolution; Co-founder and Pres. Iranian Acad. of Arts, Tehran 1999–2009; cand. for Pres. of Tehran 2009.

MOUT, Marianne Elisabeth Henriette Nicolette, PhD; Dutch historian and academic; *Professor Emeritus of Modern History and of Central European Studies, Leiden University;* b. 31 May 1945, Wassenaar; d. of Arie Mout and Maria Helena van Tooren; m. 1st Robbert Salomon van Santen (divorced 1979); m. 2nd Peter Felix Ganz 1987; ed Rijnlands Lyceum, Wassenaar, Univ. of Amsterdam, Charles Univ., Prague; research student, Czechoslovakia 1966, 1967; Asst Keeper, Jewish Historical Museum, Amsterdam 1969; Ed., Martinus Nijhoff publrs 1970; Lecturer in Modern History, Utrecht Univ. 1975–76; Sr Lecturer in Dutch History, Leiden Univ. 1976–94, Prof. of Central European Studies 1990–2010, Prof. Emer. 2010–, Prof. of Modern History 1994–2010, Prof. Emer. 2010–; Man. Ed. Tijdschrift voor Geschiedenis 1981–86; Fellow, Netherlands Inst. for Advanced Studies, Wassenaar 1987–88, 1993–94; Pres. Conseil Int. pour l'édition des oeuvres complètes d'Erasme 1998–; Pres. Soc. for Netherlandish Literature 1999–2003; Pres. Royal Netherlands Historical Soc. 2004–07; mem. Bd Inst. of Netherlands History 1989–2009; mem. Royal Netherlands Acad. of Arts and Sciences, Academia Europaea; Corresp. mem. Austrian Acad. of Sciences; Hon. mem. Soc. of Historians of the Czech Repub.; Österreichisches Ehrenkreuz für Wissenschaft und Kunst 1. Klasse (Austria). *Publications:* Komenský v Amsterodamu (with J. Polišenský) 1970, Bohemen en de Nederlanden in de zestiende eeuw 1975, Plakkaat van Verlatinge 1581 1979, Die Kultur des Humanismus 1998; numerous articles, mainly on 16th–17th century Dutch and Cen. European history of ideas and cultural history and 19th–20th century historiography; ed. and co-ed. of several books, including Gerhard Oestreich, Antiker Geist und moderner Staat bei Justus Lipsius 1989, Erasmianism Idea and Reality 1997, The World of Emperor Charles V 2004, Truth in Science, the Humanities, and Religion 2010. *Address:* Oranje Nassaulaan 27, 2361 LB Warmond, The Netherlands (home). *Telephone:* (71) 301-1407 (home). *Website:* www.universiteitleiden.nl/en/staffmembers/nicolette-mout (office).

MOUTARI, Kalla; Niger politician; *Minister of National Defence;* b. 1964, Kornaka, Dakoro Region; m. Kateri Clement; four s.; ed Univ. Abdou Moumouni, Niamey, Univ. Cheikh Anta Diop, Dakar; philosophy teacher, Tahoua City –1993; Mayor of Tessaoua 1993–96; teacher, Maradi Region –2002; worked with USAID –2011; Deputy Sec.-Gen. to the Presidency 2011–13; Gov., Zinder city 2013–16; Minister of Public Health –2016, of Nat. Defence 2016–. *Address:* Ministry of National Defence, BP 626, Niamey, Niger (office). *Telephone:* 20-72-20-76 (office). *Fax:* 20-72-40-78 (office).

MOUTAWAKIL, Nawal el-; Moroccan sports administrator, politician and fmr athlete; *Vice-President, International Olympic Committee;* b. 15 April 1962, Casablanca; m.; two c.; ed Iowa State Univ., USA; gold medallist, 400m hurdles, Olympic Games, Los Angeles 1988 (first Moroccan, African and Muslim woman to win Olympic Gold); Asst Coach, Iowa State Univ.; Dir Nat. School of Track and Field, Casablanca br. 1991; Vice-Pres. Moroccan Track and Field Fed. 1992; mem. Moroccan Nat. Olympic Cttee; Sec. of State for Sport and Youth 1997; Minister of Youth and Sports 2007–09; Sr Exec., Fondation Banque Marocaine du Commerce Exterieur; mem. Athletes' Comm., Int. Asscn Athletics Feds 1989–, mem. Council 1995–, mem. Devt Sub-Comm. for Women; mem. IOC (first Muslim woman) 1998–, mem. Electoral Coll., mem. IOC Exec. Bd 2008–12, Vice-Pres. IOC 2012–, Pres. Coordination Cttee for Games of XXXI Olympiad in 2016 in Rio de Janeiro, Brazil 2010–, mem. Radio and Television Comm. 2014–, Public Affairs and Social Development through Sport Comm. 2015–, Communications Comm. 2015–, Women in Sport Comm. 2015–; Founder-mem. and Pres. Moroccan Sport and Development Asscn 2002–; Founder-mem. Laureus World Sports Academy 2000–, Vice-Chair. 2004–; mem. Rassemblement national des indépendants; Chevalier, Ordre nat. du Mérite Exceptionnel 1983, Chevalier, Ordre nat. du Lion (Senegal) 1988, Commdr, Mérite National de l'Ordre 2004, Grand Officer, Nat. Order of Merit (Tunisia) 2005; named as one of Outstanding Arab Women 2008. *Address:* International Olympic Committee, Château de Vidy, Case postale 356, 1001 Lausanne, Switzerland (office). *Website:* www.olympic.org (office).

MOUTINOT, Laurent; Swiss lawyer and politician; b. 2 March 1953, Geneva; m. Suzanne Moutinot (deceased 2006); three c.; advocate, Geneva Bar 1978–97; Pres.

Asloca romande 1990–93, Vice-Pres. Asloca suisse 1990–97; Deputy, Grand Council of Geneva 1993–97, Leader of Parl. Group 1994–96; elected (Parti socialiste) to Council of State of Geneva, Head, Dept of Works and Housing 1997–2005, Head, Dept of Institutions 2005, Vice-Pres. 2001–02, Pres. 2002–03, 2007–08.

MOUTON, Jacques; French banker; *Honorary Chairman, Caisse Nationale des Caisses d'Epargne;* b. 1937; Chair. Supervisory Bd and Chair. Remuneration and Selection Cttee, Caisse Nationale des Caisses d'Epargne 2003–07, Hon. Chair. 2007–. *Address:* Caisse Nationale des Caisses d'Epargne, 50 avenue Pierre-Mendès, 75201 Paris Cedex 13, France (office). *Telephone:* 1-58-40-41-42 (office). *Fax:* 1-58-40-48-00 (office). *Website:* www.caisse-epargne.fr (office).

MOUTON, Jannie, BComm, CA; South African business executive; *Chairman, PSG Group Ltd;* b. 2 Oct. 1946, Carnavon; m. 1st Dana Mouton (died 2004); two s. one d.; m. 2nd Deidré Mouton; ed Univ. of Stellenbosch; started career as Financial Man., Federale Volksbeleggings Ltd; Finance Dir, Kanhym 1981–82; Co-founder and Man. Dir Senekal Mouton & Kitshoff Inc. 1982–95; f. PSG Group Ltd (fmrly PAG Ltd) 1995, currently Chair.; currently also Chair. (non-exec.) Paladin Capital Ltd, Zeder Investments Ltd; Founder-Chair. Capitec Bank 2001–07; Dir (non-exec.) Steinhoff International Holdings 2002–, Pioneer Food Group Ltd 2009–; Entrepreneur of The Year Award 2012. *Address:* PSG Group Limited, Ou Kollege, 35 Kerk Street, PO Box 7403, Stellenbosch, South Africa (office). *Telephone:* (21) 8879602 (office). *E-mail:* driesm@psggroup.co.za (office). *Website:* www.psggroup.co.za (office).

MOXLEY, John Howard, III, MD, FACP; American physician and business executive; *Managing Director, North American Health Care Division, Korn/Ferry International;* b. 10 Jan. 1935, Elizabeth, NJ; s. of John Howard Moxley, Jr and Cleopatra Mundy Moxley; m. Doris Banchik; three s.; ed Williams Coll. and Univ. of Colorado School of Medicine; hosp. posts 1961–63; Clinical Assoc., Nat. Cancer Inst., Solid Tumor Branch 1963–65; Sr Resident Physician, Peter Bent Brigham Hosp. 1965–66; mem. Lymphoma Task Force Nat. Cancer Inst. 1965–77; Instructor in Medicine and Asst to the Dean, Harvard Medical School 1966–69; Dean Univ. of Md School of Medicine and Assoc. Prof. of Medicine 1969–73; Vice-Chancellor for Health Sciences and Dean of School of Medicine, Univ. of California, San Diego and Assoc. Prof. of Medicine 1973–80; Asst Sec. of Defense for Health Affairs, Dept of Defense, Washington, DC 1979–81; Sr Vice-Pres., Corp. Planning and Alternative Services, American Medical Int. Inc. 1981–87; Pres. and CEO MetaMedical Inc., Beverly Hills, Calif. 1987–89; Man. Dir, N American Health Care Div., Korn/Ferry Int. 1989–; Dir Henry M. Jackson Foundation for the Advancement of Mil. Medicine 1983, Naval Studies Bd; Dir Nat. Fund for Medical Educ. 1986–, Chair. 1993–; Fellow, American Fed. for Clinical Research; mem. Inst. of Medicine (NAS), American Soc. of Clinical Oncology, American Medical Asscn; Sec. of Defense Medal for Distinguished Public Service and other awards. *Publications:* numerous papers in scientific journals. *Address:* Korn/Ferry International, 1900 Avenue of the Stars, Suite 2600, Los Angeles, CA 90067 (office); 2408 Latigo Drive, Solvang, CA 93463, USA (home). *Telephone:* (310) 200-1296 (office). *E-mail:* moxleyj@kornferry.com (office). *Website:* www.kornferry.com (office).

MOXON, (Edward) Richard, MB, BChir, FRS, FRCP, FMedSci; British medical doctor and academic; *Professor Emeritus of Paediatrics, University of Oxford;* b. 16 July 1941, Leeds; s. of Gerald Richard Moxon and Margaret Forster Mohun; m. Marianne Graham 1973; two s. one d.; ed Shrewsbury School, St John's Coll., Cambridge and St Thomas' Hosp. Medical School, London; with Hosp. for Sick Children, Great Ormond St, London 1969; Research Fellow in Infectious Diseases, Children's Hosp. Medical Center, Boston, Mass, USA 1971–74; Asst Prof. of Pediatrics, Johns Hopkins Hosp., Baltimore, Md, USA 1974–80, Dir Eudowood Pediatric Infectious Diseases Unit 1982–84; Action Research Prof. of Paediatrics, Univ. of Oxford 1984–2008, now Prof. Emer.; Group Leader, Molecular Infectious Diseases Group (Pathogenic Bacteria), The Weatherall Inst. of Molecular Medicine, John Radcliffe Hosp. 1988–2008; Visiting Scientist, Dept of Molecular Biology, Washington Univ., St Louis, Mo. 1990–91; Fellow, Jesus Coll. Oxford 1984–; Founder and Chair. Oxford Vaccine Group 1994–; mem. Steering Group, Encapsulated Bacteria, WHO 1987–93; Chair. MRC Sub-cttee Polysaccharide Vaccines 1986–90; Convenor, BPA Immunology and Infectious Diseases Group 1984–89; mem. American Soc. Clinical Investigation; Founding Fellow, Acad. of Medical Sciences, UK 1998; Fellow, Infectious Diseases Soc. of America, American Soc. Pediatric Research, Royal Coll. of Paediatrics and Child Health, Acad. of Medical Sciences; Mitchell Lecturer, Royal Coll. of Physicians 1992, Bazely Oration, Annual Gen. Meeting of Australian Soc. for Microbiology, Perth 1993, Blackfan Lecturer, Boston Children's Hosp. 1994, Blackfan Lecturer, Children's Hosp. Medical Alumni Council 125th Anniversary Celebration, Boston, Mass 1994, Bob Deich Memorial Lecturer, Univ. of Rochester, NY 1995, ASM Div. Lecturer, Gen. Meeting 1997, Teale Lecturer, Royal Coll. of Physicians 1998, Burroughs-Wellcome Lecturer, Univ. of Pennsylvania 1998, Dolman Lecturer, Univ. of British Columbia 1999, J.H.P. Jonxis Lecturer, Beatrix Children's Hosp., Groningen, Netherlands 2001, Anthony Dawson Lecturer, St Bartholomew's and London Hosp. 2003, Bill Marshall Award Lecturer, European Soc. of Paediatric Research, Tampere, Finland 2004, Hattie Alexander Memorial Lecturer, Columbia Univ., New York 2005, Excellence Award, European Soc. for Clinical Microbiology and Infectious Diseases, Munich 2007, Fred Griffith Review Lecturer, Soc. for Gen. Microbiology, Edinburgh 2007. *Publications:* Neonatal Infections (with D. Isaacs) 1991, A Practical Approach to Paediatric Infectious Diseases (with D. Isaacs) 1996, Longman Handbook of Neonatal Infections (with D. Isaacs) 1999; Modern Vaccines (editorial adviser) 1990, Progress in Vaccinology (ed.) 2000; more than 400 scientific articles on infections, molecular basis of bacterial virulence and vaccines published in major peer-reviewed journals. *Leisure interests:* music, literature, wine, sports. *Address:* Department of Paediatrics, The Weatherall Institute of Molecular Medicine, University of Oxford, John Radcliffe Hospital, Headington, Oxford, OX3 9DS (office); 9A North Parade Avenue, Oxford, OX2 6LX, England (home). *Telephone:* (1865) 222307 (office). *Fax:* (1865) 222444 (office). *E-mail:* richard.moxon@paediatrics.ox.ac.uk (office). *Website:* www.imm.ox.ac.uk (office).

MOYANA, Kombo James, MA, MPhil, PhD; Zimbabwean banker; *Executive Secretary, Common Market of Eastern and Southern Africa (COMESA) Clearing House;* b. 4 July 1942, Chipinge; m.; one s. three d.; ed Columbia Univ., New York, USA; Research Fellow, Inst. de Développement Economique et de Planification, Dakar 1972; Fellow, UNITAR, New York 1973; int. finance economist, Div. of Money, Finance and Devt UNCTAD, New York and Geneva 1974–80; seconded to Ministry of Econ. Planning and Devt of Govt of Zimbabwe 1980; Deputy Gov. Reserve Bank of Zimbabwe 1980, Gov. 1983–93; Alt. Gov., IMF 1983–93; Pres. Inst. of Bankers (Zimbabwe) 1985–86; Exec. Sec. Preferential Trading Area of Eastern, Cen. and Southern African States –1991; CEO Trade & Investment Bank Ltd; Chair. Asscn of African Cen. Banks 1991–93; Exec. Sec. Common Market of Eastern and Southern Africa (COMESA) Clearing House 2009–. *Leisure interest:* farming. *Address:* COMESA Centre, Ben Bella Road, Lusaka, Zambia (office). *Telephone:* (211) 229725 (office); (211) 225107 (office). *E-mail:* comesa@comesa.int (office). *Website:* www.comesa.int (office).

MOYANO, Hugo; Argentine trade union official; *President, Club Atletico Independiente;* b. 9 Jan. 1944, La Plata; Rep., Mar del Plata Div., Sindicato de Choferes de Camiones (trade union) 1962, Sec.-Gen. 1962–72, Sec.-Gen. Sindicato de Choferes de Camiones, Buenos Aires 1987–91, 1991–2003; Sec.-Gen. Mar del Plata Br., Partido Justicialista (PJ) 1983, becoming Sec. and Vice-Pres. Parl. Transport Comm.; Global Vice-Pres. Road Transport Div., Int. Fed. of Transport Workers 1998–; Sec.-Gen. Confederación Argentina de Trabajadores del Transporte 2003–05; Sec.-Gen. Confederación General del Trabajo (CGT) 2005–16; Pres. Club Atletico Independiente 2014–. *Address:* Club Atletico Independiente, Avenida Miter 470, Avellaneda, Buenos Aires, Argentina (office). *Telephone:* (11) 4229-7600 (office). *E-mail:* avellaneda@clubaindependiente.com (office). *Website:* www.clubaindependiente.com (office).

MOYERS, William (Bill) D., FAAS; American journalist and broadcaster; *Executive Editor, Public Affairs Television, Inc.;* b. 5 June 1934, Hugo, Okla; s. of Henry Moyers and Ruby Johnson; m. Judith Davidson 1954; two s. one d.; ed Univ. of Texas, Univ. of Edinburgh, UK, Southwestern Baptist Theological Seminary; Exec. Asst to Senator Lyndon Johnson 1959–60; Assoc. Dir US Peace Corps 1961–63, Deputy Dir 1963; Special Asst to Pres. Johnson 1963–66, Press Sec. to Pres. 1965–66; Publr of Newsday, Long Island, NY 1966–70; host of This Week, weekly current affairs TV programme 1970; Ed.-in-Chief Bill Moyers Journal, Public Broadcasting Service (PBS) 1971–76, 1978–81, 2007–10, Moyers & Company 2012–15; Contrib. Newsweek 1974–76; Chief Corresp. CBS Reports 1976–78, Sr News Analyst, CBS News 1981–86; Exec. Ed. Public Affairs TV Inc. 1987–; Pres. Florence and John Schumann Foundation (now Schumann Center for Media and Democracy) 1991–; mem. American Philosophical Soc.; Emmy Awards 1983–90, Gold Baton Award 1991, 1999, American Jewish Cttee Religious Liberty Award 1995, Walter Cronkite Award 1995, Fred Friendly First Amendment Award 1995, Charles Frankel Prize 1997, George Peabody Award 2000. *Television includes:* A Walk Through the 20th Century 1982–84, Joseph Campbell and the Power of Myth 1988, Becoming American: Personal Journeys 2003, Bill Moyers on Faith and Reason 2006. *Publications include:* Listening to America 1971, The Secret Government 1988, Joseph Campbell and the Power of Myth 1988, A World of Ideas 1989, Healing and the Mind 1993, Genesis: A Living Conversion 1996, Fooling with Words 1999, Moyers on America 2004, Moyers on Democracy 2008, Bill Moyers Journal: The Conversation Continues 2011. *Address:* Public Affairs Television Inc., 250 West 57th Street, Suite 718, New York, NY 10107, USA. *Website:* www.billmoyers.com.

MOYNIHAN, Brian Thomas, JD; American lawyer and banking executive; *Chairman and CEO, Bank of America Corporation;* b. 9 Oct. 1959, Marietta, Ohio; s. of; m. Susan E. Berry; three c.; ed Brown Univ., Univ. of Notre Dame Law School; with Edwards & Angell LLP, Providence, RI –1993; joined FleetBoston Financial as Deputy Gen. Counsel 1993, Exec. Vice-Pres. 1999–2004, with responsibility for brokerage and wealth man. divs 2000–04, joined Bank of America following co.'s merger with FleetBoston Financial 2004, led several lines of business, including Consumer and Small Business Banking, Pres. Global Wealth and Investment Man. 2004–08, Pres. Global Corp. and Investment Banking 2007–08, CEO Merrill Lynch after its sale to Bank of America 2008, Gen. Counsel, Bank of America Corpn 2008–09, mem. Bd of Dirs and CEO 2010–, Chair. 2014–, Chair. Global Diversity and Inclusion Council; mem. Bd of Dirs YouthBuild Boston, Boys and Girls Clubs of Boston, Nat. Museum of African American History and Culture; fmr Chair. Travelers Aid Soc. of Rhode Island, Providence Haitian Project, Inc.; Trustee, Corpn of Brown Univ. 2010–; Freedom Award, Dept of Defense 2013. *Address:* Bank of America Corporate Center, 100 North Tryon Street, Charlotte, NC 28255, USA (office). *Telephone:* (704) 386-1845 (office). *Fax:* (704) 386-6699 (office). *E-mail:* info@bankofamerica.com (office). *Website:* www.bankofamerica.com (office).

MOYNIHAN, 4th Baron, cr. 1929; **Colin Berkeley Moynihan,** MA; British business executive and organization official; b. 13 Sept. 1955, Ashtead, Surrey, England; m. Gaynor-Louise Metcalf 1992; two s. one d.; ed Monmouth School, Univ. Coll., Oxford; World Gold Medal for Lightweight Rowing, Int. Rowing Fed. 1978, World Silver Medal for Rowing 1981, Silver Medal for Rowing, Olympics 1980; Personal Asst to Chair. Tate and Lyle Ltd 1978–80, Man. Tate and Lyle Agribusiness 1980–82; CEO Ridgways Tea and Coffee Merchants 1982–83, Chair. 1983–87; Minister for Sport 1987–90; Chair. CMA Consultants 1993–; Man. Dir Ind. Power Corpn plc 1996–2001; Chair. and CEO Consort Resources Group 2000–03; Exec. Chair. Clipper Windpower Europe Ltd 2004–, Dir Clipper Windpower PLC 2005–; Dir Energreen AS, Zeropex AS, Rowan Companies Inc. 1996–; Chair. British Olympic Asscn 2005–12; Gov. Sports Aid Foundation (London and SE) 1980–82; mem. Court of Assistants, Worshipful Co. of Haberdashers; mem. Advisory Bd, Conservative Friends of Int. Devt, British Expertise; Pres. Welsh Amateur Rowing Asscn; Vice-Pres. British Wind Energy Asscn; Dir, Int. Inspiration Bd; Chair. British Ski & Snowboarding; Trustee, Canoeing Foundation; Freeman of the City of London 1978. *Leisure interests:* reading, sport, music. *Address:* House of Lords, Westminster, London, SW1A 0PW, England (office). *E-mail:* c.moynihan@cmagroup.org.uk (office). *Website:* www.buckthornpartners.com (office); www.parliament.uk/biographies/lords/lord-moynihan/924 (office).

MOYO, Jonathan, MPA, PhD; Zimbabwean politician; b. 12 Jan. 1957; m.; fmr mem. Zimbabwe African Nat. Union-Patriotic Front (ZANU-PF); Minister of State for Information and Publicity 2000–05; fmr mem. Pres. Robert Mugabe's 'Gang of Four' politicians; architect of Zimbabwe's highly controlled press regime; mem.

Parl. (ind.) for Tsholotsho 2015–17; Minister of Information and Communications Technology 2013–15; Minister of Higher and Tertiary Education, Science and Technology Development July–Nov. 2017. *Leisure interests:* philosophy, classics, music, composition, tennis, scriptwriting.

MOYO, Maj.-Gen. Sibusiso Busi, MBA, PhD; Zimbabwean politician and fmr army officer; *Minister of Foreign Affairs and International Trade;* b. 1960; ed Univ. of Zimbabwe, Zimbabwe Open Univ.; fmr mem. Zimbabwe People's Revolutionary Army (Zipra, armed wing of Zimbabwe African People's Union, Zapu); fmr leader green beret squad elite military unit; fmr commdr, mil. operations in Midlands Prov.; rank of Maj.-Gen. 2016; fmr mem. Bd of Dirs Zimbabwe Broadcasting Holdings; Minister of Foreign Affairs and Int. Trade 2017–. *Address:* Ministry of Foreign Affairs and International Trade, Munhumutapa Builindg, cnr Samora Machel Avenue and Sam Nujoma Street, POB 4240, Causeway, Harare, Zimbabwe (office). *Telephone:* (4) 794681 (office). *Fax:* (4) 705161 (office). *E-mail:* mfa@zimfa .gov.zw (office). *Website:* www.zimfa.gov.zw (office).

MOYO, S(imon) K(haya); Zimbabwean politician and diplomatist; *National Chairman, Zimbabwe African National Union-Patriotic Front (ZANU—PF);* b. 1945; fmr mem. of Parl. (ZANU—PF) for Bulilima-mangwe South, fmr ZANU (PF) Politburo Deputy-Sec. for Legal Affairs, currently Nat. Chair. ZANU—PF; Minister of Transport and Energy 1996, of Mines, Environment and Tourism 1998, Sr Minister of State 2013–; Amb. to South Africa 2000–11. *Address:* Zimbabwe African National Union-Patriotic Front (ZANU—PF), Corner Rotten Row and Samora Machel Avenue, POB 4530, Harare, Zimbabwe (office). *Telephone:* (4) 753329 (office). *Fax:* (4) 774146 (office). *Website:* www.zanupf.org .zw (office).

MOZILO, Angelo R., BSc; American financial services industry executive; b. 1938, New York, NY; ed Fordham Univ.; Co-founder Countrywide Financial Corpn 1969, Chair. and CEO –2008 (following takeover by Bank of America); Co-founder IndyMac Bank (f. as Countrywide Mortgage Investment, spun off as ind. bank 1997, collapsed and seized by fed. regulators July 2008); Chair. Countryside Home Loans Inc.; Pres. Mortgage Bankers Asscn of America (MBA) 1991–92, mem. Bd of Dirs from 1992; mem. Bd of Dirs, Jt Center for Housing Studies, Harvard Univ., The Home Depot from 2006; mem. Bd of Trustees, Nat. Housing Endowment, Fordham Univ., Gonzaga Univ., St Francis High School, Calif.; charged by US Securities and Exchange Comm. (SEC) with insider trading and securities fraud 2009, reached settlement with SEC and agreed to pay $67.5 million in fines and accept lifetime ban from serving as an officer or director of any public co. Oct. 2010, US Govt dropped its criminal investigation into facts behind civil settlement Feb. 2011; Hon. LLD (Pepperdine Univ.); Ellis Island Medal of Honor, Albert Schweitzer Award, Boy Scouts of America James E. West Fellowship Award, Jane Wyman Humanitarian Service Award, Arthritis Foundation, Special Achievement Award for Humanitarian Service, Nat. Italian American Foundation, Housing Person of the Year Award 2004; inducted into Hall of Fame, Nat. Asscn of Home Builders. *Address:* 2816 Ladbrook Way, Westlake Village, CA 91361, USA.

MPAHLWA, Mandisi Bongani Mabuto; South African politician and diplomatist; *High Commissioner to Mozambique;* b. 21 Aug. 1960; ed Mangosuthu Univ. of Tech., Univ. of London, UK; went into exile 1985, did voluntary work for African Nat. C; returned to SA 1990; Deputy Minister of Finance 1999–2004; Minister of Trade and Industry 2004–09; Amb. to Russian Fed. 2011–15, High Commr to Mozambique 2015–. *Address:* South African High Commission, Av. Eduardo Mondlane 41, CP 1120, Maputo, Mozambique (office). *Telephone:* 21243000 (office). *Fax:* 21493029 (office). *E-mail:* sahcmaputoenquiries@dirco.gov.za (office). *Website:* www.dirco.gov.za (home).

MPANGO, Philip; Tanzanian economist and politician; *Minister of Finance and Planning;* b. 14 July 1957; fmr Exec. Sec., Nat. Planning Comm.; fmr Deputy Perm. Sec., Ministry of Finance and Econ. Affairs; fmr Personal Asst to Pres. for Econ. Affairs and later Head of Pres.'s Econ. Advisory Unit; fmr Sr Economist, World Bank; Prin. Supervisor for preparation of Nat. Five-Year 2011–2016 Devt Plan; Commr-Gen. Tanzania Revenue Authority –2015; nominated mem. Nat. Ass. (parl.); Minister of Finance and Planning 2015–; Ex-Officio Mem. Bd of Govs, African Devt Bank 2015–, Multilateral Investment Guarantee Agency 2015–, World Bank Group 2015–, Trade and Devt Bank 2015–; Ex-Officio Mem. of Governing Council, East African Devt Bank 2015–; mem. Joint World Bank-IMF Devt Cttee; mem. Chama Cha Mapinduzi (CCM, Revolutionary Party of Tanzania). *Publications include:* Some Reflections on Semi-Privatization of Customs Administration in Tanzania 1996, Macro-Micro Linkages in the Fight Against Poverty: Missing Links and Enabling Bridges 2004. *Address:* Ministry of Finance and Planning, Treasury Square Building, 18 Jakaya Kikwete Road, POB 2802, 40468 Dodoma, Tanzania (office). *Telephone:* (26) 2963101 (office). *Fax:* (26) 2963109 (office). *Website:* www.mof.go.tz (office).

MPHOKO, Phelekezela; Zimbabwean agriculturalist, politician, diplomatist and fmr military commander; *Second Vice-President;* b. 11 June 1940, Gwizane, S Rhodesia (now Zimbabwe); m. Luaurinda Mphoko; one s. two d.; ed Tsholotsho Agricultural Breeding and Experimental School; studied military science and photojournalism in USSR; joined Nat. Democratic Party 1960s; Zimbabwe People's Revolutionary Army (ZIPRA) commdr in charge of logistics during Zimbabwe war of independence 1972–78; re-assigned from mil. to diplomatic missions 1978, including as Zimbabwe African People's Union (ZAPU) Rep. to Mozambique; Deputy Dir, Demobilisation Directorate, Ministry of Labour and Social Welfare early 1980s; fmr Amb. to Botswana, to Russia 2006, to South Africa 2011–14; Second Vice-Pres. 2014–, also Minister of Nat. Healing, Peace and Reconciliation 2014–; Chair. Choppies Zimbabwe (supermarket chain) –2014; mem. Zimbabwe African Nat. Union-Patriotic Front. *Leisure interests:* golf, jazz, cooking. *Address:* Office of the Vice-President, Munhumutapa Bldg, Samora Machel Avenue, Private Bag 7700, Causeway, Harare, Zimbabwe (office). *Telephone:* (4) 707091 (office). *E-mail:* info@vpmujuruoffice.gov.zw (office). *Website:* www.vpmujuruoffice.gov.zw (office).

MPOMBO, George W.; Zambian politician; mem. Nat. Ass. (Movt for Multi-party Democracy—MMD) 2001–, Minister of Energy and Water Devt 2003–05, Minister for Copperbelt Prov. 2005–06, Minister of Defence 2006–09 (resgnd). *Address:* c/o Ministry of Defence, PO Box 31931, Lusaka, Zambia (office).

MPOUHO-EPIGAT, Ernest; Gabonese politician and fmr diplomatist; b. 1967; s. of Julien Mpouho-Epigat (fmr Minister of Nat. Defence); nephew of Ali Bongo (Pres. of Gabon); ed Université Paris-1 Hautes Etudes Politiques, Tolbiac, France; fmr Chair. Société gabonaise de services (pvt. security firm); mem. Nat. Ass. (Parl.) for Bongoville; Minister of Nat. Defence 2014–15; mem. Parti Démocratique Gabonais. *Address:* c/o Ministry of National Defence, BP 13493, Libreville, Gabon (office).

MQULWANA, Koleka Anita, BA, HDipEd; South African politician and diplomatist; *High Commissioner to Kenya;* ed Univ. of the Western Cape, courses in Australia and NZ (Certificate in Int. Governance, Man. Skills, Basic Financial Skills, Procurement Policy, Risk Man. and Governance); mem. Western Cape Prov. Parl. –2011, mem. Standing Cttee on Finance 1999–2002, Standing Cttee on Public Accounts 1999–2004, Chair. Standing Cttee on Local Govt, Environmental Affairs and Devt Planning 2001–04, mem. Exec. Council (MEC) for Social Devt 2004–08, MEC for Public Works and Transport 2008–09, Spokesperson on Public Works and Transport 2009–10; High Commr to Australia (also accred to Samoa, Cook Islands, Tonga, Kiribati, Nauru and Vanuatu, Niue, Tuvalu, Palau, Marshall Islands, Federated States of Micronesia, Tokelau, Solomon Islands) 2011–15, to Kenya 2015–. *Address:* South African High Commission, PO Box 42441, Third Floor, Roshanmaer Place, Lenana Road, 00100 Nairobi, Kenya (office). *Telephone:* (20) 2827100 (office). *Fax:* (20) 2827236 (office). *E-mail:* sahc@africaonline.co.ke (office); nairobi@foreign.gov.za (office).

MRAD, Abd ar-Rahim; Lebanese politician and university administrator; *President, Lebanese International University;* mem. Lebanese Parl. 1990–2000; fmr Minister of Educ.; f. Lebanese International Univ. 2001, currently Pres.; Minister of National Defence 2004–05. *Address:* Office of the President, Lebanese International University, Mouseitbeh, PO Box: 146404, Mazraa, Beirut, Lebanon (office). *Website:* www.liu.edu.lb (office).

MRAMBA, Basil; Tanzanian politician; b. 15 May 1940; ed Makerere Univ., City Univ. Grad. School, London, UK, Harvard Grad. School of Business, USA; Man. Asst, Williamson Diamond Mwadui 1964–69; Manpower Devt Dir Nat. Devt Corpn 1969–72; Dir Gen. Small Scale Industries Org-SIDO 1973–80; mem. Parl. 1980–95; Regional Commr, Mbeya Region 1995–2000; Minister of Trade and Industry 1995–2000, 2006–08; Minister of Finance 2000–06; Minister of Infrastructure Devt 2006.

MRAMOR, Dušan, PhD; Slovenian economist, academic and politician; b. 1 Nov. 1953, Ljubljana; s. of Ivan Mramor and Marija Mramor; m. Dr Nezka Mramor Kosta; one s. one d.; ed Univ. of Ljubljana; Prof. of Finance, Faculty of Econs, Univ. of Ljubljana 2000–, Assoc. Dean, Faculty of Econs 1997–2001, Dean 2007–13, Chair. Bd of Univ. 2000–02, 2009–13, Pres. Human Resources Cttee; Recurring Visiting Prof., Cen. European Univ., Budapest, Hungary; Research Assoc. and Visiting Scholar, School of Business, Indiana Univ., USA; fmr Visiting Prof., Wirtschaftuniversität, Vienna, Austria; Head of Ministry of Finance's Group for Capital Market Devt Strategy 2001–02, Head of Advisory Group of Ministry of the Economy for the Privatisation of the Steel Industry 2001, Advisory Group for the Privatization of Insurance Cos 2002, Minister of Finance 2002–04, 2014–16; mem. Privatization Cttee of NKBM 2001–02; fmr Vice-Chair. Devt Cttee of the Prime Minister; fmr Pres. Expert Council Agency for the Securities Market; fmr Vice-Pres. Bd of Dirs SKB bank; Vice-Pres. Bd Initial Accreditation Cttee Asscn to Advance Collegiate Schools of Business; fmr Vice-Pres. European Finance Asscn; fmr mem. Expert Council Slovenian Inst. of Auditing, Co-ordinating Cttee Slovenian Asscn of Economists, Slovenian Asscn of Accountants, EIASM, Strategic Council of the Pres. of Slovenia, Slovenian Accounting Standards Bd; fmr mem. Supervisory Bd, Abanka; mem. Stranka Modernega Centra (SMC—Modern Centre Party); Best Financial Expert 2003 (award by Kapital) Best Financial Expert 2004 (Kapital), Second Place, Best Paper, Faculty of Econs, Univ. of Ljubljana 2010, Banker Magazine European Finance Minister of the Year 2016. *Publications:* numerous papers in professional journals on transition finance and economics. *Leisure interests:* skiing, basketball, mountaineering. *Address:* Faculty of Economics, University of Ljubljana, Kardeljeva ploscad 17, Ljubljana 1000, Slovenia (office). *Telephone:* (1) 5892400 (office). *Fax:* (1) 5892698 (office). *E-mail:* dusan.mramor@ef.uni-lj.si (office). *Website:* www.ef.uni-lj.si (office).

MRKIĆ, Ivan; Serbian diplomatist; b. 30 May 1953, Belgrade; m. Ivona Mrkić; two s.; ed Univ. of Belgrade; joined Fed. Secr. for Foreign Affairs 1978, Officer, Directorate for Int. Orgs 1979–82, Attaché (political affairs), Mission of the Socialist Fed. Repub. (SFR) of Yugoslavia to UN 1982–86, Adviser and later Asst Chief of Directorate, Sector for Multilateral Activities 1990–92, also Minister-Counsellor, Mission of SFR Yugoslavia to EC, Brussels 1990–92; Chef de Cabinet of Dobrica Ćosić (first Pres. of Fed. Repub. of Yugoslavia) 1992–93; Chargé d'affaires a.i., later Amb. to Cyprus 1993–99, Deputy Head of Sector for Bilateral Relations 1999, Asst Fed. Minister for Foreign Affairs and Head of Sector for Bilateral Relations 2000–01, Amb. at Fed. Ministry of Foreign Affairs 2001–03, at Ministry of Foreign Affairs of Serbia-Montenegro 2003–04, mem. Group of Ambs for special and ad hoc affairs 2004; Pres. Nat. Comm. for implementation of the Chemical Weapons Convention 2005; Amb. of Serbia to Japan 2006–11, Sec. of State, Ministry of Foreign Affairs 2011–12, Minister of Foreign Affairs 2012–14. *Address:* c/o Ministry of Foreign Affairs, 11000 Belgrade, Kneza Miloša 24–26, Serbia. *E-mail:* mfa@mfa.rs.

MROCZKOWSKI, Marek, MEconSc; Polish business executive; ed Warsaw School of Econs; with Polski Koncern Naftowy ORLEN SA 1994–2001; Pres. and CEO, POLKOMTEL SA 2001–02; Pres. and CEO, ELANA SA, Torun 2003–04; apptd CEO, Unipetrol a.s., Vice-Chair., Bd of Dirs.

MSUYA, Cleopa David, BA; Tanzanian civil servant (retd) and politician; b. 4 Nov. 1931, Chomvu Usangi, Mwanga Dist; s. of David Kilenga and Maria Ngido; m. Rhoda Christopher 1959; four s. two d.; ed Old Moshi and Tabora Secondary Schools, Makerere Univ. Coll., Uganda; Civil Service, Community Devt Officer 1956–61, Commr for Community Devt 1961–64, Prin. Sec. to Ministry of Community Devt and Nat. Culture 1964, to Ministries of Land Settlement and Water Devt 1965–67, to Ministry of Econ. Affairs and Devt Planning 1967–70 and to Treas. 1970–72; Minister of Finance 1972–75, 1983–85, for Finance, Econ. Affairs and Planning 1985–89, for Industries 1975–80, for Industries and Trade 1990–95; Prime Minister of Tanzania 1980–83, 1994–95; First Vice-Pres. 1994–95;

mem. Nat. Ass. 1995–2000; has remained active in Chama Cha Mapinduzi (CCM) party, fmr mem. Nat. Exec. Cttee; fmr Chair. Kilimanjaro Devt Forum; Gov. ADB, IMF; mem. Bd Dirs of several public corpns. *Address:* c/o Office of the Prime Minister, PO Box 239, Zanzibar, Tanzania. *Website:* ccm.or.tz.

MSUYA, Joyce, MSc, EGPM; Tanzanian microbiologist, environmental scientist and UN official; *Acting Executive Director, United Nations Environment Programme;* b. 1968; m.; two c.; ed Univ. of Strathclyde, Scotland, Univ. of Ottawa, Canada, Harvard Business School, USA, Johns Hopkins Univ., USA; joined World Bank Group (WBG) as Health Specialist 1998, apptd Advisor to the Sr Vice Pres. 2001, Coordinator for East Asia & the Pacific, World Bank Inst., China 2011, Special Rep. and Head, WBG, Republic of Korea 2014–17; Prin. Strategy Officer, Dept of Manufacturing, Agribusiness & Services, International Finance Corporation (IFC) 2005–11; Deputy Exec. Dir, UNEP 2018, Exec. Dir (Acting) Nov. 2018–, Asst Sec.-Gen., UN 2018–. *Address:* UN Environment Programme, POB.30552, 00100, Nairobi, Kenya (office). *E-mail:* unenvironment-executiveoffice@un.org (office). *Website:* www.unenvironment.org (office).

MSWATI III, HM The King of Eswatini; Makhosetive; b. (HRH Prince Makhosetive Dlamini), 19 April 1968, Manzini; s. of King Sobhuza II and Queen Ntombi Laftwala; m. to 15 wives (Emakhosikati); 30 c.; ed Sherborne School, UK; Crown Prince Sept. 1983; crowned King of Swaziland (renamed Eswatini 2018) 25 April 1986; Grand Master, Royal Order of King Sobhuza II 1986, Grand Master, Royal Order of the Ndlovukazi 2002, Grand Master, Royal Order of the Crown 2002, Grand Master, Royal Family Order of Mswati III 2002, Grand Master, Mil. Order of weSwatini 2002; Kt Grand Cross, Order of Good Hope (South Africa) 1995. *Leisure interests:* swimming, rugby. *Address:* Lozitha Palace, Mbabane, Eswatini.

MTETWA, Beatrice, LLB; Zimbabwean lawyer; ed Univ. of Botswana; lawyer, Kantor and Immerman (law firm), Harare; Dir The Zimbabwe Independent newspaper; lawyer for Foreign Corresps Asscn of Zimbabwe; Council mem. Law Soc. of Zimbabwe, currently Pres.; mem. Zimbabwe Lawyers for Human Rights; arrested for allegedly 'obstructing the course of justice' March 2013, released on bail; Hon. LLD (Rhodes Univ.) 2016; Human Rights Lawyer of the Year 2003, Cttee to Protect Journalists Int. Press Freedom Award 2005, Bindmans Law and Campaigning Award 2006, Burton Benjamin Award 2008, International Human Rights Award, ABA 2010, Inamori Ethics Prize, Case Western Reserve Univ. 2011, Int. Women of Courage Award 2014.

MU'ALLA, HH Sheikh Saud bin Rashid al-, (Ruler of Umm al-Qaiwain); United Arab Emirates ruler; b. 1 Oct. 1952; s. of Rashid bin Ahmed Al Mu'alla (Ruler of Umm al-Qaiwain); ed Cairo Univ., Egypt; apptd Third Sec., Ministry of Foreign Affairs 1973; apptd Commdr Umm al-Qaiwain Nat. Guard as Col; apptd Head of Emiri Court (Diwani) 1979; apptd by father as Crown Prince 1982; succeeded to the throne upon the death of his father 2009, mem. Supreme Council of the Union 2009–; has served as Chair. of numerous cos including National Bank of Umm al-Qaiwain, Umm al-Qaiwain Gas Co., Umm al-Qaiwain Cement Co.

MUASHER, Marwan Jamil, MS, PhD; Jordanian politician and diplomatist; *Vice-President for Studies, Carnegie Endowment for International Peace;* b. 14 June 1956, Amman; two c.; ed American Univ. of Beirut, Lebanon, Purdue Univ., USA; Asst Research Engineer, Univ. of Petroleum and Minerals, Saudi Arabia 1983–84; Dir Computer Centre, Jordan Electric Power Co. 1984; Sr Consultant Special System Co. 1984–85; Head, Computer Unit and Monitory System, Ministry of Planning 1985–87, Dir Socio-Econ. Information Centre, Nat. Information System 1987–90; Press Adviser to Prime Minister 1990–91; Head, Jordan Information Bureau, USA 1991–94; Amb. to Israel 1995–96, to USA and Mexico 1997–2002; Minister of Information 1996, of Foreign Affairs 2002–04; Deputy Prime Minister and Minister of State for Prime Ministry Affairs and Govt Performance 2004–05; Senator 2006–07; Sr Vice-Pres. for External Affairs, Communications and UN Affairs, World Bank, Washington, DC 2007–10; Vice-Pres. for Studies, Carnegie Endowment for Int. Peace 2010–; Sr Fellow, Jackson Inst. for Global Affairs, Yale Univ.; political columnist, Jordan Times 1983–90; mem. Advisory Council, The Hague Inst. for Global Justice 2011–; Al-Kawkab Medal, First Order (Jordan) 2000; Order of the Star of Jordan, Dr hc (Purdue Univ.) 1999, Jordanian Independence Medal 2000, Diplomat of the Year Award, LA Int. Affairs Council 2000. *Publications:* The Arab Center: The Promise of Moderation 2008, The Second Arab Awakening: And the Battle for Pluralism 2014. *Address:* Carnegie Endowment for International Peace, 1779 Massachusetts Avenue NW, Washington, DC 20036-2103, USA (office). *Telephone:* (202) 939-2275 (office); (202) 483-7600 (switchboard) (office). *Fax:* (202) 483-1840 (office). *E-mail:* mmuasher@ceip.org (office). *Website:* carnegieendowment.org/experts/?fa=563 (office).

MUBARAK, Fahd ibn Abdullah al-, BSc, MBA, PhD; Saudi Arabian academic and fmr central banker; b. Eastern Prov.; ed Univ. of Houston, USA; began career as Asst Prof., King Fahd Univ. of Petroleum and Minerals; six years as mem. Saudi Arabian Consultative Council (Shoura Council), fmr Vice-Chair. Econ. and Energy Cttee; fmr Gen. Man. Rana Investment Co.; Chair. Bd of Dirs Saudi Stock Exchange (Tadawul); Co-founder and shareholder Amwal Al Khaleej (alternative investment firm); fmr Chair. and Man. Dir Morgan Stanley Saudi Arabia; Gov. Saudi Arabian Monetary Agency 2011–16; fmr Dir Mobily (telecommunications co.), Majid Al Futtaim Holding LLC (also known as Majid Al Futtaim Group LLC); Ind. Dir, Saudi Hollandi Bank –2011; mem. numerous nat., econ. and charitable cttees. *Address:* c/o Saudi Arabian Monetary Agency, PO Box 2992, Riyadh 11169, Saudi Arabia (office).

MUBARAK, (Muhammad) Hosni, BMilSci, BA; Egyptian air force officer and fmr head of state; b. 4 May 1928, Kafr El-Moseilha, Minuffya Governorate; m. Suzanne Sabet; two s.; ed Mil. Acad., Air Acad.; joined Air Force 1950, Lecturer Air Force Acad. 1952–59; Commdr Cairo West Air Base 1964; Dir-Gen. Air Acad. 1967–69; Air Force Chief of Staff 1969–72; C-in-C 1972–75; promoted to Lt-Gen. 1974; Vice-Pres. of Egypt 1975–81; Pres. 1981–2011 (stepped down following popular protests); Vice-Pres. Nat. Democratic Party (NDP) 1979, Pres. 1982; mem. Higher Council for Nuclear Energy 1975; Sec.-Gen. NDP and Political Bureau 1981–82, Chair. 1982; Chair. OAU 1989–90, 1993–94, Arab Summit 1996–, GI5 1998, 2000; Pres. Emergency Arab Summit 2000, D-8 Summit 2001, COMESA Summit 2001; Order of Star of Honour 1964, 1974, Medal of the Star of Sinai of the

First Order 1983 and numerous other foreign decorations; Dr hc (Bulgaria) 1998, (Beijing) 1999, (St Johns) 1999, (George Washington) 1999; Louise Michel Prize 1990, Prize of Democratic Human Rights, Social and Political Studies Centre, Paris 1990, UN Prize of Population 1994 and numerous other awards and honours. *Leisure interest:* squash.

MUBARAK, Khaldoon Khalifa al-, BEcons; United Arab Emirates business executive; *Managing Director and CEO, Mubadala Development Company;* b. 1975, Abu Dhabi; ed Tufts Univ., Boston, USA; began career as Sales Exec., Abu Dhabi Nat. Oil Co.; currently Man. Dir and CEO Mubadala Devt Co.; mem. Abu Dhabi Exec. Council, Chair. Abu Dhabi Exec. Affairs Authority 2006–; Chair. Emirates Nuclear Energy Corpn, Abu Dhabi Motor Sport Man. Co., Abu Dhabi Media Zone Authority, Emirates Aluminium; Chair. Manchester City Football Club, UK 2008–; Deputy Chair. Urban Planning Council 2007–; mem. Abu Dhabi Council for Econ. Devt; Dir First Gulf Bank, Ferrari SpA, Aldar Properties; Co-Chair. US Chamber of Commerce's US–UAE Business Council 2007–; mem. Bd of Trustees, New York Univ.; Commdr, Ordine della Stella della solidarietà italiana 2007. *Address:* Mubadala Development Company, PO Box 45005, Abu Dhabi, United Arab Emirates (office). *Telephone:* (2) 4130000 (office). *Fax:* (2) 4130001 (office). *E-mail:* info@mubadala.ae (office). *Website:* www.mubadala.ae (office).

MUBEEN, Gen. Mohammad Abdul; Bangladeshi fmr army officer; m. Syeda Sharifa Khanom; two s. one d.; ed Y Cadet in Mirzapur Cadet Coll., Defence Services Command and Staff Coll., Nat. Defence Coll., Mirpur, Dhaka; commissioned in Regt of Infantry of Bangladesh Army 1976; served in various capacities at bn level, commanded two infantry bns and an infantry brigade; served as Brigade Maj. (Operation Staff) in an Ind. Infantry Brigade HQ, Gen. Staff Officer First Grade (Operation Staff) in Infantry Div. HQ and in Bangladesh Mil. Acad., Pvt. Sec. to Chief of Army Staff and Dir of Mil. Training Directorate at Army HQ; served as Commdt of Defence Services Command and Staff Coll.; also held appointments of Dir Gen. Bangladesh Inst. of Int. and Strategic Studies and Prin. Staff Officer, Prime Minister's Office, Armed Forces Div. 2008–09; Chief of Army Staff 2009–12 (retd); promoted to rank of Gen. 2009; commanded two Infantry Divs as GOC in Jessore and Chittagong; served as Chief of Staff (Northern Region), UN Operations in Mozambique (ONUMUZ); mem. Army Hockey team. *Leisure interests:* playing golf, keen interest in all games and sports.

MUDASSIR HUSAIN, Justice Syed J. R., BA, LLB; Bangladeshi judge (retd); b. 1 March 1940, Hobigonj; s. of Syed Md. Mumidul Husain and Syeda Honse-Ara-Akther Khatun; m. Syeda Mazida Khatun; three d. one s.; ed Dhaka Univ.; enrolled as Advocate of High Court of E Pakistan 1965; part-time Lecturer, Central Law Coll. Dhaka 1966–78; Examiner and Question Setter, Dept of Law, Univ. of Dhaka; reporter, Bangladesh Law Reports 1973–77; apptd Asst Attorney Gen. 1977; enrolled as Advocate of Appellate Div. 1980; apptd Deputy Attorney Gen. 1984; apptd Judge, High Court Div. 1992, Judge of the Appellate Div. 2002; Chief Justice, Supreme Court 2004–07 (retd); rep. World Intellectual Property Org. 2003. *Leisure interest:* reading books, watching world television, watching cricket and football. *Address:* Flat 1 – BA-RC Tower, 74 Elephant Road, Dhaka 1205, Bangladesh (home). *Telephone:* (2) 8652523 (home).

MUDAVADI, Wycliffe Musalia; Kenyan economist and politician; *Leader, Amani National Congress;* b. 21 Sept. 1960, Vihiga Dist; m.; three c.; fmr employee Tysons Ltd (property consultants firm) –1989; land economist, Nat. Housing Corpn 1984–89; mem. Parl. for Sabatia 1989–; Minister of Supplies and Marketing 1989–92, of Finance 1992–97, of Agric. 1997–99, of Transport and Communications 1999–2002, Deputy Prime Minister 2008–12, also Minister of Local Govt 2008–12; Vice-Pres. of Kenya Nov.–Dec. 2002; Nat. Vice-Chair. Kenya African Nat. Union 2002; cand. in presidential election 2013; leader Amani Nat. Congress 2015–; Founder Rainbow Alliance; mem. Inst. of Surveyors. *Address:* Amani National Congress, Amani House, Loyangalani Drive, off James Gichuru Road, Lavington, PO Box 11095, 00100 Nairobi, Kenya (office). *E-mail:* info@amani.or.ke (office). *Website:* amani.or.ke (office).

MUDD, Daniel (Dan) H., BA, MPA; American business executive; *CEO, Paladin Global;* b. 1956; s. of Roger Mudd; m.; four c.; ed Univ. of Virginia, John F. Kennedy School of Govt at Harvard Univ.; served as officer in US Marine Corps, including combat service in Beirut, Lebanon; Robert Bosch Foundation Fellowship, Germany 1989; Vice-Pres. of Business Devt, GE Capital 1991–93, Man. Dir Int. Financing 1993–95, Pres. and CEO European Fleet Services, Brussels 1995–96, Pres. Asia Pacific 1996–99, Pres. and CEO Japan 1999–2000; Vice-Chair. and COO Fannie Mae, Washington, DC 2000–04, interim CEO 2004–05, Pres. and CEO 2005–08, mem. Bd of Dirs 2000–08; mem. Bd of Dirs, Fortress Investment Group LLC 2007–12, CEO 2010–12; CEO Paladin Global; mem. Bd of Dirs, Center for the Study of the Presidency, Homes for Working Families, Hampton Univ.; mem. Bd of Mans, Univ. of Virginia; mem. Bd of Advisors, Sandboxx. *Address:* Paladin Global, 2020 K Street, NW, Suite 400, Washington, DC 20006, USA (office). *Telephone:* (202) 293-5590 (office). *E-mail:* headquarters@fanniemae.com. *Website:* www .paladincapgroup.com (office).

MUDGE, Dirk; Namibian politician; b. 16 Jan. 1928, Otjiwarongo; m. Stienie Jacobs; two s. three d.; mem. Nat. Legis. Ass. 1965–; Chair. of Turnhalle Constitutional Conf. 1977; Vice-Chair. of Nat. Party and mem. SW Africa Exec. Council Sept. 1977; formed Republican Party of SW Africa 1977; Chair. Democratic Turnhalle Alliance (now DTA of Namibia) 1977; mem. Constituent Ass. 1978–79, Nat. Ass. 1979–83; Pres. Ministers' Council 1980–83, Minister for Finance and Governmental Affairs 1985–89; mem. Nat. Ass. 1991–93; Founding Trustee, Democratic Media Trust (now Dirk Mudge Trust) 1992–2013. *Address:* c/o Dirk Mudge Trust, P.O. Box 86908, Eros, Windhoek 9000, Namibia. *Website:* dirkmudgetrust.com.

MUDIMBE, Valentin-Yves, (Hermano Mateo), PhD; Democratic Republic of the Congo academic and writer; *Newman Ivey White Professor Emeritus of Literature, Duke University;* b. 8 Dec. 1941, Likasi Jadotville, Belgian Congo (now Democratic Repub. of the Congo); ed Univ. of Lovanium, Belgian Congo, Catholic Univ. of Louvain, Belgium, Univ. of Besançon and Univ. of Paris, France; Teaching Asst in Indo-European Languages, Romance Philology and in General Linguistics, Lovanium Univ., Kinshasa, Congo 1966–68; Teaching and Research Asst to Prof. Willy Bal in Indo-European Languages, Philology and African Literature, Université de Louvain, Belgium 1968–70; Lecturer in Socio-linguistics, Lab. of

Comparative Ethnology and Sociology, Université Paris X Nanterre, France 1969–71; Asst Prof. of Indo-European Languages and Historical Linguistics of French, Lovanium Univ., Lubumbashi, Congo 1970–71; Assoc. Prof. of Indo-European Languages, Comparative Philology and General Linguistics, Nat. Univ. of Zaire 1971–74, Dean of Faculty of Philosophy and Letters 1972–74, Prof. of Classics, Indo-European Languages and Comparative Philology 1974–80; Margaret Gest Prof. of Comparative Religions, Haverford Coll. 1981–82, Ira Reid Prof. of History and Sociology 1982–83, Prof. of General Programs 1984–87; Prof. of Romance Studies and Comparative Literature Duke Univ. 1988–90, Ruth F. DeVarney Prof. of Romance Studies, Prof. of Comparative Literature, Prof. of Cultural Anthropology 1991–94, Research Prof., Program in Literature 1995–2000, Newman Ivey White Prof. of Literature 2000, now Prof. Emer.; William R. Kenan, Jr Prof., Depts of French and Italian, Comparative Literature, and Classics, Program in Modern Thought and Literature and Center for African Studies, Stanford Univ. 1995–2000; numerous visiting engagements, including Louis H. Jordan Lecturer, SOAS, Univ. of London, UK, Samuel Fischer Prof., Free Univ. of Berlin, Germany, Commonwealth Prof., Univ. of Cambridge, UK, Visiting Prof., El Colegio de Mexico, Univ. of Antioquia, Colombia, Univ. of Cologne, Germany, Univ. of Warwick, UK; Gen. Sec. Soc. for African Philosophy in N America (SAPINA) 1988–99; Chair. Int. African Inst., Univ. of London; Corresp. mem. Belgian Acad. of Overseas Sciences 1978–2006, Hon. Corresp. mem. 2006–; Chevalier de la Pléiade, Ordre de la Francophonie et du Dialogue des Cultures 1997; Dr hc (Université de Paris VII-Denis Diderot), (La Chancellerie des Universités de Paris, Sorbonne) 1997, (Katholieke Universiteit Leuven) 2006. *Publications include*: L'odeur du père 1982, The Invention of Africa 1988, Parables and Fables 1991, Le corps glorieux des mots et des êtres 1994, The Idea of Africa 1994, Tales of Faith 1997; editor: The Surreptitious Speech 1992, Nations, Identities, Cultures 1997, Diaspora and Immigration (with Sabine Engel) 1999, Cheminements 1999, The Normal & Its Orders (with Gode Iwele and Laura Kerr) 2006; co-editor: Africa and the Disciplines (with Robert H. Bates and Jean O'Barr) 1993; 70 articles; three collections of poetry, four novels. *Address*: Duke University, Literature Program, 347 Trent Hall, Campus Box 90670, Durham, NC 27708, USA (office). *Telephone*: (919) 681-6254 (office). *E-mail*: vmudimbe@duke.edu (office). *Website*: literature.duke.edu (office).

MUDRINIĆ, Ivica, BASc; Croatian business executive; *Senior Vice-President for Strategic Support, Deutsche Telekom AG*; b. 1955; ed Univ. of Toronto, Canada; began career in Product Devt Dept, Motorola Communications –1985; f. MX Engineering Inc. 1985; returned to Croatia 1990, becoming Adviser for Communications to Croatian Pres., Asst Minister for Maritime Affairs, Transport and Communications 1991–92, Minister 1992–94; Pres., Telecommunications Council 1994–96; Pres. Man. Bd, Hrvatska Radiotelevizija 1996–98; CEO, Hrvatska pošta i telekomunikacije 1998–99, Pres., T-Hrvatski Telekom (following liberalisation) 1999–, then Pres. and CEO –2013, Sr Vice-Pres. for Strategic Support, Deutsche Telekom AG (parent co.) 2013–. *Address*: Deutsche Telekom AG, Friedrich-Ebert-Allee 140, 53113 Bonn, Germany (office). *Website*: www.telekom.com (office).

MUELLER, Edward A., BS, MBA; American business executive; b. St Louis, Mo.; ed Univ. of Missouri, Washington Univ.; joined Southwestern Bell 1968, held several sr positions including Pres. and CEO Southwestern Bell, Pres. and CEO Pacific Bell 1997–99, Pres. SBC Int. Operations 1999–2000; Pres. and CEO Ameritech 2000–02; CEO Williams-Sonoma, Inc. 2003–07; CEO Qwest Communications Int., Inc., Denver 2007–11 (retd); mem. Bd of Dirs McKesson Corpn 2008–, Lead Ind. Dir 2013–.

MÜLLER, Gerd; German politician; *Federal Minister of Economic Co-operation and Development*; b. 25 Aug. 1955, Krumbach/Schwaben; m.; two c.; ed Regensburg Univ.; fmr teacher and Deputy Head, Inst. of Int. Relations, Hanns-Seidel-Stiftung, Munich; mem. European Parl. 1989–94; mem. Bundestag (Parl.) 1994–; Parl. State Sec., Fed. Ministry of Food, Agric. and Consumer Protection 2005–13; Fed. Minister of Econ. Co-operation and Devt 2013–; mem. Christlich-Soziale Union; Bayerischer Verdienstorden 2007. *Address*: Federal Ministry of Economic Co-operation and Development, Dahlmannstrasse 4, 53113 Bonn, Germany (office). *Telephone*: (228) 995350 (office). *Fax*: (228) 995353500 (office). *E-mail*: info@bmz.bund.de (office). *Website*: www.bmz.de (office); www .gerd-mueller-waehlen.de.

MUELLER, Robert Swan, III, MA, JD; American lawyer and fmr government official; *Partner, Wilmer Cutler Pickering Hale and Dorr LLP*; b. 7 Aug. 1944, New York City; s. of Robert Swan Mueller, Jr and Alice Mueller (née Truesdale); m. Ann Standish 1966; two d.; ed Princeton Univ., New York Univ. and Univ. of Virginia; Capt., US Marine Corps 1967–70; Assoc., Pillsbury, Madison & Sutro, San Francisco 1973–76; Asst US Attorney, US Attorney's Office, Northern Dist Calif., San Francisco 1976–80, Chief, Special Prosecutions Unit 1980–81, Criminal Div. 1981–82; Chief, Criminal Div. Mass. Dist, US Attorney's Office, Boston 1982–85, First Asst US Attorney in Boston 1985, US Attorney for Mass Dist 1986–87, Deputy US Attorney for Mass Dist 1987–88; Pnr, Hill & Barlow, Boston 1988–89; Asst to Attorney Gen. for criminal matters, US Dept of Justice, Washington, DC 1989–90, Asst Attorney Gen. for Criminal Div. 1990–93, Special Counsel 2017–; lawyer, Hale & Dorr, Washington, DC 1993; Interim US Attorney, Northern Dist Calif. 1998–2001; Dir FBI 2001–13; Partner, Wilmer Cutler Pickering Hale & Dorr LLP, Washington, DC 2014–; Fellow, American Coll. of Trial Lawyers 1991; Bronze Star, Purple Heart, Vietnamese Cross of Gallantry, Thomas Jefferson Foundation Medal in Law, Univ. of Virginia 2013. *Address*: Wilmer Cutler Pickering Hale and Dorr LLP, 1875 Pennsylvania Avenue, NW, Washington, DC 20006, USA (office). *Telephone*: (202) 663-6364 (office). *E-mail*: robert.mueller@ wilmerhale.com (office). *Website*: www.wilmerhale.com (office).

MUELLER-STAHL, Armin; German actor; b. 17 Dec. 1930, Tilsit, East Prussia (now Sovetsk, Russia); s. of Alfred Müller and Editta; m. Gabriele Scholz 1973; one c.; ed Berlin Conservatory; began career with music studies (violin), subsequently became actor; moved to FRG 1980; Hon. citizen of Sovetsk 2011; Hon. DHumLitt (Chicago); Bundesfilmpreis 1981, Silver Bar Award 1992. *Films include*: Heimliche Ehen 1956, Königskinder (Royal Children) 1962, ...und Deine Liebe auch 1962, Christine 1963, Nackt unter Wölfen (Naked Among Wolves) 1963, Preludio 11 1964, Alaskafüchse 1964, Tödlicher Irrtum 1970, Der Dritte (The Third) 1972, Januskopf 1972, Die Hosen des Ritters Bredow 1973, Kit & Co. 1974, Jakob, der Lügner (Jacob the Liar) 1975, Nelken in Aspik 1976, Die Flucht (The

Flight) 1977, Lola 1981, Die Flügel der Nacht 1982, Die Sehnsucht der Veronika Voss 1982, Der Westen leuchtet 1982, Trauma 1983, Viadukt (aka The Train Killer) 1983, Un dimanche de flic (A Cop's Sunday) 1983, L'homme blessé (The Wounded Man) 1983, Eine Liebe in Deutschland (A Love in Germany) 1983, Tausend Augen (Thousand Eyes) 1984, Rita Ritter 1984, Glut (Embers) 1984, Oberst Redl (Colonel Redl) 1985, Die Mitläufer 1985, Vergeßt Mozart (Forget Mozart) 1986, Bittere Ernte (Angry Harvest) 1986, Momo 1986, Der Joker (Lethal Obsession) 1987, Killing Blue (Midnight Cop) 1988, Das Spinnennetz (Spider's Web) 1989, Schweinegeld (aka C*A*S*H: A Political Fairy Tale, UK) 1989, A Hecc 1989, Music Box 1989, Avalon 1990, Kafka 1991, Bronsteins Kinder (Bronstein's Children) 1991, Night on Earth 1991, Utz 1992, The Power of One 1992, Far from Berlin 1992, Red Hot 1993, Der Kinoerzähler (The Film Narrator) 1993, The House of the Spirits 1993, Taxandria 1994, The Last Good Time 1994, Holy Matrimony 1994, A Pyromaniac's Love Story 1995, Theodore Rex (video) 1995, Shine (Australian Film Prize 1996), Conversation with the Beast 1996, Der Unhold (The Ogre) 1996, The Assistant 1997, The Game 1997, The Peacemaker 1997, The Commissioner 1998, The X-Files 1998, The Thirteenth Floor 1999, The Third Miracle 1999, Jakob the Liar 1999, The Long Run 2000, Mission to Mars (uncredited) 2000, Pilgrim 2000, The Story of an African Farm 2004, The Dust Factory 2004, Local Color 2006, Ich bin die Andere 2006, Eastern Promises 2007, Leningrad 2009, Knight of Cups 2015. *Television includes*: Fünf Patronenhülsen (Five Cartridges) 1960, Flucht aus der Hölle (mini-series) 1960, Die Letzte Chance 1962, Der Andere neben dir 1963, Wolf unter Wölfen (mini-series) 1964, Ein Lord am Alexanderplatz 1967, Columbus 64 1966, Wege übers Land (mini-series) 1968, Die Dame aus Genua 1969, Kein Mann für Camp Detrick 1970, Die Verschworenen (mini-series) 1971, Die Sieben Affären der Dona Juanita (mini-series) 1973, Das Unsichtbare Visier (series) 1973, Stülpner-Legende (series; uncredited) 1973, Die Eigene Haut 1974, Geschlossene Gesellschaft 1978, Die Längste Sekunde 1980, Collin (mini-series) 1981, Ferry oder Wie es war 1981, Ja und Nein 1981, Die Gartenlaube 1982, Ich werde warten 1982, An uns glaubt Gott nicht mehr (God Does Not Believe in Us Anymore) 1982, Ausgestoßen 1982, Der Fall Sylvester Matuska 1982, Flucht aus Pommern 1982, Ruhe sanft, Bruno 1983, Tatort - Freiwild 1984, Hautnah 1985, Gauner im Paradies 1986, Auf den Tag genau 1986, Unser Mann im Dschungel (aka Amazonas Mission) 1987, Amerika (mini-series) 1987, Franza 1987, Jokehnen oder Wie lange fährt man von Ostpreußen nach Deutschland? (mini-series) 1987, Tagebuch für einen Mörder 1988, In the Presence of Mine Enemies 1997, 12 Angry Men 1997, Jesus 1999, Crociati (Crusaders) (mini-series) 2001, Die Manns - Ein Jahrhundertroman (mini-series) 2001, The Power of Knowledge (series) 2005. *Publications*: Verordneter Sonntag (Lost Sunday), Drehtage, Unterwegs Nach Hause (On the Way Home).

MUFAMADI, Fholisani Sydney, MSc; South African politician; *Director, School of Leadership, University of Johannesburg*; b. 28 Feb. 1959, Alexandra, Johannesburg; m. Nomusa Kumalo; one s. two d.; ed Univ. of London, UK; pvt. teacher, Lamula Secondary School 1980; Gen. Sec. General and Allied Workers' Union (GAWU) 1982; Publicity Sec. United Democratic Front (UDF); Asst Gen. Sec. Congress of South African Trade Unions 1985; mem. Nat. Peace Cttee, helped draft Nat. Peace Accord 1991; mem. African Nat. Congress (ANC) Nat. Exec. Cttee, ANC Working Cttee, Cen. Cttee of South African Communist Party, Political Bureau; ANC Rep. at Transitional Exec. Council on Law and Order, Safety and Stability 1993–94; Minister of Safety and Security, Govt of Nat. Unity 1994–99, of Prov. Affairs and Local Govt 1999–2008 (resgnd); Dir School of Leadership, Univ. of Johannesburg 2011–; Hon. DSc (Igbinedion Univ., Okada). *Leisure interest*: reading. *Address*: University of Johannesburg, Auckland Park, Kingsway Campus, G22, A-Ring, Johannesburg 2006, South Africa (office). *Telephone*: (11) 4063510 (office). *E-mail*: sydneym@uj.ac.za (office). *Website*: www.uj.ac.za (office).

MUFTI, Hania, MSc; Jordanian lawyer and international organization official; b. Amman; ed in Jordan and Lebanon and Univ. of Bath, UK; more than 20 years' professional experience in human rights research and advocacy; Researcher, Middle East Research Dept, Amnesty International's Secr., London, UK 1981–97; Dir Middle East and North Africa Div., Human Rights Watch, London 2000–07; UN Chief of Human Rights Office with UN Assistance Mission for Iraq 2007–08; named by TIME magazine as one of the 100 most influential people in 2005. *Publications include*: author of numerous reports for Amnesty International, including Iraq: The World Would Not Listen 1994, Kuwait: Three Years of Unfair Trials 1994, Iraq: Human Rights Abuses in Iraqi Kurdistan Since 1991 1995, Bahrain: A Human Rights Crisis 1995. *Address*: c/o Human Rights Watch, First Floor, Audrey House, 16–20 Ely Place, London, EC1N 6SN, England. *Telephone*: 7980-540036 (mobile). *E-mail*: hrwuk@hrw.org. *Website*: www.hrw.org/london.

MUFTI, Mehbooba, BA, LLB; Indian politician; b. 22 May 1959, Akhran Nowpora, Anantnag Dist; d. of Mufti Mohammad Sayeed (fmr Chief Minister of Jammu and Kashmir) and Gulshan Nazir; m. Javed Iqbal (divorced); two c.; ed Univ. of Kashmir; mem. Jammu and Kashmir Legis. Ass. 1996–99, 2002–04, Leader, Congress Legislature Party, Jammu and Kashmir Legis. Ass. 1996–99; mem. Lok Sabha (lower house of Parl.) for Anantnag 2004–09, 2014–, Leader, Jammu and Kashmir People's Democratic Party in Lok Sabha 2014–16, mem. Standing Cttee on Empowerment of Women, Standing Cttee on Information Tech., mem. Ministry of Health and Family Welfare Consultative Cttee; Chief Minister of Jammu and Kashmir (first woman) 2016–18; mem. Jammu and Kashmir People's Democratic Party, Vice-Pres. 1999. *Leisure interests*: yoga, music. *Address*: c/o Office of the Chief Minister, Government of Jammu and Kashmir, Civil Secretariat, Srinagar, India (office).

MUGABE, Grace, DSc; Zimbabwean politician; b. (Grace Marufu), 23 July 1965, Benoni, S Africa; m. 1st Stanley Goreraza, one s.; m. 2nd Robert Mugabe (Pres. of Zimbabwe) 1996, one s. two d.; ed Christian Coll. of Southern Africa, Univ. of Zimbabwe; fmr Sec. to Pres. Robert Mugabe; mem. Zimbabwe African Nat. Union (ZANU)—Patriotic Front, Leader ZANU—PF Women's League 2014–, also mem. ZANU—PF Politburo 2014–.

MUGABE, Robert Gabriel, BA, BAdmin, BEd, MSc (Econ), LLM; Zimbabwean politician, fmr teacher and fmr head of state; b. 21 Feb. 1924, Kutama; m. 1st Sarah Mugabe (died 1992); one s. (deceased); m. 2nd Grace Marufu 1996; three c.; ed Kutama and Empandeni Mission School, Fort Hare Univ. Coll., S Africa, Univs of S Africa and London; teacher, at Drifontein Roman Catholic School, Umvuma 1952, Salisbury S Primary School 1953, in Gwelo 1954, Chalimbana Teacher

Training Coll. 1955, in Accra, Ghana 1958–60; entered politics 1960; Publicity Sec. of Nat. Democratic Party 1960–61; Publicity Sec. Zimbabwe African People's Union 1961; detained Sept.–Dec. 1962, March–April 1963; escaped to Tanzania April 1963; Co-Founder of Zimbabwe African Nat. Union (ZANU) Aug. 1963; Sec.-Gen. Aug. 1963; in detention in Rhodesia 1964–74; Pres. ZANU; mem. Politburo ZANU 1984–; Jt Leader of Patriotic Front (with Joshua Nkomo) 1976–79; contested Feb. 1980 elections as Leader of ZANU (PF) (name changed to ZANU 1984) Party, Pres. 1988–2017; Minister of Defence 1980–87, also fmrly of Public Works, Industry and Tech.; Prime Minister of Zimbabwe 1980–87; Pres. of Zimbabwe 1988–2017; Chancellor, Univ. of Zimbabwe; apptd Amb. for southern Africa, African Union 2003; Chair. African Union Ass. 2015–16; Dr hc (Ahmadu Bello Univ., Nigeria) 1980; Newsmaker of the Year Award (South African Soc. of Journalists) 1980, Africa Prize 1988; Int. Human Rights Award (Howard Univ., Washington, DC) 1981, Jawarhalal Nehru Award 1992. *Address:* c/o Zimbabwe African National Union—Patriotic Front, cnr Rotten Row St and Samora Machel Ave, Harare, Zimbabwe.

MUGLER, Thierry; French fashion designer; b. 21 Dec. 1948, Strasbourg; ed in Strasbourg and École nationale supérieure des arts décoratifs; fmr ballet dancer, Opéra du Rhin, Strasbourg; later window-dresser and clothing designer, Gudule boutique, Paris from 1972; designer of fashion collection for André Peters, London; subsequently began career as freelance clothing designer in Amsterdam, later in Paris where he launched Café de Paris collection 1973; designer of menswear and fashion accessories; launched own Thierry Mugler fashion label, Paris 1973; launched Thierry Mugler Diffusion fashion co.; opened own boutique, Place des Victoires, Paris; clothing also sold in dept stores in USA and Japan; launched range of perfumes, including Angel 1992, Angel Men (A*Men) 1996, Alien 2005, Mirror, Mirror 2007, Womanity 2010; launched Thierry Mugler Perfume Workshops 2005; completed a project for the launch of Tom Tykwer's film Perfume 2006; launched Thierry Mugler Beauty (high-end line of cosmetics) 2008; changed brand name to Mugler 2010; launched brand's first menswear collection in collaboration with Romain Kremer 2011; also directs short films, advertising films and video clips; regularly designs costumes for musical comedies, concerts, operas and the theatre (including Macbeth for the Comédie Française); has worked with artists including Robert Altman and George Michael (directed video for Michael's Too Funky 1992); also directed first advertising film for one of his fragrances, Alien; collaborated with Cirque du Soleil (directed 'Extravaganza' scene of Zumanity and cr. all the costumes and character identities) 2002; Artistic Advisor to Beyoncé 2009, cr. costumes for her 'I Am... World Tour'; also a bodybuilder. *Publications:* Thierry Mugler, Photographe 1988, Fashion Fetish Fantasy 1999. *Address:* Thierry Mugler, Westex Ltd, Unit 1, Temple House, Riverway, Harlow, Essex, CM20 2EY, England (office). *Telephone:* (1279) 774240 (office). *E-mail:* customer .relations@muglerstore.co.uk (office). *Website:* www.mugler.co.uk (office).

MUHAMMAD, Ali Nasser; Yemeni politician; b. 31 Dec. 1939, Dathina Rural Dist; active mem. of Nat. Liberation Front (NLF) 1963–67; Gov. of the Islands 1967, of Second Prov. 1968; mem. Nat. Front Gen. Command March 1968; Minister of Local Govt 1969, of Defence 1969–77, of Educ. 1974–75; mem. Front Exec. Cttee 1970; mem. Presidential Council of People's Democratic Repub. of Yemen 1971–78, Chair. June–Dec. 1978; Chair. Council of Ministers (Prime Minister) 1971–85; mem. Supreme People's Council (SPC) 1971, Chair. Presidium of SPC (Head of State) 1980–86 (overthrown in coup Jan. 1986); mem. Political Bureau of Nat. Front 1972–75, of United Political Org. Nat. Front 1975–78, of Yemen Socialist Party (YSP) 1978–86, Sec.-Gen. of YSP 1980–86; became an opposition figure in Yemeni uprising 2011, named to a 17-mem. transitional council.

MUHAMMED, Magaji, BA; Nigerian government official and diplomatist; b. 31 Dec. 1940, Dutsinma, Katsina State; ed Ahmadu Bello Univ.; Dist Officer Idoma, Wukari and Tiv Div., Prin. Asst Sec. Mil. Gov.'s Office, Kaduna 1965–75; fmr Admin., Kaduna Capital Territory, Perm. Sec. 1975; joined Civil Service 1980, Dir Project Implementation, Ministry of Industries, Dir Commercial and Industrial Incentives, Ministry of Trade and Industries; Amb. to Saudi Arabia 2000–03; Minister of Industry –2005, of Internal Affairs 2005–06 (resgnd); mem. People's Democratic Party. *Address:* c/o Ministry of the Interior, Block F, Old Federal Secretariat, Area 1, PMB 7007, Garki, Abuja; c/o People's Democratic Party, Wadata Plaza, Michael Okpara Way, Zone 5, Wuse, Abuja, Nigeria. *E-mail:* info@ peopledemocraticparty.org.

MUHAMMEDOV, Hojamuhammet; Turkmenistani economist and politician; b. 1966, Aşgabat; ed Turkmen Nat. Econ. Inst.; early career as forwarding agent, Turkmenengilazyksenagat 1983; fmr Construction Engineer, Supplies Dept, Turkmenhimsnabbyt; fmr stock-keeper, State Cttee for Logistics of Turkmenistan; Deputy Dir, later Dir, Kharytimpeks Co., also Dir Gulistan State Trading Centre 1998–2005; Deputy Chair. State Commodity and Raw Materials Exchange 2005–06, Chair. 2006; Chair. Supreme Supervisory Chamber of Turkmenistan July–Nov. 2007; Deputy Chair., Council of Ministers, responsible for Textile Industry, Trade and Chamber of Commerce and Industry 2007–13; Acting Presidential Chief of Staff March 2009–11, Presidential Chief of Staff 2011–13.

MUHITH, Abul Maal Abdul, BA (Hons), MA, MPA; Bangladeshi economist, civil servant, diplomatist and politician; b. 1934, Sylhet; s. of Abu Ahmad Abdul Hafiz and Sayed Shahar Banu Chowdhury; m. Sayed Sabia Muhith; two s. one d.; ed Sylhet MC Coll., Dhaka Univ., Univ. of Oxford, UK, Harvard Univ., USA; joined Pakistan Civil Service 1956, served in different depts of East Pakistan, Cen. Pakistan and later Bangladesh, Sec. of Planning 1972–77, Sec. of External Resource Dept, Ministry of Finance and Planning 1977–81, served as Deputy and Chief Sec. Pakistan Planning Comm.; served as diplomat, Embassy in Washington, DC, USA; retd 1981; emerged from retirement as econs and devt specialist in Ford Foundation and IFAD; Minister of Finance and Planning 1982–83; then worked as specialist of different insts of World Bank and UN; Visiting Fellow, Princeton Univ., USA 1984–85; Minister of Finance 2009–19; early proponent of Bangladesh Environment Movt; Founder-Pres. BAPA. *Publications include:* 21 books on various subjects, including admin. and liberation war affairs. *Address:* c/o Ministry of Finance, Bangladesh Secretariat, Bhaban 7, 1st 9-Storey Bldg, 3rd Floor, Dhaka 1000, Bangladesh (office).

MÜHLEMANN, Lukas, MBA; Swiss business executive; b. 1950; ed Univ. of St Gallen and Harvard Univ., USA; fmr systems engineer, IBM; man. consultant,

McKinsey & Co. 1977–94, Prin. 1982, Dir 1986, Man. Dir McKinsey Swiss offices 1989, mem. Bd Dirs McKinsey & Co., Inc., New York 1990; CEO Swiss Re 1994, Man. Dir 1994, Deputy Chair. 1996; CEO Credit Suisse Group 1997–2002, Chair. Bd of Dirs 2000–02, mem. Bd Dirs Credit Suisse, Credit Suisse First Boston; mem. Bd Tonhalle Foundation, Zurich, Zurich Opera House, Banco Gen. de Negocios; Pres. Harvard Club of Switzerland.

MUHYIDDIN, Tan Sri Dato' Haji Mohd Yassin bin; Malaysian politician; *President, Parti Pribumi Bersatu Malaysia (PPBM);* b. 15 May 1947; s. of Muhammad Yassin bin Mohammad and Hajjah Khadijah Kassim; m. Noorainee Abdul Rahman 1972; ed Univ. of Malaya, Kuala Lumpur; Man. Dir subsidiary Cos., Johor State Economic Development Corporation (PKENJ) 1974–78; mem. of Parl. for Pagoh 1978–; fmr Deputy Minister of Federal Territories, of Trade and Industry; Chief Minister of Johor 1982–95; mem. Johor State Legislative Ass. for Bukit Serampang 1986–95, also Head of Govt in, Johor; Minister of Youth and Sports 1995–99, of Domestic Trade and Consumer Affairs 1999–2004, of Agric. and Agro-Based Industry 2004–08, of Int. Trade and Industry 2008–09; Deputy Prime Minister of Malaysia 2009–15, also Minister of Education; Vice-Pres. United Malays Nat. Org. 2009–16; Pres. PPBM 2016–. *Address:* Parti Pribumi Bersatu Malaysia, Tingkat 8, Menara Yayasan Selangor, No 18A, Jalan Persiaran Barat, PJS 52, Petaling Jaya, 46200 Selangor, Malaysia (office). *Telephone:* (3) 9222 3322 (office). *E-mail:* info@bersatu.org (office). *Website:* www.pribumibersatu.org.my (office).

MUILENBERG, Dennis A., BEng, MEng, FRAeS; American aerospace engineer and business executive; *Chairman, President and CEO, The Boeing Company;* b. 1964, Orange City, Ia; ed Iowa State Univ., Univ. of Washington; joined Boeing 1985, Vice-Pres. and Program Man., Future Combat Systems 2003–06, Vice-Pres. and Gen. Man., Boeing Combat Systems Div. 2006–08, Pres., Global Services & Support, The Boeing Company 2008–09, Exec. Vice-Pres., Pres. and CEO Boeing Defense, Space & Security 2009–13, Vice-Chair. and COO The Boeing Company 2013–15, Pres. 2013–, CEO 2015–, Chair. 2016–; mem. Bd of Dirs, Caterpillar, Inc. 2011–, US-China Business Council, Congressional Medal of Honor Foundation, FIRST (For Inspiration and Recognition of Science and Technology); mem. Pres. Trump's American Manufacturing Council Jan.–Aug. 2017; mem. Asscn of the US Army Council of Trustees; Trustee, Nat. World War II Museum, Washington University, St Louis; Fellow, AIAA, Royal Aeronautical Soc. *Address:* The Boeing Company, 100 North Riverside Plaza, Chicago, IL 60606-1596, USA (office). *Telephone:* (312) 544-2000 (office). *Fax:* (312) 544-2082 (office). *E-mail:* info@boeing .com (office). *Website:* www.boeing.com (office).

MUIR, Richard John Sutherland, CMG, BA; British consultant and diplomatist (retd); b. 25 Aug. 1942, London; s. of John Muir and Edna Hodges; m. Caroline Simpson 1965; one s. one d; ed Stationers' Co. School and Univs of Reading and Strasbourg; joined FCO 1966, Second Sec., Embassy in Jeddah 1967–70, Embassy in Tunis 1970–72, at FCO 1972–75, First Sec., Embassy in Washington, DC 1975–79, Prin. Dept of Energy, FCO 1979–81, Counsellor, Embassy in Jeddah 1981–85, at FCO 1985–91, Under-Sec. and Chief Insp. Diplomatic Service 1991–94, Amb. to Oman 1994–98, to Kuwait 1999–2002 (retd); joined MEC Int. 2003, then apptd Sr Consultant (retd); fmr Dir (non-exec.) Mott Macdonald Int.; mem. Next Century Foundation. *Leisure interests:* walking, sailing, fishing, opera. *Address:* c/o MEC International Ltd, Granville House, 132—135 Sloane Street, London, SW1X 9AX, England (office).

MUIR, William (Bill) F., BEng, MBA; American business executive; b. 28 Dec. 1954, Freeport, NY; ed Cornell Univ., Harvard Univ.; joined General Motors (GM) at Treas.'s Office, New York 1983, Dir of Foreign Exchange and Int. Cash Man. 1986–87, Dir of Overseas Borrowings 1987–89, Dir of Corp. Finance and Investor Relations 1989–90, Gen. Dir of Business Devt 1990–92, Vice-Pres. of Nat. Accounts, GMAC Financial Services 1992–95, Vice-Pres. of Eastern US Operations 1995–96, Exec.-in-Charge of Operations, later Exec. Dir of Planning, GM's Delphi Automotive Systems 1996, Exec. Vice-Pres. and Chief Financial Officer GMAC Financial Services Feb. 1998–2004, Chair. GMAC's Insurance Group 1999–2004, Pres. GMAC Financial Services 2004, later Pres. and Head Dealer Financial Services Business, Ally Financial, Inc. (following rebranding of GMAC Financial Services) 2004–14, mem. Bd of Dirs, GMAC Commercial Finance 2002, Ally Bank (fmrly GMAC Bank) 2004–14. *Address:* c/o Ally Financial, PO Box 38090, Bloomington, MN 55438, USA.

MUIZ, Abdulla; Maldivian government official; fmr Deputy Attorney-Gen., then Attorney-Gen. 2011–12; apptd mem. Nat. Crime Prevention Cttee 2011.

MUIZZU, Uz Ahmed, LLB, LLM; Maldivian lawyer and fmr judge; ed Malaysiage Int. Islamic Univ., Int. Maritime Org. Law Inst.; apptd Attorney 1990; Deputy Dir of Public Prosecutions 1994–97; Chief Judge, Criminal Court of Maldives 1997–99; apptd Lead Legal Counsel, Ministry of Tourism 1999; mem. Special Majlis for Haa Alifu constituency; Founder and Man. Partner, Muizzu, Suoodh & Co. (law firm) 1994–2009, 2013–; Prosecutor Gen. 2009–13; mem. Bd of Dirs Maldives Tourism Devt Corpn Plc; mem. Law Comm. of Maldives 1994–2002. *Address:* Muizzu, Suood & Co, 2nd Floor, H. Orchidmaage, Ameeru Ahmed Magu, Male 20206, Maldives (office). *Telephone:* 3344911 (office).

MUJAMMEDOV, Hojamuhammed; Turkmenistani economist and politician; b. 1966, Aşgabat; ed Turkmen Inst. of Nat. Economy; began career 1983; worked as forwarding agent of Turkmenengilazyksenagat Asscn, Ministry of Trade and Consumers' Co-operation; various positions, including as construction engineer, as engineer of Supplies Dept of Turkmenhimsnabbyt, as stock keeper of Dept of State Cttee for Logistics; Deputy Dir and Dir, Harytimpeks Co., Ministry of Trade and Foreign Econ. Relations 1998–2005, Dir of State Trade Centre Gulistan; Deputy Chair. State commodity and Raw Materials Exchange 2005–06, Chair. 2006–07; Chair. Supreme Supervisory Chamber of Turkmenistan 2007–13; apptd Deputy Chair. Council of Ministers in charge of Trade and the Textile Industry 2007; Deputy Chair., Chief of the Govt and Presidential Staff 2012–13.

MUJAWAR, Ali Muhammad, BA, MA, PhD; Yemeni academic and politician; b. 26 April 1953, Shabwa; ed Algiers Univ., Algeria and Grenoble Univ., France; mem. Higher Studies Cttee, Business Dept, Univ. of Aden 1990–2000, Head, Business Man. Dept, Faculty of Econs 1994–96, Dean of Faculty of Oil and Minerals 1996–99, Dean, Faculty of Man. Studies 2001–03; Gen. Man. Al-Barah

Cement Factory 1999–2000; fmr Deputy Minister of Civil Service and Insurance, Minister of Fisheries 2003–06, of Electricity and Water 2006–07, Prime Minister 2007–11.

MUJEZINOVIĆ, Mustafa; Bosnia and Herzegovina politician, diplomatist and fmr electrical engineer; b. 27 Dec. 1954, Sarajevo; m. Emina Mujezinović; ed First Gen. High School, Sarajevo, Faculty of Electrical Eng, Sarajevo Univ.; Constructor, then Quality Engineer, Factory of Transformer Stations and Switchgear Plants, TTS 'Energoinvest', Sarajevo 1978–83, Head of Tech. Group, Sales Dept 1983–90, Sales Man. and mem. Man. Bd 1990–92; Pres. Municipality Stari Grad (Old Town), Sarajevo 1994–95, Mayor of Municipality Stari Grad, Sarajevo 1995–96; first Prime Minister of Sarajevo Canton 1996–98, Gov. of Sarajevo Canton 1998–2000; Amb. of Bosnia and Herzegovina to OSCE 2000–01; Dir of Privatization Fund 'Prevent Invest' 2002–04; Amb. of Bosnia and Herzegovina to Malaysia 2004–08; Advisor to Man. of Devt Bank of Fed. of Bosnia and Herzegovina 2008–09; Prime Minister of Fed. of Bosnia and Herzegovina 2009–11; Amb. to UK 2012–15; mem. Party of Democratic Action (Stranka Demokratske Akcije—SDA).

MUJICA CORDANO, José (Pepe) Alberto; Uruguayan farmer, politician and fmr head of state; b. 20 May 1935, Montevideo; s. of Demetrio Mujica and Lucy Cordano; m. Lucía Topolansky 2005; fmr mem. Movimiento de Liberación Nacional–Tupamaros guerrilla movt; fmr mem. Partido Nacional; imprisoned for 14 years during dictatorship, granted amnesty with return of democracy 1985; Founding mem. and leader Movimiento de Participación Popular (part of Frente Amplio); mem. Cámara de Senadores (parl.) –2005, 2008–18; Minister of Livestock, Agric. and Fisheries 2004–08; Frente Amplio presidential cand. 2009, Pres., Eastern Repub. of Uruguay 2010–15; Grand Collar, Nat. Order of Merit (Paraguay) 2010, Grand Collar, Order of the Sun (Peru) 2011, Order of the Aztec Eagle (Mexico) 2014. *Address:* Frente Amplio, Colonia 1367, 2°, 11100 Montevideo, Uruguay (office). *Telephone:* (2) 9026666 (office). *E-mail:* comunicacion@frenteamplio.org.uy (office). *Website:* www.frenteamplio.org.uy (office).

MUJOTA, Fehmi; Kosovo politician; ed Univ. of Prishtina; fmr mem. Kosovo Liberation Army; fmr Mayor Shtime Municipality; mem. Democratic Party of Kosovo; mem. Kosovo Ass., First Vice-Chair. Cttee for Public Services, Local Admin and Media; Minister of the Kosovo Security Force 2008–11, of Infrastructure 2011–17.

MUJURU, Joice Teurai-Ropa; Zimbabwean politician; b. (Runaida Mugari), 15 April 1955, Mount Darwin; m. Tapfumanei Ruzambu Solomon Mujuru (Nhongo) 1977 (died 2011); four d.; ed Women's Univ. in Africa; Minister of Youth, Sport and Recreation 1980–81, of Community Devt and Women's Affairs 1981–88, of Community and Co-operative Devt 1989–92, of Rural Resources and Water Devt 1996–2004; Vice-Pres. of Zimbabwe 2004–14; Second Sec. and Vice-Pres. ZANU (PF) party 2004–14 (expelled from party 2015); Gov. and Resident Minister of Mashonaland Cen. Prov. 1993–96; Fellow, Inst. of Engineers 2000–; f. Zimbabwe People First party 2016; Liberation Medal, War Veteran Order of Merit, Pride of Africa Women, Women Advancement for Economic and Leadership Empowerment in Africa 2010. *Leisure interests:* church and women's meetings, knitting, sewing, cooking, outdoor life. *Address:* No. 9 Tara Township, Ruwa (home); Box 57, Ruwa, Zimbabwe (home).

MUKAI, Chiaki, MD, PhD; Japanese astronaut, surgeon and academic; *Director, Center for Applied Space Medicine and Human Research, Japan Aerospace Exploration Agency;* b. 6 May 1952, Tatebayashi, Gunma Pref.; m. Makio Mukai; ed Keio Girls' High School, Tokyo, Keio Univ. School of Medicine; fmr Asst Prof., Dept of Cardiovascular Surgery, Keio Univ.; science astronaut, NASDA (renamed JAXA–Japan Aerospace Exploration Agency 2003) 1983–, first Japanese woman in space having logged 566 hours, Dir Space Biomedical Research Office, Human Space Technology and Astronaut Dept, Human Space System and Utilization Mission Directorate,JAXA 2007–11, Sr Adviser to JAXA Exec. Dir 2011–, Dir JAXA Center for Applied Space Medicine and Human Research (J-CASMHR) 2012–; NASA experience includes Japanese Payload Specialist, First Material Processing Test (Spacelab-J), STS-47 1985, back-up Payload Specialist, Neurolab (STS-90) Mission, flew aboard STS-65 1994, STS-95 Discovery 1998, Deputy Mission Scientist for STS-107; bd certified for medicine 1977, as cardiovascular surgeon 1989; Resident in Gen. Surgery, Keio Univ. Hosp. 1977–78; mem. Medical Staff, Shimizu Gen. Hosp., Shizuoka Pref. 1978–79, Emergency Surgery Staff, Saiseikai Kanagawa Hosp., Kanagawa Pref. 1979–80; Resident in Cardiovascular Surgery, Keio Univ. Hosp. 1980–82, Chief Resident 1982–83; mem. Medical Staff in Cardiovascular Surgery, Saiseikei Utsunomiya Hosp., Tochigi Pref. 1982–83; Asst Prof., Dept of Cardiovascular Surgery, Keio Univ. 1983–87, Visiting Assoc. Prof., Dept of Surgery 1992–98, Visiting Prof. 1999–; Visiting Scientist, Div. of Cardiovascular Physiology, Space Biomedical Research Inst., NASA Johnson Space Center 1987–88; Research Instructor, Dept of Surgery, Baylor Coll. of Medicine, Houston, Tex. 1992–; Visiting Prof., Int. Space Univ. Strasbourg, France 2004–07; apptd Vice-Pres. Tokyo Univ. of Science 2015; mem. American Aerospace Medical Asscn, Japan Soc. of Microgravity Applications, Japan Soc. of Aerospace and Environmental Medicine, Japanese Soc. for Cardiovascular and Thoracic Surgery, Japan Surgical Soc.; Hon. Citizen of Tatebayashi City 1994, Hon. Pres., Tatebayashi Children's Science Exploratorium 1995, Hon. mem. Aeromedical Asscn of Korea 1995; Legion of Honour: Chevalier, France 2015; Outstanding Service Award, Nat. Space Devt Agency of Japan 1992, 1994, Award for Distinguished Accomplishments, Tokyo Women's Foundation 1994, The Award for Distinguished Service in Advancement of Space Biology, Japanese Soc. for Biological Sciences in Space 1995, Outstanding Service Award, Soc. of Japanese Women Scientists 1996, Joe Kerwin Award, Aerospace Medical Asscn 2013, Dream's Award, The Soroptimist Japan Foundation 2013. *Leisure interests:* snow skiing, Alpine competitive skiing, bass fishing, scuba diving, tennis, golf, photography, American literature, travel. *Address:* JAXA Center for Applied Space Medicine and Human Research, Japan Aerospace Exploration Agency, 7-44-1 Jindaiji, Higashi-Machi, Chofu-shi, Tokyo 182-8522, Japan (office). *Telephone:* (281) 483-0123 (office). *Website:* www.jaxa.jp/index_e.html (office).

MUKASA, Shinji; Japanese construction industry executive; Exec. Vice-Pres. Obayashi Corpn –1997, apptd Pres. 1997, Pres. and CEO –2007; Pres. and Dir Overseas Construction Asscn of Japan Inc. (OCAJI); Dir Global Infrastructure Fund Research Foundation. *Address:* Obayashi Corporation, Shinagawa Intercity Tower B, 2-15-2 Konan, Minato-ku, Tokyo 108-8502, Japan. *E-mail:* info@obayashi.co.jp.

MUKASEY, Michael Bernard, BA, LLB; American lawyer, government official and fmr judge; *Of Counsel, Debevoise & Plimpton LLP;* b. 1941, Bronx, New York; m. Susan Mukasey 1974; one s. one d.; ed Columbia Coll., Yale Law School; Assoc., Webster Sheffield Fleishchmann Hitchcock & Brookfield (law firm), New York City 1967–72; Asst US Attorney, US Dist Court for the Southern Dist of New York 1972–76, Chief Judge, Chief Official Corruption Unit 1975–76; Assoc. then Partner, Patterson Belknap Webb & Tyler 1976–87, 2006–07; Judge, US Dist Court for the Southern Dist of New York 1988–2006, Chief Judge 2000–06 (retd); US Attorney Gen., Dept of Justice, Washington, DC 2007–09; advisor to Rudy Giuliani Republican presidential nomination campaign 2007; Of Counsel, Debevoise & Plimpton LLP, New York 2009–; part-time Lecturer, Columbia School of Law 1993–2007; mem. New York Bar; Dr hc (Brooklyn Law School) 2002; numerous awards including Learned Hand Medal, Fed. Bar Council. *Address:* Debevoise & Plimpton LLP, 919 Third Avenue, New York, NY 10022, USA (office). *Telephone:* (212) 909-6589 (office). *Fax:* (212) 909-6836 (office). *E-mail:* info@debevoise.com (office). *Website:* www.debevoise.com/michaelmukasey (office).

MUKERJEA, Pratim (Peter), MBA; British/Indian broadcasting executive; b. 1954, London; s. of Khrishna Mukerjea and Baloram Mukerjea; m. 1st Shabnam Mukerjea 1975 (divorced 1994); m. 2nd Indrani Mukerjea 2002 (divorced 2017); two s. one d.; ed business studies, Hatfield, Herts.; began career with Heinz (UK), later with British Store House and advertising agency O&M (UK office); fmr Regional Group Account Dir, DDB Needham Advertising, Hong Kong; fmr Account Dir, Ogilvy & Mather, New Delhi and London; Sales Dir (Hong Kong, later India and Middle East) Star TV 1993–97, Exec. Vice-Pres. 1997–99, CEO Star India 1999–2007; Co-founder (with Indrani Mukerjea), Chief Strategy Officer and Chair. INX Media Pvt. Ltd 2007–09; mem. Bd of Dirs ESPN STAR Sports, Hathway, Media Content and Communications Services (India) for Star News. *Address:* c/o INX Media Pvt. Ltd, Urmi Corporate Park, 1st Floor, Solaris – D, Opp. L & T Gate No. 6, Saki Vihar Road, Powai, Mumbai 400 072, India.

MUKHAMEDOV, Irek Javdatovich, OBE; Russian/Tatar ballet dancer; *Guest Principal Ballet Master, English National Ballet;* b. 8 Feb. 1960; m. Maria Zubkova; one s. one d.; ed Moscow Choreographic Inst.; joined Moscow Classical Co.; debut with Bolshoi Ballet in title role of Grigorovich's Spartacus 1981; other roles include Ivan IV in Ivan the Terrible, Jean de Brienne in Raymonda, Basil in Don Quixote, Romeo in Grigorovich's Romeo and Juliet, Boris in Grigorovich's The Golden Age; toured extensively with Bolshoi Ballet and made worldwide guest appearances; joined The Royal Ballet 1990, later becoming Sr Principal Dancer; Covent Garden debut in MacMillan's pas de deux Farewell (with Darcey Bussell) 1990; f. Irek Mukhamedov & Co. 1991–; appeared in musical The King and I, London 1995; fmrly Guest Principal Ballet Master and Character Artist, English National Ballet, now Guest Principal Ballet Master; Grand Prix, Int. Ballet Competition, Moscow 1981, Gold Medal, Int. Ballet Competition, Moscow 1981, Hans Christian Anderson Prize for Best Dancer in the World 1988, Benois de la Dance Prize 1996, Nijinsky Medal 1998. *Repertoire includes:* Coppélia, Moscow Choreographic School 1978, Romeo and Juliet, Moscow Classical Ballet 1978–81, Don Quixote (Pas de Deux) Moscow Classical Ballet 1978–81, La Fille mal gardée, Moscow Classical Ballet 1980, Spartacus, Bolshoi Ballet, Moscow 1981, Ivan the Terrible, Bolshoi Ballet 1982, Romeo and Juliet, Bolshoi Ballet 1983, The Golden Age, Bolshoi Ballet 1984, Raymonda, Bolshoi Ballet 1985, Don Quixote, Royal Ballet of Flanders 1988, The Sleeping Beauty, Paris Opera 1989, Petrushka, Bolshoi Ballet 1990, La Bayadere, Royal Ballet, London 1990, Winter Dreams, Royal Ballet, Metropolitan Opera House, New York City 1991, Manon, Royal Ballet, London 1991, Cyrano de Bergerac, Royal Ballet, London 1991, Romeo and Juliet, Royal Ballet, London 1992, Othello, Sadler's Wells Theatre, London 1994. *Plays include:* Coppélia 1978, Ivan the Terrible, Don Quixote 1978–81, Swan Lake, Romeo and Juliet 1978–81, Spartacus 1981, Ivan the Terrible 1982, The Golden Age 1984, Raymonda 1985, Cyrano de Bergerac 1988, The Sleeping Beauty, 1989, The Nutcracker 1989, Winter Dreams 1991, La Bayadere 1993, Manon 1991, La Fille Mal Gardée, The Judas Tree, Mayerling, Apollo, Fearful Symmetries 1994, played the role of King of Siam in the King and I, Giselle, Legend of Love. *Television includes:* Bolshoi Ballet: Ivan the Terrible 1990, La Bayadère - The Temple Dancer 1991, The Sandman 2000, The South Bank Show 2002. *Address:* c/o Knight Ayton Management, 114 St Martin's Lane, London, WC2N 4BE, England (office); English National Ballet, Markova House, 39 Jay Mews, London, SW7 2ES, England (office). *Telephone:* (20) 7836-5333 (office); (20) 7581-1245 (office). *Fax:* (20) 7836-8333 (office); (20) 7225-0827 (office). *E-mail:* info@knightayton.co.uk (office). *Website:* www.knightayton.co.uk (office); www.ballet.org.uk (office).

MUKHAMEJANOV, Baurzhan A., PhD; Kazakhstani politician; *Ambassador to Lithuania;* b. 26 Nov. 1960; s. of Alim Mukhamedzhanov and Kulyash Mukhamedzhanov; m. Zarema Khaidarovna Mukhamedzhanova; ed Kirov Kazakh State Univ.; worked as Sr Consultant, Head of the Sector, Deputy Head of Dept, Head, Secr. of Chair. of Supreme Soviet, Head, Legislation and Legal Due Diligence Dept of Supreme Soviet 1990–94; Deputy Head of Presidential Admin Feb.–April 1994; Head, Legislation and Legal Due Diligence Dept, Exec. Office of Pres. 1994–96; Head, Dept for Legislation, Judicial and Legal System, Exec. Office of Pres. 1996–97; Sec. of Supreme Court Council 1996–2001; Minister of Justice 1997–2000, of Internal Affairs 2005–09; mem. Supreme Court Council 2001–08; Gov. of Mangystau region 2011–13; Amb. to Lithuania (concurrently accred to Latvia) 2013–; Barys Order of the III degree 2004, Parassat Order 1999, Barys Order of the II degree 2010. *Leisure interests:* books, golf. *Address:* Embassy of Kazakhstan, Birutės g. 20a, 08117 Vilnius, Kazakhstan (office). *Telephone:* (5) 212-2123 (office). *Fax:* (5) 231-3580 (office). *E-mail:* vilnius@mfa.kz (office). *Website:* kazembassy.lt (office).

MUKHAMETSHIN, Farid Khairullovich, DScS; Russian/Tatar politician; *Chairman, State Council of Tatarstan;* b. 22 May 1947, Almetyevsk, Tatarstan; m.; two c.; ed Almetyevak Higher Professional Tech. School, Ufa Inst. of Oil; metal turner in factories; CP functionary; Sec. Almetyevsk City CP Cttee; Chair. Exec. Cttee, Almetyevsk City Soviet; Deputy Chair. Council of Ministers, Minister of Trade of Tatar ASSR 1970–91; Chair. Supreme Soviet of Tatarstan Repub.

1991–94; mem. Council of Fed. 1991–94, 1998–; Prime Minister of Tatarstan Repub. 1995–98; Chair. State Council of Tatarstan 1998–; del. to Council of Europe, Chair. Regional Comm.; Leader Tatarstan New Age political movt 1999–. *Address:* Parliament Buildings, 420060, Kazan, pl. Svobody 1, Tatarstan, Russian Federation (office). *Telephone:* (843) 267-63-00 (office). *Fax:* (843) 267-64-89 (office). *E-mail:* gossov@gossov.tatarstan.ru (office). *Website:* www.gossov.tatarstan.ru (office).

MUKHANOV, Viatcheslav F., PhD; Russian theoretical physicist and academic; *Professor, Arnold Sommerfeld Center for Theoretical Physics, Ludwig-Maximilians-Universität;* b. 2 Oct. 1956, Kanash, Chuvash ASSR, Russian SFSR; ed Moscow Inst. of Physics and Tech.; worked with G. Chibisov at Lebedev Physical Inst., Moscow 1980–81; currently Prof., Arnold Sommerfeld Center for Theoretical Physics, Ludwig-Maximilians-Universität, Germany; Oskar Klein Medal, Stockholm Univ., Sweden 2006), Tomalla Prize (Switzerland) 2009, Blaise Pascal Chair, École Normale Supérieure, Paris 2011, Amaldi Medal 2012, Cosmology Prize, Gruber Foundation (co-recipient) 2013, Max Planck Medal, Deutsche Physikalische Gesellschaft 2015. *Achievements include:* best known for the theory of Quantum Origin of the Universe Structure. *Publications:* Theory of Cosmological Perturbations (co-author) 1992, Physical Foundations of Cosmology 2005, Introduction to Quantum Effects in Gravity 2007; numerous papers in professional journals. *Address:* Arnold Sommerfeld Center for Theoretical Physics, Chair on Cosmology, Theresienstr. 37, 80333 Munich, Germany (office). *Telephone:* (89) 21804544 (office). *Fax:* (89) 21804153 (office). *E-mail:* viatcheslav.mukhanov@physik.lmu.de (office). *Website:* www.theorie.physik.uni-muenchen.de/cosmology (office).

MUKHERJEE, Pranab Kumar, LLB, MA; Indian politician and fmr head of state; b. 11 Dec. 1935, Kirnahar, Birbhum Dist, W Bengal; s. of Kamada Kinkar Mukherjee and Rajlakshmi Mukherjee; m. Suvra Mukherjee 1957 (died 2015); two s. one d.; ed Vidyasagar Coll., Univ. of Calcutta; started career as lecturer; Ed. Palli-O-Panchayat Sambad (Bengali monthly); Founder-Ed. Desher Dak (Bengali weekly) 1967–71; mem. Rajya Sabha 1969–2004, Leader 1980–88; Deputy Minister of Industrial Devt, Govt of India 1973; Deputy Minister for Shipping and Transport Jan.–Oct. 1974; Minister of State, Ministry of Finance 1974–75; Minister for Revenue and Banking 1975–77; Minister of Commerce 1980–82, 1993–95, of Finance Jan.–Sept. 1982, 1982–85, 2009–12, of External Affairs 1995–96, 2006–09, of Defence 2004–06; Pres. of India 2012–17; Deputy Chair. Planning Comm. with Cabinet rank; f. Rashtriya Samajwadi Congress 1987–; mem. Exec. Cttee Congress (I) Party 1972–73, All India Congress Cttee 1986; Treas. Congress (I) Party, mem. Working Cttee, Deputy Leader in Rajya Sabha; Pres. W Bengal Pradesh Congress Cttee 1985–2000, Nikhil Bharat Banga Sahitya Sammelan 1995–2001, 2004–12; Leader of the House, Lok Sabha 2004–12; Trustee, Bangiya Sahitya Parishad 1984–90, Bidhan Memorial Trust Kolkata 1998–; Chair. Econ. Advisory Cell 1987–89, Group 24 (ministerial group attached to IMF and World Bank) 1984, Planning Bd Asiatic Soc., Kolkata 1984–86, 1992–96, 2004–07, Cen. Election Coordination Cttee 1999–2012; mem. Cen. Parl. Bd 1978–86, Bd of Govs IMF 1982–85, World Bank 1982–85, Asian Devt Bank 1982–85, African Devt Bank 1982–85, Cen. Election Cttee 2001–12; Hon. DLitt; Best Parliamentarian Award 1997, Padma Vibhushan 2008, Bharat Ratna 2019. *Publications include:* Bangla Congress: An Aspect of Constitutional Problems in Bengal 1967, Mid-term Poll 1969, Beyond Survival: Emerging Dimensions of Indian Economy 1984, Off the Track 1987, Challenges Before the Nation 1992, Saga of Struggle and Sacrifice 1992. *Leisure interests:* reading, gardening, music. *Address:* 10 Rajaji Marg, Lutyens, New Delhi 110 006, India.

MUKHI, Jagdish, MCom, PhD; Indian academic and politician; *Governor of Assam and of Mizoram;* b. 1 Dec. 1942, Dajal Dist, Dera Gazi Khan, Punjab (now in Pakistan); s. of Shri Jesa Ram Mukhi and Laxmi Devi Mukhi; m. Prem Mukhi 1970; one s. one d.; ed Raj Rishi Coll., Alwar, Sriram Coll., Delhi Univ., Kurukshetra Univ.; started academic career teaching at Bhagat Singh Coll., Delhi Univ. 1969; elected mem. Metropolitan Council Delhi 1980, Chief Whip of Bharatiya Janta Party (BJP) 1983–89, MLA from Jank Puri in newly constituted Delhi Vidhan Sabha 1993–2014, Leader of the Opposition 1998–2008; apptd Minister of Finance, Planning and Higher Educ. 1993; Pres. BJP West Dist Delhi 1987–91, Sec., BJP Delhi Pradesh 1991–93, apptd Gen. Sec., BJP Delhi Pradesh 1993, mem. BJP Nat. Exec. 1998, apptd Nat. Sec., BJP Disciplinary Cttee 2013, in charge of BJP Affairs for Haryana State 2013; Lt-Gov. of the Andaman and Nicobar Islands 2016–17; Gov. of Assam 2017–, also of Mizoram 2019–; elected Pres. Delhi Archery Asscn and Treas., Archery Asscn of India 2002; award for being best MLA 1998–2003. *Achievements include:* participant in archery competition at World Archery Championship 2002, Commonwealth Games 2006. *Address:* Office of the Governor of Assam, Raj Bhawan, Kharguli, Guwahati 781004, Assam (office); C-4C/63, Janakpuri, New Delhi 110 058, India (home). *Website:* www.jagdishmukhi.com.

MUKHTAR, Chaudhry Ahmed, MSOM; Pakistani politician and business executive; b. 22 June 1946, Lahore; three c.; ed Forman Christian Coll.; Owner Service Shoe business and several other cos in Pakistan; sr leader of Pakistan People's Party (PPP), Gujrat Dist; Minister of Commerce in Govt of Benazir Bhutto 1993–96; arrested for fraud and misuse of authority 1998 (acquitted 2000); mem. Parl. (PPP) 1990, for Gujrat-II 2008–; Minister of Defence 2008–12; Minister of Water and Power June 2012–March 2013; Chair. Pakistan International Airlines 2008; fmr Chair. Servis Group. *E-mail:* contact@ppp-tu.com.

MUKWEGE, Denis, MD, PhD; Democratic Republic of the Congo physician; b. 1 March 1955, Bukavu; ed Univ. of Burundi, Univ. libre de Bruxelles; began career as paediatrician, Lemera Hosp. near Bukavu; medical residency, Univ. of Angers, France 1989; f. Panzi Hospital (gynaecological and obstetric hosp.) 1999, specializing in care of victims of sexual violence; in exile in Europe following assassination attempt 2012–13; returned to Congo Jan. 2013; has treated more than 50,000 survivors of rape and other sexual violence; mem. Advisory Cttee, Int. Campaign to Stop Rape and Gender Violence in Conflict; several hon. degrees; Chevalier, Légion d'Honneur 2009, Officier, Légion d'Honneur 2013; UN Human Rights Prize 2008, Olof Palme Prize 2008, Van Heuven Goedhart Award 2010, Univ. of Michigan Wallenberg Medal 2010, King Baudouin Int. Devt Prize 2011, Clinton Global Citizen Award for Leadership in Civil Society 2011, Deutscher Medienpreis (German Media Award) 2011, Sakharov Prize for Freedom of Thought 2014, Gulbenkian Prize 2015, Seoul Peace Prize 2016, Nobel Peace Prize (jtly with Nadia Murad) 2018. *Address:* Panzi Foundation, Mushununu, Bukavu 266, Sud Kivu Province, Democratic Republic of the Congo (office). *Website:* www.panzifoundation.org (office).

MULALLY, Alan Roger, BS, MS, MA; American business executive; b. 4 Aug. 1945, Oakland, Calif.; m. Jane Connell; three s. two d.; ed Univ. of Kan., Sloan School of Man., Massachusetts Inst. of Tech.; joined The Boeing Co. 1969, numerous eng and program man. positions including contribs on 727, 737, 747, 757, 767 aeroplanes, Vice-Pres. of Eng, Vice-Pres. and Gen. Man. 777 programme, Sr Vice-Pres. of Airplane Devt, Boeing Commercial Airplanes Group 1994–97, Sr Vice-Pres. The Boeing Co. and Pres. Boeing Information, Space and Defense Systems 1997–98, Exec. Vice-Pres. The Boeing Co. and Pres. Boeing Commercial Airplanes 1998–2006, CEO 2001–06; Pres. and CEO Ford Motor Co. 2006–14; mem. Bd of Dirs Google Inc. 2014–; fmr Chair. Bd of Govs Aerospace Industries Asscn; fmr Co-Chair. Washington Competitive Council; fmr mem. Advisory Bds NASA, Univ. of Washington, Univ. of Kansas, MIT; fmr mem. Scientific Advisory Bd USAF; mem. Nat. Acad. of Eng; Fellow, AIAA 1995 (Pres. –2006), Royal Acad. of Eng; Hon. FRAeS 1999; Hon. DSc (Univ. of Kansas) 2012; Industry Engineer of the Year, Nat. Soc. of Professional Engineers 1978, Tech. Man. Award, American Inst. of Aeronautics and Astronautics 1986, Univ. of Kan. Eng School Distinguished Eng Service Award 1994, Reed Aeronautics Award, American Inst. of Aeronautics and Astronautics 1996, Engineer of the Year, Design News magazine 1996, named Person of the Year by Aviation Week & Space Technology 2006, included in TIME 100 list 2009, named Person of the Year by The Financial Times ArcelorMittal Boldness in Business Awards 2011, named CEO of the Year by Chief Executive magazine 2011. *Leisure interests:* tennis and golf.

MULARONI, Antonella; San Marino lawyer, judge and politician; b. 27 Sept. 1961; ed Univ. of Bologna, Italy; qualified as lawyer and notary public 1987; Political Sec. to Sec. of State for Finance, Budget and Econ. Planning 1986–87, Dir Office for Relations with San Marino Communities Abroad, Dept of Foreign Affairs 1987–90; Deputy Perm. Rep. of Repub. of San Marino to Council of Europe 1989–90; served as lawyer and notary public 1991–2001; mem. (People's Alliance) Great and Gen. Council (Parl.) 1993–2001, 2008–; Judge European Court of Human Rights 2001–08; Sec. of State for Foreign and Political Affairs, Telecommunications and Transport 2008; Co-Captain Regent (jt head of state) April–Oct. 2013; fmr mem. San Marino Christian Democratic Party Cen. Cttee; Founding mem. People's Alliance of San Marino Democrats 1993, Co-ordinator Jan.–June 1993, Pres. of Ass. 1998–99. *Address:* c/o Office of the Captains-Regent, Contrada Omerelli, 47890 San Marino, San Marino (office).

MULARONI, Pier Marino; San Marino politician; b. 6 Sept. 1962; Capitano (mayor) of Castello di Faetano 1986–93; mem. Consiglio Grande e Generale (Parl.) 1993–; co-Capt.-Regent April–Oct. 1997; Sec. of State for Labour 2001–02, for Finance, Transport, the Budget and Relations with Azienda Autonoma di Stato Filatelica e Numismatica (AASFN) and Azienda Autonoma di Stato per i Servizi Pubblici (AASS) 2002–06, for Labour, Co-operation and Youth Policies 2007–08; founding mem. Unione per la Repubblica 2011. *Address:* c/o Secretariat of State for Labour, Co-operation and Youth Policies, Palazzo Mercuri, Contrada del Collegio 38, 47890 San Marino (office).

MULAY, Dnyaneshwar M., MA; Indian diplomatist, academic and author; *Additional Secretary, Consular Passport Visa Division and Overseas Indian Affairs, Ministry of External Affairs;* b. 5 Nov. 1958; m. Sadhna Mulay; two s. one d.; joined Foreign Service 1983, has held several positions in missions in Damascus, Mauritius, Japan and Russia, has also worked extensively in Indian Govt, Jt Sec. (HQ), Ministry of External Affairs –2009, High Commr to the Maldives 2009–13, Consul-Gen. in New York 2013–16, Additional Sec., Consular Passport Visa Division and Overseas Indian Affairs, Ministry of External Affairs 2016–; Chief Patron, India Club, Maldives 2009–; columnist for Marathi daily newspapers including Lokmat and Loksatta, and weekly Sadhana. *Publications:* Maati Pankh Aaani Aakas (autobiography; in Marathi), Russia Navya Dishanche Amantran, Swatahteel Awakash (poetry collection) (State Literary Award, Govt of Maharashtra). *Address:* Ministry of External Affairs, South Block, New Delhi 110 011, India (office). *Telephone:* (11) 24674143 (office). *Fax:* (11) 24674140 (office). *E-mail:* ascpvmea.gov.in (office). *Website:* www.mea.gov.in (office).

MULCAHY, Anne M., BA; American business executive; b. 21 Oct. 1952, Rockville Centre, NY; ed Marymount Coll.; joined Xerox Corpn, Stamford, Conn. 1976, held various sales and sr man. positions 1976–92, Vice-Pres. Human Resources 1992–95, Vice-Pres. and Staff Officer Customer Relations 1995–97, Chief Staff Officer 1997–99, Corp. Sr Vice-Pres. 1998–99, Pres. Gen. Markets Operations 1999–2000, Pres. and COO 2000–01, CEO 2001–09, also Chair. 2002–10; Chair. Bd of Trustees Save The Children Federation, Inc. 2009–; mem. Bd Dirs Johnson & Johnson, Target Corpn, The Washington Post Co., LPL Financial 2013–; Chair. Corp. Governance Task Force of the Business Roundtable; mem. Business Council; inducted into Conn. Women's Hall of Fame. *Address:* Save the Children US Headquarters, 501 Kings Hwy East, Suite 400, Fairfield, CT 06825, USA. *Website:* www.savethechildren.org.

MULCAHY, Sir Geoffrey John, Kt, BSc, MBA; British business executive; *Chairman, Javelin Group;* b. 7 Feb. 1942, Sunderland, England; s. of Maurice Mulcahy and Kathleen Mulcahy (née Blenkinsop); m. Valerie Elizabeth Mulcahy 1965; one s. one d.; ed King's School, Worcester, Univ. of Manchester, Harvard Univ.; started career in labour relations, marketing and planning with Esso Corpn; Finance Dir Norton Abrasives' European Div., then with British Sugar; joined Woolworth Holdings (now Kingfisher PLC) 1983, first as Group Financial Dir, then Group Man. Dir 1984–86, CEO 1986–93, Chair. 1990–95, Group CEO Kingfisher Group 1995–2003; Chair. Javelin Group Ltd 2003–; Dir (non-exec.), Brown & Jackson 2005–. *Leisure interest:* sailing, squash. *Address:* Javelin Group Ltd, 200 Aldersgate Street, London EC1A 4HD, England (office). *Telephone:* (20) 7961-3200 (office). *Fax:* (20) 7961-3299 (office). *E-mail:* info@javelingroup.com (office). *Website:* www.javelingroup.com (office).

MULDOON, Paul Benedict, BA, FRSL; Irish/American poet, academic and editor; *Howard G. B. Clark '21 University Professor in the Humanities and Professor of Creative Writing, Princeton University;* b. 20 June 1951, Portadown, Northern Ireland; s. of Patrick Muldoon and Brigid Regan; m. Jean Hanff Korelitz

1987; one s. one d.; ed St Patrick's Coll., Armagh, Queen's Univ., Belfast; radio and TV producer, BBC NI 1973–86; has taught at Univs of Cambridge, East Anglia, Columbia Univ., Univ. of California, Berkeley, Univ. of Massachusetts, Univ. of St Andrews, Univ. of Ulster; Lecturer, Princeton Univ. 1987–88, 1990–95, Dir Creative Writing Program 1993–2002, Prof. 1995–, Howard G. B. Clark '21 Prof. in the Humanities and Prof. of Creative Writing 1998–, Founding Chair. Lewis Center for the Arts 2006–12; Founder Princeton Poetry Festival 2009–; Visiting Prof., Bread Loaf School of English 1997–2010; Poetry Ed., The New Yorker 2007–; mem. Aosdána, American Acad. of Arts and Sciences 2000–, American Acad. of Arts and Letters 2008–; Hon. Prof. of Poetry, Univ. of Oxford 1999–2004; Eric Gregory Award 1972, Sir Geoffrey Faber Memorial Awards 1980, 1991, Guggenheim Fellowship 1990, American Acad. of Arts and Letters Award for Literature 1996, Irish Times Poetry Prize 1997, Pulitzer Prize for Poetry 2003, Griffin Prize 2003, American Ireland Fund Literary Award 2004, Shakespeare Prize 2004, Aspen Prize for Poetry 2005, European Prize for Poetry 2006, John William Corrington Award 2009, Gold Medal for Poetry 2017. *Publications include:* poetry: Knowing My Place 1971, New Weather 1973, Spirit of Dawn 1975, Mules 1977, Names and Addresses 1978, Immram 1980, Why Brownlee Left 1980, Out of Siberia 1982, Quoof 1983, The Wishbone 1984, Selected Poems 1968–83 1986, Meeting the British 1987, Madoc: A Mystery 1990, Incantata 1994, The Prince of the Quotidian 1994, The Annals of Chile (T. S. Eliot Prize) 1995, Kerry Slides 1996, New Selected Poems 1968–1994 1996, Hopewell Haiku 1997, The Bangle (Slight Return) 1998, Hay (poems) 1999, Poems 1968–1998 2001, Horse Latitudes 2006, Plan B (with Norman McBeath) 2009, Wayside Shrines 2009, Maggot 2010, The Word on the Street 2013, One Thousand Things Worth Knowing 2014; for children: The O-O's Party 1981, The Last Thesaurus 1995, The Noctuary of Narcissus Batt 1997; other: Monkeys (TV play) 1989, Shining Brow (opera libretto) 1993, Six Honest Serving Men (play) 1995, Bandanna (opera libretto) 1999, To Ireland, I (essays) 2000; ed.: The Scrake of Dawn 1979, The Faber Book of Contemporary Irish Poetry 1986, The Essential Byron 1989, Moy Sand and Gravel (Pulitzer Prize for Poetry) 2002; trans.: The Astrakhan Cloak, by Nuala Ni Dhomhnaill 1993, The Birds, by Aristophanes (with Richard Martin) 1999. *Leisure interests:* electric guitar, English longbow. *Address:* Creative Writing Program, Room 122, Lewis Center for the Arts, 185 Nassau Street, Princeton University, Princeton, NJ 08544, USA (office). *Telephone:* (609) 258-4708 (office). *E-mail:* muldoon@princeton.edu (office). *Website:* www.paulmuldoon.net.

MULET, Edmond; Guatemalan lawyer, politician, diplomatist and UN official; b. 13 March 1951, Guatemala City; s. of Augusto Mulet Descamps and Simone Lesieur; m. Karen Lind; two s.; ed Universidad Mariano Galvez; notary public; elected to Nat. Congress 1982, cand. to Nat. Constituent Ass. 1984, elected to Congress 1986–91, re-elected 1991–96; elected Sec.-Gen. Union del Centro Nacional party 1996; mem. Guatemalan-Belize Comm., first as Rep. of Congress and later as Del. from Exec. Br.; Amb. to USA 1993 (resgnd following coup d'état in Guatemala) resumed duties 1994–96, Amb. to EU, Belgium and Luxembourg 2000–06; Special Rep. of UN Sec.-Gen. in Haiti and Head of UN Stabilization Mission in Haiti (MINUSTAH) 2006–07, 2010–11 (following death of Hédi Annabi in earthquake of 12 Jan. 2010), Asst Sec.-Gen. for Peacekeeping Operations, UN 2007–10, 2011–15, Chef de Cabinet of UN Sec.-Gen. 2015–16, Head of Security Council Jt UN–OPCW Investigative Mechanism on Chemical Weapon Use in Syria 2017.

MULFORD, David Campbell, BA, MA, DPhil; American economist, investment banker and fmr diplomatist; *Vice-Chairman International, Credit Suisse Group;* b. 27 June 1937, Rockford, Ill.; m. Jeannie Simmons; two c.; ed Lawrence Univ., Boston Univ., Univ. of Oxford, UK; served as Special Asst to Sec. of Treasury as White House Fellow 1965–66; Man. Dir and Head of Int. Finance, White, Weld & Co. (investment bank) 1966–74; Sr Investment Advisor, Saudi Arabia Monetary Agency 1974–83; Under-Sec. and Asst Sec. for Int. Affairs, US Treasury Dept 1984–92; Dir, Merrill Lynch, Pierce, Fenner & Smith; Int. Chair. Credit Suisse First Boston (now Credit Suisse Group), London 1992–2003, Vice-Chair. Int. 2009–; Amb. to India 2004–09; mem. Council on Foreign Relations; affil. with Center for Strategic and Int. Studies, Washington, DC; Chevalier, Légion d'honneur 1990, Order of May for Merit (Argentina) 1993, Officer's Cross Medal for Merit (Poland) 1995; Dr hc (Lawrence Univ.) 1984; Alexander Hamilton Award, US Treasury Dept 1992, Distinguished Alumni Award, Boston Univ. 1992. *Publications:* Zambia: The Politics of Independence, 1957–1964 1967, Packing for India: A Life of Action in Global Finance and Diplomacy 2014. *Address:* Credit Suisse Group, Eleven Madison Avenue, New York, NY 10010, USA (office). *Telephone:* (212) 325-2000 (office). *Fax:* (212) 325-8057 (office). *Website:* www .credit-suisse.com (office).

MÜLIKOV, Isgender; Turkmenistani police officer and government official; *Minister of Internal Affairs;* b. 1975, Aşgabat, Turkmen SSR, USSR; ed Higher School of the Ministry of Internal Affairs of Turkmenistan; began career in state law enforcement system and held several posts within Ministry of Internal Affairs; Chief, Daşoguz Velayat Police Feb.–June 2009; Minister of Internal Affairs June 2009–. *Address:* Ministry of Internal Affairs, 744000 Aşgabat, Magtymguly Şaýoly 85, Turkmenistan (office). *Telephone:* (12) 35-13-28 (office). *Fax:* (12) 39-19-44 (office).

MULINO, José Raúl, LLL; Panamanian lawyer and politician; b. 13 June 1959; ed Univ. Santa Maria La Antigua, Tulane Univ., New Orleans, USA; Vice-Minister of Foreign Affairs 1990–93, Minister of Foreign Affairs 1993–94; mem. Nat. Council for Foreign Affairs 1994–95; Deputy Magistrate, Corte Suprema de Justicia 1994–95; Minister of the Interior and Justice 2009–10, of Public Security 2010–14; mem. Asociación Panameña de Ejecutivos de Empresa (Pres. 1989–90), Asociación Panameña de Derecho Marítimo, American Soc. of Int. Law; Hon. mem. Consejo Nacional de la Empresa Privada (Vice-Pres. 1989–90).

MULIOKELA, Wamundila; Zambian politician and business executive; b. 15 May 1942; m.; mem. Parl. 2001–06; fmr Deputy Minister of Mines and Minerals; Deputy Minister of Defence –2005, Minister of Defence 2005–06; apptd Chair. ZESCO Ltd (power utility) 2006–. *Leisure interests:* charity Work, football.

MULJADI, Kartini; Indonesian lawyer and fmr judge; *Founder and Senior Partner, Kartini Muljadi & Rekan;* b. 17 May 1930; m. Djojo Muljadi (died 1973); three c.; ed Univ. of Indonesia; judge, Special Court of Jakarta 1958–70 (retd); f. Kartini Muljadi & Rekan (law firm), Jakarta 1990, currently Sr Pnr; adviser to Indonesian Govt, Indonesian Bank Restructuring Agency, World Bank, Int. Finance Corpn; major shareholder, PT Tempo Scan (pharmaceutical co.); Trustee, Indonesian Chamber of Commerce and Industry, Indonesian Inst. of Commrs and Dirs, Indonesian AIDS Foundation; Hon. mem. Indonesian Bar Asscn, Indonesian Capital Market Arbitration Bd; Capital Markets Lifetime Achievement Award 2004. *Address:* Kartini Muljadi & Rekan, Jalan Gunawarman No. 18, Kebayoran Baru, Jakarta 12110, Indonesia (office). *Telephone:* (21) 72794535 (office). *Fax:* (21) 72794551 (office). *E-mail:* kartini.muljadi@kmuljadilaw.com (office). *Website:* www.kmuljadilaw.com (office).

MULK, Nasir-ul, BA, LLB, Barrister-at-Law; Pakistani judge and government official; b. 17 Aug. 1950, Swat, Khyber Pakhtunkhwa; s. of Seth Kamran Khan; ed Abbottabad Public School, Jehanzeb Coll., Law Coll., Univ. of Peshawar, Inner Temple, London; called to the Bar 1977, Sec.-Gen. Peshawar High Court Bar Asscn 1981, elected twice as Pres. 1990, 1993; Advocate Gen., N.W.F.P (Khyber Pakhtunkhwa) 1993–94; Judge, Peshawar High Court 1994–2004, Chief Justice 2004–05; Judge, Supreme Court 2005, Sr Justice 2013–14, Chief Justice 2014–15; Judge In Charge, Federal Judicial Acad.; Acting Chief Election Commr of Pakistan Nov. 2013–July 2014; Acting Prime Minister June–Aug. 2018; Chair. Federal Review Bd of Pakistan 2009; part-time Lecturer, Khyber Law Coll., Peshawar Univ.; fmr Visiting Scholar, Pakistan Admin. Staff Coll.; fmr mem. Judicial Comm. of Pakistan. *Leisure interest:* golf.

MULKI, Hani, MSc, PhD; Jordanian diplomatist and politician; b. 15 Oct. 1951; s. of Fawzi Mulki and Bashira Mulki; m. Sheila Mulki; two s.; ed Rensselaer Polytechnic Inst., New York, USA; fmr Sec.-Gen. Higher Council for Science and Tech.; fmr Minister of Industry and Trade, Supply, Water and Irrigation; Amb. to Egypt and Perm. Rep. to the Arab League –2004, 2008; Minister of Foreign Affairs 2004–05; mem. Senate 2005–07; Special Adviser to King of Jordan 2005–; Minister of Industry and Trade 2011; Prime Minister and Minister of Defence 2016–18; fmr Pres. Royal Scientific Soc.; Commdr, Royal Order of the Nordic Star (Sweden) 1989, Grand Cordon, Order of Istiklal 1993, Je Maintiendrai Medal (Netherlands) 1996, Grand Cordon, Order of Al Kawkab 1998, Return of the Insignia of Danish Orders 1998, Grand Officier, Ordre Nat. du Mérite (France) 1998. *Address:* 37 Damascus Street, Abdoun, Amman, Jordan (home). *Website:* www.pm.gov.jo (office).

MULLA, Habib al-, LLB, LLM, PhD; United Arab Emirates lawyer and business executive; *Founder and Executive Chairman, Habib Al Mulla & Company;* ed UAE Univ., Harvard Law School, USA, Univ. of Cambridge, UK; has held numerous prominent govt positions, including as mem. UAE Fed. Nat. Council 2000–02 and Fed. Parl. of the UAE, as mem. Legis. Cttee, in charge of reviewing federal legislation, as mem. Econ. Cttee, in charge of reviewing fiscal and economic policy of the federation, as Dir Inst. of Advanced Legal and Judicial Studies, in charge of training judges and prosecutors in Emirate of Dubai, as Chair. UAE Jurists Asscn; Founder and Exec. Chair. Habib Al Mulla & Co.; Vice-Chair. Bd of Trustees, Dubai Int. Arbitration Centre; Chair. Chartered Inst. of Arbitrators UAE Cttee; designed the legal framework establishing the Dubai Int. Financial Centre; Chair. Legis. Cttee, Dubai Financial Services Authority 2003–06; mem. ICC Inst., UAE ICC Nat. Cttee, Panel of Experts of the Broadcasting and Publs Standards Tribunal of the Tech., Electronic Commerce and Media Free Zone Authority (TECOM) in Dubai; Dir Supervisory Bd of Rasmala (Regional Investment Banking Group); Vice-Pres. Bd Govs, American Univ. in Dubai; mem. Bd of Trustees, Dubai School of Govt; Fellow Mem., Chartered Inst. of Arbitrators. *Publications:* numerous books and articles on UAE law and economy, including a two-part book on his life's work entitled Life's Harvest. *Address:* Habib Al Mulla & Co., Level 14, O14 Tower, Al Khail Road, Business Bay, PO Box 2268, Dubai, United Arab Emirates (office). *Telephone:* (4) 423-0000 (office). *Fax:* (4) 447-9777 (office). *E-mail:* habib.almulla@habibalmulla.com (office). *Website:* www.habibalmulla.com (office).

MULLALLY, Rt Rev Dame Sarah Elisabeth, DBE, BSc, MSc, DipTh; British ecclesiastic and fmr nurse; *Bishop-designate of London;* b. (Sarah Elisabeth Bowser), 26 March 1962; d. of Michael Bowser and Ann Mills; m. Eamonn Mullally 1987; one s. one d.; ed South Bank Polytechnic, London South Bank Univ., South East Inst. of Theological Educ., Univ. of Kent, Heythrop Coll., Univ. of London; various clinical nursing posts including staff nurse, later sr staff nurse, St Thomas' Hosp., London; specialist cancer care nurse, Royal Marsden Hosp.; ward sister and head of practice devt, fmr Westminster Hosp.; fmr Dir of Nursing, Chelsea and Westminster Hosp., later becoming Deputy CEO and Acting CEO; Chief Nursing Officer and Dir of Patient Experience for England, Dept of Health 1999–2004; ordained in the Church of England as deacon 2001 and as priest 2002; non-stipendiary minister (part-time minister), Parish of Battersea Fields in the Diocese of Southwark 2001–04; left post as Chief Nursing Officer to take up full-time ministry 2004; Asst Curate, St Saviour's Church, Battersea Fields 2004–06; Team Rector, Sutton team ministry, St Nicholas' Church, Sutton 2006–12; Canon Treas., Salisbury Cathedral 2012–15; consecrated as bishop July 2015; Bishop of Crediton 2015–18; Bishop-desig. of London (first female) 2018–; Ind. Gov., London South Bank Univ. 2005–15; lay mem., Council of King's Coll. London 2016–; Dir (non-exec.) Royal Marsden NHS Foundation Trust 2005–12; Fellow, London South Bank Univ. 2001, Canterbury Christ Church Univ. 2006; Dr hc (Bournemouth) 2004, (Wolverhampton) 2004, (Hertfordshire) 2005. *Address:* The Bishop of London's Office, St Michael Paternoster Royal, College Hill, London EC4R 2RL, England (office). *Telephone:* (20) 3837-5200 (office). *Website:* bishopoflondon.org (office).

MULLAN, Peter, BSc; British actor and film director; b. 2 Nov. 1954, Glasgow; ed Univ. of Glasgow; debut with Wildcat Theatre Co. 1988; Hon. MA (Caledonian Univ., Glasgow) 2000. *Film appearances include:* Riff-Raff 1990, The Bid Man 1991, Shallow Grave 1994, Braveheart 1995, Ruffian Hearts 1995, Good Day for the Bad Guys 1995, Trainspotting 1996, Fairytale: A True Story, My Name is Joe (Best Actor Award, Cannes Film Festival 1998) 1998, Duck 1998, Miss Julie 1999, Mauvaise passe 1999, Ordinary Decent Criminal 2000, The Claim 2000, Session 9 2001, The Magdalene Sisters 2002, Entering Blue Zone 2002, Young Adam 2002, Kiss of Life 2003, Kono yo no sotoe–Club Shinchugun 2004, Criminal 2004, Blinded 2004, Waves 2004, On a Clear Day 2005, Cargo 2006, Children of Men 2006, True North 2006, The Last Legion 2007, Dog Altogether 2007, Boy A 2007, Tyrannosaur 2011, Harry Potter and the Deathly Hallows-Part 2 2011, Sunshine on Leith 2013,

Welcome to the Punch 2013, Hercules 2014, Sunset Song 2015, Hector 2015. *Films written and directed include:* Good Day for the Bay Guys 1995, Fridge 1996, Orphans (Golden Lion Award, Venice Film Festival 1998) 1997, The Magdalene Sisters (Golden Lion Award, Venice Film Festival 2002) 2002, Neds (Golden Shell Winner) 2010. *Films produced include:* Caesar 2000. *Television includes:* Rab C. Nesbitt (series) 1990, Jute City (film) 1991, Nightlife (film) 1996, Cardiac Arrest (series) 1996–97, Bogwoman (film) 1997, This Little Life 2003, Shoebox Zoo 2004, The Trial of Tony Blair 2007, Scotland on Screen 2009, The Fear 2012, Top of the Lake 2013, Mum 2016–.

MULLEN, Larry, Jr; Irish musician (drums) and actor; b. 31 Oct. 1961, Dublin; ed Mount Temple School, Dublin; Founder-mem. and drummer with Feedback 1976, renamed Hype, finally renamed U2 1978–; major concerts include Live Aid Wembley 1985, Self Aid Dublin, A Conspiracy of Hope (Amnesty Int. Tour) 1986, Smile Jamaica (hurricane relief fundraiser) 1988, Very Special Arts Festival, White House, Washington, DC 1988; numerous tours world-wide; U2 have won 22 Grammy Awards, including Best Rock Performance by a Duo or Group with Vocal (for Desire) 1988, BRIT Awards for Best Int. Act 1988–90, 1992, 1998, 2001, Best Live Act 1993, Outstanding Contribution to the British Music Industry 2001, JUNO Award 1993, World Music Award 1993, Grammy Award for Song of the Year, Record of the Year, Best Rock Performance by a Duo or Group with Vocal (all for Beautiful Day) 2000, Grammy Awards for Best Pop Performance by a Duo or Group with Vocal (for Stuck In A Moment You Can't Get Out Of), for Record of the Year (for Walk On), for Best Rock Performance by a Duo or Group with Vocal (for Elevation) 2001, American Music Award for Favorite Internet Artist of the Year 2002, Ivor Novello Award for Best Song Musically and Lyrically (for Walk On) 2002, Golden Globe for Best Original Song (for The Hands That Built America, from film Gangs of New York) 2003, Grammy Awards for Best Rock Performance by a Duo or Group with Vocal, Best Rock Song, Best Short Form Music Video (all for Vertigo) 2004, Nordoff-Robbins Silver Clef Award for lifetime achievement 2005, Q Awards for Best Live Act 2005, 2016, Digital Music Award for Favourite Download Single (for Vertigo) 2005, Meteor Ireland Music Award for Best Irish Band, Best Live Performance 2006, Grammy Awards for Song of the Year, for Best Rock Performance by a Duo or Group with Vocal (both for Sometimes You Can't Make it on Your Own), for Best Rock Song (for City of Blinding Lights) 2006, Amnesty International Ambassadors of Conscience Award 2006, Golden Globe Award for Best Original Score, Motion Picture (Ordinary Love in Mandela: Long Walk to Freedom) 2014, Palm Springs Film Festival Sonny Bono Visionary Award 2014, MTV Europe Music Award for Global Icon 2017; Portuguese Order of Liberty 2005. *Films include:* Rattle and Hum 1988, Man on the Train 2011, A Thousand Times Good Night 2013. *Recordings include:* albums: Boy 1980, October 1981, War 1983, Under a Blood Red Sky 1983, The Unforgettable Fire 1984, Wide Awake In America 1985, The Joshua Tree (Grammy Award for Album of the Year, Best Rock Performance by a Duo or Group with Vocal) 1987, Rattle and Hum 1988, Achtung Baby (Grammy Award for Best Rock Performance by a Duo or Group with Vocal 1992) 1991, Zooropa (Grammy Award for Best Alternative Music Album) 1993, Passengers (film soundtrack with Brian Eno) 1995, Pop 1997, The Best Of 1980–90 1998, All That You Can't Leave Behind (Grammy Award for Best Rock Album 2001) 2000, The Best Of 1990–2000 2002, How To Dismantle An Atomic Bomb (Meteor Ireland Music Award for Best Irish Album 2006, Grammy Awards for Album of the Year, for Best Rock Album 2006) 2004, No Line on the Horizon 2009, Songs of Innocence 2014, Songs of Experience 2017. *Address:* c/o Principle Management, 30–32 Sir John Rogersons Quay, Dublin 2, Ireland (office). *E-mail:* nadine@numb.ie (office). *Website:* www.u2.com.

MULLEN, Adm. (retd) Michael (Mike) Glenn, MSc; American naval officer (retd); *Security Director, Sprint Communications, Inc.;* b. 4 Oct. 1946, Los Angeles, Calif.; m. Deborah Mullen; two s.; ed Naval Postgraduate School, Monterey, Calif., Harvard Business School; served as jr officer aboard USS Collett, USS Blandy, USS Fox, USS Sterrett, held command posts aboard USS Noxubee, USS Goldsborough, USS Yorktown, as Flag Officer commanded Cruiser-Destroyer Group Two and George Washington Battle Group, fmr Commdr US Second Fleet/NATO Striking Fleet Atlantic; non-operational posts have included Co. Officer and Exec. Asst to Commdt of Midshipmen, US Naval Acad., Annapolis, Dir Surface Officer Distribution, Bureau of Naval Personnel; posts with Chief of Naval Operations include Deputy Dir and Dir of Surface Warfare, Deputy Chief of Naval Operations for Resources, Requirements and Assessments, 32nd Vice-Chief of Naval Operations 2003–04; served as Commdr Allied Jt Force Command Naples, Chief of Naval Operations 2004–07; Chair. Jt Chiefs of Staff 2007–11; Security Dir Sprint Nextel Corpn (now Sprint Communications) 2013–; mem. Bd of Dirs General Motors Corpn; Jt Chiefs of Staff Identification Badge, Navy Surface Warfare Badge (Officer), Defense Distinguished Service Medal, Navy Distinguished Service Medal (2), Defense Superior Service Medal, Legion of Merit Decoration (6), Meritorious Service Medal, Navy and Marine Corps Commendation Medal, Navy and Marine Corps Achievement Medal, Navy Unit Commendation Ribbon, Navy Meritorious Unit Commendation Ribbon, Navy 'E' Ribbon, Navy Expeditionary Medal, Nat. Defense Service Medal (3), Armed Forces Expeditionary Medal, Viet Nam Service Medal, Global War on Terrorism Service Medal, Humanitarian Service Medal (2), Navy Overseas Service Ribbon (4), Navy Sea Service Deployment Ribbon (2), Repub. of Viet Nam Gallantry Cross Unit Citation Medal, Repub. of Viet Nam Civil Actions Unit Citation Ribbon. *Address:* Office of the Security Director, Sprint Communications, Inc., 6391 Sprint Parkway, Overland Park, KS 66251, USA (office). *Telephone:* (703) 433-4000 (office). *Website:* www.sprint.com (office).

MÜLLER, Christoph, MA, Dr iur; German diplomatist; b. 20 Dec. 1950, Starnberg, Bavaria; m.; three d.; ed Fletcher School of Law and Diplomacy, Tufts Univ., USA, Univ. of Augsburg; mil. service (alpine troops), reserve officer, Bavaria 1970–72; legal studies and practice, state examinations, research work, Augsburg and Munich 1972–79; joined Foreign Service 1981, served at Perm. Mission to NATO, Brussels 1983–85, Arms Control Directorate, Fed. Foreign Office, Bonn 1985–87, Embassy in Beijing 1988–90, served as Deputy Head of German Del. to Conf. on Disarmament, Geneva (final phase of negotiations for a global ban on chemical weapons) 1990–93, Deputy Head, Public Int. Law Div., Bonn 1993–96, Deputy Chief of Mission, Embassy in Harare, Zimbabwe 1996–98, Head of Political Dept, Embassy in New Delhi 1998–2000, Head of South Asia Desk and Task Force on Afghanistan, Fed. Foreign Office, Berlin 2000–03, Deputy Dir Gen. for Legal Affairs 2003–06, Amb. to Peru 2006–11, to Australia (also accred to Papua New Guinea, Solomon Islands and Vanuatu) 2011–16.

MÜLLER, Gerhard, Dr rer. nat; German chemist and academic; *Professor of Chemistry, University of Konstanz;* b. 7 March 1953, Rehren, Lower Saxony; ed Tech. Univ. of Munich; Postdoctoral Assoc., Univ. of California, Berkeley 1980–81; Postdoctoral Assoc., Max-Planck-Inst. für Kohlenforschung, Mulheim 1982–83; Research Assoc., Tech. Univ. of Munich 1983–89, Lecturer 1989; Prof. of Chem., Univ. of Konstanz 1990–, Vice-Dean, Dept of Chem. 1992–93, 1995–96, Dean 1993–95, 2003–05, 2008–09, Vice-Pres. of Research 1998–2000; mem. German Nat. Cttee, Int. Union of Crystallography 1994–2000, Chair. Div. of Molecular Compounds 1992–2000; Asst Ed. Zeitschrift für Naturforschung B 1986–; mem. German Chemical Soc., German Crystallographic Soc., Nat. Geographic Soc. *Publications:* more than 290 scientific papers in professional journals on organometallic chemistry. *Address:* Fachbereich Chemie, Universität Konstanz, Postfach 5560-M723, Room L703, Universitaetsstrasse 10, 78457 Konstanz, Germany (office). *Telephone:* (7531) 88-3735 (office). *Fax:* (7531) 88-3140 (office). *E-mail:* gerhard.mueller@uni-konstanz.de (office). *Website:* cms.uni-konstanz.de/mueller (office).

MÜLLER, HE Cardinal Gerhard Ludwig; German ecclesiastic and academic; b. 31 Dec. 1947, Finthen, Mainz; ed Willigis Episcopal High School, Mainz, Univs of Mainz, Munich and Freiburg; ordained priest, Archdiocese of Mainz 1978, worked as a chaplain in three parishes; Prof. of Dogmatic Theology, Ludwig Maximilian Univ. 1986–2002, now Hon. Prof.; consecrated Bishop of Regensburg 2002–12; mem. Congregation for the Doctrine of the Faith 2002–, Prefect 2012–13, 2013–17, Prefect Emer. 2017–; Pres. Pontifical Comm. 'Ecclesia Dei' 2012–13, 2013–17, Int. Theological Comm. 2012–13, 2013–17, Pontifical Biblical Comm. 2012–13, 2013–17; apptd Archbishop *ad personam* 2012; cr. Cardinal (Cardinal-Deacon of Sant'Agnese in Agone) 2014–; mem. Pontifical Council for Culture 2009–, Congregation for Catholic Educ. 2012–, Pontifical Council for Promoting Christian Unity 2012–, Congregation for the Oriental Churches 2014–; fmr Chair. Ecumenical Comm., German Bishops' Conf., fmr mem. Faith World Church of the Comm.; fmr Vice-Chair. Asscn of Christian Churches in Germany; first Pres. for the Promotion of Eastern Church Inst., Regensburg; charged with preparing the publication of the 'Opera Omnia': series of books that will collect, in a single edn, all of Pope Benedict XVI's writings; Kt Grand Cross of Merit, Sacred Mil. Constantinian Order of St George 2003; Fed. Cross of Merit, First Class (Bavaria) 2009; Dr hc (Lublin) 2004, (Pontificia Universidad Católica del Perú) 2008. *Publications:* more than 400 works on dogmatic theology, ecumenism, revelation, hermeneutics, the priesthood and the diaconate. *Address:* c/o Congregation for the Doctrine of the Faith, Piazza del S. Uffizio 11, 00193 Rome, Italy (office). *Telephone:* (06) 69895911 (office). *Fax:* (06) 69883409 (office). *Website:* www.doctrinafidei.va (office); www.vatican.va/roman_curia/congregations/cfaith (office).

MÜLLER, Herta; German (b. Romanian) writer; b. 17 Aug. 1953, Nitzkydorf, Banat, Romania; d. of Catarina Müller; m. Richard Wagner; ed Univ. of Timişoara; as a student, involved with Aktionsgruppe Banat (authors' group opposed to Nicolae Ceauşescu's rule of Romania); worked as translator in machine factory 1977–79; emigrated to Germany 1987; Heiner-Müller Guest Prof., Freie Universität Berlin 2005; has lectured in Germany, UK and USA; mem. German Acad. for Language and Poetry 1995–; Kleist Preis 1994, Aristeion Prize 1995, Int. IMPAC Dublin Literary Award 1998, Franz Kafka Preis 1999, Literature Prize, Konrad Adenauer Foundation 2004, Berliner Literaturpreis 2005, Würth Preis 2005, Nobel Prize for Literature 2009, Hoffmann-von-Fallersleben-Preis 2010. *Publications include:* Niederungen 1982, Drückender Tango: Erzählungen 1984, Der Mensch ist ein grosser Fasan auf der Welt 1986, Barfüssiger Februar: Prosa 1987, Reisende auf einem Bein 1989, Der Teufel sitzt im Spiegel 1991, Der Fuchs war damals schon der Jäger 1992, Eine warme Kartoffel ist ein warmes Bett 1992, Der Wächter nimmt seinen Kamm: vom Weggehen und Ausscheren 1993, Herztier: Roman 1994, Hunger und Seide: Essays 1995, In der Falle 1996, Heute wär ich mir lieber nicht begegnet 1997, Der fremde Blick oder Das Leben ist ein Furz in der Laterne 1999, Im Haarknoten wohnt eine Dame 2000, Heimat ist das, was gesprochen wird 2001, Der König verneigt sich und tötet 2003, Die blassen Herren mit den Mokkatassen 2005, Atemschaukel 2009 (translated as The Hunger Angel 2012), Immer derselbe Schnee und immer derselbe Onkel 2011, The Fox Was Ever the Hunter: A Novel 2016. *Address:* c/o Carl Hanser Verlag, Kolbergerstrasse 22, 81679 Munich, Germany (office). *E-mail:* info@hanser.de (office). *Website:* www.hanser-literaturverlage.de (office).

MÜLLER, K. Alex, PhD; Swiss physicist and academic; *Professor Emeritus, Physics Institute, University of Zurich;* b. 20 April 1927, Basel; ed Swiss Fed. Inst. of Tech.; Project Man., Battelle Inst., Geneva 1958–62; Lecturer, Univ. of Zurich 1962, Titular Prof. 1970, Prof. 1987–2009, Prof. Emer. 2009–; joined IBM Zurich Research Lab., Rüschlikon 1963, Man. Dept of Physics and Fellow 1973–92, Researcher 1985, Fellow Emer. 1992–98; Fellow, American Physical Soc.; mem. European Physics Soc.; Foreign Assoc. mem. NAS, Russian, Slovenian, Polish and Sachsen Acads of Sciences; Hon. mem. Swiss Physical Soc., Zurich Physical Soc., Acad. of Ceramics; Hon. DSc (Geneva) 1987, (Tech. Univ. of Munich) 1987, (Università degli Studi di Pavia) 1987, (Leuven) 1988, (Boston) 1988, (Tel-Aviv) 1988, (Tech. Univ. of Darmstadt) 1988, (Nice) 1989, (Universidad Politecnica, Madrid) 1989, (Bochum) 1990, (Università degli Studi di Roma) 1990, (Trondheim) 1992, (Metz) 1995, (Salzburg) 1995, (Regensburg) 1996, (Cottbus, Germany) 1997, (Leipzig) 2000, (Bar Ilan) 2006, (Tbilisi) 2007; with G. Bednorz: Marcel-Benoist Prize 1986, Nobel Prize for Physics (with G. Bednorz) for discovery of new superconducting materials 1987, 13th Fritz London Memorial Award, UCLA 1987, Dannie Heineman Prize, Minna James Heineman Stiftung, Acad. of Sciences, Gottingen, Germany 1987, Robert Wichard Pohl Prize, German Physical Soc. 1987, Hewlett-Packard Europhysics Prize 1988, Int. Prize for New Materials Research, American Physical Soc. 1988, Minnie Rosen Award, Ross Univ., New York 1989, Special Tsukuba Award (Japan) 1989, Int. 'Aldo Villa' Prize, Italian Ceramic Soc. 1991. *Publications:* more than 400 publs on structural phase transitions, critical and multicritical phenomena, the behaviour of ferroelectrica at low temperatures and superconductivity in cuprates. *Address:* University of Zürich, Physik-Institut, Winterthurerstr. 190, 8057 Zürich (office); Haldenstr. 54,

8909 Hedingen, Switzerland (home). *Telephone:* (44) 6355749 (office). *Fax:* (44) 6355704 (office). *Website:* www.physik.uzh.ch (office).

MÜLLER, Klaus-Peter; German banker; *Honorary Chairman of the Supervisory Board, Commerzbank AG;* b. 16 Sept. 1944, Duppach; m.; one d.; apprenticeship in banking, Bankhaus Friedrich Simon KGaA, Düsseldorf 1962–64; with Düsseldorf Br., Commerzbank AG 1966–68, New York Rep. Office and Br. 1968–73, Jt Man. Düsseldorf and Duisburg Br. 1973–82, Jt Man. New York Br. 1982–86, Exec. Vice-Pres. 1986–90, Head of Corp. Banking Dept 1990–2001, Head, East German Operations 1990, mem. Bd of Man. Dirs 1990–, Chair. Commerzbank AG 2001–08, Chair. Supervisory Bd 2008–18, Hon. Chair. 2018–; mem. of Bd Parker Hannifin Corpn 1998–2018, Linde AG 2003–, Fraport AG (Frankfurt Airport Services Worldwide) 2008–10, Fresenius SE, Fresenius Management SE 2010–, MaschmeyerRürup AG (ind. int. consultancy) 2010–, Landwirtschaftliche Rentenbank –2014; Pres. Asscn of German Banks, Berlin 2005–09; Hon. Prof., Frankfurt School of Finance and Man. 2007; Order of Merit of the Federal Republic of Germany; Dr hc (Finance Acad. of Russian Fed.) 2004. *Address:* Commerzbank AG, Kaiserpl., 60261 Frankfurt/Main, Germany (office). *Telephone:* (69) 13620 (office). *E-mail:* info@commerzbank.com (office). *Website:* www.commerzbank.com (office).

MÜLLER, Matthias; German automotive industry executive; b. 9 June 1953, Karl-Marx-Stadt (now Chemnitz), Saxony, GDR; ed high school in Ingolstadt, Munich Univ. of Applied Sciences; finished apprenticeship as toolmaker at Audi AG, Ingolstadt 1977, Jr Man., IT Dept in charge of system analysis 1984–92, with Planning Dept 1993–95, Product Man. for Audi A3 1995–2002, Co-ordinator of Audi and Lamborghini model lines 2003–07, Gen. Rep., Volkswagen AG, Wolfsburg 2007–10, Head of VW's Product Strategy, Pres. and CEO Porsche AG 2010–15, Chief Information Officer, Porsche Automobil Holding SE 2014–15, Chair. Man. Bd, Volkswagen AG 2015–18. *Address:* c/o Volkswagen AG, PO Box 1849, VHH 11th Floor, 38436 Wolfsburg, Germany (office).

MÜLLER, Michael; German printer and politician; *Governing Mayor of Berlin;* b. 9 Dec. 1964, Berlin; m.; two c.; ed Berlin Tech. Coll. for Business and Admin; worked as self-employed printer 1986–2011; mem. Berlin-Tempelhof Borough Ass. 1989–96, becoming Chair., SPD group; mem. Berlin House of Reps 1996–, directly elected Rep. for Tempelhof-Schöneberg 4 constituency 2001–, Chair. SPD Group 2001–11; Mayor of Berlin and Senator for Urban Devt and the Environment 2011–14, Governing Mayor of Berlin 2014–; mem. SPD 1981–, Chair. SPD in Tempelhof-Schöneberg 2000–04, Chair. SPD in Fed. State of Berlin 2004–12. *Address:* Governing Mayor of Berlin, Senate Chancellery, Jüdenstrasse 1, 10178 Berlin, Germany (office). *Telephone:* (30) 9026-0 (office). *Fax:* (30) 9026-2013 (office). *Website:* www.berlin.de (office).

MÜLLER, Peter; German lawyer and politician; b. 25 Sept. 1955, Illingen; m. Astrid Gercke-Müller; three s.; ed Lebach Grammar School, Univs of Bonn and Saarbrücken; trainee lawyer 1983–86, Asst Lecturer, Univ. of Saarland 1983–86, later Chair. Constitutional and Admin. Law; Judge, Saarbrücken Regional Court –1990; mem. CDU Parl. Party, Saarland Parl. 1990–; Minister Pres. of Saarland 1999–2011; Judge, Federal Constitutional Court 2011–; Dr hc (Tokyo) 2001. *Publication:* Nach dem Pisa-Shock. Plädoyers für eine Bildungreform (co-ed.) 2002, Bevölkerungsentwicklung und Grundgesetz, Ein Festschrift für Georg Ress 2005. *Leisure interests:* active footballer, plays chess and skat, clarinet and saxophone. *Address:* Federal Constitutional Court, Schlossbezirk 3, POB 1771, 76006 Karlsruhe (office); Landtag des Saarlandes, Postfach 101833, 66081 Saarbrücken, Germany (office). *Website:* www.bundesverfassungsgericht.de (office).

MULLER, Phillip Henry; Marshall Islands diplomatist and politician; b. 2 Jan. 1956; m. Yolenda deBrum; four c.; ed Rockhurst Coll., Kansas City, Mo., USA; Deputy Minister of Foreign Affairs 1982–84, Minister-in-Assistance to Pres. 1984–86, Minister of Educ. 1986–94, of Foreign Affairs 1994–99, 2012–14; mem. Nitijela (parl.) 1984–99; Public Relations and Govt Relations Consultant, GMP Assocs Inc. (eng and architectural co.) 2000–08; Amb. and Perm. Rep. to UN, New York 2008–12. *Leisure interests:* tennis, bowling, fishing. *Address:* c/o Ministry of Foreign Affairs, POB 1349, Majuro MH 96960, Marshall Islands (office).

MÜLLER, Werner, PhD; German politician and business executive; *Chairman of the Executive Board, RAG-Stiftung;* b. 1 June 1946, Essen; m.; two c.; ed Univs of Mannheim, Duisberg and Bremen; Lecturer, Univ. of Applied Sciences, Ludwigshafen 1970–72; part-time Lectureships, Univs of Mannheim and Regensburg 1970–73; Head of Market Research, Rheinisch-Westfälische electricity co. (RWE) 1973–80; Gen. Rep. and Chief Exec. VEBA AG (power co.) 1980–92, mem. Exec. Bd VEBA Kraftwerke Ruhr AG, Gelsenkirchen 1992–97; ind. industrial consultant 1997–98; apptd Adviser to Gerhard Schroder, Minister-Pres. of Lower Saxony 1991; Fed. Minister of Econ. and Tech. 1998–2002; Chair. Exec. Bd RAG AG, Essen 2003–07, also Chair. Exec. Bd RAG Beteiligungs-AG (renamed Evonik Industries AG 2007), Essen 2006–08, Chair. Bd of Execs RAG-Stiftung 2012–; Chair. Supervisory Bd, Deutsche Bahn AG 2005–10; mem. Supervisory Bd, Evonik Industries AG 2012–, RAG Corpn 2012–, RAG Deutsche Steinkohle AG 2012–. *Address:* RAG-Stiftung, Rüttenscheider Straße 1-3, 45128 Essen, Germany. *E-mail:* info@rag-stiftung.de. *Website:* www.rag-stiftung.de.

MULLIEZ, Vianney; French retail executive; *Chairman, Board of Directors and Chairman, Executive Committee (CEO), Groupe Auchan;* b. 5 March 1963, Roubaix; m.; three c.; ed Ecole des Hautes Etudes Commerciales, Paris; worked eight years with PricewaterhouseCoopers; f. MBV & Associés (accountancy firm); Dir of Finance, Auchan France 1998–2000, Dir for Int. Devt 2000–04, Pres. Immochan International (subsidiary co.) 2004, Chair. Supervisory Bd Groupe Auchan 2006–10, Chair. Bd of Dirs and Chair. Exec. Cttee (CEO) 2010–; Pres. Supervisory Bd Asscn Familiale Mulliez 2006–. *Leisure interest:* golf. *Address:* Groupe Auchan, 40 avenue de Flandre, PO Box 139, 59964 Croix Cedex, France (office). *Telephone:* (3) 20-81-68-00 (office). *Fax:* (3) 20-81-69-09 (office). *E-mail:* info@groupe-auchan.com (office). *Website:* www.groupe-auchan.com (office).

MULLIGAN, Deanna M., BS, MBA; American business executive; *President and CEO, The Guardian Life Insurance Company of America;* ed Univ. of Nebraska, Stanford Univ. Grad. School of Business; held roles of Sr Vice-Pres. at New York Life, Exec. Vice-Pres. at AXA Financial and Prin., McKinsey & Co., New York; est.

and ran own consulting firm, DMM Management Solutions, LLC, advising insurance cos on strategic and operational issues; Exec. Vice-Pres., Individual Life and Disability business, The Guardian Life Insurance Co. of America 2008–10, Pres. and COO 2010–11, mem. Bd of Dirs, Pres. and CEO 2011–; Dir and Chair. RS Investment Management Co., LLC, Trustee, RS Investment Trust and RS Variable Products Trust; mem. Bd of Dirs American Council of Life Insurers, Life Insurance Council of New York; Trustee, The American Coll.; Co-Pres. and Trustee, North Salem Open Land Foundation; fmr mem. Bd Project Renewal, Red Cross of Greater New York; mem. Partnership for New York City, The Economic Club of New York. *Address:* The Guardian Life Insurance Co. of America, 7 Hanover Square, New York, NY 10004, USA (office). *Telephone:* (212) 598-8000 (office). *Fax:* (212) 919-2170 (office). *E-mail:* info@guardianlife.com (office). *Website:* www.guardianlife.com (office).

MULLIN, Leo F., BS, MBA; American business executive; *Senior Advisor, Goldman Sachs Capital Partners;* m. Leah Mullin; one s. one d.; ed Harvard Coll., Cambridge, Harvard Univ., Harvard School of Arts and Sciences, Harvard Business School; began career as man. consultant McKinsey & Co. 1967, Partner 1973–76; Sr Vice-Pres. Strategic Planning, Consolidated Rail Corpn (Conrail), Phila 1976–81; sr man. positions First Chicago 1981–93, Pres. and COO 1993–95, also, Pres. and CEO American Nat. Bank (a subsidiary of First Chicago) 1991–93; Vice-Chair. Unicorn Corpn and Commonwealth Edison 1995–97; Chair. and CEO Delta Air Lines Inc. 1997–2004 (resgnd); currently, Sr Advisor Goldman Sachs Capital Partners; mem. Bd of Dirs Bellsouth Corpn, Johnson & Johnson 1999–2015, Juvenile Diabetes Research Foundation, Educ. Man. Corpn 2006–15, TransUnion 2012– (Chair. 2015–); Chair. Field Museum of Natural History, Chicago; Vice-Chair. Chicago Urban League; Dir, Cooper-Standard Automotive, Inc. 2005–, North American Rubber, Inc. 2005–, ACE Ltd 2007–; mem. Business Council, Atlanta Chamber of Commerce, Robert W. Woodruff Arts Center, Advisory Bd of the Carter Center; mem. Bd of Trustees, Georgia Research Alliance, Northwestern Univ. *Address:* Goldman Sachs, 200 West Street, New York, NY 10282, USA (office). *Telephone:* (212) 902-1000 (office). *Website:* www .goldmansachs.com (office).

MULLIS, Kary Banks, BS, PhD; American biochemist and academic; b. 28 Dec. 1944, Lenoir, NC; s. of Cecil Banks Mullis and Bernice Alberta Barker Fredericks Mullis; m. 4th Nancy Cosgrove Mullis; two s. one d. from two previous marriages; ed Dreher High School, Georgia Inst. of Tech., Atlanta, Univ. of California, Berkeley; Lecturer in Biochemistry, Univ. of California, Berkeley 1972; Postdoctoral Fellow, Univ. of Kansas Medical School 1973–76, Univ. of California, San Francisco 1977–79; researcher, Cetus Corp., Emeryville, Calif. 1979–86; Dir Molecular Biology Xytronyx, Inc., San Diego 1986–88; consultant on nucleic acid chemistry for more than a dozen corpns, including Angenics, Cytometrics, Eastman Kodak, Abbott Laboratories, Milligen/Biosearch, Specialty Laboratories 1987–96; Distinguished Researcher, Children's Hosp. Oakland Research Inst., Calif.; Chair. StarGene, Inc.; Vice-Pres. Histotec, Inc., Vyrex Inc.; Visiting Prof., Univ. of South Carolina; Partner in Questar International 1998; mem. Advisory Bd USA Science and Eng Festival; mem. Bd of Scientific Advisors of several cos, provides expert advice in legal matters involving DNA and frequent lecturer at colls and univs, corpns and academic meetings world-wide; known for his opposition to the HIV/AIDS hypothesis, to climate change and for his belief in astrology; Hon. DSc (Univ. of South Carolina) 1994; Dr hc in Pharmaceutical Biotechnology (Univ. of Bologna, Italy) 2004; Preis Biochemische Analytik Award 1990, William Allan Memorial Award, American Soc. of Human Genetics 1990, Preis Biochemische Analytik, German Soc. of Clinical Chem. and Boehringer Mannheim 1990, Gairdner Foundation Award 1991, Nat. Biotechnology Award 1991, R&D Magazine Scientist of the Year 1991, John Scott Award, City Trusts of Philadelphia (co-recipient) 1991, Koch Award 1992, Chiron Corpn Award 1992, Japan Prize 1992, Calif. Scientist of the Year 1992, Thomas A. Edison Award 1993, shared Nobel Prize for Chem. devising the polymerase chain reaction (PCR) technique 1993, Japanese Science and Tech. Foundation Award 1993, inducted into Nat. Inventors Hall of Fame 1998, Ronald H. Brown American Innovator Award 1998. *Publications:* Specific Enzymatic Amplification of DNA In Vitro: The Polymerase Chain Reaction 1986, The Unusual Origin of the Polymerase Chain Reaction 1990, The Polymerase Chain Reaction (co-ed.) 1994, Dancing Naked in the Mind Field (autobiog.) 1998; numerous articles in scientific journals; several major patents. *Leisure interest:* surfing. *E-mail:* lectures@karymullis.com. *Website:* www.karymullis.com.

MULLOVA, Viktoria; Russian violinist; b. 27 Nov. 1959, Moscow; d. of Yuri Mullov and Raissa Mullova; one s. two d.; ed studied in Moscow at Cen. Music School and Moscow Conservatory under Leonid Kogan; left USSR 1983; has appeared with most major orchestras and conductors and at int. festivals; f. chamber group Mullova Ensemble 1994; First Prize, Sibelius Competition, Helsinki 1980, Gold Medal, Tchaikovsky Competition, Moscow 1982, Int. Classical Music Award for Chamber Music 2011. *Recordings include:* Beethoven Violin Concerto, Mendelssohn Violin Concerto with the Orchestre Revolutionnaire et Romantique, John Eliot Gardiner, Mozart Violin Concertos Nos 1, 3 & 4, Orchestra of the Age of Enlightenment, Vivaldi Violin Concertos (Diapason D'Or of the Year 2005) 2005, Recital (with Katia Labèque) 2006, Bach's Six Solo Sonatas and Partitas 2009, The Peasant Girl 2011, Bach: Concertos 2013, Stradivarius in Rio 2014, Prokofiev 2015, Arvo Pärt with Estonian National Symphony Orchestra, Paavo Järvi 2018. *Address:* c/o Fiona Russell, Askonas Holt, 15 Fetter Lane, London, EC4A 1BW, England (office). *E-mail:* fiona.russell@askonasholt.co.uk (office); info@viktoriamullova.com (office). *Website:* www.askonasholt.co.uk/ artists/instrumentalists/violin/viktoria-mullova (office); www.viktoriamullova .com.

MULONI, Irene Nafuna, BSc, MBA; Ugandan electrical engineer and politician; *Minister of Energy and Minerals;* b. 18 Nov. 1960, Bulambuli Dist; m. Felix Muloni; one s. three d.; ed Makerere Univ., Capella Univ., USA; Man. Dir Uganda Electricity Distribution Co. Ltd 2002–11; mem. Parl. (Nat. Resistance Movt) for Bulambuli Dist 2011–; Minister of Energy and Mineral Development (now Energy and Minerals) 2011–; Founder mem. Asscn of Women Engineers, Technicians and Scientists in Uganda. *Address:* Ministry of Energy and Minerals, Amber House, Kampala Road, Kampala, Uganda (office). *Telephone:* (41) 4311111 (office). *Fax:*

(41) 4234732 (office). *E-mail:* imuloni@parliament.go.ug (office). *Website:* www .energyandminerals.go.ug (office).

MULRONEY, Rt Hon. (Martin) Brian, PC, CC, LLD; Canadian business executive, lawyer and fmr politician; *Senior Partner, Norton Rose Fulbright Canada LLP;* b. 20 March 1939, Baie Comeau, Québec; s. of Benedict Mulroney and Irene Mulroney (née O'Shea); m. Mila Pivnicki 1973; three s. one d.; ed St Thomas Coll. High School, Chatham, St Francis Xavier Univ., Antigonish, NS, Université Laval, Québec; called to Bar of Québec 1965; Partner, Ogilvy, Cope, Porteous, Montgomery, Renault, Clarke & Kirkpatrick, Montreal 1965–76, Sr Partner, Ogilvy Renault 1993– (co. merged with Norton Rose, UK to become Norton Rose Canada LLP 2011, then with US law firm Fulbright & Jaworski to become Norton Rose Fulbright Canada LLP 2013); Exec. Vice-Pres. (Corp. Affairs), Iron Ore Co. of Canada 1976–77, Pres. and Dir 1977–83; Leader, Progressive Party of Canada 1983–93, joined Conservative Party of Canada following its creation by merger of Progressive Conservatives and Canadian Alliance 2003–06; mem. Parl. 1983–93; Leader of Opposition 1983–84; Prime Minister of Canada 1984–93 (resgnd); fmr Co-Chair. UN Summit on Children; fmr Chair. Forbes Global (New York); Chair. and Dir Persona Communications, Inc., St John's; Founding Partner and Special Advisor, Teilhard Technologies Inc.; mem. Bd of Dirs Barrick Gold Corpn 1993–2014, Archer Daniels Midland Co. from 1993, Wyndham Worldwide Corpn 2006–, Blackstone Group Management LLC 2007–, Tuckamore Capital Management Inc. 2011–, Cendant Corpn, Trizec Properties Inc. 2002–, Quebecor Media 2001– (Chair. 2014–), Lion Capital LLP, London, Said Holdings Ltd, Bermuda; mem. Int. Advisory Council, JP Morgan Chase & Co., China Int. Trust and Investment Corpn, Independent News and Media PLC, Magna International; Sr Counsellor to Hicks, Muse, Tate & Furst, Dallas; Trustee The Freedom Forum Inc.; mem. Council on Foreign Relations; Grand Officier, Ordre nat. du Québec; Grand Cross with Collar, Order of Kniaz Yaroslav the Wise (Ukraine); Grand Cordon, Order of the Rising Sun (Japan); several hon. degrees, including Hon. LLD (Univ. of Western Ontario) 2007; numerous awards, including Woodrow Wilson Award for Public Service, Woodrow Wilson Int. Center for Scholars of Smithsonian Inst. 2003. *Publications:* Where I Stand 1983, Memoirs: 1939–1993 2007. *Leisure interests:* tennis, swimming. *Address:* Norton Rose Fulbright Canada LLP, Suite 2500, 1 Place Ville Marie, Montreal, PQ H3B 1R1 (office); 47 Forden Crescent, Westmount, PQ H3Y 2Y5, Canada (home). *Telephone:* (514) 847-4779 (office). *Fax:* (514) 286-5474 (office). *E-mail:* brian.mulroney@nortonrosefulbright.com (office). *Website:* www.nortonrosefulbright.com (office).

MULRONEY, David, BA; Canadian public servant and diplomatist; *Distinguished Senior Fellow, Munk School of Global Affairs, University of Toronto;* b. Nov. 1954; ed Univ. of Toronto; Asst Trade Commr, St John's Regional Office, Industry Trade and Commerce 1981–82; joined Dept of Foreign Affairs and Int. Trade 1982, Trade Commr, Embassy in Seoul 1982–85, Consul, Consulate Gen. in Shanghai 1985–88, Deputy Dir, East Asia Trade Div. 1988–90, Exec. Asst, Deputy Minister for Int. Trade 1990–92, Commercial Counsellor, High Comm. in Kuala Lumpur 1992–95, Exec. Dir Canada-China Business Council 1995–98, Exec. Dir Canadian Trade Office in Taipei 1998–2001, Asst Deputy Minister, Asia-Pacific 2001–05, Asst Deputy Minister, Bilateral Relations, Foreign Affairs Canada 2005–06; Foreign and Defence Policy Advisor to the Prime Minister in Privy Council Office 2006–07, Assoc. Deputy Minister of Foreign Affairs 2007–08, Deputy Minister of Afghanistan Task Force 2008–09; Amb. to People's Repub. of China (also accred to Mongolia) 2009–12; Distinguished Sr Fellow, Munk School of Global Affairs, Univ. of Toronto 2012–; Distinguished Fellow, Asia Pacific Foundation of Canada; Hon. Fellow, St Michael's Coll.; Queen's Diamond Jubilee Medal 2012. *Address:* Room 216, Munk School of Global Affairs, University of Toronto, 315 Bloor Street West, Toronto, ON M5S 0A7, Canada (office). *Telephone:* (416) 946-8900 (office). *E-mail:* david.mulroney@utoronto.ca (office). *Website:* munkschool.utoronto.ca/profile/david-mulroney (office).

MULUZI, Bakili; Malawi politician, business executive and fmr head of state; b. 17 March 1943, Machinga; m. Patricia Shanil 1988 (divorced 2011); seven c.; ed Huddersfield Tech. Coll., Thirsted Tech. Coll. and coll. in Denmark; clerk, colonial civil service of Nyasaland; fmr Sec.-Gen. Malawi Congress Party (resgnd 1982); mem. Parl. 1975; held various Cabinet portfolios including Educ. and Minister without Portfolio; business interests in transport, merchandise distribution and real estate; Leader, United Democratic Front 1992–; Pres. of Malawi 1994–2004; arrested on fraud and corruption charges 2006, on trial 2011; apptd Special Commonwealth Envoy to Swaziland 2014; Hon. DJur (Lincoln, MO, Glasgow); Hon. Dr rer. pol (Nat. Chengchi, Taipei). *Publications:* Democracy with a Price 2000, Mau Anga: The Voice of a Democrat 2002. *Leisure interests:* reading, watching football, assisting the needy.

MULVA, James (Jim) J., BBA, MBA; American oil industry executive (retd); b. 19 June 1946, Oshkosh, Wis.; m. Miriam Mulva; two c.; ed Univ. of Texas, Austin; served as US Navy Officer 1969–73; joined Phillips Petroleum Co. 1973, Chief Financial Officer 1990–93, Sr Vice-Pres. 1993–94, Exec. Vice-Pres. 1994, Pres. and COO 1994–99, Chair., Pres. and CEO 1999–2002, Pres. and CEO ConocoPhillips Co. (cr. following merger of Phillips Petroleum Co. and Conoco Co.) 2002–04, Chair. and CEO 2004–12; Chair. American Petroleum Inst. 2005, 2006; mem. Bd of Dirs, General Electric 2008–, General Motors Co. 2012–, Statoil ASA 2013–15; mem. Bd of Visitors, M.D. Anderson Cancer Center; mem. The Business Council, The Business Roundtable; Trustee, Boys and Girls Clubs of America; Hon. DEng (Colorado School of Mines) 2010; Petroleum Exec. of the Year 2002.

MULVANEY, John Michael (Mick), BS, JD; American lawyer, business executive and politician; *Director, Office of Management and Budget;* b. 21 July 1967, Alexandria, Va; s. of Mike Mulvaney and Kathy Mulvaney; m. Pamela West 1998; three c.; ed Georgetown Univ., Univ. of North Carolina; f. own law firm following graduation, also ran family real estate business; f. construction co.; fmr restaurant owner; mem. South Carolina State House of Reps from 45th Dist 2007–09; mem. South Carolina Senate for 16th Dist (Lancaster and York Counties) 2009–11; mem. US House of Reps from South Carolina 5th Dist 2011–17, mem. House Freedom Caucus; Dir, Office of Man. and Budget 2017–; Republican. *Address:* Office of Management and Budget, 725 17th St, NW, Washington, DC 20503, USA (office). *Telephone:* (202) 395-3080 (office). *Fax:* (202) 395-3888 (office). *Website:* www.whitehouse.gov/omb (office).

MUMBA, Rev. Nevers, MPP; Zambian politician, evangelist and diplomatist; b. 18 May 1960, Chinsali; s. of Sunday Mumba; m. Florence Mumba; five c.; ed Christ for the Nations Inst., Dallas, Tex., Regent Univ., Virginia, USA; fmr TV evangelist; Founder and fmr Pres. Victory Ministries International, Chair. Bd Victory Coll.; Co-founder and Nat. Chair. Nat. Citizen's Coalition (NCC); presidential cand. 2001; disbanded NCC and joined ruling Movt for Multiparty Democracy 2003; Vice-Pres. of Zambia 2003–04; Amb. to Canada 2009–11, also accred to Cuba and the Bahamas; apptd Pres. Movement for Multi-party Democracy (MMD) 2012; Dr hc (Univ. of Mich., Flint, USA); Ghandi, King, Ikeda Award, Morehouse Coll., Atlanta, Ga. *Television:* presenter, Zambia Shall be Saved. *Publications:* Integrity With Fire, Zambia Shall be Saved. *Leisure interest:* boxing.

MUMBENGEGWI, Simbarashe Simbanenduku, BA, DipEd; Zimbabwean diplomatist, politician and public servant; b. 20 July 1945, Chivi Dist; s. of Chivandire Davis Mumbengegwi and Dzivaidzo Shuvai Chimbambo; m. Emily Charasika 1983; one s. four d.; ed Monash Univ., Melbourne, Australia, Univ. of Zimbabwe; active in Zimbabwe African Nat. Union (ZANU) Party 1963–, in exile, Australia 1966–72, Deputy Chief Rep. in Australia and Far East 1973–76, Chief Rep. 1976–78, Chief Rep. in Zambia 1978–80, mem. Cen. Cttee 1984–94, Patriotic Front Nat. Consultative Ass. 1994–2006, Patriotic Front Cen. Cttee 2006–; elected MP 1980, 1985; Deputy Minister of Foreign Affairs 1981–82, Minister of Water Resources and Devt 1982, of Housing 1982–84, of Public Construction and Nat. Housing 1984–88, of Transport 1988–90; Perm. Rep. to UN 1990–95; Amb. to Belgium, the Netherlands and Luxembourg, Perm. Rep. to EU 1995–99; Perm. Rep. to Org. for the Prohibition of Chemical Weapons (OPCW) 1997–99, Chair. Conf. of the State Parties 1997–98, mem. Exec. Council 1997–99; Amb. to the UK and Ireland 1999–2005; Minister of Foreign Affairs 2005–17, Minister of Macro-Economic Planning and Investment Promotion Oct.–Nov. 2017, Acting Minister of Foreign Affairs 27–30 Nov. 2017, Minister of State for Presidential Affairs and Monitoring of Govt Programmes 2017–18. *Leisure interests:* reading, photography, jogging, tennis, golf.

MUMFORD, David Bryant, PhD; American (b. British) mathematician and academic; *University Professor Emeritus, Brown University;* b. 11 June 1937, Three Bridges, Sussex, England; s. of William Bryant Mumford and Grace Schiott; m. 1st Erika Jentsch 1959 (died 1988); three s. one d.; m. 2nd Jenifer Moore 1989; ed Harvard Univ., Jr Fellow, Harvard Univ. 1958–61, Prof. of Math. 1967–77, Higgins Prof. 1977–97, Prof. Emer. 1997–, Chair. Math. Dept 1981–84, MacArthur Fellow 1987–92; Univ. Prof. of Math., Div. of Applied Math., Brown Univ. 1996–, now Emer.; Pres. Int. Math. Union 1995–98; mem. NAS 1975, American Acad. of Arts and Sciences, American Philosophical Soc. 1997; Foreign mem. Accad. Nazionale dei Lincei 1991, Royal Soc. 2008, Norwegian Acad. of Sciences and Letters; Hon. Fellow, Tata Inst. of Fundamental Research 1978; Hon. mem. London Math. Soc. 1995; Hon. DSc (Warwick) 1983, (Norwegian Univ. Science and Tech.) 2000, (Rockefeller Univ.) 2001, (Brown) 2011, (Turin) 2012, (Hyderabad) 2012; Fields Medal 1974, Longuet-Higgins Prize 2005, 2009, Shaw Prize 2006, Steele Prize 2007, Wolf Prize in Math. 2008, Nat. Medal of Science 2010, BBVA Foundation Frontiers of Knowledge Award in the Basic Sciences category (with Ingrid Daubechies) 2012. *Publications:* Geometric Invariant Theory 1965, Abelian Varieties 1970, Algebraic Geometry I 1976, Two and Three Dimensional Patterns of the Face 1999, Indra's Pearls: The Vision of Felix Klein (co-author) 2002, Pattern Theory: The Stochastic Analysis of Real-World Signals (co-author) 2010. *Leisure interest:* sailing. *Address:* 282 Harts Neck Road, Tenants Harbor, ME 04860, USA (home). *Telephone:* (207) 372-8909 (home). *E-mail:* dbmumford@gmail.com (home). *Website:* www.dam.brown.edu/people/mumford.

MUMUNI, Alhaji Muhammad, LLB, LLM, BL; Ghanaian politician; b. 28 July 1949; m.; six c.; ed Univ. of Ghana, Ghana Law School; fmr Nat. Service Coordinator for the North; fmr Legal Officer, Bank for Housing and Construction; fmr Dist Magistrate; mem. Parl. for Kumbungu 1997–2004, 2012–, mem. Judiciary Cttee, Standing Orders Cttee; Minister of Employment and Social Welfare 1997–2000, of Foreign Affairs, Regional Integration and NEPAD 2009–13; Vice-Pres. 86th Session, Institutional Labour Congress, Geneva 1998. *Address:* Parliament House, Accra, Ghana (office). *Telephone:* (30) 2664042 (office). *Fax:* (30) 2665957 (office). *E-mail:* clerk@parliament.gh (office). *Website:* www .parliament.gh (home).

MUNASINGHE, Gamini Surath; Sri Lankan fmr diplomatist; ed Univ. of Ceylon, Peradeniya; Deputy High Commr to UK 1991–97, High Commr to South Africa (also accred to Namibia, Seychelles and Mauritius) 1998–2001, to Zambia 2001–03, Additional Sec., Ministry of Foreign Affairs 2002–03, High Commr to Bangladesh 2003–06; mem. Bd of Dirs Environmental Resources Investment PLC (fmrly Walker and Greig Ltd) 2007–; mem. Admin. Council Rajarata Univ. of Sri Lanka. *Address:* c/o Board of Directors, Environmental Resources Investment PLC, No.450, Taj Samudra Hotel, 25 Galle Face Centre Road, Colombo 01, Sri Lanka (office).

MUNAVVAR, Mohamed, LLM; Maldivian politician and lawyer; b. 20 Dec. 1961, Meedhoo; m.; one s. two d.; ed Majeedhiyya School, Patrice Lumumba People's Friendship Univ., Moscow, Russia, Bureau of Parl. Studies and Training, Lok Sabha Secr., New Delhi, India, Dalhousie Univ., Halifax, NS, Canada; Attorney-Gen., Repub. of the Maldives 1993–2003; MP for Addu constituency for several years; arrested Aug. 2004, transferred to house arrest Oct.–Dec. 2004 (charges withdrawn); legal adviser to Maldivian Democratic Party –2007, Pres. 2007–08 (resgnd); applied to Election Comm. for a party registration 2010.

MUNAWWAR, Ahmed, BEcons; Maldivian economist, academic and government official; ed Int. Islamic Univ. Malaysia, Macquarie Univ., Australia; fmr Lecturer (part-time) at several insts, including Maldives Coll. of Higher Educ., Modern Acad. for Professional Studies Coll., Clique Coll., Villa Coll.; served at Maldives Monetary Authority for more than ten years until 2014, including as Man. of Monetary Policy Section; Minister of State for Finance and Treasury 2014–16, Minister of Finance 2016–18; mem. Bd of Govs Asian Infrastructure Investment Bank. *Address:* c/o Ministry of Finance and Treasury, Ameenee Magu, Block 379, Malé 20-379, The Maldives (office).

MUNDA, Arjun; Indian politician; b. 5 Jan. 1968, Jamshedpur; s. of Ganesh Munda and Saira Munda; m. Meera Munda; three s.; Chief Minister of Jharkhand 2003–05 (resgnd), reappointed March 2005–Sept. 2006 (resgnd), 2010–13; Welfare

Minister, Govt of Jharkhand 2000–06, mem. Bharatiya Janata Party (Gen. Sec. 2010–), Bihar Vidhan Sabha 1995–2000, Jharkhand Vidhan Sabha 2000–09, Cttee on Energy 2009; Chair. Rural Integrated Devt Center, Jamshedpur, All Jharkhand Yoga Asscn, Shaheed Smarak Smati, Kharswan, Beenapari High School, Jamshedpur, Jharkhand Deaf and Dumb Asscn; MP 2009–. *Leisure interests:* golf, archery, music, reading, travelling, social work. *Address:* Ghorabandha, Luabasa, East Singhbhum, India (home). *Telephone:* (657) 2268292. *Fax:* (657) 2200805 (home). *E-mail:* arjun.munda@gmail.com.

MUNDELL, Rt Hon. David Gordon; British politician; *Secretary of State for Scotland;* b. 27 May 1962, Dumfries, Scotland; m. Lynda Carmichael (divorced); two s. one d.; ed Univ. of Edinburgh, Univ. of Strathclyde; Councillor (SDP), Annandale and Eskdale Dist Council 1984–86, Dumfries and Galloway Council 1986–87; worked as solicitor in private practice; Group Legal Adviser for Scotland, BT PLC 1991, becoming Head of Nat. Affairs, BT Scotland –1999; mem. Scottish Parl. (Conservative) for South of Scotland 1999–2005; MP (Conservative) for Dumfriesshire, Clydesdale and Tweeddale 2005–, mem. Scottish Affairs Cttee 2005–10; Shadow Sec. of State for Scotland 2005–10, UnderSec. of State for Scotland 2010–15, Sec. of State for Scotland 2015–; mem. Law Soc. of Scotland, mem. Social Democratic Party (SDP) 1981–88, Conservative Party 1988–; Writer to the Signet (WS). *Address:* Scotland Office, Dover House, Whitehall, London, SW1A 2AU (office); House of Commons, London, SW1A 0AA, England (office). *Telephone:* (131) 244-9010 (office). *E-mail:* david@davidmundell.com; pressoffice@scotlandoffice.gsi.gov.uk (office). *Website:* www.gov.uk/government/organisations/scotland-office (office); www.davidmundell.com.

MUNDELL, Robert Alexander, PhD; Canadian economist and academic; *University Professor of Economics, Columbia University;* b. 24 Oct. 1932, Kingston, Ont.; s. of William Campbell Mundell and Lila Teresa Mundell; m. 1st Barbara Sheff 1957 (divorced 1972); two s. one d.; m. 2nd Valerie Natsios 1998; one s.; ed Univ. of British Columbia, Univ. of Washington, Massachusetts Inst. of Tech., London School of Econs, Univ. of Chicago; Instructor, Univ. of BC 1957–58; economist, Royal Comm. on Price Spreads of Food Products, Ottawa 1958; Asst Prof. of Econs, Stanford Univ., USA 1958–59; Prof. of Econs, Johns Hopkins Univ., School of Advanced Int. Studies, Bologna, Italy 1959–61; Sr Economist, IMF 1961–63; Visiting Prof. of Econs, McGill Univ. 1963–64, 1989–90; Prof. of Int. Econs, Grad. Inst. of Int. Studies, Geneva, Switzerland 1965–75; Prof. of Econs Univ. of Chicago 1966–71; Prof. of Econs and Chair. Dept of Econs, Univ. of Waterloo, Ont. 1972–74; Univ. Prof. of Econs, Columbia Univ., New York 1974–; Ed. Journal of Political Economy 1966–71; Annenburg Distinguished Scholar in Residence, Univ. of Southern Calif. 1980; Richard Fox Visiting Prof. of Econs, Univ. of Pa 1990–91; First Rockefeller Visiting Research Prof. of Int. Econs, Brookings Inst. 1964–65; Guggenheim Fellow 1971; Marshall Lectures, Cambridge Univ. 1974; Distinguished Lecturer, Ching-Hua Inst., Taipei, Taiwan 1985; Pres. N American Econ. and Financial Asscn 1974–78; Dr hc (Univ. of Paris) 1992, (People's Univ. of China) 1995; Jacques Rueff Prize and Medal 1983, Nobel Prize for Econs 1999. *Publications:* The International Monetary System: Conflict and Reform 1965, Man and Economics 1968, International Economics 1968, Monetary Theory: Interest, Inflation and Growth in the World Economy 1971, Global Disequilibrium in the Lloyd Economy (co-author) 1989, Building the New Europe (co-author) 1991, Inflation and Growth in China (co-author) 1996; numerous papers and articles in journals. *Leisure interests:* painting, tennis, hockey, skiing, art history. *Address:* Department of Economics, Columbia University, 1031 International Affairs Building, MC 3308, 420 West 118th Street, New York, NY 10027, USA (office). *Telephone:* (212) 854-3669 (office). *Fax:* (212) 854-8059 (office). *E-mail:* ram15@columbia.edu (office). *Website:* www.columbia.edu/cu/economics (office).

MUNDIE, Craig James, BS, MS; American computer software industry executive; b. 1 July 1949, Cleveland, Ohio; m.; one d.; ed Georgia Inst. of Tech.; Software Developer, Systems Equipment Corpn (SEC), then at Data Gen. Corpn (which acquired SEC) 1972; Co-founder and CEO Alliant Computer Systems Corpn 1982–92; Gen. Man. Advanced Consumer Tech., Microsoft Corpn, Redmond, Wash. 1992–93, Vice Pres. Advanced Consumer Tech. Group 1993–96, Sr Vice Pres. Consumer Platforms Div. 1996–2001, Sr Vice-Pres. Advanced Strategies and Policies 2001–06, Chief Research and Strategy Officer 2006–12, Sr Advisor to CEO 2012–14; Pres. Mundie & Associates (consultancy) 2014–; mem. Bd of Dirs Inst. for Systems Biology, Raintree Oncology Corpn; mem. Council on Foreign Relations 2002–, President's Council of Advisors on Science and Technology 2009–, Markle Initiative for America's Economic Future; fmr mem. Nat. Security Telecommunications Advisory Cttee, Markle Foundation Task Force on Nat. Security in the Information Age; Trustee Fred Hutchinson Cancer Research Center, Seattle; mem. Advisory Bd Coll. of Computing, Ga Inst. of Tech., Aurasense Therapeutics, Madrona Venture Group.

MUNEKUNI, Yoshihide, BA; Japanese automobile executive; b. 1938, Hiroshima; ed Hosei Univ.; joined Honda Motor Co. Ltd 1966, became Dir 1984 then Exec. Vice-Pres. America Honda Motor Co. Inc. 1990–97, Pres. and Dir Honda N America Inc. 1989–90, Chair. Honda N America Inc. 1990–95, COO Automobile Sales Operations Honda Motor Co. Ltd 1995–97, Chair. and Rep. Dir 1997–2004; Chair. Japan Automobile Mfrs Asscn (JAMA) 2002–04; mem. Japan–USA Govt-Business Forum 2002; fmr Dir and Man. Exec. Officer, Japan Post Holdings Co., Ltd; Outside Dir Meiji Yasuda Life Insurance Co., Ltd 2013–; fmr mem. Advisory Bd Mitsubishi UFJ Financial Group, Inc.

MUNEOKA, Shoji; Japanese steel industry executive; *Representative Director and Chairman, Nippon Steel & Sumitomo Metal Corporation;* joined Nippon Steel Corpn in 1970, served as Dir of Sec., later Man. Dir and Vice-Pres. –2008, Rep. Dir and Pres. Nippon Steel Corpn 2008–12 (merged with Sumitomo Metal Industries Ltd to become Nippon Steel & Sumitomo Metal Corpn 2012), Rep. Dir, Chair. and CEO 2012–14, Rep. Dir and Chair. 2014–, also Chair. associated co. based in Shanghai; Chair. Japanese Iron and Steel Fed. *Address:* Nippon Steel & Sumitomo Metal Corpn, Marunouchi Park Building, 6-1, Marunouchi 2-chome, Chiyoda-ku, Tokyo 100-8071, Japan (office). *Telephone:* (3) 6867-4111 (office). *Fax:* (3) 6867-5607 (office). *E-mail:* info@nssmc.com (office). *Website:* www.nssmc.com (office).

MUNGAN, Zeren, MEconSc; Turkish-Cypriot economist and politician; b. 1956; began career as Under-Sec. of Finance, State Planning Org. 1984, held various positions including Chair., Prevention of Proceeds of Crime Comm.; Lecturer in Law and Public Finance, Anadolu Univ. 1991–2004; consultancy work as specialist in public finance; fmr CEO Turkish Cypriot Chamber of Commerce; Minister of Finance 2013–15. *Address:* c/o Ministry of Finance, Lefkoşa, Mersin 10, Turkey (office).

MUNGIU, Cristian; Romanian film director and producer; b. 27 April 1968, Iaşi; ed Univ. of Iaşi, Univ. of Film, Bucharest; fmr teacher and jurnalist; directed eight short films at film school, including The Hand of Paulista that was Romania's entry in the 1999 Student Acad. Awards, graduated from film school 1998; made several short films, then his first feature film, Occident 2002, which won prizes in several film festivals and was featured in Director's Fortnight at Cannes Film Festival 2002; formed Mobrafilms production co. 2006. *Films:* writer and dir: Zapping 2000, Nici o întâmplare 2000, Corul pompierilor 2000, Occident (aka West) 2002, Lost and Found (segment 'Turkey Girl') 2005, 4 luni, 3 săptămâni şi 2 zile (4 Months, 3 Weeks & 2 Days; also producer) (Palme d'Or, Cannes Film Festival (first Romanian dir) 2007) 2007, Amintiri din epoca de aur (Tales from the Golden Age) 2009, Dupa dealuri (Beyond the Hills) 2012, Bacalaureat (Graduation) (Best Dir, Cannes Film Festival 2016) 2016; producer: Bucuresti-Berlin 2005, Offset (exec. producer) 2006; other: Teen Knight (first asst dir) 1998, Train de vie (Train of Life; second asst dir) 1998.

MUNGUÍA PAYÉS, David Victoriano; Salvadorean army officer (retd) and government official; *Minister of National Defence;* b. 19 Aug. 1950; s. of Mariano Munguía; ed Univ. of El Salvador; fmr adviser to Christian Democratic Pres. José Napoleón Duarte; fmr army officer, rank of Col (retd); fmr Co-ordinator, Nat. Unity Movt; Minister of Nat. Defence 2009–11, 2014–, of Justice and Public Security 2011–14; numerous awards including Medalla de Oro al Mérito 1995, Medalla Escuela Militar Libertador Bernardo o Higgins. *Address:* Ministry of National Defence, Alameda Dr Manuel E. Araújo, Km 5, Carretera a Santa Tecla, San Salvador, El Salvador (office). *Telephone:* 2250-0100 (office). *E-mail:* oirmdn@faes.gob.sv (office). *Website:* www.fuerzaarmada.gob.sv/index.html (office).

MUNITZ, Barry, PhD; American academic, business executive, fmr university administrator and fmr foundation administrator; *President and CEO, Cotsen Foundation for the Art of Teaching and Academic Research;* b. 26 July 1941, Brooklyn, New York; s. of Raymond J. Munitz and Vivian LeVoff Munitz; m. Anne Tomfohrde 1987; ed Brooklyn Coll., Princeton Univ., Univ. of Leiden, Netherlands; Asst Prof. of Literature and Drama, Univ. of California, Berkeley 1966–68; Staff Assoc., Carnegie Comm. on Higher Educ. 1968–70; mem. Presidential staff, then Assoc. Provost, Univ. of Illinois 1970–72, Academic Vice-Pres. 1972–76; Vice-Pres., Dean of Faculties, Cen. Campus, Univ. of Houston 1976–77, Chancellor 1977–82; Pres. and COO Federated Devt Co. 1982–91; Vice-Chair. Maxxam Inc., LA 1982–91; Chancellor California State Univ., Long Beach 1991–98, Prof. of English Literature, UCLA 1991–98, Trustee Prof., California State Univ., LA 2006–; Pres. and CEO J. Paul Getty Trust, LA 1998–2006 (resgnd); currently Pres. and CEO Cotsen Foundation for the Art of Teaching and Academic Research, also mem. Bd of Dirs; Chair. P-16 Council 2005–10; Chair. Old Prospect Global Resources, Inc. 2010–11, SLM Corpn (parent co., known as Sallie Mae) 2011–13; Woodrow Wilson Fellow 1963, now Head of Advisory Cttee, Woodrow Wilson Nat. Fellowship Foundation; mem. Bd of Advisors, Leeds Weld and Co.; Fellow, American Acad. of Arts and Sciences; Chair. Bd of Trustees, Sierra Nevada Coll.; hon. degrees from Whittier Coll., Claremont Univ., California State Univ., Univ. of Southern California, Notre Dame Univ., Univ. of Edinburgh, UK. *Publications:* The Assessment of Institutional Leadership 1977; articles and monographs. *Address:* Cotsen Foundation for the Art of Teaching, 12100 Wilshire Blvd, Suite 920, Los Angeles, CA 90025, USA (office). *Telephone:* (310) 826-0504 (office). *E-mail:* info@cotsen.org (office). *Website:* www.cotsen.org (office).

MUNK OLSEN, Birger, DLitt; Danish professor of medieval culture and philology; *Professor, Saxo Institute, University of Copenhagen;* b. 26 June 1935, Copenhagen; m. 1st Annalise Bliddal 1964 (divorced 1988); m. 2nd Gudrun Haastrup 1994; two d.; ed Ecole Normale Supérieure, Sorbonne, Paris and Pontificia Univ. Gregoriana, Rome; Assoc. Prof. of Romance Philology, Univ. of Copenhagen 1961–68; Lecturer Univ. Paris-Sorbonne 1968–74; Prof. of Romance Philology, Univ. of Copenhagen 1974–83, Prof. of Medieval Culture and Philology 1983–; Chair. Danish Nat. Research Council for the Humanities 1987–90; Danish Rep. Standing Cttee for the Humanities, European Science Foundation 1988–92; mem. Royal Danish Acad. 1985– (Vice-Pres., Chair. Humanities Section 1989–95, Pres. 1996–2004), Danish Council for Research Planning and Policy 1987–89, Academia Europaea 1988– (Exec. Council 1989–92); Corresp. mem. Acad. des Inscriptions et Belles Lettres (Inst. de France) 1996, mem. 1998–; Vice-Pres. Soc. Int. de Bibliographie Classique 1994–99, Pres. 1999–2004; Hon. mem. Academia Româna 2000; mem. European Science and Tech. Asscn 1997–2000, Corresp. FRSE 2001; Kt, Order of the Dannebrog I; Officier, Légion d'honneur, Ordre nat. du Mérite; Commandor, Ordinul Naţional Pentru Merit (Romania); Dr hc (Paris) 2003; Prix Brunet 1984. *Publications include:* Les 'Dits' de Jehan de Saint-Quentin 1978, L'étude des auteurs classiques latins aux XI^{e}et XII^{e}siècles, Vols I–VI 1982–2014, I classici nel canone scolastico altomedievale 1991, L'atteggiamento medievale di fronte alla cultura classica 1994, La réception de la littérature classique au Moyen Age 1995. *Address:* Ny Kongensgade 20, 1557 Copenhagen V, Denmark (home); 51 rue de Tolbiac, 75013 Paris, France (office); Torshoj 9, Veddinge, 4540 Faarevejle, Denmark (home). *Telephone:* 33-91-91-81 (Copenhagen); 1-45-84-27-18 (Paris); 20-21-72-17 (Faarevejle). *E-mail:* bmo@hum.ku.dk (office).

MUNOZ, Oscar, BS, MBA; American business executive; *President and CEO, United Continental Holdings, Inc.;* b. 1959; m. Catherine Munoz; ed Univ. of Southern California, Pepperdine Univ.; held various finance positions with PepsiCo Inc. 1982–86; joined Coca-Cola Co. 1986, positions included Div. Controller, Dir of Financial Operations, Asst Corp. Controller 1986–91, Chief Financial Officer, Regional Vice-Pres. Coca-Cola Enterprises, Calif. 1991–96, Exec. Dir, Coca-Cola Co., Atlanta 1996–97; Sr Vice-Pres., Finance and Administration, US West, Denver, Colo 1997–2000; Chief Financial Officer and Vice-Pres. of Consumer Services, AT&T Corpn, New Jersey 2001–03; Chief Financial Officer and Exec. Vice-Pres., CSX Corpn, Jacksonville, Fla 2003–12, COO 2012–15, Pres. and COO Feb.–Sept. 2015; Pres. and CEO United Continental Holdings, Inc. Chicago 2015– (mem. Bd of Dirs 2004–). *Address:* United Continental Holdings

Inc., PO Box 06649, Chicago, IL 60606-0649, USA (office). *Website:* www.united.com (office).

MUÑOZ LEOS, Raúl; Mexican business executive and chemical engineer; b. 14 Oct. 1939, México; ed Nat. Univ. of Mexico (UNAM); joined Du Pont SA 1964, various sr positions in production, sales, market research, planning and admin, Exec. Vice-Pres. Du Pont Mexico –1988, Pres. (first Mexican to head co.) 1988–2000; Dir Gen. Pemex (Petróleos Mexicanos) 2000–04; mem. Bd of Dirs, Química Flúor SA, Nylon de México, Sears Roebuck and Co., Mexican Foundation for Rural Devt, Mexican Health Foundation; Nat. Vice-Pres. COPARMEX; Pres. Grupo Diálogo Inversión; fmr Pres. Mexican Inst. of Chemical Engineers; mem. Editorial Bd, El Economista; mem. Diálogo México, American Chamber of Commerce of Mexico; Trustee, UNAM Faculty of Chem., Museum of the City of Mexico, Antiguo Colegio de San Ildefonso. *Address:* c/o Petróleos Mexicanos (Pemex), Avenida Marina Nacional 329, Colonia Huasteca, 11311 México, DF, Mexico.

MUÑOZ VALENZUELA, Heraldo, BA, PhD; Chilean diplomatist and politician; b. 22 July 1948, Santiago; m. Pamela Quick; one d.; ed State Univ. of New York, USA, Harvard Univ., USA, Catholic Univ. of Chile, Univ. of Denver, USA; Nat. Supervisor, People's Stores (Almacenes del Pueblo) 1973; Co-founder Party for Democracy (PPD); mem. Political Comm. Sec. of Int. Relations, Socialist Party 1983–85; Chair. Metropolitan Santiago Region of PPD 1988–90; Jt Rep. of Socialist Party and PPD, Exec. Cttee, NO Campaign to defeat Gen. Pinochet 1988; Campaign Chief, Ricardo Lagos' senatorial race 1989; Amb. to OAS 1990–94, Pres. Environment Comm. 1991–92, Pres., Perm. Council 1993; Amb. to Brazil 1994–98; Pres., Economist Confs 1998–99; Int. Coordinator, Presidential Campaign of Ricardo Lagos 1999; Head of Int. and Defence Comm. 1999; Deputy Foreign Minister 2000–02; Minister Sec. Gen. of Govt 2002–03; Perm. Rep. to UN, New York 2003–10, mem. UN Security Council 2003–04, Pres. 2004; Asst Sec.-Gen., Asst Admin. and Regional Dir for Latin America and the Caribbean, UNDP 2010–14; Minister of Foreign Affairs 2014–18; Founder-Dir, Programa de Seguimiento de las Politicas Exteriores Latinoamericanas (PROSPEL, foreign policy Inst.), Santiago 1983–90; fmr Pres. Latinanalyst Consultores; currently Prof., Inst. of International Studies, Univ. of Chile; Fellowships from Resources for the Future, Ford Foundation, Tinker Foundation, Twentieth Century Fund, MacArthur Foundation; PhD Fellow, Brookings Inst., Washington, DC 1977; Dr hc (State Univ. of New York) 1996; Distinguished Alumnus Award, Grad. School of International Studies, Univ. of Denver 1991. *Publications include:* more than 20 books, including Latin American Nations in World Politics (co-ed.) 1998, Globalización XXI 2000, A Solitary War: A Diplomat's Chronicle of the Iraq War and Its Lessons (also in Spanish) 2008, The Dictator's Shadow: Life under Augusto Pinochet 2008; numerous essays in published academic journals including: Foreign Policy, Journal of Democracy, Journal of Interamerican and World Affairs, Latin American Research Review; contrib. to newspapers including El Mercurio, Folha de São Paulo, Los Angeles Times, Miami Herald, Página 12. *Address:* c/o Ministry of Foreign Affairs, Teatinos 180, Santiago, Chile (office).

MUNRO, Alice, BA; Canadian writer; b. 10 July 1931, Wingham, Ont.; d. of Robert E. Laidlaw and Anne Chamney; m. 1st James A. Munro 1951 (divorced 1976); three d.; m. 2nd Gerald Fremlin 1976 (died 2013); ed Univ. of Western Ontario;Foreign Hon. Mem. American Acad. of Arts and Letters 1992; Chevalier, Ordre des Arts et des Lettres 2010; Marian Engel Award, Writers' Trust of Canada 1986, Lorne Pierce Medal, Royal Society of Canada 1993, Canada-Australia Literary Prize 1994, Lannan Literary Award 1995, O. Henry Award 2001, Man Booker Int. Prize 2009, Nobel Prize for Literature 2013. *Publications include:* Dance of the Happy Shades (Gov.-Gen.'s Award for Literature 1968) 1968, A Place for Everything 1970, Lives of Girls and Women (Canadian Booksellers Asscn Int. Book Year Award 1972) 1971, Something I've Been Meaning to Tell You 1974, Who Do You Think You Are? (aka The Beggar Maid) (Gov.-Gen.'s Award for Fiction 1978) 1978, The Moons of Jupiter 1982, The Progress of Love (Gov.-Gen.'s Award for Fiction 1986) 1986, Friend of My Youth (Trillium Book Award 1990) 1990, Open Secrets (WH Smith Literary Award 1995) 1994, Selected Stories 1996, The Love of A Good Woman (Giller Prize 1998, Nat. Book Critics Circle Award 1998) 1998, Hateship, Friendship, Courtship, Loveship, Marriage 2001, Runaway (short stories) (Rogers Writers Trust Fiction Prize 2004, Giller Prize 2004) 2004, The View from Castle Rock 2006, Too Much Happiness 2009, Dear Life (Trillium Book Award 2013) 2012, Family Furnishings: Selected Stories: 1995–2014 2014, Lying Under the Apple Tree: New Selected Stories 2014. *Address:* PO Box 1133, Clinton, ON N0M 1L0, Canada; c/o William Morris Endeavor, 1325 Avenue, New York, NY 10019, USA (office). *E-mail:* admin@alicemunro.ca. *Website:* alicemunro.ca.

MUNTEAN, Mihail; Moldovan singer (tenor); b. 15 Aug. 1943, Kriva, Briceni; s. of Ion Muntean and Elizaveta Muntean; m. Rosentul Galina Andrian 1969; one s. one d.; ed Kishinev Inst. of Arts, La Scala, Italy; Prin. Tenor, Moldovan State Acad. Theatre of Opera and Ballet 1971–, Gen. Dir 1996–97; Prof. Chair of Vocal Arts, Music Acad. of Moldova 1993–; Provost, Art Inst., Mil. Acad. Stefan Cel Mare 1996–; Pres. Centre for Devt and Support of Culture Mihai Munteanu 1998–; Hon. Prof., Modern Humanitarian Inst. Moscow 1997–; Dr hc (Univ. of Arts, Iasi, Romania), (Univ. Ovidius Constanța, Romania); Verdi Award 1978, USSR People's Artist 1986, Moldovan State Award 1984, Award of the Republic 1993. *Television includes:* judge, Moldova are talent 2013–. *Opera roles include:* Lensky in Eugene Onegin, Riccardo in Un Ballo in Maschera, Don Carlo in Don Carlo, Cavaradossi in Tosca, Calaf in Turandot, Hermann in The Queen of Spades, Radames in Aida, Turiddu in Cavalleria Rusticana, Otello in Otello, Canio in Pagliacci, Manrico in Il Trovatore, Samson in Samson et Dalila, Ismael in Nabucco, Don José in Carmen, Don Alvaro in La Forza del Destino, Pinkerton in Madame Butterfly; performances and concerts throughout the world. *Leisure interests:* collecting books, family, children, music. *Address:* 16 N. Iorga str., Apt 13, 2012 Chișinău, Moldova (office). *Telephone:* 911-7577 (office); (2) 23-75-19. *Fax:* (2) 23-75-19. *E-mail:* mihai.muntean@mail.ru (home).

MÜNTEFERING, Franz; German politician; *Chairman, Advisory Board, Berlin Demography Forum;* b. 16 Jan. 1940, Neheim (now part of Arnsberg); s. of Franz Müntefering and Anna Schlinkmann; m. 1st Ankepetra Rettich 1995 (died 2008); two d.; m. 2nd Michelle Schumann 2009; apprenticeship in industrial admin. 1954–57; industrial admin. in eng firm 1957–61; mil. training 1961–62; mem. SPD 1966–, Sub-Dist Chair. Hochsauerland 1984–88, mem. Dist Exec. W Westphalia 1984–, Dist Chair. 1992–98, mem. Exec. Cttee 1991–, Fed. Business Man. 1995–99, Chair. state org. North Rhine Westphalia 1998–2001, Gen. Sec. 1999, Chair. SPD 2004–05, 2008–09; mem. Sudern City Council 1969–79; mem. Bundestag 1975–92, 1998–2013, Parl. Business Man., SPD Bundestag Parl. Group 1991–92; mem. North Rhine Westphalia Landtag 1996–98; Fed. Minister of Transport, Construction and Housing 1998–99, Vice-Chancellor and Minister of Labour and Social Affairs 2005–07 (resgnd); Co-Chair. Deutschen Gesellschaft eV 2013–; Chair. Advisory Bd, Berlin Demography Forum 2014–; mem. IG Metall (Eng TU) 1967–; Hon. Citizen of Sundern (Sauerland) 2008; Hon. Pres. Workers' Samaritan Fed. Germany 2013; Marie-Juchacz Badge, Workers' Welfare Asscn (AWO) 2006. *Publication:* Macht Politik! (co-author) 2008. *Address:* Berliner Demografie Forum, Pariser Platz 6, 10117 Berlin (office); Deutsche Gesellschaft eV, Mosse Palais, Voßstr. 22, 10117 Berlin, Germany. *Telephone:* (30) 206482110 (office). *Fax:* (30) 206482111 (office). *E-mail:* info@berlinerdemografieforum.org (office). *Website:* www.berlinerdemografieforum.org.

MUNTIANAS, Viktoras; Lithuanian engineer and politician; b. 11 Nov. 1951, Marijampolė; m. Violeta Muntianas; three c.; ed Marijampolė Secondary School No 3, Vilnius Civil Eng Inst. (now Vilnius Gediminas Tech. Univ.), Vilnius Higher School for Party Studies; Jr Research Fellow, Lithuanian Construction and Architecture Research Inst. 1978–79; construction site man., later Chief Engineer, Kaunas Construction Plant 1979–85; Deputy Chair., Exec. Cttee of Kėdainiai Dist 1986–90; Gov., Kėdainiai Dist 1990–93; Gov. AB Ūkio Bankas, Kėdainiai Br. 1994–96; Vice-Pres., Trust Vikonda 1996–97; mem., Municipal Bd, later Mayor, Kėdainiai Dist 1997–2004; mem. Seimas 2004–08; Deputy Chair. Bd of Seimas 2004–06, Speaker 2006–08, mem. Cttee on Budget and Finance 2004–06, Comm. on Anti-corruption 2004–06; mem. Ass. of Elders, Parl. Group for Relations with France, Seimo Delegacija Lietuvos ir Ukrainos Aukščiausiosios Rados Asamblėjoje; mem. CPSU –1989; mem. and Deputy Chair., Labour Party 2003–06; mem. and Chair. Civil Democracy Party 2006–. *Leisure interests:* hunting, sports, angling, horticulture.

MURAD, Ferid, BA, MD, PhD; American pharmacologist and academic; *University Professor of Biochemistry and Molecular Medicine, School of Medicine and Health Sciences, George Washington University;* b. 14 Sept. 1936, Whiting, Ind.; s. of John Murad and Henrietta Josephine Murad; m. Carol A. Leopold 1958; one s. four d.; ed DePauw Univ., Ind. and Western Reserve Univ., Cleveland, Ohio; internship and residency, Massachusetts General Hosp., Boston 1967; Dir Clinical Research Center, School of Medicine, Univ. of Virginia 1971–81, Div. of Clinical Pharmacology 1973–81, Prof. Depts of Internal Medicine and Pharmacology 1975–81; Prof., Depts of Internal Medicine and Pharmacology, Stanford Univ. 1981–89, Acting Chair. Dept of Medicine 1986–88; Chief of Medicine Palo Alto Veterans Admin. Medical Center, Calif. 1981–86; Adjunct Prof., Dept of Pharmacology, Northwestern Univ., Chicago 1988–96; Chair. Dept of Integrative Biology and Pharmacology, Univ. of Texas Medical School, Houston 1997–2010, Prof. and John S. Dunn Distinguished Chair in Physiology 1998–2010, Dir Depts of Pharmacology and Physiology, Medicine Dir Inst. of Molecular Medicine 1999–2007, Dir Emer. 2007–; Univ. Prof. of Biochemistry and Molecular Medicine, School of Medicine and Health Sciences, George Washington Univ. 2008–; Vice-Pres. Pharmaceutical Research and Devt, Abbott Laboratories 1988–92; CEO and Pres. Molecular Geriatrics Corpn, Lake Bluff, Ill. 1993–95; mem. NAS Inst. of Medicine; Fellow, American Acad. of Arts and Sciences; Hon. Citizen, Municipality of Čair, Albania 2012; Hon. mem. Acad. of Sciences and Arts of Kosovo; Hon. DSc from 11 univs; Ciba Award 1988, Albert and Mary Lasker Award for Basic Research 1996, Nobel Prize in Medicine or Physiology 1998, Baxter Award, Asscn of American Medical Colls 2000, AAMC Research Award 2002, Grisalin Award 2005. *Publications:* several books, including Discovery of Some of the Biological Effects of Nitric Oxide and its Role in Cellular Signaling (Nobel Lecture 1998) 1999; more than 405 publs. *Leisure interests:* golf, carpentry. *Address:* School of Medicine & Health Sciences, George Washington University, Ross Hall 2300 Eye Street, NW, Washington, DC 20037, USA (office). *Telephone:* (202) 994-5408 (office). *E-mail:* smhsnews@gwu.edu (office). *Website:* smhs.gwu.edu/biochemistry (office).

MURAD, Nadia; Iraqi human rights campaigner; b. 1993, Kocho, Sinjar Dist; kidnapped from home town with other Yazidi women and held captive by Islamic State for three months 2014; escaped with the help of a Muslim family to a refugee camp in Kurdish border area near Dohuk; moved to Germany under refugee programme of Govt of Baden-Württemberg 2015; f. Nadia's Initiative (works to provide advocacy and assistance to victims of genocide and human trafficking) 2016; UN Goodwill Amb. for the Dignity of Survivors of Human Trafficking 2016; Council of Europe Václav Havel Award for Human Rights 2016, Sakharov Prize for Freedom of Thought (jtly with Lamiya Aji Bashar) 2016, Nobel Peace Prize (jtly with Denis Mukwege) 2018. *Publication:* The Last Girl: My Story of Captivity, and My Fight Against the Islamic State (memoir) 2017. *E-mail:* info@nadiamurad.org (office). *Website:* nadiasinitiative.org (office).

MURAKAMI, Haruki, BA; Japanese writer; b. 12 Jan. 1949, Kyoto; m. Yoko Takahashi 1971; ed Kobe High School, Waseda Univ.; Owner, Peter Cat jazz club, Tokyo 1974–81; began writing in 1978, lived in Europe 1986–89, USA 1991–95; Visiting Scholar, Princeton Univ. 1991–93; Una's Lecturer in the Humanities, Univ. of Calif., Berkeley 1992; Writer-in-Residence, Tufts Univ. 1993–95, Harvard Univ. 2005–06; Franz Kafka Prize 2006, Jerusalem Prize 2009, Hans Christian Andersen Literature Award 2016. *Publications:* fiction: Hear the Wind Sing (Gunzo Literature Prize) 1979, Pinball 1980, A Wild Sheep Chase (Noma Literary Award for New Writers) 1982, Hard-Boiled Wonderland and The End of the World (Junichi Tanizaki Award) 1985, Norwegian Wood 1987, Dance Dance Dance 1988, South of the Border, West of the Sun 1992, Wind-Up Bird Chronicle (Yomiuri Literary Award 1996) 1994–95, Sputnik Sweetheart 1999, Kafka on the Shore 2002, After Dark 2004, 1Q84 2009, Colourless Tsukuru Tazaki and His Years of Pilgrimage 2013, Killing Commendatore 2017; short stories: Slow Boat to China 1983, A Perfect Day for Kangaloos 1983, Dead Heat 1985, The Elephant Vanishes 1986, TV People 1990, Phantoms of Lexington 1998, After the Quake 2000, Blind Willow, Sleeping Woman (Frank O'Connor Int. Short Story Award, Kiriyama Prize 2007) 2006, Men Without Women 2017; non-fiction: Underground 1997, The Place That was Promised (Kuwahara Takeo Award) 1998, What I Talk About When I Talk About Running 2008, Absolutely on Music: Conversations with Seiji Ozawa

2017; essays: A Young Reader's Guide to Short Fiction 1997; has translated works by F. Scott Fitzgerald, Raymond Carver, Truman Capote, Paul Theroux, John Irving, J. D. Salinger. *Leisure interests:* running marathons, music, jazz, classical etc. *Address:* ICM, 40 West 57th Street, New York, NY 10019, USA (office). *Telephone:* (212) 556-5600 (office). *E-mail:* vintageanchorpublicity@randomhouse.com (office). *Website:* www.icmtalent.com (office); www.randomhouse.com/features/murakami/site.php (office); www.harukimurakami.com.

MURAKAMI, Kenji; Japanese business executive; b. 1947; ed Ritsumeikan Univ.; joined Daiwa House Industry Co. Ltd 1970, held positions including Man. Hiroshima Pref. Dist, Exec. Officer, Man. Dir, Sr Man. Dir, Chief Man. Tokyo Store and Pres. Tokyo Office, apptd Rep. Dir 1997, Pres. and COO Daiwa House Industry Co. Ltd 2004–11, apptd Vice-Chair. 2011; Dir Nippon Venture Capital Co. Ltd; fmrly Pres. The Machinami Foundation 2009.

MURAKAMI, Ryunosuke (Ryū); Japanese writer and film director; b. 19 Feb. 1952, Sasebo City, Nagasaki; m. Tazuko Takahashi 1976; fmr rock band drummer, TV talk show host; writer and filmmaker. *Films include:* adaptations of many of his novels, including Almost Transparent Blue (writer and dir) 1978, Daijôbu, mai furendo (writer and dir) 1983, Raffles Hotel (writer and dir) 1989, Topâzu (writer and dir) 1992, Ôdishon (writer) 1999, Kyoko (writer and dir) 2000, Hashire! Ichiro (from novel Hashire! Takahashi) 2001, Shōwa kayō daizenshū 2003, Shikusutinain 2004, Popular! 2006, Koinrokkā Beibīzu 2008. *Publications include:* novels: Kagirinaku tōmei ni chikai burrū (trans. as Almost Transparent Blue) (Akutagawa Prize, Gunzou Prize) 1976, Hashire! Takahashi, Ôdishon, Topâzu (trans. as Tokyo Decadence), Raffles Hotel, Daijôbu, mai furendo (trans. as All Right, My Friend), Kyoko (trans. as Because of You), 69 1987, Coin Locker Babies 1995, In the Miso Soup (Yomiuri Literary Award 1998) 1997, Exodus (serialised) 1998–99, Piercing 2007, Audition 2009, Popular Hits of the Showa Era 2011; non-fiction: Ano kane de nani ga kaeta ka 2003.

MURAKAMI, Seiichiro, BA; Japanese politician; b. 11 May 1952; ed Tokyo Univ.; elected to House of Reps for Ehime Pref. 1986–; Sec. of State for Finance 1992–93, Chair. Parl. Cttee on Coal Problems 1994–95, on Finance 1997–98, Deputy Chair. Japan-Albania Parl. Friendship Asscn, Chief Sec. Japan-Cyprus Parl. Friendship Asscn; Deputy Sec.-Gen. LDP 1995–, Commr Policy Research Council 1999, Chair. Diet Affairs Cttee; Sr Vice-Minister on Finance 2000–02; Minister of State for Regulatory Reform, for Industrial Revitalization Corpn of Japan, for Admin. Reform, for Special Zones of Structural Reform and for Regional Revitalization 2004–05; Chair. Deliberative Council on Political Ethics. *Address:* c/o Liberal-Democratic Party (Jiyu-Minshuto), 1-11-23, Nagata-cho, Chiyoda-ku, Tokyo 100-8910, Japan. *Telephone:* (3) 3581-6211. *E-mail:* info@jimin.jp. *Website:* www.jimin.jp/english/profile/members/114716.html.

MURAKAMI, Takashi, MA, PhD; Japanese artist and designer; b. 1 Feb. 1962, Tokyo; ed Univ. of Fine Arts, Tokyo; trained in classical Nihon-gah style of Japanese traditional painting; pop artist whose style fuses historic Japanese painting with contemporary cartoons; made debut as modern artist with solo exhbn Takashi, Tamiya 1991; invited to participate in PS1 Int. Studio Program on Rockefeller Foundation Asian Cultural Council fellowship grant, NY 1994; f. Hirpon Factory (Kaikai Kiki—production studio) Asaka City, Saitama 1994; Guest Prof., Dept of Art, UCLA, Calif. 1998; worked for French fashion house Louis Vuitton (LV) and cr. LV 'Murakami bag' 2003; his recurring character, Mr DOB, appears on t-shirts, posters, key-chains and mugs worldwide; work has been exhibited in Asia, America and Europe; curator Super Flat exhbn (showcase of contemporary Japanese artists), Little Boy exhbn; directed artwork for Kanye West's album, Graduation, 2007; has participated in numerous group exhbns in Japan, Korea, USA, Italy, Denmark, Norway, Sweden, Finland, Austria, Australia, France, New Caledonia, Philippines 1991–; Organizer, Geisai 2002–14. *Solo Exhibitions include:* Gallery Ginza Surugadai, Tokyo 1989, Art Gallery at Tokyo Nat. Univ. of Fine Arts and Music 1991, Aoi Gallery, Osaka 1991, Rontgen Kunst Inst. 1992, Nasubi Gallery, Tokyo 1993, Gallery Koto, Okayama 1994, Emmanuel Perrotin, Paris (France) 1995, Yngtingagatan, Stockholm (Sweden) 1995, Feature Inc., NY 1996, Gavin Brown Enterprize, NY 1996, Ginza Komatsu, Tokyo 1996, Univ. of Buffalo Art Gallery, NY 1997, Blum & Poe, Santa Monica, CA 1998, Tomio Koyama Gallery, Tokyo 1998, Marianne Boesky Gallery, NY 1999, Bard Coll. Museum of Art 1999, Issey Miyake Men, Aoyama, Tokyo 2000, Grand Cen. Terminal, NY 2001, Museum of Fine Arts, Boston, 2001, Galerie Emmanuel Perrotin, Paris 2001, Museum of Contemporary Art, Tokyo 2001, Cartier Foundation, Paris 2002, Pacifico Yokohama Exhibition Hall 2003, 2004, Museum of Contemporary Art, Los Angeles 2007, Brooklyn Museum, NY 2008, Guggenheim Museum, Bilbao, Spain 2009, Gagosian Gallery, Rome, Italy 2010, Gagosian Gallery, London 2011, ALRIWAQ Doha Exhibition Space, Qatar 2012, Los Angeles County Museum of Art 2013, Mori Art Museum, Tokyo 2015–16, Museum of Contemporary Art, Chicago 2017. *Address:* c/o Kaikai Kiki New York, 5–17 46th Road, Long Island City, NY 11101, USA (office). *Telephone:* (718) 706-2213 (office). *Fax:* (718) 706-2218 (office). *E-mail:* info@kaikaikikiny.net (office). *Website:* english.kaikaikiki.co.jp (office).

MURALITHARAN, Muttiah; Sri Lankan fmr professional cricketer; b. 17 April 1972, Kandy; s. of Muttiah Sinnasamy; ed St Anthony's Coll., Kandy; right-arm off-break bowler, lower-order right-hand batsman; teams: Tamil Union Cricket and Athletic Club 1991–2009-10, Sri Lanka 1992–, Lancs. 1999, 2001, 2005, 2007, Kent 2003, Chennai Super Kings 2008–10, Victorian Bushrangers 2009–, Kochi Tuskers Kerala 2011, Glos. 2011–12, Wellington Firebirds 2011, Royal Challengers Bangalore 2012–14, Melbourne Renegades 2012–14, Jamaica Tallawahs 2013; First-class debut: 1989/90; Test debut: Sri Lanka v Australia, Colombo (RPS) 28 Aug.–2 Sept. 1992; One-Day Int. (ODI) debut: Sri Lanka v India, Colombo (RPS) 12 Aug. 1993; T20I debut: NZ v Sri Lanka, Wellington 22 Dec. 2006; played in 133 Tests, scored 1,261 runs (highest score 67) and taken 800 wickets (average 22.72), best bowling (innings) 9/51, (match) 16/220; ODIs: 350 matches, 534 wickets (average 23.08), best bowling 7/30; First-class: 232 matches, 1,374 wickets (average 19.64), best bowling (innings) 9/51, (match) 16/220; numerous records, including quickest and youngest player to reach 400 Test wickets (in 72 matches) and 500 Test wickets (in 87 matches); world's highest wicket-taker 2000, 2001; became highest wicket-taker in Test cricket when he surpassed Courtney Walsh's 519 wickets in 2004, overtook Shane Warne's 708 wickets 3 Dec. 2007; first player to take 800 Test wickets, against India, Galle 22 July 2010, announced retirement from Test cricket; most ODI wickets (534); announced retirement from int. cricket following defeat by India in Cricket World Cup final, Mumbai 2 April 2011; Head Coach, Thiruvallur Veerans 2017; Trustee, Foundation for Goodness; Wisden Cricketer of the Year 1999, CEAT Int. Cricketer of the Year 2000, rated Best Ever Test Bowler by Wisden Dec. 2002. *Website:* www.unconditionalcompassion.org.

MURALITHARAN, Vinayagamoorthy, (ColKaruna Amman); Sri Lankan politician and fmr rebel leader; b. 7 Nov. 1966, Kiran, Batticaloa Dist; m. Vidyawathi Muralitharan; one s. two d.; ed Central Coll. of Batticaloa; selected for Medical Faculty of Eastern Univ. of Sri Lanka; joined Liberation Tigers of Tamil Eelam 1983, commdr in charge of Batticaloa and Amparai Dists, Eastern Prov. 1987–2004; Founder and Leader, Tamil Makkal Viduthalai Pulikal breakaway group after defection to govt 2004 (recognized as political party 2007); mem. Parl. for United People's Freedom Alliance (UPFA) 2008–15; Minister of Nat. Integration 2009–10; apptd Deputy Minister of Resettlement 2010; Award from Mass Communicators Asscn of Sri Lanka for his special involvement in bringing peace to Sri Lanka. *Leisure interests:* listening to music, playing the guitar, playing football, reading and studying law-related books, cooking, hanging around in his home town with the people. *Telephone:* (77) 3667457 (mobile).

MURALIYEV, Amangeldy Mursadykovich; Kyrgyzstani politician; b. 7 Aug. 1947, Kum-Aryk; ed Frunze (Bishkek) Polytechnical Inst., USSR Govt Acad. of Nat. Econ.; engineer, Frunze (Bishkek) factories 1970–80; Dir heavy machine construction factory 1980–82, Kyrgizavtomash factory 1982–88; Chair., Frunze City Council (Mayor) 1988–91; Chair. State Cttee on Economy, State Sec. 1991–92; Min. Chair. Fund of State Property 1994–96; Deputy Prime Minister 1996; Gov. Osh Oblast 1996–99; Prime Minister 1999–2000; Minister of Econ. Devt, Industry and Trade (acting) 2004–06; First Deputy Prime Minister 2010; Co-ordinator Political Bd Union Party of Kyrgyzstan 2001–; Pres. Kyrgyzstan Stock Exchange 2001–04; Chair. Kyrgyz Altyn (gold co.) 2010–; mem. Kyrgyzstan Eng Acad.; Hon. Pres. Kyrgyzstan Football Fed. 1991–2008.

MURANO, Elsa Alina, BSc, MSc, DrSc; American food scientist, academic, university administrator and fmr government official; *Professor of Nutrition and Food Science, Texas A&M University;* b. (Elsa Casales), 14 Aug. 1959, Havana, Cuba; m. Dr Peter S. Murano; ed Miami Dade Coll., Florida Int. Univ., Virginia Tech Univ.; Asst Prof., Dept of Microbiology, Immunology and Preventative Medicine, Iowa State Univ. 1990–95; Assoc. Prof., Dept of Animal Science, Texas A&M Univ. 1995–97, becoming Sadie Hatfield Prof. in Agric., also Assoc. Dir Center for Food Safety, Inst. for Food Science and Eng 1995–97, Dir 1997–2001, Vice-Chancellor and Dean Coll. of Agric. and Life Sciences 2005–07, also Dir Tex. Agricultural Experiment Station (now Tex. AgriLife Research) 2005–07, Pres. Texas A&M Univ. 2008–09 (resgnd), Pres. Emer. and Prof. of Nutrition and Food Science 2009–; US Under-Sec. of Agric. for Food Safety, Washington, DC 2001–04. *Publications:* author or co-author of seven books, book chapters and monographs, numerous scholarly papers, abstracts and related materials. *Address:* Texas A&M University, Department of Nutrition & Food Science, 2254 TAMU, College Station, TX 77843-2254, USA (office). *Telephone:* (979) 845-0834 (office). *Fax:* (979) 845-5027 (office). *E-mail:* eamurano@tamu.edu (office). *Website:* nfs.tamu.edu (office).

MURAOKA, Takamitsu, PhD, FAHA; Japanese academic; *Professor Emeritus of Hebrew, University of Leiden;* b. 9 Feb. 1938, Hiroshima; s. of Yoshie Muraoka and Sachi Muraoka; m. Keiko Kageyama 1965; two s. one d.; ed Tokyo Kyoiku, The Hebrew Univ., Jerusalem; Lecturer in Semitic Languages, Dept of Near Eastern Studies, Univ. of Manchester, UK 1970–80; Prof. of Middle Eastern Studies, Chair. Dept, Melbourne Univ. 1980–91; Prof. of Hebrew, Univ. of Leiden 1991–2003, Prof. Emer. 2003–; Ed. Abr-Nahrain (Leiden) 1980–92; Visiting Prof., Univ. of Göttingen, Germany 2001–02; Research Fellow, Netherlands Inst. of Near Eastern Studies 2004–06; Assoc. Research Fellow, Kirchliche Hochschule, Wuppertal, Germany 2011–; Fellow, Hebrew Language Acad.; Hon. Prof. in Semitic Languages, Presbyterian Coll. and Theological Seminary, Seoul 2006–07; Hon. Fellow, Acad. of the Hebrew Language 2006–; Alexander von Humboldt Research Award 2001–02. *Publications:* A Greek-Hebrew/Aramaic Index to I Esdras 1982, Emphatic Words and Structures in Biblical Hebrew 1985, Classical Syriac for Hebraists 1987, A Grammar of Biblical Hebrew (with P. Joüon) 1991, 2006, Studies in Qumran Aramaic (ed.) 1992, A Greek-English Lexicon of the Septuagint (Twelve Prophets) 1993, Studies on the Hebrew of the Dead Sea Scrolls and Ben Sira (co-ed.) 1997, A Grammar of Egyptian Aramaic (with B. Porten) 1998, 2003, Classical Syriac – A Basic Grammar with a Chrestomathy 1997, 2005, Hebrew/Aramaic Index to the Septuagint Keyed to the Hatch-Redpath Concordance 1998, A Greek-English Lexicon of the Septuagint – Chiefly of the Pentateuch and the Twelve Prophets 2002, A Greek-English Lexicon of the Septuagint 2009, A Greek-Hebrew/Aramaic Two-way Index to the Septuagint 2010, A Grammar of Qumran Aramaic 2011. *Leisure interest:* angling. *Address:* Wijttenbachweg 57, 2343 XW Oegstgeest, Netherlands.

MURASIRA, Maj-Gen. Albert, BSc, MSc; Rwandan military officer and politician; *Minister of Defence;* b. 11 Nov. 1962, Maniema Prov., Democratic Repub. of the Congo; m. Marie Goretti Rafiki; three c.; ed Nat. Univ. of Rwanda, Univ. of Liverpool, UK, Ghana Inst. of Man. and Public Admin, Nat. Defence Univ. of PLA, People's Repub. of China; joined Rwandan Armed Forces 1988, commissioned 1989; Visiting Lecturer, Faculty of Applied Sciences, Nat. Univ. of Rwanda 1995–98; Dir of Planning, Ministry of Defence 1999–2004; Staff Officer, in charge of Information Tech., Communication and Information System Dept, African Union Mission in Sudan (AMIS) 2004–05; Deputy Commdt, Rwanda Military Acad., Gako 2006–07; Chief, Jt Gen. Staff in charge of Admin and Human Resource Man., Rwanda Defence Force 2007–12; CEO Zigama Credit and Saving Soc. 2012–18; Minister of Defence 2018–. *Address:* Ministry of Defence, POB 23, Kigali, Rwanda (office). *Telephone:* 252577942 (office). *Fax:* 250576969 (office). *E-mail:* info@mod.gov.rw (office). *Website:* www.mod.gov.rw (office).

MURATA, Yoshitaka; Japanese politician and government official; b. 30 July 1944, Shizuoka City; ed Univ. of Tokyo for Foreign Studies, Kyoto Univ., Univ. of Grenoble and Ecole Nat. d'Admin, France; joined Ministry of Finance 1968, seconded as Sec., Embassy in Beijing, People's Repub. of China 1974–76, Sec. to Minister of Labour 1978; Dir Office of Public Relations 1985–88, Dir Local Taxation Agency in Capital Area 1986–87, Dir Research Div., Int. Finance Bureau 1987–89; elected to House of Reps for Okayama Constituency 1990–; various positions in House include Dir Cttee on Rules and Admin, Cttee on Transport, Cttee on Finance and Monetary Affairs, Cttee on Audit and Oversight of Admin, Chair. Standing Cttee on Economy, Trade and Industry 1990–2004; various positions in Cabinet include Parl. Sec. of Econ. Planning, of Finance and of Monetary Affairs Agency 1990–2004; Chair. of Nat. Public Safety Comm. and Minister of State for Disaster Man. and for Nat. Emergency Legislation 2004–05; currently mem. Bd of Dirs Japan Investment Adviser Co. Ltd; fmr Deputy Sec.-Gen. and Dir of Transportation Div., Policy Research Council, Liberal Democratic Party (LDP). *Address:* c/o Japan Investment Adviser Company Limited, Kasumigaseki Common Gate West Tower 34F, 3-2-1 Kasumigaseki, Chiyoda-ku, Tokyo 100-0013, Japan.

MURAYAMA, Tomiichi; Japanese politician (retd); b. 3 March 1924, Oita Pref.; m. Yoshie Murayama; two d.; ed School of Political Science and Econs, Meiji Univ.; fmr sec. of a trade union of Oita Pref. Govt employees; entered local govt 1955; mem. Japanese Socialist Party (JSP), now Social Democratic Party of Japan (SDPJ), renamed Democratic League 1995, renamed Shakai Minshuto (SDP); Chair. Oita Pref. of JSP, Chair. Diet Affairs Cttee 1991–93, Chair. SDPJ 1993–96; mem. House of Reps 1972–2000; Prime Minister of Japan 1994–96; mem. Lower House's Cttee on Social and Labour Affairs; retd from politics 2000; Grand Cordon of the Order of the Paulownia Flowers 2006. *Publications:* several books on social and labour affairs. *Leisure interest:* drama appreciation. *Address:* Social Democratic Party, 2-4-3, 7F Nagatacho Building, Nagata-cho, Chiyoda-ku, Tokyo 100-0014 (office); 3-2-2 Chiyomachi, Oita, Oita 870, Japan (home). *Telephone:* (3) 3580-1171 (office); (975) 32-0033 (home). *Fax:* (3) 3580-0691. *E-mail:* sdpjmail@omnics .co.jp (office). *Website:* www.omnics.co.jp (office).

MURCH, Walter Scott; American film editor and sound designer; b. 12 July 1943, New York, NY; m. Muriel Ann (Aggie) Slater 1965; one s. three d.; ed Johns Hopkins Univ., Univ. of Southern California; worked with George Lucas, Francis Ford Coppola and Anthony Minghella as film ed. and sound designer; Hon. DLit (Emily Carr Inst. of Art and Design Vancouver) 2006; Nikola Tesla Award, Int. Press Acad. Satellite Awards 2012, Vision Award Nescens, 68th Locarno Film Festival 2015. *Films include:* The Godfather (sound-effects ed.) 1972, American Graffiti (sound designer) 1973, The Godfather, Part II (sound designer) 1974, The Conversation (ed. and sound designer) 1974, Julia (ed.) 1977, Apocalypse Now (and sound designer) (Academy Award for Best Sound) 1979, Return to Oz (dir) 1985, The Unbearable Lightness of Being (ed.) 1988, The English Patient (ed. and sound mixer) (BAFTA Award and two Academy Awards) 1996, The Talented Mr Ripley (ed.) 1999, K-19: Widowmaker (sound and ed.) 2002, Cold Mountain (sound and ed.) 2003, Jarhead (re-recording mixer, ed.) 2005, Youth Without Youth (sound re-recording mixer, ed.) 2007, Tetro (sound re-recordist, ed.) 2009, The Wolfman (ed.) 2010, Particle Fever (documentary-sound re-recording mixer, ed.) 2013, Cutaways (documentary short-sound designer, ed.) 2014, Tomorrowland: A World Beyond (ed.) 2015. *Television includes:* Seeing in the Dark (film documentary-sound mix) 2007, Hemingway & Gellhorn (film-ed.) 2012. *Publications:* In the Blink of an Eye: A Perspective on Film Editing (with Francis Ford Coppola q.v.) 1995, The Bird that Swallowed its Cage (translations of short stories by Italian writer Curzio Malapart) 2012. *Address:* c/o The Mirisch Agency, 8840 Wilshire Boulevard, Suite 100, Beverly Hills, CA 90211, USA (office). *Telephone:* (310) 282-9940 (office). *Fax:* (310) 282-0702 (office). *E-mail:* info@mirisch.com (office). *Website:* www.mirisch .com (office).

MURDOCH, Elisabeth, BA; British media executive; b. 22 Aug. 1968; d. of Rupert Murdoch (q.v.) and Anna Maria Murdoch (née Torv); m. 1st Elkin Kwesi Pianim (divorced); two d.; m. 2nd Matthew Freud 2001 (divorced 2014); one d.; ed Vassar Coll.; presentation and promotions asst, Nine Network Australia 1990–91, researcher and producer 1991–93, Man. of Programming and Promotion, Fox TV LA 1993, Programme Dir KSTU Fox 13 Salt Lake City 1993–94, Dir of Programme Acquisitions FX Cable Network LA 1994–95, Pres. and CEO, EP Communications 1995–96; Gen. Man. Broadcasting Dept, BSkyB Ltd 1996, Dir of Programming 1996–98, Man. Dir Sky Networks 1998–2000; Dir Future Publishing 2000; Co-Founder, Chair. and CEO Shine Ltd (TV production co.) 2001–14 (co. sold to 21st Century Fox 2011); Dir Freelands Group (investment fund) 2014–. *Address:* Freelands Group, 128 Wigmore Street, London, W1U 3SA, England (office).

MURDOCH, James Rupert Jacob; British/American media executive; *Co-Chief Operating Officer, Chairman and CEO, International, 21st Century Fox;* b. 13 Dec. 1972, Wimbledon, London, England; s. of Rupert Murdoch (q.v.) and Anna Maria Torv; m. Kathryn Hufschmid 2000; three c.; ed Horace Mann High School, New York, Harvard Univ.; f. record label Rawkus Entertainment 1995; joined News Corpn 1996, Pres. News Digital Media 1997–99, Exec. Vice-Pres. News Corpn 1999, mem. Exec. Cttee News Digital systems, CEO and Chair. Star TV 2000–03, Chair. and CEO Europe and Asia, News Corporation 2007–12, Exec. Chair. News International (now News UK) 2009–12 (resgnd), Dir, News Group Newspapers Ltd –2011, News International Holdings –2011, Deputy COO 2011–13 (co. restructured with News Corporation's publishing assets spun off into similarly named News Corp while existing News Corporation renamed 21st Century Fox and its legal successor 2013), Co-COO, Chair. and CEO, International, 21st Century Fox 2013–; Dir (non-exec.) BSkyB 2003, CEO 2003–07, Chair. (non-exec.) 2007–12 (resgnd), Chair. Supervisory Bd Sky Deutschland 2013–14 (remains on Supervisory Bd); mem. Bd of Dirs TrueX 2014, Vice Media 2014–, GlaxoSmithKline 2009–12, Sotheby's 2010–12. *Leisure interests:* reading, painting. *Address:* 21st Century Fox, 1211 Avenue of the Americas, New York, NY 10036, USA (office). *Telephone:* (212) 852-7000 (office). *Fax:* (212) 852-7145 (office). *Website:* www.21cf .com (office).

MURDOCH, Lachlan Keith, BA; American (b. British) media executive; *Co-Chairman, News Corp;* b. 8 Sept. 1971, London, England; s. of Rupert Murdoch (q.v.) and Anna Maria Murdoch Mann; m. Sarah O'Hare 1999; two s. one d.; ed Trinity School, Manhattan, Aspen Country Day School, Andover, Mass, Princeton Univ.; with News Corporation 1994–2005, mem. Bd of Dirs 1996–2014, Publr The Australian 1995, Gen. Man. Queensland Newspapers Ltd 1994–95, Exec. Dir 1996–99, Sr Exec. Vice-Pres. 1999–2000, Head of US Print Operations 1999–2005, Deputy COO News Corporation 2000–05, Publr New York Post 2002–05, Advisor, News Corp 2005–07, co-Chair. News Corp 2014–, Exec. Chair. 21st Century Fox 2015–; Deputy CEO News Limited 1995–97, Chair. and CEO 1997–2008; Dir Beijing PDN Xinren Information Technology Co. Ltd (People's Repub. of China)

1995; Deputy Chair. Star TV Ltd 1995–2005; Exec. Chair. Illyria Pty Ltd 2005–; Acting CEO Ten Network Holdings Ltd Feb.–April 2011, mem. Bd of Dirs 2010–12, Chair. 2012–14; Exec. Chair. DMG Radio Australia 2009–14; Deputy Chair. Prime Media Group Ltd Oct.–Nov. 2010; Chair. Nova Entertainment Group 2014–; Dir Queensland Press Ltd 1994–96, Foxtel Management Pty Ltd 1998–2005, Rovi Guides, Inc. (alternatively Gemstar-TV Guide Int. Inc.) 2001–04, Dir (non-exec.) NDS Group Ltd 2002–05; apptd Dir Beijing PDN Xiren Information Technology Co. Ltd 1996, The Herald & Weekly Times Ltd 1996, One.Tel Ltd 1999, Sky Global Networks Inc. 2000, The Partnership for New York City, Inc., NYC2012, Inc., OmniSky Corpn 2000; mem. Bd Robin Hood Foundation, New York 1999, Caffeine Inc. 2018–; Cannes Lions Media Person of the Year 2005. *Leisure interest:* rock climbing. *Address:* News Corp, 1211 Avenue of the Americas, New York, NY 10036, USA (office). *Telephone:* (212) 416-3400 (office). *Website:* newscorp.com (office).

MURDOCH, (Keith) Rupert, AC; American (b. Australian) publisher, broadcaster and media business developer; *Executive Chairman, News Corp;* b. 11 March 1931, Melbourne, Vic., Australia; s. of Sir Keith Murdoch and Dame Elisabeth Murdoch; m. 1st Patricia Booker (divorced); one d.; m. 2nd Anna Maria Torv 1967 (divorced); two s. one d.; m. 3rd Wendi Deng 1999 (divorced 2013); two d.; m. 4th Jerry Hall 2016; ed Geelong Grammar School, Vic., Worcester Coll., Oxford, UK; inherited Adelaide News 1954; built up News Corporation (Group CEO (prior to co.'s separation into two publicly traded cos in 2013) 1979–2013, Chair. 1991–2013 (co. restructured with News Corporation's publishing assets spun off into similarly named News Corp while existing News Corporation renamed 21st Century Fox and its legal successor 2013), Exec. Chair. News Corp 2013–, Chair. and CEO 21st Century Fox 2013–); has acquired newspapers, broadcasting and other interests in Australia, UK, USA, Latin America, Europe and Asia, including: Australia – newspapers: The Australian (nat.), Daily Telegraph, Sunday Telegraph, Daily Mirror (Sydney), Sunday Sun (Brisbane), The News and Sunday Mail (Adelaide), The Sunday Times (Perth); USA– New York Post; UK– newspapers: Sun, News of the World (nat., acquired 1969); acquired Times Newspapers Ltd 1981, group includes The Times, The Sunday Times, The Times Literary Supplement, The Times Educational Supplement, The Times Higher Education Supplement; Dir, Times Newspapers Holdings 1981–2012 (Chair. 1982–90, 1994–2012), News International Group Ltd –2012; magazines: Weekly Standard (US politics); film: Fox Film Entertainment; TV: British Sky Broadcasting (UK), STAR (Asia), Fox Broadcasting Co., Fox Cable Networks; other interests include lifestyle portal MySpace.com, book publr HarperCollins and ownership of 35 US TV stations; Chair. and CEO Fox Entertainment Group USA 1992–; mem. Bd of Dirs Associated Press 2008–; Commdr of the White Rose (First Class) 1985, Kt, Order of St Gregory the Great 1998. *Leisure interests:* sailing, skiing. *Address:* News Corp, 1211 Avenue of the Americas, New York, NY 10036, USA (office); News Corp Australia, 2 Holt Street, Surry Hills, Sydney, NSW 2010, Australia (office). *Telephone:* (212) 852-7017 (New York) (office); (2) 9288-3000 (Sydney) (office). *Fax:* (212) 852-7145 (New York) (office); (2) 9288-3292 (Sydney) (office). *Website:* newscorp.com (office).

MURDOCH, Hon. Tom; I-Kiribati politician; mem. Maneaba Ni Maungatabu (House of Ass.) for Kuria –2016; Minister of Finance and Economic Devt 2012–16; Gov. of the World Bank and the IMF for Kiribati 2012–16. *Address:* c/o Ministry of Finance and Economic Development, PO Box 647, Bairiki, Tarawa, Kiribati (office).

MUREKEZI, Anastase, BSc; Rwandan politician; b. 15 June 1952, Nyaruguru Dist, Southern Prov.; m. Marie Rose Byukusenge; two c.; ed Univ. de Louvain-La-Neuve, Belgium; several sr positions in Ministry of Agric. and Animal Resources; fmr ind. consultant in agri-business devt –2004; various cabinet portfolios from 2004 including Minister of State in charge of Industry and Investment Promotion, Minister of Agric. and Animal Resources and Minister of Public Service and Labour; Prime Minister 2014–17; mem. Parti Social-Démocrate (PSD), mem. Political Bureau. *Leisure interest:* playing tennis. *Address:* c/o Office of the Prime Minister, Kigali, Rwanda (office).

MURERWA, Herbert; Zimbabwean politician; b. 31 July 1941; m.; mem. Zimbabwe African Nat. Union-Patriotic Front (ZANU-PF); High Commr to UK 1984–1990; Minister of Environment and Tourism 1990–95, of Industry and Commerce 1995–96, of Finance and Econ. Devt 1996–2000, 2002, of Higher Educ. and Tech. 2000–01, of Int. Trade and Tech. 2001–02; Minister of Higher Educ. and Tech. and Acting Minister of Finance and Econ. Devt –2005, Minister of Finance and Econ. Devt 2005–07, apptd of Lands and Rural Resettlement 2009.

MUREŞAN, HE Cardinal Lucian; Romanian ecclesiastic; *Major Archbishop of Făgăraş şi Alba Iulia (Romanian);* b. 23 May 1931, Firiza (now the Ferneziu dist of Baia Mare); s. of Peter Mureşan and Maria Mureşan; ordained priest, Diocese of Maramureş 1964, Bishop of Maramureş 1990–94; Archbishop of Făgăraş şi Alba Iulia 1994–2005, Major Archbishop of Făgăraş şi Alba Iulia 2005–; Head of the Romanian Church United with Rome, Greek-Catholic; cr. Cardinal (non-voting) (Cardinal-Priest of Sant'Atanasio) 2012. *Address:* Archdiocese of Făgăraş şi Alba Iulia, Str. Petru Pavel Aron 2, 515400 Blaj AB, Romania (office). *Telephone:* (258) 712057 (office); (258) 710608 (office). *Fax:* (258) 713602 (office). *E-mail:* mitropolia@bru.ro (office). *Website:* www.bru.ro/blaj (office).

MURIGANDE, Charles, PhD; Rwandan politician and diplomatist; *Ambassador to Japan;* b. 15 Aug. 1958, Butare; ed Facultés Universitaires Notre Dame de la Paix, Namur; Scientific Adviser to Dir-Gen., Geographical Inst. of Burundi 1986–88, also Head of Computing Center, Geographical Inst. of Burundi 1986–88; Post-doctoral Fellow, Howard Univ., Washington, DC, USA 1989, later Asst Prof. and Head of Biostatistical Div., Coll. of Medicine; Spokesperson, Rwandan Patriotic Front USA; Adviser to Pres. on Foreign Affairs 1994–95; Minister of Transport and Communications 1995–97; Rector, Nat. Univ. of Rwanda 1997–98; Gen. Sec. Rwandese Patriotic Front (RPF) 1998–2002; Minister of Foreign Affairs and Regional Co-operation 2002–08, for Cabinet Affairs 2008–09, of Educ. 2009–11; Amb. to Japan 2011–. *Address:* Embassy of Rwanda, Annex Fukazawa, 1-17-17, Fukazawa, Setagaya-ku, Tokyo, 158-0081, Japan (office). *Telephone:* (3) 5752-4255 (office). *Fax:* (3) 3703-0342 (office). *Website:* www.rwandaembassy -japan.org (office).

MURILLO, Rosario; Nicaraguan government official and poet; *Vice-President;* b. 22 June 1951, Managua; m. Daniel Ortega 2005; seven c.; ed Greenway Coll., UK, Anglo-Swiss Inst. Le Manoir, Switzerland, Universidad Nacional Autónoma de Nicaragua; language teacher, Teresiano School and Inst. of Commercial Sciences 1967–69; Sec. to Pedro Joaquín Chamorro, Dir of La Prensa newspaper 1967–77; joined Sandinista Nat. Liberation Front (FSLN) 1968; arrested for political activities 1976; lived in exile in Panama, Venezuela and Costa Rica 1977–79; mem. Editorial Bd Barricade newspaper 1981–89, Ed. Ventana cultural supplement 1981–92; mem. Nat. Ass. 1984–90; Dir Inst. of Culture 1988–90; First Lady and Spokeswoman for Pres. Daniel Ortega and Dir, Social and Community Affairs 2006–16; Vice-Pres. of Nicaragua 2016–; Leonel Rugama poetry prize 1980. *Publications include:* numerous collections of poetry, including Angel in the Deluge (trans.) 1992. *Address:* Office of the President, Casa Presidencial, Managua, Nicaragua (office). *Fax:* 2266-3102 (office). *E-mail:* rosario@presidencia.gob.ni (office). *Website:* www.presidencia.gob.ni (office).

MURILLO JORGE, Marino Alberto, BEcons; Cuban politician, economist and fmr military officer; b. 19 Feb. 1961, Manzanillo; ed Coll. of Nat. Defence; fmr Dir of Audits and Econs, Ministry of Food; fmr Vice-Minister of Econs and Planning –2009; Minister for Internal Trade, of Economy and Planning 2009–11, 2014–16, Vice-Pres. Council of Ministers 2009–16; Chair. Econ. Policy Comm. 2011–14; mem. Partido Comunista de Cuba, elected to its Politburo 2011.

MURKOWSKI, Frank Hughes, BA; American banker and fmr politician; b. 28 March 1933, Seattle, Wash.; s. of Frank Michael Murkowski and Helen Murkowski (née Hughes); m. Nancy R. Gore 1954; two s. four d. including Lisa Murkowski; ed Ketchikan High School, Santa Clara Univ., Seattle Univ.; served with US Coast Guard 1955–57; with Pacific Nat. Bank of Seattle 1957–59, Nat. Bank of Alaska, Anchorage 1959–67, Vice-Pres. in Charge of Business Devt, Anchorage 1965–67; Commr, Dept of Econ. Devt, Alaska State, Juneau 1967–70; Pres. Alaska Nat. Bank of the North, Fairbanks 1971–80; Senator from Alaska 1981–2002, Chair. Cttee on Energy and Natural Resources 1995–2001; Gov. of Alaska 2002–06; Pres. Alaska State Chamber of Commerce 1977; Vice-Pres. Bd of Trade, BC (Canada) and Alaska; mem. American Bankers Asscn, Alaska Bankers Asscn (fmr Pres.); Republican. *Leisure interests:* hunting, fishing, skiing, tennis, golf.

MURKOWSKI, Lisa, BA, LLB; American politician and lawyer; *Senator from Alaska;* d. of Frank Hughes Murkowski, fmr Senator from Alaska and fmr Gov. of Alaska; m. Verne Martell; two s.; ed Georgetown Univ., Williamette Coll. of Law; worked in pvt. law practice for eight years; served as Anchorage Dist Court Attorney for two years; elected to Alaska State House of Reps 1998, 2000, 2002, served as House Majority Leader 2003; apptd Senator from Alaska 2002–04, elected 2004–; apptd Deputy Whip and Chair. Class of New Senators, sr mem. Energy and Natural Resources Cttee, mem. Appropriations Cttee (Ranking Republican mem. Interior and Environment Sub-cttee), mem. Health, Educ., Labor and Pensions Cttee, sr mem. Indian Affairs Cttee; mem. Alaska Fed. of Republican Women, Midnight Sun Republican Women, Anchorage Republican Women's Club; Republican. *Leisure interests:* skiing, fishing, camping. *Address:* 709 Hart Senate Building, Washington, DC 20510 (office); 510 L Street, Suite 600, Anchorage, AK 99501, USA. *Telephone:* (202) 224-6665 (DC) (office); (907) 271-3735 (Anchorage) (office). *Fax:* (202) 224-5301 (DC) (office); (907) 276-4081 (Anchorage) (office). *Website:* murkowski.senate.gov (office).

MŪRNIECE, Ināra, BA; Latvian journalist and politician; *Chairman (Speaker), Saeima (Parliament);* b. 30 Dec. 1970, Rīga, Latvian SSR, USSR; m. Dr Ritvars Jansons; ed Univ. Coll. of Econs and Culture, Univ. of Latvia; reporter on internal affairs and foreign policy matters for Latvijas Avīze daily newspaper 1995–2011; mem. Nacionālā Apvienība (Nat. Alliance), Chair. Parl. Group Sept.–Nov. 2014; mem. Saeima (Parl.) 2011–, Chair. Human Rights and Public Affairs Cttee 2011–14, Chair. (Speaker) 2014–. *Leisure interests:* literature, history, theatre. *Address:* Office of the Speaker, Saeima (Parliament), Jekaba iela 11, Rīga 1811, Latvia (office). *Telephone:* 6708-7487 (office); 6708-7321 (office). *Fax:* 6708-7100 (office). *E-mail:* inara.murniece@saeima.lv (office). *Website:* www.saeima.lv/en/about-saeima/work-of-the-saeima/speaker (office).

MUROMACHI, Kaneo; Japanese banking executive; *President, Mitsubishi UFJ Environment Foundation;* Sr Man.-Dir Sanwa Bank 1997–99, Pres. 1999–2001, Pres. and CEO 2001–02; Sr Adviser to UFJ Bank (created by merger of Sanwa Bank and Tokai Bank) 2004; Chair. UFJ Holdings Inc. 2004–05 (acquired by Mitsubishi UFJ Financial Group, Inc.), now Hon. Advisor, Bank of Tokyo Mitsubishi UFJ; Special mem. The Tax Comm. 2002; Dir Inamori Foundation, Foundation for Advanced Studies on Int. Devt (FASTID) 2003–; Councillor, Grad. School of Int. Man., IUJ Business School, Japan; Pres. Mitsubishi UFJ Environment Foundation. *Address:* Mitsubishi UFJ Environment Foundation, 2-4-3 Tokyo-Mitsubishi UFJ Bank Shiba Building 2F, Shiba, Minato-ku, Tokyo 105-0014, Japan (office). *Telephone:* (3) 5730-0337 (office). *Fax:* (3) 5232-0312 (office). *Website:* www.bk.mufg.jp/global/csr/contribution/foundation/eco.html (office).

MUROMACHI, Masashi, MA; Japanese engineer and business executive; b. 10 April 1950; ed Waseda Univ.; joined Toshiba Corpn 1975, Vice-Pres., Memory Div., Semiconductor Co. 2002–04, Exec. Vice-Pres. April–June 2004, Exec. Officer, Corp. Vice-Pres., Pres. and CEO June 2004–05, Exec. Officer, Corp. Sr Vice-Pres., Pres. and CEO 2005–06, Exec. Officer, Corp. Exec. Vice-Pres., Pres. and CEO 2006–07, Exec. Officer, Corp. Exec. Vice-Pres., Group CEO, Electronic Devices and Components Group 2007–08, Dir, Rep. Exec. Officer, Corp. Sr Exec. Vice-Pres., Group CEO, Electronic Devices and Components Group, Group Exec., New Lighting Systems Div., New Visual Device Div., Quality Div., Productivity and Environment Group 2008–11, Dir, Rep. Exec. Officer, Corp. Sr Exec. Vice-Pres., Group Exec., New Lighting Systems Div., Strategic Planning and Communications Group, Information and Security Group 2011–12, Sr Adviser, Toshiba Corpn 2012–13, Dir 2013–16, Chair. 2014–16, Pres. and CEO 2015–16. *Address:* c/o Toshiba Corporation, 1-1, Shibaura 1-chome, Minato-ku, Tokyo 105-8001, Japan. *E-mail:* info@toshiba.co.jp.

MURPHY, Catherine J., BS, PhD; American chemist and academic; *Peter C. and Gretchen Miller Markunas Professor of Chemistry, University of Illinois, Urbana-Champaign;* ed Univ. of Illinois, Urbana-Champaign, Univ. of Wisconsin; NSF Postdoctoral Fellow, California Inst. of Tech. 1990–92; NIH Postdoctoral Fellow 1993; Asst Prof., Dept of Chem. and Biochemistry, Univ. of South Carolina

1993–98, Assoc. Prof. 1998–2002, Prof. 2002–09, Guy F. Lipscomb Prof. of Chem. 2003–09; Peter C. and Gretchen Miller Markunas Prof. of Chem., Univ. of Illinois, Urbana-Champaign 2009–, Affiliate, Dept of Materials Science and Eng 2010–, Micro and Nanotechnology Lab. 2010–; Visiting Researcher, Dept of Chem., Univ. of Bristol, UK 2000; Harold McMaster Visiting Scientist, Coll. of Arts and Sciences, Bowling Green State Univ. 2010; Sr Ed. Journal of Physical Chemistry 2006–; mem. Editorial Advisory Bd Journal of Inorganic Biochemistry 1996–2007, Journal of Cluster Science 1997–, Langmuir 2002–, Inorganic Chemistry 2004–06, Chemistry of Materials 2004–09, NanoLetters 2005–, Chemical Communications 2005–, Journal of Colloid and Interface Science 2006–08, ACS Nano 2007–, Nanoscale 2009–; Fellow, AAAS 2008; Merck Award in Biochemistry, Univ. of Illinois 1986, Bronze Tablet, Univ. of Illinois 1986, McElvain Scholar, Univ. of Wisconsin 1986–87, Wisconsin Alumni Research Foundation Fellow 1986–87, Summer Energy Research Fellow, Electrochemical Soc. 1989, W.R. Grace & Co. Fellow, Univ. of Wisconsin 1989–90, NSF CAREER Award 1995–98, Cottrell Scholar Award 1996–2001, Alfred P. Sloan Foundation Research Fellow 1997–99, Camille Dreyfus Teacher-Scholar Award 1998–2000, Golden Key Faculty Award for the Integration of Research and Undergraduate Teaching 1998, Michael J. Mungo Award for Excellence in Undergraduate Teaching, Univ. of South Carolina 2001, Outstanding Undergraduate Research Mentor Award, Univ. of South Carolina 2003, Russell Award for Research in Science, Math. and Eng, Univ. of South Carolina 2005, Nanotech Briefs Nano 50 Award, Innovator Category 2008, Kolthoff Lectureship in Chem., Univ. of Minnesota 2009. *Publications:* Nanoparticles and Nanostructured Surfaces: Novel Reporters with Biological Applications, Proceedings of SPIE, Vol. 4258 (ed.) 2001, Biomedical Nanotechnology Architectures and Applications, Progress in Biomedical Optics and Imaging: Proceedings of SPIE, Vol. 4626 (co-ed.) 2002, Chemistry: The Central Science (12th edn) (co-author) 2012; more than 150 scientific papers in professional journals. *Address:* Department of Chemistry, University of Illinois at Urbana-Champaign, A512 Chemical & Life Sciences Laboratory, 600 South Mathews Avenue, Mail Code 712, Box 59-6, Urbana, IL 61801, USA (office). *Telephone:* (217) 333-7680 (office). *Fax:* (217) 244-3186 (office). *E-mail:* murphycj@illinois.edu (office). *Website:* www.chemistry.illinois.edu/faculty/Catherine_Murphy.html (office); www.scs.illinois.edu/murphy (office).

MURPHY, Christopher (Chris) Scott, BA, JD; American politician; *Senator from Connecticut;* b. 3 Aug. 1973, White Plains, NY; s. of Scott L. Murphy and Catherine Murphy (née Lewczyk); m. Catherine Holahan 2007; two s.; ed Williams Coll., Univ. of Connecticut School of Law, Hartford, Exeter Coll., UK; interned for US Senator Chris Dodd; campaign manager for Charlotte Koskoff's campaign against Nancy Johnson 1996; worked for Connecticut State Senate Majority Leader George Jepsen 1997–98; elected to Planning and Zoning Comm., Southington 1997; mem. Connecticut House of Reps from 81st Dist 1999–2003; practised real estate and banking law with the firm Ruben, Johnson & Morgan 2002–06; mem. Connecticut Senate from 16th Dist 2003–07, Chair. Public Health Cttee; mem. US House of Reps for 5th Congressional Dist of Conn. 2007–13, mem. Cttee on Foreign Affairs, Cttee on Oversight and Govt Reform; Senator from Connecticut 2013–, mem. Appropriations Cttee, Health, Educ., Labor, and Pensions Cttee, Foreign Relations Cttee, Democratic Steering & Outreach Cttee; Democrat; Hon. DHumLitt (Univ. of New Haven) 2013. *Address:* 136 Hart Senate Office Building, Washington, DC 20510 (office); One Constitution Plaza, 7th Floor, Hartford, CT 06103; PO Box 127, Cheshire, CT 06410, USA. *Telephone:* (202) 224-4041 (office). *Fax:* (202) 224-9750 (office). *E-mail:* info@chrismurphy.com. *Website:* www.murphy.senate.gov (office); www.chrismurphy.com.

MURPHY, Dervla Mary; Irish author and critic; b. 28 Nov. 1931, Cappoquin; d. of Fergus Murphy and Kathleen Rochfort-Dowling; one d.; ed Ursuline Convent, Waterford; American Irish Foundation Literary Award 1975, Ewart-Biggs Memorial Prize 1978, Irish American Cultural Inst. Literary Award 1985. *Publications:* Full Tilt 1965, Tibetan Foothold 1966, The Waiting Land 1967, In Ethiopia with a Mule 1968, On a Shoestring to Coorg: an Experience of South India 1976, Where the Indus is Young: a Winter in Baltistan 1977, A Place Apart 1978, Wheels Within Wheels 1979, Race to the Finish? 1981, Eight Feet in the Andes: Travels with a Mule in Unknown Peru 1983, Muddling Through in Madagascar 1985, Ireland 1985, Tales from Two Cities 1987, Cameroon with Egbert 1989, Transylvania and Beyond 1992, The Ukimwi Road: from Kenya to Zimbabwe 1993, South from the Limpopo 1997, Visiting Rwanda 1998, One Foot in Laos 1999, Through the Embers of Chaos: Balkan Journeys 2002, Through Siberia by Accident 2005, Silverland: A Winter Journey Beyond the Urals 2006, The Island That Dared 2008, A Month by the Sea: Encounters in Gaza 2013, Other Encounters 2014, Between River and Sea: Encounters in Israel and Palestine 2015. *Leisure interests:* reading, music, cycling, swimming, walking. *Address:* Lismore, Co. Waterford, Ireland.

MURPHY, Edward (Eddie) Regan; American comedian and actor; b. 3 April 1951, Brooklyn, New York; s. of Vernon Lynch (stepfather) and Lillian Lynch; m. 2nd Nicole Mitchell 1993 (divorced 2006); five c.; feature player in Saturday Night Live TV show 1980–84; film debut in 48 Hours 1982; comedy albums: Eddie Murphy 1982, Eddie Murphy: Comedian 1983, How Could It Be 1984, So Happy 1989; has also released seven record albums of comedy and songs; f. Eddie Murphy Productions (production co.) 1996; numerous awards including Mark Twain Prize 2015. *Films include:* 48 Hours 1982, Trading Places 1983, Delirious 1983, Best Defence 1984, Beverly Hills Cop 1984, The Golden Child 1986, Beverly Hills Cop II 1987, Eddie Murphy Raw 1987, Coming to America 1988, Harlem Nights 1989, 48 Hours 2 1990, Boomerang 1992, Distinguished Gentleman 1992, Beverly Hills Cop III 1994, The Nutty Professor 1996, Dr. Dolittle 1998, Holy Man 1998, Life 1998, Bowfinger 1999, Toddlers 1999, Pluto Nash 1999, Nutty Professor II: The Klumps 2000, Shrek 2001 (voice), Dr Dolittle 2 2001, Showtime 2002, I Spy 2002, Daddy Day Care 2003, Shrek 4–D 2003 (voice), Haunted Mansion 2003, Shrek 2 (voice) 2004, Dreamgirls (Golden Globe for Best Supporting Actor 2007, Screen Actors' Guild Award for Outstanding Performance by a Male Actor in a Supporting Role 2007) 2006, Norbit 2007, Shrek the Third (voice) 2007, Meet Dave 2008, Imagine That 2009, Shrek Forever After (voice) 2010, Tower Heist 2011, A Thousand Words 2012. *Address:* Eddie Murphy Productions, 152 West 57th Street, 47th Floor, New York, NY 10019, USA. *Telephone:* (212) 399-9900.

MURPHY, Gerry, MBS, PhD, FInstD, CCMI; Irish business executive; b. 1955; m.; two s.; ed Univ. Coll. Cork, Univ. Coll. Dublin; fmrly with Grand Metropolitan PLC (now Diageo), Ireland, UK and USA 1978–91; CEO Greencore Group PLC, Dublin 1991–95, Exel PLC (fmrly NFC) 1995–2000, Carlton Communications PLC 2000–03, Kingfisher PLC 2003–08; Sr Man. Dir Blackstone Group Int. Partners LLP 2008–17, Chair. 2009–; Chair. Invest Europe 2016–17, Tate & Lyle PLC 2017– (also Dir non-exec.); Dir (non-exec.) Abbey Nat. 2004, Reckitt Benckiser 2005–08, United Biscuits 2009–14, Merlin Entertainments PLC 2009–15, British American Tobacco PLC 2009–17, Intertrust NV 2013–, Ideal Shopping Direct 2015–. *Address:* Blackstone Group Int. Partners LLP, 40 Berkely Square, London, W1J5AL, England (office). *Telephone:* (20) 7451-4000 (Blackstone) (office); (20) 7758-9000 (office). *Fax:* (20) 7451-4001 (office); (20) 7758-9098 (office). *Website:* www.blackstone.com (office).

MURPHY, Glenn K., BA; Canadian retail executive; *Founder and CEO, FIS Holdings;* b. Montreal; ed Univ. of Western Ont.; began career with A.C. Nielsen; 14 years in category man., marketing, procurement and operations, Loblaw Cos Ltd, becoming Exec. Vice-Pres. Loblaws Supermarkets 1997–2000; Pres. and CEO Chapters Inc. 2000; Chair. and CEO Shoppers Drug Mart 2001–07; mem. Bd of Dirs Gap Inc. 2007–, Chair. and CEO 2007–14; currently Founder and CEO FIS Holdings, Ltd; Co-Chair. and Dir Lululemon Athletica, Inc. 2017–. *Address:* FIS Holdings, Ltd, 95 St Clair Avenue W, Suite 1400, Toronto, Ontario M4V 1X2, USA (office). *Website:* www.fis-holdings.com (office).

MURPHY, James (Jim); British politician and business strategist; b. 23 Aug. 1967, Glasgow, Scotland; m. Claire Murphy; two s. one d.; Pres. Nat. Union of Students, Scotland 1992–94, Nat. Union of Students, UK 1994–96; Dir Endsleigh Insurance 1994–96; Project Man. Scottish Labour Party 1996–97; MP for Eastwood 1997–2005, for East Renfrewshire 2005–15, mem. Public Accounts Cttee 2000–01, Parl. Pvt. Sec. to Sec. of State for Scotland 2001–02, Govt whip 2002–05, Parl. Sec. at Cabinet Office 2005–06, Minister of State for Employment and Welfare Reform 2006–07, for Europe 2007–08; Sec. of State for Scotland 2008–10; Shadow Sec. of State for Scotland May–Oct. 2010, for Defence 2010–13, for Int. Devt 2013–14; Leader, Scottish Labour Party 2014–15; Minister of the Year, awarded by the House Magazine following vote by MPs and Lords of all parties 2008. *Publication:* The 10 Football Matches That Changed The World ... and the One That Didn't 2014. *Leisure interest:* supports Glasgow Celtic Football Club. *E-mail:* jim@jimmurphy.scot (office). *Website:* www.jimmurphy.scot.

MURPHY, John Michael; British artist; b. 7 Sept. 1945, St Albans; s. of James Murphy and Maureen Murphy (née Tarrant); ed St Michael's Coll., Hitchin, Luton and Chelsea Schools of Art; has participated in several group exhbns in Britain, Europe and USA; Arts Council of GB Award 1980.

MURPHY, Kathleen A., BA, JD; American lawyer and financial services industry executive; *President, Fidelity Personal Investing, Fidelity Investments;* b. 27 Jan. 1963, Wallingford, Conn.; m. George Hornyak; one s.; ed Fairfield Univ., Univ. of Connecticut School of Law; with Aetna Financial Services 1985–2000, positions included Gen. Counsel and Chief Compliance Officer; with ING Groep NV (after acquisition of Aetna by ING) 2000–09, positions included Gen. Counsel and Chief Admin. Officer, ING US Financial Services, Group Pres. ING US Worksite and Institutional Financial Services, ING N America Insurance Corpn, Dir ING Canada Inc. 2006–08, ING Life Insurance and Annuity Co., ING USA Life Insurance and Annuity Co., ING US Foundation Bd, ING Insurance Co. of America, CEO ING US Wealth Man. 2007–09; Pres. Fidelity Personal Investing, Fidelity Investments 2009–; fmr Chair. Conn. Children's Trust Fund; mem. Bd of Dirs Nat. Conf. for Civil Justice in the Northeast, Conn. Business and Industry Asscn, Metro Hartford Alliance, American Benefits Council, Gov. of Conn.'s Prevention Partnership Program, America's Promise Alliance (also mem. Exec. Cttee), Univ. of Connecticut Foundation; Trustee, Wheeler Clinic, Boys & Girls Club of America; mem. Bd Michael Smurfit School of Business, Univ. Coll. Dublin, Ireland. *Address:* Fidelity Investments, PO Box 770001, Cincinnati, OH 45277-0003, USA (office). *Website:* www.fidelity.com (office).

MURPHY, Philip Dunton, AB, MBA; American business executive, state governor and fmr diplomatist; *Governor of New Jersey;* b. 16 Aug. 1957, Boston, Mass; m. Tammy Murphy; three s. one d.; ed Harvard Univ., The Wharton School, Univ. of Pennsylvania; spent 23 years at Goldman Sachs, headed Goldman Sachs' Frankfurt office, with oversight responsibility for activities in Germany, Switzerland and Austria, as well countries of Cen. Europe 1993–97, Pres. Goldman Sachs (Asia) 1997–99, held several sr positions before becoming a Sr Dir 2003–06 (retd); Dir Murphy Endeavors, LLC, Red Bank, NJ 2006–; Gov. of New Jersey 2018–; Nat. Finance Chair. Democratic Nat. Cttee 2006–09; Amb. to Germany 2009–13; has served on bds and/or cttees of NAACP, Local Initiatives Support Corpn, Center for American Progress, 180 Turning Lives Around and several programmes of Univ. of Pennsylvania, amongst others; Co-chaired nat. task force on 21st century public educ.; chaired task force on public sector employee benefits in NJ; fmr mem. Bd US Soccer Foundation, US Soccer Fed. World Cup Bid Cttee; Democrat. *Leisure interest:* soccer. *Address:* Office of the Governor, The State House, PO Box 001, Trenton, NJ 08625, USA (office); Washington Office of the Governor, State of New Jersey, 444 North Capitol Street, Suite 201, Washington, DC 20001, USA (office). *Telephone:* (609) 292-6000 (Trenton) (office); (202) 638-0631 (DC) (office). *Fax:* (609) 777-2922 (Trenton) (office); (202) 638-2296 (DC) (office). *E-mail:* info@state.nj.us (office). *Website:* www.nj.gov/governor (office); www.state.nj.us/governor (office).

MURPHY, William P., Jr, MD; American physician, biomedical engineer and business executive; *Chairman, Bioheart, Inc.;* b. 1923, Boston, Mass; s. of William Parry Murphy (who shared Nobel Prize in Physiology or Medicine 1934) and Harriett Adams; m.; ed Harvard Univ., Univ. of Illinois School of Medicine, Massachusetts Inst. of Tech.; cr. first invention, a residential snow blower, at high school; practised medicine at St Francis Hosp., Honolulu, Hawaii and Peter Bent Brigham Hosp., Boston; medical consultant to US Army during Korean War, cr. first dialysis machines for use during war and flexible sealed blood bags for transfusions with colleague Dr Carl Walter; f. Medical Devt Corpn (renamed Cordis Corpn 1959) 1957, purchased by Johnson & Johnson 1996; cr. first motor-driven angiographic injectors, disposable vascular diagnostic catheters, hollow-fibre artificial kidneys, medical procedural trays, physiologic cardiac pacemakers, externally programmable and dual-chamber demand pacemakers; f. Small Parts, Inc. 1963, Chair. –2005 (retd when co. acquired by Amazon.com 2005); Co-founder and CEO Hyperion, Inc., Miami 1986–2003, Chair. and CEO 1999–2004; mem. Bd of Dirs Bioheart Inc. 2003–, currently Chair.; est. FIRST (Foundation for the Inspiration and Recognition of Science and Tech.) 1989; Founding Fellow, American Soc. for Artificial Internal Organs, American Inst. for Medical and Biological Eng 1993; Award of Merit, American Roentgen Ray Society 1948, Corporate Leadership Award, MIT 1980, Distinguished Service Award, Int. Soc. for Artificial Organs 1981, 7th Frank Hastings Award, NIH 1983, Distinguished Service Award, N American Soc. of Pacing and Electrophysiology 1985, Alumnus of the Year, University of Illinois Medical Alumni Association 1987, University of Illinois Alumni Achievement Award 1994, Dean's Award for Excellence in Innovation, University of Miami, College of Engineering 1998, FIRST Founders Award 2000, Florida First Jay Malina Award, Beacon Council, Miami 2003, Lemelson-MIT Lifetime Achievement Award 2003, inducted into Nat. Inventors Hall of Fame 2008. *Publications:* more than 30 medical papers; 17 US patents issued 1952–80. *Leisure interests:* sailing antique steam-powered tugboat. *Address:* Bioheart, Inc., 13794 NW 4th Street, Suite 212, Sunrise, FL 33325, USA (office). *Telephone:* (954) 835-1500 (office). *Fax:* (954) 845-9976 (office). *E-mail:* bioheart@bioheartinc.com (office). *Website:* www.bioheartinc.com (office).

MURPHY OF TORFAEN, Baron (Life Peer), cr. 2015, of Abersychan in the County of Gwent; **Rt Hon. Paul Peter Murphy,** PC, MA; British politician; b. 25 Nov. 1948, Usk, Wales; s. of Ronald Murphy and Marjorie Murphy (née Gough); ed Oriel Coll., Oxford; man. trainee, Co-operative Wholesale Soc. 1970–71; Lecturer in History and Govt, Ebbw Vale Coll. of Further Educ. 1971–87; mem. Torfaen Borough Council 1973–87 (Chair. Finance Cttee 1976–86); Sec. Torfaen Constituency Labour Party 1974–87; MP for Torfaen 1987–2015; Opposition Front Bench Spokesman for Wales 1988–94, on NI 1994, on Foreign Affairs 1994–95, on Defence 1995–97; Minister of State, NI Office 1997–99; Sec. of State for Wales 1999–2002, 2008–09, for NI 2002–05; Chair. Intelligence and Security Cttee 2005–07; Co-Chair. British-Irish Parl. Ass. 2006–07, 2009–10, Vice-Chair. 2010–15; mem. Jt Cttee on Nat. Security Strategy 2010–; mem. (Labour), House of Lords 2015–; Hon. Fellow, Oriel Coll. Oxford, Glyndwr Univ., Wrexham; Kt of St Gregory 1997; Kt Commdr, Sacred Mil. Constantinian Order of St George; Hon. DUniv (S Wales). *Leisure interest:* music. *Address:* House of Lords, Westminster, London, SW1A 0PW, England (office). *Telephone:* (20) 7219-6193 (office). *Fax:* (20) 7219-6193 (office). *E-mail:* contactholmember@parliament.uk (office); murphypp@parliament.uk (office). *Website:* www.paulmurphymp.co.uk.

MURR, Elias; Lebanese government official, lawyer, business executive and international organization official; *President of the Board, Foundation for a Safer World, International Criminal Police Organization (INTERPOL);* b. 1962, Bteghrin; s. of Michel Murr; m. Karine Lahoud 1992; three c.; fmr Ed.-in-Chief Al-Jumhouriyah newspaper; business interests in finance and real estate; Minister of the Interior 2000–05; Deputy Prime Minister and Minister of Nat. Defence 2005–11; Pres. of the Bd Interpol Foundation for a Safer World 2013–. *Address:* Foundation for a Safer World, International Criminal Police Organization (INTERPOL), 200 quai Charles de Gaulle, 69006 Lyon, France (office). *Website:* www.interpol.int/About-INTERPOL/INTERPOL-Foundation-for-a-Safer-World (office).

MURR, Muhammad Ahmad al-; United Arab Emirates editor and government official; b. 1955, Dubai; ed Syracuse Univ., USA; worked in the field of banking man. during 1980s; fmr Ed.-in-Chief, Khaleej Times (daily newspaper); fmr Exec. Ed.-in-Chief Al Bayan (Arabic daily newspaper); fmr Deputy Chair. Dubai Cultural Council (now Dubai Culture & Arts Authority); Founder-mem. Science and Culture Symposium, Dubai, Pres. 1987–2001; fmr Dir Emirates Media Inc.; apptd to 15th Chapter of Fed. Nat. Council (Parl.) as rep. of Dubai 2011, Speaker, Fed. Nat. Council 2011–15; Emirates Appreciation Award in the field of Literature 2006. *Publications include:* numerous articles and essays, including weekly columns Awraq Al Ahad (Al Khaleej newspaper), Hadeeth Al Ethnain (Al Bayan newspaper) and Muntasaf Al Osbou (Al Reyada Wa Al Shabab magazine); around 15 collections of short stories, including Dubai Tales and The Wink of the Mona Lisa (published in English); other publs include The Wink of an Eye, Bleeding Heart, Two Neighbours, National Hopes, Wonders of the World, Kalam Al Nass: A Study of the Local Dialects, Emirates in Austrian Eyes, Around the World in 22 Days.

MURRAY, Sir Andrew (Andy) Barron, Kt, OBE; British professional tennis player; b. 15 May 1987, Dunblane, Scotland; s. of William Murray and Judy Murray (née Erskine); m. Kim Sears 2015; two d.; ed Dunblane High School, Schiller Int. School, Barcelona, Spain; right-handed (two-handed backhand); began playing tennis aged three; declined invitation to train with Rangers Football Club at their School of Excellence aged 15; moved to Barcelona to train on clay courts of Sánchez-Casal Acad. aged 15; won his first senior title at Glasgow Futures event 2003; won Jr US Open beating Sergiy Stakhovsky 2004; youngest Briton ever to play in Davis Cup 2005; turned professional 2005; played his first Asscn of Tennis Professionals (ATP) tournament with wild card to Open SEAT clay-court tournament, Barcelona 2005; advanced to doubles semifinal (with brother Jamie Murray) 2004; semifinalist, Jr Roland Garros 2005; achieved a top-10 ATP ranking for first time 16 April 2007; winner, San Jose 2006, 2007, St Petersburg 2007, 2008, Madrid 2008, Cincinnati 2008, 2011, Marseille 2008, Doha 2008, 2009, Valencia 2009, Toronto, Canada 2009, 2010, Miami 2009, 2013, Rotterdam 2009, Aegon Championships, London Queen's Club 2009, 2011, 2013, 2015, 2016, Shanghai Masters 2010, 2011, 2016, Tokyo 2011, Bangkok 2011, Brisbane Int. Title 2012, 2013, Shenzhen Open 2014, Erste Bank Open, Vienna 2014, 2016, Valencia Open 2014, BMW Open by FWU AG, Munich 2015, Mutua Madrid Open 2015, Montreal 2015, Italian Open 2016, Beijing 2016, Paris Masters 2016; finalist, Shanghai Masters 2012; Grand Slam results: winner, US Open 2012, Wimbledon 2013, 2016, finalist, US Open 2008, Australian Open 2010, 2011, 2013, 2015, 2016, Wimbledon 2012, French Open 2016, semifinalist, Wimbledon 2009, 2010, 2011, French Open 2011, 2014, 2015; winner, ATP World Tour Finals, London and year-end World No. 1 2016, semifinalist 2008, 2010; other tournaments: US Open Series Champion 2010; competed at Olympic Games, Beijing 2008; won gold medal, Olympic Games, London 2012, Rio 2016; two doubles titles (with brother Jamie), Valencia 2010, Tokyo 2011; winner (GB team), Davis Cup,

Ghent, Belgium 2015; winner Dubai Duty Free Tennis Championships 2017; became World No. 1 for first time 7 Nov. 2016; coaches: Leon Smith 1998–2004, Pato Álvarez 2003–05, Mark Petchey 2005–06, Brad Gilbert 2006–07, Miles Maclagan 2007–10, Àlex Corretja 2010–11, Ivan Lendl 2011–14, 2016–, Amélie Mauresmo 2014–16, Jonas Björkman 2015, Jamie Delgado 2016–; mem. ATP 2016–; Freeman, City of Stirling 2014, London Borough of Merton 2014; Hon. DUniv (Stirling) 2014; BBC Young Sports Personality of the Year 2004, 2016, twice named LTA's Young Player of the Year, Best ATP World Tour Match of the Year 2010, 2011, 2012, Laureus World Breakthrough of the Year Award 2013, Glenfiddich Spirit of Scotland Award for Top Scot 2013, Glenfiddich Spirit of Scotland Award for Sport 2013, BBC Sports Personality of the Year 2013, 2015, 2016, Award from Tennis Scotland 2014, Arthur Ashe Humanitarian of the Year 2014, ITF Player of the Year 2016. *Address:* XIX Entertainment, 33 Ransomes Dock, 35–37 Parkgate Road, London, SW11 4NP, England (office). *E-mail:* info@xixentertainment.com (office). *Website:* www.andymurray.com.

MURRAY, Bill; American actor and writer; b. 21 Sept. 1950, Evanston, Ill.; m. 1st Margaret Kelly 1980 (divorced 1996); four s.; m. 2nd Jennifer Butler 1997 (divorced 2008); ed Loyola Acad., Regis Coll.; mem. Second City Workshop, Chicago; performer off-Broadway Nat. Lampoon Radio Hour; appeared in radio series Marvel Comics' Fantastic Four; Emmy Award for best writing for comedy series 1977, Mark Twain Prize for American Humor 2016. *Films include:* Meatballs 1977, Mr Mike's Mondo Video 1979, Where the Buffalo Roam 1980, Caddyshack 1980, Stripes 1981, Tootsie 1982, Ghostbusters 1984, The Razor's Edge 1984, Nothing Lasts Forever 1984, Little Shop of Horrors 1986, Scrooged 1988, Ghostbusters II 1989, What About Bob? 1991, Mad Dog and Glory 1993, Groundhog Day 1993, Ed Wood 1994, Kingpin 1996, Larger Than Life 1996, Space Jam 1996, The Man Who Knew Too Little 1997, With Friends Like These 1998, Veeck as in Wreck 1998, Rushmore 1998, Wild Things 1998, The Cradle Will Rock 1999, Hamlet 1999, Company Man 1999, Charlie's Angels 2000, The Royal Tenenbaums 2001, Osmosis Jones 2001, Lost in Translation (Golden Globe, Best Actor Musical or Comedy 2004, BAFTA Award, Best Actor in a Leading Role) 2003, Coffee and Cigarettes 2003, Garfield: The Movie (voice) 2004, The Life Aquatic with Steve Zissou 2004, Broken Flowers 2005, The Lost City 2005, Garfield 2 (voice) 2006, The Darjeeling Limited 2007, Get Smart 2008, City of Ember 2008, The Limits of Control 2009, Fantastic Mr Fox (voice) 2009, Get Low 2009, Moonrise Kingdom 2012, Hyde Park on Hudson 2012, A Glimpse Inside the Mind of Charles Swan III 2012, The Monuments Men 2014, The Grand Budapest Hotel 2014, St. Vincent 2014, Aloha 2015, Rock the Kasbah 2015; co-producer, dir, actor film Quick Change 1990. *Television:* writer and regular appearances TV series Saturday Night Live 1977–80; Olive Kitteridge (mini-series) (Primetime Emmy Award for Outstanding Supporting Actor in a Limited Series or Movie 2015) 2014. *Publications include:* Cinderella Story: My Life in Golf 1999. *Leisure interest:* golf. *Address:* c/o Lina Fiks, Anchin, Block, & Anchin, 477 Madison Avenue, New York, NY 10022 (office); c/o Jessica Tuchinsky, Creative Artists Agency, 9830 Wilshire Blvd, Beverly Hills, CA 90212, USA (office).

MURRAY, John Loyola, BL, SC; Irish judge; b. 10 May 1943, Limerick; s. of John C. Murray and Catherine Casey; m. Gabrielle Walsh 1969; one s. one d.; ed Crescent Coll., Rockwell Coll., Univ. Coll. Dublin and King's Inns, Dublin; Pres. Union of Students of Ireland 1964–66; barrister-at-law 1967; Bencher, King's Inns 1986; SC, Bar of Ireland 1981; Attorney-Gen. Aug.–Dec. 1982, 1987–91; mem. Council of State 1987–91; Judge, Court of Justice of European Communities 1991–99; Judge, Supreme Court 1999–15, Chief Justice 2004–11; Hon. LLD (Limerick). *Leisure interests:* yachting, travel, art.

MURRAY, Joyce, MBA, PC; Canadian business executive and politician; *President of the Treasury Board;* b. 11 July 1954, Schweizer-Reneke, South Africa; d. of Gordon Murray and Charlotte Coe Murray; m. Dirk Brinkman 1977; two s. one d.; ed Simon Fraser Univ.; co-founder and Partner, Brinkman and Associates Reforestation Ltd 1979–; mem. Legis. Ass. 2000–, Minister of Water, Land and Air Protection 2001–04, of Man. Services 2004–05, of Digital Govt 2019–; mem. House of Commons (Liberal), Vancouver Quadra 2008–, Parliamentary Sec. to the Pres. of the Treasury Bd 2015–19, Pres. of the Treasury Bd 2019–; Chair. Northern and Western Caucus 2011–; Co-Chair. Monday Policy and Platform Caucus 2011–15; fmr Chair. Bd of Dirs, Earth Partners LP; mem. Advisory Bd, BC Forest Resources 1996–99; mem. GVRD Waste Man. Cttee; fmr mem. Standing Cttees on Nat. Defence, Trade, Health, Fisheries and Oceans, Environment and Sustainable Devt; Dean's Medal for Top MBA Grad., Simon Fraser Univ. 1992, Canada Clean50 Award 2017. *Address:* 206-2112 W Broadway, Vancouver, BC V6K 2C8, Canada (office). *Telephone:* (604) 664-9220 (office). *Fax:* (604) 664-9221 (office). *E-mail:* joyce.murray.c1@parl.gc.ca (office). *Website:* www.jmurray.liberal.ca (office).

MURRAY, Hon. Lowell, PC, BA, MA, LLD; Canadian politician; b. 26 Sept. 1936, New Waterford, Nova Scotia; s. of Daniel Murray and Evelyn Young; m. Colleen Elaine MacDonald 1981; two s.; ed St Francis Xavier Univ., NS, Queen's Univ., Ont.; fmr Chief of Staff to Minister of Justice and Minister of Public Works; Progressive Conservative Nat. Campaign Chair. in Gen. Election 1977–79, 1981–83; Senator 1979–2011, Co-Chair. Jt Senate-House of Commons Cttee on Official Languages 1980–84; Chair. Standing Cttee on Banking, Trade and Commerce 1984–86; Chair. Standing Senate Cttee on Nat. Finance 1995–96, 1999–2004, Chair. Standing Senate Cttee on Social Affairs, Science and Tech. 1997–99; Leader of Govt in the Senate 1986–93 and Minister of State for Fed.-Provincial Relations 1986–91; Minister responsible for Atlantic Canada Opportunities Agency 1987–88; Acting Minister for Communications 1988–89; mem. Bd Dirs Sony of Canada 1995–; mem. Bd Trustees Inst. for Research on Public Policy 1984–86, Trilateral Cttee 1985–86, Council of the Fed. Advisory Panel on Fiscal Imbalance 2005–06; Progressive Conservative.

MURRAY, Matt, BA, MA; American journalist; *Editor-in-Chief, Wall Street Journal;* m.; one d.; ed Northwestern Univ.; joined Dow Jones & Company as Reporter, Pittsburgh bureau 1994, joined Money & Investing Dept 1997, Sr Special Writer for General Electric 1999–2001, apptd Deputy Ed. 2001, then Deputy Nat. Ed. and Nat. News Ed., later Deputy Man. Ed. for US bureaus and corporate 2008, for foreign news and Money & Investing 2011, Deputy Ed.-in-Chief, Wall Street Journal 2013, Ed.-in-Chief 2018–. *Publications include:* The Father and the Son 1999, Strong of Heart (co-author) 2002. *Address:* Wall Street Journal, 1211 Avenue of the Americas, New York, NY 10036, USA (office). *Website:* www.wsj.com (office).

MURRAY, Patty, BA; American politician; *Senator from Washington;* b. 11 Oct. 1950, Bothell, Wash.; d. of David L. Johns and Beverly A. Johns (née McLaughlin); m. Robert R. Murray 1972; one s. one d.; ed Washington State Univ.; teacher, Shoreline Community Coll. 1984–87; campaigned against proposed closure of Wash. State Parent Educ. Programme 1980; fmr mem. Wash. State Senate; instructor, Shoreline Community Coll. Seattle 1984–88; Senator from Wash. 1993–, Chair. Veterans Affairs Cttee, Vice-Chair. Senate Democratic Policy Cttee, sr mem. Budget Cttee, Appropriations Cttee, Co-Chair. Jt Select Cttee on Deficit Reduction 2010; Democrat. *Leisure interests:* fishing, exploring Washington state's great outdoors, spending time with her family. *Address:* 448 Russell Senate Office Buidling, Washington, DC 20510, USA (office). *Telephone:* (202) 224-2621 (office). *Fax:* (202) 224-0238 (office). *Website:* murray.senate.gov (office).

MURRAY, Sir Robin MacGregor, Kt, MD, DSc, MPhil, FRS, FRCP, FRCPsych, FMedSci; British psychiatrist, institute director and academic; *Professor of Psychiatric Research, Institute of Psychiatry, King's College London;* b. 31 Jan. 1944, Glasgow, Scotland; s. of James. A. C. Murray and Helen MacGregor; m. Shelagh Harris 1970; one s. one d.; ed Univs of Glasgow and London; jr posts with Dept of Medicine, Univ. of Glasgow 1970–72, with Maudsley Hosp. 1972–75; Sr Lecturer, Inst. of Psychiatry, King's Coll., London 1978–82, Dean 1982–89, Prof. of Psychological Medicine 1989–99, Prof. of Psychiatric Research, Inst. of Psychiatry 1999–; Pres. Schizophrenia Int. Research Soc., Asscn of European Psychiatrists (now European Psychiatric Asscn) 1995–96; Joint Ed. Psychological Medicine; Visiting Prof. in Psychiatry, Univ of Sao Paulo, Brazil 1985–; Hon. Consultant, South London and Maudsley NHS Foundation Trust; Lilly Int. Fellow, Nat. Inst. for Mental Health, Bethesda, Md, USA 1976–77; Fellow, Royal Coll. of Psychiatrists; Hon. mem., Asscn of European Psychiatry 2002, Italian Soc. of Psychiatric Epidemiology 2007, Hon. Fellow, Royal Coll. of Psychiatrists 2010; Gaskell Gold Medal and Research Prize, Royal Coll. of Psychiatrists 1976, Sr Leverhulme Research Fellow, Royal Soc. 1993, Kurt Schneider Award 1994, Adolf Meyer Award 1997, Paul Hoch Award 1998, Stanley Dean Award 1999, Hilton Distinguished Investigator Award of the Nat. Alliance for Research into Schizophrenia and Depression (NARSAD) 1999, Fifth Castilla del Pino Award for Achievement in Psychiatry 2002, Psykiatriyhdistys Suomen Medal, Finnish Psychiatric Soc. 2003, ranked eighth most influential researcher in psychiatry by Thomson Reuters' Science Watch and third in schizophrenia research 1997–2007, Marsh Award for Mental Health Work, Rethink 2007, Pieter Baan Award, Dutch Asscn of Psychiatrists 2008, King's College Lifetime Achievement Award 2008. *Publications include:* Schizophrenia 1996, Psychosis in the Inner City 1998, First Episode Psychosis (co-author) 1999, Comprehensive Care of Schizophrenia 2001, An Atlas of Schizophrenia 2002, The Maudsley Handbook of Practical Psychiatry (fifth edn) 2006, Marijuana and Madness 2004, Bipolar Disorder: The Upswing in Research and Treatment 2005, Cognition and Schizophrenia: Improving Real Life Function 2006; publs on schizophrenia, depression, psychiatric genetics and epidemiology, alcoholism and analgesic abuse. *Leisure interests:* Scottish and Jamaican music, swimming. *Address:* Institute of Psychiatry, King's College London, 16 De Crespigny Park, London, SE5 8AF, England (office). *Telephone:* (20) 7848-0002. *Website:* www.kcl.ac.uk (office).

MURRAY, Simon, CBE; British banker, business executive and author; *Chairman, GEMS;* b. 25 March 1940, Leicester; s. of Patrick G. Murray and Maxine M. K. Murray; m. Jennifer A. Leila Mather 1966; one s. two d.; ed Bedford School (Sr Exec. Programme) and Stanford Business School (Stanford Exec. Program), USA; joined French Foreign Legion 1960, served for five years in 2nd Foreign Parachute Regt (2ème REP), fought in Algerian War of Independence against guerrillas of Front de Libération Nationale; Jardine Matheson & Co., Ltd 1966–73; Dir Matheson & Co., London 1973–75; Man. Dir Jardine Eng Corpn 1975–80; Founder and Man. Dir Davenham Investments Ltd 1980–84; Group Man. Dir Hutchison Whampoa Ltd 1984–93, mem. Bd Dirs –2007; pioneered mobile phones in Hong Kong and developed in the UK the mobile phone system now know as Orange; Exec. Chair. (Asia/Pacific) Deutsche Bank 1994–97; Founder and Chair. Simon Murray & Assocs; mem. Bd of Dirs and Ind. Chair. (non-exec.) Glencore International plc 2011–13; Founder and current Chair. GEMS Ltd (pvt. equity investment group) 1998–; Chair. Gleacher Partners Asia, Hong Kong, Gulf Keystone Petroleum; advisor, Bain & Co. (Asia), Inc., N.M. Rothschild & Sons Ltd, UK, China Nat. Offshore Oil Corpn; mem. Bd of Dirs Cheung Kong Holdings Ltd, Orient Overseas (International) Ltd, Wing Tai Properties Ltd, Arnhold Holdings Ltd, Richemont SA, Essar Energy plc, Omnicorp Ltd, IRC Ltd; Dir (non-exec.) Vodafone 2007–10; Officier, Ordre nat. du Mérite; Chevalier, Légion d'honneur; Hon. BA (Law) (Bath) 2005. *Achievement:* oldest man, aged 63, to walk unsupported to the South Pole 2004. *Publication:* Legionnaire: An Englishman in the French Foreign Legion 1978 (made into a film called Simon: An English Legionnaire 2002). *Leisure interests:* flying helicopters with his wife Jennifer (first woman to fly solo round the world in a helicopter), squash, jogging, reading. *Address:* GEMS Ltd, 805 Citibank Tower, Garden Road, Hong Kong Special Administrative Region, People's Republic of China (office). *Telephone:* 2838-0093 (office). *Fax:* 2838-0292 (office). *E-mail:* contact@gems.com.hk (office). *Website:* www.gems.com.hk/people/management-team.html (office).

MURSAL, Mohamed Sheikh Abdirahman; Somali politician and fmr diplomatist; *Speaker of House of the People;* b. 1957, Baidoa; ed Univ. of Science and Tech., Yemen; fmr Deputy Dist Commr; Minister of Nat. Assets and Public Procurement –2012; Amb. to Turkey 2012–15; mem. Fed. Parl., Speaker 2018–; fmr Minister of Energy and Water Resources; Minister of Defence 2017–18. *Address:* Federal Parliament, Mogadishu, Somalia (office). *E-mail:* info@parliament.gov.so (office). *Website:* www.parliament.gov.so (office).

MURSI, Muhammad, BSc, MSc, PhD; Egyptian politician and fmr head of state; b. (Muhammad Mursi Isa al-Ayyat), 8 Aug. 1951, Sharqia Governorate, northern Egypt; m. Naglaa Ali Mahmoud 1979; five c.; ed Cairo Univ., Univ. of Southern California, USA; Asst Prof., California State Univ., Northridge 1982–85; returned to Egypt to teach at Zagazig Univ. 1985, fmr Chair. Dept of Materials Science, Faculty of Eng; mem. Parl. in People's Ass. of Egypt 2000–05; arrested several times under Pres. Hosni Mubarak's regime, spent seven months in jail; a leading figure in the Muslim Brotherhood 1991–2012, mem. Guidance Office until 2011;

Chair. Freedom and Justice Party (FJP) following its founding by the Muslim Brotherhood in the wake of the Egyptian revolution 2011–12 (resgnd); stood as FJP's cand. in presidential election May–June 2012; Pres. of Egypt 2012–13; Sec.-Gen. Non-Aligned Movement 2012–; ousted by Army and placed under house arrest following mass protests calling for his resignation 3 July 2013; convicted of inciting the killing of protesters and sentenced to 20 years in prison April 2015.

MURTAGH, Peter, BA; Irish journalist; *Reporter, The Irish Times;* b. 9 April 1953, Dublin; s. of Thomas Murtagh and Olive de Lacy; m. Moira Gutteridge 1988; one s. one d.; ed The High School, Dublin, Trinity Coll., Dublin, Scandinavian Int. Man. Inst., Copenhagen, Denmark; Reporter, The Irish Times 1981–84, then Foreign Ed., Opinion Ed., Managing Ed., Reporter 1996–; Ed. Insight, The Sunday Times, London 1985; Reporter, Deputy Foreign Ed. and News Ed. The Guardian, London 1986–94; Ed. The Sunday Tribune, Dublin 1994–96; Journalist of the Year, Ireland 1983, Reporter of the Year, UK 1986, Newsbrands Ireland Journalism Awards 2016. *Publications:* The Boss: Charles J. Haughey in Government (with J. Joyce) 1983, Blind Justice – The Sallins Mail Train Robbery (with J. Joyce) 1984, The Rape of Greece – The King, the Colonels and the Resistance 1994, The Irish Times Book of the Year (ed., annually) 1999–2012, Buen Camino! – A Father/Daughter Journey from Croagh Patrick to Santiago de Compostela (with Natasha Murtagh) 2011. *Leisure interests:* family, newspapers, Ireland, motorcycling, Camino do Santiago. *Address:* The Irish Times, Tara Street, Dublin 2 (office); Penharbour, Somerby Road, Greystones, Co. Wicklow, Ireland (home). *Telephone:* (1) 6758000 (office). *Fax:* (1) 6615302 (office). *E-mail:* pmurtagh@irishtimes.com (office). *Website:* www.irishtimes.com (office).

MURTEIRA NABO, Francisco Luís, MBA; Portuguese economist and business executive; *Senior Partner, SaeR-Sociedad Estratégia e Risco, Lda.;* b. 1939, Evora; ed Instituto Superior de Economia e Gestao, Escola de Direccao e Negocios-AESE; Chief Alderman, City Hall, Lisbon 1976–81; Chair. Portuguese Radio Marconi Co. 1978–82; Vice-Pres. Sorefame 1982–83; Sec. of State for Transport 1983–85; Admin. Companhia Industrial de Portugal e Colónias 1986–87; Deputy Sec. for Educ., Health and Social Affairs, Office of Macao 1987–89, Deputy Sec. for Econ. Affairs, Admin of Macao 1989–90, Head of Govt of Territory of Macao 1990–91; Minister of Social Equipment (Public Works) 1995–96; Chair. Portugal Telecom, SGPS, SA 1996–2003 (also Chair. Exec. Cttee), CEO 1991–95; Chair. Galp Energia SGPS SA 2005–12; Pres. Câmara do Comércio e Indústria Luso-Chinesa (Portuguese-Chinese Chamber of Commerce and Industry) —2005, ELO-Portuguese Asscn for Economic Devt and Cooperation 2008–; Pres. COTEC Portugal 2003–06, Chair. Gen. Council 2006–; Chair. Superior Council of ITQB, Institute of Chemical and Biological Technology 2009–; Sr Partner, SaeR-Sociedad Estratégia e Risco, Lda. 2012–; mem. Direcção da Associação Comercial de Lisboa (Directorate of Commercial Asscn of Lisbon), Institut Européen d'Admin des Affaires (INSEAD); Chair. Proforum (Asscn for the Devt of Eng); fmr Dir (non-exec.) BPG (Banco Portugues de Gestao, SA), Companhia de Seguros Sagres, SA, Holdomnis – Gestao e Investimentos, SA, Templo – Gestao e Investimentos, SA, Seng Heng Bank, BES – Banco Espirito Santo, SA; Pres. Portuguese Economists Asscn; fmr Pres. COTEC Portugal (Asscn for Business Innovation); mem. Conselho Superior de Ciência, Tecnologia e Inovação (Supreme Council for Science, Tech. and Innovation); Trustee, Fundação Oriente; Order of Economists 2005–, Council of Public Works and Transport 2009–; Chair. Bd of Trustees Univ. of Aveiro Foundation 2009–; mem. Bd of Trustees, Fundação Oriente 2003–, Dr. Stanley Ho Foundation (Portugal) 2008– (Counselor 2010–); Grand Officer of the Military Order of Christ 1991, Grand Cross of Order of Prince Henry the Navigator 2006; Dr. hc (Macao Univ. of Science and Technology) 2010; Life Achivement Award, Deloitte Portugal 2008. *Address:* SaeR-Sociedad Estratégia e Risco, Lda., Rua Luciano Cordeiro, 123 4th Left, 1050-139 Lisbon, Portugal (office). *Telephone:* (21) 303-08-30 (office). *Fax:* (21) 303-08-39 (office). *E-mail:* i murteira.nabo@saer.pt (office). *Website:* www.saer.pt (office).

MURTHY, N(agavara) R(amarao) Narayana, CBE, BE; Indian business executive and software engineer; *Chairman Emeritus, Infosys Technologies Ltd;* b. 20 Aug. 1946, Mysore, Karnataka; s. of R. H. Kulkarni and Vimala Kulkarni; m Sudha Murthy; one s. one d.; ed Nat. Inst. of Eng, Univ. of Mysore, Indian Inst. of Tech., Kanpur; began career as Chief Systems Programmer, Indian Inst. of Man., Ahmedabad; joined Patni Computer Systems, Pune; co-f. Infosys Technologies Ltd 1981, Chair. 1981–2006, CEO 1981–2002, Exec. Chair. and Chief Mentor 2002–06, Chair. (non-exec.) 2006–11, June–Oct. 2014, Chief Mentor 2006–11, Chair. Emer. 2011–13, Oct. 2014–; Additional Dir and Exec. Chair. 2013–14; Pres. Nat. Asscn of Software and Service Cos (NASSCOM), India 1992–94; Chair. Governing Body, Int. Inst. of Information Tech., Bangalore, Bd of Mems of School of Man., Asian Inst. of Tech., Bangkok, Thailand, Asia Business Council, Hong Kong; fmr Chair. Governing Body, Indian Inst. of Man., Ahmedabad; mem. Bd of Dirs Institut Européen d'Admin des Affaires (INSEAD), Bd of Overseers Univ. of Pennsylvania's Wharton School, Bd of Trustees Cornell Univ., Business Advisory Council of Great Lakes Inst. of Man., Chennai, Bd of Trustees Singapore Man. Univ., Bd of Advisors William F. Achtmeyer Center for Global Leadership at Tuck School of Business, Bd of Govs Asian Inst. of Man. (Philippines); mem. Advisory Bds and Councils of several Univs, including Stanford Grad. School of Business, Corp. Governance Initiative at Harvard Business School, Yale Univ., Univ. of Tokyo's President's Council; mem. Bd Dirs Cen. Bd of Reserve Bank of India; Ind. mem. Bd Dirs DBS Bank of Singapore, Unilever, HSBC; Co-Chair. Indo-British Partnership; mem. Prime Minister's Council on Trade and Industry, Asia Advisory Bd of British Telecommunications plc, Bd of NDTV, India; IT adviser to several Asian countries; Foreign Fellow, American Nat. Acad. of Engineers 2010; Fellow, Indian Nat. Acad. of Engineering; Trustee Infosys Science Foundation; Hon. Fellow, Inst. of Electrical and Electronics Engineers, USA 2010, Hon. ISB Distinguished Fellowship 2016; Padma Shri 2000, Chevalier, Légion d'honneur 2008, Padma Vibushan 2008; Dr hc from several univs in India and abroad; numerous awards, including Nikkei Asia Award, Wharton School Dean's Medal, JRD Tata Corp. Leadership Award 1996–97, Distinguished Alumnus Award, Indian Inst. of Tech., Kanpur 1998, Lal Bahadur Shastri Nat. Award 2001, Indo-French Forum Medal (first recipient) 2003, Ernst & Young Global World Entrepreneur of the Year 2003, ranked first in Economic Times Corp. Dossier list of India's Most Powerful CEOs 2004, 2005, Ernst Weber Leadership Medal, IEEE 2007, Padma Vibhushan 2008, rated as Global Leader of 2009, ASME Hoover Medal 2012, Philanthropist of the Year, The Asian Awards 2013, Sayaji Ratna Award, Baroda Man. Asscn 2013,

Philanthropist of the Year, The Asian Awards 2016, Thomas Jefferson Foundation Medal for Global Innovation, Univ. of Virginia Darden School of Business 2017, Max Schmidheiny Liberty Prize. *Publication:* A Better India: A Better World (lectures) 2009. *Address:* Infosys Technologies Ltd, Corporate Headquarters, Electronic City, Hosur Road, Bangalore 560 100, India (office). *Telephone:* (80) 28520261 (office). *Fax:* (80) 28520362 (office). *E-mail:* infosys@infosys.com (office). *Website:* www.infosys.com (office).

MURTHY, Vivek Hallegere, MD, MBA; American physician and government official; *Surgeon–General;* b. 10 July 1977, Huddersfield, England; s. of Hallegere Murthy and Myetraie Murthy; ed Harvard Univ., Yale School of Medicine; Co-founder and Pres. VISIONS Worldwide, Inc. 1995–2000; Co-founder, Swasthya Community Health Partnership 1997–2002; Resident in internal medicine, Brigham & Women's Hosp. 2003–06, Attending physician 2006–; Instructor in medicine, Harvard Medical School 2006–; Co-founder and Chair., Epernicus, LLC 2007–; Co-founder and Pres., Doctors for America 2008; Chair. and Co-founder, TrialNetworks 2010; US Surgeon–Gen. 2014–; Vice-Adm., Public Health Service Commissioned Corps; mem. Advisory Group on Prevention, Health Promotion and Integrative and Public Health 2011; Samuel Huntington Public Service Award 1997, American Medical Asscn Foundation Leadership Award 2000, Yale School of Medicine Norma Bailey Berniker Prize 2003. *Address:* Office of the Surgeon–General, Tower Building Plaza, Level 1, Room 100, 1101 Wootton Parkway, Rockville, MD 20852, USA (office). *Telephone:* (240) 276-8853 (office). *Fax:* (240) 453-6141 (office). *Website:* www.surgeongeneral.gov (office).

MUSA, Said, LLB; Belizean politician and attorney-at-law; b. 19 March 1944, San Ignacio; s. of Hamid Musa and Aurora Musa (née Gibbs); m. Joan Musa; three s.; ed St John's Coll., Belize City, Manchester Univ., England; called to the Bar London 1966; worked as barrister, Gray's Inn, London 1966–67; circuit magistrate Belize 1967–68, Crown Counsel 1968–70; lawyer pvt. practice 1970–79, 1984–89, 1993–98 (Sr Counsel 1983–); Pres. Public Service Union 1969; f. People's Action Cttee, Soc. for Promotion of Educ. and Research (SPEAR) 1969; obliged to leave public service because of political activities; joined People's United Party (PUP); Chair. Fort George Div. PUP 1974–; Chair. PUP 1986–94, Deputy Leader 1994–96, Leader 1996–; Co-Founder Journal of Belizean Affairs 1972; apptd Senator to Nat. Ass. by George Price 1974; negotiator in talks to safeguard territorial integrity of Belize on independence 1975–81; mem. House of Reps for Fort George constituency 1979–84, 1993–98, 2012–; Attorney-Gen. and Minister for Educ., Sports and Culture 1979–84; Minister of Foreign Affairs, Econ. Devt and Educ. 1989–93 (negotiated recognition of Belizean sovereignty by Guatemala 1991); Leader of the Opposition 1996–98; Prime Minister of Belize 1998–2008, concurrently Minister of Finance and Foreign Affairs, then Minister of Finance and Econ. Devt 1998–2003, of Nat. Devt and the Public Service 2004–08, of Finance 2005–08; mem. Privy Council. *Publications:* People's Assemblies, People's Government; articles in nat. press. *Leisure interests:* reading, int. affairs, human rights, music, tennis. *Address:* People's United Party, 3 Queen Street, Belize City (office); 91 North Front Street, Belize City (office); 7 E Street, Belize City, Belize (home). *Telephone:* 223-2940 (office). *Fax:* 223-1149 (office). *E-mail:* mandb@btl.net (home); sahootoo@yahoo.com (home).

MUSCAT, Joseph, MA, PhD; Maltese journalist and politician; *Prime Minister;* b. 22 Jan. 1974; m. Michelle Tanti; two d.; ed Univ. of Malta, Univ. of Bristol, UK; began career as journalist with Labour Party radio station, Super One Radio; moved to Super One TV, becoming Asst Head of News 1996; Ed. maltastar.com (Labour Party online newspaper) 2001–04; columnist, l-Orizzont (Maltese-language newspaper published by Gen. Workers' Union) and it-Torca (sister Sunday title); regular contributor to The Times (English-language newspaper); mem. European Parl. (Party of European Socialists) 2004–08; mem. House of Reps (Parl.) 2008–, Leader of the Opposition 2008–13; Prime Minister 2013–; mem. Partit Laburista (PL, Labour Party), Leader 2008–; Companion of Honour, Nat. Order of Merit 2013. *Address:* Office of the Prime Minister, 55a, Transcontinental House, Zachary Street, Valletta VLT 1210, Malta (office). *Telephone:* 22001852 (office). *Fax:* 22001851 (office). *E-mail:* lawrence.gonzi@gov.mt (office). *Website:* www.opm.gov.mt (office).

MUSCATELLI, Sir Anton (Vito Antonio), Kt, MA, PhD, FRSE, FRSA, AcSS; British economist, academic and university administrator; *Principal and Vice-Chancellor, University of Glasgow;* b. 1 Jan. 1962; Sr Lecturer, Univ. of Glasgow 1984–92, Dean, Faculty of Sciences 2000–04, Prin. and Vice-Chancellor 2009–; Ed. Scottish Journal of Political Economy 1989–2003; Prin. and Vice-Chancellor Heriot-Watt Univ. 2007–09; mem. RAE Panels for Econs and Econometrics 2001, 2008; fmr mem. Research Grants Bd of ESRC and its Int. Advisory Cttee, Council of Royal Econ. Soc.; special adviser on monetary policy to House of Commons Treasury Select Cttee 2007–10; fmr consultant to EC and World Bank; Convenor of Universities Scotland 2008–10, Chair. Research and Knowledge Exchange Cttee; Vice-Pres. Universities UK 2008–10; Co-Chair. Steering Bd for creation of Nat. Centre for Univs and Business; mem. Bd Scottish Funding Council; Dir UK Nat. Centre for Univs and Business 2013–; Chair. Comm. on Econ. Growth for the Glasgow City Region 2015–; mem. Council of Econ. Advisers of First Minister of Scotland 2015–; Chair., Standing Council on Europe 2016–; mem. Bd of Dirs Russell Group of Univs 2009– (Chair. 2017–), Universitas 21 Group of Univs 2009–16, Beatson Inst. 2014–, Univs Superannuation Scheme Bd 2015–, Glasgow City Marketing Bureau 2009–16; Academician, Learned Socs of Social Sciences 2004; Hon. Fellow, Societa Italiana Degli Economisti 1996, Hon. Pres. David Hume Inst. 2014–; Hon. LLD (McGill Univ.). *Publications:* Theory and Stabilisation (co-author) 1988, Monetary Policy, Fiscal Policies and Labour Markets: Macroeconomic Policymaking in the EMU 2004; numerous papers in professional journals on monetary econs, central bank independence, fiscal policy, int. finance and macroeconomics. *Address:* University of Glasgow, Glasgow, G12 8QQ, Scotland (office). *Telephone:* (141) 330-5995 (office). *E-mail:* principal@glasgow.ac.uk (office). *Website:* www.gla.ac.uk (office).

MUSEVENI, Gen. (retd) Yoweri Kaguta; Ugandan head of state and fmr army officer; *President;* b. 1944, Ntungamo, Mbarara; s. of Amos Kaguta and Esteri Kokundeka; m. Janet Kataaha; four c.; ed Mbarara High School, Ntare School, Univ. Coll. of Dar es Salaam; Research Asst Office of fmr Pres. Milton Obote 1971; in Tanzania planning overthrow of regime of Idi Amin 1971–79; f. Front for Nat. Salvation (FRONASA) 1972; taught at Moshi Co-operative Coll., Tanzania 1972;

participated in Tanzanian invasion of Uganda 1979; Defence Minister in interim Govt of Uganda Nat. Liberation Front (UNLF) following overthrow of Amin 1979–80; following election of Dr Obote, amid allegations of ballot-rigging, in 1980, spent five years as leader of Nat. Resistance Army (NRA) waging a guerrilla war 1981–86; Pres. of Uganda (following overthrow of Govt by NRA forces) and Minister of Defence, then Pres. and C-in-C of Armed Forces 1986–; Chair. Preferential Trade Area (PTA) 1987–88, 1992–93, OAU 1990–91. *Publications include:* Selected Essays 1985, Selection of Speeches and Writings, Vol. I: What is Africa's Problem? 1992, Vol. II 1997, Sowing the Mustard Seed – The Struggle for Freedom and Democracy 1997. *Leisure interest:* football. *Address:* Office of the President, Parliament Building, PO Box 7168, Kampala, Uganda (office). *Telephone:* (41) 258441 (office). *Fax:* (41) 256143 (office). *E-mail:* aak@statehouse.go.ug (office). *Website:* www.statehouse.go.ug (office).

MUSGROVE, David Ronald (Ronnie), AA, BBA, JD; American lawyer and fmr politician; *Founding Member, Musgrove Smith Law;* b. 29 July 1956, Tocowa, Miss.; m. 1st Melanie Ballard 1977 (divorced 2001); m. 2nd Dr Melody Bounds 2007; four c.; ed Northwest Junior Coll., Univ. of Mississippi and Univ. of Mississippi School of Law; called to the Bar, Miss. State Courts, US Dist Court for the Northern and Southern Dists of Miss.; Partner, Smith, Musgrove & McCord, Miss. 1981–2000; State Senator and Lt Gov. under Kirk Fordice 1988–96; Lt Gov. State of Miss. 1996–2000, Gov. of Miss. 2000–04; unsuccessful cand. in special election for one of Miss.'s seats in US Senate 2008; Of Counsel, Copeland, Cook, Taylor & Bush, Ridgeland, Mo. 2004–10; Distinguished Visiting Lecturer, Univ. of Mississippi; Adjunct Prof., Mississippi Coll. School of Law, Jackson; Chair. Nat. Assessment Governing Bd's NAEP 12th Grade Preparedness Comm. 2009–13, 2014–, Nat. Advisory Cttee on Rural Health and Human Services 2010–, Miss. Center for Legal Services (Advisory Bd); Co-Chair. Biomass Research and Devt Tech. Advisory Cttee 2011–13; Sr Policy Scholar, Bloomberg School of Public Health Johns Hopkins Univ. 2013–; fmr Chair. Southern Regional Educ. Bd, Southern States Energy Bd, Southern Growth Policy Bd, Southern Govs Asscn; fmr Vice-Chair. Nat. Govs Asscn; mem. Bd of Dirs Mississippi Sports Hall and Fame Museum; mem. ABA, The Mississippi Bar, Mississippi Bar Foundation, Madison Co. Bar Asscn, Hinds Co. Bar Asscn, Capital Area Bar Asscn, Rotary Club; Founding Mem. Musgrove Smith Law 2014–; Fellow, Miss. Bar Foundation, Paul Harris Fellow; Distinguished Service Award, Nat. Guard Bureau, Washington, DC, Outstanding Service Award, Miss. Bar Asscn 1985. *Address:* Musgrove Smith Law, 1635 Lelia Drive, Suite 104, Jackson, MS 39216, USA (office). *Telephone:* (601) 852-1723 (office). *E-mail:* musgrove@musgrovesmith.com (office). *Website:* www.musgrovesmithlaw.com (office).

MUSHARRAF, Gen. (retd) Pervez; Pakistani politician, fmr head of state and fmr army officer; b. 11 Aug. 1943, Delhi, India; s. of Syed Musharraf Uddin; m. Sehba Farid 1968; one s. one d.; ed St Patrick's High School, Karachi, Forman Christian Coll., Lahore, Command and Staff Coll., Quetta, Nat. Defence Coll., Rawalpindi, Royal Coll. of Defence Studies, UK; spent early childhood in Turkey 1949–56; joined Pakistan Mil. Acad. 1961; commd in Artillery Regt 1964; fought in 1965 war with India (Imtiazi Sanad Gallantry Award); spent much of mil. career in Special Services Group; Company Commdr Commando Battalion Indo-Pakistan War 1971; Dir-Gen. Mil. Operations, Gen. HQ 1993–95; apptd C-in-C of Pakistani Army Oct. 1998, Chair. Jt Chiefs of Staff Cttee 1999, led mil. coup 1999, Chief of Staff 1999–2007; Chief Exec. Nat. Security Council of Pakistan 1999–2002; Pres. of Pakistan 2001–08 (resgnd); mem. Pakistan Muslim League (Quaid e Azam Group) –2010; lived in self-imposed exile in London, UK 2008–13, returned to Pakistan March 2013; Founder and Pres. All Pakistan Muslim League 2010–18; arrest warrant issued by Anti Terrorism Court and was charged with conspiracy to commit murder of Benazir Bhutto Feb. 2011; treason charges against him registered by Sindh High Court March 2011; disqualified by High Court judges from taking part in the upcoming general election and his arrest ordered by the court over an attempt to impose house arrest on judges in March 2007, April 2013, returned to Pakistan 2013, banned from int. travel 2013–16 (ban lifted). *Publication:* In the Line of Fire: A Memoir 2006. *Leisure interests:* squash, tennis, golf, reading, mil. history, rock music. *Address:* c/o All Pakistan Muslim League, Central Secretariat, House No, 01, Street No. 37, F-6/1, Islamabad, Pakistan (office).

MUSHIKIWABO, Hon. Louise, MA; Rwandan politician and international organization official; *Secretary-General, Organisation internationale de la Francophonie (OIF);* b. Kigali; m.; ed Nat. Univ. of Rwanda, Univ. of Delaware, USA; English teacher, Lycée de Kigali 1985; worked as public relations consultant, Washington, DC, USA; fmr Ed., Africa Dept, IMF; Communications Dir African Devt Bank 2006–08; Minister of Information 2008–09, of Foreign Affairs and Co-operation 2009–18; Co-founder and Pres. The Rwanda Children's Fund, Washington, DC; Sec.-Gen. Organisation int. de la Francophonie (OIF) 2019–. *Publication:* Rwanda Means the Universe 2006. *Address:* Organisation Internationale de la Francophonie, 19-21 avenue Bosquet, 75007 Paris, France (office). *Telephone:* 1-44-11-12-50 (office). *Fax:* 1-45-79-14-98 (office). *E-mail:* info@minaffet.gov.rw (office). *Website:* www.francophonie.org (office).

MUSIN, Aslan Yespulayevich; Kazakhstani government official; b. 2 Jan. 1954; ed Almaty Inst. of Econs; fmr Akim (Gov.) Aktobe and Atyrau Oblasts; Minister of Econ. Affairs and Budget Planning 2006–07; Deputy Prime Minister Jan.–Sept. 2007; Chair. Majlis (Parl.) 2007; Head Admin of the Pres. *Address:* c/o Majlis, 010000 Nur-Sultan, Parliament House, Kazakhstan (office).

MUSK, Elon, BA, BS; Canadian/American (b. South African) engineer and business executive; *CEO and Chief Technology Officer, SpaceX;* b. 28 June 1971; m. 1st Justine Musk 2000 (divorced 2008); five s.; m. 2nd Talulah Riley 2010 (divorced 2012), remarried 2014; ed Pretoria Boys High School, Univ. of Pennsylvania and Univ. of Pennsylvania Wharton School; bought first computer and taught himself to program aged ten; sold first commercial software for space game aged 12; emigrated to Regina, Sask., Canada 1989; left Canada to study business and physics in USA 1992; dropped out of grad. programme in applied physics and materials science at Stanford Univ. to co-found (with brother Kimbal Musk) Zip2 1995, acquired by Compaq's AltaVista div. 1999; co-f. X.com (online financial services and e-mail payment co.) 1999, merged with Confinity, operator of the then largest auction payments service, PayPal, under X.com as corp. name 2000, changed name to PayPal Inc. Feb. 2001, acquired by eBay Oct. 2002; f. Space Exploration Technologies (SpaceX), Hawthorne, Calif. June 2002, currently CEO and Chief Technology Officer (co. develops and manufactures space launch vehicles); Co-founder and Head of Product Design, Tesla Motors, led devt of Tesla Roadster electric sports car, CEO 2008–; primary investor and Chair. SolarCity (photovoltaics products and services startup co.) 2006–; mem. Bd of Dirs Halcyon Molecular (biotechnology co.) 2008–; Chair. Musk Foundation; Trustee, X Prize Foundation; mem. or fmr mem. Bd The Space Foundation, Nat. Acads Aeronautics and Space Eng Bd, The Planetary Soc., Stanford Eng Advisory Bd, Bd of Trustees California Inst. of Tech. (Caltech) 2010–; mem. Pres. Trump's American Manufacturing Council Jan.–June 2017 (resgnd); Hon. DUniv (Univ. of Surrey, UK) 2009; Dr hc in Design (Art Center Coll. of Design, Pasadena, Calif.) 2010; numerous awards including Global Green Product Design Award 2006, Inc Magazine Entrepreneur of the Year Award 2007, R&D Magazine Innovator of the Year 2007, AIAA George Low Award for the most outstanding contrib. in the field of space transportation in 2007–08, Nat. Conservation Achievement Award, Nat. Wildlife Fed. for Tesla Motors and SolarCity 2008, Aviation Week Laureate for the most significant achievement world-wide in the space industry 2008, Von Braun Trophy, Nat. Space Soc. 2009, World Technology Award (co-recipient) 2009, recognized as Living Legend in Aviation by the Kitty Hawk Foundation for creating the successor to the Space Shuttle (Falcon 9 rocket and Dragon spacecraft) 2010, Gold Space Medal, Fédération Aéronautique Internationale for designing the first privately developed rocket to reach orbit 2010, Automotive Exec. of the Year (world-wide) 2010, Heinlein Prize for Advances in Space Commercialization 2011, honoured as a Legendary Leader at the Churchill Club Awards 2011, Gold Medal, Royal Aeronautical Soc. 2012. *Address:* Space Exploration Technologies (SpaceX), 1 Rocket Road, Hawthorne, CA 90250, USA (office). *Telephone:* (310) 363-6000 (office). *E-mail:* media@spacex.com (office). *Website:* www.spacex.com (office); www.teslamotors.com (office); www.muskfoundation.org.

MUSLIMYAR, Fazl Hadi; Afghan politician; *Speaker, Meshrano Jirga;* b. 1969; m.; five s. two d.; ed Univ. of Jalalabad; local commdr in Nangahar Prov. during Soviet occupation; elected to Nangarhar Prov. Council 2005, Chair. 2005–09; elected Senator, Meshrano Jirga (House of Elders) 2009, First Deputy Speaker 2010, Acting Speaker 2010–11, Speaker 2011–; Dir Dawat Islami Party, Nangarhar 2010–. *Address:* Meshrano Jirga, Darul-Aman Road, Kabul, Afghanistan (office). *Telephone:* 794004000 (mobile) (office). *E-mail:* zia_shirzad@yahoo.com (office). *Website:* mj.parliament.af (office).

MUSOKE, Rt Hon Kintu; Ugandan politician, journalist and publisher; b. 5 Aug. 1938, Masaka; ed Kings Coll. Budo, Delhi Univ.; Minister of Information 1989–91; Minister for Presidency 1991–94; Minister of State for Security; Prime Minister of Uganda 1994–2000; currently Sr Adviser to Pres. of Uganda; Chair. Advisory Cttee, USA Presidential Emergency Fund for Aids Relief (PEPFAR). *Address:* PO Box 15025, Kampala, Uganda (home). *Telephone:* (41) 4257370 (home). *E-mail:* kintumusoke@hotmail.com (home).

MUSOKOTWANE, Situmbeko; Zambian economist and government official; b. 25 May 1956, Kalabo Dist, Western Prov.; m. Mate Musokotwane; two c.; ed Univ. of Zambia, Univ. of Dar es Salaam, Tanzania, Univ. of Konstanz, Germany; joined Bank of Zambia as economist 1991, later becoming Deputy Gov.; Gov. Cen. Bank of Swaziland (contracted by IMF) 1997–2000; held several cabinet positions including Adviser to Minister of Finance 2000–03, Sec. to the Treasury and Deputy Sec. to the Cabinet, Minister of Finance and Nat. Planning 2008–11; econ. adviser to Pres. of Zambia –2008; MP for Liuwa constituency; fmr Prof., Univ. of Zambia; fmr Dir ZCCM Investments Holdings plc, Bank of Zambia; fmr mem. Bd Govs, Eastern and Southern African Trade and Devt Bank; mem. Movt for Multi-party Democracy. *Address:* Movement for Multi-party Democracy, PO Box 30708, Lusaka, Zambia (office). *Telephone:* (21) 1250177 (office). *Fax:* (21) 1252329 (office). *E-mail:* info@mmdzambia.org (office). *Website:* mmdzambia.org (office).

MUSONGE, Peter Mafany, BSc, MSc; Cameroonian civil engineer and politician; *Grand Chancellor of National Orders;* b. 3 Dec. 1942, Muea-Buea; s. of John Musonge and Frida Nduma Woko; m. Anne Mojoko Mbongo 1970 (deceased); three s. one d.; ed Stanford Univ., Drexel Univ., USA; Gen. Man. Nat. Civil Eng Lab. 1980–84; Gen. Man. Nat. Civil Eng Equipment Pool 1984–87; Gen. Man. Cameroon Devt Corpn (CDC) 1988–96; Prime Minister and Head of Govt of Cameroon 1996–2004; Grand Chancellor of Nat. Orders, Office of the Presidency 2007–; Pres. Nat. Comm. for the Promotion of Bilingualism and Multiculturalism 2017–; mem. Politburo Cen. Cttee, Rassemblement démocratique du peuple camerounais (RDPC); mem. Senate, RDPC Parl. Group Leader –2017; Grand Officier de la Légion d'honneur 1999, Grand Officer, Cameroon Order of Valour 2003. *Leisure interests:* reading, sport, music. *Address:* Grand Chancellery, Presidency, Yaoundé, Cameroon (office). *Telephone:* 2220-0711 (office).

MUSONI, James; Rwandan politician and diplomatist; *Ambassador to Zimbabwe;* Commr Gen., Rwanda Revenue Authority –2005; Minister for Commerce, Industry, Investment Promotion, Tourism and Cooperatives 2005–06, of Finance and Economic Planning 2006–09, Minister of Local Govt 2009–14, Minister of Infrastructure 2014–18; Amb. to Zimbabwe 2018–; mem. Front Patriotique Rwandais. *Address:* Embassy of Rwanda, Harare, Zimbabwe (office).

MUSSELWHITE, Charlie, (Memphis Charlie, Charlie Kelly, Mussels); American blues-harp player; b. (Charles Douglas Musselwhite III), 31 Jan. 1944, Kosciusko, Miss.; s. of Charles Douglas Musselwhite, Jr and Ruth Maxine Musselwhite; m. Henrietta Musselwhite; one s. one d.; ed Memphis Tech. High School; concerts tours in USA; performed on albums with Bonnie Raitt, The Blind Boys of Alabama, Tom Waits, Mickey Hart and INXS; Presenter, weekly radio show Charlie's Back Room (KRSH); 33 Blues Music Award wins for Best Instrumentalist: Harmonica, 24 W.C. Handy Awards, Lifetime Achievement Awards (Monterey Blues Festival, San Javier Jazz Festival, Spain), Mississippi Gov.'s Award for Excellence in the Arts, Pete Pedersen Lifetime Achievement Award, Howlin' Wolf Award, Trophées France Blues 2000, 2002, inducted into Blues Music Hall of Fame 2010. *Recordings include:* Stand Back! 1967, Louisiana Fog 1968, Stone Blues 1968, Tennessee Woman 1968, Memphis, Tennessee 1970, The Harmonica According to Charlie Musselwhite 1979, Curtain Call Cocktails 1982, Mellow-Dee 1986, Ace of Harps 1990, Signature 1991, Where Have All the Good Times Gone? 1992, In My Time 1993, Memphis Charlie 1993, The Blues

Never Die 1994, Takin' Care of Business 1995, Rough News 1997, Continental Drifter 1999, Best of the Vanguard Years 2000, One Night in America 2002, Sanctuary 2004, Delta Hardware 2006, Rough Dried 2007, Get Up! (with Ben Harper) (Grammy Award for Best Blues Album 2014) 2013. *Website:* www.charliemusselwhite.com.

MUSTAFA, Isa, BA, MA, PhD; Kosovo politician; *Chairman, Lidhja Demokratike e Kosovës (Democratic League of Kosovo);* b. 15 May 1951, Prapashticë, Prishtina, Autonomous Region of Kosovo, People's Repub. of Serbia, Fed. People's Repub. of Yugoslavia; m. Qevsere Mustafa; two s. one d.; ed Univ. of Prishtina; began career as an examiner at Univ. of Prishtina 1974; Head of Municipal Govt of Prishtina 1984–88; Minister of Economy and Finance, Govt of Repub. of Kosovo, in exile, headed by Bujar Bukoshi 1991–99; warrant for his arrest issued by Serbian Govt, lived abroad as a political refugee, mainly in Germany, Switzerland, Albania, Slovenia and Croatia –1999; following Kosovo War returned home in 1999, returned to politics in 2006 as a High Political Adviser of Pres. Fatmir Sejdiu; Mayor of Prishtina 2007–13; Chair. Lidhja Demokratike e Kosovës (Democratic League of Kosovo) 2010–; Prime Minister of Kosovo 2014–17. *Address:* Lidhja Demokratike e Kosovës, 10000 Prishtina, Rruga Qafa UÇK 2b, Kosovo (office). *Telephone:* (38) 242242 (office). *Fax:* (38) 245305 (office). *E-mail:* info@ldk-ks.eu (office). *Website:* www.ldk-ks.eu (office).

MUSTAFAJ, Besnik; Albanian writer, academic, politician and diplomatist; b. 23 Sept. 1958, Bajram Curri City; m.; two c.; ed Univ. of Tirana; Prof. of Foreign Literature, Faculty of History and Philology, Univ. of Tirana 1983–91; Founding mem. Democratic Party of Albania 1990, Sec. for Int. Relations 1999–2005; elected MP 1991, Deputy Chair. Foreign Relations Comm. 2001–05, Deputy Chair. of Perm. Del. to European Parl. 2001–05; Amb. to France and Perm. Rep. to UNESCO, Paris 1992–97; Minister of Foreign Affairs 2005–07 (resgnd); Chair. Albanian Inst. for Int. Studies (think-tank); Co-founder Albanian Helsinki Cttee 1990; Founding Chair. Albanian Writers' Pen Club. *Publications include:* Vera pa kthim (The Summer of No Return) 1989, Gjinkallat e vapës (The Cicadas of the Heat) 1994, Një sagë e vogël (A Little Saga) 1995, Daullja prej letre (The Paper Drum) 1996, Boshti (The Void) 1998; several books and papers on poetry and aesthetics.

MUSTAPHA, Faisz, PC, LLB, HE; Sri Lankan lawyer and diplomatist; s. of S. M. Musthapha; m. Ameena Mustapha; ed Univ. of Ceylon; fmr lawyer; mem. Perm. Court of Arbitration 1993–; Chair. Sri Lanka Comm. on Elimination Discrimination and Monitoring Fundamental Rights; fmr Chair. and mem. Finance Comm.; mem. Sri Lanka Law Comm., Council of Legal Education, Nat. Group Sri Lanka to the Perm. Court of Arbitration-The Hague; Deputy-Pres. Bar Asscn; Chair. Sri Lanka Human Rights Comm. 2000–03; Trustee Lt-Gen. Denzil Kobbekaduwa Trust; High Commr to UK 2002–05; Pres.'s Counsel, mem. Presidential Panel of Legal/Constitutional Experts 2006–, Presidential Comm. of Inquiry into failed finance cos 2007–; mem. Bd of Dir Amana Investments Ltd.

MUSTAPHA, Shettima, BSc, PhD; Nigerian politician; b. 26 Nov. 1939, Nguru; ed Ahmadu Bello Univ., Zaria, Univ. of Cambridge, UK, Purdue Univ., USA; Commr, Borno State 1979–83; cand. for Vice-Pres. in 1983 election; held as political prisoner 1983–85; Regional Head of Jos Office, Fed. Agric. Coordinating Unit, Fed. Ministry of Agric. 1985–89, Head of Agric. Projects Monitoring and Evaluation Unit 1989–90, Minister of Agric. and Natural Resources 1990–92; Nat. Treas. People's Democratic Party 1998–2001; fmr Chair. Savannah Bank of Nigeria plc; Minister of Defence 2008–09, of the Interior 2009–10; fmr consultant to World Bank, IFAD, FAO, UNDP; Fellow, Genetics Soc. of Nigeria; mem. American Soc. of Agronomy, Agricultural Soc. of Nigeria; Hon. Fellow, Entomological Soc. of Nigeria; Officer, Order of the Fed. Repub.

MUSYOKA, (Stephen) Kalonzo, LLB; Kenyan lawyer and politician; *Leader, Wiper Democratic Movement;* b. 24 Dec. 1953, Tseikuru village, Mwingi Dist; m. Pauline Musyoka; four c.; ed Univ. of Nairobi; lawyer with Kaplan & Stratton Advocates; Sr Pnr, Musyoka & Wambua Advocates; mem. Parl. 1985, Deputy Speaker, Nat. Ass. 1988–93; Sec. Kitui branch, Kenya African Nat. Union (KANU) Party 1985–88, fmr Nat. Organizing Sec. 1988, Vice-Chair. 2002; Asst Minister for Work, Housing and Planning 1986–88; Minister of Foreign Affairs 1992–98, 2002–04; fmr Minister of Educ., Tourism and Information; Minister of the Environment and Natural Resources 2004–05; defected from KANU to launch Liberal Democratic Party just before Dec. 2002 presidential elections, leader Orange Democratic Movt—Kenya 2007–13; leader Wiper Democratic Movt 2013–; unsuccessful cand. in presidential elections 2007; Vice-Pres. of Kenya and Minister of Home Affairs 2008–13; deputy leader, Nat. Super Alliance (NASA) 2017–; Hon. DHumLitt (Kenyatta Univ.) 2008, Hon. DD (Latin Univ. of Theology, Inglewood) 2009. *Address:* Kenya National Assembly, Parliament Buildings, PO Box 41842, Nairobi (office); Wiper Democratic Movement, Wiper House, 408 Othaya Rd, PO Box 403, 00100 Nairobi, Kenya (office). *Telephone:* (20) 2663336 (office). *Fax:* (20) 336589 (office). *E-mail:* wiper@wipermovement.com (office). *Website:* wiperdmk.com (office).

MUTA, Taizo, BSc, MSc, DSc; Japanese theoretical physicist, university administrator and academic; b. 1 June 1937; ed Kyushu Univ., Tokyo Univ.; Research Assoc., Faculty of Science, Kyoto Univ. 1965–71, Asst Prof., Research Inst. for Fundamental Physics 1971–82; apptd Prof., Faculty of Science, Hiroshima Univ. 1982, mem. Senate 1991, Presidential Aide 1993–95, Dean Faculty of Science 1995–99, Vice-Pres. 1999–2001, Prof., Grad. School of Science 2000–, Pres. 2001–07; Dir Mazda Motor Corpn. *Publications include:* Foundations of Quantum Chromodynamics: An Introduction to Perturbative Methods in Gauge Theories (World Scientific Lecture Notes in Physics, Vol. 5) 1984, 1990 International Workshop of Strong Coupling Gauge Theories and Beyond, July 28–31, 1990, Nagoya, Japan 1991, International Workshop on Electroweak Symmetry Breaking: November 12–15, 1991 Hiroshima (co-author) 1992; numerous scientific papers in professional journals on the theory of elementary particles, quantum chromodynamics and dynamical symmetry breaking in quantum field theory. *Leisure interests:* astronomy, fishing, skiing.

MUTABOBA, Joseph, MPhil; Rwandan diplomatist and UN official; b. 21 Dec. 1949; m.; three c.; ed North London Univ., UK; served as Sec.-Gen. in Ministries of Foreign Affairs and of Internal Affairs, as Deputy Nat. Co-ordinator for Rwanda and Head of Peace and Security thematic group in Int. Conf. on Great Lakes Region, and as sr diplomat in Addis Ababa and Washington, DC; Perm. Rep. to UN, New York 1999–2001; Pres. of Rwanda's Special Envoy to Great Lakes Region –2009; Special Rep. of UN Sec.-Gen. for Guinea-Bissau and Head of UN Integrated Peace-building Office in Guinea-Bissau (UNIOGBIS) 2009–13, Deputy Jt Special Rep. for Political Affairs, AU-UN Hybrid Operation in Darfur (UNAMID) 2013–14. *Address:* c/o United Nations, New York, NY 10017, USA.

MUTALOV, Abdulkhashim Mutalovich, PhD; Uzbekistani politician and business executive; b. 27 April 1947, Telyau, Tashkent Region; s. of Abdurahmonov Mutal and Abdurahmonova Turihon; m. Mutalova Hurinisa; one s.; ed All-Union Inst. of Food Industry; worker, Tashkent Factory of Bread Products; army service 1965–79; Dir Akhangaran Enterprise of Bread Products 1979–86; Deputy Minister of Bread Products Uzbek SSR 1986–87, Minister 1987–91; Deputy Chair. Cabinet of Ministers 1991–92; Prime Minister of Uzbekistan 1992–96; apptd Chair. State grain co. Uzdon Makhsulot 1996; Orden Znak Pochota 1986. *Publications:* Main Directions in Formation of Free-Market Relations in Grain-Processing Enterprises of the Republic of Uzbekistan 1993. *Leisure interests:* tennis. *Address:* Turob Tula Street 28–57, Chilanzar District, Tashkent, Uzbekistan (home). *Telephone:* (712) 1394184 (home).

MUTAMBARA, Arthur, BSc, MSc, PhD; Zimbabwean politician; b. 25 May 1966; ed Univ. of Zimbabwe, Univ. of Oxford, UK, Massachusetts Inst. of Tech., USA; active in student politics in 1980s; worked as man. consultant, McKinsey and Co.; fmr Prof. of Business Strategy, Kellogg Business School, Northwestern Univ., USA; Man. Dir Africa Tech. and Business Inst. 2003–; leader of pro-Senate faction Movement for Democratic Change—Mutambara (MDC—M) 2006–; arrested for political activities, released without charge, March and May 2006; Deputy Prime Minister 2009–13. *Address:* Movement for Democratic Change, Harare, Zimbabwe (office). *E-mail:* a.mutambara@mdczim.com (office). *Website:* www.mdczim.com (office).

MUTASA, Didymus Noel Edwin; Zimbabwean politician; b. 27 July 1935, Rusape; ed Goromonzi Govt School, Univ. of Birmingham, UK; began career as clerk and admin. officer in civil service; Co-founder Southern Region Fed. Services Asscn 1960; Co-founder Cold Comfort Soc. (multi-racial farming co-operative) 1964–70; arrested 1970, held in solitary confinement, Sinoia Prison 1970–72; in exile 1972–79; Founder mem. Zimbabwe African Nat. Union (ZANU) Br., Birmingham, UK and Dist Chair. ZANU UK 1975; joined ZANU HQ, Maputo, Mozambique 1977, Deputy Sec. for Finance, ZANU Cen. Cttee 1978; mem. Parl. for Manicaland 1980–, Speaker of Parl. 1980–90, Sec. for Transport and Welfare 1984–, Minister for Political Affairs 1990, Anti-Corruption and Anti-Monopolies Programme Minister 2003–05, Minister of State for Nat. Security 2005–09, for Presidential Affairs 2009–14. *Address:* Zimbabwe African National Union—Patriotic Front, corner of Rotten Row and Samora Machel Avenue, POB 4530, Harare, Zimbabwe. *Telephone:* (4) 753329 (office). *Fax:* (4) 774146 (office). *Website:* www.zanupfpub.co.zw (office).

MUTATI, Felix C., BA; Zambian accountant and politician; b. 29 Jan. 1959; m.; ed studied in UK; began career as Asst Accountant, Zimco, South Africa; fmr Financial Dir, Nat. Hotels Devt Corpn; Chief Financial Officer, ZESCO (power co.) –1988; mem. Nat. Ass. (Parl.) for Mporokoso constituency 2001–06, for Lunte constituency 2006–16, nominated mem. 2016–, mem. Econ. Affairs, Energy and Labour Cttee 2015–16, Reforms and Modernization Cttee 2016–, Standing Orders Cttee 2016–; Minister for Energy and Water Devt 2002–04, for Commerce, Trade and Industry 2004–11, Minister of Finance 2016–18; Elder, Common Market for Eastern and Southern Africa (COMESA); Chief SADC negotiator on behalf of Eastern and Southern African region 2006–11; Chair. 10th African Growth and Opportunity Act (AGOA) Forum, Washington, DC 2010; fmr Coordinator of Least Developed Countries (LDCs) at World Trade Org. (WTO); mem. Movement for Multi-Party Democracy. *Address:* c/o Ministry of Finance, Finance Bldg, POB 50062, Lusaka, Zambia (office).

MUTAWAKIL, Wakil Ahmad; Afghan politician; b. 1971; served as spokesman and personal sec. to Taliban leader Mullah Mohammad Omar –1999; Foreign Minister in Taliban Govt of Islamic Emirate of Afghanistan 1999–2002; added to UN Security Council list of people and orgs subject to sanctions 2001; surrendered in Kandahar to govt troops following ousting of regime Feb. 2002, held for three years under house arrest in Kabul 2002–05; disowned by the Taliban 2003; later part of govt under admin of Hamid Karzai; cand. in parl. elections Sept. 2005; removed from UN Security Council sanctions list 2010.

MUTEBI II, HM; Kabaka of Buganda Ronald Edward Frederick Kimera Muwenda Mutebi; b. 13 April 1955, Mmengo; s. of Kabaka Maj.-Gen. Sir Edward Fredrick William David Walugembe Mutebi Luwangula Mutesa II (King Freddy) and Naabakyaala Sarah Nalule Kisosonkole; m. Lady Sylvia Nagginda, The Nnabagereka of Buganda 1999; one d.; two s. three d. from other unions; ed Kingsmead Preparatory School, Sussex, Bradford Public School, Reading, Magdalene Coll., Cambridge, UK; lived in exile in UK as a double-glazing salesman following overthrow of his father Mutesa II by fmr Pres. of Uganda Milton Obote 1966–86; succeeded as Head of the Royal House of Buganda on the death of his father 21 Nov. 1969; returned to Uganda following removal of Obote II regime and mil. junta that briefly replaced Obote II) 1988; crowned 36th Kabaka (King) of Buganda, marking restoration of ancient kingdom of Buganda, 31 July 1993; Assoc. Ed. African Concord. *Leisure interest:* squash. *Address:* Buganda Kingdom, Bulange House, Kabakanjagala Road, PO Box 7451, Mmengo, Kampala, Uganda. *Telephone:* (414) 274738. *Fax:* (414) 274739. *E-mail:* info@buganda.or.ug. *Website:* www.buganda.or.ug.

MUTHARIKA, Arthur Peter, LLB, LLM, JSD; Malawi lawyer, academic, politician and head of state; *President and Minister of Defence;* b. 1940, brother of Bingu wa Mutharika, (fmr Pres. of Malawi); m. (deceased); one s. two d.; ed Univ. of London, UK, Yale Univ., USA; magistrate, Dar es Salaam, Tanzania 1965; admitted to Tanzanian bar 1971; Prof. of Law, Univ. of Dar es Salaam 1968–71, UN Inst. for Training and Research Program for Foreign Service Officers from Africa and Asia, Makerere Univ., Uganda 1969, Haile Selassie Univ., Ethiopia 1970, Rutgers Univ., USA 1972; Asst Prof. of Law, Washington Univ., St Louis, USA 1972–74, Assoc. Prof. 1974–77, Prof. 1997–; Academic Visitor, London School of Econs 1980; MP for Thyolo-East constituency 2009–14; fmr Minister of Justice and Constitutional Affairs, of Educ., Science and Tech., Minister of Foreign Affairs and Int. Co-operation 2011–12, of Defence 2014–; Pres. of Malawi 2014–; currently Commdr-in-Chief Malawi Defence Force; mem. Democratic Progressive Party (DPP); Hon. DHumLitt (Addis Ababa Univ.) 2017. *Address:* Office of the President and Cabinet, Private Bag 301, Capital City, Lilongwe 3, Malawi (office). *Telephone:* 1789311 (office). *Fax:* 1788456 (office). *Website:* www.opc.gov.mw (office).

MUTHURAMAN, Balasubramanian, BTech, MBA; Indian steel industry executive; b. 26 Sept. 1944; ed Indian Inst. of Tech. (IIT), Madras, Xavier's Labour Research Inst., Jamshedpur, Advanced Man. Programme, Centre Européen d'Éducation Permanente (CEDEP)/Institut Européen d'Admin des Affaires (INSEAD), France; joined Tata Steel as grad. trainee 1966, worked in areas of Iron-making and Eng Devt for 10 years, spent 19 years in Marketing and Sales Div. rising to Vice-Pres., selected to head Cold Rolling Mill Project 1995, Exec. Dir (Special Projects) 2000–01, Man. Dir Tata Steel 2001, fmr Vice-Chair. (retd); Chair. Tata Sponge Iron Ltd, Tata Steel KZN (Pty) Ltd, SA, TM International Logistics Ltd, The Tinplate Co. of India Ltd, Natsteel Asia Pte Ltd, Natsteel Asia (S) Pte Ltd, Singapore, Millennium Steel Public Co. Ltd, Bangkok; mem. Bd Dirs Tata Inc., New York, Tata Int. Ltd, Tata Industries Ltd, Mumbai, The Dhamra Port Co. Ltd; Chair. Bd of Govs Xavier Labour Relations Inst., Jamshedpur, Nat. Inst. of Tech., Jamshedpur, Research Council of Nat. Metallurgical Lab., Jamshedpur; Pres. Indian Inst. of Metals; mem. Bd of Dirs Int. Iron and Steel Inst., Brussels (mem. Exec. Cttee), West Bengal Industrial Devt Corpn Ltd, CEDEP; mem. UN Global Compact Bd, Nat. Council of Confed. of Indian Industries; mem. Bd Govs IIT, Kharagpur; Hon. Rotarian, Jamshedpur Rotary Club (East and West), Hon. Fellow, All India Man. Asscn 2007; Distinguished Alumnus Award, IIT, Madras 1997, Tata Gold Medal, Indian Inst. of Metals 2002, CEO of the Year Award, Indian Inst. of Materials Man. 2002, Nat. HRD Network Pathfinders Award in the CEO Category 2004, CEO of the Year, Business Standard 2005, CEO with Human Resources Orientation Award, World HRD Congress at Mumbai 2005, Management Man of the Year 2006–2007 Award, Bombay Man. Asscn 2007. *Leisure interests:* playing cricket and golf, reading literature on general management, finance, marketing and business.

MUTI, Riccardo; Italian conductor; *Music Director, Chicago Symphony Orchestra;* b. 28 July 1941, Naples; s. of Domenico Muti and Gilda Sellitto; m. Cristina Mazzavillani 1969; two s. one d.; ed San Pietro Conservatory, Majella, Naples and Milan Conservatory of Music; Prin. Conductor, Maggio Musicale, Florence 1969–81; Prin. Conductor, Philharmonia Orchestra, London 1973–82, Music Dir 1979–82, Conductor Laureate 1982–; Prin. Guest Conductor, Philadelphia Orchestra 1977–80, Prin. Conductor and Music Dir 1980–92, Conductor Laureate 1992–; Music Dir, La Scala, Milan 1986–2005; Prin. Conductor, Filarmonica della Scala 1988–2005; Music Dir, Chicago Symphony Orchestra 2010–; Conductor, Teatro dell'Opera, Rome 2010–14; Founder Orchestra Giovanile Luigi Cherubini; concert tours in USA with Boston, Chicago and Philadelphia Orchestras; concerts at Salzburg, Edinburgh, Lucerne, Flanders and Vienna festivals; also conducted Berlin Philharmonic, Bayerische Rundfunk Sinfonie Orchester, Vienna Philharmonic, New York Philharmonic and Concertgebouw Amsterdam; opera: Florence, Munich, Covent Garden, La Scala, Ravenna, Vienna, Accad. di Santa Cecilia (Rome), Accademico Dell'Accademia Cherubini (Florence); Hon. mem. American Acad. of Arts & Sciences, Hon. mem. Vienna Philharmonic 2011, Hon. Dir for Life, Rome Opera 2011; Grand Golden Medal of the City of Monaco, Grand Silver Ehrenkreuz Medal (Austria), Officer Order of Merit (Germany), Verdienstkreuz (First Class, Germany) 1976, Cavaliere Gran Croce (Italy) 1991, Légion d'honneur, Hon. KBE 2000, Russian Order of Friendship 2001, Silver Medal of the Salzburg Mozarteum 2001, Knight of the Grand Cross First Class of the Order of St Gregory the Great (Holy See) 2012; Hon. PhD (Weizmann Inst. of Science); Dr hc (Pennsylvania, Philadelphia, Bologna, Urbino, Milan, Cremona, Lecce); Guido Cantelli Award 1967, Diapason d'Or, Premio Critica Discografia Italiana, Prix Académie nat. du disque 1977, Deutschen Schallplatten Prize, Bellini d'Oro, Abbiati Prize, Grand Prix du disque for La Traviata (Verdi), Requiem in C minor (Cherubini) 1982, Disco d'Oro for Music for Films, Wolf Prize 2000, Musical America Award for Musician of the Year 2010, Grammy Award for Best Classical Album (for Verdi: Requiem) 2011, Birgit Nilsson Prize 2011, Prince of Asturias Prize for the Arts 2011, Vittorio De Sica Prize for contributions to music 2012, Praemium Imperiale 2018. *Address:* RM Music SRL, Via D. Alighieri 7, 48121 Ravenna, Italy; Chicago Symphony Orchestra, Symphony Center, · 220 South Michigan Avenue, Chicago, IL 60604, USA (office). *E-mail:* info@riccardomuti .com. *Website:* www.riccardomutimusic.com/eng.

MUTKO, Vitalii Leontyevich, CandEconSci; Russian mechanical engineer and politician; *Deputy Chairman of the Government;* b. 8 Dec. 1958, Kurinskaya, nr Tuapse, Krasnodar Krai, Russia SFSR, USSR; m.; two d.; ed Leningrad (now St Petersburg) Construction Vocational School No. 226, Petrokrepost (now Shlisselburg) Nautical School, Leningrad Region, Leningrad River Vocational Coll., Leningrad Inst. of Water Transport, Faculty of Law, St Petersburg State Univ., St Petersburg State Univ. of Econs and Finance; served as seaman on ships from NW River Steam Navigation and Leningrad sea port 1977–78, originally worked on Vladimir Ilich river steamship, later transferred to work on river-sea dry cargo ship, also worked in port of Hamburg; Komsomol activist during his studies 1978, headed coll. Komsomol org., headed local trade union coll. cttee; joined CPSU 1979; following graduation, worked at Exec. Cttee of Kirov Dist Soviet of People's Deputies in Leningrad 1983, worked as an instructor and Head of Dept for Social Issues, Sec., later Chair. Exec. Cttee 1990, set up Council of Chairmen 1990; Deputy, Kirov Dist Council 1990, Head of Admin of Kirov Dist 1991; organized meetings of workers from Kirov factory against Aug. putsch conspirators 1991; Deputy Mayor of St Petersburg and Chair. of Mayor's Cttee on Social Issues 1992–95; Curator of Zenit St Petersburg Football Club 1992–95, Pres. 1995–2003; authorized rep. of Vladimir Putin in presidential elections 2000; headed electoral staff of St Petersburg Gov. cand. Valentina Matviyenko 2000; Pres. Russian Football Premier League 2001–03; Fed. Council rep. from St Petersburg Govt 2003–08, Chair. Comm. on Youth and Sport Affairs, mem. Cttee on Fed. and Regional Policy Issues, Comm. on Control of Maintenance of Activity of Fed. Council; Pres. Russian Football Union 2005, 2015–17; mem. Tech. and Devt Cttee of FIFA 2006–; Senator for St Petersburg (for second time) 2007–; mem. presidential cttee on devt of physical culture and sport, highest standard sport, and on preparation and direction of 2014 XXII Winter Olympic Games and XI Winter Paralympics in Sochi 2007–; Minister of Sport, Tourism and Youth Policy

2008–12, of Sport 2012–16; Deputy Chair. of the Govt 2016–; Pres. Special Olympics Cttee for St Petersburg, Golden Pelican (charity); Order of Honour 1994, Order of Friendship 2002; medals dedicated 'In Commemoration of the 300th Anniversary of St Petersburg', 'In Commemoration of the 1000th Anniversary of Kazan'. *Address:* Office of the Government, 103274 Moscow, Krasnopresnenskaya nab. 2, Russian Federation (office). *Telephone:* (495) 605-53-29 (office). *Fax:* (495) 605-52-43 (office). *E-mail:* duty_press@aprf.gov.ru (office). *Website:* government.ru (office).

MUTOLA, Maria Lurdes; Mozambican athlete; b. 27 Oct. 1972, Maputo; d. of João Mutola and Catarina Mutola; ed Eugene High School, Ore., USA; gold medallist, 800m, World Indoor Championships 1993, 1995, 1997, 2001, 2003, 2004, 2006; winner 800m World Cup 1992, 1994, 1998, 2002; winner 800m Grand Prix Final 1993, 1995, 1999, 2001; gold medallist, 800m, World Championships 1993, 2001, 2003; bronze medallist, 800m, Olympic Games, Atlanta 1996, gold medallist 800m, Sydney 2000; winner 800m World Athletics Final 2003; world record holder at 1,000m indoor; African record holder at 800m and 1,000m (outdoor); between 1992 and 1995 she won 42 consecutive races; won all six Golden League races 2003 winning US$1 million prize; f. Lurdes Mutola Foundation 2001; Hon. UN Amb. 2003–. *Address:* c/o Lurdes Mutola Foundation, 25th of September Avenue, Times Square Building, Block II, 1st Floor, Door 12, Maputo, Mozambique. *Website:* www .flmutola.org.mz.

MUTTER, Anne-Sophie; German violinist; b. 29 June 1963, Rheinfelden/Baden; m. 1st Dithelf Wunderlich 1989 (deceased); m. 2nd André Previn 2002 (divorced); ed studied with Prof. Aida Stucki, Winterthur, Switzerland; began musical career playing piano and violin 1969; played in Int. Music Festival, Lucerne 1976; debut with Herbert von Karajan at Pfingstfestspiele, Salzburg 1977; soloist with numerous orchestras world-wide; has given world premieres of 24 works, including works by Sebastian Currier, Henri Dutilleux, Sofia Gubaidulina, Witold Lutoslawski, Norbert Moret, Krzysztof Penderecki, Sir André Previn and Wolfgang Rihm; also plays with string trio and quartet; Guest Teacher, RAM, London 1985; est. foundation promoting gifted young string players throughout the world 1997; Hon. Pres. Mozart Soc., Univ. of Oxford 1983; Foreign Hon. mem. American Acad. of Arts and Sciences 2013; Hon. Fellow, Keble Coll., Oxford 2015; Order of Merit (Germany and Bavaria), Großes Österreichisches Ehrenzeichen (Austria), Chevalier, Ordre national de la Légion d'honneur 2009; Dr hc (Norwegian Univ. of Science and Tech.) 2012; four Grammy Awards, Youth Music Prize (FRG) for violin 1970, for piano 1970, for violin 1974, Artist of the Year, Deutscher Schallplattenpreis, Grand Prix Int. du Disque, Record Acad. Prize, Tokyo 1982, Internationaler Schallplattenpreis 1993, Herbert von Karajan Award 2003, Int. Ernst von Siemens Music Prize 2008, Leipzig Mendelssohn Prize 2008, European St Ullrichs Prize 2009, Cristobal Gabarron Award 2009, Musical America Award for Instrumentalist of the Year 2011, Brahms Prize 2011, Erich Fromm Prize 2011, Gustav Adolf Prize 2011, Atlantic Council's Distinguished Artistic Leadership Award 2012, Lutoslawski Soc. Award 2015, Foundation Albeniz Yehudi Menuhin Prize 2016, Medalla de Oro al Merito en las bellas Artes 2016, Gold Medal for Merit to Culture – Gloria Artis 2018, Polar Music Prize 2019. *Recordings include:* Mozart: Five Violin Concertos 2005, Bach, Gubaidulina: Violin Concertos (with the Trondheim Soloists) 2008, Mendelssohn's Violin Concerto 2009, Brahms: The Violin Sonatas 2010, Rihm/Currier (ECHO Klassik Award for Concerto Recording of the Year/Violin – 20th/21st Century 2012) 2011, Dvořák: Violin Concerto 2013, The Silver Album 2014, Anne-Sophie Mutter Live: The Club Album from Yellow Lounge 2015, A Portrait 2015, Schubert Forellenquintett/ Trout Quintet 2017, Hommage à Penderecki 2018. *Leisure interests:* graphic arts, sport. *Address:* Sekretariat Anne-Sophie Mutter, Ismaninger Straße 75, 81675 Munich, Germany. *E-mail:* info@anne-sophie-mutter.de. *Website:* www.anne -sophie-mutter.de.

MUXAMEJANOV, Oral B.; Kazakhstani politician; b. 11 Nov. 1948, Qostanay; m.; one s. two d.; ed Novosibirsk Inst. of Soviet Co-operative Trade, Russia, Almaty Higher Party School; worked in Oblast Consumer Products Union and Worsted Cloth Factory, Qostanay 1971–75; various positions with Komsomol (Communist Youth League) and party organs, and in regional Soviet of People's Deputies, Torgai Oblast (now Qostanay Oblast) 1975–92; Head of Regional Admin, Amangeldinsky Dist, Torgai Oblast 1992–94; Deputy, Supreme Soviet of Kazakhstan (Parl.) 1994–95 (dissolved under new constitution 1995); Head of Dept of Social-Cultural Devt, Office of the Pres. 1995–97; Inspector, Presidential Admin, becoming Head of Dept of Organizational-Control Work 1997–2004; Deputy, Majlis (Parl.) from electoral dist No 49, Qostanay Oblast 2004–07, 2007 (apptd), Chair. Majlis 2004–07, 2008–12; mem. Light of the Fatherland People's Democratic Party (Nur Otan), Leader, Parl. Fraction 2008–. *Leisure interests:* literature, poetry, fishing, billiards.

MUZAFFAR, Chandra, PhD; Malaysian political scientist, academic and international organization executive; *President, International Movement for a Just World;* b. 10 March 1947, Bedong, Kedah; m.; two d.; ed Univ. of Singapore; Lecturer, Science Univ. of Malaysia 1970–83, Sr Research Fellow 1992–97; Prof. and first Dir Centre for Civilizational Dialogue, Univ. of Malaya 1997–99; Founder-Pres. multi-ethnic social reform group Aliran Kesedaran Negara (Nat. Consciousness Movt) 1977–91; mem. Exec. Cttee Asian Comm. on Human Rights 1985; arrested by Malaysian Govt under Internal Security Act Oct. 1987, released without conditions Dec. 1987; nominated as monitor by Human Rights Watch 1988; Pres. Int. Movt for a Just World (JUST), Kuala Lumpur 1997–; Deputy Pres. Kealidan (Nat. Justice Party) 1999–2001; Chair. Bd of Trustees, 1Malaysia Foundation; mem. Bd Dirs Integrity Inst., Malaysia 2004–, and several int. NGOs; Weigand Distinguished Visitor Fellowship, Duke Univ., USA 2000; Prof. of Global Studies, Science Univ. of Malaysia 2007–12; Hon. Prof., Universidad Nacional Experimental Politecnica de la Fuerza Armada, Caracas, Venezuela 2009; Harry J. Benda Prize for distinguished scholarship on SE Asia, Asscn of Asian Studies, North America 1989, Juliet Hollister Award 'Interfaith Visionary', Temple of Understanding, New York, USA 2010. *Publications:* author or ed. of 27 books on religion, human rights, Malaysian politics, and int. relations, including Rights, Religion, and Reform 2002, Subverting Greed 2002, Muslims, Dialogue, Terror 2003, Global Ethic or Global Hegemony? 2005, Hegemony: Justice; Peace 2008, Religion and Governance 2009, Plea for Empathy 2010, Religion Seeking Justice and Peace 2010, Exploring Religion in Our Time 2011, Muslims Today 2011.

Leisure interest: reading. *Address:* International Movement for a Just World, PO Box 288, 46730 Petaling Jaya, Selangor (office); No. 1258, Jalan Telok, Section 5, Petaling Jaya 46000 Selangor, Malaysia (office). *Telephone:* (3) 7781-2494 (office); (3) 6201-5170 (home). *Fax:* (3) 7781-3245 (office). *E-mail:* cmuzaffar@just -international.org (office). *Website:* www.just-international.org (office).

MUZHENKO, Lt-Gen. Viktor Mykolayovych; Ukrainian army officer; *Chief of the General Staff and Commander-in-Chief of the Armed Forces;* b. 10 Oct. 1961, Vystupovychi, Ovruch Dist, Zhytomyr Oblast, Ukrainian SSR, USSR; ed Leningrad Higher Mil. Command School, Acad. of the Armed Forces of Ukraine, Faculty training of operational and strategic levels, Nat. Defence Acad. of Ukraine; served in Soviet Union's Transcaucasian Mil. Dist 1983, later commdr of a motorized infantry bn; Commdr Carpathian Mil. Dist 1992–2000; Chief of Staff and Deputy Div. Commdr Northern Territorial Directorate 2000–03; Chief of Staff and First Deputy Commdr of mechanized brigade of Ukrainian peacekeeping contingent of multinational force in Iraq 2003–04; Deputy Chief of Staff, Army Corps of Ukrainian Ground Forces 2005–10; Commdr 8th Army Corps 2010–12; rank of Lt-Gen. 2012; Deputy Chief of the Gen. Staff, Armed Forces of Ukraine 2012–14; First Deputy Head of Counter-terrorist Centre, Security Service of Ukraine May–July 2014; Chief of the Gen. Staff and C-in-C of the Armed Forces July 2014–; elected Deputy of Zhytomyr Oblast Council for Partiya Rehioniv (Party of Regions), but left the party Feb. 2014; entered combat during insurgency in Donbas April 2014; Order of Danylo Halytsky 2004, Medal 'For Irreproachable Service', Defender of the Motherland Medal, Medal 'For Impeccable Service', Jubilee Medal '70 Years of the Armed Forces of the USSR', Medal 'For Distinction in Military Service'. *Address:* Office of the Chief of the General Staff, Ministry of Defence, 03168 Kyiv, vul. Povitroflotskyi 6, Ukraine (office). *Telephone:* (44) 454-44-04 (office). *Fax:* (44) 226-20-15 (office). *E-mail:* admou@mil.gov.ua (office). *Website:* www.mil.gov.ua (office).

MUZITO, Adolphe; Democratic Republic of the Congo economist and politician; b. 12 Feb. 1957; ed Univ. of Kinshasa; Regional Finance Insp., Finance Inspectorate Gen. 2007; Minister of the Budget 2007–08; Prime Minister 2008–12 (resgnd); Sec.-Gen. Unified Lumumbist Party (Parti Lumumbiste Unifié—PALU) 2007–. *Address:* Parti Lumumbiste Unifié, Blvd Lumumba Pont-Matete, Matete, Kinshasa, Democratic Republic of the Congo (office). *E-mail:* partilumumbiste.rdc@gmail.com (office).

MVOUBA, Isidore; Republic of the Congo politician; *President of National Assembly;* b. 1954, Kindamba; with Chemin de fer Congo Océan 1977; mem. Parti Congolais du Travail (PCT); Presidential Campaign Dir for Denis Sassou Nguesso 1992, 2002; Minister of Youth and Sports 1992–93; Prin. Pvt. Sec. for Head of State 1997–99; Minister for Transport, Civil Aviation and the Merchant Navy 1999–2005; Minister of State for Transport and Privatization in charge of Co-ordination of Govt Action 2002–05, concurrently Prime Minister 2005–09 (post abolished); Minister of State, Co-ordinator of Basic Infrastructures, and Minister of Civil Aviation and of Maritime Trade 2009–12; Minister of State, Minister of Industrial Devt and the Promotion of the Pvt. Sector 2012–16; mem. Assemblée nationale (Parl.) as PCT MP for Kindamba constituency 2007–, Pres. 2017–.

MWAKWERE, Chirau Ali; Kenyan politician and diplomatist; b. 15 June 1945, Golini, Ziwani, Kwale Dist; m. Rose Batsigira; Amb. to Zimbabwe –2004; mem. Nat. Ass. (Parl.) for Matuga; Minister of Foreign Affairs 2004–05, of Transport 2005–10, of the Environment and Mineral Resources 2012 (apptd). *Leisure interest:* playing golf.

MWAMBA, Alexis Thambwe, LenD; Democratic Republic of the Congo lawyer and politician; *Minister of State, Minister of Justice, Keeper of the Seals, and Acting Deputy Prime Minister, Minister of Foreign Affairs and Regional Integration;* ed Univ. of Burundi, Univ. Libre de Bruxelles, Belgium; lawyer, Kinshasa Bar; fmr mem. Movt for the Liberation of Congo (resistance group); fmr Pres. Union des Démocrates Indépendants; Founding mem. Rassemblement congolais pour la Démocratie; fmr Man. Dir Société Minière du Kivu (Sominki); fmr Amb. of Zaire (now Democratic Repub. of Congo) to Italy; fmr Dir Office des Douanes et Accises (customs office); fmr Minister of Public Works, of External Trade, and of Transport; in exile in Brussels 1997; Minister of Planning and Reconstruction 2003–06; mem. Nat. Assembly (Ind.) for Kindu constituency 2006–12; Minister of Foreign Affairs 2008–12, Minister of State and Minister of Justice and Keeper of the Seals 2016–, also Acting Deputy Prime Minister and Minister of Foreign Affairs and Regional Integration 2019–. *Address:* Ministry of Justice 228 ave de Lemera, BP 3137, Kinshasa-Gombe, Democratic Republic of the Congo. *Telephone:* (12) 32432 (office).

MWAMBA, Geoffrey Bwalya; Zambian business executive and politician; b. 15 March 1959; m. Chama Mwamba; mem. Nat. Ass. for Kasama Central; Minister of Defence 2011–13; f. GBM Group, GBM Trucking and Milling Co., GBM Milling Co. Ltd; mem. Patriotic Front.

MWANAKATWE, Margaret Mhango, BBA, ACCA; Zambian chartered accountant, banking executive and politician; *Minister of Finance;* b. 1 Nov. 1961; m. Mupanga Mwanakatwe; two c.; ed Univ. of Zambia; worked as financial analyst in UK, first with MacDonald Douglas Information Systems and later with Whitbread; four years teaching accounting to MBA students in France; returned to Zambia, becoming Dir Gen. Zambia Investment Promotion Agency; Man. Dir Barclays Bank of Zambia PLC 2001–08, Man. Dir and CEO, Barclays Bank of Ghana PLC 2004–09; Man. Dir United Bank for Africa, Lagos 2009–11; mem. Nat. Ass. (parl.) (nominated) (PF) 2015, for Lusaka Central (PF) 2016–; Minister of Commerce, Trade and Industry 2015–18, Minister of Finance 2018–; Chair. Policy Monitoring and Research Centre (PMRC); Chair. Munda Wanga Botanical & Zoological Gardens, Nat. Aids Council of Zambia, Zambia Business Coalition for HIV/AIDS; Dir (non exec.) Zambia Sugar PLC 2004–, Unilever Africa Advisory Council, Zambia Venture Capital Fund, Zambia Revenue Authority, British American Tobacco (Zambia) PLC 2012–; mem. Patriotic Front (PF), mem. PF Cen. Cttee 2015–; Officer, Order of the Volta (Ghana) 2008. *Address:* Ministry of Finance, Chimanga Rd, POB 50062, Lusaka, Zambia (office). *Telephone:* (21) 1251843 (office). *Fax:* (21) 1251078 (office). *E-mail:* info@mof.gov.zm (office). *Website:* www .mof.gov.zm (office).

MWANGA, Robert, BSc, MSc, PhD; Ugandan plant scientist; *Research Scientist, International Potato Center;* b. 1954, Budhabangula, Uganda; ed Makerere Univ., Kampala (Govt Scholarship), Univ. of the Philippines, Los Baños, North Carolina State Univ., USA; root crop breeder, Kawanda Research Station 1978–83; left Uganda to work at Int. Inst. for Tropical Agric., Nigeria 1983; returned to Uganda 1986; helped develop Vitamin A-enriched orange-fleshed sweet potato (OFSP) and worked in Uganda to alleviate food insecurity and malnutrition; est. Roots and Tuber Crops Program, Namulonge Research Facility with USAID support 1986–90, 20 OFSP varieties released 1995–2013; currently Research Scientist, Int. Potato Center (Centro Internacional de la Papa), Lima, Peru; McKnight Foundation grant 1996, World Food Prize (co-recipient) 2016. *Address:* Centro Internacional de la Papa, Avenida La Molina 1895, La Molina, Apartado Postal 1558, Lima, Peru (office). *Telephone:* 3496017 (office). *E-mail:* cip@cgiar.org (office). *Website:* cipotato.org (office).

MWANSA, Kalombo T., LLB, LLM, MPhil, PhD; Zambian politician and professor of law; b. 9 Sept. 1955, Nchelenge; m. 1983; two s. two d.; ed Univ. of Zambia, Harvard Univ., USA, Univs of Cambridge and London, UK; Tutor in Law, Univ. of Zambia 1979–80, Lecturer in Law and Criminology 1983–88, Acting Dean of Law School 1992–93; Perm. Sec. Ministry of Home Affairs 1993–98; Acting Chair. Police and Prisons Service Comm. 1994–96; Perm. Sec. of Admin, Cabinet Office 1998–99; Deputy Sec. to Cabinet 1999–2002, Acting Sec. 2001, 2002; Minister of Foreign Affairs 2002–04, of Home Affairs 2004–05, 2008–09, of Mines and Mineral Devt 2005–08, of Defence 2009 (apptd); nominated mem. Parl. 2002–; Livingstone Scholar, Jesus Coll. Cambridge 1982–83; Commonwealth Scholar, SOAS 1988–92; awards from Lusaka Hindu Asscn, Law Asscn of Zambia. *Publications include:* Property Crime in Zambia, Death Penalty in Zambia, Zambia Police and Crime Prevention, Juvenile Delinquency in Zambia. *Leisure interests:* reading, vegetable gardening, soccer.

MWANZA, Rachel; Democratic Republic of the Congo actress; b. 1997; spent several years living as a street child before being cast in Rebelle after dir Kim Nguyen and producers Pierre Even and Marie-Claude Poulin saw her in a documentary film on the street kids of Kinshasa 2012. *Films include:* Rebelle (War Witch) (Silver Bear for Best Actress, Berlin Int. Film Festival, Best Actress, Tribeca Film Festival, Vancouver Film Critics' Circle and First Canadian Screen Awards) 2012, Kinshasa Kids 2012. *Television includes:* On n'est pas couché (series) 2014. *Publication:* Survivre pour le jour 2014.

MWEMWENIKARAWA, Nabuti; I-Kiribati politician; mem. Parl. for North Tarawa 1998–2002; Minister for Finance and Econ. Devt 2003–07; fmr Sec., Maurin Kiribati Party; unsuccessful cand. in 2007 presidential elections. *Address:* Maurin Kiribati Party, c/o Maneaba Ni Maungatabu, Tarawa, Kiribati (office).

MWENCHA, Erastus Jarnalese Onkundi, BA, MA, MBS; Kenyan economist and international finance official; b. 15 Nov. 1947, Kisii; m.; three s.; ed Univ. of Nairobi, York Univ., Canada; entered civil service as an economist in Industrial Survey and Promotion Centre, Ministry of Commerce and Industry 1974, Prin. Industrial Devt Officer 1980; Dir of several public enterprises 1979–83, including Kenya Medical Research Inst., Kenya Industrial Research and Devt Inst.; also served as Head of Dept of Industry and as a Sr Economist in Ministry of Commerce and Industry; apptd Sec. Industrial Sciences Advisory Council 1979; Sr Industrial Expert, Econ. Comm. for Africa 1983; Dir of Industry, Energy and Environment, Preferential Trade Area for Eastern and Southern Africa 1987–97; Acting Sec.-Gen. Common Market for Eastern and Southern Africa (COMESA) 1997–98, Sec.-Gen. 1998–2008; Deputy Chair. African Union Comm. 2008–17; fmr mem. Research Council of Nat. Council for Science and Tech.; Order of the Moran of the Burning Spear 1998. *Publications:* contrib. to The Free Trade Area of the Common Market for Eastern and Southern Africa. *Leisure interests:* playing golf, ardent Christian.

MWESIGE, Adolf Kasaija, LLB; Ugandan lawyer and politician; *Minister of Defence and Veteran Affairs;* b. 4 April 1966, Kabarole Dist; m.; ed Makerere Univ., UN Center for Human Rights, Geneva, Switzerland; Advocate, High Court of Uganda 1994–; Foreign Service Officer, responsible for legal and consular matters, Ministry of Foreign Affairs 1992–96; Managing Partner, Mwesige, Egunyu & Co. Advocates (law firm) 1996–2001; mem. Parl. for Bunyangabu 1996–; Minister of State in the Office of the Vice-Pres. 2003–05, Minister of State for Justice and Constitutional Affairs 2005–06, Minister for Gen. Duties in Office of the Prime Minister 2006–09, Minister for Local Govt 2009–11, Minister of Defence and Veteran Affairs 2016–; mem. Nat. Resistance Movt (NRM); Full mem. Uganda Law Soc., East Africa Law Soc. *Address:* Ministry of Defence, Bombo, POB 7069, Kampala, Uganda (office). *Telephone:* (41) 4270331 (office). *Fax:* (41) 4245911 (office). *E-mail:* spokesman@defenceuganda.mil.ug (office). *Website:* www.defence .go.ug (office).

MWINYI, Ali Hassan; Tanzanian teacher, diplomatist and fmr head of state; b. 8 May 1925, Kivure, Mkuranga Dist, Tanganyika; m. Siti A. Mwinyi 1960; five s. four d.; ed secondary school, Dole, Zanzibar, Zanzibar Teachers' Training Coll., Durban Univ. Inst. of Educ., South Africa, Hall Univ., UK; moved to Zanzibar as a child; primary schoolteacher at Mangapwani, Zanzibar 1945–50; Headteacher, Bumbwini Primary School 1950–54; Tutor, Zanzibar Teachers' Training Coll. 1956–61, later Prin.; joined Shiraz Party (ASP) 1964; Prin. Perm. Sec. of Educ. Zanzibar 1964–65; Asst Gen. Man. Zanzibar State Trading Corpn 1965–70; Asst Treasurer Makadara ASP Br., Zanzibar 1966–70; Chair. E African Currency Bd 1964–70, Nat. Kiswahili Council (BAKITA) 1964–77, Zanzibar Censorship Board 1964–65, Tanzania Food and Nutrition Council (LISHE); Minister of State, Office of Pres., Tanzania 1970; Minister for Health 1972–75, for Home Affairs 1975–77; Amb. to Egypt 1977–82; Minister of Natural Resources and Tourism 1982–83, of State in Vice-Pres.'s Office 1983–84; interim Pres. of Zanzibar Feb.–April 1984, Pres. April 1984; Vice-Pres. of Tanzania 1984–85, Pres. 1985–95, also fmr Minister of Defence and Nat. Service; fmr C-in-C of Armed Forces; mem. Chama Cha Mapinduzi (CCM or Revolutionary Party), Vice-Chair. 1984–90, Chair. 1990–96; Chair. Commonwealth Observer Mission to Regional and Gen. Elections in Guyana 6–19th Dec. 1997, OAU Mission to Regional and Gen. Elections in Nigeria Feb.–March 1998, Nat. Advisory Bd on the Control of HIV/AIDS; mem. Tanzania-Britain Soc.; fmr mem. Council Univ. of Dar es Salaam; Patron Tanzania Union Govt and Health Employees, Dar es Salaam Islamic Club, Tanzania Railway

Workers Union, Muslims' Asscn for the Revertees, Shinyanga Orphanage Centre, Union of Tanzania Press Club, Tanzania Heralds for Youth Services, Publishers' Asscn of Tanzania, Tanga Muslim Org., Tanzania Muslim Hajj Trust; Hon. Life mem. Tanzania Law Soc.

MWINYI, Hussein Ali, MD; Tanzanian physician and politician; *Minister of Defence and National Service;* b. 23 Dec. 1966, Zanzibar; ed Marmara Univ., Turkey, Hammersmith Hosp., UK; doctor, Ministry of Health 1993–97, specialist doctor 1997–98; Lecturer in Medicine, Hubert Kairuki Memorial Univ. 1998–2000; Deputy Minister of Health 2000–05; MP for Kwahani 2005–; Minister of State for Union Affairs 2006–08; Minister of Defence and Nat. Service 2008–12, 2014–, of Health and Social Welfare 2012–14; mem. Chama Cha Mapinduzi (CCM—Revolutionary Party of Tanzania). *Address:* Ministry of Defence and National Service, PO Box 9544, Dar es Salaam, Tanzania (office). *Telephone:* (22) 2117153 (office). *Fax:* (22) 2116719 (office). *Website:* www.modans.go.tz (office).

MYAGKOV, Andrei Vasilyevich; Russian actor; b. 8 July 1938, Leningrad; ed Leningrad Inst. of Chemical Tech., Studio-School, Moscow Art Theatre; began acting in Sovremennik Theatre 1965–77, with Moscow Art Theatre 1977–; debut as dir on stage of Moscow Art Theatre with Goodnight, Mama (Spokoinoy nochi, Mama) 1989; directed Retro 2000; USSR State Prize 1977, 1979, The Brothers Vasiliev State Prize 1979, People's Artist of the RSFSR 1986. *Theatre includes:* Aduyev in Ordinary Story, Trubetskoy in Decembrists, Repetilov in Trouble from Intelligence, Misail in Boris Godunov. *Films include:* Pokhozhdeniya zubnogo vracha (Adventures of a Dentist) 1965, Staryy dom (The Old House) 1969, Bratya Karamazovy (The Brothers Karamazov) 1969, Moya sudba 1970, Nezhdannyy gost (The Uninvited Guest) 1972, Grossmeyster 1972, Nadezhda (Hope) 1973, Utrenniy obkhod (Morning Round) 1974, Strakh vysoty (Fear of the Height) 1975, Vy mne pisali… 1976, Sluzhebnyy roman (Office Romance) 1977, Primite telegrammu v dolg 1979, Garazh 1979, Rassledovaniye 1980, 4:0 v polzu Tanechki (4:0 for Tanechka) 1982, Poslesloviye (Epilogue) 1983, Oglyanis!… (Turn Back!…) 1983, Letargiya 1983, Polosa prepyatstviy (Stripe of Obstacles) 1984, Zhestokiy romans (A Cruel Romance) 1984, Poslednyaya doroga (The Last Road) 1986, Ot zarplaty do zarplaty (From Pay to Pay) 1986, Chelovek, kotoryy bral intervyu 1986, Svobodnoye padeniye 1987, Silnee vsekh inykh veleniy (Above All Else) 1987, Kuvyrok cherez golovu 1987, Mat (Mother) 1989, Vinovata li ya… (Am I Guilty…) 1992, Na Deribasovskoy khoroshaya pogoda, ili na Brayton Bich opyat idut dozhdi (There's Good Weather in Deribasovskaya, It's Raining Again in Brighton Beach) 1992, Osenniye soblazny (Autumn Temptations) 1993, Iskusstvo umirat (The Art of Dying) 1995, Privet, duralei! (Hello, Fools!) (voice) 1996, Kontrakt so smertyu 1998, Skaz pro Fedota-streltsa (The Tale of Fedot, the Shooter) 2002, Kto prikhodit v zimniy vecher… 2007, Ironiya sudby. Prodolzhenie (The Irony of Fate 2) 2007. *Television includes:* Ironiya sudby, ili S lyogkim parom! (The Irony of Fate) (film) 1975, Dni Turbinykh 1976, Iz zapisok Lopakhina (From Lopakhin's Notes) 1977, Aktivnaya zona (Active Zone) 1979, Gonki po vertikali (Vertical Races) 1983, 32oe dekabrya 2004. *Address:* 121293 Moscow, General Yermolov str. 6, Apt 42, Russian Federation. *Telephone:* (495) 148-93-64.

MYAING, U Linn, BSc; Myanma diplomatist; b. 15 Oct. 1947, Yangon; m. Daw Thi Thi Ta; two d.; ed Defence Studies Acad.; commissioned as officer in Myanmar Navy 1967–93; Deputy Dir Americas Div., Political Dept, Ministry of Foreign Affairs 1993–94, served first as Counsellor, then as Minister Counsellor, Perm. Mission to UN and other Int. Orgs, Geneva 1994–97, Deputy Dir Gen. Ministry of Foreign Affairs, also attached as Minister, Deputy Perm. Rep. to Perm. Mission of Myanmar, Geneva 1998–99, Amb. to France (also accred to UNESCO) 1999–2001 (also accred to Belgium, the Netherlands, Switzerland and EU) 2000–01, Amb. to USA 2001–07; apptd Adviser to Bd, Serge Pun and Assocs (Myanmar) Ltd 2006.

MYASNIKOV, Vladimir Stepanovich, DrHist; Russian historian and sinologist; b. 15 May 1931, Moscow; ed Moscow State Inst. of Int. Relations; Researcher, Inst. of Sinology 1956–60, Inst. of Peoples of Asia 1963–64, Inst. of Econs of World Socialist System 1964–66; Researcher, Scientific Sec., Head of Div., Inst. of Far Eastern Studies, Russian Acad. of Sciences 1966–85, Deputy Dir from 1985, Head, Centre for Chinese and Russian Relations from 1992; Corresp. mem. Russian Acad. of Sciences 1990, mem. 1997. *Publications:* over 150 published works, books, monographs. *Address:* 117997 Moscow, Institute of Far Eastern Studies, Russian Academy of Sciences, Nakhimovsky prosp. 32 (office); 160 Moscow, Novocheremoushkinskaya str. 49, Russian Federation (home). *Telephone:* (499) 129-10-11 (office). *Fax:* (495) 718-96-56 (office). *E-mail:* ifes@ifes-ras.ru (office). *Website:* www .ifes-ras.ru (office).

MYASNIKOVICH, Mikhail Uladzimiravich, DSc; Belarusian engineer and politician; b. 6 May 1950, Novy Snov village, Nesvizhskii Raion, Minsk Oblast; m.; one s. one d.; ed Brest State Tech. Univ.; began career as Engineer, Tech. Dept, Minskproject Design Inst. 1972; Chief Engineer, Minskvodokanal Production Asscn 1973–77; Chief Engineer, Directorate for Public Service Enterprises, Minsk City Exec. Cttee 1977, Chief of Directorate 1979; Chair. Exec. Cttee, Sovietsky Dist Soviet of People's Deputies, Minsk City 1983, Deputy Chair. Minsk City Exec. Cttee 1984, Sec., Minsk City Cttee of Communist Party of Belarus 1985–86; Minister of Housing and Communal Services, Belarusian SSR (BSSR) 1986, Vice-Chair. BSSR Council of Ministers 1990, also Chair. BSSR State Cttee for Economy and Planning; Deputy Prime Minister, Repub. of Belarus (following independence) 1994–95; Head of Presidential Admin 1995–2001; Prime Minister of Belarus 2010–14 (dismissed); mem. Nat. Acad. of Sciences of Belarus, Chair. Presidium 2001–10. *Address:* c/o Office of the Council of Ministers, 220010 Minsk, vul. Savetskaya 11, Belarus. *E-mail:* contact@government.by.

MYASOYEDOV, Boris Fedorovich; Russian chemist; b. 2 Oct. 1930; m.; one s.; ed Moscow I. Mendeleyev Inst. of Chem. and Tech.; Jr, Sr Researcher, Head of Lab., Deputy Dir V. Vernadsky Inst. of Geochemistry and Analytical Chem., Corresp. mem. USSR (now Russian) Acad. of Sciences 1990, mem. 1994, ViceAcademician-Sec., Chem. and Material Studies Dept; mem. Presidium of the Scientific and Tech. Bd of Rosatom State Atomic Energy Corpn (fmrly State Atomic Energy Corpn Rosatom); research in chem. of radioactive elements, radionucleides, creation and application of chemical sensors and analysers; USSR State Prize, V. Khlopin Prize, Acad. of Sciences. *Publications:* Chemical Sensors: Possibilities and Perspectives 1990. *Leisure interests:* music, stamp collecting. *Address:* Rosatom State Atomic Energy Corporation, 119017 Moscow, Bolshaya

Ordynka str. 24 (office); Institute of Geochemistry and Analytical Chemistry, 117975 Moscow, Kosygin str. 19, Russian Federation (office). *Telephone:* (499) 949-45-35 (Rosatom) (office); (495) 137-41-47 (Inst.) (office). *Fax:* (499) 949-46-79 (Rosatom) (office); (495) 938-20-54 (Inst.) (office). *E-mail:* info@rosatom.ru (office). *Website:* www.rosatom.ru (office).

MYERS, Allan James, AC, QC, BA, LLB, BCL; Australian business executive, lawyer and university administrator; *Chancellor, University of Melbourne;* b. 17 Oct. 1947, Hamilton, Victoria; s. of John Myers and Betty Myers; m. Maria Josephine Myers; one s. two d.; ed Univ. of Melbourne, Univ. of Oxford; became a lawyer 1971; admitted to Victorian Bar 1975; Asst Prof. of Law, York Univ., Toronto 1972–73; Lecturer in Security and Taxation Law, Univ. of Melbourne 1974–88, Chancellor, Univ. of Melbourne 2017–; owner of Dunkeld Pastoral Co. (farming business) and Royal Mail Hotel, Dunkeld; fmr Asst Ed. Australian Taxation Law Review; Chair., Grattan Inst. 2009–16, Nat. Gallery of Australia 2012–18, Museum and Art Gallery of the NT 2012–; fmr mem. Bd of Trustees, Alfred Felton Bequest, Catholic Educ. Comm., Monivae Coll. Foundation, Florey Inst. of Neuroscience and Mental Health, Ian Potter Foundation (also Gov.), Newman Coll. Foundation; mem. Bd of Dirs Liberty Victoria, Grupa Żywiec, Norinvest Holding; Council mem. The Tax Inst. 1996; Hon. DUniv (Australian Catholic Univ.), Hon. DIur (Univ. of Melbourne); Centenary Medal 2001, Fellow of the Univ. of Melbourne 2015. *Address:* Keating Chambers, 15 Essex Street, London WC2R 3AA, England; 8th Floor, Raymond Priestley Building, University of Melbourne, Melbourne, VIC 3010, Australia (office). *Telephone:* (20) 7544-2600; (3) 9035-5821 (office). *Fax:* (20) 7544-2700; (3) 9347-5904 (office). *E-mail:* amyers@ keatingchambers.com; chancellor@unimelb.edu.au (office). *Website:* keatingchambers.com; unimelb.edu.au (office).

MYERS, Barton, MArch, FAIA; American/Canadian architect, planner and academic; *President, Barton Myers Associates, Inc.;* b. 6 Nov. 1934, Norfolk, Va; s. of Barton Myers and Meeta Myers (née Burrage); m. Victoria George 1959; one d.; ed Norfolk Acad., US Naval Acad. and Univ. of Pennsylvania; Registered Architect in States of Ariz., Calif., Fla, NJ and Va; Partner, A.J. Diamond & Barton Myers, Toronto 1968–75; Founder and Prin. Barton Myers Assocs, Inc., Toronto 1975–86, Barton Myers Assocs, Inc., LA 1981–; Asst Prof. of Architecture Univ. of Toronto 1968–70; mem. Advisory Cttee Nat. Capital Comm., Ottawa 1968–74; Founder and Pres. Bd of Dirs, Trace Magazine 1980–82; Visiting Prof., Harvard Grad. School of Design 1981; Sr Prof., School of Architecture and Urban Design, UCLA 1981–; mem. AIA, Soc. of Architectural Historians, GSA Nat. Register of Peer Professionals; Retired Bd mem. and Lifetime Patron Soc. of Architectural Historians; mem. Pres.'s Circle, US Naval Acad.; Past FRAIC; numerous design awards, including Royal Architectural Inst. of Canada Gold Medal 1994, several AIA awards, including Los Angeles Chapter Gold Medal 2002, USITT Distinguished Achievement Award for Architecture 2009, AIACC Distinguished Practice Award, Theater Design 2011. *Major works by Diamond & Myers Assocs include:* York Square, Toronto; Ont. Medical Asscn, Toronto; Myers & Wolf Residences, Toronto; Housing Union Bldg, Univ. of Alberta Citadel Theatre, Edmonton; Dundas-Sherborne Housing, Toronto. *Major works by Barton Myers Assocs, Inc. include:* Seagram Museum, Waterloo, Ont.; Howard Hughes Center, LA; Wang Tower, LA; Performing Arts Center, Portland, Ore.; Pasadena City Center; Music Center Expansion, LA; CBC Network HQ, Toronto; Cerritos Center for the Performing Arts, Calif.; Woodsworth Coll., Univ. of Toronto; NW Campus Housing, UCLA; Art Gallery of Ont. expansion (competition winner); York Univ. Fine Arts Bldg expansion, Toronto; New Jersey Performing Arts Center, Newark (New Jersey Golden Trowel Award, Int. Masonry Inst., Chicago Athenaeum Award 1998); The Ice House Renovation, Beverly Hills, Calif.; UCSD/Scripps Ocean Atmosphere Research Facility, La Jolla, Calif.; Univ. of New Mexico, Albuquerque (Master Devt Plan); Hall of Justice, Sacramento, Calif. (Historical Preservation Award Calif. Preservation Foundation 2002); House and studio at Toro Canyon, Montecito, Calif. (CCAIA Honor Award in Design 2000, AIA PIA Housing Award for Innovation in Housing Design 2002); 421 South Beverly Drive, Beverly Hills, Calif. (Beverly Hills Architectural Design Award 2002); Tempe Center for the Arts, Tempe, Ariz. (USITT Merit Award 2008) 2006, Montecito Residence (Santa Barbara Independent, Best Custom Home Under 5,000 sq. ft 2010, Gold Nugget Award, Best Residential over $1.5 million 2010) 2009, Dr Phillips Orlando Performing Arts Center, Orlando, Fla 2012. *Publications:* Barton Myers Selected and Current Works (in The Master Architect series) 1994, New Stage for a City (monograph) 1998, Barton Myers: 3 Steel Houses (House Design series) 2004, Barton Myers: Works of Architecture and Urbanism 2019. *Leisure interests:* travel, reading. *Address:* Barton Myers Associates, Inc., 949 Toro Canyon Road, Santa Barbara, CA 93108, USA (office). *Telephone:* (310) 208-2227 (office). *Website:* www .bartonmyers.com (office).

MYERS, (Margaret Jane) Dee Dee, BS; American business executive, consultant and fmr government official; *Executive Vice-President, Worldwide Corporate Communications and Public Affairs, Warner Bros. Entertainment Inc.;* b. 1 Sept. 1961, Quonset Point, RI; d. of Stephen George Myers and Judith Ann Burleigh; m. Todd S. Purdum; two d.; ed Univ. of Santa Clara; Press Asst, Mondale for Pres. Campaign, LA 1984, for Senator Art Torres, LA 1985; Deputy Press Sec. for LA Mayor Tom Bradley 1985–87, for Tom Bradley for Gov. Campaign 1986; Calif. Press Sec., Dukakis for Pres. Campaign, LA 1988; Press Sec., Feinstein for Gov. Campaign, LA and San Francisco 1989–90; Campaign Dir Jordan for Mayor Campaign, San Francisco 1991; Press Sec., Clinton for Pres. Campaign, Little Rock, Ark. 1991–92; Press Sec., The White House, Washington, DC 1993–94; Co-Host Equal Time, CNBC, Washington, DC 1995–97; Contributing Ed. Vanity Fair magazine, Washington, DC 1995–; Founder and Pres. Dee Dee Myers & Associates; Man. Dir The Glover Park Group (communications consultancy) 2010–14; Exec. Vice-Pres. Worldwide Corporate Communications and Public Affairs, Warner Bros. Entertainment Inc. 2014–; mem. Bd Trustees, Calif. State Univ. 1999–2004 (Vice-Chair. 2000–01); consultant to NBC TV drama The West Wing; Robert F. Kennedy Award, Emerson Coll., Boston 1993. *Film:* Contact 1997. *Publication:* Why Women Should Rule the World 2008. *Leisure interests:* running, cycling, music, major league baseball. *Address:* Warner Bros. Entertainment Inc., 4000 Warner Blvd, Burbank, CA 91522, USA. *Telephone:* (818) 954-6000 (office). *Website:* www.warnerbros.com (office).

MYERS, Mike; Canadian actor and writer; b. 25 May 1963, Toronto, Ont.; s. of Eric Myers and Bunny (née Hind) Myers; m. Robin Ruzan 1993 (divorced 2005); Canadian Comedy Award 2000. *Stage appearances:* The Second City, Toronto 1986–88, Chicago 1988–89; actor and writer: Mullarkey & Myers 1984–86. *Television includes:* John and Yoko (TV film) 1985, Saturday Night Live 1989–94 (Emmy Award for Outstanding Writing in a Comedy or Variety Series 1989), Russell Gilbert Show 1998, Dir The Bacchae (TV Film) 1999. *Films:* Wayne's World 1992, So I Married an Axe Murderer 1992, Wayne's World II 1993, Austin Powers: International Man of Mystery 1997, Meteor 1998, McClintock's Peach 1998, Just Like Me 1998, It's A Dog's Life 1998, 54 1998, Austin Powers: The Spy Who Shagged Me 1998, Pete's Meteor 1999, Shrek (voice) 2001, Austin Powers in Goldmember 2002, View from the Top 2003, Shrek 4–D (voice) 2003, Nobody Knows Anything 2003, Cat in the Hat 2003, Shrek 2 (voice) 2004, Shrek the Third (voice) 2007, The Love Guru 2008, Inglourious Basterds 2009, Shrek Forever After (voice) 2010. *Address:* c/o David O'Connor, Creative Artists Agency, 9830 Wilshire Boulevard, Beverly Hills, CA 90212, USA.

MYERS, Norman, CMG, BA, MA, PhD, FLS, FRSA; British scientist; *Fellow, Green College, Oxford;* b. 24 Aug. 1934, Whitewell, Yorks., England; s. of John Myers and Gladys Myers (née Haworth); m. Dorothy Mary Halliman 1965 (separated 1992); two d.; ed Clitheroe Royal Grammar School, Lancs., Keble Coll., Oxford, Univ. of California, Berkeley, USA; Dist Officer, Kenya Admin 1958–61; taught French and English at Delamere School for Boys, Nairobi 1961–65; freelance author and journalist, professional photographer, lecturer and broadcaster on African wildlife 1966–69; ind. scientist and consultant in Environment and Devt with focus on the tropics 1972–; has worked for many int. orgs and govt agencies; Man. Dir Norman Myers Scientific Consultancy Ltd 1982–; mem. Editorial Bd Global Environmental Change, Biodiversity and Conservation, Ecological Economics, The Environmentalist, Environmental Conservation; Environment, Development and Sustainability; Ecoscience, World Forest Resource Management, Forest Ecology and Management, Futures; Fellow, Green Coll. Oxford 2000–; Adjunct Prof. of Environmental Science, Nicholas School of the Environment, Duke Univ., USA; fmr Charles M. and Martha Hitchcock Prof., Univ. of Califonia, Berkeley; Visiting Prof., Harvard Univ., Cornell Univ., Stanford Univ.; Amb. to World Wide Fund (WWF) for Nature UK; Foreign Assoc., NAS; mem. American Asscn of Environmental and Resource Economists, American Inst. of Biological Sciences, WTO High Level Advisory Group; Fellow, AAAS, World Acad. of Art and Science; Hon. Visiting Fellow, Green Coll., Oxford; Order of the Golden Ark (Netherlands) 1983, Kt of the Golden Ark (Netherlands) 1992; hon. science degree (Univ. of Kent) 2003; Gold Medal, WWF Int. 1983, Gold Medal, New York Zoological Soc. (now the Wildlife Conservation Soc.) 1986, Volvo Environment Prize 1992, UNEP Sasakawa Environment Prize 1995, Blue Planet Prize 2001 (one of only two people world-wide to receive all three leading environmental prizes), Pew Fellow in Environment, Liveable City Award, City of London, Haas Int. Alumnus Award, Univ. of California, Berkeley. *Publications include:* The Long African Day 1972, The Sinking Ark (five scientific/literary awards) 1979, Conversion of Tropical Moist Forests (report to NAS) 1980, A Wealth of Wild Species (four book clubs and two science awards) 1983, The Primary Source: Tropical Forests and Our Future 1984, Economics of Ecosystem Management (co-ed.) 1985, The Gaia Atlas of Planet Management 1985, The Gaia Atlas of Future Worlds: Challenge and Opportunity in an Age of Change 1990, Population, Resources and the Environment: The Critical Challenges (for UN Population Fund) 1991, Tropical Forests and Climate (ed.) 1992, Ultimate Security: The Environmental Basis of Political Stability 1993, Scarcity or Abundance: A Debate on the Environment (co-author) 1994, Environmental Exodus: An Emergent Crisis in the Global Arena (co-author) 1995, Perverse Subsidies (co-author) 1998, Hotspots: Earth's Biologically Richest and Most Endangered Terrestrial Ecoregions (co-author) 1999, Towards a New Green Print for Business and Society (in Japanese) 1999, Perverse Subsidies: How Tax Dollars Undercut the Environment and the Economy (co-author) 2001, New Consumers: The Influence of Affluence on the Environment (co-author) 2004, The New Gaia Atlas of Planet Management (co-author) 2005, Institutional Roadblocks: Why Policy Processes Often Fail to Deliver (co-author) 2008; more than 300 scientific papers in professional journals on ecology, conservation biology, energy, population growth, environmental policy, environmental sociology and anthropology. *Leisure interests:* marathon running, mountaineering, professional photography.

MYERS, Gen. (retd) Richard B., BS, MBA; American air force officer (retd), business executive and academic; *Colin L. Powell Chair for National Security, Leadership, Character and Ethics, National Defense University; President, Kansas State University;* b. 1 March 1942, Kansas City, Mo.; m.; two d. one s.; ed Kansas State Univ., Auburn Univ., Air Command/Staff Coll., Ala, US Army War Coll., Pa and Harvard Univ.; commissioned 2nd Lt, USAF 1965; fighter pilot, Vietnam 1969; various assignments to Commdr US Forces, Japan and 5th Air Force, Yakota Air Base, Japan 1993–96; Asst to Chair. Jt Chiefs of Staff, The Pentagon, 1996–97; rank of Gen. 1997; Commdr Pacific Air Forces, Hickam Air Force Base, Hawaii 1997–98; C-in-C N American Aerospace Defense Command/US Space Command, Peterson Air Force Base, Colo 1998–2000; Vice-Chair. Jt Chiefs of Staff 2000–01, Chair. 2001–05 (retd); fmr mem. NATO Mil. Cttee; Colin L. Powell Chair for Nat. Security, Leadership, Character and Ethics, Nat. Defense Univ., Washington, DC 2006–; Foundation Prof. of Mil. History, Kansas State Univ. (part-time) 2006–, Pres. 2016–; Chair. Bd of Govs United Service Org.; currently Chair. Bd of Trustees Medisend Coll. of Biomedical Eng Tech., Gen. Richard B. Myers Veterans Program; mem. Bd of Dirs Northrop Grumman Corpn 2006–, Aon Corpn 2006–, Deere & Co. 2006–, United Technologies Corpn 2006–, Rivada Networks, MRI Global; mem. Defense Health Bd-Fed. Advisory Cttee to the Sec. of Defense, Office of the Sec. of Defense Policy Bd; Defense Distinguished Service Medal with Oak Leaf Cluster, Distinguished Service Medal, Legion of Merit, Distinguished Flying Cross with Oak Leaf Cluster, Meritorious Service Medal with Three Oak Leaf Clusters, Air Medal with 18 Oak Leaf Clusters, Air Force Commendation Medal, Presidential Medal of Freedom 2005. *Publications:* Eyes on the Horizon: Serving on the Front Lines of National Security 2009. *Address:* Institute for National Security Ethics and Leadership, National Defense University, 300 5th Avenue SW, Fort Lesley J. McNair, Washington, DC 20319 (office); Office of the President, Kansas State University, 110 Anderson Hall, Manhattan, KS 66506, USA (office). *Telephone:* (785) 532-6221 (Kansas) (office). *Fax:* (785) 532-7639 (Kansas) (office).

E-mail: insel@ndu.edu (office). *Website:* www.ndu.edu/INSEL (office); www.generalrichardmyers.com; www.k-state.edu (office).

MYERSON, Roger B., AB, SM, PhD; American economist and academic; *Glen A. Lloyd Distinguished Service Professor of Economics, University of Chicago;* b. 29 March 1951, Boston, Mass; m. Regina Weber Myerson; two c.; ed Harvard Univ.; Asst Prof. of Managerial Econs and Decision Sciences, Northwestern Univ. 1976–79, Assoc. Prof. 1979–82, Prof. 1982–2001; Visiting Researcher, Universität Bielefeld, Germany 1978–79; Visiting Prof. of Econs, Univ. of Chicago 1985–86, 2000–01, Prof. of Econs 2001–07, Glen A. Lloyd Distinguished Service Prof. of Econs 2007–; Assoc. Ed. Journal of Economic Theory 1983–93; mem. Editorial Bd International Journal of Game Theory 1982–92, Games and Economic Behavior 1989–97; Fellow, Econometric Soc. 1983, American Acad. of Arts and Sciences 1993, NAS 2009; Dr hc (Universität Basel, Switzerland) 2002; Nobel Prize in Econs (with Leo Hurwicz and Eric S. Maskin) 2007. *Publications:* Game Theory: Analysis of Conflict 1991, Probability Models for Economic Decisions 2005; more than 80 articles in academic journals. *Address:* Department of Economics, University of Chicago, 1126 East 59th Street, Chicago, IL 60637, USA (office). *Telephone:* (773) 834-9071 (office). *Fax:* (773) 702-8490 (office). *Website:* home.uchicago.edu/rmyerson (office).

MYHRVOLD, Nathan P., BSc, MSc, MA, PhD; American business executive; *Founder and CEO, Intellectual Ventures;* b. 3 Aug. 1959, Seattle, Wash.; ed Univ. of California, Los Angeles, Princeton Univ., Santa Monica Coll., Calif.; Postdoctoral Fellow, Dept of Applied Math. and Theoretical Physics, Univ. of Cambridge, UK 1983–84, worked with Prof. Stephen Hawking on research in cosmology, quantum field theory in curved space-time and quantum theories of gravitation; left Cambridge to co-found Dynamical Systems Research Inc., Oakland, Calif. to produce Mondrian (clone of IBM's TopView multitasking environment for DOS), co. acquired by Microsoft 1986; with Microsoft Corpn 1986–2000, held various positions within co., f. Microsoft Research 1991 and numerous tech. groups, rose to become Chief Strategist and Chief Tech. Officer; Founder and CEO Intellectual Ventures (patent portfolio developer and broker) 2000, holds large number of patents in areas of tech. and energy; Founder Modernist Cuisine 2005–; mem. Advisory Bd, Dept of Physics, Univ. of Washington, Museum of the Rockies, Montana State Univ.; Affiliate Research Assoc. of Paleontology, Museum of the Rockies, Bozeman, Mont., funds and participates in palaeontological research and yearly expeditions; mem. United Way's Million Dollar Roundtable, USA Science and Eng Festival's Advisory Bd; worked for two years as a stagier at Rover's French restaurant, Seattle, completed culinary training with chef Anne Willan at Ecole De La Varenne; has worked as Chief Gastronomic Officer for Zagat Survey (publr of Zagat restaurant guide books); mem. Bd of Trustees, Nat. Museum of Science and Industry, London; Sheffield Fellow, Yale Univ. 1998; Dr hc (Culinary Inst. of America) 2011; Hertz Foundation Fellowship for grad. study 1984, Golden Plate Award, American Acad. of Achievement 1996, Santa Monica High School Hall of Fame 1997, Software Forum Visionary Award 1998, James Madison Medal, Princeton Univ. 2005, named by Foreign Policy magazine to its list of top global thinkers 2010, Cookbook Award, Int. Asscn of Culinary Professionals 2012, James Beard Award 2012. *Achievements include:* master French chef who competed on team that won first place in several categories at World Championship of Barbecue, Memphis, Tenn. 1991. *Publications:* America 24/7 2003, Washington 24/7 2003 (wildlife photography), Modernist Cuisine: The Art and Science of Cooking 2011, Modernist Cuisine: at Home 2012, The Photography of Modernist Cuisine 2013; research has been published in scientific journals including Science, Nature, Paleobiology, Journal of Vertebrate Paleontology and the Physical Review; contrib. of articles to magazines including Harvard Business Review, The Wall Street Journal, Fortune, Time and National Geographic Traveler. *Leisure interests:* nature and wildlife photography, cuisine. *Address:* Intellectual Ventures, 3150 139th Avenue SE, Building 4, Bellevue, WA 98005, USA (office). *Telephone:* (425) 467-2300 (office). *E-mail:* info@intven.com (office). *Website:* www.intellectualventures.com (office); www.modernistcuisine.com; www.nathanmyhrvold.com.

MYINT, Ohn; Myanma politician and fmr army officer; m. Nu Nu Swe; two c.; served in Myanmar Armed Forces (Tatmadaw) –2010, including as Northern Command Commdr, Coastal Region Command Commdr, Head of Tatmadaw Bureau of Special Operations-6; left army 2010 with rank of Lt-Gen.; mem. State Peace and Devt Council (mil. junta), SPDC official for Kachin State; mem. Pyithu Hluttaw (Parl.) for Hpakant Township 2010–11; Minister for Cooperatives 2011–12, of Livestock and Fisheries 2011–16; mem. Union Solidarity and Devt Party (USDP). *Address:* Union Solidarity and Development Party, Plot 5, Yazathingaha Road, Dekkhinathiri Township, Nay Pyi Taw, Myanmar (office). *Website:* www.usda.org.mm (office).

MYINT MAUNG, U; Myanma diplomatist and administrator; b. 10 March 1921, Magwe; m.; three c.; ed Univ. of Rangoon; joined Army 1942; has held the following positions: Head of Co-operative Dept; Chief of Admin. Div. of Burma Socialist Programme Party, also mem. Party Inspection Cttee; mem. Pyithu Hluttaw (People's Congress) for Magwe Constituency; mem. Bd of Dirs People's Bank of the Union of Burma, Exec. Cttee of Burma Sports and Physical Fitness Cttee, Cen. Cttee of Burma Red Cross Soc.; Chair. Resettlement Cttee of Cen. Security and Admin. Cttee, Independence Award Cttee; Amb. and Perm. Rep. to UN, New York 1975–77; Minister of Foreign Affairs 1977–79; Amb. to China –1989; mem. State Council and Attorney-Gen. 1988.

MYNERS, Baron (Life Peer), cr. 2008, of Truro in the County of Cornwall; **Paul Myners,** CBE, FRSA; British publishing executive and government official; b. 1 April 1948, adopted by a Cornish family; m. Alison Macleod; one s. four d.; ed Univ. of London; teacher with Inner London Educ. Authority 1971–72; finance writer, Daily Telegraph 1972–75; with N. M. Rothschild (merchant bank) 1974–85; CEO Gartmore Investment Man. 1985–87, Chair. 1987–2001; Deputy Chair. Powergen 1999–2001; Exec. Dir Nat. Westminster Bank 1999–2000; Chair. Guardian Media Group 2001–08, also Publisher The Guardian and The Observer newspapers; Financial Services Sec. and Minister for the City, HM Treasury 2008–10, also Govt Spokesperson for HM Treasury in House of Lords, Chair. All Party Parl. Group on Corp. Governance 2010; mem. Financial Reporting Council 1995–2004, Company Law Review Consultative Cttee 1998–2000; Court of Dirs of Bank of England 2004–08; fmr Chair. Low Pay Comm.; Chair. Aspen Insurance Holdings, Bermuda

2002–07, Liberty Ermitage 2006–08, Autonomous Research LLP 2011– (also Partner), Cevian Capital (UK) LLP 2011– (also Partner), Platform Acquisition Holdings Ltd 2013–; Chair. Court of Govs and of Council, LSE 2015–; mem. Bd of Dirs (non-exec.), mmO2 2001, Bank of New York, Marks & Spencer 2002 (interim Chair. 2004–06); Dir RIT Capital Partners PLC 2010–, OJSC MegaFon 2013–; Sr Ind. Dir Co-operative Group (resgnd Labour Whip in House of Lords and is non-affiliated) 2013–14 (resgnd); Chair. Tate Galleries –2009; Pres. Howard League for Penal Reform 2012–; Visiting Fellow, Nuffield Coll., Oxford; Exec. Fellow, London Business School; mem. Royal Acad. Trust, United Response; Trustee, ARK (charity); Hon. Fellow, Asscn of Corp. Treasurers 2010; Dr hc (Univ. of Exeter) 2008. *Leisure interest:* London Symphony Orchestra. *Address:* House of Lords, Westminster, London, SW1A 0PW, England (office). *Telephone:* (20) 7219-5353 (office); (20) 7219-5979 (office).

MYRADOV, Gochmyrad; Turkmenistani economist, banker and politician; *Deputy Chairman of the Government;* b. 1973, Gypjak, Aşgabat Velayat (now in Ahal Velayat), Turkmen SSR, USSR; ed Turkmen State Inst. of Econs and Man.; began his career as teacher, Dept of Monetary Circulation and Credit, Turkmen State Inst. of Econs and Man. 1995–96; Expert, later Deputy Chief Accountant and Chief Accountant, Türkmenbaşi Bank (state commercial bank) 1996–2003; Deputy Chief Accountant and Head of Div., Central Bank of Turkmenistan (Türkmenis-tanyň Merkezi Banky) 2003, Deputy Chair. and Head of Operations 2003–06, First Deputy Chair. 2006–12, Chair. 2014–15; Chair., Türkmenbank—State Commer-cial Bank 'Türkmenistan' 2012–14; Head of Finance Dept for Industry, Transport and Communications, Ministry of Finance 2015–17, Deputy Minister of Finance June–July 2017, Minister of Finance July–Oct. 2017; Deputy Chair. of the Govt, responsible for Econ. Affairs, Banks and Int. Financial Orgs 2017–; Magtymguly Pyragy Medal. *Address:* Office of the President and the Council of Ministers, 744004 Aşgabat, Galkynyş köç. 20, Turkmenistan (office). *Telephone:* (12) 35-45-34 (office). *Fax:* (12) 35-51-12 (office). *E-mail:* nt@online.tm (office). *Website:* www.turkmenistan.gov.tm (office).

MYRATGULYEV, Amandurdy; Turkmenistani government official; Head of Main State Tax Service 2004–05; Deputy Prime Minister and Minister of the Economy and Finance 2005–07.

MYRDAL, Jan; Swedish writer; b. 19 July 1927, Stockholm; s. of Gunnar Myrdal and Alva Reimer; m. 1st Nadja Wiking 1948; m. 2nd Maj Lidberg 1953; m. 3rd Gun Kessle 1956 (died 2007); m. 4th Andrea Gaytan Vega 2008; one s. one d.; some hundred titles mainly in Swedish but also in English translated into some 30 languages: fiction, autobiog., travel, politics, art and literary criticism; as columnist (politics, culture), Stockholms-Tidningen 1963–66, Aftonbladet 1966–72; Chair. and Publr Folket i Bild/Kulturfront 1971–72, columnist 1972–; Hon. DLit (Upsala Coll.) 1980; Dr hc (Nankai Univ.) 1993. *Works include:* films: Myglaren 1966, Hjalparen 1968, Balzac or The Triumphs of Realism 1975, Mexico: Art and Revolution 1991; TV documentaries: Democratic Kampuchea 1978–79, Guerilla Base Area of Democratic Kampuchea 1979, China 1979, 20 films on history of political caricature and posters 1975–87. *Publications include:* (in Swedish) novels: Hemkomst 1954, Jubelvår 1955, Att bli och vara 1956, Badrumskranen 1957, Karriär 1975, Barndom 1982, En annan värld 1984; drama: Folkets Hus 1953, Moraliteter 1967, Garderingar 1969, B. Olsen 1972; travel: Resa i Afghanistan 1960, Bortom berg och öknar 1962, Turkmenistan 1966, Sidenvägen 1977, Indien väntar 1980; politics: Kina: Revolutionen går vidare 1970, Kina efter Mao Tse-tung 1977, Kampuchea och kriget 1978, Kampuchea hösten 1979, Den albanska utmaningen 1968–86, 1987, Mexico, Dröm och längtan 1996; essays: Söndagsmorgon 1965, Skriftställning 1968, Klartexter 1978, Skriftställning X 1978, Balzac und der Realismus (in German) 1978, Strindberg och Balzac 1981, Ord och Avsikt 1986, Det nya Stor, Tyskland 1992, När Västerlandet trädde fram 1992, När morgondagarna sjöng 1994, En fest i Liu Lin 1994, När morgondagarna sjöng 1994, Rölvag as an example 1995, Maj, en kärlek 1998, Om vin 1999, Gubbsjuka 2002, Meccano 2005, Sälja krig som margarin 2005; autobiography: Rescontra 1962, Samtida bekännelser 1964, Inför nedräkningen 1993, När morgondagarna sjöng 1994, En kärlek 1998, Maj: En kärlek 1998; art: Ansikte av sten, Angkor 1968, Ondskan tar form 1976, Dussinet fullt 1981, Den trettonde 1983, Franska revolutionens bilder 1989, 5 ar av frihet 1830–35 1991, När Västerlandet tradde fram 1992, André Gill 1995, Drömmen om det goda samhallet; Kinesiska affischer 1966–1976 1996; biography: August Strindberg and Ole Edvart Roelvag 1997, Johan August Strindberg 2000; (in English) Report from a Chinese Village 1965, Chinese Journey 1965, Confessions of a Disloyal European 1968, Angkor: an essay on art and imperialism 1970, Gates to Asia 1971, Albania Defiant 1976, The Silk Road 1979, China Notebook 1975–78 1979, Return to a Chinese Village 1984, India Waits 1984, Childhood 1991, Another World 1993, 12 Going on 13 1995, Red Star over India, As the Wretched of the Earth Are Rising 2012. *Leisure interests:* collecting Meccano, organizing the 50,000 vols of the Jan Myrdal Library of the Jan Myrdal Asscn. *Address:* Snidaregatan 20, 432 43 Varberg, Sweden. *Telephone:* 76-2181547 (mobile). *E-mail:* myrdal@myrdal.pp.se.

MYRZAKMATOV, Melisbek Jooshbayevich; Kyrgyzstani politician; *Leader, Uluttar Birimdigi Eldik Partiyasy (Unity of Ethnicities People's Party);* b. 18 April 1969, Papan village, Kara-Suu dist, Osh Oblast, Kyrgyz SSR, USSR; ed Osh Technological Univ.; began working as Insp., State Tax Inspectorate, Osh 1996; Deputy Dir for Commerce, Koopsnab Co. 1997–99; Pres. Eldik (charitable foundation) 2004–07; Dir Osh migrant service 2007; Deputy to Supreme Council (Jogorku Kenesh) for Ak Jol (Bright Road) party 2007–09; Acting Mayor then Mayor of Osh 2009–13 (dismissed), defeated in subsequent mayoral election Jan. 2014; Owner of Oomat Market (more than 1,500 traders) in Kara-Suu; Dir Yug Keramzitstroi brick factory and other construction materials cos; began construc-tion of Taatan-Osh trading centre (4,000 workplaces); Leader, Uluttar Birimdigi Eldik Partiyasy (Uluttar Birimdigi) (Unity of Ethnicities People's Party); where-abouts unknown when warrant for his arrest issued by state prosecutor on charges of abuse of office Nov. 2014; Hero of the Kyrgyz People Award 2010. *Address:* c/o Office of the Mayor, 732500 Osh, Lenina 221, Kyrgyzstan. *Website:* www.facebook.com/uluttarbirimdigi.

MYSEN, Bjorn O., BSc, MA, PhD; American (b. Norwegian) research scientist; *Senior Staff Scientist, Geophysical Laboratory, Carnegie Institution of Washing-ton;* b. 20 Dec. 1947, Oslo, Norway; s. of Martin Mysen and Randi Mysen; m.

Susanna Laya 1975; two c.; ed Univ. of Oslo, Pennsylvania State Univ.; Carnegie Foundation Fellow 1974–77; Sr Staff Scientist, Experimental Geochemist, Carnegie Inst., Washington, DC 1977–; Visiting Scientist, Bayerisches Geoin-stitut, Germany 1988; Research Assoc., CNRS-Orléans, France 1994; Visiting Prof., Institut de Physique du Globe, Paris, France 2001, 2004, Inst. for Study of the Earth's Interior, Univ. of Okayama at Misasa, Japan 2006–09; mem. Royal Norwegian Acad. of Science and Letters 1985; Fellow, Mineralogy Soc. of America 1991; Geochemistry Fellow, Geochemical Soc. 2008, European Geochemical Soc. 2008, Japan Geoscience Union 2017; F.W. Clarke Medal 1977, Reusch Medal 1978, ISI Highly Cited 2001, George W. Morey Award, American Ceramical Soc. 2006. *Publications:* Structure and Properties of Silicate Melts 1988, Silicate Glasses and Melts – Properties and Structure 2005; seven edited books and more than 270 other peer-reviewed scientific publs. *Address:* Geophysical Laboratory, Carnegie Institution of Washington, 5251 Broad Branch Road NW, Washington, DC 20015, USA (office). *Telephone:* (202) 478-8975 (office). *Fax:* (202) 478-8901 (office). *E-mail:* bmysen@carnegiescience.edu (office). *Website:* legacy.gl.ciw.edu/static/users/bmysen/MysenB/Research_Interests_&_CV.html (office).

MYŚLIWSKI, Wiesław; Polish writer; b. 25 March 1932, Dwikozy, nr Sando-mierz; m. Wacława Stec; one s.; ed Catholic Univ. of Lublin; worked at People's Publishing Cooperative until 1976, Ed., quarterly magazine Regiony 1975–99; Ed., fortnightly Sycyna 1994–99; numerous awards include Stanisław Piętak Prize 1968, 1973, Prize of Ministry of Culture and Art 1971, State Prize 1985, Władysław S. Reymont Prize 1997, Alfred Jurzykowski Foundation Award, New York 1998, Bogumił S. Linde Prize, Toruń-Göttingen, Polish Culture Foundation Gold Sceptre Prize 2011. *Publications include:* novels: Nagi sad (Naked Orchard) 1967, Pałac (Palace) 1970 (screenplay 1980), Kamień na kamieniu (Stone upon Stone) (Best Translated Book Award – with Bill Johnston, USA 2012) 1984, Widnokrąg (Horizon) (Nike Literary Prize 1997) 1996, Traktat o łuskaniu fasoli (Treatise on Shelling Beans) (Nike Literary Prize, Gdynia Literary Prize 2007, Grand Prix Littéraire de St Emilion, France 2011) 2006, Ostatnie rozdanie (Final Deal) 2013; screenplays: Przez dziewięć mostów (Across Nine Bridges) 1972, Klucznik (Steward) (TV) 1979, Droga (The Road) (TV) 1981, Kamień na kamieniu (Stone upon Stone) 1995; plays: Złodziej (Thief) 1973, Klucznik (Steward) 1978, Drzewo (Tree) 1988, Requiem dla gospodyni (Requiem for the Housewife) 2000. *Address:* ul. Nowoursynowska 119C, 02-797 Warsaw, Poland (home).

MYTTON, Graham Lambert, PhD, FRSA, MMRS; British consultant; b. 21 Oct. 1942, Sanderstead, Croydon; s. of Peter Mytton and Joan Jackson; m. Janet Codd 1966; two d.; ed Trinity School, Croydon, Purley Grammar School and Univs of Liverpool, Manchester and Dar es Salaam; Man. BBC Radio studio 1964–66; Research Fellow, Zambia Broadcasting 1970–73; radio producer, BBC African Service 1973–75; current affairs producer, BBC Radio Four 1976; Head, Hausa Language Section, BBC African Service 1976–82; Head, Int. Broadcasting Audience Research, BBC World Service 1982–91, Head, Audience Research and Correspondence 1991–96, Controller, Marketing 1996–98; ind. consultant and trainer in audience, opinion and market research 1998–; Dir Intermedia, Washington, DC 2001–10; Chair. InterMedia UK 2009–12; AT&T Guest Lecturer, George Washington Univ. 1995; Faculty mem., Oxford Centre for Mission Studies 2000–; various training and research projects with UNICEF, Internews, BBC Media Action, Thomson Foundation, Fondation Hirondelle, Press Now, Press Unlimited, OSCE, UN Office for the Coordination of Humanitarian Affairs and other agencies and businesses 2000–; External Examiner, Univ. of Westminster and others; Hon. Fellow, Bangladesh Marketing and Social Research Soc. 2011; Silver Medal, Market Research Soc. 1997, Wally Langschmidt Memorial Lecturer, SABC, Johannesburg 1999, Piet Smit PAMRO Achiever of the Year Award 2012. *Publications include:* Mass Communications in Africa 1983, Global Audiences (ed.) 1993, Handbook on Radio and TV Audience Research 1993, 1999, Manuel de recherche sur l'audience de la radio et de la télévision 2000, Media Audience Research 2016, Media Audience Research: A Guide for Professionals 2016; several articles in academic journals on audience research, broadcasting and devt issues. *Leisure interests:* stamp collecting, singing, bird watching, jazz. *Address:* Roffeys, Coldharbour, Dorking, Surrey, RH5 6HE, England (office). *Telephone:* (1306) 712122 (office). *Fax:* (1306) 712958 (office). *E-mail:* gmytton@gn.apc.org (office).

MZEMBI, Walter, PhD; Zimbabwean engineer and politician; b. 16 March 1964; m. Barbra Hernandes Mzembi; seven c.; ed Northern Tech. Coll., Zambia, Univ. Azteca, Mexico, Aldersgate Univ. Coll., Philippines; Inspector of Mines, Govt of Zimbabwe 1988–89; Area Man., Total Zimbabwe Management Devt Programme 1990–97; Divisional Engineer, Mitchell Cotts Engineering (mining co.) 1991–94; Gen. Man., Stewarts and Lloyds (water eng co.) 1994–97; Marketing Dir, Agro-Venture (agro industry co.) 1998–2000; mem. House of Ass. (parl.) for Masvingo South Constituency 2004–; Deputy Minister of Water Resources and Devt 2006–08, Minister of Tourism & Hospitality Industry 2009–17, Minister of Foreign Affairs Oct.–Nov. 2017; mem. Exec. Council, UN World Tourism Org. (UNWTO) 2009–13, Chair., UNWTO Regional Comm. for Africa 2013–17; Pres. Africa Travel Asscn (three terms); mem. Zimbabwe African Nat. Union—Patriotic Front (ZANU—PF); Fellow, Zimbabwe Inst. of Engineers 2011, Eng Inst. of Zambia 2011; African Investor Tourism Investment Awards African Tourism Minister of the Year 2011, African Investor Tourism Investment Awards Lifetime Achieve-ment Award 2016. *Address:* c/o Ministry of Foreign Affairs, Munhumutapa Bldg, cnr Samora Machel Ave and Sam Nujoma St, POB 4240, Causeway, Harare, Zimbabwe (office).

MZIMELA, Sizakele (Siza) Petunia, BA; South African business executive; *Independent Non-executive Chairman, Cargo Carriers Ltd;* b. 1967; m.; two c.; ed Univ. of Swaziland, Gordon Inst. of Business Science; worked in Small Business and Retail Div., Standard Bank 1991–94; Corp. Planning Analyst, Total SA 1994–96; Research Analyst, South African Airways (Pty) Ltd 1996, later Man. Market Devt, Sr Man., Alliances, Regional Gen. Man. Africa and the Middle East 2000–01, Exec. Vice-Pres. for Global Passenger Services 2001–02, for Global Sales and Voyager 2002–03, CEO South African Airways 2010–12, CEO South African Express Airways 2003–10; mem. Bd of Dirs Cargo Carriers Ltd 2008–, Ind. Non-exec. Chair. 2015–; mem. Bd of Dirs Ansys Ltd 2013–. *Address:* Cargo Carriers Ltd, 11a Grace Road, Mountain View, Observatory 2198, Johannesburg, South Africa (office). *Website:* www.cargocarriers.co.za (office).

N

NA-RANONG, Kittiratt, BEcons, MBA; Thai financial services industry executive and government official; b. 3 Aug. 1958; ed Assumption Coll., Chulalongkorn Univ., Sasin Graduate Inst. of Business Admin; began career in corp. lending div., Thai Farmers' Bank (now Kasikorn Bank); worked in trading, research and asset man. divs of Securities One (broker), Bangkok 1987; sr roles in several securities firms, including Exec. Dir and Chief Investment Officer, Univentures Pcl, Chair. Cathay Asset Management Co. Ltd, Pres. First Asia Securities Pcl, Pres. One Asset Management Ltd; Pres. Stock Exchange of Thailand 2001–06; Deputy Dir for Academic Affairs, Sasin Graduate Inst. of Business Admin, Chulalongkorn Univ. 2006–10; Chancellor Shinawatra Univ. 2010–11; Deputy Prime Minister and Minister of Commerce 2011–12, Deputy Prime Minister and Minister of Finance 2012–14; Vice-Chair. High-Level Experts and Leaders Panel on Water and Disasters; Pres. Thailand Chess Asscn; fmr Chair. Nat. Econs Research Council; managed Thai nat. football team for Asian Cup 2007; Dir Mass Rapid Transit Authority of Thailand, State Enterprises Capital Policy Cttee, Vayupak Fund Cttee; Knight Grand Cordon (First Class), Most Noble Order of the Crown of Thailand 2011. *Address:* Thailand Chess Association, Chalerm Prakiat Building, 20th Floor, Sports Authority of Thailand, No. 286, Ramkhamhaeng Road, Hua Mark Sub-District, Bangkapi District, Bangkok 10240, Thailand. *E-mail:* kittirattn@gmail.com.

NÄÄTÄNEN, Risto Kalervo, PhD; Finnish psychologist and academic; *Professor of Cognitive Neuroscience, University of Tartu;* b. 14 June 1939, Helsinki; s. of Prof. Esko K. Näätänen and Rauni Näätänen (née Raudanjoki); m. Marjatta Kerola 1960; three s.; ed Univ. of Helsinki; Asst Dept of Psychology, Univ. of Helsinki 1965–69, Prof. of Psychology 1975–98, Dir Cognitive Brain Research Unit 1991–2006, Brain Research Centre 2001–07 (retd); Researcher, Acad. of Finland 1969–75, Research Prof. 1983–95, Acad. Prof. 1995–2007; Prof. of Cognitive Neuroscience, Univ. of Tartu, Estonia 2007–;Visiting Prof., Århus Univ., Denmark 2008–14; Scientific Organizer (with Prof. G. Rizzolatti) of European Science Foundation Winter School 1990; Fellowships, Dept of Psychology, UCLA, USA 1965–66, Univ. of Dundee, UK 1979–80, Univ. of Marburg, Germany 1980–81, Neurosciences Inst., New York 1985–86, Inst. for Advanced Study, Berlin 1988–89; Vice-Pres. Fed. of European Psychophysiology 1994–96, Pres. 1996–2000; mem. Brain Research Soc. of Finland (Pres. 1983–91), Int. Brain Research Org. (mem. Governing Council 1985–91), Nordic Psychophysiology Soc. (Pres. 1992–95), Advisory Council, Int. Asscn for the Study of Attention and Performance; Fellow, World Innovation Foundation 2005, Asscn for Psychological Science 2011; mem. Finnish Acad. of Science and Letters 1980–, Academia Europaea 1991– (mem. Council 2000–); Foreign mem. Russian Acad. of Sciences 1994–, Royal Swedish Acad. of Sciences 2008–; Kt (First Class), Order of the White Rose of Finland, Commdr, Order of the Lion of Finland 2012; Dr hc (Jyväskylä) 2000, (Tartu) 2000, (Barcelona) 2007, (St Petersburg) 2008, (Helsinki) 2010; Purkinje Medal (Prague) 1988, Finnish Cultural Foundation Prize 1990, State Traffic Safety Medal 1992, Distinguished Contributions Award, Soc. of Psychophysiological Research, Washington, DC 1995, First Science Prize (Finland) 1997, 20th Anniversary Award, Int. Soc. of Psychophysiology, Montreal, Canada 2002, Grand Medal of Univ. of Tartu 2010, Main Scientific Prize, Finnish Acad. of Science and Letters 2011, Golden Medal, Finnish Psychological Asscn 2012. *Publications:* Selective Attention and Evoked Potentials 1967, Road-User Behaviour and Traffic Accidents (with H. Summala) 1976, Attention and Brain Function 1992, The Orienting Response in Information Processing (with E.N. Sokolov, J.A. Spinks & H. Lyytinen); numerous articles. *Leisure interests:* sports, the Green Movement, traffic safety. *Address:* Institute of Psychology, University of Tartu, Näituse 2, Room 211, 50409 Tartu, Estonia (office); Mäkipellontie 12 D, 00320 Helsinki, Finland (home). *E-mail:* risto.naatanen@ut.ee (office); risto.naatanen@helsinki.fi. *Website:* www.psychology.ut.ee (office).

NABARRO, David, BA, MA, MSc, CBE, FRCP; British physician, public health official and UN official; *Special Adviser to the Secretary-General on 2030 Agenda for Sustainable Development, United Nations;* b. 26 Aug. 1949, London; s. of Sir John David Nunes Nabarro and Lady Joan Nabarro; m. Gillian Frances Holmes 2002; one s. one d.; two s. one d. from previous relationship; ed Worcester Coll., Oxford, Univ. Coll. Hosp., Univ. of London; qualified as physician 1973; began career as Medical Officer, Save the Children Fund, later postings include Relief Expedition, N Iraq 1974–75, Dist Medical Officer, Dhankuta, E Nepal 1977–79, Regional Medical Adviser, S Asia, Kathmandu, Nepal 1982–85; House Officer, later Sr House Officer with Nat. Health Service 1975–77; Lecturer in Nutrition and Public Health, London Univ. 1980–82; Sr Lecturer in Int. Health, Liverpool Univ. Medical School 1985–89, also Hon. Consultant, Mersey Regional Health Authority; Regional Health and Population Adviser, E Africa, British Govt Overseas Devt Admin (ODA) 1989–90, Chief Health and Population Adviser and Head of Health and Population Div., ODA 1990–97 (renamed British Govt Dept for Int. Devt, DFID 1997) 1997–99; Project Man., Roll Back Malaria, WHO, Geneva 1999–2000, Exec. Dir Office of the Dir-Gen., WHO 2000–02, Exec. Dir Sustainable Devt and Sr Policy Adviser to Dir-Gen. 2002–03, Rep. of Dir-Gen. for Health Action in Crises 2003–05; Sr Co-ordinator for Avian and Pandemic Influenza, UN Devt Group, New York 2005–14; Deputy UN System Co-ordinator for Global Food Security Crisis 2008–14, Special Rep. of Sec.-Gen. on Food Security and Nutrition, UN 2009–, Co-ordinator, Scale Up Nutrition Movt 2011–15, Sr System Coordinator for Ebola Virus Disease, UN 2014–, Special Envoy of Sec.-Gen. on Ebola, UN 2014–15, Special Adviser to the Sec.-Gen. on 2030 Agenda for Sustainable Devt 2015–. *Address:* Office of the Secretary-General, United Nations, New York, NY 10017, USA (office). *Website:* www.un.org/sustainabledevelopment (office); www.davidnabarro.com.

NABÉ, Louceny; Guinean central banker and fmr politician; *Governor, Banque Centrale de la République de Guinée;* fmr Contracts Man., AU Metals Co. sarl; Minister of Mines 2008–09; Gov. Banque Centrale de la République de Guinée 2010–. *Address:* Office of the Governor, Banque Centrale de la République de Guinée, 12 blvd du Commerce, BP 692, Kaloum, Conakry, Guinea (office). *Telephone:* 30-41-26-51 (office). *Fax:* 30-41-48-98 (office). *E-mail:* gouv.bcrg@eti-bull.net (office). *Website:* www.bcrg-guinee.org (office).

NABIULLINA, Elvira Sakhipzadovna, PhD; Russian economist, government official and central banker; *Governor, Bank Rossii—Central Bank of the Russian Federation;* b. 29 Oct. 1963, Ufa, Bashkir ASSR (now Repub. of Bashkortostan), Russian SFSR, USSR; ed M.V. Lomonosov Moscow State Univ.; Chief Specialist, Russian Union of Industrialists and Businessmen on econ. policy 1992–94; Deputy Head, Dept of Econ. Reform 1994–96, Head of Dept 1996–97; Deputy Minister of the Economy 1997–98; Vice-Pres. Bd of Dirs Promtorgbank 1998–99; Exec. Dir Euroasian (rating service) 1999; First Deputy Minister of Econ. Devt and Trade 2000–07, Minister of Econ. Devt 2007–12; Econ. Adviser to Pres. Putin 2012–13; Gov. Bank Rossii—Cen. Bank of the Russian Fed. 2013–; Vice-Pres. Fund Centre of Strategic Devt 1999–2000, Pres. 2003–05, Head of Research Group 2005–07; Head of Advisory Council of Organizing Cttee on Preparation and Maintenance of Presidency of the Russian Fed. in G8 2005–06; fmr mem. Pres.'s Expert Council on Priority Nat. Projects and Demography; World Fellow, Yale Univ., USA 2007; named by Euromoney magazine as Cen. Bank Gov. of the Year 2015, Cen. Banker of the Year (Europe), The Banker magazine 2016, 2017. *Address:* Bank Rossii—Central Bank of the Russian Federation, 107016 Moscow, ul. Neglinnaya 12, Russian Federation (office). *Telephone:* (495) 771-91-00 (office). *Fax:* (495) 771-48-30 (office). *E-mail:* webmaster@cbr.ru (office). *Website:* www.cbr.ru (office).

NACHTWEY, James, FRPS; American photojournalist and war photographer; b. 1948, Syracuse, NY; ed Leominster High School and Dartmouth Coll.; influenced by imagery from Viet Nam War and American Civil Rights Movt; became self-taught photographer; held a series of odd jobs, including as a truck driver; also worked on merchant ships; started work as newspaper photographer, NM 1976; moved to New York and began working as freelance photographer 1980; worked for Black Star 1980–85; contract photographer, Time magazine 1984–; covered first overseas assignment in NI 1981; worked in SA, Latin America, Middle East, Russia, Eastern Europe, fmr Soviet Union shooting pictures of war, conflict and famine, and images of sociopolitical issues (pollution, crime and punishment) in Western Europe and USA; covered elections in SA 1994, invasion of Iraq 2003, tsunami in SE Asia 26 Dec. 2004; made series of photographs about attacks on World Trade Center 11 Sept. 2001; compiled a photo essay on effects of Sudan conflict on civilians; has worked on extensive photographic essays in El Salvador, Nicaragua, Guatemala, Lebanon, West Bank and Gaza, Israel, Indonesia, Thailand, India, Sri Lanka, Afghanistan, the Philippines, South Korea, Somalia, Sudan, Rwanda, SA, Russia, Bosnia, Chechnya, Kosovo, Romania, Brazil and USA; mem. Magnum Photos 1986–2001; Co-founding mem. VII Photo Agency 2001; Hon. DFA (Massachusetts Coll. of Art); numerous honours and awards, including Common Wealth Award, Martin Luther King Award, Dr Jean Mayer Global Citizenship Award, Henry Luce Award, Robert Capa Gold Medal (five times), World Press Photo Award (twice), Magazine Photographer of the Year (seven times), Int. Center of Photography Infinity Award (three times), Leica Award (twice), Bayeaux Award for War Corresps (twice), Alfred Eisenstaedt Award, Canon Photo Essayist Award, W. Eugene Smith Memorial Grant in Humanistic Photography, Dan David Prize, Dan David Foundation and Tel-Aviv Univ. 2003, Heinz Foundation Achievement Award 2006, TED (Tech. Entertainment Design) Prize (co-recipient) 2007. *Address:* c/o TIME magazine, 1271 Avenue of the Americas, New York, NY 10020-1393, USA (office). *Telephone:* (212) 522-1212 (office). *Fax:* (212) 522-0602 (office). *Website:* www.time.com (office); www.jamesnachtwey.com.

NADAL PARERA, Rafael (Rafa); Spanish professional tennis player; b. 3 June 1986, Manacor, Majorca; s. of Sebastian Nadal and Ana Maria Parera; ed coached by Toni Nadal; began playing tennis aged four; turned professional 2001; played his only jr Grand Slam event at Wimbledon in 2002 and reached semi-finals; won first ATP match defeating Ramon Delgado in Majorca to become the ninth player in open era to win an ATP match before 16th birthday; became second-youngest player to be ranked among world's top 100 singles players 2003; reached fourth round at Australian Open 2005, semi-finalist 2008, winner 2009, finalist 2012, 2014, 2017; winner, French Open 2005, 2006, 2007, 2008, 2010, 2011, 2012 (beating Bjorn Borg's previous record of six titles), 2013 (first male player to win eight titles at the same Grand Slam tournament), 2014, 2017; runner-up, Wimbledon 2006, 2007, 2011, winner 2008, 2010; quarter-finalist, US Open 2006, semi-finalist 2008, 2009, winner 2010, 2013, runner-up 2011; semi-finalist, Masters Cup 2006, 2007; gold medal, men's singles, Olympic Games, Beijing 2008; runner-up, Barclays ATP World Tour Finals, London 2010, 2013; clay-court winning streak of 81 matches (longest among male players in open era) April 2005–May 2007; World No. 1 18 Aug. 2008–5 July 2009, 7 June 2010–3 July 2011, 7 Oct. 2013–7 July 2014, 21 Aug. 2017–; winner, Monte-Carlo Rolex Masters 2012, Barcelona Open 2012, 2013, 2016, Internazionali BNL d'Italia, Rome 2012, 2013, Brasil Open 2013, Abierto Mexicano Telcel, Acapulco 2013, BNP Paribas Open, Indian Wells 2013, Mutua Madrid Open 2013, 2014, Coupe Rogers, Montreal 2013, Western & Southern Open, Cincinnati 2013, Qatar ExxonMobil Open, Doha 2014, Rio Open presented by Claro hdtv Rio de Janeiro 2014, Stuttgart 2015, Hamburg Open 2015, Monte Carlo Masters 2016; doubles winner: (with Juan Monaco), Qatar ExxonMobil Open, Doha 2015; became seventh man to complete a Career Grand Slam after winning US Open 13 Sept. 2010; ATP Newcomer of the Year 2003, asteroid 128036 Rafaelnadal named in his honour 2003, ATP Most Improved Player 2005, Laureus World Newcomer of the Year 2006, Prince of Asturias Award 2008, BBC Overseas Sports Personality of the Year 2010, Laureus Sportsman of the Year Award 2011, Amb. of the Year, Int. Tennis Writers Asscn 2018. *Publication:* Rafa (with John Carlin) 2012. *Leisure interests:* playing PSP, soccer and golf, fishing, going out with friends in Majorca. *Address:* c/o Carlos Costa, IMG, Via Augusta, 200 4th Floor, 08021 Barcelona, Spain (office). *Telephone:* (93) 2003455 (office). *Fax:* (93) 2005924 (office). *E-mail:* kc@rafaelnadal.com. *Website:* www.rafaelnadal.com.

NADAR, Shiv; Indian business executive, engineer and philanthropist; *Chairman and Chief Strategy Officer, HCL Technologies;* b. 18 July 1945, Tamil Nadu; s. of Sivasubramaniya Nadar and Vamasundari Devi; m. Kiran Nadar; one d.; ed Madurai American Coll., P.S.G. Coll. of Tech.; Systems Analyst, Cooper Eng; Sr Man. Trainee, DCM Ltd 1968; f. Hindustan Computers Ltd (later HCL) 1976, CEO

HCL Technologies Ltd 1991, currently Chair. and Chief Strategy Officer; mem. Exec. Bd Indian School of Business, Hyderabad; mem. Public Health Foundation of India, Global Charter The Indus Entrepreneurs; Founder S.S.N. Coll. of Eng, Chennai 1996; Hon. Fellow, All India Man. Asscn 2006; Dr hc (Madras) 2007; CNBC Business Excellence Award 2005, Ernst & Young Entrepreneur of the Year Award 2007, Padma Bhushan 2008. *Address:* HCL Technologies Ltd, A10/11, Sector 3, Noida 201 301, India (office). *Telephone:* (120) 2520917 (office). *Fax:* (120) 2526907 (office). *E-mail:* webhost@hcl.in (office). *Website:* www.hcl.in (office).

NADELLA, Satya, BS, MSCS, MBA; American (b. Indian) computer industry executive; *CEO, Microsoft Corporation;* b. (Satyanarayana Nadella), 1967, Hyderabad, AP, India; s. of B. N. Yugandhar; m. Anupama Venugopal 1992; one s. two d.; ed Hyderabad Public School, Begumpet, Manipal Inst. of Tech., Karnataka (then affiliated to Mangalore Univ.), Univ. of Wisconsin-Milwaukee, Univ. of Chicago Booth School of Business; mem. tech. staff, Sun Microsystems –1992; joined Microsoft 1992, later Vice-Pres. Microsoft Business Div., Sr Vice-Pres., Research and Devt, for Online Services Div. 2007–11, Pres. Server and Tools Business 2011–14, Exec. Vice-Pres. Cloud and Enterprise Group 2011–14, CEO Microsoft Corpn 2014–. *Leisure interests:* cricket, poetry. *Address:* Microsoft Corporation, 1 Microsoft Way, Redmond, WA 98052-8300, USA (office). *Telephone:* (425) 882-8080 (office). *Fax:* (425) 936-7329 (office). *E-mail:* info@microsoft.com (office). *Website:* www.microsoft.com (office).

NADER, Ralph, AB, LLB; American lawyer, author and consumer advocate; b. 27 Feb. 1934, Winsted, Conn.; s. of Nadra Nader and Rose Bouziane; ed Princeton and Harvard Univs; admitted to Conn. Bar 1958, Mass Bar 1959, also US Supreme Court; served in US Army 1959; est. law practice in Hartford, Conn. 1959; Lecturer in History and Govt, Univ. of Hartford 1961–63; Founder and fmr Head of Public Citizen Inc. 1980; Lecturer, Princeton Univ. 1967–68; Co-founder Princeton Project 55 1989; launched political movt Democracy Rising 2001; Green Party cand. for US presidential election 1996, 2000, ind. cand. 2004, 2008; f. Clean Water Action Project, Disability Rights Center, Public Interest Research Groups (PIRGs), Center for Study of Responsive Law, Center for Auto Safety, Pension Rights Center, Project for Corp. Responsibility; Contributing Ed. Ladies Home Journal 1973–81, syndicated columnist, In the Public Interest 1972–; f. The Multinational Monitor (monthly magazine); mem. ABA; Nieman Fellows Award 1965–66, Woodrow Wilson Award, Princeton Univ. 1972, inducted into Automotive Hall of Fame 2016. *Film appearance:* (as himself) Fun with Dick and Jane 2005. *Publications include:* Unsafe at Any Speed 1965, Who Runs Congress? 1972, The Consumer and Corporate Accountability 1974, Taming the Giant Corporation (co-author) 1976, The Menace of Atomic Energy (with John Abbotts) 1979, The Lemon Book 1980, Who's Poisoning America? 1981, The Big Boys 1986, Winning the Insurance Game (co-author) 1990, Good Works 1993, No Contest: Corporate Lawyers and the Perversion of Justice in America 1996, The Ralph Nader Reader 2000, Crashing the Party 2002, Civic Arousal 2004, It Happened in the Kitchen: Recipes for Food and Thought, Why Women Pay More (with Frances Cerra Whittelsley), Children First! A Parent's Guide to Fighting Corporate Predators, The Seventeen Traditions 2007, Only the Super-Rich Can Save Us! 2009, Getting Steamed to Overcome Corporatism 2011, The Seventeen Traditions 2012, The Seventeen Solutions 2012, Unstoppable: The Emerging Left-Right Alliance to Dismantle the Corporate State 2014. *Address:* PO Box 19312, Washington, DC 20036, USA. *E-mail:* info@nader.org. *Website:* www.nader.org.

NADINGAR, Emmanuel; Chadian politician; b. 1951; Deputy Chief of Staff, Govt of Chad –2004; Minister of Nat. Defence, Veterans and Victims of War 2004–07, of Petroleum 2007–08, Minister-del. to the Prime Minister, responsible for Decentralization 2008–10; Prime Minister of Chad 2010–13.

NAEEM, Mohamed Monaza; Maldivian business executive and politician; f. Monaza Contracting Co. Pvt. Ltd 1978; MP for Laamu Atoll, Chair. Business Cttee of Special Majlis 2007; Founder and Leader Maldivian Nat. Congress 2007–10; apptd Minister of State for Home Affairs 2011; sr mem. People's Asscn. *Address:* Naeem & Sons Trading Pvt. Ltd, 1/7, First Floor, M. Velidhooge, Dhambu Goalhi, Malé, Maldives (office). *Telephone:* 3316921 (office). *Fax:* 3316922 (office). *E-mail:* info@monaza.mv (office). *Website:* www.monaza.mv (office).

NAEEM, Mohammad; Pakistani physicist; *Chairman, Pakistan Atomic Energy Commission;* joined Pakistan Atomic Energy Comm. (PAEC) 1972, has served in various positions including as Dir PAEC Pakistan Welding Inst., Mem. (Fuel Cycle), Chair. PAEC 2015–; Chair. Bd of Govs Pakistan Inst. of Eng and Applied Sciences; Sitara-i-Imtiaz, Hilal-i-Imtiaz. *Address:* Pakistan Atomic Energy Commission, Near K-Block, POB 1114, Islamabad, Pakistan (office). *Telephone:* (51) 9209032 (office). *Fax:* (51) 9204908 (office). *E-mail:* sipr@paec.gov.pk (office). *Website:* www.paec.gov.pk (office).

NAEGLE, Sue; American television executive; *Chief Content Officer, Annapurna Pictures;* b. Rockaway, NJ; m. Dana Gould; three adopted d. from China; ed Indiana Univ.; began career in post room of United Talent Agency, LA 1991, became agent 1994, Co-head of TV Dept and Partner 1999; Pres. Entertainment Div., HBO (Time Warner co.) 2011–13, oversaw series programming and specials; formed own production Co. Naegle Ink; Head, Annapurna Pictures 2016–19, Chief Content Officer 2019–; College of Arts and Sciences Distinguished Alumni Award 2015. *Address:* Annapurna Pictures, 812 North Robertson Boulevard, West Hollywood, CA 90069, USA (office). *Telephone:* (310) 724-8936 (office). *Fax:* (310) 388-1550 (office). *Website:* annapurna.pictures (office).

NAEK, Farooq Hamid, LLB, MA; Pakistani lawyer and politician; ed Univ. of Karachi, Sindh Muslim Law Coll.; enrolled as advocate 1970, as advocate of Supreme Court 1976, as advocate of High Court 1976; fmr Asst Dir, Directorate of Labour and Social Welfare, Govt of Sindh; Civil Judge and First Class Magistrate 1971–75; resigned from judicial service after serving as civil judge for two years and became active mem. Pakistan People's Party mid-1970s; Deputy Attorney Gen. 1994–96; Senator from Karachi 2003–15, Chair. of Senate 2009–12; Fed. Minister of Law, Justice, Parl. Affairs and Human Rights 2008–09, of Law and Justice 2012–13; successfully defended fmr Prime Minister Benazir Bhutto and her husband Asif Ali Zardari in numerous cases filed by earlier govts in courts in Pakistan, UK, Switzerland and Spain; arrested leading demonstration against rule of Gen. Zia Ul Haq 1983, remained in Cen. Prison, Karachi for six months along with ten other lawyers, declared Prisoner of Conscience by Amnesty International; elected Gen. Sec. Karachi Bar Asscn 1983, elected Pres. 1989; mem. Sindh Bar Council 1984–89 (re-elected 1990–94), twice elected Vice-Chair. 1986, 1993; mem. Pakistan Bar Council 1997–2010. *Address:* Suite-5, 3rd Floor, Shafiq Plaza, Block-A, Sarwar Shaheed Road, Karachi, Pakistan. *E-mail:* naek_law786@hotmail.com.

NAFISI, Azar, PhD; Iranian writer and academic; *Executive Director, Dialogue Project, School of Advanced International Studies, Johns Hopkins University;* b. 1 Dec. 1955; d. of Ahmad Nafisi and Nezhat Nafisi; m.; one d.; ed Univ. of Oklahoma, USA; fmrly teacher, Tehran Univ., Allemeh Tabatabai Univ.; fmrly Visiting Fellow, Univ. of Oxford; currently Visiting Prof. and Exec. Dir Dialogue Project, School of Advanced Int. Studies, Johns Hopkins Univ., Washington, DC. *Publications include:* Anti-Terra: A Study of Vladimir Nabokov's Novels 1994, Reading 'Lolita' in Tehran: A Memoir in Books 2003, La Voce Verde 2006, Things I've Been Silent About 2009, The Republic of Imagination 2014; contrib. numerous chapters and articles on promotion of democracy, human rights in Muslim societies, women's rights, literature, culture. *Address:* Paul H. Nitze School of Advanced International Studies, Johns Hopkins University, The Rome Building, Room 731, 1619 Massachusetts Avenue NW, Washington, DC 20036, USA (office). *Telephone:* (202) 663-5785 (office). *E-mail:* anafisi@jhu.edu (office); info@azarnafisi.com (office). *Website:* www.sais-jhu.edu (office); www.azarnafisi.com.

NAG, Rajat Mohan, BTech, MSc, MBA, MSc; Canadian engineer, economist and financial analyst; b. 12 Sept. 1948, Sylhet, Bangladesh; s. of Rohini Mohan Nag and Asha Lata Nag; m. Shikha Nag; one s. one d.; ed Indian Inst. of Tech., Delhi, Univ. of Saskatchewan, London School of Econs, UK; worked as Supervising Engineer, later Economist, later Chief Economist in an eng firm in Canada for agricultural, water, energy and mining projects; fmr Sr Financial Analyst for Bank of Canada; fmr Visiting Lecturer in Financial and Econ. Analysis, Carleton Univ., McGill Univ., Concordia Univ.; joined Asian Devt Bank (ADB) as Project Economist in Agric. Dept 1986, assigned to ADB's Nepal Resident Mission 1991–94, held various sr positions in ADB's Programs Dept (West) and in Financial Sector and Industry Div., Infrastructure Dept (West), mem. man. cttee that formulated proposals for re-organization of ADB operations 2001, Deputy Dir Programs Dept (West) 2000–02, Dir-Gen. for SE Asia and Mekong Depts 2002–06, Special Advisor to ADB Pres. on Regional Econ. Co-operation and Integration 2005–06, Dir-Gen. newly amalgamated SE Asia Dept 2006, Man. Dir-Gen. ADB 2006–13; Chair. Look East Council, Indian Chamber of Commerce 2014–; Visiting Prof., Strategy and Devt Issues, Asian Inst. of Man., Philippines 2014–; Visiting Prof., Emerging Markets Inst., China 2014–17, Distinguished Prof. 2017–; mem. Bd of Dirs Partnership for Transparency 2015–, Bd of Govs. Action for Autism 2015–; Sr Fellow, Emerging Markets Forum, USA 2014–; Fellow, Nat. Council of Applied Economic Research, India 2014–. *Leisure interest:* involved with various community and charitable orgs.

NAGAE, Shusaku; Japanese business executive; *Chairman, Panasonic Corporation;* served as Dir of Project Sales Operations, Tokyo HQ, Panasonic Corpn, Dir of Electrical Construction Materials Marketing Business Unit and Sr Man. Dir, Exec. Vice-Pres. Panasonic Electric Works Co. Ltd April–June 2010, Pres. in charge of Lighting Co. and Panasonic Ecology Systems Co. Ltd 2010–11, Sr Man. Exec. Officer, Panasonic Corpn 2011–12, Pres. Eco Solutions Co. Jan. 2012–, Exec. Vice-Pres., Panasonic Corpn June 2012–13, Chair. 2013–. *Address:* Panasonic Corporation, Corporate Headquarters, 1006 Oaza Kadoma, Kadoma-shi, Osaka 571-8501, Japan (office). *Telephone:* (6) 6908-1121 (office). *Fax:* (6) 6908-2351 (office). *E-mail:* info@panasonic.net (office). *Website:* panasonic.net (office).

NAGAI, Kiyoshi, PhD, FRS; Japanese biologist and academic; *Senior Research Scientist, Structural Studies Division, Medical Research Council Laboratory of Molecular Biology;* b. 25 June 1949, Osaka; s. of Otoji Nagai and Naoko Nagai; m. Yoshiko Majima 1974; one s. one d.; ed Osaka Univ. Morimoto Lab.; Research Scientist, MRC Lab. of Molecular Biology 1981–, Jt Head of Structural Studies 2001–10, Sr Research Scientist 2010–; Research Group Leader, Nagai Group (molecular mechanism of pre-mRNA splicing); Fellow, Darwin Coll. Cambridge 1993–; Novartis Medal and Prize, Biochemical Soc. 2000. *Publications:* RNA-Protein Interaction (co-ed. with Iain Mattaj) 1995); numerous publs in scientific journals. *Leisure interests:* reading, playing cello in chamber groups. *Address:* Structural Studies Division, MRC Laboratory of Molecular Biology, Hills Road, Cambridge, CB2 0QH, England (office). *Telephone:* (1223) 402292 (office). *Fax:* (1223) 213556 (office). *E-mail:* kn@mrc-lmb.cam.ac.uk (office). *Website:* www2.mrc-lmb.cam.ac.uk (office).

NAGAI, Koji, BA; Japanese financial services executive; *Group CEO, Nomura Holdings, Inc.;* ed Chuo Univ.; joined Nomura 1981, later Deputy Pres. of domestic unit, Pres. Nomura's domestic brokerage –2012, apptd Sr Corp. Man. Dir Nomura Securities Co. 2008, Exec. Man. Dir and Exec. Vice-Pres. 2009, Co-Chief Opertaing Officer and Deputy Pres. 2011, Pres. 2012–17, Sr Man. Dir 2013, Chair. 2017–, Group CEO Nomura Holdings, Inc. Aug. 2012–. *Address:* Nomura Holdings, Inc., 1-9-1, Nihonbashi, Chuo-ku, Tokyo 103-8645, Japan (office). *Telephone:* (3) 3211-1811 (office). *E-mail:* info@nomura.co.jp (office). *Website:* www.nomura.co.jp (office).

NAGAMOOTOO, Moses Veerasammy, JP; Guyanese journalist, lawyer and politician; *Prime Minister and First Vice-President;* b. 30 Nov. 1947, Whim Village, Berbice County; s. of Gangama (Chunoo) and Nagamootoo Ramaswamy; m. Sita Nagamootoo; four c.; ed Univ. of Guyana, Univ. of the West Indies; began career as teacher 1964–70; Gen. Sec., Union of Guyanese Journalists 1970–92; attorney at law; mem. Nat Ass. (PPP) 1992–2001, 2006–11, (AFC) 2011–15, mem. Select Cttee on Constitutional Reform 1996–2001, mem. Foreign Relations, Standing Orders and Constitutional Reform Cttees 2006–09; Minister of Information 1992–93, Minister of Local Govt & Regional Devt 1995–2000; Prime Minister and First Vice-Pres. 2015–; Dir, Guyana Airways Corpn 1994–98; Founder and Exec. mem., Caribbean Asscn of Media Workers 1986–92; Exec. mem. Guyana Bar Asscn 2005–06; Exec. mem. Fed. of Latin American Journalists; Vice-Pres. Int. Org. of Journalists 1990–96; mem. People's Progressive Party (PPP) 1964–2011; mem. Alliance for Change 2011–, currently Vice-Pres. *Publications:* Hendree's Cure (novel), For the Fighting Front: Anthology of Revolutionary Poems (Ed.), Fragments from Memory 2015. *Address:* Office of the Prime Minister, Oranapai

Towers, Wights Lane, Kingston, Georgetown, Guyana (office). *Telephone:* 226-6955 (office). *Fax:* 226-7573 (office). *E-mail:* opm@networksgy.gy (office).

NAGANO, Kent; American conductor; *General Music Director and Chief Conductor, Hamburg State Opera;* b. 22 Nov. 1951, Berkeley, Calif.; m. Mari Kodama; one d.; ed studied under Ozawa, Boulez and Bernstein; first achieved int. recognition when he conducted Boston Symphony Orchestra in performance of Mahler's Symphony No. 9 1984; conducted US premiere of Messiaen's The Transfiguration; debut at Paris Opera conducting world premiere of Messiaen's St François d'Assise; debut, Metropolitan Opera, New York conducting Poulenc's Dialogues des Carmélites 1994; Music Dir, Berkeley Symphony Orchestra, Calif. 1978–2008, Opéra de Lyon 1988–98, Hallé Orchestra 1991–2000; Artistic Dir, Deutsches Symphonie-Orchester Berlin 2000–06; Prin. Conductor and Music Dir, Los Angeles Opera 2001–06; Music Dir, Montreal Symphony Orchestra 2006–, Bayerische Staatsoper 2006–13; Prin. Guest Conductor and Artistic Adviser, Gothenburg Symphony Orchestra 2013–; Gen. Music Dir and Chief Conductor, Hamburg State Opera and Philharmonic Orchestra 2015–; Officier, Ordre des Arts et des Lettres 1992, Order of the Rising Sun, Gold Rays 2009, Gov.-Gen.'s Meritorious Service Decoration 2018; Grammy Awards for Busoni's Dr Faust with Opéra Nat. de Lyon, Prokofiev's Peter and the Wolf with the Russian Nat. Orchestra, Saariaho's L'Amour de Loin with Deutsches Symphonie-Orchester Berlin (Best Opera Recording 2011), Bayerischer Verdienstorden 2013, ECHO Klassik Award for Opera Recording (for Honegger and Ibert: L'Aiglon) 2016, ECHO Klassik Conductor of the Year Award 2017. *Publication:* Erwarten Sie Wunder 2014. *Address:* c/o HarrisonParrott, The Ark, 201 Talgarth Road, London, W6 8BJ, England (office). *E-mail:* jasper.parrott@harrisonparrott.co.uk (office). *Website:* www.osm.ca; www.kentnagano.com.

NAGANO, Tsuyoshi; Japanese business executive; *President and CEO, Tokio Marine Holdings, Inc.;* b. 9 Nov. 1952; joined Tokio Marine 1975, Exec. Officer and Gen. Man. Nagoya Production Dept III, Tokai Div., Tokio Marine 2003–04, Exec. Officer and Gen. Man. Nagoya Production Dept III, Tokio Marine & Nichido 2004–06, Man. Exec. Officer, Tokio Marine & Nichido 2006–08, Man. Dir and Gen. Man. Corp. Planning Dept, Tokio Marine & Nichido 2008–09, Dir, Tokio Marine Holdings, Inc. 2008–09, Sr Man. Dir Tokio Marine & Nichido 2010–11, Sr Man. Dir Tokio Marine Holdings, Inc. 2011–12, Sr Man. Dir and Gen. Man. Int. Business Devt Dept 2012–13, Exec. Vice-Pres., Tokio Marine & Nichido 2012–13, Exec. Vice-Pres. and Gen. Man. Int. Business Devt Dept, Tokio Marine Holdings, Inc. 2012–13, Pres. and CEO Tokio Marine & Nichido 2013–, Tokio Marine Holdings, Inc. 2013–, Chair. Bd Tokio Marine & Nichido 2016–. *Address:* Tokio Marine Holdings Inc., Nichido Building Shinkan, 1-2-1 Marunouchi, Chiyoda-ku, Tokyo, 100-0005, Japan (office). *Telephone:* (3) 6212-3333 (office). *E-mail:* ir@tokiomarinehd.com (office). *Website:* www.tokiomarinehd.com (office).

NAGAO, Makoto, MEng, PhD; Japanese academic and engineer; b. 4 Oct. 1936; ed Kyoto Univ.; pioneer of natural language processing and intelligent image processing tech.; led research developing first machine translation systems and digital library systems; Asst Prof., Faculty of Eng, Kyoto Univ. 1961–67, Lecturer 1967–68, Assoc. Prof. 1968–73, Prof. 1973–, Dir Data Processing Centre 1986–90, Dean Faculty of Eng 1997, Pres. Kyoto Univ. 1997–2003; Visiting Assoc. Prof., Dept of Informatics, Grenoble Univ. 1969–70; Pres. Japan Asscn of Nat. Univs 2001–03; Pres. Nat. Inst. of Information and Communications Tech. (NICT) 2004–07, Nat. Diet Library 2007–12; Pres. Japanese Cognitive Science Soc. 1988–90, Int. Asscn for Machine Tech. (IAMT) 1991–93, Asia-Pacific Asscn for Machine Tech. 1992–96, Asscn for Nat. Language Training 1994–96, Inst. of Electronics, Information and Communication Engineers (IEICE) 1998–99, Information Processing Soc. of Japan (IPSJ) 1999–2000, Japan Library Asscn 2002–; mem. Science Council of Japan 2000–03; Fellow, IEEE 1999; Order of Cultural Merit 2018; Hon. DSc (Univ. of Nottingham, UK) 1999; IEEE Emmanuel R. Piore Award 1993, Bunka-shou Culture Prize 1994, IEICE Distinguished Achievement and Contribs Award 1997, IPSJ Contribs Award 1997, IAMT Medal of Honour 1997, Japanese Govt Purple Ribbon Medal 1997, JSAI Achievement Award 1998, NHK Broadcast Cultural Award 1998, C&C Prize 1999, Takayanagi Kinen-shou Memorial Award 2000, Asscn for Computational Linguistics Lifetime Achievement Award 2003, Japan Prize for Information and Media Tech. 2005. *Publications:* in English: A Structural Analysis of Complex Aerial Photographs 1980, Machine Translation: How Far Can It Go? 1989, Knowledge and Inference 1990; in Japanese: Engineering for Pattern Recognition and Language Understanding 1989, Artificial and Human Intelligence 1992, Digital Library 1994, Natural Language Processing (co-author) 1996, What Is Understanding? 2001. *Address:* 39-1 Kitaikeda, Iwakura, Sakyo, Kyoto, Japan (home).

NAGASE, Jinen; Japanese politician; b. 3 Oct. 1943; joined Ministry of Labour 1966, Sec. to Minister of Labour 1982–84, Dir Employment Security Bureau, Measures for the Aged Dept, Employment Measures Div. 1984–86, Dir Labour Relations Bureau, Labour Legislation Div. 1986–88 (resgnd from Ministry); mem. House of Reps for Toyama Pref. 1st Dist (LDP) 1990–, Deputy Chair. LDP Diet Affairs Cttee 1994, State Sec. for Health and Welfare 1995–96, Dir LDP Environment Div. 1996, Chair. LDP Social Affairs Div. 1996, Dir LDP Labour Admin Div. 1997, Deputy Sec.-Gen. LDP and Chief Dir House Cttee on Health and Welfare 1998, Sr State Sec. for Labour 1999–2000, Chair. House Standing Cttee on Judicial Affairs 2000, Sr State Sec. for Justice 2000–01, Sr Vice-Minister of Justice 2001–02, Chief Dir House Cttee on Health, Labour and Welfare 2002–03, Chief Deputy Chair. Policy Research Council 2004, Dir Jt Meeting of Both Houses on the Reform of Pension and Other Social Security Systems 2005, Deputy Chief Cabinet Sec. 2005–06, Minister of Justice 2006–07. *Address:* c/o Ministry of Justice, 1-1-1, Kasumigaseki, Chiyoda-ku, Tokyo 100-8977, Japan.

NAGASHIMA, Shigeo, BA; Japanese professional baseball player and manager (retd); b. 20 Feb. 1936, Chiba Pref.; s. of Toshi Nagashima and Chiyo Nagashima; m. Akiko Nishimura 1965 (deceased 2007); two s. two d.; ed St Paul's Univ., Tokyo; professional baseball player, Tokyo Yomiuri Giants 1958–74, retd with lifetime average of .305 and 444 career home runs with 1,522 RBIs 1974, Man. 1975–81, 1993–2001, currently Hon. Lifetime Man.; Rookie of the Year 1958, Most Valuable Player of the Year (five times), Japan Professional Sports Grand Prize 1971, Matsutaro Shoriki Award 1994, People's Honor Award, Japan 2013. *Leisure interest:* golf.

NAGATO, Masatsugu, BA; Japanese business executive; *President and CEO, Japan Post Holdings Company Ltd;* b. 18 Nov. 1948; ed Hitotsubashi Univ.; fmr Man. Exec. Officer and Head of the Americas, Mizuho Corporate Bank (subsidiary of Mizuho Financial Group, Inc.); Exec. Vice-Pres., then Deputy Pres. Fuji Heavy Industries Ltd 2010–15; Vice-Chair., then Chair. Citibank Japan Ltd –2015; Pres. and CEO Japan Post Bank Co. Ltd 2015–16, Pres. and CEO Japan Post Holdings Co. Ltd 2016–, mem. Bd of Dirs, Japan Post Insurance Co. 2016–, Japan Post Co. Ltd 2016–. *Address:* Japan Post Holdings Company Ltd, 1-3-2 Kasumigaseki, Chiyoda-ku, Tokyo 100-8798, Japan (office). *Telephone:* (3) 3504-4411 (office). *Fax:* (3) 3504-5399 (office). *E-mail:* info@japanpost.jp (office). *Website:* www.japanpost.jp (office).

NAGATSUMA, Akira, LLB; Japanese lawyer and politician; b. 14 June 1960, Nerima, Tokyo; ed Keio Univ., Tokyo; began career with NEC Corpn; fmr reporter, Nikkei Business magazine; mem. House of Reps for Tokyo No. 7 constituency 2000–, fmr mem. Parl. Cttee on Health, Labour and Welfare; mem. Democratic Party of Japan (DPJ), Deputy Chair. DPJ Policy Research Cttee; fmr Next (Shadow) Cabinet Minister of State for Pensions and Deputy Chief Cabinet Sec.; Minister of Health, Labour and Welfare, also Minister of State for Pension Reform 2009–10. *Leisure interests* watching movies, karaoke, football, camp. *Address:* Democrats Nagatsumaakira Office, Yubinbango, Tokyo 164-0011, Japan (office). *Telephone:* (3) 5342-6551 (office). *Fax:* (3) 5342-6552 (office). *E-mail:* Akiraattonaga.Tv (office). *Website:* naga.tv (office).

NAGAYAMA, Osamu; Japanese business executive; *Chairman, Sony Corporation;* b. 1947; ed Faculty of Business and Commerce, Keio Univ.; joined Long-Term Credit Bank of Japan 1971, worked at London Br. 1975–78; joined Chugai Pharmaceutical Co. Ltd 1978, Dir, Pharmaceutical Sales and Marketing Div. and Int. Business Div. 1983–85, Deputy Gen. Man. Pharmaceutical Research and Devt Div. and mem. Bd of Dirs 1985–86, Deputy Gen. Man. Personal Healthcare Div. 1986–87, Sr Vice-Pres. 1987–89, Deputy Pres. 1989–92, Pres. Chugai Pharmaceutical Co. Ltd 1992–2012, COO –2012, Chair., Pres. and CEO 2012–; Dir, Sony Corpn 2010–, Vice-Chair. 2012–13, Chair. 2013–; Ind. Dir, Nomura Partners Funds, Inc.–The Japan Fund 2005–; mem. Exec. Cttee Roche. *Address:* Sony Corporation, 1-7-1 Konan, Minato-ku, Tokyo 108-0075, Japan (office). *Telephone:* (3) 6748-2111 (office). *Fax:* (3) 6748-2244 (office). *E-mail:* info@sony.net (office). *Website:* www.sony.net (office); www.sony.com (office).

NAGAYASU, Katsunori; Japanese business executive; *Senior Advisor, Bank of Tokyo-Mitsubishi UFJ Limited;* ed Univ. of Tokyo; joined Mitsubishi Bank in Kyoto br. 1970, Deputy Gen. Man., Planning Dept 1992–96, became part of Planning Dept of Bank of Tokyo-Mitsubishi (following merger with Bank of Tokyo) 1996, Dir 1997; Man. Dir Nippon Trust Bank Ltd 2000–01; Man. Dir Mitsubishi Trust & Banking Corpn and its Bank 2001–02; Dir and Man. Officer Mitsubishi Tokyo Financial Group Inc. 2004; served as Gen. Man. Trust Business Planning Div. and Co-Gen. Man. Corp. Business Planning Div. of Integrated Corp. Banking Business Group of Mitsubishi Trust & Banking Corpn, Dir, Bank of Tokyo-Mitsubishi UFJ Ltd (subsidiary of Mitsubishi UFJ Financial Group, Inc.) 1997–2000, Rep. Dir 2002–, Man. Dir 2002–04, Chief Exec. Commercial Banking Business Unit 2004–05, Sr Man. Dir Bank of Tokyo-Mitsubishi UFJ Ltd Jan.–May 2005, Deputy Pres. Business & Systems Integration Div. 2005–08, Pres. 2008–10, Dir, Mitsubishi UFJ Financial Group, Inc. 2001–04, 2008–13, Group Head of Integrated Corp. Banking Business Group 2004–06, Chief Planning Officer and Deputy Pres. Mitsubishi UFJ Financial Group, Inc. 2006–07, Chief Compliance Officer 2007–08, Pres., CEO and Rep. Dir Mitsubishi UFJ Financial Group, Inc. 2010–13, Chair. Bank of Tokyo-Mitsubishi UFJ Ltd 2012–16 mem. Audit and Supervisory Bd 2014–, Sr Advisor 2016–; Dir Mitsubishi Tokyo Financial Group, Inc. (subsidiary of Mitsubishi UFJ Financial Group, Inc. and holding co. of Mitsubishi Trust & Banking Corpn) 2001–04, Man. Officer 2004–06; Dir, Acom Co. Ltd 2006–, UnionBanCal Corpn 2012–, Isetan Mitsukoshi Holdings, Ltd 2014–, Kirin Holdings Co., Ltd 2016–, Mitsubishi Electric Corpn 2016–; External Audit and Supervisory Bd mem., Nippon Steel & Sumitomo Metal Corpn; Chair. Japanese Bankers Asscn 2009. *Address:* Bank of Tokyo-Mitsubishi UFJ, 7-1, Marunouchi 2-chome, Chiyoda-ku, Tokyo 100-8388, Japan (office). *E-mail:* info@bk.mufg.jp (office). *Website:* www.bk.mufg.jp/global (office).

NAGEL, Andrés; Spanish artist; b. 15 Aug. 1947, San Sebastián; qualified as an architect; subject of books 'Nagel' by Edward Lucie-Smith 1992 and 'Una Decada' by Lluisa Borrás 2003. *Address:* Caserío Parada 36, 20015 San Sebastián, Guipúzcoa, Spain (office). *Website:* www.andresnagel.com.

NAGEL, Günter; German landscape architect; b. 2 Feb. 1936, Dresden; s. of Heinrich Nagel and Erna Nagel (née Hempel); m. Helga Jähnig 1962; one c.; ed Dresden, Humboldt Univ., Berlin and Berlin Tech. Univ.; Scientific Asst, Garden and Landscape Design, Berlin Tech. Univ. 1962–70, lectureship in Design, Garden and Landscape; freelance landscape architect; lectureships at Fine Arts Univ., Berlin (Prof. 1974) and Tech. Univ. Brunswick 1970–74; Prof. and Dir Inst. for Park Planning and Garden Architecture, Univ. of Hanover 1977–2000, Vice-Pres. of the Univ. 1986–88 Prof. Emer. 2001–, Founding mem. Center for Garden Art and Landscape Architecture 2001–; mem. German Soc. for Garden Design and Preservation of Natural Resources; mem. Deutscher Werkbund; mem. Bd of Trustees, Fritz Schumacher Foundation, Karl Foerster Foundation; Dir Acad. of Arts, Berlin, German Acad. of Town and Country Planning. *Publications:* Staatsbibliothek der Stiftung Preußischer Kulturbesitz 1972, Staatliches Institut für Musikforschung und Instrumentenmuseum 1973, Gärten in Cornwall 1975, Villa von der Heydt, Sitz der Stiftung Preußischer Kulturbesitz 1976, Freiräume in der Stadtentwicklung 1978, Erholungsraum Stadtlandschaft 1980, Bildungsstätte der IG Metall 1981, Stadtumbau Grunfunktionen im Hamburger Hafen 1983, Gestaltung und Nutzung des Freiraums Strasse 1985, Verbesserung des Wohnumfeldes 1985, Qualität öffentlicher Freiräume 1986, Museen Stiftung Preußischer Kulturbesitz 1987, Tagungszentrum Messe 1988, Haus Arbeitssicherheit 1992, Fachbereich Chemie, Universität Hannover 1993, Uferräume des Mittellandkanals 1995, Spiel-und Sportpark am Kronsberg 1997. *Address:* c/o Institut für Grünplanung und Gartenarchitektur, Universität Hannover, Herrenhäuser Strasse 2, 30419 Hannover, Germany.

NAGEL, Thomas, BA, BPhil, PhD, FBA; American academic; *Professor of Philosophy and Law, School of Law, New York University;* b. 4 July 1937,

Belgrade, Serbia; s. of Walter Nagel and Carolyn Baer Nagel; m. 1st Doris Blum 1968 (divorced 1972); m. 2nd Anne Hollander 1979; ed Cornell and Harvard Univs and Univ. of Oxford, UK; Asst Prof. of Philosophy, Univ. of California, Berkeley 1963–66; Asst Prof. of Philosophy, Princeton Univ. 1966–69, Assoc. Prof. 1969–72, Prof. 1972–80; Prof. of Philosophy, New York Univ. 1980–, Prof. of Philosophy and Law 1986–, Fiorello LaGuardia Prof. of Law 2001–03, Univ. Prof. 2002–; Visiting Prof., Rockefeller Univ. 1973–74, Univ. of Pittsburgh 1976, Universidad Nacional Autonoma de Mexico 1977, Univ. of the Witwatersrand 1982, UCLA 1986–87, All Souls Coll., Oxford 1990, Univ. of California, Berkeley 2004; Fellow, American Acad. of Arts and Sciences 1980–; Corresp. Fellow, British Acad. 1988–; Hon. Fellow, Corpus Christi Coll., Oxford 1992–; Hon. DLitt (Oxford) 2008, Hon. DrIur (Harvard) 2010; Dr hc (Bucharest) 2010; Mellon Distinguished Achievement Award, Andrew Mellon Foundation 2006, Rolf Schock Prize in Logic and Philosophy, Royal Swedish Acad. of Sciences 2008, Balzan Prize in Moral Philosophy 2008. *Publications include:* The Possibility of Altruism 1970, Mortal Questions 1979, The View from Nowhere 1986, What Does It All Mean? 1987, Equality and Partiality 1991, Other Minds 1995, The Last Word 1997, The Myth of Ownership (with Liam Murphy) 2002, Concealment and Exposure & Other Essays 2002, Secular Philosophy and the Religious Temperament: Essays 2002–08, Mind and Cosmos 2012. *Address:* Department of Philosophy, Law, 5 Washington Place, New York, NY 10003, USA (office). *Telephone:* (212) 998-6225 (office). *Fax:* (212) 995-4179 (office). *E-mail:* thomas.nagel@nyu.edu (office). *Website:* philosophy.fas.nyu.edu (office).

NAGGAR, Zaghloul Raghib el-, PhD; Egyptian geologist and academic; *Chairman, Committee of Scientific Notions in the Quran;* b. 17 Nov. 1933; ed Cairo Univ., Univ. of Wales, UK; taught at Ain Shams Univ., Cairo, King Saud Univ., Riyadh, Univ. Coll. of Wales, Aberystwyth, Kuwait Univ., Univ. of Qatar, Doha; fmr Prof. of Geology, King Fahd Univ. of Petroleum and Minerals, Dhahran; now at Arab Devt Inst.; Chair., Cttee of Scientific Notions in the Quran (part of Egyptian Supreme Council of Islamic Affairs); mem. Geological Soc., London, Geological Soc. of Egypt, American Soc. of Petroleum Geologists, Tulsa; Fellow, Inst. of Petroleum, London, Islamic Acad. of Sciences, mem. Council 1994; Secondary Educ. Award (Egypt), Best Papers Award (Arab Petroleum Congress) 1970. *Publications:* more than 150 scientific articles, 45 books in Arabic, French and English. *Address:* c/o Islamic Academy of Sciences, PO Box 830036, Amman, Jordan (office). *Telephone:* 5522104 (office). *Fax:* 5511803 (office). *Website:* www.elnaggarzr.com.

NAGUIB, Patriarch Antonios; Egyptian ecclesiastic and academic; *Patriarch Emeritus of Alexandria (Coptic);* b. 7 March 1935, Minya; ed interritual seminary of Maadi, Cairo, Pontifical Urbanian Coll., Rome; ordained to Coptic Catholic priesthood 1960; served as pastor for a year at Fikryak, Minya; returned to Rome and obtained a licentiate in theology 1962 and in scripture 1964; Prof. of Sacred Scripture in Maadi seminary from 1964; worked with group of Protestant and Orthodox specialists preparing Arabic trans. of the Bible; Bishop of Minya, Egypt 1977–2002 (resgnd); Patriarch of Alexandria of the Copts 2006–13, Bishop of Alexandria of the Copts 2006–13, Patriarch Emer. 2013–; named Relator Gen. (Recording Sec.) of Special Ass. of Synod of Bishops for the Middle East, held at the Vatican Oct. 2010; cr. Cardinal 2010; participated in Papal Conclave (one of four cardinal-electors from outside the Latin Church) 2013. *Address:* Patriarcat Copte Catholique, BP 69, 34 Rue Ibn Sandar, Saray El Koubbeh, 11712 Cairo, Egypt (office). *Telephone:* (2) 2571740 (office). *Fax:* (2) 4545766 (office).

NAGY, Peter Alan, BFA; American artist, curator and gallery owner; *Founder and Director, Nature Morte Gallery;* b. 11 Nov. 1959, Bridgeport, Conn.; s. of Paul Louis Nagy and Kathleen Marie Furdon Nagy; Co-founder Nature Morte Gallery, New York 1982–88, currently Founder and Co-Dir; moved to Delhi, India 1992, re-opened Nature Morte, Delhi 1997, opened Nature Morte, Berlin 2008–14, Kolkata 2006–09, Gurgaon 2011–14; fmr Pnr, BosePacia Gallery, New York. *Address:* Gallery Nature Morte, A1 Neeti Bagh, New Delhi 110 049, India (office). *Telephone:* (11) 41740215 (office). *Fax:* (11) 41764608 (office). *E-mail:* info@naturemorte.com (office). *Website:* www.naturemorte.com (office).

NAHLES, Andrea Maria, MA; German politician; *Chairman, Sozialdemokratische Partei Deutschlands;* b. 20 June 1970, Mendig, Rhineland-Pfalz; m. Marcus Frings; one d.; ed Univ. of Bonn; mem. Bundestag (Parl.) 1998–2002, 2005–, SPD Parl. Leader 2017–; Fed. Minister of Labour and Social Affairs 2013–17; mem. SPD, State Chair. Young Socialists, Rhineland-Pfalz 1993, Nat. Chair., Young Socialists 1995–99, mem. SPD Party Exec. 1997–, mem. SPD Präsidium 2003–, Deputy Chair. SPD 2007–09, Sec.-Gen. 2009–13, Chair. 2018–; co-f. Forum Demokratische Linke 21 2000; mem. IG Metall (trade union); mem. Euro Solar (European Asscn for Renewable Energy). *Address:* Sozialdemokratische Partei Deutschlands, Willy-Brandt-Haus, Wilhelmstr. 141, 10963 Berlin, Germany (office). *Telephone:* (30) 25991500 (office). *Fax:* (30) 25991507 (office). *Website:* www.spd.de (office); www.andrea-nahles.de.

NAHM, Werner, PhD, FRS, MRIA; German mathematical physicist and academic; *Director and Senior Professor, School of Theoretical Physics, Dublin Institute for Advanced Studies;* b. 21 March 1949, Münster; ed Johann Wolfgang Goethe Univ., Frankfurt am Main, Ludwig Maximilian Univ., Munich, Univ. of Bonn; Postdoctoral Researcher, Univ. of Bonn 1972–75, Heisenberg Fellow 1982–86, Prof. 1989–2002; Fellow and mem. staff, CERN 1976–82; Assoc. Prof., Univ. of California, Davis, USA 1986–89; Sr Prof., Dublin Inst. for Advanced Studies, Ireland 2002–, Dir School of Theoretical Physics; External Scientific mem. Max Planck Inst. for Math., Bonn; mem. Acad. of Sciences and Literature, Mainz; Gothenburg Lise Meitner Prize, Chalmers Univ. of Tech. 2012, Max Planck Medal, Deutsche Physikalische Gesellschaft 2013. *Publications:* numerous papers in professional journals. *Address:* Room 403, School of Theoretical Physics, Dublin Institute for Advanced Studies, 10 Burlington Road, Dublin 4, Ireland (office). *Telephone:* (1) 6140143 (office). *Fax:* (1) 6680561 (office). *E-mail:* nahm@mpim-bonn.mpg.de (office). *Website:* www.dias.ie (office); www.mpim-bonn.mpg.de (office).

NAHODHA, Shamsi Vuai, BA, LLB; Tanzanian politician; b. 28 Nov. 1962, Zanzibar; ed Dar es Salaam Univ.; mem. Chama Cha Mapinduzi (CCM) 2000–; Chief Minister, Supreme Revolutionary Council of Zanzibar 2000–10 (post abolished); mem. Parl. 2010–, mem. Foreign Affairs, Security and Defense Cttee 2015–18; Minister of Home Affairs 2010–12; Minister of Defence and Nat. Service 2012–13; Branch Vice-Pres., Commonwealth Parl. Asscn. *Address:* POB 2182, Zanzibar, Tanzania (office). *Telephone:* (77) 3550063 (office). *E-mail:* s.nahodha@bunge.go.tz (office). *Website:* parliament.go.tz (office); ccm.or.tz (office).

NAHYAN, Sheikh Abdullah bin Zayed al-; United Arab Emirates government official and diplomatist; *Minister of Foreign Affairs and International Co-operation;* b. 30 April 1972; s. of Zayed bin Sultan al-Nahyan; m. HH Sheikha Alyazia bint Saif Al Nahyan; four s. one d.; ed United Arab Emirates Univ.; Under-Sec., Ministry of Information and Culture 1995–97, Minister of Information and Culture 1997–2006; Minister of Foreign Affairs and International Co-operation 2006–; mem. Council of Ministers; Chair. UAE Football Asscn 1993–2001, Emirates Media Inc. 1999–, Nat. Media Council 2006–, Educ. and Human Resources Council; Chair. Bd of Dirs, Abu Dhabi Fund for Devt (ADFD) 2005–, Emirates Foundation for Youth Devt; Deputy Chair. Perm. Cttee on Borders; Chair. Bd of Trustees, Emirates Diplomatic Acad.; mem. Nat. Security Council; mem. Bd, Nat. Defense Coll.; Hon. KCMG 2011. *Leisure interests:* reading, history, scuba diving, football, cycling, classical music. *Address:* Ministry of Foreign Affairs, PO Box 1, Abu Dhabi, United Arab Emirates (office). *Telephone:* (2) 2222000 (office). *Fax:* (2) 2222000 (office). *E-mail:* info@mofa.gov.ae (office). *Website:* www.mofa.gov.ae (office).

NAHYAN, Sheikh Hamdan bin Zayed bin Sultan al-, BA; United Arab Emirates politician; *Ruler's Representative in Western Region of Abu Dhabi;* b. 1963, Al Ain; s. of Sheikh Zayed bin Sultan al-Nahyan (founder and Pres. of UAE) and Sheikha Fatima bint Mubarak Al Ketbi; m. Shamsa bint Hamdan bin Mohammed an-Nahyan; six s.; ed United Arab Emirates Univ.; Minister of State for Foreign Affairs 1990–2006; Deputy Prime Minister and Minister of Public Works 1997–2009; Ruler's Rep. in Western Region of Abu Dhabi 2009–; Chair. Emirati German Friendship Soc., Red Crescent Authority, Emirates Camel Racing Fed.; Pres. Abu Dhabi Univ. Bd of Trustees; fmr Pres. UAE Football League; Hon. Chair. Al-Jazira Club, Chair. Hon. Panel. *Address:* Office of the President of the United Arab Emirates and Ruler of Abu Dhabi, Manhal Palace, PO Box 280, Abu Dhabi, United Arab Emirates (office). *Telephone:* (2) 6652000 (office). *Fax:* (2) 6651962 (office).

NAHYAN, HH Sheikh Hamed bin Zayed al-; United Arab Emirates royal and government official; *Managing Director, Abu Dhabi Investment Authority;* third s. of Sheikha Mouza, one of several wives of UAE's founder, Sheikh Zayed bin Sultan al-Nahyan; half brother of HH Sheikh Khalifa bin Zayed al-Nahyan, (Pres. of UAE), younger brother of Sheikh Ahmed bin Zayed al-Nahyan; currently Chair. Abu Dhabi Crown Prince's Court and Chair. Higher Corpn of Specialized Economy Zones (ZonesCorp); Man. Dir Abu Dhabi Investment Authority 2010–. *Address:* Abu Dhabi Investment Authority, 211 Corniche, PO Box 3600, Abu Dhabi, United Arab Emirates (office). *Telephone:* (2) 415-0000 (office). *Fax:* (2) 415-1000 (office). *E-mail:* info@adia.ae (office). *Website:* www.adia.ae (office).

NAHYAN, HH Sheikh Khalifa bin Zayed al-, (Ruler of Abu Dhabi); United Arab Emirates; *President;* b. 25 Jan. 1948, al-Ain; s. of HH Sheikh Zayed bin Sultan al-Nahyan and HH Sheikha Hassa bint Mohammed bin Khalifa an-Nahyan; m. Shamsa bint Suhailal-Mazrouei; apptd Rep. of Ruler of Abu Dhabi in Eastern Region of Abu Dhabi and Head of Courts Dept in Al-Ain on his father's accession as Ruler of Abu Dhabi 1966, Crown Prince of Abu Dhabi and Head of Abu Dhabi Defence Force 1969; Prime Minister of Abu Dhabi and Minister of Defence and Finance 1971–74, first Chair. Abu Dhabi Exec. Council 1974; Deputy Prime Minister of UAE 1973; Supreme Commdr UAE Armed Forces 1976; Chair. Supreme Petroleum Council late 1980s–, Abu Dhabi Fund for Devt, Abu Dhabi Investment Authority, Research and Wildlife Devt Agency; Pres. of UAE and Ruler of Emirate of Abu Dhabi 2004–. *Leisure interests:* falconry, fishing, reading history and poetry. *Address:* Office of the President of the United Arab Emirates and Ruler of Abu Dhabi, Manhal Palace, PO Box 280, Abu Dhabi, United Arab Emirates (office). *Telephone:* 6652000 (office). *Fax:* 6651962 (office).

NAHYAN, HH Sheikh Mansour bin Zayed bin Sultan al-, BA; United Arab Emirates royal, government official and business executive; *Chairman, International Petroleum Investment Company;* b. 20 Nov. 1970, Trucial States, Abu Dhabi; s. of HH Sheikh Zayed bin Sultan al-Nahyan and Sheikha Fatima; half brother of Khalifa bin Zayed al-Nahyan (Pres. of UAE and Emir of Abu Dhabi); m. Sheikha Alia bint Mohammed bin Butti al-Hamed mid-1990s; one s.; m. Sheikha Manal bint Mohammed bin Rashid al-Maktoum 2005; three c.; mem. of ruling family of Abu Dhabi; apptd Chair. Presidential Office for UAE 1997, apptd by his half brother as First Minister of Presidential Affairs following merger of Presidential Office and Presidential Court; apptd Chair. Ministerial Council for Services; Deputy Prime Minister 2009–; apptd Chair. Nat. Centre for Documentation and Research 2000; apptd Deputy Chair. Abu Dhabi Educ. Council 2005; apptd Chair. Emirates Foundation 2005, Abu Dhabi Food Control Authority 2005, Abu Dhabi Fund for Devt 2005, First Gulf Bank –2006, Abu Dhabi Judicial Dept 2006, Khalifa bin Zayed Charity Foundation 2007, Emirates Investment Authority 2007–, Emirates Horse Racing Authority; mem. Supreme Petroleum Council 2005–; Chair. International Petroleum Investment Co. 2005–; mem. Bd of Dirs Abu Dhabi Investment Council 2005–; Owner of Manchester City Football Club 2008–; mem. Bd of Trustees, Zayed Charitable and Humanitarian Foundation. *Achievements:* an accomplished horse rider, has won several Endurance Racing tournaments held in the Middle East. *Address:* International Petroleum Investment Company, PO Box 7528, Sheikh Zayed the 1st Street, Al Muhairy Centre, Office Tower, 10th Floor, Abu Dhabi, United Arab Emirates (office). *Telephone:* (2) 6336555 (office). *Fax:* (2) 6330111 (office). *E-mail:* info@ipic.ae (office). *Website:* www.ipic.ae (office).

NAHYAN, HH Sheikh Mohammed bin Zayed al-, (Crown Prince of Abu Dhabi); United Arab Emirates government official; *Deputy Supreme Commander of the UAE Armed Forces;* b. 1961; s. of Zayed bin Sultan al-Nahyan and Fatima bint Mubarak al-Ketbi; m.; nine c.; ed Royal Mil. Acad. Sandhurst, UK; Deputy Crown Prince of Abu Dhabi 2003–04, Crown Prince of Abu Dhabi 2004–; Chief of Staff of Armed Forces of UAE 1993–2005, Deputy Supreme Commdr UAE Armed Forces 2005–; Chair. Exec. Bd 2004–; mem. Abu Dhabi Exec. Council, Deputy Chair. 2004–; mem. Supreme Petroleum Council; Chair. Abu Dhabi Council for Econ. Devt, Abu Dhabi Educ. Council 2005–; Head of Mubadala Devt Co. 2002–,

UAE Offsets Group; Pres. Emirates Centre for Strategic Studies and Research; Special Adviser to his brother Sheikh Khalifa bin Zayed al-Nahyan; numerous decorations. *Address:* Abu Dhabi Council for Economic Development, PO Box 44484, Abu Dhabi, United Arab Emirates (office). *Telephone:* (2) 6913300 (office). *Fax:* (2) 6913400 (office). *E-mail:* info@adced.ae (office). *Website:* www.adced.ae (office).

NAHYAN, HE Sheikh Nahayan Mabarak al-; United Arab Emirates university chancellor and politician; *Minister of State for Tolerance;* b. 1951; Chancellor, United Arab Emirates Univ. 1976–2013, Higher Colls of Tech. 1988–2013, Abu Dhabi Petroleum Univ. –2013, Zayed Univ. –2013; Minister of Higher Educ. and Scientific Research 1990–2004, of Educ. 2004–13, of Culture, Youth and Community Devt 2013–17; Minister of State for Tolerance 2017–; Chair. Union Nat. Bank, Abu Dhabi Group (construction co.), Bank Alfalah Ltd; Hilal-i-Pakistan Award, Pres. of Pakistan. *Address:* General Secretariat of the Cabinet, PO Box 899, Abu Dhabi, United Arab Emirates (office). *Fax:* (2) 6777399 (office). *Website:* uaecabinet.ae (office).

NAHYAN, Sheikh Sultan bin Zayed bin Sultan al-; United Arab Emirates government official and army officer; b. 1955, Al Ain, Abu Dhabi, Trucial States; s. of Zayed bin Sultan al-Nahyan; m. Shamsa bint Mohammed bin Khalifa an-Nahyan; ed in Abu Dhabi, Lebanon, Sandhurst Mil. Acad., UK; Commdr Western Mil. Dist 1976; Gen. Commdr UAE Armed Forces 1978; now Deputy Commdr Abu Dhabi Defence Forces; Deputy Prime Minister 1990–97, 1997–2009; Pres.'s Rep.; Chair. Culture and Media Centre, Emirates Heritage Club, Zayed Centre for Co-ordination and Follow-up 1999–2003; mem. Supreme Petroleum Council, Abu Dhabi Investment Authority. *Address:* Culture and Media Centre, Al Khaleej Al Arabi Street (30th Street), Villa 4/417, PO Box 5727, Abu Dhabi, United Arab Emirates. *Telephone:* (2) 6666130. *Fax:* (2) 6663088. *E-mail:* administration@cmc .ae. *Website:* www.cmc.ae.

NAIDENOV, Angel Petrov; Bulgarian politician and fmr merchant seaman; b. 28 Sept. 1958, Kardzhali; m. Nina Naidenova (divorced); ed Nikola Vaptsarov Naval Acad., Varna, G. S. Rakovski Nat. Defence Acad., Sofia; worked for shipping cos Parahodstvo Bulgarski Morski Flot AD, Varna and Navigation Maritime Bulgare (NAVIBULGAR); fmr Ship's Mate and specialist, Darzhavno Stopansko Obedinenie Voden Transport, Varna (state-owned shipping group); fmr specialist, Deputy Dir and Dir, Darzhavno Stopansko Predpriyatie Despred, Haskovo (Despred State Econ. Enterprise); Mayor of Dimitrovgrad 1990–94; Gov. of Haskovo Region 1995–97; mem. Narodno Sobranie (Nat. Ass., parl.) for Constituency No 14 (Pernik) (BSP) 1995–2013, fmr Deputy Chair. Parl. Cttees on Nat. Security, Foreign Affairs and Defence, Chair. Parl. Cttee on Defence 2005–09, Chair. Parl. Group of Coalition for Bulgaria 2005–09, Deputy Chair. 2009–13; Minister of Defence 2013–14; mem. Bulgarian Socialist Party (BSP), mem. Exec. Office of BSP Nat. Council, also Party Spokesperson.

NAIDOO, Beverley, BA (Hons), PGCE, PhD; South African/British author; b. (Beverley Trewhela), 21 May 1943, Johannesburg, South Africa; d. of Ralph Henry Trewhela and Evelyn Levison; m. Nandhagopaul Naidoo 1969; one s. one d.; ed Univ. of Witwatersrand, Univ. of York, Univ. of Southampton; NGO worker, SA 1964; detained without trial, SA 1964; teacher, London then Dorset, UK 1969–89; educ. adviser on English and cultural diversity, Dorset 1990–97; writer 1985–; Hon. Visiting Fellow, School of Educ., Univ. of Southampton 1992–2006; Hon. DLitt (Southampton) 2002, (Exeter) 2007; Hon. DUniv (Open Univ.) 2003. *Play:* The Playground, Polka Theatre, London 2004. *Radio:* The Other Side of Truth (BBC) 2003. *Publications:* Censoring Reality: An Examination of Non-fiction Books on South Africa 1985, Journey to Jo'burg (The Other Award 1985) 1985, Chain of Fire (Vlag en Wimpel Award 1991) 1989, Through Whose Eyes? Exploring Racism: Reader, Text and Context 1992, Letang and Julie (series – illustrator Petra Rohr-Rouendaal) 1994, No Turning Back (Josette Frank Award, Child Study Children's Book Cttee Award 1998, African Studies Asscn Children's Book Award for Older Readers 1998) 1995, Where Is Zami? (illustrator Petra Rohr-Rouendaal) 1998, The Other Side of Truth (Arts Council Writers Award 1999, Carnegie Medal for Children's Literature 2000, Smarties Book Prize Silver Medal 2000, Jane Addams Book Award (older children category) 2002, Sankei Children's Book Award 2003) 2000, Out of Bounds (Jane Addams Peace Asscn Book Award for Older Children 2004, African Studies Asscn Children's Africana Book Award (Older Readers) 2004, Parents' Choice Silver Honor Award 2003) 2001, Baba's Gift (with Maya Naidoo, illustrator Karin Littlewood) 2003, The Great Tug of War and Other Stories 2003, Web of Lies 2004, Burn My Heart (African Studies Asscn Children's Africana Book Award (Honor Book Older Readers) 2010) 2007, Call of the Deep 2008, S is for South Africa (with photographer Prodeepta Das) (African Studies Asscn Children's Africana Honor Book for Young Children 2011) 2011, Aesop's Fables (illustrator Piet Grobler) (Parents Choice Silver Award 2011), Death of an Idealist: In Search of Neil Aggett 2012. *Leisure interests:* reading, theatre, walking. *Address:* c/o Hilary Delamere, The Agency, 24 Pottery Lane, London, W11 4LZ, England (office). *Telephone:* (20) 7727-1346 (office). *Fax:* (20) 7727-9037 (office). *E-mail:* info@theagency.co.uk (office). *Website:* www.theagency.co.uk (office); www.beverleynaidoo.com.

NAIDOO, Jayaseelan (Jay); South African trade union official, banker and business executive; b. 20 Dec. 1954, Durban; m. Lucie Pagé 1992; two s. one d.; ed Sastri Coll., Durban and Univ. of Durban-Westville; mem. SASO 1977; involved in community orgs, Natal 1976–79; studies interrupted by political events 1978; Organizer Fed. of South African Trade Unions (FOSATU) 1980; Gen. Sec. Sweet Food & Allied Workers Union 1982, Congress of South African Trade Unions (COSATU) 1985–93; mem. Parl. (ANC) 1994–99; Minister, Office of the Pres., Govt of Nat. Unity 1994–96, Minister of Posts and Telecommunications and Broadcasting 1996–99; Co-founder The J and J Group 1999–2010; Chair. Devt Bank of Southern Africa 2000–10, Global Alliance for Improved Nutrition (GAIN) 2003–15; Commr, UN Broadband Comm. 2010–12; mem. Bd Dirs Mo Ibrahim Foundation 2013–, Old Mutual Life Assurance Company of South Africa (Omlacsa) 2007–09; mem. UN Scaling up Nutrition Lead Group 2012–, Health Advisory Comm. Clinton Global Initiative 2007–; Chevalier, Légion d'honneur 2006. *Leisure interests:* jazz, skiing cross-country, family, cuisine.

NAIDU, Muppavarapu Venkaiah, BA, BL; Indian politician; *Vice-President;* b. 1 July 1949, Chavatapalem, Nellore Dist, Andhra Pradesh; s. of Rangaiah Naidu and Ramanamma Naidu; m. M. Usha; one s. one d.; ed V.R. Coll., Coll. of Law, Andhra Univ.; fmr agriculturalist; political activist, imprisoned during Nat. Emergency 1975–77; Pres. Youth Wing of Janata Party, Andhra Pradesh (AP) 1977–80, State Univ. of Bharatiya Janata Party (BJP—Indian People's Party) 1988–93, Student Union, Andhra Univ. 1973–74; Vice-Pres. Youth Wing of All-India BJP 1980–83, Leader of BJP Legis. Party, AP 1980–85, Gen. Sec. All-India BJP 1993–2002, Pres. BJP 2002–04; mem. AP Legis. Ass. for Udayagiri 1978–83, 1983–85; mem. Rajya Sabha for Karnataka 1998–16, for Rajasthan 2016–17; Minister of Rural Devt 2000–02, Minister of Parl. Affairs 2014–16, of Urban Devt 2014–17, of Housing and Urban Poverty Alleviation 2014–17, of Information and Broadcasting 2016–17; Vice-Pres. of India 2017–; Pres. Governing Council, UN-Habitat. *Address:* Vice-President's Secretariat, 6 Maulana Azad Road, New Delhi 110011, India (office). *Telephone:* (11) 23018684 (office). *E-mail:* officemvnaidu@ gmail.com (office); vpindia@nic.in (office). *Website:* mvenkaiahnaidu.net (office); vicepresidentofindia.nic.in (office).

NAIDU, Hon. Nara Chandrababu, MA; Indian politician and business executive; *Chief Minister of Andhra Pradesh;* b. 20 April 1950, Naravari Palle, Madras State (now in Andhra Pradesh); s. of N. K. Naidu and Smt. Ammanamma Naidu; m. Nara Bhuvaneswari; one s.; ed Sri Venkateswara Univ., Tirupathi; mem. Andhra Pradesh Legis. Ass. 1978, re-elected 1989, 1994; Minister 1978–83; Gen. Sec. and Co-ordinator Telugu Desam Party 1989–94; Minister of Finance and Revenue 1994–95; Chief Minister of Andhra Pradesh 1995–2004, 2014–; Pres. Telugu Desam Party (Telugu Nation); f. Heritage Foods; fmr Chair. State Karshak Parishad; fmr Dir A. P. Small Scale Industries Devt Corpn; Co-chairperson Nat. Task Force on Information Tech.; Businessperson of the Year Award, The Economic Times 1998, IT Man of the Year Award, Computer World 1999, named South Asian of the Year, Time Asia magazine 1999. *Address:* Office of the Chief Minister, Government of Andhra Pradesh, C-Block, 6th Floor, AP Secretariat, Hyderabad Begumpet, opp. Grand Kakatiya, Hyderabad 500 034, India (office). *Telephone:* (40) 23456698 (office). *Fax:* (40) 2345498 (office). *E-mail:* cmap@ap.gov .in (office). *Website:* www.aponline.gov.in (office).

NAIK, A(nil) M(anibhai); Indian business executive; *Non-Executive Chairman, Larsen & Toubro Limited;* b. 9 June 1942, Ambabari, now in Daman, Maharashtra; ed Birla Vishwakarma Mahavidhyalaya Eng Coll., Vallabh Vidyanagar, Gujarat; joined Larsen & Toubro Ltd (eng co. and one of India's largest cos) as a jr engineer 1965, Gen. Man. 1985–89, Vice-Pres. (Operations) and mem. Bd of Dirs 1989–95, Pres. (Operations) 1995–99, Man. Dir and CEO 1999–2003, Chair. and Man. Dir 2003–14, Group Exec. Chair. 2014–17, Non-Exec. Chair. 2017–; Chair. Indian Inst. of Man. Soc., Ahmedabad 2012–16; Chair. and Pres. Kharel Educ. Soc.; led Indian industry's del. to 17th Congress of World Energy Council, Houston, USA 1998; mem. del. led by Prime Minister Atal Behari Vajpayee, along with key Cabinet colleagues; participated in India-EU Summit, Copenhagen Oct. 2002, Sixth India-EU Business Summit, New Delhi Sept. 2005; Sr mem. Confed. of Indian Industry Nat. Council; mem. Bd of Trade, Ministry of Commerce, Govt of India; mem. Bd of Govs Indian Inst. of Man., Ahmedabad; mem. Bd of Trustees Indian Business Trust for HIV/AIDS; Fellow, Indian Nat. Acad. of Engineers; Hon. Consul Gen. for Denmark; Kt, Order of the Dannebrog (Denmark) 2008, Order of the Dannebrog–Knight First Class; Dr hc (Sardar Patel Univ.) 2011, (Gujarat Technological Univ.) 2013; JRD Tata Corp. Leadership Award, All India Man. Asscn 2004, Exec. of the Year Award, Indian Asscn of Secs & Admin. Professionals 2004, Lifetime Achievement Excellence Award for Best Corp. Man. of the Decade, Foundation of Indian Industry & Economists 2004, Sankara Ratna Award, Sankara Nethralaya 2005, Man. Man of the Year Award, Bombay Man. Asscn 2005, Outstanding Chief Exec. Award, Indian Inst. of Industrial Eng 2005, IEI Eng Personality Trophy, Inst. of Engineers India 2008, Distinguished Alumnus, Birla Vishwakarma Mahavidyalaya (also known as BVM Eng Coll.), Vallabh Vidyanagar, Gujarat 2008, V. Krishnamurthy Award for Excellence, Centre for Org. Devt, Hyderabad 2008, Entrepreneur of the Year Award (Professional Category), Ernst & Young 2008, Transformational Leader Award, Indian Merchants' Chamber and Asian Centre for Corp. Governance & Sustainability 2008, Gujarat Garima (Pride of Gujarat) Award, Govt of Gujarat 2009, Business Leader of the Year, The Economic Times 2009, Gujarat Garima Award 2009, Lakshya Business Visionary Award, Nat. Inst. of Industrial Eng, Mumbai 2009, Padma Bhushan 2009, Infrastructure Leader of the Year Award, CNBC TV18 2012, Padma Vibhushan 2019. *Achievements include:* instrumental in setting up Larsen & Toubro Public Charitable Trust (conducts skill training at Mumbai, Lonavala, Aurangabad, Latur and Kharel). *Address:* Larsen & Toubro Ltd, L&T House, Ballard Estate, PO Box 278, Mumbai 400 001, India (office). *Telephone:* (22) 67525856 (office). *Fax:* (22) 67525858 (office). *E-mail:* ccd@lth .ltindia.com (office). *Website:* www.larsentoubro.com (office).

NAILATIKAU, Ratu Epeli, OBE; Fijian government official, diplomatist, army officer and fmr head of state; *Speaker of Parliament;* b. 5 July 1941, Levuka, Ovalau; s. of Ratu Edward Cakobau and Vasemaca Tuiburelevu; m. Adi Koila Mara; one s. one d.; ed Levuka Public School and Queen Victoria School; completed mil. training in New Zealand, seconded to 1st Bn, Royal New Zealand Infantry Regt in Sarawak, Malaysia 1966, Brig.-Gen., Fiji Infantry Regt 1987–88, Commdr of Armed Forces 1982–88; fmr High Commr to UK; Amb. to Denmark, Egypt, Germany, Israel and Holy See, to the Pacific 1998–99; Perm. Sec. for Foreign Affairs and External Trade 1999–2000; Deputy Prime Minister 2000–01; Minister for Fijian Affairs 2000–01; Speaker of House of Reps 2001–06, Chair. Parl. Appropriations and House Cttees 2001–06, Speaker of Parl. 2019–; Minister of Foreign Affairs and Trade 2007 (in Cdre Josaia Bainimarama's interim govt), Minister of Foreign Affairs, International Co-operation and Civil Aviation 2007–08, of Prov. Devt and Multi-Ethnic Affairs 2008–09; Vice-Pres. of Fiji April–July 2009, Acting Pres. July–Nov. 2009, Pres. 2009–15; LVO, Meritorious Service Decoration, Venerable Order of the Hosp. of St John of Jerusalem. *Address:* Parliament of the Republic of Fiji, POB 2352, Government Building, Suva, Fiji (office). *Telephone:* 3225600 (office); 3305811 (office). *E-mail:* info@ parliament.gov.fj (office). *Website:* www.parliament.gov.fj/speaker-of-parliament.

NA'IM, Abdullahi Ahmed An-, LLB, Dip.Crim., PhD; Sudanese/American academic; *Charles Howard Candler Chaired Professor of Law, Emory University;* b. 19 Nov. 1946, Shendi, Sudan; ed Univ. of Khartoum, Univs of Cambridge and Edinburgh, UK; Lecturer and Assoc. Prof. of Law, Univ. of Khartoum 1976–85;

Rockefeller Fellow, Columbia Univ. Center for Study of Human Rights 1981–82; Visiting Prof., UCLA 1985–87; Fellow, Woodrow Wilson Int. Center for Scholars 1987–88; Ariel F. Sallows Prof. of Human Rights, Univ. of Saskatchewan, Canada 1988–91; Olof Palme Visiting Prof., Uppsala Univ., Sweden 1991–92; Visiting Fellow, Harvard Law School Human Rights Program 1991; Scholar-in-Residence, Ford Foundation Office for Middle East and N Africa, Cairo, Egypt 1992–93; Prof. of Law and Sr Fellow of Law and Religion Program, Emory Univ., Atlanta 1995–, Charles Howard Candler Chaired Prof. of Law 1999–; Visiting Prof., Utrecht Univ. 1999, Harvard Law School 2003; Wiarda Chair, Faculty of Law, Utrecht Univ. 2005–06; Global Legal Scholar, Univ. of Warwick School of Law, UK 2007–09; Scholar-in-Residence, Ford Foundation, New York May–Dec. 2007; Extraordinary Prof., Human Rights Centre, Univ. of Pretoria, South Africa 2009; Exec. Dir Human Rights Watch/Africa, Washington, DC 1993–95; Commr Int. Comm. of Jurists; mem. Bd Urban Morgan Inst. for Human Rights, Cairo Inst. for Human Rights Studies, Int. Council on Human Rights Policy, Geneva, Global Rights, Washington, DC 2009–; mem. Editorial Bd Human Rights Quarterly, International Politics; Dr hc (Univ. catholique de Louvain) 2009; Dr J.P. van Praag Award of Dutch Humanist Ethical Soc. 1999, Marion Creekmore Award for Internationalization, Emory Univ. *Publications:* Sudanese Criminal Law: The General Principles of Criminal Responsibility 1985, The Second Message of Islam by Ustadh Mahmoud Mohamed Taha (English trans.) 1987, Toward an Islamic Reformation: Civil Liberties, Human Rights and International Law 1990, Human Rights in Africa: Cross-Cultural Perspectives (co-ed.) 1990, Cry of the Owl by Francis Deng (Arabic trans.) 1991, Human Rights in Cross Cultural Perspectives: Quest for Consensus (ed.) 1992, Human Rights and Religious Values (co-ed.) 1995, Proselytization and Communal Self-Determination in Africa (ed.) 1999, The Politics of Memory: Truth, Healing and Social Justice (ed.) 2002, Cultural Transformation and Human Rights in Africa (ed.) 2002, Human Rights Under African Constitutions (ed.) 2003, African Constitutionalism and the Role of Islam 2006, Islam and the Secular State 2008; numerous writings, including 60 articles and 28 short articles and book reviews. *Address:* School of Law, Emory University, 1301 Clifton Road, Atlanta, GA 30322, USA (office). *Telephone:* (404) 727-1198 (office). *E-mail:* Abduh46@law.emory.edu (office). *Website:* www.law.emory.edu (office).

NAIR, Dileep, BMechEng, MPA; Singaporean banker, diplomatist and fmr UN official; b. 12 July 1950, Singapore; ed McGill Univ., Montreal, Canada, Kennedy School of Govt, Harvard Univ., USA; with Housing and Devt Bd 1974–79; joined Admin. Service 1979, various posts including Dir in charge of expenditure control, Deputy Sec. Ministry of Trade and Industry 1986–89, Ministry of Defence 1989–97; CEO Post Office Savings Bank of Singapore 1997–98, Man. Dir Devt Bank of Singapore 1998–2000; Under-Sec.-Gen. for Internal Oversight Services, UN 2000–05; Consul-Gen. in Dubai 2005–11, Amb. to Laos 2011–13, High Commr to Ghana (resident in Singapore) 2013–17; fmr Vice-Pres. Singapore Indian Devt Asscn; Ind. Dir Keppel Data Centre REIT 2014–, Thakral Corp. 2015–, Singapore Reinsurance 2015–; mem. Hindu Advisory Bd; mem. Bd of Govs Raffles Inst.; Colombo Plan Scholar 1969–73; Friendship Medal, Govt of Laos 2013.

NAIR, G. Madhavan, BSc; Indian engineer; b. 31 Oct. 1943, Thiruvanathapuram; ed Coll. of Eng, Univ. of Kerala; Head of Payload Integration Section, Thumba Equatorial Rocket Launching Station, Trivandrum 1967–72; Project Man. Telecommand System, Vikram Sarabhai Space Centre (VSSC), Trivandrum 1972–74, Head, Electronics Systems 1980–84, Project Engineer, SLV-3 Project 1974–80, Assoc. Project Dir Polar Satellite Launch Vehicle 1984–88, Project Dir 1988–95, Programme Dir ILVP, VSSC, Trivandrum 1994–96, Dir Liquid Propulsion Systems Centre, Trivandrum 1995–99, Dir VSSC 1999–2003; Chair. Indian Space Research Org. (ISRO) 2003–09; Sec. to Dept of Space, Govt of India 2003–09; Chair. Space Comm. 2003–09, Chair. Governing Body, Nat. Remote Sensing Agency, Hyderabad 2003–08; Chair. Antrix Corpn, Bangalore 2003–09; Pres. Astronautical Soc. of India 2004, Aeronautical Soc. of India 2005; Vice-Pres., Scientific Activities Cttee, Int. Acad. of Astronautics 2006–07, Pres. 2009–15; Gen. Pres. 97th Indian Science Congress 2009–10; Sr Assoc. Nat. Inst. of Advanced Studies 2004–07; Pres. Intersputnik Bd 2005; Chair. Research Council of Nat. Aerospace Laboratories 2007–10; Chair. Centre for Management Devt 2010–; Chair. Bd of Govs Indian Inst. of Tech., Patna –2012; mem. System Soc. of India, Working Cttee of Current Science Asscn 2004–06, Int. Acad. of Astronautics 2004; joined Bharatiya Janata Party 2018; Fellow, Indian Nat. Acad. of Eng 2009–10, Astronautical Soc. of India, Nat. Acad. of Sciences; Hon. Fellow, Aeronautical Soc. of India 2007, Indian Soc. for Non-Destruction Testing; Hon. DPhil (Punjab Technical Univ.) 2003; Dr hc (Indian Inst. of Tech., Delhi) 2004, (Univ. of Mysore, G.J. Univ., Hissar) 2006; Hon. DSc (Sri Venkateswara Univ., Indian Inst. of Tech., Delhi) 2004, (Rani Durgavati Vishwavidyalaya, Indira Gandhi Nat. Open Univ., Delhi, Rani Durgavati Vishwavidyalaya, Jabalpur) 2005, (Cochin Univ. of Science and Tech., Kochi) 2006, (Univ. of Kerala, Rajiv Gandhi Technical Univ., Bhopal) 2007, (SRM Univ., Chennai) 2008, (Pandit Ravishankar Shukla Univ., Raipur, Karnatak Univ., Dharwad, Indian Inst. of Tech., Bombay, Indian Inst. of Tech., Kharagpur) 2009, (Vishvesariah Technological Univ., Belgaum) 2010, (Ch. Charan Singh Univ., Meerut) 2010, (Amity Univ., Gurgaon, Delhi) 2015; Nat. Aeronautical Award 1994, FIE Foundation Award 1994, Shri Om Prakash Bhasin Award 1995, Swadeshi Sastra Puraskar Award 1995, Padma Bhushan 1998, Vikram Sarabhai Memorial Gold Medal 2003, Personality of the Decade Award 2004, Melpadom Attumail Georgekutty Award 2004, Raja Sir Muthiah Chettiar Endowment Award 2004, 10th Science and Tech. Award 2003–04, Sathyabama Deemed Univ. 2005, Benedict Mar Gregorios Award, Asscn of Mar Ivanios Coll. Old Students 2005, Dr Yelavarthy Nayudamma Memorial Award 2004 2005, H.K. Firodia Award 2005, Shri Balvantbhai Parekh Award, Indian Planetary Soc. 2006, Best R&D Man of the Year, Corporate Excellence Award 2005 2006, Lokmanya Tilak Award 2006, Sree Chithira Thirunal Award, Sasthra Ratna Purskara 2006, Gold Medal from the Prime Minister 2007, 9th Sri Chandrasekarendra Saraswathi Nat. Eminence Award 2006, Dr A.S.G. Jayakar Award, Science India Forum, Muscat and Indian Inst. of Scientific Heritage, Oman Chapter 2007, Shankar Ratna Award 2007, Bharat Shiromani Award 2006, 2007, M. M. Chugani Award 2006, 2008, Raja Rammohan Puraskar Award 2008, NDTV Indian of the Year Award 2009, Kururamma Award 2009, Yashwantrao Chavan Nat. Award 2008, 2009, Chanakya Award 2009, A.V. Rama Rao Tech. Award 2009, M.P. Birla Memorial Award 2009, Padma Vibhushan 2009.

NAIR, Mira; Indian film director and producer; b. 15 Oct. 1957, Bhubaneswar, Orissa; m. 1st Mitch Epstein; m. 2nd Mahmood Mamdan; one s.; ed Irish Catholic boarding school, Simla, Univ. of Delhi and Harvard Univ., USA; performed with experimental theatre co., Calcutta (now Kolkata); began career as documentary and feature film maker at Harvard Univ.; Asst Prof., School of the Arts, Columbia Univ., New York; Founder Mirabai Films 1989; est. Maisha Film Lab, Kampala, Uganda 2004; Govt of India Padma Bhushan 2012; New Generation Award, Los Angeles Film Critics' Asscn 1988, Asian Media Award 1992, India Abroad Person of the Year 2007, Faith Hubley Web of Life Award, Rochester-High Falls Int. Film Festival 2004, Padma Bhushan 2012. *Films:* Jama Masjid Street Journal 1979, So Far from India 1983, India Cabaret (American Film Festival Award for Best Documentary of 1985) 1985, Children of Desired Sex (documentary), Salaam Bombay! (Cannes Film Festival Camera d'Or Award for Best First Feature by a New Dir, Prix du Publique, Lilian Gish Award, Los Angeles Women in Film Festival 1988, three awards at Montreal World Film Festival 1988, Nat. Film Award 1989) 1988, Mississippi Masala (three awards at Venice Film Festival, Critics Special Award, São Paulo Int. Film Festival 1991, Golden Osella Award 1991, Best Director, Italian Nat. Syndicate of Film Journalists 1992, Independent Spirit Award for Best Feature 1993) 1991, Buddha, The Day the Mercedes Became a Hat 1993, The Perez Family 1996, Kama Sutra 1996, My Own Country 1998, The Laughing Club of India 1999, Monsoon Wedding (Laterna Magica Prize, Golden Lion Award, Venice Film Festival 2001, Audience Award, Canberra Short Film Festival 2001, Zee Cine Award 2002) 2001, Hysterical Blindness 2002, 11'09"01–September 11 2002 (UNESCO Award 2002), Vanity Fair 2005, The Namesake (Golden Aphrodite Award 2006) 2006, Migration 2007, 8 2008, New York I Love You 2009, Amelia 2009, The Reluctant Fundamentalist 2012, Words with Gods 2014, Queen of Katwe 2016. *E-mail:* assistant@mirabaifilms.com (office). *Website:* www.mirabaifilms.com (office).

NAJDER, Zdzisław Marian, PhD; Polish civic leader and author; b. 31 Oct. 1930, Warsaw; s. of Franciszek Najder and Józefa Najder (née Kowalska); m. Halina Paschalska 1965; one s.; ed Warsaw Univ., Univ. of Oxford, UK; Asst Inst. for Literary Research of Polish Acad. of Sciences 1952–57; Sr Asst Aesthetics, Warsaw Univ. 1958–59; on staff, Twórczość (monthly) 1957–81; taught Polish literature at Columbia and Yale Univs, USA 1966 and Univ. of California, Berkeley, USA 1966–67; Prof. of Philosophy, Univ. of California, Davis 1967–68, Regents' Prof. 1968–69; Prof. of English Literature, Northern Illinois Univ., USA 1971–72; Visiting Scholar, Stanford Univ., Calif. 1974–75; adviser to Solidarity Trade Union 1980–90; Visiting Fellow, St Antony's Coll., Oxford, UK 1981, 1988; Head, Polish section of Radio Free Europe, Munich 1982–87; charged with spying, sentenced to death in absentia by Warsaw Mil. Tribunal 1983, stripped of Polish citizenship 1985, sentence revoked 1989, case dismissed 1990; mem. editorial staff, Kontakt, Paris 1988–91; Chair. Nat. Civic Cttee 1990–92; Chief Adviser to the Prime Minister 1992; Pres. Civic Inst. 1991–97, Atlantic Club 1991–93; Chair. Joseph Conrad Soc. (Poland) 1994–; Prof. of English Literature, Univ. of Opole 1997–2003; Adviser to Chair. Cttee for European Integration 1998–2001; Prof., European Acad., Kraków 2005–; mem. Polish Writers' Union 1956–83, PEN Club 1957–, Polish Writers' Asscn 1989–Nat. Council for European Integration 1999–2004; f. Polish Agreement for Independence 1976; Founder and Pres. Club of Weimar 2005–; Commdr's Cross, Order of Polonia Restituta 1983, Commdr, Ordre nat. du Mérite 1991, Chevalier, légion d'honneur 2004; Juliusz Mieroszewski Award 1982, Prize of Modern Language Asscn 1984, Polish PEN Club Prize 1988, Adama Mickiewicza, Weimar Triangle 2009. *Publications:* studies and essays including Conrad's Polish Background 1964, Nad Conradem 1965, Values and Evaluations 1975, Życie Conrada-Korzeniowskiego 1981, Ile jest dróg? 1982, Wymiary polskich spraw 1990, Jaka Polska 1993, Z Polski do Polski poprzez PRL 1995, Conrad in Perspective: Essays on Art and Fidelity 1997, W sercu Europy 1998, Sztuka i wierność 2000. *Leisure interests:* travel, walks in forest, 12th-century Romanesque art. *Telephone:* (22) 8448536 (home). *Fax:* (22) 8448536 (home). *E-mail:* zdzislaw.najder@list.pl (home).

NAJEEB, Fazeel, BA (Econs), MA; Maldivian economist, lawyer and fmr central banker; b. Fuahmulah; ed Univs of Sunderland, Hull and London, UK; Investment Promotion Officer, then Ass. Dir Investment, then Deputy Dir Investment, then Deputy Dir Int. Co-operation, then Dir Int. Co-operation, Ministry of Trade –2008; pursued PhD studies in intellectual property law in UK 2008; Gov. and Chair. Maldives Monetary Authority 2008–13; apptd Minister of Foreign Affairs 2017.

NAJJAR, Iyyad Ibrahim; Syrian film producer and trade union official; b. 1972; Founder Clacket Productions, Damascus (TV and film production co.); also First Deputy Chief, Arab Union for Goods Freight and Logistics (trade union), Syrian Regional Office. *Address:* Clacket Productions, POB 5894, Mezze Highway, Farabi Street, Building 4, Damascus, Syria (office). *Telephone:* (11) 6124446 (office). *E-mail:* info@clacketproductions.com (office). *Website:* www.clacketproductions.com (office).

NAJJAR, Mohammad Mostafa, MEng; Iranian politician; b. 1956, Tehran; ed Khajeh Nasir Toosi Univ., Industrial Man. Univ.; joined Revolutionary Cttees (Revolutionary Police) 1979 and Islamic Revolutionary Guard Corps 1979; Deputy Man. Dir Sasad (defence industry org.) 1976–2007; Minister of Defence 2005–09, Minister of the Interior 2009–13.

NAJMIDDINOV, Safarali Mahsudinovich; Tajikistani politician; ed Tajik State Univ.; fmr Chief Accountant and Head of Dept of Finance, State Cttee of Statistics; Head of Trade Dept, Municipality of Dushanbe 1982–92; Deputy Minister of Trade 1991–2000; Minister of Finance 2000–13; fmr Dir Agency of Social Insurance and Pension.

NAKADAI, Tatsuya; Japanese actor; b. 13 Dec. 1932, Tokyo; m. Tomoye Ryu 1957 (died 1996); ed Haiyuza Actors' Training School; worked with Masaki Kobayashi and Akira Kurosawa; stage work comprises both shingeki (modern theatre) featuring a highly acclaimed Hamlet and roles in other Shakespeare, Gorky, Ibsen and Chekhov adaptations, and avant-garde, including work with Kobo Abe's theatre group; Order of the Rising Sun, Fourth Class, Gold Rays with Rosette 2003; Person of Cultural Merit 2007, Asahi Prize 2013, Kawakita Award 2013. *Theatre includes:* Hamlet 1964, Yotsuya Kaidan 1968, Othello 1971, Richard III 1974, The Lower Depths 1975, Oedipus the King 1978, Macbeth 1982, Cyrano de Bergerac 1990, Death of a Salesman 2000, The Merry Wives of Windsor 2001,

Don Quixote 2008, John Gabriel Borkman 2010, Bluebeard's Castle 2013, Barrymore 2014, Romeo and Juliet 2014. *Films include:* Shichinin no samurai (Seven Samurai) 1954, Kabe atsuki heya (The Thick-Walled Room) 1956, Hi no tori 1956, Fukuaki no seishun 1956, Sazae-san 1956, Oshidori no mon (Lovebirds' Gate) 1956, Ôban 1957, Arakure (Untamed) 1957, Hikage no musume 1957, Zoku Ôban: Fû unhen 1957, Kiken na eiyu (A Dangerous Hero) 1957, Zokuzoku Ôban: Dôto uhen 1957, Sazae-san no seishun (Sazae's Youth) 1957, Kuroi kawa (Black River) 1957, Haha sannin (A Boy and Three Mothers, USA) 1958, Kekkon no subete (All About Marriage) 1958, Buttuke honban (Go and Get It) 1958, Enjo (Conflagration) 1958, Hadaka no taiyo (Naked Sun) 1958, Yajû shisubeshi 1959, Kagi (The Key) 1959, Ginza no onéchan (Three Dolls in Ginza, USA) 1959, Anyakôro 1959, Ningen no joken I (No Greater Love) 1959, Ningen no joken II (The Road to Eternity) 1959, Musume tsuma haha (Daughters, Wives and a Mother) 1960, Aoi yaju (The Blue Beast, USA 1965) 1960, 'Minagoroshi no uta' yori kenjû-yo saraba! (Get 'em All, USA 1961) 1960, Qnna ga kaidan o agaru toki (When a Woman Ascends the Stairs) 1960, Qginsama (Love Under the Crucifix, USA 1965) 1960, Yojimbo (The Bodyguard) 1961, Tsuma to shita onna to shite (As a Wife, As a Woman) 1961, Ningen no joken III (A Soldier's Prayer) 1961, Eien no hito (Immortal Love) 1961, Tsubaki Sanjûrô 1962, Karami-ai (The Inheritance, USA 1964) 1962, Yushu heiya (Madame Aki) 1963, Tengoku to jigoku (Heaven and Hell) 1963, Shiro to kuro (Pressure of Guilt) 1963, Gojuman-nin no isan (Legacy of the 500,000) 1963, Miren 1963, Onna no rekishi (A Woman's Life) 1963, Seppuku (Harakiri, USA) 1964, Jigoku sakusen 1964, Kaidan (Ghost Story) 1964, Chi to suna (Fort Graveyard) 1965, Saigô no shinpan 1965, Dai-bosatsu tôge (The Sword of Doom, USA) 1966, Tanin no kao (The Face of Another) 1966), Jinchoge (Daphne), Yotsuya kaidan 1966 (Illusion of Blood) 1966, Gohiki no shinshi (Cash Calls Hell) 1966, Satsujin kyo jidai (The Age of Assassins) 1967, Kojiro 1967, Jôi-uchi: Hairyô tsuma shimatsu (Samurai Rebellion) 1967, Tabiji 1967, Oggi a me... domani a te! (Today We Kill, Tomorrow We Die!) 1968, Kiru (Kill!, USA) 1969, Rengo kantai shirei chôkan: Yamamoto Isoroku (Admiral Yamamoto) (narrator) 1968, Nikudan (The Human Bullet) 1968, Goyokin (Official Gold) 1969, Eiko e no 5,000 kiro (5,000 Kilometres to Glory) 1969, Nihonkai daikasen (Battle of the Japan Sea) 1969, Hitokiri (Tenchu!, USA 1970) 1969, Tengu-to (Blood End) 1969, Jigokuhen (Portrait of Hell) 1969, Ezo yakata no ketto (Duel at Ezo) 1970, Bakumatsu (The Ambitious) 1970, Buraikan (Outlaws) 1970, Zatôichi abare-himatsuri (Blind Swordsman's Fire Festival) 1970, Tenkan no abarembo (Will to Conquer, USA 1971) 1970, Inochi bonifuro (At the Risk of My Life) 1971, Gekido no showashi: Okinawa kessen (The Battle of Okinawa) 1971, Shussho Iwai (Prison Release Celebration) 1972, Ôshô 1973, Kanashimi no Belladonna (Belladonna) (voice) 1973, Ningen kakumei (The Human Revolution, USA) 1973, Asayake no uta (Rise, Fair Sun, USA 1975) 1973, Karei-naru ichizoku 1974, Seishun no mon (The Gate of Youth, USA 1976) 1975, Tokkan (Battle Cry) 1975, Wagahai wa neko de aru (I Am a Cat) 1975, Kinkanshoku 1975, Banka 1976, Fumô chitai 1976, Sugata Sanshiro 1977, Jo-oh-bachi (Queen Bee) 1978, Kumokiri nizaemon (Bandit vs. Samurai Squad) 1978, Hi no tori (The Firebird) 1978, Buru kurisumasu (Blue Christmas) 1978, Yami no karyudo (Hunter in Darkness) 1979, Kagemusha (Kagemusha the Shadow Warrior), 203 kochi (The Battle of Port Arthur) 1980, Nihon no atsui hibi bôsatsu: Shimoyama shigen (Willful Murder) 1981, Kirûin Hanako no shôgai (Onimasa) 1982, Uchû senkan Yamato: Kanketsuhen (Final Yamato) (narrator) 1983, Ran (Chaos) 1985, Shokutaku no nai ie (The Empty Table) 1985, Atami satsujin jiken 1986, Hachiko monogatari 1987, Yushun (Oracion, USA) 1988, Return From the River Kwai 1988, Ni-ni-roku (Four Days of Snow and Blood, USA 1989, Kagerô 1991, Goh-hime (Basara – The Princess Goh) 1992, Toki rakujitsu (The Distant Setting Sun) 1992, Yao shou du shi (The Wicked City) 1992, Kozure Ôkami: Sono chîsaki te ni 1993, Gekko no natsu (Summer of the Moonlight Sonata 1993, East Meets West 1995, Miyazawa Kenji son ai 1996, Ame agaru (After the Rain) 1999, Kin'yû fushoku rettô: Jubaku (Jubaku: Spellbound) 1999, Sukedachiya sukeroku (Vengeance for Sale) 2001, Shiroi inu to Waltz wo (To Dance with the White Dog) 2002, Hi wa mata noboru 2002, Ashura no gotoku (Like Asura) 2003, Yamato 2005, The Inugamis 2006, Listen to My Heart 2009, Haru's Journey 2010, Zatoichi: The Last 2010, Japan's Tragedy 2012, Until the Break of Dawn 2012, Yakusoku: Nabari dokubudôshu jiken shikeishû no shôgai 2013, The Human Trust 2013, The Tale of Princess Kaguya (voice) 2013, Giovanni's Island (voice) 2014, Gun Woman 2014. *Television includes:* Shurushuru (film) 1966, Shin heike monogatari (series) 1972, Aokiôkami narukichiomoase no shôgai (film) 1980, Taikoki (film, narrator) 1987, Bujinesuman no chichi yori musuko e no 30-tsuu no tegami (series) 1990, Hideyoshi (series) 1996, Crying Out Love, in the Center of the World (series) 2004, Hoshi ni negaio: 7jô ma de umareta 410man no hoshi (film) 2005, Shin ningen kousaten (series) 2006, Gaku (film) 2012, Zainin no uso (mini-series) 2014.

NAKAGAWA, Junko; Japanese business executive; *Executive Managing Director and Chief Financial Officer, Nomura Holdings, Inc.;* ed Kobe Univ.; joined Nomura Securities Co. 1988, held various sr positions in underwriting and finance divs, led several key projects, including Nomura's listing on New York Stock Exchange 2001, left co. to accompany her husband overseas 2004, returned as Pres. Nomura Healthcare Support and Advisory 2008–10, Co-Deputy Chief Financial Officer (CFO), Nomura Holdings, Inc. 2010–11, Exec. Man. Dir and CFO (first woman) 2011–. *Address:* Nomura Holdings, Inc., 9-1 Nihonbashi 1-chome, Tokyo 103-8645, Japan (office). *Telephone:* (3) 5255-1000 (office). *Fax:* (3) 3274-4496 (office). *E-mail:* info@nomura.com (office). *Website:* www.nomura.com (office).

NAKAGOME, Kenji; Japanese insurance industry executive; *President and Representative Director, T&D Holdings, Inc.;* b. 1954; joined Taiyo Life 1976, Gen. Man. Gen. Affairs Dept March–July 2001, Dir of Taiyo Life 2001–, Man. Dir Taiyo Life 2003–04, Man. Dir T&D Holdings 2004–06, Dir and Man. Exec. Officer Taiyo Life and T&D Holdings, Inc. 2006–07, Dir and Sr Exec. Officer Taiyo Life and T&D Holdings, Inc. 2007–08, Rep. Dir and Sr Exec. Officer Taiyo Life 2008–09, Dir of T&D Holdings, Inc., Pres. and Rep. Dir Taiyo Life 2009–11, Pres. and Rep. Dir T&D Holdings, Inc. 2011–. *Address:* T&D Holdings Inc., 2-7-9 Nihonbashi, Chuo-Ku, Tokyo 103-0027, Japan (office). *Telephone:* (3) 3231-8685 (office). *Fax:* (3) 3231-8893 (office). *E-mail:* info@td-holdings.co.jp (office). *Website:* www.td-holdings.co.jp (office).

NAKAJIMA, Shigehiro; Japanese business executive; fmr Sr Vice-Pres. and Corp. Vice-Pres., Fujifilm Corpn, Dir, Fujifilm Holdings Corpn 2010–16, Exec. Vice-Pres. 2011–, Pres. and COO 2012–16, Vice-Chair. and Rep. Dir 2016; Dir, Pres. and COO Fujifilm USA, Inc., Dir, Fuji Xerox Co. Ltd.

NAKAMITSU, Izumi, LLB, MSc; Japanese UN official; *Under-Secretary-General and High Representative for Disarmament Affairs, UN;* b. 1963; m.; two d.; ed Waseda Univ., Tokyo, Georgetown Univ., Washington, DC; began UN career with UN High Commr for Refugees (UNHCR) in Turkey 1991, worked in office of Asst High Commr for Policy and Operations Sergio Vieira de Mello, and in UNHCR field operations in fmr Yugoslavia, Turkey and northern Iraq; mem. UN Reform Team of fmr Sec.-Gen. Kofi Annan; Dir, Policy, Evaluation and Training Div., UN Dept of Peacekeeping 2008–12, Dir Asia and Middle East Div. 2012–14; Asst Admin., UNDP Crisis Response Unit 2014–17; Special Adviser Ad Interim on Follow-up to the Summit on Addressing Large Movements of Refugees and Migrants 2016–17; Under-Sec.-Gen. and High Rep. for Disarmament Affairs 2017–; Chef de Cabinet and Dir of Planning and Coordination, Int. Inst. for Democracy and Electoral Assistance, Stockholm 1998–2004; Prof. of Int. Relations, Hitotsubashi Univ., Tokyo 2005–08; fmr mem. Foreign Exchange Council, Japanese Ministry of Foreign Affairs; fmr Visiting Sr Adviser on Peacebuilding, Japan Int. Cooperation Agency. *Address:* United Nations Office for Disarmament Affairs, UN Plaza, Room S-3185, New York, NY 10017, USA (office). *Fax:* (212) 963-4066 (office). *E-mail:* UNODA-web@un.org (office). *Website:* www.un.org/disarmament/about/ (office).

NAKAMURA, Kenzo, PhD; Japanese physicist and academic; *Head, Physics Division 3, Institute of Particle and Nuclear Studies, High Energy Accelerator Research Organization (KEK);* ed Univ. of Tokyo; Research Assoc., Physics Dept, Univ. of Tokyo 1973–84, Inst. for Cosmic Ray Research 1988–95; Assoc. Prof., Nat. Lab. for High Energy Physics (KEK) 1984–88, Head, Experimental Planning and Program Coordination Div. 1995, currently Head, Physics Div. 3, Inst. of Particle and Nuclear Studies, High Energy Accelerator Research Org. (KEK); mem. Kamiokande Collaboration and Super-Kamiokande Collaboration 1987–; Asahi Prize (Super-Kamiokande Group) for discovery of neutrino mass 1998. *Publications:* numerous articles in scientific journals. *Address:* KEK-IPNS, Room No. 4-307 (Building No. 4), 1-1 Oho, Tsukuba, Ibaraki 305-0801, Japan (office). *Telephone:* (29) 864-5435 (office). *Fax:* (29) 864-2580 (office). *E-mail:* kenzo.nakamura@kek.jp (office). *Website:* legacy.kek.jp (office).

NAKAMURA, Kuniharu; Japanese business executive; *Chairman, Board of Directors, Sumitomo Corporation;* joined Sumitomo Corpn 1974, Gen. Man. Motor Vehicles Dept No. 1, Motor Vehicles Dept No. 3, Motor Vehicles Business Planning and Co-ordination Dept, Planning and Admin Dept, Transportation and Construction Systems Business Unit, Exec. Officer and Gen. Man. Corp. Planning and Co-ordination Dept 2005–07, Man. Exec. Officer and Gen. Man. 2007–08, Man. Exec. Officer and Gen. Man. Corp. Planning and Co-ordination 2008–09, Sr Man. Exec. Officer and Gen. Man. Mineral Resources, Energy, Chemical and Electronics Business Unit April–June 2009, Rep. Dir, Sr Man. Exec. Officer and Gen. Man. 2009–12, Rep. Dir, Exec. Vice-Pres. and Gen. Man. April–June 2012, Rep. Dir, Pres. and CEO Sumitomo Corpn June 2012–18, Chair. Bd of Dirs 2018–. *Address:* Sumitomo Corporation, 8-11 Harumi 1-chome, Chuo-ku, Tokyo 104-8610, Japan (office). *Telephone:* (3) 5166-5000 (office). *Fax:* (3) 5166-6292 (office). *E-mail:* info@sumitomocorp.co.jp (office). *Website:* www.sumitomocorp.co.jp (office).

NAKAMURA, Kunio; Japanese electronics industry executive; b. 5 July 1939, Shiga; ed Osaka Univ.; joined Matsushita Electric Industrial Co. Ltd 1962, Dir Tokyo Special Sales Office, Corp. Consumer Sales Div. 1985–89, Dir Corp. Man. Div. for the Americas and Chair. Matsushita Electric Corpn of America 1993–97, Man. Dir 1996–97, Sr Man. Dir 1997–2000, Pres. Matsushita Electric Industrial Co. Ltd 2000–06, Chair. 2006–12 (renamed Panasonic Corpn Oct. 2008), Pres. Panasonic Co. 1989–92, Pres. Panasonic UK Ltd 1992–93; Pres. AVC Co. 1997–2000.

NAKAMURA, Kuniwo; Palauan politician and fmr head of state; Vice-Pres. of Palau 1989–92; Pres. of Palau 1993–2001; Leader Ta Belau Party.

NAKAMURA, Mitsuyoshi; Japanese business executive; *Chairman and Representative Director, Kajima Corporation;* has spent most of career as marketer involved in business devt with Kajima Corpn, Sr Man. Dir 2002–05, Pres. and Rep. Dir 2005–15, Chair. 2015–. *Address:* Kajima Corpn, 3-1 Motoakasaka 1-chome, Minatu-ku, Tokyo 107-8388, Japan (office). *Telephone:* (3) 3403-3311 (office). *Fax:* (3) 3470-1444 (office). *E-mail:* info@kajima.co.jp (office). *Website:* www.kajima.co.jp (office).

NAKAMURA, Mutsuo, LLB, LLM, LLD; Japanese academic and fmr university administrator; b. 7 Feb. 1939; ed Hokkaido Univ.; Instructor of Law, Hokkaido Univ. 1963–70, Assoc. Prof. 1970–74, Prof. 1974–2001, mem. Senate 1984–88, Dean Faculty of Law 1988–90, Vice-Pres. Hokkaido Univ. 1997–99, Pres. 2001–07; Chair. Promotion Cttee, Hokkaido Univ. Initiative for Sustainable Devt 2005–07; Officier des Palmes académiques 2004. *Publication:* Ainu minzoku hōsei to kenpō 2018.

NAKAMURA, Shuji, BE, MS, PhD; Japanese engineer, academic and entrepreneur; *Professor of Materials, University of California, Santa Barbara;* b. 22 May 1954, Ehime; ed Univ. of Tokushima; Research and Devt (R&D) Dept, Nichia Chemical Industries Ltd 1979–89; Visiting Research Assoc., Dept of Electrical and Computer Eng, Univ. of Florida 1988–89; Prof., Materials Dept, Univ. of California, Santa Barbara (UCSB) 1999–, Cree Chair in Solid State Lighting & Displays, also Research Dir UCSB Solid State Lighting & Energy Electronics Center; co-Founder Soraa Inc.; mem. Nat. Acad. of Eng 2003; Order of Culture Award (Japan) 2014; Dr hc (Univ. of Mass Lowell) 2018; numerous awards, including Sakurai Award 1995, Nishina Memorial Award 1996, Okochi Memorial Award 1997, Julius-Springer Prize for Applied Physics 1999, Takayanagi Award 2000, Carl Zeiss Research Award 2000, Honda Award 2000, Crystal Growth and Crystal Technology Award 2000, Asahi Award 2001, Optical Soc. of America Nick Holonyak Award 2001, Franklin Institute Medal in Eng 2002, Millennium Tech. Prize 2006, Harvey Prize, Technion, Israel (co-recipient) 2009, Technology & Engineering Emmy Award, Nat. Acad. of Television Arts & Sciences 2012, named Silicon Valley Intellectual Property Law Asscn Inventor of the Year 2012, Nobel Prize in Physics (co-recipient with Isamu Akasaki and Hiroshi Amano for the invention of blue light-emitting diodes (LEDs)) 2014, Charles Stark Draper Prize, Nat. Acad. of Inventors 2015, Global Energy Prize (Russia) 2015, Mountbatten

Medal 2017, Zayed Future Energy Prize 2018. *Achievement:* inventor of solid-state white lights made from LEDs and violet laser diodes. *Publications:* more than 550 papers in scientific journals; more than 300 Japanese and 200 US patents. *Address:* Materials Department, University of California, Santa Barbara, CA 93106-5055, USA (office). *Telephone:* (805) 893-5552 (office). *Fax:* (805) 893-8983 (office). *E-mail:* shuji@engineering.ucsb.edu (office). *Website:* www.materials.ucsb .edu/people/faculty/shuji-nakamura (office); ssleec.ucsb.edu/nakamura (office).

NAKAMURA, Toshikazu, PhD; Japanese clinical professor of medicine; *Professor and Chairman, Division of Molecular Regenerative Medicine, Osaka University Graduate School of Medicine;* ed Osaka Univ. Grad. School of Science; Assoc. Prof., School of Medicine, Univ. of Tokushima 1980–88; Prof., Faculty of Science, Kyushu Univ. 1988–93; Prof., Biomedical Research Centre, Osaka Univ. Medical School 1993–2001, Prof., Div. of Molecular Regenerative Medicine, Osaka Univ. Grad. School of Medicine 2001–; Princess Takamatsu Cancer Research Award, Academic Award, Mochida Memorial Foundation, Osaka Science Award, Inoue Prize for Science, and other awards. *Publications:* numerous articles in scientific and medical journals. *Address:* Division of Molecular Regenerative Medicine, Course of Advanced Medicine, B7, Osaka University Graduate School of Medicine, Suita, Osaka 565-0871, Japan (office). *Telephone:* (6) 6879-3783 (office). *Fax:* (6) 6879-3789 (office). *E-mail:* nakamura@onbich.med.osaka-u.ac.jp (office). *Website:* www .med.osaka-u.ac.jp (office).

NAKAMURA, Yuji; Japanese diplomatist; b. Sept. 1944, Tokyo; m. Kazuko Nakamura; ed Tokyo Univ.; joined Ministry of Foreign Affairs 1966, Counsellor, Third Dept, Cabinet Legislation Bureau 1981–83, Dir Cen. and Eastern Europe Div., European and Oceanian Affairs Bureau 1983–85; posted to Germany 1985, Minister, Embassy in Bonn 1990–91, Minister, Embassy in Vienna 1991, fmr Consul-Gen. in Sydney; fmr Dir-Gen., Int. Affairs Dept, House of Councillors; Amb. to Switzerland 2002–05 (also accred to Liechtenstein 2003–05), to Italy (also accred to Albania) 2006–08. *Address:* Ministry of Foreign Affairs, Kasumigaseki 2-2-1, Chiyoda-ku, Tokyo 100-8919, Japan (office). *Telephone:* (3) 3580-3311 (office). *Fax:* (3) 3581-2667 (office). *E-mail:* webmaster@mofa.go.jp (office). *Website:* www .mofa.go.jp (office).

NAKANE, Chie; Japanese social anthropologist and academic; *Professor Emerita, University of Tokyo;* b. 30 Nov. 1926, Tokyo; d. of Minoru Nakane and Chiyo Nakane; ed Univ. of Tokyo; lived in China in 1940s; embarked on career investigating Asian societies including Japan, India, China and Tibet; Prof. of Social Anthropology, Inst. of Oriental Culture, Univ. of Tokyo (first woman prof.) 1979–87, Dir Inst. 1980–82, Prof. Emer. 1987–; Visiting Prof., Univ. of Chicago, USA, SOAS, London, UK; Prof.-at-Large, Cornell Univ., USA; mem. Japan Acad. (first and only woman mem.) 1995; Dir, Oriental Library and Art Museum of Seikado, Tokyo 2010–; Fellow, Center for Advanced Studies in Behavioral Sciences USA 1973–74; Hon. Fellow, Royal Anthropological Inst. of Britain and Ireland 1975; Foreign mem. American Philosophical Soc. 1977; mem. UNESCO World Comm. on Culture and Devt 1993–95, Pres. Japan Nat. Comm. of UNESCO 1995–96; mem. Jury, Rolex Awards for Enterprise 1980, 2002; Hon. mem., Royal Anthropological Inst. of GB and Ireland 1975, Gold Medal of Int. Union for Anthropological and Ethnological Sciences 2005; Imperial Order of Culture 2001; Japan Foundation Award 1987. *Publications:* Garo and Khasi – A Comparative Study in Matrilineal Systems 1967, Kinship and Economic Organization in Rural Japan 1967, Japanese Society 1970, Social Anthropology – A Comparative Study of Asian Societies 1987, Recent Trends in Mongolian, Tibetan and Vietnamese Studies (ed.), Acta Asiatica 76 1999, Caste, Its Diversity and Fluidity (article) 2002, Development Processes of Tibet Politico-Religious Systems (article) 2007. *Leisure interest:* oil painting. *Address:* The Japan Academy, 7–32 Ueno Park, Tokyo 110-0007, (office); 1404 Takanawa, 4-24-55, Minato-ku, Tokyo 108-0074, Japan (home). *Telephone:* (3) 3822-2101 (office); (3) 3473-4321 (home). *Fax:* (3) 3822-2105 (office). *Website:* www.japan-acad.go.jp (office).

NAKANISHI, Hiroaki, BSc, MSc; Japanese business executive; *Representative Executive Officer and Chairman, Hitachi Ltd;* ed School of Eng, Tokyo Univ., Dept of Computer Science, Stanford Univ., USA; joined Hitachi as engineer in Computer Control Design Dept, Omika Works 1970, served in increasingly responsible man. and eng positions in Information and Telecommunications Systems Group, as well as Chief Exec. for Europe, Gen. Man. Global Business 2003, Vice-Pres. 2003–04, Sr Vice-Pres. Hitachi Ltd 2004–09, Chief Exec. for North America 2005–06, Exec. Vice-Pres. 2006–09, Exec. Chair. Hitachi Global Storage Technologies Inc. 2007–10, Exec. Dir 2010–, Exec. Vice-Pres. Hitachi America Ltd, Chair. –2007, CEO Hitachi Global Storage Technologies, Inc. of Hitachi America Ltd and Hitachi Ltd 2006–09, Rep. Exec. Officer, in charge of Power Systems Business, Industrial Systems Business, Automotive Systems Business and Production Tech. and Gen. Man. Supervisory Office of Monozukuri, Supervisory Office for Transportation Systems and Corp. Quality Assurance Div., Hitachi Ltd 2009–14, Pres. 2010–14, Chair. and CEO 2014–16, Rep. Exec. Officer and Chair. 2016–, also Exec. Vice-Pres. and Exec. Officer, Hitachi America Ltd; Sr Vice-Pres., Exec. Officer and Gen. Dir North America and Exec. Officer, Hitachi China Ltd, Exec. Vice-Pres. Babcock-Hitachi K.K. *Address:* Hitachi Ltd, 6-6 Marunouchi 1-chome, Chiyoda-ku, Tokyo 100-8280, Japan (office). *Telephone:* (3) 3258-1111 (office). *Fax:* (3) 3258-2375 (office). *E-mail:* ir@hdq.hitachi.co.jp (office). *Website:* www.hitachi.com (office).

NAKANISHI, Shigetada, PhD; Japanese biochemist and academic; *Director, Osaka Bioscience Institute;* b. 7 Jan. 1942, Ogaki; ed Kyoto Univ.; earned degree in medicine; Post-doctoral Fellow, Nat. Cancer Inst., NIH, Bethesda, Md, USA 1971; returned to Kyoto Univ. as Asst Prof., Dept of Medical Chemistry 1974–81, Prof. Dept of Biological Sciences, Graduate School of Medicine and Faculty of Medicine 1981–2005, Prof. Dept of Molecular and System Biology, Graduate School of Biostudies 1999–2005, Dean faculty of Medicine 2000–02, Prof. Emer. 2005–; Dir Osaka Bioscience Inst. 2005–; mem. NAS 2000–; Person of Cultural Merit 2006; Bristol-Myers Squibb Award for Distinguished Achievement in Neuroscience Research 1995, Keio Medical Science Prize (co-recipient) 1996, Gruber Neuroscience Prize, The Peter and Patricia Gruber Foundation 2007. *Achievements include:* pioneered research into communication between nerve cells in the brain; with research team unravelled molecular detail of information transfer and processing, and provided pharmacologists with many new possibilities for drug design. *Publications:* Systems Biology: The Challenge of Complexity (co-ed.) 2009; numerous scientific papers in professional journals. *Address:* Osaka Bioscience

Institute, 6-2-4 Furuedai, Suita, Osaka 565-0874, Japan (office). *Telephone:* (6) 6872-4850 (office). *Fax:* (6) 6871-6686 (office). *E-mail:* nakanishi@obi.or.jp (office). *Website:* www.obi.or.jp (office).

NAKANO, Kazuhisa, BA; Japanese business executive; *Representative Director and Chairman, Idemitsu Kosan Company Limited;* ed Waseda Univ.; joined Idemitsu Kosan Co. Ltd 1971, served as Pres. Idemitsu Oil & Gas Co. Ltd (subsidiary), Vice-Pres. and Rep. Dir Idemitsu Kosan Co. Ltd 2007–09, Pres. and Rep. Dir 2009–13, Rep. Dir and Chair. 2013–. *Address:* Idemitsu Kosan Co. Ltd, 1-1, Marunouchi 3-chome, Chiyoda-ku, Tokyo 100-8321, Japan (office). *Telephone:* (3) 3213-3115 (office). *Fax:* (3) 3213-9354 (office). *E-mail:* info@idemitsu.com (office). *Website:* www.idemitsu.com (office).

NAKAO, Takehiko, BA, MBA; Japanese international organization official; *Chairman and President, Asian Development Bank;* b. 5 March 1956, Osaka; m. Asako Ishibashi; two s.; ed Univ. of Tokyo, Univ. of California, Berkeley; joined Ministry of Finance 1978, with Research Div., Int. Finance Bureau 1978–80, Research Div., Tax Bureau 1982–84, Dir Izumiotsu Local Tax Office 1984–85; Loan Officer, Export-Import Bank of Japan 1985–87, Deputy Dir, Investment Advisory Div., Security Bureau 1987, Deputy Dir, Int. Taxation Div. 1987–89, First Tax Div. 1989–90, Research Div. 1990–91, Int. Org. Div. 1991–93; Adviser, Policy Devt and Review Dept, IMF 1994–97; Deputy Dir Coordination Div., Ministry of Finance 1993–94, Special Officer in charge of Asian monetary cooperation 1997–98, Dir Int. Org. Div., Int. Bureau 1998–2000, Budget Examiner, Budget Bureau 2000–02, Devt Policy Div. 2002–04, Coordination Div. 2004–05; Minister, Embassy in Washington, DC 2005–07; Vice-Minister of Finance for International Affairs, Ministry of Finance 2011–13; Chair. and Pres. Asian Devt Bank 2013–; Visiting Prof., Univ. of Tokyo 2010–11; Rep. at G-7 and G-20 summits 2012. *Publications include:* International Taxation System 1989, America's Economic Policy: Can it Sustain its Strength? 2008. *Address:* Asian Development Bank, 6 ADB Avenue, 1550, Mandaluyong City, Philippines (office). *Telephone:* (2) 6324444 (office). *Fax:* (2) 6362444 (office). *Website:* www.adb.org (office).

NAKASONE, Hirofumi; Japanese politician; b. 28 Nov. 1945; s. of Yasuhiro Nakasone (fmr Prime Minister of Japan); ed Keio Univ.; with Asahi Chemical Industry Co. Ltd 1968; Sec. to Prime Minister Yasuhiro Nakasone 1983; mem. House of Councillors (Liberal Democratic Party—LDP) 1986–; Parl. Vice-Minister, Ministry of Int. Trade and Industry 1990; Chair. Standing Cttee on Commerce and Industry, House of Councillors 1993, Cttee on Orgs Involved with Women's Issues, Social Educ. and Religion, LDP 1995; Head Deputy Chair. LDP Diet Affairs Cttee, House of Councillors 1996; Chair. Standing Cttee on Rules and Administration, House of Councillors 1997; Chair. LDP Policy Bd, House of Councillors 1998, Special Cttee on Managing Debts of Japan Nat. Railway Settlement Corpn and Reform of Nat. Forestry Services 1998; Minister of Educ., Science, Sports and Culture and Minister of State for Science and Tech. 1999–2000; Minister of Foreign Affairs 2008–09. *Address:* c/o Liberal Democratic Party, 1-11-23, Nagatacho, Chiyyoda-ku, Tokyo 100-8910, Japan (office). *Telephone:* (3) 3581-6211 (office). *E-mail:* koho@ldp.jimin.or.jp (office). *Website:* www.jimin.jp (office).

NAKASONE, Yasuhiro; Japanese politician; b. 27 May 1918, Takasaki, Gunma Prov.; s. of Matsugoroh Nakasone and Yuku Nakasone; m. Tsutako Kobayashi 1945; one s. (Hirofumi Nakasone) two d.; ed Tokyo Imperial Univ.; fmr mem. House of Reps (fmr Minister of State, Dir-Gen. of Science and Tech. Agency; Chair. Nat. Org. LDP, Jt Cttee on Atomic Energy, Special Cttee on Scientific Tech., Chair. LDP Exec. Council 1971–72, Sec.-Gen. LDP 1974–76, Chair. 1977–80; Minister of Transport 1967–68; Minister of State and Dir-Gen. Defence Agency 1970–71; Minister of Int. Trade and Industry 1972–74; Minister of State and Dir-Gen. of Admin. Man. Agency 1980–82; Prime Minister of Japan 1982–87; Chair. and Pres. Int. Inst. for Global Peace 1988–89, Inst. for Int. Policy Studies 1988–; after involvement in Recruit affair resigned from LDP, rejoined April 1991. *Publications include:* Ideal of Youth, Frontier in Japan, The New Conservatism, Human Cities – A Proposal for the 21st Century 1980, Tenchiyujou (autobiog.) 1996. *Leisure interests:* golf, swimming, painting. *Address:* 3-22-7, Kamikitazawa, Setagaya-ku, Tokyo, Japan (home). *Telephone:* (3) 3304-7000 (home).

NAKATA, Hideo; Japanese film director; b. 19 July 1961, Okayama; ed Univ. of Tokyo; began career as Asst Dir, Nikkatsu Studios; worked under supervision of Masaru Konuma; directorial debut with God's Hand (TV film) 1992; adapted horror novel Ringu by Suzuki Koji into feature film 1998. *Films include:* Curse, Death & Spirit (video) 1992, Don't Look Up/Ghost Actress (also writer) 1996, Ringu 1998, Chaos 1999, Ringu 2 (also writer) 1999, Sadistic and Masochistic 2000, Sleeping Bride 2000, Dark Water (also writer) 2002, Last Scene 2002, Samara: The Ring 2 2005, The Eye 2006, Out 2006, The Entity 2006, Kaidan 2007, Death Note: L Change the World 2007, Foreign Filmmakers' Guide to Hollywood (documentary) 2009, The Incite Mill 2009, Chatroom 2010, The Complex 2013, Life After 3.11 (documentary) 2013, Monsterz 2014, Words with Gods (segment 'Sufferings') 2014. *Television includes:* God's Hand (film) 1992, Gakkô no kaidan F (film) 1997, Kaiki Daisakusen – Second File (mini-series) 2007, The Complex: Prologue (series) 2013, Shinigami kun (mini-series) 2014. *Address:* c/o United Talent Agency, 9336 Civic Center Drive, Beverly Hills, CA 90210, USA (office). *Telephone:* (310) 273-6700 (office). *Fax:* (310) 247-1111 (office). *Website:* www.unitedtalent.com (office).

NAKATANI, Gen; Japanese politician; b. 14 Oct. 1957; ed Nat. Defense Acad.; served in Japan Ground Self-Defence Force; Sec. to Minister of State for Defence 1985, to Minister of Health and Welfare 1985–86, to Minister of Finance 1996; mem. House of Reps (lower house of Parl.) for Kochi 1st Dist 1990–, Parl. Sec. for Nat. Land 1995, for Posts and Telecommunications 1997, Sr State Sec. for Home Affairs 2000, Minister of State for Defence 2001, Minister of Defence and Minister in charge of Security Legislation 2014–16.

NAKAYAMA, Nariaki; Japanese politician; b. 7 June 1943; m. Kyoko Nakayama; ed Univ. of Tokyo; entered Ministry of Finance 1966, Chief of Ebara Tax Office 1971, Head of Budget Bureau 1978, Dir Tokai Local Finance Bureau 1980, Dir for Minister's Secr. 1982; with World Bank, Washington, DC, USA 1975; mem. House of Reps for Miyazaki Pref. 1986–, Chair. Cttee on Commerce and Industry 1999, Special Cttee on Disasters 2000, Cttee on Health, Labour and Welfare 2003; Parl. Vice-Minister for Educ. 1990; Dir Environment Div., LDP 1992, Commerce and Industry Div. 1996, Chair. Cttee on Commerce and Industry 1999, Special Cttee on Disasters 2000, Cttee Health, Labour and Welfare 2003, Deputy Chair. Research

Comms 2002, Deputy Sec.-Gen. 2003; Vice-Minister of Int. Trade and Industry 2000–01, of Economy, Trade and Industry 2001–04; Minister of Educ., Culture, Sports, Science and Tech. 2004–05; Minister of Land, Infrastructure and Transport Sept. 2008 (resgnd).

NAKAYAMA, Taro, MD, PhD; Japanese politician; b. 27 Aug. 1924, Osaka; ed Osaka Medical Coll.; mem. Osaka Pref. Ass. 1955–68; mem. House of Councillors 1968–86, Parl. Vice-Pres. Labour Party 1971; Chair. Cttee on Cabinet 1976, Chair. Cttee on Rules and Admin 1979; Dir-Gen. Prime Minister's Office 1980; Chief Okinawa Devt Agency 1980; Chair. Parl. Affairs Cttee of LDP 1982, LDP Financial Cttee 1988, LDP Political Reform HQ 1998, LDP Research Comm. on Foreign Affairs 1999; mem. Gen. Council of LDP 1998–; mem. House of Reps 1986–; Minister of Foreign Affairs 1989–91; Chair. Research Comm. on Constitution of House of Reps 2000–; Chair. Asian Population and Devt Asscn and Chair. or Pres. numerous int. parliamentarians' friendship leagues including Japan–India Parliamentarians' Friendship League; Grand Cordon, First Order of Rising Sun, 1997. *Publications:* five books including Scientific Strategy for the Post-Oil Age 1979. *Address:* 1-7-1 Nagata-Cho, Chiyoda-ku, Tokyo, Japan.

NALBANDYAN, Edvard, PhD; Armenian diplomatist and politician; b. 16 July 1956, Kirovakan (now Vanadzor, Lori Marz), Armenian SSR, USSR; s. of Vardanush Nalbandyan; m.; one d.; ed Moscow State Inst. of Int. Relations, Inst. of Oriental Studies, USSR State Acad. of Sciences; worked at USSR Embassy in Beirut 1978–83, at USSR Ministry of Foreign Affairs, Moscow 1983–86, Counsellor, USSR Embassy (then Russian Fed. Embassy) in Cairo 1986–92, Chargé d'affaires a.i. in Cairo 1992–93, Amb. to Egypt 1994–98, to France 1999–2008; Special Rep. of the Pres. of Armenia to Int. Org. of La Francophonie 2006; Minister of Foreign Affairs 2008–18; Commdr, Légion d'honneur 2001, Grand Officier 2011; Grand Cross of St Gregory (Holy See) 2003, Second Degree Medal 'For Services Contributed to the Motherland' 2012; First Degree Medal 'For Services Contributed to the Motherland' 2015; Order of Friendship (Russian Fed.) 2016; Order Pro Merito Melitensi, Sovereign Mil. Hospitaller Order of St John of Jerusalem of Rhodes and of Malta 2016; Award of Friendship of Nations (USSR) 1982, Mkhitar Gosh Medal 2001, La Grande Médaille de la Ville de Paris 2015, Gold Medal of the Human Rights League of Spain 2016. *Address:* c/o Ministry of Foreign Affairs, 0010 Yerevan, V. Sargsyan poghots 3, Hanrapetutyun Hraparak, Government Building 2, Armenia (office).

NALLET, Henri Pierre; French politician; *President, Fondation Jean Jaurès;* b. 6 Jan. 1939, Bergerac (Dordogne); s. of Jean Nallet and France Lafon; m. Thérèse Leconte 1963; one s.; ed Inst. d'Etudes Politiques, Bordeaux; Sec.-Gen. Jeunesse Étudiante Catholique 1963–64; Inst. de Formation des Cadres Paysans 1965–66; Féd. Nat. des Syndicats d'Exploitants Agricoles (FNSEA) 1966–70; Dir of Research, Dept of Econ. and Rural Sociology, Inst. Nat. de Recherche Agronomique (INRA) 1970–81; agricultural adviser, Secr. Gen. of Presidency of Republic 1981–85; Minister of Agric. 1985–86; Socialist Deputy to Nat. Ass. 1986–88; Minister of Agric. and Forestry 1988–90, Garde des Sceaux, Minister of Justice 1990–92; Conseiller-Gen. of Yonne 1988–2001; Mayor of Tonnerre 1989–2000; Conseiller d'état 1992–; Deputy for Yonne 1997–99; Pres. Del. of Nat. Ass. to EU; mem. Parl. Ass. of Council of Europe and of WEU; Consultant IBRD 1992–, EU 1992–; Vice-Chair. European Socialist Party 1997–2003; Nat. Sec. for Int. Affairs of Socialist Party 1999–2003; Directeur Général Relations Extérieures Groupe de Recherche Servier; Pres. World Council of Nutrition 1985–87; Vice-Pres. Fondation Jean Jaurès 1997–13, Pres. 2013–; Officier Légion d'honneur 2001, Commander of the Legion of Honor 2015. *Publications:* Tempête sur la justice 1992, Les Réseaux multidisciplinaires. La Documentation française 1999, Le multilateralisme: une réforme possible 2004. *Address:* 22 rue Garnier, 92578 Neuilly-sur-Seine Cedex, France. *E-mail:* fondation@jean-jaures.org (office). *Website:* www.jean-jaures.org (office).

NAM, Joong-soo, BBA, MBA, PhD; South Korean telecommunications executive; ed Seoul Nat. Univ., Univ. of Massachusetts and Duke Univ. Fuqua School of Business, USA; joined KT Corpn 1981, Vice-Pres. IMT-2000 Business Group –2001, Chief Financial Officer 2001–03, Pres. and CEO KT Freetel Co. (mobile affiliate) 2003–05, Pres. and CEO KT Corpn 2005–09; apptd Pres. Daelim University Coll. 2013; currently outside Dir Poongsan Corp.

NAM, Young-sun, BA; South Korean business executive; b. 2 April 1953; ed Yonsei Univ.; joined Korea Plastics 1978; Dir for Planning and Co-ordination, Planning Team, Hanwha Gen. Explosives 1997–99, Div. Man., Floor Covering Business Div., Hanwha L&C, Hanwha Gen. Explosives 1999–2003, Man. Dir, Marketing Team, Hanwha Restructuring HQ 2003–04, Officer in Charge, Hanwha Corpn/Explosives Div. 2004–05, Rep. Dir, Hanwha Corpn/Explosives Div. and Treasury Team 2005. *Address:* c/o Hanwha Chemical Corpn, Hanwha Building, 1 Changgyo-dong, Chung-ku, Seoul 100-797, Republic of Korea (office).

NAMALIU, Rt Hon. Sir Rabbie Langanai, KCMG, PC, BA, MA; Papua New Guinea politician; *Chairman, Kramer Ausenco;* b. 3 April 1947, Raluana, E New Britain Prov.; s. of Darius Namaliu and Utul Ioan Namaliu; m. 1st Margaret Nakikus 1978 (died 1993); two s. one step-d.; m. 2nd Kelina Tavul 1999; one s.; ed Keravat High School, Univ. of Papua New Guinea, Univ. of Victoria, BC, Canada; fmr Tutor, Lecturer in History and Fellow, Univ. of Papua New Guinea; Prin. Pvt. Sec. to Chief Minister 1974; fmr Prov. Commr, E New Britain and Chair. Public Services Comm.; held sr positions in Office of Prime Minister and Leader of Opposition under Mr Somare; MP (Pangu Pati) for Kokopo Open 1982–2007, Speaker 1994–97; Minister for Foreign Affairs and Trade 1982–84, for Primary Industry 1984–85; Deputy Leader, Pangu Pati 1985–88, Leader 1988–92; Prime Minister 1988–92; Sr Minister for State 1997–98, for Petroleum and Energy 1998–99; Minister of Foreign Affairs and Immigration 2002–06, of Finance 2006–07, of the Treasury 2007; Chancellor PNG Univ. of Natural Resources and Environment 2007–11; Chair. Kina Asset Management Ltd 2008–, Dir (non-Exec.) Kina Securities Ltd 2009–, Chair. 2011–; Pres. African Caribbean Pacific Council of Ministers 1984; Co-Pres. ACP/EEC Jt Council of Ministers 1984; Dir (non-Exec.) Marengo Mining Ltd 2008–, Kramer Ausenco 2010– (also Chair.), Bougainville Copper Ltd 2011–; mem. PNG Advisory Bd, InterOil 2011–; Vacation Scholar, ANU 1968; Visiting Fellow, Center for Pacific Studies, Univ. of California, Santa Cruz, USA 1976; Hon. MA, LLD (Victoria, BC) 1983; Independence Medal 1975, Queen's Silver Jubilee Medal 1977, Pacific Man of the Year 1988. *Leisure interests:*

reading, fishing, walking, golf. *Address:* Kramer Ausenco, Rue Pl, Telikom Depot, 4 Mile, Port Moresby, Papua New Guinea (office). *Telephone:* 3256033 (office). *Website:* www.kramerausenco.com (office).

NAMBIAR, Vijay K., MA; Indian diplomatist and UN official; b. Aug. 1943, Poona (now Pune); m. Malini Nambiar; two d.; ed Univ. of Bombay; joined Foreign Service 1967, early years specializing in Chinese language and serving in Hong Kong and Beijing; subsequent posts included Belgrade, Yugoslavia in mid-1970s; numerous bilateral and multilateral postings in Beijing, Belgrade and New York in 1970s and 1980s, also Jt Sec. (Dir-Gen.) for E Asia 1988 and multilateral affairs at New Delhi HQ 1980s; Amb. to Algeria 1985–88, to Afghanistan 1990–92, to Malaysia 1993–96, to China 1996–2000, to Pakistan 2000–01; Perm. Rep. to UN, New York 2002–04; Deputy Nat. Security Adviser (DNSA) and Head, Nat. Security Council Secr. 2005–06; Under-Sec.-Gen. and Special Adviser to UN Sec.-Gen., New York 2006–07, Chef de Cabinet (Chief of Staff), UN Sec.-Gen. 2007–12, Special Adviser to the UN Sec.-Gen. on Myanmar 2010–16, also Acting Special Rep. of the Sec.-Gen. on Sexual Violence in Conflict 2012; Chancellor's Gold Medal, Univ. of Bombay 1965.

NAMGYEL, Maj.-Gen. Vetsop; Bhutanese diplomatist, army officer and government official; *Ambassador to India;* b. 15 Aug. 1952, Paro Dist; m. Daw Zam; one s. two d.; ed St Joseph's College, West Bengal, India; commissioned from Indian Mil. Acad.; joined Royal Bhutan Army, selected to Royal Body Guards 1973, apptd ADC to King Jigme Singye Wangchuk 1974, served as ADC to King for 35 years, as a mem. of Royal Secr., as Officer of Royal Body Guards, promoted to rank of Col 1989, to Maj.-Gen. 2005; mem. del. to Summits of Non-Aligned Movement 1976–89, del. to SAARC Summits 1985–97; Amb. to India 2009–; Druk Yugyel Medal 2004, Druk Thuksey Medal 2010. *Address:* Embassy of Bhutan, Chandragupta Marg, Chanakyapuri, New Delhi 110 021, India (office). *Telephone:* (11) 26889807 (office). *Fax:* (11) 26876710 (office). *E-mail:* bhutan@vsnl.com (office).

NAMI, Özdil, BA, MBA; Turkish-Cypriot politician; *Minister of Economy and Energy;* b. 23 May 1967, London, UK; m.; one c.; ed Boğaziçi Univ., Univ. of California, Berkeley, USA; Lecturer in Econs, Eastern Mediterranean Univ. 1993–97, Near East Univ., European Univ. of Lefke; Chair. Cyprus Asscn of Businessmen 2001–03; mem. Legis. Ass. (Parl.) 2003–; Minister of Foreign Affairs 2013–15, of Economy and Energy 2018–; Special Rep. of Pres. Mustafa Akıncı in Cyprus reunification talks 2015–18; mem. Turkish Cypriot Chamber of Commerce 2000–01; mem. Parl. Ass., Council of Europe 2005; mem. Cumhuriyetçi Türk Partisi (Republican Turkish Party). *Address:* Ministry of Economy and Energy, Lefkoşa, Mersin 10, Turkey (office).

NAMOLOH, Maj.-Gen. (retd) Charles Dickson Ndaxu Phillip; Namibian military officer (retd), diplomatist and government official; *Minister of Safety and Security;* b. 28 Feb. 1950, Odibo, Ovamboland (now Ohangwena Region); s. of Phillip Hidishange Namoloh and Fransiska Kaimba Nghihangakenwa; ed St Mary's Mission Anglican School, Indira Gandhi Univ., Delhi, Nasser High Mil. Acad., Egypt, Vystrel Field Acad., Moscow, Naval Post Graduate School, Monterey, USA; fighter with People's Liberation Army of Namibia (Plan) 1975–77, Plan Chief of Staff for NE front 1977–79, Plan Chief of Staff 1979–89; Chief of Staff, Namibian Defence Force 1990–95; Amb. to Angola 1995–2003; High Commr to India 2003–05; mem. Nat. Ass. 2005–; Minister of Defence 2005–12, of Regional and Local Govt, Housing and Rural Devt 2012–15, of Safety and Security 2015–; Head of Politics, Security and Defence Cttee, South African Devt Community; Swapo Highest Medal of Ongulumbashe 1989, Order of the Eagle 2004. *Address:* Ministry of Safety and Security, Brendan Simbwaye Square, Goethe Street, PMB 13281, Windhoek, Namibia (office). *Telephone:* (61) 2846111 (office). *Fax:* (61) 272487 (office). *Website:* www.mss.gov.na (office).

NAN, Zhenzhong; Chinese journalist and politician; b. May 1942, Lingbao, He'nan Prov.; ed Zhengzhou Univ.; joined Xinhua News Agency 1964, fmrly Vice-Chief, then Chief Shandong Br., Xinhua News Agency, Assoc. Ed. then Ed.-in-Chief, Office of Gen. Editing 1986, Vice-Pres. Xinhua News Agency 1993–2000, Ed.-in-Chief 2000–07 (retd); Vice-Chair. All-China Journalists' Asscn; joined CCP 1978; Del., 13th CCP Nat. Congress 1987–92, 14th CCP Nat. Congress 1992–97, 15th CCP Nat. Congress 1997–2002, 16th CCP Nat. Congress 2002–07; Deputy, 9th NPC 1998–2003, 10th NPC 2003–08, mem. 11th NPC Standing Cttee 2008–13; Vice-Chair. 11th NPC Foreign Affairs Cttee 2008–13; awarded title China's Prominent Journalist of the Year 1984, winner, first Fan Chanjiang News Awards 1991. *Publications:* The Responsibility System of Agricultural Production in China 1981, I Learn to Be a Journalist 1985, The Eyes of a Correspondent 1988, The Reflections of a Correspondent 1993, Selected Works by Nan Zhenzhong 1996, The Ability to Discover 1999, The Strategic View of a Correspondent 1999, On Success – A Discussion with Young Journalists 2003.

NANDAN, Shri Rohit, MA; Indian civil servant (retd) and airline industry executive (retd); b. 27 Jan. 1957, Uttar Pradesh; joined the Admin. Service 1982, Exec. Magistrate, Land Revenue Man. and Dist Admin 1984–85, Additional Dist Magistrate 1985–86, Project Dir 1986–88, Collector and Dist Magistrate, Farukhabad 1990–91, Collector and Dist Magistrate, Mainpuri 1991–93; Jt Sec., Ministry of Home Affairs 1988–90, Special Sec. 1994–95; Dir Personnel and Gen. Admin March–July 1991, Staff Officer 2001–02; Special Sec., Ministry of Information and Broadcasting 1995–96, March–June 1997, Sec. June–Sept. 1997, Dir and Sec., Information Tech. Dept 2002–03; Dir Ministry of Culture 1996–97; Sec., Industries 1997–2000; Sec., Disabled Welfare Dept, Ministry of Social Justice and Empowerment 2003–07; Personal Sec. to Chief Minister of UP Handicapped Welfare Dept June–Nov. 2007; Personal Sec., Rural Devt Dept, Ministry of Rural Devt 2007–09; Jt Sec., Ministry of Civil Aviation 2009–11, Chief Man. Dir 2011; Chair. and Man. Dir Air India Ltd 2011–15; Sec., Ministry of Skill Devt and Entrepreneurship 2015–17 (retd).

NANDI-NDEITWAH, Neitumbo; Namibian politician; *Deputy Prime Minister and Minister of International Relations and Co-operation;* b. 29 Oct. 1952, Onamutai, Oshana region; m. Epaphras Denga Ndeitwah; ed Keele Univ., UK, Glasgow Coll. of Tech.; joined SWAPO 1966, Deputy Sec.-Gen. 1996, mem. Politburo 1996, later Sec. for Information and Mobilisation; went into exile in Zambia 1974, worked at SWAPO HQ, Lusaka 1974–75, SWAPO Deputy Rep. in Zambia 1976–78, Chief Rep. in Zambia 1978–80; returned to Namibia 1989; mem. Nat. Ass. (SWAPO) 1990–; Deputy Minister of Foreign Affairs 1990–96, Dir-Gen.

of Women's Affairs in Office of the Pres. 1996, Minister of Women's Affairs and Child Welfare 2000, of Information and Broadcasting 2005, of Environment and Tourism 2010–12, of Foreign Affairs (renamed Int. Relations and Co-operation 2015) 2012–, Deputy Prime Minister 2015–; Pres. Namibian Nat. Women's Org. 1991–94; mem. Bd Namibian Econ. Policy Research Unit 1998–. *Address:* Ministry of International Relations and Co-operation, Government Bldgs, Robert Mugabe Avenue, PMB 13347, Windhoek, Namibia (office). *Telephone:* (61) 2829111 (office). *Fax:* (61) 223937 (office). *E-mail:* headquarters@mfa.gov.na (office). *Website:* www.mirco.gov.na.

NANO, Fatos Thanas, PhD; Albanian politician and economist; b. 16 Sept. 1952, Tirana; m. Xhoana Nano; three c.; ed Tirana Univ.; Lecturer in Political Economy, Faculty of Econs, Tirana Univ. 1978–; mem. Parl. 1991–2005; Sec.-Gen. Council of Ministers 1990, Deputy Chair. Jan.–Feb. 1991, Chair. (Prime Minister) Feb.–June 1991; Chair. Socialist Party of Albania (Partia Socialiste e Shqipërisë) 1991–2005, elected Hon. mem. 2012; stripped of immunity from prosecution to face charges of embezzlement July 1993; convicted of misappropriation of state funds, of dereliction of duty and of falsifying state documents April 1994; sentenced to 12 years' imprisonment; declared political prisoner of conscience by Amnesty International, Int. Parl. Union and Council of Europe Parl. Ass.; released and pardoned March 1997, found non-guilty by Tirana Court 2001; Prime Minister of Albania 1997–98, 2002–05; Founder Movt for Solidarity 2007; unsuccessful cand. in presidential elections 2007; . *Address:* c/o Partia Socialiste e Shqipërisë, Tirana, Albania.

NAOSHIMA, Masayuki; Japanese politician; b. 23 Oct. 1945, Osaka Pref.; ed Kobe Univ.; began career with Toyota Motor Corpn; fmr Vice-Chair. Confed. of Japan Automobile Workers Unions; mem. House of Councillors 1992–, Chair. Parl. Cttee on Land and Transport; fmr mem. Democratic Socialist Party; mem. Democratic Party of Japan (DPJ) 1998–, Sec.-Gen. DPJ Parl. Caucus 2001, Chair. DPJ Policy Research Cttee 2007; fmr Next (Shadow) Chief Cabinet Sec.; Minister of Economy, Trade and Industry 2009–10. *Leisure interests:* reading, swimming.

NAOURI, Jean-Charles; French financier and business executive; *Chairman, President and CEO, Groupe Rallye;* b. 8 March 1949, Bone, Algeria; m. Gabriel Naouri; three c.; ed Ecole Normale Supérieure (Sciences), Harvard Univ., USA Nat. School of Directors; began career at Treasury Dept; apptd Chief of Staff to Minister of Social Affairs and Nat. Solidarity 1982–84, to Minister of Economy, Finance and Budget 1984–86; Founder and Chair. Foncière Euris (pvt. equity fund) 1987, has roles in several cos by Euris including Censor, Fimalac 2002–, Chair. Casino Group 2003–, CEO 2005–, Man. SCI Penthièvre 2003–, Chair., Pres. and CEO Groupe Rallye, Chair. Finatis; Vice-Pres. Fondation Euris; mem. Bd of Dirs, HSBC France; mem. Supervisory Bd, Groupe Marc de Lacharrière, Companhia Brasileira de Distribuição; Man. Partner, Rothschild et Compagnie Banque; Special Rep. of France for econ. relations with Brazil 2013–; Chevalier, Légion d'honneur 2004, Officier 2013. *Address:* Groupe Rallye, 83 rue du Faubourg Saint Honoré, 75008 Paris (office); Groupe Casino, 24 rue de la Montat, 42100 Saint Etienne (office); Finatis, 83 rue du Faubourg Saint Honoré, 75008 Paris, France (office). *Telephone:* 1-44-71-13-62 (Paris) (office); 4-77-45-31-31 (Saint Etienne) (office). *Fax:* 1-44-71-13-60 (Paris) (office). *E-mail:* info@rallye.fr (office); contact-finatis@euris.fr (office). *Website:* www.rallye.fr (office); www.groupe-casino.fr (office); www.finatis.fr (office).

NAPIER, Iain J. G., FCMA; British business executive; *Chairman, John Menzies PLC;* fmr mem. Bd of Dirs Bass PLC, CEO Bass Leisure, then CEO Bass Brewers and Bass International Brewers; Vice-Pres., UK and Ireland, Interbrew SA 2000–01; CEO Taylor Woodrow Int. Housing and Devt 2002–07; apptd Vice-Chair. Imperial Tobacco Group PLC 2000, Chair. 2007–14; Chair. McBride PLC 2007–, John Menzies PLC 2010–; mem. Bd of Dirs Molson Coors Brewing Co. 2008–, William Grant & Sons Holdings Ltd 2009–. *Address:* John Menzies PLC, 2 Lochside Avenue, Edinburgh Park, EH12 9DJ, Scotland (office). *Website:* www.johnmenziesplc.com (office).

NAPIER, John; British stage designer; b. 1 March 1944; s. of James Edward Thomas Napier and Florence Napier (née Godbold); m. 1st Andreanne Neofitou; one s. one d.; m. 2nd Donna King; one s. one d.; ed Hornsey Coll. of Art, Cen. School of Arts and Crafts; Designer and Co-Dir Siegfried & Roy Show, Las Vegas 1990; fmr Guest Lecturer, New York Film School; fmr Assoc., Royal Shakespeare Co., Assoc. Designer 1976; Visiting Chair, St Catherine's Coll., Oxford 2001; mem. British Soc. of Theatre Designers; Hon. Fellow, London Inst. 2001, University of the Arts, London; Designer of the Year Award 1977, Drama Desk Awards 1983, 1987, BAFTA Award 1983, Outer Critics Circle Award 1987, London Critics Theatre Award 1989, Royal Designer for Industry, Royal Soc. of Arts 1996, London Critics Circle Award 1997, four Olivier Awards, Tony Award 1982, 1983, 1987, 1995. *Production designs include:* A Penny for a Song, Fortune and Men's Eyes, The Ruling Class, The Fun War, Muzeeka, George Frederick (ballet), La Turista, Cancer, Isabel's a Jezebel, Mister, The Foursome, The Lovers of Viorne, Lear, Jump, Sam Sam, Big Wolf, The Devils (ENO), The Party, Knuckle, Kings and Clowns, Lohengrin (Covent Garden), Macbeth, Richard III, Hedda Gabler, Twelfth Night, The Greeks, Nicholas Nickleby, Cats, Starlight Express, Time, Les Misérables, Miss Saigon, Sunset Boulevard, Burning Blue, Jesus Christ Superstar, Idomeneo (Glyndebourne), Who's Afraid of Virginia Woolf?, An Enemy of the People, Peter Pan, Martin Guerre, Candide, Jane Eyre, Nabucco (Metropolitan Opera), South Pacific, Skellig 2003, Aladdin (Old Vic), Equus 2007 (and New York transfer 2008), Disconnect, Birdsong, Don Giovanni (Welsh Nat. Opera) 2011. *Leisure interests:* photography, sculpture. *Address:* c/o Macnaughton Lord Representation, 2nd Floor, 16 Crucifix Lane, London, SE1 3JW, England (office). *Telephone:* (20) 7407-9201 (office). *E-mail:* info@mlrep.com (office); info@johnnapierstages.com (office). *Website:* www.johnnapierstages.com (office).

NAPIER, John Alan, MA (Econ); British business executive; b. 22 Aug. 1942; s. of William Napier and Barbara Napier (née Chatten); m. 1st Gillian Reed 1961; two s. one d.; m. 2nd Caroline Denning 1992; one d. two step-s. one step-d.; ed Colchester Royal Grammar School and Emmanuel Coll., Cambridge; jr and middle man. positions, Int. Publishing Corpn and Reed International 1960–69; Man. Dir Index Printers 1969–72; Man. Dir QB Newspapers 1972–76; Exec. Dir (Australia) James Hardie Industries 1976–86; Group Man. Dir AGB PLC 1986–90; Group Man. Dir Hays PLC 1991–98; Chair. Booker PLC 1998–2000; Exec. Chair. Kelda Group PLC 2000–02, Chair. (non-exec.) 2002–; Chair. Yorkshire and Humber Rural Affairs Forum 2002–; Chair. Royal & Sun Alliance Insurance Group (RSA) plc 2003–12. *Leisure interests:* rural matters, outdoor activities, people, philosophy. *Address:* c/o Royal & Sun Alliance Insurance Group plc, 9th Floor, One Plantation Place, 30 Fenchurch Street, London, EC3M 3BD, England.

NAPIER, HE Cardinal Wilfrid Fox, OFM, BPh, BTh, MA; South African ecclesiastic; *Archbishop of Durban;* b. 8 March 1941, Swartberg; s. of Thomas D. Napier and Mary Davey; ed Little Flower School, Ixopo, Natal, Nat. Univ. of Ireland, Galway and Catholic Univ., Louvain, Belgium; ordained priest of Order of Friars Minor 1970; Asst Pastor, St Anthony's Parish, Lusikisiki 1971; Parish Priest, St Francis Parish, Tabankulu 1973; Apostolic Admin., Diocese of Kokstad 1978; Bishop of Kokstad 1981–92; Archbishop of Durban 1992–; cr. Cardinal (Cardinal-Priest of San Francesco d'Assisi ad Acilia) 2001; participated in Papal Conclave 2005, 2013; Vice-Pres. S African Catholic Bishops' Conf. 1984, Pres. 1988–94, 2003–06, First Vice-Pres. 1994, Chair. Dept for Finance; mem. Pontifical Council for the Pastoral Care of Health Care Workers 2012–, Secr. for the Economy 2014–; Hon. LLD (Nat. Univ. of Ireland, Galway) 1995. *Leisure interests:* gardening, tennis, golf, DIY mechanics, fishing. *Address:* Archbishop's House, 154 Gordon Road, Durban 4001 (office); PO Box 47489, Greyville 4023, South Africa. *Telephone:* (31) 3031417 (office). *Fax:* (31) 231848 (office). *E-mail:* chancery@durban-archdiocese.co.za (office).

NAPIERALSKI, Grzegorz Bernard, MA; Polish politician; b. 18 March 1974, Szczecin; m. Małgorzata Juras; two d.; ed Mechanics School, Szczecin, Univ. of Szczecin; Sec. of Szczecin br. of Social Democracy of the Repub. of Poland (later became Democratic Left Alliance—SLD) 1995–99, Vice-Chair. 2004–05, Sec.-Gen. 2005–08, Chair. 2008–11; became aide to Voivod in Zachodniopomorskie Voivodship 2002; mem. Sejm (Parl.) 2004–15, Chair. SLD Parl. group 2009–11; unsuccessful cand. in presidential election 2010; Co-Founder Biało-Czerwoni Party 2015; mem. Senate for Constituency No. 98 2015–; mem. Nat. Economy and Innovation Cttee. *Address:* Office of Grzegorz Napieralski, 71–410 Szczezin, ul. Niedzialkowskiego 21, Room 303, Poland (office). *Telephone:* (91) 8238758 (office). *E-mail:* biuro@grzegorznapieralski.pl (office). *Website:* www.sld.org.pl (office); www.grzegorznapieralski.pl.

NAPOLITANO, Giorgio; Italian politician and fmr head of state; b. 29 June 1925, Naples; m. Clio Maria Bittoni; two s.; ed Univ. of Naples Frederico II; joined Italian Communist Party (PCI) 1945, mem. Nat. Cttee, subsequently responsible for Comm. for Southern Italy 1956, then Sec. for Naples and Caserta, coordinator of Party Sec.'s Office and Political Office 1966–69, responsible for culture and later econ. policy and int. relations during 1970s and 80s; joined Democratic Party of the Left (later Democrats of the Left) following dissolution of PCI, 1981; elected to Chamber of Deputies 1953, Pres. 1992–94; Minister of the Interior 1996–98; MEP 1999–2004; Senator for Life 2005–; Pres. of Italy 2006–15 (resgnd); Dr hc (Università degli Studi di Bari) 2004; Dan David Prize 2010. *Publications:* Movimento Operaio e Industria di Stato 1962, Intervista sul PCI (jtly) 1975, In Mezzo al Guado 1979, Oltre i Vecchi Confini 1988, Europa e America dopo l'89 1992, Dove va la Repubblica – Una Transizione Incompiuta 1994, Europa Politica 2002, Dal PCI al Socialismo Europeo: Un'Autobiografia Politica 2005.

NAPOLITANO, Janet Ann, BS, JD; American lawyer, university administrator and fmr government official; *President, University of California;* b. 29 Nov. 1957, New York, NY; d. of Leonard Michael Napolitano and Jane Marie Napolitano (née Winer); ed Santa Clara Univ., Univ. of Virginia Law School; grew up in Pittsburgh, Pa and Albuquerque, NM; served as a clerk for Judge Mary M. Schroeder on US Court of Appeals for the Ninth Circuit; Assoc., Lewis & Roca (law firm), Phoenix, Ariz. 1984–89, Partner 1989–93, attorney 1997–98; US Attorney, Phoenix 1993–97; Attorney-Gen. of Ariz. 1999–2002; Gov. of Ariz. (first woman) 2003–09; Sec. of Homeland Security, Washington, DC 2009–13 (resgnd); Pres. Univ. of California (system of 10 campuses) 2013–; mem. Ariz. Bar Asscn, Maricopa Co. Bar Asscn, American Judicature Soc., Ariz. Women Lawyers' Asscn, Ariz. Women's Forum, Charter 100; Fellow, Ariz. Bar Foundation; Democrat; Truman Scholar from NM, Santa Clara Univ. 1977, Leader of Distinction, Anti-Defamation League, Woman of Distinction, Crohns and Colitis Disease Foundation, Women Making History Award, Nat. Museum of Women's History. *Publications:* numerous contribs to legal journals. *Leisure interests:* hiking, trekking, whitewater rafting, travel, reading, film, sports including basketball, tennis and softball. *Address:* Office of the President, University of California, Franklin Building, 1111 Franklin Street, Oakland, CA 94607-5200, USA (office). *E-mail:* president@ucop.edu (office). *Website:* www.universityofcalifornia.edu (office).

NARA, Yoshitomo, BFA, MFA; Japanese artist; b. 5 Dec. 1959, Hirosaki, Aomori Prefecture; ed Musashino Art Univ., Aichi Prefectural Univ. of Fine Arts and Music, Kunstakademie Düsseldorf; worked as a professional artist, Cologne 1993–2000; Visiting Prof. Univ. of California 1998; works as professional artist, Tokyo 2000–; Founder The Little Art Club in the Blue Woods 2012; Nagoya City Art Award 1995. *Publications include:* Drawing File 2005, Nobody Knows 2005, Slash with a Knife 2005, From the Depth of My Drawer 2005, Ceramic Works 2010, A to Z 2006, Nara Life 2017. *Address:* c/o Stephen Friedman Gallery, 25–28 Old Burlington Street, London, W1S 3AN, England. *Telephone:* (20) 7494-1434. *E-mail:* info@stephenfriedman.com. *Website:* www.stephenfriedman.com.

NARANG, Gopi Chand, MA, PhD; Indian academic and writer; *Professor Emeritus, University of Delhi;* b. 11 Feb. 1931, Dukki, Baluchistan, British India; s. of Dharam Chand Narang and Tekan Bai; m. Manorma Narang; two s.; ed Univ. of Delhi, Indiana Univ., USA; Urdu writer; Lecturer, St Stephen's Coll., Delhi 1957–58; Lecturer, Univ. of Delhi 1959–61, Reader of Urdu 1961–74, Prof. of Urdu 1985–2005, Prof. Emer. 2005–; Prof. and Head, Jamia Millia Islamia Univ. 1974–85, Acting Vice-Chancellor 1981–82; Visiting Prof., Univ. of Wisconsin at Madison, USA 1963–65, Univ. of Minnesota 1968–70, Univ. of Oslo, Norway 1997; Chair Prof., Central Univ., Hyderabad 2011–13; Vice-Pres. Sahitya Akademi 1998–2002, Pres. 2003–07, Fellow 2007–; mem. Nat. Book Trust 1997–2007; mem. Advisory Bd T.V. Urdu Channel, Doordarshan 2008–; mem. Advisory Cttee on Culture, Govt of India 2008–; mem. Cen. Advisory Bd of Educ., Govt of India 2009–; Fellow, Royal Asiatic Soc., London, UK 1963–72; Hon. DLitt (Central Univ. of Hyderabad) 2007, (Aligarh Muslim Univ.) 2009, (Manulana Azad Nat. Urdu Univ.) 2009; Ghalib Award 1962, 1985, Nat. Award 1977, Iqbal Centenary Gold Medal

1977, Mir Award 1977, Urdu-Hindi Sahitya Cttee Award 1985, Amir Khusrau Award 1987, Canadian Acad. of Urdu Language and Literature Award 1987, Padma Shri 1991, Rajiv Gandhi Award 1994, Sahitya Akademi Award 1995, Rockefeller Foundation Fellowship 1997, Khwaja Ashkar Husain Award 2000, Indira Gandhi Memorial Fellowship 2002–04, Bapu Reddy Jaatheeya Sahiti Puraskaram 2003, Zainabia Trust Award 2003, Padma Bhushan 2004, Mazzini Gold Medal, Italian Govt 2005, Sahir Ludhianvi Award 2005, Bahadurshah Zafar Award 2010, Iqbal Samman 2012, Moortidevi Award of Jnanpith 2012, Sitara-e Imtiaz, Govt of Pakistan 2012, Kusumanjali Sahitya Samman 2013. *Publications:* in Urdu: Hindustani Qisson se Makhuz Urdu Mansnawiyan 1959, 2002, Imla Nama 1974, Puranon ki Kahaniyan 1976, Wazahati Kitabiyat 1976, Safar Ashna 1982, Iqbal ka Fan 1983, Usloobiyat-e-Mir 1985, Naya Urdu Afsana 1986, Saniha-e-Karbala bataur She'ri Isti'ara 1986, Amir Khusrau ka Hindavi Kalaam 1987, Urdu ki Nai Kitab 1989, Adabi Tanqeed aur Usloobiyaat 1989, Qaari Asaas Tanqeed 1992, Saakhtiyaat, Pas-Saakhtiyaat aur Mashriqi She'riyaat 1995, Urdu Maba'd-e-Jadidiyat par Mukalama 1998, Urdu Ghazal aur Hindustani Zehn-o-Tahzib 2002, Hindustan ki Tehreek-e-Azadi aur Urdu Shairi 2004, Taraqqi Pasandi Jadidiyat Ma'bad Jadidiyat 2004, Jadidiat ke Baad 2005, Anis-o-Dabir 2005, Wali Dakni 2005, Urdu Zaban aur Lisaniyaat 2006, Sheriyat Tashkeel o Tanqeed 2009, Dekhna Taqreer ki Lazzat 2010, Khwaja Ahmad Faruqi ke Khutoot Gopi Chand Narang ke Naam 2010, Kaghaz-e Atish Zadah 2011, Tapishnama-e Tamanna 2012, Ghalib: Maani-afrini, Jadliyati Waza', Shunyata aur Sheriyat 2013, Kulliyat-e-Hindavi Amir Khusrau 2017; in English: as ed.: Karkhandari Dialect of Delhi 1961, Readings in Literary Urdu Prose 1967, Anthology of Modern Urdu Poetry 1981, Contribution of Writers to Indian Freedom Movement 1985, Rajinder Singh Bedi: Selected Short Stories 1989, Krishnan Chander: Selected Short Stories 1990, Balwant Singh: Selected Short Stories 1996, Urdu Language and Literature: Critical Perspectives 1991, Encyclopedia of Indian Literature (four vols) 1987–94, Masterpieces of Indian Literature (three vols) 1997, Let's Learn Urdu 2000, Ghalib: Innovative Meaning and the Ingenious Mind 2017; in Hindi: Samrachnavad, Uttar-Samrachnavad evam Prachya Kavyashastra 2000, Urdu Kaise Likhen 2001, Urdu Par Khulta Dareecha 2004. *Address:* D-252 Sarvodaya Enclave, New Delhi 110 017, India (home). *Telephone:* (11) 26511460. *E-mail:* narang_5@yahoo.co.in (home). *Website:* gopichandnarang.com.

NARASIMHAM, Maidavolu; Indian government official; b. 3 June 1927, Bangalore; s. of M. Seshachelapati; m. Shanthy Sundaresan; one s.; ed Presidency Coll., Madras and St John's Coll., Cambridge, UK; joined Reserve Bank of India, Bombay 1950, Sec. 1967, Gov. May–Nov. 1977; Chief of S Asia Div., IMF 1960–63, Exec. Dir of IMF for India, Bangladesh and Sri Lanka 1980–82; Exec. Dir IBRD 1978–80; Additional Sec. Ministry of Finance 1972, Sec. Banking Dept 1976–78, Sec. Dept of Econ. Affairs 1982; Finance Sec., Govt of India 1983; Prin. Admin. Staff Coll. of India, Hyderabad 1983–85, apptd Chair. 1991; Vice-Pres. Asian Devt Bank, Manila 1985–88; Norton Prize, Madras Univ., Padma Vibhushan 2000, Telugu Talli Award 2001, Lifetime Achievement Award 2001. *Publications include:* World Economic Environment and Prospects for India 1988, Economic Reforms: Development and Finance 2002, From Reserve Bank to Finance Ministry and Beyond: Some Reminiscences 2002. *Leisure interests:* reading, music. *Address:* 'Sukruti', 8-2-681/7, Road No. 12, Banjara Hills, Hyderabad 500 034, India (home). *Telephone:* (40) 23396511 (home).

NARASIMHAN, Ekkadu Srinivasan Lakshmi, BSc, LLB, MA; Indian lawyer, diplomatist and politician; *Governor of Andhra Pradesh and of Telangana;* b. 1946; m. Vimala Narasimhan; ed Madras Univ., Madras Law Univ., Nat. Defence Coll., Delhi; joined Indian Police Service in 1968, served in various capacities in Police and Intelligence Bureau services, Head of Intelligence Bureau –2006; served in Ministry of External Affairs, first Sec., Embassy in Moscow 1981–84; fmr Dir-Gen. of Police in Chhattisgarh; Gov. of Chhattisgarh 2007–10, of Andhra Pradesh 2009–, also of Telangana 2014– (following division of Andhra Pradesh and creation of new state Telengana). *Address:* Office of the Governor, Raj Bhavan Rd, Hyderabad, Andhra Pradesh, India (office). *Telephone:* (40) 23310521 (office). *Fax:* (40) 23312650 (office). *E-mail:* governor@ap.nic.in (office).

NARASIMHAN, Mudumbai Seshachalu, PhD, FRS; Indian mathematician and academic; *Honorary Fellow, Tata Institute of Fundamental Research;* b. 1932, Thandarai, Tamil Nadu; ed Loyola Coll., Chennai, Univ. of Bombay; fmr Prof. at Tata Inst. of Fundamental Research, Mumbai mid-1960s–1992, now Hon. Fellow; Head of Research Group in Math., Int. Centre for Theoretical Physics, Trieste 1992; pioneer of study of moduli spaces of holomorphic vector bundles on projective varieties; Chevalier de l'Ordre National du Mérite; Dr hc (Chennai Math. Inst.); Shanti Swarup Bhatnagar Prize for Math. 1975, Third World Acad. Award for Math. 1987, Padma Bhushan 1990, King Faisal Int. Prize for Science, King Faisal Foundation (co-recipient) 2006. *Address:* Tata Institute of Fundamental Research, Homi Bhabha Road, Mumbai 400 005, India (office). *Telephone:* (22) 22782000 (office). *Fax:* (22) 22804610 (office). *E-mail:* webmaster@tifr.res.in (office). *Website:* www.tifr.res.in (office).

NARAYAN, Shovana, MA; Indian dancer and government official; m. Dr Herbert Traxl; ed Miranda House, Univ. of Delhi; officer, Indian Audits and Accounts Service 1976–2010; f. Asavari Centre of Dance; fmr Deputy Dir-Gen. Bharat Sanchar Nigam Ltd; fmr Special Dir-Gen. Organising Cttee Commonwealth Games 2010; Visiting Lecturer, Univ. of Vienna, Austria; holds two annual dance festivals; mem. Delhi Public School Soc. 1998–; Padma Shri 1992, Sangeet Natak Akademi Award 1999–2000, Parishad Samman, Govt of Delhi 1992, Indira Priyadarshini Award, Rajiv Gandhi Puraskar 1992, Rajdhani Ratna Award 1992, Kalpana Chawla Excellence Award 2011, Guru ML Koser Award 2013, Shaksiyat Award 2015, Baba Allauddin Khan Award 2015, Bihar Gaurav Puraskar, Oisca Award, Dadabhai Naoroji Award, IMM Award for Excellence. *Dance performances include:* Festival of Arts of India, Théâtre de la ville, Paris 1973, Sanskritik Festival of Arts of India, UK 1976, 1978, 1986, Festival of Arts of India, Switzerland 1976, 1980, Reykjavik Icelandic Arts Festival 1982, India Festival, Festival of Arts of India 1987–88, Salzburg Landestheatre, Austria, 1987, Carinthian Summer Festival, Villach, Austria, Finkenstein Summer Festival, Programmes in Sweden, Netherlands, Belgium, Germany and Poland 1999, World Hindi Conf., London, Manchester, Netherlands 1999, int. festivals in Africa (Algeria, Ghana, Zambia, Kenya, Namibia), in Europe (Germany, Austria, Netherlands, Slovenia, Sweden, Belgium, Poland, Italy, Hungary, Czech Repub.), in SE Asia (Singapore, Thailand, Indonesia, Malaysia), in Middle East (Syria, Abu Dhabi, Dubai), in Cen. Asia (Uzbekistan: Tashkent, Bukhara, Kazakhstan: Almaty, Kyrgyzstan: Bishkek, Frunze, Turkmenistan: Ashgabat), in South Asia (Nepal, Sri Lanka and Bangladesh) during the period 1976–2000, Thailand 2003, Asian Alaskan Dance Festival 2003, Nepal, Bangladesh 2006. *Publications include:* Indian Classical Dances, Performing Arts in India: A Policy Perspective, Indian Theatre and Dance Traditions, Kathak: Rhythmic Echoes and Reflections, The Dance Legacy of Patliputra, Kathak, Sterling Book of Indian Classical Dances, Folk Dance Traditions of India, Meandering Pastures of Memories 2006, Krishna in Performing Arts 2007. *Leisure interest:* charity work. *Address:* T2-LL-103 Commonwealth Games Village, Near Akshardham Temple, New Delhi 110 092, India. *E-mail:* shov02@gmail.com; info@shovananarayan.in. *Website:* www.shovananarayan.com.

NARAYANAN, Mayankote Kelath, BA (Econs); Indian government official; b. 10 March 1934, New Delhi; s. of C. B. Nair and M.K. Kallianikvity Amma; m. Padmini Narayanan; one s. one d.; Head of Indian Intelligence Bureau 1987–90, 1991–92; apptd Special Adviser to Prime Minister Manmohan Singh with rank of Minister of State 2004, Nat. Security Adviser to the Prime Minister 2005–10; Gov. of West Bengal 2010–14 (resgnd), acting Gov. of Sikkim 2010; Padmashree Award 1992. *Address:* 10 Teen Murti Lane, New Delhi 110 011, India (home). *Telephone:* (11) 23019856 (home).

NARAYANASAMY, V., BA, LLB; Indian lawyer and politician; *Chief Minister of Puducherry;* b. 30 May 1947, Puducherry; s. of Velu Narayanasamy and Iswary Narayanasamy; m. Kalai Selvi 1977; one s. one d.; ed Tagore Arts Coll., Annamalai Univ.; began practising law 1973; mem. Rajya Sabha (Indian Nat. Congress) 1985–97, 2003–09; Minister of State, Planning and Parl. Affairs and mem. (ICT) Planning Comm. 2008–09; mem. Lok Sabha 2009–14; Union Minister of State, Personnel, Public Grievances and Pensions and Prime Minister's Office Jan.–Oct. 2011, of State, Parl. Affairs Jan.–July 2011; Chief Minister of Puducherry 2016–; fmr Gen. Sec., All India Congress Cttee (AICC); fmr Pres. All India Backward Classes Employees Fed.; fmr Cultural Sec., Constitution Club; mem. India-China Soc. *Address:* Chief Minister's Secretariat, Goubert Salai (Beach Road), Puducherry 605 001 (office); 5, Ellaiamman Koil Street, Puducherry 605 001, India (home). *Telephone:* (413) 2333399 (office); (413) 2339099 (home). *Fax:* (413) 2333135 (office); (413) 2339099 (home). *E-mail:* cm.pon@nic.in (office); samyselvi@sansad.nic.in. *Website:* www.py.gov.in (office).

NARDELLI, Robert (Bob) L., BS, MBA; American business executive; b. 17 May 1948, Old Forge, Pa; m. Sue Nardelli 1971; four c.; ed Western Illinois Univ., Univ. of Louisville; with General Electric (GE) Corpn 1971–88; Exec. Vice-Pres. and Gen. Man. Case Corpn, Racine, Wis. 1988–91; returned to GE and served in various exec. positions, including CEO Canadian Appliance Mfg Co., Toronto 1991–92, GE Transportation Systems, Erie, Pa 1992–95, GE Power Systems 1995–2000, Sr Vice-Pres. GE and mem. Bd of Dirs GE Capital Corpn; Pres. Home Depot Inc. 2000–02, Pres. and Chair. 2002–07 (resgnd); Chair. and CEO Chrysler LLC, Auburn Hills, Mich. 2007–09; CEO, Cerberus Capital Management 2009–12, now Sr Advisor to CEO; CEO Remington Outdoor Company, Inc. 2009–12; Advisor, Starboard Value LP; mem. Bd of Dirs Newpage Holdings 2010–, Pep Boys 2015–, The Coca-Cola Co. 2002–05; mem. Pres.'s Council on Service and Civic Participation 2003; mem. Advisory Bd Univ. of Louisville Grad. School of Business; Dr hc (Univ. of Louisville) 2001, (Siena Coll.) 2001, (Western Illinois Univ.) 2002; Nat. Italian American Foundation Special Achievement Award in Business 2002. *Address:* Cerberus Capital Management, LP, 875 3rd Avenue, New York, NY 10022, USA. *Website:* www.cerberuscapital.com.

NAREV, Ian M., BA, LLB (Hons), LLM, LLM; New Zealand business executive; *Managing Director and CEO, Commonwealth Bank Group;* m.; three c.; ed Univ. of Auckland, Univ. of Cambridge, UK, New York Univ. (Hauser Scholar), USA; fmr Ed.-in-Chief Univ. of Auckland Law Review; lawyer specializing in mergers and acquisitions –1998; Partner, McKinsey & Co., worked in New York, Sydney and Auckland offices 1998–2007, Global Partner 2003–07, Head of New Zealand office 2005–07, joined Commonwealth Bank Group 2007, Group Head of Strategy 2007–09, Group Exec., Business and Pvt. Banking 2009–11, Man. Dir and CEO 2011–; mem. Bd of Dirs Commonwealth Bank Foundation (Chair.), Financial Markets Foundation for Children; Chair. Springboard Trust; Trustee, Louise Perkins Foundation; Amb. for Australian Indigenous Educ. Foundation. *Address:* Commonwealth Bank of Australia, Level 7, 48 Martin Place, Sydney 1155, Australia (office). *Telephone:* (2) 9378-2000 (office). *Fax:* (2) 9378-3317 (office). *E-mail:* info@commbank.com.au (office). *Website:* www.commbank.com.au (office).

NARIMAN, Fali Sam, BA, LLB; Indian lawyer and politician; *President Emeritus, Bar Association of India;* b. 10 Jan. 1929, Rangoon, Burma (now Myanmar); m. Bapsi F. Nariman 1955; one s. one d.; ed St Xavier's Coll., Bombay, Govt Law Coll., Bombay; advocate, High Court of Bombay 1950; Sr Advocate, Supreme Court of India 1971–; Additional Solicitor Gen. of India 1972–75; mem. Rajya Sabha (Parl.) 1999–2005 (mem. Rules Cttee, Ethics Cttee, Consultative Cttee for Ministry of External Affairs, Standing Cttee of Parl. on External Affairs); Founder Chair. Law Asscn for Asia and the Pacific (LAWASIA) Standing Cttee on Human Rights 1979, Pres. LAWASIA 1985–87; Pres. Bar Asscn of India 1991, now Pres. Emer., Int. Council for Commercial Arbitration 1994–2002; Chair. Exec. Cttee Int. Comm. of Jurists, Geneva 1995–97; Co-Chair. Int. Bar Asscn Human Rights Inst. 2001–03; Vice-Chair. Int. Court of Arbitration of the ICC, Paris 1989–2002; mem. Delhi Legal Aid and Advice Bd 1981–, London Court of Int. Arbitration 1988–2005, Advisory Council of Jurists of the Asia-Pacific Forum of Nat. Human Rights Insts 1999, Press Comm. of India, Advisory Bd of UNCTAD, Governing Council Body of Nat. Law School Univ., Bangalore, Gen. Council of West Bengal Nat. Univ. of Judicial Sciences, Kolkata; Founding mem. People's Union for Civil Liberties; Leader, Indian Del. of Lawyers to 59th Int. Law Asscn Conf., Belgrade, Serbia and to Int. Bar Asscn Conf., Berlin, Germany; Hon. mem. Int. Comm. of Jurists, Geneva 1998–; several nat. and int. awards, including Kinlock Forbes Gold Medal and Prize for Roman Law and Jurisprudence 1950, Padma Bhushan 1991, named a Living Legend of the Law by the Int. Bar Asscn 1995, Global Medal Laurel 1998, Peter Gruber Foundation Justice Prize 2002, Padma Vibhushan 2007, Lal Bahadur Shastri Nat. Award 2018. *Publications include:* India's Legal System: Can It Be Saved? 2006; numerous articles on politics, religion, the constitution and human rights. *Address:* Bar Association of

India, 93 Lawyers Chambers, Supreme Court of India, New Delhi 110 001, India (office). *Telephone:* (11) 26862980 (office). *Fax:* (11) 26964718 (office). *E-mail:* fnariman@hathway.com.

NARLIKAR, Jayant Vishnu, PhD, ScD (Cantab.); Indian cosmologist and academic; *Professor Emeritus, Inter-University Centre for Astronomy and Astrophysics;* b. 19 July 1938, Kolhapur; s. of Prof. Vishnu Vasudeva Narlikar and Sumati Narlikar; m. Mangala S. Rajwade 1966; three d.; ed Banaras Hindu Univ. and Fitzwilliam Coll., Cambridge, UK; Berry Ramsey Fellow, King's Coll., Cambridge 1963–69, Sr Research Fellow 1969–72, Grad. Staff mem., Inst. of Theoretical Astronomy, Univ. of Cambridge 1966–72, Prof., Tata Inst. of Fundamental Research 1972–89; mem. Science Advisory Council to the Prime Minister 1986–90; Founder-Dir Inter-Univ. Centre for Astronomy and Astrophysics (IUCAA), Pune 1988–2003, Homi Bhabha Prof. 1998–2003, Prof. Emer. 2003–; Pres. Cosmology Comm. of Int. Astronomical Union 1994–97; Fellow, Indian Nat. Science Acad., Indian Acad. of Sciences, Nat. Acad. of Sciences (India); Assoc., Royal Astronomical Soc., London, Acad. of Sciences for the Developing World; Hon. Prof., Jawaharlal Nehru Centre for Advanced Scientific Research 1990–99; Dr hc from several Indian univs and from Univ. of Natal, South Africa; Tyson Medal 1960, Smith's Prize 1962, Padma Bhushan 1965, S. S. Bhatnagar Award 1978, Rashtrabhushan Award of FIE Foundation 1981, Rathindra Award 1985, INSA Vainu Bappu Award 1988, INSA Indira Gandhi Award for Science Popularization 1990, UNESCO Kalinga Award for Science Popularization 1996, Padma Vibhushan 2004, Janssen Medal, French Astronomical Soc., Maharashtra Bhushan 2011. *Radio:* series for children in Marathi (All India Radio) early 1980s. *Television:* Brahmand (The Universe) (series on nat. channel in Hindi) 1990s. *Publications include:* articles on cosmology, general relativity and gravitation, quantum theory, astrophysics etc. in the Proceedings of the Royal Soc., London, The Monthly Notices of the Royal Astronomical Soc., London, The Astrophysical Journal, Nature, Observatory and scientific articles in various magazines; Action at a Distance in Physics and Cosmology (with Sir F. Hoyle) 1974, The Structure of the Universe 1977, General Relativity and Cosmology 1978, The Physics Astronomy Frontier (with Sir F. Hoyle) 1980, Violent Phenomena in the Universe 1982, The Lighter Side of Gravity 1982, Introduction to Cosmology 1983, From Black Clouds to Black Holes 1985, Gravity Gauge Theories and Quantum Cosmology (with T. Padmanabhan) 1986, The Primeval Universe 1988, Highlights in Gravitation and Cosmology 1989, Philosophy of Science: Perspectives from Natural and Social Sciences 1992, Seven Wonders of the Cosmos 1999, Quasars and Active Galactic Nuclei: An Introduction 1999, The Scientific Edge 2003, A Different Approach to Cosmology 2000, Current Issues in Cosmology 2006, Facts and Speculations in Cosmology 2008, An Introduction to Relativity 2010. *Leisure interests* reading, going for walks, listening to music. *Address:* Inter-University Centre for Astronomy and Astrophysics, Post Bag 4, Ganeshkhind, Pune University Campus, Pune 411 007, India (office). *Telephone:* (20) 25604100 (office). *Fax:* (20) 25604698 (office). *E-mail:* jayant@iucaa.ernet.in (office). *Website:* www.iucaa.ernet.in (office).

NARRO ROBLES, José, MD; Mexican physician, government official and university administrator; b. 5 Dec. 1948, Saltillo, Coahuila; two c.; ed Universidad Nacional Autónoma de México, Univ. of Birmingham, UK; fmr Gen. Dir of Health Services of Mexico City; fmr Sec.-Gen. Mexican Inst. of Social Security; fmr Under-Sec. of Migratory Services and Population, Ministry of the Interior (Secretaría de Gobernación), later Under-Sec. of Health, Fed. Secr. of Health; Dir Faculty of Medicine, Universidad Nacional Autónoma de México 2003–07, Rector Universidad Nacional Autónoma de México 2007–15; apptd Sec. of Health 2016; Adviser to WHO; mem. Academia Nacional de Medicina (Nat. Acad. of Medicine); Dr hc (Univ. of Birmingham) 2012.

NARRUHN, Alexander, BBA, MA; Micronesian banking executive; *Chairman, Federated States of Micronesia Banking Board;* ed National Univ., USA; joined Office of Chuuk Attorney Gen. 1998, Deputy Admin., FSM Social Security Admin 1999–2000, Admin. 2000–; mem. Federated States of Micronesia Banking Bd 2003–, later Acting Chair., now Chair.; Sec., Bd for FSM Petro Corpn; mem. Asia Pacific Asscn of Fiduciary Studies. *Address:* Federated States of Micronesia Banking Board, POB 1887, Kolonia, Pohnpei, FM 96941, Federated States of Micronesia (office). *Telephone:* 320-2015 (office). *Fax:* 320-5433 (office). *E-mail:* fmbb@mail.fm (office).

NARS, Kari, DrSc; Finnish banker; b. 21 Aug. 1940, Pietarsaari; m.; two c.; ed Univ. of Helsinki, Helsinki Swedish School of Econs; economist, Bank of Finland 1964–66, Sec. of Bank 1967, Head Foreign Exchange Policy Dept 1972–75, Dir (Int.) 1977–83; Exec. Man. Dir Bank of Helsinki 1984–85; Economist, IMF, Washington, DC 1967–71; Dir Council of Econ. Orgs 1975–76; Dir of Finance, Ministry of Finance 1986–91, 1994; Exec. Dir EBRD, London 1991–94; Chair Admin. Cttee, Social Devt Fund of Council of Europe 1993, fmrly Pres. Governing Bd, Council of Europe Devt Bank; Alt. Gov. for Finland, IMF 1981–82; mem. Bd Nordic Investment Bank 1989–91; Co-Chair. Govt Borrowers' Forum 1988–91. *Publications include:* Corporate Foreign Exchange Strategies 1980, Foreign Financing and Foreign Exchange Strategy (co-author) 1981, Financial Sector Study on Mozambique – A World Bank Study (co-author) 1992, Cross Currency Swaps (contrib.) 1992, Money and Happiness 2006, Swindling Billions 2006; numerous articles and speeches.

NARUHITO, HIM The Emperor of Japan, MA; ruler; b. 23 Feb. 1960, Tokyo; s. of fmr Emperor Akihito (q.v.) and Empress Michiko; m. Masako Owada (now Empress Consort Masako) 1993; one d.; ed Gakushuin Univ., Merton Coll., Oxford, UK; invested as Crown Prince following the death of his grandfather, Emperor Shōwa in 1989, 23 Feb. 1991; succeeded 1 May 2019, following the abdication of his father; mem. IOC 1998–; Patron Global Water Partnership, Japanese Olympic Games Cttee –1998; Hon. Vice-Pres. Japanese Red Cross Soc. 1994; Hon. Pres. Third World Water Forum 2003, Expo 2005, UN Sec.-Gen.'s Advisory Bd on Water and Sanitation; Hon. Mem. World Comm. on Water for the 21st Century; Grand Cordon, Order of the Chrysanthemum 1980; Grand Cross, Order of Christ (Portugal) 1993, Grand Decoration of Honour in Gold with Sash, Decoration of Honour for Services to the Repub. of Austria 1999, Collar, Order of al-Khalifa (Bahrain), Grand Cordon, Order of Leopold (Belgium), Kt, Order of the Elephant (Denmark) 2004, Kt Grand Cross, Order of Merit of the Italian Repub., Grand Cross, Order of the Crown (Netherlands), Kt Grand Cross, Order of St Olav (Norway), Necklace of Merit (Qatar), Grand Cross, Order of Charles III (Spain) 2008, Kt Grand Cross with Collar, Order of the Crown of Tonga 2008, Coronation Medal of HM King George Tupou V 2008, Kt, Royal Order of the Seraphim (Sweden), Grand Collar, Royal Order of Pouono (Tonga), Hon. Grand Commdr, Order of the Defender of the Realm (Malaysia) 2012, Coronation Medal of HM King Tupou VI 2015, Kt, Order of the Gold Lion of the House of Nassau (Luxembourg) 2017; hon. degree from Univ. of Oxford; Golden Medal of Merit of the Japanese Red Cross, Golden Medal of Honorary Mem. of the. *Publications:* Temuzu to tomoni: Eikoku no ninenkan 1993, The Thames and I: A Memoir of Two Years at Oxford (with Hugh Cortazzi) 2006; several papers. *Leisure interests:* music, playing viola and violin, jogging, hiking, mountaineering, tennis. *Address:* The Imperial Palace, 1-1 Chiyoda, Chiyoda-ku, Tokyo 100, Japan. *Telephone:* (3) 32131111.

NARVEKAR, Prabhakar R., BCom, MCom; American (b. Indian) international civil servant; *Vice-Chairman, Centennial Group of Consultants;* b. 5 Jan. 1932, Mumbai; s. of Ramkrishna Manjunath Narvekar and Indira Narvekar; m. (wife deceased); one s. one d.; ed Bombay, Columbia and Oxford Univs; Research Asst IMF 1953; subsequently held various positions in Asian and European Depts of IMF; Dir Asian Dept, IMF 1986–91, Special Adviser to Man. Dir 1991–94, Deputy Man. Dir 1994–97; Special Adviser to Pres. of Indonesia 1998; Sr Adviser to the Pres. Nikko Securities, Japan 1997–2004; currently Vice-Chair. and Founding Dir Centennial Group of Consultants. *Leisure interest:* reading. *Address:* Centennial Group, Watergate Office Building, 2600 Virginia Avenue, NW, No. 231, Washington, DC 20037 (office). *Telephone:* (202) 393-6663 (office). *Fax:* (202) 393-6556 (office). *E-mail:* narvekarpr@yahoo.com (home). *Website:* www.centennial-group.com (office).

NARYSHKIN, Sergei Yevgenyevich; Russian engineer and government official; *Director, Foreign Intelligence Service;* b. 27 Oct. 1954, Leningrad (now St Petersburg), Russian SFSR, USSR; m.; two c.; ed Leningrad Inst. of Mechanics, Petersburg Int. Man. Inst.; apptd Deputy Vice-Rector of Leningrad Polytechnical Inst. 1982; served in USSR Embassy in Brussels 1980s; worked in Cttee for Economy and Finance, Office of the Mayor of St Petersburg 1992–95; Head of Foreign Investments Dept, Promstroibank 1995–97; with Leningrad Oblast Govt, positions including Head Investments Dept, Head of Int. Affairs Cttee 1997–98; Chair. Cttee for External Economic and Int. Relations, Leningrad Oblast Govt 1998–2004; Deputy Head of Govt Staff, Russian Fed. 2004, Chief of Staff 2004–07, Deputy Prime Minister responsible for external econ. activity 2007–08; Head of Presidential Admin 2008–11; Chair. Historical Truth Comm. 2009–12; Chair. State Duma 2011–16; apptd Chair. Channel One 2004; Dir Foreign Intelligence Service (SVR) 2016–; apptd Deputy Chair. Rosneft 2004; fmr Dir, Sovkomflot. *Address:* Foreign Intelligence Service, 101000 Moscow, Russia (office). *Telephone:* (499) 245-33-68 (office); (499) 255-79-38 (office). *Fax:* (499) 255-25-29 (office). *E-mail:* svr@gov.ru (office). *Website:* www.svr.gov.ru (office).

NASCIMBENE, Norma Ester; Argentine diplomatist; *Ambassador to Canada;* m. Amb. Alberto Juan Dumont; two d.; ed Nat. Inst. of the Foreign Service; served at Embassy in Lagos 1979–81, Perm. Mission to UN, Geneva 1981–86, worked at Antarctica Dept, Ministry of Foreign Affairs, other postings have included to UK, Geneva, Italy, rank of Amb. 2009, Dir-Gen. for Foreign Policy, Ministry of Foreign Affairs 2010, later Under-Sec. for Foreign Policy, then Special Envoy of Minister of Foreign Affairs to several Caribbean countries, Adviser to Sec. for Foreign Relations 2012–13, Amb. to Canada 2014–. *Address:* Embassy of Argentina, 81 Metcalfe Street, 7th Floor, Ottawa, ON K1P 6K7, Canada (office). *Telephone:* (613) 236-2351 (office). *Fax:* (613) 235-2659 (office). *E-mail:* ecana@mrecic.gov.ar (office). *Website:* www.ecana.mrecic.gob.ar (office).

NASCIMENTO, Lopo Fortunato Ferreira do; Angolan fmr politician; *Director (non-executive), Sonangol EP;* b. 10 July 1940, Luanda; s. of Vaz I. do Nascimento and Arminda F. do Nascimento; m. Maria do Carmo Assis 1969; two s. two d.; ed Commercial Inst., Luanda; mem. Presidential Collegiate in transitional govt before independence from Portugal Jan.–Nov. 1975; Prime Minister of Angola 1975–78; Minister of Internal Trade 1977–78, of Foreign Trade 1979–82, of Planning 1980–86; Deputy Exec. Sec. UN ECA, Addis Ababa 1979; Head Fifth Mil. Region 1986–90; Gov. Huila Prov. 1986–90; Presidential Adviser for Special Political Affairs 1990; Head Govt Del. at negotiations on a peace agreement for Angola 1991; Minister of Territorial Admin. 1991; Sec.-Gen. Movimento Popular de Libertação de Angola –1993; Deputy Speaker of Parl.; fmr MP and Chair. Nat. Centre for Social and Devt Studies; retd 2013; Dir (non-exec.) Sonangol EP 2018–. *Leisure interests:* music, writing, walking. *Address:* Sonangol EP, Rua Rainha Ginga, No 29–31, Baixa de Luanda, Distrito das Ingombotas, Municipio de Luanda, Luanda, 1316 (office); 47 Ambuíla Street, PO Box 136, Luanda, Angola (home). *Telephone:* (222) 444229 (home); 92-3642051 (mobile). *Fax:* (2) 443088 (home). *E-mail:* loponascimento1@netcabo.ao. *Website:* www.sonangol.co.ao.

NASCIMENTO, Milton; Brazilian singer, songwriter, composer and musician (piano, accordion, guitar, bass guitar); b. 26 Oct. 1942, Rio de Janeiro; one s.; DJ, announcer, dir, Rádio Três Pontas, early 1960s; composer 1963–; played Carnegie Hall 1994; collaborations with Art Blakey, Laudir De Oliviera, Deodato, João Gilberto, Herbie Hancock, Airto Moreira, Flora Purim, Charlie Rouse, Wayne Shorter, Roberto Silva; Chevalier des Arts et des Lettres 1984, Ordem do Rio Branco 1985; Dr hc (Universidade Federal de Ouro Preto) 2000; Festival of Brazilian Popular Music Best Performer 1965, Villa-Lobos Prize 1977, Santos Dumont Medal 1998, Sisac Gold Medal, Chile 2000, Latin Grammy Awards for Best Brazilian song (for Tristesse) 2004, (for A Festa) 2005, Gold Medal, Acad. des Arts, Sciences et Belles-Lettres (France) 2006. *Recordings include:* albums: Milton Nascimento (aka Travessia) 1967, Courage 1968, Milton Nascimento 1969, Milton 1970, Clube Da Esquina (Lo Borges) 1972, Milagre Dos Peixes 1973, Native Dancer 1974, Minas 1975, Geraes 1976, Clube Da Esquina Dois 1978, Journey To Dawn 1979, Sentinela 1980, Caçador De Mim 1981, Missa Dos Quilombos 1982, Anima 1982, Encontros E Despedidas 1985, A Barca Dos Amantes 1986, Yauarete 1987, Miltons 1988, Taxi 1990, O Planeta Blue Na Estrada Do Sol 1991, Angelus 1993, Amigo 1995, Nascimento (Grammy Award for Best World Music Record of the Year 1998) 1997, Tambores De Minas – Ao Vivo 1998, Crooner (Latin Grammy Award for Best Brazilian Contemporary Pop Album 2000) 1999, Gil e Milton (with Gilberto Gil) 2001, Pietá 2002, Bossas Novas (with Jobim Trio) 2008, . . .E a Gente Sonhando 2010, Tamarear 2015. *E-mail:* milton@miltonnascimento.com.br. *Website:* www.miltonnascimento.com.br.

NASEEM, Ahmed; Maldivian diplomatist and politician; b. 1948; m.; one s. three d.; ed Wesley Coll., Sri Lanka; joined govt service 1967, served in numerous positions including Sec., Ministry of Foreign Affairs, Under-Sec. Ministry of Fisheries (later Deputy Minister); fmr Perm. Rep., UN, New York; fmr First Sec., Embassy in Washington, DC; Dir-Gen. of Investments, Foreign Investment Services Bureau 1998–2005; Minister of State for Foreign Affairs 2008–11, Minister of Foreign Affairs 2011–12; fmr mem. Bd of Dirs Regional Centre for Strategic Studies, Sri Lanka, Maldives Asscn of Tourism Industry; joined Maldivian Democratic Party 2005.

NASEER, Umar; Maldivian business executive, politician and fmr police officer; ed English Prep School, Malé; conscripted into Nat. Security Service, later sent to Scotland Yard, London, UK for police training, promoted to Sergeant on return, later transferred to Maldives Water Supply Unit; opened fire safety equipment dealership Alarms Pvt. Ltd; unsuccessful cand. in parl. elections for Malé constituency; started tour co. Whale Submarine to promote underwater sightseeing, later sold his share of co. to Qasim Ibrahim; Co-founder and Pres. Islamic Democratic Party 2005–10; Vice-Pres. Dhivehi Rayyithunge Party Sept.–Dec. 2010 (expelled); currently Interim Vice-Pres., Progressive Party of Maldives; Minister of Home Affairs 2013–16.

NASERI, Muhammad Ashraf; Afghan politician; *Governor of Zabul Province;* b. Paktia Prov.; ed Kabul Univ.; teacher in Dawat aw Jahad Univ., Peshawar; worked in UN Office on Project Services (UNOPS); fmr mem. Ittihad-e Islami; Gov. Badghis Prov. 2007–09; Gov. Zabul Prov. 2009–. *Address:* Office of the Governor, Qalat, Zabul Province, Afghanistan (office).

NASH, David, OBE, RA; British sculptor; b. 14 Nov. 1945, Surrey; s. of Lt-Col W. C. E. Nash and Dora Nash (née Vickery); m. Claire Langdown 1972; two s.; ed Brighton Coll., Kingston Art School and Chelsea School of Art; has exhibited widely in Britain, Europe, USA and Japan; first exhbn Briefly Cooked Apples, York Festival 1973; works in over 100 public collections including Tate Gallery and Guggenheim Museum; Research Fellow, Dept of Visual and Performing Arts, Univ. of Northumbria 1999–2002; Hon. Fellow, Univ. of Wales (Cardiff) 2003; Dr hc (Kingston) 1999; Hon. DH (Glamorgan) 2002. *Publications:* Forms into Time 1996, The Sculpture of David Nash 1996, Twmps 2000, Black and Light 2001, The Return of Art to Nature 2003, Pyramids Rise, Spheres Turn, Cubes Stay Still, David Nash 2008, David Nash at the Yorkshire Sculpture Park 2010, David Nash: A Natural Gallery 2013. *Address:* Capel Rhiw, Blaenau Ffestiniog, Gwynedd, LL41 3NT, Wales; c/o Annely Juda Fine Art, 23 Dering Street, London, W1S 1AW, England. *Telephone:* (20) 7629-7578 (London). *Fax:* (1766) 831179 (Blaenau Ffestiniog); (20) 7491-2139 (London).

NASH, Ronald Peter, CMG, LVO, BA, MCIL; British fmr diplomatist and consultant; b. 18 Sept. 1946; m.; three s.; ed Univ. of Manchester; joined FCO 1970, Personnel Operations Dept 1970, Western Orgs Dept 1970–72, full-time Russian language training 1972–73, Second, later First Sec., Chancery, Moscow 1974–76, First Sec., UK Del., Vienna 1976–79, Western European Dept, FCO 1979–81, UN Dept 1981–83, First Sec. (Information), New Delhi 1983–86, Deputy Head of E European Dept, FCO 1986–87, Deputy Head of Mission, Vienna 1988–92, Deputy High Commr, Colombo 1992–95, Coordinator, London Peace Implementation Conf. for Bosnia 1995, Head of Human Rights Policy Dept, FCO 1996–99, Amb. to Nepal 1999–2002, to Afghanistan 2002–03, High Commr to Trinidad and Tobago 2003–06 (retd); consultant to various pvt. sector, govt and int. orgs 2006–; mem. Chartered Inst. of Linguists.

NASH, Steve, OC, OBC, BA; Canadian professional basketball player (retd); b. 7 Feb. 1974, Johannesburg, SA; s. of John Nash and Jean Nash; m. Alejandra Nash (née Amarilla); two d.; ed St Michael's Univ. School, Santa Clara Univ., USA; plays point guard; selected 15th overall in Nat. Basketball Asscn (NBA) draft by Phoenix Suns 1996, played with Suns 1996–98, moved to Dallas Mavericks 1998–2004, returned to Phoenix Suns 2004–12, with Los Angeles Lakers 2012–15 (retd); Capt. Canadian Men's Basketball Team, Olympic Games, Sydney 2000, qualifying stages of Athens Olympics 2004; Gen. Man. Canada's sr men's basketball team 2012–; f. Steve Nash Foundation 2001, Steve Nash Sports Club, Vancouver 2007, Meathawk (production co.); Co-owner Vancouver Whitecaps (Major League Soccer team); Order of British Columbia 2006; Dr hc (Univ. of Victoria) 2008; NBA West Conference Player of the Year 1995, 1996, NBA Most Valuable Player Award 2005, 2006, All-Star 2002, 2003, 2005, 2006, 2007, 2008, All-NBA First Team 2005, 2006, 2007, Second Team 2008, 2010, Third Team 2002, 2003, Lou Marsh Trophy 2004, Lionel Conacher Award 2002, 2005, 2006, Canada's Most Influential Sports Figure, The Globe and Mail 2006, J. Walter Kennedy Citizenship Award 2007. *Address:* The Steve Nash Foundation, 9400 Sugar Circle, Anchorage, Alaska 99507, USA. *Website:* www.stevenash.org; www.basketball.ca.

NASHAAT, Soha, MBA; Egyptian/Syrian banking executive; *Strategic Advisor to the Executive Chairman, SHUAA Capital psc;* b. Kuwait; m. Javier Fernandez; ed Columbia Univ. and Univ. of San Francisco, USA; Product Man. Merrill Lynch, New York 1991–97, Sales Man., Merrill Lynch Int. Private Client Group, Buenos Aires 1997–2000, Head of Int. Private Client Group in Middle East 2000–06; CEO Barclays Wealth Middle East and N Africa 2006–11, Sr Advisor and mem. Bd of Dirs Barclays Wealth Switzerland 2011–14; Strategic Advisor to Exec. Chair., SHUAA Capital, Dubai 2014–; mem. Bd of Dirs Foundation for Renewable Energy and Environment, Int. Cttee for Barnard Coll., Columbia Univ.; Middle East Excellence Award Inst. Award for Woman Banker of the Year 2007. *Address:* SHUAA Capital psc, Level 31, Emirates Towers Sheikh Zayed Road, PO Box 31045, Dubai, United Arab Emirates (office). *Telephone:* 43303600 (office). *Fax:* 43303550 (office). *E-mail:* info@shuaa.com (office). *Website:* www.shuaa.com (office).

NASHEED, Mohamed (Anni), BSc; Maldivian journalist, politician and fmr head of state; *President, Maldivian Democratic Party;* b. 17 May 1967, Malé; m. Laila Ali Abdulla; two d.; ed Overseas School of Colombo, Sri Lanka, Dauntsey's School, Wilts. and John Moores Univ., UK; fmr journalist for Sangu magazine; arrested several times for political reasons, declared prisoner of conscience by Amnesty International 1991; arrested and sentenced several times for criticism of the govt; Dir Safari Tours Maldives 1994–98; mem. Parl. 1999–2001; apptd Dir Oriental Acad. Centre 2001; Co-founder and mem. Gen. Council, Maldivian Democratic Party (MDP) 2003, Pres. 2014–; fmr Chair.; Pres. of the Maldives 2008–12 (resgnd); cand. in presidential election 2013; convicted of a terrorism charge by a criminal court and sentenced to 13 years in prison March 2015, left for UK 2016, returned 2018 following stay of conviction; Hon. mem. International PEN, Hon. Fellow, Liverpool John Moores Univ.; Anna Lindh Award 2009, UN Champions of Earth Award 2010, James Lawson Award, Int. Center on Nonviolent Conflict, Tufts Univ. 2012. *Film:* The Island President (documentary) 2011. *Publications include:* Dhagadu Dhahanan: Internal Feuding and Anglo-Dhivehi Relations 1800–1900 1995, Maldives: Historical Overview of Dhivehi Policy, Hithaa Hithuge Gulhuu. *Leisure interests:* tennis, music, reading, writing. *Address:* Maldivian Democratic Party, H. Sharasha, 2nd Floor, Sosun Magu, Malé 20-059, Maldives (office). *Telephone:* 3340044 (office). *Fax:* 3322960 (office). *E-mail:* secretariat@mdp.org.mv (office). *Website:* www.mdp.org.mv (office); raeesnasheed.com.

NASHID, Ahmed; Maldivian business executive; *Chairman, ADK Group of Companies;* opened small medical clinic with a single doctor and attached pharmacy 1987; opened ADK Pharmacy 1990; Founder-chair. ADK Group of Companies 1987–; expanded medical, clinical and pharmaceutical operations under ADK Co. Pvt. Ltd, ADK Enterprises Pvt. Ltd; est. ADK Hospital (first pvt. hospital in the Maldives); Founder-mem. Jumhooree Party (Republican Party); fmr Chair. Horizon Fisheries Pvt. Ltd. *Address:* ADK Hospital, Sosun Magu, Malé 20040, Maldives (office). *Telephone:* 3313553 (office). *Fax:* 3313554 (office). *E-mail:* info@adkenterprises.com (office). *Website:* www.adkhospital.mv (office).

NASIM, Anwar, PhD; Pakistani geneticist and academic; b. 7 Dec. 1935, Pasrur; ed Univ. of the Punjab, Univ. of Edinburgh, UK; Lecturer, Govt Coll., Multan and Lahore 1957–62; Research Officer, Atomic Energy of Canada Ltd, Chalk River 1966–73; Sr Research Officer, Nat. Research Council of Canada 1973–89; Adjunct Prof., Carleton Univ., Ottawa 1984–89, Univ. of Ottawa 1983–89; Prin. Scientist and Head, Molecular Genetics Group, Biology and Medical Research Dept, King Faisal Specialist Hosp. and Research Centre, Riyadh 1989–93; Exec. Sec. Pakistan Acad. of Sciences 1994–96, Pres. 2015–17; Science Adviser, OIC Standing Cttee on Scientific and Technological Co-operation (COMSTECH) 1996–11; Fellow, Third World Acad. of Sciences 1987, Islamic Acad. of Sciences 1998, Pakistan Acad. of Medical Sciences 2000; Foreign Fellow, Pakistan Acad. of Sciences 1988; Gold Medal, MSc (Punjab); Civil Award Prime of Performance in Molecular Genetics 1995, Award for Outstanding Service, Overseas Pakistanis Inst. 1995, Sitara-e-Imtiaz Civil Award in Molecular Genetics 1999. *Publications:* Repairable Lesions in Microorganisms (co-author) 1984, Recombinant DNA Methodology (co-author) 1985, Molecular Biology of the Fission Yeast (co-author) 1989, Genetic Engineering and Biotechnology (co-author) 1990, Genetic Engineering – State of the Art (monograph) 1992, Biotechnology for Sustainable Development (co-author) 1995; more than 100 scientific papers published in int. journals since 1965. *Leisure interests:* reading literature, music. *Address:* 237, Street 23, F-11/2, Islamabad (home). *Telephone:* (51) 2299838 (home). *E-mail:* anwar_nasim@yahoo.com (home).

NASR, Ramsey; Dutch poet, writer, actor and musical theatre director; b. 28 Jan. 1974, Rotterdam; ed Studio Herman Teirlinck, Antwerp; actor, Het Zuidelijk Toneel 1995–90; leading parts in several films and TV series; also dir of musical theatre productions, including Mozart's The Abduction from the Seraglio; numerous poetry performances at int. festivals; City Poet of Antwerp 2005; Dichter des Vaderlands (Poet Laureate) 2009–13; Dr hc (Antwerp); Mary Dresselhuys Prize for outstanding acting performance 2000, Hugues C. Pernath Prize (biennial prize for best vol. of poetry) 2004, Journalist for Peace, Humanistic Peace Council 2006, Humanistic Peace Council Journalist for Peace 2006. *Plays:* theatrical monologues (as writer and actor): De doorspeler – Geen lied (Taalunie Toneelschrijfprijs—Playwright's Prize for Best Theatre Text) 2000; other: Leven in Hel – de operette (libretto writer, actor, singer, director), Il Re Pastore, opera by Mozart (trans./adaptation, dir), Een totale Entführung (adaptation/trans., dir of new adaptation of Mozart's The Abduction from the Seraglio). *Films include:* as actor: Frans en Duits 1995, Thuisfront 1998, De man met de hond 1998, Mariken 2000, Liefje 2001, Magonia 2001, The Enclave 2002, Hotel Bellevue 2003, Armando 2004, Mon ange 2004, Live! 2005, Het echte leven 2008, Goltzius and the Pelican Company 2011. *Television:* actor in series De Enclave – Overspel. *Publications:* poetry collections: 27 gedichten & Geen lied 2000, onhandig bloesemend (Hugues C. Pernath Prize) 2004, onze-lieve-vrouwe-zeppelin 2006, tussen lelie en waterstofbom 2009, anthology of poetry in English: Heavenly Life (trans. David Colmer) 2010; prose: Kapitein Zeiksnor & De Twee Culturen (novella) 2001; music theatre: Twee libretto's 2002; essays and opinion articles: Van de vijand en de muzikant 2006; travel diaries: Homo safaricus 2009, In de gouden buik van Boeddha (Burma/Myanmar) 2010; contrib. of articles to newspapers and journals. *Address:* c/o Uitgeverij De Bezige Bij, Van Miereveldstraat 1, 1071 Amsterdam, Netherlands (office). *Telephone:* (20) 305-9810 (office). *E-mail:* info@debezigebij.nl (office). *Website:* www.ramseynasr.nl.

NASR, Seyyed Hossein, MS, PhD; Iranian academic; *University Professor of Islamic Studies, George Washington University;* b. 7 April 1933, Tehran; s. of Valiallah Nasr and Ashraf Kia; m. Soussan Daneshvari 1958; one s. one d.; ed Massachusetts Inst. of Tech. and Harvard Univ.; Teaching Asst Harvard Univ. 1955–58, Visiting Prof. 1962, 1965; Assoc. Prof. of History of Science and Philosophy, Tehran Univ. 1958–63, Prof. 1963–79, Dean, Faculty of Letters 1968–72, Vice-Chancellor 1970–71; Chancellor (Pres.) Aryamehr Univ. 1972–75; First Prof. of Islamic Studies, American Univ. of Beirut 1964–65; Prof. of Islamic Studies, Temple Univ. 1979–84; Univ. Prof. of Islamic Studies, George Washington Univ. 1984–; Visiting Prof., Harvard Univ. 1962, 1965, Princeton Univ. 1975, Univ. of Utah 1979; A.D. White Prof.-at-Large, Cornell Univ. 1991–98; Founder and first Pres. Iranian Acad. of Philosophy 1974–79; mem. Inst. Int. de Philosophie, Greek Acad. of Philosophy, Royal Acad. of Jordan; Dr hc (Uppsala) 1977, (Lehigh) 1996; Gifford Lecturer, Univ. of Edinburgh 1981, The Library of Living Philosophers dedicated to his thought 2001. *Publications:* more than 50 books and 500 articles in Persian, Arabic, English and French in leading int. journals. *Leisure interests:* classical music (both Western and Eastern), tennis, hiking. *Address:* 709R Gelman Library, The George Washington University, Washington, DC 20052, USA (office). *Telephone:* (202) 994-5704 (office). *Fax:* (202) 994-4571 (office). *E-mail:* msirat@gwu.edu (office). *Website:* www.nasrfoundation.org (office).

NASRALLAH, Sheikh Hasan; Lebanese ecclesiastic and political leader; *Secretary-General, Hezbollah;* b. 31 Aug. 1960, Beirut; s. of Abdul Karim Nasrallah; m. Fatima Yassin; five c. (one deceased); at age 15 joined Amal movt, Bassouriyeh, 1975, then moved to Najaf, Iraq to study at Hawza (Islamic Seminary); forced to leave Iraq and returned to Lebanon to study with Amal leader Sheikh Abbas al-Musawi; elected Amal political del. Biqaa; resgnd from Amal and joined Hezbollah 1982, chief exec. and mem. Consultative Council, Beirut 1987–89, moved to Qom, Iran to resume studies 1989; returned briefly to Lebanon then back to Tehran to represent Hezbollah 1989; Sec.-Gen. Hezbollah 1992–. *E-mail:* hizbollahmedia@hizbollah.org. *Website:* www.moqawama.org/english; www.hizbollah.org.

NASREEN, Taslima, BS, MD, MB; Bangladeshi/Swedish writer and physician; b. 25 Aug. 1962, Mymensingh, East Pakistan (now Bangladesh); d. of Rajab Ali and Edul Wara; m. 1st Rudra Mohammad Shahidullah 1982 (divorced 1986); m. 2nd Nayeemul Islam Khan (divorced 1991); m. 3rd Minar Mahmood 1991 (divorced 1992); ed Mymensingh Medical Coll., Dhaka Univ.; practised as a gynaecologist and anaesthesiologist 1986–93; columnist, Khoborer Kagoj 1989; books banned in Bangladesh and Indian state of West Bengal 1993–2004, first fatwa (death threat) pronounced against her 1993; forced to leave Bangladesh for Sweden 1994, later in Germany, USA, France and India; further fatwas issued against her in India 2004–08, forced to leave there 2008, returned to India then relocated to USA after death threats 2015; Fellowship, Carr Centre for Human Rights Policy, John F. Kennedy School of Government, Harvard Univ., New York Univ. 2009; lectures on human rights world-wide; Hon. Citizen, Esch, Luxembourg, Metz, France, Thionville, France 2011; Dr hc (Ghent Univ., Belgium) 1995, (American Univ. in Paris) 2005, (Université Catholique de Louvain, Belgium) 2010, (Paris Diderot Univ.) 2011; Ananda Puroshkar, India 1992, Kurt Tucholsky Prize, Sweden 1994, Feminist of the Year, USA 1994, Human Rights Award, French Govt 1994, Edit de Nantes Award, France 1994, Monismanien Prize, Sweden 1995, Sakharov Prize, European Parl. 1995, Int. Humanist Award, Int. Humanist and Ethical Union 1996, Erwin Fischer Award 2002, UNESCO Prize 2004, Grand Prix International Condorcet-Aron 2005, Prix Simone de Beauvoir 2008, Citoyenne d'honneur, France 2008, Woodrow Wilson Fellowship, USA, Crossing Border Award 2009, Prins Global Scholars Fellowship, New York Univ., USA 2009, Medal of Honour, City of Lyon, France 2009, Acad. Award, Royal Acad. of Arts, Science and Literature (Belgium) 2013. *Publications include:* Shikore Bipul Khudha 1986, Nirbashito bahire Ontore 1989, Amar Kichu Jay Ashe Ne 1990, Atole Ontorin 1991, Nirbachito Kolam 1991, Nosto meyer nosto goddo 1992, Oporpokkho 1992, Shodh 1992, Balikar Gollachut 1992, Nimontron 1993, Laija (novel) 1993, Phera 1993, Choto choto dukkho kotha (selected columns) 1994, Bhromor koio gia 1994, Nirbashito Narir Kobita 1996, Amar Meyebela (autobiog.) 1999, Jolopodyo 2000, Utal Hawa (autobiog.) 2002, Forashi Premik 2002, Dwihkandita (autobiog.) 2003, Ko 2003, Sei Sob Ondhokar (autobiog.) 2004, Khali Khali Lage 2004, Kicchukhan Thako 2005, Ami bhalo nei, tumi bhalo theko prio desh (autobiog.) 2006, Minu (short stories) 2007, Narir Kono Desh Nei 2007, Bhalobaso? Cchai Baso 2008, Bondini 2008, Shorom 2009, Nei, kichu nei (autobiog.) 2010, Nirbasan 2012, Sakal ghriho haralo jar 2016, Bhabnaguli 2018, Golpo 2018. *E-mail:* taslima.nasrin@gmail.com; email@taslimanasrin.com. *Website:* taslimanasrin.com.

NASSER, Jacques A. (Jac), AO; Australian business executive; *Chairman, BHP Billiton;* b. 12 Dec. 1947, Amyoun, Lebanon; m.; ed Royal Melbourne Inst. of Tech.; with Ford of Australia 1968–73, mem. financial staff, N American Truck operations, Ford Motor Co. 1973, profit analysis, product programming Ford Motor Co., Australia 1973–75, various positions, Int. Automotive Operations, Ford Motor Co. 1975–87, Dir, Vice-Pres. Finance and Admin., Autolatina jt venture, Brazil and Argentina 1987–90, Pres., CEO Ford of Australia 1990–93, Chair. Ford of Europe 1993–96, Vice-Pres. Ford Motor Co. 1993–96, CEO 1999–2001, Chair. Ford of Europe, Pres. Ford Automotive Operations, Exec. Vice-Pres. 1996–2002; Sr Partner, One Equity Partners LLC (JPMorgan Chase & Co.) 2002–10, Advisory Partner (non-exec.) 2010–14, Chair. (non-exec.), Polaroid Holding Co. 2002–05 (after acquisition of Polaroid by One Equity Partners); mem. Bd of Dirs, BHP Billiton Ltd, Melbourne, Australia and BHP Billiton Plc 2006–, Chair. 2010–; Dir (non-exec.), BSkyB Ltd 2002–12, Brambles Industries 2004–08, Quintiles Transnational Corpn –2008, 21st Century Fox 2013–, Koç Holding AŞ 2015–; mem. Int. Advisory Bd, Allianz AG 2001–; Order of the Cedar (Lebanon); Hon. DTech (RMIT Univ. of Melbourne); Centenary Medal (Australia), Ellis Island Medal of Honor for outstanding contribs to American Society 2008. *Leisure interest:* opera. *Address:* BHP Billiton Ltd, BHP Billiton Centre, 180 Lonsdale Street, Melbourne, Vic. 3000, Australia (office). *Telephone:* (3) 9609-3333 (office); 1300-55-4757 (office). *Fax:* (3) 9609-3015 (office). *Website:* www.bhpbilliton.com (office).

NASSER, Maher, BSc; Palestinian UN official; b. 19 Oct. 1962, al-Bireh, West Bank (now Palestine); m.; three c.; ed Bir Zeit Univ., Warwick Business School, Univ. of Warwick; began career with Arab Thought Forum (non-govt org.), Jerusalem; more than 29 years working in UN System, including positions in Gaza, Jerusalem, Amman, Cairo, Vienna and New York City, roles include Public Information Officer and Spokesperson, UNRWA, Gaza and Jerusalem 1987–91, Assoc. Information Officer, UN Drug Control Programme, Vienna 1992–94, with UNRWA, Vienna 1994–96, later in charge of donor liaison, representation and media relations, UNRWA HQ, Amman 1996, Chief of New York Liaison Office, UNRWA 2001–06, joined UN Dept of Public Information (DPI), as Dir, UN Information Centre in Cairo 2006–08, becoming Dir, UN Information Service in Vienna 2008–11, Acting Head, DPI, New York April–Aug. 2012, 2014–15, Acting Under-Sec.-Gen. for Global Communications April–Sept. 2017; mem. Bd of Trustees UN Int. School 2013–15; attended Madrid Middle East Peace Conf. 1991; Dir, UN Outreach Div. 2011.

NASSER, Nassir bin Abdulaziz al-; Qatari diplomatist and fmr UN official; b. 15 Sept. 1953, Doha; m. Muna Rihani; one s.; joined Ministry of Foreign Affairs (MFA) 1971, Attaché, Embassy in Beirut 1972–74, mem. Qatari Del. to Org. of the Islamic Conf. 1974–75, Gen. Counsellor, Embassy in Dubai 1975–81, with MFA 1981–85, Deputy Foreign Minister 1984–85, Minister at Perm. Mission to UN, New York 1986–93, Amb. to Jordan 1993–98, Amb. and Perm. Rep. to UN, New York 1998–2011, Vice-Pres. UN Gen. Ass. 2002–03, Chair. Group of 77 2004, Pres. Security Council Dec. 2006, Pres. High-level Cttee on South–South Cooperation 2007–09, Chair. Special Political and Decolonization Cttee 2009–10, Pres. UN Gen. Ass. 2011–12; High Rep. of the Sec.-Gen. for the Alliance of Civilizations, UN 2013–18; mem. Bd of Advisers, New York Univ. Center for Dialogues; Hon. Fellow, Foreign Policy Asscn, New York 2009; Grand Officer, Order of Merit (Italy) 2004, Medal of Grand Commdr of Order of Makarios III (Cyprus) 2007, Nat. Order of Doctor José Matias Delgado (El Salvador) 2007, Commdr, Nat. Order (Côte d'Ivoire) 2008; Dr hc (Chongqing Univ.) 2007, (Fordham Univ.), (Int. Islamic Univ. of Malaysia) 2014, (Al-Farabi Kazakh Nat. Univ.) 2017; Medal of Independence (Jordan) 1998, High Honour Awards (Italy) 2005, Humanitarian Award, UNA 2012.

NĂSTASE, Adrian, LLM, PhD; Romanian academic and politician; b. 22 June 1950, Bucharest; s. of Marin Năstase and Elena Năstase; m. Daniela Miculescu 1985; two s.; ed Bucharest Univ.; Research Fellow, Inst. of Legal Research, Bucharest 1973–90; Prof. of Public Int. Law, Bucharest Univ. 1990–, Titu Maiorescu, Dimitrie Cantemir and Nicolae Titulescu pvt. univs 1992–; Assoc. Prof. of Public Int. Law, Univ. of Paris (Sorborne) 1994–; Minister of Foreign Affairs 1990–92; Speaker, Chamber of Deputies 1992–96, Deputy Speaker 1996; Exec. Pres. Social Democracy Party of Romania 1992–97, First Vice-Pres. 1997–2000, Pres. 2001–06 (resgnd); Prime Minister of Romania 2000–04; Vice-Chair. Camera Deputaţilor (Chamber of Deputies) 1996–2000, Chair. 2004–06 (resgnd); apptd mem. Romanian Parl. Del. to Parl. Asscn Council of Europe 1996; Vice-Pres. Asscn of Int. Law and Int. Relations, Bucharest 1977; Dir of Studies, Int. Inst. of Human Rights, Strasbourg 1984; Pres. Titulescu European Foundation 1990–92 (Hon. Pres. 1992–); Exec. Pres. Euro-Atlantic Centre, Bucharest 1991–92; mem. Bd of Dirs Inst. for East-West Studies, New York 1991–97; mem. Human Rights Information and Documentation System; mem. French Soc. of Int. Law 1984–, American Soc. of Int. Law 1995–; indicted by Romanian prosecutors on corruption charges Jan. 2009, sentenced by Supreme Court to four years in prison for taking bribes 2014, also sentenced to three years for blackmail to run concurrently, released 2014; Order of Diplomatic Service Merit 1991, Gwanghwa Medal (Repub. of Korea) 1991, Grande Croix de Mérite, Sovereign Order of Malta 1992; Nicolae Titulescu Prize, Romanian Acad. 1994, The Political Man of 1995, Turkish Businessmen's Asscn, Global Leader for Tomorrow Prize 1993. *Publications include:* Human Rights: An End-of-the-Century Religion 1992, International Law: Achievements and Prospects (co-author) 1992, Human Rights, Civil Society, Parliamentary Diplomacy 1994, Public International Law (co-author) 1995, Nicolae Titulescu – Our Contemporary 1995, Parliamentary Humour 1996, International Economic Law II 1996, Romania and the New World Architecture 1996, Documenta universales I (with law documents) 1997, 1998, The Treaties of Romania (1990–1997) 1998, Documenta universales II: The Rights of Persons Belonging to National Minorities 1998, Battle for the Future 2000, Contemporary International Law – Essential Texts 2001; more than 240 articles and papers. *Leisure interests:* hunting, music, modern art, collecting antiques, gardening, tennis. *E-mail:* contact@adriannastase.ro. *Website:* www.adriannastase.ro.

NĂSTASE, Andrei; Moldovan lawyer and politician; *Chairman, Demnitate şi Adevăr (DA—Dignity and Truth);* b. 6 Aug. 1975, Mândreşti, Moldovan SSR, USSR; m.; two c.; ed Faculty of Law, Alexandru Ioan Cuza Univ., Iaşi, Romania; taught at school in Mândreşti 1982–92; lawyer 2002–; a leader of protest movt in Moldova Sept. 2015; Chair. Consiliului Marii Adunări Naţionale; joined Partidului Forţa Poporului (PFP—Party Strength People) Dec. 2015, party renamed Demnitate şi Adevăr (DA—Dignity and Truth), Chair. Dec. 2015–. *E-mail:* info@demnitate-adevar.md (office). *Website:* www.demnitate-adevar.md (office).

NĂSTASE, Ilie; Romanian fmr professional tennis player; b. 19 July 1946, Bucharest; m. 1st; one d.; m. 2nd Alexandra King 1984; m. 3rd Amalia Năstase 2004 (divorced 2010); nat. champion (13–14 age group) 1959, (15–16 age group) 1961, (17–18 age group) 1963, 1964; 58 ATP singles titles: Salisbury, USA 1970, 1974, 1976, Rome 1970, 1973, Richmond, USA 1971, Hampton, USA 1971, Nice 1971, 1972, Monte Carlo 1971, 1972, 1973, Båstad, Sweden 1971, Wembley, UK 1971, Tennis Masters Cup, Paris 1971, Baltimore 1972, Omaha 1972, 1973, Madrid 1972, 1973, 1974, 1975, Düsseldorf 1972, Toronto 1972, US Open 1972, South Orange, USA 1972, 1975, 1976, Seattle 1972, London 1972, Tennis Masters Cup, Barcelona 1972, Calgary 1973, Washington 1973, 1974, Barcelona 1973, 1975, Florence 1973, French Open 1973, Queen's Club, London 1973, Gstaad, Switzerland 1973, Cincinnati 1973, Torneo Godó-Barcelona 1973, 1974, Paris 1973, Tennis Masters Cup, Boston 1973, Bournemouth, UK 1974, Cedar Grove, USA 1974, Valencia 1975, Tennis Masters Cup, Stockholm 1975, Atlanta 1976, La Costa, USA 1976, Pepsi Grand Slam, Myrtle Beach 1976, Honolulu Challenge Cup 1976, Las Vegas Challenge Cup 1976, Mexico City 1977, Aix en Provence 1977, Miami 1978, Montego Bay Challenge Cup, Jamaica 1978; winner of doubles, French Open (with Ion Ţiriac) 1970, mixed doubles, Wimbledon (with Rosemary Casals) 1970, 1972, doubles, Wimbledon (with Jimmy Connors q.v.) 1973, doubles, US Open (with Jimmy Connors) 1975; winner Tour Finals 1971, 1972, 1973, 1975; winner of ILTF Grand Prix 1972, 1973; won 108 pro titles in his career; played 130 matches for the Romanian team in the Davis Cup; elected to Nat. Council of Romania's Social Democracy Party (Partidul Social Democrat—PSD) 1995; PSD cand. in elections for Mayor of Bucharest 1996; Pres. Romanian Tennis Fed.; currently competes on Delta Tour of Champions; rank of Maj.-Gen.; mem. Laureus World Sports Acad.; Chevalier, Légion d'honneur 2009; Best Romanian Sportsman of the Year 1969, 1970, 1971, 1973, Int. Tennis Hall of Fame 1991, ranked 28th by Tennis Magazine on its list of 40 Greatest Players of the Tennis Era 2005. *Publications:* Breakpoint 1986; wrote several novels in French 1980s. *Address:* Clubul sportiv Steaua, Calea Plevnei 114, Bucharest, Romania.

NASUTION, Darmin, PhD; Indonesian government official and fmr central banker; *Coordinating Minister for Economic Affairs;* b. 21 Dec. 1948, Tapanuli; ed Fakultas Ekonomi Universitas Indonesia, Univ. of Paris (Sorbonne), France; held several sr ministerial posts including Asst Minister of Trade and Industry Co-ordinator, Asst Minister for Production and Distribution Co-ordinator, Asst to Co-ordinating Minister for Devt Supervision and Admin. Reform; Dir-Gen. Financial Insts, Bank Indonesia 2000–05, Chair. Capital Market and Financial Inst. Supervisory Agency 2006, Dir-Gen. of Taxation 2006–09, Sr Deputy Gov. Bank Indonesia 2009, Acting Gov. then Gov. 2010–13; Co-ordinating Minister for Econ. Affairs 2015–; mem. Bd of Dirs FEUI LPEM 1989–93. *Address:* Office of the Coordinating Minister for Economic Affairs, Building Wardhana Jl. No.2-4 East Lapangan Banteng, Jakarta 10710, Indonesia (office). *Telephone:* (21) 3521835 (office). *Fax:* (21) 3511643 (office). *E-mail:* humas@ekon.go.id (office). *Website:* www.ekon.go.id (office).

NATADZE, Nodar, (Nodar Tskhireli); Georgian politician and academic; b. 27 May 1929, Tbilisi; s. of Revas Natadze and Tina Natadze (née Tatiana); m. Nana Gadyatska 1968; two s.; Philologist Inst. of Philosophy, Georgian Acad. of Sciences; Leader Popular Front of Georgia (now People's Front of Georgia) 1989–; Ed.-in-Chief Sakartvelo; mem. Supreme Council (Parl.) of Georgia 1989–90, 1990–91, 1992–95; mem. Tskhumi-Abkhazian Acad. of Sciences. *Leisure interests:* mountaineering, skiing, literary criticism.

NATARAJAN, Jayanthi, BA, BL; Indian lawyer and politician; b. 7 June 1954, Madras (now Chennai); d. of Dr C. R. Sundararajan; m. V. K. Natarajan 1974; one s.; ed Ethiraj Coll. and Madras Law Coll.; mem. Rajya Sabha (Council of States, Parl.) 1986–2001, 2008–; Co-founder Tamil Maanila Congress 1996, Leader 1997–2001; Minister of State for Civil Aviation and Parl. Affairs 1997–98, for Environment and Forests 2011–13; fmr Spokesperson, All India Congress Cttee; Fellow, Inst. of Politics, Kennedy School of Govt 2001; resgnd from Congress party 2015; Trustee Tamil Nadu Congress Committee Trust –2015 (resgnd). *Leisure interests:* playing veena, reading. *Address:* 'Badri', 47 Warren Road, Mylapore, Chennai 600 004, India (home). *Telephone:* (44) 24992440 (home).

NATBILADZE, Nikoloz, PhD; Georgian business executive, politician and fmr diplomatist; *Managing Director—CIS Countries, Suez Capital Ltd;* b. 17 Nov. 1971, Tbilisi; m.; two d.; ed Georgian Tech. Univ.; Sr Expert at Foreign Relations and Investment Dept, Ministry of Industry 1993–95; Regional Dir for CIS countries, Lone Star Corpn 1995–96; Tech. Supervisor, Municipal Infrastructure Devt Project 1996–97; Deputy Dir Tbilisi-London Insurance Co. Ltd 1997–98; Gen. Dir British-Caucasian Insurance Co. (BCI), Chair. Supervisory Bd and Hon. Pres. 1998–2004; Chair. Supervisory Bd ENERGOTRANS Ltd 2002–04; Dir Econ. Security Dept, Nat. Security Council 2004–05, Deputy Sec. 2005; Deputy Minister of Foreign Affairs 2005–07; Amb. to Azerbaijan 2007–11, to Spain 2011–12 (resgnd); currently Man. Dir—CIS Countries, Suez Capital Ltd; Chair. Georgian Philatelists Union; Orden de Honor (Spain) 2012; World Young Entrepreneurs Millennium Award 2000. *E-mail:* info@suez.holdings (office). *Website:* www .suezcap.org (office).

NATH, Amar, BE, MA; Indian civil servant and government official; *Joint Secretary, Exploration Division, Ministry of Petroleum and Natural Gas;* ed Nat. Inst. of Technology, Kurukshetra Univ., Duke Univ., USA; worked as Man. Trainee, Steel Authority of India Ltd; fmr Probationary Officer, State Bank of India; Officer, Trainee Admin. Service 1994–95; worked in Govt of Rajasthan 1995–96; Sec., Dept of Industrial Devt, Dept of Labour and Man. Dir, Pondicherry Distilleries Ltd, Govt of Pondicherry 1998–99; Sec., Dept of Planning and Programme Implementation, Dept of Econs and Statistics, Dept of Tourism, Govt of Arunachal Pradesh 1999–2003, also served as Deputy Commr/Dist Magistrate Govt of Arunachal Pradesh; Sec., Delhi Subordinate Services Selection Bd 2003–05; CEO Chandigarh Housing Bd and Dir Dept of Rural Devt 2005–08, also served as Sub-Div. Magistrate and officer in charge of various depts, Chandigarh Admin; Vice-Chair., Delhi Agricultural Marketing Bd 2008–11; Admin. of Union Territory of Lakshadweep 2011–12; CEO Delhi Urban Shelter Improvement Board 2012–15; Sec., Dept of Health and Family welfare, Govt of Nat. Capital Territory of Delhi –2016; Jt Sec., Exploration Div., Ministry of Petroleum and Natural Gas 2016–. *Address:* Ministry of Petroleum and Natural Gas, Shastri Bhavan, Dr Rajendra Prasad Road, New Delhi 110 001, India. *Telephone:* (11) 23382583. *Fax:* (11) 23383100. *E-mail:* amar.nath94@nic.in. *Website:* petroleum.nic.in.

NATH, Indira, MD, FRCPath, FAMS, FNASc, FASc; Indian immunologist and academic; *Professor Emeritus, Raja Ramanna Fellow and Chairman, Research Advisory Committee, Institute of Pathology, Indian Council of Medical Research;* b. 14 Jan. 1938; m.; one d.; ed All India Inst. of Medical Sciences; studied leprosy and immunology at MRC Lab. and Royal Coll. of Surgeons, UK; Nuffield Postdoctoral Fellow, UK 1971–72; mem. Faculty, Dept of Biotechnology, All India Inst. of Medical Sciences, New Delhi, 1972–87, Prof. and Head 1987–98, Indian Nat. Science Acad. Sr Scientist 1998–2003; Dean, School of Medicine, Asian Inst. of Medicine, Science and Tech. 2004–05; Dir LEPRA-Blue Peter Research Centre, Hyderabad 2006–08; Prof. Emer., Raja Ramanna Fellow and Chair. Research Advisory Cttee, Inst. of Pathology, Indian Council of Medical Research, New Delhi 2009–; Country Rep. to UN Comm. on Science and Tech. for Devt (UNCSTD) 2003–05; served on several ICSU cttees including Cttee on Science and Social Responsibility 2003, Scoping Group on Health 2006–07; mem. Science Advisory Cttee of Govt of India 2003–08; Fellow, Indian Acad. of Sciences 1988– (mem. Council 1992–94, Vice-Pres. 2001–03), Indian Nat. Science Acad., Nat. Acad. of Sciences (India), Nat. Acad. of Medical Sciences (India), Acad. of Sciences for the Developing World (TWAS), Royal Coll. of Pathologists (UK); Padmashri 1999, Silver Banner (Italy) 2002, Chevalier, Ordre nat. du Mérite 2003; Hon. DSc (Pierre and Marie Curie Univ., Paris) 2003; S.S. Bhatnagar Award, Council for Scientific and Industrial Research 1983, Kshanika Award, ICMR 1984, Nitya Anand Endowment Lecturer 1987, Clayton Memorial Lecturer 1988, Shri Om Prakash Bhasin Foundation Award 1990, Basanti Devi Amir Chand Award, ICMR 1994, Cochrane Research Award (UK) 1995, RD Birla Award 1995, Padma Shri 1999, L'Oréal-UNESCO For Women in Science Award 2002, K.K. Shastri Oration 2006, Prof. R C Mehrotra Memorial Life Time Achievement Award, Indian Science Congress Asscn 2012. *Publications:* numerous articles in scientific and medical journals on leprosy. *Address:* Institute of Pathology (ICMR), Safdarjang Hospital Campus, PO Box 4909, New Delhi 110 029 (office); 707 Sarvapriya Apartments, Sarvapriya Vihar, New Delhi 110 016, India (home). *Telephone:* (11) 26517707 (home). *Fax:* (11) 26100754 (office). *E-mail:* indiranath@gmail.com; indiran@hotmail.com. *Website:* www.icmr.nic.in (office).

NATH, Kamal, BCom; Indian politician; *Chief Minister of Madhya Pradesh;* b. 18 Nov. 1946, Kanpur; m. Alka Nath; two s.; ed Doon School, Dehra Dun, St Xavier's Coll., Calcutta (now Kolkata); joined Indian Nat. Congress 1968 as youth worker; mem. Lok Sabha (lower house of Parl.) for Chhindwara 1980–96, 1998–; mem. Del. to UN Gen. Ass. 1982–83; Minister of Environment and Forests 1991–95, of Textiles 1995–96, of Commerce and Industry 2004–09, of Road Transport and Highways 2009–11, of Urban Devt and of Parl. Affairs 2011–14, Chief Minister of Madhya Pradesh 2018–; Sec.-Gen. Indian Nat. Congress; mem. Congress Working Cttee; Pres. Bd Govs Inst. of Man. Tech.; Chair. Madhya Pradesh Devt Council; Patron, Child Devt Council of Madhya Pradesh; Dr hc (Rani Durgavati Univ., Jabalpur) 2006. *Address:* Office of the Chief Minister, Ballabh Bhavan, Mantralaya, Bhopal 462 004 (office); No. 1 Tughlak Road, New Delhi 110 011, India (home). *Telephone:* (755) 2441581 (office); (11) 23792233 (home). *E-mail:* kncmmp@gmail.com (home).

NATOCHIN, Yury Victorovich, DSc; Russian physiologist and academic; *Principal Scientist, Sechenov Institute of Evolutionary Physiology and Biochemistry, Russian Academy of Sciences;* b. 6 Dec. 1932, Kharkov, USSR (now Ukraine); s. of Victor Natochin and Frida Kohan; m. 1957; one s. one d.; ed Novosibirsk High Medical School; Jr, then Sr Researcher, Sechenov Inst. of Evolutionary Physiology and Biochemistry, St Petersburg 1959–64, Head of Lab. 1964–2015, Prin. Scientist 2015–; Dean, Medical Faculty, St Petersburg State Univ. 1995–2002, Prof. of Physiology 1996–; Acad.-Sec. Dept of Physiology, Russian Acad. of Sciences 1996–2002, 2011–; Ed.-in-Chief Russian Journal of Physiology 1995–2013; main research in physiology of the kidney, functional nephrology, molecular physiology; Hon. mem. Hungarian Physiology Soc. 1984; Hon. Prof., St Petersburg State Univ. 1999; Dr hc (Inst. of Experimental Medicine, St Petersburg) 2012, (Pirogov Centre, Moscow) 2012, (Medical Mil. Acad., St Petersburg) 2012; L.A. Orbeli Prize 1980, Jan Parkinje Gold Medal 1982, S. Rach Medal 1986, S. Korolev Medal 1992, Science Prize of Govt of Russia 1997, I. Pavlov Gold Medal 2001, Triumph Prize 2009, A. Knorre Medal 2016. *Publications include:* Ion-Regulating Function of the Kidney 1976, Physiology of the Kidney 1982, Problems of Evolutional Physiology of Water-Salt Balance 1984, Kidney 1997, Fluid and Electrolyte Regulation in Spaceflight 1998, Introduction in Nephrology 2007. *Leisure interests:* photography, poetry, travelling. *Address:* Sechenov Institute of Evolutionary Physiology and Biochemistry, 194223 St Petersburg, 44 M. Thorez prospekt (office); 8/2 Vernosty str., Apt 25, St Petersburg, Russia (home). *Telephone:* (812) 552-30-86 (office). *Fax:* (812) 552-30-86 (office). *E-mail:* natochin@iephb.ru (office). *Website:* www.iephb.ru (office).

NATTIEZ, Jean-Jacques, OC, LèsL, MèsL, PhD, FRSC; Canadian (b. French) musicologist and academic; *Professor Emeritus of Musicology, Faculty of Music, University of Montreal;* b. 30 Dec. 1945, Amiens, France; ed Amiens Conservatoire, Université d'Aix-en-Provence, Université de Paris VIII-Vincennes, France; naturalized Canadian 1975; Prof., Depts of Linguistics and French Studies, Univ. of Montreal 1970–72, apptd Prof. of Musicology, Faculty of Music 1972, later Prof. Emer.; Co-Ed. first six issues of CUMR 1980–85; fmr Ed. Circuit periodical; pioneer in br. of musicology known as musical semiology (analysis of music dealing with musical meaning, sometimes inspired by structural linguistics); Co-Ed. series Musique/Passé/Présent, Christian Bourgois publishing house, Paris 1981; Musical Dir Joliette-Lanaudière Symphony Orchestra 1984–87; currently Gen. Ed. five-volume Encyclopedia of Music; contrib. to EMC; in field of ethnomusicology, has produced several recordings of Inuit (Canada), Ainu (Japan) and Baganda (Uganda) music; Gen. Curator That's Opera! exhbn, Brussels to commemorate bicentenary of the founding of Milanese publishing house Ricordi 2008; fmr Researcher-in-Residence, Univ. of Oxford, UK; held Alphonse-Dupront Chair, Univ. Paris-Sorbonne 2008; mem. RSC 1988; mem. Ordre nat. du Québec 2001, Chevalier 2011, Kt, Order of Academic Palms 2018; Killam Research Fellowship 1988–90, Dent Medal, Royal Musical Asscn (England) for his complete works 1988, Prix André-Laurendeau pour les sciences humaines, Asscn canadienne française pour l'avancement des sciences 1989, Molson Prize 1990, Prix Léon-Gérin pour les sciences sociales du Gouvernement du Québec 1994, Fumio Koizumi Prize for Ethnomusicology 1996, Prize for Teaching Excellence, Univ. of Montreal in 2004, Killam Prize (Humanities), Canada Council for the Arts 2004, Venezia Prize, Italian Chamber of Commerce 2009, Medal of Acad. des lettres du Québec 2009, Gold Medal, Research Council of Canada Humanities "for Lifetime Achievement in research" 2009. *Recordings include:* Inuit Games and Songs (UNESCO's Musical Sources series) (Grand prix du disque de l'Acad. Charles-Cros 1979) 1978, Jeux vocaux des Inuit (Inuit du Caribou, Netsilik et Igloolik); contributed to Chants des Aïnou 1982, LP edn of oral music recordings made by Romanian ethnomusicologist Constantin Brailoïu in the 1950s, under the title Collection universelle de musique populaire enregistrée (Grand prix Charles-Cros 1987) 1985. *Publications:* Fondements d'une sémiologie de la musique 1975, Tétralogies 1983, Proust musicien 1984, Music and Discourse 1987, Wagner androgyne 1990; has edited texts by composer Pierre Boulez and published several major articles on the composer; Opera (novel); has published three collections of articles: De la sémiologie à la musique 1988, Le combat de Chronos et d'Orphée and La musique, la recherche et la vie; more than 150 papers. *Address:* Bureau B-504, Faculté de musique, Université de Montréal, 200 avenue Vincent-d'Indy, CP 6128, succursale Centre-ville, Montréal, PQ H3C 3J7, Canada (office). *Telephone:* (514) 844-4212 (office). *Fax:* (514) 844-1164 (office). *E-mail:* jean-jacques.nattiez@umontreal.ca (office). *Website:* www.musique.umontreal.ca/personnel/nattiez_jj.html (office).

NATTRASS, E. M. B. (Sue), AO, FAIM, FAIAM; Australian arts administrator, artistic director and trustee; b. (Elizabeth Margaret Barrett Nattrass), 15 Sept. 1941, Horsham, Vic.; d. of John Elliott Nattrass and Elizabeth Claven Saul; ed Univ. of Melbourne and Melbourne Business School; Stage Man., Lighting Designer and Production Dir 1963–79; Gen. Man. J. C. Williamson Productions Ltd 1980–83; Dir Playbox Theatre Co. 1981–84; Theatre Operations Man., Victorian Arts Centre 1983–88, Deputy Gen. Man. 1988–89, Gen. Man. 1989–96; Artistic Dir Melbourne Int. Festival of the Arts 1997–99; Exec. Dir, Producer Services, Millmaine Entertainment 2000–04; CEO and Artistic Dir Adelaide Festival 2002; Owner, The Yarts Consulting 2004–16; Pres. Australian Entertainment Industry Asscn 1994–2003; Councillor, Victorian Coll. of Arts 1989–2004, Deputy Pres. 1992–2002, Pres. 2002–04; Dir John Truscott Design Foundation 1994–2016, Leadership Vic. 1996–2003, Theatre Royal Hobart 2000–08, Fed. Square Pty Ltd 2000–08, Harold Mitchell Foundation 2000–09, Melbourne Football Club 2004–08; Adjunct Prof. and Chair. Academic Advisory Bd of Arts and Entertainment Management Course, Deakin Univ. 2009–12; Patron Victorian Theatres Trust 2000–, The Song Room Inc. 1999–2007; mem. Drama Advisory Panel, Vic. Ministry for the Arts 1983–85, 1987–88, mem. Bicentennial Arts and Entertainment Cttee 1987–88; mem. Ministerial Advisory Cttee, Queen Victoria Women's Centre 1993–94, Patron 1994–2001; mem. Melbourne and Olympics Parks Trust 2000–12, Brian Stacey Memorial Trust 2003–17, Sydney

Opera House Trust 2006–12, Australian Int. Cultural Council 2009–13; Chair. Collections Council of Australia 2004–09, City of Melbourne Cultural Devt Bd 2007–13; Bd mem. Melbourne Workers' Theatre 2010–13; George Fairfax Fellow, Deakin Univ. 2009; Hon. DLitt; Premier Award, The Age 2001 Performing Arts Awards, St Michael's Medal 1996, Vic. Day Award for Community and Public Service 1999, Centenary Medal 2001, Dame Elisabeth Murdoch Cultural Leadership Award 2006, The Green Room Award for Lifetime Achievement 2007, J.C. Williamson Award for outstanding contrib. to Australian live performance industry 2008. *Leisure interests:* cooking, walking, staring at trees, the bush, people and what makes them tick, medicine, sport. *Address:* The Yarts Consulting, 19 Myross Avenue, Ascot Vale, Vic. 3032, Australia. *Telephone:* (3) 9370-7062. *E-mail:* sue@theyarts.com.au.

NATUMAN, Joe; Ni-Vanuatu politician; *Deputy Prime Minister;* b. 24 Nov. 1952, Tanna; ed Univ. of the South Pacific, Univ. of Papua New Guinea; Public Relations Sec., Chief Minister's Office 1980; Asst Sec. for Foreign Affairs with responsibility for Australia and S Pacific 1982; Pvt. Sec., Prime Minister's Office 1983; Pvt. Sec. to Prime Minister Ham Lini Vanuaroroa 1984; First Sec., Prime Minister's Office 1987–91; Asst Registrar, Univ. of South Pacific, Suva 1991–95; mem. Parl. for Tanna 1995–; Minister for Judicial Services, Culture and Women's Affairs 1996, for Lands, Energy, Geology and Mines 1997, for Educ. 1998, 2004, for Internal Affairs 2002, 2007–08; Prime Minister 2014–15, Deputy Prime Minister 2016–; mem. Vanua'aku Pati (VP). *Address:* Parliament of Vanuatu, PMB 9052, Port Vila, Vanuatu (office). *Website:* www.parliament.gov.vu (office).

NATUVA, Col Timoci Lesi, MA; Fijian military officer and government official; b. 1957, Navuso village, Naitasiri; m. Mereani Natuva; four c.; ed Deakin Univ., Australia, Royal Australian Naval Staff Coll., Asia Pacific Center for Security Studies and Naval Post-Graduate School, USA; career in mil., including as Co. Commdr, 2nd Fiji Infantry Bn, Sinai (peacekeeping operation following peace treaty between Egypt and Israel) 1989–90, Chief Operations Officer, Civil Mil. Affairs, UNTAET, East Timor, mil. adviser to UN Sec.-Gen. in Afghanistan and Pakistan 1992–93, Chief of Staff, UNIFIL, Lebanon 2001, Commdr, Fiji Contingent, UNTAET, Contingent Commdr, 1st Fiji Infantry Regt, UNAMI, Iraq 2007; Minister for Works, Transport and Public Utilities 2013–14, for Immigration, Nat. Security and Defence 2014–16 (resgnd); Fellow, Australian Defence Coll. of Strategic Studies.

NATYNCZYK, Gen. (retd) Walter J., BBA, CD; Canadian army officer and government official; *Deputy Minister for Veterans' Affairs;* b. 1958, Winnipeg; m. Leslie Natynczyk; two s. one d.; ed Royal Roads Mil. Coll., Collège militaire royal, Canadian Forces Command and Staff Coll., All Arms Tactics Course, UK, US Army War Coll., Pa; joined Canadian Forces 1975; served in numerous regimental command positions, becoming CO Royal Canadian Dragoons; four years with Royal Canadian Dragoons on NATO duty, Germany; Squadron Commdr, Royal Mil. Coll., Kingston, Ont. 1983–86; six months UN peace-keeping duties, Cyprus 1984; one-year mission with British forces for UN as Sector SW Chief of Operations, Bosnia-Herzegovina 1994, later Chief of Land Operations, UNPROFOR HQ, Zagreb, Croatia, Canadian Contingent Commdr, Bosnia-Herzegovina 1998; fmr Deputy Commanding Gen., III Corps and Fort Hood, Texas, USA; deployed with III Corps to Baghdad, Iraq 2004, serving first as Deputy Dir of Strategy, Policy and Plans, later Deputy Commanding Gen. of Multi-National Corps; fmr Asst Dir to Nat. Defence HQ Secr., Ottawa; Vice-Chief of Defence Staff 2006–08, Chief of Defence Staff 2008–12 (retd); Pres. Canadian Space Agency 2013–14; Deputy Minister for Veterans' Affairs 2014–; attained rank of Lt-Gen. 2006, Gen. 2008; Order of Mil. Merit, Meritorious Service Cross 2006. *Leisure interests:* jogging and sailing. *Address:* Veterans Affairs Canada, 66 Slater Street, 14th Floor, Ottawa, Ont. K1A 0P4, Canada (office). *E-mail:* information@vac-acc.gc.ca (office). *Website:* www.veterans.gc.ca (office).

NAUGHTIE, (Alexander) James, MA; British journalist; b. 9 Aug. 1951, Aberdeen, Scotland; s. of Alexander Naughtie and Isabella Naughtie; m. Eleanor Updale 1986; one s. two d.; ed Univ. of Aberdeen and Syracuse Univ., USA; journalist, The Scotsman (newspaper) 1977–84; with The Guardian 1984–88, becoming Chief Political Corresp. 1985; Laurence Sterne Fellow, The Washington Post, Washington, DC 1981; Presenter, The World at One, BBC Radio 1988–94, The Proms, BBC Radio and TV 1991–, Today, BBC Radio 4 1994–2015, Book Club BBC Radio 4 1998–; mem. Council, Gresham Coll. 1997–; Hon. LLD (Aberdeen), (St Andrews), Hon. DUniv (Stirling). *Publications include:* The Rivals 2001, The Accidental American: Tony Blair and the Presidency 2004, The Making of Music: A Journey with Notes 2007, The New Elizabethans 2012, The Madness of July (novel) 2014, Paris Spring (novel) 2016. *Leisure interests:* books, opera. *Address:* BBC News Centre, Broadcasting House, London, W1A 1AA, England. *Telephone:* (20) 8624-9644. *Website:* www.bbc.co.uk/radio4/today.

NAUMAN, Bruce, MFA; American artist; b. 6 Dec. 1941, Fort Wayne, Ind.; ed Univ. of Wisconsin, Madison and Univ. of California, Davis, studied with Italo Scango, William Wiley, Robert Arneson, Frank Owen, Stephen Kaltenbach; Instructor, San Francisco Art Inst. 1966–68, Univ. of California, Irvine 1970; has participated in numerous group exhbns in USA and Europe; work in many perm. collections, including Whitney Museum, Los Angeles County Museum of Art, Tate Modern (London); first solo exhbn 1966; Dr hc (San Francisco Art Inst.) 1989; Artist Fellowship Award, Nat. Endowment for the Arts 1968, Max Beckmann Prize (Frankfurt) 1990, Wolf Prize 1993, Aldrich Prize 1995, ranked ninth in ArtReview magazine's Power 100 list 2005. *Publications include:* Pictures of Sculptures in a Room 1966, Clear Sky 1968, Burning Small Fires 1968, Bruce Naumann 1988, Bruce Naumann Prints 1989.

NAUMANN, Gen. Klaus, OBE; German army officer (retd); b. 25 May 1939, Munich; m. Barbara Linke; one s. one d.; joined Bundeswehr 1958, Col staff of German Mil. Rep., NATO Mil. Cttee, Brussels 1981–84; Brigade Commdr Armoured Infantry Brigade, Ellwangen 1984–86; Brig. Dept Head of Force Planning, Gen. Staff, Ministry of Defence 1986–88; Maj.-Gen., Head of Defence Policy and Operations staff 1988–90; adviser in two-plus-four negotiations on German Unification 1990; Lt-Gen., Commdr first German corps April–Oct. 1991; Insp.-Gen. of the Bundeswehr 1991; Chair. NATO Mil. Cttee 1996–99; currently Participant, European Leadership Network; mem. Int. Advisory Bd Worldsecurity.network.com; Great Distinguished Service Cross 1993, Commdr Legion of Merit

1993, Grand Officier, Légion d'honneur 1994, Grosses Bundesverdienstkreuz mit Stern 1998, Commdr's Cross of Merit (FRG), Gold Cross of Honour of Fed. Armed Forces, Gran Cruz de la Orden del Mérito Militar con Distintivo Blanco (Spain), KBE (Mil.) (UK), Grootofficier, Kroonorde (Belgium), Commdr's Cross, Legion of Merit (USA), Grand Cross, 2nd Class, Order of Merit (Austria), Kommandor m/ Stjerne av den Kongelige Norske Fortjenstorden (Norway), Defence Medal, 1st Class (Hungary), Grand Officier, Ordre de Leopold (Mil.) (Belgium), Grootofficier, Orde van Oranje-Nassau (Netherlands), Commdr's Grand Cross of the Order of the Lion of Finland. *Publication:* Die Bundeswehr in einer Welt im Umbruch; numerous articles in newspapers and journals. *Leisure interests:* politics, history, art, photography, Latin American culture. *Address:* European Leadership Network, Suite 7, Southbank House Black Prince Road, London, SE1 7SJ, England (office). *Website:* www.europeanleadershipnetwork.org/klaus-naumann_91.html (office).

NAUMANN, Michael, DPhil; German publisher and editor; *Rector, Barenboim-Said Akademie;* b. 8 Dec. 1941, Köthen; s. of Eduard Naumann and Ursula Naumann (née Schönfeld); m. Christa Wessel 1969 (divorced); one s. one d.; ed Univ. of Munich, Queen's Coll., Oxford, UK; Asst Prof., Univ. of Bochum 1971–76; Florey Scholar, Queen's Coll. Oxford 1976–78; Ed., Foreign Corresp. Die Zeit, Hamburg 1978–82; Sr Foreign Ed., Der Spiegel, Hamburg 1982–84; Publr Rowohlt Verlag, Reinbek 1984–95; Pres. and CEO Henry Holt and Co., New York 1996–98; Minister of State for Culture 1998–2000; Chief Ed. and Publisher, Die Zeit 2001–07; unsuccessful SPD cand. for Hamburg mayoral elections 2008; Ed., Cicero (magazine) 2010–12; Rector Barenboim-Said Acad., Berlin 2012–; Trustee, Thomson Reuters 2010–; Commdr, Légion d'honneur. *Publications include:* Der Abbau einer Verkehrten Welt 1969, Amerika liegt in Kalifornien 1983, Strukturwandel des Heroismus 1984, Die Geschichte ist offen 1990, Die schönste Form der Freiheit 2001, Glück gehabt 2017. *Leisure interests:* books, motorcycling, sailing. *Address:* Barenboim-Said Akademie GmbH, Französische Str. 33D, 10117 Berlin, Germany (office). *Telephone:* (30) 209671723 (office). *E-mail:* info@barenboimsaid.de (office). *Website:* www.barenboimsaid.de (office).

NAUMI, Najeeb an-, PhD; Qatari lawyer and politician; b. 21 March 1954, Doha; m.; four s. one d.; ed Alexandria Univ., Egypt, Univ. of Dundee, UK; legal adviser, Qatar Gas and Petrochemical Co. 1981–88, Diwan Amiri 1988–92; Minister and Legal Adviser, Office of HH The Heir Apparent and Minister of Defence 1992–95; Minister of Justice 1995–97; advocate and legal consultant 1997–. *Publication:* International Legal Issues Arising under the United Nations Decade of International Law 1995. *Leisure interests:* boating, Internet, reading, writing. *Address:* PO Box 9952, Doha, Qatar (office). *Telephone:* (974) 4311124 (office). *Fax:* (974) 44311124 (office).

NAUMOV, Vladimir Naumovich; Russian film director and screenwriter; *CEO, Soyuz-Navona Film Production Company;* b. 6 Dec. 1927, Leningrad (now St Petersburg); s. of Naum Naumov and Agnia Burmistrova; m. Natalia Belokhvostikova; one s. one d.; ed Dept of Directing, State Inst. of Cinematography (under I. A. Savchenko); Artistic Dir workshop unit at Mosfilm 1961–89 (with A. Alov until 1983); Chair. Bd Mosfilm Studios Co. 1989–; Prof. VGIK 1980–; currently CEO Soyuz-Navona film production co.; Head of Dept, Nesterova Univ.; Pres. Nat. Film Acad.; Sec. Nat. Union of Cinematographers; Academician, European Film Acad.; mem. Bd Mosfilm Cinema Concern; Order of Honour 1971, Order of the Red Banner of Labour 1972, Order of the Friendship of Peoples 1987, Order for Merit to the Fatherland 4th class 1997, Golden Cross for the Resurrection of Russia, Order for Merit to the Fatherland 2nd class 2007, Meritorious Art Worker 1965, People's Artist of the RSFSR 1974, People's Artist of USSR 1983, USSR State Prize 1984, First Degree Peacemaker Award for charity work 2007, Golden Eagle Award for outstanding contrib. to world cinematography 2008. *Films include:* (in collaboration with Alov to 1983) Uneasy Youth 1955, Pavel Korchagin (based on Ostrovsky's novel How the Steel Was Tempered) 1957, Wind 1959, Peace to Him Who Enters (two prizes at 22nd Venice Film Festival) 1961, The Coin, A Nasty Story (based on Dostoevsky) 1966 (banned, shown 1989), Flight (based on M. Bulgakov's play) 1971, How the Steel Was Tempered (TV series) 1974, Legend about Til (three prizes at All-Union Festival, First Prize Int. Festival Haugesunde, Norway, Int. Festival Brussels) 1976, Tehran-43 (Golden Prize at 12th Int. Film Festival, Moscow, Golden Prize All-Union Festival) 1981, The Shore (First Prize at 17th Int. Film Festival, Kiev) 1984, Alov 1984 (documentary), The Choice 1987, The Law 1989, Ten Years of Confinement 1990, The White Holiday (two prizes Int. Film Festival Rimini 1995) 1994, Nardo's Mystery (aka White Dog's Dream) (Moscow Film Festival Prize 1998) 1998, Clock without Hands (Russian 'Window to Europe' Film Festival Prize 2000, Grand Gold Pegasus Prize from the Moscow Film Festival 2001, Moscow Mayor's Prize 2001) 2000, Joconda on Asphalt 2007. *Publications:* Alexandr Alov Vladimir Naumov 1989, Vladimir Naumov Natalia Belokhvostikova In Frame 2000. *Leisure interests:* paintings and graphics. *Address:* Mosfilm, Mosfilmovskaya Street 1, Moscow, Russia (office); 123056 Moscow, Bolshaya Gruzinskaya 39, Apt 214, Russia. *Telephone:* (903) 723-15-16 (office); (903) 721-73-49 (office); (499) 253-87-32 (home); (499) 143-49-26 (office). *E-mail:* n.v.naumova@mail.ru (office).

NAUMOVSKI, Vasko, MA, LLM, PhD; Macedonian lawyer, academic, politician and diplomatist; *Ambassador to USA;* b. 1980, Skopje; ed SS Cyril and Methodius Univ., Iustinianus Primus Law School, Skopje, Rheinische-Friedrich-Wilhelms Univ., Bonn, Germany; mem. staff, Faculty for Int. Relations, Policy and European Studies, New York Univ., Skopje 2005–, Asst Prof. of Int. Law and Law within the EU 2008–; has participated in several int. scientific confs in Europe and USA; Deputy Prime Minister, responsible for European Integration 2009–11; Asst Prof., SS Cyril and Methodius Univ. 2011–14; Amb. to USA 2014–; scholarships from Konrad Adenauer Foundation (Germany), from US State Dept for study in USA. *Publications:* numerous scientific papers on European integration and int. law. *Leisure interests:* skiing, hiking. *Address:* Embassy of North Macedonia, 2129 Wyoming Avenue NW, Washington, DC 20008, USA (office). *Telephone:* (202) 667-0501 (office). *Fax:* (202) 667-2131 (office). *E-mail:* vasko.naumovski@mfa.gov.mk (office); usoffice@macedonianembassy.org (office). *Website:* www.macedonianembassy.org (office); www.mfa.gov.mk (office).

NAVALNYI, Aleksei Anatolyevich; Russian lawyer, politician and political activist; b. 4 June 1976, Butyn, Odintsovo Dist, Moscow Oblast, Russian SFSR, USSR; s. of Anatoliy Navalnyi; m. Yuliya Navalnaya; two c.; ed Peoples' Friendship

Univ. of Russia, Finance Univ. under the Govt of the Russian Fed., Yale Univ., USA; joined Russian United Democratic Party Yabloko 2000, mem. Fed. Political Council, elected to regional council of Moscow br. 2002, expelled from Yabloko "for causing political damage to the party; in particular, for nationalist activities" 2007; minor stockholder in several Russian state-related corpns; gained prominence within Russian media as a critic of state corruption from 2009; has organized large-scale demonstrations against alleged electoral fraud; writes regularly articles in several publs, including Forbes Russia; arrested, convicted and sentenced to 15 days in jail "for defying a government official" Dec. 2011; helped lead anti-Putin rally following the latter's election as Pres. March 2012, arrested along with Sergei Udaltsov following another anti-Putin rally and given 15-day jail sentence May 2012; f. Foundation for the Combating of Corruption (FBK) 2011, projects include RosPil (analysis of govt contracts), RosVybory (election monitoring); accusations of embezzlement and fraud brought against him by Russian federal authorities 2012, found guilty July 2013, sentenced to five years' imprisonment, but released on bail; announced his intention to run for Pres. of Russia April 2013; placed second in election to Mayor of Moscow Sept. 2013; placed under house arrest Feb. 2014, extended for a further period of six months April 2014, sentenced to a further suspended prison term of three and a half years Dec. 2014, released from a Moscow detention centre having served a 15-day sentence for distributing leaflets for an opposition rally March 2015; European Court of Human Rights (ECHR) ruled that Russia had violated his right to a fair trial and ordered the Govt to pay him 56,000 euros in legal costs and damages Feb. 2016; announced candidacy for presidential election Dec. 2016; Supreme Court overturned 2013 sentence and sent verdict back to Lenin Dist Court in Kirov for review Nov. 2016, latter repeated its sentence of 2013 (previously annulled by ECHR ruling) and charged him with a five-year suspended sentence Feb. 2017, Navalny announced he will pursue annulment of sentence that contravenes ECHR ruling Feb. 2017; mem. Bd, Aeroflot 2012–13; Chair. Progress Party 2013–; named by Russian business newspaper Vedomosti as Person of the Year 2009, World Fellow, Yale Univ.'s World Fellows Program 2010. *Address:* Foundation for the Combating of Corruption (Fond borby s korruptsiei), 109240 Moscow, ul. Nikoloyamskaya 26, korp 1-1A, Russian Federation. *Telephone:* (499) 653-75-52. *E-mail:* navalny_en@livejournal.com (office); fbk@fbk.info. *Website:* navalny.com; fbk.info; rosyama.ru.

NAVARRE, Christophe, BBA; Belgian business executive; *President, Vinexpo;* b. 1958; ed Univ. of Liège, INSEAD (France) European Marketing Programme; joined Continental Bank 1980; moved to Exxon where he held marketing and sales positions with the Esso group; joined Interbrew 1989, headed several different Italian and French subsidiaries; Pres. and CEO JAS Hennessy & Co., LVMH 1997–2001, CEO Moët Hennessy (Wines and Spirits div. of LVMH) 2001–17; f. SCP Neptune Int.; Pres. Vinexpo 2017–; Dir JetSmarter, Inc. 2017–, Vivino 2017–; mem. Bd Comité Colbert; mem. Advisory Bd Heineken NV 2009–; Chevalier, Légion d'honneur; Commdr, Ordre du Mérite agricole; Officier, Ordre de la Couronne (Belgium). *Address:* Vinexpo, 2 cours du XXX Juillet, 33074 Bordeaux, France (office). *Telephone:* 5-56-56-00-22 (office). *Website:* www.vinexpo.com (office).

NAVARETTE LÓPEZ, Jorge Eduardo; Mexican economist, diplomatist and academic; *Researcher, Programa Universitario de Estudios del Desarrollo (PUED), Universidad Nacional Autónoma de México (UNAM);* b. 29 April 1940, Mexico City; one s.; ed Nat. Autonomous Univ. of Mexico (UNAM); Prof., Nat. School of Econs and Nat. School of Political and Social Sciences, UNAM 1964–71, Head of Research on Int. Affairs, 2004, then with Centro de Investigaciones Interdisciplinarias en Ciencias y Humanidades (CEIICH), currently Researcher, Programa Universitario de Estudios del Desarrollo (PUED); various positions with Foreign Trade Nat. Bank 1966–72; Ed. Comercio Exterior; with Secr. of Finance and Public Credit –1972; Amb. to Venezuela 1972–75, to Austria 1975–77, to Yugoslavia 1977–78, to UK 1986–89, to People's Repub. of China 1989–93, to Chile 1993–95, to Brazil 1997–2001, to Germany 2002–04; Rep. of Mexico at Int. Conf. for Co-operation and Devt, Paris 1976–77; Deputy Perm. Rep. to UN and Vice-Pres. Econ. and Social Council 1978–79, Perm. Rep. to UN 2001–02; Under-Sec. for Econ. Affairs, Secr. of Foreign Relations 1979–86; Under-Sec. for Policy and Devt, Secr. of Energy 1995–97; fmr consultant for Inter-American Bank and UNDP; fmr Perm. Rep. to UNIDO; fmr mem. Bd of Govs IAEA; fmr mem. South Comm. *Publications include:* The International Transference of Technology: The Mexican Case (with Gerardo Bueno and Miguel Wionczek) 1969, Mexico: The Economic Policy of the New Government 1971, The Latin American External Debt 1986, and other books on China, the int. oil market and Mexican foreign policy. *Address:* Programa Universitario de Estudios del Desarrollo (PUED), Planta baja del edificio Unidad de Posgrado Costado Sur de la Torre II Humanidades Campus central de Ciudad Universitaria Coyoacán, México 04510, DF, Mexico (office). *E-mail:* jorgeeduna@gmail.com. *Website:* www.pued.unam.mx (office).

NAVARRO, Peter, BA, MPA, PhD; American economist, academic, writer and government official; *Director, National Trade Council;* b. 15 July 1949; m. Leslie Lebon; ed Tufts Univ., Harvard Univ.; served in US Peace Corps, Thailand 1973–76; Policy Analyst, Urban Services Group (consulting firm), Washington, DC 1976–77; Policy Analyst, Massachusetts Energy Office 1988, US Dept of Energy 1979–80; Research Assoc., Energy and Environmental Policy Center, Harvard Univ. 1981–85; Lecturer, Univ. of California, San Diego 1985–86; Asst Prof. of Business and Govt, Univ. of San Diego 1986–88; Prof. of Econs and Public Policy, Univ. of California, Irvine 1989–; policy advisor to Donald Trump during presidential campaign 2016; Dir, Nat. Trade Council 2017–. *Film:* Death By China (documentary) 2012. *Publications include:* books: The Policy Game 1984, If It's Raining in Brazil, Buy Starbucks 2001, When the Market Moves, Will You Be Ready? 2003, What the Best MBAs Know 2005, The Well-Timed Strategy: Managing the Business Cycle for Competitive Advantage 2006, The Coming China Wars 2008, Always a Winner 2009, Seeds of Destruction (with Glenn Hubbard) 2010, Death by China: Confronting the Dragon – A Global Call to Action 2011, Crouching Tiger: What China's Militarism Means for the World 2015; numerous articles in newspapers and journals. *Address:* National Trade Council, The White House Office, 1600 Pennsylvania Avenue, NW, Washington, DC 20500, USA (office). *Telephone:* (202) 456-1414 (office). *Fax:* (202) 456-2461 (office). *E-mail:* pn@peternavarro.com. *Website:* www.whitehouse.gov (office); www.peternavarro.com.

NAVARRO, Samuel Lewis, BA, MBA; Panamanian politician and business executive; *Chairman, Latin American Board, Georgetown University;* b. 1957, Panama City; s. of Gabriel Lewis Galindo; m. 1st; two c.; m. 2nd Anagrethel González; two c.; ed Georgetown and American Univs, USA; Founder, Partido de Solidaridad 1993, est. alliance with Partido Revolucionario Democrático 1999, left to serve as running mate to presidential cand. Martín Torrijos 2004; Vice-Pres. of Panama and Minister of Foreign Affairs 2004–09; Pres. and Dir Empaques de Colón (family business) 1985–2001, Grupo ELE 1985–2001, Northsound Corpn, Inc. 1985–2001; mem. Bd of Dirs Panama Canal Authority 1997–2001; currently Pres. Calder International (Panamanian real estate co.); also currently Man. Partner, VH Propertis; Chair. Latin American Bd, Georgetown Univ. 2015–; mem. Bd of Dirs Georgetown Univ.; fmr mem. Bd of Dirs Distribuidora de Productos de Papel, Inmobiliaria Costa Azul, Cervecería Nacional, Red Crown Corpn; mem. Bd of Counselors, McLarty Associates. *Address:* Georgetown University Latin American Board, 3700 O Street, NW, 433 Hariri Building, Washington, DC 20057, USA (office). *Telephone:* (202) 687-1695 (office). *E-mail:* latinamericanboard@georgetown.edu (office). *Website:* latinamericanboard.com (office).

NAVARRO GARCÍA, Andrés; Dominican Republic architect, urban planner, writer, academic and government official; *Minister of Education;* b. 4 Feb. 1964, Bonao, La Vega Prov. (now Monseñor Nouel Prov.); ed Universidad Autónoma de Santo Domingo, Universidad Nacional Autónoma de México; Dir Nat. Urban Devt Policy (CONAU) 1998; Dir-Gen. Urban Planning, Nat. Dist City Council 2002, Tech. Sec. 2008–12, Sec.-Gen. 2012–14; Deputy Program Dir for the Reform and Modernization of the State – PARME 2005–08; Dir of Cabinet, Ministry of Public Works April–Sept. 2014; Minister of Foreign Affairs 2014–16, of Educ. 2016–. *Address:* Ministry of Education, Avda Máximo Gómez, esq. Santiago 2, Gazcue, Santo Domingo, DN, Dominican Republic (office). *Telephone:* 688-9700 (office). *Fax:* 689-8688 (office). *E-mail:* mlibreacceso@see.gob.do (office). *Website:* www.see.gob.do (office); andresnavarrogarcia.blogspot.com.

NAVARRO GONZÁLEZ, Alberto; Spanish diplomatist and government official; *Head of Delegation and Ambassador of the European Union to the Dominican Republic;* b. 27 March 1955, Santa Cruz de Tenerife, Canary Islands; joined Diplomatic Service 1980, served in Embassy in Tegucigalpa, Honduras, Prague, Czechoslovakia and Mission of Spain to the European Communities, later served as Deputy Dir-Gen. for Co-ordination of Community Programs of Co-operation, as Dir-Gen. for Community, Legal and Institutional Co-ordination and Dir-Gen. Chief of Staff, Minister of Foreign Affairs, apptd Dir Dept for Humanitarian Aid (ECHO) 1997, and later Chief of Staff of Sec.-Gen., High Rep. for the Common Foreign and Security Policy of the Council of EU, Javier Solana, Amb. and Head of EC in Brazil 2003–04, Sec. of State for the EU 2004–08, Amb. to Portugal 2008–10, to Morocco 2010–13, currently Head of Del. and Amb. of EU to Dominican Repub. *Address:* Delegation of the European Union to the Dominican Republic, Ave. Abraham Lincoln 1063, Ensanche Serrallés, Santo Domingo, Dominican Republic (office). *Telephone:* 227-0525 (office). *Fax:* 227-0509 (office). *E-mail:* delegation-dominican-rep@eeas.europa.eu (office). *Website:* eeas.europa.eu/delegations/dominican (office).

NAVARRO NAVARRO, Miguel; Spanish sculptor and set designer; b. 29 Sept. 1945, Mislata, Valencia; s. of Vicente Navarro Lopez and Valentina-Francisca Navarro Hernandez; ed Escuela Superior de Bellas Artes de San Carlos, Valencia; began career as a painter; from 1972 devoted himself mainly to sculpture; works in public spaces include public fountains, Valencia 1984, Turis (Valencia) 1986, Minerva Paranoica (sculpture), Castellón 1989, Torre del Sonido (sculpture), Universidad Carlos III, Getafe 1990, Fraternitat (sculpture), Barcelona 1992, Boca de Luna (fountain), Brussels 1994, Casco Industrial (sculpture) Bilbao 1999, Vigía (sculpture) Las Palmas 2000, Cabeza con Luna Menguante, Mislata 2001, La Mirada (sculpture) Vitoria-Gasteiz 2002, Palera (sculpture), Malaga 2002, Palas Fundición (sculpture) Ceuti, Murcia 2003, El Parotet, Valencia 2003, Conexion, Bilbao 2006, Mantis, Murcia 2007, Valvula con alberca, Zaragoza 2008, Almassil, Mislata (Valencia) 2010; works in public collections including Guggenheim Museum, New York, Fundació Caixa de Pensions, Barcelona, Instituto Valenciano de Arte Moderno, Valencia, Museo Nacional Centro de Arte Reina Sofía, Madrid, Fondation Lambert, Brussels, Diputación Prov. de Valencia, Centre Georges Pompidou, Paris, Museu d'Art Contemporani, Barcelona, Colección Argentaria, Madrid, Colección Banco de España, Madrid, Fundación Coca Cola España, Madrid, Fundazion ICO, Madrid, Universidad Politécnica de Valencia, Museo de Arte Contemporáneo Sofía Imbert, Caracas, Mie Prefectural Art Museum, Japan; has designed sets for plays including Fernando Sabater's Vente a Sinopia and Calderon de la Barca's Absalon; Premio Nacional de Artes Plásticas 1986, Premio Alfons Roig, Valencia 1987, Premio CEOE a las Artes 1990, Premio Nacional de la Asociación de Críticos de Arte ARCO 95 1995, Premio Valencianos para el Siglo XXI 2001, Distinción de la Generalidad Valenciana al Merito Cultural 2002, Julio Gonzalez Int. Prize, IVAM. *Leisure interests:* cooking, countryside. *Address:* c/o San Martín 13, 46920 Mislata, Valencia, Spain. *Telephone:* (6) 3792624. *E-mail:* info@cifo.org.

NAVASKY, Victor Saul, AB, LLB, JD; American writer, editor and academic; *Chairman, Columbia Journalism Review;* b. 5 July 1932, New York, NY; s. of Macy Navasky and Esther Goldberg; m. Anne Landey Strongin 1966; one s. two d.; ed Swarthmore Coll., Yale Univ. Law School; Special Asst to Gov. G. Mennen Williams, Mich. 1959–60; Founding Ed. and Publr Monocle quarterly 1961–65; Ed. New York Times Magazine 1970–72, wrote monthly column (In Cold Print) for The New York Times Book Review; Ed.-in-Chief The Nation magazine 1978–94, Editorial Dir and Publr 1995–2007, Publr Emer. 2007–; George Delacorte Prof. of Magazine Journalism, Grad. School of Journalism, Columbia Univ. 1999–, Dir Delacorte Center of Magazines, Chair. Columbia Journalism Review; Visiting Scholar, Russell Sage Foundation 1975–76; Ferris Visiting Prof. of Journalism, Princeton Univ. 1976–77; Visiting Prof. of Social Change, Swarthmore Coll. 1982; Fellow, John F. Kennedy School of Govt, Harvard Univ. 1994, Freedom Forum Media Studies Center 1995; mem. Man. Bd Swarthmore Coll. 1991–94; fmr mem. Bd Authors Guild, Cttee to Protect Journalists, Bd of Govs New School for Social Research; fmr Vice-Pres. PEN; mem. American Acad. of Arts and Sciences; numerous hon. degrees; Guggenheim Fellow 1975–76, Carey McWilliams Award, American Political Science Assn 2001. *Play:* Starr's Last Tape (with Richard R.

Lingeman) 1999. *Publications include:* Kennedy Justice, Naming Names (Nat. Book Award), The Experts Speak: The Definitive Compendium of Authoritative Misinformation, A Matter of Opinion (George Polk Book Award 2005, Ann M. Sperber Prize 2006) 2005, Mission Accomplished: The Experts Speak about Iraq (with Christopher Cerf) 2008; numerous articles and reviews published in magazines and journals of opinion. *Address:* Room 802, Columbia Graduate School of Journalism, 2950 Broadway, New York, NY 10027 (office); 33 West 67th Street, New York, NY 10023, USA (home). *Telephone:* (212) 854-5751 (office). *E-mail:* vic@thenation.com (office). *Website:* www.journalism.columbia.edu (office).

NAVICKAS, Vytas, PhD; Lithuanian economist and politician; b. 14 March 1952, Lazdijai Dist; m. Raimonda; two d.; ed Vilnius Univ.; Research Fellow, Inst. of Econs, Lithuanian Acad. of Sciences 1975–89; Lecturer, Vilnius Univ., Vilnius Pedagogical Univ. and Vilnius Gediminas Tech. Univ. 1983–90, 1997–2004; Head of Div. for Econ. Reforms, Council of Ministers 1989; Minister of the Economy 1990–91, 1995–96, 2006–08, Deputy Minister 1991–95; Dir UAB Draudos Asistavimas 1996–2004; Pres. Vilnius Chamber of Commerce, Industry and Crafts 2001–05; mem. Lithuanian Peasant Nationalists' Union.

NAVRACSICS, Tibor, PhD; Hungarian lawyer, political scientist, academic, politician and EU official; *Commissioner for Education, Culture, Youth and Sport, European Union;* b. 13 June 1966, Veszprém; m. Anikó Prevoz; two d.; ed Eötvös Loránd Univ., Budapest; Tribunal Clerk, Municipal Court, Veszprém 1990–92; Lecturer, Dept of Social Sciences, Univ. of Veszprém 1990–92; Research Fellow, Regional Ass. of Veszprém Co. 1992–93; Lecturer, Dept of Sociology and Political Sciences, Dániel Berzsenyi Teacher's Coll., Szombathely 1992–98; Asst Prof., Dept of Political Sciences, Univ. of Econs, Budapest 1993–97, Assoc. Prof. 1997–2001; Sr Assoc. Prof., Dept of Political Sciences, Eötvös Loránd Univ. 2001–; Head of Communications Dept (Viktor Orbán's Cabinet), Prime Minister's Office 1998–99, Head of Dept for Press and Information 1999–2002; Head of Dept for Political Analyses, Parl. Group of Fidesz—Hungarian Civic Union 2002–03, Chief of Pres.'s Cabinet 2003–06; Leader of programme-creating team (referred to as Civic Governance) 2004–; mem. Parl. 2006–, Head of Parl. Group of Fidesz—Magyar Polgári Szövetség (Hungarian Civic Alliance) 2006–10; Deputy Prime Minister and Minister of Public Admin and Justice 2010–14, Acting Minister of Nat. Devt 2011, Minister of Foreign Affairs and Trade June–Sept. 2014; Commr for Educ., Culture, Youth and Sport, European Comm. (EC), Brussels Nov. 2014–19; Sec.-Gen. Hungarian Asscn of Political Scientists 1998–2000; Vice-Pres. Asscn of the Hungarian Inst. for Political Science 1996–; Ed. Periodical Comitatus 1992–93; mem. Editorial Bd Politikatudományi Szemle (Political Science Review) 1999–; mem. of the Presidency, Hungarian Asscn of Political Science 2001–; mem. Political Sciences Asscn; Scholarship of the Soros Foundation 1994–96, CEEPUS Scholarship, Univ. of Zagreb 1995, Leverhulme Research Fellow/Scholarship, European Inst., Univ. of Sussex, Brighton, UK 1996–97, Winner, OTKA Competition: The Democracy in Central Eastern Europe 1996–99, Jean Monnet Scholarship 1998–2001, elected Teacher of the Year by the students of Eötvös Loránd Univ. 2007. *Publications include:* Európai belpolitika (Internal Politics in the European Union) 1996, Political Analysis of the European Union 1996, Political Communication (with István Hegedűs, Mihály Szilágyi and Sipos Balázs) 2004. *Address:* European Commission, 200 Rue de la Loi/Wetstraat 200, 1049 Brussels, Belgium (office). *Telephone:* (2) 299-11-11 (switchboard) (office). *E-mail:* cab-navracsics-contact@ec.europa.eu (office). *Website:* ec.europa.eu (office).

NAVRATILOVA, Martina; American/Czech fmr professional tennis player; b. (Martina Šubertová), 18 Oct. 1956, Prague, Czech Repub.; d. of Miroslav Navratil and Jana Navratilova; m. longtime partner Julia Lemigova 2014; two d.; left-handed, one-handed backhand; professional since 1975, the year she defected to USA; ranked No. 1 July 1978, 1982–85; Wimbledon singles champion 1978, 1979, 1982, 1983, 1984, 1985, 1986, 1987, 1990, finalist 1988, 1989, 1994; (doubles 1976, 1979, 1982, 1983, 1984, 1985); French champion 1982, 1984; Australian champion 1981, 1983, 1985; Avon champion 1978, 1979, 1981; US Open champion 1983, 1984, 1986, 1987; 57 Grand Slam titles (18 singles, 37 women's doubles, 2 mixed doubles); won 167 singles and 177 doubles titles (more than any other player, male or female; World No. 1 for 332 weeks at retirement (Nov. 1994); 19 Wimbledon titles (1995); set professional women's record for consecutive victories 1984; won 100th tournament of career 1985; only player to win 100 matches at Wimbledon 1991; record of 158 wins (Feb. 1992) in singles beating the record of Chris Evert Lloyd; Pres. WTA (Women's Tennis Asscn) 1979–80, 1983–84, 1994–95; World Champion 1980; played Fed. Cup for Czechoslovakia 1973, 1974, 1975, for USA 2003; 1,442 victories, 219 defeats; designer own fashion wear; made comeback (in doubles only) 2000; winner Mixed Doubles, Australian Open 2003, Wimbledon 2003 (at age 46 years and 6 months, oldest winner of a Grand Slam title); retd 2006; Dr hc (George Washington Univ.) 1996; WTA Player of the Year 1978, 1979, 1982, 1983, 1984, 1985, 1986, ITF World Champion 1979, 1982, 1983, 1984, 1985, 1986, Female Athlete of the Decade for the 1980s, Nat. Sports Review, Sportswomen of the Year 1982–84, Women's Sports Foundation, Int. Tennis Hall of Fame 2000, named by The Tennis Channel as the second greatest female tennis player of all time, behind Steffi Graf 2012, among the first class of inductees into the Nat. Gay and Lesbian Sports Hall of Fame 2013. *Television:* I'm a Celebrity... Get Me Out of Here! (ITV) 2008. *Publications include:* Being Myself (autobiog.) 1985, The Total Zone (novel with Liz Nickles) 1994, The Breaking Point (with Liz Nickles) 1996, Killer Instinct (with Liz Nickles) 1998, Shape Yourself 2006. *Leisure interests:* golf, snowboarding, skiing, basketball. *Address:* c/o IMG, 1360 East 9th Street, Cleveland, OH 44114, USA (office). *Website:* www.martinanavratilova.com.

NAWAR, Ahmed, BFA, PhD; Egyptian arts administrator; b. 3 June 1945, el-Shin, Gharbia dist; s. of Mohamed Ismail Nawar and Fakiha Karam Mostafa Ghali; m. Wafaa Mossallem 1969; three d.; ed Cairo Univ. and St Fernando Acad., Madrid, Spain; apptd Prof. of Graphics, Faculty of Fine Art, Helwan Univ. 1967, Prof. Emer. 2008–, Gen. Supervisor, Cultural Centre for Sciences and Arts 2008–; Founder and Dean, Faculty of Fine Art, Menia Univ. 1983–88; Head, Nat. Centre for Fine Arts, Ministry of Culture 1988–2006; Head, Museums Service, Higher Council for Antiquities 1994–99; Gen. Supervisor Nubia Savings Fund 1996–98; Art Adviser to People's Ass. 1999–2008, Banque Misr 2007–10; mem. Bd Gen. Authority of Cultural Palaces 1991–2005, Chair. 2008–; Chair. Bd Soc. of Art Lovers 2007–; Moderator, Art Cttee 2012–, mem. Advisory Cttee 2012–; mem. Bd

Cairo Opera House 1990–2005; mem. Higher Cttee, Egypt's Who's Who, Alexandria Library 2008–; State Order of Arts and Sciences, First Class 1979, Order of Merit (Spain) 1992, Officier, Ordre des Arts et des Sciences 1995; Nobel Gold Medal 1986, Medal of Honour, Russia 2006. *Address:* 78 el-Shishiny Street, off Al-Mariyoutiyah Canal Street, Al-Hram, Giza (studio); 54 Dimashk Street, Madinat al-Mohandeseen, Flat 16, Giza, Egypt (home). *Telephone:* (2) 7448336. *E-mail:* nawarart@hotmail.com. *Website:* www.ahmednawar.net.

NAWAWI AYOB, Ahmad, PhD; Malaysian botanist, academic and fmr university vice-chancellor; *Professor Emeritus, Institute of Biological Sciences, University of Malaya;* b. 11 Feb. 1937, Perak; m.; two c.; ed Queen's Univ., Belfast, Northern Ireland; Demonstrator in Botany, Mycology and Plant Pathology, Queen's Univ., Belfast 1963–65; botanist and plant pathologist, Ministry of Agric., Malaysia 1966–67; Post-doctoral Research Fellow, Wageningen Agricultural Univ., Nether-lands 1970, Queen's Univ. Belfast 1971–72; Lecturer in Botany, Univ. of Malaya 1967–74, Assoc. Prof. 1974–78, now Emer., Head Dept of Botany 1974–75, Prof. of Botany 1978, Dean Faculty of Sciences 1976–78, Acting Deputy Vice-Chancellor 1977, Deputy Vice-Chancellor for Finance and Devt 1983–86, Acting Vice-Chancellor 1986, Deputy Vice-Chancellor 1991; Pres. Malaysian Soc. for Micro-biology 1986–87; fmr Pres. Malaysian Soc. for Applied Biology; mem. Council Malaysian Agricultural Research and Devt Inst., Malaysian Nat. Science Council 1981–, Man. Cttee Nat. Scientific Research and Devt Trust Fund 1981–, Council Nat. Inst. of Public Admin.; mem. Acad. of Sciences Malaysia; Fellow, Islamic Acad. of Sciences, Malaysian Acad. of Sciences; Hon. DSc (Portsmouth), (Belfast) 1995; Johan Mangku Negara 1982, Datuk Paduka Cura Si Manja Kini 1986, Dato Paduka Cura Simanja Kini (DPCM). *Publications:* over 60 specialized publs. *Address:* Institute of Research Management and Consultancy, IPS Building, University of Malaya, 50603 Kuala Lumpur, Malaysia (office). *Telephone:* (3) 79674370 (office). *Fax:* (3) 79674178 (office). *E-mail:* nawawi@um.edu.my (office). *Website:* www.ippp.um.edu.my (office).

NAWAZ KHAN, Lt-Gen. (retd) Khalid; Pakistani army officer (retd) and business executive; *Managing Director, Fauji Foundation;* b. Dera Ismail Khan, Khyber Pakhtunkhwa; ed Command and General Staff Coll., Fort Leavenworth, US, Armed Forces War Coll. (National Defence Univ.); commissioned in the Pakistan Army in 1975 with Sword of Honour; worked as command of an Infantry Div. and Corps deployed along the Line of Control; Commdt, Command and Staff Coll., Quetta; Commdr X corps, Rawalpindi –2013; Man. Dir Fauji Foundation, Fauji Oil Terminal & Distribution Co. Ltd; Chair. Askari Bank Ltd 2015–, Fauji Cement Co. Ltd (Construction Materials) 2015–, Fauji Fertilizer Co. Ltd (Agricultural Chemicals) 2015–, Fauji Fertilizer Bin Qasim Ltd (Agricultural Chemicals), Mari Petroleum Co. Ltd (Oil & Gas Exploration and Production) 2015–, Askari Cement Ltd; Pres. Foundation Univ., Vice-Chair. Bd of Govs; Hilal-e-Imtiaz (Military), Sitara-i-Esar. *Leisure interests:* golf. *Address:* Fauji Founda-tion Head Office, 68 Tipu Road, Chaklala, Rawalpindi 46000, Pakistan (office). *Telephone:* (51) 5951821 (office). *E-mail:* info@fauji.org.pk (office). *Website:* www .fauji.org.pk (office).

NAYDENOV, Radi, MA; Bulgarian diplomatist and government official; b. 1962, Sofia; ed Univ. of Nat. and World Economy, Sofia, participated in specialization programmes at Foreign Ministries of FRG, France, USA, etc.; entered diplomatic service 1992; Deputy Minister of Defence 2001; Chief of Staff of fmr King of Bulgaria, Simeon Saxe-Coburg-Gotha, Prime Minister of Bulgaria 2002–05; Amb. to Austria 2005–12, Perm. Sec., Ministry of Foreign Affairs 2011–12, Amb. to Germany 2012–17, Minister of Foreign Affairs 2017.

NAYLOR, Christopher David, OC, MD, DPhil, FRSC, FRCPC, FCAHS; Canadian medical researcher and fmr university administrator; *Professor of Medicine and President Emeritus, University of Toronto;* b. 26 Oct. 1954, Woodstock, Ont.; m. Ilse Treurnicht; ed Univ. of Toronto, Univ. of Oxford, UK, Univ. of Western Ontario; fmr Sr Scientist, Medical Research Council of Canada; mem. Faculty, Univ. of Toronto 1987–, Dean of Medicine and Vice-Provost, Relations with Health Care Insts 1999–2005, Pres. Univ. of Toronto 2005–13, Pres. Emer. 2013–; Founding CEO Inst. for Clinical Evaluative Sciences 1991–98; Chair. Nat. Advisory Cttee on SARS and Public Health 2003, Nat. Advisory Cttee on Healthcare Innovation 2014–15, Nat. Advisory Cttee to Review Support for Fundamental Science 2016–17; mem. Editorial Oversight Cttee, Journal of the American Medical Association 2017–; fmr mem. Editorial Bd, Journal of the American Medical Association, Canadian Medical Association Journal, British Medical Journal, Journal of Health Services Research and Policy, Health Affairs, Journal of General Internal Medicine, among others; fmr Gov. Canadian Insts of Health Research; fmr mem. Bd, Mount Sinai Hosp., St Michael's Hosp., Univ. Health Network, Sunnybrook Health Science Centre, Toronto Rehabilitation Inst., Asscn of Univs and Colls of Canada, Council of Ontario Univs; Trustee, The Aga Khan Univ. 2013–; Fellow, Royal Coll. of Physicians and Surgeons of Canada, Canadian Acad. of Health Sciences; mem. US Nat. Acad. of Medicine; Hon. DSc (Univ. of Manitoba) 2009; Hon. LLD (Western Univ.) 2011, (Univ. of Calgary) 2017; Royal Australasian Coll. of Physicians John Dinham Cottrell Medal 1996, Royal Coll. of Physicians and Surgeons of Canada G. Malcolm Brown Award 1996, Medical Research Council of Canada Michael Smith Award 1999, Canadian Cardiovascular Soc. Research Achievement Award 2002, R.D. Defries Award, Canadian Public Health Asscn 2005, inducted into Canadian Medical Hall of Fame 2016, F.N.G. Starr Medal, Canadian Medical Asscn 2016. *Publications:* more than 300 scholarly works. *Leisure interests:* jazz piano, golf. *Telephone:* (416) 901-9480 (office). *E-mail:* david.naylor@utoronto.ca (office).

NAYLOR, Sir Robert, Kt, BSc; British health services executive; b. 1950, Manchester; ed Univ. of Greenwich; began career as graduate trainee, later Hosp. Admin. Nat. Hosp., Queen Square, London; CEO Birmingham Heartlands & Solihull National Health Service (NHS) Trust (now Heart of England NHS Foundation Trust—HEFT) 1985–2000; CEO Univ. Coll. London Hosps 2000–16; Chair. Shelford Group 2013–14; Sr Assoc. Fellow, Univ. of Warwick Inst. of Governance and Public Man.; mem. Bd of Dirs NHS Providers; mem. NHS Confederation Policy Bd, NHS Procurement and Efficiency Bd; Dr hc (Univ. of Greenwich) 2009. *Leisure interests:* football (Manchester United), opera, scuba diving.

NAYYER HUSSAIN BOKHARI, Syed, BA, LLB; Pakistani lawyer and politician; b. 23 Dec. 1952, Rawalpindi; m.; one s. two d.; ed Gordon Coll., Univ. of the Punjab; joined Pakistan People's Party (PPP) 1968, Gen. Sec. 1983–87, Pres. PPP Islamabad 1987–; apptd mem. of Nat. Ass. 2002, Deputy Chief Whip 2002–07; Advocate, High Court 1981, Supreme Court 2010; Admin. People's Works Program, Islamabad Dist 1989–90; mem. Bd of Man. Bait-ul-Mal 1994–96; elected to Senate, Leader of the House 2009–12, Chair. 2012–15 (retd); Gen. Sec., Islamabad Bar Asscn 1982–83, apptd Pres. 1984, 1992 and 2000.

NAZARBAEV, Nursultan Abishulı, DSc; Kazakhstani politician and fmr head of state; *Leader of the Nation and Chairman, National Security Council;* b. 6 July 1940, Chemolgan, Kaskelen Dist, Almatı Oblast, Kazakh SSR, USSR; s. of Abish Nazarbaev and Aizhan Nazarbaeva; m. Sara Kunakaeva 1962; three d.; ed Qarağandi Metallurgical Combine, Russian Acad. of Management and Higher Party School of Cen. Cttee CPSU; mem. CPSU 1962–91; worked for Qarağandi Metallurgical Plant 1960–64, 1965–69; Sec. Temirtau City Cttee of Kazakh CP 1969–84; Sec. Party Cttee of Qarağandi Metallurgical Combine 1973–77; Second, then First Sec. Qarağandi Oblast Cttee of Kazakh CP 1977–79; Sec. Cen. Cttee of Kazakh CP 1979–84; Chair. Council of Ministers of Kazakh SSR 1984–89; USSR People's Deputy 1989–91; First Sec. Cen. Cttee of Kazakh CP 1989–91; Chair. Kazakh Supreme Soviet 1989–90; Exec. Pres. Kazakh SSR 1990–91; Pres. Repub. of Kazakhstan 1991–2019; Elbasy (hon. status, Leader of the Nation) 2019–; Chair. Nat. Security Council; Chair. Nur Otan (Light of the Fatherland People's Democratic Party) 2007–; Chair. World Kazakh Union 1992–; mem. Int. Eng Acad. 1993, Acad. of Social Sciences of the Russian Fed. 1994, Nat. Acad. of Sciences of the Repub. of Kazakhstan 1995; Hon. Citizen of Temirtau 1991, Duluth, USA 1991, Almatı 1995; Diploma of Freeman of Municipality of Bucharest 1998; Hon. Prof., Al-Farabi Kazakh State Nat. Univ., M.V. Lomonosov Moscow State Univ. 1996; Hon. mem. Belarusian Acad. of Sciences 1996, Nat. Acad. of Applied Sciences of Russia 1997; numerous decorations, including Order of the Red Banner of Labour, Kt, Order of St Andrew (Russia), Grand Collar, Order of Vytautas the Great (Lithuania), Collar of the Order of the Star of Romania, Kt Grand Cross with Grand Cordon, Order of Leopold (Belgium), Grand Cordon, Order of the Chrysanthemum (Japan), Grand Cordon, Order of the Nile (Egypt), Kt Grand Cross, Order of Merit (Hungary), Medal of Astana (Kazakhstan), Order of Prince Daniil of Moscow (First Class) 1996, Order of the Golden Eagle (Kazakhstan) 1996, The First Class of the Order of Prince Yaroslav the Wise (Ukraine) 1997, Cavaliere di Gran Croce con Gran Cordone (Italy) 1998, GCMG 2000, Order of the White Eagle (Poland) 2002, Kt Grand Cross with Grand Cordon, Order of the White Rose (Finland) 2008, Grand Croix, Ordre de la Légion d'honneur 2008, Grand Cross, Order of the Lion (Finland) 2009, Order of Liberty (Ukraine) 2010, Order of Friendship (China) 2019; Dr hc (Kazakh Inst. of Man., Economy and Forecasting) 1995, (Bilkent Univ., Ankara) 1998; Hon. DrIng (Tokai Univ.) 2016; Capri Award (Italy) 1992, Rukhaniyat Man of the Year 1993, Gold Medal of Guild of Econ. Devt and Marketing of the City of Nuremberg (Germany) 1993, Award of Crans-Montana Int. Forum 1996, star No. Perseus RA 3h 23v Osd 40* 43 named after him 1997, Medal No. 1 of Al-Farabi Kazakh State Nat. Univ. 1998, Award for Int. Understanding, Indian Fund Unity Int. 1998, Award For Service to Turkish World 1998, Gold Medal and Diploma for Special Contrib. to Devt of CIS Aviation, Int. Aviation Comm. 1998, Peace Dove Prize, UNESCO Club of Dodecanese Islands (Greece) 1999, Man of the Century Award, Abylai Khan Int. Fund 2000, Man of the Year Nat. Award (State Policy category) 2012. *Publications:* Steel Profile of Kazakhstan, With Neither the Right nor the Left, Strategy of Resource Saving and Market Transition, Strategy of Formation and Development of Kazakhstan as a Sovereign State, Market and Social-and-Economic Development, On the Threshold of the XXIst Century, Eurasian Union: Ideas, Practice, Prospects 1994–1997, In the Flood of History, The Epicenter of Peace, Manifesto: The World—The 21st Century 2016, and others; numerous scientific articles and articles on econs. *Leisure interests:* tennis, water-skiing, horses, reading history books. *Address:* c/o Office of the President, 010000 Nur-Sultan, Beibitshilik kösh. 11, Kazakhstan (office).

NAZARBAEVA, Dariğa Nursultanqizi, Dr rer. pol; Kazakhstani politician and media executive; *Chairman, Senate;* b. 7 May 1963, Temirtaw, Qarağandi Oblast, Kazakh SSR, USSR; d. of Pres. Nursultan Nazarbaev; m. Rahat Aliev (divorced 2007); four c.; ed Moscow M.V. Lomonosov State Univ., Kazakh S.M. Kirov State Univ., Almatı (now Al-Farabi Kazakh National Univ.), Russian Presidential Acad. of Public Service; Vice-Pres. State TV & Radio Corpn 1994–95; Dir Khabar TV Information Agency 1994–95, Gen. Dir 1995–98, Pres. 1998–2001, Chair. Council of Dirs 2001–04; Founder and Chair. Asar (Mutual Help) Republican Party, later Otan (Fatherland) Republican Political Party, following merger 2003–06, Deputy Chair. Nur Otan Xalıqtıq Demokratïyalıq Partïyası (Nur Otan—Light of the Fatherland People's Democratic Party) 2006–07; Deputy in Ass. (Majlis) 2004–07, 2012–, Head of Social and Cultural Devt Cttee –2014, Head of Nur Otan faction in Majlis, Deputy Chair. of Majlis 2014–15; Deputy Prime Minister 2015–16; mem. Senate 2016–, Chair. 2019–; Head Public Council, Kazakh Foreign Ministry 2017–; Dir Foundation of the First Pres. of Kazakhstan, Leader of the Nation 2007–12; Chair. Eurasian Media Forum 2001; Leader, Congress of Journalists of Kazakhstan; Chair., Supervisory Bd of Int. Inst. for Modern Politics, Kazakhstan; mem. Bd, Int. TV Acad., New York; Pres. Eurasian Centre for Strategic Studies, Russia; Vice-Pres. Eurasian TV Acad., Russia; Co-Chair. Eurasian TV Forum Organizing Cttee; Assoc. mem. Int. Econ. Acad. Eurasia; Vice-Pres. Children's Charitable Fund Bobek 1992–94; mem. Nat. Comm. of Repub. of Kazakhstan for UNESCO; fmr Pres. Sports Gymnastics Fed. of Repub. of Kazakhstan; jury mem., second season of SuperStar KZ; Parasat, Barys Second Degree, Ordre des Arts et des Lettres; Silver Medal of the 20th Anniversary of the Interparliamentary Ass. of the CIS, Medal of Nur Otan People's Democratic Party, Medal of the Constitutional Council of Repub. of Kazakhstan, Medal of the Nat. Bank of Repub. of Kazakhstan. *Publications:* Democratization of Political Systems in the Commonwealth of Independent States 1997, The Eurasian Commonwealth 2000, From the Union Towards the Commonwealth (ed. and co-author) 2001, Ten Years of the Commonwealth of Independent States: Experience, Problems, Future Prospects (co-author) 2001. *Leisure interest:* amateur opera singer. *Address:* Senate (Senat) 010000 Nur-Sultan, Abay d-lı 33, Parliament House (office); Nur Otan, 050000 Almaty, Abylai khana 79, Kazakhstan. *Telephone:* (7172) 74-72-39 (office); (727)

279-78-00. *Fax:* (7172) 24-26-19 (office); (727) 279-40-66. *E-mail:* partyotan@ nursat.kz. *Website:* www.parlam.kz (office); nurotan.kz.

NAZARE, Alexandru; Romanian politician; b. 25 June 1980; ed Nat. School of Political and Admin. Studies, Bucharest, European Coll. of Liberal Arts, Berlin; Minister Counsellor, Ministry of European Integration 2005–07; Counsellor, Del. of Democratic Liberal Party-European People's Party to the European Parl. 2007–08; mem. European Parl. 2008–09, Parl. Adviser Aug.–Oct. 2009; Sec. of State, Dept for European Affairs 2009–10; Sec. of State, Ministry of Finance April–Nov. 2010, Ministry of Transport 2010–12; Minister of Transport and Infrastructure Feb.–May 2012.

NAZARENKO, Tatyana Grigorievna; Russian painter; *Professor of Art, Moscow Surikov State Fine Arts Institute;* b. 24 June 1944, Moscow; m.; two s.; ed Moscow Surikov State Fine Arts Inst.; worked in studio of USSR Acad. of Fine Arts 1969–72; mem. USSR (now Russian) Union of Painters 1969; works in numerous major museums world-wide and in numerous pvt. collections; Assoc., Russian Acad. of Fine Arts 1998, Full mem. and mem. Bd of Dirs 2001–; Prof. of Art, Moscow Surikov State Fine Arts Inst. 1999–; Acad. of Arts Silver Medal 1987, Russian State Prize 1993, Moscow Govt Prize 1999, Honored Artist of Russia 2003, Triumph Prize 2008. *Television:* Artist's Portrait: Life and Work of Tatiana Nazarenko, 'Kultura' (Russian TV), Classics in Contemporary Art, 'Kultura' (Russian TV). *Publication:* Vanishing Reality 2006. *Address:* c/o Volga Art Gallery, 125009 Moscow, Bolshoi Gnezdnikovsky per. 10, Russia. *Telephone:* (495) 629-75-18; (925) 507-45-58. *E-mail:* tatyana@nazarenko-art.ru. *Website:* www.nazarenko-art.ru; volga-gallery.com.

NAZAREWICZ, Witold (Witek), MSc, PhD, Dr habil., FInstP; American (b. Polish) physicist and academic; *James McConnell Distinguished Professor in Physics, University of Tennessee;* b. 26 Dec. 1954, Warsaw, Poland; s. of Ryszard Nazarewicz and Hanna Blonska; m. Krystyna Nazarewicz; one s. one d.; ed Warsaw Univ. of Tech., Inst. for Nuclear Research, Warsaw, Warsaw Univ.; Teaching Asst, Warsaw Univ. of Tech. 1977–81; Asst Prof., Warsaw Univ. 1981–88, Assoc. Prof. 1988–91, Prof. 1994–; Visiting Research Fellow, Lund Univ., Sweden 1982–84, Visiting Prof. 1990; Visiting Research Fellow, Niels Bohr Inst., Copenhagen, Denmark 1984–85; Visiting Prof., Jt Inst. for Heavy Ion Research, Oak Ridge, TN, USA 1985–86, 1991–95, Scientific Dir, Oak Ridge Nat. Lab. Holifield Radioactive Ion Beam Facility 1996–; Visiting Prof., Florida State Univ. 1986, 1991, Cologne Univ., Germany 1987, KTH (Royal Inst. of Tech.), Stockholm, Sweden 1988; Visiting Sr Lecturer, Univ. of Liverpool, UK 1988–89; Visiting Prof., Univ. of Lund, Sweden 1990, Kyoto Univ., Japan 1992, Univ. of Liverpool 1995; Prof. of Physics, Univ. of Tennessee, Knoxville 1995–; James McConnell Distinguished Prof. in Physics 2012–; mem. Editorial Bd, Physical Review C 1994–96, Reports on Progress in Physics 2001–06, Reviews of Modern Physics 2006–, European Physical Journal A 2006–; mem. numerous expert panels; mem. Bd of Physics and Astronomy, Nat. Research Council 1996–99, Nat. Advisory Cttee, Inst. for Nuclear Theory, Seattle 1996–98; Co-Chair., later Chair. RIA Steering Group 2000–04; mem. and Chair. RIA Users Organization Exec. Cttee 2004–05; mem. Bd Mazurian Lakes Confs on Physics, Warsaw 2006, Steering Cttee Japan US Theory Inst. for Physics with Exotic Nuclei 2006–, Jefferson Lab. Program Advisory Cttee 2007–; Chair. Bd Zdzisław Szymanski Prize, Warsaw Univ. 2002–; Scientific Expert, Scientific Advisory Bd for Finnish Centre of Excellence in Nuclear and Accelerator Based Physics, Univ. of Jyvaskyla 2006–; mem. European Physical Soc. 1992–95, Polish Physical Soc.; Fellow, American Physical Soc. 1994, Inst. of Physics 2004, AAAS 2009; Univ. of Tennessee-Battelle Corp. Fellow, ORNL 2013; Carnegie Centenary Prof. (Scotland, UK) 2008; Hon. Guest Prof., Peking Univ. 2013–15; Hon. DUniv (Univ. of the West of Scotland) 2009; Individual Scientific Award, Polish Ministry of Educ. 1982, 1987, 1989, Individual Scientific Award, Polish Nuclear Energy Comm. 1983, Individual Scientific Award, Polish Physical Soc. 1986, Lockheed Martin Tech. Achievement Award 1999, Univ. of Tennessee Battelle Tech. Achievement Award 2000, Coll. of Arts and Sciences Sr Research/ Creative Achievement Award 2001, Univ. of Tennessee Research and Creative Achievement Award 2002, Tom W. Bonner Prize, American Physical Soc. 2012, Distinguished Scientist Award, Oak Ridge Nat. Lab. 2012. *Publications:* author of editor of five books, nine review papers and more than 350 refereed research papers on theoretical nuclear physics, nuclear structure, and the many-body problem, listed by ISI among the most highly cited in physics. *Leisure interest:* map collecting. *Address:* Department of Physics and Astronomy, University of Tennessee, 104 South College, Knoxville, TN 37996-1200 (office); Oak Ridge National Laboratory, 8W Building 6025, 1 Bethel Valley Road, Oak Ridge, TN 37830, USA (office). *Telephone:* (865) 974-4375 (Knoxville) (office); (865) 574-4580 (Oak Ridge) (office). *Fax:* (865) 974-7843 (Knoxville) (office). *E-mail:* witek@utk .edu (office). *Website:* www. phys.utk.edu/faculty/faculty-nazarewicz.html (office).

NAZARIAN, Garen A., MA; Armenian diplomatist; *Deputy Foreign Minister;* b. 29 Nov. 1966, Yerevan; m. Siranush Nazarian-Shahnazarova; two c.; ed Faculty of Oriental Studies, Yerevan State Univ., Faculty of Int. Relations, Moscow Diplomatic Acad.; worked in Dept on Mil.-Political Problems, Ministry of Foreign Affairs 1991–92, at Embassy of Armenia, Moscow 1992–94; Chief of Secr., Ministry of Foreign Affairs 1994–96; Perm. Rep. to UN and other Int. Orgs, Geneva 1996–2002; Adviser to Minister of Foreign Affairs 2002–05; Amb. to Iran 2005–09; Perm. Rep. to UN, New York 2009–14, Deputy Foreign Minister 2014–; apptd Vice-Pres. World Conf. against Racism, Racial Discrimination, Xenophobia and Related Intolerance, Durban, South Africa 2001; apptd Chair. 8th Meeting of the State Parties to the UN Convention against Torture 2002; Chair. UN Comm. on the Status of Women 2009–11; fmr mem. Armenian-American Inter-Governmental Comm. *Leisure interests:* skiing, music. *Address:* Ministry of Foreign Affairs, 0010 Yerevan, Hanrapetutyun Hraparak, Govt Bldg 2, Armenia (office). *Telephone:* (10) 62-00-00 (office). *Fax:* (10) 62-00-62 (office). *E-mail:* info@mfa.am (office). *Website:* www.mfa.am (office).

NAZAROV, Talbak Nazarovich, DEconSc; Tajikistani politician and academic; b. 15 March 1938, Danghara, Kulyab District; s. of Khojaev Nazar and Ismailova Hanifa; m. Tatyana Grigorievna Teodorovich 1959; one s. one d.; ed Leningrad (now St Petersburg) Inst. of Finance and Econs, USSR; Asst, then Deputy Dean of Econs Faculty, Tajik State Univ. 1960–62, Head of Dept, Dean 1965–80, Rector 1982–88; Chair. Supreme Soviet Tajik SSR 1986–88; Minister of Public Educ. 1988–90; USSR People's Deputy 1989–92; First Deputy Chair. Tajikistan Council of Ministers, Chair. State Planning Cttee 1990–91; Minister of Foreign Affairs 1994–2006, Amb.-at-Large 2006–; mem. Presidium, Acad. of Sciences 1980–, currently Vice-Pres.; Merited Worker of Science and many other awards and medals. *Publications:* books and articles on Tajikistan's economy and external policies. *Leisure interests:* reading fiction and political literature. *Address:* 33 Rudaki Avenue, 734025 Dushanbe, Tajikistan (office).

NAZDRATENKO, Yevgeny Ivanovich; Russian politician; b. 16 Feb. 1949, Severo-Kurilsk, Sakhalin Region; m.; two s.; ed Far East Inst. of Tech.; served with Pacific Fleet; Head of sector Bor Co.; mechanic, Vice-Pres., Pres. Primorsk Mining Co., Vostok 1980–93; Peoples' Deputy of Russian Fed. 1990–93; Head of Admin. Primorsk Territory 1993–95, Gov. 1995–2001; mem. Council of Fed. of Russia 1996–2001; Chair. State Cttee for Fisheries 2001–03; apptd Deputy Sec. Russian Security Council 2003; Dr hc (St Petersburg Mining Univ., Seoul Univ.); Order for Personal Courage 1994, Hon. Citizen of Russia 1995.

NAZIF, Ahmad Mahmoud Muhammad, BSc, MA, PhD; Egyptian computer engineer and government official; b. 8 July 1952, Alexandria; m.; two s.; ed Cairo Univ., McGill Univ., Canada; Prof. of Computer Eng, Cairo Univ. 1994; Exec. Man. IDSC 1989–95; apptd Minister for Communications and Tech. 1999; Prime Minister 2004–11 (dismissed); First Order Medal of Science and Art. *Address:* 2 Magles El Shaab Street, Kasr El Aini St., Cairo, Egypt.

NAZIR-ALI, Rt Rev. Michael James, BA, BLitt, MLitt, ThD, DHLitt, DD; British/Pakistani ecclesiastic and academic; *Founder and Director, Oxford Centre for Training, Research, Advocacy and Dialogue (OXTRAD);* b. 19 Aug. 1949, Karachi, Pakistan; s. of James Nazir-Ali and Patience Nazir-Ali; m. Valerie Cree 1972; two s.; ed St Paul's High School, Karachi, St Patrick's Coll., Karachi, Univ. of Karachi, Fitzwilliam Coll. Cambridge, Ridley Hall, Cambridge, St Edmund Hall, Oxford, Australian Coll. of Theology with assistance from the Centre for World Religions, Harvard etc.; Tutorial Supervisor in Theology, Univ. of Cambridge 1974–76; Asst Curate, Holy Sepulchre, Cambridge 1974–76; Tutor then Sr Tutor, Karachi Theological Coll. 1976–81; Assoc. Priest Holy Trinity Cathedral, Karachi 1976–79; Priest-in-Charge St Andrew's Akhtar Colony, Karachi 1979–81; Provost Lahore Cathedral 1981–84; Bishop of Raiwind 1984–86; fmr Visiting Lecturer, Selly Oak Colls, Birmingham; Asst to Archbishop of Canterbury; Co-ordinator of Studies for 1988 Lambeth Conf. 1986–89; Gen. Sec. Church Mission Soc. 1989–94; Asst Bishop, Diocese of Southwark 1990–94; Canon Theologian, Leicester Cathedral 1992–94; Bishop of Rochester 1994–2009; mem. House of Lords 1999–2009; Founder and Dir OXTRAD (Oxford Centre for Training, Research, Advocacy and Dialogue) 2009–; Chair. Mission Theological Advisory Group 1992–2001, Chair. Governing Council, Trinity Coll. Bristol 1996–2009; Dir Oxford Centre for Mission Studies, Christian Aid; mem. Design Group for 1998 Lambeth Conf., Anglican Roman Catholic Int. Comm. 1991–2010, Bd of Mission Gen. Synod, Church of England 1992–94, 1996–2000, Human Fertilization and Embryology Authority 1998–2003 (Chair. of Ethics and Law Cttee); Visiting Prof. of Theological and Religious Studies, Univ. of Greenwich 1996–; mem. Archbishop's Council 2001–06, House of Bishops' Standing Cttee 2001–06, Anglican-Roman Catholic Jt Working Group 2001–, Chair. Working Party on Women in the Episcopate, Chair. House of Bishops' Theological Group, Lecturer Royal Coll. of Defence Studies; Paul Harris Fellow, Rotary International 2005; Sr Fellow, Wycliffe Hall Oxford; Visiting Bishop, Anglican Communion, SC, USA; Visiting Faculty, London School of Theology, Oxford Centre for Mission Studies, Lahore Coll. of Theology; Hon. Fellow, St Edmund Hall, Oxford 1998, Fitzwilliam Coll., Cambridge 2006; Hon. DLitt (Bath, Greenwich, Westminster); Hon. DD (Kent) 2004, (Nashotah House, USA) 2010; Radio Pakistan Prize for English Language and Literature 1964, Burney Award (Cambridge) 1973, 1975, Oxford Soc. Award for Grads 1973, Langham Scholarship 1974, Shaikh Yamani Gold Medal in Islamic Studies 2008. *Publications:* Islam, a Christian Perspective 1983, Frontiers in Christian–Muslim Encounter 1987, Martyrs and Magistrates: Toleration and Trial in Islam 1989, The Roots of Islamic Tolerance: Origin and Development 1990, From Everywhere to Everywhere 1991, Mission and Dialogue 1995, The Mystery of Faith 1995, Citizens and Exiles 1998, Shapes of the Church to Come 2001, Understanding My Muslim Neighbour 2002, Conviction and Conflict 2006, The Unique and Universal Christ 2008, Triple Jeopardy for the West 2012, Faith, Freedom and the Future 2016; contrib. to The Jesus Accounts on the 4 Gospels (DVD) 2009, to Jesus: The Son of God and to Jesus: Dead and Buried; various monographs and numerous articles on Islam, Christianity, mission, inter-faith dialogue, Anglican and ecumenical affairs, public policy and int. affairs. *Leisure interests:* cricket, hockey, table tennis, reading and writing poetry. *Address:* 70 Wimpole Street, London, W1G 8AX, England (office). *Telephone:* (20) 3327-1139 (office). *E-mail:* oxtrad@gmail.com (office). *Website:* www.michaelnazirali.com

NCUBE, Mthuli, PhD; Zimbabwean economist, politician and fmr banker; *Minister of Finance and Economic Development;* b. 1963, Lubane Dist; m.; four c.; ed Selwyn Coll., Cambridge; fmr lecturer in Finance, London School of Econs; Dean, Faculty of Commerce Law and Management, also Dean and Prof. of Finance, Wits Business School, Univ. of Witwatersrand 2005–07, currently HSBC Distinguished Prof. of Banking and Finance, Univ. of Witwatersrand Graduate School of Business Admin; Chief Economist and Pres., African Devt Bank (ADB) 2007–14; Prof. of Public Policy, Blavatnik School of Govt, Univ. of Oxford 2014–, also Visiting Prof. in African Studies, Saïd Business School, Univ. of Oxford; f. Barbican Holdings, Selwyn Capital (financial services cos); fmr Head of Asset Allocation Strategy and Manager, Investec Global Managed Fund; Head of Quantum Global Research Lab, Switzerland 2016–18; Minister of Finance and Econ. Devt 2018–; Gov. African Capacity Building Foundation; mem. African Econ. Research Consortium (AERC), currently Chair.; mem. Bd of Dirs OMFIF (ind. think tank for central banking), Global Devt Network (GDN); fmr mem. Bd of Dirs South African Financial Services Bd (FSB); Chair. Nat. Small Business Advisory Council, South Africa 2009–10; mem. World Econ. Forum (WEF) Global Agenda Council on Poverty and Econ. Devt, WEF Advisory Council on Sustainable Infrastructure; mem. OECD Expert Group on Rethinking the Future of Devt Aid. *Publications include:* Development Dynamics: Lessons from Zimbabwe 1992, African Financial Markets and Monetary Policy 2009, Monetary Policy and the Economy in South Africa 2013, Quantitative Easing and its Impact 2013, Africa's Middle Class 2014, The Oxford Companion of the Economics of South Africa (co-ed.) 2015, Inclusive Growth in Africa 2015, Infrastructure in Africa 2017, Global

Uncertainty and Exchange Rates 2018. *Address:* Ministry of Finance and Economic Development, Blocks B, E and G, Composite Bldg, cnr Samora Machel Ave and Fourth St, Private Bag 7705, Causeway, Harare, Zimbabwe (office). *Telephone:* (24) 2794572 (office). *Fax:* (24) 2792750 (office). *Website:* www .zimtreasury.gov.zw (office).

NCUBE, Most Rev. Pius Alick Mvundla, LTh; Zimbabwean RC ecclesiastic; b. (Mvundla Ncube), 1 Jan. 1947, Mtshabezi, Gwanda; s. of Amos Ncube and Ivy Mkwananzi; ed Chishawasha Major Seminary, Harare, Lateran Univ., Rome, Italy; ordained Priest, Bulawayo 1973, Parish Priest, St Patrick's 1986–90, St Mary's Cathedral 1990–95; Vicar Gen., Archdiocese of Bulawayo 1995–98, Archbishop of Bulawayo 1998–2007 (resgnd); adultery lawsuit filed against him, leading to his resignation as Archbishop July 2007; outspoken critic of Pres. Robert Mugabe; Human Rights Award, Lawyers Cttee for Human Rights, New York 2003. *Radio:* one week per month of morning and evening prayers on nat. radio 1990–98; interviews on human rights issues. *Publications include:* Imfundiso. Yebandla. Elikhatholike (Catholic catechism). *Leisure interests:* reading, writing articles. *Address:* 73 Marigold Road, North Trenance, Bulawayo, Zimbabwe. *Telephone:* (9) 204951; 23-226932 (mobile).

NCUBE, Welshman, MPhil, LLB; Zimbabwean politician, academic and judge; *President, Movement For Democratic Change;* b. 7 July 1961, Gweru; m. Thobekile Ncube; five c.; ed Univ. of Zimbabwe; Prof. of Law, Univ. of Zimbabwe 1992–; serves as Advocate of High Court and Supreme Court of Zimbabwe; Pres. Movt for Democratic Change (MDC) 1999–2011, Co-leader pro-Senate faction of MDC (MDC—Ncube) 2006–; Pres. United Movt for Democratic Change (UMDC) 2014–; mem. of House of Ass. of Zimbabwe for Bulawayo North East 2000–13, Chair. Parl. Legal Cttee; charged with high treason over alleged plot to assassinate Pres. Robert Mugabe 2002, found not guilty; Minister of Industry and Commerce 2009–13; unsuccessful cand. in presidential election 2013; mem. Bd of Trustees, Amani Trust; mem. Advisory Bd, ZimRights; mem. Zimbabwe Lawyers for Human Rights; Dr hc (Oslo) 2005. *Publications include:* numerous books and articles on family law, women's law, human rights law and constitutional law. *Address:* Movement for Democratic Change, 11 Creswick Road, Hillside, Harare, Zimbabwe (office). *Telephone:* (4) 747071 (office).

NCUBE, Trevor Vusumuzi, BA; Zimbabwean journalist and media executive; *Owner, M&G Media Ltd;* b. 9 Sept. 1962, Bulawayo; m. 2nd Nyaradzo Ncube; two c.; ed Univ. of Zimbabwe; Teacher, Pumula High School, Bulawayo 1983; Asst Ed., The Financial Gazette 1989–91, Exec. Ed. 1991–96; Ed.-in-Chief and Group Editorial Dir, Zimbabwe Independent 1996–2000, CEO 2000; Owner, M&G Media Ltd 2002–, also CEO, Mail and Guardian, Johannesburg 2002–; Chair. ALPHA Media Holdings (AMH), Harare; Ind. Non-Exec. Dir, Moneyweb Holdings Ltd, South Africa 2008–; Vice-Chair., Zimbabwe Chapter, Commonwealth Press Union (CPU) 1998–99, Acting Chair., CPU 1999; Vice-Pres., Zimbabwe Econ. Soc. 1989–91; Dir Modus Publications Pvt Ltd 1992–96; Zimbabwe Ed. of the Year 1994, Int. Publishers Asscn Freedom Prize Award 2007, German Africa Foundation Award 2008, Kenya Nation Media Group Life Achievement Award 2010, Media Inst. of Southern Africa Press Freedom Award 2012. *Address:* M&G Media Ltd, Grosvenor cnr, 195 Jan Smuts Avenue, Rosebank, Johannesburg 2193, South Africa (office). *Telephone:* (11) 2507300 (office). *Fax:* (11) 2507300 (office). *E-mail:* newsdesk@mg.co.za (office). *Website:* mg.co.za (office).

NDAGIJIMANA, Uzziel, MSc, PhD; Rwandan economist and politician; *Minister of Finance and Economic Planning;* ed Warsaw Univ., Poland, Warsaw School of Econs; Lecturer, Faculty of Econs, Social Sciences and Man., Nat. Univ. of Rwanda 1999–2002, Vice Rector, Nat. Univ. of Rwanda 2007–11; Rector, School of Finance and Banking, Kigali 2002–07; Perm. Sec., Ministry of Health 2011–14; Minister of Finance and Econ. Planning 2018–; fmr Chair. Econ. Advisory Council of the Pres., Audit Cttee of Inter-Univ. Council for East Africa; fmr mem. Bd of Dirs Nat. Bank of Rwanda, Prime Holdings, Nat. Inst. of Statistics of Rwanda, Student Financing Agency for Rwanda, School of Finance and Banking, Kigali. *Publications:* numerous papers in nat. and int. journals. *Address:* Ministry of Finance and Economic Planning, blvd de la Révolution, opp. Kigali City Council, POB 158, Kigali, Rwanda (office). *Telephone:* 252596002 (office). *Fax:* 252577581 (office). *E-mail:* mfin@minecofin.gov.rw (office). *Website:* www.minecofin.gov.rw (office).

NDAYIZEYE, Domitien; Burundian politician and fmr head of state; b. 2 May 1953, Murango, Kayanza Prov.; Sec.-Gen. opposition pro-Hutu party Front pour la démocratie au Burundi (FRODEBU); Vice-Pres. of Burundi, responsible for Political and Admin. Affairs 2001–03; Pres. of Burundi 2003–05; arrested in Bujumbura in relation to his alleged role in a coup plot earlier in the year Aug. 2006, acquitted Jan. 2007; president cand. but later withdrew from contest 2010.

NDEBELE, Njabulo Simakahle, PhD; South African academic, writer and university administrator; *Chancellor, University of Johannesburg;* b. 4 July 1948, Johannesburg; m. Kathleen Mpho; one s. two d.; ed Univs of Botswana, Lesotho and Swaziland, Univ. of Cambridge, UK, Univ. of Denver, USA; Head of Dept, Nat. Univ. of Lesotho, Dean of Humanities Faculty 1987, Pro-Vice-Chancellor 1988–90; Chair. and Head of Dept of African Literature, Wits Univ. 1991; Vice-Rector, Univ. of the Western Cape 1992–93; Vice-Chancellor and Prin. Univ. of the North 1993–98, Scholar-in-Residence, Ford Foundation 1998–2000; Vice-Chancellor and Prin. Univ. of Cape Town 2000–08; Chancellor Univ. of Johannesburg 2012–; Chair. South African Broadcasting Policy Project, Ministry of Post, Telecommunications and Broadcasting 1997, South African Univs Vice-Chancellors' Asscn –2000; Chair., Nelson Mandela Foundation, Mandela Rhodes Foundation; mem. Exec. Bd AA4, AC4; Bd mem. and Chair. Inst. for Democracy in Africa; Hon. Fellow, Churchill Coll., Cambridge 2007; Dr hc (Natal Univ.) 1999, (Chicago State Univ.) 1996, (Vrije Univ. Amsterdam), (Soka Univ., Japan), (Wesleyan Univ.) 2005, (Univ. of Cambridge) 2006, (Univ. Coll. London) 2006, (Univ. of Michigan) 2008, (Univ. of Stellenbosch) 2008, (Univ. of Witwatersrand) 2009, (Durban Univ. of Tech.) 2012, (Univ. of Pretoria) 2013; Lincoln Univ. Pres.'s Award, Nat. Univ. of Lesotho 50th Anniversary Distinguished Service Award, NOMA Award for Publishing in Africa 1984, Sanlam Award for Outstanding Fiction, Pringle Prize for Outstanding Criticism, Lifetime Achievement Award, Nat. Research Foundation 2009. *Publications include:* Fools and Other Stories 1983, Bonolo and the Peach Tree 1991, Rediscovery of the Ordinary 1991, The Prophetess 1992, Sarah, Rings and I 1993, South African Literature and Culture: Rediscovery of the

Ordinary 1994, Death of a Son 1996, The Cry of Winnie Mandela (novel) 2004, Telling Tales (contrib. to charity anthology) 2004, Fine Lines from the Box 2007. *Leisure interests:* bird watching, computer simulation games. *Address:* Office of the Chancellor, University of Johannesburg, PO Box 524, Auckland Park, 2006 (office); Glenara, Burg Road, Rondebosch 7700, Cape Town, South Africa (home). *Telephone:* (11) 5594555. *Website:* www.uj.ac.za (office); www.njabulondebele.co.za.

NDEBELE, Sibusiso; South African diplomatist; b. 17 Oct. 1948, KwaZulu-Natal; m. Zama Ndebele; three c.; ed Eshowe Teachers' Training and High School, Univ. of Zululand, Univ. of South Africa; apptd Publicity Sec., South African Students Org., Univ. of Zululand 1972; Asst Librarian, Univ. of Swaziland 1974–76; imprisoned on Robben Island for his role in struggle against apartheid 1977–87; Research Fellow, Town and Regional Planning, Univ. of KwaZulu-Natal 1987; Regional Sec. African Nat. Congress (ANC) 1990–98, Prov. Deputy Chair., ANC, KwaZulu-Natal, Durban 1996–98, Prov. Chair. 1998–2008, mem. Nat. Exec. Cttee, ANC 1997–; mem. Kwazulu-Natal Prov. Legislature 1994–2015; Premier of KwaZulu-Natal Prov. 2004–09; Minister of Transport 2009–12; Minister of Correctional Services 2012–14; Chancellor Univ. of Zululand 2014–; High Commr to Australia (also accred to Samoa, Cook Islands, Tonga, Kiribati, Nauru, Vanuatu, Niue, Tuvalu, Palau, Marshall Islands, Federated States of Micronesia, Tokelau, Solomon Islands) 2015–17; Dir, 2010 FIFA World Cup Local Organizing Cttee 2010; Founder African Renaissance Trust; Trustee, Educ. Devt Trust 1980–94; Hon. Dr of Admin (Univ. of Zululand) 2005; COMTO Award 2000.

NDEREBA, Catherine; Kenyan athlete; b. (Wincatherine Nyambura Ndereba), 21 July 1972, Nyeri; m. Anthony Maina 1996; one d.; ed Ngorano Secondary School, Nairobi; long distance and marathon runner; rep. Kenya at women's relay race in Seoul, S Korea 1995; won individual bronze and team gold medals at World Half-Marathon Championships 1999; ran world's fastest times at 5000m (15:09), 12,000m (38:37), 15000m (48:52) and 10 miles (53:07) 1999; marathon debut in Boston Marathon, finishing sixth 1999; runner-up, New York Marathon 1999, 2003; won both Boston and Chicago Marathons 2000, 2001; gold medal, World Championships Marathon 2003 (Championship Record time of 2 hours, 23 minutes, 55 seconds); silver medal, Olympic Games marathon, Athens 2004, Beijing 2008; set the then women's world marathon record time of 2 hours, 18 minutes, 47 seconds in Chicago Marathon Oct. 2001; ranked No. 1 by Runner's World for three consecutive years; works as telephone operator at a Kenyan prison; Runner's World magazine Road Runner of the Year 1996, 1998, Running Times Road Racer of the Year 1996, 1998, 1999, IAAF Athlete of the Year 2001, Asscn of Int. Marathon and Road Races (AIMS)/ASICS Golden Shoe World Athlete of the Year Award 2001. *Address:* c/o Lisa Buster, IAAF Authorized Athlete Representative President, Promotion in Motion International Limited, 1039 Colin Drive, Royersford, PA 19468-3137, USA (office). *Telephone:* (610) 948-5966 (office). *E-mail:* lbuster.pmi@comcast.net (office). *Website:* www.marathonchamps.com (office).

NDIAYE, Mankeur; Senegalese diplomatist and politician; *Special Representative of Secretary-General, Multidimensional Integrated Stabilization Mission in Central African Republic, United Nations;* b. 15 March 1960, Dagana, Saint-Louis region; m.; two s. one d.; ed Teaching Middle School Gen. Dagana, École Normale St Louis, École Normale Supérieure de Dakar, Nat. School of Admin and Magistracy (ENAM) Diplomatic Section, courses at UN Conf. on Trade and Devt, UN Inst. for Training and Research and Institut des Hautes Études de Defense Nationale de Paris; teacher in charge of Goudoudou Diobé School (Dept of Matam) 1982–83; Lecturer, Coll. of Educ., Middle Neuville, St Louis 1983–86; Head of Div. of Personnel and Social Affairs, Ministry of Foreign Affairs 1991–93, Deputy Dir-Gen. Admin and Equipment and Deputy Dir Dept of Credit, Dir of Cabinet of the Minister Del. to the Prime Minister of the African Econ. Integration 1993–95, mem. Bd of Dirs Solidarity Fund and Devt Intervention in Econ. Community of West African States (FOSIDEC), mem. Bd of Dirs ECOWAS Fund (Fund Econs of West Africa) became EBID (Bank for Investment and Devt of ECOWAS); Dir Cabinet of the Minister Del. to the Minister of Economy, Finance and Planning 1995; Tech. Adviser to the Minister of State, Minister of Foreign Affairs and Senegalese Abroad 1995–97; Second, then First Counsellor, Perm. Mission of Senegal to the UN, New York 1997–2003, Vice-Pres. Comm. on the Status of Women, mem. NGO Cttee of the UN and of several working groups of the UN Gen. Ass., mem. numerous official dels at int. confs or official state visits, Dir of Cabinet of the Minister of State, Minister of Foreign Affairs 2003–09, rank of Amb. 2003, Interim Dir of Cabinet Oct.–Nov. 2009, Amb. to France 2009–12; Minister of Foreign Affairs and Senegalese Nationals Abroad 2012–17; Special Rep. of Sec.-Gen., Multidimensional Integrated Stabilization Mission in Cen. African Repub. (MINUSCA), rank of Deputy Sec.-Gen. 2019–; Fellow, ENAM Diplomatic Section 1991; Chevalier, Ordre du Mérite. *Publications:* numerous articles on int. affairs and African issues. *Leisure interests:* running, playing chess and draughts. *Address:* Department of Peacekeeping Operations, Room S-3727B, United Nations, New York, NY 10017, USA (office). *Website:* peacekeeping.un.org (office).

NDIAYE, Souleymane Ndéné, LLM; Senegalese lawyer and politician; b. 6 Aug. 1958, Kaolack; m.; four c.; Mayor of Guinguinéo 2002–; Minister of Civil Service, Labour, Employment and Professional Orgs March–Aug. 2005; Dir of Cabinet, Office of the Pres. Aug. 2005–07; mem. Nat. Ass. 2007–; Minister of State for the Environment and Protection of Nature June–July 2007, for Maritime Economy July 2007–09; Prime Minister of Senegal 2009–12; Head, African Union Election Observation Mission to observe the presidential and legislative elections in Central African Republic 2015; Head, National Union for the People 2015–.

NDIMIRA, Pascal-Firmin; Burundian politician; b. 9 April 1956, Muyinga, Ngozi Prov.; ethnic Hutu; fmr univ. rector, IBRD official; Minister of Agric. 1994–95; Head of Nat. Council for Unity 1987–93; Prime Minister of Burundi 1996–98 (position abolished); mem. Union pour le Progrès Nat. (UPRONA). *Address:* c/o Union pour le Progrès National (UPRONA), BP 1810, Bujumbura, Burundi. *Telephone:* 22225028. *Website:* www.uprona.org.

NDONG, Jean Eyeghé; Gabonese politician; b. 12 Feb. 1946, Libreville; nephew of Léon M'ba, fmr Pres. of Gabon; m. Gisèle Biyoghé 1971; six c.; ed École des Hautes Études en Sciences Sociales, Paris and Université de Paris X Nanterre, France; Admin. Dir Nat. Social Security Fund (CNSS) 1984–90, Deputy Dir-Gen. 1990–91; Deputy Dir-Gen. Nat. Social Guarantee Fund 1991–96; mem. Nat. Ass. for Libreville constituency 1996–2001; mem. Senate 2002; Sec. of State for Finance 1996, later Minister-Del. to Minister of State, Minister of Economy, Finance, Budget and Privatization; Prime Minister and Head of Govt 2006–09; fmr mem. Gabonese Democratic Party, First Vice-Pres. –2009; mem. Nat. Union party, Vice-Pres. 2010–; mem. Senate 2014–. *Address:* Senate, Libreville, Gabon (office).

N'DONG, Léon; Gabonese diplomatist; b. 15 Feb. 1935, Libreville; s. of Jean-Martin Bikègne and Marthe Kemeboune; m. Chantal Annette Bekale 1971; four s. one d.; ed School of Law and Econ. Sciences, Rennes, France; Under-Sec.-Gen. of Ministry of Foreign Affairs, later Sec.-Gen.; Teacher, Nat. School of Admin. 1969–72; Amb. to Cen. African Repub. and Sudan 1972–73, to Morocco 1973–74, to UN Office at Geneva 1974–76, to UN 1976–80, to UK 1980–86, to FRG 1986–90 (also accred to Norway, Denmark, Finland and Sweden); Amb. du Gabon, Diplomatic Adviser to Prime Minister 1990–99; High Commr, Office of Prime Minister 1997–; Commdr de l'Etoile Equatoriale, Grand Cordon of Order of the Brilliant Star (China), Commdr, Order of Devotion (Malta), Commdr Nat. Order of Dahomey, Order of Nile (Sudan), Ordre Nat. du Mérite (Gabon), Diplomatic Order of Repub. of Korea, Ordre de la Pléïade (France), Grand Officier Etoile Equatoriale, Grand Officier Ordre du Mérite, Officier Courtoisie française. *Leisure interests:* swimming, walking, music, reading, fishing, gardening. *Address:* BP 848, Libreville, Gabon. *Telephone:* (241) 263175; (241) 071952.

NDONG SIMA, Raymond; Gabonese economist and politician; b. 23 Jan. 1955, Oyem, Woleu-Ntem Prov.; began career as Research Asst, Ministry of Planning and the Economy 1983, assigned to cabinet of Minister 1986, Dir-Gen. Econs Dept 1992, responsible for structural adjustment and relations with IMF and World Bank –1994; Dir-Gen. Hévégab (state-owned rubber co.) 1994–98; Minister for Agric., Fisheries and Rural Devt 2009; mem. Assemblée Nationale (Parl.) for Kyé constituency 2011–; Prime Minister 2012–14; mem. Parti démocratique gabonais. *Address:* c/o Office of the Prime Minister, BP 546, Libreville, Gabon (office).

NDONGOU, Jean-François; Gabonese politician; *President, National Council of Communication;* b. 1960; apptd Minister 1999, several portfolios including Minister for Relations with Parl. and Constitutional Insts, Deputy Minister for Foreign Affairs, Co-operation, Francophony and Regional Integration –2007, Deputy Prime Minister for Social Affairs, Welfare, Nat. Solidarity and Poverty Reduction 2007, Minister of the Interior, Local Authorities, Immigration and Security, in charge of Civil Defence and Nat. Defence 2009–10, Minister of the Interior, Public Security, Immigration and Decentralization 2010–14; Pres. National Council of Communication 2014–.

N'DOUR, Youssou; Senegalese singer, songwriter and government official; b. Oct. 1959, Dakar; s. of Elimane N'Dour and Ndeye Sokhna Mboup; m. 1st Mami Camara (divorced), four c.; m. 2nd Aida Coulibaly, two d.; mem. Sine Dramatic 1972, Orchestre Diamono 1975, The Star Band (house band of Dakar nightclub, the Miami Club) 1976–79; formed band Etoile de Dakar (changed name to Super Etoile 1982) 1979–; has performed with Peter Gabriel, Paul Simon, Bob Dylan, Branford Marsalis; sings in English, French, Fulani, Serer and native Wolof; apptd Goodwill Amb. to UN, UNICEF, Int. Bureau of Work; Owner, Jololi Records recording studio, radio station, Thoissane nightclub, Dakar; f. political group Fekke ma ci bolle (I am involved) Nov. 2011, announced candidacy for presidential election 2012, subsequently barred from standing by Constitutional Council ruling; Minister of Tourism and Culture 2012–13, apptd Minister-Counsellor to the Presidency 2013; Dr hc (Yale Univ.) 2011; Best African Artist 1996, African Artist of the Century 1999, MOBO Award for Best African Act 2005. *Recordings include:* albums: A Abijan 1980, Xalis 1980, Tabaski 1981, Thiapathioly 1983, Absa Gueye 1983, Immigrès 1984, Nelson Mandela 1985, Inedits (1984–1985) 1988, The Lion 1989, African Editions Vols 5–14 1990, Africa Deebeub 1990, Jamm La Prix 1990, Kocc Barma 1990, Set 1990, Hey You: The Essential Collection 1988–90, Eyes Open 1992, The Guide 1994, Gainde–Voices From The Heart Of Africa (with Yande Codou Sene) 1996, Lii 1996, Immigrès/Bitim Rew 1997, St Louis 1997, Special Fin D'annee Plus Djamil 1999, Rewmi 1999, Joko: From Village to Town 2000, Le Grand Bal, Bercy 2000, Le Grand Bal 1 & 2 2001, Batay 2001, Birth of a Star 2001, Nothing's In Vain (Coono Du Réér) 2002, Et Ses Amis 2002, Sant Allah (Homage to God) 2003, Egypt (BBC Radio 3 World Music Award for Album of the Year 2005) 2004, Rokku Mi Rokka 2007, I Bring What I Love 2010, Etoile de Dakar/Once Upon a Time in Senegal 2010, Dakar-Kingston 2010, Mbalakh Dafay Wakh 2011, Fatteliku 2014, Senegaal Rek 2016, Africa Rekk 2016. *Film roles include:* Picc Mi 1992, Amazing Grace 2006. *Leisure interest:* football. *Address:* Youssou N'Dour Head Office, 8 Route des Almadies Parcelle, BP 1310, Dakar, Senegal. *Telephone:* 33-865-1039. *Fax:* 33-865-1068. *E-mail:* yncontact@yahoo.fr.

N'DOURO, Issifou Kogui, PhD; Benin government official; b. Bembereke; ed Université Louis Pasteur, Strasbourg, France; consultant to UNSO Tree Planting Project, FAO 1979–83, Nat. Dir UNSO /UNDP Multi-purpose Tree Planting Project 1983–87; Deputy Dir-Gen. Ministry of Rural Devt and Cooperative Action 1987–90, Deputy Chief of Staff 1990–91; fmr Finance Dir Organisation Internationale de la Francophonie; fmr Dir Office of Minister of Rural Devt; Minister of Nat. Defence 2006–12; Minister of State for Presidential Affairs 2012–13.

NDULU, Benno J., PhD; Tanzanian economist and central banker; ed North-western Univ., USA; began career as econs teacher; Prof., Univ. of Dar es Salaam early 1980s; Research Dir, later Exec. Dir African Econ. Research Consortium, Nairobi; African Country Dir, World Bank, Dar es Salaam; Deputy Gov., Bank of Tanzania (Benki Kuu Ya Tanzania) –2008, Gov. and Chair. 2008–18; fmr Chair. Tanzania Revenue Authority; Dr hc (Int. Inst. of Social Studies, The Hague). *Publications include:* Agenda for Africa's Economic Renewal (co-author) 1996, New Directions in Development Economics 1996, Regional Integration and Trade Liberalization in Africa (co-author) 1999, Challenges of African Growth (co-author) 2007; numerous articles in The Journal of Development Studies. *Address:* c/o Bank of Tanzania, 10 Mirambo Street, PO Box 2939, Dar es Salaam, Tanzania (office).

NDUNGANE, Most Rev. Njongonkulu Winston Hugh, MTh, DD, AFTS; South African ecclesiastic; *Anglican Archbishop Emeritus of Cape Town;* b. 2 April 1941, Kokstad; s. of Foster Ndungane and Tingaza Ndungane; m. 1st Nosipo Ngcelwane 1972 (died 1986); 2nd Nomahlubi Vokwana 1987; one step-s. one step-d.; ed Lovedale High School, Univ. of Cape Town, Fed. Theological Seminary and King's Coll., London, UK; Rector St Nicholas Church, Matroosfontein, Cape Town

1980–81; Prov. Liaison Officer, Johannesburg 1982–84; Prin., St Bede's Theological Coll. Umtata 1985–86; Exec. Officer, Church of the Prov. of Southern Africa (Anglican) 1987–91; Bishop of Kimberley and Kuruman 1991–96; Archbishop of Cape Town and Metropolitan of the Anglican Church of Southern Africa 1996–2007, Archbishop Emer. 2007–; f. African Monitor 2006; mem. Bd SABC, Johannesburg 1992–96; Chair. Hearings into Poverty in S Africa; Patron Jubilee 2000 1998–; Order of the Baobab in Silver 2008; Hon. DD (Rhodes) 1997, (Protestant Episcopal Theological Seminary, Virginia) 2000; Hon. DHumLitt (Worcester State Coll., Mass) 2000; Hon. DScS (Natal) 2001. *Publications:* The Commuter Population for Claremont, Cape 1973, Human Rights and the Christian Doctrine of Man 1979, Primate Speaks Out on Debt and Arms 1997, Oppression, Faith and the Future 1997, Address[es] by the Archbishop of Cape Town 1999, A World with a Human Face: A Voice from Africa 2003; newspaper articles. *Leisure interests:* music, walking. *Address:* c/o Bishopscourt, 20 Bishopscourt Drive, Claremont 7708, South Africa. *E-mail:* archbish@bishopscourt-cpsa.org.za.

NDUWIMANA, Martin, MD; Burundian politician and physician; b. Mugamba, Prov. of Bururi; Prof. of Paediatrics, Univ. of Burundi; fmr Dir Nat. Centre for Public Health; fmr MP for Bururi Prov.; First Vice-Pres. of Burundi in charge of Political and Admin. Affairs 2005–07 (resgnd); mem. East African Legis. Ass. 2012–17; mem. Union pour le progresse nationale (Uprona). *E-mail:* docrmartin@yahoo.fr (office). *Website:* www.eala.org (office).

NEAL, Hon. Sir Eric James, Kt, AC, CVO, CEng, CPEng, FAIM; Australian state governor, business executive and chartered engineer; b. 3 June 1924, London, England, UK; s. of James Neal and May Neal (née Johnson); m. Thelma Joan Bowden 1950; two s.; ed South Australian School of Mines; Dir Boral Ltd 1972–92, Chief Exec. 1973–82, Man. Dir 1982–87; Dir Oil Co. of Australia NL 1982–87, Chair. 1984–87; Dir Westpac Banking Corpn 1985–92, Chair. 1989–92; Dir Atlas Copco Australia Ltd 1987–96, Chair. 1990–96; Dir Metal Manufactures Ltd 1987–96, Chair. 1990–96; Dir Wormald Int. Ltd 1978–85, John Fairfax Ltd 1987–88, Cola-Cola Amatil Ltd 1987–96, BHP 1988–94; Gov. S Australia 1996–2001; Chancellor The Flinders Univ. of S Australia 2002–10; Chair. State Govt's Veterans Advisory Council 2009–16; Nat. Pres. Australian Inst. of Co. Dirs 1990–93, currently Fellow; mem. Gen. Motors Australia Advisory Council 1987–94; Chief Commr Council of City of Sydney 1987–88; Life Fellow, Australian Inst. of Building; Int. Trustee, The Duke of Edinburgh's Award Int. Foundation 1987–97; Chair. of Trustees, Sir David Martin Foundation 1991–94; Patron, Soccer Club Blacks, Adelaide Univ. 2007–, Freemasons Foundation Centre for Men's Health –2012; KStJ; Hon. DEng (Sydney) 1989, Hon. DUniv (S Australia) 1996, (Flinders) 2001; numerous awards and medals. *Leisure interests:* reading, walking, motor boating, sailing, naval and eng history, opera. *Address:* 82/52 Brougham Place, North Adelaide 5006, Australia (home). *Telephone:* (8) 8361-7014 (home). *Fax:* (8) 8267-1715 (home). *E-mail:* nj@internode.on.net.

NÉAOUTIYNE, Paul; New Caledonian politician; b. 1952, St Michel Village; ed Univ. of Lyon; teacher of econs at secondary coll. in Nouméa until 1980; jailed for participation in pro-independence demonstration 1980; reinstated as teacher 1983; Aide to Jean-Marie Tjibaou (Pres. Northern Regional Council) 1985; Leader, Party of Kanak Liberation (Palika); Mayor of Poindimie; mem. Northern Prov. Govt; Leader Parti de Libération Kanak (PALIKA) (merged with Kanak Socialist Nat. Liberation Front 1984).

NEARY, J. Peter, DPhil, FBA, MRIA; Irish economist and academic; *Professor of Economics, University of Oxford;* b. 11 Feb. 1950, Drogheda, Co. Louth; s. of Peter Neary and Anne Loughran; m. 1st Frances Ruane 1972 (divorced); two s.; m. 2nd Mairéad Hanrahan 1997; two d.; ed Clongowes Wood Coll., Co. Kildare, Univ. Coll., Dublin, Univ. of Oxford; Jr Lecturer, Trinity Coll. Dublin 1972–74, Lecturer 1978–80; Heyworth Research Fellow, Nuffield Coll. Oxford 1976–78; Prof. of Political Economy, Univ. Coll. Dublin 1980–2006; Prof. of Econs, Univ. of Oxford 2006–, Professorial Fellow, Merton Coll. Oxford 2006–; Visiting Prof., Princeton Univ., USA 1980, Univ. of California, Berkeley, USA 1982, Queen's Univ., Ont., Canada 1986–88, Univ. of Ulster at Jordanstown 1992–93; Research Assoc. Centre for Econ. Performance, LSE 1993–2003; Dir de Recherche, Ecole Polytechnique, Paris 1999–2000; mem. Council Royal Econ. Soc. 1984–89, European Econ. Asscn 1985–92, Econometric Soc. 1994–99; Co-Ed. Journal of International Economics 1980–83; Assoc. Ed. Economic Journal 1981–85, Econometrica 1984–87, Review of Economic Studies 1984–93, Economica 1996–2000; Ed. European Economic Review 1986–90; Pres. Irish Econ. Asscn 1990–92, Int. Trade and Finance Soc. 1999–2000, European Econ. Asscn 2002, Econs Section, BAAS 2005; Pres.-Elect Royal Econ. Soc. 2016–17; mem. Academia Europaea 1989–; Fellow, Centre for Econ. Policy Research, London 1983, Econometric Soc. 1987, European Econ. Asscn 2004; Royal Irish Acad. Gold Medal in the Social Sciences 2006, Advanced Grant, European Research Council 2012–17. *Publications:* Measuring the Restrictiveness of International Trade Policy (with J. E. Anderson) 2005; three edited books and more than 100 publs on econs, especially int. econs. *Leisure interests:* family, friends, travel, reading, music. *Address:* Department of Economics, University of Oxford, Manor Road Building, Manor Road, Oxford, OX1 3UQ, England (office). *Telephone:* (1865) 271085 (office). *Fax:* (1865) 271094 (office). *E-mail:* peter.neary@economics.ox.ac.uk (office). *Website:* users.ox.ac.uk/~econ0211 (office).

NEARY, Martin Gerard James, LVO, MA, DMus, FRCO; British conductor and organist; b. 28 March 1940, London, England; s. of Leonard W. Neary and Jeanne M. Thébault; m. Penelope J. Warren 1967; one s. two d.; ed City of London School, Gonville & Caius Coll., Cambridge; Asst Organist, St Margaret's Westminster 1963–65, Organist and Master of Music 1965–71; Prof. of Organ, Trinity Coll. London 1963–72; Organist and Master of Music, Winchester Cathedral 1972–87; Founder and Conductor Martin Neary Singers 1972–; Conductor Waynflete Singers 1972–87; Organist and Master of Choristers, Westminster Abbey 1988–98; has led Westminster Abbey Choir on tours to France, Germany, Switzerland, Hungary, USA, Russia, Ukraine; Guest Conductor, Australian Youth Choir 1999–; Founder and Conductor, Millennium Consort Singers 2007, including appearances at Disney Hall, Los Angeles; Pres. Cathedral Organists Asscn 1985–88, Organists' Charitable Trust 1988–, Royal Coll. of Organists 1988–90, 1996–98; Chair. Church Services Cttee, Musicians Benevolent Fund 1993–98, Herbert Howells Soc. 1993–; Artistic Dir Paulist Boy Choristers of California 1999–2003; many organ recitals and broadcasts in UK (including First Night of the Proms 2004), Europe, USA, Canada, the Far East and Australia; many choral premières; guest conductor English Chamber Orchestra, London Symphony Orchestra, Netherlands Chamber Choir, Netherlands Radio Choir, Nat. Lutheran Choir, University Voices Canada; Hon. RAM; Hon. FTCL; Hon. Fellow, Royal School of Church Music. *Compositions include:* Responses, carol arrangements, All Saints Mass, Mass of the Redeemer, O Worship the Lord, Joy and Woe, Christmas Recordings. *Recordings:* numerous recordings. *Publications:* edns of early organ music, contribs to organ journals. *Leisure interest:* watching cricket. *Address:* 44 Radipole Road, Fulham, London, SW6 5DL, England. *Telephone:* (20) 7736-5268. *E-mail:* martin@mneary.co.uk.

NEBENZIA, Vassily Alekseevich; Russian diplomatist; *Permanent Representative to United Nations;* b. 26 Feb. 1962, Volgograd; s. of Alexei Andreevich Nebenzia and Antonina Timofeevna Nebenzia; m. Lyudmila Ruslanovna Kasintseva; one s.; ed Moscow State Inst. of Int. Relations; Attaché, Embassy of USSR in Thailand 1988–90, Third, later Second Sec., Int. Orgs Dept, Ministry of Foreign Affairs (MFA), Moscow 1990–92, Head, Int. Orgs Dept 1993–96; Sr Adviser, Perm. Mission of Russian Fed. to UN, New York 1996–2000; Head, Int. Orgs Dept, MFA 2000–03, Deputy Dir 2003–06; Deputy Perm. Rep. of Russian Fed. to UN and other Int. Orgs, Geneva 2006–12; Dir, Dept for Humanitarian Cooperation and Human Rights, MFA 2012–13; Deputy Minister of Foreign Affairs 2013–17; Perm. Rep. to UN, New York 2017–; Order For Services to the Fatherland (II degree), Order of Friendship. *Address:* Permanent Mission of the Russian Federation to the United Nations, 136 East 67th Street, New York, NY 10065, USA (office). *Telephone:* (212) 861-4900 (office). *Fax:* (212) 628-0252 (office). *E-mail:* press@russiaun.ru (office). *Website:* russiaun.ru (office).

NÉBIÉ, B(édializoum) Moussa; Burkinabè diplomatist and politician; *Special Representative of African Union (AU) to Central African Republic (CAR) and Head of the African Union Mission for CAR and Central Africa (MISAC);* b. 8 Sept. 1959, Pouni, Centre-Ouest Region; m.; one c.; ed Univ. de Ouagadougou, Ecole Nat. d'Admin et de Magistrature, Inst. des Relations Int. du Cameroun; joined Ministry of Foreign Affairs 1987, with Political Affairs Directorate 1987–88, Acting Head, Dept of Refugees 1988–89, Second Counsellor, Perm. Mission of Burkina Faso in New York 1991–94, Dir of Multilateral Cooperation 1994–99, Acting Dir-Gen. of Int. Co-operation 1999–2000, Minister–Counsellor and Chargé d' affaires, Perm. Mission of Burkina Faso in Geneva 2003–08, Amb. to Egypt (also accred to Sudan, Israel, Jordan and Syria) 2008–13, Minister-Del., Ministry of Foreign Affairs and Regional Co-operation, responsible for Regional Co-operation 2014–15, Minister of Foreign Affairs and Regional Co-operation 2015–16; Special Rep. of African Union (AU) to Central African Repub. (CAR) and Head of African Union Mission for CAR and Central Africa (MISAC) 2017–; represented Burkina Faso in all sessions of UN Gen. Ass. 1988–2007; fmr Lecturer, Ecole Nat. d'Admin et de Magistrature and Univ. Libre du Burkina.

NEČAS, Petr, DrScNat; Czech politician; b. 19 Nov. 1964, Uherské Hradiště; m. Radka Nečasová (divorced); two s. two d.; ed Gymnasium in Uherské Hradiště, Masaryk Univ., Brno; mil. service, helicopter regt in Prostejov 1988–89; technologist and research engineer, Tesla Rožnov 1988–92; mem. Občanská demokratická strana (ODS—Civic Democratic Party) 1991–, Jt Vice-Chair. 1999–2004, First Deputy Chair. 2004–10, Leader 2010–13; mem. Parl. for Zlín 1992–; mem. Parl. Cttee for Foreign Affairs 1992–96; Deputy Minister of Defence 1995–96; Chair. Parl. Cttee for Defence and Security 1996–2002; Vice-Chair. Parl. Cttee for European Affairs 2002–06; Deputy Prime Minister and Minister for Labour and Social Affairs 2006–09; Prime Minister 2010–13 (resgnd); Minister of Defence 2012–13; charged with bribery Feb. 2014. *Leisure interest:* history. *Address:* Na Příkopě 814/36, 755 01 Vsetín, Czech Republic (home). *Website:* www.petr-necas.cz.

NECHAEV, Andrey Alekseevich, PhD; Russian politician, economist, academic, banker and journalist; b. 2 Feb. 1953, Moscow; s. of Aleksey Nechaev and Marseliesa Nechaev; m. 1st Elena Belyanova 1975; one d.; m. 2nd Margarita Kitova 1986; m. 3rd Svetlana Sergienko 1997; ed Moscow State Univ.; Researcher, USSR Acad. of Sciences 1979–90, Deputy Dir Inst. of Econ. Policy, Acad. of Nat. Economy 1990–91; First Deputy Minister of Economy and Finance of Russia 1991–92; Minister of Economy 1992–93; mem. Security Council of Russia 1992–93; apptd Pres. Russian Financial Corpn 1993, Moscow Finance Club 1994; mem. Political Consultative Council under Pres. of Russia 1996–2000, Scientific Council under Security Council of Russia 1997–2002; mem. Expert Council under Chair. Financial Control Chamber of Russia, Nat. Econ. Council; Prof., Russian Acad. of Econs; Pres. Int. Youth Exchanges Foundation (Coordinator Russian-German youth exchanges); mem. Russian Union of Journalists, Political Council 'Right Deal' (political party), Council of Moscow Banks Union; mem. Acad. of Nat. Sciences, Int. Acad. of Informatization, Acad. of Security and Defence, Advisory Bd RBC-TV; Order of State Statistical Comm. 2002, Order of Ministry of Internal Affairs 2003, Leader of Russian Economy 2003, 2005, Public Order Glory of Russia 2003; State Medal 1997, 2003, Public Recognition Prize 2001, Honour Staff of Ministry of Economy and Trade 2003, Best Pen of Russia Prize, Honour Bookkeeper and Accounter. *Radio:* author and presenter of 'Financial Club' and 'Credit of Trust' radio programmes, econ. analyst on Russian radio. *Television:* author and presenter of 'Money Matter' programme; econs expert on main Russian channels. *Publications:* 250 books and publs on econs and econ. policy. *Leisure interests:* journalism, publicity, politics, history, theatre, travelling, tennis, gardening. *E-mail:* nechaev@rusfincorp.ru (home); rfc@rusfincorp.ru (office).

NECHAEV, Sergei; Russian diplomatist; *Ambassador to Germany;* b. 2 June 1953; m.; one s.; ed Lomonosov Moscow State Univ., Diplomatic Acad. of Russian Foreign Ministry; joined diplomatic service 1977; postings to USSR Embassy, Berlin DDR 1977–80, Consulate-Gen., Erdenet, Mongolia 1982–86; Russian Embassy, Germany 1992–96, 1999–2001, Consul-Gen., Bonn 2001–03; Amb. to Austria 2010–15; Dir, Third European Dept, Ministry of Foreign Affairs 2015–18; Amb. to Germany 2018–. *Address:* Embassy of the Russian Federation, Unter den Linden 63-65, 10117 Berlin, Germany (office). *Telephone:* (30) 2291110 (office). *Fax:* (30) 2299397 (office). *E-mail:* infokonsulat@russische-botschaft.de (office). *Website:* russische-botschaft.ru (office).

NEDVĚD, Pavel; Czech fmr professional footballer; b. 30 Aug. 1972, Cheb, Czechoslovakia (now Czech Repub.); s. of Vaclav Nedvěd and Ana Nedvěd; left winger/attacking midfielder; youth player for TJ Skalná 1977–85, RH Cheb

1985–86, Škoda Plzeň 1986–90, VTJ Tábor 1990–91, Dukla Prague 1991–92; sr player for Dukla Prague (19 league appearances, three goals) 1991–92, Sparta Prague (98 league appearances, 23 goals) 1992–96 (won Czechoslovak League 1992/93, Czech Gambrinus Liga 1993/94, 1994/95, Czech Repub. Football Cup 1996), Lazio, Italy (138 appearances, 33 goals) 1996–2001 (won Coppa Italia 1997/98, 1999/2000, Supercoppa Italiana 1998, 2000, UEFA Cup Winners' Cup 1998/99, UEFA Super Cup 1999, Serie A 1999/2000), Juventus, Italy (244 appearances, 51 goals) 2001–09 (won Serie A 2001/02, 2002/03, 2004/05, 2005/06, Supercoppa Italiana 2002, 2003, Serie B 2006/07); 83 caps and 17 goals for Czech Repub. 1994–2006 (silver medal, UEFA Euro 1996, bronze medal, UEFA Euro 2004); retd 2009; mem. Bd of Dirs Juventus Football Club SpA; Czech Player of the Year 1998, 2000, 2001, 2003, 2004, 2008, Czech Athlete of the Year 2003, World Soccer Magazine Player of the Year 2003, Serie A Footballer of the Year 2003, Serie A Foreign Footballer of the Year 2003, Ballon d'Or (European Footballer of the Year) 2003, Champions League Best Midfielder 2003, Sportske Novosti Award 2003, Czech Player of the Decade 2003, UEFA Team of the Year 2003, 2004, 2005, Golden Foot 2004, named to FIFA 100. *Address:* Juventus Football Club SpA, C.so Galileo Ferraris 32, 10128 Turin, Italy. *E-mail:* info@pavelnedved.cz. *Website:* www.pavelnedved.cz.

NEEDLEMAN, Jacob, PhD; American philosopher and academic; *Professor of Philosophy, San Francisco State University;* b. 6 Oct. 1934, Philadelphia, Pa; s. of Benjamin Needleman and Ida Needleman; m. 1st Carla Satzman 1959 (divorced 1989); one s. one d.; m. 2nd Gail Anderson 1990; ed Research Assoc., Rockefeller Inst., New York 1960–61, Harvard Coll., Yale Univ.; Assoc. Prof. of Philosophy, San Francisco State Univ. 1962–66, Prof. 1967–; Dir Center for the Study of New Religions, Grad. Theological Union, Berkeley, Calif. 1977–83; Vice-Pres. Audio Literature Co. 1987–; Rockefeller Humanities Fellow, Fulbright Scholar. *Publications include:* The New Religions 1970, A Sense of the Cosmos 1975, Lost Christianity 1980, The Heart of Philosophy 1982, The Way of the Physician 1985, Sorcerers 1986, Money and the Meaning of Life 1991, A Little Book on Love 1996, Time and the Soul 1998, The American Soul 2002, The Wisdom of Love 2005, Why Can't We Be Good 2007, What Is God? 2009, An Unknown World: Notes on the Meaning of the Earth 2012, Necessary Wisdom 2013, I Am Not I 2016. *Address:* San Francisco State University, Department of Philosophy, 1600 Holloway Avenue, San Francisco, CA 94132, USA (office). *Telephone:* (415) 338-1596 (office). *E-mail:* jacob.needleman@gmail.com (home). *Website:* www.jacobneedleman.com.

NEESON, Liam, OBE; British actor; b. 7 June 1952, Ballymena, Co. Antrim, Northern Ireland; m. Natasha Richardson 1994 (died 2009); two s.; ed St Mary's Teachers' Coll., London, Queen's Univ., Belfast; worked as forklift operator, then as architect's asst; acting debut with Lyric Players' Theatre, Belfast, in The Risen 1976. *Theatre includes:* Of Mice and Men (Abbey Theatre Co., Dublin), The Informer (Dublin Theatre Festival), Translations (Nat. Theatre, London), The Plough and the Stars (Royal Exchange, Manchester), The Judas Kiss. *Films include:* Excalibur 1981, Krull 1983, The Bounty 1984, The Innocent 1985, Lamb 1986, The Mission 1986, Duet for One 1986, A Prayer for the Dying 1987, Suspect 1987, Satisfaction 1988, High Spirits 1988, The Dead Pool 1988, The Good Mother 1988, Next of Kin 1989, Darkman 1990, The Big Man 1990, Under Suspicion 1991, Husbands and Wives 1992, Leap of Faith 1993, Ethan Frome 1993, Ruby Cairo 1993, Schindler's List 1993, Nell 1994, Rob Roy 1995, Before and After 1996, Michael Collins (Best Actor Evening Standard Award 1997) 1996, Les Misérables 1998, The Haunting 1999, Star Wars: Episode 1 – The Phantom Menace 1999, Gun Shy 2000, K-19: The Widowmaker 2002, Gangs of New York 2002, Love Actually 2003, Kinsey (Best Actor, Los Angeles Film Critics' Asscn) 2004, Kingdom of Heaven 2005, Batman Begins 2005, The Proposition 2005, Breakfast on Pluto 2005, The Chronicles of Narnia: The Lion, the Witch and the Wardrobe (voice) 2005, Seraphim Falls 2006, Taken 2008, The Other Man 2008, The Chronicles of Narnia: Prince Caspian (voice) 2008, Gake no ue no Ponyo (aka Ponyo on the Cliff) (voice: English version) 2008, Fallout 3 (video game) 2008, Five Minutes of Heaven 2009, Chloe 2010, Clash of the Titans 2010, The Chronicles of Narnia: The Voyage of the Dawn Treader (voice) 2010, The Next Three Days 2010, The Grey 2012, Wrath of the Titans 2012, Battleship 2012, Taken 2 2012, The Gentleman Prizefighter 2012, Jeff Wayne's Musical Version of the War of the Worlds Alive on Stage! The New Generation 2013, Khumba (voice) 2013, Third Person 2013, The Nut Job (voice) 2014, A Walk Among the Tombstones 2014, The Lego Movie (voice) 2014, Non-Stop 2014, A Million Ways to Die in the West 2014, A Walk Among the Tombstones 2014, Taken 3 2014, Run All Night 2015, Entourage 2015, Ted 2 2015, Operation Chromite 2016, Silence 2016, Mark Felt: the Man Who Brought Down the White House 2017, The Commuter 2018. *Television includes:* An Audience with Mel Brooks 1983, A Woman of Substance 1983, Ellis Island (mini-series) 1984, Arthur the King 1985, If Tomorrow Comes (mini-series) 1986, Hold the Dream 1986, Sweet As You Are 1987, Sworn to Silence 1987, The American Film Institute Salute to Steven Spielberg 1995, Out of Ireland (voice) 1995, Riverdance: The New Show (video) 1996, Kiss Me Goodnight, The Great War and the Shaping of the 20th Century (mini-series) (voice) 1996, Comic Relief VIII 1998, Empires: The Greeks – Crucible of Civilization (narrator) 2000, The Endurance: Shackleton's Legendary Antarctic Expedition (voice) 2000, Inside the Space Station (voice) 2000, The Man Who Came to Dinner 2000, The Greeks (mini-series) (voice) 2001, Revenge of the Whale 2001, Nobel Peace Prize Concert (host) 2001, Uncovering the Real Gangs of New York 2002, The Maze (voice) 2002, Martin Luther (voice) 2002, Evolution (mini-series) (narrator) 2002, Liberty's Kids: Est. 1776 (series) (voice) 2002, Happy Birthday Oscar Wilde 2004, Patrick (voice) 2004, The Simpsons (voice) 2005, The Big C 2010, The Garden's Defining Moments (mini-series) 2015. *Address:* c/o Ed Limato, ICM, 8942 Wilshire Boulevard, Beverly Hills, CA 90211-1934, USA (office). *Telephone:* (310) 550-4000 (office). *Website:* www.icmtalent.com (office).

NEEWOOR, Anund Priyay, BA (Hons); Mauritian diplomatist and international organization official; b. 26 June 1940; m. Chandranee Neewoor 1971; two s. one d.; ed Delhi Univ., Makerere Univ., Uganda; teacher, Prin. Northern Coll. (secondary school), Mauritius 1964–67; joined Ministry of External Affairs, Tourism and Emigration (in charge of UN affairs and West Asia affairs) 1970; Admin. Asst, Civil Service 1972; Second Sec., High Comm., London 1973–75, First Sec., High Comm., New Delhi 1975–81, Minister-Counsellor, Embassy in Washington, DC 1982, Amb. to Pakistan 1983, High Commr to India 1983–93, Amb. to USA 1993–96, Amb. in Ministry of External Affairs in charge of Multilateral Econ. Affairs 1996, Sec. for Foreign Affairs 1996–99, Amb. and Perm. Rep. to UN, New York 1999–2001, apptd Sec. for Foreign Affairs 2005; Commdr, Order of the Star and Key of the Indian Ocean (CSK) 2003, Grand Officer (GOSK) 2008. *Leisure interests:* reading, sports. *Address:* 17 Avenue des Dodos, Sodnac, Quatre Bornes, Mauritius (home). *E-mail:* apneewoor@hotmail.com.

NEFEDOV, Oleg Matveyevich, DSc; Russian chemist; *Head of Laboratory of Carbene and Small Ring Chemistry, N.D. Zelinksky Institute of Organic Chemistry, Russian Academy of Sciences;* b. 25 Nov. 1931, Dmitrov, Moscow region; s. of Matvey Kondrat'evich Nefedov and Mariya Adolfovna Teodorovich; m. Galina Gimelfarb 1954; one s. one d.; ed D.I. Mendeleev Inst. of Chem. and Tech.; worked as jr then sr researcher; Prof. of Chem. and Head, Lab. of Carbene and Small Ring Chem., N.D. Zelinsky Inst. of Organic Chem., USSR (now Russian) Acad. of Sciences 1968–, now Head of Dept; Corresp. mem. USSR (now Russian) Acad. of Sciences (RAS) 1979–87, mem. 1987–, Academic Sec. Div. of Gen. and Applied Chem. 1988–91, Vice-Pres. RAS 1988–2001, Rector Higher Chemical Coll. 1990–, Counsellor, RAS 2001–; Prof., Lomonosov Moscow State Univ. 2009–; Ed.-in-Chief Mendeleev Communications 1990–, Russian Chemical Bulletin 1991–, Russian Chemical Reviews 1995–; Chair. Nat. Cttee of Russian Chemists 1996–; mem. IUPAC Bureau and Exec. Cttee 1999–2008; Pres. Mendeleev Congresses on Gen. and Applied Chem., Tashkent 1989, Minsk 1993, St Petersburg 1998, Kazan 2003, Moscow 2007; USSR People's Deputy 1989–91; mem. Academia Europaea 1991, Academia Scientiarum et Artium Europaea (Austria) 1991, Asia-Pacific Acad. of Materials (India); Foreign mem. Georgia Acad. of Sciences 1996, Nat. Acad. of Sciences of Ukraine 2000; Hon. Prof., Harbin Polytechnic Inst., China 2000, D.I. Mendeleev Russian Chemical Tech. Univ. 2001; Hon. FRSC 1991; USSR State Prize 1983, 1990, ND Zelinsky Prize 1987, Prize of USSR and Hungarian Acads 1988, N. Semyonov Prize 1991, A. Karpinsky Prize 1993, D.I. Mendeleev Gold Medal 1998, Russian Fed. State Prize in Science and Tech. 2002, A.M. Butlerov Prize 2003. *Publications:* The Structure of Cyclopropane Derivatives 1986, Chemistry of Carbenes and Small-sized Cyclic Compounds (ed.) 1989, Carbenes Chemistry 1990; more than 700 articles and 201 patents on physical organic chemistry, small ring chemistry, organic synthesis and organometallic chemistry. *Leisure interests:* sport, gathering mushrooms. *Address:* N.D. Zelinsky Institute of Organic Chemistry, 119991 Moscow, GSP-1, Leninsky prospekt 47, Russian Federation (office). *Telephone:* (499) 137-29-44 (office). *Fax:* (495) 135-53-28 (office). *E-mail:* nefedov@ras.ru (office). *Website:* www.ioc.ac.ru (office).

NEGERI SEMBILAN, Yang di-Pertuan Besar; Tuanku Muhriz ibni al-Marhum Tunku Munawir, LLB; Malaysian; b. 14 Jan. 1948; s. of Tuanku Munawir ibni al-Mmarhum Tuanku Abdul Rahman and Tunku Ampuan Durah binti al-Marhum Tunku Besar Burhanuddin; m. Tuanku Aishah Rohani Tengku Besar Mahmud; three s.; ed Tuanku Muhammad and Tunku Besar Schools, Tampin, King George V School, Seremban, Negeri Sembilan, Aldenham School and Univ. Coll. of Wales at Aberystwyth (now the Univ. of Wales, Aberystwyth), UK; named Tunku Besar (Heir Presumptive) 1960, bypassed by the Council of Undangs to become Yang di-Pertuan Besar on the death of his father in 1967 for his uncle, Tuanku Jaafar ibni Abdul Rahman; proclaimed 11th Yang di-Pertuan Besar of Negeri Sembilan 29 Dec. 2008; began career in int. bank in Malaysia, became a dir and shareholder of a co. licensed as brokers in interbank foreign exchange and in currency deposits market 1973–86; chair. and shareholder of a Malaysian jt venture with a worldwide advertising agency 1981–92; chair. and dir of a jt venture co. involved in the manufacturing of building products 1995–98; dir and shareholder of an electrical eng and construction co. 1995–; mem. Bd of Dirs Bangkok Bank 2006–.

NEGGA, Ruth, BA; Ethiopian/Irish actress; b. 7 Jan. 1982, Addis Ababa; d. of Norra Negga; partner Dominic Cooper 2010–; ed Trinity Coll., Dublin. *Plays include:* Duck, Traverse Theatre, Edinburgh 2003, Phèdre (Irish Times Theatre Award for Best Actress), Nat. Theatre London 2009, Titus Andronicus (Ian Charleson Award 2009), The Project Theatre, Hamlet 2010–11, Playboy of the Western World, Old Vic Theatre London 2011. *Films include:* Feature film: Capital Letters 2004, Breakfast on Pluto 2005, Colour Me Kubrick 2005, Jacob 2010, Fury 2012, World War Z 2013, Jimi: All Is by My Side 2013, Noble 2014, Of Mind and Music 2014, Iona 2015, Warcraft 2016, Loving (African-American Film Critics Asscn Award for Best Actress 2017, Palm Springs Int. Film Festival Rising Star Award 2017) 2016. *Television includes:* Doctors (series) 2004, Love is the Drug (series) 2004, Criminal Justice (mini-series) 2008, Personal Affairs (series) 2009, Five Daughters (mini-series) 2010, Love/Hate (series) 2010–11, Misfits (series) 2010, The Nativity (mini-series) 2010, Shirley (IFTA Award for Best Actress in a TV Film 2012) 2011, Secret State (mini-series) 2012, Marvel's Agents of S.H.I.E.L.D (series) 2013–15, Preacher (series) 2016–. *Address:* c/o Markham, Froggatt & Irwin, 4 Windmill Street, London, W1T 2HZ, England (office). *Telephone:* (20) 7636–4412 (office). *Fax:* (20) 7637–5233 (office). *E-mail:* admin@markhamfroggattirwin.com (office). *Website:* www.markhamfroggattandirwin.com (office).

NEGISHI, Akio, BSc; Japanese business executive; *Director, President and Representative Executive Officer, Meiji Yasuda Life Insurance Company;* b. 1958; ed Waseda Univ.; joined Meiji Yasuda Life Insurance Co. 1981, Gen. Man. Shiga Regional Office 2003–04, Gen. Man. Shiga Regional Office, Meiji Yasuda Life Insurance Co. 2004–05, Gen. Man. Corp. Planning and Research Dept 2005–07, Gen. Man. Marketing Planning and Research Dept 2007–09, Exec. Officer and Gen. Man. Marketing Planning and Research Dept 2009–11, Exec. Officer 2011–12, Man. Exec. Officer 2012–13, Dir, Pres. and Rep. Exec. Officer 2013–. *Address:* Meiji Yasuda Life Insurance Company, 1-1, Marunouchi 2-chome, Chiyoda-ku, Tokyo 100-0005, Japan (office). *Telephone:* (3) 3283-8293 (office). *Fax:* (3) 3215-8123 (office). *E-mail:* info@meijiyasuda.co.jp (office). *Website:* www.meijiyasuda.co.jp (office).

NEGISHI, Ei-ichi, BS, PhD; Japanese chemist and academic; *Herbert C. Brown Distinguished Professor of Chemistry, Purdue University;* b. 14 July 1935, Changchun (fmr capital of Japanese-controlled Manchukuo, now capital of Jilin, China); m. Sumire Negishi (died 2018); ed Univ. of Tokyo, Univ. of Pennsylvania; research chemist, Teijin Ltd 1958–60, 1963–66; Postdoctoral Assoc., Purdue Univ., West Lafayette, Ind. 1966–68, Asst to Nobel laureate Herbert C. Brown 1968–72, Prof. of Chem. 1979–99, Herbert C. Brown Distinguished Prof. of Chem. and Teijin Ltd Dir of the Negishi-Brown Inst. 1999–; Asst Prof., Syracuse Univ. 1972–76,

Assoc. Prof. 1976–79; Visiting Prof., Univ. of California, Santa Cruz 1980, Univ. of Tokyo 1987, Nat. Univ. of Singapore 2000; First Burroughs-Welcome Visiting Prof., Duke Univ., Durham, NC 1994; mem. ACS 1979–, AAAS 1975–80, 1992–94, Japan Chemical Soc. 1985–; Chair. NIH Medicinal Chem. Study Section 1986–90 (Ad hoc mem. 1980, 1985, 1994), ACS Purdue Section 1986; Co-Chair. Pre-OMCOS-8 Symposium 1995, OMCOS-8 1995; mem. IUPAC-OMCOS Int. Scientific Cttee 1993–; Guest Ed. Tetrahedron Symposium-in-print 1995; Co-Guest Ed. Journal of Organometallic Chemistry Special Issue 1998, Special Issue, 2002; mem. Editorial Advisory Bd Organometallics 1999–2001; consultant, Hoffmann-LaRoche & Co., Basel, Switzerland 1983–2002, Kaneka, Takasago, Japan 1991–2003; consultant to Pres. of Hokkaido Univ., Japan 2002; Fullbright-Smith-Mund Scholarship 1960–63, Harrison Fellowship 1962–63, Visiting Lectureship, sponsored by Western Swiss Univs (seven invited lectures) 1983, Syntex Distinguished Lecturer, Univ. of Colorado, Boulder 1985, John E. Mahler Lecturer, Univ. of Texas, Austin 1986, John S. Guggenheim Memorial Foundation Fellowship 1987, Nat. Science Council Lectureship, Taiwan 1987, NSF Special Creativity Extension Award 1988–90, Robert A. Welch Foundation Lectureship 1989, NATO Invited Lecturer, Ankara Univ., Turkey 1991, Alan R. Day Award (POCC) 1996, J.C. Karcher Lecturer, Univ. of Oklahoma 1996, The Chemical Soc. of Japan Award 1996, K. Nakamoto Distinguished Lectureship, Marquette Univ. 1997, Sr Researcher Award, Alexander von Humbolt Foundation 1998–2001, ACS Organometallic Chem. Award 1998, Herbert N. McCoy Award 1998, RSC Sir Edward Frankland Prize Lectureship 2001, inclusion of the Negishi Cross-Coupling in Merck Index, 13th edn 2001, Weissberger-Williams Lectureship, Eastman Kodak, Rochester, NY 2002, Sigma Xi Award, Purdue Univ. 2003, Professional/Scholarly Publishing Div. Award (Chem.), Asscn of American Publrs 2003, Merck Frosst Award Lectureship, Univ. of Waterloo 2004, Roche Distinguished Lectureship, Colorado State Univ., Fort Collins 2005, Merck-Frosst Award Lecturer, Univ. of Montreal 2006, Merck-Frosst Award Lecturer, Univ. of California, Irvine 2006, Yamada-Koga Prize (Japan) 2007, Gold Medal of Charles Univ., Prague, Czech Repub. 2007, ACS Award for Creative Work in Synthetic Organic Chem. 2010, Nobel Prize in Chem. (jtly with Richard Heck and Akira Suzuki) "for palladium-catalyzed cross couplings in organic synthesis" 2010. *Publications:* Handbook of Organopaladium Chemistry for Organic Synthesis, two vols (ed.) 2002; more than 400 papers in professional journals; several patents. *Address:* Room WTHR 465B, H.C. Brown Laboratories of Chemistry, Purdue University, 560 Oval Drive, West Lafayette, IN 47907-2084, USA (office). *Telephone:* (765) 494-5301 (office); (765) 463-4439 (home). *Fax:* (765) 496-3380 (office); (765) 494-0239 (office). *E-mail:* negishi@purdue.edu (office). *Website:* www.chem.purdue.edu (office).

NEGISHI, Takashi, PhD; Japanese economist and academic; *Emeritus Professor, Tokyo University;* b. 2 April 1933, Tokyo; s. of Setsuko Negishi and Suteta Negishi; m. Aiko Mori 1964; one d.; ed Univ. of Tokyo; Research Asst, then Research Assoc., Stanford Univ., Calif. 1958–60; Research Asst, Univ. of Tokyo 1963–65, Assoc. Prof. 1965–76, Prof. 1976–94, Prof. Emer. 1994–, also Dean, Faculty of Econs 1990–92; Prof., Aoyama Gakuin Univ. 1994–2002, Toyo Eiwa Univ. 2002–06; Fellow Econometric Soc. 1966–, Vice-Pres. 1992–93, Pres. 1994; Pres. Japan Asscn of Econs and Econometrics 1985; Pres. The Soc. for the History of Econ. Thought, Japan 1997–99; mem. Exec. Cttee Int. Econ. Asscn 1989–92, Science Council of Japan 1985–88, Japan Acad. 1998–; Foreign Hon. mem. American Econ. Asscn 1989; Distinguished Fellow, History of Econs Soc. 2005; Japan Acad. Prize 1993, Order of Culture 014. *Television:* Introduction to History of Economic Thought, Univ. of the Air, Japan 2001. *Publications:* General Equilibrium Theory and International Trade 1972, Microeconomic Foundations of Keynesian Macro Economics 1979, Economic Theories of a Non-Walrasian Tradition 1985, History of Economic Theory 1989, The Collected Essays of Takashi Negishi 1994, 2000. *Address:* 1-3-1-2003, Motoazabu, Minato-ku, Tokyo 106-0046, Japan. *Telephone:* (3) 3440-0630. *E-mail:* tnegishi@bk9.so-net.ne.jp.

NEGMATULLAEV, Sabit, DTechSc; Tajikistani physicist; b. 16 Sept. 1937, Ura-Tube; ed Tajik Polytech. Inst.; mem. CPSU 1966–91; jr researcher, Tajik Inst. of Seismic Resistance, Construction and Seismology of Seismology, Tajik Acad. of Sciences, Scientific Sec. 1964–65, Vice-Dir 1965–69, Dir 1969, then Hon. Dir, apptd Head, Geophysical Service 2008; mem. Tajik Acad. of Sciences 1987, Pres. 1988–95; Chair. Scientific-Publishing Council of Acad. of Sciences; mem. Cen. Cttee CPSU 1990–91.

NEGOITĂ, Liviu Gheorghe, LLB; Romanian lawyer and politician; b. 22 March 1962, Brăila; ed Univ. of Bucharest; mem. Democratic Liberal Party (DLP) 1997–; mem. Camera Deputaţilor (Chamber of Deputies) 1996–2000, 2000–04, fmr Leader DLP Parl. Group, mem. several parl. cttees; Mayor of Bucharest Sector 3 2004–12; Prime Minister Desig. 2009 (stepped down before taking office Dec. 2009). *Address:* c/o Partidul Democrat Liberal, 011825 Bucharest, Al. Modrogan 1, Romania.

NEGRI, Barjas, PhD; Brazilian politician; *Mayor of Piracicaba;* b. 8 Dec. 1950, Santo Amaro, São Paulo; s. of Affonso Negri Neto and Hirce Rodrigues Negri; m. Sandra Regina Bonsi; one s. two d.; ed Methodist Univ. of Piracicaba; Prof. of Econs, Univ. of Piracicaba 1974–95; Researcher and Lecturer, UNIVCAMP Univ. 1986; Sec. of Educ., São Paulo State Parl. 1979–82, Sec. of Planning 1993–94; Sec. Dept of Educ., Fed. Govt 1995–96; Sec. Dept of Health 1997–2001, Minister for Health 2002; Mayor of Piracicaba 2005–12, 2016–. *Address:* Prédio da Prefeitura Municipal, Rua Amadeu Amaral, 255, 13380 Piracicaba São Paulo, Brazil (office). *Website:* www.piracicaba.sp.gov.br (office).

NEGRITOIU, Misu, MS, PhD; Romanian politician, economist and banker; b. 25 May 1950, Dăbuleni, Dolj Co.; s. of Marin Negritoiu and Floarea Negritoiu; m. Paulina Urzica 1977; one s. one d.; ed Bucharest Acad. of Econ. Studies, Law School, Bucharest Univ., HDS Hertfordshire Univ.; foreign trade economist and later foreign trade co. dir 1973–90; fmr Minister-Counsellor, Embassy in Washington; Pres. Romanian Devt Agency 1990–92; Deputy Prime Minister and Chair. Council for Strategy and Econ. Reform Co-ordination 1993; Chief Econ. Adviser to Pres. of Romania 1994–96; mem. Parl. 1996–97; mem. Club of Rome, Vice-Pres., Romanian Div. 1998–2008; Exec. Dir Wholesale Banking, ING Bank Romania 1997–2006, Gen. Man. 2006–10, CEO ING Bank Romania 2010–12, Chair. 2012–14, Pres. (also non-Exec. Pres.) Consultative Bd 2012–14; Chair. Advisory Bd Maastricht School of Man. 2012–; Pres. Financial Supervisory Authority 2014–18; Sr Advisor EY Romania 2018–; Prof., Acad. of Econ. Studies, School of Political Studies and Public Admin., Bucharest; Chair. Grad. School of Man., MBA Canadian Programme; Pres. Forum for European Integration; mem. Romanian Econ. Soc. (SOREC), Romanian Asscn for Energy Policy (APER), American Asscn for Arbitration, Centre for European Policy Studies, Econ. Policy Forum, Faculty for Int. Econs and Business, Business Advisory Council, South-East European Co-operation Initiative/Stability Pact, ASPEN Int; Banker of the Year, Bucharest Business Week magazine 2004, Banker of the Year, Piata Financiara magazine 2006, Best Banker, Bucharest Business Week magazine 2008. *Publications:* Jumping Ahead – Economic Development and FDI 1996, International Finance (textbook) 1994, Management in International Trade 1997; numerous studies and articles on int. and domestic econ. issues, presentations to int. and domestic confs and seminars. *Leisure interest:* golf. *Address:* 16 Dionisie Fotino Street, Apt 3, Bucharest 1, Romania (home). *Telephone:* (21) 2091103 (office). *Website:* www.ey.com (office).

NEGROPONTE, John Dimitri, BA; American diplomatist and academic; *Vice-Chairman, McLarty Associates;* b. 21 July 1939, London; s. of Dimitri J. Negroponte and Catherine C. Negroponte; m. Diana Mary Villiers 1976; two s. three d.; ed Phillips Exeter Acad., NH, Yale Univ., New Haven, Conn.; entered Foreign Service 1960, Amb. to Honduras 1981–85; Asst Sec. of State for Oceans and Int. Environmental Scientific Affairs 1985–87; Deputy Asst to Pres. for Nat. Security Affairs 1987–89; Amb. to Mexico 1989–93, to the Philippines 1993–96; Special Co-ordinator for post-1999 US Presence in Panama 1996–97; Exec. Vice-Pres. Global Markets McGraw-Hill 1997–2001; Perm. Rep. to UN 2001–04; Amb. to Iraq 2004–05; Dir of Nat. Intelligence 2005–07; Deputy Sec. of State 2007–09; Brady-Johnson Distinguished Fellow in Grand Strategy and Sr Lecturer in Global Affairs, Jackson Inst., Yale Univ. 2009–16; J. B. and Maurice C. Shapiro Prof. of Int. Affairs, George Washington Univ. 2016–; Vice-Chair. McLarty Associates (strategic advisory firm), Washington, DC 2009–; Chair. Emer. Council of the Americas/Americas Soc., New York 2009–, Intelligence and Nat. Security Alliance (INSA) 2013–; Co-Chair. US-Philippines Soc. 2012–; Bd Advisor, Libra Group, London and New York; mem. Council on Foreign Relations, American Acad. of Diplomacy, Sec. of State's Foreign Affairs Policy Bd 2011–17; Sec. of State's Distinguished Service Award 2005, 2009, Pres.'s Nat. Security Medal 2009. *Leisure interests:* swimming, skiing, reading, history. *Address:* McLarty Associates, 900 17th Street, NW, Washington, DC 20006, USA (office). *Telephone:* (202) 419-1420 (office). *Fax:* (202) 419-1421 (office). *E-mail:* jnegroponte@maglobal.com (office). *Website:* www.yale.edu/jackson (office); www.maglobal.com (office).

NEGRUŢA, Veaceslav; Moldovan economist and politician; b. 4 March 1972, Delacău, Grigoriopol; m.; two c.; ed Acad. of Econ. Studies of Moldova; Head of Macroeconomic and Financial Analyses Unit, Ministry of Finance 1994–97; Macroeconomist, Centre for Strategic Research and Reforms, World Bank/UNDP 1997–99; Sr State Adviser to Prime Minister Ion Sturza 1999; Dir Dept of Monetary Policy and Research, Nat. Bank of Moldova 2000–01; Sr Economist, KPMG Barents Group LLC/Bearing Point, USAID Moldovan Fiscal Reform Project 2001–05; Deputy Exec. Dir Moldova CASE (Centre of Social-Economic Analyses) Foundation 2003–07; worked as financial consultant 2005–09; Minister of Finance 2009–13; Consultant to UNEP/Jt Integrated Local Devt Programme, Chisinau 2014; mem. Liberal Democratic Party of Moldova; sentenced to three years probation by Rascani District Court in 2015 for abuse of power while Minister of Finance. *Website:* vnegruta.wordpress.com/author/vnegruta.

NEGUS, Anthony (Tony) William, AO, APM, MPPA; Australian diplomatist and fmr police commissioner; b. Cowra, New South Wales; m.; three c.; ed Charles Sturt Univ., Australian Inst. of Police Man., Harvard Univ. Leadership Program, USA; served with Australian Fed. Police for 32 years, Commr 2009–14; High Commr to Canada 2015–17; has served on law enforcement bds, including as Chair. Australian Crime Comm.; Australian Police Medal 2005, Indonesian Nat. Police Meritorious Service Star 2012, Int. Police and Public Safety 9/11 Medal (USA) 2012, Interpol Medal 2014.

NEHER, Erwin; German research scientist and academic; *Research Director, Max-Planck-Institut für biophysikalische Chemie, Göttingen;* b. 20 March 1944, Landsberg; s. of Franz Xaver Neher and Elisabeth Neher (née Pfeiffer); m. Dr Eva-Maria Neher 1978; three s. two d.; ed Tech. Univ. Munich, Univ. of Wisconsin-Madison, USA; Research Assoc., Max-Planck-Institut für Psychiatrie, Munich 1970–72, Max-Planck-Institut für biophysikalische Chemie, Göttingen 1972–75, 1976–83, Research Dir 1983–; Research Assoc., Yale Univ., New Haven, Conn., USA 1975–76; Fairchild Scholar, California Inst. of Tech. 1988–89; elected Foreign mem. Royal Soc. 1994; Dr hc (Univ. of Pavia) 2000; shared Nobel Prize for Medicine 1991; several nat. and int. scientific awards; Bundesverdienstkreuz mit Stern und Schulterband 1998. *Publications:* Elektronische Messtechnik in der Physiologie 1974, Single Channel Recording (ed.) 1983. *Address:* Max-Planck-Institut für biophysikelische Chemie, Am Fassberg 11, 37077 Göttingen, Germany (office). *Telephone:* (551) 2011630 (office). *Fax:* (551) 2011688 (office). *E-mail:* eneher@gwdg.de (office). *Website:* www.mpibpc.gwdg.de (office).

NEHWAL, Saina; Indian professional badminton player; b. 17 March 1990, Hisar, Haryana; d. of Dr Harvir Singh Nehwal and Usha Rani; ed St Ann's Coll., Mehdipatnam; took part in Jr Asian Championship, Hwacheon, Repub. of Korea aged 14; turned professional 2003; winner, Czech Jr Open 2003, Asian Satellite Tournament 2005, 2006, Philippines Open 2006, Indian Nat. Championships 2007, 2008, Indian Int. Challenge 2007, Yonex Chinese Taipai Open 2008, World Jr Badminton Championships (first Indian), Pune 2008, 2010, Indonesian Open Super Series (first Indian) 2009, 2010, Nat. Games of India (gold medal) 2007, Commonwealth Youth Games (gold medal) 2008, Indian Open Grand Prix 2009, 2010, Badminton Asia Championships (bronze medal) 2010, Singapore Open Super Series 2010, Commonwealth Games (gold medal) 2010, Hong Kong Super Series 2010, Swiss Open Grand Prix Gold trophy 2011, 2012, Indonesia Open Super Series Premier (silver medal) 2011, 2012, Malaysia Open Grand Prix Gold (silver medal) 2011, Denmark Open 2012, Indian Super Series 2015; represented India (quarterfinalist) at Beijing Olympics 2008, London Olympics (bronze medal) 2012; mem. IOC Athletes Comm. 2016–; Most Promising Player, Badminton World Fed. 2008, Sports Illustrated India Sportsperson of the Year 2009, MSN Sportsperson of the Year 2009, Rajiv Gandhi Khel Ratna Award 2010, Padma Bhushan 2016. *Address:* Globosport India Pvt. Ltd, 1st Floor, 2nd Cross, Amarjyoti

Layout, off Intermediate Ring Road, Domlur, Bangalore 560 071, India. *Telephone:* (80) 41154214. *Fax:* (80) 41154043130. *E-mail:* info@globosportworld.com.

NEI, Masatoshi, BS, MS, PhD; American (b. Japanese) biologist and academic; *Carnell Professor, Department of Biology, Temple University;* b. 2 Jan. 1931, Miyazaki; m. Nobuko Nei; one s. one d.; ed Miyazaki and Kyoto Univs, Univ. of California, Davis and North Carolina State Univ., USA; Asst Prof., Kyoto Univ. 1958–62, Hon. Advisory mem. Soc. for the Study of Molecular Biology and Evolution 2011; Geneticist, Nat. Inst. of Radiological Sciences, Chiba 1962–65, Head, Population Genetics Lab. 1965–69; Assoc. Prof. of Biology, Brown Univ., Providence, RI 1969–71, Prof. of Biology 1971–72; Prof. of Population Genetics, Center for Demographic and Population Genetics, Univ. of Texas, Houston 1972–90, Acting Dir 1978–80; Distinguished Prof. of Biology, Pennsylvania State Univ. 1990–94, Dir Inst. of Molecular Evolutionary Genetics 1990–15, Evan Pugh Prof. of Biology 1994–15; Laura Carnell Prof., Dept of Biology, Temple Univ. 2015–; Visiting Prof. of Biology, Tokyo Inst. of Tech. 2001; Assoc. Ed. Theoretical Population Biology 1973–84, Genetics 1977–85, Journal of Heredity 1995–2007; Ed. Molecular Biology and Evolution 1983–93; mem. Editorial Bd Journal of Molecular Evolution 1979–2001, Proceedings of the National Academy of Sciences (USA) 2003–15; mem. Bd of Overseers, Harvard Univ. 1988–94; mem. Advisory Bd Gene Geography 1985–97, Gene: Evolutionary Genomics 2004–11; mem. NAS 2003– (mem. Nat. Research Council Cttee 1994–96), American Genetic Assn (Pres. 1999), Soc. for Molecular Biology and Evolution (Pres. 1994); Hon. mem. Genetics Soc. of Japan 1989, Japan Soc. of Human Genetics 1996, Japan Soc. for Histocompatibility and Immunogenetics 2000, Japan Soc. of Animal Genetics and Breeding 2001; Dr hc (Miyazaki Univ.) 2002; Japan Soc. of Human Genetics Award 1977, Kihara Prize, Genetics Soc. of Japan 1990, P.R. Krishnaiah Memorial Lecture, Pennsylvania State Univ. 1999, Masatoshi Nei Annual Lecture, est. for the Soc. for Molecular Biology and Evolution 2000, Certificate of Award 'Highly Cited Researchers', Inst. for Scientific Information 2000, Wilhelmine E. Key Invitational Lecture, Annual Meeting of American Genetic Assn 2001, Int. Prize for Biology, Japan Soc. for the Promotion of Sciences 2002, Barbara Bowman Award, Texas Geneticist Soc. 2003, Thomas Hunt Morgan Medal, Genetics Soc. of America 2006, Masatoshi Nei Legacy Symposium held at the Molecular Biology and Evolution Soc. meeting, Tempe, Ariz. 2006, Kyoto Prize, Inamori Foundation (co-recipient) 2013. *Publications:* more than 260 articles in scientific journals. *Address:* Temple University, Department of Biology, SERC Bldg, 1925 N 12th Street, Philadelphia, PA 19122, USA (office). *Telephone:* (215) 204-5233 (office). *Fax:* (215) 204-4438 (office). *Website:* igem.temple.edu/labs (office).

NEID, Silvia; German football coach and fmr professional football player; b. 2 May 1964, Walldürn, Baden-Württemberg; midfielder; as a youth played with SV Schlierstadt 1975–80; sr career: played with Klinge Seckach 1980–83, SSG Bergisch Gladbach 1983–85 (Fußball-Bundesliga (women) 1984, Frauen DFB Pokal 1984), TSV Siegen 1985–86 (Fußball-Bundesliga (women) 1987, 1990, 1991, 1992, 1994, 1996, Frauen DFB Pokal 1986, 1987, 1988, 1989, 1993); mem. Germany Women's Nat. Football Team 1982–96 (won UEFA Women's Championship 1989, 1991, 1995, runners-up, FIFA Women's World Cup 1995), managed Under-19 Germany Women's Nat. Football Team, winning World Championship 2004, runners-up, Women's Championship, Asst Coach Germany Women's Nat. Football Team 1996–2005, Head Coach 2005–16, as coach has won the World Cup 2007, bronze medal, Summer Olympics, Beijing 2008, European Championship 2009, gold medal, Women's Olympic Football Tournament, Rio 2016; Bundesverdienstkreuz am Bande 2007, Verdienstorden des Landes Nordrhein-Westfalen 2011, Verdienstorden des Landes Baden-Württemberg 2013; FIFA World Coach of the Year 2010, 2013, Best FIFA Women's Coach 2016. *Address:* Deutscher Fußball-Bund, Hermann-Neuberger-Haus, Otto-Fleck-Schneise 6, 60528 Frankfurt am Main, Germany (office). *Telephone:* (69) 67880 (office). *Fax:* (69) 6788266 (office). *E-mail:* info@dfb.de (office). *Website:* www.dfb.de (office).

NEIL, Andrew Ferguson, MA; British publisher, broadcaster, editor and business executive; *Chairman, Spectator Magazine Group;* b. 21 May 1949, Paisley, Renfrewshire, Scotland; s. of Maj. James Neil and Mary Ferguson; m. Susan Nilsson 2015; ed Paisley Grammar School, Univ. of Glasgow; with Conservative Party Research Dept 1971–72; with The Economist 1973–83, Ulster, Political then Industrial Corresp. 1973–79, American Corresp. in New York and Washington, DC 1979–82, UK Ed. 1982–83; Ed. The Sunday Times 1983–94; Exec. Ed. Fox TV News, USA 1994; Exec. Chair. Sky TV 1988–90; Publr The Scotsman, Scotland on Sunday, Edinburgh Evening News 1996–2006; Publr, The Business 1999–2007; regular anchor and TV commentator UK and USA; anchor, The Daily Politics (BBC 2) 2003–, This Week (BBC 1) 2003–19, Straight Talk with Andrew Neil (BBC News Channel) 2004–09, Sunday Politics (BBC 1) 2012–17, Politics Live 2018–; Contrib. Ed. Vanity Fair, New York 1994–2007; Chair. The Spectator and Apollo magazines 2004–; Chair. World Media Rights (WMR) 2005–15, ITP Magazines (Dubai) 2005–; led consortium of investors to acquire Peters, Fraser & Dunlop (PFD) literary agency 2008, Chair. 2008–10; Founder and Dir Glenburn Enterprises; Lord Rector Univ. of St Andrews 1999–2002; Hon. DLit (Napier Univ.) 1998; Hon. DUniv (Paisley) 2001; Hon. LLD (St Andrews) 2002. *Publications include:* The Cable Revolution 1982, Britain's Free Press: Does It Have One? 1989, Full Disclosure 1996, British Excellence 1999, 2000, 2001. *Leisure interests:* dining out in New York, London, Dubai and Côte d'Azur, cycling when not chairing companies. *Address:* 22 Old Queen Street, London, SW1H 9HP, England (office). *Telephone:* (845) 299-7225 (office); (20) 7961-0000 (office). *E-mail:* afneil@icloud.com.

NEILAND, Brendan Robert, MA; British artist and professor of painting; b. 23 Oct. 1941, Lichfield, Staffs.; s. of Arthur Neiland and Joan Whiley; m. Hilary Salter 1970; two d.; ed St Philip's Grammar School, Birmingham, St Augustine's Seminary, Ireland, Birmingham School of Art and Royal Coll. of Art, London; painter and printmaker; best known for his paintings of reflections in modern city buildings; gallery artist, Angela Flowers Gallery 1970–78, Fischer Fine Art 1978–92, Redfern Gallery 1992–; solo and group shows throughout Europe, Middle East, USA and Australia; Lecturer in Fine Art, Univ. of Brighton 1983–96, Prof. of Painting 1996–98; Keeper (Dir), Royal Acad. Schools 1998–2004 (resgnd), expelled from membership of RA 2005; Visiting Prof. of Fine Art, Loughborough Univ. 1999; Daler Rowney Award, Royal Acad. Summer Exhbn 1989. *Publication:* Upon Reflection 1997. *Leisure interests:* cricket, golf, fine wines. *Address:* c/o Redfern Gallery, 20 Cork Street, London, W1S 3HL; 2 Granard Road, London, SW12 8UL, England (home); Crepe, La Grévé sur Mignon, 17170 Courcon, France. *Telephone:* (20) 7734-1732 (Redfern Gallery); (20) 8673-4597 (home); (5) 46-01-62-97 (Courcon). *E-mail:* neilands@talktalk.net. *Website:* www.brendanneiland.com.

NEILL, Sam, DCNZM, OBE; New Zealand actor; b. (Nigel Neill), 14 Sept. 1947, Omagh, Co. Tyrone, Northern Ireland, UK; m. Noriko Watanabe; one d.; one s. by Lisa Harrow; ed Univ. of Canterbury; toured for one year with Players Drama Quintet; appeared with Amamus Theatre in roles including Macbeth and Pentheus in The Bacchae; joined NZ Nat. Film Unit playing leading part in three films 1974–78; moved to Australia 1978, to England 1980; owns a small family wine-producing business called Two Paddocks at Gibbston, Central Otago in the South Island of NZ. *Films include:* Ashes 1975, Landfall 1975, Sleeping Dogs 1977, The Journalist 1979, Just Out of Reach 1979, My Brilliant Career 1979, The Final Conflict (Omen III) 1981, Possession 1981, Attack Force Z 1982, From a Far Country, Enigma 1983, Le Sang des Autres 1984, Robbery Under Arms 1985, Plenty 1985, For Love Alone 1986, Peter Kenna's The Good Wife 1987, A Cry in the Dark 1988, Dead Calm 1989, La révolution française 1989, The Hunt for Red October 1990, Shadow of China 1990, Death in Brunswick 1990, Until the End of the World 1991, Memoirs of an Invisible Man 1992, Hostage 1992, The Piano 1993, Jurassic Park 1993, Sirens 1993, Country Life 1994, The Jungle Book 1994, In the Mouth of Madness 1994, Restoration 1995, Children of the Revolution 1996, Victory 1996, Snow White: A Tale of Terror 1997, Event Horizon 1997, The Horse Whisperer 1998, The Revengers' Comedies 1998, Molokai: The Story of Father Damien 1999, Bicentennial Man 1999, My Mother Frank 2000, The Dish 2000, The Magic Pudding (voice) 2000, Jurassic Park III 2001, The Zookeeper 2001, Dirty Deeds 2002, Perfect Strangers 2003, Yes 2004, Wimbledon 2004, Little Fish 2005, Irresistible 2006, Angel 2007, My Talks with Dean Spanley 2008, Skin 2008, In Her Skin 2009, Under The Mountain 2009, Daybreakers 2009, Legend of the Guardians: The Owls of Ga'Hoole (voice) 2010, The Dragon Pearl 2011, The Hunter 2011, The Vow 2012, Escape Plan 2013, Mariah Mundi and the Midas Box 2013, A Long Way Down 2014, The Daughter 2015, Hunt for the Wilderpeople 2016, Thor: Ragnarok 2017, Peter Rabbit 2018. *Television includes:* Lucinda Brayford (series) 1980, Young Ramsay (series) 1980, The Sullivans (series) 1980, Ivanhoe (film) 1982, Reilly: Ace of Spies (mini-series) 1983, The Country Girls (film) 1984, Kane and Abel (mini-series) 1985, Strong Medicine (film) 1986, Amerika (mini-series) 1987, Leap of Faith (film) 1988, Fever (film) 1991, One Against the Wind (film) 1991, Family Pictures (film) 1993, The Rainbow Warrior (film) 1993, The Simpsons (series) 1994, In Cold Blood (film) 1996, Merlin (mini-series) 1998, The Games (series) 1998, Sally Hemings: An American Scandal (film) 2000, Submerged (film) 2001, Framed (film) 2002, Dr Zhivago (film) 2002, Stiff (film) 2004, Jessica (film) 2004, To the Ends of the Earth (mini-series) 2005, Mary Bryant (mini-series) 2005, To the Ends of the Earth (mini-series) 2005, Sci Fi Inside: 'The Triangle' (film) 2005, The Triangle (mini-series) 2005, Merlin's Apprentice (mini-series) 2006, Two Twisted (series) 2006, The Tudors (series) 2007, Crusoe (series) 2008–10, Iron Road (mini-series) 2009, Happy Town 2010, Rake (series) 2010, Ice (mini-series) 2011 Alcatraz (series) 2012, Peaky Blinders (series) 2013, Harry (series) 2013, The Ordained (film) 2013, Peaky Blinders (series) 2013–14, Old School 2014, Tutankhamun (mini-series) 2016. *Address:* c/o ICM, 10250 Constellation Boulevard, Los Angeles, CA 90067, USA (office). *Telephone:* (310) 550-4000 (office). *Fax:* (310) 550-4100 (office). *Website:* www.icmtalent.com (office); www.twopaddocks.com.

NEILSON, Kerr, BCom; Australian investment fund manager; b. 1950, Johannesburg, South Africa; m. Judith Neilson (divorced 2015); two c.; ed Univ. of Cape Town; early career as stockbroker in London; with Banker's Trust, SA, moved to Australia to work for Banker's Trust Asset Man. Div. 1984; f. Platinum International Fund 1994, Chief Investment Officer –2013, CEO 1994–2018.

NEIVA TAVARES, Ricardo; Brazilian diplomatist; b. 16 Aug. 1958, Rio de Janeiro; ed Rio Branco Inst., Brasília, École Nationale d'Admin, France, Univ. of Brasília; Asst Chief, Div. of Europe, Ministry of External Relations 1980–83, 1985–86, Second, then First Sec., Embassy in Paris 1986–89, First Sec., Embassy in Tokyo 1989–93, Adviser to Under-Sec.-Gen. of Planning and Econ. Policy, Ministry of External Relations 1993, Adviser to Sec.-Gen. Dir 1993–95, Counsellor, Perm. Mission to UN, New York 1995–98, Counsellor, Dir in Canberra 1998–2001, Co-ordinator-Gen. of Econ. Orgs 2001–03, Dir of Press and Spokesman for Minister of State 2003–06, Special Adviser to Minister of State for Foreign Affairs 2006–08, Amb., Perm. Mission to EU, Brussels 2008–13, to Italy 2013–16; apptd Perm. Rep. to UN, Vienna 2016–18; Grand Cross, Ordine di Rio Branco; Grand Officer, Ordine al Merito Militare, Ordine al Merito Navale, Ordine al Merito Aeronautico; Alta Distinzione, Ordine al Merito Giudiziario Militare; Medaglia del Pacificatore; Grand Officer, Order of Orange Nassau (Netherlands); Commdr, Royal Order of Merit (Norway); Commdr, Ordine Al Alaoui (Morocco); Chevalier, Légion d'honneur, Ordre nat. du Mérite. *Publication:* As Organizações Não-Governamentais nas Nações Unidas 1999.

NEJAD-HOSSEINIAN, Seyed Mohammad Hadi, MS, PhD; Iranian diplomatist and politician; b. 2 Jan. 1947, Karbala; s. of Hossein Nejad Hosseinian and Razie Haj Tarkhani; m. Fatemeh Tadbir; two s. two d.; ed Tehran Univ., George Washington Univ., USA; Adviser to Deputy Prime Minister 1979–81; Deputy Minister, Plan and Budget Org. 1981; Minister for Roads and Transportation 1981–85; Deputy Minister of Oil 1985–89, 1994–97, 2002–07; Minister for Heavy Industry 1989–94; Amb. and Perm. Rep. to UN, New York 1997–2002; Sec.-Gen. Asian Parl. Ass. 2007–17. *Publications:* International Business, Environments and Operations (2 vols, trans. from English), Dolate Dolatgera: Challenges and Road Map for the Next Government, Competition among Dolat abad and Mardom shar.

NEKIPELOV, Alexander Dmitriyevich, DrEcon; Russian economist, academic and business executive; *Director, Moscow School of Economics, Lomonosov Moscow State University;* b. 16 Nov. 1951, Moscow; m. Elena Nekipelova; one d.; ed Moscow State Univ.; jr researcher, sr researcher, Head of Sector, Deputy Dir, Inst. of Int. Econ. and Political Studies, Russian Acad. of Sciences 1973–98, Dir 1998–; Dir Moscow School of Econs, Lomonosov Moscow State Univ. 2004–; mem. Russian Acad. of Sciences 1997–, Vice-Pres. 2001–; Ind. Dir, Rosneft from 2006–15, Deputy Chair. April–June 2011, Chair. June 2011–15; mem. Bd of Dirs, OJSC Zarubezhneft, OJSC AK Transneft; Co-Chair. Bd of Trustees Nat. Investment

Council; Medal of Order for Service to Motherland, and other state awards. *Publications:* four scientific works and more than 200 academic papers published in Russia and abroad, including monograph Essays on Economics of Postcommunism 1996, The General Theory of Market Economy 2017. *Leisure interest:* chess. *Address:* Moscow School of Economics, 119992 Moscow, 1, Building 61, Leninskie Gory, M.V. Lomonosov MSU, Russia (office). *Telephone:* (495) 510-52-67 (office). *E-mail:* mail@mse-msu.ru (office). *Website:* www.mse-msu.ru (office).

NEKVASIL, Lt-Gen. (retd) Jiří, MSc; Czech army officer (retd) and diplomatist; b. 24 April 1948, Benešov; m. 1st Jaroslava Papeová; m. 2nd Danuše Kadlečková; two s. three d.; m. 3rd Nanuli Kobaladze; two s. three d.; ed Tech. Inst. Liptovský Mikuláš, Mil. Acad., Kalinin, Acad. of Gen. Staff of Mil. Forces, Moscow, NATO Defence Coll., Rome; Second in Command, Czech AF and Anti-Air Defence System 1990–92, Commdr of Gen. Staff 1993–98, Adviser to Ministry of Defence 1998–99; Amb. to Georgia 2000–04, to Mongolia 2004–07, to Afghanistan 2007–10; Order of Red Star (Czechoslovakia) 1985, Commdr, Legion of Merit 1996, Legion d'honneur 1996, Bundeswehr Gold Cross (Germany) 1998, Gold Cross (Austria) 1998. *Leisure interests:* mushrooming, tennis, gardening, photography.

NELIDOV, Andrey Vitalievich, DEcon, PhD; Russian engineer and politician; b. 12 June 1957, Leningrad (now St Petersburg); ed Leningrad Inst. of Water Transportation; Soviet Army service 1978–80; Equipment Engineer, Deputy Chief of Procurement Dept, Leningrad Experimental Research Plant, Leningrad Inst. of Water Transportation 1980–85; Sr Engineer, Housing Services Enterprises, Petrograd Dist Housing Admin 1985–88; car mechanic, Leningrad 1988–89; Marketing Dir and Dir-Gen., Nord-Kemp Co. (scientific mfr), later Deputy Dir-Gen. for Forestry, Nord-Kemp Jt Stock Co. 1989–96, Chair. Bd of Dirs Aug.–Oct. 1999; Chair. Timber Processing Complex Cttee, St Petersburg 1996–99; Chair. Lesnaya Birzha (timber yard), St Petersburg 1999–2000; Dir-Gen. White Sea Onego Shipping Co. Inc., Petrozavodsk 2000–02; mem. St Petersburg Region Legis. Ass. 2002–04, Vice-Chair. 2004–06; Repub. of Karelia Rep. to Russian Fed. Ass., Moscow and mem. Council 2006–10; Pres. Repub. of Karelia 2010–12 (resgnd); Order of Honour 2007, Council of Russian Fed. 15 Year Medal 2008, 300 Years of Russian Navy Jubilee Medal 1996, Letter of Award of Federal Ass. of the Russian Fed. 2010.

NELISSEN, Roelof J., MA; Dutch politician and banker; b. 4 April 1931, Hoofdplaat, Zeeland Prov.; m. A. M. van der Kelen; three s. one d.; ed grammar school at Dongen and Faculty of Law, Catholic Univ. of Nijmegen; various posts in employers' asscns, Amsterdam and The Hague 1956–69; mem. Second Chamber, States-Gen. (Parl.) 1963–70; Minister of Econ. Affairs 1970–71; First Deputy Prime Minister, Minister of Finance 1971–73; mem. Bd of Man. Dirs Amsterdam-Rotterdam Bank NV 1974–, Vice-Chair. 1979–82, Chair. 1983–92; Chair. Bd of Man. Dirs ABN-AMRO Holding NV 1990–92; Commdr, Order of Orange-Nassau 1973. *Address:* PO Box 552, 1250 AN Laren, Netherlands.

NELLIGAN, Kate; Canadian actress; b. (Patricia Colleen Nelligan), 16 March 1950, London, Ont.; d. of Patrick Joseph Nelligan and Alice Nelligan (née Dier); m. Robert Reale 1989 (divorced); one s.; ed St Martin's Catholic School, London, Ont., York Univ., Toronto and Cen. School of Speech and Drama, London, UK; professional stage debut as Corrie in Barefoot in the Park, Little Theatre, Bristol 1972; other parts there and at Theatre Royal for Bristol Old Vic 1972–73 include: Hypatia in Misalliance, Stella Kowalski in A Streetcar Named Desire, Pegeen Mike in The Playboy of the Western World, Grace Harkaway in London Assurance, title role in Lulu, Sybil Chase in Private Lives; London debut as Jenny in Knuckle, Comedy Theatre 1974; joined Nat. Theatre Co. at Old Vic 1975 to play Ellie Dunn in Heartbreak House, also in Plenty and Moon for the Misbegotten 1984; As You Like It for RSC, Stratford; Serious Money, Broadway 1988, Spoils of War 1988, Eleni; Evening Standard Best Actress Award 1978. *Films include:* The Count of Monte Cristo, The Romantic Englishwoman 1975, Dracula 1979, Mr. Patman 1980, Agent 1980, Eye of the Needle 1981, Without a Trace 1983, Eleni 1985, Il Giorno prima 1987, White Room 1990, The Prince of Tides 1991, Frankie and Johnny (BAFTA Award for Best Actress in a Supporting Role 1991) 1991, Shadows and Fog 1992, Fatal Instinct 1993, Wolf 1994, Margaret's Museum (Genie Award for Best Actress in a Supporting Role) 1995, How to Make An American Quilt 1995, Up Close and Personal 1996, U.S. Marshals 1998, Stolen Moments (voice), Boy Meets Girl 1998, The Cider House Rules 1999, Blessed Stranger 2000, Premonition 2007. *Television includes:* The Onedin Line (series) 1971, The Arcata Promise 1974, Count of Monte Cristo 1975, The Lady of the Camellias 1976, Bethune 1977, Measure for Measure 1979, Licking Hitler, Thérèse Raquin (mini-series) 1980, Forgive Our Foolish Ways 1980, Victims 1982, Kojak: The Price of Justice 1987, Love and Hate: The Story of Colin and Joanne Thatcher 1989, Golden Fiddles (mini-series) 1990, Three Hotels 1991, Old Times 1991, Terror Stalks the Class Reunion 1992, The Diamond Fleece (Gemini Award for Best Actress in a Dramatic Program or Mini-Series 1993) 1992, Liar, Liar 1992; Shattered Trust: The Shari Karney Story 1993, Spoils of War 1994, Million Dollar Babes 1994, A Mother's Prayer 1995, Captive Heart: The James Mink Story 1996, Calm at Sunset 1996, Love is Strange 1999, Swing Vote 1999, Blessed Stranger: After Flight 111 2000, Walter and Henry 2001, A Wrinkle in Time (mini-series) 2003, Human Cargo (mini-series) 2004, In From the Night 2005, Eleventh Hour 2008, Law & Order: Special Victims Unit 2010. *Leisure interests:* reading, cooking. *Address:* c/o Innovative Artists, 235 Park Avenue South, Suite 7, New York, NY 10003, USA. *Telephone:* (212) 253-6900.

NELSON, Bill, JD; American politician; b. 29 Sept. 1942, Miami, Fla; s. of C. W. Nelson and Nannie Nelson; m. Grace H. Cavert 1972; one s. one d.; ed Yale Univ., Univ. of Virginia; served with US Army Reserves 1965–75, US Army 1968–71, attained rank of Capt.; admitted to the Bar, Fla; pvt. law practice, Melbourne, Fla 1970–79; mem. Fla House of Reps 1972–78; mem. US House of Reps, Washington, DC 1979–91, Chair. Space Sub-cttee of Science, Space and Tech. Cttee (flew with crew on 24th flight of NASA Space Shuttle); Fla State Treas., Insurance Commr and Fire Marshall, 1995–2000; Senator from Florida 2001–19, mem. Commerce, Budget and Finance Cttee, Intelligence Cttee, Aging Cttee. *Address:* c/o 716 Hart Senate Building, Washington, DC 20510, USA (office).

NELSON, Brendan, AO; Australian diplomatist, physician and politician; *Director, Australian War Memorial;* b. 19 Aug. 1958, Melbourne; m. Gillian Nelson; three c.; ed Flinders Univ.; Gen. Practitioner, Hobart, Tasmania 1985–95;

Dir Hobart and Launceston After Hours Medical Services 1987–91; Tasmanian State Pres. Australian Medical Asscn 1990–92, Fed. Vice-Pres. 1991–93, Fed. Pres. 1993–95; MP for Bradfield (Liberal) 1996–2009, Chair. House of Reps Standing Cttee on Employment, Educ. and Workplace Relations 1998; Chair. Sydney Airport Community Forum –2000; Parl. Sec. to Minister for Defence 2000–01; Minister for Educ., Science and Training 2001–06, for Defence 2006–07; Fed. Parl. Leader, Liberal Party of Australia 2007–08; Amb. to Belgium, Luxembourg, the EU and NATO 2010–12; Dir Australian War Memorial 2012–; Amb. for Legacy Australia, Invictus Games for disabled veterans, Soldier On, Defence Reserve Forces Council; mem. Advisory Bd Australian Genome Project; Fellow Royal Soc. of NSW 2017–; Patron Lifeline ACT, Trish MS Research, Weary Dunlop Foundation; Hon. Fellow, Royal Australasian RACP, Hon. Life Membership, Returned and Services League of Australia NSW Branch; Dr hc (Flinders Univ.) 2011, (Australian Nat. Univ.) 2017; AMA Gold Medal for Distinguished Service to Medicine and Humanity 1995, Sydney Univ. John Lowenthal Medal, Paul Harris Fellow, Distinguished Research Fellow, Australian Nat. Univ. *Leisure interests:* music, motorcycles, tennis. *Address:* Australian War Memorial, GPO Box 345, Canberra ACT 2601, Australia (office). *Telephone:* (2) 6243-4211 (office). *E-mail:* brendan.nelson@awm.gov.au (office). *Website:* www.awm.gov.au (office).

NELSON, David Daniel, BA, MA; American diplomatist and business executive; *Senior Manager, Global Government Affairs and Policy, General Electric Company;* b. 1956, Minn.; m. Gloria Nelson; one s.; ed Univ. of Wisconsin, Univ. of Maryland; has served in various Foreign Service positions including Jr Political Officer, Embassy in Montevideo 1982–84, Econ. Officer, Embassy in Quito 1987–89, Embassy in Bonn 1990–93, Dir Office of Monetary Affairs, Bureau of Econ., Energy and Business Affairs 1997–2000, Minister Counselor for Econs, Embassy in Berlin 2001–03, Sr Co-ordinator, Sea Island G-8 Summit 2003–04, Dir Office of Terrorism Finance and Sanctions 2004–07, Exec. Asst to Under-Sec. for Econs 2007–08, Prin. Deputy Asst Sec. of State, Econ., Energy and Business Affairs 2008, Acting Asst Sec. 2009, Amb. to Uruguay 2010–11, fmr Dir Iraq Reconstruction Task Force; Sr Man., Global Govt Affairs and Policy, General Electric Co. 2011–. *Address:* General Electric Company, 1299 Pennsylvania Avenue, NW, Suite 1100, Washington, DC 20004-2407, USA (office). *Website:* www .ge.com (office).

NELSON, E. Benjamin (Ben), MA, JD; American lawyer, organization executive and fmr politician; b. 17 May 1941, McCook, Neb.; s. of Benjamin E. Nelson and Birdella Nelson; m. Diane Nelson (née Gleason); two s. two d. (one deceased) from previous m.; one step-s. one step-d.; ed Univ. of Nebraska; Instructor, Dept of Philosophy, Univ. of Neb. 1963–65; Dir of Compliance Neb. Dept of Insurance 1965–72, Dir 1975–76; admitted to Neb. Bar 1970; Gen. Counsel, Cen. Nat. Insurance Group of Omaha 1972–74, Exec. Vice-Pres. 1977, Pres. 1978–79, Pres. and CEO 1980–81; Exec. Vice-Pres. Nat. Asscn of Insurance Commrs 1982–85, CEO 2013–16; Attorney of Counsel, Kennedy, Holland DeLacy and Svoboda, Omaha 1985–90; Gov. of Nebraska 1990–99; Senator from Nebraska 2001–13 (retd), mem. Agric., Nutrition and Forestry, Armed Services Cttee, Appropriations Cttee, Rules and Admin Cttee; mem. of Counsel Lumson, Dugan and Murray 1999; Chair. Nat. Educ. Goals Panel 1992–94, Govs Ethanol Coalition (also f.) 1991, 1994, Midwestern Govs Conf. 1994; fmr Chair. Interstate Oil and Gas Compact Comm., Western Govs Asscn and Co-Lead Gov. on Int. Trade; Pres. Council of State Govts 1994; Chair. Nat. Resources Cttee and Co-Lead Gov. on Federalism, Nat. Govs Asscn; Co-Chair. Nat. Summit on Federalism 1995; fmr Vice-Chair. Democratic Govs Asscn; Democrat; Hon. LLD (Creighton Univ.) 1992, (Peru State Coll.) 1993; Hon. DHumLitt (Coll. of St Mary) 1995; numerous awards. *Leisure interests:* spending time with my family, hunting and fishing, reading and collecting clocks.

NELSON, Jennifer (Jenny), BA, PhD, FRS; Irish physicist and academic; *Professor of Physics, Imperial College London;* ed Univs of Cambridge and Bristol, UK; Greenpeace Research Fellowship, Imperial Coll. London, UK 1989–92, 1996–97, EPSRC Advanced Research Fellowship 1997–2003, Prof. of Physics 2006–; Industry Fellowship, Royal Soc. 2010–13; External Sr Fellowship, Freiburg Inst. for Advanced Studies 2011–12; Joule Prize and Medal, Inst. of Physics 2009, Wolfson Merit Award, Royal Soc. 2010, Armourers and Brasiers' Co. Prize and Medal, Royal Soc. 2012, Faraday Medal and Prize, Inst. of Physics 2016. *Publications:* The Physics of Solar Cells 2003; several book chapters and more than 200 papers in peer-reviewed journals. *Address:* Room H/1007, EXSS General Section, Department of Physics, Faculty of Natural Sciences, Imperial College, 10th Floor, Huxley Building, South Kensington Campus, London, SW7 2BB, England (office). *Telephone:* (20) 7594-7581 (office). *E-mail:* jenny.nelson@imperial .ac.uk (office). *Website:* www.imperial.ac.uk/physics (office).

NELSON, John Frederick, CBE, FCA (ACA); British chartered accountant and banking executive; b. 26 July 1947; s. of George Frederick Nelson and Betty Violet Roddick; m. Caroline Vivien Hannam 1976; two s. one d.; qualified as a chartered accountant 1970; with Kleinwort Benson 1971–86, worked in UK and USA, Vice-Pres. 1973–75, mem. Bd of Dirs 1980–86; joined Lazard Brothers 1986, Man. Dir 1986–98, ran Corp. Finance Div. 1986–99, Vice-Chair. 1990–99, also Chair. Lazard SpA, Italy and Man. Dir Lazard Freres, New York; Chair. Credit Suisse First Boston Europe 1999–2002; Deputy Chair. Kingfisher plc 2002–11; Chair. Lloyd's 2011–17; Dir (non-exec.) Woolwich plc 1998–2000, BT Group 2002–08, Hammerson plc 2004–13 (Chair. (non-exec.) 2005–13), JP Morgan Cazenove and Cazenove Group 2008–10; Chair. London Investment Banking Asscn 2001–02; Sr Adviser, Charterhouse Capital Partners LLP 2006–; Dir ENO 2002–10; Trustee, Nat. Gallery 2010–. *Leisure interests:* sailing, opera.

NELSON, M. Bruce, BBA; American business executive; b. 1945; m. La Vaun Nelson; one s. one d.; ed Idaho State Univ.; man. positions with Boise Cascade, BT Office Products USA; Pres. and CEO Viking Inc. –1998; Pres. and CEO Viking Office Products (following merger of Viking and Office Depot 1998) 1998–2000, Pres. Office Depot International Inc. 1998–2000, CEO Office Depot Inc. 2000–04 (resgnd); mem. Advisory Council Idaho State Univ., Exec.-in-Residence 2001; Distinguished Alumnus Award, Idaho State Univ. 2001; Entrepreneur Business Leader of the Year, Florida Atlantic Univ. 2001.

NELSON, Marilyn Carlson; American business executive; *Chairman, Carlson Companies;* b. 1939, Minneapolis, Minn.; m. Glen Nelson; ed Smith Coll., Mass,

Univ. of Paris (Sorbornne), France, Inst. des Hautes Etudes Economiques Politiques, Geneva, Switzerland; began career as Securities Analyst with PaineWebber; Dir of Community Relations, Carlson Co. Inc. 1968–88, Sr Vice-Pres. 1989–91, COO 1997–2003, Chair. and CEO 1998–2008, Chair. 2008–; Co-founder and mem. Minn. Women's Econ. Roundtable 1974–; mem. Bd of Dirs First Bank System 1978–97, Nat. Tourism Org. 1996–98, Exxon Mobil Corpn 1991–, US West Inc., Singapore Tourism Bureau 1999–, Travel Industry Asscn of America 2000–09, Juran Center for Leadership in Quality 1999–2005, Univ. of Minnesota Foundation 1999–; Chair. Nat. Women's Business Council 2002–05, Pres.'s Cttee on Trade and Industry 2002, Scandinavia Today celebration in USA; Co-Chair. Annual Meeting, Davos, Switzerland 2004, US Travel Advisory Bd; mem. Bd of Dirs Mayo Clinic 2001–, Chair. 2010–; mem. Minn. Orchestral Asscn 1972–, Business Roundtable, Int. Business Council, World Travel and Tourism Council, World Econ. Forum 2000–; Bd mem. Cttee Encouraging Corp. Philanthropy 2004–, Overseers Curtis L. Carlson School of Man. 1999–; Del., White House Conf. on Tourism 1996, Kennedy Center for Performing Arts 2009–; Distinguished Visiting Prof., Johnson & Wales Univ.; Leader Gov.'s Task Force to bring 1992 Super Bowl to Minnesota; fmr Pres. United Way of Minneapolis; fmr Chair. New Sweden '88; fmr Bd mem. United Way of America 1984–90; Chavalier, Légion d'honneur, Royal Order of the North Star (First Class) (Sweden), Order of the White Rose (Finland), Commdr, Royal Norwegian Order of Merit; Hon. DBA (Johnson & Wales Univ.); Hon. DHumLitt (Coll. of St Catherine), (Gustavus Adolphus Coll.); Hon. DJur (Univ. of Minnesota); Outstanding Business Leader 1996, ranked by Travel Agent magazine as The Most Powerful Woman in Travel 1997–2004, Woodrow Wilson Award for Corp. Citizenship, Woodrow Wilson Int. Center 2000, Penn State Hotel and Restaurant Soc. Hospitality Exec. of the Year 2000, FIRST magazine Responsible Capitalism Award, London, UK 2001, Businesswoman of the World, Business Women's Network 2001, American Hotel & Lodging Asscn Cutting Edge Award 2001, Int. Hotel Investment Forum Lifetime Achievement Award, Berlin, Germany 2002, Great Swedish Heritage Award, Swedish Council of America 2002, inducted into Travel Industry Asscn of America's Hall of Fame 2003, inducted into Sales and Marketing Execs Int. Hall of Fame 2003, Swedish-American of the Year, King Carl XVI Gustaf and Queen Silvia of Sweden 2003, Businesswoman of the Year, US Commerce Dept's Small Business Admin 2005, 18th Annual Lucia Trade Award, Swedish-American Chamber of Commerce 2005, UN.GIFT/End Human Trafficking Now! Business Leader Award 2010. *Address:* Carlson Companies, 701 Carlson Parkway, Minnetonka, MN 55305-8212, USA (office). *Telephone:* (763) 212-1272 (office). *Fax:* (763) 212-2219 (office). *E-mail:* mnelson@carlson.com (office). *Website:* www.carlson.com (office).

NELSON, Ronald (Ron) L., BA, MBA; American car rental industry executive; *Executive Chairman, Avis Budget Group, Inc.;* ed Univ. of California, Berkeley, Univ. of California, Los Angeles; Exec. Vice-Pres., Chief Financial Officer and mem. Bd of Dirs, Paramount Communications, Inc. (fmrly Gulf & Western Industries, Inc.) 1987–94; Co-COO DreamWorks SKG 1994–2003; Pres., Chief Financial Officer and mem. Bd of Dirs, Cendant Corpn 2003–06, Chair. and CEO Avis Budget Group, Inc. (formed after Cendant separated into four ind. businesses in 2006) 2006–15, Exec. Chair. 2015–; mem. Bd of Dirs Convergys Corpn 2008–, Hanesbrands Inc. 2008–; Warren Bennis Award for Excellence in Leadership 2013. *Address:* Avis Budget Group Inc., 6 Sylvan Way, Parsippany, NJ 07054, USA (office). *Telephone:* (973) 496-3500 (office). *Fax:* (888) 304-2315 (office). *Website:* www.avisbudgetgroup.com (office).

NELSON, Willie Hugh; American country and western singer, musician and songwriter; b. 30 April 1933, Abbott, Tex.; m. Annie Marie Nelson; three s. four d.; ed Baylor Univ.; fmr salesman, announcer, host and DJ, country music shows in Tex.; bass player, Ray Price's band; formed own band; appearances at Grand Ole Opry, Nashville and throughout USA 1964–; tours to NZ, Australia, USA, Canada, Europe, Japan; annual Fourth of July picnics throughout USA 1972–; performed with Frank Sinatra, Neil Young, Dolly Parton, Linda Ronstadt, ZZ Top, Waylon Jennings, Ray Charles, Santana, Joni Mitchell, Kris Kristofferson, Bob Dylan, Patsy Cline; six Grammy (NARAS) Awards, eight CMA Awards, Nashville Songwriters' Asscn Hall of Fame 1973, Nat. Acad. of Popular Music Lifetime Achievement Award 1983, three ACM Awards, Tex Ritter Songwriting Award (with Kris Kristofferson) 1984. *Film appearances:* Electric Horseman 1980, Honeysuckle Rose 1980. *Compositions include:* Crazy (performed by Patsy Cline), Hello Walls (performed by Faron Young). *Recordings include:* albums: The Sound In Your Mind 1976, The Troublemaker 1976, Willie Nelson and His Friends 1976, To Lefty From Willie 1977, Willie Before His Time 1978, Wanted/The Outlaw 1978, The Willie Way 1978, Stardust 1978, One For The Road 1979, Willie And Family Live 1979, Pretty Paper 1979, Willie Sings Kristofferson 1979, San Antonio Rose 1980, Honeysuckle Rose 1980, Family Bible 1980, Tougher Than Leather 1983, City Of New Orleans 1984, Me And Paul 1985, Highwayman 1985, The Promised Land 1986, Partners 1986, Island In The Sea 1987, Seashores Of Old Mexico 1987, What A Wonderful World 1988, A Horse Called Music 1989, Highwayman II 1990, Born For Trouble 1990, Clean Shirt Waylon And Willie 1991, Across The Borderline 1993, Six Hours At Pedernales 1994, Healing Hands Of Time 1994, Just One Love 1995, Spirit 1996, How Great Thou Art 1996, Christmas With Willie Nelson 1997, Hill Country Christmas 1997, Teatro 1998, Nashville Was The Roughest 1998, Night And Day 1999, Forever Gold 2000, Me And The Drummer 2000, Milk Cow Blues 2000, Rainbow Connection 2001, Joy 2001, The Great Divide 2002, All The Songs I've Loved Before 2002, Crazy: The Demo Sessions 2003, Picture In A Frame (with Kimmie Rhodes) 2003, It Always Will Be 2004, Countryman 2005, Songbird 2006, Last Of The Breed (with Merle Haggard and Ray Price) 2007, Moment Of Forever 2008, Two Men With The Blues (with Wynton Marsalis) 2008, Willie And The Wheel (with Asleep at the Wheel) 2009, American Classic 2009, Country Music 2010, Remember Me Volume 1 2011, Heroes 2012, Let's Face the Music and Dance 2013, To All the Girls... 2013, Band of Brothers 2014, December Day 2014, Summertime: Willie Nelson Sings Gershwin (Grammy Award for Best Traditional Pop Vocal Album 2017) 2016, For the Good Times: A Tribute to Ray Price 2016, God's Problem Child 2017, My Way (Grammy Award for Best Traditional Pop Vocal Album 2019) 2018. *Address:* c/o Mark Rothbaum and Associates Inc., PO Box 2689, Danbury, CT 06813-2689, USA (office); 12400 St Hwy 71 West, Suite 350, Austin, TX 78738, USA. *Telephone:* (203) 792-2400 (office). *E-mail:* info@willienelson.com. *Website:* www.willienelson.com.

NELSONS, Andris; Latvian conductor; *Music Director, Boston Symphony Orchestra;* b. 18 Nov. 1978, Rīga; s. of Irēna Nelsone; m. Kristine Opolais (q.v.) 2011 (divorced 2018); one d.; ed Emils Darzins Music School, Latvian Acad. of Music, St Petersburg Conservatory, Russia, pvt study with Mariss Jansons, master-classes with Neeme Järvi and Jorma Panula; began career as trumpeter with Latvian Nat. Opera Orchestra; Asst Conductor Latvian Nat. Opera 2001–03, Prin. Conductor 2003–07; Prin. Conductor, Nordwestdeutsche Philharmonie, Herford 2003–08; Music Dir City of Birmingham Symphony Orchestra 2008–15, Boston Symphony Orchestra 2014–; Chief Conductor, Gewandhaus-orchester Leipzig 2015–, Music Dir-Desig. 2017, Music Dir 2018–; regular guest appearances with Berliner Philharmoniker, Wiener Philharmoniker, Het Koninklijk Concertgebouworkest, Symphonieorchester des Bayerischen Rundfunks and Philharmonia Orchestra; regular guest at Royal Opera House Covent Garden, Wiener Staatsoper and the Metropolitan Opera New York; Latvian Grand Music Award 2001, Preis der deutschen Schallplattenkritik, ECHO Klassik as Conductor of the Year, Int. Shostakovich Days Annual Award 2019. *Recordings include:* Strauss, Also sprach Zarathustra, Don Juan, Till Eulenspiegels lustige Streiche with City of Birmingham Symphony Orchestra, Wagner, Overture to Tannhäuser, Sibelius Symphony No. 2 with Boston Symphony Orchestra, Wagner, Der fliegende Holländer with Concertgebouw Orkest 2015, Shostakovich: Under Stalin's Shadow: Symphony No. 10 (Grammy Award for Best Orchestral Performance 2015) 2015, Tchaikovsky: Slavonic March, Manfred Symphony 2015, Abrahamsen: Let Me Tell You 2016, Dvorak & Schumann: Piano Concertos 2016, Strauss: Oboe Concerto 2017, Wagner: Lohengrin 2018, Shostakovich: Symphonies Nos 4 & 11 (Grammy Award for Best Orchestral Performance 2019) 2018, Shostakovich Under Stalin's Shadow: Symphonies Nos 6 & 7 2019. *Address:* c/o Karen McDonald, KD SHMID, 40 St Martin's Lane, London, WC2N 4ER, England (office). *Telephone:* (20) 7395-0915 (office). *Fax:* (20) 7395-0911 (office). *E-mail:* karen.mcdonald@kdschmid.co.uk (office). *Website:* www.kdschmid.de (office); www.bso.org; www.gewandhausorchester.de; www.andrisnelsons.com.

NEMBANG, Subas Chandra, BA, BL; Nepalese barrister and politician; b. 11 March 1953; m.; fmr Minister of Law, Justice and Parl. Affairs; fmr mem. Standing Cttee; Leader of Communist Party of Nepal (Unified Marxist-Leninist—UML), mem. Cen. Cttee; Sr Most Advocate, Supreme Court of Nepal; Speaker of the Interim Parl. ('Legislature-Parl.') –2008, Chair. Security Special Cttee, House of Reps Proclamation Implementation Special Cttee, Business Man. Advisory Cttee, Chair. Constituent Ass. (Speaker) 2008–12, 2014–15, Deputy Leader UML Parl. Party 2016–. *Address:* Constituent Assembly, Singh Durbar, Kathmandu, Nepal (office). *Telephone:* (1) 4200159 (office). *Fax:* (1) 4222923 (office). *E-mail:* info@can.gov.np (office); nepal.ipu@can.gov.np (office). *Website:* www.can.gov.np (office).

NĚMCOVÁ, Miroslava; Czech politician; *Leader, Civic Democratic Party;* b. 17 Nov. 1952, Nové Město na Moravě; m. Vladimír Němec; one s.; ed Secondary Agricultural and Technical School, Havlíčkův Brod; officer, Czech Statistical Office 1972–92; bookshop owner in Žďár nad Sázavou 1992–2007; mem. Civic Democratic Party (Občanská demokratická strana—ODS) 2010–12, fmr Deputy Chair., Leader 2013–; Alderman in Žďár nad Sázavou 1994–97; fmr mem. Žďár City Council; cand. for office of Deputy, became leader of ODS in Southern Region; mem. Chamber of Deputies for Highlands (Vysočina) 1998–2010, for Prague 2013–, Chair. (Speaker) 2010–13. *Leisure interests:* literature, film, music, art, flowers, travelling. *Address:* Civic Democratic Party (Občanská demokratická strana), Truhlářská 1106/9, 110 00 Prague 1 (office); Poslanecká sněmovna (Chamber of Deputies), Sněmovní 4, 118 26 Prague 1 (office); Constituency Office, Doudlebska 1699/5, 140 00 Prague 4, Czech Republic. *Telephone:* (2) 34707111 (office). *Fax:* (2) 34707103 (office). *E-mail:* hk@ods.cz (office); miroslava.nemcova@ods.cz (office); nemcovam@psp.cz (office). *Website:* www.ods.cz (office); www.psp.cz (office); www.miroslavanemcova.cz.

NÉMETH, János, PhD Habil.; Hungarian academic and lawyer; b. 31 July 1933, Újpest; s. of János Németh and Erzsébet Németh (née Nemes); m. Izabella Vass 1959, two d.; ed Eötvös Loránd Univ. of Budapest; jr legal official in law firm 1957, teacher at Dept of Civil Procedural Law at Eötvös Loránd Univ. 1957–2003, Vice-Chancellor 1993–97, Head of Dept and Prof. 1994–2003, Prof. Emer. 2004–; Ed. Hungarian Law (journal) 1991–; Chief Ed. Pres. Comm. for Hungarian Lawyers Asscn 1991–; Chair. Editorial Bd European Law (review) 2001–, JogOk (Lawyer's Training) 2005–06; mem. of Nat. Legal Comm. of Hungarian Acad. of Sciences, Nat. Legal Cttee of Experts for Doctorates at Hungarian Acad. of Sciences 2005–08; Sr Partner Békés-Németh-Vékás and Co. law firm 1986–; Chair. of Nat. Electoral Cttee 1990–97; judge, Constitutional Court of Hungary 1997–98, Pres. 1998–2003; Arbitrator, Arbitration Court attached to Hungarian Chamber of Commerce and Industry; Cross of Honours with Spurs of Hungarian Repub. 1995, Order of the Rising Sun (Japan) 2002, Grand Cross of Honours of Hungarian Repub. 2003, Grand Gold Honours on Sash for Service to Repub. of Austria 2004. *Publications:* more than 100 legal publs. *Leisure interest:* hunting. *Address:* ELTE Polgári Eljárásjogi Tanszék, 1053 Budapest, Egyetem tér 1–3 (office); Brassó köz 8, 1112 Budapest, Hungary (home). *Telephone:* (1) 411-6522 (office). *Fax:* (1) 411-6522 (office). *E-mail:* nemethj@ajk.elte.hu (office).

NÉMETH, Miklós; Hungarian politician; b. 24 Jan. 1948, Monok; s. of András Németh and Margit Németh (née Stajz); m. Erzsébet Szilágyi 1971; two s.; ed Karl Marx Univ. of Budapest; Lecturer in Political Economy, Karl Marx Univ. 1971–77; Deputy Section Head, Nat. Planning Office 1977–81; worked on staff, later as deputy leader, of HSWP Cen. Cttee Dept of Political Economy, Dept Leader 1987–88; mem. of Cen. Cttee, Secr. 1987–88; mem. Political Cttee 1987–88; mem. Parl. 1988–90; Prime Minister of Hungary 1988–90; apptd to four-mem. Presidium of HSWP 1989; mem. Presidium, HSP Oct.–Dec. 1989 (resgnd); Vice-Pres. (Personnel and Admin) EBRD, London, UK 1991–2000. *Leisure interests:* sailing, tennis, classical music.

NEMITSAS, Takis; Cypriot fmr politician, industrialist and business administrator; *President, Takis & Louki Nemitsas Foundation;* b. 2 June 1930, Limassol; s. of Xanthos Nemitsas and Vassiliki Nemitsa; m. 1st Daisy Petrou 1958 (died 1983); three d.; m. 2nd Louki Loucaides 1986; ed English and Commercial courses in Cyprus, courses abroad in business admin and marketing; mem. House of Reps 1976–81; fmr Pres. Parl. Cttee on Commerce and Industry; Minister of Commerce, Industry and Tourism 1988–93; Exec. Chair. and Man. Dir Nemitsas Group 1993–95, Chair. Bd of Dirs 1995–, Pres. Takis & Louki Nemitsas Foundation; fmr mem. Bd Bank of Cyprus, Cyprus Employers' and Industrialists' Fed., Chamber of Commerce and Industry, Cyprus Tourism Org.; Grand Cross of Leopold II (Belgium), Grand Officer Kt of the Order of Merit (Italy). *Publications:* Environmental Policy and the EU, Recycling of Scrap Metal in Cyprus. *Leisure interest:* swimming. *Address:* 159 Leontiou A' Str., Maryvonne Building, Office 104, PO Box 50124, 3601 Limassol (office); Thera Complex, 2 Megalou Alexandrou Str., Pyrgos, 4534 Limassol, Cyprus (home). *Telephone:* (25) 569222 (office); (25) 636844 (home). *Fax:* (25) 569275 (office); (25) 636050 (home). *E-mail:* foundation@nemitsas.org (office). *Website:* www.nemitsasfoundation.org (office).

NEMYRYA, Hryhoriy, BA, PhD; Ukrainian academic and politician; b. 5 April 1960, Donetsk; m.; one s.; ed Donetsk State Univ., Kyiv Shevchenko Univ.; began career as Lecturer, Dept of History, Donetsk State Univ., becoming Head Centre for Political Research 1992–96; Nat. Forum Foundation Fellow, Centre for Strategic and Int. Studies, Washington, DC, USA 1994; Dean, Mohyla Acad., Kiev 1996–98; fmr Deputy Head European Integration Faculty, Nat. Acad. of Public Admin; fmr Head Centre for European and Int. Studies, Shevchenko Univ.; Chair. George Soros Int. Renaissance Foundation, Kyiv 2002; fmr Ed. Noval Bezpeka (New Security); mem. Tymoshenko Bloc, Adviser to Yuliya Tymoshenko 2005–; mem. Verkhovna Rada (Supreme Council, Parl.) 2006–; Deputy Prime Minister for European and Int. Integration 2007–10; mem. Socialist Group, Council of Europe 2006–. *Address:* Verkhovna Rada, Grushevsky 5, 01008 Kyiv, Ukraine (office). *Telephone:* (44) 253-32-17 (office). *Fax:* (44) 253-32-17 (office). *E-mail:* Nemyria.Hrihorii@rada.gov.ua (office). *Website:* www.kmu.gov.ua/control (office).

NENCHEV, Nikolay Nankov, LLM; Bulgarian lawyer and politician; b. 11 Aug. 1966, Yambol; m.; two c.; ed New Bulgarian Univ.; mem. Man. Bd Bulgarian Agrarian Nat. Union 1992, Chair. Bulgarian Agrarian Nat. Union Youth Org. 1994, Chair. Bulgarian Agrarian Nat. Union 2011; Chef de Cabinet of Vice-Pres. Todor Kavaldjiev 1997–2002; Asst Prof., New Bulgarian Univ., Risk Assessment and Security Studies Center 2003; Founder, European Integration Asscn 2006; Lawyer AgoraLaw Firm 2008; mem. Nat. Ass. (parl.) for 17-Plovdiv Okrag 2014–; Minister of Defence 2014–17; mem. Reformatorsky Blok.

NENE, Nhlanhla Musa, BCom; South African economist and politician; b. 5 Dec. 1958; m.; three c.; ed Univ. of Western Cape; active in student politics since 1979; 15 years as Regional Admin. Man., Metropolitan Life Insurance; mem. Nat. Ass. (Parl.) for KwaZulu-Natal 1999–2015, Chair. Jt Budget Cttee; Deputy Minister of Finance 2008–14, Minister of Finance 2014–15, Feb.–Oct. 2018; Chair. Kwangcolosi Child and Family Care 2007–, Ntunjambili Hospital Bd 2013–; Chair. Supervisory Bd, Arise BV –2017; Chair. Bd of Govs, African Devt Bank 2018–; Dir (non-exec.) Allan Gray 2016–; Resident Adviser, Thebe Investment Corpn 2016–; mem. ANC, ANC Local Govt Councillor and Caucus Chair. 1996–99, ANC Regional Sec., Ukhahlamba Region 1997–2000; mem. Devt Cttee, World Bank and IMF 2018–. *Leisure interests:* reading, jogging, tennis.

NEOH, Anthony Francis, LLB, QC, JP; Chinese lawyer; b. 9 Nov. 1946, Hong Kong; ed Univ. of London, UK; teacher 1964–66; Hong Kong Civil Service 1966–79; pvt. practice, Hong Kong Bar 1979–95, Calif. Bar 1984–95; Hong Kong public service in educ., health etc. 1985–; Chair. Securities and Futures Comm., Hong Kong 1995–98; mem. Hong Kong SAR Basic Law Cttee 1997–2008; People's Repub. of China public service in teaching, Govt advisory work etc., including Chief Adviser to China Securities Regulatory Comm. 1998–2004; Visiting Scholar, Harvard Univ., USA 1990–91; Chair. IOSCO Tech. Cttee 1996–98; Sr Advisor to Bd, Bank of China (Hong Kong) 2001–05, Dir 2004– (also Chair. Risk Policy Cttee), Bank of China Ltd 2004–13; fmr Arbitrator, China Int. Econ. and Trade Arbitration Comm.; Sr Econ. Advisor, Fujian Provincial Govt, Tianjin City Govt; Nomura Visiting Prof. of Int. Financial Systems, Harvard Law School, USA 2004; Vice-Chair. Exec. Cttee, School of Law, Chinese Univ. of Hong Kong 2005–, mem. Exec. Cttee, Council of Chinese Univ. of Hong Kong, Advisory Bd of the Faculty; Dir China Shenhua Energy Co. Ltd 2004–10, China CITIC Bank 2014–, Industrial and Commercial Bank of China Ltd 2015–, China Life Insurance Ltd 2016–; Hon. Legal Advisor, Shenzhen Municipal Govt, Fellow, Hong Kong Securities Inst., Academician, Int. Euro-Asian Acad. of Sciences 2009; Hon. DIur (Chinese Univ. of Hong Kong) 2003, DScS (Open Univ. of Hong Kong) 2013, (Lingnan Univ.) 2016. *Leisure interests:* reading, music. *Address:* 12th Floor, The Landmark, 15 Queen's Road Central, Hong Kong Special Administrative Region, People's Republic of China. *Telephone:* 28409201. *Fax:* 28101872.

NEPAL, Chiranjibi, PhD; Nepalese economist, academic and central banker; *Governor and Chairman, Nepal Rastra Bank;* b. Palpa dist; ed Banaras Hindu Univ., India; taught at Tribhuvan Univ. and Kathmandu Univ. for 28 years; fmr Exec. Dir Nepal Industrial Development Corpn, Chief of IT Park; Chair. Securities Board of Nepal, Sebon 2007–09; Chief Econ. Adviser at Finance Ministry, then Chief Econ. Adviser to Prime Minister Sushil Koirala –2015; also served as Chief Adviser to Fed. of Nepalese Chambers of Commerce and Industry; Gov. and Chair. Nepal Rastra Bank (central bank) 2015–. *Address:* Office of the Governor, Nepal Rastra Bank, Central Office, Baluwatar, POB 73, Kathmandu, Nepal (office). *Telephone:* (1) 4410158 (office). *Fax:* (1) 4410159 (office). *E-mail:* fxm@nrb.org.np (office). *Website:* www.nrb.org.np (office).

NEPAL, Madhav Kumar; Nepalese politician; b. 6 March 1953, Rautahat Dist; s. of Mangal Kumar Upadhyaya and Durgadevi Upadhyaya; m. Gayatri Nepal; one s. one d.; ed Thakur Ram Campus, Birgunj, Tribhuvan Univ.; dropped surname Upadhyaya since it indicates caste; joined Communist movt 1969; became mem. Dist Cttee Nepal Revolutionary Org. (Marxist-Leninist) 1971; elected mem. Bureau All Nepal Communist Revolutionary Co-ordination Cttee (Marxist-Leninist) 1975, latter f. Communist Party of Nepal (Marxist-Leninist) 1978, elected mem. Politburo 1978–, mem. Communist Party of Nepal (Unified Marxist Leninist—UML), Gen. Sec. 1993–2008, Head of Foreign Dept 2008–09, mem. Standing Cttee; Deputy Prime Minister during CPN (UML) minority govt as well as Leader of Opposition in Nat. Ass. 1995; arrested during crackdown on anti-govt protest 2001; Prime Minister of Nepal 2009–10 (resgnd); mem. Constituent Ass. 2009–, Chair. Constitutional Cttee 2009–, won second Constituent Ass. Elections in 2013, then again in 2017; known in Nepal as Ma-Ku-Ne. *Address:* c/o Prime Minister's Office, Singha Durbar, PO Box 43312, Kathmandu, Nepal. *E-mail:* bishnurijal@gmail.com; info@opmcm.gov.np. *Website:* www.madhavnepal.com.

NERI, Romulo L., MBA; Philippine government official and business executive; b. 1 Feb. 1950; ed Ateneo de Manila, Coll. of Business Admin, Univ. of the Philippines, Grad. School of Man., Univ. of California, Los Angeles, USA; fmr Eugenio Lopez Assoc. Prof. for Corp. Financial Man., Asian Inst. of Man.; fmr Corp. Planning and Finance Officer, Canlubang Sugar Estate, Canlubang Pulp and Manufacturing Corpn, C-J Yulo and Sons Inc., Philippine Nat. Oil Co., Luzon Stevedoring Corpn, Mobil Oil Philippines Inc.; Dir-Gen. Nat. Econ. and Devt Authority –2005, 2007–08; Dir-Gen. House of Reps Congressional and Budget Office –2005; Sec. of the Budget and Man. 2005–07; Pres. Social Security System 2008–; Chair. Comm. on Higher Educ. 2007–08. *Address:* c/o National Economic and Development Authority, NEDA-sa-Pasig Building, 12 St Josemaria Escriva Street, Pasig City, 1605 Metro Manila, Philippines.

NERITANI, Adrian, LLB, LLM, MALD; Albanian lawyer and fmr diplomatist; *Member, International Law, Immigration, and Business Law Groups, Norris McLaughlin & Marcus, P.A.;* b. 26 Oct. 1967, Lushnjë; m.; two c.; ed Univ. of Tirana, Univ. of Malta, John Marshall School of Law, USA; Lecturer, Luigi Gurakuqi Univ. 1989–91; Desk Officer, US Desk, Ministry of Foreign Affairs 1991–93, China and the Far East Desk 1993–97; First Sec. and Chargé d'affaires a.i., Embassy in Beijing 1997–98; ind. consultant on immigration issues, trade and int. business 2000–01; lawyer, Cullison & Cullison, P.C, Chicago, Ill. 2003–06; Amb. and Perm. Rep. to UN, New York 2006–09; fmr Adjunct Prof., John Marshall School of Law, Chicago; currently mem. International Law, Immigration, and Business Law Groups, Norris McLaughlin & Marcus, P.A. (law firm), New York; also currently Of Counsel, Newton Arbitration, New York; apptd to Panel of Arbitrators of Int. Centre for Settlement of Investment Disputes (ICSID) 2011; apptd by UN Sec.-Gen. Ban Ki-moon as mem. of ind. panel leading the Joint Investigative Mechanism (JIM) tasked with identifying those responsible for use of chemical weapons in Syria 2015. *Address:* Norris McLaughlin & Marcus, P.A., 875 Third Avenue, 8th Floor, New York, NY 10022, USA (office). *Telephone:* (212) 444-2255 (office). *E-mail:* aneritani@hotmail.com. *Website:* www.nmmlaw.com (office).

NERLOVE, Marc L., MA, PhD; American academic; *Distinguished University Professor Emeritus of Agricultural and Resource Economics, University of Maryland;* b. 12 Oct. 1933, Chicago, Ill.; s. of Samuel Henry Nerlove and Evelyn Nerlove (née Andelman); two d.; ed Univ. of Chicago and Johns Hopkins Univ.; First Lt, US Army 1957–59; Analytical Statistician, US Dept of Agric., Washington, DC 1956–57; Visiting Lecturer, Dept of Political Economy, Johns Hopkins Univ. 1958; Assoc. Prof., Univ. of Minnesota, Minneapolis 1959–60; Prof., Stanford Univ. 1960–65, Yale Univ. 1965–69; Prof. of Econs, Univ. of Chicago 1969–74; F.W. Taussig Research Prof., Harvard Univ. 1967–68; Visiting Prof., Northwestern Univ., 1973–74, Cook Prof. 1974–82; Prof. of Econs, Univ. of Pennsylvania 1982–86, Univ. Prof. 1986–93; Prof. of Agric. and Resource Econs, Univ. of Maryland, College Park 1993–2011, Distinguished Univ. Prof. Emer. 2011–; mem. NAS 1979; Fellow and Past Pres. Econometric Soc.; Fellow, American Statistical Asscn 1964; Distinguished Fellow, American Agricultural Econ. Asscn 1993; John Bates Clark Medal 1969, P.C. Mahalinobis Medal 1975. *Publications:* Dynamics of Supply 1958, Distributed Lags and Demand Analysis 1958, Estimation and Identification of Cobb-Douglas Production Functions 1965, Analysis of Economic Time Series: A Synthesis 1979, Household and Economy: Welfare Economics of Endogenous Fertility 1987; numerous articles. *Address:* Department of Agricultural and Research Economics, 2200 Symons Hall, University of Maryland, College Park, MD 20742 (office); 7026 Hunter Lane, Hyattsville, MD 20782, USA (home). *Telephone:* (301) 405-1388 (office); (301) 779-3214 (home). *Fax:* (301) 314-9091 (office). *E-mail:* mnerlove@umd.edu (office). *Website:* www.arec.umd.edu (office).

NERO, Franco; Italian actor; b. (Francesco Sparanero), 23 Nov. 1941, Parma; m. Vanessa Redgrave (q.v.) 2006; two s. *Films include:* Wild, Wild Planet 1965, The Bible: In the Beginning 1966, Django 1966, Camelot 1967, The Mercenary 1968, The Day of the Owl 1968, Mafia 1968, Un detective 1969, Battle of the Neretva 1969, A Quiet Place in the Country 1969, Vendetta, Companeros 1970, Tristana 1970, The Virgin and the Gypsy 1970, Confessions of a Police Commissioner to the District Attorney 1971, Vacation 1971, Pope Joan 1972, Deaf Smith & Johnny Ears 1973, Victory March 1976, Last Days of Mussolini 1975, Force Ten from Navarone 1978, The Man With Bogart's Face 1980, Il giorno del Cobra 1980, Mimi 1983, Enter the Ninja 1981, The Salamander 1981, Querelle 1982, Kamikaze '89 1982, Red Bells Part I: Mexico on Fire 1982, Red Bells Part II: I Saw the Birth of a New World 1983, The Repenter 1985, The Girl 1987, Sweet Country 1987, Die Hard 2 1990, Breath of Life 1990, Jonathan degli orsi 1994, The Innocent Sleep 1996, The Versace Murder 1998, Talk of Angels 1998, White Smoke 2002, Ultimo stadio 2002, Die 8. Todsünde: Das Toskana-Karussell 2002, Cattive inclinazioni 2003, Post coitum 2004, Guardiani delle nuvole 2004, Forever Blues 2005, Hans 2006, Amore e libertà – Masaniello 2006, Two Families 2007, Mineurs 2007, Márió, a varázsló 2008, Bastardi 2008, La rabbia 2008, Bathory: Countess of Blood 2008, Ti stramo: Ho voglia di un'ultima notte da manuale prima di tre baci sopra il cielo 2008, Elena (short) 2008, Killing Is My Business, Honey 2009, Palestrina – princeps musicae (documentary) 2009, Angelus Hiroshimae 2010, Letters to Juliet 2010, Prigioniero di un segreto 2010, Rasputin (narrator) 2010, Cars 2 (voice) 2011, New Order 2012, Canepazzo 2012, A Memória que me Contam 2012, The Woods 2012, Django Unchained 2012, Cadences obstinées 2013, Father 2013, Dark Sea 2014, Dante's Hell Documente (Italian version, voice) 2014, Mamula 2014. *Television includes:* The Legend of Valentino (film) 1975, 21 Hours at Munich (film) 1976, The Pirate (film) 1978, Wagner (series) 1983, The Last Days of Pompeii 1984, Garibaldi: The General (mini-series) 1987, Young Catherine (film) 1991, Das Babylon Komplott (film) 1993, The Dragon Ring (film) 1994, Love, Lies, Passions (mini-series) 2003, The Uncrowned Heart (film) 2003, Summer Solstice (film) 2005, The Holy Family (film) 2006, Der Fürst und das Mädchen (series) 2007, Il sangue e la rosa (series) 2008, A Night at the Grand Hotel (film) 2008, Mein Herz in Chile (film) 2008, Four Seasons (mini-series) 2008, Augustine: The Decline of the Roman Empire (film) 2010, Law & Order: Special Victims Unit (series) 2011. *Address:* c/o Anne Alvares Correa, 34 rue Jouffroy d'Abbans, 75017 Paris, France (office). *Telephone:* 1-42-67-80-85 (office). *Fax:* 1-44-09-00-27 (office). *E-mail:* arac2@wanadoo.fr (office). *Website:* www.agence-annealvarescorrea.com/artiste.cfm/297008-franco_nero.html (office).

NERURKAR, Hemant M., BTech; Indian steel industry executive; *Chairman, TRL Krosaki Refractories Limited;* b. 20 Oct. 1948; ed Coll. of Eng, Pune Univ., several man. courses in India and overseas, including CEDEP in France; joined Tata Steel 1982, held various positions, including Chief Metallurgist, Sr Deputy Man. (LD-2 Projects), Deputy Gen. Man. (Steel and Primary Mills), Gen. Man. (Marketing), Sr Gen. Man. (Supply Chain) and COO (Steel), Vice-Pres. (Flat Products) 2002–07, COO (Steel) 2007–09, Exec. Dir, India and SE Asia, Tata Steel Ltd April 2009–13, Man. Dir Oct. 2009–13; Chair. TM International Logistics Ltd, Kolkata, Tata Metaliks Ltd 2008–09, Kolkata, Centennial Steel Co. Ltd, Mumbai, JAMIPOL Ltd, Jamshedpur, Igarashi Motors India Ltd, TM Int. Logistics Ltd, NCC Ltd; Vice-Chair. Tata Steel (Thailand) Public Co. Ltd, Bangkok 2008–10; Chair. TRL Krosaki Refractories Ltd 2011–; fmr Chair. Hooghly Met Coke & Power Co. Ltd, Gopalpur Special Econ. Zone Ltd; fmr Chair. Global Research and Devt Bd, Tata Steel Europe Ltd; mem. Bd of Dirs NatSteel Asia Pte Ltd, NatSteel Holdings Pte Ltd, Singapore, Tata BlueScope Steel Ltd, Pune; Dir World Steel Asscn, Belgium 2009–, CEDEP, France; fmr Dir Tata Ryerson Ltd, Dhamra Port Co. Ltd, Jajpur Cluster Development Ltd, New Millennium Iron Corp.; fmr Dir (non-exec.) Crompton Greaves Consumer Electricals Ltd; Dir (non-exec.) Adani Enterprises Ltd 2016–, Tube Investments of India Ltd 2017–; Pres. Jamshedpur Kennel Club; Vice-Pres. (Ferrous Div.), Indian Inst. of Metals; Vice-Chair. Man. Cttee Indian Cancer Soc., Jamshedpur Br.; mem. CII Nat. Cttee on Steel, Internal Security Task Force of CII Eastern Region (also Chair.), Inst. for Steel Devt and Growth (INSDAG), Man. Cttee Tata Steel Rural Devt Soc.; Special Invitee, All India Man. Asscn; Chair. Bd of Govs XLRI, Jamshedpur; mem. Bd of Govs Xavier Inst. of Man., Bhubaneshwar; mem. All India Man. Asscn Governing Council, Gen. Body of the Sports Authority of India 2010–, amongst others; Dr hc (KIIT Univ., Bhubaneswar), (Maxwell Foundation); NMD Award 1987, Visveswaraya Award 1988, SAIL Gold Medal 1989, Steel 80s Award 1990, SMS Demag Excellence Award 2002, Tata Gold Medal 2004, CEO with HR Orientation Award, Asia's Best Employer Brand Awards 2010, CEO of the Year Award, Indian Inst. of Materials Management (IIMM) 2011, Maharashtra Excellence Award 2012. *Address:* TRL Krosaki Refractories Ltd, 1102, Gd-itl Tower, B-8, Subhas Place, Pitampura, New Delhi 110 034, India (office). *Telephone:* (11) 27355933 (office). *Website:* www .trlkrosaki.com (office).

NESBØ, Jo, MBA; Norwegian crime novelist, singer and songwriter; b. 29 March 1960, Oslo; fmr freelance journalist; fmr mem. De Tusen Hjem, Di Derre; numerous concerts; currently crime writer, creator of Harry Hole series of detective novels. *Recordings:* albums: with Di Derre: Den Derre 1992, Jenter and Sånn 1994. *Publications:* Harry Hole novels: Flaggermusmannen (The Bat) (Riverton Prize for Best Norwegian Crime Novel of the Year 1997, Glass Key Award for Best Nordic Crime Novel of the Year 1998) 1997, Kakerlakkene (The Cockroaches) 1998, Rødstrupe (The Redbreast) (Norwegian Booksellers' Prize for Best Novel of the Year 2000, Norwegian Book Clubs' Award for Best Norwegian Crime Novel Ever Written 2004) 2000, Sorgenfri (Nemesis) (Mads Wiel Nygaards Bursary 2002) 2002, Marekors (The Devil's Star) (Finnish Acad. of Crime Writers Special Commendation for Excellence in Foreign Crime Writing 2007) 2003, Frelseren (The Redeemer) 2005, Snømannen (The Snowman) (Norwegian Booksellers' Prize for Best Novel of the Year 2007, Norwegian Book Club Prize for Best Novel of the Year 2008) 2007, Panserhjeerte (The Leopard) 2009, Gjenferd (Phantom) 2011, Police 2013, Tørst (The Thirst) 2017; Doktor Proktor novels: Doktor Proktors prompepulver (trans. as Doctor Proctor's Fart Powder) 2007, Doktor Proktors Tidsbadekar (trans. as Doktor Proktor's Time Bathtub) 2008, Doctor Proctor and the Armageddon: Maybe 2010; other novels: Stemmer fra Balkan (trans. as Figures in the Balkans) 1999, Det hvite hotellet (trans. as The White Hotel) 2007, Hodejegerne (trans. as Headhunters) 2008, The Son 2014, Blood on Snow 2015, Midnight Sun (Blood on Snow 2) 2015; short stories: Karusellmusikk 2001. *Address:* c/o Solomonsson Agency, Svartensgatan 4, 116 20 Stockholm, Sweden (office). *Telephone:* (8) 22-32-11 (office). *E-mail:* info@ salomonssonagency.com (office). *Website:* www.salomonssonagency.com (office); www.jonesbo.com.

NESTERENKO, Evgeni, DipEng; Russian/Austrian singer (bass) and teacher; b. 8 Jan. 1938, Moscow, USSR; s. of Evgeni Nesterenko and Velta Baumann; m. Ekaterina Alexeyeva 1963 (died 2014); one s.; ed Leningrad Eng Inst. and Leningrad Conservatory with V. Lukanin; debut as General Ermolov in War and Peace, Maly Theatre, Leningrad 1963; soloist with Leningrad Maly Opera and Ballet Theatre 1963–67; soloist with Kirov Opera 1967–71; teacher of solo singing, Leningrad Conservatory 1967–72, Moscow Conservatory 1975–93, Konservatorium Wien 1993–2003; soloist with the Bolshoi 1971–2003; mem. staff, Moscow Musical Pedagogical Inst. 1972–74; Chair. of Singing at Moscow Conservatoire 1975–93, Prof. 1981–93; USSR People's Deputy 1989–91; seasons at Budapest 1970, Vienna Staatsoper 1975, Metropolitan Opera 1975, Teatro Colón, Buenos Aires 1975, La Scala, Milan 1977, Covent Garden 1978, Verona Festival 1978, Munich 1978, Estonia 1980, Japan 1983, Barcelona 1984, Bregenz Festival 1986, Savonlinna Festival 1987, Hamburg 1986, Orange Festival 1990, Antwerp 1993, Hong Kong 2002, São Paulo 2006; mem. Int. Acad. of Creative Endeavours, Moscow 1991; People's Artist of the USSR 1976, Viotti d'Oro Prize, City of Vercelli (Italy) 1981, Lenin Prize 1982, Melodia Golden Disc, USSR 1984, Giovanni Zenatello Prize, Verona (Italy) 1986, Hero of Labour 1988, Chaliapin Prize 1992, Wilhelm Furtwängler Prize (Germany) 1992, Austrian Kammersänger 1992, Casta Diva Prize 2001, Golden Pegasus Theatre Prize (Poland) 2004, Centaur with Gold Flower 2009. *Roles include:* Boris Godunov, Ivan Khovansky and Dosifey (Khovanshchina), Igor and Khan Konchak (Prince Igor), Mephistopheles (Faust), Grigori (Quiet Flows the Don), General Ermolov and Kutuzov (War and Peace), Filippo II (Don Carlo), Attila, Zaccaria (Nabucco), Don Pasquale, Sarastro (Magic Flute), Bluebeard, Gremin (Eugene Onegin), Ivan Susanin, Old Convict (Lady Macbeth), Don Basilio, Enrico VIII, Moses, Water-Sprite (Rusalka), Don Bartolo. *Recordings:* Glinka's Ruslan and Lyudmila and Ivan Susanin, Tchaikovsky's Mazeppa, Iolanta and Eugene Onegin, Rachmaninov's Francesca da Rimini and Aleko, Songs by Shostakovich and Mussorgsky, Suite on Poems of Michelangelo and 14th Symphony by Shostakovich, Verdi Requiem, Nabucco, Attila and Trovatore, Gounod's Faust, Dvořák's Rusalka, Donizetti's Don Pasquale and L'Elisir d'amore, Bela Bartók's Bluebeard's Castle; videos: Verdi's Attila, Rachmaninov's Aleko, Mussorgsky's Boris Godunov and Khovanshchina, Glinka's A Life for the Tsar. *Publications:* Evgeni Nesterenko, Thoughts on My Profession 1985, Evgeni Nesterenko, Memoirs of a Russian Bass 2011. *Leisure interests:* tea collecting and testing.

NESTERIKHIN, Yuri Yefremovich; Russian nuclear physicist; *Head, Synchrotron and Applied Electronics Divisions, National Research Centre ('Kurchatov Institute');* b. 10 Oct. 1930, Ivanovo; s. of Yefrem Nesterikhin and Maria Morozova; m. 1954; one s. one d.; ed Moscow Lomonosov State Univ.; mem. CPSU 1960–91; Jr Researcher, Inst. of Atomic Energy 1954–61; Sector Head and Head of Lab., Inst. of Nuclear Physics (Siberian Br.) 1961–65; Prof. 1970; Corresp. mem., USSR (now Russian) Acad. of Sciences 1970, Full mem. 1981–; Dir, Inst. of Automation and Electrometrics, Siberian Br. of Acad. of Sciences 1967–87; Head of Synchrotron and Applied Electronics Divs, Kurchatov Inst., Moscow 1987– (renamed Nat. Research Centre ('Kurchatov Inst.') 2010); Dir Multimedia Centre, Acad. of Nat. Economy 1992–; mem. Bd Ranet (jt stock co.) 1992–95; Chair. Moscow Physics and Tech. Inst. 2001–; Deputy Chair. Scientific Council for Cybernetics; most important works on plasma physics and thermonuclear synthesis; USSR Council of Ministers Prize. *Publications:* Methods of Speed Measurements in Geodynamics and Plasma Physics 1967; several other works on nuclear physics and automation of research. *Leisure interest:* sauna. *Address:* National Research Centre ('Kurchatov Institute'), 123182 Moscow, Akademika Kurchatova pl. 1 (office); 117071 Moscow, Leninski Prosp. 13, Apt 93, Russian Federation. *Telephone:* (499) 196-70-38 (office); (495) 237-43-47 (home). *Fax:* (495) 420-22-66. *E-mail:* presscentr@kiae .ru (office).

NESTEROVA, Natalia Igorevna; Russian painter; *Professor of Scenography, Russian Institute of Theatre Arts-GITIS;* b. 23 April 1944, Moscow; one s.; ed Moscow Surikov State Fine Arts Inst.; mem. USSR (now Russian) Union of Painters; Stage Designer, Bolshoi Theatre 1958; participated in over 60 exhbns including solo exhbns in Moscow 1989, 1997, 2017, 2018, New York 1990, 1991, 2017, Chicago 1991, Montréal 1992, Berlin 1993, Tallinn 1997; Prof. of Scenography, Russian Institute of Theatre Arts-GITIS 1992–, Corresponding Mem. 1998; works in collections of Tretyakov Gallery, Moscow, Ludwig Collection, Germany, Guggenheim Museum, New York, Art Museum, Warsaw, Gallery Maya Polsky, Chicago; Honored Artist of the Russian Fed. 1994; State Prize of Russia 1992, 1998, Triumph Award 2003. *Address:* Russian Institute of Theatre Arts, Faculty of Scenography, Moscow, Zemlyanoy Val Street 66/20, Russia (office). *Telephone:* (495) 915-31-73 (office). *E-mail:* art@gitis.net (office). *Website:* www .gitis.net (office).

NESTOR, Eiki; Estonian mechanical engineer and politician; b. 5 Sept. 1953, Tallinn; m. Anu Nestor; two s.; ed Tallinn Univ. of Tech.; Head of Div., Keila Motor Depot 1976–82; Chief Insp. of Occupational Health and Safety, Motor Transport and Road Workers' Trade Union 1982–89; Deputy Chair., then Chair. Estonian Transport and Road Workers' Trade Union 1989–92; mem. Sotsiaaldemokraatlik Erakond (SDE—Estonian Social Democratic Party) 1994–, Leader 1995–96; mem. State Ass. (Riigikoku—Parl.) 1992–, Chair. (Speaker) 2014–19; Minister without Portfolio in charge of Regional Affairs 1994–95, Minister of Social Affairs 1999–2002; cand. in presidential election 2016; mem. Tallinn City Council 1996–99; mem. Bd of Trustees, Tallinn Univ. of Tech.; Order of the Nat. Coat of Arms, Fifth Class 2001; Grand Cross, Order of the White Rose of Finland 2016. *Publications:* articles in the Estonian press. *Leisure interests:* sports, music. *Address:* c/o State Assembly (Riigikogu), Lossi plats 1A, Tallinn 15165, Estonia (office). *Website:* eikinestor.blogspot.com.

NETANYAHU, Benjamin, MSc; Israeli politician and diplomatist; *Prime Minister and Minister of Defence;* b. 21 Oct. 1949, Tel-Aviv; s. of Benzion Netanyahu and Tzila Segal; m. 1st Miriam Weizmann 1972 (divorced 1978); m. 2nd Fleur Cates 1981 (divorced 1984); m. 3rd Sara Ben-Artzi 1991; three c.; ed Massachusetts Inst. of Tech., USA; Man. Consultant, Boston Consulting Group 1976–78; Exec. Dir Jonathan Inst., Jerusalem 1978–80; Sr Man. Rim Industries, Jerusalem 1980–82; Deputy Chief of Mission, Israeli Embassy in Washington, DC 1982–84; Perm. Rep. to UN, New York 1984–88; mem. Knesset 1988–; Deputy Minister of Foreign Affairs 1988–91; Deputy Minister, Prime Minister's Office 1991–92; Prime Minister of Israel and Minister of Housing and Construction 1996–99; Minister of Foreign Affairs 2002–03, 2012–13, 2015–18, of Finance 2003–05; Prime Minister of Israel 2009–, also Minister of Econ. Strategy, of Pensioner Affairs and of Health 2009–13, Minister of Public Diplomacy and Diaspora Affairs 2013, Minister of Defence 2018–; Leader of Likud 1993–99, 2005–. *Publications include:* Yoni's Letters (ed.) 1978, Terror: Challenge and Reaction (ed.) 1980, Terrorism: How the West Can Win (ed.) 1986, International Terrorism: Challenge and Response (ed.) 1991, A Place Among the Nations: Israel and the World 1993, Fighting Terrorism: How Democracies Can Defeat Domestic and International Terrorism 1995, A Durable Peace 2000. *Address:* Office of the Prime Minister, PO Box 187, 3 Kaplan Street, Kiryat Ben-Gurion, Jerusalem 91950 (office); Likud (Consolidation), 38 Rehov King George, Tel-Aviv 61231, Israel (office). *Telephone:* 2-6705510 (office); 3-5630666 (Likud) (office). *Fax:* 2-6703398 (office); 3-5282901 (Likud) (office). *E-mail:* pm_eng2@pmo.gov.il (office); likud@likud.org.il (office). *Website:* www .pmo.gov.il (office); www.likud.org.il (office).

NETREBKO, Anna; Austrian (b. Russian) singer (soprano); b. 18 Sept. 1971, Krasnodar, Russia; m. Yusif Eyvazov; one s.; ed Rimsky-Korsakov Conservatory; debut at Mariinsky Opera Theatre, St Petersburg 1994, as Susanna; roles include Glinka's Ludmila with Kirov Opera, Gilda in Rigoletto and Kundry in Parsifal at St Petersburg; first appearance at Salzburg Festival 1998; tours with Kirov Opera as Pamina and Bizet's Micaela; sang Gilda at Washington 1999 and New York, Mimi at San Francisco 1999–2000 and New York; concerts with Rotterdam Philharmonic Orchestra include London Proms and Teresa in Benvenuto Cellini, Royal Festival Hall 1999; sang Natasha in War and Peace at St Petersburg and London 2000; other roles include Zerlina and Louisa in Prokofiev's Betrothal in a Monastery at San Francisco, Rosina, Pamina and Xenia in Boris Godunov, Mozart's Servilia at Covent Garden 2002, Donna Anna in Don Giovanni at Salzburg 2003 and Covent Garden 2007, Violetta in La Traviata at Salzburg 2005, Norina in Don Pasquale in New York 2005, and Elvira in I Puritani 2006; role debuts as Leonora in Il trovatore at Berlin Staatsoper, in title role of Puccini's Manon Lescaut, Lady Macbeth in Bavarian State Opera's Macbeth, Marguerite in Gounod's Faust at Covent Garden, Vienna's Staatsoper and Festspielhaus, Baden-Baden 2013; title role in Giovanna d'Arco, La Scala 2015; Violetta in La Traviata at Teatro alla Scala 2017, Opéra National de Paris 2018; Order of Friendship 2018;

First Prize, All-Russian Glinka Vocal Competition, Moscow 1993, Third Prize, Rimsky-Korsakov Int. Competition for Young Opera Singers, St Petersburg 1996, Costa Diva Prize 1998, Golden Sophit Prize, St Petersburg 1999, 11 ECHO Klassik Awards including Female Singer of the Year 2004, 2005, 2014, 2016, Russian State Prize 2005, Bambi Award 2006, Classical BRIT Award for Singer of the Year 2007, Musician of the Year, Musical America Awards 2008, People's Artist of Russia 2008, Opera News Award 2016, Int. Opera Award for Best Female Singer 2017. *Repertoires include:* Elsa (Lohengrin), Adriana Lecouvreur, Aida, Magdalena (Andrea Chénier), Tosca, Susanna (Le nozze di Figaro), Donna Anna Netrebko (Don Giovanni), Violetta (La traviata), Mimi (La bohème), Juliette (Roméo et Juliette), Amina (La sonnambula), Lucia di Lammermoor, Norina (Don Pasquale), Adina (L'elisir d'amore), Natasha Rostova (War and Peace), Iolanta, Tatiana (Eugene Onegin), Anna Bolena, Lady Macbeth. *Recordings include:* Glinka's Ruslan and Ludmila, Mozart Album 2006, Souvenirs 2008, In the Still of Night 2010, Rossini's Stabat Mater (Gramophone Editor's Choice Award 2011), Anna Netrebko – Live at the Metropolitan Opera 2011, Anna Netrebko – Verdi 2013, Four Last Songs 2014, Puccini's Manon Lescaut 2016, Verismo 2016, Romanza (with Yusif Eyvazov) 2017. *Address:* c/o Judith Neuhoff, Centre Stage Artist Management, Stralauer Allee 1, 10245 Berlin, Germany (office). *E-mail:* arina .koreniushkina@umusic.com (office). *Website:* www.annanetrebko.com (home).

NEUBERGER, Baroness (Life Peer), cr. 2004, of Primrose Hill in the London Borough of Camden; **Rabbi Julia Babette Sarah Neuberger,** DBE, MA; British rabbi, author, broadcaster and politician; *Senior Rabbi, West London Synagogue;* b. 27 Feb. 1950, London, England; d. of Walter Schwab and Alice Schwab; m. Anthony John Neuberger 1973; one s. one d.; ed South Hampstead High School, Newnham Coll. Cambridge and Leo Baeck Coll. London; Rabbi, South London Liberal Synagogue 1977–89, currently Sr Rabbi, West London Synagogue; Lecturer and Assoc. Fellow, Leo Baeck Coll. 1979–97; Assoc. Newnham Coll. Cambridge 1983–96; Sec. and Chief Exec. The King's Fund 1997–2004; Chancellor Univ. of Ulster 1994–2000; Chair. Rabbinic Conf. Union of Liberal and Progressive Synagogues 1983–85; Camden and Islington Community Health Services Nat. Health Service (NHS) Trust 1993–97; mem. Policy Planning Group, Inst. of Jewish Affairs 1986–90, NHS Complaints Review 1993–94, Gen. Medical Council 1993–2001, Council, Univ. Coll. London 1993–97, MRC 1995–2000, Council, Save the Children Fund 1995–96; Visiting Fellow, King's Fund Inst. 1989–91; Chair. Patients Asscn 1988–91, Royal Coll. of Nursing Comm. on Health Service; mem. Nat. Cttee Social Democratic Party 1982–88, Funding Review of BBC 1999, Cttee on Standards in Public Life 2001–04; Civil Service Commr 2001–02; mem. Bd of Visitors, Memorial Church, Harvard Univ. 1994–2000, Bloomberg Prof. of Philanthropy and Public Policy, Divinity School 2006; Prime Minister's Champion for Volunteering 2007–09; Chair. Liberal Judaism –2011, One Housing Group, Advisory Panel Judicial Diversity –2010; other public and charitable appointments; Harkness Fellow, Commonwealth Fund of New York; Visiting Fellow, Harvard Medical School 1991–92; Chair. Responsible Gambling Strategy Bd –2011, Responsible Gambling Fund –2011; Trustee, Runnymede Trust 1990–97; fmr Trustee, Imperial War Museum, British Council, Booker Prize Foundation, Jewish Care; Chair. W & L Schwab Charitable Trust; mem. House of Lords (Liberal Democrat) 2004–11, (Crossbench) 2011–; Hon. FRCP 2004; Hon. Fellow, Royal Coll. of Gen. Practitioners, Royal Coll. of Psychiatrists, City and Guilds Inst.; Hon. Fellow, Mansfield Coll. Oxford; Dr hc (Open Univ., City Univ. London, Humberside, Ulster, Stirling, Oxford Brookes, Teesside, Nottingham, Queen's Belfast, Aberdeen). *Radio:* Pause for Thought (BBC Radio 2). *Television:* Presenter, Choices (BBC) 1986, 1987. *Publications:* The Story of Judaism 1986, Days of Decision (ed., four vols) 1987, Caring for Dying Patients of Different Faiths 1987, Whatever's Happening to Women? 1991, A Necessary End (co-ed. with John White) 1991, Ethics and Healthcare: The Role of Research Ethics Committees in the UK 1992, The Things That Matter 1993, On Being Jewish 1995, Dying Well: A Health Professional's Guide to Enabling a Better Death 1999, Hidden Assets: Values and Decision-Making in the NHS Today (co-ed. with Bill New) 2002, The Moral State We're In 2005, Not Dead Yet: A Manifesto for Old Age 2008, Is That All There Is? Thoughts on Leaving a Legacy 2011; contribs to various books on cultural, religious and ethical factors in nursing; contribs journals and newspapers, including Nursing Times, Jewish Chronicle, Times, Irish Times, The Independent, Guardian, Telegraph, Sunday Express, Mail on Sunday, Evening Standard. *Leisure interests:* riding, sailing, Irish life, opera, setting up the old girls' network, children, theatre, family. *Address:* House of Lords, Westminster, London, SW1 0PW, England (office). *Telephone:* (20) 7219-2716 (office); (20) 7535-0255 (office). *E-mail:* paolachurchill@googlemail.com (office); paola.churchill@wls.org .uk (office).

NEUGER, Tim; German art dealer and gallery curator; *Co-Founder, neugerriemschneider;* Co-founder and Co-dir, with Burkhard Riemschneider, neugerriemschneider, Berlin, represents artists including Ai Weiwei, Pawel Althamer, James Benning, Billy Childish, Keith Edmier, Olafur Eliasson, Andreas Eriksson, Noa Eshkol, Mario García Torres, Isa Genzken, Thilo Heinzmann, Sharon Lockhart, Renata Lucas, Michel Majerus, Antje Majewski, Mike Nelson, Jorge Pardo, Elizabeth Peyton, Tobias Rehberger, Simon Starling, Thaddeus Strode, Rirkrit Tiravanija, Pae White. *Address:* neugerriemschneider, Linienstraße 155, 10115 Berlin, Germany (office). *Telephone:* (30) 288772-77 (office). *E-mail:* mail@ neugerriemschneider.com (office). *Website:* www.neugerriemschneider.com (office).

NEUHAUSER, Duncan von Briesen, PhD, MBA, MHA; American professor of epidemiology and biostatistics; *The Charles Elton Blanchard MD Professor of Health Management Emeritus, Medical School, Case Western Reserve University;* b. 20 June 1939, Philadelphia, Pa; s. of Edward B. D. Neuhauser and Gernda von Briesen Neuhauser; m. Elinor Toaz Neuhauser 1965; one s. one d.; ed Harvard Univ. and Univs of Michigan and Chicago; Research Assoc. (Instructor), Center for Health Admin. Studies, Univ. of Chicago 1965–70; Asst Prof., then Assoc. Prof., Harvard School of Public Health 1970–79; Assoc. Chair., Program for Health Systems Man., Harvard Business School 1972–79; Consultant in Medicine, Massachusetts Gen. Hosp. 1975–80; Prof. of Epidemiology and Biostatistics, Case Western Reserve Univ. 1979–, Prof. of Organizational Behavior 1979–, Prof. of Medicine 1981–, Keck Foundation Sr Research Scholar 1982–, Prof. of Family Medicine 1990–, Charles Elton Blanchard MD Prof. of Health Man. 1995–2011, Emer. 2011–; Adjunct Prof. of Nursing, Vanderbilt Univ. 1998–; mem. bioscientific medical staff, Cleveland Metropolitan Gen. Hosp. 1981–2012; Adjunct mem., Medical Staff, Cleveland Clinic Foundation 1984–99; Co-Dir Health Systems Man. Centre, Case Western Reserve Univ. 1985–2012; Ed. Medical Care 1983–97, Health Matrix 1982–90, Non-Profit Management and Leadership 2012–14; mem. Inst. of Medicine (NAS) 1983–; Visiting Prof. of Health Man., Karolinska Inst., Stockholm, Sweden 2002–; Festschrift Issue of Medical Care, Aug. 1998, The Duncan Neuhauser PhD Endowed Chair in Community Health Improvement created at Case Western Reserve Univ. 2003. *Achievements include:* est. annual Duncan Neuhauser Curricular Innovation Award, Acad. of Health Care Improvement 2009; conference room at Medical Management Centre, Karolinska Inst., dedicated in his name 2011. *Publications:* (co-author) Health Services in the US 1976, The Efficient Organization 1977, The Physician and Cost Control 1979, Clinical Decision Analysis 1980, Competition, Co-operation or Regulation 1981, The New Epidemiology 1982, Coming of Age 1984, 1995, Clinical CQI 1995, Health Services Management 1997 (nine edns); numerous scientific papers in professional journals. *Leisure interests:* sailing, curling. *Address:* Department of Epidemiology and Biostatistics, Medical School, Case Western Reserve University, 10900 Euclid Avenue, Cleveland, OH 44106-4945 (office); PO Box 932, Blue Hill, ME 04614, USA (home). *Telephone:* (216) 368-3726 (office); (207) 374-2292 (Blue Hill) (home). *Fax:* (216) 368-3970 (office). *E-mail:* dvn@case.edu (office).

NEUKIRCHEN, Karl-Josef (Kajo), Dr rer. pol; German business executive; *Partner, Kajo Neukirchen GmbH;* b. 17 March 1942, Bonn; Chair. Man. Bd Klöckner-Humboldt-Deutz AG, Cologne –1988, Hösch AG, Dortmund 1991–92; Chair. Supervisory Bd Klöckner-Werke AG Duisburg 1992–95, Dynamit Nobel AG 1994–, FAG Kugelfischer Georg Schäfer AG, Vossloh AG, Sixt AG; CEO Metallgesellschaft AG 1993–2004; Partner, Kajo Neukirchen GmbH; mem. Exec. Bd German Lung Foundation. *Address:* Kajo Neukirchen Management und Beteiligungs GmbH, Bockenheimer Landstraße 24, 60323 Frankfurt am Main, Germany (office). *Telephone:* (69) 7137478-0 (office). *Fax:* (69) 713747829 (office). *E-mail:* info@kaneco.de (office). *Website:* (office).

NEUMEIER, John, BA; American/German choreographer and ballet director; *Chief Choreographer, Ballet Director and Ballettintendant, The Hamburg Ballet;* b. 1942, Milwaukee, Wis.; s. of Albert Neumeier and Lucille Neumeier; ed Marquette Univ., Milwaukee; dance training in Milwaukee, Chicago, Royal Ballet School, London and in Copenhagen with Vera Volkova; soloist, The Stuttgart Ballet 1963; Ballet Dir Frankfurt 1969; Ballet Dir and Chief Choreographer, Hamburg Ballet 1973–, Balletintendant 1996–; Prof., City of Hamburg 1987; f. John Neumeier ballet centre, Hamburg 1989; f. a ballet training school in Hamburg 1978; appears as soloist, notably in The Chairs with Marcia Haydée, a ballet cr. for them by M. Béjart; danced lead role of St Matthew Passion 1981; est. John Neumeier Foundation 2006; f. Germany's Nat. Youth Ballet 2011; Hon. mem. Semper Oper (Germany) 2002; Hon. Citizen of Hamburg 2007; Bundesverdienstkreuz; Chevalier, Légion d'honneur, des Arts et des Lettres; Medal of the Kt's Cross of the Dannebrog in Gold 2000; Order of Friendship of the Russian Fed. 2012; Hon. DFA (Marquette); Golden Camera Award for TV series of his Ballet Workshops 1978, Dance Magazine Award 1983, Deutscher Tanzpreis 1988, Diaghilev Prize 1988, Benois de la Danse 1992, Medal of Honour (City of Tokyo) 1994, Carina-Ari Gold Medal (Sweden) 1994, Nijinsky Medal (Polish Ministry of Culture) 1996, Min-On Int. Award for Arts (Tokyo) 1997, European Prince Henrik of Denmark Award 2000, Danza Magazine Award for production of Messiah 2001, Bayerischers Theaterpreis for production of Nijinsky 2001, Gold Mask (Russia) 2002, Wilhelm Hausen Prize (Denmark) 2002, Medal for Art and Science, Hamburg 2003, Kt of the Region of Knox, Pres. of France, Jacques Chirac 2003, Porselli Prize (Italy) 2004, Hans Christian Andersen Ambassador 2004–05, Saeculum Prize for his life's work, Dresden 2005, Steffen Kempe Prize 2005, Golden Mask for Moscow's Best Contemporary Dance Production 2005, Portugaleser in Silver, Hamburg 2006, Nijinsky Award for Lifetime Achievement 2006, Citizen of the Year Hamburg 2006, German Critic Prize for Life Achievement 2007, Herbert von Karajan Music Prize 2007, German Anniversary Dance Prize 2008, Kyoto Prize 2015, Prix Benois de la Danse Lifetime Achievement Award (Russia) 2016. *Works choreographed include:* Romeo and Juliet, The Nutcracker 1971, Daphnis and Chloë 1972, Third Symphony of Gustav Mahler 1975, Illusions-Like Swan Lake 1976, A Midsummer Night's Dream 1977, Sleeping Beauty, Lady of the Camellias 1978, St Mathew Passion 1981, Giselle 1983, Sixth Symphony of G. Mahler 1984, Peer Gynt 1989, Fifth Symphony of G. Mahler 1989, Requiem 1991, A Cinderella Story 1992, Odyssee 1995, Vivaldi Or What You Will 1996, Sylvia 1997, Images from Bartók 1998, Messias 1999, Nijinsky 2000, Giselle 2000, Sounds of Empty Pages, Winterreise 2001, The Seagull 2002, Death in Venice 2003, Preludes CV 2003, The Little Mermaid, a homage to Hans Christian Andersen for his 200th birthday celebrations 2005, Songs of the Night 2005, Parzival Episodes and Echo 2006, Christmas Oratorio 2007, Verklungene Feste 2008, Le Pavillon d'Armide 2009, Orpheus 2009, Purgatorio 2011, Liliom 2011, Christmas Oratorio I–VI 2013, Tatiana 2014, The Song of the Earth 2015, Peer Gynt 2015, Duse 2015, Turangalîla 2016. *Films:* The Legend of Joseph, Lady of the Camellias, Illusions – Like 'Swan Lake' (DVD), The Little Mermaid (DVD), St Matthew Passion (DVD), Christmas Oratorio I–VI (DVD), Tatiana (DVD). *Television includes:* series of ballet workshops (also on DVD), Wendungen (String Quintet in C Major by Franz Schubert), The Chairs (WDR), Third Symphony of Gustav Mahler (ZDF), Othello (ZDF), Scenes of Childhood (NDR3), Death in Venice (ARTE), St Matthew Passion (SWR), Tatiana (France Télévisions, Mezzo and NHK Japan. *Publications:* John Neumeier Unterwegs 1972, John Neumeier und das Hamburg Ballett 1977, Matthäus-Passion 1983, John Neumeier Traumwege 1980, 10 Jahre – John Neumeier und das Hamburg Ballett 1983, 20 Jahre – John Neumeier und das Hamburg Ballett 1993, My Favourite Pictures for John 1998, John Neumeier 2004, In Bewegung 2007, John Neumeier: Pictures from a Life (text by Horst Koegler) 2010. *Address:* Hamburg Ballet, Ballettzentrum Hamburg, Caspar-Voght-Str. 54, 20535 Hamburg, Germany (office). *Telephone:* (40) 211188-16 (office). *Fax:* (40) 211188-17 (office). *E-mail:* presse@hamburgballett.de (office). *Website:* www .hamburgballett.de (office).

NEUPERT, Walter, PhD, MD; German biochemist, physician, cell biologist and academic; *Max Planck Fellow, Max Planck Institute of Biochemistry;* b. 24 Oct. 1939, Munich; ed Univ. of Munich; Asst Prof., Inst. of Physiological Chem., Univ. of Munich 1969–72, Privatdozent 1972–77, Prof. and Chair. Adolf Butenandt Inst. of Physiological Chem., Molecular Biology, Biochemistry and Cell Biology

1983–2010; Assoc. Prof., Inst. of Biochemistry, Univ. of Göttingen 1977–79, Prof. and Chair. Inst. of Biochemistry 1979–83; Max Planck Fellow, Max Planck Inst. of Biochemistry, Martinsried/Munich 2008–; Bundesverdienstkreuz (Fed. Cross of Merit), First Class 2000, Bayerischer Verdienstorden (Bavarian Cross of Merit) 2003, Bayerischer Maximiliansorden für Wissenschaft und Kunst 2008; Ferdinand Springer Lecturer, Fed. of European Biochemical Socs 1991, Bernard Axelrod Lecturership in Biochemistry 1992, Heinrich Wieland-Prize 1993, Feldberg Foundation Prize 1996, E.C. Slater Lecturer 1997, Gairdner Foundation Prize 1998, Schleiden Medal, German Acad. of Sciences Leopoldina 1999, Otto Warburg Medal, German Soc. for Biochemistry and Molecular Biology 2000, E.B. Wilson Award, American Soc. for Cell Biology 2000, Felix Wankel Animal Protection Prize 2003, Fawcett Lecturer, Harvard Univ. 2007, Otto Warburg Lecturer, Univ. of Bayreuth 2010, The W.P. and D.N. Harris German-Dartmouth Distinguished Visiting Professorship, Dartmouth, NH 2010, Ernst Jung Gold Medal 2015. *Publications include:* numerous papers in professional journals. *Address:* Max Planck Institute of Biochemistry, Am Klopferspitz 18, 82152 Martinsried, Germany (office). *Telephone:* (89) 8578-0 (office). *Fax:* (89) 8578-3777 (office). *E-mail:* neupert@biochem.mpg.de (office). *Website:* www.biochem.mpg.de (office).

NEUVILLE, Colette Jeannine Michelle Claude, LenD; French lawyer, organization executive and economist; *President, Association de défense des actionnaires minoritaires (Adam);* b. 21 Jan. 1937, Coutances (Manche); d. of Pierre Wacongne and Suzanne Wacongne (née Piquot); m. Christian Neuville 1961; one s. four d.; ed Lycée de jeunes filles et Ecole Saint-Julien, Le Mans, Faculté de droits, Caen, Faculté de droit et de sciences économiques, Paris; economist with Kléber Colombes group 1959–60; with NATO 1960–63; with Nat. Office of Irrigation, Rabat, Morocco 1963–68; with Financial Agency, Loire Bretagne 1968–69; Founder-Pres. Asscn de défense des actionnaires minoritaires (Adam) 1991–; mem. Supervisory Council Paribas 1995–2000; Dir (non-exec.) Eurotunnel plc 2005–, mem. Jt Bd 2005–, Dir Eurotunnel SA 2007–. *Leisure interests:* music, walking in the mountains. *Address:* Adam, 4 rue Montescot, BP 208, 28004 Chartres Cedex, France.

NEUVO, Yrjö A., PhD, FIEEE; Finnish electronics engineer and academic; *Professor and Research Director, Aalto University;* b. 21 July 1943, Turku; s. of Olavi Neuvo and Aune Neuvo (née Vaisala); m. Tuula Halsas 1968; two s. one d.; ed Cornell Univ., NY, USA and Helsinki Univ. of Tech.; Acting Prof., Helsinki Univ. of Tech. 1975–76; Prof. of Electronics, Tampere Univ. of Tech. 1976–92; Sr Research Fellow, Acad. of Finland 1979–80, Research Prof. 1984–; Visiting Prof., Univ. of California 1981–82; Sr Vice-Pres., Tech. and Chief Tech. Officer, Nokia Corpn 1993–2005; Prof. and Research Dir, Univ. of Aalto 2005–; Chair. ARTEMIS JTI Governing Bd 2007–08; mem. Bureau, European Science and Tech. Ass. 1994–97; Gen. Chair. IEEE Int. Symposium on Circuits and Systems 1988, IEEE Int. Conf. on Communications 2001; mem. Governing Bd (and its Exec. Cttee), European Inst. of Innovation and Tech. 2008–12, Advisory Bd of Future Internet PPP 2012–14; mem. Bd of Dirs, Vaisala Corpn, Metso Minerals Oy 2006–13, and three high tech start-ups; Commdr Order of Lion of Finland 1992; four hon. doctorates, including Hon. MD (Tampere Univ. of Tech.) 1992; IEEE Bicentennial Award 1986, Asscn in Finland Hon. Prize 1988, Nokia Prize 1989, Asteroid 1938 DN named after him. *Publications:* more than 300 scientific publs on computer eng and new technologies. *Address:* Aalto University, PO Box 15600, 00076 Aalto, Finland (office). *E-mail:* yrjo.neuvo@aalto.fi (office). *Website:* people.aalto.fi/en/yrjo_neuvo (office).

NEVANLINNA, (Eero) Olavi, DipEng, DTech; Finnish academic; *Professor Emeritus, Department of Mathematics and Systems Analysis, Aalto University;* b. 17 April 1948, Helsinki; m. Marja Lähdesmäki 1968; three s. one d.; ed Helsinki Univ. of Technology; Asst Prof. of Math., Alto Univ. 1971–74, Prof. 1980–2016, Prof. Emer. 2016–, Vice-Rector 2003–05, Sr Advisor 2016–; Sr Researcher Acad. of Finland 1975–77; Assoc. Prof. of Applied Math., Oulu Univ. 1978–79; Research Prof., Acad. of Finland 1986–92; Visiting Prof. at several US univs and ETH, Zurich; Chair. Rolf Nevanlinna Inst. 1989–90; Chair. Supervisory Bd Suomi Mutual Life Assurance Co. 1996–98; Pres. Int. Council for Industrial and Applied Math. 1999–2003, Past Pres. 2003–05; Chair. Council of Finnish Acads. 2012–13, 2016–, Vice-Chair. 2014–16; mem. Bd Emil Aaltonen Foundation 1994– (Chair. 2009–), Pohjola Insurance Co. Ltd 1997–99, Finnish Acad. of Technology 2008–14 (Pres. 2009–14), Technology Acad. Finland 2009–15 (Vice-Chair. 2010–15), Council of Finnish Foundations 2012; mem. Editorial Bd BIT, Finnish Acad. of Tech. Sciences 1984, Finnish Acad. of Sciences and Letters 1986 (mem. Bd 2000–), Nat. Cttee in Math. 1984–. *Publications:* Convergence of Iterations for Linear Equations 1993, Meromorphic Functions and Linear Algebra 2003. *Address:* Department of Mathematics and Systems Analysis, Aalto University, Otakaari 1, Espoo, Room M 306, PO Box 11100, 00076 FI, Aalto, Finland (office). *Telephone:* (50) 5750474 (office); (40) 0448055 (mobile). *Fax:* (9) 8632048 (office). *Website:* math.aalto.fi (office).

NEVES, José Maria Pereira, BA; Cabo Verde politician; b. 28 March 1960, Santa Catarina, Santiago; three s.; ed São Paulo School of Business and Admin; consultant in organizational devt and human resources man. 1987–96; Dir Nat. Public Admin Training Centre 1988–89; Co-ordinator Admin Reform and Modernization Projects 1987–88; mem. Parl. 1996–; Mayor of Santa Catarina 2000–01; Chair. Partido Africano da Independência de Cabo Verde 2000–; Prime Minister of Cabo Verde 2001–16; Asst Prof. of Man., Higher Educ. Inst.; Marechal Floriana Peixoto Merit Award, Brazil 2005, Patrons of Century Ruby Cross 2006. *Leisure interests:* reading, walking, music. *Address:* c/o Gabinete do Primeiro Ministro, Palácio do Governo, Várzea, CP 16, Praia, Santiago, Cabo Verde (office).

NEVES DA CUNHA, Aécio; Brazilian politician; *President, Partido da Social Democracia Brasileira;* b. 10 March 1960, Belo Horizonte; s. of Aécio Ferreira da Cunha and Inês Maria Neves; grandson of fmr Brazilian Pres. Tancredo Neves; m. 1st Andrea Falcão (divorced); one d.; m. 2nd Letícia Weber; one s. one d.; ed Pontifícia Universidade Católica de Minas Gerais; Sec. to Tancredo Neves 1980–85; Fed. Deputy for Minas Gerais 1986–2002, Pres. Chamber of Deputies 2001–02; co-f. Partido da Social Democracia Brasileira 1988, Leader in Chamber of Deputies 1997–2001, Pres. 2013–; Gov. Minas Gerais 2002–10; mem. Senado Federal for Minas Gerais 2011–; unsuccessful cand. in presidential election 2014. *Address:* Senado Federal, National Congress Building, Praça dos Três Poderes, 70165-900 Brasilia, Brazil. *Telephone:* (61) 3303-4141. *Website:* www.senado.gov.br.

NEVILLE, Anne, OBE, BEng (Hons), PhD, CEng, MIM, FIMechE, FREng, FRSE; British engineer and academic; *RAEng Chair in Emerging Technologies and Deputy Head, School of Mechanical Engineering, University of Leeds;* ed Univ. of Glasgow; Prof. of Tribology and Surface Eng, Univ. of Leeds 2003–, currently RAEng Chair in Emerging Technologies and Deputy Head, School of Mechanical Eng; mem. Soc. of Tribologists and Lubrication Engineers (USA), Inst. of Corrosion; EPSRC Advanced Fellow 1999–2004; Fellow, Royal Acad. of Eng 2010; Research Merit Award, Royal Soc. 2011, Leverlhulme Medal, Royal Soc. 2016. *Publications:* several book chapters and numerous papers in professional journals on corrosion and tribo-corrosion, lubrication and wear, mineral scaling, surgical technologies and tribology; two patents. *Address:* 136 School of Mechanical Engineering, University of Leeds, Leeds, LS2 9JT, England (office). *Telephone:* (113) 343-6812 (office). *E-mail:* a.neville@leeds.ac.uk (office). *Website:* engineering.leeds.ac.uk (office).

NEVO, Ruth, PhD; Israeli painter and fmr professor of English literature; b. 8 July 1924, Johannesburg, SA; d. of Benjamin Weinbren and Henrietta Weinbren (née Goldsmith); m. Natan Nevo 1952; three s.; ed Univ. of the Witwatersrand, Hebrew Univ.; tutor, Dept of English, Hebrew Univ. 1952, Prof. 1973, Renee Lang Prof. of Humanities 1982–90, Prof. Emer. 1990–; full-time painter 1987–; nine solo exhbns 1987–2005; mem. Israel Acad. 1985–, Israel Asscn of Painters and Sculptors 1989–, Int. Asscn of English Profs, Int. Shakespeare Asscn. *Publications:* The Dial of Virtue 1963, Tragic Form in Shakespeare 1972, Comic Transformations in Shakespeare 1980, Shakespeare's Other Language 1987; trans. Selected Poems by Bialik 1981, Travels by Amichai 1986, The Challenge of Poetry 2008. *Address:* c/o Department of English, Hebrew University, Mount Scopus, Jerusalem, Israel. *E-mail:* ruth.nevo@mail.huji.ac.il.

NEWBERY, David Michael Garrood, CBE, PhD, ScD, FBA; British economist and academic; *Professor Emeritus of Economics, University of Cambridge;* b. 1 June 1943, Bucks., England; m. Terri E. Apter 1975; two d.; ed Portsmouth Grammar School, Trinity Coll. Cambridge; Economist, Treasury of Tanzanian Govt 1965–66; Asst Lecturer, Faculty of Econs and Politics, Univ. of Cambridge 1966–71, Lecturer 1971–86, Reader in Econs 1986–88, Prof. of Applied Econs (Prof. of Econs from 2004) 1988–2008, Prof. Emer. of Econs 2008–, Dir Dept of Applied Econs 1988–2003, Fellow, Churchill Coll. 1966–, currently Dir Cambridge Electricity Policy Research Group; Div. Chief, World Bank 1981–83; Pres.-elect, Int. Asscn for Energy Econs 2012, Pres. 2013; currently Research Fellow, Control and Power Research Group, Imperial Coll. London; Vice-Pres. European Econ. Asscn 1994–95, Pres. 1996; Vice-Chair. Cambridge Econ. Policy Assocs; occasional consultant to the World Bank; mem. Monopolies and Mergers Comm. (later Competition Comm.) 1996–2002; fmr Chair. Dutch electricity market surveillance cttee; mem. Academic Panel of Dept for Environment, Food and Rural Affairs (Defra); Fellow, Econometric Soc. 1989; Dr hc (Antwerp) 2004; Frisch Medal, Econometric Soc. 1990, Harry Johnson Prize (jtly), Canadian Econ. Asscn 1993, Int. Asscn for Energy Econs 2002 Outstanding Contribs to the Profession Award 2003. *Publications:* Project Appraisal in Practice (co-author) 1976, The Theory of Commodity Price Stabilization: A Study in the Economics of Risk (with J. E. Stiglitz) 1981, The Theory of Taxation for Developing Countries (with N. H. Stern) 1987, Hungary: An Economy in Transition (with I. Székely) 1993, Tax and Benefit Reform in Central and Eastern Europe 1995, A European Market for Electricity? (co-author) 1999, Privatization, Restructuring and Regulation of Network Utilities 2000, Hungary: An Economy in Transition (co-author) 2008; numerous articles. *Address:* Faculty of Economics, Sidgwick Avenue, Cambridge, CB3 9DE (office); 9 Huntingdon Road, Cambridge, CB3 0HH, England (home). *Telephone:* (1223) 335248 (office). *Fax:* (1223) 335299 (office). *E-mail:* dmgn@cam.ac.uk (office); david.newbery@econ.cam.ac.uk (office). *Website:* www.econ.cam.ac.uk/faculty/newbery (office).

NEWBIGGING, Sir David Kennedy, Kt, OBE; British business executive; b. 19 Jan. 1934, Tientsin, China; s. of D. L. Newbigging, CBE, MC, Bar and L. M. Newbigging; m. Carolyn S. Band 1968; one s. two d.; ed Oundle School; joined Jardine, Matheson & Co. Ltd 1954, Dir 1967, Man. Dir 1970, Chair. and Sr Man. Dir 1975–83; Chair. Hong Kong & Kowloon Wharf & Godown Co. Ltd 1970–80; Chair. and Man. Dir Hong Kong Land Co. Ltd 1975–83; Dir Hong Kong & Shanghai Banking Corpn 1975–83; Dir Hong Kong Electric Holdings Ltd 1975–83, Chair. 1982–83; Dir Hong Kong Telephone Co. Ltd 1975–83; Chair. Jardine, Fleming & Co. Ltd 1975–83; Dir Rennies Consolidated Holdings Ltd 1975–83, Safmarine and Rennies Holdings Ltd 1984–85, Provincial Insurance PLC 1984–86 (Deputy Chair. Provincial Group PLC 1985–91); Deputy Chair. Ivory & Sime PLC 1990–95, Chair. 1992–95 (Dir 1987–95); Dir NM UK (Chair. 1990–93), Rentokil Group PLC 1986–94 (Chair. 1987–94), PACCAR (UK) Ltd 1986–97, Mason Best International Ltd 1986–90 (Chair. 1987–90), International Financial Markets Trading Ltd 1986–93, United Meridian Corpn 1987–97, Thai Holdings Ltd 1989–91, Merrill Lynch and Co. Inc., USA 1997–2007, Ocean Energy Inc., USA 1998–, PACCAR Inc., USA 1999–; Deputy Chair. Benchmark Group PLC 1996–2004; Chair. Redfearn PLC March–Dec. 1988, Faupel PLC 1994–2005 (Dir 1989–2005), London Capital Holdings PLC March–Dec. 1994, Talbot Holdings Ltd 2003–07; Dir Wah Kwong Shipping Holdings Ltd 1992–99, Lloyd's Market Bd 1993–95, Friends' Provident Life Office 1993–2001 (Deputy Chair. 1996–98, Chair. 1998–2001, Chair. Friends Provident PLC 2001–05); Chair. Equitas Holdings Ltd 1995–98, Maritime Transport Services Ltd 1993–95; Trustee, Cancer Research UK 2001–10 (Deputy Chair. Council of Trustees 2002–04, Chair. 2004–10), King Mahendra UK Trust for Nature Conservation 1988–; Chair. of Trustees, Wilts Community Foundation 1991–97; Chair. of Council, Mission to Seafarers (fmrly Mission to Seaman) 1993–; Chair. Academic Partnerships International Ltd 2012–15; mem. Legis. Council of Hong Kong 1978–82, mem. Exec. Council 1980–84; mem. Int. Council, Morgan Guaranty Trust Co. of New York 1977–85, Supervisory Bd DAF Trucks NV 1997–99; mem. British Coal Corpn (fmrly Nat. Coal Bd) 1984–87, CIN Man. 1985–87; DL of Wilts. 1994–, High Sheriff of Wilts. 2003–04; Liveryman, Worshipful Co. of Grocers. *Leisure interests:* most outdoor sports, Chinese art. *Address:* 119 Old Church Street, London, SW3 6EA, England (home). *Telephone:* (20) 7352-1558 (home). *E-mail:* david@newbigging.co (home).

NEWBY, Sir Howard Joseph, KCB, CBE, BA, PhD, AcSS, FRSA; British sociologist, academic and university vice-chancellor; *Vice-Chancellor, University of Liverpool;* b. 10 Dec. 1947, Derby, England; s. of Alfred J. Newby and Constance A. Potts; Lecturer in Sociology, Univ. of Essex 1972–75, Sr Lecturer 1975–79; Prof. of Sociology, Univ. of Wisconson, USA 1979–83, Univ. of Essex 1983–88; Chair. Econ. & Social Research Council 1988–94, Chief Exec. 1994; Vice-Chancellor, Univ. of Southampton 1994–2001; mem. Rural Devt Comm. 1991–99, S & W Regional Health Authority 1994–96, European Sciences and Technology Asscn 1997–; Chair. Centre for Exploitation of Science and Tech. 1995, Cttee of Vice-Chancellors and Prins 1999–2001; Pres. BAAS 2001–02; Chief Exec. Higher Educ. Funding Council for England 2001–06; Vice-Chancellor, Univ. of the West of England 2006–07, Univ. of Liverpool 2008–; visiting appointments include Univs of New South Wales 1976, Sydney, Australia 1976, Wisconsin, USA 1977–78, Newcastle 1983–84; ten hon. degrees. *Publications include:* Community Studies (co-author) 1971, The Deferential Worker 1977, Property, Paternalism and Power (co-author) 1978, Green and Pleasant Land? 1979, The Problem of Sociology (co-author) 1983, Country Life 1987, The Countryside in Question 1988, Social Class in Modern Britain 1988 (co-author), The National Trust: The Next 100 Years 1995. *Leisure interests:* family life, gardening, Derby County, railway enthusiasms. *Address:* Office of the Vice-Chancellor, University of Liverpool, Liverpool, L69 3BX, England (office). *Telephone:* (151) 794-2000 (office). *E-mail:* howard.newby@liverpool.ac.uk (office). *Website:* www.liv.ac.uk (office).

NEWCOMBE, John David, AO, OBE; Australian fmr professional tennis player; b. 23 May 1944, Sydney, NSW; s. of George Ernest Newcombe and Lillian Newcombe; m. Angelika Pfannenberg (fmr German pro tennis player) 1966; one s. two d.; ed Sydney Church of England Grammar School; winner Wimbledon Singles Championship 1967 (last amateur), 1970, 1971, US Singles Championship 1967, 1973, Australian Singles Championship 1973, 1975, World Championship Tennis Crown 1974, Wimbledon Doubles Championship 1965–66, 1968–70, 1974; won 73 pro titles; played with Australian Davis Cup Team 1963–67, 1973–76, Capt. (non-playing) 1994–2000; set up a tennis camp, the John Newcombe Tennis Ranch, in Tex. 1968; Pres. Asscn of Tennis Professionals (Int.) 1976–78, Nat. Australia Day Council 1981–91; Chair. Player Devt Bd, Tennis Australia 1985–94; Hon. Life mem. Australian Wheelchair Tennis Asscn; Dr hc (Bond, Queensland) 1999; inducted into Int. Tennis Hall of Fame 1986. *Television:* has appeared as a commentator for various networks on numerous tennis tournaments in Australia, USA and UK. *Publications:* The Family Tennis Book 1975, The Young Tennis Player 1981, Bedside Tennis 1983, Newk 2002, No-one's Indestructible 2003, The Power Within 2012. *Leisure interests:* skiing, water-skiing, golf, fishing. *Address:* c/o Tennis Australia, Batman Avenue, Melbourne, Vic. 3000, Australia.

NEWELL, Mike, MA (Cantab.); British film director; b. 1942, St Albans, Herts.; s. of Terence William Newell and Mollie Louise Newell; m. Bernice Stegers 1979; one s. one d.; ed Univ. of Cambridge; trainee dir, Granada TV 1963; Dir European premiere of Tennessee Williams' The Kingdom of the Earth, Bristol Old Vic. *Films as director:* The Man in the Iron Mask 1976, The Awakening 1979, Bad Blood 1980, Dance with a Stranger (Prix de la Jeunesse, Cannes) 1984, The Good Father (Prix Italia 1985) 1985, Amazing Grace and Chuck 1986, Soursweet 1987, Common Ground 1990, Enchanted April 1991, Into the West 1992, Four Weddings and a Funeral (BAFTA Award for Best Film and Best Achievement in Direction 1995, Cesar Award for Foreign Film) 1994, An Awfully Big Adventure 1994, Donnie Brasco 1997, Pushing Tin 1998, Mona Lisa Smile 2003, Harry Potter and the Goblet of Fire 2005, Love in the Time of Cholera 2007, Prince of Persia 2010, Great Expectations 2012, The Guernsey Literary and Potato Peel Pie Society 2018. *Films as executive producer:* Photographing Fairies 1997, 200 Cigarettes 1999, Best Laid Plans 1999, High Fidelity 2000, Traffic 2000, I Capture the Castle 2003. *Television films:* Ready When You Are, Mr McGill, Tales out of School, Birth of a Nation (Prix Futura, Berlin), The Melancholy Hussar, Lost Your Tongue, Baa Baa Black Sheep, Common Ground (for CBS), Blood Feud (for Fox) 1983. *Television work includes:* Mr and Mrs Bureaucrat, Destiny, The Gift of Friendship, Brassneck (play), Just Your Luck (play). *Leisure interests:* reading (anything but fiction), walking. *Address:* c/o ICM, 3rd Floor, Marlborough House, 10 Earlham Street, London, WC2H 9LN, England (office). *Telephone:* (20) 7836-8564 (office). *Website:* www.icmtalent.com (office).

NEWLAND, Martin, BA, MA (Theol); British newspaper editor; b. 26 Oct. 1961, Port Harcourt, Nigeria; m.; four c.; ed Univ. of London; News Ed., The Catholic Herald 1987–89; Reporter, News Ed. and Home Ed., The Daily Telegraph 1989–98, Ed. 2003–05; Deputy Ed. The National Post, Canada 1998–2002; Founder and Ed.-in-Chief, The National, Abu Dhabi Media Co. 2007–09, Exec. Dir Abu Dhabi Media Co. 20011–14, Adviser to Chair. 2014–15; Consultant, Int. Media Investments, UAE 2016–17. *Leisure interest:* working out in the gym. *Address:* c/o International Media Investments FZ LLC, 769555, Dubai, United Arab Emirates.

NEWMAN, Frank Neil, BA; American banking executive; *Chairman, Promontory Financial Group China Ltd;* b. 20 April 1942, Quincy, Mass; m. Lizabeth Newman; one s.; ed Harvard Univ.; Man. Peat Marwick Livingston & Co. 1966–69; Vice-Pres. Citicorp 1969–73; Exec. Vice-Pres., Chief Financial Officer Wells Fargo Bank 1973–86; Vice-Chair., Chief Financial Officer Bank America Corp. 1986–93; Under-Sec. of the Treasury for Domestic Finance 1993–94, Deputy Sec. of the Treasury 1994–95; Sr Vice-Chair. Bankers Trust Co. 1995–96, Chair., Pres. and CEO 1996–99, resgnd as Chair., now Chair. Emer.; CEO Shenzhen Development Bank Co. Ltd (renamed Ping An Bank Co. Ltd following merger with Ping An Bank Co. Ltd 2012) from 2005; Founding Chair. and CEO, Promontory Financial Group China Ltd, now Chair.; Vice-Chair. of Asia, Global Strategic Associates LLC; fmr Vice-Chair. The Broad Center for Man. of School Systems, Los Angeles; mem. Bd Deutsche Bank 1999, Dow Jones & Co., Korea First Bank, GUS; Alexander Hamilton Award (US Treasury Dept). *Address:* Promontory Financial Group, LLC, 801 17th Street, NW, Suite 1100, Washington, DC 20006 (office); Global Strategic Associates LLC, 150 East 58th Street, 24th Floor, New York, NY 10155, USA (office). *Telephone:* (202) 384-1200 (Promontory Financial Group) (office); (212) 308-6423 (office). *E-mail:* fnewman@promontory.com (office). *Website:* www.promontory.com (office); www.globalstrategicassociates.com (office).

NEWMAN, Kevin, BA; Canadian broadcast journalist; b. 2 June 1959, Toronto, Ont.; m. Cathy Kearns; one s. one d.; ed Univ. of Western Ontario; corresp., Global News, Global TV Network, Toronto, Parl. Bureau, Ottawa 1983–87; later with CTV Nat. News, CBC The National, CBC Midday; joined ABC (American Broadcasting Corpn) News, New York 1994, positions including Substitute Anchor and Corresp., World News Tonight with Peter Jennings, Sr Corresp., Nightline, Co-host, Good Morning America; Anchor and Exec. Ed., Global National with Kevin Newman, Global TV Network, BC 2001–10; Co-anchor, CTV 2011–, Host and Man. Ed. W5 (series) 2016–; fmr Instructor in Broadcast Journalism, Ryerson Univ. School of Journalism; Rogers Communication Lecturer, Univ. of Western Ontario 1999; mem. Bd of Dirs Communitech 2011; Hon. LLD (Univ. of Western Ontario) 2011; Emmy Award for Outstanding News and Documentary Program Achievement 2000, Emmy Award for Outstanding Coverage of a Breaking News Story 2000, George Foster Peabody Award for ABC 2000 Millennium Coverage 2000, Women's Sport Foundation Award for Outstanding Network TV Journalism 2000, Leo Award for Best Anchor 2002, 2003, Canadian Radio and TV News Dirs Asscn Best Breaking News Coverage Award 2001, Best Continuing Coverage Award 2001. *Publication:* All Out: A Father and Son Confront the Hard Truths That Made Them Better Men (Memoir) (co-author) 2015. *Address:* CTV Television Network, PO Box 9, Station O, Toronto, ON M4A 2M9, Canada. *Telephone:* (416) 384-5000. *E-mail:* w5@ctv.ca (office). *Website:* www.ctvnews.ca.

NEWMAN, Maurice Lionel, AC, AM; Australian banker, business executive and government official; *Chairman, Prime Minister's Business Advisory Council;* b. 20 March 1938, Ilford, England; s. of J. Newman; m. 1st 1963 (divorced); two s.; m. 2nd Jeanette Newman 1994; ed Univ. of Sydney; Partner, Bain & Co. 1966–73, Man. Dir Bain & Co. Group 1983–85; Man. Dir Deutsche Bank Australia Group (fmrly Deutsche Morgan Grenfell Group) 1984, Exec. Chair. 1985–99, Chair. Deutsche Asset Management (Australia) Ltd 1997–2000, Chair. Deutsche Bank Asia Pacific Advisory Bd and Dir, Deutsche Bank Asia Pacific 1999–2001; Chair. Australian Stock Exchange Ltd (merged with Sydney Futures Exchange to form Australian Securities Exchange—ASX Ltd 2006) 1994–2008, Australian-Taiwan Business Council from 1995, East Asia and Oceanic Stock Exchange Fed. 1995–96, Axiom Funds Man. Ltd from 1997, Benchmark Securities Man. Ltd from 1997, Commercial Investment Trust from 1998, Financial Sector, Advisory Council from 1998, Acrux Ltd 1999–2003, Melon Pastoral Pty Ltd; Dir, Financial Futures Market from 1990, Securities Industry Research Centre Australia; Chair. Nat. Judging Panel for Innovation in Local Govt 1997–98, Commonwealth Govt's Nat. Year 2000 Steering Cttee 1997–2000, Sydney Legacy Citizen's Cttee 1998–2004, Fed. Treas.'s Financial Sector Advisory Council 1998–2007, Business Mature Age Workforce Advisory Group 2000–01, Sydney Convention & Visitors Bureau 2001–07, Tourism NSW 2002–07; Co-Chair. Singapore Australia Business Alliance Forum 1999–2002; mem. Consultative Cttee on Relations with Japan 1984–87, Business Advisory Panel est. by the Minister for Multicultural Affairs 1997–2002, NSW Premier's Major Events Bd 2002–04; Commr, Nat. Comm. of Audit 1996; Trustee, Stock Exchange Superannuation and Accumulation Fund 1990–; mem. Bd of Dirs Australian Broadcasting Corpn 2000–04, Chair. 2006–12; Chancellor Macquarie Univ. 2002–08, now Hon. Prof. and Hon. Chair. Macquarie University Foundation Patrons; Chair. Prime Minister's Business Advisory Council 2013–; mem. Australian Inst. of Co. Dirs; Civil Patron, Royal Australian Naval Reserve, Professional Studies Program 2005–09. *Leisure interests:* cycling, horse riding, tennis. *Address:* Prime Minister's Business Advisory Council, Parliament House, Canberra, ACT 2600 (office); 35 Burran Avenue, Mosman, NSW 2088, Australia (home). *Telephone:* (2) 6271-5111 (office). *Fax:* (2) 6271-5414 (office). *Website:* www.pm.gov.au/media/2013-12-04/prime-ministers-business-advisory-council (office).

NEWMAN, Nanette; British actress and writer; b. 29 May 1934, Northampton, England; d. of Sidney Newman and Ruby Newman; m. Bryan Forbes 1955 (died 2013); two d.; ed Sternhold Coll., London, Italia Conti Stage School, Royal Acad. of Dramatic Art. *Film appearances include:* The L-Shaped Room 1962, The Wrong Arm of the Law 1962, Seance on a Wet Afternoon 1963, The Wrong Box 1965, The Whisperers 1966, The Madwoman of Chaillot 1968, The Raging Moon (Variety Club Best Actress Award) 1971, The Stepford Wives 1974, International Velvet 1978, Restless Natives 1985, The Mystery of Edwin Drood 1993. *Television appearances include:* The Fun Food Factory, London Scene, Stay with Me Till Morning, Jessie, Let There Be Love, Late Expectations, The Endless Game 1988, Ideal Home Cooks, Newman Meets (series), Celebrations (series). *Publications:* God Bless Love 1972, Lots of Love 1973, Fun Food Factory 1976, All Our Love 1978, The Root Children 1978, Amy Rainbow 1980, That Dog 1980, Reflections 1981, Dog Lovers Coffee Table Book 1982, Cat Lovers Coffee Table Book 1983, My Granny Was a Frightful Bore 1983, 2004, Christmas Cookbook 1984, Cat and Mouse Love Story 1984, The Best of Love 1985, Pigalev 1985, Archie 1986, The Summer Cookbook 1986, Small Beginnings 1987, Bad Baby 1988, Entertaining with Nanette Newman 1988, Charlie the Noisy Caterpillar 1989, Sharing 1989, ABC 1990, 123 1991, Cooking for Friends 1991, Spider, The Horrible Cat 1992, There's a Bear in the Bath 1993, There's a Bear in the Classroom 1996, Take 3 Cooks 1996, Up to the Skies and Down Again 1999, To You with Love 1999, Bad Baby Good Baby 2002, Small Talk 2004, Ben's Book 2005, Eating In 2005. *Leisure interests:* needlepoint, china painting. *Address:* c/o Chatto & Linnit Ltd, 123A King's Road, London, SW3 4PL, England (office). *Telephone:* (20) 7352-7722 (office).

NEWMAN, Thomas Montgomery, MMus; American composer; b. 29 Oct. 1955, Los Angeles, Calif.; s. of Alfred Newman; m. Ann Marie Zirbes; three c.; ed Univ. of Southern California, Yale Univ.; mem. Broadcast Music, Inc. *Compositions include:* several works for concert stage, including symphonic work Reach Forth Our Hands commissioned in 1996 by Cleveland Orchestra, At Ward's Ferry, Length 180 ft., concerto for double bass and orchestra commissioned in 2001 by Pittsburgh Symphony, chamber work It Got Dark, commissioned by Kronos Quartet in 2009, with Rick Cox released 35 Whirlpools Below Sound, collection of avant-garde electronic soundscapes 2014. *Compositions for film include:* Summer's End 1984, Reckless 1984, Revenge of the Nerds 1984, Grandview, USA 1984, Desperately Seeking Susan 1985, Girls Just Want to Have Fun 1985, The Man with One Red Shoe 1985, Real Genius 1985, Gung Ho 1986, Jumpin' Jack Flash 1986, Light of Day 1987, The Lost Boys 1987, Less Than Zero 1987, The Great Outdoors 1988, The Prince of Pennsylvania 1988, Cookie 1989, Men Don't Leave 1990, Welcome Home, Roxy Carmichael 1990, Career Opportunities 1991, Naked Tango 1991, The Rapture 1991, Deceived 1991, The Linguini Incident 1991, Fried Green Tomatoes 1991, The Player 1992, Whispers in the Dark 1992, Scent of a

Woman 1992, Flesh and Bone 1993, Josh and S.A.M. 1993, Threesome 1994, The Favor 1994, Corrina, Corrina 1994, The Shawshank Redemption 1994, The War 1994, Little Women 1994, Unstrung Heroes 1995, How to Make an American Quilt 1995, Up Close & Personal 1996, Phenomenon 1996, American Buffalo 1996, The People vs Larry Flynt 1996, Mad City 1997, Red Corner 1997, Oscar and Lucinda 1997, The Horse Whisperer 1998, Meet Joe Black 1998, American Beauty (Grammy Award, BAFTA 2000) 1999, The Green Mile 1999, Erin Brockovich 2000, My Khmer Heart 2000, Pay It Forward 2000, In the Bedroom 2001, The Execution of Wanda Jean 2002, The Salton Sea 2002, Road to Perdition 2002, White Oleander 2002, Finding Nemo 2003, Lemony Snicket's A Series of Unfortunate Events 2004, Cinderella Man 2005, Jarhead 2005, Little Children 2006, The Good German 2006, Nothing is Private 2007, Wall-E 2008, Revolutionary Road 2009, Brothers 2009, The Debt 2010, Skyfall (BAFTA 2013, Grammy Award for Best Score Soundtrack for Visual Media 2014) 2012, Side Effects 2013, Saving Mr. Banks 2013, The Judge 2014, Bridge of Spies 2015, Finding Dory 2016. *Compositions for television include:* The Paper Chase (series) 1978, The Seduction of Gina (film) 1984, Amazing Stories (episode 'Santa 85') 1985, Heat Wave (film) 1990, Against the Law (series) 1990, Those Secrets (film) 1992, Citizen Cohn (film) 1992, Arli$$ (series) 1996, Boston Public (series theme) 2000, Six Feet Under (series theme, Emmy Award) 2001, Angels in America (mini-series) 2003, Katedralen 1.z 2004, The Newsroom (series) 2012, Lauren (series) 2013. *Address:* c/o Gorfaine/Schwartz Agency Inc., 4111 West Alameda Avenue, Suite 509, Burbank, CA 91505, USA (office). *Telephone:* (818) 260-8500 (office). *Website:* www .gsamusic.com (office).

NEWSOM, Gavin, BA; American politician; *Governor of California;* b. 10 Oct. 1967, San Francisco; s. of William Newsom and Tessa Newsom; m. 1st Kimberly Guilfoyle 2001 (divorced 2006); m. 2nd Jennifer Siebel 2008; four c.; ed Santa Clara Univ.; opened first business, PlumpJack Wine Shop 1992, gen. partner in several business ventures including Squaw Valley Inn, PlumpJack Man. Group; Pres. Parking and Traffic Comm., San Francisco 1996, mem. Bd of Supervisors 1997–2003; Mayor of San Francisco 2004–11; Lt-Gov. of Calif. 2011–19, Gov. of Calif. 2019–; Democrat. *Address:* Office of the Governor, State Capitol, Suite 1173, Sacramento, CA 95814, USA. *Telephone:* (916) 445-2841 (office). *Fax:* (916) 558-3160 (office). *E-mail:* gavin@gavinnewsom.com. *Website:* www.gov.ca.gov; www .gavinnewsom.com.

NEWSOME, William T., III, BS, PhD; American neuroscientist and academic; *Professor, Department of NeurobiologyHarman Family Provostial Professor, Stanford University;* b. 5 June 1972, Live Oak, FL; ed Stetson Univ., California Inst. of Tech.; Postdoctoral Researcher, Nat. Eye Inst. 1980–84; Asst Prof., Dept of Neurobiology and Behavior, State Univ. of New York, Stony Brook 1984–88; Assoc. Prof., Dept of Neurobiology, Stanford Univ. School of Medicine 1988–93, Prof. 1993–, Dept Chair 2005–08, Dir Neurosciences Grad. Program 2000–05, BioX NeuroVentures 2008–13, Harman Family Provostial Prof. 2013–; Investigator, Howard Hughes Medical Inst. 1997–, Chevy Chase, Md; mem. NAS 2000, American Philosophical Soc. 2011, American Acad. of Arts and Sciences 2017; Hon. DSc (State Univ. of New York Coll. of Optometry) 2012; Rank Prize in Optoelectronics 1992, Spencer Award, Columbia Univ. Coll. of Physicians and Surgeons 1994, Guggenheim Fellowship 1995, Distinguished Scientific Contrib. Award, American Psychological Asscn 2002, Dan David Prize (Brain Sciences), Dan David Foundation and Tel-Aviv Univ. 2004, Karl Spencer Lashley Award, American Philosophical Soc. 2010, Pepose Award, Brandeis Univ. 2015. *Publications:* numerous scientific papers in professional journals on the neural mechanisms underlying visual perception, visually based decision-making, and related issues in cognitive neuroscience. *Address:* Department of Neurobiology, Clark Center, W-123, Stanford University School of Medicine, Stanford, CA 94305-5125 (office); 12 Summit Road, Woodside, CA 94062, USA (home). *Telephone:* (650) 725-5814 (office). *Fax:* (650) 725-3958 (office). *E-mail:* bnewsome@stanford.edu (office). *Website:* monkeybiz.stanford.edu (office).

NEWSON, Marc Andrew, CBE, RDI; Australian designer; *Director, Marc Newson Ltd;* b. 20 Oct. 1963, Sydney, NSW; s. of Paul Newson and Carol Conomos; m. Charlotte Stockdale 2008; two c.; ed Sydney Coll. of the Arts; staged first exhbn at Rosyln Oxley Galery, Sydney 1986; designed first of pod series of watches 1986; designer, Idée Co., Tokyo, Japan 1987–91; set up studio in Paris, France 1991; began to work for Flos for Lighting, Cappellini and Moroso 1991; est. Ikepod Watch Co. (jt venture) 1991; designed Shiseido Men's Toiletries Range, Paris 1992; Visiting Prof. European Inst. of Design, Milan, Italy 1992, Vitra Design Museum Summer Workshop, Germany 1992; designed Gluon Chair and TV Chair for Moroso 1993, Helice Lamp for Flos 1993, Gello Table for 3 Suisses 1994; co-f. Ikepod, Switzerland (with Oliver Ike) 1994; set up Marc Newson Ltd, London 1997, currently Dir; designs include Glassware for Iittala, Finland 1998, MNO1 Aluminium Bicycle for Biomega, Denmark 1999, O21C Concept Car for Ford Motor Co. (Concept Car Design Award, Tokyo Motor Show 1999) 1999, Hair Care Products for Vidal Sassoon, New York 2000, Lever House Restaurant and Bar, New York 2002, interiors of Hotel Puerta America, Madrid 2005, Qantas first class lounges in Melbourne and Sydney, Qantas 'Skybed' business class seat and Airbus 380 Economy Class Seat (Australian Int. Design Award of the Year 2009), Riva Aquariva speedboat 2010; design work for Nike, Idée-Sputnik 2000; est. Partnership with Syn to develop products for Japanese market 2000; Artistic Dir Sydney New Year's Eve fire works display 2011; joined Apple, Inc. 2014–; works in several major museum collections, including MoMA, New York, Design Museum, London, Victoria and Albert Museum, London, Centre Georges Pompidou, Paris, Vitra Design Museum; Adjunct Prof., Sydney Coll. of the Arts, Hong Kong Polytechnic Univ.; Royal Designer for Industry (UK) 2006; Chair. Int. Design Council, London Design Museum 2018; Hon. Dr of Visual Arts (Sydney) 2010; Australian Crafts Council Award 1984, Visual Arts Bd Grant, Australia Council 1988, Prix du créateur de l'année, Salon du Meuble, Paris 1993, Top 50 Designers Award, I.D. Magazines 1998, Sydney Design Convention Award 1999, Red Dot Design Award (Germany) 1999, 2006, George Nelson Design Award (USA) 1999, Compasso D'Oro Award, X1X Premio (Italy) 2000, Design Innovationen 2000, Design Zentrum Nordrhein Westfalen, Germany, 2000, Chicago Athenaeum Good Design Award 2001, 2003 (twice), 2005, 2006, 2009, 2010, Australian Design Award 2003, 2009 (twice), Elle Decoration Design Awards, UK 2003, ADI Compasso d'Oro Award 2004, Good Design Award (G Mark) (Japan) 2004, L'Observateur du Design Award, Paris 2005, Time Out Awards NY Reader's Choice, Best New Restaurant

Design 2005, Classic Design Awards, Homes & Gardens with V&A Museum 2005, Product Innovation Award, Bathroom & Kitchen Magazine 2005, Design & Decoration Awards, best bathroom product (UK) 2005, SIFA Awards, Berlin 2005, included in TIME magazine's 100 Most Influential People in the World 2005, Designer of the Year Award, Design Miami/ Basel 2006, Australian Travel Innovator Award 2007, Australian Int. Design Awards 2008, Skytrax World Airline Award 2008, London Design Medal, London Design Festival 2008, Man of the Year Award, for Design, GQ Germany 2008, Wallpaper Design Award, Smeg Ovens & Hobs 2009, Condé Nast Traveller Innovation & Design Award 2009, Lifetime Achievement Award, The Design Awards (UK) 2010, Lucky Strike Designer Award 2011, GQ Man of the Year (Creative Icon) 2015. *Designs include:* Lockheed Lounge 1984, Orgone Lounge, Charlotte Chair, Sugar Guppy Lamp 1987, Black Hole Table and Felt Chair 1988, Wood Chair for House of Fiction Exhbn, Sydney 1988, Embryo Chair for Powerhouse Museum, Sydney 1988, Andoni Shop Interior, Sydney 1988, Pod Bar Interior, Tokyo 1989, Orgone Fibreglass Chair and Lounge, Sydney 1989, Carbon Fibre Mystery Clock 1990, Event Horizon Table 1991, Interiors of Hysterie and Skoda Boutiques, Germany 1992, Seaslug Watch 1994, Interior of Coast Restaurant, London 1995, Hemipode Watch 1996, Interior of Syn Recording Studio, Tokyo 1996, Interior of Komed Restaurant, Cologne 1996, Falcon 900B Business Jet, London 1999, Llama Apartments Project, Brisbane 2000, Interior of Lever Bar, New York 2000, Miniature Lockheed Lounge 2000, Magnum Presentation Set for Dom Perignon 2006 and Black Box 2010, new range for Smeg (appliances) 2009–10, Caroma Marc Newson Bathroom Collection (Good Design of the Year Award 2014, Good Design Award – Housing and Building category 2014) 2013, Apple Watch Sport, Apple Watch, Apple Watch Edition 2015, Decanter design for Hennessy's new Cognac, James Hennessy 2015, Montblanc M pen 2015. *Museum collections:* Art Gallery of S Australia, Adelaide, Carnegie Museum, Pittsburgh, Design Museum, London, Musée des Arts Decoratifs, Paris, Powerhouse Museum, Sydney, San Francisco Museum of Modern Art, Vitra Design Museum, Weil am Rhein (Germany). *Publication:* Marc Newson 1999. *Address:* Marc Newson Ltd, 7 Howick Place, London, SW1P 1BB, England (office). *Telephone:* (20) 7932-0990 (office). *Fax:* (20) 7630-6017 (office). *E-mail:* pod@marc-newson.com (office). *Website:* www.marc -newson.com (office).

NEWTON, Christopher, CM, BA, MA; Canadian (b. British) actor, director and author; *Artistic Director Emeritus, The Shaw Festival;* b. 11 June 1936, Deal, Kent, England; s. of Albert E. Newton and Gwladys M. Emes; ed Sir Roger Manwood's School, Sandwich, Kent and Univ. of Leeds, UK, Illinois and Purdue Univs, USA; actor, Stratford Festival, New York; Founding Artistic Dir, Theatre Calgary, Calgary, Alberta 1968–71; Artistic Dir, Vancouver Playhouse and Founder (with Powys Thomas), The Playhouse Acting School 1973–79; Artistic Dir, The Shaw Festival, Niagara-on-the-Lake 1979–2002, Artistic Dir Emer. 2002–; Hon. Fellow, Ryerson Univ., Royal Conservatory of Music; Hon. LLD (Brock Univ., Guelph, Toronto); Hon. DLitt (Wilfrid Laurier Univ.); Hon. DHL (State Univ. of NY at Buffalo); Gov.-Gen.'s Award, Molson Prize, Gascon-Thomas Award, Chalmers Award, Barbara Hamilton Memorial Award 2017. *Plays directed include:* (for the Shaw Festival) Heartbreak House, Cavalcade, Man and Superman, Pygmalion, The Importance of Being Earnest, Easy Virtue, The Doctor's Dilemma, Lady Windermere's Fan, Caesar and Cleopatra, The Return of the Prodigal; (for Melbourne Theatre Co.) Misalliance; (for Vancouver Playhouse) She Stoops to Conquer, Hamlet, Julius Caesar, The Taming of the Shrew; (for Theatre Calgary) An Inspector Calls; (for YPT) Great Expectations; (for Stratford Festival) Much Ado About Nothing. *Operas directed include:* (for Canadian Opera Co.) Madama Butterfly, Patria I, The Turn of the Screw, Albert Herring; (for Nat. Arts Centre and Vancouver Opera) The Barber of Seville; (for Opera Hamilton) I due Foscari. *Publications:* plays: You Two Stay Here the Rest Come with Me, Slow Train to St Ives, Trip, The Sound of Distant Thunder, The Lost Letter (adaptation). *Leisure interest:* landscape architecture. *Address:* Shaw Festival, Box 774, Niagara-on-the-Lake, ON L0S 1J0 (office); 22 Prideaux Street, PO Box 609, Niagara-on-the-Lake, ON L0S 1J0, Canada (home). *Telephone:* (905) 468-2153 (office); (905) 468-4169 (home). *E-mail:* c_newton@sympatico.ca (home). *Website:* www.shawfest.com (office).

NEWTON, Thandiwe (Thandie) Melanie; British actress; b. 6 Nov. 1972, London, England; d. of Nick Newton and Nyasha Newton; m. Oliver Parker 1998; one s. two d.; ed Downing Coll., Cambridge. *Films include:* Flirting 1991, The Young Americans 1993, Bloody Weekend 1994, Interview with the Vampire: The Vampire Chronicles 1994, Loaded 1994, Jefferson in Paris 1995, The Journey of August King 1995, The Leading Man 1996, Gridlock'd 1997, Besieged 1998, Beloved 1998, Mission: Impossible II 2000, It Was an Accident 2000, The Truth About Charlie 2002, Shade 2003, The Chronicles of Riddick 2004, Crash (BAFTA Award for Best Actress in a Supporting Role 2006) 2005, The Pursuit of Happyness 2006, Norbit 2007, Run Fat Boy Run 2007, RocknRolla 2008, W. 2008, How to Lose Friends & Alienate People 2008, 2012 2009, Huge 2010, Vanishing on 7th Street 2010, For Colored Girls 2010, Retreat 2011, Good Deeds 2012, Half of a Yellow Sun 2013, The Slap 2015, Gringo 2018, Solo: A Star Wars Story 2018, The Death and Life of John F. Donovan 2018. *Television:* Pirate Prince (film) 1991, In Your Dreams (film) 1996, ER (series) 2003–09, American Dad! (series) 2006, Rogue (series) 2013–15, Westworld (series) (Emmy Award for Outstanding Supporting Actress In A Drama Series 2018, Critics' Choice Award for Best Supporting Actress in a Drama Series 2019) 2016, Line of Duty 2017. *Address:* c/o WME Entertainment, 9601 Wilshire Boulevard, Beverly Hills, CA 90210-5213, USA (office). *Telephone:* (310) 285-9000 (office). *Website:* wmeentertainment.com (office).

NEWTON-JOHN, Olivia, AO, OBE; British singer and actress; b. 26 Sept. 1948, Cambridge, England; d. of Brin Newton-John and Irene Born; m. 1st Matt Lattanzi 1984; one d.; m. 2nd John Easterling 2008; Co-owner Koala Blue 1982–; UNEP Goodwill Amb. 1989–; numerous awards including Grammy Awards for Best Female Country Vocal Performance 1973, for Record of the Year 1974, for Best Female Pop Vocal Performance 1974, American Music Awards for Favorite Female Country Artist 1974, 1975, for Favorite Female Pop/Rock Artist 1974, 1975, 1976, 1982, Humanitarian Award, US Red Cross 1999, People's Choice Awards, Medal of the Order of Australia 2010. *Albums include:* If Not For You 1971, Let Me Be There (American Music Award for Favorite Country Album 1974) 1974, Music Makes My Day 1974, Long Live Love 1974, If You Love Me Let Me Know (No. 1, USA) 1974, Have You Never Been Mellow (American Music Award for Favorite Pop/Rock

Album 1975) 1975, Clearly Love 1975, Come On Over 1976, Don't Stop Believin' 1976, Making A Good Thing Better 1977, Greatest Hits 1978, Grease (film soundtrack) (American Music Award for Favorite Pop/Rock Album 1978) 1978, Totally Hot 1979, Xanadu (film soundtrack) 1980, Physical 1981, 20 Greatest Hits 1982, Olivia's Greatest Hits Vol. 2 1983, Two Of A Kind 1984, Soul Kiss 1986, The Rumour 1988, Warm And Tender 1990, Back To Basics: The Essential Collection 1971–92 1992, Gaia – One Woman's Journey 1995, More Than Physical 1995, Greatest Hits 1996, Olivia 1998, Back With A Heart 1998, Highlights From The Main Event 1999, Greatest Hits: First Impressions 1999, Country Girl 1999, Best Of Olivia Newton John 1999, Love Songs: A Collection: One Woman's Live Journey 2000, Grace and Gratitude 2007, Christmas Collection 2010, Magic 2011, This Christmas 2012, Liv On (with Beth Nielsen Chapman and Amy Sky) 2016. *Films include:* Grease 1978, Xanadu 1980, Two of a Kind 1983, It's My Party 1995, Sordid Wives 1999, 1 a Minute (documentary) 2009, A Few Best Men 2012. *Television includes:* It's Cliff Richard (BBC series). *Publication:* LivWise: Easy Recipes for a Healthy, Happy Life 2011. *Leisure interests:* horse riding, songwriting, cycling, astrology, conservation, animals. *Address:* c/o Fitzgerald Hartley Co., 34 North Palm Avenue, Suite 100, Ventura, CA 93001, USA (office). *Website:* www.olivianewton-john.com.

NEY, Martin, LLB, MA, PhD; German lawyer and diplomatist; *Ambassador to India;* m. Dr Gabriele Ney; two s.; ed Univ. of Würzburg, Univ. of Geneva, Switzerland, Univ. of Oxford (Rhodes Scholar), UK; Jr Lecturer in Constitutional and Public Int. Law, Univ. of Würzburg 1983–86; began diplomatic career in Legal Dept of Fed. Foreign Office, Bonn 1986, Head of Cultural and Press Section, Embassy in Bangkok 1988–90, acted as legal adviser and chaired legal cttee in final round of negotiations on external aspects of German unification ('2+4-Negotiations') 1990–91, Exec. Asst to State Sec., Fed. Foreign Office 1991–93, Counsellor for Politico-Mil. Affairs, Embassy in Washington, DC 1993–97, Deputy Head of Econ. Section, Embassy in Tokyo 1997–98, Head of Political Dept, Embassy in Tokyo 1998–2001, European Corresp., Fed. Foreign Office 2001–05, Amb. and Sr Deputy High Rep. for Bosnia and Herzegovina, Sarajevo 2005–06, Commr for the UN, Human Rights and Humanitarian Aid, Fed. Foreign Office 2006–07, Deputy Perm. Rep. to UN, New York (rank of Amb.) 2007–10, Deputy Dir-Gen., Legal Affairs, Fed. Foreign Office 2010–12, Legal Adviser of Fed. Foreign Office 2012–15, Amb. to India 2015–; mem. Toenissteiner Kreis 1984, Atlantik-Bruecke 2001. *Achievements include:* Co-Prin. Flautist of First German Airforce Band during mil. service 1974–76, performed as soloist with Sarajevo Symphony Orchestra in Nat. Theatre, gave solo concerts in Wiener Musikverein several times, has performed frequently with Frankfurter Solisten (chamber ensemble of Frankfurt Opera orchestra) 2005–, performed as soloist with Nürnberger Philharmoniker in UN Gen. Ass. 2010. *Recordings:* four concerts with Frankfurter Solisten recorded on CD. *Leisure interests:* tennis, sailing, playing chamber music. *Address:* German Embassy, 6/50G Shanti Path, Chanakyapuri, New Delhi 110 021, India (office). *Telephone:* (11) 44199199 (office). *Fax:* (11) 26873117 (office). *E-mail:* info@new-delhi.diplo.de (office). *Website:* www.new-delhi.diplo.de (office).

NEYNSKY, Nadezhda; Bulgarian politician; b. (Nadezhda Nikolova Mihaylova), 9 Aug. 1962, Sofia; m. 1st Kamen Mikhailov (divorced 2006); two d.; m. 2nd Svetlin Neynski; ed Spanish Language High School, Sofia, St Kliment Ohridski Univ. of Sofia, John F. Kennedy School of Govt, Harvard Univ., USA; freelance journalist 1986–88; trans. of Spanish poetry and English literature 1988–90; Head of Foreign Relations, Dept of the Radical Democratic Party 1990–91; gained US Congress Foreign Policy and Public Relations Certificate through working in office of Rep. David Drier (Republican) 1991; Spokesperson and Chief of the Press Centre, Union for Democratic Forces during election campaign 1991; Spokesperson of centre-right cabinet and Chief of the Govt Press Centre 1991–93; took public relations course, BBC, London, UK 1993; Deputy Chair. Union of Democratic Forces 1994–97, Chair. 2002–05; Chair. Right Alternative Union 2006–; Vice-Pres. European People's Party (EPP), Co-Chair. EPP's Foreign Relations Cttee 1999–2006, Vice-Pres. SME Central, SME Union of the EPP 2007–11; mem. Parl. (37th Nat. Ass.), mem. Foreign Policy Cttee, mem. Bulgarian Del. to the Council of Europe, Chair. Cttee for Parl. and Public Relations 1994–97, 38th Nat. Ass. 1997, 39th Nat. Ass., mem. Foreign Policy, Defence and Security Cttee 2001–05, Chair. Parl. Group of the United Democratic Forces 2002–05, 40th Nat. Ass., mem. Foreign Affairs Cttee, European Affairs Cttee 2005–09, Deputy Speaker, Nat. Ass. 2008–09; Minister of Foreign Affairs 1997–2001; mem. European Parl. (Group of the European People's Party (Christian Democrats) 2009–, mem. Cttee on Budgets, Del. to EU-Russia Parl. Co-operation Cttee, Del. for Relations with the NATO Parl. Ass., Substitute mem. Cttee on Foreign Affairs, Sub-cttee on Security and Defence, Del. for Relations with the Maghreb countries and the Arab Maghreb Union; Chair. Inst. for Democracy and Stability in South-East Europe 2004–; mem. Int. Advisory Cttee to the Democracy Coalition Project, in partnership with Bertelsmann Foundation, Freedom House and Ghana Centre for Democratic Devt 2006, Advisory Group for Southern Leaders' Round Tables to the Special Unit for South–South Cooperation 2006; Chair. Small and Medium Enterprises in Bulgaria 2007; mem. Nat. Union of Civil Soc. 2012; Order of the Kingdom of Denmark (First Class), Medal awarded by Repub. of Malta, Chevalier, Légion d'honneur, Cross of the Order for Public Service (Spain); Special Golden Distinction of US Acad. of Achievements, Badge of Honour, Venice, B'nai B'rith Medal of Tolerance. *Address:* European Parliament, Bâtiment Altiero Spinelli, 03F142, 60 rue Wiertz, 1047 Brussels, Belgium (office). *Telephone:* (2) 284-52-42 (office). *Fax:* (2) 284-92-42 (office). *E-mail:* nadezhda.neynsky@europarl.europa.eu (office). *Website:* www.europarl.europa.eu (office); www.nadezhdaneynsky.eu.

NEZVAL, Jiří; Czech automobile executive; b. 5 April 1941, Brno; s. of František Nezval and Květa Nezvalová; m. Silva Moltašová 1963; two d.; ed Railway Coll. Žilina and Polytechnic Inst. Brno; designer and design office man. in automation of rail transport, Prague; involved in Czechoslovak Scientific and Tech. Soc., Peace Movt; Fed. Minister of Transport 1990–92; mem. Civic Movt Party 1991–93, Free Democrats Party 1993– (merged with Liberal Nat. Social Party 1995); apptd Dir Denzel Praha Co. 1992; Chair. Union of Motor Car Importers 1995; Exclusive Mitsubishi dealership in Czech Repub. 1997–. *Leisure interests:* computer art, man. systems, reading books, sports (skiing, cycling, volleyball).

NFUBEA, Ricardo Mangue Obama; Equatorial Guinean lawyer and politician; mem. Democratic Party of Equatorial Guinea (PDGE); fmr State Minister for Labour and Social Security; Minister of State in charge of the Civil Service and Admin. Co-ordination 2003; Deputy Prime Minister 2004–06, Prime Minister 2006–08 (resgnd).

NG, Andrew Y., MSc, PhD; American computer scientist; *Co-Founder and Co-Chairman, Coursera, Inc.;* b. 18 April 1976, UK; m. Carol E. Reiley 2014; ed Carnegie Mellon Univ., Massachusetts Inst. of Tech., Univ. of California, Berkeley; Asst Prof., Dept of Computer Science and Dept of Electrical Eng, Stanford Univ. 2002–09, Assoc. Prof. 2009–15, Adjunct Prof. of Computer Science 2015–, Dir Stanford Artificial Intelligence Lab., led devt of Stanford main MOOC (Massive Open Online Courses) platform 2011; Founder, Google Brain project, Google, Inc. 2011–12; Co-founder and Co-Chair. Coursera, Inc. 2012–; Vice Pres. and Chief Scientist, Baidu, Inc. 2014–17; Founder, deeplearning.ai (online education platform) 2017–; Chair. Bd of Dirs Woebot Labs Inc. 2017–; Founder and CEO Landing Al 2017–; mem. Bd of Dirs drive.ai (tech. co.) 2017–; Int. Jt Conf. on Artificial Intelligence Computers and Thought Award 2009. *Publications include:* author and co-author of over 150 published papers on machine learning, robotics. *Address:* Coursera, Inc., 381 E Evelyn Ave, Mountain View, CA 94041 (office); Computer Science Department, Stanford University, Room 156, Gates Building, Stanford, CA 94305-9010, USA. *Telephone:* (650) 725-2593 (Stanford) (office). *Fax:* (650) 725-1449 (Stanford) (office). *E-mail:* ang@cs.stanford.edu (office). *Website:* www.andrewng.org.

NG, Eng Hen, MBBS, MCh, FRCSE; Singaporean physician and politician; *Minister of Defence;* b. 10 Dec. 1958, Singapore; m. Ivy Lim Swee Lian 1982; two s. two d.; ed Nat. Junior Coll., Nat. Univ. of Singapore, M.D. Anderson Cancer Center, Houston, USA; Consultant Surgeon, Singapore Gen. Hosp. 1992–97; pvt. practice, Mount Elizabeth Hosp. 1997–2001; MP for Bishan-Toa Payoh Group Representation Constituency 2001–; Minister of State for Educ. and Manpower 2002–04, Minister of Manpower and Second Minister for Educ. 2004–07, Minister of Manpower 2005–07, Second Minister for Defence 2005–11, Minister of Educ. 2008–11, of Defence 2011–; Chair. Bd of Govs, SAFRA (Singapore Armed Forces Reservist Asscn); mem. People's Action Party; Founder-mem. Breast Cancer Foundation, Singapore 1998; Fellow, Singapore Acad. of Medicine 1990, American Soc. of Surgical Oncology 1992, American Soc. of Clinical Oncology 1999; Clinical Fellow, Surgical Oncology, Univ. of Texas MD Anderson Cancer Center 1990. *Leisure interests:* jogging, golf, reading. *Address:* Ministry of Defence, Gombak Drive, off Upper Bukit Timah Road, Mindef Bldg, Singapore 669645, Singapore (office). *Telephone:* 67608844 (office). *Fax:* 67646119 (office). *Website:* www.mindef.gov.sg (office).

NGANFUAN, Augustine Kpehe; Liberian economist and politician; ed Univ. of Liberia, Simon Grad. School of Business, Univ. of Rochester, USA; Pres. Univ. of Liberia Student Union 1998–99; fmrly with Cen. Bank of Liberia; Prof. of Auditing and Accounting, Univ. of Liberia; Dir-Gen., Bureau of Budget, Ministry of Finance –2008; Minister of Finance 2008–12, of Foreign Affairs 2012–15.

NGAUJAH, Sahr, MA; American theatre director, actor and musician; b. 1978; m. Ayesha Ngaujah; ed Dasarts Theatre School, Amsterdam; early career in dance, music and acting with Freddie Hendricks Youth Ensemble of Atlanta, later also Asst Dir; fmr Theatre Dir and Developer, Lef Club, ACT Festival, Rotterdam; collaborator, Made n da Shade theatre co., Amsterdam; Art Dir, Bajah+The Dry Eye Crew (Sierra Leone hip-hop act). *Films include:* How I Spent My Summer Vacation 1997, A Lesson Before Dying (TV film) 1999, Big Ain't Bad 2002, The Signal 2007, Stomp the Yard 2007, The Jailhouse 2009, Blood Done Sign My Name 2010, Freeheld 2015. *Plays include:* The Eternal Curse on the Reader of These Pages (touring Rotterdam, Amsterdam and London), Conversations of Ice, title role in Fela! The Musical (Broadway) (Audelco Award 2008, Obie Award 2008) 2008–09, (Nat. Theatre, London) 2010–11, The Painted Rocks at Revolver Creek (Broadway) 2015, Fela! (Broadway) 2015. *Television includes:* House of Payne (series) 2007–10, Last Resort (series) 2012–13, The Blacklist (series) 2014–15.

NGCOBO, S. Sandile, BProc, LLB, LLM; South African judge and academic; b. 1 March 1953, Durban; m. Zandile Ngcobo; two s. one d.; ed Univ. of Zululand, Univ. of Natal, Durban, Int. Law Inst. at Georgetown Law Center, Washington, DC and Harvard Law School, USA; in detention 1976–77; worked in Maphumulo magistrate's office 1977–78; articled clerk, then assoc. attorney, KK Mthiyane & Co. law firm, Durban 1978–82; attorney at law, Legal Resources Centre, Durban 1982–86; law clerk and research assoc. of the late Hon. A Leon Higginbotham Jr, fmr Chief Judge of US Court of Appeals for the Third Circuit, USA 1986–87; Visiting Foreign Attorney, Pepper, Hamilton & Scheetz, Phila, Pa Aug.–Nov. 1987, Assoc. Attorney 1989–92; Acting Dir Legal Aid Services Clinic, Univ. of Natal, Durban 1988–92, also taught course on race legislation; practised as advocate in Durban 1988–89, 1992–94; lectured part-time in constitutional litigation 1994; Acting Judge of Supreme Court, Cape of Good Hope Prov. Div. April–Aug. 1996, Judge Sept. 1996–97; Acting Judge of Labour Appeal Court Jan.–Dec. 1997; apptd Acting Judge Pres. of Labour Court and Labour Appeal Courts 1999; Judge in Constitutional Court of S Africa 1999–2011, Chief Justice of S Africa 2009–11; Visiting Prof. of Law, Harvard Law School and Columbia Law School, USA; mem. Industrial Court of KwaZulu 1993; Co-ordinator Equal Opportunities Project, Centre for Socio-Legal Studies, Univ. of Natal, Durban 1993; a Presiding Officer of Ind. Election Comm.'s Electoral Tribunal 1994; Samuel Rubin Visiting Prof. of Law, Columbia Law School, USA 2006–08; apptd to serve on Amnesty Cttee of Truth and Reconciliation Comm. 1998; mem. and Chair. Rules Bd for Courts of Law 1998–2004; Trustee Centre for Socio-Legal Studies, Univ. of Natal 1993–98, Dehler Foundation; Hon. Prof. of Law, Univ. of Cape Town 1999; scholarship from Barclays Bank 1973–76, Fulbright Scholarship 1985, Human Rights Fellowship, Harvard Law School 1986. *Publications:* numerous papers on topics such as justice, the Truth and Reconciliation Comm., housing segregation and gender equality. *Address:* c/o Constitutional Court, Private Bag X 1, 1 Hospital Street, Constitution Hill, Braamfontein 2017, South Africa (office).

NGENZEBUHORO, Frederic; Burundian politician; mem. Union pour le Progrès nat. (UPRONA, main Tutsi party); Minister of Information, then of Communication, then of Sports and Culture, then of Transport under Pres. Pierre Buyoya 1987–93; Deputy Pres. Nat. Ass. 1998–2004; Vice-Pres. of Burundi 2004–05. *Address:* c/o Union pour le Progrès national, BP 1810, Bujumbura, Burundi. *Telephone:* 22225028. *Website:* www.uprona.org.

NGHIMTINA, Col Erkki; Namibian politician; *Minister of Labour, Industrial Relations and Employment Creation;* fmr Man. Dir Prin. Bank for Devt and Agricultural Credit; Minister of Defence 1997–2005, of Works and Transport 2010–15, Minister of Labour, Industrial Relations and Employment Creation 2015–; Most Brilliant Order of the Sun, Second Class 2014. *Address:* Ministry of Labour, Industrial Relations and Employment Creation, 32 Mercedes Street, Khomasdal, PMB 19005, Windhoek, Namibia. *Telephone:* (61) 2066111. *Fax:* (61) 212323. *Website:* www.mol.gov.na.

NGIRENTE, Edouard, PhD; Rwandan economist and politician; *Prime Minister;* b. 1973, Gakenke Dist, Northern Prov.; m.; two c.; ed Nat. Univ. of Rwanda, Catholic Univ. of Louvain, Belgium, Facultés Univ. St-Louis, Brussels; lecturer, Nat. Univ. of Rwanda –2010; fmr Dir-Gen. in charge of planning, later Sr Advisor, Ministry of Finance and Econ. Planning; Advisor to Exec. Dir, World Bank, Washington, DC 2011–17; Prime Minister 2017–; mem. Parti Social-Démocrate. *Address:* Office of the Prime Minister, POB 1334, Kigali, Rwanda (office). *Telephone:* 252586902 (office). *Fax:* 252583714 (office). *E-mail:* webinfos@primature.gov.rw (office). *Website:* www.primature.gov.rw (office).

NGÔ, Bao Châu, PhD (Habil.); Vietnamese/French mathematician and academic; *Francis and Rose Yuen Distinguished Service Professor, University of Chicago;* b. 28 June 1972, Hanoi; s. of Prof. Ngo Huy Can and Tran Luu Van Hien; m. Nguyen Bao Thanh; three c.; ed École Normale Supérieure, Université Paris-Sud, Université Paris-Nord; mem. CNRS, Paris 13 Univ. 1998–2005; Prof., Université Paris-Sud 11 2005–; works at Inst. for Advanced Study, Princeton, NJ, USA 2007–, Hanoi Inst. of Math. 2007–; Francis and Rose Yuen Distinguished Service Prof., Univ. of Chicago, USA 2010–; Scientific Dir Vietnam Inst. for Advanced Study 2011–; mem. Editorial Bd, Grundlehren der mathematischen Wissenschaften, Inventiones Mathematicae, Compositio Mathematica, Acta Mathematica Vietnamica, Vietnam Journal of Mathematics; Fellow, American Math. Soc. 2012; Chevalier, Légion d'honneur 2010; Dr hc (Vietnamese Nat. Univ.); Clay Research Award 2004, invited address at Int. Congress of Mathematicians, Madrid 2006, Prix Sophie Germain, Acad. des sciences 2007, Oberwolfach Prize 2007, invited plenary address at Int. Congress of Mathematicians, Hyderabad 2010, Fields Medal (co-recipient) 2010. *Publications:* numerous papers in professional journals on algebraic geometry, group theory and automorphic representations. *Address:* Department of Mathematics, Eckhart 303, 5734 University Avenue, Chicago, IL 60637-1514, USA (office). *Telephone:* (773) 702-7385 (office). *Fax:* (773) 702-9787 (office). *E-mail:* ngo@uchicago.edu (office). *Website:* www.math.uchicago.edu (office).

NGO, Gen. Xuan Lich; Vietnamese army officer and politician; *Minister of National Defence;* b. 20 April 1954, Yen Bac commune, Duy Tien Dist; ed Military Culture College, Politics and Military Acad.; Deputy Commdr 14th Battalion, 320th Div., 308th Div. 1972–73, Squadron Leader 14th Battalion, 55th Regt, 341st Div., 4th Corps 1973–74, promoted to Lt 1974, Lt Commdr and Political Commr 1974–78, Sr Lt and Political Bureau Asst 1978–81, Deputy Political Commr, Deputy Regimental Political Commr 667th Regt, 779th Regt, 346th Div. 1985–87, promoted to Maj. 1987, Sec. Regimental Party Cttee 1987–88, Deputy Regt Commdr Political Regt 462, 392nd Div., Military Region 1 1987–88, promoted to Lt-Col 1988, to Col 2000, Head Military Region 3 2003–04, promoted to Maj.-Gen. 2004, Deputy Political Commdr Military Region 3 2004–06, Political Commdr 2006–07, promoted to Lt-Gen. 2007, Deputy Dir Political Bureau, Vietnam People's Army 2007–11, Dir 2011–16, Gen. 2016; mem. Cao Bang Province Party Cttee 1973–, Commissar 1985–87, Deputy Sec. 2000–03, mem. Standing Cttee 2003–04, Sec. Party Cttee 2004–07, mem. Party Cen. Cttee 2007–11, Sec. 2011–16; Asst Gen. Dept of Politics 1988–94, Deputy Dir and Head Political Affairs Dept 1994–2000, also Deputy Dir-Gen. Org. Dept, Gen. Politics Dept, Dir-Gen. Policy Dept 2000–03; mem. Standing Cttee, Cen. Military Comm. 2011–16, Deputy Sec. 2016–; Minister of Nat. Defence 2016–. *Address:* Ministry of National Defence, 7 Nguyen Tri Phuong, Ba Dinh District, Hanoi, Viet Nam (office). *Telephone:* (69) 696154 (office). *Fax:* (24) 37334163 (office). *E-mail:* info@mod.gov.vn (office). *Website:* www.mod.gov.vn (office).

NGOMA, Angélique; Gabonese politician; b. 19 March 1964, Libreville; ed Institut Nat. des Sciences de Gestion, Libreville, École Normale Nat. d'Apprentissage, Paris, France; Dir Coll. d'Enseignement technique commercial, Owendo 1991–93; Dir Ecole Nat. de Commerce, Port-Gentil 1993–94; mem. Parti démocratique gabonais (PG), Leader, Union des femmes du PDG; mem. Assemblée Nationale (Parl.) for Nyanga constituency 1996–; Sr Commr, Ministry of Educ., Youth and Sport 1995–97, Sec. of State, Ministry of Social Affairs 1997–2000, Ministry of Health 1999, Minister of Family, Children's Welfare and Women's Advancement 1999–2007, of Health and Public Hygiene, also responsible for Family and Women's Advancement 2007–08, Minister of Social Affairs and the Fight against AIDS 2008–09, also Minister of Protection of Widows and Orphans –Oct. 2009, Minister of Nat. Defence 2009–11, of Labour, Employment and Social Provision and Govt Spokesperson 2011–13. *Address:* Assemblee Nationale, Palais Léon MBA, Boulevard Triomphal Omar Bongo, BP 29, Libreville, Gabon (office). *Website:* www.assemblee-nationale.ga (office).

NGOWENUBUSA, Dieudonné; Burundian politician; b. 8 Sept. 1964, Ngagara; Minister of Finance 2005–06, of Devt Planning and Nat. Reconstruction 2007; Dir-Gen. Hôpital populaire de Mirango II; mem. Conseil nat. pour la défense de la democratie-Forces pour la défense de la democratie (CNDD-FDD).

NGOY MUKENA, Aimé, DSc; Democratic Republic of the Congo politician; *Minister of Hydrocarbons;* ed Univ. of Lausanne, Univ. of Geneva, Switzerland; Gov., Katanga Prov. 2001–04; mem. Assemblée Nationale (Parl.) 2006–11; mem. Bd of Dirs Société nationale des Chemins de fer du Congo 2011; fmr Prof. of Political Philosophy, Univ. of Lubumbashi; Minister of Nat. Defence, War Veterans and Rehabilitation 2014–15, of Hydrocarbons 2015–; mem. People's Party for Reconstruction and Democracy, fmr Exec. Sec. for Interior Affairs and Decentralization. *Address:* Ministry of Hydrocarbons, Kinshasa, Democratic Republic of the Congo (office). *Website:* hydrocarbures.gouv.cd (office).

NGRÉBADA, Firmin; Central African Republic politician; *Prime Minister;* b. 24 May 1968, Bangui; m.; ed Univ. of Bangui; Deputy Chief of Staff to Pres. 2008–13, then Chief of Staff 2014–19; Prime Minister 2019–. *Address:* Office of the Prime Minister, BP 932, Bangui, Central African Republic (office). *Telephone:* 21-61-59-23 (office). *Website:* primature.govcf.org (office).

NGUBANE, (Baldwin Sipho) Ben, MB, ChB; South African physician, politician and business executive; b. 22 Oct. 1941, Camperdown; m. Sheila Buthelezi; four c.; ed St Francis Coll., Marrianhill, Durban Medical School, Univ. of Witwatersrand, Natal Medical School; fmr Latin teacher; mem. Inkatha Freedom Party Cen. Cttee Exec. 1977; elected mem. KwaZulu Legis. Ass. 1978; led KwaZulu Govt del. to Constitutional negotiations; Minister of Health, KwaZulu Govt 1991–94, Premier 1997–99; Minister of Arts, Culture, Science and Tech. 1994–96, 1999–2004; Amb. to Japan 2004–08; Chair. South African Broadcasting Corpn, Johannesburg 2009–13 (resgnd); Chair. Land Bank 2010–14; Chair. Eskom Holdings SOC Ltd 2015–17; mem. Council Univ. of Zululand; mem. Nat. Boxing Bd of Control 1991; Grand Cordon of Order of the Rising Sun (Japan) 2010. *Leisure interests:* tennis, reading, photography. *Address:* c/o Eskom Holdings SOC Ltd, Megawatt Park, Maxwell Drive, Sunninghill, Sandton (office); Empangeni, KwaZulu-Natal, South Africa (home).

N'GUESSAN, Pascal Affi; Côte d'Ivoirian politician; b. 1953, Bouadikro; ed Lycée Moderne de Dimbokro, Lycée Technique d'Abidjan; Dir of Studies and Work Placements, École Nat. Supérieure des Postes et Télécommunications 1989–93; Vice-Pres. Union des villes et commune de Côte d'Ivoire (UVICOCI) 1990–95; mem. nat. directorate, Front populaire ivoirien—FPI (Ivorian Popular Front) 1990–, Pres. 2001–11; Special Adviser to the Regional Dir, Ci-Télécom, Bouaké 1993–97; Head Dept of Resources and Standards, Côte d'Ivoire Télécom 1997–2000; Campaign Man. for Laurent Gbagbo in presidential elections 2000; Minister of Industry and Tourism 2000; Prime Minister of Côte d'Ivoire 2000–03; Minister for Planning and Devt 2000–03; arrested following capture of Laurent Gbagbo April 2011; Officier du mérite sportif 1995.

NGUYEN, Duc Doan; Vietnamese business executive; *Chairman, Hoang Anh Gia Lai Joint Stock Company;* b. 1962, Nhon My, An Nhon dist, Binh Dinh Prov.; m. Hoàng; began career as forest products developer, f. Hoang Anh 1993, renamed Hoang Anh Gia Lai Jt Stock Co. 2006, currently Chair. Hoang Anh Gia Lai Group, also Chair. Hoang Anh Gia Lai Football Club; also owns rubber plantations and tourist resorts. *Leisure interest:* football. *Address:* HAGL Joint Stock Company, 15 Truong Chinh Street, Phu Dong Ward, Pleiku City, Gia Lai Province, Viet Nam (office). *Telephone:* (592) 225888 (office); (592) 3820288 (office). *Fax:* (592) 222335 (office); (592) 2211726 (office). *E-mail:* contact@hagl.com.vn (office); hoa.pleiku@dng.vnn.vn (office). *Website:* www.hagl.com.vn (office).

NGUYEN, Dy Nien; Vietnamese politician; b. 9 Dec. 1935, Hoang Anh, Hoang Hoa, Thanh Hoa Prov.; m.; three d.; ed Banaras Hindu Univ., India; mem. Nat. Liberation Movt 1951; joined Ministry of Foreign Affairs 1954, postings to Consulate Gen. in New Delhi 1956–59, 1964–69, work in Asia and at Ministry of Foreign Affairs 1970–72, Chargé d'affaires a.i. in Canberra 1973–75, Asst Dir Ministry of Foreign Affairs 1976–79, Deputy Dir, then as Acting Dir of Asia 4 1980–81, Chief's Office, Dept of State 1982–83, Asst Minister of Foreign Affairs 1984–86, Deputy Minister of Foreign Affairs 1987–2000, Minister of Foreign Affairs 2000–06; Deputy, Nat. Ass. 2002–06; apptd mem. Cen. Cttee, CP of Viet Nam 1991; Pres. Viet Nam Nat. Comm. for UNESCO 1987, Nat. Cttee for Overseas Vietnamese 1995; mem. Council of Defence 2002–07 (retd); Medal of the American Struggle against the First Div., Labour Medal First Class; Coat 40-year Party.

NGUYEN, Minh Triet, BS; Vietnamese politician and fmr head of state; b. 8 Oct. 1942, Ben Cat dist, Binh Duong Prov.; m. Tran Thi Kim Chi; ed Nguyen Ai Quoc Party School, Saigon Univ.; taught Math. in Saigon; active in Sai Gon Students Movt 1960–63; mem. Cadre of Cen. Cttee of the People's Revolutionary Youth Union and Youth Mobilization of Party Cen. Cttee's Dept for S Vietnam, also Sec. Agency's Youth Union 1963–73, Deputy Dir Office of Youth Union and Deputy Chief Youth Union Cen. Cttee's Bd for Voluntary Young People 1974–79; apptd additional mem. Party Cttee of Song Be Prov., Perm. Deputy Sec. 1989–91; mem. Party Cen. Cttee 1991–; Deputy, Nat. Ass. 1991–2006; apptd mem. Politburo 1997; Dir Cen. Party Cttee's Comm. for Mass Mobilization 1997–2000; Sec. Ho Chi Minh City Party Cttee 1997–2000, Gen. Sec. 2000–06; Pres. of Viet Nam 2006–11. *Address:* c/o Dang Cong San Viet Nam (Communist Party of Viet Nam), 1 Hoang Van Thu, Hanoi, Viet Nam.

NGUYEN, Phu Trong; Vietnamese politician and head of state; *President and General Secretary, Communist Party of Viet Nam;* b. 14 April 1944, Dong Hoi Commune, Dong Anh Dist, Hanoi; ed Vietnam Nat. Univ., Hanoi, USSR Acad. of Social Sciences, Ho Chi Minh Nat. Political Admin. Inst.; mem. Dang Cong San Viet Nam (CP of Viet Nam, fmrly Viet Nam Workers' Party) 1968–, mem. Cen. Cttee 1994–, mem. Political Bureau 1997–, Gen. Sec. 2011–, Sec. Hanoi CP Cttee 2000–06; Pres. of Viet Nam 2018–; Ed.-in-Chief Tap chi Cong San (Communist Review) 1991–96; Deputy, Quoc Hoi (Nat. Ass.) 2002–, Chair. 2006–11. *Address:* Dang Cong San Viet Nam (Communist Party of Viet Nam), 1A Hung Vuong, Hanoi, Viet Nam (office). *E-mail:* dangcongsan@cpv.org.vn (office). *Website:* www.cpv.org.vn (office); nguyenphutrong.net.

NGUYEN, HE Cardinal Pierre Van Nhon; Vietnamese ecclesiastic; b. 1 April 1938, Da Lat, Lam Dong; ordained priest, Archdiocese of Da Lat 1967; consecrated Coadjutor Bishop of Da Lat 1991–94, Bishop of Da Lat 1994–2010; Coadjutor Archbishop of Hanoi April–May 2010, Archbishop of Hanoi May 2010–18; cr. Cardinal (Cardinal-Priest of San Tommaso Apostolo) 2015. *Address:* c/o Toa Tong Giam Muc, 40 Pho Nha Chung, Hoan Kiem, Hanoi, Viet Nam (office).

NGUYEN, Quoc Cuong, BA, MA; Vietnamese government official and diplomatist; m.; one s. one d.; ed Univ. of Foreign Affairs, Fletcher School of Law and Diplomacy, Tufts Univ., Maxwell School of Public Admin, Syracuse Univ., Vietnam Exec. Leadership Program, Kennedy School of Govt, Harvard Univ., USA; joined Ministry of Foreign Affairs 1981, worked as an officer at China Dept and as a researcher at Inst. of Int. Relations, Second Sec., Embassy in Beijing 1990–93, Minister Counsellor and Deputy Chief of Mission, Embassy in Ottawa 2002–05, Deputy Dir-Gen. Dept of Multilateral Econ. Co-operation 2005–07, Head of Political and Security Section of APEC Viet Nam 2006, Secr., Dir-Gen. and Exec. Asst to Deputy Prime Minister cum Minister of Foreign Affairs 2007–08; Asst Minister of Foreign Affairs 2008, Deputy Minister of Foreign Affairs in charge of relations of Viet Nam with European countries, and Press and Information Affairs, also Chief Negotiator with the Vatican 2008–11; Amb. to USA 2011–14. *Address:* Ministry of Foreign Affairs, 1 Ton That Dam, Ba Dinh District, Hanoi, Viet Nam. *Telephone:* (4) 37992000. *Fax:* (4) 38231872. *E-mail:* banbientap@mofa.gov.vn. *Website:* www.mofa.gov.vn.

NGUYEN, Sinh Hung, PhD; Vietnamese economist and politician; b. 18 Jan. 1946, Nam Dan, Nghe An; previous posts include accountant in Finance Ministry, econ. researcher in Bulgaria, Deputy Dir then Dir Treasury, Vice-Minister of Finance, Minister of Finance –2006; Standing Deputy Prime Minister 2006–11; Chair. Nat. Ass. (Quoc Hoi) 2011–16; mem. Cen. Standing Cttee Dang Cong San Viet Nam (CP of Viet Nam), also mem. Political Bureau (Politburo). *Website:* nguyensinhhung.net.

NGUYEN, Tam Chien, MA; Vietnamese diplomatist; b. 20 Jan. 1948, Nghe An Prov.; m. Nguyen Thi Lien Huong; two s. one d.; ed Eng Univ. and Moscow Diplomatic Acad., USSR; joined Ministry of Foreign Affairs 1972, staff mem., Embassy in Moscow 1972–73, Desk Officer, Soviet Union Dept, Hanoi 1973–85, Attaché in Moscow 1975–79, returned to Soviet Union Dept 1979, with Policy Planning Dept 1984–88, Deputy Dir-Gen. 1988–90, Dir-Gen. 1990–92, Amb. to Japan 1992–96, Asst Minister of Foreign Affairs 1996–97, Vice-Minister of Foreign Affairs, in charge of Econ. Affairs and Multilateral Affairs, Int. and Regional Orgs 1997–2001, rank of Amb. 2000, Amb. to USA 2001–07; currently Pres. Vietnam-US Friendship Soc.

NGUYEN, Tan Dung, LLB; Vietnamese politician and fmr central banker; b. 17 Nov. 1949, Ca Mau City, Ca Mau Prov.; m. Tran Thanh Kiem; three c.; served in Viet Nam People's Army 1961–81; mem. CP of Viet Nam 1968–, mem. Cen. Police Party Cttee 1995–96, mem. Politburo 1997–; Deputy 10th, 11th, 12th and 13th Nat. Ass.; Deputy Minister of Public Security 1995–96; First Deputy Prime Minister of Viet Nam 1997–2006; Gov. State Bank of Viet Nam and Sec. State Bank of Viet Nam's Party Cttee 1998–99; Prime Minister of Viet Nam 2006–16, also Vice-Pres. Nat. Defence and Security Council.

NGUYEN, Thanh Chau, MA; Vietnamese diplomatist; b. 17 Sept. 1945, Phu Tho; m.; two c.; ed Australian Nat. Univ.; Lecturer, Inst. of Int. Relations, Ministry of Foreign Affairs, Hanoi, Second Sec., Perm. Mission to UN, New York 1983–86, various positions with Viet Nam Comm. for UNESCO including Sec.-Gen. 1987–92, Amb. to Australia (also accred to NZ, Papua New Guinea, Vanuatu and Fiji) 1992–96, Dir Int. Orgs Div., Ministry of Foreign Affairs 1996–2000, Perm. Rep. to UN, New York 2000–04. *Address:* c/o Ministry of Foreign Affairs, 1 Ton That Dam, Ba Dinh District, Hanoi, Viet Nam.

NGUYEN, Thi Doan, PhD; Vietnamese economist, academic and politician; b. 11 Jan. 1951, Ha Nam Prov.; ed Univ. of Commerce, Hanoi, Sofia Econ. Univ., Bulgaria; joined CP of Viet Nam 1981; mem. Nat. Ass. representing Ha Nam Prov.; mem. 10th Cen. Cttee, CP of Viet Nam 2006; fmr Deputy Sec., Party Cttee of Block-I Cen. Agencies; mem. Party Cen. Cttee's Comm. for Inspection 1998, Deputy Perm. Head –2007; Vice-Pres. of Viet Nam 2007–16; Government Leadership Award, Global Summit of Women 2015. *Address:* Dang Cong San Viet Nam (Communist Party of Viet Nam), 381 Doi Can Street, Ba Dinh District, Hanoi, Viet Nam (office). *Telephone:* (80) 48161 (office). *Fax:* (80) 44175 (office). *E-mail:* dangcongsan@cpv.org.vn (office). *Website:* www.cpv.org.vn (office).

NGUYEN, Van Binh; Vietnamese economist and fmr central banker; *Chief Economist, Executive Committee of the Communist Party of Viet Nam;* b. 4 March 1961, Phu Tho; ed Cen. Inst. for Math. Econs, USSR Acad. of Sciences; joined Foreign Econ. Relations Dept, State Bank of Viet Nam 1986, becoming Deputy Head of Int. Financial Insts Dept, Deputy Head of Int. Project Man. and Int. Co-operation Dept 1996, Chief Insp., Deputy Gov. 2008–11, Gov. 2011–16; Vice-Pres. and Acting Chair. Int. Investment Bank, Moscow 2001–05; mem. Exec. Cttee CP of Viet Nam, Chief Economist 2016–. *Address:* Central Economic Committee, A4, Nguyen Canh Chan Street, Ba Dinh District, Hanoi, Viet Nam (office).

NGUYEN, Van Giau, DEcon; Vietnamese fmr central banker and politician; b. 8 Dec. 1957, An Giang Prov.; Dir An Giang Br. of Viet Nam Bank for Agriculture and Rural Development (Agribank) 1988–90, Deputy Gen. Dir Agribank 1991–96, Gen. Dir 1996–97; Deputy Gov. State Bank of Viet Nam 1998–2003, Gov. 2007–11; mem. Party Cen. Cttee, Deputy Party Sec., Ninh Thuan Prov. 2003–05, Party Sec. 2005–07; Chair. Nat. Ass. Econ. Cttee 2011–16; mem. Standing Cttee, Nat. Ass. 2016–. *Address:* Parliamentary Public House, No.2 Hoang Cau Street, O Cho Dua Ward, Dong Da District, Hanoi, Viet Nam.

NGUYEN, Van Tho; Vietnamese diplomatist; fmr Pres. Dept for External Relations, Ministry of Foreign Affairs, Deputy Minister of Foreign Affairs –2008, Chair. ASEAN Cttee, Beijing 2010, Amb. to People's Repub. of China 2008–15. *Address:* Ministry of Foreign Affairs, 1 Ton That Dam, Ba Dinh District, Hanoi, Viet Nam (office). *Telephone:* (4) 37992000 (office). *Fax:* (4) 38231872 (office). *E-mail:* banbientap@mofa.gov.vn (office). *Website:* www.mofa.gov.vn (office).

NGUYEN, Xuan Phuc, BEcons; Vietnamese party official and politician; *Prime Minister;* b. 20 July 1954, Quang Nam Prov.; ed Hanoi Nat. Econ. Univ., Vietnam Nat. Admin. Acad., Nat. Univ. of Singapore; with Quang Nam-Da Nang Econ. Bd 1978–79; mem. Dang Cong San Viet Nam (Communist Party of Viet Nam) 1983–, mem. Politburo 2011–; various party roles in Quang Nam Prov. 1980–93, becoming Chief of Office of Provincial People's Cttee, perm. mem., Provincial Party Cttee (17th and 18th sessions) 1997–2001, Deputy Chair., Provincial People's Cttee 1997–2001; Dir Tourism Dept and Dir of Planning and Investment, Quang Nam-Da Nang Prov. 1993–96; Dir of Industrial Zones Man. Bd, Quang Nam Prov. 1997–2001; mem. 11th Nat. Ass. (Parl.) 2002–07, 13th Nat. Ass. 2011–16, mem. Economy and Budget Cttee; Minister and Chair., Govt Office 2007–11; Deputy Prime Minister 2011–16, Prime Minister 2016–; Chair., Cttee on HIV/AIDS 2011–14. *Address:* Office of the Prime Minister, Hanoi, Viet Nam (office). *Website:* nguyenxuanphuc.chinhphu.vn (office).

NGWENYA, Sindiso Ndema, BSc, MSc; Zimbabwean international organization official; b. 16 April 1951; m.; three c.; ed Middlesex Polytechnic, Univ. of Birmingham, UK; Corp. Planning Officer, Ethiopia Airlines 1979–80; Planning Officer, Nat. Railways of Zimbabwe 1980–83; Sr Transport Expert, Common Market for Eastern and Southern Africa (COMESA) 1994–98, Asst Sec.-Gen., in charge of Programming 1998–2008, Sec.-Gen. 2008–18; mem. Interim Cttee Food,

Agric. and Natural Resources Policy Analysis Network 2007; Southern Africa Trust Drivers of Change Award (Govt category) 2010. *Address:* c/o COMESA Secretariat, COMESA Centre, Ben Bella Road, PO Box 30051, 101101 Lusaka, Zambia (office).

NHASSÉ, Alamara; Guinea-Bissau politician; *President, Partido da Reconciliação Nacional;* b. 2 June 1957; fmr Pres. Partido para a Renovação Social (PRS); apptd Minister of Agriculture, Water, Forestry and Hunting 2000, of Agriculture and Fisheries 2001, of Internal Admin. 2001; Prime Minister of Guinea-Bissau 2001–02; currently Pres. Partido da Reconciliação Nacional (PRN).

NHEK, Bun Chhay; Cambodian politician; *Chairman, Khmer National United Party;* b. 7 Feb. 1958; Second Vice-Pres. of the Senate 1999–2004; Acting Head of State July 2004; Deputy Prime Minister 2004–13; Minister of Defence 2004–06; apptd Sec.-Gen. United Nat. Front for an Ind., Neutral, Peaceful and Co-operative Cambodia Party (Funcinpec) 2006; currently Chair. Khmer Nat. United Party.

NI, Runfeng; Chinese business executive; b. 1944, Rongcheng, Shandong Prov.; ed Dalian Eng Coll.; Dir, later Gen. Man., later Chair. Changhong Machinery Factory, Sichuan Prov. 1985, Gen. Man. Changhong Electronics Corpn 1995–2000, Chair. 1996–2004; mem. CCP; Del., 14th CCP Nat. Congress 1992–97; Deputy, 8th NPC 1993–98; Alt. mem. 15th CCP Cen. Cttee 1997–2002; named Prof.-grade Sr Engineer, named Most Outstanding Man. by All-China Fed. of Trade Unions 1990, Nat. Wuyi Labour Medal 1990, Awarded Special Governmental Subsidy 1991, Nat. Model Worker, State Council 1995, Nikkei Asian Prize 1998, honoured as Man. Guru by Int. Statistics Conf. 1998, Award for Achievement of Asian Entrepreneurs 1998. *Address:* c/o Changhong Electronics Corporation, Chengdu, Sichuan Province, People's Republic of China.

NIAM, Chiang Meng, MPA; Singaporean business executive and fmr government official; *Chairman, MediaCorp Pte Ltd;* ed Nat. Univ. of Singapore, Harvard Univ.; Vice-Pres. (News) TV Corpn of Singapore (now MediaCorp Pte Ltd) 1994–97, mem. Exec. Bd 2011–, mem. Bd of Dirs 2016–18, Chair. 2018–; Perm. Sec., Ministry of Community Devt, Youth and Sports 2005–11, Ministry of Information, Communications and the Arts, Ministry of Law, Prime Minister's Office; also served as Deputy Sec., Ministry of Health; Chair., Media Devt Authority of Singapore 2011–16 (also mem. Bd of Dirs); Maritime and Port Authority of Singapore 2016–; Ind. Dir SMRT Corpn Ltd; mem. Bd of Dirs, Keppel Land Ltd 2003–10, SMRT Trains Ltd, SMRT Road Holdings Ltd, Housing and Devt Bd 2002–04, Nat. Arts Council, Nat. Heritage Bd, Singapore Broadcasting Authority, The Esplanade Corpn Ltd; Public Admin Medal (Silver) 1995, Public Admin Medal (Gold) 2001. *Address:* MediaCorp Pte Ltd, 1 Stars Avenue, Singapore 138507, Singapore (office). *Telephone:* 63333888 (office). *Fax:* 62515628 (office). *E-mail:* tellmediacorp@mediacorp.com.sg (office). *Website:* www.mediacorp.sg (office).

NIANG, Madické, LLM; Senegalese lawyer and politician; b. 1953; ed Univ. of Abidjan, Côte d'Ivoire; legal practice, chambers of Bassine Niang 1982–85; Adviser to Pres. Abdoulaye Wade 2000; Minister of Housing 2002–03, of Energy and Mines 2003–07, of Mines, Industry and Energy Feb.–Mar 2007, of Mines and Industry 2007–08, Minister of Justice and Keeper of the Seals 2008–09, Minister of Foreign Affairs 2009–12; mem. Bd Caisse des Règlements Pécuniaires des Avocats (legal deposit fund) 1991, Sec. 1995; mem. Bd Ordre des Avocats du Sénégal 1992; mem. World Jurist Asscn. *Publications:* Pour que triomphe la vérité: l'assassinat de Maître Babacar Seye 2002, Sénégal, affaire maître Sèye: les pièges de l'acharnement 2006.

NIASSE, Cheikh Moustapha; Senegalese politician, UN official and company director; *President, National Assembly;* b. 4 Nov. 1939, Keur Madiabel; ed Lycée Faidherbe, St Louis, Univ. of Dakar, Univ. of Paris, France, Nat. School of Admin, Dakar; Dir for Information and Press Affairs, Ministry of Information 1968–69; Dir de Cabinet at Presidency 1970–78; Minister of Town Planning, Housing and Environment March–Sept. 1978, of Foreign Affairs 1978–84; Minister of Foreign Affairs of the Confed. of Senegambia 1982–84; fmr Minister of State, Minister of Foreign Affairs and Senegalese Abroad; presidential cand. 2000, 2007, 2012; Prime Minister of Senegal 2000–01; UN Special Envoy to Peace Process of the Democratic Repub. of the Congo 2002; Political Sec. Union Progressiste Sénégalaise until 1984; Founder and Sec.-Gen. Alliance des forces de progrès 1999–; Pres. Nat. Ass. (Parl.) 2012–; mem. bd of dirs several pvt.-sector cos world-wide. *Address:* Office of the President, National Assembly, pl. Soweto, BP 86, Dakar (office); Alliance des forces de progrès, rue 1, angle rue A, point E, BP 5825, Dakar, Senegal (office). *E-mail:* admin@afp-senegal.org (office); afp.net@yahoo.fr (office). *Website:* www.afp-senegal.org (office).

NIBIGIRA, Ezéchiel, BA; Burundian politician and fmr diplomatist; *Minister of Foreign Affairs;* ed Hope Africa Univ., Bujumbura; Chief Election Campaign Man. for Pres. Pierre Nkurunziza 2010; fmr Leader Imbonerakure (CNDD-FDD youth wing); Amb. to Kenya –2014; Dir-Gen., Autorité Maritime, Portuaire et Ferroviaire (maritime, port and rail authority) 2014; Dir, Direction Nat. du Contrôle des Marchés Publics (Nat. Directorate for Public Procurement Control) 2015; fmr mem. Nat. Ass. (Parl.) for Bujumbura rural constituency, fmr Chair. Finance Cttee; Minister of Foreign Affairs 2018–; mem. Conseil Nat. pour la Défense de la Démocratie—Forces pour la Défense de la Démocratie (CNDD—FDD). *Address:* Ministry of Foreign Affairs, ave de la Liberté, Bujumbura, Burundi (office). *Telephone:* 22222150 (office). *Website:* www.diplobdi.org (office).

NIBLETT, Robin, CMG, BA, MPhil, DPhil; British political scientist and academic; *Director, Chatham House;* b. 1962; ed Univ. of Oxford; Research Assoc., Political-Mil. Studies Program, Center for Strategic and Int. Studies (CSIS) 1988–92, European Rep. 1992–97, Dir Strategic Planning 1997–2001, Exec. Vice-Pres. 2001–07, Dir Europe Program 2004–07; Politics Lecturer, Univ. of Oxford 1995–98; Dir Chatham House (Royal Inst. of Int. Affairs) 2007–. *Publications include:* Rethinking European Order (co-ed.) 2001, Ready to Lead? Rethinking America's Role in a Changed World, Chatham House 2009, America and a Changed World: A Question of Leadership (ed.) 2010, The Chatham House-YouGov Survey 2011: British Attitudes Towards the UK's International Priorities 2011, Hard Choices Ahead: The Chatham House-YouGov Survey 2012, Britain, Europe and the World: Rethinking the UK's Circles of Influence 2015, Britain, the EU and the Sovereignty Myth 2016; contribs to International Affairs, The

Washington Quarterly, The World Today, Strategic Europe: A Carnegie Europe Series, Royal Elcano Institute. *Address:* Office of the Director, Royal Institute of International Affairs, Chatham House, 10 St James's Square, London, SW1Y 4LE, England (office). *Telephone:* (20) 7314-2798 (office). *Fax:* (20) 7957-5710 (office). *E-mail:* kburnet@chathamhouse.org (office). *Website:* www.chathamhouse.org (office).

NIBLOCK, Robert A., BA; American accountant and business executive; *Chairman, President and CEO, Lowe's Companies, Inc.;* b. 1963, Fla; m. Melanie Niblock; two c.; ed Univ. of North Carolina-Charlotte; certified public accountant; began career with Ernst & Young 1984–93; joined Lowe's Companies Inc. as Dir of Taxation 1993, Vice-Pres. and Treas. 1997–99, Sr Vice-Pres. 1999–2000, Sr Vice-Pres. and Chief Financial Officer 2000–01, Exec. Vice-Pres. and Chief Financial Officer 2001–03, Pres. 2003–06, mem. Bd of Dirs 2004–, Chair. and CEO 2005–11, Chair., Pres. and CEO 2011–; mem. Bd of Dirs Retail Industry Leaders Asscn 2003– (Vice-Chair. 2006–07, Chair. 2008–09), ConocoPhillips 2010– (mem. Audit and Finance Cttee). *Address:* Lowe's Companies, Inc., 1000 Lowe's Boulevard, Mooresville, NC 28117, USA (office). *Telephone:* (704) 758-1000 (office). *Fax:* (336) 658-4766 (office). *E-mail:* info@lowes.com (office). *Website:* www.lowes.com (office).

NICA, Dan, PhD; Romanian telecommunications engineer and politician; b. 2 July 1960, Panciu, Vrancea Co.; m.; one c.; ed Faculty of Electronics and Telecommunications, Iasi, specializations in man. and communications in France, Sweden, Austria and Canada; various positions at Galati Co. Telecommunications Directorate 1985–96, Dir Galati Co. Telecommunications Directorate 1991–96; Assoc. Prof., Univ. 'Lower Danube' for Telecommunications and Data Transmission 1993–96; mem. Partidul Social Democrat (PSD—Social Democratic Party) Cen. Exec. Bureau 1999–2004, Pres. Galati Municipal PSD Org. 1997–2003, First Vice-Pres. PSD Galati Co. Org. 1999–2003, Pres. 2003–, mem. PSD Co-ordinating Bureau 2004–05, Vice-Pres. PSD and Pres. Dept of Transportation and Communications 21 April 2005, Vice-Pres. PSD and Co-ordinator Dept of Transport and Communications 2006–; mem. Chamber of Deputies (PSD) for Galati Electoral Ward 1996–, mem. Parl. Comm. for Industries and Services, mem. Parl. Groups of Friendship with Egypt, Syria and Sweden, mem. Parl. Comm. for Public Admin, Territory Man. and Ecological Balance 2000–04, Vice-Pres. Comm. for Communication and Information Tech. 2004–08; Minister of Communication and Information Tech. 2000–04; Deputy Prime Minister and Minister of the Interior and Admin. Reform 2008–09; Pres. Romania-Bavaria Governmental Comm. 2001–04; Minister of Communications and the Information Soc. 2012–14; mem. UN Information and Communication Technologies Task Force 2002–04, Nat. Council for Science and Tech. Policy; Kt, Steaua României Nat. Order (Order of the Star of Romania) 2002; Prize for Excellence for the promotion of Romanian IT industry abroad, CHIP Review 2002, Prize for Excellence for the promotion and development of e-governance and transparency, ARIES 2003, 'Ion Irimescu – 100' Homage Medal, Ministry of Culture and Denominations 2003, Personalitatea anului (Personality of the Year) Prize, eFinance Review 2004. *Publications include:* Government, Citizen, IT Society 2001, Le Gouvernement électronique (Concepts Appliqués en Roumanie) (Tudor Tanasescu Prize, Romanian Acad. 2007) 2005. *Address:* Partidul Social Democrat, 011346 Bucharest 1, Şos. Kiseleff 10, Romania (office). *Telephone:* (31) 4135155. *E-mail:* psd@psd.ro (office). *Website:* www.psd.ro (office).

NICA, Marius, BA, MSc, MBA; Romanian government official and business executive; b. 27 Nov. 1980, Brasov Sânpetru; ed Acad. of Information, Bucharest, Nat. School of Political and Admin. Studies, Acad. of Econ. Sciences, Faculty of Business Admin in German; Officer, Ministry of Defence 2003–08; Adviser-Collaborator to Rovana Plumb MEP, European Parl., Brussels, Belgium 2008–12; Admin., SC Holding Group International Trading Srlcalea Mosilor, No. 268–270, Bucharest 2011–13; Dir of Cabinet, Ministry of Environment and Water 2012–13; Chair. Romanian Nat. Lottery Co. 2013–14; Sec.-Gen., Ministry of Environment and Climate Change 2013–14, Ministry of Labour, Family, Social Protection and Elderly 2014–15; Minister of European Funds March–Nov. 2015.

NICHOLAS, Sir David, Kt, CBE; British television executive and editor; b. 25 Jan. 1930, Tregaron; m. Juliet Davies 1952; one s. one d.; ed Neath Grammar School, Univ. Coll. of Wales, Aberystwyth; Nat. Service 1951–53; journalist with Yorkshire Post, Daily Telegraph, Observer; joined ITN (Ind. TV News) 1960, Deputy Ed., Ed. 1963–77, Ed. and CEO 1977–89, Chair. 1989–91; Dir (non-exec.) Channel 4 TV 1992–97; Chair. Sports News TV 1996–2003; Visiting Ed. 10 US Schools of Journalism 1992–99; Hon. LLD (Univ. Coll. of Wales, Aberystwyth) 1990; Hon. DHumLitt (Univ. of Southern Illinois). *Leisure interests:* walking, sailing, golf. *Address:* Lodge Stables, 2F Kidbrooke Park Road, London, SE3 0LW, England (home). *Telephone:* (20) 8319-2823 (home). *E-mail:* dnicholas1@btinternet .com (home).

NICHOLAS, Peter M., MSc; American medical device industry executive; *Chairman, Boston Scientific Corporation;* s. of Nicholas John Nicholas; brother of Nicholas John Nicholas, Jr; m.; three c.; ed Duke Univ., Univ. of Pennsylvania Wharton School; Founder, Chair. and CEO Boston Scientific 1979–99, Chair. 1999–; fmr Chair. Bd of Trustees, Duke Univ.; Fellow, American Acad. of Arts and Sciences (Vice-Chair. Academy Trust); mem. American Acad. of Achievement; Founder Nicholas School of the Environment, Duke Univ.; Phoenix Lifetime Achievement Award, Ellis Island Medal of Honor. *Address:* Boston Scientific Corporation, 1 Boston Scientific Place, Natick, MA 01760-1537, USA (office). *Telephone:* (508) 650-8000 (office). *Fax:* (508) 647-2393 (office). *Website:* www .bostonscientific.com (office).

NICHOLL, Elizabeth (Liz), CBE, OBE; British sports administrator; *Chief Executive, UK Sport;* fmr Welsh int. netball player; Chief Exec. England Netball for 16 years, including a period as Championship Dir World Netball Championships 1995; Dir of Elite Sport, UK Sport 1999–2009, COO 2009–10, Chief Exec. 2010–. *Address:* UK Sport, 21 Bloomsbury Street, London, WC1B 3HF, England (office). *Telephone:* (20) 7211-5150 (office). *Fax:* (20) 7211-5246 (office). *E-mail:* liz .nicholl@uksport.gov.uk (office). *Website:* www.uksport.gov.uk (office).

NICHOLLS OF BIRKENHEAD, Baron (Life Peer), cr. 1994, of Stoke D'Abernon in the County of Surrey; **Donald James Nicholls,** PC, MA, LLB (retd); British judge; b. 25 Jan. 1933, Bebington, Cheshire; s. of William Greenhow Nicholls and Eleanor J. Nicholls; m. Jennifer Mary Thomas 1960; two s. one d.; ed Birkenhead

School, Univ. of Liverpool and Trinity Hall, Cambridge; Nat. service 1951–53 (2nd Lt, Royal Army Pay Corps); called to Bar, Middle Temple 1958; in practice at Chancery Bar, London 1958–83; QC 1974; Judge, High Court of Justice, Chancery Div. 1983–86; Lord Justice of Appeal 1986–91; Vice-Chancellor, Supreme Court 1991–94; a Lord of Appeal in Ordinary 1994–2007, Second Sr Lord of Appeal 2002–07; Chair. Lord Chancellor's Advisory Cttee on Legal Educ. and Conduct 1996–97, Jt Cttee on Parl. Privilege 1997–99; a non-perm. Judge, Hong Kong Court of Final Appeal 1998–2004; Hon. Fellow, Trinity Hall, Cambridge 1986; Treas. Middle Temple 1997; Hon. LLD (Liverpool) 1987. *Leisure interests:* history, music, walking.

NICHOLS, Leigh (see KOONTZ, Dean Ray).

NICHOLS, Peter Richard, CBE, FRSL; British playwright; b. 31 July 1927, Bristol; s. of Richard G. Nichols and Violet A. Poole; m. Thelma Reed 1960; one s. two d. (and one d. deceased); ed Bristol Grammar School, Bristol Old Vic School, Trent Park Training Coll.; actor, mostly in repertory 1950–55; schoolteacher 1958–60; mem. Arts Council Drama Panel 1973–75; Playwright-in-Residence, Guthrie Theatre, Minneapolis; Visiting Writer, Nanyang Coll., Singapore 1994; directed revivals of Joe Egg and Forget-Me-Not Lane (Greenwich), National Health (Guthrie, Minneapolis) and first productions of Born in the Gardens (Bristol), A Piece of My Mind (Southampton), Blue Murder (Bristol), Nicholodeon (Bristol); Tony Award, New York 1985, several SWET and four Evening Standard Drama Awards, Ivor Novello Award for Best Musical 1977. *Plays include:* A Day in the Death of Joe Egg 1967, The National Health 1969, Forget-Me-Not Lane 1971, Chez Nous 1973, The Freeway 1974, Privates on Parade 1977, Born in the Gardens 1979, Passion Play 1980, Poppy (musical) 1982, A Piece of My Mind 1986, Blue Murder 1995, So Long Life 2000, Nicholodeon 2000, Lingua Franca 2010. *Films:* Catch Us If You Can 1965, Georgy Girl 1967, Joe Egg 1971, The National Health 1973, Privates on Parade 1983. *Radio:* Something In The Air, Jam Yesterday. *Television:* plays include Walk on the Grass 1959, Promenade 1960, Ben Spray 1961, The Reception 1961, The Big Boys 1961, Continuity Man 1963, Ben Again 1963, The Heart of the Country 1963, The Hooded Terror 1963, When the Wind Blows 1964, The Brick Umbrella 1968, Daddy Kiss It Better 1968, The Gorge 1968, Hearts and Flowers 1971, The Common 1973, Greeks Bearing Gifts (Inspector Morse series) 1991. *Publications:* Feeling You're Behind (memoirs) 1984, Nichols: Plays One and Two 1991, Diary 1969–71, Diary Selection 2000; all listed plays published separately; archive now available in Manuscripts Dept, British Library. *Leisure interests:* listening to jazz, looking at cities. *Address:* c/o Alan Brodie Representation, Fairgate House, 6th Floor, 78 New Oxford Street, London, WC1A 1HB, England (office). *Telephone:* (20) 7253-6226 (office). *E-mail:* abr@alanbrodie .com (office).

NICHOLS, HE Cardinal Vincent Gerard, STL, PhL, MA; British ecclesiastic; *Archbishop of Westminster;* b. 8 Nov. 1945, Crosby, Merseyside; s. of Henry Joseph Nichols and Mary Russell; ed St Mary's Coll., Crosby, Gregorian Univ., Rome, Manchester Univ. and Loyola Univ., Chicago; Chaplain St John Rigby VI Form Coll., Wigan 1972–77; priest in inner city of Liverpool 1978–81; Dir Upholland Northern Inst., Lancs. 1981–84; Gen. Sec. Catholic Bishops' Conf. of England and Wales 1984–91; Auxiliary Bishop of Westminster 1992–2000; Archbishop of Birmingham 2000–09, of Westminster 2009–; Pres. Catholic Bishops' Conference of England and Wales 2009–; Chancellor St Mary's Univ., Twickenham 2013–; cr. Cardinal (Cardinal-Priest of Santissimo Redentore e Sant'Alfonso in Via Merulana) 2014–; Adviser to HE Cardinal Hume and Archbishop Worlock at the Int. Synods of Bishops 1980, 1983, 1985, 1987, 1990, 1991; Del. of Bishops' Conf. to Synod of Bishops 1994, 1999; Bailiff Grand Cross of Honour and Devotion, Sovereign Military Hospitaller Order of St John of Jerusalem of Rhodes and of Malta. *Publications include:* Promise of Future Glory: Reflections on the Mass 1997, Missioners, Priest and People Today 2007, St John Fisher, Bishop and Theologian in Reformation and Controversy 2011, Hope in Action: Reaching Out to a World in Need 2017, Faith Finding a Voice 2018, Gospel in Art 2018. *Address:* Archbishop's House, Ambrosden Avenue, London, SW1P 1QJ, England (office). *Telephone:* (20) 7798-9033 (office). *Fax:* (20) 7798-9077 (office). *E-mail:* cardinalnichols@rcdow.org.uk (office). *Website:* www.rcdow.org.uk/archbishop (office).

NICHOLSON, Arnold Joseph, QC; Jamaican lawyer and politician; b. 28 Feb. 1942, Rock River, Clarendon; s. of Arnold A. Nicholson and Bernice Nicholson; m. Yvonne Nicholson; two s.; ed Univ. Coll. of the West Indies, Middle Temple Inn of Court, London, Univ. of London, UK; early career in banking 1964–68; called to the Bar 1972, practised law in Jamaica and Grenada 1972–92; MP for W Central St Andrew 1989–97; Parl. Sec. in Ministry of Educ. and Culture 1992–95, Minister of State, Ministry of Legal Affairs Jan.–Sept. 1995, Attorney-Gen. 1995–2007; apptd to Senate 1998; Minister of Justice 2001, of Foreign Affairs and Foreign Trade 2012–16. *Leisure interests:* reading, music, cricket and dancing.

NICHOLSON, Sir Bryan Hubert, Kt, GBE, MA, FRSA, CBIM, FCIM; British business executive; *Senior Adviser, Penfida Partners Limited;* b. 6 June 1932, Rainham, Essex; s. of Reginald H. Nicholson and Clara Nicholson; m. Mary E. Harrison 1956; one s. one d. (and one s. deceased); ed Palmers School, Grays, Oriel Coll. Oxford; man. trainee, Unilever 1955–58; Dist Man. Van den Berghs 1958–59; Sales Man. Three Hands/Jeyes Group 1960–64; joined Sperry Rand 1964, Sales Dir UK Remington Div. 1964–66, Gen. Man. Australia, Remington Div. 1966–69, Man. Dir UK and France, Remington Div. 1969–72; Dir Operations, Rank Xerox (UK) 1972–76, Dir Overseas Subsidiaries 1976, Exec. Dir 1976–84, Chair. Rank Xerox (UK) and Rank Xerox GmbH 1979–84; Chair. Manpower Services Comm. 1984–87, The Post Office 1987–92; Chair. BUPA 1992–2001, Varity Holdings Ltd (now Varity Europe Ltd) 1993–96, Cookson Group PLC 1998–2003; Sr Adviser, Penfida Partners LLP 2006–; Pres. Involvement and Participation Asscn 1990–94; Chair. CBI Vocational Educ. and Training Task Force 1988–89, CNAA 1988–91, Nat. Council for Vocational Qualifications 1990–93, CBI Educ. and Training Affairs Cttee 1990–93, Industrial Soc. 1990–93, Deputy Pres. CBI 1993–94, Pres. 1994–96; Dir (non-exec.) GKN 1990–2000, Varity Corpn, USA 1993–96, LucasVarity 1996–99, Equitas Holdings Ltd 1996–2005, Newsquest PLC 1997–99, Action Centre for Europe Ltd 1997–2004, Accountancy Foundation 2000–04; mem. Nat. Econ. Devt Council 1985–92; Pres. Oriel Soc. 1988–92; Vice-Pres. Nat. Children's Home 1990–2002, Industrial Trust 1999–2010; Deputy Chair. Educ. Devt International 2003–04, Chair. 2004–05; Chancellor, Sheffield Hallam Univ. 1992–2001;

Pro-Chancellor and Chair. Council The Open Univ. 1996–2004; Chair. United Oxford and Cambridge Univ. Club 1995–97, Financial Reporting Council 2001–05, Goal PLC 2001–02; mem. Int. Advisory Bd, Active International 2001–; mem. Public Interest Oversight Bd, International Fed. of Accountants; mem. Exec. Cttee, The Pilgrims 2016–; Trustee, International Accounting Standards Cttee Foundation 2006–12; Pres. Young Epilepsy (fmrly Nat. Centre for Young People with Epilepsy) 2005–11, Life Vice-Pres. 2011–; Fellow, Open Univ. 2006; Patron, Inst. of Financial Accountants 2012–16; Hon. FCGI 1988; Hon. Fellow, Oriel Coll. Oxford 1989, Manchester Metropolitan Univ. 1990, Scottish Vocational Ed. Council 1994, Scottish Qualifications Authority 1997; Hon. Companion, Inst. of Personnel and Devt 1994; Hon. FCA 2011; Dr hc (CNAA) 1994, (Open Univ.) 1994, (Sheffield Hallam) 2001; Hon. DLitt (Glasgow Caledonian) 2000. *Leisure interests:* tennis, bridge, opera, political history. *Address:* Point Piper, Lilley Drive, Kingswood, KT20 6JA, England. *Telephone:* (1737) 832208. *Fax:* (1737) 832208. *E-mail:* bryanhnicholson@aol.com.

NICHOLSON, Jack; American actor and film director; b. 22 April 1937, Neptune, NJ; s. of John Nicholson and Ethel May Nicholson; m. Sandra Knight 1961 (divorced 1966); two d.; f. Proteus Films Inc. (production co.); Commdr des Arts et des Lettres; American Film Inst. Lifetime Achievement Award 1994, Cecil B. De Mille Award 1999, Kennedy Center Honor 2001. *Films:* The Cry-Baby Killer 1958, Teenage Lovers 1960, The Wild Ride 1960, Too Soon to Love 1960, The Little Shop of Horrors 1960, Studs Lonigan 1960, The Broken Land 1962, The Raven 1963, The Terror 1963, Ensign Pulver 1964, Flight to Fury 1964, Back Door to Hell 1964, Ride the Whirlwind (also writer and producer) 1965, The Shooting (also producer) 1967, Hell's Angels on Wheels 1967, The Trip (screenplay) 1967, Head (co-scriptwriter, co-producer) 1968, Psych-Out 1968, Easy Rider (Acad. Award for Best Supporting Actor) 1969, The Rebel Rousers 1970, On a Clear Day You Can See Forever 1970, Five Easy Pieces 1971, Drive, He Said (dir) 1971, A Safe Place 1971, Carnal Knowledge 1971, The King of Marvin Gardens 1972, The Last Detail 1973, Chinatown 1974, The Passenger 1974, Tommy 1974, The Fortune 1975, One Flew over the Cuckoo's Nest (Acad. Award for Best Actor 1976) 1975, The Missouri Breaks 1976, The Last Tycoon 1976, Goin' South (also dir) 1978, The Shining 1980, The Postman Always Rings Twice 1981, Reds 1981, The Border 1982, Terms of Endearment (Acad. Award for Best Supporting Actor) 1984, Prizzi's Honor 1984, Heartburn 1985, The Witches of Eastwick 1986, Broadcast News 1987, Ironweed 1987, Batman 1989, The Two Jakes (also dir) 1989, Man Trouble 1992, A Few Good Men 1992, Hoffa 1993, Wolf 1994, The Crossing Guard 1995, Mars Attacks! 1996, The Evening Star 1996, Blood and Wine 1996, As Good As It Gets 1997, The Pledge 2001, About Schmidt (Golden Globe for Best Dramatic Actor 2003) 2002, Anger Management 2003, Something's Gotta Give 2003, The Departed 2006, The Bucket List 2007, How Do You Know 2010. *Television:* Matinee Theatre (series) 1956, Mr. Lucky (series) 1960, The Barbara Stanwyck Show (series) 1960, Tales of Wells Fargo (series) 1961, Sea Hunt (series) 1961, Bronco (series) 1961, Little Amy (film) 1962, Hawaiian Eye (series) 1962, Dr Kildare (series) 1966, Voyage to the Bottom of the Sea (series) 1966, The Andy Griffith Show (series) 1966–67, The Guns of Will Sonnett (series) 1967, Elephant's Child (film) 1986. *Address:* c/o Bresler Kelly and Associates, 11500 West Olympic Boulevard, Suite 510, Los Angeles, CA 90064, USA (office).

NICHOLSON, Pamela (Pam) M., BA; American business executive; *President and CEO, Enterprise Holdings;* b. St Louis, Mo.; ed Univ. of Missouri; joined Enterprise Rent-A-Car as man. trainee in St Louis 1981, Asst Br. Man. 1982, transferred to Southern California group 1982, rose through ranks to become Regional Vice-Pres. 1994, returned to St Louis to become Corp. Vice-Pres. 1994–97, Gen. Man. Enterprise's New York group 1997–99, Sr Vice-Pres., North American operations 1999–2003, Exec. Vice-Pres. and COO Enterprise Rent-A-Car 2003–08, Pres. and COO Enterprise Holdings 2008–13, Pres. and CEO 2013–, mem. Bd of Dirs Crawford Group (parent co.), Enterprise Rent-A-Car Foundation, ERAC USA Finance LLC (subsidiary); mem. Bd of Dirs Energizer Holdings, Inc. (now Edgewell Personal Care Co.) 2002–14, Hyatt Hotels Corpn 2014–, Humane Soc. of Missouri; mem. Bd Trustees St Louis Regional Chamber and Growth Asscn. *Address:* Enterprise Holdings, 600 Corporate Park Drive, St Louis, MO 63105, USA (office). *Telephone:* (314) 512-1000 (office). *Fax:* (314) 512-4706 (office). *E-mail:* info@enterprise.com (office). *Website:* www.enterpriseholdings.com (office); www.enterprise.com (office); www.erac.com (office).

NICHOLSON, The Hon. Robert (Rob) Douglas, PC, QC, BA; Canadian lawyer and politician; b. 1952, Niagara Falls, Ont.; m. Arlene Nicholson; three c.; ed Queen's Univ., Univ. of Windsor; fmr Niagara Regional Councillor, Conservation Authority Dir, Niagara Escarpment Commr; MP for Niagara Falls 1983–93, 2004–; Parl. Sec. to the Leader of the Govt in the House of Commons 1989–90, to the Attorney-Gen. 1989–93; Minister for Science and Minister responsible for Small Business 1993; fmr Transport Critic; Chief Opposition Whip 2005; Leader of the Govt in the House of Commons and Minister for Democratic Reform 2006–07; Opposition Critic for Justice 2015–; Minister of Justice and Attorney-Gen. of Canada 2007–13, Minister of Nat. Defence 2013–15, of Foreign Affairs Feb.–Oct. 2015; mem. Upper Canada Law Soc. *Address:* House of Commons, Ottawa, ON K1A 0A6, Canada (office). *Telephone:* (613) 995-1547 (office). *Fax:* (613) 992-7910 (office). *E-mail:* rob.nicholson@parl.gc.ca (office). *Website:* www.parl.gc.ca (office); www.robnicholson.ca.

NICHOLSON, Robin, CBE, MA (Cantab.), MSc (Lon), RIBA, FRSA; British architect; *Senior Practice Partner, Cullinan Studio;* b. 27 July 1944, Hertford, Herts.; s. of Gerald Nicholson and Margaret Hanbury; m. Fiona Mary Bird; three s.; ed Eton Coll., Magdalene Coll. Cambridge, Bartlett School, Univ. Coll., London; worked for James Stirling Chartered Architects, London 1969–76; Boza Lührs Muzard, Santiago, Chile 1973; Polytechnic of North London 1976–79; Partner, Cullinan Studio (fmrly Edward Cullinan Architects) 1980–90, now Sr Practice Partner; Vice-Pres. RIBA 1992–94; Comm. for Architecture and the Built Environment Commr 2002–10, Jt Deputy Chair. 2008–10; Dir Nat. House-Building Council 2007–14; Chair. Dept for Children, Schools and Families Zero Carbon (Schools) Task Force 2009–10; Chair. Cambridgeshire Quality Panel 2010–; Convenor, The Edge 1996–; Founder-mem. Movement for Innovation Bd 1998–2001; mem. Eco-Town Design Review Panel, Comm. for Architecture and the Built Environment, Nat. House-Bldg Council Foundation Expert Panel 2011–; Hon. Fellow, Inst. of Structural Eng 2002, Chartered Inst. of Building Services

2013, Hon. Prof. Univ. of Nottingham 2013; RIBA Student Design Prize 1969, Happold Medal, Happold Trust and Construction Industry Council 2013. *Publications:* Innovations in Healthcare Design 1995, The Cost of Bad Design 2006. *Leisure interests:* gardening, making things. *Address:* Cullinan Studio, 5 Baldwin Terrace, London, N1 7RU, England (office). *Telephone:* (20) 7704-1975 (office). *E-mail:* robin.nicholson@cullinanstudio.com (office). *Website:* www.cullinanstudio .com (office).

NICHOLSON, Sir Robin Buchanan, Kt, BA, MA, PhD, FRS, FREng, FIM, MInstP; British metallurgist, academic and businessman; *Member of Council, University of Exeter;* b. 12 Aug. 1934, Sutton Coldfield, West Midlands, England; s. of Carroll Nicholson and Nancy Nicholson; m. 1st Elizabeth Mary Caffyn 1958 (died 1988); one s. two d.; m. 2nd Yvonne Appleby 1991; ed Oundle School and St Catharine's Coll., Cambridge; Demonstrator in Metallurgy, Univ. of Cambridge 1960–64, Lecturer 1964–66, Fellow of Christ's Coll. 1962–66; Prof. of Metallurgy, Univ. of Manchester 1966–72; Dir of Research Lab., Inco Europe Ltd 1972–76, Dir 1975–81, Man. Dir 1976–81; Co.-Chair. Biogen NV 1979–81; Chief Scientist, Cen. Policy Review Staff 1981–83; Chief Scientific Adviser, Cabinet Office 1983–86; Chief. Exec., Chair. Electro-Optical Div., Pilkington PLC 1986–96, Dir Pilkington PLC (fmrly Pilkington Bros PLC) 1986–96, Pilkington Optronics Ltd 1991–98; Dir Rolls-Royce 1986–2005, BP PLC 1987–2005; Chair. Centre for Exploitation of Science and Tech. 1987–90, Advisory Council on Science and Tech. 1990–93; Pres. Inst. of Materials 1997–98; mem. Council for Science and Tech. 1993–2000; mem. Council Univ. of Exeter 2005–; fmr Pro Chancellor UMIST; Fellow, Royal Acad. of Eng, Royal Soc. (mem. Council 1983–85); Hon. DSc (Cranfield, Aston) 1983, (Manchester) 1985, (Nottingham) 2000; Hon. DMet (Sheffield) 1984; Hon. DEng (Birmingham) 1986; Rosenhain Medal, Inst. of Metals 1971, Platinum Medal, Metals Soc. 1981. *Publications:* Precipitation Hardening (co-author) 1962, Electron Microscopy of Thin Crystals (co-author) 1965, Strengthening Methods in Crystals (co-ed. and contrib.) 1971. *Leisure interests:* family life, gardening, music. *Address:* Penson Farm, Diptford, Totnes, Devon, TQ9 7NN, England. *E-mail:* pensonfarm@aol.com (home).

NIČIĆ, Radovan; Serbian politician; b. 1971, Čaglavica; ed Univ. of Prishtina; worked at Inst. for the Protection of Cultural Monuments, City of Prishtina 1990s; mem. Nat. Ass. (Serbian Radical Party); Speaker, 'Ass. of the Union of Municipalities of Kosovo and Metohija', Mitrovica 2008; Pres. 'Municipal Ass. of Prishtina' 2008.

NICKELL, Sir Stephen (Steve) John, Kt, CBE, BA, MSc, FBA, FES; British economist and academic; *Honorary Fellow, Nuffield College, Oxford;* b. 25 April 1944; s. of John Edward Hilary Nickell and Phyllis Nickell; m. Susan Elizabeth Pegden; one s. one d.; ed Merchant Taylors' School, Pembroke Coll., Cambridge, London School of Econs; math. teacher, Hendon Co. School 1965–68; Lecturer, LSE 1970–77, Reader 1977–79, Prof. of Econs 1979–84, School Prof. of Econs 1998–2005; Prof. of Econs, Dir Inst. of Econs and Statistics and Fellow, Nuffield Coll., Oxford 1984–98, Hon. Fellow 2003–06, 2012–, Warden Nuffield Coll. 2006–12; Chair. Nat. Housing and Planning Advice Unit, Dept for Communities and Local Govt 2006–09, Advisory Cttee on Civil Costs, Ministry of Justice 2007–12; mem. Academic Panel, HM Treasury 1981–89, Council of Royal Econ. Soc. 1984–94 (Pres. Royal Econ. Soc. 2001–04), Econ. and Social Research Council 1990–94; External mem. Monetary Policy Cttee Bank of England 2000–06; mem. Econ. Research Advisory Panel, Welsh Ass. Govt 2004–10, Bd of the UK Statistics Authority 2008–10, UK Budget Responsibility Cttee 2010–; Fellow, Econometric Soc. 1980, European Econ. Asscn 2004, Soc. of Labor Economists 2007; Foreign Hon. mem. American Econ. Asscn 1997, American Acad. of Arts and Sciences 2006; Hon. Fellow, Pembroke Coll., Cambridge 2006; Hon. DSc (Warwick) 2008; ISI Highly Cited Researcher 2003, IZA Prize for Labor Econs 2008, DIW Senior Prize (best scientific publ. using German Socio-Econ. Panel 2007–08) 2009. *Publications:* The Investment Decisions of Firms (co-author) 1978, The Rise in Unemployment (co-ed.) 1987, The Performance of the British Economy (co-author) 1988, The Nature of Unemployment in Britain: Studies of the DHSS Cohort (co-ed.) 1989, Unemployment: Macroeconomic Performance and the Labour Market (co-author) 1991 (second edn 2005), The Unemployment Crisis 1994, The Performance of Companies 1995, Combating Unemployment (co-author) 2011; numerous articles in learned journals. *Leisure interests:* reading, cricket, riding, cooking. *Address:* Nuffield College, New Road, Oxford, OX1 1NF, England (office). *E-mail:* steve .nickell@nuffield.ox.ac.uk (office). *Website:* www.nuffield.ox.ac.uk (office).

NICKLAUS, Jack William; American professional golfer; b. 21 Jan. 1940, Columbus, Ohio; s. of L. Charles Nicklaus and Helen Nicklaus (née Schoener); m. Barbara Bash 1960; four s. one d.; ed Ohio State Univ.; professional golfer 1961–; won US Amateur Championship 1959, 1961; US Open Championship 1962, 1967, 1972, 1980, US Masters 1963, 1965, 1966, 1972, 1975, 1986, US PGA Championship 1963, 1971, 1973, 1975, 1980, The Open Championship 1966, 1970, 1978; by 1973 had won more major championship titles (totals now: 18 as professional, two as amateur) than any other player; Australian Open Champion six times, World Series winner five times, record three times individual winner World Cup, six times on winning team; rep. USA in six Ryder Cup matches; 97 tournament victories, 76 official tour victories, 58 times second, 36 times third; joined Seniors Tour 1990; won US Sr Open; 136 tournament appearances 1996; played in 154 consecutive majors 1999; has also designed over 100 golf courses in 26 countries; Co-Chair. The First Tee's Capital Campaign, More Than A Game 2000; Capt. US team, President's Cup 2003; f. Nicklaus Design (golf course design co.); Founder and Chair. Nicklaus Children's Health Care Foundation; Hon. LLD (St Andrews) 1984; five times US PGA Player of the Year; Golfer of the Century 1988, Athlete of the Decade Award 1970s, Golf World's Golf Course Architect of the Year 1993, Presidential Medal of Freedom 2005. *Publications:* My Story 1997 and numerous books about golf. *Leisure Interests:* fishing, hunting, tennis. *Address:* Nicklaus Design, 11780 US Highway 1, Suite 500, North Palm Beach, FL 33408, USA (office). *Telephone:* (561) 227-0300 (office). *Fax:* (561) 227-0548 (office). *Website:* www.nicklaus.com (office).

NICKLES, Donald Lee (Don); American business executive and fmr politician; *Chairman and CEO, Nickles Group LLC;* b. 6 Dec. 1948, Ponca City, Okla; s. of Robert Nickles and Coeweene Nickles; m. Linda Morrison 1968; one s. three d.; mem. Nat. Guard 1971–76; Vice-Pres. and Gen. Man. Nickles Machine Co. 1972–80; mem. Okla State Senate 1978–80, US Senator from Oklahoma (Republican) 1981–2005, Chair. Nat. Republican Senatorial Cttee 1989–91, Republican Policy Cttee 1991–96, Asst Majority Leader 1996–2001, Senate Minority Whip 2001–03, Chair. Senate Budget Cttee 2003–05; Founder, Chair. and CEO Nickles Group LLC (lobbyist firm), Washington, DC 2005–; mem. Bd of Dirs Fortress America Acquisition Corpn 2005–09, Chesapeake Energy Corpn 2005–, Valero Energy Corpn 2005–, National Asscn of Insurance Commrs 2007–. *Film:* featured in the film Traffic giving his opinion on the war on drugs. *Address:* Nickles Group LLC, 601 13th Street NW, Suite 250 North, Washington, DC 20005, USA (office). *Telephone:* (202) 742-6980 (office); (202) 637-0214 (office). *E-mail:* mail@ nicklesgroup.com (office). *Website:* www.nicklesgroup.com (office).

NICKS, Stephanie (Stevie); American singer and songwriter; b. 26 May 1948, Phoenix, Ariz.; m. Kim Anderson 1983 (divorced 1984); fmr mem. Fritz (with Lindsey Buckingham); mem. duo, Buckingham Nicks (with Lindsey Buckingham) 1971–74; mem. Fleetwood Mac 1975–93, 1997–; solo artist 1978–; tour with The Pretenders 2016; numerous world-wide tours and concert appearances; American Music Award for Favorite Pop/Rock Group 1978, Billboard Award for Group of the Year 1977, BRIT Award for Outstanding Contribution 1998, Grammy Hall of Fame Award 2003. *Recordings include:* albums: with Lindsey Buckingham: Buckingham Nicks 1973; with Fleetwood Mac: Fleetwood Mac 1975, Rumours (Billboard Award for Album of the Year 1977, American Music Award for Favorite Pop/Rock Album 1978, Grammy Award for Album of the Year 1978) 1977, Tusk 1979, Fleetwood Mac Live 1980, Mirage 1982, Tango In The Night 1987, Behind The Mask 1990, The Dance 1997, Say You Will 2003, Pious Bird Of Good Omen 2004; solo: Bella Donna 1981, The Wild Heart 1983, Rock A Little 1985, The Other Side Of The Mirror 1989, Street Angel 1994, Maybe Love Will Change Your Mind 1994, Trouble In Shangri-La 2001, The Divine 2001, The Soundstage Sessions 2009, In Your Dreams 2011, 24 Karat Gold 2014. *Website:* www.stevienicksofficial .com.

NICKSON, Baron (Life Peer), cr. 1994, of Renagour in the District of Stirling; **David Wigley Nickson,** KBE, CBE, FRSE; British business executive (retd); b. 27 Nov. 1929, Eton, Berks., England; s. of Geoffrey W. Nickson and Janet M. Nickson; m. 1st Helen L. Cockcraft 1952; three d.; m. 2nd Eira Drysdale 2013; ed Eton and Royal Mil. Acad. Sandhurst; man. trainee, Wm. Collins, Publrs, Glasgow 1954, Dir 1961, Jt Man. Dir 1967, Vice-Chair. 1976, Vice-Chair. and Group Man. Dir 1979–82, Dir (non-exec.) 1982–85; Dir (non-exec.) Scottish & Newcastle Breweries PLC 1981–95, Deputy Chair. 1982, Chair. 1983–89; Dir (non-exec.) General Accident Fire & Life Assurance Corpn PLC, Edinburgh Investment Trust PLC 1983–94; Pres. CBI 1986–88; Chair. Top Salaries Review Body 1989–95; Chair. Atlantic Salmon Trust 1989–96 (Vice-Chair. 1985–88), Sec. of State for Scotland's Atlantic Salmon Task Force 1996, Scottish Devt Agency 1989–90, Scottish Enterprise 1990–92; Deputy Chair. Clydesdale Bank PLC 1989–91 (Chair. 1991–98), General Accident 1993–98; Chancellor Glasgow Caledonian Univ. 1993–2002; mem. House of Lords 1994–2015 (retd); Pres. Assoc of District Salmon Fishery Bds 1996–2011; Vice-Lord Lt of Stirling and Falkirk 1997–2004; Hon. DL; Hon. DUniv (Stirling) 1986, (Glasgow) 1993; Hon. DBA (Napier) 1990, (Paisley) 1991. *Leisure interests:* fishing, birdwatching, shooting, the countryside. *Address:* The River House, Doune, Perthshire, FK16 6DA, Scotland. *Telephone:* (1876) 841614. *Fax:* (1876) 841062.

NICOL, Peter Franz, MBE; British fmr professional squash player; b. 5 April 1974, Inverurie, Scotland; s. of Patrick Nicol; professional debut 1992; World No. 1 ranking for 60 months Feb. 1998–Sept. 2004; major singles titles include US Open 1994, Canadian Open 1995, Mahindra International 1995, 1996, 1997, Al-Ahram International 1997, 2000, 2001, Kuwait Open 1997, British Open 1998, 2002, Commonwealth Games 1998, 2006, PSA Super Series Final 1999, 2000, 2001, Hong Kong Open 1999, 2000, 2002, World Open 1999, 2001, Flanders Open 2000, Irish Open 2000, 2001, PSA Masters 2000, Tournament of Champions 2001, 2003, Scottish Open 2001, Qatar Classic 2001, 2003, YMG Capital Classic 2001, Memorial US Open 2002, British Nat. Championship 2003; 67 appearances for Scotland (66 wins, 1 defeat); switched allegiance from Scotland to England 2001 (qualified for England May 2002); doubles gold for England (with Lee Beachill) Commonwealth Games 2002, 2006; winner (with England team) European Team Championships 2003; retd 2006; Co-Founder and Dir Eventis Sports Marketing Ltd 2002–; f. Nicol Champions Acad. 2006–; Co-Founder SquashSkills; Team Amb. Commonwealth Games Council for England 2010; Dr hc (Robert Gordon Univ., Aberdeen). *Leisure interests:* golf, shopping. *Address:* c/o Melissa Winstanley, Nicol Champions Academy. *Telephone:* (678) 523-7393. *E-mail:* melissa@ nicolchampionsacademy.com. *Website:* www.nicolchampionsacademy.com.

NICOLĂESCU, Gheorghe-Eugen; Romanian economist and politician; b. 2 Aug. 1955, Grădiştea, Giurgiu County; m.; two c.; ed Bucharest Acad. of Econ. Studies; began career with Ministry of Tourism, worked at several hotels including Athénée Palace, Bucharest, as Technologist 1976, Commodities Economist 1978–82, Economist 1982–85; Computer Analyst, Ministry of Industry and Resources equipment factory 1985–87, Economist, Supplies Div. 1987–90; Head of Supplies, Ratmil (mil. equipment co.) 1990–91, Supplies Economist 1991–92, Head of Budget and Econ. Analysis 1992–94, Econ. Dir 1994–97, Gen. Dir 1997–99; Asst Sec.-Gen., Ministry of Public Finance 1999–2000; mem. Chamber of Deputies for Mureş County 2000–08, for Calarasi 2008–; Minister of Health 2005–08; Asst Prof., Spiru Haret Univ. 2000–01, Bucharest Acad. of Econ. Studies 2001–02;Vice-Pres. Chamber of Financial Auditors of Romania; mem. Partidul Naţional Liberal 1997–. *Address:* Partidul Naţional Liberal, 011866 Bucharest 5, Bd. Aviatorilor 86, Romania (office). *Telephone:* (21) 2310795 (office). *Fax:* (21) 2310796 (office). *E-mail:* dre@pnl.ro (office). *Website:* www.pnl.ro (office).

NICOLAOU, Kyriacos Costa, BSc, PhD; Cypriot/American chemist and academic; *Harry C. and Olga K. Wiess Professor of Chemistry, Wiess School of Natural Sciences, Rice University;* b. 5 July 1946, Karavas, Cyprus; ed Bedford Coll., London and Univ. Coll., London, UK; Research Assoc., Columbia Univ., USA 1972–73; Research Assoc., Harvard Univ. 1973–76; Asst Prof. of Chem., Univ. of Pennsylvania 1976–80, Assoc. Prof. 1980–81, Prof. 1981–88, Rhodes-Thompson Prof. of Chem. 1988–89; Prof. of Chem., Univ. of California, San Diego 1989; Chair. Dept of Chem. and Darlene Shiley Chair. in Chem., Scripps Research Inst., La Jolla, Calif. 1989, also Aline W. and L. S. Skaggs Prof. of Chemical Biology 1996; Harry C. and Olga K. Wiess Prof. of Chem., Wiess School of Natural Sciences, Rice Univ. 2013–; mem. editorial bds of numerous journals; mem. NAS 1996, ACS,

German Chemical Soc., European Chemical Soc., German Acad. of Sciences Leopoldina 2009, American Philosophical Soc. 2011; Foreign mem. Acad. of Athens 2001; Fellow, American Acad. of Arts and Sciences 1993, AAAS 1999, Nat. Acad. of Investors 2015; Hon. mem. Pharmaceutical Soc. of Japan 1996, Israel Chemical Soc. 2009; Hon. Life Fellow, Singapore Nat. Inst. of Chem. 2011; Honorary Fellowship, Honorary Fellowship, Chemical Research Society of India, India, 2004, Indian Academy of Sciences, India, 2007; Order of the Commdr of Honour (Greece) 1998; Hon. MA (Univ. of Pennsylvania) 1980; Hon. DSc (Univ. Coll., London) 1994; Hon. PhD (Univ. of Athens) 1995, (Univ. of Thessaloniki) 1996, (Univ. of Cyprus) 1997, (Univ. of Crete) 1998, (Univ. of Alcala) 1998, (Agric. Univ. of Athens) 2000, (Univ. of Rome, La Sapienza) 2003; numerous awards, including US Sr Scientist Award, Alexander von Humboldt Foundation 1987, ACS Award for Creative Work in Synthetic Organic Chem. 1993, RSC Rhone-Poulenc Medal 1995, Max Tischler Prize, Harvard Univ. 2000, RSC Centenary Medal 2000, Ernst Schering Prize 2001, Nagoya Medal of Organic Chem., Nagoya Univ. (Japan) 2001, Greek American Scientists, Engineers, and High Tech Entrepeneurs Award 2001, Tetrahedron Prize for Creativity in Organic Chem. (Int.) 2002, ACS Nobel Laureate Signature Award for Grad. Educ. in Chem. (shared with Phil S. Baran) 2003, Aristeio Bodossaki Prize, Bodossaki Foundation (Greece) 2004, Burckhardt-Helferich Prize (Germany) 2006, ACS Arthur C. Cope Award 2005, ACS Western Regional Meeting Award of Excellence 2007, ACS (Auburn Section) G.M. Kosolapoff Award 2006, ISHC Sr Award in Heterocyclic Chem. (Int.) 2007, August Wilhelm von Hofmann-Denkmünze Award (Germany) 2008, Charles Chandler Medal, Columbia Univ. 2008, San Diego BioPharma Achievement Award 2009, Lampousa Lifetime Achievement Award, Cypriot American Asscn 2009, Science Award, Ministry of Educ. and Culture (Cyprus) 2010, Benjamin Franklin Medal in Chem., The Franklin Inst. 2011, ACS (NJ Section) Creativity in Molecular Design and Synthesis Award 2011, Wolf Prize in Chem. (co-recipient) 2016. *Publications:* Selenium in Natural Products Synthesis (co-author) 1984, Classics in Total Synthesis (co-author) 1996, Handbook of Combinatorial Chemistry, Vols 1 and 2 (co-ed.) 2002, Classics in Total Synthesis II (co-author) 2003, Molecules That Changed The World (co-author) 2008, Classics in Total Synthesis III (co-author) 2011; more than 770 publs and 65 patents. *Address:* Department of Chemistry, BioScience Research Collaborative, Rice University, 6500 Main Street, Houston, TX 77005, USA (office). *Telephone:* (713) 348-8860 (office). *Fax:* (713) 348-8865 (office). *E-mail:* kcn@rice.edu (office). *Website:* nicolaou.rice.edu (office).

NICOLAS, Alrich; Haitian sociologist, economist, academic, diplomatist and politician; *Professor of Macro-Economics, Université Quisqueya;* b. 1956; ed Free Univ., Berlin, Germany; fmr Dean, Latin America Inst., Free Univ., Berlin; fmr Visiting Prof., Costa Rica; fmr Chief, Strategy and Policy Unit, Haiti, UNDP; Amb. to Germany (also accred to Denmark) 1996–2005, Minister of Foreign Affairs 2008–09; Prof. of Macro-Econs, Université Quisqueya, Founder and Dir Centre haïtien d'études et de recherches économiques et sociales (CHERIES) 2012–. *Publications:* numerous articles in scholarly journals on economy and culture. *Address:* Université Quisqueya, 218 Avenue Jean-Paul II, Haut de Turgeau, Port-au-Prince, Haiti (office). *Website:* www.uniq.edu.ht (office).

NICOLAS, Gwenael, MA; French interior designer and product designer; *President, Curiosity Inc.;* b. 6 June 1966, Rosporden; ed Ecole supérieure d'art graphique et d'architecture d'intérieure, Royal Coll. of Art, London; freelancer in Japan 1991; Pres. Curiosity Inc. 1998–; Nintendo Game Boy Advance Design Consultant 2000; American Inst. of Architecture Citation 1998, I.D. Magazine Distinction 1999, 2000, I.F. Design Award 2003, Japan Display Design Award 2005, 2006, Ku/Kan Prize 2009. *Achievements:* Tag Heuer Shops, Tokyo, New York, London, Sony LCD TV 'Capujo', Sony Showroom, Tokyo 2003, Nissan Booth, Tokyo Motor Show 2004, 2005. *Publication:* Curiosity 2002. *Address:* Curiosity Inc., 2-13-16, Tomigaya, Shibuya-ku, Tokyo 151-0063, Japan (office). *Telephone:* (3) 5452-0095 (office). *Fax:* (3) 5454-9691 (office). *E-mail:* nicolas@curiosity.jp (office). *Website:* www.curiosity.jp (office).

NICOLI, Eric Luciano, CBE, BSc; British business executive; *Chairman, YO! Sushi Ltd;* b. 5 Aug. 1950, Pulham Market, Norfolk, England; s. of Virgilio Nicoli and Ida Nicoli; m. Rosalind West 1977; one s. one d.; ed Diss Grammar School, Norfolk, King's Coll. London; worked briefly in market research, then various positions with Rowntree Marketing Dept 1972–80; Sr Marketing Controller Biscuit Div., United Biscuits 1980–81, Marketing Dir Biscuits 1981–84, and Confectionery 1982–84; UK Business Planning Dir 1984, Man. Dir UB Frozen Foods 1985, UB Brands 1986–89, apptd. to Bd of UB (Holdings) PLC 1989, CEO European Operations 1989–90, Group CEO United Biscuits (Holdings) PLC 1991–99, Acting Chair. 2001; Non-Exec. Dir EMI Group PLC 1993–99, Exec. Dir and Chair. 1999–2007, CEO Jan.–Aug. 2007; Chair. (non-exec.) Tussauds Group Ltd 1999-2007, HMV Media Group PLC 2001–04, Vue Entertainment 2006–10, R&R Music 2008, Nick Stewart & Associates Ltd 2008–, Wentworth Media and Arts 2013–, uSwitch Ltd 2013–15, Centtrip 2015–, YO! Sushi 2015–; Chair. Per Cent Club 1993–, EMI Music Sound Foundation 2003–07; mem. Bd of Dirs Akazoo 2008–, Greencore Group plc 2010–; Deputy Chair. Business in the Community 1991–2003; Hon. degree (Brunel) 2011. *Leisure interests:* all sports (especially golf), music, food. *Address:* YO! Sushi Ltd, 95 Farringdon Road, London, EC1R 3BT, England. *Telephone:* (20) 7841-0700. *Website:* yosushi.com.

NICOLL, Roger, BA, MD; American neuroscientist and academic; *Professor of Cellular and Molecular Pharmacology, University of California, San Francisco;* b. 15 Jan. 1941, Camden, NJ; m.; one c.; ed Lawrence Univ., Univ. of Rochester Medical School, Nat. Insts of Health; Research Fellow, Public Health Service, Nat. Inst. of Mental Health Lab. of Neuropharmcology, Bethesda, Md 1965–66, Research Assoc. (Mil.) 1969–73; Intern in Medicine, Univ. of Chicago Hosps and Clinic 1968–69; Research Assoc. Prof., State Univ. of NY, Lab. of Neurobiology, Buffalo 1973–75; Asst Prof., Depts of Pharmacology and Physiology, Univ. of California, San Francisco 1975–76, Assoc. Prof. 1977–80, Prof. 1980–, currently Prof. of Cellular and Molecular Pharmacology, Interim Dept Chair. 1991–93; Visiting Assoc. Prof., Salk Inst. for Biological Studies 1976; mem. Editorial Bd Current Opinion in Neurobiology 1991–, Hippocampus 1993–, Molecular and Cellular Neurobiology 1996–, Physiological Reviews 1998–; mem. NAS 1994–, American Acad. of Arts and Sciences 1999–; numerous awards including Gruber Neuroscience Prize, Peter and Patricia Gruber Foundation (co-recipient) 2006, Ralph W. Gerard Prize in Neuroscience, Soc. for Neuroscience (co-recipient) 2014.

Publications: numerous scientific papers in professional journals on the cellular and molecular mechanisms underlying learning and memory in the mammalian brain. *Address:* UCSF MC 2140, Genentech Hall, Room N-272D, 600 16th Street, San Francisco, CA 94143-2140, USA (office). *Telephone:* (415) 476-2018 (office). *E-mail:* roger.nicoll@ucsf.edu (office); nicoll@cmp.ucsf.edu (office). *Website:* nicolllab.ucsf.edu (office); keck.ucsf.edu/neurograd (office).

NICULESCU, Alexandru A.; Romanian diplomatist; b. 1 Jan. 1941, Bucharest; s. of Alexandru Niculescu and Elisabeth Niculescu; m.; three c.; ed Polytechnical Inst. and Univ. of Law, Bucharest; Chargé d'affaires a.i., Perm. Mission to UN, Geneva 1990–91, Deputy Perm. Rep. 1991–95, Dir Div. for UN and Specialized Agencies, Ministry of Foreign Affairs, Bucharest 1995–98, Deputy Perm. Rep., UN, New York 1999–2000, Amb. and Perm. Rep. 2001–03, Chair. Second Cttee (Econ. and Int. Financial Co-operation), UN Gen. Ass. at the Millennium Session 2000–01, currently with Administrative Affairs Office, Embassy in Prague; Nat. Order 'Serviciu Credincios' 2002. *Publications:* Diplomacy and Destiny 2005; essays and articles on world econ. relations, globalization and UN system's activities. *Leisure interests:* literature, music, economic literature (on globalization). *Address:* 13A Dumbrava Rosie Street, Apt 6, Sector 2, Bucharest, Romania. *Telephone:* (1) 2117877. *E-mail:* alniculescu@hotmail.com; alexandru.niculescu@rouemb.cz.

NIE, Major-Gen. Haisheng; Chinese astronaut; b. 13 Oct. 1964, Zaoyang, Hubei Prov.; m. Nie Jielin; one d.; served as fighter pilot in PLA Air Force; attained rank of Lt-Col; selected to be astronaut, Shenzhou Program 1998; support crew for Shenzhou 5, (China's first manned space mission) 2003; debut space flight on board Shenzhou 6, with astronaut Fei Junlong (q.v.), launched from Jiuquan Satellite Launch Centre, Gobi Desert (China's second space mission) 12 Oct. 2005; attained rank of Major Gen.; Commdr, Shenzhou 10 mission 11–26 June 2013. *Address:* China National Space Administration, Fucheng Road, Haidian District, Beijing 100048, People's Republic of China. *E-mail:* webmaster@cnsa.gov.cn. *Website:* www.cnsa.gov.cn.

NIEBEL, Dirk, MPA; German politician; b. 29 March 1963, Hamburg; m. Andrea Niebel 1990; three s.; ed Univ. of Mannheim; paratrooper, Bundeswehr (airborne infantry), Calw 1984–92; Placement Officer, Fed. Employment Office, Heidelberg 1993–98; mem. CDU 1979–81; mem. FDP 1990–, Sec.-Gen. 2005–09; mem. Bundestag (Parl.) for Heidelberg-Weinheim constituency 1998–2013, FDP Parl. Group Speaker on Labour Market Policy 1998–2009, mem. Parl. Cttee on Labour and Social Affairs; Fed. Minister of Econ. Co-operation and Devt 2009–13; Vice Pres. German-Israeli Asscn 2000–10; Deputy Chair. German-Israeli Parl. Friendship Group; mem. Bd of Trustees Friedrich Naumann Foundation for Freedom 2003–, Pres. Friedrich Ebert Memorial 2009–. *Address:* c/o Federal Ministry of Economic Co-operation and Development, Dahlmannstr. 4, 53113 Bonn, Germany (office). *Website:* www.dirk-niebel.de (office).

NIEDERAUER, Duncan L., BA, MBA, CBE; American business executive; *Founding Partner, Communitas Capital Partners;* b. 7 Sept. 1959; m.; three c.; ed Colgate Univ., Emory Univ.; joined Goldman Sachs & Co. 1985, joined Equities Div. 1987, relocated to HQ of Spear, Leeds & Kellogg (subsidiary) 2000, Man. Dir and Co-head, Equities Div. Execution Services, Goldman Sachs & Co. 1985–2007; Pres. and Co-COO New York Stock Exchange (now NYSE Euronext Inc.) and Head, US Cash Markets April–Nov. 2007, CEO 2007–14, mem. Man. Cttee April 2007–; Ind. Dir Realogy Holdings Corpn 2016–, Chair. Compensation Cttee 2016–; Founding Partner Communitas Capital Partners 2017–, Co-Chair. Investment Cttee; Co-Founder Mountain Top Advisory Group; Non-Exec. Chair. Scenic Advertisement; mem. Colgate Univ. Alumni Corpn Bd of Dirs, also Alumni Trustee 2006–; mem. Bd First Republic Bank 2015–; mem. Bd of Dirs Fantex Holdings Inc. 2015–, Paxos Trust Co. 2016–; fmr mem. Bd of Mans, Archipelago Holdings LLC; fmr mem. Bd of Dirs EzeCastle Software. *Address:* Communitas Capital Partners, 575 5th Avenue, 14th Floor, New York, NY 110017, USA (office). *Telephone:* (646) 867-7295 (office). *E-mail:* info@communitascapital.com (office). *Website:* www.communitascapital.com (office).

NIEDERHUBER, John Edward, MD; American surgeon, academic, researcher and institute director; *Executive Vice-President and CEO, Inova Translational Medicine Institute and Inova Health System;* b. 21 June 1938, Steubenville, Ohio; s. of William Henry Niederhuber and Helen (Smittle) Niederhuber; one s.; ed Bethany Coll., W Va, Ohio State Univ. School of Medicine; NIH Academic Trainee in Surgery, Univ. of Michigan 1969–70, completed training in surgery 1973, mem. Faculty 1973–87, apptd Prof. of Microbiology/Immunology and Prof. of Surgery 1980; Visiting Fellow, Div. of Immunology, Karolinska Inst., Stockholm, Sweden 1970–71; Visiting Prof., Dept of Molecular Biology and Genetics, Johns Hopkins Univ. School of Medicine, Baltimore, Md 1986–87, Prof. of Surgery, Oncology, and Molecular Biology and Genetics 1987–91; Emile Holman Prof. of Surgery, Prof. of Microbiology and Immunology, and Chair. Dept of Surgery, Stanford Univ. 1991–97; Prof. of Surgery and Oncology, Univ. of Wisconsin School of Medicine 1997–2002, Dir Univ. of Wisconsin Comprehensive Cancer Center 1997–2002; Chair. Nat. Cancer Advisory Bd (NCAB) 2002–05; apptd COO and Deputy Dir for Translational and Clinical Sciences, Nat. Cancer Inst. (NCI) 2005, Dir NCI 2006–10, external adviser to NCI, mem. NCI Cancer Centers Review Cttee 1984–86, mem. NCI Div. of Cancer Treatment's Bd of Scientific Counselors 1986–91 (Chair. 1987–91), mem. NCAB's Sub-cttee to Evaluate the Nat. Cancer Program (Cttee to Assess Measures of Progress Against Cancer) and Chair. Molecular Medicine Panel 1993–95, Lab. Investigator supported by NCI and NIH, Leader, Lab. of Tumor and Stem Cell Biology (part of Cell and Cancer Biology Br. of NCI's Center for Cancer Research); holds clinical appointment on NIH Clinical Center Medical Staff; Exec. Vice-Pres. and CEO Inova Translational Medicine Inst. and Inova Health System 2010–; currently Prof. of Oncology and Surgery, School of Medicine, Johns Hopkins Univ., Co-Dir Johns Hopkins Clinical Research Network; mem. Bd C-Change; mem. CEO Roundtable, fmr Co-Chair. Task Force to develop a plan for future oncology devt; Pres. Asscn of American Cancer Insts 2001–03; Founding mem. and Exec. Cttee mem. American Coll. of Surgeons Oncology Co-operative Group; mem. American Coll. of Surgeons Comm. on Cancer 1983–95, Chair. 1989–90, General Motors Cancer Research Foundation Kettering Prize Selection Cttee 1988–89, GMCRF Awards Assembly 1988–92, 1998–2002, Burroughs-Wellcome Foundation Translational Research Advisory Cttee 1999–2006; Chair. American Soc. of Clinical Oncology Surgical Oncology Task

Force Strategic Planning Process 2001–02, ASCO Public Policy and Practice Cttee 2002, 2003; mem. 10 scientific journal editorial bds, including Journal of Clinical Oncology 1993–95; mem. Soc. of Surgical Oncology 1978 (Pres. 2001–02); mem. NAS Inst. of Medicine 2008; numerous hon. professorships; Hon. DSc (Bethany Coll.) 2007; US Public Health Service Career Devt Award, Nat. Inst. of Allergy and Infectious Diseases, Distinguished Faculty Service Award, Univ. of Michigan, Alumni Achievement Award, Ohio State Univ. Coll. of Medicine 1989, Distinguished Alumni Award in Medicine, Bethany Coll. 1995, Professional Achievement Award, Ohio State Univ. 2007, Annual Heritage Award, Soc. of Surgical Oncology 2009. *Achievements include:* recognized for pioneering work in hepatic artery infusion chemotherapy and was first to demonstrate feasibility of totally implantable vascular access devices. *Publications:* editor of four books, including Clinical Oncology; author or co-author of more than 180 publs. *Address:* Inova Translational Medicine Institute, 3300 Gallows Road Claude Moore, Bldg, 2nd Floor, Falls Church, VA 22042, USA. *Telephone:* (703) 776-8199 (office). *Website:* inova.org (office).

NIELSEN, Holger Kirkholm, PhD; Danish politician; b. 23 April 1950, Ribe; ed Univ. of Aarhus, Univ. of Belgrade; mem. Folketing (Parl.) 1981, 1984, 1987–; mem. European Affairs Cttee, Econ. and Political Affairs Cttee, Foreign Policy Cttee; mem. Socialist People's Party, Chair. 1991–2005; mem. Parliamentary Bureau 2007–; Minister of Taxation 2012–13, of Foreign Affairs 2013–14. *Address:* c/o Ministry of Foreign Affairs, Asiatisk Pl. 2, 1448 Copenhagen K, Denmark (office).

NIELSEN, Jakob, PhD; American (b. Danish) software designer; *Principal, Nielsen Norman Group;* b. 5 Oct. 1957, Copenhagen; s. of Gerhard Nielsen and Helle Nielsen; m. Hannah Kain; ed Tech. Univ. of Denmark, Copenhagen; fmr researcher, Aarhus Univ., Tech. Univ. of Denmark, Bellcore, IBM; Distinguished Engineer, Sun Microsystems 1994–98; Co-founder and Prin., Nielsen Norman Group; mem. editorial bd of several professional journals, including Morgan Kaufmann Publrs, ACM Interactions, Behaviour & Information Technology, Personal and Ubiquitous Computing; inducted into Scandinavian Interactive Media Hall of Fame 2000, inducted into Asscn for Computing Machinery (ACM) Computer-Human Interaction Acad. 2006, Lifetime Achievement Award, Special Interest Group on Computer–Human Interaction 2013. *Publications:* Usability Engineering 1994, Multimedia and Hypertext: The Internet and Beyond 1995, Designing Web Usability: The Practice of Simplicity 2000, Homepage Usability: 50 Websites Deconstructed 2001, Prioritizing Web Usability 2006, Eyetracking Web Usability 2008, Mobile Usability 2012; more than 70 US patents; author of monthly newsletter on web design. *Address:* Nielsen Norman Group, 48105 Warm Springs Boulevard, Fremont, CA 94539, USA (office). *Telephone:* (415) 682-0688 (office). *E-mail:* nielsen@nngroup.com (office). *Website:* www.nngroup.com (office).

NIELSEN, Jens, MSc, PhD; Danish academic; *Founding Head of Department, Department of Biology and Biological Engineering, Chalmers University of Technology;* b. 17 Nov. 1962, Horsens; ed Tech. Univ. of Denmark; Research Asst, School of Eng, Univ. of Western Ontario 1986; Assoc. Research Prof., Dept of Biotechnology, Tech. Univ. of Denmark (DTU) 1990–95, Deputy Dir, Center for Process Biotechnology 1995–2000, Assoc. Prof. 1996–98, Prof. BioCentrum 1998–2008, Dir, Center for Process Biotechnology 2001–03, Founding Dir, Center for Microbial Biotechnology 2004–07; Prof. & Scientific Dir, Novo Nordisk Foundation Centre for Biosustainability 2011–, Chief Science Officer 2013–; Founding Chair. Danish Biotechnological Forum 1994–99; Visiting Prof. Dept of Chemical Eng, MIT 1995–96; Adjunct Prof. Dept of Biotechnology, Norwegian Univ. of Science and Tech. (NTNU) 2005–11; Prof. Dept of Chemical and Biological Eng, Chalmers Univ. of Tech., Sweden 2008–, Founding Head of Dept, Dept of Biology and Biological Eng 2015–; Adjunct Prof. Dept of Biotechnology, Royal Inst. of Tech. (KTH), Sweden 2012–17, mem. Bd Center for BioProcess Tech. 2001–03; Adjunct Prof. Beijing Univ. of Chemical Tech. (BUCT) 2016–; mem., Danish Soc. for Engineers 1986–, American Asscn for Advancement of Sciences 1996–, Soc. of Industrial Microbiology, USA 2001–, American Chemical Soc. 2004–, Int. Metabolic Eng Soc. 2012–; mem., Acad. of Tech. Sciences, Denmark 1997, Royal Danish Acad. of Science and Letters 2010, Royal Swedish Acad. of Eng Sciences 2010, Royal Soc. of Arts and Sciences in Gothenburg 2012, Royal Swedish Acad. of Sciences 2014; Foreign mem. Nat. Acad. of Eng, USA 2010; mem. World Council for Industrial Biotechnology, World Econ. Forum 2010–; Hon. Prof., Beijing Univ. of Chemical Tech. 2014, Dalian Inst. for Chemical Physics, Chinese Acad. of Science 2015, East China Univ. of Science and Tech., Shanghai 2017; Merck Award for Metabolic Eng 2004, Amgen Biochemical Eng Award 2011, Charles D. Scott Award 2012, Norblad-Exstrand Medalj 2013, Gaden Award 2016, Gold Medal, Royal Swedish Acad. of Eng Sciences 2017. *Publications include:* numerous articles and journals published. *Address:* Department of Biology and Biological Engineering, Chalmers University of Technology, Kemigården 4, 412 96 Gothenburg, Sweden (office). *Telephone:* (1) 772-38-04 (office). *Fax:* (1) 772-38-01 (office). *E-mail:* nielsenj@chalmers.se (office). *Website:* www.chalmers.se (office).

NIELSEN, Kirstjen Michele, BS, JD; American lawyer and government official; b. 14 May 1972; ed Georgetown Univ., Univ. of Virginia School of Law; Legis. Corresp., US Senator Connie Mack III 1994–97; Assoc., Corp. Practice Group and Int. Working Group, Haynes and Boone LLP, Dallas/Fort Worth 1999–2002; Dir, Office of Legis. Policy, Transportation Security Admin, Dept of Homeland Security 2002–04; Special Asst to the Pres. and Sr Dir for Prevention, Preparedness and Response, White House Homeland Security Council 2003–07; Pres. and Gen. Counsel, Homeland and Nat. Security Solutions, Civitas Group LLC 2007–12; Pres., Sunesis Consulting LLC, Washington DC 2012–17; Civilian Expert, NATO 2015–17; Chief of Staff to John F. Kelly, Dept of Homeland Security Jan.–July 2017; White House Deputy Chief of Staff Sept.–Dec. 2017; Sec. of Homeland Security 2017–19 (resgnd); Sr mem., Resilience Task Force, Center for Cyber and Homeland Security, George Washington Univ. 2010–; mem. Catastrophic Risk Global Agenda Council, World Econ. Forum (WEF) 2011–14, Chair., WEF Global Agenda Council on Risk and Resilience 2014–16, mem. WEF Global Risks Report Advisory Bd 2016–17; mem. Advisory Bd, Cyber Inst., Nat. Cybersecurity Center 2016–17. *Address:* c/o Department of Homeland Security, 245 Murray Lane SW, Washington, DC 20528, USA (office).

NIELSON, Poul, MPolSci; Danish civil servant, academic and fmr politician; *Adjunct Professor, Department of History, International and Social Studies,*

University of Aalborg; b. 11 April 1943, Copenhagen; m. Anne-Marie Nielson 1967; three c.; ed Univ. of Aarhus; Chair. Nat. Social Democratic Students Org. 1966–67; mem. Social Democratic Foreign Affairs Cttee 1965–79 (Chair. 1974–79, 2009–17); mem. Parl. 1971–73, 1977–84, 1986–99; Head of Section, Ministry of Foreign Affairs 1974–79, 1984–85; Chair. Danish European Movt 1977–79; Chair. Parl. Commerce Cttee 1979; Minister of Energy 1979–82; Asst Prof., Danish School of Public Admin. 1985–86; CEO LD-Energy Inc. 1988–94; Minister for Devt Co-operation 1994–99; EU Commr for Devt and Humanitarian Aid 1999–2004; mem. UN Sec.-Gen.'s Advisory Bd on Water and Sanitation 2004–15; Adjunct Prof., Dept of History, Int. and Social Studies, Univ. of Aalborg 2005–; Special Adviser, Labour Market Issues for the Nordic Council of Ministers 2015–17; mem. Bd of Dirs Vestas Inc. 1987–94. *Publications:* Power Play and Security 1969, The Wage Earners and the Company Act 1974, Politicians and Civil Servants 1987, En hel Nielson (memoirs) 2011. *Leisure interests:* photography, gardening, table tennis. *Address:* University of Aalborg, Department of History, International and Social Studies, 9220 Aalborg East, Denmark (office). *Telephone:* 72-30-08-00 (Danish Social Democratic Party) (office); 24-26-14-17 (office). *E-mail:* poulnielson@gmail.com (home).

NIEMCZYCKI, Zbigniew Marian; Polish entrepreneur and business executive; *Chairman, Curtis Group;* b. 23 Jan. 1947, Nisko; m. Katarzyna Frank; one d. three s.; ed Warsaw Univ. of Tech.; Owner and Chair. Curtis Group; Founder and Chair. Polish Eagles Aviation Foundation; Pres. Bd Polish Business Roundtable; Vice-Pres. Main Council Business Centre Club; mem. Council of European Integration affiliated to Prime Minister's Office, Council to the Rector of Warsaw Univ.; Hon. Citizen, City of Mtawa 2011; Commdr's Cross, Order of St Gregory with Star (Second Class) 1992, Kt's Cross, Order of Polonia Restituta, Pope John Paul II 1998; Oscar Heart, Cardiosurgery Devt Foundation, Businessman of the Year 1992, Leader of Polish Business 1992. *Leisure interests:* piloting helicopters and planes, tennis. *Address:* Curtis Group, ul. Wołoska 18, 02-675 Warsaw, Poland (office). *Telephone:* (22) 640-27-06 (office). *Fax:* (22) 640-27-18 (office). *E-mail:* info@curtisgroup.pl (office). *Website:* www.curtisgroup.pl (office).

NIETO MONTESINOS, Jorge; Peruvian sociologist, political analyst and politician; b. 29 Oct. 1951, Arequipa; ed Pontifical Catholic Univ. of Peru, Latin American Faculty of Social Sciences; fmr mem. Partido Comunista Revolucionario Trinchera Roja; fmr Pres. Centro Internacional para la Cultura Democrática, Mexico City; fmr Rep. of Peru to UNESCO and Dir UNESCO Global Governance Unit; fmr consultant to UN; regular lecturer at univs in Europe and Latin America; Minister of Culture July–Dec. 2016; Minister of Defence 2016–17 (resgnd); Dir Nat. Emergency Operations Center (COEN) 2017–. *Publications:* several books including Incertidumbre, Cambio y Decisión, Ética y política en el siglo XXI. Etnicidad y política en América Latina, Ciudades multiculturales y cultura de paz, Desarrollo económico y cultura de paz. *Address:* c/o Ministry of Defence, Edif. Quiñones, Avda de la Peruanidad s/n, Jesús María, Lima 1, Peru (office).

NIGHTINGALE, Anthony John Liddell, CMG; British business executive; b. Nov. 1947, Yorkshire; ed Univ. of Cambridge; joined Jardine Matheson Group 1969, served in several exec. positions, mem. Bd of Dirs Jardine Matheson Holdings 1994–, Man. Dir 2006–12, Chair. and Man. Dir Jardine Matheson Ltd 2006–12, Chair. Jardine Cycle & Carriage, Jardine Motors, Jardine Pacific; Man. Dir Dairy Farm, Hongkong Land, Jardine Strategic, Mandarin Oriental; Commr Astra International; Chair. Business Facilitation Advisory Cttee est. by Financial Sec. in Hong Kong; Chair. The Sailors Home, Missions to Seamen, Hong Kong, Hong Kong-APEC Trade Policy Study Group; Hong Kong Rep. to APEC Business Advisory Council; Vice-Pres. Real Estate Developers' Asscn of Hong Kong; mem. Bd of Dirs Schindler Holding Ltd, Prudential PLC 2013–, China Xintiandi Ltd, Vitasoy Int. Holdings Ltd, UK ASEAN Business Council; mem. Greater Pearl River Delta Business Council, Employers' Fed. of Hong Kong, Securities and Futures Comm. Cttee on Real Estate Investment Trusts; non-official mem. Comm. on Strategic Devt. *Address:* Jardine Matheson Ltd, 48th Floor, Jardine House, GPO Box 70, Hong Kong Special Administrative Region, People's Republic of China (office). *Telephone:* 2843-8288 (office). *E-mail:* jml@jardines.com (office). *Website:* www.jardines.com (office).

NIGHTINGALE, (William) Benedict Herbert, BA; British writer and theatre critic; b. 14 May 1939, London; s. of R. E. Nightingale and Hon. Mrs Nightingale (née Gardner); m. Anne B. Redmon 1964; two s. one d.; ed Charterhouse School, Magdalene Coll., Cambridge, Univ. of Pennsylvania, USA; gen. writer, The Guardian 1963–66; Literary Ed., New Society 1966–67; Theatre Critic, New Statesman 1968–86; Prof. of English, Theatre and Drama, Univ. of Michigan 1986–89; Chief Drama Critic, The Times 1990–2010 (retd); Sunday Theatre Critic, New York Times 1983–84. *Publications include:* Charities 1972, Fifty British Plays 1982, Fifth Row Center 1986, The Future of the Theatre 1998, What's So Flinking Bunny 2010, Great Moments in the Theatre 2012, Les Misérables: From Stage to Screen (with Martyn Palmer) 2013; numerous articles on cultural and theatrical matters in British and American journals. *Leisure interests:* music, literature, watching soccer. *Address:* 40 Broomhouse Road, London, SW6 3QX, England.

NIGHY, Bill; British actor; b. 12 Dec. 1949, Caterham, Surrey, England; s. of Alfred Nighy and Catherine Whittaker; fmr partner Diana Quick; one d.; ed John Fisher Grammar, Purley; Theatre Managers Best Actor 1996, Barclays Best Actor Award 2004. *Stage appearances include:* Arcadia, Rosencrantz & Guildenstern, Entertaining Mr Sloane, Speak Now, Under New Management, Freedom of the City, Comings and Goings, Illuminations, Map of the World, The Seagull, Skylight, Blue Orange, Mean Tears, King Lear, Pravda, Betrayal, Skylight (Best Actor, Barclays Theatre Award 1996), A Kind of Alaska, Blue/Orange, The Vertical Hour 2006. *Film appearances include:* Eye of the Needle 1981, Curse of the Pink Panther 1983, The Little Drummer Girl 1984, The Phantom of the Opera 1989, Mack the Knife 1990, Being Human 1993, True Blue 1996, Indian Summer 1996, Fairy Tale – A True Story 1997, The Bass Player 1998, The Canterbury Tales (voice) 1998, Still Crazy (Best Comedy Performance, Evening Standard Peter Sellers Award 1998) 1998, Guest House Paradiso 1999, The Magic of Vincent 2000, Blow Dry 2001, The Lawless Heart (Best Supporting Actor, LA Critics' Circle Award 2004) 2001, Lucky Break 2001, AKA 2002, I Capture the Castle (Best Supporting Actor, LA Critics' Circle Award 2004) 2003, Love Actually (London Film Critics' Award 2004, Best Supporting Actor, LA Critics' Circle Award 2004, BAFTA Award for Best Actor in a Supporting Role 2004) 2003, Underworld 2003, Shaun of the Dead 2004, Enduring Love 2004, The Magic Roundabout (voice) 2005, The Hitchhiker's Guide to the Galaxy 2005, The Constant Gardener 2005, Underworld: Evolution 2006, Pirates of the Caribbean: Dead Man's Chest 2006, Stormbreaker 2006, Flushed Away (voice) 2006, Notes on a Scandal 2006, Hot Fuzz 2007, Pirates of the Caribbean: At World's End 2007, Slapper 2008, Valkyrie 2008, Underworld: Rise of the Lycans 2009, The Boat That Rocked 2009, G-Force 2009, Wild Target 2010, Harry Potter and the Deathly Hallows: Part 1 2010, The Best Exotic Marigold Hotel 2011, Total Recall 2012, About Time 2013, I, Frankenstein 2014, Pride 2014, The Second Best Exotic Marigold Hotel 2015, Dad's Army 2016, Their Finest 2016. *Radio:* Lord of the Rings 1981, No Commitments, Bleak House, Private Lives 2010, numerous others. *Television includes:* Auf Wiedersehen Pet, Insiders, Kavanagh Series III, Wycliffe, Peak Practice, Bergerac, Antonia and Jane 1991, The Cat Bought It In, South of the Border, Under the Skin, Dreams of Leaving, Soldiers Talking Cleanly, Fat, Standing in for Henry; Agony (series) 1979, Fox 1980, Easter 2016 1982, Reilly: The Ace of Spies (mini-series) 1983, The Last Place on Earth (mini-series) 1985, Hitler's S.S.: Portrait in Evil 1985, Thirteen at Dinner (film) 1985, Making News (series) 1989, Absolute Hell 1991, The Men's Room (mini-series) 1991, A Masculine Ending 1992, Eye of the Storm (mini-series) 1993, Unnatural Causes 1993, Don't Leave Me This Way 1993, The Maitlands 1993, Kiss Me Kate (series episode) 1998, Longitude 2000, The Inspector Lynley Mysteries: Well Schooled in Murder 2002, Ready When You Are Mr. McGill 2003, The Lost Prince (Best Actor, Broadcasting Press Guild Award 2003) 2003, State of Play (series) (Best Actor, Broadcasting Press Guild Award 2003, BAFTA Award for Best Actor in a Television Drama 2004) 2003, The Canterbury Tales (mini-series, The Wife of Bath's Tale) 2003, The Young Visiters (sic) (Best Actor, Broadcasting Press Guild Award 2003) 2003, Life Beyond the Box: Norman Stanley Fletcher (narrator) 2003, He Knew He Was Right (mini-series) 2004, Gideon's Daughter (Golden Globe Award for Best Actor in a mini-series or film made for TV 2007) 2005, The Girl in the Café 2005, The Armstrongs (series) 2006, Page Eight 2011, Turks & Caicos 2014, Salting the Battlefield 2014. *Leisure interests:* reading, rhythm and blues. *Address:* c/o Markham, Froggatt & Irwin Ltd Personal Management, 4 Windmill Street, London, W1T 2HZ, England (office). *Telephone:* (20) 7636-4412 (office). *Fax:* (20) 7637-5233 (office). *Website:* www.markhamfroggattandirwin.com (office).

NIGMATULIN, Nurlan Zayrollaulı, PhD; Kazakhstani politician, government official and business executive; *Chairman, Majlis (Assembly);* b. 31 Aug. 1962, Qarağandi, Kazakh SSR, USSR; m. Baimurzayeva Venera; three s.; ed Qarağandi Polytechnic Inst.; Deputy Akim (Gov.) of Astana 1999–2002; Vice-Minister of Transport and Communications 2002–04; Deputy Chief of Presidential Admin 2004–06; Akim (Gov.) of Qarağandi Oblast 2006–09; mem. Political Council, Nur Otan Xalıqtıq Demokratïyalıq Partïyası (Light of the Fatherland People's Democratic Party) 1999–2000, Chair. Astana City Br. 2000–02, First Deputy Chair. Nur Otan 2009–; Chair. (Speaker), Majlis (Parl.) 2012–14, 2016–; Head, Exec. Office of the Pres. 2014–16; mem. Bd of Dirs, CJSC Nat. Information Technologies 2002–03; Chair. Astana Int. Airport 2002–03, KazakhTelecom 2003, Air Astana 2007; Kurmet Order 2004; II Degree Barys Order 2009; Medal '10 Years of Astana City' 2008; Medal '20 Years of the Independence of the Republic of Kazakhstan' 2011; Order of the First Pres. of the Repub. of Kazakhstan 2015. *Leisure interests:* tennis, football. *Address:* Office of the Chairman, Majlis, 010000 Nur-Sultan, Parliament House (office); Nur Otan, 050000 Almatı, Kunaev kösh. 12/1, Kazakhstan. *Telephone:* (7172) 74-71-42 (office); (7172) 55-55-62. *Fax:* (7172) 24-26-19 (office); (727) 279-40-66. *E-mail:* smimazh@parlam.kz (office); partyotan@nursat.kz. *Website:* www.parlam.kz (office); nurotan.kz.

NIGMATULIN, Robert I., MS, PhD, DrSc; Russian mechanical engineer and academic; *Director, P.P. Shirsov Institute of Oceanology, Russian Academy of Sciences;* b. 17 June 1940; m. 1968; two c.; ed Bauman Tech. Univ., Lomonosov Univ., Moscow; Jr Researcher, Inst. of Mechanics, Lomonosov Univ., Moscow 1963–70, Sr Researcher 1970–74, Prof. and Scientific Chief of Lab. 1974–86, currently Prof.; Vice-Dir Inst. of North Devt Problems and Inst. of Thermophysics, Siberian Br. of Russian Acad. of Sciences, Tyumen 1986–90, Dir Tyumen Inst. of Mechanics of Multiphase Systems 1990–95; Prof. and Chair. Dept of Mechanics, Tyumen Univ. 1986–93; Deputy in State Duma 1999–2003, Chair. Highest Ecology Council; Pres. Ufa (Bashkortostan) Br., Russian Acad. of Sciences 1993–2006, Scientific Chief, Inst. of Mechanics, Ufa Br. 2006–; mem. Presidium Russian Acad. of Sciences 2006–; Dir P.P. Shirsov Inst. of Oceanology, Moscow 2006–; Visiting Scholar and Prof., Centre for Multiphase Research, Rensselaer Polytechnic Inst. 1993–2006; Visiting Prof., Univ. of Pierre and Marie Curie, Paris 1993, 1996, Isaac Newton Inst., Cambridge 2000; Academician, Russian Acad. of Sciences 1991–, Bashkortostan Acad. of Sciences 1991–; mem. Russian Nat. Cttee of Theoretical and Applied Mechanics 1976–, Cen. Asia Acad., Uzbekistan 1993–, Int. Eastern Petroleum Acad., Azerbaijan 1993–; Fellow, Islamic World Acad. of Sciences 2009; Hon. mem. Acad. of Natural Sciences of Russian Fed. 1995, Acad. of Sciences of Tatarstan 2007; Order of Honour (Decree of the Pres. of Russia) 2000; Lenin Komsomol Prize 1973, USSR State Prize 1983, Gold Medal, Nat. Econ. Achievements Exhbn 1989, First Prize, Siberian Br. of Russian Acad. of Sciences 1990, Makeev Medal, Russian Fed. of Astronautica 1996, Tsiolkovski Gold Medal, Russian Fed. of Astronautica 2000. *Publications:* eight books, 200 papers and 20 preprints; 13 patents. *Address:* P.P. Shirsov Institute of Oceanology, 36, Nahimovski prospect, 117997 Moscow, Russia (office). *Telephone:* (495) 124-59-96 (office). *Fax:* (495) 124-59-83 (office). *Website:* www.ocean.ru (office); www.nigmatulin.ru.

NIGO; Japanese fashion designer, music producer and DJ; b. (Tomoaki Nagao), 23 Dec. 1970; ed Bunka Fashion Coll., Tokyo; fashion student, magazine stylist, DJ early 1990s; DJ of Japanese hip hop group Teriyaki Boyz; began making T-shirts and selling them at parties and DJ shows; opened store Nowhere with Jun Takahashi 1993; set up A Bathing Ape fashion label 1993, label now has stores across Japan and in Hong Kong, Taiwan, London, New York; built Ape Sounds the studio and f. The Bapesounds music label; f. A Bathing Ape fashion label 1993 with stores across Japan and in Hong Kong and London, opened New York store 2005, Los Angeles (closed 2010); with Pharrell Williams, responsible for helping produce the Billionaire Boys Club and Ice Cream Footwear brands; Creative Dir for Uniqlo's UT brand; also has interests in music, art, cafés, hairstyling; f. Bapesta!!Wrestling (professional wrestling), Bape Gallery; Best Producer Award,

Tokyo Art Dirs Club (ACD) 2002, one of 30 Best Asian Heroes, Time Asia 2004, Style Award, MTV Asia Awards 2005. *Television:* Nigoldeneye (MTV Japan). *Broadcasts:* (B)ape TV, live show Bape Heads Show. *Recordings include:* Ape Sounds 2000, Return of the Ape Sounds 2005.

NIINILUOTO, Ilkka, BSc, MSc, PhD; Finnish philosopher, mathematician, academic and fmr university administrator; *Professor Emeritus, University of Helsinki;* b. 12 March 1946, Helsinki; s. of Yrjö Niiniluoto and Marja Niiniluoto; m. Ritva Pelkonen; three c.; ed Univ. of Helsinki, Stanford Univ., USA; Teaching Asst, Dept of Philosophy, Univ. of Helsinki 1969–71, Assoc. Prof. of Math. 1973–77, Docent of Theoretical Philosophy 1974–81, Acting Prof. of Theoretical Philosophy 1977–81, Prof. 1981–2014, Prof. Emer. 2014–, Chair. Dept of Philosophy 1983–88, 1992, 1995–2000, Vice-Dean, Faculty of Arts 1988–89, 1991, 1995–98, Dean 1990, 1993–94, Vice-Rector 1998–2003, Rector 2003–08, Chancellor 2008–13; Research Asst, Dept of Philosophy, Acad. of Finland 1971–73; Chair. Finnish Cultural Foundation 1993–94, Helsinki Inst. of Physics 1998–2003; Pres. Philosophical Soc. of Finland 1975–2015, Finnish Soc. for Science Studies 1985–86, Fed. of Finnish Learned Socs 2000–14, Finnish Council of Univ. Rectors 2006–07; mem. Finnish Acad. of Science 1985–, British Soc. for the Philosophy of Science; Foreign mem. Russian Acad. of Sciences; Academician of Science 2017 Dr hc (Univ. of Art and Design) 2007, (Turku School of Econs) 2016; Public Information Award, Univ. of Helsinki 1986, Chydenius Award 1990, Warelius Award 2015. *Publications:* Is Science Progressive? 1984, Truthlikeness 1987, Critical Scientific Realism 1999; numerous journal articles. *Address:* PO Box 24, Unioninkatu 40A, 00014 Helsinki, Finland (office). *Telephone:* (9) 5884252 (office). *E-mail:* ilkka.niiniluoto@helsinki.fi (office). *Website:* www.helsinki.fi (office).

NIINISTÖ, Jussi, MA, PhD; Finnish academic and politician; *Minister of Defence;* b. 27 Oct. 1970, Helsinki; s. of Lauri Niinistö and Leena Niinistö; m. 1st Kati Niinistö 1993 (divorced 2014); three c. m. 2nd Leena Sharma 2015; ed Univ. of Helsinki; Researcher, Nat. Archives 2003; Heritage Work Sec., Heritage Foundation of Finnish Freedom War Invalids 2003–11; Ed.-in-Chief, Vapaussoturi magazine 2006–11; Lecturer in History, Univ. of Helsinki and Nat. Defence Univ. 2004–; mem. Nurmijärvi Municipal Council 2009–15, Helsinki City Council 2017–; mem. Eduskunta (Parl.) for Uusimaa 2011–, Gen. Sec., Finns Party Parl. Group 2005–11, Chair. Defence Cttee 2011–; Minister of Defence 2015–; mem. NATO Parl. Ass. 2011–; mem. Forum for Int. Affairs 2011–; mem. Perussuomalaiset (Finns Party), First Vice-Chair. 2013–; mem. Bd of Dirs KUUMA 2013–15; mem. Bd JRT Foundation 2018–; Golden Mem., Tradition of the War of Liberty 2005, Reserve Officer Perennialist 2017, Merit Officer, Finnish Peacekeeping Fed. 2018, Hon. Military Intelligence Officer 2019; Sininen Risti (Blue Cross) 2001, Ordre de la Libération (France) 2014, Hon. Cross, Front Veterans Asscn 2015, Commdr, Grand Cross, Ostrobothnian Order 2018, Commdr Mark, White Rose of Finland 2018; Medal of Voluntary Defence Work 2000, Fed. of Finnishism Silver Award 2013, Golden Merit 2018, Merit Medal, War Veteran Union 2014, Silver Reserve Medal, Tampere Reserve 2014, Earth Defense Medal with Swords 2015, Special Class Medal of Merit, Reserve Asscn 2015, Medal of Honor, Finnish Nat. Defence League Guild 2016, Military Medal 2017, Gunman Medal with Buckle 2018, Golden Reserve Medal, Finnish Reserve Officers Asscn 2018, 1st Division Medal of Honor 2018. *Publications include:* several books on Finnish history; contrib. numerous articles on history, social affairs to professional journals. *Address:* Ministry of Defence, Eteläinen Makasiinikatu 8, POB 31, 00131 Helsinki, Finland (office). *Telephone:* (9) 16001 (office). *Fax:* (9) 088244 (office). *E-mail:* jussi.niinisto@defmin.fi (office). *Website:* www.defmin.fi (office); www.jussiniinisto.fi.

NIINISTÖ, Sauli Väinämö, LLM; Finnish politician, lawyer and head of state; *President;* b. 24 Aug. 1948, Salo; m. 1st (wife deceased); two s.; m. 2nd Jenni Haukio; own law office in Salo 1978–88; Sr Sec., Turku Court of Appeal 1976; mem. Salo City Council 1977–92, Chair. 1989–92, mem. City Bd 1977–88; mem. Nat. Coalition Party (KOK) Council 1979–81, Party Chair. 1994–2001; mem. Parl. 1987–2003, 2007–11, Chair. Constitutional Cttee of Parl. 1993–95, Speaker 2007–11; Deputy Prime Minister 1995–2001; Minister of Justice 1995–96, of Finance 1996–2003; Vice-Pres. EIB 2003–07; Pres. of Finland 2012–; Chair. European Democratic Union 1998–2002, Econ. and Financial Affairs Council and the Eurogroup 1999; apptd Gov. for Finland, World Bank 2001; mem. Bd of Govs EBRD 1996–2003, Chair. 1999–2000. *Address:* Office of the President, Mariankatu 2, 00170 Helsinki, Finland (office). *Telephone:* (9) 661133 (office). *Fax:* (9) 638247 (office). *E-mail:* presidentti@tpk.fi (office). *Website:* www.presidentti.fi (office).

NIKAI, Toshihiro; Japanese politician; *Secretary-General, Liberal Democratic Party;* b. 17 Feb. 1939; ed Faculty of Law, Chuo Univ.; Sec. to Saburo Endo 1961; mem. Wakayama Prefectural Ass. 1975; mem. House of Reps (Wakayama 3rd Dist; elected eight times) 1983–, Chair. Standing Cttee on Construction 1997, Special Cttee on Postal Privatization 2005; State Sec. of Transportation 1990, 1993; Dir Election Div., New Frontier Party 1995; Minister of Transport and Dir-Gen. Hokkaido Devt Agency 1999, 2000; Sec.-Gen. and Rep. New Conservative Party 2002; joined Liberal Democratic Party (LDP) 2003, Chair. Special Cttee on Tourism, Dir-Gen. Election Bureau 2004–05, Chair. Diet Affairs Cttee 2006, Chair. Gen. Council 2007–08, 2014–, Sec.-Gen. 2016–; Minister of Economy, Trade and Industry 2005–06, 2008–09. *Address:* Liberal Democratic Party, 1-11-23, Nagata-cho, Chiyoda-ku, Tokyo 100-8910, Japan (office). *Telephone:* (3) 3581-6211 (office). *Fax:* (3) 5511-8855 (office). *E-mail:* koho@ldp.jimin.or.jp (office). *Website:* www.jimin.jp (office).

NIKOIAN, Samvel; Armenian politician; b. 13 Feb. 1958, Sarnaghbyur, Ani region (now Shirak Prov.); m.; three c.; ed State Eng Univ. of Armenia, Armenian Br. of Marxism-Leninism Univ. adjunct to USSR Cen. Cttee; worked as engineer-constructor 1982–90, later as Sr Engineer, Head of Div., Deputy Head of Production Unit and Head of Production Unit in Yerevan Hydro Apparatus Plant; Deputy Chief Engineer, Yerevan Experimental Machinery Plant 1995; Head of Div. in Chamber of Commerce and Industry of Armenia 1995–98; Deputy Dir 'Haymamul' (Armenian Media) CJSC 1998–2001; involved in production of ammunition and its delivery during the years of Artsakh freedom fighting; mem. Nat. United Party acting underground in USSR; mem. Republican Party of Armenia (RPA), Chair. RPA Org. Cttee 2001–03, Sec. RPA Faction 2007–09, mem. Foreign Relations Cttee 2008–09, mem. Bd; mem. 'Yerkrapah' Volunteer Union 1997–; Deputy (RPA) in Nat. Ass. 2003–, mem. Standing Cttee on Foreign Relations, mem. ad-hoc Cttee Studying the Effectiveness of the Use of Loans, Credits, Grants and Humanitarian Aid Received from Foreign States and Int. Orgs, mem. Armenian del. of OSCE Parl. Ass., Head of Armenian del. of Inter-parl. Union 2008–, Deputy-Chair. Nat. Ass. 2009–11, Chair. (Speaker) 2011–12; Medal of 'Andranik Ozanyan' of the Armenian Armed Forces 2005, Commemorative Medal from the Prime Minister 2006. *Address:* Azgayin Zhoghov (National Assembly), 0095 Yerevan, Marshal Baghramian Street 19, Armenia (office). *E-mail:* samvel.nikoyan@parliament.am (office). *Website:* www.parliament.am (office).

NIKOLAISHVILI, Col Ramaz; Georgian economist and politician; b. 17 June 1965, Tbilisi; m.; three c.; ed Polytechnic Inst. of Georgia, Ivane Javakhishvili Tbilisi State Univ.; served in various man. positions in Operations Div., Georgian Nat. Tax Inspectorate 1994–2000; Deputy Head of Special Tasks Div., Special Legion 2000–03; Deputy Head of Information and Analytical Dept of Financial Police Div., Ministry of Finance 2003–04, Head of Statistical and Information Service of Financial Police 2004–05, Head of Tbilisi Main Div. of Financial Police Investigation Dept 2005–07, Head of Tbilisi Main Div. of Revenue Service Investigation Dept 2007–08; Gov. Lanchkhuti, Ozurgeti and Chokhatauri Dists 2008; Deputy Minister of Defence 2008; Chair. Nat. Roads Dept 2008–10; Minister of Regional Devt and Infrastructure 2010–12, resgnd in order to run for parl. election; Mem. of Parl. 2012–; Medal of Honour 2007, Order of Honour 2009, Presidential Order of Excellence 2010, St George's Order of Victory 2012; Engineer of the Year, Union Scientific and Engineering Asscn of Georgia 2010. *Address:* Parliament of Georgia, Room No. C-209, C-217, 26, Abashidze Street, 4600 Kutaisi, Georgia (office). *Telephone:* (32) 2-28-92-73 (office); (32) 2-28-15-77 (office). *E-mail:* rnikolaishvili@parliament.ge (office).

NIKOLAYEV, Army Gen. Andrei Ivanovich; Russian politician and fmr army officer; b. 21 April 1949, Moscow; m. Tatyana Yuryevna Nikolayeva; two s.; ed Moscow Gen. Troops Commdg School of RSFSR Supreme Soviet, M. Frunze Mil. Acad., Gen. Staff Acad.; commdr of platoon, co., regt; First Deputy Head Main Admin. of Gen. HQ of USSR Armed Forces; First Deputy Head of Gen. HQ of Russian Army 1992–94; C-in-C of Border troops of Russian Fed. 1994–; Head of Fed. Border Troops Service 1995–97; mem. State Duma (Parl.) 1998–2003; Chair. Cttee of Defence 2000–03; Adviser to the Pres. on Military and Naval Matters 2004; f. Union of People's Power and Labour 1998. *Leisure interests:* theatre, organ music. *Address:* c/o Office of the President, 103132 Moscow, Staraya pl. 4, Russia.

NIKOLAYEV, Mikhail Yefimovich; Russian/Yakut politician; b. 13 Nov. 1937, Ordzhonikidze Region, Yakutia; m.; three c.; ed Omsk Veterinary Inst., Higher CP School; worked as veterinarian, then Sec. Zhigan Regional Comsomol Cttee, First Sec. Yakut Comsomol Cttee, Sec., then First Sec. Verkhneviluysk Regional CP Cttee 1971–75; Deputy Chair. Council of Ministers Yakut ASSR 1975–79; Minister of Agric. 1979–85; Sec. Yakut Regional CP Cttee 1985–89; Chair. Presidium of Supreme Soviet Yakut ASSR 1989–91; Pres. Repub. of Sakha (Yakutia) 1991–2001; mem. Council of Fed. of Russia 1993, Rep. Sakha-Yakutia Rep. In Council of Fed. 2001, Deputy Chair. 2002; Order of Red Banner of Labour, Order of Friendship, Order for Prominent Services to the Fatherland and other honours. *Publications include:* My People are My Republic 1992, The Arctic: The Pain and Hope of Russia 1994, The Arctic. XXI Century 1999.

NIKOLIĆ, Tomislav; Serbian politician and fmr head of state; b. 15 Feb. 1952, Kragujevac; s. of Radomir Nikolić and Živadinka Nikolić (née Đoković); m. Dragica Ninković; two s.; ed Univ. of Belgrade; Deputy, Fed. Ass. of Serbia and Montenegro 1991–2006, mem. Cttee on Constitutional Charter Issues, Cttee on Foreign Affairs; mem. del. to Parl. Ass. of Council of Europe; Vice-Pres. of Serbia 1998, of Serbia and Montenegro 1999; unsuccessful presidential cand. for Srpska Napredna Stranka (SNS—Serbian Progressive Party) 2000, 2003, 2004, 2008; Co-founder (with Vojislav Šešelj) and Vice-Pres. Srpska Radikalna Stranka (SRS—Serbian Radical Party), Acting Leader 2003–08; Speaker, Serbian Parl. 8–13 May 2007; Leader, SNS 2008–12; Pres. of Serbia 2012–17; Hon. Citizen of Čačak, Serbia 2013, of Trebinje, Bosnia and Herzegovina 2013, of Berane, Montenegro 2015, of Beijing 2017; Order of Makarios III (Cyprus) 2013; Order of State (Ukraine) 2013; Order of the Redeemer (Greece) 2013; Order of Glory (Armenia) 2014; Order of José Marti (Cuba) 2015; Nat. Order of Merit (Algeria) 2016; Order of Friendship, First Degree (Kazakhstan) 2016; Order of Prince Henry (Portugal) 2017. *Publications:* (13 political books, all in Serbo-Croatian): Neither Victory Nor Defeat, All for Kosovo and Metohija, Abducted Victory, Šešelj for President, Through the Darkness of the Media, The Letter with an Address, In the Grip of Hatred, I Spoke, The Parliamentary Walk on Torture, Neo-Communist Parliament, Since the Beginning, When the Government Falls, Milošević Falls, The Trenches in the National Assembly.

NIKOLSKY, Boris Vassilyevich; Russian politician; b. 1 May 1937, Moscow; m.; two c.; ed Moscow Inst. of Agric. Eng, Higher School Cen. Cttee CPSU; master, chief engineer in a factory; Deputy Chair. Moscow Municipal Exec. Cttee on problems of energy and eng 1976–82; Sec. Moscow City CP Cttee 1982–84; Sec., then Second Sec. Cen. Cttee of Georgian CP 1984; First Deputy Chair. Moscow City Planning Cttee 1989; First Deputy Chair. Moscow City Construction Cttee 1990–91; Deputy Prime Minister Moscow Govt 1991–92, First Deputy Chair. 1992–2002; apptd Moscow Rep. to Council of Fed. 2002.

NIKONENKO, Sergey Petrovich; Russian actor, film director and scriptwriter; b. 16 April 1941, Moscow; s. of Peter Nikonenko and Nina Nikonenko; m. Yekaterina Voronina-Nikonenko; one s.; ed All-Union Inst. of Cinematography; mem. Union of Cinematographers 1968–; f. Yesenin Cultural Foundation 1994–; Order of the Badge of Honour 1971, Order of the Honour 2011; Comsomol Prize 1976, A. Dovzhenko Medal 1988, Grand Prix. Int. Film Festival in Oberhausen (Germany), People's Artist of Russia 1991. *Film appearances include:* War and Peace 1965–67, Wings 1966, They Are Ringing, Open the Door 1966, Strange People 1969, Journalist, I Have Come This Way, Crime and Punishment, White Explosion 1969, Sing a Song, Poet 1971, Inspector of Road Police 1982, Unfinished Piece for a Mechanical Piano 1976, Winter Evening in Gagry 1986, Tomorrow Was War 1987, The Red Wine of Victory 1990, Family Man 1991, Unwilling to Marry 1992, Time of the Dancer 1996, Kids of Monday 1997, Sinful Love 1997, Chinese Service 1999, Classic 1998, Istinnyye proishestviya (True Stories) 2002, Interesnyye muzhchiny (Interesting Men) 2003 Attack on Leningrad 2009, O chyom govoryat muzhchiny (What Men Talk About) 2010. *Films directed include:* Gypsy's

Happiness, Birds Above the Town, Love, Wait, Lyonya, I Want Your Husband. *Television appearances include:* Kamenskaya 2000, Igry v podkidnogo (Tricky Games) 2001, Nevozmozhnye zelyonye glaza 2002, In the Service of My Country 2003, Gibel' imperii (The Fall of the Empire) 2005. *Leisure interests:* classical literature and music, opera music, painting. *Address:* Sivcev-Vrasheu 44/14, 119002 Moscow (office); Sivtsev Vrazhek str. 44, Apt. 20, 121002 Moscow, Russia (home). *Telephone:* (495) 244-03-44 (office); (495) 241-78-72 (home).

NIKONOV, Vyacheslav Alekseyevich, DrHis; Russian politician, academic and consultant; *President, Polity Foundation;* b. 5 June 1956, Moscow; s. of Aleksey Dmitrievich Nikonov and Svetlana Vyacheslavovna Molotova; grandson of Vyacheslav Molotov; m. 1st Viktoria Makarovna Kostyuk 1976; m. 2nd Olga Mikhailovna Rozhkova 1987; three s.; ed Moscow State Univ.; researcher, Moscow State Univ.; on staff Admin. Cen. Cttee CPSU 1989–90; on staff of Pres. Gorbachev 1990–91; Asst to Chair. USSR State Security Cttee (KGB) 1991–92; Prof. of Political Science, California Inst. of Tech., USA 1992; counsellor, Dept of Political Problems, Int. Foundation of Econ. and Social Reforms (Foundation Reforma) 1992–93; mem. State Duma (Parl.) 1994–96, 2011–, Chair. Sub-cttee on Int. Security and Arms Control 1994–95; Dean of History and Political Science, Moscow Int. Univ. 2001–; Pres. Polity Foundation 1993–, Unity for Russia Foundation 2003–; Head, Int. Cooperation and Public Diplomacy Cttee, Public Council of the Russian Fed. 2006–; Deputy Chair. Editorial Bd Russia in Global Affairs 2002; Ed.-in-Chief Strategy for Russia Journal 2003–; mem. Bd of Dirs Council on Foreign and Defense Policy, Russian Public Policy Center; mem. Advisory Council Carnegie Endowment (Moscow Br.). *Publications include:* Republicans: From Eisenhower to Nixon 1984, Iran-Contra Affair 1988, Republicans: From Nixon to Reagan 1989, The Age of Change: Russia in the 90s as Viewed by a Conservative 1999, Contemporary Russian Politics (ed.) 2003, 2005, Agenda for Russia 2004 (ed.), Russia in Contemporary Politics 2005 (ed.), Agenda for Russia 2005 (ed.), Molotov: Youth 2005, A Code to Politics 2006. *Leisure interests:* reading, gardening. *Address:* Polity Foundation, 101000 Moscow, Bolshoy Zlatoustinsky per. 8/7, Russia (office). *Telephone:* (495) 206-81-49 (office). *Fax:* (495) 206-86-61 (office). *E-mail:* info@polity.ru (office). *Website:* www.polity.ru (office).

NIKŠIĆ, Nermin (Dževad); Bosnia and Herzegovina lawyer and politician; *Chairman, Socijaldemokratska Partiya BiH (SDP BiH—Social Democratic Party of Bosnia and Herzegovina);* b. 27 Dec. 1960, Konjic; s. of Džemal Nikšić and Amila Nikšić; m. Nadja Nikšić; one s. one d.; ed Univ. of Mostar; employed in Dept of Urban Planning, Construction and Housing and Utilities, municipality of Konjic 1988, later Dept of Hotel Inspection, Chief Inspector 1990–92, Asst Head of Legal Affairs 1992–95, Chair. Exec. Bd, Municipality of Konjic 1995–98, apptd Deputy Mayor of Konjic 2000, resgnd after being elected to Parl.; mem. House of Reps of Fed. of Bosnia and Herzegovina 2000–07; mem. Socijaldemokratska Partija BiH (SDP BiH—Social Democratic Party of Bosnia and Herzegovina) 1993–, Pres. Konjic Municipal Br. 1994, Pres. Herzegovina-Neretva Canton Br. 2007, SDP Gen. Sec. 2007–; Prime Minister, Fed. of Bosnia and Herzegovina 2011–15; Chair. Socijaldemokratska Partija BiH (Social and Democratic Party of Bosnia and Herzegovina) 2014–. *Leisure interest:* sport. *Address:* Socijaldemokratska Partija BiH (Social and Democratic Party of Bosnia and Herzegovina), 71000 Sarajevo, Alipašina 41, Bosnia and Herzegovina (office). *Telephone:* (33) 563910 (office). *Fax:* (33) 563913 (office). *E-mail:* predsjednik@sdp.ba (office). *Website:* sdp.ba (office).

NILEKANI, Nandan M., BEng, BTech; Indian business executive and government official; *Chairman, Infosys Limited;* b. 2 June 1955, Bangalore, Karnataka; s. of Mohan Rao Nilekani and Durga Nilekani; m. Rohini Nilekani; two c.; ed Indian Inst. of Tech., Bombay (now Mumbai); Co-founder and mem. Bd of Dirs Infosys Technologies Ltd 1981–, later Man. Dir, Pres. and COO, CEO, Pres. and Man. Dir 2002–07, Co-Chair. 2007–09, Chair. 2017–; Chair. (with rank of cabinet minister) Unique Identification Authority of India 2009–14; Co-founder India's Nat. Asscn of Software and Service Cos (NASSCOM), Bangalore Chapter of The IndUS Entrepreneurs (TiE); Chair. Govt of India's IT for the Power Sector task force, Bangalore Agenda task force; Co-Chair. Business Leaders Dialogue, Initiative for Social Innovation Through Business, Aspen Inst., Advisory Bd IIT Bombay Heritage Fund; currently Pres. Governing Body, Nat. Council of Applied Economic Research; mem. Asia Pacific Regional Advisory Bd, London Business School, Global Advisory Council, The Conf. Bd, World Econ. Forum Foundation Bd 2006–, Bd of Govs Indian Inst. of Tech. Bombay, Review Cttee Jawaharlal Nehru Nat. Urban Renewal Mission; Hon. DIur (Rotman School of Man., Univ. of Toronto) 2011; Padma Bhushan 2006; Alumnus Award, Indian Inst. of Tech. 1999, Fortune Asian Businessman of the Year (co-recipient) 2003, Corporate Citizen of the Year Award, CNBC Asia Business Leader Awards 2004, Asia Business Leaders Awards 2004, Joseph Schumpeter Prize 2005, Forbes Businessman of the Year for Asia 2007, Legend in Leadership Award, Yale Univ. 2009, Transformational Idea of the Year Award, NDTV Indian of the Year 2011 Social & Economic Innovation Award 2014. *Publications:* Imagining India: Ideas for the New Century (Indiaplaza Golden Quill Readers' Choice Award for Non-fiction) 2009, Rebooting India: Realizing a Billion Aspirations 2015. *Address:* Infosys Ltd, Electronics City, Hosur Road, Bengaluru 560 100; National Council of Applied Economic Research, Parisila Bhawan, 11, Indraprastha Estate, New Delhi 110 002 (office); 856, 13th Main, III Block, Koramangala, Bangalore 560 034, India (home). *Telephone:* (80) 2852 0261 (Infosys, Bengluru) (office); (11) 23379861 (office); (80) 25536150 (home). *Fax:* (80) 2852 0362 (Infosys, Bengluru) (office); (11) 23370164 (office); (80) 25534654 (home). *Website:* www.infosys.com; www.ncaer.org (office); .

NILES, Thomas Michael Tolliver, MA; American diplomatist; b. 22 Sept. 1939, Lexington, Ky; s. of John Jacob Niles and Rena Niles (née Lipetz); m. Carroll C. Ehringhaus 1967; one s. one d.; ed Harvard Univ. and Univ. of Kentucky; Foreign Service Officer, Dept of State 1962; posts in Moscow, Belgrade and Brussels; Amb. to Canada 1985–89, to Greece 1993–97; Perm. Rep. to the EEC, Brussels 1989; Vice-Pres. Nat. Defense Univ. 1997–98 (retd); Pres. US Council for Int. Business 1998–2005, Pres. Emer. 2005–, now mem. Bd of Dirs; mem. Bd of Dirs Jacobs Eng Group Inc., Internet Corpn for Assigned Names and Numbers (ICANN) 2003–05; Superior Honor Award, Dept of State 1982, 1985. *Address:* United States Council for International Business, 1212 Avenue of the Americas, New York, NY 10036, USA (office). *Telephone:* (212) 354-4480 (office). *Fax:* (212) 575-0327 (office). *E-mail:* info@uscib.org (office). *Website:* www.uscib.org (office).

NIMATALLAH, Yusuf A., PhD; Saudi Arabian economist; b. 1 Jan. 1936; ed American Univ., Beirut and Univ. of Massachusetts, USA; with Banque de l'Indochine 1952–57; Teaching Asst in Econs, Univ. of Massachusetts 1963–65; Prof. of Monetary and Int. Econs, Univ. of Riyadh (King Saud Univ. 1982–) 1965 (on leave 1973); Adviser to Minister of Finance on Money and Banking, Oil Finance and Planning 1967–73; Adviser to Sultan of Oman on Oil, Finance, Money and Banking; Deputy Chair. and Pres. Cen. Bank of Oman 1975–78; Deputy Chair. UBAF Arab American Bank, New York 1976–78; Exec. Dir Fund for Saudi Arabia 1979–89; currently Chair. and CEO Injaz Money Exchange Co. (Yousuf Abdul Wahab Niamatullah Co.) Jeddah. *Address:* Injaz Money Exchange Company, PO Box 7039, Behind Al Shoalah Centre 88, Moh Taweel Street, 21462 Jeddah, Saudi Arabia. *Telephone:* (2) 667-6025. *Fax:* (2) 665-8858.

NIMETZ, Matthew, LLB, MA; American diplomatist, lawyer, business executive and UN official; *Personal Envoy of the Secretary-General for the Greece-FYROM talks, United Nations;* b. 17 June 1939, Brooklyn, NY; m. Gloria S. Lorch; one s. one d.; ed Williams Coll., Balliol Coll. Oxford, UK, Harvard Univ.; called to Bar, NY 1966, DC 1968; law clerk to Justice John M. Harlan, Supreme Court 1965–67; Staff Asst to Pres. Johnson 1967–69; Assoc. with Simpson Thatcher and Bartlett LLC, New York 1969–74, Pnr 1974–77; Pnr, Paul, Weiss, Rifkind, Wharton & Garrison LLC 1981–2000; Man. Dir General Atlantic Pnrs (now General Atlantic) LLC, Greenwich, Conn. 2000–; Counsellor, Dept of State 1977–80, Acting Co-ordinator of Refugee Affairs 1979–80; Presidential Envoy to Greece–Macedonian Negotiations 1994–95, Chair. 1997, Personal Envoy of UN Sec.-Gen. for Greece-FYROM Talks 1999–; Commr Port Authority of NY and NJ 1975–77; Dir and Chair. World Resources Inst. 1982–94; Chair. UN Devt Corpn 1986–94, Carnegie Forum in USA, Greece and Turkey 1996–98, Centre for Democracy and Reconciliation in SE Europe 1997–; mem. Bd of Dirs Charles H. Revson Foundation 1990–98, NY State Nature Conservancy 1997–; Dir Inst. Public Admin. 1999–; mem. NY State Advisory Council on State Productivity 1990–92; mem. Bd of Trustees, Cen. European Univ., Budapest, Hungary 1998–, Asscn of Bar of City of NY, Council on Foreign Relations; Trustee, William Coll. 1981–96; Rhodes Scholar, Balliol Coll. Oxford, UK 1962; Hon. LLD (Williams Coll.) 1979. *Address:* Office of the Secretary-General, United Nations, 405 E 42nd Street, New York, NY 10017, USA (office). *Telephone:* (212) 963-1234 (office). *Fax:* (212) 963-1234 (office). *Website:* www.un.org (office).

NIMLEY, Thomas Yaya; Liberian politician; b. 5 Nov. 1956, Pleebo, Maryland County; Minister of Foreign Affairs 2003–06; Chair. Movt for Democracy in Liberia (MODEL); mem. Bd of Dirs Liberia Telecommunications Corpn 2014–. *Address:* Cnr 18th Street and Tubman Blvd, Sinkor, Monrovia, Liberia. *Website:* www.libtelco.com.lr.

NIMROD, Elvin, MA, DJur; Grenadian politician; b. 1943, Carriacou; ed Brooklyn Coll., John Jay Coll. of Criminal Justice, New York, New York Law School, USA, Hugh Wooding Law School, Port-of-Spain, Trinidad and Tobago; teacher, Mt Pleasant Govt Primary School, Carriacou; called to the Bar, Grenada 1993; mem. House of Reps for Carriacou and Petite Martinique 1999–; Minister of Labour 1999, of Foreign Affairs and Int. Trade and of Carriacou and Petit Martinique Affairs 1999–2008, also of Legal Affairs 1999–2007, Deputy Prime Minister 2013–, also Minister for Legal Affairs, Labour, Local Govt and Carriacou and Petite Martinique Affairs 2013–16, of Foreign Affairs 2016–18; fmr Attorney-Gen. of Grenada; fmr Chair. New Nat. Party (NNP). *Address:* c/o Ministry of Foreign Affairs and International Business, Ministerial Complex, 4th Floor, Botanical Gardens, Tanteen, St George's, Grenada (office).

NIN NOVOA, Rodolfo; Uruguayan politician; *Minister of Foreign Affairs;* b. 25 Jan. 1948, Montevideo; m. Patricia Damiani; three s. one d.; active in Agricultural Soc. of Cerro Largo and Fed. of Rural Uruguay during 1970s; elected Nat. Party rep. for Cerro Largo 1982; Mayor of Cerro Largo 1985–95; left Nat. Party 1994; Co-founder Encuentro Progresista party 1994, Vice-Pres. Encuentro Progresista–Frente Amplio 1995; Founder Alianza Progresista 738 political alliance 1999, currently Leader; Senator 2000–05, 2010–, Pres., Chamber of Senators 2005–10, mem. various senate cttees including Budget Cttee (Vice-Chair. 2002) 2000–04, Livestock, Agric. and Fisheries (Vice-Chair. 2002) 2000–04, Admin. Affairs (Vice-Chair. 2002) 2000–04; Vice-Pres. of Uruguay 2005–10; Minister of Foreign Affairs 2015–. *Address:* Ministry of Foreign Affairs, Avda 18 de Julio 1205, 11100 Montevideo (office); Alianza Progresista 738, Col. 1831, Montevideo, Uruguay (office). *Telephone:* (2) 9022132 (ministry) (office); (2) 4016365 (Alianza Progresista) (office). *Fax:* (2) 9021349 (ministry) (office). *E-mail:* webmaster@mrree.gub.uy (ministry) (office); a738@alianza738.org.uy (office). *Website:* www.mrree.gub.uy (ministry) (office); www.alianza738.org.uy (office).

NING, Frank Gaoning, BA, MBA; Chinese business executive; *Chairman, Sinochem Group;* b. 1958, Shandong Prov.; m.; one d.; ed Shandong Univ., Univ. of Pittsburgh, USA; previous positions include Gen. Man. China Resources Enterprise Ltd 1990–99, Chair. 1999–2004; fmr Chair. China Resources Land Ltd, fmr Vice-Chair. and Pres. China Resources (Holdings) Ltd, China Resources Nat. Corpn; Chair. China Nat. Cereals, Oils and Foodstuffs Corpn (COFCO) 2005–15; Chair. Sinochem Group 2015–; Chair. Hong Kong Building and Loan Agency Ltd; Deputy Chair. China Vanke Co. Ltd; mem. Bd of Dirs, HIT Investments Ltd, SAB Miller; mem. Asia Business Council; mem. Cen. Comm. for Discipline Inspection of the CCP 2012–; 13th Five-Year Plan Nat. Devt Planning Expert Panel; Co-Chair. APEC Business Advisory Council (ABAC); Chair. APEC China Business Council; Exec. Dir ICC; CCTV China Econ. Person of the Year three times, named Asian Corp. Dir by Corporate Governance Asia, named Asia Business Leader of the Year by CNBC Asia Pacific 2009. *Address:* Sinochem Group, 11/F Central Tower, Chemsunny World Trade Centre, 28 Fuxingmennei Street, 100031 Beijing, People's Republic of China (office). *Telephone:* (10) 59568888 (office). *Fax:* (10) 59568890 (office). *E-mail:* webmaster@sinochem.com (office). *Website:* www.sinochem.com (office).

NINOVA, Korneliya Petrova; Bulgarian jurist and politician; *Chairman, Balgarska Sotsialisticheska Partiya (Bulgarian Socialist Party);* b. 16 Jan. 1969, Krushovitsa, Vratsa Oblast; ed Sofia Univ. (now Sofia St Clement of Ohrid Univ.); worked as a trainee judge at Sofia City Court 1995; consultant jurist at Sofia Municipal Office 1995–96; Examining Magistrate, Sofia Investigation Service 1996–97; Exec. Dir Tekhnoimpeks Co. 1997–2005, also Chair. Technoimporteksport in preparation of privatization of two subsidiary cos; Deputy Minister of the Economy and Energy 2005–07; mem. Balgarska Sotsialisticheska Partiya (BSP—Bulgarian Socialist Party), Chair. 2016–; mem. (BSP), 41st, 42nd and 43rd Nat. Ass. for 26-Sofia Oblast, Deputy Chair. BSP Parl. Group. *Address:* Balgarska Sotsialisticheska Partiya, 1000 Sofia, ul. Positano 20, Bulgaria (office). *Telephone:* (2) 810-72-00 (office). *Fax:* (2) 981-21-85 (office). *E-mail:* korneliya.ninova@parliament.bg (office); bsp@bsp.bg (office). *Website:* www.bsp.bg (office); www.parliament.bg/en/MP/2384 (office).

NIRENBERG, Louis, PhD; American mathematician and academic; b. 28 Feb. 1925, Hamilton, Ont., Canada; s. of Zuzie Nirenberg and Bina Katz; m. Susan Blank 1948 (deceased); one s. one d.; ed McGill and New York Univs; Instructor, New York Univ. 1949–51, Asst Prof. 1951–54, Assoc. Prof. 1954–57, Prof. 1957, now Prof. Emer.; Dir Courant Inst. of Math. Sciences 1970–72; mem. NAS, American Acad. of Arts and Sciences, American Philosophical Soc., Accad. dei Lincei, Acad. des sciences, Istituto Lombardo, Accad. di Scienze e Lettere; Hon. Prof., Nankai Univ., Zhejiang Univ.; Hon. mem. European Acad. of Sciences 2004; Hon. DSc (McGill Univ., Univ. of Pisa, Univ. of Paris, Dauphine, McMaster Univ., British Coumbia); Bôcher Memorial Prize 1959, Crafoord Prize, Royal Swedish Acad. of Sciences 1982, Steele Prize, American Math. Soc. 1994, 2014, Nat. Medal of Science 1995, Chern Medal 2010, Abel Prize (co-recipient), Norwegian Acad. of Science and Letters 2015. *Publications:* Functional Analysis 1961, Lectures on linear partial differential equations. In: Conference Board of the Mathematical Sciences of the AMS 1973, Topics in Nonlinear Functional Analysis 1974, Partial differential equations in the first half of the century. In Jean-Paul Pier Development of Mathematics 1900–1950 1994; various papers in mathematical journals. *Leisure interests:* classical music, reading, cinema, walking. *Address:* 251 Mercer Street, New York, NY 10012 (office); 221 West 82nd Street, New York, NY 10024, USA (home). *Telephone:* (212) 998-3192 (office); (212) 724-1069 (home). *Fax:* (212) 995-4121 (office); (212) 724-1069 (home). *E-mail:* nirenberg@cims.nyu.edu (office); nirenl@cims.nyu.edu (office). *Website:* www.math.nyu.edu/faculty/nirenl (office).

NISAR, Mian Saqib, BA, LLB; Pakistani lawyer and judge; *Chief Justice, Supreme Court of Pakistan;* b. 18 Jan. 1954, Lahore; ed Government Coll., Univ. of Punjab; apptd Advocate, Dist Court 1980; Advocate, Lahore High Court 1982–91, Sec.-Gen. Lahore High Court Bar Asscn 1991–92, Justice 1998–2010; Advocate, Supreme Court of Pakistan 1994–98, Justice 2010–16, Chief Justice 2016–; Fellow, Supreme Court Bar Asscn 1992; Law Sec. of Pakistan 1997–99; mem. Del. to Int. Youth Conf., Libya 1973; Rep. Int. Conf. on Pakistan and India at Fifty, UK; Head, Pakistani Del. to Ministerial-level Conf. on Asia Region Transitional Crimes, Philippines, Pakistani Del. on Human Rights, Switzerland; fmr Part-Time Lecturer, Punjab Law Coll., Pakistan Coll. of Law. *Address:* G-5/2 Constitution Avenue, Islamabad, Pakistan (office). *Telephone:* (51) 9220581 (office). *Fax:* (51) 9213452 (office). *E-mail:* mail@supremecourt.gov.pk (office). *Website:* www.supremecourt.gov.pk (office).

NISH, David, BAcc; British business executive; b. 5 May 1960, Barrhead, Glasgow; m. Caroline Nish 1983; two c.; ed Paisley Grammar School, Univ. of Glasgow; fmr Pnr, Price Waterhouse; Finance Dir Scottish Power plc 1999–2005, subsequently Exec. Dir Infrastructure Div.; mem. Bd of Dirs Standard Life plc 2006–15, Group Finance Dir 2006–09, Chief Exec. 2010–15; mem. Bd of Dirs (non-exec.), Thus plc 2001–02, Royal Scottish Nat. Orchestra 2002–08, Northern Foods plc 2005– (Chair. Audit Cttee), Vodafone plc 2015–, London Stock Exchange Group plc 2015– (Chair. Audit Cttee), HSBC Holdings 2016– (mem. Audit Cttee, Remuneration Cttee, Nomination & Corp. Governance Cttee), Zurich Insurance Group Ltd 2016– (mem. Audit Cttee, Risk and Investment Cttee), UK Green Investment Bank plc; mem. Bd and Deputy Chair. Asscn of British Insurers, Chair. Long Term Savings and Life Insurance Cttee; mem. UK Strategy Cttee of TheCityUK, Financial Services Advisory Bd of the Scottish Govt; mem. Govt Employers Pension Task Force 2004–05; mem. Inst. of Chartered Accountants of Scotland; Scottish Business Awards Finance Dir of the Year 2000, 2009. *Leisure interests:* travel, trekking, rugby, cycling.

NISHANI, Bujar Faik, MA; Albanian politician and fmr head of state; b. 29 Sept. 1966, Durrës; m. Odeta Nishani; two c.; ed Ushtarake Skënderbej Mil. Acad., Univ. of Tirana, Univ. of Texas at San Antonio, USA; Lecturer, Ushtarake Skënderbej Mil. Acad. 1988–93; with Foreign Relations Dept, Ministry of Defence 1993–94; with NATO Relations Dept, Ministry of Foreign Affairs 1994–96; mem. Cabinet of Ministry of Defence 1996–97; Freelance Chair. European-Atlantic Mil. Forum 1997–99; mem. Partia Demokratike e Shqipërisë (PDSh—Democratic Party of Albania) 2001–12, Gen. Sec., Tirana br. 2001–03, mem. Nat. Council 2004–, mem. Chairmanship 2005–, Sec. Nat. Council Comm. 2005–; mem. Municipal Council of Tirana 2003–; mem. Parl. for Constituency 34 in Tirana 2005–12 (re-elected 2009), mem. DPA Parl. Group 2005–12; Minister of the Interior 2007–09, 2011–12, of Justice 2009–11; Pres. of Albania 2012–17; mem. Bd Goethe Inst. 1997; Hon. Citizen of Libohova 2013, of Shkodër 2016; Kt Grand Cross, Order of Merit of the Italian Repub. 2014; Order of Stara Planina, First Class 2016; Cross of Merit, Order pro Merito Melitens 2016; Raoul Wallenberg Award (USA) 2015.

NISHANK, Ramesh Pokhriyal, MA, PhD; Indian writer and politician; b. 15 Aug. 1958, Pinani, Uttar Pradesh; s. of Parmanand Pokhriyal and Vishwambhari Devi Pokhriyal; m. Kusum Kanta Pokhriyal 1985 (died 2012); three d.; entered politics in 1991; mem. Vidhan Sabha (state ass.) of Uttar Pradesh 1991–92, 1993–2000, 2000–02, 2007–14; Minister of Devt of Uttaranchal 1997–98; Minister for Culture and Religion 1998–2000, of 12 Dept including Finance, Revenue, Planning etc. 2000–02; State Minister of Health, Family Welfare, Science and Tech., Biotechnology and Language 2007–09; Chief Minister of Uttarakhand 2009–11 (also Leader of House, Uttarakhand Legislative ass.); MP, 16th Lok Sabha, Haridwar Parliamentary Constituency 2014–, mem. Public Accounts Cttee 2014–16, Standing Cttee on Rural Devt 2014–, Consultative Cttee, Ministry of Health and Family Welfare 2014–, Gen. Purposes Cttee 2015–, Chair. Cttee on Govt Assurances 2014–; mem. Bharatiya Janata Party; Chief Ed. Seemant Varta; Hon. DSc (Int. Open Univ., Sri Lanka) 2007; Hon. DLitt (Int. Open Univ., Sri Lanka) 2009; numerous honours and awards, honoured for his literary work by Univ. of Hamburg, Germany 2008. *Publications include:* has written more than 20 books including several collections of poems including Samarpan 1983, Navaankur 1984, Mujhe vidhata banana hai 1985, Roshni ki ek kiran 1986, Tum bhi mere saath chalo 1986, Desh hum na jalne denge 1988, Bus ek hi ichha 1989, Jeevan path mein 1989, Matrabhoomi ke liye 1992, Kya nahi ho sakta 1993, Koi mushkil nahin 2005, Ae Vatan Tere Liye 2006, Khade hue prashn (Sahitya Bharti Samman Award) 2007, Ek aur Kahani 2007, Nishant 2008, Sangharsh Jaari Hai 2009, Apna Paraya 2010. *Address:* Lok Sabha, Parliament House Annexe, New Delhi 110 001 (office); 37/1, Vijay Colony, Rabindranath Tagore Marg, Dehradun 248001, India (home). *Telephone:* (11) 23017465 (office); (135) 2740104 (home). *Fax:* (11) 23792107 (office). *E-mail:* nishankramesh@gmail.com (office). *Website:* www.rameshpokhriyalnishank.com (office).

NISHI, Yoshio, BSc, PhD; Japanese electrical engineer, materials scientist and academic; *Professor, Electrical Engineering (Research) and Professor, Materials Science and Engineering (Courtesy), Stanford University;* ed Waseda Univ., Univ. of Tokyo; Researcher, R&D Dept, Toshiba Corpn –1986; Dir Silicon Process Lab., Hewlett-Packard, USA 1986, then est. ULSI Research Lab.; Sr Vice-Pres. and Dir R&D for the semiconductor group, Texas Instruments, Inc., USA 1995, est. Kilby Center; Prof., Dept of Electrical Eng (Research) and Prof., Dept of Material Science and Eng (Courtesy), Stanford Univ., USA 2002–, Dir Stanford Nanofabrication Facility of Nat. Nanotechnology Infrastructure Network of the US; Dir of Research, Center for Integrated Systems; Affiliated mem. Science Council of Japan; mem. Japan Soc. of Applied Physics, Electrochemical Soc.; Life Fellow, IEEE 1987; Fellow International, Japan Soc. of Applied Physics 2012; IEEE Jack Morton Award 1995, IEEE Robert Noyce Medal 2002, Lifetme Achievement Award, SEMI 2008, Charles Stark Draper Prize, Nat. Acad. of Eng (co-recipient) 2014. *Publications:* coauthor/editor of nine books; more than 200 papers in professional journals on semiconductor device physics and silicon interfaces; more than 70 patents in USA and Japan. *Address:* Paul G. Allen 103, 420 Via Palou, Stanford University, Stanford, CA 94305-4070, USA (office). *Telephone:* (650) 723-9508 (office). *Fax:* (650) 725-0991 (office). *E-mail:* nishiy@stanford.edu (office). *Website:* profiles.stanford.edu/yoshio-nishi (office); nanodevice.stanford.edu/people.html (office).

NISHIDA, Atsutoshi, MA; Japanese electronics industry executive; b. 29 Dec. 1943; ed Waseda Univ., Tokyo Univ.; joined Toshiba Corpn 1975, Sr Vice-Pres. Toshiba Europe 1984, Pres. Toshiba America Information Systems Inc. 1992, Gen. Man. Personal Computer Div. 1995, Vice-Pres., Deputy Group Exec. Information Equipment Group 1997, Vice-Chair. Toshiba America Inc., Pres. Toshiba America Information Systems Inc. 1997–99, Corp. Vice-Pres., Exec. Vice-Pres. Digital Media Equipment & Services Co. 1998–2000, Gen. Man. Corp. Devt Centre, Electronic Commerce Strategy Planning Div. 2000–01, Corp. Sr Vice-Pres. 2000–03, Pres. and CEO Digital Media Network Co. 2001–03, CEO Digital Products Group 2003, Pres. and CEO Personal Computer and Network Co., Dir, Corp. Exec. Vice-Pres. 2003–05, Pres. and CEO Toshiba Corpn 2005–09, Chair. 2009–14; Akira Inoue Award for EHS Excellence. *Address:* c/o Toshiba Corpn, 1-1, Shibaura 1-chome, Minato-ku, Tokyo, 105-8001, Japan. *E-mail:* info@toshiba.co.jp.

NISHIDA, Tsuneo; Japanese diplomatist and academic; *Professor and Director, Institute for Peace Science, Hiroshima University;* m. Keiko Nishida; ed Higher Diplomatic Service Examination, Ministry of Foreign Affairs, Univ. of Tokyo, Faculty of Law; joined Ministry of Foreign Affairs 1970, First Sec., Embassy in Moscow 1981–86, Dir Eastern Europe Div., European and Oceanic Affairs Bureau 1986–87, Dir Legal Affairs Div., Treaties Bureau 1987–89, Counsellor, Embassy in Washington, DC 1989–92, Dir Press Div. 1992–93, Dir Russian Div., European and Oceanic Affairs Bureau 1993–94, Deputy Dir-Gen. European and Oceanic Affairs Bureau 1994–96, Deputy Dir-Gen. Econ. Co-operation Bureau 1996–98, Councillor, Cabinet Secr. April–July 1998, Asst Vice-Minister July 1998–99, Consul-Gen. in Los Angeles 1999–2001, Dir-Gen. Econ. Co-operation Bureau 2001–02, Deputy Vice-Minister for Foreign Policy/Dir-Gen. Foreign Policy Bureau 2002–05, Deputy Minister for Foreign Affairs 2005–07, Amb. to Canada 2007–10, Amb. and Perm. Rep. to UN, New York 2010–13; currently Prof. by special appointment and Dir, Inst. for Peace Science, Hiroshima Univ.; mem. Bd of Dirs EastWest Inst.; mem. Council, United Nations Univ.; Hon. Advisor, Terasaki Center for Japanese Studies, UCLA. *Address:* Institute for Peace Science, Hiroshima University, Higashisenda-machi 1-1-89, Naka-ku, Hiroshima 730-0053, Japan (office). *Telephone:* (8) 2542-6975 (office). *Fax:* (8) 2542-0585 (office). *E-mail:* heiwa@hiroshima-u.ac.jp (office). *Website:* home.hiroshima-u.ac.jp/heiwa (office).

NISHIHARA, Haruo, LLD; Japanese professor of law and academic administrator; b. 13 March 1928, Tokyo; s. of Keiichi Nishihara and Makoto Tateyama Nishihara; m.; one s.; ed Waseda Univ.; Asst, School of Law, Waseda Univ. 1953–59, Asst Prof. 1959–63, Assoc. Prof. 1963–67, Prof. from 1967, Dean School of Law and mem. Bd of Trustees 1972–76, Exec. Dir 1978–80, Vice-Pres. 1980–82, Pres. and mem. Bd of Trustees 1982–95; fmr Pres. Kokushikan Univ.; Hon. LLD (Korea Univ.) 1985, (Earlham Coll.) 1988; Hon. DUniv (Sydney) 1989; Educational Man. Prize, De La Salle Univ. 1988. *Publications:* Das Abge Nderte Japanische Strafgesetzbuch Vom 10. August 1953 (trans.) 1954, On the Theory of 'mittelbare Täterschaft' 1962, Traffic Accidents and the Principle of Trust 1962, Particular Aspects of Criminal Law 1974, 1983, General Aspects of Criminal Law 1977, What Governs the Criminal Law? 1979, Kyu Keiho: Meiji 13-nen (Nihon rippo shiryo zenshu) 1994, Die Idee des Lebens im japanischen Strafrechtsdenken: Vortrag und Ansprachen anlässlich der Verleihung der Ehrendoktorwürde durch die Juristische . . . 2. Juli 1996 1997, Hanzai jikko koiron 1998. *Leisure interests:* swimming, skiing. *Address:* c/o Kokushikan University, 4-28-1 Setagaya, Setagaya-ku, Tokyo 154-8515 (office); 619-18 Nohgaya-cho, Machida-shi, Tokyo, Japan. *E-mail:* info@kokushikan.ac.jp.

NISHIKAWA, Yoshifumi; Japanese financial executive; b. 1939; ed Osaka Univ.; Pres. Sumitomo Bank 1997–2001, Pres. and CEO Sumitomo Mitsui Financial Group (Sumitomo Mitsui Banking Corpn) 2001–05, Hon. Advisor 2005–; Chair. Nat. Banking Asscn 2003–05; Pres. and CEO Japan Post Holdings Co. Ltd 2007–10, Dir Japan Post Network Co. Ltd, Japan Post Service Co. Ltd and Japan Post Bank Co. Ltd; Special Advisor, Ichiryu Assocs Inc. 2010; Dir, Panasonic Corpn (fmrly Matsushita Electric Industrial Co. Ltd 2005–07, Nippon Venture Capital Co. Ltd, Daiichi Pharmaceutical Co. Ltd; Outside Dir, Internet Initiative Japan Inc. 2005–07, Daiichi Sankyo Co. Ltd 2005. *Leisure interest:* supporting Hanshin Tigers baseball team. *Address:* c/o Ichiryu Associates Inc., Iidabasi Masumoto Bldg, 3F, 1-21, Ageba-cho, Sinjyuku-ku, Tokyo, Japan (office).

NISHIMATSU, Chikara; Japanese business executive; b. 3 Nov. 1931, Osaka; m. Michiko Yamada 1959; two s. one d.; ed Pratt Inst.; joined Itochu Co., Ltd 1959, mem. Bd Dirs 1984–91, Gen. Man. Itochu Asian Operations 1985, Man. Dir 1986, Gen. Man. Itochu Europe and Africa Operation 1989–91; Pres. and CEO Matsubo Co. Ltd (fmrly. known as Matsuzaka Co. Ltd) 1992–98, Chair. and CEO 1998–2000, Adviser 2000–02; CEO The Mirai Creative Co. Inc.

NISHIMATSU, Haruka; Japanese airline industry executive; b. 5 Jan. 1948, Hamamatsu, Shizuoka Pref.; m.; one s. one d.; ed Tokyo Univ.; joined Japan Airlines 1972, assigned to Flight Crew Training Dept in charge of preparing schedules for pilot trainees; moved to Finance Dept 1974 and held several positions in finance and investor relations –1980, Traffic Div., Admin in charge of budgets for airport offices 1980–83, worked in Corp. Planning 1983–87, Admin Man., Frankfurt, Germany 1987–91, returned to Finance Dept 1991, Dir 1999–2001, Exec. Officer, Finance and Investor Relations 2003–05, Sr Vice-Pres., Finance and Investor Relations 2005–06, Sr Man. Dir, Finance and Investor Relations 2006, Pres. and CEO 2006–10. *Leisure interests:* golf, reading.

NISHIMI, Toru; Japanese retail industry executive; joined Marubeni Corpn 1972, Corp. Vice-Pres., later Corp. Sr Vice-Pres., Marubeni Corpn –2006, served as CEO and Pres. Marubeni Canada Ltd and as COO and Exec. Vice-Pres. Marubeni America Corpn, COO Finance and Logistics Business Div., mem. Bd of Dirs Marubeni-Itochu Steel Inc. 2006–10; Vice-Pres. The Daiei Inc. retail group Sept.–Oct. 2006, Pres. Oct. 2006–10; Pres. and Rep. Dir, Katakura Chikkarin Co. Ltd 2010–14. *Address:* Katakura Chikkarin Co. Ltd, 1-13-5 Kudanshita-Kita, Chiyoda-ku, Tokyo 102-0073, Japan (office). *Telephone:* (3) 5216-6611 (office). *Fax:* (3) 5216-6621 (office). *Website:* www.chikkarin.co.jp (office).

NISHIMURA, Hidetoshi; Japanese business executive; Sr Man. Exec. Officer Nissho Iwai Corpn –2002, Pres. 2002, Pres. and CEO 2002–03, Pres. and Co-CEO Nisho Iwai-Nichimen Holdings Corpn (est. as holding corpn of Nichimen Corpn and Nissho Iwai Corpn 2003) 2003–04 (cos merged to form Sojitz Corpn 2004); fmr Gov. Ehime Pref., also Vice-Gov. in charge of Educ. and Foreign Affairs. *Address:* c/o Sojitz Corporation, 1-23 Shiba 4-chome, Minato-ku, Tokyo 108-8408, Japan.

NISHIMURA, Hiroshi; Japanese insurance executive; *Advisor, Mitsui Mutual Life Insurance Company Limited;* joined Mitsui Mutual Life Insurance Co. Ltd 1967, Dir and Gen. Man. Gen. Accounting Div. 1996–99, Sr Dir 1998–2009, Gen. Man. Marketing Dept 1999–2000, Gen. Man. Corp. Planning Dept 2000–01, Pres. and Rep. Dir 2001–09, Adviser 2009–, negotiated jt pension man. venture and marketing collaborations with Sumitomo Life 2001; Dir, Sanki Engineering Co. Ltd 2004–. *Address:* Mitsui Mutual Life Insurance Co. Ltd, 1-2-3 Ohtemachi, Chiyoda-ku, Tokyo 100-8123, Japan (office). *Telephone:* (3) 3211-6111 (office). *Fax:* (3) 3215-1580 (office). *Website:* www.mitsui-seimei.co.jp (office).

NISHIMURA, Kiyohiko G., PhD; Japanese economist, academic and fmr central banker; *Professor, National Graduate Institute for Public Policy;* b. 30 March 1953, Tokyo; s. of Giichi Nishimura and Sumiko Otsuka; m. Yukiko Kurihata 1979; two d.; ed Univ. of Tokyo, Yale Univ., USA; Arthur Okun Research Fellow, Brookings Inst., USA 1981–82; Assoc. Prof. of Econs, Univ. of Tokyo 1983–94, Prof. 1994–2005, 2013–17, Dean, Grad. School of Econs and Chair. Faculty of Econs 2013–15, Prof. Emer. and Distinguished Project Research Fellow 2017–; Assoc. Ed. Economic Studies Quarterly 1989–93; Research Assoc. US-Japan Center, New York Univ. 1989–2008; Dir Tokyo Centre for Econ. Research 1990–91; Prof. Nat. Graduate Inst. for Public Policy 2016–; Visiting Scholar, MIT, USA 1991–92; Visiting Research Fellow, Inst. for Int. Econ. Studies, Sweden 1993; Visiting Prof., Louis Pasteur Univ. 1994, Århus Univ., Denmark 1996, Univ. of Copenhagen, Denmark 1998; Special mem. Econ. Council, Japanese Govt 1994–98; mem. Regulatory Reform Cttee, Japanese Govt 1999–2001, Council Japanese Econ. Asscn 1999–2005, Statistic Council, Japanese Govt 2003–05, Financial System Council, Japanese Govt 2003–05; mem. Policy Bd Bank of Japan 2005–08, Deputy Gov. 2008–13; Chair. Statistics Comm., Japanese Govt 2014–; Co-Ed. Journal of Industry, Competition and Trade 2000–; Sr Advisor, Asian Econ. Panel 2001–; Exec. Research Fellow, Cabinet Office, Japanese Govt 2003–05; Fellow, East Asian Econ. Asscn 2005; mem. Int. Academic Advisory Council, Jeffrey Cheah Inst. on Southeast Asia 2014–; mem. Bd of Dirs Cookpad Inc. 2014–17, Minnano Wedding Co. 2017–; Emperor's Medal of Honour with Purple Ribbon 2015; Nikkei Prize 1993, Japan Economist's Prize 1997, Nakahara Prize, Japanese Econ. Asscn 1998, Prize of the Japan Asscn for Real Estate Sciences 2005, Telecom Social Science Award, 2006. *Publications:* Stock and Land Prices in Japan 1990, The Distribution System in Japan (co-ed.) 1991, Imperfect Competition, Differential Information and Microfoundations of Macroeconomics 1992, Macroeconomics of Price Revolution 1996, The Grief of a Prairie Dog (socioeconomic essays) 1998, The Distribution in Japan 2002, The Japanese Economy: Inconspicuous Structural Transformation 2004, Advancement of Information and Communication Technology and Its Impacts on the Japanese Economy 2004, Socially-Oriented Investment Trusts – Beyond Private Finance Initiative 2004, Information Technology Innovation and the Japanese Economy 2010, Economics of Pessimism and Optimism 2017. *Leisure interest:* photography. *Address:* 7-22-1, Roppongi, Tokyo 106-8677 (office). *Telephone:* (3) 6439-6000 (office). *Fax:* (3) 6439-6010 (office). *Website:* www.grips.ac.jp/list/en/facultyinfo/nishimura-kiyohiko/ (office).

NISHIO, Shinji; Japanese petroleum industry executive; *Executive Consultant, JX Holdings, Inc.;* joined Nippon Oil Co. 1964, positions include Dir of Accounting, Chief Dir of First Man. Admin, Chief Dir of Second Man. Admin, Man. Dir and Vice-Pres., Exec. Vice-Pres. and Chief Financial Officer, Nippon Oil Corpn –2005, Pres. 2005–12, also Rep. Dir, Chair. and Rep. Dir, JX Holdings, Inc. (following incorporation of Nippon Oil Corpn and Nippon Mining Holdings in JX Holdings, Inc. through a share transfer) 2010–12, Exec. Consultant 2012–. *Address:* JX Holdings, Inc., 2-6-3, Ote-machi, Chiyoda-ku, Tokyo 100-0004, Japan (office). *Telephone:* (3) 3502-1131 (office). *Fax:* (3) 3502-9352 (office). *E-mail:* info@hd.jx-group.co.jp (office). *Website:* www.hd.jx-group.co.jp (office).

NISHIOKA, Takashi; Japanese manufacturing executive; b. 5 March 1936; joined Mitsubishi Heavy Industries Ltd 1959, mem. Bd 1992–, Man.-Dir 1995–98, Exec. Vice-Pres. 1998–99, Pres. 1999–2003, Chair. 2003–08, Sr Adviser 2008–, also mem. Bd Mitsubishi Motors Corpn 2003–14, Rep. Dir and Chair. 2006–14, led negotiations with Caterpillar Inc. to est. jt venture Shin Caterpillar Mitsubishi Ltd 2003, Chair. Mitsubishi Aircraft Corpn –2010; mem. Bd of Dirs Japan Post Holdings Co. Ltd 2006–13, Chair. 2009–13; Dir, Seiryo Electric Corpn. *Address:* c/o Mitsubishi Motors Corpn, 2-16-4 Konan, Minato-ku, Tokyo 108-8410, Japan. *E-mail:* info@mitsubishi-motors.co.jp.

NISHIZAWA, Jun-ichi, BS, DEng, FIEE; Japanese electrical engineer, academic and university administrator; *Professor (Special Appointment), Sophia University;* b. 12 Sept. 1926, Sendai; s. of Kyosuke Nishizawa and Akiko (née Ishii) Nishizawa; m. Takeko Hayakawa 1956; one s. two d.; ed Tohoku Univ.; Research Asst, Electrical Communication Research Inst., Tohoku Univ. 1953–54, Asst Prof. 1954–62, Prof. 1962–90, Dir 1983–86, 1989–90, Pres. of Univ. 1990–96; Dir Semiconductor Research Inst., Sendai 1968–2004; Pres. Iwate Prefectural Univ. 1998–2005; Chair. Japan Atomic Industrial Forum 2000–06, Eng Acad. of Japan; Pres. Tokyo Metropolitan Univ. 2005–09; Prof. (Special Appointment), Sophia Univ., Tokyo 2009–; mem. Japan Acad.; Foreign mem. Polish Acad. of Sciences, Russian Acad. of Sciences, Korea Acad. of Science and Tech., Serbian Acad. of Eng, Nat. Acad. of Eng; Life mem. IEEE; Hon. Citizen of Sendai City 1984, First Hon. Citizen of Miyagi Pref. 1990; Person of Cultural Merits (Bunka-Korosha), conferred by Japanese Govt 1983, Order of Cultural Merits from the Emperor 1989; Dr hc (Humboldt Univ., Berlin) 1989; Dirs Award of Japanese Science and Tech. Agency 1965, 1970, Invention Prize by the Emperor 1966, Matsunaga Memorial Award 1969, Okochi Memorial Tech. Prize 1971, Japan Acad. Prize 1974, Science and Tech. Merits Award 1975, Purple Ribbon Medal conferred by Japanese Govt 1975, Achievement Award from Inst. of Electronics and Communication Engineers of Japan 1975, Dir Award of Patent Agency 1980, Okochi Memorial Tech. Prize 1980, IEEE Jack A. Morton Award 1984, Honda Prize 1986, Laudise Prize of Int. Org. of Crystal Growth 1989, Power Conversion and Intelligent Motion (PCIM) Award 1989, Kenneth J. Button Prize 1993, Harushige Inoue Award 1993, The Okawa Prize 1996, IEEE Edison Medal 2000. *Publications:* Semiconductor Devices 1961, Semiconductor Materials 1968, Optoelectronics 1977; approx. 615 patents in Japan, 345 patents abroad. *Leisure interests:* classical music, reading, pottery, pictures (especially Impressionist school). *Address:* Sophia University, 7-1 Kioi-cho, Chiyoda-ku, Tokyo 102-8554, Japan (office). *Telephone:* (3) 3238-3024 (office). *Fax:* (3) 3238-3137 (office). *Website:* www.sophia.ac.jp (office).

NISHIZAWA, Ryue; Japanese architect; b. 1966, Tokyo; has worked with Kazuyo Sejima at their architects' office SANAA in Tokyo since 1995; their architecture has been described as "translucent minimalism", in which glass walls and thin, white textiles divide interior from exterior; Rolf Schock Prize in the Visual Arts, Royal Swedish Acad. of Sciences (co-recipient) 2005, Pritzker Prize (co-recipient) 2010. *Works include:* Gifu Kitagata Apartment Bldg, Motosu 1994–98, N-Museum, Nakahechi 1995–97, O-Museum, Iida 1995–99, K Bldg, Hitachi 1996–97, M-House, Tokyo 1996–97, Park Café, Koga 1996–98, Multi-Media Workshop, Oogaki 1996–97, Weekend House, Usui-gun 1997–98, New Campus Center for Illinois Inst. of Tech., Chicago 1997–98, Museum für Zeitgenössische Kunst, Sydney 1997–2001, Day Care Centre for the Elderly, Yokohama 1997–2000, S-House, Okayama 1997, Centre for the Contemporary Arts, Rome 1998–99, Stadstheater, Almere 1998, Renovation of the Antique Quarter, Salerno 1998, pvt. residence, Kamakura 1999–2001, Contemporary Art Museum, Kanazawa 1999, Wochenendhaus, Japan 2000, Christian Dior Shop, Tokyo-Minato-ku 2004, Museum of Contemporary Art, Kanazawa 2004, new bldg for The New Museum, New York 2006, Towada Art Center, Japan 2008, Teshima Art Museum, Japan 2010, Garden and House, Japan 2013. *Address:* Sanaa Ltd/Kazuyo Sejima, Ryue Nishizawa & Associates, 7-A Shinagawa-Soko, 2-2-35-6B, Higashi-Shinagawa, Shinagawa-ku, Tokyo 140-0002, Japan (office). *Telephone:* (3) 34500117 (office). *Fax:* (3) 34501757 (office). *E-mail:* sanaa@sanaa.co.jp (office); office@ryuenishizawa.com (office). *Website:* www.sanaa.co.jp (office); www.ryuenishizawa.com (office).

NISKALA, Markku, MPA; Finnish Red Cross official (retd); b. 5 Dec. 1945; m. Anita Niskala; ed Tampere Univ.; worked for Student Health Foundation 1969–70; Dist Sec., Red Cross, Helsinki 1970, various positions in Red Cross Soc. of Finland 1970–78, Rep. of League of Red Cross and Red Crescent Socs, Zambia, Tanzania and Zimbabwe 1978–81, oversaw implementation of S African Programme –1985, Head of Europe Dept, Int. Fed. of Red Cross and Red Crescent Socs (IFRC) Secr., Geneva 1985–87, missions to Tanzania, Zambia, Zimbabwe and Ethiopia, IFRC 1987–88, Sec.-Gen. Finnish Red Cross 1988–2003, Chair. Comm. of the Financing of Int. Cttee of Red Cross 1992–, Acting Sec.-Gen. IFRC July–Nov. 2003, Sec.-Gen. Nov. 2003–08, mem. Standing Comm. 2007–08; Chair. Kepa (devt org.) 2010–11; Golden Order of Merit, Japanese Red Cross Soc. 2008, Cross of Merit, Finnish Red Cross Soc. 2008.

NISSIM, Moshe Binyamin, LLB, MJ; Israeli lawyer and politician; *Head of Law Office, Moshe Nissim, Rinkov, Senderovitch;* b. 10 April 1935, Jerusalem; s. of Isaac Nissim (Chief Rabbi of Israel) and Victoria Nissim; m.; five c.; ed Hebrew Univ. of Jerusalem; mem. Knesset (Parl.) 1959–96, as rep. of Union of Gen. Zionists 1959, subsequently as rep. of Gahal faction of the Liberal Party, then of the Likud Bloc, has served on Defence, Foreign Affairs and Security, Constitution Law and Legislation, Labour and Housing Cttees; Co-Chair. Likud Group 1975–79, Chair. Exec. Cttee 1978–; Minister without Portfolio 1978–80, 1988–89; Minister of Justice 1980–86, of Finance 1986–88, of Trade and Industry 1989–92; Deputy Prime Minister 1990–92; currently Head of Law Office, Moshe Nissim, Rinkov, Senderovitch; mem. Public Comm. on the Status and Authority of Attorney Gen.; Chair. several comms; Dr hc (Ben-Gurion Univ.). *Publications include:* numerous articles in monthly and quarterly journals. *Address:* 12 Aba Hilel Street, Ayalon Tower, Ramat-Gan 5250606 (office); 4 Shalom Aleichem Street, Jerusalem 92148, Israel (home). *Telephone:* 3-6133333 (office); 2-5619414 (home). *Fax:* 3-6133334 (office); 2-5617155 (home). *E-mail:* nrs@nrs-law.com (office). *Website:* www.nrs-law.com (office).

NISSINEN, Mikko; Finnish artistic director, teacher, ballet dancer and choreographer; *Artistic Director, Boston Ballet;* b. 1962, Helsinki; ed Stanford Univ., USA; began dance training at Finnish Nat. Ballet School 1973; began performing as soloist 1977; joined Kirov Ballet School 1979; performer with Dutch Nat. Ballet and Basel Ballet; Prin. Dancer, San Francisco Ballet, USA 1986–96; guest artist at numerous int. galas; Artistic Dir, Marin Ballet, San Rafael, Calif., USA 1996–98, Alberta Ballet, Calgary, Canada 1998–2001; Artistic Dir, Boston Ballet and Boston Ballet Center for Dance Educ. 2001–; mem. Artistic Cttee, New York Choreographic Inst.; mem. Advisory Bd, Albert Schweitzer Fellowship, Armitage Gone!

Dance; First Prize, Nat. Ballet Competition, Kuopio 1978, UN Asscn of Greater Boston Leadership Award 2007, Finlandia Foundation Arts and Letters Award 2008, Amb. for the Arts Award 2009. *Dance:* as choreographer: The Nutcracker, Alberta and Boston Ballets 2003, Swan Lake, Boston Ballet 2004, Raymonde (Act III), Alberta and Boston Ballets. *Address:* Boston Ballet, 19 Clarendon Street, Boston, MA 02116-6100, USA (office). *Telephone:* (617) 695-6950 (office). *Fax:* (617) 695-6995 (office). *Website:* www.bostonballet.org (office).

NIȚA, Constantin, PhD; Romanian economist, academic and politician; b. 27 Nov. 1955; ed Theoretical High School No. 1, Paşcani, Iaşi Co., Faculty of Econ. Studies, Iaşi, Faculty of Law, Iaşi, Faculty of Econ. Sciences, Iaşi; Economist, Export and Distribution Dir, Braşov Truck Plant 1978–83; Economist, ICE Braşov Car 1983–86; Head of BTT Braşov 1986–93; Dir Pîrîul Rece Resort, Braşov 1990–93; Dir-Gen. Valea Prahovei Representation and Protocol Dept 1993–97; Dir SC Nimpex SRL, Braşov 1997–2000; mem. Social Democratic Party (PSD) (Partidul Social Democrat) 1994–, Vice-Pres. Braşov Municipal PDSR Org. 1994–97, Pres. Braşov PSD Co. Org. 1997–, mem. PSD Nat. Council 1997–, mem. PSD Exec. Bureau 1998–2004, mem. PSD Exec. Cttee 2005–06; mem. Chamber of Deputies 2000–, Sec. 2000–03, Vice-Pres. 2003–04, Deputy Leader, PSD Parl. Group 2004–08, Vice-Pres. Special Cttee of Chamber of Deputies and Senate for the Exercise of Parl. Control over the Foreign Intelligence Service 2004–07, mem. Cttee for Defence, Public Order and Nat. Security 2008–; Minister, Ministry of Small and Medium-Sized Enterprises, Trade and Business Environment 2008–09; Minister of the Economy –2014; Lecturer, Transylvania Univ. of Braşov 1998–2001, Assoc. Prof., Faculty of Econ. Sciences 2010–; Reader, Faculty of Econ. Sciences, George Barițiu Univ. of Braşov 2001–05, Prof. 2005–; Pres. Braşov Economists Club Asscn; Ed. Convorbiri economice review; Founding mem. ASCOT (Trade and Tourism Employees' Asscn), Braşov, Transilvania Braşov Regional Foundation, Foundation for Political, Admin. and Civic Educ. (FEPAC), Braşov, 'Pro Braşov' Asscn, Asscn for the Construction of the Nasterea Domnului Cathedral, Braşov; Kt, Nat. Order 'Faithful Service' 2004. *Publications:* Dictionary of Marketing and Business (co-author) 1999, Marketing Audit (co-author) 1999, Industrial Marketing (co-author) 1999, Romania's Tourism Market (co-author) 2000, Practical Guide for Business Correspondence Drafting Methods (co-author) 2005, Marketing Bases 2004; several book chapters, reviews and articles in professional journals. *Website:* constantinnita.wordpress.com.

NITIWUL, Dominic Aduna Bingab, MBA, LLM; Ghanaian politician; *Minister of Defence;* b. 4 Nov. 1977, Chamba, Northern Region; m.; four c.; ed Univ. of South Wales, Univ. of Westminster; MP for Bimbilla 2002–05, 2009–, Deputy Minority Leader of Parl. 2012–16; mem. Pan-African Parl. 2013–; Minister of Defence 2017–; mem. New Patriotic Party. *Address:* Ministry of Defence, POB CT139, Cantonments, Accra, Ghana (office). *Telephone:* (30) 2776115 (office). *E-mail:* info@mod.gov.gh (office). *Website:* www.mod.gov.gh (office).

NITTVE, Lars; Swedish museum director, art historian, academic and writer; *Executive Director, M+ Museum of Visual Culture, West Kowloon Cultural District Authority;* b. 17 Sept. 1953, Stockholm; m. Shideh Shaygan; one c. from previous m.; fmr Stockholm newspaper critic; fmr journalist for Artforum; Sr Curator Moderna Museet (nat. contemporary art museum) 1986–89, Dir 2001–09, also Deputy Chair. Bd Dirs; Dir Rooseum, Malmö 1990–95, Louisiana Museum of Modern Art, Humlebæk, Denmark 1995–98, Tate Modern, London 1998–2001; Exec. Dir M+ Museum of Visual Culture, West Kowloon Cultural Dist Authority 2011–; Prof., Umeå Univ. 2010–; mem. Royal Swedish Acad. of Fine Art; HM The King's Medal in Gold, 12th Size in the Order of the Serafim's Ribbon 2010; Hon. PhD (Umeå Univ.). *Address:* M+, West Kowloon Cultural District Authority, 29/F, Tower 6, The Gateway, 9 Canton Road, Tsim Sha Tsui, Kowloon, Hong Kong Special Administrative Region, People's Republic of China (office). *Telephone:* 2200-0008 (office). *Fax:* 2895-0016 (office). *E-mail:* lars.nittve@wkcda.hk (office). *Website:* www.wkcda.hk (office).

NIU, Maosheng; Chinese government official (retd); b. Oct. 1939, Beijing; ed Beijing Agricultural Inst.; joined CCP 1961; sent to the countryside 1963–65; Sec., later Deputy Dir Office, Bureau for Water Resources and Meteorology, Beijing 1965–73 (mem. CCP Party Cttee), Dir Water Conservancy Man. Div.; Deputy Dir Water Conservancy Bureau, Beijing 1973–82 (Deputy Sec. CCP Party Cttee); Sec. CCP Miyun Co. Cttee, Beijing 1982–85; Vice-Chair. and Gen. Man. China Water Resources Devt Corpn 1980s; First Deputy Dir, later Dir Yellow River Man. Cttee, Ministry of Water Resources 1980s; mem. CCP Beijing Municipal Cttee 1982–85; Sec.-Gen. State Flood Control and Drought Relief HQ 1985–88, Deputy Head 1993–98; Vice-Minister of Water Resources 1988–93, Minister 1993–98; Head, Leading Group, Construction Comm. for Diverting Water from the South to the North Project 1998; Vice-Gov. Hebei Prov. 1998, Acting Gov. 1998–99, Gov. 1999–2002; mem., 15th CCP Cen. Cttee 1997–2002, 16th CCP Cen. Cttee 2002–07; mem. Standing Cttee 10th CPPCC Nat. Cttee 2003–08, Chair. CPPCC Sub-cttee of Ethnic and Religious Affairs 2003–08. *Leisure interests:* painting, calligraphy.

NIU, Qun; Chinese actor (retd) and government official (retd); b. Dec. 1949, Tianjin; m. Liu Su 1982 (divorced 2007); one s.; joined PLA 1971; actor, Zhanyou Art Troupe of PLA Beijing Mil. Command 1974–93, China Broadcasting Art Troupe 1993; performed comic dialogues with Feng Gong; Vice-Mayor Mengcheng Co., Anhui Prov. 2001; mem. National United Asscn of China; numerous prizes. *Publications:* In Various Ingenious Names (five cassettes of comic dialogues).

NIU, Ximing, MA; Chinese economist and banking executive; *Chairman, Bank of Communications;* b. Aug. 1956; ed Harbin Inst. of Tech.; worked at Qinghai Br. of The People's Bank of China 1983–86, served as an official and Deputy Div. Chief of Industrial and Commercial Credit Div.; served successively from 1986 to 2009 as Vice-Pres. then Pres. of Xining Br. of Industrial and Commercial Bank of China Ltd, Qinghai Prov., a temporary transferred official, Div. Chief of Div. 1, a Deputy Dir, a Dir and Gen. Man. of Industrial and Communication Credit Dept, Industrial and Commercial Bank of China Ltd, Pres. of Beijing Br. of Industrial and Commercial Bank of China Ltd, an Asst to Pres. of Industrial and Commercial Bank of China Ltd (and Pres. Beijing Br. concurrently), Vice-Pres. Industrial and Commercial Bank of China Ltd, an Exec. Dir and Vice-Pres. Industrial and Commercial Bank of China Ltd; Exec. Dir, Vice-Chair. and Pres. Bank of Communications 2009–13, Exec. Dir, Chair. and Pres. May–Oct. 2013, Exec. Dir and Chair. Oct. 2013–. *Address:* Bank of Communications, 188 Yinchengzhong Road, Shanghai 200120, People's Republic of China (office). *Telephone:* (21) 95559 (office). *E-mail:* 95559@bankcomm.com (office). *Website:* www.bankcomm.com (office).

NIWA, Toshiyuki, BA, MALD; Japanese diplomatist and UN official; m.; four c.; ed Waseda Univ., Fletcher School of Law and Diplomacy, USA; worked in pvt. sector; joined UNDP 1971, served in various positions including UN Resident Co-ordinator and UNDP Resident Rep. in Yemen 1980–83, Nepal 1983–88, Thailand and Dir UN Border Relief Operation (UNBRO) for displaced Cambodians along Thai–Cambodian border 1988–90, Asst Sec.-Gen. and Asst Admin. and Dir Bureau for Finance and Admin. 1990–97, Acting Assoc. Admin. 1994; Exec. Co-ordinator for Common Services at UN Secr. 1977, responsible for common services, Asst Sec.-Gen. for Cen. Support Services, Asst Sec.-Gen. 1998–2003, Exec. Dir Capital Master Plan 2003–04; Deputy Exec. Dir UNICEF 2004–07 (retd); Head of Japan Election Observation Mission during legis. elections in Nepal 2008. *Address:* c/o Ministry of Foreign Affairs, Kasumigaseki 2-2-1, Chiyoda-ku, Tokyo 100-8919, Japan.

NIWA, Uichiro; Japanese business executive and diplomatist; b. 29 Jan. 1939, Nagoya; ed Nagoya Univ.; joined Itochu Corpn (gen. trading co. involved in aerospace, electronic, multimedia, chemicals, energy, finance, automobile and textiles industries) 1966, Pres. and CEO 2000–04, Chair. 2004–10; Co-Chair. Japan-hailand Trade and Econ. Cttee, Japan Business Fed.; Chair. Japan Asscn of the UN World Food Programme; apptd Pres. Keidanren Cttee on Agric. Policy 2000; Amb. to People's Repub. of China 2010–12; Chair. Soc. of Global Business 2014–; Visiting Prof. Waseda Univ. *Publications include:* Shin Nippon kaikoku ron (Toward a New Opening of Japan). *Address:* Society of Global Business, Shinjuku Gyoen-mae, Annex Building 2F, 4-34, Yotsuya, Shinjuku-ku, Tokyo 160–0004, Japan. *Telephone:* (3) 5269-4745. *E-mail:* info@s-gb.net.

NIWA, Yuya; Japanese politician; b. 20 April 1944, Niihari; ed Keio Univ.; mem. House of Reps; fmr Parl. Vice-Minister for Health and Welfare; fmr Health and Welfare Minister; fmr Chair. LDP Policy Research Council; Minister for Health and Welfare 1999–2000; mem. Liberal Democratic Party. *Address:* Liberal Democratic Party, 1-11-23, Nagata-cho, Chiyoda-ku, Tokyo 100-8910, Japan (office). *Telephone:* (3) 3581-6211 (office). *Fax:* (3) 5511-8855 (office). *E-mail:* koho@ldp.jimin.or.jp (office). *Website:* www.jimin.jp (office).

NIWANO, Rev. Nichiko; Japanese religious leader; *President, Rissho Kosei-kai;* b. 1938; s. of Nikkyo Niwano; ed Rissho Univ.; entered Rissho Kosei-kai 1968, later Head, Dissemination Dept, later Pres. Rissho Kosei-kai Seminary, Pres. Rissho Kosei-kai 1991–; Pres. Niwano Peace Foundation, World Conf. on Religion and Peace, Asian Conf. on Religion and Peace; Chair. Shinshuren; chaired a plenary session during the Millennium World Peace Summit of Religious and Spiritual Leaders 2000. *Publications:* Modern Meditations: The Inward Path; My Father, My Teacher. *Address:* Rissho Kosei-kai, 2-11-1, Wada Suginami-ku, Tokyo 166-8537, Japan (office). *Telephone:* (3) 3380-5185 (office). *Fax:* (3) 3381-9792 (office). *E-mail:* info@rk-world.org (office). *Website:* www.rk-world.org (office).

NIXON, Gordon M., CM, O.Ont., BComm; Canadian banking executive; b. 1957, Montreal; m.; three c.; ed Queen's Univ., Kingston, Ont.; began investment banking career with Dominion Securities, 1979, with Fixed Income and Govt Finance Divs 1979–86, Head of Operations, Japan 1986–89, Man. Dir Investment Banking, Royal Bank of Canada (following RBC's acquisition of Dominion) 1989–95, Head of Global Investment Banking 1995–98, Head of Banking RBC Financial Group 1998–99, CEO RBC Dominion Securities 1999–2001, apptd mem. Exec. Cttee RBC Financial Group 1999, Pres. and CEO RBC Financial Group 2001–14; Dir RBC and Chair. Group Man. Cttee; Chair. MaRS; Co-Chair. The Toronto Region Immigrant Employment Council; Dir and Past Chair. Canadian Council of Chief Execs; mem. Bd of Dirs The Int. Monetary Conf.; Chair. Queen's Univ. Capital Campaign; Hon. LLD (Queen's Univ., Dalhousie Univ.); Rotary Foundation Paul Harris Fellowship, Queen's Golden Jubilee Medal 2002, Outstanding CEO of the Year Award, Canadian Business Leader Award, included in Barron's list of the World's Best CEOs, Honouree of the Public Policy Forum, CIJA/UJA Words and Deeds Leadership Award, Learning Partnership Champion of Public Educ. Tribute, American Banker Innovator of the Year Award.

NIXON, Jeremiah Wilson (Jay), BA, JD; American lawyer and politician; b. 13 Feb. 1956, De Soto, Mo.; s. of Jeremiah 'Jerry' Nixon and Betty Lea Nixon (née Willson); m. Georganne Wheeler; two s.; ed Univ. of Missouri, Columbia; Partner, Nixon, Nixon Breeze & Roberts (law firm) 1981–86; mem. Mo. State Senate from Dist 22 1986–93; Attorney-Gen. for State of Mo. 1993–2009; Gov. of Missouri 2009–17; helped found Missouri Foundation for Health 2000; Democrat. *Address:* c/o Office of the Governor, Room 218, Capitol Building, PO Box 720, Jefferson City, MO 65102, USA (office).

NIXON, John Forster, PhD, DSc, FRS; British scientist and academic; *Professor Emeritus of Chemistry, University of Sussex;* b. 27 Jan. 1937, Whitehaven, Cumbria, England; s. of Edward Forster Nixon, MBE and Mary Nixon (née Lytton); m. 'Kim' Smith 1960; one s. one d.; ed Univs of Manchester and Cambridge; Research Assoc. in Chem., Univ. of Southern California 1960–62; ICI Fellow, Inorganic Chem. Dept, Univ. of Cambridge 1962–64; Lecturer in Inorganic Chem., Univ. of St Andrews 1964–66; Lecturer in Chem., Univ. of Sussex 1966, Reader 1976, Subject Chair. in Chem. 1981–84, Prof. of Chem. 1986–, now Research Prof., Dean School of Chem. and Molecular Sciences 1989–92; Visiting Assoc. Prof. of Chem., Univ. of Victoria, BC 1970–71; Visiting Prof., Simon Fraser Univ., Vancouver BC 1975; Chair. Downland Section, Chemical Soc. 1973–74; mem. Int. Cttee on Phosphorus Chem. 1983–, Inorganic Chem. Panel Science and Eng Research Council Cttee 1986–89, Int. Cttee Inorganic Ring Systems (IRIS) 2002–06, Main Group Element Council 2002–06; elected Titular mem. IUPAC Comm., Inorganic Nomenclature 1985; Royal Soc.-Leverhulme Sr Research Fellow 1993; Visiting Prof., Indian Inst. of Science, Bangalore 2002, 2005–06, IISER Trivandrum 2010; Visiting Fellow, ANU, Canberra 2004; RSC Corday-Morgan Medal and Prize 1973, RSC Main Group Element Prize 1985, RSC Tilden Lectureship 1991–92, RSC Ludwig Mond Lectureship and Prize 2003, Alexander von Humbold Prize Winner 2001–02, 2009–12, Geza Zemplen Medal, Budapest Inst. of Tech. 2003, Alexander Von Humboldt Awardee, Univ. of Regensburg, Germany 2009–14, numerous invited lectures to int. confs and univ. depts. *Publications:* Phosphorus: The Carbon Copy (co-author) 1998 and about 400 publs in chemical journals. *Leisure interests:* walking, theatre, music, watching cricket, playing tennis. *Address:* Chemistry Department, School of Life Sciences, University of Sussex, Brighton, Sussex, BN1 9RQ (office); Juggs Barn, The Street, Kingston, Lewes, Sussex, BN7 3PB, England (home). *Telephone:* (1273) 483993 (home). *Fax:* (1273) 876876 (office). *E-mail:* j.nixon@sussex.ac.uk (office). *Website:* www.sussex.ac.uk/profiles/1954 (office).

NIXON, Patrick Michael, CMG, OBE; British diplomatist (retd); b. 1 Aug. 1944, Reading, Berks.; m. Elizabeth Carlton 1968; four s.; ed Downside School, Magdalene Coll., Cambridge; joined Diplomatic Service 1965, served Middle East Centre for Arab Studies, Lebanon, Cairo, Lima, Tripoli, British Information Services, New York 1980–83; Asst, later Head Near East and N Africa Dept, FCO 1983–87; Amb. to Qatar 1987–90; Counsellor, FCO 1990–93; High Commr in Zambia 1994–97; Dir FCO 1997–98; Amb. to UAE 1998–2003; Regional Co-ordinator, Coalition Provision Authority, Southern Iraq 2004; Gov., All Hallows School 2003–12 (Chair. 2005–12), Downside School 2005–12. *Address:* The Old Vicarage, Maiden Bradley, Warminster, Wilts., BA12 7HN, England (home). *Telephone:* (1985) 844242 (home). *E-mail:* patricknixon82@gmail.com (home).

NIYOYANKANA, Lt-Gen. Germain; Burundian politician; commdr during civil war; Armed Forces Chief of Staff, Nat. Defence Force 2004–05; Minister of Nat. Defence and War Veterans 2005–10; mem. Union pour le progresse nationale (Uprona).

NIYUNGEKO, Vincent; Burundian politician; Chiefs of General Staff 1996–2002; Minister of Defence 2002–05.

NIZAMI, Farhan Ahmad, CBE, BA (Hons), MA, DPhil; Indian/British professor of history; *Director, Oxford Centre for Islamic Studies;* b. 25 Dec. 1956; s. of Khaliq Nizami and Razia Nizami; m. Farah Deba Ahmad 1983; one s. one d.; ed Aligarh Muslim Univ., Wadham Coll., Oxford (Overseas Scholar); mem. Faculties of Modern History and Oriental Studies, Univ. of Oxford, Rothman's Fellow in Muslim History, St Cross Coll., Oxford 1983–85, Fellow 1985–97, Emer. Fellow 1997–, Founding Dir Oxford Centre for Islamic Studies 1985–, Sec., Bd of Trustees 1985–, Prince of Wales Fellow, Magdalen Coll., Oxford 1997–, Gov. Magdalen Coll. School, Oxford 2005–10; Series Ed. Makers of Islamic Civilization 2004–; Founding Ed. Journal of Islamic Studies, Oxford University Press 1990–; mem. Bd of Dirs, Oxford Trust for Islamic Studies 1998–2014; Dir Oxford Inspires 2002–03; Chair. Oxford Endeavours 2003–; mem. Council, Al-Falah Programme, Univ. of California, Berkeley 1997–2004, Advisory Council, Wilton Park 2000–04, Court of Oxford Brookes Univ. 2000–10, Advisory Bd, Dialogues Project, New York Univ. 2003–15, Archbishop of Canterbury's Reference Group for Christian–Muslim Relations 2001–04, Academic Consultative Cttee, Cumberland Lodge 2003–12, Steering Cttee C-100, World Econ. Forum, Davos 2003–07, Int. Advisory Panel, World Islamic Econ. Forum, Malaysia 2004–08, Int. Jury, Sharjah Prize for Arab Culture, UNESCO 2012–17, Int. Advisory Bd, Universiti Tun Abdul Razak 2013–16, Int. Advisory Panel, Universiti Teknologi, Malaysia 2013–, Advisory Council, UN Alliance of Civilizations 2015–; Scholar Consultant to the Christian-Muslim Forum 2005–09; Patron Oxford Amnesty Lectures 2003–; Order of the Crown of Brunei (Class IV) 1992; Univ. Medal for standing First in Order of Merit 1977, 1979, Begam Khursheed Nurul Hasan Gold Medal for Standing First in Order of Merit 1977. *Publication:* Makers of the Islamic Civilization (series ed.) 2004–. *Leisure interests:* reading, cricket. *Address:* Oxford Centre for Islamic Studies, Marston Road, Oxford, OX3 0EE, England (office). *Telephone:* (1865) 278731 (office). *Fax:* (1865) 248942 (office). *E-mail:* farhan.nizami@oxcis.ac.uk (office). *Website:* www.oxcis.ac.uk (office).

NIZIGAMA, Clotilde; Burundian politician and international organization official; fmr Dir-Gen. Office Nat. Pharmaceutique (ONAPHA); Minister of the Economy, Finance and Co-operation and Devt 2007–12; fmr mem. Bd of Govs, African Development Bank, Eastern and Southern African Trade and Development Bank; currently Deputy Sec. Gen., Communauté Economique des Etats de l'Afrique Centrale (CEEAC) (Economic Community of Central African States) 2013–16; mem. Conseil nat. pour la défense de la démocratie—Force pour la défense de la démocratie (CNDD—FDD).

NJIE, Mambury, BA, MSc; Gambian economist, politician and fmr diplomatist; *Minister of Finance and Economic Affairs;* b. 27 June 1962; ed World Bank Econ. Devt Inst., Zimbabwe, East Stroudsburg Univ., Pa, Columbia Univ., Harvard Univ., USA; Jr Economist, Special Studies Unit, Ministry of Finance and Trade 1988–89, Policy Analyst, Office of the Pres. 1989, Economist, Dept of State for Finance and Econ. Affairs 1990–92, later becoming Prin. Economist; Econ. Counsellor, Gambian Embassy in Taiwan and the Philippines 1996, Acting Head of Mission 1997, Amb. to Taiwan and the Philippines 1997–2001; Perm. Sec. in Office of the Pres. 2001–04; Man. Dir of Social Security and Housing Finance 2004; Chair. Gambia Nat. Petroleum Co. 2005–06; Sec.-Gen. and Head of Civil Service of The Gambia 2005–06; Amb. to UAE 2008–10; Minister of Econ. Planning and Industrial Devt 2010–11, of Finance and Econ. Affairs 2011–12, 2018–, of Foreign Affairs, Int. Co-operation and Gambians Abroad April–Aug. 2012; apptd Chair. Governing Council, West African Insurance Inst. 2011; apptd Chair. ECOWAS Bank for Investment and Devt 2011; Managing Dir Gambia Nat. Petroleum Corpn 2017–18; Gov. Islamic Devt Bank, IMF, World Bank, African Devt Bank; mem. Bd of Dirs Nat. Water and Electricity Co. Ltd 2001–04, Jammeh Foundation for Peace 2002–06, Ocean Bay Hotel and Resort 2004–05, CFAO Gambia 2004–05, Gambia Agricultural Marketing Co. 2004–05, Trust Bank Ltd 2004–05, Skye Bank 2008–09 (Chair. Jan.–July 2010); Thomas Jefferson Int. Fellow, USAID 1992–93; arrested on two counts of economic crime and neglect of duty 2014, acquitted July 2014, re-arrested Oct. 2014; Order of Brilliant Star with Grand Cordon (Repub. of China) 2001, Insignia of Officer of Nat. Order of the Repub. of The Gambia 2005. *Leisure interests:* sports, soccer, travelling, community work. *Address:* Ministry of Finance and Economic Affairs, The Quadrangle, POB 9686, Banjul, Gambia (office). *Telephone:* 4227221 (office). *Fax:* 4227954 (office). *E-mail:* info@mof.gov.gm (office). *Website:* www.mof.gov.gm (office).

NJIE-SAIDY, Isatou, MSc; Gambian teacher and politician; b. 5 March 1952, Kuntaya, North Bank Div.; m.; four c.; ed Yundum Teacher's Training Coll., Research Inst. for Man. Science, RVB, The Netherlands, Univ. Coll. of Swansea, Univ. of Wales, UK; schoolteacher 1970–76; Sr Business Advisory and Training Officer, Indigenous Business Advisory Services 1976–83; Deputy Exec. Sec.,

Women's Bureau (arm of Nation's Women's Council) 1983–89; Minister of Health, Social Welfare and Women's Affairs 1996, Vice-Pres. and Minister of Women's Affairs 1997–2017.

NJOROGE, Patrick Ngugi, BA, MA, PhD; Kenyan economist, international organization official and central banker; *Governor, Central Bank of Kenya;* b. 1961, Nairobi; ed Univ. of Nairobi, Yale Univ., USA; Planning Officer, Ministry of Planning 1985–87, Economist, Ministry of Finance 1993–94; Economist, later Sr Economist IMF 1995–2005, Mission Chief for Dominica 2005–06, Deputy Div. Chief, Finance Dept 2006–12, Advisor to Deputy Man. Dir 2012–15; Gov. Central Bank of Kenya 2015–; African Central Bank Gov. of the Year 2016, Central Banker of the Year, The Banker Magazine 2018. *Address:* Central Bank of Kenya, City Square, Haile Selassie Avenue, POB 60000, 00200 Nairobi, Kenya (office). *Telephone:* (20) 22861000 (office). *Fax:* (20) 340192 (office). *E-mail:* comms@centralbank.go.ke (office). *Website:* www.centralbank.go.ke (office).

NJUE, HE Cardinal John, MA; Kenyan ecclesiastic; *Archbishop of Nairobi;* b. 1944, Kiriari Village, Mukangu Sub-Ngandori, Embu Dist; s. of Joseph Nyaga Kibariki and Monica Ngima Nyaga; ed Nguviu Intermediate School, Kyaweru, Nkubu Jr Seminary, Pontifical Urbanian Univ. and Pontifical Lateran Univ., Rome; ordained priest of Embu 1973; served in Kariakomu Parish, Meru South Dist, Meru Diocese 1973–75; apptd Prof. of Philosophy and Dean of Students at St Augustine Sr Seminary, Mabanga, Bungoma 1975, Rector 1978–82; went to USA and undertook spiritual renewal programme course for six months; appointed Father-in-Charge of Chuka Parish (first African priest to be assigned in the parish as Parish Priest after Consolata Missionaries left) 1982; Rector St Joseph's Philosophicum Seminary, Nairobi 1985–86; Bishop of Embu 1986–2002; Coadjutor Archbishop of Nyeri 2002–07; Apostolic Admin. of Vicariate of Isiolo –2006; Archbishop of Nairobi 2007–; currently Apostolic Admin. of Catholic Diocese of Muranga; cr. Cardinal (Cardinal-Priest of Preziosissimo Sangue di Nostro Signore Gesù Cristo) 2007; Chair. Seminary Episcopal Comm. for Major Seminaries in Kenya 1987–91, Kenya Episcopal Conf. 1997–2003, Kenya Episcopal Conf. Justice and Peace Comm., Devt and Social Services Dept of Kenya Catholic Secr.; mem. Congregation for Catholic Educ. 2013. *Address:* Archdiocese of Nairobi, PO Box 14231, Nairobi, Kenya (office). *Telephone:* (2) 441919 (office). *Fax:* (2) 447027 (office).

NKAMBULE, Christian Muzie; Swazi diplomatist; *High Commissioner to UK;* m.; joined Ministry of Foreign Affairs (MFA) 1989, First Sec., Embassy in Brussels 1989–96, Consul-Gen., High Comm. in South Africa 1996–2000, apptd Head Trade Promotion Unit, Ministry of Foreign Affairs (MFA) 2000, Deputy Chief of Mission, Embassy in Washington, DC, USA 2003–07, Counsellor, High Comm. in Kuala Lumpur, Malaysia, later Deputy Head of Mission and Chargé d'affaires, Chief of Protocol, MFA, High Commr to Mozambique 2014, to UK 2017–. *Address:* Swaziland High Commission, 20 Buckingham Street, London SW1E 6LB, England (office). *Telephone:* (20) 7630-6611 (office). *Fax:* (20) 7630-6564 (office). *E-mail:* enquiries@swaziland.org.uk (office). *Website:* www.gov.sz (office).

NKATE, Jacob, LLB; Botswana politician, lawyer and diplomatist; ed Univ. of Botswana, Univ. of Edin., UK; Attorney at Law, Magistrate Grade I, Francistown and Palapye 1986–88; Attorney at Law and pvt. practitioner 1988–95; mem. of Parl. 1994–; Asst Minister of Finance and Devt Planning 1997–99; Minister of Lands, Housing and Environment 1999–2002; Minister of Trade and Industry 2002–05, of Educ. 2005–09; CEO Botswana Export Development and Investment Authority (BEDIA) 2009; pvt. practice as lawyer –2012; Amb. to Japan 2012–17; del. to numerous int. and multilateral confs including Commonwealth and Trade Conf., UK and S Korea, IPU and UNESCO Conf. in Educ. Science, UNEP Governing Council, Malmo; Chair. Parl. Law Reform; mem. Presidential Task Force on Vision 2016; Gov. and Chair. African Devt Bank.

NKOANA-MASHABANE, Maite Emily; South African diplomatist and politician; *Minister of Rural Development and Land Reform;* b. 30 Sept. 1963, Ga-Makanye, Limpopo; m. Norman Mashabane (died 2007); activist during apartheid era in United Democratic Front; apptd South African High Commr to India and Malaysia in 1990s; fmr mem. Limpopo Local Govt and Housing Exec. Council; mem. Nat. Exec. Cttee of African Nat. Congress (ANC) 2007–; Minister of Int. Relations and Co-operation 2009–18, of Rural Devt and Land Reform 2018–. *Address:* Department of Rural Development and Land Reform, Private Bag X833, Pretoria 0001 (office); 184 Jeff Masemola St, Pretoria 0001 (office). *Telephone:* (12) 3128911 (office). *Fax:* (12) 3236072 (office). *Website:* www.drdlr.gov.za (office).

NKOGHE BEKALÉ, Julien; Gabonese politician; *Prime Minister;* b. 23 Aug. 1958, Libreville; mem. Nat. Ass. (parl.) for Komo Mondah constituency; Minister for Oil, Gas and Hydrocarbons 2009, for Transport and Equipment 2011; fmr Minister of Labour and Employment, of SMEs and Handicrafts; Prime Minister 2019–; mem. Gabonese Democratic Party. *Address:* Office of the Prime Minister, Immeuble du 2 décembre, Avenue Jean Paul II, BP 95, Libreville, Gabon (office). *Telephone:* (1) 77-56-24 (office). *Fax:* (1) 77-20-04 (home). *Website:* www.primature.gouv.ga (office).

NKOSI, Mxolisi, MA; South African diplomatist and fmr trade union leader; *Ambassador to Belgium, Luxembourg and the European Union;* b. 26 June 1967, Soweto; ed Univ. of Pretoria; trained as a teacher; student and youth activist in Soweto, holding several leadership positions in Azanian Students' Congress and in South African Students' Congress; fmr Deputy Gen. Sec., South African Democratic Teachers Union (affiliate of Congress of South African Trade Unions); mem. Prov. Exec. Cttee, South African Communist Party; Chief Dir, Dept of Int. Relations and Co-operation 2003–07, Deputy Dir-Gen. Africa Br. –2012, Amb. to Belgium (also accred to Luxembourg and the EU, Brussels) 2012–. *E-mail:* eu.political@saembassy.be (office). *Website:* www.southafrica.be (office).

NKUHLU, Wiseman Lumkile, BCom, MBA; South African accountant, academic and university administrator; *Chancellor, University of Pretoria;* b. 5 Feb. 1944, Cala, Eastern Cape; Nondima Mahlulo; four c.; ed Univs of Fort Hare and Cape Town, New York Univ., USA; qualified as Chartered Accountant (first black African) 1976; moved to Umtata to manage an audit practice and to lecture in Dept of Accounting, Univ. of Transkei, Sr Lecturer, later Prof. and Head of Dept of Accounting 1977–82, Vice-Prin. Univ. of Transkei 1983–87, Prin. and Vice-Chancellor 1987–91; served articles with Hoek Wiehahn & Cross, Pnr in charge of

Umtata office (merged with Price Waterhouse, now PricewaterhouseCoopers 1988), resigned from partnership to join Ind. Devt Trust 1990, Chief Exec. for three years; Econ. Adviser to Nat. African Federated Chamber of Commerce 1989–93; served as Econ. Adviser to Pres. T. M. Mbeki and as Chief Exec. of Secr. of new Partnership for Africa's Devt 2000–05; Chancellor Univ. of Pretoria 2007–; Chair. Devt Bank of Southern Africa 1993–2000; Chair. Pan-African Capital Holdings (Pty) Ltd, MEEG Bank, Eastern Cape 1998–2009, Metropolitan Ltd 2007–09; Chair. KPMG South Africa 2018–; Chair. (non-exec.) Bigen Africa (Pty) Ltd, Kagiso Trust Investments; mem. Bd of Dirs Standard Bank, South African Breweries, Old Mutual, Tongaat Hulett, BMW and JCI 1989–2000, AngloGold Ashanti (Pty) Ltd, Datatec Ltd; first Chair. Council on Higher Educ. 1998–2002; Pres. Black Management Forum 1992–95, South African Inst. of Chartered Accountants 1998–2000, now mem. Advisory Bd, Int. Org. of Employers, Geneva 2008–11; mem. Global Financial Crisis Advisory Panel (est. jtly by Int. Accounting Standards Bd and Financial Accounting Standards Bd) 2009–; Chevalier, Légion d'honneur 2005, Grand Counsellor, Order of the Baobab 2008; Dr hc (Free State, Stellenbosch, Cape Town, Pretoria, Nelson Mandela Metropolitan, Witwatersrand, Fort Hare); several awards, including merit awards from Nat. African Federated Chamber of Commerce, Asscn of Advancement of Black Accountants, Black Man. Forum, Pres. of Convocation Medal, Univ. of Cape Town 2004. *Publications:* various articles on socio-economic devt issues. *Address:* Office of the Chancellor, University of Pretoria, Private Bag X20, Hatfield, Pretoria 0028, South Africa (office). *Telephone:* (12) 4203111 (office). *Fax:* (12) 4204555 (office). *E-mail:* ssc@up.ac.za (office). *Website:* www.up.ac.za (office).

NKUNIKA, Lt-Col (retd) Bizwayo Newton; Zambian army officer (retd), diplomatist and politician; m.; seven c.; ed Kim Il-Sung Military Univ., North Korea; served in Zambian army 1972–93; joined Diplomatic Service 1993, first posting as Deputy High Commr to Nigeria, followed by positions as High Commr to South Africa and Amb. to Egypt; Perm. Sec., Ministry of Works and Supply 2002–10; High Commr to South Africa 2010–11, to UK (also accred as Amb. to Ireland and the Holy See (Vatican City)) 2012–13, to Nigeria 2013–15; cand. (ind.) for mem. Parl. from Lundazi 2016.

NKURUNZIZA, Maj.-Gen. Pierre, BA; Burundian politician and head of state; *President;* b. 18 Dec. 1963, Mwumba, Ngozi Prov.; s. of Eustache Ngabisha; m.; three s.; ed Gitega Secondary School, Univ. of Burundi, Bujumbura; began career as sports teacher, Vugizo and Muramvya Secondary Schools 1991; fmr Asst Lecturer, Faculty of Physical Educ. and Sports, Univ. of Burundi and ISCAM Mil. Acad. of Burundi; coached Army Football Team, Muzinga, and Union Sporting (first div. football team); forced into exile following inter-ethnic clashes 1995; joined Hutu rebellion Conseil Nat. Pour la Défense de la Démocratie–Forces pour la Défense de la Démocratie (CNDD-FDD—Nat. Council for the Defence of Democracy-Forces for the Defence of Democracy) 1995, elected Leader of CNDD-FDD 2001; signed ceasefire accord with Govt Nov. 2003; Minister of State for Good Governance 2004–05; Pres. of Burundi 2005–; Hon. PhD (Latin Univ. of Theology, Calif., Univ.); several int. awards, including Accord Peace Prize, Durban 2006, Interfaith Peacebuilding Peace Prize 2007, Oscar de Paix, Assis Pax International, Model Leader for a New Africa Award, African Forum on Religion and Govt 2009, Rising Star of Africa Award, Unity International Foundation (India) 2010, Peace and Sports International Award 2011. *Address:* Office of the President, Boulevard de l'Indépendance, Bujumbura, BP 1980, Burundi. *Telephone:* 22226063. *E-mail:* pierre.nkurunziza@burundi.gov.bi (office). *Website:* presidence.gov.bi (office).

NNAJI, Genevieve; Nigerian actress, model and singer; b. 3 May 1979, Mbaise, Imo State; ed Methodist Girls' Coll., Yaba, Univ. of Lagos; grew up in Lagos; began career as child actress in TV soap opera Ripples aged eight; debut in Nigerian film industry with film Most Wanted 1998; signed recording contract with EKB Records (Ghana) 2004; launched clothing line, St. Genevieve 2008 (donates proceeds to charity); Member of the Order of the Federal Republic 2011; numerous awards, including Best Actress of the Year, City People Awards 2001, Best Actress in a Leading Role, African Movie Acad. Awards 2005. *Album:* debut album One Logologo Line (mix of R&B, Hip-Hop and Urban music). *Films include:* Most Wanted 1998, Camouflage 1999, Love Boat 2001, Death Warrant 2001, Valentino 2002, Sharon Stone 2002, Runs! 2002, Power of Love 2002, Formidable Force 2002, Battle Line 2002, Above Death: In God We Trust 2003, Blood Sister 2003, Break Up 2003, Butterfly 2003, By His Grace 2003, Church Business 2003, Deadly Mistake 2003, Emergency Wedding 2003, Emotional Tears 2003, For Better for Worse 2003, Honey 2003, Jealous Lovers 2003, Keeping Faith: Is That Love? 2003, Last Weekend 2003, Late Marriage 2003, Love 2003, My Only Love 2003, Not Man Enough 2003, Passion & Pain 2003, Passions 2003, Player: Mr. Lover Man 2003, Private Sin 2003, Sharon Stone in Abuja 2003, Super Love 2003, The Chosen One 2003, Women Affair 2003, Bumper to Bumper 2004, Critical Decision 2004, Dangerous Sister 2004, Goodbye New York 2004, He Lives in Me 2004, Into Temptation 2004, My First Love 2004, Never Die for Love 2004, Promise Me Forever 2004, Stand by Me 2004, Treasure 2004, Unbreakable 2004, We Are One 2004, Darkest Night 2005, Games Women Play 2005, Rip-Off 2005, Girls Cot 2006, 30 Days 2006, Letters to a Stranger 2007, Warrior's Heart 2007, Beautiful Soul 2008, Broken Tears 2008, Critical Condition 2008, River of Tears 2008, My Idol 2008, Silent Scandal 2009, Ijé: The Journey 2010, Tango with Me 2010, Bursting Out 2010, Mirror Boy 2011, Half of a Yellow Sun 2013, Doctor Bello 2013. *Address:* 213 Igbosere Road, 4th Floor, Lagos, Nigeria.

NOAH, Harold Julius, MA, PhD; American (b. British) academic; *Gardner Cowles Professor Emeritus of Economics and Education, Teachers College, Columbia University;* b. 21 Jan. 1925, London; s. of Abraham Noah and Sophia Cohen; m. 1st Norma Mestel 1945 (divorced 1966); m. 2nd Helen Claire Chisnall 1966; two s. two d.; ed Stratford Grammar School, London School of Econs, King's Coll. London, Teachers Coll. Columbia Univ., New York; Asst Master then Head of Econs, Henry Thornton School, London 1949–60; Asst, later Assoc. and Gardner Cowles Prof. of Econs and Educ., Teachers Coll., Columbia Univ., New York 1964–87, now Prof. Emer., also Dean 1976–81; Prof. of Educ., State Univ. of New York, Buffalo 1987–91; has received numerous academic honours and awards. *Publications include:* Educational Financing and Policy Goals for Primary Schools: General Report (with Joel Sherman) 1979, The National Case Study: An Empirical Comparative Study of Twenty-one Educational Systems (with Harry Passow and others) 1976, Canada: Review of National Policies for Education 1976, International Study of Business/Industry Involvement in Education 1987, Secondary School Examinations: International Perspectives on Policies and Practice 1993, Doing Comparative Education: Three Decades of Collaboration (with Max Eckstein) 1998, Fraud in Education: The Worm in the Apple 2001. *Leisure interests:* chess, reading German, French and Russian literature. *Address:* Teachers College, Columbia University, New York, NY 10027, USA (office). *E-mail:* hjnoah@gmail.com (office).

NOAKES, Baroness (Life Peer), cr. 2000, of Goudhurst in the County of Kent; **Sheila Valerie Noakes,** DBE, LLB, FCA; British chartered accountant and company director; b. (Shelia Valerie Masters), 23 June 1949, London, England; d. of Albert Frederick Masters and Iris Sheila Ratcliffe; m. Colin Barry Noakes 1985; ed Univ. of Bristol; joined Peat Marwick Mitchell & Co. 1970; seconded to HM Treasury 1979–81; Partner, KPMG (fmrly Peat Marwick Mitchell & Co., then KPMG Peat Marwick) 1983–2000; seconded to Dept of Health as Dir of Finance, Nat. Health Service Man. Exec. 1988–91; Dir Bank of England 1994–2001, Chair. Cttee of Non-Exec. Dirs 1998–2001; mem. Council, Inst. of Chartered Accountants in England and Wales 1987–2002 (Pres. 1999–2000), Inland Revenue Man. Bd 1992–99, Chancellor of Exchequer's Pvt. Finance Panel 1993–97; Dir (non-exec.), Royal Bank of Scotland Group PLC, Carpetright PLC 2001–, Severn Trent plc 2008–; Dir Social Market Foundation 2002–05; mem. Bd ENO 2000–08; Gov. London Business School 1998–2001, Eastbourne Coll. 2000–06, Marlborough Coll. 2000–02; Trustee, Reuters Founders Share Co. 1998–; Hon. LLD (Bristol) 2000; Hon. DSc (Buckingham) 2001; Hon. DBA (London Guildhall) 1999. *Leisure interests:* opera, early classical music, horse racing, skiing. *Address:* House of Lords, Westminster, London, SW1A 0PW, England (office). *Telephone:* (20) 7219-5353 (office). *Fax:* (20) 7219-5979 (office). *E-mail:* noakess@parliament.uk (office).

NOAM, Eli M., BA, MA, PhD, JD; American economist, lawyer, academic and author; *Garrett Professor of Public Policy and Business Responsibility, Columbia Business School and Director, Institute for Tele-Information, Columbia University;* b. 22 Aug. 1946, Jerusalem, Israel; m. Nadine Strossen 1980; ed Harvard Univ. and Harvard Law School; mil. service in Israel 1966–68, 1973; Visiting Asst Prof., Princeton Univ. 1975–76; Prof. of Econs and Finance, Columbia Business School, Columbia Univ. 1976–, Founder and Dir Inst. for Tele-Information 1983–87, 1991–, Garrett Prof. of Public Policy and Business Responsibility 2012–, Faculty mem. School of Public and Int. Affairs, taught at Columbia Law School; Commr, New York State Public Service Comm. 1987–90; Virtual Visiting Prof., Univ. of St Gallen, Switzerland 1998–2002; mem. numerous panels including NAS Cttee on Future of Broadband Communications, Comm. on the Status of Women in Computing, New York Gov.'s Task Force on New Media and the Internet; mem. numerous bds and advisory bds, including Electronic Privacy Information Center, European Inst. on the Media, France Telecom Scientific Advisory Bd, Intek Corpn, Minority Media Telecommunications Council, Oxford Internet Inst.; mem. Editorial Bd The Communications Review, Information Law Series, New Media, Telecommunications Policy, Telematics, Transborder Data Report, Utility Policy, Communications and Strategies, International Journal of Media Management, Info: The International Journal of Information; columnist for Financial Times online edn; Trustee, Jones Int. Univ. (online coll.); Dr hc (Munich) 2004, (Marseilles) 2008. *Publications:* Telecommunications Regulation: Today and Tomorrow (ed.) 1982, Video Media Competition: Regulation, Economics, and Technology (ed.) 1985, Services in Transition: The Impact of Information Technologies on the Service Sector (co-ed.) 1986, Law of International Telecommunications in the United States (co-ed.) 1988, The Cost of Libel (co-ed.) 1989, Technologies without Boundaries (ed.) 1990, Television in Europe 1991, Telecommunications in Europe 1992, The Telecommunications Revolution (co-ed.) 1992, The International Market for Film and Television (co-ed.) 1992, Asymmetric Deregulation (co-ed.) 1992, Privacy in Telecommunications: Markets, Rights, and Regulations 1994, Telecommunications in the Pacific Basin (co-ed.) 1994, Private Networks and Public Objectives (co-ed.) 1996, Globalism and Localism in Telecommunications (co-ed.) 1997, Telecommunications in Western Asia 1997, Public Television in America 1998, Telecommunications in Latin America 1998, Telecommunications in Africa 1999, The New Investment Theory of Real Options and its Implication for Telecommunications Economics (co-ed.) 1999, Interconnecting the Network of Networks 2001, Internet Television (co-ed.) 2004, Competition for the Mobile Internet (co-ed.) 2004, Telecommunications Meltdown (co-author) 2005, Mobile Media: Content and Services for Wireless Communications (co-ed.) 2006, Media Ownership and Concentration in America 2009, Broadband Networks, Smart Grids and Climate Change (co-author) 2013; Gen. Ed. Business, Government and Society, Columbia Univ. Press Book series; over 400 articles in econ., legal, communications and other journals. *Address:* Columbia Institute for Tele-Information, Graduate School of Business, Uris Hall, Suite 1A, 3022 Broadway, Columbia University, New York, NY 10027 (office); Riverside Drive, Apt 51, New York, NY 10027 (home); 346 Kent Road, New Milford, CT 06776, USA (home). *Telephone:* (212) 854-4222 (office); (212) 864-3776 (NY) (home); (845) 354-6626 (CT) (home). *Fax:* (212) 854-1471 (office); (212) 851-1846 (NY) (home); (860) 354-3026 (CT) (home). *E-mail:* noam@columbia.edu (office). *Website:* www.citi.columbia.edu/elinoam (office).

NOBLE, Adrian Keith, BA; British theatre director; b. 19 July 1950; s. of William John Noble and Violet Ena Noble (née Wells); m. Joanne Pearce 1991; one d. one s.; ed Chichester High School for Boys, Univ. of Bristol, London Drama Centre; Resident Dir then Assoc. Dir Bristol Old Vic 1976–79; Resident Dir RSC 1980–82, Assoc. Dir 1982–90, Artistic Dir 1991–2003; Guest Dir Royal Exchange Theatre, Man. 1980–81; Visiting Prof., London Inst. 2001; Hon. Bencher, Middle Temple; Hon. DLitt (Birmingham) 1994, (Bristol) 1996, (Exeter) 1999, (Warwick) 2001. *Film directed:* A Midsummer Night's Dream 1995. *Stage productions include:* Ubu Rex 1977, A Man's a Man 1977, A View from a Bridge 1978, Titus Adronicus 1978, The Changeling 1978, Love for Love 1979, Timon of Athens 1979, Recruiting Officer 1979, The Duchess of Malfi (Best Dir, Plays and Players) 1980, Dr Faustus 1981, The Forest (Best Revival, Drama Awards) 1981, A Doll's House (Best Dir, Best Revival, Critics' Awards) 1981, King Lear 1982, Antony and Cleopatra 1982, A New Way to Pay Old Debts 1983, The Comedy of Errors 1983, Measure for Measure 1983, Henry V 1984, The Winter's Tale 1984, As You Like It 1985, Mephisto 1986, The Art of Success 1986, Macbeth 1986, Kiss Me Kate 1987, The Plantagenets 1989, The Master Builder 1989, The Fairy Queen (Aix-en-Provence), Three Sisters 1990, Henry IV Parts 1 and 2 1991, The Thebans 1991, Hamlet, The

Winter's Tale 1992, Travesties, King Lear, Macbeth 1993, A Midsummer Night's Dream 1994, Romeo and Juliet 1995, The Cherry Orchard 1995, Little Eyolf 1996, Cymbeline 1997, Twelfth Night 1997, The Tempest 1998, The Lion, the Witch and the Wardrobe 1998, The Seagull, The Family Reunion 2000, The Return of Ulysses (Aix-en-Provence) (Grand Prix des Critiques) 2000, The Secret Garden 2000–01, Chitty Chitty Bang Bang 2002, Pericles 2002, Brand 2003, A Woman of No Importance 2003, The Home Place (Dublin and London) 2005; opera: Don Giovanni (Kent Opera) 1983, The Faery Queen (Aix-en-Provence Festival) (Grand Prix des Critiques) 1989, Falstaff (Gothenburg Opera) 2005, Così fan tutte (Opera de Lyon) 2006, The Marriage of Figaro (Opera de Lyon) 2007, Macbeth (Metropolitan Opera) 2007; others: Alcina (Vienna State Opera) 2010, The Captain of Köpenick (Royal Nat. Theatre, London) 2013, Don Carlo (Bolshoi Theatre, Moscow) 2013, Hänsel and Gretel (Vienna State Opera) 2015. *Address:* c/o Independent Talent Group Limited, 40 Whitfield Street, London, W1T 2RH, England (office). *Telephone:* (20) 7636-6565 (office). *Website:* www.independenttalent.com (office).

NOBLE, Denis, CBE, PhD, FRS; British scientist and academic; *Professor Emeritus of Physiology, University of Oxford;* b. 16 Nov. 1936, London; s. of George Noble and Ethel Rutherford; m. Susan Jennifer Barfield 1965; one s. (adopted) one d.; ed Emanuel School and Univ. Coll. London; Asst Lecturer, Univ. Coll. London 1961–63; Fellow, Lecturer and Tutor in Physiology, Balliol Coll. Oxford 1963–84, Praefectus, Balliol Grad. Centre 1971–89, Burdon Sanderson Prof. of Cardiovascular Physiology and Professorial Fellow, Univ. of Oxford 1984–2004, apptd Dir of Computational Physiology 2004, now Prof. Emer. of Physiology; Visiting Prof., Univ. of Alberta 1969–70; Ed., Progress in Biophysics 1967–; Founder-Dir, Oxsoft Ltd 1984–, Physiome Sciences Inc. 1994–; Chair. Jt Dental Cttee 1984–90; Pres. Medical Section, British Asscn 1992; Gen. Sec. Int. Union of Physiological Sciences 1993–2001, Pres. 2009–17; Hon. Sec. Physiological Soc. 1974–80, Foreign Sec. 1986–92; Fellow, Univ. Coll., London 1986; Adjunct Prof., Xi'an Jiaotong Univ., China 2003–07; Visiting Prof., Osaka Univ., Japan 2006–11; Founder-Fellow, Acad. of Medical Sciences 1998; Founder and performer, Oxford Trobadors; Hon. FRCP; Hon. mem. Acad. de Médecine de Belgique, American Physiological Soc., Academia Europaea 1989, Japanese Physiological Soc. 1998, The Physiological Soc. 1999; Hon. DSc (Sheffield) 2004, (Warwick) 2008; Dr hc (Bordeaux) 2005; Darwin Lecturer, British Asscn 1966, Scientific Medal, Zoological Soc. 1970, Nahum Lecturer, Yale Univ. 1977, British Heart Foundation Gold Medal and Prize 1985, Lloyd Roberts Lecturer 1987, Bowden Lecturer 1988, Alderdale Wyld Lecturer 1988, Pierre Rijlant Prize, Belgian Royal Acad. 1991, Baly Medal, Royal Coll. of Physicians 1993, Pavlov Medal Russian Acad. of Science 2004, Hodgkin-Huxley-Katz Prize, Physiological Soc. 2004, Mackenzie Prize, British Cardiac Soc. 2005, Gordon Moe Lecturer, Cardiac Electrophysiology Soc. 2010. *Publications:* Initiation of the Heartbeat 1975, Electric Current Flow in Excitable Cells 1975, Electrophysiology of Single Cardiac Cells 1987, Goals, No Goals and Own Goals 1989, Sodium-Calcium Exchange 1989, Logic of Life 1993, Ionic Channels and the Effect of Taurine on the Heart 1993, Ethics of Life 1997, The Music of Life 2006, The Selected Papers of Denis Noble CBE, FRS, A Journey in Physiology towards Enlightenment 2012, Dance to the Tune of Life 2016; scientific papers mostly in Journal of Physiology. *Leisure interests:* Occitan language and music, Indian and French cooking, classical guitar. *Address:* Department of Physiology, Anatomy and Genetics, Parks Road, Oxford, OX1 3PT (office); 49 Old Road, Oxford, OX3 7JZ, England (home). *Telephone:* (1865) 272528 (office); (1865) 762237 (home). *Fax:* (1865) 282504 (office). *E-mail:* denis.noble@dpag.ox.ac.uk (office). *Website:* www .dpag.ox.ac.uk/team/h-n/denis-noble (office); www.musicoflife.website (home).

NOBLE, Ronald Kenneth, BA, JD; American lawyer, law enforcement executive and academic; *Professor of Law, New York University;* b. 1956, Fort Dix, New Jersey; ed Univ. of New Hampshire, Stanford Univ. Law School; fmr Asst to US Attorney, then Deputy Asst to Attorney-Gen., Dept of Justice; Pres. Financial Action Task Force (26 mem. multi-nat. org. est. to fight money-laundering by G7) 1989; Chief Law Enforcement Officer, US Treasury Dept 1989–96, responsible for The Secret Service, Customs Service, Bureau of Alcohol, Tobacco and Firearms, Fed. Law Enforcement Training Center, Financial Crimes Enforcement Network, Office of Foreign Assets Control and Criminal Investigation Div. of Internal Revenue Service; currently Prof. of Law, New York Univ. School of Law, also Faculty Dir of Root-Tilden-Kern Scholarship Program; fmr mem. Exec. Cttee INTERPOL, Sec.-Gen. 2000–14; Chevalier, Légion d'honneur 2008. *Address:* New York University, School of Law, 40 Washington Square S, New York, NY 10012, USA (office). *Telephone:* (212) 998-6702 (office). *Fax:* (212) 995-4526 (office). *E-mail:* ronald.noble@nyu.edu (office). *Website:* www.law.nyu.edu (office).

NOBOA BEJARANO, Gustavo, PhD; Ecuadorean politician and academic; b. 21 Aug. 1939, Guayaquil; m. Marta Baquerizo; six c.; teacher of social sciences and politics 1962–; fmr Rector of Catholic Univ. of Guayaquil; fmr Rector of Public Univ. of Guayaquil; Gov. of Guayas Prov. 1983; mem. of peace comm. on border dispute with Peru 1996; Vice-Pres. of Ecuador 1998–2000, Pres. 2000–02; investigated for allegedly mishandling $126 million in govt bonds to bail out state-run banks during his presidency; granted asylum by Govt of Dominican Repub. 2003–05; Order of St Sylvester, Commdr, State of the Vatican 1979, Order of San Gregorio Magno 1996, Order of Merit, Chile 2000, Order of Isabel la Católica, Spain 2001, Order of the Cross of the South, Brazil 2001, Order of the Condor of the Andes, Bolivia 2001, Order of the Sun, Peru.

NOBOA PONTÓN, Alvaro Fernando; Ecuadorean business executive and politician; *President, Noboa Corporation;* b. 21 Nov. 1950, Guayaquil; s. of Luis Noboa Naranjo; m. Anabella Azín; three s.; ed Le Rosey School, Switzerland, State Univ. of Guayaquil; est. first business Promandato Global SA 1973; f. La Verdad (monthly magazine) 1986, Banco del Litoral 1990, Global Financing Co. and other investment cos 1992, joined these cos with Banco del Litoral to form Grupo de Empresas Ab. Alvaro Noboa P. 1994; inherited portion of Noboa Corpn following death of father 1994, Pres. Noboa Corpn (controls 105 cos in Ecuador, Europe, USA and NZ with interests in coffee, bananas, real estate and flour) 1995–, cos include Bonita Bananas (largest banana co. in Ecuador, four shipping cos, one bank, two insurance cos, La nica (edible oils), Valdez (sugar refinery), Los Alamos and 14 other banana plantations, mines, media cos and other Ecuadorean businesses; Pres. Monetary Bd 1996; presidential cand. for Partido Roldosista Ecuatoriano (PRE) 1998, for Partido Renovador Institucional Acción Nacional (PRIAN) 2002, 2006 (also Founder and Leader); f. Fundación Cruzada Nueva Humanidad

(charity) 1977. *Address:* Corporacion Noboa, El Oro y La Ria, Guayaquil (office); Partido Renovador Institucional de Acción Nacional (PRIAN), Quito, Ecuador. *Website:* www.alvaronoboa.com (office); www.prian.org.ec.

NÓBREGA SUÁREZ, Tobías, DEcon; Venezuelan economist and politician; b. 30 Jan. 1961, Puerto Cabello, Carabobo; ed Univ. Central de Venezuela, Univ. Complutense de Madrid, Spain; Lecturer, Dept of Econs, Univ. Central de Venezuela 1986–97; Chief Economist, Central Hipotecaria 1988, Asociácion Bancaria de Venezuela 1995–97, Asociácion de Gobernadores de Venezuela 1993–98; ind. financial consultant 1986–, also financial adviser to Nat. Govt and several regional govts; Dir Oficina de Asesoría Económica del Parlamento Nacional (OAEF) 2000; adviser to numerous parl. cttees, including Parl. Finance Sub-cttee 2000; Minister of Finance 2002–04. *Publications:* numerous articles in econ. journals.

NODA, Seiko; Japanese politician; *Minister of Internal Affairs and Communications;* b. 3 Sept. 1960, Kitakyushu, Fukuoka; m. Yosuke Tsuruho 2001 (divorced 2007); one s.; ed Futaba Acad. Secondary School, Jonesville High School, Michigan, USA, Sophia Univ., Bulgaria; mem. staff, Imperial Hotel 1983–87; elected mem. Gifu Prefectural Ass. 1987; mem. for Gifu No. 1 Dist, House of Rep. (LDP) 1993–; Parl. Vice-Minister of Posts and Telecommunications, Minister 1998–99; Minister of State for Science and Tech. Policy and Food Safety, Consumer Affairs, Space Policy 2008–09; Minister of Internal Affairs and Communications 2017–, also Minister in charge of Women's Empowerment and Minister of State for the Social Security and Tax Number System 2017–; currently Chair. LDP General Council; adviser to Sake Mfrs Asscn; Pres. Sake-Loving Female Diet Members Club. *Publications include:* (in Japanese) I am Seeing 1987, Under the Pretext of Reform 1994, Things I Want to Get Across to the People – Politics Spoken with Sincerity 1996, Japan Will Win the Post-IT Era! – Proposals of Seven Leading Figures (co-author) 2001, I Want to Give Birth 2004, Who is Taking Away Our Future – Fighting the Declining Birthrate 2005, Easy-to-understand Guide to the Revised Child Prostitution/Pornography Law (co-author) 2005. *Leisure interests:* reading, watching movies, karaoke, using the computer. *Address:* Ministry of Internal Affairs and Communications, 2-1-2, Kasumigaseki, Chiyoda-ku, Tokyo 100-8926, Japan (office). *Telephone:* (3) 5253-5111 (office). *Fax:* (3) 3504-0265 (office). *Website:* www.soumu.go.jp (office).

NODA, Tetsuya, MA; Japanese printmaker and academic; *Professor Emeritus, Tokyo University of the Arts (formerly Tokyo National University of Fine Arts and Music);* b. 5 March 1940, Kumamoto Pref.; s. of Tesshin Noda and Sakae Noda; m. Dorit Bartur; one s. one d.; ed Tokyo Univ. of the Arts (fmrly Tokyo Nat. Univ. of Fine Arts and Music); Visiting Artist, Alberta Univ., Canada 1984, Betzalel Art Acad., Israel 1985, Canberra Art School, Australia 1990, Columbia Univ., USA 1998; Prof., Tokyo Nat. Univ. of Fine Arts and Music (renamed Tokyo Univ. of the Arts) 1990–2007, Prof. Emer. 2007–; Cultural Envoy, Japanese Govt Agency of Cultural Affairs 2010–, to Hebrew Univ., Israel 2011, London Metropolitan Univ.; mem. Int. Jury for the British Int. Print Biennale 1976, Korean Int. Print Biennale 1996, Space Int. Print Biennale, Seoul 2002, First Int. Print Biennale, Istanbul 2008, Edmonton Print Int. 2008, 2nd Bangkok Triennale Int. Print and Drawing Exhbn 2008; Hon. DLitt (London Metropolitan); prizes include Int. Grand Prize (Tokyo Int. Print Biennale) 1968, Grand Prize (Ljubljana Int. Print Biennale) 1977 and Grand Prize of Honour 1987, Grand Prize (Norwegian Int. Print Biennale) 1978, Friends of Bradford Art Galleries and Museum Prize (British Int. Print Biennale) 1986, Gen Yamaguchi Memorial Grand Prize, City of Numazu 1993; Medal of Purple Ribbon (Japanese Govt). *Publications:* Tetsuya Noda – The Works III 1992–2000 2001. *Leisure interest:* gardening. *Address:* 2-12-4 Kikkodai-cho, Kashiwa-shi, Chiba-ken 277-0031, Japan (home). *Telephone:* (471) 63-5332 (home). *Fax:* (471) 63-5332 (home). *E-mail:* tetsuyanoda@hotmail.com (home).

NODA, Yoshihiko; Japanese politician; b. 20 May 1957, Funabashi, Chiba Pref.; ed Waseda Univ., Matsushita Inst. of Govt and Man.; mem. Chiba Prefectural Ass. 1987–93; mem. House of Reps Japan New Party (now Democratic Party of Japan—DPJ) 1993–, Pres. 2011–12, Chair. Diet Affairs Cttee 2002, 2005, Public Relations Cttee 2007; Acting Sec.-Gen. DPJ 2009; Sr Vice-Minister of Finance 2009, Minister of Finance 2010–11; Prime Minister 2011–12. *Address:* Democratic Party of Japan, 1-11-1, Nagata-cho, Chiyoda-ku, Tokyo 100-0014, Japan (office). *E-mail:* Post@ Nodayoshi.gr.jp (office). *Website:* www.dpj.or.jp; www.nodayoshi.gr.jp (office).

NODDLE, Jeffrey (Jeff), BA; American retail executive; s. of Robert Noddle and Edith Noddle; ed Univ. of Iowa; began career as Dir of Retail Operations, JM Jones Div., Supervalu Inc. 1976, held various positions including Merchandising Dir, Vice-Pres. Marketing JM Jones Div. –1982, Pres. Fargo and Miami Divs 1982–85, Corp. Vice-Pres. Merchandising, Supervalu Inc. 1985–88, Sr Vice-Pres. Marketing 1988–92, Corp. Exec. Vice-Pres. Marketing 1992–93, Corp. Exec. Vice-Pres. and Pres. 1993–95, COO Distribution Food Cos 1995–2000, Pres. and COO 2000–01, Pres. and CEO 2001–02, Chair. and CEO Supervalu Inc. 2002–09, Exec. Chair. 2009–10 (retd); mem. Bd of Dirs General Cable Corpn 1998–2004, Donaldson Co. Inc. 2000–, Ameriprise Financial Inc. 2005–, Clorox Co. 2013–; fmr Chair. Food Marketing Inst.; fmr mem. Bd Ind. Grocers Alliance Inc., Sarah W. Stedman Center for Nutritional Studies, Duke Univ. Medical Center; mem. Exec. Cttee, Minneapolis Business Partnership; mem. Bd of Overseers, Univ. of Minnesota Carlson School of Man.; Chair. Greater Twin Cities United Way 2009; National Bridge Award, Chicago United 2005, Executive of the Year, Minneapolis/St Paul Business Journal 2008, Herbert Hoover Award, Food Marketing Inst. 2009, named the Network of Executive Women's Outstanding Champion for 2009, inducted into Minnesota Grocers Asscn's Hall of Fame 2009.

NOE PINO, Hugo, PhD; Honduran economist, diplomatist and politician; b. 11 Jan. 1955, Tegucigalpa; s. of Roberto Noe and Elidia Pino; m. Vivian Bustamante; two s. one d.; ed Universidad Nacional Autonoma de Honduras (UNAH), Univ. of Texas at Austin, USA; fmr teaching Asst, Dept of Econs, Univ. of Tex.; Pres. Cen. Bank of Honduras 1994–97; Dir Master's Programme in Econs for Cen. American and Caribbean Region, UNAH; Pres. Asscn of Economists of Honduras; mem. Editorial Council of various magazines published in Honduras; Spokesman of Shadow Cabinet 1993; Amb. to USA –1999; mem. Partido Liberal (PL), campaign man. for successful presidential cand. José Manuel (Mel) Zelaya Rosales 2005; Minister of Finance Jan.–July 2006. *Publications:* An Assessment of the

Campesino Associative Enterprise of Isletas 1987, Honduras: Structural Adjustment and Agrarian Reform 1992. *Leisure interests:* reading, music.

NOEM, Kristi, BA; American politician; *Governor of South Dakota;* b. 30 Nov. 1971, Watertown, SDak; d. of Ron Arnold and Corrine Arnold; m. Bryon Noem 1992; one s. two d.; ed South Dakota State Univ.; mem. State House of Reps, SDak 2007–11, also fmr Asst Majority Leader; mem. US House of Reps 2011–19; Gov. of SDak 2019–; Pres. 4-H Leaders Asscn, Hamlin Co.; mem. of numerous caucuses including Defence Communities, Gen. Aviation, Medical Tech., Rural Health, Tourism & Travel; Young Leader Award, State of SDak 2003. *Leisure interests:* hunting, raising cattle, horses. *Address:* Office of the Governor, 500 E Capitol Avenue, Pierre, SD 57501, USA (office). *Telephone:* (605) 773-3212 (office). *Fax:* (605) 773-4711 (office). *Website:* www.sd.gov/governor (office).

NOFAL, María Beatriz, MA, PhD; Argentine economist, politician and academic; b. 7 Oct. 1952, Mendoza; ed Universidad Nacional de Cuyo, Inst. of Social Studies, Netherlands, Univ. of Paris, France, Johns Hopkins Univ., Baltimore, Md, USA; Assoc. Prof., Johns Hopkins Univ. 1983–84, MIT 1985; Prof., Univ. of Bologna based in Buenos Aires 1999; Visiting Prof., Univ. of Toronto, Canada 2004; Prof., Universidad Católica Argentina 2005; Under-Sec. of Industrial Devt, Industry and Foreign Trade Secr., Ministry of Economy 1986–89; Pres. of ECO-AXIS, SA consultants 1993–99, 2002–06; Congresswoman (Unión Cívica Radical) 1999–2002; Pres. Nat. Agency for Investment Devt (ANDI) 2006–10; Pres. Int. Women's Forum Argentina Chapter 2008–12, mem. Bd 2011–13; Dir, Arthur D. Little (consultancy firm), Argentina 1999–2000; Dir (non-exec.), Nobleza Piccardo/British American Tobacco 2006; mem. Interamerican Dialogue (US-based think tank) 2001–; adviser to Argentine Council for Int. Relations (CARI); Ed. and Prin. Author Mercosur Journal 1995–99. *Publications include:* Absentee Entrepreneurship and the Dynamics of the Motor Vehicle Industry in Argentina 1989; numerous articles in newspapers, magazines and professional journals. *Address:* Ministry of Economy and Production, Hipólito Yrigoyen 250, C1086AAB, Buenos Aires, Argentina (office); Inter-American Dialogue, 1211 Connecticut Avenue NW, Suite 510, Washington, DC 20036, USA. *Telephone:* (11) 4349-5000 (Buenos Aires) (office); (202) 822-9002 (Washington, DC). *Fax:* (202) 822-9553 (Washington, DC). *E-mail:* sagpya@mecon.gov.ar (office). *Website:* www.mecon.gov.ar (office); www.thedialogue.org.

NOGAMI, Tomoyuki, PhD; Japanese educationalist, university administrator and academic; b. 1946; ed Hiroshima Univ.; Research Assoc., Faculty of Educ., Hiroshima Univ. 1979–80; Lecturer, Faculty of Home Econs, Hiroshima Women's Univ. 1980–83, Assoc. Prof. 1983–86; Visiting Scholar, Teachers' Coll., Columbia Univ., New York 1986–88; Assoc. Prof., Faculty of Educ., Kobe Univ. 1988–92, Prof., Faculty of Human Devt 1992–94, Dir Research Centre for Human Science 1994–96, Prin. Kindergarten/Akashi Elementary School/Akashi Jr High School attached to Faculty of Human Devt 1996–98, Dean Faculty of Human Devt 1998–2001, Dean Grad. School of Cultural Studies and Human Science 2001, apptd Pres. Kobe Univ. 2001; mem. Japanese Nat. Comm. for UNESCO 2003.

NOGAMI, Yoshiji; Japanese diplomatist (retd) and research institute director; b. 19 June 1942; m. Geraldine Nogami; three s.; ed Univ. of Tokyo; joined Ministry of Foreign Affairs 1966, held positions as Dir-Gen. Econ. Affairs Bureau, Deputy Minister, later Vice-Minister for Foreign Affairs 2001, Consul-Gen. in Hong Kong, Amb. to OECD, Paris, to UK 2004–08, Adviser to the Cabinet 2008; Sr Visiting Fellow, Chatham House (Royal Inst. of Int. Affairs) 2002; apptd Pres. and Dir-Gen. Japan Inst. of Int. Affairs 2009–13(then Dir), Chair. Japan Nat. Cttee for Pacific Econ. Cooperation; Exec. Adviser, Mizuho Corporate Bank.

NOGHAIDELI, Zurab; Georgian business executive, academic and politician; b. 22 Oct. 1964, Kobuleti, Ajara; s. of Nazi Katamadze; m. Nino Tsintsabadze; one s.; ed Moscow M.V. Lomonosov State Univ., USSR (now Russian Fed.); Asst, Inst. of Geography, Acad. of Sciences of Georgia, Batumi 1988–89; Guest Researcher, Inst. of Geology, Acad. of Sciences of Estonia, Tallinn 1989–91; Sr Researcher and Head of Lab., Niko Berzenishvili Research Inst., Acad. of Sciences of Georgia, Batumi 1989–92; Exec. Sec. Georgia Greens 1992–93; mem. Parl., Chair. Cttee of Environment Protection and Natural Resources 1992–95, Chair. Cttee of Tax and Revenue 1999–2000; Co-ordinator Office of the Chair. 1995–99; Int. Sec., Citizens' Union of Georgia 1995–98; mem. Supreme Council, Adjara Autonomous Rep. 1996–98; Minister of Finance 2000–02, 2004–05; Prime Minister of Georgia 2005–07 (resgnd); mem. Bd People's Bank of Georgia 2002–03; Partner, Solidary Responsibilities Soc. Damenia, Varshalomidze, Noghaideli and Kavtaradze April–Nov. 2003; Chair. Kala Capital (investment co.) 2007; Chair. Int. School of Econs Business Council, Tbilisi State Univ. 2008.

NOGOYBAYEV, Bolotbek, CandJur; Kyrgyzstani politician; b. 10 Nov. 1955, Telman village, Panfilov Dist; m. Mariya Boronbayevna Nogoybayeva; two s. one d.; ed Kyrgyz State Univ.; served in Soviet Army 1973–75; served in various policing roles including police officer, Inspector and Head, Criminal Investigation Dept, Dept of Transport, Pishpek (now Bishkek) office 1976–85, Head, Transport Police Div. 1987–90; Dir Internal Affairs Dept, Sverdlov region 1990–95; Deputy Head of Internal Affairs, Talas Oblast 1995–96; Head, Criminal Investigation Dept, Ministry of Internal Affairs 1996–98; Head of Internal Affairs, Osh Oblast 1998–99; Deputy Minister of Internal Affairs 1999–2001, 2002–05; Chief Inspector, Kyrgyz Security Council Feb.–Aug. 2005; Dir Kyrgyz Drug Control Agency 2005–07; Minister of Internal Affairs 2007–08. *Publications:* Narcotics: Theory and Practice of Counteraction; numerous articles on drug control.

NOGRALES, Karlo Alexei Bendigo, JUD; Philippine politician; *Cabinet Secretary;* b. 3 Sept. 1976, Davao City; s. of Prospero Nograles and Rhodora Burgos Bendigo Nograles; m. Marga Maceda Montemayor; three c.; ed Ateneo de Davao Univ., Philippine Science High School (Main Campus), Ateneo de Manila Univ., Ateneo de Manila Law School; mem. House of Reps. (Parl.) from Davao City's 1st Dist 2010–18; Cabinet Sec. 2018–; mem. PDP–Laban (political party) 2017–; fmr mem. Nat. Unity Party (NUP); mem. Integrated Bar of the Philippines, Davao City 2004–; mem. Global Organization of Parliamentarians Against Corruption (GOPAC), South East Asian Parliamentarians Against Corruption (SEAPAC), Hijos de Davao, Philconsa; Outstanding Congressman Award, Superbrands Marketing Int. 2012, 2015, Golden Globe Award for Excellence in Public Service 2015, 2016. *Address:* Cabinet Secretariat, Malacañang Palace Compound, J. P. Laurel Street, San Miguel, Manila, Philippines (office). *E-mail:* kaka_nograles@yahoo.com. *Website:* karlonograles.ph.

NOGUCHI, Teruhisa, PhD; Japanese business executive; b. 22 Oct. 1924, Chiba Pref.; m.; one s. three d.; ed Schools of Medicine, Kanazawa and Tokyo Univs; with Nihon Soda Co. 1949–72; with Teijin Ltd 1972–79, Dir 1973, Dir Teijin Inst. for Biomedical Research 1976; with Suntory Ltd 1979–92, Dir 1979, Exec. Man. Pharmaceutical Div. 1981, Sr Man. Dir 1987–, Chief Exec. 1991; fmr Exec. Vice-Pres. Yamanouchi Pharmaceutical Co. Ltd; Pres. and CEO Tenox Inst., Medico Frontier Inst.; Adjunct Prof., The Rockefeller Univ. 1984–; Fellow, American Acad. of Microbiology; several prizes and awards. *Publications include:* Biochemistry of Interferons 1982, New Trends in Neuro-Science 1984. *Leisure interests:* fine arts, golf.

NOHRIA, Nitin, BTech, PhD; Indian chemical engineer, academic and university administrator; *Dean and George F Baker Professor of Administration, Harvard Business School;* b. 1962, Mumbai; s. of Kewal Nohria; m. Monica Norhia; two d.; ed Indian Inst. of Tech., Bombay, Sloan School of Man., Massachusetts Inst. of Tech., USA; Asst Prof., Harvard Business School 1988–93, Assoc. Prof. 1993–99, Richard P. Chapman Prof. of Business Admin 1999, Co-Chair. Leadership Initiative 2009, Dean, Harvard Business School 2010–, Dir Div. of Research 2003–04, Sr Assoc. Dean of Faculty Devt 2006–09, Head of Organizational Behavior unit 1998–2002, George F Baker Prof. of Admin; Visiting Faculty mem. London Business School 1996; Distinguished Alumnus Medal, Indian Inst. of Tech. 2007. *Publications include:* co-author or co-editor of 16 books, including Networks and Organizations: Structure, Form, and Action, Building the Information Age Organization, Beyond the Hype: Rediscovering the Essence of Management, Differentiated Network: Organizing Multinational Corporations for Value Creation (George R. Terry Award, Academy of Management 1998) 1997, Portable MBA Desk Reference, Breaking the Code of Change, Arc of Ambition: Defining the Leadership Journey (co-author) 2000, Master Passions: Emotion, Narrative, and the Development of Culture, Driven: How Human Nature Shapes Our Choices (co-author) 2001, Changing Fortunes: Remaking the Industrial Corporation (co-author) 2002, What Really Works: The 4+2 Formula for Sustained Business Success (co-author) 2003, In Their Time: The Greatest Business Leaders of the 20th Century, Paths to Power: How Insiders and Outsiders Shaped American Business Leadership (co-author) 2006, Handbook of Leadership Theory and Practice (co-ed.) 2010; over 50 journal articles, book chapters, cases, working papers and notes. *Address:* Office of the Dean, Harvard Business School, Soldiers Field, Boston, MA 02163, USA. *Website:* www.hbs.edu/dean.

NØJGAARD, Morten, DPhil; Danish academic; *Romance Editor, Orbis Litterarum;* b. 28 July 1934, Holbaek; s. of Niels Nøjgaard and Annie Nøjgaard (née Bay); m. Stina Lund 1962; two s. two d.; secondary school teacher, Roedovre Statskole 1960–63; Research Scholar, Univ. of Copenhagen 1963–65; Prof. of Romance Philology, Univ. of Southern Denmark, Odense 1966–2004; Chief Ed. Orbis Litterarum 1968–99, Romance Ed. 1999–; Pres. Asscn of French Prof. 1962–63, Alliance Française, Odense 1970–; mem. Soc. of Letters (Lund, Sweden) 1978, Royal Danish Acad. of Science 1982, Royal Norwegian Acad. of Science 1991, Royal Swedish Acad. of Antiquities 1997; Ordre du Mérite 1980; Fnske Bladfond Research Award 1975. *Publications:* La Fable Antique, (Vols I–II) 1964–67, Elévation et Expansion. Les deux dimensions de Baudelaire 1973, An Introduction to Literary Analysis 1975, Romain-Gary-Emile Ajar, Homo Duplex 1986, Les Adverbes français, Vol. I 1992, Vol. II 1993, Vol. III 1995, Plaisir et vérité, Le paradoxe de l'évaluation littéraire 1993, Le Temps de la littérature. Sur Paul Ricoeur et les paradoxes du temps raconté 1999, Temps, réalisme et description: Essais de théorie littéraire 2004; numerous scientific articles. *Address:* University of Southern Denmark, Campusvej 55, 5230 Odense M (office); Åløkken 48, 5250 Odense SV, Denmark (home). *Telephone:* 65-50-10-00 (office); 20-49-85-95 (home). *Fax:* 65-93-51-41 (office). *E-mail:* mno@sdu.dk (office). *Website:* www.humaniora.sdu.dk (office).

NOJI, Kunio; Japanese business executive; *Chairman, Komatsu Ltd;* b. 17 Nov. 1946, Fukui Pref.; m.; two d.; ed School of Eng Science, Osaka Univ.; joined Komatsu Ltd 1969, Gen. Man. Production Control Dept, Tech. Div. 1993–95, Plant Man. Chattanooga Manufacturing Operation, Komatsu Dresser Co. (currently Komatsu America Corpn) 1995–97, Gen. Man. Information Systems Div. 1997–99, Dir June 1997, Exec. 1999–2000, Exec. Officer and Pres. Production Div. and Vice-Pres. e-Komatsu Tech. Centre April–June 2000, Sr Exec. Officer, Pres. Production Div. and Vice-Pres. e-Komatsu Tech. Centre 2000–01, Man. Dir and Pres. Production Div. and e-Komatsu Tech. Centre 2001–03, Dir and Sr Exec. Officer, Pres. of Construction and Mining Equipment Marketing Div. 2003–05, Dir and Sr Exec. Officer, Supervising Construction and Mining Equipment Business and e-Komatsu Tech. Centre 2005–06, Dir and Sr Exec. Officer, Supervising Construction and Mining Equipment Business, e-Komatsu Tech. Centre and Komatsu Way April–July 2006, Dir and Sr Exec. Officer, Gen. Man. of Komatsu Way Dept, Supervising Construction and Mining Equipment Business and e-Komatsu Tech. Centre 2006–07, Dir and Sr Exec. Officer, Pres. of Production Div. and Gen. Man. Komatsu Way Dept, Supervising Construction and Mining Equipment Business and e-Komatsu Tech. Centre Jan.–June 2007, Pres. and CEO Komatsu Ltd 2007–, Chair. Komatsu Ltd 2013–; mem. Bd of Dirs NEC Corpn 2013–. *Leisure interests:* golfing, mountain climbing. *Address:* Komatsu Ltd, 2-3-6, Akasaka, Minato-ku, Tokyo 107-8414, Japan (office). *Website:* www.komatsu.com (office).

NOJIMA, Hideo; Japanese retail executive; b. 19 Jan. 1957, Kumamoto; s. of Eijiro and Mariko Nojima; m. Mariko Yoshida 1994; two c.; fmrly with Okadaya Corpn; fmr Man. Dir AEON Co. Ltd, later Sr Man. Dir, Chair. and Rep. Dir 2006–08, part-time Auditor AEON Environmental Foundation as of 2012; Kodaira Memorial Prize 2001, Takagi Prize 2001.

NOKA, Flamur, MD; Albanian physician and politician; b. 3 March 1971, Kukës; m.; two c.; held positions within Democratic Party of Albania (DPA), including Organizing Sec. 2005, mem. Nat. Council of DPA; mem. (DPA) Ass. of Repub. of Albania for Kukës dist 2009–; Minister of the Interior 2012–13. *Address:* c/o Ministry of the Interior, Sheshi Skënderbej 3, Tirana, Albania. *Telephone:* 69-4133588 (mobile). *E-mail:* minister@moi.gov.al.

NOKED, Orit, LLB; Israeli lawyer and politician; b. 25 Oct. 1952, Jerusalem; m.; three c.; ed Hebrew Univ. of Jerusalem; attained rank of staff sergeant while serving in Israeli Army; admitted to Israeli Bar 1977; legal adviser of the Kibbutz Movt 1986–92, Dir Legal Dept 1996–2002; unsuccessful cand. for Knesset (Parl.) 1999, mem. Knesset 2002–13, served on Finance Cttee, Cttee on the Status of Women, Cttee on the Rights of the Child, Labour, Welfare and Health Cttee, Cttee for the Appointment of Judges; Asst to Shimon Peres, Deputy Prime Minister and Minister for Devt of the Negev and Galilee Jan.–Nov. 2005, headed Team for Settlement-Related Issues in Outlying Areas; Deputy Minister of Industry, Trade, and Labour –2011; Minister of Agric. and Rural Devt 2011–13; mem. Labour Party 2002–11, Independence 2011–; with Balter, Guth, Aloni & Co. Law Offices 2013–; mem. Jewish Nat. Fund's directorate, Agricultural Asscn's Secr., Nat. Council for Environmental Quality, Bd of Israel Lands Admin, Kibbutz Shefayim. *Address:* Balter, Guth, Aloni & Co. Law Offices, 96 Yigal Alon Street, 67891 Tel-Aviv, Israel (office). *Telephone:* 3-5111111 (office). *E-mail:* onoked@bgalaw.co.il (office). *Website:* bgalaw.co.il (office).

NOLAN, Christopher Jonathan James; British/American director, writer and producer; b. 30 July 1970, London; m. Emma Thomas 1997; three c.; ed Haileybury Coll., Herts., UK, Univ. Coll., London; filmed several short films in his univ. film soc., London; short film Tarantella shown on Image Union, an ind. film and video showcase featured on PBS 1989; short film Larceny shown during Cambridge Film Festival in 1996; Visionary Award, Palm Springs Int. Film Festival 2003. *Films directed:* Doodlebug (as Chris Nolan; also writer, cinematographer, ed. and set designer) 1997, Following (also writer, producer, cinematographer and ed.) (Silver Hitchcock, Dinard British Film Festival 1999, Best Dir Award, Newport Int. Film Festival 1999, Tiger Award, Rotterdam Int. Film Festival 1999, Black & White Award, Slamdance Film Festival 1999) 1998, Memento (also screenplay) (CinéLive Award, Critics' Award and Jury Special Prize, Deauville Film Festival 2000, Prize of the Catalan Screenwriter's Critic and Writer's Asscn, Sitges-Catalonian Int. Film Festival 2000, Boston Soc. of Film Critics' Award for Best Screenplay 2001, ALFS Award for British Screenwriter of the Year, London Critics' Circle Film Awards 2001, Los Angeles Film Critics' Asscn Award for Best Screenplay 2001, SEFCA Award for Best Original Screenplay, Southeastern Film Critics' Asscn Awards 2001, Waldo Salt Screenwriting Award, Sundance Film Festival 2001, Toronto Film Critics' Asscn Award for Best Screenplay 2001, AFI Screenwriter of the Year 2002, Bram Stoker Award for Best Screenplay 2002, Critics' Choice Award for Best Screenplay, Broadcast Film Critics' Asscn Awards 2002, Chicago Film Critics' Asscn Award for Best Screenplay 2002, Chlotrudis Award for Best Dir 2002, Russell Smith Award, Dallas-Fort Worth Film Critics' Asscn Awards 2002, Edgar for Best Motion Picture, Edgar Allan Poe Awards 2002, Florida Film Critics' Circle Award for Best Screenplay 2002, Independent Spirit Awards for Best Dir and Best Screenplay 2002, Sierra Award for Best Screenplay, Las Vegas Film Critics' Soc. Awards 2002, MTV Movie Award for Best New Filmmaker 2002, Online Film Critics' Soc. Award for Best Breakthrough Filmmaker 2002, Phoenix Film Critics' Soc. Awards for Best Newcomer and Best Original Screenplay 2002) 2000, Insomnia (ALFS Award for British Dir of the Year, London Critics' Circle Film Awards 2003) 2002, Cinema16: British Short Films (video) 2003, Batman Begins (also screenplay) (Saturn Award for Best Writing, Academy of Science Fiction, Fantasy & Horror Films, USA 2006) 2005, The Prestige (also screenplay and producer) (Empire Award for Best Dir 2007) 2006, The Dark Knight (also story and producer) 2008, Inception (also screenplay, story and producer) (Hugo Award for Best Dramatic Presentation, Long Form 2011) 2010, The Dark Knight Rises (also story, screenplay and producer) 2012, Interstellar (also writer and producer) 2014, Dunkirk (also writer and producer) 2014. *Films produced:* Man of Steel (also writer) 2013, Transcendence 2014, Batman v Superman: Dawn of Justice 2016, Justice League 2017. *Address:* c/o Dan Aloni, WME, 9601 Wilshire Blvd, Beverly Hills, CA 90212, USA (office). *Website:* www.christophernolan.net.

NOLAN, Philip, MBA, PhD; British telecommunications executive; *Chairman, Associated British Ports (ABP);* b. Oct. 1953, Enniskillen, Northern Ireland; ed Queen's Univ., Belfast, London Business School; fmr Lecturer in Geology, Univ. of Ulster; with British Petroleum (BP) Exploration –1996, numerous roles including Man. of Acquisitions and Disposals; Dir Transco East Area, BG Group 1996–97, Man. Dir Transco 1997–2000, CEO 1999–2000, mem. Bd BG Group 1998–2000; CEO Lattice Group (fmrly part of the BG Group) 2000–02, Eircom plc 2002–06, Irish Man. Inst. 2006–12; Chair. Sepura plc 2007–10, Infinis Ltd 2007–10, Ulster Bank Ltd 2007–17, John Laing Group plc 2010–18, Affinity Water Ltd 2013–18, Associated British Ports (ABP) 2017–; Sr Advisor, Warburg Pincus LLC; mem. Bd of Dirs De La Rue plc 2001–09, Providence Resources plc 2004–16, EnQuest plc 2012–17, The Ireland Funds, British Gas, Queen's Univ. of Belfast Foundation. *Address:* Associated British Ports, 2nd Floor, 25 Bedford Street, London, WC2E 9ES, England (office). *Telephone:* (20) 7430-1177 (office). *Fax:* (20) 7406-7896 (office). *Website:* www.abports.co.uk (office).

NOLTE, Nick; American film actor; b. 8 Feb. 1941, Omaha, Neb.; m. Rebecca Linger 1984 (divorced 1995); one s.; pnr Clytie Lane; one d.; ed Pasadena City Coll., Phoenix City Coll.; f. Kingsgate Films Inc. (production co.). *Films include:* Return to Macon County 1975, The Deep 1977, Who'll Stop the Rain 1978, North Dallas Forty 1979, Heartbeat 1980, Cannery Row 1982, 48 Hours 1982, Under Fire 1983, The Ultimate Solution of Grace Quigley 1984, Teachers 1984, Down and Out in Beverly Hills 1986, Weeds 1987, Extreme Prejudice 1987, Farewell to the King 1989, New York Stories 1989, Three Fugitives, Everybody Wins, Q & A 1990, Prince of Tides 1990, Cape Fear 1991, Lorenzo's Oil 1992, Blue Chips 1994, I'll Do Anything 1994, Love Trouble 1994, Jefferson in Paris 1994, Mulholland Falls 1996, Mother Night 1996, Afterglow 1997, Affliction 1998, U-Turn, Breakfast of Champions 1998, The Thin Red Line 1998, Trixie 2000, The Golden Bowl 2000, Investigating Sex 2001, Double Down 2001, The Good Thief 2003, Hotel Rwanda 2004, Neverwas 2005, Over the Hedge (voice) 2006, Paris, je t'aime 2006, A Few Days in September 2006, Off the Black 2006, Peaceful Warrior 2006, The Spiderwick Chronicles 2007, Tropic Thunder 2008, Arcadia Lost 2009, Arthur 2011, Warrior 2011, The Company You Keep 2012, Gangster Squad 2013, Parker 2013, Hateship Loveship 2013, The Trials of Cate McCall 2013, A Walk in the Woods 2015. *Television includes:* Rich Man, Poor Man (mini-series) 1976, Luck (series) 2011–12, Gracepoint (mini-series) 2014. *Address:* Kingsgate Films, Inc., 18954 West Pico, 2nd Floor, Los Angeles, CA 90035; Creative Artists Agency, Inc., 2000 Avenue of the Stars, Los Angeles, CA 90067; 6153 Bonsall Drive, Malibu, CA 90265, USA.

NOMAKUCHI, Tamotsu, MS, PhD; Japanese business executive and institute director; *President, National Institute of Advanced Industrial Science and Technology;* b. 18 Nov. 1940, Kagoshima; ed Kyoto Univ., Osaka Univ.; joined Mitsubishi Electric Corpn 1965, various positions including researcher Cen. Research Laboratory, Dir Mitsubishi Information Tech. Research and Devt Centre 1996–97, mem. Bd of Dirs 1997–, Sr Vice-Pres. and Vice-Pres. of Corp. Research and Devt 1997–2001, Exec. Vice-Pres. and Vice-Pres. of Information Systems & Network Services 2001–02, Pres. and CEO Mitsubishi Electric Corpn 2002–06, Chair. 2006–10; currently Pres. Nat. Inst. of Advanced Industrial Science and Tech.; Chair. Echonet Consortium; Vice-Chair. Bd of Councillors, Nippon Keidanren (Japan Business Fed.) 2008–; mem. Intellectual Property Strategy Headquarters, Japan 2009; Intellectual Property Achievement Award 2015. *Address:* National Institute of Advanced Industrial Science and Technology, 1-3-1 Kasumigaseki, Chiyoda-ku, Tokyo 100-8921, Japan (office). *Telephone:* (3) 5501-0900 (office). *E-mail:* info@aist.go.jp (office). *Website:* www.aist.go.jp (office).

NOMIYAMA, Akihiko, LLB; Japanese business executive; *Honorary Executive Consultant, JX Holdings, Incorporated;* b. 15 June 1934, Fukuoka Pref.; one s. one d.; ed Tokyo Univ.; joined Nippon Mining Co. 1957, assignments in budget control, corp. financing, Gen. Man. Admin. Dept, Petroleum Operation 1981–92, Man. Dir Japan Energy Corpn (formed from merger with Kyodo Oil Co.) 1992–96, apptd Pres., CEO and Dir 1996, Chair. and Rep. Dir Nippon Mining Holdings Inc. –2006, Special Adviser 2006–10 (co. formed JX Holdings, Inc. with Nippon Oil Corpn 2010), Hon. Exec. Consultant, JX Holdings, Inc. 2010–; Dir, Mizuho Financial Group, Inc. 2007–; Vice-Chair. Petroleum Asscn of Japan. *Leisure interests:* golf, classical music. *Address:* JX Holdings, Inc., 6-3 Otemachi 2-chome, Chiyoda-ku, Tokyo 100-8162, Japan (office). *Telephone:* (3) 6275-5208 (office). *Website:* www.hd.jx-group.co.jp/english (office); www.noe.jx-group.co.jp/english (office).

NOMURA, Tetsuya; Japanese construction industry executive; joined Shimizu Corpn (contractor in eng and construction projects) 1961, served in various exec. roles including Man. of Kyushu Office, Man. Dir, Sr Man. Dir and Vice-Pres., Pres. and CEO –2007, Chair. and Rep. Dir 2007, led negotiations with NTT Data Corpn to est. jtly funded corpn NTT Data Billing Service 2002; Dir Global Industrial and Social Progress Research Inst. (GISPRI) 2003, Japan Productivity Centre for Socio-Econ. Devt (JPC-SED) 2003. *Address:* c/o Shimizu Corporation, Seavans South, 1-2-3 Shibaura, Minato-ku, Tokyo 105-8007, Japan (office).

NOMURA, Yoshihiro; Japanese legal scholar and academic; *Professor Emeritus of Civil Law, Meiji-Gakuin University;* b. 3 Jan. 1941, Nagoya City; s. of Akio Nomura and Michiko Nomura; m. 1966; three s. one d.; ed Univ. of Tokyo; Asst Researcher in Law, Univ. of Tokyo 1963; Lecturer, Tokyo Metropolitan Univ. 1966–67, Assoc. Prof. 1967–77, Prof. of Civil and Environmental Law 1977; later Prof. of Civil Law, Meiji-Gakuin Univ., now Prof. Emer. *Publications:* Automobile Accident Damages 1970, Environmental Law 1981. *Leisure interest:* nature watching. *Address:* Faculty of Law, Meiji-Gakuin University, 1-2-37 Shirokanedai, Minato-ku, Tokyo 108-8636, Japan (office). *Telephone:* (35) 421-5209 (office). *Fax:* (35) 421-5692 (office). *Website:* www.meijigakuin.ac.jp/law (office).

NONAKA, Tomoyo, BA, MA; Japanese television journalist and business executive; *Chairman, Gaia Initiative;* b. 18 June 1954; ed Sophia Univ., Tokyo, Univ. of Missouri at Columbia, USA; worked as TV anchor on Japan Broadcasting Corpn (NHK) programme International News Weekly (Kaigai Weekly) 1979–92; main newscaster for TV Tokyo's World Business Satellite programme 1992–96; has served as mem. of numerous advisory and discussion councils, including at Ministry of Finance, Ministry of Posts and Telecommunications (now Ministry of Public Man., Home Affairs, Posts and Telecommunications) and Ministry of Educ. and Science and Tech. Agency (now Ministry of Educ., Culture, Sports, Science and Tech.); mem. Council on the Financial System, Ministry of Finance, Council on Science and Tech.; mem. Bd of Dirs, Sanyo Electric Co. Ltd 2002–07, Chair. and CEO 2005–06, Chair. 2006–07; Founder and Chair. Gaia Initiative (non-profit org.) 2007–; mem. Bd of Dirs, Asahi Breweries 2002–07; Exec. mem. Advisory Bd, Mitsui Fudosan Co. Ltd 2001–. *Publications include:* Ganbare, Jibun! (Do the Best for Yourself!), Iron John no Kokoro (The Shadow of Iron John) (trans.). *Address:* Gaia Initiative, 6-10-45-305 Akasaka, Minato-ku, Tokyo 107-0052, Japan (office). *Telephone:* (3) 5574-7716 (office). *Fax:* (3) 5574-7718 (office). *E-mail:* info@gaiainitiative.org (office). *Website:* www.gaiainitiative.org (office).

NONG, Duc Manh; Vietnamese politician; b. 11 Sept. 1940, Cuong Loi, Na Ri Dist, Bac Kan Prov.; s. of Nông Van Lai and Hoang Thi Nhi; m.; one s.; ed Hanoi Higher School, Hanoi Foreign Languages Coll., Forestry Inst., Leningrad, USSR, Nguyen Ai Quoc High-Level Party School; worked as a forestry supervisory technician in Bac Kan Forestry Service 1962–63, Deputy Chief of Bach Thong wood exploitation team 1963–65, Deputy Head Bac Thai prov. forestry inspection bd 1971–73, Dir Phu Luong State Forestry Camp, Bac Thai Prov. 1973–74, Deputy Dir Prov. Forestry Service and Dir Construction Co. of the Forestry Service 1976–77, Dir 1977–80; Deputy Chair. Bac Thai Prov. People's Cttee 1980–83, Chair. 1983–86; elected Deputy Chair. Nat. Ass. Nationalities Council, 8th Nat. Ass., Chair. Nat. Ass. 1992–2001; mem. Dang Cong San Viet Nam (CP of Viet Nam) 1963, mem. Prov. Party Exec. Cttee for Bac Thai 1977, mem. Standing Bd, Prov. Party Cttee, Deputy Sec. Party Cttee for Bac Thai Prov. 1983–86, Sec. 1986, Alt. mem. to Cen. Cttee, Full mem. 1989, Dir Nationalities Comm. 1989–91, elected mem. Political Bureau 1991, 1996, Gen. Sec. CP of Viet Nam 2001–11. *Address:* Dang Cong San Viet Nam, 1 Hoang Van Thu, Hanoi, Viet Nam (office). *E-mail:* cpv@hn.vnn.vn (office). *Website:* www.cpv.org.vn (office).

NONGXA, Loyiso G., BSc, BSc (Hons), MSc, DPhil (Oxon.); South African mathematician, academic and university administrator; *Vice-President, International Mathematical Union;* b. 22 Oct. 1953, Indwe, Eastern Cape; s. of Arthur Tamsanqa Nongxa and Tuddie Ruth Nongxa; m. Nomthunzi Jacobs; three c.; ed Healdtown Coll., Eastern Cape, Univ. of Fort Hare, Balliol Coll., Oxford (Rhodes Scholar), UK; Lecturer, Dept of Math., Univ. of Fort Hare 1978–82; Lecturer, Dept of Math. and Computer Sciences, Nat. Univ. of Lesotho 1982–85; Sr Lecturer, Dept of Pure and Applied Math., Univ. of KwaZulu-Natal 1986–90; Prof. of Math. and Dean of Faculty of Natural Sciences, Univ. of the Western Cape, Belville 1990–2000; Vice-Prin. and Dept Vice-Chancellor—Research, Univ. of the Witwatersrand 2000–03, Vice-Chancellor and Prin. 2003–13 (first black Vice-Chancellor in its history); Founding Vice-Pres. Int. Mathematical Union (IMU) 2018–;

currently Chair. Nat. Research Foundation of South Africa (NRF); Visiting Fellow, Harvard Univ., Univ. of Illinois; Visiting Researcher, Univ. of Colorado, Univ. of Hawaii, Univ. of Connecticut, Baylor Univ., USA; Chair. TENET Bd, NRF; mem. Rhodes Scholarships Selection Cttee, South Africa Netherlands Programme for Alternative Devt, South African Univ. Vice-Chancellors' Asscn, Higher Educ. South Africa; mem. South African Math. Soc., American Math. Soc., SAUVCA Research Cttee, Nat. Research Foundation; Univ. of Fort Hare Council Prize for best performance by an undergraduate student at the Univ. 1976, Rhodes Scholarship 1978, South Africa/Harvard Fellowship. *Achievements include:* South Africa's first African Rhodes Scholar to graduate from Univ. of Oxford with a doctoral degree in math. 1982. *Publications:* numerous papers in professional journals on Abelian group theory and universal algebra. *Leisure interest:* watching football. *Address:* International Mathematical Union, Secretariat, Hausvogtei-platz 11A, 10117 Berlin, Germany (office). *Telephone:* (30) 20372430 (office). *E-mail:* imu.info@mathunion.org (office). *Website:* www.mathunion.org (office).

NONIS, Christantha (Chris) Nicholas Anthony, FMedSci; Sri Lankan physician, business executive and fmr diplomatist; *Chairman, Mackwoods Group of Companies;* ed trained in medicine at Royal Free Hosp., Univ. of London, Harvard Medical School, postgraduate studies at Addenbrooke's Hosp., Cambridge and Royal Brompton Hosp. and Hammersmith Hosp., London; previously lived in UK for 28 years; succeeded as Chair. of family business, Mackwoods, a Sri Lankan co. est. in 1841 2005–, range of industries, including health care, agribusiness and plantations, infrastructure devt, energy, tourism and financial services, including stockbroking and fund management; High Commr to UK 2011–14; currently Chair. Mackwoods Group of Companies, also Chair. Mackwoods Research Foundation, Mendis-Mackwoods Charity Fund; Trustee, Sriyani Nonis Charitable Trust; mem. Bd Ramphal Centre for Commonwealth Policy Studies, Commonwealth Business Council, Advisory Council of Asia House; fmr mem. Peace and Reconciliation Cttee of Ceylon Chamber of Commerce; mem. Royal Coll. of Physicians. *E-mail:* drchrisnonis@gmail.com. *Website:* drchrisnonis.com.

NOONAN, Michael, BA, HDipEd; Irish politician; b. 21 May 1943, Limerick; m. Florence Knightly (deceased); three s. two d.; ed St Patrick's Teacher Training Coll., Univ. Coll. Dublin; began career as teacher, Crescent Coll., Limerick; mem. Limerick Co. Council 1974–81; mem. Dáil Éireann (Fine Gael) for Limerick East 1981–2011, for Limerick City 2011–, mem. Fine Gael Front Bench 2004–07, Front Bench Spokesman on Finance 1997–2001, Leader of the Opposition 2001–02; Minister of Health 1994–97, of Justice 1982–86, of Industry, Commerce and Trade 1986–87, of Energy 1987, for Finance 2011–17; mem. Fine Gael. *Address:* Fine Gael, 51 Upper Mount St, Dublin D02 W924, Ireland (office). *Telephone:* (1) 6198444 (office). *E-mail:* finegael@finegael.com (office). *Website:* www.finegael.ie (office).

NOOR, Gen. Ata Mohammad; Afghan military commander and government official; b. 5 Jan. 1964, Qalander Shah Colony, Mazar e Sharif; m. 1992; six c.; ed Bakhter High School, studied political science at univ. in Tajikistan; fought Soviet occupation in Mazar-i-Sharif as Mujahed mil. officer under the command of Ustad Zabiullah 1980s, following assassination of Ustad Zabiullah was selected as Deputy Commdr of Mujahed forces that belonged to Zabiullah 1987; his forces captured Balkh from forces of communist govt 1993; rank of Lt-Gen. 1993; apptd Chief of Politics and Mil. of Jamiat e Mili Islami (Islamic Soc.) and mem. High Comm. of Islamic Govt of Afghanistan 1993; apptd Commdr 7th Army Corps 1994; led troops to recapture northern provs 2001; promoted to Gen. 2002; Gov. of Balkh Prov. 2004–14, Acting Gov. 2014–18; umerous honours and awards including Medal of Educ., Ministry of Educ., Shining Star of Educ., Educ. Presidency, title of Man of Peace, Univ. of Mazar e Sharif, honoured by Ministry of Information, Culture and Tourism and by Ministry of Women's Affairs, n. *Address:* c/o Office of the Governor, Mazar-i-Sharif, Balkh Province, Afghanistan (office).

NOOR, Tan Sri Datuk Mohamad Yusof, MA, PhD; Malaysian politician and teacher; b. 5 Feb. 1941, Raja, Terangganu; m.; two c.; ed Islamic Coll., Klang, Selangor, Al Azhar Univ., Ein Shams Univ. and Univ. of Cairo; secondary school teacher 1969–70; Insp. of Secondary Schools, Terengganu State 1970; Prin., Sultan Zainal Abidin Secondary Religious School 1970; Lecturer and Head of Coll., Nat. Univ. of Malaysia 1974, Dean, Faculty of Islamic Studies 1975–79, Deputy Vice-Chancellor for Student Affairs 1980–84; mem. Senate 1987–90; Deputy Minister responsible for Islamic Affairs, Prime Minister's Dept 1984; mem. House of Reps from 1987; mem. Supreme Council, UMNO 1987–; Minister, Prime Minister's Dept 1987; Minister of Public Enterprises 1990–95; apptd to State Govt Meetings 1995–99; Chair. Religious Council for Fed. Territory; fmr Chair. Majlis Amanah Rakyat (Indigenous People's Trust Council), MRSM Besut, Fed. Land Devt Authority –2010, Universiti Sains Islam Malaysia (fmrly Islamic Univ. Malaysia) 2000–12; many other appointments in Islamic and religious field; KMN, PPT, JMN, DPMT, SPMT, DSSA, PSM from various states in Malaysia; Star of al-Uloom wal Funun (Egypt) 1988; Nat. Personality Maal. *Publications:* books and numerous articles in fields of educ. and Islamic affairs. *Address:* c/o Universiti Sains Islam Malaysia, Bandar Baru Nilai, 71800, Nilai, Negeri Sembilan, Malaysia. *E-mail:* helpdesk@usim.edu.my.

NOOR AL-HUSSEIN, HM Queen, BA; Jordanian public servant and international humanitarian activist; b. (Lisa Najeeb Halaby), 23 Aug. 1951, USA; d. of Najeeb Halaby; m. King Hussein I of Jordan 1978 (died 1999); two s.: HRH Prince Hamzah (b. 29 March 1980), HRH Prince Hashim (b. 10 June 1981) two d.: HRH Princess Iman (b. 24 April 1983), HRH Princess Raiyah (b. 9 February 1986); ed attended schools in Los Angeles, Washington, DC and New York City, Concord Acad., Mass, Princeton Univ., USA; architectural and urban planning projects in Australia, Iran and Jordan 1974–78; f. in Jordan: Royal Endowment for Culture and Educ. 1979, annual Arab Children's Congress 1980, annual int. Jerash Festival for Culture and Arts 1981 (also Chair.), Noor Al-Hussein Foundation 1985 (also Chair.), King Hussein Foundation (also Chair.) 1999; Chair. UN Univ. Int. Leadership Inst. (UNU/ILI), Amman; UN Expert Adviser 2004–05; Founding mem. Int. Comm. on Peace and Food 1992; Pres. United World Colls 1995; mem. Int. Eye Foundation, Int. Council Near East Foundation, Int. Comm. on Missing Persons, The Mentor Foundation, Hunger Project; Trustee, Refugees International, Conservation International, WWF International, Aspen Inst. 2004–; Adviser, Women Waging Peace and Seeds of Peace; Patron Royal Soc. for the Conservation of Nature, World Conservation Union 1988, Int. Campaign to Ban Landmines, Landmine Survivors Network (also Chair.) 1998, Int. Alert's Women and Peace-building Campaign, Council of Women World Leaders' Advisory Group 2004–; Hon. Pres. Jordan Red Crescent, Birdlife International 1996–2004 (Hon. Pres. Emer. 2004–); Hon. Chair. Petra Nat. Trust, SOS Children's Asscn, McGill Middle East Program in Civil Society and Peace Building; Kt Grand Cordon with Collar, Order of al-Hussein bin Ali, Kt Grand Cordon, Supreme Order of the Renaissance, Kt Grand Cordon, Order of the Star of Jordan; Grand Cross of the Decoration of Honour for Services to the Repub. of Austria, Gold, Dame Grand Cross, Order of the Most Esteemed Family Order of Brunei, First Class, Kt Grand Cross, Order of the Elephant (Denmark), Grand Cross, Order of the Virtues, Supreme Class (Egypt), Grand Croix, Légion d'honneur, Grand Cross, Order of Merit of the Italian Repub., Dame Grand Cross, Order of Charles III (Spain), Dame Grand Cross, Order of Isabella the Catholic (Spain), Mem. Grand Cross, Order of the Seraphim (Sweden), Dame Grand Cross, Venerable Order of St John (UK); numerous hon. doctorates, numerous int. awards and decorations for the promotion educ., culture, women and children's welfare, sustainable community devt, environmental conservation, human rights, conflict resolution, cross-cultural understanding and world peace, Woodrow Wilson Award 2015. *Publications:* Hussein of Jordan 2000, Leap of Faith: Memoirs of an Unexpected Life 2002. *Leisure interests:* skiing, water skiing, tennis, horse riding, reading, gardening, photography, biking, sailing. *Address:* Office of Her Majesty Queen Noor, Bab Al Salam Palace, Amman, Jordan. *Telephone:* (6) 551-5191. *Fax:* (6) 464-7961. *E-mail:* noor@queennoor.jo. *Website:* www.noor.gov.jo.

NOOR YACOB, Y.Bhg Dato' Muhamad; Malaysian diplomatist, government official and international organization official; *Chairman, Malaysia Automotive Institute;* ed Univ. of Malaya, Univ. of Wisconsin and Advanced Man. Programme, Harvard Business School, USA; Asst Sec., Int. Affairs Div., Ministry of Plantation Industry and Commodities 1974–84; Trade Commr (Commodities), Malaysian High Comm., London 1984–87; Prin. Asst Sec., Ministry of Plantation Industry and Commodities 1987–96; Head of Planning and Policy Research and Chief Information Officer, Ministry of Human Resources 1996–2001, concurrently Dir of Electronic Labour Exchange Project; Deputy Sec.-Gen., Ministry of Women, Family and Community Devt 2001–03; Amb. and Perm. Rep. to WTO, Geneva 2003–09, Chair. WTO Negotiating Group on Trade Facilitation 2004–05, Chair. WTO Dispute Settlement Body 2006, Chair. Gen. Council 2007; Exec. Dir APEC 2010–12; currently Chair. Malaysia Automotive Inst.; also currently Dir, Asia Pacific Centre for Econ. Diplomacy; Adjunct Prof., Inst. of Malaysian and Int. Studies, Universiti Kebangsaan Malaysia; fmr Chair. Exec. Cttee Int. Rubber Study Group, Man. Bd Int. Tin Research Inst.; fmr Vice-Chair. Int. Cocoa Council; Excellent Public Service Award, Ministry of Plantation Industry and Commodities 1995, Kesatria Mangku Negara, HM King of Malaysia 1996, Darjah Indera Mahkota Pahang (carries the title Dato'), HRH Sultan of Pahang 2006, Johan Mangku Negara, HM King of Malaysia 2006. *Address:* Office of the Chairman, Malaysia Automotive Institute, Office No.12, Jalan Menara U8/6 Bukit Jelutong, 40150, Shah Alam, Selangor, Malaysia (office). *Telephone:* (11) 12284803 (office). *E-mail:* muhdnoor@gmail.com (office). *Website:* www.mai.org.my (office).

NOORISTANI, Muhammad Yosuf, MA, PhD; Afghan government official; b. 1948; ed Kabul Univ., Arizona State Univ., USA; fmr Asst Prof. of Anthropology, Kabul Univ.; Researcher, Arizona State Univ. 1975–78; Sr Cultural Specialist, US Information Service Afghan Program, Peshawar 1988–90; Project Coordinator, Basic Educ. for Afghan Refugees, Peshawar, Pakistan 1992–96; consultant and coordinator for several research and humanitarian aid orgs –2001; Chief of Media and Spokesman for Interim Admin, Kabul Jan.–June 2001; Minister of Irrigation and Environment during first Interim Admin 2001–02; Deputy Minister of Defence 2005–08; Gov. Herat Prov. 2009–10; Chair. Independent Election Comm. 2013–16 (resgnd); Founding mem. Writers' Union of Free Afghanistan 1985–88; Dr hc (Arizona State Univ.) 2003.

NOOTEBOOM, Cornelis (Cees) Johannes Jacobus Maria; Dutch writer and poet; b. 31 July 1933, The Hague; m. 1st Fanny Lichtveld 1957 (divorced); m. 2nd Simone Sassen; fmrly worked in banking; worked for Elsevier magazine 1957–60, de Volkskrant newspaper 1961–68; Travel Ed., Avenue; Hon. mem. Modern Language Asscn, USA 1997; Chevalier, Légion d'honneur 1991, Commdr, Ordre des Arts et des Lettres; Hon. DLitt (Katholieke Universiteit Brussel) 1998, Dr hc (Freie Universität Berlin) 2008; Prijs van de dagbladjournalistiek 1969, Cestoda-prijs 1982, Preis zum 3 Oktober 1990, Constantijn Huygensprijs 1992, Hugo Ball Preis 1993, Aristeion Prijs 1993, Premio Grinzane Cavour 1994, Dirk Martens-prijs 1994, Goethe-prijs 2002, Oostenrijkse staatsprijs 2002, P. C. Hooftprijs 2004, Prijs der Nederlandse Letteren 2009. *Plays include:* De zwanen van de Theems (ANV-Visser Neerlandia-prijs 1960) 1959, Gyges en Kandaules. Een konings-drama 1982. *Publications include:* fiction: Philip en de anderen (Anne Frank-prijs 1957) 1954, De verliefde gevangene 1958, De koning is dood 1961, De ridder is gestorven (Lucy B. en C. W. van der Hoogtprijs 1963) 1963, Rituelen (F. Bordewijkprijs 1981, Mobil Pegasus Literatuurprijs 1982) 1980, Een lied van schijn en wezen 1981, Mokusei 1982, In Nederland (Multatuliprijs 1985) 1984, De Boeddha achter de schutting. Aan de oever van de Chaophraya 1986, Ina Rilke 1991, Allerzielen 1998, Paradijs Verloren 2004, 's Nachts kommen de vossen (Goulden Uil Prize 2010) 2009, Roads to Berlin 2012; poetry: De doden zoeken een huis 1956, Koude gedichten 1959, Het zwarte gedicht 1960, Ibicenzer gedicht (Poëzieprijs van de gemeente Amsterdam) 1960, Gesloten gedichten (Poëzieprijs van de gemeente Amsterdam 1965) 1964, Gemaakte gedichten 1970, Open als een schelp – dicht als een steen (Jan Campertprijs 1978) 1978, Aas 1982, Vuurtijd, Ijstijd. Gedichten 1955–1983 1984, Het gezicht van het oog 1989, Zo kon het zijn (Gedichtendagprijzen 2000) 1999, Bitterzoet, honderd gedichten van vroeger en zeventien nieuwe 2000, Met andere woorden 2004, Die schlafenden Götter 2005; non-fiction: Een middag in Bruay 1963, Een nacht in Tunesië 1965, Een ochtend in Bahia 1968, De Parijse beroerte 1968, Bitter Bolivia, Maanland Mali 1971, Een avond in Isfahan 1978, Waar je gevallen bent, blijf je 1983, De zucht naar het Westen 1985, De wereld een reiziger 1989, Berlijnse notities 1990, Vreemd water 1991, Het volgende verhaal 1991, De omweg naar Santiago (Preis für Reiseliter-atur des Landes Tirol 1996) 1992, Zurbaránk 1992, De ontvoering van Europa (essay) 1993, De koning van Suriname 1993, Van de lente de dauw. Oosterse reizen 1995, De filosoof zonder ogen: Europese reizen 1997, Terugkeer naar Berlijn 1997, Nootebooms Hotel 2002, Het geluid van Aijn naam. Reizen door de Islamitische wereld 2005, Rode regen 2007, Verleden als eigenschap. Kronieken 1961/1968

2008, Berlin 1989/2009 2009, Het raadsel van het licht 2009, Scheepsjournaal 2010, Brieven aan Poseidon 2012. *Address:* c/o De Bezige Bij, PO Box 75184, 1070 AD Amsterdam; c/o Arbeiderspers, Herengracht 370-372, 1016 CH Amsterdam, The Netherlands. *E-mail:* info@debezigebij.nl; *Website:* www.debezigebij.nl; www .ceesnooteboom.com.

NOOYI, Indra K., BS, MBA, MPPM; Indian/American business executive; b. 28 Oct. 1955, Chennai, India; m. Rajkishan Nooyi 1981; two d.; ed Madras Christian Coll., Indian Inst. of Man., Calcutta, Yale School of Man.; early position as Product Man., Johnson & Johnson, Mettur Beardsell Ltd; spent six years at Boston Consulting Group; fmr Pres. and Dir of Corp. Strategy and Planning, Motorola; Sr Vice-Pres. of Strategic Planning and Strategic Markets, Asea Brown Boveri 1990–94; Sr Vice-Pres. PepsiCo Inc. 1994–2001, Chief Financial Officer 2000–06, Pres. 2001–06, CEO 2006–18, Chair. 2007–19, mem. Bd of Dirs PepsiCo, PepsiCo Foundation; Chair. USA-India Business Council 2008–; apptd to US-India CEO Forum by Pres. Obama; mem. Pres.'s Strategic and Policy Forum Jan.–Aug. 2017; mem. Bd of Dirs Schlumberger Ltd 2015–, Amazon.com, Inc. 2019–; mem. Bd US-China Business Council, US-India Business Council, The Consumer Goods Forum, Catalyst, Lincoln Center for the Performing Arts, The Peterson Inst. for Inst. of Int. Econs, Grocery Mfrs Asscn, Tsinghua Univ.; Successor Fellow, The Yale Corpn 2002; Fellow, American Acad. of Arts and Sciences 2008; Hon. LLD (Babson Coll.) 2004, (Wake Forest Univ., Univ. of Warwick, Miami Univ.) 2011; Dr hc (New York Univ.) 2008, (Duke Univ.) 2009, (North Carolina State Univ.) 2013, (Cranfield Univ.) 2018; Woman Pioneer Award 2003, Padma Bhushan Award 2007, Barnard Medal of Honor, Barnard Coll. 2019, CEO of the Year, Global Supply Chain Leaders Group 2009, Ellis Island Medal of Honor 2017. *Address:* c/o PepsiCo Inc., 700 Anderson Hill Road, Purchase, NY 10577, USA (office). *Telephone:* (914) 253-2000 (office). *Website:* www.pepsico.com (office).

NORBU, Lyonpo Wangdi, BEcons; Bhutanese politician and civil servant; b. 15 June 1954, Galing, Trashigang Dist; m. Aum Pem Zangmo; one s. one d.; ed Scotch Coll., Australia, Univ. of Western Australia; joined Ministry of Finance 1977, has held various posts including Dir Dept of Budget and Accounts, Auditor Gen. Royal Audit Authority, Finance Sec., Minister of Finance 2003–07 (resgnd), 2008–13; mem. Nat. Ass. (Druk Phuensum Tshogpa) from Bartsham-Shongphu constituency 2008–; fmr Chair. Royal Monetary Authority, Chair. 2010–11; Vice-Chair. Gross Nat. Happiness Comm.; Red Scarf (Dasho) 1998, Orange Scarf (Lyonpo) 2003. *Address:* National Assembly, Gyelyong Tshokhang, POB 139, Thimphu, Bhutan (office). *Telephone:* (2) 336907 (office). *E-mail:* wnorbu@nab.gov.bt (office). *Website:* www.nab.gov.bt (office).

NORDAL, Salvör, BA, MPh, PhD; Icelandic academic; *Ombudsman for Children;* b. 21 Nov. 1962, Reykjavik; two s.; ed Univ. of Iceland, Univ. of Stirling, UK, Univ. of Calgary, Canada; journalist, Morgunbladid (newspaper) 1984–85; Gen. Man. Reykjavík Arts Festival and Reykjavík Film Festival 1985–86, Iceland Ballet 1989–94; Lecturer (part-time), Dept of Ethics, Univ. of Iceland 1998, Dir Centre for Ethics 2001–17, Asst Prof. in Philosophy 2015–17; Ombudsman for Children 2017–; Co-Ed. Hugur, Journal of the Icelandic Philosophy Society 2000–02; mem. Nat. Animal Research Cttee 2001–07, Univ. Hospital Ethics Cttee 2004–08, Icelandic Journalists Asscn Ethics Cttee 2005, Nat. Bioethics Cttee 2008; mem. Working Group on Ethics, Special Investigation Comm. of Icelandic Parl. 2009–10; mem. Constitutional Council (Stjórnlagaráð) 2010–, Chair. 2011–13; Chair. Reykjavík Acad. 2000–01, Art Gallery of Univ. of Iceland; Ombudsman for Children 2017–; mem. Nordic Bioethics Cttee 2011–16; mem. Bd Hagar hf Retail co. *Publications:* numerous essays and articles in professional journals. *Address:* Ombudsman for Children, Kringlan 1, 103 Reykjavík, Iceland (office). *Telephone:* 5528999 (office). *E-mail:* salvorn@barn.is (office). *Website:* www.barn.is (office).

NORDBERG, Bert, BElecEng; Swedish business executive; *Chairman, Vestas Wind Systems A/S;* b. 1956, Malmö; ed Malmö Univ., courses in Int. Man., Marketing and Finance, Institut Européen d'Admin des Affaires (INSEAD), France; engineer in Swedish Marines, Berga 1980; various positions with Data General Corpn and Digital Equipment Corpn, Sweden 1985–96; Head of Enterprise Services, Ericsson 1996–99, Exec. Vice-Pres. Ericsson Services 1999–2000, apptd Exec. Vice-Pres. Div. Global Services July 2000, Head of Business Unit Global Services 2001–02, Head of Business Unit Systems 2002–03, Sr Vice-Pres. Group Function Sales and Marketing Jan.–April 2004, Exec. Vice-Pres. Group Function Sales and Marketing, Telefonaktiebolaget LM Ericsson 2004–07, Exec. Vice-Pres. and Head of Ericsson Silicon Valley 2008–09, Head of Sales and Marketing and Exec. Vice-Pres. Ericsson Group cos Redback and Entrisphere –2008, Exec. Vice-Pres. and Chair. 2008–09, Pres. and CEO Sony Ericsson 2009–12, Chair. Sony Mobile May–Dec. 2012; Chair., Vestas Wind Systems A/S 2016–; Litos reprotryck i Malmo AB; mem. Bd Remuneration Cttee, Saab 2016–. *Address:* Vestas Wind Systems, Hedeager 42, 8200 Aarhus N, Denmark (office). *Telephone:* 97-30-00-00 (office). *Website:* www.vestas.com (office).

NORDENBERG, Mark A., BA, JD; American teacher, university administrator and academic; *Chairman, Institute of Politics, University of Pittsburgh;* b. Duluth, Minn.; m. Dr Nikki Pirillo Nordenberg; two s. one d.; ed Thiel Coll., Univ. of Wisconsin Law School; joined Law Faculty, Univ. of Pittsburgh 1977, Dean School of Law 1985–93, Interim Provost and Sr Vice-Chancellor for Academic Affairs 1993–94, apptd Distinguished Service Prof. of Law 1994, Interim Chancellor 1995, Chancellor and CEO Univ. of Pittsburgh 1996–2013, now Chancellor Emer. and Chair. Inst. of Politics; Chair. Citizens Advisory Cttee on Efficiency and Effectiveness of City-County Govt; fmr mem. US Advisory Cttee on Civil Rules, Pa Civil Procedural Rules Cttee; Founding mem. Technology Collaborative, Pittsburgh Life Sciences Greenhouse (Co-Chair. both bds); mem. Asscn of American Univs, Pa Asscn of Colls and Univs, Univ. of Pittsburgh Medical Center, Allegheny Conf. on Community Devt, Pittsburgh Council on Higher Educ., Mellon Financial Corpn, Pittsburgh Post-Gazette Dapper Dan Charities, Pittsburgh-Wuhan Friendship Cttee Inc.; Univ. of Pittsburgh School of Law's Excellence-in-Teaching Award (first recipient) 1984, Chancellor's Distinguished Teaching Award 1985, Vectors Pittsburgh Person of the Year in Educ. 1997, selected by Vectors Pittsburgh as Pittsburgh's Overall Person of the Year 1998, Person of Vision Award, Pittsburgh Vision Services 2003, endowed Chancellor Mark A. Nordenberg Univ. Chair (est. to honour his 10 years of leadership) 2005, Chief Exec. Leadership Award, Council for Advancement and Support of Educ., District II 2006, Nellie Leadership Award, Three Rivers Youth 2006, Kesher Award, Edward and Rose Berman Hillel Jewish

Univ. Center (co-recipient) 2006, Presidential Leadership Award, Gordie Foundation 2009, Louis and Barbara Thiel Distinguished Service Award, Thiel Coll. 2014, Chairman's Award, Carnegie Science Center (co-recipient) 2014. *Publications:* has published books, articles and reports on civil litigation. *Address:* Institute of Politics, University of Pittsburgh, 4227 Fifth Avenue, 710 Alumni Hall, 260, Pittsburgh, PA 15260, USA (office). *Telephone:* (412) 624-1837 (office). *E-mail:* norden@pitt.edu (office). *Website:* www.iop.pitt.edu (office).

NORDH, Sture, BPA; Swedish trade union official; b. 3 June 1952, Skellefteå; m. Gudrun Nordh (née Nygren); one s. one d.; ed Univ. of Umeå; Union Sec. Swedish Union of Local Govt Employees (SKTF) 1975–79, Gen. Sec. 1979–83, Pres. 1983–96; State Sec. Ministry of Labour 1996–98; Deputy Dir-Gen. Nat. Inst. of Working Life 1999; Pres. Swedish Confed. of Professional Employees (TCO) 1999–2011. *Publication:* Future of the Welfare State (co-author with Bengt Westerberg). *Leisure interests:* skiing, literature. *Address:* Gyllenstiernsg. 10, 115 26 Stockholm, Sweden. *Telephone:* (8) 661-34-23. *Fax:* (8) 662-16-75. *E-mail:* sture .nordh@telia.com.

NORDHAGEN, Per Jonas, DPhil; Norwegian professor of history of art; *Professor Emeritus, University of Bergen;* b. 30 Oct. 1929, Bergen; s. of Rolf Nordhagen and Elisabeth M. Myhre; m. Inger K. Noss 1978; one s. four d.; ed Univ. of Oslo; Lecturer, Univ. of Oslo 1962; Assoc. Prof., Univ. of Bergen 1969; Dir Norwegian Inst. Rome 1973; Sr Lecturer, Univ. of Oslo 1977; Prof. of History of Art, Univ. of Bergen 1986–2000, Prof. Emer. 2000–; mem. Norwegian Acad. of Sciences. *Publications:* The Frescoes of John VII (705–707 AD) in S. Maria Antiqua, Rome 1968, Frescoes of the Seventh Century 1978, Collected Papers in the History of Byzantine and Early Medieval Art 1990, The Wooden Architecture of Bergen 1994, The Technique of Early Christian and Byzantine Mosaics 1997, Roberto Longhi: Connoisseurship as a Science 1999, Architecture of Norway (AD 1000–1900) 2003, Iconoclasm: Rupture or Interlude? 2005, Ernst Kitzinger's Thesis on the 'Perennial Hellenism' of Constantinople 2007, The Birth of the Byzantine Cross-Domed Church as a Receptacle for Pictorial Decoration 2011, Icons Before Iconoclasm 2011, In the Iconographer's Studio 2015, John VII and Monotheletic Iconography 2016, Byzantium, The Enigmatic 7th Century 2017, Three Botanical Excursions with my Father 2017. *Leisure interests:* skiing, hiking, books, botany. *Address:* Heien 6, 5037 Bergen, Norway. *E-mail:* pjnordhagen@ gmail.com.

NORDLUND, Roger; Åland Islands politician; *Deputy Chairman (Vice-Lantråd) of the Landskapsregering;* b. 19 Nov. 1957; mem. Lagting (Åland Parl.) 1983–87, Ålands landskapsstyrelse, sedan 2004; Chair. Åländsk Ungcenter 1979–85, Åländsk Center (Åland Centre Party) 1986–87, 1997–; Minister of Educ. and Culture 1991–95; Deputy Chair. Landskapsregering (Deputy Premier—Vice-lantråd) 1995–99, 2011–, Chair. (Premier—Lantråd) 1999–2007. *Address:* Pb 1060, 22111 Mariehamn, Åland Islands, Gulf of Bothnia, Finland (office). *Telephone:* (18) 25370 (office). *Fax:* (18) 19155 (office). *E-mail:* roger.nordlund@ regeringen.ax (office). *Website:* www.regeringen.ax (office).

NORDMANN, François, LLB; Swiss diplomatist (retd); b. 13 May 1942, Fribourg; m. Myriam Nordmann; ed Univs of Fribourg and Geneva; joined Dept of Foreign Affairs 1971, mem. Political Secr. and Diplomatic Sec., Councillor, Observer Mission to UN 1980–84, Amb. to Guatemala (also accred to Costa Rica, Honduras, Nicaragua, El Salvador, Panama) 1984–87, Head, Perm. Del. to UNESCO, Paris 1987–94, Dir Int. Orgs 1992–94, Amb. to UK 1994–99, Amb. and Perm. Rep. to Int. Orgs, Geneva 1999–2002; Amb. and Perm. Rep. to UN, New York 2002–04, Amb. to France 2004–07; Chair. Festival international de films de Fribourg 2015–; mem. Advisory Bd, Centre for Int. Governance, Geneva. *Address:* Festival International de Films de Fribourg, Esplanade de l'Ancienne-Gare 3, Case postale 550, 1701 Fribourg, Switzerland. *E-mail:* info@fiff.ch. *Website:* www.fiff.ch.

NORDSTRÖM, Anders, MD; Swedish physician and international organization official; b. 9 March 1960; m.; two c.; ed Karolinska Institut; worked with Swedish Red Cross in Cambodia and Int. Cttee of the Red Cross in Iran; worked for Swedish Int. Devt Co-operation Agency (SIDA) for 12 years, including three years as Regional Advisor, Zambia and four years as Head of Health Div., Stockholm; Interim Exec. Dir Global Fund to Fight AIDS, Tuberculosis and Malaria 2002; Asst Dir-Gen. for Gen. Man., WHO 2003–06, Acting Dir-Gen. 2006–07; Dir-Gen. Swedish Int. Devt Cooperation Agency (Sida) 2008–10; Amb. for Global Health 2012–15.

NORDSTRÖM, Lars G.; Swedish business executive; *Chairman, Vattenfall AB;* b. 1943; ed Uppsala Univ.; with Skandinaviska Enskilda Banken 1970–93, Exec. Vice-Pres. 1989–93; Exec. Vice-Pres. and mem. Group Exec. Man., Nordbanken 1993–98, CEO 1998–2000, Exec. Vice-Pres. and mem. Group Exec. Bd, MeritaNordbanken 1998–99; Exec. Vice-Pres. and mem. Group Exec. Cttee, Nordic Baltic Holding 1999–2000; Exec. Vice-Pres. and Head of Retail Banking, Nordea 2000–02, mem. Group Exec. Man. 2000–02, Pres. and Group CEO 2002–07, Vice Chair. Bd of Dirs Nordea Bank Abp 2017–; Group CEO and Pres. Posten Norden AB 2008–11; mem. Bd of Dirs and Chair. Vattenfall AB 2011–; mem. Bd of Dirs TeliaSonera 2006–10; fmr Chair. Finnish-Swedish Chamber of Commerce; mem. Bd of Dirs Viking Line Abp 2006–, Swedish-American Chamber of Commerce; Chair. Swedish Royal Opera 2005–09; fmr mem. Royal Swedish Acad. of Eng Sciences. *Address:* Vattenfall AB, Evenemangsgatan 13, 169 79 Solna, Sweden (office). *Telephone:* (8) 739-50-00 (office). *Fax:* (8) 17-85-06 (office). *E-mail:* press@ vattenfall.com (office). *Website:* www.vattenfall.com (office).

NORMAN, Archie John, BA, MA, MBA; British business executive and fmr politician; b. 1 May 1954, London; s. of Archibald Percy Norman and Aleida Elizabeth Norman; m. Vanessa Peet 1982; one d.; ed Univ. of Minnesota, USA, Emmanuel Coll. Cambridge, Harvard Business School USA; with Citibank N.A. 1975–77; Partner, McKinsey & Co. Inc. 1984–86; Group Finance Dir Kingfisher PLC 1986–91; Chief Exec. Asda Group PLC 1991–96, Chair. 1996–97; MP for Tunbridge Wells 1997–2005; Shadow Foreign Affairs Post 1999–2000; Shadow Spokesman on Environment, Transport and the Regions 2000–01; Vice-Chair. Conservative Party 1997–98, Chief Exec. and Deputy Chair. 1998–99; Chair. ITV plc 2010–16; Deputy Chair. Coles Group, Australia 2007–; Chair.-Desig. Marks & Spencer (2017–); Chair. (non-exec.) French PLC 1999–2001, Energis 2002–05, HSS Hire Group 2007–; Sr Adviser, Lazard 2004–; Founder and Chair. Aurigo Management Partners LLP (pvt. equity firm) 2006–; Adviser to Bd of Wesfarmers

2009–; mem. Bd of Dirs (non-exec.) Geest 1988–91, British Rail 1992–94, Railtrack 1994–2000, Holmes Place 2003–06; UK Retailer of the Year 1995, Yorks. Businessman of the Year 1995, Marketing Soc. Hall of Fame 1996, Inst. of Turnaround Professionals Lifetime Achievement Award 2010. *Leisure interests:* farming, music, opera, tennis, football. *Address:* Aurigo Management Partners, LLC, 11 St Margarets Drive, Twickenham, Middlesex, TW1 1QL, England.

NORMAN, Donald (Don) A., BS, MS, PhD; American design consultant, author and academic; *Co-founder and Principal, Nielsen Norman Group;* b. 25 Dec. 1935, New York, NY; s. of Noah N. Norman and Miriam F. Norman; m. Julie J. Norman; two s. one d.; ed Massachusetts Inst. of Tech., Univ. of Pennsylvania; Jr Faculty mem. Center for Cognitive Studies, Harvard Univ.; joined Dept of Psychology, Univ. of California, San Diego, fmr Chair. Dept of Psychology and Dept of Cognitive Science, now Prof. Emer. of Cognitive Science (recalled) and Dir Design Lab; acted as consultant on Three Mile Island nuclear accident, realized his unique combination of eng and psychology could be combined in study of design; research moved to study of aviation safety and computers, then to everyday items; Exec. at Apple Computer (Vice-Pres. Advanced Tech. Group), Hewlett-Packard and Cardean Learning Systems, UNext; Breed Prof. Emer. of Design and Prof. of Electrical Eng and Computer Science, Northwestern Univ., Evanston, Illinois; currently Dir Design Lab., Univ. of California, San Diego; fmr Visiting Distinguished Prof. of Design, Korea Advanced Inst. of Science and Tech. (KAIST), Daejeon, S Korea; Co-founder and Prin., Nielsen Norman Group, Palo Alto, Calif.; Founding mem. and Fellow, Cognitive Science Soc.; Charter Fellow, American Psychological Soc.; Fellow, American Acad. of Arts and Sciences, Asscn for Computational Machinery, American Psychological Asscn, Design Research Soc.; mem. Industrial Design Soc. of America, Nat. Acad. of Eng; Dr hc (Univ. of Padua), (Tech. Univ. of Delft), (Univ. of San Marino); Franklin V. Taylor Award, American Psychological Asscn, Presidential Citation and Lifetime Achievement Award, ACM Human-Computer Interaction Group, Benjamin Franklin Medal in Computer and Cognitive Science, The Franklin Inst. 2006. *Publications include:* Human Information Processing: An Introduction to Psychology (co-author) 1975, Memory and Attention 1977, Learning and Memory 1982, Direct Manipulation Interfaces (co-author) 1985, User Centered System Design: New Perspectives on Human-Computer Interaction (co-ed) 1986, The Design of Everyday Things (originally under the title The Psychology of Everyday Things) 1988 (revised edn 2013), Turn Signals Are the Facial Expressions of Automobiles 1992, Things That Make Us Smart: Defending Human Attributes in the Age of the Machine 1993, The Invisible Computer: Why Good Products Can Fail, the Personal Computer Is So Complex and Information Appliances Are the Solution 1999, Emotional Design 2003, The Design of Future Things 2007, Living with Complexity 2011. *E-mail:* dnorman@ucsd.edu (office). *Website:* www.jnd.org (office).

NORMAN, Gregory (Greg) John, AO; Australian professional golfer; *Chairman and CEO, Great White Shark Enterprises, Inc.;* b. 10 Feb. 1955, Queensland; s. of M. Norman; m. Laura Andrassy 1981 (divorced 2006); one s. one d.; m. Chris Evert 2008 (divorced 2010); ed Townsville Grammar School, High School, Aspley, Queensland; turned professional 1976; won West Lake Classic, Australia 1976, Martini Int., Kuzuhz Int., Japan 1977, NSW Open, South Seas Classic, Fiji 1978, Martini Int., Hong Kong Open 1979, Australian Open, French Open, Scandinavian Open 1980, Australian Masters, Martini Int., Dunlop Masters 1981, Dunlop Masters, State Express Classic, Benson & Hedges Int. 1982, Australian Masters, Nat. Panasonic NSW Open, Hong Kong Open, Cannes Invitational, Suntory World Match Play Championship 1983, Canadian Open, Victorian Open, Australian Masters, Toshiba Australian PGA Championship 1984, Toshiba Australian PGA Championship, Nat. Panasonic Australian Open 1985, European Open, British Open, Suntory World Matchplay Championship, Panasonic-Las Vegas Invitational, Kemper Open 1986, Australian Masters, Nat. Panasonic Australian Open 1987, Palm Meadows Cup, Australia, PGA Nat. Tournament Players Championship, Australia, Panasonic NSW Open, Lancia Italian Open 1988, Australian Masters, PGA Nat. Tournament Players Championship 1989, Australian Masters, The Memorial Tournament 1990, Canadian Open 1992, British Open, Taiheyo Masters, Japan 1993, Johnnie Walker Asian Classic, The Players Championship 1994, Australian Open, Memorial Tournament, Canon Greater Hartford Open 1995, Doral-Ryder Open, S African Open 1996, World Championship, FedEx St Jude Classic 1997, Greg Norman Holden Int. 1998, Franklin Templeton Shootout 1998, Skins Game 2001; apptd Australian Amb. for Sport by Prime Minister 1998; currently Chair. and CEO Great White Shark Enterprises, Inc.; mem. Bd GPS Industries, LLC 2003–15; mem. Advisory Bd Falconhead Capital, LLC; inducted into World Golf Hall of Fame 2001. *Publications:* My Story 1983, Shark Attack 1988, Greg Norman's Instant Lessons 1993, Greg Norman's Better Golf 1994. *Leisure interests:* family, fishing, hunting, scuba diving. *Address:* Great White Shark Enterprise Inc., 2041 Vista Parkway, Level 2, West Palm Beach, FL 33411, USA. *Telephone:* (561) 640-7000 (office). *Website:* www.shark.com (office).

NORMAN, Jessye, MMus; American singer (soprano); b. 15 Sept. 1945, Augusta, Ga; d. of Silas Norman and Janie Norman (née King); ed Howard Univ., Peabody Conservatory, Univ. of Michigan; operatic debut, Deutsche Oper Berlin 1969; debut La Scala, Milan 1972, Royal Opera House, Covent Garden 1972; American operatic debut, Hollywood Bowl 1972; performer at Lincoln Center 1973–; tours in N and S America, Europe, Middle East, Australia; int. festivals including Aix-en-Provence, Aldeburgh, Berliner Festwochen, Edin., Flanders, Helsinki, Lucerne, Salzburg, Tanglewood, Spoleto, Hollywood Bowl, Ravinia; with leading orchestras from USA, UK, Israel, Australia; other performances include La Voix Humaine, Orchestre nat. de Lyon 2002; Founder and Pres. L'Orchidée Inc.; mem. Bd of Dirs Ms. Foundation, New York Botanical Garden, Nat. Music Foundation, City-Meals-on-Wheels (New York City); Trustee, Paine Coll., Augusta, Ga; spokesperson for Partnership for the Homeless; Fellow, American Acad. of Arts and Sciences; Commdr des Arts et des Lettres 1984; more than 30 hon. degrees including Hon. MusDoc (Howard) 1982, (Univ. of the South, Sewance) 1984, (Univ. of Michigan) 1987, (Edinburgh) 1989; Hon. DMus (Cambridge) 1989; Vocal Winner, Int. Musikwettbewerb, Bayerischer Rundfunk (Germany) 1968, Grand Prix du Disque (Acad. du Disque Français) 1973, 1976, 1977, 1982; Deutsche Schallplatten Preis für Euryanthe 1975; Cigale d'Or (Aix-en-Provence Festival) 1977; Grammy Award 1980, 1982, 1985, Musician of the Year (Musical America) 1982, IRCAM Record Award 1982, Alumna Award (Univ. of Michigan) 1982, Edison Award for Lifetime Achievement, Amsterdam 2006, Grammy Lifetime Achievement Award 2006, Nat. Medal of Arts 2009, NAACP Spingarn Award 2013, Wolf Prize in Arts 2015, Glenn Gould Prize 2018. *Publication:* Stand Up Straight and Sing! 2014. *Leisure interests:* reading, cooking, houseplant growing, fashion designing. *Address:* 244 Mount Airy Road West, Croton On Hudson, NY 10520-3311, USA.

NORMAN, Marsha, BA, MA; American playwright and writer; *Co-director of Playwrights Program, Juilliard School;* b. 21 Sept. 1947, Louisville, Ky; d. of Billie Williams and Bertha Conley; m. 1st Michael Norman 1969 (divorced 1974); m. 2nd Dann C. Byck Jr 1978 (divorced); m. 3rd Timothy Dykman 1987; one s. one d.; ed Agnes Scott Coll. and Univ. of Louisville; Rockefeller Playwright-in-Residence grantee 1979–80; American Acad. and Inst. for Arts and Letters grantee; Instructor, MFA in Theatre Program, Stony Brook Southampton, State Univ. of New York at Stony Brook; currently Co-Dir of Playwrights Program, Juilliard School; fmr Vice-Pres. Dramatists Guild of America; Co-founder The Lilly Awards; mem. Bd of Dirs, Writers Guild of America East Foundation; Margo Jones Award (with Christopher Durang) 2003–04, inducted into Coll. of Arts and Sciences Hall of Honor, Univ. of Louisville 2007, William Inge Distinguished Lifetime Achievement in Theatre Award 2011, inducted into Theatre Hall of Fame 2016, Career Achievement Award, Dramatists Guild of America 2016, Nat. Endowment for the Arts, Literature Award, American Acad. and Inst. of Arts and Letters, Lifetime Achievement Award, Guild Hall Acad. of Arts and Letters. *Plays include:* Getting Out (Newsday Oppenheimer Award) 1977, Third and Oak 1978, Circus Valentine 1979, Merry Christmas 1979, The Holdup 1980, 'Night, Mother (Pulitzer Prize for Drama 1983) 1982, Traveler in the Dark 1984, The Fortune Teller 1987, Sarah and Abraham 1987, The Secret Garden (musical) (Tony Award 1991, Drama Desk Award for Outstanding Book of a Musical) 1991, D. Boone 1991–92, Loving Daniel Boone 1992, The Red Shoes 1992, Trudy Blues 1995, Love's Fire 1998, 140 1998, Last Dance 2003, The Color Purple (musical) (Tony Award) 2005, The Master Butchers Singing Club 2010. *Television plays:* It's the Willingness 1978, In Trouble at Fifteen 1980, The Laundromat 1985, The Pool Hall 1989, Face of a Stranger 1991. *Publication:* The Fortune Teller (novel) 1987. *Address:* c/o John Buzzetti, WME Entertainment, 9601 Wilshire Boulevard, Beverly Hills, CA 90210-5213, USA (office); MFA in Theatre Program, Stony Brook Southampton, Chancellors Hall, 239 Montauk Highway, Southampton, NY 11968, USA (office). *Telephone:* (310) 285-9000 (office); (631) 632-5071 (office). *Fax:* (310) 285-9010 (office). *Website:* www.wma.com (office); www.stonybrook.edu/southampton/mfa/theatre (office); www.juilliard.edu (office); www.marshanorman.com. *E-mail:* mnorman@juilliard.edu (office); info@marshanorman.com.

NORODOM RANARIDDH, Prince; Cambodian politician; b. 2 Jan. 1944; s. of King Norodom Sihanouk; m. 1968; two s. one d.; ed Univ. of Aix-Marseilles, France; worked with resistance leaders during early 1970s, arrested, acquitted on charges of engaging in terrorism 1971, returned to France in mid-1970s to teach at alma mater; Supreme Commander ANS 1985, C-in-C and Chief of Staff 1986; Pres. United Nat. Front for an Ind., Neutral, Peaceful and Co-operative Cambodia (FUNCINPEC); Hon. Pres. Cambodian Royalist Youth Movement; Co-Chair. Provisional Nat. Govt of Cambodia, also Minister of Nat. Defence, Interior and Nat. Security June–Sept. 1993; mem. Nat. Ass. 1993 (fmr Pres.); Co-Prime Minister and mem. Throne Council Sept.–Oct. 1993; First Prime Minister of Royal Govt of Cambodia 1993–97; Chair. Nat. Devt Council 1993–97; found guilty of conspiracy with Khmer Rouges to overthrow the Govt, sentenced to 30 years' imprisonment; in exile; returned from exile May 1998; Prof. of Public Law; Grand Officer of the Royal Order of Cambodia 1992, Grand Officer de l'Ordre de la Pléiade 2000, Grand Order of Nat. Merit 2001, Order of Sovatara 2001. *Leisure interest:* aviation. *Address:* FUNCINPEC, Head Office 59, Street 1, Village 2, Sangkat Chroy Chang Va, Khan Chroy Chang Va, Phnom Penh, Cambodia (office). *Telephone:* (15) 504559 (office). *E-mail:* info@funcinpecparty.info (office). *Website:* www.funcinpecparty.info (office).

NORODOM SIHAMONI, HM King of Cambodia; b. 14 May 1953, Phnom Penh; s. of HM King Norodom Sihanouk and HM Queen Norodom Monineath Sihanouk; ed Norodom School, Descartes High School, Phnom Penh, Prague High School, Nat. Conservatory of Prague, Acad. of Musical Art, Prague, Czechoslovakia (now Czech Repub.); studied dance, music, theatre and cinematography; Prof. of Classical Dance and Artistic Pedagogy, Marius Petipa Conservatory, Gabriel Faure Conservatory, W. A. Mozart Conservatory, Paris 1981–2004; Pres. Khmer Dance Asscn, France 1984–2004; Dir-Gen. and Artistic Dir Deva Ballet Group 1984–2004; Dir-Gen. and Artistic Dir Khmer Cinematographic Soc. 'Khemara Pictures' 1990–2004; Amb. and Perm. Rep. to UN 1992–2004; Amb. to UNESCO 1993–2004; elevated to rank of Sdech Krom Khun (Great Prince) 1994; crowned King of Cambodia (following abdication of his father) Oct. 2004; mem. High Council of Francophone Countries 2004; Foreign Assoc. mem. Acad. des Inscriptions et Belles-Lettres 2008; Hon. Citizen of the City of Prague 2006; Grand Collier, Ordre Nat. de l'Independence, Grand Cross, Royal Order of Monisaraphon; Grand Officier, Légion d'honneur 2004, Grand Croix 2010; Grand Cross, Royal Order of Cambodia, Grand Cordon, Order of the Chrysanthemum 2010; Silver Medal of the City of Paris. *Address:* Royal Palace, Phnom Penh, Cambodia. *E-mail:* cabinet@norodomsihanouk.info. *Website:* www.norodomsihamoni.org.

NORONHA NASCIMENTO, Luís António; Portuguese judge (retd); b. 2 Dec. 1943, Porto; m. Maria Clara Nascimento; early career as Asst to Public Prosecutor for Comarcas de Paredes, Pombal e Santo Tirso; Judge for Trancoso, Marco de Canavezes, Vila Nova de Famalicão, Vila Nova de Gaia and Porto; Judge Court of Appeal, Lisbon –1994; mem. Superior Council of Magistrates 1989–90, Vice-Pres. 2001–; Judge Supreme Court of Justice 1994–98, Vice-Pres. 1998–2006, Pres. 2006–13 (retd); mem. Portuguese Asscn of Judges 1984–88, Pres. 1992–96. *Address:* c/o Supremo Tribunal da Justiça, Praça do Comércio, 1149-012 Lisbon, Portugal.

NORRBACK, Johan Ole; Finnish diplomatist and politician; b. 18 March 1941, Övermark; m. Vivi-Anna Lindqvist 1959; two c.; teacher 1966–67; Dist Sec. Swedish People's Party in Ostrobothnia 1967–71; Exec. Man. Prov. Union of Swedish Ostrobothnia 1971–91; Political Sec. to Minister of Communications 1976–77; mem. Parl. 1979–87, 1991–99; mem. Exec. Cttee Svenska Folkpartiet (SFP) (Swedish People's Party) 1983–89, Chair. 1990–99; Minister of Defence 1987–90, of Educ. and Science 1990–91, of Transport and Communications 1991–95, for Europe and Foreign Trade 1995–99; Amb. to Norway 1999–2003, to Greece 2003–07; apptd Amb. for Baltic Sea Issues, Ministry for Foreign Affairs

2007, Special Adviser to the Prime Minister on border obstacles between Nordic countries 2007–, Chair. Steering Group for the Implementation of Baltic Sea Action Plan (BSAP) 2008–. *Address:* Ministry of Foreign Affairs, Merikasarmi, Laivastokatu 22, PO Box 176, 00023 Helsinki (office); c/o Svenska Folkpartiet (SFP), Simonsgatan 8A, 00100 Helsinki, Finland. *Telephone:* (9) 5350000 (office). *Fax:* (9) 629840 (office). *E-mail:* ole.norrback@formin.fi (office). *Website:* formin.finland.fi (office).

NORRINGTON, Sir Roger Arthur Carver, Kt, CBE, FRCM, FRAM; British conductor; b. 16 March 1934; s. of Sir Arthur Norrington and Edith Joyce Carver; m. 1st Susan Elizabeth McLean May 1964 (divorced 1982); one s. one d.; m. 2nd Karalyn Mary Lawrence 1986; one s.; ed Dragon School, Oxford, Westminster School, Clare Coll. Cambridge, Royal Coll. of Music; freelance singer 1962–72; Prin. Conductor, Kent Opera 1966–84; Guest Conductor with numerous British, American and European orchestras, appearances at BBC Proms and City of London, Bath, Aldeburgh, Edin. and Harrogate festivals; regular broadcasts UK, Europe, USA; f. Schütz Choir of London 1962; Musical Dir London Baroque Players 1975, London Classical Players 1978–97, Orchestra of St Luke's, New York 1990–94; Prin. Conductor, Bournemouth Sinfonietta 1985–89; Chief Conductor, Camerata Salzburg 1997–2006; Prin. Conductor, Radio Sinfonieorchester, Stuttgart 1998–2011, Zurich Chamber Orchestra 2011–15; Chief Guest Conductor, Orchestre de Chambre de Paris; Conductor Emer., Orchestra of the Age of Enlightenment; conducted Stuttgart Radio Symphony Orchestra at BBC Proms, London 2016; Co.-Dir Early Opera Project 1984–90, Historic Arts 1986–90; Visiting Prof., Royal Coll. of Music; Cavaliere, Ordine al Merito della Repubblica Italiana, Ehrenkreuz Erster Klasse (Austria) 1999; Ehrenkreuz Erste Klasse (Germany) 2011; Hon. DMus (Kent) 1994, (York) 2013; ECHO Klassik Award for Symphonic Recording of the Year – 19th Century (for Elgar Enigma Variations) 2012. *Leisure interests:* reading, walking, sailing.

NORRIS, David, MA, FSA, FRAM, FRCO; British pianist, broadcaster and academic; *Professor of Musical Performance, University of Southampton;* b. 16 June 1953, Northampton; s. of Albert Norris and Margaret Norris; two s.; ed Keble Coll. Oxford, Royal Acad. of Music, and privately in Paris; Prof., RAM 1977–89; Dir Petworth Festival 1986–92; Artistic Dir Cardiff Festival 1992–95; Chair. Steans Inst. for Singers, Chicago 1992–98; Gresham Prof. of Music, London 1993–97; apptd Prof., Royal Coll. of Music 2000, Visiting Prof. 2014–; Lecturer in Music and Head of Keyboard, Univ. of Southampton 2000–07, Prof. of Musical Performance 2007–; gave world premieres of Schubert's First Song Cycle and Elgar's Piano Concerto; Hon. Fellow, Keble Coll., Oxford 2006, Fellow, Soc. of Antiquaries of London 2015; First Gilmore Artist Award 1991. *Compositions include:* oratorios: Prayerbook, Turning Points; other: Piano Concerto, Symphony, HengeMusic for saxophones, organ, film and poetry; song cycles, cantatas. *Recordings include:* complete piano music of Elgar, Dyson and Quilter, and the World's First Piano Concertos; Prayerbook 2012, DON Piano Concerto 2016. *Radio:* Playlist (BBC Radio 4 series), regular contrib. to Building a Library (BBC Radio 3). *Television:* 'Chord of the Week' for BBC 2's Proms Extra; appearances in programmes on Elgar (including 'Imagine' on the Piano Concerto), Parry, Vaughan Williams, Holst, Music & Royalty, etc. *Leisure interests:* naval and detective fiction. *Address:* Music, Building 2, Highfield Campus, University of Southampton, Southampton, SO17 1BJ, England (office). *Telephone:* 7957-322091 (mobile) (office). *E-mail:* info@davidowennorris.com (home). *Website:* www.davidowennorris.com (home).

NORRIS, Elwood (Woody); American inventor and engineer; *Chief Scientist, Turtle Beach Corporation;* b. Barrelville, Cumberland, Md; m.; eleven c.; ed Univ. of New Mexico; joined USAF 1956, trained as Nuclear Weapons Specialist, Monzano Base, New Mexico; cameraman, American Broadcasting Corpn (ABC) TV network, Albuquerque 1958; joined Tech. Staff, Univ. of Wash. 1959, Dir Eng Experiment Station –1970; worked for Heath Technic Corpn 1970s; f. American Tech. Corpn (LRAD Corpn since 2010), San Diego 1980, Chair. 1980–2010; Founder and CEO Parametric Sound Corpn (fmr subsidiary of LRAD Corpn) 2010–12; currently Chief Scientist Turtle Beach Corpn (merger of Parametric Sound and Voyetra Turtle Beach); licensed pilot; Lemelson-MIT Inventor of the Year Award 2005. *Achievements include:* inventions include Transcutaneous Doppler System (precursor to sonogram) 1967, tone arm, unidrectional microphone, virtual speaker, electrostatic transducer, holographic transparent speaker, magnetic film, ear-mounted speaker/microphone device (designed for NASA astronaut helmets, now used for cell phone headsets), Flashback®, HyperSonic Sound®, AirScooter® ultralight helicopter, hydrogen-poweres automobiles, artificial hip alarm; holds 47 US patents and over 300 patents world-wide. *Leisure interest:* flying aeroplanes. *Address:* Turtle Beach Corporation, 100 Summit Lake Drive, Suite 100, Valhalla, NY 10595, USA (office). *Telephone:* (914) 345-2255 (office). *E-mail:* woody@woodynorris.com. *Website:* corp.turtlebeach.com (office); hypersound.com (office); www.woodynorris.com.

NORRIS, Sir Ralph James, Kt, KNZM; New Zealand banking executive; b. 1949, Auckland; ed Lynfield Coll.; began career as commercial cadet, Mobil Oil NZ 1967–69; joined Auckland Savings Bank (ASB) Ltd 1969, Man. Dir and CEO 1991–2001; mem. Bd of Dirs Air New Zealand Ltd 1998–2005, Man. Dir and CEO 2002–05; Head of Int. Financial Services, Commonwealth Bank of Australia 1999–2001, Man. Dir and CEO 2005–11; Chair. Australian Bankers' Asscn, CommFoundation Pty Ltd; fmr Chair. NZ Bankers Asscn, Business Roundtable, Hosting Cttee of Asia-Pacific Econ. Council CEO Summit; Chair. Contact Energy, RANQX Holdings; mem. Bd of Dirs Fletcher Building Ltd 2001–05, 2014, (Chair. 2014–), Team NZ Defence 2003, Business Council of Australia, Financial Markets Foundation for Children; fmr mem. Prime Minister's Enterprise Council, Prime Minister's Y2K Task Force, Pacific Basin Econ. Council; mem. Starship Foundation Trust, Knowledge Wave Trust, Northern Lifeguard Services Trust; Fellow, NZ Inst. of Man.; Amb., Australian Indigenous Educ. Foundation; Hon. Fellow, NZ Computer Soc., Inst. of IT Professionals; Distinguished Companion, NZ Order of Merit 2006, Kt, NZ Order of Merit; NZ Exec. of the Year Award 1997, 2004.

NORRIS, Steve, FRSA; British film producer; *CEO, Apollo Productions;* b. 1959, Harefield, England; fmrly with The Rank Org.; fmr exec., Columbia Pictures, Warner Brothers, Enigma, USA 1989–99; fmr Vice-Pres. Producers' Alliance for Cinema and TV, Chair. Film Cttee; British Film Commr 1998–2006; Man. Dir of Film, Framestore 2006–13; Exec. Producer, Pinewood Films Ltd; CEO Apollo Productions 2013–; has consulted for several key industry clients including nat. govts; fmr mem. Council, BAFTA, Producers Alliance for Cinema and Television, British Screen Advisory Council, amongst others; Chair. UK Screen (trade body for UK film, TV and commercial sector cos); Hon. mem. Production Guild of GB; several awards, including Golden Globe for The Burning Season. *Films include:* Memphis Belle 1990, Being Human 1994, War of the Buttons 1994, Le Confessionnal (Canadian Academy Award for Best) 1995, Diane & Me 1997, My Life So Far 1999, Freakdog 2008, Me and Orson Welles 2008, Triangle 2009, Heartless 2009, harry Brown 2009, Ghost Machine 2009, A Fantastic Fear of Everything 2012, Last Passenger 2013, Dom Hemingway 2013, Belle 2013, Powder Room 2013, Camera Trap (documentary) 2014, Robot Overlords 2014, Posh 2014. *Television includes:* The Burning Season (film) 1994. *Address:* Apollo Productions, Pinewood Studios, Pinewood Road, Iver Heath, Bucks., SL0 0HH, England. *E-mail:* julia@apolloprods.com. *Website:* www.apolloprods.com.

NORRIS, Steven, MA; British politician and business executive; *Chairman, BNP Paribas Real Estate UK;* b. 24 May 1945, Liverpool; s. of John Francis Birkett and Eileen Winifred Walsh; m. 1st Peta Veronica Cecil-Gibson 1969 (divorced); two s.; m. 2nd Emma Courtney 2000; one s.; ed Liverpool Inst. High School, Worcester Coll., Oxford; Berks. Co. Councillor 1977–85; various man. positions in industry –1983; MP for Oxford E 1983–87, for Epping Forest 1988–97; Parl. Pvt. Sec. to William Waldegrave, Minister of State, Dept of Environment 1985–87, to Nicholas Ridley, Sec. of State for Trade and Industry 1990, to Kenneth Baker, Home Sec. 1991–92; Minister for Transport in London 1992–96; Dir-Gen. Road Haulage Asscn 1997–99; Conservative cand. for Mayoralty of London 2000, 2004; Vice-Chair. Conservative Party 2000–01; mem. Bd Transport for London –2001; Sr Partner, Park Place Communications 2003–; Chair. The Internet Corporation Ltd (Amris eRecruitment) 2000–; Exec. Chair. Jarvis plc 2004–10; Group Chair. AMT-Sybex Group Ltd 2004–12; Chair. Saferoad UK 2004–13, Soho Estates Ltd 2010–, Virtus Data Centres Ltd 2010–, BNP Paribas Real Estate UK 2013–, Driver Group 2015–; Pres. ITS UK 2002–; Partner, Norris McDonough LLP 2013–; mem. Bd of Dirs initiate Consulting Limited 2001–, Cubic Corpn 2014–; Chair. East Side Young Leaders Acad., British Urological Foundation; Companion Inst. of Civil Engineers; Trustee London Action Trust; Freeman of the City of London; Liveryman of the Worshipful Co. of Coachmakers and Coach Harness Makers, Worshipful Co. of Carmen; Craftowning Freeman of Co. of Watchmen and Lightermen of City of London. *Publication:* Changing Train 1996. *Leisure interests:* football, opera, reading. *Address:* BNP Paribas Real Estate UK, 5 Aldermanbury Square, London, EC2V 7BP, England (office). *Telephone:* (20) 7338-4000 (office). *E-mail:* realestate.press@bnpparibas.com (office). *Website:* www.realestate.bnpparibas.co.uk (office).

NORSHTEIN, Yuri Borisovich; Russian film director, animator and scriptwriter; b. 15 Sept. 1941, Andreyevka, Penza Region; s. of Berko Leibovich Norshtein and Basya Girshevna Krichevskaya; m. Francesca Alfredovna Yarbusova; one s. one d.; ed Soyuzmultfilmstudio courses; debut as film dir of 25 October, the First Day (co-dir with Arkady Tyurin) 1968; cutout film The Battle at Kerzhenets (co-dir with I. Ivanov-Vano) 1971; later with his wife (art dir Yarbusova): The Fox and the Hare 1973, The Heron and the Crane 1974, Hedgehog in Mist 1975, Tale of Tales 1979, The Overcoat 2003; People's Artist of Russia 1996, Order of the Rising Sun (Japan) 2004; USSR State Prize 1979, Grand Prix, Zagreb Animation Festival 1980, Tale of Tales voted best animated film of all time in int. survey, LA Animation Olympiad 1984, Tarkovsky Prize 1989, Ind. Triumph Prize 1995, Breakthrough Prize for 'Russian Sugar' (commercial), First Open Russian Festival of Animated Film 1996, Tale of Tales again voted by large int. jury to be the greatest animated film of all time, Zagreb World Festival of Animated Films 2002. *Other films include:* shorts: Dve skazki 1962, Kto skazal myau? 1962, Mister Tvister 1963, Levsha 1964, Kanikuly Bonifatsiya 1965, My Green Crocodile 1966, The Mitten 1967, Ostorozhno, shchuka! 1968, Komediant 1968, Seasons 1969, Pismo 1970, General Toptygin (TV) 1971, Mama 1972, Cheburashka 1972, Chasy s kukushkoy (TV) 1973, Aybolit i Barmaley (TV) 1973, Avrora (TV) 1973, Shapoklyak 1974, 38 popugaev 1976, Ya k vam lechu vospominanem 1977, I s vami snova ya 1980, O sport, ty – mir! (documentary) 1981, Osen 1982, Winter Days 1982. *Address:* 1-i Voykovsky pro., korp. 1, Apt 16, podbezhd 1-a, Moscow, Russian Federation. *Telephone:* (926) 611-55-25. *Website:* norshteyn.ru.

NORTEN, Enrique, BArch, MArch; Mexican architect and teacher; *Principal, TEN Arquitectos (Taller de Enrique Norten Arquitectos, SC);* b. 27 Feb. 1954, Mexico City; ed Universidad Iberoamericana, Mexico City, Cornell Univ., USA; f. TEN (Taller de Enrique Norten) Arquitectos 1986, currently Prin., involved in projects of different types and scales, including furniture design, single-family houses, residential, cultural and institutional bldgs, as well as landscape and master planning, opened New York office 2003; Prof. of Architecture, Universidad Iberoamericana, Mexico City 1980–90; Coordinator of Grad. Urban Design Program 1983–85; has held Miller Chair, Univ. of Pennsylvania, Phila 1998–; fmr holder of O'Neal Ford Chair in Architecture, Univ. of Texas at Austin; fmr Lorch Prof. of Architecture, Univ. of Michigan; fmr Eero Saarinen Visiting Prof. of Architectural Design, Yale School of Architecture; fmr Distinguished Visiting Prof., Cornell Univ.; fmr Visiting Prof., UCLA Dept of Architecture and Urban Design, Yale School of Architecture, Sci-Arc, Rice Univ., Univ. of Houston, Columbia Univ., Pratt Inst., Parsons School of Design; fmr Elliot Noyes Visiting Design Critic, Harvard Univ.; has lectured world-wide and is a regular speaker at Urban Age Conf.; has participated on int. juries and award cttees, including the World Trade Center Site Memorial Competition in New York City and Holcim Foundation Awards for Sustainable Construction; mem. Bd Trustees, Deutsche Bank 2006–; mem. Bd Mexican Cultural Inst. of New York 2007–, Americas Soc./Council of the Americas 2008–; Hon. mem. AIA 1999; Hon. Mention, I Bienal de Arquitectura Mexicana 1990, Grant for Creators and Intellectuals, Nat. Council for Culture and the Arts (CONACULTA) 1990, Medalla a la Excelencia Profesional Colegio de Arquitectos de México 1990, Architectural Record Awards (House 'O') 1992, Hon. Mention, II Bienal de Arquitectura Mexicana 1992, Latin American Award, Bienal de Arquitectura de Buenos Aires 1993, Consejo Internacional de Críticos de Arquitectura 1993, Progressive Architecture Award, P/A Awards 1994, Hon. Mention, III Bienal de Arquitectura Mexicana 1994, Progressive Architecture Award, P/A Awards 1995, First Prize, IV Bienal de Arquitectura Mexicana 1996, Hon. Mention, IV Bienal de Arquitectura Mexicana 1996, Hon. Mention, P/A Awards (Museum of Natural History) 1996, Ciudad de México Award, Departamento del DF 1997, Progressive Architecture Award, P/A Awards 1999, Creador Artístico 2000, Grant, CONACULTA 2000, Sistema Nacional de Creadores de Arte Gold Mention 2000, Quorum Design Award 2000, Graphic Design for the Book TEN Arquitectos 2000, Hon. Mention, VI Bienal de Arquitectura Mexicana 2000, Hon. Mention, P/A Awards (JVC Convention & Exhbn Center) 2000, DuPont Benedictus Awards for Innovation in Architectural Glass, DuPont Benedictus (House IA) 2001, AIA Gold Medal 2002, Gold Medal, Soc. of American Registered Architects 2003, 'Leonardo da Vinci' World Award of Arts, World Cultural Council 2005, Design Awards 2006, Hon. Mention, IX Bienal de Arquitectura Mexicana (House C) 2006, 'Legacy Award', Smithsonian Latino Center, Smithsonian Inst. 2007, Hon. Mention, CAF Office Bldg Competition, Caracas, Venezuela 2008, Excellence in Architecture and Design Award, PODER – The Boston Consulting Group Business Awards 2008, Design and Construction Excellence Program, NYC DC, New York 2009, Calli de Cristal, Colegio de Arquitectos de Nuevo Léon, Mexico, XV Bienal de Arquitectura CANL 2009, Careers 2014 Award, Coll. of Architects, Mexico City 2014, Richard J. Neutra Medal for Professional Excellence 2015. *Projects include:* Nat. School of Theater at Nat. Center of the Arts, Churubusco, Mexico City, Televisa Mixed Use Bldg, Mexico City (first Mies van der Rohe Pavillion Award for Latin American Architecture, Barcelona 1998), House RR, Mexico City (Design Excellence in Housing, Boston Soc. of Architects 2004), Hotel HABITA (AR Awards for Emerging Architecture 2001, DuPont Benedictus Awards for Innovation in Architectural Glass, DuPont Benedictus 2001, Latin American Bldg of the Year, World Architecture Awards 2002, RIBA Worldwide Architecture Award 2002, Mention, XIII Bienal de Arquitectura de Quito, Ecuador 2002, Silver Medal, VII Bienal de Arquitectura Mexicana 2002, Business Week/Architectural Record Award 2003, AIA Architecture Award, New York Chapter Design Awards 2003), Educare in Zapopan, Jalisco (Hon. Mention, VII Bienal de Arquitectura Mexicana (Educare) 2002 2002, First Prize of Int. Design, XIII Bienal de Arquitectura de Quito, Ecuador 2002, AIA Architecture Award, New York Chapter Design Awards 2003), Princeton Parking Structure (Gold Medal, AIA/New Jersey Design Awards 2002), Parque España Residential Bldg, Colonia Condesa, Mexico City (Design Excellence in Housing, Boston Soc. of Architects 2004, Guggenheim Museum, Guadalajara (Project Citation, AIA New York Chapter 2006) 2005, One York Residential Bldg, New York City 2009, Orange County Great Park (AIA Inst. Honor Award for Regional and Urban Design) 2009, Americano Hotel, High Museum of Villahermosa, Nat. Lab. of Genomics for Biodiversity, Univ. Museum of Chopo, Amparo Museum, Emblematic Monument of the 150th Anniversary of the Battle of Puebla, anta Fe Eurocenter, Business School Campus, Livingston Rutgers Univ., New Jersey, Mercedes House in New York. *Commissions include:* Guggenheim Museum, Guadalajara, Xochimilco Master Plan and Aquarium, Mexico City (AIA Inst. Merit Award, New York Chapter Design Awards 2009), new vision for Rutgers Univ.'s Coll. Avenue Campus and Livingston Campus, New Brunswick, NJ, plan for the recovery of a 4½ mile stretch of the New Orleans Riverfront, New Orleans, La, Chopo Museum, Mexico City, Nat. Lab. of Genomics, Irapuato, Guanajuato, Mexico, Cassa Residential Bldg at 45th Street, New York City, High Line Hotel, New York City, 580 Carroll Street Residential Bldg, Brooklyn, NY, 1.3 million square feet Clinton Park, New York City. *Publications:* several monographs, including TEN Arquitectos 1998, Enrique Norten: Temas y Variaciones 2004, Working: Enrique Norten/TEN Arquitectos 2007; numerous articles in nat. and int. publs. *Address:* TEN Arquitectos, 127 W 25th Street, New York, NY 10001, USA (office); TEN Arquitectos, Cuernavaca 114/PB, Colonia Condesa, 06140 Mexico City DF, Mexico (office). *Telephone:* (212) 620-0794 (New York) (office); (55) 5211-8004 (Mexico City) (office). *Fax:* (212) 620-0798 (New York) (office); (55) 5286-1735 (Mexico City) (office). *E-mail:* ten@ten-arquitectos.com (office). *Website:* www.ten-arquitectos .com (office).

NORTH, Alastair Macarthur, OBE, PhD, DSc; British chemist and academic (retd); b. 2 April 1932, Aberdeen, Scotland; s. of Norman R. North and Anne North; m. Charlotte Muriel Begg 1957; two s. two d.; ed Univs of Aberdeen and Birmingham; Lecturer, Dept of Inorganic, Physical and Industrial Chem., Univ. of Liverpool 1959–67; apptd to Burmah Chair of Physical Chem., Univ. of Strathclyde 1967, Dean, School of Chemical and Materials Science 1972–75, Vice-Prin. of the Univ. 1976–80; Pres., Asian Inst. of Tech. 1983–96; Visiting Prof. Chiang Mai Univ. 1984–2003, Mahidol Univ., Bangkok 1989–; mem. several nat. cttees on formation of science policy; Commdr des Palmes académiques; Commdr, Order of King Leopold II (Belgium); Prasidda Prabala Gorkha Dakshin Bahu (Nepal); Hon. ScD (Politechnika Lodzka), Hon. PhD (Ramkhamhaeng Univ.), Hon. DUniv (Strathclyde), Hon. DTech (AIT), Hon. LLD (Aberdeen), Dr hc (Inst. Nat. Polytechnique de Toulouse). *Leisure interest:* gardening. *Address:* 79/78 Soi 7/1 Mooban Tararom, Ramkhamhaeng Soi 150, Sapansoong, Bangkok 10240, Thailand (home). *Telephone:* (2) 373-2818 (home). *Fax:* (2) 373-3052 (home).

NORTH, Anthony (see KOONTZ, Dean Ray).

NORTH, Oliver Laurence; American fmr marine officer, radio and television show host and author; *Honorary Chairman, Freedom Alliance;* b. 7 Oct. 1943, San Antonio, Tex.; s. of Oliver Clay North and Ann Theresa North (née Clancy; m. Betsy Stuart 1967; four c.; ed Ockawamick High School, State Univ. of NY at Brockport, US Naval Acad., Annapolis; served with US Marines for 22 years, platoon commdr in Viet Nam; marine instructor 1969; leader marine mission, Turkey 1980; mem. Nat. Security Council staff as Deputy Dir for Political Mil. Affairs 1981–86; dismissed Nov. 1986 because of involvement with secret operation to sell arms to Iran and diversion of proceeds from the sales to aid anti-govt 'Contra' guerrillas in Nicaragua; rank of Lt-Col 1983, retd from Marines 1988; found guilty on three counts May 1989, appeal court reversed one count 1990, three convictions set aside 1990; cleared of all charges 1991; mem. Bd of Dirs Nat. Rifle Asscn (Pres. 2018–); co-f. Freedom Alliance 1990, now Hon. Chair.; radio show host 1995–; TV host War Stories with Oliver North; writes a nationally syndicated newspaper column through Creators Syndicate; Silver Star Medal, Bronze Star Medal with Combat 'V', Purple Heart Medal (twice), Combat Action Ribbon, Presidential Service Badge; Dr hc (Liberty Univ.) 1988. *Television:* received story credit for an episode of The Americans (series) 2014. *Publication:* Under Fire: An American Story 1991, One More Mission: Oliver North Returns to Vietnam (co-author) 1993, Mission Compromised (novel) 2002, The Jericho Sanction (co-author) 2004, True Freedom: The Liberating Power of Prayer (co-author) 2004, War Stories: Operation Iraqi Freedom 2005, The Assassins (co-author) 2006, War Stories III: The Heroes Who Defeated Hitler 2006, War Stories with Oliver North: Red Tails – The Saga of the Tuskegee Airmen 2007, American Heroes 2008, American Heroes: In the Fight Against Radical Islam 2009, American Heroes in Special Operations 2010, Heroes Proved: A Novel 2012, American Heroes: On the Homefront 2013, Counterfeit Lies (novel) 2014. *Address:* c/o Freedom Alliance, 22570 Markey Court, Suite 240, Dulles, VA 20166, USA. *Telephone:* (703) 444-7940. *Fax:* (703) 444-9893. *Website:* freedomalliance.org; olivernorth.com.

NORTH, Sir Peter Machin, Kt, CBE, QC, MA, DCL, FBA; British academic and lawyer; b. 30 Aug. 1936, Nottingham, Notts.; s. of Geoffrey Machin North and Freda Brunt North (née Smith); m. Stephanie Mary Chadwick 1960; two s. one d.; ed Oakham School, Rutland, Keble Coll., Oxford; Teaching Assoc., Northwestern Univ. Law School, Chicago 1960–61; Lecturer, Univ. Coll. of Wales, Aberystwyth 1961–63, Univ. of Nottingham 1964–65; Fellow and Tutor in Law, Keble Coll. Oxford 1965–76; Chair. Faculty of Law, Univ. of Oxford 1971–75; Prin. Jesus Coll., Oxford 1984–2005; Pro-Vice-Chancellor Univ. of Oxford 1988–93, 1997–2005, Vice-Chancellor 1993–97; Ed. Oxford Journal of Legal Studies 1987–92; Law Commr for England and Wales 1976–84; mem. Lord Chancellor's Advisory Cttee on Legal Educ. 1973–75, Council of Man., British Inst. of Int. and Comparative Law 1976–, Econ. and Social Research Council Cttees 1982–87, Council, Univ. of Reading 1986–89, Finance Cttee, Oxford University Press 1993–2008 (Chair. 2005–08), Sr Salaries Review Body 2004–12, Accountancy Investigation and Discipline Bd Tribunal 2005–13; Chair. Conciliation Advisory Cttee 1985–88, Road Traffic Law Review 1985–88, Ind. Review of Parades and Marches in Northern Ireland 1996–97, Ind. Cttee for Supervision of Standards of Telephone Information Services 1999–2006, Review of Drink and Drug Driving Law 2009–10; mem. Inst. de droit int.; Visitor, Ashmolean Museum, Oxford 2004–08; Hon. Bencher, Inner Temple; Hon. Fellow, Keble Coll. Oxford, Jesus Coll. Oxford, Univ. Coll. of N Wales, Bangor, Trinity Coll., Carmarthen, Univ. of Wales, Aberystwyth; Hon. LLD (Reading) 1992, (Nottingham) 1996, (Aberdeen) 1997, (New Brunswick) 2002; Hon. DHumLitt (Arizona) 2005. *Publications:* Occupier's Liability 1971 (second edn 2014), Modern Law of Animals 1972, Chitty on Contracts (ed.) 1968–89, Private International Law of Matrimonial Causes 1977, Contract Conflicts (ed.) 1982, Cases and Materials on Private International Law (with J. H. C. Morris) 1984, Cheshire and North's Private International Law (ed.) 1970–2008, Private International Law Problems in Common Law Jurisdictions 1993, Essays in Private International Law 1993, Civil Liability for Animals 2012. *Telephone:* (1865) 557011 (home). *E-mail:* peter.north@jesus.ox.ac.uk.

NORTH, Richard Conway, FCA, ACA; British accountant and business executive; b. 20 Jan. 1950; joined Coopers and Lybrand 1971, seconded to New York 1976–78, seconded to Midland Bank plc 1981–82, Partner 1983–91; Group Finance Dir The Burton Group PLC 1991–94, later Chair.; Group Finance Dir Bass PLC (later Six Continents plc) 1994–2003, Chief Exec., Hotels Div. 2002; Chair. Britvic Soft Drinks 1996–2004; CEO InterContinental Hotels Group PLC 2003–04; mem. Bd of Dirs Woolworths Group PLC 2006–11, Chair. 2007–08; Chair. Payments Council 2010–14; Dir (non-Exec.) Asda PLC 1997–99, Leeds United plc 1998–2002, FelCor Lodging Trust 1998, Logica plc 2002–04, Majid al Futtaim Group LLC 2006; mem. Bd of Dirs Mecom Group PLC 2007–09; mem. Senate Inst. of Chartered Accountants in England and Wales 1991–2000, Hundred Group Cttee 1996–2000, Exec. Cttee World Travel and Tourism Council 2003–04. *Leisure interests:* golf, tennis, sailing, football, opera. *Address:* 8 St Simon's Avenue, Putney, London, SW15 6DU, England.

NORTHAM, Ralph Shearer, BSc, MD; American physician, politician and fmr army officer; *Governor of Virginia;* b. 13 Sept. 1959; s. of Wescott B. Northam and Nancy B. Shearer; m. Pam Thomas; one s. one d.; ed Virginia Mil. Inst., Eastern Virginia Medical School; served as medical officer, US Army 1984–92 (left with rank of major); fmr Chief Neurological Resident, Johns Hopkins Hosp.; Paediatric Neurologist, Children's Hosp. of the King's Daughters, Norfolk 1992–; mem. Virginia Senate from 6th Dist 2008–14; Lt-Gov. of Virginia 2014–18, Gov. 2018–; Asst Prof. of Neurology, Eastern Virginia Medical School; Democrat. *Address:* Office of the Governor, Patrick Henry Building, 3rd Floor, 1111 East Broad Street, Richmond, VA 23219, USA (office). *Telephone:* (804) 786-2211 (office). *Fax:* (804) 371-6351 (office). *E-mail:* info@governor.virginia.gov (office). *Website:* www .governor.virginia.gov (office); ralphnortham.com.

NORTHFLEET, Ellen Gracie, LLB; Brazilian judge; b. 16 Feb. 1948, Rio de Janeiro; d. of José Barros Northfleet and Helena Northfleet; m. (divorced); one d.; ed Universidade do Estado da Guanabara, Universidade Federal do Rio Grande do Sul; Public Prosecutor (1st Level) 1980–89; Prof. of Law, Universidade Federal do Rio Grande do Sul 1983–87, Universidade do Vale do Rio dos Sinos 1987–; mem. Fed. Public Ministry 1973–89; mem. Regional Electoral Tribune, Rio Grande do Sul 1989–2000, Pres. 1997–2000; apptd Justice Supreme Federal Court 2000, Vice-Pres. 2004, Pres. 2006–08; Minister for Supreme Fed. Tribunal 2000–04, Vice-Pres. 2004–06, Pres. 2006–08; Pres. Nat. Justice Council 2006–08; Fulbright Scholar, American Univ., Washington DC 1991–92; mem. Fulbright Alumni Asscn of Brazil; Jurist in Residence, Library of Congress, USA 1992; mem. Bd of Dirs World Justice Project; mem. Governing Bd Int. Council for Commercial Arbitration; Hon. mem. Fed. Judiciary of the USA 2006; Santos Dumont Medal 1977, Grand Official of the Order of Merit 2001, Grand Cross of the Order of Rio Branco 2006, numerous other decorations. *Publications:* numerous articles in professional journals. *Address:* c/o Supremo Tribunal Federal, Praça dos Três Poderes, 70175-900 Brasília, DF, Brazil.

NORTON, Edward Harrison, BA; American actor, screenwriter, film director and producer; b. 18 Aug. 1969, Boston, Mass; s. of Edward Mower Norton, Jr and Lydia Robinson 'Robin' Norton (née Rouse); m. Shauna Robertson 2011; one s.; ed Wilde Lake High School, Md, Yale Univ., Columbia School for Theatrical Arts, Md; fmr consultant, Enterprise Foundation, Osaka, Japan, currently mem. Nat. Bd; mem. Signature Theatre Repertory Co. 1994–, performed in premiere of Edward Albee's Fragments, mem. Bd 1996–; Co-founder Class 5 Films (production co.). *Play:* Burn This (Obie Award). *Films include:* Primal Fear (Golden Globe, Best Supporting Actor) 1996, Everyone Says I Love You 1996, The People vs. Larry Flynt 1996, American History X 1998, Rounders 1998, Fight Club 1999, Keeping the Faith (also dir and producer), The Score, Death to Smoochy, Red Dragon 2002, The 25th Hour 2001, Frida 2002 (also co-wrote screenplay), The Italian Job 2003,

Down in the Valley 2004, Kingdom of Heaven 2005, The Illusionist 2006, The Painted Veil 2006, Pride and Glory 2007, The Incredible Hulk 2008, Pride and Glory 2008, The Invention of Lying 2009, Leaves of Grass (also producer) 2010, Stone 2010, Moonrise Kingdom 2012, The Dictator 2012, The Bourne Legacy 2012, The Grand Budapest Hotel 2014, Birdman 2014, Sausage Party (voice) 2016. *Television includes:* host, National Geographic's Strange Days on Planet Earth. *Website:* www.edward-norton.org.

NORTON, Gale Ann, BA, JD; American lawyer and fmr government official; *President, Norton Regulatory Strategies;* b. 11 March 1954, Wichita, Kan.; d. of Dale Bentsen Norton and Anna Jacqueline Norton (née Lansdowne); m. John Goethe Hughes 1990; ed Univ. of Denver; lawyer, Colorado 1978, Supreme Court 1981; judicial clerk, Colorado Court of Appeals 1978–79, Sr Attorney, Mountain States Legal Foundation 1979–83; Nat. Fellow, Hoover Inst., Stanford Univ. 1983–84; Asst to Deputy Sec., Dept of Agric., Washington, DC 1984–85; Assoc. Solicitor, Dept of Interior 1985–87; pvt. law practice 1987–90; Attorney-Gen., Colorado 1991–99; Sr Counsel, Brownstein, Hyatt & Farber, PC 1999–2001; Sec. of the Interior, Washington, DC 2001–06; Gen. Counsel, Royal Dutch Shell 2006–10; Pres. Norton Regulatory Strategies 2011–; Corp. Dir American Transmission Co. 2012–; Transportation Law Program Dir, Univ. of Denver 1978–79; Lecturer, Univ. of Denver Law School 1989; mem. Bd of Dirs, Federalist Soc. and Univ. of Colorado Energy Inst.; Chair. Environmental Comm. of Republican Nat. Lawyers Asscn, Nat. Park Foundation 2001–06, Migratory Bird Conservation Comm. 2001–06; fmr Chair. Nat. Asscn of Attorneys Environmental Cttee; Co-Chair. Nat. Policy Forum Environmental Council; Policy Analyst, Presidential Council on Environmental Quality 1985–88; Founding mem., Conservation Leadership Council 2012–; Hon. DEng (Colorado School of Mines); Hon. PhD (Univ. of Denver); Trailblazer Award, Colo Women's Bar Asscn, Conservation Patriot Award, Nat. Fish and Wildlife Foundation, Western Business Roundtable Spirit of the West Award, Ind. Inst. Award for Inspired Leadership, Boone and Crockett Club Conservation Award, American Recreation Coalition Coleman Outdoor Award, Outstanding Alumni Award, Univ. of Denver Law School 2014. *Publications:* chapters in several books; articles in various legal journals. *Leisure interests:* skiing, travel, golf. *Address:* Norton Regulatory Strategies, PO Box 460971, Aurora, CO 80046, USA (office).

NORTON, Hugh Edward, BA; British business executive; b. 23 June 1936, London, England; s. of Lt-Gen. Edward F. Norton and I. Joyce Norton; m. 1st Janet M. Johnson 1965 (died 1993); one s.; m. 2nd F. Joy Harcup 1998; ed Winchester Coll., Trinity Coll., Oxford; joined British Petroleum Co. 1959, Exploration Dept 1960, in Abu Dhabi, Lebanon and Libya 1962–70, subsequently held appointments in Supply, Cen. Planning, Policy Planning, Regional Directorate Middle East and Int. and Govt Affairs Depts; Man. Dir BP's assoc. cos, Singapore, Malaysia, Hong Kong 1978–81, Dir of Planning 1981–83, Regional Dir for Near East, Middle East and Indian subcontinent 1981–86, Dir of Admin. 1983–86, Man. Dir and CEO BP Exploration Co. 1986–89, Chair. 1989–95, Man. Dir The British Petroleum Co. PLC 1989–95; Chair. BP Asia Pacific Pvt. Co. Ltd 1991–95; Dir (non-exec.), Inchcape PLC 1995–2004; Ind. Dir (non-exec.), Standard Chartered PLC 1995– (Sr Ind. Dir (non-exec.) 2003–06), Standard Chartered Bank Australia 1995–; Sr Ind. Dir (non-exec.), Standard Chartered Bank (Thai) Public Co. Ltd 1995–; Lasmo PLC 1997–; mem. Council Royal Inst. of Econ. Affairs 1991–, Chancellor's Court of Benefactors, Univ. of Oxford. *Leisure interests:* painting, ornithology, tennis, travel. *Address:* Standard Chartered Bank Australia, Level 1, 345 George Street, Sydney, NSW 2000, Australia. *Telephone:* (2) 9232-9333. *Fax:* (2) 9232-9345. *E-mail:* info@standardchartered.com. *Website:* www.standardchartered.com/au.

NORVIK, Harald J., MS; Norwegian business executive; b. 21 June 1946, Vadsø; ed Norwegian School of Econs and Business Admin., Bergen; Adviser, Nat. Inst. of Tech. 1971–73; Group Sec. for Industrial and Financial Affairs 1973–75; trainee course, Ministry of Foreign Affairs 1975–76; Personal Sec. to Prime Minister 1976–79; Minister of Petroleum and Energy 1979–81; Dir of Finance Aker mek. Verksted A/S 1981–85, Sr Exec. Vice-Pres. 1985–86; Pres. Astrup Hoyer A/S 1986–87; Pres. and Chair. Exec. Bd Statoil Group 1988–99; Chair. and Partner, Econ Management AS 2002–08, strategic adviser 2008–10; alternating Chair. Bd of Dirs SAS Norge ASA, Scandinavian Airlines System (SAS); Chair. Telenor ASA 2007–12; fmr Chair. Supervisory Bd Den Norske Bank; Advisor Exec. Bd, PriceWaterhouseCoopers; mem. Bd of Dirs DeepOcean Group Holding AS 2011–, ConocoPhillips, Petroleum Geo-Services ASA; Commdr Order of the Lion of Finland (1st Class), Grosses Bundesverdienstkreuz. *Address:* c/o PriceWaterhouseCoopers, 1128 Sixteenth Street North West, Washington, DC, USA.

NOSSAL, Sir Gustav Joseph Victor, AC, CBE, MB, BS, PhD, FRS, FRCP, FRACP, FRCPA, FRCPath, FRSE, FTSE, FAA; Australian medical research scientist and academic; *Professor Emeritus, University of Melbourne;* b. 4 June 1931, Bad Ischl, Austria; s. of R. I. Nossal and I. M. C. Lowenthal; m. Lyn B. Dunnicliff 1955; two s. two d.; ed St Aloysius Coll., Sydney, Univs of Sydney and Melbourne; Jr and Sr Resident Officer, Royal Prince Alfred Hosp., Sydney 1955–56; Research Fellow, The Walter and Eliza Hall Inst. of Medical Research, Melbourne 1957–59, Deputy Dir (Immunology) 1961–65, Dir 1965–96; Asst Prof., Dept of Genetics, Stanford Univ. School of Medicine, Calif., USA 1959–61; Prof. of Medical Biology, Univ. of Melbourne 1965–96, Prof. Emer. 1996–; Chair. WHO Global Programme for Vaccines and Immunization 1992–2002; Pnr, Foursight Assocs Pty Ltd 1996–; Dir CRA Ltd 1977–97; Pres. Australian Acad. of Science 1994–98; Foreign Assoc. NAS; mem. or hon. mem. many other nat. and foreign acads and learned socs; Hon. FRACOG; Hon. LLD (Monash, Melbourne); Hon. MD (Mainz, Newcastle, Leeds, Univ. of Western Australia); Hon. DSc (Sydney, Queensland, ANU, Univ. of New South Wales, La Trobe, McMaster, Oxford); Robert Koch Gold Medal, Albert Einstein World Award of Science, Emil von Behring Prize, Rabbi Shai Shacknai Prize, Burnet Medal of the Australian Acad. of Science, Australian of the Year 2000, Australia Post 6th Annual Australian Legends Award and many other awards and prizes. *Publications include:* Antibodies and Immunity 1968, Antigens, Lymphoid Cells and Immune Response 1971, Medical Science and Human Goals 1975, Nature's Defences (1978 Boyer Lectures), Reshaping Life: Key Issues in Genetic Engineering 1984, Immunology: the Making of a Modern Science 1988, Diversity and Discovery 2007; 540 publs on immunology. *Leisure interests:* golf, literature. *Address:* Department of Pathology, University of Melbourne, Melbourne, Vic. 3010 (office); 46 Fellows Street, Kew, Vic. 3101, Australia (home). *Telephone:* (3) 8344-6946 (office); (3) 9853-8256 (home). *E-mail:* gnossal@bigpond.net.au (home).

NOSSOL, Most Rev. Archbishop Alfons, PhD; Polish ecclesiastic and professor of theology; *Archbishop ad personam of Opole;* b. 8 Aug. 1932, Brożec, Opole Prov.; ed Higher Ecclesiastic Seminary in Opole Silesia, Catholic Univ. of Lublin (KUL); ordained priest, Opole 1957; Lecturer, Higher Ecclesiastic Seminary, Opole Silesia 1962–; Lecturer, Catholic Univ. of Lublin 1968, Asst Prof. 1976, Head, Second Dept of Dogmatic Theology 1977, Prof. 1981, Head Ecumenical Inst. 1983; Prof., Theological Dept, Jan Gutenberg Univ., Mainz 1977; Prof., Pontifical Theology Dept, Wrocław 1978; Prof., Diocesan Theology and Pastoral Inst., Opole 1981; Bishop of Opole 1977–14; Archbishop ad personam of Opole 1999–; High Chancellor and Prof., Opole Univ. Theological Dept 1994–; mem. Main Council Polish Episcopate; mem. Scientific Council of the Episcopate of Poland; Chair. Episcopate Cttee for Ecumenism; Vice-Leader Episcopate Cttee for Catholic Learning; mem. Christian Unity Pontifical Council, int. cttees for theological dialogue with the Orthodox Church and the Lutheran Church; mem. European Acad. of Science and Art, Salzburg; Commdr's Cross, Order of the Rebirth of Poland 2008, Great Cross of Merit 2009, Star, Order of Merit of the Fed. Repub. of Germany 2009, Zasłużony Kulturze Gloria Artis 2009, Order Ecce Homo 2011, Grand Cross, Order of the Rebirth of Poland 2013; Dr hc (Munster) 1991, (Mainz) 1992, (Opole) 1995, (Christian Acad. of Theology, Warsaw) 1997, (Bamberg) 1998, (Olomuniec) 2000, (Wrocław) 2007; Nagroda im. Karola Miarki 1994, Lux ex Silesia 1996, Augsburger Friedenspreis 1997, Kulturpreis Schlesien des Landes Niedersachsen 2001, Commanderies Missio Reconciliationis 2003, Jan Karski Eagle Award 2003, Wojciech Korfanty 2004, Fundacja na rzecz Nauki Polskiej 2005, Silesian Szmaragdu 2006, Deutscher Nationalpreis 2010, Klaus Hemmerlego 2010, Medal of Silesia 2011, Totus Prize. *Publications:* Theology for the Service of Faith 1968, Cognito Dei experimentalis 1974, Karol Barth Christology 1979, Truth and Love 1982, Towards a Civilization of Love 1984, Theology Closer to Life 1984, Der Mensch braucht Theologie 1986, Love the Victor of Truth 1987, Gelebte Theologie Heute 1991, By Truth to Love 1994, Love Rejoices Together with Truth 1996, Ecumenism as Imperative of Christian Conscience 2001, Brücken bauen Wege zu einem christlichen Europa von Morgen 2002. *Leisure interests:* classical literature, philosophy, the history of art. *Address:* Kuria Diecezjalna, ul. ul. Jan Pawła II 3, 25-013 Kielce, Poland (office). *Telephone:* -(41) 344-54-25 (home). *Fax:* (41) 341-56-56 (office). *E-mail:* kuriakie@kielce.opoka.org.pl. *Website:* diecezja.kielce.pl (office).

NOTE, Kessai H.; Marshall Islands politician and fmr head of state; b. 7 Aug. 1950, Ailinglablab Atoll; m. Mary Neimoj Yamamura; five c.; ed Vudal Coll., Papua New Guinea, Univ. of the South Pacific; began career as agricultural economist with Div. of Agric.; Senator from Jabat, fmr Speaker of Nitijela (Parl.); Pres. of the Marshall Islands 2000–08; unsuccessful cand. in 2008 presidential election; Minister of Foreign Affairs Jan.–Feb. 2016; fmr Vice-Chair. Air Marshall Islands; fmr Pres. Marshall Islands Sport Council; fmr Dir Marshall Islands Community Action Agency, Nat. Telecommunications Authority, Foreign Investment Bd; mem. United Democratic Party (UDP). *Address:* c/o Ministry of Foreign Affairs, PO Box 1349, Majuro, MH 96960, Marshall Islands (office).

NOTEBAERT, Richard C. (Dick), BA, MBA; American business executive; m. Peggy Notebaert; two c.; ed Univ. of Wisconsin; began career with Amitech Corpn 1969, various positions including Pres. Amitech Mobile Communications 1986–89, Pres. Indiana Bell 1989–92, Pres. Amitech Services 1992–93, Pres. and COO Amitech Corpn 1993–94, Pres. and CEO 1994, Chair. and CEO 1994–99; Pres. and CEO Tellabs 2000–02; Chair. and CEO Qwest Communications International Inc. 2002–07 (retd); mem. Bd Dirs AON Corpn 1998–, American Electric Power Co., Inc. 2011–, Cardinal Health Inc. 1999–2015; fmr mem. Bd Dirs Sears and Roebuck & Co.; mem. Bd of Trustees Univ. of Notre Dame 1997–, Chair. 2007–; fmr mem. Business Council, Reliability and Interoperability Council, Nat. Security Telecommunications Advisory Cttee (NSTAC), US Dept of State; fmr Vice-Chair. Civic Cttee of Commercial Club of Chicago; fmr Co-Chair. Alexis de Tocqueville Soc., United Way; Prin. Merrick Ventures LLC; mem. Exec. Advisory Bd The Edgewater Funds; Member of Board of Investors at Merrick Ventures, LLC. mem. Bd Execs Club of Chicago; Trustee, Univ. of Notre Dame; Distinguished Alumni Award, Univ. of Wisconsin 1999. *Address:* Merrick Ventures LLC, 350 North Orleans Street, #10, Chicago, IL 60654, USA.

NOTEBOOM, Ben J.; Dutch business executive; b. 4 July 1958; Dir of Asst Man., Zurel Holding 1982–84; Dow Chemical 1984–93; joined Randstad 1993, later held series of sr man. positions and started in-house services, with Europe-wide responsibility from 2000, mem. Exec. Bd 2001–14, Chair. Exec. Bd and CEO 2003–14, also responsible for Randstad in the Netherlands, Group HR, Group Marketing and Communications, Business Concept Devt, Group Legal and Public Affairs; mem. Supervisory Bd Corporate Express NV (fmrly Buhrmann NV) 2005–, Coastwide Laboratories, Inc., Koninklijke Ahold NV 2009–; mem. Supervisory Bd Aegon 2015–, Chair. Remuneration Cttee, mem. Risk Cttee. *Telephone:* (office). *E-mail:* info@aegon.com (office). *Website:* www.aegon.com (office).

NOTLEY, Rachel Anne, BA, LLB; Canadian lawyer and politician; b. 17 April 1964, Edmonton, Alberta; d. of Grant Notley and Sandra Mary Notley (néeWilkinson); m. Lou Arab; one s. one d.; ed Univ. of Alberta, Osgoode Hall Law School; early career as lawyer with Alberta Union of Provincial Employees; Occupational Health and Safety Officer, Health Sciences Asscn of BC, Vancouver 1994; fmr ministerial adviser to Attorney-Gen. of BC; lawyer with Nat. Union of Public and General Employees, Edmonton 2002; mem. Alberta Legis. Ass. for Edmonton-Strathcona 2008–; Premier of Alberta 2015–19; Leader of the Opposition in Alberta 2019–; mem. Alberta New Democratic Party, Leader 2014–. *Address:* Legislature Building, Room 307, 10800 97th Avenue, Edmonton, AB T5K 2B6, Canada (office). *Website:* www.albertandp.ca/rachel_notley_leader.

NOTT, Rt Hon. Sir John William Frederic, KCB, PC, BA; British fmr politician and business executive; b. 1 Feb. 1932; s. of Richard Nott and Phyllis Nott (née Francis); m. Miloska Sekol 1959; two s. one d.; ed Bradfield Coll. and Trinity Coll., Cambridge; Lt with 2nd Gurkha Rifles, (regular officer) 1952–56; Pres. Cambridge Union 1959; called to the Bar, Inner Temple 1959; MP for St Ives, Cornwall 1966–83; Minister of State at Treasury 1972–74; Sec. of State for Trade 1979–81, for Defence 1981–83; Man. Dir, Lazard Brothers 1983–90, Chair. and

CEO 1985–90; Chair., Hillsdown Holdings PLC 1993–99 (Dir 1991–), Maple Leaf Foods Inc., Toronto 1993–95; Deputy Chair., Royal Insurance PLC 1986–89; Chair. (non-exec.), Etam 1991–95; Dir, Apax Partners & Co. Capital 1996–. *Publications:* Here Today, Gone Tomorrow: Recollections of an Errant Politician 2002, Mr Wonderful Takes a Cruise 2004, Mr Wonderful Seeks Immortality: The Diary of a Restless Man 2014. *Leisure interests:* farming, fishing, golf. *Address:* 31 Walpole Street, London, SW3 4QS, England. *Telephone:* (20) 7730-2351. *Fax:* (20) 7730-9859.

NOTTAGE, Bernard Jonathon, MD; Bahamian physician and politician; b. 23 Oct. 1945; m. Portia Butterfield; two s.; ed Univ. of Aberdeen and Royal Coll. of Obstetricians and Gynaecologists, UK; fmr consultant in obstetrics and gynaecology, Princess Margaret Hosp., Nassau; mem. House of Ass. (PLP) for Garden Hills 1987–92, for Bain Town and Grants Town 2012–17; apptd to Senate 2005, Leader of Opposition Business 2007; Minister of Health and Nat. Insurance 2006, Minister of Nat. Security and Leader of Govt Business in House of Ass. 2012–17; Chair. Nat. Insurance Bd 1982–87; Pres. Central American and Caribbean Athletic Confed. 1982–90; fmr Pres. Scottish Univs Athletic Asscn, Bahamas Asscn of Athletic Asscns, Medical Asscn of the Bahamas, Bahamas Doctors' Union, Bahamas Family Planning Asscn; mem. Progressive Liberal Party (PLP) –1998, 2005–; Chair. Centre for Positive Change 1998–2006; CEO Coalition for Democratic Reform 2000–05; inducted into Central American and Caribbean Athletic Confed. Hall of Fame 2008. *Achievements include:* represented Bahamas in athletics (200 metres) at 1966 Commonwealth Games, 1967 Pan American Games, 1968 Mexico Summer Olympic Games and 1970 Commonwealth Games. *Address:* c/o Ministry of National Security, East Hill Street POB N-3746, Nassau, Bahamas (office).

NOTTAGE, Lynn; American playwright; b. 2 Nov. 1964, Brooklyn, New York; d. of Wallace Nottage and Jeannette Nottage; m. Tony Gerber; two c.; ed Brown Univ., Yale Univ. School of Drama; Visiting Lecturer, Yale Univ. School of Drama 2001–; also Assoc. Prof., Theatre Dept, Columbia School of the Arts; Bd mem. BRIC Arts/Media/Brooklyn, Voice and Vision, New Black Fest, Dramatists Guild; fmr Artist Trustee, Sundance Inst.; NEA/TCG residency grant 1999, Manhattan Theatre Club Fellowship, New Dramatists Fellowship, New York Foundation for the Arts Fellowship 2000, 2004, Audelco Award for Best Production of the Year and Best Playwright 2004, American Theatre Critics'/Steinberg New Play Award 2004, PEN/Laura Pels Award for Drama 2004, John Gassner Award for Best Playwright 2004, Outer Critics' Circle Award for Best Play 2004, Guggenheim Foundation Fellowship 2005, Nat. Black Theatre Festival August Wilson Playwriting Award 2005, Lucille Lortel Foundation Fellowship 2007, MacArthur Genius Award 2007, Obie Award for Playwriting 2009, Outer Critics' Circle Award 2009, Lucille Lortel Award 2009, New York Drama Critics' Circle Award 2009, Jeff Award 2009, Audelco 2009, Steinberg Distinguished Playwrights' Award, Dramatists' Guild Hull-Warriner Award, inaugural Horton Foote Prize for Outstanding New American Play, Helen Hayes Award, Lee Reynolds Award, Jewish World Watch iWitness Award. *Plays include:* Poof! (Heideman Award) 1993, Crumbs from the Table of Joy 1995, Mud, River, Stone 1998, Becoming American 2002, Snapshot 2002, Las Meninas (AT&T OnStage Award) 2002, Intimate Apparel (New York Drama Critics' Circle Award for Best Play 2004, AT&T OnStage Award) 2003, A Walk Through Time (children's musical), Por'Knockers, Fabulation (Obie Award for Playwriting 2005) 2003, Give Again? 2006, Point of Revue 2006, A Stone's Throw, Ruined (Manhattan Theatre Club, New York) (Pulitzer Prize for Drama) 2009, By The Way, Meet Vera Stark 2011, Our War 2014, In Your Arms 2015, Sweat (Pulitzer Prize for Drama 2017) 2015. *Publications:* Poof! 1993, Crumbs From the Table of Joy 1998, Mud, River, Stone 1999, Las Meninas 2004, Intimate Apparel/Fabulation 2006, Ruined 2009, By The Way, Meet Vera Stark 2013. *Address:* c/o Oliver Sultan, Creative Artists Agency, 405 Lexington Avenue, 19th Floor, New York, NY 10174, USA (office). *Telephone:* (212) 277-9000 (office). *Fax:* (212) 277-9099 (office). *E-mail:* osultan@caa.com (office); info@lynnnottage.net (home). *Website:* www.caa.com (office); www.lynnnottage.net.

NOTTEBOHM, Fernando, BA, PhD; American (b. Argentine) neuroscientist and academic; *Dorothea L. Leonhardt Professor, Head of the Laboratory of Animal Behavior, The Rockefeller University;* b. 1940, Buenos Aires, Argentina; ed Univ. of California, Berkeley; joined Faculty, The Rockefeller Univ., New York 1967, Asst Prof. 1967–76, Prof. 1976–, Dir Field Research Center for Ecology and Ethology 1981–2016, Dorothea L. Leonhardt Prof. and Head of Lab. of Animal Behavior 1996–; mem. NAS, Soc. for Neuroscience, American Philosophical Soc.; Fellow, American Acad. of Arts and Sciences, AAAS; Kenneth Caik Research Award, St John's Coll. Cambridge (UK) 1983, Karl Spencer Lashley Award (co-recipient) 1983, 2005, Charles A. Dana Award (co-recipient) 1983, 1992, Lewis S. Rosensteil Award for Distinguished Work in the Basic Medical Sciences (co-recipient) 2004, French Fondation Ipsen Neuronal Plasticity Prize 2004, MERIT Award, Nat. Insts of Mental Health 2004, Pattison Award for Distinguished Research in the Neurosciences 2004, Benjamin Franklin Medal in Life Science, The Franklin Inst. 2006, Sven Berggren Lecture and Prize, Royal Physiographic Soc., Lund 2006, Mortimer D. Sackler, MD Prize 2011. *Achievement:* most famous for providing definitive proof that neurogenesis occurs in the vertebrate brain. *Publications:* more than 135 scientific papers in professional journals. *Address:* Laboratory of Animal Behavior, The Rockefeller University, 1230 York Avenue, New York, NY 10065, USA (office). *Telephone:* (212) 327-8000 (office). *E-mail:* fernando.nottebohm@rockefeller.edu (office). *Website:* lab.rockefeller.edu/nottebohm (office).

NOUGAYRÈDE, Natalie; French journalist and editor; b. 29 May 1966, Dijon; ed educated in UK and Canada, Institut d'Etudes Politiques, Strasbourg, Centre de formation des journalistes, Paris; as a journalist, specialized in int. issues, including Eastern Europe and the post-Soviet space; began career as corresp. in Prague, Czechoslovakia for Libération newspaper and the BBC 1991, then as corresp. in the Caucasus for Libération and RFI; reporter in Caucasus region, covering Georgia, Azerbaijan and Ukraine 1993–95; Ed. Portraits pages of Libération 1995–96; Eastern Europe Corresp. for Le Monde newspaper in Ukraine and Russia 1996–2001, Moscow Corresp. 2001–05, Diplomatic Corresp. 2005–13, Dir and Ed.-in-Chief Le Monde 2013–14 (resgnd); Prix de la Presse diplomatique 2004, Prix Albert-Londres for her reporting on Chechnya and the hostage crisis in Beslan 2005. *Address:* c/o Le Monde, 80 boulevard Auguste Blanqui, 75707 Paris Cedex 13, France.

NOUR, Momtaz Saed Abu El-, BCom; Egyptian politician; b. 16 Dec. 1948; m.; ed Ain Shaims Univ.; joined Ministry of Finance 1972, Gen. Man. Int. Org. Div. 1990–96, Head of Cen. Treasury Dept in the State Gen. Budget Sector 1996–2003, Head of Minister of Finance Office Sector 2003–08, Councillor to the Minister of Finance 2008–11, Pvt. Adviser to the Minister of Finance 2011, Deputy Minister of Finance 2011, Minister of Finance 2011–13; mem. Bd of Dirs Nat. Investment Bank; fmr mem. Bd of Dirs Egyptian Postal Authority, South Cairo Electricity Distribution Co.

NOUVEL, Jean; French architect; b. 12 Aug. 1945, Fumel, Lot-et-Garonne; s. of Roger Nouvel and Renée Barlangue; m. Catherine Richard 1992; one d.; two s. by Odile Fillion; ed Ecole des Beaux Arts, Paris; has headed own architectural practice since 1970; amongst major completed buildings are: Arab World Inst., Paris 1987, Lyon Opera House, Cartier Foundation, Paris 1994, The Galeries Lafayette dept store, Berlin, Lucerne Culture and Congress Centre, Tours Conf. Centre, The Hotel, Lucerne, Andel office bldg, Prague, Nantes Justice Centre, Dentsu Tower, Tokyo, tech. centre, Wismar, museum of archaeology, Périgueux, Agbar office tower, Barcelona 2003, extension to Queen Sophia museum, Madrid 2005, Quai Branly Museum, Paris 2006, Guthrie Theater, Minneapolis 2006, Brembo's research and devt centre, Richemont Corpn HQ, Geneva, swimming pool of Les Bains des docks, Le Havre, Symphonic House, Copenhagen 2009, apartment bldg, 40 Mercer Street, Soho, New York, apartment bldg, Chelsea, New York, Ferrari factory in Maranello Modena, Pavilion B, Fiera di Genova; commission to design 10th Serpentine Gallery Pavillion, Theatre 'Archipel', Perpignan, One New Change, London 2010, Doha 9 skyscraper, Doha, Qatar 2012, City Hall, Montpellier 2012, Philharmonic Hall, Paris 2015, Le Nouvel Residences, Kuala Lumpur 2016, Louvre Museum, Abu Dhabi 2017; current projects under study or construction include sea centre museum, Le Havre, office bldg Horizons, Boulogne Billancourtan, two apartment bldgs, Ibiza, Spain, hotel in Barcelona, Tour de Verre, New York, a mixed use high-rise bldg in Sydney, two apartment bldgs in Singapore, the Grand Paris with Jean Marie Duthilleul and Michel Cantal-Dupart, Nat. Qatar Museum, design showroom RBC, Montpellier, two office bldgs in the dist of Brussels Midi train station, Foundation Imagine, Paris, police station and extension of Charleroi Danses, Charleroi; Architect Man. l'Île Seguin; Chevalier, Ordre nat. du Mérite, des Arts et des Lettres; Officier, Légion d'honneur; Dr hc (Univ. of Buenos Aires) 1983, (RCA, London) 2002, (Higher Inst. of Art, Cuba) 2006, (Université catholique de Louvain) 2013; hon. fellowships in AIA; Gold Medal, French Acad. of Architecture, RIBA Royal Gold Medal, Aga Khan Prize for the Arab World Inst., Nat. Grand Prize for Architecture, Francesco Borromini Int. Architecture Prize for Lucerne Culture and Congress Centre (Italy) 2001, Praemium Imperiale Career Prize, Japan Art Asscn 2001, Wolf Prize in the Arts 2005, Arnold W. Brunner Memorial Prize in Architecture 2005, Int. Highrise Award for the Agbar tower 2006, Pritzker Prize 2008, Special Jury Prize, AFEX 2018. *Address:* Ateliers Jean Nouvel, 10 Cité d'Angoulême, 75011 Paris, France (office). *Telephone:* 1-49-23-83-83 (office). *Fax:* 1-43-14-81-10 (office). *E-mail:* info@jeannouvel.fr (office). *Website:* www.jeannouvel.com (office).

NOVÁK, Jiří, JUDr; Czech politician and lawyer; *Partner, Brož & Sokol & Novák Attorneys at Law;* b. 11 April 1950, Hranice, Přerov Dist; m.; one s. one d.; ed J.E. Purkyně (now Masaryk) Univ., Brno; practising lawyer 1976–89; mem. Standing Comm. of the Presidium of Czech Nat. Council for Prison System Issues 1989–92; Deputy to Czech Nat. Council Feb.–June 1990; mem. Presidium, Czech Nat. Council 1990–92; Chair. Cttee on Law and Constitution of Czech Nat. Council 1990–92; Minister of Justice, Czech Repub. 1992–96; Chair. Legis. Council of Govt of Czech Repub. Feb.–July 1992; mem. Parl. 1996–98; Chair. Parl. Cttee for Petitions 1996–98; Vice-Chair. Interdepartmental Antidrug Comm. 1996; mem. Civic Democratic Party 1991–98; advocate 1998–, currently Partner, Brož & Sokol & Novák Attorneys at Law. *Address:* Nám. T.G. Masaryka 15, 750 02 Přerov, Czech Republic (home). *Telephone:* (2) 24941946 (home). *Fax:* (2) 24941940 (office). *E-mail:* advokati@akbsn.eu (office). *Website:* www.akbsn.eu (office).

NOVAKOVIC, Phebe N.; American business executive; *Chairman and CEO, General Dynamics Corporation;* fmr Deputy Assoc. Dir Office of Man. and Budget, US Dept of Defense, Washington, DC, later Special Asst to Sec. and Deputy Sec. of Defense –2001; joined General Dynamics Corpn 2001, Vice-Pres., Strategic Planning 2002–05, Sr Vice-Pres., Planning and Devt 2005–10, Exec. Vice-Pres., Marine Systems 2010–12, Pres. and COO General Dynamics Corpn May–Dec. 2012, Chair. and CEO 2013–; Dir, Abbott Diabetes Care, Inc., Abbott Laboratories 2010–. *Address:* General Dynamics Corporation, 2941 Fairview Park Drive, Suite 100, Falls Church, VA 22042, USA (office). *Telephone:* (703) 876-3000 (office). *Fax:* (703) 876-3125 (office). *E-mail:* info@generaldynamics.com (office). *Website:* www.generaldynamics.com (office).

NOVALIĆ, Fadil; Bosnia and Herzegovina business executive and politician; *Prime Minister, Federation of Bosnia and Herzegovina;* b. 25 Sept. 1959, Gradačac, Socialist Repub. of Bosnia and Herzegovina, Socialist Fed. Repub. of Yugoslavia; m.; three d.; ed Univ. of Sarajevo; volunteer soldier, 107th Brigade, army of Bosnia-Herzegovina, Gradačac during war in Bosnia 1992–95; Head of Devt, TMD Gradača (automotive parts mfr) 1983–90, Dir and Chair. 1990–96, Gen. Man. TMD Automotive Industry (part of CIMOS TMD) 2001–13; mem. Council, Faculty of Econs, Univ. of Sarajevo; mem. Supervisory Bd Wagner-Automotive, Furniture dd Gradačac; Prime Minister, Fed. of Bosnia and Herzegovina 2015–; mem. Stranka Demokratske Akcije (Party of Democratic Action). *Address:* Office of the Federation Prime Minister, 71000 Sarajevo, Alipašina 41, Bosnia and Herzegovina (office). *Telephone:* (33) 650457 (office). *Fax:* (33) 664816 (office). *E-mail:* premijer@fbihvlada.gov.ba (office). *Website:* www.fbihvlada.gov.ba (office).

NOVELLI, Hervé; French politician; *Mayor of Richelieu;* b. 6 March 1949, Paris; ed Univ. of Paris-Dauphine; began his career at Chambre Syndicale de la Sidérurgie Française (French Steel Industry Employers' Asscn); Chair. and Man. Dir family-owned prosthesis and orthesis maker based in Richelieu (Indre-et-Loire Dist) 1982–2006; Head of Minister's Office, Ministry of Industry, the Post Office and Tourism 1986–90; apptd Gen. Sec. Republican Party 1990, subsequently became mem. Exec. Bureau; mem. Nat. Ass. 1993–97, 2002–07, 2010–12, elected Deputy to Nat. Ass. for Indre-et-Loire Dist 1993, re-elected for UMP party 2002,

2007; joined Audace Pour l'Emploi group made up of 50 mems Parl. with entrepreneurial backgrounds 1993; elected to Conseil Général (deliberative ass.) as Rep. of Richelieu canton 1997, Vice-Pres. Conseil Général 1998–2001; Co-founder and first Gen. Del. Démocratie Libérale party 1998; mem. European Parl. 1999–2002 (resgnd); Municipal Councillor of Joué-lès-Tours 1995–2001, of Richelieu, Indre-et-Loire 2001–; Deputy Mayor of Richelieu 2001–08, Mayor 2008–; elected mem. Conseil Régional (governing body) of Centre region 2004 (resigned when appointed to Govt 2007); Pres. Les Réformateurs (asscn formed under aegis of UMP) 2002–; Co-founder Euro 92 Inst. to prepare French businesses for European Single Market 1988; Minister of State for Businesses and Foreign Trade 2007–09, for Commerce, Arts and Crafts, Small and Medium Businesses, Tourism and Services 2009–10; Co-founder Wikipme. *Website:* www.wikipme.fr.

NOVELLO, Antonia Coello, MD, MPH, DPhil; American paediatrician and public health official; b. 23 Aug. 1944, Fajardo, Puerto Rico; m. Joseph Novello 1970; ed Univ. of Michigan, Univ. of Puerto Rico, Johns Hopkins Univ.; intern, Mott Children's Hosp., Univ. of Michigan, Ann Arbor 1970–71; Univ. of Michigan Medical Center 1971–73, postgraduate training in nephrology, Dept of Internal Medicine 1973–74; postgraduate training, Dept of Pediatrics, Georgetown Univ. 1974–75; pvt. practice in pediatrics, Springfield, Va 1976–78; entered US Public Health Service 1978; various posts at NIH, Bethesda, Md 1978–90, Deputy Dir Nat. Inst. of Child Health and Human Devt 1986–90; apptd Clinical Prof. of Pediatrics, Georgetown Univ. Hosp., Washington, DC 1986, 1989, Uniformed Services Univ. of the Health Services, Bethesda 1989; Adjunct Prof. of Pediatrics and Communicable Diseases, Univ. of Michigan, of Int. Health, Johns Hopkins School of Public Health; Surgeon-Gen., US Public Health Service (first woman and first Hispanic) 1990–93; UNICEF Special Rep. for Health and Nutrition 1993–96; Visiting Prof. of Health Policy and Man., Johns Hopkins Univ. School of Hygiene and Public Health 1996–99 (also Special Dir for Community Health Policy); New York State Commr of Health 1999–2007, Pres. Health Research, Inc.; mem. Alpha Omega Alpha, American Soc. of Nephrology, American Soc. of Pediatric Nephrology, American Pediatrics Soc., Soc. for Pediatric Research; Fellow, American Acad. of Pediatrics; numerous professional appointments, memberships and affiliations; 50 hon. doctorates; recipient of numerous awards, including Surgeon Gen.'s Exemplary Service Medallion and Medal, USPHS Distinguished Service Medal, Army Legion of Merit, Coast Guard Meritorious Medal, US Dept of the Navy Distinguished Public Service Award, American Medical Asscn Nathan B. Davis Award, Congressional Hispanic Caucus Medal, Johns Hopkins Soc. of Scholars Award and Univ. Alumni Asscn's Woodrow Wilson Award for Distinguished Govt Service, Elizabeth Blackwell Award, Univ. of Michigan Medical Center Alumni Award and Alumna Council Athena Award, Public Health Service Commissioned Officer's Asscn Health Leader of the Year Award, Ellis Island Medal of Honor, Elizabeth Ann Seton Award, Charles C. Shepard Science Award for Scientific Excellence, American Medical Women's Asscn Leadership Award, Nat. Council of La Raza Pres.'s Award, Nat. Council of Alcohol and Drug Dependency Golden Key Award, American Acad. of Pediatrics Excellence in Public Service Award, Healthy American Fitness Leaders Award, Nat. Women's Hall of Fame, Ronald McDonald Children's Charities Award of Excellence, Hispanic Hero Award, Miami Children's Hosp. Int. Hall of Fame, Women at Work Science Award, Award for Leadership, Hispanic Heritage Awards 1998, James Smithson Bicentennial Medal 2002. *Leisure interest:* collecting antique furniture. *Address:* 5438 Coral Ridge Drive, Grand Blanc, MI 48439, USA. *E-mail:* novello.antonia@gmail.com.

NOVIKOV, Arkady; Russian restaurateur; b. 1962, Moscow; m. Nadezhda Advokatova; two c.; ed Culinary Coll. No. 174, G.V. Plekhanov Econs Acad.; started career as chef, Universitetsky restaurant; deputy chef, Havana restaurant, later chef, Olympic Lights restaurant; Chef, Hard Rock Cafe, Gorky Park Green Theatre 1990; opened Sirena fish restaurant 1992, followed by White Sun of the Desert 1997; Founder and Owner Yolki-Palki chain of over 60 restaurants 1996–; est. Vogue Café in jt venture with Condé Nast; opened Gallery restaurant 2004, Cantinetta Antinori 2004, numerous other restaurants; f. Rodnik NT to open and operate chain of grocery stores in Moscow 2004; opened his first restaurant in London 2011; Founding Dir Fed. of Restaurateurs and Hoteliers; TV presenter, The Candidate 2005. *Website:* www.novikovrestaurant.co.uk/arkady-novikov.

NOVIKOV, Sergey Petrovich; Russian mathematician and academic; *Distinguished University Professor, Department of Mathematics, University of Maryland;* b. 20 March 1938, Gorky (now Nizhniy Novgorod); s. Petr Novikov and Ludmila Keldysh; m. Eleonora Tsoi 1962; one s. two d.; ed Moscow Univ., Steklov Math. Inst.; Prof., Moscow Univ. 1966–; Head, Dept, Landau Inst. for Theoretical Physics 1975–2014, Chair. Dept of Geometry and Topology, Moscow Univ. 1984–; Head, Dept, Steklov Math. Inst. 1983–; Distinguished Univ. Prof., Univ. of Maryland, USA 1997–; Corresp. mem. USSR (now Russian) Acad. of Sciences 1966–, mem. 1981–; Foreign Assoc., NAS 1994, European Acad. of Sciences 2003; Hon. mem. London Math. Soc. 1987, Serbian Acad. of Art and Science 1988, Academia Europaea 1993, Pontifical Acad. of Sciences 1996, Montenegro Acad. of Art and Science 2011; Dr hc (Athens) 1989, (Tel-Aviv) 1999, (Loughborough) 2016; Moscow Math. Soc. Prize 1964, Lenin Prize 1967, Field's Medal, Int. Math. Union 1970, Lobachevsky Int. Prize, USSR Acad. of Sciences 1981, Wolf Foundation Prize in Math. 2005, Bogoliubov Gold Medal, Russian Acad. of Sciences 2008, Euler Medal, Russian Acad. of Sciences 2013, Pogorelov Prize, Ukrainian Acad. of Sciences (NANU) 2013. *Publications:* Algebraic and Differential Topology 1960–70, Theory of Solitons: Topological Phenomena in Physics 1974–2003, Riemannian Geometry and Poisson Structures 1983–90, Discrete Systems 1997. *Leisure interest:* history. *Address:* University of Maryland, College Park, IPST, MD 20742, USA (office); Landau Institute for Theoretical Physics, Kosygina 2, 117334 Moscow, Russia (office). *Telephone:* (301) 405-4836 (College Park) (office); (495) 137-32-44 (Moscow) (office); (495) 135-12-24 (Moscow) (home); (301) 779-7472 (USA) (home). *Fax:* (301) 314-9363 (USA) (office). *E-mail:* novikov@iumd.edu (office). *Website:* www.umd.edu/researchandfaculty/novikov.php (office).

NOVITSKY, Gennady; Belarusian politician and construction engineer; b. 2 Jan. 1949, Mogilev; m.; two s.; ed Belarus State Polytechnic Inst. Acad. of Social Sciences; foreman, supervising foreman, Head of Construction Div., Mogilev Construction Trust No. 12 1971–77; worked in econ. man. and as a party exec. 1977–94, Chief Engineer of Mogilev Region Agricultural Construction Enterprise, Instructor and Head of Construction Dept at Mogilev Region CP Cttee, Head of Mogilev Agricultural Construction Enterprise Bd; Minister of Architecture and Construction 1994–97; Deputy, later Acting Prime Minister 1997–2001; Prime Minister 2001–03; Chair. Council of the Repub., Nat. Ass. of Repub. of Belarus 2003–11, apptd Chair. Standing Cttee 2011; Certificate of Honour, Council Ministers, Repub. of Belarus. *Leisure interests:* simple sports like jogging.

NOVOSELOV, Sir Konstantin (Kostya) Sergeevich, Kt, MSc, PhD, FRS; Russian/British physicist and academic; *Royal Society Research Professor, University of Manchester;* b. 23 Aug. 1974, Nizhny Tagil, Russian SFSR, USSR; ed Moscow Physical-Technical Univ., High Magnetic Field Lab., Univ. of Nijmegen, the Netherlands; Researcher, Inst. for Microelectronics Tech., Chernogolovka 1997–99; Researcher, High Magnetic Field Lab., Univ. of Nijmegen 1999–2001; Researcher, Univ. of Manchester 2001–05, Leverhulme Research Fellow 2005–06, Royal Soc. Research Fellow 2007–14, Prof. of Physics 2010–13, Langworthy Prof. of Physics 2013–, Royal Soc. Research Prof. 2014–; Hon. FInstP 2011, Hon. FRSC 2011; Hon. DSc (Manchester) 2011; Early Career Fellowship, Leverhulme Trust 2004, Nicholas Kurti European Prize 2007, Univ. of Manchester Researcher of the Year 2008, Young Scientist Prize, Int. Union of Pure and Applied Science 2008, Technology Review-35 Young Innovator 2008, Europhysics Prize (jtly) 2008, Nobel Prize in Physics (with Andre Geim) 2010, Leverhulme Medal, Royal Soc. 2013, Onsager Medal 2014, Carbon Medal 2016, Dalton Medal 2016. *Achievements include:* best known for his discovery, with Andre Geim, of two-dimensional crystals made of carbon atoms (and most notably graphene) in 2004 at Univ. of Manchester; original jt paper on graphene in Science in 2004 acknowledged by ISI citation index as "one of the most cited recent papers in the field of Physics". *Publications:* more than 250 peer-refereed research papers, including many in Nature and in Science, on condensed matter physics. *Address:* Room 2.09, Schuster Building, The School of Physics and Astronomy, University of Manchester, Manchester, M13 9PL, England (office). *Telephone:* (161) 275-4119 (office). *E-mail:* kostya@manchester.ac.uk (office). *Website:* www.physics.manchester.ac.uk (office); www.condmat.physics.manchester.ac.uk/people/academic/kostyanovoselov (office).

NOVOTNÝ, Petr; Czech actor, writer and producer; b. 6 Aug. 1947, Olomouc; m. Miroslava Novotný; four c.; ed Charles Univ., Prague; mem. Laterna Magika Theatre, Prague; Owner Firma 6P and Amfora Football Club. *Awards:* Best Comedian and Best Programme (Novotný), TYTY Awards 1999, Most Popular Male Actor, TYTY Awards 2000. *Theatre productions directed:* Sugar (Some Like It Hot), Gypsies Go to Heaven, Libuse (opera) 1995, Hello Dolly! 1996, My Fair Lady, Evita 1999, Pokuseni sv. Antonina 2001. *Television includes:* Big Ear; writer and presenter of numerous programmes. *Leisure interests:* football, cooking. *Address:* Firma 6P—Petr Novotný, s.r.o, Koterovská 833, 15500 Prague 5, Czech Republic (office). *Telephone:* 721658090 (office). *E-mail:* fialkalenka@hotmail.com (office).

NOWAK, Rev. Arkadiusz; Polish ecclesiastic and charity worker; b. 28 Nov. 1966, Rybnik; ed Pontifical Faculty of Theology, Warsaw, Szczecin Univ.; mem. Camillian Order (Ordo Clericorum Regularium Ministrantium Infirmis—OSCam.) 1985–; opened first AIDS hospice in Poland; Dir Centre of Re-adaptation Ministry of Health, Konstancin (brs in Piastów and Anielin) 1990–; ordained priest 1993; Co-founder Polish Humanitarian Aid Foundation Res Humanae 1993–; Adviser on Issues of AIDS and Drugs to Minister of Health 1995–2001, Plenipotentiary 2001; co-Fonder Pres. Inst. of Patient Rights and Health Educ. 2004; Order of the Smile 1995; numerous prizes include Medal of St Georges (Tygodnik Powszechny Award) 1993, Award for Acting Against Intolerance, Xenophobia and Racialism (Finland), Global Leader for Tomorrow, World Econ. Forum 2000, UN Award for Breaking the Silence on HIV/AIDS 2000.

NOWINA-KONOPKA, Piotr Maria, MSc (Econs), PhD; Polish politician, economist and diplomatist; b. 27 May 1949, Chorzów; s. of Mikołaj Nowina-Konopka and Anna Nowina-Konopka; m. Wanda Nowina-Konopka 1975; two d.; ed Higher School of Econs, Sopot, Univ. of Gdańsk; Asst, Gdańsk Tech. Univ. 1972–74; post-doctoral studies, Univ. of Gdansk 1975–77; Deputy Head, Centre of Revocatory Maritime Chamber, Gdynia 1977–79; Lecturer, Foreign Trade Econs Inst. of Gdańsk Univ. 1979–89; Co-founder and Sec. Catholic Intelligentsia Club in Gdańsk 1980–81; mem. Solidarity Independent Self-governing Trade Union 1980–90, aide to Pres. Lech Wałęsa 1982–89, Press Spokesman 1988–89, Chief of Press 1989; mem. Civic Cttee attached to Lech Wałęsa 1988–91; Lecturer, Gdańsk Theology Inst. 1988–89; Minister of State in Chancellery of Pres. of Poland 1989–90; Sec.-Gen. Democratic Union 1990–94; Union for Freedom Sec. for Foreign Affairs 1994–98; Deputy to Sejm (Parl.) 1991–2001, Vice-Chair. Cttee for the European Treaty 1992–97, Deputy Chair. Jt Parl. Cttee Poland-European Parl. 1993–97; Sec. of State Office of the Cttee for European Integration 1998; Sec. of State in Chancellery of Prime Minister 1998–99; Vice-Rector Coll. of Europe, Bruges/Warsaw 1999–2004; adviser to Nat. Parl. of Georgia 2005–06; Dir for Relations with Nat. Parls, European Parl. 2006–09; Dir European Parl. Liaison Office with US Congress, Washington, DC 2010–12; Amb. to the Holy See 2013–16; Prof., Giedroyć Coll., Warsaw 2006–; mem. Foreign Affairs Comm. 1991–2001; Pres. Robert Schuman Foundation 1996, now mem. Bd of Founders; Deputy Chief Negotiator for negotiations with EU 1998–99; Chevalier, Ordre nat. du Mérite, Officer, Légion d'honneur, Verdienstkreuz Erste Klasse des Verdienstordens, Officer, Polonia Restituta, Commdr, Ordre de Roi Leopold (Belgium). *Publications:* weekly columnist in Wprost, political articles in different books/periodicals. *Leisure interests:* family life, reading, social sciences, yachting, riding, skiing.

NOWITZKI, Dirk Werner; German professional basketball player; b. 19 June 1978, Würzburg; s. of Jörg-Werner Nowitzki and Helga Nowitzki; ed Röntgen Gymnasium, Würzburg; power forward for the Dallas Mavericks, Nat. Basketball Asscn (NBA), USA; played for DJK Würzburg basketball club 1994–98; drafted ninth overall by the Milwaukee Bucks in 1998 NBA Draft and immediately traded to Mavericks 1998–, led team to 11 consecutive NBA Playoffs 2000/01–10/11, including an NBA Finals appearance 2006 and franchise's first championship 2011; led German nat. basketball team to a bronze medal in FIBA World Championship 2002, silver medal in EuroBasket 2005; f. Dirk Nowitzki Foundation (charity aiming to fight poverty in Africa); Euroscar European Basketball Player of the Year 2002–06, 2011, Gazzetta dello Sport 2002–06, 2011, Mister Europa European Player of the Year, Superbasket magazine 2005, FIBA Europe

Basketball Player of the Year 2005, 2011; All-NBA First Team 2005–07, 2009, NBA All-Star 2002–12, 2014–15, FIBA World Championship Most Valuable Player (MVP) 2002, EuroBasket MVP 2005, NBA MVP (first European player) 2007, NBA Finals MVP 2011, Silbernes Lorbeerblatt 2011, German Sports Personality of the Year 2011, Naismith Legacy Award 2012, Magic Johnson Award 2014. *Leisure interests:* reading, playing the saxophone. *Address:* Dirk Nowitzki Foundation, c/o Dallas Mavericks, The Pavilion, 2909 Taylor Street, Dallas, TX 75226, USA; c/o Helga Nowitzki, Am Kirschberg 18, 97218 Gerbrunn, Germany. *Website:* www.mavs.com; www.dirk-nowitzki-foundation.org.

NOWOTNY, Ewald, DrIur; Austrian economist, academic, central banker and fmr politician; *Governor, Oesterreichische Nationalbank;* b. 1944, Vienna; m.; one s.; ed Vienna Univ. of Econs, Inst. for Advanced Studies, Vienna, Univ. of Vienna; Asst, Inst. of Econs and Finance, Johannes Kepler Univ., Linz 1968–73; mem., later Chair., Österreichischen Postsparkasse 1971–79; mem. Nationalrat (Parl., SPÖ) 1979–99, mem. Finance Cttee 1985–99; Visiting Prof., Harvard Univ. 1971–72, Technische Universität Darmstadt 1972; Prof., Inst. für Finanzwissenschaften, Univ. of Linz 1973–82; Prof., Vienna Univ. of Econs 1982–, Vice-Rector 2003–04; Vice-Pres. and mem. Bd of Man. European Investment Bank (EIB), Luxembourg 1999–2003; CEO BAWAG PSK Group 2006–07; mem. Gen. Council, Oesterreichische Nationalbank 2007–08, Gov. 2008–; mem. Governing Council, European Central Bank; Grosses Goldenes Ehrenzeichen für Verdienste um die Republik Österreich; Hon. DEcon (Alpen-Adria Univ., Klagenfurt) 2008. *Publications include:* Der öffentliche Sektor: Einführung in die Finanzwissenschaft 2009; numerous contribs to econ. journals. *Address:* Office of the Governor, Oesterreichische Nationalbank, Otto-Wagner-Pl. 3, 1090 Vienna, Austria (office). *Telephone:* (1) 404-20 (office). *Fax:* (1) 404-23-99 (office). *E-mail:* gouverneur@oenb.at (office). *Website:* www.oenb.at (office).

NOWRA, Louis; Australian writer and scriptwriter; b. 12 Dec. 1950; m. Mandy Sayer; Dr hc (Griffiths Univ.) 1996; Literature Board Grants 1975, 1977, 1979, 1980, 1981, 1982; Prix Italia 1990, NSW Premier's Literary Prize 1992, Victoria Premier's Prize 1994, Australian Literary Soc. Gold Medal 1994, The Australia/Canada Award 1994, The Green Room Award for Best New Play 1995, Courier-Mail Book of the Year 2000, Winner, Green Room Awards, New Australian Opera (Librettist) – Midnight Son, Patrick White Literary Award 2013. *Radio:* Albert Names Edward 1975, The Song Room 1980, The Widows 1984, Summer of the Aliens 1989, Sydney 1993, Moon of the Exploding Trees 1995, The Divine Hammer 2001, Jez 2006, Far North 2008, Light of Darkness 2010, Echo Point 2012, The Wedding in Venice 2012. *Films:* Map of the Human Heart 1992, Heaven's Burning 1997, K-19: The Widowmaker 2002, Black and White 2002, Rain of the Children 2008. *Plays:* Kiss The One-Eyed Priest 1973, Death of Joe Orton 1974, Inner Voices 1977, Visions 1979, Beauty and the Beast 1980, Lulu 1981, The Prince of Homburg 1982, Spellbound 1983, The Golden Age 1985, The Song Room 1987, Capricornia 1988, Byzantine Flowers 1989, Cos 1992, Crow 1994, Jungle 1995, Radiance 1998, Language of the Gods 1999, The Woman with Dog's Eyes 2004, The Marvellous Boy 2005, The Emperor of Sydney 2006, This Much is True 2017. *Television:* Displaced Persons 1985, Hunger 1986, The Last Resort (TV series) 1988, Twisted Tales Directly From My Heart to You 1996, The Straits 2014, First Australians 2018. *Publications:* The Misery of Beauty 1976, The Cheated 1978, Albert Names Edward 1975, Inner Voices 1978, Visions 1979, Inside The Island/The Precious Woman 1981, The Song Room 1982, Sunrise 1983, The Golden Age 1985, Palu 1987, Capricornia 1988, The Watchtower 1992, Summer of the Aliens 1992, Cosi 1992, Radiance 1993, The Temple 1993, Crow 1994, The Incorruptible 1995, Cosi (Australian Film Inst. Award for Best Adapted Screenplay 1996) 1996, Red Nights 1997, The Jungle 1998, Language of the Gods 1999, The Twelfth of Never 1999, Byzantine Flowers 2000, Radiance 2000, In the Gutter... Looking at the Stars (anthology, co-ed.) 2000, Abaza 2001, Warne's World 2002, Walkabout 2003, Shooting the Moon 2004, Chihuahuas, Women and Me 2005, Bad Dreaming 2007, The Boyce Trilogy Includes: The Woman with Dog's Eyes, The Marvellous Boy, The Emperor of Sydney 2007, Ice 2008, Into That Forest 2012, Kings Cross: A Biography 2013, Woolloomooloo: A Biography 2017. *Leisure interests:* cricket, mycology. *Address:* c/o HLA Management, PO Box 1536, Strawberry Hills, NSW 2012, Australia (office). *Telephone:* (2) 9549-3000 (office). *Fax:* (2) 9310-4113 (office). *E-mail:* hla@hlamgt.com.au (office). *Website:* www.hlamgt.com.au (office).

NOYCE, Phillip; Australian film director; b. 29 April 1950, Griffith, NSW; ed Univ. of Sydney, Australian Film and Television School. *Films include:* That's Showbiz 1973, Castor and Pollux (Rouben Mamoulien Award, Sydney Film Festival) 1974, God Knows Why But It Works 1975, Backroads (writer, dir and producer) 1977, Newsfront 1978, Heatwave 1982, Echoes of Paradise (1987), Dead Calm 1989, Blind Fury 1989, Patriot Games 1992, Sliver 1993, Clear and Present Danger 1994, The Saint 1997, The Bone Collector 1999, Rabbit Proof Fence (dir and producer) 2002, The Quiet American 2002, Catch a Fire 2006, Salt 2010, Mary and Martha 2013, The Giver 2014, Roots (segment) 2016. *Television includes:* The Dismissal (mini-series) 1983, Cowra Breakout (mini-series) 1984, The Hitchhiker (various episodes) 1983, Tru Calling (series pilot) 2003. *Address:* c/o Endeavor Talent Agency, 9701 Wiltshire Boulevard, #1000, Beverly Hills, CA 90212, USA (office); c/o The Cameron Creswell Agency Pty Ltd, 5/2 New McLean Street, Edgcliff, NSW 2027, Australia (office).

NOYER, Christian; French civil servant and fmr central banker; b. 6 Oct. 1950, Soisy-sous-Montmorency, Val d'Oise; ed Univs of Rennes and Paris, Inst. of Political Science, Ecole Nat. d'Admin; mil. service as naval officer 1972; joined French Treasury 1976, Chief of Banking Office, then of Export Credit Office 1982–85, Deputy Dir in charge of Int. Multilateral Issues 1988–90, then of Debt Man., Monetary and Banking Issues 1990–92, Dir of Dept responsible for public holdings and public financing 1992–93, Dir of Treasury 1993–95; Financial Attaché, French Del. to EC, Brussels 1980–82; Econ. Adviser to Minister for Econ. Affairs and Finance Edouard Balladur 1986–88, Chief of Staff to E. Alphandéry 1993, to Jean Arthuis 1995–97; Dir, Ministry for Econ. Affairs, Finance and Industry 1997–98; Alt. Gov., IMF and World Bank 1993–95; Vice-Pres., European Cen. Bank 1998–2002; Gov., Banque de France 2003–15, Hon. Gov. 2015–; Alt. mem. European Monetary Cttee 1988–90, mem. 1993–95, 1998; Alt. mem. G7 and G10 1993–95; mem. Working Party No. 3 OECD 1993–95; Chair. Paris Club of Creditor Countries 1993–97; mem. European Econ. and Financial Cttee 1999–2002; Chair. BIS, Basel, Switzerland 2010–15; Commdr, Légion d'honneur, des Arts et des Lettres; Chevalier, Ordre nat. du Mérite; Commdr, Ordre Nat. du Lion, Grand Officier, Ordre Nat. du Mérite (Senegal); Great Cross, Orden del Mérito (Spain); Officier, Ordre Nat. de la Valeur (Cameroun). *Publications:* Banks: The Rules of the Game 1990; various articles. *Leisure interest:* sailing. *Address:* 9 rue de Valois, 75001 Paris, France (office). *Telephone:* 1-42-92-65-71 (office).

NOYORI, Ryōji, MEng, PhD; Japanese scientist and academic; b. 3 Sept. 1938, Kobe; m. Hiroko Oshima; two s.; ed Kyoto Univ.; Research Assoc. Dept of Industrial Chem., Kyoto Univ. 1963–68; Assoc. Prof., Dept of Chem., Nagoya Univ. 1968–72, Prof. 1972–2003, Dir Chemical Instrument Center 1979–91, Dean Grad. School of Science 1997–99, Dir Research Center for Materials Science 2000–03, Distinguished Prof. 2004–; Pres. RIKEN (scientific research inst.) 2003–15; Dir ERATO Molecular Catalysis Project, Research Devt Corpn of Japan 1991–96; Science Adviser, Ministry of Educ., Science and Culture 1992–96, mem. Scientific Council 1996–2003; Prof. Inst. for Fundamental Research on Organic Chem., Kyushu Univ. 1993–96; Cttee Chair. Research for the Future Program on Advanced Processes, Japan Soc. for the Promotion of Science 1996–2002; Pres. Soc. of Synthetic Organic Chem. 1997–99; Visiting Prof. at numerous int. univs; mem. editorial bd of 30 learned journals; mem. numerous professional bodies including Chemical Soc. of Japan, Pharmaceutical Soc. of Japan, ACS, RSC (UK); numerous hon. degrees, including Hon. Dr (Univ. of Rennes 1) 2000, (Technical Univ. of Munich) 2005, (RWTH Aachen Univ., Germany) 2005; numerous awards and prizes, including Chemical Soc. of Japan Award 1985, Japan Acad. Prize 1995, Wolf Prize (jtly) 2001, Nobel Prize in Chem. (jt recipient) 2001, The Luigi Sacconi Medal 2002, Gold Medal, Scientific Partnership Foundation, Russia 2003, Molecular Chirality Award, Molecular Chirality Research Org. 2006, The Amedeo Avogadro Gold Medal, The Italian Chemical Soc. 2006, The Centenary Medal, The Royal Soc. of Canada 2009, Lomonosov Gold Medal, Russian Acad. of Sciences 2009, and several ACS awards. *Address:* Department of Chemistry, Graduate School of Science, Nagoya University, Furo-cho, Chikusa, Nagoya, Aichi, 464-8602 (office); 1105 Luxembourg House, 8-9, Yonban-cho, Chiyoda, Tokyo 102-0081, Japan (home). *Telephone:* (52) 789-2956 (Nagoya University) (office). *Fax:* (52) 783-4177 (Nagoya University) (office). *E-mail:* noyori@chem3.chem.nagoya-u.ac.jp (office). *Website:* www.nagoya-u.ac.jp/en/ (office).

NOZARI, Gholamhossein, BS, MA; Iranian petroleum industry executive; b. 1954; responsible for air defence in southern Iran during Iran–Iraq War; fmr Head of Security, Nat. Iranian South Oil Co.; fmr mem. Cen. Council, Islamic Republic Party; fmr Deputy Chair. Majlis Energy Comm., fmr mem. Majlis Devt Comm.; fmr Man. Dir Nat. Iranian Cen. Oil Co., then Man. Dir Nat. Iranian Oil Co. –2007; Minister of Petroleum 2007–09.

NOZIÈRES, Philippe Pierre Gaston François; French physicist; *Emeritus, Institut Laue-Langevin;* b. 12 April 1932, Paris; s. of Henri Nozières and Alice Noël; m. Catherine Michel 1982; one d. (one s. and one d. by previous m.); ed Ecole Normale Supérieure and Princeton Univ., USA; Prof. of Physics, Univ. of Paris 1961–72; Physicist, Institut Laue-Langevin (ILL) 1972–76, currently Emer.; Prof. of Physics, Grenoble Univ. 1976–83; Prof. of Statistical Physics, Collège de France 1983–2001; mem. Acad. des Sciences (Inst. de France); Foreign Assoc. NAS; Holweck Prize 1976, Prix du CEA (Acad. des Sciences) 1979, Wolf Prize 1985, Gold Medal CNRS 1988, Feenberg Medal 2000. *Publications:* papers on theoretical and statistical physics. *Address:* ILL, 71 avenue des Martyrs, CS 20156, 38042 Grenoble Cedex 9, France (office); 15 route de Saint Nizier, 38180 Seyssins, France (home). *Telephone:* (4) 76-20-72-74 (office); (4) 76-21-60-28 (home). *Fax:* (4) 76-88-24-16 (office). *E-mail:* nozieres@ill.fr (office).

NOZOE, Kuniaki, BA; Japanese business executive; ed Waseda Univ.; joined Fujitsu Ltd 1971, has held several exec. positions including Corp. Sr Vice-Pres. Fujitsu Ltd –2007, Corp. Vice-Pres., Group Support, and Corp. First Sr Vice-Pres. 2007–, Corp. Sr Exec. Vice-Pres. April–June 2008, Pres. and Rep. Dir, Fujitsu Ltd June 2008–10; mem. or fmr mem. Bd of Dirs, Fujitsu Frontech Ltd, Asscn of Radio Industries and Businesses. *Address:* c/o Fujitsu Headquarters, Shiodome City Center, 1-5-2 Higashi-Shimbashi, Minato-ku, Tokyo 105-7123, Japan. *E-mail:* info@fujitsu.com.

NQAKULA, Charles; South African politician; b. 13 Sept. 1942; m. Nosiviwe Mapisa-Nqakula; ed Cradock, Lovedale; fmr waiter, wine steward; fmr clerk, Dept of Bantu Educ.; journalist, Midland News 1966; Political Reporter, Imvo Zabantsundu 1973; with Daily Dispatch, London 1976; placed under banning order 1981, declared prohibited immigrant, forbidden to enter S Africa 1982; est. Veritas News Agency, Zwelitsha 1982; Publicity Sec. United Democratic Front (UDF) 1983; fmr underground operative African Nat. Congress (ANC), mem. Nat. Exec. Cttee 1994; granted amnesty 1991; mem. S African Communist Party (SACP), Deputy Gen. Sec. 1991, later Gen. Sec., Chair.; Parl. Counsellor to Pres. –2001; Deputy Minister of Home Affairs 2001–02; Minister of Safety and Security 2002–08, of Defence 2008–09; mem. Union of Black Journalists, Vice-Pres. 1976; Vice-Pres. Writers' Asscn of S Africa (later Media Workers' Asscn of S Africa) 1979; High Commr to Mozambique 2012; mem. Nat. Ass. 2014–, Chair. Joint Standing Cttee on Intelligence 2016–. *Leisure interests:* composing choral music, writing poetry. *Address:* ANC Constituency Office, 45 Main Street, Kirkwood 6120, South Africa (office). *Telephone:* (21) 4033922 (office). *E-mail:* cnqakula@parliament.gov.za (office). *Website:* www.pa.org.za (office).

NSANZE, Augustin, PhD; Burundian politician, diplomatist, historian and academic; b. 1953, Kibumbu, Mbuye; m.; ed Univ. of Burundi, Univ. of Paris, France; Instructor, Lycée Clarte-Notre Dame, Bujimbura 1978–79; Lecturer, Univ. of Burundi 1979–90, Prof. 1987–90, Advisor to Dir of Dept of Scientific Research 1989, Chief of Scientific Research Service 1990; First Advisor to Pres. on social and cultural issues 1992–98; Consultant on the history of Burundi, UNESCO 1998; Researcher, Univ. of Lieden 1999; Research Asst, Univ. of Laval, Canada 2001–03; Counsellor, Perm. Mission to UN, New York 2004–06; Amb. to Ethiopia (also accred to Djibouti) and Rep. to African Union and Econ. Comm. for Africa 2006–08; Amb. and Perm. Rep. to UN, New York 2008–09; Minister for External Relations 2009–11. *Publications:* several books and academic articles. *Address:* c/o Ministry of External Relations and International Co-operation, Bujumbura, Burundi.

NSEREKO, Daniel David Ntanda, LLB, MCJ, LLM, JSD; Ugandan judge and academic; *Judge, Appeals Chamber, Special Tribunal for Lebanon;* b. 27 Nov.

1941, Masaka; s. of Obadiya Yese Busuulwa and Tolofaayina Ndagire Busuulwa; m. Helen Yvonne Dingle Nsereko; five c.; ed Univ. of East Africa, Dar es Salaam, Tanzania, Howard Univ. School of Law, Washington, DC, USA, The Hague Acad., Netherlands, New York Univ. School of Law, USA; pupil advocate with Kiwanuka & Co., Advocates, Kampala 1968; Advocate, High Court of Uganda 1972–, included on List of Counsel eligible for appointment to represent accused or victims before Int. Criminal Court 2007; Lecturer in Law, Makerere Univ., Kampala 1971–75, Sr Lecturer in Law 1975–78; full-time pvt. law practice, Kampala 1978–82; expert consultant, Crime Prevention and Criminal Justice Br. of UN Centre for Social Devt and Humanitarian Affairs, New York, USA 1983–84, Social Affairs Officer, UN Centre for Social Devt and Humanitarian Affairs 1983; Sr Lecturer in Law, Univ. of Botswana, Gaborone 1984–92, Head of Dept of Law 1985–93, Assoc. Prof. of Law 1992–96, Prof. of Law 1996–; Walter S. Owen Visiting Prof. of Law, Univ. of British Columbia, Canada 1993–94; Visiting Scholar, Max Planck Inst. for Foreign and Int. Criminal Law, Freiburg, Germany 1995, 2006; Judge, Trial Div., Int. Criminal Court, The Hague 2008–09, Div. 2009–12; Judge, Appeals Chamber, Special Tribunal for Lebanon 2012–; mem. Advisory Cttee on Nomination of Judges of the ICC 2012–; served as Amnesty International Trial Observer to Swaziland 1990, Amnesty International mission to Swaziland to investigate allegations of human rights abuses and to inspect prison conditions 1991, Amnesty International Trial Observer to Ethiopia 1996, Head of an Amnesty International del. to Lesotho to investigate allegations of human rights and humanitarian law violations and inspecting prison conditions following S African and Botswana mil. intervention 1998; mem. Exec. Cttee Uganda Red Cross Soc. 1975–80, Bd Int. Soc. for Reform of Criminal Law, Vancouver, Canada 1988–, Advisory Exec. War Crimes Research Office, American Univ., Washington, DC 2006–; mem. Editorial Council Journal of Church and State 1985–, Editorial Bd Journal Violence, Aggression and Terrorism 1986–90, Criminal Law Forum: An International Journal 1990–, University of Botswana Law Journal 2005–; mem. Int. Advisory Bd Int. Doctorate School of Excellence, Univ. of Cologne, Germany 2006–; mem. Uganda Law Soc. 1972– (mem. Law Council (Exec. Cttee) 1975–80), East African Law Soc. 2004–; Fellow, Inst. of Int. Law and Int. Relations Research, The Hague Acad. of Int. Law 1982; Medal of Int. Soc. for Reform of Criminal Law 1996. *Publications:* Police Powers and the Rights of the Individual in Uganda 1973, The International Protection of Refugees (doctoral dissertation) 1975, Antigone: A Greek Play by Sophocles (trans. into the Luganda language) 1989, English–Luganda Law Dictionary 1993, Eddembe Lyaffe (Our Rights; treatise written in the Luganda language) 1995, Criminal Law and Procedure in Uganda (in, International Encyclopaedia of Laws) 1996, Criminal Procedure in Botswana: Cases and Materials (third edn) 2002, Constitutional Law in Botswana (in, International Encyclopaedia of Laws) 2002, Legal Ethics in Botswana: Cases and Materials (with K. Solo) 2004, Criminal Law and Procedure in Botswana 2007; several book chapters and reviews and numerous articles in professional journals. *Address:* Special Tribunal for Lebanon, PO Box 115, 2260 AC Leidschendam, The Netherlands (office). *Telephone:* (70) 800-3550 (office). *E-mail:* stl-pressoffice@un .org (office). *Website:* www.stl-tsl.org (office).

NSHUTI, Paul Manasseh, PhD; Rwandan academic and government official; *Co-founder, University of Kigali;* ed Univ. of Aberdeen, UK; worked in Kenya as a sr academic at Catholic Univ. of Eastern Africa; also taught at Strathmore Coll. (now Strathmore Univ.); Minister of Commerce, Industry, Investment, Tourism and Co-operation 2004–05, of Finance and Econ. Planning 2005–06; Presidential Advisor c. 2011; Chair. Crystal Ventures Ltd (business arm of ruling Rwandan Patriotic Front) –2013; Co-founder Univ. of Kigali 2013–, also Chair. Bd of Promoters; fmr Chair. Bd of Govs., School of Finance and Banking (SFB), Kigali. *Publication:* A Text Book of Principles of Auditing. *Address:* University of Kigali, KN 3 Road, PO Box 2611, Kigali, Rwanda (office). *Telephone:* 788304804 (office). *E-mail:* universityofkigaliuok@gmail.com (office). *Website:* www.uok.ac.rw (office).

NSIBAMBI, Apolo Robin, BSc, MSc, PhD; Ugandan politician; b. 27 Nov. 1938; s. of Simeon Nsibambi; m. 1st Rhoda Nsibambi (deceased); m. 2nd Esther Nsibambi; ed Univ. of London, UK, Univ. of Chicago, USA, Univ. of Nairobi, Kenya; Dean, Faculty of Social Science, Makerere Univ. 1978–83, 1985–87, Head, Dept of Political 1987–90, Dir Makerere Inst. of Social Research 1994–96, Chancellor of Makerere Univ. 2003–07; Minister of Public Service 1996–98, of Educ. and Sports 1998–99; Prime Minister of Uganda 1999–2011; mem. Nat. Resistance Movt. *Address:* c/o Office of the Prime Minister, PO Box 341, Kampala, Uganda.

N'SINGA UDJUU ONGWABEKI UNTUBE, Joseph; Democratic Republic of the Congo politician; *President, Union chrétienne pour le renouveau et la justice;* b. (Joseph N'Singa Udjuu), 29 Oct. 1934, Nsontin, Bandundu Prov.; s. of Nshue O. N'singa and Monkaju Medji; m. Mbu Modiri Marie; four s. four d.; ed Kokoro and Kabue Seminaries, Bandundu Prov., Univ. of Lovanium (now Kinshasa); Juridical adviser of the provisional Govt, Inongo, Bandundu Prov. 1963; Provincial Minister of the Interior (Home Affairs) and Information 1963–64; elected Nat. Deputy 1964; Vice-Minister of the Interior (Home Affairs) 1965, of Justice 1965; Minister of Justice 1966–69; Minister of State for Home Affairs 1968; Minister of State at the Presidency Sept. 1970; Chair. Nat. Inst. of Social Security 1975–80; Co-founder and mem. Cen. Cttee, Mouvement Populaire de la Révolution (MPR) 1980–83 (Exec. Sec. 1981–83), First Vice-Pres. 1980–83; Chair. 1990–91; Prime Minister (first State Commissary) 1981; Pres. Judiciary Council 1987–90; mem. Sovereign Nat. Conf. and elected Counsellor of the Repub. during Nat. Conf.; mem. transition Parl.; Minister of Transportation 1994–95, of Justice 1995–96, of Reconstruction and Planning 1997; participant at nat. consultation assizes conf., Kinshasa 2000; mem. Jt Comm. Cttee in charge of Law Review 2001; Founder and Pres. own political party Union chrétienne pour le renouveau et la justice (UCRJ); Grand Cordon of the Leopard Nat. Order, Commdr of the Belgian King Leopold II Cross, Commdr of the Cen. African Repub. Order of Merit. *Leisure interests:* walking, jogging. *Address:* 68 Avenue Uvira, #5 Commune de Gombe, Kinshasa, Democratic Republic of the Congo (home). *E-mail:* nsinga5@hotmail.com.

NTAHOMVUKIYE, Emmanuel, lic.en.droit; Burundian magistrate and politician; *Minister of National Defence and War Veterans;* b. 1969, Murirwe, Gitega Prov.; s. of Bernard Kayoya and Therese Berahino; ed Univ. of Burundi; began career as magistrate, Makamba regional court 1998–2002, Bururi regional court 2002–04; Inspector of Justice 2004–08; Adviser to Supreme Court 2008–09; Pres.

Anti-Corruption Court 2009–11; Inspector of Justice, Special Court of Land and Other Assets 2011–14; Minister of Nat. Defence and War Veterans 2015–. *Address:* Ministry of National Defence and War Veterans, Bujumbura, Burundi (office).

NTIBANTUNGANYA, Sylvestre; Burundian politician; b. 8 May 1956, Nyamu-tobo; m. 1st Eusebie Ntibantunganya (deceased); m. 2nd Pascasie Minani; one s. two d.; ed Nat. Audiovisual Inst. Paris, Nat. Univ. of Rwanda; worked for Burundi State TV and Radio 1984–87; joined Nat. Secr. Unity for Nat. Progress (UPRONA); in exile in Rwanda 1979–83; Founding mem. Sahwanya-Frodebu Party, mem. Exec. Cttee 1991, Leader 1993; Chief Ed. Aube de la Démocratie (Frodebu Party newspaper) until 1993; Deputy for Gitega 1993; Minister for External Relations 1993; fmr Speaker of Parl.; Pres. of Burundi 1994–96; Chair. Nat. Security Council 1996; mem. Senate 2002. *Publications:* Une démocratie pour tous les Burundais 1999.

NTISEZERANA, Gabriel; Burundian economist, fmr central banker and politician; *President, Senate;* m.; three c.; Customers Officer, Credit Dept, Interbank Burundi s.a. in charge of business portfolio 1993–99, Man. Cen. Market Br. 1999–2000, Head of Asian Area br. Jan.–Aug. 2001; Chair. Banque nationale de développement économique (Nat. Bank for Econ. Devt) –2006; Gov. Cen. Bank 2006–07, Gov. for Burundi, IMF 2006; mem. Conseil nat. pour la défense de la démocratie-Forces pour la défense de la démocratie (CNDD-FDD—Nat. Council for the Defence of Democracy-Forces for the Defence of Democracy); Second Vice-Pres. of Burundi 2007–10; Pres. Senate 2010–. *Address:* Office of the President, Senate, Bujumbura, Burundi (office).

NTOUTOUME EMANE, Jean-François; Gabonese politician; b. 6 Oct. 1939; mem. Fang ethnic group from Estuaire Prov.; worked at Ministry of Finance; Personal Adviser to Pres. Omar Bongo 1976–90; Minister of Civil and Commercial Aviation –1984, of Commerce and Consumer Affairs 1984–87; elected to Nat. Ass. for Gabonese Democratic Party (PDG) 1990–2007; Minister of State Control, Decentralization, Territorial Admin and Regional Integration 1994, declined the position; led negotiations with the opposition that resulted in the Paris Accords 1994; Minister of State for the Land-Survey Register, Housing, Lodgings, Urban Affairs and Spatial Planning 1997–99; campaign manager for Pres. Bongo during his re-election campaign 1998; Prime Minister of Gabon and Head of Govt 1999–2006; Mayor of Libreville 2008–14; Hon. Vice-Pres. PDG 2008. *Address:* c/o Parti Démocratique Gabonais (PDG), Immeuble PETROGAB, BP 268, Libreville, Gabon.

NTSAY, Christian; Malagasy business executive, consultant and politician; *Prime Minister;* b. 27 March 1961, Diégo-Suarez; m.; two c.; ed Univ. d'Antananarivo, Centres d'Etudes Financières, Economiques et Bancaires, Paris/Marseilles; Jr Auditor, Sud Marine Enterprise (shipyard), Marseilles 1985–86; Admin. and Financial Dir, also Deputy Gen. Man. and later Gen. Man., SECREN Shipyard, Madagascar 1986–92; Nat. Coordinator, ILO/UNDP Tech. Cooperation Project, Madagascar 1992–98; Gen. Man., Solima Oil Co., Madagascar 1993–97; Founding Pres. Radio Frequency Plus Madagascar and Compagnie Madagascar Distribution Services 1993–2001; Chair. Bd of Dirs SMTH (Hilton) and CCM (Andilana Beach) (tourism establishments) 1996–2002; Exec. Chair. Entreprendre Madagascar 1997–2007; worked as nat. and int. consultant in fields of int. trade, devt, nutrition, employment for several int. orgs including UNDP, World Bank, UN Population Fund and EU 1998–2007; int. consultant to ILO in the fields of employment and enterprise for Senegal, Cameroon, Comoros, Madagascar, Mauritania, Democratic Repub. of Congo, Benin and Mauritius 1999–2007; Minister of Tourism 2002–03; ILO Rep. in Antananarivo for Comoros, Madagascar, Mauritius and Seychelles 2008–18; Prime Minister 2018–. *Address:* Office of the Prime Minister, BP 248, Palais d'Etat Mahazoarivo, 101 Antananarivo, Madagascar (office). *Telephone:* (20) 2264498 (office). *Fax:* (20) 2233116 (office). *E-mail:* stp-ca@primature.gov.mg (office). *Website:* www.primature.gov.mg (office).

NTUMUKE, Gen. (retd) Atanasio Salvador; Mozambican politician and fmr army officer; *Minister of National Defence;* b. Cabo Delgado; fmr Commdr in Frente de Libertação de Moçambique (Frelimo) guerrilla army during war for Mozambican independence 1980s, including as Commdr, First Motorized Infantry Brigade and Mil. Commdr, Maputo Prov.; Minister of Nat. Defence 2015–. *Address:* Ministry of National Defence, Av. Mártires de Mueda 280, CP 3216, Maputo, Mozambique (office). *Telephone:* 21492081 (office). *Fax:* 21491619 (office). *E-mail:* mdn@mdn.gov.mz (office). *Website:* www.mdn.gov.mz (office).

NUAIMI, Ali ibn Ibrahim an-, MS; Saudi Arabian government official and fmr oil industry executive; b. 1935, Eastern Prov.; m. 1962; four c.; ed Int. Coll. Beirut, American Univ., Beirut and Lehigh Univ., Pennsylvania and Stanford Univ., USA; Asst Geologist, Exploration Dept, Aramco 1953, Hydrologist and Geologist 1963–67, worked in Econs and Public Relations Dept 1967–69, Vice-Pres. Aramco 1975, Sr Vice-Pres. 1978, Dir 1980, Exec. Vice-Pres., Operations 1982, Pres. 1984, CEO 1988; Minister of Petroleum and Mineral Resources 1995–2016. *Leisure interests:* hunting, hiking. *Address:* c/o Ministry of Petroleum and Mineral Resources, PO Box 247, Al Ma'ather Street, Riyadh 11191, Saudi Arabia.

NUAIMI, HH Sheikh Humaid bin Rashid an-, (Ruler of Ajman); United Arab Emirates; b. 1931, Ajman; s. of Sheikh Rashid bin Humaid an-Nuaimi; at least four s.; Ruler of Ajman 6 Sept. 1981–; mem. Supreme Council of UAE 1981–; Patron, Sheikh Humaid bin Rashid Prizes for Culture and Science 1983–. *Address:* Ruler's Palace, PO Box 1, Ajman, United Arab Emirates.

NUAIMI, Rashid Abdullah an-, BEng; United Arab Emirates politician; ed Univ. of Cairo, Egypt; began career at Dept of Oil and Industrial Affairs, Abu Dhabi; joined Emirati Ministry of Foreign Affairs, worked in various capacities –1975, Dir of Political Affairs Dept 1975–76, Undersecretary for Foreign Affairs 1976–77, Minister of State for Foreign Affairs 1977–90, Minister of Foreign Affairs of UAE 1990–2005.

NUDER, Pär, LLM; Swedish politician; *Chairman, Skistar AB;* b. 27 March 1963, Täby; m.; two d.; ed Stockholm Univ.; mem. Österåker Municipal Exec. Cttee 1982–94; Chair. Stockholm Co. Br. Swedish Social Democratic Youth League 1986–89, mem. Nat. Exec. Cttee 1989–90; Political Adviser to Minister for Justice 1986–87, to Prime Minister's Office 1988–91, to Prime Minister 1994–96, 1996–97; Alt. mem. Riksdag 1988–94, mem. 1994, mem. Parl. Cttee on Justice 1994–97;

Political Sec. Social Democratic Parl. Party Group 1992–94, mem. Exec. Cttee, Stockholm Co. Br. of Social Democratic Party (SDP) 1992–94; Vice-Pres. Bd Nat. Swedish Art Museums 1995–97; Exec. mem. Prime Minister's Advisory Council for Baltic Sea Co-operation 1996–2000; Chair. Task Force on Organized Crime in the Baltic Sea Area 1996–2000; State Sec., Prime Minister's Office 1997–2002; Minister for Policy Co-ordination 2002–04, for Finance 2004–06; Chair. Vasallen AB 2001–02, AP3 2011–, AMF Insurance 2015–, Skistar AB 2017–; econ. adviser to SDP –2010 Sr Counselor, Albright Stonebridge Group 2010–; Columnist, Hemsö Fastighets AB 2010–; mem. Bd of Dirs, Vin & Sprit AB 2001–02, Fabege AB 2010–; Visiting Fellow, Harvard Univ. 2007. *Address:* Skistar AB, 780 67 Sälen, Sweden (office). *Telephone:* (46) 280-880-50 (office). *E-mail:* info@skistar.com (office). *Website:* www.skistar.com (office).

NUHIU, Agim, DrIur; Macedonian (ethnic Albanian) academic and government official; b. 24 Aug. 1977, Slatino, Tetovo; m.; two c.; ed State Univ. of Tetovo, Univ. of Tirana; Docent and Assoc. Dean, Faculty of Law, State Univ. of Tetova 2015–16; mem. Bashkimi Demokratik për Integrim/Demokratska Unija za Integracija (BDI—Democratic Union for Integration); Co-ordinator Justicia legal journal; Scientific Ed., Ulpianus journal and Chair. Scientific Research Forum, Asscn of Albanians Lawyers in Macedonia; mem. Comm. for Protection Against Discrimination; Minister of Internal Affairs 2016–17. *Address:* c/o Ministry of Internal Affairs, 1000 Skopje, ul. Dimče Mirčev 9, North Macedonia (office). *Telephone:* (2) 3117222 (office). *Fax:* (2) 3112468 (office). *E-mail:* kontakt@mvr.gov.mk (office). *Website:* www.mvr.gov.mk (office).

NUHODŽIĆ, Mevludin; Montenegrin politician; *Minister of Internal Affairs;* b. 29 Aug. 1959, Bijelo Polje, Socialist Repub. of Montenegro, Socialist Fed. Repub. of Yugoslavia; ed Faculty of Political Science and Faculty of Law; mem. Presidency of Demokratska Partija Socijalista Crne Gore (Democratic Party of Socialists of Montenegro); held posts of Minister without Portfolio, Dir of Joint Activities of State Authorities, Dir of Property and Dels of Four Seats in Parl.; mem. Skupština (Parl.), Chair. Security and Defence Cttee, mem. Cttee on Int. Relations and Emigrants, mem. Anti-corruption Cttee, Head of Del. to Parl. Ass. of NATO; Minister of Internal Affairs 2016–. *Address:* Ministry of Internal Affairs, 81000 Podgorica, bul. Svetog Petra Cetinjskog 22, Montenegro (office). *Telephone:* (20) 241590 (office). *Fax:* (20) 246779 (office). *E-mail:* mevludin.nuhodzic@skupstina .me (office); kabinet@mup.gov.me (office). *Website:* www.mup.gov.me (office).

NUJOMA, Sam; Namibian fmr head of state; *Founding President of the Republic of Namibia and Founding Father of the Namibian Nation;* b. (Samuel Shafiihuma Nujoma), 12 May 1929, Etunda Village, Ongandjera Dist; s. of Daniel Uutoni Nujoma and Helvi Mpingana Kondombolo; m. Kovambo Theopoldine Katjimune 1956; three s. one d.; ed Okahaol Finnish Mission School, St Barnabas School, Windhoek; with State Railways until 1957; Municipal Clerk, Windhoek 1957; clerk in wholesale store 1957–59; elected Leader of Ovamboland People's Org. (OPO) 1959; arrested Dec. 1959; went into exile 1960; Founder, with Herman Toivo ja Toivo and Pres. SWAPO (SW Africa People's Org.) April 1960–2007; appeared before UN Cttee on SW Africa June 1960; set up SWAPO provisional HQ in Dar es Salaam, Tanzania March 1961; arrested on return to Windhoek and formally ordered out of the country March 1966; turned to armed struggle after rejection by Int. Court of Justice of SWAPO complaint against S Africa Aug. 1966; gave evidence at UN Security Council Oct. 1971; led SWAPO negotiations at numerous int. negotiations culminating in implementation in March 1989 of UN Resolution 435 providing for independence of Namibia; returned to Namibia Sept. 1989; mem. Constituent Ass. 1989–90; Pres. of Namibia 1990–2005, also Minister of Home Affairs 1995–96; Fellow, Inst. of Governance and Social Research – Jos, Plateau State, Nigeria 2003–; apptd Founding Chancellor, Univ. of Namibia 1993; Hon. Prof., China Univ. of Geosciences 2006; Grand Master, Order of Merit Grand Cruz (Brazil), Companion of the Order of Star of Ghana 2004; Hon. LLD (Ahmadu Bello Univ., Nigeria) 1982, (Lincoln Univ., USA) 1990, (Ohio Central State Univ., USA) 1993, (State Univ. of NJ, USA) 1997; Hon. DTech (Fed. Univ. of Tech., Minna) 1992; Hon. DEd (Univ. of Namibia) 1993; Hon. DSc (Abubakar Tafawa Balewa Univ., Nigeria) 2003; Dr hc (Academic Council, Russian Econ. Acad.) 1998, (People's Friendship Univ. of Russia), (Copperbelt Univ.) 2014, (Univ. of Kinshasa) 2014; Lenin Peace Prize 1973, Frederic Joliot Curie Gold Medal 1980, Ho Chi Minh Peace Award 1988, Indira Gandhi Peace Prize 1990, Africa Prize for Leadership for Sustainable End to Hunger, New York 1995, Order of Friendship Award (Viet Nam) 2000, International Kim Il Sung Prize (India) 2008, Sir Seretse Khama SADC Medal 2010, African Union 'Son of Africa' Award for lifetime achievement in the promotion of peace and dignity on the African continent 2015. *Publications:* To Free Namibia 1994, Where Others Wavered: My Life in SWAPO and My Participation in the Liberation Struggle of Namibia (autobiography) 2001. *Address:* Sam Nujoma Foundation, Private Bag 13220, Robert Mugabe Avenue, Windhoek, Namibia (office). *Telephone:* (61) 377700 (office). *Fax:* (61) 253098 (office). *E-mail:* jnauta@iway.na (office). *Website:* www.samnujomafoundation.org (office).

NUJOMA, Uutoni Daniel, LLB; Namibian politician; *Minister of Land Reform;* b. 8 Sept. 1952, Kapako; s. of Sam Nujoma (fmr SWAPO leader and Pres. of Namibia); ed Univ. of Warwick, UK, Lund Univ., Sweden; grew up in exile in Angola; mem. SWAPO Cen. Cttee 2002–; mem. Nat. Ass. (Parl.) 2005–; Deputy Minister of Justice 2005–10; Minister of Foreign Affairs 2010–12; Minister of Justice 2012–15, of Land Reform 2015–. *Address:* Ministry of Land Reform, 55 Robert Mugabe Avenue, PMB 13343, Windhoek, Namibia (office). *Telephone:* (61) 2965371 (office). *Fax:* (61) 254737 (office). *Website:* www.mlr.gov.na (office).

NUKAGA, Fukushiro; Japanese politician and fmr journalist; b. 1944; ed Waseda Univ.; fmr political and econ. reporter for Sankei Shimbun; fmr mem. Ibaraki Prefectural Ass.; mem. LDP, fmr Chair. Policy Research Council (Jiyu-Minshuto); mem. for Kitakanto Block, House of Reps; fmr Deputy Chief Cabinet Sec.; Dir-Gen. Defence Agency 1998–2000, of Econ. Planning Agency 2000–01; Minister of State for Defence 2005–06; Minister of Finance 2007–08. *Address:* Liberal Democratic Party, 1-11-23, Nagata-cho, Chiyoda-ku, Tokyo 100-8910, Japan (office). *Telephone:* (3) 3581-6211 (office). *E-mail:* koho@ldp.jimin.or.jp (office). *Website:* www.jimin.jp (office).

NUMAN, Yasin Said; Yemeni politician; b. 1 Jan. 1947; fmr Deputy Prime Minister and Minister of Fisheries; Prime Minister of Democratic Republic of Yemen 1986–90, Minister of Labour and Civil Service 1986; Gen. Sec. Yemeni Socialist Party (Al-Hizb Al-Ishtiraki Al-Yamani) 2005–15.

NUMATA, Sadaaki; Japanese diplomatist (retd); b. 1943, Hyogo Pref.; m. Kyoko Numata; one s. one d.; ed Tokyo Univ., Univ. Coll., Oxford, UK; served in Embassy in London 1968–70, positions at Ministry of Foreign Affairs, Tokyo dealing with econ. co-operation, then N American affairs 1970–76, served in Embassy in Jakarta, Indonesia 1976–78, Politico-Mil. Officer, Embassy in Washington, DC 1978–82, Dir, First Int. Orgs (GATT) Div., Econ. Affairs Bureau, Tokyo 1982–84, Dir Japan–US Security Div., N American affairs Bureau 1984–85, Dir First N America Div. 1985–87, Deputy Japanese Rep. to Conf. on Disarmament, Geneva 1987–88, Deputy Head of Mission, Embassy in Canberra, Australia 1989–91, Deputy Spokesman of Foreign Ministry, Tokyo 1991–94, Deputy Head of Mission, Embassy in London 1994–98, Foreign Ministry Spokesman and Dir-Gen. for Press and Public Information, Tokyo 1998–2000, Amb. to Pakistan 2000–02, Amb. in Charge of Okinawan Affairs 2003–04, Amb. to Canada 2005–07; Exec. Dir Centre for Global Partnership, Japan Foundation for Global Partnership 2007–09; Advisor, Kajima Corpn; Vice-Chair. English-Speaking Union of Japan 2008–11, Chair. 2011–; Chair. Hon. Bd of Advisors, Canadian Chamber of Commerce Japan; mem. Advisory Cttee on Int. Broadcasting Programmes, NHK; Counsellor, Foreign Press Center/Japan. *Leisure interests:* singing folk songs, fly fishing, skiing. *Address:* English-Speaking Union of Japan, Fujikage-Building, 9th Floor, Motoakasaka 1-1-5, Minato-ku, Tokyo 107-0051, Japan (office). *Telephone:* (3) 3423-0970 (office). *Fax:* (3) 3423-0971 (office). *E-mail:* esuj@esuj.gr.jp (office). *Website:* www.esuj.gr.jp (office).

NUNES FERREIRA, Aloysio; Brazilian lawyer and politician; b. 5 April 1945, São José do Rio Preto; m. Gisele Nunes; ed Univ. de São Paulo, Univ. Paris VII, Univ. Paris I; Public Prosecutor, State of São Paulo 1981; mem. São Paulo Legis. Ass. 1982–90; Deputy Gov., State of São Paulo 1991–94; mem. Chamber of Deputies for São Paulo 1995–2005; Sec.-Gen. of Presidency of the Repub. 1999; Minister of Justice 2001; mem. Senate for São Paulo 2011–17, Pres., Senate Cttee on Foreign Relations and Nat. Defence 2015–17, Chair. Jt Cttee on Intelligence Activities of Nat. Congress 2016–17, Govt Leader in Senate 2016–17; Minister of Foreign Affairs 2017–19; mem. Partido del Movimiento Democrático Brasileño (PMDB) 1980–97; mem. Partido de la Socialdemocracia Brasileña (PSDB) 1997–. *Address:* c/o Ministry of Foreign Affairs, Esplanada dos Ministérios, Bloco H, Brasília DF, 70170-900, Brazil (office).

NÚÑEZ DE REYES, Gabriela, MEconSc; Honduran economist, politician and central banker; m. Juan Carlos Reyes; ed Univ. Nacional Autonoma de Honduras, State Univ. of New York at Albany, USA; Financial Analyst, Banco Cen. de Honduras 1985–94, later Pres.; Tech. Sec., UDAPE (econ. policy analysis unit) 1993–95, Under-Sec. of Finance 1995–96, Honduras Rep. at IDB, IMF and World Bank 1996–98, Minister of Finance 1998–2002, Gov. Banco Central de Honduras (Central Bank of Honduras) 2006–07, Minister of Finance 2009–10; currently Deputy (Liberal) National Congress, Leader Parl. Group of Partido Liberal de Honduras; fmr Vice-Pres. Banco Atlántida; mem. Bd of Dirs Asociación de Instituciones Bancarias de Honduras. *Address:* Congreso Nacional de Honduras, Calle Bolivar, Tegucigalpa, MDC, Honduras (office). *Website:* www .congresonacional.hn/bancada_liberal/gabrielanunez (office).

NÚÑEZ FÁBREGA, Fernando; Panamanian journalist, economist and politician; b. 1946; s. of Emilio Núñez Portuondo and Olga Fábrega y Fábrega; ed Univ. of Missouri, USA; fmr Pres. Société Panamericane de Bourse, Andorra; fmr Man. Dir El Siglo (daily newspaper); fmr Exec. Vice-Pres. Vision Group (news media conglomerate in Spanish, based in London); several diplomatic postings including Consul Gen. in Tampa, Fla, USA, Vice-Consul in Nassau, Bahamas and Sec. Gen., Consulate in Maracaibo, Venezuela; fmr Sec.-Gen., Ministry of Agric.; Exec. Sec., Consejo Nacional de Transparencia contra la Corrupción (anti-corruption agency) 2009–11 (resgnd); Gov. Coclé Prov. 2011–13; Minister of Foreign Affairs 2013–14 (resgnd); fmr Pres. Nat. Broadcasting Asscn of Panama.

NUÑEZ, Marianela; Argentine ballet dancer; *Principal Dancer, The Royal Ballet;* b. 23 March 1982, Buenos Aires; ed The Royal Ballet Upper School; began training with Teatro Colón Ballet School at the age of six, joined Teatro Colón Co. at the age 14; joined The Royal Ballet 1998, promoted to First Soloist 2000, Principal Dancer 2002–; dance partner with Maximiliano Guerra in Uruguay, Spain, Italy and Japan 1997; toured as guest ballerina with Teatro Colón in Europe and USA; appeared as guest artist with Vienna State Opera Ballet, American Ballet Theatre, La Scala, Milan, Ballet Estable del Teatro Colón, Ballet Argentino de La Plata Australian Ballet; performed in Petipa's Diana and Acteon, and Raymonda, Balanchine's Agon, Nijinska's Les Biches; created roles in Will Tuckett's Love's Fool, Mark Baldwin's Towards Poetry, Matthew Hart's Acheron's Dream 2000, Javier De Frutos' The Misty Frontier 2001, David Bintley's Les Saisons 2003, Christopher Wheeldon's Danse à grande vitesse 2006, Tuckett's The Seven Deadly Sins 2007; Best Female Dancer, Critics' Circle National Dance Awards 2005, 2012, Konex de Platino for Best Dancer of the Decade 2009, Olivier Award for Outstanding Achievement in Dance 2013. *Ballet includes:* by Kenneth MacMillan: Soirée Musicale (Lead Female) 1997, The Dying Swan 2007, Romeo and Juliet (Juliet) 2008, Mayerling (Mitzi Caspar and Princess Louise), Manon (Lescaut's Mistress), Concerto, Elite Syncopations; by Frederick Ashton: Cinderella, La fille mal gardée, Les Rendezvous, Dante Sonata, La Valse, Ondine, Daphnis, Chloë; lead roles: Christopher Wheeldon's Alice's Adventures in Wonderland, Balanchine's Ballo della Regina, The Royal Ballets's The Prince of the Pagodas (Princess Belle Rose); others: Macmillan's Enigma Variations (Isabel Fitton), Nijinsky's L'Aprés-Midi d'un Faune (Nymph), Coppélia (Swanilda and Aurora), Checkmate (Black Queen), Giselle (Myrtha), Swan Lake (Odette/Odile), The Nutcracker (Sugar Plum Fairy), Don Quixote (Kitri), Onegin (Olga and Tatiana), La Bayadère (Third Shadow Solo, Nikiya and Gamzatti), Sleeping Beauty (Fairy of Vitality, Lilac Fairy and Aurora) (producer), Apollo (Polyhimnia), Carmen (Carmen); Stephen Baynes' Beyond Bach (with Inaki Urlezaga), Antony Tudor's The Leaves Are Fading, Nacho Duato's Por Vos Muero, William Forsythe's In the middle, somewhat elevated, Jiří Kylián's Sinfonietta. *Address:* Royal Opera House, Bow Street, Covent Garden, London, WC2E 9DD, England (office). *Website:* www.roh.org.uk.

NUNN, Hon. Samuel Augustus (Sam), LLB; American lawyer and politician; *Co-Chairman, Nuclear Threat Initiative;* b. 8 Sept. 1938, Macon, Ga; s. of Samuel Augustus Nunn and Elizabeth Cannon Nunn; m. Colleen O'Brien 1965; one s. one d.; ed Georgia Inst. of Tech., Emory Univ. and Emory Univ. Law School, Atlanta; pvt. law practice 1964–72; mem. Georgia House of Reps 1968–72; US Senator from Georgia (Democrat) 1972–97, mem. Armed Services Cttee, Govt Affairs Cttee, Small Business Cttee; Sr Partner, King & Spalding, Atlanta 1997 (now retd); currently Co-Chair. Nuclear Threat Initiative, Washington, CEO –2017; Distinguished Prof., Sam Nunn School of Int. Affairs, Georgia Inst. of Tech.; Chair. Bd of Trustees, Center for Strategic and Int. Studies, Washington, currently Chair. Emer.; mem. Bd of Dirs, ChevronTexaco Corpn, The Coca-Cola Co., Dell Inc., General Electric Co., Internet Security Systems. Inc., Scientific-Atlanta Inc., Hess Corpn 2012–; mem. Supervisory Council, Int. Luxembourg Forum on Preventing Nuclear Catastrophe, Bd of Advisors, Nat. Bureau of Asian Research; teamed up with fmr Senator Fred Thompson to promote a new film, Last Best Chance, on the dangers of excess nuclear weapons and materials 2005; Kt Commdr, Order of Merit (FRG) 2013; US Senator John Heinz Award for Greatest Public Service by an Elected or Appointed Official, Jefferson Awards 1996, Chairman's Medal, Heinz Awards (jtly) 2004, Hessian Peace Prize 2008, Georgia Trustee, Georgia Historical Soc. in conjunction with the Gov. of Georgia 2011, Inaugural recipient of Ivan Allen Jr Prize for Social Courage, Georgia Inst. of Tech. and Georgia Tech's Ivan Allen Coll. of Liberal Arts 2011, Lone Sailor Award, US Navy Veterans Memorial 2014. *Film:* Nuclear Tipping Point (documentary) 2010. *Leisure interests:* golf, reading. *Address:* Nuclear Threat Initiative, 1747 Pennsylvania Avenue NW, Seventh Floor, Washington, DC 20006 (office); The Sam Nunn School of International Affairs, 781 Marietta Street NW, Atlanta, GA 30318 (office); Center for Strategic and International Studies, 1616 Rhode Island Avenue NW, Washington, DC 20036, USA (office). *Telephone:* (202) 296-4810 (NTI) (office); (404) 894-3195 (Georgia Tech) (office); (202) 887-0200 (CSIS) (office). *Fax:* (202) 296-4811 (NTI) (office); (404) 894-1900 (Georgia Tech) (office); (202) 775-3199 (CSIS) (office). *E-mail:* contact@nti.org (office). *Website:* www.nti.org/about/leadership-staff/sam -nunn (office); www.inta.gatech.edu/mission/senator-sam-nunn (office); csis.org/ expert/sam-nunn (office).

NUNN, Sir Trevor Robert, Kt, CBE; British theatre director; *Director Emeritus, Royal Shakespeare Company;* b. 14 Jan. 1940, Ipswich; s. of Robert Alexander Nunn and Dorothy May Nunn (née Piper); m. 1st Janet Suzman (q.v.) 1969 (divorced 1986); one s.; m. 2nd Sharon Lee Hill 1986 (divorced 1991); two d.; m. 3rd Imogen Stubbs 1994; one s. one d.; ed Northgate Grammar School, Ipswich and Downing Coll. Cambridge; Trainee Dir Belgrade Theatre, Coventry; Assoc. Dir Royal Shakespeare Co. 1964–86, Artistic Dir 1968–78, CEO 1968–86, Jt Artistic Dir 1978–86, Dir Emer. 1986–; f. Homevale Ltd and Awayvale Ltd; Artistic Dir Royal Nat. Theatre 1996–2001; Cameron Mackintosh Prof. of Contemporary Theatre, Univ. of Oxford 2010–11; toured USA, Australia with own version of Hedda Gabler 1975; mem. Arts Council of England 1994–; Hon. LittD (Warwick) 1982; Hon. MA (Newcastle-upon-Tyne) 1982; Hon. DLitt (Suffolk) 1997; Laurence Olivier Award for Outstanding Achievement 2002. *Productions:* Tango 1965, The Revenger's Tragedy (London Theatre Critics' Best Dir Award) 1965, 1969, The Taming of the Shrew, The Relapse, The Winter's Tale (London Theatre Critics' Best Dir Award) 1969, Hamlet 1970, Henry VIII 1970, Roman Season: Antony and Cleopatra (Soc. of Film and TV Arts Award 1975), Coriolanus, Julius Caesar, Titus Andronicus 1970, Macbeth 1974, 1976, Hedda Gabler (own version) 1975, Romeo and Juliet 1976, The Comedy of Errors (Ivor Novello Award for Best British Musical of 1976 (Lyrics), Soc. of West End Theatre Award for Best Musical of the Year 1977) 1976, Winter's Tale (co-dir) 1976, King Lear (co-dir) 1976, Macbeth 1976, The Alchemist 1977, As You Like It 1977, Every Good Boy Deserves Favour 1977, Three Sisters 1978, The Merry Wives of Windsor 1979, Once in a Lifetime (Plays and Players Award 1978, 1979 for Best Production (Dir), Sydney Edwards Award for Best Dir, Evening Standard Drama Awards 1978, 1979) 1979, Juno and the Paycock 1980, The Life and Adventures of Nicholas Nickleby (Laurence Olivier Award for Best Dir 1980, Tony Award for Best Direction of a Play 1982, Soc. of West End Theatres Awards, including Best Dir, Best New Play, Evening Standard Award, Best Dir, Drama Award for Best Dir, Mr. Abbott Award (Broadway) 1980 (with John Caird) (New York 1981), Cats (Tony Award for Best Direction of a Musical 1983) 1981, All's Well That Ends Well (Drama Desk Award for Outstanding Director of a Play 1983) 1981, Henry IV (Parts I & II) 1981, 1982, Peter Pan (with John Caird) 1982, Starlight Express 1984, Les Misérables (with John Caird) (Tony Award for Best Direction of a Musical 1987) 1985, Chess 1986, The Fair Maid of the West 1986, Aspects of Love 1989, Othello 1989, The Baker's Wife 1989, Timon of Athens 1991, The Blue Angel 1991, Measure for Measure 1991, Heartbreak House 1992, Arcadia 1993, Sunset Boulevard 1993, Enemy of The People 1997, Mutabilitie 1997, Not About Nightingales (Drama Desk Award for Outstanding Dir of a Play 1999) 1998, Oklahoma! 1998, Betrayal 1998, Troilus and Cressida 1999, The Merchant of Venice 1999, Summerfolk (Laurence Olivier Award for Best Dir 2000) 1999, Love's Labour's Lost 2002, We Happy Few 2004, The Woman in White 2004, Acorn Antiques: The Musical! 2005, Porgy and Bess 2006, Katya Kabanova 2007, The Seagull 2007, King Lear 2007, Gone with the Wind 2008, Inherit the Wind 2009, A Little Night Music 2009, Aspects of Love 2010, Birdsong 2010, Flare Path 2011, The Lion in Winter 2011, A Chorus of Disapproval 2012. *Films:* Hedda (dir and adaptation), Lady Jane (dir) 1985, Twelfth Night: Or What You Will (dir and adaptation) 1996. *Operas:* Idomeneo 1982, Porgy and Bess 1986, Così fan tutte 1991, Peter Grimes 1992, Katya Kabanova 1994, Sophie's Choice 2002, Porgy and Bess 2006. *Television:* Antony and Cleopatra 1975, Comedy of Errors 1976, Every Good Boy Deserves Favour 1979, Macbeth 1978, Shakespeare Workshops Word of Mouth (written and directed by T. Nunn) 1979, Three Sisters 1981, The Life and Adventures of Nicholas Nickleby (mini-series) 1982, Othello 1990, Porgy and Bess 1993, Oklahoma! 1999, The Merchant of Venice 2001, King Lear 2008. *Publication:* British Theatre Design 1989. *Address:* c/o Royal Shakespeare Company, Royal Shakespeare Theatre, Waterside, Stratford-upon-Avon, Warwicks., CV37 6BB, England.

NURBERDIYEVA, Akja; Turkmenistani politician; b. 1957, Aşgabat, Turkmen SSR, USSR; m.; two s.; ed Turkmen State Art Inst., Management Acad., Moscow, Russia; higher education in pedagogical faculty, candidates's degree in philosophy; mem. Türkmenistanyň Demokratik Partiýasy (Democratic Party of Turkmeni-

stan), Sec. Ahal Velayat br.; mem. Majlis (Parl.) 1994–, Vice-Chair. 2003–06, Acting Chair. 2006–07, Chair. 2007–18; Chair. Nat. Centre of Trade Unions of Turkmenistan 2005–07; Gurbansoltan-Eje Order, 20 Years of Independence of Turkmenistan Medal, Magtymguly Pyragy Medal. *Address:* c/o Office of the Chairman, Majlis, 744000 Aşgabat, Garaşyslyk Şaýoly 110, Turkmenistan (office).

NURGALIYEV, Col-Gen. Rashid Gumarovich, PhD; Russian politician and security officer; *Deputy Secretary of the Security Council;* b. 8 Oct. 1956, Jetikar, Kazakh SSR, USSR; m.; two s.; ed Kuusinen State Univ., Petrozavodsk; ethnic Tatar; physics teacher, Nadvoitsy 1979–81; with KGB, and its successor, since 1981, Head of Anti-Terrorist Dept, Karelian Republican KGB 1991–95, Chief Inspector, Fed. Counterespionage Service (FSB) 1995–98, Head, Office for Drug Trafficking Control, Dept of Econ. Security 1999–2000, Deputy Dir, Head of Inspectors Admin 2000–02; First Deputy Minister of Internal Affairs 2002–03, Head of Criminal Militia Service 2002–03, Minister of Internal Affairs 2003–12; Deputy Sec. Security Council 2012–; Hon. Citizen of the Repub. of Karelia; Order of Merit for the Fatherland (Third and Fourth Classes), Order of Honour, Order of Saint Blessed Prince Dimitry Donskoy Great (First Class) (Russian Orthodox Church) 2005, Order of Akhmad Kadyrov (Chechen Repub.) 2006, Medal 'In Commemoration of the 1000th Anniversary of Kazan', Medal for Distinction in Mil. Service (Second Class), Medal of Merit in the conduct of national census, Jubilee Medal '100 Years of the Trans-Siberian Railway', Medal 'In Commemoration of the 300th Anniversary of Saint Petersburg', Jubilee Medal '70 Years of the Armed Forces of the USSR', Medal for Strengthening Mil. Co-operation (Defence), Medal '200 Years of the Ministry of Defence', Medal 'For Military Merit' (MIA), Medal 'For Impeccable Service' (First Class); Yuri Andropov Award. *Address:* Security Council of Russian Federation, 103132 Moscow, Ipatyevskii per. 4/10, Russia (office). *Telephone:* (495) 206-35-96 (office). *Website:* www.scrf.gov.ru (office); state .kremlin.ru/security_council (office).

NURMAHMADZODA, Jamshed; Tajikistani accountant, banking executive and central banker; *Chairman, National Bank of Tajikistan (Bonki Millii Tojikiston);* b. 14 Dec. 1960, Kurgan tyube; m.; four c.; ed Tajik State Univ.; Controller-Auditor, Ministry of Finance 1983–88, in Communist Dist 1988–90, Chief Controller-Auditor 1990–93, Deputy Head of Finance 1993–94, Head of State Financial and Audit Control Dept 1994–2001, Head of Sector, State Financial Control Dept 2001–06, Deputy Minister of Finance 2006–12; Deputy Head, Soghd Region 2012–13; Chair. Amonatbonk (State Savings Bank) 2013–15; Chair. Nat. Bank of Tajikistan (Bonki Millii Tojikiston) 2015–, also currently mem. Bd of Govs IMF; Hon. Financier, Repub. of Tajikistan 2011; Certificates of Merit, Ministry of Finance. *Address:* National Bank of Tajikistan (Bonki Millii Tojikiston), 734003 Dushanbe, Xiyoboni Rudaki 107A, Tajikistan (office). *Telephone:* (44) 600-32-01 (office). *Fax:* (44) 600-32-35 (office). *E-mail:* info@nbt.tj (office). *Website:* www.nbt.tj (office).

NURMURATOV, Mamarizo, PhD; Uzbekistani economist and central banker; *Chairman, Central Bank of the Republic of Uzbekistan;* b. 1960, Samarqand Viloyat, Uzbek SSR, USSR; ed Tashkent Inst. of Nat. Economy, Leningrad Econ. and Finance Inst.; Teacher, Tashkent Inst. of Nat. Economy 1982–85, Asst Prof. 1989–93, also Asst Prof. Tashkent Financial Inst. 1989–93; joined Central Bank of the Repub. of Uzbekistan 1993, becoming Dir, Centre for Scientific Research, Deputy Chair. Bd of Dirs, First Deputy Chair., Adviser to Chair. 2006–17, Chair. 2017–; Minister of Finance 2000–04; mem. Senate (upper house of Oliy Majlis, parl.) 2017–, Chair. Senate Budget and Economic Reform Cttee –2017; Hokim (Gov.) Samarqand Viloyat 2004–06. *Address:* Central Bank of the Republic of Uzbekistan, 100001 Tashkent, O'zbekiston shoh ko'ch. 6, Uzbekistan (office). *Telephone:* (71) 200-00-44 (office). *Fax:* (71) 233-35-09 (office). *E-mail:* info@cbu.uz (office). *Website:* www.cbu.uz (office).

NURSE, Sir Paul Maxime, Kt, BSc, PhD, FRS; British university president and scientist; *Director, Francis Crick Institute;* b. 25 Jan. 1949, Norfolk; s. of Maxime Nurse and Cissie Nurse (née White); m. Anne Teresa Talbott 1971; two d.; ed Harrow Co. Grammar School, Univ. of Birmingham, Univ. of East Anglia; Research Fellow, Dept of Zoology, Univ. of Edin. 1974–78; Sr Research Fellow, School of Biology, Univ. of Sussex 1980–84; Head Cell Cycle Control Lab., Imperial Cancer Research Fund (ICRF), London 1984–87; Iveagh Prof. of Microbiology, Univ. of Oxford 1987–91; Dir of Research (Labs) and Head Cell Cycle Lab., ICRF 1993–96, Dir-Gen. ICRF 1996–2002, Dir-Gen. (Science) and CEO Cancer Research UK 2002–03; Pres. Rockefeller Univ., New York, USA 2003–11; Dir Francis Crick Inst. (fmrly UK Centre for Medical Research and Innovation) 2011–; mem. EMBO 1987–; Chancellor, Univ. of Bristol 2017–; Pres. Genetical Soc. 1990–93; mem. Academia Europaea 1991; Foreign Assoc. NAS 1995–, Chinese Acad. of Sciences 2015; Fellow, Royal Soc. 1989– (Pres. 2010–15), Acad. of Medical Sciences 1998–; Hon. FRCP, Hon. FRCPath 2000, Hon. mem. American Acad. of Arts and Sciences 2006, Royal Irish Acad., Hon. Fellow British Acad., Royal Acad. of Engineering; Chevalier, Légion d'honneur 2002; Dr hc numerous univs; Fleming Lecturer, Soc. of Gen. Microbiology 1984, Florey Lecturer, Royal Soc. 1990, Marjory Stephenson Lecturer, Soc. of Gen. Microbiology 1990, Feldberg Prize for Medical Research (UK/Germany) 1991, CIBA Medal, Biochemical Soc. 1991, Louis Jeantet Prize for Medicine in Europe (Switzerland) 1992, Gairdner Foundation Int. Award (Canada) 1992, Royal Soc. Wellcome Medal 1993, Jiménez Díaz Memorial Award and Medal (Spain) 1993, Purkyne Medal, Czech Acad. 1994, Pezcoller Award for Oncology Research (Italy) 1995, Royal Soc. Medal 1995, Dr Josef Steiner Prize, Switzerland 1996, Dr H.P. Heineken Prize for Biochemistry and Biophysics (Netherlands) 1996, Alfred P. Sloan, Jr Prize and Medal, General Motors Cancer Research Foundation 1997, Berkan Judd Award (USA) 1998, Albert Lasker Award for Basic Medical Research (USA) 1998, Nobel Prize in Physiology or Medicine 2001, Copley Medal 2005, Henry G. Friesen International Prize in Health Research 2015, inducted into Chinese Acad. of Sciences 2018. *Publications:* The Romanes Lecture for 2003 2004; numerous articles in scientific journals concerned with cell and molecular biology. *Leisure interests:* gliding, motorcycling, running, astronomy, talking. *Address:* Francis Crick Institute, 1 Midland Road, London, NW1 1AT, England (office). *Telephone:* (20) 3796-2495 (office). *E-mail:* paul .nurse@crick.ac.uk (office). *Website:* www.crick.ac.uk (office).

NUSSBAUM, Martha Craven, MA, PhD; American academic; *Ernst Freund Distinguished Service Professor of Law and Ethics, University of Chicago;* b. 6 May 1947, New York, NY; d. of George Craven and Betty Craven; m. Alan J. Nussbaum

1969 (divorced 1987); one d.; ed New York and Harvard Univs; Jr Fellow, Soc. of Fellows, Harvard Univ. 1972–75, Asst Prof. of Philosophy and Classics 1975–80, Assoc. Prof. 1980–83; Assoc. Prof. of Philosophy and Classics, Brown Univ. 1984–85, Prof. of Philosophy, Classics and Comparative Literature 1985–87, David Benedict Prof. 1987–89, Prof. 1989–95; Visiting Prof. of Law, Univ. of Chicago 1994, Prof. of Law and Ethics 1995–96, Prof. of Philosophy 1995–, Prof. of Divinity 1995–, Ernst Freund Prof. of Law and Ethics 1996–99, Ernst Freund Distinguished Service Prof. of Law and Ethics 1999–, Assoc. mem. Classics Dept 1996–, Assoc. mem. Dept of Political Science 2003–, Founder and Co-ordinator, Center for Comparative Constitutionalism 2002–; Founding and Past Pres. Human Development Devt and Capability Asscn; Past Pres. American Philosophical Asscn; Visiting Prof., Jawaharlal Nehru Univ., New Delhi, India 2004; mem. American Acad. of Arts and Sciences, American Philosophical Asscn (Chair. Cttee on Status of Women 1994–97); elected Corresp. Fellow, British Acad. 2008; Kt, Order of the White Rose of Finland (First Class) 2012; 60 honorary degrees from various Univ. including Dr hc (Knox Coll.) 2003, (Bucknell Univ.) 2010, (Mount Holyoke Coll.) 2011, (Lawrence Univ.) 2013; Brandeis Creative Arts Award 1990, PEN Spielvogel-Diamondstein Award 1991, NY Univ. Distinguished Alumni Award 2000, Grawemeyer Award in Educ. 2002, Barnard Medal of Distinction 2003, Prince of Asturias Award for Social Sciences 2012, Philip Quinn Prize, American Philosophical Asscn 2015, Kyoto Prize in Arts and Philosophy, Inamori Foundation 2016, Don M. Randel Award for Humanistic Studies 2017, Berggruen Prize 2018 and numerous other awards. *Publications include:* Aristotle's De Motu Animalium 1978, Language and Logic (ed.) 1983, The Fragility of Goodness 1986, Love's Knowledge 1990, Essays on Aristotle's De Anima (ed. with A. Rorty) 1992, The Therapy of Desire 1994, The Quality of Life (ed. with A. Sen) 1993, Passions and Perceptions (ed. with J. Brunschwig) 1993, Women, Culture and Development (ed. with J. Glover) 1995, Poetic Justice 1996, For Love of Country 1996, Cultivating Humanity 1997, Sex and Social Justice 1998, Hiding from Humanity: Disgust, Shame and the Law 2004, Liberty of Conscience 2008, From Disgust to Humanity: Sexual Orientation and Constitutional Law 2010, Not for Profit: Why Democracy Needs the Humanities 2010, Creating Capabilities: The Human Development Approach 2011, The New Religious Intolerance: Overcoming the Politics of Fear in an Anxious Age 2012, Political Emotions: Why Love Matters for Justice 2013, Creating Capabilities: The Human Development Approach 2013, Anger and Forgiveness: Resentment, Generosity, Justice 2016, Aging Thoughtfully: Conversations about Retirement, Romance, Wrinkles, and Regret (with Saul Levmore) 2017, The Monarchy of Fear: A Philosopher Looks at Our Political Crisis 2018; has also edited 21 books. *Leisure interests:* music, running, hiking. *Address:* Law School, Room 520, University of Chicago, 1111 East 60th Street, Chicago, IL 60637, USA (office). *Telephone:* (773) 702-3470 (office). *Fax:* (773) 702-0730 (office). *E-mail:* martha_nussbaum@law.uchicago.edu (office). *Website:* www.law.uchicago.edu/faculty/nussbaum (office).

NUSSLE, James (Jim) Allen, BA, JD; American lawyer, fmr politician and fmr government official; *President and CEO, Credit Union National Association;* b. 27 June 1960, Des Moines, Ia; m. 1st Leslie Jeanne Harbison 1986 (divorced 1996); one s. one d.; m. 2nd Karen Chiccehitto 2001; ed Luther Coll., Drake Univ.; called to the Bar, Iowa 1985, States Attorney for Delaware Co., Ia 1986–90; mem. US House of Reps for Ia 2nd Dist 1991–2007 (retd), Chair. House Budget Cttee 2001–07; ran unsuccessfully for Gov. of Ia 2006; Dir US Office of Man. and Budget 2007–09; Founder and Pres. Nussle Group (consultancy), Alexandria, Va 2009–14; Pres. and COO Growth Energy 2010–13; Pres. and CEO Credit Union Nat. Asscn 2014–; mem. Bd of Dirs Portfolio Recovery Associates, Inc. 2013–, Thrivent Mutual Funds 2011–, PRA Group Inc. 2013–, Nat. Down Syndrome Soc. 2009–; Co-Chair. Cttee for a Responsible Federal Budget 2009–14; Special Advisor, Avista Capital Partners 2009–; mem. Advisory Council (US Programs), Bill and Melinda Gates Foundation 2011–14; mem. Steering Cttee, Fix the Debt Campaign 2012–; Republican. *Address:* Credit Union National Association, PO Box 431, Madison, WI 53701-0431, USA (office). *Telephone:* (202) 508-6745 (office). *E-mail:* jnussle@cuna.coop (office). *Website:* www.cuna.org (office).

NÜSSLEIN-VOLHARD, Christiane, PhD, FRS; German scientist and academic; b. 20 Oct. 1942, Magdeburg; d. of Rolf Volhard and Brigitte Volhard (née Haas); ed Univ. of Tübingen; Research Assoc., Lab. of Dr Schaller, Max-Planck-Inst. für Virusforschung, Tübingen 1972–74; Postdoctoral Fellow (EMBO Fellowship), Lab. of Prof. Dr W. Gehring, Biozentrum Basel, Switzerland 1975–76, Lab. of Prof. Dr K. Sander, Univ. of Freiburg 1977; Head of Group, European Molecular Biology Lab. (EMBL), Heidelberg 1978–80; Group Leader, Friedrich-Miescher-Laboratorium, Max-Planck-Gesellschaft, Tübingen 1981–85, Scientific mem. Max-Planck-Gesellschaft and Dir Max-Planck-Institut für Entwicklungsbiologie, Tübingen 1985–90, Dir Dept of Genetics 1990–2015, Emer. 2015–; mem. Scientific Council of the European Research Council (ERC) 2005–12; Chancellor, Order Pour le mérit 2013–; Head of the Curatorium, Int. Hugo Wolf Acad., Stuttgart 2010–; f. Christiane Nüsslein-Volhard Stiftung 2004; mem. NAS; Grosses Verdienstkreuz mit Stern 1996, mit Stern und Schulterband 2005; Ordre pour le Mérite 1997; Hon. ScD (Yale) 1990, (Oxford) 2005; Dr hc (Utrecht) 1991, (Princeton) 1991, (Harvard) 1993; Albert Lasker Medical Research Award, New York 1991, Prix Louis Jeantet de Médicine, Geneva 1992, Ernst Schering Prize, Berlin 1993, Nobel Prize in Medicine (co-recipient) 1995. *Publications:* 135 Zebra Fish: A Practical Approach 2002; numerous scientific articles. *Address:* Max-Planck-Institut für Entwicklungsbiologie, Spemannstrasse 35, 72076 Tübingen, Germany (office). *Telephone:* (7071) 601489 (office). *Fax:* (7071) 601384 (office). *E-mail:* christiane.nuesslein-volhard@tuebingen.mpg.de (office). *Website:* www.eb.tuebingen.mpg.de/research/emeriti/research-group-colour-pattern-formation.html (office); www.cnv-stiftung.de.

NUTBEAM, Don, PhD, FFPH; British public health scientist, academic and university administrator; m.; two c.; ed Univ. of Southampton; Head of Public Health, UK Dept of Health 2000–03; Academic Provost, Univ. of Sydney 2003–09; Vice-Chancellor Univ. of Southampton 2009–15; has worked as an adviser and consultant for WHO over 20 years and as consultant and team leader in projects for the World Bank; Fellow, Faculty of Public Health. *Publications include:* two public health text books; more than 100 papers in peer-reviewed journals on public health intervention, health literacy and adolescent health behaviour. *Leisure interests:* sport, especially football, rugby, skiing, tennis and golf, vegetable gardening.

Address: c/o Office of the Vice-Chancellor, University of Southampton, University Road, Southampton, Hants., SO17 1BJ, England (office).

NUTT, Jim, BFA; American artist; b. 28 Nov. 1938, Pittsfield, Mass.; s. of Frank E. Nutt and Ruth Tureman Nutt; m. Gladys Nilsson 1961; ed School of Art Inst. of Chicago, Washington Univ. and Univ. of Pennsylvania; first Hairy Who exhibition, Hyde Park Art Center, Chicago 1966; Prof. of Art, Calif. State Univ., Sacramento 1968–75, School of Art Inst. of Chicago 1990; Cassandra Foundation Award 1969, Nat. Endowment for the Arts Award 1975, 1990. *Address:* c/o David Nolan Gallery, 527 West 29th Street, New York, NY 10001, USA. *Website:* www.davidnolangallery.com/artists/jim-nutt.

NWANZE, Kanayo F., BSc, MSc, PhD; Nigerian agricultural scientist and international organization official; ed Univ. of Ibadan, Kansas State Univ., USA; experience in poverty reduction through agric., rural devt and research world-wide since late 1970s; Dir-Gen. Africa Rice Centre (WARDA) for ten years; held sr positions at several research centres affiliated to Consultative Group on Int. Agricultural Research (CGIAR), Chair. Centre Dirs' Cttee, helped establish Alliance of CGIAR Centres; Vice-Pres. IFAD, Rome, Italy 2007–09, Pres. 2009–17; apptd FAO Special Amb. for Zero Hunger 2017; has served on exec. bds of various insts; mem. several scientific asscns; DSc hc (Warwick) 2015; Officier, Ordre de Mérite du Niger 2013, Nat. Order of the Repub. of Gambia 2014, Grand Officer, Ordre Nat. du Bénin 2014; Dr M.S. Swaminathan Award for Environment Protection 2014. *Achievements include:* instrumental in introducing and promoting New Rice for Africa (NERICA), a high-yield, drought- and pest-resistant rice variety developed specifically for the African landscape. *Publications:* numerous publs and articles in scientific journals.

NYAKLYAEU, Uladzimer; Belarusian poet, writer, journalist, editor and politician; b. 11 July 1946, Smarhon, Grodno Region; s. of Prokofiy Neklyayev and Anastasiya Mahyer; m. 1st Ludmila Nyaklyaeu 1965; one d. one step-c.; m. 2nd Volha Nyaklyaeu 1999; ed Higher State Communications Coll., Minsk Pedagogical Inst., Moscow Literature Inst.; began working in Vladivostok, Taishet and Norilsk following graduation; returned to Belarus 1967, worked as a radio mechanic at Minsk TV custom shop –1971; literature worker, Znamya Yunosti newspaper 1972–75; Ed. Theatrical Minsk bulletin 1975–87; Chief Ed. main editorial bd of literature and drama programmes, Belarusian TV 1978–87; Chief Ed. Krynitsa magazine 1987–98; Chief Ed. Litaratura i Mastatstva weekly 1996–99; left Belarus to lived in Poland for political reasons June 1999, also lived in Finland, returned to Minsk 2003; initiator of civil campaign 'Tell the Truth!' 2010; opposition leader and presidential cand. 2010; beaten unconscious by men in black uniform in Minsk before the closure of the polls 19 Dec. 2010, spent more than a month in custody following the post-election street protest before being released and placed under house arrest 28 Jan. 2011; given a two-year suspended sentence for his role in a protest in Minsk on 19 Dec. 2010 following announcement of Pres. Lukashenka's re-election May 2011; barred by court from leaving Minsk without written permission and from travelling outside Belarus for duration of sentence, also barred from attending public gatherings and meetings, ordered to present himself at a police station once a week, and told to stay at home between 8 pm and 6 am; attended OSCE conf. on human rights in Warsaw and thereafter summoned by the police Sept. 2011; named a prisoner of conscience by Amnesty International who called for his immediate and unconditional release; exempted by Leninski Dist Court in Minsk from serving two-year imprisonment sentence July 2013; mem. Union of Writers of USSR 1978; Order of the Badge of Honour 1986; First Prize, First Int. Festival of Slavic Poetry 'Singing Letters', Tver, Russia 2009. *Publications include:* Adkryccio (Disovery) 1976, Vynachodcy viatrou (Inventors of the Winds) (Prize of Lenin Komsomol) 1979, Znak achovy (The Sign of Protection) 1983, Mestnoe vremja (Local Time) 1983, Naskroz (Throughout) 1985, Halubinaja posta (Pigeon Mail) 1987, Derevo boli (The Tree of Pain) 1989, Prosca (Proshcha) (State Award of Belaru 'Janka Kupala') 1996, Vybranaje (Selected Works) 1998, Labuch (Musician) (novel) 2003, Tak (Yes) 2004, Centar Europy (The Centre of Europe) (prose works) 2009, Kon (Con) 2010.

NYAMDORJ, Tsendiin, LLB, PhD; Mongolian lawyer and politician; *Minister of Justice and Home Affairs;* b. 1956, Aimag Uws; ed Leningrad Univ.; Div. Prosecutor and Head of Div., State Gen. Authority of Prosecutor 1981–88; First Deputy, Gen. Prosecutor's Office of Mil. Affairs 1988–90; First Deputy Minister of Justice 1990–92; mem. State Great Khural (Parl.) 1992–, Chair. (Speaker) 2005–07, Deputy Chair. 2016–; Minister of Justice and Home Affairs 2000–05, 2008, 2017–; mem. Mongolian People's Revolutionary Party. *Address:* Ministry of Justice and Home Affairs, Government Bldg 5, Khudaldaany Gudamj 6/1, Chingeltei District, Ulaanbaatar, Mongolia (office). *Telephone:* (51) 267533 (office). *E-mail:* info@moj.gov.mn (office). *Website:* www.mjia.gov.mn (office).

NYAMITWE, Alain Aimé; Burundian diplomatist and politician; b. 1971, Ngagara; ed Univ. of Burundi; lived in Belgium mid-1990s; long career within Ministry of External Relations, including as Chef de cabinet, fmr Amb. to Nigeria, Deputy Head, Perm. Mission to UN and other Int. Orgs in Geneva, Perm. Rep. to Econ. Community of W African States (ECOWAS), Amb. to Ethiopia, Djibouti and Chad and Perm. Rep. to African Union and UN Econ. Comm. for Africa 2013–15, Minister of External Relations and Int. Co-operation 2015–18. *Publication:* J'ai échappé au massacre de l'Université du Burundi 1995. *Address:* c/o Ministry of External Relations and International Co-operation, ave de la Liberté, Bujumbura, Burundi (office).

NYAN WIN, Maj.-Gen.; Myanma government official; b. 22 Jan. 1953; m. Myint Myint Soe; three c.; ed Defence Services Acad.; fmr mem. of staff, Office of Strategic Studies; served as Commdt, Command and Gen. Staff Coll.; Deputy Chief of Defence Services Training –2004; Minister of Foreign Affairs 2004–11; mem Regional Hluttaw for Zigon Township 2010; Chief Minister of Bago Region 2011–16; mem. Nat. Convention Convening Comm.

NYANDA, Gen. Siphiwe, (Gebhuza), BA, MSc; South African army officer (retd); b. 22 May 1950, Soweto; s. of Henry Nyanda and Betsy Nyanda; m. Sheila Mathabe; two s. five d.; ed Orlando High School, Soweto, Univ. of S Africa, Univ. of London, UK; fmrly sports journalist; trained in fmr GDR and USSR as platoon commdr, artilleryman and in intelligence; mem. African Nat. Congress (ANC), fmrly guerrilla fighter for ANC, Commissar of Transvaal Region 1979–86, mem. Nat. Exec. Cttee 1991–96, 2007–; Deputy Chief, S African Nat. Defence Force

1997–98, Chief 1998–2005; Minister of Communications 2009–10; Parl. Counsellor to Pres. Jacob Zuma 2010–; Chief of Staff, Mkhonto we Sizwe 1992–94; Chevalier, Légion d'honneur and other decorations; Mil. Merit Medal 1995, Gold Star of South Africa 1998, American Legion of Honor, Star of South Africa. *Publications:* articles in newspapers and ANC publs. *Leisure interests:* reading, watching soccer, playing golf, aerobics, chess. *Address:* 15 Westminster Avenue, Bryanstown, South Africa (home). *Telephone:* (11) 4632778 (home). *Fax:* (11) 4632847 (home). *E-mail:* s.nyanda@mweb.co.za (home).

NYCZ, HE Cardinal Kazimierz; Polish ecclesiastic; *Archbishop of Warsaw and Bishop of Poland, Faithful of Eastern Rites;* b. 1 Feb. 1950, Stara Wieś, Gmina Wilamowice dist, Bielsko Co., Silesian Voivodeship; ed Lyceum of Maria Skłodowska-Curie, Czechowice-Dziedzice, Major Seminary of Kraków, Faculty of Theology of Papieska Akademia Teologiczna (Pontifical Acad. of Theology), Kraków, Catholic Univ. of Lublin; ordained deacon, Diocese of Kraków 1972; ordained priest, Diocese of 1973; vicar in a parish of St Elisabeth, Jaworzno 1973–75; Vice-Rector Major Seminary of Kraków 1987–88; Auxiliary Bishop of Kraków and Titular Bishop of Villa Regis 1988–2004; apptd Chair. Cttee for Catholic Educ. 1999; served as Chair. Comm. for Educ. of Conf. of the Polish Episcopate; Bishop of Koszalin-Kołobrzeg 2004–07; Archbishop of Warsaw 2007–; Bishop of Poland, Faithful of Eastern Rites 2007–; cr. Cardinal (Cardinal-Priest of Santi Silvestro e Martino ai Monti) 2010; participated in Papal Conclave 2013. *Address:* Archdiocese of Warsaw, 00-246 Warsaw, ul. Miodow 17–19, Poland (office). *Telephone:* (22) 531-72-00 (office). *Fax:* (22) 635-43-24 (office). *E-mail:* info@ archidiecezja.warszawa.pl (office). *Website:* www.archidiecezja.warszawa.pl (office).

NYE, John Frederick, MA, PhD, FRS, FInstP; British physicist and academic; *Professor Emeritus of Physics, University of Bristol;* b. 26 Feb. 1923, Hove, Sussex; s. of Haydn Percival Nye and Jessie Mary Nye (née Hague); brother of Peter Hague Nye; m. Georgiana Wiebenson 1953; one s. two d.; ed Stowe School, King's Coll., Cambridge; Demonstrator, Dept of Mineralogy and Petrology, Univ. of Cambridge 1949–51; mem. of Tech. Staff, Bell Telephone Labs, NJ 1952–53; Lecturer in Physics, Univ. of Bristol 1953–65, Reader 1965–69, Prof. 1969–88, Prof. Emer. 1988–; Pres. Int. Glaciological Soc. 1966–69, Int. Comm. of Snow and Ice 1971–75; Foreign mem. Royal Swedish Acad. of Sciences 1977; glacier in Palmer Peninsula, Antarctica officially named Nye Glacier 1963, Seligman Crystal Int. Glaciological Soc. 1969, Antarctic Service Medal (USA) 1974, Charles Chree Medal and Prize, Inst. of Physics 1989. *Publications:* Physical Properties of Crystals 1957, Natural Focusing and Fine Structure of Light 1999; numerous papers in scientific journals on glaciers, physics of ice, waves and math. catastrophes. *Leisure interest:* gardening. *Address:* University of Bristol, H.H. Wills Physics Laboratory, Royal Fort, Tyndall Avenue, Bristol, BS8 ITL (office); 45 Canynge Road, Bristol, BS8 3LH, England (home). *Telephone:* (117) 973-3769 (home). *E-mail:* john.nye@bristol .ac.uk (office). *Website:* www.phy.bris.ac.uk (office).

NYE, Joseph Samuel, Jr, BA, PhD, FBA; American political scientist, academic and fmr government official; *University Distinguished Service Professor, Harvard University;* b. 19 Jan. 1937, NJ; s. of Joseph Nye and Else Ashwell; m. Molly Harding 1961; three s.; ed Princeton and Harvard Univs, Univ. of Oxford, UK; joined as Instructor, then Asst Prof., later Assoc. and Full Prof. of Govt, Harvard Univ. 1964–95, Dir Centre for Int. Affairs 1978–93, Assoc. Dean of Int. Affairs 1989–92, Dean and Don K. Price Prof. of Public Policy, John F. Kennedy School of Govt 1995–2004, Univ. Distinguished Service Prof. 2004–, mem. of the bd, Belfer Center for Science and Int. Affairs; Deputy Under-Sec. Dept of State, Washington, DC 1977–79, fmr Chair. Nat. Security Council Group on Nonproliferation of Nuclear Weapons, Chair. Nat. Intelligence Council 1992–94; Asst Sec. of Defense for Int. Security Affairs 1994–95; Commr, Global Comm. on Internet Governance; Visiting Prof. Carnegie Endowment for Int. Peace, Institut Universitaire des Hautes Etudes Internationales 1968, School of Int. Affairs, Carleton Univ. 1973; Winant Visiting Prof., Balliol Coll., Univ. of Oxford 2005, Visiting Fellow, All Souls Coll. 2001; mem. Trilateral Comm., Chair. N American branch; mem. Council, Int. Inst. of Strategic Studies; mem. Council on Foreign Relations, Defense Policy Bd, Foreign Affairs Policy Bd 2014; Fellow, American Acad. of Arts and Sciences, American Acad. of Diplomacy, Aspen Inst., British Acad., Woodrow Wilson Int. Center, Smithsonian Inst.; Visiting Fellow, Theodore Roosevelt Fellow, American Acad. of Political and Social Science; Hon. Fellow, Exeter College, Oxford 1996, Hon. Patron, Univ. Philosophical Society, Trinity Coll., Dublin 2005; Palmes Academiques, Le Premier Ministre, France 2003; hon. degrees from 10 Coll. Univ.; Dept of State Distinguished Honor Award 1979, Intelligence Distinguished Service Award 1994, Dept of Defense Distinguished Service Medal 1995, Charles E. Merriman Award, American Political Science Asscn 2003, Woodrow Wilson Award, Princeton Univ. 2004, Dr Jean Mayer Global Citizenship Award, Tufts Univ. 2004, Foreign Policy Distinguished Scholar Award, Int. Studies Asscn. *Publications include:* Power and Independence (co-author) 1977, The Making of America's Soviet Policy (co-author and ed.) 1984, Hawks, Doves and Owls (co-author and ed.) 1985, Nuclear Ethics 1986, Fateful Visions (co-ed.) 1988, Bound to Lead: The Changing Nature of American Power (co-ed.) 1990, Understanding International Conflicts: An Introduction to Theory and History 1993 (fourth edn) 2002, Governance in a Globalizing World 2000, The Paradox of American Power 2002, Soft Power: The Means to Success in World Politics 2004, Power in a Global Information Age 2004, The Power Game (novel) 2004, The Powers to Lead 2008, The Future of Power 2011, Presidential Leadership and the Creation of the American Era 2013, Is the American Century Over? 2015. *Leisure interests:* fly fishing, skiing, hiking, hunting, gardening. *Address:* John F. Kennedy School of Government, Harvard University, Mailbox 124, 79 John F. Kennedy Street, Cambridge, MA 02138-5801, USA (office). *Telephone:* (617) 495-1123 (office). *Fax:* (617) 496-3337 (office). *E-mail:* joseph_nye@hks.harvard.edu (office). *Website:* www.hks.harvard.edu/about/faculty-staff-directory/joseph-nye (office); joenye .com.

NYEMBEZI-HEITA, Nonkululeko (Nku) Merina Cheryl, MSc, MBA; South African business executive; *CEO, IchorCoal NV;* b. 22 March 1960, Pietermaritz-burg, KwaZulu-Natal; d. of Aubrey Vulindlela Nyembezi and Dibiya Merina; m. Sam Ndahupula Heita; one s. one d.; ed Univ. of Manchester Inst. of Science and Tech. and Open Univ., UK, California Inst. of Tech., USA; engineer, IBM, Research Triangle Park, NC, USA 1984–86, moved to S Africa, Account Sales Rep.,

IBM SA 1986–93, Regional Man. 1993–98, also involved in establishment of IBM in Namibia; CEO Alliance Capital SA 1998–2005, Chair. Alliance Capital Namibia; Corp. Strategy Officer and Head of Mergers and Acquisitions, Vodacom Group 2005–08; CEO ArcelorMittal SA Ltd 2008–14; CEO and mem. Man. Bd, IchorCoal NV 2014–; Chair. Bond Exchange of South Africa Ltd 2004–; Dir (non-exec.), JSE Securities Exchange, Macsteel International, Bigen Africa 2003–, JSE Ltd 2009– (Ind. Chair. (non-exec.) 2014–), Old Mutual PLC 2012–; Ind. Dir (non-exec.), Exxaro Resources Ltd 2006–08; Anglo-American Prize Scholarship. *Leisure interests:* reading, walking, Pilates, yoga, listening to jazz and classical music. *Address:* IchorCoal NV, An der Wuhlheide 232, 12459 Berlin, Germany (office). *Telephone:* (30) 65668160 (office). *Fax:* (30) 65668169 (office). *E-mail:* info@ ichorcoal.com (office). *Website:* www.ichorcoal.com (office).

NYEMBO, Deogratias Mutombo Mwana; Democratic Republic of the Congo central banker; *Governor, Banque Centrale du Congo;* b. 8 Aug. 1964, Kongolo; m.; three c.; ed Univ. of Kinshasa; apptd Bureau Chief, Directorate Change, Banque Centrale du Congo 1991, Deputy Dir in charge of Operations 2003–05, Deputy Head, Accounting Dept 2005–08, Dir Foreign Services Directorate 2008–10, Head, Directorate of Banking Operations and Markets 2010–13, Gov. 2013–; currently mem. Bd of Govs IMF. *Address:* Banque Centrale du Congo, 563 Blvd Colonel Tshatshi au nord, BP 2697, Kinshasa, Democratic Republic of the Congo (office). *Telephone:* 992320001 (mobile). *E-mail:* info@bcc.cd (office). *Website:* www.bcc.cd (office).

NYEMBO SHABANI, DSc (Econ); Democratic Republic of the Congo politician, economist and academic; b. 5 Aug. 1937, Kayanza; ed Inst. Saint Boniface, Elisabethville (now Lubumbashi) and Univ. Catholique de Louvain, Belgium; Dir, Bureau of Econ. Co-operation attached to the Prime Minister's Office 1964–65; Research in Econs, Univ. Catholique de Louvain 1967–76; Prof., Faculty of Econ. Science, Nat. Univ. of Zaïre Oct. 1976; State Commr for Nat. Econ. and Industry Feb.–Aug. 1977, for Nat. Econ. 1977–78, for the State Portfolio (Investments) 1978–80, for Agric. and Rural Devt 1980–81, 1983–84, for Econ., Industry and Foreign Trade 1982–83, for Finance and Budget 1986–88, for Agric. 1988–89; Pres. Gécamines Holdings 1985. *Publications:* L'industrie du cuivre dans le monde, Le progrès économique du Copperbelt Africain, Bruxelles, La Renaissance du Livre 1975.

NYLANDER, Dag Halvor, Cand.jur; Norwegian lawyer and diplomatist; b. 1969; s. of Gro Nylander; ed Univ. of Oslo, Univ. of Aix-Marseille; joined Ministry of Foreign Affairs (MFA) as trainee 1997, served with Embassy in Buenos Aires 1999–2001, Perm. Mission to UN, New York 2001–04, Head of Mission in Bogota 2006–08, Special MFA Envoy 2009–11, Norwegian Special Envoy to Colombia peace process 2012–16; UN Sec.-Gen.'s Personal Rep. on the Border Controversy between Guyana and the Bolivarian Repub. of Venezuela 2017; Deputy Judge, Fosen, N Norway 2005–06; Lawyer, Moltke Advokatfirma DA 2011; Lawyer, Waterfront Management AS 2011–12.

NYMAN, Michael, CBE; British composer; b. 23 March 1944, London; ed Royal Acad. of Music, King's Coll. London; composer, writer and music critic 1968–78; lecturer 1976–80; f. MN Records label 2005–; f. Michael Nyman Band 1976; Hon. DLitt. *Film and television soundtracks:* Peter Greenaway films: 5 Postcards from Capital Cities 1967, Vertical Features Remake 1976, Goole by Numbers 1976, A Walk Through H: The Reincarnation of an Ornithologist 1978, 1–100 1978, The Falls 1980, Act of God 1980, Terence Conran 1981, The Draughtsman's Contract 1982, The Coastline 1983, Making a Splash 1984, A Zed and Two Noughts 1985, Inside Rooms: 26 Bathrooms, London & Oxfordshire 1985, Drowning by Numbers 1988, Fear of Drowning 1988, Death in the Seine 1988, The Cook, The Thief, His Wife and Her Lover 1989, Hubert Bals Handshake 1989, Prospero's Books 1991; other films: Keep It Downstairs 1976, Tom Phillips 1977, Brimstone and Treacle 1982, Nelly's Version 1983, Frozen Music 1983, The Cold Room 1984, Fairly Secret Army 1984, The Kiss 1985, L'ange frénétique 1985, I'll Stake My Cremona to a Jew's Trump 1985, The Disputation 1986, Ballet méchanique 1986, Le miraculé 1987, The Man Who Mistook His Wife for a Hat 1987, Monsieur Hire 1989, Out of the Ruins 1989, Le mari de la coiffeuse 1990, Men of Steel 1990, Les enfants volants 1990, Not Mozart: Letters, Riddles and Writs 1991, The Final Score 1992, The Fall of Icarus 1992, The Piano 1993, Ryori no tetsujin 1993, Mesmer 1994, A la folie (Six Days, Six Nights) 1994, Carrington 1995, Anne no nikki (The Diary of Anne Frank) 1995, Der Unhold (The Ogre) 1996, Enemy Zero 1996, Gattaca 1997, Titch 1998, Ravenous 1999, How to Make Dhyrak: A Dramatic Work for Three Players and Camera, Truncated with Only Two Players 1999, Wonderland 1999, Nabbie no koi (Nabbie's Love) 1999, The End of the Affair 1999, The Claim 2000, Act Without Words I 2000, That Sinking Feeling 2000, La Stanza del figlio 2001, Subterrain 2001, 24 heures de la vie d'une femme 2002, The Man with a Movie Camera 2002, The Actors 2003, Nathalie… 2003, Charged 2003, Ident (Channel 5) 2004, Man on Wire 2007, The Eleventh Year 2009, The Trip 2010, 2 Graves 2010, Everyday 2012. *Other compositions:* orchestral: A Handsome, Smooth, Sweet, Smart, Clear Stroke: Or Else Play Not At All 1983, Taking a Line for a Second Walk 1986, L'Orgie Parisienne 1989, Six Celan Songs 1990, Where the Bee Dances 1991, Self Laudatory Hymn of Inanna and Her Omnipotence 1992, The Upside-Down Violin 1992, MGV (Musique à Grande Vitesse) 1993, On the Fiddle 1993, Concerto for Harpsichord and Strings 1995, Concerto for Trombone 1995, Double Concerto 1996, Strong on Oaks, Strong on the Causes of Oaks 1997, Cycle of Disquietude 1998, a dance he little thinks of 2001, The Draughtsman's Contract for Orchestra 2001, Dance of the Engines 2002, Gattaca for Orchestra 2003, The Claim for Orchestra 2003, The Piano: Concert Suite 2003, Violin Concerto 2003; chamber music: First Waltz in D, Bell Set No. 1 1974, 1–100 1976, Waltz in F 1976, Think Slow, Act Fast 1981, 2 Violins 1981, Four Saxes (Real Slow Drag) 1982, I'll Stake My Cremona to a Jew's Crump 1983, Time's Up 1983, Child's Play 1985, String Quartet No. 1 1985, Taking a Line for a Second Walk 1986, String Quartet No. 2 1988, String Quartet No. 3 1990, In Re Don Giovanni 1991, Masque Arias 1991, Time Will Pronounce 1992, Songs for Tony 1993, Three Quartets 1994, H.R.T. 1995, String Quartet No. 4 1995, Free for All 2001, Five Who Figured Four Years Ago 2002, Mapping 2002, Yellow Beach 2002, 24 Hour Sax Quartet 2004, For John Peel 2004; instrumental: Shaping the Curve 1990, Six Celan Songs 1990, Flugelhorn and Piano 1991, For John Cage 1992, The Convertibility of Lute Strings 1992, Here to There 1993, Yamamoto Perpetuo 1993, On the Fiddle 1993, To Morrow 1994, Tango for Tim 1994, Elisabeth Gets Her Way 1995, Viola and

Piano 1995, Titch 1997, Fourths, Mostly (for organ) 2001; dramatic works: Strange Attractors, The Princess of Milan, A Broken Set of Rules 1984, Basic Black 1984, Portraits in Reflection 1985, And Do They Do 1986, The Man Who Mistook His Wife for a Hat 1986, Miniatures/Configurations 1988, Letters, Riddles and Writs 1991, Noises, Sounds and Sweet Airs 1994, Facing Goya 2000, Man and Boy: Dada (opera) 2004, Love Counts 2004; vocal: A Neat Slice of Time 1980, The Abbess of Andouillets 1984, Out of the Ruins 1989, Polish Love Song 1990, Shaping the Curve 1991, Anne de Lucy Songs 1992, Mozart on Mortality 1992, Grounded 1995, The Waltz Song 1995, The Ballad of Kastriot Rexhepi 2001, Mosè 2001, A Child's View of Colour 2003, Acts of Beauty 2004; with Michael Nyman Band: In Re Don Giovanni 1977, The Masterwork/Award-Winning Fishknife 1979, Bird List Song 1979, Five Orchestral Pieces Opus Tree 1981, Bird Anthem 1981, M-Work 1981, Love is Certainly, at Least Alphabetically Speaking 1983, Bird Work 1984, The Fall of Icarus 1989, La Traversée de Paris 1989, The Final Score 1992, AET (After Extra Time) 1996, De Granada a la Luna 1998, Orfeu 1998, The Commissar Vanishes 1999, Man with a Movie Camera 2001, Compiling the Colours (Samhitha) 2003, Three Ways of Describing Rain (Sawan; Rang; Dhyan) 2003, Zeit und Ziel 1814–2002, Manhatta 2003; dance: Flicker 2005. *Films:* Cine Opera 2009, Nyman with a Movie Camera 2010. *Recordings include:* film soundtracks, The Piano Sings 2005. *Publications:* Libretto for Birtwistle's Dramatic Pastoral, Down by the Greenwood Side 1968–69, Experimental Music: Cage and Beyond 1974; contribs: critical articles to journals, including The Spectator. *E-mail:* myriam@michaelnyman.com (office); office@michaelnyman.com. *Website:* www .michaelnyman.com.

NYRUP RASMUSSEN, Poul, MA; Danish politician; b. 15 June 1943, Esbjerg, Western Jutland; s. of Olof Nyrup Rasmussen and Vera Nyrup Rasmussen; m. 1st (divorced); m. 2nd (divorced); m. 3rd Lone Dybkjar; one c. (deceased); ed Esbjerg Statsskole and Univ. of Copenhagen; worked for Danish Trade Union Council in Brussels for a year; Chief Economist, Danish Trade Union Council 1981; Man. Dir Employees' Capital Pension Fund 1986–88; Deputy Chair. SDP 1987–92, Chair. 1992–2002; mem. Folketing (Parl.) 1988–2004; Prime Minister 1993–2001; MEP 2004–09, Pres. Party of European Socialists 2004–11; fmr Pres. Global Progressive Forum; mem. Club of Madrid. *Publications:* grådighedens tid (In a Time of Greed) 2007. *Leisure interests:* music, spending time with his wife and grandchild. *E-mail:* poul@nyrup.dk. *Website:* www.nyrup.dk.

NYUSI, Filipe Jacinto, MA; Mozambican engineer, politician and head of state; *President;* b. 9 Feb. 1959, Namaua, Mueda, Cabo Delgado; s. of Jacinto Nhussi Chimela and Angelina Daima; Isaura Nyusi; four c.; ed Mil. Acad., Brno, Czechoslovakia, Univ. of Manchester, UK, Indian Inst. of Man., Ahmadbad; Exec. Dir CMF-Norte, Mozambique Ports and Railways 1992–2007, mem. Bd of Dirs 2007–; Minister of Nat. Defence 2007–14; Pres. of Mozambique 2015–; Pres. Clube Ferroviário de Nampula (football club) 1993–2002; Fellow, Africa Leadership Initiative; mem. Frente de Libertação de Moçambique (Frelimo), mem. Cen. Cttee 2012–; Hon. Mention in Czechoslovakia 1990. *Leisure interests:* singing, football. *Address:* Office of the President, Avenida Julius Nyerere 1780, Maputo (office); Frente de Libertação de Moçambique (Frelimo), Rua Pereira do Lago 229, Maputo, Mozambique (office). *Telephone:* (21) 491928 (office); (21) 491121 (office). *Fax:* (21) 492065 (office). *E-mail:* gabimprensa@teldata.mz (office); sg@frelimo.org .mz (office). *Website:* www.presidencia.gov.mz (office); www.frelimo.org.mz (office).

NZAMBIMANA, Lt-Col Édouard; Burundian politician and army officer; b. 20 Dec. 1945; Minister of Public Works, Transport and Equipment 1974–76; participated in coup that overthrew Pres. Micombero Nov. 1976; Prime Minister 1976–78 and Minister of Planning 1976–78, of Agric., Livestock and Rural Devt 1978, of Foreign Affairs and Co-operation 1978–82; later Chair. Union Commerciale d'Assurances et de Réassurance (UCAR). *Address:* Union Commerciale d'Assurances et de Réassurance, BP 3012, Bujumbura, Burundi. *Telephone:* 223638. *Fax:* 223695. *E-mail:* info@ucar.bi.

NZAPAYÉKÉ, André; Central African Republic government official, international banking official and diplomatist; *Ambassador to South Africa;* b. 20 Aug. 1951, Bangassou; ed Univ. of Amsterdam, The Netherlands; Minister of Rural Devt 1990s; f. COSSOSIM (research consultancy), Bangui; postings with several int. orgs, including World Bank, UN, Luxembourg Devt Corpn; Governance and Institutional Reforms Expert, African Devt Bank, Tunis 2001–09, Chair., Staff Council 2009–10, Exec. Dir 2010–12; Vice-Pres. Banque de Développement des Etats de l'Afrique Centrale (Central African States Devt Bank) 2012–14; Prime Minister Jan.–Aug. 2014; Amb. to South Africa 2014–. *Address:* Embassy of the Central African Republic, 209 Eastwood, opp. Eastwood Village, Stanza Bopape Street, Arcadia 0083, South Africa (office). *Telephone:* 0780336843 (mobile) (office). *E-mail:* carembassysa@gmail.com (office).

NZÉ NFUMU, Agustín; Equatorial Guinean diplomatist and politician; b. 18 May 1949, Otong Ntam, Añisok; m. Josefina Mifumu (died 2009); several c.; ed Centro Laboral La Salle, Univ. of Cairo, Egyptian Foreign Ministry, OAU HQ, Addis Ababa, Ethiopian, English courses in Cairo, Ethiopian Foreign Ministry/ Protocol Div.; training courses on int. relations in Egypt and Ethiopia 1960s; returned to Equatorial Guinea as trans. in Ministry of Foreign Affairs 1970, Chief of Dept of Protocol and Trans. 1971–79; political exile in Cameroon Feb. 1979, invited to return home Aug. 1979; Tech. Dir of Protocol, Ministry of Foreign Affairs 1980, Amb./Advisor to the Pres. for Protocol and Foreign Languages 1981, Delegated Minister of External Affairs responsible for Francophone Affairs 1992–93, Minister of Culture, Tourism and Francophone Affairs 1993–96; Diplomatic Adviser and Personal Rep. of the Pres. at Perm. Council of Francophone nations 1996; Gen. Sec., Partido Democrático de Guinea Ecuatorial (Democratic Party of Equatorial Guinea) 1996–2003, mem. Nat. Council and Exec. Cttee; Minister of State for Information, Tourism and Culture 2003–04; elected mem. Chamber of Reps 2004; Amb. to UK 2005–12; Minister of Information, Press and Radio 2012–13; mem. Senate 2013–; Pres. Academia Ecuatoguineana de la Lengua Española 2015–; Founder and Ed. La Gaceta De Guinea Ecuatorial magazine, El Correo De Guinea Ecuatorial; Corresp. mem. Spanish Royal Acad. of Language; Cross of the Ind. Order, Commdr, Guinea Equatorial Ind. Order, Commdr, Order of the Day of Cen. African Repub.; Award '12 de Octubre' for literature, Spanish Cultural Centre, Malabo 1985, El Quijote Award, Equatorial Guinea Press Asscn 2009. *Publications:* Macias, Verdugo o Victima 2003, Eyom Ndong, de la Tribu Mikanfung 2005; editorials and articles in La Gaceta De Guinea Ecuatorial magazine, CEIBA magazine and other nat. newspapers. *Leisure interests:* watching TV, reading and music.

NZIBO, Yusuf Abd ar-Rahman, BA, MPhil, MBA, PhD; Kenyan banking executive, historian and diplomatist (retd); *Commissioner, Independent Electoral and Boundaries Commission;* b. 27 Nov. 1951, Nairobi; m.; four c.; ed Univ. of Nairobi, Strayer Coll., Univ. of Glasgow, UK; Lecturer, Univ. of Nairobi 1979–89; Deputy Man. Dir Industrial Devt Bank Ltd, Nairobi 1989–92, Man. Dir 1992–96; Commr-Gen. Kenya Revenue Authority Feb. 1996; Amb. to the Netherlands and Czech and Slovak Repubs 1998–2000, to Mexico, Colombia and USA 2000–04, to Saudi Arabia, Kuwait, Yemen, Oman and Bahrain 2004–06 (retd); Co-founder and first Man. Dir Gulf African Bank Ltd 2006; Commr Independent Electoral and Boundaries Comm., Nairobi 2011–; mem. Kenya Inst. of Man., Inst. of Bankers, Asscn of African Devt Finance Insts, World Ass. of Small and Medium Enterprises, Aga Khan Foundation and Giants Int; Order of the Grand Warrior, Moran of the Burning Spear. *Publications:* several articles on Latin American history, diplomacy, History of Swahili-Speaking Community of Nairobi. *Leisure interests:* computers, charity work, walking, satellite TV. *Address:* Independent Electoral and Boundaries Commission, University Way, Anniversary Towers, 6th Floor, Nairobi 00100, Kenya (office). *Telephone:* (20) 2769000 (office). *E-mail:* info@iebc .or.ke (office). *Website:* www.iebc.or.ke (office); www.nzibo.com.

NZOMUKUNDA, Alice; Burundian politician; b. 12 April 1966; trained as accountant; elected mem. Parl. for Bujumbura, First Vice-Pres. of Nat. Ass. 2007–08; Second Vice-Pres. of Burundi in charge of Econ. and Social Affairs 2005–06 (resgnd); Founder and Leader, Alliance Démocratique pour le Renouveau 2008; Vice-Pres. for Southern Africa, Africa Liberal Network 2012. *Address:* c/o Alliance Democratique pour le Renouveau, Bwiza, 4ème Avenue, BP 3055, Bujumbura, Burundi.

O

O'NEILL, Michelle, MLA; Northern Irish politician; *Leader, Sinn Féin (Northern Ireland);* b. 10 Jan. 1977; d. of Brendan Doris; m. Paddy O'Neill; two c.; political adviser to MLA Francie Molloy, NI Ass. 1998–2005; mem. Dungannon and South Tyrone Borough Council 2005–10, becoming Mayor 2010–11; MLA for Mid Ulster 2007–; NI Minister of Agric. and Rural Devt 2011–16, of Health 2016–17; mem. Sinn Féin, Leader, Sinn Féin in Northern Ireland 2017–. *Address:* Sinn Féin, 53 Falls Road, Belfast, BT12 4PD, Northern Ireland (office). *Telephone:* (28) 9034-7350 (office). *Fax:* (28) 9022-3001 (office). *E-mail:* admin@sinnfein.ie (office). *Website:* www.sinnfein.ie (office).

OAKDEN, Edward Anthony, CMG; British government official and diplomatist; *Ambassador to Jordan;* b. 3 Nov. 1959; m. Dr Florence Eid; three d.; ed School of Oriental and African Studies, London; Repub. of Ireland Dept, FCO 1981–82, Third Sec. (Chancery), Embassy in Baghdad 1984–85, Second Sec. (Chancery), Embassy in Khartoum 1985–88, Pvt. Sec. to the Amb., Embassy in Washington, DC 1988–92, Asst Head of EC Dept (External), FCO 1992–94, Asst Head of Eastern Adriatic Unit 1994–95, Pvt. Sec. to Prime Minister 1995–97, Deputy Head of EU Union Dept (Internal), FCO 1997–98, Deputy Head of Mission, Embassy in Madrid 1998–2002, Head of Security Policy Dept, FCO 2002, Dir for Defence and Strategic Threats and Envoy for Counter-Terrorism 2002–06, Amb. to UAE 2006–10, Man. Dir, Sectors Group, UK Trade and Investment (UKTI) 2010–12, Man. Dir Strategic Trade, UKTI 2012–13, Dir Middle East, FCO, with responsibility for Gulf countries, Iraq and Iran 2013–15, Amb. to Jordan 2015–. *Address:* British Embassy, POB 87, Abdoun, Amman 11118, Jordan (office). *Telephone:* (6) 5909200 (office). *Fax:* (6) 5909279 (office). *E-mail:* amman.enquiries@fco.gov.uk (office). *Website:* ukinjordan.fco.gov.uk (office).

OAKLEY, Ann, BA, MA, PhD; British sociologist, writer and academic; *Professor of Social Policy and Founding Director, Social Science Research Unit, Institute of Education, University of London;* b. 17 Jan. 1944, London, England; d. of Richard Titmuss and Kay Titmuss; m. Robin Oakley; three c.; ed Chiswick Polytechnic, Somerville Coll., Oxford, Bedford Coll., London; Research Fellow, Bedford Coll., Univ. of London 1974–79, Univ. of Oxford 1979–84; Deputy Dir Thomas Coram Research Unit, Univ. of London 1985–90; Prof. of Social Policy 1991–, Dir Social Science Research Unit, Inst. of Educ., Univ. of London 1990–2005, Founding Dir Social Science Research Unit 2005–; Academician, Acad. of Social Sciences 2009–; Leverhulme Emer. Fellow, Leverhulme Trust 2012; Hon. Prof., Univ. Coll. London 1996–2005; Hon. Fellow, Somerville Coll., Oxford 2001–; Hon. DLitt (Salford) 1995; Hon. DSc (Edinburgh); Lifetime Achievement Award, British Sociological Asscn 2011. *Publications include:* novels: The Men's Room (adapted for TV 1991) 1988; as Rosamund Clay: Only Angels Forget 1990; as Ann Oakley: Matilda's Mistake 1991, The Secret Lives of Eleanor Jenkinson 1992, Scenes Orginating in the Garden of Eden 1993, A Proper Holiday 1996, Overheads 1999; two short stories; non-fiction: Sex, Gender and Society 1972, Housewife 1974, The Sociology of Housework 1974, The Rights and Wrongs of Women (co-ed.) 1976, Becoming a Mother (also published as From Here to Maternity 1981) 1979, Women Confined: Towards a Sociology of Childbirth 1980, Subject Women 1981, Miscarriage (with A. McPherson and H. Roberts) 1984, The Captured Womb: A History of the Medical Care of Pregnant Women 1984, Taking It Like a Woman 1984, What is Feminism? (co-ed.) 1986, Telling the Truth about Jerusalem: Selected Essays 1986, Helpers in Childbirth: Midwifery Today (with S. Houd) 1990, Social Support and Motherhood: The Natural History of a Research Project 1992, Essays on Women, Medicine and Health 1993, Young People, Health and Family Life (with others) 1994, The Politics of the Welfare State (co-ed.) 1994, Evaluating Social Interventions: A Report on Two Workshops (co-ed.) 1996, Man and Wife: Richard and Kay Titmuss, My Parents' Early Years 1996, Who's Afraid of Feminism? (co-ed.) 1997, The Gift Relationship: From Human Blood to Social Policy (co-ed.) 1997, Welfare Research: A Critical Review (co-ed.) 1998, Experiments in Knowing: Gender and Method in the Social Sciences 2000, Welfare and Being: Richard Titmuss's Contribution to Social Policy (co-ed.) 2001, Gender on Planet Earth 2002, The Ann Oakley Reader 2005, Fracture: Adventures of a Broken Body 2007, A Critical Woman: Barbara Wootton, Social Science and Public Policy in the Twentieth Century 2011. *Leisure interests:* cycling, grandchildren. *Address:* c/o The Sayle Literary Agency, 1 Petersfield, Cambridge, CB1 1BB, England (office); Social Science Research Unit, Institute of Education, University of London, Room 102, 18 Woburn Square, London, WC1H 0NR, England (office). *Website:* www.sayleliteraryagency.com (office); www.ioe.ac.uk/SSRU (office); www.annoakley.co.uk. *Telephone:* (20) 7612-6380 (office). *Fax:* (20) 7612-6400 (office). *E-mail:* a.oakley@ioe.ac.uk (office).

OATES, Joyce Carol, (Lauren Kelly, Rosamond Smith), MA; American writer, poet, publisher and academic; *Roger S. Berlind '52 Professor in the Humanities, Professor of Creative Writing, Emerita, Princeton University;* b. 16 June 1938, Lockport, New York; d. of Frederic J. Oates and Caroline Bush; m. 1st Raymond J. Smith 1961 (died 2008); m. 2nd Charles Gross 2009; ed Syracuse Univ. and Univ. of Wisconsin; instructor, Univ. of Detroit 1961–65, Asst Prof. of English 1965–67; mem. Faculty, Dept of English, Univ. of Windsor, Ont. 1967–78; publr (with Raymond Joseph Smith) Ontario Review 1974–; Writer-in-Residence, Princeton Univ. 1978–81, apptd Prof. 1987, now Roger S. Berlind '52 Prof. in the Humanities and Prof. of Creative Writing, Emer.; mem. American Acad., Inst. of Arts and Letters; Guggenheim Fellow 1967–68; mem. Bd of Trustees, John Simon Guggenheim Memorial Foundation 1997–2016; Dr hc (Mount Holyoke Coll.) 2006, (Univ. of Pennsylvania) 2011; O. Henry Prize Story Award 1967, 1973, Rea Award for Short Story 1990, Elmer Holmes Bukst Award 1990, Ivan Sandrof Lifetime Achievement Award, Nat. Book Critics' Circle 2009, Nat. Humanities Medal 2010, Fernanda Pivano Award 2011, Mailer Prize for Lifetime Achievement 2012, PEN Center USA Award for Lifetime Achievement 2012, Poets and Writers Distinguished Lifetime Award 2014, Barnes & Nobel Writers for Writers Award 2014. *Plays include:* Three Plays: Ontological Proof of My Existence, Miracle Play, The Triumph of the Spider Monkey 1980, Twelve Plays 1991, The Perfectionist and Other Plays 1995. *Publications include:* novels: With Shuddering Fall 1964, A Garden of Earthly Delights (M.L. Rosenthal Award 1968) 1967, Expensive People 1968, Them 1969, Wonderland 1971, Do with Me What You Will 1973, The Assassins: A Book of Hours 1975, Childworld 1976, Son of the Morning 1978, Unholy Loves 1979, Cybele 1979, Bellefleur 1980, A Sentimental Education 1981, Angel of Light 1981, A Bloodsmoor Romance 1982, Mysteries of Winterthurn 1984, Solstice 1985, Marya: A Life 1986, You Must Remember This 1987, American Appetites 1989, Because It is Bitter and Because It is My Heart 1990, Black Water 1992, Foxfire 1993, What I Lived For 1994, Zombie (Bram Stoker Award for Best Novel 1996) 1995, First Love: A Gothic Tale 1996, We Were the Mulvaneys 1996, Man Crazy 1997, My Heart Laid Bare 1998, Come Meet Muffin 1998, The Collector of Hearts 1999, Broke Heart Blues 1999, Blonde: A Novel 2000, Middle Age: A Romance 2002, I'll Take You There 2002, Big Mouth and Ugly Girl 2002, The Tattooed Girl 2004, Rape: A Love Story 2004, I Am No One You Know 2004, The Falls (Prix Femina Etranger 2005) 2004, Mother, Missing 2005, The Gravedigger's Daughter 2007, My Sister, My Love: The Intimate Story of Skyler Rampike 2008, Little Bird of Heaven 2009, A Fair Maiden 2010, Blonde 2011, Mudwoman 2012, Two or Three Things I Forgot to Tell You 2012, The Accursed 2013, Carthage 2014, The Sacrifice 2015, The Man Without a Shadow: A Novel 2016, A Book of American Martyrs 2017, Hazards of Time Travel 2018; short story collections: By the North Gate 1963, Upon the Sweeping Flood and Other Stories 1966, The Wheel of Love 1970, Cupid and Psyche 1970, Marriages and Infidelities 1972, A Posthumous Sketch 1973, The Girl 1974, Plagiarized Material 1974, The Goddess and Other Women 1974, Where Are You Going, Where Have You Been?: Stories of Young America 1974, The Hungry Ghosts: Seven Allusive Comedies 1974, The Seduction and Other Stories 1975, The Poisoned Kiss and Other Stories from the Portuguese 1975, The Triumph of the Spider Monkey 1976, Crossing the Border 1976, Night-Side 1977, The Step-Father 1978, All the Good People I've Left Behind 1979, Queen of the Night 1979, The Lamb of Abyssalia 1979, A Middle-Class Education 1980, A Sentimental Education 1980, Last Day 1984, Wild Saturday and Other Stories 1984, Wild Nights 1985, Raven's Wing 1986, The Assignation 1988, Heat and Other Stories 1991, Where is Here? 1992, Haunted Tales of the Grotesque 1994, Faithless: Tales of Transgression 2001, The Female of the Species 2006, High Lonesome: New & Selected Stories 1966–2006 2006, Wild Nights! 2008, Museum of Doctor Moses 2008, Sourland 2010, Give Me Your Heart 2011, The Maiden and Other Nightmares 2011, Black Dahlia and White Rose (Bram Stoker Award for Best Fiction Collection 2013) 2012, Evil Eye: Four Novellas of Love Gone Wrong 2013, High Crime Area: Tales of Darkness and Dread 2014, Lovely, Dark, Deep 2014, The Doll Master and Other Tales 2016, Beautiful Days 2018; poetry: Women in Love and Other Poems 1968, Anonymous Sins and Other Poems 1969, Them (Nat. Book Award 1970) 1969, Love and its Derangements 1970, Wooded Forms 1972, Angel Fire 1973, Dreaming America and Other Poems 1973, The Fabulous Beasts 1975, Seasons of Peril 1977, Women Whose Lives are Food, Men Whose Lives are Money 1978, Celestial Timepiece 1980, Nightless Nights: Nine Poems 1981, Invisible Women: New and Selected Poems 1970–1982 1982, Luxury of Sin 1984, The Time Traveller: Poems 1983–1989 1989, Tenderness 1996; non-fiction: The Edge of Impossibility: Tragic Forms in Literature 1972, The Hostile Sun: The Poetry of D. H. Lawrence 1973, New Heaven, New Earth: The Visionary Experience in Literature 1974, The Stone Orchard 1980, Contraries: Essays 1981, The Profane Art: Essays and Reviews 1983, Funland 1983, On Boxing 1987, (Woman) Writer: Occasions and Opportunities 1988, George Bellows: American Artist (biog.) 1995, The Faith of a Writer: Life, Craft, Art 2004, Black Girl/White Girl 2006, The Journals of Joyce Carol Oates, 1973–1982 2007, In Rough Country: Essays and Reviews 2010, A Widow's Story: A Memoir 2011, The Lost Landscape: A Writer's Coming of Age 2015; Ed.: Scenes from American Life: Contemporary Short Fiction 1973, The Best American Short Stories 1979 (with Shannon Ravenel) 1979, Night Walks: A Bedside Companion 1982, First Person Singular: Writers on Their Craft 1983, Story: Fictions Past and Present (with Boyd Litzinger) 1985, Reading the Fights (with Daniel Halpern) 1988, The Oxford Book of American Short Stories 1993, The Best American Mystery Stories 2006; as Rosamond Smith: The Lives of the Twins 1987, Kindred Passions 1988, Soul-Mate 1989, Nemesis 1990, Snake Eyes 1992, You Can't Catch Me 1995, Double Delight 1997, Starr Bright Will Be with You Soon 1999, The Barrens 2001, Beasts 2003; fiction in nat. magazines. *Address:* c/o Steven Barclay Agency, 12 Western Avenue, Petaluma, CA 94952, USA (office); New South Building, Floor 6, Department of Creative Writing, Princeton University, Princeton, NJ 08544, USA (office). *Telephone:* (707) 773-0654 (office); (609) 258-8561 (office). *Fax:* (707) 778-1868 (office). *E-mail:* steven@barclayagency.com (office); jcsmith@princeton.edu (office). *Website:* barclayagency.com (office); arts.princeton.edu/academics/creative-writing (office).

OBADIA, Nathalie, MA; French art dealer; ed Univ. Panthéon-Assas, Institut d'études politiques de Paris (Sciences-Po); worked as a sr dir at Galerie Daniel Templon, Paris 1988–93; opened own gallery Rue de Normandie in the Marais 1993; has introduced artists including Huma Bhabha, Guy Ben-Ner, Cameron Jamie, Frank Nitsche and Chloe Piene; Galerie Obadia opened in Oct. 2008, joined by Sarkis, a French artist from Turkey with second gallery opening in Brussels; mem. bureau of the French professional cttee of art galleries, Vice-Chair. 2005–08; takes part in numerous int. art fairs, including Fiac (Paris), Armory Show (New York), Art Brussels (Brussels), Frieze (London), Art Forum (Berlin) and Art Basel (Basel); Officier des Arts et des Lettres 2009. *Publication:* a monograph on Martin Barré, published in partnership with Thea Westreichand Ethan Wagner, including the English trans. of the reference text by Yve-Alain Bois. *Address:* Galerie Obadia, 18 rue du Bourg-Tibourg, 75004 Paris, France (office). *Telephone:* 1-53-01-99-76 (office). *E-mail:* nathalie.obadia@galerie-obadia.com (office). *Website:* www.galerie-obadia.com (office).

OBAID, Thoraya Ahmed, BA, MA, PhD; Saudi Arabian fmr UN official; b. 2 March 1945, Baghdad, Iraq; m. Mahmoud Saleh; two d.; ed Mills Coll. and Wayne State Univ., USA; mem. League of Arab States working group for formulating Arab Strategy for Social Devt 1984–85; mem. Editorial Bd Journal of Arab Women 1984–90; mem. Int. Women's Advisory Panel, Int. Planned Parenthood Fed. 1993; Chair. UN Inter-agency Task Force on Gender, Amman 1996; mem. UN Inter-agency Gender Mission to Afghanistan Nov. 1997, UN Strategic Framework Mission to Afghanistan 1997; Assoc. Social Affairs Officer (Women and Devt), Econ. and Social Comm. for W Africa (ESCWA) Social Devt and Population Div. (SDPD) 1975–81, Women and Devt Programme Man., ESCWA SDPD 1981–92,

Chief of ESCWA SDPD 1992–93, Deputy Exec. Sec. ESCWA 1993–98; Dir Div. for Arab States and Europe, UN Population Fund (UNFPA) 1998–2000, Exec. Dir and Under-Sec.-Gen. UNFPA 2001–10; mem. Middle East Studies Asscn, Al-Nahdha Women's Philanthropic Asscn; Order of Dionisio de Herrera (Honduras) 2005; Dr hc of Law (Mills Coll.) 2002, (Kwansei Gakuin Univ., Japan) 2004; George P. Younger Award, UN Cttee of Religious NGOs 2002, Medal and Key to the City of Managua, Nicaragua 2003, Pedro Joaquin Chamorro Award, Nicaragua 2003, Second Century Award for Excellence in Health Care, Columbia Univ. 2003, Commemorative Medal, Bulgaria 2006, Louis B. Sohn Human Rights Award 2009.

OBAIDI, Gen. Abd al-Qader Jasim al-; Iraqi army officer and government official; b. 1947, Ramadi; fmr Gen. in Iraqi army under Saddam Hussein, rejoined army 2003, served as Commdr of Operations Centre, then Mil. Commdr in western Iraq, then Commdr infantry commando units; Minister of Defence 2006–10.

OBAMA, Barack Hussein, Jr, BA, JD; American lawyer, politician and fmr head of state; b. 4 Aug. 1961, Honolulu, Hawaii; s. of Barack Obama, Sr and Ann Dunham; m. Michelle Obama (née Robinson) 1992; two d.; ed Punahou School, Hawaii, Occidental Coll., Columbia Univ., Harvard Law School; family lived in Hawaii and Indonesia; Ed.-in-Chief, Harvard Law Review (first African-American) and mem. Exec. Bd Black Law Students Asscn, Harvard Univ.; writer and financial analyst, Business Int. Corpn 1984–85; Dir Developing Communities Project, Chicago 1985–88; worked for Bill Clinton's presidential election campaign as Dir Ill. Project Vote 1992; Assoc., Davis, Miner, Barnhill & Galland, PC (law firm), Chicago 1993–96, Of Counsel 1996–2004; Sr Lecturer, Univ. of Chicago Law School 1993–2004; mem. Ill. State Senate for 13th Senate Dist, S Chicago 1997–2005, Chair. Public Health and Welfare Cttee, mem. Judiciary Cttee, Revenue Cttee; lost Democratic primary for US House of Reps to incumbent Congressman Bobby Rush 2000; Senator from Ill. (third-ever African-American mem. of Senate) 2005–08; Pres. of USA (first African-American) 2009–17; fmr Chair. Chicago Lawyers Cttee for Civil Rights under the Law, Chicago Annenberg Challenge; mem. Ill. Bar Asscn, Cook Co. Bar Asscn; Democrat; Hon. LLD (Knox Coll.) 2005, (Northwestern Univ.) 2005, (Univ. of Massachusetts) 2006, (Xavier Univ.) 2006, (Southern New Hampshire Univ.) 2007, (Harvard Univ.) 2007, (Wesleyan Univ.) 2008, (Univ. of Notre Dame) 2009, (Hampton Univ.) 2010, (Rutgers Univ.) 2016, Hon. ScD (Howard Univ.) 2016; Grammy Award for Best Spoken Word Album (for audio-book version of The Audacity of Hope) 2008, named by TIME magazine as its Person of the Year 2008, Nobel Peace Prize 2009, Robert F. Kennedy Human Rights Ripple of Hope Award 2018, numerous other awards and honours. *Publications:* Dreams from My Father 1995, The Audacity of Hope 2006, Of Thee I Sing: A Letter to My Daughters 2010.

OBAMA, Michelle LaVaughn Robinson, BA, JD; American lawyer and fmr first lady; b. 17 Jan. 1964, Chicago, Ill.; d. of Fraser Robinson III and Marian Shields Robinson; m. Barack Obama 1992; two d.; ed Whitney Young High School, Chicago, Princeton Univ., Harvard Law School; Assoc., Sidley Austin (law firm), Chicago 1988–91; Asst to Chicago Mayor Richard M. Daley 1991–93, also Asst Commr of Planning and Devt; Exec. Dir Public Allies, Chicago 1993–96; Assoc. Dean of Student Services, Univ. of Chicago 1996–2002; Exec. Dir for Community Affairs, Univ. of Chicago Hosps 2002–05, Vice-Pres. for Community and External Affairs 2005–09; First Lady of USA 2009–17; mem. Bd of Dirs Chicago Council on Global Affairs; numerous awards and honours. *Publications include:* American Grown 2012, Becoming 2018.

OBAMA ASUE, Francisco Pascual Eyegue; Equatorial Guinean politician; *Prime Minister;* has held several ministerial portfolios including fmr Minister of State for Agric., Livestock and Rural Devt, Minister of Health and Social Welfare, of Educ. and Science, apptd Minister of Youth and Sports 2011, Second Deputy Prime Minister for Social Sector 2015–16, Prime Minister, in charge of Admin. Co-ordination 2016–; mem. Partido Democrático de Guinea Ecuatorial (PDGE). *Address:* Office of the Prime Minister, Malabo, Equatorial Guinea (office).

OBASANJO, Gen. (retd) Olusegun Mathew Okikiola Aremu, (OBJ); Nigerian politician, UN official, fmr army officer and fmr head of state; b. 5 March 1937, Abeokuta, Ogun State; m. 1st Oluremi Akinbwon; two s. four d.; m. 2nd Stella Abebe (died 2005); ed Abeokuta Baptist High School and Mons Officers' Cadet School, UK; joined Nigerian Army 1958, commissioned 1959; served in Congo (now Democratic Repub. of the Congo) 1960; promoted Capt. 1963, Maj. 1965, Lt-Col 1967, Col 1969, Brig. 1972, Lt-Gen. 1976, Gen. 1979; Commdr Eng Corps 1963, later Commdr 2nd Div. (Rear), Ibadan; GOC 3rd Infantry Div. 1969; Commdr 3rd Marine Commando Div. during Nigerian Civil War, accepted surrender of Biafran forces Jan. 1970; Commdr Eng Corps 1970–75; Fed. Commr for Works and Housing Jan.–July 1975; Chief of Staff, Supreme HQ 1975–76; mem. Supreme Mil. Council 1975–79; Head of Fed. Mil. Govt and C-in-C of Armed Forces 1976–79; mem. Advisory Council of State 1979; arrested March 1995, interned 1995; Pres. of Nigeria and C-in-C of Armed Forces 1999–2007; Chair. Bd of Trustees, People's Democratic Party 2007; apptd UN Special Envoy for the Democratic Repub. of the Congo 2008; UN Special Rep. of Sec.-Gen. for the Great Lakes Region Dec. 2008–12; mem. Sec.-Gen.'s High-Level Advisory Bd on Mediation, UN 2017–; fmr Chair. African Union; Chair. Africa Leadership Forum and Foundation; Co-Chair. Eminent Persons Group on S Africa 1985; Chair. Advisory Council for Inaugural Intra-African Trade Fair (IATF2018), African Export-Import Bank 2018–; Fellow, Univ. of Ibadan 1979–81; Chief Promoter, Olusegun Obasanjo Presidential Library Foundation; mem. Ind. Comm. on Disarmament and Security 1980, mem. Exec. Cttee Inter-Action Council of fmr Heads of Govt; Grand Commdr, Order of the Fed. Repub. of Nigeria 1980; Hon. DHumLitt (Howard), Hon. LLD (Maiduguri) 1980, (Ahmadu Bello Univ., Zaria) 1985, (Ibadan) 1988, Dr hc (Namibia), (Bowen); Human Rights Prize, Friedrich–Ebert Foundation, Germany 1996, Indira Gandhi Peace Prize, India. *Publications include:* My Command 1980, Africa in Perspective 'Myths and Realities' 1987, Nzeogwu 1987, Africa Embattled 1988, Constitution for National Integration and Development 1989, Not My Will 1990, Elements of Development 1992, Elements of Democracy 1993, Africa: Rise to Challenge 1993, Hope for Africa 1993, Guide to Effective Prayer 1999, This Animal Called Man 1999, Women of Virtue 1999, A New Dawn 2000, Exemplary Youth in a Difficult World 2002, I See Hope 2002, Sermons from Prison 2002, My Watch Vols 1-3. *Leisure interests:* table tennis, squash, reading, writing. *Address:* African Export-Import Bank, P.O. Box 613 Heliopolis, Cairo 11757, Egypt (office); Olusegun Obasanjo Presidential Library

Foundation, Presidential Blvd, Oke-Mosan Abeokuta, Ogun State, Nigeria (office). *Telephone:* (2) 24515201 (office). *E-mail:* info@afreximbank.com (office); ortesev@yahoo.com (office); obasanjonig@yahoo.com (office). *Website:* www.afreximbank .com.

OBAYASHI, Takeo, MS; Japanese construction industry executive; *Chairman, Obayashi Corporation;* s. of Yoshiro Obayashi; m.; ed Keio Univ., Stanford Univ., Calif., USA; trained as civil engineer; joined Obayashi Corpn 1977, apptd Dir 1983, Rep. Dir 1989–, Vice-Pres. 1997–2003, Vice-Chair. 2003–07, Chair. 2007–; Chair. Obayashi Foundation; Man.-Dir Kansei Asscn of Corp. Execs; Vice-Chair. Osaka Chamber of Commerce and Industry; mem. Bd, Kansei Econ. Fed., Bd of Councillors, Int. Inst. for Advanced Studies Foundation, Bd of Visitors, Stanford Inst. for Int. Studies, Research Governance Cttee, Stanford Japan Center, Japanese Cttee of Honour, Royal Acad. of Arts, London, Int. Council, Tate Gallery, London, UK, Advisory Group, Asian Art Fairs Ltd; Trustee and mem. Council, Museum of Modern Art; Hon. Consul of the Repub. of Lithuania 2008–. *Address:* Obayashi Corporation, Shinagawa Intercity Tower B, 2-15-2 Konan, Minato-ku, Tokyo 108-8502, Japan (office). *Telephone:* (3) 5769-1906 (office). *Fax:* (3) 5769-1910 (office). *E-mail:* info@obayashi.co.jp (office). *Website:* www.obayashi .co.jp (office).

OBEID, Jean, BA; Lebanese politician; b. 8 May 1939, Alma, Zghorta; m. Loubna Emile El-Boustani; two s. three d.; ed Collège de Frères-Pères Carmélites-Lycée Officiel, Tripoli, St Joseph's Univ., Beirut; journalist, Magazine and Isbouh El Arabi 1959–62, Lissan Al Hal 1960–63, Al Nahar 1963–66, Assayad 1963–66, Ed. Assayad 1966–72; began political career 1973; adviser to Pres. Elias Sarkis of Lebanon 1973; counsellor and presidential del. to Summit of Non-Aligned States, New Delhi, India 1983; participated in Inter-Lebanese Nat. Reconciliation Conf., Geneva, Switzerland; Deputy of the Chouf 1991; Deputy for Tripoli, N Lebanon 1992; Minister of State 1993; Deputy for N Lebanon 1996–2004; Minister of Nat. Educ., Sports and Youth 1996–2003, of Foreign Affairs and Emigrants 2003–04; unsuccessful cand. for Pres. of Lebanon 2007.

OBEID SALIM, Lt-Gen. Mustafa Osman; Sudanese military commander and government official; long career in Sudanese Armed Forces, becoming Chief of Staff of Ground Forces 2010, Chief of Staff of Sudanese Armed Forces 2013–16; Acting Minister of Defence June –Aug. 2015.

OBEIDAT, Ahmad Abdul-Majeed; Jordanian lawyer and politician; b. 18 Nov. 1938, Hartha, Irbid; m.; five c.; ed Salahiyah School and Univ. of Baghdad; teacher, Minister of Educ. 1957; Customs Officer, Ministry of Finance 1962; First Lt-Gen., Security Service 1962–64; Asst Dir-Gen. Intelligence Service 1964–74, Dir 1974–82; Minister of the Interior 1982–84; Prime Minister of Jordan and Minister of Defence 1984–85; Partner, Law and Arbitration Centre 1985–; fmr Deputy Speaker of the Senate from 1984; attorney and legal consultant in pvt. practice as of 1985; launched Nat. Front for Reform 2011; Pres. Jordan Environment Soc.; Chair. Bd of Trustees, Nat. Centre for Human Rights 2003–08; Founder and mem. Jordan Environment Soc. 1986–2003, currently Bd of Trustees; Founding mem. and Chair. Jordan Nat. Soc. for Consumer Protection 1989; Chair. Royal Cttee for Drafting the Nat. Charter 1990–91; Deputy Chair. Royal Human Rights Comm. 2000–, Royal Comm. for Judicial Reform 2000–; mem. Bd of Trustees, Arab Anti-Corruption Org.; mem. Jordan Bar Asscn 1985; UNDP Goodwill Amb. 1990. *Address:* Law and Arbitration Centre, PO Box 926544, Amman, Jordan. *Telephone:* 672222.

OBEIDI, Khaled al-, PhD; Iraqi engineer, academic, politician and fmr army officer; b. Mosul; ed Eng Acad. of Yugoslavia and Univ. of Belgrade, Yugoslavia; worked in Air Force with specialist eng structures and aircraft turbine engines 1984–2003, served as an officer in Saddam Hussein's mil.; Lecturer, Jt Chiefs of Staff Coll. 1996; mem. Muttahidoon (The Uniters for Reform); Deputy in Iraqi Parl. for Mosul; Minister of Defence 2014–16 (resgnd).

OBENG, Letitia Eva, BSc, MSc, PhD, FRSA; Ghanaian scientist, research director and environmental manager; b. (Takyibea Asihene), 10 Jan. 1925, Anum; d. of Rev. E. V. Asihene and Dora Asihene; m. George A. Obeng 1953; two s. one d.; ed Achimota Coll., Univs of Birmingham and Liverpool, Imperial Coll., Univ. of London, UK; Lecturer, Coll. of Science and Tech., Kumasi 1952–59; Research Scientist, Nat. Research Council, Ghana 1960–62; mem. research staff, Ghana Acad. of Sciences 1963–65; built and served as first Dir, Inst. of Aquatic Biology, Council for Scientific and Industrial Research, Ghana 1965–74; Project Co-Man., Ghana Govt/UNDP Volta Lake Research Project; Sr Programme Officer and Chair. Soil and Water Task Force, UNEP, Nairobi 1974–80; Regional Dir and Rep. of UNEP to Africa 1980–85; Dir Environmental Man. Services 1986; Chair. Global Water Partnership 2008–12; mem. Exec. Council, Africa Leadership Forum 1991, Bd of Stockholm Environment Inst., PANOS 1986–95; Distinguished Int. Visitor, Radcliffe Coll., USA 1992; mem. Bd of Dirs WaterAid America 2012–, Int. Water Man. Inst. 2013–; Affiliate mem. Africa Leadership Forum, Royal Soc. (UK), New York Acad. of Sciences 1995, Int. Rice Research Inst., Int. Irrigation Man. Inst., Stockholm Environment Inst.; Fellow, Ghana Acad. of Arts and Sciences (fmr Pres.); Trustee, Bd of Int. Rice Research Inst., Int. Irrigation Man. Inst., Human Ecology Foundation; Star of Ghana 2006; Silver Medal, Royal Soc. of Arts, Ghana Council for Scientific and Industrial Research (CSIR) Award 1997, Ghana Govt Award for Biological Sciences 1998, CSIR Bldg named The Letitia Obeng Block 1998; featured on nat. commemorative postage stamp. *Publications:* Man-made Lakes (ed.) 1969, Environment and the Responsibility of the Privileged, Environment and Population, The Right to Health in Tropical Agriculture; Parasites: The Sly and Sneaky Enemies Inside You 1997, Ephraim Amu – A Portrait of Cultured Patriotism, Kwame Mkrumah and the Sciences 2005, A Silent Heritage 2010; scientific articles; book chapters. *Leisure interests:* poetry, painting flowers, Akan culture and traditions.

OBENG, Lt-Gen. Seth Kofi, MSc; Ghanaian army officer; b. 26 Jan. 1945, Lagos, Nigeria; s. of Nicholas Emmanuel Obeng and Dina Kwaley Obeng; m. Barbara Baaba Obeng; six c.; ed US Command and Staff Coll., Fort Leavenworth, Kansas, London School of Econs, UK, Nat. Defence Coll., Delhi, India (Postgraduate Diploma in Int. and Comparative Politics); commissioned into Ghanaian Army as artillery officer 1965, various sr command and staff appointments including Commdt Mil. Acad. and Training School and Ghana Armed Forces Command and Staff Coll. as well as Chief of Staff/Gen. HQ; Defence Adviser, Ghana High Comm.,

London 1984–88; Chief Staff Officer, Army HQ 1988–89; Man. Dir State Housing Corpn (now State Housing Co. 1989–92, 1992–93; Deputy Force Commdr Econ. Community of West African States (ECOWAS) Monitoring Group in Liberia 1994–96; Force Commdr UN Observer Mission to Angola 1998–99; Force Commdr UN Interim Force in Lebanon (UNIFIL) 1999–2001; Chief of Defence Staff 2001–05; Chair. ECOWAS Defence and Security Comm., mem. ECOWAS Council of the Wise 2006–, mem. Bd of Govs Small Arms and Light Weapons Contol Programme; Under-Sec.-Gen., UN Secr. 2006–, mem. Follow Up Cttee of the Greentree Agreement of 12th June 2006; Special Adviser on Mil. Affairs to African Union Chair. 2007; apptd by ECOWAS Comm. as mem. of Mediation Team to help resolve political and constitutional crisis in Niger Nov. 2009; has participated in several ECOWAS Observer Missions in Nigeria, Sierra Leone (as Head of Mission), Guinea (Conakry), Côte d'Ivoire, Liberia (Special Envoy of the Pres. of ECOWAS Comm.) 2011; ECOMOG Medal (Liberia) 1996, MONUA Medal (Angola) 1999, UNIFIL Medal 2001; Commdr, Nat. Legion of Cedars (Lebanon) 2001, Officer Nat. Order of Côte d'Ivoire 2002, Meritorious Service Medal (USA) 2004, Order of the Star of Ghana 2006, Commdr, Nat. Order of Merit (Niger) 2012; ECOWAS Award 1996, Int. Officer Hall of Fame (USA) 2004, Ghana Mil. Acad. Jubilee Award for outstanding contrib. to Int. Peace Support Operations from Vice-Pres. of Ghana and Chair. Armed Forces Council 2010. *Leisure interests:* reading, keeping fit, football, hockey, volleyball. *Telephone:* 24-2861246 (mobile). *E-mail:* sethobeng@gmail.com (office).

OBERHELMAN, Douglas (Doug) R., BA; American business executive; b. 25 Feb. 1953; ed Millikin Univ.; joined Caterpillar 1975, held a variety of positions, including Sr Finance Rep. based in S America for Caterpillar Americas Co., Region Finance Man. and Dist Man. for the co.'s N American Commercial Div., Man. Dir and Vice-Gen. Man. for Strategic Planning at Caterpillar Japan Ltd, Tokyo, Japan, Vice-Pres. 1995, served as Caterpillar's Chief Financial Officer 1995–98, Vice-Pres. with responsibility for Engine Products Div. 1998–2002, Group Pres. and mem. Exec. Office 2002–09, Vice-Chair. and CEO-elect 2009–10, mem. Bd of Dirs and CEO 2010–16, Chair. 2010–17; mem. Bd of Dirs Eli Lilly & Co., Illinois Chapter, The Nature Conservancy, Asscn of Equipment Mfrs, Nat. Asscn of Mfrs, Manufacturing Inst., Wetlands America Trust; fmr mem. Bd of Dirs Ameren Corpn (Chair. Audit Cttee and mem. Nominating and Governance Cttee and the Public Policy Cttee), South Side Bank, Millikin Univ. (Chair. Bd of Trustees), Easter Seals (Chair.). *Address:* c/o Caterpillar Inc., 100 NE Adams Street, Peoria, IL 61629, USA.

OBERMANN, René; German business executive; *CEO, Ziggo;* b. 5 March 1963, Düsseldorf; m.; two d.; ed Univ. of Muenster; traineeship with BMW AG 1984–86; f. ABC Telekom (subsequently Hutchison Mobilfunk), Muenster 1986, Man. Partner 1991, Chair. Man. Bd 1994–98; Man. Dir of Sales, T-Mobile Deutschland 1998–2000, CEO T-Mobile International AG (holding co. for Deutsche Telekom AG mobile operations) 2000–02, mem. Man. Bd responsible for European operations 2001–02, responsible for mobile operations 2002–06, also responsible for mobile communications strategic business area, CEO Deutsche Telekom AG 2006–13, responsible for innovation 2012–13; CEO Ziggo 2014–; Chair. VAM – Verband der Anbieter von Mobilfunkdiensten (Asscn of Mobile Communications Service Providers) 1995–96; Presidium mem. BITKOM German industry asscn 2007–; mem. Supervisory Bd E.ON AG 2011–, Senate of the Fraunhofer Gesellschaft 2011–. *Address:* Ziggo, Atoomweg 100, 3542 AB Utrecht, The Netherlands (office). *Telephone:* (88) 7170717 (office). *Website:* www.ziggo.com (office).

OBERMEIER, Georg, DPhil; German business executive; b. 21 July 1941, Munich; m.; ed Ludwig-Maximilians-Universität, Munich; with Knorr-Bremse GmbH 1964–72; Bayernwerk AG, Munich, latterly Dir of Finance and Org. 1973–89; apptd mem. Man. Bd VIAG AG 1989–98, Chair. 1995–98; Chair. Ryhag, Vienna 1999–2001; fmr Chair. Supervisory Bd Isar-Amperwerke AG, Munich, Rheinhold & Mahla AG, Munich, SKW Trostberg AG, Trostberg; Vice-Chair. and mem. Supervisory Bd Kühne & Nagel International AG 1992–2011; Chair. Supervisory Bd Gigaset AG (fmrly Arques Industries AG) 2007–09, 2009–10; mem. or fmr mem. Supervisory Bd Bayernwerk AG, Munich, Didier-Werke AG, Wiesbaden, Gerresheimer Glas AG, Düsseldorf, Klöckner & Co. AG, Duisburg, Schindellegi, Mobil Oil AG, Hamburg, Schmalbach-Lubeca AG, Brunswick, Thomassen & Drijver Verblifa NV, Deventer, Thyssengas GmbH, Duisburg, VAW Aluminium AG, Berlin/Bonn, SKW Stahl-Metallurgie Holding GmbH 2006–; mem. Int. Advisory Bd and Jt Advisory Council, Allianz SE; mem. Supervisory Cttee Energie-Control GmbH, Spaten-Franziskaner KGaA, Munich. *Address:* c/o Allianz SE, Koeniginstrasse 28, 80802 Munich, Germany.

OBI, Onyeabo C., LLB, FCIArb; Nigerian international business lawyer; b. 20 Nov. 1938, Ogidi; s. of Chief Z. C. Obi; m. Evelyn Nnenna Obioha 1967; two s. three d.; ed London School of Econs, UK; called to the Bar, Gray's Inn, London 1962; in pvt. practice as barrister and solicitor of Supreme Court of Nigeria 1963–; Dir Nigerian Rubber Bd 1977–79; Senator, Fed. Repub. of Nigeria 1979–83; mem. of Council (and Vice-Chair. Cttee on Procedures for Settling Disputes), Section on Business Law, Int. Bar Asscn 1986–92; mem. Advisory Cttee on Rules of the Supreme Court of Nigeria (by appointment of Hon. Chief Justice) 1986–92; mem. Panel of Arbitrators held at Int. Center for Settlement of Investment Disputes, World Bank, Washington, DC, USA 2009–. *Leisure interest:* short walks. *Address:* Western House (13th Floor), 8–10 Broad Street, PO Box 4040, Lagos, Nigeria (office). *Telephone:* (1) 263-0843 (office); (1) 743-2365 (office); (1) 263-4604 (office). *Fax:* (1) 263-7609 (office). *E-mail:* abobi@hyperia.com (office); niger.lex@gmail.com (office).

OBIALA, Edmund, MESc; Polish/Australian civil and structural engineer; b. 9 Feb. 1946, Poland; m. Grażyna Guth; ed Poznań Univ. of Tech., Bydgoszcz Univ. of Tech.; geodesist Pomeranian Mil. Dist 1966–72; construction designer, head of designer team, Eltor, Bydgoszcz 1972–78; research worker, Ibmer Warsaw, constructed works in Bydgoszcz 1977–80; mem. staff, Civil and Civic Pty Ltd, Sydney 1982–88, Multiplex Constructions Pty Ltd 1988–2000; apptd Operations Dir Bovis Lend Lease Ltd 2000; Adviser, Ministry of Sport and led construction 2006–07; Award for Excellence, Concrete Inst. of Australia 1999, Grand Award for Excellence in Arboriculture, Nat. Arborist Asscn 1999, British Construction Award for Olympic Stadium in Sydney 2000, Structural Special Award 2000, Green Apple Award 2004. *Works:* constructions designed include Nat. Bank of Australia, Sydney 1982–85, sports stadium Parramatta and football stadium,

Sydney 1985–88, Chiefley Tower, Coles Myer Centre and re-building of Chelsea football team stadium, London 1988–2000. *Achievements:* project dir on major constructions including Olympic Stadium, Sydney 1994–99, Wembley Stadium 1999–2001, Chelsea Stadium 1999–2001, Munich City Tower 2001–02, Everton Stadium, Liverpool 2002–03, Chapelfield Shopping Centre, Norwich 2003–. *Leisure interests:* cinema, literature, tennis, volleyball. *Address:* 42 Wherry Road, Norwich, NR1 1WS, England (home). *Telephone:* (1603) 766584 (home). *E-mail:* eobiala@onetel.com (home); gguth@onetel.net (home).

OBIANG EYANG, Miguel Engonga; Equatorial Guinean economist and politician; Gen. Dir of Budget, Ministry of Finance and Budget 2013–15, Minister of Finance and the Budget 2015–18.

OBIANG MANGUE, Col Teodoro (Teodorín) Nguema; Equatorial Guinean politician; *First Vice-President, in charge of National Defence and State Security;* b. 25 June 1969; s. of Teodoro Obiang Nguema Mbasogo (Pres. of Equatorial Guinea) and Constancia Okomo; ed Pepperdine Univ., USA; Adviser to the Presidency 1990s; fmr Minister of Agric. and Forestry; Second Vice-Pres., in charge of Defence and Security 2012–16, First Vice-Pres., in charge of Nat. Defence and State Security 2016–; Owner, Radio Televisión Asonga (broadcasting co.). *Address:* Office of the Vice-President, Malabo, Equatorial Guinea (office). *Website:* presidencia-ge.org (office).

OBIANG NGUEMA MBASOGO, Gen. (retd) Teodoro; Equatorial Guinean politician, fmr army officer and head of state; *President and Supreme Commander of the Armed Forces;* b. 5 June 1942, Acoacán, Spanish Guinea; s. of Santiago Nguema Eneme and María Mbasogo Ngui; m. Constancia Mangue; one s.; ed Mil. Acad., Zaragoza, Spain; held various positions, including Gov. of Bioko, Leader of the Nat. Guard, Head of Black Beach Prison; fmr Deputy Minister of Defence; overthrew his uncle fmr Pres. Macias Nguema in coup; Pres. of Equatorial Guinea 1979–; Supreme Commdr of the Armed Forces 1979–; Minister of Defence 1986; Chair. African Union 2011–12; mem Partido Democrático de Guinea Ecuatorial (PDGE—Democratic Party of Equatorial Guinea); Grand Collar of the Order of Lakandula (Philippines) 2006, Grand Officer, Hon. Order of the Yellow Star (Suriname). *Address:* Oficina del Presidente, Malabo, Equatorial Guinea (office).

O'BRIEN, Conan Christopher, AB; American comedian, television writer and talk show host; b. 18 April 1963, Brookline, Mass; s. of Thomas Francis O'Brien and Ruth O'Brien (née Reardon); m. Elizabeth Ann (Liza) Powel 2002; one s. one d.; ed Brookline High School, Harvard Univ.; was Man. Ed. of school newspaper; wrote for Harvard Lampoon humour magazine, later Pres. Harvard Lampoon; moved to Los Angeles following graduation to join writing staff of HBO's Not Necessarily the News 1985–87; performed regularly with improvisational groups, including The Groundlings; was hired as writer for Saturday Night Live (SNL) 1988–92, put on improvisational comedy revue in Chicago, with fellow SNL writers Bob Odenkirk and Robert Smigel, called Happy Happy Good Show, occasionally appeared as an extra in sketches, returned to host the show 2001; co-wrote TV pilot Lookwell, NBC 1991; writer and producer for The Simpsons 1991–93 (credited as writer or co-writer of four episodes); host, Late Night with Conan O'Brien 1993–2009, The Tonight Show with Conan O'Brien 2009–10, Conan 2010–; ordained as a minister by the Universal Life Church Monastery 2011. *Films include:* Space Ghost: Coast to Coast (as himself) 1994, Mr. Show with Bob and David 1995, The Single Guy (TV) 1996, Good Money 1996, Arli$$ 1996, Spin City (TV) 1998, Futurama 1999, Storytelling 2001, Vanilla Sky 2001, Sugar & Spice (cameo in end credits) 2001, Andy Richter Controls the Universe (TV) 2003, End of the Century 2003, Bewitched (as himself) 2005, Robot Chicken 2005, The Denial Twist (the White Stripes music video) 2005, O'Grady (TV) 2006, The Office (cameo) 2006, Queer Duck (as himself) 2006, 30 Rock (as himself) 2007, 2009, Robot Chicken: Star Wars (TV; voice) 2007, Robot Chicken: Star Wars Episode II (TV; voice) 2008, The Backyardigans 2009. *TV writer/producer:* Not Necessarily the News (writer 5 episodes) 1983–85, The Rich Hall Show (writer) 1987, The Wilton North Report (series writer and producer) 1987, Saturday Night Live (aka NBC's Saturday Night, aka SNL 25; writer 73 episodes) 1987–91, Lookwell (writer and producer) 1991, Best of Saturday Night Live: Special Edition (writer) 1992, The Simpsons (writer 4 episodes; producer 52 episodes) 1991–93, Saturday Night Live: The Best of Phil Hartman (writer) 1998, Late Night with Conan O'Brien: 5th Anniversary Special (writer) 1998, Saturday Night Live: 25th Anniversary (writer; uncredited) 1999, 50 Years of NBC Late Night (writer) 2001, The Greg Giraldo Show (exec. producer) 2002, Beat Cops (exec. producer) 2003, Late Night with Conan O'Brien: 10th Anniversary Special (writer) 2003, Foster Hall (exec. producer) 2004, Saturday Night Live: The Best of Jon Lovitz (writer; uncredited) 2005, Marsha Potter Gets a Life (exec. producer) 2005, Haskett's Chance (exec. producer) 2006, The 58th Annual Primetime Emmy Awards (writer) 2006, Andy Barker, P.I. (creator and exec. producer 6 episodes) 2007, Wildlife (exec. producer) 2007, Late Night with Conan O'Brien (writer 1,494 episodes; producer 7 episodes) 1993–2008, Man of Your Dreams (exec. producer) 2008, The Tonight Show with Conan O'Brien (writer 51 episodes; also consulting producer) 2009, Outnumbered (series; exec. producer) 2009, Operating Instructions (exec. producer) 2009. *Address:* c/o WME Entertainment, 9601 Wilshire Boulevard, Beverley Hills, CA 90210-5213, USA (office). *Telephone:* (310) 285-9000 (office). *Fax:* (310) 285-9010 (office). *Website:* www.wma.com (office).

O'BRIEN, David P., OC, BA, BCL; Canadian business executive; b. 9 Sept. 1941, Montreal; s. of John Lewis and Ethel O'Brien (née Cox); m. Gail Baxter Cornell 1968; two s. one d.; ed Loyola Coll., McGill Univ.; Assoc. Ogilvy Renault 1967, later Pnr; joined Petro-Canada 1978, positions including Exec. Vice-Pres. 1985–89; Pres. and CEO Noverco Inc. 1989; with PanCanadian Petroleum 1990–95, Chair., Pres. and CEO –1995; Pres. and COO Canadian Pacific Ltd 1995–96, Chair., Pres. and CEO 1996–2001; Chair. and CEO PanCanadian Energy Corpn 2001–02, Chair. EnCana Corpn (following merger of PanCanadian Energy Corpn and Alberta Energy Co.) 2002–13; joined Bd of Dirs, Royal Bank of Canada 1996, Chair. 2004–13; mem. Bd Dirs Fairmont Hotel and Resorts, Inco Ltd, TransCanada Pipelines Ltd, Molson Inc., C. D. Howe Inst.; Hon. DCL (Bishops Univ.) 1998, Hon. BA (Mount Royal Coll.) 2000.

O'BRIEN, Derek, BA; Indian television presenter and author; b. 13 March 1961, Kolkata; s. of Neil O'Brien and Joyce O'Brien; m. 1st Rila Banerjee 1991 (divorced); m. 2nd Tonuca O'Brien; one d.; ed St Xavier's Collegiate School, Kolkata, St

Columba's School, Delhi, Scottish Church Coll., Kolkata; early career as journalist for Sportsworld; worked for Ogilvy and Mather advertising firm; f. Derek O'Brien & Assocs Pvt. Ltd 1991 (direct marketer and developer of quiz shows); Host, Brand Equity Quiz 1991–, Cadbury Bournvita Quiz Contest 1992–, Mind Grind (Pakistan) 2008–; conducts inter-school quiz contests in India, UAE, Oman, Kuwait, Qatar, Saudi Arabia, Bahrain, Bangladesh, Pakistan and Nepal; joined All India Trinamool Congress (political party) 2005, fmr Spokesperson; Chair. Passenger Services Cttee, Indian Railways 2009–; Hero Honda Indian TV Acad. Award (Best Anchor of a Game/Quiz Show) 2003. *Publications include:* Penguin India Reference Yearbook (ed.), Bournvita Book of Knowledge (ed.), C B Book Of Knowledge (Vols 1–13), Discover with Derek (Vols 1–3) GK with Derek—Box Set (Vols 1–6) 2004, Ultimate Quiz Challenge 2005, Essential Knowledge Quiz Book 2006, Penguin CNBC Business YRBK-07 2007, The Ultimate India Quiz Book 2007, Derek's Picks 2008, Penguin CNBC TV18 Business Yearbook 2010. *Leisure interests:* horses, cricket. *Address:* Derek O'Brien & Associates Pvt. Ltd, 23E Ahiripukur 1st Lane, Kolkata 700 019, West Bengal (office); 7/2Y Jamir Lane, Ballygunge, Kolkata 700 019, West Bengal, India (home). *Telephone:* (33) 22804093 (office); (33) 22804094 (office); (33) 4404126 (home). *Fax:* (33) 22804092 (office); (33) 4405844 (home). *E-mail:* shows@derek.co.in (office). *Website:* www.derek.co.in (office).

O'BRIEN, Edna; Irish writer; b. 15 Dec. 1930, Tuamgraney, Co. Clare; d. of Michael O'Brien and Lena Cleary; m. Ernest Gébler 1954 (divorced 1964); two s.; ed convents, Pharmaceutical Coll. of Ireland; qualified as a pharmacist 1950; Writer-in-Resident, New York Univ. 1997–98; Adjunct Prof. of Creative Writing, Univ. Coll. Dublin 2006–; apptd mem. Aosdána 1996; Hon. DBE 2018; Hon. DLitt (Queen's) 1999, (Limerick) 2004; Irish PEN Lifetime Achievement Award 2001, Ulysses Medal, Univ. Coll. Dublin 2006, American Nat. Arts Gold Medal 2002, Bob Hughes Lifetime Achievement Award, Irish Book Awards 2009, Charleston-Chichester Award for a Lifetime's Excellence in Short Fiction 2015, elected Saoi of Aosdána 2015, PEN/Nabokov Award for Achievement in Int. Literature 2018, John B. Keane Lifetime Achievement Award 2018. *Television:* numerous screenplays. *Publications include:* The Country Girls 1960 (Kingsley Amis Award 1962), The Lonely Girl 1962, A Cheap Bunch of Flowers (play) 1962, Girls in Their Married Bliss 1963, August is a Wicked Month 1964, Casualties of Peace 1966, The Love Object 1968, A Pagan Place (Yorkshire Post Novel Award 1971) 1970, Zee & Co. (play) 1971, Night 1972, A Scandalous Woman (short stories) 1974, Mother Ireland 1976, Johnny I Hardly Knew You (novel) 1977, Arabian Days 1977, Mrs. Reinhardt and other stories 1978, Virginia (play) 1979, Mrs. Reinhardt 1981, James and Nora (non-fiction) 1981, The Dazzle (children's book), Returning: A Collection of New Tales 1982, A Christmas Treat 1982, A Fanatic Heart (Selected Stories) 1985, Madame Bovary (play) 1987, Vanishing Ireland 1987, Tales for the Telling (children's book) 1987, The High Road (novel) 1988, On the Bone (poetry) 1989, Blood Memory (play) 1989, Scandalous Woman and Other Stories 1990, Lantern Slides (stories) (Los Angeles Times Book Prize 1990) 1990, Time and Tide (novel) (Writers' Guild of GB Award 1993) 1992, House of Splendid Isolation (novel) (European Prize for Literature 1995) 1994, Down by the River (novel) 1997, Maud Gonne (screenplay) 1996, James Joyce 1999, Wild Decembers 1999, Love's Lessons (short stories) (Literary Award of the American Ireland Fund 2000) 2000, In the Forest (novel) 2002, Iphigenia (play) 2003, Triptych (play) 2004, The Light of Evening (novel) 2006, Byron in Love (biography) 2009, Haunted (play) 2010, Saints and Sinners (short stories) (Frank O'Connor Int. Short Story Award 2012) 2012, Country Girl (memoir) (Irish Book Award (Non-Fiction 2012) 2012, The Love Object: Selected Stories of Edna O'Brien 2013, The Little Red Chairs (novel) 2015. *Leisure interests:* reading, walking, meditating. *Address:* c/o Curtis Brown, Haymarket House, 28–29 Haymarket, London, SW1Y 4SP, England (office). *Telephone:* (20) 7393-4400 (office). *E-mail:* info@curtisbrown.co.uk (office). *Website:* www.curtisbrown.co.uk (office).

O'BRIEN, HE Cardinal Edwin Frederick, BA, MDiv, MA, DST; American ecclesiastic; *Grand Master, Equestrian Order of the Holy Sepulchre of Jerusalem;* b. 8 April 1939, Bronx, New York; s. of Edwin Frederick O'Brien, Sr and Mary Winifred O'Brien; ed Our Lady of Solace School, St Mary's High School, Katonah 1953–57, St Joseph's Seminary, Yonkers, Pontifical North American Coll., Rome, Angelicum Univ.; ordained priest, Archdiocese of New York 1965; served as civilian chaplain at US Mil. Acad., West Point –1970; army chaplain with rank of Capt. 1970, chaplain at Fort Bragg, North Corolina with 82nd Div. 1970–71, in Viet Nam with 173rd Airborne Brigade and 1st Cavalry Brigade 1971–72; post chaplain at Fort Gordon, Ga 1972–73; Vice-Chancellor Archdiocese of New York and Assoc. Pastor, St Patrick's Cathedral 1976–81; co-ordinated Pope John Paul II's visit to New York 1979; Archdiocesan Dir of Communications 1981–83; Pvt. Sec. to Cardinal Cooke and then to Cardinal John Joseph O'Connor 1983–85; rank of Hon. Prelate of His Holiness 1986; Rector, St Joseph's Seminary, Yonkers 1985–89, 1994–97, Pontifical North American Coll., Rome 1990–94; apptd Auxiliary Bishop of New York and Titular Bishop of Thizica 1996, Coadjutor Archbishop of USA, Mil. and Titular Archbishop of Thizica 1997–98; Archbishop of USA Mil. 1997–2007; Archbishop of Baltimore 2007–11, Apostolic Admin. of Baltimore 2011–12; Pro-Grand Master of the Equestrian Order of the Holy Sepulchre of Jerusalem 2011–12, Grand Master 2012–; cr. Cardinal (Cardinal-Deacon of San Sebastiano al Palatino) 2012; participated in Papal Conclave 2013; Premio Benifacio VIII, St Pio Award. *Address:* Equestrian Order of the Holy Sepulchre of Jerusalem, Borgo Spirito Santo 73, 00193 Rome, Italy (office). *Telephone:* (06) 69892943 (office); (06) 69892901 (office). *Fax:* (06) 69892930 (office). *E-mail:* gm@oessh.va (office). *Website:* www.oessh.va/content/ordineequestresantosepolcro/en.html (office).

O'BRIEN, Grant; Australian business executive; m. Mary O'Brien; three c.; with Woolworths since 1980s starting as an Accountant in Purity (Supermarkets) in Tasmania (div. of Woolworths Ltd), held positions as COO Australian Food and Petrol, Dir New Business Devt 2008–10, Gen. Man. Woolworths Liquor, Nat. Operations Man. Freestanding Liquor, Sr Business Man. Marketing Supermarkets, and Marketing and Merchandise Man. for Purity –2010, COO for Australia Food and Petrol, with responsibility for Supermarket Operations, Online and Petrol 2010–11, mem. Bd of Dirs, Deputy CEO and CEO-designate April–Oct. 2011, Man. Dir and CEO Oct. 2011–15 (resgnd); Dir, Global Consumer Goods Forum, Avner Nahmani Pancreatic Cancer Research Fund; mem. Business Council of Australia. *Address:* c/o Woolworths Ltd, PO Box 8000, Baulkham Hills, NSW 2153, Australia.

O'BRIEN, Gregory Michael St Lawrence, BA, MA, PhD; American academic and fmr university chancellor; *President, The Higher Education Group, Inc.;* b. 7 Oct. 1944, New York; s. of Henry Joseph O'Brien and Mary Agnes O'Brien (née McGoldrick); m. Mary K. McLaughlin 1968; two d.; ed Lehigh Univ., Pa and Boston Univ.; Dean and Prof., School of Social Welfare, Univ. of Wisconsin-Milwaukee 1974–78; Provost and Prof. of Psychology, Univ. of Michigan-Flint 1978–80; Prof. of Psychology, Univ. of South Florida 1980–83, Prof. of Social Work 1980–83, Prof. of Man. 1986–87, Vice-Pres. for Academic Affairs 1980–83, Provost 1983–87; Chancellor, Univ. of New Orleans 1987–2003; Pres. Argosy Univ. Systems 2004–07, now Pres. Emer.; consultant, Schiller International Univ. 2009–10; Pres. The Higher Education Group, Inc. (consultancy) 2010–; Chair. Metro Council Govts Metrovision 1992–94; Vice-Chair. State of Louisiana Film and Video Comm. 1993–94 (mem. 1993–2003); Supt New Orleans Public Schools 1999–2000; mem. Bd of Dirs WLAE-TV (PBS), Bank One New Orleans Region, Entergy New Orleans, Nat. Coalition for Advanced Manufacturing, Nat. Asscn of State Univs and Land-Grant Colls; mem. Kellogg Comm. on Future of Land Grant Colls and State Univs 1996–98, State of Louisiana Econ. Devt Council 1997; Advisory mem. Business Council New Orleans and the River Region; mem. Bd of Dirs The Chamber/New Orleans and the River Region 1988–2003; mem. NCAA (Chair. and Pres. Comm. 1992–93), Nat. Asscn of Social Workers, Nat. Conf. on Social Welfare, Society General Systems Research, American Psychological Asscn, American Public Health Asscn, Metrovision Partnership Foundation 1992–93, Council on Social Work Educ. (presidential task force on structure of the asscn), Industrial Relations Research Asscn; Fellow, American Coll. of Mental Health Admins (Founding Fellow, Pres. 1984–86); Trustee, Sofia Univ.; Nat. Inst. of Mental Health Fellow 1968–69, Gambit Weekly's New Orleanian of the Year 1999. *Publications:* contrib. of chapters to books and articles to professional journals. *Address:* The Higher Education Group, Inc., 900 Gulf Shore Drive, Unit 1021, Destin, FL 32541, USA (office). *Website:* www.thehighereducationgroup.com (office).

O'BRIEN, Patricia, BA, MA, BL, LLB; Irish lawyer and diplomatist; *Ambassador to France;* b. 8 Feb. 1957; m.; three c.; ed Trinity Coll., Dublin, Kings Inns, Dublin, Univ. of Ottawa, Canada; lawyer, Irish Bar 1979–88; called to Bar of England and Wales 1986; fmr lawyer, Bar of BC, Canada; Lecturer, Dept of Law, Univ. of British Columbia 1989–92; fmr Sr Legal Adviser to Irish Attorney-Gen.; fmr Legal Counsellor, Irish Perm. Representation to EU, Brussels; Legal Adviser, Dept of Foreign Affairs, Dublin 2003–08; Under-Sec.-Gen. for Legal Affairs and Legal Counsel, UN 2008–13; Amb. and Perm. Rep. to UN, Geneva 2013–17, Amb. to France 2017–; Fellow, Soc. for Advanced Legal Studies, Inst. of Advanced Legal Studies, London. *Address:* Embassy of Ireland, 12 ave Foch, 75116 Paris, France (office). *Telephone:* 1-44-17-67-00 (office); 1-44-17-67-50 (office). *Fax:* (22) 7335009 (office). *E-mail:* paris@dfa.ie (office). *Website:* www.embassyofireland.fr (office).

O'BRIEN, Patrick Karl, BSc (Econ), MA, DPhil, FRSA, FRHistS, FBA; British historian and academic; *Professor of Global Economic History, London School of Economics;* b. 12 Aug. 1932, London; s. of William O'Brien and Elizabeth O'Brien Stockhausen; m. Cassy Cobham 1959; one s. two d.; ed London School of Econs, Nuffield Coll. Oxford; Lecturer, SOAS, Univ. of London 1963–70; Reader in Econs and Econ. History, Univ. of London 1967–70; Univ. Lecturer in Econ. History and Faculty Fellow, St Antony's Coll. Oxford 1970–84, Univ. Reader in Econ. History and Professorial Fellow 1984–90; Prof. of Econ. History, Univ. of London 1990–98, then Prof. Emer.; Dir Inst. of Historical Research, Univ. of London 1990–98, Sr Research Fellow 1998–99; Prof. of Global Econ. History, LSE 2009–13; Fellow, Academia Europaea; Dr hc (Carlos III Univ., Madrid) 1999, (Uppsala) 2000. *Publications include:* The Revolution in Egypt's Economic System 1966, The New Economic History of Railways 1977, Two Paths to the 20th Century: Economic Growth in Britain and France 1978, The Economic Effects of the Civil War 1988; more than 100 articles. *Leisure interests:* theatre, Western art, foreign travel. *Address:* Department of Economic History, Room E488, London School of Economics, Houghton Street, Aldwych, London, WC2A 2AE (office); 13 Woodstock Close, Oxford, OX2 8DB, England (home). *Telephone:* (20) 7955-6586 (office); (1865) 512004 (home). *Fax:* (20) 7955-7730 (office). *E-mail:* p.o'brien@lse.ac.uk (office). *Website:* www.lse.ac.uk (office).

O'BRIEN, Rt Hon. Sir Stephen Rothwell, Kt, PC, KBE, MA; British lawyer, politician and UN official; b. 1 April 1957, Mtwara, Tanganyika (now Tanzania); s. of David H. O'Brien and Rothy O'Brien; m. Gemma O'Brien; two s. one d.; ed Sedbergh School, Sedbergh, Cumbria, Emmanuel Coll., Cambridge, Coll. of Law; qualified as solicitor 1983, practised at Freshfields (City of London) 1983–88; Group Company Sec., Int. Dir and Dir of Strategy and Corp. Affairs, Redland PLC 1988–98; MP for Eddisbury (Conservative) 1999–2015, mem. House of Commons Select Cttee on Educ. and Employment 1999–2001, mem. Educ. sub-Cttee 1999–2001, Chair. All Party Groups on Malaria and Neglected Tropical Diseases, Tanzania, Primary Headache Disorders; Parl. Pvt. Sec. to Rt Hon Francis Maude Feb.–Sept. 2000, Parl. Pvt. Sec. to Rt Hon Michael Ancram (Chair. of Conservative Party) 2000–01, Opposition Whip 2001–02, Shadow Paymaster Gen. 2002–03, Shadow Sec. of State for Industry 2003–05, Shadow Minister for Skills May–Dec. 2005, Shadow Minister for Health and Social Care 2005–10, Parl. Under-Sec. of State for Int. Devt 2010–12, Prime Minister's Envoy and Special Rep. for Sahel at FCO 2012–15; Under-Sec.-Gen. for Humanitarian Affairs and Emergency Relief Co-ordinator, UN Office for Co-ordination of Humanitarian Affairs 2015–17; Assoc., British-Irish Inter-Parl. Body 2001; Champions Award for Malaria Leadership, Washington DC 2014. *Address:* c/o Office for the Co-ordination of Humanitarian Affairs, 405 East 42nd Street, New York, NY 10017, USA (office).

OBRIST, Hans Ulrich; Swiss gallery curator; *Co-Director, Exhibitions and Programmes and Director of International Projects, Serpentine Galleries, London;* b. 1968, Zurich; Founder and Curator, Robert Walser migratory museum, Vienna, Austria 1993–2000; Curator, Musée d'Art Moderne de la Ville de Paris, France 2000–06; Lecturer, Arts Faculty, Univ. IUAV, Venice, Italy 2001–; Co-Dir Exhbns and Programmes and Dir of Int. Projects, Serpentine Gallery, London 2006–. *Publications include:* A Brief History of Curating 2008, Everything You Always Wanted to Know About Curating But Were Afraid to Ask 2011, Ai Weiwei Speaks 2011, Do It: The Compendium 2013, Think Like Clouds 2014, along with new vols of the Conversation Series. *Address:* Serpentine Galleries, Kensington Gardens, London, W2 3XA, England (office). *Telephone:* (20) 7298-1543 (office); (20) 7298-1508 (PA) (office). *Fax:* (20) 7402-4103 (office). *E-mail:* information@serpentinegallery.org (office). *Website:* www.serpentinegallery.org (office).

OBSITNIK, Vincent, BS, MBA; American business executive and diplomatist (retd); *President and CEO, East West Ventures LLC;* b. 24 Jan. 1938, Moravany, Slovakia; m. Annemarie Harden; four s.; ed Linden High School, NJ, US Naval Acad., American Univ., Washington, DC, IBM Advanced Man. School, Sands Point, Long Island, NY, IBM Int. Man. School, La Hulpe, Belgium, Unisys Exec. Program, Wharton School, Univ. of Pennsylvania, Phila; moved to USA with parents prior to occupation of Czechoslovakia by Nazi Germany 1938; served as officer in USN in destroyers and submarines 1959–64; fmr Pres. Systems Devt Div., Unisys Corpn; fmr Vice-Pres. Int. Litton Corpn; spent 27 years at IBM Corpn, responsible for Marketing, Sales, Mfg, Eng and Program Man., spent eight years with IBM World Trade Corpn with mfg responsibilities in Europe, Latin America and Asia; Founder and Pres. International Investments, Inc.; Pres. and CEO East West Ventures LLC; apptd by Pres. George W. Bush to US Comm. for Preservation of America's Heritage Abroad 2001–06, to US Presidential Del. for Austrian State Treaty Anniversary 2005, to US Presidential Del. for Commemoration of 65th Anniversary of Tragedy in Babyn Yar in Ukraine 2006; Amb. to Slovakia 2007–09. *Leisure interests:* running marathons, playing tennis and squash. *Address:* 6849 Grenadier Blvd, #904, Naples, FL 34108, USA (home).

OBUCHI, Yuko, MA; Japanese politician; b. 11 Dec. 1973, Tokyo; d. of Keizo Obuchi (fmr Prime Minister) and Chizuko Ono; m.; two s.; ed Seijo Univ., Waseda Univ.; worked for Tokyo Broadcasting System Holdings, Inc. 1996–98; Sec. to her father (Prime Minister Keizo Obuchi) 1998–2000; mem. House of Reps (lower house of Parl.) for Gunma No. 5 constituency 2000–, Chair. Educ., Culture, Sports, Science and Tech. Cttee –2014; Sr Vice-Minister of Finance 2012, Minister of Economy, Trade and Industry Sept.–Oct. 2014 (resgnd); mem. Liberal Democratic Party (LDP). *Leisure interests:* cooking, theatre. *Address:* Liberal Democratic Party, 1-11-23, Nagata-cho, Chiyoda-ku, Tokyo 100-8910 (office); The House of Representatives, 1-7-1, Nagata-cho, Chiyoda-ku, Tokyo 100-0014, Japan (office). *Telephone:* (3) 3581-6211 (LDP) (office). *Fax:* (3) 5511-8855 (LDP) (office). *E-mail:* koho@ldp.jimin.or.jp (office); webmaster@shugiin.go.jp (office). *Website:* www.jimin.jp (LDP) (office).

OBUKHOV, Alexey Aleksandrovich, PhD; Russian diplomatist (retd); b. 12 Nov. 1937, Moscow; s. of Alexander Ivanovich Obukhov and Klaudia Ivanovna Obukhov; m. Olga Obukhov; two s.; ed Moscow Inst. of Int. Relations and Univ. of Chicago; joined Ministry of Foreign Affairs 1965; served in Embassy in Thailand; took part in Soviet-American Strategic Arms Limitation Talks on Threshold Test Ban Treaty (TTBT), Moscow 1974; Deputy Dir US Dept, Ministry of Foreign Affairs 1980–86; mem. Soviet negotiating team in arms control talks, responsible for negotiations on long-range strategic weapons, subsequently for negotiations on medium-range nuclear weapons, Geneva 1985; Deputy Head Soviet Del., Nuclear and Space Talks, Geneva 1987, Head 1988; Head, Dept of USA and Canada, Ministry of Foreign Affairs 1989–90; Deputy Minister of Foreign Affairs 1990–91; Amb. to Denmark 1992–96; Amb.-at-Large 1996–2002; Head of Del. to Russian-Lithuanian talks on border issues 1996–2012; Head of Del. to Joint Russian-Lithuanian Comm. on Demarcation 2005–12; Chair. Cttee of Sr Officers (CSO) of the Barents Euro/Arctic Council 2000–01, CSO of the Council of Baltic Sea States 2001–02; Order of the Red Banner 1988; Harold Weill Medal for Outstanding Contrib. to Peace and Understanding through the Rule of Law, New York Univ. 1988, Medal of Merit, Russian Acad. of Arts 2006. *Publications:* Russia and Denmark: Painters of the Royal Courts from Catherine the Great to Margrethe II and numerous texts on diplomatic affairs. *Leisure interests:* art, photography. *Address:* 117049 Moscow, 40/7/71 Bolshaya Yakimanka str. (home). *Telephone:* (495) 238-00-48 (home). *Fax:* (495) 238-00-48 (home). *E-mail:* moscowsuper@mtu-net.ru (home).

OCAMPO, José Antonio, PhD; Colombian academic and UN official; *Professor of Professional Practice, Columbia University;* b. 20 Dec. 1952; m. Ana Lucía Lalinde; three c.; ed Univ. of Notre Dame, Yale Univ., USA; researcher, Centre for Devt Studies, Universidad de los Andes 1976–80, Dir 1980–82; at Foundation for Higher Educ. and Devt 1983–93, Deputy Dir 1983–84, Exec. Dir 1984–88, Sr Researcher and mem. Bd of Dirs; Minister of Agric. 1993–94, of Planning 1994–96, of Finance and Public Credit 1996–97; Exec. Sec. UN Econ. Comm. for Latin America and the Caribbean 1998–2003; UN Under-Sec.-Gen. for Econ. and Social Affairs 2003–07; Co-Dir UNDP/OAS Project 'Agenda for a Citizens' Democracy in Latin America' 2008–10; Chair. Cttee for Devt Policy, UN Econ. and Social Council 2013–15, 2016–; Goodwill Amb. for Social Protection, ILO 2015–; mem., Comm. of Experts, UN Gen. Ass. on Reforms of the Int. Monetary and Financial System 2009; Prof. of Professional Practice, Columbia Univ., New York 2007–, Dir Econ. and Political Devt Concentration, School of Int. and Public Affairs 2007–, Co-Pres. Initiative for Policy Dialogue, mem. Cttee on Global Thought; Nat. Dir Employment Mission 1985–86; Adviser, Colombian Foreign Trade Bd 1990–91, Colombian Nat. Council of Entrepreneurial Asscn; mem. Exec. Bd Inst. of Latin American Studies 2009–16; mem. Tech. Comm. on Coffee Affairs, Public Expenditure Comm., Advisory Comm. for Fiscal Reform, Mission on Intergovernmental Finance; consultant to IBRD, IDB and UN; mem. Colombian Acad. of Econ. Science 1987; Visiting Fellow, Univ. of Oxford, Yale Univ.; Grand Cross, Order of Boyacá, 1997, Order of Merit of Chile 2003; Alejandro Angel Escobar Colombian Nat. Science Prize 1988, Leontief Prize for Advancing the Frontiers of Economic Thought 2008. *Publications:* author or ed. of over 40 books. *Address:* School of International and Public Affairs, Columbia University, 116th and Broadway, New York, NY 10027, USA (office). *Telephone:* (212) 854-6339 (office). *E-mail:* jose.ocampo@sipa.columbia.edu (office). *Website:* sipa.columbia.edu (office).

OCANTE DA SILVA, Aristides; Guinea-Bissau politician; *Minister of State, Minister of the Civil Service, State Reform, Labour and Social Security;* fmr Minister of Energy, of Natural Resources and Environment 2005, of Nat. Educ., Culture and Science –2009, Minister of Nat. Defence 2009–11, of the Civil Service, Employment and Modernization of the State 2011–12, Minister of State, Minister of the Civil Service, State Reform, Labour and Social Security 2013–; mem. Partido Africano da Independência da Guiné e Cabo Verde. *Address:* Ministry of the Civil Service, State Reform, Labour and Social Security, Bissau, Guinea-Bissau.

O'CATHAIN, Baroness, cr. 1991 (Life Peer), of The Barbican in the City of London; **Detta O'Cathain,** OBE, BA, FCIM; British economist, business executive and parliamentarian; b. 3 Feb. 1938, Cork, Ireland; d. of Caoimhghin O'Cathain and Margaret Prior; m. William Ernest John Bishop 1968 (died 2001); ed Loreto School, Rathfarnham, Co. Dublin, Laurel Hill, Limerick, Univ. Coll. Dublin; Asst Economist, Aer Lingus 1961–66; Group Economist, Tarmac Ltd 1966–69; Econ. Adviser, Rootes Motors Ltd 1969–72; Sr Economist, Carrington Viyella 1972; Market Planning Dir, British Leyland 1973–76; Corp. Planning Exec., Unigate PLC 1976–81; Head of Strategic Planning, Milk Marketing Bd 1981–83, Dir and Gen. Man. 1983, Man. Dir Milk Marketing 1984–88; Man. Dir Barbican Centre, London 1990–95; Dir (non-exec.), Midland Bank PLC 1984–93, Tesco PLC 1985–2000, Sears PLC 1987–94, British Airways 1993–2004, BET PLC 1994–96, BNP Paribas (UK) PLC 1995–2005, Thistle Hotels 1996–2003; Pres. Chartered Inst. of Marketing 1998–2001, Southeast Water PLC 1998, Allders PLC 2000–03, William Baird PLC 2000–02; Commdr, Royal Norwegian Order 1992, Commdr, Order of Lion of Finland 1992, Order of Azerbaijan 2010. *Leisure interests:* music, reading, swimming, gardening. *Address:* House of Lords, Westminster, London, SW1A 0PW, England (office). *Telephone:* (20) 7219-0662 (office). *Fax:* (20) 7219-0785 (office). *E-mail:* ocathaind@parliament.uk (office).

OCCHETTO, Achille; Italian politician; b. 3 March 1936, Turin; joined Italian Communist Party (PCI) and Young Communists' Fed. 1953, apptd Nat. Sec. Young Communists 1962, Sec. PCI Palermo 1969, subsequently Regional Sec. for Sicily; moved to Rome, held succession of party posts 1976; mem. Chamber of Deputies 1976–2001; Deputy Leader PCI (name changed to Partito Democratico della Sinistra 1991) 1987–88, Gen. Sec. 1988–94, mem. –1998; Senator 2001–06, Alternate Chair. Cttee on Rules of Procedure and Immunities, Cttee on Migration, Refugees and Population; mem. European Parl. 2004 (resgnd), 2006–07; mem. Democrats of the Left 1994–2007, Democratic Left 2007–09, Left Ecology Freedom party (Sinistra Ecologia Libertà) 2009–. *Address:* c/o Sinistra Ecologia Libertà, via Arenula 29, 00186 Rome, Italy. *Telephone:* (06) 44700403. *Fax:* (06) 4455832. *E-mail:* selnazionale@sxmail.it; achille@achilleocchetto.it. *Website:* www.sinistraecologialiberta.it.

OCHIAI, Yoichi, PhD; Japanese computer scientist, media artist and academic; *Assistant Professor, Faculty of Library, Information and Media Science, University of Tsukuba;* b. 16 Sept. 1987; s. of Nobuhiko Ochiai; currently Asst Prof., Faculty of Library, Information and Media Science and Head of Digital Nature Group, Univ. of Tsukuba; Sr Research Fellow, jiseCHI Co. Ltd; CEO Pixie Dust Technologies, Inc.; mem. Bd, Virtual Reality Consortium, Mitou Foundation; World Tech. Award (IT Hardware) 2015. *Publications:* numerous papers in professional journals. *Address:* University of Tsukuba, Ibaraki-ken, Tsukuba-shi, 1 Chome-1-2, Kasuga 305-0003, Japan (office). *Telephone:* (3) 5770-2666 (office). *E-mail:* ochyai.manage@gmail.com (office). *Website:* digitalnature.slis.tsukuba.ac.jp (office).

OCHIRBAT, Punsalmaagin, DSc; Mongolian politician; *President, Ochirbat Fund;* b. 23 Jan. 1942, Tudevtei Dist, Zavkhan Prov.; s. of Gonsiin Gendenjav and Tsogtiin Punsalmaa; m. Sharaviin Tsevelmaa 1965; two d.; ed Mining Inst. of USSR; apptd official at Ministry of Industry 1966, Chief Engineer, Sharyn Gol coal mine 1967, Deputy Minister, Ministry of Fuel and Power Industry and Geology 1972–76, Minister 1976; Chair. State Cttee External Econ. Relations 1985–87, Minister 1987; elected mem. Mongolian People's Revolutionary Party (MPRP) Cen. Cttee 17th, 18th and 19th Party Congresses and at 1990 Extraordinary Congress; resgnd from MPRP 1991; elected Deputy to Great People's Hural 9th, 10th and 11th elections, Chair. 1990; Pres. of Mongolia 1990–97, C-in-C of the Armed Forces 1993–97; Pres. Ochirbat Fund 1997–; Prof. and Adviser, School of Mining Eng 1999–; mem. Constitutional Court of Mongolia 2005–16; Altan Gadas 1972, Mu Gung Hwa (Repub. of Korea) 1991, Liberty Award (USA) 1995. *Publications:* Black Gold, Art of Management, Organisation and Management of Fuel and Energy Complex, Heavenly Hour, Without the Right to Mistakes, Ecolog-Steady Development. *Address:* Olympic Street 14, Sky Plaza, 3rd Floor of Office Building 1, Ulaanbaatar 210648, Mongolia (office). *Telephone:* (11) 327233 (office). *Fax:* (11) 327233 (office). *E-mail:* pobmongolia@magicnet.mn (office). *Website:* www.ochirbatfoundation.mn (office).

OCHOJSKA-OKOŃSKA, Janina; Polish charity administrator; *Chairman, Polska Akcja Humanitarna;* b. 12 March 1955, Gdańsk; m. Michał Okoński; ed Nicolaus Copernicus Univ., Toruń; Asst, Astrophysics Lab. of Astronomy Centre of Polish Acad. of Sciences (PAN), Toruń 1980–92; co-f. EquiLibre Foundation 1989, Co-founder and Dir Warsaw br. 1992–94; Co-founder and Chair. Polska Akcja Humanitarna (Polish Humanitarian Org.) 1994–; Order of the Smile awarded by Polish children 1995; EU Woman of Europe 1994, Feliks Civic Prize, Gazeta Wyborcza 1994, St George Medal, Tygodnik Powszechny magazine 1994, Pax Christi Int. Peace Award 1995, Woman of the Year, Poland 1995, Atsushi Nakata Memorial, Japan 1996, Romers' Foundation Award, Canada 1997, European German Culture Award 1999, Life Guide Award, Lublin Archdiocese's Youth Council 2000, Jt Winner, Twój Styl Magazine poll for the 50 Most Influential Women in Poland 2000, 2001, Gold Medal of Voluntary Fire Brigades of Poland, Winner, first Jan Karski Freedom Award for Valour and Compassion, American Center of Polish Culture, Washington, DC 2002. *Leisure interests:* music, books, cooking. *Address:* Polska Akcja Humanitarna, 00-031 Warsaw, ul. Szpitalna 5 lok. 3, Poland (office). *Telephone:* (22) 8288882 (office). *Fax:* (22) 8319938 (office). *E-mail:* pah@pah.org.pl (office). *Website:* www.pah.org.pl (office).

OCKRENT, Christine; Belgian journalist and broadcaster; b. 24 April 1944, Brussels; d. of Roger Ockrent and Greta Bastenie; m. Bernard Kouchner (q.v.); one s.; ed Collège Sévigné, France, Univ. of Cambridge, UK, Institut d'Etudes Politiques de Paris, France; journalist, Information Office, EEC 1965–66; Researcher, NBC News, USA 1967–68; producer and journalist, CBS News, USA 1968–77; journalist and producer, FR3, France 1976–80; Ed. and Anchor, news programme on Antenne 2 1980–85; Chief Ed. RTL 1985–86; Deputy Dir-Gen. TF1 1986–87; Ed., anchor and producer, news programmes on Antenne 2 1988–92, on France 3 1992–95; Chief Ed. L'Express 1995–96; Deputy Dir BFM 1996–2000; Ed.-in-Chief Dimanche Soir programme France 3 1996–98; Ed.-in-Chief and Presenter, France Europe Express 1997; currently columnist, Int. Herald Tribune, El Pais, The Guardian, Prospect magazine, and several other European newspapers; Pres. BFMbiz.com; mem. Bd of Dirs Int. Crisis Group, French Council on Foreign Relations, European Council on Foreign Relations, Centre for European Reform,

Human Rights Watch France, Reporters sans Frontières, Women's Forum for the Economy and Soc.; Officer, ordre de Leopold (Belgium), Chevalier, Légion d'honneur 2000, Officier Légion d'honneur 2007, Ordre national du Merite; James Cameron Memorial Lecturer 2014. *Publications include:* Dans le secret des princes 1986, Duel 1988, Les uns et les autres 1993, Portraits d'ici et d'ailleurs 1994, La mémoire du cœur 1997, Les grands patrons (co-author) 1998, L'Europe racontée à mon fils, de Jules César à l'euro 1999, La double vie d'Hillary Clinton 2000, Françoise 2003. *Leisure interests:* riding, skiing, tennis. *Address:* The Guardian, Kings Place, 90 York Way, London, N1 9GU, England. *E-mail:* christine.ockrent@guardian.co.uk. *Website:* www.guardian.com/profile/christine-ockrent.

O'CONNELL, Robert J., MA; American insurance executive; b. 6 May 1943, New York; ed Univ. of Pennsylvania; with American Int. Group Inc. (AIG) 1989–98; joined MassMutual Life Insurance 1998, Pres. and CEO 1999–2000, Chair., Pres. and CEO 2000–05; mem. Bd of Dirs, Oppenheimer Acquisition Corpn, DLB Acquisition Corpn, American Council of Life Insurance, Life Office Man. Asscn, US Chamber of Commerce, CM Life Insurance Co. 1999, Yankee Holding Corpn (fmrly Yankee Candle Co. Inc.) 2004–05. *Address:* c/o Massachusetts Mutual Life Insurance Co., 1295 State Street, Springfield, MA 0111-0001, USA. *E-mail:* info@massmutual.com.

O'CONNOR, Gordon, PC, OMM, CD, BSc, BA; Canadian politician and fmr military officer; b. 18 May 1939, Toronto, Ont.; m.; two c.; ed Concordia and York Univs; fmr mil. officer, Second Lt Armour Br., later Brig.-Gen.; fmr Sr Assoc., Hill and Knowlton Canada; MP for Carleton-Mississippi Mills 2004–, mem. Standing Cttee on Nat. Defence and Veterans Affairs, Sub-cttee on Veterans Affairs; fmr Official Opposition Critic for Nat. Defence; Minister of Nat. Defence 2006–07, of Nat. Revenue 2007–08; Minister of State and Chief Govt Whip 2008–13; Order of Mil. Merit (Canada). *Address:* Room 1100, La Promenade, 151 Sparks Street, Ottawa, ON K1A 0A6, Canada (office). *Telephone:* (613) 992-1119 (office). *Fax:* (613) 992-1043 (office). *E-mail:* gordon.oconnor@parl.gc.ca (office). *Website:* www.gordonoconnor.ca.

O'CONNOR, Sandra Day, BA, LLB; American lawyer and judge (retd); b. 26 March 1930, El Paso, Tex.; d. of Harry A. Day and Ada Mae Day (née Wilkey); m. John Jay O'Connor III 1952 (died 2009); three s.; ed Stanford Univ.; pvt. law practice, Phoenix, Ariz. 1959–65; served in Ariz. Senate 1969–75, Majority Leader 1972–75; Superior Court Judge, Ariz. 1975–79, Judge of Appeals 1979–81; Assoc. Justice, US Supreme Court 1981–2006 (retd); mem. Nat. Bd, Smithsonian Assocs 1981–, Exec. Bd, Cen. European and Eurasian Law Initiative (ABA) 1990–; Chancellor Coll. of William and Mary 2005–11; mem. Bd of Trustees, Rockefeller Foundation 2006–; mem. Iraq Study Group, US Inst. of Peace 2006; Harry Rathbun Visiting Fellow, Office for Religious Life, Stanford Univ. 2008; f. iCivics.org 2009; mem. ABA, State Bar of Ariz., State Bar of Calif., Maricopa Co. Bar Asscn, Ariz. Judges' Asscn, Nat. Asscn of Women Judges, Ariz. Women Lawyers' Asscn; Fellow, American Acad. of Arts and Sciences 2007; 15th Hendrick Fellow by the US Coast Guard Acad. 2009; 25 hon. degrees, including Dr hc (Yale Univ.) 2006; numerous awards, including Elizabeth Blackwell Award, Hobart and William Smith Coll. 1985, Service to Democracy Award, American Ass. 1982, Fordham-Stein Prize, Fordham Univ. 1992, Award of Merit, Stanford Law School 1990, Nat. Women's Hall of Fame, Seneca Falls, NY 1995, ABA Medal 1997, Sylvanus Thayer Award, US Mil. Acad. 2005, Harry F. Byrd Jr. '35 Public Service Award, Virginia Mil. Inst. 2008, Franklin Award, Nat. Conf. on Citizenship 2008, Presidential Medal of Freedom 2009, Brigham-Kanner Property Rights Prize 2011. *Publications:* Lazy B: Growing Up on a Cattle Ranch in the American Southwest 2002, The Majesty of Law: Reflections of a Supreme Court Judge 2003, Chico (children's book) 2005, Finding Susie (children's book) 2009, Out of Order: Stories from the History of the Supreme Court 2013. *Website:* www.icivics.org.

O'CONNOR, Sean; South African business executive; *CEO and President, INTL FCStone Inc.;* ed Univ. of Stellenbosch, Univ. of Cape Town; qualified as Chartered Accountant in SA; began career with Standard Bank as investment banking exec., spent 14 years as mem. man. team that est. bank's int. operations, CEO Standard New York Securities 1994–2002, Exec. Dir Standard Bank London Ltd (subsidiary of Standard Bank of South Africa) 1999–2002; mem. Bd of Dirs and CEO Int. Assets Holding Corpn (INTL) 2002– (merged with FCStone Sept. 2009), Pres. 2015–. *Address:* INTL FCStone Inc., 708 Third Avenue, 15th Floor, New York, NY 10017, USA (office). *Telephone:* (212) 485-3500 (office). *Fax:* (212) 485-3505 (office). *E-mail:* info@intlfcstone.com (office). *Website:* www.intlfcstone.com (office).

O'CONNOR, Sinéad; Irish singer, songwriter and musician (guitar, piano, keyboards, percussion, low whistle); b. (Sinéad Marie Bernadette O'Connor), 8 Dec. 1966, Glenageary, Co. Dublin; d. of John O'Connor and Marie O'Connor; m. 1st John Reynolds (divorced); one d. (by John Waters); m. 2nd Nicholas Sommerland 2002; one c. with Frank Bonadio 2007; m. 3rd Steve Cooney 2010 (divorced 2011); m. 4th Barry Herridge 9 Dec. 2011 (divorced 26 Dec. 2011); ed Dublin Coll. of Music; mem. Ton Ton Macoute 1985–87; refused to accept Grammy Award for Best Alternative Album 1991; now Tridentine priest Mother Bernadette Mary; MTV Award for Best Video, MTV Award for Best Single (both for Nothing Compares 2 U) 1990, MTV Award for Best Female Singer 1990, Rolling Stone Artist of the Year Award 1991, BRIT Award for Best Int. Solo Artist 1991. *Recordings include:* albums: The Lion and the Cobra 1987, I Do Not Want What I Have Not Got (Grammy Award for Best Alternative Album 1991) 1990, Am I Not Your Girl? 1992, Universal Mother 1994, Gospeloak 1997, Sean-Nós Nua 2002, Throw Down Your Arms 2005, Theology 2007, How About I Be Me (And You Be You)? 2012, I'm Not Bossy, I'm the Boss 2014. *Video films:* Value of Ignorance 1989, The Year of the Horse 1991. *Television:* Hush-a-Bye-Baby. *Website:* www.sineadoconnor.com.

O'CONNOR-CONNOLLY, Julianna, JP; Cayman Islands lawyer and politician; b. Cayman Brac; ed Univ. of Liverpool, UK; mem. Legis. Ass. for Cayman Brac and Little Cayman 1996–, Speaker 2001–03, 2013–17; Minister of Community Affairs, Sports, Women, Youth and Culture 1997, Minister for Planning, Communications, Dist Admin and Information Tech. 2003–05, Minister of Finance, Dist Admin, Works, Lands and Agric. 2009–; Deputy Premier of Cayman Islands 2009–12, Premier (first woman) 2012–13; Founding mem. United Democratic Party 2001. *Address:* Legislative Assembly, 33 Fort Street, POB 890, George Town, Grand Cayman KY1-1103, Cayman Islands (office). *Telephone:* 949-4236 (office). *Fax:* 949-9514 (office). *Website:* www.legislativeassembly.ky (office).

ODA, Beverley (Bev) J., PC, BA; Canadian politician (retd) and broadcasting executive; b. 27 July 1944, Thunder Bay, Ont.; ed Univ. of Toronto; joined TVO 1973; various positions in broadcasting industry; Commr CRTC 1987–93; Sr Vice-Pres., Industry Affairs, CTV Inc. 1999; fmr Chair. Lakeridge Health Hosp. Network, Co-Chair. Task Force on Diversity on Canadian TV; MP for Durham 2004–12; Minister of Canadian Heritage and Status of Women 2006–07, of Int. Co-operation 2007–12; Queen's Golden Jubilee Medal 2002, Canadian Broadcasters Hall of Fame 2003. *Website:* www.bevoda.ca.

ODA, Shigeru, LLB, LLM, JSD, LLD; Japanese international judge, lawyer and academic; *Professor Emeritus, Tôhoku University;* b. 22 Oct. 1924; s. of Toshio Oda and Mioko Oda; m. Noriko Sugimura 1950; one s. one d.; ed Univ. of Tokyo, Yale Univ.; Research Fellow, Univ. of Tokyo 1947–49; Asst Prof. Tôhoku Univ. 1950–53, Assoc. Prof. 1953–59, Prof. 1959–76, Prof. Emer. 1985–; Tech. Adviser, Atomic Energy Comm. 1961–64; Special Asst to Minister for Foreign Affairs 1973–76; mem. Science Council of Ministry of Educ. 1969–76, of Council for Ocean Devt in Prime Minister's Office 1971–76, Advisory Cttee for Co-operation with UN Univ. 1971–76; Judge, Int. Court of Justice 1976–85, 1985–94, 1994–2003, (Vice-Pres. 1991–94); del. to UN Confs on Law of the Sea 1958, 1960, 1973–75; Rep. at 6th Gen. Conf. of Inter-Governmental Oceanographic Comm., UNESCO 1969; consultative positions with bodies concerned with marine questions; Counsel for FRG before Int. Court of Justice 1968; Ed.-in-Chief, Japanese Annual of International Law 1973–77; Assoc. Inst. de Droit Int. 1969 (mem. 1979, Hon. mem. 2003); mem. Curatorium, Hague Acad. of Int. Law 1989–2004, fmr. mem. Bd of Dirs, Int. Devt Law Inst., Rome, Int. Council of Arbitration for Sport, Lausanne 1994–2006; mem. Japan Acad. 1994–; Hon. mem. American Soc. of Int. Law 1975, Inst. of Int. Law 2001; Hon. Citizen of the City of Sendai 2004; Grand Order of the Sacred Treasure, Medal of Cultural Merit (both by Emperor of Japan), Govt of Japan 2004; Hon. DJur (Bhopal) 1980, (New York Law School) 1981. *Publications:* in Japanese: International Law of the Sea 1956–85 (eight vols), International Law and Maritime Resources 1971–75, Judicial Decisions relating to International Law before Japanese Courts 1978; in English: International Control of Sea Resources 1962, International Law of Sea Resources 1969, The International Law of Ocean Development (four vols) 1972–79, The Law of the Sea in Our Times (two vols) 1977, The Practice of Japan in International Law 1961–70 1982, The International Court of Justice 1987, 1993, Fifty Years of the Law of the Sea 2002, Sixty Years as Scholar and Judge of International Law 2009; various articles. *Address:* c/o Japan Academy, Ueno Koen 7-32, Taito-ku, Tokyo, 110-0007 (office); Akashicho 8-2-704, Chuo-ku, Tokyo 104-0044, Japan (home). *Telephone:* (3) 3822-2101 (office); (3) 5550-6694 (home). *Fax:* (3) 3822-2105 (office); (3) 5550-6694 (home). *E-mail:* oda.icj@bma.biglobe.ne.jp (home).

ODAGIRI, Joe, (Odajo); Japanese actor and singer; b. (Jô Odagiri), 16 Feb. 1976, Tsuyama City, Okayama; m. Yuu Kashii 2008; one s.; ed Fresno State Univ., USA. *Films include:* Kamen Rider Kuuga 2000, Platonic Sex 2001, Terrors 2001, Satorare 2002, Mokka no Kobito 2002, Azumi (Japan Acad. Award for Best New Actor) 2003, Bright Future (Japanese Professional Movie Award) 2003, Kaikyo wo wataru violin 2004, Pacchigi! 2004, Blood and Bones (Blue Ribbon Best Supporting Actor Award 2004, Japan Acad. Award for Best Supporting Actor 2004, Kinema Junpo Best Supporting Actor Award 2004, Mainichi Film Concours Award for Best Supporting Actor 2004, Nikkan Sports Film Ishihara Yujiro New Actor Award 2004) 2004, Black Kiss 2004, In the Pool 2005, HAZARD 2005, House of Himiko (Yokohama Film Festival Best Actor Award 2005, Kinema Junpo Best Actor Award 2005) 2005, Shinobi: Heart Under Blade 2005, Scrap Heaven 2005, Princess Raccoon 2005, Big River 2006, The Uchôten Hotel 2006, Jikou Keisatsu 2006, Retribution 2006, Mushishi 2006, The Pavilion Salamandre 2006, Sway 2006, Tokyo Tower: Mom and Me and Sometimes Dad 2007, Sad Vacation 2007, Adrift in Tokyo 2007, Plastic City 2008, Dream 2008, The Warrior and the Wolf 2009, Air Doll 2009, I Wish 2011, My Way 2011, Real 2013, Mr. Go 2013, The Human Trust 2013, Present for You 2013; as writer and dir: Looking for Cherry Blossoms 2009. *Television includes:* Kamen Raidâ Kûga (series) 2000, Sitto no nioi (mini-series) 2001, Hatsu taiken (series) 2002, Satoukibi batake no uta (film) 2003, Prayer Beads (series) 2004, Shinsengumi!! Hijikata Toshizô saigo no ichi-nichi (film) 2004, Kaikyou o wataru baiorin (film) 2004, Fukigen na jiin (series) 2005, Kaette kita jikô keisatsu (series) 2007, Boku no imôto (series) 2009, Atami no Sôsakan (series) 2010, Hei no naka no chûgakkô (film) 2010, Kazoku no uta (series) 2012, Toshi densetsu no onna (series) 2012, Yae no sakura (series) 2013, Airport 2013 (film) 2013, River's Edge: The Ohkawabata Detective Agency (mini-series) 2014. *Recordings:* albums: White 2006, Black 2006. *Address:* c/o Dongyu, JPL 6F, Shibuya 2-10-15, Shibuya-ku, Tokyo, 150-0002, Japan (office). *Telephone:* (81) 3-3400-2131 (office). *Fax:* (81) 3-3400-2132 (office). *E-mail:* contact@dongyu.co.jp (office). *Website:* www.dongyu.co.jp/English/profile/odagiri.html (office); www.odagiri-joe.com (home).

ODDSSON, Davíð; Icelandic politician, journalist and fmr central banker; *Editor, Morgunblaðið;* b. 17 Jan. 1948, Reykjavík; s. of Oddur Ólafsson and Ingibjörg Kristín Lúðvíksdóttir; m. 1st Ástríður Thorarensen 1951; one s.; m. 2nd Þorsteinn Daviðsson 1971; ed Reykjavík Coll., Univ. of Iceland; Chief Clerk Reykjavík Theatre 1970–72; parl. reporter for Morgunblaðið newspaper 1973–74, Ed. Morgunblaðið 2009–; worked for Almenna bokafelagid publishing co. 1975–76; Office Man., Reykjavik Health Insurance Fund 1976–78, Man. Dir 1978–82; mem. Reykjavik City Council 1974–99; Mayor of Reykjavik 1982–91; Vice-Chair. Independence Party 1989–91, Chair. 1991–; mem. Parl. 1991–; Prime Minister of Iceland 1991–2004; Minister of Statistical Bureau of Iceland; Minister of Foreign Affairs 2004–05; Gov. Cen. Bank of Iceland 2005–09; cand. in presidential election 2016; Chair. of Exec. Cttee Reykjavik Arts Festival 1976–78; Hon. LLD (Univ. of Manitoba) 2000. *Publications:* plays: For My Country's Benefit (Nat. Theatre 1974–75), Icelandic Confabulations (Reykjavik Theatre 1975–76); TV dramas: Robert Eliasson Returns From Abroad 1977, Stains on the White Collar 1981; short stories: A Couple of Days Without Gudny 1997, Stolen from the Author of the Alphabet 2002; essay The Independence Movement 1981; trans. A Small Nation Under the Yoke of a Foreign Power by Anders Küng-Estonia 1973. *Leisure interests:* bridge, salmon fishing, forestry. *Address:* Morgunblaðið, Hádegismóum

2, 110 Reykjavik, Iceland (office). *Telephone:* 5691100 (office). *Fax:* 5691110 (office). *Website:* www.mbl.is (office).

O'DEA, Willie, LLM, CA; Irish politician; b. 1 Nov. 1952, Limerick; m. Geraldine Kennedy; ed Patrician Brothers Coll., Ballyfin, Co. Laois, Univ. Coll. Dublin (UCD), Kings Inns, Inst. of Certified Accountants; fmr barrister and accountant; fmr Lecturer, UCD and Univ. of Limerick; TD Limerick 1982–, Minister of State at Dept of Justice 1992–93, at Depts of Justice and Health 1993–94, at Dept of Educ. 1997–2002, at Dept of Justice, Equality and Law Reform with special responsibility for Equality Issues 2002–04, Minister for Defence 2004–10; regular columnist, Sunday Independent and other nat. newspapers. *Address:* 2 Glenview Gardens, Farranshone, Limerick, Ireland. *E-mail:* willie.odea@oireachtas.ie. *Website:* www.willieodea.ie.

ØDEGÅRD, Knut, LittD; Norwegian poet, writer, critic and diplomatist; *Consul General, Republic of Macedonia;* b. 6 Nov. 1945, Molde; m. Thorgerdur Ingólfsdóttir 1981; two d.; ed Univ. of Oslo; poetry critic, Aftenposten newspaper 1968–2009, Vårt Land 2009–; Publr Noregs Boklag 1975–77; Cinema and Cultural Dir, Kristiansund Municipality 1977–78; Cultural Dir, Sør-Trøndelag Co. 1978–84; Man. Dir Scandinavian Centre, Nordens Hus, Reykjavík 1984–89; Founder and Pres. Bjornson Festivalen, Norwegian Festival of Int. Literature 1992–2002; Consul, Repub. of Slovakia 1995–97; Consul-Gen., Repub. of Macedonia 1997–; Pres. Bjornstjerne Bjornson Acad., Norwegian Acad. of Literature and Freedom of Expression 2003–14; mem. Icelandic Soc. of Authors, Literary Acad. of Romania, Norwegian Soc. of Authors, European Acad. of Poetry (Sec.-Gen. 2009–12), The Norwegian Acad. 2015–; Norwegian State Scholar for Life 1989–; knighted by Pres. of Iceland 1987, Grand Kt Commdr, Order of the Icelandic Falcon 1993, Int. Order of Merit 1993, Kt, Norwegian Order of Literature 1995, knighted by King of Norway 1998, Kt, Equestrial Order of Holy Sepulchre of Jerusalem (Vatican) 2009; Jan Smrek Int. Poetry Award, Slovakia 2008, Bastian Prize 1984, Anders Jahre Cultural Prize 2001, Dobloug Prize, Swedish Acad. 2010, Golden Key of Smederevo 2014. *Publications include:* poetry: Bee-buzz, Salmon Leap 1968, Cinema Operator 1991, Ventriloquy 1994, Selected Poems 1995, Missa 1998, The Stephensen House 2003, Look-out 2005, It Flowered So Insane 2009; books of prose and essays, a play, two non-fiction books about Iceland 1992, 1998 and a book about St Olaf 2011; works trans. into 33 languages. *Address:* Postboks 326, 6401 Molde, Norway. *Telephone:* 71-21-59-91 (office). 91-83-86-67 (office). *E-mail:* knutode@mimer.no (office).

ODEH, Ayman, LLM; Jordanian lawyer and politician; b. 1961; ed Univ. of Jordan, Miami Univ., USA; practising lawyer 1985–2007; mem. various legal cttees including Jordan First Comm. Anti-Corruption Cttee, We Are All Jordan Cttee; Minister of Justice 2007–10; apptd Minister of State for Prime Ministry Affairs and Legislation 2011.

ODEIN AJUMOGOBIA, Henry, LLB; Nigerian lawyer and fmr politician; ed Univ. of Lagos; Asst Lecturer, Dept of Commercial and Industrial Law, Univ. of Lagos 1979–80; with Fred Egbe & Co., Solicitors 1980–83, Nigerian LNG Consultants 1983; Founding Partner, Ajumogobia & Okeke (legal practice), Lagos 2003–; Attorney-Gen. and Commr of Justice 2003–07; Fed. Minister of State for Petroleum 2007–09, Fed. Minister of Foreign Affairs 2010–11; mem. ICC International Court of Arbitration, Paris; Sr Advocate of Nigeria 2003. *Address:* Ajumogobia & Okeke, 2nd Floor, Sterling Towers, 20 Marina, Lagos, Nigeria (office). *Telephone:* (1) 2719368 (office). *E-mail:* odein@ajumogobiaokeke.com (office). *Website:* www.ajumogobiaokeke.com (office).

ODEMBO ABSALOM, Elkanah, BS, MS; Kenyan business executive and fmr diplomatist; ed Bowdoin Coll. and Univ. of Texas, USA; fmr Research Officer for African Medical Research Foundation; fmr East Africa Rep. for World Neighbors; fmr consultant to Ford Foundation's Coordinator of Africa Philanthropy Initiative; Founding Dir Ufadhili Trust (Centre for Philanthropy and Social Responsibility); Chair. Kenya Community Devt Foundation, Kenya Nat. Council of Non-Governmental Orgs (NGOs); Lead facilitator for the Kenya Poverty Reduction Strategy Paper Consultation Process; mem. Selection Cttee for UNDP Africa 2000 Project; Founding mem. NGO Coalition for East Africa; mem. Nat. Advisory Cttee for Health Research, NGO Co-ordination Bd of Kenya, Nat. Cttee for Social Dimensions of Devt; Amb. to France –2010, to USA 2010–13; Vice-Pres., African Region, World Council of Credit Unions, Nairobi 2013–14; Country Dir CARE Int. 2015–18; fmr Synergos Sr Fellow; Fellow, Africa Leadership Initiative.

ODENBERG, Mikael; Swedish politician; *Chairman, Karolinska Institutet;* b. 14 Dec. 1953, Stockholm; m. Catherine Odenberg; two s. two d.; ed Östra Real Upper Secondary School, Stockholm, Stockholm Univ., Stockholm School of Econs, Reserve Officer Training, Nat. Defence Coll.; Maj. (reserve) in Swedish Marines; Local Govt Ombudsman, Swedish Young Conservatives and Moderate Party, Nacka 1972–73; Sec. Moderate Youth (MUF) 1978; Deputy Sec. to Stockholm City Commr (real estate, town-planning and highways depts) and Sec. to Moderate City Council Group 1979–85; self-employed 1985–2004; mem. Riksdag (Parl.) 1987, 1990, 1991–2006, mem. Cttee on Housing 1991–94, Cttee on Industry and Trade 1994–98, Cttee on Labour Market and Cttee on EU Affairs 1998–2002, Deputy Chair. Cttee on Industry and Trade 2002–03, mem. War Del. 2003–, Leader Moderate Party Parl. Group 2003–06, Deputy Chair. Cttee on Finance 2003–06, mem. Advisory Council on Foreign Affairs 2003–06, mem. Riksdag Bd 2003–06, mem. Parl. Review Comm. 2003–06; Minister for Defence 2006–07; Leader Moderate Party's group on healthcare matters, Stockholm Co. Council 1988–91; Dir-Gen. Svenska kraftnät 2008–16; Chair. Univ. Bd, Karolinska Institutet 2016–. *Address:* Karolinska Institutet, 171 77 Stockholm, Sweden (office). *Telephone:* (8) 524-80-00 (office). *Website:* www.ki.se (office).

ODENT, Michel, MD; French obstetrician and writer; *Director, Primal Health Research Centre, London;* b. 7 July 1930, Bresles, Oise; m. Nicole Odent; two s. (one deceased) one d.; ed Univ. of Paris; developed and led surgical unit and maternity unit at the Pithiviers state hosp. 1962–85; commissioned by WHO to report on planned home birth in industrialized countries 1986–90; moved to London, UK 1990; Founder and Dir Primal Health Research Centre, London, for study of long-term consequences of early experiences; introduced concepts of home-like birthing rooms and birthing pools in maternity hosps 1970s; Contributing Ed. Midwifery Today, USA. *Achievements:* author of the first article in the medical literature about the use of birthing pools (Lancet 1983), of the first article about the initiation

of lactation during the hour following birth, and of the first article applying the 'Gate Control Theory of Pain' to obstetrics. *Publications:* 12 books, published in 22 languages, including Birth Reborn 1984, Primal Health 1986, The Scientification of Love 2001, The Farmer and the Obstetrician 2002, The Caesarean 2004, The Functions of the Orgasms 2009, Childbirth in the Age of Plastics 2011, Childbirth and the Future of Homo Sapiens 2013, Do we Need Midwives? 2015; more than 90 medical articles. *Address:* 72 Savernake Road, London, NW3 2JR, England (office). *Telephone:* (20) 7485-0095 (office); (20) 7475-0095 (home). *Fax:* (20) 7267-5123 (office). *E-mail:* modent@aol.com (home). *Website:* www.wombecology.com (home); www.primalhealthresearch.com (home).

ODGERS, Sir Graeme David William, Kt, MA, MBA; British business executive; b. 10 March 1934, Johannesburg, SA; s. of William Arthur Odgers and Elizabeth Minty (née Rennie); m. 1st Diana Patricia Berge 1957 (died 2012); one s. three d. (one deceased); m. 2nd Susan Tait 2014; ed St John's Coll., Johannesburg, Gonville and Caius Coll., Cambridge, Harvard Business School, USA; Investment Officer, IFC, Washington, DC 1959–62; Man. Consultant, Urwick Orr & Partners Ltd 1962–64; Investment Exec., Hambros Bank Ltd 1964–65; Dir, Keith Shipton Ltd 1965–72, C.T. Bowring (Insurance) Holdings Ltd 1972–74; Chair. Odgers & Co. Ltd (Exec. Recruitment Consultants) 1970–74; Dir, Industrial Devt Unit, Dept of Industry 1974–77; Assoc. Dir (Finance), General Electric Co. 1977–78; Group Finance Dir, Tarmac PLC 1979–86, Group Man. Dir 1983–86, Dir (non-exec.) 1986–87; Dir (non-exec.), Dalgety PLC 1987–93; part-time Bd mem., British Telecommunications PLC 1983–86, Govt Dir 1984–86, Deputy Chair. and Chief Finance Officer 1986–87, Group Man. Dir 1987–89; Chief Exec., Alfred McAlpine 1990–93; Chair., Monopolies and Mergers Comm. 1993–97; Dir (non-exec.), Southern Electric PLC 1998–99; Dir, Scottish and Southern Energy PLC 1999–2004; Chair., Locate in Kent Ltd 1998–2005, Kent Econ. Bd 2001–09; DL, Co. of Kent 2002–09; Chair., later Pres. New Marlowe Theatre Devt Trust 2007–18; Hon. Fellow, Christ Church Univ. 2010; Freedom of City of Canterbury 2015; Hon. LLD (Greenwich) 2004, (Kent) 2005; Invicta Award, Co. of Kent 2009. *Leisure interest:* golf. *Address:* Cramond House, Harnet Street, Sandwich, Kent, CT13 9ES, England (home). *Telephone:* (1304) 621038 (home). *E-mail:* graemedwodgers@gmail.com (home).

ODIER, Patrick, BA (Econ), MBA; Swiss banking executive; *Chairman, Swiss Bankers Association;* b. 1955; ed Univ. of Geneva, Univ. of Chicago, USA; joined Lombard Odier & Cie (pvt. bankers) 1982, completed training in Zurich, New York and Montreal, Man. Partner 1986–2008, Sr Man. Partner, Lombard Odier Group, Geneva 2008–, Chair. Bank Lombard Odier & Co Ltd 2014–; Chair. Swiss Bankers Asscn 2009–; Vice-Chair. economiesuisse (Swiss fed. of trade and industry); mem. Bd several Swiss and int. academic insts and non-profit orgs. *Address:* Swiss Bankers Association, Aeschenplatz 7, PO Box 4182, 4002 Basel, Switzerland (office). *Telephone:* (61) 2959393 (office). *Fax:* (61) 2725382 (office). *E-mail:* office@sba.ch (office). *Website:* www.swissbanking.org (office); www.lombardodier.com.

ODIERNO, Gen. (retd) Raymond (Ray) T., BSc, MS, MA; American army officer (retd); *Chairman, Eastern Airlines LLC;* b. 8 Sept. 1954, Rockaway, NJ; s. of Ray Odierno and Helen Odierno; m. Linda Burkarth; two s. one d.; ed US Mil. Acad., West Point, North Carolina State Univ., Naval War Coll.; began army career with US Army Europe and US Seventh Army, Germany, becoming Platoon Leader and Survey Officer, 1st Bn, US 41st Field Artillery Brigade, 56th Field Artillery Brigade, and ADC to Commdg Gen.; Exec. Officer, 2nd Bn, 3rd Field Artillery and later Div. Artillery, 3rd Armored Div., Operation Desert Storm 1990–91; fmr Chief of Staff, US States V Corps, US Army Europe; Commdr, US 4th Infantry Div. (4th ID) 2001–04; Asst to Chair. of Jt Chiefs of Staff and Sr Mil. Adviser to Sec. of State, Washington, DC 2004–06; Commdg Gen., US III Corps, Iraq, also Commdg Gen. Multi-Nat. Force—Iraq, Baghdad 2008–10, Commdg Gen., US Forces—Iraq, Operation Iraqi Freedom Jan.-Oct. 2010; Commdr, US Jt Forces Command, Norfolk, Va 2010–11; Chief of Staff of US Army 2011–15 (retd); Sr Advisor, JP Morgan Chase & Co 2015–; Chair. and Alt. Gov. Florida Panthers 2017–; Chair. Eastern Airlines LLC 2016–; decorations include four Defense Distinguished Service Medals, two Army Distinguished Service Medals, Defense Superior Service Medal, six Legions of Merit, Bronze Star Medal, Defense Meritorious Service Medal, four Meritorious Service Medals, Army Commendation Medal, Army Achievement Medal, Combat Action Badge; Orders of Mil. Merit from Brazil, Colombia, Romania and Italy; Officier, Légion d'honneur; numerous medals, including Army Distinguished Service Medal, Defense Superior Service Medal, Legion of Merit, Bronze Star, State Department Sec.'s Distinguished Service Award. *Website:* easternairlines.aero (office).

ODINGA, Raila Amollo, MSc; Kenyan politician; b. 7 Jan. 1945, Nyanza; s. of Jaramogi Odinga and Mary Emma Odinga; m. Ida Anyango Oyoo; four c.; ed Herder Inst., Leipzig, Otto von Guericke Tech. Univ., Magdeburg, Germany; Asst Lecturer, Dept of Mechanical Eng, Univ. of Nairobi 1971–72; f. Spectre Ltd (later East African Spectre Ltd) eng co. 1971; Group Standards Man. Kenya Bureau of Standards 1974–78, Deputy Dir 1978–82; detained without trial following coup attempt by Kenya Air Force personnel 1982–88, re-arrested and detained 1988, 1990, spent four months in political asylum in Norway 1991; Co-founder Forum for the Restoration of Democracy 1991; MP for Langata 1992–2013, joined Nat. Devt Party 1996, joined Liberal Democratic Party 2002; unsuccessful cand. in presidential elections 1997, 2007, 2013, 2017; Minister for Energy 2001–02, Minister for Roads and Public Works 2002–05; Prime Minister 2008–13; Pres. People Ass. 2018–; Co-founder Orange Democratic Movt 2005, Leader 2007–; Dr hc (Univ. of Nairobi) 2008, (Florida A&M Univ.) 2012, (Limkokwing Univ. of Creative Technology, Malaysia) 2012. *Address:* Orange Democratic Movement, Orange House, Menelik Road, Kilimani, POB 42242, 00202 Nairobi, Kenya (office). *Telephone:* (20) 2053481 (office). *E-mail:* info@odm.co.ke (office). *Website:* www .odm.co.ke (office).

ODIO BENITO, Elizabeth; Costa Rican politician, lawyer, judge and inter-national arbitrator; b. 15 Sept. 1939, Puntarenas; d. of Emiliano Odio Madrigal and Esperanza Benito Ibañez; ed Colegio Superior de Señoritas, Univ. of Costa Rica, Univ. of Buenos Aires; Minister of Justice and Attorney-Gen. 1978–82; Minister of Justice 1990–94; Second Vice-Pres. of Costa Rica and Minister of Environment and Energy 1998–2002; Perm. Rep. to UN, Geneva 1993; mem. Sub-comm. for Prevention of Discrimination and Minorities Protection, Human Rights Comm., UN 1980–83, Special Rapporteur, Sub-comm. on Discrimination and

Intolerance Based on Religion or Creed 1983–86; Vice-Pres. Criminal Tribunal for the Fmr Yugoslavia 1993–95, Judge, Int. Tribunal for the Fmr Yugoslavia (ICTY) 1993–98; mem. Admin. Tribunal, IDB 1997–98; mem. and Vice-Pres. Bd of Dirs Univ. para la Paz, UNESCO 1999–, Pres. Working Group on Optional Protocol for the Int. Convention against Torture 1998; mem. Costa Rican Nat. Group to Perm. Court of Arbitration 2000–03; Judge, Trial Div., Int. Criminal Court, The Hague 2003–12 (served term as Second Vice-Pres. 2003–06); Prof., Univ. of Costa Rica 1986–94, Vice-Pres. of Academic Affairs 1988–90, Prof. Emer. 1994–; Prof. Inter-American Inst. of Human Rights, Costa Rica 1992–; Visiting Prof., Univs of Strasbourg, France 1986, Utrecht, Netherlands 1995, Zaragoza, Spain 1996, Leiden, The Netherlands 1998, Barcelona, Spain 1998; mem. Costa Rican Law Asscn, Steering Cttee Asser Inst., The Hague, Bd Dirs Inter-American Inst. of Human Rights, Int. Comm. of Jurists; Dr hc (St Edward's Univ.) 2004. *Address:* PO Box 2292/1000, San José, Costa Rica. *Telephone:* 2809654 (home). *Fax:* 2536984 (home). *E-mail:* eodio@racsa.co.cr (home).

ODLAND, Steve, BBA, MM; American business executive; *President and CEO, The Conference Board, Inc.;* ed Univ. of Notre Dame, Kellogg School of Management at Northwestern Univ.; with Quaker Oats Co. 1981–96; Sr Vice-Pres., Gen. Man. Snacks Div., Sara Lee 1996–98, Pres. Foodservice Div. 1997–98; Exec. Ahold USA 1998–2000; Chair., CEO, Pres. and Dir AutoZone Inc. 2001–05; Chair. and CEO Office Depot Inc. 2005–10; Adjunct Prof., grad. schools of business, Florida Atlantic Univ., Lynn Univ. 2010–11; CEO Cttee for Econ. Devt 2011–18, Pres. 2013–18; Pres. and CEO The Conference Board, Inc. 2018–; mem. Bd of Dirs General Mills Inc.; fmr Commr, Nat. Surface Transportation Policy and Revenue Study Comm.; fmr US Presidential Appointee, Pres.'s Council on Service and Civic Participation; mem. or fmr mem. Business Roundtable (Chair. Corp. Governance Task Force 2004–06), Cttee on Capital Markets Regulation, Advisory Council, Inst. for Corp. Ethics, Advisory Council, Univ. of Notre Dame Mendoza Coll. of Business, Florida Council of 100; publishes a blog on www.forbes.com. *Address:* The Conference Board, Inc., 845 Third Avenue, New York, NY 10022-6600, USA (office). *Telephone:* (212) 759-0900 (office). *Website:* www.conference-board.org (office).

ODLING-SMEE, John Charles, CMG, MA; British economist (retd); b. 13 April 1943, Leeds, Yorks., England; s. of Rev. Charles William Odling-Smee and Katherine Hamilton Odling-Smee (née Aitchison); m. Carmela Veneroso 1996; ed Durham School, St John's Coll., Cambridge; Jr Research Officer, Dept of Applied Econs, Cambridge 1964–65; Asst Research Officer, Inst. of Econs and Statistics, Oxford 1968–71, 1972–73; Econ. Research Officer, Govt of Ghana 1971–72; Sr Research Officer, Centre for Urban Econs LSE 1973–75; Econ. Adviser, Cen. Policy Review Staff, Cabinet Office 1975–77; Sr Econ. Adviser, HM Treasury 1977–80; Sr Economist, IMF 1981–82; Under-Sec., HM Treasury 1982–89; Deputy Chief Econ. Adviser, HM Treasury 1989–90; Sr Adviser, IMF 1990–91, Dir IMF European II Dept 1992–2003 (dept dissolved), retd 2004. *Publications:* Housing Rent Costs and Subsidies 1978, British Economic Growth 1856–1973 1982; various articles in books and learned journals. *Address:* 3506 Garfield Street, NW, Washington, DC 20007, USA. *E-mail:* jodlingsmee@juno.com.

ODOKI, Hon. Benjamin Joses, LLB; Ugandan lawyer; b. 23 March 1943, Busia; m. Veronica Odoki; three s. one d.; ed King's Coll. Budo, Kampala, Univ. of Dar-es-Salaam; State Attorney 1969–72; Advocate, High Court of Uganda 1970; Dir Law Devt Centre 1974–78; Judge, High Court of Uganda 1978–81, Dir Public Prosecution 1981–84; Judge, Supreme Court 1986–2001; Chair. Uganda Constitutional Comm. 1989–93; Chair. Judicial Service Comm. 1996–2000; Chief Justice of Uganda 2001–13; Gen. Ed. Uganda Law Focus 1974–78, Ed.-in-Chief Uganda Law Reports 1974–78; mem. Editorial Advisory Bd Commonwealth Law Bulletin 2005, then Hon. Bd; Independence Medal 1974, Order of Merit, Uganda Law Soc. 1998, Distinguished Jurist Award (Nigeria) 2002. *Publications include:* A Guide to Criminal Procedure in Uganda 1990, An Introduction to Juridicial Conduct and Practice 1992, A Guide to the Legal Profession in Uganda 1992, Criminal Investigation and Prosecutions 1999. *Leisure interests:* music, fine art, drama. *Address:* Plot 4 Philip Road, Kololo, Kampala, Uganda (home). *Telephone:* (41) 343576 (home). *E-mail:* bodoki2000@yahoo.com (home).

O'DONNELL, Baron (Life Peer), cr. 2012, of Clapham in the London Borough of Wandsworth; **Augustine Thomas (Gus) O'Donnell,** Kt, GCB, KCB, CB, BA, MPhil; British economist and civil servant; *Chairman, Frontier Economics;* b. 1 Oct. 1952, South London, England; s. of James O'Donnell and Helen O'Donnell (née McLean); m. Melanie Timmis 1979; one d.; ed Salesian Coll., Battersea, Univ. of Warwick and Nuffield Coll., Oxford; Lecturer, Dept of Political Economy, Univ. of Glasgow 1975–79; economist, HM Treasury 1979–85; First Sec. (Econ.) Embassy in Washington, DC 1985–88; Sr Econ. Adviser, HM Treasury 1988–89, Press Sec. to Chancellor of the Exchequer 1989–90; Press Sec. to Prime Minister John Major 1990–94; Under-Sec. (monetary group) HM Treasury 1994–95, Deputy Dir Macroeconomic Policy and Prospects Directorate 1995–96, Minister (Econs), Embassy in Washington, DC; Exec. Dir IMF, World Bank 1997–98, Man. Dir Macroeconomic Policy and Prospects Directorate 1998–2002; Head of Govt Econ. Service, HM Treasury 1998–2002, Perm. Sec. (with responsibility for Euro entry tests) 2002–05; Sec. to Cabinet, Head of Home Civil Service and Perm. Sec. of Cabinet Office 2005–11; Pres. Inst. for Fiscal Studies 2016–; Chair. Bd of Trustees, Pro Bono Econs 2016–; mem. (Crossbench), House of Lords 2012–; Visiting Fellow, Nuffield Coll., Oxford; Visiting Prof. LSE, Univ. Coll. London; Chair. Frontier Economics 2013–; Adviser, TD Bank 2012–; Dir (non-exec.) and Strategic Advisor, Brookfield Asset Man. 2013–; Trustee, The Tablet newspaper, The Economist Trust; Hon. mem. British Acad.; Dr hc (Warwick), (Glasgow), (Strathclyde). *Publications:* The O'Donnell Review of the Revenue Departments, Reforming Britain's Economic and Financial Policy (ed.), Microeconomic Reform in Britain (ed.); various articles in econ. journals and contrib. to Scotland's Future (ed. A. Goudie). *Leisure interests:* football, cricket, tennis, golf. *Address:* Frontier Economics, 71 High Holborn, London, WC1V 6DA, England (office). *Telephone:* (20) 7031-7000 (office). *Fax:* (20) 7031-7001 (office). *E-mail:* lisa.garment@frontier-economics.com (office). *Website:* www.parliament.uk/biographies/lords/lord-o'donnell/4255 (office).

O'DONNELL, Christopher (Chris) Eugene; American actor; b. 26 June 1970, Winnetka, Ill.; m. Caroline Fentress 1997; five c.; f. George Street Pictures (production co.). *Films:* Men Don't Leave 1990, Fried Green Tomatoes at the Whistle Stop Cafe 1991, School Ties 1992, Scent of a Woman 1992, The Three Musketeers 1993, Blue Sky 1994, Circle of Friends 1995, Mad Love 1995, Batman Forever 1995, The Chamber 1996, In Love and War 1996, Batman and Robin 1997, Cookie's Fortune 1999, The Bachelor (producer and actor) 1999, Vertical Limit 2000, 29 Palms 2002, Kinsey 2004, The Sisters 2005, Kit Kittredge: An American Girl 2008, Max Payne 2008, A Little Help 2010, Cats & Dogs: The Revenge of Kitty Galore 2010. *Television includes:* The Practice (series) 2003, The Amazing Westerbergs (film) 2004, Two and a Half Men (series) 2004, Head Cases (series) 2005, Grey's Anatomy (series) 2006, The Company (mini-series) 2007, NCIS: Los Angeles (series) 2009–15. *Address:* c/o Josh Lieberman, Creative Artists Agency, 2000 Avenue of the Stars, Los Angeles, CA 90067, USA (office); George Street Pictures, 4000 Warner Blvd, Building 81, Room 203, Burbank, CA 91522. *Telephone:* (424) 288-2000 (office); (818) 954-4361. *Fax:* (424) 288-2900 (office). *Website:* www.caa.com (office).

O'DONNELL, Daniel, MBE; Irish singer; b. 12 Dec. 1961, Kincasslagh, Co. Donegal; m. Majella McLennan 2002; backing vocalist for sister Margo O'Donnell early 1980s; tours of UK and Ireland 1985–, Australia and NZ 1993–, USA 2003–; numerous live appearances. *Radio:* numerous interviews in Ireland, UK, USA and Australia. *Television:* series, Ireland, Pledges (PBS TV, USA), participant, Strictly Come Dancing 2015. *Recordings include:* albums: Two Sides Of Daniel O'Donnell 1985, I Need You 1986, Don't Forget To Remember 1987, The Boy From Donegal 1987, Love Songs 1988, From The Heart 1988, Thoughts Of Home 1989, Favourites 1990, The Last Waltz 1990, The Very Best Of... 1991, Follow Your Dream 1992, Christmas With Daniel 1994, Especially For You 1994, The Classic Collection 1995, Irish Collection 1996, Timeless (with Mary Duff) 1996, Songs Of Inspiration 1996, Country Collection 1997, This Is Daniel O'Donnell 1997, I Believe 1997, Love Hope & Faith 1998, Greatest Hits 1999, Faith And Inspiration 2000, Live Laugh Love 2001, Heartbreakers 2002, Songs Of Love 2002, Irish Album 2002, Yesterday's Memories 2002, Dreaming 2002, The Daniel O'Donnell Show 2003, Welcome To North America 2003, Date With (live) 2003, Daniel In Blue Jeans 2003, Daniel O'Donnell And Friends (live) 2003, At The End Of The Day 2003, The Jukebox Years 2004, Welcome To My World 2004, Until The Next Time 2006, Together Again (with Mary Duff) 2008, Country Boy 2008, Peace In The Valley 2009, O Holy Night 2010. *Videos include:* Daniel O'Donnell Live In Concert 1988, Thoughts Of Home 1989, TV Show Favourites 1990, An Evening With Daniel O'Donnell 1990, Follow Your Dream 1992, Daniel And Friends Live 1993, Just For You 1994, The Classic Concert 1995, Christmas With Daniel 1996, The Gospel Show, Live At The Point 1997, Give A Little Love 1998, Peaceful Waters 1999, Faith And Inspiration 2000, Live Laugh Love 2001, The Daniel O'Donnell Show 2001, Shades Of Green 2002, Songs Of Faith 2003, Daniel in Blue Jeans 2003, At the End of the Day 2003, The Jukebox Years 2004, Welcome to My World 2004, Teenage Dreams 2005, From Daniel with Love 2006, Until the Next Time 2006, Together Again (with Mary Duff) 2007, Country Boy 2008, Peace in the Valley 2009, O Holy Night 2010, Moon Over Ireland 2011, Songs from the Movies and More 2012, A Picture of You 2013, Stand Beside Me 2014. *Publications:* My Story (autobiog.) 2000, Daniel O'Donnell: My Pictures and Places 2004. *Website:* www.danielodonnell.org.

O'DONNELL, Edward B., BA, MA; American economist, diplomatist and business executive; *Director of International Business Development, American Business Development Group International;* b. Memphis, Tenn.; m.; three c.; ed Southern Methodist Univ., American Univ. and Univ. of Heidelberg, Germany; served with US Army 1968–72; joined Foreign Service 1975, positions included West German and East German Desk Officer, Econ. Counsellor, Embassy in Vienna, Commercial Officer, US Mission in Berlin, Chargé d'affaires a.i. and Deputy Chief, Embassy in Panama, Econ. and Commercial Officer, Embassies in Bogotá and Asunción, Prin. Officer and Consul-Gen., Frankfurt, Germany; served as Exec. Asst to three Under-Secs and as Special Asst to two Dirs of Policy Planning Staff, US State Dept; fmr Dir Dept of State Liaison Office to US House of Reps; Special Envoy for Holocaust Issues, US State Dept 2003–06; currently Special Negotiator, US Mission to OAS; Dir Int. Business Devt, American Business Devt Group Int., Columbia, SC 2007–; returned to Dept of State for 90 days to assist with transition of Sec. Hillary Clinton's new leadership team 2009. *Address:* American Business Development Group International, 1201 Gervais Street, Columbia, SC 29201, USA (office). *Telephone:* (803) 929-1414 (office). *Website:* www.abdg.com (office).

O'DONNELL, Norah, BA, MA; American journalist and television presenter; *Co-Host, CBS This Morning;* b. 23 Jan. 1974, Washington, DC; m. Geoff Tracy 2001; one s. two d.; ed Douglas MacArthur High School, San Antonio, Tex., Georgetown Univ.; grew up in San Antonio, Tex., Landstuhl, Germany, Seoul, South Korea and Washington, DC; worked as staff reporter, Roll Call; worked as a contrib. and analyst for MSNBC, joined NBC News 1999, Chief Washington Corresp. for MSNBC and contributing corresp. for NBC News' Today and Weekend Today programmes, White House Corresp. for NBC 2003–05, was also regular contrib. to all of NBC News platforms and served as substitute anchor on 9:00 AM hour of Today –2011; joined CBS News as Chief White House Corresp. 2011, also serves as primary substitute anchor for Face The Nation and reports for all CBS News broadcasts and platforms, Co-host, with Charlie Rose and Gayle King, CBS This Morning 2012–; Sigma Delta Chi Award for Breaking News Coverage 2001, Emmy Award as part of NBC News' election night coverage 2008. *Address:* CBS News, 555 West 57th Street, New York, NY 10019, USA (office). *Telephone:* (212) 975-4114 (office). *Website:* www.cbsnews.com/cbsthismorning (office).

O'DONOGHUE, John, BCL, LLB; Irish barrister and fmr politician; b. 28 May 1956, Cahirciveen, Co. Kerry; m. Kate Ann Murphy; two s. one d.; ed Christian Brothers' Secondary School, Cahirciveen, Univ. Coll., Cork, Inc. Law Soc. of Ireland; began career as solicitor, Cahirciveen; mem. Dáil Éireann (lower house of parl.) 1987–2011, Chair. 2007–09; Minister of State, Dept of Finance 1991–92; fmr Fianna Fáil Spokesperson on Justice; Minister of Justice, Equality and Law Reform June 1997–2002, for Arts, Sport and Tourism 2002–07; qualified as Barrister 2014–; mem. Kerry Co. Council (Chair. 1990–91), mem. Kerry Co. Library Cttee, Kerry Fisheries and Coastal Man. Cttee, Southern Health Bd Psychiatric Services Cttee, Caherciveen Social Services Cttee. *Leisure interests:* English literature, history, Gaelic games, horse racing. *Address:* c/o The Bar of

Ireland, Garranearagh Caherciveen, County Kerry, Dublin, Ireland (office). *Telephone:* (087) 7438847 (office). *E-mail:* john.odonoghue@lawlibrary.ie (office).

ODUBER, Nelson Orlando; Dutch politician; b. 7 Feb. 1947; m. Glenda Oduber; three s.; ed St Antonius Coll., Santa Cruz, Admin. Acad. of Brabant, Tilburg, Univ. of Utrecht; Teacher, Governmental Org. and mem. Exams Preparatory Cttee 1973–75; mem. Cttee of the Kingdom to prepare the independence of Suriname 1973–75; Deputy in charge of Dept for Legis. and Constitutional Affairs 1975–85; Vice-Pres. Consultative Cttee for Independence of Aruba 1978–85; mem. Kingdom Cttee for political restructuring of Antilles 1978–80; Leader Movimento Electoral di Pueblo (MEP) (People's Electoral Movt); Prime Minister of Aruba 1989–94, 2001–09, also Minister of Gen. Affairs 1989–94, 2001–09; Ordén Francisco de Miranda (Venezuela) 1989, Order of the Liberatador First Class (Venezuela) 1991, Kt, Order of Orange Nassau 1995; Man of the Year (Diario) 1980, Gold Award for contributing to educ. of Aruba 1983, Politician of the Year by readers of Extra 1990, Man of the Year (MEP) 1993, Man of the Year 2001. *Leisure interests:* swimming, gardening, keeping fit. *Address:* Nayostraat 5, Oranjestad (home); MEP, Nayostraat 5, Oranjestad, Aruba. *Telephone:* (297) 5824206 (home).

ODUNTON, Nii Allotey, MS; Ghanaian mining engineer, administrative officer and international organization official; b. 14 June 1951; m. Nijama Odunton (deceased); four c.; ed Achimeta Secondary School, Accra, Henry Krumb School of Mines, Columbia Univ., USA; Mine Planning Officer, Bethlehem Steel Corpn, Morgantown, Pa 1974–75; Econ. Affairs Officer, Dept of Int. Econ. Social Affairs, UN Secr., New York 1980–83, held several other UN positions 1984–88 including Chief of Mineral Resources Section and Ocean Econs and Tech. Br., First Officer in Charge, UN Office for Law of the Sea, Kingston, Jamaica 1988–; Adviser to Minerals Comm. of Govt of Ghana 1984–87; Interim Dir-Gen. and Programme Co-ordinator, Int. Seabed Authority 1996–2008, Head of Office of Resources and Environmental Monitoring 2008, Deputy to Sec.-Gen. 2008, Sec.-Gen. 2009–16, Perm. Observer to UN, New York; mem. American Inst. of Mining, Metallurgical and Petroleum Engineers, Ghana Inst. of Engineers; African Scholarship Programme of American Univs Award 1969, 1969–72, Henry Krumb Research Fellow 1972, Henry Krumb Fellow 1974–75.

ŌE, Kenzaburō, BA; Japanese writer; b. 31 Jan. 1935, Ehime, Shikoku; m. Yukari Itami 1960; two s. one d.; ed Tokyo Univ.; first stories published 1957; first full-length novel Pluck the Flowers, Gun the Kids 1958; represented young Japanese writers at Peking (now Beijing) 1960; travelled to Russia and Western Europe writing a series of essays on Youth in the West 1961; Commdr, Légion d'honneur 2002; Hon. DLit (Harvard) 2000; Shinchosha Literary Prize 1964, Tanizaka Prize 1967, Europelia Arts Festival Literary Prize 1989, Nobel Prize for Literature 1994. *Publications include:* fiction: Shisha no ogori (trans. as The Catch) (Japanese Soc. for the Promotion of Literature Akutagawa Prize) 1958, Memushiri kouchi (trans. as Nip the Buds, Shoot the Kids) 1958, Miru mae ni tobe 1958, Our Age (in trans.) 1959, Screams (in trans.) 1962, The Perverts (in trans.) 1963, Nichijo seikatsu no boken 1963, Kojinteki na taiken (trans. as A Personal Matter) 1964, Adventures in Daily Life (in trans.) 1964, Man'en gannen no futtoburu (trans. as The Silent Cry) 1967, Football in The First Year of Mannen (in trans.) 1967, Warera no kyoki o iki nobiru michi o 1969, Pinchi ranna chosho (trans. as The Pinch Runner Memorandum) 1976, Shosetsu no hoho 1978, Natsukashii toshi e no tegami 1986, M/T to mori no fushigi no monogatari 1986, A Healing Family (in trans.) 1996, A Quiet Life (in trans.) 1998, Torikaeko (trans. as The Changeling) 2000, Jibun no Ki'no Sitade (trans. as Under My Tree) 2000, Sakokushiteha Naranai 2001, Iigataki Nagekimote 2001, Ureigao no Douij 2002, Rouse Up, O Young Men of the New Age (in trans.) 2002, Somersault (in trans.) 2003, Bouryoku ni Sakaratte kaku (trans. as Writing against Violence) 2003, Atarasii hito' no houe 2003, Nihyakunen no kodomo 2003, Telling Tales (contrib. to charity anthology) 2004, Sayounara, Watashi no Hon yo! 2005, Routashi Anaberu rī souke dachitu mimakaritu (trans. as The Beautiful Annabel Lee was Chilled and Killed) 2007, Suishi (trans. as Death by Water) 2009, Bannen Youshiki shū (trans. as In Late Style) 2013; non-fiction: Hiroshima noto (trans. as Hiroshima Notes) 1963, Okinawa noto 1970, Chiryo noto 1990, Japan, the Ambiguous and Myself (the Nobel Prize speech and other lectures) 1995. *Address:* 585 Seijo-machi, Setagaya-ku, Tokyo, Japan. *Telephone:* 482-7192.

OEHLEN, Albert; German artist; b. 17 Sept. 1954, Krefeld; m. Esther Freund; three c.; ed Hochschule für bildende Künste Hamburg; Prof., Kunstakademie Düsseldorf 2000–09; mem. Lord Jim Lodge (artists' group).

OELZE, Christiane; German singer (soprano); b. 9 Oct. 1963, Cologne; m. Bodo Primus; one d.; ed studied with Klesie Kelly-Moog and Erna Westenberger; began singing in opera 1990; recital tours USA, S America, Japan; has worked with numerous major int. conductors and has appeared on all important European concert stages and at int. festivals, including Salzburg Festival; roles include Despina (Ottawa), Pamina (Leipzig, Lyon, Hamburg, Munich), Konstanze (Salzburg, Zurich), Anne Trulove (Glyndebourne), Regina (in Mathis der Maler, Covent Garden), Zdenka (Covent Garden), Zerlina (Covent Garden), Ännchen (in Der Freischütz, Covent Garden), Mélisande (Glyndebourne), Servilia (in La Clemenza di Tito, Covent Garden), Susanna (Salzburg), Ilia (in Idomeneo, Glyndebourne), Igluno (Palestina, Covent Garden), Sophie (in Rosenkavalier, Hamburg); Prof., Robert-Schumann-Hochschule, Dusseldorf, Germany 2003–08; conducts regular master-classes, including at Arosa Music Acad., Switzerland 2011–; winner, several lieder competitions, including Hugo-Wolf-Wettbewerb 1987, Hochschule Wettbewerb für Lied-Duo 1988. *Recordings include:* several solo recitals, concert arias, Mass in C minor (Mozart), Christmas Oratorio, St John and St Matthew Passions, Webern songs and cantatas, Le nozze di Figaro and many others. *Television:* Pelléas et Mélisande, Glyndebourne 1999. *E-mail:* kontakt@christianeoelze.de. *Website:* www.christianeoelze.com.

OESTREICHER, Rev. Canon Paul, MA, DD; British/New Zealand/German clergyman and journalist; b. 29 Sept. 1931, Meiningen, Germany; s. of Paul Oestreicher and Emma Oestreicher (née Schnaus); m. 1st Lore Feind 1958 (died 2000); two s. (one deceased) two d.; m. 2nd Barbara Einhorn 2002; ed Otago and Victoria Univs, NZ, Bonn Univ., FRG, Lincoln Theological Coll., UK; emigrated to New Zealand with parents 1939; Ed. Critic student newspaper, Otago Univ. 1952–53; Humboldt Research Fellow, Bonn Univ. 1955, Berlin 1992; studied industrial mission (Opel, Gen. Motors), Rüsselsheim 1958–59; ordained in Church of England 1959; freelance journalist and broadcaster in FRG and UK 1959–; Curate in Dalston, London 1959–61; Programme Producer, Religious Dept, BBC Radio 1961–64; Assoc. Sec., Dept of Int. Affairs, British Council of Churches, with special responsibility for East–West relations 1964–69, Hon. Sec. East–West Relations Cttee 1969–81, Asst Gen. Sec. and Div. Sec. for Int. Affairs 1981–86; Vicar, Church of the Ascension, Blackheath, London 1968–81; Dir of Lay Training, Diocese of Southwark 1969–72; mem. Gen. Synod of Church of England 1970–86, 1996–97, Int. Affairs Cttee 1965–2001; mem. Exec. Council Amnesty International (UK Section) 1969–80, Chair. 1974–79; Founder and Trustee, Christian Inst. (of Southern Africa) Fund 1974–94, Chair. Trustees 1983–94; Hon. Chaplain to Bishop of Southwark 1975–80; Hon. Canon of Southwark Cathedral 1978–83, Canon Emer. 1983–86; Public Preacher, Diocese of Southwark 1981–86; Dir Int. Ministry of Coventry Cathedral 1986–97, Canon Residentiary 1986–97, Canon Emer. 1998–; int. consultant 1997–2000; Chair. Christians Aware 1999–2000; mem. Council Keston Coll. 1975–83; mem. Nat. Council Campaign for Nuclear Disarmament 1980–82, Vice-Chair. 1983–85, Vice-Pres. 1985–; mem. Religious Soc. of Friends (Quakers) 1982; Quaker Chaplain, Univ. of Sussex 2002–09; Hon. Citizen of Meiningen 1995; Bundesverdienstkreuz (Cross of Merit First Class), Germany 1995, Verdienstorden of Free State of Saxony 2004; Hon. DLitt (Coventry); Hon. LLD (Sussex); Hon. DD (Otago); Wartburg Prize for Promotion of European Unity 1997, City of Coventry Distinguished Citizen Award 2002. *Publications:* Ed.: Gollwitzer: The Demands of Freedom (English edn) 1965, The Christian Marxist Dialogue 1969, (with J. Klugmann) What Kind of Revolution 1969, The Church and the Bomb (co-author) 1983, The Double Cross 1986; trans. Schulz: Conversion to the World 1967; contrib. to British Council of Churches working party reports on Eastern Europe and Southern Africa. *Address:* 97 Furze Croft, Furze Hill, Brighton, BN3 1PE, England (home); 42/8 Leeds Street, Wellington, 6011, New Zealand (home). *Telephone:* (1273) 728033 (England) (home). *E-mail:* paul.oestreicher.nz@gmail.com (home).

OETTINGER, Günther H.; German lawyer, politician and EU official; *Commissioner for Digital Economy and Society, European Commission;* b. 15 Oct. 1953, Stuttgart; m. Inken Oettinger; one s.; ed Tübingen Univ.; mem. Town Council, Ditzingen 1980–94; practised as a lawyer 1984–2005; mem. CDU, Chair. Baden-Württemberg Junge Union (CDU youth div.) 1983–89, Chair. Baden-Württemberg CDU 2005–09, Chair. CDU Fed. Cttee for Media Politics; mem. Landtag (regional ass.), Baden-Württemberg 1984–09, Minister-Pres. of Baden-Württemberg 2005–09; Commr for Energy, EC 2010–14, for Digital Economy and Soc. 2014–. *Address:* European Commission, 200 Rue de la Loi/Wetstraat 200, 1049 Brussels, Belgium (office). *Telephone:* (2) 299-11-11 (switchboard) (office). *Fax:* (2) 295-01-38 (office). *Website:* ec.europa.eu/commission_2010-2014/oettinger/index_en.htm (office); www.guenther-oettinger.de.

O'FARRELL, Anthony (Tony) Gilbert, PhD, MRIA; Irish mathematician and academic; *Professor Emeritus of Mathematics, Maynooth University;* b. 28 May 1947, Dublin; s. of Patrick O'Farrell and Sheila O'Farrell (née Curtis); m. Lise Pothin 1972; three s. one d.; ed Univ. Coll. Dublin, Brown Univ., USA; Meteorological Officer, Irish Meteorological Service 1967–68; Fellow and Teaching Asst, Brown Univ., USA 1970–73; Asst Prof., UCLA 1973–75; Prof. of Math., Maynooth Coll. (now Maynooth Univ.) 1975–2013, Prof. Emer. 2013–, also Head of Dept, Head of Computer Science 1992–95; Research Assoc., Dublin Inst. for Advanced Studies 1979–; mem. Irish Math. Soc. (Pres. 1982–84, Sec. 1984–85, 1987–89), London Math. Soc., Soc. Mathématique de France –2012, American Math. Soc., Math. Asscn of America, Irish Meteorological Soc.; Fellow, Inst. of Math. and its Applications –2012; Nat. Univ. Travelling Studentship 1969. *Publications:* six books: numerous research papers. *Leisure interests:* literature, walking, music. *Address:* Department of Mathematics and Statistics, Maynooth University, Maynooth, W23 HW31, Co. Kildare, Ireland (office). *Telephone:* (1) 7083914 (office). *Fax:* (1) 7083913 (office). *E-mail:* anthony.ofarrell@mu.ie (office). *Website:* www.maynoothuniversity.ie/faculty-science-engineering/our-people/anthony-g-ofarrell (office).

OFER, Idan, BA, MBA; Israeli business executive; *Principal, Quantum Pacific Group;* b. 5 May 1955; s. of Sammy Ofer and Aviva Ofer; ed Haifa Univ., London School of Business, UK; spent 15 years in Hong Kong, Singapore and USA in shipping and offshore oil storage industries, est. and managed Tanker Pacific Man.; Co-founder and Adviser, Synergy Ventures; Chair. Tower Semiconductor Ltd –1999; Chair. Israel Corpn Ltd ('Israel Corp.') 1999–2010, mem. Bd of Dirs 1999–2013; Chair. ZIM Integrated Shipping Services Ltd, Project Better Place 2007–; currently Principal, Quantum Pacific Group; mem. Bd of Dirs Israel Chemicals, Zim Israel Navigation Co. Ltd, Dead Sea Works, and other subsidiaries and related cos of Israel Corp. and Ofer Group; also engaged in several venture capital and energy projects, including Chair. Energy Horizons and Ofer Power Stations and Dir of Yozma Venture Capital and Ofer Hi-Tech; mem. Advisory Bd Council on Foreign Relations, John F. Kennedy School of Govt at Harvard Univ., Aspect Enterprise Solutions Ltd; Fellow, London School of Business 1999. *Address:* Quantum Pacific Capital Ltd, 19/F, Cheung Kong Center, 2 Queens Road Central, Hong Kong (office). *E-mail:* contact@qpshipping.com (office). *Website:* www.qpshipping.com (office); quantumpacificcapital.com (office).

OFFORD, Robin Ewart, MA, PhD; British medical scientist, biochemist and academic; *Executive Director, Mintaka Foundation for Medical Research;* b. 28 June 1940, Stondon, Beds.; s. of Frank Offord and Eileen Offord; m. Valerie Wheatley 1963; one s. two d.; ed Dame Alice Owen's School, London, Peterhouse, Univ. of Cambridge; scientific staff (part-time), UKAEA 1959–62; grad. student, MRC Lab. for Molecular Biology 1962–65, on scientific staff 1965–66; scientific staff, Lab. of Molecular Biophysics, Oxford 1966–72; Fellow, Univ. Coll., Oxford 1968–73, Univ. Lecturer in Molecular Biophysics, Univ. of Oxford 1972–80, Tutor in Biochemistry and Official Fellow, Christ Church Coll., Oxford 1973–80; Prof., Dir Dept of Medical Biochemistry, Univ. of Geneva 1980–2005, Prof. Emer. 2005–, Pres. Pre-Clinical Medicine 1994–2000; Dir Geneva Bioinformatics SA 1999–2000; Pres. and Exec. Vice-Chair. GeneProt Inc. 2000–01; Chair. Scientific and Econ. Advisory Bd Eclosion SA 2003–; Co-founder and Exec. Dir Mintaka Foundation for Medical Research 2005–; Chair. Bd of Trustees, Torrey Pines Inst. for Molecular Studies 2009–; mem. Council, American Peptide Soc. 1999–, Sec. 2003–11, Pres. 2013–15; mem. Bd of Trustees, Fondation Eclosion Genève 2012–; Agefi Man. of the Year Award (Switzerland) 2002, Makineni Award, American Peptide Soc.

2005, Tribune de Genève Personality of the Year-Society 2008, Innovation Award, Geneva Univ. Hosps 2014, two prizes at Global Healthcare Innovation Acad., Calgary 2016. *Publications:* author, co-author or ed. six scientific books; author or co-author of approx. 200 articles in scientific journals. *Leisure interests:* scuba diving (PADI Master Instructor), windsurfing, cross-country skiing, comparative linguistics. *Address:* Mintaka Foundation, 31 route Pré-Marais, 1233 Bernex, Switzerland (office). *Telephone:* (79) 293-5781 (office). *Website:* www.mintakafoundation.org (office).

OFORI-ATTA, Ken, BA, MBA; Ghanaian business executive, investment banker and government official; *Minister of Finance;* b. 1959, Kibi; m. Angela Ofori-Atta; ed Columbia Univ. and Yale Univ., USA; worked with Salomon Brothers and Morgan Stanley; co-f. Databank Financial Services Ltd 1990, Exec. Chair. 1990–2012; Minister of Finance 2017–; Chair. Bd of Govs, African Capacity Building Foundation 2018–; Co-Founder Aspen Global Leadership Network African Leadership Initiative; mem. Bd of Dirs Enterprise Group Ltd 2010–15, Bank of Kigali Ltd 2015, Trust Bank Ltd, Int. Bank of Liberia, Acumen Fund; Fellow, Aspen Inst.; mem. President's Ghana Investors' Advisory Council; named Global Leader of Tomorrow by World Econ. Forum, Davos. *Address:* Ministry of Finance, POB M40, Accra, Ghana (office); African Capacity Building Foundation, 2 Fairbairn Drive, Mount Pleasant, Harare, Zimbabwe (office). *Telephone:* (30) 2665587 (office). *Fax:* (30) 2666079 (office). *E-mail:* minister2009@mofep.gov.gh (office). *Website:* www.mofep.gov.gh (office); www.acbf-pact.org (office).

OGANDAGA, Jean-Marie; Gabonese politician; *Minister of Economy, Forecasting and Development Programming;* Minister of Economy, Forecasting and Devt Programming 2018–, fmr Minister of Civil Service and Modernization of Public Service, responsible for State Reform. *Address:* Ministry of Economy, Forecasting and Development Programming, Immeuble Arambo, BP 747, Libreville, Gabon (office). *Telephone:* 01-79-55-27 (office). *Fax:* 01-72-18-18 (office). *Website:* www.economie.gouv.ga (office).

OGATA, Sadako, PhD; Japanese international organization official; b. 16 Sept. 1927; one s. one d.; ed Univ. of Sacred Heart, Tokyo, Georgetown Univ., Univ. of California, Berkeley, USA; Minister, Japan's Mission to UN 1978–79; UN special emissary investigating problems of Cambodian refugees on Thai-Cambodian border; rep. of Japan on UN Comm. for Human Rights 1982–85; fmr Chair. Exec. Bd UNICEF; Prof., Sophia Univ. Tokyo 1980–87, Dir Inst. of Int. Relations 1987–88, Dean, Faculty of Foreign Studies 1989–90, currently Prof. Emer.; UN High Commr for Refugees 1991–2000; Co-Chair. Comm. for Human Security 2001–03; Prime Minister's Special Rep. for Afghanistan 2002–04; mem. UN High Level Panel on Threat, Challenges and Change 2003–04, Chair. Advisory Bd on Human Security 2003–; Pres. Japan Int. Co-operation Agency 2003–12, Special Advisor to Pres. 2012–; Advisor, Minister of Foreign Affairs 2012–; Co-Chair. Global Coalition for Africa 2004; mem. Independent Comm. on Int. Humanitarian Issues 1982–83, Trilateral Comm. 1983, Comm. on Global Governance 1992–96; mem. Int. Advisory Bd Council of Foreign Relations, Int. Cttee of the Red Cross 2003–07; Ford Foundation Scholar-in-Residence 2002; currently Distinguished Fellow, Foreign Policy, Global Economy and Development; Dr hc (Harvard) 1994; Hon. DCL (Oxford) 1998; Grand Officer, Order of Orange-Nassau 2008; Hon. DCMG 2011; UNESCO Houphouët-Boigny Peace Prize 1996, Ramon Magsaysay Award for Int. Understanding 1997, Seoul Peace Prize 2000, Delta Prize for Global Understanding 2002, J. William Fulbright Prize for Int. Understanding 2002, Eleanor Roosevelt Val-Kill Medal 2002, Indira Gandhi Prize 2002, Great Negotiator Award, Harvard 2005, Woodrow Wilson Award for Public Service 2007. *Publications:* The Turbulent Decade: Confronting the Refugee Crises of the 1990s 2005, Defiance in Manchuria: The Making of Japanese Foreign Policy, 1931–1932. *Address:* Shinjuku Maynds Tower, 1-1 Yoyogi, 2-chome, Shibuya-ku, Tokyo 151-8558, Japan.

OGAWA, Seiji, BS, PhD; Japanese neuroscientist; *Director, Ogawa Laboratories for Brain Function Research;* b. 19 Jan. 1934; ed Univ. of Tokyo, Stanford Univ., USA; pioneer in devt of nuclear magnetic resonance (NMR) and functional magnetic resonance imaging (fMRI) of brain; Research Assoc., Radiation Research Labs, Mellon Inst., Pittsburgh, USA 1962–64; Postdoctoral Fellow, Stanford Univ. 1967–68; mem. Tech. Staff, Biophysics Research (later Biological Computation Research) Dept, Bell Labs, AT&T, Murray Hill, NJ 1968–80, Distinguished mem. of Tech. Staff and Prin. Investigator, Biophysics Research 1984–96; Distinguished mem. of Tech. Staff and Prin. Investigator, Bell Labs, Lucent Technologies 1996–2001; Visiting Prof., Dept of Biophysics and Physiology, Albert Einstein Coll. of Medicine, Yeshiva Univ., Bronx, NY 2001; Dir Ogawa Labs for Brain Function Research, Hamano Life Science Research Foundation, Tokyo 2001–; Distingushed Prof. and Dir of fMRI Researcher Neuroscience Research Inst., Gachon Univ. of Medicine and Science, Korea 2008–; mem. US Nat. Acad. of Sciences -Inst. of Medicine; Fellow, Int. Soc. for Magnetic Resonance in Medicine 1997; mem. Inst. of Medicine, NAS 2000, Soc. for Neuroscience; Hon. mem. Japanese Soc. of Magnetic Resonance in Medicine 2004, Japanese Soc. of Nuclear Magnetic Resonance 2004; Eastman Kodak Award in Chem. 1967, Gold Medal Award, Soc. of Magnetic Resonance in Medicine 1995, Biological Physics Prize, American Physical Soc. 1996, Nakayama Prize, Nakayama Foundation for Human Science 1998, Asahi Prize, Asahi-Shinbun Cultural Foundation 1999, Japan Int. Prize, Japan Foundation for Science and Tech. 2003, Gairnder Int. Award, Gairdner Foundation, Canada 2003, Int. Soc. of Magnetic Resonance Prize 2007, Olli V. Lounasmaa Memorial Prize of Finland 2008, Keio Medical Science Prize 2017. *Publications:* numerous articles in scientific journals. *Address:* Ogawa Laboratories for Brain Function Research, Hamano Life Science Research Foundation, 12 Daikyo-cho, Shinjuku-ku, Tokyo 160-0015, Japan (office). *Telephone:* (3) 5919-3991 (office). *Fax:* (3) 5919-3993 (office). *E-mail:* info@hlsrf.or.jp (office). *Website:* www.hlsrf.or.fp (office).

OGI, Adolf; Swiss politician, international consultant, fmr head of state and UN official; b. 18 July 1942, Kandersteg; s. of Adolf Ogi and Anna Ogi; m.; two c.; ed Ecole Supérieure de Commerce, La Neuveville, Swiss Mercantile School, London; Man. Soc. for the Devt and Improvement of Meiringen and the Hasli Valley 1963–64; joined Swiss Ski Asscn 1964, Tech. Dir 1969–74, Dir 1975–81; Maj. in Army 1981–83, Staff Liaison Officer 1984–87; mem. Swiss People's Party 1978–, Chair. 1984–87; mem. Parl. 1979–; mem. Fed. Council 1987, Vice-Pres. 1999; Head Fed. Dept of Transport, Communications and Energy 1988–95; Pres. of Switzerland Jan.–Dec. 1993, Jan.–Dec. 2000; Special Adviser to UN Sec.-Gen. on Sport for Devt and Peace 2001–07; Head Fed. Mil. Dept 1995–97, Fed. Dept of Defence, Civil Protection and Sports 1998–2002; Chair. Candidature Cttee for Winter Olympic Games Sion 2006 1998–99; Vice-Chair. Int. and European Cttee, Int. Ski Fed. 1971–83; Dir-Gen. and mem. of Bd Intersport Schweiz Holding AG 1981–; mem. Int. Olympic Truce Cttee; mem. Bd of Dirs NGO Right to Play International; Hon. Prof., Vassil Levski Nat. Sports Acad. of Sofia 2004; Hon. Pres. Swiss Olympic Asscn; Hon. mem. Swiss Ski Asscn; Citizen of Honour, Kandersteg 1992, Fraubrunnen 1999, Sion 2000, Crans Montana, Gondo, Ferden, Kippel, Wiler, Blatten; Dr hc (Univ. of Berne, Int. Univ. in Geneva, Geneva School of Diplomacy and Int. Relations, American Coll. of Greece); European Solar Prize, Human Rights Prize (Switzerland), Swiss Lifetime Award 2012, Karl-Schmid Prize, Fed. Inst. of Tech., Zurich 2002, Olympic Order, IOC 2003, Max Petitpierre Prize, Max Petitpierre Foundation, Bern 2004, Hon. Award, Credit Suisse Sports Award 2007, European Cultural Communication Prize, Pro Europe Foundation 2012. *Address:* Bureau Ogi, Worbstrasse 140, 3073, Gümligen, Switzerland (office). *Telephone:* (31) 9525477. *E-mail:* info@adolfogi.ch (office).

OGILVIE, Dame Bridget Margaret, AC, DBE, ScD, FRS, FIBiol, FRCPath, FMedSci; Australian scientist and academic; b. 24 March 1938, Glen Innes, NSW; d. of John Mylne Ogilvie and Margaret Beryl McRae; ed New England Girls School, Armidale, NSW, Univ. of New England, NSW, Univ. of Cambridge; Fellow, Wellcome Animal Health Trust 1963–66; mem. scientific staff MRC 1966–81; mem. staff of The Wellcome Trust (various capacities) 1979–, Dir 1991–98; Visiting Prof., Univ. Coll. London 1997–; Chair. Governing Body, Inst. for Animal Health 1997–2003, Cttee on Public Understanding of Science 1998–2002, British Library Advisory Cttee for Science and Business 1999–2002, Asscn of Medical Research Charities 2002–, Medicines for Malaria Venture 1999–2006, Lister Inst. Governing Body 2002–; High Steward Univ. of Cambridge 2002–; Dir (non-exec.) Lloyds Bank 1995–96, Lloyds TSB Group PLC 1996–2000, Zeneca Group PLC 1997, AstraZeneca 1999–2006; mem. UK Council for Science and Tech. 1993–2000, Advisory Council for Chem., Univ. of Oxford 1997–2001, Australian Health and Medical Research Strategic Review 1998, Australian Acad. of Science 2008–; Trustee, Nat. Museum of Science and Industry 1992–2002, Royal Coll. of Veterinary Surgeons Trust Fund 1998–2001, Nat. Endowment for Science and Tech. and the Arts 1998–2002, Cancer Research Campaign 2000–02, Research UK 2002–; Ian McMaster Fellow 1971–72; Vice-Chair. Sense About Science; Hon. mem. British and American Socs of Parasitology, British Veterinary Asscn; Hon. MRCP; Hon. FRCP; Hon. Assoc. Royal Coll. of Veterinary Surgeons; Hon. Fellow, Univ. Coll. London, Girton Coll., Cambridge, St Edmunds Coll., Cambridge, Royal Australasian Coll. of Physicians, Inst. of Biology, Royal Soc. of Medicine; Foundation Hon. Fellow, Royal Veterinary Coll.; Hon. MD (Newcastle); Hon. DSc (Nottingham, Salford, Westminster, Bristol, Glasgow, ANU, Buckingham, Dublin, Nottingham Trent, Oxford Brookes, Greenwich, Auckland, Durham, Kent, Exeter, London, Leicester, Manchester, St Andrews, Wollongong); Hon. LLD Trinity Coll., Dundee; Dr hc (Edin.); Univ. Medal (Univ. of New England); Inaugural Distinguished Alumni Award (Univ. of New England); Lloyd of Kilgerran Prize 1994, Wooldridge Memorial Medal 1998, Australian Soc. of Medical Research Medal 2000, Kilby Award 2003, Duncan Davies Memorial Medal 2004, Ralph Doherty Memorial Medal, Queensland Inst. of Medical Research 2006. *Publications:* various scientific papers, reviews, book chapters on the immune response to parasitic infections of man and animals 1964–84. *Leisure interests:* the company of friends, looking at landscape, swimming, walking, music, gardening. *Address:* c/o Medical Administration, University College London, Gower Street, London, WC1E 6BT, England. *Telephone:* (20) 7679-6939. *Fax:* (20) 7383-2462. *E-mail:* rachel.chapman@ucl.ac.uk.

OGILVIE THOMPSON, Julian, MA; South African business executive (retd); b. 27 Jan. 1934, Cape Town; s. of the Hon. Newton Ogilvie Thompson and Eve Ogilvie Thompson; m. the Hon. Tessa M. Brand 1956; two s. two d.; ed Diocesan Coll., Rondebosch and Worcester Coll., Oxford; Dir (non-exec.) De Beers Consolidated Mines Ltd 1966–2006, Chair. 1985–97, Deputy Chair. 1998–2001; Chair. Mineral and Resources Corpn 1982–99; Deputy Chair. Anglo-American Corpn of South Africa Ltd 1983–90, Chair. 1990–2002, Chair. Anglo-American PLC 1999–2002; Dir Anglogold Ltd 1998–2004; Rhodes Trustee 2002–14, Emer. 2014–; Trustee, Mandela-Rhodes Foundation 2003–; Commdr, Order of Leopold (Belgium), Grand Official, Order of Bernardo O'Higgins (Chile), Presidential Order of Honour (Botswana); Hon. LLD (Rhodes Univ.); Rhodes Scholar 1953. *Leisure interests:* golf, fishing, shooting. *Address:* PO Box 61631, Marshalltown 2107 (office); Froome, Froome Street, Athol Ext. 3, Sandton, Gauteng, South Africa (home). *Telephone:* (11) 274-2043 (office); 884-3925 (home). *Fax:* (11) 643-2720 (office). *E-mail:* odonnellt@coson.co.za (office).

OGILVY, HRH Princess Alexandra, the Hon. Lady, KG, GCVO; b. 25 Dec. 1936; d. of Duke of Kent (fourth s. of King George V) and Princess Marina (d. of Prince Nicholas of Greece); m. Sir Angus James Bruce Ogilvy (second s. of the 12th Earl of Airlie, KT, GCVO, MC) 1963 (died 2004); one s. one d.; ed Heathfield School, Ascot; Chancellor, Univ. of Lancaster 1964–2004; Col-in-Chief, the King's Own Royal Border Regt –2006, The Queen's Own Rifles of Canada –2010, Canadian Scottish Regt (Princess Mary's); Col-in-Chief, The Light Infantry –2007; Deputy Col-in-Chief, Queen's Royal Lancers (now The Royal Lancers) 1993–; Royal Col, Third Battalion, The Rifles; Patron and Air Chief Commdt, Princess Mary's Royal Air Force Nursing Service; Patron, Queen Alexandra's Royal Naval Nursing Service; Pres. or Patron of many charitable and social welfare orgs; rep. HM Queen Elizabeth II at independence celebrations of Nigeria 1960 and St Lucia 1979, 150th anniversary celebrations, Singapore 1969; Hon. Royal Col The Royal Yeomanry (Territorial Army Voluntary Reserves); Hon. Liverywoman, Worshipful Co. of Clothworkers; Royal Hon. Freeman, Worshipful Co. of Barbers; Hon. Freeman, City of Lancaster, City of London; Hon. Fellow, Royal Coll. of Physicians and Surgeons of Glasgow, Royal Coll. of Anaesthetists, Royal Coll. of Obstetricians and Gynaecologists, Royal Coll. of Physicians; decorations from Mexico, Peru, Chile, Brazil, Japan, Finland, Luxembourg, Netherlands, Canada; hon. degrees (Queensland, Hong Kong, Mauritius, Liverpool); Hon. DMus (Lancaster) 2005. *Address:* Buckingham Palace, London, SW1A 1AA, England. *Telephone:* (20) 7024-4270 (office). *Fax:* (20) 7839-3371 (office).

O'GRADY, Frances, BA; British trade union executive; *General Secretary, Trades Union Congress;* b. 9 Nov. 1959, Oxford; two c.; ed Milham Ford School, Univ. of Manchester, Middlesex Polytechnic, London; has spent career as trade unionist and campaigner; employed in a range of jobs from shop work to the voluntary sector; worked for Transport and General Workers Union on campaigns to prevent abolition of the Agricultural Wages Bd and for introduction of nat. minimum wage, equal pay for women, and on a range of industrial wage claims; Campaigns Officer, Trades Union Congress (TUC) 1994–97, Head of New Unionism campaign 1997–99, launched the TUC's Organising Acad., Head of TUC's org. dept 1999–2003, Deputy Gen. Sec. TUC 2003–12, Gen. Sec. (first woman) 2013–; fmr mem. Resolution Foundation's Comm. on Living Standards, Low Pay Comm., High Pay Comm. *Address:* Trades Union Congress, Congress House, Great Russell Street, London, WC1B 3LS, England (office). *Telephone:* (20) 7467-1215 (office). *E-mail:* info@tuc.org.uk (office). *Website:* www.tuc.org.uk (office).

OGUNLESI, Adebayo O., BA, MBA, JD; Nigerian lawyer and banking executive; *Chairman and Managing Partner, Global Infrastructure Partners;* b. 20 Dec. 1953, Ibadan; s. of Theophilus O. Ogunlesi; m. Amelia Quist-Ogunlesi; two s.; ed Lincoln Coll., Oxford, Harvard Law School, Harvard Business School; law clerk to Assoc. Justice Thurgood Marshall, US Supreme Court 1980–81; Attorney, Cravath, Swaine & Moore (law firm), New York 1982–83; joined First Boston (investment bank) as advisor on Nigerian gas project 1983, worked in Project Finance Group, becoming Head of Global Energy Group, Credit Suisse First Boston (CSFB) 1997–2002, Global Head, CSFB Investment Banking Div. 2002–04, Chief Client Officer, CSFB 2004–06, mem. Exec. Bd and Man. Cttee 2002, Exec. Vice Chair. and Chief Client Officer, CSFB 2004–06; f. Global Infrastructure Partners (GIP) (private equity firm) 2006, currently Chair. and Man. Partner; fmr lecturer, Harvard Law School, Yale School of Org. and Man.; mem. Bd of Dirs Goldman Sachs 2012–, Lead Dir 2014–; mem. Dist of Columbia Bar Asscn. *Address:* Global Infrastructure Partners, 12 East 49th Street, New York, NY 10017, USA (office). *Telephone:* (212) 315-8100 (office). *Website:* www.global-infra.com (office).

OH, Byung-wook; South Korean business executive; *President and CEO, Hyundai Samho Heavy Industries;* joined Hyundai Heavy Industries 1974, COO, Offshore & Eng and Industrial Plant & Eng Divs and Sr Exec. Vice-Pres., Hyundai Heavy Industries Co. Ltd 2006–09, Pres. 2009–10, Pres. and CEO Hyundai Samho Heavy Industries Co. Ltd 2010–; Chair. The Korea Shipbuilders' Asscn (KOSHIPA) 2009. *Address:* Hyundai Samho Heavy Industries Co. Ltd, 1700 Yongdang-Ri, Samho-Eup, Jeollanam-Do, Yeongam 526-701, Republic of Korea (office). *Telephone:* (61) 460-2641 (office). *Fax:* (61) 460-3707 (office). *E-mail:* asteam@hshi.co.kr (office). *Website:* www.hshi.co.kr (office).

OH, Yeon-cheon, BA, MPA, PhD; South Korean economist, academic and university administrator; *President, Seoul National University;* ed Seoul Nat. Univ., New York Univ., USA; passed the 17th Sr Civil Service Examination for Admin. Service 1975; Chief Researcher, Korea Econ. Research Inst. 1982–83; Asst Prof., Assoc. Prof. and Prof., Grad. School of Public Admin, Seoul Nat. Univ. (SNU) 1983–2010, Dean, Grad. School of Public Admin 2000–04, Pres. SNU 2010–; Visiting Prof., Univ. of Berlin, Germany 1991–92; Pres. Korea Taxation Asscn 1997; Cttee mem., Planning and Budget Bd 1998–99; consultant to World Bank on privatization 1999; Chair. Korea Congressional Devt Foundation, Nat. Ass. 2000–06, Public Enterprise Evaluation Task Force, Ministry of Planning and Finance 2001–03, Information and Communication Policy Review Cttee 2003–07, Korea Evaluation Inst. of Industrial Tech., Ministry of Commerce 2005–09, Cttee of Industry Devt Advisory Cttee, Ministry of Knowledge and Econs 2007–09, Korea Biotech R&D Group 2008–10, Korea Childhood Leukemia Foundation 2009–; Pres. Korea Academic Asscn of Public Choice 2007; Order of Service Merit (Red Stripes) 2005. *Publications:* Fiscal Policy and Economic Well-being (co-ed.) 1989, A Theory of Korean Local Public Finance 1989, A Theory of Korean Taxation 1992, Prospect for Fiscal Policy and Directions for Property Tax 1996, Strong Market and Responsible Government 2009; numerous papers in professional journals. *Address:* Office of the President, Seoul National University, Building 60, 1 Gwanak-ro, Gwanak-gu, Seoul 151-742, Republic of Korea (office). *Telephone:* (2) 880-7137 (office). *Fax:* (2) 889-7515 (office). *E-mail:* snuop@snu.ac.kr (office). *Website:* www.useoul.edu (office).

O'HALI, Abdulaziz A., PhD; Saudi Arabian business executive; b. 1935; one s. three d.; ed Univ. of Puget Sound, Tacoma, Wash. and Claremont Grad. School, Calif.; entered govt service 1957, held various posts, including Mil. Advisory Dir, Prime Minister's Office, Acting Dir of Planning and Budgeting, Dir Cultural and Educ. Directorate, Ministry of Defense and Aviation; retd with rank of Col 1979; founding shareholder United Saudi Commercial Bank, Nat. Industrialization Co. 1983; Chair. Saudi Investment Bank; Man. Dir Gulf Center Man. Consultants; mem. Jt Econ. and Tech. Comm. of Saudi Arabia and USA, of Saudi Arabia and Germany.

O'HANLON, Rory, MB, BCh, BAO, DCH; Irish politician (retd) and physician; b. 7 Feb. 1934, Dublin; s. of Michael O'Hanlon and Anna Mary O'Hanlon; m. Teresa Ward 1962; four s. two d.; ed Blackrock Coll. Dublin and Univ. Coll. Dublin; mem. Dáil 1977–2011; mem. Monaghan Co. Council 1979–87; Minister of State, Dept of Health and Social Welfare Oct.–Dec. 1982; Minister of Health 1987–91, for the Environment 1991–92; Chair. Fianna Fáil Parl. Party 1994–2002; Deputy Speaker of Dáil 1997–2002, Ceann Comhairle (Speaker) 2002–07; Fellow, Royal Acad. of Medicine; mem. British-Irish Parl. Group 1992–2002, Jt Cttee on Foreign Affairs 1993–97. *Leisure interests:* swimming, reading, walking, computers.

OHANYAN, Col-Gen. Seyran, PhD; Armenian government official and fmr army officer; b. 1 July 1962, Shushi (Şuşa), Nagornyi Karabakh Autonomous Oblast, Azerbaijan SSR, USSR; m.; three s. one d.; ed high school, Mrgashen Village, Nairi dist (now Kotayk Marz), Armenian SSR, Baku Higher Jt Command Coll., Azerbaijan SSR; began mil. service serving as Platoon Commdr with USSR motorized rifle platoon, GDR 1987–88, Co. Commdr 1987–88; Co. Commdr, 366th motorized rifle regt, Stepanakert 1988–89, Battalion Deputy Commdr 1989–90, Battalion Commdr 1990–92; Chief of Staff of Self-Defence Forces, 'Repub. of Nagornyi Karabakh' 1992–94, First Deputy Commdr of Defence Army 1994–98; Commdr 5th Army Corps of Armenia 1998–99; rank of Maj.-Gen. 1995, Lt-Gen. 2000, Col-Gen. 2007; Minister of Defence, 'Repub. of Nagornyi Karabakh'

1999–2000, Minister of Defence and Commdr of Defence Army 2000–07; Chief of Staff, Armenian Armed Forces 2007–08; Minister of Defence 2008–16; 70th Anniversary of USSR Armed Forces, For Perfect Service, For Excellency, Soviet Union Marshal Zhukov (all from USSR); Hero of Artsakh, Golden Eagle, Combat Cross, 1st Degree, For the Liberation of Shushi (Nagornyi Karabakh); Combat Cross, 1st Degree, Tigranes the Great, For Service to the Motherland, For Perfect Service, 1st and 2nd Degrees, Drastamat Kanayan, Marshal Baghramyan, For the Strengthening of Co-operation, Maternal Gratitude, Coat of Arms. *Address:* c/o Ministry of Defence, 0044 Yerevan, Bagrevand poghots 5, Armenia. *E-mail:* modpress@mil.am.

O'HARE, Joseph Aloysius, MA, PhL, STL, PhD; American RC priest, editor and fmr university president; b. 12 Feb. 1931, New York; ed Berchmans Coll., Cebu City, Philippines, Woodstock Coll. and Fordham Univ., USA, Ateneo de Manila Univ., Philippines; entered the Jesuits 1948, ordained 1961; Instructor in Humanities, Ateneo de Manila Univ. 1955–58, Assoc. Prof. in Philosophy 1967–72; Assoc. Ed. America Magazine, New York 1972–75, 2003–09, Ed.-in-Chief 1975–84; Pres. Fordham Univ. 1984–2003 (retd); mem. Mayor's Cttee on Appointments 1986–89, Charter Revision Comm. of the City of New York 1986–88; apptd Chair. Campaign Finance Bd 1988, reappointed 1994, 1999; fmr Pres. Regis High School; numerous hon. degrees. *Leisure interests:* contemporary fiction, Irish folk music.

O'HARE, Kevin, CBE; British ballet director and fmr professional ballet dancer; *Director, The Royal Ballet;* b. Kingston upon Hull, England; born to Irish parents; ed Vera Skelton School of Dance, Louise Browne Yorkshire Ballet Scholarship Centre, Royal Ballet School, London, Royal Danish Ballet (exchange programme); as a child, appeared with his brother in the film Bugsy Malone with Jodie Foster; joined Sadler's Wells Ballet 1984, Prin. 1990, remained with the co. (now called Birmingham Royal Ballet) until his retirement from dancing 2000; worked with Frederick Ashton, Kenneth MacMillan, David Bintley and Sir Peter Wright; studied co. man. and worked at RSC, returned to Birmingham Royal Ballet as Co. Man. 2001–04; Co. Man., The Royal Ballet 2004–09, Admin. Dir 2009–12, Artistic Dir 2012–. *Address:* The Royal Ballet, Covent Garden, London, WC2E 9DD, England (office). *Telephone:* (20) 7240-1200 (office). *E-mail:* info@roh.org.uk (office). *Website:* www.roh.org.uk (office).

OHASHI, Nobuo; Japanese business executive; Sr Man.-Dir Kawasaki Steel Corpn 1990; Pres. Techno-Research Corpn (subsidiary of Kawasaki Steel Corpn) 1991; mem. Bd of Dirs (Dir, Gen. Man. Seoul Br.), Mitsui & Co. Ltd 1994–97, Rep. Dir, Exec. Man. Dir, COO Foods Unit 1997–99, Rep. Dir, Sr Exec. Man. Dir, Gen. Man. Corp. Planning Div. 1999–2000, Rep. Dir, Exec. Vice-Pres. 2000–02, Rep. Dir, Exec. Vice-Pres., Group Pres. Consumer Products and Services Group 2002, Rep. Dir, Chair. and Exec. Dir 2002–04, Chair. and Dir 2004–09; Chair. Japan-India Business Co-operation Cttee; mem. Exec. Cttee Japan-US Business Council 2004; mem. Bd of Dirs, The Angel Foundation 2002.

OHATA, Akihiro; Japanese engineer and politician; b. 5 Oct. 1947; m.; two c.; ed Musashi Inst. of Tech.; began career as engineer in power plant design team, Hitachi Ltd 1971; elected to Ibaraki Prefectural Ass. 1986; mem. House of Reps (lower house of parl.) for Ibaraki No. 5 Constituency 1990–, Chair. Fundamental Nat. Policies Cttee 2009–10, Disciplinary Cttee 2015–16; Minister of Economy, Trade and Industry 2010–11, of Land, Infrastructure, Transport and Tourism Jan.–Sept. 2011; Founding mem. Democratic Party of Japan, Sec.-Gen. 2013–15, Vice-Pres. 2015–. *Leisure interests:* kendo (second-degree black belt), cinema, mountain trekking, swimming. *Address:* Democratic Party of Japan (DPJ) 1-11-1, Nagata-cho, Chiyoda-ku, Tokyo 100-8901, Japan (office). *Website:* www.oohata.com.

OHENE, Elizabeth Akua, BA; Ghanaian journalist and politician; b. 24 Jan. 1945, Ho; ed Mawuli High School, Univ. of Ghana, Indiana Univ., USA; work experience with newspapers in USA; reporter, staff writer, columnist, leader writer, then Ed. The Daily Graphic and Mirror 1967–82; f. Talking Drum Publications 1986, Publr and Ed.; joined BBC, London, UK 1986, worked successively as Producer of Radio Programmes, Presenter, Sr Producer World Service and BBC Domestic Radio, researcher and columnist, Focus on Africa Magazine, Deputy Ed. African Service for English Daily Programmes, Ed. Focus on Africa Programme, Dir Operational Budget, Corresp. 1993–94; conducted training programmes for BBC in SA, Nigeria, Liberia, Senegal, Sierra Leone, Kenya, Ethiopia and Somalia; Minister of State for Media Relations 2001–02; Govt Spokesperson 2002–03; Minister of State in charge of Tertiary Educ. 2003–08; mem. Int. Women Media Foundation, Bd Int. Comm. of Investigative Journalists, CNN Africa Journalist of the Year Competition 1997–; Order of the Volta; Hon. DLitt (Univ. of Mines and Tech.). *Address:* c/o Ministry of Education, Youth and Sports, POB M45, Accra, Ghana.

OHIN, Elliot, MBA; Togolese business executive and government official; b. 3 Oct. 1951, Lomé; m.; three c.; ed Sullivan Univ., USA and Ecole Superieure des Ingenieurs Commerciaux en Informatique, France; Commercial Engineer, Athena Informatique, Paris, France 1986–92; Dir PNC Bank, Louisville, Kentucky, USA 2001–07; Dir Marathon Petroleum Corpn, Louisville 2007–10; Minister of State, Minister of Foreign Affairs and Co-operation 2010–13; mem. Union of Forces for Change.

OHLSSON, Mikael, MSc; Swedish retail executive; b. 27 Dec. 1957; m.; two s. one d.; ed Linköping Tekniske Högskola; joined IKEA in 1979, worked in carpet dept, Linköping Br., becoming Store Man., IKEA Sundsvall Br. 1981–84, Training and Devt Man. IKEA Sweden 1984–86, Marketing Man. IKEA Sweden 1986–88, Country Man. IKEA Belgium 1988–91, Country Man. IKEA Canada 1991–95, mem. IKEA Exec. Man. Group 1995, Man. Dir IKEA Sweden 1995–2000, Regional Man. IKEA (various regions) 2000–09, Regional Man. for Retail, S Europe and N America –2009, Pres. and CEO, Inter IKEA Systems B.V. 2009–13; mem. Bd of Dirs, Volvo Cars 2013–18 (Vice-Chair. 2015–18), Ikano SA, Tesco PLC, Lindengruppen AB.

OHMORI, Kazuo; Japanese business executive; *Chairman, Sumitomo Corporation;* joined Sumitomo Corpn 1971, Gen. Man., Transportation Project and System Dept, thereafter Gen. Man., Ship and Marine Project Dept, Corp. Officer, Gen. Man., Ship, Aerospace and Transportation Systems Div. 1996–2003, Exec.

Officer and Gen. Man., Ship, Aerospace and Transportation Systems Div. 2003–05, Man. Exec. Officer and Asst Gen. Man., Transportation and Construction Systems Business Unit, Gen. Man., Ship, Aerospace and Transportation Systems Div. 2005–06, Man. Exec. and Gen. Man., Transportation and Construction Systems Business Unit, Rep. Dir, Man. Exec. and Gen. Man. 2006–07, Rep. Dir, Sr Man. Exec. and Gen. Man. 2007–09, Rep. Dir, Exec. Vice-Pres. and Gen. Man. 2009–12, Rep. Dir and Asst to Pres.'s Office April–June 2012, Special Adviser June 2012–13, Chair. Sumitomo Corpn 2013–. *Address:* Sumitomo Corporation, 8-11 Harumi 1-chome, Chuo-ku, Tokyo 104-8610, Japan (office). *Telephone:* (3) 5166-5000 (office). *Fax:* (3) 5166-6292 (office). *E-mail:* info@sumitomocorp.co.jp (office). *Website:* www.sumitomocorp.co.jp (office).

OHNISHI, Minoru; Japanese business executive; b. 28 Oct. 1925, Hyogo Pref.; s. of Sokichi Ohnishi and Mitsu Ohnishi; m. Yaeko Yui 1951; two s.; ed School of Econs, Tokyo Univ.; joined Fuji Photo Film Co. Ltd 1948, Man. Tokyo Sales Dept of Consumer Products Div. 1957–61, Sales Dept of Industrial Products Div. 1961–62, Fukuoka Br. Office 1962–64, Exec. Vice-Pres. Fuji Photo Film USA Inc. 1964–68, Man. Export Sales Div. Fuji Photo Film Co. Ltd 1968–76, Dir 1972–, Man. Dir 1976–79, Sr Man. Dir 1979–80, Pres. 1980–96, Chair. and CEO 1996–2002, Chair. 2003–12; Pres. Photo-Sensitized Materials Mfrs Asscn of Japan 1980–96; mem. Photography Soc. of Japan (fmr Chair.); Hall of Fame Award, Int. Photographic Council 2004. *Leisure interests:* golf, reading.

OHNO, Hideo, PhD; Japanese physicist and academic; *President, Tohoku University;* ed Univ. of Tokyo; began career as Lecturer, then Assoc. Prof., Dept of Electrical Eng, Hokkaido Univ.; fmr Prof. of Lab. for Nanoelectronics and Spintronics, Research Inst. of Electrical Communication, currently Dir Research Inst. of Electrical Communication, Centre for Spintronics Integrated Systems, Spintronics Research Network, Tohoku Univ., Distinguished Prof., Principal Investigator, WPI Advanced Inst. for Materials Research, Prof. Centre for Innovative Integrated Electronic Systems, Pres. 2017–; Visiting Scientist, IBM T.J. Watson Research Center 1988–90; currently leading an IT-Program of Research Revolution 2002, Development of Universal Low-Power Spin Memory project, Ministry of Educ., Culture, Sports, Science and Tech.; Leader of Exploratory Research for Advanced Tech. (ERATO) Project 'Semiconductor Spintronics', Japan Science and Tech. Corpn; Fellow, Inst. of Physics 2004–, Japan Soc. of Applied Physics (JSAP) 2007, American Physical Soc. 2012; Hon. Prof. Inst. of Semiconductors, Chinese Acad. of Sciences 2007; Japan IBM Science Award 1998, IUPAP Magnetism Prize 2003, Japan Acad. Prize 2005, Presidential Prize for Research Excellence, Tohoku Univ. 2005, Agilent Technologies Europhysics Prize 2005, Outstanding Achievement Award, JSAP 2011, IEEE David Sarnoff Award 2012, Compound Semiconductor Electronics Achievement Award, JSAP 2014. *Publications:* more than 300 papers in professional journals on spintronics, physics and the application of semiconductor quantum structures, and semiconductor crystal growth. *Address:* Tohoku University, 2-1-1 Katahira, Aoba-ku, Sendai 980-8577, Japan (office). *Telephone:* (22) 217-5553 (office); (22) 217-5555 (Lab.) (office). *Fax:* (22) 217-5553 (office). *E-mail:* ohno@riec.tohoku.ac.jp (office). *Website:* www.riec.tohoku.ac.jp/lab/ohno/index-e.html (office); www.ohno.riec.tohoku.ac.jp (office).

OHNO, Naotake; Japanese business executive; *President and Chief Operating Officer, Daiwa House Industry Company Ltd;* b. 1948; joined Daiwa House Industry 1971, served in various positions including Head of Marketing, Exec. Man. Dir, Man. Dir, Man., Kinki District and Gen. Man. of Osaka Branch, Dir 2000–, Exec. Vice-Pres. 2007–11, Pres. and COO Daiwa House Industry Co. Ltd 2011–. *Address:* Daiwa House Industry Co. Ltd, 3-3-5 Umeda, Kita-ku, Osaka 530-8241, Japan (office). *Telephone:* (6) 6346-2111 (office). *Fax:* (6) 6342-1419 (office). *E-mail:* info@daiwahouse.com (office). *Website:* www.daiwahouse.com (office); www.daiwahouse.co.jp (office).

OHNO, Shigeru; Japanese energy industry executive; Dir Japan Nuclear Fuel Ltd 1997; fmr Chair. Kyushu Electric Power Co. Inc.; Chair. Fukuoka Venture Market Asscn; fmr Chair. Kyushu Industrial Tech. Centre; mem. Kyushu Economy Int.; Auditor, Nisseki Plasto Co. Ltd 2002; Hon. mem. Bd of Dirs Asian-Pacific Children's Convention (APCC), Fukuoka 2003–. *Address:* c/o Kyushu Electric Power Company Inc., 1-82 Watanabe-dori, 2-chome, Chuo-ku, Fukuoka 810-8720, Japan.

OHNO, Yoshinori; Japanese politician; b. 16 Oct. 1935; ed Univ. of Tokyo, Univ. of Pennsylvania, USA (Fulbright Exchange Student); joined Ministry of Finance 1958, First Sec., Perm. Del. of Japan, Geneva, Switzerland 1971–75, Dir Int. Orgs Section, Int. Finance Bureau 1976; mem. House of Reps 1986–2012, Chair. Standing Cttee on Transport 1997, Standing Cttee on Rules and Admin 2002, Research Comm. on Annuities System 2003; Parl. Vice-Minister of Posts and Telecommunications 1990; Dir Nat. Defence Div., LDP 1994; Sr State Sec. for Finance 1999–2000, for Science and Tech. 2000–01; Sr Vice-Minister of Educ., Culture, Sports, Science and Tech. 2001–04; Minister of State for Defence 2004–05; Chair. Research Comm. on Finance and Banking Systems, LDP, Deputy Chair. Research Comm. on Tax System; Order of Merit of Duarte, Sanchez and Mella, Légion d'honneur 2011, Grand Cordon, Order of the Rising Sun 2013. *Address:* Room #432, 1st Members' Office Building, 2-2-1, Nagata-cho, Chiyoda-ku, Tokyo 100-8981, Japan (office). *Telephone:* (3) 3508-7132 (office). *Fax:* (3) 3502-5870 (office).

OHSAN BELLEPEAU, (Agnès) Monique, GOSK; Mauritian politician, journalist and news broadcaster; b. 3 May 1942, grand-d. of Bartholomée Ohsan, founding mem. of Mauritian Labour Party; m. Yves Joseph Bellepeau (died 2010); two c.; fmr news announcer, Mauritius Broadcasting Corpn; Parl. Pvt. Sec. 1997–2000; fmr mem. Parti Travailliste (Labour Party), Pres. 2007–10; Vice-Pres. of Mauritius (first woman) 2010–16, Acting Pres. March–July 2012, May–June 2015; Grand Officer, Star and Key of the Indian Ocean 2009.

OHSUMI, Yoshinori, BSc, PhD; Japanese cell biologist and academic; *Honorary Professor, Frontier Research Centre, Tokyo Institute of Technology;* b. 9 Feb. 1945, Fukuoka; ed Tokyo Univ.; Postdoctoral Fellow, The Rockefeller Univ., USA 1974–77; Research Assoc., Tokyo Univ. 1977–86, Lecturer 1986–88, Assoc. Prof. 1988–96, began work on identifying the genes connected with autophagy 1988; Prof., Nat. Inst. for Basic Biology, Okazaki, Aichi Pref. 1996–2009, Prof. Emer. 2009–; Prof., Grad. Univ. for Advanced Studies, Hayama 2004–09, Prof. Emer. 2009–; Prof., Frontier Research Centre, Tokyo Inst. of Tech. 2009–14, Hon. Prof. 2014–; mem. European Molecular Biology Org. 2013; Fujihara Award 2005, Japan Acad. Prize 2006, Asahi Prize 2008, Kyoto Prize for Basic Science, Inamori Foundation (co-recipient) 2012, Thomson Reuters Citation Laureate 2013, Int. Prize for Biology, Japan Soc. for Promotion of Science 2015, Meister Award, Japan Endocrine Soc. 2015, Gairdner Int. Award (Canada) 2015, Keio Medical Science Prize 2015, Wiley Prize in Biomedical Sciences 2016, Nobel Prize in Physiology or Medicine 2016, Paul Janssen Award for Biomedical Research 2016, Breakthrough Prize in Life Sciences 2017. *Publications include:* numerous papers in professional journals. *Address:* Frontier Research Centre, Tokyo Institute of Technology, S2-2, 4259 Nagatsuta-cho, Midori-ku, Yokohama 226-8503, Japan (office). *Telephone:* (45) 924-5113 (office); (45) 924-5879 (office). *Fax:* (45) 924-5121 (office). *E-mail:* kenkik.suzu@jim.titech.ac.jp (office). *Website:* www.fcrc.titech.ac.jp/english (office); www.ohsumilab.aro.iri.titech.ac.jp (office).

OHTA, Tomoko Harada, PhD; Japanese geneticist and academic; *Professor Emerita, National Institute of Genetics;* b. (Tomoko Harada), 7 Sept. 1933, Aichi-Ken; d. of Mamoru Harada and Hatsu Harada; m. Yasuo Ohta 1960 (divorced 1972); one d.; ed Tokyo Univ., North Carolina State Univ., USA; researcher, Kihara Inst. for Biological Research 1958–62; Postdoctoral Fellow, Nat. Inst. of Genetics 1967–69, Researcher 1969–76, Assoc. Prof. 1976–84, Prof. 1984–97, Prof. Emer. 1997–, Head of Dept of Population Genetics 1988–97; Vice-Pres. Soc. for the Study of Evolution 1994; Foreign mem. NAS 2002; Fellow, AAAS 2000; Foreign Hon. mem. American Acad. of Arts and Sciences 1984; Order of Culture 2016; Saruhashi Prize 1981, Japan Acad. Prize 1985, Weldon Memorial Prize, Oxford Univ. 1986, Person of Cultural Merit 2002, Crafoord Prize in Biosciences (Ecology), Royal Swedish Acad. of Sciences (co-recipient) 2015. *Publications:* Theoretical Aspects of Population Genetics (co-author) 1971, Evolution and Variation of Multigene Families, Lecture Notes in Biomathematics Vol. 37 1980; articles in professional journals. *Leisure interest:* reading. *Address:* 20–20 Hatsunedai, Mishima-shi, Shizuoka-ken 411-0018 (home); National Institute of Genetics, Mishima 411-8540, Japan (office). *E-mail:* tohta@nig.ac.jp (office). *Website:* www.nig.ac.jp (office).

OHTANI, Monshu Koshin, MA; Japanese ecclesiastic; *Monshu (Head Priest) Emeritus, Jodo Shinshu Hongwanji-ha;* b. 12 Aug. 1945, Kyoto; s. of Kosho Ohtani and Yoshiko Ohtani; m. Noriko Tanaka 1974; two s. two d.; ed Tokyo Univ. and Ryukoku Univ.; ordained Priest of Jodo Shinshu Hongwanji-ha Aug. 1960, Monshu (Head Priest) Apparent 1970–77, Monshu 1977–2014, Monshu Emer. 2014–; Pres. Japan Fed. of Prison Chaplains 1996–; Pres. Kyoto Chapter, UNA of Japan 2006–; Pres. Japan Buddhist Fed. 1978–80, 1988–90, 2002–04. *Publications:* The Buddha's Wish for the World 2009, The Buddha's Call to Awaken 2012, The Buddha's Gift to the World 2014. *Leisure interests:* classical music, skiing. *Address:* Horikawa-dori, Hanayacho-sagaru, Shimogyo-ku, Kyoto 600-8501, Japan (home). *Telephone:* (75) 371-5181 (office). *Fax:* (75) 351-1211 (office). *Website:* www.hongwanji.or.jp (office).

OHTSUBO, Fumio, MA; Japanese business executive; *Executive Advisor, Panasonic Corporation;* ed Kansai Univ., Osaka; joined Matsushita Electric Industrial Co. in 1971, mem. Bd of Dirs 1998–2013, Vice-Pres. Audio and Video Sector (now Panasonic AVC Networks Co.) 1998–2000, Man. Dir 2000–03, Pres. Panasonic AVC Networks Co., Business Group Exec. AVC Network Business Group, and in Charge of Storage Device Business Jan.–June 2003, Sr Man. Dir Matsushita Electric Industrial Co. Ltd –2006, Pres. and Rep. Dir Matsushita Electric Industrial Co. Ltd 2006–12 (renamed Panasonic Corpn Oct. 2008), Chair. 2012–13, Exec. Advisor, also responsible for Storage Device Business 2013–; Chair. Exec. Bd Japan Electronics and Information Tech. Industries Asscn; Outside Dir Teijin Ltd 2016–. *Address:* Panasonic Corpn, Corporate Headquarters, 1006 Oaza Kadoma, Kadoma-shi, Osaka 571-8501, Japan (office). *Telephone:* (6) 6908-1121 (office). *Fax:* (6) 6908-2351 (office). *E-mail:* info@panasonic.net (office). *Website:* panasonic.net (office).

OHURUOGU, Christine Ijeoma, MBE; British athlete; b. 17 May 1984, Newham, East London; ed Univ. Coll., London; sprinter; specializes in 400m, Commonwealth, World and Olympic Champion; bronze medal, 400m, European Jr Championships 2003; AAA Champion in 400m 2004; semi-finalist in 400m, Olympic Games, Athens 2004, also took part in 4×400m relay team that finished 4th; silver medal, 400m and 4×400m relay, European Under 23 Championships 2005; semi-finalist in 400m, World Championships, Helsinki 2005, bronze medal, 4×400m relay; gold medal, 400m, Commonwealth Games, Melbourne 2006; banned from athletics for one year for missing three out-of-competition drugs tests 2006, also banned by British Olympic Asscn from competing at future Olympic Games for GB, appealed to Court of Arbitration for Sport, original decision upheld, appealed against her Olympic ban which was overturned Nov. 2007; gold medal, 400m, bronze medal, 4×400m relay, World Championships, Osaka 2007, World Championships, Moscow 2013; gold medal, Olympic Games, Beijing 2008, silver medal, 400m, Olympic Games, London 2012; gold medal, 4×400m, World Indoor Championships, Istanbul 2012; gold medal, 4×400m, European Indoor Championships, Gothenburg 2013; bronze medal, 4×400m Indoor World Championship 2014; bronze medal 4×400m Commonwealth Games 2014; bronze medal 4×400m World Championships, Beijing 2015; bronze medal 4×400m Olympic Games, Rio de Janeiro 2016; retd from competitive athletics 2018; first British female to win two World Championship titles, first British female to win three global titles, first British athlete to win three global titles in the same event; mem. Newham and Essex Beagles Athletics Club; coached by Lloyd Cowan 2004–16. *E-mail:* info@chrissyo.com. *Website:* www.chrissyo.com.

OIKE, Kazuo, BSc, DSc; Japanese geophysicist and university administrator; b. 1940, Tokyo; ed Kyoto Univ.; Research Assoc., Disaster Prevention Research Inst., Kyoto Univ. 1963–73, Assoc. Prof. 1973–88, Prof. of Seismology, Grad. School of Science 1988–2003, Dean Grad. School of Science 1997–99, Dir Fmr Research Centre for Sports Science 2001–03, Vice-Pres. Kyoto Univ. 2001–03, Pres. 2003–08; f. observation network of microearthquakes in Inner Zone of south-western Japan to study stress field. *Publications:* numerous scientific papers in professional journals. *Address:* Kyoto University, Yoshida-Honmachi, Sakyo-ku, Kyoto 606-8501, Japan (office). *Telephone:* (75) 753-7531 (office). *Fax:* (774) 334598 (home). *E-mail:* koryu52@mail.adm.kyoto-u.ac.jp (office); konamazu@infoseek.to (office). *Website:* www.kyoto-u.ac.jp (office); homepage2.nifty.com/cat-fish.

OISHI, Katsuro; Japanese insurance industry executive; Dir and Gen. Man. Investment Planning Dept, Taiyo Mutual Life Insurance Co. 1999–2004, Rep. Dir and Pres. Taiyo Life Insurance Co. 2004–09, Rep. Dir and Chair. 2009–13, Advisor 2013–, Dir T&D Holdings Inc. (holding co. for Taiyo Life Insurance Co., Daido Life Insurance Co. and T&D Financial Life Insurance Co.) 2004–13. *Address:* Taiyo Life Insurance Co., 11-2 Nihonbashi 2-chome, Chuo-ku, Tokyo 103-0027, Japan. *E-mail:* info@td-holdings.co.jp.

OJEDA Y EISELEY, Jaime de, LLB; Spanish diplomatist; *Ambassador-in-Residence, Shenandoah University;* b. 5 Aug. 1933; ed Univ. of Madrid, Int. Acad. of The Hague, Naval War Coll. of Madrid and Sr Centre for Nat. Defence Studies (CESEDEN), Madrid; Prof. of Political Law, Complutense Univ. of Madrid 1958; joined diplomatic service 1958; served Washington, DC 1962–69; Minister-Counsellor, Beijing 1973–76; Consul-Gen. of Spain in Hong Kong and Macao 1976–79; Fellow, Center for Int. Relations, Harvard Univ. 1979–80; Deputy Perm. Rep. to North Atlantic Council 1982–83, Perm. Rep. to NATO 1983–90; Amb. to USA 1990–97; Pres. Sr Council on Foreign Affairs 1997–98; Amb.-in-Residence Shenandoah Univ. 1998–; Great Cross, Mil. Merit, Great Cross, Civil Merit, Kt Order of Carlos III. *Publications:* El 98 en el Congreso y en la Prensa de los Estados Unidos 1999; trans. Alice in Wonderland (Lewis Carroll) 1971, Through the Looking Glass (Lewis Carroll) 1974, Spain and America: The Past and the Future 1994. *Leisure interests:* music, botany, sailing. *Address:* 1460 University Drive, Winchester, VA 22643 (office); 3770 Leeds Manor Road, Markham, VA 22643, USA (home). *Telephone:* (540) 665-4696 (office); (540) 364-2275 (home). *Fax:* (540) 665-4698 (office); (540) 364-9281 (home). *E-mail:* wsherdow@su.edu (office).

OJO, Chief Bayo, LLB, LLM, BL, Dip ICArb, FCIArb, SAN; Nigerian lawyer, politician and chartered arbitrator; *Principal Partner, Bayo Ojo & Company;* b. Ife-Ijumu, Kogi State; ed Univ. of Lagos, Royal Inst. of Public Admin, London, London School of Econs, UK; began career as civil servant, Ilorin, fmr Kwara State; called to Nigerian Bar 1978; fmr State Counsel, Ministry of Justice, Kwara State; Head of Chambers, Oniyangi & Co. 1983–86; Prin. Partner, Bayo Ojo & Co. (law firm) 1986–; Minister of Justice and Attorney-Gen. 2005–07; Solicitor of Supreme Court of England and Wales; Chair. Nigeria Legal Aid Council; fmr Pres. Nigeria Bar Asscn, also mem. Nat. Exec. Cttee; mem. UN Int. Law Comm. 2007; Sr Advocate of Nigeria (SAN); Fellow, Chartered Inst. of Arbitrators, UK. *Address:* Bayo Ojo & Co., ITF House, 4th Floor, 6 Adetokunbo Ademola Crescent, Wuse 2, Abuja, Nigeria (office). *Telephone:* 8191-432366 (mobile) (office). *Fax:* (9) 5232317 (office). *E-mail:* info@bayoojoandco.org (office). *Website:* www.bayoojoandco.org (office).

OKA, Motoyuki; Japanese business executive; *Senior Adviser, Sumitomo Corporation;* b. 15 Sept. 1943; joined Sumitomo Corpn (gen. trading co.) 1966, served as Gen. Man. Tubular Products Import and Export Dept No. 1 and Gen. Man., Sumitomo Corpn of America, Houston Office, Dir and Gen. Man. Iron and Steel Div. No. 3 and Gen. Man. Planning and Co-ordination Div. 1994–98, Man. Dir and Gen. Man. Planning and Co-ordination Div., Responsible for Personnel Div., C&C System Div. 1998–2001, Sr Man. Dir Responsible for Legal Div., Personnel and Gen. Affairs Div., Planning and Co-ordination Div. April–June 2001, Pres. and CEO Sumitomo Corpn 2001–07, Chair. 2007–12, Sr Adviser 2012–; Outside Dir, Japan Tobacco Inc. 2012–; Dir, NEC Corpn 2013–; Chair. Int. Market Cttee, Japan Foreign Trade Council 2001–. *Address:* Sumitomo Corpn, 8-11 Harumi 1-chome, Chuo-ku, Tokyo 104-8610, Japan (office). *Telephone:* (3) 5166-5000 (office). *Fax:* (3) 5166-6292 (office). *E-mail:* info@sumitomocorp.co.jp (office). *Website:* www.sumitomocorp.co.jp (office).

OKA, Takeshi, PhD, FRS, FRSC; Canadian/American (b. Japanese) scientist and academic; *Robert A. Millikan Distinguished Service Professor Emeritus of Chemistry, Astronomy and Astrophysics, Enrico Fermi Institute, University of Chicago;* b. 10 June 1932, Tokyo, Japan; s. of Shumpei Oka and Chiyoko Oka; m. Keiko Nukui 1960; two s. two d.; ed Univ. of Tokyo; Fellow, Japan Soc. for Promotion of Science 1960–63; Postdoctoral Fellow, Nat. Research Council of Canada 1963–65; Research Physicist, Herzberg Inst. of Astrophysics 1965–81; Prof. of Chem. and Astronomy and Astrophysics, Enrico Fermi Inst., Univ. of Chicago, USA 1981–, Robert A. Millikan Distinguished Service Prof. 1989–2003, Prof. Emer. 2003–; Fellow, American Acad. of Arts and Sciences, American Physical Soc.; Hon. DSc (Waterloo) 2001, (Univ. Coll. London) 2004; Steacie Prize 1972, Plyler Prize 1982; Meggers Award 1997, Lippincott Award 1998, Wilson Award 2002, Davy Medal 2004. *Leisure interest:* history of science. *Address:* Department of Chemistry, Astronomy and Astrophysics, University of Chicago, 5735 S Ellis Avenue, Chicago, IL 60637, USA (office). *Telephone:* (773) 702-7070 (office). *Fax:* (773) 702-0805 (office). *E-mail:* t-oka@uchicago.edu (office). *Website:* www.fermi.uchicago.edu (office).

OKABE, Hiromu, BSc; Japanese business executive and economist; ed Faculty of Econs, Nagoya Univ., Aichi; joined Denso Corpn 1960, held various positions in Accounting Dept and Corp. Planning Dept, Head of Planning Centre No. 2 (Electrical Products), Head of Corp. Planning 1989–95, apptd Dir 1989, Man.-Dir in charge of Engine Electrical Systems Product Div. 1995–96, Pres. and CEO 1996–2003, Vice-Chair. 2003–04, Chair. 2004–09, Special advisor 2011–; Dir, Nagoya Railroad Co. Ltd 2007–; fmr Corporate Auditor, Toyota Boshoku Corp.; Japanese Prime Minister's Award for a Treatise on Econs 1971. *Leisure interests:* reading, writing, playing the traditional board game Go. *Address:* Nagoya Railroad Co. Ltd, 1-2-4 Meieki, Nagoya, Aichi 450-8501, Japan (office). *Telephone:* (52) 588-0813 (office). *Fax:* (52) 588-0815 (office). *Website:* www.meitetsu.co.jp (office).

OKABE, Keiichiro; Japanese oil industry executive; b. 1946; fmr Pres. AOC Holdings; Pres. and CEO Cosmo Oil Co. Ltd –2004, Rep. Dir and Chair. 2004–12, fmr Hon. Chair.; Chair. Japan Oil Asscn 2000, Petroleum Asscn of Japan 2002–; Pres. Qatar Petroleum Devt Co., also Dir; mem. Business Leaders' Inter-Forum for Environment 2002; mem. Bd Auditors Tokyo Broadcasting System Inc. (TBS) 2003–; mem. Bd of Dirs Japan Co-operative Centre for the Middle East. *Address:* Qatar Petroleum Devt Co., IBA Building, 2nd floor, room 202, C-Ring Road, POB 8923, Doha, Qatar (office). *Telephone:* 44669340 (office). *Fax:* 44669321 (office). *Website:* www.qpd-jp.com.

OKABE, Masahiko; Japanese business executive; joined Nippon Express Co. Ltd 1961, various positions within Corp. Admin and Human Resources Depts, Gen.-Man. Chugoku Regional Br. Office 1995–97, Man.-Dir Nippon Express Co. Ltd 1997–99, Pres. 1999–2001, Pres. and CEO 2001–05, Chair. and Rep. Dir 2005–09, Chair. and Dir 2009–; Co-Chair. Cttee on Transportation, Nippon Keidanren 2003–. *Address:* Nippon Express Company Ltd, 1-9-3 Higashi-Shimbashi, Minato-ku, Tokyo 105-8322, Japan (office). *Telephone:* (3) 6251-1111 (office). *Website:* www.nittsu.co.jp (office).

OKADA, Akashige; Japanese banking executive; Pres. Sakura Bank –2001; Chair. Sumitomo Mitsui Banking Corpn 2001–05; Chair. and Rep. Dir Sumitomo Mitsui Financial Group Inc. 2004–05; apptd Dir Sony Corpn 2002 (also Chair. Compensation Cttee 2004), Mitsui & Co. Ltd, Kao Corpn 2002; mem. Japan Cttee, Pacific Basin Econ. Council; Auditor Toray Science Foundation.

OKADA, Katsuya; Japanese lawyer and politician; b. 14 July 1953; ed Univ. of Tokyo and Harvard Univ., USA; entered Ministry of Int. Trade and Industry; joined Takeshita faction of LDP; joined Shinsheito 1993; later mem. Shinshinto and Taiyo Party, then Minseito, finally Democratic Party of Japan, DPJ, following merger with Minseito 1998–, Pres. 2004–05 (resgnd) 2014–16, Vice-Pres. 2006–10, Sec.-Gen. 2010–11; mem. House of Reps for Mie Pref.; Minister for Foreign Affairs 2009–10, Deputy Prime Minister and Minister for Total Reform of Social Security and Tax Jan.–Dec. 2012. *Address:* Democratic Party of Japan, 1-11-1, Nagata-cho, Chiyoda-ku, Tokyo 100-0014, Japan (office). *Telephone:* (3) 3595-9988 (office). *Fax:* (3) 3595-9961 (office). *E-mail:* dpjenews@dpj.or.jp (office). *Website:* www.dpj.or.jp (office).

OKADA, Motoya, MBA; Japanese retail executive; *President, Representative Executive Officer and Group CEO, AEON Company Limited;* ed Babson Coll., USA; mem. Bd of Dirs, Jusco Co. Ltd (retail co.) 1990–92, Man. Dir 1992–95, Sr Man. Dir 1995–97, Pres. and CEO 1997–2009 (renamed AEON Co. Ltd 2001), Pres., Rep. Exec. Officer and Group CEO 2009–, Pres. Talbots Japan Co. Ltd (subsidiary of AEON) 1990–97, mem. Bd of Dirs, AEON Co. (Malaysia) Berhad, The Talbots, Inc. 1993–; Chair. Mycal; mem. Bd of Dirs, CIES – The Food Business Forum 2000–. *Address:* AEON Co. Ltd, 1-5-1 Nakase, Mihama-ku, Chiba-shi, Chiba 261-8515, Japan (office). *Telephone:* (4) 3212-6042 (office). *Fax:* (4) 3212-6849 (office). *E-mail:* info@aeon.info (office). *Website:* www.aeon.info (office).

OKAFUJI, Masahiro; Japanese business executive; *Representative Director, President and CEO, ITOCHU Corporation;* b. 1949, Osaka Pref.; ed Tokyo and Osaka Univs; joined ITOCHU 1974, positions include Vice-Pres., Pres. of Fibre Co., Dir of Brand Marketing Business, Exec. Officer 2002, Man. Exec. Officer, Sr Man. Dir, Pres. of Textiles and Man. Dir ITOCHU Corpn 2004–06, Sr Man. Dir 2006–10, Rep. Dir, Pres. and CEO 2010–. *Address:* ITOCHU Corporation, 5-1 Kita-Aoyama 2-chome, Minato-ku, Tokyo 107-8077, Japan (office). *Telephone:* (3) 3497-2121 (office). *Fax:* (3) 3497-4141 (office). *E-mail:* info@itochu.co.jp (office). *Website:* www.itochu.co.jp (office).

OKALIK, Paul, BA, LLB; Canadian politician; b. 26 May 1964, Pangnirtung, NWT; s. of Auyaluk; m.; two c.; ed Carleton Univ., Univ. of Ottawa; first Inuit law grad.; called to the Bar 1999; mem. Nunavut Legis. Ass. 1999–; first Premier of Nunavut, Minister of Exec. and Intergovernmental Affairs and Minister of Justice 1999–2008, Minister of Health –2016 (resgnd). *Leisure interests:* hunting, fishing, golf. *Address:* Nunavut Legislative Assembly, PO Box 1200, Iqaluit, NU X0A 0H0, Canada (office). *Telephone:* (867) 975-5017 (office). *Fax:* (867) 975-5112 (office). *Website:* www.assembly.nu.ca (office).

OKAMOTO, Kunie; Japanese insurance company executive; *Chairman, Nippon Life Insurance Company;* ed Univ. of Tokyo; joined Nippon Life Insurance Co. 1969, Dir 1999, Man. Dir 1999–2002, Sr Man. Dir 2002–05, Pres. 2005–11, Chair. 2011–; Corp. Auditor, Sapporo Holdings Ltd, UFJ Holdings, Inc. June–Sept. 2005, Mitsubishi Financial UFJ Group 2005–, Tokyu Corpn 2005–; Dir Kintetsu Corpn 2010–; External Corp. Auditor, Daicel Chemical Industries Ltd; Vice-Chair. Life Insurance Asscn of Japan. *Address:* Nippon Life Insurance Co., 3-5-12 Imabashi, Chuo-ku, Osaka 541-8501, Japan (office). *Telephone:* (6) 6209-5525 (office). *Fax:* (3) 5510-7340 (office). *E-mail:* info@nissay.co.jp (office). *Website:* www.nissay.co.jp (office).

OKAMOTO, Tao; Japanese fashion model and actress; b. 22 May 1985, Tokyo; signed with Elite model agency 2006, catwalk debut at spring Emanuel Ungaro and Martin Grant shows, Paris 2006; has modelled for Vogue, Dolce & Gabbana, Julien Macdonald, Yves Saint Laurent, Ralph Lauren. *Film:* The Wolverine 2013, Crossroads 2015, Batman v Superman: Dawn of Justice 2016, Manhunt 2017. *Television:* Chi no wadachi (mini-series) 2014, Hannibal 2015, The Man in the High Castle 2015. *Address:* c/o The Society Management, 156 5th Avenue, 8th Floor, New York, NY 10010, USA (office). *Website:* taookamoto.com (office).

OKAMOTO, Tsuyoshi; Japanese business executive; *Director and Chairman, Tokyo Gas;* b. 23 Sept. 1947; joined Tokyo Gas 1970, Dir, Sr Exec. Officer, Chief Exec. of Corp. Communication Div. and in charge of Compliance Dept, Internal Audit Dept 2006–07, Rep. Dir, Exec. Vice-Pres., and in charge of Personnel Dept, Sec. Dept, Gen. Admin Dept, Compliance Dept and Internal Audit Dept 2007–09, Rep. Dir, Exec. Vice-Pres., and in charge of Personnel Dept, Sec. Dept, Gen. Admin Dept and Compliance Dept 2009–10, Rep. Dir Tokyo Gas 2010–, fmr Pres., Chair. 2014–; apptd Dir Japan Post Bank Co. Ltd 2016. *Address:* Tokyo Gas, 1-5-20 Kaigan, Minato-ku, Tokyo 105-8527, Japan (office). *Telephone:* (3) 3344-9100 (office). *E-mail:* tgir@tokyo-gas.co.jp (office). *Website:* www.tokyo-gas.co.jp (office).

OKAMURA, Tadashi, LLB; Japanese electronics industry executive; b. 26 July 1938, Tokyo; ed Univ. of Tokyo; joined Toshiba Corpn 1962, Gen.-Man. Marketing Planning Div. 1989–93, Group Exec. Information Processing and Control Systems Group 1993–94, Dir 1994–, Vice-Pres. 1994–96, Sr Vice-Pres. 1996–2000, Pres. and CEO Toshiba Corpn 2000–05, Chair. 2005–09, apptd Adviser 2009, currently Hon. Adviser; apptd Chair. Japan Chamber of Commerce and Industry 2007, Tokyo Chamber of Commerce and Industry 2007. *Address:* Toshiba Corporation, 1-1 Shibaura 1-chome, Minato-ku, Tokyo 105-8001, Japan (office). *Telephone:* (3) 3457-4511 (office). *Fax:* (3) 3455-1631 (office). *Website:* www.toshiba.com (office).

OKAMURA, Tomio; Czech/Japanese business executive and politician; *Leader, Svoboda a Přímá Demokracie (Freedom and Direct Democracy);* b. 4 July 1972, Tokyo, Japan; s. of Matsuo Okamura and Helena Okamurova; divorced; one s.; moved with family from Japan to fmr Czechoslovakia at age five; worked as commentator, BBC public radio, Prague 2004–05; f. businesses including Miki (travel agency) and Japa (food shop); mem. Presidium, Asscn of Czech Travel

Agencies and Agencies (AČCKA) 2004–, Vice-Pres. 2009–14; three years as judge, Den D (Czech version of BBC TV programme Dragons' Den); mem. Senate (ind.) for Dist 80, Zlín Region 2012–13; f. Úsvit Přímé Demokracie (Dawn of Direct Democracy) 2013; mem. Chamber of Deputies (Poslanecká Sněmovna, lower chamber of parl.) 2013–; f. Svoboda a Přímá Demokracie (Freedom and Direct Democracy) 2015, Leader. *Publications:* Czech Dream (autobiography) 2010, The Art of Governance (essays) 2011, Art of Living 2012, Great Japanese Cookbook 2013, The Art of Direct Democracy 2013. *Address:* Svoboda a Přímá Demokracie, Sněmovní 1, 118 00 Prague, Czech Republic (office). *E-mail:* info@spd.cz (office). *Website:* www.spd.cz (office); www.tomio.cz.

OKANLA, Moussa, PhD; Benin politician and academic; b. 2 Sept. 1950; m.; ed Univ. of Michigan, USA; Professor in Political Science, Univ. of Abomey-Calavi 1983–2013; Benin Rep., African and Afroamerican Inst., New York 1987–94; Specialist in Democracy and Governance for USAID regional office, Abidjan, Côte d'Ivoire 1994–98; Governance Adviser, UNDP, Cotonou 1999–2000; Deputy Dir, later Dir, Benin School of Public Admin 2001–03; Program Officer, PGDP (Danish-funded governance programme) 2004–07; Minister of Foreign Affairs, African Integration, Francophony and Beninese Diaspora 2007–08; Prof. in Int. Relations, African Politics and Political Econs, Houdegbe North American Univ. Benin 2010–; Chair. Group of Least Developed Countries, UNDP; Commdr, Ordre Nat. du Bénin 2012.

OKAWA, Ryuho; Japanese religious leader; *Leader, Kofuku-no-Kagaku;* b. 7 July 1956, Tokushima Pref.; ed Univ. of Tokyo, Graduate Center, City Univ. of New York, USA; attained enlightenment 23 March 1981, realized his identity as El Cantare, saviour of humanity; f. Kofuku-no-Kagaku (Inst. for Research in Human Happiness) 1986; f. Happiness Realization Party 2009, Happy Science Acad. 2010; holds numerous open lecture sessions with large audiences that are broadcast by satellite throughout Japan. *Publications include:* more than 400 books including The Starting Point of Happiness – A Practical and Intuitive Guide to Discovering Love, Wisdom, and Faith 2001, Love, Nurture, and Forgive – A Handbook on Adding New Richness in Your Life 2002, An Unshakeable Mind – How to Cope with Life's Difficulties and Turn Them into Food for Your Soul 2002, A Revolution of Happiness – The Power of Thought to Change the Future, The 'Inability to Attain Happiness' Syndrome – Say Good-bye to a Life of Gloom, Work and Love – Become a True Leader in the Business World, Invincible Thinking – Become a Master of Your Own Destiny 2003, The Science of Happiness 2009. *Address:* Kofuku-no-Kagaku, 1-6-7 Togoshi, Shinagawa-ku, Tokyo, 142-0041, Japan (office). *Telephone:* (3) 6384-5770 (office). *Fax:* (3) 6384-5776 (office). *E-mail:* tokyo@happy-science.org (office). *Website:* www.happy-science.org; www.kofuku-no-kagaku.or.jp (office).

OKAYAMA, Norio; Japanese electronics industry executive; fmrly with Juki Corpn; Dir Sumitomo Electric Industries Ltd 1991–95, Man. Dir 1995–99, Pres. 1999–2004, Chair. 2004–08; mem. Bd of Dirs Dunlop Co. 2000–, Optoelectronic Industry and Tech. Devt Asscn (OITDA); Acting Pres. Int. Cablemakers Fed. 2006. *Address:* c/o Sumitomo Electric Industries Ltd, 5-33 Kitahama 4-chome, Chuo-ku, Osaka 541-0041, Japan. *E-mail:* info@global-sei.com.

OKAZAKI, Tsuneko, MSc, DSc; Japanese molecular biologist, cellular biologist, academic and business executive; *Professor Emerita, Department of Molecular Biology, Faculty of Science, Nagoya University;* b. (Tsuneko Hara), 7 June 1933, Nagoya; d. of Takima Hara and Hama Hara; m. Reiji Okazaki; two s.; ed Nagoya Univ., studies in USA; Fellowship with J. L. Strominger at Washington Univ., St Louis, Mo., USA 1960–61; Fellowship with A. Kornberg at Stanford Univ., USA 1961–63; mem. Faculty, Dept of Molecular Biology, Faculty of Science, Nagoya Univ. 1963–97, Prof. 1997–2002, Visiting Prof. 2002–08, now Prof. Emer.; Prof. and Visiting Prof., Div. of Artificial Chromosome Project, Inst. for Comprehensive Medical Science, Fujita Health Univ., Toyoake, Aichi 1997–2008; Dir JSPS Stockholm Office, Sweden; CEO Chromo Research Inc., Nagoya 2008–13; Order of the Sacred Treasure 2008; Person of Cultural Merit 2015; L'Oréal-UNESCO For Women in Science Award 2000, Purple Ribbon Prize 2000. *Achievements include:* co-discoverer of Okazaki Fragments of DNA; discoverer of Primer RNA for DNA synthesis; elucidation of detail mechanisms of discontinuous way of DNA synthesis; construction of human artificial chromosome. *Publications include:* numerous articles in scientific journals on mechanisms of DNA replication and the human artificial chromosome.

OKAZAKI, Yoichiro; Japanese engineering executive; b. 16 Dec. 1942; joined Mitsubishi Heavy Industries Ltd 1965, Deputy Gen. Man., Sagamihara Machinery Works 1995–97, Chief Engineer, Gen. Machinery & Components HQ 1997, Pres. Mitsubishi Caterpillar Forklift America Inc. 1997–2001, Dir and Chief Co-ordinator, Gen. Machinery & Components HQ 1999–2000, Gen. Machinery & Special Vehicle HQ 2000–01, Dir, Gen. Man. then Man. Dir 2001–04; Chair., Pres. and CEO Mitsubishi Motors Corpn 2004–05; Dir Shin Caterpillar Mitsubishi Ltd 2001, Mitsubishi Heavy Industries Ltd 2004–05; mem. Hon. Cttee FISITSA.

OKÇAL, Arslan Hakan, BA; Turkish diplomatist; *Ambassador to South Korea;* b. 25 Feb. 1954, Istanbul; m. Pınar Okçal; one s. two d.; ed Univ. of Ankara, Diplomatic Acad. of Ministry of Foreign Affairs, NATO Defence Coll., Italy; joined Ministry of Foreign Affairs (MFA) 1978, mil. service, Second Lt, Turkish Air Force HQ, Ankara 1980–81, Vice-Consul, Consulate General in Benghazi, Libya 1981–83, Vice-Consul, then Consul, Consulate General in Münster, FRG 1983–87, First Sec., Admin. and Financial Dept, MFA 1987–89, NATO Defence Coll., Rome, Feb.–July 1989, First Sec. and Counsellor, Turkish Del. to NATO, Brussels, Aug. 1989–92, Consul Gen. in Komotini, Greece 1992–95, Head of North America Dept, MFA 1995–97, First Counsellor and Minister Counsellor, Embassy in Bonn 1997–99, Minister Counsellor, Embassy in Berlin 1999–2001, Deputy Dir-Gen. for Research, MFA 2001–04, Amb. to Nigeria (also accred to Liberia, Sierra Leone, Ghana, Togo, Benin, Niger, Kamerun, Equatorial Guinea, São Tomé and Príncipe and to Econ. Community of West African States—ECOWAS) 2004–08, to Macedonia 2008–10, Dir-Gen. for the Balkans and Cen. Europe, MFA 2010–13, Amb. to South Korea (also accred to North Korea) 2014–. *Address:* Embassy of Turkey, Vivien Building 4-52, Seobinggo-ro 51-gil, Yeongsan-gu, Seoul 140-240, Republic of Korea (office). *Telephone:* (2) 3780-1600 (office). *Fax:* (2) 797-8546 (office). *E-mail:* embassy.seoul@mfa.gov.tr (office). *Website:* www.seul.be.mfa.gov.tr (office).

OKDAH, Farouk Abd el-Baky el-, BS, MS, MBA, PhD; Egyptian economist and central banker; b. 10 Aug. 1946; m.; two c.; ed Ain Shams Univ., Cairo Univ., The Wharton School, Univ. of Pennsylvania, USA; instructor in Accounting and Finance, The Wharton School, Univ. of Pennsylvania 1978–82; Asst Vice-Pres., Middle East Div., later Vice-Pres. and Africa Dist Man., Irving Trust Co., New York 1984–88; Vice-Pres., Regional Man. and Adviser, Bank of New York 1989–2002; Man. Dir, Int. Co. for Leasing 'Incolease' 1997–2002; Chair. and CEO Nat. Bank of Egypt Jan.–Dec. 2003; advisor to Gov., Cen. Bank of Egypt Dec. 1998–2001, Gov. 2003–13; Gov. African Devt Bank, Arab Monetary Fund; Alt. Gov. IMF; Chair. Nat. Bank of Egypt, London, Union de Banques Arabes et Françaises; mem. Bd of Dirs Egypt Air Holding Co. 1998–; Dir British Arab Commercial Bank Ltd 2003–10; mem. Bd of Dirs Egyptian Banking Fed., Arab Bankers Asscn–N America (also Treas.) 1987–89.

OKE, Timothy Richard, OC, FRSC, PhD; Canadian/British geographer and academic; *Professor Emeritus of Geography, University of British Columbia;* b. 22 Nov. 1941, Kingsbridge, Devon, England; s. of Leslie Oke and Kathleen Oke; m. Margaret 1967; one s. one d.; ed Lord Wandsworth Coll., Univ. of Bristol and McMaster Univ.; Asst Prof., McGill Univ. 1967–70; Asst Prof., Univ. of British Col 1970–71, Assoc. Prof. 1971–78, Prof. of Geography 1978–, now Prof. Emer., also Head, Dept of Geography 1991–96; Ed.-in-Chief, Atmosphere-Ocean 1977–80; Hooker Distinguished Visiting Prof., McMaster Univ. 1987; Visiting Fellow, Keble Coll. Oxford 1990–91; Research Scholar (Rockefeller Foundation) Bellagio, Italy 1991; consultant to WMO and other orgs; Founder and Pres. Int. Asscn for Urban Climate 2000–03; Fellow, Royal Canadian Geographical Soc., Canadian Meteorological and Oceanographic Soc. 2003, American Meteorological Soc. 2004; Dr hc (Łódź) 2005; Pres.'s Prize, Canadian Meteorological Soc. 1972, Killam Prize 1988, Award for Scholarly Distinction, Canadian Asscn of Geographers 1986, Guggenheim Fellow 1990, American Meteorological Soc. Outstanding Achievement in Biometeorology Award 2002, Patterson Medal, Meteorological Service of Canada, Environment Canada 2002, Luke Howard Award, Int. Asscn for Urban Climate 2004, Massey Medal, Royal Canadian Geog Soc. 2005, Helmut E. Landsberg Award, American Meteorological Soc. 2006, Founder's Medal, Int. Asscn for Urban Climate 2012. *Publications:* Boundary Layer Climates 1978, Vancouver and its Region 1992, The Surface Climates of Canada 1997; more than 200 articles on the climate of cities. *Leisure interests:* golf, music, walking, art. *Address:* Department of Geography, University of British Columbia, 1984 West Mall, Vancouver, BC, V6T 1Z2, Canada (office). *Telephone:* (604) 822-2900 (office). *Fax:* (604) 822-6150 (office). *Website:* www.geog.ubc.ca (office).

O'KEEFE, John, BA, MA, PhD, FRS, FMedSci; American/British neuroscientist and academic; *Professor of Cognitive Neuroscience and Director, Sainsbury Wellcome Centre for Neural Circuits and Behaviour, University College London;* b. 18 Nov. 1939, New York; ed City Coll. of New York, USA, McGill Univ., Canada; originally attended Univ. Coll. London, UK as US Nat. Insts of Mental Health Postdoctoral Fellow 1967, awarded professorship 1987, currently Prof. of Cognitive Neuroscience and inaugural Dir Sainsbury Wellcome Centre for Neural Circuits and Behaviour and Head of Dept; Feldberg Foundation Prize 2001, Grawemeyer Award in Psychology (co-recipient) 2006, British Neuroscience Asscn Award for Outstanding Contrib. to British Neuroscience 2007, European Journal of Neuroscience Award, Fed. of European Neuroscience Socs 2008, Gruber Prize in Neuroscience 2008, Louisa Gross Horwitz Prize (with Edvard Moser and May-Britt Moser) 2013, Kavli Prize, Norwegian Acad. of Science and Letters (co-recipient) 2014, Nobel Prize in Medicine or Physiology (co-recipient with Edvard and May-Britt Moser) 2014. *Achievements include:* known for his discovery of place cells in the hippocampus and that they show temporal coding in the form of theta phase precession. *Publications:* numerous papers in professional journals on the neural basis of cognition and memory, in particular, spatial cognition and memory. *Address:* The Sainsbury Wellcome Centre, Faculty of Life Sciences, University College London, Gower Street, London, WC1E 6BT (office); Institute of Cognitive Neuroscience and Department of Anatomy, University College London, Alexandra House, 17 Queen Square, London, WC1N 3AR, England (office). *Telephone:* (20) 7679-1307 (office). *Fax:* (20) 7679-1306 (office). *E-mail:* j.okeefe@ucl.ac.uk (office). *Website:* www.ucl.ac.uk/cdb/research/okeefe (office).

O'KEEFE, Sean Charles, BA, MPA; American academic, space research administration official and fmr university administrator; *University Professor and Howard G. and S. Louise Phanstiel Chair in Strategic Management and Leadership, Maxwell School of Citizenship and Public Affairs, Syracuse University;* b. 27 Jan. 1956, Monterey, Calif.; s. of Patrick Gordon O'Keefe and Patricia O'Keefe (née Carlin); m. Laura McCarthy O'Keefe; three c.; ed Loyola Univ. New Orleans, Syracuse Univ.; fmr staff dir and professional staff mem. Defense Subcttee of Senate Appropriations Cttee; Comptroller, Dept of Defense 1989, Sec. of the Navy 1992–93; Prof. of Business Admin., Sr Vice-Pres. for Research, Dean of Grad. School, Pennsylvania State Univ. 1993–96; Louis A. Bantle Prof. of Business and Govt Policy, Maxwell Grad. School of Citizenship and Public Affairs, Syracuse Univ., NY 1996–2001, Univ. Prof. and Howard G. and S. Louise Phanstiel Chair in Strategic Man. and Leadership 2014–; Dir Nat. Security Studies, Syracuse Univ. and Johns Hopkins Univ. 1996–2001; Deputy Dir Office of Man. and Budget March–Dec. 2001; Admin. NASA Dec. 2001–05 (resgnd); Chancellor Louisiana State Univ. 2005–08; CEO EADS North America (subsidiary of European Aeronautic Defence and Space Co. NV) 2009–14, Chair. 2012–14; Vice-Chair. Exec. Cttee, Nat. Defense Industrial Asscn –2011, Chair. 2011–; Distinguished Sr Advisor Center for Strategic and Int. Studies (CSIS) 2014–; mem. Bd of Dirs Computer Sciences Corporation (now DXC Technology) 2014–15, Airbus Group, Inc. –2014, CSRA Inc. 2015–18; mem. Bd of Advisors Naval Postgraduate School; Fellow, Nat. Acad. of Public Admin, Int. Acad. of Astronautics; survived a plane crash nr Aleknagik, Alaska 2010; Hon. Engineer of the Year Award, Engineer's Council 2005; Distinguished Public Service Award 1993, Chancellor's Award for Public Service, Syracuse Univ. 1999, Public Service Award, Dept of the Navy 2000, Navigator Award, Potomac Inst. for Policy Studies 2005, inducted into Louisiana Political Hall of Fame 2007, Arents Award for Excellence in Public Service, Syracuse Univ. 2011, Asteroid 78905 Seanokeefe named in his honour. *Publications:* The Defense Industry in the Post-Cold War Era: Corporate Strategies and Public Policy Perspectives (co-author) 1998, Keeping the Edge: Managing Defense for the Future (contrib.) 2000; several journal articles. *Address:* Maxwell School of Citizenship and Public Affairs, Syracuse University, 309 Eggers Hall, Syracuse,

NY 13244-1020, USA (office). *Telephone:* (315) 443-8583 (office). *E-mail:* scokeefe@maxwell.syr.edu (office). *Website:* www.maxwell.syr.edu (office).

O'KEEFFE, Michael, BSc, PhD, DSc; American (b. British) chemist and academic; *Regents' Professor Emeritus and Research Professor Emeritus of Chemistry, Arizona State University;* b. 3 April 1934, Bury St Edmunds, Suffolk; ed Univ. of Bristol, UK; Research Scientist, Mullard Research Labs and Philips Research Labs, UK 1958–60; Postdoctoral Assoc., Indiana Univ., USA 1960–63; Asst Prof., Arizona State Univ. 1963–66, Assoc. Prof. 1966–70, Prof. 1970–94, Regents' Prof. and Research Prof. of Chem. 1994, now Prof. Emer. *Publications:* three books, including Crystal Structures: Patterns & Symmetry (with Bruce Hyde); more than 280 papers in professional journals. *Address:* PSC-208, Physical Sciences Building, Department of Chemistry and Biochemistry, Arizona State University, Tempe, AZ 85287-1604, USA (office). *Telephone:* (480) 965-3670 (office). *Fax:* (480) 965-2747 (office). *E-mail:* mokeeffe@asu.edu (office). *Website:* chemistry.asu.edu/faculty/M_Okeeffe.asp (office); www.public.asu.edu/~rosebudx/okeeffe.htm (office).

OKEKE, Francisca Nneka, PhD, FAS; Nigerian physicist, space scientist and academic; *Professor of Physics, University of Nigeria, Nsukka;* Visiting Research Fellow, Univ. of Natal, South Africa 1998; Prof. of Physics, Univ. of Nigeria, Nsukka 2000–, Head of Dept of Physics and Astronomy (first woman) 2003–06, Dean, Faculty of Physical Sciences 2008–10 (first woman); research visits to Harvard Smithsonian Centre, USA 2004, Morgan State Univ., USA 2003, etc.; Fellowship Int. Award (as Fellow, Japan Soc. for Promotion of Science), Univ. of Tokyo 1999–2000, Visiting Assoc., CPTEC Brazil, Laureate for Africa and Arab States, L'Oréal-UNESCO Awards for Women in Science 2013. *Publications:* several physics textbooks and numerous papers in professional journals. *Address:* Department of Physics and Astronomy, Faculty of Physical Sciences, University of Nigeria, Nsukka, Nigeria (office). *Telephone:* 803-5079686 (mobile) (office). *E-mail:* francisca.okeke@unn.edu.ng (office); franciscaokeke@yahoo.com (home). *Website:* www.unn.edu.ng/profile/prof-francisca-nneka-okeke (office).

O'KENNEDY, Michael, MA; Irish politician and barrister; b. 21 Feb. 1936, Nenagh, Co. Tipperary; s. of Eamonn O'Kennedy and Helena (Slattery) O'Kennedy; m. Breda Heavey 1965; one s. two d.; ed St Flannan's Coll., Ennis, Univ. Coll. Dublin, King's Inns, Dublin; practised as barrister 1961–70, as Sr Counsel 1973–77, 1982–; mem. Senate 1965–69, 1993–, Front Bench Spokesman on Educ. and Justice, Senate Statutory Instruments Cttee on the Constitution until 1967; mem. Dáil for N Tipperary 1969–80, 1982–93, 1997–2002; presidential cand. 1997; Parl. Sec. to Minister of Educ. 1970–72, Minister without Portfolio 1972–73, Minister for Transport and Power 1973; Opposition Spokesman on Foreign Affairs 1973–77; Minister for Foreign Affairs 1977–79, of Finance and Public service 1979–80, for Economic Planning and Devt 1979–80; mem. Comm. of European Communities 1980–82; Commr for Personnel, Consumer Affairs, Environment 1981–82; Opposition Spokesman for Finance 1982–87, Minister of Agric. 1987–92; Pres. Bd of Govs. European Investment Bank 1980; mem. All-Parties Cttee on Irish Relations, Chair. 1973–80; mem. Informal Cttee on Reform of Dáil Procedure until 1972, Dáil and Senate Joint Cttee on Secondary Legislation of EEC 1973–80, Anglo-Irish Parl. Body 1993– (Co-Chair. 1997–); mem. Inter-Parl. Union, mem. Exec. of Irish Council of European Movt; Pres. EEC Council of Ministers July–Dec. 1979; Pres. EC Council of Agric. Ministers Jan.–June 1990; Pres. Re-negotiation EEC/ACP at 2nd Lomé Convention 1979; Nat. Trustee Fianna Fáil. *Leisure interests:* reading, philosophy, history, politics, drama, music, sports. *Address:* Gortlandroe, Nenagh, Co. Tipperary, Ireland. *Telephone:* (67) 31366 (home).

OKETA, Gazmend; Albanian engineer and politician; b. 14 Dec. 1968, Durrës; s. of Nuri Oketa; m.; two c.; ed General High School 'Gjergj Kastrioti', Durrës, Faculty of Civil Eng, Tirana Polytechnic Univ., Siegen Univ., Germany; Prof., Faculty of Civil Eng, Tirana 1994–95; Specialist of World Bank project on water supply rehabilitation, Durrës 1995–97; designing engineer and pvt. admin. in pvt. construction enterprises 1997–2003; adviser to Voith Siemens (Austria), project on Bistrica hydroelectric power station rehabilitation 2003–04; mem. Democratic Party of Albania (Partia Demokratike e Shqipërisë), Deputy Head of DPA, Durrës Br. 2004, Head of DPA and Spokesman Nov. 2005; mem. Durrës Municipal Council 2003–05; mem. Parl. for Durrës City, Zone No. 29 2005–, mem. Parl. Comm. for Legal Issues, Public Admin and Human Rights; Successive Pres. Cen. European Initiative Parl. Dimension Jan. 2006; Deputy Prime Minister 2007–08; Minister of Defence 2008–09. *Address:* c/o Partia Demokratike e Shqipërisë, Rruga Punëtorët e Rilindjes 1, Tirana, Albania (office). *Telephone:* (4) 2228091 (office). *Fax:* (4) 2223525 (office). *E-mail:* profsberisha@albaniaonline.net (office). *Website:* www.partiademokratike.al (office).

OKIHARA, Takamune; Japanese banking executive; *Chairman, Mitsubishi UFJ Financial Group Inc.;* Exec. Officer, Sanwa 2001–02; Exec. Officer, UFJ Bank Ltd 2002–03, Sr Exec. Officer 2003–04, Pres. and CEO 2004–05, Man. Officer and Group Head of Integrated Corp. Banking Business Group, Mitsubishi UFJ Financial Group, Inc. 2005–06, Deputy Pres. and Chief Exec., Commercial Banking Business Unit, Bank of Tokyo-Mitsubishi UFJ Ltd 2006–08, Deputy Chair. Bank of Tokyo-Mitsubishi UFJ Ltd 2008–10, Chair. Mitsubishi UFJ Financial Group, Inc. 2010–; Dir UFJ Central Leasing Co. Ltd 2005–, Bank of Tokyo-Mitsubishi UFJ Ltd 2006–, UFJ Holdings Inc. *Address:* Mitsubishi UFJ Financial Group Inc., 7-1, Marunouchi 2-chome, Chiyoda-ku, Tokyo 100-8330, Japan (office). *Telephone:* (3) 3240-8111 (office). *Fax:* (3) 3240-8203 (office). *Website:* www.mufg.jp (office).

OKITUNDU, Léonard She, LLB; Democratic Republic of the Congo politician, diplomatist and lawyer; b. 26 March 1946; s. of Dovell Okitundu and Kitenge Avoki; ed Congo Univ., Lovanium Univ. of Kinshasa, Univ. of Lausanne, Switzerland; lawyer, Amnesty International (Swiss chapter), Offices of Legal Consultation, Caritas–Switzerland, Caritas–GENEVE 1982–97; legal consultant to numerous int. human rights orgs; Amb. (itinerant) of Democratic Repub. of the Congo 1997; Minister of Human Rights 1998, of Foreign Affairs and Int. Co-operation 2001–02; Deputy Prime Minister and Minister of Foreign Affairs and Regional Integration 2016–19; mem. Vaud SOS–Asylum, Swiss League of Human Rights, Swiss Cttee for the Defence of the Right of Asylum (CSDDA), European Network of Lawyers Defending the Right of Asylum (ELENA); Chief of Staff to Pres. Joseph Kabila 2003–06; mem. Sénat for Sankuru 2006–. *Address:* c/o Ministry of Foreign Affairs and Regional Integration, Place de l'Indépendance, BP 7100, Kinshasa-Gombé, Democratic Republic of the Congo (office).

OKOGIE, HE Cardinal Anthony Olubunmi, STL, DD; Nigerian ecclesiastic; *Archbishop Emeritus of Lagos;* b. 16 June 1936, Lagos; s. of Prince Michael Okogie and Lucy Okogie; ed St Gregory's Coll., Lagos, St Theresa Minor Seminary, Ibadan, St Peter and St Paul's Seminary, Ibadan, Urban Univ., Rome; ordained priest 1966; Acting Parish Priest, St Patrick's Church, Idumagbo, Lagos; Asst Priest, Holy Cross Cathedral, Lagos; Religious Instructor, King's Coll., Lagos; Dir of Vocations, Archdiocese of Lagos; Man. Holy Cross Group of Schools, Lagos; Master of Ceremonies, Holy Cross Cathedral; broadcaster of religious programmes, NBC-TV; apptd Titular Bishop of Mascula 1971; Auxiliary Bishop of Oyo Diocese 1971–72; Auxiliary Bishop to the Apostolic Admin., Archdiocese of Lagos 1972–73; Archbishop of Lagos 1973–2012, Archbishop Emer. 2012–; cr. Cardinal (Cardinal-Priest of Beata Vergine Maria del Monte Carmelo a Mostacciano) 2003; participated in Papal Conclave 2005, 2013; Vice-Pres. Catholic Bishops' Conf. of Nigeria 1985–88, Pres. 1988–94; Nat. Pres. Christian Asscn of Nigeria 1988–96; mem. Prerogative of Mercy, Religious Advisory Council; Commdr, Order of the Niger 1999. *Leisure interests:* reading, watching films, table tennis. *Address:* Archdiocese of Lagos, 19 Catholic Mission Street, PO Box 8, Lagos, Nigeria (office). *Telephone:* (1) 2635729 (office). *Fax:* (1) 2633841 (office). *E-mail:* arclagos@yahoo.com.

OKONJO-IWEALA, Ngozi, AB, PhD; Nigerian economist, politician and international organization official; b. 13 June 1954; m. Ikemba Iweala; four c.; ed Harvard Univ., Massachusetts Inst. of Tech., USA; joined World Bank 1982, various positions including Economist, Country Dir in E Asia Region responsible for Malaysia, Cambodia, Laos and Mongolia 1997–99, Dir of Operations Middle East Region 2001–02, Vice-Pres. and Corp. Sec., World Bank Group 2002–03, Man. Dir 2007–11; Adviser on Econ. Issues to Pres. of Nigeria 2000; Minister of Finance and Economy (first woman) 2003–06, 2011–15, of Foreign Affairs (first woman) June–Aug. 2006 (resgnd); Distinguished Visiting Fellow, Global Economy and Devt Program, Brookings Inst., Washington, DC 2007; Founder NOI-Gallup polls; Co-founder African Inst. for Applied Econs, Enugu (apptd Chair.), Makeda Fund; mem. bd of Dirs Twitter Inc. 2018–; mem. bd several NGOs and think-tanks, including DATA, World Resources Inst., Clinton Global Initiative, Nelson Mandela Inst. and African Insts of Science and Tech., Mo Ibrahim Foundation Governance Prize Cttee, Friends of the Global Fund Africa; Hon. LLD (Brown Univ.) 2006, (Colby Coll.) 2007, Hon. DHumLitt (Northern Caribbean Univ., Jamaica), Dr hc (Trinity Coll., Dublin); Euromarket Forum Award for Vision and Courage 2003, Time Magazine European Hero 2004, This Day Nigeria Minister of the Year 2004, 2005, Euromoney Magazine Global Finance Minister of the Year 2005, Financial Times/The Banker African Finance Minister of the Year 2005. *Publications include:* The Debt Trap in Nigeria: Towards a Sustainable Debt Strategy (co-ed.), several papers in devt journals.

OKOUNKOV, Andrei Yurovich, PhD; Russian mathematician and academic; *Samuel Eilenberg Professor of Mathematics, Columbia University;* b. 26 July 1969, Moscow; two d.; ed Moscow State Univ.; fmr Research Fellow, Dobrushin Math. Lab., Inst. for Problems of Information Transmission, Russian Acad. of Sciences; has taught at Inst. for Advanced Study in Princeton and Univ. of Chicago; Asst Prof., Univ. of California, Berkeley –2002; Prof., Princeton Univ. 2002–10; Samuel Eilenberg Prof. of Math., Columbia Univ., New York 2010–; Sloan Research Fellowship 2000, Packard Fellowship 2001; European Math. Soc. Prize 2004, Fields Medal (co-recipient) 2006. *Publications:* numerous papers in professional journals on probability, representation theory, algebraic geometry and math. physics. *Leisure interests:* cooking, playing football and ping-pong, reading. *Address:* Columbia University, Mathematics Department, Room 617, MC 4416, 2990 Broadway, New York, NY 10027, USA (office). *Telephone:* (212) 854-3988 (office). *Fax:* (212) 854-8962 (office). *E-mail:* okounkov@math.columbia.edu (office). *Website:* www.math.columbia.edu (office).

OKOUR, Abdul Rahim, BA; Jordanian politician; b. 1939; ed Univ. of Damascus; worked as secondary school teacher for two years; fmr Lecturer, Howwara Coll., Yarmouk Univ.; served 22 years in various civil service positions; mem. House of Reps, Majlis al-Umma for eight years; fmr mem. Consultative Council, Irbid Governorate; fmr mem. Islamic Action Front (IAF); apptd Minister of State for Parl. Affairs 2007, of Awqaf (Religious Endowments) and Islamic Affairs 2011.

OKPAKO, David Tinakpoevwan, PhD, CBiol, FIBiol, FNIBiol, FAAS, FAS, FRPharmS; Nigerian pharmacologist and pharmacist; b. 22 Nov. 1936, Owahwa, Delta; s. of Okun Okoro-Okpako Tsere and Obien Rebayi-Tsere; m. Kathleen Gweneth Jones-Williams 1967; one s. one d.; ed Urhobo Coll. Effurun, Nigerian Coll. of Arts, Science & Tech. Ibadan, Univ. of Bradford and Univ. Coll., London; Visiting Fellow, Corpus Christi Coll., Cambridge 1973–74, 1983–84; Prof. and Head, Dept of Pharmacology and Therapeutics, Univ. of Ibadan 1978–81, 1986–87, Dean, Faculty of Pharmacy 1987–91; Pres. W African Soc. for Pharmacology 1987–90; Foundation Pres. Nigeria Inst. of Biology 1990–92; Chair. Council, Nigerian Field Soc. 1991–2000; Visiting Prof., Univ. of the Western Cape, SA 1995–96; Visiting Fellow, Humanities Research Centre, ANU, Canberra 1996, Fitzwilliam Coll., Cambridge 1997; Visiting Scientist, Research Inst. Hosp. for Sick Children, Univ. of Toronto; now working as consultant pharmacist and pharmacologist. *Publications:* Principles of Pharmacology – A Tropical Approach 1991, 2001, Pharmacological Methods in Phytotherapy Research, Vol. 1. Selection, Preparation and Pharmacological Evaluation of Plant Material (with E. M. Williamson and F. J. Evans) 1996; articles in professional journals; several book chapters. *Leisure interests:* golf, tennis, reading, fishing. *Address:* PO Box 20334, University of Ibadan Post Office, Oyo Road, Ibadan (office); 22 Sankore Avenue, University of Ibadan, Ibadan, Nigeria (office). *Telephone:* (234) 28107602 (home). *E-mail:* dpc@skannet.com.ng (office).

OKREPILOV, Vladimir V., Dr.sc.oec; Russian economist; *General Director, TEST-St Petersburg;* b. 23 Feb. 1944, Leningrad; m.; two s.; ed Leningrad State Inst. of Mechanics; engineer, sr engineer-constructor, Leningrad factory of radiotechnology equipment 1965–70; Komsomol and CP service 1970–79; Chief Engineer, Research-Production Co. Mendeleyev VNIIM 1979–86; Dir Leningrad Centre of Standardization and Metrology of USSR State Cttee of Standards

1986–90; Gen. Dir TEST-St Petersburg 1986–; Prof., Head of Chair, St Petersburg Univ. of Econs and Finance; Pres. St Petersburg Br. of Acad. of Quality Problems; mem. Presidium Russian Acad. of Sciences 2003–, Acad. of Electrotechnological Sciences, St Petersburg Acad. of Eng, Int. Acad. of Ecological Sciences, Security of Man and Nature; Corresp. mem. Russian Acad. of Sciences 2000–; Merited Worker of Science and Tech. of Russian Fed., Order of Friendship of Peoples 1988, Order for Merits to the Fatherland, Fourth Grade 1997; hon. prize for merits in standardization 1984, State Prize of Russian Fed. 1997, Prize of Pres. of Russian Fed. for Educ. 2002. *Publications include:* more than 300 scientific publs. *Address:* Kurlyandskaya str. 1, St Petersburg 190103, Russia (office). *Telephone:* (812) 251-39-50 (office). *Fax:* (812) 251-41-08 (office). *E-mail:* letter@rustest.spb.ru (office). *Website:* www.rustest.spb.ru (office).

OKRI, Ben, OBE, FRSL, FRSA; Nigerian/British novelist, poet, essayist and short-story writer; b. 15 March 1959, Minna; s. of Silver Okri and Grace Okri; ed John Donne's School, Peckham, London, Children's Home School, Nigeria, Christ High School, Urhobo Coll., Univ. of Essex, UK; staff writer and librarian, Afriscope magazine 1978; Poetry Ed. West Africa magazine 1983–86; broadcaster with BBC 1983–85; Fellow Commoner in Creative Arts, Trinity Coll., Cambridge 1991–93; Visiting Prof. School of English, Univ. of Leicester 2012–; mem. Int. PEN, a Vice-Pres. English Centre of Int. PEN 1997–; mem. Bd Royal Nat. Theatre of GB 1999–2006; mem. Soc. of Authors, RSL (mem. of Council 1999–2004); Hon. Fellow, Mansfield Coll., Oxford 2014; Hon. DLitt (Westminster) 1997, (Essex) 2002, (Exeter) 2004, (SOAS, London) 2010; Dr hc (Universiteit voor het Algemeen Belang, Belgium) 2009; Hon. Dr of Arts (Bedfordshire) 2010; Aga Khan Prize for Fiction, Paris Review (for The Dream-Vendor's August) 1987, The Crystal Award, World Econ. Forum) 1995, Grinzane for Africa Mainstream Prize 2008, Int. Literary Award of Novi Sad, Serbia 2008. *Plays:* In Exilus (The Studio, Royal Nat. Theatre of GB) 2001, The Heart's Tent is Broken (Tristam Bates Theatre) 2011. *Television:* Great Railway Journey: London to Arcadia 1996. *Film:* (writer) N–The Madness of Reason 2014. *Publications include:* Flowers and Shadows 1980, The Landscapes Within 1982, Incidents at the Shrine (Commonwealth Writers Prize (Africa Region) 1987) 1986, Stars of the New Curfew 1988, The Famished Road (Booker Prize 1991, Premio Letterario Internazionale, Chianti Ruffino-Antico Fattore 1993, Premio Grinzane Cavour 1994) 1991, An African Elegy (poetry) 1992, Songs of Enchantment 1993, Astonishing the Gods 1995, Birds of Heaven (essays) 1996, Dangerous Love (novel) (Premio Palmi 2000) 1996, A Way of Being Free (non-fiction) 1997, Infinite Riches (novel) 1998, Mental Fight (epic poem) 1999, In Arcadia (novel) 2002, Starbook (novel) 2007, Tales of Freedom 2009, A Time for New Dreams (poetic essays) 2011, Wild (poetry) 2012, The Age of Magic (novel) 2014. *Leisure interests:* chess, music, travel, theatre, cinema, art, walking, good conversation, silence. *Address:* Rider Books, 20 Vauxhall Bridge Road, London SW1V 2SA (office); The Marsh Agency, 50 Albemarle Street, London, W1S 4BD, England (office). *Website:* www.marsh-agency.co.uk (office); benokri.co.uk.

OKRUASHVILI, Irakli; Georgian lawyer and politician; b. 6 Nov. 1973, Tskhinvali, South Ossetian Autonomous Oblast, Georgian SSR; s. of Koba Okruashvili and Eter Giguashvili; m. Irina Gordeladze; one d.; ed Tbilisi State Univ.; leading specialist, Elections Cen. Comm. 1995; consultant, TACIS project, State Service Div. 1996; lawyer, Korzadze, Svanidze & Okruashvili, Okruashvili & Partners 1996–2000; Lecturer in Int. Trade Law, Tbilisi State Univ. 1997–2001; Deputy Minister of Justice 2000–01; mem. Tbilisi Sakrebulo (City Ass.) 2002–, Head of Revision Comm. Nov. 2002; Pres.'s plenipotentiary in Shida Kartli Mkhare (region) Nov. 2003; Gen. Prosecutor Jan.–June 2004; Minister of Internal Affairs June–Dec. 2004, of Defence Dec. 2004–06, of Econ. Devt Nov. 2006; f. Movt for a United Georgia 2007, resgnd his position and joined with several politicians in Georgia to establish the Georgian Party Oct. 2010; mem. Georgian Young Lawyers' Asscn, World Lawyers' Asscn, Lawyers' Int. Asscn; sentenced in absentia to 11 years' imprisonment on corruption charges March 2008; granted asylum in France April 2008; returned to Georgia and arrested upon arrival at Tbilisi airport Nov. 2012, cleared of bribe-taking and extortion charges and released from court on bail Jan. 2013, awaiting trial on charges of negligence in Tbilisi City Court; candidacy for election as Mayor of Gori rejected by Cen. Electoral Comm. 2014. *Leisure interest:* hunting.

OKTAY, Fuat, MBA, PhD; Turkish politician and academic; *Vice-President;* b. 1964, Çekerek, Yozgat; m.; three c.; ed Çukurova Univ., Wayne State Univ., Detroit, USA; worked formanagement consultancies including KOSGEB and automotive industries including Ford, General Motors, Chrysler; fmr Vice-Dean and Head of Man. Dept, Beykent Univ.; Deputy Dir-Gen. responsible for strategic planning, business devt, sales, marketing, production planning and information tech., Turkish Airlines 2008–12; Chair. Disaster and Emergency Man., Presidency 2012–16; Undersecretary to Prime Ministry 2016–18; Vice-Pres. 2018–; mem. Steering Cttee for Turkish–English, Turkish–German and Turkish–Spanish Business Councils, Foreign Economic Relations Bd. *Address:* Cumhurbaşkanlığı Külliyesi, 06560 Beştepe, Ankara, Turkey (office). *Telephone:* (312) 5255555 (office). *Fax:* (312) 5255831 (office). *E-mail:* contact@tccb.gov.tr (office). *Website:* www.tccb.gov.tr (office).

OKU, Masayuki; Japanese banking executive; *Chairman and Representative Director, Sumitomo Mitsui Financial Group, Inc.;* joined Sumitomo Bank Corpn 1968, Dir 1994–, later Deputy Pres. and Head of Corp. Banking Unit and Head of Int. Banking Unit, Sumitomo Mitsui Banking Corpn (unit of Sumitomo Mitsui Financial Group Inc.), Man. Dir 1998–99, Man. Exec. Officer 1999–2001, Sr Man. Dir and Sr Exec. Officer 2001–02, Sr Man. Dir Sumitomo Mitsui Financial Group, Inc. 2002–05, Chair. 2005–, Pres. Sumitomo Mitsui Banking Corpn 2005–, Pres. and Rep. Dir Sumitomo Mitsui Banking Corpn (SMBC) Friend Securities Co. Ltd; Chair. Japanese Bankers Asscn; Exec. Dir Nikko Cordial Securities Inc.; Standing Auditor, Nankai Electric Railway Co. Ltd 2008–; Dir, Panasonic Corpn 2008–, Mitsui Oil Exploration Co. *Address:* Sumitomo Mitsui Financial Group, Inc., 1-2, Yurakucho 1-chome, Chiyoda-ku, Tokyo 100-0006, Japan (office). *Telephone:* (3) 5512-3411 (office). *Fax:* (3) 5512-4429 (office). *E-mail:* info@smfg.co.gp (office). *Website:* www.smfg.co.jp (office).

OKUDA, Hiroshi; Japanese automotive industry executive; *Senior Advisor, Toyota Motor Corporation;* b. 29 Dec. 1932; ed Hitotsubashi Univ.; fmr Exec. Dir Toyota Motor Corpn, Pres. and CEO 1995–99, Chair. 1999–2006, mem. Bd and Sr Advisor 2006–07, Sr Advisor 2007–; Chair. Nippon Keidanren (Japan Fed. of Employers' Asscns) 1999–2006, Japan Automobile Mfrs Asscn from 2000; mem. Prime Minister's Econ. Strategy Council of Japan 1998. *Achievement:* holds a 4th dan black belt in Judo. *Leisure interests:* reading, watching films. *Address:* Toyota Motor Corporation, 1 Toyota-cho, Toyota, Aichi 471-8571, Japan (office). *Telephone:* (565) 28-2121 (office). *Fax:* (565) 23-5800 (office). *Website:* www.toyota-global.com (office).

OKUDA, Norihiro, LLB; Japanese diplomatist; *Ambassador to Saudi Arabia;* b. 19 Aug. 1952; ed Univ. of Tokyo; joined Ministry of Foreign Affairs (MFA) 1975, intensive study programme in Arabic language (Egypt) 1976–79, Second Sec., Embassy in Cairo 1979–81, Staff mem., First Middle East Div., Middle Eastern and African Affairs Bureau, MFA 1981–83, Deputy Dir, Energy Affairs Div., Econ. Affairs Bureau 1983–85, Deputy Dir overseeing Ministry of Transport, Man. and Co-ordination Agency, Prime Minister's Office 1985–87, First Sec., Perm. Mission to UN New York 1987–90, First Sec., later Counsellor (Political Affairs), Embassy in Riyadh 1990–92, Legal Co-ordinator, Legal Affairs Div., Treaties Bureau, MFA 1992–93, Dir, Second Middle East Div., Middle Eastern and African Affairs Bureau 1993–95, Dir, Grant Aid Div., Econ. Co-operation Bureau 1995–97, Counsellor (Congressional Affairs), Embassy in Washington, DC 1997–99, Head of Chancery, Washington, DC 1999–2000, Deputy Dir-Gen. for Gen. Affairs, Econ. Affairs Bureau, MFA 2000–02, Deputy Dir-Gen., Middle Eastern and African Affairs Bureau 2002–04, Amb. to Afghanistan 2004–06, Dir-Gen., Middle Eastern and African Affairs Bureau, MFA 2006–08, Amb. and Perm. Rep. to UN, New York 2008–10, Amb. to Egypt 2010–13, to Canada 2013–15, to Saudi Arabia 2015–. *Address:* Embassy of Japan, PO Box 4095, Riyadh 11491, Saudi Arabia (office). *Telephone:* (11) 488-1100 (office). *Fax:* (11) 488-0189 (office). *E-mail:* info@jpn-emb-sa.com (office). *Website:* www.ksa.emb-japan.go.jp (office).

OKUDA, Takashi; Japanese business executive; joined Sharp Corpn 1978, Gen. Man. Global Procurement Dept, Global Procurement Operations Group 1996–97, Gen. Man. Global Procurement, Sharp Electronics (Malaysia) Sdn Bhd (SEM) and Gen. Man. Singapore Br. 1997–2000, Gen. Man. Procurement and Quality of Audio-Visual Systems Group 2000–01, Gen. Man. Visual Systems Div., Audio-Visual Systems Group 2001–02, Deputy Gen. Man. Audio-Visual Systems Group and Gen. Man. Visual Systems Div. 2002–05, Gen. Man. Audio-Visual Systems Group from 2005, later Gen. Man. Int. Production Planning Group, Exec. Officer and Gen. Man. Strategic Business Promotion of Growing Markets, Exec. Man. Officer, Gen. Man. Global Business, Admin and Manufacturing Promotion and Gen. Man. Global Business Group –2012, Rep. Dir, Pres. and CEO Sharp Corpn 2012–13; Dir, Permasteelisa SpA 2011–. *Address:* c/o Sharp Corpn, 22-22 Nagaike-cho, Abeno-ku, Osaka 545-8522, Japan. *E-mail:* info@sharp.co.jp.

OKULOV, Valery Mikhailovich; Russian pilot and business executive; b. 22 April 1952, Kirov; m. Yelena Yeltsin (d. of fmr Pres. Boris Yeltsin); one s. two d.; ed Acad. of Civil Aviation; navigator, instructor, Sverdlovsk aviation team 1976–85; leading navigator, First Deputy Gen. Dir Aviation Co. Aeroflot (now Aeroflot Russian Airlines JSC) 1996–97, Gen. Dir 1997–2009, also Chair. of Man. Bd; mem. Bd of Dirs JSC United Aircraft Corpn 2010–; fmr mem. Bd of Govs Int. Air Transport Asscn. *Leisure interest:* boating.

OKURUT, Mary Karooro, MA, DipEd; Ugandan lecturer, novelist and politician; *Minister for General Duties, Office of the Prime Minister;* b. 12 July 1954, Bushenyi; d. of Erinesti Karooro; m. Stanislaus Okurut (died 2014); five s. three d.; ed Makerere Univ.; Lecturer, Dept of Literature, Makerere Univ. 1981–93; Press Sec. to Pres. Museveni 1994–96; Commr Educ. Service Comm. 1996–99; mem. Parl. (Nat. Resistance Movt) for Bushenyi Dist 2001–; Minister of Information and Nat. Guidance 2011–12, of Gender, Labour and Social Devt 2012–15, of Security 2015–16, Minister for General Duties, Office of Prime Minister 2016–; Founder Uganda Women Writers Asscn; Woman Writer of the Millennium 1999. *Publications include:* The Invisible Weevil 1998, A Woman's Voice (Ed.) 1998, The Official Wife (Nat. Book Trust of Uganda 2004) 2003, The Switch 2016. *Address:* Office of the Prime Minister, Plot 9–11, Apollo Kaggwa Road, POB 341, Kampala, Uganda (office). *Telephone:* (41) 7770500 (office). *Fax:* (41) 4341139 (office). *E-mail:* ps@opm.go.ug (office). *Website:* opm.go.ug (office).

OKWO-BELE, Jean-Marie, MD, MPH; Democratic Republic of the Congo physician, epidemiologist, public health official and international organization official; *Director, Department of Immunization, Vaccines and Biologicals, World Health Organization;* b. 23 Feb. 1957, Bandundu, Belgian Congo (now Democratic Repub. of the Congo—DRC); ed Univ. of Zaïre Kinshasa Campus (now Univ. of Kinshasa), Johns Hopkins School of Hygiene and Public Health (now the Johns Hopkins Bloomberg School of Public Health), USA; Expanded Programme on Immunization (EPI) Man. at prov. and nat. levels, within EPI-Combatting Child Communicable Diseases Div., Dept of Health, DRC 1982–89; Medical Officer with WHO/African Region 1989–2002; Regional Adviser, Vaccine-Preventable Disease Unit, WHO African Regional Office 1993–2002; Chief of Immunization Activities, UNICEF HQ, New York, USA 2002–04; Dir Dept of Immunization, Vaccines and Biologicals, WHO, Geneva, Switzerland 2004–; directed Polio Eradication Initiative in Africa 1993–2002; ensured oversight and co-ordination of devt of WHO/UNICEF Global Immunization Vision and Strategy for 2006–2015 (adopted by World Health Ass. 2005). *Address:* World Health Organization, Avenue Appia 20, 1211 Geneva 27, Switzerland (office). *Telephone:* (22) 791-21-11 (office). *Fax:* (22) 791-31-11 (office). *E-mail:* info@who.int (office). *Website:* www.who.int (office).

OLAFSSON, Thröstur; Icelandic government official and business consultant; b. 4 Oct. 1939, Husavík; m. 1st Monika Büttner 1966 (divorced); m. 2nd Thorunn Klemenzdóttir 1975; three s. one d. (and one s. deceased); ed Akureyri Gymnasium, Free Univ. of Berlin, Ruhr Univ., Bochum, Germany; economist, Nat. Bank of Iceland 1968–69, Civil Servants' Org. 1969–71; specialist adviser to Minister of Industry 1971–73; Man. Dir Mál og Menning (publishing co.) 1973–80; Asst to Minister of Finance 1980–83; Man. Dir, Gen. Workers and Transport Union 1983–88; Exec. Dir Mikligarður Ltd 1989–90; Political Asst to Minister of Foreign Affairs 1991–95; Chair. Cen. Bank of Iceland 1994–98; Sec.-Gen. Social Democratic Party's Parl. Group 1995–97; consultant 1997–98; Chair. Icemarkt Ltd 1989–99, Icelandic Int. Devt Agency 1991–95, Social Housing Co. Felagsbustadir Ltd, Minjavernd (Icelandic Heritage Inst.), Reykjavik Forestry Soc. 2007; Gen. Man. Iceland Symphony Orchestra 1998–2009; mem. Bd Edda Ltd (publishing co.); mem. Admin. Council of Europe Devt Bank 1995–2004. *Publications:* numerous articles on Icelandic econs and politics. *Leisure interests:* music, literature, skiing, forestry.

OLARREAGA, Manuel; Uruguayan academic; b. 1 June 1937, Salto; s. of Manuel Olarreaga and Hilda Leguisamo; m. Marina Rico 1966; three s.; ed Univ. of Paris; Minister-Counsellor, Uruguay's Perm. Del. to GATT 1982–87; First Exec. Sec. Latin American and Caribbean Program of Commercial Information to Support Foreign Trade 1988–91; Co-ordinator, Admin. Secr., Mercado Común del Sur, (Mercosur) 1991–96, Head Regulations Div. 1997–2003, Ed. Official Bulletin of Mercosur 1997–2003; apptd Prof. of Int. Marketing, Catholic Univ. of Uruguay 1993; Chair. Cttee of Countries Participating in Protocol Relating to Trade between Developing Countries, GATT; Deputy Chair. 18th, 19th and 20th Consultative Groups, UNCTAD-GATT Int. Trade Centre. *Publications:* several publs on int. trade. *Leisure interests:* reading, collecting antique keys. *Address:* Tomás Diago 769, Apartment 601, CP 11300, Montevideo, Uruguay (home). *Telephone:* (2) 710-24-33 (home). *E-mail:* olarreaga@hotmail.com.

ÓLASON, Vésteinn, PhD; Icelandic academic and university administrator; *Professor Emeritus, University of Iceland;* b. 14 Feb. 1939, Höfn; s. of Óli K. Gudbrandsson and Adalbjörg Gudmundsdóttir; m. Unnur Alexandra Jónsdóttir 1960; one s. one d.; ed Menntaskólinn Laugarvatni, Univ. of Iceland Háskóli Íslands, Univ. of Iceland; Lecturer in Icelandic Language and Literature, Univ. of Copenhagen 1968–72; Lecturer in Comparative Literature, Univ. of Iceland 1972–80, Docent in Icelandic Literature 1980–85, Prof. of Icelandic Literature 1991–2009, Dean, Faculty of Arts 1993–95, Prorektor 1993–94, Dir Árni Magnússon Inst. 1999–2009, now Prof. Emer.; Prof. of Icelandic, Univ. of Oslo 1985–91; mem. Icelandic Soc. of Sciences and Letters 1983–, Norwegian Acad. of Sciences and Letters 1994–, Icelandic Research Council 1994–, Royal Gustaf Adolf Acad. of Letters 1999–, Royal Norwegian Soc. of Sciences and Letters 2000–, Soc. of Antiquaries London 2005–; Hon. mem. Soc. of Antiquaries of London 2005; Iceland Literary Prize for Non-Fiction 1993, Gad Rausing Prize, Royal Swedish Acad. of Letters, History and Antiquities 2010. *Publications include:* Sagnadansar: Edition and Study 1979, The Traditional Ballads of Iceland 1982, Islensk Bókmenntasaga I–II (History of Icelandic Literature 870–1720) 1992–93, Dialogues with the Viking Age: Narration and Representation in the Sagas of the Icelanders 1998, Eddukvæði: Edition and Study with Jonas Kristjansson 2014; more than 100 articles in professional publs. *Address:* Klapparsti gur 5, 101 Reykjavik, Iceland. *Telephone:* 8917062. *E-mail:* vesteinn@hi.is.

OLAYAN, Khaled S., BS, MBA; Saudi Arabian business executive; *Chairman, Olayan Group;* b. 4 July 1945, Unayzah; s. of Suliman Saleh Olayan; m. Dunia Master of Science Al-Saawi 1984; three c.; ed in Saudi Arabia and Lebanon, Menlo Coll., Calif. and American Univ., Washington, DC, USA; following return to Saudi Arabia, worked with Ministry of Finance 1973, Nat. Economy; Vice-Pres. Gen. Contracting Co., Saudi Arabia 1974–75; joined The Olayan Group 1974, Exec. Vice-Pres. 1976–77, Vice-Chair. Olayan Financing Co. 1978–79, Chair. Olayan Group 2002–, Olayan Saudi Holding Co. (OSHCO) 1980, serves on bds of numerous Olayan joint ventures; has also been on bds of several outside cos; mem. Bd of Dirs Dhahran Int. Exhibition Co. 1984–90, Saudi Livestock Transport Co. 1986–92, Saudi Refrigerated Transportation Co. 1986–94, Riyad Bank 1989–95, Saudi Cement Co. 1992, Man. Dir 1995; apptd to Eastern Prov. Council 1997; mem. Bd of Dirs Saudi British Bank (SABB) 2002–, Chair. 2009–. *Leisure interests:* reading (especially the works of Naguib Mahfouz, Ahmed Shawky, Ilya Abumadi and Taha Hussein, as well as historical stories, biographies and poetry, especially the works of Khaled Al-Faisal), sports, travelling, meeting people. *Address:* Olayan Financing Co., PO Box 8772, Riyadh 11492, Saudi Arabia (office). *Telephone:* (1) 474-9000 (office). *Fax:* (1) 474-9108 (office). *E-mail:* info@olayan.com (office). *Website:* www.olayan.com (office).

OLAYAN, Lubna Suliman, BSc, MBA; Saudi Arabian business executive; *CEO and Deputy Chairperson, Olayan Financing Group;* b. 4 Aug. 1955; d. of Suliman Saleh Olayan and Maryam bint Jassim Al Abdulwahab; sister of Khaled S. Olayan; m. John Xefos; three d.; ed Cornell and Indiana Univs, USA; CEO and Deputy Chair. Olayan Financing Co. 1986–, mem. Bd of Dirs Olayan Investments Co. Establishment; Co-Chair. Arab World Competitiveness Forum, Geneva, Switzerland 2002; Dir (non-exec.) WPP 2005–; mem. Bd Chelsfield Plc (UK) 1996–2004, Saudi Hollandi Bank 2004–; mem. Int. Council of Institut Européen d'Admin des Affaires (INSEAD) 1997– (mem. Bd of Dirs INSEAD 2006–), Arab Business Council of World Econ. Forum, Int. Business Council of World Econ. Forum 2005–, Advisory Bd Effat Coll., Jeddah 2006–; mem. Int. Advisory Bds Council on Foreign Relations 2005–, Rolls Royce 2006–, Citigroup 2007–; mem. Bd Al Fanar 2006–, Down Syndrome Charitable Asscn, Riyadh 2005–; mem. Bd of Trustees, Arab Thought Foundation, Beirut 2002–, King Abdullah Univ. for Science and Tech. (KAUST) 2005–, Cornell Univ. 2007–; spokesperson for women's rights in the Middle East, first woman to speak at a 'mixed' conf. in Saudi Arabia, Jeddah Econ. Conf. 2004; Co-Chair. World Econ. Forum, Davos, Switzerland 2005; Middle East Award for Distinguished Businesswoman (UAE) 2003, named Female Exec. of the Year, Arabian Business Achievement Awards 2004, Arab Bankers Asscn of North America Achievement Award 2004, Distinguished Arabic Woman Award in the Businesswomen Sector in the Arab World, Sec.-Gen. Arab League, Cairo 2004. *Address:* Olayan Financing Group, PO Box 8772, Riyadh, Saudi Arabia (office). *Telephone:* (1) 477-9000 (office). *Fax:* (1) 478-9207 (office). *Website:* www.olayan.com (office).

OLAZÁBAL, José María; Spanish professional golfer; b. 5 Feb. 1966, Hondarribia (Fuenterrabía), Gipuzkoa, Basque Country; s. of Gaspar Olazábal and Julia Olazábal; won Italian Open, Spanish Open and British Boys' Amateur Championships 1983, Belgian Int. Youth Championship 1984, Spanish Open Amateur Championship 1984, British Youths' Amateur Championship 1985; turned professional 1985; winner Ebel European Masters Swiss Open 1986, Sanyo Open 1986, Volvo Belgian Open 1988, German Masters 1988, Tenerife Open 1989, KLM Dutch Open 1989, Benson & Hedges International Open 1990, 2000, Carroll's Irish Open 1990, Lancome Trophy 1990, NEC World Series of Golf 1990, 1994, Open Catalonia 1991, Epson Grand Prix of Europe 1991, The International (USA) 1991, Turespana Open de Tenerife 1992, Open Mediterrania 1992, Turespana Open Mediterrania 1994, US Masters 1994, 1999, Volvo PGA Championship 1994, Turespana Masters Open de Canarias 1997, Dubai Desert Classic 1998, Open de France 2001, Omega Hong Kong Open 2001, Buick

Invitational 2002, Mallorca Classic 2005; mem. European Ryder Cup Team 1987, 1989, 1991, 1993, 1997, 1999, Capt. of winning European Ryder Cup Team, Medinah Country Club, Ill., USA 2012, Vice-Capt. at Gleneagles, Scotland 2014 (winners); golf-course designer (15 designed); Prince of Asturias Award for Sports 2013. *Leisure interests:* cinema, music, hunting, wildlife, ecology. *Website:* www .europeantour.com/europeantour/players/playerid=729.

OLBRYCHSKI, Daniel; Polish actor; b. 27 Feb. 1945, Łowicz; m. 1st Monika Dzienisiewicz-Olbrychska 1967 (divorced 1977); one s.; m. 2nd Zuzanna Lapicka 1978 (divorced 1988); one d.; m. 3rd Krystyna Demska 2003; one s. with Barbara Sukowa; ed State Higher School of Drama, Warsaw; actor, Nat. Theatre 1969–77; best known for leading roles in several Andrzej Wajda films; mem. Polish Film Union; Officier des Arts et des Lettres 1986; State Prize (Second Class) 1974; numerous awards at Polish and foreign film festivals, including Stanislavsky Award at 29th Moscow Int. Film Festival 2007. *Roles include:* Koral in Wounded in the Forest 1964, Rafał Olbromski in Ashes 1965, boxer in Boxer 1966, Marek in Jowita 1967, Daniel in All for Sale 1968, Azja in Michael Wołodyjowski 1969, Angel of Death in Agnus Dei 1970, Tadeusz in Landscape After Battle 1970, Bolesław in The Birch Wood (Best Actor, 7th Moscow Int. Film Festival) 1971, Wit in Family Life 1971, Pan Młody in The Wedding 1972, Mateusz in Pilatus und Andere 1972, Kmicic in The Deluge 1974, Karol Borowiecki in The Promised Land 1975, Przybyszewski in Dagny 1976, Wiktor in The Maids of Wilko 1978, Jan in Little Tin Drum 1978, Saint-Genis in The Trout 1982, Pisarz in Flash-Back 1983, Love in Germany 1983, I'm Against 1985, Leon in Rosa Luxemburg 1986, Scope in Ga-ga 1986, Michał Kątny in Siekierezada 1986, Pitt in Tiger's Fight 1987, The Unbearable Lightness of Being 1988, Borys in Pestka 1995, Old Tuchajbej in With Fire and Sword 1998, Gerwazy in Last Foray in Lithuania 1999, Seweryn in It's Me, the Thief 2000, Szymon Gajowiec in The Spring to Come 2001, Prince of Elfs in The Hexer 2001, Konrad Sachs in Gebürtig (2002) 2002, Dyndalski in The Revenge 2002, Piastun in Stara basn. Kiedy slonce bylo bogiem 2003, Nitschewo 2003, Break Point 2004, Anthony Zimmer 2005, The Turkish Gambit 2005, Dwie strony medalu 2007, Taras Bulba 2008, A Man and His Dog 2009, Czas honoru as Doctor 2009–11, Salt as Vasily Orlov 2010, Józef Piłsudski in Battle of Warsaw 1920 2011, Hans Kloss: Stawka większa niż śmierć 2012. *Stage appearances:* Hamlet 1970, Rhett in Gone With the Wind, Rodric in Cyd 1985, Cześnik in Revenge 1998. *Television:* Raskolnikow in Crime and Punishment 1980, Chello 1985, Kean 1993, Milady (TV) 2004. *Leisure interests:* tennis, horses, family life.

OLDENBURG, Claes Thure, BA; American (b. Swedish) artist; b. 28 Jan. 1929, Stockholm, Sweden; s. of Gösta Oldenburg and Sigrid E. Oldenburg (née Lindforss); brother of Richard Oldenburg; m. Patricia Joan Muschinski 1960 (divorced 1970); m. Coosje van Bruggen 1977 (died 2009); ed Yale Coll. and Art Inst. of Chicago; arrived in USA 1929 (naturalized 1953); moved to New York City 1956; took up fabrication on large scale 1969; has worked in partnership with Coosje van Bruggen 1976–; mem. American Acad. of Arts and Letters, American Acad. of Arts and Sciences; Dr hc (Oberlin Coll.) 1970, (Art Inst. of Chicago) 1979, (Bard Coll.) 1995, (RCA) 1996, (Nova Scotia Coll. of Art and Design—NSCAD Univ.) 2005, (Coll. for Creative Studies, Detroit) 2005, (Pennsylvania Acad. of Fine Arts) 2011; Skowhegan Medal for Sculpture 1972, Brandeis Univ. Sculpture Award 1976, Art Inst. of Chicago Sculpture Award 1976, Medal American Inst. of Architects 1977, Wilhelm Lehmbruck Sculpture Award 1981, Wolf Foundation Prize for the Arts 1989, Brandeis Univ. Creative Arts Award for Lifetime Artistic Achievement 1993, Lifetime Achievement Award, Int. Sculpture Center, New York 1994, Distinction in Sculpture, New York 1994, Rolf Schock Foundation Stockholm 1995, Nathaniel S. Saltonstall Award, Boston 1996, National Medal of Arts, Washington, DC 2000, Partners in Educ. Award, Solomon R. Guggenheim Museum 2002, Medal Award, School of the Museum of Fine Arts, Boston 2004. *Public sculptures with Coosje van Bruggen include:* Trowel I, Rijkmuseum Kröller-Müller, Otterlo, The Netherlands 1971–76, Crusoe Umbrella, Nollen Plaza, Civic Center of Greater Des Moines, Ia 1979, Balancing Tools, Vitra International AG, Weil am Rhin, Germany 1984, Spoonbridge and Cherry, Minneapolis Sculpture Garden, Walker Art Center, Minn., Bicyclette Ensevelie Parc de la Villette, Paris 1990, Bottle of Notes, Central Gardens, Middlesbrough, UK 1993, Shuttlecocks, Nelson-Atkins Museum of Art, Kansas City, Mo. 1994, Saw Sawing, Tokyo Int. Exhbn Centre 1996, Soft Shuttlecocks, Guggenheim Foundation 1996, Ago, Filo e Nodo, Piazzale Cadorna, Milan 2000, Flying Pins, Eindhoven, Netherlands 2000, Dropped Clone, Neumarkt Galerie, Cologne, Germany 2001, Cupid's Span, San Francisco 2002, Big Sweep, Denver, Colo 2006. *Publications include:* Store Days 1967, Notes in Hand 1971, Raw Notes 1973, Multiples in Retrospect 1991; with Coosje van Bruggen: Claes Oldenburg: Sketches and Blottings Toward the European Desk Top 1990, Large Scale Projects 1994, Claes Oldenburg Coosje van Bruggen 1999, Down Liquidambar Lane: Sculpture in the Park 2001, Images á la Carte 2004. *Address:* 556 Broome Street, New York, NY 10013-1517, USA (office). *Telephone:* (212) 966-2290 (office). *Fax:* (212) 226-4315 (office). *E-mail:* office@oldenburgvanbruggen.com (office). *Website:* www.oldenburgvanbruggen .com (office).

OLDFIELD, Bruce, OBE; British fashion designer; *Managing Director, Bruce Oldfield Ltd;* b. 14 July 1950, brought up in Dr Barnardo's charity home, Ripon; ed Ripon Grammar School, Sheffield City Polytechnic, Ravensbourne Coll. of Art and St Martin's Coll. of Art; designed for Henri Bendel, New York and other stores 1973–74; freelance comms include film wardrobe for Charlotte Rampling 1974–75; first collection 1975; est. couture div. 1978; opened London boutique and redeveloped ready-to-wear collection with couture collection 1984–, opened Bruce Oldfield Wedding boutique at 34 Beauchamp Place, Knightsbridge 2009; British Rep., Australian Bicentennial Wool Collection Fashion Show, Sydney Opera House 1988; lectures: Fashion Inst., New York 1977, Los Angeles Co. Museum 1983, Int. Design Conf., Aspen, Colo (speaker and show) 1986; Vice-Pres. Barnardo's 1998–; mem. panel, Whitbread Literary Awards 1987; organized Bruce Oldfield for Barnardo's gala evenings attended by HRH The Princess of Wales 1985, 1988; Northern Personality of the Year Variety Club 1985; Gov. London Inst. 1999–2002; Trustee, Royal Acad. of Arts 2000–02; Hon. Fellow, Sheffield Hallam Univ. 1987, RCA 1990, Hatfield Coll. Durham 1991; Hon. DCL (Univ. of Northumbria at Newcastle) 2001; Hon. DUniv (Univ. of Cen. England) 2005; Hon. DL (Hull) 2009. *Television:* A Journey into Fashion (Tyne Tees TV documentary) 1990. *Publications:* Bruce Oldfield's Season (contrib.) 1987, Bruce Oldfield: Rootless (autobiog.) 2004. *Leisure interests:* music, reading, gardening, working, cooking, playing piano. *Address:* 27 Beauchamp Place, London, SW3 1NJ, England. *Telephone:* (20) 7584-1363. *Fax:* (20) 7761-0351. *E-mail:* hq@bruceoldfield.com (office). *Website:* www.bruceoldfield.com.

OLDMAN, Gary; British actor; b. 21 March 1958, New Cross, S London; m. 1st Lesley Manville; one s.; m. 2nd Uma Thurman (q.v.) 1991 (divorced 1992); m. 3rd Donya Fiorentino (divorced 2001); two c.; m. 4th Alexandra Edenborough 2008 (divorced 2015); m. 5th Gisele Schmidt 2017; ed Rose Bruford Drama Coll.; studied with Greenwich Young People's Theatre; acted with Theatre Royal, York and then with touring co.; appeared at Glasgow Citizens Theatre in Massacre at Paris, Chinchilla, Desperado Corner, A Waste of Time; London stage appearances: Minnesota Moon, Summit Conference, Real Dreams, The Desert Air (RSC), War Play I, II, III (RSC), Serious Money (Royal Court), Women Beware Women (Royal Court), The Pope's Wedding; appeared in The Country Wife, Royal Exchange Theatre, Manchester; Co-founder SE8 Group (production co.) 1995. *Films include:* Sid and Nancy 1986, Prick Up Your Ears 1987, Track 29 1988, Criminal Law 1988, We Think the World of You 1988, Chattahoochee 1989, State of Grace 1990, Rosencrantz and Guildenstern are Dead 1990, JFK 1991, Dracula 1992, True Romance 1993, Romeo is Bleeding 1993, Léon 1994, Immortal Beloved 1994, Murder in the First 1995, The Scarlet Letter 1995, Basquiat 1996, Nil by Mouth (producer, BAFTA Award) 1997, The Fifth Element 1997, Air Force One 1997, Lost in Space 1998, Anasazie Moon 1999, Plunkett & Macleane (exec. producer) 1999, The Contender (also exec. producer) 2000, Nobody's Baby 2001, Hannibal 2001, Interstate 60 2002, The Hire: Beat the Devil 2002, Tiptoes 2003, Sin 2003, Harry Potter and the Prisoner of Azkaban 2004, Who's Kyle? 2004, Dead Fish 2004, Batman Begins 2005, Harry Potter and the Goblet of Fire 2005, BackWoods 2006, The Legend of Spyro: A New Beginning (video game, voice) 2006, Harry Potter and the Order of the Phoenix 2007, The Legend of Spyro: The Eternal Night (video game, voice) 2007, The Legend of Spyro: Dawn of the Dragon (video game, voice) 2008, The Dark Knight 2008, Call of Duty: World at War (video game, voice) 2008, The Unborn 2009, Rain Fall 2009, A Christmas Carol 2009, Planet 51 (voice) 2009, The Book of Eli 2010, Tinker, Tailor, Soldier, Spy 2011, The Dark Knight Rises 2012, Lawless 2012, Guns, Girls and Gambling 2012, Paranoia 2013, RoboCop 2014, Dawn of the Planet of the Apes 2014, Child 44 2015, Man Down 2015, Criminal 2016, Darkest Hour (Golden Globe Award for Best Performance By An Actor In A Motion Picture, Drama 2018, Academy Award for Best Actor in a Leading Role 2018) 2017. *Television includes:* Remembrance, Meantime (Channel 4); Honest, Decent and True (BBC); Rat in the Skull (Central), The Firm, Heading Home, Fallen Angels. *Address:* c/o Douglas Urbanski, Douglas Management Inc., PO Box 691763, West Hollywood, CA 90069, USA (office); SE8 Group, 12 Great James Street, Camden, London, WC1N 3DR, England (office). *Telephone:* (310) 285-6090 (office). *Fax:* (310) 285-6097 (office). *Website:* www.douglasmanagementgroup.com (office).

OLDSTONE, Michael Beauregard Alan, MD, PhD; American neuropharmacologist and academic; *Professor, Department of Immunology and Microbial Science, Scripps Research Institute;* b. New York; m. Elizabeth Hoster Oldstone; ed Univ. of Maryland School of Medicine and Johns Hopkins McCullom Pratt Inst. of Biochemistry; Intern, Medicine, Univ. Hospital, Baltimore, Md 1962, Resident, Medicine 1963–64, Chief Resident, Neurology 1965–66; Postdoctoral Fellow, Dept of Experimental Pathology, Scripps Research Inst. 1966–69, Asst mem., Exp. Pathology 1969–71, Assoc. mem. of Immunopathology 1972–76, mem. Dept of Immunology 1977–89, Prof., Molecular and Integrative Neurosciences Dept 1989–2008, Prof., Dept of Immunology and Microbial Science 2008–, apptd Head, Div. of Virology and mem. Dept of Neuropharmacology 1989, currently Head, Viral-Immunobiology Lab., currently also Adjunct Prof., Dept of Neurosciences, School of Medicine, Univ. of California, San Diego; Resident Scholar (Prof.), Coll. of Arts and Sciences, Univ. of Alabama; mem. Nat. Advisory Cttee, PEW Scholars Program in the Biomedical Sciences, WHO Cttee for the Eradication of Poliomyelitis and Measles Virus; Ed. Virology; mem. Editorial Bd Current Topics in Microbiology and Immunology, Journal of Experimental Medicine, Immunity; mem. Inst. of Medicine of NAS 1996–, NAS 2008–, American Asscn of Physicians, American Soc. for Clinical Investigation, Scandinavian Soc. of Immunology; Fellow, American Acad. of Microbiology, AAAS; Burroughs Wellcome Professorship Award, Cotzias Award 1986, Abraham Flexner Award 1988, Rous-Whipple Award 1993, Biomedical Science Award, Karolinska Inst. (Sweden) 1994, J. Allyn Taylor Int. Prize in Medicine 1997, R.E. Dyer Lectureship and Directors Award, NIH 2000, Pioneer in NeuroVirology Award, Int. Soc. for NeuroVirology 2003, Excellence in Mentoring Award, American Asscn of Immunologists 2011. *Publications:* HIV and Dementia 1995, Transgenic Models of Human Viral and Immunology Disease 1995, Arenaviruses I: The Epidemiology, Molecular and Cell Biology of Arenaviruses 2002, Arenaviruses II: The Molecular Pathogenesis of Arenavirus Infections 2002; numerous articles in scientific journals. *Address:* Scripps Research Institute, Department of Immunology & Microbial Science (IMM-6), 10550 N Torrey Pines Road, La Jolla, CA 92037, USA (office). *Telephone:* (858) 784-8054 (office). *Fax:* (858) 784-9981 (office). *E-mail:* mbaobo@scripps.edu (office). *Website:* www.scripps.edu (office).

OLE-MOIYOI, Onesmo K.; Kenyan molecular biologist and immunologist; b. Tanzania; ed Harvard Coll. (Aga Khan Scholar) and Harvard Medical School, USA; looked after Maasai village cattle herd of 800 cows as a boy; Head of Biochemistry and Molecular Biology Lab. and Leader in Programme on Pathophysiology and Genetics, Int. Lab. for Research on Animal Diseases, Int. Livestock Research Inst., Nairobi 1987–2001; est. Inst. of Molecular and Cell Biology, Nairobi; Dir of Research and Partnerships, Int. Centre of Insect Physiology and Ecology (now African Insect Science for Food and Health—ICIPE), Nairobi 2001–07; fmr Asst Prof. and Capps' Scholar, Harvard Medical School; fmr Visiting Prof., Harvard School of Public Health; mem. Science Council for the Consultative Group of Int. Agricultural Research, Steering Cttees of HUGO (Human Genome Org.), among other appointments; Chair. Kenyatta Univ. Council in Kenya 2007, Kenya Agricultural Research Inst. 2009–14; Elder of the Order of the Burning Spear; Dr hc (Soka Univ., Japan); Kilby Int. Award 2003.

O'LEARY, Hazel, BA, JD; American lawyer, academic administrator and fmr government official; b. 17 May 1937, Newport News, Va; d. of Russell Reid and Hazel Palleman; m. John F. O'Leary 1980 (deceased); one s.; ed High School of Fine and Performing Arts, Newark, NJ, Fisk Univ., Rutgers Univ. Law School; fmr prosecutor, then an Asst Attorney-Gen., NJ; fmr mem. staff US Dept of Energy and Fed. Energy Admin.; Vice-Pres. and Gen. Counsel, O'Leary Assocs (consultants on energy econs and planning) 1981–89, 1997–2000; joined Northern States Power Co., Minn. 1989, subsequently Exec. Vice-Pres.; US Sec. of Energy 1993–97; COO Blaylock & Pnrs (investment banking firm), New York 2001–02; Pres. Fisk Univ., Nashville 2004–13; Dir Alchemix Corp., AES Corpn, ICF Kaiser Int. Inc.; Ind. Dir ITC Holdings Corp. 2007–16, Erin Energy Corpn 2010–16. *Address:* 4215 Harding Pike, Apt 301, Nashville, TN 37205-2029, USA.

O'LEARY, Michael Kevin; Irish airline industry executive; *CEO, Ryanair Holdings PLC;* b. 20 March 1961, Kanturk, Co. Cork; s. of Ted O'Leary and Ger O'Leary; m. Anita Farrall 2003; four c.; ed Clongowes Wood Coll., Co. Kildare, Trinity Coll. Dublin; trainee with Stokes Kennedy Crowley (later KPMG) 1984–86; Dublin property developer and financial adviser to Tony Ryan; Dir Ryanair Holdings PLC 1988–91, Deputy CEO 1991–93, COO 1993–94, CEO 1994–; breeds Aberdeen Angus cattle and horses at his Gigginstown House Stud, Co. Westmeath, his horses War of Attrition won the Cheltenham Gold Cup 2006, Rule the World won Grand Nat. 2016 and Tiger Roll won Grand Nat. 2018; European Businessman of the Year, Fortune Magazine 2001. *Leisure interests:* horse riding, farming, watching rugby, Manchester City Football Club. *Address:* Ryanair Ltd, Corporate Head Office, Airside Business Park, Swords, Co. Dublin, Ireland (office). *Telephone:* (1) 9451212 (office). *E-mail:* info@ryanair.com (office). *Website:* www.ryanair.com (office).

OLECHNOWICZ, Paweł, BEcons, PhD; Polish business executive; *Chairman, President and CEO, Grupa LOTOS SA;* b. 2 Jan. 1952, Puszcza Obalska; s. of Leon Olechnowicz and Janina Olechnowicz (née Rodziewicz); m. Krystyna Olechnowicz 1975; one s.; ed Acad. of Mining and Metallurgy, Krakow, INSEAD, Fontainebleau, France, Tech. Univ., Gdansk; Technologist, Zamech Mechanical Works, Elblag 1976–77, Foreman, Metallurgical Dept, 1977–80, Man. 1980–90, Gen. Man. Elzam and Zamech 1990, CEO ABB Zamech Ltd 1990–96, Dir Power Generation Div. 1993–96, Vice-Pres. Cen. and E Europe Power Generation Div. 1996–98; Vice-Pres. and Deputy CEO, ZML Kęty SA 1999–2000; Dir Pawel Olechnowicz Consulting 2001; Chair., Pres. and CEO Grupa Lotos SA (fmrly Rafineria Gdanska), Gdansk 2002–; mem. Polish Tech. Cttee, Det Norske Veritas Classification AS, Norway 1993–; Chair. Supervisory Bd Rekoenergo, Warsaw 1991; mem. Polish Council for Econ. Devt, Warsaw 1993; Dir Business Forum, Polish Higher Educ.; mem. Polish Centre Club, Int. Inst. of Man. Devt; Orderu Odrodzenia Polski 2011. *Leisure interests:* chess, sports, playing guitar and piano. *Address:* Grupa Lotos SA, ul. Elbląska 135, 80–718 Gdansk, Poland (office). *Telephone:* (58) 3087111 (office). *Fax:* (58) 3018838 (office). *E-mail:* lotos@grupalotos.pl (office). *Website:* www.lotos.pl (office).

OLECHOWSKI, Andrzej, MA, PhD; Polish politician, economist and writer; b. 9 Sept. 1947, Kraków; m. Irena Olechowska 1951; two s.; ed Cen. School of Planning and Statistics, Warsaw; Assoc. Econ. Affairs Officer, UNCTAD Multilateral Trade Negotiations Project, Geneva 1973–78; Head, Dept of Analysis and Projections, Foreign Trade Research Inst. Warsaw 1978–82; Econ. Affairs Officer, UNCTAD, Geneva 1982–84; Economist, IBRD, Washington, DC 1985–87; Adviser to Gov. Nat. Bank of Poland 1987; Dir World Bank Co-operation Bureau, Nat. Bank of Poland 1988; Dir Ministry of Foreign Econ. Relations 1988–89; Deputy Gov. Nat. Bank of Poland 1989–91; Sec. of State, Ministry of Foreign Econ. Relations and Chief Negotiator of Asscn Treaty with EU and Cen. European Free Trade Agreement 1991–92; Minister of Finance Feb.–May 1992; Sr Adviser, EBRD 1992–93; Econ. Adviser to Pres. of Repub. 1992–93, 1995; Minister of Foreign Affairs 1993–95; Chair. Bank Handlowy 1991–96, 1998–2000; presidential cand. 2000; Chair. Program Council, Civic Platform (Platforma Obywatelska—PO, a centrist political movt) 2001–04; fmrly European Deputy Chair. Trilateral Comm., now Chair. Polish Group; also currently Prof. Vistula Univ.; mem. Bd of Dirs Bank Handlowy, Euronet, MCI; mem. Advisory Bd Baltic Devt Forum, ACE, Citigroup Europe, Macquarie European Infrastructure Funds; Officer's Cross of Order of Polonia Restituta 2011; Kisiel Award 2000. *Publications include:* Wygrac przyszlosc; publs on int. trade and foreign policy. *Address:* ul. Traugutta 7/9, 00-067 Warsaw, Poland (office). *Telephone:* (22) 629-80-70 (office). *Fax:* (22) 692-50-09 (office). *E-mail:* a.olechowski@olechowski.pl (office). *Website:* www.olechowski.pl (office).

OLEKAS, Juozas; Lithuanian physician and politician; b. 30 Oct. 1955, Krasnoyarsk Krai, Russian SFSR, USSR; m. Aurelija Olekas; one s. two d.; ed Kaunas Medical Inst., Vilnius Univ.; worked at hosp. in Vilnius 1980–90; physician and sr researcher, Vilnius Univ. Microsurgery Centre 1982–89; participated in Sąjūdis (Lithuanian Movt for Reconstruction), elected mem. Seimas (Sąjūdis) 1988, People's Deputy of USSR 1989; mem. Lithuanian Del., Supreme Council of USSR 1989–91; Minister of Health 1990–92 (resgnd), 2003–04; surgeon, Vilnius Ambulance Univ. Hosp. 1993–94; Chief Physician, Vilnius Univ. Hosp. 1994; staff mem. Stomatology Clinic, Medical Faculty, Vilnius Univ. Hosp. 1994–99; mem. Social Democratic Party 1989–, mem. Seimas 1996–; Minister of Nat. Defence 2006–08, 2012–16; mem. Org. Comm., European Regional Bureau of WHO 1992–93; Chair. Lithuanian Trade Union Centre 1997; Medal of Independence 2000; Commdr's Cross, Order of Orange-Nassau (Netherlands) 2008, Order of the Cross of Terra Mariana (Second Class) (Estonia) 2013; Nat. Award of Lithuania 1998. *Publications include:* Gyvoji medicinos istorija (The History of Medicine Live) (compiler) 2004, Burnos, veido ir žandikaulių chirurgija (Mouth, Face and Jaws Surgery) (supervisor and co-author) 2008, Tikra Lauryno nesuaugusios lūpytės gydymo istorija (The True Story of Healing Little Laurynas's Cleft Lip) (educational book for children) 2009, Mažasis Ungutas. Išblaškyti ir sujungti likimai (Malyy Ungut: Fates Scattered and Connected) (co-author and ed.) 2013, Lietuva ir NATO: 10 metų kartu" (Lithuania and NATO: 10 Years Together) (co-author and ed.) 2014; more than 100 scientific articles. *Leisure interests:* gardening, sport, dancing, theatre. *Address:* Social Democratic Party, Barboros Radvilaites g. 1, Vilnius 01124 (office); Seimas, Gedimino pr. 53, Vilnius 01109, Lithuania. *Telephone:* (5) 239-6060 (Seimas) (office); (5) 261-5420 (office). *Fax:* (5) 239-6289 (Seimas) (office). *E-mail:* priim@lrs.lt (office); info@lsdp.lt (office). *Website:* www.lrs.lt; www.lsdp.lt (office).

OLESEN, Poul; Danish physicist and academic; *Professor Emeritus of Theoretical Physics, The Niels Bohr Institute, University of Copenhagen;* b. 28 April 1939, Ålborg; s. of Viktor Olesen and Herdis Olesen; m. Birgitte Sode-Mogensen

1984; ed Univ. of Copenhagen; Research Assoc., Univ. of Rochester, NY, USA 1967–69; Research Assoc., CERN, Geneva, Geneva 1969–71, Visiting Fellow 1985; Assoc. Prof. of Theoretical Physics, The Niels Bohr Inst., Copenhagen 1971–97, Prof. 1997–2009, Prof. Emer., The Niels Bohr Inst. 2009–, Chair. Research Cttee 1993–95, 2005–08, mem. Governing Body 1996–99; mem. Faculty of Science Council, Univ. of Copenhagen 1989–2005, Exec. Cttee 1990–93, Research Cttee 1998–2003; mem. Royal Danish Acad.; Hermer Prize. *Publications:* articles in int. journals on theoretical physics. *Leisure interests:* mountain biking. *Address:* The Niels Bohr Inst., Blegdamsvej 17, 2100 Copenhagen, Ø (office); Malmmosevej 1, 2840 Holte, Denmark (home). *Telephone:* 31-42-16-16 (office). *Fax:* 35-32-50-16 (office). *E-mail:* polesen@nbi.ku.dk (office). *Website:* www.nbia.dk (office).

OLI, K. P. Sharma; Nepalese politician; *Prime Minister;* b. 22 Feb. 1952, Terhathum Dist; s. of Mohan Prasad Oli and Madhumaya Oli; m.; mem. CP of Nepal 1970–, mem. Area Cttee 1970, Dist Cttee 1971, Head, Jhapa Movt Organizing Cttee 1972; imprisoned 1973–87; named Founding Leader Communist Party of Nepal (Marxist-Leninist) 1976, mem. Cen. Cttee 1987, Head of Lumbini zone –1990; Founding Leader Communist Party of Nepal (Unified Marxist-Leninist—UML) 1991, Chief, Cen. Dept of Int. Affairs 1992, Cen. Dept of Publicity 1993, Dept of Parl. Affairs 1995–2008, Cen. Dept of Party School, Chair. 2014–; mem. Standing Cttee and Head of Foreign Dept 1992–; Founder and Pres. Nat. Democratic Youth Fed. 1990; mem. House of Reps for Jhapa Dist 1991–2002, 2006–, Leader of Opposition 1999–2002; Minister for Home Affairs 1994–95; Deputy Prime Minister and Minister for Foreign Affairs 2006–07; mem. Constituent Ass. from Jhapa 2013–15, elected Leader of Parl. Party 2014; Prime Minister 2015–16, 2018–; mem. Presidium of Afro-Asian Peoples' Solidarity Org. (AAPSO) in Nepal 1994–2000, Pres. 2000. *Address:* Office of the Prime Minister, Singha Durbar, POB 23312, Kathmandu (office); Communist Party of Nepal (Unified Marxist-Leninist), Madan Nagar, Balkhu, POB 5471, Kathmandu (office); Balkot-4, Bhaktapur, Nepal (home). *Telephone:* (1) 4278081 (Communist Party) (office); (1) 4211000 (Office of the PM) (office); (1) 6630563 (home). *Fax:* (1) 4278084 (Communist Party) (office); (1) 4211065 (Office of the PM) (office). *E-mail:* uml@ntc.net.np (Communist Party) (office); sharmaoli@gmail.com. *Website:* www.cpnuml.org (Communist Party) (office); www.opmcm.gov.np (Office of the PM) (office); www.kpsharmaoli.com.

OLIPHANT, Patrick (Pat), DHumLitt; American political cartoonist, artist and sculptor; b. 24 July 1935, Adelaide, Australia; copyboy, press artist, Adelaide Advertiser 1953–55, cartoonist 1955–64; cartoonist, Denver Post 1964–75, Washington Star 1975–81; ind. cartoonist syndicated through Universal Press Syndicate 1980; retd in 2015; came out of retirement in 2017, published two images on Donald Trump; Hon. LHD (Dartmouth Coll.) 1981; Pulitzer Prize 1967, Reuben Award 1968, 1972, Nat. Cartoonist of Year Award 1971, 1973, 1974, 1984, 1989, 1990, 1991, Washington Journalism Review 'Best in the Business' Award 1985, Thomas Nast Prize (Germany), Premio Satira Politica of Italy. *Publications include:* The Oliphant Book 1969, Four More Years 1973, An Informal Gathering 1978, Oliphant, A Cartoon Collection 1980, The Jellybean Society 1981, Ban This Book 1982, But Seriously Folks 1983, The Year of Living Perilously 1984, Make My Day! 1985, Between Rock and a Hard Place 1986, Up to Here in Alligators 1987, Nothing Basically Wrong 1988, What Those People Need is a Puppy 1989, Oliphant's Presidents: Twenty-Five Years of Caricature 1990, Fashions for the New World Order 1991, Just Say No 1992, Waiting for the Other Shoe to Drop 1994, Off to the Revolution 1995, Maintain the Status Quo 1996, So That's Where They Came From 1997, Are We There Yet? 1999, Now We'll Have to Spray for Politicians! 2000, When We Can't See the Forest for the Bushes 2001, Leadership: Cartoon and Sculptures from the Bush Years 2008. *Address:* Universal Press Syndicate, 4520 Main Street, Suite 700, Kansas City, MO 64112 (office); c/o Susan Conway Gallery, 1214 Thirtieth Street NW, Washington, DC 20007, USA (office). *Telephone:* (505) 670-6266 (office). *E-mail:* susancconway@gmail.com (office). *Website:* www.ucomics.com/patoliphant (home).

OLIVA NEYRA, Carlos Augusto, PhD; Peruvian politician and economist; *Minister of Economy and Finance;* ed Universidad del Pacífico, Georgetown Univ.; Economist, Banco Interamericano de Desarrollo 1992–2000, External Adviser 2000–10; Deputy Minister of Economy and Finance 2011–15, Minister of Economy and Finance 2018–; Dir Banco Central de Reserva 2015–16, Master Program in Public Man., Universidad del Pacífico 2015–; Exec. Dir Governa 2002–11; Project Man., Basel Inst. on Governance, Switzerland 2015–; mem. Bd of Dirs Centro Nacional de Planeamiento Estratégico (Ceplan) 2015–. *Address:* Ministry of Economy and Finance, Jirón Junín 319, 4°, Circado de Lima, Lima 1, Peru (office). *Telephone:* (1) 3115930 (office). *E-mail:* postmaster@mef.gob.pe. *Website:* www.mef.gob.pe.

OLIVER, Jamie, MBE; British chef, restaurateur, television personality and cookery writer; b. (James Trevor Oliver), 27 May 1975; m. Jools Oliver 2000; two s. three d.; ed Westminster Catering Coll.; began cooking at parents' pub/restaurant The Cricketers, Clavering, Essex; fmr Head Pastry Chef, The Neal Street Restaurant; fmr Chef, The River Café; numerous TV series; advertising contract with Sainsbury's Co.; cookery show tour The Happy Days Tour, UK, NZ and Australia 2001; designed range of cooking and tableware for Royal Worcester; Consultant Chef, Monte's Restaurant, London; est. restaurant Fifteen, London 2003; est. Jamie's Italian chain of restaurants 2008; opened Barbecoa 2011; sometimes known as The Naked Chef; British Book Awards Outstanding Achievement Award 2006. *Television includes:* Presenter, The Naked Chef (Optomen TV) 1998–99, Pukka Tukka (Channel 4) 2000, Oliver's Twist 2002, Jamie's Kitchen 2002, Jamie's School Dinners (Channel 4, UK and internationally) 2005, Jamie's Great Italian Escape (Channel 4) 2005, Jamie's Kitchen Australia 2006, Jamie's Chef 2007, Jamie at Home 2007, Jamie's Fowl Dinners 2008, Jamie's Ministry of Food 2008, What's Cooking? with Jamie Oliver (video game) 2008, Jamie Saves Our Bacon (Channel 4) 2009, Jamie's American Roadtrip (Channel 4) 2009, Jamie's Family Christmas (Channel 4) 2009, Jamie Oliver's Food Revolution (ABC; aired in UK on Channel 4 as Jamie's American Food Revolution) (Emmy Award for Outstanding Reality Programme 2010) 2010–, Jamie Does… (Channel 4) 2010, Jamie's 30 Minute Meals (Channel 4) 2010–11, Jamie's Dream School 2011; other: twice guest-hosted Channel 4's The Friday Night Project, two appearances in 'Star in a Reasonably-Priced Car' segment of BBC 2's Top Gear, second British celebrity chef to appear as a challenger on Iron Chef America, starred as a judge in series Oprah's Big Give (ABC) 2008. *Publications include:* The Naked Chef (three cookery books), Jamie's Kitchen 2002, Jamie's Dinners 2004, Jamie's Italy 2005, Cook with Jamie 2006, Jamie at Home 2007, Jamie's Ministry of Food 2008, Jamie's America 2009, Jamie Does… 2010, Jamie's 30-Minute Meals: A Revolutionary Approach to Cooking Good Food Fast 2010, 5 Ingredients: Quick and Easy Food (Non-Fiction: Lifestyle Book of the Year, British Book Awards 2018) 2017. *Address:* 19–21 Nile Street, London, N1 7LL, England (office). *Telephone:* (20) 7566-1770 (office). *Fax:* (20) 7251-2749 (office). *Website:* www.jamieoliver.com (office).

OLIVER, Joseph (Joe), PC, BA, BCL, MBA; Canadian lawyer, politician and fmr investment banker; *Distinguished Senior Fellow, Montreal Economic Institute;* b. 20 May 1940, Montreal; m. Golda Goldman; two s.; ed McGill Univ., Rotman School of Man., Harvard Graduate School of Business; called to Quebec Bar; early career as investment banker with Merrill Lynch; sr positions with other investment dealers; fmr Exec. Dir Ontario Securities Comm.; Pres. and CEO Investment Dealers Asscn of Canada 1995–2007; mem. House of Commons for Eglinton-Lawrence (Conservative Party) 2011–15; Minister of Natural Resources 2011–14, of Finance 2014–15; Distinguished Sr Fellow, Montreal Econ. Inst. 2016–; Chair. Advisory Bd, Origin Merchant Partners 2016–; fmr Chair. Advisory Cttee, Int. Council of Securities Asscn; fmr Chair. Consultative Cttee, Int. Asscn of Securities Comms; mem. Canadian Inst. of Chartered Business Valuators; fmr Dir Canadian Securities Inst. Research Foundation. *Address:* Montreal Economic Institute, 910 Peel Street, Suite 600, Montreal, PQ H3C 2H8, Canada (office). *Telephone:* (514) 273-0969 (office). *Website:* www.iedm.org (office).

OLLIER, Patrick; French politician; *Mayor of Rueil-Malmaison;* b. 17 Dec. 1944, Périgueux, Dordogne; m. (divorced) one s.; pnr Michèle Alliot-Marie (q.v.); Founding mem. Union des jeunes pour le progrès 1965; participated in presidential campaign of Jacques Chaban-Delmas 1974; attached to Mayor of Rueil-Malmaison (Hauts-de-Seine) 1983–89; Deputy (RPR) for Hautes-Alpes 1988–2002, Vice-Pres. Nat. Ass. 1998–2002, Deputy (Union pour un Mouvement Populaire) for Hauts-de-Seine 2002–10, Pres. Nat. Ass. March–June 2007; Mayor of La Salle les Alpes (Hautes-Alpes) 1989–2001; mem. Conseil général, Hautes-Alpes 1992–2001; Pres. Cttee on Econ. Affairs, the Environment, and Territory, Head of French-Libyan Friendship Group; Mayor of Rueil-Malmaison, Hauts-de-Seine 2004–; apptd Political Advicer, UMP 2009, Vice-Pres. 2013; Minister in the Office of the Prime Minister, in charge of Relations with Parl. 2010–12; Del.-Gen. to Relations with the Parl. Groups 2015; Pres. Metropole of Greater Paris 2016; Hon. mem. Rotary-Club of Rueil-Malmaison. *Address:* Mairie de Rueil-Malmaison, 13 boulevard Foch, 92501 Rueil-Malmaison Cedex (office); 12 rue Hervet, 92500 Rueil-Malmaison, France (home). *Telephone:* 1-47-32-65-65 (office). *E-mail:* infos@patrick-ollier.com (office); contact@patrickollier2012.fr (office). *Website:* www.mairie-rueilmalmaison.fr (office); www.patrick-ollier.com (office).

OLLILA, Jorma Jaakko, MPolSci, MSc (Econs), MSc (Eng); Finnish business executive; *Advisory Partner, Perella Weinberg Partners;* b. 15 Aug. 1950, Seinäjoki; m. Liisa Annikki (née Metsola); two s. one d.; ed Univ. of Helsinki, London School of Econs, UK and Helsinki Univ. of Tech.; rank of Sr Lt; Account Man., Corporate Bank, Citibank N.A., London UK 1978–80; Account Officer, Citibank Oy 1980–82, mem. Bd of Man. 1983–85; Vice-Pres. Int. Operations, Nokia 1985–86, mem. Group Exec. Bd 1986–, Sr Vice-Pres. Finance 1986–89, Deputy mem. Bd of Dirs 1989–90, Pres. Nokia Mobile Phones 1990–92, Pres. and CEO Nokia 1992–99, Chair. Group Exec. Bd 1992–2006, mem. Bd Nokia Corpn 1995–2006, Chair. and CEO 1999–2006, Chair. 2006–12; Chair. (non-exec.), Royal Dutch Shell plc 2006–15, Chair. Nomination and Succession Cttee; Chair. Bd MTV Oy 1993–97; mem. Bd of Dirs Oy Dipoli Ab 1990–94, ICI PLC 1992–2000, Otava Books and Magazines Group Ltd 1996–, UPM-Kymmene 1997–; Dir (non-exec.) Ford Motor Co. 2000–; mem. Supervisory Bd, Oy Rastor AB 1992–93, Tietotehdas Oy 1992–95, Industrial Mutual Insurance Co., Pohjola Insurance Co. Ltd 1992–97, NKF Holding NV 1992–99, Pension-Varma Mutual Insurance Co. 1993–98, Sampo Insurance Co. Ltd 1993–2000, Merita Bank Ltd (fmr Union Bank of Finland Ltd) 1994–2000; Chair. Nat. Union of Finnish Students 1973–74; mem. Planning Bd for Defence Economy 1992–96; mem. Bd and Exec. Cttee Confed. of Finnish Industries and Employers 1992–2002, Deputy Chair. Bd 1995–2002; Chair. Supervisory Bd Finnish Foreign Trade Asscn 1993–98; Chair. Bd of Dirs and Supervisory Bd Finnish Business and Policy Forum 2004–, Research Inst. of the Finnish Economy 2004–; Vice-Chair. Bd, Finnish Section, Int. Chamber of Commerce 1993–97, Advisory Cttee Helsinki Univ. of Tech. 1993–95 (Chair. 1996–); Chair. Bd of Dirs, Outokumpu Oyj 2013–, Miltton Oy 2015–; Advisory Partner, Perella Weinberg Partners 2006–; mem. Bd Econ. Information Bureau 1993–97; mem. Exec. Bd Asscn for the Finnish Cultural Foundation 1993–99; mem. Council, Centre for Finnish Business and Policy Studies 1993–2001, Helsinki School of Econs and Business Admin 1993–98; mem. Supervisory Bd Foundation for Pediatric Research 1993–98, WWF Finland 1995–97; mem. Science and Tech. Policy Council of Finland 1993–2002; mem. Council of Supervisors, Research Inst. of the Finnish Economy 1993–2000; mem. Dean's Council, John F. Kennedy School of Govt, Harvard Univ. 1995–; Overseas Advisory Trustee, The American-Scandinavian Foundation 1994–; mem. Int. Bd United World Coll. 1995–; mem. European Round Table of Industrialists 1997– (Chair. 2005–09), GBDe Business Steering Cttee 1999–; Hon. Citizen of Beijing 2002; Hon. Fellow, LSE 2003; Hon. mem. IEEE 2003; Kt, First Class, Order of White Rose of Finland 1991, Commdr, 1st Class 1996; Commdr, Order of Orange-Nassau 1995, Order of White Star (Estonia) 1995, Officer's Cross, Order of Merit (Hungary) 1996; Commdr's Cross, Order of Merit of FRG 1997, Commdr's Cross, Order of Merit of the Repub. of Poland 1999, Commdr Grand Cross, Order of the Lion of Finland 2005, Hon. CBE 2008; Hon. PhD (Helsinki) 1995; Hon. DSc (Helsinki Univ. of Tech.) 1998. *Publication:* published his memoirs 2013. *Website:* www.pwpartners.com (office).

OLMERT, Ehud, BA, LLB; Israeli politician and lawyer; b. 30 Sept. 1945, Binyamina; m.; four c.; ed Hebrew Univ. of Jerusalem; served in Israeli Defense Force (IDF) as combat infantry unit officer; mil. corresp. for IDF journal Bamachane; mem. Likud Party; mem. Knesset 1973–98, 2003–, mem. Foreign Affairs and Security Cttee 1981–88; Minister without Portfolio responsible for Minority Affairs 1988–90; Minister of Health 1990–92; Mayor of Jerusalem 1993–2003; Vice-Prime Minister and Minister of Industry, Trade, Labor and Communications 2003–05, Vice-Premier and Minister of Finance 2005–06; left

Likud party to join newly formed Kadima party Dec. 2005; Acting Chair. of Kadima Jan.–April 2006, Chair. April 2006–08; Acting Prime Minister Jan.–April 2006, Prime Minister and Minister for Social Affairs April 2006–08 (resgnd), Minister of Finance April–July 2007; acquitted of a series of corruption charges 2012, found guilty in retrial 2015, sentenced to eight months in prison. *Address:* Kadima, Petach Tikva, Tel-Aviv, Israel (office). *Telephone:* 3-9788000 (office). *Fax:* 3-9788020 (office). *Website:* www.kadima.org.il (office).

OLOFSSON, Lars, BBA; Swedish business executive; b. 19 Dec. 1951, Kristianstad; ed Univ. of Lund; began career with Nestlé SA, Vevey, Switzerland as Product Man. for Findus frozen products 1976, worked at Nestlé France and held various commercial and marketing positions 1981–92, apptd Gen. Man. France Glaces Findus 1992, then became Pres. Pripps-Procordia Sweden, then led the Dairy and Dietetic Products Div. of Sopad Nestlé, apptd Gen. Man. Nestlé Nordic Markets 1995, apptd CEO Nestlé France 1997, Exec. Vice-Pres. Nestlé Group, responsible for Zone Europe 2001–08, Exec. Vice-Pres. in charge of Strategic Business Units, Marketing and Sales, Nestlé 2005–08; mem. Bd of Dirs and CEO Carrefour Group 2009–12, Chair. 2011–12, Chair. Carrefour Foundation; apptd Co-Chair. Consumer Goods Forum 2010; Chevalier du Mérite agricole; Chevalier, Légion d'honneur 2003, Officier 2011.

OLOVSSON, Ivar (Olov Göte), DrSc; Swedish chemist and academic; *Professor Emeritus of Inorganic Chemistry, University of Uppsala;* b. 15 Oct. 1928, Rödön; s. of Erik Olovsson and Anna Andersson; m. Kristina Jonsson 1950; three s. one d.; ed Univ. of Uppsala; Teaching Asst, Univ. of Uppsala 1953–57, Asst Prof. 1961–64, Assoc. Prof. 1965–69, Prof. of Inorganic Chem. 1969–93, Prof. Emer. 1993–; Research Assoc., Univ. of California, Berkeley 1957–59, 1964–65, Visiting Miller Prof. 2002; Guest Prof., Lab. de Cristallographie, Grenoble 1977–78, Univ. of Konstanz 1982–83, 1999; mem. Royal Soc. of Sciences 1970 (Pres. 1996–97), Royal Swedish Acad. of Sciences 1974; Kt of Northern Star 1975, Chevalier des Palmes académiques 1981; Gold Medal, Royal Acad. of Sciences of Sweden 1961, Gold Medal, Swedish Chem. Soc. 1965, María Sklodowska-Curie Medal, Polish Chem. Soc. 2003. *Publications include:* From a Grain of Salt to the Ribosome – The History of Crystallography as Seen Through the Lens of the Nobel Prize 2014, Snow, Ice and Other Wonders of Water – A Tribute to the Hydrogen Bond 2016; about 90 scientific papers, mainly in field of structural chem. *Leisure interests:* outdoor life, mountaineering, skiing, music. *Address:* Ångström Laboratory, Department of Chemistry, PO Box 538, 751 21 Uppsala (office); Murkelvägen 27, 756 46 Uppsala, Sweden (home). *Telephone:* (18) 30-22-76 (home). *E-mail:* ivar.olovsson@gmail.com (office). *Website:* www.kemi.uu.se (office).

OLSEN, Matthew G., BA, JD; American lawyer, academic and fmr government official; *Lecturer on Law, Harvard Law School;* m.; three c.; ed Univ. of Virginia, Harvard Law School; Fed. Prosecutor, US Attorney's Office for Dist of Columbia 1994–2006, Chief of Nat. Security Section 2005–06; Special Counsel to Dir of FBI 2004–05; Deputy Asst Attorney-Gen., Nat. Security Div. 2006–09; Assoc. Deputy Attorney-Gen., Dept of Justice, also Special Counselor to Attorney-Gen. and Exec. Dir Guantanamo Review Task Force 2009–11, served as Acting Asst Attorney-Gen. for Nat. Security during presidential transition of Barack Obama; Gen. Counsel, Nat. Security Agency (NSA) –2011; Dir Nat. Counterterrorism Center 2011–14; Nat. Security Contrib. 2014–; f. IronNet Cybersecurity 2014; Lecturer on Law, Harvard Law School 2015–, Fellow 2017–; Adjunct Prof. Univ. of Virginia 2017–; Prin. WestExec Advisors 2018–. *Address:* Harvard Law School, Langdell Library 305, Cambridge, MA 02138, USA (office). *Telephone:* (617) 495-4610 (office). *E-mail:* matthew.g.olsen@gmail.com (office). *Website:* hls.harvard.edu (office).

OLSEN, Øystein, Cand. oecon; Norwegian economist and central banker; *Governor, Norges Bank;* b. 8 Jan. 1952; ed Univ. of Oslo; with Research Dept, Statistics Norway 1977–90, 1991–94, Head of Research Dept 1996–99, Dir-Gen. Statistics Norway 2005–10; Researcher, Lawrence Berkeley Lab., Univ. of California, Berkeley, USA 1985–86; with ECON Centre for Economic Analysis, Oslo 1990–91; Prof., Norwegian School of Man. 1993–99; Deputy Dir-Gen., Econ. Policy Dept, Ministry of Finance 1994–96, Dir-Gen. 1999–2005; Gov. Norges Bank (central bank) 2011–. *Address:* Office of the Governor, Norges Bank, Bankplassen 2, POB 1179 Sentrum, 0107 Oslo, Norway (office). *Telephone:* 22-31-60-00 (office). *Fax:* 22-41-31-05 (office). *E-mail:* central.bank@norges-bank.no (office). *Website:* www.norges-bank.no (office).

OLSON, Hon. Lyndon Lowell, Jr; American insurance executive, politician and diplomatist; *Chairman, Hill+Knowlton Strategies for the United States;* b. 7 March 1947, Waco, Tex.; m. Kay Woodward Olson 1982; ed Baylor Univ., Baylor Law School, Tex.; mem. Texas State House of Reps 1973–78; Chair. Cttee on Higher Educ., House Standing Cttee on Local Govt; Chair. Texas State Bd of Insurance 1979–81, 1983–87; fmr CEO Nat. Group of Insurance Cos 1987; helped negotiate US–Israeli Free Trade Agreement; led Trade Del. on Financial Services to Russia and China 1985; Pres. and CEO Travelers Insurance Holdings and Associated Madison Cos (predecessors of Citigroup) 1990–98, sr adviser to the Chair. of Citigroup Inc. 2002–08; Chair. Hill+Knowlton Strategies for the US 2011–; Amb. to Sweden 1997–2001; Pres. Nat. Asscn of Insurance Commrs 1982; Pres. and CEO Travellers Insurance Holdings Inc. 1990–98, Assoc. Madison Cos Inc.; Commr and Vice-Chair. US Advisory Comm. on Public Diplomacy; Vice-Chair. Lyndon B. Johnson Foundation; mem. Bernard and Audre Rapoport Foundation; Chair. Scott & White Health Plan; Chair. and Trustee, Texas Scottish Rite Hosp. for Children, Dallas; fmr Chair. Swedish American Chamber of Commerce, New York; mem. Bd of Dirs First Acceptance Corp. 2004–, Energy Future Holdings Corpn 2007–; mem. Bd of Trustees, Baylor Coll. of Medicine, Austin Presbyterian Theological Seminary 2009–; fmr Trustee, American Scandinavian Foundation, New York; mem. Council on Foreign Relations, Council of American Ambs; Elder Cen. Pres. Church, Tex.; Democrat; Order of the Polar Star (Sweden) 2007; Dr hc (Umeå Univ); Gates of Jerusalem Award (Israel), Baylor Young Outstanding Alumni Award 1999, Distinguished Public Official (Texas Medical Asscn), Ellis Island Medal of Honor in 2001, Swedish-American of the Year Award, King Carl XVI Gustaf 2002, The Swedish-American of 2002, Vasa Order of America 2002, Price Daniel Distinguished Public Service Award, Baylor Univ. 2002, Anson Jones Award, Fort Worth Scottish Rite Foundation 2007. *Address:* Hill+Knowlton Strategies, 825 3rd Avenue, New York, NY 10022, USA (office). *Telephone:* (212) 885-0300 (office). *E-mail:* lyndon.olson@hkstrategies.com (office). *Website:* www.hkstrategies.com (office).

OLSON, Maynard V., BS, PhD; American chemist, geneticist and academic; *Professor of Genome Sciences and of Medicine, University of Washington;* ed California Inst. of Tech., Stanford Univ.; chemist at Dartmouth Coll. 1970–74; Visiting Scholar and Research Assoc., Dept of Genetics, Univ. of Washington 1974–79, rejoined Dept of Molecular Biotechnology 1992–, currently Prof. of Genome Sciences and of Medicine and Adjunct Prof. of Computer Science and Eng; joined Faculty, Washington Univ., St Louis 1979; fmr Investigator, Howard Hughes Medical Inst.; mem. NAS 1994; Genetics Soc. of America Medal 1992, Gairdner Foundation Int. Award 2002, Gruber Genetics Prize, The Peter and Patricia Gruber Foundation 2007. *Achievements include:* one of main architects of Human Genome Project; created a method to break the yeast genome into manageable pieces for analysis; his pioneering work paved way for analysis of entire human genome. *Publications:* numerous scientific papers in professional journals. *Address:* Fluke Hall 316, University of Washington, Box 352145, Seattle, WA 98195, USA (office). *Telephone:* (206) 685-7346 (office). *Fax:* (206) 543-0754 (office). *E-mail:* mvo@u.washington.edu (office). *Website:* www.genome.washington.edu/UWGC (office).

OLSON, Richard, AB; American diplomatist; *Special Representative for Afghanistan and Pakistan;* m. Deborah K. Jones; two d.; ed Brown Univ.; joined Foreign Service 1982, overseas postings have included Embassies in Mexico City, Kampala, Tunis, Riyadh, Addis Ababa, Baghdad and Abu Dhabi 1999–2001, Consul Gen., Consulate Gen. in Dubai 2001–03, served at Operations Center, State Dept (twice), NATO Desk, Dir Office of Israel and Palestinian Affairs, Dir Office of Iraqi Affairs, Deputy Chief of Mission, US Mission to NATO, Brussels 2006–08, Amb. to UAE 2008–11, Co-ordinating Dir for Devt and Econ. Affairs, Embassy in Kabul 2011–12, Amb. to Pakistan 2012–15, US Special Rep. for Afghanistan and Pakistan 2015–; Superior Honor Award (three times), Dept of State, Exceptional Civilian Service Award, Sec. of Defence. *Address:* Office of the Special Representative for Afghanistan and Pakistan, Department of State, 2201 C Street, NW, Washington, DC 20520, USA (office). *Telephone:* (202) 647-4000 (office). *Fax:* (202) 647-6738 (office). *Website:* www.state.gov/s/special_rep_afghanistan_pakistan (office).

OLSSON, Christian; Swedish fmr athlete; b. (John Christian Bert Olsson), 25 Jan. 1980, Gothenburg; competed in high jump and triple jump; Programme Seller, World Championships, Gothenburg Stadium 1995; coached by Viljo Nousiainen 1995–99, Yannick Tregaro 1999–; professional debut 1999; equalled world record at World Indoor Championships 2004; winner Gold Medal for triple jump, Grand Prix, Athens 2002, European Championships, Munich 2002, Golden League, Monaco 2002, World Athletics Final, St Denis 2002, Monaco 2003, World Championships, Paris 2003, World Indoor Championships, Birmingham 2003, Budapest 2004, Super Grand Prix, Gateshead 2003, 2004, Stockholm 2003, 2004, Olympic Games, Athens 2004, Bergen 2004, Rome 2004, Zurich 2004, St Denis 2004, European Championships, Gothenburg 2006; winner Silver Medal for triple jump, World Championships, Edmonton 2001, Goodwill Games Brisbane 2001, Grand Prix, Stockholm 2001, 2002, Golden League, Oslo 2002, St Denis 2002, Brussels 2002; winner Bronze Medal for triple jump, Golden League, Zurich 2002; personal bests: Triple jump (Indoor) 17.83m, (Outdoor) 17.79m, High jump (Indoor) 2.28m, (Outdoor) 2.24m, Long jump (Outdoor) 7.69m; Flagbearer for Sweden, Summer Olympics, Beijing 2008; mem. Örgryte IS Club; retd from professional competition 2012; Best Sports Achievement of the Year, Swedish Sports Awards 2001, European Athletic Asscn Athlete of the Year 2003, Waterford Crystal European Athlete of the Year Trophy 2003, 2004. *Leisure interests:* cars, reading, computer games, music. *Address:* c/o Svenska Friidrottsförbundet, Heliosgatan 3, 120 30 Stockholm, Sweden. *Website:* www.iaaf.org/athletes/sweden/christian-olsson-172059.

OLSSON, Hans-Olov, MBA; Swedish automobile industry executive; *Vice-Chairman, Volvo Car Corporation;* b. 1941, Snäcke, Ånimskogs parish; m. Monica Olsson; two d.; ed Univ. of Gothenburg, Harvard Univ., Vevey, Switzerland; joined Volvo Corpn 1966, systems engineer responsible for production control, logistics and procurement 1966–69, Man. of Material and Production Control 1969–72, Production Man. of Final Ass. Plant, Volvo Truck Corpn, Gothenburg 1972–74, Project Man., Chesapeake Plant, Volvo Car Corpn, VA 1974–77, Gen. Plant Man., Component Supply, Volvo Daisland Plant 1977–80, Dir of Area Overseas, Global Sales and Marketing Div. 1984–87, Vice-Pres. of Div. 1987–89, est. Volvo Business Univ. 1989, Pres. of Volvo Japan, Tokyo 1990–96, Pres. of Volvo Cars Market Area Europe, Brussels, Belgium 1996–98, Pres. and CEO Volvo Cars N America, Rockleigh, NJ 1998–2000, Pres. and CEO Volvo Car Corpn 2000–05; Sr Vice-Pres. and Chief Marketing Officer, Ford Motor Co. 2005–06; Vice-Chair., Volvo Car Corpn 2010–; mem. Bd Svenskt Näringsliv (Confed. of Swedish Enterprises); Dir, Lindab AB –2010, Lindab International AB 2001–10, Höganäs AB 2006–, Elanders AB 2007–. *Leisure interests:* jogging, golf, gardening, skiing. *Address:* Volvo Car Corporation, PVH50, 50200, 405 31 Göteborg, Sweden (office). *Website:* www.volvocars.com (office).

OLSSON, Karl Erik; Swedish politician and farmer; b. 23 Feb. 1938, Häglinge, Kristianstad; m. Sonja Olsson; three c.; ed Colls of Agric.; farmer, Nygård Farm 1963–; Chair. Nat. Centre Party Youth League 1971–74; mem. Centre Party Nat. Bd 1981–92, Asst Vice-Chair. 1986–87, Vice-Chair. 1987–92; mem. Parl. 1976–79, 1985–95; mem. Bd Nuclear Power Inspectorate 1977–91, Foundation for Promotion of Literature 1980–91, Swedish Univ. of Agric. Sciences 1986–91; Chair. Standing Cttee on Agric. 1985–91; Minister of Agric. 1991–94; mem. European Parl. 1995–2004, mem. European Liberal, Democrat and Reform Party Group (ELDR), Bureau European Parl., Cttee on Agric. and Rural Devt, Cttee on Fisheries, Substitute Cttee on Environment, Public Health and Consumer Policy, mem. Del. to EU–Czech Repub. Jt Parl. Cttee, Substitute Del. to EU–Bulgaria Jt Parl. Cttee; Chair. Häglinge Church Council 1983–2009, Kristianstad Council of Agric. 1997–2009, Swedish Mutual Guarantee Asscn 2004–09, Swedish Asscn for Sr Citizens 2008–14; mem. ELDR Group Bureau, Exec. Bd Global Crop Diversity Trust, FAO, Rome, Advisory Council to Nat. Bd of Health and Welfare; mem. Royal Swedish Acad. for Agric. and Forestry 1999–; Hon. AgrD; Gold Medal, Chamber of Agric. *Publications:* Bonde i lokalsamhället 1973, Tankar 1978, Naturresurserna och framtiden 1984, Sverige behöver en Livskraftig Landsbygd 1985, Europeiskt jordbruk i battre takt med naturen 1998, Jordbruk, Handel och Utreckling 2006. *Address:* Nygård 2116, 282 73 Sösdala, Sweden (home). *Telephone:* (451) 63091 (home); 720-677517 (mobile) (home). *E-mail:* karl.erik.olsson@hotmail.com (home). *Website:* www.haglingenygard.se (home).

OLTEANU, Bogdan, MBA; Romanian banker and politician; b. 29 Oct. 1971, Bucharest; s. of Dănuț Florin Olteanu and Ecaterina Olteanu; m. Cristina Oteanu; two c.; ed Univ. of Bucharest, Romanian Banking Inst. and City Univ., Seattle, USA; mem. Nat. Liberal Party (Partidul Național Liberal—PNL) 1991–2009, Pres. Youth Section 1998–2000, Alt. mem. Standing Bureau 2001–02, Chair. Court of Honour and Arbitration 2002; Sec.-Gen. Org. of Liberal Students 1993–96; Adviser to State Minister, Ministry of Industry and Commerce 1997; lawyer, Bogdan Olteanu Law Firm 1998–; Govt Minister responsible for relations with Parl. 2004–06; mem. Camera Deputaților (Chamber of Deputies) 2004–09, Chair. 2006–08, Vice-Chair. 2008–09, mem. Culture, Arts, Mass Information Means Cttee (Chair. 2004–05) 2004–06, Investigation of Abuses, Corrupt Practices and Petitions Cttee 2006–07, Defence, Public Order and Nat. Security Cttee 2007; Vice-Gov. Nat. Bank of Romania 2009–16 (resgnd); Kt Grand Officer of the Order of Crown.

OLUTOYIN AGANGA, Olusegun; Nigerian economist and politician; b. 1955, Lagos State; m.; four c.; ed Univ. of Ibadan, Univ. of Oxford, UK; with Ernst & Young, London 1989–2001; Man. Dir Goldman Sachs, London, UK 2001–10; Minister of Finance 2010–11, of Trade and Investment 2011–13, of Industry, Trade and Investment 2013–15; co-f. Nigerian Leadership Initiative 2006; Commdr, Order of Niger 2011.

OLVER, Sir Richard (Dick) Lake, Kt, BSc, FREng, FICE; British engineer and business executive; b. 2 Jan. 1947; m. Pamela Larkin 1968; two d.; ed City Univ., London; joined British Petroleum (BP) 1973, apptd Vice-Pres. BP Pipelines Inc., BP North America 1979, Div. Man. of Corp. Planning 1985, Gen. Man. Gas, BP Exploration Europe 1988, Chief of Staff to Chair., Head of Corp. Strategy 1990, CEO BP Exploration USA 1992, Deputy CEO BP Exploration 1995, CEO BP Exploration and Production Div. 1998–2002, apptd Deputy Group CEO BP plc 2003–04; Chair. BAE Systems plc 2004–14; Dir (non-exec.) Reuters, then Thomson Reuters PLC 1997–2007; Sr Adviser, Clayton, Dubilier & Rice, HSBC; mem. Prime Minister's Business Advisory Group and India/UK CEO Forum, GLF Global Leadership Foundation, Trilateral Comm.; currently mem. Supervisory Bd, Sand Hill Petroleum B.V.; UK Business Amb.; Fellow, Royal Acad. of Eng 2005, mem. Council 2006–09; Hon. DSc (City Univ.) 2004, (Cranfield Univ.) 2006; Non-Exec. Dir (NED) of the Year Award, NED Awards sponsored by The Sunday Times 2012. *Leisure interests:* grandchildren, education, sailing, ballet, fine arts. *Address:* c/o Sand Hill Petroleum B.V., Atrium, Strawinskylaan 3051, 1077 ZX, Amsterdam, The Netherlands. *Telephone:* (20) 3012198 (office). *Fax:* (20) 3012202. *Website:* www.shpbv.eu.

OMAAR, Mohamed Abdullahi, MA, PhD; Somali politician; b. 1 July 1953; s. of Abdullahi Omaar; ed Univ. of Nottingham, Univ. of Birmingham, UK; taught at Brunel Univ., London and then at Inst. of Educ., Univ. of London; worked as Sr Educ. Policy Adviser for Birmingham City Council, UK; Minister for Higher Educ. and Heritage, 'Somaliland' –2010, Minister of Foreign Affairs 2010–12; mem. Kulmiye Party, fmr Foreign Affairs Spokesman; cand. for Pres. of Somalia 2012.

O'MAHONY, W. I. (Liam), BE, BL, MBA, FIEI; Irish business executive; *Chairman, Smurfit Kappa Group plc;* b. 1947; began career as civil engineer in Repub. of Ireland and UK; joined CRH plc 1971, worked in Middle East, Africa and USA for CRH Cos, sr man. positions include COO of US Operations, Man.-Dir Repub. of Ireland and UK Group Cos 1991–94, mem. Bd of Dirs 1992–2011, Chief Exec. Oldcastle Inc., USA 1994–2000, Dir 2000–, Group Chief Exec. 2000–08; mem. Bd of Dirs Smurfit Kappa Group plc 2007–, Chair. 2008–; mem. The Irish Man. Inst. Council, Harvard Business School European Advisory Bd, USA. *Address:* Smurfit Kappa Group, Beech Hill, Clonskeagh, Dublin 4, Ireland (office). *Telephone:* (1) 202-7000 (office). *Website:* www.smurfitkappa.com (office).

O'MALLEY, Bert W., MD; American biologist and academic; *Tom Thompson Distinguished Service Professor and Chairman, Department of Molecular and Cellular Biology, Baylor College of Medicine;* b. Pittsburgh, Pa; ed Univ. of Pittsburgh School of Medicine; Resident, Duke Univ. 1963–65; Clinical Assoc., NIH, Bethesda, Md 1965–67, Head of Molecular Biology Section 1967–69; Luscious Birch Prof. and Dir Reproductive Biology Center, Vanderbilt Univ. 1969–73; Tom Thompson Distinguished Service Prof. of Molecular and Cellular Biology, Baylor Coll. of Medicine 1973–, also Chair. Dept of Molecular and Cellular Biology; mem. NAS, Inst. of Medicine, Endocrine Soc. (Pres. 1985); Fellow, AAAS, American Acad. of Arts and Sciences, American Acad. of Microbiology; several hon. doctorates, including (Karolinska Inst., New York Univ., Nat. Univ. of Ireland, Univ. of Maryland, Univ. of Pittsburgh, Univ. of Athens, Greece); Ernst Oppenheimer Award, British Endocrine Soc. Award, Carl G. Hartman Award 2007, Nat. Medal of Science 2008, Ernst Schering Prize 2011. *Publications:* more than 600 publs; holder of 19 patents. *Address:* Baylor College of Medicine, Interdepartmental Program in Cell and Molecular Biology, One Baylor Plaza, Room N204Q, Houston, TX 77030, USA (office). *Telephone:* (713) 798-6205 (office). *Fax:* (713) 798-5599 (office). *E-mail:* berto@bcm.edu (office). *Website:* www.bcm.edu (office).

O'MALLEY, Desmond Joseph, BCL; Irish politician, solicitor and banker; b. 2 Feb. 1939, Limerick; s. of Desmond J. O'Malley and Una O'Malley; m. Patricia McAleer 1965; two s. four d.; ed Crescent Coll., Limerick, Nat. Univ. of Ireland; practised as solicitor 1962; mem. Dáil (House of Reps) for Limerick East 1968–2002; mem. Limerick Corpn 1974–77; Parl. Sec. to Taoiseach (Prime Minister) and to Minister for Defence 1969–70; Minister for Justice 1970–73; Opposition Spokesman on Health 1973–75, on Industry and Commerce 1975–77; Minister for Industry and Commerce 1977–81, 1989–92, for Energy 1977–79; Opposition Spokesman on Industry and Commerce 1981–82; Minister for Trade, Commerce and Tourism 1982; Opposition Spokesman on Energy 1983–84; fmrly Fianna Fáil (expelled 1984); Co-founder and Leader of Progressive Democrats Party 1985–93; Chair. Foreign Affairs Cttee, Irish Parl. 1997–2002; Alt. Dir for Denmark, Ireland, Lithuania and Macedonia, EBRD 2003–10; Hon. LLD (Univ. of Limerick) 2003. *Publication:* Conduct Unbecoming: A Memoir 2014. *Leisure interests:* golf, horse racing.

O'MALLEY, Martin Joseph, JD; American lawyer and politician; *Visiting Professor, Carey Business School, Johns Hopkins University;* b. 18 Jan. 1963, Washington, DC; m. Catherine Curran (Katie) O'Malley 1990; two s. two d.; ed Gonzaga Coll. High School, Catholic Univ. of America, Univ. of Maryland School of Law; worked for Gary Hart for Pres. campaign; named by US Congresswoman Barbara Mikulski as her state field dir for her primary and gen. election campaigns for US Senate 1986, served as Legis. Fellow in Senator Mikulski's office 1987–88; Asst State's Attorney for City of Baltimore 1988–90; cand. for Maryland State Senate in 43rd Dist 1990; mem. Baltimore City Council for 3rd Dist 1991–99, served as Chair. Legis. Investigations Cttee, Taxation and Finance Cttee; Mayor of Baltimore 1999–2006; Gov. of Maryland 2007–15; Visiting Prof., Carey Business School, Johns Hopkins Univ. 2015–; announced candidacy for Democratic nomination for Pres. of US 2015; Democrat; named by Esquire Magazine as The Best Young Mayor in the Country 2002, named by TIME magazine as one of America's Top 5 Big City Mayors 2005. *Address:* Johns Hopkins Carey Business School, 100 International Drive, Baltimore, MD 21202, USA (office). *E-mail:* martin.omalley@jhu.edu (office). *Website:* carey.jhu.edu (office).

O'MALLEY, HE Cardinal Sean Patrick, OFM Cap.; American ecclesiastic; *Archbishop of Boston;* b. 29 June 1944, Lakewood, Ohio; ordained priest of Order of Friars Minor Capuchin 1970; Coadjutor Bishop of St Thomas, US VI 1984–85, Bishop of St Thomas 1985–92; Bishop of Fall River, Mass 1992–2002; Bishop of Palm Beach, Fla 2002–03; Archbishop of Boston 2003–; cr. Cardinal (Cardinal-Priest of Santa Maria della Vittoria) 2006; participated in Papal Conclave 2013; mem. Pontifical Comm. for the Protection of Minors 2014–; Grand Cross, Order of Prince Henry (Portugal) 1985, Commdr 2016. *Address:* Cardinal's Residence, 2121 Commonwealth Avenue, Boston, MA 02135-3192, USA (office). *Telephone:* (617) 782-2544 (office). *Fax:* (617) 782-8358 (office). *Website:* www.rcab.org (office).

O'MALLEY, Thomas D., BA; American business executive; *Executive Chairman, PBF Energy Company LLC;* b. 1942, Staten Island, New York; m. Mary Alice Lucey; four c.; ed Manhattan Coll.; mailroom employee, Philipp Brothers 1963–66, commodities trader, Europe, Salomon Inc. 1966–75, various exec. roles at Salomon Inc. and its predecessor cos, Philbro/Salomon and Philipp Brothers, including Vice-Chair., Chief Exec. of oil-trading div., Chair. Phibro Energy, mem. parent co.'s Bd of Dirs and Exec. Cttee 1975–86; Chair. and CEO Argus Resources 1986–88, Chair. Comfed Bancorp (a holding of Argus) 1988–89; Pres. Tosco Corpn 1989–90, 1993–97, Chair. and CEO 1990–2001, Vice-Chair. Phillips Petroleum Co. (following acquisition of Tosco Corpn) 2001–02; Chair. Premcor Inc. 2002–05, Sr Exec. Jan.–Sept. 2005, CEO 2002–04, Pres. 2002–03; Pres. and CEO Argus Services Corpn 2005–06; CEO Petroplus Holdings 2006–08, Chair. 2008–11; Exec. Chair. PBF Energy Inc. 2011–, Chair. PBF Holding Co. LLC 2012–; mem. Exec. Cttee American Fuel and Petrochemical Manufacturers; mem. Bd of Trustees, Florida Polytechnic Univ. 2015–; fmr Chair. Bd of Trustees, Manhattan Coll.; Dr hc (Manhattan Coll.) 2012; Refining Leadership Award, Harts, Mercantile Exchange's Director's Award for Global Vision, Humanitarian Award, Nat. Conference of Christians and Jews, Ellis Island Medal of Honor, Manhattan Coll. De La Salle Medal 1994. *Address:* PBF Energy Company LLC, 1 Sylvan Way, Parsippany, NJ 07054, USA (office). *Telephone:* (973) 455-7500 (office). *E-mail:* info@pbfenergy.com (office). *Website:* www.pbfenergy.com (office).

OMAMO, Raychelle Awuor, LLB; Kenyan lawyer, diplomatist and politician; *Secretary for Defence;* b. 6 July 1963, Nairobi; d. of William Odongo Omamo (fmr Minister of Agric.); ed Univ. of Kent at Canterbury, UK; 27 years' experience as advocate, High Court of Kenya, becoming Sr Counsel; fmr Amb. to Portugal, Vatican City and Serbia, fmr Perm. Rep. of Kenya to UNESCO, Amb. to France –2013; Sec. (Minister) for Defence 2013–; Dir Mo-Consult Ltd (consultancy firm); fmr mem. bds and governing councils of several non-profit orgs; legal counsel for numerous govt task forces and comms including Task Forces on Establishment of the Truth and Reconciliation Comm. for Kenya and on Review of Landlord and Tenant Legislation; Assisting Counsel to Ndungu Comm. on Illegal/Irregular Allocation of Public Land; fmr Chair. Law Soc. of Kenya (first woman); fmr Vice-Pres. E African Law Soc. *Address:* Ministry of State for Defence, Ulinzi House, Lenana Road, POB 40668-00100, Nairobi, Kenya (office). *Telephone:* 2721100 (office). *E-mail:* info@mod.go.ke (office). *Website:* www.mod.go.ke (office).

OMAND, Sir David Bruce, Kt, GCB, KCB, BA; British civil servant (retd); b. 15 April 1947, Glasgow, Scotland; s. of J. Bruce Omand and Esther Omand; m. Elizabeth Wales 1971; one s. one d.; ed Glasgow Acad., Corpus Christi Coll., Cambridge; Asst Prin., Ministry of Defence 1970, Pvt. Sec. to Chief Exec. (Procurement Exec.) 1973, Asst Pvt. Sec. to Sec. of State 1973–75, 1979–80, Prin. 1975, Asst Sec. 1981, Pvt. Sec. to Sec. of State 1981–82; Asst Under-Sec. of State (Man. Strategy) 1988–91, Deputy Under-Sec. of State (Policy) Ministry of Defence 1993–96, Dir Govt Communications HQ 1996–97; Perm. Under-Sec. of State, Home Office 1998–2001; Defence Counsellor FCO UK Del. to NATO, Brussels 1985–88; Chair. Centre for Man. and Policy Studies, Cabinet Office 2001–02, Perm. Sec. Cabinet Office, also Security and Intelligence Co-ordinator 2002–05 (retd); Visiting Prof., King's Coll. London 2005–; Deputy Chair. Windsor Leadership Trust; mem. Bd Natural History Museum 2006–14, now Trustee; currently Vice-Pres., Royal United Services Inst.; currently also Visiting Prof., War Studies Dept, King's Coll. London; British Soc. for History and Math. Prize 2003. *Publication:* Securing the State 2010. *Leisure interests:* opera, walking. *Address:* Royal United Services Institute for Defence and Security Studies, Whitehall, London, SW1A 2ET, England (office). *Telephone:* (20) 7747-2600 (office). *Website:* www.rusi.org (office).

OMAR, Abdisalan Hadliye, BSc, MPA, PhD; Somali/American economist and politician; ed Boston Coll., Oklahoma State Univ., Univ. of Tennessee; moved to USA at age 16; fmr Lecturer, Univ. of Tennessee; Research Assoc., ACRC Systems, New York 1987; Sr Budget Analyst for Public Safety and Educ., Washington, DC Budget Office 1992, Chief Financial Officer for DC Public Schools (DCPS) 1996, Chief Business Officer, DCPS 2007; Deputy Chief Financial Officer, DC Govt 1997, Chief of Staff, DC municipality 1999; consultant in municipal finances, World Bank 2001–02; Dir UNDP Governance and Financial Services Program, Somalia 2002–06; Gov. Cen. Bank of Somalia Jan.–Sept. 2013; Minister of Foreign Affairs 2015–17.

OMAR, Yusuf Garaad, BA; Somali journalist, diplomatist and politician; b. 26 June 1960, Mogadishu; ed Somali Nat. Univ., Fletcher School of Law and Diplomacy, Tufts Univ.; Broadcast and News Ed., Radio Mogadishu, Somali Broadcasting Service 1983–90; Dissemination Officer, Red Cross Int. Cttee, Mogadishu and Berbera 1987–90; Freelance Reporter with BBC 1991–92; worked for BBC World Service 1992–2012, becoming Head of Somali Service 2000–12, also Acting Head of Africa Service 2002–03; Sr Trainer in journalism and production, World Service Trust (now BBC Coll. of Journalism) 1997; cand. in presidential election 2012; Consultant, Rift Valley Inst. 2013; Exec. Dir, Nat. Civic Forum (ind. non-partisan org.) 2014–; Sr Consultant for strategic communications to Pres. of Somalia 2014–15; Dir, Horn Media & Communications Ltd 2015–17; Perm. Rep. of Somalia to UN, New York 2016–17; Minister of Foreign Affairs and Int. Co-operation 2017–18.

O'MEARA, Mark Francis; American professional golfer; b. 13 Jan. 1957, Goldsboro, NC; m. Alicia O'Meara; one s. one d.; ed Long Beach State Univ.; professional golfer 1980–; won US Amateur Championship 1979, Greater Milwaukee Open 1984, Bing Crosby Pro-Am 1985, Hawaiian Open 1985, Fuji Sankei Classic 1985, Isuzu Kapalua International (unofficial PGA Tour event) 1985, Australian Masters 1986, Lawrence Batley International 1987, AT&T Pebble Beach Nat. Pro-Am 1989, 1990, 1992, 1997, RMCC Invitational (with Curtis Strange) 1989, H-E-B Tex. Open 1990, Walt Disney World/Oldsmobile Classic 1991, Tokai Classic 1992, Argentine Open 1994, Fred Meyer Challenge (with John Cook) 1994, 2000, Honda Classic 1995, Bell Canada Open 1995, Mercedes Championships 1996, Greater Greensboro Open 1996, Buick Invitational 1997, US Masters 1998, The Open Championship 1998, Cisco World Match Play Championship (European unofficial event) 1998, Skins Game (US unofficial event) 1998, 2002, World Cup of Golf (with Tiger Woods) 1999, Dubai Desert Classic 2004, Champions Challenge (with Mike Reid) 2007, Liberty Mutual Insurance Legends of Golf (with Nick Price) 2010, Constellation Energy Senior Players Championship 2010; best finish 2002, second in Buick Invitational and second in Buick Open; mem. Ryder Cup team 1985, 1989 (tie), 1991 (winners), 1997, 1999 (winners), Alfred Dunhill Cup team 1985, 1986, 1987, 1996 (winners), 1997, 1998, 1999, Presidents Cup team 1996 (winners), 1998, World Cup team 1999 (winners); Hon. mem. Royal Birkdale Golf Club 2013; All-American Rookie of Year, Long Beach State Univ. 1981, PGA Tour Player of the Year 1998. *Leisure interests:* golf course consulting, hunting, fishing. *Address:* Mark O'Meara Design, 12386 North Deer Mountain Blvd, Deer Mountain, UT 84036, USA. *Telephone:* (877) 663-1998. *Fax:* (435) 333-1999. *E-mail:* info@markomearadesign.com. *Website:* www.markomearadesign.com; www.pgatour.com/players/player.01887 .html.

OMI, Koji; Japanese politician; b. 14 Dec. 1932, Gunma Pref.; ed Faculty of Commercial Science, Hitotsubashi Univ.; joined Ministry of Int. Trade and Industry (MITI) 1956, Consul, Consulate Gen., New York 1970–74, Dir S Asia and Eastern Europe Div., Trade Policy Bureau 1974, Dir Small Enterprise Policy Div., Small and Medium Enterprise Agency (SMEA) 1978, Dir Admin. Div., Science and Tech. Agency 1979–81, Dir-Gen. Guidance Dept, SMEA 1981–82 (retd from MITI); elected mem. House of Reps 1983, Parl. Vice-Minister for Finance 1990; Dir-Gen. Research and Investigation Bureau, LDP 1991–92, Dir-Gen. Commerce and Industry Policy Bureau 1992–93, Dir-Gen. Science and Tech. Policy Bureau 1993–94, LDP Deputy Sec.-Gen. 1994–95; Chair. House Standing Cttee on Finance 1995, Sec.-Gen. Research Council for Promotion of Science and Tech.-oriented Nation, LDP 1996, Dir Special Cttee on Taxation System Problems and Relatives Matters 1996, mem. Standing Cttee on Budget 1996, Deputy Chair. Policy Research Council, LDP 1996–97, Dir-Gen. Election Bureau, LDP 1998–99, Dir Interest Group Policy Div., LDP 1999–2000, Acting Chair. Party Org. HQ, LDP 1999–2000, Acting Sec.-Gen., LDP 2000–01, Chair. LDP Research Comm. to Promote Research and Establish a Nation of Innovative Science and Tech. 2002, Deputy Chair. LDP Gen. Council 2004, Chair. LDP Research Comm. on Oil, Resources and Energy 2005; Minister of State for Econ. Planning 1997–98, Minister of State for Okinawa and Northern Territories Affairs and Minister of State for Science and Tech. Policy 2001, Minister of Finance 2006–07. *Address:* Liberal-Democratic Party (Jiyu-Minshuto), 1-11-23, Nagata-cho, Chiyoda-ku, Tokyo 100-8910, Japan (office). *Telephone:* (3) 3581-6211 (office). *E-mail:* koho@ ldp.jimin.or.jp (office). *Website:* www.jimin.jp (office).

OMI, Shigeru, MD, PhD; Japanese molecular biologist, academic and fmr international organization executive; *President, Japan Community Health Care Organization;* b. 11 June 1949, Tokyo; m.; one s. one d.; ed American Field Service scholarship to Potsdam Central High School, New York, Keio Univ., Jichi Medical School; Medical Officer, Div. of Medical Affairs, Bureau of Public Health, Tokyo Metropolitan Govt (assigned as sole doctor on remote Pacific islands) 1978–87; Researcher, Div. of Immunology, Jichi Medical School 1987–89, Prof. of Public Health 2009–12; Deputy Dir Office of Medical Guidance and Inspection, Bureau of Health Insurance, Ministry of Health and Welfare 1989–90; Medical Officer and Regional Adviser, Expanded Programme on Immunization, WHO Regional Office for the Western Pacific 1990–95, Dir Div. of Communicable Disease Prevention and Control 1995–98, Dir WHO Regional Office for Western Pacific 1999–2009, Dir Emer. 2009–, Pres. 66th World Health Ass. 2013, WHO mem. Exec. Bd, 2013–; Chair. Nat. Advisory Group for Infectious Disease Control in Japan 2013; Pres. JAPAN Community Health Care Org. 2014–; Exec. Ed. Polio Eradication in the Western Pacific Region 2002; Hon. Fellow, Hong Kong Coll. of Community Medicine 2002, Hon. mem. Keio Univ. 2004; Dr hc (Mongolian Nat. Medical Univ.) 2002; 37th Kojima Award 2001, Polio Eradication Champion Award, Rotary Int. 2009. *Publication:* SARS: How a Global Epidemic Was Stopped (ed.) 2006. *Website:* www.jcho.go.jp (office).

OMIDYAR, Pierre M., BS; French/American internet executive; b. Paris, France; m. Pam Omidyar; three c.; ed Tufts Univ.; family moved to Washington, DC, when he was a child; joined Claris (Apple Computer subsidiary) and wrote MacDraw application 1988–91; co-f. Ink Development (later renamed eShop and acquired by Microsoft) 1991; software engineer, General Magic 1991–96; Founder eBay 1995, Chair. 1998–2015; Co-Founder Omidyar Network (charity), now Chair. and CEO, now part of Omidyar Group; est. (with Tufts Univ.) Univ. Coll. of Citizenship and Public Service; f. Honolulu Civil Beat (local news service) 2010, now Publr and CEO; Co-founder Peer News Inc. (operating as Ginx) 2008; Fellow, American Acad.

of Arts and Sciences 2009–; Trustee, Tufts Univ., Santa Fe Inst., Punahou School; Carnegie Medal of Philanthropy 2011. *Address:* Omidyar Network, 1991 Broadway, Suite 200, Redwood City, CA 94063, USA. *Website:* www.omidyar.com; www .civilbeat.com.

OMIYA, Hideaki; Japanese business executive; *Chairman, Mitsubishi Heavy Industries;* joined Mitsubishi Heavy Industries in 1969, served in several exec. positions including Deputy Head of Industrial Machinery Div. and Head of Air Conditioning and Refrigeration Systems Div., apptd Exec. Vice-Pres. 2005, mem. Bd of Dirs and Sr Exec. Vice-Pres. 2007–08, Pres. and CEO Mitsubishi Heavy Industries 2008–13, Chair. 2013–, mem. Bd of Dirs 2016–; Outside Dir Seiko Epson Corp., Mitsubishi Corpn 2016–. *Address:* Mitsubishi Heavy Industries, 16-5, Konan 2-chome, Minato-ku, Tokyo 108-8215, Japan (office). *Telephone:* (3) 6716-3111 (office). *Fax:* (3) 6716-5800 (office). *E-mail:* info@mhi.co.jp (office). *Website:* www.mhi.co.jp (office).

OMIYI, Basil Efoise; Nigerian oil industry executive; joined Shell Petroleum Devt Co. of Nigeria Ltd (SPDC) as petroleum engineer 1970, worked in Nigeria, UK and the Netherlands, apptd to Bd of SPDC as Gen. Man. Relations and Environment 1996–99, External Affairs Dir 1999–2002, Production Dir 2002–04, Man. Dir Shell Petroleum Devt Co. of Nigeria Ltd (first Nigerian) 2004–09.

OMOROGBE, Oluyinka Osayame, LLB, LLM, BL, MCIArB; Nigerian academic, legal practitioner and energy consultant; *Nabo Graham Douglas Distinguished Professor, Nigerian Institute of Advance Legal Studies;* b. (Oluyinka Osayame Ighodaro), 21 Sept. 1957, Ibadan; d. of Samuel O Ighodaro and Irene E. B. Ighodaro; m. Allan Omorogbe 1984; one s. two d.; ed Univ. of Ife, London School of Econs, UK; Nat. Youth Service 1979–80; pvt. legal practitioner 1980–81; Lecturer, Dept of Jurisprudence and Int. Law, Univ. of Benin 1983–90, Head of Dept 1988–89; Sr Lecturer, Univ. of Lagos 1990–; Dir Centre for Petroleum, Environment and Devt Studies, Lagos 1996–; e-publr and consultant 2001–; Prof., Dept of Public and Int. Law, Ibadan Univ. 2002–09, Dean 2005–09; Corpn Sec. and Legal Adviser, Nigerian Nat. Petroleum Corpn 2009–11; currently Nabo Graham Douglas Distinguished Prof. of Law, Nigerian Inst. of Advance Legal Studies, Abuja; mem. Exec. Cttee Petroleum Energy and Mining Law Asscn of Nigeria 1986; mem. Acad. Advisory Group, Section on Energy and Natural Resources Law, Int. Bar Asscn, African Soc. of Int. and Comparative Law; mem. Oil and Gas Sector Reform Implementation Cttee (OGIC) 1999; Treas. Nigerian Soc. of Int. Law 1994–97, Gen. Sec. 1997. *Publications:* The Oil and Gas Industry: Exploration and Production Contracts 1997, Oil and Gas Law in Nigeria 2000; numerous articles on petroleum and energy law and int. econ. law in int. journals and books. *Leisure interests:* cooking, baking, handicrafts. *Address:* Univ. of of Lagos Campus, PMB 12820, Lagos, Nigeria (office). *E-mail:* info@nials.edu.ng. *Website:* www.nials.edu .ng (office).

OMRAN, Mohammed Hassan, BEng; United Arab Emirates telecommunications industry executive; *Chairman, Emirates Telecommunications Corporation (Etisalat);* ed Cairo Univ., Egypt; joined Emirates Telecommunications Corpn PJSC (Etisalat) 1977, Area Man., Ras al-Khaimah 1982–84, Deputy Gen. Man. Etisalat 1984–99, Sr Exec. Vice-Pres. 1999–2004, CEO 2004–05, Chair. 2005–; Chair. Canar Telecommunications Co., Thuraya Telecommunications Co. 2007–; Lifetime Achievement Award, Abu Dhabi Econ. Forum 2008, Outstanding Achievement Award, CEO Magazine 2008, Chair. of the Year, Int. Business Awards 2010, Chair. of the Year, World Communications Awards 2010, Lifetime Achievement Award, Middle East Business Leaders Awards 2010. *Address:* Emirates Telecommunications Corporation, Etisalat Building, intersection of Zayed The 1st Street and Sheikh Rashid Bin Saeed Al Maktoum Street, PO Box 3838, Abu Dhabi, United Arab Emirates (office). *Telephone:* (2) 6283333 (office). *Fax:* (2) 6317000 (office). *E-mail:* info@etisalat.ae (office). *Website:* www.etisalat.ae (office).

OMRANA, Abderrahim, PhD; Moroccan economist and banker; b. 1947, Quezane; m.; three c.; with Govt Gen. Inspection Dept 1970; Head of Mission, Treasury Dept, Ministry of Finance 1973; Asst Lecturer, Univ. of Rabat 1974, Sr Lecturer 1975–78; Exec. Attaché, Banque Nationale pour le Développement Economique 1975–78; Lecturer, Univ. of Dakar, Senegal 1978–79; Deputy Dir-Gen. African Centre for Monetary Studies and Fed. of African Cen. Banks 1978–87; Dir-Gen. ICOMA and NASCOTEX 1989–95; Bank Sec., Islamic Devt Bank 1996–2001, 2003–, Dir-Gen. Fund for Municipal Equipments 2001–03, later Adviser to Bank Pres. *Publications:* three books on finance, accountancy and modern econs and more than 100 articles on econs and finance. *Address:* Islamic Development Bank, PO Box 5925, Jeddah 21432, Saudi Arabia (office). *Telephone:* (2) 6361400 (office). *Fax:* (2) 6366871 (office). *E-mail:* idbarchives@isdb.org (office). *Website:* www.isdb.org (office).

ŌMURA, Satoshi, MS, PhD; Japanese biochemist, bioorganic chemist and academic; *Distinguished Emeritus Professor and Special Coordinator, Research Project for Drug Discovery from Natural Products, Kitasato Institute;* b. 12 July 1935, Yamanashi Pref.; ed Yamanashi Univ., Univ. of Tokyo, Tokyo Univ. of Science; Research Assoc., Yamanashi Univ. 1963–65; Researcher, Kitasato Inst. 1965–71, Prof. and Exec. Vice-Pres. 1984–90, Prof. and Pres. 1990–2008, Pres. Emer. 2008–12, Distinguished Emer. Prof. 2013–, also Special Coordinator, Research Project for Drug Discovery from Natural Products, Assoc. Prof., School of Pharmaceutical Sciences, Kitasato Univ. 1968–75, Prof. 1975–84, Prof., Kitasato Inst. for Life Sciences 2001–02, also Prof., Grad. School of Infection Control Sciences 2002–07; Max Tishler Prof. of Chem., Wesleyan Univ., USA 2005–; Pres. Joshibi Univ. of Art and Design 2007–; mem. Editorial Bd Journal of Antibiotics 1973–, Ed.-in-Chief 2004–13; mem. Japan Acad. 2001, American Chemical Soc., Japanese Biochemical Soc., Acad. des sciences 2002, Russian Acad. of Sciences 2004, Soc. for Industrial Microbiology and Biotechnology, USA; Hon. Prof., Chinese Acad. of Medical Science 1985, Shenyang Pharmaceutical Univ. (China) 1997, Jinan Univ., China 2006; Hon. mem. American Soc. of Biochemistry and Molecular Biology 1986, Robert Koch Inst. (Germany) 1994, Chemical Soc. of Japan 1998, Pharmaceutical Soc. of Japan, Japanese Soc. of Chemotherapy, Soc. for Actinomycetes (Japan) 2005, Japan Soc. for Bioscience, Biotechnology and Agrochemistry 2009; Special Hon. mem. Japanese Soc. for Bacteriology 2003; Distinguished Hon. mem. Japanese Soc. for Bacteriology 2002; Hon. FRSC (UK) 2005; Hon. Citizen of Nirasaki-City, Yamanashi, Japan 2001; Chevalier, Ordre nat. du Mérite 1992, Légion d'honneur 2007, Order of the Sacred Treasure, Gold and Silver Star (Nat. Medal of Japan) 2011, Person of Cultural Merit 2012; Hon. DSc (Lajos Kossuth Univ., Hungary) 1991, (Wesleyan Univ., USA) 1994; numerous awards, including Japan Acad. Prize 1990, Robert Koch Gold Medal (Germany) 1997, Nakanishi Prize 2000, Tetrahedron Prize 2010, Arima Award 2011, Person of Cultural Merit (Japan) 2012, Norman R. Farnsworth ASP Research Achievement Award (American Soc. of Pharmacognosy) 2013, Canada Gairdner Global Health Award 2014, Nobel Prize in Physiology or Medicine (co-recipient with William C. Campbell and Youyou Tu) 2015. *Publications:* MacRolide Antibiotics: Chemistry, Biology and Practice (ed.) 1984, The Search for Bioactive Compounds from Microorganisms (ed.) 1992; co-author of 42 books; more than 1,150 research papers. *Leisure interests:* golf, cross-country skiing, Japanese art. *Address:* Kitasato Institute for Life Sciences, Kitasato University, 9-1, Shirokane 5-chome, Minato-ku, Tokyo 108-8642, Japan (office). *Telephone:* (3) 5791-6101 (office). *Fax:* (3) 444-8360 (office). *E-mail:* omuras@insti.kitasato-u.ac.jp (office); omura-s@kitasato.or.jp (office). *Website:* www.kitasato.or.jp (office); www.satoshi-omura.info.

OMURA, Yukiko, BA (Econs), MA; Japanese banker, international business consultant and international organization official; b. Paris, France; ed Int. School of Geneva, Queen Mary, Univ. of London, UK, Boston Univ., USA; began career as project economist with IDB; spent ten years with J.P. Morgan, Tokyo, New York and London; fmrly Head of Emerging Markets, Asia, Lehman Brothers, Head of Credit Business, Asia; fmrly Head of Global Fixed Income and Derivatives UBS Japan; fmrly Head of Global Markets and Global Debt, Dresdner Bank, Japan; Founder, CEO and Exec. Dir HIV/AIDS Prevention Fund, London 2002–04; Exec. Vice-Pres. Multilateral Investment Guarantee Agency (MIGA), World Bank Group 2004–09; Vice-Pres. IFAD 2010–12; mem. Bd of Dirs GuarantCo Ltd, Pvt. Infrastructure Devt Group 2013–; mem. Advisory Bd CG/LA Infrastructure, LLC, Washington, DC 2008–, Columbus Frontiers Investment Man. NV 2012–, Amatheon Holding NV 2013–. *Address:* CG/LA Infrastructure LLC, 1827 Jefferson Place NW, Washington, DC 20036, USA (office). *Telephone:* (202) 776-0990 (office). *Fax:* (202) 776-0994 (office). *E-mail:* info@cg-la.com (office). *Website:* www.cg-la.com (office).

OMURALIEV, Maj.-Gen. Taalaybek; Kyrgyzstani army officer and politician; Deputy Chief, Maintenance Dept, Ministry of Defence, fmr Chief of Gen. Staff of Armed Forces; First Deputy Minister of Defence –2011, Minister of Defence 2011–14.

ONA ONDO, Daniel; Gabonese economist and politician; b. 10 July 1945, Oyem; m.; seven c.; ed Univ. de Picardie, Univ. Paris 1 (Panthéon-Sorbonne 2), France; Assoc. Prof., Faculty of Law and Social Sciences, Omar Bongo Univ., Libreville; fmr Technical Adviser to Minister of Planning and Devt; apptd Adviser to Pres. Omar Bongo 1990; mem. Nat. Ass. (Parl.) for Woleu Dist No 4 1996–, First Vice-Pres., Nat. Ass. 2007–14; Minister-Del. under Minister of Health and Population 1997; Minister of Culture, Arts, Popular Educ., Youth and Sports 1999–2002, of Nat. Educ. 2002, of Posts and Telecommunications 2005; Prime Minister and Head of Govt 2014–16; mem. Parti démocratique gabonais. *Address:* Parti démocratique gabonais, Immeuble PETROGAB, BP 268, Libreville, Gabon (office). *Telephone:* 01-70-31-21 (office). *Fax:* 01-70-31-46 (office). *Website:* www.gabon-pdg.org.

ONAIYEKAN, HE Cardinal John Olorunfemi, Lic. Sacr. Scrip., PhD; Nigerian ecclesiastic; *Archbishop of Abuja;* b. 29 Jan. 1944, Kabba, Kogi State; s. of Bartholomew Onaiyekan and Joann Onaiyekan; ed Mount St Michael's Secondary School, Aliade, Benue State, Ss. Peter & Paul Major Seminary, Bodija, Ibadan, completed his religious studies in Rome; ordained priest, Archdiocese of Lokoja 1969; taught at St Kizito's Coll., Isanlu 1969–71; Rector St Clement Jr Seminary, Lokoja 1971–77; Vice-Rector Ss. Peter & Paul 1977–82; Titular Bishop of Thunusuda 1982; Auxiliary Bishop of Ilorin 1982–84, Bishop of Ilorin 1984–90; Coadjutor Bishop of Abuja 1990–92, Bishop of Abuja 1992–94, Archbishop of Abuja 1994–; cr. Cardinal (Cardinal-Priest of San Saturnino) 2012; Apostolic Administrator, Diocese of Ahiara 2013–14; mem. Int. Theological Comm. 1980–85, Int. Catholic/Methodist Dialogue Comm. 1980–85, Inter-Denominational Faith and Order Comm. 1994–2006, Nigeria Interreligious Council; Vice-Pres. Catholic Bishops Conf. of Nigeria 1994–2000, Pres. 2000–07; Pres. Symposium of Episcopal Conf. of Africa and Madagascar 2003–07, Asscn of Episcopal Conf. of Anglophone West Africa 2004–07, Christian Asscn of Nigeria 2007–10; apptd Synod Father for Ordinary Gen. Ass. of Synod of Bishops on New Evangelization 2012; fmr Co-Pres. African Council of Religious Leaders; mem. Congregation for Doctrine of the Faith 2013–, Presidential Cttee of Pontifical Council for the Family 2013–, Congregation for Divine Worship and Discipline of the Sacraments 2016–; named Pax Christi Int. Peace Laureate 2012. *Publications:* The Priesthood in Pre-monarchial Ancient Israel and among the Owe-Yoruba of Kabba: A Comparative Study (dissertation) 1976, The Shariah in Nigeria: A Christian Ciew, in Bulletin on Islam & Christian-Muslim Relations in Africa 1987. *Address:* Archbishop's House, Area 3, Section 2, PO Box 286, Garki, Federal Capital Territory, Abuja, Nigeria (office). *Telephone:* (803) 451-1635 (office).

ONANGA-ANYANGA, Parfait; Gabonese diplomatist and UN official; *Special Envoy of the Secretary-General, Horn of Africa, United Nations;* b. 1960; m.; three c.; ed Univ. of Paris I Pantheon-Sorbonne, Univ. Omar Bongo, Libreville; served as First Counsellor for Disarmament and Political Affairs, Perm. Mission to UN, New York; has held several exec. positions in the UN including Acting Sec., UN Standing Advisory Cttee for Security Questions in Cen. Africa, Prep. Comm. of Comprehensive Nuclear Test-Ban Treaty Org., Vienna and New York 1988–2004, Chef de Cabinet to Pres., 59th session of UN Gen. Ass. 2004, Special Adviser to Pres., 60th and 61st sessions of UN Gen. Ass. 2005–07, Dir UN Deputy Sec.-Gen.'s Office 2007–12, Special Rep. of Sec.-Gen. for Burundi and Head of UN Office in Burundi (BNUB) 2012–14, with UN Dept of Political Affairs 2015, Coordinator of UN HQ Response to Boko Haram crisis 2015, Special Rep. of Sec.-Gen. and Head, Multidimensional Integrated Stabilization Mission in Cen. African Repub. (MINUSCA) 2016–18, Special Envoy of Sec.-Gen. for the Horn of Africa 2019–. *Website:* www.un.org (office).

ONDAATJE, Michael, OC, BA, MA; Canadian (b. Sri Lankan) writer, poet and filmmaker; b. 12 Sept. 1943, Colombo, Sri Lanka; s. of Philip Mervyn Ondaatje and Enid Doris Gratiaen; m. Linda Spalding; two s.; ed Dulwich Coll., UK, Bishop's

Univ., Queen's Univ. and Univ. of Toronto; has taught at Univ. of Western Ontario, York Univ., Univ. of Hawaii at Manoa, Brown Univ., Univ. of Toronto; Founding Trustee, Griffin Trust for Excellence in Poetry; Foreign Hon. mem. American Acad. of Arts and Letters. *Films include:* Sons of Captain Poetry 1970, Carry on Crime and Punishment 1970, The Clinton Special: A Film About The Farm Show 1974. *Publications include:* poetry: The Dainty Monsters 1967, The Man with Seven Toes 1968, The Collected Works of Billy the Kid (Gov.-Gen.'s Award) 1970, There's a Trick with a Knife I'm Learning to Do (Gov.-Gen.'s Award) 1979, Secular Love 1984, The Cinnamon Peeler 1991, Handwriting 1998; fiction: In the Skin of a Lion (City of Toronto Book Award) 1988, The English Patient (shared Booker Prize for Fiction 1992, Gov.-Gen.'s Award, Golden Booker 2018) 1992, Running in the Family 1993, The Collected Works of Billy the Kid 1996, Coming through Slaughter 1996, Anil's Ghost (Prix Médicis, Giller Prize, Gov.-Gen.'s Award, Kiriyama Pacific Rim Book Prize, Irish Times Int. Prize for Fiction 2001) 2000, The Conversations 2004, The Story 2005, Divisadero (Gov.-Gen.'s Literary Award) 2007, Divisadero 2008, The Cat's Table 2011, Warlight 2018. *Address:* Steven Barclay Agency, 12 Western Avenue, Petaluma, CA 94952, USA; 2275 Bayview Avenue, Toronto, ON N4N 3M6, Canada. *Website:* barclayagency.com/ondaatje.html.

ONDAATJE, Sir (Philip) Christopher, Kt, CBE, OC, FRGS, FRSL; Canadian/British banker and author; *Chairman, The Ondaatje Foundation;* b. 22 Feb. 1933, Kandy, Ceylon (now Sri Lanka); s. of Philip Mervyn Ondaatje and Enid Doris Gratiaen; m. Valda Bulins 1959; one s. two d.; ed Blundell's School, Tiverton, Devon; Nat. and Grindlays Bank, London 1951–55; Burns Bros & Denton, Toronto 1955–56; Montrealer Magazine and Canada Month Magazine 1956–57; Maclean-Hunter Publishing Co. Ltd, Montreal 1957–62; Financial Post, Toronto 1963–65; Pitfield Mackay, Ross & Co. Ltd, Toronto 1965–69; Founder Pagurian Corpn Ltd 1967–89, Loewen, Ondaatje, McCutcheon & Co. Ltd 1970–88; Chair. The Ondaatje Foundation 1975–; major donor to Ondaatje Wing, Nat. Portrait Gallery, London 2000 and to Ondaatje Theatre, Royal Geographical Soc.; mem. Advisory Bd Royal Soc. of Portrait Painters; Life mem. Somerset Co. Cricket Club; Trustee, Portrait Fund, Nat. Portrait Gallery 2002–10; mem. Canadian Olympic Bobsled Team 1964; Hon. Vice-Pres. Royal Geographical Soc.; Hon. LLD (Dalhousie) 1994, Hon. DLit (Buckingham) 2003, (Exeter) 2003, (Macquarie) 2011. *Publications:* Olympic Victory 1964, The Prime Ministers of Canada (1867–1985) 1985, Leopard in the Afternoon 1989, The Man-Eater of Punanai 1992, Sindh Revisited 1996, Journey to the Source of the Nile 1998, Hemingway in Africa 2003, Woolf in Ceylon 2005, The Power of Paper 2006, The Glenthorne Cat 2008, The Last Colonial 2011. *Leisure interests:* golf, tennis, adventure, writing, photography. *Address:* Glenthorne, Countisbury, nr Lynton, N Devon, EX35 6NQ, England. *Website:* www.ondaatje.com.

ONDEKANE, Jean-Pierre; Democratic Republic of the Congo politician; fmr leader rebel forces; Minister of Defence, Demobilization and War Veterans' Affairs 2003–05.

ONDOA, Christine Joyce Dradidi, MD; Ugandan paediatrician and politician; *Adviser to President on Health;* b. 21 Oct. 1968, Adjumani Dist; one s.; ed Makerere Univ.; paediatrician, Arua Hosp. 2000–09; Medical Supt and Sr Consultant, Jinja Hosp. 2009–10; Exec. Dir Mbarara Hosp. 2010–11; Minister of Health 2011–13; Adviser to Pres. on Health 2013–. *Address:* Office of the President, Parliament Building, POB 7168, Kampala, Uganda (office). *Telephone:* (41) 4258441 (office). *Fax:* (41) 4256143 (office). *E-mail:* aak@statehouse.go.ug (office). *Website:* www.statehouse.go.ug (office).

ONDONGO, Gilbert; Republic of the Congo politician; b. 1960, Owando; Adviser to Pres. on the Economy, Finance and Budget 1997–2002, Sec. of State under Minister of the Economy, Finance and Budget 2002–05, Minister of Labour, Employment and Social Security 2005–09, of Finance, the Budget and Public Portfolio 2009–16; mem. Assemblée nationale (Parti Congolais du Travail) for Owando constituency 2012–; mem. PCT, mem. Political Bureau 2011–. *Address:* Assemblée nationale, Palais du Peuple, cnr aves des Huileries et blvd Triomphale, Lingwala I, Kinshasa, Republic of the Congo (office). *E-mail:* info@assemblee-nationale.cd (office). *Website:* www.assemblee-nationale.cd.

ONDZOUNGA, Rufin Pacôme; Gabonese politician; fmrly with financial insts Paribas-Gabon and BGFI Bail; fmr Gen. Man. and CEO Banque de l'habitat du Gabon; Minister of Housing and Town Planning 2009–11, also of the Environment and Sustainable Devt July–Dec. 2010, of Nat. Defence 2011–14.

O'NEAL, E. Stanley, BS, MBA; American business executive; b. 7 Oct. 1951, Roanoke, Ala; m. Nancy A. Garvey; two c.; ed Kettering Univ., Harvard Univ.; joined Treasury Dept, General Motors 1978; Dir of Investment Banking, Merrill Lynch 1986–91, Man. Dir of High Yield Finance and Restructuring 1991–95, Head of Capital Markets Group 1995–98, Exec. Vice-Pres. and Co-head of Corp. and Institutional Client Group 1997–99, Pres. US Pvt. Client Group 1999–2001, COO, mem. Bd of Dirs and Exec. Man. Cttee, Merrill Lynch 2001–07, CEO 2002–07, Chair. 2003–07 (retd); Co-head CICG 1997–, Chief Financial Officer 1998–2000, Pres. 2000–; Vice-Chair. Securities Industry Asscn; mem. Advisory Cttee New York Stock Exchange; mem. Bd of Dirs Platform Specialty Products Corpn 2013–, General Motors Corpn 2001–06; mem. Bd Nat. Urban League, McDonald House of New York, Catalyst, Buckley School; mem. Advisory Council, Bronx Preparatory Charter School; named among Most Influential Black Americans, Ebony magazine 2006.

O'NEAL, Hon. Ralph T., OBE; British Virgin Islands business executive and politician; b. 15 Dec. 1933; m. Edris O'Neal; ed Oxford Univ.; mem. Virgin Islands Party, Leader 1995–2014; mem. House of Ass. (Parl.) for 7th Dist (Ind.) 1975–79, for 9th Dist (Virgin Islands Party) 1979–2015; Leader of the Opposition 1986–88, 2003–07, 2011–14; fmr civil servant and mem. of govt in various capacities; Deputy Premier (Chief Minister) –1995; Premier and Minister of Finance 1995–2003, 2007–11; fmr Dir British Virgin Islands Red Cross; Founding mem. Rotary Club, Tortola. *Leisure interest:* watching cricket. *Address:* Virgin Islands Party (VIP), Road Town, Tortola VG1110, British Virgin Islands (office). *E-mail:* info@viparty.com (office).

O'NEAL, Rodney, MEng; American business executive; *President and CEO, Delphi Corporation;* b. 1953; ed Kettering Univ., Stanford Univ.; joined General

Motors (GM) 1971, Inland Div. 1976–91, Dir of Industrial Eng, Chevrolet-Pontiac-GM of Canada Group 1991–92, Dir of Mfg, Delphi Corpn (GM subsidiary spun off from parent 1999) 1992–94, Gen. Dir of Warehousing & Distribution, GM Service Parts Operations 1994–97, Vice-Pres. GM 1997, also Gen. Man. Delphi Interior Systems 1997–98, Vice-Pres. Delphi 1998–2000, also Pres. Delphi Interior Systems 1998–2000, Exec. Vice-Pres. Safety, Thermal & Electrical Architecture Sector 2000–03, Pres. Dynamics, Propulsion, and Thermal Sector 2003–05, mem. Bd of Dirs, Pres. and COO Delphi Corpn 2005–07, Pres. and CEO 2007–; mem. or fmr mem. Bd of Dirs Goodyear Tire & Rubber Co., Sprint/Nextel; fmr mem. Bd of Dirs Inroads Inc., Michigan Mfrs Asscn, Woodward Governor Co.; mem. Advisory Bd Focus: HOPE (charity); mem. Exec. Leadership Council. *Address:* Delphi Corpn, 5725 Delphi Drive, Troy, MI 48098-2815, USA (office). *Telephone:* (248) 813-2000 (office). *Fax:* (248) 813-2673 (office). *E-mail:* info@delphi.com (office). *Website:* www.delphi.com (office).

O'NEAL, Ryan; American actor; b. (Charles Patrick Ryan O'Neal), 20 April 1941, Los Angeles, Calif.; s. of Charles O'Neal and Patricia O'Neal (née Callaghan); m. 1st Joanna Moore 1963 (divorced 1967), one s. one d. Tatum O'Neal (q.v.); m. 2nd Leigh Taylor-Young 1967, one s.; one s. by Farrah Fawcett; ed US Army High School, Munich, Germany, UCLA Theatre Arts. *Films include:* The Big Bounce 1969, Love Story (David di Donatello Award 1972) 1970, The Wild Rovers 1971, What's Up, Doc? 1972, The Thief Who Came to Dinner 1973, Paper Moon 1973, Oliver's Story 1978, The Main Event 1979, So Fine 1981, Partners 1982, Irreconcilable Differences 1983, Fever Pitch 1985, Tough Guys Don't Dance 1986, Chances Are 1989, Faithful 1996, Hacks 1997, Burn Hollywood Burn 1997, Zero Effect 1998, Coming Soon 1999, The List 2000, People I Know 2002, Gentleman B. 2003, Malibu's Most Wanted 2003, Waste Land (short) 2007, Slumber Party Slaughter 2012, Knight of Cups 2014. *Television includes:* Dobie Gillis, Two Faces West, Perry Mason, The Virginian, This is the Life, The Untouchables, My Three Sons, Bachelor Father, Empire, Peyton Place, Epoch 2000, Miss Match (series) 2003, Desperate Housewives (series) 2005, Bones 2006–13, 90210 (series) 2010, Ryan & Tatum: The O'Neals (series) 2011. *Leisure interest:* boxing. *Address:* 21368 Pacific Coast Highway, Malibu, CA 90265, USA. *Telephone:* (310) 277-7351 (office). *Fax:* (310) 456-8310 (home).

O'NEAL, Shaquille Rashaun, BA, MBA; American professional basketball player (retd) and television presenter; b. 6 March 1972, Newark, NJ; s. of Philip A. Harrison and Lucille O'Neal; m. Shaunie Nelson 2002; four c.; two c. from previous relationships; ed Louisiana State Univ., Univ. of Phoenix; centre; drafted in first round (first overall) by Orlando Magic 1992, played 1992–96; signed as free agent LA Lakers 1996, played 1996–2004; traded to Miami Heat 2004–08, with Phoenix Suns 2008–09, Cleveland Cavaliers 2009–10, Boston Celtics 2010–11 (retd); mem. four Nat. Basketball Asscn (NBA) championship teams (with Lakers 2000, 2001, 2002, with Heat 2006); Most Valuable Player in NBA Finals 2000, 2001, 2002; NBA Most Valuable Player 2000; 15-time NBA All-Star team 1993–98, 2000–07, 2009; NBA Rookie of the Year 1993; NBA scoring champion 1995, 2000; mem. gold-medal winning World Championship team 1994, US Olympic team, Atlanta 1996; commentator, Inside The NBA on Turner Network Television 2011–; Hon. US Deputy Marshal 2006; named one of 50 Greatest Players in NBA History 1996. *Films:* Blue Chips 1994, Kazaam 1996, Steel 1997, Freddy Got Fingered 2001, The Wash 2001, The Kid & I 2005, Scary Movie 4 2006, The House Bunny 2008. *Music:* has released five rap albums; owns record label Twism. *Publications:* Shaq Talks Back: The Uncensored Word on My Life and Winning in the NBA 2001. *Website:* shaq.com.

O'NEAL, Tatum; American actress; b. 5 Nov. 1963, Los Angeles, Calif.; d. of Ryan O'Neal and Joanna Moore; m. John McEnroe 1986 (divorced 1994); two s. one d. *Films include:* Paper Moon (Acad. Award for Best Supporting Actress) 1973, The Bad News Bears 1976, Nickelodeon 1976, International Velvet 1978, Little Darlings 1980, Circle of Two 1980, Prisoners 1981, Certain Fury 1985, Little Noises 1991, Basquiat 1996, The Scoundrel's Wife 2002, The Technical Writer 2003, My Brother 2006, Saving Grace B. Jones 2009, The Runaways 2010, Last Will 2010, This Is 40 2012, Mr. Sophistication 2013, Sweet Lorraine 2014, Squirrels to the Nuts 2015. *Television includes:* 15 and Getting Straight (film) 1989, Woman on Trial: The Lawrencia Bembenek Story (film) 1993, Sex and the City (series) 2003, 8 Simple Rules (series) 2004, Law & Order: Criminal Intent (series) 2004, Rescue Me (series) 2004–11, Wicked Wicked Games (series) 2006–07, Fab Five: The Texas Cheerleader Scandal (film) 2008. *Achievements include:* youngest person to ever win a competitive Acad. Award (1973). *Publication:* A Paper Life 2004. *Address:* c/o Innovative Artists, 1999 Avenue of the Stars, Suite 2850, Century City, CA 90067, USA (office).

O'NEIL, William Andrew, CMG, CM, BASc, FRSA, FREng, PEng; Canadian international public servant and engineer; b. 6 June 1927, Ottawa, Ont.; s. of Thomas Wilson O'Neil and Margaret O'Neil (née Swan); m. Dorothy Muir 1950; one s. two d.; ed Univ. of Toronto; engineer, Fed. Dept of Transport, Ottawa 1949–53, Resident Engineer, Special Projects Br. 1954; Div. Engineer, St Lawrence Seaway Authority 1955–59, Regional Dir 1960–63, Dir of Construction 1964–70; Deputy Admin., Marine Services, Canadian Marine Transportation Admin. 1970–79; Commr, Canadian Coast Guard and Deputy Admin., Marine Admin. 1975–89; Pres. St Lawrence Seaway Authority 1980–89; Chair. Council Int. Maritime Org. 1980–89, Sec.-Gen. 1990–2003; mem. Bd of Govs World Maritime Univ. 1983–; Chair. Governing Bd, Int. Maritime Law Inst., Malta 1991–2004; Canadian del. to Perm. Int. Asscn of Navigation Congresses 1984–90; Chair. Canadian Cttee Lloyd's Register of Shipping 1987–88; Chancellor World Maritime Univ. 1991–2004; Dir Canarctic Shipping Co.; Pres. Seaway Authority, Int. Bridge Corpn, Inst. of Chartered Shipbrokers 2004–, Videotel 2004–; mem. Bd Thousand Islands Bridge Authority 1980–90; mem. Asscn of Professional Engineers of Ont., American Soc. of Civil Engineers; Foreign mem. Royal Acad. of Eng (UK); Hon. Cdre, Canadian Coast Guard; Hon. mem. Canadian Maritime Law Asscn, Hon. Co. of Master Mariners (UK), Int. Maritime Pilots Asscn, Int. Fed. of Shipmasters' Asscns, NUMAST (Nat. Union of Marine Aviation and Shipping Transport Officers) (UK), Soc. of Naval Architects and Marine Engineers (USA), Singapore, Int. Asscn of Lighthouse Authorities, Co. of Master Mariners (India) 1998; Hon. Fellow, The Nautical Inst. (UK) 1996, Royal Inst. of Naval Architects 1998, Royal Inst. of Navigation; Hon. Titular mem. Comité Maritime Int.; Commdr, Ordre Nat. des Cèdres (Lebanon) 1995, Grand Cross, Orden Vasco Núñez de Balboa (Panama) 1998; Hon. Diploma, Canadian Coast Guard Coll.; Hon. LLD (Malta) 1993, (Memorial Univ. of Newfoundland) 1996; Hon. DSc (Nottingham Trent) 1994 (World Maritime Univ.) 2004; Eng Medal, Asscn of Professional Engineers of Ont. 1972, Distinguished Public Service Award, US Govt, Admirals' Medal 1994, Seatrade Personality of the Year Award 1995, NUMAST Award (UK) 1995, Professional Engineers Ont. Gold Medal 1995, mem. Eng Alumni Hall of Distinction, Univ. of Toronto 1996, Silver Bell Award, Seamen's Church Inst. New York 1997, Vice-Adm. Jerry Land Medal, Soc. of Naval Architects and Marine Engineers, USA 1999, Cdre Award, Conn. Maritime Asscn 1998, Dioscun Prize, Lega Navale Italiana (Italy) 1998, Halert C. Shepheard Award (USA) 2000, Medal for Distinguished Services to Directorate Gen. for Maritime Affairs, Colombia 2001, CITIS Lifetime Achievement Award UK 2002, Freeman of Worshipful Co. of Shipwrights (hc) UK 2002, Golden Jubilee Medal, Canada 2002, '15 November 1817 Medal', Uruguay 2002. *Leisure interests:* reading, swimming, golf. *Address:* 2 Dean Wood Close, Woodcote, RG8 0PW, England. *Telephone:* (1491) 682897. *Fax:* (1491) 682625. *E-mail:* bill.oneil@imo.org.

O'NEILL, Brendan, MA, PhD, FCMA; British business executive; b. 6 Dec. 1948; s. of John Christopher O'Neill and Doris Monk; m. Margaret Maude O'Neill 1979; one s. two d.; ed Churchill Coll., Cambridge, Univ. of East Anglia; with Ford Motor Co. 1973–75, British Leyland 1975–81, BICC PLC 1981–83; Group Financial Controller Midland Bank 1983–87; Dir of Financial Control Guinness PLC 1987, Finance Dir 1988–90, Man. Dir Int. Regulation, United Distillers 1990–92, Guinness Brewing Worldwide 1993–97, CEO Guinness Diageo PLC 1997–98; COO ICI PLC 1998–99, CEO 1999–2003, Dir 1998–2003; mem. Bd of Dirs EMAP PLC 1995–2002, Diageo 1997–98, Tyco Int. Ltd 2003–, Rank Group PLC 2005–07, Aegis Group Plc 2005–09, Endurance Specialty Holdings Ltd 2005–14, Informa Plc 2008– (Chair. Audit Cttee, mem. Remuneration Cttee), Towers Watson and Co. 2010–; Life Gov., Imperial Cancer Research Fund 1994–2002; Trustee, Cancer Research UK 2002–; Fellow, Chartered Inst. of Man. Accountants. *Leisure interests:* music, reading.

O'NEILL, Michael E., BA, MBA; American banker; *Chairman, Citigroup Inc.;* b. 31 Oct. 1946, Santa Monica, Calif.; m. Trish O'Neill; two s.; ed Princeton Univ., Colgate W. Darden Grad. School of Business Admin, Univ. of Virginia; Lt with Marine Corps 1969–71; worked with Continental Bank 1974–84, in Belgium, Hong Kong and London (as Country Man.); ind. consultant 1985–88; returned to Continental Bank as Chief Financial Officer heading merger negotiations with BankAmerica; responsible for pvt. equity business BankAmerica Corpn following 1994 merger, Vice-Chair., Chief Financial Officer 1995, then Pres. Prin. Investing and Wealth Man. and mem. Policy Cttee Transition (fmr Chair.); Group Chief Exec. and Dir Barclays PLC and Barclays Bank PLC Feb.– April 1999; mem. Bd of Dirs Bank of Hawaii Corpn 2000–04, Chair. and CEO 2000–04; mem. Bd of Dirs Citibank N.A. 2009–, Citigroup Inc. 2009–, Chair. Citi Holdings Oversight Cttee 2009–, Citibank N.A. 2011–, Citigroup Inc. 2012–; Trustee, Hawaii Pacific Univ., Honolulu Acad. of Arts; mem. Econ. Advisory Council, Fed. Reserve Bank of San Francisco. *Address:* Citigroup Inc., 399 Park Avenue, New York, NY 10043, USA (office). *Telephone:* (212) 559-1000 (office). *Fax:* (212) 793-3946 (office). *E-mail:* info@citigroup.com (office). *Website:* www.citigroup.com (office).

O'NEILL, Paul H., MPA; American business executive and fmr government official; *Chairman, Value Capture;* b. 4 Dec. 1935, St Louis, Mo.; s. of John Paul O'Neill and Gayland Elsie Irvin; m. Nancy Jo Wolfe 1955; one s. three d.; ed Fresno State Coll., Indiana Univ., Claremont Grad. School and George Washington Univ.; computer systems analyst, US Veterans Admin.; later engineer, Morris-Knudsen, Anchorage, Alaska; mem. staff, Office of Man. and Budget 1967–77, Deputy Dir 1974–77; Vice-Pres. Planning, International Paper Co. 1977, Sr Vice-Pres. Planning and Finance 1981, Sr Vice-Pres. paperboard and packaging Div. 1983, Pres. 1985–87; Chair. and CEO Aluminum Co. of America (Alcoa) 1987–99, Chair. 1999–2000; Sec. of Treasury 2001–02; Co-founder and CEO Pittsburgh Regional Healthcare Initiative 2002–05, mem. Bd of Dirs 2002–; Founder and Chair. Value Capture (hosp. consulting firm) 2005–; fmr Co-leader, Pittsburgh's Riverlife Task Force; Ed., Pittsburgh Post-Gazette; fmr Dir Manpower Demonstration Research Group, Alcoa, Lucent Technologies, Eastman Kodak Co., RAND Corpn (fmr Chair.), American Enterprise Inst.; mem. Dean's Advisory Council, Heinz Coll., Carnegie Mellon Univ.; Dr hc (Clarkson Univ.) 1993. *Address:* Value Capture, One North Shore Center 12 Federal Street, Suite 100, Pittsburgh, PA 15212, USA (office). *Telephone:* (412) 553-2299 (office). *E-mail:* poneillpa@aol.com. *Website:* valuecapturellc.com (office).

O'NEILL, Peter Charles Paire, CMG; Papua New Guinea politician and fmr accountant; *Prime Minister;* b. 13 Feb. 1965, Pangia Dist; s. of Brian O'Neill; ed Ialibu High School, Goroka High School, Univ. of Papua New Guinea; Certified Practising Accountant 1989; Pres. Papua New Guinea Inst. of Certified Practising Accountants 1990; Pnr, Pratley and O'Neill Accounting Firm 1991–92; Exec. Chair. Pangia Enterprises Ltd 1993–97, Papua New Guinea Banking Corpn (PNGBC) 1997–99, Motor Vehicle Insurance Ltd 1997–99, Pacific MMI Insurance Ltd 1997–99, Finance Pacific Ltd 1997–99, Port Moresby Private Hosp. Ltd 1997–99, Remington Technologies Ltd 1999; MP for Ialibu-Pangia 2002–; Minister for Labour and Industrial Relations 2002–03, for Public Service and Leader of Govt Business 2003–04; Leader, People's Nat. Congress Party 2004–; Minister for Public Service 2007–10, for Finance and Treasury 2010–11, Works Minister 2011; Prime Minister 2011–; Minister of Finance Feb.–Aug. 2012. *Address:* Office of the Prime Minister, PO Box 639, Waigani, NCD, Papua New Guinea (office). *Telephone:* 3277316 (office). *Fax:* 3277328 (office). *E-mail:* chiefsectogov@pmnec.gov.pg (office). *Website:* www.pm.gov.pg (office).

O'NEILL, Robert John, AO, MA, BE, DPhil, FASSA; Australian historian, academic and fmr army officer; *Professor Emeritus, Australian National University;* b. 5 Nov. 1936, Melbourne, Vic.; s. of Joseph Henry O'Neill and Janet Gibbon O'Neill; m. Sally Margaret Burnard 1965; two d.; ed Scotch Coll. Melbourne, Royal Mil. Coll. of Australia, Melbourne Univ., Brasenose Coll. Oxford; served in Australian Army 1955–68, Fifth Bn, Royal Australian Regt, Viet Nam (despatches) 1966–67, Maj. 1967–68 (resgnd); Rhodes Scholar, Vic. 1961; Official Australian Historian for the Korean War 1969–82; Sr Fellow in Int. Relations, ANU 1969–77, Professorial Fellow 1977–82, Head of Strategic and Defence Studies Centre 1971–82, Prof. Emer. 2013–; Dir IISS, London 1982–87, Chair. Council 1996–2001;

Chichele Prof. of the History of War, Univ. of Oxford 1987–2001, Dir Grad. Studies, Modern History Faculty 1990–92, Fellow, All Souls Coll. 1987–2001; Trustee, Imperial War Museum 1990–2001, Deputy Chair. 1996–98, Chair. 1998–2001; Gov. Ditchley Foundation 1989–2001, Int. Peace Acad. 1990–2001; Chair. Centre for Defence Studies, Centre for Australian Studies, Univ. of London 1990–95; Chair. Council of Australian Strategic Policy Inst. 2001–05; Deputy Chair. Grad. School of Govt, Univ. of Sydney 2001–05, Planning Dir, US Studies Centre 2006–07; Dir The Shell Transport and Trading Co. 1992–2002 and three mutual funds of Capital Group, Los Angeles 1992–2013, The Lowy Inst. 2001–12; mem. Advisory Bd Investment Co. of America 1988–2010; mem. Commonwealth War Graves Comm. 1990–2001, The Rhodes Trust 1995–2001; Fellow, Australian Inst. of Int. Affairs 2008; Hon. Fellow, Brasenose Coll. Oxford; Hon. Col 5th (V) Bn, The Royal Greenjackets 1993–99; mentioned in despatches, Viet Nam 1967; Hon. DLitt (ANU) 2001; Nat. Volunteer's Award 2012. *Publications include:* The German Army and the Nazi Party 1933–39 1966, Vietnam Task 1968, General Giap: Politician and Strategist 1969, The Strategic Nuclear Balance (ed.) 1975, The Defence of Australia: Fundamental New Aspects (ed.) 1977, Insecurity: The Spread of Weapons in the Indian and Pacific Oceans (ed.) 1978, Australian Dictionary of Biography Vols 7–12, 1891–1939, 1979–91 (co-ed.), New Directions in Strategic Thinking (co-ed.) 1981, Australia in the Korean War 1950–53: Vol. I Strategy and Diplomacy 1981, Vol. II Combat Operations 1985, Australian Defence Policy for the 1980s (co-ed.) 1982, Security in East Asia (ed.) 1984, The Conduct of East–West Relations in the 1980s (ed.) 1985, New Technology and Western Security Policy (ed.) 1985, Doctrine, the Alliance and Arms Control (ed.) 1986, East Asia, the West and International Security (ed.) 1987, Security in the Mediterranean (ed.) 1989, The West and the Third World (co-ed.) 1990, Securing Peace in Europe 1945–62 (co-ed.) 1992, War, Strategy and International Politics (co-ed.) 1992, Alternative Nuclear Futures 1999, Osprey Essential History series (ed.) 2000–14; articles in numerous journals. *Leisure interests:* local history, walking.

O'NEILL, Terence (Terry) Patrick; British photographer; b. 30 July 1938, London, England; s. of Leonard Victor O'Neill and Josephine Mary O'Neill; m. 1st Vera Day; one s. one d.; m. 2nd Faye Dunaway (q.v.) 1983–86; one s.; m. 3rd Laraine Ashton; ed Gunnersbury Grammar School; fmr modern jazz drummer in leading London jazz clubs; army service as physical training instructor; subsequently took up photography, took first photographs of Beatles and Rolling Stones early 1960s; went to Hollywood 1962; has photographed leading actors and actresses, rock and classical musicians, political and sports personalities, members of British and other royal families; work published in The Sunday Times, Time, Life, Newsweek, Tatler, Elle, Paris Match, Stern etc. and other newspapers and magazines, in 52 countries and used on about 500 front covers world-wide a year; Centenary Medal, Royal Photographic Soc. "in recognition of a sustained, significant contribution to the art of photography" 2011, The Terry O'Neill Award named in his honour. *Film:* Mommie Dearest (exec. producer) 1981, Aria (stills photography) 1987. *Publication:* Legend S. *Leisure interests:* music, food, wine, art in all forms, literature. *E-mail:* info@terryo.co.uk. *Website:* www.terryo.co.uk.

O'NEILL, Thomas C., BComm, FCPA, FCA; Canadian chartered accountant and business executive; *Chairman, BCE Inc. and Bell Canada;* ed Queen's Univ.; chartered accountant 1970; client service partner for numerous multinationals, specializing in dual Canadian and US listed cos 1975–85; fmr Chair. and CEO Price Waterhouse Canada, then CEO PricewaterhouseCoopers LLP, Canada 1998–2000, COO PricewaterhouseCoopers LLP, Global 2000–02, CEO PricewaterhouseCoopers Consulting Jan.–May 2002, Chair. May–Oct. 2002; mem. Bd of Dirs BCE (Bell Canada Enterprises) Inc. 2003–, Chair. 2009–, Chair. Audit Cttee, also Chair. Bell Canada; mem. Bd of Dirs Adecco SA, Bank of Nova Scotia, Loblaw Cos Ltd, Nexen Inc.; fmr Vice-Chair. Bd Govs Queen's Univ. and past mem. Advisory Council of Queen's Univ. School of Business; mem. Bd St Michael's Hosp.; Fellow, Inst. of Corp. Dirs 2008; Hon. LLD (Queen's Univ.); ICAO Award of Outstanding Merit 2013. *Address:* BCE Inc., 1 Carrefour Alexander Graham Bell, Building A, 4th Floor, Verdun, PQ H3E 3B3, Canada (office). *Telephone:* (514) 870-8777 (office). *Fax:* (514) 786-3970 (office). *E-mail:* bcecomms@bce.ca (office). *Website:* www.bce.ca (office).

O'NEILL OF BENGARVE, Baroness (Life Peer), cr. 1999, of The Braid in the County of Antrim; **Onora Sylvia O'Neill,** CH, CBE, BA, PhD, FBA, FMedSci; British philosopher and academic; *Emeritus Professor of Philosophy, Cambridge University;* b. 23 Aug. 1941, Aughafatten, Northern Ireland; d. of Sir Con O'Neill and Lady Garvey (née Rosemary Pritchard); m. Edward Nell 1963 (divorced 1976); two s.; ed St Paul's Girls' School, London, Somerville Coll., Oxford, Harvard Univ., USA; Asst Prof., Barnard Coll., Columbia Univ. 1970–76, Assoc. Prof. 1976–77; Lecturer, Univ. of Essex 1977–78, Sr Lecturer 1978–82, Reader 1982–87, Prof. 1987–92; Prin. Newnham Coll., Cambridge 1992–2006; Chair. Nuffield Foundation 1998–2010, Equality and Human Rights Comm. 2012–16; Chair. Royal Irish Acad.'s Strategic Review Cttee May–Oct. 2012, Advisory Bd, Inst. of Philosophy, Insts of Advanced Study, Univ. of London; Pres. British Acad. 2005–09; mem. Council, Royal Inst. of Philosophy, Foundation for Science and Tech., British-Irish Asscn; Trustee, American Univ. of Sharjah, Sense about Science; Foreign mem. American Philosophical Soc. 2003, Leopoldina 2004, Norwegian Acad. of Sciences 2006; Fellow, Wissenschaftskolleg, Berlin 1989–90; Foreign Hon. mem. American Acad. of Arts and Sciences 1993, Austrian Acad. of Sciences 2002; Hon. Bencher of Gray's Inn 2002; Hon. MRIA 2003; Hon. FRS; Dr hc (East Anglia) 1995, (Essex) 1996, (Nottingham) 1999, (Aberdeen) 2001, (Dublin) 2002, (Oxford) 2003, (Ulster) 2003, (London) 2003, (Bath) 2004, (Stirling) 2005, (Queen's Univ. Belfast) 2005, (Edinburgh) 2006, (Cambridge) 2007, (Newcastle) 2008, (Lancaster) 2008, (York) 2009, (Harvard) 2010, (Glasgow) 2010, (Univ. Coll. London) 2010, (Nat. Univ. of Ireland) 2011 Pour le Mérite Order 2014, Verdienstorden der Bundesrepublik Deutschland 2016; Fritz Thyssen Stiftung Kant Prize 2015, Holberg Prize 2017, Berggruen Prize 2017. *Radio:* The Reith Lectures 2002. *Publications:* Faces of Hunger: An Essay on Poverty, Development and Justice 1986, Constructions of Reason: Explorations of Kant's Practical Philosophy 1989, Towards Justice and Virtue: A Constructive Account of Practical Reasoning 1996, Bounds of Justice 2000, Autonomy and Trust in Bioethics 2002, A Question of Trust 2002, Rethinking Informed Consent in Bioethics (with Neil Manson) 2007, Constructing Authorities: reason, politics and interpretation in Kant's philosophy 2015, Justice across Boundaries: whose obligations? 2016; numerous articles in learned journals. *Leisure interests:* walking, talking. *Address:* House of Lords, Westminster, London, SW1A 0PW, England (office). *Telephone:* (20) 3117-0220 (office). *E-mail:* oon20@cam.ac.uk (home); sue.thomson@equalityhumanrights.com (office).

ONG, Beng Seng; Singaporean hotel industry executive; *Owner and Managing Director, Hotel Properties Ltd;* b. Malaysia; m. Christina Fu; one s. one d.; family relocated to Singapore when aged four; began career when joined insurance firm for ships; joined Kuo Int. 1975; Founder, Owner and Man. Dir Hotel Properties Ltd (Hotel Properties Pte Ltd 1980–82) 1982– with 18 hotels in nine countries in Asia, Australia and Europe; acquired NatSteel through 98 Holdings consortium 2003; credited as one of the people most responsible for bringing Singapore Grand Prix to the country. *Address:* Hotel Properties Ltd, 50 Cuscaden Road, #08-01, HPL House, 249724 Singapore (office). *Telephone:* 6734-5250 (office). *Fax:* 6732-0347 (office). *E-mail:* contactus@hotelprop.com.sg (office). *Website:* www.hotelprop.com (office); www.hplhotels.com (office).

ONG, John Doyle, LLB, MA; American business executive and fmr diplomatist; *Senior Visiting Policy Fellow, RTI International;* b. 29 Sept. 1933, Uhrichsville, Ohio; s. of Louis Brosee and Mary Ellen Ong (née Liggett); m. Mary Lee Schupp 1957; two s. one d.; ed Ohio State Univ., Harvard Univ.; admitted to Ohio Bar 1958; Asst Counsel, B.F. Goodrich Co., Akron 1961–66, Asst to Pres. Int. B.F. Goodrich Co., Akron 1966–69, Vice-Pres. 1969–70, Pres. 1970–72, Group Vice-Pres. 1972–73, Exec. Vice-Pres. 1973–74, Vice-Chair. 1974–75, Pres. 1975–84, Dir 1975–77, COO 1978–79, Chair., Pres. and CEO 1979–84, Chair. 1984–97, CEO 1984–96, Chair. Emer. 1997–; Amb. to Norway 2002–05; Sr Visiting Policy Fellow, RTI Int. 2006–; fmr mem. Bd of Dirs Cooper Industries, The Kroger Co., Ameritech Corpn, Nat. Alliance for Business; Chair. Ohio Business Roundtable 1994–97; Pres. Bd of Trustees, Western Reserve Acad., Hudson, Ohio 1977–95; Trustee, John S. and James L. Knight Foundation 1995–, Univ. of Chicago 1991–, Ohio Historical Soc. 1998–; Dr hc (Ohio State Univ., Kent State Univ., Univ. of Akron, South Dakota State Univ.); Humanities Award of Distinction, Ohio State Univ., Alumni Medal, Ohio State Univ. *Leisure interests:* fishing, hunting. *Address:* RTI International, 701 13th Street, NW, Suite 750, Washington, DC 20005-3967 (office); 230 Aurora Street, Hudson, OH 44236, USA (home). *Telephone:* (202) 728-2080 (office). *Fax:* (202) 728-2095 (office). *E-mail:* johndong@aol.com; listen@rti.org (office). *Website:* www.rti.org (office).

ONG, Keng Sen; Singaporean theatre director; *Artistic Director, TheatreWorks (Singapore) Ltd;* ed Nat. Univ. of Singapore, Tisch Schools of the Arts, New York Univ.; trained as lawyer; Artistic Dir TheatreWorks (Singapore) Ltd 1988–; f. Arts Networks Asia 1999; Co-Artistic Dir 'In Transit' Arts Festival (annual three-week festival) Berlin 2002–03; mem. Int. Council of Asia Soc. of New York; Artist-in-Residence, New York Univ. Asian Pacific and American Studies Programme/Inst. 2002, Vienna Schauspielhaus 2003, Leverhulme Artist-in-Residence, Inst. for Advanced Studies in the Humanities, Univ. of Edinburgh 2008; Singapore Young Artist Award 1992, Singapore Cultural Medallion Award 2003, Distinguished Artist Award, Int. Soc. of Performing Arts 2003, Excellence for Singapore Award, Singapore Totalisator Bd 2003. *Productions include:* A Language of Their Own, New York Shakespeare Festival 1995, Lear, Tokyo 1997, The Silver River, Spoleto Festival, Charleston 2000, The Continuum: Beyond the Killing Fields, Int. Festival of Arts and Ideas, Yale Univ. and Singapore 2001, The Myths of Memory, Vienna 2003. *Address:* TheatreWorks (Singapore) Ltd, 72-13 Mohamed Sultan Road, Singapore 239007 (office). *Telephone:* 67377213 (office). *Fax:* 67377013 (office). *E-mail:* tworks@singnet.com.sg (office). *Website:* www.theatreworks.org.sg (office).

ONG, Romualdo Añover, BSc; Philippine fmr diplomatist; b. 25 April 1939, Manila; s. of Juan Salido Ong and Adelaida Añover; m. 1st Cecilia Hidalgo 1964 (deceased); m. 2nd Farita Aguilucho 1994; two s. two d.; ed Ateneo de Manila and Univ. of the Philippines; joined Ministry of Foreign Affairs 1968; served Bonn 1972–75, Geneva 1975–79, Minister Counsellor, Beijing 1979–82; Special Asst to Deputy Minister for Foreign Affairs 1983; Asst Minister for ASEAN Affairs 1984–85; Sr Econ. Consultant, Tech. Secr. for Int. Econ. Relations/Bd. of Overseas Econ. Promotion 1985; Amb. to Australia (also accred to Vanuatu) 1986–89; Asst Sec. for Asian and Pacific Affairs, Dept of Foreign Affairs, Manila 1990–93; Amb. to Russia 1993–94, to People's Repub. of China 1994–2000, to Malaysia 2003–04; Dir Foreign Service Inst. 2000; mem. Bd of Dirs First Metro Investment Corpn 2005–12, PBC Capital Investment Corpn 2006–, First Metro Asia Focus Equity Fund, Inc. 2012–, Paradigm Global Growth Fund, Inc. 2016–. *Leisure interests:* reading, car driving, basketball, hiking, movies, listening to music. *Address:* c/o Board of Directors, First Metro Investment Corporation, 20th Floor, GT Tower International, Ayala Avenue corner HV Dela Costa, Makati City, Philippines.

ONGERI, Samson Kegengo, MB, DCH, MRCP; Kenyan physician, politician and diplomatist; *Senator for Kisii County;* b. 23 Feb. 1938, Kisii; ed Univ. of Bombay, India, Univ. of London, UK; Lecturer, Univ. of Nairobi 1973–88, becoming Prof., Dept of Paediatrics and Child Health; Council Chair., OUN 1993–97; mem. Nat. Ass. (Parl.) for Nyaribari Masaba constituency 1989–92, 1998–2002, 2008–13; fmrly with Ministries of Health and Local Govt; Minister for Tech. Training and Applied Tech. 1988–92, for Educ. 2008–12, of Foreign Affairs 2012–13; Senator for Kisii County 2017–; mem. Nat. Dialogue Reconciliation team led by Kofi Annan (following post-election violence) 2008; Pres. Multilateral Fund of the Ozone Layer; Perm. Rep. of Kenya to UNEP 1993–97, becoming Vice-Chair. UNEP Governing Council; fmr Chair., Conf. of Ministers of Education of the African Union; Chair. Kenya Athletic Asscn 1976–84, Ongeri Foundation (promoting health, educ., environment and devt issues); fmr Chair. Kenya Inst. of Educ., Kenya Nat. Trading Co.; fmr Co-Chair., Asscn of Devt of Educ. in Africa; Amb. and Perm. Rep., UN Human Settlement Programme, Nairobi; mem. Kenya African Nat. Union 2007–13; Elder of the Order of the Golden Heart of Kenya (EGH), Elder of the Burning Spear (EBS), Ordre Nationale Burkinabe 2012; IAAF Veteran's Pin. *Address:* Senate, KICC Bldg, 1st Floor, POB 41842, 00100 Nairobi, Kenya (office). *Telephone:* (20) 3261304 (office). *E-mail:* csenate@parliament.go.ke (office). *Website:* www.parliament.go.ke (office).

ONGPIN, Roberto V., CPA, MBA; Philippine business executive and fmr government official; *Chairman, Alphaland Corporation;* m.; four c.; ed Ateneo de Manila Univ., Harvard Business School, USA; with SyCip Gorres Velayo & Co.

1964–79, becoming Man. Pnr; Minister of Trade and Industry 1979–86; f. AIA Capital (financial advisory firm) 1987; CEO ISM Communications Corpn 2001–13; Chair. Alphaland Corpn 2009–; Founder and Chair. PhilWeb Corpn 2000–; Chair. Macondray Plastics Inc 2009–; Vice-Chair. SCMP Group Ltd, South China Morning Post; mem. Bd of Dirs Shangri-La Asia Ltd 2003–, Philex 2007–, Petron Corpn 2008–, San Miguel Corpn 2009–, Philippine Bank of Communications Inc 2011–, PAL Holdings, Inc. 2012–. *Address:* Alphaland Corporation, The Penthouse, Alphaland Southgate Tower 2258, Chino Roces Avenue, corner Edsa Makati, Metro Manila, Philippines (office). *Telephone:* (2) 3372031 (office). *Website:* www.alphaland.com.ph (office).

O'NIONS, Sir (Robert) Keith, Kt, MA, PhD, FRS; British geochemist, academic and university administrator; b. 26 Sept. 1944, Birmingham, England; s. of William Henry O'Nions and Eva Stagg; m. Rita Bill 1967; three d.; ed Univ. of Nottingham, Univ. of Alberta; Postdoctoral Fellow, Univ. of Alberta, Canada 1969–70; Unger Vetlesen Postdoctoral Fellow, Univ. of Oslo, Norway 1970–71; Demonstrator in Petrology, Univ. of Oxford 1971–72, Lecturer in Geochemistry 1972–75; Assoc. Prof. and Prof. of Geology, Columbia Univ., New York, USA 1975–79; Royal Soc. Research Prof., Univ. of Cambridge 1979–95; Fellow, Clare Hall Cambridge 1980–95; Prof. of Physics and Chem. of Minerals, Univ. of Oxford 1995–2003; Chief Scientific Adviser, Ministry of Defence 2000–04; Dir-Gen. Research Councils 2004–08; Head, Inst. for Security Science and Tech., Imperial Coll. London 2008–10, Rector, Imperial Coll. London 2010–13, Pres. and Rector 2012–14; mem. UK Govt's Council of Science and Tech. 1998–2000; Trustee, then Chair. Natural History Museum 1996–2005; Fellow, St Hugh's Coll. Oxford 1995–2003; mem. Norwegian Acad. of Sciences 1980; Fellow, American Geophysical Union 1979, Indian Nat. Science Acad. 2001; hon. doctorates from 11 univs; J.B. Macelwane Award 1979, Bigsby Medal 1983, Holmes Medal 1995, Lyell Medal 1995, Urey Medal 2001. *Publications:* numerous publs in scientific journals on geochemistry.

ONKELINX, Laurette, BL; Belgian lawyer and politician; b. 2 Oct. 1958, Ougrée; ed Univ. of Liège; Lecturer in Admin. Sciences 1982–85; barrister, Liège 1981–; Deputy for Liège (Parti Socialiste—PS) 1987–95, Municipal Councillor, Seraing 1995–2001, elected Senator 1995, elected Deputy for Brussels-Halle-Vilvoorde 2003, Pres. PS Parl. Group 2014–; Minister for Social Integration, Health and Environment 1992–93, Minister-Pres. in Govt of Communauté française in charge of Civil Service, Childhood and Promotion of Health 1993–95, Minister-Pres. in charge of Educ., Audiovisual, Youth Help and Promotion of Health 1995–99, apptd Deputy Prime Minister and Minister for Employment (later Employment and Equal Opportunities) 1999, then also Minister of Mobility and Transport 2003; Deputy Prime Minister and Minister for Justice 2003–07; Minister of Social Affairs and Public Health 2007 (resgnd), reappointed Dec. 2007, resgnd March 2008, Deputy Prime Minister and Minister of Social Affairs and Health March–Dec. 2008 (resgnd), reappointed Dec. 2008–11, Dec. 2011–14; Vice-Pres. PS 2014–; Chair. Brussels Tourism Agency 2015–. *Publications:* Continuons le débat, Théâtre du jeune public. *Address:* Parti Socialiste (PS) (Socialist Party), Maison du PS, 13 blvd de l'Empereur, 1000 Brussels, Belgium (office). *Telephone:* (2) 548-32-11 (office). *Fax:* (2) 548-32-90 (office). *E-mail:* info@ps.be (office); info@laurette-onkelinx.be. *Website:* www.ps.be (office); www.laurette-onkelinx.be.

ONODERA, Itsunori, MPolSci; Japanese academic and politician; b. 5 May 1960, Kesennuma, Miyagi Pref.; m.; two s.; ed Tokyo Univ. of Marine Science and Tech., Matsushita Inst. of Govt and Man., Univ. of Tokyo; began career with Miyagi Prefectural Govt 1983; Special Lecturer, later Asst Prof. and Guest Prof., Tohoku Fukushi Univ. 1994–98, Assoc. Prof. 2002; mem. House of Reps (lower house of Parl.) for Miyagi No. 6 constituency (LDP) 1997–2000 (resgnd), 2003–, Dir Special Cttee on Prevention of Int. Terrorism and Japan's Co-operation and Support, mem. Cttee on Foreign Affairs; Parl. Sec. for Foreign Affairs 2004–05, Sr Vice-Minister for Foreign Affairs 2007; Minister of Defence 2012–14, 2017–18; Visiting Research Fellow, School of Advanced Int. Studies, Johns Hopkins Univ., USA Sept. 2000; mem. LDP, Deputy Dir Fisheries Div., Policy Research Council 1999, Foreign Affairs Div., Deputy Chair. Diet Affairs Cttee 2006. *Address:* c/o Ministry of Defence, 5-1, Ichigaya, Honmura-cho, Shinjuku-ku, Tokyo 162-8801, Japan (office). *Website:* www.itsunori.com.

ONODERA, Tadashi, BEng; Japanese business executive; *Chairman, KDDI Corporation;* b. 3 Feb. 1948; ed Tohuko Univ.; began career as electronic engineer Microwave Div., Nippon Telegraph and Telephone Public Corpn 1970; joined DDI Corpn 1984, Dir and Gen. Man. Microwave Eng Dept, Network Communications Group and Mobile Communications Group 1989–95, Man. Dir and Sr Gen. Man. Eng Group 1995–97, Exec. Vice-Pres. and Sr Gen. Man. Eng Group 1997–98, Exec. Vice-Pres., Chief Engineer and Sr Gen. Man. Mobile Communications Group 1998–2000, Exec. Vice-Pres. and Deputy Operating Officer Mobile Communications Sector 2000–01, Pres. KDDI Corpn (following merger of DDI Corpn, KDD Corpn and IDO Corpn 2000) 2001–05, Pres. and Chair. 2005–10, Chair. 2010–; Dir, Kyocera Corpn 2013–, Daiwa Securities Group Inc. 2014–. *Address:* KDDI Corpn, Garden Air Tower, 3-10-10, Iidabashi, Chiyoda-ku, Tokyo 102-8460, Japan (office). *Telephone:* (3) 6678-0692 (office). *Fax:* (3) 6678-0305 (office). *E-mail:* info@kddi.com (office). *Website:* www.kddi.com (office).

ONORIO, Teima, MA; I-Kiribati politician; d. of Rota Onorio; MP for Arorae constituency 1998–2002; Vice-Pres. of Kiribati 2003–16, also Minister of Commerce, Industry and Co-operatives 2007–08, for Educ., Youth and Sport Devt 2008, for Internal and Social Affairs 2012–16.

ONWUMECHILI, Ozo Ochendo Cyril Agodi, PhD, DSc; Nigerian physicist, academic and administrator; b. 20 Jan. 1932, Inyi; s. of Nwaime Onwumechili and Akuviro Onwumechili (née Orji); m. Cecilia Bedeaka (née Anyadibe) 1958; two s. one d.; ed King's Coll., Lagos, Univ. Coll., Ibadan and Univ. of London, UK; Dir of chain of observatories 1960–66; Dean, Faculty of Science, Univ. of Ibadan 1965–66; Prof. and Head of Dept, Univ. of Nigeria 1966–73, 1976–78, Dean, Faculty of Science 1970–71, Dean, Faculty of Physical Sciences 1973–76, 1978; Visiting Prof. of Geophysics, Univ. of Alaska 1971–72; Consultant, Inst. for Space Research, Nat. Research Council of Brazil 1972; Vice-Chancellor, Univ. of Ife, Ile-Ife 1979–82; Deputy Pres. Anambra State Univ. of Tech., Enugu 1983–84, Pres. 1984–85, Vice-Chancellor 1985–86; Consultant UN Econ. Comm. for Africa 1987, Commonwealth Science Council 1988; Vice-Chair. Div. II Int. Asscn of Geomagnetism and Aeronomy 1987–91, Chair. Interdivisional Comm. 1991–95; mem. Int. Scientific Programmes Cttee, Int. Symposia on Equatorial Aeronomy 1972–, UN Advisory Cttee on Science and Tech. for Devt 1981–83; Chair. Man. Cttee UNESCO African Network of Scientific and Technological Insts (ANSTI) 1985–90; Vice-Pres. Asscn of African Univs 1984–89, Consultant 1990–2002, Chair. Scientific Cttee 1993–; mem. American Geophysical Union, Soc. for Terrestrial Magnetism and Electricity of Japan; Fellow, UK and Nigerian Inst. of Physics 1969; Foundation Ed.-in-Chief Nigerian Journal of Science 1964–67; Visiting Prof. of Physics, Univ. of Wales at Cardiff 1987–88; Foundation Fellow and fmr Pres. Nigerian Acad. of Science; UK Chartered Physicist 1986; Fellow, African Acad. of Sciences 1987, Third World Acad. of Sciences 1989; Foundation Fellow, Science Asscn of Nigeria 1974; Hon. DSc (Ife) 1977, (Enugu State Univ.) 1992, (Univ. of Nigeria) 2001. *Publications:* Geomagnetic Variations in the Equatorial Zone 1967, University Administration in Nigeria: The Anambra State University of Technology Approach I 1991, Cost Effectiveness and Efficiency in African Universities 1993, The Equatorial Electrojet 1997, Igho Enwe Eze?: The 2000 Ahiajoku Lecture; numerous scientific articles. *Leisure interests:* swimming, table tennis, lawn tennis. *Address:* PO Box 9059, Uwani, Enugu, Nigeria; 69 Lansdowne Drive, Hackney, London, E8 3EP, England. *Telephone:* (20) 7249-3260 (London); (42) 254987 (Enugu).

ONYEAMA, Geoffrey, BA, MA, LLM; Nigerian lawyer, politician and fmr international organization official; *Minister of Foreign Affairs;* b. 2 Feb. 1956; m.; three c.; ed Columbia Univ., USA, Univ. of London, St John's Coll., Cambridge, UK; called to the English Bar, Grey's Inn 1981; admitted as Barrister-at-Law, Supreme Court of Nigeria 1983; Research Officer, Nigerian Law Reform Comm. 1983–84; Law Practitioner, Mogboh and Assocs, Enugu 1984–85; joined World Intellectual Property Org. (WIPO) 1985, various roles including Asst Programme Officer for Devt Cooperation and External Relations, Bureau for Africa and W Asia 1985–86, Programme Officer 1986–90, Sr Programme Officer for Devt Cooperation and External Relations, Bureau for Africa 1990–96, Sr Counsellor for Devt Cooperation and External Relations, Bureau for Africa 1996–98, Deputy Dir, Cooperation for Devt, Bureau for Africa 1998–99, Acting Dir 1999–2006, Asst Dir-Gen., Coordination Sector for External Relations, Industry, Communications and Public Outreach 2006–09, also in charge, various WIPO external offices 2006–12, Deputy Dir-Gen., WIPO 2009–14; Minister of Foreign Affairs 2015–. *Address:* Ministry of Foreign Affairs, Sir Tafawa Balewa House, Federal Secretariat, PMB 130, Abuja, Nigeria (office). *Telephone:* (9) 5230570 (office). *E-mail:* omaduekwe@nigeria.gov.ng (office). *Website:* www.foreignaffairs.gov.ng (office).

ONYSZKIEWICZ, Janusz, DMath; Polish mathematician and government official; *Chairman, International Board of Directors, International Centre for Democratic Transition;* b. 18 Dec. 1937, Lvov; s. of Stanislaw Onyszkiewicz and Franciszka Onyszkiewicz; m. 1st Witoslawa Boretti (died 1967); m. 2nd Alison Chadwick (died 1978); m. 3rd Joanna Jaraczewska 1983; two s. three d.; ed Univ. of Warsaw; Asst, Math. Engines Inst., Polish Acad. of Sciences, Warsaw 1958–61; Asst, later Sr Asst, Faculty of Math., Informatics and Mechanics, Math. Inst., Univ. of Warsaw 1963–67, Lecturer 1967–75, now Sr Lecturer; Lecturer, Univ. of Leeds, UK 1976–79; mem. Polish Teachers' Union (ZNP) 1969–80, Ind. Self-governing Trade Union of Science, Tech. and Educ. Workers 1980, Deputy Chair. Br. at Warsaw Univ. Sept.–Oct. 1980; adviser to Interfactory Founding Cttee of Solidarity Ind. Self-governing Trade Union – Mazovia Region, subsequently mem. Presidium of Nat. Comm. of Solidarity Trade Union, Bd and Press Spokesman of Mazovia Region of Solidarity Trade Union; Press Spokesman Nat. Understanding Comm. and First Nat. Congress of Solidarity Trade Union 1980–81; interned 1981–82; arrested April 1983, released under amnesty July 1983; sentenced to six weeks' confinement May 1988; Press Spokesman Nat. Exec. Comm., Solidarity Trade Union; mem. Civic Cttee attached to Lech Wałęsa (q.v.) 1988–91; participant Round Table debates, mem. team for mass media and opposition press spokesman Feb.–April 1989; Deputy to Sejm (Parl.) 1989–2001; Vice-Minister of Nat. Defence 1990–92, Minister 1992–93, 1997–2000, Chair. Defence Cttee, Council of Ministers 1997–99; mem. European Parl. 2004–09, Vice-Pres. Foreign Affairs Cttee 2007–09; currently Chair. Int. Bd of Dirs Int. Centre for Democratic Transition, Budapest; mem. Democratic Union Parl. 1991–94, Freedom Union Parl. 1994; Vice-Pres. Polish Asia-Pacific Council 1996; mem. Nat. Council Freedom Union 1996; mem. Euro-Atlantic Asscn 1994– (Pres. 1994–98); currently Sr Fellow, Centre for Int. Relations; Pres. Polish Mountaineering Fed. 2001–; Great Cross of Gedymin (Lithuania), Great Cross of King Leopold II (Belgium); Hon. DSc (Leeds) 1991; Gold Medal (For Outstanding Sporting Achievements), Manfred Wörner Medal. *Achievements include:* mountaineer and speleologist, participant in mountaineering expeditions in Himalayas, Hindu Kush, Karakoram, Pamir. *Publications:* 15 works on foundations of math., including Complete Abstract Logics 1979; Zdobycie Gasherbrumów (co-author) 1977. *Leisure interests:* climbing, caving, tourism, classical music. *Address:* International Centre for Democratic Transition, 1022 Budapest, Árvácska u. 12, Hungary (office). *Telephone:* (1) 438-0820 (office). *Fax:* (1) 438-0821 (office). *Website:* www.icdt.hu (office).

OPENG, Datuk Amar Abang Johari Abang, MBA; Malaysian politician; *Chief Minister of Sarawak;* b. 4 Aug. 1950, Limbang, Sarawak; s. of Tun Abang Openg Abang Sapiee and Toh Puan Masniah Abdulrahman; m. Datin Amar Juma'ani Tuanku Bujang; two c.; ed Sekolah Menengah Kebangsaan St Joseph, Brunel Univ., UK; fmr Exec. Officer, Corp. Relations Div., Malaysia Airlines; mem. Sarawak State Legis. Ass. for Satok 1981–, Chief Political Sec. to Chief Minister 1982–84; Asst Minister of Regional and Community Devt 1984–87, Minister of Industrial Devt 1987–2000, Minister of Tourism 2000, Minister of Housing 2004, Minister of Housing and Urbanization 2009, Minister of Housing and Minister of Tourism 2011, Deputy Chief Minister, Minister of Housing and Urbanization and Minister of Tourism, Arts and Culture 2016–17, Chief Minister of Sarawak 2017–; Acting Pres. Pesaka Bumiputera Bersatu party; Pres. Sarawak United Nat. Youth Org. *Address:* Office of the Chief Minister, 22nd Floor, Wisma Bapa Malaysia Petra Jaya, 93502 Kuching, Sarawak, Malaysia (office). *Telephone:* (82) 440801 (office). *Fax:* (82) 444566 (office). *E-mail:* cmo@sarawak.gov.my (office). *Website:* www.cm.sarawak.gov.my (office).

OPERTTI BADÁN, Didier, PhD; Uruguayan lawyer, politician and international organization official; b. 23 April 1937, Montevideo; m.; four c.; ed Univ. of Uruguay; fmr Asst Prof. of Int. Pvt. Law, Univ. of Uruguay, Prof. of Int. Relations 1986; Dir Office of Codification and Devt of Int. Law, Gen. Secr., OAS 1979–81,

Perm. Rep. to OAS 1988–93, Pres. OAS Perm. Council's Comm. of Juridical and Political Matters 1989, Pres. OAS Perm. Council 1990; Dir Diplomatic Law Advisory Council, Ministry of Foreign Affairs 1985–88; Prof. of Int. Pvt. Law, Int. Law Acad., The Hague; Prof. of Int. Pvt. Law, Catholic Univ. of Uruguay 1994; Minister of the Interior 1995–98, of Foreign Affairs 1998, 2000–05; Sec.-Gen., Latin-American Integration Asscn (Asociación Latinoamericana de Integración—ALADI) 2005–08; Pres. 53rd Session of UN Gen. Ass. 1998–2000; Special Counsellor for MERCOSUR issues to IDB and Inst. for Integration of Latin America and the Caribbean 1993–94; mem. UN Law Comm.; fmr mem. Uruguayan Nat. Group of Perm. Court of Arbitration; Founder and Bd mem. Int. Law Asscn of Uruguay; mem. and Dir Uruguayan Comparative Law Inst.; mem. Lawyers Asscn of Uruguay, Portuguese-Spanish American Int. Law Inst., Int. Law Asscn of Argentina, Int. and Comparative Law Acad. of Brazil. *Publications:* Exhortos y embargo de bienes extranjeros: Medios de cooperación judicial internacional 1976, Contratos comerciales internacionales: Ultimos desarrollos teorico-positivos en el ambito internacional 1997. *Address:* c/o Asociación Latinoamericana de Integración, Cebollati 1461, Casilla 577, CP 11200, Montevideo, Uruguay. *Telephone:* (2) 410-1121.

OPIE, Julian Gilbert, BA; British artist; b. 12 Dec. 1958, London, England; s. of Roger G. Opie and Norma Opie; m. Aniela Opie; one s. three d.; ed Magdalen Coll. School, Oxford, Chelsea School of Art, London and Goldsmiths' School of Art, London; has exhibited widely in UK and internationally, with major museum exhbns, including shows at Kunstverein, Cologne, Hayward Gallery and ICA, London, Lehnbachhaus, Munich, K21, Dusseldorf, MAK, Vienna, Mito Tower, Japan, CAC, Malaga and IVAM, Valencia, MOCAK, Kraków, Tidehalle, Helsinki, as well as Dehli Triennial, Venice Biennial and Documenta; represented by 12 galleries world-wide, including Lisson and Alan Cristea, London, Barbara Krakow, Boston, Bob van Orsouw, Zurich, Gerhardsen Gerner, Oslo and Germany, Krobath, Vienna, Kukje, Seoul, Mario Sequeira, Portugal, Patrick De Brock, Brussels, Sakshi, Mumbai, Maho Kubota, Japan and Valentina Bonomo, Rome; has presented numerous public projects in cities around the world, notably in Dentsu Bldg, Tokyo 2002, City Hall Park, New York 2004, Mori Building, Omotesando Hill, Japan 2006, River Vltava, Prague 2007, Pheonix Art Museum, USA 2007, Dublin City Gallery, Ireland 2008, Seoul Square, South Korea 2009, Regent's Place, London 2011, Calgary, Canada, The Lindo Wing, St Mary's Hosp., London and, more recently, perm. installations at SMETS, Belgium, PKZ, Zurich, Arendt and Medernach, Brussels, Tower 535, Hong Kong, Tapei, Taiwan and Takamatsu City, Japan; Best Illustration for Best of Blur, Music Week CADS. *Publications include:* Julian Opie, Kunstverein Cologne: Catalogue of Works 1984, Julian Opie Drawings, ICA, London, Julian Opie New Works, Lisson Gallery, The Complete Edtions Vols 1 & 2, Alan Cristea Gallery. *Address:* c/o Lisson Gallery, 52–54 Bell Street, London, NW1 5DA, England (office). *E-mail:* info@julianopie.com. *Website:* www.julianopie.com.

OPIE, Lionel Henry, MD, PhD, MRCP, FACC, FRSSA; South African cardiologist and academic; *Professor Emeritus of Medicine, Hatter Institute for Cardiology Research, Cape Heart Group, University of Cape Town;* b. 6 May 1933, Hanover, SA; s. of Prof. William Henry Opie and Marie Opie (née Le Roux); m. Carol June Sancroft Baker 1969; two d.; ed Diocesan Coll., Rondebosch, Cape Town, Univ. of Cape Town, Univ. of Oxford, UK; Intern, Groote Schuur Hosp. 1956; Sr House Officer, Dept of Neurology, Radcliffe Infirmary, Oxford 1957–59; House Physician (Endocrinology), Hammersmith Hosp., London 1959; Asst in Medicine, Peter Bent Brigham Hosp., Boston, Mass, USA, Samuel A. Levine Fellow in Cardiology, Harvard Medical School 1960–61; Asst Resident in Medicine, Toronto Gen. Hosp., Canada 1961–62; Consultant Physician, Karl Bremer Hosp. and Univ. of Stellenbosch, SA; Out-Patient Asst Physician, Radcliffe Infirmary, Wellcome Research Fellow, Dept of Biochemistry, Univ. of Oxford 1964–66; part-time Registrar, Hammersmith Hosp., London 1966–67; Research Fellow, Dept of Biochemistry, Imperial Coll., London 1966–68; Sr Registrar in Medicine (Cardiology), Hammersmith Hosp. 1967–69, Consultant in Medicine 1969; Sr Specialist Physician, Groote Schuur Hosp. 1971; Assoc. Prof. of Medicine, Univ. of Cape Town 1975, Dir MRC Research Unit for Ischaemic Heart Disease (now Hatter Inst., Cape Heart Centre) 1976, Personal Chair in Medicine, Prof. of Medicine 1980, now Prof. Emer., Dir Hypertension Clinic 1979; Visiting Prof., Div. of Cardiovascular Medicine, Stanford Univ. School of Medicine, Calif., USA 1991–94; British Heart Foundation Sr Fellow and Visiting Prof. St Thomas' Hosp., London 1992; Pres. Southern Africa Cardiac Soc. 1980–82; Chair. Council on Cardiac Metabolism, Int. Soc. and Fed. of Cardiology 1980; Pres. Southern Africa Hypertension Soc. 1986; Chair. Cttee Cardiovascular Drugs, Int. Soc. and Fed. Cardiology 1990; mem. British Cardiac Soc., Physiological Soc. (UK), SA Socs of Cardiology, Pharmacology, Biochemistry and Hypertension, Int. Hypertension Soc.; Dr. hc (Univ. of Stellenbosch) 2012. *Publications:* over 300. *Address:* Hatter Institute for Cardiology Research, Cape Heart Centre, Faculty of Health Sciences, University of Cape Town, 7925 Observatory (office); 66A Dean Street, Newlands 7700, South Africa (home). *Telephone:* 471250 (office); 6853855 (home). *Website:* web.uct.ac.za/depts/chc/hatter/intro.htm (office).

OPIYO, Nicholas; Ugandan human rights lawyer; *Executive Director, Chapter Four Uganda;* b. 15 Nov. 1980, Gulu; ed Uganda Christian Univ.; began career as interpreter for Int. Criminal Court's investigation into war crimes committed by Lord's Resistance Army (LRA); Rights Monitoring and Policy Advocate Officer, Foundation for Human Rights Initiative 2006–07; Founder and Exec. Dir, Chapter Four Uganda (human rights org.) 2013–; Advocate and Consulting Assoc. (Human Rights), Akijul (Enabling Change), Kampala; Visiting Scholar, Center for African Studies, Stanford Univ. 2015, Univ. of California at San Francisco 2016; key facilitator on Nat. Consultations on Juba Peace Process (negotiations between Ugandan Govt and LRA); several high-profile cases, including as lead attorney on constitutional case that overturned Uganda's Anti-Homosexuality Act 2014; regular appearances in the Ugandan media; took part in US-Africa Leadership Summit organized by the White House, Washington 2014; fmr Sec.-Gen., Bar Asscn of Kampala (forced to resign 2014); Hon. Sec. Uganda Law Soc. 2013–14; EU Sakharov Fellow 2016; Human Rights Watch Alison Des Forges Award for Extraordinary Activism 2015, German Africa Foundation Prize 2017. *Address:* Chapter Four Uganda, Plot 2, Wampewo Avenue, Kampala, Uganda (office). *Telephone:* (790) 916614 (office). *E-mail:* info@chapterfouruganda.com (office). *Website:* chapterfouruganda.com (office).

OPOLAIS, Kristīne; Latvian singer (soprano); b. 12 Nov. 1979, Rēzekne; m. Andris Nelsons (q.v.) 2011 (divorced 2018); one d.; ed Jāzeps Vītols Latvian Acad. of Music, studied with sopranos Regina Frinberga and Lilija Greidāne and vocal coach Margarita Gruzdeva, and with Margreet Honig at Sweelinck Conservatory, Amsterdam; started career as mem. chorus with Latvian Nat. Opera 2001–03, soloist 2003–07, operatic stage debut as Musetta in La Bohème, Riga 2003; debut at Staatsoper Unter den Linden, Berlin, as title role in Tosca 2006; debut at Teatro alla Scala, Milan as Pauline in The Gambler 2008, at Wiener Staatsoper as Mimi in La Bohème 2008, at Bavarian State Opera as title role in Dvorak's Rusalka 2010, at Royal Opera, Covent Garden as Cio Cio San in Madama Butterfly 2011; debut at Metropolitan Opera, New York as Magda in La Rondine 2013; title role in Manon Lescaut at Covent Garden 2013–14 and Metropolitan Opera 2016; title role in Rusalka, Metropolitan Opera 2017; opera repertoire includes Puccini roles (Tosca, Musetta, Mimi, Butterfly, Magda), Tatyana in Eugene Onegin, Rusalka, Jenufa, Violetta in La traviata, Tamara in The Demon; has worked with leading conductors, including Daniel Barenboim, Riccardo Chailly, Antonio Pappano, Daniel Harding, Louis Langrée, Andris Nelsons, Gianandrea Noseda, Marco Armiliato, Marc Minkowski, Fabio Luisi, Kirill Petrenko, Alain Altinoglu and Kazushi Ono; concert repertoire includes Verdi's Requiem, Wagner's Wesendonck Lieder, Strauss' Vier letzte Lieder, and Mahler's 4th Symphony; concert performances have included appearances at Salzburg Festival, Tanglewood, BBC Proms, with orchestras including Symphonieorchester des Bayerischen Rundfunks, WDR Sinfonieorchester Köln, Tonhalle Orchester Zürich, Stockholm Philharmonic and Filarmonica della Scala, Royal Danish Orchestra; regular guest with City of Birmingham Symphony Orchestra; Paul Sakss Singers Award 2004, Latvian Annual Theatre Award for Best Opera Artist 2005, Latvian Cultural Foundation Award 2005, Latvian Great Music Award 2006, 2007. *Recordings include:* Puccini: Suor Angelica 2012, Tchaikovsky: Eugene Onegin (with Orchestra and Chorus of the Comunitat Valenciana) 2013, Simon Boccanegro (recording from Vienna Konzerthaus conducted by Massimo Zanetti) 2013, Manon Lescaut (RoH recording with Jonas Kaufmann, conducted by Antonio Pappano) 2015. *Address:* c/o Askonas Holt Ltd, 15 Fetter Lane, London, EC4A 1BW, England (office). *Telephone:* (20) 7400-1700 (office). *Website:* www.askonasholt.co.uk (office); kristineopolais.com.

OPPENHEIMER, Nicholas (Nicky) Frank, MA; South African business executive; b. 8 June 1945, Johannesburg; s. of Harry F. Oppenheimer and Bridget Oppenheimer (née McCall); m. Orcillia M. L. Lasch 1968; one s.; ed Harrow School, UK and Christ Church, Oxford, UK; apptd Chair. The Diamond Trading Co. Ltd 1985, Chair. De Beers Consolidated Mines Ltd 1998–2012 (retd), also Exec. Chair. De Beers Centenary AG, Dir De Beers Industrial Corpn Ltd, E. Oppenheimer & Son (Pty) Ltd; Dir (non-exec.) Anglo-American Corpn of South Africa Ltd –2011; f., Greene and Partners Investments (venture capital firm) 1999; Hon. DTech (Technikon Witwatersrand) 2003. *Leisure interests:* squash, golf, cricket, flying.

OPREA, Gabriel, DIur; Romanian politician and fmr army officer; b. 1 Jan. 1961, Fundulea, Călăraşi Co.; m.; two c.; ed Active Officers' Mil. School, Sibiu, Faculty of Law, Univ. of Bucharest, Nat. Coll. of Defence; officer, Ministry of Defence 1983–90; Vice-Pres. Nat. Coll. of Defence 2000, Deputy Dir 2000–01, Prof. 2001; Sec. of State and Pres. Nat. Admin of State Reserves 2001–02; thesis adviser, Alexandru Ioan Cuza Police Acad. 2002; Prefect, Bucharest 2002–03; Del. Minister of Public Admin 2003–04; mem. Chamber of Deputies for Ilfov Co. 2004–; mem. Partidul Social Democrat (PSD—Social Democratic Party) 2003–09, Pres. PSD Ilfov 2004–09, PSD Defence Dept 2006–09; Minister of Interior and Admin. Reform Dec. 2008–Jan. 2009 (resgnd), Nov.–Dec. 2009, Minister of Nat. Defence 2009–12; Prof., Nat. Intelligence Acad. 2008–; Deputy Prime Minister 2012–15; Minister of Internal Affairs 2014–15; Interim Prime Minister June–July 2015; Exec. Pres. Uniunea Naţională pentru Progresul României (UNPR—Nat. Union for the Progress of Romania) 2010–16, 18–; rank of four-star Gen. in the reserves 2009; Kt, Nat. Order of the Star of Romania 2000; Nat. Order of Faithful Service 2001. *Address:* Uniunea Naţională pentru Progresul României (National Union for the Progress of Romania), 011413 Bucharest 1, Str. Gheorghe Bratianu 7, Romania. *Telephone:* (31) 4327774 (office). *Fax:* (31) 4327774 (office). *E-mail:* secretariat@unpr.eu (office). *Website:* www.unpr.eu (office).

OPRESCU, Sorin Mircea; Romanian physician and politician; b. 7 Nov. 1951, Bucharest; m. (divorced); one c.; ed Faculty of Medicine, Univ. of Bucharest; surgical intern 1975–78; physician, M. Kogălniceanu Int. Airport, Constanţa 1978–79; Trainee Univ. Asst, Surgery Clinic of Brancovenian Clinic Hosp. 1978, Univ. Asst 1982; surgeon, Bucharest Univ. Hosp. 1985–90, Primary Surgeon, Clinic for Higher Digestive Surgery 1990–94, Dir Bucharest Univ. Hosp. 1994–; Lecturer, Carol Davila Univ. of Medicine and Pharmacy 1996–2000, Univ. Prof. and Chair of Surgery 2000–; Adviser to Minister of Health 1993–94; Adviser to Gen. Council of Bucharest 1996–2000; Deputy Mayor of Bucharest 2000; mem. Senate 2000–08; mem. Social Democrat Party 1990–2008, Pres. Bucharest br. 2006–08; Mayor of Bucharest (Ind.) 2008–15 (suspended); arrested on charges of corruption Sept. 2015. *E-mail:* sorin@sorinoprescu.ro. *Website:* sorinoprescu.ro; sorinoprescu.wordpress.com.

OQILOV, Oqil Ghaybulloyevich; Tajikistani politician and engineer; b. 2 Feb. 1944, Leninobod (now Khujand); m.; three c.; ed Moscow Inst. of Construction and Eng; various posts in construction orgs, Leninobod (now Sugdh) Viloyat 1960–76; worked for CP 1976–93; Minister of Construction of Tajikistan 1993–94; Deputy Prime Minister 1994–96; First Deputy Chair. Leninobod Viloyat 1996–99; Prime Minister 1999–2013, also Minister of Construction; mem. People's Democratic Party of Tajikistan. *Address:* People's Democratic Party of Tajikistan, 734000 Dushanbe, Xiyoboni Rudaki 107, Tajikistan (office). *Telephone:* (372) 21-05-45 (office). *Fax:* (372) 21-25-36 (office). *E-mail:* admin@hhdt.tj (office).

ORABI, Muhammad al-, MBA; Egyptian diplomatist; b. 26 Jan. 1951, Heliopolis, Cairo; m.; one d.; ed Cairo Univ.; Attaché, Ministry of Foreign Affairs (MFA) 1976–78, Second Sec., Embassy in Kuwait 1978–82, in Cabinet of State Minister for Foreign Affairs and Pvt. Sec. to Minister 1982–84, First Sec., Embassy in London 1984–88, Official MFA Spokesperson 1988–89, Counsellor, Embassy in Washington, DC 1989–93, Minister Plenipotentiary and Deputy Head of Mission, Embassy in Tel-Aviv 1994–98, Dir Office of Minister of Foreign Affairs 1998–2001, Amb. to Germany 2001–08, Asst Minister of Foreign Affairs for Econ. Affairs and Int. Co-operation 2008–11, Minister of Foreign Affairs June–July 2011 (resgnd); Grosses Bundesverdientstkreuz (Germany).

ORAM, Jacob David Philip; New Zealand fmr professional cricketer; b. 28 July 1978, Palmerston North, Manawatu; m. Mara Tait-Jamieson 2008; one s.; all-rounder; left-handed batsman; right-arm fast-medium pace bowler; played for Central Districts Stags 1997–2014, New Zealand 2001–12, Chennai Super Kings 2008–09, Rajasthan Royals 2011–12, Uva Next 2012, Chittagong Kings 2013, Mumbai Indians 2013; First-class debut: 1997/98; Test debut: NZ v India, Wellington 12–14 Dec. 2002; One-Day Int. (ODI) debut: NZ v Zimbabwe, Wellington 4 Jan. 2001; T20I debut: S Africa v NZ, Johannesburg 21 Oct. 2005; played in 33 Test matches, scored 1,780 runs (average 36.32) and took 60 wickets (average 33.05) with five centuries, six half-centuries, highest score 133 against South Africa, Centurion 2006, best bowling 4/41 against India, Hamilton 2002; played in 160 ODIs, scored 2,434 runs (average 24.09) and took 173 wickets (average 29.17) with one century, 13 half-centuries, highest score 101 not out against Australia, Perth 2007, and two five-wicket performances, best bowling 5/26 against India, Auckland 2002; played in 36 T20Is, scored 474 runs (average 20.60) and took 19 wickets (41.73), with two fifties, highest score 66 not out against Australia, Perth 2007, best bowling 3/33 against Colombo 2009; played in 85 First-class matches, scored 4,158 runs (average 33.83) and took 155 wickets (average 26.82) with eight centuries and 18 fifties, highest score 155, and three five-wicket performances, best bowling 6/45; took a hat trick against Sri Lanka in a Twenty20 Int. in Colombo 2 Sept. 2009; announced retirement from Test cricket 13 Oct. 2009; name inscribed on Lords Honours Bd for his Test century against England 2008.

ORAYEVSKY, Victor Nikolayevich, DPhysMathSc; Russian physicist; b. 9 March 1935, Poltava, Ukraine; ed Kharkov State Univ.; Jr Researcher, Inst. of Nuclear Physics, USSR Acad. of Sciences (Siberian br.) 1958–65, Head of Div. Inst. of Earth Magnetism, Ionosphere and Radiowaves Propagation (IZMIRAN) 1979–89, Dir 1989–, Head of int. Sputnik projects; Sr Researcher, Inst. of Physics, Ukrainian Acad. of Sciences 1965–70, Head of Div., Inst. of Nuclear Studies 1970–74; Head of Scientific Production Div., Energia Co. 1974–79, Head of Lab., Head of Dept 1979–89; mem. Int. Acad. of Astronautics, New York Acad. of Sciences, Russian Acad. of Sciences, Int. Acad. of Informatics; State Prize of Ukrainian SSR, USSR State Prize 1987, Merited Worker of Science, Russian Fed. 1996. *Address:* IZMIRAN, 142092 Troitsk, Moscow, Russia (office). *Telephone:* (495) 334-01-20 (office).

ORAZBAY, Askhat T.; Kazakhstani international organization official and diplomat; *Ambassador to Iran;* b. 2 Dec. 1960; Sec.-Gen. Econ. Co-operation Org. 2004–06; fmr Amb. to Turkmenistan, Amb. to Indonesia –2019, Amb. to Iran 2019–. *Address:* Embassy of the Republic of Kazakhstan, 83 Hadionot Street, Daroush, Tehran, Iran (office). *Telephone:* (21) 22565933 (office). *Fax:* (21) 22546400 (office). *E-mail:* tehran@mfa.kz (office). *Website:* www.mfa.kz/kz/tehran (office).

ORAZMUKHAMEDOV, Nury Orazovich; Turkmenistani politician and diplomatist; b. 1949, Mary; ed Turkmenistan Polytech. Inst.; master, engineer, Chief Engineer, Turkmencentrstroi 1971–; Head of Ashkhabad construction units; Deputy Chair. State Construction Cttee 1990–91; Minister of Construction 1991–94, of Construction and Architecture 1994–95; Head of Admin. Khikim Ashkhabad Feb. 1995; Amb. to Russian Fed. 1996–2000, to Moldova 2000. *Address:* Ministry of Foreign Affairs, 744000 Aşgabat, Archabil av. 108, Turkmenistan (office). *Telephone:* (12) 445622 (office). *Fax:* (12) 218675 (office). *E-mail:* mfatm@online.tm (office). *Website:* www.mfa.gov.tm (office).

ORBAN, Leonard; Romanian engineer and politician; b. 28 June 1961, Braşov; brother of Ludovic Orban; m.; one c.; ed Faculty of Mechanical Eng, Univ. of Braşov, Faculty of Man., Acad. of Econ. Studies, Bucharest; engineer, Inst. of Research for Machine Mfg Tech., Bucharest, Enterprise for Special Industrial Constructions, Bucharest, Tractor Mfg Co. Miercurea Ciuc 1986–93; Parl. Counsellor on European and Int. affairs, Chamber of Deputies, Romanian Parl. 1993–2001; Deputy Chief Negotiator for accession to EU 2001–04, Chief Negotiator 2004–05; State Sec., Ministry of European Integration 2005–06; Head of Romanian del. for negotiating accession to European Econ. Area 2006–; nominated as Romania's cand. for EC Oct. 2006, European Commr for Multilingualism 2007–10; Minister of European Affairs 2011–12; Co-ordinator, Elaboration of Romanian Post Accession Strategy for 2007–13; mem. several governmental cttees related to Romania's EU accession negotiations, including European Integration Exec. Cttee, State Aid Cttee, Cttee for the Man. of EU Funds, Romanian Steel Sector Restructuring; mem. Romanian Social and Econ. Council; Kt of 'Steaua Romaniei' Nat. Order (Star of Romania) 2002. *Publications:* articles and analyses in nat. and foreign newspapers and magazines on European integration and European affairs 2001–. *Leisure interests:* foreign policy, classical music, reading, cinema.

ORBAN, Ludovic; Romanian politician; *President, Partidul Naţional Liberal (National Liberal Party);* b. 25 May 1963, brother of Leonard Orban; m. Mihaela Orban; one c.; ed Univ. of Brasov, Nat. School of Political and Admin. Studies; mem. Bucharest City Council for Sector 3 Bucharest 1992–96; Sec. of State and Head of Govt Public Information Dept 1999–2000; Sec. of State and Pres., Nat. Agency of Civil Servants 2000–01; Deputy Mayor of Bucharest 2004–07; Minister of Transport 2007–08; mem. Chamber of Deputies (lower house of parl.) for No. 41 Bucharest 2008–16, Vice-Pres. (Deputy Speaker) 2009–11; mem. Partidul Naţional Liberal (Nat. Liberal Party), Pres. 2017–. *Address:* Partidul Naţional Liberal, 011866 Bucharest 1, Aleea Modrogan 1, Romania (office). *Telephone:* (21) 2310795 (office). *Fax:* (21) 2310796 (office). *E-mail:* dre@pnl.ro (office). *Website:* pnl.ro (office).

ORBÁN, Viktor, LLD, PhD; Hungarian politician and lawyer; *Prime Minister;* b. 31 May 1963, Székesfehérvár; s. of Győző Orbán; m. Anikó Lévai; two s. three d.; ed Eötvös Loránd Univ., Budapest and Pembroke Coll., Oxford, UK; worked as sociologist for Man. Training Inst., Ministry of Agric. and Food 1987–88; researcher, Middle Europe Research Group 1989–91; co-f. Hungarian opposition group Fidesz (Fed. of Young Democrats) 1988, Spokesman 1989, Chair. Fidesz 1993–2000, 2003–; represented Fidesz political Sub-cttee of Opposition Round Table Discussion 1989; mem. Parl., Leader Fidesz Parl. Group 1990–94; Prime Minister 1998–2002, 2010–; Chair. Parl. Cttee on European Integration Affairs 1994–98; Pres. New Atlantic Initiative Hungarian Cttee 1996–98; Vice-Pres. Liberal Int. 1992–2000 (mem. Bureau 1993–2002), Christian Democrat and People's Parties Int. 2001–, European People's Party 2002–; Hon. Senator, European Acad. of Sciences and Arts 2000; Hon. Citizen of Esztergom 2006; Grande Croix, Ordre nat. du Mérite 2001, Papal Grand Cross of the Order of St Gregory the Great 2004; Freedom Prize, American Enterprises Inst. and the New Atlantic Initiative 2001, Vesek and Maria Polák Prize 2001, Franz Josef Strauss Prize 2001, Capo Circeo Prize 2001, Förderpreis Soziale Marktwirtschaft, German Club of Econs 2002, Mérite Européen Prize, European Peoples's Party 2004, Goce Delchev Award, United Macedonian Diaspora 2014. *Film:* played bit part of a footballer in Hungarian family film 'Szegény Dzsoni és Árnika' 1983. *Publications include:* National Policy 1988–1998, Egy az ország 2007 (translated into Polish as Ojczyzna jest jedna 2009), Rengés-Hullámok 2010. *Leisure interests:* playing football (signed player and financier of Felcsút Football Club), music (favourite band is Creedence Clearwater Revival). *Address:* Office of the Prime Minister, 1357 Budapest, Pf. 6, Hungary (office). *Telephone:* (1) 795-6978 (office). *Fax:* (1) 795-0381 (office). *E-mail:* miniszterelnok@mk.gov.hu (office); orbanviktor@orbanviktor.hu. *Website:* www.kormany.hu/en/the-prime-minister (office); www.orbanviktor.hu.

ORDE, Sir Hugh Stephen Roden, Kt, OBE, QPM, BA; British police officer; b. 27 Aug. 1958, London, England; s. of Thomas Orde and Stella Orde; ed Univ. of Kent; joined London Metropolitan Police 1977, apptd Sergeant, Brixton 1982, Police Staff Coll. 1983, Insp., Greenwich 1984–90, Chief Insp., Deputy Asst Commdr SW London 1990, Chief Insp., Hounslow 1991–93, Supt Territorial Support 1993–95, Commdr (Community Safety and Partnership) 1997–98, Commdr (Crime), S London 1998–99, Deputy Asst Commr attached to Commr's Pvt. Office, New Scotland Yard 1999–2002; Chief Constable, Police Service of NI 2002–09; Pres. Asscn of Chief Police Officers 2009–15; Visiting Prof., Univ. of Ulster; Hon. LLD (Kent) 2008, (Ulster) 2010; Queen's Police Medal for Distinguished Service 2010, Queen Elizabeth II Golden Jubilee Medal 2002, Diamond Jubilee Medal 2012. *Leisure interests:* marathon running, wine, gardening.

ORDJONIKIDZE, Iosif Nikolaevich; Georgian engineer and politician; b. 9 Feb. 1948, Borjomi; m.; two c.; ed Georgian Polytechnic Inst.; engineer, Tbilisi Aviation plant 1971–73, Sec. Komsomol Cttee 1973–76; First Sec. Regional Komsomol Cttee of Georgia 1976–83; Sec. USSR Cen. Komsomol Cttee 1983–90; Chair. Union of Innovation Enterprises 1990–91; Deputy Premier for Int. and External Econ. Relations, Govt of Moscow 1991–2001, Deputy Mayor 2001; Order of the Red Banner of Labour, Order of Friendship of Nations, Badge of Honour.

OREFFICE, Paul F(austo), BS; American business executive; *Chairman Emeritus, National Parkinson Foundation Inc.;* b. 29 Nov. 1927, Venice, Italy; s. of Max Oreffice and Elena Oreffice (née Friedenberg); m. Franca Giuseppina Ruffini 1956; one s. one d.; ed Purdue Univ.; joined Dow Chemical Int., Midland, Mich. 1953, Mediterranean Area Sales Man., Milan, Italy 1955–56, Man. Dow Quimica do Brazil, São Paulo 1956–63, Gen. Man. Dow Int., Spain 1963–65, Gen. Man. Dow Chemical Latin America 1965–67, Pres. Dow Chemical Inter-American Ltd 1967–69, Financial Vice-Pres. The Dow Chemical Co. 1969–75, Dir Dow Chemical Co. 1971–, Pres. Dow Chemical USA 1975–78, Chair. Exec. Cttee Dow Chemical Co. 1978–87, Pres. and CEO 1978–86, Chair., Pres. and CEO 1986–87, Chair. Bd 1987–92; Dir Cigna Corpn, Northern Telecom Ltd 1983, The Coca-Cola Co. 1985, Morgan Stanley Group Inc. 1987; Chair. American Enterprise Inst., Bd of Overseers Inst. for Civil Justice; mem. Bd of Govs Nat. Parkinson Foundation, fmrly Chair. now Chair. Emer.; mem. The Business Council; Encomienda del Mérito Civil (Spain) 1966; Hon. DEng (Purdue) 1976; Hon. Dr of Industrial Man. (Lawrence Inst. of Tech.); Hon. DSc (Saginaw Valley State Coll.); Hon. DBA (Tri-State Univ.). *Leisure interests:* tennis, bridge, golf, various other sports. *Address:* c/o National Parkinson Foundation Inc., 1501 NW 9th Avenue, Bob Hope Road, Miami, FL 33136-1494, USA (office). *Website:* www.parkinson.org (office).

O'REILLY, Sir Anthony (John Francis), Kt, BCL; Irish business executive; *President Emeritus, Independent News and Media PLC;* b. 7 May 1936, Dublin; s. of John Patrick O'Reilly and Aileen O'Reilly (née O'Connor); m. 1st Susan Cameron 1962 (divorced); three s. three d.; m. 2nd Chryss Goulandris 1991; ed Belvedere Coll., Dublin, Univ. Coll., Dublin; qualified as solicitor 1958; Demonstrator and Lecturer, Univ. Coll., Cork 1960–62; Personal Asst to Chair., Suttons Ltd, Cork 1960–62; Dir Robert McCowen & Sons Ltd, Tralee 1961–62; Gen. Man. Bord Bainne (Irish Dairy Bd) 1962–66; Man. Dir and CEO, Cómhlucht Siúicre Éireann Teo. (Irish Sugar Co.) 1966–69; Jt Man. Dir Heinz-Erin Ltd 1967–70, Man. Dir H. J. Heinz Co. Ltd, UK 1969–71, Sr Vice-Pres. N America and Pacific, H. J. Heinz Co. 1971–72, Exec. Vice-Pres. and COO 1972–73, Pres. and COO 1973–79, Chair. 1978–2000, Pres. 1979–90, CEO 1979–98; Chair. Ind. Newspapers PLC 1980–2009, Chair. and CEO Independent News and Media PLC 2000–04, CEO 2004–09, Pres. Emer. 2009–; f. O'Reilly Foundation; Chair. Waterford Wedgwood PLC 1993–2009 (resgnd); Chair. European Advisory Bd Bankers Trust 1992, Fitzwilton PLC, Atlantic Resources, Dublin, Eircom PLC 2001; numerous other commercial appointments; Fellow, BIM, RSA; Dr hc (Bradford) 1991; Hon. LLD (Leicester) 1992. *Publications:* Prospect 1962, Developing Creative Management 1970, The Conservative Consumer 1971, Food for Thought 1972. *Leisure interests:* tennis, rugby. *Address:* Independent News and Media, Independent House, 2023 Bianconi Avenue, Citywest Business Park, Citywest Business Campus, Naas Road, Dublin 2 (office); Castlemartin, Kilcullen, Co. Kildare, Ireland (home). *Telephone:* (1) 4663200 (office). *Fax:* (1) 4663222 (office). *Website:* www.independentnewsmedia.com (office).

O'REILLY, David J., BEng; American/Irish petroleum company executive (retd); b. Jan. 1947, Dublin, Ireland; ed Univ. Coll., Dublin; joined Chevron Research Co. 1968, Sr Vice-Pres. and COO Chevron Chemical Co. 1989–91, Vice-Pres. Chevron 1991–98, Pres. Chevron Products Co. 1994–98, mem. Bd of Dirs Chevron Corpn 1998–2010, Vice-Chair. Chevron Corpn 1998–99, Chair. and CEO 2000–10 (retd); fmr mem. American Petroleum Inst., Peterson Inst. for Int. Econs, The Business Council, The Business Roundtable, JPMorgan Int. Council, World Econ. Forum's Int. Business Council, Nat. Petroleum Council, American Soc. of Corp. Execs, Bd of Trustees Eisenhower Fellowships, King Fahd Univ. of Petroleum, Minerals Int. Advisory Bd; Order of Kurmet 2002.

ORELLANA MERCADO, Angel Edmundo, DJur; Honduran diplomatist and legal executive; b. 20 Oct. 1948, Honduras; m.; ed Universidad Autónoma de Honduras, Univ. of Bologna, Italy; Asst to Legal Counsel of Nat. Housing Inst.

1968; Legal Counsel of Tech. Secr. of Council for Econ. Planning 1976–79; Dir Honduran Pre-Investment Fund 1980–84; Dir-Gen. Admin. Reform of State Secr. for Planning, Co-ordination and Budget 1985–88; Pty Magistrate of Court of Appeals, Admin. Jurisdiction 1989–94; Attorney-Gen. 1994–99; Perm. Rep. to UN, New York 1999–2001; mem. Faculty of Law and Social Sciences, Universidad Nacional Autónoma de Honduras 1976; Hon. Consul in Genoa, Italy 1974–75; mem. Admin. Law Comm., Honduran Bar Asscn 1980–91; Vice-Chair. for Co-ordination, Comm. on Judicial Reform 1988–93; Co-ordinator Cttee on Admin. Oversight of the Judiciary 1988–93; Minister of the Interior 2007–08, for Foreign Affairs 2008–09, of Nat. Defence 2009. *Publications include:* numerous articles and books; participated in promulgation of several bills.

OREN, Michael B., BA, MA, PhD; Israeli (b. American) historian, academic, author and diplomatist; b. (Michael Bornstein), 20 May 1955, upstate NY, USA; m. Sally Oren 1982; two s. one d.; ed Columbia Univ., New York, Princeton Univ., NJ; grew up in NJ; youth activist in Zionist youth groups including USY; made first trip to Israel with youth movt Habonim Dror, working on Kibbutz Gan Shmuel 1970; adviser to Israeli del. to UN headed by Yehuda Blum 1978–79; emigrated to Israel and joined Israel Defense Forces (IDF) 1979, served as paratrooper in Lebanon War 1982; Israeli Liaison Officer to US Sixth Fleet during Gulf War 1991; Army Spokesman in IDF Reserves during Israel–Lebanon conflict 2006, Gaza operation Jan. 2009; Media Relations Officer during Israel–Gaza conflict 2008–09; Israeli Emissary to Jewish refuseniks in USSR, Israeli Govt's Dir of Inter-Religious Affairs; Visiting Prof., Harvard and Yale Univs 2006, Georgetown Univ.'s School of Foreign Service (as part of the Faculty associated with the Program for Jewish Civilization) 2008–09; continued teaching at Yale Univ. 2007; apptd by Pres. George W. Bush to serve on Hon. Del. to accompany him to Jerusalem for 60th anniversary of State of Israel May 2008; Amb. to USA 2009–13 (forfeited US citizenship to accept post); currently mem. Knesset (Kulanu Party), also Deputy Minister in Prime Minister's Office; fmr Lady Davis Fellow, Hebrew Univ.; fmr Moshe Dayan Fellow, Tel-Aviv Univ.; fmr Distinguished Fellow, Shalem Center, Jerusalem; fmr Contributing Ed., The New Republic, Shalem Center's quarterly journal, Azure; fellowships from US Deps of State and Defense, and from UK and Canadian Govts. *Achievements include:* gold medal-winning athlete in Maccabiah Games. *Publications:* Six Days of War: June 1967 and the Making of the Modern Middle East (Los Angeles Times History Book of the Year Award, Nat. Council of the Humanities Award, Nat. Jewish Book Award) 2002, Reunion (novel) 2003, Power, Faith, and Fantasy: The United States in the Middle East, 1776 to 2006 2007, New Essays on Zionism (co-ed.) 2007; articles and essays on Middle Eastern history and current political issues. *Address:* Knesset, Kiryat Ben-Gurion, Jerusalem 91950, Israel (office). *Telephone:* 2-6753333 (Knesset) (office); 3-7446974 (Kulanu) (office). *Fax:* 2-6753665 (Knesset) (office). *E-mail:* mshenkar@knesset.gov.il (office); info@kulanu-party.co.il (office). *Website:* www.kulanu-party.co.il (office); www.knesset.gov.il (office).

OREPIĆ, Vlaho, BSc; Croatian politician and fmr naval officer; b. 16 Nov. 1968, Ploče; ed Faculty of Maritime Studies, Dubrovnik, Faculty of Kinesiology, Zagreb (Sr Fitness Coach), Split Naval Mil. Acad. (Mechanical Engineer), Olympic Acad. of the Croatian Olympic Cttee (WKF-accredited karate coach), Blago Zadro Command and Staff School – Maritime Dept; first Commdr of naval port of Ploče 1991–93; Asst Chief of Staff for Operations, Operational Group Sinj 1993–96; Head of Operational Dept at HQ of VPS South 1996; also worked as karate coach and sports fitness trainer; returned to Croatian Navy –2014, attained rank of Capt.; Pres. Community of Sports Asscns of City of Ploče 2007; Vice-Pres. County Community Sports 2014; Minister of the Interior 2016–17; mem. Most Nezavisnih Lista (MOST—Bridge of Ind. Lists); several medals and awards, including Croatian Pistol Award from Chief of the Gen. Staff. *Address:* c/o Ministry of the Interior, 10000 Zagreb, ul. grada Vukovara 33, Croatia (office). *Telephone:* (1) 6122129 (office); (1) 6122405 (office). *Fax:* (1) 6122452 (office). *E-mail:* ministar@mup.hr (office). *Website:* www.mup.hr (office).

ORESHARSKI, Plamen Vasilev, PhD; Bulgarian politician; b. 21 Feb. 1960, Dupnitsa; m. Elka Georgieva; one s.; ed Univ. of Nat. and World Economy; Vice-Dean Finance Dept, Univ. of Nat. and World Economy 1992–93, Vice-Chancellor and Prof., Teaching on Finance Man., Investments, Investment Analysis 2003–05; Dir State Treasury and Debt Directorate, Ministry of Finance 1993–97, Deputy Minister 1997–2001, Minister of Finance 2005–09; mem. Sayuz na Demokratichnite Sili (SDS—Union of Democratic Forces), Deputy Chair. and mem. SDS Nat. Exec. Bd –2003 (resgnd), SDS nominee for Mayor of Sofia at 2003 elections, candidature withdrawn; mem. Nat. Ass. (Koalitsiya za Balgariya/Balgarska Sotsialisticheska Partiya—Coalition for Bulgaria/Bulgarian Socialist Party) 2009–13; Prime Minister of Bulgaria 2013–14 (resgnd); cand. in presidential election 2016; Pres. Man. Bd Sofiabank 1996–97; mem. Man. Bd Bulgarian Stock Exchange 1995–99, State Saving Bank 1996–97, Bulbank 1997–2000, Bulgarian Consolidation Co. 1997–2000; Emerging Markets magazine Finance Minister of the Year Award 2007, Person of the Year, Int. Tribunal for Crimes against Disabled People 2007, Knight of Book, Bulgarian Book Asscn 2007. *Publications:* Investment Analysis, Finance; more than 100 articles, reviews and comments. *Leisure interests:* mountaineering, badge collecting from various public events. *Address:* Balgarska Sotsialisticheska Partiya (Bulgarian Socialist Party), 1000 Sofia, ul. Positano 20, Bulgaria (office). *Telephone:* (2) 810-72-00 (office). *Fax:* (2) 981-21-85 (office). *E-mail:* bsp@bsp.bg (office). *Website:* www.bsp.bg (office).

OREŠKOVIĆ, Tihomir (Tim), BSc, MBA; Croatian/Canadian pharmaceutical industry executive and politician; *Senior Vice-President and Chief Financial Officer, Business Efficiency, Teva Pharmaceutical Industries;* b. 1 Jan. 1966, Zagreb; s. of Dane Orešković and Đurđa Orešković; m. Sanja Dujmović; two s. two d.; ed McMaster Univ., Canada; moved with parents to Hamilton, Canada 1966; began career with Eli Lilly pharmaceutical co. 1992, Assoc. Vice-Pres., Business and New Product Devt, Eli Lilly & Co. 1995–97, Dir Strategic Planning 1997–99, Chief Financial Officer (CFO), Eli Lilly Export SA 1999–2003, Assoc. Vice-Pres., Govt and Econ. Affairs 2003–05; CFO and Vice-Pres., Specialty Products, Novopharm (now Teva Canada) 2005–09, CFO, Eastern Europe, Middle East, Israel, Africa, Teva Pharmaceuticals 2009–12, Pres. Pliva Croatia and Gen. Man., Southeast Europe 2012–15, CFO, Europe 2014–15, CFO, Global Generic Medicines April–Dec. 2015; named as compromise, non-partisan cand. of Domoljubna Koalicija (Patriotic Coalition) and Most Nezavisnih Lista (MOST—Bridge of Ind. Lists) Dec. 2015; Prime Minister of Croatia Jan.–Oct. 2016; Ind.; Senior Vice-Pres. and Chief Financial Officer, Business Efficiency, Teva Pharmaceutical Industries 2017–. *Address:* Teva Pharmaceutical Industries, 5 Basel St., Petach Tikva, 49131, Israel (office). *Telephone:* 3-9267267 (office). *Fax:* 3-9234050 (office). *Website:* www.tevapharm.com (office).

ORGAN, (Harold) Bryan; British artist; b. 31 Aug. 1935, Leicester; s. of Harold Victor Organ and Helen Dorothy Organ; m. 2nd Sandra Mary Mills 1982; ed Loughborough Coll. of Art, Royal Acad. Schools, London; Lecturer in Drawing and Painting, Loughborough 1959–65; represented: Kunsthalle, Darmstadt 1968, Mostra Mercato d'Arte Contemporanea, Florence 1969, 3rd Int. Exhbns of Drawing Germany 1970, São Paulo Museum of Art, Brazil; works in pvt. and public collections in England, France, Germany, Italy, Switzerland, USA, Canada, Brazil; Hon. MA (Loughborough) 1974; Hon. DLitt (Leicester) 1985. *Portraits include:* Sir Michael Tippett 1966, David Hicks 1968, Mary Quant 1969, Princess Margaret 1970, Sir Roy Strong 1971, Elton John 1973, Lester Piggott 1974, Jimmy Lindley 1974, Geoff Lewis 1974, Willie Carson 1974, Tony Murray 1974, Joe Mercer 1974, Harold Macmillan, 1st Earl of Stockton 1980, HRH The Prince of Wales 1980, Diana, Princess of Wales 1981, Alfred Thompson (Tom) Denning, Baron Denning 1982, James Callaghan, Baron Callaghan of Cardiff 1982, HRH The Duke of Edinburgh 1983, François Mitterrand 1985, Richard Attenborough (later Lord Attenborough) 1985, 2003, Lord Jenkins 2002, Martin Johnson 2004, Alan Sugar, Baron Sugar 2010. *Leisure interest:* cricket. *Address:* c/o Redfern Gallery, 20 Cork Street, London, W1X 2HL (home); The Stables, Marston Trussell, nr Market Harborough, Leics., LE16 9TX, England (home). *Telephone:* (20) 7734-1732 (London) (home). *E-mail:* art@redfern-gallery.com (home). *Website:* www.redfern-gallery.com/artists/32-bryan-organ.

O'RIORDAN, Timothy, OBE, MA, PhD, FRSA, FBA, DL; British environmental scientist and academic; *Professor Emeritus of Environmental Sciences, University of East Anglia;* b. 21 Feb. 1942, Edinburgh, Scotland; s. of Kevin O'Riordan and Norah O'Riordan (née Joyce); m. Ann Philip 1968 (died 1992); two d.; ed Univs of Edinburgh and Cambridge, Cornell Univ., USA; Asst Prof., Dept of Geography, Simon Fraser Univ. Vancouver, BC 1967–74; Visiting Lecturer, Univ. of Canterbury, NZ 1970; Visiting Assoc. Prof., Clark Univ., Worcester, Mass, USA 1972; Reader, Univ. of East Anglia 1974, Prof. of Environmental Sciences 1980–2005, Prof. Emer. 2005–; Chair. Environment Cttee Broads Authority 1989–99, Environment Science and Soc. Programme, European Science Foundation 1989–; Adviser, Environmental Research Directorate 1996–97; mem. Environmental Advisory Council, Dow Chemical 1992–97, Eastern Group PLC 1995–98; mem. UK Sustainable Devt Comm. 2000–07; Trustee, Soil Asscn 2005–; DL of Norfolk 1998; Sheriff, City of Norwich 2009–10; Gill Memorial Prize, Royal Geographical Soc. *Publications:* Environmentalism 1976, Countryside Conflicts 1986, Sizewell B: An Anatomy of the Inquiry 1987, The Greening of the Machinery of Government 1990; ed. Interpreting the Precautionary Principle 1994, The Politics of Climate Change in Europe 1996, Ecotaxation 1996, The Transition to Sustainability in Europe 1998, Environmental Science for Environmental Management 2000, Globalism, Localism and Identity 2001, Reinterpreting the Precautionary Principle 2001, Biodiversity, Sustainability and Human Communities 2002, Tipping Points for a Precarious Future 2013. *Leisure interests:* classical double bass playing, jogging, cycling, swimming, intuition. *Address:* Wheatlands, Hethersett Lane, Colney, Norwich, Norfolk, NR4 7TT, England (home). *Telephone:* (1603) 810534 (home). *E-mail:* t.oriordan@uea.ac.uk (office). *Website:* www.uea.ac.uk/env (office).

ORITA, Masaki, LLB; Japanese academic and fmr diplomatist; *Professor, Faculty of Law, Chuo University;* b. 29 July 1942, Tokyo; s. of Saburo Orita and Saeko Orita; m. Masako Orita; one s.; ed Univ. of Tokyo, St Catherine's Coll., Oxford, UK; diplomatic postings to UK 1967–69, USSR 1975–77, OECD, Paris 1977–79, Washington, DC 1984–87; Exec. Asst to Prime Minister 1989–92; Consul-Gen., Hong Kong 1992–94, Dir-Gen. Treaties Bureau and N American Affairs Bureau, Ministry of Foreign Affairs 1994–97, Amb. to Denmark (also accred to Lithuania) 1997–2001, Insp. Gen., Ministry of Foreign Affairs 2001, Amb. to UK 2001–04, Special Envoy (Europe) for UN Reform, Ministry of Foreign Affairs 2005; currently Prof., Faculty of Law, Chuo Univ.; Chair. Inst. of Int. Affairs; mem. Bd of Dirs, Japan Centre for Conflict Prevention; mem. Japanese chapter, Int. Law Asscn; Hon. Fellow, St Catherine's Coll., Oxford; Commdr, Order of Orange (Netherlands) 1991; Grand Cross, Order of the Dannebrog (Denmark) 1998. *Publications:* several articles. *Address:* Faculty of Law, Chuo University, 742-1 Higashinakano Hachioji-shi, Tokyo 192-0393 (office). *Telephone:* (42) 674-2211 (switchboard) (office). *Fax:* (42) 674-2214 (office). *Website:* global.chuo-u.ac.jp/english/academics/faculties/law (office).

ORLOV, Aleksey Maratovich; Russian politician; b. 9 Oct. 1961, Elista, Repub. of Kalmykia, Russia; ed Moscow State Inst. of Int. Relations; Perm. Rep. of Repub. of Kalmykiya, S Russia, to Pres. of Russian Fed. 1995–2003, 2010–, First Deputy Chair. Repub. of Kalmykiya 2003–10; Head of Repub. of Kalmykiya 2010–19. *Address:* c/o Government House, 358000 Elista 18, Pushkin Street, Republic of Kalmykiya, Russia (office).

ORLOV, Alexandre; Russian diplomatist; b. 17 March 1948; m.; two s. one d.; ed Moscow State Inst. of Int. Relations; entered Ministry of Foreign Affairs of USSR 1971, various posts, including Minister Counsellor, Embassy in Paris 1993–98, Dir First Dept European Affairs, Ministry of Foreign Affairs 1998–2001, Perm. Rep. to Council of Europe, Strasbourg 2001–07, Dir Dept of Relationships to Federated Entities, Parl. and non-governmental orgs, Ministry of Foreign Affairs 2007–08, Amb. to France (also accred to Monaco) 2008–17.

ORLOV, Viktor Petrovich, CandGeolSc, DEconSc; Russian politician and geologist; b. 23 March 1940, Chernogorsk, Krasnoyarsk Region; s. of Petr Orlov and Eva Orlova; m.; three d.; ed Tomsk State Univ., Acad. of Nat. Econ. at USSR Council of Ministers; geologist, Chief Geologist, Team Leader, W Siberian Geological Survey 1968–75; Chief Engineer Geological Exploration, Iran 1975–78; Chief Geologist, Deputy Head Geological Div., Amalgamation Tsentrgeologiya 1979–81, Dir-Gen. 1986–90; Deputy Head Geology and Production Depts, Ministry of Geology Russian Fed. 1981–84, 1986; Deputy Minister of Geology USSR 1990–91; First Deputy Chair. State Cttee on Geology Russian Fed. 1991–92; Chair. Cttee on Geology and Use of Mineral Resources Russian Fed. 1992–96; Minister of Natural Resources Russian Fed. 1996–98, 1998–99; Pres.

Russian Geological Soc. 2000–01; mem. Council of Fed., Fed. Ass. of the Russian Fed., Rep., Admin, Koryak Autonomous Area 2001–12; Laureate, RF State Prize in Science and Eng 2001; Honoured Geologist of Russia 1990, Order for Services to the Native Land, IVth degree, 2001. *Publications:* Geological Forecasting 1991, Iron-Ore Base of Russia 1998, Mineral Resources and Geological Service of Russia during the Economic Reforms 1999, Reforms in Geology 2000; more than 200 scientific articles. *Leisure interests:* fishing, hunting. *Address:* Russian Geological Society, Zvenigorodskoye Shosse 9, 123022 Moscow (office); Palana, Portova str. 22, 684620 Kamchatka region, Karyak autonomous district, Russia (office). *Telephone:* (495) 292-75-43 (Geological Soc.) (office); (495) 259-79-53; (8415-43) 3-13-80 (Palana) (office). *Fax:* (495) 292-75-43.

ORMAN, Susan Lynn (Suze), BA; American financial adviser, television host, author, producer and magazine columnist; b. 5 June 1951, Chicago, Ill.; d. of Morry Orman and Ann Orman; m. Kathy Travis 2010; ed Univ. of Illinois at Urbana-Champaign; Account Exec., Merrill Lynch 1980–83; Vice-Pres. of Investments, Prudential Bache Securities 1983–87; opened own financial planning firm, Suze Orman Financial Group, Emeryville, Calif. 1987, mem. Bd of Dirs 1987–97; contributing ed. to "O" The Oprah Magazine, Costco Connection Magazine; contrib., The Philadelphia Inquirer, Lowes MoneyWorks, Your Business at Home Magazine; host, weekly The Suze Orman Show (CNBC) 2001–15; host, QVC Network 'Financial Freedom' Hour 1999–2009; regular guest on The View, Larry King Live, and The Oprah Winfrey Show; motivational speaker; Hon. DHumLitt (Univ. of Illinois) 2009; The Suze Orman First Book Award est. by Books for a Better Life to honour first-time authors of self-improvement books 2002, Crossing Borders Award, Feminist Press 2003, American Women in Radio and Television (AWRT) Gracie Allen Award for The Suze Orman Show (National/Network/Syndication Talk Show category) 2003, Day Time Emmy Award in category of Outstanding Service Show Host for her PBS Special, AWRT Gracie Allen Award for The Suze Orman Show (Individual Achievement: Program Host category) 2005, 2006, Day Time Emmy Award for her PBS Special, The Money Show for the Young Fabulous & Broke (Outstanding Service Show Host category) 2006, AWRT Gracie Allen Award for The Suze Orman Show (Outstanding Talk Show category) 2007, 2008, 2009, Amelia Earhart Award 2008, CableFAX Program Award for Best Show or Series in the Talk Show/Commentary for The Suze Orman Show 2008, Vito Russo Media Award, Gay & Lesbian Alliance Against Defamation 2009, Touchstone Award from Women in Cable Telecommunications 2010. *Television:* co-produced and hosted six PBS Specials (based on her New York Times bestselling books). *Publications:* You've Earned It, Don't Lose It 1995, The 9 Steps to Financial Freedom 1997, Suze Orman's Financial Guidebook 1998, The Courage to Be Rich (Books for a Better Life Motivational Book Award 1999) 1999, Ask Suze Library System (nine-vol. set) 2000, The Road to Wealth 2001, The Laws of Money, the Lessons of Life 2003, The Money Book for the Young, Fabulous and Broke 2005, Women & Money: Owning the Power to Control Your Destiny 2007 (Spanish edn) 2007, Suze Orman's 2009 Action Plan 2009, Suze Orman's 2010 Action Plan: New Rules for New Times 2010; US Patent for her Ultimate Protection Portfolio design 2006; several non-book products, primarily CD-ROM-based services that offer educ. and various financial services, usually in conjunction with her books and writings, including Suze Orman's FICO Kit 2002, Suze Orman's Protection Portfolio 2002, Suze Orman's Will & Trust Kit 2005, Suze Orman's Insurance Kit 2007, Suze Orman's Identity Theft Kit 2008, Suze Orman's Save Yourself Retirement Program 2009, The Money Class, Learn To Create Your New American Dream 2011. *E-mail:* info@suzeorman.com. *Website:* www.suzeorman.com.

ORMOND, Julia; British actress; b. 4 Jan. 1965, Epsom, Surrey; m. 1st Rory Edwards 1989 (divorced 1994); m. 2nd Jon Rubin 1999 (divorced 2008); one c.; ed Guildford High School, Cranleigh School, Farnham Art School and Webber Douglas Acad.; worked in repertory, Crucible Theatre, Sheffield, Everyman Theatre, Cheltenham and on tour with Royal Exchange Theatre, Manchester; appeared in Faith, Hope and Charity (Lyric, Hammersmith), Treats (Hampstead Theatre); West End debut in Anouilh's The Rehearsal (Almeida), My Zinc Bed (Royal Court) 2000; Founding Chair. and Co-Chair. FilmAid International, currently Chair. Emer., mem. UK Bd of Trustees; UN Goodwill Amb. 2005; Crystal Award, World Econ. Forum 2003. *Films include:* The Baby of Mâcon 1993, Nostradamus 1994, Captives 1994, Legends of the Fall 1994, First Knight 1995, Sabrina 1995, Calling the Ghosts (producer) 1996, Smilla's Sense of Snow 1997, The Barber of Siberia 1998, The Prime Gig 2000, Resistance 2003, Inland Empire 2006, I Know Who Killed Me 2007, Surveillance 2008, The Argentine 2008, Kit Kittredge: An American Girl 2008, La Conjura de El Escorial 2008, The Curious Case of Benjamin Button 2008, My Week with Marilyn 2011, Chained 2012, The East 2013, Exploding Sun 2013, Unity (narrator) 2014. *Television includes:* Traffik (Channel 4 mini-series) 1989, Capital City (series) 1989, Ruth Rendell Mysteries: The Best Man to Die 1990, Young Catherine 1991, Stalin 1992, Animal Farm (voice) 1999, Varian's War 2001, Iron Jawed Angels 2004, Beach Girls 2005, The Way 2006, Mr. and Mrs. Smith 2007, Temple Grandin 2010, Law & Order: Criminal Intent 2011, Mad Men 2012–15, Witches of East End (series) 2013–14, Incorporated 2016–17, Howards End 2017. *Address:* c/o Gersh Agency Inc., 9465 Wilshire Blvd, 6th floor, Beverly Hills, CA 90212, USA (office); c/o FilmAid International UK, Flat 2, 9 Colville Terrace, London, W11 2BE, England. *Telephone:* (310) 274-6611 (office); (20) 7727-1030. *E-mail:* info@gershla.com (office). *Website:* www.gershagency.com (office); www.filmaidinternational.org.

ORMOND, Richard Louis, CBE, MA; British museum director and art historian; b. 16 Jan. 1939, Bath; s. of Conrad E. Ormond and Dorothea Gibbons; m. Leonée Ormond 1963; two s.; ed Marlborough Coll., Brown Univ., USA and Christ Church, Oxford; Asst Keeper, Nat. Portrait Gallery 1965–75, Deputy Dir 1975–83; Head of Picture Dept Nat. Maritime Museum 1983–86, Dir Nat. Maritime Museum 1986–2000; Chair. Watts Gallery 1985–; Kress Prof., Nat. Gallery of Art, Washington, DC 2001–02; Deputy Chair. Museums Training Inst. 1994–97; Dir J. S. Sargent Catalogue Raisonné project 2000–; Pres. Friends of Leighton House; fmr Trustee, Mariners Museum Newport News. *Publications:* J. S. Sargent 1970, Catalogue of Early Victorian Portraits in the National Portrait Gallery 1973, Lord Leighton 1975, Sir Edwin Landseer 1982, The Great Age of Sail 1986, F.X. Winterhalter and the Courts of Europe 1987, Frederic, Lord Leighton (co-author) 1996, Sargent Abroad (co-author) 1997, John Singer Sargent: The Early Portraits (co-author) 1998, John Singer Sargent (co-author) 1998, Sargent (co-author) 1998, Sargent e l'Italia (co-author) 2001, John Singer Sargent:

Portraits of the 1890s (co-author) 2002, John Singer Sargent: The Later Portraits (co-author) 2004, John Singer Sargent: Figures and Landscapes (co-author) 2006, John Singer Sargent: Venetian Figures and Landscapes (co-author) 2009, Edwin Landseer: The Private Drawings 2009, Sargent and the Sea (co-author) 2009, John Singer Sargent: Figures and Landscapes 1883–1899 (co-author) 2010, G F Watts: The Hall of Fame (co-author) 2012, John Singer Sargent: Figures and Landscapes 1900-1907 (co-author) 2012, John Singer Sargent: Figures and Landscapes 1908-1913 (co-author) 2014, Sargent: Portraits of Artists and Friends (co-author) 2015, John Singer Sargent: Figures and Landscapes 1914–1925 (co-author) 2016. *Leisure interests:* opera, theatre, cycling. *Address:* 8 Holly Terrace, London, N6 6LX, England (home). *Telephone:* (20) 7839-3125 (home). *E-mail:* rormond@ceoexpress.com (office).

ORMOS, Mária, DSc; Hungarian historian and academic; b. 1 Oct. 1930, Debrecen; d. of János Ormos and Elza Förster; one s. one d.; ed Kossuth Lajos Univ., Debrecen; Asst Lecturer, Historic Science Inst. 1963; Univ. Prof., Eötvös Loránd Univ., Budapest 1982; Prof. of History then Prof. Emer., Janus Pannonius Univ. (now Univ. of Pécs), Rector 1984–92, f. Foundation of the Univ. of Pécs 1992; mem. Nat. Cttee of Historians; Pres. Italian-Hungarian Mixed Cttee of Historians; Vice-Pres. Asscn d'histoire des relations internationales; mem. Hungarian Acad. of Sciences 1993 (mem. of Presidium), European Acad. of Arts, Sciences and Humanities; Széczhenyi Prize 1995, Szentgyörgyi Prize 1995, Leo Sziliard Prize 2000, Deák Ferenc Prize 2000, Pulitzer Prize 2000, Hazám-díj 2003, Grastyán-díj 2004, Húszéves a Köztársaság Díj 2009, Miklós Radnóti Anti-Racist Prize 2010. *Publications:* Franciaország és a keleti biztonság 1931–36 (France and the Eastern Security) 1969, Europai Fasizmusok 1919–1939 (co-author) 1976, Merénylet Marseille-Ben (Assassination in Marseille) 1984, Mussolini: Politikai eletrajz (Mussolini: A Political Portrait) 1987, Nacizmus, Fasizmus (Nazism and Fascism) 1987, Never as Long as I Shall Live 1989, Civitas fidelissima 1921 1990, From Padua to the Trianon 1918–1920 1991, Hitler 1993, Documents diplomatiques français sur l'histoire du Bassin des Carpates 1918–1932: août 1919–juin 1920 (co-author) 1995, Magyarország a világháborúk korában 1914–45 (Hungary in the Age of the World Wars 1914–45) 1997, Európa a nemzetközi Küzdőtéren. Felemelkedés és hanyatlás 1814–1945 (Europe in the International Arena. Rise and Decline) (co-author) 1998, Hitler–Sztálin (Hitler-Stalin) (co-author 1999), Documents diplomatiques français sur l'histoire du Bassin des Carpates: 1918–1932 (co-author) 1999, Kozma Miklós, Egy magyar Médiavezér (Nikolaus Kozma, Life of Hungarian Media Leader) 2000, Hungary Governments and Politics 1848–2000 (co-ed.) 2001, Gazdasagi Vilagvalsag Magyar Visszhangja: 1929–1936 2004, Hungary in the Age of the Two World Wars: 1914–1945 2008, Hommage à Kosáry Domokos 2009, From the cathedral to the death row. Péter Agoston, 1874-1925 2011, Discovery and Conquest of the Earth: Western Europe at the top 2016, Hopes and disappointments (memoir) 2017. *Leisure interests:* music, books, theatre.

ORNSTEIN, Donald Samuel, PhD; American mathematician and academic; *Professor Emeritus of Mathematics, Stanford University;* b. 30 July 1934, New York; s. of Harry Ornstein and Rose Ornstein (née Wisner); m. Shari Richman 1964; two s. one d.; ed Swarthmore Coll. and Univ. of Chicago; mem. Inst. for Advanced Study, Princeton, NJ 1956–58; Instructor, Univ. of Wisconsin 1958–60; Asst Prof., Stanford Univ. 1960–63, Sloan Fellow and Assoc. Prof. 1963–65, Assoc. Prof. 1965–66, Prof. of Math. 1966–, now Emer.; Visiting Prof., Cornell Univ. and New York Univ. (Courant Inst.) 1967–68, Hebrew Univ., Jerusalem 1975–76, Math. Sciences Research Inst., Berkeley 1983–84; mem. NAS 1981, American Acad. of Arts and Sciences 1991; Fellow, American Math. Soc. 2012; Bôcher Prize 1974. *Publications:* Ergodic Theory Randomness and Dynamical Systems 1974; mathematical papers in many journals since 1959. *Address:* Department of Mathematics, Stanford University, Office 384-B, 450 Serra Mall, Building 380, Stanford, CA 94305-2125 (office); 857 Tolman Drive, Stanford, CA 94305, USA (home). *Telephone:* (650) 721-1720 (office). *Fax:* (415) 725-4066 (office). *E-mail:* ornstein@math.stanford.edu (office). *Website:* math.stanford.edu (office).

OROZCO, Esther, PhD; Mexican biologist and academic; *Professor Emeritus, National Polytechnic Institute (Cinvestav-IPN);* b. 25 April 1945, Est. Pascual Orozco, Chihuahua; m. Tomás Sánchez; one s. one d.; ed Universidad Autónoma de Chihuahua, Centre for Research and Advanced Studies, Nat. Polytechnic Inst. (Cinvestav-IPN); conducted postdoctoral research for short periods at MRC, London and Netherlands Cancer Inst., Amsterdam; fmr Visiting Prof., Harvard School of Public Health, Weizmann Inst. of Science, Israel, School of Medicine, Univ. of Virginia, Cancer Nat. Inst., Netherlands; Assoc. Prof., Dept of Genetics and Molecular Biology, Centre for Research and Advanced Studies, Nat. Polytechnic Inst. (Cinvestav-IPN), Investigator and Prof. of Experimental Pathology, est. Multidisciplinary Program of Molecular Biomedicine; Howard Hughes Medical Inst. Int. Research Scholar 1991–96, Howard Hughes Medical Inst. Foreign Prof., currently Prof. Emer.; fmr Rector, Autonomous Univ. of Mexico City mem. Mexican Acad. of Sciences, Instituto de las Mujeres, Nat. Researcher System (Level E), The World Acad. of Sciences (TWAS), World Science Forum; unsuccessful cand. (Revolutionary Democratic Party–PRD) for Gov. of Chihuahua (first woman) 1998; Dir-Gen. Inst. of Science and Tech., Mexico City; Int. Fellow, Howard Hughes Medical Inst.; Nat. Emer. Research Fellow of Conacyt, Mexico; Premio Nacional Miguel Otero, Secr. of Health 1985, Pasteur Medal, Institut Pasteur and UNESCO 1997, L'Oreal/UNESCO Award for Women in Science (Latin American) for discovery of mechanisms and control of infections by amoebae in the tropics 2006, Medal for Scientific Merit, Asamblea Legislativa, Mexico City 2006. *Publications:* numerous scientific papers in professional journals. *Leisure interests:* writing, reading, theatre. *Address:* Centro de Investigación y de Estudios Avanzados del IPN, Av. Instituto Politécnico Nacional, 2508 Col. San Pedro, Apartado Postal 14-740, 07000 Mexico City, DF, Mexico (office). *Telephone:* (52) 5061-3800 (ext 5650) (office). *Fax:* (52) 5061-7108 (office). *E-mail:* esther@cinvestav.mx (office). *Website:* www.cinvestav.mx (office); www.icyt.df.gob.mx; www.estherorozco.net.

OROZCO, Gabriel; Mexican artist; b. 27 April 1962, Jalapa, Veracruz; s. of Mario Orozco Rivera and Cristina Fèlix Romandía; m. Maria Gutierrez 1994; one s.; ed Escuela Nacional de Arte Plasticas, Mexico City, Circulo de Bellas Artes, Madrid, Spain; gained reputation with his exploration of drawing, photography, sculpture and installation early 1990s; works include Sleeping Dog 1990, Recaptured Nature 1991, Crazy Tourist 1991, My Hands are my Heart 1991, Yielding Stone 1992,

Empty Shoe Box 1993, Home Run 1993, La DS 1993, Yogurt Caps 1994, Working Tables 1996, Black Kites 1997, Lintels 2001, Samurai Tree Paintings 2004, Corplegados 2011; terracotta ceramics featured at Documenta XI 2002; lives and works in New York, Paris and Mexico City; Seccio Espacios Alternativos Prize, Salon Nacional de Artes Plasticas, Mexico City 1987, DAAD Artist-in-Residence grant, Berlin 1995, German Blue Orange Prize 2006. *Leisure interests:* football (soccer), throwing boomerangs. *Address:* c/o Marian Goodman Gallery, 24 West 57th Street, New York, NY 10019, USA. *Telephone:* (212) 977-7160. *Fax:* (212) 581-5187. *E-mail:* info@mariangoodman.com. *Website:* www.mariangoodman.com/artists/gabriel-orozco.

ORPO, Petteri, MSc; Finnish politician; *Minister of Finance;* b. 3 Nov. 1969, Köyliö; s. of Hannu Orpo and Maija Orpo; m. Niina Kanniainen-Orpo; two c.; ed Turku Univ.; Gen. Sec., Univ. of Turku 1994–96; mem. Turku City Council 1996–2000, 2005–; Gen. Sec., Fed. of Univ. Students in Finland 1997–98; Exec. Dir, Coalition of SW Finland 1998–2001; Special Adviser, Ministry of Internal Affairs 2002–03; Business Services Dir, Turku Adult Educ. Centre 2005–07; Vice-Pres., SW Finland Regional Council 2009–12; mem. Eduskunta (parl.) for SW Finland 2007–; Minister of Agric. and Forestry 2014–15, of the Interior 2015–16, Minister of Finance 2016–; mem. Nat. Coalition Party, Deputy Sec. 2003–05, Chair. 2016–; mem. Bd of Govs., EIB; mem. (ex-officio) Bd of Govs., European Stability Mechanism, Asian Infrastructure Investment Bank, EBRD, Multilateral Investment Guarantee Agency, Nordic Investment Bank, World Bank; Jt mem. World Bank-IMF Devt Cttee. *Address:* Ministry of Finance, Snellmaninkatu 1a, Helsinki, Finland (office). *Telephone:* (295) 16001 (office). *Fax:* (9) 16033123 (office). *E-mail:* valtiovarainministerio@vm.fi (office). *Website:* www.vm.fi (office); orpo.fi.

ORR, Adrian, BA, MA; New Zealand economist and central banker; *Governor, Reserve Bank of New Zealand;* b. 1963, Taupo; m. Sue Orr; three c.; ed Waikato Univ., Leicester Univ., UK; began career as Research Assoc. and Tutor, City Univ. Business School, London; Research Economist, New Zealand Inst. of Econ. Research 1988–89; mem. Econs Team, Nat. Bank of New Zealand 1989–92, Chief Economist 1995–97; Economist, OECD, Paris 1992–95; Chief Analyst, New Zealand Treasury 1995; Chief Man., Econs Dept, Reserve Bank of New Zealand (RBNZ) 1997–2000, Deputy Gov. and Head of Financial Stability Dept 2003–07, Gov., RBNZ 2018–; Chief Economist, Westpac 2000–03; CEO, New Zealand Super Fund (sovereign wealth fund) 2007–18; Chair. Inst. for Study of Competition and Regulation 1998–2005; Deputy Chair. Int. Forum of Sovereign Wealth Funds 2013–; Vice-Chair. and mem. Bd of Dirs Pacific Pensions Inst.; mem. Expert Advisory Group, World Bank Treasury; mem. Bd of Dirs Emory Center for Alternative Investments, Emory Univ., Atlanta, Georgia; mem. Bd of Dirs Kai Waho (tourism body), Lake Taupo Funds Ltd 1995–2005. *Address:* Reserve Bank of New Zealand, 2 The Terrace, POB 2498, Wellington 6011, New Zealand (office). *Telephone:* (4) 472-2029 (office). *Fax:* (4) 473-8554 (office). *E-mail:* rbnz-info@rbnz .govt.nz (office). *Website:* www.rbnz.govt.nz (office).

ORR, Christopher John, MBE, MA, RCA, RA; British artist; *Professor Emeritus of Printmaking, Royal College of Art;* b. 8 April 1943, London, England; s. of Ronald Orr and Violet Townley; m. Catherine Terris 1985; one s. one d.; ed Ravensbourne Coll. of Art, Hornsey Coll. of Art, Royal Coll. of Art; worked as artist and teacher, latterly as a tutor and Visiting Lecturer, RCA 1976–, Prof. and Course Dir of Printmaking 1998–2008, Prof. Emer. 2008–; solo touring exhbns The Complete Chris Orr 1976, Many Mansions 1990; numerous exhbns world-wide; Fellow, Royal Soc. of Painters and Printmakers; elected Royal Academician 1995. *Publications:* Many Mansions 1990, The Small Titanic 1994, Happy Days 1999, Semi-antics 2001, The Disguise Factory 2003, City of Holy Dreams 2006, The Multitude Diaries 2008. *Telephone:* (20) 7738-1203. *E-mail:* info@chrisorr-ra.com. *Website:* www.chrisorr-ra.com.

ORR, Robert C., PhD, MPA; American government official, UN official and academic; *Special Adviser to Secretary-General on Climate Change, United Nations;* m. Audrey Choi; two c.; ed Woodrow Wilson School, Princeton Univ., Univ. of California Los Angeles; served in sr posts in Govt including Deputy to US Amb. to UN, Dir US UN Washington Office, Dir Global and Multilateral Affairs, Nat. Security Council 1996–2001; Co-Dir Bipartisan Comm. Center for Strategic and Int. Studies, Washington 2001–03, also for Asscn of US Army; Asst Sec.-Gen. for Strategic Planning, UN 2004–14, Special Adviser to Sec.-Gen. on Climate Change; currently Dean School of Public Policy, Univ. of Maryland; fmr Exec. Dir Belfer Center for Science and Int. Affairs, Kennedy School of Govt, Harvard Univ. *Publications include:* Keeping the Peace: Multidimensional UN Operations in Cambodia and El Salvador 1997, Winning the Peace: an American Strategy for Post-Conflict Reconstruction 2004. *Address:* University of Maryland School of Public Policy, 2101 Van Munching Hall, College Park, MD 20742, USA (office). *Telephone:* (301) 405-3103 (office). *Fax:* (301) 403-4675 (office). *E-mail:* rorr1@umd .edu (office). *Website:* www.publicpolicy.umd.edu (office).

ORSENNA, Érik (see ARNOULT, Érik).

ORSI, Giuseppe, CBE, PhD, FRAeS; Italian business executive; b. 24 Nov. 1945, Piacenza; m. Rita Orsi; two s.; ed Milan Polytechnic Univ., Wharton School, Univ. of Pennsylvania, USA; served as an officer in Italian Air Force, a qualified civil pilot; joined SIAI Marchetti 1973, later Product Support Dir; joined Agusta Corpn as staff to Marketing & Strategy Dir 1984–87, Sales Dir Agusta's Aircraft Div. 1987–89, Pres. and CEO Agusta Aerospace Corpn (North American subsidiary headquartered in Philadelphia) 1989–94, Chair. EHI Inc. (jt Agusta and Westland co. incorporated in USA) 1989–94, Sr Vice-Pres. of Govt Sales and Programs Agusta 1994–97, relocated to Italy with responsibility for worldwide military sales, Deputy Gen. Man. Agusta, responsible for Marketing and Sales 1997–99, Co-Gen. Man. Agusta 1999–2001, mem. Man. Cttee of JV, Agusta and Westland merged 2001, Man. Dir Marketing and Sales org. of AgustaWestland world-wide 2001–02, Man. Dir Agusta SpA 2002–11, CEO AgustaWestland NV 2004–11; apptd CEO Finmeccanica SpA May 2011, Chair. Dec. 2011; arrested on bribery allegations 2013; Freeman of the City of London 2010.

ORSZAG, Peter Richard, AB, MS, PhD; American economist, business executive and fmr government official; *Vice-Chairman of Investment Banking and Managing Director, Lazard Freres & Co LLC;* b. 16 Dec. 1968, Boston; m. 1st Cameron Hamill 1997 (divorced 2006); two c.; pnr Claire Milonas; one c.; m. 2nd Bianna Golodryga 2010; one c.; ed Princeton Univ., London School of Econs, UK; Research Officer, Centre for Econ. Performance, London School of Econs 1992–93, mem. Professional Research Staff 1994–95; Econ. Adviser, Macroeconomic and Fiscal Unit, Ministry of Finance, Russian Fed., Moscow 1993; Staff Economist, Council of Econ. Advisers, Washington, DC 1993–94, Sr Adviser 1996; Sr Econ. Advisor, Nat. Econ. Council 1997, Special Asst to Pres. Clinton for Econ. Policy 1998; consultant, McKinsey & Co. 1998; Pres. Sebago Assocs Inc. 1998–2007, Sr Dir 2002–07; Dir Congressional Budget Office, Washington, DC 2007–08; Dir Office of Man. and Budget 2009–10 (resgnd); Distinguished Visiting Fellow, Council on Foreign Relations 2010; Vice-Chair. Global Banking, Citigroup Inc. 2010–13; Vice Chair. of Investment Banking and Man. Dir, Lazard Freres & Co. LLC 2016–, Global Co-Head, Healthcare 2016–; Head, North American M&A 2018–, also mem. Opinion Cttee; Dir Competition Policy Assocs Inc. 2003–07; Sr Fellow in Economic Studies, Brookings Inst. 2001–07, Joseph A. Pechman Fellow in Tax and Fiscal Policy 2001–07, Co-Dir Tax Policy Center 2003–07, Dir The Hamilton Project 2005–07, Deputy Dir of Econ. Studies 2006–07; Dir Retirement Security Project, Pew Charitable Trust 2004–07; Dir CBO 2007–08; Dir of Office of Man. and Budget, Obama Admin 2009–10; Lecturer, Univ. of California, Berkeley 1999–2000; Research Prof., Georgetown Univ. 2005–07; Columnist, The New York Times Sept. 2010 – Jan 2011, Bloomberg View 2011–2018, Bloomberg Opinion 2018–; mem. Bd of Dirs, Peterson Inst. for Int. Economics, Mt. Sinai Medical Center, Robert Wood Johnson Foundation, Russell Sage Foundation, New Visions for Public Schools, ideas42; mem. Inst. of Medicine, Nat. Acad. of Science; Dr hc (Rennselaer Polytechnic Inst.) 2010; John Glover Wilson Memorial Prize in Economics, Princeton Univ. 1991, First Annual Good Governance Award, Mosbacher Inst., Texas A&M Univ. 2011. *Publications:* American Economic Policy in the 1990s (co-ed.) 2002, Protecting the American Homeland: A Preliminary Analysis (co-author) 2002, Protecting the American Homeland: One Year On (co-author) 2003, Saving Social Security: A Balanced Approach (co-author) 2005, Aging Gracefully: Ideas to Improve Retirement Security in America (co-author) 2006, Protecting the Homeland 2006/7 (co-author) 2006; numerous articles. *Website:* www.peterorszag.com.

ORTEGA GAONA, Amancio; Spanish retail executive; b. 28 March 1936, León; fmr shop assistant; f. Confecciones Goa (mfrs of bathrobes) 1963, f. Zara (chain of fashion stores, 1,500 outlets world-wide) 1975, now majority shareholder and fmr Chair. Inditex group (Industrias de Diseño Textil SA) (now mem. Bd), including Zara, Massimo Dutti and Pull and Bear and other brands. *Address:* Industria de Diseño Textil, SA, Avenida de la Diputación, 15142 Arteixo, A Coruña, Spain (office). *Website:* www.inditex.com (office).

ORTEGA MARTÍNEZ, Jesús; Mexican politician; b. 5 Nov. 1952, Aguascalientes; m. Angélica de la Peña; ed Instituto Politécnico Nacional; fmr mem. Partido Socialista de los Trabajadores; fmr mem. Partido Mexicano Socialista; mem. Chamber of Deputies 1979–82, 1988–91; mem. Senate (upper house) 2000; Founding mem. Partido de la Revolución Democrática, Sec.-Gen. 1996–99, Pres. 2008–11, Nat. Coordinator, New Left 2012–. *Address:* Partido de la Revolución Democrática, Avda Benjamín Franklin 84, Col. Escandón, 11800 México DF, Mexico (office). *Telephone:* (55) 1085-8000 (office). *Fax:* (55) 1085-8144 (office). *E-mail:* comunicacion@prd.org.mx (office); jesus.ortega@prd.org.mx (office). *Website:* www.prd.org.mx (office).

ORTEGA SAAVEDRA, José Daniel; Nicaraguan politician, fmr resistance leader and head of state; *President;* b. 11 Nov. 1945, La Libertad, Chontales; s. of Daniel Ortega and Lidia Saavedra; m. Rosario Murillo; seven c.; ed Univ. Centroamericano, Managua; joined Frente Sandinista 1963; active in various underground resistance movt against regime of Anastasio Somoza from 1959, was imprisoned several times and tortured for revolutionary activities; ed. El Estudiante, official publ of Frente Estudiantil Revolucionaria and directed org. of Comités Cívicos Populares in Managua 1965; mem. Nat. Directorate of FSLN (Sandinista Liberation Front) 1966–67; imprisoned 1967–74; resumed position with FSLN and with José Benito Escobar, became involved in further revolutionary activities; fought on front in two-year mil. offensive which overthrew Somoza regime 1979; mem. Junta of Nat. Reconstruction Govt 1979, Co-ordinator of Junta 1981–85, Pres. of Nicaragua 1985–90, 2007–; presidential cand. 2001; Gen. Sec. FSLN. *Address:* Office of the President, Casa Presidencial, Managua, Nicaragua (office). *Fax:* 2266-3102 (office). *E-mail:* daniel@presidencia.gob.ni (office). *Website:* www.presidencia.gob.ni (office).

ORTEGA Y ALAMINO, HE Cardinal Jaime Lucas; Cuban ecclesiastic; *Archbishop Emeritus of San Cristóbal de la Habana;* b. 18 Oct. 1936, Jagüey Grande, Matanzas; ed Arturo Echemendía School, Matanzas, Advanced Inst. for Secondary Studies of Matanzas, Diocesan Seminary of San Alberto Magno, Seminary of Foreign Mission in Quebec, Canada; ordained priest 1964; Coadjutor Vicar of Cárdenas 1964, detained in work camp 1966, released 1967; Parish Priest of Jagüey Grande 1967 and also of Cathedral of Matanzas, also responsible for Parish of Pueblo Nuevo in city and another two churches outside it; Pres. Diocesan Comm. for Catechesis; taught moral theology part-time at Sts Charles and Ambrose Interdiocesan Seminary, Havana; Bishop of Pinar del Rio 1979; Archbishop of San Cristóbal de la Habana 1981–16, now Archbishop Emer.; Pres. Cuban Conf. of Catholic Bishops 1988–98, 2001, took part in fourth Gen. Conf. Latin-American Bishops, Santo Domingo; Founder Caritas Cuba 1991; Vice-Pres. Latin American Episcopal Council 1995–99; cr. Cardinal (Cardinal-Priest of Santi Aquila e Priscilla) 1994; participated in Papal Conclave 2005, 2013; attended Special Ass. for America of World Synod of Bishops, Vatican City 1997; Special Papal Envoy to Nat. Eucharistic Congress of El Salvador, San Salvador 2000; Dr hc (St John's Univ., New York); hon. degrees from Barry and St Thomas Univs, Fla, Univ. of San Francisco, Calif., Providence Coll., RI, Boston Coll., Mass 2001. *Address:* Apartado 594, Calle Habana 152, Havana 10100, Cuba (office). *Telephone:* (7) 624000 (office). *Fax:* (7) 338109 (office).

ORTEZ COLINDRES, Enrique, LLD; Honduran lawyer, diplomatist and politician; b. 29 Oct. 1931, Tegucigalpa; s. of Enrique Ortez Pinel; m. 1st Hilda Sequeira 1959; two s. one d.; m. 2nd Patricia d'Arcy Lardizabal 1995; one d.; diplomatic postings include Sec., Embassy in Paris 1955, Rep. to Org. of Cen. American States, Perm. Rep. to UN, New York in 1970s; Dir, later Pres. Banco Centroamericano de Integracion Economico; mem. Partido Liberal; Minister of Foreign Affairs June–July 2009; Minister of the Interior and Justice 2009.

Publications: La Republica Federal de Centro America a la luz del derecho internacional publico 1963, Integracion politica de Centroamerica 1975.

ORTIZ, Cristina; Brazilian pianist; b. 17 April 1950, Bahia; d. of Silverio M. Ortiz and Moema F. Ortiz; m. Jasper W. Parrott 1974; two d.; ed Conservatório Brasileiro de Música, Rio de Janeiro, Académie Internationale de Piano (with Magda Tagliaferro), France, Curtis Inst. of Music, (with Rudolf Serkin), USA; New York recital debut 1971; London debut with LSO and André Previn 1973; has appeared in concerts with the Vienna Philharmonic, Berlin Philharmonic, the Concertgebouw, Chicago Symphony, New York Philharmonic, Israel Philharmonic, Los Angeles Philharmonic, leading British orchestras and has undertaken many tours of North and South America, the Far East, New Zealand and Japan; appeared with NHK Symphony, the Bergen Philharmonic and Philharmonia under Janowski 1997; played with conductors including Previn, Mehta, Kondrashin, Ashkenazy, Leinsdorf, Chailly, Masur, Salonen, Colin Davis, Janssons, Fedoseyev, Zinman, Rattle, Järvi and Fürst; First Prize, Van Cliburn Int. Competition, Texas 1969. *Leisure interests:* tennis, swimming, reading, hiking, holidaying, horse riding. *E-mail:* cristina.ortiz.name@gmail.com. *Website:* www.cristina.ortiz.name.

ORTIZ, Juan José Imbroda; Spanish politician and head of government; *Mayor-President of Melilla;* b. 24 June 1944, Melilla; First Deputy Mayor, Melilla Ass. 1979–83, Deputy 1995–; tax adviser 1979–98; worked for Commercial Distributions Co. 1988–97; mem. People's Party of Spain 2000–; Senator for Melilla in Cortes Generales 2000–04; Mayor-Pres. of Melilla 2000–. *Address:* Plaza de España, s/n, Primera Planta, Ala Izquierda, Palacio de la Asamblea 52001 Melilla, Spain (office). *Telephone:* (95) 2699100 (office). *Fax:* (95) 2692230 (office). *E-mail:* presidencia@melilla.es (office). *Website:* www.melilla.es (office).

ORTIZ DE LA CADENA, Fausto, MBA; Ecuadorean economist and government official; ed Universidad Católica de Guayaquil; served as State Treas. 2005, Sub-Sec. of Public Credit 2005; Deputy Minister of the Economy 2005–07, Minister of the Economy and Finance 2007–08 (resgnd); mem. Alianza País (Patria Altiva i Soberana). *Address:* Alianza País, Avenida Los Shyris N34-368 y Portugal, Quito, Ecuador (office). *Telephone:* (2) 224-3299 (office). *Fax:* (2) 600-1029 (office). *E-mail:* comunicacion@35pais.com.ec (office). *Website:* movimientoalianzapais.com.ec (office).

ORTIZ DE ZEVALLOS MADUEÑO, Felipe, BA, MA; Peruvian economist, academic, business executive, diplomatist and diplomatist; *Chairman, Grupo APOYO;* b. 28 Aug. 1947, Lima; ed Universidad Nacional de Ingeniería, Lima, Univ. of Rochester, NY and Owner-Pres. Man. Program, Harvard Business School, USA; worked as consulting engineer in Peru 1970–77; f. APOYO (consultancy and publishing firm) 1977, currently Chair. Grupo APOYO; ind. mem. of Bd of several businesses, educational and cultural insts, including Buenaventura Mining Co., Credicorp; Chair. Eisenhower Fellowship's Nominating Cttee Peru, mem. Eisenhower Fellowship's Advisory Int. Council; Founder-Dir Inst. of Econ. Devt, ESAN (Grad. School of Business Admin), Lima 1979–82; Chair. Nat. Devt Corpn (CONADE) and Inversiones Cofide (holding cos of all state-owned enterprises) 1982; Pres. Annual Conf. of Execs 1985; Visiting Scholar, Inst. of Latin American Studies, Univ. of Texas, Austin, USA 1983, 1984; Prof., Econs Dept, Universidad del Pacífico 1978–, Pres. Universidad del Pacífico 2004–06; Amb. to USA 2006–09; Independent Dir Cementos Pacasmayo SAA 2014–; guest columnist in magazines; Instituto Peruano de Administracion de Empresas Award 1990, Eisenhower Exchange Fellowship 1996, Jerusalem Award of Journalism 1998, Manuel J. Bustamante de la Fuente Prize 2008. *Publications:* The Peruvian Puzzle 1989, Respuestas para los 90s (Answers to the 90s) (with Pedro Pablo Kuzcynski) 1990, In the Shadow of the Debt (co-author) 1992, A Mitad de Camino (Half Way Through) 1992, El Reto 2001: Competir y Crear Empleo (The 2001 Challenge: Compete and Create Employment) (with Pedro Pablo Kuczynski) 2001; numerous articles in nat. and int. journals. *Leisure interests:* reading, swimming, collecting art. *Address:* Grupo APOYO, Camino Real 390, Torre Central Piso 11, San Isidro, Lima 27, Peru (office). *Telephone:* (1) 513-3030 (office). *Website:* www.apoyo.com (office).

ORTIZ MARTÍNEZ, Guillermo, BA, MSc, PhD; Mexican economist, academic, fmr central banker and fmr government official; *Chairman, BTG Pactual Casa de Bolsa Mexico;* b. 21 July 1948, Mexico City; s. of Gen. Leopoldo Ortiz Sevilla and Graciela Martínez Ostos; m. Margie Simon de Ortiz; three d.; ed Universidad Nacional Autónoma de México, Stanford Univ., USA; economist, Ministry of the Presidency of Mexico 1971–72; Deputy Man., later Man. Econ. Research Dept, Banco de México 1977–84; Under-Sec. of Finance and Public Credit, Fed. Govt 1988–94, Exec. Dir IMF 1984–88; Sec. of Telecommunications and Transportation –1994, of Finance and Public Credit 1994–97; Gov. Banco de México 1998–2009, mem. Bd of Dirs BIS, Basel, Switzerland (Chair. March–Dec. 2009), also chaired Cen. Bank Governance Forum; Founder and Pres. Guillermo Ortiz & Asociados (econ. advisory and consulting firm) 2009–11; Chair. Grupo Financiero Banorte-Ixe 2011–14; Chair. BTG Pactual Casa de Bolsa Mexico 2016–; mem. Group of Thirty; Chair. External Panel for the Review of the IMF Risk Man. Framework 2010–11, mem. External Advisory Group for the IMF's Triennial Surveillance Review –2014; Chair. Advisory Bd, Grupo Financiero Banorte-Ixe –2015, Advisor First Reserve 2015–; mem. Bd of Dirs, Mexichem, Asur, Vitro, Chedraui, Weatherford Int., Geneva; mem. Int. Advisory Council, Zurich Insurance Group Ltd, Advisory Council, Bombardier Inc.; fmr mem. Group of Thirty; dir of several int. orgs, including Per Jacobsson Foundation, Int. Econ. Forum of the Americas/Conf. of Montreal, Globalization and Monetary Policy Inst., Fed. Reserve Bank of Dallas; mem. Council of Global Financial Regulation, Advisory Council, Swift Inst., Bd of China's Int. Finance Forum, Advisory Bd, Centre for Financial Stability; decorations from Govts of France, Spain, Germany, Japan and Brazil; Rodrigo Gómez Prize, Man of the Year, Top Central Banker, Good Neighbor Award, Best Central Bank Governor for Latin America, Central Banker of the Year, Legacy Award. *Publications:* three books and numerous papers on topics in econs and finance in specialized journals and magazines in Mexico and abroad. *Address:* BTG Pactual Casa de Bolsa Mexico, Paseo de los Tamarindos 400-A, Bosques de las Lomas CP, 05120 Mexico City, DF, Mexico (office). *Telephone:* (55) 3692-2200 (office). *Website:* www.btgpactual.com (office).

OSAFO-MAAFO, Yaw, BSc; Ghanaian engineer, banker, economist and politician; b. (Samuel Yaw Osafo-Maafo), 24 Dec. 1942, Akim Awisa; s. of Nana Kwabena Maafo and Mary Boateng; m. Anna Osafo-Maafo; four c.; ed Kwame Nkrumah Univ. of Science and Tech., Metal Eng Inst., USA, Les Aspin Centre for Govt, Marqutee Univ., USA; Process and Quality Control Engineer, VALCO-Tema 1967–69; Sr Investment Promotions Officer, Capital Investment Bd 1969–76; Dir Ghana Investment Centre, Frankfurt, Germany 1972–76; Sr Investment Promotions Officer, Capital Investment Bd (now Ghana Investment Promotion Centre) 1969–76; Chief Operations Man., Bank for Housing and Construction 1976–79, Man. Dir 1979–89; Man. Dir Nat. Investment Bank 1990–92; Sr Consultant, Consultancy Man. Enterprise 1992–94, Dir of Training 1993–96; mem. Parl. for Akim Oda Constituency 1997–2009; Minister of Finance and Econ. Planning 2001–04, of Educ. and Sports 2005–06; Sr Minister (non-Cabinet) 2017–; CEO Econ. and Man. Consultancy 2006; mem. Consultative Ass. which drafted 1992 constitution for Repub. of Ghana; fmr mem. first World Bank financial sector mission to Uganda; Chair. W African Monetary Zone Convergence Council; Founding Deputy Chair. Ghana Stock Exchange; dir numerous corp. bodies including Nat. Trust Holding Co., Nestlé Ghana Ltd, Redco Ltd, PSCP (Gh) Ltd, Plant Pool Ltd, Consultant Man. Enterprise, Donewell Insurance Co., Divestiture Implementation Cttee, Nat. Devt Planning Comm.; Dir Asante Kotoko Football Club; mem. Ghana Inst. of Engineers; Fellow, Ghana Inst. of Engineers; mem. Methodist Conf.; mem. New Patriotic Party (NPP), mem. NPP Manifesto Cttee; Hon. Fellow, Ghana Inst. of Architects; Order of the Volta Companion. *Leisure interests:* reading, football. *Address:* Government of Ghana, PO Box 745, Accra, Ghana (office). *Telephone:* (30) 2228054 (office). *E-mail:* info.isd@isd.gov.gh (office).

OSBORN, Frederic (Derek) Adrian, CB, BA, BPhil; British government official; *President, Stakeholder Forum for a Sustainable Future;* b. 14 Jan. 1941, Dorset; s. of Rev. George Osborn and Betty Osborn; m. Caroline Niebuhr Tod 1971; one s. one d.; ed Leys School, Cambridge and Balliol Coll., Oxford; with Ministry of Housing and Local Govt 1965–70, Dept of Transport 1975–77, Dept of Environment 1977–95, Dir-Gen. (Deputy Sec.) 1990–95; Chair. European Environment Agency 1995–99; Chair. UNED, UK (name changed to Stakeholder Forum for Our Common Future 2002, renamed Stakeholder Forum for a Sustainable Future 2004) 1996–99, currently Pres.; Chair. Earth Centre 1996–, Joseph Rowntree Foundation Steering Group on Reconciling Environmental and Social Objectives 1998–, UK Round Table on Sustainable Devt 1999–; mem. of Bd England and Wales Environment Agency 1996–98, Severn Trent PLC 1998–; Special Adviser House of Commons Environmental Audit Cttee 1998–99; Chair. Jupiter Global Green Investment Trust 2001–; mem. Royal Soc. for Protection of Birds 1996–; mem. Bd of Trustees, Green Alliance; Visiting Fellow, Green Coll., Oxford 1996–97; Visiting Prof., School of Public Policy, Univ. Coll., London 1998–. *Publications include:* Earth Summit II 1998; contribs to Journal of Environmental Law. *Leisure interests:* music, reading. *Address:* Stakeholder Forum for a Sustainable Future, #60, 49 Effra Road, London, SW2 1BZ, England (office). *Telephone:* (20) 7930-8752 (office). *E-mail:* info@stakeholderform org (office). *Website:* www.stakeholderforum.org (office).

OSBORN, Mary, PhD; British biologist and academic; *Professor, Max Planck Institute for Biophysical Chemistry;* b. 16 Dec. 1940, Darlington; d. of Philip James and Gertrude Annie Osborn; m. Klaus Weber 1972; lab. work in USA; Prof., Max Planck Inst. for Biophysical Chem. (Karl Friedrich Bonhoeffer Inst.), Göttingen 1975–; Hon. Prof. in the Medical Faculty, Univ. of Göttingen 1989–, mem. Research Cttee 2007–; Pres. Exec. Cttee Int. Union of Biochemistry and Molecular Biology 2003–06; Chair. European Tech. Assessment Network expert working group on gender balance in research policy 1998; mem. Editorial Advisory Bd Encyclopedia of Human Biology; mem. Helmholtz Soc. Senate, European Strategy Forum on Research Infrastructures Group A, Descartes Prize Grand Jury of the EC; mem. Bd of Trustees, Swedish Foundation on the Environment 1994–97; Fed. Cross of Merit (1st Class), Germany 2014; Dr hc (Pomerian Medical Acad., Sczeczin, Poland) 1997; Meyenburg Prize 1987, L'Oréal-UNESCO For Women in Science Award 2002, Dorothea Schlözer Medal, Univ. of Göttingen 2007. *Publications:* numerous articles in scientific journals. *Address:* Max-Planck-Institut für biophysikalische Chemie, Am Faßberg 11, 37077 Göttingen, Germany (office). *Telephone:* (551) 201-1486 (office). *E-mail:* mosborn@gwdg.de (office). *Website:* www.mpibpc.mpg.de (office).

OSBORNE, Rt Hon. George Gideon Oliver, CH, PC; British politician and journalist; *Editor, London Evening Standard;* b. 23 May 1971, London; s. of Sir Peter Osborne, 17th Baronet; m. The Hon. Frances Victoria Howell 1998; one s. one d.; ed St Paul's School, London, Magdalen Coll., Oxford; fmr Jt Ed. Isis (Univ. of Oxford magazine); Dean Rusk Scholar (for a semester), Davidson Coll., N Carolina, USA; first job providing data entry services to Nat. Health Service; worked briefly for Selfridges and as freelance journalist; joined Conservative Research Dept in 1994, later Head of Political Section; Special Adviser, Minister of Agric., Fisheries and Food 1995–97; worked in Political Office, No. 10 Downing Street, Political Sec. to Leader of the Opposition and Sec. to Shadow Cabinet 1997–2001; Chair. David Cameron's Conservative Party leadership election campaign 2005; MP (Conservative) for Tatton, Cheshire 2001–17, mem. Public Accounts Select Cttee 2001–04, Transport Select Cttee 2002–03, Opposition Whip (Commons) April–Oct. 2003, Shadow Chief Sec. to the Treasury 2004–05, Shadow Chancellor of the Exchequer 2005–10, Chancellor of the Exchequer and First Sec. of State 2010–16; Ed. London Evening Standard 2017–; Adviser (part time) BlackRock (fund manager) 2017–; Kissinger Fellow, McCain Inst. for Int. Leadership 2017–; Vice-Pres. East Cheshire Hospice; Trustee, Arts and Business; Hon. Pres. The British Youth Council; Macmillan Cancer Relief Champion 2005. *Address:* London Evening Standard, 2 Derry Street, London, W8 5TT, England (office). *Telephone:* (20) 3367-7000 (office). *E-mail:* editor@standard.co.uk (office). *Website:* www.standard.co.uk (office); www.georgeosborne.co.uk.

OSBOURNE, (John) Ozzy; British musician and singer; b. 3 Dec. 1948, Aston, Warwicks., England; m. 1st Thelma Osbourne; two d.; m. 2nd Sharon Arden 1982; two d. one s.; mem. and lead singer, Black Sabbath (fmrly Polka Tulk, then Earth) 1967–77, reunion tour 1998–99; solo artist with backing group Blizzard of Ozz 1979; cr. annual touring festival Ozzfest 1996; numerous live performances and festival appearances; Grammy Awards for Best Metal Performance (for I Don't Want to Change the World) 1994, (for Iron Man) 2000, (for God is Dead?) 2014,

Nordoff-Robbins O2 Silver Clef Award (with Sharon Osbourne) 2006, MTV Europe Music Award for Global Icon 2014. *Television includes:* The Osbournes (series) 2002–05, Osbournes Reloaded (series) 2009, Ozzy & Jack's World Detour (series) 2016. *Recordings include:* albums: with Black Sabbath: Black Sabbath 1969, Paranoid 1970, Master Of Reality 1971, Black Sabbath Vol. 4 1972, Sabbath Bloody Sabbath 1973, Sabotage 1975, Technical Ecstasy 1976, Never Say Die! 1978, Reunion 1998, 13 2013; solo: Blizzard Of Ozz 1980, Diary Of A Madman 1981, Speak Of The Devil 1982, Bark At The Moon 1983, The Ultimate Sin 1986, Tribute 1987, No Rest For The Wicked 1988, Just Say Ozzy 1990, No More Tears 1991, Live & Loud 1993, Ozzmosis 1995, The Ozzman Cometh 1997, OzzFest Vol. 1 1997, Down To Earth 2001, Live At Budokan 2002, X-Posed 2002, Under Cover 2005, Black Rain 2007, Scream 2010, Ozzy Live 2011, Memoirs of a Madman 2014. *Publication:* I Am Ozzy (autobiog.) 2009. *Address:* Sharon Osbourne Management, 9292 Civic Centre Drive, Beverly Hills, CA 90210, USA (office). *Website:* www.ozzy.com; www.ozzfest.com.

OSEI, Isaac, BSc, MA; Ghanaian economist, diplomatist, politician and business executive; *Managing Director, Tema Oil Refinery;* b. 29 March 1951; s. of Nana Osei Nkwantabisa I and Rosina Eunice Osei (née Inkumsah); m. Marian Osei; two s. two d.; ed Achimota School, Univ. of Ghana, Legon, Econ. Inst., Univ. of Colorado, USA, Williams Coll., Mass, USA; Asst Econ. Planning Officer, Ministry of Finance and Econ. Planning 1970s; Founder and Man. Consultant, Ghanexim Econ. Consultants Ltd; fmr consultant to numerous official orgs. including Govt of Ghana, USAID, World Bank, UNCTAD, Japan Int. Co-operation Agency, Dept for Int. Devt; Man. Dir Intravenous Infusions Ltd, Koforidua; fmr Chief, Commercial Operations Dept, Ghana Tourist Devt Co. Ltd; High Commr to UK 2001–06; Chair. Bd of Govs Commonwealth Secr. 2003–05; Chief Exec. Ghana Cocoa Bd (COCOBOD) 2006–08; mem. Parl. for Subin constituency (New Patriotic Party) 2009–17; Man. Dir Tema Oil Refinery (TOR) 2017–; Officer, Order of the Volta. *Leisure interest:* football (from a distance). *Address:* Tema Oil Refinery, Heavy Industrial Area, Tema, Ghana (office). *E-mail:* info@torghana.com (office). *Website:* www.tor.com.gh (office).

OSEI-ADJEI, Akwasi, MSc; Ghanaian politician; b. 29 Dec. 1949, Onwe, Ashanti Region; m.; five c.; ed De Montfort Univ., UK; trained and qualified as an accountant, worked at Ozze Ghana Ltd; mem. Parl. for Ejisu/Juabeng constituency 1996–2007; fmr Deputy Minister of Foreign Affairs, Regional Integration and New Partnership for Africa's Devt (NEPAD), Minister of Foreign Affairs, Regional Integration and NEPAD 2007–09; arrested and charged with conspiracy and contravening the Public Procurement Act July 2009, acquitted by the Court of Appeal April 2012; mem. New Patriotic Party. *Address:* New Patriotic Party, C912/2 Duade Street, Kokomlemle, PO Box 3456, Accra, Ghana (office). *Telephone:* (21) 2264288 (office). *Fax:* (21) 2229048 (office). *E-mail:* info@newpatrioticparty.org (office). *Website:* www.newpatrioticparty.org (office).

O'SHEA, Sir Timothy Michael Martin, Kt, BSc, PhD, FRSE; British university principal and professor of computer science; *Professor Emeritus of Digital Education, University of Edinburgh;* b. 28 March 1949, Hamburg, Germany; s. of John Patrick O'Shea and Elisabeth Hedwig Oberhof; m. Eileen Scanlon 1982; two s. two d.; ed Royal Liberty School Havering, Univs of Sussex and Leeds; postgraduate research, Univ of Texas at Austin, USA and Univ. of Edinburgh; Founder, Computer Assisted Learning Research Group, Open Univ. 1978; Lecturer, Inst. of Educational Tech. 1980–82, Sr Lecturer 1983–87, Prof. of Information Tech. and Educ. 1987–97, Pro-Vice-Chancellor for Quality Assurance and Research 1994–97, Visiting Research Prof. 1997; Master of Birkbeck Coll. and Prof. of Information and Communication Technologies 1998–2002; Gov. Literary Inst. 1998–2000, SOAS 1998–2002, St George's Medical School, Univ. of London 2000–02; Curator, School of Advanced Study, Univ. of London 1999–2002; Provost, Gresham Coll. 2000–02; Pro-Vice-Chancellor Univ. of London 2001–02; Prin. and Vice-Chancellor, Univ. of Edinburgh 2002–18, Prof. Emer. of Digital Educ. 2018–; Visiting Scientist, Xerox PARC and Visiting Scholar, Univ. of California, Berkeley 1986–87; Chair. NATO programme on Advanced Educational Tech. 1988–90; Chair. London Metropolitan Network Ltd 1999–2002; Chair. HERO Ltd 2000; Dir, Edexcel Foundation 1998–2001 (mem. Exec. Cttee 1998–2001), Univs and Colls Staff Devt Agency 1999–2000; Chair. Information Systems Sector Group, Cttee of Vice-Chancellors and Principals 1999; mem. Higher Educ. Funding Council for England Cttee on Equal Opportunities, Access and Lifelong Learning 1998, Jt Information Systems Cttee 2000–13 (Chair.); mem. Bd Universities UK 2001–18; Pres. Pyschology Section, BAAS 1991–92; Chair. Artificial Intelligence Soc. 1979–82; mem. Council, Royal Coll. of Music 2001; Chair. Scottish Inst. for Enterprise 2009–17; Chair. Edinburgh Festival Fringe Soc. 2012–, Newbattle Abbey Coll. 2012–17; Visiting Prof., Learning Teaching Innovation, Open Univ. 2017; mem. Advisory Bd, Coursera Univ. 2013–17 (Chair. 2016–17), Inst. for Cultural Diplomacy 2014–; mem. Scottish Govt Financial Services Advisory Bd 2014–17, Digital Public Services Sponsor Bd 2015–17; mem. Univ. Council for All-Parl. Univ. Group 2013–18; mem. Governing Council, Confucius Inst. Headquarters 2007–18, Scottish Funding Council's Research and Knowledge Exchange Cttee 2016–17; Convener, Univ. Scotland's Research and Knowledge Exchange Cttee 2016–; Fellow, Birkbeck, Univ. of the Highlands and Islands, Millennium Inst., European Co-ordinating Cttee on Artificial Intelligence, Acad. of Social Sciences, Royal Acad. of Eng; Trustee, Eduserv 1999–2000, Carnegie Trust for Univs of Scotland 2002–18; Hon. DUniv (Heriot-Watt) 2008, (Strathclyde) 2011; Hon. LLD (McGill) 2011; Dr hc (St Petersburg Univ. of Humanities and Social Sciences) 2013; Univ. of London Union Laurel for his services to part-time students, outstanding contrib. awards from Govt of Japan and of People's Repub. of China for promoting academic co-operation between Scotland and those countries. *Television:* The Learning Machine (series presenter and author) 1985. *Publications include:* Self-Improving Teaching Systems 1979, Learning and Teaching with Computers (co-author) 1983, Artificial Intelligence: Tools, Techniques and Applications (co-author) 1984, Advances in Artificial Intelligence (ed.) 1985, Intelligent Knowledge-based Systems: An Introduction (co-ed.) 1987, Educational Computing (co-ed.) 1987, New Directions in Educational Tech. (co-ed.) 1992. *Leisure interests:* hill walking, especially on the Pentlands and the north Kilkenny countryside, avid reader of history books, active mem. Oyster Club of Edinburgh and Caledonian Club of London. *Address:* Moray House School of Educ., University of Edinburgh, Holyrood Campus, Edinburgh, EH8 8AQ, Scotland (office). *Telephone:* (131) 651-6138 (office). *E-mail:* toshea@ed.ac.uk (office).

OSHEROFF, Douglas Dean, PhD; American physicist and researcher; *Emer. Prof. of Physics and Applied Physics and J.G. Jackson and C.J. Wood Emer. Prof. of Physics, Standford University, California;* b. 1 Aug. 1945, Aberdeen, Wash.; s. of William Osheroff and Bessie Anne Osheroff (née Ondov); m. Phyllis S. K. Liu 1970; ed California Inst. of Tech., Cornell Univ.; mem. tech. staff, Bell Labs, Murray Hill, NY 1972–82, Head Solid State and Low Temperature Physics Research Dept 1982–87; apptd Prof. of Physics and Applied Physics 1987 and J.G. Jackson and C.J. Wood Prof. of Physics 1992, Stanford Univ., Calif., Chair. Physics 1993–96, currently Emer. Prof. of Physics and Applied Physics and J.G. Jackson and C.J. Wood Emer. Prof. of Physics; co-discoverer of superfluidity in liquid ^{3}He 1971, nuclear antiferromagnetic resonance in solid ^{3}He 1980; Fellow, American Physical Soc., American Acad. of Arts and Sciences, NAA; Simon Memorial Prize, British Inst. of Physics (co-recipient) 1976, Oliver E. Buckley Solid State Physics Prize 1981, John D. and Catherine T. MacArthur Prize Fellow 1981, Nobel Prize for Physics (co-recipient) 1996. *Address:* Room 150, Department of Physics, Stanford University, Varian Physics Building, 382 Via Pueblo Mall, Stanford, CA 94305-4060, USA. *Telephone:* (650) 723-4228 (office). *Fax:* (650) 725-6544 (office). *E-mail:* osheroff@stanford.edu (office). *Website:* web.stanford.edu/dept/physics/people/faculty/osheroff_douglas%20-%20Copy.html (office).

OSHII, Mamoru; Japanese film director; b. 8 Aug. 1951, Tokyo; ed Fine Arts School, Dept of Educ., Tokyo Liberal Arts Univ. (Tokyo Gakugei Daigaku); involved in anti-ANPO (US–Japan Security Treaty) student movt 1970s; began directing short films 1976; joined Tatsunoko Productions 1977; made film On the Roof using permeable light filming process; worked for Studio Pierrot under supervision of Nagayuki Toriumi 1980–84; joined Headgear as writer and dir 1980s; cr. Patlabor franchise with Masami Yuuki, Kenji Kawaï and Akemi Tadaka. *Films directed include:* Darossu 1983, Urusei Yatsura 1: Only You 1983, Urusei Yatsura 2: Beautiful Dreamer 1984, Angel's Egg 1985, The Red Spectacles 1987, Twilight Q Episode 2: Meikyu Bukken File 538 1987, Mobile Police Patlabor 1988, Patlabor: The Movie 1989, Stray Dogs: Kerberos Panzer Cops 1991, Talking Head 1992, Patlabor 2: The Movie (Best Animated Film, Mainichi Film Concours 1993) 1993, Ghost in the Shell (Feature Film Award, Animation Kobe 1996) 1995, Avalon (Best Feature Film, London Sci-Fi Film Festival 2002) 2001, Ghost in the Shell 2: Innocence (Feature Film Award, Animation Kobe 2004, 25th Nihon SF Taisho Award 2004, Orient Express Award, Sitges - Catalan Int. Film Festival 2004) 2004, Open Your Mind (short) 2005, Tachiguishi retsuden 2006, The Women of Fast Food (segments The Assault Girl, The Golden Fish Girl) (also exec. producer) 2007, Ghost in the Shell 2.0 2008, The Sky Crawlers (Best Animated Film, Mainichi Film Concours 2008, Future Film Festival Digital Award, Venice Film Festival 2008) 2008, Kill (also exec. producer) 2008, Assault Girls 2009, Halo Legends (video) (creative dir segment The Duel) 2010, 28½ mousou no kyojin 2010, 009: The Reopening (short) 2010, The Last Druid: Garm Wars 2014, The Next Generation Patoreibā: Shuto kessen 2015, Nowhere Girl 2015. *Screenplays include:* Urusei Yatsura 1: Only You 1983, Urusei Yatsura 2: Beautiful Dreamer 1984, When All's Said and Done 1984, Angel's Egg 1985, The Red Spectacles 1987, In the Aftermath 1988, Legend of a Wolf-Dog 1988, StrayDog: Kerberos Panzer Cops 1991, Talking Head 1992, Seraphim 1995, Jin Roth: The Wolf Brigade 1998, Ghost in the Shell 2: Innocence 2004, Tachiguishi retsuden 2006, The Women of Fast Food 2007, Kill 2008, Musashi: The Dream of the Last Samurai (also producer) 2009, Assault Girls 2009. *Television series:* The Wonderful Adventures of Nils 1980, Urusei Yatsura (Those Obnoxious Aliens) 1981–84, Mrs Pepperpot 1983, Blood: The Last Vampire (supervising producer) 2000, Mini-Pato 2002, Blood+ (series) (producer and co-planner) 2005, Ani*Kuri15 (series) (also writer) 2007, The Next Generation: Patlabor (also writer) 2014, Sand Whale and Me (mini-series) 2017. *Website:* www.oshiimamoru.com.

OSHIMA, Kenzo; Japanese diplomatist; *Senior Vice-President, Japan International Co-operation Agency;* b. 1943; m.; two c.; ed Tokyo Univ.; served in diplomatic posts in Australia, France, India, USA and at Perm. Mission to UN; Dir-Gen. Econ. Co-operation Bureau, Ministry of Foreign Affairs; Sec.-Gen. Secr. for Int. Peace Co-operation HQ, Office of the Prime Minister –2000; UN Under-Sec.-Gen. for Humanitarian Affairs and Emergency Relief Co-ordinator 2001–03; Amb. to Australia 2003; Perm. Rep. to UN 2004–07; Sr Vice-Pres. Japan Int. Co-operation Agency 2007–. *Address:* Japan International Co-operation Agency, 6th–13th floors, Shinjuku Maynds Tower 2-1-1 Yoyogi, Shibuya-ku, Tokyo 151-8558, Japan (office). *Telephone:* (3) 5352-5311 (office). *E-mail:* oshima.kenzo@jica.go.jp (office). *Website:* (office).

OSHIMA, Tadamori; Japanese politician; *Speaker, House of Representatives;* b. 6 Sept. 1946, Hachinohe, Aomori Prefecture; m.; two s.; ed Keio Univ.; worked at Mainichi Shimbun 1965–74; elected to Ass. Aomori Prefecture 1975; elected to House of Reps (LDP) 1983–, Chair. Steering Cttee 1999–2000; Deputy Sec. of the Cabinet 1992–2003; later Vice-Chair., Parl. Cttee, LDP, Deputy Sec.-Gen. 1993–95; Minister for Educ., Minister for Science and Tech. Agency July–Dec. 2000, Minister of Agric., Forestry and Fisheries 2002; Speaker, House of Rep. 2015–. *Address:* House of Representatives, 1-7-1, Nagata-cho, Chiyoda-ku, Tokyo 100-0014 (office); Liberal Democratic Party, 1-11-23, Nagata-cho, Chiyoda-ku, Tokyo 100-8910, Japan (office). *Telephone:* (3) 3581-3111 (office); (3) 3581-6211 (LDP) (office). *Fax:* (3) 5511-8855 (LDP) (office). *E-mail:* webmaster@shugiin.go.jp (office); koho@ldp.jimin.or.jp (office). *Website:* www.shugiin.go.jp/internet/index.nsf/html/index_e.htm (office); www.jimin.jp (office); www.morry.jp.

OSHIOMHOLE, Adams Aliyu; Nigerian trade union official and regional governor; *Chairman, All Progressive Congress;* b. 4 April 1952; s. of Aishetu Oshiomhole; m. 1st Clara Oshiomhole (deceased 2010); five c.; m. 2nd Lara Fortes 2015; ed Ruskin Coll., Oxford, UK and Nat. Inst. for Policy and Strategic Studies, Kuru; began career as shop steward at textile factory; Pres. Nigeria Labour Congress 1999; Chair. Governing Bd Nigerian Social Insurance Trust Fund Scheme; Gov. Edo State 2008–16; Chair. All Progressives Congress (APC) 2018–; mem. Action Congress of Nigeria. *Address:* All Progressive Congress, 40 Blantyre Street, off Adetokunbo Ademola Street, Wuse II, Abuja, Nigeria (office). *E-mail:* info@apc.com.ng (office). *Website:* apc.com.ng (office).

OSHO, Pierre, MA; Benin politician; b. 5 May 1945, Porto Novo; m.; six c.; ed Acad. of Grenoble, Univ. of Dakar, Univ. of Aix-en-Provence, France; Prof. of History and Geography, Coll. Père Aupiais, Cotonou 1968–70, Coll. d'Enseignement Moyen Général de Gbégamey, Cotonou 1970–73; Dir of Information and

Propaganda (MISON) 1976–78; mem. Cen. Cttee, Party of Popular Revolution 1979–90; Chief of Dist of Klouékanmey, Prov. of Mono 1978–84; Peoples' Commr, Nat. Ass. 1980–90; Pres. Comm. on Govt and Ass. Relations 1980–84; Dir Nat. Centre of Revolutionary Educ. 1982–84; Sec.-Gen. Perm. Cttee of Nat. Ass. 1984–89; Pres. Comm. on Constitutional Affairs 1989–90; Dir Cabinet of Pres. of Benin 1989–91; with Dept of Research of Human and Social Sciences 1991–96; Minister of Foreign Affairs and Co-operation 1996–98; Minister to Pres. of Benin 1998–2001; Minister of Nat. Defence 2001–06 (resgnd); del. to int. and multilateral confs.

OSIPOV, Victor Ivanovich, MS, PhD; Russian engineer, geologist and hydrogeologist; *Scientific Adviser, Sergeev Institute of Environmental Geoscience, Russian Academy of Sciences;* b. 15 April 1937, Bashkortostan; ed Moscow State Univ.; Dir scientific station 1959–61; Lecturer, Prof., Moscow State Univ. 1964–90, Hon. Prof. 1999–; Deputy Dir Inst. of Lithosphere 1990; mem. Russian Acad. of Sciences 1991–, Dir Scientific Centre for Eng, Geology and Environment, Russian Acad. of Sciences 1991–2015 (now Sergeev Inst. of Environmental Geoscience), Scientific Adviser 2015–; main research in eng geology, environmental protection; Hon. Prof., Geological Inst., Acad. of Science of China 1996; State Prize 1988, Moscow Major Prize 2002, Nat. Ecological Prize 2004, Russian State Medal 2008, Hans Cloos Medal 2012. *Publications:* more than 650 articles in scientific journals. *Leisure interests:* travelling, sports (skiing), gardening, fishing. *Address:* Sergeev Institute of Environmental Geoscience, PO Box 145, Ulansky per. 13, Building 2, 101000 Moscow, Russia (office). *Telephone:* (495) 623-31-11 (office). *Fax:* (495) 623-18-86 (office). *E-mail:* direct@geoenv.ru (office). *Website:* www.geoenv.ru (office).

OSIPOV, Yuri Sergeyevich, DPhys-MathSc; Russian mathematician and technician; *Advisor, Russian Academy of Sciences;* b. 7 July 1936, Tobolsk; m.; one d.; ed Urals State Univ.; Corresp. mem. USSR (now Russian) Acad. of Sciences 1984, mem. 1987, Pres. 1991–2013, Advisor 2013–; staff mem., Inst. of Mechanics and Math., Urals Scientific Cen. Acad. of Sciences 1959, Dir 1990–93; Prof., Urals Univ. 1961–70; fmr Head of Chair of Moscow State Univ.; Dir Steklov Math. Inst. 1993–; mem. American Math. Soc., American Acad. of Arts and Sciences, Mongolian Acad. of Sciences, Armenian Acad. of Sciences, Santiago Univ., Chile; mem. Bd of Dirs Skolkovo Foundation 2010–, OJSC LSR Group 2014–15; mem. Supervisory Bd Russian Council on Foreign Affairs 2011–; Order of Merit for the Fatherland of 3rd Degree 1996, 2nd Degree 1999, 1st Degree 2006, 4th degree 2013, Demidov Prize 2010, Commdr, Ordre national de la Légion d'honneur 2011; Dr hc (Bar-Ilan Univ., Israel), (Santiago Univ., Chile); Lenin Prize 1976, USSR State Prize. *Publications:* more than 150 works on the theory of math., differential equations and their application. *Address:* Russian Academy of Sciences, Leninsky prospekt 14, 119991 GSP-1, Moscow; Steklov Mathematical Institute, 42 Vavilov Street, 117966 Moscow, Russia. *Telephone:* (495) 954-35-06 (Acad.); (495) 135-22-91 (Inst.). *Website:* www.ras.ru.

OSKANYAN, Vardan, BS, MSc, MA; Armenian diplomatist and politician; *Founder and Director, Civilitas Foundation;* b. 7 Feb. 1955, Syria; m. Nani Oskanyan; two s.; ed Yerevan Polytechnic Inst., Tufts Univ., Mass, Harvard Univ., Fletcher School of Law and Diplomacy, USA; Founder and Ed. Armenian Int. Magazine 1990; on staff, Armenian Ministry of Foreign Affairs 1992–; Deputy Head, Middle East Dept, Head, Dept of N America 1992–94; prin. negotiator in Misk process on Nagorno-Karabakh conflict 1994–97; Visiting Asst Prof. of Int. Relations, American Univ. of Armenia 1994–96; Deputy Foreign Minister 1994–96, First Deputy Foreign Minister 1996–98, Minister of Foreign Affairs 1998–2008; f. Civilitas Foundation 2008; f. Unity party 2016, Chair. 2016–, contested legislative elections as part of 'Ohanyan-Raffi-Oskanyan' alliance 2017. *Publication:* Speaking to be Heard: A Decade of Speeches 2009. *Address:* Civilitas Foundation, 0010 Yerevan, One Northern Avenue, Suite 30, Armenia (office). *Telephone:* (10) 50-01-19 (office). *Fax:* (10) 50-01-12 (office). *E-mail:* info@civilitasfoundation.org (office). *Website:* www.civilitasfoundation.org (office).

OSKARSON, Peter, (Dhyan Manyu); Swedish theatre director and actor; b. 13 June 1951, Stockholm; s. of Per-Otto Oskarson and Margareta Du Rietz; m. 1st Kajsa Reingardt 1979; m. 2nd Gunilla Kindstrand 1983 (divorced 2002); one s. four d.; m. 3rd Sofie Livebrant 2004; one d.; ed Swedish Actors' School, Acad. of Dramatic Arts, Stockholm; Artistic Dir Skånska Teatern Landskrona 1973–82, Folkteatern Gävleborg 1982–90; Head, Helsingegården, inst. for theatre and popular arts, N Scandinavia 1990–2004; Artistic Dir Orion Theatre 1993–2000; Gen. Man. Folkteatern Gävleborg 1997–2006; Artistic Adviser, Peking Opera, Anhui, Hefei, China 1996–2000; Artistic Dir World Theatre Project 1999–; Artistic Dir Holy Fools of Katarina Church 2009–; Artistic Leader, The Scania Anatomical 2012–15; theatre plays produced also at Royal Opera House and at Royal Dramatic Theatre, Stockholm, Drottningholm Theatre, Staatsoper, Stuttgart, Intiman, Seattle, USA, Oper der Stadt, Bonn, Festwochen, Vienna, Schwetzingen Festspiele, Swedish TV, Nationaltheater Mannheim, Royal Opera House, Copenhagen etc.; mem. Swedish Theatre Acad. 1993–, Swedish World Culture Forum 1998–2001, Framtidens Kultur 2003–06; Medal of Honour, Landskrona Municipality; Alf Sjöberg Prize, Swedish Acad. Theatre Prize, Svenska Dagbladet Thalia Prize, Expressen Theatre Prize, Gävle and Gävleborg Culture Prize, Malmö Thalia Prize, Gefledagblad Culture Prize, Olof Hogberg Prize, Sture Linnér Prize, Poul Reumert Prize for Best Opera. *Plays:* Monsters by Niklas Rådström 2014, Faust 1 2 by Goethe 2015, Migrants by Vilhelm Moberg 2016, Romeo and Juliet by Shakespeare 2017, On a Hill in Wales 2018, Schlagt Sie Tot! 2019. *Address:* Manyu Dream Sharing, Köpmangatan 9, 111 31 Stockholm, Sweden (office). *E-mail:* posk@me.com. *Website:* www.oskarson.se.

OSLON, Alexander A., CandTechSci; Russian engineer and institute director; *President, All-Russian Foundation for Public Opinion;* b. 19 March 1952, Zlatoust, Chelyabinsk region; m.; one d.; ed Tula State Polytechnic Inst.; worked as engineer, then Chief Constructor, GSKTB 1974–87; Researcher, All-Union Centre of Public Opinion Studies 1988–90, Deputy Dir 1990–92; Co-founder and Pres. All-Russian Foundation for Public Opinion 1992–; mem. Man. Bd, Inst. of Contemporary Devt. *Publications include:* numerous articles in the press on results of public pools of population and methodical problems of sociological studies. *Address:* All-Russian Foundation for Public Opinion, 123242 Moscow, Kapranov per. 3, Russian Federation (office). *Telephone:* (495) 745-87-65 (office). *Fax:* (495) 745-89-03 (office). *E-mail:* fom@fom.ru (office). *Website:* fom.ru (office).

OSMAN, Abukar Dahir, MBA; Somali civil servant and diplomatist; *Permanent Representative to United Nations;* ed Illinois State Univ., Franklin Univ., Columbus, Univ. of Wisconsin; worked in Ministry of Nat. Planning, Dir Somali Nat. Documentation Centre 1987–88; Documentation Specialist, UN Centre for Human Rights, Tirana 1996–98; Case Man., Franklin County Dept of Job and Family Services, OH, USA 1999–2005, Social Program Specialist 2005–07, Supervisor Adult Medical Unit 2007–12; Chief of Staff to Prime Minister of Transitional Fed. Govt 2010–11; Perm. Sec., Ministry of Interior and Nat. Security 2012–14; Chief of Staff, Office of the Pres. 2014–17; Perm. Rep. to UN 2017–. *Address:* Permanent Mission of Somalia, 425 E 61st Street, Suite 702, New York, NY 10021, USA (office). *Telephone:* (212) 688-9410 (office). *Fax:* (212) 759-0651 (office). *E-mail:* somalia@un.int (office). *Website:* www.un.int/somalia (office).

OSMAN, Ahmed, LLM; Moroccan politician and diplomatist; b. 3 Jan. 1930, Oujda; s. of Muhammad Osman and Sofia Malti; m. HRH Princess Lalla Nezha (sister of King Hassan II) 1964 (deceased 1977); one s.; ed Royal High School, Rabat, Univ. of Rabat and Univ. of Bordeaux, France; Head of the Legal Section, Royal Cabinet 1956; joined Ministry of Foreign Affairs 1957; Sec.-Gen. Ministry of Nat. Defence 1959–61; Amb. to FRG 1961–62; UnderSec.-of-State for Industry and Mines 1963–64; Pres. and Gen. Man. Moroccan Navigation Co. 1964–67; Amb. to USA, Canada and Mexico 1967–70; Minister of Admin. Affairs 1970–71; Dir of Royal Cabinet 1971–72; Prime Minister 1972–79; Parl. Rep. for Oujda 1977–; Leader Rassemblement nat. des indépendants 1978–2007; mem. Nat. Defence Council 1979–; Minister of State 1983; Pres. Chamber of Reps. 1984–92; participated in UN sessions 1957, 1958, 1960, 1961, 1968, Conf. on Maritime law 1958, Conf. of the League of Arab States 1961; Kt Grand Cordon of the Order of the Throne, Kt Grand Cross of the Order of the British Empire, Order of St Michael and St George, Order of Merit of the Fed. Repub. of Germany 1962. *Leisure interests:* bridge, sports, reading, swimming. *Address:* Rassemblement national des indépendants, 6 rue Laos, avenue Hassan II, Rabat, Morocco.

OSMAN, Salih Mahmoud; Sudanese lawyer and human rights activist; b. 1957, Darfur; m.; for over 30 years has defended people who were allegedly arbitrarily detained and tortured by Sudanese govt; Lawyer, Sudanese Org. Against Torture 2003, also works with Amal Center for Rehabilitation of Torture Victims, Nyala; imprisoned Feb.–Sept. 2004; mem. Parl., Nat. Democratic Alliance 2006; mem. Bd of Dirs Darfur Peace and Devt Org.; Human Rights Defender Award, Human Rights Watch 2005, International Human Rights Award 2006, Sakharov Prize 2007.

OSMAN ALI, Ahmed; Djibouti central banker; *Governor, Banque Centrale de Djibouti;* ed Institut d' Etude Bancaire de Tours and Université François Rabelais, France; fmr teacher, Grandes Ecoles de Commerce et de Gestion, France; joined Banque Centrale de Djibouti 1989, rising to Exec. Dir, Gov. Banque Centrale de Djibouti 2013–, mem. Bd of Govs IMF; Pres. Development Funds Administration Bd, Agence Djiboutienne du Développement Social. *Address:* Banque Centrale de Djibouti, BP 2118, Avenue Saint Laurent du Var, Djibouti (office). *Telephone:* 21352751 (office). *Fax:* 21356288 (office). *E-mail:* bndj@intnet.dj (office). *Website:* www.banque-centrale.dj (office).

OSMANI, Bujar, MD; Macedonian doctor and politician; *Deputy Prime Minister, responsible for European Integration;* b. 11 Sept. 1979, Skopje, Socialist Repub. of Macedonia, Socialist Fed. Repub. of Yugoslavia; ed SS Cyril and Methodius Univ. of Skopje; ethnic Albanian; worked as a doctor at the Public Hosp., Skopje; mem. Bashkimi Demokratik për Integrim/Demokratska Unija za Integracija (BDI—Democratic Union for Integration); apptd Minister of Health 2008; Deputy Prime Minister, responsible for European Integration 2017–. *Address:* Office of the Prime Minister, 1000 Skopje, Ilindenska b.b. 2, North Macedonia (office). *Telephone:* (2) 3118022 (office). *Fax:* (2) 3112561 (office). *E-mail:* primeminister@primeminister.gov.mk (office). *Website:* www.vlada.mk (office).

OSMIĆ, Zekerijah (Mevludin); Bosnia and Herzegovina economist and politician; b. 2 Aug. 1956, Brčko; m.; three c.; ed Brčko Univ.; began career as math. and physics teacher, Brčko elementary school 1976–80; Professional Sec., Youth and Cooperatives Centre, Brčko 1981–83, Dir 1983–88; engaged in private enterprise 1988–92; Head of Logistics Centre, Govt of Brčko-Rahić 1992–96, Sec. for Economy and Deputy Mayor for Economy and Finance 1996–98; mem. Nat. Ass. of Republika Srpska (Serbian Democratic Party) 1998–2006; Adviser on Economy and Finance to Mayor of Brčko Dist 2006–08; Head, Public Records Div., Govt of Brčko Dist 2008–12; Minister of Defence 2012–15.

OSMOND, Charles Barry, PhD, FRS, FAA; Australian biologist and academic; b. 20 Sept. 1939, Cooranbong, NSW; s. of Edward Charles Osmond and Joyce Daphne Osmond (née Krauss); m. 1st Suzanne Ward 1962 (divorced 1983); one s. one d.; m. 2nd Cornelia Gauhl 1983; ed Morisset Central and Wyong High Schools and Univs of New England and Adelaide; Postdoctoral Fellow, UCLA 1965–66, Univ. of Cambridge 1966–67; Research Fellow, Dept of Environmental Biology, Research School of Biological Sciences, ANU 1967, subsequently Fellow, Sr Research Fellow, Prof. of Biology 1978–87, Dir Research School of Biol. Sciences 1991–98, Prof., Photo Bioenergetics Group 1998–2001, currently Hon. Visiting Fellow, Div. of Plant Sciences; apptd Prof. of Plant Science, Inst. of Conservation Biology and Environmental Man., Univ. of Wollongong 2011, later Hon. Prof.; Exec. Dir Biological Science Center, Desert Research Inst., Univ. of Nevada 1982–86; Arts and Sciences Distinguished Prof., Dept of Botany, Duke Univ. 1987–91; Pres. and CEO Biosphere 2 Center, Columbia Univ. 2001–03; Sr Fulbright Fellowship, Univ. of Calif., Santa Cruz 1973–74; Guest Prof., Technical Univ., Munich 1974; Overseas Fellow, Churchill Coll., Cambridge 1980; mem. Australian Nat. Comm. for UNESCO 1980–82; Treasurer, Int. Soc. of Photosynthesis Research 1999–2007; mem. Council, Australian Acad. of Sciences 1982–85, Deutsche Akad. der Naturforscher, Leopoldina 2001; Life mem. Australian Soc. of Plant Scientists 2008; Goldacre Award Australian Soc. of Plant Physiologists 1972, Edgeworth David Medal, Royal Soc. of NSW 1974, Inaugural Distinguished Alumnus, Univ. of New England 1994, Clarke Medal (Botany), Royal Soc. of NSW 1997, Research Prize, Alexander von Humboldt Foundation, Univs of Darmstadt and Göttingen 1997–2000. *Publications:* numerous publs in plant physiology. *Address:* PO Box 3252, Weston Creek, ACT 2611, Australia (home). *Telephone:* (2) 6287-1487 (home). *E-mail:* osmond.barry@gmail.com.

OSMOND, Donald (Donny) Clark; American singer; b. 9 Dec. 1957, Ogden, Utah; m. Debra Glenn 1978; five c.; ed Brigham Young Univ.; singer with The Osmonds 1963–80; solo artist 1971–78, 1988–; also duo with sister Marie; head of own TV production co., Night Star 1980s; fmr host of two daily internationally syndicated radio shows, The Donny Osmond Radio Show and Donny's 8-Track Playback; nightly performances at Las Vegas Flamingo Hotel, 2010–12; f. Donny Osmond Home (home furnishings brand); Georgie Award for Best Vocal Team (with Marie Osmond) 1978. *Television includes:* Donny and Marie (show) 1976–79, Osmond Family (show) 1980, Dancing With The Stars (winner) 2009. *Films include:* Goin' Coconuts 1978, College Road Trip 2008. *Theatre includes:* Joseph and his Amazing Technicolour Dreamcoat, Toronto, Canada 1992–93, Beauty and the Beast, New York 2006. *Recordings include:* albums: with The Osmonds: Homemade 1971, Osmonds 1971, Crazy Horses 1972, Phase-III 1972, The Osmonds Live 1972, The Plan 1973, Love Me For A Reason 1974, Around The World: Live In Concert 1975, The Proud One 1975, Brainstorm 1976, The Osmond Christmas Album 1976, Osmond Family Christmas 1991; solo: The Donny Osmond Album 1971, To You With Love, Donny 1971, Portrait of Donny 1972, Too Young 1972, My Best To You 1972, A Time For Us 1973, Alone Together 1973, Donny Osmond Superstar 1973, Donny 1974, I'm Leaving It All Up To You (with Marie Osmond) 1974, Love Me For A Reason 1974, Make The World Go Away (with Marie Osmond) 1975, Donny and Marie – Featuring Songs From Their Television Show (with Marie Osmond) 1976, Donny and Marie: New Season (with Marie Osmond) 1976, Deep Purple (with Marie Osmond) 1976, Disco Train 1976, Donald Clark Osmond 1977, Goin' Coconuts (with Marie Osmond) 1978, Winning Combination 1978, Donny Osmond 1989, Eyes Don't Lie 1990, Christmas At Home 1998, This Is The Moment 2001, Somewhere In Time 2002, What I Meant To Say 2004, Love Songs of the '70s 2007, From Donny with Love 2008, Duets (with Marie Osmond) 2009, The Entertainer 2010, Donny & Marie (with Marie Osmond) 2011, The Soundtrack of My Life 2014. *Publication:* Life is Just What You Make of It (autobiography) 2005. *Website:* www.donnyosmond.com; donny.com.

OSMONOV, Kurmanbek Ergeshovich; Kyrgyzstani politician and lawyer; b. 1 March 1953, Kara-Kulja; m. Zhakin Chymbayeva; two s. two d.; ed Kyrgyz State Univ.; Deputy Minister for Justice, subsequently First Deputy Minister 1991–94; Judge Constitutional Court 1994–2000; mem. Jogorku Kenesh (parl.) 2000–02; First Deputy Prime Minister of Kyrgyzstan and Minister of Justice 2002–04; Chair. of the Supreme Court 2004–08; Honoured Lawyer of Kyrgyz Repub.; Dank Medal (highest nat. award). *Publications:* several books on development and court reform in Kyrgyzstan. *Leisure Interests:* music, chess, cars. *Address:* 26 Keldibek Karboz Uulu Street, Orto-sai, Bishkek, Kyrgyzstan (home). *Telephone:* (312) 55-01-37 (home).

OSORI, Ayisha, LLB, LLM, MC/MPA; Nigerian lawyer, consultant and organization official; *Board Chairperson, Open Society Initiative West Africa;* ed Univ. of Lagos, Harvard Law School, Sloan School of Man. at Massachusetts Inst. of Tech., Kennedy School of Govt at Harvard Univ., USA; called to Nigerian Bar 1998, NY State Bar 2000; Assoc., Arthur Andersen, Lagos 1998–2000; Vice-Pres., Corp. Services, Ocean & Oil Holdings Nigeria Ltd 2002–06; Regulatory Affairs Man., British American Tobacco (BAT) Nigeria 2006–09, Area Regulation and Compliance Counsel, West Africa Area 2006–12; CEO The Nigerian Women's Trust Fund 2012–15, currently mem. Bd of Dir; Chair. Bd Open Soc. Initiative W Africa 2012–; hosted and co-produced a local radio programme Women Talk Politics 2010–11; wrote a weekly column, Pedestrian Lawyer, in Thisday's The Lawyer for more than three years; writes a weekly column for Leadership newspaper Nigerian Citizen; lead consultant and nat. co-ordinator for the World Bank DFID Gender Dialogue Sessions; Dir, Advocates for Change & Social Justice Initiative; fmr Eisenhower Fellow. *Publication:* Social Studies For Primary Schools (co-author) (series) 2007. *Address:* Open Soc. Initiative W Africa, 32/Plot 1266, Amazon Street Off Alvan Ikoku Way Ministers Hill, Maitama, Abuja, Nigeria (office). *Telephone:* (9) 6576016 (office). *E-mail:* osiwa-abuja@osiwa.org (office). *Website:* www.osiwa.org/osiwa_member (office).

OSORIO CHONG, Miguel Ángel, LLB; Mexican lawyer and politician; b. 5 Aug. 1964, Pachuca, Hidalgo State; s. of Eduardo Osorio Hernández and María Luisa Chong Chávez; m. Laura Vargas; one s. one d.; ed Univ. Autónoma del Estado de Hidalgo; held several positions with Pachuca municipal govt including Chief Clerk, Pachuca City Hall, Sec. of Govt, Sec. of Social Devt, Regional Devt Sec.; mem. Cámara Federal de Diputados (Parl.) for Pachuca constituency 2003–05, Deputy Coordinator of Parl. Partido Revolucionario Institucional—PRI Group; Gov., Hidalgo State 2005–11; Coordinator of Political Dialogue and Agreement, Office of Pres.-elect Enrique Peña Nieto 2012; Sec. (Minister) of the Interior 2012–18. *Address:* c/o Secretariat of State for the Interior, Abraham González 48, Col. Juárez, Del. Cuauhtémoc, 066000 México DF, Mexico (office).

OSPEL, Marcel; Swiss banker; b. 8 Feb. 1950; ed Higher School of Econs and Man., Basel; joined Dept of Planning and Marketing Swiss Bank Corpn (SBC) 1977, with SBC Capital Markets, London, New York 1980, Dir 1987, mem. Enlargement Group 1990, CEO Capital Markets and Treasury 1992, SBC Warburg 1995, Group Pres. 1996; Man. Dir Capital Markets Div., Merrill Lynch Capital Markets 1984–87; Pres. and Group CEO Swiss Bank Corpn (SBC) 1996–98; Group CEO UBS AG 1999–2001, Chair. 2001–08 (resgnd); Dr hc (Univ. of Rochester) 2005.

OSPINA BERNAL, Camilo, LLB; Colombian lawyer, academic and government official; *Founding Partner and Director, Opebsa Compañía de Abogados S.A.S;* b. 23 Dec. 1959, Bogotá; m. Gloria Hoyos; one s. one d.; ed Colegio Mayor de Nuestra Señora del Rosario; Vice-Dean, Faculty of Law, Colegio Mayor de Nuestra Señora del Rosario 1990–91; legal adviser, Ministry of Finance and Public Credit 1991–92, Sec.-Gen. Budget Directorate 1992–94; consultant, UNDP 1994–95; Legal Adviser to the Pres. 2002–05; Minister of Nat. Defence 2005–06; Perm. Rep. of Colombia to OAS, Washington, DC 2006–09; apptd mem. Drafting Cttee of Law 1508 2012; Founding Partner and mem. Soc. of Constitutional Rights, Sec. 1997–99; currently Founding Partner and Dir Opebsa Compañía de Abogados S.A.S. *Address:* Opebsa Compañía De Abogados S.A.S, Av. 9 Nª 113-52, Oficina 1705, Bogotá, DC, Colombia. *Telephone:* (1) 637-1288 (office). *E-mail:* info@opebsa.com. *Website:* www.opebsa.com (office).

OSSINOVSKI, Jevgeni, BA, MA, MSc; Estonian politician; *Chairman, Sotsiaaldemokraatlik Erakond;* b. 15 March 1986, Kohtla-Järve, Estonian SSR, USSR; s. of Oleg Ossinovski; m. Triinu Ossinovski 2014; ed Tallinn Secondary School, Univ. of Tartu, Univ. of Warwick and London School of Econs, UK; mem. Sotsiaaldemokraatlik Erakond (SDE—Estonian Social Democratic Party), fmr Spokesperson for integration and migration policy and integration issues between ethnic Estonians and ethnic Russians in Estonia, fmr Int. Sec. and Party Rep. in Party of European Socialists Presidency, Chair. SDE 2015–; mem. Riigikogu (Parl.) for Party List Electoral Dist No. 7 (Ida-Viru Co.) 2011–, mem. Cttee on Foreign Affairs, Cttee on EU Affairs; specialist on Russian political affairs; Minister of Education and Research 2014–15, of Health and Labour 2015–18. *Address:* Sotsiaaldemokraatlik Erakond (Estonian Social Democratic Party), Toompuiestee 16, Tallinn 10137, Estonia (office). *Telephone:* 611-6040 (SDE) (office). *Fax:* 611-6050 (SDE) (office). *E-mail:* riigikantselei@riigikantselei.ee (office); kantselei@sotsdem.ee (office). *Website:* www.sotsdem.ee (office).

OSSOUKA RAPONDA, Rose Christiane; Gabonese economist and politician; *Minister of State, Minister of National Defence and Territorial Security;* b. 1964, Libreville; ed Institut gabonais de l'économie et des finances, Libreville; fmr Dir Gen. of Economy and Deputy Dir Gen., Banque de l'habitat du Gabon; Minister of Budget, Public Accounts and Public Service 2012–14; Municipal Councillor for 3rd Dist, Libreville City Council 2014, Mayor of Libreville 2014–19; Minister of State, Minister of Nat. Defence and Territorial Security 2019–; mem. Parti démocratique gabonais. *Address:* Ministry of National Defence, BP 13493, Libreville, Gabon (office). *Telephone:* 01-76-35-79 (office). *Fax:* 01-77-86-92 (office). *Website:* www.defense-nationale.gouv.ga (office).

OST, Friedhelm, Dipl. rer. pol.; German politician and business executive; *Chairman, PKS Kommunikations- und Strategieberatung GmbH;* b. 15 June 1942, Castrop-Rauxel; s. of Franz Ost and Barbara Ost; m. Erika Herrmann 1968; three s. two d.; ed Univs of Freiburg and Cologne; research asst of a major bank 1966–69; Speaker, Bundesverband Deutscher Banken 1969–72; Econ. Ed., moderator and commentator, Zweites Deutsches Fernsehen (ZDF) 1973–85; State Sec. and Head, Govt Press and Information Dept 1985–89; Econ. and Political Adviser to German Fed. Chancellor and freelance journalist and public relations consultant 1989–90; Gen. Man. Wirtschaftsvereinigung Bergbau –1990; mem. CDU 1980–; mem. Bundestag 1990–2002, Chair. Econ. Cttee 1991–98; Adviser, Frankfurter Rothschild GmbH 1997–; fmr Gen. Rep. Deutsche Vermögensberatungs AG; currently Chair. PKS Kommunikations- und Strategieberatung GmbH; mem. Bd of Govs Univ. of Haifa, Israel; mem. Russian Acad. of Sciences; Fed. Cross of Merit, Grand Cross, Order of Merit of the Italian Repub. 1986, Grand Cross of the Falcon 1988, Grand Cross of the Portuguese Order of Merit 1989. *Leisure interests:* football, tennis. *Address:* PKS Kommunikations- und Strategieberatung GmbH, Reinhardtstr. 34, 10117 Berlin 32, Germany (office). *Telephone:* (30) 25797223 (office); (2224) 78291. *Fax:* (30) 25797225 (office); (2224) 75633. *E-mail:* friedhelm.ost@t-online.de. *Website:* www.pks-gmbh.net (office).

OSTEN, Suzanne Carlota; Swedish playwright and theatre and film director; b. 20 June 1944, Stockholm; d. of Carl Otto Osten and Gud Osten; m.; one d.; ed Lund Univ.; started directing while a student 1963; Founder Fickteatern fringe theatre group performing in schools, prisons, public areas, etc. 1967–71; joined City Theatre, Stockholm 1971; Founder and Artistic Dir, Unga Klara Stadsteatern ind. repertory co. 1975–2014; began directing films 1980; Prof. of Directing, Dramatic Inst., Stockholm 1995–2009; Film Amb., Swedish Film Inst. 2014–; Dr hc (Lund) 2000; Nat. Theatre Critics Prize 1982, Prix d'Assitej 1985, Tage Danielsson-priset 1990, Paris-Creteil Prize 1993, Expressens Theatre Prize 2002, Assitej Int. Prize 2002, Berns Prize, Swedish PEN 2002, Expressens teaterpris 2002, Natur & Kulturs kulturpris 2003, Svenska Akademiens teaterpris 2003, TCO:s kulturpris 2007, Moa-priset (jtly) 2007, Habets Pris 2009, Regeringsmedalj 2014, among numerous others. *Plays include:* as writer and dir: Medea's Children 1975, The Haga-Princesses 1976, The Hunt for Snores 1976, Lazarillo 1977, Prince Carefree 1977, The Children from Mount Frostmo 1978, The Pork Horses 1981, The Frontier 2000; as dir: The Vampire 1975, The Sweaty Tiger 1978, Unga Klara tells Life 1982, The Smile of Hades 1982, A Clean Girl 1983, Hitler's Childhood 1 1984, Hitler's Childhood 2 1984, The Danton Affair 1986, Everybody – But Me 1987, The Toad Aquarium 1988, In the Summer House 1988, R 1990, The Piggle 1991, The Dolphin 1992, Preparation for Suicide 1994, Mirad 1994, Money 1994, Lilacs 1914 1996, Irina's New Life 1996, The Girl, the Mother and the Trash 1998, Difficult People 1999, Time of Darkness 2002, The Main Thing 2002. *Films include:* Ei inspelat, Mamma 1982, Bröderna Mozart (Guldbagge Award for Direction 1986) 1986, Livsfarlig film 1988, Skyddsängeln 1990, Tala det är så mörkt 1992, Bara du och jag 1994, Bengbulan 1996, Besvärliga Människor 2001.

ØSTERGAARD, Morten, MSc; Danish politician; b. 17 June 1976, Aarhus; s. of Bent Østergaard Kristensen and Ingrid Bayer Kristensen; m. Line Østergaard; two c.; ed Conval High School, USA, Risskov Amtsgymnasium, Univ. of Aarhus; Marketing Man., Dafolo A/S, Aarhus 2001–05; mem. Det Radikale Venstre (Danish Social Liberal Party), Vice-Chair. 2002–05, mem. Parl. Man. Group 2006–, Vice-Chair. Parl. Group 2007–11, Parl. Group Leader 2014–; Temporary mem. Folketing (Parl.) for Århus Co. 21–27 Jan. 2002, 20–26 April 2002, 25–31 Jan. 2003, Jan.–Feb. 2004, mem. Folketing (Parl.) for Aarhus Co. constituency 2005–07, for East Jutland greater constituency 2007–; Minister for Science, Innovation and Higher Educ. 2011–14, for Taxation Feb.–Sept. 2014, for Econ. Affairs and the Interior Sept. 2014–15. *Publication:* Digital forkalkning: en debatbog om digital forvaltning i Danmark (co-author) 2004. *Address:* Det Radikale Venstre, Christiansborg, 1240 Copenhagen K, Denmark (office). *Telephone:* 33-37-47-47 (office). *E-mail:* radikale@radikale.dk (office); morten.ostergaard@ft.dk. *Website:* www.radikale.dk (office).

OSTERWALDER, Konrad, PhD; Swiss physicist and university administrator; *Professor Emeritus, Department of Mathematics, Eidgenössische Technische Hochschule (ETH), Zürich;* b. 3 June 1942, Frauenfeld, Thurgau; m.; three c.; ed Eidgenössische Technische Hochschule (ETH) Zürich, Univ. of Zürich, Harvard Grad. School for Higher Educ., USA; Asst Prof. of Math. Physics, Harvard Univ. 1973–76, Assoc. Prof. 1976–78; Prof. of Math. Physics, ETH Zürich 1977–2007, Head Dept of Math. 1986–90, Head, Planning Cttee 1990–95, Rector 1995–2007, Prof. Emer., Dept of Math. 2007–; Guest Prof., Univ. of Austin, Tex., Univ. of Cambridge, UK, IHES, Bures-sur-Yvette, France, Max-Planck-Institut für Physik und Astrophysik, Munich, Università La Sapienza, Rome, Università di Napoli, Tokyo Univ., Weitzmann Inst., Rehovot, Israel; Rector UNU, Tokyo 2007–13; Founder-Pres. UNITECH Int.; Chair. Univ. Council, Tech. Univ., Darmstadt, Germany; mem. Admin. Cttee, Ecole Polytechnique de France, Educ. Cttee, Ecole des Mines, Paris, Conseil d'Orientation Statégique, ParisTech, Consiglio dell'Università della Svizzera, Italy, Academic Council, Int. Council on Systems Eng; mem. Swiss Acad. of Tech. Sciences 2000; Fellow, Alfred P. Sloan Foundation 1974–78, American Mathematical Soc. 2012–; Hon. mem. Riga Tech. Univ. 2002; Dr hc (Tech. Univ., Helsinki) 2003; J. Bauer Prize 1959, 1960, ETH Medaille, Kern Prize 1970, Matteo Ricci Award 2009, Leonardo da Vinci Medal 2010. *Address:* Department of Mathematics, Leonhardstrasse 27, 8092 Zurich, Switzerland (office). *Telephone:* 446322370 (office). *E-mail:* konrad.osterwalder@math.ethz.ch (office). *Website:* www.ethz.ch (office).

ÖSTLING, Leif, MEng, BEcons; Swedish business executive; b. 25 Sept. 1945, Luleå; ed Chalmers Univ. of Tech., Univ. of Göteborg; joined Scania 1972, Head of Strategic Planning 1977–81, Marketing Man., Scania Nederland BV 1981–83, Pres. Scania Nederland 1983–88, Man. Scania Div. (part of Saab-Scania) 1988, Pres. and CEO Scania AB 1994–2012; mem. Bd of Man. Volkswagen AG with responsibility for Commercial Vehicles 2012–15; Chair. Confederation of Swedish Enterprise 2016–17; Chair. ISS A/S 2005; Dir SKF AB 2005, Vice-Chair. 2006–08, Chair. 2008; mem. Bd Confed. of Swedish Enterprise (Chair. 2016–17), Asscn of Swedish Eng Industries; Dr hc (Royal Inst. of Technology) 2003, (Luleå Univ. of Technology) 2003; Gustaf Dalén medaljen 2012.

OSTOJIĆ, Ranko; Croatian lawyer and politician; b. 3 Oct. 1962, Split; ed Univ. of Split; held various positions in Split-based cos; mem. Socijaldemokratska Partija Hrvatske (SDP—Social Democratic Party of Croatia) 1990–2000, 2004–; served as Asst to the Minister of the Interior 2001–04, held post of Dir of Police; mem. 6th Sabor (Parl.) 2007–11, Chair. Parl. Cttee for Internal Affairs and Nat. Security; unsuccessful cand. for Mayor of Split 2009; Minister of Internal Affairs 2011–16; Deputy Prime Minister 2013–16.

OSTRIKER, Jeremiah Paul, PhD, FAAS; American astronomer, astrophysicist and academic; *Professor, Columbia University;* b. 13 April 1937, New York; s. of Martin Ostriker and Jeanne Sumpf; m. Alicia S. Suskin 1958; one s. two d.; ed Harvard Univ. and Univ. of Chicago; Postdoctoral Fellow, Univ. of Cambridge, UK 1964–65; Research Assoc. and Lecturer, Princeton Univ. 1965–66, Asst Prof. 1966–68, Assoc. Prof. 1968–71, Prof. 1971–, Chair. Dept of Astrophysical Sciences and Dir Observatory 1979–95, Charles A. Young Prof. of Astronomy 1982–2002, Provost, Princeton Univ. 1995–2001, Dir, Princeton Inst. for Computational Science and Eng 2005–09, Charles A. Young Prof. Emer. 2012–; Plumian Prof. of Astronomy and Experimental Physics, Inst. of Astronomy, Univ. of Cambridge 2001–04; Prof. of Astronomy, Columbia Univ. 2012–; mem. Editorial Bd and Trustee, Princeton Univ. Press 1982–84, 1986; mem. NAS 1974 (mem. Council 1992–95, mem. Bd of Govs 1993–95, Treas. 2008–16), American Acad. of Arts and Sciences 1975, American Astronomical Soc., Int. Astronomical Union, American Philosophical Soc. 1994; Assoc. mem. Royal Astronomical Soc. 1994; Foreign mem. Royal Netherlands Acad. of Arts and Sciences, Royal Soc. (London); Trustee, American Museum of Nat. History 1997–2004; Hon. FRAS 1994; Hon. DSc (Chicago) 1992, (Princeton) 2017; NSF Fellow 1960–65, Alfred P. Sloan Fellowship 1970–72, Helen B. Warner Prize, American Astronomical Soc. 1972, Sherman Fairchild Fellowship of CalTech 1977, Henry Norris Russell Prize 1980, Vainu Bappu Memorial Award, Indian Nat. Science Acad. 1993, Karl Schwarzschild Medal, Astronomische Gesellschaft (Germany) 1999, US Nat. Medal of Science 2000, Golden Plate Award, American Acad. of Achievement 2001, Gold Medal, Royal Astronomical Soc. 2004, Catherine Wolfe Bruce Gold Medal 2011, James Craig Watson Medal 2012, White House Champion of Change 2013, Cosmology Prize, Peter Gruber Foundation (co-recipient) 2015. *Publications:* Heart of Darkness, Unraveling the Mysteries of the Invisible Universe 2013; papers in scientific journals. *Leisure interest:* squash. *Address:* Room #1024, Pupin Hall Department of Astronomy, Columbia University, 550 West 120th Street, New York, NY 10027, USA (office). *Telephone:* (212) 854-2150 (office). *E-mail:* jpo@astro .columbia.edu (office). *Website:* www.astro.columbia.edu/profile?uid=jOstriker (office).

OSTROUMOVA, Olga Mikhailovna; Russian actress; b. 21 Sept. 1947, Buguruslan; ed Moscow Inst. of Theatre Arts; actress, Moscow Theatre of Young Spectators until 1973, Moscow Theatre on Malaya Bronnaya 1973–83, Moscow Mossoviet Theatre 1983–; Silver Nymph Prize, Sorrento and Naples 1973, USSR Official State Prize 1979, RSFSR Merited Actress 1982, Golden Dovzhenko Medal 1982, Peoples' Actress of Russian Fed. 1993. *Films include:* Garage, Stop Kidding, Fate, Snake's Spring, We'll Live up to Monday 1969, Dawns Here Are Quiet 1972, Destiny 1977, Garazh 1979, Earthly Love, Vassily and Vassilisa 1981, There Was No Sorrow 1982, Ya sdelal vsyo, chto mog 1986, The Time of Sons 1986, The Spy 1987, Tower 1987, The Charming Traveller 1990, Very Faithful Wife 1992, Zmeiny istochnik 1997, Ne valyai duraka 1997, Novogodnie priklyucheniya 2002, Photo 2003, Syn 2004, Admiral 2008. *Television includes:* Whilom at California 1978, Engineer Barkasov's Crazy Day 1983, My Sister Lucy 1985, Days and Years of Nikolai Batygin (mini-series) 1987, Zhenshchiny, kotorym povezlo (mini-series) 1989, Po tu storonu volkov (mini-series) 2002, Zachem tebe alibi? (mini-series) 2003, Bednaya Nastya (mini-series) 2003, Zhenshchiny v igre bez pravil (mini-series) 2004, Karusel (series) 2005, Ne rodis krasivoy (series) 2005, Morpekhi (series) 2011. *Music:* (CDs) Tribute to Vladimir Visotsky 2000, A Song about Earth, A Novel about Girls 2002. *Theatre includes:* White Guard, Madame Bovary, At the Threshold of the Tsardom, Cherry Orchard 2001, A Husband, a Wife and a Lover, The Eternal Husband (Dostoevsky) 2003. *Leisure interest:* travelling. *Address:* Moscow Mossoviet Theatre, 103050 Moscow, B. Sadovaya str. 16 (office); 121002 Moscow, Arboit str. 17, 4, Apartment 9, Russia (home). *Telephone:* (495) 299-33-77 (office); (495) 202-01-88 (home).

OSTROVSKY, Mikhail Arkadievich, DBiolSc; Russian physiologist, biophysicist and academic; *Head of Laboratory, Institute of Biochemical Physics;* b. 22 Feb. 1935, Leningrad (now St Petersburg); m. Raisa Brook; two s.; ed Moscow State Univ.; jr then sr researcher, Inst. of Higher Nervous Activity and Neurophysiology 1959–70, Head of Sensory Reception Lab., Inst. of Biochemical Physics USSR (now Russian) Acad. of Sciences 1970–, currently Head of Lab., Inst. of Biochemical Physics; Prof., Moscow State Univ. 1977–, currently Head of Dept of Molecular Physiology; Visiting Prof., Univ. of Maryland, Coll. Park, USA 1994–; Corresp. mem. USSR (now Russian) Acad. of Sciences 1990, mem. 1994; Ed. Russian Sensory Systems 1987–; Chair. Expert Comm. on Physiology and Medicine of Russian Foundation for Basic Research 1992–; mem. Int. Brain Research Organization 1980, Russian Pavlov Physiological Soc. 1976, Int. Eye Research Asscn 1989; mem. Bd and Chair. Cttee for Relations with E European Neuroscience Asscns; Sechenov Golden Medal, Russian Acad. of Sciences 2000. *Publications:* more than 100 articles and papers on photoreception, visual pigments, phototransduction, eye screening pigments, light damage to eye structures. *Address:* ul. Kosygina 4, 119334 Moscow, Russia. *Telephone:* (495) 135-70-73 (office); (499) 939-73-57 (lab.); (495) 434-15-35 (home). *Fax:* (499) 137-41-01. *E-mail:* ostrovsky@sky.chph.ras.ru (office).

OSTROWSKI, Hartmut; German business executive; *Chairman of Supervisory Board, DSC Arminia Bielefeld eV;* b. 25 Feb. 1958, Bielefeld; m.; one s. one d.; ed Univ. of Bielefeld; Asst to Bd of Dirs, Bertelsmann Distribution GmbH, Gütersloh, Germany 1982–83, Dept Head 1983–86, Exec. Dept Head 1986–88, Head of Business Unit 1990–92, Man. Dir 1992–95, Chair. 1995–96, mem. Exec. Bd Bertelsmann Industrie AG (now Bertelsmann Arvato AG) 1996–2002, Chair. 2002–07, Deputy mem. Exec. Bd Bertelsmann AG, Gütersloh 2001–02, mem. 2002–11, Chair. and CEO 2008–11, mem. Supervisory Bd –2015; Man. Dir Security Pacific Eurofinance, Inc., Munich 1988–90; Sr Adviser, Greenhill & Co. Inc. 2012; Chair. Supervisory Bd DSC Arminia Bielefeld eV (sports club) 2013–. *Address:* Arminia Bielefeld eV, SchücoArena, Melanchthonstrasse 31a, 33615 Bielefeld, Germany (office). *Telephone:* (05) 21966110 (office). *Fax:* (05) 219661111 (office). *E-mail:* kontakt@arminia-bielefeld.de (office).

OSTRY, Sylvia, CC, OC, OM, PhD, FRSC; Canadian economist and academic; *Distinguished Research Fellow in International Studies, Munk Centre for International Studies, University of Toronto;* b. (Sylvia Knelman), Winnipeg, Man.; d. of Morris J. Knelman and B. Knelman (née Stoller); m. Bernard Ostry; two s.; ed McGill Univ., Montreal, Univ. of Cambridge, UK; Chief Statistician, Statistics Canada 1972–75; Deputy Minister of Consumer and Corp. Affairs and Deputy Registrar Gen. 1975–78; Chair. Econ. Council of Canada 1978–79; Head, Econ. and Statistics Dept, OECD 1979–83; Deputy Minister (Int. Trade) and Co-ordinator for Int. Econ. Relations, Dept of External Affairs 1984–85; Amb., Multilateral Trade Negotiations and Personal Rep. of the Prime Minister, Econ. Summit, Dept of External Affairs 1985–88; Per Jacobsson Foundation Lecture, Washington 1987; Sr Research Fellow, Univ. of Toronto 1989–90; Volvo Distinguished Visiting Fellow, Council on Foreign Relations, New York 1989; Chair. Centre for Int. Studies, Univ. of Toronto 1990–97, Distinguished Research Fellow 1997–; Chancellor, Univ. of Waterloo 1991–97; Western Co-Chair. Blue Ribbon Comm. for Hungary's Econ. Devt 1990–94; Chair. Council Canadian Inst. for Int. Affairs 1990–94; mem. Int. American Dialogue, Advisory Bd Inst. of Int. Econs, Washington, DC, Academic Advisory Council of Deputy Minister for Int. Trade; Founding mem. Pacific Council on Int. Policy; mem. Emer. Group of Thirty Consultative Group on Int. Econ. and Monetary Affairs, Inc. (G-30), Washington, DC; mem. several learned socs and professional orgs; Fellow, American Statistical Asscn; 19 hon. doctorates 1971–2003; The Per Jacobsson Foundation Lecture, Washington, DC 1987, Outstanding Achievement Award, Govt of Canada 1987, Public Policy Forum honouree, Testimonial Dinner 1991, Hon. Assoc. Award, Conf. Bd of Canada 1992, Sylvia Ostry Foundation annual lecture series launched 1992, Career Achievement Award, Canadian Policy Research 2000, Couchiching Award for Public Policy Leadership 2010. *Publications include:* International Economic Policy Co-ordination (with Michael Artis) 1986, Governments and Corporations in a Shrinking World: The Search for Stability 1990, The Threat of Managed Trade to Transforming Economies 1993, Rethinking Federalism: Citizens, Markets and Governments in a Changing World (co-author) 1995, The Halifax G7 Summit: Issues on the Table (co-ed. with Gilbert Winham) 1995, Who's On First? The Post Coldwar Trading System 1997, The Future of the World Trading System 1999, Business, Trade and the Environment 2000, The Changing Scenario in International Governance 2000, The World Trading System: In Dire Need of Reform 2003, Global Integration: Currents and Counter Currents (in The World Trade Organization: Legal, Economic and Political Analysis) 2005, The WTO and Global Governance 2008, Economic Integration in the Americas 2008, The World Trade Organization: System Under Stress 2008; articles on labour econs, demography, productivity, competition policy. *Leisure interests:* films, theatre, contemporary reading. *Address:* Munk Centre for International Studies, University of Toronto, Room 361S, 1 Devonshire Place, Toronto, ON M5S 3K7, Canada (office). *Telephone:* (416) 946-8927 (office); (416) 946-8839 (office). *Fax:* (416) 946-8915 (office). *E-mail:* sylvia.ostry@utoronto.ca (office). *Website:* www.utoronto.ca/cis/ostry (office).

O'SULLIVAN, (Alfred) John, CBE, BA (Hons); British editor, journalist, author and foundation executive; *Editor, Quadrant Magazine;* b. 25 April 1942, Liverpool; s. of Alfred M. O'Sullivan and Margaret O'Sullivan (née Corner); m. Melissa Matthews O'Sullivan; ed Queen Mary Coll. and Bedford Coll., Univ. of London; jr tutor, Swinton Conservative Coll. 1965–67, Sr Tutor 1967–69; Conservative parl. cand. 1970; Ed. Swinton Journal 1967–69; London Corresp. Irish Radio and TV 1970–72; editorial writer and parl. sketchwriter, Daily Telegraph 1972–79; Ed. Policy Review 1979–83; Asst Ed. Daily Telegraph 1983–84; columnist, The Times 1984–86, Assoc. Ed. 1986–87; Editorial Page Ed. New York Post 1984–86; Ed.-in-Chief Nat. Review 1988–97, Ed.-at-Large 1998–, Fellow, National Review Inst.; columnist, Sunday Telegraph 1988–, Independent on Sunday 1990–91; Editorial Consultant, Hollinger 1998–2001; Ed.-in-Chief, United Press International 2001–04; Exec. Ed., Radio Free Europe/Radio Liberty 2008–11; Ed., The National Interest 2004–06, Quadrant Magazine 2015–; Assoc. Ed., Hungarian Review 2014–; Dir, Danube Inst. 2014–16, Pres. 2016–; Dir of Studies, Heritage Foundation 1979–83; Special Adviser to UK Prime Minister Margaret Thatcher 1987–88; Founder and Co-Chair. The New Atlantic Initiative, American Enterprise Inst. 1996–; Pres. Danube Inst., Budapest; mem. Exec. Advisory Bd Margaret Thatcher Foundation, Advisory Council Social Affairs Unit, Hon. Bd Civic Inst., Prague; Fellow, Inst. of Politics, Harvard Univ. 1983; Sr Fellow, Hudson Inst. 2006–09, Nixon Center 2003–05; Hon. LLD (Lewis and Clark Coll.). *Publication:* The President, the Pope, and the Prime Minister: Three Who Changed the World. *Leisure interests:* reading, cinema, theatre, dining out, walking around cities. *Address:* Quadrant Magazine Ltd, PO Box 82, Balmain, NSW 2041, Australia (office); Danube Institute, 1067 Budapest, Eötvös u. 24, Hungary (office). *Telephone:* (2) 9818-1155 (Balmain) (office); (1) 269-1041 (Budapest) (office). *E-mail:* johnosullivan@quadrant.org.au (office); john.osullivan@danubeinstitute.hu (office). *Website:* quadrant.org.au (office); www.danubeinstitute.hu (office).

O'SULLIVAN, David, BA; Irish international civil servant and diplomatist; b. 1 March 1953, Dublin; s. of Gerald O'Sullivan and Philomena Boland; m. Agnes O'Hare; one s. one d.; ed Trinity Coll. Dublin, Collège d'Europe, Bruges; Dept of Foreign Affairs, Dublin 1976–79; mem. staff External Relations, EC 1979–81, First Sec. (Econ. and Commercial), Del. of EC in Japan 1981–85; mem. Cabinet of Commr P. Sutherland 1985–89; Head of Unit (Educ. and Youth, Training) 1989–92; mem. Cabinet of Commr P. Flynn 1993–96, Deputy Head 1994–96; Dir Social Affairs, European Social Fund 1996–98, Social Affairs, Man. of Resources 1998–99; Dir-Gen. DGXXII (Educ., Training and Youth) 1999; Head of Cabinet of Pres. of Comm. 1999–2000; Sec.-Gen. European Comm. 2000–05, Dir-Gen. for Trade 2005–10, for External Relations Oct.–Dec. 2010, COO European External Action Service 2010–14; EU Amb. to USA 2014–19; Visiting Prof., European Coll. of Parma; Dr hc (Dublin Inst. of Tech.) 2005, (Trinity Coll. Dublin) 2014; European of the Year, Irish Council of the European Movt 1999, American Chamber of Commerce EU Transatlantic Business Award 2014. *Leisure interests:* tennis, fitness, cinema, music, scuba-diving, yoga.

O'SULLIVAN, Kevin, BSc; Irish journalist; *Environment, Agriculture and Science Editor, The Irish Times;* b. 1960, Tramore, Co. Waterford; m. Ger O'Sullivan; two s. one d.; ed Univ. Coll. Dublin, Nat. Inst. of Higher Educ., Dublin (now Dublin City Univ.); began career as freelance journalist and Founder, Copywrite News Agency 1983–84; reporter, Tuam Herald, Co. Galway 1984–86; Sr Journalist, Connacht Tribune Newspaper Group 1986–96; joined The Irish Times 1997, becoming Environmental and Food Science Corresp. 1997–99, Deputy/Asst News Ed. 2000–01, Special Projects Ed./Asst Ed. 2000–04, Acting Northern Ed. (based in Belfast) May–June 2001, Acting Foreign Ed. Spring 2003, Founding Ed. of Healthplus supplement 2004–05, Night Ed. 2005–06, News Ed. 2006–11, Ed. 2011–17, Environment, Agriculture and Science Ed. 2017–. *Telephone:* 868121759 (mobile) (office); (1) 6758000 (office). *Address:* The Irish Times, Irish Times Building, 24–28 Tara Street, Dublin 2, Ireland (office). *Fax:* (1) 6758322 (office). *E-mail:* kosullivan@irishtimes.com (office). *Website:* www.irishtimes.com (office).

O'SULLIVAN, Patrick, MSc, FCA; British chartered accountant and business executive; *Chairman, Saga plc;* b. April 1949; ed Trinity Coll., Univ. of Dublin, London School of Econs; experience includes positions at Bank of America, Goldman Sachs, Financial Guaranty Insurance Co. (subsidiary of GE Capital), Barclays/BZW; Chief Exec. Eagle Star Insurance Co. 1998–2002; Group Finance Dir, Zurich Financial Services 2002–07, Vice-Chair. 2007–09; Chair. (non-exec.) Old Mutual plc 2010–18, also Chair. Nomination Cttee; Chair. Saga plc 2018–; Dir (non-exec.) COFRA Group (Switzerland), Man Group plc, Bank of Ireland; fmr mem. Bd of Dirs COFRA Holding AG, Inst. for United States Studies, London Univ. *Address:* Saga plc, Enbrook Park, Sandgate, Folkestone, Kent, CT20 3SE, England (office). *Telephone:* (13) 0377-1111 (office). *Website:* corporate.saga.co.uk (office).

O'SULLIVAN, Paul, BA (Hons); Australian diplomatist; *Political Adviser, Government of Australia;* b. 3 Feb. 1948, Sydney, NSW; m. Merrilyn O'Sullivan; three s.; ed Marcellin Coll., Randwick, Univ. of Sydney; joined Dept of Foreign Affairs 1971, served in Embassies in Rome, Washington, DC and Cairo, Amb. and Perm. Rep. to UN for Disarmament Issues, Geneva 1991–94, held range of sr positions in Dept of Foreign Affairs and Trade, including First Asst Sec., Americas and Europe Div. 1994–95, First Asst Sec., Int. Orgs and Legal Div. 1995–96, Deputy Chief of Mission, Washington, DC 1996–98, Amb. to Germany 1999–2003, Deputy Sec., Dept of Foreign Affairs and Trade 2003–04; Sr Adviser (Int.), Office of Prime Minister John Howard 2004–05; Dir-Gen. Australian Security and Intelligence Org. 2005–09; High Commr to New Zealand 2009–12; Political Adviser, Govt of Australia 2013–. *Address:* Department of Prime Minister and Cabinet, 1 National Circuit, Barton, ACT 2600, Australia (office). *Telephone:* (2) 6271-5111 (office). *Fax:* (2) 6271-5414 (office). *Website:* www.dpmc.gov.au (office).

O'SULLIVAN, Ronald (Ronnie) Antonio, OBE; British professional snooker player and business executive; b. 5 Dec. 1975, Wordsley, West Midlands, England; one s. one d. with Jo Langley and one d. from a previous relationship; ed Wanstead High School; grew up in Chigwell, Essex; first century break (117) aged ten, maximum (147) break aged 15; amateur titles: British Under-16 Championship 1988, IBSF World Under-21 Championship 1991, Jr Pot Black 1991; turned professional 1992; won his first 38 ranking matches as a professional (record); winner of 25 ranking titles: UK Championship 1993, 1997, 2001, 2007, 2014, British Open 1994, Asian Classic 1996, German Open 1996, German Masters 2012, Scottish Open 1998, 2000, China Open 1999, 2000, World Snooker Championship 2001, 2004, 2008, 2012, 2013, European Open 2003, Irish Masters 2003, 2005, Welsh Open 2004, 2005, Grand Prix 2004, Northern Ireland Trophy 2008, Shanghai Masters 2009; minor-ranking event titles: Players Tour Championship 2011, Kay Suzanne Memorial Trophy 2011; non-ranking event titles: Nescafé Extra Challenge 1993, Benson and Hedges Championship 1993, The Masters 1995, 2005, 2007, 2009, Charity Challenge 1996, European League 1997, Riley Superstar International 1997, Scottish Masters 1998, 2000, 2002, Champions Cup 2000, Irish Masters 2001, 2007, Premier League Snooker 1997, 2001, 2002, 2005, 2006, 2007, 2008, 2009, 2011, 2012; winner, Nations Cup (with Team England) 2000; youngest winner of a ranking title 1993 (aged 17); fmr World No. 1; has made a record 15 maximum (147) breaks, including the fastest (5:08 in first round of World Championship 1997), only player to score six century breaks in a World Championship final and achieved a total of 131 centuries at the Crucible, beating Stephen Hendry's record of 127 May 2013; holds record for scoring the most century breaks (1,000 as of March 2019); known for his rapid playing style and nicknamed 'The Rocket'; Founder and Owner Viva la Diva lingerie shop, London 2003; launched Ronnie O'Sullivan Int. Ltd 2010; named World Snooker Player of the Year 2012, voted Snooker Writers Player of the Year 2012, inducted into the Hall of Fame 2012. *Publication:* The Autobiography of Ronnie O'Sullivan 2003. *Leisure interests:* Arsenal Football Club, motor racing. *Website:* www.ronnieosullivan.tv.

O'SULLIVAN, Sonia, BA; Irish/Australian athlete; b. 28 Nov. 1969, Cobh, Co. Cork; d. of John O'Sullivan and Mary O'Sullivan; m. Nick Bideau; two d.; ed Villanova Univ., USA; gold medal, 1500m, silver medal, 3000m, World Student Games 1991; holds seven nat. (Irish) records; set new world record (her first) in 2000m TSB Challenge, Edinburgh 1994, new European record in 3000m, TSB Games London 1994, gold medal in 3000m, European Athletic Championships, Helsinki 1994; winner, Grand Prix 3000m, second overall 1993; silver medal, 1500m, World Championships, Stuttgart 1993; gold medal, 5000m, World Championships, Gothenburg 1995; gold medal, World Cross Country Championships 4km, 8km 1998; gold medal, European Championships 5000m, 10,000m 1998; silver medal, 5000m Olympic Games, Sydney 2000; silver medal, 5000m, 10,000m European Championships, Munich 2002; winner BUPA Great South Run, Portsmouth 2002 (new world 10-mile record); winner Great BUPA Ireland Run, Dublin 2003; silver medal (with Ireland team), European Cross Country Championships 2003; ran London Marathon for the first time 2005, finished 8th; chosen for the Australian team for the 5000m in Commonwealth Games, Melbourne 2006, unable to compete due to a hamstring injury; flag bearer for Irish team, Sydney Olympic Games 2000, Ireland Chef de Mission, London Olympic Games 2012; Female Athlete of the Year 1995, Texaco Sports Star of the Year (Athletics) 2002. *Publications:* Running to Stand Still 2001, Sonia: My Story 2008. *Leisure interests:* cycling, swimming, reading, movies, food and cooking. *Telephone:* (1) 4278400. *E-mail:* info@nkmanagement.ie.

OSZKÓ, Péter, PhD; Hungarian lawyer, management consultant and government official; *Chairman and CEO, PortfoLion Kockázati Tőkealap-kezelő Zrt.;* b. 22 March 1973; ed Eötvös Loránd Univ.; Marketing Dir and Chair. Bd of Trustees, ELTE Student Foundation 1995–97; Man. Dir HÖOK Kht 1997–99, Vice-Pres. Asscn of Student Councils 1997–99; Man. Dir Agora Universitatis Kht 1997–99; adviser to KPMG Hungary 1996–2000, Tax Man. 2000, Man. KPMG, London 2000–01; Sr Attorney and Head of Tax Group, Freshfields Bruckhaus Deringer Budapest 2001–04; Tax Partner, Deloitte Hungary Inc. 2004–06, Head of Tax Dept 2006–07, Chair. and CEO 2007–09; Minister of Finance 2009–10; currently Chair. and CEO PortfoLion Kockázati Tokealap-kezelo Zrt, Szombathely; teaching at Faculty of Financial Law, ELTE AJTK 1998–; Ed. Hungarian 'Collega' Journal (page of financial law) 1997–2000; mem. Bd of Trustees Pro Facultati Iuridica Foundation 1997–; mem. Bd American Chamber of Commerce 2007–, Jt Venture Asscn 2008–; Head of Tax Working Party, Reform Alliance 2008–09. *Publication:* Verlag Dashöfer's financial issues (co-author) 1998–2000; numerous articles on taxation and other financial matters. *Address:* PortfoLion Kockázati Tőkealap-kezelő Zrt., Babér u. 9., 1131 Budapest, Hungary (office). *E-mail:* info@portfolion.hu (office). *Website:* www.portfolion.hu (office).

OTA, Akihiro, MEng; Japanese journalist and politician; b. 6 Oct. 1945, Shinshiro, Aichi Pref.; ed Kyoto Univ.; began career as journalist with Komei Shimbun (newspaper of New Komeito political party), becoming parl. reporter and leader writer; mem. House of Reps (lower house of Parl.) for Tokyo No. 12 constituency 1993–2009, 2012–; Minister of Land, Infrastructure, Transport and Tourism 2012–15; fmr mem. New Frontier Party (Shinshinto), Deputy Sec.-Gen. 1994 (party dissolved 1997); mem. New Komeito, Pres. 2006–09.

ŌTA, Hiroko, BA; Japanese economist, academic and government official; *Professor of Public Finance Policy, National Graduate Institute for Policy Studies (GRIPS);* b. 2 Feb. 1954, Kagoshima, Kagoshima Pref.; ed Faculty of Social Sciences, Hitotsubashi Univ.; with Mikimoto Corpn 1976–81; Research Fellow, Japan Inst. of Life Insurance 1981–93; Guest Lecturer, Econs Dept, Osaka Univ. 1993–96; Assoc. Prof., Grad. School of Political Science, Saitama Univ. 1996–97; Assoc. Prof., Nat. Grad. Inst. for Policy Studies 1997–2001, Prof. of Econs 2001, 2005–06, 2008–, Vice-Pres. 2009–11; Dir of Policy Analysis, Cabinet Office 2002–03, Deputy Dir-Gen. for Econ. Research 2003–04, Dir-Gen. 2004–05; Minister of State for Econ. and Fiscal Policy 2006–08 (resgnd). *Address:* National Graduate Institute for Policy Studies, 7-22-1 Roppongi, Minato-ku, Tokyo 106-8677, Japan (office). *Telephone:* (3) 6439-6000 (office). *Fax:* (3) 6439-6010 (office). *Website:* www.grips.ac.jp/list/en/facultyinfo/ota_hiroko (office).

OTA, Hiroshi; Japanese business executive; fmr Deputy Sr Gen. Man. Sales HQ, Sr Gen. Pharmaceutical Marketing Dept and Sr Exec. Officer Suzuken Co. Ltd, later Man. Dir Suzuken Co. Ltd, mem. Bd of Dirs, Pres. and CEO 2007–16.

OTAFIIRE, Kahinda, BA; Ugandan politician and army officer; *Minister of Justice and Constitutional Affairs;* b. 29 Dec. 1950, Mitooma Dist; m. Fridah Nayebale; ed Makerere Univ.; Youth Officer 1975–76; Foreign Service Officer, Ministry of Foreign Affairs 1976–80; Chief Political Commissar, Nat. Resistance Army 1981–84, Nat. Political Commissar 1984–86; Commr Internal Affairs Interim Admin 1985–86, Minister of State for Internal Affairs 1986–88, Presidential Asst (Security) 1988–92, Dir-Gen. External Security Org. 1992–94, Constituent Ass. Delegate 1994–95, Minister of State for Security 1994–95, for Local Govt 1996–98, Deputy Minister for Local Govt 1996–2001, Political Head, Congo Mil. Expedition 1998–2001, Minister of State for Regional Cooperation 2001–03, Minister of Water, Land and Environment 2003–06, of Local Govt 2006–09, of Trade and Industry 2009–11, of Justice and Constitutional Affairs and Attorney-Gen. 2011–; mem. Parl. (Nat. Resistance Movt) for Ruhinda Co. 1996–; Major Gen. Uganda People's Defence Force. *Leisure interests:* reading, teaching. *Address:* Parliament of Uganda, PO Box 7171, Parliamentary Avenue, Kampala, Uganda (office). *Telephone:* (48) 543199 (office). *E-mail:* kotafiire@parliament.go.ug (office). *Website:* www.parliament.go.ug (office).

OTAJANOV, Nodir; Uzbekistani business executive and politician; *Deputy Prime Minister responsible for the Development of Foreign Trade Activity, Export Potential, Mechanical Engineering, the Automotive, Electro-technical, Defence and Cotton Processing Industries, Light Industry and the Standardization of Production;* b. 24 Jan. 1967, Namangan, Uzbek SSR, USSR; m.; two c.; ed Andijon Agric. Inst., Namangan Eng and Pedagogical Inst., Banking and Finance Acad. of the Repub. of Uzbekistan; Head of Dept, Finance Directorate, Namangan Viloyat 1993–2002; Dir of Dept, Ministry of Finance 2002–07; Chair. O'zavtosanoatleasing Leasing Co. 2007–10; Chair. O'zqishloqkhujalikmashleasing Leasing Co. 2010–16; Deputy Chair. and Chief Engineer, O'zagrosanoatmashholding Holding Co. (Uz Agro Technical Industry Holding) 2016, Chair. 2016; Chair. O'zagrotexsanoatxolding Jt-Stock Co. 2016–; Deputy Prime Minister, responsible for Devt of

Foreign Trade Activity, Export Potential, Mechanical Eng, Automotive, Electrotechnical, Defence and Cotton Processing Industries, Light Industry and the Standardization of Production 2017–. *Address:* Office of the Cabinet of Ministers, 100078 Tashkent, Mustaqillik maydoni 5, Uzbekistan (office). *Telephone:* (71) 239-86-76 (office). *Fax:* (71) 239-84-63 (office). *Website:* www.gov.uz (office).

OTAKA, Tadaaki; Japanese conductor; *Permanent Conductor, NHK Symphony;* b. 8 Nov. 1947, Kamakura; s. of Hisatada Otaka and Misaoko Otaka; m. Yukiko Otaka 1978; ed Toho Gakuen Music School, Toho Gakuen Music Acad., Vienna Acad., Austria; began studying violin 1951; apptd Chief Conductor, Tokyo Philharmonic Orchestra 1971, Conductor Laureate 1991–; Chief Conductor, Sapporo Symphony 1981–86, apptd Prin. Conductor 1998, apptd Music Dir 2004, Hon. Music Dir 2015–; Prin. Conductor, BBC Welsh Symphony Orchestra (now BBC Nat. Orchestra of Wales) 1987–95, Conductor Laureate 1996–; Chief Conductor, Yomiuri Nippon Symphony Orchestra 1992–98; apptd Music Adviser and Prin. Conductor, Kioi Sinfonietta, Tokyo 1995, Hon. Conductor Laureate 2003–; Dir Britten Pears Orchestra 1998–2001; Perm. Conductor, NHK Symphony, Tokyo 2010–; Prin. Guest Conductor, Melbourne Symphony 2009–12; Artistic Dir New Nat. Theatre, Tokyo 2010–14; Chief Conductor, Osaka Philharmonic Orchestra 2017–; has conducted BBC Proms, and orchestras including City of Birmingham Symphony, Royal Liverpool Philharmonic, Royal Scottish Nat., Bournemouth Symphony, BBC Symphony, London Symphony, London Philharmonic, Rotterdam Philharmonic, Bamberg Symphony, Strasbourg Philharmonic, Bergen Philharmonic and Singapore Symphony; Hon. Fellow, Welsh Coll. of Music and Drama 1993; Hon. CBE 1997; Dr hc (Univ. of Wales) 1993; Second Prize, Min-On Conductors Competition 1969, Suntory Music Award 1992, Elgar Medal 2000. *Recordings include:* numerous recordings with BBC Nat. Orchestra of Wales including works by Takemitsu and Franck, and Britten's Peter Grimes with Yomiuri Nippon. *Leisure interests:* fishing, tennis, cooking. *Address:* c/o Rona Eastwood, Askonas Holt Ltd, 15 Fetter Lane, London, EC4A 1BW, England; NHK Symphony Orchestra 2-16-49 Takanawa, Minato-ku, Tokyo, 108-0074, Japan (office). *E-mail:* rona.eastwood@askonasholt.co.uk. *Website:* www.askonasholt.co .uk/artists/conductors/tadaaki-otaka; www.nhkso.or.jp/en (office). *Telephone:* (3) 5793-8111 (office). *Fax:* (3) 3443-0278 (office).

OTARI, Muhammad Naji al-; Syrian politician; b. 1944, Aleppo; ed studied architecture, diploma in town planning from the Netherlands; Head of Aleppo City Council 1983–87; fmr Gov. of Hums; mem. Ba'ath Party Cen. Cttee 2000, mem. Regional Command 2000; Deputy Prime Minister for Services Affairs 2000–03; Speaker of People's Ass. (Parl.) March–Sept. 2003; Prime Minister of Syria 2003–11 (resgnd with rest of cabinet at Pres.'s request following popular protests); Pres. Aleppo's eng syndicate 1989–93.

OTÁROLA PEÑARANDA, Luis Alberto; Peruvian lawyer, academic and politician; *Executive Chairman, National Commission for Development and Life Without Drugs (DEVIDA);* b. 12 Feb. 1967, Huaraz; s. of Huaracino Saturnino Otárola Caceres and Chacasina Olga Penaranda Mazzini; ed Univ. San Martín de Porres, Lima, American Inst. of Human Rights, San José, Costa Rica; Adviser to Ministry of Defence 2002–03; Deputy Minister of Econ. Affairs and Admin of Ministry of Defence 2003–04; Deputy Minister of Internal Order, Ministry of the Interior Aug.–Dec. 2011; Minister of Defence 2011–12; Presidential Adviser to the Head of State 2012–14; Exec. Chair. Nat. Comm. for Devt and Life Without Drugs (DEVIDA) 2014–; Prin. Prof., Academia de la Magistratura; Prof. of Constitutional Law, ESAN; fmr Lecturer in Law, Univ. of Lima and Peruvian Naval War Coll.; fmr visiting lecturer at several int. univs; Ad-hoc Public Prosecutor for cases arising from Judgments of Inter-American Court of Human Rights; Founder and Prin. Attorney, Estudio Otárola & Priale Abogados SCRL law firm. *Publications:* La Constitución Explicada; Democracia y Corrupción en el Perú; La Constitución de 1993. Estudio y reforma a quince años de su vigencia. *Address:* DEVIDA, Avenida Benavides 2199, B Lima 18, Peru (office). *Telephone:* (1) 207-4800 (office). *E-mail:* devida@devida.gob.pe (office). *Website:* www.devida.gob.pe (office).

OTHAIMEEN, Yousef bin Ahmed al-, BA, MA, PhD; Saudi Arabian charity administrator, politician and international organization official; *Secretary-General, Organization of Islamic Cooperation (OIC);* ed King Saud Univ., Ohio Univ., American Univ., Washington, DC; fmr lecturer, later Asst Prof., King Saud Univ.; fmr Sec.-Gen., King Abdullah bin Abdul-Aziz Foundation for Housing Devt; fmr Dir-Gen., Prince Salman Charity Soc. for Orphans' Care; fmr Asst Deputy Minister for Social Welfare and for Rehabilitation of the Handicapped, Ministry of Labour and Social Affairs, fmr Adviser to Minister of Labour and Social Affairs, Minister of Social Affairs 2007–15; Chair. Government Disabled Services Coordination Cttee; fmr Dir-Gen. of Cabinet and Chief Adviser, Org. of Islamic Cooperation (OIC), Sec.-Gen. OIC 2016–; fmr mem. Bd of Trustees Prince Salman Centre for Disability Research; fmr mem. Bd of Dirs Saudi Arabia Social Charity Fund. *Address:* Organization of Islamic Cooperation (OIC), Medina Rd, Sary St, POB 178, Jeddah 21411, Saudi Arabia (office). *Telephone:* (12) 651-5222 (office). *Fax:* (12) 651-2288 (office). *Website:* www.oic-oci.org (office).

OTHMANI, Saâdeddine el-, MD; Moroccan psychiatrist and politician; *Prime Minister;* b. 16 Jan. 1956, Inezgane; ed Hassan II Univ., Casablanca, Univ. Mohammed V, Rabat; gen. medical practitioner 1987–94; psychiatrist, Berrechid City Hosp. 1994–97; mem. Majlis al-Nuab (Parl.) for Mohammedia 1997–2007, Vice-Pres. Foreign Affairs Cttee 2001–02; Minister of Foreign Affairs and Co-operation 2012–13; Prime Minister 2017–; mem. Conseil Maghrébin de la Choura (Union du Maghreb Arabe) 2002–; mem. Parti de la justice et du développement (Sec.-Gen. 2004–08). *Publications include:* several books on psychiatry and Islamic law. *Address:* Office of the Prime Minister, Palais Royal, Touarga, Rabat, Morocco (office). *Telephone:* (53) 7219400 (office). *Fax:* (53) 7768656 (office). *E-mail:* courrier@pm.gov.ma (office). *Website:* www.pm.gov.ma (office).

OTI, John Paterson; Solomon Islands politician; *High Commissioner to Fiji;* desk officer, Ministry of Foreign Affairs 1983–1990; Provincial Sec., Ministry of Provincial Govt 1991–93; apptd Political Analyst for Prime Minister Francis Billy Hilly 1994; Special Sec. to Leader of the Opposition 1995–97; mem. Parl. for Temotu and Nende 1997–; Deputy Speaker Nat. Parl. Feb.–Dec. 2005; Minister for Foreign Affairs 1997–2000, 2006–07; Minister of Communications, Aviation and Meteorology 2004–05; Deputy Prime Minister Nov.–Dec. 2007; Sec.-Gen., Ownership, Unity and Responsibility Party 2010–; High Commr to Fiji 2012–; served as "special envoy" to Melanesian Spearhead Group; mem. Solomon Islands Alliance for Change, Public Accounts Cttee 2000–01 (Chair. 2002). *Address:* Solomon islands High Commission, Plaza 1, Level 3, Downtown Blvd, PO Box 2647, Government Buildings,Suva, Fiji; National Parliament, PO Box G19, Honiara, Solomon Islands (office). *Telephone:* 28520 (office). *Fax:* 24272 (office). *Website:* www.parliament.gov.sb (office).

O'TOOLE, Shane, BArch; Irish architectural historian and critic; b. 5 July 1955, Dublin; s. of James Patrick O'Toole and Caroline Louise O'Toole (née Hannan); m. Maeve O'Neill 1984 (separated 2011); one s. one d.; ed Franciscan Coll., Gormanston, Co. Meath, Univ. Coll., Dublin (UCD); Lynch O'Toole Walsh Architects, Dublin 1979–86; Project Man. Energy Research Group, UCD 1986–92; Co-Founder and Dir urban design consortium Group 91 Architects 1990–99; Shane O'Toole Architect 1991–97, 2008–; Co. Architect, Tegral Bldg Products Ltd 1994–2008; architecture critic, The Sunday Times 1999–2009; Adjunct Sr Lecturer, UCD 2014–16, Adjunct Assoc. Prof. 2016–; Pres. Architectural Asscn of Ireland 1982–83; Vice-Pres. Royal Inst. of the Architects of Ireland 1988, 1997; Founder and Sec., DoCoMoMo Ireland 1990–2012, Treas. 2014–17; Dir Irish Architectural Archive 2002–, Chair. Collections Devt Cttee 2015–; Fellow, Salzburg Global Seminar 2005; inaugural Curator and Dir Irish Architecture Foundation 2005–06; mem. CICA (Int. Cttee of Architectural Critics) 2008–; Adviser to Mies van der Rohe Award for European Architecture 1992–, to 20th-Century Architecture: Ireland book 1995–97, to Nation Building (TV series on architecture in Ireland 1922–2000) 2000, to Veronica Rudge Green Prize in Urban Design (Harvard Prize in Urbanism), Harvard Univ. Grad. School of Design 2000–04, to New Trends of Architecture in Europe and Asia-Pacific Exhbn 2002–07, to Royal Irish Acad. Irish Architecture 1600–2000 research project 2008–13, to European Prize for Urban Public Space 2012–; Judge, European Prize for Contemporary Architecture 2003, World Architecture Festival 2008–11, 2018; Hon. mem. Architectural Asscn of Ireland 1995; Hon. Fellow, Royal Inst. of the Architects of Ireland 2016; Int. Fellow, RIBA 2017; Silver Medal Sofia Biennale 1987, Grand Prix Kraków Biennale 1989, Irish Bldg of the Year Award 1996, Architectural Asscn of Ireland Downes Medal 1996, European Architectural Award (RIBA) 1997, Int. Union of Architects Sir Patrick Abercrombie Prize for town planning and territorial devt 2002, Gold Medal Commendation, Royal Inst. of the Architects of Ireland 2003, Int. Bldg Press Architectural Critic/Architecture Writer of the Year 2008, 2009, 2010, CICA Book Award 2011, 2014, 2017 and other prizes and awards. *Achievements:* Co-Dir Architectural Framework Plan for Regeneration of Temple Bar, Dublin 1992–2000; Co-Designer The Ark, Europe's first cultural centre for children 1992–95; represented in architecture exhbns including 40 Under 40: Emerging British Architects, UK and USA 1988–89, The New Breed, Sydney 1988, Making a Modern Street, Zurich 1991, 20 Young Architects of the World, London 1993, Presenting Architecture, Dublin 2005, Collection Building, Dublin 2006, Group 91: 15 Years On, Belfast 2006, Notebooks and Narratives: The Secret Laboratory, Belfast, Cork and Dublin 2010–11, Group 91, Dublin 2011, Made in Europe, Venice 2014, Capstones Shift, Dublin 2016; cr. exhbns, The Pillar Project, Dublin 1988, Tales from Two Cities: Emerging Architects in Dublin and Edinburgh (Edin., Dublin, Berlin, London) 1994, Master of All the Muses: Michael Scott 1905–2005 (Cork, Dublin) 2005, Irish Commr, Venice Biennale 2004, 2006, North by Northwest: Liam McCormick 1916–1996 (Dublin, Belfast, Letterkenny, Greencastle) 2008, (Derry) 2009, New Irish Architecture: Rebuilding the Republic, Leuven 2011, Ireland at the Venice Architecture Biennale 2000–2010, Shankill Castle 2011, Restless Pencil: Noel Moffett 1912–94, Dublin 2012. *Film:* contrib. to Drawing on Life 2013, Kevin Roche: The Quiet Architect 2017, Dreaming Squares 2018. *Radio:* contrib. to RTÉ documentary series The Architect's Eye 2006, to RTÉ Arts Tonight documentary on Sam Stephenson Architect (PPI Award) 2011. *Television:* contrib. to RTÉ documentary series Nation Building 2000, Designing Ireland 2015. *Publications:* Kevin Roche Architect 1983, Aldo Rossi: Selected Writings and Projects 1983, Collaboration: The Pillar Project 1988, The Architect and the Drawing 1989, Making a Modern Street 1991, Tales from Two Cities 1994, Transformation of an Institution 2004, SubUrban to SuperRural 2006, North by Northwest (co-author) 2008, One Hundred & One Hosannas for Architecture 2017, Architecture Ireland 2018. *Leisure interests:* family, football, films, food, good buildings, a glass or two of wine. *Address:* Shankill Castle, Paulstown, Co. Kilkenny, Ireland (home). *Telephone:* 85-7686590 (mobile) (office). *E-mail:* shane_otoole@hotmail.com (home).

OTORBAYEV, Djoomart; Kyrgyzstani economist, academic and politician; b. 18 Aug. 1955, Frunze (now Bishkek), Kyrgyz SSR, USSR; ed Leningrad (now St Petersburg) State Univ., Russian SFSR; Lecturer, Sr Lecturer, Prof., Kyrgyz State Univ. 1985–96; Visiting Prof., Eindhoven Univ., The Netherlands 1992–96; Prof., Kyrgyz-Russian Slavonic Univ. 1996–2005; Chief Rep. of Philips Electronics Corpn in Cen. Asia 1996–99, Vice-Pres. of Representation 1999–2002; Special Rep. of Pres. of Kyrgyzstan for attracting investment 2001–04, and for econ. assistance to Afghanistan 2001–05; Deputy Prime Minister, responsible for the Economy 2002–05; f. Investment Round Table 2001; Sr Adviser for Caucasus and Cen. Asia, EBRD, London, UK 2006–12; First Deputy Prime Minister 2012–14, Acting Prime Minister 25 March–3 April 2014, Prime Minister of Kyrgyzstan 3 April 2014–1 May 2015; mem. Ata Meken Sotsialisttik Sayasiy Partiyasy (Fatherland Socialist Political Party). *Address:* Ata Meken Sotsialisttik Sayasiy Partiyasy (Fatherland Socialist Political Party), 720040 Bishkek, Ibraimova 108, Kyrgyzstan (office). *Telephone:* (312) 89-55-12 (office). *Fax:* (312) 66-46-38 (office). *E-mail:* pr@ atameken.kg (office). *Website:* atameken.kg (office).

OTOUNGA OSSIBADJOUO, Mathias, MEcon; Gabonese politician; *Minister of Sports, Tourism and Recreation;* b. 22 Feb. 1960, Okondja, Sebe-Brikolo; m.; five c.; ed Univ. Omar Bongo, Libreville, Univ. Mohamed V de Rabat, Morocco, Ecole Nat. des Douanes Françaises; Banking Exec., Banque Internationale pour le Commerce et l'Industrie du Gabon, SA (BICIG) Jan.–July 1987; Chef du Cabinet, Ministry of Economy and Finance 1990–94; Adviser on Fiscal and Customs Affairs, Ministry of Mines and Petrol 1994–96; Consultant, M2O Consult 1990–2012; with CAISTAB (stabilization fund) 2006; Deputy Chef du Cabinet to Pres. of the Repub. 2012–15; Minister of Nat. Defence 2015–16, of the Budget and Public Accounts Oct. 2016–Aug. 2017; of Sports, Tourism and Recreation 2017–; mem. Parti Democratique Gabonais (mem. political bureau). *Address:* Ministry of Sports, Tourism and

Recreation, BP 2150, Libreville, Gabon (office). *Telephone:* 01-74-00-19 (office). *Fax:* 01-74-65-89 (office). *Website:* www.jeunesse-sports.gouv.ga (office).

OTSUKA, Mutsutake; Japanese transport industry executive; b. 5 Jan. 1943, Beijing, China; ed Tokyo Univ.; began career with Japanese Nat. Railways 1965, various positions 1965–87; Man. Dir East Japan Railway Co. 1987–97, Vice-Pres. 1997–2000, Pres. and CEO JR East (formed during privatization of railways) 2000–06, Chair. East Japan Railway Co. 2006–12, apptd Advisor 2012; Corp. Auditor, Electric Power Devt Co. Ltd. *Leisure interests:* music, golf. *Address:* c/o East Japan Railway Co., 2-2 Yoyogi 2-chome, Shibuya-ku, Tokyo 151-8578, Japan (office). *Telephone:* (3) 5334-1310 (office). *Fax:* (3) 5334-1297 (office). *E-mail:* info@jreast.co.jp (office). *Website:* www.jreast.co.jp (office).

OTT, Hans Rudolf, PhD; Swiss physicist and academic; *Professor Emeritus, Eidgenössische Technische Hochschule, Zurich;* b. 4 July 1940, Berne; m. Marie-Louise Ott (née Gruaz); one s.; ed Eidgenössische Technische Hochschule (ETH), Zurich; Asst, ETH, Zurich 1971, Admin. Dir, Dept of Physics 1976–88, Prof. of Physics 1986–2008, Prof. Emer. 2008–, Deputy Chair., Dept of Physics 1999–2001, Chair. 2001–05, also Head, Inst. for Solid State Physics 1990–93, 1998–99; Head of Research, Paul Scherrer Inst. (PSI), Villigen 1988–91, also Dir and Chair. of Research Cttee 1991–2008; Vice-Chair., Comm. C5, IUPAP 1996–2002; Pres. Physikalische Gesellschaft, Zurich 1994–97; Sec. of Comm., Int. Inst. of Refrigeration 1976–86; mem. Council European Physical Soc. 1993–96 (mem. Cttee for Low Temperature Physics, IUPAP 1987–92, Chair. Condensed Matter Div. 1998–2005); mem. Exec. Bd Int. Council for Science (ICSU) (Treas.) 2008–; Co-Ed. Physica C 1988–2004; Assoc. Ed. Reviews of Modern Physics 1994–99; Ed.-in-Chief European Physical Journal B 2004–09; mem. Research Council, Swiss Nat. Science Foundation 1997–2007; Chair. Platform Math., Astronomy and Physics, Swiss Acad. of Natural Sciences 2007–12; Pres. Albert Einstein Soc., Bern 2008–; Foreign mem. Finnish Acad. of Sciences 2005–; Fellow, American Physical Soc. 1989–, World Innovation Foundation 2004–; Hon. mem. Physical Soc., Zurich 2003, Swiss Physical Soc. 2005; European Physical Soc. Hewlett-Packard Europhysics Prize 1989, American Physical Soc. Int. Prize for New Materials 1990. *Publications:* several books and more than 600 articles in scientific journals. *Address:* Laboratorium für Festkörperphysik, ETH Hönggerberg Office, HPF F 16.4, Otto-Stern-Weg 1, 8093 Zurich, Switzerland (office). *Telephone:* (1) 633-2311 (office). *E-mail:* ott@phys.ethz.ch (office). *Website:* www.dscm.ethz.ch/people/otth (office).

OTTER, Clement Leroy (Butch), BA; American business executive, politician and fmr state governor; b. 3 May 1942, Caldwell, Ida; m. 1st Gay Simplot 1964 (divorced 1992); four c.; m. 2nd Lori Easley 2006; ed St Teresa's Acad. (now Bishop Kelly High School), Boise, Saint Martin's Univ., Boise Jr Coll. (now Boise State Univ.), Coll. of Idaho (now Albertson Coll. of Idaho); served in Ida. Army Nat. Guard's 116th Armored Cavalry 1968–73, received specialized training at Fort Knox, Ky; mem. Bd of Dirs J.R. Simplot Co., later Dir Food Products Div., later Pres. Simplot Livestock, Pres. Simplot Int. –1993; mem. Ida. State House of Reps from Canyon Co. 1973–76, served as Deputy Majority Whip; cand. for Gov. of Ida. 1978; remained active in Ida. Republican Party, including its Cen. Cttee, served as Chair. Canyon Co. Republican Party; Lt-Gov. of Ida. 1987–2001; mem. US House of Reps for Ida. First Congressional Dist 2001–06; Gov. of Idaho 2007–19 (retd); mem. Nat. Rifle Asscn, Maple Grove State Grange, Ida. Cowboys Asscn, American Legion, Ida. 4-H Million Dollar Club; Grand Slam mem. Ducks Unlimited; Lifetime mem. Safari Club International; Republican; Dr hc (Mindanao State Univ., Philippines, Albertson Coll. of Idaho). *Address:* c/o Office of the Governor, State Capitol, PO Box 83720, Boise, ID 83720, USA (office).

OTTO, Michael, Dr rer. pol; German business executive; *Chairman of the Supervisory Board, Otto Group;* b. 12 April 1943, Kulm, Westpreußen; joined Otto Group 1971, mem. Exec. Bd Merchandise 1971–81, Chair. Exec. Bd and CEO 1981–2007, Chair. Supervisory Bd 2007–; mem. Bd of Dirs Axel Springer Verlag AG, Berlin; Chair. Council WWF Deutschland; Chair. Bd of Trustees Soc. for Politics and Industry, Werner Otto Foundation for Medical Research; Founder and Chair. Bd of Trustees Michael Otto Foundation for Environmental Protection, Foundation for Sustainable Agriculture and Forestry (FSAF); Hon. Senator, Univs of Hamburg and Greifswald 2000; Bundesverdienstkreuz mit Stern 2006; Ehrendoktorwürde der HH (Leipzig Grad. School of Man.) 2012; Manager of the Year 1986, 2001, Hamburg Senate Alfred Töpfer Medal 1996, German Environ-ment Award 1997, Corp. Ethics Award 2000, German Business Ethics Network Business Ethics Award, Sustainability Leadership Award 2002, Jewish Museum Berlin Prize for Understanding and Tolerance 2004, BAUM Sustainability Special Award 2005, Vernon A. Walters Award, Atlantik-Brücke 2005, German Incor-poraters Prize (for life's work) 2006, Int. Lifetime award 2006, Theodor Heuss Award 2010, UNESCO Children in Need Support Award 2010, Walter-Scheel-Award 2011, Heinz Sielmann Award 2011, Int. TÜV Rheinland Global Compact Award 2011, Business Hall of Fame, Manager Magazin 2012, Ehrenbürger der Freien und Hansestadt Hamburg 2013, Steiger-Award 2013, Bayrischer Verdien-storden 2015. *Address:* Otto GmbH & Co. KG, Werner-Otto-Strasse 1-7, 22179 Hamburg, Germany (office). *Telephone:* (40) 64610 (office). *E-mail:* info@ottogroup.com (office). *Website:* www.ottogroup.com (office).

OTUDEKO, Oba, BA, FCA, FCIB, FCIS; Nigerian business executive and fmr banker; *Chairman, Honeywell Group;* b. 18 Aug. 1943; m.; ed Leeds Coll. of Commerce, UK; f. Honeywell Group (fmrly Honeywell Enterprises) in early 1980s, currently Chair.; Gen. Man. and Acting CEO Cooperative Bank, Ibadan –1983 (retd); currently also Chair. Airtel Nigeria, Fan Milk of Nigeria Plc; Pres. and Chair. of Council, Nigerian Stock Exchange 2006–09; fmr Chair. Nat. Maritime Authority, FBN Bank (UK) Ltd, Nigeria–South Africa Chamber of Commerce, Vee-Networks; f. Oba Otudeko Foundation 2003; apptd Chair. Digital Africa Conf. Exhibition 2013; mem. Bd of Dirs Cen. Bank of Nigeria 1990–97, Guinness Nigeria Plc 1999–2003, British American Tobacco Ltd 2001–04, Ecobank Transnational Inc. 2002–10; fmr mem. Bd NEPAD Business Group; mem. Constituent Ass. responsible for drafting new constitution 1988–89; mem. of Council, Manufactur-ers Asscn of Nigeria, Africa Regional Advisory Bd, London Business School, UK (also mem. Office of Distinguished Friends); fmr Chancellor, Onabanjo Univ.; Fellow, Inst. of Chartered and Corporate Accountants, UK, Inst. Chartered Secs and Admins of Nigeria; Paul Harris Fellow, Rotary Int.; Chancellor, Olabisi Onabanjo Univ. (fmrly Ogun State Univ.) 2001–10; Hon. Citizen of Dallas, Texas,

USA, Hon. Citizen of Meziara, Lebanon; mem. Order of the Fed. Repub. 2000, Officer, Order of the Fed. Repub. 2003, Commdr, Order of the Fed. Repub. 2011; Hon. DSc (Olabisi Onabanjo Univ.), (Crescent Univ.), (Ajayi Crowther Univ.) CEO of the Year, African CEO 2016, Vanguard Lifetime Achievement Award 2018. *Address:* Honeywell Group, 6B Mekunwen Road, Off Oyinkan Abayomi Drive, Ikoyi, Lagos, Nigeria (office). *Telephone:* (1) 2900525 (office). *E-mail:* info@honeywellgroup.com (office). *Website:* www.honeywellgroup.com (office).

OTUNBAYEVA, Roza Isakovna, CPhilSc; Kyrgyzstani diplomatist, politician and fmr head of state; b. 23 Aug. 1950, Frunze (now Bishkek); d. of Isak Otunbayev and Salika Daniyarova; one s. one d.; ed Lomonosov Moscow State Univ.; Assoc. Prof., Kyrgyz State Univ. 1975–81; Sec., Regional CP Cttee in Frunze (now Bishkek) 1981–83, Second Sec., City CP Cttee 1983–86; Deputy to the Chair., Council of Ministers, Minister of Foreign Affairs of Kyrgyz SSR 1986–89; Exec. Sec., USSR Comm. on UNESCO 1989–90, Chair. 1990–91; Amb. of USSR to Malaysia 1991–92; Vice-Prime Minister and Minister of Foreign Affairs of Repub. of Kyrgyzstan Feb.–May 1992; Amb. of Kyrgyzstan to USA 1992–94 (also accred to Canada); Minister of Foreign Affairs 1994–97; Amb. to UK 1997–2002; Deputy Special Rep. of UN Sec.-Gen. for Georgia (to regulate conflict between Georgia and Abkhazia) 2002–04; Co-Chair. Ata-Jurt (Homeland Idealistic Democratic Political Party) 2004–06, amongst leaders of 'Tulip Revolution' that led to overthrow of Pres. Akayev 2005, Acting Minister of Foreign Affairs March–Sept. 2005; mem. Parl. (Kyrgyzstandyn Sotsial-Demokratiyalyk Partiyasy (Social Democratic Party of Kyrgyzstan) 2007–10, Leader of Opposition; Chair. Cen. Exec. Cttee 2009; Chair. Interim Govt of Nat. Trust (following overthrow of Pres. Kurmanbek Bakiyev) April–May 2010, Acting Pres. of Kyrgyzstan May–July 2010, Pres. July 2010–Dec. 2011, also Head of Interim Govt May–Dec. 2010; Co-Chair. Banner (Asaba) Party of Nat. Revival 2006–07; mem. Sec.-Gen.'s High-Level Advisory Bd on Mediation, UN 2017–; mem. Advisory Bd (Moscow Br.), Carnegie Endowment for Int. Peace; Founder 'Roza Otunbayeva Initiative' Int. Social Fund 2012; Hon. Prof. at numerous univs., including Shanghai Univ. of Political Science and Law, China, Ganjavi Univ., Azerbaijan, several Kyrgyz univs.; Commdr, Légion d'honneur; Order of the Polar Star (Mongolia); Int. Women of Courage Award, US Dept of State 2011. *Leisure interests:* reading political and fiction literature, painting, music, skiing, yoga, trekking. *Address:* 'Roza Otunbayeva Initiative' International Public Foundation, 720040 Bishkek, Kyrgyzstan (home). *Telephone:* (312) 66-03-68 (home). *E-mail:* office@roza.kg (home). *Website:* www.roza.kg.

OU, Francisco H. L., BA; Taiwanese diplomatist and politician; b. 5 Jan. 1940, Hsinchu; ed Nat. Chengchi Univ.; Officer, Dept of Cen. and S American Affairs, Ministry of Foreign Affairs 1964–67, Third Sec., Embassy in Lima 1967–71, Second Sec. 1971, Section Chief, Dept of Cen. and S American Affairs, Ministry of Foreign Affairs 1971–73, Deputy Dir-Gen. 1973–75, Dir-Gen. 1981–84, Dir Far East Commercial Office, Santiago, Chile 1975–81, Amb. to Nicaragua 1984–85, to Guatemala 1990–96, 2003–08, Dir Commercial Office, Argentina 1986–90, Vice-Minister of Foreign Affairs 1996–2000, Minister of Foreign Affairs 2008–09; Rep. Taipei Econ. and Cultural Office, Spain 2000–03. *Address:* Ministry of Foreign Affairs, 2 Kaitakeland Blvd, Taipei 10048, Taiwan (office). *Telephone:* (2) 23482999 (office). *Fax:* (2) 23805678 (office). *E-mail:* eyes@mofa.gov.tw (office). *Website:* www.mofa.gov.tw (office).

OU, Jinping, BS, MS, PhD; Chinese engineer and fmr university administrator; b. 15 April 1959; ed Xiangtan Univ., Wuhan Univ. of Tech., Harbin Inst. of Tech.; Asst Prof. of Civil Eng, Harbin Inst. of Tech. 1985–87, Assoc. Prof. 1987–90, Prof. 1990, Dean, School of Civil Eng 1997–2000; Prof., Dept of Civil Eng, Dalian Univ. of Tech. 1988–, also Univ. Pres. 2006–12; Deputy, 11th NPC 2008; mem. Chinese Acad. of Eng 2003–; winner of first Feng Kang Prize for Scientific Computing. *Address:* c/o Dalian University of Technology, 2 Linggong Road, Ganjingzi Qu, Dalian 116024, Liaoning Province, People's Republic of China.

OUALALOU, Fathallah, DèsSc; Moroccan economist and politician; b. 26 March 1942, Rabat; m.; four c.; ed Lycée Moulay Youssef, Univ. of Rabat, Univ. of Paris; began career as Research Asst, Centre Universitaire de Recherche Scientifique, also Pres. Union Nationale des Etudiants; Lecturer, Law Dept, Univs of Rabat, Casablanca and Ecole Nat. d'Admin 1968; mem. Groupe de Rabat; Co-founder Socialist Union of Popular Forces (Union socialiste des forces populaires) 1972, mem. Political Bureau 1989–, Leader Parl. Group 1984–98; Minister of Economy, Finance, Privatization and Tourism 1998–2002, of Finance and Privatization 2002–07; Mayor of Rabat 2009–15; mem. Nat. Bureau, Syndicat Nat. de l'Enseignement Supérieur; Co-founder Asscn des économistes marocains 1972, Pres. 1982–; Pres. Union des économistes Arabes; mem. Chambre des Représen-tants. *Publications:* numerous articles on econ. theory and Maghreb economies. *Address:* Union Socialiste des Forces Populaires (USFP), 9 al-Araâr Avenue, Hay Riad, Rabat, Morocco (office). *Telephone:* (53) 7565511 (office). *Fax:* (53) 7565510 (office). *E-mail:* usfp@usfp.ma (office). *Website:* usfp.org.ma (office).

OUATTARA, Alassane Dramane, DSc; Côte d'Ivoirian politician, financial official and head of state; *President;* b. 1 Jan. 1942, Dimbokro; s. of Dramane Ouattara and Nabintou Cissé; m. Dominique Ouattara 1991; four c.; ed Drexel Inst. of Tech., Phila and Univ. of Pennsylvania, USA; Economist, IMF 1968–73; sr staff mem. in charge of missions Banque Centrale des Etats de l'Afrique de l'Ouest (BCEAO) 1973–75, Special Adviser to Gov. and Dir of Research 1975–82, Vice-Gov. 1983–84, Gov. 1988–90; Dir African Dept, IMF 1984–88, Counsellor to Man. Dir 1987–88; Prime Minister of Côte d'Ivoire and Minister of Economy and Finance 1990–93; Deputy Man. Dir IMF 1994–99; Pres. UNCTAD 1979–80; mem. Bd of Dirs Global Econ. Action Inst.; Expert Adviser Comm. on Transnat.Corpns; Hon. Gov. BCEAO; apptd Pres. Rassemblement des républicains (RDR) 1999; in exile in Gabon; being also a citizen of Burkina Faso he was barred from standing in 2000 presidential elections of Côte d'Ivoire; granted Côte d'Ivorian citizenship 2002; declared winner of presidential election by election comm. and formally recognized by UN Security Council as winner Dec. 2010, Pres. of Côte d'Ivoire 2011– (sworn in 6 May), apptd Minister of Defence 2012; Commdr Ordre du Lion du Sénégal, Ordre du Mono du Togo, Ordre Nat. du Niger, Grand Officier Ordre Nat. de Côte d'Ivoire. *Address:* Office of the President, 01 BP 1354, Abidjan, Côte d'Ivoire (office). *Telephone:* 20-22-02-22 (office). *Fax:* 20-21-14-25 (office).

OUDÉA, Frédéric; French business executive and fmr civil servant; *CEO, Société Générale;* b. 3 July 1963; ed Ecole Polytechnique, Ecole Nationale d'Admin; held several posts in French sr civil service, including in Audit Dept of Ministry of Finance, Ministry of Economy and Finance, Budget Ministry and in Cabinet of Ministry of Treasury and Communication 1987–95; Deputy Head, then Head of Corp. Banking arm, Société Générale, London, UK 1995–97, Head of Global Supervisory and Devt of Equities 1998–2001, Deputy Chief Financial Officer, Société Générale Group 2002–03, Chief Financial Officer 2003–March 2008, Deputy CEO March–May 2008, CEO May 2008–, Chair. 2009–15, mem. Nomination Cttee; Chair. Fédération Bancaire Française 2011–12. *Address:* Société Générale, 29 boulevard Haussmann, 75009 Paris, France (office). *Telephone:* 1-42-14-20-00 (office). *E-mail:* info@socgen.com (office). *Website:* www.societegenerale.com (office).

OUDEMAN, Marjan J., LLM; Dutch lawyer, business executive and university administrator; *President of the Executive Board, Utrecht University;* b. 7 July 1958, Beverwijk; ed Univ. of Groningen; began career as company lawyer at Koninklijke Hoogovens 1982, moved to Finance Dept and rose to become Dir of canning factory, following merger with British Steel to become Corus, responsible for European Steel, later mem. Exec. Cttee of European part of Tata Steel Group (fmrly Corus) and Exec. Dir Strip Div. –2010; mem. Exec. Cttee AkzoNobel 2010–13, responsible for Organizational Devt and Human Resources; Pres. Exec. Bd Utrecht Univ. 2013–; Commr, Dutch Railways 2005–13; Chair. Supervisory Bd HKS Scrap Metals BV; Gov. of Training Mans., Ashorne Hill Man. Coll.; mem. Exec. Bd VNO NCW; mem. Bd Foundation Sail Amsterdam, Foundation Cttee for Concertgebouw; mem. Steering Cttee of Artis, Bd of Nat. Fund 4 and 5 May, Recommendation Cttee of Young Entrepreneurs, Ronald McDonald Kinderfonds, October Knowledge Month; fmr mem. Innovatieplatform; ranked first by FEM Business magazine on list of most powerful businesswomen in the Netherlands Nov. 2005, chosen by Aside magazine as one of ten most influential women in the Netherlands and as most important woman in business category 2009. *Address:* Utrecht University, Heidelberglaan 8, PO Box 80125, 3508 Utrecht TC, Netherlands (office). *Telephone:* (30) 2535150 (office). *Fax:* (30) 2537745 (office). *E-mail:* m.j.oudeman@uu.nl (office); c.krapels@uu.nl (office). *Website:* www.uu.nl (office).

OUÉDRAOGO, Ablassé, DEcon; Burkinabè economist, international organization official and politician; *President, Le Faso Autrement;* b. 30 June 1953, Burkina Faso; ed Univ. of Nice, France; Deputy Resident Rep. of UNDP, Kinshasa 1991–93; Head of Regional Office for E Africa of UN Sudano-Sahélienne Office (also accred to OAU, ECA, UNEP) 1993–94; Minister of Foreign Affairs 1994–99; Special Adviser to Pres. of Burkina Faso 1999; Jt Deputy Dir-Gen. WTO 1999–2000; apptd Regional Adviser for Africa, African Devt Bank 2006; Special Envoy of the African Union in Madagascar 2009; currently Pres. Le Faso Autrement political party; Officer of Nat. Order of Burkina Faso 1997; Officer of Equatorial Order of Gabon 2000. *Publications:* Réflexions sur la crise industrielle en France 1979, Les firmes multinationales et l'industrialisation des pays en voie de développement 1981. *E-mail:* info@lefasoautrement.org (office). *Website:* www.lefasoautrement.org (office).

OUÉDRAOGO, Kadré Désiré; Burkinabè politician, economist and banker; b. 1953; m. Solange Ouedraogo; ed Haute Ecole, Paris, Université Paris I (Sorbonne), France; fmr Deputy Exec. Sec. Econ. Community of West African States (ECOWAS) in charge of Econ. Affairs; fmr Gov. of Cen. Bank of West African States; Prime Minister of Burkina Faso 1996–2000; Amb. to the EU (also accred to Belgium, Luxembourg, Netherlands and UK), Brussels 2001–12; Pres. Econ. Community of West African States (ECOWAS) Comm., Abuja, Nigeria 2012–16; Grand Officier, Ordre Nat. du Burkina Faso 1996. *Address:* 01 BP 3474, Ouagadougou 01, Burkina Faso (home).

OUÉDRAOGO, HE Cardinal Philippe Nakellentuba; Burkinabè ecclesiastic; *Archbishop of Ouagadougou;* b. 25 Jan. 1945, Konéan; ordained priest, Diocese of Kaya 1973; consecrated Bishop of Ouahigouya 1996–2009; Archbishop of Ouagadougou 2009–; cr. Cardinal (Cardinal-Priest of Santa Maria Consolatrice al Tiburtino) 2014–. *Address:* Archdiocese of Ouagadougou, 01 BP 1472, Ouagadougou 01, Burkina Faso (office). *Telephone:* 306704 (office). *Fax:* 307275 (office).

OUELLET, Hon. André, PC, BA, LLL; Canadian lawyer and fmr politician; b. 6 April 1939, St-Pascal, Québec; s. of Albert Ouellet and Rita Turgeon; m. Edith Pagé 1965; two s. two d.; ed Pensionnat St-Louis de Gonzague, Québec Seminary, Ottawa and Sherbrooke Univs; MP for Papineau 1967–93; Parl. Sec. to Minister for External Affairs 1970, to Minister for Nat. Health and Welfare 1971; Postmaster Gen. 1972–74; Minister for Consumer and Corp. Affairs 1974–76, 1980–84, for Urban Affairs 1976–79, for Public Works 1978–79, for Canada Post Corpn 1980–83, for Labour 1983, for Regional Econ. Devt 1983–84; Pres. Privy Council 1984; Govt Leader of Commons 1984; Opposition Transport Critic 1984; Opposition External Affairs Critic 1987; Opposition Critic for Fed. Provincial Relations 1990; Minister for Foreign Affairs 1993–96; Chair. Canada Post Corpn 1996–99, Pres. and CEO 1999–2004. *Leisure interests:* tennis, swimming, squash, skiing, reading and collecting works of art.

OUELLET, HE Cardinal Bishop Marc, PSS; Canadian ecclesiastic; *Prefect of the Congregation for Bishops;* b. 8 June 1944, Lamotte; ed Collège de Berthier, Ecole Normale of Amos, Univ. of Laval, Major Seminary of Montreal, Pontifical Univ. San Tommaso d'Aquino, Pontifical Gregorian Univ., Rome, Italy; ordained priest of Soc. of Priests of St Sulpice 1968; entered Soc. of Priests of St Sulpice 1972, held several teaching positions in Colombia, Montreal and Edmonton; Prof., John Paul II Inst. for Studies on Marriage and the Family 1997–2001; Sec. Pontifical Council for Promoting Christian Unity 2001–03; Titular Archbishop of Acropolis 2001–02; Archbishop of Quebec City 2002–10; cr. Cardinal (Cardinal-Priest of Santa Maria in Traspontina) 2003; participated in Papal Conclave 2005, 2013; Prefect of the Congregation for Bishops 2010–13, 2013–; Pres. Pontifical Comm. for Latin America 2010–; Consultor, Congregation for the Doctrine of Faith, Congregation for Divine Worship; Sec. Comm. for Religious Relations with Jews; mem. Perm. Interdiscasteral Comm. for the Eastern Churches in Europe, Pontifical Acad. of Theology; mem. Editorial Bd Rivista Internazionale Communio (N American edn); mem., XIth Gen. Ordinary Ass. of Synod of Bishops, Vatican City 2005, Congregation for the Oriental Churches 2012; cr. Cardinal Bishop 2018. *Address:* Congregation for Bishops, Palazzo della Congregazioni, Piazza Pio XII 10, 00193 Rome, Italy (office). *Telephone:* (06) 69884217 (office). *Website:* www.vatican.va/roman_curia/congregations/cbishops/index.htm (office).

OULD ABDEL AZIZ, Gen. Mohamed; Mauritanian army officer and head of state; *President;* b. 20 Dec. 1956, Akjoujt; ed Royal Military Acad., Meknès, Morocco; joined army in 1977, attained rank of Second-Lt 1980, Capt. 1988, Maj. 1994, Lt-Col 1988, Col 2004, Gen. 2007; Commdr Presidential Guard (Bataillon de la Sécurité présidentielle) 1987–91; Chief of Staff to Pres. Sidi Ould Cheikh Abdallahi 2007–08; Pres. High Council of State (following coup d'etat of 6 Aug. 2008) 2008–09; Leader, Union for the Republic 2009 (resgnd); Pres. of Mauritania 2009–; Chair. African Union 2014–15. *Address:* Office of the President, BP 184, Nouakchott, Mauritania (office). *Telephone:* 525-26-36 (office). *Fax:* 525-26-36 (office).

OULD AHMED IZID BIH, Isselkou, MMath; Mauritanian mathematician, academic and politician; b. 12 Oct. 1961, Amourj; m.; five c.; ed Univ. of Orléans, France; Math. Coordinator, Faculty of Science and Tech, Univ. of Nouakchott 1995–2003, Pres., Univ. of Nouakchott 2007–10; Vice-Dean of Student Affairs, Ajman Univ., UAE 2004–06; Attaché, Civil Cabinet of the Pres. 1998–03, Dir, Cabinet of the Pres. 2010–13; Minister of Higher Educ. and Scientific Research 2013–14, of Equipment and Transport 2015, of Foreign Affairs and Co-operation 2016–18; Pres., Conseil Nat. de Régulation (fmrly Autorité des Régulations des Télécommunications) 2015; Assoc. mem. Int. Centre of Theoretical Physics, Italy 1997–2002; mem. Centre de Mathématiques Pures et Appliquées, Nice, France 1998–; mem. Union pour la République, Pres. 2014. *Address:* c/o Ministry of Foreign Affairs and Co-operation, BP 230, Nouakchott, Mauritania (office).

OULD BÉCHIR, Mohamed Salem; Mauritanian engineer and politician; *Prime Minister;* b. 17 Dec. 1962, Aïoun el Atrouss; m.; two c.; ed Compiègne Univ. of Tech., Pierre Mendès Univ., Grenoble Inst. of Econs and Energy Policy; joined SONELEC (nat. water and electricity co.) 1986, Project Engineer 1987–88, Head, Nouakchott new power plant 1988–96, Electricity Tech. Dir, SONELEC, later Tech. Dir SOMELEC (Mauritanian Electricity Co.) (following division of SONELEC) 1996–2005, Gen. Man., SOMELEC 2009–13; Dir of Electricity, Ministry of Energy and Oil Feb.–May 2007; Sec.-Gen., Ministry of Hydraulics, Energy, Information Tech. and Communication 2007–08; Sec.-Gen., Ministry of Hydraulics and Energy May 2008–Oct. 2009; Sec.-Gen., Ministry of Hydraulics and Sanitation Oct. 2008–Sept. 2009; Minister of Hydraulics and Sanitation 2013–15; Minister of Petroleum, Energy and Mines 2015–16; Dir Gen., Nat. Soc. of Industry and Mines (SNIM) 2016–18; Prime Minister 2018–. *Address:* Office of the Prime Minister, BP 237, Nouakchott, Mauritania (office). *Telephone:* 45-25-33-37 (office). *Website:* www.primature.gov.mr (office).

OULD CHEIKH AHMED, Ismail, BEcons, MA; Mauritanian economist, diplomatist, politician and fmr UN official; *Minister of Foreign Affairs and Co-operation;* b. 1960, Nouakchott; ed Univ. of Montpellier, France, Univ. of Manchester, UK, Maastricht Graduate School of Governance, Netherlands; several positions with UNICEF including as Dir of Change Man. in New York, Deputy Regional Dir for Eastern and Southern Africa in Nairobi and Rep. in Georgia, UN Resident Coordinator, Humanitarian Coordinator and UNDP Resident Rep. in Syria 2008–12, in Yemen 2012–14, Deputy Special Rep. and Deputy Head of UN Support Mission in Libya (UNSMIL) 2014, Special Rep. for UN Mission for Ebola Emergency Response (UNMEER) Jan.–April 2015, UN Special Envoy for Yemen 2015–18; Minister of Foreign Affairs and Co-operation 2018–. *Address:* Ministry of Foreign Affairs and Co-operation, BP 230, Nouakchott, Mauritania (office). *Telephone:* 45-25-26-82 (office). *Fax:* 45-25-28-60 (office). *E-mail:* info@maec.gov.mr (office). *Website:* www.diplomatie-mr.com (office).

OULD DAHI, Abdel Aziz, PhD; Mauritanian government official and central banker; *Governor, Banque Centrale de Mauritanie;* b. 12 June 1966, Louga; m.; three c.; ed Ecole Polytechnique Fédérale de Lausanne, Switzerland, Univ. of Dakar, Senegal, Univ. of Orléans, France, Univ. of Nouakchott, Mauritania; Project Man., Balance of State Employees, Ministry of Finance 1992–97, IT Focal Point, UN Devt Programme, Mauritania 1997–98, Dir Internet Centre of Admin, Secr. Gen. of Govt 1998–2000, Nat. Coordinator, IT Transition to the Year 2000 programme 1999–2000, Mission Officer and Dir Internet Centre Govt, Sec. of State to Prime Minister for New Techs 2000–07; Minister of Civil Service and Modernisation of Admin 2007–08; consultant to several missions to countries in Africa 2008–09; Dir-Gen. Nat. Health Insurance Fund 2009–15; Gov. Banque Centrale de Mauritanie 2015–. *Publications include:* Towards e-governance, for a new digital administration (co-author). *Address:* Banque Centrale de Mauritanie, ave de l'Indépendance, BP 623, Nouakchott, Mauritania (office). *Telephone:* 45-25-22-06 (office). *Fax:* 45-25-27-59 (office). *E-mail:* info@bcm.mr (office). *Website:* www.bcm.mr (office).

OULD DIAY, Mokhtar; Mauritanian politician; *Minister of Economy and Finance;* b. 28 Dec. 1973, Moudjéria; m.; five c.; ed Nat. Inst. of Statistics and Applied Econs, Morocco, Univ. of Toulouse, France; Labor Market Data Officer, Nat. Employment Policy Project 1998–2003; Head of Monitoring and Evaluation, Educ. and Training Project and Dir, Office of Special Studies in the field of statistics and econs; Adviser to the Minister of Educ. 2003–10; Dir-Gen. of Taxation 2010–15; Minister of Finance 2015–, of Economy 2016–. *Address:* Ministry of Finance, 303 Ilôt C, BP 5150, Nouakchott, Mauritania (office). *Telephone:* 44-48-04-59 (office). *E-mail:* ouldmodou@gmail.com (office). *Website:* www.economie.gov.mr (office).

OULD HAMADI, Hamadi Ould Baba; Mauritanian engineer and government official; b. 31 Dec. 1948, Moudjéria; one c.; ed Ecole Nat. d'Admin.; Deputy Head, Hydraulic Div., Nouadhibou, Ministry of Equipment 1967–78; Sec.-Gen. FIAP 1983–90; Consultant 1992–2007; Minister of Nat. Defence 2009, of Foreign Affairs and Co-operation 2011–13, of Fisheries and the Maritime Economy 2013–14. *Address:* Union Pour la République, Nouakchott (office). *Telephone:* 524-03-10 (office). *E-mail:* communication.upr15@gmail.com (office). *Website:* www.upr.mr (office).

OULD MEÏMOU, Hamadi, DESS; Mauritanian politician and fmr diplomatist; b. 31 Dec. 1957, Timbedra; m.; three c.; ed univs in Tunisia and France; Dir, Union des Banques de Developpement (UBD) 1987–89, Dir, UBD Nouadhibou (fisheries finance agency) 1989–93; Dir, Industry Dept, Ministry of Mines and Industry

1993–97; Dir-Gen., Banque de l'Habitat de Mauritanie 1997–2000; Dir-Gen., Nat. Social Security Fund (CNSS) 2000–03; Commr for Human Rights, Poverty Reduction and Integration (rank of minister) 2003–05; mem. Nat. Ass. (Parl.) 2006–07, Chair. Finance Cttee 2006–07; Amb. to Kuwait 2007–12, to Ethiopia 2012–14, also Perm. Rep. to African Union, UN Econ. Comm. for Africa and UNEP 2012–14; Minister of Foreign Affairs and Co-operation 2015–16.

OULD SIDI MOHAMED, Zahabi, DEA; Malian politician, UN official and fmr resistance fighter; b. 1 Oct. 1957, Goundam; ed École nationale d'Admin, Bamako, Univ. of Paris-IV (Sorbonne), France; Deputy Dir, aid programme in N Mali, Aide de l'Eglise Norvégienne (non-govt org.) 1985–90; with Front islamique arabe de l'Azawad (armed rebel group) 1990s, prin. negotiator at peace talks with govt 1992; several postings with UN in Congo, Haïti, Somalia, Côte d'Ivoire and S Sudan 1996–2013; Minister of Foreign Affairs and Int. Co-operation 2013–14.

OULD TAH, Sidi, PhD; Mauritanian economist and politician; *Director-General, Arab Bank for Economic Development in Africa;* b. 11 May 1964, Mederdra; ed Nice-Sophia-Antipolis Univ., Paris VII Univ.; started as expert at Mauritanian Bank for Devt and Commerce 1984–86; Financial Analyst, Food Security Comm. 1986; Admin. and Finance Man. Municipality of Nouakchott 1987; Advisor to Dir-Gen. Internal Auditing Dept in "Nouakchott" Port Authority 1988–96; Financial Analyst Arab Authority for Agric., Investment and Devt (AAAID) 1996–99; served as Investment Promotion Office, later as Technical Asst to Pres. Islamic Devt Bank 1999–2006; Econ. adviser to Prime Minister and Pres. 2006–08; Minister of Economy and Finance 2008, of Econ. Affairs and Devt 2009–15; Chair. Council of Ministers, G5-Sahel 2014–15; Dir-Gen. Arab Bank for Econ. Devt in Africa (BADEA) 2015–; fmr Head Nat. Statistics Council; fmr mem. Bd of Govs IBRD. *Address:* Arab Bank for Economic Development in Africa, PO Box 2640, Khartoum, Sudan (office). *Telephone:* (183) 773646 (office). *Fax:* (183) 770600 (office). *E-mail:* badea@badea.org (office). *Website:* www.badea.org (office).

OUMAROU, Mamane; Niger politician and diplomatist; b. 1945; m.; Prime Minister of Niger Jan.–Nov. 1983, 1988–90; mem. Mouvement Nat. de la Soc. de développement (MNSD); fmr Amb. to Saudi Arabia; apptd Mediator of the Repub. 2008.

OUMAROU, Seyni; Niger politician; *President, Mouvement national pour la société de développement;* b. 9 Aug. 1950, Tillabéri; m.; six c.; Dir-Gen. Nigerien Paper Transformation Enterprise (ENITRAP) 1987–98; mem. Mouvement nat. pour la soc. de développement—Nassara (MNSD—Nassara), Pres. Tillabéry regional council 2007–08, Pres. MNSD 2008–; apptd Special Adviser to the Prime Minister 1995; Minister of Trade and Industry 1999–2004; Minister of State for Equipment 2004–07; Prime Minister of Niger 2007–09; Pres. Nat. Ass. 2009–10; cand. in presidential election 2016. *Address:* Mouvement national pour la société de développement, rue Issa Beri 30, corner boulevard de Zarmaganda, Porte 72, BP 881, Niamey, Niger (office). *Telephone:* 20-73-39-07 (office). *Fax:* 20-72-41-74 (office). *E-mail:* presi@mnsd-nassara.org (office).

OUSELEY, Baron (Life Peer) cr. 2001, of Peckham Rye in the London Borough of Southwark; **Herman (George) Ouseley,** Kt, Diploma in Municipal Management; British civil servant and race relations adviser; b. 24 March 1945, Georgetown, British Guiana (now Guyana); m. Margaret Ouseley; two c.; ed William Penn School, Dulwich, Catford Coll.; came to UK aged 11; town planning man. 1963–70; social care man. for the elderly 1970–73; community relations exec. 1973–79; Race Relations Adviser, London Borough of Lambeth 1979–81, Asst CEO 1984–86; Dir Policy Unit, GLC 1981–84; Dir of Educ. ILEA 1986–88, Chief Exec. 1988–90; Chief Exec. London Borough of Lambeth 1990–93; Chair. Comm. for Racial Equality 1993–2000, Policy Research Inst. on Ageing and Ethnicity 1997–2010; Man. Dir Different Realities Partnership Ltd 2000–06; mem. Council, Policy Studies Inst. 1988–90, Inst. of Race Relations 1990–2011, Inst. of Educ., Univ. of London 1995–, Football Asscn (Chair. Race Equality Advisory Group) 2008–12; mem. Advisory Council Prince's Youth Business Trust 1993–98; Chair., Presentation Educ. and Employment Charitable Trust 1997–99, Kick It Out 1993–2018, Preset Educ. and Training Trust; Pres. Local Govt Asscn 2002–05; mem. (Crossbench) House of Lords 2001–; Dir (non-exec.), Focus Consultancy Ltd 2001–10, Brooknight Security Ltd, Manchester United Foundation 2006–; Patron Presentation Housing Asscn 1990–2002, Daneford Trust 2001–, Nat. Black Police Asscn 2007–15; 14 hon. degrees, including Dr hc (Edinburgh) 1999. *Publications:* The System 1981, pamphlets and articles on local govt, public services, employment, training and race equality issues. *Address:* House of Lords, Westminster, London, SW1A 0PW, England. *Telephone:* (20) 7219-8725. *E-mail:* ouseleyh@parliament.uk.

OUSMANE, Kane; Mauritanian mining engineer, politician and business executive; *CEO, International Mining & Infrastructure Corporation PLC;* ed Polytechnique, Paris, France; fmr Vice-Pres. for Corp. Man., African Devt Bank; Gov. Banque centrale de Mauritanie –2008; Man. Dir Societe Nationale Industrielle et Minière 2008–09; Minister of Finance 2009–10; fmr Dir of Infrastructure, Minière de Guinée Holdings Ltd, then Dir (non-Exec.) Afferro Mining Inc.; Deputy Chair. African Iron Ore Group –2012; CEO Int. Mining & Infrastructure Corpn PLC 2013–. *Address:* International Mining & Infrastructure Corporation PLC, 40 New Bond Street, London, W1S 2RX, England (office). *Website:* www.imicplc.com (office).

OUSSEINI, Brig.-Gen. Mamadou; Niger army officer and politician; b. 1 Jan. 1953, Gouré; m.; six c.; ed Ecole Mil. Préparatoire Technique, Bingerville, Côte d'Ivoire, Acad. Mil. d'Antsirabé, Madagascar, Ecole d'application de l'infanterie, Montpellier, France, École d'état-major, Compiègne, Coll. Inter-Armées de Défense, Paris; joined army 1974, command roles include fmr Deputy Officer, 2nd Agadez Compagnie saharienne motorisée (CSM), Deputy Commdr, 4th CSM, 3rd Zinder CSM, Commdr 3rd Zinder CSM, 6th Dirkou CSM, Préfet (Police Commr) of Dosso, of Diffa, Head of Garde Républicaine, Commdr, Presidential Guard, Land Army Adviser, Ministry of Nat. Defence, Sec.-Gen. Ministry of Nat. Defence, Defence Attaché, Embassy in Nigeria, Deputy Chief of Gen. Staff of Land Army, Chief of Gen. Staff of Land Army –2010, Minister of Nat. Defence 2010–11; rank of 2nd Lt 1977, Lt 1979, Capt. 1984, Commdr 1990, Lt-Col 1995, Col 2000, Brig.-Gen. 2006; Grand Officier, Ordre Nat. du Niger.

OUTLULE, Samuel Otsile, BPA; Botswana diplomatist; *Ambassador to France and European Union;* b. 8 July 1957; m.; three c.; ed Gaborone Campus, Univ. of Botswana and Swaziland, Inst. of Devt Man., Gaborone, Ranche House Coll., Harare, German Foundation for Int. Devt, Berlin; Foreign Affairs Officer, Ministry of Foreign Affairs 1982–85; served at High Comm. in Harare 1985–89, Counsellor, High Comm. in London 1993–95; First Sec. to Perm. Mission to UN, New York 1989, Political Counsellor and Alternate Rep. to Security Council 1995; Deputy Dir for Africa and Middle E, Ministry of Foreign Affairs 1997–99, Dir of Int. Relations 1999–2000; Clerk to Cabinet and Sr Pvt. Sec. to Pres. Mogae 2000–05; Perm. Rep. to UN, New York 2005–08; Foreign Sec., Ministry of Foreign Affairs 2008–09; Perm. Sec., Ministry of Youth, Sport and Culture 2009–11; Amb. to EU 2011–. *Address:* Permanent Delegation of the Republic of Botswana to the European Union, 169, avenue de Tervuren, 1150 Brussels, Belgium (office). *Telephone:* (2) 735-20-70 (office). *Website:* en.unesco.org (office).

OUYAHIA, Ahmed; Algerian politician and diplomatist; b. 2 July 1952, Bouadnane; m.; two c.; military service 1976–78; Sec., Ministry of Foreign Affairs 1979–81; Counsellor, Embassy in Abidjan 1981–84; Counsellor, Perm. Mission to UN, New York 1984–89, Deputy Rep. to Security Council 1988–89; Counsellor, Office of the Minister of Foreign Affairs 1989–90, Dir-Gen. Dept of African Affairs, Ministry of Foreign Affairs 1990–91; Amb. to Mali 1992–93; Sec. of State for Cooperation and N African Affairs 1993–94; Dir of Cabinet to the Presidency 1994–95; Prime Minister of Algeria 1995–98, 2003–06 (resgnd), 2008–12, 2017–19 (resgnd); Deputy, Nat. Ass. 1997–; Minister of Justice 2000–02; Minister of State, Personal Rep. of the Pres. of the Repub. 2002–03; Sec.-Gen. Rassemblement nat. démocratique (RND) 1999–2013. *Address:* Rassemblement national démocratique (RND), Cité des Asphodèles, BP 10, Ben Aknoun, Algiers, Algeria (office). *Telephone:* (21) 91-64-10 (office). *Fax:* (21) 91-47-40 (office). *E-mail:* rnd@rnd-dz .org (office). *Website:* www.rnd-dz.org (office).

OUYANG, Ziyuan, MSc; Chinese scientist; *Honorary Chief Director, Chinese Society of Mineralogy, Petrology and Geochemistry;* b. 9 Oct. 1935, Jian City, Jiangxi Prov.; ed Beijing Coll. of Geology, Inst. of Geology, Beijing, Univ. of Science and Tech., Beijing, Inst. of Atomic Energy; Asst Prof., Inst. of Geology Chinese Acad. of Sciences 1960–66, Assoc. Prof., Inst. of Geochemistry 1966–78, Prof., Vice-Dir then Dir 1978–94, Prof. 1994–, Dir Bureau of Resources and Environmental Sciences 1991–93; Vice-Pres. People's Congress of Guizhou Prov. 1993–; Chair. Asscn for Science and Tech. Guizhou Prov. 1993–; Standing Vice-Pres. Chinese Soc. of Mineralogy, Petrology and Geochemistry 1976–94, apptd Chief Dir 1994, currently Hon. Chief Dir; Guest Prof., Beijing, Nanjing and other univs 1993–; Vice-Pres. Chinese Soc. of Space Sciences; Chair. Cttee of Space Chem. and Space Geology, Assoc. Ed.-in-Chief Journal of Space Science, Chinese Journal of Geochemistry 1980–; Ed.-in-Chief Journal of Environmental Science, Journal of Geology-Geochemistry, Bulletin of Mineralogy, Petrology and Geochemistry 1985–; Vice-Pres. Chinese Soc. of Geology 1992–96; Academician, Chinese Acad. of Sciences 1991–; Asteroid 8919 Ouyangziyuan named in his honour; First-Class Award of Natural Science Prize, Chinese Acad. of Sciences Nat. Science Conf. Prize, Nat. Outstanding Science Worker 2010. *Publications:* Progress of Selenology Research, Space Chemistry, Progress of Geology and Geochemistry during the 1980s, Progress of Mineralogy, Petrology and Geochemistry Research in China, Riddle of Dinosaur Depopulation, Formation and Evolution of the Planets and the Earth. *Leisure interests:* music, literature, tourism, photography. *Address:* Chinese Society for Mineralogy, Petrology and Geochemistry, 99 Lincheng West Road, Guanshanhu Hu 550002 Guiyang, Guizhou Province, People's Republic of China (office). *Telephone:* (851) 85895849 (office). *Fax:* (851) 5891379 (home). *E-mail:* csmpg@vip. skleg.cn (home); kydhtb@263.net (home). *Website:* csmpg.gyig .cas.cn (office).

OVCHINNIKOV, Vladimir Pavlovich; Russian pianist and academic; *Professor of Piano and Director, Central Music School, Moscow Conservatory;* b. 1 Jan. 1958, Beleby, Urals; ed studied with Anna Artobolevskaya and at Moscow Conservatory with Alexey Nasedkin; London debut, Barbican Hall 1987; has since given recitals in UK, Europe, USA, Canada and Japan and appeared with BBC Symphony, BBC Philharmonic, Royal Philharmonic, Royal Scottish Nat., Royal Liverpool Philharmonic, Ulster Orchestra, Netherlands Philharmonic, Netherlands Radio Symphony Orchestra, Bournemouth Symphony, Chicago Symphony, Danish Radio Symphony, Hague Residentie, Hallé, Leipzig Gewandhaus, Montreal Symphony, Nat. Symphony of Wales, Philharmonia, Polish Nat. Radio Orchestra, Slovak Philharmonic, Zurich Tonhalle, Russian State Symphony Orchestra, Moscow Philharmonic, Moscow Radio Symphony, St Petersburg Philharmonic and other major orchestras; Lecturer in Keyboard Studies, Royal Northern Coll. of Music, UK from 1994; Prof. of Piano, Moscow Conservatory, Dir Cen. Music School 2011–; Guest Prof. of Piano, Sakuyo Univ., Japan; Chair. Jury, Int. Russian Rotary Children's Music Competition 2011; Second Place, Montreal Int. Music Competition 1980, Jt Second Prize (with Peter Donohoe, no first prize awarded), Moscow Tchaikovsky Competition 1982, First Prize, Leeds Int. Piano Competition 1987, Nat. Artist of Russia 2005. *Recordings include:* Shostakovich's Piano Concerto No. 1 coupled with Mussorgsky's Pictures at an Exhibition; Rachmaninoff's Études-Tableaux; Liszt's Transcendental Études; Prokofiev's Piano Sonatas; Sonatas for Violin and Piano by Grieg (with violinist Vinnitsky); Liszt, Tchaikovsky, Taneyev, Rubinstein for Gold Club. *Address:* Schmidt Artists International, Inc., 59 East 54th Street, Suite 83, New York, NY 10022, USA (office); Moscow Conservatory, Bolshaya Nikitskaya str. 13/6, 125009 Moscow, Russian Federation (office). *Telephone:* (212) 421-8500 (office). *Fax:* (212) 421-8583 (office). *E-mail:* info@ schmidtart.com (office); spravka@mosconsv.ru (office). *Website:* www.schmidtart .com/artists/vladimir_ovchinnikov (office); www.mosconsv.ru (office).

OVCHINNIKOV, Col-Gen. Vyacheslav Victorovich; Russian army officer; b. 25 Oct. 1946, Tambov Region; m.; two s.; ed Leningrad Artillery Higher School, Kalinin Mil. Artillery Acad.; various posts in internal troops; service in Dept of Internal Affairs; fmr Deputy Head of Gen. Staff, Ministry of Internal Affairs, Head Dept of Punishments 1989–99, Deputy Minister of Internal Affairs 1999; Commdt of Stepanakert during Karabakh Conflict 1992, of N Osetia during Osetia-Ingush Conflict, of Grozny during mil. operations in Chechnya; First Deputy C-in-C Internal Troops, Ministry of Internal Affairs 1999, C-in-C 1999–2000, Adviser to Dir-Gen. Rosoboronexport Co. 2001; Order for Personal Courage, Order for Service to Motherland and numerous other medals.

OVELAR, Blanca, MEd, PhD; Paraguayan politician; b. (Blanca Margarita Ovelar de Duarte), 2 Sept. 1957, Concepcion; d. of Vicente Ovelar Lamas and

Edemilda Valiente; m. Ramón Duarte Rodas; three s.; Minister of Educ. 2002–07; selected as cand. for 2008 presidential election by Asociación Nacional Republicana—Partido Colorado (now Asociación Nacional Republicana); mem. Senate 2013–; Best Grad. Teacher of Primary Ed., Gold Medal of the Presidency of the Repub. *Publications:* Introduction to Basic Skills 1994, articles on education in values 1996–2000, articles on national reality 2009, Policy Papers 2009–10. *Address:* Cámara de Senadores, Congreso Nacional, 14 de Mayo e/ Avda. República, Asunción (office); Teniente 2do Jorge Martinez N° 1140, c/ Dr. Sosa Barrio Madame Lynch, c.p: 1732, Asunción, Paraguay. *Telephone:* (21) 414-5280 (office). *E-mail:* bovelar@senado.gov.py (office). *Website:* www.senado.gov.py (office).

OVERY, Richard James, PhD, FRHistS, FBA, FRSA; British historian and academic; *Professor of History, University of Exeter;* b. 23 Dec. 1947, London; s. of James Herbert Overy and Margaret Grace Overy (née Sutherland); m. 1st Tessa Coles 1969 (divorced 1976); m. 2nd Jane Giddens 1979 (divorced 1992); m. 3rd Kim Turner 1992 (divorced 2004); one s. five d.; ed Sexey's Blackford Grammar School, Somerset, Gonville & Caius Coll., Cambridge; Research Fellow, Churchill Coll., Cambridge 1972–73; Fellow and Coll. Lecturer, Queen's Coll., Cambridge 1973–79; Asst Univ. Lecturer, Univ. of Cambridge 1976–79; Lecturer in History, King's Coll., London 1980–88, Reader in History 1988–92, Prof. of Modern History 1992–2004, Fellow 2003–; Prof. of History, Coll. of Humanities, Univ. of Exeter 2004–; Chair. Research Bd, RAF Museum London; mem. European Acad. for Sciences and Arts; T.S. Ashton Prize 1983, Cass Prize for Business History 1987, Samuel Eliot Morison Prize for lifetime contrib. to mil. history, Soc. for Mil. History 2001, James Doolittle Award for a lifetime contrib. to aviation history 2010, Cundill Award for Historical Literature 2014. *Publications include:* William Morris, Viscount Nuffield 1976, The Air War 1939–1945 1980, The Nazi Economic Recovery 1982, Goering: The Iron Man 1984, The Origins of the Second World War 1987, The Road to War 1989, War and Economy in the Third Reich 1994, The Interwar Crisis 1919–1939 1994, Why the Allies Won 1995, The Penguin Atlas of the Third Reich 1996, The Times Atlas of the Twentieth Century 1996, Bomber Command 1939–1945 1997, Russia's War 1998, The Times History of the World (Gen. Ed.) 1999, The Battle 2000, Interrogations: The Nazi Elite in Allied Lands 1945 2001, The Dictators: Hitler's Germany and Stalin's Russia (Second Prize, Wolfson Prize for History 2004, Hessell-Tiltman Prize for History (jtly) 2005) 2004, What Britain Has Done: September 1939–May 1945 A Selection of Outstanding Facts and Figures 2007, The Morbid Age 2009, 1939: Countdown to War 2009, The Battle of Britain Experience 2010, Goering: Hitler's Iron Knight 2011, A Chronicle of the Third Reich 2011, The Bombing War: Europe 1939-1945 2013, The History of War in 100 Battles 2014, The Birth of the RAF 1918: The World's First Air Force 2018; contrib. to scholarly books and professional journals. *Leisure interests:* opera, art, antiquities. *Address:* College of Humanities, University of Exeter, Amory Building, Rennes Drive, Exeter, Devon, EX4 4RJ, England (office). *Fax:* (1392) 263291 (office). *E-mail:* r.overy@exeter.ac.uk (office). *Website:* humanities.exeter .ac.uk/history/staff/overy (office).

OVETT, Stephen Michael James (Steve), OBE; British fmr athlete; b. 9 Oct. 1955, Brighton, Sussex, England; m. Rachel Waller 1981 (divorced 2006); two s. two d.; pnr Carolyn Schuwalow; ed Varndean School, Brighton Coll. of Art; middle distance runner; European Jr Champion at 800m 1973; European Champion at 1500m, Prague 1978 and silver medallist at 800m Rome 1974, Prague 1978; competed at Olympic Games, Montreal 1976, finished 5th in 800m, reached semifinal of 1,500m; Moscow 1980, won gold medal at 800m and bronze medal at 1,500m; gold medal, Int. Asscn of Athletics Feds (IAAF) World Cup, Düsseldorf 1977, Rome 1980; gold medal, 5,000m, Commonwealth Games, Edinburgh 1986; set four world records; holder of record for greatest number of mile/1,500m victories (45 to 1980); also winner of major titles at 5,000m; holds UK record for the two miles, set in 1978; Track and field TV commentator for ITV, later for IAAF, for CBC since 1992; part of BBC's on-location commentary team for Commonwealth Games, Melbourne 2006; lives in Australia; BBC Sports Personality of the Year 1978, bronze statue of him erected in Preston Park, Brighton 1987. *Publication:* Ovett: An Autobiography. *Leisure interest:* art.

OVIA, Jim, BSc, MBA; Nigerian business executive; b. 4 Nov. 1951, Agbor; m.; ed Southern Univ., USA, Northeast Louisiana Univ. (now Univ. of Louisiana at Monroe), USA, Harvard Business School, USA; Bank Clerk, Barclays Bank (now Union Bank) 1973; part-time Computer Operator, Baton Rouge and Trust Co., Louisiana 1977; Financial Analyst, Int. Merchant Bank 1980, Sr Man. 1987; Head, Corporate Finance Dept, Merchant Bank of Africa 1987–90; Co-founder Zenith Bank plc 1990, Group Man. Dir and CEO 1990–2010; Pres. Nigeria Internet Group 2001–03; Founder Visafone Communications Ltd 2007–, also mem. Bd of Dirs; Chair. Quantum Luxury Properties Ltd, Nigerian Software Devt Initiative, Nat. Information Technology Advisory Council, Cttee on Nigeria Polio-Immunisation Action Group; Proprietor, Univ. of Information and Communication Tech., Agbor, Delta State; Founder-Chair. Youth Empowerment and ICT Foundation, Mankind United to Support Total Education; mem. Bd of Dirs Africa Finance Corpn, Transnational Corpn of Nigeria plc, American Int. School, Lagos 2001–03; mem. Governing Council, Nigerian Investment Promotion Comm. 1999–2007, Governing Council, Lagos State Univ., Hon. Int. Investor Council, Digital Bridge Inst.; mem. Bd of Trustees, Redeemer's Univ. for Nations; Order of the Fed. Repub. 2000; Hon. DSc (Lagos State Univ.) 2005; Zik Award 1999, Business Day's Award for top 10 bankers in Nigeria. *Address:* c/o Board of Directors, Visafone Communications Ltd., 4th Floor, Zenon House, 2, Ajose Adeogun Street, Victoria Island, Lagos, Nigeria.

OVITZ, Michael, BA; American entertainment industry executive; *Owner, Broad Beach Ventures LLC;* b. Dec. 1946, Chicago, Ill.; m. Judy Reich 1969; three c.; ed Birmingham High School and UCLA; tour guide at Universal Studios while at coll.; joined William Morris Agency, Beverly Hills 1968; with three others formed Creative Artists Agency (CAA) 1975, Pres. 1975–95; Pres. Walt Disney Co. 1995–97; private investor 1997–98; Head Livent Inc. Toronto 1998–99; Founder, CEO Artists Man. Group 1998–2002; Founder and Prin., CKE Assocs 1999–2002; now invests in startup technology and media cos, real estate and other ventures; Owner Broad Beach Ventures (portfolio of more than 30 cos) 2010–; mem. Bd of Dirs Museum of Modern Art, Bd of Advisors of Andreessen Horowitz; fmr mem. Bd of Dirs D.A.R.E. America, J. Crew Group Inc., Gulfstream Aviation, Opsware;

Chair. Exec. Bd UCLA Hosp. and Medical Center; Trustee, Museum of Modern Art, New York; mem. Bd of Advisors UCLA School of Theater, Film and Television, Exec. Advisory Bd Pediatric AIDS Foundation, Nat. Bd of Advisors for the Children's Scholarship Fund; mem. Council on Foreign Relations; considered amongst the world's top 200 art collectors, contemporary pieces include works by Pablo Picasso, Jasper Johns, Willem de Kooning, Barnett Newman, Mark Rothko and many others; Top 100 People of the Advertising Century, Ad Age. *Publications:* Who is Michael Ovitz ? 2018. *Address:* c/o Board of Advisors, UCLA School of Theater, Film and Television, 102 East Melnitz Hall, Box 951622, Los Angeles, CA 90095-1622, USA. *E-mail:* info@michaelovitz.com. *Website:* www.michaelovitz .com.

OVSYANNIKOV, Dmitrii Vladimirovich; Russian government official and business executive; *Governor and Chairman of the Government, Sevastopol City;* b. 21 Feb. 1977, Omsk, Russian FSFR, USSR; m.; four c.; ed Udmurt State Univ., Izhevsk, Tolyatti Acad. of Man., Tolyatti, Samara Oblast, Russian Acad. of State Service at the Office of the Presidency of the Russian Fed., Higher School of Econs, Moscow; worked in manufacturing sector in Izhevsk (Udmurt Repub.) and Chaikovskii (Perm Oblast—now Perm Krai), Fed. Insp. in Kirov Oblast 2001–04, in Udmurt Repub. 2004–; Deputy Gen. Dir, Chepets Mechanical Factory (Atomic Energy Sector), Glazov, Udmurt Repub. 2007–10; Deputy Man. Dir, Dir of Econs and Finance, Perm Motor Plant 2010–; Deputy Head, Financial and Econ. Dept, United Engine Corpn 2013–14; Head, Dept of Regional Industrial Policy, Ministry of Industry and Trade 2014–15; Deputy Minister of Industry and Trade 2015–16; Acting Gov. and Acting Chair. of the Govt, Sevastopol City 2016–17, Gov. and Chair. 2017–; Order 'For Merits Before Fatherland' 2016. *Address:* Office of the Governor, 299011 Sevastopol, ul. Lenina 2 (office). *Telephone:* (8692) 54-42-14 (office). *Fax:* (8692) 54-20-53 (office). *E-mail:* pravitelstvo@sevastopol.gov.ru (office). *Website:* en.kremlin.ru/catalog/persons/483/events (office); sevastopol.gov .ru (office).

OWADA, Hisashi, BA, LLB; Japanese judge, academic and fmr diplomatist; b. 18 Sept. 1932, Shibata, Niigata Pref.; s. of Takeo Owada and Shizuka Tamura; m. Yumiko Egashira 1962; three d. (one d. Masako Owada; m. Crown Prince Naruhito of Japan); ed Univ. of Tokyo, Univ. of Cambridge, UK; entered Foreign Service 1955, served in various posts in Ministry of Foreign Affairs, Tokyo and embassies in Moscow and Washington, DC, Pvt. Sec. to Minister of Foreign Affairs 1971–72, Pvt. Sec. to Prime Minister Takeo Fukuda 1976–78, Minister-Plenipotentiary, Embassy in Moscow 1981–84, Dir-Gen. Treaties Bureau and Office for Law of the Sea 1984–87, Deputy Vice-Minister, Ministry of Foreign Affairs 1987–88, Amb. to OECD, Paris 1988–89, Deputy Minister, Ministry of Foreign Affairs 1989–91, Vice-Minister of Foreign Affairs 1991–93, Adviser to Minister of Foreign Affairs 1993–94, 1999–2003, Amb. and Perm. Rep. to UN, New York 1994–98 (twice served as Pres. Security Council); Sr Adviser to Pres. of World Bank, Washington, DC 1999–2003; Adjunct Prof., Univ. of Tokyo 1963–88; Visiting Prof., Harvard Univ. 1979–81, 1987, 1989, 1999–2002, New York Univ. Law School 1994–; Prof., Waseda Univ. 1999–2003; Pres. Japan Inst. of Int. Affairs 1999–2003; Judge, Int. Court of Justice 2003–18, Pres. 2009–12; Associé de l'Institut de Droit Int.; mem. Bd of Dirs Nuclear Threat Initiative, UN Foundation; Al-Istiqlal Order, First Class (Jordan) 1990; Officier, Légion d'honneur 1992; Grand Cross, Order of Merit (FRG) 1994; Hon. LLD (Keiwa Univ., Banaras Hindu Univ., Waseda Univ.). *Publications include:* US–Japan Economic Interaction in an Independent World 1981, Japanese Perspectives on Asian Security 1982, Practice of Japan in International Law 1984, From Involvement to Engagement: A New Course for Japanese Foreign Policy 1994, Diplomacy 1997, A Treatise on International Relations 2003. *Leisure interests:* music, skiing, mountain walking. *Address:* c/o International Court of Justice, Peace Palace, Carnegieplein 2, 2517 KJ, The Hague, The Netherlands (office). *Telephone:* (70) 3022323 (office). *Fax:* (70) 3649928 (office). *E-mail:* info@icj -cij.org (office). *Website:* www.icj-cij.org (office).

OWEN, Clive; British actor; b. 3 Oct. 1964, Keresley, Warwicks.; m. Sarah-Jane Fenton; two d.; ed Royal Acad. of Dramatic Arts. *Films include:* Vroom 1988, Close My Eyes 1991, Century 1993, The Turnaround 1994, The Rich Man's Wife 1996, Bent 1997, Croupier 1998, Greenfingers 2000, The Hire: Ambush 2001, The Hire: Chosen 2001, The Hire: The Follow 2001, The Hire: Star 2001, The Hire: Powder Keg 2001, Gosford Park 2001, A Day in the Death of Joe Egg 2001, Beyond Borders 2002, The Bourne Identity 2002, The Hire: Hostage 2002, The Hire: Beat the Devil 2002, The Hire: Ticker 2002, I'll Sleep When I'm Dead 2003, Beyond Borders 2003, King Arthur 2004, Closer (Best Supporting Actor, Golden Globe Awards 2005, Best Actor in a Supporting Role, BAFTA Awards 2005) 2004, Sin City 2005, Derailed 2005, Inside Man 2006, Children of Men 2006, Shoot 'Em Up 2007, Elizabeth: The Golden Age 2007, The International 2009, Duplicity 2009, The Boys are Back 2009, Intruders 2011, Shadow Dancer 2012, Blood Ties 2013, Words and Pictures 2013, Last Knights 2015, The Confirmation 2016, Valerian and the City of a Thousand Planets 2017, Ophelia 2018, Gemini Man 2019. *Television includes:* Precious Bane 1989, Capital City (series) 1989, Lorna Doone 1990, Chancer (series) 1990, The Magician 1993, Class of '61 1993, Nobody's Children 1994, An Evening with Gary Lineker 1994, Doomsday Gun 1994, The Return of the Native 1994, Bad Boy Blues 1995, Sharman (series) 1996, The Echo 1998, Split Second 1999, Second Sight 1999, Second Sight: Parasomnia 2000, Second Sight: Kingdom of the Blind 2000, Second Sight II: Hide and Seek 2000, Hemingway & Gellhorn 2012, The Knick (series) 2014–15. *Stage appearances include:* Design for Living 1994, Closer 1997. *Address:* c/o Creative Artists Agency, 9830 Wilshire Blvd, Beverly Hills, CA 90212- 1825, USA.

OWEN, Baron (Life Peer), cr. 1992, of the City of Plymouth; **David Anthony Llewellyn Owen,** CH, PC, MA, MB, BChir, FRCP; British politician and fmr business executive; b. 2 July 1938, Plymouth, Devon; s. of John William Morris Owen and Mary Llewellyn; m. Deborah Schabert 1968; two s. one d.; ed Bradfield Coll., Sidney Sussex Coll., Cambridge, St Thomas' Hosp.; trained as a doctor specializing in neurology; house appointments, St Thomas' Hosp. 1962–64, Neurological and Psychiatric Registrar 1964–66, Research Fellow, Medical Unit 1966–68; MP for Sutton Div. of Plymouth 1966–74, for Devonport Div. of Plymouth 1974–92; Parl. Pvt. Sec. to Minister of Defence, Admin. 1967; Parl. Under-Sec. of State for Defence, RN 1968–70; Opposition Defence Spokesman 1970–72, resgnd over party policy on EEC 1972; Parl. Under-Sec. of State, Dept of Health and Social Security (DHSS) March–July 1974; Minister of State, DHSS 1974–76, FCO

1976–77; Sec. of State for Foreign and Commonwealth Affairs 1977–79; Opposition Spokesman for Energy 1979–80; co-f. Social Democratic Party (SDP) 1981; Chair. Parl. Cttee 1981–82; Deputy Leader SDP 1982–83, Leader 1983–87, 1988–92; now Ind. Social Democrat; mem. House of Lords 1992–; mem. Palme Comm. on Disarmament and Security Issues 1980–89, Ind. Comm. on Int. Humanitarian Issues 1983–88; EC Co-Chair. Int. Conf. on fmr Yugoslavia 1992–95, Carnegie Comm. on Preventing Deadly Conflict 1994–2000; Chair. Global Natural Energy 1996–2006, New Europe 1999–2005, Europe Steel 2000–15, Yukos Int. 2002–05; mem. Bd of Dirs, Abbott Laboratories Inc. 1996–2011; Dir (non-exec.), Coats Viyella 1994–2001, Intelligent Energy 2003–05, Hyperdynamics Corpn 2009–14; Dir Center for Int. Health and Co-operation; Chancellor Univ. of Liverpool 1996–2009; Pres. River Thames Soc.; Freeman, City of Plymouth 2000. *Publications:* Ed.: A Unified Health Service 1968; contrib.: Social Services for All 1968; author: The Politics of Defence 1972, In Sickness and in Health – The Politics of Medicine 1976, Human Rights 1978, Face the Future 1981, A Future that Will Work 1984, A United Kingdom 1986, Personally Speaking to Kenneth Harris 1987, Our NHS 1988, Time to Declare (autobiog.) 1991, Seven Ages (poetry) 1992, Balkan Odyssey 1995, The Hubris Syndrome: Bush, Blair and the Intoxication of Power 2007 (revised edn 2012), In Sickness and in Power 2008 (revised edn 2016), Time to Declare: Second Innings (updated and abridged autobiog.) 2009, Nuclear Papers 2009, Europe Restructured: The European Crisis and Its Aftermath 2012, Bosnia-Herzegovina: The Vance-Owen Peace Plan 2013, Health of the Nation – NHS in Peril 2014, The Hidden Perspective – The Military Conversations 1906–1914 2014, Cabinet's Finest Hour – The Hidden Agenda of May 1940 2014, British Foreign Policy After Brexit 2017, Hubris: The Road to Donald Trump, Power, Populism, Narcissism 2018; articles in The Lancet, Neurology, Clinical Science and Brain. *Leisure interest:* sailing. *Address:* House of Lords, Westminster, London, SW1A 0PW (office); 78 Narrow Street, Limehouse, London, E14 8BP, England (home). *Telephone:* (1442) 872617 (office); (20) 7987-5441 (home). *Fax:* (1442) 876108 (home). *E-mail:* davidowen@lorddavidowen.co.uk (office). *Website:* www.parliament.uk/biographies/lords/lord-owen/992 (office); www.lorddavidowen.co.uk.

OWEN, Michael James; British fmr professional football player and commentator; b. 14 Dec. 1979, Chester, Cheshire; s. of Terence Owen and Jeanette Owen; m. Louise Bonsall 2005; one s. three d.; ed Hawarden High School, Flintshire, Wales, Idsall High School, Shifnal, Shropshire; striker; youth player, Liverpool Football Club 1991–96, sr player 1996–2004 (306 games, 179 goals), scored during debut against Wimbledon May 1997 (youngest ever Liverpool player to score), 21 goals in European competition (club record), won FA Cup 2001, Football League Cup 2001, 2003, FA Community Shield 2001, UEFA Cup 2001, European Super Cup 2001, FA Youth Cup 1996; player for Real Madrid, Spain 2004–05 (43 games, 19 goals), Newcastle United 2005–09 (Capt. 2008–09) (74 games, 30 goals), Manchester United 2009–12 (49 games, 17 goals), won League Cup 2009–10, FA Community Shield 2010, Premier League 2010–11, Stoke City 2012–13 (eight games, one goal); player for England U-20 team 1997 (four caps, three goals), England U-21 team 1997 (one cap, one goal), England team 1998–2008 (89 caps and 40 goals, scored hat-trick in 5–1 victory over Germany in World Cup qualifier 2001, won FA Summer Tournament 2004), England B team 2006–07 (two caps, no goals); lead co-commentator, BT Sport's football coverage 2013–; Professional Footballers' Asscn Young Player of the Year 1998, Premier League jt top scorer: 1998, 1999, BBC Sports Personality of the Year 1998, Ballon d'Or (European Footballer of the Year) 2001, Domestic Team of the Decade – Premier League 10 Seasons Awards (1992/93–2001/02), named to FIFA 100, Golden Foot 2017. *Film appearance:* Goal II: Living the Dream 2006. *Publication:* Michael Owen: Off the Record 2004. *Leisure interests:* golf, table-tennis, snooker. *Address:* BT Correspondence Centre, Providence Row, Durham, DH98 1BT, England. *Telephone:* (20) 7356-5000. *Website:* home.bt.com.

OWEN, Robert John Richard, MA; British financial industry official; *Chairman, International Securities Consultancy Ltd;* b. 11 Feb. 1940, London; s. of Thomas R. Owen and Margaret Fletcher; m. Beatrice M. Voelker 1962 (divorced); two s. one d.; ed Repton School and Oriel Coll., Oxford; Foreign Office 1961–68, served in British Embassy, Washington, DC 1964–68; HM Treasury 1968–70; Morgan Grenfell & Co. Ltd 1970–79, Dir 1973; Dir Merchant Banking Div. Lloyds Bank Int., Ltd 1979–82, Dir Far East Div. 1982–84; Dir of Investment Banking, Lloyds Bank PLC and Chair. Lloyds Merchant Bank, Ltd 1984–88; Adviser to Hong Kong Govt on implementation of Securities Review Cttee Report 1988–89; Chair. Securities and Futures Comm. of Hong Kong 1989–92; Dir European Capital Co. Ltd 1992–, Regulatory Bd and Council of Lloyd's of London 1993–95; Deputy Chair. Nomura Int. Ltd, Hong Kong 1993– (now Sr Adviser), Capital Ltd, Crosby Ltd; Chair. Crosby Capital Ltd 2001, KASB Funds Ltd; mem. Bd of Dirs Singapore Stock Exchange 2004–13 (now Adviser), IB Daiwa Corpn, Yaohan Int. Holdings 1993, Int. Securities Consultancy Ltd 1995– (now Chair.), Regent Pacific Group Ltd 1998, ECK and Partners Ltd 1999, TechPacific Ltd 1999–2004, Citibank, Hong Kong 2005; fmr Adviser, Dubai Financial Services Authority; Gov. Repton School; mem. Regulatory Council, Dubai Int. Financial Centre 2002–. *Leisure interests:* mountain walking, collecting oriental paintings and carvings. *Address:* International Securities Consultancy Ltd, 9th Floor, Carfield Commercial Building, 75-77 Wyndham Street, Central, Hong Kong Special Administrative Region, People's Republic of China (office). *Telephone:* 28773417 (office). *Fax:* 28770914 (office). *E-mail:* info@isc-global.com (office). *Website:* www.isc-global.com (office).

OWEN-JONES, Sir Lindsay, KBE, BA, MBA; British business executive; *Honorary President, L'Oréal;* b. 17 March 1946, Wallasey; s. of Hugh A. Owen-Jones and Esmee Owen-Jones (née Lindsay); m. 1st; one d.; m. 2nd Cristina Furno 1994; ed Univ. of Oxford and European Inst. of Business Admin (INSEAD); Product Man. L'Oréal 1969, Head, Public Products Div., Belgium 1971–74, Man. SCAD (L'Oréal subsidiary), Paris 1974–76, Marketing Man. Public Products Div., Paris 1976–78, Gen. Man. SAIPO (L'Oréal subsidiary, Italy) 1978–81, Pres. COSMAIR Inc. (exclusive L'Oréal agent) USA 1981–83, apptd mem. Bd of Dirs 1984 (resgnd 2013), Vice-Pres. L'Oréal Man. Cttee 1984, Pres. and COO 1984–88, Chair. and CEO 1988–2006, Chair. 2006–11, now Hon. Pres.; mem. Bd of Dirs Banque Nat. de Paris 1989–, Lafarge 1993–2001, Air Liquide Canada, Inc. 1994–; Fellow, Worcester Coll., Oxford; Officier, Légion d'honneur; Hon. DSc (Cranfield School of Man.); named by Futuro magazine as Best European Manager 2002, Challenges magazine Best Manager of the Last 20 Years 2002, Le Nouvel Economiste magazine Manager of the Year 2002. *Leisure interest:* sailing. *Address:* L'Oréal, 41 rue Martre, 92117 Clichy Cedex, France (office). *Telephone:* 1-47-56-70-00 (office). *Fax:* 1-47-56-80-02 (office). *E-mail:* info@loreal.com (office). *Website:* www.loreal.com (office).

OWENS, James W., PhD; American economist and business executive; b. Elizabeth City, NC; ed North Carolina State Univ.; Corp. Economist, Caterpillar Inc. 1972–75, Chief Economist, Caterpillar Overseas SA, Geneva 1975–80, Man. Accounting and Product Source Planning Dept, Peoria, Ill. 1980–87, Man. Dir, P. T. Natra Raya, Indonesia 1987–90, Corp. Vice-Pres. 1990, also Pres. Solar Turbines Inc., San Diego 1990, Vice-Pres. and Chief Financial Officer, Caterpillar Corp. Services Div., Peoria 1993–95, Group Pres. Caterpillar Inc. 1995–2004, Chair. and CEO 2004–10 (retd); mem. Bd of Dirs IBM Corp., Alcoa Inc. 2005–, Morgan Stanley 2011–; Sr Advisor, Kohlberg Kravis Roberts & Co. LP 2011–; Chair. Exec. Cttee Peterson Inst. for Int. Econs; mem. Bd of Trustees North Carolina State Univ.; mem. Council on Foreign Relations, Business Roundtable, Global Advisory Council to The Conf. Bd, New York, Community Advisory Bd, St Francis Medical Center, Peoria; Watauga Medal, North Carolina State Univ.

OWENS, William (Bill) F., BA, MPA; American business executive and fmr state official; *Chairman of the Supervisory Board, Credit Bank of Moscow;* b. 22 Oct. 1950, Fort Worth, Tex.; m. Frances Owens; two s. one d.; ed Austin State Univ., LBJ School of Public Affairs, Univ. of Texas; fmrly with Touche Ross & Co., Gates Corpn; served as Exec. Dir Colorado Petroleum Asscn and Exec. Vice-Pres. Rocky Mountain Oil and Gas Asscn; mem. Colorado House of Reps 1983–89, Colorado Senate 1989–95, Colorado State Treas. 1994–99, Gov. of Colorado 1999–2007; fmr Vice-Chair. RBS Greenwich Capital Markets, Inc.; Partner, JCB Group 2007–; Man. Dir Renew Strategies, LLC, Front Range Resources; Chair. Supervisory Bd, Credit Bank Of Moscow OAO 2013–; mem. Bd of Dirs Key Energy Services Inc. 2007–, Federal Signal Corpn 2011–, Bill Barrett Corpn 2010–, Cloud Peak Energy, Inc. 2010–; mem. Bd of Dirs FESCO Transport Group 2007–12. *Publications:* contrib. to professional journals. *Address:* Credit Bank Of Moscow, 107045 Moscow, 2 Str. 1, Per. Lukov, Russia (office). *Website:* mkb.ru (office).

OWONO EDU, Marcelino; Equatorial Guinean politician; b. 1963, Mongomo; ed studied econs in Ukraine; several posts within Ministry of Economy and Finance, including as Dir-Gen. of Financial Control, Dir-Gen. of Autonomous Entities, Dir-Gen. of Imports and Contribution, Dir-Gen. of Budgets, Minister of Finance and the Budget 2003–08, 2012–15, of Mines, Industry and Energy 2008–12; Alt. Gov. for Equatorial Guinea, ADB Group.

OWUSU-AGYEMANG, Hackman, MSc; Ghanaian politician and economist; *Chairman, Ghana Cocoa Board;* b. 22 Nov. 1941, Effiduase-Koforidua; ed St Augustine's Coll., Cape Coast, Kwame Nkrumah Univ. of Science and Tech., Kumasi, Inst. of Social Studies, The Hague, Netherlands, Wye Coll., Univ. of London, UK; economist, Ministry of Agric. 1965–68, Sr Agricultural Economist 1968–70; economist, Econ. Analysis Div., FAO, Rome, Field Programme Officer, FAO-Regional Co-operation and Liaison Officer for Africa 1970–84; FAO Rep. in Zambia, Trinidad and Tobago 1979–84; Chief FAO Regional Bureau for Africa, Italy 1984; mem. New Patriotic Party (NPP) 1982–; mem. Parl. for New Juaben 1996–; Shadow Minister of Foreign Affairs 2000–01, Minister 2001–03; Minister of the Interior 2003–05, for Water Resources, Works and Housing 2005–07; Chair. Ghana Cocoa Bd 2017–. *Address:* Cocoa House, 41 Kwame Nkrumah Avenue, PO Box 933, Accra, Ghana (office). *Telephone:* (21) 661872 (office). *Fax:* (21) 661681 (office). *Website:* cocobod.gh (office).

OXBURGH, Baron (Life Peer), cr. 1999, of Liverpool in the County of Merseyside; **Ernest Ronald Oxburgh,** Kt, KBE, PhD, FRS; British geologist/geophysicist; b. 2 Nov. 1934, Liverpool, England; s. of Ernest Oxburgh and Violet Bugden; m. Ursula Mary Brown 1934; one s. two d.; ed Liverpool Inst., Univ. of Oxford and Princeton Univ., USA; Departmental Demonstrator, Univ. of Oxford 1960–61, Lecturer in Geology 1962–78, Fellow, St Edmund Hall 1964–78, Emer. Fellow 1978, Hon. Fellow 1986; Prof. of Mineralogy and Petrology, Univ. of Cambridge 1978–91, Head of Dept of Earth Sciences 1980–88; Chief Scientific Adviser, Ministry of Defence 1988–93; Rector Imperial Coll. of Science, Tech. and Medicine 1993–2001; Fellow, Trinity Hall, Cambridge 1978–82, Hon. Fellow 1983; Pres. Queens' Coll., Cambridge 1982–89, Hon. Fellow 1989; Chair. D1 Oils PLC 2007–09, Falck Renewables 2008–10; mem. Bd of Dirs, Shell Transport and Trading Co. 1996–2005 (Chair. 2004–05), Nirex 1996–97; Sherman Fairchild Distinguished Scholar, California Inst. of Tech. 1985–86; Pres. European Union of Geosciences 1985–87, Geological Soc. of London 2000–01, Carbon Capture and Storage Asscn 2005–15; mem. Nat. Cttee of Inquiry into Higher Educ. (Dearing Cttee) 1996–97; mem. (Crossbench), House of Lords 1999–, Chair. House of Lords Select Cttee on Science and Tech. 2001–04; Trustee, Natural History Museum 1993–2002, Chair. of Trustees 1999–2002; Chair. SETNET 2001–05; Foreign mem. Venezuelan Acad. of Sciences 1992, Deutsche Akad. der Naturforscher Leopoldina 1994, Australian Acad. of Sciences 1999, NAS 2001, American Philosophical Soc. 2006; Hon. mem. Geologists Asscn; Hon. FREng 2002; Hon. Citizen of Singapore 2012; Officier des Palmes académiques 1995; Hon. DSc (Paris) 1986, (Leicester) 1990, (Loughborough) 1991, (Edin.) 1994, (Birmingham, Liverpool) 1996, (Southampton) 2003, (John Moores Univ.) 2006, (Newcastle) 2007, (Leeds) 2009, (Wyoming) 2011, (St Andrews) 2013; Bigsby Medal, Geological Soc. of London 1979, Public Service Medal of Singapore 2009, Sir Geo Thompson Gold Medal, Inst. of Measurement and Control 2010, Melchett Award, Energy Inst. 2014. *Publications:* The Geology of the Eastern Alps (ed. and contrib.) 1968, Structural, Metamorphic and Geochronological Studies in the Eastern Alps 1971 and contribs to Nature, Journal of Geophysical Research, Tectonophysics, Journal of the Geological Soc. of London and other learned journals. *Leisure interests:* reading, various sports. *Address:* House of Lords, Westminster, London, SW1A 0PW, England (office). *Telephone:* (20) 7219-5353 (office). *Fax:* (20) 7219-5979 (office). *E-mail:* oxburghe@parliament.uk (office). *Website:* www.parliament.uk/biographies/lords/lord-oxburgh/2494 (office).

ØYE, Harald Arnljot, MSc, DTech; Norwegian chemist and academic; *Professor Emeritus, Norwegian University of Science and Technology;* b. 1 Feb. 1935, Oslo; s. of Leiv C. Øye and Ingrid H. Øye; m. Tove Stiegler 1963; two s. one d.; ed Norwegian Inst. of Tech.; Postdoctoral Fellow, Argonne Nat. Lab., Illinois, USA

1963–64; Assoc. Prof., Inst. of Inorganic Chem., Norwegian Inst. of Tech. 1965–72, Prof. and Head of Inst., Norwegian Univ. of Science and Tech. (fmrly Norwegian Inst. of Tech.) 1973–90, 1992–98, Prof., Chem. Dept, later Dept of Materials Tech. 1999–2006, Prof. Emer. 2006–; Pres. Norwegian Acad. of Tech. Sciences 1985–92, Hon. Fellow 1993–; guest scientist at various insts in Germany, Italy, USA, France, New Zealand, Switzerland, UK; Brotherton Distinguished Prof., Univ. of Leeds 1985; Hon. Prof., North-Eastern Univ., Shenyang, People's Repub. of China; Kt First Class, Royal Norwegian Order of St Olav; Prize for Outstanding Research, Research Council of Norway 1997, Guldberg-Waage Medal, Norwegian Chemical Soc. 1998, Max Bredig Award, Electrochemical Soc., USA 1998, Royal Norwegian Soc. of Sciences and Letters Gunnerus Gold Medal 2004. *Publications include:* Cathodes in Aluminium Electrolysis (with M. Sørlie) 1991; more than 400 publs on electrowinning of aluminium and magnesium, characterization of silicon, carbon technology, transport properties, molten salt chem., spectroscopy and thermodynamics of high temperature systems. *Leisure interests:* reading, outdoor activities. *Address:* Department of Materials Technology, Norwegian University of Science and Technology, 7491 Trondheim (office); Steinhaugen 5, 7049 Trondheim, Norway (home). *Telephone:* 73-93-75-58 (office); 73-93-75-58 (home). *Fax:* 73-59-39-92 (office). *E-mail:* oye@material.ntnu.no (office). *Website:* www.ntnu.edu/employees/haoye (office).

OYÉ-MBA, Casimir, LLD; Gabonese banker and politician; b. 20 April 1942, Nzamaligue Village, Libreville; s. of Ange Mba and Marie-Jeanne Nse; m. Marie-Françoise Razafimbelo 1963; three s. three d.; ed Univs of Rennes and Paris, France; trainee, Banque Centrale, Libreville 1967–69, Asst Dir 1969–70, Dir 1970–73; Nat. Dir Banque pour le Gabon 1973–76; Asst Dir-Gen. Banque Centrale 1977–78; Gov. Banque des Etats de l'Afrique Centrale 1978–90; Prime Minister of Gabon 1990–94; Minister of Foreign Affairs and Co-operation 1994–99; fmr Minister of State for Planning and Devt; Sr Minister of Mining, Oil, Energy and Water 2007–09; Alt. Gov. IMF for Gabon 1969–76; apptd Pres. Assn des Banques Centrales Africaines 1987; elected mem. Parl. for Komo-Mondah dist 1990, re-elected 1996, 2001, 2006; mem. political bureau, Gabonese Democratic Party 1991; Campaign Man. for Pres. Omar Bongo 1993; Gabon mem. Bd of Govs of World Bank 1999; mem. Ntoum City Council; unsuccessful presidential cand. 2009; Commdr, Légion d'honneur; Gabon, Cameroon, Congo, Equatorial Guinea and Cen. African Repub. decorations. *Leisure interests:* football, tennis, cinema, reading, travelling. *E-mail:* casimir.oyemba@yahoo.fr (home). *Website:* www.oyemba.org (office).

OYELOWO, David Oyetokunbo, OBE; British actor, writer and director; *Co-Director, Inservice Productions;* b. 1 April 1976, Oxford, England; s. of Stephen Oyelowo; m. Jessica Oyelowo 1998; four c.; ed Model Coll., Lagos, Nigeria, Highbury Grove Boys, Islington Sixth Form Centre, London Acad. of Music and Dramatic Art; left drama school early to do work on BBC TV series Maisie Raine 1998; joined the RSC 1999, played Henry VI 2000, first black actor to play an English King at the RSC, mem. Bd of Dirs RSC 2005–; Amb. for the Prince's Trust 2003–; Co-Dir Inservice Productions; London Acad. of Music and Dramatic Art Scholarship of Excellence, Ian Charleson Award for Best Newcomer 2001, Gold Award for Achievement beyond Further Educ., GAB (Gathering of Africa's Best) Award for Excellence. *Plays:* The Suppliants (Gate Theatre, London) 1998; Oroonoko, Volpone, Antony and Cleopatra (RSC) 1999; Henry VI Parts 1, 2, 3 (RSC) 2001, Richard III, The Godbrothers (Bush Theatre London), Prometheus Bound (Sound Theatre, London, Classic Stage Co., New York); Dir: The Man of Mode (Pavilion Theatre), The White Devil (Pavilion Theatre). *Films include:* Dog Eat Dog 2001, Tomorrow La Scala! 2002, A Sound of Thunder 2005, Spice of Life 2005, The Best Man 2005, Derailed 2005, American Blend 2006, Shoot the Messenger 2006, The Last King of Scotland 2006, As You Like It 2006, Chess 2008, Who Do You Love 2008, Rage 2009, Change in the Wind (voice) 2010, Rise of the Planet of the Apes 2011, The Help 2011, 96 Minutes 2011, Red Tails 2012, Middle of Nowhere 2012, The Paperboy 2012, Lincoln 2012, Jack Reacher 2012, The Butler 2013, Nightingale 2014, Default 2014, Interstellar 2014, A Most Violent Year 2014, Selma 2014, Five Nights in Maine 2015, Captive 2015, A United Kingdom 2016, Queen of Katwe 2016, Nina 2016, Queen of Katwe 2016, Gringo 2018, Chaos Walking 2019. *Television includes:* Maisie Raine (series) 1998, Brothers and Sisters (series) 1998, Spooks 2002–04, Tomorrow La Scala (film) 2002, As Time Goes By 2005, Mayo (series) 2006, Born Equal (film) 2006, Five Days (series) 2007, A Raisin in the Sun (film) 2008, The Passion (mini-series) 2008, The No. 1 Ladies' Detective Agency (series) 2008, Sweet Nothing in My Ear (film) 2008, Small Island (film) 2009, Blood and Oil (film) 2010, Glenn Martin DDS (series) 2010–11, The Good Wife (series) 2011, Complicit (film) 2013, Star Wars Rebels (series) 2014, Nightingale (mini-series) (Critics' Choice Television Award for Best Actor in a Movie/Miniseries) 2014, Robot Chicken (series) (voice) 2014; writer: Graham & Alice (BBC). *Radio:* The Faerie Queen (BBC), Man Talk, Woman Talk (BBC), Oroonoko (BBC), The Word (BBC). *Publications:* Actors on Shakespeare: Henry VI 2003. *Leisure interests:* drawing, film, tennis, football, travel, writing. *Address:* c/o Hamilton Hodell Management, 66–68 Margaret Street, London, W1W 8SR, England. *Telephone:* (20) 7636-1221. *Fax:* (20) 7636-1226.

ÖYMEN, Onur Başaran, PhD; Turkish diplomatist and politician; b. 18 Oct. 1940, Kadıköy, Istanbul; s. of Münir Raşit Öymen and Nebahat Öymen; m. Nedret Gürsel 1971; one s. one d.; ed Galatasay Lisesi, Istanbul, Univ. of Ankara; joined Ministry of Foreign Affairs 1964; mil. service 1964–66; Second Sec. NATO Dept, Ministry of Foreign Affairs 1966–68, First Sec. Perm. Del. to Council of Europe, Strasbourg 1968–72, Chief of Section, Policy Planning Dept, Ministry of Foreign Affairs 1972–74, Counsellor Turkish Embassy, Nicosia 1974–78; Special Adviser to Minister of Foreign Affairs 1978–80; Counsellor, Turkish Embassy, Prague 1980–82, Madrid 1982–84; Head Policy Planning Dept, Ministry of Foreign Affairs 1984–88; Amb. to Denmark 1988–90, to Germany 1990–95; Under-Sec. Ministry of Foreign Affairs 1995–97; Perm. Rep. to NATO 1997–2002; mem. Grand Nat. Ass. of Turkey (Parl.) 2002–; Deputy Leader, Cumhuriyet Halk Partisi (CHP—Republican People's Party) 2003–10; mem. IISS, London, UK; Bureaucrat of the Year, Nokta Review 1995, Diplomat of the Year, Assn of Turkish Industrialists and Business 1995, 1996, 1997; Abdi Ipekçi Special Peace Award, Milliyet newspaper 1997, Politician of the Year Award, Nokta Dergisi 2005. *Publications:* Türkiye 'nin Gücü (Turkish Strength) 1998 (trans. into Turkish of Science and Common Sense by Oppenheimer), Geleceği Yakalamak: Küreselleşme ve Devlet Reformu (Catch the Future: Globalization and Government Reform) 2000, Silahsız Savaş: Bir Mücadele Sanatı Olarak Diplomasi (Unarmed War: Diplomacy as a Fighting Art) 2002, Ulusal Çıkarlar: Küreselleşme Çağında Ulus Devleti Korumak (National Interests: Protecting the Nation State in the Age of Globalization) 2005, Çıkış Yolu (Exit Path) 2008. *Address:* TBMM, 06543 Bakanlıklar, Ankara, Turkey (office). *E-mail:* assembly@tbmm.gov.tr (office). *Website:* www.tbmm.gov.tr/develop/owa/milletvekillerimiz_sd.bilgi?p_donem=23&&p_sicil=6335 (office); www.onuroymen.com.

OYUN, Sanjaasurengin, DPhil; Mongolian geologist and politician; *President, United Nations Environment Assembly (UNEA);* b. 18 Jan. 1964, Ulan Bator; m.; three c.; ed Univ. of Cambridge, UK, Charles Univ., Prague, Czech Repub.; worked as exploration geologist on surveys in Mongolia and for Rio Tinto-Zinc; elected mem. Mongolian Great Khural (Parl.) 1998; Founder and Chair. Civil Will Party (Irgenii Zorig Nam) 2000–; Minister of Foreign Affairs 2007–08; Pres., UN Environment Ass. (UNEA) 2014–; Founder and Head of Zorig Foundation. *Address:* United Nations Environment Programme, United Nations Avenue, Gigiri, PO Box 30552, 00100, Nairobi, Kenya (office). *Telephone:* (20) 7621234 (office). *Website:* www.unep.org (office).

OZAWA, Ichiro, BA; Japanese politician; b. 24 May 1942, Mizusawa, Iwate Pref.; s. of Saeki Ozawa and Michi Ozawa; m. Kazuko Fukuda 1973; three s.; ed Keio Univ.; mem. House of Reps representing Iwate Prefecture 1967–; Minister of Home Affairs 1985–87; fmr Deputy Chief Cabinet Sec.; fmr Dir-Gen. Liberal-Democratic Party (LDP) Election Bureau; Sec.-Gen. LDP 1989–91; Chair. Cttee on Rules and Admin.; left LDP 1993; Co-Founder and Sec.-Gen. Shinseito (Japan Renewal Party) 1993–94; Sec.-Gen. Shinshinto (New Frontier Party) 1994–95, Pres. 1995–97; Founder and Pres. Jiyuto (Liberal Party) 1998–2003 (resgnd), Acting Pres. Democratic Party of Japan (DPJ) (after merger with Liberal Party) 2003–04, Vice-Pres. 2004–05, Pres. 2006–09, Sec.-Gen. 2009–10; f. People's Life First (PLF) 2012 (dissolved). *Publication:* Blueprint for a New Japan 1993. *Leisure interests:* fishing, Go. *Address:* c/o Democratic Party of Japan (DPJ), 1-11-1, Nagata-cho, Chiyoda-ku, Tokyo, 100-0014 (office); 2-38 Fukuro-machi, Mizusawa-shi, Iwate-ken 023-0814, Japan (home).

OZAWA, Sakihito, LLB; Japanese politician; b. 31 May 1954, Yamanashi Pref.; ed Tokyo Univ., Grad. School of Political Science, Saitama Univ.; began career in foreign currency exchange dept, Bank of Tokyo Ltd 1981; mem. House of Reps for Yamanashi 1st Dist constituency 1993–, Chief Dir Parl. Cttee on Financial Affairs 2006; fmr mem. Japan New Party; mem. Democratic Party of Japan 1996–, various party roles including Deputy Chair. Diet Affairs Cttee 1996, Deputy Chair. Policy Research Council 1998, Deputy Sec.-Gen. 1998, 2006, Chief of Office of Party Pres. 2001, Deputy Chief, Global Warming Prevention HQ 2008; Next (Shadow) Minister of Information and Communication 1999, Shadow Minister of the Economy, Trade and Industry 2002; Minister of the Environment 2009–10. *Address:* c/o Democratic Party, 1-11-1, Nagata-cho, Chiyoda-ku, Tokyo 100-0014, Japan.

OZAWA, Seiji; Japanese conductor; b. 1 Sept. 1935, Shenyang, China; m. 1st Kyoko Edo; m. 2nd Vera Ilyan; one s. one d.; ed Toho School of Music, Japan with Prof. Hideo Saito, Tanglewood, USA and in Berlin under Herbert von Karajan; Asst Conductor (under Leonard Bernstein), New York Philharmonic 1961–62 (including tour of Japan 1961); Guest Conductor, San Francisco Symphony, Detroit Symphony, Montréal, Minneapolis, Toronto and London Symphony Orchestras 1961–65; Music Dir Ravinia Festival, Chicago 1964–68; Music Dir Toronto Symphony Orchestra 1965–69, San Francisco Symphony Orchestra 1970–76, Boston Symphony Orchestra 1973–2002 (now Music Dir Laureate), Vienna State Opera 2002–10; Co-founder, Saito Kinen Orchestra 1987, Saito Kinen Festival Matsumoto 1992, Tokyo Opera Nomori 2005; toured Europe conducting many of the major orchestras 1966–67; Salzburg Festival 1969; toured USA, France, FRG, China 1979, Austria, UK 1981, Japan 1981, 1986, toured England, Netherlands, France, Germany, Austria and Belgium 1988; est. International Music Acad., Geneva 2005; makes frequent guest appearances with leading orchestras of America, Europe and Japan; has conducted opera at Salzburg, Covent Garden, La Scala, Vienna Staatsoper and Paris Opera; conducted world premiere, Messiaen's St Francis of Assisi, Paris 1983; Hon. mem. Vienna Staatsoper 2007; Chevalier, Légion d'Honneur 1999, Order of Friendship (Russia) 2011; Hon. DMus (Univ. of Mass., New England Conservatory, Wheaton Coll., Norton, Mass.); Dr hc (Univ. of Paris—Sorbonne) 2004; First Prize, Int. Competition of Orchestra Conductors, France 1959, Koussevitsky Prize for outstanding student conductor 1960, Laureate, Fondation du Japon 1988, Inouye Award 1994, Japan Art Assn Praemium Imperiale 2011, Tanglewood Medal 2012, Kennedy Center Honoree 2015, Grammy Award for Best Opera Recording 2016. *Leisure interests:* golf, tennis, skiing. *Address:* c/o Ronald A. Wilford, Columbia Artists Management Inc., 5 Columbus Circle at 1790 Broadway, New York NY 10019-1412, USA (office). *Website:* www.saito-kinen.com.

ÖZAYDINLI, F. Bülend; Turkish business executive; *Executive Chairman, Migros Ticaret AS;* b. 1949, Eskişehir; ed Izmir Maarif Coll., American Univ. of Beirut, Lebanon; Asst Man. Oyak 1972–76; Regional Man. Motorlu Araçlar Tic. AS 1976–79; Asst Gen. Man. Oyak 1979–87; Investments Co-ordinator, Migros Türk TAS 1987–88; Asst Gen. Man. Maret AS 1988–90; Gen. Man. Migros Türk TAS 1990–2001; Deputy CEO Koç Holding AS 2001, CEO 2002–07, also mem. Bd of Dirs; Chair. Migros Turk TAS (now Migros Ticaret AS) 2008–; Pres. Fiat Group 2001. *Address:* Migros Ticaret AS, Ataturk Mahallesi Turgut Ozal Bulvari No:7, Atasehir, Istanbul 34758, Turkey (office). *Telephone:* (216) 5793000 (office). *Website:* www.migros.com.tr (office).

OZBEK, (Ibrahim Mehmet) Rifat, BA; Turkish/British couturier; b. 8 Nov. 1953, Istanbul; s. of Melike Osbek and Abdulazim Mehmet Ismet; pnr Erdel Karaman; ed St Martin's School of Art, London; moved to London 1970s; worked with Walter Albini for Trell; went to Italy following graduation and designed clothes for Monsoon Co.; launched O for Ozbek (now Future Ozbek) 1984, began to show yearly collections in Milan and New York and, more recently, in Paris; launched own perfume 'Ozbek' 1995, and later a second perfume called 'Ozbek 1001'; began presenting collections for Pollini 2004; launched new business 'Yastik' (cushion) 2010; interior designer for Robin Birley's nightclub (Rupert's), opened 2011; lives between London, Istanbul and Bodrum; Woman Magazine Designer Award 1986, British Fashion Council Designer of the Year 1988, 1992, British

Glamour Award 1989. *Address:* Şakayık Sokak, Olcay Apt No. 13/1, Teşvikiye, Şişli, Istanbul, Turkey; c/o Georgina Daley, 8 Holland Street, London, W8 4LT, England. *Telephone:* (212) 240-8731 (Istanbul); (20) 3538-7981 (London). *E-mail:* info@yastikbyrifatozbek.com; georgina.daley@yastiklondon.co.uk. *Website:* www.yastikbyrifatozbek.com.

ÖZERSAY, Kudret, PhD; Turkish-Cypriot politician; *Deputy Prime Minister and Minister of Foreign Affairs, 'Turkish Republic of Northern Cyprus';* b. 16 Dec. 1973, Alaminyo, Larnaca; m.; ed Ankara Univ., Univ. of London Inst. of Advanced Legal Studies; Research Asst, Ankara Univ. 1996–2002; worked in Dept of Political Science and Int. Relations, Eastern Mediterranean Univ. 2003–, becoming Assoc. Prof. and Prof. 2015; Visiting Prof., Faculty of Law, Univ. of Oxford 2008; worked for OSCE (supervising post-war elections in Bosnia and Herzegovina) 1997; mem. Turkish-Cypriot Cttee on Int. Treaties 2002–03, 2003–04; mem. Turkish-Cypriot negotiation team during Annan Plan negotiations; Special Rep. of Pres. Derviş Eroğlu 2010–12; cand. in presidential election 2015; mem. Ass. of the Repub. (parl.) from Lefkoşa Dist 2018–; Deputy Prime Minister and Minister of Foreign Affairs 2018–; Founding Pres. People's Party (HP) 2016. *Address:* Ministry of Foreign Affairs, Selçuklu Cad., Lefkoşa (Nicosia), Mersin 10, Turkey (office). *Telephone:* 2283241 (office). *Fax:* 2284290 (office). *E-mail:* info@mfa.gov.ct.tr (office). *Website:* mfa.gov.ct.tr (office); www.kudretozersay.com.

ÖZGÜRGÜN, Hüseyin; Turkish-Cypriot politician; b. 1965, Nicosia; m.; two c.; ed Ankara Univ.; fmr professional football player; mem. Ass. of the Repub. (Parl.) 1998–; mem. Parl. Ass., Council of Europe 2004–09; Deputy Prime Minister and Minister of Foreign Affairs 2009–13; Prime Minister, 'Turkish Repub. of Northern Cyprus' 2016–18; Pres., Nat. Unity Party (Ulusal Bırlık Partisi, UBP) 2013–. *Address:* c/o Prime Minister's Office, Selçuklu Road, Lefkoşa (Nicosia), Mersin 10, Cyprus (office).

OZICK, Cynthia, MA; American writer and poet; b. 17 April 1928, New York; d. of William Ozick and Celia Regelson; m. Bernard Hallote 1952; one d.; ed New York Univ., Ohio State Univ.; mem. PEN, Authors League, American Acad. of Arts and Sciences, American Acad. of Arts and Letters; Founder-mem. Acad. Universelle des Cultures; Guggenheim Fellow 1982; Dr hc (Yeshiva) 1984, (Hebrew Union Coll.) 1984, (Williams Coll.) 1986, (Hunter Coll.) 1987, (Jewish Theological Seminary) 1988, (Adelphi) 1988, (State Univ. of NY) 1989, (Brandeis) 1990, (Bard Coll.) 1991, (Spertus Coll.) 1991, (Seton Hall Univ.) 1999, (Rutgers Univ.) 1999, (Asheville) 2000, (New York) 2001, (Bar-Ilan) 2002, (Baltimore Hebrew Univ.) 2004, (Georgetown) 2007; Mildred and Harold Strauss Living Award, American Acad. of Arts and Letters 1983, Rea Award for short story 1986, Harold Washington Literary Award, City of Chicago 1997, John Cheever Award 1999, Lotos Club Medal of Merit 2000, Lannan Foundation Award 2000, Koret Foundation Award for Literary Studies 2001, Mary McCarthy Award, Bard Coll. 2007, Nat. Humanities Medal 2007, PEN/Malamud Prize 2008, PEN/Nabokov Prize 2008. *Publications include:* Trust 1966, The Pagan Rabbi and Other Stories (Edward Lewis Wallant Award 1971) 1971, Bloodshed and Three Novellas 1976, Levitation: Five Fictions 1982, Art & Ardor: Essays 1983, The Cannibal Galaxy 1983, The Messiah of Stockholm 1987, Metaphor & Memory: Essays 1989, The Shawl 1989, Epodes: First Poems 1992, What Henry James Knew, and Other Essays on Writers 1993, Blue Light (play) 1994, Portrait of the Artist as a Bad Character and Other Essays on Writing 1995, The Shawl (novel) 1996, Fame & Folly: Essays (PEN/Spiegel-Diamonstein Award for the Art of the Essay 1997) 1996, The Puttermesser Papers (novel) 1997, The Best American Essays (ed.) 1998, Quarrel & Quandary (essays) (Nat. Critics' Circle Award for Criticism 2001) 2000, Heir to the Glimmering World (novel published as The Bear Boy in UK) 2004, Collected Stories 2006, A Din in the Head: Essays 2006, Dictation: A Quartet 2008, Foreign Bodies 2010, Critics, Monsters, Fanatics, and Other Literary Essays 2016, Letters of Intent: Selected Essays 2018; contrib. of fiction to numerous periodicals and anthologies, including New Criterion, New Yorker, Harper's, Partisan Review, Yale Review, New York Times Magazine, Best American Short Stories, O. Henry Prize Stories, Best American Essays, The Oxford Book of Jewish Short Stories, Norton Anthology of Jewish American Literature. *Address:* c/o Rogers, Coleridge & White Ltd, 20 Powis Mews, London, W11 1JN, England (office). *Website:* www.rcwlitagency.com/authors/ozick-cynthia (office).

OZIM, Igor; Slovenian/German violinist and academic; *Professor of Violin, Universität Mozarteum;* b. 9 May 1931, Ljubljana, fmr Yugoslavia (now Slovenia); s. of Rudolf Ozim and Marija Kodric; m. Wonji Kim-Ozim; ed Akad. za glasbo Ljubljana, Royal Coll. of Music, UK, studied with Prof. Max Rostal; Prof. of Violin, Akad. za glasbo Ljubljana 1960–63, Staatliche Hochschule für Musik, Cologne 1963–96, Berne Conservatoire 1985–96, Hochschule für Musik, Vienna 1996–, currently Universität Mozarteum, Salzburg; mem. trio with Walter Grimmer and Ilse Dorati-von Alpenheim which performed and recorded all of Mozart's and Schubert's works –1995; Pres. Cen. Cttee European String Teachers' Asscn; mem. jury, Int. Violin Competition Henri Marteau 2017; Dr hc; First Prize, Int. Carl-Flesch Competition, London 1951, Munich 1953. *Leisure interests:* photography, table tennis. *Address:* Department of Strings, Universität Mozarteum, Mirabellplatz 1, 5020 Salzburg, Austria (office). *Telephone:* (662) 61-98-0 (office). *E-mail:* igor.ozim@moz.ac.at (office). *Website:* www.moz.ac.at (office).

ÖZKÖK, Gen. Hilmi; Turkish army officer; b. 4 Aug. 1940, Turgutlu, Manisa; m. Özenç Özkök; two c.; ed Işıklar Mil. High School, Turkish Mil. Acad., Field Artillery School, Army War Coll., NATO Defence Coll.; Artillery 3rd Lt 1959; Platoon Leader and Anti-Aircraft Battery Commdr 1972; Chief of Operations and Training Br., 15th Training Brigade; Staff Officer, Plan and Policy Dept of Shape, HQ; Chief of Defence Research Section, Plan and Policy Dept of Shape, HQ; Dir Exec. Office of Sec.-Gen. of Nat. Security Council; Commdr Cadet Regiment, Turkish Mil. Acad.; rank of Brig.-Gen. 1984; Chief of Planning and Operations Dept, Turkish Gen. Staff (TGS) 1984–86; Commdr 70th Infantry Brigade 1986–88; rank of Maj.-Gen. 1988; Commdr 28th Infantry Div. 1988–90; Chief of Personnel, Dept of TGS 1990–92; rank of Lt-Gen. 1992; Chief of Turkish Mil. Del. to NATO, Brussels 1992–95; Commdr 7th Corps 1995–96; rank of Gen. 1996; Command of Allied Land Forces South-Eastern Europe 1996–98; Deputy Chief of TGS 1998–99; 1st Army Commdr 1999–2000; Commdr of Turkish Army 2000–02; Chief of the Gen. Staff 2002–06; fmr mem. NATO Mil. Cttee; Turkish Armed Forces Medal of Honour, Turkish Armed Forces Medal of Distinguished Service, Medal of Distinguished Service and Self-Sacrifice, Chevalier, Ordre nat. du Mérite, Legion of Merit (USA), Medal of Nishan-i-Imtiaz (Pakistan), Great Cross for Military Merit (Spain), Tong-Il Medal (Repub. of Korea), Eagle Golden Medal (Albania). *Leisure interests:* photography, poetry.

ÖZPETEK, Ferzan; Turkish/Italian film director and screenwriter; b. 3 Feb. 1959, Istanbul; Hon. Citizen of the City of Lecce 2010; Medal of Merit (Italy) 2008. *Films directed:* Hamam (Hamam: The Turkish Bath, UK) (also screenplay) (Golden Orange for Best Film and Best Direction, Antalya Int. Film Festival, Italian Nat. Syndicate of Film Journalists Silver Ribbon Award for Best Producer) 1997, Harem Suaré (also screenplay) 1999, His Secret Life 2001, Le fate ignoranti (The Ignorant Fairies) (also screenplay) (Austin Gay & Lesbian Int. Film Festival Award for Best Feature, New York Lesbian and Gay Film Festival Award for Best Feature) 2001, La finestra di fronte (The Window Opposite) (also screenplay) (David di Donatello Award 2003, also won awards for Best Film, Best Direction, Best Leading Actor and Actress) 2003, Cuore sacro (also screenplay) 2005, Saturn in Opposition (also writer) 2007, A Perfect Day (also screenplay) 2008, L'Aquila 2009 – Cinque registi tra le macerie (video documentary short) (segment 'Nonostante tutto è Pasqua') 2009, Loose Cannons (also writer) 2010, Magnifica presenza (A Magnificent Haunting) (also written by) 2012, Allacciate le cinture (also screenplay/story) 2014; other films include: Scusate il ritardo (first asst dir) 1983, Son contento (first asst dir) 1983, Il tenente dei carabinieri (asst dir) 1986, Noi uomini duri (asst dir) 1987, Il volpone (The Big Fox) (asst dir) 1988, Mortacci (first asst dir) 1989, Ultrà (asst dir) 1991, La scorta (The Escort) (asst dir) 1993, Anche i commercialisti hanno un'anima (asst dir) 1994, Il branco (The Pack) (asst dir) 1994, Vite strozzate (asst dir) 1996. *Television includes:* Qualcosa di biondo (film) (second asst dir) 1984, Il maestro del terrore (The Prince of Terror) (film) (asst dir) 1988, The Man Who Didn't Want to Die (film) (asst dir) 1988, School of Fear (film) (asst dir) 1989. *Website:* www.ferzanozpetek.com.

ÖZSOYLU, Şinasi, (Nasih), MD; Turkish physician; *Professor of Paediatrics and Haematology, Fatih University, Ankara;* b. 29 July 1927, Erzurum; s. of Ahmet Fazil Ozsoylu and Azime Ozsoylu; m. Selma Ozsoylu; two s. one d.; ed Istanbul Univ.; paediatrician, Washington Univ. Medical School, St Louis, USA 1960; haematologist, Harvard Univ. Medical School, Boston, Mass 1963; Assoc. Prof. of Paediatrics, Hacettepe Univ., Ankara 1964–69, Prof. 1969–94, Head of Haematology 1970–94, of Paediatrics 1976–77; Prof. of Paediatrics and Haematology, Fatih Univ., Ankara 1996–; Visiting Prof., Md Univ. Medical School, Baltimore 1972; mem. Turkish Medical Soc. 1953–, Turkish Paediatrics Soc. 1958–, Turkish Haematology Soc. 1974–, Int. Paediatrics Soc. 1974–; Pres. European Soc. of Haematology and Immunology 1991–93; Fellow Islamic Acad. of Sciences 1989–; Ed. Turkish Journal of Medical Sciences 1989–94, Hon. Ed. 1994–; Ed. Yeni Tip Dergisi 1994–; invited to speak at numerous specialist congresses; Hon. mem. American Pediatric Soc. 1992–; Hon. Fellow, American Acad. of Pediatrics 1995–; numerous awards and prizes including Exceptional Scientific Achievement Award, Hacettepe Univ. 1991. *Publications:* several hundred papers on paediatrics, haematology, liver disorders, etc. *Leisure interests:* gardening, music. *Address:* Kenedi Cad. No. 148/14, GOP 06700, Ankara, Turkey (home); Fatıh University, Medical School Hospital, Alpaslan Turkes Cad. No. 57, Emek. 06510, Ankara (office). *Telephone:* (312) 2126262 (office); (312) 2121804 (office); (312) 4280975 (home). *Fax:* (312) 2213276 (office). *E-mail:* sinasi.ozsoylu@hotmail.com (office).

OZZIE, Raymond (Ray) E., BS; American software industry executive; b. 20 Nov. 1955, Chicago, Ill.; m. Dawna Bousquet 1982; one s. one d.; ed Main Township High School South, Park Ridge, Ill., Univ. of Ill.; Programmer, Protection Mutual Insurance Co. 1972–73; Technician, Dept of Nuclear Eng, Univ. of Ill. 1974, System Programmer, PLATO project, 1974–79; Co-founder Urbana Software Enterprises 1998–79; with Data Gen. Corpn 1979–81; Co-founder Microcosm Corpn 1981; with Software Arts 1981–82; with Lotus Devt 1982–84, led team that developed Lotus Symphony; Founder and Pres. Iris Assocs (back by Lotus), developed Lotus Notes 1984–97; Founder, Chair. and CEO Groove Networks Inc. (provider of collaboration software for the virtual office), Beverly, Mass 1997–2005, Chief Tech. Officer, Microsoft Corpn, Redmond, Wash. (after acquisition of Groove Networks by Microsoft) 2005–06, Chief Software Architect 2006–10 (resgnd); Founder and CEO Talko 2012–; mem. Nat. Acad. of Eng, Nat. Research Council; mem. and Gov. for IT and Telecommunications, World Econ. Forum; mem. Int. Council, John F. Kennedy School of Govt, Harvard Univ.; Person of the Year, PC Magazine 1995, W. Wallace McDowell Award, IEEE Computer Soc. 2000; named one of seven Windows Pioneers by Microsoft; inducted into Computer Museum Industry Hall of Fame and InfoWorld Hall of Fame. *Website:* ozzie.net; www.talko.com.

P

PÄÄBO, Svante, PhD; Swedish biologist and academic; *Director, Max Planck Institute for Evolutionary Anthropology;* b. 20 April 1955, Stockholm; s. of Sune Bergström and Karin Pääbo; ed Uppsala Univ.; worked in School of Interpreters, Swedish Defense Forces 1975–76; Researcher, Dept of Biochemistry, Univ. of California, Berkeley, USA 1987–90; Docent in Medical Genetics, Univ. of Uppsala 1990, Guest Prof. of Comparative Genomics 2003–15; Prof. of General Biology, Univ. of Munich 1990–98; Founding Dir, Max Planck Inst. for Evolutionary Anthropology, Leipzig, Germany 1997–, Hon. Prof. of Genetics and Evolutionary Biology, Univ. of Leipzig 1999–; Chair. Scientific Advisory Bd Uppsala Centre for Comparative Genomics 2005–; mem. Editorial Bd PLoS Biology 2003–; mem. Academia Europaea, Swedish Royal Acad. of Sciences, Deutsche Akademie der Naturforscher Leopoldina, Halle, Saxonian Acad. of Sciences, Leipzig; Foreign mem. Finnish Soc. of Sciences and Letters, NAS, American Acad. of Arts and Sciences, USA 2011, Royal Acad. of Eng, Stockholm 2013; Corresponding mem. Croatian Acad. of Sciences and Arts 2012; Foreign Assoc., Académie des Sciences, Institut de France 2016; Grad. Univ. of the Chinese Acad. of Sciences, Beijing 2008; Hon. mem. Croatian Anthropological Soc. 2010; Order of Pour le Mérite (Civil Class) 2008, Order of Terra Mariana, 3rd Class (Estonia) 2008, Verdienstorden der Bundesrepublik Deutschland 2009, HM The King's Medal 2012; Dr hc (Zurich, Helsinki, Royal Inst. of Tech., Stockholm, Karolinska Inst., Stockholm); Hon. DrMed (Karolinska Inst., Stockholm) 2012; Hon. DSc (NUI Galway) 2015; Leibniz Prize German Science Foundation 1992, Max Delbrück Medal, Berlin, Germany 1998, Carus Medal and Prize, Halle and Schweinfurt, Germany 1999, Rudbeck Prize, Uppsala, Sweden 2000, Leipzig Science Prize 2003, Ernst Schering Prize, Berlin 2003, Louis-Jeantet Prize for Medicine 2005, Virchow Medal 2005, Gorjanovic-Kramberger Medal 2008, Kistler Prize 2009, Theodor Bücher Medal, Fed. of European Biochemical Socs 2010, Newcomb-Cleveland Prize, American Acad. of Arts and Sciences 2011, Biochemical Analysis Prize 2011, Heisse Kartoffel, Leipzig 2012, Gruber Genetics Prize 2013, Learning Ladder Prize 2014, Allen Distinguished Investigator 2014, Lomonosov Gold Medal, Russian Acad. of Sciences (co-recipient) 2015, Breakthrough Prize in Life Sciences (co-recipient) 2015. *Achievements include:* pioneer in study of ancient DNA and a founder of palaeogenetics; has worked extensively on the Neanderthal genome. *Publications include:* Neanderthal Man: In Search of Lost Genomes 2014; numerous book chapters and articles and papers in scientific journals. *Address:* Max Planck Institute for Evolutionary Anthropology, Deutscher Platz 6, Level 3, Room U3.92, 04103 Leipzig, Germany (office). *Telephone:* (341) 3550501 (office). *Fax:* (341) 3550555 (office). *E-mail:* paabo@eva.mpg.de (office). *Website:* www.eva.mpg.de/genetics/staff/paabo (office).

PAAR, Vladimir, DSc; Croatian physicist and academic; *Professor of Physics, Zagreb University;* b. 11 May 1942, Zagreb; s. of Vladimir Paar and Elvira Paar; m. Nada Paar-Pandur 1968; three s. one d.; ed Zagreb Univ.; Research Assoc., Zagreb Univ. 1973–76, Prof. 1981–; Visiting Prof. in Copenhagen, Julich, Paris, Moscow, Munich, Amsterdam, Livermore (Calif.) and Rio de Janeiro; participation in numerous int. confs; mem. Croatian Acad. of Arts and Sciences 1992, Croatian Physical Soc., European Physical Soc. *Television:* Deterministic Chaos, Energy Crisis, Physics in Educ. *Publications:* author and ed. of 21 books and more than 500 papers on atomic nucleus structure, symmetry, supersymmetry and deterministic chaos, energetics and scientific econ. devt. *Leisure interests:* soccer, tennis, presenting science in the media. *Address:* Theoretical Physics Department, Faculty of Science, University of Zagreb, Bijenicka 32, 10000 Zagreb (office); Croatian Academy of Sciences and Arts, Zrinski trg 11, 10000 Zagreb, Croatia. *Telephone:* (1) 4605555 (office). *Fax:* (1) 4680336 (office). *E-mail:* paar@hazu.hr (office); vpaar@phy.hr (office). *Website:* info.hazu.hr/vladimir_paar_biografija (office).

PAASIO, Pertti Kullervo, MSc; Finnish politician and organization official; b. 2 April 1939, Helsinki; s. of Rafael Paasio and Mary Wahlman; m. Kirsti Johansson 1967; two s. two d.; ed Turku Univ.; regional organizer, Nuoret Kotkat (Young Falcons) 1963–66; mem. Turku City Council 1965–91, 2003–06; Pres. Council of Jäsenä 1965–90, 2001–08; Sec. for Tourism, City of Turku 1967–73; Political Sec. Ministry of Finance 1972; Head of Turku Labour Exchange 1973–87; Vice-Pres. Int. Falcon Movt 1975–81; Chair. Young Falcons Fed. 1978–81; Political Sec. to Prime Minister 1975; mem. Parl. 1975–79, 1982–96; mem. Exec. Cttee Social Democratic Party of Finland 1978–91; mem. Presidential Electoral Coll. 1978, 1982, 1988; Leader, Social Democratic Parl. Group 1984–87; Chair. Social Democratic Party 1987–91; Deputy Prime Minister and Minister for Foreign Affairs 1989–91; Chair. Parl. Cttee for Foreign Affairs 1991–96; mem. European Parl. 1996–99, Quaestor 1997; Chair. Finland Soc. 1998–2010. *Publications:* Minä ja Mr. Murphy (Me and Mr. Murphy) 1996, Punatulkku ja sikarodeo (Bullfinch and Sikarodeo) 1998, Brussels baanalla (Brussels Baanalla) 2000. *Leisure interests:* photography, caravanning. *Address:* Eerikinkatu 30, 20100 Turku, Finland.

PABLO ROSSO, Pedro, MD; Chilean paediatrician, academic and university administrator; *Professor Emeritus, Pontificia Universidad Católica de Chile;* b. 27 Aug. 1941, Spotorno, Italy; s. of José Pablo Rosso and Laura Pablo Rosso; m. Mary Rose Streeter, two s. one d.; ed Scuola Italiana de Valparaíso, Scuola Italiana de Santiago, Pontificia Universidad Católica de Chile; Paediatrician, Roberto del Río Hosp., Santiago 1966–69; Paediatrician, Weill Cornell Medical Coll., Cornell Univ., NY 1970–72; Asst Prof. and Researcher, Coll. of Physicians and Surgeons, Columbia Univ., New York 1972–75, Assoc. Prof. of Paediatrics 1978, Dir Growth and Devt Div. 1982–84; Prof., Faculty of Medicine, Pontificia Universidad Católica de Chile 1984–2012, f. Centro de Investigaciones Médicas 1990, Dean, Faculty of Medicine 1991, Rector, Pontificia Universidad Católica 2000–10, Prof. Emer. 2012–; fmr Visiting Prof., Universidad de Puerto Rico, Universidad de San Marcos, Lima; Pres., Asscn of Chilean Medical Faculties 1996–2000; Vice-Pres. Federación Internacional de Escuelas de Medicina de Universidades Católicas 1994–96; mem. Academia Chilena de Medicina 1999–; Cavalier, Order of Merit of Repub. of Italy 2008; Ligures del Mundo Special Prize 2003, US March of Dimes/Birth Defect Foundation Agnes Higgins Prize, McCollum Award, American Inst. of Nutrition, Agnes Higgins Award. *Publications:* more than 120 publs. *Address:* Pontificia Universidad Católica de Chile, 8320000 Santiago, Chile (office). *Telephone:* (2) 354-2000 (office). *Website:* www.puc.cl (office).

PABRIKS, Artis, PhD; Latvian politician, political scientist and academic; *Minister of Defence;* b. 22 March 1966, Jūrmala; ed Univ. of Latvia, Univ. of Århus, Denmark; Research Asst, Acad. of Sciences 1988–90; External Lecturer, Univ. of Århus, Denmark 1994; Lecturer, Univ. of Latvia 1995–99; First Rector, Vidzeme Univ. Coll. 1996–97, Asst Prof. 1996–2001, Assoc. Prof. 2001–; Policy Analyst, Latvian Centre for Human Rights and Ethnic Studies 2001–03, Political Educ. Foundation 2003–04; mem. Saeima (Parl.) 2004–, Chair. Foreign Affairs Comm.; Parl. Sec., Ministry of Foreign Affairs 2004, Minister of Foreign Affairs 2004–07; Deputy Prime Minister and Minister of Defence 2010–11, Minister of Defence 2011–14, 2019–; Deputy mem. for Latvia, European Comm. against Racism and Intolerance, Council of Europe 2002–; mem. Editorial Bd, Baltic Review magazine 2002–; mem. Soc. for a Different Politics (SCP); Visiting Prof., Bosphorus (Boğaziçi) Univ., Istanbul 2009–10; Prof., Rīga Int. School of Econs and Business Admin 2011–; Great Commdr, Order of Duke Gediminas. *Leisure interest:* karate (black belt). *Address:* Ministry of Defence, K. Valdemāra iela 10–12, Rīga 1473, Latvia (office). *Telephone:* 6733-5114 (office). *Fax:* 6721-2307 (office). *E-mail:* kanceleja@mod.gov.lv (office). *Website:* www.mod.gov.lv (office).

PACARI VEGA, Nina, BA, JD; Ecuadorean lawyer and politician; b. (María Estela Vega), 9 Oct. 1960, Imbabura-Cotopaxi; ed Universidad Cen. del Ecuador; Legal Advisor, Confed. of Indigenous Nationalities of Ecuador (CONAIE) 1989; elected mem. Nat. Ass. 1998–2003, Vice-Pres. (first native Quécha-Indian in position) 1999–2000, Acting Pres. 2000–03; Minister of Foreign Affairs 2003 (resgnd); mem. UN Perm. Forum on Indigenous Issues 2005–07; Judge, Constitutional Court of Ecuador 2007; mem. Faculty, Univ. of Ambato; mem. Inter-American Dialogue; Best Congresswoman of the Year, TC Television 1998.

PACE, Gen. (retd) Peter, MBA; American management consultant and military officer (retd); *Chairman, Haystax Technology, Inc.;* b. 5 Nov. 1945, Brooklyn, New York; m.; one s. one d.; ed US Naval Acad., George Washington Univ., Harvard Univ., Nat. War Coll.; Rifle Platoon Leader, then Asst Operations Officer, 1st Marine Div. in Viet Nam 1968–69; various positions 1969–71, including Head, Infantry Writer Unit, Marine Corps Inst., White House Social Aide; CO Marine Corps Recruiting Station, Buffalo, NY 1980–83, 2nd Battalion, 1st Marines 1983–85; assigned to Combined/Jt Staff, Seoul 1986, served as Chief, Ground Forces Br., then Exec. Officer to the Asst Chief of Staff; Chief of Staff, 2nd Marine Div., Camp Lejeune 1991–92, Asst Div. Commdr 1992; Pres. Marine Corps Univ., Commanding Gen. Marine Corps Schools, Marine Corps Combat Devt Command, Quantico, Va 1992; Deputy Commdr Marine Forces, Somalia 1992–93, Deputy Commdr Jt Task Force, Somalia 1993–94; Deputy Commdr/Chief of Staff, US Forces, Japan 1994–96; Dir for Operations, Jt Staff, Washington, DC 1996–97; Commdr US Marine Corps Forces, Atlantic/Europe/South 1997–2000; C-in-C US Southern Command 2000–01; Vice-Chair. Jt Chiefs of Staff 2001–05, Chair. 2005–07; apptd Pres. and CEO SM&A Strategic Advisors Inc. (man. consultancy) 2008; Chair. Haystax Technology Inc. 2014–; mem. Bd of Dirs Marine Corps Law Enforcement Foundation, Webroot Inc. 2015–; Distinguished Visiting Research Scholar, Fordham Univ.; Adjunct Faculty mem., Georgetown Univ.; Legion of Merit, Combat Action Ribbon; Defense Distinguished Service Medal, Defense Superior Service Medal, Bronze Star Medal with Combat V, Defense Meritorious Service Medal, Meritorious Service Medal with Gold Star, Navy Commendation Medal with Combat V, Navy Achievement Medal with Gold Star, Presidential Medal of Freedom 2008. *Address:* Haystax Technology, Inc., 8251 Greensboro Drive, Suite 1111, McLean, VA 22102, USA (office). *Telephone:* (571) 297-3800 (office). *Fax:* (703) 442-4720 (office). *E-mail:* info@haystax.com (office). *Website:* www.haystax.com (office).

PAČES, Vaclav, PhD, DrSc; Czech biochemist and academic; *Chairman, Academy of Sciences of the Czech Republic;* b. 2 Feb. 1942, Prague; m. Magdalena Tomková Pačes 1966; two s.; ed Charles Univ., Czechoslovak Acad. of Sciences; joined Inst. of Molecular Genetics 1977, Head of Lab. 1986, Docent 1992–95, Full Prof. 1995, Dir 1999–2005; apptd Chair. Czech Soc. for Biochemistry and Molecular Biology 1990, now Sec.-Gen.; Chair. Czech Acad. of Sciences 2005–09; at Yale Univ. 1990–91, has also conducted research at Univs of Chicago, Seville, Bristol and Japan; mem. Czech Soc. of Arts and Sciences (SVU), Fellow 2004–; mem. European Acad. of Sciences and Arts, European Molecular Biology Org. (EMBO); recipient of several prizes including State Prize for Science 1989, Prize for Popularization of Science 1992, State medal for science 2008, Acad. medal De Scientia et Humanitate Optime Meritis 2009, Medal of Acad. of Sciences, Slovakia 2009, Gregor Mendel Medal 2012. *Publications:* Molecular Biology of the Gene 1982, Molecular Genetics 1983, Antibiotics: Mechanism of Action and Resistance (co-author) 1987, Highlights of Modern Biochemistry 1989; more than 100 original papers. *Address:* Institute of Molecular Genetics, Academy of Sciences of the Czech Republic, Vídenska 1083, 14220 Prague 4, Czech Republic (office). *Telephone:* (224) 229610 (office). *Fax:* (224) 240512 (office). *E-mail:* vpaces@img.cas.cz. *Website:* www.cas.cz (office).

PACHACHI, Adnan, PhD; Iraqi politician and diplomatist (retd); b. (Adnan Muzahim al-Pachachi), 14 May 1923, Baghdad; m. Selwa Pachachi 1946; three d.; ed Victoria Coll., Alexandria, Egypt, American Univ., Beirut, Lebanon, Georgetown Univ, Washington, DC, USA; Perm. Rep. to UN 1959–65, 1967–69; Minister of Foreign Affairs 1965–67; left Iraq to settle in UAE 1971, Minister of State in Govt of Abu Dhabi 1971–93, Personal Rep. of the Pres. of Pres. 1974–90, returned to Iraq 2003; Founder and Pres. Ind. Democratic Movt 2003–06; led Iraqi del. to UN Security Council July 2003; mem. Iraq Governing Council 2003–04, Pres. Jan. 2004; mem. Parl. 2006–10; decorations from Italy and Morocco. *Publications:* Muzahim Pachachi – Political Career (in Arabic) 1990, Voice of Iraq in the UN 1959–1969 – Personal Record 1991. *Leisure interests:* music, swimming, theatre, visiting art galleries and exhibitions. *E-mail:* adnan@pachachi.org (office).

PACHAURI, Rajendra Kumar, MS, DEcon, DEng; Indian economist, academic, research director and international organization official; b. 20 Aug. 1940, Nainital;

s. of A. R. Pachauri; m. Saroj Pachauri; three d.; ed North Carolina State Univ., USA; Asst Prof., North Carolina State Univ. 1974–75, Visiting Faculty mem., Dept of Econs and Business 1976–77; mem. Sr Faculty, Admin. Staff Coll. of India 1975–79, Dir Consulting and Applied Research Div. 1979–81; Dir The Energy Research Inst. (TERI), New Delhi 1982–2001, Dir-Gen. 2001–15; Visiting Prof., Resource Econs, Univ. of West Virginia 1981–82; Sr Visiting Fellow, Resource Systems Inst., East-West Center, USA 1982; Visiting Fellow, Energy Dept, IBRD 1990; Pres. Int. Asscn for Energy Econs 1988, Chair. 1989–90; Pres. Asian Energy Inst. 1992–; Adviser on Energy and Sustainable Man. of Natural Resources to the Admin., UNDP 1994–99; Adviser, Int. Advisory Bd, Toyota Motor Corpn, Japan 2006–09; Vice-Chair. Intergovernmental Panel on Climate Change (IPCC) 1997, Chair. 2002–15 (resgnd); Dir-Gen. Energy and Resources Inst., New Delhi; Chancellor TERI Univ.; Dir Yale Climate and Energy Inst.; mem. Bd of Dirs Int. Solar Energy Soc. 1991–97, Inst. for Global Environmental Strategies 1999–, Indian Oil Corpn Ltd 1999–2003, Nat. Thermal Power Corpn Ltd 2002–05, GAIL (India) Ltd 2003–04, Oil and Natural Gas Corpn Ltd 2006–09; McCluskey Fellow, Yale Univ., USA Sept.–Dec. 2000; mem. Advisory Bd, Clinton Climate Initiative, USA 2010–; mem. High Panel on Peace and Dialogue among Cultures, UNESCO, France 2009–; mem. Bd of Govs, Shriram Scientific and Industrial Research Foundation 1987–90; mem. Exec. Cttee, India Int. Centre, New Delhi, mem. Bd of Trustees 1985–; Vice-Pres. Bangalore Int. Centre; mem. Governing Council, India Habitat Centre, New Delhi 1987–, Pres. 2004–06; mem. Court of Govs, Admin. Staff Coll. of India 1979–81; mem. Advisory Bd on Energy, reporting directly to Prime Minister 1983–88, World Energy Council 1990–93, Nat. Environmental Council, under Prime Minister 1993–99, Oil Industry Restructuring Group, 'R' Group, Ministry of Petroleum and Natural Gas 1994, Econ. Advisory Council to Prime Minister 2001–04, Prime Minister's Advisory Council on Climate Change 2007–; Hon. Prof., HEC Paris 2009; Officier, Legion d'honneur 2006, Commdr, Order of the White Rose (Finland) 2010, Order of the Rising Sun, Gold and Silver Star (Japan) 2010; Dr hc (Ritsumeikan Univ.) 2007, (Univ. of Liege) 2008, (Univ. of Athens) 2009, Hon. DHumLitt (Yale Univ.) 2008, (Brandeis Univ.) 2009, Hon. DSc (Kumaun Univ.) 2008, (Rani Durgavati Vishwavidyalaya, Jabalpur) 2008, (Univ. of New South Wales) 2008, (Univ. of Warwick) 2009, (Univ. of Kalyani) 2009, (Illinois Univ.) 2009, (Gustavus Adolphus Coll., Minnesota) 2009, Hon. ScD (Univ. of East Anglia) 2008; Millennium Pioneer Award 2000, Padma Bhushan 2001, Intergovernmental Panel on Climate Change awarded Nobel Peace Prize (shared with Al Gore) 2007, NDTV Global Indian Award 2007, Padma Vibhushan 2008, IIFA Global Leadership Award 2008, GQ Global Indian of the Year Award 2009. *Publications include:* The Dynamics of Electrical Energy Supply and Demand 1975, Energy and Economic Development in India 1977, International Energy Studies 1980, Energy Policy for India: An Interdisciplinary Analysis 1980, National Energy Data Systems (co-author) 1984, The Political Economy of Global Energy 1985, Global Energy Interactions 1986, Global Warming and Climate Change: Perspectives from Developing Countries (co-ed.) 1990, Role of Innovative Technologies and Approaches for India (co-ed.) 1991, Global Warming: Mitigation Strategies and Perspectives from Asia and Brazil (co-ed.) 1991, Energy-Environment-Development (co-ed.) 1991, Global Warming: Collaborative Study on Strategies to Limit CO2 emissions in Asia and Brazil (co-ed.) 1992, Contemporary India 1992, Climate Change in Asia and Brazil: The Role of Technology Transfer (co-ed. with Preety Bhandari) 1994, Population, Environment and Development (ed. with Lubina F. Qureshy) 1997, Energy in the Indian Sub-Continent (co-ed. with Gurneeta Vasudeva) 2000, Directions, Innovations, and Strategies for Harnessing Action for Sustainable Development 2001, Business Unusual: Championing Corporate Social Responsibility (ed) 2004, Petroleum Pricing in India: Balancing Efficiency and Equity (co-author) 2005, The Promises and Challenges of Biofuels for the Poor in Developing Countries 2006, CITIES: Steering Towards Sustainability 2009; scientific papers and newspaper articles. *Leisure interests:* cricket, flying, golf. *Address:* 160 Golf Links, New Delhi 110 003, India (home). *Telephone:* (11) 4634663 (home).

PACHECO, Abel; Costa Rican psychiatrist, writer and fmr head of state; b. (Abel Pacheco de la Espriella), 22 Dec. 1933, San José; ed Nat. Autonomous Univ. of Mexico, Louisiana State Univ., USA; fmr TV commentator and producer of documentaries; Pres. Partido Unidad Social Cristiana (PUSC); Pres. of Costa Rica 2002–06. *Publications:* series of novels, six books on Costa Rica and several popular songs. *Address:* c/o Partido Unidad Social Cristiana (PUSC), Del Restaurante Kentucky Fried Chicken 75 metros al sur, frente a la Embajada de España, Paseo Colón, Apdo 10.095, 1000 San José, Costa Rica (office).

PACHECO, José Condungua António; Mozambican politician; *Minister of Foreign Affairs and Cooperation;* b. 10 Sept. 1958, Búzi Dist, Sofala Prov.; s. of António Pacheco and Madalena Machami Pacheco; m.; ed Escola de Regentes Agrícolas de Manica, Wye Coll., Univ. of London; Prov. Dir of Agriculture, Zambezia Prov. 1981–90; Nat. Dir of Rural Devt 1990–95; Deputy Minister of Agriculture and Fisheries 1995–98; Gov. of Cabo Delgado 1998–2005; Minister of Interiors 2005–09, Jan.–Oct. 2010, of Agriculture 2010–14, of Agriculture and Food Security 2015–17, of Foreign Affairs and Cooperation 2017–; mem. Frelimo Party 1979–, Political Comm.; apptd mem. Bd of Dirs Sociedade Argelino-Moçambicana de Florestas (SAMOFOR) 1984; mem. Bd of Dirs, then Chair. Bd of Dirs Instituto Nacional de Desenvolvimento da Indústria Local 1992–94. *Leisure interests:* sports, reading, music. *Address:* Ministry of Foreign Affairs and Cooperation, Avenue 10 de Novembro 640, Maputo, Mozambique (office). *Telephone:* 21327000 (office). *Fax:* 21327020 (office). *E-mail:* minec@minec.gov.mz (office). *Website:* www.minec.gov.mz (office).

PACHECO MATTE, Máximo, MBA; Chilean economist, business executive and politician; b. 12 Feb. 1953, Santiago; s. of Máximo Pacheco and Adriana Matte; m. Soledad Flanagan 1976; four d.; ed Univ. of Chile; Man. Banco Osorno; Man. Planning, Banco Talca; Gen. Man. Leasing Andino 1983–90; mem. Bd of Dirs Cabildo SA 1982–90, Jucosa 1987–90; Pres. Chilean Leasing Asscn 1984–90; Faculty mem. Univ. de Chile; COO Codelco-Chile; Exec. Vice-Pres. for Chile and Latin America, Carter Holt Harvey 1994–2000, Exec. Pres. International Paper-Latinamerica 2000–04, named Exec. Pres. International Paper-Brazil 2004, named Sr Vice-Pres. International Paper Co. 2004, Sr Vice-Pres. and Pres. IP Europe, Middle East, Africa & Russia 2010–13; Minister of Energy 2014–15.

PACHTA-REYHOFEN, Georg, Dipl-Ing, Dr techn; German engineer and business executive; b. 28 June 1955; ed Vienna Univ. of Tech.; worked as a univ. asst at Inst. for Internal Combustion Engines and Automotive Eng, Vienna Univ. of Tech. 1981–86; joined MAN Group at ÖAF Gräf und Stift AG, Vienna (now MAN Sonderfahrzeuge AG) 1986, held various positions –1995, Tech. Dir MAN A.S., Ankara (now MAN Türkiye) 1996–99, mem. Exec. Bd 1998–99, Head of Engine Devt, MAN Nutzfahrzeuge AG, Nuremberg 1999–2001, apptd mem. Exec. Bd MAN Nutzfahrzeuge Group 2001, Exec. Bd MAN SE 2006, Chair. Exec. Bd MAN Diesel SE –2009, CEO MAN SE and MAN Nutzfahrzeuge AG 2010–15.

PACINO, Al (Alfredo James); American actor; b. 25 April 1940, New York, NY; s. of Salvatore Pacino and Rosa Pacino; ed High School for the Performing Arts, New York, The Actors Studio; worked as messenger and cinema usher; Co-artistic Dir The Actors Studio, Inc., New York 1982–83; mem. Artistic Directorate Globe Theatre 1997–; Broadway début in Does a Tiger Wear a Necktie? 1969; appeared with Lincoln Center Repertory Co. as Kilroy in Camino Real 1970; other New York appearances include The Connection, Hello Out There, Tiger at the Gates and The Basic Training of Pavlo Hummel 1977, American Buffalo 1981 (UK 1984), Julius Caesar 1988, Salome 1992; appearances at Charles Playhouse, Boston, include: Richard III 1973 (repeated on Broadway 1979), Arturo Ui 1975, Rats (director) 1970; f. Chal Productions (production co.); Nat. Soc. of Film Critics Award (for The Godfather), British Film Award (for The Godfather Part II) Tony Award 1996, American Film Inst. Lifetime Achievement Award 2007, Kennedy Center Honor 2016. *Films include:* Me, Natalie 1969, Panic in Needle Park 1971, The Godfather 1972, Scarecrow 1973, Serpico 1974, The Godfather Part II 1974, Dog Day Afternoon 1975, Bobby Deerfield 1977, And Justice For All 1979, Cruising 1980, Author! Author! 1982, Scarface 1983, Revolution 1985, Sea of Love 1990, Dick Tracy 1991, The Godfather Part III 1990, Frankie and Johnny 1991, Glengarry Glen Ross 1992, Scent of a Woman (Acad. Award for Best Actor 1993) 1992, Carlito's Way 1994, City Hall 1995, Heat 1995, Donnie Brasco 1996, Looking for Richard 1996 (also producer, Dir), Devil's Advocate 1997, The Insider 1999, Chinese Coffee 1999, Man of the People 1999, Any Given Sunday 1999, People I Know 2002, Insomnia 2002, Simone 2002, The Recruit 2003, The Merchant of Venice 2004, Two for the Money 2005, 88 Minutes 2007, Ocean's Thirteen 2007, Righteous Kill 2008, The Son of No One 2011, Stand Up Guys 2012, Salomé 2013, The Last Act 2014, Manglehorn 2014, Danny Collins 2015, Misconduct 2016. *Television includes:* Angels in America (Golden Globe for Best Actor in a Mini-Series or TV Movie 2004, Screen Actors Guild Award for Best Actor in a Miniseries 2004, Emmy Award for Outstanding Lead Actor in a Miniseries 2004) 2003, You Don't Know Jack (film) (Emmy Award for Outstanding Lead Actor 2010, Golden Globe Award for Best Performance by an Actor in a Mini-Series or Movie Made for TV 2011) 2010, Phil Spector (film) 2013. *Address:* c/o Rick Nicita, Creative Artists Agency, 2000 Avenue of the Stars, Los Angeles, CA 90067, USA (office); Chal Productions, 301 West 57th Street, Suite 49A, New York, NY 10017, USA (office). *Telephone:* (424) 288-2000 (office); (212) 247-0227. *Fax:* (424) 288-2900 (office). *Website:* www.caa.com (office).

PACKER, James Douglas; Australian media company executive; *Co-Chairman, Melco Crown Entertainment;* b. 8 Sept. 1967; s. of Kerry Francis Packer and Roslyn Packer; m. 1st Jodie Meaves 1999; m. 2nd Erica Baxter 2007; ed Cranbrook School, Sydney; worked as a 'jackeroo' on a family-owned cattle station, Newcastle Walters; joined family business as magazine sales rep.; Dir Publishing & Broadcasting Ltd (PBL) 1991–, Man. Dir 1996–98, Exec. Chair. 1998–, inherited co. after father's death and split into two public cos, Consolidated Media Holdings Ltd and Crown Ltd, Dir Australian Consolidated Press Group Ltd 1991–2018, Gen. Man. 1993–2018, fmr Jt CEO Consolidated Press Holdings Ltd, Chair. Crown Ltd (now Crown Resorts Ltd) –2015, Exec. Dir 2007–15, 2017–18; currently Co-Chair. Melco Crown Entertainment, Alon, Las Vegas; Chair. Burswood Ltd; Dir Nine Network Australia Ltd 1992–, Huntsman Corpn (Utah) 1994–, Optus Vision Pty Ltd 1995–, Valassas Inserts, USA, Ecorp Ltd 1999–, Challenger International 1999–, Crown Ltd 1999–2015, Hoytes Cinemas Ltd 1999–, Qantas Ltd 2004–07, Foxtel. *Address:* Melco Crown Entertainment, 1/F unit A1 Flower City Building, 199–207 Rua de Evora, Taipa, Macau (office). *Telephone:* (2) 9282-8000 (office). *Fax:* (2) 9282-8828 (office). *E-mail:* info@melco-crown.com (office). *Website:* www.pbl.com.au (office).

PACKER, Sir Richard John, KCB, MSc; British fmr government official and author; b. 18 Aug. 1944, Bexley, England; s. of George Packer and Dorothy Packer; m. 1st Alison Sellwood; two s. one d.; m. 2nd Baroness (Lucy) Neville-Rolfe; four s.; ed City of London School and Univ. of Manchester; joined Ministry of Agric., Fisheries and Food (MAFF) 1967; on secondment, First Sec., Office of Perm. Representation to EEC 1973–76; Prin. Pvt. Sec. to Minister, MAFF 1977–78, Asst Sec. 1979–85, Under-Sec. 1985–89, Deputy Sec. 1989–93, Perm. Sec. 1993–2000; Dir (non-exec.) Express Foods (later Arla Foods) PLC 2002–07. *Publications:* The Politics of BSE 2006, Life to 70 2016. *Leisure interests:* philosophy, history, arts, sport. *Address:* 113 St George's Road, London, SE1 6HY, England (home).

PACKER, William John; British artist, art critic and teacher; b. 19 Aug. 1940, Birmingham; s. of Rex Packer and Molly Wornham; m. Clare Winn 1965; three d.; ed Windsor Grammar School, Wimbledon School of Art; Nat. Diploma in Design (Painting); secondary school teacher 1964–67; part-time art school lecturer 1967–77; art critic, Art & Artists 1969–74, Financial Times 1974–2004; first exhibited Royal Acad. 1963; mem. Fine Art Bd of Council for Nat. Academic Awards and Specialist Adviser 1976–83, Specialist Adviser 1983–87; mem. Advisory Cttee to Govt Art Collection 1977–84, Crafts Council 1980–87; sole selector first British Art Show (Arts Council) 1979–80; external examiner at various art schools 1980–2000; mem. New English Art Club 2006; Trustee, Heatherley's School of Art 2008–14; Hon. Fellow, RCA; Hon. RBA; Hon. RBS; Hon. PS; inaugural Henry Moore Memorial Lecturer, Florence 1986. *Publications:* Art of Vogue Covers 1980, Fashion Drawing in Vogue 1983, Henry Moore 1985, John Houston 2003, Sarah Raphael 2013, Mary Newcomb: Drawing from Observation (co-author) 2018. *Leisure interests:* France, books, singing. *Address:* 60 Trinity Gardens, London, SW9 8DR, England (home). *Telephone:* (20) 7733-4012 (home). *E-mail:* williampacker@hotmail.com (home); williampacker19@gmail.com (home).

PACOLLI, Behgjet Isa; Kosovo/Swiss business executive and politician; *First Deputy Prime Minister and Minister of Foreign Affairs;* b. 30 Aug. 1951, Marevc, Kosovo, Autonomous Region of Kosovo, People's Repub. of Serbia, Fed. People's

Repub. of Yugoslavia; s. of Isa Pacolli and Nazmije Pacolli; m. 1st Anna Oxa 1999 (divorced 2002); m. 2nd Maria (Masha) Pacolli; one s. four d.; ed Institut für Aussenhandel, Univ. of Hamburg, Germany, Institut Mösinger, Zurich, Switzerland; emigrated to Hamburg, Germany 1970s; mil. service in Fmr Yugoslavia; fmr Man. Interplastica (eng co.), Switzerland; f. Mabetex Project Management (construction co.) 1990, now Pres. and CEO Mabetex Group, Lugano, Switzerland; Founder and Leader, Aleanca Kosova e Re (AKR—New Kosovo Alliance) 2006–; mem. (AKR) Ass. of Kosovo 2007–; Pres. of Kosovo 22 Feb.–30 March 2011 (resgnd after his election was declared to have occurred by unconstitutional means); First Deputy Prime Minister of Kosovo 2011–14, 2017–, also Minister of Foreign Affairs 2017–; Int. Councillor, Center for Strategic and Int. Studies, Washington, DC (think-tank); Chief Exec. Lajm (The News); Hon. Citizen of Lezhë, Albania, of Astana, Kazakhstan, of Baton Rouge, La, USA, Hon. Diplomat of Liberia; Highest honours of Russian Fed., of Peru, Cavaliere della Pace (Cavalier of Peace), Int. Union for Peace 2010; hon. titles from Technology Univ., Rochester, NY, USA; Dr hc (European Univ. of Tirana); Certificate of Thanks from American Univ. in Kosovo, Honours of TMK, Recognition from Nelson Mandela Foundation, Recognition from Pres. Clinton, Gusi Peace Prize (Philippines), Chancellor's Gold Medal, Gov. of Louisiana, Key of New Orleans, copy of the key of City of Tirana on the occasion of state visit to Albania 2011. *Address:* Ministry of Foreign Affairs, 10000 Prishtina, Rruga Luan Haradinaj, Kosovo (office); Mabetex Group Headquarters, Via Cattori 7, 6902 Lugano, Switzerland. *Telephone:* (38) 20011087 (Ministry) (office); (91) 9850101. *Fax:* (38) 213985 (Ministry) (office); (91) 9930636. *E-mail:* mfa@rks-gov.net (office); avdii@hotmail.com (office); info@mabetex.com. *Website:* www.mfa-ks.net (office); www.mabetex.com; www.behgjetpacolli.com.

PACQUEMENT, Alfred; French museum administrator (retd); b. 27 Dec. 1948, Paris; ed Université Paris Nanterre; Curator, Centre Nat. d'Art Contemporain 1971–72, with Ministry of Cultural Affairs 1973, Exhbns Dir Musée Nat. d'Art Moderne (MNAM) 1974–81, Curator 1982–87, Attached to Ministry of Culture 1987–89, Dir Galerie Nat. du Jeu de Paume 1990–93, Dir for 'Arts plastiques', Ministry of Culture 1993–96, Dir École Nationale Supérieure des Beaux-Arts 1996–2000, Dir MNAM, Centre Pompidou 2000–13 (retd); Pres. Int. Cttee for Museums and Collections of Art (CIMAM). *Address:* c/o Musée National d'Art Moderne, Place Georges Pompidou, 75004 Paris, France.

PACQUIAO, Emmanuel (Manny) Dapidran; Philippine professional boxer, politician, actor and singer; b. 17 Dec. 1978, Kibawe, Bukidnon, Mindanao; s. of Rosalio Pacquiao and Dionesia Dapidran-Pacquiao; m. Maria Geraldine (Jinkee) Jamora 2000; three s. two d.; ed Notre Dame of Dadiangas Univ., General Santos City, Devt Acad. of the Philippines –Grad. School of Public and Devt Man.; dropped out of high school and left home aged 14; began amateur boxing and made the Philippine nat. amateur boxing team aged 14; amateur record of 64 fights, 60 wins, 4 losses; began professional boxing career aged 16 (light flyweight); currently fights in welterweight div.; World Boxing Council (WBC) Flyweight Champion 1998–99 (stripped); Lineal Flyweight Champion 1998–99; Int. Boxing Fed. (IBF) Super Bantamweight Champion 2001–03 (vacated); The Ring Magazine Featherweight Champion 2003–05 (vacated); WBC Super Featherweight Champion March–July 2008 (vacated); The Ring Super Featherweight Champion March–July 2008 (vacated); WBC Lightweight Champion 2008–09 (vacated); Int. Boxing Org. (IBO) Light Welterweight Champion 2009–10; The Ring Light Welterweight Champion 2009–10 (vacated); World Boxing Org. (WBO) Welterweight Champion (Super Champion) 2009–12; WBC Light Middleweight Champion 2010–11 (stripped); WBO Welterweight Champion (Super Champion) 2014–15; regional and int. championships: OPBF Flyweight Champion 1997–98 (vacated), WBC Super Bantamweight Champion Int. title 1999–2001 (vacated), WBC Super Featherweight Champion Int. title 2005–08 (won world title), WBO Welterweight Champion Int. title 2013–14 (won world title); lost to five-div. world champion Floyd Mayweather (q.v.) by unanimous points decision in richest title fight in history, billed as The Fight of the Century, Battle for Greatness or Legacy, at MGM Grand Garden Arena, Las Vegas 2 May 2015; sustained right shoulder injury prior to fight, requiring surgery and up to 12 months recovery; 65 total fights, 57 wins (38 by knockout), 6 losses (3 knockouts, 3 decisions), 2 draws; rated by The Ring Magazine as the No. 1 pound-for-pound boxer in the world 2008–12; first boxer to win seven world titles in seven different weight divs; flagbearer for The Philippines at Beijing Olympics (non-participant) 2008; player and Head Coach, Kia Carnival Basketball team 2014–; Chair. People's Champ Movt 2009–; mem. (People's Champ Movt, then with Nacionalista Party, then with Partido Demokratiko Pilipino-Lakas ng Bayan, then United Nationalist Alliance), House of Reps for Sarangani, Lone Dist 2010–; entered Reserve Force of Philippine Army as a Sergeant 2006, rank of Tech. Sergeant 2006, Master Sergeant 2007, special rank of Sr Master Sergeant 2009, also designated as Command Sergeant Maj. of 15th Ready Reserve Div. 2009, rank of Lt Col 2011; has appeared in several films and TV shows; has also turned to singing as part of his entertainment career and has recorded two albums; Hon. mem. Boston Celtics 2010; Champion for Life (Kampeon Habambuhay) 2006, Order of Lakandula 2006, Officer (Pinuno), Philippine Legion of Honor 2008, Grand Cross with Gold Distinction (Datu), Order of Sikatuna 2009; Hon. DH (Southwestern Univ.) 2009; Presidential Medal of Merit 2003, Ring Magazine Fighter of the Year 2006, 2008, Boxing Writers Asscn of America Fighter of the Year 2006, 2008, WBC Emer. Champion, Five-Time PSA Sportsman of the Year, World Boxing Hall of Fame 2007, Univ. Athletic Asscn of the Philippines Hon. Award for Sports Excellence 2008, BoxingScene.com Fighter of the Year 2008, Sports Illustrated Boxer of the Year 2008, SecondsOut.-com Fighter of the Year 2008, TheSweetScience.com Boxer of the Year 2008, WBC Boxer of the Year 2008, Yahoo Sports Fighter of the Year 2008, ESPN Star's Champion of Champions 2008, ESPY Awards Best Fighter 2009, Bleacher Report 2010, Fighter of the Year, World Boxing Org. 2010, Gabriel 'Flash' Elorde Memorial 'Quintessential Athlete' Award 2011, Reader's Digest Asia Pacific Most Trusted Personality 2013, PublicAffairsAsia HP Gold Standard Award for Communicator of the Year 2014. *Recordings include:* albums: Laban Nating Lahat Ito 2006, Pac-Man Punch 2007; several singles. *Address:* c/o Top Rank, Inc., 748 Pilot Road, Las Vegas, NV 89119, USA (office); c/o Krista Gem J. Mercado, Room SWA-403, House of Representatives, HOR Complex, Constitution Hills, Quezon City 1126, The Philippines (office). *E-mail:* info@toprank.com (office). *Website:* www.toprank.com (office); www.congress.gov.ph/members/search

.php?id=pacquiao-e (office); mp8.ph. *Telephone:* (632) 931-5001 (office). *Fax:* (632) 932-0535 (office).

PADAR, Ivari, BA; Estonian politician; b. 12 March 1965, Navi village, Võru county; m.; one s. one d.; ed Tartu Univ.; began career as transport worker, Võru Dairy Factory 1984–88; carpenter, Võru Dept of Repairs and Construction 1988–90; teacher, Võru School 1990–92; Deputy Mayor of Võru 1993–94; Asst to Chancellor of the Exchequer 1995–97; Dir-Gen. AS HT Hulgi (customs warehouse) 1997–99; Minister of Agric. 1999–2002, of Finance 2007–09; Chair. Võru City Council 2002–03; Advisor AS Tallink Duty Free 2002–03; mem. Riigikogu (Parl.) 2002–09; mem. Estonian Social Democratic Party (Sotsiaaldemokraatlik Erakond) 1999–, Chair. 2003–10; mem. European Parl. (Group of the Progressive Alliance of Socialists and Democrats) 2009–14, 2017–; mem. Farmers Union of Võru Co. (Chair. 1994–95); Hon. Pres. Estonian Asscn of Equestrian Sports; Hon. mem. Estonian Grilling Union, Eesti Lihakasvatajate Selts, Eesti Noortalunike Ühing, Eesti Sporthobuste Kasvatajate Selts; Order of the Nat. Coat of Arms (Third Class) 2011; Friend of the Press, Estonian Newspaper Asscn 2008. *Address:* European Parliament, 60 rue Wiertz, 1047 Brussels, Belgium (office). *Telephone:* (2) 284-55-46 (office). *E-mail:* ivari.padar@europarl.europa.eu (office). *Website:* www.padar.ee.

PADDA, Bali; British business executive; *CEO and President, Lego Group;* b. 1956, Punjab, India; m.; one s. one d.; ed Gordon School, Gravesend, Kent; moved to UK with parents 1968; moved to USA with family 1999; with Customer Services Dept, GlaxoSmithKline PLC 1998–2000; Vice-Pres., Supplier Relations, The Timberland Co. 2001–02; Sr Dir Market Oriented Packing, Lego Group 2002–03, Head of Global Logistics 2003–05, Head of Global Supply Chain 2005–06, Exec. Vice-Pres. Global Supply Chain 2006–11, Chief Operating Officer 2011–16, Interim Exec. Vice-Pres. of Human Resources 2015–16, CEO and Pres. Lego Group (first non-Danish) Jan. 2017–Oct. 2017. *Address:* The Lego Group, Aastvej 1, 7190 Billund, Denmark (office). *Telephone:* 79-50-60-70 (office). *Website:* www.lego.com (office).

PADILLA, James (Jim) J., BChemEng, MChemEng, MEconSc; American automobile industry executive (retd); *Chairman, Magellan Fuel Solutions Inc.;* b. 1947, Detroit, Mich.; ed Univ. of Detroit; joined Ford Motor Co. as Quality Control Engineer 1966; held various man. positions in product eng and manufacturing including manufacturing operations man. for Ford Escort and Mercury Tracer, Ford Contour and Mercury Mystique, Ford Taurus and Mercury Sable car lines 1976–92, Dir of Eng and Manufacturing, Jaguar Cars 1992–94, Dir of performance luxury vehicle lines 1994–96, Pres. S American Operations 1996–98, Group Vice-Pres. for Global Manufacturing 1999, for Quality 2001, Group Vice-Pres. N America 2001–02, Pres. N American Operations 2002, then Exec. Vice-Pres. and Pres. the Americas, COO and Chair. Automotive Operations 2004, Pres. and COO Ford Motor Co. 2004–06 (retd); currently Chair. Magellan Fuel Solutions Inc.; Dir Azure Dynamics Corpn 2007–12; mem. US Dept of Commerce Manufacturing Council; Fellow, Nat. Acad. of Eng; Distinguished Eagle Scout; Ohtli Award (Mexico) 2004. *Address:* Magellan Fuel Solutions Inc., 2711 Centerville Road., Suite 400, Wilmington, DE 19808, USA (office). *E-mail:* info@magellanfuel.com (office). *Website:* www.magellanfuel.com (office).

PADILLA DE LEÓN, Gen. (retd) Freddy; Colombian army officer, government official and diplomatist; b. 10 Oct. 1948, Montería, Córdoba; m. Miriam Hodges de Padilla; ed Escuela Militar de Cadetes Gen. José María Córdova, Pontificia Univ. Javeriana, Univ. de Chile; Prof. of Mil. Geography and Geopolitics, Academia de Guerra del Ejército de Chile 1999; joined Colombian army 1966, attained rank of Brig.-Gen. 1997, Maj.-Gen. 2001, Gen. 2004, Gen. (Four Stars) 2009; Jt Gen. Chief of Staff 2003–06, Commdr Gen. of Mil. Forces 2006–10, also Minister of Nat. Defence 2009–10; Amb. to Austria 2010–13 (resgnd); Gran Oficial de la Legión de Honor 2008; numerous awards including Orden de Boyacá, Orden de la Democracia, Servicios Distinguidos en Orden Público.

PADOAN, Pier Carlo; Italian economist, international organization executive, academic and government official; ed Univ. of Rome; has held various academic positions in Italian and foreign univs including at Univ. of Rome, College of Europe (Bruges), Université Libre de Bruxelles, Univ. of Urbino, Universidad de La Plata and Univ. of Tokyo; Italian Exec. Dir at IMF, Washington, DC, with competence also for Greece, Portugal, San Marino, Albania and Timor Leste, served as mem. Bd and chaired several Bd Cttees, was also in charge of European Coordination; Econ. Adviser to Prime Ministers Massimo D'Alema and Giuliano Amato, in charge of int. econ. policies 1998–2001; Pres. of Econs, Univ. La Sapienza, Rome and Dir Fondazione Italianieuropei (policy think-tank) 2001–07; Deputy Sec.-Gen. OECD 2007–13, in charge of relations with other int. orgs, also Chief Economist 2009; Minister of Economy and Finance 2014–18; mem. Partito Democratico 2018–. *Address:* Partito Democratico, Via Sant'Andrea delle Fratte 16, 00187 Rome, Italy (office). *Website:* www.partitodemocratico.it (office).

PADRINO LÓPEZ, Vladimir; Venezuelan military commander and politician; *Minister of Defence;* ed Mil. Acad. of Venezuela; commanded Mortar Personnel, Antonio Ricaurte Infantry Bn, Rubio, Táchira State, Col, Simon Bolivar Infantry Bn Fuerte Tiuna 2002, later Chief of Jt Staff of Strategic Defence, apptd Commdr-in-Chief of Armed Forces 2013; Minister of Defence (also Strategic Operational Commdr of Bolivarian Nat. Armed Forces) 2014–. *Address:* Ministry of Defence, Edif. 17 de Diciembre, planta baja, Base Aérea Francisco de Miranda, La Carlota, Caracas, Venezuela (office). *Telephone:* (212) 607-1603 (office). *E-mail:* prensafuerzaarmada@gmail.com (office). *Website:* www.mindefensa.gob.ve (office).

PADVA, Genrikh Pavlovich; Russian lawyer; *Managing Partner, Padva & Partners;* b. 20 Feb. 1931, Moscow; s. of Pavel Padva and Eva Rappoport; ed Moscow Inst. of Law; Kalinin Pedagogical Inst.; mem. Kalinin Bar 1953, Presidium 1965–71, of Moscow Bar 1971–, of the Presidium 1986, Dir Research Inst. of Bar; one of founders of the USSR (now Russian) Union of Barristers, Deputy-Chair. of the Exec. Board 1990; Vice-Pres. of the Int. Asscn of Lawyers 1990, acted as a barrister on major political and economic trials in 1970s, was a lawyer for many dissidents, rendered legal advice to the families of Andrei Sakharov, singer Vladimir Vysotsky, Pavel Borodin; represented Mikhail Khodorkovsky in criminal proceedings; investigated some major econ. and criminal cases in late 1980s–1990s, a founder and Dir-Gen. of Russian-American Int. Lawyers Co.; Man. Partner Padva & Partners, Attorneys at Law; currently Vice-Pres.

International Union (Commonwealth) of Advocates; mem. Central Council of the Russian Lawyers Asscn, Academic Council, Federal Chamber of Advocates of Russia; Honoured Barrister of Russian Fed., F.N. Plevako Gold Medal. *Publications:* articles in specialized journals and newspapers on legal problems. *Address:* Padva & Partners, Bolshoi Golovin 6, Moscow 107045, Russia (office). *Telephone:* (495) 737-43-03 (office). *Fax:* (495) 737-43-08 (office). *E-mail:* padva@col.ru (office). *Website:* padvapartners.com (office).

PAE, Chong-yeul, BA; South Korean electronics industry executive; b. 18 Feb. 1943; m.; four c.; began career as jr economist, Research Dept, Bank of Korea 1969–76; Asst Adviser on Econ. Policy, Office of Pres. of Repub. of Korea 1973–75; Man. Planning Dept, Samsung Corpn 1976–83, Pres. Samsung Pacific Int. Inc., LA, USA 1983, Pres. Samsung America Inc., NY 1983–87, Sr Exec. Man.-Dir Sales and Marketing, Semiconductor Div., Samsung Electronics Co. Ltd 1988–90, Vice-Pres., Office of Chair., Samsung Group 1991–93, Pres. and CEO Samsung Corpn Ltd 2001; Exec. Vice-Pres. Joong-ang Daily News 1994–98; Pres. and CEO Cheil Communications Inc. 1998–2001.

PAEK, Ryong-chon; North Korean government official and central banker; *Governor, Central Bank of the DPRK;* b. 1962; s. of Paek Nam-sun (fmr Minister of Foreign Affairs); fmr Deputy Dir, Cabinet Secr.; mem. N Korean del. to working-level talks on inter-Korean econ. co-operation, Seoul 2002, and inter-Korean Jt Summit, Gwangju 2006; Gov. Central Bank of DPRK 2011–; Alt. mem. Korean Workers' Party Cen. Cttee. *Address:* Office of the Governor, Central Bank of the DPRK, Munsudong, Seungri Street 58-1, Central District, Pyongyang, Democratic People's Republic of Korea (office). *Telephone:* (2) 3338196 (office). *Fax:* (2) 3814624 (office). *E-mail:* kcb_idkb@co.chesin.com (office).

PAENIU, Rt Hon Bikenibeu, BAgr, MSc; Tuvaluan politician and economist; b. 10 May 1956, Bikenibeu, Tarawa; m. Foketi Paeniu; two s. two d.; ed King George V School, Tarawa, Univ. of S Pacific, Suva and Univ. of Hawaii; worked in Agric. Div. Tuvalu; later Asst Economist, South Pacific Comm. Nouméa; returned to Tuvalu 1988; MP 1989–2006; Prime Minister of Tuvalu 1989–93, 1996–99; Minister for Finance and Econ. Planning and Industries –2006.

PAES, Leander Adrian; Indian professional tennis player; b. 17 June 1973, Goa; s. of Vece Paes and Jennifer Paes; m. Rhea Pillai; one d.; ed Madras Christian Coll. Higher Secondary School, St Xavier's Coll., Kolkata; winner, Davis Cup (singles) 1993, 1994, 1995, 1997, 2007, (doubles) 1995, 1997, 1998, 2005, 2007, Atlanta Olympics (bronze medal) (men's singles) 1996, ATP Championships (men's singles), Newport 1998, Wimbledon and French Open Championships (men's doubles) 1999, Wimbledon (mixed doubles) 1999, French Open (men's doubles) 2001, Asian Games (gold medal), Busan 2002, Australian Open, Wimbledon (mixed doubles) 2003, US Open (men's doubles) 2006, Asian Games (two gold medals) (men's doubles, mixed doubles), Doha 2006, US Open (mixed doubles) 2008, French Open, US Open (men's doubles) 2009, 2013, US Open (mixed doubles runner-up) 2009, Australian Open (mixed doubles) 2010, 2015, Commonwealth Games (bronze medal) (men's doubles), New Delhi 2010; Dir Leander Sport Pvt. Ltd; Rajiv Gandhi Khel Ratna 1996–97, Arjuna Award 1998, Padma Shri 2001, Padma Bhushan 2014. *Address:* Leander Sport Private Limited, 4121/B, 19th A Main, 6th Cross, HAL II Stage Extension, Bangalore 560 038, India (office). *E-mail:* ara@leandersport.com (office). *Website:* www.leandersport.com (office).

PAES de SOUSA, Rômulo, PhD; Brazilian epidemiologist, public policy adviser and international organization official; *Director, UNDP World Centre for Sustainable Development (RIO + Centre);* ed Universidade Federal do Pará, Universidade Federal de Minas Gerais, Univ. of London; Reader, Post-Graduation Program of Social Sciences, PUC Minas 2002–08; Nat. Sec. of Evaluation and Information Man., Ministério do Desenvolvimento Social e Combate à Fome 2004–07, Deputy Minister of Social Devt 2009–12; Strategic Evaluation Adviser, Unimed-BH 2007–09; Sr Int. Assoc., Inst. of Devt Studies, Univ. of Sussex 2012–13; Dir UNDP World Centre for Sustainable Devt (RIO+ Centre) 2013–; Sr Investigator, Fiocruz 2018–; Research Assoc., Government Studies Center, Federal Univ. of Rio Grande do Sul; Assoc. Prof., International Relations Institute, Pontifical Catholic Univ. of Rio de Janeiro; fmrly worked as adviser and consultant for FAO, IADB, PAHO, World Bank, DFID; Hon. Assoc., Inst. of Development Studies, Univ. of Sussex, Hon. Prof., Government School of the Oswaldo Cruz Foundation (Fiocruz). *Publications include:* Senior Development Fellowship Report 2013, Evaluating Social Protection Policies: Lessons from Brazil 2013, books on epidemiology, on monitoring and policy evaluation, and several articles in scientific journals. *Address:* RIO+ Centre, Palácio do Itamaraty, Avenida Marechal Floriano, 196, Centro, 20080-002, Rio de Janeiro, RJ, Brazil (office). *Telephone:* (21) 99114-1154 (office). *E-mail:* rio.mais@undp.org (office). *Website:* riopluscentre.org (office).

PAET, Urmas, BA; Estonian journalist and politician; b. 20 April 1974, Tallinn; m. Tiina Paet; three d.; ed Univ. of Tartu, Univ. of Oslo, Norway; ed., Chief Editorial Office for Int. News, Estonian Radio 1991–92, ed., News Editorial Office 1993–94; reporter, News Editorial Office, AS Postimees 1994–98, Sr Ed. and Political Journalist 1998–99; mem. and Adviser, Estonian Reform Party 1999–; Dist Elder, Nõmme (Dist of Tallinn) 1999–2003; Minister of Culture 2003–05, of Foreign Affairs 2005–14. *Leisure interests:* cycling, skiing, theatre, cinema, literature. *Address:* Estonian Reform Party, Tõnismagi 9, Tallinn 10119, Estonia (office). *Telephone:* 680-8080 (office). *Fax:* 680-8081 (office). *E-mail:* info@reform.ee (office). *Website:* www.reform.ee (office).

PAGAN, Adrian Rodney, BEcons, PhD, FASSA, FES, AO; Australian economist and academic; *Professor Emeritus of Economics, University of Sydney;* b. 12 Jan. 1947, Mungindi, Qld; m.; two c.; ed Queensland Univ., Australian Nat. Univ.; Visiting Research Fellow, Princeton Univ., USA 1973; Lecturer, then Sr Lecturer, ANU, 1974–80, Sr Research Fellow 1980–83, Sr Fellow 1983–88, Adjunct Prof. 1989–90, Prof. of Econs, Research School of Social Sciences 1992–2006; Prof. of Econs, Univ. of Rochester, USA 1986–90, 1992–95, Wilson Prof. of Econs 1990–92; Sr Research Fellow, Nuffield Coll., Oxford 2003–; Prof. of Econs, Queensland Univ. of Tech. 2005–10; Prof. of Econs, Australian School of Business, Univ. of New South Wales 2007–09; Distinguished Research Prof., Univ. of Tech., Sydney 2010; Prof. of Econs, Univ. of Sydney 2011–12, then Prof. Emer. of Econs; Visiting Prof., Inst. of Advanced Studies, Vienna, Austria 1982, Yale Univ., USA 1985, Johns Hopkins Univ., USA 1996, 2000–, UCLA, USA 1997; mem. Bd Reserve Bank of Australia 1995–2000; Professorial Assoc., Univ. of Melbourne 1996–99; Professorial Fellow, Nuffield Coll. and Visiting Prof. of Econs, Univ. of Oxford, UK 2000–02; numerous assoc. editorships and editorial bd memberships; Fellow, Centre of Operations Research and Econometrics 1977–78, Econometric Soc. 1985, Journal of Econometrics 1990; Hon. Professorial Fellow, Australian Nat. Univ. 2016–; University of Queensland Scholarship, Esso Prize in Accounting, Brinds Prize in Econs, Univ. Medal (Queensland), Medallist Fellow and Socio-Econ. Systems Medal, Modelling and Simulation Soc. of Australia 1997, Distinguished Fellow Award, Econ. Soc. of Australia 1999, Centenary Medal 2003. *Publications include:* The Theory of Economic Policy (with A. J. Preston) 1982, The Effects of Inflation (co-ed. with P. K. Trivedi) 1983, Non-Parametric Econometrics (with A. Ullah) 1999, Quantitative Macroeconomic Modeling with Structural Vector Autoregressions: An Eviews Implementation (with Sam Ouliaris and J. Restrepo) 2016; numerous journal articles on macro-econ. modelling and its uses in policy analysis and for the explanation of business cycles. *Address:* 61 Albert Street, Williamstown, Vic. 3016, Australia (home). *Telephone:* (4) 1647-2474 (home). *E-mail:* adrian.pagan@sydney.edu.au (office). *Website:* www.sydney.edu.au (office).

PAGANI, Rémy; Swiss writer and politician; b. 21 April 1954, Geneva; m.; two c.; active in local politics 1974–87; Union Sec., Syndicat interprofessionnel de travailleuses et travailleurs (SIT) 1987–97; Perm. Sec., Syndicat des Services Publics (trade union) 1997–2007; Deputy, Geneva City Council 1997–2005; apptd mem. Exec. Council, City of Geneva 2007, Head of Building and Town Planning Dept, Mayor of Geneva 2009–10, 2012–13; mem. À gauche toute! coalition. *Publications:* Les beaux jours reviendront, Entre chien et loup, Confession d'un commissaire de police, Étrange balade. *Website:* remy-pagani.isuisse.com.

PAGBALHA, Geleg Namgyai; Chinese administrator; *Honorary President Buddhist Association of China;* b. Feb. 1940, Litang Co., Sichuan Prov.; was confirmed by the Qangdin Lamasery as 11th incarnation of a living Buddha 1942; Vice-Chair. Qamdo Prefectural People's Liberation Cttee, Tibet Autonomous Region 1950; Vice-Chair. Tibet Autonomous Regional Preparatory Cttee 1956, Vice-Chair. Religious Affairs Cttee, Chair. Ethnic Affairs Cttee; sent to do manual labour 1966–76; Vice-Chair. People's Govt of Tibet Autonomous Region 1979–83; Acting Chair. Tibet Autonomous Region People's Congress 1983–86; Vice-Chair. Tibetan Autonomous Region Cttee of CPPCC and Vice Chair. Standing Cttee of Tibetan Autonomous Regional People's Congress 1983–88; Vice-Chair. 3rd CPPCC Nat. Cttee 1959–64, 4th CPPCC Nat. Cttee 1964–78, mem. Presidium 4th NPC 1975–78, Vice-Chair. 5th CPPCC Nat. Cttee 1978–83, mem. Presidium 5th NPC 1978–83, Exec. Chair. 6th CPPCC 1983–88, Vice-Chair. 7th CPPCC Nat. Cttee 1988–92, 10th CPPCC Nat. Cttee 2003–08, 11th CPPCC Nat. Cttee 2008–13, 12th CPPCC Nat. Cttee 2013–18; Deputy, 2nd NPC 1959, 3rd NPC 1964, 4th NPC 1975, 5th NPC 1978, Vice-Chair. Standing Cttee 8th NPC 1993–98, 9th NPC 1998–2003; Chair. CPPCC, Tibetan Autonomous Region 1993–; Vice-Pres. Buddhist Asscn of China 1993–2002, Hon. Pres. 2002–; Pres. China Tibet Devt Foundation. *Address:* Buddhist Association of China, 25 Fuchengmennei Dajie, Xicheng Qu, Beijing, People's Republic of China (office).

PAGE, Ashley, OBE; British classical dancer, choreographer, artistic director and opera director; b. (Ashley John Laverty), 9 Aug. 1956, Rochester, Kent, England; s. of John H. Laverty and Sheila R. Medhurst; m. Nicola J. Roberts; one s. one d.; ed St Andrew's, Rochester, Royal Ballet, Lower and Upper Schools; joined Royal Ballet Co. 1975, soloist 1980, Prin. 1984, House Choreographer; leading roles in classical and modern repertoire; cr. numerous roles for MacMillan, Ashton and other leading choreographers; Choreographer, Royal Opera House 1984; with numerous cos in London, Europe; Artistic Dir, Scottish Ballet 2002–12; freelance with numerous comms 2012–, including for San Francisco Ballet, Warsaw Ballet, Royal Ballet of Flanders, Glyndebourne Opera, New Year's Concert in Vienna 2013, 2014, Rambert, Vienna State Ballet, Scottish Opera, Nevill Holt Opera, Staatstheater Darmstadt, Nat. Ballet of Croatia, Tulsa Ballet, Joffrey Ballet/Chicago; Dr hc (Royal Conservatoire of Scotland); Frederick Ashton Choreographer Award 1982, Frederick Ashton Memorial Comm. Award 1990, Time Out Dance Award 1994, Olivier Award for Best New Dance Production 1995, TMA Award for Outstanding Achievement in Dance (with Scottish Ballet) 2004, Herald Angel Award (for Scottish Ballet Dances Balanchine, Edinburgh Festival) 2005, Herald Archangel for five Edinburgh Festival programmes with Scottish Ballet 2011, De Valois Award For Outstanding Achievement 2012. *Productions include:* 19 works for the Royal Ballet, two for the Dutch Nat. Ballet, four for the Rambert Dance Co. and several for Dance Umbrella, West Australian Ballet and other cos, six works for Scottish Ballet (including four full-length). *Films:* (all dance): Savage Water (Channel 4) 1989, Soldat (BBC) 1990; (art film): Pull – Dance for the Camera with Bruce McLean 1998. *Leisure interests:* visual arts, film, music, reading, theatre, travel, photography, driving, family, friends. *Address:* c/o Loesje Sanders Ltd, The Old Rectory, Church Road, Limpenhoe, Norwich, NR13 3JB, England (office). *Telephone:* (1394) 385260 (office). *E-mail:* info@loesjesanders.org.uk (office); ashleypage3@me.com (office).

PAGE, Geneviève, (pseudonym of Geneviève Bonjean); French actress; b. 13 Dec. 1927, Paris; d. of Jacques Bonjean and Germaine Lipmann; m. Jean-Claude Bujard 1959; one s. one d.; ed Lycée Racine, Paris, Univ. of Paris (Sorbonne), Conservatoire nat. d'art dramatique, École du Louvre; prin. actress in the Comédie Française, the Jean-Louis Barrault company and TNP Jean Vilar; has appeared in many famous classical and tragic stage roles, including Les larmes amères de Petra von Kant (Critics' Prize for Best Actress 1980), La nuit des rois, L'aigle à deux têtes, Angelo, tyran de Padoue 1984, Perséphone 1988, Mère Courage 1988, Le balcon 1991, Paroles de poètes 1992, La peste 1992, La femme sur le lit 1994 (Colombe Prix, Plaisir du Théâtre Best Actress), Les grandes forêts 1997, 2009, Delicate Balance 1998, Le martyre de Saint Sébastien 2005; Chevalier du Mérite sportif, du Cèdre du Liban, Officier des Arts et des Lettres 2006, Officier de la Légion d'honneur 2013. *Films include:* Ce siècle a cinquante ans, Pas de pitié pour les femmes, Fanfan la tulipe, Lettre ouverte, Plaisirs de Paris, Nuits andalouses, L'étrange désir de M. Bard, Cherchez la femme, L'homme sans passé, Foreign Intrigue, The Silken Affair, Michael Strogoff, Un amour de poche, Song Without End, Le bal des adieux, El Cid, Les égarements, Le jour et l'heure, L'honorable correspondence, Youngblood Hawke, Le majordome, Les corsaires, Trois chambres à Manhattan, Grand Prix, Belle de jour, Mayerling, A Talent for Loving, The Private Life of Sherlock Holmes, Les Gémeaux, Décembre, Buffet froid, Beyond Therapy 1987, Les bois noirs 1991, Lovers 1999, Last Night 1999, Eye of the

Beholder 2000, Eye 2000, Rien que du bonheur 2002, Britannicus (as Agrippine) 2011. *Television includes:* La nuit des rois 1962 (Best Actress TV, Quatre Siècles de Théâtre français 2002), La chambre 1964, La chasse aux hommes 1976, Athalie 1980, Les gens ne sont pas forcément ignobles 1990, Mémoire en fuite 2001. *Music includes:* Jeanne au Boucher-Persephone, Le Martyre de St-Sebastien, Oedipus Rex, Histoire du Soldat. *Publications include:* Pour l'amour du Grec, Les Femmes et l'Amour. *Leisure interests:* ancient artefacts, skiing, tennis, riding, skin diving. *Address:* 52 rue de Vaugirard, 75006 Paris, France.

PAGE, Lawrence (Larry) Edward, MS; American computer scientist, internet industry executive and entrepreneur; *CEO, Alphabet Inc.;* b. 26 March 1973, Lansing, Mich.; s. of Dr Carl Victor Page and Gloria Page; m. Lucinda Southworth 2007; two c.; ed East Lansing High School, Univ. of Michigan, Stanford Univ.; co-f. (with Sergey Brin) Google Inc. 1998, Co-Pres. and CEO 1998–2001, Pres., Products 2001–11, CEO 2011–15, CEO Alphabet Inc. (holding co. containing Google and new ventures) 2015–; mem. Nat. Advisory Cttee, Univ. of Michigan Coll. of Eng; mem. Nat. Acad. of Eng 2004; mem. Bd of Trustees, X PRIZE; Fellow, Marconi Foundation at Columbia Univ. 2004; Hon. MBA (IE Business School) 2003, Dr hc (Univ. of Michigan) 2009; named a World Econ. Forum Global Leader for Tomorrow 2002, Marconi Prize (with Sergey Brin) 2004, Economist Innovation Award (with Sergey Brin) 2005. *Film:* Broken Arrows (exec. producer) 2009. *Address:* Alphabet Inc., 1600 Amphitheatre Parkway, Mountain View, CA 94043, USA (office). *Telephone:* (650) 253-0000 (office). *Fax:* (650) 253-0001 (office). *Website:* www.google.com (office); plus.google.com/+LarryPage/posts.

PAGE, Lyman Alexander, Jr, BS, PhD; American physicist, cosmologist and academic; *Henry DeWolf Smyth Professor of Physics and Chairman, Department of Physics, Princeton University;* b. 24 Sept. 1957, San Francisco, Calif.; m. Lisa Olson; three s.; ed Bowdoin Coll., Massachusetts Inst. of Tech.; took a job operating a cosmic ray station in McMurdo Sound, Antarctica 1978, spent two months at South Pole helping to make solar observations; worked as painter, rigger and boat carpenter while sailing a 37-foot ketch along the east coast of the USA and around Caribbean 1980–82; currently Henry DeWolf Smyth Prof. of Physics, Princeton Univ., Chair. Dept of Physics; mem. NAS 2006; Fellow, American Acad. of Arts and Sciences 2004; NASA Grad. Student Researchers Program Fellowship 1987–89, Princeton Eng Council Teaching Award 1992, 1994, NSF NYI Award 1993, Research Corpn Cottrell Scholar 1994, David & Lucile Packard Fellowship 1994, Primakoff Lectureship 2003, Marc Aaronson Lectureship and Prize 2003, Philips Lectureship 2006, Shaw Prize in Astronomy (co-recipient) 2010, Cosmology Prize, Peter Gruber Foundation (co-recipient) 2015, Breakthrough Prize in Fundamental Physics 2018. *Achievements include:* one of the original co-investigators for the Wilkinson Microwave Anisotropy Probe that measured the cosmic background radiation. *Publications:* numerous papers in professional journals. *Address:* Department of Physics, Princeton University, PO Box 708, 217 Jadwin Hall, Princeton, NJ 08544-0708, USA (office). *Telephone:* (609) 258-5578 (office). *Fax:* (609) 258-6853 (office). *E-mail:* page@princeton.edu (office). *Website:* www .princeton.edu/physics (office); phy-page-imac.princeton.edu/~page (office).

PAGLIA, Camille, BA, MPhil, PhD; American academic and writer; *University Professor of Humanities and Media Studies, University of the Arts;* b. 2 April 1947, Endicott, NY; d. of Pasquale Paglia and Lydia Paglia; ed State Univ. of New York at Binghamton, Yale Univ.; mem. Faculty, Bennington Coll. 1972–80; Visiting Lecturer, Wesleyan Univ. 1980, Yale Univ. 1980–84; Asst Prof., Philadelphia Coll. of Performing Arts (now Univ. of the Arts) 1984–87, Assoc. Prof. 1987–91, Prof. of Humanities 1991–2000; Univ. Prof. of Humanities and Media Studies 2000–. *Publications include:* Sexual Personae: Art and Decadence from Nefertiti to Emily Dickinson 1990, Sex, Art and American Culture: Essays 1992, Vamps and Tramps: New Essays 1994, Alfred Hitchcock's The Birds 1998, Break, Blow, Burn: Camille Paglia Reads Forty-Three of the World's Best Poems 2005, Glittering Images: A Journey Through Art from Egypt to Star Wars 2012, Free Women, Free Men: Sex, Gender, Feminism 2017, Provocations: Collected Essays on Art, Feminism, Politics, Sex, and Education 2018. *Telephone:* (212) 421-1700 (literary agent) (office). *Fax:* (212) 980-3671 (literary agent) (office). *Website:* www.uarts.edu (office).

PĄGOWSKI, Andrzej; Polish graphic designer; b. 19 April 1953, Warsaw; ed Faculty of Poster Design, Acad. of Fine Arts, Poznań; est. own graphic studio 1990–; illustrator of books, covers of compact discs; designer of posters, TV and film billboards, TV programme credits, satirical drawings; has designed over 1,000 posters since 1977, including Husband and Wife and series highlighting dangers of alcohol, tobacco and drug abuse; began co-operation with various magazines as their artistic dir 1986; Art Dir Polish edn of Playboy from 1992 for several years; works in numerous pvt. and public collections, including Metropolitan Museum, New York; Owner and Creative Dir KreacjaPro Co. 1989–; numerous awards include Silver Medal, Biennale Polish Poster 1983, 1993, First Prize, Int. Competition for the Best Film and TV Poster, Los Angeles 1980–93, Silver Hugon, Golden and Silver Badge (twice), Int. Competition Film Poster, Chicago 1982–87, Annual Award of Hollywood Reporters for film posters 1986, Clio Poland Award 1993. *Address:* Andrzej Pągowski Studio P, ul. Balaton 8, 01-981 Warsaw (office); KreacjaPro, ul. Lektykarska 4c/3, 01-687 Warsaw, Poland. *Telephone:* (22) 8649293 (Studio) (office); (22) 8339303 (KreacjaPro) (office). *Fax:* (22) 8649290 (Studio) (office); (22) 8328655 (KreacjaPro) (office). *E-mail:* ap@kreacjapro.pl (office); biuro@kreacjapro.pl (office). *Website:* www.kreacjapro.pl (office); www .pagowski.pl.

PAHAD, Aziz Goolam Hoosein, MA; South African politician; *Special Envoy to Middle East, Ministry of International Relations and Co-operation;* b. 25 Dec. 1940, Schweizer-Reneke, Western Transvaal; s. of Goolam Hoosein Ismail Pahad and Amina Pahad; m. Sandra Pahad 1994; two s. one d.; ed Cen. Indian High School, Johannesburg, Univ. of Witwatersrand, Univ. Coll., London, and Univ. of Sussex, UK; in exile 1964–90; worked in London office of African Nat. Congress (ANC) from 1968, later mem. ANC Revolutionary Council until its dissolution in 1983; rep. of ANC Revolutionary Council in Angola and Zambia; mem. ANC Nat. Exec. Cttee 1985–; Deputy Head, ANC Dept of Int. Affairs 1991; mem. Nat. Peace Exec. Cttee 1991–92; mem. Sub-Council on Foreign Affairs of Transitional Exec. Council 1993–94; MP 1994–2008; Deputy Minister of Foreign Affairs 1994–2008, Special Envoy to Middle East 2014–. *Leisure interests:* listening to music, watching sport, reading. *Address:* Ministry of International Relations and Co-operation,

Union Bldgs, East Wing, 1 Government Avenue, Arcadia, Pretoria 0002, South Africa (office). *Telephone:* (12) 3511000 (office). *Fax:* (12) 3291000 (office). *E-mail:* minister@foreign.gov.za (office). *Website:* www.dfa.gov.za (office).

PAHADIA, Jagannath, MA, LLB; Indian government official; b. 15 Jan. 1932, Bhusawar, Bharatpur Dist; m. Smt. Shanti Devi Pahadia; two s. five d.; ed M.S.J. Coll., Bharatpur, Maharaja Coll., Jaipur and Law Coll., Rajasthan Univ.; mem. Lok Sabha (Parl.) for Bayana constituency (Indian Nat. Congress) 1957–77, 1980–84; mem. Rajya Sabha (upper house of parl.) 1965, mem. Congress Party Parl. Exec. Cttee and Sec. Parl. Congress Party 1967–68; Union (Nat.) Minister of Finance 1967–69, Deputy Minister of Food and Agric. 1970–71, of Supply 1971, of Communications 1973–76, of Labour 1976–77, Union Minister of State for Finance 1980; Chief Minister of Rajasthan 1980–81; Gov. of Bihar 1989–90, of Haryana 2009–14; mem. Indian Nat. Congress Party. *Address:* Indian National Congress, 24 Akbar Road, New Delhi 110 011, India (office). *Telephone:* (11)-23019080 (office). *Fax:* (11)-23017047 (office). *E-mail:* connect@inc.in (office). *Website:* www .inc.in (office).

PAHANG, HM The Sultan of; Abdullah Ri'ayatuddin al-Mustafa Billah Shah ibni Sultan Ahmad Shah al-Musta'in Billah; Malaysian head of state; *Yang di-Pertuan Agong (Supreme Ruler);* b. 30 July 1959, Pekan; s. of Paduka Ayahanda Sultan Ahmad Shah of Pahang and Tengku Ampuan Afzan; m. 1st Tunku Hajjah Azizah Aminah Maimunah Iskandariah 1986; four s. two d.; m. 2nd Cik Puan Julia Rais 1991; three d.; ed Davis Coll., London, Worcester Coll. and Queen Elizabeth Coll., Oxford, Royal Mil. Acad., Sandhurst; Lt-Col, 505 Rejimen Askar Wataniah (Territorial Army Regt) 1999, Col 2000, Brig.-Gen. 2004; Tengku Mahkota (Crown Prince) of Pahang 1975–2019, Regent of Pahang 1979–84, 2016; proclaimed Sultan of Pahang 15 Jan. 2019; elected Yang di-Pertuan Agong (Supreme Ruler of Malaysia) 31 Jan. 2019; C-in-C of the Malaysian Armed Forces 2019–; Pres. Asian Hockey Asscn, Football Asscn of Malaysia 2013–17; mem. FIFA Council 2015–19; Chancellor, Univ. Kuala Lumpur, Univ. Malaysia Pahang, Univ. of Automotive Malaysia; numerous decorations including Grand Knight, Order of Sultan Ahmad Shah of Pahang 1980, Sultan of Brunei Golden Jubilee Medal 2017, Grand Master, Order of the Crown of the Realm 2019, Grand Master, Order of Merit of Malaysia 2019. *Address:* Istana Abu Bakar, Pekan, Pahang, Malaysia (office). *Website:* www.dirajapahang.my (office).

PAHIMI PADACKÉ, Albert; Chadian politician; b. 15 Nov. 1966, Mayo-Kebbi Ouest; fmr Minister of Finance; Minister of Trade –1997; Sec. of State for Finance 2001; Minister of Mines, Energy and Oil 2001; mem. Nat. Ass. for Pala constituency 2002–; cand. in presidential election May 2006; Minister of Agric. –2007, Minister of Justice 2007–08, Minister of Posts, Information Technologies and Communications 2008; Prime Minister 2016–18 (resgnd); mem. Rassemblement Nat. pour la Démocratie au Tchad—le Réveil, currently Leader.

PAHLAVI, Farah Diba, fmr Empress of Iran; b. 14 Oct. 1938; d. of Sohrab and Farida Diba; m. HIM Shah Mohammed Reza Pahlavi 1959 (died 1980); two s. two d.; ed Jeanne d'Arc School and Razi School, Tehran and Ecole Spéciale d'Architecture, Paris; Foreign Assoc. mem. Fine Arts Acad., France 1974; fmr Patron, Farah Pahlavi Asscn (admin. of Social Educ. Asscn), Iran Cultural Foundation and 34 other educational, health and cultural orgs; left Iran 1979, living in Egypt 1980–. *E-mail:* fpahlavi@hotmail.com. *Website:* www.farahpahlavi .org.

PAHOR, Borut, BA; Slovenian politician and head of state; *President;* b. 2 Nov. 1963, Postojna, Socialist Repub. of Slovenia, Socialist Fed. Repub. of Yugoslavia; m. Tanja Pečar; one s.; ed Nova Gorica Grammar School, Faculty of Sociology, Political Sciences and Journalism, Univ. of Ljubljana; mem. League of Communists –1990; mem. Združena Lista Socialnih Demokratov (United List of Social Democrats—renamed Socialni Demokrati—Social Democrats 2005) 1990–2012, Deputy Leader 1993–97, Leader 1997–2012; Ind. 2012–; Deputy to Nat. Ass. 1992–2004, mem. Comms for EU Affairs and the Supervision of Intelligence and Security Services 1992–96, Cttee on Defence 1992–96, Vice-Pres. Cttee on International Relations 1996–97, Chair. Slovenian Del. to the Parl. Ass. of the Council of Europe 1996–97, mem. Constitutional Comm 1996–97, Exec. Cttee of Inter-Parl. Union 1996–97, Pres. Nat. Ass. 2000–04; mem. European Parl. (Socialist Group) 2004–08, Vice-Chair. of Del. to EU-Croatia Jt Parl. Cttee, mem. Cttee Budgetary Control, on Constitutional Affairs; Prime Minister 2008–Sept. 2011, Acting Prime Minister Sept. 2011–Feb. 2012; Pres. of Slovenia 22 Dec. 2012–. *Leisure interest:* sport. *Address:* Office of the President, 1000 Ljubljana, Erjavčeva 17, Slovenia (office). *Telephone:* (1) 4781209 (office); (1) 4781357 (office). *E-mail:* gp.uprs@up-rs.si (office). *Website:* www.up-rs.si (office).

PAHR, Willibald P., DrIur; Austrian diplomatist and politician; b. 5 June 1930, Vienna; m. Ingeborg Varga 1960; one s. one d.; ed Univ. of Vienna and Coll. of Europe, Bruges, Belgium; Asst in Inst. of Int. Law and Int. Relations, Univ. of Vienna 1952–55; served in Fed. Chancellery 1955–76, Head of Section 1968, Head of Dept 1973, Dir-Gen. 1975–76; Fed. Minister for Foreign Affairs 1976–83; Amb. to FRG 1983–85; Sec.-Gen. World Tourism Org. 1986–88; Special Commr for Refugees and Migration, Austrian Ministry of the Interior 1990–95; fmr Chair. Int. Centre for Migration Policy Devt (ICMPD), then Chair. Advisory Bd. *Publications:* Der österreichische Status der dauernden Neutralität 1967, several articles in Revue des Droits de l'Homme, numerous articles on current int. problems in various periodicals; co-ed. Grundrechte, die Rechtsprechung in Europa (journal).

PAI, Ajit Varadaraj, BA, JD; American lawyer and government official; *Chairman, Federal Communications Commission;* b. 10 Jan. 1973, Buffalo, NY; s. of Varadaraj Pai and Radha Pai; m. Janine Van Lancker; one s. one d.; ed Harvard Univ., Univ. of Chicago; clerk for Martin Leach-Cross Feldman, US Dist Court for Louisiana Eastern Dist 1997–98; Trial Attorney (Attorney Gen.'s Honors Program), Antitrust Div., Telecommunications Task Force, US Dept of Justice 1998–2001; Assoc. Gen. Counsel, Verizon Communications Inc. 2001–03; Deputy Chief Counsel to US Senate Judiciary Cttee's Sub-Cttee on Admin. Oversight and the Courts 2003–04; Sr Counsel, Office of Legal Policy 2004–05, Chief Counsel to Sub-Cttee on the Constitution, Civil Rights and Property Rights 2005–07; Deputy Gen. Counsel, later Assoc. Gen. Counsel and Special Advisor to Gen. Counsel, Federal Communications Comm. (FCC) 2007–11, Commr, FCC 2012–, Chair. 2017–; Partner, Jenner & Block, LLP 2011–12; Republican. *Address:* Federal Communications Commission, 445 12th Street, SW, Washington, DC 20554, USA (office). *Telephone:* (202) 418-1440 (office). *Fax:* (866) 418-0232 (office). *E-mail:* mbinfo@fcc.gov (office). *Website:* www.fcc.gov (office).

PAIGE, Elaine, OBE; British singer and actress; b. (Elaine Bickerstaff), 5 March 1948, Barnet, England; d. of Eric Bickerstaff and Irene Bickerstaff; ed Aida Foster Stage school; Variety Club Award for Showbusiness Personality of the Year and Recording Artist of the Year 1986, BASCA Award 1993, Lifetime Achievement Award, Nat. Operatic and Dramatic Asscn 1999. *Theatre includes:* West End, London appearances in Hair 1968, Jesus Christ Superstar 1973, Grease (played Sandy) 1973, Billy (played Rita) 1974, Evita (created role of Eva Perón) (Soc. of West End Theatre Award for Best Actress in a Musical 1978) 1978, Cats (created role of Grizabella) 1981, Abbacadabra (played Carabosse) 1983, Chess (played Florence) 1986, Anything Goes (played Reno Sweeney) 1989, Piaf 1993–94, Sunset Boulevard (played Norma Desmond) 1995–96, The Misanthrope (played Célimène) 1998, The King and I (played Anna) 2000, The Drowsy Chaperone (Novello Theatre, London) 2007. *Recordings include:* albums: Sitting Pretty 1978, Elaine Paige 1981, Stages 1983, Cinema 1984, Love Hurts 1985, Christmas 1986, Memories: The Best Of Elaine Paige 1987, The Queen Album 1988, Elaine Paige: The Collection 1990, Love Can Do That 1991, An Evening With Elaine Paige 1991, Elaine Paige And Barbara Dickson 'Together' 1992, Romance And The Stage 1993, Piaf 1994, Encore 1995, Performance 1996, From A Distance 1997, On Reflection 1998, Centre Stage: The Best of Elaine Paige 2004, Essential Musicals 2006, Elaine Paige and Friends 2010, Celebrating a Life Onstage 2012, The Ultimate Collection 2014, I'm Still Here 2015, Elaine Paige Presents the Musicals 2016; contributions to soundtrack recordings, including Nine, Anything Goes, Chess, Cats, Evita, Billy, The King And I; appears on: Tim Rice Collection: Stage and Screen Classics 1996, Christmas with the Stars Vol. 2 1999. *Leisure interests:* antiques, gardening, skiing, tennis. *Website:* www.elainepaige.com.

PAIGE, Richard (see KOONTZ, Dean Ray).

PAIGE, Roderick (Rod), PhD; American educational administrator and fmr government official; b. 1933, Monticello, Miss.; m. Stephanie Nellons-Paige; one s.; one d.; ed Jackson State Univ., Indiana Univ.; mem. Bd of Educ., Houston Ind. School Dist 1989, Pres. 1992; Supt of Schools 1994; Dean Coll. of Educ. Texas Southern Univ.; US Sec. of Educ. 2001–05; apptd Public Policy Scholar, Woodrow Wilson Int. Center for Scholars 2005; mem. Bd of Dirs Universal Tech. Inst., The Broad Foundation, American Coll. of Educ., Patten Univ., Strake Foundation, Blue Cure Foundation, Texas Charter Schools Asscn, Nat. Council of Economic Education's Comm. on the Skills of the American Workforce; consultant, Greater New Orleans Educ. Foundation; mem. Bd of Trustees, Thomas B. Fordham Foundation 2005–; Richard R. Green Award 1998, Outstanding Urban Educator Award 1999, McGraw Prize in Educ. 2000, Supt of the Year Award 2000, 2001, Lifetime Achievement Award, Urban Houston Network 2015. *Publications:* The War Against Hope: How Teachers' Unions Hurt Children, Hinder Teachers, and Endanger Public Education 2007, The Black-White Achievement Gap: Why Closing It Is the Greatest Civil Rights Issue of Our Time (with Elaine Witty) 2010. *Website:* www.rodpaige.com.

PAIHAMA, Gen. Kundi; Angolan politician and army general; *Governor of Huambo Province;* b. 1958; with Angolan armed forces, also seconded to the Portuguese army; fmr Councillor of Benguela; fmr Minister of the Interior; Gov. of Huíla Prov. 1992–99, also of the City of Luanda; Minister of State Security 1998; elected to Congress (MPLA) 1998; Minister of Nat. Defence 1999–2010, Former Combatants and War Veterans 2010–14; Gov. of Huambo Prov. 2014–. *Website:* www.huambo.gov.ao.

PAIK, Kun-woo; South Korean pianist; b. 10 March 1946, Seoul; ed Juilliard School, USA, studied with Rosina Levine, studied in London with Ilona Kabos and in Italy with Guido Agosti and Wilhelm Kempf; interpreter of piano works of Ravel, Liszt, Scriabin and Prokofiev; has played with orchestras throughout N America and Europe, including Indianapolis Symphony, Rotterdam Philharmonic, Royal Philharmonic, London Symphony, BBC Symphony (soloist, Last Night of the Proms 1987), Orchestre Nat. de France, Polish Radio Nat. Symphony; Music Dir Festival International de Musique de Dinard-Emerald Coast 1993–2014; mem. jury, Tchaikovskyi Competition, Moscow 2007; recitals at maj. European music festivals; Chevalier, Ordre des arts et des lettres 2000, Eun-gwan (Silver Crown), Order of Cultural Merit 2010; winner, Naumburg Competition, Gold Medal, Busoni Int. Piano Competition, three Diapason d'Or awards. *Recordings:* numerous recordings, including complete Prokofiev piano concerti (Diapason d'Or and Nouvelle Académie du disque awards). *Address:* Kajimoto, Tokaido Ginza Bldg., 6-4-1 Ginza, Chuo-ku, Tokyo 104-0061, Japan (office). *E-mail:* inquiry@kajimotomusic.com (office).

PAIN, Emil Abramovich, PhD; Russian sociologist; *Director-General, Center of Ethnopolitical and Regional Studies (CEPRS);* b. 6 Dec. 1948, Kiev; m.; one s.; ed Voronezh State Univ., Moscow State Univ.; researcher on problems of regional sociology and ethnology, problems of nat. conflicts, Voronezh State Univ. and Inst. of Ethnography USSR (now Russian) Acad. of Sciences 1974–91; during perestroika was expert of Deputies' Comm. on Deported Peoples and Problems of Crimea Tartars 1989–91; Chief Adviser Int. Asscn of Foreign Policy 1991–92; Dir-Gen. Cen. Ethnopolitical and Regional Studies (CEPRS) 1993–; mem. Pres.'s Council 1993–97; mem. Expert-Analytical Dept of Pres. of Russia 1994–98; Adviser to Pres. 1996–99; Prof. Inst. of Int. Relations 1992–99, Moscow Univ. 1999–, Inst. of Sociology, Russian Acad. of Sciences; fmr Galina Starovoitova Fellow, Kennan Inst. for Advanced Russian Studies. *Publications:* Russia between the Nation and Empire 2004; numerous articles on relations between nations, prevention of social conflicts, sociology and ethnology. *Address:* CEPRS, Krzhizhanovskogo str. 24/35 Korp. 5, Suite 522, 117259 Moscow, Russia. *Telephone:* (495) 128-56-51 (office); (495) 431-56-07 (home). *Fax:* (495) 128-56-51 (office); (495) 431-56-07 (home).

PAJAZITI, Zenun; Kosovo politician; b. 12 Sept. 1966, Gjilan; m.; two s. one d.; ed Tech. Faculty, Univ. of Prishtina, Prishtina School of Politics, completed Int. Visitor Leadership Programme course on Accountability and Ethics in Govt and Business, sponsored by US Dept of State/US Office, Prishtina; served with Emergency Cttee of Kosovo in Prishtina with responsibility for displaced persons; worked as Programme Devt Co-ordinator with Int. Medical Corps 1999–2000; mem. Advisory Bd for Kosovo Action Together 2000–, Exec. Dir 2005–08; Jt Head, Dept of Sports within Jt Interim Admin. Structure (highest level advisory body to UN Interim Admin Mission in Kosovo—UNMIK) March–Nov. 2000, Head Nov. 2000–04; entered Govt of Kosovo 2004, served in Office of the Prime Minister as Head of Govt Liaison Office with UNMIK and Special Rep. of Sec.-Gen. and Co-ordinator for Standards; consultant, Public Administration International 2005–07, engaged in Support for European Integration and Standards Process (UK Dept for Int. Devt-funded project); Minister of Internal Affairs 2008–10; mem. Partia Demokratike e Kosovës (Democratic Party of Kosovo); Pres. Bd of Volleyball Fed. of Kosovo; Vice-Pres. Olympic Cttee of Kosovo; has participated in int. seminars in Albania, Italy, Turkey and other countries.

PAJTIĆ, Bojan, SJD; Serbian politician; b. 2 May 1970, Senta, Vojvodina; s. of Lazar Pajtić and Anđelija Pajtić; m. Vesna Pajtić; two s.; ed Univ. of Novi Sad Law School; worked briefly in Novi Sad Dist Court; joined Nat. Party of Milan Paroški, changed to Demokratska Stranka (DS—Democratic Party) 1996, Spokesman for Novi Sad City Bd of DS, then Pres. Prov. Party Cttee, mem. Cen. Cttee Presidium, later Vice-Pres., Pres. DS 2014–16; Councillor, City of Novi Sad 2000–04, Vice-Pres. and mem. Exec. Bd, City of Novi Sad 2001–04; mem. Nat. Ass. of Repub. of Serbia and Pres. Nat. Ass., Chief Party Whip 2003–04, Head of Democratic Party in Nat. Ass. 2004; Chair. Exec. Council (Govt) of Vojvodina 2004–09, Pres. 2009–16. *Address:* Demokratska Stranka (Democratic Party), 11000 Belgrade, Terazije 3/IV, Serbia (office). *Telephone:* (11) 3443003 (office). *Fax:* (11) 2444864 (office). *E-mail:* info@ds.org.rs (office). *Website:* www.ds.org.rs (office).

PAK, Gil-yon; North Korean diplomatist; b. 1943; m.; three c.; ed Univ. of Int. Relations; joined Ministry of Foreign Affairs 1964, served as Officer, Consul in Singapore and Myanmar, Section Chief, Deputy Dir, Dir of Ministry 1978–83, Vice-Minister 1983–84, 1996–; Perm. Rep. to UN, New York 1984–96, 2001–08; Order of Kim Il Sung 1992.

PAK, Pong-ju; North Korean government official; b. 23 Oct. 1939; Vice-Dir Party Light Industry Dept 1992–98, 2010–12, Dir 2012; Dir Chemical Industry 1998–2003; Premier of Democratic People's Repub. of Korea 2003–07, 2013–19; mem. Korean Workers' Party, mem. Presidium 2016–. *Address:* Korean Workers' Party, Pyongyang, Democratic People's Republic of Korea (office). *Website:* www.rodong.rep.kp (office).

PAK, Se Ri; South Korean fmr golfer; b. 28 Sept. 1977, Daejeon, Repub. of Korea; won 30 tournaments in Repub. of Korea as amateur; turned professional 1996; moved to USA 1997; became youngest player to capture four major tournments; 22 other Ladies Professional Golf Asscn (LPGA) victories; finished second in LPGA prize money 1998, 2001–2003; first woman in 58 years to make cut in men's golf tournament, SBS Super Tournament on Korean tour (finished tenth overall); 25 LPGA wins; retd 2016; flag bearer in opening ceremony of Winter Olympic Games, Pyeongchang 2018; Rolex Rookie of the Year 1998, Golf Writers Asscn of America Player of the Year 1998, Repub. of Korea Order of Merit 1998, Vare Trophy 2003, LPGA Heather Farr Award 2006, inducted into World Golf Hall of Fame 2007. *Leisure interests:* playing video games, watching television, shopping.

PAK, Su-gil; North Korean politician; mem. Korean Workers' Party, fmr Chair. North Hamgyong Prov. People's Cttee; apptd Vice-Premier and Minister of Finance 2009.

PAK, Ui-chun; North Korean diplomatist and government official; b. 1932; began diplomatic career with posting at Embassy in Cameroon 1972; fmr Amb. to Algeria, Syria and Lebanon; Amb. to Russian Fed. 1998–2006; Minister of Foreign Affairs 2007–14.

PAK, Gen. Yong-sik; North Korean military officer and politician; *Minister of the People's Armed Forces;* fmr official, Ministry of People's Security; fmr Vice-Dir Gen. Political Dept, Korean People's Army; Vice-Chair. special investigation cttee on missing Japanese nationals 2014; Minister of the People's Armed Forces 2015–; attained rank of Maj.-Gen. 1999, Lt-Gen. 2009, Gen. 2015. *Address:* Ministry of the People's Armed Forces, Pyongyang, Democratic People's Republic of Korea (office).

PAKENHAM, Hon. Sir Michael, Kt, KBE, CMG, MA; British consultant and fmr diplomatist; *Senior Adviser, Access Industries;* b. 3 Nov. 1943, Oxford; s. of Earl of Longford and Elizabeth Pakenham, Countess of Longford; brother of Antonia Fraser (q.v.); m. Mimi Doak; two d.; ed Ampleforth Coll., N Yorks., Trinity Coll. Cambridge, Rice Univ., Tex., USA; joined FCO 1965, served in Warsaw, New Delhi, Paris, Washington, DC; seconded to Cabinet Office 1971–74; Counsellor British Representation to EU 1987–91; Amb. to Luxembourg 1991–94; Deputy Sec. to Cabinet, Chair. Jt Intelligence Cttee and Intelligence Co-ordinator 1997–2000; Amb. to Poland 2000–03; Sr Adviser, Access Industries 2004–, Signet Asset Management 2004–06, Droege & Co. (Dusseldorf) 2006–08; European Security Project Consultant, Thales International 2004–06; Deputy Chair. King's Coll. London Council 2005–; Chair. Pakenvest Int.; Vice-Chair. King's Coll. London 2009–, also mem. Governing Council; Dir (non-exec.) Westminster Group 2008–; Trustee Chevening Estate, Inst. for Strategic Dialogue; Patron The Longford Trust. *Leisure interests:* golf, tennis, museums, military history. *Address:* Cope House, 15B Kensington Palace Gardens, London, W8 4QG, England (office). *Telephone:* (20) 7908-9966 (office). *E-mail:* mpakenham@accind.co.uk (office). *Website:* www.accessindustries.com (office).

PAKSAS, Rolandas; Lithuanian politician, engineer and fmr head of state; b. 10 June 1956, Telšiai; s. of Feliksas Paksas and Elena Paksienė; m. Laima Paksienė; one s. one d.; ed Žemaitės Secondary School, Telšiai, Vilnius Inst. of Civil Eng, Leningrad Inst. of Civil Aviation; flight instructor –1984; Chair. Vilnius Darius ir Girenas Aero Club, Aviation Dept, Voluntary Nat. Defence Service 1985–92; Pres. Construction Co. Restako 1992–97; elected to Vilnius City Council, Mayor of Vilnius 1997–99, 2000, elected to Vilnius City Council 2007–09; Prime Minister of Lithuania 1999–2000 (resgnd), 2000–01; Adviser Pres. of Lithuania and Plenipotentiary of Pres. for Special Assignments 1999–2000; elected Chair. newly founded Liberal Democratic Party 2002 (later renamed Order and Justice Party); Pres. of Lithuania 2003–04, charged with violating the constitution and his oath of office March 2004, impeached April 2004; fmr Chair. Lithuanian Liberal Union; mem. European Parl. 2009–, Vice-Chair. Europe of Freedom and Democracy political group. *Leisure interest:* aviation. *Address:* Order and Justice Party, Gedimino Avenue 10/1, Vilnius 01103 (office). *Telephone:* (5) 269-1618 (home). *Fax:* (5) 269-1618 (office). *E-mail:* tt@tvarka.lt (office). *Website:* www.tvarka.lt (office).

PÁL, László; Hungarian electrical engineer and politician; b. 5 Sept. 1942, Budapest; m.; two c.; ed Inst. of Energetics, Moscow, Political Acad., Budapest; Research Inst. for Electrical Eng 1966–69; mem. Nat. Cttee for Technological Devt 1969–89; State Sec. Ministry of Industry 1989–90; mem. Parl. 1990–97; Minister for Industry and Trade 1994–95; Dir and Head of Power Machinery Production, Ganz Holding Rt. –2002; fmr Chair. MOL Rt. (Hungarian Oil and Gas Co.); CEO Magyar Villamos Müvek Reszvenytarsag (MVM—nat. electricity co.) 2002–11; mem. several MTESZ (Fed. of Tech. and Scientific Socs) and GTTSZ (Fed. of Econ. and Scientific Socs) asscns; mem. Energetic Cttee of Hungarian Acad. of Sciences, AGORA Asscn, Bd AISEC Hungary; Pro Inventore Prize, Borbála Prize, Lóránd Eötvös Award 1986, János Neumann Award 1988. *Address:* c/o Magyar Villamos Muvek Zrt., Szentendrei út 207–209, 1031 Budapest, Hungary. *E-mail:* info@mvm.hu.

PÁL, Lénárd; Hungarian physicist; *Research Professor Emeritus, Centre for Energy Research, Hungarian Academy of Sciences;* b. 7 Nov. 1925, Gyoma; s. of Imre Pál and Erzsébet Varga; m. Angela Danóci 1963; one d.; ed Budapest and Moscow Univs; Dept Head, Cen. Research Inst. for Physics, Budapest 1953–56, Deputy Dir 1956–69, Dir 1970–74, Dir-Gen. 1974–78; Prof. of Nuclear Physics, Eötvös Lóránd Univ., Budapest 1961–77, 1989–98; Pres. State Office for Tech. Devt 1978–80, 1984–85, Nat. Atomic Energy Comm. 1978–80, 1984–85; mem. Science Policy Cttee, Council of Ministers 1978–85; Sec. Cen. Cttee Hungarian Socialist Workers' Party 1985–88; currently Research Prof. Emer., Centre for Energy Research, Hungarian Acad. of Sciences; fmr Vice-Pres. IUPAP; Corresp. mem. Hungarian Acad. of Sciences 1961–73, mem. 1973, Gen. Sec. 1980–84, Pres. Intercosmos Council 1980–84; Foreign mem. Acad. of Sciences of the USSR 1976, of GDR 1982, of Czechoslovakia 1983, Russian Acad. of Sciences 1996; mem. Leibniz Soc. eV 1994; Gold Medal, Order of Labour 1956, 1968, Red Banner Order of Labour (USSR) 1975, Red Banner of Work 1985; Kossuth Prize 1962, Memorial Medal 25th Anniversary of the Liberation 1970, Kurtchatov Memory Medal (USSR) 1970, Gold Medal of the Hungarian Acad. of Sciences 1975, Eötvös Lóránd Physical Soc. Medal 1976, Wigner's Award 2001. *Publications:* Science and Technical Development 1987, Science and Technology Policies in Finland and Hungary 1985, Foundation of Probability Calculus and Statistics 1995, Neutron Fluctuations, a Treatise on the Physics of Branching Processes; approx. 275 articles in Hungarian and foreign scientific journals. *Leisure interests:* hunting, angling.

PALA, Ano; Papua New Guinea politician; Parl. Clerk –2007; mem. Nat. Parl. for Rigo constituency 2007–; Parl. Sec. to Puka Temu (Deputy Prime Minister) –2010; Attorney-Gen. and Minister of Justice 2010, Minister for Foreign Affairs, Trade and Immigration 2011–12, Minister of Transport 2013–14, Minister of Justice and Attorney-Gen. 2014–17; mem. Nat. Alliance Party.

PALACIO, Alfredo, MD; Ecuadorean politician, cardiologist and fmr head of state; b. 22 Jan. 1939, Guayaquil; m. Maria Beatriz Paret; four s.; ed Colegio San José La Salle, Universidad de Guayaquil; residency at Case Western Reserve Univ., USA, worked at various hosps in USA 1969–74, including Mount Sinai Hosp., Cleveland, OH 1969–71, Veterans Admin. Hosp., Missouri 1971–72, Barnes Hosp., Washington Univ. 1972–74; Dir Nat. Inst. of Cardiology 1980–; Prin. Prof. of Cardiology, Faculty of Medicine, Univ. of Guayaquil 1989–2003, Prof. of Public Health 2001–03; Minister of Public Health 1994–96; Vice-Pres. of Ecuador 2003–05, Pres. 2005–07; fmr Regional Dir Ecuador Inst. of Social Security (IESS); Fellow, American Coll. of Cardiology, American Coll. of Chest Physicians, American Coll. of Physicians; mem. American Acad. of Sciences, Ecuador Acad. of Medicine, and numerous other medical socs; Dr hc (Johns Hopkins Univ.) 2007; Commdr, Al Mérito Atahualpha, Ministry of Nat. Defence 1995, Recognition of Merit, Ecuador Nat. Civil Defence 1996, Recognition of Merit, Gran Cruz, Pres. of Ecuador 1996; American Medical Asscn Award 1976, Eugenio Espejo Award, Quito Municipality 1982, Scientific Merit Award, Guayaquil Municipality 1982, 1987. *Publications include:* Atlas de Ecocardiografía Bidimensional 1981, Atlas of 2D Echocardiography 1983, Cardiopatía Isquémica (ed.) 1985, Estudio Guayaquil 1991, Hacia un Humanisco Científico 1997. *Address:* c/o Office of the President, Palacio Nacional, García Moreno 1043, Quito, Ecuador (office).

PALACIO DEL VALLE LERSUNDI, Ana Isabel; Spanish lawyer, politician and international organization official; b. 22 Aug. 1948, Madrid; d. of Luis María de Palacio y de Palacio, 4th Marqués de Matonte, and Luisa Mariana del Valle-Lersundi y del Valle; ed Complutense Univ., Madrid; early career as lawyer in pvt. practice, held numerous sr positions in Madrid Bar; MEP (PPE, PP) 1994–2002; Chair. Cttee on Legal Affairs and the Internal Market, European Parl. 1994–2002, Justice and Home Affairs Cttee 1994–2002, Conf. of Cttee Chairs 1994–2002; Minister of Foreign Affairs 2002–04; mem. Parl. 2002–06, Chair. Jt Parl. Cttee for European Affairs 2004–06; Sr Vice-Pres. and General Counsel, World Bank Group, Washington, DC 2006–08, also Sec.-Gen. Int. Centre for the Settlement of Investment Disputes; joined Areva as Sr Vice-Pres. for Int. Affairs and Marketing 2008; mem., Consejo de Estado, Madrid 2012–; mem. Int. Advisory Bd, Council on Foreign Relations, New York; First Vice-Pres., later Pres.-elect, Council of Bars and Law Socs of the EU, Brussels; Pres. Acad. of European Law; mem. Bd Council on Foreign Relations, Fundación para el Análisis y los Estudios Sociales, Fundacion para las Relaciones Internacionales y el Diálogo Exterior, CSIS Initiative for Renewed Transatlantic Partnership, Transatlantic Policy Network; mem. Bd of Govs, Law Soc. of Madrid; Trustee, Carnegie Corpn, New York; Hon. mem. Bar of England and Wales (including the Inner Temple); Hon. Co-Chair. World Justice Project; Ramer Award for Diplomatic Excellence, American Jewish Cttee 2004. *Address:* Consejo de Estado, C/ Mayor 79, 28013, Madrid (office); Palacio & Partners SC, Plaza de las Salesas 3, 28004 Madrid, Spain. *Telephone:* (91) 5166240 (office). *Fax:* (91) 5166244 (office). *E-mail:* info@consejo-estado.es (office). *Website:* www.consejo-estado.es (office).

PALAITIS, Raimundas, BSc; Lithuanian politician; b. 23 Oct. 1957, Palanga; s. of Algirdas and Genovaitė; m. 1st (died 2004); two s. one d.; m. 2nd Vilija Venckutė-Palaitienė 2006; ed Palanga Secondary School (now Palanga Old Gymnasium), Vilnius Univ.; programmer, Palanga br. of Kaunas Inst. of Cardiology 1980–89; launched own business 1989; also employed at the Palanga Communications Unit and Municipality 1989; Founder and Dir JSC Klaipėdos vertybiniai popieriai 1997–2000; mem. Lithuanian Liberal Union 1994–2003, Liberal and Cen. Union 2003–; mem. Palanga City Municipality Bd 1995–2000, Mayor of Palanga April–Nov. 2000; mem. Seimas (Parl.) 2000–08; Minister of the Interior 2008–12 (resgnd). *Leisure interests:* music, sport. *Address:* Gedimino pr. 53, Vilnius, Lithuania.

PALANISWAMY, Edappadi K., BSc; Indian politician; *Chief Minister of Tamil Nadu;* b. 12 May 1954, Siluvampalayam village, Edappadi, Salem Dist; m. Radha Palaniswamy; one s.; mem. Tamil Nadu Legis. Ass. for Edappadi 1989–2006, 2011–16; mem. Lok Sabha (lower house of parl.) from Tiruchengode 1998–99; Tamil Nadu Minister for Highways and Minor Ports 2011–16, for Public Works, Highways and Minor Ports 2016–17; Chief Minister of Tamil Nadu 2017–; mem. All India Anna Dravida Munnetra Kazhagam (AIADMK-AMMA), Pres. 2016–. *Address:* Government of Tamil Nadu, Namakkal Kavignar Maaligai, Fort St George, Chennai 600 009, Tamil Nadu, India (office). *Telephone:* (044) 25672345 (office). *Fax:* (044) 25670930 (office). *E-mail:* cmcell@tn.gov.in (office). *Website:* www.tn.gov.in (office).

PALAU, Luis; American evangelist and writer; b. 27 Nov. 1934, Maschwitz, Buenos Aires, Argentina; s. of Luis Palau, Sr; m. Patricia Marilyn Scofield 1961; four s.; ed St Alban's Coll., Buenos Aires, Multnomah School of the Bible, Portland, Ore., USA; mem. staff, Bank of London, Buenos Aires and Córdoba 1952–59; moved to USA 1960; worked as interpreter for Billy Graham 1962; began Spanish radio broadcasts as missionary in Colombia 1967; began evangelistic ministry as part of Overseas Crusades 1968; made crusade broadcasts to all Latin America 1975; named Pres. Overseas Crusades 1976; f. Luis Palau Evangelistic Asscn 1978; first major crusade in USA, San Diego 1981; hosted three daily radio programmes: an English show carried by 900 stations in 23 countries and two Spanish programmes carried by 880 stations in 25 countries 2003; visited China and attended Beijing church service along with Pres. George W. Bush 2005; Dr hc (Talbot Theological Seminary) 1977, (Wheaton Coll.) 1985. *Publications:* Where is God when Bad Things Happen?, What to Do when You Don't Want to Go to Church, Heart after God 1978, My Response 1985, Time To Stop Pretending 1985, So You Want To Grow 1986, Calling America and the Nations to Christ 1994, God is Relevant, High Definition Life, A Friendly Dialogue between an Atheist and a Christian 2005; 26 books and booklets in Spanish; works have been translated into 30 languages. *Leisure interest:* family. *Address:* Luis Palau Association, PO Box 50, Portland, OR 97207, USA (office). *Telephone:* (503) 614-1500 (office). *Fax:* (503) 614-1599 (office). *E-mail:* info@palau.org (office). *Website:* www.palau.org (office).

PALECKIS, Justas Vincas; Lithuanian diplomatist and politician; b. 1 Jan. 1942, Samara (Kuibyshev), Russia; s. of Justas Paleckis and Genovaite Paleckiene; m. Laima Paleckienė; two s. one d.; ed Univ. of Vilnius, Diplomatic Univ. of the Ministry of Foreign Affairs, USSR; contrib. Komjaunimo Tiesa (daily), Head of Dept 1960, 1963–66; Third Sec. USSR Embassy to Switzerland; Second, First Sec., Counsellor, USSR Embassy to GDR 1969–83; Deputy Dir, Dir of sector Lithuanian CP Cen. Cttee 1983–89; Sec., Ind. Lithuanian CP Cen. Cttee 1989–90; Deputy Chair. Foreign Affairs Cttee, Lithuanian Repub. Supreme Council (Parl.) 1990–92; Lecturer, Inst. of Journalism, Vilnius State Univ. 1990–93; Lecturer, Inst. of Int. Relations and Political Science, Vilnius State Univ. 1993–95; adviser on Foreign Affairs to Lithuanian Pres. 1993–96; rank of Amb. 1993–; Amb. to UK 1996–2001 (also accred to Portugal and Ireland 1997–2001); Deputy Minister of Foreign Affairs 2002–04; mem. European Parl. (Socialist Group) 2004–14, Vice-Chair. Sub-cttee on Security and Defence, mem. Cttee on Foreign Affairs, Substitute mem. Cttee on the Environment, Public Health and Food Safety, Temporary Cttee on Climate Change, Del. to EU-Russia Parl. Cooperation Cttee, Del. to EU-Fmr Yugoslav Repub. of Macedonia Jt Parl. Cttee, Del. to EU–Bulgaria Jt Parl. Cttee; Kt, Royal Swedish Order of the Northern Star 1994, Lithuanian Independence Medal 2000, Commdr, Order of Merit (Lithuania) 2003. *Publications:* Swiss Pyramids 1974, At the Foot of Swiss Pyramids 1985, Life in a Triangle. Vilnius-Brussels-Strasbourg 2007. *Leisure interests:* reading, theatre, gardening, tennis, swimming. *Address:* Europos Parlamento nario Justo Paleckio biuras, Pylimo g. 12-10, 01118 Vilnius (office); K. Donelaicio 20-5, 2000 Vilnius, Lithuania (home). *Telephone:* (5) 2663056 (office); (5) 2635445 (home). *Fax:* (5) 2663058 (office). *E-mail:* biuras@paleckis.lt (office). *Website:* www.paleckis.lt.

PALECZNY, Piotr; Polish pianist and academic; *Artistic Director, Duszniki International Chopin Festival;* b. 10 May 1946, Rybnik; m.; one s.; ed State Higher School of Music, Warsaw, studied under Prof. Jan Ekier; soloist with orchestras including Warsaw Nat. Philharmonic Orchestra, Polish Radio Nat. Symphony Orchestra, Chicago Symphony, American Symphony, Royal Philharmonic, Concertgebouw, BBC London Orchestra, Yomiuri Nippon, Tonhalle Zürich, RAI Roma, Santa Cecilia, Mexico Nat., Buenos Aires Nat., Gewandhaus, Nat. Orchestra Madrid; has performed in major concert halls, including Carnegie Hall, Avery Fisher Hall and Alice Tully Hall, New York, Orchestra Hall, Chicago, Suntory Hall, Tokyo, Teatro Colon, Buenos Aires, Gewandhaus, Leipzig, Concertgebouw, Amsterdam, Royal Festival Hall, London; Artistic Dir Duszniki Int. Chopin Festival, Duszniki Zdrój 1993–, Int. Ignacy Jan Paderewski Piano Competition, Bydgoszcz 2004–; Prof. of Piano Performance, Frederick Chopin Acad. of Music, Warsaw; judge, int. music competitions in Warsaw, Paris, Santander, Tokyo, Hamamatsu, Prague, Taipei, Cleveland, London; judge, Sendai Int. Music Competition, Japan 2010, Prix Amadèo de Piano 2011; f. master courses in music, Bordeaux, Amsterdam, Paris, Buenos Aires, Tokyo, Lugano, Warsaw; Kt's Cross, Order of Polonia Restituta, Gold Cross of Merit, Order of the Aguila Azteca (Mexico); winner, competitions in Sofia 1968, Munich 1969, Warsaw 1970, Pleven 1971, Bordeaux 1972, Grand Prix VIII Chopin Competition 1970, granted title of Prof. by Pres. of Poland 1998, Gloria Artis Gold Medal 2005. *Recordings include:* K. Szymanowski Concert Symphony No. 4, complete Ballads, Sonatas, and Concertos by Chopin, The Best of Fryderyk Chopin ('Fryderyk 1999' Award, Polish Phonographic Acad.), works by Paderewski, Szymanowski, Lutosławski. *Address:* International Chopin Festival, 57-340 Duszniki-Zdrój, Rynek 10, Poland (office). *Telephone:* (74) 8669280 (office). *E-mail:* chopin@festival.pl (office). *Website:* festival.pl/en (office); konkurspaderewskiego.pl/en.

PALESE, Peter, MSc, PhD; American microbiologist and academic; *Horace W. Goldsmith Professor and Chairman, Department of Microbiology, Mount Sinai School of Medicine;* ed Univ. of Vienna, Austria; Postdoctoral Fellow, Roche Inst. of Molecular Biology 1970–71; apptd Asst Prof., Dept of Microbiology, Mount Sinai School of Medicine, New York 1971, currently Horace W. Goldsmith Prof., Chair. Dept of Microbiology 1987–, also Prof., Medicine, Infectious Diseases; Visiting

Assoc. Prof., Dept of Microbiology and Immunology, UCLA School of Medicine 1976; Pres. Harvey Soc. 2003–04, American Soc. of Virology 2005–06; Co-Founder and Scientific Advisor, Vivaldi Biosciences, Inc. 2006–; mem. NAS 2000, German Acad. of Sciences Leopoldina 2006, Inst. of Medicine 2012–; Corresp. mem. Austrian Acad. of Sciences 2002; mem. Editorial Bd NAS; Ed. Journal of Virology; Fellow, American Acad. of Arts and Sciences 2014; Dr hc (Baylor Coll. of Medicine) 2014; Robert Koch Prize, Berlin 2006, Charles C. Shepard Science Award 2006, 2008, Wilhelm Exner Medal, Austrian Asscn for SME (Oesterreichischer Gewerbeverein—OGV) (jtly) 2007, European Virology Award 2010, Sanofi–Institut Pasteur Award 2012, Beijerinck Virology Prize, Royal Netherlands Acad. of Arts and Sciences 2015. *Achievements include:* built "the first genetic maps for influenza A, B and C viruses, identified the function of several viral genes, . . .defined the mechanism of neuraminidase inhibitors (which are now FDA-approved antivirals)" and "pioneered the field of reverse genetics for negative-strand RNA viruses". *Publications:* numerous papers in professional journals on host-virus interactions, vaccines and antivirals, and virulence factors of RNA viruses. *Address:* Mount Sinai School of Medicine, 1 Gustave L. Levy Place, Box 1124, New York, NY 10029-6500 (office); Mount Sinai School of Medicine, Annenberg Building, Floor 16, Room 16–20, 1468 Madison Avenue, New York, NY 10029, USA (office). *Telephone:* (212) 241-7318 (office). *Fax:* (212) 722-3634 (office). *E-mail:* peter.palese@mssm.edu (office). *Website:* www.mssm.edu/research/labs/palese-laboratory (office).

PALIHOVICI, Liliana, BA, MA, MA; Moldovan politician; b. 26 Nov. 1971, Horodişte, Călăraşi dist; m. Sergiu Palihovici; two c.; ed Moldovan State Univ., Centre for Grad. Studies, Acad. of Public Admin; Prof. of History, School Mircea Eliade 1993–95; specialist in youth issues, Youth Div., Dept of Youth, Ministry of Educ. 1995–2001, Head of Directorate, Youth and Sport Dept 2001–03; consultant, UNICEF project co-ordinating socio-econ. empowerment of youth 2004–07; World Bank Consultant, Co-ordinator of Youth Voices Group 2007–08; Grants Co-ordinator, Acad. of Educational Devt 2008; mem. Parl. 2009–17, Deputy Speaker 2010–17, Acting Chair. (Speaker) April–May 2013; Head, Nat. Del. to Parl. Ass. of the Council of Europe (PACE); Pres. Institutum Virtutes Civilis' Ass.; f. Women 4 Leadership Project 2018; mem. Nat. Security, Defense and Public Order Cttee; mem. Initiative Group, Liberal Democratic Party 2007–09; mem. Alliance for European Integration 2009–; Order of the Repub. *Address:* Institutum Virtutes Civilis, 2001 Chişinău, Strada Bulgară nr.1, Moldova (office). *Telephone:* (22) 27-25-00 (office). *E-mail:* ivc.moldova@gmail.com (office). *Website:* palihovici.pldm.md (office); www.ivcmoldova.org (office); www.palihovici.pldm.md.

PALIKOT, Janusz Marian, MA; Polish politician and business executive; *Leader, Twój Ruch (Your Movement);* b. 26 Oct. 1964, Biłgoraj; m. 1st Maria Nowińska (divorced); two s.; m. 2nd Monika Kubat; one s. one d.; ed John Paul II Catholic Univ. of Lublin, Warsaw Univ.; entrepreneur and fmr Co-owner Polmos Lublin SA (vodka business) and Ambra SA; mem. Civic Platform 2005–10; mem. Sejm (Parl.) for 6 – Lublin 2005–; Founder and Leader, Ruch Poparcia (Movt of Support—later renamed Ruch Palikota—Palikot's Movt) 2010–13, Twój Ruch (Your Movt) 2013–. *Publications:* Myśli o nowoczesnym biznesie (with Krzysztof Obłój) 2003, Płoną koty w Biłgoraju (autobiog.) 2007, Poletko Pana P. 2008, Pop-polityka 2009, Ja Palikot (interview by Cezary Michalski) 2010, Kulisy Platformy (interview by Anna Wojciechowska) 2011. *Address:* Twój Ruch (Your Movement), 00-029 Warsaw, ul. Nowy Świat 39, Poland (office). *Telephone:* 731-537500 (mobile). *E-mail:* biuro@twojruch.eu (office). *Website:* www.twojruch.eu (office); palikot.blog.onet.pl.

PALIN, Michael Edward, CBE, BA, FRGS; British actor, writer and traveller; b. 5 May 1943, Sheffield, Yorks., England; s. of Edward Palin and Mary Palin; m. Helen M. Gibbins 1966; two s. one d.; ed Birkdale School, Sheffield, Shrewsbury School, Brasenose Coll. Oxford; Pres. Transport 2000, Royal Geographical Soc. 2009–11; Vice-Pres. Michael Palin Centre for Stammering Children; Dr hc (Sheffield) 1992, (Queen's Univ., Belfast) 2000; Michael Balcon Award for outstanding contrib. to cinema (with Monty Python), BAFTA 1987, Travel Writer of the Year, British Book Awards 1993, Lifetime Achievement Award, British Comedy Awards 2002, BCA Illustrated Book of the Year Award 2002, BAFTA Special Award for Outstanding Contrib. to TV 2005, British Book Award for Outstanding Achievement 2009, BAFTA Fellowship Award 2013. *Musical theatre:* Monty Python's Spamalot 2006. *Films:* actor and co-author: And Now for Something Completely Different 1970, Monty Python and the Holy Grail 1974, Monty Python's Life of Brian 1979, Time Bandits 1980, Monty Python's The Meaning of Life 1982; actor, writer and co-producer: The Missionary 1982; actor, co-scriptwriter: American Friends 1991; actor: Jabberwocky 1976, A Private Function 1984, Brazil 1985, A Fish Called Wanda (Best Supporting Film Actor, BAFTA Award 1988) 1988, American Friends (also writer) 1991, The Wind in the Willows 1996, Fierce Creatures 1997, Not the Messiah (He's a Very Naughty Boy) 2010, The Death of Stalin 2017. *Television includes:* actor and writer: Monty Python's Flying Circus, BBC TV 1969–74, Ripping Yarns, BBC TV 1976–79; actor: Three Men in a Boat, BBC 1975, GBH (Channel 4 TV) 1991; writer: East of Ipswich, BBC TV 1987, Number 27, BBC TV, The Weekend (play for stage) 1994; TV series: contrib. to Great Railway Journeys of the World, BBC TV 1980, 1993; presenter, Around the World in 80 Days 1989, Pole to Pole 1992, Palin's Column 1994, Full Circle 1997, Michael Palin's Hemingway Adventure 1999, Sahara 2002, Himalaya with Michael Palin 2004, Michael Palin's New Europe 2007, Around the World in 20 Years 2008, Brazil with Michael Palin 2012; art documentaries (presenter): Palin on Redpath 1997, The Bright Side of Life 2000, The Ladies Who Loved Matisse 2003, Michael Palin and the Mystery of Hammershoi 2005, Michael Palin in Wyeth's World 2013. *Publications include:* Monty Python's Big Red Book 1970, Monty Python's Brand New Book 1973, Bert Fegg's Nasty Book for Boys and Girls (fiction) (with Terry Jones, illustrated by Martin Honeysett, Frank Bellamy *et al.*) 1974, Montypythonscrapbook 1979, Dr Fegg's Encyclopaedia of All World Knowledge 1984, Limericks 1985, Around the World in 80 Days 1989, Pole to Pole 1992, The Weekend (play) 1994, Hemingway's Chair (fiction) 1995, Full Circle 1997, Michael Palin's Hemingway Adventure 1999, Sahara 2002, The Pythons Autobiography (co-author) 2003, Himalaya (British Book Award for TV & Film Book of the Year 2005) 2004, Diaries 1969–1979: The Python Years 2006, New Europe 2007, Diaries 1980–88: Halfway to Hollywood – The Film Years 2009, The Truth (fiction) 2012, Brazil 2012, Travelling to Work: Diaries 1988–98 2014, Monty Python at Work 2014; for children: Small Harry and the Toothache Pills 1981, Limericks or The Limerick Book 1985, Cyril and the House of Commons 1986, Cyril and the Dinner Party 1986, The Mirrorstone (with Alan Lee and Richard Seymour) 1986. *Leisure interests:* reading, running, railways. *Address:* c/o Mayday Management, 34 Tavistock Street, London, WC2E 7PB, England (office). *Telephone:* (20) 7497-1100 (office). *Fax:* (20) 7497-1133 (office). *Website:* www.palinstravels.co.uk.

PALIN, Sarah Louise, BS; American television host and fmr politician; b. 11 Feb. 1964, Sandpoint, Ida.; d. of Charles 'Chuck' Heath and Sarah 'Sally' Heath (née Sheeran); m. Todd Palin; two s. three d.; ed Wasilla High School, Hawaii Pacific Univ., North Idaho Coll., Univ. of Idaho, Matanuska-Susitna Coll.; family moved to Alaska while an infant; worked as sportscaster for KTUU-TV and KTVA-TV in Anchorage and as sports reporter for Mat-Su Valley Frontiersman; mem. Wasilla, Alaska City Council 1992–96; Mayor and Man. of Wasilla 1996–2002; unsuccessful cand. for Lt-Gov. of Alaska 2002; Chair. Alaska Oil and Gas Conservation Comm. 2003–04 (resgnd); fmr Pres. Alaska Conf. of Mayors; also served on Interstate Oil and Gas Compact Comm.; Gov. of Alaska 2006–09 (resgnd); Republican nominee for Vice-Pres. of US 2008; political commentator, Fox News Channel 2010–2013, June 2013–15; mem. Bd Valley Hosp., Iditarod Parent-Teacher Asscn; fmr mem. American Man. Asscn, Alaska Outdoor Council, Alaska Miners Asscn, Alaska Resource Devt Council, Youth Court Steering Cttee, Salvation Army Bd; Lifetime mem. Nat. Rifle Asscn; fmr coach, Valley Youth Sports, ice hockey team man.; Hon. mem. Rotary; State Chamber 'Top 40 Under 40' Award, American Public Works Asscn Alaska Chapter Person of the Year, Distinguished Alumni Achievement Award, Alumni Asscn of North Idaho Coll. 2008. *Television:* host, Sarah Palin's Alaska 2010, Amazing America 2014–. *Publications include:* Going Rogue: An American Life (memoir) 2009, America by Heart 2010. *Leisure interests:* hunting, fishing, snow machining, running. *Address:* SarahPAC, PO Box 7711, Arlington, VA 22207, USA. *Website:* www.sarahpac.com.

PALIS, Jacob, PhD; Brazilian mathematician and academic; *Director Emeritus, Instituto de Matemática Pura e Aplicada (IMPA);* b. 15 March 1940, Uberaba; s. of Jacob Palis and Sames Palis; m. Suely Lima; three c.; ed Fed. Univ. of Rio de Janeiro, Univ. of California, Berkeley, USA; Prof., Instituto de Matemática Pura e Aplicada (IMPA), Rio de Janeiro 1971–, Dir 1993–2003, Dir Emer. 2003–; Visiting Prof. Univ. of Warwick, Inst. des Hautes Etudes Scientifiques, France, Univ. of Dijon, Ecole Polytechnique, Paris, City Univ. of New York, Steklov Inst., Moscow, ETH-Zurich, Univs of Nagoya, Tokyo, Kyoto, Toulouse, Rome, Paris-Orsay, Nice, Collège de France 1969–94; Chair. Int. Center for Theoretical Council (ICTP), Trieste, Italy 2003–05, mem. Scientific Cttee 1993–2005; mem. Exec. Bd Int. Math. Union 1982–91, Sec. 1991–99, Pres. 1999–2002; mem. Exec. Bd Int. Council for Science 1993–96, Vice-Pres. 1996–99; mem. Scientific Advisory Cttee, ETH, Zürich 1990–2006, Scientific and Strategic Council, Collège de France 2003–08; Founding Mem. Latin American and Caribean Math. Union 1995; Guggenheim Fellow 1993; mem. Brazilian Acad. of Sciences 1970 (Vice-Pres. 2004–07, Pres. 2007–16), Third World Acad. of Sciences (now Acad. of Sciences for the Developing World) 1991 (Sec.-Gen. 2004–06, apptd Pres. 2006), Indian Acad. of Sciences 1995, Chilean Acad. of Sciences 1997, Mexican Acad. of Sciences 2001, US Nat. Acad. of Sciences 2002, French Acad. of Sciences 2002, European Acad. of Sciences 2004, Norwegian Acad. of Sciences 2005, Russian Acad. of Sciences 2006; Hon. mem. Peruvian Math. Soc.; Chevalier de la Légion d'honneur 2005; Dr hc (State Univ. of Rio de Janeiro) 1993, (Univ. of Chile) 1996, (Univ. of Warwick) 2000, (Univ. of Santiago de Chile) 2000, (Universidad de la Habana) 2001, (Universidad de Ingenieria, Peru) 2003; Prize Moinho Santista 1976, Math. Prize, Third World Acad. of Sciences 1988, Grand-Croix National Order of Scientific Merit, Brazil, 1994, Nat. Prize for Science and Tech., Brazil 1990, Inter-American Prize for Science, OAS 1995, Prize Mexico for Science and Technology 2001, Trieste Science Prize in Math. (co-winner with C.S. Seshadri) 2006; honoured for contribution to science by Brazil UNESCO in its 60th annniversary 2006. *Publications:* Geometric Theory of Dynamical Systems (with W. de Melo) 1982, Hyperbolicity and Sensitive-Chaotic Dynamics and Homoclinic Bifurcations, Fractal Dimensions and Infinitely Many Attractors (with F. Takens) 1994, Jacob Palis–Selected Works 2014; numerous scientific papers. *Address:* Instituto Matemática Pura e Aplicada, Estrada Dona Castorina 110, Jardim Botânico, 22460-320 Rio de Janeiro, RJ, Brazil (office). *Telephone:* (21) 2529-5136 (office). *Fax:* (21) 2529-5019 (office). *E-mail:* jpalis@impa.br (office). *Website:* w3.impa.br/~jpalis (office).

PALLANT, John, BA; British advertising executive; *Founder and Creative Director, Brouhaha Creative Ltd;* b. 10 Aug. 1955; s. of Dennis Pallant and Doreen Pallant (née Hirst); ed St John's Coll., Southsea, Univ. of Reading; copywriter, Griffin & George Ltd 1977, Acroyd Westwood Assocs 1977, Collett Dickenson Pearce 1980, Gold Greenless Trott 1982, Boase Massimi Politt 1978, copywriter and creative group head 1983; copywriter, Saatchi & Saatchi 1988, Group Head 1991, Deputy Creative Dir and Exec. Bd Dir 1995, Creative Dir 1996–97, Jt Exec. Creative Dir 1997–98, Deputy Exec. Creative Dir 1999–2002, Regional Creative Dir Europe, Middle East and Africa 2003–17; Founder and Creative Dir Brouhaha Creative Ltd 2017–; numerous awards, including Cannes Gold Lions, D&AD Silver Pencils, Black Pencil and New York One Show Best of Show Award. *Leisure interest:* kickboxing. *Address:* Brouhaha Creative Ltd, 37 Warren Street, London, W1T 6AD, England (office).

PALLASMAA, Juhani Uolevi; Finnish architect and academic; *Principal, Juhani Pallasmaa Architects;* b. 14 Sept. 1936, Hämeenlinna; s. of Harry Alexander Pallasmaa and Aili Pallasmaa (née Kannisto); m. 1st 1957; two d.; m. 2nd Hannele Jäämeri 1980; one s. one d.; ed Helsinki Univ. of Tech.; Dir Exhbn Dept, Museum of Finnish Architecture, Helsinki 1968–72, 1974–83, Dir of Museum 1978–83; Rector Coll. of Crafts and Design, Helsinki 1970–72; Assoc. Prof., Haile Selassie Univ., Addis Ababa, Ethiopia 1972–74; Prin., Juhani Pallasmaa Architects, Helsinki 1983–; State Artist Prof., Helsinki 1983–88; Prof., Faculty of Architecture, Univ. of Tech., Helsinki 1991–97; Eero Saarinen Visiting Prof., Yale Univ., New Haven, Conn., USA 1993; Raymond E. Maritz Visiting Prof. of Architecture, Washington Univ., St Louis, Mo., USA 1999–2004; Thomas Jefferson Visiting Prof., Univ. of Virginia, USA 2002; Visiting Prof., Univ. of Florida, USA 2009; Plym Distinguished Prof., Univ. of Illinois, USA 2010; Walton Critic, Catholic Univ. of America, Washington, DC, USA 2011; participant in numerous exhbns of architecture and visual arts, designer numerous nat. and int. exhbns of architecture and visual arts, on town planning, architecture, design and visual arts; Dr hc (Helsinki Univ. of Industrial Arts) 1993, (Helsinki Univ. of Tech.) 1998, (Estonian Art Acad.) 2004, (Washington Univ.) 2013, (Ion Mincu Univ.) 2014; Kt, Order of White Rose 1988, Commdr, Order of the White Rose 1997; Finnish State Award for Architecture 1992, Helsinki City Culture Award 1993, Russian Fed. Architecture Award 1996, Fritz Schumacher Prize for Architecture, Germany 1997, Int. Union of Architects Jean Tschumi Prize for Architectural Criticism 1999, Finland Award 2000, Arnold W. Brunner Prize for Architecture, American Acad. of Arts and Letters 2009, Award for Merit, A. Kordelin Foundation 2010, Dean's Medal, Washington Univ. 2012, The Schelling Prize for Architectural Criticism 2014. *Publications include:* Language of Wood 1987, Animal Architecture 1995, The Melnikov House 1996, The Eyes of the Skin: Architecture and the Senses 1996, 2005, Alvar Aalto, Villa Mairea 1938–39 1998, Architecture of Image: Existential Space in Cinema 2001, Sensuous Minimalism 2002, Encounters: Architectural Essays 2005, The Thinking Hand: Existential and Embodied Wisdom in Architecture 2009, Conversaciones con Alvar Aalto 2010, Una arquitectura de la humildad 2010, The Embodied Image: Imagination and Imagery in Architecture 2011, Understanding Architecture (with Robert McCarter) 2012, Mind in Architecture: Neuroscience, Embodiment and the future of design (with Sarah Robinson) 2015, Abitar 2017. *Leisure interests:* philosophy and psychology of artistic phenomena. *Address:* Tehtaankatu 13 B 29, 00140 Helsinki (office); Huvilakatu 14 A 8, 00150 Helsinki, Finland (home). *Telephone:* (9) 669740 (office); (9) 666625 (home). *Fax:* (9) 669741 (office). *E-mail:* jpallasmaa@gmail.com (office). *Website:* www.pallasmaa.fi (office).

PALMER, Andrew Clennel, PhD, FRS, FREng, FICE; British civil engineer and academic; *Professor of Civil Engineering, National University of Singapore;* b. 26 May 1938, Colchester; s. of Gerald Basil Coote Palmer and Muriel Gertrude Palmer (née Howes); m. Jane Rhiannon Evans 1963; one d.; ed Cambridge Univ., Brown Univ., USA; Lecturer, Univ. of Liverpool 1965–67, Univ. of Cambridge 1968–75; Chief Pipeline Engineer, R. J. Brown & Assocs 1975–79, Vice-Pres. Eng 1982–85; Prof. of Civil Eng, Univ. Manchester Inst. of Science and Technology 1979–82; Man. Dir and Tech. Dir Andrew Palmer and Associates Ltd (consultancy) 1985–96; Research Prof. of Petroleum Eng, Univ. of Cambridge 1996–2005, Fellow, Churchill Coll., Cambridge 1996–; Visiting Prof., Div. of Engineering and Applied Sciences, Harvard Univ. 2002–03; apptd Keppel Chair. Prof., Nat. Univ. of Singapore 2006, currently Prof. of Civil Eng; Founder and Man. Dir Bold Island Eng (consultancy), Singapore; Trustee, American Univ. of Sharjah, UAE; Dr hc (Clarkson Univ.) 2007. *Publications include:* Structural Mechanics 1976, Subsea Pipeline Engineering (with R. A. King) 2004; papers in learned journals. *Leisure interests:* travel, languages, glassblowing. *Address:* Department of Civil and Environmental Engineering, National University of Singapore, 1 Engineering Drive 2, E1A 07-03, Singapore 117576 (office); #12-06 Block C, 111 Clementi Road, Singapore 129792, Singapore. *Telephone:* 65164601 (office). *E-mail:* ceepalme@nus.edu.sg (office). *Website:* www.nus.edu.sg (office); andrewcpalmer.com.

PALMER, Frank Robert, MA, DLitt, FBA; British academic; *Professor Emeritus of Linguistic Science, University of Reading;* b. 9 April 1922, Westerleigh, Glos., England; s. of George Samuel Palmer and Gertrude Lilian Palmer (née Newman); m. Jean Elisabeth Moore 1948; three s. two d.; ed Bristol Grammar School, New Coll., Oxford, Merton Coll., Oxford; Lecturer in Linguistics, SOAS, Univ. of London 1950–60; Prof. of Linguistics, Univ. Coll. of North Wales, Bangor 1960–65; Prof. of Linguistic Science, Univ. of Reading 1965–87, Dean, Faculty of Letters and Social Sciences 1969–72, Prof. Emer. 1987–; Vice-Pres., Philological Soc.; Chair. Linguistics Asscn (GB) 1965–68, Ed. Journal of Linguistics 1969–79, Linguistic Soc. of America Prof., Buffalo, USA 1971; Distinguished Visiting Prof., Univ. of Delaware, Newark, USA 1982; mem. Academia Europaea 1992; Hon. DLitt 1997. *Publications include:* The Morphology of the Tigre Noun 1962, A Linguistic Study of the English Verb 1965, Selected Papers of J. R. Firth (1951–58) (ed.) 1968, Prosodic Analysis (ed.) 1970, Grammar 1971, 1984, The English Verb 1974, 1987, Semantics 1976, 1981, Modality and the English Modals 1979, 1990, Mood and Modality 1986, 2001, Studies in the History of Western Linguistics in Honour of R. H. Robins (co-ed.) 1986, Grammatical Roles and Relations 1994, Grammar and Meaning: Essays in Honour of Sir John Lyons (ed.) 1995, Modality in Contemporary English (co-ed.) 2003, English Modality in Perspective (co-ed.) 2004. *Leisure interests:* gardening, crosswords. *Address:* 'Whitethorns', Roundabout Lane, Winnersh, Wokingham, Berks., RG41 5AD, England (home). *Telephone:* (118) 978-6214 (home). *E-mail:* llspalmf@reading.ac.uk.

PALMER, Sir Geoff (Godfrey) Henry Oliver, Kt, OBE, PhD, DSc, FRSA, FRSM; British (b. Jamaican) academic; *Professor Emeritus of Brewing, Heriot-Watt University;* b. 1940, St Elizabeth, Jamaica; m.; three c.; ed Kingston Senior School, Univ. of Leicester, Heriot-Watt Univ.; researcher and later Sr Scientist, Brewing Research Foundation, British Brewing Soc., Surrey 1968–77; Lecturer, Heriot-Watt Univ. 1977–, Prof. of Brewing 1989–, now Emer.; Visiting Prof., Kyoto Univ., Japan; mem. Exec. and Hon. Pres. Edinburgh and Lothian Racial Equality Council; American Soc. of Brewing Chemists Award 1998, Good Citizen of Edinburgh Award 2002. *Publications:* The Enlightenment Abolished, Mr White and the Ravens; over 150 scientific papers. *Leisure interests:* reading, pop music, travel. *Address:* 23 Waulkmill Drive, Penicuik, EH26 8LA, Scotland. *E-mail:* geoff.palmer4@btinternet.com.

PALMER, Rt Hon. Sir Geoffrey Winston Russell, KCMG, QC, PC, AC, BA, LLB, JD; New Zealand lawyer, academic and fmr politician; *Barrister, Harbour Chambers;* b. 21 April 1942, Nelson; s. of Leonard R. Palmer and Jessie P. Palmer; m. Margaret E. Hinchcliff 1963; one s. one d.; ed Nelson Coll., Victoria Univ. of Wellington and Univ. of Chicago; solicitor, Wellington 1964–66; Lecturer in Political Science, Victoria Univ. 1968–69; Prof. of Law, Univ. of Iowa and Univ. of Virginia, USA 1969–73; Prof. of English and New Zealand Law, Victoria Univ. 1974–79, Prof. of Law 1991–95; Prin. Asst to Australian Nat. Comm. of Inquiry on Rehabilitation and Compensation 1973; Visiting Fellow, Wolfson Coll., Oxford 1978; MP for Christchurch Cen. 1979–90; Deputy Leader, New Zealand Labour Party 1983–89; Deputy Prime Minister, Minister of Justice and Attorney-Gen. 1984–89; Minister for the Environment 1987–90; Prime Minister of New Zealand 1989–90; Minister in Charge of New Zealand Security Intelligence; Prof. of Law, Victoria Univ. 1991–95; Prof. of Law, Univ. of Iowa 1991–95, Ida Beam Distinguished Visiting Prof. of Law 1991; Partner, Chen, Palmer & Partners, Wellington 1994–2005; Pres. New Zealand Law Comm. 2005–10; currently Barrister, Harbour Chambers; also currently Distinguished Fellow, Faculty of Law, Victoria Univ. of Wellington; Global Affiliated Prof., Univ. of Iowa; Master of the Bench, Middle Temple 2016; Dr hc (Victoria Univ. of Wellington, Washington Univ. of St Louis, Hofstra Univ., Univ. of Glasgow); UNEP Global 500 Laureate 1991. *Publications include:* Unbridled Power?: An Interpretation of New Zealand's Constitution and Government 1979, Compensation for Incapacity: A Study of Law and Social Change in Australia and New Zealand 1979, Environmental Politics: A Greenprint for New Zealand 1990, New Zealand's Constitution in Crisis 1992, Public Law in New Zealand (with Mai Chen) 1993, Environment: The International Challenge 1995, Bridled Power 1997, A Constitution for Aotearoa New Zealand (co-author) 2016. *Leisure interests:* cricket, golf, playing the trumpet, fishing. *Address:* Harbour Chambers, Level 10, Equinox House, 111 The Terrace, PO Box 10-242, Wellington (office); 63 Roxburgh Street, Mount Victoria, Wellington, New Zealand (home). *Telephone:* (4) 4992684 (office); (4) 8015185 (home). *Fax:* (4) 4992705 (office). *E-mail:* geoffrey@geoffreypalmer.co.nz (office); marina.kapua@legalchambers.co.nz (office). *Website:* www.harbourchambers.co.nz (office).

PALMER OF CHILDS HILL, Baron (Life Peer), cr. 2011, of Childs Hill in the London Borough of Barnet; **Monroe Edward Palmer,** OBE, BA, FCA; British politician and chartered accountant; *Deputy Speaker, House of Lords;* b. (Monroe Polikoff), 30 Nov. 1938, London, England; s. of Will Polikoff and Sybil Polikoff; m. Susette Palmer; three c.; ed Orange Hill Grammar School; Councillor for Childs Hill, London Borough of Barnet 1986–94, 1998–2014, Chair. Audit Cttee 2010–14; Jt Treas. Liberal Parl. Party and Liberal Party 1977–83, Treas., London Region, Liberal Democrats 2008–10; contested (Liberal) Hendon South in Gen. Election 1979, 1983, 1987, (Liberal Democrat) Hastings and Rye 1992, 1997; mem. (Liberal Democrat), House of Lords 2011–, Deputy Speaker 2018–; fmr Dir Barnet Homes; fmr Treas. Disablement Asscn of Barnet; Nat. Chair. Liberal Democrat Friends of Israel 1987–2010, Vice-Pres. 2010–16, Pres. 2016–. *Leisure interests:* horse riding, fishing, reading, politics. *Address:* House of Lords, Westminster, London, SW1A 0PW, England (office). *Telephone:* (20) 7219-2561 (office); (20) 8455-5140 (home). *E-mail:* palmerm@parliament.uk (office). *Website:* www.parliament.uk/biographies/lords/lord-palmer-of-childs-hill/4214 (office).

PALMIERI, Stefano; San Marino accountant and politician; b. 18 Sept. 1964, Serravalle; m.; two s.; Accountant, Savings Bank of San Marino 1985–2003; f. Biancoazzurro Movement 2003; mem. Popular Alliance 2006–; MP Consiglio Grande e Generale 2006–2012, 2016–; Co-Captain-Regent Oct. 2009–April 2010, April–Oct. 2018; mem. Council of XII 2009–, Comm. for Foreign Affairs and Finance; Kt, Grand Cross of the Order of Saint-Charles (Monaco) 2010. *Website:* www.sanmarino.sm (office).

PALMISANO, Samuel J. (Sam), BA; American business executive; *Chairman, Center for Global Enterprise;* b. 29 July 1951, Baltimore, Md; m. Gaier Notman; three s. three d.; ed The Johns Hopkins Univ., Baltimore, Md; joined Int. Business Machines Corpn (IBM), Baltimore, Md 1973, subsequently Sr Man. Dir of Operations, IBM Japan, Pres., CEO ISSC (IBM subsidiary) 1993, mem. Worldwide Man. Council IBM 1994, in charge of IBM's strategic outsourcing business 1995, Sr Vice-Pres. and Group Exec. Enterprise Systems Group, IBM Global Services, Personal Systems Group, mem. Corp. Exec. Cttee 1998, Pres. and COO 2000–02, Pres. and CEO IBM Corpn 2002–11, Chair. 2003–12; currently Chair. Center for Global Enterprise; Ind. Advisor, Bloomberg Philanthropies 2013–; mem. Bd of Dirs Gannett Co. Inc.; Co-Chair. Council of Competitiveness' Nat. Innovation Initiative; mem. American Acad. of Arts and Sciences; Hon. Fellow, London Business School 2006; Hon. DHumLitt (Rensselaer Polytechnic Inst.) 2005; Distinguished Business Leadership Award, Atlantic Council 2009, inaugural Deming Cup, W. Edwards Deming Center for Quality, Productivity and Competitiveness at Columbia Business School 2010. *Address:* Center for Global Enterprise, 200 Park Avenue, Suite 1700, New York, NY 10166, USA (office). *Telephone:* (646) 632-4742 (office). *Website:* www.thecge.net (office).

PALOCCI, António Filho; Brazilian physician and politician; b. 4 Oct. 1960; s. of António Palocci and Antonia de Castro Palocci; m. Margareth Rose Silva Palocci; one s. two d.; ed Univ. of São Paulo; physician specializing in preventive medicine; mem. Partido dos Trabalhadores 1980–, Municipal Party Exec. 1988–89, Regional Party Directorate 1990–91 (Pres. 1997–99), Nat. Party Directorate 1996–97, Deputy Leader 2000; Pres. Rocha Lima Centre, Univ. of São Paulo 1981; Regional Dir DCE Alexandre Vanucci Leme, Univ. of São Paulo 1982; Pres. Ass. Resident Physicians of Ribeirão Pret 1984–85; Regional Dir SIMESP 1985; Pres. Regional CUT Ribeirão Preto 1985; Regional Dir Sanitary Monitoring Service São Paulo 1986–88; Mayor of Ribeirão Preto 1993–96, 2001–02; Fed. Deputy 1999–2000, 2007–; Co-ordinator Govt transition team Oct.–Dec. 2002; Minister of Finance 2003–06; Pres. Conselho Monetário Nacional 2003–06; Cabinet Chief (Chief of Staff) Jan.–June 2011 (resgnd); UNICEF Child and Peace Prize 1995, Juscelino Kubitschek Prize, Serviço Brasileiro de Apoio às Micro e Pequenas Empresas–SEBRAE 1996. *Publications include:* Saúde do trabalhador (Health of the Worker) 1994, A reforma do Estado e os municípios: a experiência de Ribeirão Preto (State and City Reform: The Experience of Ribeirão Preto) 1996, Sobre Formigas e Cigarras (autobiography) 2007.

PALOMÉROS, Gen. Jean-Paul; French air force officer and international organization official; b. 1953; m. Agnes Paloméros; five c.; ed Royal Air Force Staff Coll., UK; Commdr SPA 124 Jeanne d'arc squadron on Mirage F1, USA, 30th Fighter Squadron in Reims 1990, Cazaux Air Base 1996–98, Head 2/12 Picardy squadron, Epervier operation, Chad 1987, Deputy Commdr Air Force, Vicenza, Italy 1993, Head, Studies and Strategic Plans Dept, Air Force staff 1998, Chair. Capability Devt Cttee, Jt Staff 2002, Deputy Chief of Staff, Air Force 2005–09, Chief of Staff, Air Force 2009–12, Supreme Allied Commdr Transformation, NATO 2012–15; apptd Gen. Sec. Coherence Officers Jt Staff Coll. 2001; attained rank of Brig.-Gen. 2000, Maj.-Gen. 2005; Grand Officier, Légion d'honneur 2009, Officier, Ordre national du Mérite, Grand Cross, Order of the Redeemer (Greece), Santos-Dumont Medal of Merit (Brazil); Aeronautical Medal, Overseas Medal, Meritorious Service Medal (Singapore), Guatemalan Armed Forces Cross (with two crossed sabres); Curtis Prize. *Leisure interests:* jogging, swimming, opera, poetry. *Address:* c/o Allied Command Transformation, 7857 Blandy Road, Suite 100, Norfolk, VA 23551-2490, USA (office).

PÁLSSON, Thorsteinn; Icelandic politician, diplomatist and journalist; b. 29 Oct. 1947, Selfoss; m. Ingibjörg Rafnar; three c.; ed Commercial Coll., Reykjavik and Univ. of Iceland; Chair. Vaka (student's union) 1969–70; Ed. Vísir 1975; Dir Confed. of Icelandic Employers 1979–83; mem. Parl. 1983–99; Chair. Independence Party 1983–91; Minister of Finance 1985–87, Prime Minister of Iceland 1987–88, Minister of Fisheries 1991–99, of Justice 1991–99, also of Ecclesiastical Affairs –1999; Amb. to UK 1999–2002, to Denmark 2003–05; Co-Ed. Fréttablaðið (daily newspaper) 2006–09.

PALTRIDGE, Garth William, BSc, PhD, DSc, FAA; Australian atmospheric physicist; b. 24 April 1940, Brisbane, Queensland; s. of T. B. Paltridge and A. T. Savage; m. Kay L. Petty 1965; one s. one d.; ed Brisbane Boys' Coll., Univs of Queensland and Melbourne; Postdoctoral Fellow, New Mexico Inst. of Mining and Tech. 1965; Sr Scientific Officer, Radio and Space Research Station, Ditton Park, Bucks., UK 1966–67; Research Scientist, CSIRO Div. of Meteorological Physics 1967–81, Chief Research Scientist 1981–89; Exec. Dir PIECE, Australian Inst. of Petroleum 1980; Sr Visiting Scientist, Nat. Climate Program Office 1989–90; Prof. and Dir Inst. of Antarctic and Southern Oceans Studies (IASOS) and CEO Antarctic Co-operative Research Centre, Univ. of Tasmania 1991–2002, Prof. Emer. and Hon. Research Fellow 2002–; Visiting Fellow, ANU; WMO Research Prize. *Publications:* Radiative Processes in Meteorology and Climatology (co-author) 1976, The Climate Caper: Facts and Fallacies of Global Warming 2009; 100 research papers on environmental topics. *Leisure interests:* golf, history, furniture and cabinet making. *Address:* c/o Institute of Antarctic and Southern Ocean Studies, University of Tasmania, Private Bag 77, Hobart, Tasmania 7001 (office); 9 Waymouth Avenue, Sandy Bay, Tasmania 7005, Australia (home). *E-mail:* secretary@iasos.utas.edu.au (office).

PALTROW, Gwyneth; American actress; b. 27 Sept. 1972, Los Angeles, Calif.; d. of Bruce Paltrow and Blythe Danner; m. 1st Chris Martin 2003 (divorced 2014); one s. one d.; m. 2nd Brad Falchuk 2018; ed Spence School, New York and Univ. of California, Santa Barbara. *Films include:* Shout 1991, Hook 1991, Malice 1993, Flesh and Bone 1993, Mrs. Parker and the Vicious Circle 1994, Jefferson in Paris 1995, Se7en 1995, Moonlight and Valentino 1995, Hard Eight 1996, The Pallbearer, Seven 1995, Emma 1996, Sydney 1996, Great Expectations 1998, Sliding Doors 1998, Hush 1998, A Perfect Murder 1998, Shakespeare in Love (Academy Award for Best Actress 1999) 1998, The Talented Mr. Ripley 1999, Duets 2000, Bounce 2000, The Intern 2000, The Anniversary Party 2001, The Royal Tenenbaums 2001, Shallow Hal 2001, Possession 2002, View from the Top 2003, Sylvia 2003, Sky Captain and the World of Tomorrow 2004, Proof 2005, Infamous 2006, Love and Other Disasters 2006, Running with Scissors 2006, The Good Night 2007, Iron Man 2008, Two Lovers 2008, Iron Man 2 2010, Country Strong 2010, Contagion 2011, Avengers Assemble 2012, Thanks for Sharing 2012, Iron Man 3 2013, Mortdecai 2015, Avengers: Infinity War 2018. *Television includes:* High (film) 1989, Cruel Doubt (film) 1992, Deadly Relations (film) 1993, Spain… On the Road Again 2008, The Marriage Ref 2010, Glee (series) 2010–11, 2014, Web Therapy 2014, The Politician (series) 2019–. *Play:* Proof (Donmar Warehouse, London) 2002. *Address:* c/o Rick Kurtzman, Creative Artists Agency, 2000 Avenue of the Stars, Los Angeles, CA 90067, USA (office). *Telephone:* (424) 288-2000 (office). *Fax:* (424) 288-2900 (office). *Website:* www.caa.com (office).

PALTSEV, Mikhail Alexandrovich, DrMed; Russian pathologist; *Vice-Director, National Research Centre, Kurchatov Institute;* b. 9 Nov. 1949, Russia; m.; one d.; ed 1st Moscow Sechenov Inst. of Medicine; Prof., Moscow Sechenov Acad. of Medicine; active as pathology anatomist and organizer of medical sciences; Pres. Moscow Medical Academy of I.M. Sechenov 1987–2009; mem. Presidium Russian Acad. of Sciences, Russian Div., Int. Acad. of Science, Int. Acad. of Pathology, European Soc. of Pathology; Pres. Asscn of Medical and Pharmaceutical Educ.; Ed.-in-Chief Molecular Medicine, Pathology Archives; mem. Int. Acad. of Pathology, Exec. Cttee European Soc. of Pathology; Rector and Head of Pathology Dept, Moscow Sechenov Acad. of Medicine 1990–2010; Vice-Pres. Russian Academy of Medical Sciences (RAMS) 2006–11; Vice Dir in medical and biological studies, Nat. Research Centre, Kurchatov Inst. 2011–; Hon. Prof., Moscow State Univ. 2004; Order of Friendship Between Peoples, USSR State Prize 1991, Order for Service to the Fatherland, Rank IV 1999; Russian Govt's Prize 2000, 2006, 2008, 2011, The President of RF award 2002, D.S. Sarkisov Award, RAMS 2001, V.S. Gulevich Award, RAMS 2007, A.I.Strukov Award, RAMS (2010). *Publications:* Pathological Anatomy (with N. Anichkov) 2001, 2005, Pathology (textbook, co-author) 2002, Intercellular Interactions (co-author) 2003. *Address:* Nat. Research Centre, Kurchatov Inst., Akademika Kurchatova pl, 123182 Moscow, Russia (office). *Telephone:* (499) 196-99-61 (office), *E-mail:* paltsev_ma@nrcki.ru (office). *Website:* eng.nrcki.ru (office).

PALUCKAS, Gintautas; Lithuanian politician and local government official; *Chairman, Lietuvos Socialdemokratų Partija (Lithuanian Social Democratic Party);* b. 19 Aug. 1979, Panevėžys, Lithuanian SSR, USSR; ed Panevėžys Juozas Balčikonis Gymnasium, Faculty of Math. and Computer Science and Int. Business School, Faculty of Law, Vilnius Univ.; Chief Specialist, Repub. of Lithuania State Social Insurance Fund (SODRA) 2003–05; Asst to Justas Paleckis, MEP 2005–07; Admin Dir, Vilnius City Municipality 2007–09, LSDP cand. for Mayor of Vilnius 2015, mem. Municipality Council and Deputy Mayor of Vilnius 2015–; mem. Lietuvos Socialdemokratų Partija (LSDP—Lithuanian Social Democratic Party) 2004–, Vice-Pres. Vilnius Br. 2006–, Exec. Sec. LSDP Council and mem. Bd 2013–, Chair. LSDP 2017–. *Publications:* several articles and reviews in the press on political matters. *Address:* Lietuvos Socialdemokratų Partija, Barboros Radvilaites g. 1, Vilnius 01124, Lithuania (office). *Telephone:* (5) 261-3907 (office). *Fax:* (5) 261-5420 (office). *E-mail:* info@lsdp.lt (office). *Website:* www.lsdp.lt (office).

PALUMBO, Baron (Life Peer), cr. 1991, of Walbrook in the City of London; **Peter Garth Palumbo,** MA; British property developer; b. 20 July 1935, London; s. of Rudolph Palumbo and Elsie Palumbo; m. 1st Denia Wigram 1959 (died 1986), one s. two d.; m. 2nd Hayat Morowa 1986, one s. two d.; ed Eton Coll. and Worcester Coll., Oxford; Gov. LSE 1976–94; Hon. mem. Emmanuel Coll., Cambridge 1994–; Trustee, Mies van der Rohe Archive 1977–, The Tate Gallery 1978–85, Whitechapel Art Gallery Foundation 1981–87; Trustee and Hon. Treas. Writers and Scholars Educational Trust 1984–99; Chair. The Tate Gallery Foundation 1986–87, Painshill Park Trust Appeal 1986–96; Chair. The Arts Council of GB 1989–94; Chair. Pritzker Architecture Prize Jury 2004–; Chancellor Univ. of Portsmouth 1992–2007; mem. bd and Dir Andy Warhol Foundation for the Arts 1994–97; Trustee Natural History Museum 1994–2007, Design Museum 1995–2005; mem. Council, Royal Albert Hall 1995–99; Gov. RSC 1995–2000, Whitgift School 2002–; Hon. FRIBA 1986; Hon. Fellow Inst. of Structural Eng 1994; mem. Livery, Salters' Co. 1965; Dr hc (Portsmouth) 1993; Nat. Order of Southern Cross, Brazil; Cranbrook Patronage of the Arts Award, Detroit, USA 2002. *Leisure interests:* music, travel, gardening, reading. *Address:* House of Lords, London, SW1A 0PW, England. *Telephone:* (20) 7219-5353. *Website:* www.lordpeterpalumbo.com.

PAMFILOVA, Ella Aleksandrovna; Russian politician; *Chairperson, Central Electoral Commission of the Russian Federation (Tsentralnaya izbiratelnaya komissiya Rossiiskoi Federatsii);* b. 12 Sept. 1953, Almalyk, Uzbekistan; d. of Aleksandr Lekomtsev and Polina Lekomtseva; m. 1st Nikita Leonidovich Pamfilov 1976 (divorced 1993); one d.; m. 2nd; ed Moscow Inst. of Power Eng; foreman at cen. factory Mosenergo, Chair. of trade union at factory 1981–89; USSR People's Deputy 1989–91; Sec. Comm. of Supreme Soviet on Privileges Jan.–Nov. 1991; Russian Fed. Minister for Social Security 1991–94; mem. State Duma (Parl.) 1993–99, mem. Cttee on Security 1995–98; Chair. Council on Social Policy under Presidential Admin. 1994; Founder and Head Movt for Healthy Russia 1996; Chair. Movt for Civic Dignity 2001–14; Chair. Presidential Comm. on Human Rights 2002–04; Chair. Civil Society Insts and Human Rights Council 2004–10 (resgnd); High Commr for Human Rights 2014–16; Chair. Central Electoral Commission of the Russian Federation (Tsentralnaya izbiratelnaya komissiya Rossiiskoi Federatsii) 2016–; fmr Public Policy Scholar, Kennan Inst., Woodrow Wilson Int. Center for Scholars, USA; Pres. Acad. Revival; Order of the Russian Orthodox Church of the Holy Martyr Tryphon 1998, Order For Merit to the Fatherland 2003, Chevalier, légion d'honneur 2006, Order of Honour 2010. *Leisure interest:* gardening. *Address:* Central Electoral Commission of the Russian Federation (Tsentralnaya izbiratelnaya komissiya Rossiiskoi Federatsii), 109012 Moscow, B. Cherkassii per. 9, Russia (office). *Telephone:* (495) 606-79-61 (office). *Fax:* (495) 606-97-69 (office). *E-mail:* info@cikrf.ru (office). *Website:* www.cikrf.ru (office).

PAMPURO, José Juan Bautista, MD; Argentine politician and physician; b. 28 Dec. 1949, Buenos Aires; m.; three d.; ed Univ. of Buenos Aires; Sec. of Health, Lanús Municipality 1983–87; elected Nat. Deputy for Justice, Buenos Aires Prov. 1987–91; Minister of Health and Social Action, Buenos Aires Prov. 1991–92; in pvt. medical practice 1992–95; Gov. of Buenos Aires 1995–99; re-elected Nat. Deputy 1999–2002; Gen. Coordinator for Pres. Eduardo Duhalde 2002; Sec.-Gen. of the Nat. Presidency 2002–04; Minister of Defence 2004–05; Provisional Pres. of the Senate 2006–11; apptd Vice-Pres. Banco de la Provincia de Buenos Aires 2011.

PAMUK, Orhan; Turkish novelist and academic; *Robert Yik-Fong Tam Professor of the Humanities, Columbia University;* b. 7 June 1952, Istanbul; m. Aylin Turegen 1982 (divorced 2001); one d.; ed Robert Coll., Istanbul Technical Univ., Inst. of Journalism at Istanbul Univ.; Visiting Scholar, Columbia Univ. 1985–88, Robert Yik-Fong Tam Prof. of the Humanities 2006–; jury mem. Cannes Film Festival 2007; mem. American Acad. of Arts and Sciences 2008–, Chinese Acad. for Social Sciences 2008–; Hon. mem. American Acad. of Arts and Letters 2005; Officier, Légion d'honneur 2012; Dr hc (American Univ. of Beirut) 2003, (Georgetown Univ.) 2007, (Bogaziçi Univ.) 2007, (Tilburg Univ.) 2007, (Free Univ. of Berlin) 2007, (Univ. of Bucharest) 2008, (Madrid Univ.) 2008, (Univ. of Rouen) 2009, (Univ. of Tirana) 2010, (Yale Univ.) 2010, (Sofia Univ.) 2011, (Brera Acad., Italy) 2017, (St Petersburg State Univ.) 2017; Prix de la Découverte Européenne 1991, Ricardo-Huch Prize 2005, Nobel Prize in Literature 2006, Distinguished Humanist Award, Washington Univ. 2006, Puterbaugh Award 2006, Ovid Award 2008, Norman Mailer Lifetime Achievement Award 2010, Sonning Prize (Denmark) 2012, Helena Vaz da Silva European Award for Raising Public Awareness on Cultural Heritage 2014, Tabernakul Prize (FYR Macedonia) 2014. *Publications include:* Cevdet Bey ve Ogullari (Cevdet Bey and His Sons) (First Prize, Milliyet Press Novel Contest 1979, Orhan Kemal Novel Prize 1983) 1983, Sessiz Ev (The Quiet House) (Madarali Novel Prize, Turkey 1984, in translation Prix de la découverte européene 1991) 1983, Beyaz Kale (trans. as The White Castle) (Independent Foreign Fiction Prize 1990) 1985, Kara Kitap (trans. as The Black Book) (Prix France Culture 1995) 1990, Gizli Yuz (screenplay of Kara Kitap) 1992, Yeni Hayat (trans. as The New Life) 1995, My Name is Red (Prix du Meilleur Livre Etranger, France 2002, Premio Grinzane Cavour, Italy 2002, Int. IMPAC Dublin Literary Award 2003) 2000, Istanbul 2003, Snow (Prix Médicis Etranger, France 2005) 2004, Istanbul: Memories of a City 2006, Istanbul: City of a Hundred Names 2007, Other Colours (essays) 2007, Masumiyet Müzesi (trans. as The Museum of Innocence) 2008, Manzaradan Parçalar 'Hayat, Sokaklar, Edebiyat' 2010, The Naive and the Sentimental Novelist 2011, The Innocence of Objects (Mary Lynn Kotz Award 2014) 2012, I Am a Tree 2014, A Strangeness in My Mind 2015, Kırmızı Saçlı Kadın (trans. as The Red-Haired Woman) 2016; contrib. to various newspapers and magazines. *Address:* School of the Arts, Columbia University, 305 Dodge Hall, 2960 Broadway, New York, NY 10027, USA (office). *E-mail:* op2114@columbia.edu. *Website:* arts.columbia.edu (office); www.orhanpamuk.net.

PAN, Hong; Chinese film actress; b. 4 Nov. 1954, Shanghai; m. Mi Jingshan (divorced 1990); ed Shanghai Drama Acad.; mem. 5th Nat. Cttee, Fed. of Literary and Art Circles 1988–; Vice-Chair. China Film Asscn, China Film Performance Academic Soc.; mem. CPPCC Nat. Cttee; mem. Jury 5th Shanghai Int. Film Festival 2001. *Films include:* Troubled Laughter 1979, Sunray Through Clouds 1980, At Middle Age (3rd Golden Rooster Best Actress Award 1983) 1982, The Last Empress 1985, The Trouble-shooters 1988, Well (8th Golden Rooster Best Actress) 1988, The Last Aristocrats 1989, The Single Woman 1991, Woman-TAXI-Woman 1991, Shanghai Fever (14th Golden Rooster Best Actress, Hundred Flowers Award Best Actress) 1994, Up For the Raising Sun 1997, Destination – 9th Heaven 1997, So Young 2013. *Television includes:* Secret Murder, Amazing Cases 2003, Beijing My Love 2005, Qing Tian Ya Men 2006, Embroiderer Lan Xin 2007, Ancestral Temple 2008.

PAN, Wenent P., BS, PhD; Taiwanese oil industry executive; *Chairman and CEO, Gintech Energy Corporation;* ed Nat. Taiwan Normal Univ., Univ. of Wyoming, USA; fmrly with ACE Chemical Co. and Fluid Properties Research Inst.; joined CPC Corpn, Taiwan (fmrly Chinese Petroleum Corpn), held various roles including Man. of Process Research, Dir of Corp. Planning, Vice-Pres. then Pres. 1996–2004, Chair. 2006–09, also Vice-Chair. Kuo Kuang Power Co. (subsidiary co.) 1997–2004, Chair. 2004–09; Chair. and CEO Gintech Energy Corpn 2009–; Chair. ROC-Australia Business Council, Sino-Indonesia Cultural and Econ. Asscn, Indonesia Cttee of Chinese Int. Econ. Cooperation Asscn; fmr Pres. Chinese Asscn for Energy Econs; mem. Bd of Dirs Taiwan High Speed Rail Corpn 2009–, CTCI Group 2012– (Chair. CTCI Foundation), U-Ming Marine Transport Corpn –2016. *Address:* Gintech Energy Corporation, No. 21, Kebei 1st Road, Hsinchu Science Park, Zhunan 350, Taiwan. *Telephone:* (6) 37586198 (office). *Fax:* (6) 37586199 (office). *Website:* www.gintechenergy.com.

PANAGIOTOPOULOS, Panos; Greek journalist, lawyer and politician; b. 1957, Athens; m. Maouzi Tsaldari; one s.; ed Technical Univ. of Athens, Athens Law School, Univ. of Vincennes, Paris, French Inst. of Athens; mil. service in Greek Air Force; active in ONNED and DAP-NDFK (student org. of Nea Demokratia), mem. leadership of ONNED and Ed. Demokratike Protoporia newspaper; mem. Steering Cttee (Youth Dept) of Nea Demokratia, participated in Govt Comm. programme responsible for Youth and Drugs 1984–85; mem. Political Council of New Democracy; mem. (New Democracy) of the Vouli (Parl.) for Athens B 2000–; Minister for Employment and Social Protection in first govt of Kostas Karamanlis March 2004; served as Govt Gen. Rapporteur for the Revision of the Constitution; Parl. Spokesman for New Democracy 2007–09, Spokesman for New Democracy 2009–11, responsible for Foreign Policy 2011–12; Minister of Nat. Defence following formation of coalition govt with Panhellenic Socialist Movt (PASOK) and Democratic Left (Dimokratiki Aristera) June 2012–13; Minister of Culture and Sports 2013–14; Chair. Special Parl. Cttee on the ratification of the Treaty of Lisbon; had successful TV and print journalism career; legal career as prosecuting lawyer with own law office in Athens, specializing in criminal and corp. affairs; news reporter on Greek television; mem. Journalists Union of Athens Daily Newspapers, Athens Bar Asscn; fmr Dir News SKY 100, 4 FM, STAR TV News; fmr Dir of Information and Broadcasting, ET1 and ANT1 TV; Founding mem. Athens radio station; political ed. and columnist at several newspapers; numerous awards, including Greek Television Award 1992, Botsis Foundation Award, Prize of the Greek Christian Literature Soc., Honour of the Panhellenic Asscn of Reserve Forces. *Address:* c/o Ministry of Culture and Sports, Andreas Papandreou 37, 151 80 Maroussi, Greece. *Website:* www.panospanagiotopoulos.gr.

PANARITI, Edmond, DipVetMed, PhD; Albanian veterinary surgeon, academic and politician; *Minister of Agriculture, Rural Development and Water Administration;* b. 1 June 1960, Tirana; m. Narin Panariti; two c.; ed Univ. of Agriculture, Tirana; Researcher, Dept of Radio-biology, Inst. of Veterinary Research, Tirana 1984–89, Head of Dept of Environmental Toxicology 1992–95, Deputy Dir Inst. of Veterinary Research 1998–2006; Postgraduate Researcher on Environmental Toxicology, ETH, Zurich, Switzerland 1989–92; Lecturer and Researcher, Univ. of Kentucky, USA 1995–96, Univ. of Mississippi 2000–01; Head of Food Safety Section, Inst. of Public Health 1996–98; Lecturer and Researcher on Analytical Toxicology, Veterinary Univ. of Hanover, Germany 2004–05; Officer and Project Co-ordinator, WHO 2009–11; mem. Tirana Municipal Council 2011, Deputy Mayor of Tirana 2011–12; Minister of Foreign Affairs 2012–13; Minister of Agric., Rural Devt and Water Admin 2013–; mem. Socialist Movement for Integration 2004–, Sec. for Agric. and Environment 2006–08, Chair. Nat. Steering Cttee 2008–; Chair. Cttee of European Ministers, Council of Europe –2012; Hon. DMV (Univ. of Perugia, Italy) 2015. *Publications:* two textbooks and numerous articles. *Address:* Ministry of Agriculture, Rural Development and Water Administration, Sheshi Skënderbej 2, 1001 Tirana, Albania (office). *Telephone:* (4) 2232796 (office). *Fax:* (4) 2227924 (office). *E-mail:* edmond.panariti@bujqesia.gov.al (office). *Website:* www .bujqesia.gov.al (office).

PANDA, Ramakanta, MCh; Indian cardiothoracic and vascular surgeon; *Chief Consultant Cardiovascular Thoracic Surgeon, Vice-Chairman and Managing Director, Asian Heart Institute;* b. (Ramakant Madanmohan Panda), Sundargarh, Orissa; s. of Sarla Panda; m. Sanghamitra Panda; two c.; ed SCB Medical Coll., Orissa, All India Inst. of Medical Sciences; fmr Sr Registrar, Harefield Hosp. UK; Fellowship in Cardiovascular and Thoracic Surgery, Cleveland Clinic, Ohio, USA, fmr Assoc. Staff Surgeon; f. Asian Heart Inst. 2003, currently Chief Consultant Cardiovascular Thoracic Surgeon, Vice-Chair. and Man. Dir; fmr Consultant Cardiothoracic Surgeon, Jaslok Hosp., Breach Candy Hosp., Lilavati and Nanavati Hosp.; f. Sarla Madan Charitable Trust, Asian Heart Inst., Mumbai; Rashtriya Samman, Central Bd of Taxes, Bank of Baroda Sun Lifetime Achievement Award 2009, Lifetime Achievement Award, World Congress on Clinical, Preventive & Geriatric Cardiology 2009, Padma Bhushan 2010, Think Odisha Legend Leadership Award 2011. *Achievements include:* under his leadership, his surgical team has performed more than 16,000 bypass surgeries, has also performed more than 900 repeat (redo) bypass surgeries as well as more than 2,000 surgeries on patients considered high risk by surgical definition. *Publications:* several scientific publications in nat. and int. journals. *Address:* Asian Heart Institute, Bandra Kurla Complex, Bandra (E), Mumbai 400 051, India (office). *Telephone:* (22) 66986601 (office). *Fax:* (22) 66986639 (office). *E-mail:* rp@ahirc.com (office). *Website:* www.asianheartinstitute.org (office).

PANDAY, Basdeo, BLL, BSc (Econs); Trinidad and Tobago politician; b. 25 May 1933, Prince's Town; m. 1st Norma Mohammed (died 1981); one d.; m. 2nd Oma Ramkisson; three d.; ed Lincoln's Inn, Univ. of London, UK; entered politics as mem. of Workers' and Farmers' Party 1966; trade union legal adviser; Pres.-Gen. All Trinidad Sugar and Gen. Workers' Trade Union 1973, Sugar Industry Staff Asscn 1975; founder mem. United Labour Front (ULF); Leader of the Opposition 1976–86, 1989–95, 2001–10; Minister of Foreign Affairs 1986–91; mem. Nat. Alliance for Reconciliation (NAR), expelled 1988; Founder United Nat. Congress (UNC), Leader 1989–2005, 2006–10; Prime Minister of Trinidad and Tobago 1995–2001; Chief Admin. Basdeo Panday Foundation; Pravasi Bharatiya Samman (India) 1986. *Address:* Basdeo Panday Foundation, 78–81 Southern Main Road, Exchange Village, Couva; La Fantasie Gardens, St Ann's, Port of Spain, Trinidad and Tobago (home). *Telephone:* 636-3507. *E-mail:* basdeopandayfoundation@gmail .com.

PANDE, Arvind, MA; Indian business executive; b. 7 Sept. 1942; ed Allahabad Univ., Univ. of Cambridge, UK; Adviser to Exec. Dir for India, Bangladesh and Sri Lanka, IBRD 1971–74; Dept of Econ. Affairs, Ministry of Finance 1974–78; Special

Sec., Govt of Madhya Pradesh 1978–81; Jt Sec. to Prime Minister of India 1981–86; Dir (Corp. Planning) Steel Authority of India Ltd (SAIL) 1986–90, (Personnel and Corp. Planning) 1990–93, Vice-Chair. 1993–97, Chair. (CEO) 1997–2002; Chair. Indian Iron and Steel Co. Ltd; fmrly Dir HDFC Bank Ltd (ADR), Exec. Dir 2003–11; Pres. Nat. HRD Network; Council mem. Indian Inst. of Metals, Confed. of Indian Industry; mem. Bd of Govs Int. Man. Inst.; Dir Int. Iron and Steel Inst., Belgium; mem. Bureau of Indian Standards; Chair. IVRCL Infrastructures and Projects Ltd 2003–06; Chair. (non-exec.) Burnpur Cement Ltd 2006–09; mem. Bd of Dirs Era Infra Eng Ltd 2005–15, Coal India Ltd 2007–10, Essar Steel India Ltd 2013–, Ind. Dir VISA Steel Ltd –2010. *Address:* c/o Essar Steel India Ltd., Essar House, 11, Keshavrao Khadye Marg, Mahalaxmi, Mumbai 400034, Maharashtra (office); E-148(Ff), East Of Kailash, New Delhi 110065, India (home).

PANDE, Kabinga J.; Zambian journalist and politician; fmr Head Public Relations, Zambian Cen. Bank; fmr Pres. Africa Travel Asscn; Minister of Science, Tech. and Vocational Training 2005, of Tourism, Environment and Natural Resources 2005–07, of Foreign Affairs 2007–11; currently mem. Parl. for Kasempa; Deputy Chair. Movt for Multi-party Democracy. *Address:* National Assembly, Parliament Road, POB 31299, Lusaka 10101, Zambia (office). *Telephone:* (1) 292425 (office); 977-639630 (mobile). *Fax:* (1) 292252 (office). *E-mail:* pkabinga@ parliament.gov.zm (office); info@parliament.gov.zm (office). *Website:* www .parliament.gov.zm (office).

PANDE, Mrinal; Indian journalist, editor and broadcasting executive; b. 1946, Tikamgarh, Madhya Pradesh; d. of Gaura Pant Shivani; m.; two d.; ed Allahabad Univ.; taught at Univs of Allahabad, Delhi and Bhopal; Ed. Vama (women's magazine) 1984–87; Ed.-Anchor (Hindi news), Star News and Doordarshan; Chief Ed. Hindustan (Hindi daily) 2000–09; Chair. Prasar Bharati (public service broadcaster) 2010–14; currently columnist, The Indian Express; Contrib., Scoll.in; fmr Sec.-Gen. Eds Guild of India; Founder-Pres. Indian Women's Press Corps; Life Mem. Centre for Women's Development Studies; Trustee Wildlife Trust of India; Padmashree 2006, Lifetime Achievement Award, Red Ink Awards 2014. *Television:* Baaton Baaton Mein (host). *Publications include:* The Subject is Woman 1991, Daughter's Daughter 1993, That Which Ram Hath Ordained 1993, Devi, Tales of the Goddess in Our Time 2000, My Own Witness 2001, The Other Country: Dispatches from the Mofussil 2012, Dhvaniyon ke aalok mein stree 2016. *Address:* E-148 (FF), East of Kailash, New Delhi 110 065, India. *E-mail:* mrinal .pand@gmail.com. *Website:* indianexpress.com/profile/columnist/mrinal-pande.

PANDE, Prithivi Bahadur; Nepalese banker; *Chairman, Nepal Investment Bank Ltd.;* m. Pratima Pande; one s.; worked at Central Bank of Nepal –1990; Gen. Man. Rastra Banijya Bank 1990, then Exec. Dir Himalayan Bank (first pvt. sector commercial bank in Nepal) 1991–2001; led consortium of investors to buy Credit Agricole shares in Nepal Indosuez Bank Ltd, renamed Nepal Investment Bank Ltd 2002, Chair. 2002–, Chief Exec. Dir 2002–12; Chair. Himalayan Infrastructure Fund (pvt. equity fund). *Address:* Nepal Investment Bank Ltd, Durbar Marg, PO Box 3412, Kathmandu, Nepal (office). *Telephone:* (1) 4228229 (office). *Fax:* (1) 4226349 (office); (1) 4228927 (office). *E-mail:* info@nibl.com.np (office). *Website:* www.nibl.com.np (office).

PANDEY, Mahendra Bahadur, MEd, LLB; Nepalese politician, academic and diplomatist; b. 1948, Nuwakot Dist; m. Bhim Kumari Thapa; one s. one d.; ed Tribhuwan Univ.; Assoc. Prof. of English, Tribhuvan Univ. 1975–95; joined Communist Party of Nepal 1977, Chief Whip, Communist Party of Nepal (Unified Marxist-Leninist) (UML) 2006–07, Chief, Education and Human Resource Dept, Communist Party of Nepal (Unified Marxist-Leninist) 2011–; elected to House of Reps 1999; Minister of Foreign Affairs 2014–15; Mem. Sec., Social Welfare Council 1995.

PANDEY, Ramesh Nath; Nepalese politician; b. Feb. 1944; mem. Nepalese Del. to UN 1962, 1968, Leader of Del. 2005; fmr Minister of Population and Devt, Information, Communication and Gen. Admin; fmr Minister for Industry and Communication; fmr Minister of State for Tourism, Labour and Social Welfare; fmr Govt Spokesman; mem. Parl.; Minister of Foreign Affairs 2005–06; arrested 2006 after King Gyanendra ceded control of govt; currently political analyst.

PANDEY, Surendra; Nepalese sociologist and politician; b. 25 Aug. 1958; elected mem. Upper House, Nat. Ass.; mem. Communist Party of Nepal (Unified Marxist-Leninist), mem. Politburo; Minister of Finance 2009–11, also Gov. for Nepal in Asian Devt Bank.

PANDIT, Vikram S., BS, MS, MBA, PhD; American (b. Indian) banking executive; b. 14 Jan. 1957, Nagpur, Maharashtra, India; s. of Shankar Pandit and Shailaja Pandit; m. Swati Pandit; one s. one d.; ed Dadar Parsee Youths Ass. High School, Mumbai, Gannon Univ., Columbia Univ., New York; moved to USA to study aged 16; Prof., Indiana Univ., Bloomington 1986–90; worked for 20 years with Morgan Stanley & Co., becoming Man. Dir 1990–94, Head of Equity Derivatives 1994–2000, also Man. Dir 1997–2000, Co-pres. and COO Institutional Securities Div. 2000–03, Pres. and COO Institutional Securities & Investment Banking Group 2003–05; Founder and Chair. Old Lane LP (hedge fund) 2005–07; Chair. and CEO Citigroup Alternative Investments 2007, Chair. and CEO Institutional Clients Group 2007, mem. Bd of Dirs and CEO Citigroup Inc. 2007–12 (resgnd); mem. Bd of Dirs Columbia Univ., Columbia Business School, Indian School of Business, Trinity School, NASDAQ 2000–03; fmr mem. Bd of Dirs New York City Investment Fund, American India Foundation; Padma Bhushan 2008, named Banker of the Year by Euromoney magazine 2010. *Address:* c/o Citigroup Inc., 399 Park Avenue, New York, NY 10043, USA.

PANDITHAGE, A(beyakumar) Mohan; Sri Lankan business executive; *Chairman and CEO, Hayleys PLC;* s. of P. D. Alexander; began career with Hayleys as a man. trainee 1969, apptd a Dir of Hayleys Advantis 1981, Man. Dir 1988, Group Exec. Dir 1996, elected mem. Bd of Dirs 1998, Deputy Chair. Hayleys PLC and CEO Hayleys Advantis Ltd 2007–09, Chair. and CEO Hayleys PLC 2009–; mem. American Bureau of Shipping, SRILPO (Trade Facilitation) Cttee, mem. of several Chambers of Commerce; mem. Bd of Dirs Sri Lanka Port Man. Consultancy Services Ltd; mem. Presidential Cttee on Maritime Matters; fmr Chair. and Vice-Chair. Ceylon Asscn of Ships' Agents; fmr mem. Bd of Dirs Sri Lanka Ports Authority, Jaya Container Terminals Ltd; Hon. Consul of Mexico to Sri Lanka 2011; Best Shipping Personality, Inst. of Chartered Shipbrokers, Sri Lanka 2004.

Address: Hayleys Group, 400 Deans Road, Colombo 10, Sri Lanka (office). *Telephone:* (11) 2696331 (office). *Fax:* (11) 2699299 (office). *E-mail:* info@cau.hayleys.com (office). *Website:* www.hayleys.com (office).

PANDOLFI, Filippo Maria, PhD; Italian politician (retd); b. 1 Nov. 1927, Bergamo; ed Università Cattolica del Sacro Cuore, Milan; fmr co. dir; mem. Chamber of Deputies for Brescia-Bergamo 1968–89; mem. Comm. on Finance and the Treasury; fmr Under-Sec. of State in Ministry of the Budget; Minister of Finance 1976–78, of the Treasury 1978–80, of Trade and Industry 1980–81, 1982–83, of Agric. and Forestry 1983–88; EEC Commr for Science, Research, Telecommunications and Information Tech. 1989–93; mem. Group of 10, Luigi Sturzo Inst. from 2000; Christian Democrat; Cavaliere di Gran Croce dell'Ordine al Merito della Repubblica Italiana 2003. *Leisure interests:* ancient Christian literature, opera and classical music, climbing.

PANENIĆ, Tomislav; Croatian politician and government official; b. 12 March 1973, Nürtingen, Germany; m. Anica Panenić; two d.; ed Faculty of Econs, Osijek; volunteer in Homeland War 1991–92; worked for several years in pvt. sector; Head of Devt Agency, Office of Int. Co-operation, TINTL 2005–07; Vukovar-Srijem Programme Co-ordinator of World Bank, Ministry of Regional Devt 2007–10; Mayor of Tompojevci 2010–15; Pres. Local Action Groups, Srem 2011; mem. Co. Cttee, Pilot Project Land Consolidation, Ministry of Agric. 2004–09; Rep. of European LEADER Asscn for Rural Devt, Brussels 2011–13; mem. Man. Bd, Croatian Network for Rural Devt 2011–13, also Pres.; mem. Bd and Treas., Int. Orgs Danube Competence Centre 2012; mem. Most Nezavisnih Lista (MOST) (Bridge of Independent Lists); Minister of the Economy Feb.–Oct. 2016; owner of farmland and four vineyards.

PANETTA, Leon E., BA, JD; American lawyer, academic, fmr government official and fmr politician; *Chairman, Panetta Institute for Public Policy, California State University;* b. 28 June 1938, Monterey, Calif.; s. of Carmelo Panetta and Carmelina Panetta; m. Sylvia Varni 1962; three s.; ed Santa Clara Univ.; served US Army 1964–66; Legis. Asst to Senator Thomas Kuchel, Washington, DC 1966–69; Dir Office of Civil Rights 1969–70; Exec. Asst to Mayor of New York 1970–71; Pnr, Panetta, Thompson and Panetta (law firm), Monterey, Calif. 1971–76; mem. US House of Reps 1977–93, Washington, DC, mem. House Agric. Cttee 1977–93, Budget Cttee 1979–85 (Chair. 1989–92), Vice-Chair. New Mem. Caucus 1977, Caucus of Vietnam Era Veterans in Congress, mem. Pres.'s Comm. on Foreign Language and Int. Studies; Head of Office of Man. and Budget 1993–94; Chief of Staff to Pres. Bill Clinton 1994–97; Founder and Co-Dir Panetta Inst. for Public Policy, California State Univ., Monterey Bay 1998–2009, Chair. 2013–, also Distinguished Scholar to the Chancellor, Calif. State Univ. System, Presidential Prof., Santa Clara Univ.; Dir CIA 2009–11; Sec. of Defense 2011–13; Chair. Pew Oceans Comm., Co-Chair. Jt Ocean Cttee Initiative; Co-Chair. Calif. Council on Base Support and Retention, Calif. Forward Leadership Council; mem. Iraq Study Group, US Inst. of Peace 2006; mem. Ind. Task Force on Immigration and America's Future; fmr mem. Bd of Dirs Blue Shield, Zenith, Nat. Marine Sanctuary Foundation, Bread for the World, Close Up, BP America's Public Policy Inst. of Calif., Oracle 2015–; mem. Bd of Visitors Santa Clara Univ. School of Law; fmr mem. Advisory Bd Fleishman–Hillard Int.; Trustee, Monterey Bay Aquarium; Democrat; numerous awards including John H. Chafee Coastal Stewardship Award, Julius A. Stratton Award for Coastal Leadership and Distinguished Public Service Medal, Center for the Study of the Presidency, Army Commendation Medal, NEA Lincoln Award, A. Philip Randolph Award, Smithsonian Inst. Nat. Portrait Gallery Paul Peck Presidential Award, Nat. Marine Sanctuary Foundation Lifetime Achievement Award, Natural Resources Defense Council Forces for Nature, Nat. Hospice Foundation Silver Anniversary Honouree. *Publications:* Bring Us Together 1971, Worthy Fights 2014. *Address:* Panetta Institute for Public Policy, 100 Campus Centre, Building 86E, California State University, Monterey Bay, Seaside, CA 93955, USA (office). *Telephone:* (831) 582-4200 (office). *Fax:* (831) 582-4082 (office). *E-mail:* info@PanettaInstitute.org (office). *Website:* www.panettainstitute.org (office).

PANFILOV, Gleb Anatolyevich; Russian film director; b. 21 May 1934, Magnitogorsk; m. Inna Mikhailovna Churikova; one s.; graduated from Sverdlovsk Polytechnic Inst. as a chemical engineer and Mosfilm Studios (course in directing); work as Dir in Sverdlovsk, Leningrad (now St Petersburg), Moscow 1976–; RSFSR People's Artist 1984, RSFSR State Prize 1985, Golden Prize, 13th Moscow Int. Film Festival, Hon. Prize for contrib. to cinema; 22nd Moscow Int. Film Festival 2000. *Stage productions include:* (Lenkom Theatre): Hamlet 1986, Sorry (A. Galin) 1992, The Romanovs: An Imperial Family 2000. *Films include:* National Militia (short) 1958, Vstavay v nash stroy! (documentary short) 1959, No Path Through Fire (scenario: Yevgeniy Gabrilovich) (Grand Prix Locarno 1969) 1968, Nachalo 1970, I Wish to Speak 1975, Proshu slova 1977, Tema (full version was not released for nine years when it won the Golden Bear at 37th Berlin Int. Film Festival 1986) 1979, Valentina 1981, Vassa Zheleznova 1983, Hamlet 1989, The Mother 1990, The Romanovs: An Imperial Family 2000, Bez vini vinovatiye 2008, Khranit vechno 2008; as writer: Utomlyonnye solntsem 2: Predstoyanie 2010, Utomlennye solntsem 2 2011. *Television includes:* Ubit ne na voyne (short) 1962, Nina Melovizinova (short) 1962, The Case of Kurt Clausewitz (film) 1963, The First Circle (mini-series) 2006; as writer: Utomlennye solntsem 2 (mini-series) 2011. *Address:* Universitetski Prosp. 6, Korp. 4, Apt 68, 117333 Moscow, Russia. *Telephone:* (495) 137-89-67.

PANGALOS, Theodoros, PhD; Greek politician, economist and lawyer; b. 17 Aug. 1938, Elefsis; m.; three s. two d.; ed Univ. of Athens, Univ. of Paris IV (Paris-Sorbonne), France; Co-founder Grigoris Lambrakis Youth Movt; stood as EDA cand. in 1964 election; active in dissident movt during mil. dictatorship; deprived of Greek citizenship by junta 1968; lecturer and researcher specializing in econ. devt, programming and town and country planning, Sorbonne, Paris and Head of Econ. Devt Inst. 1969–78; practises as lawyer in Athens; legal adviser to trade unions; active in movt to protect environment; Socialist mem. Parl. for Attica 1981–2012; Deputy Minister of Commerce 1982–84, of Foreign Affairs 1984–89, 1993–94; Minister of Transport and Communications 1994, of Foreign Affairs 1996–99, of Culture April–Nov. 2000; Deputy Chair. of Govt (Deputy Prime Minister), responsible for Co-ordination of Foreign Policy and Defence Cttee and the Econ. and Social Policy Cttee 2009–12; Rep. of Greek Del. to WEU Ass. and Council of Europe 2001–09; mem. Political Council and Head of Int. Affairs and

Defence section, Panhellenic Socialist Movt (PASOK); Visiting Prof. at various insts; 17 awards or honours from various countries. *Publications:* several works on econs, sociology and philosophy. *Address:* c/o Office of the Prime Minister, Maximos Mansion, Herodou Atticou 19, 106 74 Athens; 16–18 Pireos Street, 104 31 Athens, Greece (home). *Telephone:* (1) 5231142 (home). *Fax:* (1) 5231178 (home). *E-mail:* pangalos@otenet.gr (home). *Website:* www.pangalos.gr.

PANGESTU, Prajogo, (Pang Djun Phen); Indonesian business executive; *President Commissioner, PT Barito Pacific Tbk;* b. 1951; m. Herlina Tjandinegara; three c.; Dir Djajanti Timber Group, Kalimantan 1969–76, Pres. Dir 1977–93; mem. Bd of Commrs PT Astra International 1993–98; Pres. Dir PT Chandra Asri 1990–99; f. Barito Pacific Group, Pres. Commr PT Barito Pacific Tbk 1993–; Pres. Commr PT Tri Polyta Indonesia Tbk; Propr Transpacific Group; other business interests include PT Mangole Timber Producers, PT Chandra Asri Petrochemical Centre (CAPC) (jt venture). *Address:* PT Barito Pacific Tbk, Wisma Barito Pacific, Tower B, Lt.8 Jl. Letjen S. Parman Kav. 62-63, Jakarta 11410, Indonesia (office). *Telephone:* (21) 5306711 (office). *Fax:* (21) 5306680 (office). *E-mail:* corpsec@barito.co.id (office). *Website:* www.barito.co.id (office).

PANIĆ, Milan; Serbian business executive and fmr politician; *Owner, MP Global Enterprises;* b. 20 Dec. 1929, Belgrade; one s. two d.; ed Univ. of Belgrade, Univ. of South Carolina, USA, and Heidelberg Univ., Germany; emigrated to USA 1956; Founder and Chair. ICN Pharmaceuticals Inc. 1960–2002; returned to Yugoslavia 1991; Prime Minister of Yugoslavia July–Dec. 1992; cand. for Presidency of Serbia 1992; Founder and Owner of MP Global Enterprises 2003–; Dir Galenica Co., Belgrade and Moscow; mem. Bd Fund for Interdisciplinary Scientific Research (ISRF); Corresp. mem. California Inst. of Tech.; mem. American Nuclear Soc., Swiss Chemical Soc., Int. Soc. of Haemotherapy; mem. Bd Freedoms Foundation of Valley Forge; Wall Street Journal European of the Year. *Leisure interests:* tennis, cycling (fmr Yugoslav Champion). *Address:* MP Global Enterprises, 650 Town Center Drive, No. 660, Costa Mesa, CA 92626 (office); 1050 Arden Road, Pasadena, CA 91106, USA (home). *Telephone:* (714) 384-4000 (office). *Fax:* (714) 384-4010 (office). *Website:* www.milanpanic.com (office).

PANIGORO, Arifin, BEng; Indonesian business executive and politician; *Adviser, Medco Group;* b. 14 March 1945, Bandung; m.; two c.; ed Institut Teknologi Bandung, Inst. of Business Admin, France; Founder Meta Epsi Drilling Co. (Medco), currently Adviser, Medco Group, majority shareholder, Bank Saudara (part of Medco Group); fmr mem. House of Reps (parl.); fmr Chair. Partai Demokrasi Indonesia Perjuangan; mem. Indonesia Petroleum Asscn, Indonesian Engineer Asscn; Dr hc (Bandung Inst. of Tech.) 2010. *Address:* Medco Group, Medco Building III, 3rd Floor, Jl. Ampera Ray,a 18-20 Cilandak, Pasar Minggu South, Jakarta 12560, Indonesia (office). *Telephone:* (21) 7821671 (office). *Fax:* (21) 7821771 (office). *Website:* www.medcogroup.com (office).

PANITCHPAKDI, Supachai, MA, PhD; Thai banker, UN official and fmr government official; b. 30 May 1946, Bangkok; m. Sasai; one s. one d.; ed St Gabriel's Coll., Netherlands School of Econs (now Erasmus Univ.), Rotterdam; worked in Research Dept, Int. Finance Div., and Financial Insts Supervision Dept, Bank of Thailand 1974–86; elected mem. Thai Parl. 1986, Deputy Minister of Finance 1986–88; Dir and Adviser, then Pres. Thai Military Bank 1988–92; apptd Senator 1992, then Deputy Prime Minister of Thailand 1992–95, Deputy Prime Minister and Minister of Commerce 1997–99; Dir-Gen. WTO 2002–05; Sec.-Gen. UNCTAD 2005–Aug. 2013; Visiting Prof., Int. Inst. for Man. Devt, Lausanne 2001; Knight Grand Cordon (Special Class) of the Most Exalted Order of the White Elephant. *Publications include:* Globalization and Trade in the New Millennium 2001, China and the WTO: Changing China, Changing World Trade (with Mark Clifford) 2002. *Address:* c/o United Nations Conference on Trade and Development (UNCTAD), Palais des Nations 8-14, Avenue de la Paix, 1211 Geneva 10, Switzerland.

PANJIKIDZE, Maia, PhD; Georgian philologist, academic, diplomatist and politician; b. 16 Oct. 1960; m.; two s.; ed Tbilisi Javakhishvili State Univ., Friedrich Schiller Univ., Jena, GDR; Lecturer and Prof. of Philology, later Prof., Guram Tavartkiladze Univ. 2010–11; joined Foreign Service and was promoted to various high-level positions in Ministry of Foreign Affairs, including First Sec. 1994, Deputy Minister 2004, Amb. to Germany 2004–07, to The Netherlands 2007–10; mem. Qartuli Ocneba (Georgian Dream) political coalition, Spokesperson and Head of Cen. Office of coalition Feb.–Oct. 2012; Minister of Foreign Affairs 2012–14 (resgnd); Founder and fmr Chair. Union of German Language Teachers of Georgia. *Publications:* several works on German language and literature. *Address:* c/o Ministry of Foreign Affairs, 0108 Tbilisi, Sh. Chitadze 4, Georgia. *E-mail:* inform@mfa.gov.ge.

PANKE, Helmut, PhD; German business executive; b. 31 Aug. 1946, Storkow, Fürstenwalde; ed Univ. of Munich; Researcher, Swiss Inst. for Nuclear Research, simultaneous teaching role at Univ. of Munich 1976–78; worked as consultant, McKinsey & Co. in Düsseldorf and Munich 1978–82; joined Bayerische Motoren Werke (BMW) AG as Head of Planning and Controlling, Research and Devt 1982, then served in several man. positions in corp. planning, organization and corp. strategy, Head of Corp. Strategy and Co-ordination 1990–93, Chair. and CEO BMW (US) Holding Corpn 1993–96, mem. Bd of Man. (Personnel and Information Tech.) 1996–99, mem. Bd of Man. (Finance) 1999–2002, Chair. Bd of Man. BMW AG 2002–06; mem. Supervisory Bd Bayer AG 2006–; mem. Bd of Dirs Microsoft Corpn 2003–, UBS AG, Singapore Airlines. *Address:* c/o Supervisory Board, Bayer AG, Kaiser-Wilhelm-Allee 1, Leverkusen, Nordrhein-Westfalen, 51373, Germany.

PANNEERSELVAM, Thiru O., BA; Indian politician and state official; *Deputy Chief Minister of Tamil Nadu;* b. 14 Jan. 1951, Periyakulam, Theni Dist; s. of Ottakara Thevar; m. Vijayalakshmi Panneerselvam; three c.; ed Haji Karutha Ravuthar Kavuthiya Arts Coll., Uthamapalayam; mem. All India Anna Dravida Munnetra Kazhagam party; elected from constituency of Bodinayakkanur, Theni Dist; Chair. Periyakulam Municipality 1996–2001; won assembly elections from Periyakulam 2001; Revenue Minister May–Sept. 2001; elected Leader of Opposition 2006; Chief Minister of Tamil Nadu 2001–02 (resgnd), 2014–15 (resgnd), Dec. 2016–Feb. 2017, Deputy Chief Minister of Tamil Nadu 2017–; Minister for Public Works, Prohibition and Excise March–Dec. 2002, Minister for Public Works, Prohibition, Excise and Revenue 2002–06; mem. Tamil Nadu Legis. Ass. 2006–11; Minister for Finance and Public Works Dept 2006–14. *Address:* Office of the Chief

Minister, Government of Tamil Nadu, Secretariat, Fort St George, Chennai 600 009, India (office). *Telephone:* (44) 25672345 (office). *Fax:* (44) 25671441 (office). *E-mail:* cmcell@tn.gov.in (office). *Website:* www.tn.gov.in (office).

PANNI, Marcello; Italian conductor and composer; b. 24 Jan. 1940, Rome; s. of Arnaldo Panni and Adriana Cortini; m. Jeanne Colombier 1970; one d.; ed Accad. di Santa Cecilia, Rome under Goffredo Petrassi and Conservatoire Nat. Supérieur, Paris under Manuel Rosenthal; conducting debut, Festival of Contemporary Music, Venice 1969; has since achieved renown in field of avant-garde music conducting first performances of works by Berio, Bussotti, Cage, Feldman, Donatoni, Clementi, Sciarrino, Glass and others at all major European festivals and for Italian Radio; regular guest conductor for Accad. di Santa Cecilia, the Italian radio orchestras and other European orchestras performing full range of baroque, classical and modern works; opera debut with The Barber of Seville, Hamburg 1977 and has since conducted opera in all the principal opera houses in Europe; American debut with Elisir d'amore, Metropolitan Opera, New York 1988; conducted world premiere of Bussotti's Cristallo di Rocca (opera) at La Scala 1983; Bolshoi debut with Macbeth, Moscow 2003; Musical Dir Bonn Opera House 1994–97, Nice Opera House 1997–2001; Artistic Dir San Carlo Opera House, Naples 2001–02; Artistic Dir Accad. Filarmonica Romana 2001–04, 2007–09; Musical Dir Orchestra Sinfonica Tito Schipa, Lecce 2008–11; Milhaud Prof. of Composition and Conducting, Mills Coll., Oakland, Calif. 1980–84; mem. Accad. di Santa Cecilia 2003–. *Works include* symphonic and chamber music and music for experimental theatrical works; operas and sacred music: Hanjo (one act) 1994, Il giudizio di Paride (one act) 1996, The Banquet (one act) 1998, Missa brevis 2002, Garibaldi en Sicile (two acts) 2005, Apokàlypsis (oratorio) 2009. *Leisure interests:* arts, sport. *Address:* 3 Piazza Borghese, 00186 Rome, Italy (home). *Telephone:* (06) 6873617 (home). *Fax:* (06) 6873617 (office). *E-mail:* marcellopanni@yahoo.it (office).

PANNICK, Baron (Life Peer), cr. 2008, of Radlett in the County of Hertfordshire; **David Philip Pannick,** QC, BCL, MA; British barrister; b. 7 March 1956, London, England; s. of Maurice A. Pannick and Rita L. Pannick; m. Denise Sloam 1978 (died 1999); two s. one d.; m. Nathalie Trager-Lewis 2003; one s. two d.; ed Bancroft's School, Essex and Hertford Coll., Oxford; called to the Bar 1979, QC 1992; Fellow, All Souls Coll. Oxford 1978–; Jr Counsel to the Crown (Common Law) 1988–92; columnist on law, The Times 1991–; Bencher of Gray's Inn 2001; mem. (Crossbench), House of Lords 2008–, mem. Constitution Cttee 2008–13, 2016–; Chair. British Legal Friends of the Hebrew Univ. 2008–; Hon. Fellow, Hertford Coll., Oxford, Hebrew Univ. of Jerusalem; Hon. LLD (Hertfordshire) 1998. *Publications:* Sex Discrimination Law 1985, Judges 1987, Advocates 1992, Human Rights Law and Practice (co-author with Lord Lester of Herne Hill) 1999, 2004, 2009. *Leisure interests:* theatre, cinema, Arsenal Football Club. *Address:* House of Lords, Westminster, London, SW1A 0PW (office); Blackstone Chambers, Temple, London, EC4Y 7BH, England (office). *Telephone:* (20) 7219-3107 (House of Lords) (office); (20) 7583-1770 (Blackstone Chambers) (office). *Fax:* (20) 7219-5353 (House of Lords) (office); (20) 7822-7222 (Blackstone Chambers) (office). *E-mail:* davidpannick@blackstonechambers.com (office).

PANNONE, Rodger John, DL, FRSA; British solicitor; b. 20 April 1943, Minehead, Somerset, England; s. of Cyril Pannone and Violet Weeks; m. Patricia Todd 1966; two s. one d.; ed St Brendan's Coll. Bristol and Coll. of Law, London and Manchester Polytechnic; articled clerk, Casson and Co. Salford; joined W.H. Thompson 1969, later Partner; joined Conn Goldberg (later Pannone & Partners, now Pannone Part of Slater & Gordon) 1973, Sr Partner 1991–2003 (retd), Consultant 2003–10; Co-founder Pannone Law Group, Asscn of Personal Injury Lawyers (first Sr Fellow, now Hon. Life mem.); lecturer and broadcaster on legal affairs; mem. Lord Chancellor's Advisory Cttee on Civil Justice; fmr mem. Supreme Court Rule Cttee; Chair. Forensic Science Service; Chair. Gov. Coll. of Law, Council of Univ. of Manchester; mem. Council Law Soc. of England and Wales, Deputy Vice-Pres., Vice-Pres. and Pres. 1993–94; Fellow, Manchester Metropolitan Univ.; DL Greater Manchester; Hon. mem. Canadian Bar Asscn, Hon. Fellow, Soc. of Chiropodists, Univ. of Birmingham 1998; Hon. DLitt (Salford), Hon. LLD (Nottingham Trent), Hon. LittD (Manchester); voted one of the top solicitors of the last 20 years, first Outstanding Achievement Award, Manchester Law Soc. 2010. *Publications:* legal articles. *Leisure interests:* walking slowly, food and drink.

PANOU, Themis; Greek actor; b. (Themistoklis Panou), 1960, Istanbul, Turkey; ed Univ. of Athens, Drama School 'E. Chatzikou'; teaches acting improvisation at Univ. of Athens; mem. Nat. Theatre of Greece 2000–, European Film Acad., Int. Theatre Inst., Asscn of Greek Actors. *Films include:* Ermineia (short) 1985, The Jaws of Death (short) 1996, Black Milk 1999, Edge of Night 2000, Men Don't Cry (short) 2001, Brazilero 2001, A Touch of Spice 2003, Utopia 2004, Lista gamou 2006, Illustration 2006, One Night Together (short) (Best Actor Award, 32nd Festival of Drama) 2009, Miss Violence (Volpi Cup for Best Actor, Venice Film Festival) 2013, Lines 2016. *Television includes:* Erhontai oi Amerikanoi (series) (writer) 1993, Matomena homata (series) 2008, Karyotakis (series) 2009. *Publications:* translations from Greek to Turkish: Ichneftes Sophocles for show directed by D. Avdeliodi, Festival Izmir 2010, Fiakas of D. Misitzi, in Greek trilogy Midas by Güngör Dilmen; writings have been published in magazine Cistern to an Apple; narratives entitled Suddenly published by Rodakio. *Address:* Metonos 51, Holargos, 15561 Athens, Greece. *Telephone:* (210) 6523825; 694-6682685 (mobile). *E-mail:* themispan@yahoo.gr.

PANOV, Alexander Nikolayevich, CandHistSc; Russian diplomatist; b. 6 July 1944, Moscow; m. 1967; one d.; ed Moscow Inst. of Int. Relations; diplomatic service 1968–; trans., attaché Embassy in Tokyo 1968–71; teacher, Asst Prof., Moscow Inst. of Int. Relations 1971–77; Third, Second Sec., Perm. Mission to UN, New York 1977–82; First Sec., Second Far East Dept USSR Ministry of Foreign Affairs 1982–83; First Sec., Counsellor, Embassy in Tokyo 1983–88; Deputy Chief, Chief of Div., Deputy Chief, Dept of Countries of Pacific Ocean and SE Asia, USSR Ministry of Foreign Affairs 1988–90, Chief 1990–92; Amb. to Repub. of Korea 1992–94; Deputy Minister of Foreign Affairs 1994–96; Amb. to Japan 1996–2003, to Norway 2004–06; apptd Rector of the Diplomatic Acad., Ministry of Foreign Affairs 2006; Order of Merit. *Publications:* Postwar Reforms in Japan 1945–52, Japanese Diplomatic Service, Beyond Distrust to Trust; articles in periodicals. *Leisure interest:* photography. *Address:* Ministry of Foreign Affairs, 119200 Moscow, Smolenskaya-Sennaya pl. 32/34, Russia (office). *Telephone:* (499) 244-16-06 (office). *Fax:* (499) 244-91-57 (office). *E-mail:* ministry@mid.ru (office). *Website:* www.mid.ru (office).

PANSIERI, Flavia, PhD; Italian diplomatist and UN official; b. 17 May 1951, Milan; m. Peter Marshall; one d.; ed Milan, Venice and Beijing Univs; began UN career with UNDP in China 1983, responsible for UN Volunteers (UNV) and TOKTEN programmes, as well as for projects in energy sector, continued with UNDP in Bangladesh 1987–90 and Myanmar 1990–93, posted to Laos as Dir UN Office on Drugs and Crime (UNOCD), served at UNOCD HQ in Vienna 1995–98, Deputy Exec. Dir UNIFEM, New York 1998–2001, took charge of Country Div. of Regional Bureau for Arab States at UNDP 2001–04, UN Resident Co-ordinator and Resident Rep. of UNDP in Yemen 2004–08, Exec. Co-ordinator UNV 2008–13; Deputy High Commr for Human Rights 2013–15. *Address:* Office of the United Nations High Commissioner for Human Rights (OHCHR), Palais des Nations, 1211 Geneva 10, Switzerland (office). *Telephone:* (22) 9179220 (office). *E-mail:* infodesk@ohchr.org (office). *Website:* www.ohchr.org (office).

PANTEV, Plamen Ilarionov, PhD; Bulgarian research institute director and academic; *Founder-Director, Institute for Security and International Studies;* b. 31 July 1952, Gradets, Vidin Dist; s. of Ilarion Pantev and Sofiana Panteva; m. Tatyana Panteva; one d.; ed Sofia Univ. 'St Kliment Ohridsky', Nat. Defence Coll., Stockholm, George C. Marshall Centre for European Security Policy, Garmisch-Partenkirchen; fmr Researcher, Columbia Univ., New York, Johns Hopkins Univ., Washington, DC and Harvard Univ., USA 1988–89, WEU Inst. for Security Studies, Paris, Istituto Affari Internazionali, Rome 1992, Netherlands Inst. for International Relations, Clingendael, The Hague 1993; Founder-Dir Inst. for Security and International Studies, Sofia 1994–; currently Prof. of Law and Int. Relations, Dir MA Program in Int. Security and fmr Vice-Dean, Law School, Sofia Univ. 'St Kliment Ohridsky', responsible for Int. Relations Dept 2006–11; Lecturer, NATO Defence Coll., Rome, Italy 2002, Henry L. Stimpson Center, Washington, DC 2003, Diplomatic Acad., Vienna July 2004, Texas A&M Univ. March 2006; Co-Chair. Study Group on Regional Stability in SE Europe 2002–10, Consortium of Defence Acad and Security Studies Insts of PfP Countries; mem. Supreme Testimonial Comm.'s Specialized Council in International Relations at Council of Ministers of Bulgaria –2011; Ed.-in-Chief, Balkan and Black Sea Regional Profiles (electronic periodicals) –2005; mem. International Studies Asscn, International Advisory Bd, Journal of International Negotiation –2011, Europe's World Journal, Contemporary Law (in Bulgarian) 2007–15; mem. EU Non-Proliferation Consortium; mem. Acad. of Political Science, New York 2011, IISS, London 2013, VANGA Foundation 2013; Ford Foundation/WEU Inst. for Security Studies Fellow, Istituto Affari Internazionali, Rome, Italy 1992, Erazmus Fellowship, Netherlands Inst. for International Relations, Clingendael, The Hague 1993, NATO Individual Fellow 1995–97, USIA Fellow, Univ. of Michigan 1997, Fellowship, Swedish Nat. Defence Coll. 2000, 2010, Hon. Plaque of Austrian NDA, Individual Coin by the PfP Consortium 2010. *Radio:* commentator, Bulgarian nat. Radio. *Television:* commentator, Bulgarian Nat. TV. *Publications include:* 20 books and more than 150 articles on int. and regional security, int. law, relations and negotiations, foreign policy and civil-mil. relations in Bulgarian, English, Italian, German, French, Russian, Ukrainian, Polish, Bahasa (Indonesian). *Leisure interests:* music, swimming, mountain walking, cinema. *Address:* PO Box 231, Institute for Security and International Studies, 1c Krasno selo bl. 194, ent. B ap. 36, 1618 Sofia (office); 1c 'Buxton', bl. 1, ent. A, ap. 11, 1618 Sofia, Bulgaria (home). *Telephone:* 88-8289605 (mobile) (office). *E-mail:* plamen.pantev@abv.bg (office); isis.pantev@gmail.com (office). *Website:* www.isis-bg.org (office).

PANTÓ, György; Hungarian geochemist and academic; *Professor Emeritus Instituti, Institute for Geochemical Research;* b. 1936, Budapest; s. of Endre Pantó and Ilona Botár; m. Márta Juhász; one s. one d.; ed Loránd Eötvös Univ.; mine geologist, Hungarian Mineral and Ore Mines 1959–62; postgraduate scholarship, Hungarian Acad. of Sciences 1962–65, Sr Researcher, Inst. for Geochemical Research 1965–76, Dir 1976–2000, now Prof. Emer. Instituti; Dir-Gen. Hungarian Acad. of Sciences Research Centre for Earth Sciences 1998–2005; mem. Hungarian Acad. of Sciences, Pres. Earth Sciences Section 1999–2005; Foreign mem. Serbian Acad. of Arts and Sciences; mem. Editorial Bd Acta Geologica Hungarica; Commdr's Cross, Order of Merit of the Hungarian Repub. 2006; Eminent Worker of Geological Research, Cen. Geological Office 1976, Vendl Mária Medal, Hungarian Geological Soc. 1986, Szèchenyi Prize 2000. *Publications:* numerous articles, books and contribs on geochemistry; several patents. *Leisure interests:* gardening, tourism. *Address:* Room 220, Institute for Geochemical Research, Hungarian Academy of Sciences, Budaörsi út 45, 1112 Budapest, Hungary (office). *Telephone:* (1) 319-3137 (office). *Fax:* (1) 319-3137 (office). *E-mail:* panto@geochem.hu (office). *Website:* www.geochem.hu/people/panto_eng.html (office).

PANTON, Seymour; Jamaican judge; *Judge, Mechanism for International Criminal Tribunals;* called to the Bar, Lincoln's Inn, London 1968; held posts in Jamaica including Deputy Clerk of Courts, Clerk of Courts, Crown Counsel (Acting) in Dir of Public Prosecutions Office, Resident Magistrate, Puisne Judge; fmr Legal Asst to Attorney-Gen., Sr Counsel and Judge of Grand Court, Cayman Islands; Appeal Judge, Court of Appeal, Jamaica 1999–07, Pres. 2007–16 (retd); fmr mem. Bench and Bar Consultative Cttee, Asscn of Resident Magistrates (Vice-Pres.), Commonwealth Magistrates and Judges Asscn; mem. Commonwealth Secretariat Arbitral Tribunal 2008–; Judge, Mechanism for Int. Criminal Tribunals 2016–; Chair. Compensation Cttee; Assoc. Tutor, Norman Manley Law School 1986–93; Examiner, Deputy Clerk of Courts Qualifying Exams 1986–96; Fulbright Grant 1990, Outstanding Service Awards from Rusea's Old Students' Asscn 1990, Cornwall Bar Asscn 1995, Jamaican Govt 2006. *Address:* Mechanism for International Criminal Tribunals, Haki Road, Plot No. 486, Block A, Lakilaki Area, Arumeru District, PO Box 6016, Arusha, Tanzania (office). *Website:* www.unmict.org (office).

PANWAR, Lalit K., BSc, MSc, PhD; Indian government official; *Vice-Chancellor, Institute of Leadership Development;* b. 11 July 1955; City Magistrate, Bikaner 1982–83; Collector and Dist Magistrate, Jaisalmer 1985–88; Dir of Primary and Secondary Educ., Bikaner 1988–91, of Art, Culture and Tourism 1991–95; mem. Bd of Revenue, Ajmer 1995–96; Divisional Commr, Jodhpur 1996–98; Sec. to Chief Minister 1998–2000; Sec., Tourism, Art and Culture Dept 2003–04, Mines and Petroleum Dept 2004; Commr Jaipur Devt Authority 2004–05; Prin. Sec., Urban

Devt and Housing Dept 2005, Urban Governance Dept 2005–07, Labour and Employment 2007, School and Sanskrit Educ. 2009–10; Chair. and Man. Dir India Tourism Devt Corpn Ltd 2010–13; apptd Sec., Ministry of Minority Affairs 2013; apptd Chair. Rajasthan Public Service Comm. 2015; Vice-Chancellor, Inst. of Leadership Devt Skill Univ. 2017–. *Address:* Inst. of Leadership Devt 6/2, Jamdoli, Jaipur 302 031, Rajasthan, India (office). *Telephone:* (141) 5184222 (office). *Fax:* (141) 5184215 (office). *E-mail:* info@ildindia.org (office). *Website:* www.ildindia.org (office).

PANYARACHUN, Anand; Thai business executive, fmr diplomatist and fmr politician; *Chairman, Siam Commercial Bank;* b. 9 Aug. 1932, Bangkok; s. of Maha Ammat Tri Phya Prichanusat (Sern Panyarachun) and Khunying Prichanusat (Pruek Chotikasathien); m. M. R. Sodsee Chakrabandh; two d.; ed Bangkok Christian Coll., Dulwich Coll., Univ. of Cambridge, UK; joined Ministry of Foreign Affairs 1955, Sec. to Foreign Minister 1959, First Sec., Perm. Mission to UN, New York 1964, Counsellor 1966, concurrently Amb. to Canada and Acting Perm. Rep. to UN 1967–72 (Perm. Rep. 1972–75), concurrently Amb. to USA 1972–75, Amb. to FRG 1977–79, Head, Ministry of Foreign Affairs 1976; accused of being a Communist after coup, suspended but exonerated and reinstated; fmr Chair. Saha-Union Group (industrial conglomerate); fmr Chair. Fed. of Thai Industries 1990; Prime Minister of Thailand 1991–92; elected mem. Constitution Drafting Ass. 1997, Chair. Drafting Cttee; Chair. UN High-Level Panel on Threats, Challenges and Change, Steering Cttee Asia Pacific Leadership Forum on HIV/AIDS and Devt; mem. Advisory Group Anti-Corruption Issues for the East Asia and Pacific Region, World Bank; UNICEF Amb. 1996–; Dir Siam Commercial Bank 1984–, currently Chair.; Chair. Thailand Devt Research Inst., Council of Trustees Thailand Environment Inst., Council of Asian Univ. of Science and Tech., Bd of Trustees of Asian Inst. of Tech.; Dir Sime Darby Berhad 1982–98; mem. Int. Advisory Bd American Int. Group, Unocal Asia Pacific Ventures, Toyota Motor Corpn; mem. Asian Advisory Bd The Carlyle Group –2003; Hon. KBE 1996; Order of Diplomatic Service Merit (South Korea) 1970, Ringtang Jasa (First Class) Indonesia 1971, Kt Grand Cordon (Special Class) of the Most Noble Order of the Crown of Thailand 1988, Grand Officier de l'Ordre de la Couronne, 2nd class (Belgium) 1990, Kt Grand Commdr (Second Class, higher grade) of the Most Illustrious Order of Chula Chom Klao 1991, Kt Grand Cordon (Special Class) of the Most Exalted Order of the White Elephant 1992, Grand Cordon of the Order of the Rising Sun (Japan) 1991, Commdr, Grand Cross of the Royal Order of the Polar Star (Sweden) 2007; 25 hon. degrees from univs in Thailand, USA, Canada, Hong Kong and Japan; Royal Cypher Medal (Third Class), Ramon Magsaysay Award for Government Service 1997. *Address:* Siam Commercial Bank PCL, 9 Ratchadaphisek Road, SCB Park, Chatuchak, Bangkok 10900, Thailand (office). *Telephone:* (2) 311-4076 (office). *Fax:* (2) 332-5613 (office). *E-mail:* anandp1932@gmail.com (office). *Website:* www.scb.co.th (office).

PAOCHINDA, Gen. Anupong; Thai army officer and government official; *Minister of the Interior;* b. 10 Oct. 1949, Bangkok; m. Kunlaya Paochinda; two c.; ed Amnuay Silpa School, Armed Forces Acads Preparatory School, Bangkok, Chulachomklao Royal Mil. Acad., Nakhon Nayok Prov., Ramkhamhaeng Univ., Nat. Inst. of Devt Admin, Bangkok; fmr commdr of several army divs, including 21st Infantry Regt (Queen's Guard), 2nd Infantry Div. (King's Guards), 1st Infantry Div. (King's Guards); fmr Commdr 1st Army Area; Deputy Sec.-Gen., Council for Nat. Security (junta that staged the coup d'état and deposed caretaker govt of Prime Minister Thaksin Shinawatra) 2006; Deputy Commdr in Chief, Royal Thai Army 2006–07, Commdr in Chief 2007–10; Minister of the Interior 2014–. *Address:* Ministry of the Interior, Thanon Atsadang, Bangkok 10200, Thailand (office). *Telephone:* (2) 222-1141 (office). *Fax:* (2) 223-8851 (office). *E-mail:* webmaster@moi.go.th (office). *Website:* www.moi.go.th (office).

PAOLILLO, Felipe H.; Uruguayan lawyer, diplomatist and UN official; *Professor of International Law, Universidad ORT Uruguay;* b. 8 Oct. 1931; Prof. of Int. Public Law, Univ. of Uruguay 1967–74, 1985–87, 1995; Prof., Universidad ORT Uruguay, Montevideo 1995–96, Prof. of Int. Law 2005–; Assoc. Prof. New York Univ. School of Law 1977–84; Dir Diplomatic Acad. of Uruguay, Ministry of Foreign Affairs 1985–87; Amb. and Perm. Rep. to UN, New York 1987–90, 2000–01, 2003, Amb. to Holy See and FAO 1996–2000; Chair. UN Gen. Ass. Credentials Cttee 2002; Vice-Pres. Ass. of States Parties, Int. Criminal Court, The Hague 2002–05; Legal counselor to Govt of El Salvador on int. boundaries matters 2005–08; fmr Co-Chair. UN Open-ended Informal Consultative Process on Oceans and the Law of the Sea (UNICPOLOS); consultant to OAS on dispute between Guatemala and Belize 2006–07; mem. Inst. of Int. Law; mem. Permanent Court of Arbitration 1993–2005, Interamerican Judicial Cttee 2001–04; mem. Institut de Droit International, Societe Française pour Ie Droit International, Instituto Hispano-Luso-Americano de Derecho Internacional, Asociaci6n Uruguaya de Derecho Internacional. *Publications include:* numerous articles in professional journals. *Address:* Faculty of Law, Universidad ORT Uruguay, Cuareim 1451, Montevideo, Uruguay (office). *Website:* www.ort.edu.uy (office).

PAOLINELLI, Alysson; Brazilian agronomist, academic and politician; b. 10 July 1936, Bambuí, Minas Gerais; ed Fed. Agricultural Univ. of Lavras; Prof. of Agric., Fed. Agricultural Univ. of Lavras 1960–67, Dean 1967–71; Sec. of Agric. for Minas Gerais 1971–74; Minister of Agric. for Brazil 1974–79; Chair. Bank of the State of Minas Gerais 1979–82, 1983–86; affiliated with Partido Social Democrático (PSD) 1954–64, Aliança Renovadora Nacional (ARENA) 1971–79, Partido Democrático Social (PDS) 1980–84, Partido da Frente Liberal (PFL) 1985–; elected Fed. Deputy for Minas Gerais in 1986 elections as part of Nat. Constituent Ass. 1987–91; currently consultant in agribusiness; Pres. Brazilian Asscn for Agricultural Educ. 1970–71; Chair. Confederação Nacional da Agricultura 1987–90; Sec. of Agric., Livestock and Food Supply 1991–94; Pres. Nat. Forum on Agric. 1992–93; mem. Bd of Dirs Verde AgriTech PLC 2014–; Commr for EXPO '90 Brazil –Int. Fair of Horticulture and Gardens, Osaka, Japan 1989; Medal Marechal Rondon 1969, Medalha da Inconfidência, Govt of Minas Gerais 1971, Awards of Merit Naval, Aviation and Mil., Fed. Govt 1974, Merit of Santos Dumont 1974, Medal of Merit of Brasilia, DF Govt 1974, Medal Almirante Tamandaré 1974, Order of Rio Branco 1974, Maua Order of Merit 1976, Order of the Sacred Treasure (Japan) 1977; Personality of the Year in Agrobusiness, Ministry of Agric. 2006, World Food Prize 2006.

PAOLUCCI, Antonio; Italian art historian and museum director; b. 1939, Rimini; m. Giulia 1966; one s.; ed student of Roberto Longhi; began his career at Soprintendenza per i Beni Culturali for Venice Region 1969–80; fmr Supt Polo Museale Fiorentino; worked for Mantova-Brescia-Cremona Region 1984–86; Dir Office of Hard Stones and the restoration laboratory in Florence 1986–88, Dept of Artistic Affairs of Tuscany 1988; Minister of Culture 1995–96; supervised comm. in charge of restoration of Basilica of St Francis of Assissi after the earthquake in 1997; was at centre of controversy concerning restoration of Michelangelo's David in Florence 2003; Dir Museums in Florence 2004–06, Vatican Museums 2007–17; Pres. Accad. Carrara, Bergamo. *Publications:* more than 300 articles in various journals, including Paragone, Bollettino d'Arte, and of monographic studies on Palmezzano, Signorelli, as well as other Florentine artists and monuments.

PAPACONSTANTINOU, George, BSc, MA, PhD; Greek economist, writer and politician; *Chairman, GSP Advisory;* b. 30 Oct. 1961, Athens; m. Jacoline Vinke; two s.; ed London School of Econs, UK, New York Univ., USA; Sr Economist, OECD, Paris 1988–98; Adviser on Information Soc. issues to fmr Prime Minister Costas Simitis 1998–2000; Special Sec. for the Information Society, Ministry of Economy and Finance 2000–02; mem. Council of Econ. Advisors 2002–04; mem. Bd OTE (telecoms co.) 2002–04; Greek Rep. to EU Econ. Policy Cttee 2002–04; co-ordinated 'Lisbon Strategy' for econ. and social reforms during Greek Presidency of EU 2003; econ. adviser to Panhellenic Socialist Movt (PASOK) Pres. George Papandreou 2004–07; mem. Bd Inst. for Strategic and Devt Studies (PASOK's think-tank) 2005–08; mem. Nat. Council of PASOK 2005–09, Press Spokesman 2008–09; taught Econs at Athens Univ. of Econs and Business 2003–07; advised EC on research and information society issues, participating in various int. research projects 2003–07; mem. Vouli (Parl.) for Pref. of Kozani 2007–09; mem. European Parl. 2009; Minister of Finance 2009–11, of the Environment, Energy and Climate Change 2011–12; Founder and Chair. GSP Advisory 2013–; part-time Prof., European Univ. Inst., Fiesole, Italy 2018–. *Publication:* Game Over: The Inside Story of the Greek Crisis 2016. *Telephone:* (694) 4455580 (office). *E-mail:* gsp@gsp-advisory.com (office); g.papaconstantinou@eui.eu (office). *Website:* www.gsp-advisory.com (office); www.gpapac.com (office); www.stg.eui.eu (office).

PAPADEMOS, Lucas Demetrios, PhD; Greek economist, banker and politician; *Senior Fellow, Center for Financial Studies, Goethe University Frankfurt;* b. 11 Oct. 1947, Athens; m. Sana Ingram 1977; ed Athens Coll., Massachusetts Inst. of Tech., USA; Asst Prof., then Assoc. Prof. of Econs, Columbia Univ., New York, USA 1975–84; Prof. of Econs, Univ. of Athens 1988–; Sr Economist, Fed. Reserve Bank of Boston, USA; Econ. Adviser, Bank of Greece 1985–93, Head of Econ. Research Dept 1988–92, Deputy Gov. 1993–94, Gov. 1994–2002; Vice-Pres. European Cen. Bank 2002–10; adviser to Prime Minister George Papandreou Jan.–Nov. 2011; Prime Minister of Greece (following resignation of Papandreou to allow formation of a provisional coalition govt to avert political crisis caused by country's debt crisis) 2011–12; mem. Cttee of Alts of Govs of EC Cen. Banks 1985–93, Council of Econ. Advisers 1985–88, 1991–94, Trilateral Comm. 1998–, EMI and various bds; Visiting Prof. of Public Policy, Kennedy School of Govt, Harvard Univ., USA; Sr Fellow, Center for Financial Studies, Goethe Univ. of Frankfurt 2010–; mem. Acad. of Athens 2006; Grand Commdr, Order of Honour 1999. *Publications:* numerous articles on macroeconomic theory, the structure and functioning of financial markets, monetary analysis and policy as well as on subjects concerning the economic performance, financial stability and economic policy in the EU. *Address:* Center for Financial Studies, House of Finance, Goethe University Frankfurt, Theodor-W.-Adorno-Platz 3, 60323 Frankfurt am Main, Germany. *Website:* www.ifk-cfs.de.

PAPADONGONAS, Alexandros; Greek politician and naval officer; b. 11 July 1931, Tripolis; s. of Dionisios Papadongonas and Vasiliki Papadongonas; m. Niki Maidonis 1976; one s. one d.; ed Greek Naval Acad., Naval War Coll., US Naval Schools, NATO Defence Coll.; has served on Greek fleet vessels and submarines and has held staff positions; organized with other Navy officers Movt of Navy against the dictatorship; arrested May 1973 and removed from service; returned to Navy July–Nov. 1974; mem. Vouli (Parl.) 1974–93; Minister of Merchant Shipping 1974–77, 1992–93, of Communications 1977–80; Deputy Minister of Defence 1990–91; mem. Council of Europe 1982–89, 1991; Pres. Greek Del. to Parl. Ass. of OSCE 1993–; Pres. and mem. Bd of Dirs Yacht Club of Greece 2012–; mem. North Atlantic Ass.; New Democracy Party; Medal of Mil. Valour; Commdr, Order of the Phoenix; Officer Order of George I. *Leisure interests:* sailing, scuba diving, underwater archaeology. *Address:* Yacht Club of Greece, 18 Karagiorgi Servias str. 185 33 Piraeus (office); 11 Nikis Street, Athens 105 57, Greece (home). *Telephone:* (210) 417-9730 (office); (210) 325-5150 (home). *E-mail:* noe@ycg.gr (office). *Website:* www.ycg.gr (office).

PAPAIOANNOU, Miltiades; Greek politician and lawyer; b. 1946, Kalavryta, Achaia; ed Panteio Univ., Law Faculty of Athens; Panhellenic Socialist Movt (PASOK) MP; Deputy Minister, Ministry of Internal Affairs 1982–85, Minister of Justice 1985, Deputy Minister, Prime Minister's Dept and Govt Spokesman 1985–86, Gen. Sec. Ministry of Nat. Economy 1993–96; Minister of Labour and Social Security 1998–2000; Minister of State 2000–02; Minister of Justice, Transparency and Human Rights 2011–12; mem. Exec. Bureau and Cen. Cttee PASOK. *Publications:* numerous articles on politics, econs, public admin, local govt and regional devt.

PAPALOIZOU, John Christopher Baillie, DPhil, FRS; British astrophysicist, applied mathematician and academic; *Emeritus Professor, University of Cambridge;* b. 4 May 1947, London, England; ed Univ. Coll., London, Univ. of Sussex, Brighton; fmr Prof. of Math. and Astronomy and Dir Astronomy Unit, Queen Mary, Univ. of London; Prof., Dept of Applied Math. and Theoretical Physics, Univ. of Cambridge, now Emer. Prof.; Asteroid 17063 Papaloizou named in his honour; Brouwer Award Winner 2004. *Achievements include:* co-discovered, with Jim E. Pringle, the Papaloizou-Pringle instability 1984. *Publications:* numerous scientific papers in professional journals on the theory of accretion disks, with particular application to the formation of planets, radial-orbit instability, toroidal modes in stars and different instabilities in accretion disks. *Address:* c/o Department of Applied Mathematics and Theoretical Physics, Centre for Mathematical Sciences, Wilberforce Road, Cambridge, CB3 0WA, England (office). *Telephone:* (1223) 765000 (office). *Fax:* (1223) 765900 (office). *Website:* damtp.cam.ac.uk (office).

PAPANDREOU, Georgios (George) A., BA, MSc; Greek politician; *President, Socialist International;* b. 16 June 1952, Saint Paul, Minn., USA; s. of Andreas Papandreou and Margaret Papandreou (née Chant); m. 1st Evanthia Zissmidides 1976–87; one s.; m. 2nd Ada Papapanos; one d.; ed King City Secondary School, Canada, Athens Coll., Amherst Coll. and York High School, Elmhurst, Ill., USA, Stockholm Univ., Sweden, London School of Econs, UK; mem. Parl. (Panhellenic Socialist Movt—PASOK) for Achaia (Patrias) 1981–96, for First Dist of Athens 1996–2012, for Achaea 2012–; Under-Sec. for Cultural Affairs 1985–87; Minister of Educ. and Religious Affairs 1988–89, 1994–96; Deputy Minister of Foreign Affairs 1993–94, Alt. Minister of Foreign Affairs 1996–99, Minister of Foreign Affairs 1999–2004, 2009–10; unsuccessful presidential cand. 2004; Leader of the Opposition 2004–09; Prime Minister and Chair. of the Govt 2009–11 (resgnd to allow formation of a provisional coalition govt to avert political crisis caused by country's debt crisis); mem. Cen. Cttee PASOK 1984–2015, Exec. Cttee 1987–88, mem. Exec. Office and Political Bureau 1996–2015, Leader, PASOK 2004–12; Founder and Leader, Kinima Dimokraton Sosialiston (To Kinema—Movt of Democratic Socialists) 2015–; Govt Co-ordinator for 2004 Athens Olympic bid 1997; mem. Socialist International (Vice-Pres. 2005–06, Pres. 2006–); mem. Bd Foundation of Mediterranean Studies for Research and Self-Educ., Cambridge Foundation for Peace; Fellow, Center for Int. Affairs, Harvard Univ. 1992–93; Distinguished Prof., Center for Hellenic Studies, Georgia State Coll. of Arts and Science 2006; decorations from numerous countries, including Commdr, Order of Prince Yaroslav the Wise (Ukraine) 1996, Grand Cross, Order of the Lion (Finland) 1996, Grand Commdr, Order of the Polish Repub. 1996, Grand Cross, Order of Civil Merit (Spain) 1998, Grand Cross, Order of the Polar Star (Sweden) 1999, Grand Cross, Order of the White Star (Estonia) 1999, Grand Cross, Order of Honour, First Class (Austria) 1999, Grand Cross, Order of Merit (Germany) 2000, Grand Cross, Order of Isabella the Catholic (Spain) 2001, Grand Cross, Order of the Crown (Belgum) 2001, Grand Cross, Order of Infante Dom Henrique (Portugal) 2002, Grand Cross, Order of Pius IX (Vatican) 2002, Grand Commdr, Order of Merit (Hungary) 2003, Grand Cross, Order of Merit (Italy), Gran Cruz El Sol de Peru 2003; Hon. LLD (Amherst Coll.) 2002; Botsis Foundation for Promotion of Journalism Award 1988, SOS against Racism Award 1996, Abdi Ipekci Special Award for Peace and Friendship (Turkey) 1997, Statesman of the Yea Award, Eastwest Inst. (USA) 2000, Jackie Robinson Humanitarianism Award, US Sport Acad. 2002, Defender of Democracy, Parliamentarians for Global Action 2003, Open Fields Award, Truce Foundation (USA) 2006, Quadriga Award, Werkstatt Deutschland (Germany) for The Power of Veracity (transparency regarding the state of the Greek economy) 2010. *Address:* Kinima Dimokraton Sosialiston (To Kinema) (Movement of Democratic Socialists), Athens, Greece (office); Socialist International, Maritime House, Old Town, Clapham, London, SW4 0JW, England. *Telephone:* (210) 3700000 (office); (20) 7627-4449. *Fax:* (210) 3811852 (office); (20) 7720-4448. *E-mail:* tokinima@tokinima.gr (office); dialogue@politicalforum.gr (office); secretariat@socialistinternational.org. *Website:* www.tokinima.gr (office); www.socialistinternational.org; www.papandreou.gr.

PAPANTONIOU, Ioannis, PhD; Greek politician; b. 27 July 1949, Paris, France; m.; two s. one d.; ed Univ. of Athens, Univ. of Wisconsin, USA, Univ. of Paris, France and Univ. of Cambridge, UK; Lecturer, Dept of Econs, Univ. of Athens, Researcher Centre of Planning and Econ. Research 1977–78; staff mem. Econs Dept OECD, Paris 1978–81; Panhellenic Socialist Movt (PASOK) MEP 1981–84; Special Adviser to Prime Minister on EC Affairs; Deputy Minister for Nat. Economy 1985–89, Minister of Trade 1989; apptd mem. Parl. for first Dist of Athens 1989; Deputy Minister for Nat. Economy 1985–86, 1987–89; Minister for Commerce 1993–94; Minister for Nat. Economy 1994–96, for Nat. Economy and Econs 1996–2001, of Nat. Defence 2001–04.

PAPARIGA, Alexandra (Aleka), BA; Greek politician; b. 5 Nov. 1945, Athens; widowed; one d.; ed Univ. of Athens; joined CP of Greece (KKE) in 1968 during mil. dictatorship (1967–74), mem. Cen. Cttee, KKE 1978–, mem. Politburo 1986–, Gen. Sec. Cen. Cttee 1991–2013; mem. of the Vouli (Parl.) 1993–; mem. Bureau of City Cttee of Athens Party Org. (KOA), then active in women's movt; Founding mem. Women's Fed. of Greece (OGE), helped organize nat. events for Int. Women's Day; leading cadre of women's movt –1981, then active in KOA –1991; participated in int. congresses of World Women Democratic Fed. and UNO. *Publications:* two books on women's emancipation. *Address:* Communist Party of Greece (KKE), Leoforos Irakliou 145, Nea Ionia, 142 31 Athens, Greece (office). *Telephone:* (210) 2592111 (office). *Fax:* (210) 2592298 (office); (210) 3232821 (office). *E-mail:* cpg@int.kke.gr (office); cpg.kke@gmail.com (office). *Website:* inter.kke.gr (office); www.kke.gr (office).

PAPATHANASIOU, Ioannis; Greek business executive and politician; b. 1 Jan. 1954, Athens; m. Ileana Iliopoulou; two d.; ed Tech. Univ. of Athens; Pres. and Man. Dir J.D. Papathanassiou SA –2002; mem. Bd of Dirs Athens Chamber of Commerce and Industry 1982–88, Sec.-Gen. 1988–93, Pres. 1994–2000; adviser to Minister of Commerce, Industry and Energy 1991–92; Vice-Pres. DEPA (Public Gas Enterprises) 1992–93; mem. New Democracy party; mem. Vouli (Parl.) 2002– (re-elected 2004, 2007, 2009); Deputy Minister of Devt 2004–07, of the Economy and Finance 2007–09, Minister of the Economy and Finance Jan.–Oct. 2009. *Website:* www.papathanassiou.gr.

PAPAZIAN, Vahan; Armenian politician, diplomatist, historian and orientalist; b. 26 Jan. 1957, Yerevan; s. of Hagop Papazian and Ophelia Papazian; m. Anahit Papazian; two s.; ed Yerevan State Univ.; researcher, Inst. of History, Armenian Acad. of Sciences 1980–91; Counsellor to Pres. of Armenia 1991–92; Chargé d'affaires of Armenia to France 1992–93; Minister of Foreign Affairs 1993–96; on staff, Acad. of Sciences 1996–98; Amb. to France 1997–98; apptd Prof. of Political Sciences, Yerevan State Univ. 1998. *Publications:* works on history of Armenian-Iranian relations and trade routes in Middle Ages, politics.

PAPOULIAS, Karolos, PhD; Greek politician, lawyer and fmr head of state; b. 4 June 1929, Ioannina, Epirus; s. of Maj.-Gen. Gregorios Papoulias; m. May Panou Papoulia; three d.; ed Nat. and Kapodistrian Univ. of Athens, Univ. of Madrid, Spain, Ludwig Maximilian Univ. of Munich and Univ. of Cologne, Germany; fmr pole-vault and volleyball champion; fmr practising lawyer in Athens; lived in Germany 1962–74; Founding mem. Socialist Democratic Union which mobilized Greeks living in Western Europe against the mil. coup 1967; worked for Greek radio programme of Deutsche Welle; mem. Greek democratic del. at Gen. Ass. of Council of Europe during period of mil. dictatorship in Greece; mem. Parl. 1977–2004; mem. Cen. Cttee Panhellenic Socialist Movt (PASOK); Sec.-Gen. Centre for Mediterranean Studies, Athens; Deputy Minister for Foreign Affairs 1981–84, Alt. Minister 1984–85, Minister of Foreign Affairs 1985–89, 1993–96; Alt. Minister for Defence 1989–90; Pres. of Greece 2005–15; Founder and fmr Pres. Asscn for Greek Linguistic Heritage; Chair. Nat. Sports Asscn 1985–; fmr Pres. Ethnikos athletic union; Kt, Order of the Elephant (Denmark), Kt Grand Cross with Grand Cordon, Order of Merit of the Italian Repub. 2006, Grand Star of the Decoration of Honour for Services to the Repub. of Austria 2007, Kt Grand Cross, Grand Order of King Tomislav (Croatia) 2007, Kt, Order of the Seraphim (Sweden) 2008, Kt, Order of the White Eagle (Poland) 2013. *Address:* c/o Office of the President, Odos Vassileos Georgiou 2, 100 28 Athens, Greece. *E-mail:* publicrelationsoffice@presidency.gr.

PAPOUTSIS, Christos; Greek economist and politician; b. 11 April 1953, Larissa; m. Ioulia Taliouri; one d.; ed Univ. of Athens; Pres. Greek Nat. Union of Students 1978–80; Special Adviser on Public Admin, Ministry of Presidency of Govt 1981–84; mem. Exec. Bureau Pan-Hellenic Socialist Movt (PASOK), Leader PASOK Del. to European Parl., mem. Political Council for Foreign Affairs, Security and Defence Policy; mem. European Parl. 1984–95, Vice-Pres. Socialist Group 1987–89; mem. Presidium, Party of European Socialists 1988–; Commr for Energy and Euratom Supply Agency, Small and Medium Enterprises (SME) and Tourism, European Comm. 1995–99; Minister of Mercantile Marine 2000–01; mem. Parl. 2000–12, PASOK Parl. Spokesman 2007–; Minister of Citizen Protection 2010–12; Advisor to the Exec. Dir World Bank Group 2013–; Highest Mark of Distinction with Cross (Austria), Gran Official, Orden Libertador Bernardo O'Higgins (Chile). *Publications:* European Journeys 1994, The Colour of the Future 1998, For Europe in the 21st Century 1999. *Address:* World Bank Group, 1818 H Street, NW Washington, DC 20433, USA (office). *Telephone:* (202) 473-1000 (office).

PAPPANO, Sir Antonio (Tony), Kt; British conductor and pianist; *Music Director, The Royal Opera, Covent Garden;* b. 30 Dec. 1959, Epping, Essex; m. Pam Bullock 1995; ed studied in USA with Norma Verrilli, Arnold Franchetti and Gustav Meier; Répétiteur and Asst Conductor New York City Opera, Gran Teatro del Liceo, Barcelona, Frankfurt Opera, Lyric Opera of Chicago early to mid-1980s; asst to Daniel Barenboim for Tristan und Isolde, Parsifal and the Ring cycle at Bayreuth Festival 1986; opera conducting debut with Norwegian Opera, Oslo 1987; Music Dir, Norwegian Opera 1990–92; Covent Garden debut conducting La Bohème 1990; Vienna Staatsoper debut conducting new production of Wagner's Siegfried 1993; season 1996 included the original Don Carlos in Brussels and at the Paris Théâtre du Châtelet; season 1997 Salome at Chicago and Eugene Onegin at the Metropolitan; Prin. Guest Conductor Israel Philharmonic Orchestra 1997–2000; seasons 1999–2001 Lohengrin at Bayreuth; Music Dir, Théâtre Royal de la Monnaie, Brussels 1992–2002, conducting a wide variety of titles; Music Dir, Royal Opera, Covent Garden 2002–; new productions of Ariadne auf Naxos, Wozzeck, Madama Butterfly and Pagliacci, revival of Falstaff 2002–03; Don Giovanni, Aida, Lady Macbeth of Mtsensk, Faust and Peter Grimes in 2003–04; Das Rheingold and Die Walküre 2005; Music Dir Orchestra dell'Accad. Nazionale di Santa Cecilia, Rome 2005–; 2008 performances at ROH included Don Giovanni, La fanciulla del West, Les contes d'Hoffmann; 2009 included Lulu, La Traviata, Il barbiere di Siviglia, Tristan und Isolde; 2010 Simon Boccanegra, Les Pêcheurs de perles; 2011 Turnage's new opera Anna Nicole, Werther, Macbeth and Tosca, among others; 2012 Die Meistersinger von Nürnberg, Le nozze di Figaro, Les Troyens, Otello; has conducted major orchestras, including Berlin Philharmonic Orchestra, Boston Symphony Orchestra, Chicago Symphony Orchestra, Cleveland Orchestra, London Symphony Orchestra, Los Angeles Philharmonic Orchestra, Orchestre de Paris, Oslo Philharmonic Orchestra, Munich Philharmonic Orchestra; Commendatore of Italian Repub. 2008, Cavaliere di Gran Croce, Order of Merit of Italian Repub. 2012; Olivier Award for Outstanding Achievement in Opera 2003, Royal Philharmonic Soc. Award for best conductor 2005, Assoc. Naz. Critici Musicali Premio Abbiati Prize for Conductor 2006, Inc. Soc. of Musicians Distinguished Musician Award 2012, Int. Opera Awards Best Conductor 2013, Bruno Walter Prize, Royal Philharmonic Soc. Gold Medal 2015, ECHO Klassik Award for Conductor of the Year 2016. *Recordings include:* many recordings as conductor including Puccini's La Rondine (Gramophone Award for Best Opera Recording and Record of the Year 1997), Il Trittico 1999, Britten's The Turn of the Screw (Choc du Monde de la Musique, Prix de l'Acad. du Disque Lyrique, Grand Prix Int., Orphées d'Or) 1999, Werther 1999, Manon (Gramophone Award for Best Opera Recording) 2001, Rachmaninov's Piano Concertos 1 & 2 2005, Madame Butterfly 2009, Verdi's Messa da Requiem 2009, Wagner: Tristan and Isolde 2011, Rossini: William Tell 2011, Tosca (Puccini) (BBC Music Magazine DVD Performance Award 2014), Nessun Dorma: The Puccini Album (with Jonas Kaufmann) 2015, Szymanowski: Król Roger (DVD) 2015, Schumann (with Orchestra dell'Accademia Nazionale di Santa Cecilia) 2016, Brahms: Violin Concerto, Bartok: Violin Concerto (with Janine Jansen and London Symphony Orchestra) 2016, Verdi's Aida (BBC Music Magazine Recording of the Year Award and Opera Award 2016, Gramophone Classical Music Award for Opera 2016) 2016, Verismo (with Anna Netrebko) 2016; recordings as pianist: recordings with Rockwell Blake, Barbara Bonney and Han-Na Chang; Joyce & Tony – Live From Wigmore Hall (with Joyce DiDonato) (Best Classical Solo Vocal Album 2016, Int. Classical Music Award for Vocal Recital 2016) 2015. *Television includes:* Pappano's Classical Voices (BBC series) 2015. *Address:* c/o Nicholas Mathias, IMG Artists, Capital Tower, 91 Waterloo Road, London, SE1 8RT, England (office); Royal Opera House, Bow Street, Covent Garden, London, WC2E 9DD, England (office). *Telephone:* (20) 7957-5800 (office); (20) 7240-1200 (office). *E-mail:* nmathias@imgartists.com (office); info@roh.org.uk (office). *Website:* imgartists.com/artist/antonio_pappano (office); www.roh.org.uk (office).

PAPPAS, Spyros; Greek lawyer, judge, academic and EU official; *Managing Partner, Pappas & Associates;* b. (Spyridon Pappas), 1 Jan. 1953, Athens; m. Frady Karkanis; one s. one d.; ed Univ. of Athens, Panteios School of Econ. and Political Studies, Univ. of Paris, Directorate for European Affairs, Institut Européen d'Admin des Affaires (INSEAD), Brookings Inst., Washington, DC, USA; fmr naval Petty Officer; barrister, Athens 1976; Auditor Council of State 1978, Judge in Supreme Admin. Court 1983; Special Adviser in Prime Minister's Legal Office 1981; mem. Cen. Comm. for Drafting of Laws 1982; est. Nat. Centre of Public

Admin., Sec.-Gen. 1985; est. Inst. of Permanent Training 1985; Assoc. Prof., European Inst. of Public Admin, Maastricht 1988, Dir of Faculty 1989, Dir-Gen. 1990, Prof. of European Law 1992; Dir-Gen. for Consumer Policy, EC 1995, for Information, Communication, Culture and Audiovisual Media 1997–99, for Educ. and Culture 2000; Founder and Man. Partner, Pappas & Associates (legal practice), Brussels 2004–; Chair. Centre of European Culture 2010–15, Centre of Social Responsibility in the Digital Age 2011; Chair. Bd of Govs, Int. East-West Acad.; Pres. Hellenic Network Belgium ARGO 2015; mem. Supreme Council Church of Greece 1984, Comm. of Information on National Affairs, Inst. for Admin. Studies, Asscn of the Judges of the Council of State, Inst. of Public Admin., Cttee for Drafting of the Encyclopedia of Admin., Centre for European Policy Studies Int. Advisory Council, Scientific Council of Academia Istropolitana Bratislava Inst. of Advanced Studies, Foundation for Hellenic Culture; assoc. mem. Asscn of European Magistrates for Democracy and Liberty (MEDEL); Substitute Bd mem. Open Univ., Athens; cr. European Centre of Judges and Lawyers 1992; mem. Athens Bar, Brussels Bar; Hon. title of State Scholar 1971–73; Hon. Fellow, European Coll. of Sport Science, Univs of Cologne and Jyväskylä 2000; Hon. mem. Asscn of European Journalists, The Hague 2000; Officer, Order of Merit (Luxembourg) 1994; Distinction of the Pan-Greek Dissertation 1968, First Prize, Foundation for Admin. Law 'Michel Stassinopoulos' 1976, Scholar of the Council of Europe 1977, Medal of Honour, European Inst., Łódź 1998. *Publications:* La constitution de la Grèce de 1975 1976, Le régime de planification en Grèce 1977, Le Tribunal de Première Instance 1990, Tendances actuelles et évolution de la jurisprudence de la cour de justice des Communautés européennes: suivi annuel (ed.) Vol. I 1993, Vol. II 1995, Procédures administratives nationales: préparation et mise en oeuvre des décisions communautaires: études comparatives (ed.) 1994, EC Competition Law: Financial Aspects (Co-Ed.) 1994, The Changing Role of Parliaments in the European Union (co-ed.) 1995, The European Union's Common Foreign and Security Policy: The Challenges of the Future 1996, Politiques publiques dans l'Union européenne 1996, Digital Television and EU Audiovisual Policy 1999, The New European Governance 2001, The Institutional Alteration of the Right of Initiative of the European Commission 2003, A New Era of Competition Policy? – Competition DG and the Control of the Court of Justice of the European Communities 2004, Morale and Change in the EU 2005, Pro-Action versus Reaction within the EU 2005, Competitiveness and Data Protection 2005, The Lisbon Strategy and its Implementation 2006, When Competition Law is a Commercial Tool 2006, Implementation of Competition Rules in Mergers and Protection of Personal Data 2007, Is European Audiovisual Policy a Driver to European Identity or a Carrier to Further Globalization? 2007, La crise grecque: dégénérescence ou régénération de l'intégration européenne? 2010, Case law of the European Civil Service Tribunal: Restarting or Continuation?, in The European Union Civil Service Tribunal (CST) 2005–2010, Proceedings of the Colloquim organized on the occasion of the 5th Anniversary of the CST, Luxembourg, 1 Oct. 2010, Human Rights Law Journal, Vol. 31 No. 1 2011, Google and the Credibility of EU Data Protection Laws 2012, Towards EU State Aid Modernisation: What Role Do Member States and the Market Play in State Aid Cases? 2012, Tobacco Taxation: Those Member States That Do Not Apply the Law 2015, EU Needs Leadership 2015, Sine qua non for the Development of a Responsible, Independent and Stable Public Administration 2016. *Leisure interests:* music, reading, gardening, swimming, cycling. *Address:* Pappas & Associates, 49–51 rue Stévin, 1000 Brussels, Belgium (office). *Telephone:* (2) 23-15-704-5 (office). *Fax:* (2) 23-15-708 (office). *E-mail:* contact@pappaslaw.eu (office). *Website:* www.pappaslaw.eu (office).

PAPUC, Gheorghe; Moldovan politician and military officer; b. 6 May 1954, Frăsineşti; m.; three c.; ed Inst. of Econs and Law, Moscow, Legal Inst., Ministry of Internal Affairs of Russian Fed.; various military positions in Soviet and Moldovan armed forces to brigade command level 1973–97; Head of Advanced Courses, Ministry of the Interior, fmr USSR 1989–92; Minister of Internal Affairs 2002–08, Oct. 2008–Sept. 2009; sentenced to 4 years of imprisonment 2015, released from prison after Supreme Court acquitted him.

PARADIS, The Hon. Christian; Canadian lawyer, politician and business executive; *Senior Vice-President for Strategic Development, GardaWorld Corporation;* b. 1 Jan. 1974, Thetford Mines, Québec; m. Julie Paradis; three c.; ed Université de Sherbrooke, Université Laval; mem. House of Commons (Conservative) for Mégantic–L'Érable 2006–15; Parl. Sec. to Minister of Natural Resources 2006–07, Sec. of State for Agric. and Agri-food 2007–08, Minister of Public Works and Govt Services 2008–10, of Natural Resources 2010–11, of Industry 2011–13, of Int. Devt 2013–15, also Minister for La Francophonie 2013–15; Pres. Global Development Solutions Canada, Inc. 2015–; Sr Vice-Pres. for Strategic Development, Protective Services, GardaWorld Corpn (security services) 2016–; mem. Bd of Dirs Canadian Wildlife Foundation, Canada World Youth. *Address:* GardaWorld Corporation, 1390 Barre Street, Montreal, PQ H3C 1N4, Canada (office). *Telephone:* (514) 281-2811 (office). *Website:* www.garda-world.com (office).

PARAMONOVA, Tatyana Vladimirovna, CandSci; Russian banker and business executive; *CEO, Insurance Company ZHASO, JSC;* b. 24 Oct. 1950; one s.; ed G.V. Plekhanov Inst. of Nat. Economy; economist, later Head of Div., USSR State Bank 1972–92; Deputy Chair. Cen. Bank of Russian Fed. 1992–94, 1995–97, Acting Chair. 1994–95, First Deputy Chair. 1998–2007, also IMF Alt. Gov. for Russian Fed.; worked in various Moscow commercial banks 1992, 1997–98; Adviser to Pres. of JSC Russian Railways; CEO JSC Zhaso (insurance co.) 2009–; Deputy Chair. Transcapitalbank CJSC 2012–; Dr hc (G.V. Plekhanov Inst. of Nat. Economy); Order of Merit 2000; Merited Economist of the Russian Fed. 1999. *Publications:* more than 120 research papers on economics. *Address:* Insurance Company ZHASO, JSC, 105066 Moscow, ul. Dobroslobodskaya, 19, Russia (office). *E-mail:* zhaso@zhaso.ru (office). *Website:* www.zhaso.ru (office).

PARAS BIR BIKRAM SHAH DEV; Nepalese royal; b. 30 Dec. 1971, Kathmandu; s. of King Gyanendra Bir Bikram Shah Dev and Queen Komal Rajya Laxmi Devi Shah; m. Himani Rajya Laxmi Devi Shah 2000; one s. two d.; ed St Joseph's Coll., Darjeeling, India, Budhanilkantha School, Schiller Int. Univ., UK; proclaimed Crown Prince of Nepal 26 Oct. 2001, heir-apparent to throne of Nepal until monarchy was abolished and replaced by secular fed. repub. May 2008; Chair. Council of Royal Reps during state visits; Coordinator, Zoo Devt Cttee, King Mahendra Trust for Nature Conservation –2001, Chair. King Mahendra Trust for

Nature Conservation 2001–; conferred title of Grand Master of all Orders of the Kingdom of Nepal 2006; Shubha Rajyabhisheka Padaka 1975, Gaddi Aarohan Ko Rajat Mahotsav Padaka, 2028–2053 B.S. 1997, Vishista Seva Padaka 1999, Birendra-Aishwarya Seva Padaka 2001, Suprasiddha Prabala Gorkha Dakshina Bahu 2001, Daivi Prakopa Piditoddhara Padaka 2003, Maha Ujjvala Keertimaya Nepal-Shreepada (First Class) 2004, Birendra-Mala 2006, Ati Maha Gauravamaya Supradeepta Birendra Prajatantra Bhaskara 2006. *Leisure interests:* horse riding, music, composing poems.

PARASKEVA, Rt Hon Janet, BA, JP; British civil servant; *Chairman, Child Maintenance and Enforcement Commission;* b. 28 May 1946; d. of Antonis Paraskeva and Doris Paraskeva (née Fowler); m. Alan Hunt 1967 (divorced 1983); two d. two step s.; ed Worcester Coll. of Educ., Open Univ., UK; teacher 1967–71; self-employed toy maker 1970–73; several positions in youth work 1972–78; Head of Youth Work Unit, Nat. Youth Bureau 1978–81; HM Insp. of Schools Dept of Educ. and Science (now Dept for Educ. and Employment) 1983–88; Dir Nat. Youth Bureau 1988–91; CEO Nat. Youth Agency 1991–95; Dir Nat. Lotteries Charities Bd, England 1995–2000; CEO Law Soc. of England and Wales 2000–06; First Civil Service Commr 2006–10; Chair. Olympic Lottery Distributor 2006–; Chair. Child Maintenance and Enforcement Comm. 2007–; mem. UK Govt Torture Inquiry 2010–. *Publications:* articles in youth, educ. and law journals and periodicals and in Times Education Supplement. *Leisure interests:* golf, riding, gardening. *Address:* Office of the Chairman, Child Maintenance and Enforcement Commission, London, SW1P 9NT, England (office). *Telephone:* (20) 7853-8001 (office). *E-mail:* cmec@dwpdevelopment.net (office). *Website:* www.childmaintenance.org (office).

PARAVAĆ, Borislav; Bosnia and Herzegovina politician; b. 18 Feb. 1943, Kostajnica, Doboj Municipality; m. Dragica Paravać; two c.; ed Univ. of Zagreb; certified accountant and financial auditor; Mayor of Doboj 1990–2000; mem. Republika Srpska Parl. 1996–2002; First Deputy Chair. Parl. House of Reps 2002; Serb mem. Presidency (tripartite) of Bosnia and Herzegovina 2003–06, Chair. April–June 2003, Oct. 2004–June 2005. *Address:* c/o Socijaldemokratska Partija BiH, 71000 Sarajevo, Alipašina 41, Bosnia and Herzegovina. *E-mail:* predsjednik@sdp.ba.

PARAYRE, Jean-Paul-Christophe; French building and civil engineering executive; b. 5 July 1937, Lorient; s. of Louis Parayre and Jeanne Parayre (née Malarde); m. Marie-Françoise Chaufour 1962; two s. two d.; ed Lycées in Casablanca (Morocco) and Versailles, Ecole Polytechnique, Paris, Ecole Nat. des Ponts et Chaussées; Engineer, Dept of Highways 1963–67; Tech. Adviser, Ministry of Social Affairs 1967, Ministry of Econ. and Finance 1968; Dir of Mech. Industries at Ministry of Industry and Research 1970–74; Chief Adviser to Pres. and Gen. Man. Banque Vernes et Commerciale 1974; Man. of Planning, Automobile Div. of Peugeot 1975; Man. Automobile Div. of Peugeot-Citroën 1976, Chair. Bd of Dirs Peugeot SA 1977–84, mem. advisory Bd 1984; mem. Supervisory Bd Soc. Dumez 1977–84 (Dir-Gen. 1984, Chair. 1988–90, Pres. 1991–92); Pres., Dir-Gen. Fided Financière (affil. to Dumez) 1985; Vice-Pres., Dir-Gen. Lyonnaise des Eaux-Dumez 1990–92, Vice-Pres. 1990–93; Pres. Supervisory Bd Razel 1991; Pres. Bolloré Technologies Jan.–Sept. 1994, Scac-Delmas-Vieljeux 1994, Pres. Saga 1996–99; Vice-Pres. Bolloré Group 1994–99; Dir Bolloré Investissement 1994, Carillion PLC 1999, Stena UK 1999; Chair. Advisory Bd Vallourec 2000; Officier, Légion d'honneur, Commdr Ordre nat. du Mérite. *Leisure interests:* golf, tennis.

PARDEE, Arthur Beck, BS, MA, PhD; American biochemist and academic; *Professor Emeritus of Biological Chemistry and Molecular Pharmacology, Harvard Medical School;* b. 13 July 1921, Chicago, Ill.; s. of Charles A. Pardee and Elizabeth Beck; m. Ruth Sager (died 1997); three s. from previous m.; m. Ann Goodman; ed Univ. of California, Berkeley, California Inst. of Tech.; Postdoctoral Fellow, Univ. of Wisconsin 1947–49; Instructor, Asst and Assoc. Prof., Univ. of Calif., Berkeley 1949–61; Sr Postdoctoral Fellow, Pasteur Inst. 1957–58; Prof. of Biochemical Sciences and Donner Prof. of Science, Princeton Univ. 1961–75; Prof. of Biological Chem. and Molecular Pharmacology, Harvard Medical School, Boston 1975–97, Prof. Emer. 1997–; Prof. Emer., Harvard Univ. 1998–; Chief, Div. Cell Growth and Regulation, Dana Farber Cancer Inst. 1975–98; mem. ACS, American Soc. of Biological Chemists (Treasurer 1964–70, Pres. 1980), American Asscn for Cancer Research (Pres. 1985), American Acad. of Arts and Sciences, American Soc. of Microbiologists, Japanese Biochemical Soc.; mem. Council American Cancer Soc. 1967–71; Fellow, Int. Inst. for Advanced Studies Nara, Japan 1999, American Philosophical Soc. 2001; Hon. Faculty mem. Nanjing Univ. 1999; Dr hc (Paris) 1993; ACS Paul Lewis Award 1960, Krebs Medal, Fed. of European Biochemical Socs 1973, Rosensteil Award, Brandeis Univ. 1975, Princess Takamatsee Award (Japan) 1990, Boehringer Bioanalytica Award 1998, Ludwig Award 2002, and numerous other honours and awards. *Publications:* Experiments in Biochemical Research Techniques (co-author) 1957; more than 500 articles on subjects including bacterial physiology and enzymology in synchronous cultures, cell division cycle events, growth regulation in cancer and normal cells, enzymology of DNA synthesis, repair of damaged DNA . *Leisure interests:* music, tennis, travel, art. *Address:* Dana Farber Cancer Institute, 44 Binney Street, Boston, MA 02115 (office); 987 Memorial Drive, Unit 271, Cambridge, MA 02138, USA (home). *Telephone:* (617) 632-3372 (office). *Fax:* (617) 632-4680 (office). *E-mail:* arthur-pardee@fci.harvard.edu (office). *Website:* hms.harvard.edu/hms/home.asp (office).

PARDLO, Gregory, BA, MFA; American poet and academic; b. 1968, Philadelphia, Pa; m. Ginger Romero Pardlo; two d.; ed Rutgers Univ.; served in US Marine Corps Reserve; worked in a restaurant in Copenhagen; ran blues and jazz bar with grandfather, Pennsauken, New Jersey; mem. Cave Canem (writers' collective); fmr Asst Prof. of Creative Writing, George Washington Univ.; fmr teacher, Medgar Evers Coll., The New School Univ., John Jay Coll., Hunter Coll., New York Univ.; Teaching Fellow, Undergraduate Writing Program, Columbia Univ.; Assoc. Ed. Callaloo (literary journal); Contributing Ed. Painted Bride Quarterly; currently Faculty, Master of Fine Arts in Creative Writing, Rutgers Univ.; Guggenheim Fellowship 2017, other fellowships from New York Foundation for the Arts, Cave Canem Foundation, MacDowell Artist's Colony, Seaside Inst., Lotos Club Foundation, City Univ. of New York. *Publications include:* poetry collections: Totem (American Poetry Review / Honickman First Book Prize 2007) 2007, Digest (Pulitzer Prize for Poetry 2015) 2014; Air Traffic: A Memoir of Ambition & Manhood in America (memoir) 2018; trans.: Pencil of Rays and Spike Mace by

Niels Lyngsø 2006; poems, reviews, and translations have appeared in The Best American Poetry 2010, 2014, The American Poetry Review, Callaloo, Poet Lore, Harvard Review, Ploughshares. *Telephone:* (856) 668-4980 (office). *E-mail:* gregory@pardlo.com; mfa@camden.rutgers.edu (office). *Website:* www.mfa.camden.rutgers.edu/faculty (office); www.pardlo.com.

PARDO, Jorge, BFA; Cuban sculptor and architect; b. 1963, Havana; ed Art Center Coll. of Design, Univ. of Illinois, USA; collections at Museum of Contemporary Art, Los Angeles, Museum of Modern Art, New York, Tate Gallery, London, Cooper-Hewitt, Nat. Design Museum, New York, Harvard Univ. Art Museums, Mildred Lane Kemper Art Museum, St Louis, Stedelijk Museum voor Actuele Kunst, Belgium, Smithsonian American Art Museum, Washington, DC; Fellow, John D. and Catherine T. MacArthur Foundation 2010–. *Telephone:* (323) 225-4700. *E-mail:* jps@jorgepardosculpture.com. *Website:* www.jorgepardosculpture.com.

PARED PÉREZ, Vice-Adm. Sigfrido; Dominican Republic naval officer and government official; b. 2 Dec. 1957, Santo Domingo; twice Head of Nat. Investigations Directorate; Sec. of State for Armed Forces 2004–06; Dir of Migration/Immigration Dept 2009–11; Minister of the Armed Forces 2012–14; Grand Cross of Mil. Merit with White Distinction, Medal of Honour for Merit of the Nat. Guard and Honour Star of Carabobo (Venezuela), Grand Cross of Naval Merit (Spain), Order of Nat. Security (China), Order of Naval Merit Medal Naval Merit 1990, Order of Naval Merit Distinguished Service Medal (Category 2) 1991, Honour Grad., Course in Command and Staff in Mil. Inst. of Higher Educ. 1993, Grand Cordon, Order of Juan Pablo Duarte 1994, Order of Naval Merit Service Medal (1st, 2nd and 3rd Category) 1994, Order of Naval Merit Medal to Naval Merit) 1997, Order of Naval Merit Distinguished Service Medal) 1997, Grand Cross of Mil. Merit with White Distinction (Spain) 1999, Order of Naval Merit Medal of Honour) 2000, Medal of Honour for Merit of the Nat. Guard (Venezuela) 2003, Star of Honour Single Class Carabobo (Venezuela) 2005, Grand Cross of Naval Merit (Spain) 2006, Order of Naval Merit Medal Honour, First Class 2009, Order of Air Merit 2009; Medal of Merit for Public Servants 2011, Order of Naval Merit Distinguished Service Medal 2011, Order of the Resplendent Banner with Grand Cordon 2013.

PAREDES RANGEL, Beatriz Elena; Mexican politician and diplomatist; b. 18 Aug. 1953, Tlaxcala; ed Nat. Autonomous Univ. of Mexico (UNAM); Tlaxcala state deputy (Partido Revolucionario Institucional—PRI) 1974–77; adviser to Gov. of Tlaxcala 1978–80; Under-Sec. for Agrarian Reform 1982; Gov. of Tlaxcala (first woman) 1987–92; Amb. to Cuba 1993; unsuccessful cand. for presidency of PRI 2002; unsuccessful campaign for mayoralty of Mexico City, representing alliance of PRI and Partido Verde Ecologista de Mexico (PVEM) 2006; Pres. PRI Nat. Exec. Cttee 2007–11; Amb. to Brazil 2012–16; fmr mem. Chamber of Deputies and Senate; fmr Pres. Nat. Comm. of Integral Devt and Social Justice for Indigenous Peoples; fmr Pres. Colosio Trust Fund; Vice-Pres. Socialist Int.; fmr Pres. Parlatino (Latin American Parl.), currently mem. Consulting Council; Orden de la Solidaridad (Cuba) 1994, Gran Cruz, Orden del Soberano Congreso Nacional de Guatemala 2001, Gran Cruz de Isabel la Católica (Spain) 2002, Ordem Nacional do Cruzeiro do Sul (Brazil) 2003. *Music:* two CDs: El Loco Afán, Corazón Gemelo. *Publications:* Acaso la Palabra, Con la Cabeza Descubierta; regular contrib. to journal El Universal. *Leisure interests:* music and poetry.

PAREKH, Deepak Shantilal, BCom, CA; Indian business executive and banker; *Chairman, Housing Development Finance Corporation Ltd;* b. 18 Oct. 1944; s. of Shantilal Parekh; m. Smita Parekh; two s.; ed Sydenham Coll., Mumbai, Inst. of Chartered Accountants in England & Wales; began career with Ernst & Young Management Consultancy Services, New York 1970; worked with Grindlays Bank for three years; Asst Rep. for South Asia, Chase Manhattan Bank for three years; Deputy Gen. Man., Housing Development Finance Corpn Ltd 1978–85, Man. Dir 1985–93, Chair. 1993–; Chair. (non-exec.) Infrastructure Development Finance Co. Ltd 1997, GlaxoSmithKline Pharmaceuticals Ltd, Siemens Ltd; mem. Bd of Dirs Mahindra & Mahindra Ltd, Indian Hotels Co. Ltd amongst others; mem. Int. Bd WNS (Holdings) (USA), DP World (UAE); mem. Advisory Bd of several Indian and multinational corpns; Chevalier, Légion d'honneur 2010, Bundesverdienstkreuz 2014; Businessman of the Year, Business India 1996, JRD Tata Corp. Leadership Award, All India Man. Asscn, Padma Bhushan 2006, Lifetime Achievement Award, Econ. Times 2006, Best Non-Exec. Dir, Asian Centre for Corp. Governance 2006, IMC Juran Quality Medal 2008, Outstanding Business Leader of the Year 2008, NDTV Business Leader of the Year Award 2008, Lifetime Achievement Award, CNBC Awaaz Crisil Real Estate Awards 2008, Priyadarshni Acad. Award 2008, Qimpro Platinum Award, Corp. Award for Lifetime Achievement, Econ. Times, AIMA Man. India Award 2010, Most Inspiring Business Leader Award, NDTV Profit, Lifetime Achievement Award, Confed. of Real Estate Developers Asscn 2010, Lifetime Achievement Award, Finance Asia magazine, Hong Kong, first int. recipient of Outstanding Achievement Award, Inst. of Chartered Accountants in England and Wales 2010. *Address:* Housing Development Finance Corporation Ltd, Ramon House 169, Backbay Reclamation, H T Parekh Marg, Churchgate, Mumbai 400 020, India (office). *Telephone:* (22) 66316000 (office). *Fax:* (22) 22811203 (office). *E-mail:* investorcare@hdfc.com (office). *Website:* www.hdfc.com (office).

PARENGKUAN, August; Indonesian journalist, editor, media executive and diplomatist; b. 1 Aug. 1943, Surabaya, East Java; journalist, Kompas 1965–81, Ed. of Political Affairs 1981–87, Deputy Man. Ed. 1989–90, Man. Ed. 1990–92, Deputy Chief Ed. of Kompas 1992–93, Exec. Ed. of Kompas and concurrently Deputy Chief Ed. 1993–2000, Dir of Communications, Kompas Gramedia Group (KKG) 2000, Pres. TV7 2001, Sr Vice-Pres. KKG 2002; Amb. to Italy 2012–17.

PARENT, Mary Campbell; American producer; *Vice Chair (Worldwide Production), Legendary Entertainment;* b. 1968, Santa Barbara, Calif.; began career as agent trainee, Int. Creative Man. (ICM); Dir of Devt then Production Vice-Pres. New Line Cinema 1994–97; Sr Vice-Pres. of Production Universal Pictures 1997–2000, Exec. Vice-Pres. of Production 2000–01, Co-Pres. of Production 2001–03, Vice-Chair. Worldwide Production 2003–05; Producer Stuber/Parent 2006–08; Chair. Worldwide Motion Picture Group Metro-Goldwyn-Mayer Inc. 2008–10, also mem. Office of CEO; co-f. Disruption Entertainment (subsidiary of Paramount Pictures) 2011, Vice Chair. (Worldwide Production) Legendary Entertainment 2016–. *Films produced include:* Set It Off 1996, Trial and Error 1997, Pleasantville 1998, You, Me and Dupree 2006, The Kingdom 2007, Welcome Home, Roscoe Jenkins 2008, Role Models 2008, Love Happens 2009, Pacific Rim 2013, Noah 2014, Godzilla 2014, The SpongeBob Movie: Sponge Out of Water 2015, The Revenant (BAFTA Award for Best Film 2016) 2015, Monster Trucks 2016, Kong: Skull Island 2017, Same Kind of Different as Me 2017, Pacific Rim Uprising 2018, Pokémon Detective Pikachu 2019. *Address:* Legendary Entertainment, 2900 W Alameda Avenue, Burbank, CA 91505, USA (office). *Telephone:* (818) 688-7003 (office). *Website:* www.legendary.com (office).

PARET, Peter, PhD, DLit, LittD, DH, DPhil; American historian and academic; *Andrew W. Mellon Professor Emeritus in the Humanities, Institute for Advanced Study;* b. 13 April 1924, Berlin, Germany; s. of Dr Hans Paret and Suzanne Aimée Cassirer; m. Isabel Harris 1961; one s. one d.; ed Univ. of California, Berkeley, Univ. of London, UK; Research Assoc. Center of Int. Studies, Princeton Univ. 1960–62; Visiting Asst Prof., Univ. of Calif., Davis 1962–63, Assoc. Prof. 1963–66, Prof. of History 1966–69; Prof. of History, Stanford Univ. 1969–77, Raymond A. Spruance Prof. in Int. History 1977–86; Andrew W. Mellon Prof. in the Humanities, Inst. for Advanced Study, Princeton 1986–97, Andrew W Mellon Prof. Emer. 1997–; Lees Knowles Lecturer, Univ. Cambridge 2008; mem. American Philosophical Soc., Historische Kommission zu Berlin; Fellow, American Acad. of Arts and Sciences, Leo Baeck Inst.; Hon. Fellow, LSE, Clausewitz Gesellschaft; Great Cross, German Order of Merit; four hon. degrees; Thomas Jefferson Medal, Samuel Eliot Morison Medal, Moncado Prizes. *Publications:* Guerrillas in the 1960s (with John Shy) 1961, French Revolutionary Warfare 1964, Yorck and the Era of Prussian Reform 1966, The Berlin Secession 1980, Makers of Modern Strategy (ed.) 1986, Art as History 1988, Carl von Clausewitz: On War (ed. and trans. with Michael Howard) 1976, 1984, Clausewitz and the State 1985, Carl von Clausewitz, Historical and Political Writings (ed. and trans.) 1991, Understanding War 1992, Persuasive Images (with Beth Lewis and Paul Paret) 1992, Sammler, Stifter und Museen (ed. with Ekkehard Mai) 1993, Imagined Battles 1997, German Encounters with Modernism 2001, An Artist against the Third Reich: Ernst Barlach, 1933–38 2003, 1806: The Cognitive Challenge of War 2009. *Address:* School of Historical Studies, Institute for Advanced Study, Einstein Drive, Princeton, NJ 08540, USA (office). *Telephone:* (609) 734-8344 (home). *Fax:* (609) 683-5027 (home). *E-mail:* paret@ias.edu (office). *Website:* www.hs.ias.edu (office).

PARETSKY, Sara N., BA, MBA, PhD; American writer; b. 8 June 1947, Ames, Ia; d. of David Paretsky and Mary E. Edwards; m. Courtenay Wright 1976; three c.; ed Univs of Kansas and Chicago; Man. Urban Research Center, Chicago, Ill. 1971–74, CNA Insurance Co., Chicago 1977–85; writer of crime novels 1982–; Pres. Sisters in Crime, Chicago 1986–88; Dir Nat. Abortion Rights Action League, Ill. 1987–90; Pres. Mystery Writers of America 2015; Grand Master, Mystery Writers of America 2011; mem. Crime Writers' Asscn; Hon. DLit (Columbia Coll.), (Elmhurst Coll.), (DePaul Univ), (Univ of Kansas) 2015; Ms Magazine Woman of the Year 1987, CWA Silver Dagger Award 1988, Diamond Dagger for Lifetime Achievement, British Crime Writers Asscn 2002. *Publications include:* Indemnity Only 1982, Deadlock (Friends of American Writers Prize 1985) 1984, Killing Orders 1986, Bitter Medicine 1987, Toxic Shock (British Crime Writers' Asscn Silver Dagger for Fiction 1988) 1987, Blood Shot 1988, Burn Marks 1990, Guardian Angel 1992, A Woman's Eye (ed.) 1992, Tunnel Vision 1994, Women on the Case 1997, Hard Time 2000, Total Recall 2002, Blacklist 2003 (British Crime Writers' Asscn Gold Dagger for Fiction 2004), Fire Sale 2006, Writing in an Age of Silence 2007, Bleeding Kansas 2008, Hardball 2009, Body Work 2010, Breakdown 2012, Critical Mass 2013, Brush Black 2015, Fallout 2017, Shell Game (Sue Grafton Memorial Award 2019) 2018; numerous short stories and articles. *Leisure interests:* walking, singing, making the perfect cappuccino. *Address:* c/o Dominick Abel Literary Agency, Inc., 146 West 82nd Street, Apartment 1A, New York, NY 10024, USA (office); 1507 E 53rd Street, Chicago, IL 60615, USA (office). *Telephone:* (212) 877-0710 (office). *E-mail:* dominick@dalainc.com (office); viwarshawski@mindspring.com (office). *Website:* www.saraparetsky.com.

PARFITT, David John; British film, theatre and television producer; *Director/Partner, Trademark Films Limited;* b. 8 July 1958, Reading, Berks.; s. of William Parfitt and Maureen Collinson; m. 1st Susan Coates (divorced 1993); one s.; m. 2nd Elizabeth Barron 1996; two s.; ed Bede Grammar School, Sunderland, Barbara Speake Stage School, London; actor 1970–88; producer 1985–; Man. Dir Renaissance Theatre Co. 1987–, Trademark Films Ltd 1999–; mem. Bd Chicken Shed Theatre Trust 1997–2011; mem. Council of BAFTA 2000–16, mem. Bd of Trustees 2006–11, Chair. of Film 2004–07, Deputy Chair. BAFTA 2007–08, Chair. 2008–10; Chair. Film London 2010–17; mem. Bd of Govs, Dulwich Coll. 2018–; Dr hc (Sunderland) 2000, Hon. Dr of Drama (Royal Scottish Acad. of Music and Drama) 2001. *Plays (as producer):* Public Enemy, John Sessions' Napoleon, Twelfth Night, Much Ado About Nothing, Hamlet, As You Like It, Scenes from a Marriage, A Midsummer Night's Dream, King Lear, Travelling Tales, Uncle Vanya, Coriolanus, Les Liaisons Dangereuses, Elling, A Bunch of Amateurs, The Wipers Times, Trial by Laughter. *Films include:* Henry V 1989, Peter's Friends 1992, Swan Song 1992, Much Ado About Nothing 1993, Mary Shelley's Frankenstein 1994, The Madness of King George (BAFTA Best British Film 1995) 1994, Twelfth Night 1996, The Wings of the Dove 1997, Shakespeare in Love (BAFTA Best Film 1998, Golden Globe Award for Best Musical or Comedy 1998, Academy Award for Best Film 1998) 1998, Gangs of New York (production consultant) 2001, I Capture the Castle 2003, Chasing Liberty 2004, My Talks with Dean Spanley (exec. producer) 2008, A Bunch of Amateurs 2008, My Week with Marilyn 2011, The Truth About Stanley (short) (exec. producer) 2012, Loving Vincent (exec. producer) 2016, Red Joan 2018. *Television:* as producer: Twelfth Night 1988, Look Back in Anger 1989, Parade's End (series) 2012, Wipers Times 2013, Glyndebourne: The Untold History 2014, Birth of an Opera: Danielle de Niese on The Barber of Seville 2016. *Address:* Trademark Films, 11 Trinity Rise, London, SW2 2QP, England (office). *Telephone:* (20) 3322-8900 (office). *E-mail:* mail@trademarkfilms.co.uk (office). *Website:* www.trademarkfilms.co.uk (office).

PARISI, Arturo Mario Luigi; Italian politician and academic; b. 13 Sept. 1940, San Mango Piemonte, Salerno, Campania; ed Nunziatella Mil. School, Univ. of Sassari; worked as forester and teacher at training centre for industrial workers while attending univ.; Sec., then Nat. Vice-Pres. Youth Dept, Azione Cattolica, also mem., Exec. Cttee, Int. Fed. of Catholic Youth Movt 1963–68; academic posts have included Asst Lecturer of Statistics, Univ. of Sassari, Researcher, Cattaneo Inst., Bologna 1968, Asst Prof. of Ecclesiastical Law, Univ. of Parma, Asst Prof. of History of Religious Insts, Univ. of Florence; First Prof. of Sociology of Religions, then full Prof. of Sociology of Political Phenomena, Cattaneo Inst., Bologna 1971–, also currently Dir Cattaneo Inst.; mem. Chamber of Deputies for Bologna 1999–2001, for Sardinia 2001–; mem. Partito Democratico 2007–; Minister of Defence 2006–08; political adviser to Romani Prodi; Under-Sec., Presidency of Council of Ministers 1996; active in I Democratici movt 1999; Co-founder and Nat. Vice-Pres. Democrazia è Libertà – La Margherita 2001, Pres. of party in Fed. Ass. 2004–07; Vice-Pres. Il Mulino Asscn, also ed. of journal; fmr Pres. Italian Soc. of Electoral Studies; served as expert to govt cttee and parl. comm. on domestic terrorism 1987–88; active in movt for Institutional Reforms and Ulivo movt. *Address:* Partito Democratico, Piazza Saint'Anastasia 7, 00186 Rome, Italy (office). *Telephone:* (06) 675471 (office). *Fax:* (06) 67547319 (office). *E-mail:* arturoparisi@arturoparisi.it (office). *Website:* www.partitodemocratico.it (office); www.arturoparisi.it.

PARISI, Giorgio, PhD; Italian theoretical physicist and academic; *Professor, University of Rome;* b. 4 Aug. 1948, Rome; m.; two c.; ed Univ. of Rome; Researcher, Laboratori Nazionali di Frascati 1971–81, on leave of absence to Columbia Univ., USA 1973–74, to Institut des Hautes Études Scientifiques 1976–77, to École Normale Supérieure, Paris 1977–78; Prof., Univ. of Rome 1981–; Prof. of Theoretical Physics, Univ. of Roma II, 'Tor Vergata' 1981–92; currently also Prof. of Quantum Theories, Univ. of Rome I, 'La Sapienza'; mem. or fmr mem. various editorial bds and of various scientific cttees, including Scientific Cttee, INFM, French Nat. Research Panel; Head of Italian Del. to IUPAP; Dir CNR-INFM Research and Devt Centre SMC (Statistical Mechanics and Complexity), Rome; Fellow, Accad. dei Lincei, Acad. des sciences, Accad. dei XL, NAS, American Philosophical Soc.; Laurea hc in Philosophy (Urbin Univ.); Feltrinelli Prize for Physics, Accad. dei Lincei 1986, Boltzmann Medal 1992, Italgas Prize 1993, Dirac Medal and Prize, Inst. of Physics (UK) 1999, Italian Prime Minister's Prize 2002, Enrico Fermi Prize 2003, Dannie Heineman Prize 2005, Nonino Prize 2005, Galileo Prize 2006, Microsoft Award 2007, Lagrange Prize 2009, Max Planck Medal, Deutsche Physikalische Gesellschaft 2011, Nature Award for Mentoring in Science 2013. *Publications:* Statistical Field Theory 1988, Spin Glass Theory and Beyond 1988, Field Theory, Disorder and Simulations (co-author) 1992; more than 500 papers in professional journals. *Address:* Piazzale Aldo Moro n° 2, Rome 00185, Italy (office). *Telephone:* (06) 49913481 (office). *Fax:* (06) 4463158 (office). *E-mail:* giorgio.parisi@roma1.infn.it (office). *Website:* chimera.roma1.infn.it/GIORGIO/index.html (office).

PARISOT, Laurence; French business executive; *Chairman and Managing Director, French Unit, Citibank, Inc.;* b. 31 Aug. 1959, Luxeuil-les-Bains; d. of Michel Parisot and Janine Parisot; ed Institut d'études politiques de Paris, Univ. of Nancy 11, Sciences Po, Paris; inherited Optimum (France's leading maker of cupboard doors) from her father; Asst to Alain Lancelot, Pres. Centre d'Etudes de la Vie Politique Française (CEVIPOF) 1983–85; Dir-Gen. Louis Harris France (polling co.) 1986–90; Chair. and CEO IFOP (polling co.) 1990–2007, Vice-Chair. 2008–17; mem. Exec. Council, Medef, le Mouvement des Entreprises de France 2003, Pres. 2005–13; CEO Gradiva 2017–18; Chair. and Man. Dir French Unit, Citibank Inc. 2018–; mem. Bd of Dirs BNP-Paribas 2006–18, Coface 2007–14; mem. Comité des Sages, Samu Social, Fives 2013–15; mem. Bd of Trustees, Michelin SCA 2005–15; Chevalier, Légion d'honneur, Officier, Ordre nat. du Mérite, Commdr du Ouissam Al Alaoui (Morocco). *Publications:* Besoin d'Air 2007, Un piège Bleu Marine 2012. *Address:* Citibank Europe Plc, French Branch, 21–25, Rue Balzac, 75406 Paris, France (office).

PARIVODIĆ, Milan, LLM, PhD; Serbian lawyer, academic and politician; *Principal Attorney, Parivodić Advokati;* b. 1966, Belgrade; m. Alexandra Parivodić; two d.; ed Faculty of Law, Univ. of Belgrade, University College London, UK; Lecturer in Civil Law and Property Law, Faculty of Law, Univ. of Belgrade 1991–2004; pvt. law practice 2004–06; Minister of Int. Econ. Relations 2004–07, Co-ordinator Ministry of Finance 2006–07; Head, Serbian WTO accession 2005–07; advisor for economy and law to the Prime Minister of Serbia 2007–08; Pnr. Wolf Theiss 2007–09; currently, Principal Attorney, Parivodić Advokati; Prof. Int. Commercial and Contract Law, European Centre for Peace and Development (ECPD), Faculty for Peace, UN(O); mem. Editorial Advisory Bd Journal of International Franchising; Sec.-Gen. Serbian chapter of Association Internationale pour la Protection de la Propriété Intellectuelle—Int. Asscn for Protection of Intellectual Property; mem. Democratic Party of Serbia, Crown Council of HRH Prince Alexander of Serbia, Economic Advisory Council, Serbian Orthodox Patriarch Bd of Dir Vojvodjanska Banka; Grand Cross of the Serbian Royal Order of the White Eagle. *Publications:* Exclusive Distribution in the Laws of Yugoslavia and the European Community 1996, Law of International Franchising 2003; numerous articles on int. trade law, contract law, intellectual property law, competition law, distribution law in professional journals. *Address:* Parivodić Advokati, Patrijarha Varnave 15, 11000 Belgrade, Serbia (office). *Telephone:* (11) 3087963; 611333331 (mobile). *E-mail:* Milan.Parivodic@investmentserbia.com. *Website:* parivodic.com.

PARK, Bong-heum, MA (Econ); South Korean business executive; *Chairman, Samsung Life Insurance Company Limited;* ed Duke Univ., USA; fmrly worked for Bank of Korea; Ind. Dir (non-exec.), Samsung Life Insurance Co. Ltd 2011–, currently also Chair.; Ind. Dir, SK Gas Ltd. *Address:* Samsung Life Insurance Co. Ltd, 150 Taepyung-ro 2-ga, Jung-gu, Seoul 100-716, Republic of Korea (office). *Telephone:* (2) 1588-3114 (office). *Fax:* (2) 751-8021 (office). *E-mail:* info@samsunglife.com (office). *Website:* www.samsunglife.com (office).

PARK, Chan-wook; South Korean filmmaker; b. 23 Aug. 1963, *Films directed:* Simpan (Judgement) (also screenplay) 1999, Gongdong gyeongbi guyeok JSA (Joint Security Area) (also screenplay) 2000, Boksuneun naui geot (Sympathy for Mr Vengeance) (also screenplay) 2002, Yeoseot gae ui siseon (If You Were Me) (also screenplay) 2003, Oldboy (also screenplay) (Grand Prix, Cannes Film Festival 2004) 2003, Three... Extremes (also screenplay) 2004, Chinjeolhan Geumja-ssi (Sympathy for Lady Vengeance) (Bangkok Film Festival Golden Kinaree Award for Best Director 2006) 2005, I'm A Cyborg 2006, Crush and Blush 2008, Bak-jwi (Thirst) (Jury Prize, Cannes Film Festival) 2009, Stoker 2013, The Handmaiden 2016. *Film screenplays:* Anarchists 2000, The Humanist 2001.

PARK, Geun-hye; South Korean politician and fmr head of state; b. 2 Feb. 1952, Gumi, northern Gyeongsang Prov.; d. of Park Chung-hee (Pres. of South Korea 1961–79); ed Sogang Univ.; worked for Yukyoung Foundation and Saemaeum Hosp.; served as dir in sr citizen welfare centre; Dir Korean Cultural Foundation 1993; Dir Jeongsu Scholarship Fund 1994; mem. Grand Nat. Party (GNP) (renamed Saenuri Party 2012) 1998–2002, 2003–, Vice-Pres. 2000–02, Chair. 2004–06, 2011–12; mem. Nat. Ass. for Daegu 1998–2012, as Proportional Representation mem. Parl. May–Dec. 2012; Pres. of South Korea (first woman) 2012–16 (suspended following impeachment proceedings 8 Dec. 2016, impeachment upheld by Constitutional Court March 2017); Chair. Preparatory Cttee Korean Coalition for the Future 2001, Leader 2002 (merged with GNP 2003); mem. Korean Literature Asscn 1994; Hon. Pres. Korean Girl Scouts 1974. *Publications include:* six books on family and literature.

PARK, Han-woo; South Korean business executive; *Representative Director, President and Co-CEO, Kia Motors Corporation;* ed Dankook Univ.; fmr Exec. Vice-Pres., Hyundai Motor Co., Sr Exec. Dir of Admin and Chief Financial Officer, Hyundai Motor India –2012, CEO and Man. Dir Hyundai Motor India Ltd 2009–12, Chief Financial Officer and Exec. Vice-Pres., Kia Motors Corpn –2014, Rep. Dir, Pres. and Co-CEO 2014–, Rep. Dir, Hyundai Card Co. Ltd. *Address:* Kia Motors Corporation, Hyundai Kia Buillding, Seoul 137130, Republic of Korea (office). *Telephone:* (2) 3464-1114 (office). *E-mail:* info@kia.com (office). *Website:* www.kia.com/worldwide (office).

PARK, Keun-hee; South Korean business executive; currently Vice-Chair. and CEO Samsung Life Insurance Co. Ltd. *Address:* Samsung Life Insurance Co. Ltd, 150 Taepyung-ro 2-ga, Jung-gu, Seoul 100-716, Republic of Korea (office). *Telephone:* (2) 1588-3114 (office). *Fax:* (2) 751-8021 (office). *E-mail:* info@samsunglife.com (office). *Website:* www.samsunglife.com (office).

PARK, (Nicholas Wulstan) Nick, CBE, BA; British animated film director; b. 6 Dec. 1958, Preston, Lancs., England; ed Sheffield Art School and Nat. Film and TV School, Beaconsfield; joined Aardman Animations 1985, Partner 1995–; best known as the creator of Wallace and Gromit and Shaun the Sheep. *Films include:* Wallace & Gromit: A Grand Day Out (BAFTA Awards for Best Short Animated Film) 1989, Creature Comforts (Academy Award for Best Animated Short Film) 1990, Wallace & Gromit: The Wrong Trousers (Academy Award for Best Animated Short Film) 1993, Wallace & Gromit: A Close Shave (Academy Award for Best Animated Short Film) 1995, Chicken Run (co-dir) 2000, Wallace & Gromit: The Curse of the Were-Rabbit (BAFTA Best British Film 2006, Academy Award for Best Animated Feature Film 2006) 2005, Wallace & Gromit's Grand Adventures: Fright of the Bumblebees (video game) 2009, Shaun the Sheep Movie 2015. *Television:* Creature Comforts (series) 2003–05, Shaun the Sheep (series) 2007–09, Wallace & Gromit in A Matter of Loaf and Death (short; writer) (BAFTA Best Short Animation 2009) 2008, Wallace and Gromit's World of Invention (series) 2010. *Website:* www.aardman.com.

PARK, Seung, PhD; South Korean fmr central banker, economist and academic; b. 16 Feb. 1936; ed Seoul Nat. Univ. and State Univ. of New York, USA; economist at Bank of Korea 1961–76, Gov. 2002–06, fmr mem. Monetary Bd; Assoc. Prof., Chung-Ang Univ. 1976, Prof. 1982–88, 1990, Dean Coll. of Politics and Econs 1984–87, Dean Grad. School 1988; Pres. Korea Int. Econ. Asscn 1986; Sr Sec. for Econs, Presidential Secr. 1988; Minister of Construction 1988–89; Chief Dir Korea Nat. Housing Corpn 1993–96; Chief Dir Korea Transport Inst. 1997; Chair. Korea Econ. Asscn 1999; Head, Public Funds Man. Cttee –2002. *Publications:* author of five books.

PARK, Tae-hwan; South Korean swimmer; b. 27 Sept. 1989, Seoul; ed Kyunggi High School, Dankook Univ.; began swimming aged five, began competitive swimming aged 17, won several medals in junior competitions; selected by Korean Swimming Fed. as mem. of nat. team based in Taereung, Seoul 2003; Asian Games Doha, 2006: gold medal, 200m freestyle, 400m freestyle, 1,500m freestyle, bronze medal, 4×100m freestyle relay, 4×200m freestyle relay, 4×100m medley relay; Pan Pacific Championships, Victoria 2006: gold medal, 400m freestyle, 1,500m freestyle, silver medal, 200m freestyle; Olympic Games, Beijing 2008: gold medal, 400m freestyle, silver medal, 200m freestyle; World Championships, Shanghai 2011: gold medal, 400m freestyle; Windsor 2016: gold medal, 200m freestyle, 400m freestyle, 1500m freestyle; Olympic Games, London 2012: silver medal, 200m freestyle, 400m freestyle; trains in Melbourne, Australia; Goodwill Amb. for 'Dynamic Korea'; coach Michael Bohl 2010–; voted Most Valuable Player at Asian Games, Doha 2006, World Pacific Rim Swimmer of the Year 2006. *Address:* Korea Swimming Federation, RM 510 Olympic Center #88, Ohryun-Dong Songpa-ku, 138-749 Seoul, Republic of Korea. *Telephone:* (2) 4204236. *Fax:* (2) 4206934. *E-mail:* korswim@chol.com. *Website:* swimming.sports.or.kr.

PARK, Y. H., BA, MA, PhD; South Korean surgeon and business executive; *Chairman, Doosan Corporation;* ed Kyunggi High School, Dept of Surgery, School of Medicine, Seoul Nat. Univ.; full-time medical doctor at Brigham and Women's Hosp., Harvard Medical School, Boston; apptd Pres. 11th and 12th Seoul Nat. Univ. Hosp. 1998, Chair. Hosp. Man. Cttee, Korean Red Cross 2005; Chair. Yonkang Foundation 2005–; Chair. Doosan Corpn 2007–; Vice-Chair. Fed. of Korean Industries 2007–; mem. Bd of Trustees, Chung-Ang Univ. Foundation 2008–; Chair. Korea Arts and Culture Educ. Centre 2009–. *Address:* Doosan Corporation, Doosan Tower 18-12, Euljiro 6-ga, Jung-gu, Seoul 100-730, Republic of Korea (office). *Telephone:* (2) 3398-0114 (office). *Fax:* (2) 3398-1135 (office). *E-mail:* info@doosan.com (office). *Website:* www.doosan.com (office).

PARK, Yong-sung, MBA; South Korean business executive and international organization official; *Chairman, Doosan Heavy Industries and Construction Company;* b. 11 Sept. 1940, Seoul; ed School of Commerce, Seoul Nat. Univ., Leonard N. Stern School of Business, New York Univ., USA; fmr mem. Exec. Bd ICC 1998–2003, Vice-Chair. 2003–05, Chair. 2005–06; currently Chair. Doosan Heavy Industries and Construction Co.; Chair. Korean Chamber of Commerce and Industry (KCCI); fmr mem. Int. Olympic Cttee, Pres. South Korea Olympic Cttee 2008–13; Pres. Int. Judo Fed. 1995–2007. *Address:* Doosan Heavy Industries and Construction Company, 1303–22 Seocho-Dong, Seocho-Gu, Seoul 137-920, Republic of Korea (office). *Telephone:* (2) 513-6114 (office). *Fax:* (2) 513-6200 (office). *Website:* www.doosanheavy.com.

PARK, Yongmaan, BA, MBA; South Korean business executive; *CEO, Doosan Group;* b. 5 Feb. 1955, Seoul; s. of Park Du-byeong; two s.; ed Kyunggi High School, Seoul National University, Boston University, USA; joined Doosan Engineering and Construction 1982, Pres. and CEO Doosan Corpn 1998–2000, 2001–09, Chair. and CEO Doosan Infracore 2007–, CEO Doosan Corpn 2009–12, Chair. and CEO Doosan Group 2016–; Vice-Chair. Seoul Chamber of Commerce and Industry 2009–; Chair. for Korea, Korea-Spain Econ. Cooperation Council 2000–. *Address:* Doosan Corpn, Doosan Tower 18-12, Euljiro 6-ga, Jung-gu, Seoul 100-730, South Korea (office). *Telephone:* (2) 3398-0114 (office). *Fax:* (2) 3398-1135 (office). *E-mail:* info@doosan.com (office). *Website:* www.doosan.com (office).

PARK, Young-ho, MBA; South Korean business executive; *Vice-Chairman, SK China;* ed Seoul Nat. Univ.; worked at Posco Research Inst. –2000; joined SK Holdings Co. Ltd 2000, Pres. and Co-CEO SK Holdings Co. Ltd 2007–10, Vice-Chair. SK China 2010–. *Address:* SK China, SK Holdings Co. Ltd, 99 Seorin-Dong, Jongru-Gu, Seoul 110-110, Republic of Korea (office). *Telephone:* (2) 2121-5114 (office). *Fax:* (2) 2121-7001 (office). *E-mail:* Byc778@sk.com (office). *Website:* www.sk.com.cn (office).

PARKANOVÁ, Vlasta, JUDr; Czech lawyer and politician; b. 21 Nov. 1951, Prague; m. Zdeněk Parkan; one d.; ed Charles Univ.; began legal career specialising in commercial law 1975–88; co-f. Civic Forum, Tábor 1989; mem. Fed. Ass. 1990–93; various positions within Ministry of Foreign Affairs and Ministry of Interior 1992–96; mem. Parl. 1996–2013, Vice-Chair. Chamber of Deputies 2011–12; Minister of Justice 1997–98, Deputy Chair. Cttee on Defence and Security 1998–2002, Minister of Defence 2007–09; Vice-Chair. Constitution and Legal Cttee 1998–2002, Chair. 2003–06; mem. Perm. Del. of Parl. of Czech Repub. to NATO 1998–2006; mem. Civic Democratic Alliance (ODA) 1991–98; mem. Christian Democratic Party (KDU-ČSL) 2001–09.

PARKER, Sir Alan William, Kt, CBE; British film director, producer and writer; b. 14 Feb. 1944, Islington, London, England; s. of William Leslie Parker and Elsie Ellen Parker; m. 1st Annie Inglis 1966 (divorced 1992); three s. one d.; m. Lisa Moran 2001; one s.; ed Dame Alice Owen's School, Islington; advertising copywriter 1965–68; TV commercials dir 1968–78; Founding mem. and Chair. Directors Guild of GB 1982–86; Chair. British Film Inst. 1998–99, Film Council 1999–2012; Pres. Fed. of European Film Dirs 2013–; Visiting Prof., Southampton Solent Film School; Hon. Fellow, Nat. Film and Television School; Officier des Arts et des Lettres 2005; Hon. DArts (UAE) 1999, (Sunderland) 2005, (Southampton Solent) 2012; BAFTA Michael Balcon Award for Outstanding Contrib. to British Film, Directors Guild of GB Lifetime Achievement Award, BAFTA Fellowship 2013. *Screenplay:* Melody (also original story). *Wrote and directed:* Our Cissy (short) 1974, Footsteps (short) 1974, Bugsy Malone 1976, No Hard Feelings (TV film) 1976, Angel Heart 1987, A Turnip Head's Guide to the British Cinema, Come See the Paradise 1990, The Road to Wellville (also producer) 1994, Evita (also actor and producer) 1996, Angela's Ashes (also actor and producer) 1999. *Directed:* The Evacuees (TV film) 1974, Midnight Express (also actor) 1978, Fame 1980, Shoot the Moon 1982, Pink Floyd The Wall 1982, Birdy 1984, Mississippi Burning (Nat. Review Bd Best Dir Award) 1988, Renegade MTV Special (TV film) 1990, The Commitments (also actor) (BAFTA Award for Best Dir) 1991 The Life of David Gale (also actor and producer) 2003. *Publications:* (novels) Bugsy Malone 1976, Puddles in the Lane 1977, The Sucker's Kiss 2003; (cartoon) Hares in the Gate 1983, Making Movies 1998, Will Write and Direct for Food 2005. *Leisure interests:* painting, cartooning, Arsenal FC. *Address:* c/o Independent Talent Group, 40 Whitfield Street, London, W1T 2RH, England. *Telephone:* (20) 7636-6565. *Fax:* (20) 7323-0101. *Website:* www.alanparker.com.

PARKER, Cornelia, OBE, RA; British artist; b. 1956, Cheshire; ed Gloucestershire Coll. of Art and Design, Wolverhampton Polytechnic, Univ. of Reading; Int. Artist-in-Residence, Two Rooms, Auckland 2010, Artist-in-Residence, Jupiter Artland, Edinburgh 2009, Brontë Parsonage Museum, Yorks. 2006, part of Illuminate festival 2006, For-site Residency, Nevada City, Calif. 2005, Artist-in-Residence, Science Museum, London 1998–99, Int. Artist-in-Residence, ArtPace Foundation for Contemporary Art, San Antonio, Tex., 1997, Koopman Chair, Jose Loff Gallery, Hartford Art School, Conn. 1997, Sr Fellow in Fine Art, Cardiff Inst. 1992–95, Henry Moore Sculpture Residency, Wimbledon School of Art 1991–92, Sculpture Residency and Commission, Forest of Dean, Gloucestershire 1988, Artist-in-Residence, Crewe & Alsager Coll., Cheshire 1980; Visiting Fellow, Lady Margaret Hall, Oxford 2016–; Dr hc (Univ. of Wolverhampton) 2000, (Univ. of Birmingham) 2005, (Univ. of Gloucestershire) 2008; First Prize, Midland View Stoke City Art Gallery & Museum 1980, Southern Arts Award 1983, Greater London Arts Award 1985, British School at Rome Award 1989, Henry Moore Scholarship, Wimbledon School of Art 1991–92, Int. Asscn of Art Critics Prize (USA) 1998, Best Show by an Emerging Artist, for Mass: Colder Darker Matter at Deitch Projects, New York 1998, The Hugh Casson Drawing Prize, RA Summer Exhbn 2011, Artist of the Year, Apollo Magazine 2016, Official Artist for the UK General Election 2017. *Television:* Date With An Artist – 1997 Turner Prize (Channel 4) 1997, Artist ties up Rodin's lovers (BBC News) 2003, Tate Modern: Different Dimensions, Tate Modern and Nat. Gallery, Series 1 Episode 5 (Channel 4) 2008, Vic Reeves' Turner Prize Moments (Channel 4) 2011, Cornelia Parker Night (Sky Arts) 2011. *Publications:* Cold Dark Matter: An Exploded View, Essay by Adrian Searl, London: Chisenhale Gallery 1991, Avoided Object (with Guy Brett, Stuart Cameron, Antonia Payne and Jonathon Watkins) 1996, Contemporary Art 1992, Cornelia Parker (with Bruce Ferguson and Jessica Morgan) 2000, On Second Thoughts – Cornelia Parker 2003, Brontean Abstracts 2006. *Address:* c/o Frith Street Gallery, 59–60 Frith Street, London, W1D 3JJ, England (office). *Telephone:* (20) 7494-1550 (office). *Fax:* (20) 7287-3733 (office). *E-mail:* info@frithstreetgallery.com (office). *Website:* www.frithstreetgallery.com (office).

PARKER, Eugene N., PhD; American physicist (retd) and academic; *S. Chandrasekhar Distinguished Service Professor Emeritus, Department of Astronomy and Astrophysics, University of Chicago;* b. 10 June 1927, Houghton, Mich.; s. of Glenn H. Parker and Helen M. Parker; m. Niesje Meuter 1954; one s. one d.; ed Michigan State Univ. and California Inst. of Tech.; Instructor, Dept of Math. and Astronomy, Univ. of Utah 1951–53, Asst Prof., Dept of Physics 1953–55; joined Univ. of Chicago 1955, Prof., Dept of Physics 1962–95, Prof., Dept of Astronomy and Astrophysics 1967–95, now S. Chandrasekhar Distinguished Service Prof. Emer.; mem. NAS 1967–, Norwegian Acad. of Sciences 1988–, Int. Astronomical Union; Hon. DSc (Michigan State Univ.) 1975; Dr hc (Utrecht) 1986; Space Science Award, AIAA 1964, John Adam Fleming Award, American Geophysical Union 1968, Henryk Arctowski Medal, NAS 1969, Henry Norris Russell Lecture, American Astronomical Soc. 1969, George Ellery Hale Award, Solar Physics Div. American Astronomical Soc. 1978, Sydney Chapman Medal, Royal Astronomical Soc. 1979, Distinguished Alumnus Award, Calif. Inst. of Tech. 1980, James Arthur Prize Lecture, Harvard Smithsonian Center for Astrophysics 1986, US Nat. Medal of Science 1989, William Bowie Medal, American Geophysical Union 1990, Karl Schwarzschild Medal (FRG) 1990, Gold Medal, Royal Astronomical Soc. 1992, Bruce Medal, Astronomical Soc. of the Pacific 1997, ADION Medal, Observatoire de Nice 1997, James Clark Maxwell Prize, American Physical Soc. 2003, Kyoto Prize, Inamori Foundation 2003, Outstanding Alumni Award, Michigan State Univ. 2004. *Publications include:* Interplanetary Dynamical Processes 1963, Cosmical Magnetic Fields 1979, Spontaneous Current Sheets in Magnetic Fields 1994. *Leisure interests:* hiking, history, wood-carving. *Address:* Department of Astronomy and Astrophysics, University of Chicago, 5640 South Ellis Avenue, Chicago, IL 60637, USA (office). *Telephone:* (773) 702-7847 (office). *Fax:* (773) 702-6645 (office). *E-mail:* parker@odysseus.uchicago.edu (office). *Website:* astro.uchicago.edu (office).

PARKER, Sir (Thomas) John, Kt, GBE, DSc (Eng), FREng; British business executive; *Non-Executive Chairman, Anglo American plc;* b. 8 April 1942, Downpatrick, Northern Ireland; s. of Robert Parker and Margaret Elizabeth Parker (née Bell); m. Emma Elizabeth Blair 1967; one s. one d.; ed Belfast Coll. of Tech., Queen's Univ., Belfast; Ship Design Staff, Harland and Wolff PLC 1963–69, Ship Production Man. 1969–71, Production Drawing Office Man. 1971–72, Sales and Projects Dept Gen. Man. 1972–74; Man. Dir Austin & Pickersgill 1974–78; mem. Bd for Shipbuilding (Marketing and Operations), British Shipbuilders 1978–80, Corpn Deputy Chief Exec. 1980–83; Chair. and CEO Harland and Wolff Holdings PLC 1983–93, Dir (non-exec.) 1993–94; Chair. Harland-MAN Engines 1983–93; mem. Industrial Devt Bd for NI 1983–87; mem. Gen. Cttee Lloyds Register of Shipping 1983– (Chair. Tech. Cttee 1996–); mem. Bd QUBIS 1984–93, British Coal 1986–93; Deputy Chair. Babcock Int. Group PLC 1993–94, Chief Exec. 1993–2000, Chair. 1994–2001; Jt Chair. (non-exec.) Mondi Group (following its demerger from Anglo American plc) –2009; Deputy Chair. DP World (Dubai); Chair. (non-exec.) Lattice Group PLC (merged with National Grid Group to become National Grid Transco PLC 2002, renamed National Grid PLC 2005) 2000–11, Firth Rixson PLC 2001–04, Anglo American plc 2009–; Chair. RMC Group plc 2002–05; Sr Non-Exec. Dir (Chair.) Court of the Bank of England 2005–09; Dir (non-exec.) GKN PLC 1993–2008, BG PLC 1997–2000, Carnival PLC and Carnival Corpn, Inc. 2003–, P&O Princess Cruises PLC (Chair. P&O Group PLC 2005–08), European Aeronautic Defence and Space Co. (EADS) NV 2007–; fmr Dir (non-exec.) British Coal Corpn Brambles Industries plc; Pres. Royal Acad. of Eng; Vice-Pres. Royal Inst. of Naval Architects 1985–93, Pres. 1996–99; Chair. Council of European Shipbuilders Asscn 1993; Chancellor Univ. of Southampton –2011; Visiting Fellow, Univ. of Oxford; Fellow, Inst. of Marine Engineers; Hon. Fellow, Inst. of Marine Eng, Science and Tech. (IMarEST), Royal Inst. of Naval Architects; Hon. DSc (Trinity Coll. Dublin, Ulster, Abertay), Hon. ScD, Hon. DUniv; Man. of the Year Award, Ireland 1986, Inst. of Energy Melchett Medal 2003, and other awards. *Publications:* A Profile of British Shipbuilders 1979, British Shipbuilders: A Period of Constructive Change (Marintec Conf., Shanghai) 1981, The Challenge of Change in Shipbuilding Today (ICCAS '85 Conf., Trieste) 1985. *Leisure interests:* reading, music, ships, sailing. *Address:* Anglo American plc, 20 Carlton House Terrace, London, SW1Y 5AN, England (office). *Telephone:* (20) 7968-8888 (office). *Fax:* (20) 7968-8500 (office). *E-mail:* info@angloamerican.com (office). *Website:* www.angloamerican.com (office).

PARKER, Mark G., BS; American business executive; *Chairman, President and CEO, Nike, Inc.;* b. 21 Oct. 1955, Poughkeepsie, NY; s. of Meg Parker and Bruce Parker; m. Kathy Parker; three c.; ed Pennsylvania State Univ.; Designer and Devt Man., Nike, Inc., Exeter, NH 1979–80, Man. Advanced Product Design, Exeter 1980–81, Dir Design Concepts and Eng 1981–82, Dir Footwear Design 1982–83, Man. Running and Fitness Footwear Marketing 1983–85, Head Special Design Project Teams 1985–87, Divisional Vice-Pres. Footwear Research, Design and Devt 1987–88, Corporate Vice-Pres. Research, Design and Devt 1988–93, Vice-Pres. Consumer Product Marketing 1993–98, Vice-Pres. and Gen. Man. Global Footwear 1998–2001, Pres. Nike Brand 2001–06, CEO and Pres. Nike Inc. 2006–, Chairman 2016–. *Address:* Nike, Inc., 1 Bowerman Drive, Beaverton, OR 97005-6453, USA (office). *Telephone:* (503) 671-6453 (office). *Fax:* (503) 671-6300 (office). *E-mail:* info@nikebiz.com (office). *Website:* www.nike.com (office).

PARKER, Michael D., CBE, BChemEng, MBA; American/British business executive; m. Noreen Parker; one s. one d.; ed Univ. of Manchester and Manchester Business School, UK; joined Dow Chemical Co. 1968, later served with Dow Int. Research and Devt, Freeport, Tex., field sales post, Birmingham, UK 1972, Dist Sales Man. 1975, Product Marketing Man. for Epoxy Resins, Dow Europe, later Dir Marketing for Inorganic Chemicals, then Dir Marketing for Organic Chemicals, Commercial Dir Functional Products Dept, Dow Europe 1983, Gen. Man. Specialty Chemicals Dept, Dow USA, Midland, Mich. 1984, Commercial Vice-Pres. Dow Pacific, Hong Kong 1987, Pres. 1988–93, Group Vice-Pres. (Chemicals and Hydrocarbons) 1993–95, Pres. Dow N America 1995–96, mem. Bd of Dirs 1995, mem. Exec. Cttee Bd, Chair. Corp. Operating Bd, Exec. Vice-Pres. 1996–2000, Pres. and CEO 2000–02, also mem. Bd of Dirs and Exec. Cttee Dow Corning Corpn 2000–02, mem. Mems Cttee of Dow Agrosciences; CEO British Nuclear Fuels plc 2003–09; mem. Bd of Dirs SNC-Lavalin, PV Crystalox Solar PLC, Invensys PLC, Tianhe Chemicals PLC (Sr Ind. Dir); Chair. Liverpool Vision, Street League (charity); Trustee Royal Soc. for the Prevention of Accidents; mem. Manchester Business School Advisory Bd. *Address:* c/o Liverpool Vision, 10th Floor, The Capital, 39 Old Hall Street, Liverpool, L3 9PP, England.

PARKER, Robert M., Jr, BA, LLB; American writer and wine critic; *Publisher, The Wine Advocate;* b. 23 July 1947, Baltimore, Md; m. Patricia Parker 1969; one d.; ed Univ. of Maryland, Univ. of Maryland Law School; Attorney, Sr Attorney and later Asst Gen. Counsel for Farm Credits, Bank of Baltimore 1973–84; Founder,

Writer and Publr The Wine Advocate 1978–; Contributing Ed. Food and Wine Magazine; wine critic for L'Express magazine (first non-French holder of post); Hon. Citizen of Châteauneuf du Pape 1995; Chevalier, Ordre nat. du Mérite 1993, Chevalier, Légion d'honneur 1999, Commendatore, Nat. Order of Merit (Italy) 2002, Officier, Légion d'honneur 2005, Gran Cruz de la Orden del Mérito Civil (Spain) 2011; Loyola Coll. Marylander of the Year Award 1992, James Beard Foundation Wine and Spirits Professional of 1997, Distinguished Alumnus Award, Univ. of Maryland 2006, inducted into Culinary Inst. of America's Vintners Hall of Fame 2013. *Publications include:* Bordeaux (Glenfiddich Award 1986, Int. Asscn of Cooking Professionals Award for second edn 1992, Goldene Feder Award (Germany) for third edn 1993, Moët-Hennessy Wine and Vine Communication Award for French edn 1993) 1985, Parker's Wine Buyer's Guide 1987, The Wines of the Rhône Valley and Provence (Tastemaker's Award, USA 1989, Wine Guild's Wine Book of the Year Award, UK 1989) 1987, Burgundy (Moët-Hennessy Wine and Vine Communication Award for French edn 1993) 1990, World's Greatest Wine Estates: A Modern Perspective 2006, Wines Of The Rhône Valley 2010; contribs to The Field. *Address:* The Wine Advocate, Inc., PO Box 311, Monkton, MD 21111, USA (office). *Telephone:* (410) 329-6477 (office). *Fax:* (410) 357-4504 (office). *E-mail:* wineadvocate@erobertparker.com (office). *Website:* www .erobertparker.com.

PARKER, Sarah Jessica; American actress and fashion designer; b. 25 March 1965, Nelsonville, Ohio; m. Matthew Broderick (q.v.) 1997; one s. two d.; Lifetime Achievement Award (Performing Arts), Guild Hall 2016. *Stage appearances include:* The Innocents 1976, The Sound of Music 1977, Annie 1978, The War Brides 1981, The Death of a Miner 1982, To Gillian on Her 37th Birthday 1983–84, Terry Neal's Future 1986, The Heidi Chronicles 1989, How To Succeed in Business Without Really Trying 1996, Once Upon A Mattress 1996, Wonder of the World 2001. *Films include:* Rich Kids 1979, Somewhere Tomorrow 1983, Firstborn 1984, Footloose 1984, Girls Just Want to Have Fun 1985, Flight of the Navigator 1986, LA Story 1991, Honeymoon in Vegas 1992, Hocus Pocus 1993, Striking Distance 1993, Ed Wood 1994, Miami Rhapsody 1995, If Lucy Fell 1996, Mars Attacks! 1996, The First Wives Club 1996, Extreme Measures 1996, A Life Apart: Hasidism in America 1997, 'Til There Was You 1997, Isn't She Great 1999, Dudley Do-Right 1999, State and Main 2000, Life Without Dick 2001, Strangers with Candy 2005, Family Stone 2005, Failure to Launch 2006, Slammer 2007, Smart People 2008, Sex and the City: The Movie 2008, Did You Hear About the Morgans? 2009, Sex and the City 2 2010, New Year's Eve 2011, Escape from Planet Earth (voice) 2013, All Roads Lead to Rome 2015. *Television includes:* Equal Justice 1990–91, The Sunshine Boys (film) 1995, Sex and the City (four Golden Globe Awards for Best Actress in a TV series 2000, 2001, 2002, 2004, three Screen Actors Guild Awards for Outstanding Performance by a Female Actor in a Comedy Series 2001, 2002, 2004, Emmy Award for Outstanding Comedy Series 2001, Emmy Award for Outstanding Lead Actress in a Comedy 2004) 1998–2004, Stories from My Childhood (series, narrator) 1998, Who Do You Think You Are? 2010, Glee (series) 2012–13, Divorce (series) 2016. *Address:* c/o Jane Berliner, Creative Artists Agency, 2000 Avenue of the Stars, Los Angeles, CA 90067, USA. *Telephone:* (424) 288-2000. *Fax:* (424) 288-2900. *Website:* www.caa.com.

PARKER, Sean N.; American internet industry executive; b. 3 Dec. 1979, Herndon, Va; s. of Bruce Parker and Diane Parker; m. Alexandra Lenas 2013; one s. one d.; Analyst, UUNET 1996–98; co-f. Napster, Inc. (peer-to-peer file-sharing computer service) with Shawn Fanning 1999 (Napster closed down following legal challenges 2001); Founder and Pres. Plaxo, Inc. (online address book and social networking service) 2001–04; Founding Pres., Facebook, Inc. 2004–06, Founder and Chair. Causes on Facebook 2006; Man. Partner, Founders Fund (venture capital fund), San Francisco 2006–14; Co-f. Project Agape 2007; Co-founder and Exec. Chair. Airtime Media Inc. 2010–; Founder and Chair. Economic Innovation Group, Washington, DC; Founder and Pres. Sean N. Parker Foundation (philanthropic fund) 2015–; Exec. Chair. Brigade; mem. Bd of Dirs Spotify 2009–, Gowalla, Ooma, Inc., Yammer 2009–; Oliver R. Grace Award for Distinguished Service in Advancing Cancer Research, Cancer Research Inst. *Address:* Sean N. Parker Foundation, 1 Letterman Drive, Bldg C, # 420, San Francisco, CA 94129-2402, USA (office). *Telephone:* (650) 804-7100 (office). *E-mail:* info@parker.org (office). *Website:* parker.org (office).

PARKER, Trey; American screenwriter, film director and producer; b. (Randolph Severn Parker III), 19 Oct. 1969, Conifer, Colo; collaborated with Matt Stone on short animation, Jesus vs Frosty 1992, later remade as animated Christmas card for FoxLab, titled The Spirit of Christmas 1995; Co-creator and Exec. Producer, South Park animation (with Matt Stone) 1997–, and other films and TV series. *Films include:* Jesus vs Frosty (writer, dir, producer) 1992, American History (writer, dir) (Student Acad. Award) 1992, Your Studio and You (writer, dir) 1995, The Spirit of Christmas (writer, dir, producer) 1995, For Goodness Sake II (dir) 1996, Alferd Packer: The Musical (aka Cannibal! The Musical) (writer, dir, producer) 1996, Orgazmo (writer, dir, producer) 1997, South Park: Bigger Longer & Uncut (writer, dir, producer) (Los Angeles Film Critics Award, New York Film Critics Award, MTV Movie Award) 1999, How's Your News? (exec. producer) 1999, Team America: World Police (writer, dir, producer) 2004. *Film appearances include:* BASEketball 1998, provides voices for many characters in his animation films and television series. *Television includes:* South Park (series writer, dir, producer) 1997–, That's My Bush! (series writer, dir, producer) 2001, Kenny vs Spenny (producer) 2007. *Recordings include:* albums: Chef Aid: The South Park Album, South Park: Bigger, Longer and Uncut (soundtrack), Mr Hankey's Christmas Classics, Timmy and the Lords of the Underworld, The Book of Mormon (Grammy Award for Best Musical Theater Album 2012) 2011. *Play:* The Book of Mormon (Tony Award for Best Musical 2011, WhatsOnStage Award for Best New Musical 2014, Olivier Award for Best New Musical 2014) 2011. *Address:* c/o Paramount Studios, 5555 Melrose Avenue, Hollywood, CA 90038, USA. *E-mail:* news@southparkstudios.com. *Website:* www.southparkstudios.com.

PARKER, W(illiam) Douglas (Doug), BA, MBA; American airline executive; *Chairman and CEO, American Airlines Group, Inc. and American Airlines;* m. Gwen Parker; three c.; ed Albion Coll., Owen Grad. School of Man. at Vanderbilt Univ.; held several financial management positions with American Airlines 1986–91; Vice-Pres. and Asst Treas., and Vice-Pres. of Financial Planning and Analysis, Northwest Airlines 1991–95; Sr Vice-Pres. and Chief Financial Officer,

America West Airlines from 1995, later Exec. Vice-Pres. (Corporate Group) and COO, CEO 2001–05, apptd Chair., Pres. and CEO (merged with US Airways 2005), Chair. and CEO US Airways 2005–13, Chair. and CEO American Airlines Group, Inc. and American Airlines (following merger of US Airways and American Airlines) 2013–; mem. Bd of Dirs, Valley of the Sun United Way. *Address:* American Airlines Group, Inc., PO Box 619616, MD 5675, Dallas/Fort Worth Airport, TX 75261-9616, USA (office). *Telephone:* (817) 963-1234 (office). *Website:* www.aa.com (office).

PARKHOMENKO, Sergey Borisovich; Russian journalist; b. 13 March 1964, Moscow; m.; two s.; ed Moscow State Univ.; Head of Div. Teatre (magazine) 1985–90; political observer, Nezavisimaya Gazeta 1990–92; mem. Bd Segodnya (newspaper) 1993–95; Co-founder Moscow Charter for Journalists 1994; Ed.-in-Chief Itogi (magazine) 1996–2001, IT Weekly (journal) 2002, Real Itogi 2002, Yezhenedel'ny zhurnal 2003, Vokrug sveta 2009–11; elected mem. Russian Opposition Coordination Council 2012; Co-founder League of Voters (opposition movt) 2012, Dissernet 2013; mem. Russian PEN 2014–.

PARKIN, Stuart S. P., MA, PhD, FRS; British physicist and academic; *Director, Max Plank Institute of Microstructure Physics;* b. 9 Dec. 1955, Watford, Herts.; ed Univ. of Cambridge; Research Student, Cavendish Lab., Cambridge 1977; Research Fellow, Trinity Coll., Cambridge 1979–85; Royal Soc. European Exchange Fellowship, Univ. Paris-Sud, Lab. de Physique des Solides, France 1980–81, Visiting Prof. 1988; IBM World Trade Fellowship, IBM Research Lab., Almaden Research Center, San José, Calif., USA 1982, Adjunct Research Staff Mem. 1983, Research Staff Mem. 1984, mem. IBM Acad. of Tech. 1997–, IBM Fellow 1999, Man. of Magnetoelectronics, Dir IBM-Stanford Spintronic Science and Applications Center 2004–15; Consulting Prof., Dept of Applied Physics, Stanford Univ. 1997–2015, Nat. Taiwan Univ. 2007; Dir Max Planck Inst. of Microstructure Physics, Halle 2014–; Prof., Inst. of Physics, Martin Luther Univ. Halle-Wittenberg 2014–; Visiting Chair Prof., Taipei, Taiwan 2007; Distinguished Visiting Prof., Dept of Electrical and Computer Eng, Nat. Univ. of Singapore 2007; Distinguished Research Chair Prof., Nat. Yunlin Univ. of Science and Tech., Douliou, Taiwan; Distinguished Visiting Prof., Eindhoven Univ. of Tech. 2008; mem. Advisory Bd Journal of Physics: Condensed Matter 1993–96; Assoc. Ed. Materials Letters 1993–2006; Chief Ed. Spin Journal 2010; mem. Editorial Advisory Bd Advanced Materials 2008; mem. Admin. Cttee IEEE Magnetics Soc. 2010, Scientific Advisory Bd IFW Dresden, Germany 2010, Standing Cttee on Tech. Insight (TIGER), Nat. Acads 2009, Condensed Matter and Materials Research Cttee, Nat. Acads 2010; mem. NAS 2008, Nat. Acad. of Eng 2009, German Nat. Acad. of Sciences, Leopoldina 2015; Fellow, American Physical Soc., Cambridge Philosophical Soc., Inst. of Physics, London, Materials Research Soc., IEEE, AAAS, American Acad. of Arts and Sciences; Corresp. Fellow, Royal Soc. of Edinburgh 2016; Hon. Prof., Univ. Coll. London 2009, Hon. Fellow, Indian Acad. of Sciences 2012, Trinity Coll., Cambridge 2014; Dr hc (RWTH Aachen Univ.) 2007, (Eindhoven Univ. of Tech.) 2008, (Univ. Regensburg) 2011, (Technische Universität Kaiserslautern) 2013; numerous IBM Patent Achievement Awards, Inst. of Physics Charles Vernon Boys Prize 1991, American Physical Soc. Int. Prize for New Materials 1994, European Physical Soc. Hewlett-Packard Europhysics Prize 1997, American Inst. of Physics Prize for Industrial Application of Physics 1999–2000, R&D Magazine's first Innovator of the Year 2001, Humboldt Research Award 2004, Economist Magazine's 'No Boundaries' Award for Innovation 2007, IEEE Daniel E. Noble Award 2008, Johannes Gutenberg Research Award 2008, IUPAP Magnetism Prize and Neel Medal 2009, Dresden Barkhausen Award 2009, Swan Medal, Inst. of Physics, London 2013, Millennium Tech. Prize 2014. *Publications:* more than 525 scientific papers in refereed journals; 113 issued patents. *Address:* Max Planck Institute of Microstructure Physics, Weinberg 2, 06120 Halle, Germany (office). *Telephone:* (345) 5582657 (Halle) (office). *E-mail:* stuart.parkin@mpi-halle.mpg.de (office); stuart.parkin@icloud.com (office). *Website:* www.mpi-halle.mpg.de (office).

PARKINSON, Bradford W., BS, SM, PhD; American engineer, inventor and academic; *Edward C. Wells Professor Emeritus, School of Engineering, Stanford University;* b. 16 Feb. 1935, Wis.; m. Virginia Parkinson; ed US Naval Acad., MIT, Stanford Univ.; served in USAF 1957–78, retd with rank of Col; instructor, Air Force Test Pilot School, Edwards Air Force Base, Calif.; Head, Dept of Astronautics and Computer Science, USAF Acad., Colo; cr. and managed NAVSTAR GPS Jt Program Office 1972–78; Edward C. Wells Prof. of Aeronautics and Astronautics, W.W. Hansen Experimental Physics Lab., Stanford Univ. 1995–, now Emer.; fmr Prof., Colorado State Univ.; Chair. Bd of Trustees, The Aerospace Corpn; Co-Chair. JPL Advisory Council; Pres. Comm. on Air Safety and Security, Royal Inst. of Navigation (RION); mem. Nat. Acad. of Engineers 1990, AAAS, Int. Acad. of Astronautics 1997, ASME, Nat. Acad. of Eng 2013; Fellow, RION 1990, AIAA 1990, Inst. of Navigation 1999, IEEE 2004; Hon. Fellow, Royal Inst. of Navigation 2015; Legion of Merit; Defense Dept Superior Performance Award for Best Program Dir in USAF 1977, Discover Innovation Award, NASA Distinguished Public Service Medal, IEEE Simon Ramo Award, Von Karman Lectureship and Aerospace Contrib. to Soc. Medal, AIAA, Gold Medal, RION 1983, Engineer of the Year for Silicon Valley, AIAA 1985, Thurlow Award, ION 1986, Kirschner Award, IEEE 1986, Burka Award, ION 1987, Johannes Kepler Award, ION 1991, Distinguished Public Service Medal, NASA 1994, Pioneer Award, AESS/IEEE 1994, GPS Hall of Fame Award, NAVSTAR Jt Program Office 1995, Magellanic Premium Award, American Philosophical Soc. 1997, Sperry Award, IEEE 1998, Hall of FAME, NASA 1998, Discover Innovation Award for Communications, Discover Magazine 2002, Simon Ramo Award, IEEE 2002, Charles Stark Draper Prize, Nat. Acad. of Eng 2003, Gold Medal Award, ASME 2004, Nat. Inventors Hall of Fame 2004, Goddard Astronautics Award, AIAA 2006, Marconi Prize 2016. *Invention:* Global Positioning System (GPS) (co-inventor with Roger L. Easton and Ivan A. Getting). *Publications:* numerous articles in scientific journals; seven US patents. *Address:* W.W. Hansen Experimental Physics Laboratory, Stanford University, Stanford, CA 94305-4085 (home); 2360 Camino Edna, San Luis Obispo, CA 93401, USA (home). *Telephone:* (650) 725-4105 (office). *Fax:* (650) 725-8312 (office). *E-mail:* brad.parkinson@stanford.edu (office). *Website:* profiles .stanford.edu/bradford-parkinson (office).

PARKINSON, Mark Vincent, BA, JD; American lawyer, politician and business executive; *President and CEO, American Health Care Association and National*

Center for Assisted Living (AHCA/NCAL); b. 24 June 1957, Wichita, Kan.; s. of Henry Filson and Barbara Ann Horton (née Gilbert); m. Stacy Abbott 1983; three s.; ed Wichita Heights High School, Wichita State Univ., Univ. of Kansas; Assoc., Payne & Jones (law firm), Olathe, Kan. 1984–86; Co-founder and Partner, Parkinson, Foth & Reynolds (law firm) 1986–96; mem. Kan. State House of Reps 1990–92, Kan. State Senate 1992–96; Chair. Kan. Republican Party 1999–2003; mem. Democratic Party 2006–; Lt-Gov. of Kan. 2007–09, Gov. of Kan. 2009–11; Pres. and CEO American Health Care Asscn and Nat. Center for Assisted Living (AHCA/NCAL) 2011–; Chair. Shawnee Area Chamber of Commerce 2004–05; mem. ABA, Kansas Bar Asscn, Johnson Co. Bar Foundation (fmr Pres.), Kansas Mentors Leadership Council; named by Topeka Capital Journal as Kansan of the Year 2009, Caring Award, Kan. Advocates for Better Care 2010. *Leisure interests:* travel, running, films. *Address:* American Health Care Association, 1201 L Street, NW, Washington, DC 20005, USA (office). *Telephone:* (202) 842-4444 (office). *Fax:* (202) 842-3860 (office). *E-mail:* info@ahcancal.org (office). *Website:* www.ahcancal .org (office).

PARKINSON, Sir Michael, Kt, CBE; British television and radio presenter and writer; b. 28 March 1935, Barnsley; m. Mary Heneghan 1959; three s.; ed Barnsley Grammar School; began career as journalist with local paper, then worked on The Guardian, Daily Express, Sunday Times, Punch, The Listener, others; joined Granada TV as interviewer/reporter 1965; joined 24 Hours (BBC) as reporter; Exec. Producer and Presenter, London Weekend TV 1968; Presenter Cinema 1969–70, Tea Break, Where in the World 1971, host own chat show 'Parkinson' 1971–82, 1998–2004, The Boys of '66 1981, Presenter TV-AM 1983–84, Give Us a Clue 1984–92, All Star Secrets 1984–86, The Skag Kids 1985, Desert Island Discs (BBC Radio 4) 1986–88, The Help Squad 1991–92, Ghostwatch 1992, Parkinson on Sport (BBC Radio 5) 1994–97, Going for a Song 1995–99, A League Apart, 100 Years of Rugby League (BBC 2) 1995, Parkinson: The Interviews 1995–97, Parkinson's Sunday Supplement (BBC Radio 2) 1996–2007, Auntie's All-Time Greats 1997, Parkinson's Choice (BBC Radio 2) 1999–2004; columnist for Daily Mirror 1986–90, for Daily Telegraph 1991–2007; Parkinson One-to-One 1987–88; Parkinson (ITV) 2004–07; Ed. Catalyst 1988; has worked extensively on Australian TV; Founder and Dir Pavilion Books 1980–97; Pres. Sports Journalists' Asscn 2005–15; Chancellor, Nottingham Trent Univ. 2008–14; Dr hc (Lincs. and Humberside) 1999; Sports Feature Writer of the Year, British Sports Journalism Awards 1995, 1998, Fellow, BFI for contrib. to TV 1997, Yorks. Man of the Year 1998, Sony Radio Award 1998, Sports Writer of the Year, British Press Award 1998, BAFTA Award for Best Light Entertainment (for 'Parkinson') 1999, Media Soc. Award for Distinguished Contrib. to Media 2000. *Publications include:* Football Daft 1968, Cricket Mad 1969, Sporting Fever 1974, George Best: An Intimate Biography 1975, A–Z of Soccer (Jt author) 1975, Bats in the Pavilion 1977, The Woofits 1980, Parkinson's Lore 1981, The Best of Parkinson 1982, Sporting Lives 1992, Sporting Profiles 1995, Michael Parkinson on Golf 1999, Michael Parkinson on Football 2001, Parky: My Autobiography 2008. *Leisure interests:* cricket, golf. *Website:* www.michaelparkinson.tv.

PARKS, Suzan-Lori, BA; American playwright and academic; *Arts Professor, Rita and Burton Goldberg Department of Dramatic Writing, Tisch School of the Arts, New York University;* b. 10 May 1963, Fort Knox, Ky; m. Paul Oscher; ed John Carroll School, Mount Holyoke Coll.; Guggenheim Foundation Fellow 2000; Master Writer Chair., Public Theater, New York 2008–; taught at California Inst. of the Arts, Yale School of Drama; Arts Prof., Goldberg Dept of Dramatic Writing, Tisch School of the Arts, New York Univ. 2008–; Master Writer Chair, Public Theater, New York; Dr hc (Brown Univ.) 2004; Herb Alpert Award in the Arts 1996, John Simon Guggenheim Foundation fellowship 2000, MacArthur Foundation Award 2001, Eugene McDermott Award in the Arts, Council for the Arts at MIT 2006, Academy of Achievement Golden Plate Award 2007, Dorothy and Lillian Gish Prize 2015, Windham-Campbell Prize for Drama 2018, Steinberg Distinguished Playwright Award 2018. *Plays include:* The Sinner's Place 1984, Imperceptible Mutabilities in the Third Kingdom (Obie Award for Best New American Play) 1989, Betting on the Dust Commander 1990, The Death of the Last Black Man in the Whole Entire World 1990, Devotees in the Garden of Love 1992, The America Play 1994, Venus 1996, In the Blood 1999, Fucking A 2000, Topdog/ Underdog (Pulitzer Prize for Drama 2002) 2001, 365 Days/365 Plays 2006, Ray Charles Live! A New Musical (NAACP Theatre Award 2008) 2007, Father Comes Home from the Wars (Parts 1, 2 and 3) (Edward M. Kennedy Prize for Drama Inspired by American History 2015) 2009, The Book of Grace 2010. *Plays for radio:* Pickling 1990, Third Kingdom 1990, Locomotive 1991. *Screenplays:* Girl 6 1996, Their Eyes Were Watching God 2005, The Great Debaters (co-writer) 2007. *Publication:* Getting Mother's Body: A Novel 2003. *Address:* Rita and Burton Goldberg Department of Dramatic Writing, 721 Broadway, New York, NY 10003, USA (office). *Telephone:* (212) 998-1940 (office). *E-mail:* slp7@nyu.edu (office). *Website:* tisch.nyu.edu/dramatic-writing (office). www.suzanloriparks.com.

PARKS, Timothy Harold, BA, MA; British writer, educator and translator; *Professor of English Literature, Università IULM, Milan;* b. 19 Dec. 1954, Manchester, England; m. Rita Baldassare; three d.; ed Univ. of Cambridge, Harvard Univ., USA; teacher of trans. studies, Università IULM, Milan, Prof. of English Literature 2006–; mem. Authors' Soc.; Somerset Maugham Award 1986, Betty Trask Prize 1986, Rhys Prize 1986, John Floria Prize for Best Trans. from Italian. *Publications include:* novels: Tongues of Flame 1985, Loving Roger 1986, Home Thoughts 1987, Family Planning 1989, Cara Massimina 1990, Goodness 1991, Italian Neighbours 1992, Juggling the Stars 1993, Shear 1993, Mimi's Ghost 1995, An Italian Education 1996, Europa 1997, Adultery and Other Diversions 1999, Destiny 2000, A Season with Verona 2002, Judge Savage 2003, Rapids 2005, Cleaver 2006, Dreams of Rivers and Seas 2008, Sex is Forbidden (The Server) 2012; short stories: Keeping Distance 1988, The Room 1992; non-fiction: Translating Style: The English Modernists and their Italian Translations 1999, Hell and Back: Reflections on Writers and Writing from Dante to Rushdie 2001, Medici Money: Banking, Metaphysics and Art in Fifteenth-Century Florence 2005, The Fighter 2007, Teach Us to Sit Still 2010, Italian Ways: On and Off the Rails from Milan to Palermo 2013; numerous trans. from Italian; contrib. of numerous articles, reviews and talks to BBC Radio 3. *Address:* Istituto di Anglistica, Università IULM, Via Carlo Bo, 20143 Milan, Italy (office). *Website:* tim-parks .com.

PARMELIN, Guy; Swiss wine producer and politician; *Member, Federal Council and Head of Federal Department of Defence, Civil Protection and Sports;* b. 9 Nov. 1959, Bursins; m. Caroline Parmelin; ed Ecole cantonale d'agriculture de Marcelin; wine producer, Vaud canton; mem. Grand Conseil de Vaud (cantonal legislature) 1994–2003; mem. Nat. Council 2003–15, mem. Social Security and Health Cttee, Environment, Spatial Planning and Energy Cttee; mem. Fed. Council 2016–, Head, Fed. Dept of Defence, Civil Protection and Sports 2016–; Vice-Chair. Fed. of Swiss Agricultural Cooperatives (FENACO); mem. Swiss People's Party (SVP), Pres. Vaud Canton SVP 2000–04. *Leisure interests:* classical music, opera. *Address:* Federal Department of Defence, Civil Protection and Sports, Schwanengasse 2, 3003 Bern, Switzerland (office). *Telephone:* 584622111 (office). *E-mail:* postmaster.vbs@gs-vbs.admin.ch (office). *Website:* www.vbs.admin .ch (office); www.guyparmelin.ch.

PARMIGGIANI, Claudio; Italian artist; b. 1 March 1943, Lussara, Reggio Emilia; ed Istituto Statale di Belle Arti, Modena; first solo exhbn at Libreria Feltrinelli, Bologna 1965; progression from conceptual works, including installations, photo-works and books, towards use of assemblage; first Delocazioni appear 1970, works realized with use of powder, fire and smoke; realized series of works using plaster models of ancient works of art early 1960s; among the more significant later works are the Iconostasi of statues and veiled canvases 1980s (presented for the first time at Galleria Stein, Milan 1989); realized Il faro d'Islanda (perm. work) in most deserted part of Iceland 2000; realized Teatro dell'arte e della guerra in Teatro Farnese in Parma (labyrinth of shattered crystals) 2006; most recent work includes Ex-voto at Louvre Museum; lives and works in Bologna. *Address:* c/o Galerie Serge Leborgne, 108 rue Vieille-du-Temple, Paris - 3, France (office). *Telephone:* 1-42-74-53-57 (office).

PARNELL, Sean R., BBA, JD; American lawyer and politician; b. 19 Nov. 1962, Hanford, Calif.; s. of Pat Parnell and Thelma Parnell; m. Sandra Parnell 1987; two d.; ed East Anchorage High School, Pacific Lutheran Univ., Univ. of Puget Sound School of Law (now Seattle Univ. School of Law); family moved to Alaska aged 10; attorney 1987–, admitted to practise law in Alaska and Washington, DC; owned small law practice in Anchorage for many years; mem. Alaska State House of Reps 1992–96 (re-elected 1994), mem. Finance Cttee; mem. Alaska State Senate 1996–2000, mem. Energy Council, served on and then co-chaired Senate Finance Cttee and numerous budget sub-cttees; left Senate to become Dir of Governmental Relations in Alaska for Conoco Phillips oil co.; joined lobbying firm Patton Boggs (had earlier represented Exxon Mobil in Exxon Valdez oil spill litigation) 2005–06; adviser on oil and gas issues to Gov. Sarah Palin 2006–09; Lt-Gov. of Alaska 2008–09; campaigned to be elected to US House of Reps 2008; Gov. of Alaska 2009–14; f. Navigate North Consultants, Anchorage 2015; f. pvt. law practice in Palmer, Alaska 2015; Republican. *Leisure interest:* outdoor activities. *Address:* Law Offices of Sean R. Parnell, PC, 610 South Bailey Street, Suite 200, Palmer, AK 99645, USA (office). *Telephone:* (907) 746-9700 (office). *E-mail:* information@ parnellaklaw.com (office). *Website:* www.parnellaklaw.com (office).

PAROLIN, HE Cardinal Pietro; Italian ecclesiastic and diplomatist; *Secretary of State, Roman Curia;* b. 17 Jan. 1955, Schiavon, Prov. of Vicenza; ed Pontifical Gregorian Univ., Pontifical Ecclesiastical Acad.; ordained priest of Vicenza 1980; entered diplomatic service of Holy See 1986, served for three years in Nunciature of Nigeria, in Nunciature of Mexico 1989–92, Country Dir for Spain, Andorra, Italy, San Marino, Apostolic Nuncio to Venezuela 2009–13; Undersecretary for Relations with States 2002–09; consecrated by Pope Benedict XVI 2009; Titular Archbisop of Aquipendium 2009–; Pres. Interdicasterial Comm. on Particular Churches 2013–, Interdicasterial Comm. for the Church in Eastern Europe 2013–; Protector of Pontifical Ecclesiastical Acad. 2013–; Sec. of State 2013–; cr. Cardinal (Cardinal-Priest of Santi Simone e Giuda Taddeo a Torre Angela) 2014–; Kt Grand Cross, Order of Merit of the Italian Repub. 2005. *Address:* Secretariat of State, Palazzo Apostolico Vaticano, 00120 Città del Vaticano, Rome, Italy (office). *Telephone:* (06) 69883913 (office). *Fax:* (06) 69885255 (office). *Website:* www .vatican.va/roman_curia/secretariat_state (office).

PAROUBEK, Jiří, MA; Czech politician (retd); b. 21 Aug. 1952, Olomouc; m. 1st Zuzana Paroubková 1979 (divorced 2007); m. 2nd Petra Paroubková 2007; one s. one d.; ed Prague School of Econs; economist, pvt. sector 1976–90; Sec.-Gen. Czechoslovak Social Democrats 1990; financial consultant 1991–98; various positions in the Czech Social Democratic Party (CSSD) Prague Regional Exec. 1993–95, Vice-Chair. 2001–03, Vice-Chair. CSSD 2005–06, Chair. 2006–10; Deputy Mayor for Finance, Prague 1998–2004; Minister of Regional Devt 2004–05; Prime Minister of Czech Repub. 2005–06; Chair. Editorial Bd, Trend; contrib. to several daily newspapers; f. Nat. Socialists—21st Century Left 2011–13; retd from politics 2014. *Website:* www.paroubek.cz.

PARRA GIL, Antonio; Ecuadorean lawyer, politician and diplomatist; ed Univ. of Salamanca; fmr Asst Sec. of State in Ministries of Educ. and Public Works; Minister of Foreign Affairs 2004–05; Amb. to Spain 2005–07.

PARRATT, James Roy, DSc, DSc (Med), PhD, FRSE, FESC, FRCPath, FRPharmS; British professor of cardiovascular pharmacology; *Professor Emeritus, University of Strathclyde;* b. 19 Aug. 1933, London, England; s. of James J. Parratt and Eunice E. King; m. Pamela J. Lyndon 1957; two s. one d.; ed St Clement Danes Holborn Estate Grammar School, London and Univ. of London; Nigerian School of Pharmacy 1958–61; Dept of Physiology, Univ. Coll. Ibadan, Nigeria 1961–67; Univ. of Strathclyde, Glasgow 1967–, Reader 1970, Personal Prof. 1975, Prof. of Cardiovascular Pharmacology 1983–, now Prof. Emer., Head, Dept of Physiology and Pharmacology 1986–90, Chair. School of Pharmacy and Pharmacology 1988; Visiting Prof. Albert-Szent-Györgyi Medical Univ., Szeged 1995–; Vice-Pres. European Shock Soc.; mem. Council, Int. Soc. for Heart Research (European Section); Emer. Fellow, Leverhulme Trust 2002–03; Szent-Györgyi Research Fellow, Szeged Univ. 2003; Fellow, Royal Pharmacology Soc., Inst. of Biology, Int. Soc. for Heart Research; Hon. mem. Hungarian Pharmacological Soc., Slovak Medical and Cardiological Socs, Czech Cardiological Soc.; Hon. MD (Albert-Szent-Gyorgyi Univ. Medical School); Gold Medal, Univ. of Szeged, Hungary, Gold J.E. Purkyne Medal, Acad. of Sciences of the Czech Repub. *Leisure interests:* active within Baptist denomination in Scotland and in Christian mission, music. *Address:* Strathclyde Institute of Pharmacy and Biomedical Sciences, University of Strathclyde, 161 Cathedral Street, Glasgow, G4 0RE (office); 16 Russell Drive,

Bearsden, Glasgow, G61 3BD, Scotland (home). *Telephone:* (141) 548-2125 (office); (141) 942-7164 (home). *E-mail:* j.r.parratt@strath.ac.uk (office). *Website:* spider .science.strath.ac.uk/sipbs/staff.php?limit=emeritus (office).

PARRIS, Matthew Francis, BA, MA; British author, broadcaster and fmr politician; b. 7 Aug. 1949, Johannesburg, S Africa; s. of Leslie F. Parris and Theresa E. Parris (née Littler); civil partnership with Julian Glover; ed Waterford School, Swaziland, Clare Coll., Cambridge and Yale Univ.; FCO 1974–76; with Conservative Research Dept 1976–79; MP (Conservative) for W Derbyshire 1979–86; Parl. Sketch Writer for The Times 1988–2001; columnist, The Times 1988–, The Spectator 1992–; mem. Broadcasting Standards Council 1992–97, Bd of Index On Censorship 2008–16; various awards for writing and journalism. *Radio includes:* presenter, Great Lives series (BBC Radio 4) 2007–. *Television includes:* presenter, Weekend World (LWT) 1986–88. *Publications:* Inca Kola (travel) 1990, Chance Witness (memoir) 2001, expanded and updated edn 2013, Great Parliamentary Scandals (with Kevin Maguire) 2004, A Castle in Spain 2005, Mission Accomplished (with Phil Mason) 2007, Scorn 2008, Parting Shots (with Andrew Bryson) 2010, The Spanish Ambassador's Suitcase, and Other Stories (with Andrew Bryson) 2012; various books about politics, insult and scandal; various collections of journalism. *Address:* The Spout, Gratton, Bakewell, Derbyshire, DE45 1LN; c/o The Times, Pennington Street, London, E1 9XN, England.

PARROTT, Andrew Haden, BA; British conductor and musicologist; *Artistic Director, Taverner Consort, Choir and Players;* b. 10 March 1947, Walsall, W Midlands, England; s. of R. C. Parrott and E. D. Parrott; m. 1st Emma Kirkby 1971; m. 2nd Emily Van Evera 1986; one d.; ed Queen Mary's Grammar School, Walsall, Merton Coll., Oxford; Dir of Music, Merton Coll., Oxford 1969–71; Founder, Conductor and Artistic Dir, Taverner Consort, Choir and Players 1973–; Music Dir and Prin. Conductor, London Mozart Players 2000–06; Music Dir, New York Collegium 2002–10; BBC Promenade Concerts debut 1977; fmr musical asst to Sir Michael Tippett; freelance orchestral and operatic conductor; occasional writer, lecturer and continuo player; Open Postmastership, Merton Coll. 1966–69; Leverhulme Fellowship 1984–85; Hon. Research Fellow, Royal Holloway, Univ. of London 1995; Hon. Sr Research Fellow, Univ. of Birmingham 2000–; York Early Music Festival Lifetime Achievement 2014. *Recordings include:* more than 60 recordings of medieval and renaissance music and major works by Monteverdi, Purcell, Vivaldi, Bach, Handel, Mozart, Beethoven and 20th-century composers, including Trauer-Music for Prince Leopold 2011, Monteverdi's L'Orfeo 2013, Taverner's Western Wind mass 2016 (Gramophone Award). *Publications include:* New Oxford Book of Carols (co-ed.) 1992, The Essential Bach Choir 2000 (German edn 2003), Composers' Intentions? 2015; articles in Early Music and other journals. *Address:* c/o Rayfield Allied, Southbank House, Black Prince Road, London, SE1 7SJ, England (office). *Telephone:* (20) 3176-5500 (office). *E-mail:* info@rayfieldallied.com (office). *Website:* www.rayfieldallied.com/artists/andrew -parrott (office).

PARROTT, Jasper William, BA; British impresario and agent; *Executive Chairman and Head of Tours/Projects, Harrison/Parrott Limited;* b. 8 Sept. 1944, Stockholm, Sweden; s. of Prof. Sir Cecil Parrott and of Lady Parrott; m. Cristina Ortiz; two d.; ed Tonbridge School, Peterhouse Cambridge; joined Ibbs & Tillett Ltd 1965–69; f. Harrison Parrott Ltd 1969, Chair. and Jt Man. Dir 1987–2013, Exec. Chair. and Head of Tours/Projects 2013–; Dir Japan Festival 1991, Swiss Festival in UK 1991; Dir Rambert Dance Co. 1993–98; Hon. Trustee Kew Foundation, Royal Botanical Gardens 1991–; Co-Dir Simdi Now, Turkish Festival of Arts, Berlin 2004; Int. Adviser, Sakip Sabanci Museum, Istanbul 2005–07; Dir Polyarts UK 2004–; consultant, The Icelandic Nat. Concert and Conf. Centre 2007–11. *Publication:* Beyond Frontiers: Vladimir Ashkenazy. *Leisure interests:* reading, theatre, history, tennis, landscape and water gardening, languages. *Address:* Harrison/Parrott Ltd, 5–6 Albion Court, Albion Place, London, W6 0QT, England (office). *Telephone:* (20) 7313-3527 (office). *Fax:* (20) 7221-5042 (office). *E-mail:* jp@harrisonparrott.co.uk (office). *Website:* www .harrisonparrott.com (office).

PARRY, Eric Owen, MA, RA, RIBA; British architect; *Principal, Eric Parry Architects;* b. 24 March 1952, Kuwait; s. of Eric Parry and Marion Parry; ed Univ. of Newcastle upon Tyne, Royal Coll. of Art, London, Architectural Asscn, London; Founder and Prin. Eric Parry Architects 1983–, est. Eric Parry Assocs 1983, including Eric Parry Architects Ltd 1990; Lecturer, Univ. of Cambridge 1983–97, Harvard Univ. Grad. School of Design 1988, Univ. of Houston 1988, 1990, Tokyo Inst. of Tech. 1996; mem. RIBA Awards Group 2001–04, Chair. 2002–04; mem. Arts Council of England (ACE) Architecture Unit 1991–2003, ACE Lottery Architecture Advisory Cttee 1991–99, ACE Visual Arts Panel 1996–2003; mem. Council, Architectural Asscn 1995– (Pres. 2005–07); mem. Royal Acad. Architecture Cttee, RIBA Library Cttee, Canterbury Cathedral Fabric Advisory Cttee, Council of the British School at Rome, Mayor's Design Advisory Group; External Examiner, Univ. of Kent at Canterbury, John Moore's Univ., Cardiff Univ. and Univ. Coll., London; Hon. mem. Librarian Architectural Asscn; Hon. Dr of Arts (Bath) 2012. *Architectural works include:* Artists' Studio, London 1986–88, Stockley Park Office Bldg W3, London 1989–91, Foundress Court, Pembroke Coll. Cambridge (RIBA Award 1998) 1993–98, Damai Suria Luxury Apartments, Kuala Lumpur 1996–97, Southwark Information Centre, London Bridge (RIBA Award 1999) 1997–99, Mandarin Oriental, Hyde Park, London (FX Int. Interior Award for the Spa 2001) 1997–2000, 30 Finsbury Square, London 1999–2002, King Edward Court, Paternoster Square (HQ for London Stock Exchange) 2000–03, St Martin-in-the-Fields, London 2002–08, 50 New Bond Street and 14 St George Street, London 2004–09, 5 Aldermanbury Square, London EC2 2007, Eagle Place, London, SW1 2008–13, 7–8 St James's Square, London 2010–15, Holburne Museum of Art extension, Bath 2011. *Publications include:* On Certain Possibilities of the Irrational Embellishment of a Town (co-author with Peter Carl) 1999, Eric Parry Architects Vol. 1 2002, Eric Parry Architects Vol. 2 2012, Context: Architecture and the Genius of Place 2015. *Leisure interests:* walking, drawing, general cultural pursuits. *Address:* Eric Parry Architects Ltd, 28–42 Banner Street, London, EC1Y 8QE, England (office). *Telephone:* (20) 7608-9600 (office). *Fax:* (20) 7608-9601 (office). *E-mail:* eric.p@ericparryarchitects.co.uk (office). *Website:* www.ericparryarchitects.co.uk (office).

PARRY, Martin, OBE, PhD; British environmentalist and academic; *Visiting Professor, Centre for Environmental Policy, Imperial College London;* b. 12 Dec. 1945; s. of John Fyson Parry and Frances Joan Stewart; m. Cynthia Jane Mueller 1968; two d.; ed Durham and West Indies Univs, Univ of Edinburgh; Lecturer, Univ of Birmingham 1973–85, Sr Lecturer 1986–88, Reader in Resource Management 1988–89, Prof. of Environmental Management 1989–91; Prof. of Environmental Man. and Dir Oxford Univ. Environmental Change Unit 1991–94, also Professorial Fellow, Linacre Coll.; Prof. of Environmental Man., Dept of Geography, Univ. Coll. London 1996–99, also Dir Jackson Environment Inst.; Prof. of Environmental Science and Dir Jackson Environment Inst., Univ. of East Anglia 1999–2002; Co-Chair. Working Group II, Intergovernmental Panel on Climate Change (IPCC) 2002–08; Visiting Prof., Centre for Environmental Policy, Imperial Coll. London, also Visiting Fellow, Graham Inst.; Project Dir Climate Impacts Project, Int. Inst. for Applied Systems Analysis, Laxenburg, Austria 1983–85; Chair. UK Climate Change Review Group 1989–96; Ed. Global Environmental Change (journal) 1992–2004; Peek Award, Royal Geographical Soc. 1991, Gerbier-Mumm Int. Award, WMO 1993. *Publications:* Climatic Change, Agric. and Settlement 1976, Climate Change and World Agriculture 1990, Economic Implications of Climate Change in Britain 1995. *Leisure interests:* riding, sailing. *Address:* Centre for Environmental Policy, Imperial College London, Natural Sciences Building, 13 Prince's Gardens, South Kensington Campus, London, SW7 2AZ, England (office). *E-mail:* m.parry@imperial.ac.uk (office); martin@mlparry .com. *Website:* www.imperial.ac.uk/environmental-policy (office); www.mlparry .com.

PARSEKAR, Laxmikant Yashwant, BEd, MSc; Indian politician; b. 4 July 1956, Harmal village, Pernem region, Goa; s. of Yashwant Parsekar and Smt. Chandrabhaga Parsekar; m.; ed Bombay Univ.; started career as volunteer for Rashtriya Swayamsevak Sangh (RSS) (non-govt org.), Pernem region; fmr Prin., Harmal Panchakroshi Secondary School, Harmal; began working for Bharatiya Janata Party (BJP) late 1980s, Sec. BJP Goa Unit 1989–90, Gen. Sec. 1994–99, Pres. BJP Goa Unit 2010–12; mem. Goa Legis. Ass. from Mandrem constituency 2002–17, Chair. Budget Cttee 2002–04, Petitions Cttee 2004–05, Library Cttee 2010–11; Goa State Minister of Health, Panchayat and Rural Devt 2012–14; Chief Minister of Goa 2014–17 (resgnd).

PARSON, Michael L. (Mike); American politician and fmr law enforcement officer; *Governor of Missouri;* b. 17 Sept. 1955, Wheatland, Missouri; m. Teresa Parson; one s. one d.; ed Univ. of Maryland, Univ. of Hawai'i at Mānoa; served in US Army 1975–81; fmr gasoline station owner and farmer; Sheriff, Polk County, Iowa 1992–2004; mem., Missouri House of Reps. (Republican) 2005–11, mem. several cttees including Chair., House Cttee on Rules 2004, on Governmental Accountability and Fiscal Oversight 2013–14, Vice-Chair., Small Business, Insurance and Industry Cttee 2011–14, Chair. 2015; Lt-Gov. of Mo. 2017–18, Gov. 2018–; mem. Bd, Jobs for America's Graduates 2018–; mem. American Legion, Nat. Rifle Asscn, Nat. Sheriffs' Asscn; Republican. *E-mail:* mike@ mikeparson.com (office). *Website:* www.mikeparson.com (office); governor.mo.gov (office). *Address:* Office of the Governor, 201 W Capitol Avenue, Room 216, POB 720, Jefferson City, MO 65102, USA (office). *Telephone:* (573) 751-3222 (office).

PARSONS, Charles Dacre, PhD; American philosopher and academic; *Edgar Pierce Professor Emeritus of Philosophy, Harvard University;* b. 13 April 1933, Cambridge, Mass; s. of Talcott Parsons and Helen Walker Parsons; m. Marjorie Louise Wood 1968; one s. one d.; ed Harvard Coll., King's Coll., Cambridge, UK, Harvard Univ.; Jr Fellow, Soc. of Fellows, Harvard Univ. 1958–61, Santayana Fellow 1964–65; Asst Prof. of Philosophy, Cornell Univ. 1961–62, Harvard Univ. 1962–65; Assoc. Prof. of Philosophy, Columbia Univ. 1965–69, Prof. 1969–89, Chair. Dept of Philosophy 1976–79, 1985–89; Prof. of Philosophy, Harvard Univ. 1989–91, Edgar Pierce Prof. of Philosophy 1991–2005, Prof. Emer. 2005–; Visiting Prof. of Philosophy, UCLA 2002, 2005, 2007, 2009; Ed. The Journal of Philosophy 1966–90, Consulting Ed. 1990–; Sec. Asscn for Symbolic Logic 1971–76, Vice-Pres. 1986–89, Pres. 1989–92; Vice-Pres. Institut Int. de Philosophie 2012–15; Foreign mem. Norwegian Acad. of Science and Letters 2002–; Fellow, Nat. Endowment for the Humanities 1979–80, American Acad. of Arts and Sciences 1982–, Center for Advanced Study in The Behavioral Sciences 1994–95; Guggenheim Fellow 1986–87. *Publications:* Mathematics in Philosophy 1983, Kurt Gödel, Collected Works, Vols III–V (co-ed.) 1995, 2003, Mathematical Thought and its Objects 2008, Hao Wang, Logician and Philosopher (co-ed.) 2011, From Kant to Husserl 2012, Philosophy of Mathematics in the Twentieth Century 2014; articles on logic and philosophy. *Address:* Department of Philosophy, Emerson Hall, Harvard University, Cambridge, MA 02138 (office); 22 Hancock Street, Cambridge, MA 02139, USA (home). *Telephone:* (617) 495-2191 (office). *E-mail:* parsons2@fas.harvard.edu (office). *Website:* philosophy.fas.harvard.edu/people/charles-parsons (office).

PARSONS, Nigel; British media executive; *Senior Partner, NZN Media Consultants;* b. 27 May 1951, Dorset, England; Lt Col Parsons and Mrs F. A. Parsons; m. Zoulfia Parsons; four c.; ed Framlingham Coll., Suffolk, Portsmouth Univ. (Certificate of Journalism); previous roles as journalist/producer at BBC Radios 1–4, BBC World Service Radio and TV and WTN (Worldwide Television News), conceived and oversaw launch of global broadcaster Al Jazeera English, also managed TV start-up news network teams, EBC in Switzerland, Middle East Broadcasting and Telecampione in Italy; Vice-Pres. (Eastern European and fmr USSR markets), WTN; Dir of Associated Press TV News (APTN, cr. when Associated Press bought WTN); Man. Dir Al Jazeera English, Doha, Qatar 2004–09; Sr Partner, NZN Media Consultants 2009–11; CEO Continental Broadcasting Ltd, Lagos, Nigeria 2011–16; Sr Partner, NZN Media Consultants 2016–. *Leisure interests:* reading, skiing, diving. *Address:* 456 Merton Road, London, SW18 5AE, England (office). *Telephone:* 7768-728234 (mobile) (office). *E-mail:* nigel.parsons@gmail.com (home).

PARSONS, Peter John, MA, FBA; British academic (retd); b. 24 Sept. 1936, Surbiton, Surrey, England; s. of Robert John Parsons and Ethel Ada Parsons (née Frary); m. Barbara Montagna Macleod 2006; ed Raynes Park County Grammar School and Christ Church, Oxford; Lecturer in Documentary Papyrology, Univ. of Oxford 1960–65, Lecturer in Papyrology 1965–89, Regius Prof. of Greek 1989–2003, now Prof. Emer., Student (Fellow), Christ Church, Oxford 1964–2003; J. H. Gray Lecturer, Univ. of Cambridge 1982; Hon. PhD (Berne) 1985, (Athens) 1995; Hon. DLitt (Milan) 1994. *Publications:* The Oxyrhynchus Papyri (jtly) Vols XXXI 1966, XXXIII and XXXIV 1968, LIV 1987, LIX 1992, LX 1994, LXVI 1999, LXVIII 2003, (solely) Vol. XLII 1973, Supplementum

Hellenisticum (with H. Lloyd-Jones) 1983, City of the Sharp-nosed Fish 2007; articles in learned journals. *Leisure interests:* music, cinema, cooking, eating. *Address:* Ioannou Centre for Classical and Byzantine Studies, 66, St Giles, Oxford, OX1 3LU, England (office). *Telephone:* (1865) 422132 (home). *E-mail:* peter.parsons@classics.ox.ac.uk (office).

PARSONS, Richard (Dick) Dean, JD; American lawyer and business executive; *Senior Advisor, Providence Equity Partners LLC;* b. 4 April 1948, Brooklyn, NY; m. Laura Ann Bush; three c.; ed Univ. of Hawaii, Albany Law School, Union Univ.; began career with various positions in state and fed. service, including counsel for NY Gov. Nelson Rockefeller and Sr White House aide under Pres. Gerald Ford; Founder and Man. Partner, Patterson, Belknap, Webb & Tyler 1979–88; COO Dime Bancorp Inc. 1988–90, Chair. 1990–94; joined Time Warner Inc., mem. Bd of Dirs 1991–2008, apptd Pres. 1995, Co-COO –2002, CEO 2002–07, Chair. 2003–08; mem. Bd of Dirs Citigroup Inc. 1996–2012, Lead Dir and Chair. Nomination and Governance Cttee –2009, Chair. Citigroup Inc. 2009–12; Sr Advisor, Providence Equity Partners LLC 2009–; apptd interim CEO Los Angeles Clippers professional basketball team 2014; Chair.-elect Bd of Trustees, The Rockefeller Foundation Board 2015–16, Chair. 2016–; Chair. Jazz Foundation of America 2007–, Apollo Theatre Foundation; Co-Chair. Pres.'s Comm. to Strengthen Social Security 2001; Chair. Emer., New York City Partnership; Co-Chair. Advisory Bd Smithsonian Inst. of African American History and Culture, New York City Comm. for Econ. Opportunity; econ. adviser, Pres. Barack Obama's transition team 2008–09; mem. Bd of Dirs Estée Lauder, Teach for America; mem. Pres.'s Council on Jobs and Competitiveness; mem. Bd of Dirs Comm. on Presidential Debates; Trustee, Museum of Modern Art, American Museum of Natural History. *Address:* Providence Equity Partners LLC, 9 West 57th Street, Suite 4700, New York, NY 10019, USA (office). *Telephone:* (212) 588-6700 (office). *E-mail:* info@jazzfoundation.org (office). *Website:* www.provequity.com (office).

PARSURAMEN, Armoogum (Dassen), GOSK, BA (Hons); Mauritian politician and international organization official; *Founder-President, Global Rainbow Foundation;* b. 30 June 1951; m.; ed Friendship Coll., Goodlands, Univ. of Mauritius; fmr Chair. Parti Socialiste Mauricien (PSM); Vice-Pres. MSM from 1986; mem. MSM/PMSD/Labour Party Govt –1990, MSM/MMM Govt from 1990; mem. Legis. Ass. 1982–95, Chair. Public Accounts Cttee 1982–83; Minister of Educ., Arts and Culture 1983–92, of Educ. and Science 1992–95; Sr Adviser, The World Bank 1997–98; Dir Div. for Secondary Educ., UNESCO, Paris 1998–2000, Dir and Rep., Regional Bureau for Educ. in Africa 2000–04, Sec. Exec. Bd and Gen. Conf. 2004–09, Dir and Rep., Cluster Office, New Delhi 2009–11; Founder-Pres. Global Rainbow Foundation (charitable trust) 2011–; Chair. Advisory Bd Amity Inst. of Higher Educ. 2012–; fmr Chair. Mauritius Ex-Servicemen Welfare Fund; mem. Local Govt Comm., Select Cttee on Industrial Relations Act; Hon. Freedom of the Dist of Pamplemousses-Riviere du Rempart 1984; Hon. Chair. Gandhi Ashram, Petit-Raffray 2012; Grand Officer of the Star and Key of the Indian Ocean 2010; Officier des Arts et des Lettres 2011; Outstanding Int. Leader in Tech. Vocational Educ. and Training, Wolansky Award Fund and Int. Vocational Educ. and Training Asscn 2002, honoured by UNESCO Exec. Bd Decision 182 EX/PLEN/DR.3 2009. *Address:* Global Rainbow Foundation, Old Mill Road, Morc Swan, Pereybere, Mauritius (office). *Telephone:* 2691501 (office); 591-83767 (mobile). *E-mail:* chairman@globalrainbowfoundation.org (office). *Website:* www.grftrust.org (office).

PÄRT, Arvo; Estonian composer; b. 11 Sept. 1935, Paide; m. Eleonora Pärt; ed composition studies with Heino Eller at Tallinn Conservatory; sound engineer, Estonian Radio 1958–67; freelance composer 1967–; first creative period starting with neoclassicist piano music 1958–68; experiments with serial techniques, aleatoricism ("incorporation of chance into the process of creation"), collage and sonic fields; his piece Credo from this period caused scandal in Soviet Estonia and was immediately banned 1968; new artistic re-orientation 1968–76; studied Gregorian chant, Notre Dame School and classic vocal polyphony; long silence broken by Symphony No. 3 1971 (sole work from this period); Für Alina 1976, first composition in tintinnabuli technique; emigrated to Vienna, Austria 1980; contract with Universal Edition; grant from German Academic Exchange Service (DAAD) 1981, moved to Berlin; began collaboration with ECM label and producer Manfred Eicher 1984; Int. Arvo Pärt Centre est. in Laulasmaa, Estonia 2010 (holds composer's personal archive); returned to Estonia where he resides 2010–; mem. Serbian Acad. of Sciences and Arts 2009, Estonian Acad. of Sciences (Academician for Music), Tallinn 2011, Pontifical Council for Culture, Vatican City 2011; Hon. Citizen of Rakvere 1995, Paide 2009; Hon. mem. Royal Swedish Acad. of Music 1991, American Acad. of Arts and Letters 1996, Royal Acad. of Sciences, Letters and Fine Arts (Belgium) 2001, Royal School of Church Music (UK) 2003, Accad. Nazionale di Santa Cecilia (Italy) 2004, Int. Soc. for Contemporary Music (ISCM) 2014; Hon. title 'Borderlander' from Borderland Foundation, Sejny, Poland 2003; Archon of Ecumenical Patriarchate 2013; Honoured Artist of Music, Int. Asscn of People in Music 2017; Second Class Order, Nat. Coat of Arms (Estonia) 1998, Commdr, Ordre des Arts et des Lettres 2001, Estonian Nat. Honour First Class 2006, Cross of Honour for Science and Art First Class (Austrian) 2008, Coat of Arms of Tallinn 2011, Chevalier, Légion d'honneur 2011, Estonian Evangelical Lutheran Church Cross of Merit First Class 2015, Austrian Decoration for Science and Art 2015; Dr hc (Estonian Acad. of Music) 1989, (Sydney) 1996, (Tartu) 1998, (Durham) 2002, (Nat. Univ. of Gen. San Martín, Argentina) 2003, (Freiburg) 2007, (Liège) 2009, (St Andrews) 2010, (Pontifical Inst. for Sacred Music) 2011, (Lugano) 2012, (St Vladimir's Orthodox Theological Seminary) 2014, (Oxford) 2016, (Fryderyk Chopin Univ. of Music, Poland) 2018; DAAD Fellowship (German Academic Exchange Service), Berlin 1981, Ind. Russian Arts Award 'Triumph', Moscow 1997, Culture Award (Estonia) 1998, Herder Prize (Germany) 2000, Composition Award for choral work, C.A. Seghizzi, Gorizia, Italy 2003, Composer of the Year, Musical America 2005, European Church Music Prize (Germany) 2005, Int. Prize 'Baltic Star', St Petersburg 2007, Int. Brückepreis Award, European City of Görlitz/Zgorzelec 2007, Léonie Sonning Music Prize (Denmark) 2008, Lifelong Achievement Award (Estonia) 2009, Lifelong Achievement Award, Int. Istanbul Music Festival 2010, Baltic Image Enhancement Award (USA) 2010, Homage to Arvo Pärt by Konrad Adenauer Fund (Germany) 2011, Prize of Int. Festival Cervantino (Mexico) 2012, Estonian Music Council Composition Award 2012, Orlando-di-Lasso-Medaille (Germany) 2013, Praemium Imperiale (Japan) 2014, Tallinn Black Nights Film Festival (PÖFF) Lifetime Achievement Award 2015, Estonian Culture Endowment Annual Award 2016, Medal of the Pontifical Council for Culture 'Per Arte ad Deum' 2016, Ratzinger Prize, Joseph Ratzinger-Benedict XVI Vatican Foundation 2017, Gloria Artis Medal, Polish Ministry of Culture and Nat. Heritage 2018. *Compositions include:* for chamber or symphony orchestra: Symphony No. 1 (Polyphonic) 1963, Symphony No. 2 1966, Symphony No. 3 1971, Symphony No. 4 (Classic Brit Award: Composer of the Year 2011) 2008, Nekrolog 1960, Perpetuum mobile 1963, Collage über B-A-C-H 1964, Pro et contra (concerto for violoncello and orchestra) 1966, Wenn Bach Bienen gezüchtet hätte ... 1976–2001, Cantus in Memory of Benjamin Britten 1977–80, Fratres for different ensembles 1977, Tabula rasa for two violins or one violin and one viola, prepared piano and orchestra (Estonia SSR annual music award 1978) 1977, Festina lente 1986–90, Silouan's Song, 'My Soul Yearns after the Lord ...' 1991, Trisagion 1992–94, Mein Weg 1999–2000, Orient & Occident (Classical Brit Award: Contemporary Music Award 2003) 2000, Lamentate, Homage to Anish Kapoor and His Sculpture 'Marsyas' for piano and orchestra 2002, La Sindone 2005–15, Für Lennart in memoriam 2006, 'These Words ...' 2008, Silhouette, Hommage à Gustave Eiffel 2009, Swansong 2013, Sequentia 2014, Greater Antiphons 2015; for choir and orchestra: Our Garden (First Prize, Composers Forum, Moscow 1962) 1959, Credo 1968, Stabat Mater 1985–2008, Te Deum 1985–92, Miserere 1989–92, Berliner Messe for different instrumentation 1990–2002, Litany, Prayers of St John Chrysostom for each hour of the day and night 1994–96, Como cierva sedienta 1998–2002, Cantique des degrés 1999–2002, Cecilia, vergine romana 2000–02, Salve Regina 2011, In principio 2003, Adam's Lament (Tõnu Kaljuste, Sinfonietta Riga, Latvian Radio Choir, Vox Clamantis, Tallinn Chamber Orchestra, Estonian Philharmonic Chamber Choir, soloists Tui Hirv and Rainer Vilu, Grammy Award for Best Choral Performance 2014) 2010; chamber music: Quintettino 1964, Sarah Was Ninety Years Old 1976–89, In spe (later: An den Wassern zu Babel... for different ensembles) 1976, Pari intervallo (later for different ensembles) 1976, Arbos for different ensembles 1977, Fratres for different ensembles 1977, Summa for different ensembles 1977, Spiegel im Spiegel for different ensembles 1978, De profundis 1980, Passio (Edison Classical Music Award 1989) 1982, Es sang for langen Jahren 1984, Ein Wallfahrtslied/Pilgrims' Song 1984, Psalom for different ensembles 1985, Mozart-Adagio 1992–2005, My Heart's in the Highlands 2000, Salve Regina 2001, Estonian Lullaby for different ensembles 2002, Christmas Lullaby for different ensembles 2002, L'abbé Agathon for different ensembles 2004, Vater unser 2005–11, Sei gelobt, du Baum 2007, Alleluia-Tropus 2008, Missa brevis 2009; for choir a cappella: Solfeggio 1963, Missa syllabica for different ensembles 1977, Summa for different ensembles 1977, Sieben Magnificat-Antiphonen 1988–91, Magnificat 1989, Dopo la vittoria 1996–98, Kanon pokajanen 1997, Triodion 1998, Zwei Beter 1998, Which Was the Son of ... 2000, Peace upon You, Jerusalem 2002, Most Holy Mother of God 2003, Da pacem Domine for different ensembles (Estonian Philharmonic Chamber Choir, conductor Paul Hillier, Grammy Award for Best Choral Performance 2007) 2004, Habitare fratres in unum 2012, Virgencita 2012–13, Drei Hirtenkinder aus Fatima 2014, Kleine Litanei 2015, And I heard a voice... 2017; for piano: Partita 1958, Two Sonatinas 1958–59, Diagramme 1964, Für Alina 1976, Variations for the Healing of Arinushka 1977, Hymn to a Great City 1984–2004, Für Anna Maria 2006; for organ: Trivium 1976, Pari intervallo 1976–80, Annum per annum 1980, Mein Weg hat Gipfel und Wellentäler 1989. *Address:* c/o Universal Edition AG, Boesendorferstrasse 12, 1010 Vienna, Austria (office). *Telephone:* (1) 337-23-0 (office). *Fax:* (1) 337-23-400 (office). *E-mail:* office@universaledition.com (office); info@arvopart.ee (office). *Website:* www.universaledition.com/paert (office); www.arvopart.ee.

PARTON, Dolly Rebecca; American singer, songwriter and actress; b. 19 Jan. 1946, Sevier County, Tenn.; d. of Robert Lee Parton and Avie Lee Parton (née Owens); m. Carl Dean 1966; Owner, Dollywood Entertainment Complex, including Dollywood Theme Park; Country Music Asscn Awards for Vocal Group of the Year (with Porter Wagoner) 1968, for Vocal Duo of the Year 1970, 1971, for Female Vocalist of the Year 1975, 1976, for Country Star of the Year 1978, for Nashville Metronome Award 1979, for People's Choice 1980, received Lifetime Achievement Award 2016, ACM Female Vocalist of the Year 1980, ACM Vocal Event of the Year and Video of the Year (both for When I Get Where I'm Going, with Brad Paisley) 2006, Kennedy Center Honor 2006, US Songwriters' Hall of Fame Johnny Mercer Award 2007, Grammy Lifetime Achievement Award 2011, Grammy Award for Best Country Duo/Group Performance (for Jolene; with Pentatonix) 2017. *Films include:* Nine to Five 1980, The Best Little Whorehouse in Texas 1982, Rhinestone 1984, Steel Magnolias 1989, Straight Talk 1991, The Beverly Hillbillies 1993, Frank McKlusky, C.I. 2002, Miss Congeniality 2: Armed and Fabulous 2005, Joyful Noise 2012. *Stage:* as score writer: Nine to Five: The Musical, Broadway 2009. *Recordings include:* albums: Here You Come Again (Grammy Award 1978), Real Love 1985, Just the Way I Am 1986, Heartbreaker, Great Balls of Fire, Rainbow 1988, White Limozeen 1989, Home for Christmas 1990, Eagle When She Flies 1991, Slow Dancing with the Moon 1993, Honky Tonk Angels 1994, The Essential Dolly Parton 1995, Just the Way I Am 1996, Super Hits 1996, I Will Always Love You and Other Greatest Hits (with others) 1996, Hungary Again 1998, Grass is Blue 1999, Best of the Best-Porter 2 Doll 1999, Halos and Horns 2002, Those Were The Days 2006, Backwoods Barbie 2008, Better Day 2011, Blue Smoke 2014. Pure and Simple 2016, I Believe in You 2017. *Compositions include:* Nine to Five (Grammy Award 1981). *Radio includes:* Grand Ole Opry, WSM Radio, Cass Walker Program. *Publications include:* Dolly: My Life and Other Unfinished Business 1994, Dream More: Celebrate the Dreamer in You 2012. *Address:* PO Box 150307, Nashville, TN 37215, USA. *Website:* www.dollypartonmusic.net.

PARTRIDGE, Dame Linda, DBE, CBE, BA, DPhil, FRS, FRSE, FMedSci; British biometrist and academic; *Director, Institute of Healthy Ageing, University College London;* b. 18 March 1950, Bath, England; d. of George Albert Partridge and Ida Partridge (née Tucker); m. 1st Vernon French (divorced 1989); m. 2nd Michael John Morgan 1996; ed Convent of Sacred Heart, Tunbridge Wells, Univ. of Oxford; NERC Post-doctoral Fellow, Univ. of York 1974–76; Demonstrator then Lecturer, Reader, Prof. of Evolutionary Biology, Univ. of Edinburgh 1976–93; Weldon Prof. of Biometry, Univ. Coll. London 1993–, NERC Research Prof. 1997–2002, Biotechnology and Biological Sciences Research Council Professorial Fellowship 2002–07, Dir Inst. of Healthy Ageing 2008–; Founding Dir Max Planck Inst. for Biology of Ageing, Cologne; mem. European Acad. of Sciences 2005, European Molecular Biology Org. 2006; Hon. DSc (St Andrews) 2004; London

Zoological Soc. Frink Medal 2000, American Soc. of Naturalists Sewall Wright Award 2002, Sewall Wright Award, American Soc. of Naturalists 2003, Longevity Prize, Fondation IPSEN 2004, The Lord Cohen Medal, British Soc. for Research on Ageing 2004, Medal of the Asscn for the Study of Animal Behaviour 2005, Living Legend, Help the Aged 2008, Thomassen a Thuessink Medal, Univ. of Groningen, Netherlands 2009, Darwin-Wallace Medal, Linnean Soc. of London 2009, Women of Outstanding Achievement Award for Science Discovery, Innovation and Entrepreneurship, UKRC for Women 2009, Royal Soc. Croonian Prize Lecturer 2009. *Leisure interests:* sailing, gardening, tennis, natural history. *Address:* Department of Genetics, Evolution and Environment, Darwin Building, University College London, Gower Street, London, WC1E 6BT, England (office). *Telephone:* (20) 7679-4380 (office). *Fax:* (20) 7679-7096 (office). *Website:* www.ucl.ac.uk/iha (office).

PARTRIDGE, Sir Michael John Anthony, KCB, MA, CB; British civil servant; b. 29 Sept. 1935, Stourbridge, Worcs.; s. of Dr John Henry Partridge and Ethel Green; m. Joan Elizabeth Hughes 1968; two s. one d.; ed Merchant Taylors' School, St John's Coll., Oxford; joined Home Civil Service (Ministry of Pensions and Nat. Insurance—MPNI) 1960, Pvt. Sec. to Perm. Sec. 1962–64, Prin. MPNI 1964–71, Asst Sec. 1971–76, UnderSec. 1976–81, Deputy Sec. 1981–83; Deputy Under-Sec. of State, Home Office 1983–87; Second Perm. Sec. Dept of Health and Social Security 1987–88; Perm. Sec. Dept of Social Security 1988–95; Sr Treas. Methodist Church Finance Div. 1980–96; Hon. Fellow St John's Coll. Oxford 1991–; Dir (non-exec.) Methodist Ministers' Pensions Trust 1992–2010, Epworth Investment Man. 1995–2011, Commercial Gen. and Norwich Union and Aviva 1996–2003, Stationery Office 1997–99; Gov. Middx Univ. 1992–2014, Chair. Bd of Govs 1996–2002, Pro-Chancellor 2001–; Vice-Chair. Magdi Yacoub Research Foundation 2001–14; mem. Council Sheffield Univ. 2001–03; Gov. Merchant Taylors' School 1992–99; Chair. Stationery Office Pension Scheme 2002–; Chair. Bd of Govs Heathfield School 2004–11; Pres. Old Merchant Taylors' Soc. 2002–03; Trustee Harefield Hosp. Heart Transplant Trust 1992–2003; Liveryman Merchant Taylors' Co. 1987; Hon. DUniv (Middlesex) 2015. *Publication:* Serta Scissorum 2012. *Leisure interests:* do-it-yourself, Greece, reading, skiing. *Address:* 27 High View, Pinner, Middx, HA5 3NZ, England (home). *Telephone:* (20) 8868-0657 (home). *E-mail:* michael@partridges.org.uk (home).

PARTS, Juhan, BL; Estonian politician; b. 27 Aug. 1966, Tallinn; m. Merle Parts; one s. one d.; ed Tallina First Secondary School, Univ. of Tartu; Deputy Sec.-Gen., Ministry of Justice 1992–98; Auditor Gen. 1998–2002; Chair. Res Publica Party 2002–05 (merged with Isamaaliit to form Isamaa ja Res Publica Liit (IRL—Union of Pro Patria and Res Publica) 2006); Prime Minister of Estonia 2003–05 (resgnd); Minister of Econ. Affairs and Communications 2007–14; IRL cand. for Prime Minister in parl. elections March 2015. *Leisure interest:* football (mem. FC Toompea). *Address:* Isamaa ja Res Publica Liit, Paldiski mnt. 13, Tallinn 10137, Estonia (office). *Telephone:* 624-0400 (office). *E-mail:* info@irl.ee (office). *Website:* www.irl.ee (office).

PARUBIY, Andriy Volodymyrovych; Ukrainian politician; *Chairman, Verkhovna Rada (Supreme Council);* b. 31 Jan. 1971, Chervonohrad, Lviv Oblast, Ukrainian SSR, USSR; ed Lviv Univ.; independence activist –1991, arrested for organizing an unsanctioned rally 1989; co-f. with Oleh Tyahnybok Sotsial-natsionalna Partiya Ukrainy (Social-Nat. Party of Ukraine) 1991, mem. 1991–2004; participated in 'Orange Revolution' 2004; mem. Nasha Ukraina (Our Ukraine) 2004–12, Fronta Zmin (Front of Changes) 2012, Batkivshchyna (Fatherland) 2012–14; Founding mem. Narodny Front (People's Front) 2014–; commdt of Euromaidan 2013–14, co-ordinated volunteer security corps for the mainstream protesters; Sec. Nat. Security and Defence Council of Ukraine Feb.–Aug. 2014 (resgnd); mem. Verkhovna Rada (Supreme Council) 2007–, Deputy Chair. 2014–16, Chair. 2016–. *Address:* Office of the Chairman, Verkhovna Rada, 01008 Kyiv, vul. M. Hrushevskoho 5 (office). *Telephone:* (44) 255-21-15 (office). *Fax:* (44) 253-32-17 (office). *E-mail:* umz@rada.gov.ua (office). *Website:* www.rada.gov.ua (office).

PARVANOV, Georgi Sedefchov, MA, PhD; Bulgarian historian and fmr head of state; b. 28 June 1957, Sirishnik, Pernik Dist; m. Zorka Petrova; two s.; ed Secondary School of Math., Pernik, St Clement of Ohrid Univ. of Sofia; researcher, Inst. of History, Bulgarian CP (BCP—became Bulgarian Socialist Party—BSP 1990) 1981–91, conducted research on the nat. question and history of social democracy in Bulgaria, Sr Research Assoc. 1989–92, Dir Centre for History and Policy Studies with the Supreme Council of the Bulgarian Socialist Party (BSP) 1992–96; joined BCP 1981 first party post 1991, Deputy Chair. Supreme Council 1994–96, Chair. 1996–2001; mem. Narodno Sobraniye (Parl.) for Kurdjali (Southern Bulgaria) 1994–2001, Chair. Parl. Group for Friendship with Greece and mem. Parl. Cttee on Radio and Television 1994–97, Parl. Group of the Democratic Left, Parl. Group of Coalition for Bulgaria 1997–2001; Pres. of Bulgaria 2002–12; fmr Chair. Parl. Group on Friendship between Bulgaria and Greece; initiated Bulgarian Christmas Charity Campaign 2003–08; Founder and Chair. Alternative for Bulgarian Revival 2014–17; Heydar Aliyev Order (Azerbaijan), Grand Cordon of the Leopold (Belgium), Grand Cross, Order of the Southern Cross (Brazil), Collar of the Order of the Cross of Terra Mariana (Estonia), First Class with Chain, Order of the Three Stars (Latvia), Grand Cross with Golden Chain, Order of Vytautas the Great (Lithuania), Grand Cross, Order of Saint-Charles (Monaco) 2004, Kt Grand Cross, Order of St Olav (Norway); Dr hc (Prešov Univ., Baku Univ., Yerevan State Univ.); Grand Gold Medal, Tomáš Garrigue Masaryk Univ., Brno, Czech Repub. *Publications:* numerous scientific articles, monographs and books, including Dimitar Blagoev and the Bulgarian National Problem 1879–1917 1988, From Bouzloudja to the Corona Theatre–An Attempt at a New Reading of Pages from the BSP's Social Democratic Period 1995, The Bulgarian Social Democracy and the Macedonian Issue at the End of the 19th Century up to 1918 1997, November 10: Before and After 2001. *Address:* c/o Alternative for Bulgarian Revival, 1000 Sofia, ul. Vrabcha 23, NDK, Bulgaria. *E-mail:* abvpresscenter@gmail.com. *Website:* www.abv-alternativa.bg.

PARVEEN, Abida; Pakistani singer; b. 1954, Larkana, Sindh; d. of Ghulam Haider; m. Ghulam Hussain Sheikh (deceased); one s. two d.; ed attended father's music school; studied classical music with Salamat Ali Khan; debut on Hyderabad Radio Station; repertoire includes classical music, ghazals, traditional Sufiana kalaam and Punjabi folk music; worldwide tours and performances before heads of

state; made recordings of original works of Sufi poets; President's Award for Pride of Performance 1982, Sitara-i-Imtiaz Award 2005, Lifetime Achievement Award, Kaladharmi Begum Akhtar Academy of Ghaza, India 2012. *Recordings include:* Pakistani Sufi Songs 1995, The Best of Abida Parveen 1997, Ho Jamalo 2000, Songs of the Mystics 2000, Tere Ishq Nachaya 2001, Raqs-e-Bismil 2001, Faiz by Abida 2001, Jahan E. Khusrau 2001, Visal – The Meeting Mystic Poets from the Hind & Mind 2002, Baba Bulleh Shah 2003, Mere Dil Se 2005, Ishq: l'Amour Absolu (Supreme Love) 2005, Svar Utsav 2006, Abida Parveen-The Sufi Queen 2011, Treasures Vol 1 2012, Lal De Rang Vich Rangi Aan 2012, Sufiana Safar 2012, Tera Lal Sakhi Mera Lai Sakhi 2012, Shaane-e-Ali 2012, Ghazal Ka Safar Vol 2 2013, Ru-e-Ali 2013, Treasures Vol 2 2014, Tasawwuf 2014.

PASCAL, Amy Beth; American film industry executive; b. 25 March 1958, Los Angeles, Calif.; m. Bernard Weinraub; one s.; ed Univ. of California, Los Angeles; worked for producer Tony Garnett at Kestral Films (affiliated to Warner Bros); Vice-Pres. of Production, 20th Century Fox 1986–87; Studio Exec., Columbia Pictures 1987–94, Pres. 1996–99, Chair. 1999–2003, Vice-Chair. Sony Pictures Entertainment 2002–06, Chair. Sony Pictures Entertainment Motion Picture Group 2003–, Co-Chair. Sony Pictures Entertainment 2006–15, resgnd and announced plans to establish film production co.; Pres. of Production, Turner Pictures 1994–96; mem. Exec. Bd UCLA School of Theater, Film and Television; Trustee, RAND Corpn, American Film Inst. *Films:* appeared in Intimate Portrait: Jennifer Lopez (TV documentary) 2002; Peter Pan (co-producer) 2003. *Address:* Sony Pictures Entertainment, 10202 West Washington Boulevard, Culver City, CA 90232, USA (office). *Telephone:* (310) 244-4000 (office). *Fax:* (310) 244-2626 (office). *Website:* www.sonypictures.com (office).

PASCAL, Jean-Baptiste Lucien, LenD; French banker; b. 26 Nov. 1930, Bordeaux; s. of Ernest Pascal and Paule de Battisti; m. Christiane Gardelle 1962; three s. (one deceased); ed Univ. of Paris; attached to Banque Nat. pour le Commerce et l'Industrie 1954; Head of Supplies Mission for the Devt of Algeria and Jt Govt Commr for Crédit Populaire de France in Algeria 1959; Head of Bureau for Financial Co-operation to Sec. of State for Algerian Affairs 1963; mem. Crédit Commercial de France (CCF) 1965, Deputy Dir Cen. Admin. CCF 1967, Dir Gen. d'Interbail 1971, Dir Cen. Admin. 1973, Admin. Dir-Gen. 1974, Vice-Pres. Dir-Gen. d'Interbail 1978–96; Dir Crédit Commercial de France 1977; Pres. Dir-Gen. Banque Hervet 1986–89; Pres. Admin. Council SOFEC 1991; Pres. GOBTP 1993–97, Pres. Conseil de Surveillance du GOBTP 1997–99, Interbail 1996 (Chair. Bd of Dirs 1996–97); Dir French Asscn of Financial Cos, Vice-Pres. 1995–97; Chevalier, Légion d'honneur. *Publication:* La Décolonisation de l'Europe: Querelle des Continents 1964. *Leisure interests:* alpinism, hunting. *Address:* 14 rue Jules Claretie, 75116 Paris, France (home).

PASCHKE, Fritz, DTechSc; Austrian electrical engineer and academic; *Professor Emeritus, Technical University of Vienna;* b. 2 March 1929, Graz/Goesting; s. of Eduard Paschke and Stefanie Mittellehner; m. Gertrud P. Kutschera 1955; two d.; ed Tech. Univs of Graz and Vienna; Asst, Tech. Univ. Vienna 1953–55; consultant, New York 1955–56; mem. tech. staff, RCA David Sarnoff Research Center 1956–61; Components Div. Siemens AG, Munich 1961–66; Prof. of Gen. Electronics, Tech. Univ. Vienna 1965–97, Prof. Emer. 1997–, Dean, School of Electrical Eng 1970–71, Rector/Pro-Rector 1971–76, Head, Inst. für Allgemeine Elektrotechnik und Elektronik 1980–97; Vice-Pres. Austrian Nat. Science Foundation 1974–82; Dr hc (Budapest) 1974; Großes Ehrenzeichen des Landes Kärnten 2008; Ludwig Boltzmann Award 1977, HE Cardinal Innitzer Award 1984, Erwin Schrödinger Award (Austrian Acad.) 1988, City of Vienna Award for Science and Tech. 1988, Leonardo da Vinci Medal, Soc. Européenne pour la Formations des Ingénieurs 1996, Johann Joseph Ritter von Prechtl-Medaille 1998. *Leisure interests:* art, hiking, swimming. *Address:* Technical University of Vienna, Karlsplatz 13, 1040 Vienna, Austria (office). *Telephone:* (1) 58801-36653 (office). *Fax:* (1) 58801-36699 (office). *E-mail:* fritz.paschke@tuwien.ac.at (office); fritz.paschke@chello.at. *Website:* www.isas.tuwien.ac.at (office).

PASCHKE, Karl Theodor; German diplomatist, UN official and academic; *Lecturer in International Affairs, Willy Brandt School of Public Policy, University of Erfurt;* b. 12 Nov. 1935, Berlin; s. of Adolf Paschke and Adele Cornill; m. Pia-Irene Schwerber 1963; one s. one d.; ed Univs of Munich and Bonn; Consul, New Orleans, La, USA 1964–68; Deputy Chief of Mission, Embassy in Kinshasa 1968–71; Dean, Foreign Office Training School, Bonn 1972–77; Press Counsellor, Washington, DC 1977–80; Spokesman, German Foreign Office, Bonn 1980–84; Amb. to UN Orgs, Vienna 1984–86; Minister, Embassy in Washington, DC 1987–90; Dir-Gen. for Personnel and Man., Foreign Office, Bonn 1990–94; Under-Sec.-Gen. for Internal Oversight Services, UN, New York 1994–99, Special Insp., Foreign Office 2000, Special Envoy for UN Secr. and Managerial Reform 2006; fmr Chair. Cttee on Budget and Finance, Ass. of States Parties, Int. Criminal Court, The Hague; fmr mem. Bd of Advisors, Comprehensive Nuclear-Test-Ban Treaty Org.; Lecturer in Int. Affairs, Willy Brandt School of Public Policy, Univ. of Erfurt; Hon. Citizen, New Orleans, Los Angeles, Washington, DC. *Publications include:* Reform der Attache-Ausbildung 1975, Apfelindianer 2015 (trans. as Apple Indian 2017). *Leisure interest:* music, especially jazz. *Address:* Denglerstrasse 46, 53173 Bonn, Germany (home). *Telephone:* (228) 9562032 (home). *Fax:* (228) 9562083 (home). *E-mail:* kpaschke@t-online.de.

PASCOE, B. Lynn, BA, MA; American diplomatist and UN official; b. 1943, Missouri; m. Diana Pascoe; two d.; ed Univ. of Kansas, Columbia Univ.; served on Soviet and China Desks; postings to embassies in Moscow, Hong Kong, Bangkok, Beijing (twice) and Taiwan; Prin. Deputy Asst Sec., East Asian and Pacific Bureau, State Dept; Deputy Chief of Mission, Embassy in Beijing; Deputy Exec. Sec., US Dept of State; Special Asst to Deputy Sec. of State; Dir American Inst., Taiwan 1993–96; Sr Adviser, Bureau of E African and Pacific Affairs and at US Mission to UN; Special Negotiator for Nagorno-Karabakh and Regional Conflicts; Co-Chair. OSCE Minsk Group; apptd Amb. to Malaysia 1999; Deputy Asst Sec. for European and Eurasian Affairs, US Dept of State 2001–04; Amb. to Indonesia 2004–07; Under-Sec.-Gen. for Political Affairs, UN 2007–12.

PASCUA CERRATO, Marlon; Honduran business executive and politician; fmr Vice-Pres. Comisión para la Defensa y Promoción de la Competencia (Nat. Comm. for the Defence of Competition); mem. Congreso Nacional (Parl.) for Francisco

Morazán constituency 2002–06; Minister of Defence 2010–14; mem. Partido Nacional.

PASCUAL, Ramon, PhD; Spanish physicist and academic; *Professor of Theoretical Physics, Universitad Autónoma de Barcelona;* b. 4 Feb. 1942, Barcelona; s. of Josep Pascual and Montserrat Pascual; m. Maria Lluisa Roca 1966; two s. one d.; Junta de Energía Nuclear, Madrid 1963–64; Teaching Asst Univ. of Valencia 1964–67; Asst Prof. of Quantum Mechanics, Univ. Complutense de Madrid 1967–70; Prof. of Math. Physics, Univ. of Zaragoza Jan.–Sept. 1970; Prof., Univ. Autónoma de Madrid 1970–71; Prof. of Theoretical Physics, Univ. Autónoma de Barcelona 1971–, Dean, Faculty of Science 1976–79, Vice-Rector for Academic Affairs 1979–80, Rector 1986–90; Visiting Scientist, CERN, Geneva, Switzerland 1969, 1970, 1977, 1978, 1981, 1983, 1986, Faculty of Science, Paris (Orsay) 1972, 1975, Rutherford Appleton Lab., Oxford, UK 1975; Chair. Exec. Cttee, ALBA Synchrotron Light Source 2003–16, also Hon. Pres.; mem. Catalan, Spanish and European Physical Soc.; mem. and fmr Pres. Reial Acadèmia Ciencies i Artes de Barcelona; St George Cross 2011, Order of Alfonso X the Wise 2016; Narcís Monturiol Prize 1991. *Publications:* more than 40 articles in scientific journals etc. *Address:* Universitat Autónoma de Barcelona, Edificio C, 08193 Bellaterra, Barcelona, Spain (office). *Telephone:* (93) 170-2717 (office); (93) 592-4444 (office). *Fax:* (93) 581-3213 (office). *E-mail:* pascual@ifae.es (office). *Website:* www.ifae.es (office); www.cells.es.

PASECHNIK, Col Leonid Ivanovich; Ukrainian military commander and separatist leader; 'Head', 'Lugansk People's Republic'; b. 15 March 1970; s. of Ivan Sergeyevich Pasechnik; ed Donetsk Mil.-Political Coll.; worked for Security Service of Ukraine (SBU) in Luhansk Oblast 1993–2013, becoming Chief of Stakhanov Interdistrict Dept 2010–14; retd from SBU (rank of Col) 2013; Minister of State Security, self-proclaimed 'Lugansk People's Repub.' 2014–; Acting 'Head', 'Lugansk People's Repub.' 2017–18, Head 2018–; Medal For Mil. Service to Ukraine 2007. *Address:* 'Government of the Lugansk People's Republic', 91000 Lugansk, pl. Geroyev VOV 3, Ukraine (office). *Telephone:* (642) 58-19-88 (office). *Website:* glava-lnr.info (office).

PASHA, Lt-Gen. Ahmed Shuja; Pakistani military officer and intelligence official; b. 18 March 1952; Second Lt, Frontier Force Regiment, PMA Long Course 1974; Chief Instructor, Command and Staff Coll.; Contingent and Sector Commdr, UN Mission in Sierra Leone 2001–02; promoted to Maj.-Gen., posted as GOC 8th Infantry Div., Sialkot 2003; Commdt, Command and Staff Coll., Quetta 2005; Dir-Gen. of Mil. Operations 2006–08; Dir-Gen. Inter-Services Intelligence 2008–12 (retd); Hilal-e-Imtiaz (Mil.).

PASHINYAN, Nikol Vovayi; Armenian politician and journalist; *Prime Minister;* b. 1 June 1975, Ijevan, Tavush Marz, Armenian SSR, USSR; s. of Vova Pashinyan; m. Anna Hakobyan; one s. three d.; worked with Dprutyun, Hayastan, Lragir and Molorak (newspapers); f. Oragir newspaper 1998, shut down in 1999; Ed.-in-Chief, Haykakan Zhamanak 1999–2012; political prisoner 2009–11; mem. Armenian Nat. Congress 2012–13; elected mem. Azgayin Zhoghov (Nat. Ass.) 2012, Chair. Ethics Comm. 2012–13; Founding mem. Kaghakatsiakan Paymanagir (KP—Civil Contract) 2013; Leader, Yelq dashinq (Exit Alliance) (principally comprising KP, Lusavor Hayastan—Bright Armenia and Hanrapetutyun Kusaktsutyun—Republican Party) 2016–; Prime Minister May–Oct. 2018, Jan. 2019–; Acting Prime Minister Oct. 2018–Jan. 2019. *Address:* Office of the Prime Minister, 0077 Yerevan, Marshal Baghramyan poghota 26, Armenia (office). *Telephone:* (10) 52-53-94 (office). *Fax:* (10) 52-53-94 (office). *E-mail:* hotline@gov.am (office). *Website:* www.primeminister.am (office); www.gov.am (office).

PASHTUN, Mohammad Yousef, BSc, MA; Afghan politician and engineer; *Senior Advisor to President on Construction, Mines, Water & Energy;* b. 15 Nov. 1946, Kandahar; s. of Brig. Mohammad Ghani Khan; m. Qamar Angaar Pashtun; two s. three d.; ed Ahmad Shah Baba High School, Kabul Univ., American Univ. of Beirut, Lebanon; worked in Dar-ul-Handasa Design & Construction Co.; took refuge in Pakistan during Soviet occupation 1980s; fmr Lecturer, Eng Faculty, Kabul Univ.; Minister of Urban Affairs 2002–03; Gov. of Qandahar Prov. 2003–04; Minister of Urban Devt and Housing 2004–10; Sr Advisor to Pres. on Construction, Mines, Water & Energy 2010–; currently Chair. Kabul New City Devt. *Address:* Office of the President, Gul Khana Palace, Presidential Palace, Kabul, Afghanistan (office). *Telephone:* (20) 2141135 (office). *Website:* www.president.gov.af (office).

PASINETTI, Luigi Lodovico, MA, PhD; Italian economist and academic; *Professor Emeritus of Economics, Università Cattolica del Sacro Cuore, Milan;* b. 12 Sept. 1930, Zanica (Bergamo); s. of Giovanni Pasinetti and Romilda Arzuffi; m. Carmela Colombo 1966; one s.; ed Università Cattolica del Sacro Cuore, Milan, Univ. of Cambridge, UK, Harvard Univ., USA, Univ. of Oxford, UK; Research Fellow, Nuffield Coll., Oxford 1960–61; Fellow and Lecturer in Econs, King's Coll., Cambridge 1961–75; Lecturer, then Reader in Econs, Univ. of Cambridge 1961–76; Prof. of Econs, Università Cattolica del Sacro Cuore 1964–2003, Chair. Econs Dept 1980–83, Prof. Emer. 2004–; Wesley Clair Mitchell Visiting Research Prof. of Econs, Columbia Univ., New York 1971, 1975; Visiting Research Prof., Indian Statistical Inst., Calcutta and New Delhi 1979; Visiting Prof. of Econs, Univ. of Ottawa, Carleton Univ. 1981, Kyoto Univ. 1984, Univ. of Southern California 1985; Visiting Fellow, Gonville & Caius Coll., Cambridge 1989; McDonnell Distinguished Scholars Fellow, WIDER, the UN Univ., Helsinki 1991, 1992; Visiting Prof., Univ. of Sydney 1993; Visiting Fellow, Trinity Coll. Cambridge 1997, 1999; mem. Council and Exec. Cttee, Int. Econ. Asscn 1980–99 (Hon. Pres. 2005); Pres. Italian Econ. Asscn 1986–89 (Hon. Pres. 1990), Confed. of European Econ. Asscns 1990–91, 1994–95 (Pres. 1992–93), European Soc. for the History of Econ. Thought 1995–97 (Hon. Pres. 2002); Fellow, Econometric Soc. 1978–; mem. Accad. Nazionale dei Lincei, Rome 1986–, Inst. Lombardo Accad. di Scienze e Lettere, Milan 1995–; Hon. Fellow, Gonville & Caius Coll., Cambridge 1999–; Hon. Pres. European Asscn for Evolutionary Political Economy 1989, Italian Econs Asscn 1990–, European Soc. for the History of Economic Thought 2002–, Italian Asscn for the History of Political Economy 2003–, Italian Asscn for the History of Econ. Thought 2004–, Int. Econ. Asscn 2005–; Dr hc (Univ. of Fribourg, Switzerland) 1986; St Vincent Prize for Econs 1979, 2002, Gold Medal (First Class) for Educ., Culture and Arts 1982, 'La Madonnina' Int. Prize (Econs section), Milan 1987, Special Prize for Culture (Econs section), Presidency of the Council of

Ministers 1996, Invernizzi Prize for Econs 1997. *Publications include:* Growth and Income Distribution 1974, Lectures on the Theory of Production 1977, Structural Change and Economic Growth 1981, Structural Change and Adjustment in the World Economy (with P. Lloyd) 1987, Structural Economic Dynamics 1993, Economic Growth and the Structure of Long-Term Development (with R. M. Solow) 1994, The Impact of Keynes in the 20th Century (with B. Schefold) 1999, Keynes and the Cambridge Keynesians: A 'Revolution in Economics' to be Accomplished 2007 (Italian version 2010, Japanese trans. 2017); numerous articles on income distribution, capital theory, econ. growth and structural econ. dynamics, and on the econ. crisis of 2011–12. *Leisure interests:* tennis, climbing, music, reading. *Address:* Faculty of Economics, Università Cattolica del Sacro Cuore, Largo A. Gemelli 1, 20123 Milan, Italy (office). *Telephone:* (02) 72342470 (office). *Fax:* (02) 72342406 (office). *E-mail:* llp@unicatt.it (office). *Website:* docenti.unicatt.it/eng/luigi_lodovico_pasinetti (office); www.unicatt.it/docenti/pasinetti (office).

PASLOSKI, Darrell, BPharm; Canadian pharmacist and politician; m. Tammie Pasloski; four c.; ed Univ. of Saskatchewan; propr of two pharmacies, Whitehorse 1991–; mem. Yukon Party, Leader 2011–16; mem. Yukon Legis. Ass. for Mountainview (Yukon Party) 2011–16; Premier of Yukon 2011–16, also Minister responsible for Exec. Council Office, Minister of Finance, Minister responsible for Yukon Energy Corpn and for Yukon Devt Corpn; fmr Dir MacBride Museum, Swim Yukon, Mountainview Golf Course; Yukon Chamber of Commerce Business Person of the Year 2009. *Leisure interests:* ice hockey, hiking, fishing, hunting, camping. *Address:* c/o Government of Yukon, Box 2703, Whitehorse, YK Y1A 2C6, Canada (office).

PASQUAL, Lluís, BA; Spanish theatre and opera director; b. (Lluís Pasqual Sánchez), 5 June 1951, Reus, Tarragona, Catalonia; ed Universitat Autònoma de Barcelona, Institut del Teatre, Barcelona; Founder and Dir Lliure Theatre, Barcelona 1976, Co-Dir 1998–2000, Dir 2011–; worked in Poland; Asst to Giorgio Strehler, Italy 1978; Dir Centro Dramático Nacional, Teatro María Guerrero, Madrid 1983–89; Dir Odéon, Théâtre de l'Europe, Paris 1990–96; Dir Venice Theatre Biennale 1995–96; Commr, Projecte Ciutat del Teatre, Barcelona City Council 1997–99; fmr Artistic Dir Teatro Arriaga, Bilbao; Chevalier des Arts et des Lettres 1984, Officier 1991; Chevalier, Légion d'honneur 1996; Nat. Theatre and Dance Prize 1984, Ciutat de Barcelona Prize 1985, Generalitat de Catalunya Prize 1988, Nat. Theatre Prize, Spanish Ministry of Culture 1991, Paris Chamber of Commerce Prize 1995, Egyptian Ministry of Culture's Hon. CIFET Prize 1995, Comunidad de Madrid Prize 2002, Max de Teatro Award 2003. *Plays directed include:* Luces de Bohemia (Valle Inclán) 1984, Sans Titre (Lorca) 1990, Le Balcon (Genet) 1991, Tirano Banderas (Valle Inclán) 1992, Le Chevalier d'Olmédo (Lope de Vega) 1992, El Público (Lorca) 1986, The Tempest (Shakespeare), Teatro San Martin, Buenos Aires 2001, Waiting for Godot (Beckett, in Spanish) 2001, Hamlet (Shakespeare) and The Tempest (Shakespeare), Teatro Arriaga, Bilbao, later at Spanish Theatre of Madrid 2006, Perpetual Peace (Juan Mayorga), María Guerrero Theatre of Madrid 2008, The House of Bernarda Alba (Lorca), Teatre Nacional de Catalunya 2009, Celebration of Harold Pinter, Lliure Barcelona 2010–11. *Operas directed include:* (Teatro de la Zarzuela, Madrid); Samson et Dalila (Saint-Saëns) 1982, Falstaff (Verdi) 1983, Don Carlo (Verdi) 1985, Il Trittico (Puccini) 1987, Il Turco in Italia (Rossini) 1990; La Vera Storia (Berio), Paris 1985, Maggio Musicale, Florence 1986, Falstaff, Bologna 1987. *Television include:* Lletres catalanes (series) 1979, Al vostre gust (film) 1984, Lorenzaccio, Lorenzaccio (film) 1989, Un dels últims vespres de carnaval (film) 1991, Capvespre al jardí (film) 1994, 44e edición de los premios Ondas (Special) 1997, I Premios Max de las artes escénicas (Special) 1998, Núria Espert. Una mujer de teatro 2012. *Address:* c/o Matthias Vogt Artistic Management, 211 Gough Street, Suite 115, San Francisco, CA 94102, USA (office); c/o Teatre Lliure, plaça margarida xirgu, 1, 08004 Barcelona, Spain.

PASSACANTANDO, Franco, DEcon; Italian economist; *Managing Director for Relations with International Institutions, Banca d'Italia (Bank of Italy);* b. 7 Aug. 1947, Rome; m. Miriam Veronesi 1987; three s. one d.; ed Rome and Stanford Univs; Head, Money Market Div., Research Dept, Banca d'Italia (Bank of Italy) 1981–85, Task Force on the Reform of the Italian Payment System 1986–89, Dir Monetary and Financial Sector, Research Dept 1990–95, Head of Asset Man. Dept 2003–06, Man. Dir Cen. Banking, Markets and Payment Systems Area 2006–12, Man. Dir for Relations with Int. Insts 2012–; Exec. Dir World Bank Group 1995–2003, Chair. Budget Cttee, Audit Cttee, Steering Cttee; mem. T2S Project Steering Cttee, Cen. European Bank; mem. Cttee on Payment and Settlement Systems, BIS; mem. Econ. and Financial Cttee, EC; mem. Working Party 3, OECD; G7 Deputy; G20 Deputy; Chair. OTC Derivatives Regulators' Forum 2013–; Fulbright, Einaudi and Stringher fellowships. *Publications:* White Paper on the Payment System in Italy 1988, Le Banche e il Finanziamento delle Imprese 1997, Governance Reforms at the World Bank 2002, Building an International Framework for Monetary Stability: The Case of Italy 1979–1994 1996, The Loss of Confidence in Bank Money in the Great Depression; and articles on monetary policy in professional journals. *Leisure interests:* making movies, art. *Address:* Banca d'Italia, Via Nazionale, 91, 00184 Rome, Italy (office). *Telephone:* (06) 47923515 (office). *Fax:* (06) 47923883 (office). *E-mail:* franco.passacantando@bancaditalia.it (office). *Website:* www.bancaditalia.it (office).

PASSERA, Corrado, MBA; Italian banking executive and government official; b. 30 Dec. 1954, Como; m. Cecilia Canepa; one s. one d.; ed Bocconi Univ., Milan, Wharton School, Univ. of Pennsylvania; Sr Engagement Man., McKinsey & Co., Milan 1980–85; with CIR SpA, Milan 1985–66, COO 1988–90; Deputy Chair. Credito Romagnolo 1988–95; COO Arnoldo Mondadori Editore SpA 1990–91; Deputy Chair. and CEO Gruppo Espresso–Repubblica, Rome 1991–92; Man. Dir and Co-CEO Olivetti SpA, Ivrea 1992–96; Man. Dir and CEO Banco Ambrosiano Veneto 1996–98; Man. Dir and CEO Poste Italiane 1998–2002; Man. Dir and CEO Banca Intesa SpA (fmrly IntesaBci) 2002–06, Man. Dir and CEO Intesa Sanpaolo (following merger between Banca Intesa and Sanpaolo IMI) 2007–11; Minister of Econ. Devt, Infrastructure and Transport (in Mario Monti's 'govt of technocrats') 2011–13; Dir RCS MediaGroup, Bocconi Univ.; Dir and mem. Exec. Cttee Italian Bankers' Asscn (ABI); mem. Advisory Bd Scuola Normale, Pisa, Int. Advisory Bd Wharton School, Gen. Council Fondazione Giorgio Cini; mem. Int. Business Council, World Econ. Forum, Geneva; Cavaliere, Ordine al Merito del Lavoro 2006;

Int. Business Hon. Degree (MIB School of Man. of Trieste) 2001, Man. Eng Hon. Degree (Politecnico of Bari) 2004. *Publications include:* Ricomincio da cinque 2016.

PASSOS COELHO, Pedro Manuel Mamede; Portuguese economist and politician; b. 24 July 1964, Coimbra; s. of António Passos Coelho and Maria Rodrigues Santos Mamede; m. 1st Fátima Padinha, two d.; m. 2nd Laura Ferreira, one d.; ed Univ. of Lisbon, Lusíada Univ.; mem. Assembleia da República (Parl.) for Lisbon 1991–99, for Vila Real 2011–; mem. Partido Social Democrata (PSD), Vice-Chair. PSD Parl. Group 1996–99, Vice-Pres. PSD 2005–06, Pres. 2010–; Prime Minister 2011–15; consultant, Tecnoforma 2000–04. *Publication:* Mudar 2010. *Address:* c/o Office of the Prime Minister, Presidency of the Council of Ministers, Rua da Imprensa à Estrela 4, 1200-888 Lisbon, Portugal (office).

PASSY, Solomon Isaac, MS, PhD; Bulgarian politician and academic; b. 22 Dec. 1956, Plovdiv; s. of Isaac Passy; m.; two s. one d.; ed Sofia Univ. 'St Kliment Ohridski'; in opposition to anti-Muslim policy of the Communist regime 1985–89; Asst Prof. of Math. Logic and Computer Science, Sofia Univ. 'St Kliment Ohridski' and at Bulgarian Acad. of Sciences 1984–94; participant in Nat. Round Table for transition to democracy 1989–90; activist of Ecoglasnost opposition movt 1989; Co-founder and mem. Coordinating Council of UDF 1990–91; Founding Pres. and CEO Atlantic Club of Bulgaria (first pro-Atlantic NGO in a non-NATO mem. state) 1991–2001, Hon. Pres. 2001–; Founder and Spokesman, Green Party of Bulgaria 1989; Mem. Grand Nat. Ass. (Green Party, Union of Democratic Forces—UDF) 1990–91, (Nat. Movt Simeon II) 2005, Chair. Foreign Affairs, Defence and Security Cttee, 39th Nat. Ass. July 2001, Foreign Affairs Cttee, 40th Nat. Ass. 2005–09, Bulgaria–USA caucus, 40th Nat. Ass. 2005–09; Minister of Foreign Affairs 2001–05; Vice-Pres. Nat. Movt Simeon II 2005, mem. Political Council 2002–05; apptd Chair.-in-Office Org. for Security and Co-operation in Europe 2004; Special Adviser on NATO accession to Govt of Macedonia 2007; mem. 2nd, 3rd, 4th and 13th Bulgarian Antarctic Expeditions to Livingston Island, Antarctica 1993–2005; Leader, Bulgarian Del. for the Audience with Pope John Paul II 1994; Vice-Chair. Atlantic Treaty Asscn, Paris 1996–99; Hon. Citizen of Nedelino 2003, of State of Tex., USA 2004; Orden Infante Don Enrique (Grã-Cruz) (Portugal) 2002; Orden del Mérito Civil (Gran Cruz) (Spain) 2003; Order of Léopold II (Grand Cross) (Belgium) 2004; Ordine della Stella della Solidarieta' Italiana (I classe) (Italy) 2006; Orden de Isabel la Catolica (Gran Cruz) (Spain) 2006; Dr hc (South-West Univ. of Bulgaria) 2005; Balkan Peace Award 2004. *Publications:* numerous scientific articles on math. logic and computer science. *Address:* The Atlantic Club of Bulgaria, 1404 Sofia, I111, Bulgaria Blvd, 5th floor, Office 14, Bulgaria (office). *E-mail:* office@atlantic-club.org. *Website:* www.atlantic-club.org.

PASTERNAK, Anne, MA; American gallery director; *Shelby White and Leon Levy Director, Brooklyn Museum;* b. 1965; m. Mike Starn; one d.; ed Univ. of Massachusetts, Hunter Coll., New York; fmr Dir Stux Galleries, Boston and New York; fmr Curator, Real Art Ways, Hartford, Conn.; Co-founder and Dir BRAT (arts org.); Pres. and Artistic Dir Creative Time, New York 1994–2015; Shelby White and Leon Levy Dir Brooklyn Museum 2015–; Advisor, Nat. Asscn of Artists Orgs, Public Art Seminar (SESC), São Paulo, Brazil, Artists' Museum, Negev, Israel, Hallwalls Contemporary Arts Center; fmr guest critic, Yale Univ.; Lecturer, School of Visual Arts, New York; panel mem. Pew Center for Arts and Heritage 2002, Philadelphia Exhbns Initiative 2009; mem. Bd White Columns (gallery) 1994–97. *Publications:* numerous essays in cultural publs; Creative Time: The Book 2007; contribs to Columbia Journal of American Studies, New York Times Magazine, Art New England, Journal of Contemporary Art. *Address:* Brooklyn Museum, 200 Eastern Parkway, Brooklyn, NY 11238-6052, USA (office). *Telephone:* (718) 638-5000 (office). *E-mail:* information@brooklynmuseum.org (office). *Website:* www.brooklynmuseum.org (office).

PASTOR, Ana, MBA; Spanish politician; *President, Congress of Deputies;* b. (Ana María Pastor Julián), 11 Nov. 1957, Cubillos del Pan, Zamora; m.; ed Univ. of Salamanca; Dir-Gen., Gen. Mutuality of Civil Servants 1996–99; Under-Sec., Ministry of Educ. and Culture 1999–2000, of Presidency 2000–01, of Interior 2001–02; mem. Congress of Deputies (Pontevedra, People's Party) 2000–, apptd Second Vice-Pres., Pres. 2016–; fmr Minister of Health, Social Services and Equality 2002–04, Minister of Public Works, Transport and Housing 2011–16; currently mem. People's Party. *Address:* Congress of Deputies, Carrera de Floridablanca s/n, 28071 Madrid, Spain (office). *Telephone:* (91) 3906000 (office). *Fax:* (91) 4298707 (office). *E-mail:* informacion@congreso.es (office). *Website:* www.congreso.es (office).

PASTORE, Oscar, PhD; Paraguayan economist and international organization official; ed Nat. Univ. of Asunción, Univ. of Chile, Univ. del Empresa, Uruguay; taught for more than 20 years at univs in Paraguay, Uruguay and Brazil, including Univ. Americana, Paraguay (fmr Dean, Faculty of Econs), Univ. de la Empresa, Fed. Univ. of Latin American Integration (UNILA), Brazil; various positions in Technical Dept, Associação Latino-Americana de Livre Comércio/Associação Latino-Americana de Integração (LAIA) 1961–98, Adviser to LAIA Sec.-Gen. 2009–11; mem. Bd of Experts, Cartagena Agreement (establishing Andean Community) 1972; Head of Admin and Finance, also Coordinator and Adviser to Secr., MERCOSUR 1999–2006, Coordinator, MERCOSUR Secr. 2012–14, Dir MERCOSUR Secr. 2014–16. *Address:* c/o MERCOSUR, Edif. Mercosur, Luis Piera 1992, 1°, 11200 Montevideo, Uruguay (office). *Website:* www.mercosur.int (office).

PASTORELLI, Jean, LenD; Monegasque civil servant, diplomatist and politician; *President, Grimaldi Forum;* b. 20 June 1942, Monaco; m.; two c.; ed Institut d'Etudes Politiques, Diplome d'Etudes Supérieures de la Faculté de Droit de Paris, Ecole Nationale d'Admin (Fonctionnaire Etranger), Paris; joined Secr., Dept of Finance and Economy 1969; Dir Budget and Treasury 1978–88; Govt Counsellor for Finance and the Economy 1988–95; Pres. Radio Monte Carlo 1995–2000, Monaco Telecom 1997–99; Perm. Del. to Posteurop 1995–; Perm. Del. to ITU, UPU 1995–2004; Pres. Tele Monte Carlo 1995–, Monte Carlo Radiodiffusion (MCR) 1995; Minister Plenipotentiary 1995; Perm. Del. to UNESCO 2003, to French-speaking community 2003; Perm. Rep. at IAEA 2003; Nat. Authority for Principality of Monaco to Org. for Prohibition of Chemical Weapons 2003, Perm. Rep. 2003; Pres. EUTELSAT Ass. of Parties 2001–04, INTELSAT Ass. of Parties (ITSO) 2002–04; Amb. to Belgium, the Netherlands and Grand Duchy of Luxembourg 2003–07; Head of Mission to European Communities 2003–07, apptd Observer within Int. Criminal Court 2003; Govt Counsellor for External Relations 2007–08; Amb. to France 2008–11; Pres. Grimaldi Forum 2011–; Commdr, Ordre de Saint-Charles. *Address:* Grimaldi Forum, 10 Avenue Princesse Grace, 98000 Monte Carlo, Monaco (office). *Telephone:* 99992000 (office). *Fax:* 99992001 (office). *E-mail:* gf@grimaldiforum.mc (office). *Website:* www.grimaldiforum.com (office).

PASTRANA ARANGO, Andrés, LLD; Colombian journalist, diplomatist and fmr head of state; b. 17 Aug. 1954, Bogotá; s. of Misael Pastrana Borrero (fmr Pres. of Colombia) and María Cristina Arango de Pastrana; m. Nohra Puyana Bickenbach; one s. two d.; ed Colegio San Carlos de Bogotá, Colegio Mayor de Nuestra Señora del Rosario Law School, Harvard Univ.; Founder and Man. Dir Revista Guión (political magazine) 1978–79; Man. Dir Datos y Mensajes SA News Broadcasting Co. 1979–80; Dir TV Hoy News 1980–87; Councillor Bogotá City Council 1982–86, Chair. Jan.–April 1983, 1984–85; Mayor of Bogotá 1988–90; Senator 1991–93; Founder and Presidential Cand. of Nueva Fuerza Democrática 1994; Pres. of Colombia 1998–2002; Amb. to USA 2005–06 (resgnd); mem. Int. Union of Local Authorities, Exec. Cttee 1989, Pres. Latin American Chapter 1988–89; Vice-Pres. Latin American Union of Capital Cities; Co-Dir World Mayors' Conf. on Drug Addiction, New York 1989, Madrid 1990; Sec.-Gen. Union of Latin American Parties 1992, now Hon. Pres.; Adviser to UN Univ., Tokyo 1994; Founder and Dir UN Leadership Acad., Jordan; fmr Chair. Bogotá Telephone Co., Bogotá Aqueduct and Sewerage Co., Electricity and Public Utilities Co. of Bogotá, Inst. for Urban Devt, Dist Planning; mem. Bd of Dirs Int. Foundation for Electoral Systems; Nat. Police Distinguished Service Order, UNESCO Order, Grand Cross, Civilian Order of Merit 1988, Order of Merit, Colombian Publishing Industry 1988, Civilian Defence Order 1989, Order of Santa Bárbara, Colombian Navy 1990, José María Córdova Order of Mil. Merit 1990; Colombian Jr Chamber Exec. of the Year 1981, King of Spain Int. Journalism Award 1985, Simón Bolívar Nat. Journalism Award 1987, King of Spain Nat. Journalism Award 1987, Bogotá Circle of Journalists Nat. Award 1987. *Publication:* La Palabra Bajo Fuego 2005, Memorias olvidadas 2013, Hacia la formulación de un derecho ecológico (Towards the formulation of an ecological law).

PASTUKHOV, Boris Nikolayevich; Russian politician; b. 10 Oct. 1933, Moscow; m. Janna Pastukhova; two d.; ed Bauman Higher Tech. Coll., Moscow; mem. CPSU 1959–91; First Sec. Bauman Regional Komsomol Cttee, Moscow 1959–61; Second Sec. Moscow City Komsomol Cttee 1961–62, First Sec. 1962–64; Second Sec. All-Union Komsomol Cttee 1964–77, First Sec. 1977–82; Chair. USSR State Cttee for Publishing, Printing and Bookselling, USSR Goskomizdat 1982–86; mem. Presidium, Supreme Soviet of the USSR 1978–83; USSR Amb. to Denmark 1986–89, to Afghanistan 1989–92; Deputy Foreign Minister of Russia 1989–96; First Deputy Foreign Minister 1996–98; mediator in negotiations between Georgia and Abkhazia; Minister for CIS Affairs 1998–99; Chair. Govt Cttee on CIS; apptd mem. State Duma (Otechestvo) 1999, re-elected 2003 (United Russia); mem. Cttee on Connections with Compatriots 2000.

PASTUSIAK, Longin, PhD; Polish politician and academic; *Professor, Vistula University;* b. 22 Aug. 1935, Łódź; s. of Josef Pastusiak and Sabina Pastusiak; m. Anna Ochab; one s. one d.; ed Warsaw Univ., American Univ., Univ. of Virginia, USA; Prof. and Head Dept, Polish Inst. of Int. Affairs 1963–93; Deputy to Sejm (Parl.) 1991–2001, Vice-Chair. Foreign Affairs Cttee 1993–2001; Head, Polish Del. to WEU Ass. 1993–; Head, Polish Del. to NATO Parl. Ass. 1993–, Vice-Pres. 2002–; Senator 2001–05, Pres. of the Senate 2001–05; Prof. of Int. Relations, Gdansk Univ. 1994–2005; Prof., Vistula Univ., Warsaw 2005–, Higher School of Communications and Mass Media, Warsaw 2005–; Visiting Prof., Appalachian State Univ., USA; Silver Cross of Merit 1972, Kt's Cross 1985, Order of Merit (Lithuania) 2004, Grand Commdr's Cross (Lithuania) 2004, Order of Polonia Restituta 2015; Dr hc (Naval Mil. Acad. Gdynia, Poland) 2003, Hon. DHumLitt (Appalachian State Univ.) 2004; Parliamentarian of the Year 1997, numerous scholarly awards. *Television:* various programmes on Polish public and pvt. TV. *Publications include:* more than 90 books, including Poland–Canada 1945–1961 1994, United States Diplomacy, 18th and 19th Century 1997, Chicago: Portrait of the City 1997, Will the World Come to an End? 1999, From the Secrets of the Diplomatic Archives: Polish–American Relations 1948–1954 1999, Ladies of the White House 2000, Presidents of the USA 2002; 800 scholarly publs and more than 3,000 articles in daily and weekly journals on American history and foreign policy, German studies, East–West relations, Polish foreign policy, Polish–American relations and theoretical aspects of int. relations. *Leisure interest:* tennis. *Address:* al. Niepodleglosci 151, Apartment 21, 02-555 Warsaw, Poland (home). *Telephone:* (22) 8495044 (home). *Fax:* (22) 8495044 (home). *E-mail:* longin.pastusiak@mac.com (home).

PASWAN, Ram Vilas, BL, MA; Indian politician; *Minister of Consumer Affairs, Food and Public Distribution;* b. 5 July 1946, Shaharbanni, Bihar; s. of Jamun Paswan and Siya Devi; m. 1st Raj Kumari; two d.; m. 2nd Reena Sharma-Paswan; one s. one d.; ed Kosi Coll., Khagaria, Patna Univ.; mem. Bihar Legis. Ass. 1969; Gen. Sec. Lok Dal, Bihar 1974; mem. Lok Sabha 1977–, Leader of the House 1996; Gen. Sec. Janata Party 1987–88, Janata Dal 1988–90; Sec. Nat. Front 1988–90; Minister of Labour and Welfare 1989–90, of Railways 1996–98, of Communications 1999–2001, of Coal and Mines 2001–02, of Chemicals and Fertilizers and of Steel 2004–09, of Consumer Affairs, Food and Public Distribution 2014–; Pres. Lok Jan Shakti Party (formed following split from Janata Dal (United) 2000–; mem. Court of Jawaharlal Nehru Univ. 1998–99. *Leisure interests:* playing chess, social work. *Address:* Ministry of Consumer Affairs, Food and Public Distribution, 179 Krishi Bhavan, New Delhi 110 001 (office); Shaharbanni, Tola, Bellai, Khagaria 851 204, India (home). *Telephone:* (11) 23070637 (office). *Fax:* (11) 23386098 (office). *E-mail:* secy-food@nic.in (office). *Website:* fcamin.nic.in (office).

PASZTOR, Janos, BSc, MSc; Hungarian scientist and UN official; *Senior Advisor to the Secretary-General on Climate Change, United Nations;* b. 1955; ed Massachusetts Inst. of Tech., USA; Dir Energy for My Neighbour Programme, World Council of Churches 1979–83; Assoc. Scientist, Beijer Inst. of Ecological Econs, Stockholm Oct.–Dec. 1983; Sr Programme Officer, Energy World Comm. on Environment and Devt (Brundtland Comm.) 1984–86; Programme Officer (Energy), UNEP 1986–89; Assoc. Scientist, Stockholm Environment Inst., Boston, Mass, USA 1989–90; Sr Programme Officer, UN Conf. on Environment and Devt (Earth Summit '92) 1990–92; various sr positions with UN Framework Convention on Climate Change (UNFCCC) 1993–2006; Dir Environment Man. Group, UNEP 2007; Dir UN Sec.-Gen.'s Climate Change Support Team 2008–10, Exec. Sec., Sec.-

Gen.'s High-level Panel on Global Sustainability 2011–12, Asst Sec.-Gen. on Climate Change 2015–16, Sr Advisor to Sec.-Gen. on Climate Change 2016–; Acting Exec. Dir Conservation, and Dir of Policy and Science, World Wide Fund for Nature (WWF) Int. 2012–14. *Address:* Office of the Secretary-General, United Nations, New York, NY 10017, USA (office). *Telephone:* (212) 963-1234 (office). *Fax:* (212) 963-4879 (office). *Website:* www.un.org/sg (office).

PATABENDIGE DON, HE Cardinal Albert Malcolm Ranjith, BTh; Sri Lankan ecclesiastic; *Archbishop of Colombo;* b. 15 Nov. 1947, Polgahawela; s. of Don William and Mary Winifreeda; ed De La Salle Coll., Mutwal, St Aloysius Seminary, Borella, Nat. Seminary, Kandy, Pontifical Urbanian Univ. and Pontifical Biblical Inst., Rome, Hebrew Univ. of Jerusalem, Israel; ordained priest, Diocese of Colombo 1975; Asst Pastor in Pamunugama 1978, later served as Pastor in Payagala and Kalutara; est. Seth Sarana (centre for poor relief), Archdiocese of Colombo; named Nat. Dir Pontifical Mission Socs 1983; revived Soc. of the Holy Childhood; also served as Diocesan Co-ordinator for Human Devt; Auxiliary Bishop of Colombo 1991–95; Titular Bishop of Cabarsussi 1991–2004; Vicar Gen. in charge of Parochial Apostolate and Lay Apostolate 1991–95; Sec.-Gen. Catholic Bishops' Conf. of Sri Lanka, Chair. Organizing Cttee for the Beatification of Venerable Joseph Vaz; first Bishop of Ratnapura 1995–2001; Adjunct Sec. Congregation for the Evangelisation of Peoples 2001–04; Pres. Pontifical Mission Socs 2001–04; Apostolic Nuncio (first Sri Lankan) to Indonesia and Timor-Leste 2004–05; Titular Archbishop of Umbriatico 2004–; Sec. Congregation for Divine Worship and the Discipline of the Sacraments 2005–09; Archbishop of Colombo 2009–; cr. Cardinal (Cardinal-Priest of San Lorenzo in Lucina) 2010; participated in Papal Conclave 2013. *Address:* Archbishop's House, 976 Gnanartha Pradeepaya Mawatha, Colombo 8, Sri Lanka (office). *Telephone:* (11) 2695471 (office). *Fax:* (11) 2692009 (office). *E-mail:* info@archdioceseofcolombo .com (office). *Website:* www.archdioceseofcolombo.com (office).

PATAIL, Hon. Tan Sri Abdul Gani, LLB (Hons); Malaysian lawyer; *Attorney-General;* b. 6 Oct. 1955; m. 1st YBhg. Puan Sri Datin Seri; m. 2nd Panglima Maimun Datuk Haji Arif; ed Univ. of Malaya; began legal career as a Deputy Public Prosecutor in Kota Kinabalu, Sabah 1980; promoted to Sr Fed. Counsel for Sabah 1985; moved to Attorney-Gen.'s Chambers, Kuala Lumpur 1994, Sr Public Prosecutor 1994–95, 2000–01, Head of Advisory and Int. Div. 1995–97, Commr of Law Revision 1997–2000, Attorney-Gen. 2002–; involved in numerous high-profile cases, led prosecution of fmr Deputy Prime Minister Anwar Ibrahim in trials involving corruption and sodomy 1998. *Address:* Attorney-General's Chambers, 45 Persiaran Perdana, Precint 4, 62100 Putrajaya, Malaysia (office). *Telephone:* (603) 8872-2000 (office). *Fax:* (603) 8890-5670 (office). *E-mail:* pro@agc.gov.my (office). *Website:* www.agc.gov.my (office).

PATAKI, George Elmer, BA, JD; American lawyer, politician and fmr state official; *Counsel, Chadbourne & Parke LLP;* b. 24 June 1945, Peekskill, NY; s. of Louis P. Pataki and Margaret Pataki (née Lagana); m. Elizabeth Rowland 1973; two s. two d.; ed Peekskill High School, Yale Univ., Columbia Univ. Law School; Assoc. Dewey Ballantine PC (law firm), New York 1970–74; Partner, Plunkett & Jaffee PC (law firm), White Plains and New York; Co-Owner, Pataki's Farm, Peekskill, NY; Mayor of Peekskill 1981–84; mem. NY State Ass. 1985–92; mem. NY State Senate 1993–94; Gov. of NY State 1994–2007; Counsel, Chadbourne & Parke LLP (law firm), New York 2007–; Founder, Pataki-Cahill Group 2007–; Republican. *Address:* Chadbourne & Parke LLP, 1301 Avenue of the Americas, New York, NY 10019-6022, USA (office). *Telephone:* (212) 408-5145 (office). *E-mail:* gpataki@chadbourne.com (office). *Website:* www.chadbourne.com/gpataki (office).

PATARADZE, Zurab; Georgian economist, diplomatist and politician; *Ambassador to Azerbaijan;* b. 12 Feb. 1973, Batumi, Ajaran ASSR, Georgian SSR, USSR; m.; three c.; ed Tbilisi State Univ., Batumi State Univ.; Sr Auditor, Savings Bank Batumi Br. 1994–96; joined civil service 1996, Investigative Service Inspector, Fight Against Organized Crime, Ministry of the Interior Criminal Police Dept 1996–2000, Chief Specialist, Foreign Policy Research and Analysis Centre, Ministry of Foreign Affairs (MFA) April–May 2000, Second Sec., Consular Econ. Activity and Visa Div., MFA Consular Dept 2000–01, Second Sec., Dept of Consular Affairs 2001–04, Second Sec. in charge of consular service, Embassy in Moscow 2004–08, Consular Officer, Georgian interests section, Swiss Embassy in Moscow 2008–09, Consul-Gen., Thessaloniki 2009–10, Consul-Gen., Istanbul 2011–12, Amb. to Turkey 2012–13, Amb. to Kazakhstan 2013–16, Amb. to Azerbaijan 2018–; Chair. of the Govt, Autonomous Repub. of Ajara 2016–18. *Address:* Embassy of Georgia, 1069 Baku, Y. Huseynov küç. 15, Azerbaijan (office). *Telephone:* (12) 497-45-60 (office). *Fax:* (12) 497-45-61 (office). *E-mail:* bakuemb@ mfa.gov.ge (office). *Website:* azerbaijan.mfa.gov.ge (office).

PATCHETT, Ann, BA, MFA; American writer; b. 2 Dec. 1963, Los Angeles, Calif.; ed Sarah Lawrence Coll., Univ. of Iowa Writers' Workshop; Writer-in-Residence, Allegheny Coll. 1989–90; Yaddo Fellow 1990; Millay Fellow 1990; Resident Fellow, Fine Arts Work Center, Provincetown 1990–91; Visiting Asst Prof., Murray State Univ. 1992; Bunting Fellow, Mary Ingram Bunting Inst., Radcliffe Coll. 1993; Guggenheim Fellowship 1994; Nashville Banner Tenn. Writer of the Year Award 1994, Peggy V. Helmerich Distinguished Author Award 2014. *Publications include:* The Patron Saint of Liars (Univ. of Iowa James A. Michener/Copernicus Award for a book in progress 1989, American Library Asscn Notable Book 1992) 1992, Taft (Janet Heidinger Kafka Prize) 1994, The Magician's Assistant 1997, Bel Canto (PEN/Faulkner Award 2002, Orange Prize 2002) 2001, Truth and Beauty (biography) 2004, Run 2007, What Now? 2008, State of Wonder 2011, This Is the Story of a Happy Marriage 2013, Commonwealth 2016; contribs to anthologies and to periodicals, including The New York Times Magazine, Chicago Tribune, Boston Globe, Vogue, GQ, Elle, Gourmet. *Address:* c/o Author Mail, 11th Floor, HarperCollins Publishers, 10 East 53rd Street, New York, NY 10022, USA (office). *Website:* www.annpatchett.com (office).

PATE, John Stewart, DSc, PhD, FAA, FRS; British scientist and academic; *Professor Emeritus of Botany, University of Western Australia;* b. 15 Jan. 1932; s. of H. S. Pate and M. M. Pate; m. Elizabeth L. Sloan 1959 (died 2004); three s.; ed Campbell Coll. Belfast and Queen's Univ. Belfast; lecturer in Botany, Univ. of Sydney 1957–60; lecturer in Botany, Queen's Univ. Belfast 1960–65, then Reader, Personal Chair. in Plant Physiology 1970–83; Prof. of Botany, Univ. of W Australia 1974–2001, Prof. Emer. 2001–; Hon. DSc (Univ. of W Australia); Australian

Minerals and Energy Research Foundation Award 1999, Commonwealth Centenary Medal 2003. *Publications:* Restionaceae and Allied Families of Australia 1999 (co.-ed.); over 350 books, research articles, reviews, chapters for textbooks and conf. proceedings. *Leisure interests:* music, reading, nature study, writing nature books, committed Christian. *Address:* Department of Plant Sciences, University of Western Australia, Nedlands, WA 6009 (office); 681 Mount Shadforth Road, Denmark, WA 6333, Australia. *Telephone:* (9) 848-1096 (office).

PATEL, A. K., MB; Indian politician and medical practitioner; b. 1 July 1931, Vadu, Mehsana Dist, Gujarat; s. of Kalidas Patel; m. Divaben Patel; two s. one d.; ed B. J. Medical Coll., Ahmedabad; mem. Gujarat Legis. Ass. –1984; mem. for Mehsana, Lok Sabha 1984–99, Minister of State for Chemicals and Fertilizers 1998–99; Pres. Bharatiya Janata Party, Gujarat 1982–85; mem. Rajya Sabha 2000–06; Man. Trustee, SRST Gen. Hosp., Vijapur, Asha Educ. Trust, Girls' Coll., Vijapur; Trustee St Joseph Public School, Vijapur. *Leisure interests:* reading, swimming, riding, sports. *Address:* nr T. B. Hospital, Bhavsor, Vijapur 384 001, India (home). *Telephone:* (27) 6320080 (home).

PATEL, Anandiben, MEd; Indian politician, fmr teacher and state governor; *Governor of Madhya Pradesh and of Chhattisgarh;* b. 21 Nov. 1941, Mehsana Dist, Gujarat; m. Mafatbhai Patel; two c.; ed M. G. Panchal Science Coll., Pilvai; Math. and Science Teacher, Mohinba Kanya Vidhyalaya school 1968–98, Prin. 1988–99; mem. Bharatiya Janata Party (BJP) 1987–; mem. Rajya Sabha (upper house of Parl.) 1994–98; mem. Gujarat Legis. Ass. 1998–2002, Gujarat Minister of Educ. and Women and Child Welfare 1998, of Road and Building, Revenue, Urban Devt and Urban Housing, Disaster Man. and Capital Projects 2007–14; Chief Minister of Gujarat (first woman) 2014–16; Gov. Madhya Pradesh Jan. 2018–, also of Chhattisgarh Aug. 2018–; fmr Chair. Sahiyar Mahila Credit Soc.; Founder Gramshree Trust and Dir Gramshree Women Empowerment Section 25 Company. *Address:* Raj Bhavan, Malviya Nagar, Bhopal 462003, Madhya Pradesh, India. *Telephone:* (755) 408-0204 (office). *Website:* www.bjp.org.

PATEL, Bhavesh V. (Bob), BS, MBA; American (b. Indian) business executive; *Chairman of the Management Board and CEO, LyondellBasell Industries;* ed Ohio State Univ. and Fox School of Business and Man., Temple Univ.; with Chevron Corpn and its affiliates 1990–2010, Gen. Man., Olefins and Natural Gas Liquids, Chevron Phillips Chemical Co. –2010, also served as Gen. Man., Asia-Pacific region, based in Singapore; Sr Vice-Pres., Olefins & Polyolefins (O&P) – Americas, LyondellBasell March–Nov. 2010, Sr Vice-Pres., O&P – Europe, Asia and Int. (O&P EAI) Nov. 2010–13, Exec. Vice-Pres., O&P EAI 2013–14, also responsible for manufacturing operations outside of the Americas, mem. Man. Bd LyondellBasell Industries 2014–, Chair. and CEO 2015–; mem. Exec. Cttee and Bd of Dirs, American Chem. Council. *Address:* LyondellBasell Industries, PO Box 2416, 3000 CK Rotterdam (office); LyondellBasell Industries, Groot Handelsgebouw – Entrance A, Stationsplein 45, 3013 AK Rotterdam, The Netherlands (office). *Telephone:* (10) 275-5500 (office). *Fax:* (10) 275-5599 (office). *E-mail:* info@ lyondellbasell.com (office). *Website:* www.lyondellbasell.com (office).

PATEL, Dev; British actor; b. 3 April 1990, Harrow, Middx, England; s. of Raj Patel and Anita Patel; partner Freida Pinto 2009–14; ed Longfield Middle School, Whitmore High School, Rayners Lane Acad. of Taekwon-do. *Films include:* Slumdog Millionaire (Black Reel Award for Best Actor 2008, Black Reel Award for Best Breakthrough Performance 2008, British Ind. Film Award for Most Promising Newcomer 2008, Chicago Film Critics Asscn Award for Most Promising Performer 2008, Nat. Board of Review Award for Best Breakthrough Performance 2008, Phoenix Film Critics Soc. Award for Break Out On Camera 2008, Washington, DC Area Film Critics Asscn Award for Best Breakthrough Performance 2008, Critics' Choice Award for Best Young Performer (Actor/Actress) 2009, Richard Attenborough Film Award for Best Breakthrough 2009, Richard Attenborough Film Award for Rising Star of the Year 2009) 2008, The Last Airbender 2010, The Best Exotic Marigold Hotel 2011, Cherry 2012, The Road Within 2014, The Second Best Exotic Marigold Hotel 2015, Chappie 2015, The Man Who Knew Infinity 2016, Only Yesterday (voice) 2016, Lion (AACTA Int. Award for Best Supporting Actor 2016, Best Supporting Actor, Santa Barbara Int. Film Festival 2017, BAFTA Award for Best Supporting Actor 2017) 2016. *Television includes:* Skins (series) 2007–08, Mister Eleven (mini-series) 2009, True Jackson, VP (series) 2010, The Newsroom (series) 2012–13. *Achievements include:* competed regularly in both nat. and int. Taekwon-do championships, including Action Int. Martial Arts Asscn World Championships, Dublin 2004, won a bronze medal; bronze medal, World Championships 2004; gained a 1st dan black belt 2006. *Address:* c/o Sarah Spear, Curtis Brown Ltd, 28–29 Haymarket, London, SW1Y 4SP, England (office). *Telephone:* (20) 7393-4466 (office). *Fax:* (20) 7393-4401 (office). *E-mail:* spearclissoldoffice@curtisbrown.co.uk (office). *Website:* www .curtisbrown.co.uk (office).

PATEL, Dinsha Jhaverbhai; Indian politician; b. 25 May 1937, Itola, Baroda Dist, Gujarat; s. of Jhaverbhai Patel and Hiraben J. Patel; m. Kundanben Dinsha Patel; started political career as youth leader 1956; mem. Nagar Palika (municipal council), Nadiad, Gujarat 1972–82; mem. Gujarat Legis. Ass. 1975–96; Minister of Public Works and Parl. Affairs, Govt of Gujarat 1990–95; mem. Lok Sabha (lower house of Parl.) for Kheda constituency (Gujarat) 1996–2014; Union Cabinet Minister of State for Petroleum and Natural Gas 2006–09, Minister of State (Ind. Charge) for Micro, Small and Medium Enterprises 2009–11, Minister of State for Mines 2011–12, Minister of Mines 2012–14; mem. Exec. Cttee Gujarat Cricket Asscn. *Leisure interests:* hockey, cricket. *Address:* c/o Ministry of Mines, 'A' Wing, 3rd Floor, Shastri Bhavan, Dr Rajendra Prasad Road, New Delhi, India.

PATEL, Nadir, BA, MBA; Canadian civil servant and diplomatist; *High Commissioner to India;* ed Wilfrid Laurier Univ., New York Univ., USA, London School of Econs, UK, Ecole des hautes études commerciales de Paris, France; began career at Canada Customs and Revenue Agency 1990, served in various roles in offices in Kitchener-Waterloo, Ottawa and Montreal, Departmental Asst to the Minister, Dir of Ministerial Services, Agency Adviser to the Minister and Sec. to the Bd of Man. 1997–2003; transferred to Privy Council Office 2003, Chief of Staff to Nat. Security Adviser to Prime Minister, Assoc. Sec. to Cabinet and Deputy Minister to Deputy Prime Minister 2003–05, Sr Policy Adviser to Clerk of the Privy Council and Sec. to Cabinet 2005–06; Canada's Chief Air Negotiator 2006–09; Consul-Gen. in Shanghai 2009–11, Asst Deputy Minister for Corp. Planning,

Finance and Information Tech. and Chief Financial Officer, Foreign Affairs, Trade and Development Canada 2011–15, High Commr to India 2015–. *Address:* Canadian High Commission, 7/8 Shanti Path, Chanakyapuri, New Delhi 110 021, India (office). *Telephone:* (11) 41782000 (office). *Fax:* (11) 41782020 (office). *E-mail:* delhi@international.gc.ca (office). *Website:* www.canadainternational.gc.ca/india-inde (office).

PATEL, Praful Khodabhai; Indian politician; *Administrator of Daman and Diu, and Dadra and Nagar Haveli;* b. 28 Aug. 1957, Mehsana District, Gujarat; started career in construction sector; MLA, 27-Himmatnagar Constituency, Vidhansabha, Gujarat 2007–12; Minister of State for Home Affairs, Gujarat 2010–12; currently mem. Bhartiya Janata Party (BJP), Pres. BJP Sabarkantha Dist, Gujarat 2010–; Admin., Daman and Diu, and Dadra and Nagar Haveli 2016–; active social worker and worked with Rotary club, Lions Club, Red Cross Soc. and other social organizations. *Leisure interests:* travelling, reading, mountaineering, rescue in natural calamities, adventure touring to unexplored places and research. *Address:* Office of the Administration of Daman and Diu, Administrator's Bungalow, Moti Daman, Daman 396 210, India (office). *Telephone:* (260) 2231707 (office); (260)-2230700 (office). *E-mail:* administrator-dd-dnh@nic.in (office). *Website:* daman.nic.in (office); www.prafulpatel.in.

PATEL, Praful Raojibhai Chaturbhai; British campaigner and business executive; *President, Que Capital Limited;* b. 7 March 1939, Jinja, Uganda; s. of Raojibhai Chaturbhai Patel and Maniben Jivabhai Lalaji Patel; ed Govt Secondary School and London Inst. of World Affairs, Univ. Coll., London; Gen. Sec. Uganda Students' Union 1956–58; Del. to Int. Youth Ass., New Delhi 1958; arrived in UK as student, then commenced commercial and financial services activities 1962; Pres. Nava Kala India Socio-Cultural Centre, London 1962–75; Hon. Sec. All-Party Parl. Cttee on UK Citizenship 1968–82; Founder and Council mem. UK Immigration Advisory Service 1970–82; Chair. Bd of Trustees, Swaminarayan Hindu Mission, UK 1970–76; mem. Uganda Resettlement Bd 1972–74; Hon. Sec. Uganda Evacuees Resettlement Advisory Trust 1974–2000; Jt Convener Asian Action Cttee 1976; mem. Indian Govt Consultative Cttee on Non-Resident Indian Investments 1986–91; adviser to His Holiness Pramukh Swami Maharaj on NGO activities, continues to support the activities of Worldwide Swaminarayan Fellowship; initiator of many inter-faith dialogues with spiritual leaders in India and abroad, including organizing many recitations of Hindu scriptures; fmr Gov. City Lit Coll., London; cand. (Labour) for Brent N constituency 1986; organized historic trip of His Holiness Sant Shri Morari Bapu to Kailas Manasarovar, Tibet, China in 1997; Dir Indo-British Cultural Exchange 2002–; Chair. 40th Anniversary British Uganda Asian Celebration Cttee 2012–; Pres. Que Capital Ltd 2013–; fmr Chair. Asia Fund Ltd; Chair. and Trustee, Manava Trust 1979–; Trustee and Gen. Sec. Int. Ayurveda Foundation, UK 2002–; involved in industrial, cultural and educational projects affecting immigrants in UK; spokesman for Asians in UK following restrictions of immigration resulting from Commonwealth Immigrants Act 1968; active campaigner for civil and human rights issues, co-operation between Third World countries and investments in India; mem. British Labour Party, Charter '88 Movt, UK Democratic Audit; UK Del. to Indo-British Conf. on Democracy and Human Rights organized by Rajiv Gandhi Foundation, New Delhi; specialist on immigration, citizenship and race-relation issues; Trustee, The Charutar Arogya Mandal Trust, UK 1980, India Overseas Trust 2002–, Kailas Manasarovar Trust 2002–; Queen's Scout 1956, Asian Times Award for achievement 1986, Neasden Swaminarayan Mandir Award. *Dance:* Nritya Natika Ramayana (producer) 1982. *Film:* Kailas Manasarovar Yatra (producer). *Publications:* numerous articles in newspapers and journals on political, immigration, race relations and business related issues. *Leisure interests:* cricket, campaigning and lobbying, current affairs, promoting traditional Ayurveda medicines, inter-faith co-operation, passionate about his unique collection of more than 3,000 Ganesh Murtis (idols) and Hindu artifacts. *Address:* 60 Bedford Court Mansions, Bedford Avenue, London, WC1B 3AD, England (home); Praful Patel Associates, Readymoney Mansion, 3rd Floor, 43 Veer Nariman Road, Mumbai, 400023 India (office); Que Capital Ltd, Office 1905, INDEX Tower, Dubai International Financial Centre, PO Box 506581, Dubai, United Arab Emirates (office). *Telephone:* (20) 7580-0897 (London) (home); (22) 22049248 (India) (office); (4) 818-4014 (Dubai) (office). *Fax:* (20) 7436-2418 (London) (home); (22) 22048938 (India) (office); (4) 432-5783 (Dubai) (office). *E-mail:* prcpatel@vsnl.com (home); praful.patel@quecap.com (office). *Website:* www.quecap.com (office); www.prafulpatel.co.uk.

PATEL, Priti Sushil; British politician; b. 29 March 1972, London; d. of Sushil Patel; m. Alex Sawyer 2004; one s.; ed Keele Univ., Univ. of Essex; mem. Referendum Party 1995–97, Head, Referendum Party Press Office 1995–97; worked for Conservative Party Research Dept, Conservative Central Office, becoming Deputy Press Sec. to Leader of the Opposition William Hague 1998; with Corp. Relations Dept, Diageo PLC 2003–07; contested for seat as MP for Nottingham North 2005; Consultant, Weber Shandwick (public relations co.) 2007–10; MP for Witham (Conservative) 2010–, mem. Public Admin Select Cttee 2011–14; Exchequer Sec. to the Treasury 2014–15, Minister of State for Employment 2015–16, Sec. of State for Int. Devt 2016–17; mem. Vote Leave Campaign Cttee 2016; mem. 1922 Cttee Exec. 2012–16, mem. Prime Minister's Policy Bd 2013–17. *Publication:* Britannia Unchained: Global Lessons for Growth and Prosperity (co-author) 2012. *Address:* House of Commons, London, SW1A 0AA, England (office). *Telephone:* (20) 7219-3528 (House of Commons) (office). *E-mail:* priti.patel.mp@parliament.uk (office). *Website:* www.priti4witham.com (office).

PATEL, Urjit R., BA, M.Phil., PhD; Indian economist, international organisation official and central banker; b. 28 Oct. 1963, Kenya; s. of Ravindra Patel; ed Yale Univ., USA, Univ. of Oxford and London School of Econs, UK; joined IMF 1990, posted at India desk 1991–94, country mission in India 1992–95; Advisor, Reserve Bank of India 1995–97; Pres. Business Devt, Reliance Industries Ltd 1997–2006; apptd Exec. Dir Infrastructure Devt Finance Co. Ltd 1997; Consultant, Ministry of Finance, Dept of Econ. Affairs, New Delhi 1998–2001; Dir Gujarat State Petroleum Corpn, Multi Commodity Exchange of India Ltd 2005–08; Non-Resident Sr Fellow, Brookings Inst. 2009; Advisor, Energy and Infrastructure, Boston Consulting Group –2013; Deputy Gov. Reserve Bank of India 2013–16, Gov. 2016–18; Dir Nat. Housing Bank 2015–16; mem. Integrated Energy Policy Cttee, Govt of India 2004–06, advisory bd, Bank of International Settlement 2017–. *Leisure interests:* reading, traveling. *Address:* c/o Reserve Bank of India, Central Office Building, Shahid Bhagat Singh Road, POB 10007, Mumbai 400 001, India (office). *Telephone:* (22) 22661602 (office). *Fax:* (22) 22658269 (office). *E-mail:* helpprd@rbi.org.in (office). *Website:* www.rbi.org.in (office).

PATERSON, David Alexander, BA, JD; American academic and fmr politician; b. 20 May 1954, Brooklyn, NY; s. of Basil Paterson and Portia Paterson (née Hairston); m. Michelle Paige 1992; one s. one step-d.; ed Hempstead High School, Columbia Univ., New York, Hofstra Law School; born legally blind; worked for Queens Dist Attorney's Office (failed NY Bar examination); joined campaign staff of David Dinkins for Manhattan Borough Pres. 1985; won selection process to serve remainder of term in NY State Senate for 30th Senate Dist following death of Senator Bogues 1985, youngest senator when elected aged 31, won seat for first full term representing 29th Dist 1986–2007; ran in Democratic primary for office of New York Public Advocate 1993; elected by Democratic Caucus of Senate as Minority Leader (first non-white state legis. leader and highest-ranking black elected official in history of NY State) 2002; mem. Democratic Nat. Cttee, Bd Democratic Legis. Campaign Cttee; selected as running mate by NY Attorney-Gen. and Democratic Party nominee Eliot Spitzer in NY gubernatorial election 2006; Lt-Gov. of NY (first legally blind lt-gov.) 2006–08, Gov. of NY (first African American) 2008–10; Guest Lecturer, New York Univ. 2011–; fmr Adjunct Prof., Columbia Univ. School of Int. and Public Affairs; mem. Bd of Dirs Achilles Track Club; mem. Nat. Asscn for the Advancement of Colored People (mem. Bd of Dirs Mid-Manhattan Br.), Allen Black Bar Asscn, New York State Bar Asscn, Metropolitan Cttee of 100 (legal adviser), Martin Luther King Democratic Club; mem. Bd of Trustees, American Foundation for the Blind; Community Service Award, New Hampshire Hairston Clan 1984, Achievement Award, Courtsman A.A., Inc. 1986, named Senator of Year, New York State Nat. Org. of Women 1989, Migel Award, American Foundation for Blind 1996, named to The Power 150, Ebony magazine 2008. *Publications:* numerous articles in professional journals. *Leisure interests:* playing basketball, New York sports teams, theatre, history.

PATERSON, Rt Rev. John Campbell, BA, LTh; New Zealand ecclesiastic; b. 4 Jan. 1945, Auckland; s. of Thomas Paterson and Mary Paterson; m. Marion Reid Anderson 1968; two d.; ed King's Coll., Univ. of Auckland, St John's Coll.; asst curate, Whangarei 1969–71; vicar, Waimate N Maori pastorate 1971–76; Priest-in-Charge, Hokianga 1973–74, Bay of Islands 1974–75; Chaplain, Queen Victoria School 1976–82; Asst Priest, Maori Mission 1976–82; Sec. Bishopric of Aotearoa 1978–87; Prov. Sec. 1986–92; mem. Anglican Consultative Council 1990–96, Chair. 2002; Gen. Sec. of Anglican Church, Aotearoa, Polynesia and NZ 1992–95, Presiding Bishop and Primate of Anglican Church, Aotearoa, Polynesia and NZ 1998–2004; Bishop of Auckland 1995–2010; Cross of St Augustine 2010 Outstanding Old Collegian Award King's Coll. 2000, Univ. of Auckland Distinguished Alumni Award 2004. *Publications:* He Toenga Whatiwhatinga 1984. *Leisure interests:* literature, music. *Address:* Bishopscourt, PO Box 37242, Parnell 1033, New Zealand (home). *Telephone:* (9) 302-7202 (home). *Fax:* (9) 377-6962 (home).

PATERSON, Katherine Womeldorf; American children's writer; b. 31 Oct. 1932, Qing Jiang, People's Republic of China; m. John Barstow Paterson 1962 (died 2013); four c.; ed King Coll., Union Theological Seminary; Nat. Amb. to Young People's Literature, Library of Congress 2010–11; currently Vice-Pres. Nat. Children's Book and Literacy Alliance; mem. Bd of Trustees Vermont Coll. of Fine Arts; Hon. lifetime mem. Int. Bd of Books for Young People, Alida Cutts lifetime mem. The US Board on Books for Young People; Dr hc (St Mary of the Woods), (Univ. of Maryland), (Hope Coll.), (Otterbein Coll.), (Presbyterian Coll.), (King Coll.), (Norwich Univ.), (Saint Michael's Coll.), (Shenandoah Coll. and Conservatory), (Washington and Lee Univ.), (Mount Saint Vincent Univ., Canada); Union Theological Seminary Union Medal, New York, Univ. of Southern Mississippi Medallion 1983, Univ. of Minnesota Kerlan Award 1983, Keene State Coll. Children's Literature Award 1987, Catholic Library Asscn Regina Medal 1988, New England Book Award 1992, Tulsa Public Library Anne V. Zarrow Award 1993, Education Press Friend of Education Award 1993, Hans Christian Andersen Medal for Writing 1998, New York Public Library Lion 1998, Library of Congress Living Legend Award 2000, Boston Public Library Literary Light 2000, Astrid Lindgren Memorial Award 2006, NSK Neustadt Prize for Children's Literature 2007, Laura Ingalls Wilder Medal 2013, E. B. White Award, American Acad. of Arts and Letters 2019. *Publications include:* novels: Bread and Roses, Too, Bridge to Terabithia (Newbery Medal 1978, Lewis Carroll Shelf Award 1978, Janusz Korczak Medal, Poland 1981, Silver Pencil Award, Netherlands 1981, Grand Prix des Jeunes Lecturs, France 1986, Colorado Blue Spruce Young Adult Book Award 1986), Come Sing, Jimmy Jo, The Day of the Pelican, Flip-Flop Girl, The Great Gilly Hopkins (Nat. Book Award 1979, Newbery Honor Award 1979, Jane Addams Children's Book Award 1979, Christopher Award 1979), Jacob Have I Loved (Newbery Medal 1981), Jip, his Story (Scott O'Dell Award for Historical Fiction 1997), Lyddie (Int. Bd of Books for Young People Honor Book 1994, IBBY Honor Book), The Master Puppeteer (Nat. Book Award for Childrens Literature 1977, MWA Edgar Allen Poe Special Award 1977), Of Nightingales that Weep (Children's Literature Asscn Phoenix Award 1994), Park's Quest, Preacher's Boy (Jefferson Cup of Virginia Library Asscn), Rebels of the Heavenly Kingdom, The Same Stuff as Stars (Paterson Prize 2003, Jane Addams Award 2003, Judy Lopez Memorial Award 2003), Sign of the Chrysanthemum, My Brigadista Year; picture books: The Angel and the Donkey, Blueberries for the Queen, Celia and the Sweet, Sweet Water, The King's Equal, The Tale of the Mandarin Ducks (Boston Globe/Horn Book Picture Book Award 1991), The Wide-Awake Princess; non-fiction: Consider the Lilies, Gates of Excellence, Images of God, The Invisible Child, A Sense of Wonder, The Spying Heart, Who Am I?. *Address:* c/o HarperCollins Publishers, Elsinore House, 195 Broadway, New York, NY 10007, USA (office). *Website:* www.harpercollins.com (office); katherinepaterson.com.

PATERSON, Mervyn Silas, FAA, ScD; Australian geophysicist and academic; *Professor Emeritus and Visiting Fellow, Research School of Earth Sciences, Australian National University;* b. 7 March 1925, South Australia; s. of Charles Paterson and Edith M. Michael; m. Katalin Sarosy 1952; one s. one d.; ed Adelaide Tech. High School, Univ. of Adelaide, Univ. of Cambridge, UK; Researcher, Aeronautical Research Labs, Melbourne 1945–53; mem. Faculty, ANU 1953–, Prof., Research School of Earth Sciences 1987–90, Prof. Emer. and Visiting Fellow 1990–; Consultant, Australian Scientific Instruments Pty Ltd; Fellow, American

Mineralogical Soc., American Geophysical Union; Hon. Fellow, Geological Soc. of America 1987; Walter H. Bucher Medal, American Geophysical Union 2004. *Publications include:* Experimental Rock Deformation: The Brittle Field 1978; about 110 research papers in rock deformation and materials science. *Leisure interests:* walking, reading. *Address:* J6, 218, Research School of Earth Sciences, Australian National University, Acton, ACT 2601, Australia (office). *Telephone:* (2) 6125-2497 (office). *Fax:* (2) 6125-0738 (office). *E-mail:* mervyn.paterson@anu.edu.au (office). *Website:* rses.anu.edu.au/people/mervyn-paterson (office).

PATERSON, Rt Hon. Owen William, PC, MA; British politician; b. 24 June 1956, Whitchurch, Salop.; m. The Hon. Rose Ridley 1980; two s. one d.; ed Abberley Hall School, Radley Coll., Corpus Christi Coll., Cambridge, Nat. Leathersellers Coll. (now British School of Leather Tech. at Univ. of Northampton); joined British Leather Co. (family leather business) 1979, Sales Dir 1983–94, Man. Dir 1994–99; Dir Parsons & Sons (leather co.), Halesowen 1990s; contested Wrexham constituency 1992; MP for N Shropshire 1997–, mem. (Select Cttees), Welsh Affairs 1997–2001, European Standing Cttee A 1998–2001, Welsh Grand Cttee 1998–2000, European Scrutiny 1999–2000, Agric. 2000–01; Opposition Whip 2000–01; Parl. Pvt. Sec. to Iain Duncan Smith as Leader of the Opposition 2001–03; Shadow Minister for Environment, Food and Rural Affairs 2003–05, for Transport 2005–07; Shadow Sec. of State for NI 2007–10; Sec. of State for NI 2010–12, for Environment, Food and Rural Affairs 2012–14; Vice-Pres. Conservatives Against a Fed. Europe 1998–2001; mem. 92 Group 1997–, Conservative Friends of Israel 1997–, Conservative Way Forward 1997–, Conservative 2000 1997–, No Turning Back Group 1998–, Exec. 1922 Committee 2000; Founding Chair. UK 2020 (think tank) 2014–; Pres. Cotance (European Tanners' Confed.) 1996–98; mem. Inter-Parl. Union 1997–, Commonwealth Parl. Asscn 1997–, Advisory Bd European Foundation 1998–; Conservative; Liveryman of the Leathersellers' Co. *Leisure interests:* horses, racing and eventing, trees, architecture, history. *Address:* House of Commons, Westminster, London, SW1A 0AA, England (office). *Telephone:* (20) 7219-5185 (office); (1978) 710073 (Constituency). *Fax:* (20) 7219-3955 (office). *E-mail:* patersono@parliament.uk (office); owen@shellbrook.demon.co.uk. *Website:* www.owenpaterson.org.

PATERSON, William (Bill), BA (Hons), FAIM; Australian diplomatist; m.; three c.; ed Univ. of Melbourne; sr career officer with Dept of Foreign Affairs and Trade, postings to Vienna, Baghdad and Dhaka, later Counsellor, Embassy in Washington, DC, Chief of Staff to Foreign Minister Alexander Downer 2000, later Minister at Embassy in Tokyo, Amb. to Thailand 2004–08, First Asst Sec., Int. Security Div., Canberra and Australian Amb. for Counter-Terrorism 2008–13, Amb. to South Korea 2013–16; Dir Australia–Korea Business Council; Public Service Medal 2003, Humanitarian Overseas Service Medal 2005. *Address:* Australia Korea Business Council, PO Box 24430, Melbourne Vic. 3001, Australia (office). *E-mail:* info@akbc.com.au; bill.paterson49@gmail.com (office). *Website:* akbc.com.au (office).

PATERSON, William Edgar, OBE, MSc, PhD, FRSE, FRSA, FAcSS; British academic; *Honorary Professor of German and European Politics, Aston University;* b. 26 Sept. 1941, Blair Atholl, Scotland; s. of William Edgar Paterson and Winnie Paterson (née McIntyre); m. 1st Jacqueline Cramb 1964 (died 1974); two s.; m. 2nd Phyllis MacDowell 1979; one d. one step-s. one step-d.; ed Morrison's Acad., Univ. of St Andrews, London School of Econs; Lecturer in Int. Relations, Univ. of Aberdeen 1967–70; Volkswagen Lecturer in German Politics, Univ. of Warwick 1970–75, Sr Lecturer 1975–82, Reader 1982–89, Prof. and Chair. of Dept 1989–90; Salvesen Prof. and Dir of Europa Inst., Univ. of Edin. 1990–94; Dir Inst. for German Studies, Univ. of Birmingham 1994–2008, now Emer. Prof. in German Politics; currently Hon. Prof. in German and European Politics, Aston Centre for Europe, Aston Univ.; Chair. Asscn for the Study of German Politics 1974–76, Univ. Asscn for Contemporary European Studies 1989–94; Vice-Chair. German-British Forum 1996, Chair. 2005–13; mem. Econ. and Social Research Council Research Priorities Bd 1994–99, British Königswinter Cttee 1995–, Kuratorium Allianz Kulturstiftung 2001–04; Co-Ed. German Politics 1991–2001, Journal of Common Market Studies 2003–08; Academician, Acad. of Learned Socs in Social Sciences 2000; Bundesverdienstkreuz (Germany) 1999; Lifetime Award, Asscn for the Study of German Politics 2004, Lifetime Award, Univ. Asscn for Contemporary European Studies 2007, Special Recognition Award for excellence in German politics, European integration and the study of German-British relations, Political Studies Asscn. *Publications include:* The Federal Republic of Germany and the European Community (with Simon Bulmer) 1987, Government and the Chemical Industry (with Wyn Grant) 1988, Developments in German Politics II 1996, The Kohl Chancellorship (with Clay Clemens) 1998, The Future of the German Economy (with Rebecca Harding) 2000, Developments in German Politics 3 2003, Governance in Contemporary Germany: The Semisovereign State Revisited (co-ed.) 2005, Germany's Gathering Crisis (co-ed) 2009, Research Agendas in European Union Studies (co-ed) 2010, Developments in German Politics 4 2014; 20 other books and over 120 articles in learned journals. *Leisure interest:* walking. *Address:* 220 Myton Road, Warwick, CV34 6PS, England (home). *Telephone:* (1926) 492492 (home). *E-mail:* w.paterson@aston.ac.uk (office).

PATEY, Sir William Charters, Kt, KCMG, MA; British diplomatist (retd); b. 11 July 1953, Edinburgh, Scotland; s. of William Maurice Patey and Christina Kinnell Patey; m. Vanessa Morrell 1978; two s.; ed Trinity Acad., Edinburgh, grammar school, Univ. of Dundee; joined FCO 1975, Aid and Financial Relations Dept 1975–76, Rhodesia Dept 1976–77, Commercial Attaché, Abu Dhabi 1978–81, Second Sec., Tripoli 1981–84, Perm. Under-Sec./Dir-Gen. Offices, FCO 1984–85, Near East and N African Dept 1986–87, Middle Eastern Dept 1987–88, First Sec., Canberra 1988–92, Deputy Head, UN Dept, FCO 1992–94, Overseas Insp. 1994–95, Deputy Head of Mission and Consul-Gen., Riyadh 1995–98, Head, Middle Eastern Dept, FCO 1998–2002, Amb. to Sudan 2002–05, to Iraq 2005–06, Dir Comprehensive Spending Review Programme, FCO 2006–07, Amb. to Saudi Arabia 2007–10, to Afghanistan 2010–12 (retd); Partner, The Ambassador Partnership LLP; Adviser on Int. Affairs, Control Risks 2012–; mem. Bd of Dirs WCP Consultants, HSBC Middle East and HBME 2012–; Chair. Swindon Town Football Club 2012–13; Hon. Fellow, Univ. of Exeter 2013; Hon. LLD (Univ. of Dundee) 2017; Iraq Civilian Service Medal 2006, Afghanistan Civilian Service Medal 2012. *Leisure interests:* cinema, theatre, golf, supports QPR Football Club and Hibernian Football Club. *Telephone:* (20) 7979-2105 (office). *E-mail:* william.patey@controlrisks.com (office); williampatey@hotmail.com (home).

PATHMANATHAN, Selvarasa, (Shanmugam Kumaran Tharmalingam); Sri Lankan rebel leader; b. 6 April 1955, Kankesanthurai, Jaffna Dist; ed Nadeswara Coll., Kankesanthurai, Mahajana Coll., Thellipalai, Jaffna Univ.; left Sri Lanka and fled to India after outbreak of civil war in 1983, began procuring arms and equipment for Liberation Tigers of Tamil Eelam (LTTE) (Tamil separatist group), in exile in Malaysia 1987–90, in Thailand 1990; apptd Head of Dept of Int. Relations, Jan. 2009, Chief LTTE Int. Spokesman during last months of civil war in 2009, apptd Leader, LTTE July 2009, detained Aug. 2009, released from prison 2012.

PATIASHVILI, Jumber Ilich; Georgian politician; b. 5 Jan. 1940, Lagodekhi, Kakheti Oblast; m.; two c.; ed Tbilisi Agricultural Inst.; worked for the Komsomol (V.I. Lenin Young Communist League) from 1966, subsequently for Communist Party; Dir Land Inst. of Georgia 1980–2000; apptd First Sec. Communist Party of Georgian SSR 1985–89 (resgnd after Soviet troops killed demonstrators in Tbilisi); cand. for presidency 1995, 2000; Founder and Leader of Unity Alliance (Ertoba) (social-democratic party which contested gen. election as part of Jumber Patiashvili-Unity bloc 2003).

PATIL, Dnyandeo Yashwantrao (D. Y.), MA, LLB, PhD; Indian educationalist and government official; b. 22 Oct. 1935, Ambap village, Kolhapur, Maharashtra; ed Shivaji Univ., Kolhapur; mem. Kolhapur Municipal Council (Indian Nat. Congress) 1957–62; mem. Maharashtra Vidhan Sabha (state legis. ass.) for Panhala Vidhan Sabha constituency 1967–78; Founding Pres. D.Y. Patil Educational Acad., Ramrao Adik Educ. Soc., Dr D.Y. Patil Pratishthan, D.Y. Patil Educ. Soc., Continental Medicare Foundation; Gov. of Tripura 2009–13, of Bihar 2013–14, also acting Gov. of West Bengal July 2014; mem. Indian Nat. Congress party; Dr hc (Nottingham Trent Univ., UK) 2000; Padma Shri 1991, Manapatra Award, Kolhapur Municipal Corpn 2000, Special Award, Fourth Zorostanian Dental Congress 2000, Vocational Excellence Award, Rotary Int. Dist 3140 2000, Rajiv Gandhi Award 2007. *Address:* c/o Office of the Governor, Raj Bhavan, Patna 800 022, India.

PATIL, Pratibha Devisingh, LLB, MA; Indian politician and fmr head of state; b. 19 Dec. 1934, Jalgaon, Mahar; d. of Narayanrao Patil and Gangaji Patil; m. D. R. Shekhawat; one s. one d.; ed Mooljee Jetha Coll., Jalgaon, Govt Law Coll., Mumbai; mem. Maharashtra Legis. Ass. 1962–85, Deputy Minister 1967–72, Cabinet Minister for Social Welfare 1972–74, for Public Health and Social Welfare 1974–75, for Prohibition, Rehabilitation and Cultural Affairs 1975–76, for Educ. 1977–78, for Urban Devt and Housing 1982–83; Deputy Chair. Rajya Sabha (Council of States, Parl.) 1986–88; mem. Lok Sabha 1991; Gov. of Rajasthan 2004–07; Pres. of India 2007–12; Vice-Chair. Nat. Fed. for Co-operative Urban Banks and Credit Soc.; Chair. Bhartiya Granin Mahila Sangh, Mahar; Organizer, Women Home Guards, Jalgaon Dist 1962; mem. Standing Cttee, All India Women's Council; Convener, Women's Conf., Delhi. *Leisure interest:* social service. *Address:* RAIGAD Bungalow, Near C I D Office, Pashan Road, Pune 411 008, India (home). *Telephone:* (20) 25639222. *E-mail:* deshmukh.jaydip85@gmail.com. *Website:* pratibhapatil.nic.in.

PATIL, Shivraj Vishwanath, BS, LLM; Indian politician; b. 12 Oct. 1935, Chakur, Latur dist (Marathwada region) of Bombay State, British India; s. of Vishwanath Rao and Bhagiriti Bai; m. Vijaya Patil (deceased); one s. one d.; ed Osmania Univ., Hyderabad, Univ. of Bombay (now Mumbai); Pres. Latur Municipality 1967–69, 1971–72; mem. Maharashtra Legis. Ass. 1972–79; mem. Lok Sabha (Parl.) 1980, Speaker, Lok Sabha 1991–96; Minister of State, including Defence, Commerce, Science and Tech., Space and Tourism portfolios 1980–89; Minister of Home Affairs 2004–08 (resgnd); Gov. of Punjab and Admin. of Chandigarh 2010–15; Acting Gov. of Rajasthan 2010–12; mem. Indian Nat. Congress party; Hon. Prof. of Law. *Leisure interests:* reading, painting, farming, swimming, horse-riding, shooting.

PATIL, Shriniwas Dadasaheb, BA, MA, LLB; Indian politician and fmr civil servant; b. 11 April 1941, Tehsil Patan, Maharashtra; s. of Dadasaheb Ramchandra Patil and Anusaya Dadasaheb Patil; m. Rajanidevi Patil; one s.; ed Univ. of Poona, Govt Law Coll., Bombay; joined Maharashtra Public Service Comm. as Deputy Collector (Dist Commr) 1965, served as sub-divisional officer in several dists 1965–71, 1973–75, seconded as Man. Dir Sangamner Cooperative Sugar Factory 1971–73 and as Sr Personnel Man., Hindustan Antibiotics Ltd 1975–77; CEO Pimpri Chinchwad Municipality 1977–78; promoted to Indian Admin. Services 1979; Dir of Sugar, Maharashtra State 1985–87; Collector and Dist Magistrate, Beed 1987–88, Pune 1988–92, Commr, Pimpri Chinchwad Municipal Corpn and Chair., Pimpri Chinchwad New Township Devt Authority 1992–95; Chair., Nagpur Improvement Trust 1996–99; mem. Lok Sabha (Parl.) for Karad constituency 1999–2009; Gov. of Sikkim 2013–18; mem. Nationalist Congress Party 1999–. *Address:* c/o Raj Bhavan, Gangtok 737 103, India (office). *Website:* www.shriniwaspatil.com.

PATIÑO AROCA, Ricardo Armando, PhD; Ecuadorean economist and politician; b. 1955, Guayaquil; m. Miriam Alcívar; one d.; ed Autonomous Metropolitan Univ. of Iztalapa, Mexico, Univ. of Guayaquil and Int. Univ., Andalucía, Spain; Head, Econ. Planning Dept Nat. Agrarian Reform Inst. in southern Nicaragua 1980–81; mem. Econs Dept, Univ. of Guayaquil; fmr Coordinator Inter-Ministerial Comm. on Employment; fmr consultant ILO; Deputy Minister of the Economy 2005–07, Minister of the Economy and Finance 2007, of Coastal Affairs 2007, Co-ordinating Minister for Politics 2007–10, Minister of Foreign Relations, Trade and Integration 2010–16, of Nat. Defence 2016–17; Dir Acción Política del Movimiento Patria Altiva y Soberana (PAÍS) 2006.

PATNAIK, Naveen, BA; Indian politician; *Chief Minister of Odisha;* b. 16 Oct. 1946, Cuttack; s. of Biju Patnaik and Gyan Patnaik; ed Doon School, Dehradun, Univ. of Delhi; mem. Lok Sabha 1997–2000; State Minister of Steel and Mines 1998–99, of Mines and Minerals 1999–2000, of Water Resources, Information and Tech. 2000–02, of Home 2000–, of Agric. 2000–04, 2012–, of Gen. Admin 2000–, of Works 2001–02, 2009–, of Parl. Affairs 2001–02, of Housing 2001–02, 2012–, of Health and Family Welfare 2001–02, of Rural Devt 2001–02, of Finance 2002–04, of Planning and Co-ordination 2002–06, 2007–08; Founder-Pres. Biju Janata Dal

1998–; Chief Minister of Odisha 2000–; mem. Library Cttee, Standing Cttee on Commerce, Gen. Purpose Cttee; Founding mem. Indian Nat. Trust for Art and Cultural Heritage. *Publications include:* A Second Paradise, A Desert Kingdom, The Garden of Life. *Leisure interests:* reading, watching programmes on culture, history and environment. *Address:* Office of the Chief Minister, Government of Odisha, Bhubaneswar (office); Naveen Nivas, Aerodrome Road, Bhubaneswar, 751 001, India (home). *Telephone:* (674) 2590299 (home); (674) 2531100 (office). *Website:* www.naveenpatnaik.com.

PATO, Rimbink, OBE, LLB; Papua New Guinea lawyer, business executive and politician; *Minister for Foreign Affairs and Trade;* m. Joyce Pato; three c.; ed Glasgow Caledonian Univ.; fmr property investor; Exec. Chair. Finance Pacific Ltd; Propr, Pato Lawyers (private law firm); Chair. Lutheran Univ. of Papua New Guinea; mem. Nat. Parl. (United Party) for Wapenamanda Open constituency 2012–; Minister for Foreign Affairs and Immigration 2012–17, of Foreign Affairs and Trade 2017–, also of Correctional Services, Community Devt, Youth and Religion 2017–. *Address:* Department of Foreign Affairs and Trade, POB 422, Waigani 131, NCD, Papua New Guinea (office). *Telephone:* 3014158 (office). *Fax:* 3277480 (office). *Website:* www.parliament.gov.pg (office).

PATON, Borys Yevgenovych, DTechSc; Ukrainian metallurgist; *President, Ukraine National Academy of Sciences;* b. 27 Nov. 1918, Kyiv; s. of Yevgen Oskarovych Paton and Natalya Viktorivna Paton; m. Olga Borysivna Milovanova 1948; one d.; ed Kiev Polytechnic Inst.; Dir E. O. Paton Electric Welding Institute of Ukrainian SSR (now Ukraine) Acad. of Sciences 1953–; Corresp. mem. Ukrainian SSR (now Ukraine) Acad. of Sciences 1951–58, mem. 1958–, Pres. 1962–; mem. USSR (now Russian) Acad. of Sciences 1962, mem. Presidium 1963–91; Pres. Int. Engineering Acad. 1991–; mem. CPSU 1952–91, cand. mem. Cen. Cttee of CPSU 1961–66, mem. 1966–91; mem. Central Cttee of CP of Ukraine 1960–91; Deputy to USSR Supreme Soviet 1962–89; Vice-Chair. Soviet of the Union USSR Supreme Soviet 1966–89; Deputy to Ukrainian SSR Supreme Soviet 1959–90, mem. of Pres. 1963–80; People's Deputy of the USSR 1989–91; mem. of editorial bd and ed.-in-chief of several scientific and tech. journals; Foreign mem. of Acads of Science of 10 countries; Honoured Scientist of Ukrainian SSR 1968, Honoured Inventor of USSR 1983; more than 10 hon. doctorates; State Prize of the USSR 1950, Lenin Prize 1957, State Prize of the Ukraine 2004, Order of Liberty 2012, numerous other awards. *Publications include:* numerous books and articles in professional journals; more than 1,000 patents 1942–2004. *Leisure interest:* swimming. *Address:* E.O. Paton Electric Welding Institute, 11 Bozhenko Street, Kyiv 150, 03680, Ukraine (home). *Telephone:* (44) 287-31-83 (home). *Fax:* (44) 528-04-86 (home). *E-mail:* office@paton.kiev.ua. *Website:* www.paton.kiev.ua.

PATRICK, Danica Sue; American racing driver and model; b. 25 March 1982, Beloit, Wis.; d. of T. J. Patrick and Beverly Patrick; m. Paul Edward Hospenthal 2005; grew up in Roscoe, Ill.; began go-karting competitively aged ten, won first World Karting Asscn championship aged 12; moved to Milton Keynes, UK aged 16 to advance her racing career, racing in British nat. series events against drivers including future Formula 1 world champion Jenson Button (q.v.); raced in Formula Ford, Formula Vauxhall and earned a second-place in Formula Ford Festival (highest finish by a woman) 1998–2001; finished 2nd Formula Ford Festival, Brands Hatch, UK 2000; winner Pro Div. Long Beach Grand Prix Toyota Pro-Celebrity Race 2002; third in Toyota Atlantic Championship; with Rahal Letterman Racing –2006; with Andretti Green Racing 2007–10, Andretti Autosport 2010–; earned ten top-five finishes in 12 races including best finish (second) at Portland 2004; finished fourth Indianapolis (Indy) 500 2005; won Indy Japan 300 2008 (first woman to win an Indy car race); came third in Indianapolis 500 2009 (personal best and highest finish by a woman in event's history); currently drives #7 GoDaddy.com Honda/Dallara for Andretti Autosport; began racing in NASCAR Nationwide Series, driving #7 GoDaddy.com Chevrolet Impala for JR Motorsports part-time 2010; also has equity stake in her #7 team; has hosted several shows on Spike TV, including the Powerblock 2004; featured in Girl Racers documentary 2005; Gorsline Scholarship Award for top upcoming road racing driver 2001, Indianapolis 500 Rookie of the Year 2005, IndyCar Series Rookie of the Year 2005, IndyCar Most Popular Driver 2005–07, 2009. *Television:* acting debut in episode of CSI: New York Feb. 2010 (played a racing driver suspected of murder). *Publication:* Danica: Crossing the Line 2006. *Address:* Andretti Green Racing, 7615 Zionsville Road, Indianapolis, IN 46268, USA (office). *Telephone:* (317) 872-2700 (office). *E-mail:* DanicaMedia7@GoDaddy.com. *Website:* www .andrettigreenracing.com; www.danicaracing.com.

PATRICK, Deval Laurdine, JD; American lawyer, business executive and politician; *Managing Director, Bain Capital;* b. 31 July 1956, Chicago, Ill.; s. of Pat Patrick and Emily Patrick; m. Diane Bemus 1984; two d.; ed Milton Acad., Harvard Coll., Harvard Law School; worked with UN in Africa 1978; Pres. Legal Aid Bureau, Harvard Law School; worked as law clerk for Judge Stephen Reinhardt, US Court of Appeals for the Ninth Circuit; attorney for Nat. Asscn for the Advancement of Colored People (NAACP) Legal Defense and Educational Fund, New York City; attorney, Hill & Barlow 1986–90, Partner 1990; apptd Asst Attorney-Gen. for Civil Rights 1994; adviser to post-apartheid S Africa and helped to create their civil rights laws; attorney, Day, Berry & Howard 1997; apptd by Fed. Dist Court to serve as Chair. Task Force to oversee implementation of terms of race discrimination settlement at Texaco, apptd Vice-Pres. and Gen. Counsel, Texaco, New York City; Exec. Vice-Pres., Gen. Counsel and Corp. Sec. Coca-Cola Co., Atlanta 2000–04 (resgnd); Gov. of the Commonwealth of Massachusetts 2007–15; Man. Dir Bain Capital 2015–; mem. Bd of Dirs United Airlines 2004–06; Crown Fellow, Aspen Inst.; Democrat. *Publications:* A Reason to Believe: Lessons from an Improbable Life 2011 Faith in the Dream: A Call to the Nation to Reclaim American Values 2012. *Address:* Bain Capital, John Hancock Tower, 200 Clarendon Street, Boston, MA 02116, USA (office). *Telephone:* (617) 516-2000 (office). *Website:* www.baincapital.com (office); www.devalpatrick.com.

PATRIOTA, Antonio de Aguiar; Brazilian diplomatist and politician; *Ambassador to Italy;* b. 27 April 1954, Rio de Janeiro; m. Tania Cooper Patriota; two s.; ed Univ. of Geneva, Switzerland and Rio Branco Inst.; Adviser to Head of UN Div., Ministry of Foreign Affairs 1980–82, mem. Perm. Mission to Int. Orgs, Geneva 1983–87, Political Counsellor, Embassy in Beijing 1987–88, Head of Econ. Section, Embassy in Caracas 1988–90, Adviser to Sec.-Gen. for Political Affairs, Ministry of Foreign Affairs 1990–92, Deputy Diplomatic Adviser to Pres. of Brazil 1992–94,

Political Counsellor, Perm. Mission to UN, New York 1994–99, mem. Brazilian del. to UN Security Council 1995, 1998–99, Minister Counsellor, Perm. Mission to Int. Orgs, Geneva 1999–2003, Deputy Perm. Rep. to WTO 2001–02, Sec. for Diplomatic Planning, Office of the Minister of Foreign Affairs 2003, Chief of Staff 2004, Under-Sec.-Gen. for Political Affairs 2005–07, Amb. to USA 2007–09, Sec.-Gen., Ministry of Foreign Affairs 2009–10, Minister of Foreign Affairs 2011–13 (resgnd), Perm. Rep. to UN, New York 2013–16, Amb. to Italy 2016–; several decorations from Brazil, France, Norway and Morocco. *Address:* Embassy of Brazil, Palazzo Pamphili, Piazza Navona 14, 00186 Roma, Italy (office). *Telephone:* (06) 683981 (office). *Fax:* (06) 6867858 (office). *E-mail:* brasemb.roma@itamaraty.gov.br (office). *Website:* roma.itamaraty.gov.br (office).

PATRONI GRIFFI, Filippo; Italian lawyer and government official; *President, Council of State;* b. 27 Aug. 1955, Naples; Judge, Admin. Court of Basilicata 1984; Legal Adviser to Minister of State Holdings 1987, to Minister for Social Affairs 1989, to Minister of the Budget and Econ. Planning 1989–92, to Prime Minister and later Head, Legis. Office of Minister for Public Admin 1993–98, Chef de Cabinet of Minister for Institutional Reforms 1998–99, Legal Adviser to Minister for Heritage 2002, Legal Adviser, Nat. Centre for Information Tech. in Public Admin (CNIPA) 2003–05; Head, Dept for Legal Affairs of Presidency of the Council of Ministers 2006–08; Chef de Cabinet of Minister for Public Admin Reforms and Innovation 2008–09; Minister for Public Admin 2011–13; Sec. of State to the Prime Minister and Sec., Council of Ministers 2013–14; Pres., Council of State 2018–; mem. Central Tax Comm. 2007; mem. editorial bd several journals including Giurisdizione amministrativa, Rivista italiana di diritto pubblico comunitario, Rivista dello sport, Federalismi.it, Il lavoro nelle pubbliche amministrazioni; Commdr, Order of Merit 1991, Officer, Order of Merit 2005, Kt Grand Cross, Order of Merit 2013. *Publications:* contributions to various legal journals. *Address:* Council of State, Spada Palace, Piazza Capo di Ferro 13, 00186 Rome, Italy (office). *Website:* www.governo.it (office); www.giustizia-amministrativa.it (office).

PATRUSHEV, Col-Gen. Nikolai Platonovich, PhD; Russian government security official; *Secretary, Security Council;* b. 11 July 1951, Leningrad (now St Petersburg), Russian SFSR, USSR; m.; two s.; ed Leningrad Inst. of Vessel Construction (now the State Marine Tech. Univ. of St Petersburg); on staff KGB, Kareliyan ASSR 1974; in Leningrad Oblast 1974–92; Minister of Security, Repub. of Kareliya 1992–94; Head Dept of Self-Protection, Fed. Security Service 1994–98, Deputy Dir, then Head, Dept of Econs 1998–99, Dir 1999–; Head of Presidential Control Dept May–Aug. 1998; Deputy Head Admin. of Russian Presidency Aug.–Oct. 1998; Deputy Dir Fed. Security Service of Russia (FSB), Head of Econ. Security Dept 1998, First Deputy Dir April–Aug. 1999, Dir Aug. 1999–2008; Sec. Security Council of Russian Fed. 2008–; Hon. Citizen of the Repub. of Kareliya; Hero of the Russian Fed., Order of Merit for the Fatherland (First Class) 2006, (Second Class, Third Class and Fourth Class), Order of Courage, Order of Mil. Merit, Order of Naval Merit, Order of Honour, Jubilee Medal '300 Years of the Russian Navy', Medal 'In Commemoration of the 850th Anniversary of the Foundation of Moscow', Jubilee Medal '60 Years of the Armed Forces of the USSR', Jubilee Medal '70 Years of the Armed Forces of the USSR', Medal Anatoly Koni, Medal for Strengthening Mil. Cooperation (Defence) three times, Medal 'Diligence in carrying out engineering tasks' (Defence), Medal for distinction in military service (MOD) (First Class), Meritorious Service (Second Class), Medal of Honour (Belarus) 2001, Order of Bohdan Khmelnitsky (Third Class) (Ukraine) 2001, Medal 'For Services to Stavropol Krai' (Stavropol Krai) 2003, Order of the Cross (First Class) (Armenia) 2003, Order of Saint Blessed Prince Dimitry Donskoy the Great (First Class) (Russian Orthodox Church) 2005. *Achievements include:* joined expedition of polar explorer, Arthur Chilingarov, that flew on two helicopters to Antarctica and visited S Pole and Amundsen-Scott station Jan. 2007. *Address:* Security Council of Russian Federation, 103132 Moscow, Ipatyevskii per. 4/10, Russia (office). *Telephone:* (495) 206-35-96 (office). *Website:* www.scrf.gov.ru (office).

PATRY, Gilles G., CM, MASc, PhD; Canadian engineer, academic and university administrator; *Professor and President Emeritus, University of Ottawa;* ed Univ. of Ottawa, Univ. of California, Davis; began career as consulting engineer 1971–78; Prof. of Civil Eng, École Polytechnique de Montréal 1978–83; Prof. of Civil Eng, McMaster Univ. 1983–93; f. Hydromantis Inc. 1985; Dean, Faculty of Eng, Univ. of Ottawa 1993, Vice-Pres. (Academic) 1997, Pres. and Vice-Chancellor 2001–08, Prof. and Pres. Emer. 2008–; mem. Bd of Dir Univ. of Ottawa Heart Inst. 2001–08; Assoc. Ed., Journal of Environmental Engineering and Science 2001–05; Pres. and CEO Canada Foundation for Innovation 2010–17; Exec. Dir U15 Group of Canadian Research Univs. 2017–; mem. Bd of Dir Hydromantis Holding Inc. 1993–2001, British Columbia Freshwater Inst. (BCFI) 2002–04, Ottawa Centre for Research and Innovation (OCRI) 2002–08 (mem. Exec. Cttee 2004–06), Ontario Centres of Excellence Inc. 2005–10, Canadian Merit Scholarship Foundation 2006–10, Canadian Water Network (Réseau canadien de l'eau) 2009–10, Royal Canadian Mint 2018–; mem. Council Nat. Research Council of Canada 2002–08 (mem. Audit Cttee 2004–10), Advisory Bd Canadian Research Knowledge Network 2009–10; mem. Review Panel, Innovation centres, Ministerio de educacion, Chile 2011–13; Genome Canada 2017–18; Fellow, Canadian Acad. of Eng 2002–; Visiting Scholar, Georgia Institute of Technology Jan.–April 2009; Chevalier, Ordre de la Pléiade 2009, mem. Order of Canada 2010, Order of Ontario 2011; Hon. LLD (Waterloo) 2008, Hon. DSc (McMaster) 2009, Dr hc (INSA, Lyon) 2016, (Western) 2017, (Carleton) 2018; co-author of paper selected as one of the 10 most significant ground-breaking papers in the 40-year history of Water Research 2006, Alumnus of the Year Award, Faculty of Eng, Univ. of Ottawa 2008, Community Builder Award, United Way Ottawa 2009, 26th John W. Hodgins Memorial Lecturer, McMaster Univ. 2009, Water Research Award. *Publications:* more than 125 journal and conf. papers. *Address:* University of Ottawa, STE Building, 800 King Edward blvd, Ottawa, ON K1N 6N5, Canada (office). *E-mail:* gilles.patry@uottawa .ca (office). *Website:* gillespatry.net (office).

PATTAMA, Noppadon, LLB (Hons), BA, LLM, MA; Thai lawyer and politician; b. 23 April 1961, Nakorn Rachasima; m.; one d.; ed Thammasat Univ., Univs of Oxford and London, UK; practised as barrister in Bangkok 1983–; called to the Bar, Lincoln's Inn, London 1991; Sec. to Leader of the Opposition Chuan Leekpai 1995–96; mem. Parl. (Democrat Party) 1996–2000, mem. Standing Cttee on Foreign Affairs, House of Reps 1996–2000; Parl. Sec. to Minister of Foreign Affairs

1999–2001; defected to Thai Rak Thai party 2006; Vice-Minister of Natural Resources and Environment 2006; legal adviser to fmr Prime Minister Thaksin Shinawatra (deposed in mil. coup Sept. 2006) Nov. 2006; mem. People's Power Party (successor to Thai Rak Thai) 2007–08, Pheu Thai Party 2008–; Minister of Foreign Affairs Feb.–July 2008; Pres. Thai Students' Asscn in UK (Samaggi Samagom) 1988–89; participant in The Ship for Southeast Asian Youth Programme 1981; Fulbright Scholarship to study in USA 1982, Ananda Mahidol Scholarship to study law in UK, King of Thailand 1984. *Publications:* book: I'm Not a Traitor 2008. *Address:* c/o Pheu Thai Party, 1770 Thanon Petchaburi Tat Mai, Bang Gapi, Huay Kwang, Bangkok 10310, Thailand (office). *Website:* www.ptp.or.th (office).

PATTEN, Brian, FRSL; British poet and author; b. 7 Feb. 1946, Liverpool, Merseyside; s. of Ireen Stella Bevan; Regents Lecturer, Univ. of California, San Diego; performance work and lectures worldwide for British Council; Freedom of the City of Liverpool 2000; Hon. Fellow, John Moores Univ. 2002, Open Univ. 2014; Hon. DLitt (Liverpool) 2006; Cholmondeley Award for Poetry 2002. *Radio:* various, including History of 20th-Century Poetry for Children, BBC Radio 2000, The Dittisham Nativity, BBC Radio 2005, Lost Voices, BBC Radio series 2009, 2010, 2011, 2017. *Publications include:* poetry: The Mersey Sound 1967, Little Johnny's Confession 1967, The Home Coming 1969, Notes to the Hurrying Man 1969, At Four O'Clock in the Morning 1971, Walking Out: The Early Poems of Brian Patten 1971, Love Poems 1981, New Volume 1983, Gargling With Jelly 1985, Storm Damage 1988, Grinning Jack: Selected Poems 1990, Thawing Frozen Frogs 1990, Armada 1996; as ed: Clare's Countryside: A Book of John Clare 1981, Selected Poems 2007, New Collected Love Poems 2007, View From The Boathouse Window 2010; children's fiction: Grizzelda Frizzle and Other Stories 1992, The Magic Bicycle 1993, Impossible Parents 1994, Frognapped! and Other Stories 1994, The Utter Nutters 1995, The Blue and Green Ark 1999, Juggling with Gerbils 2000, Little Hotchpotch 2000, The Impossible Parents Go Green 2001, The Story Giant 2001 (adapted for the stage 2017), View From The Boathouse Window 2009, The Big Snuggle-up 2011, Thawing Frozen Frogs 2012, Can I Come Too? 2013; children's books as ed: The Puffin Book of 20th Century Children's Verse 1991, Ben's Magic Telescope 2003, The Puffin Book of Modern Children's Verse 2006, Monster Slayer (Beowulf for children) 2016, The Book of Upside Down Thinking (adaptations into poetry of Sufi stories) 2018. *Leisure interests:* river cruising/travel. *Address:* c/o Rogers, Coleridge & White Literary Agency, 20 Powis Mews, London, W11 1JN, England (office). *Telephone:* (18) 0372-2389 (office). *Fax:* (20) 7229-9084 (office). *E-mail:* info@rcwlitagency.co.uk (office); words@brianpatten.co.uk (office). *Website:* www.rcwlitagency.co.uk (office); www.brianpatten.co.uk.

PATTEN, Pramila, LLB, LLM; Mauritian lawyer and UN official; *Special Representative of the Secretary-General on Sexual Violence in Conflict, United Nations;* b. 29 June 1958; ed Ealing Coll. of Higher Educ., Univ. Coll. London; called to the Bar, Gray's Inn, London; practising barrister at law 1982–86; Legal Adviser, Ministry of Labour and Industrial Relations 1982–86; Dist Court Magistrate 1986–88; Lecturer, Faculty of Law, Univ. of Mauritius 1987–92; mem. Int. Women's Rights Action Watch 1993–2002; Head, Patten & Co. Chambers (law firm), Port Louis 1995–; Adviser to Ministry of Women's Rights, Child Devt & Family Welfare 2000–04, to Ministry of Justice and Human Rights 2005–06; mem. UN Convention on the Elimination of all Forms of Discrimination Against Women (CEDAW) 2003–; apptd by UN Sec.-Gen. as Commr, Int. Comm. of Inquiry into massacre in Guinea Conakry 2009; mem. Advisory Panel, UN Econ. Comm. for Africa African Women's Rights Observatory 2010–; mem. High Level Advisory Group for Global Study on UN Security Council resolution 1325 on Women, Peace and Security 2014–; Special Rep. of the Sec.-Gen. on Sexual Violence in Conflict 2017–. *Publications:* numerous publications on human rights. *Address:* Office of the Secretary-General, United Nations, New York, NY 10017, USA (office). *Telephone:* (212) 963-1234 (office). *Fax:* (212) 963-4879 (office). *Website:* www.un.org/sg (office).

PATTEN OF BARNES, Baron (Life Peer), cr. 2005, of Barnes in the London Borough of Richmond; **Christopher Francis Patten**, CH, PC; British politician and government official; b. 12 May 1944, Cleveleys, Lancs., England; s. of Francis Joseph Patten and Joan McCarthy; m. Mary Lavender Thornton 1971; three d.; ed St Benedict's School, Ealing, Balliol Coll., Oxford; worked in Conservative Party Research Dept 1966–70, Dir 1974–79; seconded to Cabinet Office 1970; at Home Office, then personal asst to Lord Carrington, Party Chair. 1972–74; MP for Bath 1979–92; Parl. Pvt. Sec. (PPS) to Leader of the House 1979–81, to Social Services Sec. 1981–83; Parl. Under-Sec. for Northern Ireland 1983–85; Minister of State for Educ. 1985–86; Overseas Devt Minister 1986–89; Sec. of State for the Environment 1989–90; Chancellor of the Duchy of Lancaster and Chair. of the Conservative Party 1990–92; Gov. of Hong Kong 1992–97; Chair. Comm. charged with reform of Royal Ulster Constabulary 1998–99; EU Commr for External Relations 1999–2004; Chair. BBC Trust 2011–14 (resgnd); Co-Chair. UK-India Round Table, Int. Crisis Group 2004–11; Pres. Medical Aid for Palestinians 2010–11; Chancellor, Newcastle Univ. 1999–2009, Univ. of Oxford 2003–; mem. Bd of Dirs Russell Reynolds Assocs; mem. Int. Advisory Bd BP; mem. European Advisory Bd Bridgepoint; European Adviser, Hutchinson Whampoa Ltd; mem. EDF Stakeholder Advisory Panel; Int. Adviser to Praemium Imperiale, Japan Art Asscn; mem. Bd of Overseers, Sabanci Univ.; Trustee, the Tablet Journal; Hon. FRCP (Edin.) 1994; Hon. Fellow, Balliol Coll., Oxford 1999; several hon. degrees from British and foreign univs, including Hon. DCL (Newcastle) 1999; Coolidge Travelling Scholarship, USA 1965. *Publications:* The Tory Case 1983, Letters to Hong Kong 1997, East and West: The Last Governor of Hong Kong on Power Freedom and the Future 1998, Not Quite the Diplomat: Home Truths About World Affairs 2005, Cousins and Strangers: America, Britain, and Europe in a New Century 2006, What Next? Surviving the 21st Century 2008. *Leisure interests:* reading, tennis, gardening. *Address:* House of Lords, Westminster, London, SW1A 0PW, England. *Telephone:* (20) 7219-5353. *Fax:* (20) 7219-5979.

PATTERSON, Gavin E.; British business executive; *CEO, BT Group plc;* b. 1967, Altrincham, Greater Manchester; m. Karen Patterson; four c.; ed Emmanuel Coll., Cambridge; with Procter and Gamble 1991–2000, rose to become European Marketing Dir; with Telewest (now Virgin Media) 2000–04, latterly as Man. Dir Consumer; joined BT as Group Man. Dir BT Retail's Consumer div. 2004, Chief Exec. BT Retail May 2008–13, mem. Bd of Dirs BT Group plc June 2008–, launched

BT Infinity, led BT as Founder-Partner in YouView, cr. BT Sport 2013, CEO BT Group plc 2013–; Pres. Advertising Asscn 2011–; Dir (non-exec.) British Airways; Trustee, British Museum; mem. Advisory Bd, Cambridge Judge Business School; mem. Thirty Club; Fellow, Marketing Soc. *Leisure interest:* Liverpool Football Club. *Address:* BT Group plc, BT Centre, 81 Newgate Street, London, EC1A 7AJ, England (office). *Telephone:* (20) 7356-5000 (office). *E-mail:* info@btplc.com (office). *Website:* www.btplc.com (office).

PATTERSON, Henry (Harry), (Martin Fallon, James Graham, Jack Higgins, Hugh Marlowe), BSc, FRSA; British/Irish novelist; b. 27 July 1929, Newcastle upon Tyne; s. of Henry Patterson and Rita Higgins Bell; m. 1st Amy Margaret Hewitt 1958 (divorced 1984); one s. three d.; m. 2nd Denise Leslie Ann Palmer 1985; ed Roundhay School, Leeds, Beckett Park Coll. for Teachers, London School of Econs; NCO, The Blues 1947–50, tried numerous jobs including clerk and circus tent hand 1950–58; schoolmaster, lecturer in liberal studies, Leeds Polytechnic, Sr Lecturer in Educ., James Graham Coll. and Tutor in School Practice, Leeds Univ. 1958–72; full-time writer from age of 41; Hon. DUniv (Leeds Metropolitan Univ.) 1995; Hon. DLitt (Univ. of London) 2014. *Publications include:* as Martin Fallon: The Testament of Caspar Schultz 1962, Year of the Tiger 1963, The Keys to Hell 1965, Midnight Never Comes 1966, Dark Side of the Street 1967, A Fine Night for Dying 1969, Day of Judgement 1979; as Hugh Marlowe: Seven Pillars to Hell 1963, Passage by Night 1964, A Candle for the Dead (aka The Violent Enemy) 1966; as James Graham: A Game for Heroes 1970, The Wrath of God 1971, The Khufra Run 1972, The Run to Morning 1974; as Harry Patterson: Sad Wind from the Sea 1959, Cry of the Hunter 1960, The Thousand Faces of Night 1961, Comes the Dark Stranger 1962, Wrath of the Lion 1963, Pay the Devil 1963, The Dark Side of the Island 1963, A Phoenix in Blood 1964, Thunder at Noon (aka Dillinger) 1964, The Graveyard Shift 1965, Iron Tiger 1966, Brought in Dead 1967, Hell is Always Today 1968, Toll for the Brave 1971, To Catch a King (aka The Judas Gate) 1979; as Jack Higgins: East of Desolation 1968, In the Hour Before Midnight 1969, Night Judgement at Sinos 1970, The Last Place God Made 1971, The Savage Day 1972, The Eagle has Landed 1975, Storm Warning 1976, The Valhalla Exchange 1976, A Prayer for the Dying 1977, Solo (aka The Cretan Lover) 1980, Luciano's Luck 1981, Touch the Devil 1982, Exocet 1983, Confessional 1985, Night of the Fox 1986, Walking Wounded (play) 1987, Memoirs of a Dance Hall Romeo 1989, A Season in Hell 1989, Cold Harbour 1989, The Eagle Has Flown 1990, Eye of the Storm (aka Midnight Man) 1992, Thunder Point 1993, On Dangerous Ground 1994, Angel of Death 1995, Sheba 1995, Drink With the Devil 1996, The President's Daughter 1996, The Violent Enemy 1997, Flight of Eagles 1998, The White House Connection 1999, Day of Reckoning 1999, Midnight Runner 2001, Edge of Danger 2001, The Keys of Hell 2002, Bad Company 2003, Without Mercy 2005, Death Run (with Justin Richards) 2007, Sure Fire (juvenile, with Justin Richards) 2007, The Killing Ground 2008, Rough Justice 2008, A Darker Place 2009, Wolf at the Door 2009, The Judas Gate 2011, A Devil is Waiting 2012, The Death Trade 2014, Rain on the Dead 2015, The Midnight Bell 2016, The Wrath of God/The Last Place God Made 2017. *Leisure interests:* tennis, old movies.

PATTERSON, James, BA, MA; American writer and fmr advertising executive; b. 22 March 1947, Newburgh, NY; m. Susan; one s.; ed Manhattan Coll., Vanderbilt Univ.; wrote first novel 1976; joined J. Walter Thompson as jr copywriter 1971, subsequently Exec. Creative Dir, CEO, Chair. 1990–96; f. ReadKiddoRead.com; Edgar Award, International Thriller of the Year Award, Children's Choice Award for Author of the Year. *Publications include:* The Thomas Berryman Number (MWA Edgar Award) 1976, The Season of the Machete 1977, The Jericho Commandment (aka See How They Run) 1979, Virgin 1980, Black Market 1986, The Midnight Club 1989, The Day America Told the Truth: What People Really Believe About Everything that Matters (non-fiction, with Peter Kim) 1991, Along Came a Spider 1993, The Second American Revolution 1994, Kiss the Girls 1995, Hide & Seek 1996, Jack & Jill 1996, Miracle on the 17th Green (with Peter de Jonge) 1996, Cat & Mouse 1997, When the Wind Blows 1998, Pop Goes the Weasel 1999, Cradle and All (revised version of Virgin) 2000, Roses are Red 2000, Suzanne's Diary for Nicholas 2001, 1st to Die 2001, Violets are Blue 2001, 2nd Chance (with Andrew Gross) 2002, Four Blind Mice 2002, The Beach House (with Peter de Jonge) 2002, The Jester 2003, The Lake House 2003, The Big Bad Wolf 2003, 3rd Degree 2003, Sam's Letters to Jennifer 2004, London Bridges 2004, Honeymoon 2005, 4th of July 2005, Mary Mary 2005, Maximum Ride: The Angel 2005, The 5th Horseman (with Maxine Paetro) 2006, Judge and Jury 2006, Lifeguard (with Andrew Gross) 2006, Thriller (short stories) (ed) 2006, Maximum Ride: School's Out Forever (with Peter De Jonge) 2006, Cross 2006, Step on a Crack (with Michael Ledwidge) 2007, The Beach Road (with Peter De Jonge) 2007, The 6th Target (with Maxine Paetro) 2007, Maximum Ride: Saving the World and Other Extreme Sports (children's fiction) 2007, The Quickie (with Michael Ledwidge) 2007, Double Cross 2007, You've Been Warned 2007, 7th Heaven 2008, Maximum Ride: The Final Warning 2008, Sundays at Tiffany's 2008, Sail 2008, The Dangerous Days of Daniel X 2008, Against All Odds (non-fiction), Cross Country 2008, 8th Confession (with Maxine Paetro) 2009, Max: A Maximum Ride Novel 2009, Swimsuit 2009, Alex Cross's Trial 2009, Run for Your Life 2009, The Murder of King Tut (with Martin Dugard) 2009, I, Alex Cross 2009, Worst Case 2010, 9th Judgement (with Maxine Paetro) 2010, Private (with Maxine Paetro) 2010, Daniel X: Demons and Druids 2010, The Postcard Killers (with Liza Marklund) 2010, Don't Blink 2010, The Gift (with Ned Rust) 2010, Tick Tock 2011, The Christmas Wedding 2011, Kill Alex Cross 2011, Witch and Wizard: The Fire (with Jill Dembowski) 2011, Private Games (with Mark Sullivan) 2012, Private: #1 Suspect (with Maxine Paetro) 2012, 11th Hour (with Maxine Paetro) 2012, Guilty Wives (with David Ellis) 2012, Middle School: Get Me Out of Here (with Chris Tebbetts) 2012, I, Michael Bennett (with Michael Ledwidge) 2012, Nevermore: The Final Maximum Ride Adventure 2012, Zoo (with Michael Ledwidge) 2012, Confessions of a Murder Suspect (with Maxine Paetro) 2012, NYPD Red (with Marshall Karp) 2012, Daniel X: Armageddon (with Chris Grabenstein) 2012, I Funny (with Chris Grabenstein) 2012, Merry Christmas, Alex Cross 2012, Private Berlin (with Mark Sullivan) 2013, The Kiss (with Jill Dembowski) 2013, Cross My Heart 2013, Gone 2013, 12th of Never (with Maxine Paetro) 2013, Alex Cross, Run 2013, Hope to Die 2014, NYPD Red 2 (with Marshall Karp) 2014, Burn 2014, Unlucky 13 (with Maxine Paetro) 2014, NYPD Red 3 (with Marshall Karp) 2015, Private Vegas 2015, Cross Justice 2015, Cross the Line 2016, Alex Cross vs The People 2017, The President is Missing (with Bill Clinton) 2018, Not So Normal

Norbet 2018. *Address:* c/o Author Mail, Hachette Book Group USA, 1290 Avenue, New York, NY 10104, USA (office). *Website:* www.jamespatterson.com.

PATTERSON, The Most Hon. Percival James, BA, LLB, ON, PC, QC; Jamaican international consultant; *President, Heisconsults;* b. 10 April 1935, Cross Road, St Andrew; s. of Henry Patterson and Ina James; m. (divorced); one s. one d.; ed Univ. of West Indies, London School of Econs; called to Bar, Middle Temple 1963, Jamaican Bar 1963; party organizer, People's Nat. Party (PNP) 1958–60, mem. party exec. 1964–2006, Vice-Pres. 1969–82, Chair. 1983–92, Pres. 1992–2006; mem. nominated to Senate 1967; Leader of Opposition Business in Senate 1969–70; mem. House of Reps for S.E.Westmoreland 1969–80, 1989–2006; Minister for Industry and Tourism 1972–77, Deputy Prime Minister 1978–92, also Minister of Foreign Affairs and Foreign Trade 1978–80, Minister for Devt, Planning and Production 1989–90, for Finance and Planning 1990–91, of Defence 1992–2006; Prime Minister 1992–2006; Adviser to Govt of Belize 1982; currently Pres. Heisconsults; Pursell Trust Scholarship, Leverhulme Scholarship; Gran Cruz Placa De Oro, Order of Francisco Morazán (Honduras) 1990, Order of Águila Aztec (Mexico) 1990, Order of San Martín (Argentina) 1992, Great Cross of the Order of Bernado O'Higgins (Chile) 1992, Order of the Liberator Simon Bolivar (Venezuela) 1992, Order of Gran Cruz Gonzalo Jiménez de Quesada (Colombia) 1994, Order of Jose Marti (Cuba) 1997, Order of the Volta (Ghana) 1999, Gran Cruz Placa, Order Juan Mora Fernández (Costa Rica) 2001, Grand Cross, Nat. Order of Civil Merit (Spain) 2006, Order of Excellence (Guyana) 2006, Order of Belize 2006, Grand Cross, Order of Cruzeiro do Sul (Brazil) 2006, Order of the Caribbean Community 2009, Order of the Companions of O.R. Tambo (Gold) (South Africa) 2012; Hon. DLitt (Northeastern, Boston) 1994, (Connecticut) 2003, (Igbinedion Univ., Nigeria) 2007, Hon. LLD (Brown) 1998; FAO Agricola Medal 2001, Distinguished Service Award, Caribbean Tourism Org. 2005, Diggs Award for Foreign Affairs (Congressional Black Caucus) 2005, Chancellor's Medal, Univ. of the West Indies 2006, Living Legends Award, Economic Community of West African States, African Communications Agency, Ghana 2007, Andrew Young Medal for Capitalism and Social Progress 2007, Northern California Caribbean-American Heritage Month Cttee Award 2007, Jamaican Bar Asscn Award 2007, Caribbean Bar Asscn Govt Service Award 2007, Pinnacle Award, Org. of Nat. Coalition on Caribbean Affairs 2007, Lifetime Achievement Award, Hanover Homecoming Foundation 2008, EC Honour 2009. *Publications:* My Political Journey: Jamaica's Sixth Primie Minister 2018. *Leisure interests:* jazz, Jamaican music, spectator sports including cricket, boxing, track and field events, tennis. *Address:* Heisconsults, Sagicor Life Jamaica Centre (10th Floor), 28-48 Barbados Avenue, Kingston 5, Jamaica (office). *Telephone:* 929-57014 (office). *Fax:* 929-5705 (office). *E-mail:* pjpatterson@heisconsults.com (office).

PATTERSON, Walter Cram, MSc; Canadian/British energy analyst and writer; *Associate Fellow, Chatham House;* b. 4 Nov. 1936, Winnipeg, Man., Canada; s. of Walter Thomas Patterson and Thirza Helen Cram; m. Cleone Susan Davis 1966; two d.; ed Kelvin High School, Winnipeg, Univ. of Manitoba; Ed. Your Environment 1970–73, European Ed. Bulletin of the Atomic Scientists 1979–81; First 'Energy Campaigner' Friends of the Earth 1972–78; ind. analyst, writer 1978–93; with Gorleben Int. Review 1978–79; course tutor, Open Univ. 1981–91; series adviser, BBC TV Drama Edge of Darkness 1984–85; specialist adviser, House of Commons Select Cttee on Environment 1985–86, on Energy 1991–92; Assoc. Fellow, Energy and Environmental Programme, Royal Inst. of Int. Affairs (now Chatham House) 1991–93, Sr Research Fellow 1993–2000, Assoc. Fellow 2001–; Visiting Fellow, Sussex Energy Group, Univ. of Sussex 2006–; founding mem. Int. Energy Advisory Council 2015–; Fellow, Energy Inst.; Companion, Inst. of Energy 1991; Melchett Medal, Inst. of Energy 2000, Scientific American 50 Energy Policy Leader 2004. *Publications:* Nuclear Power 1976–86, The Fissile Society 1977, Coming to a Boil 1978, The Plutonium Business 1984, Going Critical 1985, Advanced Coal-Use Technology 1987, The Energy Alternative 1990, Coal-Use Technology in a Changing Environment 1990, Coal-Use Technology: New Challenges, New Responses 1993, Power from Plants 1994, Rebuilding Romania: Energy, Efficiency and the Economic Transition 1994, Electric Futures 1997, Transforming Electricity 1999, Keeping the Lights On 2007, Electricity Vs Fire 2015. *Leisure interests:* baseball, beer, computers, languages, music, orchids, epiphyllums, playing with the family, travel. *Address:* Little Rushmoor, High Bois Lane, Amersham, Bucks., HP6 6DQ (home); Chatham House, St James's Square, London, SW1Y 4LE, England (office). *Telephone:* (1494) 726748 (home); 7971-840036 (mobile) (office). *E-mail:* waltpattersn@gn.apc.org (home); walt@waltpatterson.org (home). *Website:* www.waltpatterson.org (home); www.chathamhouse.org.uk (office).

PATTISON, Jim, OC; Canadian business executive; *Managing Director, Chairman and CEO, The Jim Pattison Group;* b. Luseland, Sask.; m. Mary Pattison; three c.; ed Univ. of BC; paid univ. tuition fees washing cars and selling cars to fellow students; bought General Motors automobile dealership 1961, Owner, Man. Dir, Chair. and CEO The Jim Pattison Group 1961–; bought CJOR radio station 1965; Owner Ripley's Believe It or Not!, Overwaitea Food Group (including Save-On-Foods) and Buy-Low Foods grocery stores, Canadian Fishing Co., News Group; Dir The Toronto Dominion Bank, Canadian Pacific Ltd, Livent Inc.; Chair. and Pres. Vancouver EXPO '86; mem. Bd Trustees Ronald Reagan Presidential Foundation; Order of British Columbia 1990; Gov. Gen.'s Commemorative Medal 1992; inducted into Canadian Business Hall of Fame 1996, one of eight inaugural laureates of Canadian Professional Sales Asscn Sales Hall of Fame. *Leisure interests:* playing the piano, organ and trumpet. *Address:* Jim Pattison Group, 1055 W. Hastings Street, Suite 1600, Vancouver, BC V6E 2H2, Canada (office). *Telephone:* (604) 688-6764 (office). *Fax:* (604) 687-2601 (office). *Website:* www.jimpattison.com (office).

PATTISON, Sir John Ridley, BSc, MA, DM, FRCPath, FMedSci; British fmr medical scientist; b. 1 Aug. 1942; s. of Tom Frederick Pattison and Elizabeth Pattison; m. Pauline Evans 1965; one s. two d.; ed Barnard Castle School, Univ. Coll. Oxford, Middlesex Hosp. Medical School; Asst Lecturer in Pathology, later Lecturer in Virology, Middx Hosp. Medical School 1970–75; Lecturer, later Sr Lecturer in Virology, St Bartholomew's and London Hosp. Medical Colls 1976–77; Prof. of Medical Microbiology, King's Coll. Hosp. Medical School 1977–84, Univ. Coll. London 1984–2004, Dean 1990–98, Vice-Provost 1994–99; Dir of Research and Devt, Dept of Health and Nat. Health Service 1999–2004; consultant, GlaxoSmithKline, Legal & General; mem. MRC 1992–2004, Sr Medical Advisor 1996–99; mem. Spongiform Encephalopathy Advisory Cttee 1994–95, Chair. 1995–99; mem. Council, International Journal of Experimental Pathology 1979–2001, Soc. of Gen. Microbiology 1981–87; mem. Bd Inst. of Child Health 1992–96, Inst. of Neurology 1995–97; mem. Man. Cttee King's Fund 1993–, Deputy Chair. 1994–99; Founder-fellow, Acad. of Medical Science 1998; Ed.-in-Chief Epidemiology and Infection 1980–94; Hon. Fellow, Imperial Coll. London, Univ. Coll. London; hon. degrees (Middlesex, Southampton, Durham). *Publications include:* Principles and Practice of Clinical Virology (co-ed. five edns) 1987–2006, Practical Guide to Clinical Virology (co-ed.) 1989, Practical Guide to Clinical Bacteriology (co-ed.) 1995; numerous papers on medical virology. *Address:* 17 Broadwater Lane, Towcester, NN12 6YF, England (home). *Telephone:* (1327) 352116 (home); 7747-441313 (mobile) (home). *E-mail:* portsea200@btopenworld.com (home).

PATTON, Paul E., BEng; American politician, government official and university administrator; *Chancellor and Interim President, University of Pikeville;* b. 6 May 1937, Fallsburg, Ky; m. Judi Conway; four c.; ed Univ. of Kentucky; early career as owner of coal co. –1979; Deputy Sec. of the State Transportation Cabinet 1979–80; Chair. Ky Democrats 1981–83; Co. Judge Exec., Pike Co. 1981–91; Lt-Gov. of Ky 1991–95, Gov. of Ky 1995–2003; Chair. Ky Council on Postsecondary Educ. 2009–; Pres. Pikeville Coll. (now Univ. of Pikeville) 2009–13, now Chancellor and Interim Pres., also Distinguished Visiting Lecturer in Public Policy and Leadership; served numerous terms Pike Co. Democrats Exec. Comm.; mem. Bd Overseers Bellarmine Coll.; Chair. Pikeville/Pike Co. Industrial and Econ. Authority; fmr Chair. Nat. Ind. Coal Operators Asscn; fmr mem. Bd of Dirs Kentucky Coal Asscn, Kentucky Deep Mine Safety Comm.; Fellow, Univ. of Kentucky; mem. Big Sandy Regional Econ. Development Bd; Democrat; Univ. of Kentucky Hall of Distinguished Alumni 2010. *Address:* Office of the President, University of Pikeville, 147 Sycamore Street, Pikeville, KY 41501, USA (office). *Telephone:* (606) 218-5261 (office). *E-mail:* pep@upike.edu (office). *Website:* ww.upike.edu (office).

PATTULLO, Sir (David) Bruce, Kt, CBE, BA, FCIBS, FRSE; British banker (retd); b. 2 Jan. 1938, Edinburgh; s. of Colin Pattullo and Elizabeth Bruce; m. Fiona Nicholson 1962; three s. one d.; ed Rugby School and Hertford Coll. Oxford; Gen. Man. Bank of Scotland Finance Co. Ltd 1973–77; Dir British Linen Bank Ltd 1977–98, Chief Exec. 1977–78; Deputy Treas. Bank of Scotland 1978, Treas. and Gen. Man. (Chief Exec.) 1979–88, Dir 1980–98, Group Chief Exec. 1988–96, Deputy Gov. 1988–91, Gov. 1991–98; Chair. Cttee of Scottish Clearing Bankers 1981–83, 1987–89; three hon. degrees; Bilsland Prize, Inst. of Bankers in Scotland 1964. *Leisure interests:* tennis, hill walking. *Telephone:* (131) 339-6012 (home).

PAU, Louis-François, DSc, MBA, PhD; French business executive and academic; *Professor of Mobile Business, Rotterdam School of Management;* b. 29 May 1948, Copenhagen, Denmark; s. of Louis Pau and Marie-Louise Von Jessen; m. 1st Miki Miyamoto 1983 (divorced 1990); one d.; m. 2nd Maria Joukovskaia; one d.; ed Ecole Nat. Supérieure de l'Aéronautique et de l'Espace (renamed Institut Supérieur de l'Aéronautique et Espace), Paris Univ. (VI and IX), Inst. d'Etudes Politiques, Paris, Int. Inst. for Man. Devt, Switzerland, Institut Européen d'Admin des Affaires, Fontainebleau (INSEAD); dancer, Royal Ballet, Copenhagen 1957–66; served in Air Force 1970–72; Asst Prof., Tech. Univ., Denmark 1972–74; Prof. and Dept Head, Ecole Nat. Supérieure Télécommunications, Paris 1974–82; Assoc. Prof., MIT, USA 1977–78; Science and Tech. Counsellor, French Embassy, Washington, DC 1979–82; Professorial Lecturer, Univ. of Maryland, College Park, Md 1980–82; Sr Scientist, Battelle Memorial Inst. 1982–86; Research Prof., Tech. Univ., Denmark 1986–90; CSK Prof., Univ. of Tokyo 1988–90; Tech. Dir, Digital Equipment Corpn (Europe) (later Hewlett Packard (Europe)) 1990–95; Chief Tech. Officer, Ericsson Network Systems Div., Sweden 1995–2011; Prof. of Mobile Business, Rotterdam School of Man. 2001–; Adjunct Prof., Copenhagen Business School 2003–; Vodacom Chair Prof., Gordon Inst. of Business, Johannesburg, SA 2010–11; Chair. Upgötva AB (Sweden) 2015–; mem. Bd of Dirs, SCF Technologies A/S 2006–12; consultant to several int. corpns; adviser to several govts and govt agencies in USA, Asia and Europe; mem. Nat. Research Foundation Scientific Advisory Bd, Singapore 2000–17, ASTRI Tech. Advisory Bd, People's Repub. of China 2004–, review bds in EU and USA; mem. review panel, Czech Research Agency 2018–; Vice-Pres. (Tech.) Int. Fed. of Automatic Control 1982–86; Fellow, IEEE, Japan Soc. of Promotion Sciences, British Computer Soc.; numerous awards and prizes. *Publications:* 10 authored and 12 edited books; more than 350 papers on computers and communications, management science, aerospace tech. and financial/econ. models. *Leisure interests:* ballet, flying, travel. *Address:* T-9, Rotterdam School of Management, PO Box 1738, 3000 DR Rotterdam, The Netherlands (office). *Telephone:* (10) 590-13-39 (office). *E-mail:* lpau@nypost.dk (office).

PAUDEL, Bishnu Prasad; Nepalese politician; *Deputy General Secretary, Communist Party of Nepal (Unified Marxist-Leninist) (UML);* b. 20 Nov. 1959, Putalibazar-12, Syangja; s. of Devi Lal Paudel and Revati Paudel; m.; mem. House of Reps (CP of Nepal—Unified Marxist-Leninist) from Palpa 1994–99; Minister of Youth, Sports and Culture 1996; mem. Constituent Ass. (CP of Nepal—Unified Marxist-Leninist) (UML) from Rupandehi–4 2008–17, Chair. Cttee for Studying Constitutional Archives, Disputes and Consensus 2013–14; Minister of Water Resources 2009, of Defence 2011, of Finance 2015–16; Gov. Asian Development Bank 2015–16; mem. Communist Party of Nepal (Unified Marxist-Leninist) 1978–, mem. Central Cttee 1990–2015, Standing Cttee 2003–15, Sec., Central Cttee 2009–14, currently Deputy Gen. Sec. *Address:* Communist Party of Nepal (Unified Marxist-Leninist) (UML), Dhumbarahi Kathmandu (office); Butwal, 10 Rupandehi, Nepal (home). *Telephone:* (1) 4015979 (office). *Website:* www.cpnuml.org (office).

PAUDYAL, Leela Mani, MBA; Nepalese government official; b. 9 May 1962, Baletaksar-5, Gulmi; m.; two c.; ed Tribhuwan Univ.; joined Civil Service 1988; Accounts Officer, Office of the Comptroller-Gen. 1988–96; Under-Sec. (Admin), Ministry of Local Devt 1996–97; Jt Sec., Ministry of Industries, Commerce and Supplies 1997–2000; Dir-Gen., Dept of Cottage and Small Industries 2000–03; Jt Sec., Ministry of Industries, Commerce and Supplies May–Oct. 2003; Consular-Gen. for Tibet Autonomous Region of China, Lhasa 2003–07; Jt Sec., Ministry of Gen. Admin (Reserve) 2007–08; Sec., Ministry of Culture, Tourism and Civil Aviation 2007–08, Ministry of Information and Communications 2008–09, Office of

Prime Minister and Council of Ministers 2009–12, Ministry of Home Affairs May–Sept. 2011; Chief Sec. 2012–15. *Leisure interests:* travelling, yoga, meditation.

PAUGAM, Anne; French civil servant and international organization official; *CEO, Agence Française de Développement;* b. Oct. 1966; ed Institut d'études politiques de Paris (Sciences Po), Ecole nationale d'admin; joined Inspectorate Gen. of Finance 1993, Insp. Gen. of Finances 2010–13; joined World Bank, Washington, DC via Young Professionals' Program 1997, held positions related to strategic management, then operational functions, in charge of public sector reform projects at World Bank's office in Rabat; Tech. Adviser, then Deputy Dir, Cabinet of Minister for Co-operation and Francophonie 2001–02, worked on devt finance issues (Inter-ministerial Cttee on Int. Co-operation and Devt, Monterrey Conf.); joined Agence Française de Développement (AFD) 2002, held positions in strategic management (creation and management of the Strategic Steering and Forward-looking Dept) and operations (Dir Dept that finances projects in the education, vocational training and health sectors), later apptd Sec.-Gen. and mem. Exec. Cttee responsible for budget, resources, finance and risks, CEO (first woman) 2013–. *Address:* Agence Française de Développement, 5 rue Roland Barthes, 75598 Paris Cedex 12, France (office). *Telephone:* 1-53-44-31-31 (office). *Fax:* 1-44-87-99-39 (office). *E-mail:* site@afd.fr (office). *Website:* www.afd.fr (office).

PAUGET, Georges, MA, PhD; French banking executive; b. 1947, Rumilly, Haute-Savoie; ed Univs of Lyon and Bordeaux; joined Groupe Crédit Agricole SA 1973, early man. positions with Aude Regional Bank and Caisse Nationale de Crédit Agricole, then internal auditor and then project leader in Group Control and Audit, Cen. Sec. then Sr Gen. Man. Unicrédit; CEO Haute Saône et du Territoire de Belfort Regional Bank 1985–87, Pyrénées-Atlantique 1987–92, Pyrénées-Gascogne Regional Bank 1992–2002; Deputy CEO Crédit Agricole SA 2003–05, CEO and Chair. Exec. Cttee 2005–10, Perm. Rep. on Supervisory Bd of Fonds de Garantie des Dépôts, and COO, mem. Exec. Cttee and Dir Regional Banks Div.; Chair. and CEO Le Crédit Lyonnais 2003–10, now Hon. Chair.; Chair. Calyon –2010; Chair. Amundi Group 2011; Vice-Chair. Club Méditerranée, now Ind. mem.; Lead Dir Valeo SA, also Chair. Section for Appointments, Compensation and Man., mem. Strategy Cttee; mem. Supervisory Bd Eurazeo; mem. Bd of Dirs Paris-Europlace, Valeo; mem. Exec. Cttee Fédération Bancaire Française, Chair. –2009; fmr Chair. Union des Assurances Fédérales. *Publication:* Faut-il brûler les banquiers? 2009. *Website:* www.valeo.com/fr/georges-pauget (office).

PAUK, György; British (b. Hungarian) violinist; *Professor of Violin, Royal Academy of Music;* b. 26 Oct. 1936, Budapest, Hungary; s. of Imre Pauk and Magdolna Pauk; m. Susan Mautner 1959; one s. one d.; ed Franz Liszt Acad. of Music, Budapest under Ede Zathureczky, Leo Weiner and Zoltán Kodály; concerts all over Eastern Europe 1952–58 and world-wide; settled in The Netherlands 1958–61, England 1961–; Prof. of Violin, RAM 1987–; Artistic Dir Mozart Bicentenary Festival, London 1991; Prof. of Violin, Winterthur-Zürich Konservatorium of Music 1994–2000; Prof. Emer., Franz Liszt Acad. of Music, Budapest; jury mem. at int. violin competitions; master-classes world-wide; Hon. mem. and Prof., Guildhall School of Music and Drama, London 1987; Hon. RAM 1990; highest civilian award, Hungarian Govt 1998; Paganini Prize 1956, Sonata Competition Prize, Munich 1957, Jacques Thibaud Prize 1959, Grand Prix for Bartók Records (Ovation Magazine, USA) 1982, Best Record of 1983 (Gramophone Magazine), Bartók-Pasztory Prize (Hungary). *Recordings include:* numerous concertos, the complete violin/piano music of Mozart and Schubert, Handel and Brahms sonatas, Mozart string quintets, all Bartók's music for solo, duo and sonatas; first performances of Penderecki's violin concerto, UK, Japan, Sir Michael Tippett's Triple Concerto, London 1980, Lutosławski's Chain 2, UK, Netherlands, Hungary, with composer conducting, Sir Peter Maxwell Davies' violin concerto, Switzerland, Germany, William Mathias violin concerto, England. *Leisure interests:* football, tennis, theatre, reading, swimming, grandchildren. *Address:* Royal Academy of Music, Marylebone Road, London, NW1 5HT, England (office). *Telephone:* (20) 7873-7395 (office). *E-mail:* strings@ram.ac.uk (office). *Website:* www.ram.ac.uk (office).

PAUL, Christian; French politician; b. 23 March 1960, Clermont-Ferrand (Puy-de-Dôme); Deputy to Nat. Ass. for Nièvre (3ème) 1997–, mem. Comm. des affaires sociales; Sec. of State for Overseas, Ministry of the Interior 2000–02; Founding mem. Nouveau Parti Socialiste (New Socialist Party); left party, along with Arnaud Montebourg, to create Rénover Maintenant (Renew Now) within Socialist party; Pres. Parc Régional du Morvan; mem. Comm. nationale des comptes de la formation professionnelle, Comm. du dividende numérique; temporary mem. Conseil d'admin de l'Ecole nationale admin; mem. Municipal Council of Lormes, Nièvre 1995–2008, Gen. Council of Nièvre 1994–2004; Vice-Pres. Regional Council of Burgundy 2004–10; mem. Communauté de communes des Portes du Morvan. *Publications:* Le défi numérique des territoires 2007, Pour la République européenne (with Stéphane Collignon) 2008. *Address:* Assemblée nationale, 126 rue de l'Université, 75355 Paris 07 SP (office); 1 rue des Teureaux, 58140 Lormes, France. *Telephone:* 1-40-63-68-11 (office); (3) 86-22-89-50. *Fax:* (3) 86-22-58-32. *E-mail:* christian.paul@orange.fr (office); cpaul@christianpaul.fr. *Website:* www.assemblee-nationale.fr (office); www.christianpaul.fr.

PAUL, Evans; Haitian politician, radio commentator and fmr playwright; b. 26 Nov. 1955, Port-au-Prince; m. Irène Ridoré; ed Nat. Conservatory of Dramatic Arts; Founding Dir KPK Konbit Pitit Kay (theatre co.) 1977–98; Host, radio show Konbit Pitit Kay, Radio Cacique 1977–80; Co-founder Komite Inite Demokratik 1986 (renamed Konfederasyon Inite Demokratik 1987, Party Konvansyon Inite Demokratik 1995); Mayor of Port-au-Prince 1990–91 (forced to step down following coup d'état, reinstated 1994–95); Prime Minister of Haiti 2014–16; fmr Prof. of Dramatic Arts and Social Sciences, Ecole Normale Methodist. *Address:* c/o Office of the Prime Minister, 33 boulevard Harry S. Truman, BP 6114, Port-au-Prince, Haiti.

PAUL, Krishan Kant, MSc, PhD; Indian politician, government official and fmr police commissioner; b. 8 July 1948; m. Omita Paul; ed Punjab Univ.; joined Indian Police Service 1970, allocated to Arunachal Pradesh-Goa-Mizoram-Union Territories Div., Supt of Police, Andaman and Nicobar Islands, later Chief of Police, Arunachal Pradesh, served in Intelligence Bureau and Research and Analytical Wing, Commr, Delhi Police 2004–07 (retd); mem. Union Public Service Comm. 2007–13; Gov. of Meghalaya 2013–14, of Mizoram Sept.–Dec. 2014, of Manipur 2014–15, of Uttarakhand 2014–18; Acting Gov. of Nagaland July 2014; Special Duty Medal (Andaman and Nicobar), Pres.'s Police Medal for Distinguished Services, Sangram Medal, Paschim Star. *Leisure interest:* cricket. *Address:* c/o Raj Bhavan, Dehradun 248 001, India (office).

PAUL, Randal (Rand) Howard, BS, MD; American ophthalmologist and politician; *Senator from Kentucky;* b. 7 Jan. 1963, Pittsburgh, Pa; s. of Ronald Ernest Paul and Carolyn (Carol) Paul (née Wells); m. Kelley Ashby 1990; three s.; ed Baylor Univ., Duke Univ. School of Medicine; internship, Georgia Baptist Medical Center 1989; resident in ophthalmology, Duke Univ. Medical Center 1990–93; staff mem. Greenview Regional Hosp., Bowling Green, Ky, Bowling Green Medical Center, Logan Co. Memorial Hosp., Russellville, TJ Sampson Hosp., Glasgow; ophthalmologist, Graves-Gilbert Clinic; practising ophthalmologist in Bowling Green 1993–, est. own clinic 2007; Founder and Chair. Kentucky Taxpayers United 1994–; Founder Southern Kentucky Lions Eye Clinic, 1995; Senator from Kentucky 2011–, mem. Energy and Natural Resources Cttee 2011–, Homeland Security and Governmental Affairs Cttee 2011–, Small Business and Entrepreneurship Cttee 2011–; mem. Lions Clubs International (fmr Pres.); unsuccessful cand. for Republican party nomination for US Pres. 2015–16; Melvin Jones Fellow Award for Dedicated Humanitarian Services, Lions Clubs International, Lion of the Year Award, Bowling Green Lions, Fines E. Davis Fellow Award for Dedicated Humanitarian Service, Gov.'s Appreciation Award for Sight Conservation, Outstanding Service and Commitment to Seniors, Twilight Wish Foundation 2002, Center for the Nat. Interest Distinguished Service Award 2014. *Address:* 167 Russell Senate Office Building, Washington, DC 20510, USA (office). *Telephone:* (202) 224-4343 (office). *Website:* www.paul.senate.gov (office).

PAUL, Baron (Life Peer), cr. 1996, of Marylebone in the City of Westminster; **Swraj Paul,** MSc, FRSA; British business executive; *Chairman, Caparo Group Limited;* b. 18 Feb. 1931, India; s. of Payare Paul and Mongwati Paul; m. Aruna Vij 1956; three s. one d. (and one d. deceased); ed Punjab Univ., Massachusetts Inst. of Tech., USA; joined family-owned Apeejay Surrendra Group as Partner 1953; moved to UK and est. Natural Gas Tubes Ltd 1966; Founder Indo-British Asscn 1975; Founder-Chair., Caparo Group Ltd 1978–, Ambika Paul Foundation 1978–, Theirworld 2002–15; Amb. for British Business 1998–2010; Chancellor, Univ. of Wolverhampton 1999–; Deputy Speaker, House of Lords 2008–10, Deputy Chair. of Cttees 2008–10, suspended from membership Oct. 2010–Feb. 2011; Resigned Labour Whip Oct. 2010; mem. London Devt Agency 2000–08, London 2012 2003–05; Hon. PhD (American Coll. of Switzerland, Leysin) 1986; Hon. DSc (Econ.) (Hull) 1992; Hon. DLitt (Westminster) 1996; Hon. DHL (Chapman) 1996; Hon. DUniv (Bradford) 1997, (Central England) 1999; Hon. DSc (Buckingham) 1999; Padma Bhushan 1983, Corp. Leadership Award, MIT 1987, Freedom of the City of London 1998, Asian Business Awards Lifetime Achievement Award 2008, Int. Indian of the Decade 2013. *Publications:* Indira Gandhi 1984, Beyond Boundaries 1998. *Address:* Caparo House, 103 Baker Street, London, W1U 6LN (office); House of Lords, Westminster, London, SW1A 0PW, England. *Telephone:* (20) 7486-1417 (office). *Fax:* (20) 7224-4109 (office). *E-mail:* lp@caparogrp.com (office). *Website:* www.caparo.com (office); www.parliament.uk/biographies/lords/lord-paul/3163.

PAUL, Vivek, BE, MBA; American (b. Indian) business executive; b. 1958; m.; three c.; ed BITS, Pilani, Univ. of Massachusetts; fmrly with Pepsi and Bain & Co.; joined Gen. Electric (GE) 1989, Pres. and CEO medical equipment joint venture in India, then global head Computerized Tomography business 1995–99, Pres. and CEO Wipro GE Medical Systems Ltd 1993–95, Vice-Chair. Wipro, Bangalore, India 1999–2005, Pres. and CEO global IT, product engineering, and business process services; Pnr, Texas Pacific Group (TPG), Man. Dir Ventures 2005–2008; Founder KineticGlue (cloud-based software co. 2008, sold co. 2013; Consulting Professor of Radiology, Molecular Imaging Program, Stanford Univ.; Dir Electronic Arts, Inc. 2008–. *Address:* c/o Molecular Imaging Program, Stanford University, The James H Clark Center 318 Campus Drive, East Wing, 1st Floor, Stanford, CA 94305-5427, USA (office).

PAULA GUTIÉRREZ, Francisco de, MA, PhD; Costa Rican economist, academic, fmr politician and fmr central banker; *Professor of Economics and Finance, INCAE Business School;* ed Univ. of Costa Rica, Univ. of Pennsylvania, USA; Lecturer in Econs, Univ. of Costa Rica 1972–86; Economist, Banco Centroamericano de Integración Ecónomico, Tegulcigalpa, Honduras 1973–74; Adviser to Pres. of Costa Rica 1974–76, to Exec. Cttee, Banco Central de Costa Rica 1974–76; Economist, Wharton Econometric Forecasting Associates, Philadelphia, Pa 1981–84; Dir Consejeros Económicos y Financieros SA (CEFSA) 1984; mem. Comisión Internacional para la Reconstrucción y el Desarrollo de Centroamérica 1987–89; Minister of Finance 1996–98; Dir Banco Central de Costa Rica 1989–90, 1996–98, Pres. 2002–10; Prof. of Econs and Finance, INCAE Business School 1986–; Pres. Grupo Financiero SAMA 1998–; Dir Banco de Fomento Agrícola 1985–87, Productos de Concreto 1985–86, RICALIT SA 1986–96, Atlas Eléctrica 1990–96, ACORDE 1993–95, FUNDES 1993–96, Banco de COFISA 1993–96, Corporación INCSA 1998–, El Financiero (periodical) 1998–. *Publications:* numerous specialist papers on economics. *Address:* INCAE Business School, Campus Walter Kissling, 960-4050 Alajuela, Costa Rica (office). *Telephone:* 243-72153 (office). *Fax:* 433-9820 (office). *E-mail:* Francisco.Gutierrez@incae.edu (office). *Website:* www.incae.edu/ES/facultad/Francisco.Gutierrez (office).

PAULAUSKAS, Artūras; Lithuanian politician; b. 23 Aug. 1963; m. Jolanta Paulauskienė; one s. one d. (and two s. from previous m.); ed Vilnius State Univ.; Deputy Prosecutor, Kaisiadoris 1979–82; Prosecutor, Varena 1982–87; instructor, Cen. Cttee CP 1987; Deputy Prosecutor-Gen. of Lithuania 1987–90, Prosecutor-Gen. 1990–95; barrister 1997–2000; cand. in presidential elections 1997, 1998, 2014; est. The New Union (Social Liberals) Party, Leader 2006–; mem. Seimas (Parl.) of Lithuania 2000–08, Speaker 2000–06; Acting Pres. of Lithuania 6 April–12 July 2004; Minister of Environment Jan.–Nov. 2008. *Leisure interests:* sport, reading. *Address:* New Union (Social Liberals), Gedimino pr. 10/1, Vilnius 01103, Lithuania (office). *Telephone:* (5) 210-7600 (office). *Fax:* (5) 210-7602 (office). *E-mail:* arturas.paulauskas@lrs.lt (office); centras@nsajunga.lt (office). *Website:* www.nsajunga.lt (office); www.paulauskas.lt.

PAULINO SEM, Lt-Gen. (retd) Rubén Darío; Dominican Republic military officer (retd) and government official; *Minister of Defence;* b. 21 Sept. 1962,

Santiago de los Caballeros; s. of Bruno Paulino Minier and Dulce María Sem Estrella de Paulino; m. Lesbi Lizardo de Paulino; six c.; ed Academia Militar de las Fuerzas Armadas 'Batalla de las Carreras' (AMFA); long mil. career, including as Intelligence Officer, 2nd Infantry Brigade 1988, Intelligence Man., N Region 1992, Commanding Officer, B Co., 2nd Infantry Bn 1993, Commdr, 2nd Infantry Bn 1995, Commanding Officer, 3rd Co. 1996, Exec. Officer, 6th Infantry Brigade 2000, Staff Officer, 1st Infantry Brigade 2000, served in Mil. Cartographic Inst. 2002, Dir Fuel Control Special Div. 2004, Deputy Dir Armed Forces Vocational Schools 2007, Commdr, MRM Mil. Complex 2008, Commdr, 6th Infantry Brigade 2008, 4th Infantry Brigade 2008–09, 2nd Infantry Brigade 2009, Personnel Dir Ministry of Defence Aug.–Dec. 2009, Dir of Civil Affairs 2009, Dir-Gen., Voice of the Armed Forces (radio station) 2010, Dir-Gen., Voluntary Mil. Service Program 2010, Commdr-Gen. of the Army 2012–14, Deputy Minister of Defence, responsible for Mil. Affairs 2014–16, Minister of Defence 2016–; Dir-Gen. of Immigration 2015–16; numerous awards including Juan Pablo Duarte Grand Mil. Cordon 1998, Order of Mil. Merit (White Ribbon) 2010, (Blue Ribbon) 2011, CFAC Award and Golden Cross Medal (First Class) 2013, Order of Mil. Merit with Blue Ribbon (First Class) 2014, XXXV Anniversary Commemorative Medal (Army of Nicaragua) 2014, Order of Merit with White Ribbon (First Class) 2014. *Address:* Ministry of Defence, Plaza de la Bandera, Avda 27 de Febrero, esq. Avda Luperón, Santo Domingo DN, Dominican Republic (office). *Telephone:* 530-5149 (office). *Fax:* 531-0461 (office). *E-mail:* directorrev@j2.mil.do (office). *Website:* www.mide.gob.do (office).

PAULRAJ, Arogyaswami J., BE, PhD; Indian/American electrical engineer, academic and entrepreneur; *Professor Emeritus (Research) of Engineering and Marconi Society Fellow, Department of Electrical Engineering, Stanford University;* b. Pollachi, nr Coimbatore, Tamil Nadu; m. Nirmala Paulraj; ed Nat. Defence Acad., Indian Navy Training Schools, Naval Coll. of Eng, Indian Inst. of Tech., Delhi; served with Indian Navy 1961–91, Deputy Electrical Officer, INS Darshak 1968–69; Research Scholar, Indian Inst. of Tech. 1969–71; Staff Officer, Naval HQ, New Delhi 1971–72; Project Leader, Indian Inst. of Tech. 1972–73; Research Fellow, Loughborough Univ. of Tech., UK 1974–75; Div. Head, Naval Physical and Oceanographic Lab., Cochin 1976–83; Visiting Scientist, Stanford Univ., USA 1984–86; Founding Dir Centre for Artificial Intelligence and Robotics, Bangalore 1986–88, Founding Dir Centre for Devt of Advance Computing, Bangalore 1988–90, Chief Scientist (Founding Dir), Cen. Research Lab., Bharat Electronics, Bangalore 1988–91; Visiting Scientist, Stanford 1992–93, Prof. (Research) 1993–2010, Prof. Emer. 2010–; Distinguished Prof., Indian Inst. of Tech., Madras 2014–; Visiting Prof., Beijing Univ. of Posts and Telecommunications 2012–, Imperial Coll. London 2013–; Founder and Chief Tech. Officer, Iospan Wireless Inc., San Jose, USA 1998–2003; Co-founder and Chief Tech. Officer, Beceem Communications Inc., San Jose 2004–10; Sr Advisor, Broadcom Corpn, USA 2010–14; Chief Tech. Officer, Rasa Networks Inc., USA 2014–15; Visiting Prof., Imperial Coll., London, UK 2013–, Beijing Univ. of Posts and Telecommunications, People's Repub. of China 2012–; mem. US Nat. Acad. of Eng 2006; Assoc. mem. The World Acad. of Sciences (TWAS) 2007; Foreign mem. Royal Swedish Acad. of Eng Sciences 2008; Fellow, Inst. of Electronics and Telecommunications Engineers (India) 1987, Inst. of Engineers (India) 1990, IEEE 1990, Indian Acad. of Eng 1998, AAAS 2010, Indian Nat. Acad. of Sciences 2016; Foreign Fellow, Nat. Acad. of Sciences (India) 2011, Indian Acad. of Sciences 2014; Foreign mem., Chinese Acad. of Eng 2015; Chief of Naval Staff Medal 1973, Vishist Seva Medal 1974, V.K. Jain Memorial Gold Medal (Navy) 1974, Ati Vishist Seva Medal 1983, Padma Bhushan 2010; VASVIK Gold Medal (Industry Innovation) 1982, Scientist of the Year, Govt of India 1985, IEEE SPS Distinguished Lectureship 1996, IEEE SP Soc. Tech. Achievement Award 2003, IEEE Alexander Graham Bell Medal 2011, Marconi Prize and Fellowship 2014, several IEEE Best Paper awards. *Achievements include:* pioneer of wireless technology known as MIMO (multiple input, multiple output) that increases performance of wireless systems. *Publications include:* Communication, Control, Signal Processing and Computing (co-ed.) 1997, Introduction to Space-Time Wireless Communications (co-author) 2003, Introduction to MIMO Wireless (co-author) 2006, Distributed Space-Time Systems (co-ed.) 2008; 18 book chapters, more than 140 papers in professional journals and more than 60 patents. *Address:* Room 232, David Packard Electrical Engineering 350 Serra Mall, MC 9510, Stanford, CA 94305-9510, USA (office). *E-mail:* apaulraj@stanford .edu (office). *Website:* web.stanford.edu/~apaulraj (office).

PAULS, Raymond; Latvian composer and jazz pianist; b. 12 Jan. 1936, Riga; m. Lana Paula; one d.; ed Latvian Conservatory; Artistic Dir and Chief Conductor, Latvian State Radio and TV 1985–88; Chair. Latvian State Cttee for Culture, later Minister of Culture 1988–93 (first non-communist minister in USSR since 1920s); Counsellor to Pres. 1993–97; mem. Parl. (Saeima) 1998–; Hon. mem. Latvian Acad. of Sciences 1992; People's Artist of USSR 1985; Three Star Order (Third Class) 1995; Latvian State Prize 1979. *Compositions:* musical stage works: Pāri, kas dabonas (Lovers Who Get It) 1976, Māsa Kerija (Sister Carry) 1978, Nāc pie puikām (Come to the Boys) 1982, Vella būšana (A Matter of the Devil) 1987, Meža gulbji (Forest Swans) 1995, Legenda par Zaļo Jumpravu (The Legend of the Green Maiden) 2000; ballets: Kubas melodijas (Melodies of Cuba) 1963, Ritmi, ritmi (Rhythms, Rhythms) 1979, Vitrāžas (Stained Glass Panels) 1979; music for 30 theatre performances, including: Īsa pamācība mīlēšanā (A Short Instruction in Love), Atjautīgā aukle (The Ingenious Nanny), Šerloks Holmss (Sherlock Holmes), Brands (Brand), Džons Neilands (John Neiland), Elizabete – Anglijas karaliene (Elizabeth – Queen of England), Grāfs Monte Kristo (The Count of Monte Cristo), Dāmu paradīze (Paradise of Ladies), Melanholiskais valsis (The Melancholic Waltz) etc. and for puppet theatre performances Runčuks Punčuks (The Belly Tomcat), Velniņi (The Two Imps), Ceturtais skriemelis (The Fourth Vertebra) etc.; music for radio performances and plays; music for more than 30 films, including Vella kalpi (Servants of the Devil), Vella kalpi Vella dzirnavās (The Servants of the Devil in the Windmill of the Devil), Tauriņdeja (The Butterfly Dance), Melnā vēža spīlēs (In the Pincers of the Black Lobster), Dāvana vientuļai sievietei (A Present for a Lonely Woman), Mans draugs: nenopietns cilvēks (My Friend the Rattlebrain), Teātris (The Theatre), Limuzīns Jāņu nakts krāsā (A Limousine in the Colour of a Summer Solstice Night), Liktendzirnas (The Hand-Mill of Fate), for the series Ilgais ceļš kāpās (The Long Way through the Dunes) etc.; choral music: 3 Songs for choir and piano 1972, 10 arrangements of Latvian folk songs for boys choir 1980, Song Cycle with the lyrics of Aspazija for boys choir 1980, Baltās dziesmas (The White Songs) for boys choir and instrumental ensemble 1981, Song Cycle for choir and piano 1984, Cycle Vītola stabules dziesmas (Songs of a Willow Pipe) for boys choir 1984, Mazs, laimīgs zēns (A Small and Happy Boy): ten songs for boys choir and piano with lyrics by M. Karēms 1985, Cycle Pērļu zvejnieks (Pearl Hunter) for boys choir and tenor 1986; cycles of light music songs: Vecās Rīgas vitrāžas (The Stained Glass Panels of the Old Rīga) 1971, Five Songs with lyrics by D. Avotiņa 1972, Oriental Motifs 1982, City Romance 1983, Melnais kliedziens (The Black Cry) 1985, Cycle with lyrics by Rainis 1985; more than 500 songs; children's music: approx. 70 songs for children; jazz music: Suite Portreti (Portraits) 1962, A Rhapsody for piano and light music orchestra 1964, Suite Iespaidi (Impressions) 1965, Suite Dienvidu akvareļi (The Water-Colours of the South) 1965, Kalnu skices (Mountain Sketches) 1966, Five Improvisations in the spirit of Latvian folk songs 1967, Suite Melnās krāsas (Black Colours) 1967, Jazz Expressions 1970 and other works; instrumental music: approx. 300 works, including instrumental versions of songs, arrangements of folk songs, versions on familiar themes, arrangements of classical composer works. *Recordings include:* more than 90 albums, including Cinema 1982, U morya zhizn' moya 1995, Na Rozhdestvo 1995, Izbrannoe 1995, Nostal'giya. Instrumental'naya muzika 1996, Dva maestro 1997, My Favourite Melodies/So Many Stars. *Address:* Veidenbaum Str. 41/43, Apt 26, 6001 Rīga, Latvia. *Telephone:* 6227-5588.

PAULSON, Henry (Hank) Merritt, Jr, BA, MBA; American investment banker and fmr government official; *Chairman, Paulson Institute;* b. 28 March 1946, Palm Beach, Fla; s. of Henry Merritt and Marianna Paulson (née Gallaeur); m. Wendy Judge 1969; one s. one d.; ed Dartmouth Coll., Harvard Univ. Business School; Staff Asst to Asst Sec. of Defense (Comptroller), Pentagon, Washington, DC 1970–72; Staff Asst to Pres.'s Domestic Council, The White House, Washington, DC 1972–73; Assoc. Goldman Sachs & Co., Chicago 1974–77, Vice-Pres. 1977–82, Pnr, Investment Banking Dept 1982–, pnr in charge of investment banking, Midwest Region 1984–90, Man. Cttee Co-Head Investment Banking Div., Vice-Chair., COO 1990–99, CEO and Chair. 1999–2006; US Sec. of the Treasury 2006–09; Distinguished Visiting Scholar, Johns Hopkins School of Advanced Int. Studies, Washington, DC 2009–, Fellow, Bernard Schwartz Forum on Constructive Capitalism; Trustee Chicago Symphony Orchestra; Dir The Peregrine Fund Inc.; Vice-Chair. Nature Conservancy and Co-Chair. of Latin American Conservation Council of Nature Conservancy, Risky Business Project; Founder and Chair. Paulson Inst., Univ. of Chicago. *Publications:* On the Brink: Inside the Race to Stop the Collapse of the Global Financial System 2010, Dealing with China 2015. *Leisure interests:* skiing, fishing, canoeing, tennis, visiting wildlife habitats. *Address:* Paulson Institute, 5711 South Woodlawn Avenue, Chicago, IL 60637, USA (office). *Website:* www.paulsoninstitute.org (office).

PAULY, Daniel, PhD; French marine biologist and academic; b. 2 May 1946, Paris; ed Univ. of Kiel, Germany; Project Asst, German Soc. for Technical Cooperation (GTZ) 1974–76; Research Asst, Dept of Fishery Biology, Inst. for Marine Sciences, Kiel 1978–79; Post-Doctoral Fellow, Int. Center for Living Aquatic Resources Man. (ICLARM), Manila 1979–80, Assoc. Scientist 1980–85, Sr Scientist 1985–94; Prof. of Fisheries, Univ. of British Columbia, Vancouver 1994–, Project Leader of Sea Around Us Project, Dir Fisheries Centre 2003–08; mem. Bd of Oceana; earned place in Scientific American 50 2003, labelled by New York Times as an "iconoclast" 2003, Int. Cosmos Prize 2005, Volvo Environment Prize, Volvo Environment Foundation (co-recipient) 2006, ECI Prize 2007, Ted Danson Ocean Hero Award 2007, Ramon Margalef Prize in Ecology 2008, Albert Ier Grand Medal in Science 2016, Ocean Award 2017. *Achievements include:* early in his career, worked in tropics and developed new methods for estimating fish populations; developed concept of shifting baselines in 1995; published seminal paper on Fishing Down Marine Food Webs in Science 1998; developed important models and tools, including the Marine Trophic Index, Ecopath Modelling Model, and global database FishBase. *Publications:* author of several books and more than 500 scientific papers in professional journals on studies of human impacts on global fisheries. *Address:* AERL Room 333, Fisheries Centre, Aquatic Ecosystems Research Laboratory, University of British Columbia, 2202 Main Mall, Vancouver, BC V6T 1Z4, Canada (office). *Telephone:* (604) 822-1201 (office). *E-mail:* d.pauly@fisheries.ubc.ca (office). *Website:* www.fisheries.ubc.ca (office).

PAUZE, Jean-Charles, BEng, MSc (Econ), MBA; French business executive; b. 1947; ed IDN-EC Lille, Institut Européen d'Admin des Affaires (INSEAD); began career with Total 1971–74; joined Alfa Laval Group 1974, held several positions, CEO Alfa Laval France 1981–84, CEO Brand & Luebbe (subsidiary in Germany) 1984–86; Chair. and CEO Clestra-Hauserman, Strafor Facom Group 1986–91, Chair. and CEO Steelcase Strafor 1991–98; Chair. Man. Bd Guilbert (PPR Group) 1998–2002; CEO Rexel 2002–12, Chair. Man. Bd 2007–12; Chair. Remuneration Cttee IMCD Group 2014–; mem. Bd of Dirs Bunzl PLC. *Address:* Head Office, IMCD Group, Wilhelminaplein 32, 3072 DE Rotterdam, The Netherlands (office). *Telephone:* (10) 2908684 (office). *Fax:* (10) 2908680 (office).

PAVLIS, Pavol, MTech; Slovak politician; b. 12 Jan. 1961, Bratislava; m.; four c.; ed Slovak Technical Univ.; Researcher, Head of Section, Research Inst. of Computer Tech., Žilina 1984–90; Head Specialist, SLUVIS Foreign Trade Enterprise 1990–92; CEO Port Service Bratislava Ltd 1992–2006; mem. Supervisory Bd, Fond národného majetku (Nat. Property Fund of the Slovak Repub.) 2003–06; mem. Nat. Council (Parl.) 2006–10, 2010–12, mem. Standing Cttee for Econ. Policies 2006–10, Standing Cttee for Agric. and Environment 2010–12; State Sec., Ministry of the Economy 2012–14, Minister of Economy 2014–15; mem. Smer-Sociálna demokracia (Smer-SD, Direction-Social Democracy).

PAVLOPOULOS, Prokopis K., PhD; Greek lawyer, academic, politician and head of state; *President;* b. 10 July 1950, Kalamata; m. Vlassia Peltsemi; one s. two d.; ed Univ. of Athens, Panthéon-Assas Univ., Paris; Sec. to Pres. 1974; Alt. Minister for the Presidency and Govt Spokesman 1989; legal adviser to Pres. 1990–95; political adviser to Chair. Nea Demokratia (ND—New Democracy) party 1995, Press and Information Officer 1996; mem. Parl. (ND) 1996–, ND Parl. Spokesman 2000–, mem. Standing Cttee on Public Admin., Public Order and Justice, Special Standing Cttee on Institutions and Transparency, Cttee for Revision of Constitution, Cttee on Public Enterprises, Banks and Public Utilities; Minister of the Interior, Public Admin and Decentralization 2004–07, of the Interior and Public Order 2007–09; Pres. of Greece 13 March 2015–; Visiting Prof., Univ. of Paris II 1986; Prof. of Admin. Law, Univ. of Athens 1989; fmr mem. Bd Greek Culture Foundation; fmr Vice-Chair. Greek State Radio and TV Co. (ERT

SA). *Publications include:* The Constitutional Safeguard for Plea in Abatement, The Civil Responsibility of the Government. *Address:* Office of the President, Odos Vassileos Georgiou 2, 100 28 Athens (office); 36 Michalakopoulou str., 115 28, Athens, Greece. *Telephone:* (210) 7283111 (office); (210) 3390201 (office); (210) 3616926 (office). *Fax:* (210) 7248938 (office); (210) 3390507 (office). *E-mail:* ppavlopoulos@prokopispavlopoulos.gr (office); pavp@hellasnet.gr; publicrelationsoffice@presidency.gr (office). *Website:* www.presidency.gr (office).

PAVLOVSKY, Gleb Olegovich; Russian journalist, editor and political scientist; b. 5 March 1951, Odessa; m.; one s. four d.; ed Odessa State Univ.; with Samizdat 1972–86; Co-founder and mem. Bd Poiski (magazine) 1978–80; arrested for anti-Soviet activity and sentenced to three years in exile in Komi Repub. 1982; Chair. Postfactum (information agency) 1988–93; Vice-Chair. Kommersant publishing house 1991–92; mem. Editorial Bd Obshchaya Gazeta 1993–; Ed.-in-Chief Twentieth Century and World; Co-Publr Sreda (Russian-European review) 1995–96; Co-founder and Ed.-in-Chief Russian Journal internet magazine 1997; Ed.-in-Chief Peredely Blasti magazine 1994–95; Co-founder and Ed. Europe publishing house 2005; Founder and Pres. Foundation for Effective Politics 1995–2009; took part in election campaign of Pres. Vladimir Putin 2000; involved in Ukrainian presidential election supporting defeated cand. Viktor Yanukovych 2004; adviser to Presidential Admin of Russian Fed. –2011; hosted weekly TV news commentary, Real Politics, shown on NTV Russia 2005–08; Founder and Ed.-in-Chief gefter.ru blog 2012. *Address:* Foundation for Effective Politics, Zubovsky blvd 4 entr. 8, 119021 Moscow, Russia (office). *Telephone:* (495) 745-52-25 (office).

PAVĻUTS, Daniels, BA, MPA; Latvian politician and academic; b. 14 May 1976, Jūrmala; ed Jāzeps Vītols Latvian Acad. of Music, City Univ., London, UK, John F. Kennedy School of Govt, Harvard Univ., USA; Exec. Dir Int. Boys' Choir Festival 'Rigas Doms' 1997–2001; Adviser to the Dir on Man. and Communication, Latvian Nat. Opera 2001; Brand Dir DDB LATVIJA Ltd 2001–03; State Sec., Ministry of Culture 2003–06; mem. Bd, ZENO Consulting 2007–11, Latvian Chamber of Commerce and Industry 2008–10; mem. Man. Team and Head of Corp. Affairs, Swedbank AS 2010–11; Minister of the Economy 2011–14; Visiting Lecturer, Stockholm School of Econs, Rīga 2007–. *Address:* Stockholm School of Economics, Strelnieku iela 4A, Rīga 1010, Latvia (office). *Telephone:* 6701-5800 (office). *Fax:* 6783-0249 (office). *E-mail:* office@sseriga.edu (office). *Website:* www.sseriga.edu (office).

PAWAR, Sharadchandra Govindrao, BCom; Indian politician; *President, Nationalist Congress Party;* b. 12 Dec. 1940, Baramati, Pune; s. of Govindrao Jijaba Pawar and Shardabai G. Pawar; m. Pratibha Pawar 1967; one d.; ed Brihan Maharashtra Coll. of Commerce, Pune; Head, State Level Youth Congress; Gen. Sec. Maharashtra Pradesh Congress Cttee; elected to State Legis. 1967, held Portfolios of Home and Publicity and Rehabilitation, Minister of State and Educ. and Youth Welfare, Home, Agric. and Industries and Labour; Chief Minister of Maharashtra 1978–80, 1993–95; Minister of Defence 1991–93; Minister of Agric. 2004–14; Minister of Consumer Affairs, Food and Public Distribution 2004–11, of Food Processing Industries 2011–14; Pres. Nat. Congress (opposition) 1981–86; rejoined Congress (I) 1986; fmr Pres. Congress Forum for Socialistic Action; Sec. Defence Cttee; mem. Lok Sabha (lower house of parl.) for Baramati 1984–85, 1991–2009, for Madha 2009–14; mem. Rajya Sabha (upper house of parl.) for Maharashtra 2014–; Leader of Opposition 1998–99; Founder-Pres. Nationalist Congress Party 1999–; Pres. Maharashtra Kabbadi Asscn, Maharashtra Olympic Asscn, Agricultural Devt Foundation, Mumbai Cricket Asscn, Garware Club House, Maharashtra Kustigir Parishad, Nehru Centre, Vasantdada Sugar Inst., Bd of Control for Cricket in India 2005–08; Vice-Pres. Int. Cricket Council 2008–12, Pres. 2010–12, Organizing Pres. ICC Cricket World Cup 2011; Dr hc (Lawrence Technological Univ., USA); Outstanding Parliamentarian Award 2003. *Leisure interests:* sports, reading, travelling. *Address:* Nationalist Congress Party, 10, Bishambhar Das Marg, New Delhi 110 001 (office); Ramalayan, 44-A Pedder Road, Mumbai 400 026, India (home). *Telephone:* (22) 23659191 (home). *E-mail:* sharadpawar.sp@gmail.com (home).

PAWLAK, Waldemar, MSc; Polish politician and business executive; b. 5 Sept. 1959, Model, Mazowieckie Voivodship; m. Elżbieta Pawlak; two s. one d.; ed Warsaw Univ. of Tech.; computer teacher in Pacyna 1984; farm man. 1984; mem. United Peasant Party (ZSL) 1984–90; Deputy to Sejm (Parl.) 1989–; mem. Polish Peasant Party (PSL) 1992– (Chair. 1992–97, 2005–12); Chair. Council of Ministers (Prime Minister) June–July 1992, 1993–95; Chair. Union of Volunteer Fire Brigades with rank of Brig.-Gen. 1992–; Pres. Warszawska Gielda Towarowa Spolka Akcyjna (WGT) S.A. (commodity exchange) Warsaw 2001–05; Deputy Prime Minister and Minister of the Economy 2007–12. *Leisure interests:* philosophy, information science, computers. *Address:* Polish People's Party (PSL), 00-924 Warsaw, ul. Kopernika 36/40, Poland (office). *Telephone:* (22) 6206020 (office). *Fax:* (22) 6543583 (office). *E-mail:* biuronkw@psl.org.pl (office). *Website:* www.psl.pl (office).

PAWLENTY, Timothy James (Tim), BA, JD; American fmr politician; *President and CEO, Financial Services Roundtable;* b. 27 Nov. 1960, St Paul, Minn.; s. of Eugene Pawlenty and Virginia Pawlenty (née Oldenburg); m. Mary Elizabeth Anderson 1987; two d.; ed Univ. of Minnesota; fmr labour law attorney, Rider Bennett, LLP, Minneapolis for 15 years, served as Lead Counsel for Minneapolis School Dist for ten years, later Partner; fmr prosecutor, Hennepin Co.; fmr Vice-Pres. Wizmo Inc.; Chair. Eagan Planning Comm. 1988–89; mem. Eagan City Council 1990–92; mem. for Dist 38B, Minnesota House of Reps 1993–2003, Majority Leader 1999–2003; Gov. of Minn. 2003–11; unsuccessful cand. for Republican US presidential nomination 2011; Pres. and CEO Financial Services Roundtable 2012–; Chair. Midwest Govs Asscn 2006–07, Nat. Govs Asscn 2007–08; Republican. *Publications:* Minnesota's Capitol: A Centennial Story (contrib.), Courage to Stand: An American Story 2011. *Address:* Financial Services Roundtable, 600 13th Street, NW, Suite 400, Washington, DC 20005, USA (office). *Telephone:* (202) 289-4322 (office). *E-mail:* info@fsroundtable.org (office). *Website:* fsroundtable.org (office).

PAWLIK, Kurt, PhD, PrivDoz; Austrian academic; *Professor Emeritus of Psychology, University of Hamburg;* b. 16 March 1934, Vienna; ed Univ. of Vienna; Prof. of Psychology and Dept Dir, Univ. of Hamburg, Germany 1966–, now Prof. Emer.; Founder and Ed.-in-Chief European Psychologist journal; Ed. Methods of

Psychology monograph series; Co-Ed. Research Texts in Psychology monograph series (more than 60 vols) and several scientific journals including American Psychologist; Pres. German Soc. of Psychology 1972–74, Int. Social Science Council 1998–2000, J. Jungius Soc. of Science 1999–; Sec.-Gen. Int. Union of Psychological Science 1984–92, Pres. 1992–96, 2000–02; Ordinary Mem. Academia Europaea 1990–; Hon. mem. German Soc. of Psychology 2002–, Acad. of Sciences, Hamburg; Fellow, Chinese Psychological Soc. 2004–, Asscn of Psychological Science; Austrian Cross of Honours (First Class) in Science and Arts 1999; Outstanding Psychologist Award, American Psychological Asscn 2012. *Publications include:* International Handbook of Psychology (co-ed.) 2000; 17 books and more than 180 research papers. *Leisure interests:* music, theatre, skiing. *Address:* University of Hamburg, Department of Psychology, Von Melle Park 11, LD 20146 Hamburg, Germany (office). *Telephone:* (40) 428384722 (office); (40) 6072210 (home). *Fax:* (40) 428386591 (office); (40) 6072334 (home). *E-mail:* pawlik@uni-hamburg.de (office).

PAWSON, John; British architect; b. 6 May 1949, Halifax; s. of Jim Pawson and Winifred Ward; m. Catherine Berning 1989; two s.; ed Eton; lived three years in Japan before studying architecture; pvt. architectural practice 1981–; pvt. bldgs designed include Neundorf House, Majorca, Klein Apartment, NY; commercial bldgs designed include Calvin Klein Store, Madison Avenue, NY, Jigsaw clothes store, Bond St, London, Cathay Pacific Lounges, Chek Lap Kok Airport, Hong Kong, Novy Dvur Monastery, Czech Rep., Sackler Crossing, Royal Botanic Gardens, Kew, Christopher Kane Store, London; Blueprint Architect of the Year 2005, RSA Royal Designer for Industry 2005, Region Skane Award 2006, Stephen Lawrence Prize 2008, RIBA Nat. Award 2008, RIBA Arts and Leisure Regional Award 2008, RIBA London Special Award 2008, Interior Designer of the Year, German Design Council 2014. *Publications:* Minimum 1996, Living and Eating (with Annie Bell) 2001, Themes and Projects 2002, Leçons du Thoronet 2006, John Pawson: Plain Space (with Alison Morris) 2010. *Address:* John Pawson Ltd, Unit B, 70–78 York Way, London, N1 9AG, England (office). *Telephone:* (20) 7837-2929 (office). *Fax:* (20) 7837-4949 (office). *E-mail:* email@johnpawson.com (office). *Website:* www.johnpawson.com (office).

PAXMAN, Jeremy Dickson, MA; British broadcast journalist, writer and television presenter; b. 11 May 1950, Leeds, Yorks., England; s. of Arthur Keith Paxman and Joan McKay Dickson; one s. two d.; ed Malvern Coll., St Catharine's Coll., Cambridge; journalist, NI 1973–77; reporter, BBC TV Tonight and Panorama programmes 1977–85, presenter, Breakfast Time (BBC 1) 1986–89, Newsnight (BBC 2) 1989–2014, Univ. Challenge 1994–, Start the Week, Radio 4, 1998–2002; Contributing Ed. weekend edition of Financial Times 2014–; Fellow, St Edmund Hall, Oxford; Vice-Pres. The Wild Trout Trust 2004–, The London Library; Patron Sustrans; Hon. Fellow, St Catharine's Coll. Cambridge 2001; Dr hc (Leeds) 1999, (Bradford) 1999, (Open Univ.) 2006; TV Soc. Award for Int. Reporting, Richard Dimbleby Award, BAFTA 1996, 2000, Royal TV Soc. Interview of the Year 1997, Presenter of the Year 2001, 2007, Voice of the Viewer and Listener Presenter of the Year 1994, 1997, 2005, Variety Club Media Personality of the Year 1999. *Publications:* A Higher Form of Killing (co-author) 1982, Through the Volcanoes: A Central American Journey 1985, Friends in High Places: Who Runs Britain? 1990, Fish, Fishing and the Meaning of Life 1994, The Compleat Angler 1996, The English: A Portrait of a People 1998, The Political Animal: An Anatomy 2002, On Royalty 2006, The Victorians: Britain Through the Paintings of the Age 2009, Empire: What Ruling the World Did to the British 2011, Great Britain's Great War 2013; numerous articles in newspapers and magazines. *Leisure interests:* fly-fishing, daydreaming. *Address:* c/o Capel & Land, 29 Wardour Street, London, W1V 6PS, England (office). *Website:* www.bbc.co.uk/programmes/b006t6l0.

PAXSON, Christina Hull, MA, PhD; American economist, academic and university administrator; *President, Brown University;* ed Swarthmore Coll., Columbia Univ.; Lecturer, Princeton Univ. 1986–87, Asst Prof. 1987–94, Assoc. Prof. 1994–97, Prof. of Econs and Public Affairs 1997–2012, Hughes-Rogers Prof. of Econs and Public Affairs 2007–12, Faculty Chair. MPA Program, Woodrow Wilson School 1997–99, Founding Dir Center for Health and Wellbeing 2000–09 (included directorship of Princeton's Health Grand Challenges programme 2007–09), Assoc. Chair. Dept of Econs 2005–08, Chair. 2008–09, Dean of Woodrow Wilson School of Public and Int. Affairs 2009–12; Prof. of Econs and Public Policy and Pres. Brown Univ. 2012–; Visiting Prof., Wharton School, Univ. of Pennsylvania 1999; Sr Ed. The Future of Children 2004–12; mem. Bd of Dirs Federal Reserve Bank of Boston 2016–; mem. Bd of Assoc. Eds, Journal of Development Economics 1995–99; mem. Bd of Eds, American Economic Review 1996–2000; Vice-Pres. American Econs Asscn 2012, mem. Exec. Cttee 2012–13; mem. Council on Foreign Relations 2012–, Bd of Trustees, MDRC 2011–12, Bd of Trustees, Center for Health Care Strategies 2002–12 (Chair. 2010–12), American Acad. of Arts and Sciences 2017–; Sr Fellow, Bureau for Research and Econ. Analysis of Devt 2005–; teaching awards from Woodrow Wilson School MPA students 1991/92, 1992/93, 1993/94, 1994/95, 1995/96, H. Gregg Lewis Prize for best paper published in Journal of Labor Economics (co-recipient) 1996–97, Kenneth Arrow Award for best paper in health economics (co-recipient) 2003. *Publications:* numerous papers in professional journals; Pathways to Diversity and Inclusion: An Action Plan for Brown University 2016. *Address:* Office of the President, Brown University, Box 1860, 1 Prospect Street, Providence, RI 02912, USA (office). *Telephone:* (401) 863-2234 (office). *Fax:* (401) 863-7737 (office). *E-mail:* president@brown.edu (office). *Website:* www.brown.edu/about/administration/president (office).

PAYETTE, Julie, OC, CQ, BEng, MSc; Canadian business executive, engineer and fmr astronaut; *Governor General;* b. 20 Oct. 1963, Montréal; m. 1st François Brissette (divorced); m. 2nd Billie Flynn (divorced); one c.; ed United World Coll. of the Atlantic, South Wales, McGill Univ., Univ. of Toronto; Systems Engineer, Science Eng Div., IBM Canada 1986–88; Research Asst, Univ. of Toronto 1988–90; Visiting Scientist, Communications and Science Dept, IBM Zurich Research Lab., Switzerland 1991; Research Engineer, Speech Research Group, Bell-Northern Nortel Research, Montréal 1992; selected as astronaut by Canadian Space Agency (CSA) 1992, becoming Chief Astronaut 2000–07, completed two spaceflights, STS-96 on board Space Shuttle Discovery 27 May–6 June 1999, and STS-127 on board Space Shuttle Endeavour 15–31 July 2009; Technical Specialist, NATO Int. Research Study Group on speech processing 1993–96; Capsule Communicator, NASA Mission Control Center, Houston 1998; fmr Technical Adviser, Mobile

Servicing System robotics system, Int. Space Station; Scholar, Woodrow Wilson Int. Center for Scholars, Washington, DC 2011–13; Chief Operating Officer, Montréal Science Centre 2013–16; Gov. Gen. of Canada Oct. 2017–; Dir Nat. Bank of Canada 2014; mem. Int. Olympic Cttee Women in Sports Comm.; carried Olympic flag at opening ceremony of Olympic Winter Games, Vancouver 2010; mem. Ordre des ingénieurs du Québec, Natural Sciences and Engineering Research Council (NSERC) of Canada 1995; Fellow Canadian Acad. of Eng, Int. Acad. of Astronautics; 27 hon. doctorates; Knight, Nat. Order of Québec 2000, Knight, Ordre de la Pléiade, Org. int. de la Francophonie 2001, Officer, Order of Canada 2010; Queen Elizabeth II Diamond Jubilee Medal 2012. *Leisure interests:* piano and singing (has sung with Montréal Symphonic Orchestra Chamber Choir, Piacere Vocale, Basel, Switzerland and Tafelmusik Baroque Orchestra Choir, Toronto). *Address:* Office of the Governor General, 1 Sussex Drive, Ottawa, ON K1A 0A1, Canada (office). *Telephone:* (613) 993-8200 (office). *Fax:* (613) 998-8760 (office). *Website:* www.gg.ca (office).

PAYNE, Alexander, BA, MFA; American film director and screenwriter; b. 10 Feb. 1961, Omaha, Neb.; s. of George Payne and Peggy Payne (née Constantine); m. Sandra Oh 2003 (divorced); ed Stanford Univ. and Univ. of California, Los Angeles; fmr employee at Universal Pictures; completed several shorts for Propaganda Films and screened on Playboy Channel; feature film debut with Citizen Ruth (co-wrote screenplay with Jim Taylor) 1996. *Films include:* Carmen (short) 1985, Inside Out 1991, The Passion of Martin (thesis film, dir) 1989, Inside Out (dir and screenwriter) 1992, Citizen Ruth (dir and screenwriter) (First Prize, Munich Film Festival) 1996, Election (dir and co-screenwriter with Jim Taylor) (Best Screenplay Award: WGA, New York Film Critics' Circle and Ind. Spirit, Best Film and Best Dir, Ind. Spirit Awards) 1999, Jurassic Park III (screenplay) 2001, About Schmidt (dir and co-screenwriter with Jim Taylor) (Best Movie of the Year, Los Angeles Film Critics' Asscn 2002, Golden Globe for Best Screenplay 2003) 2002, Sideways (dir) (Los Angeles Film Critics' Asscn Best Movie of the Year, Golden Globe Award for Best Screenplay 2005, BAFTA Award for Best Adapted Screenplay 2005, Writers' Guild of America Award for best adapted screenplay 2005, Acad. Award for Best Writing, Adapted Screenplay 2005, Ind. Spirit Awards for Best Dir, Best Screenplay 2005) 2004, Paris, je t'aime (segment) 2006, I Now Pronounce You Chuck and Larry (co-screenwriter) 2007, The Descendants (dir) (Dallas-Fort Worth Film Critics Asscn Award for Best Dir and Best Screenplay 2011, Florida Film Critics Circle Award for Best Adapted Screenplay 2011, Acad. Award for Best Writing, Adapted Screenplay 2012) 2011, Nebraska 2013. *Television includes:* Hung (also exec. producer 2009–11) 2009.

PAYNE, Anthony Edward, BA, FRCM; British composer; b. 2 Aug. 1936, London; s. of Edward Alexander Payne and (Muriel) Margaret Payne; m. Jane Manning (q.v.) 1966; ed Dulwich Coll., London and Durham Univ.; freelance musical journalist, musicologist, lecturer, etc. with various publs and BBC Radio, active in promoting new music, serving on Cttee of Macnaghten Concerts (Chair. 1967) and Soc. for the Promotion of New Music (Chair. 1969–71), composed part-time 1962–73; full-time composer 1973–; Composition Tutor, London Coll. of Music 1983–85, Sydney Conservatorium 1986, Univ. of Western Australia 1996; Milhaud Prof., Mills Coll., Oakland, Calif., USA 1983; Artistic Dir Spitalfields Festival; Creative Arts Fellow, Royal Coll. of Music 2007–08; Professorial Fellow, Univ. of East Anglia 2012–13; mem. Cttee Asscn Frank Bridge Trust; Vice-Pres. Delius Trust; Hon. mem. Royal Philharmonic Soc. 1999; Hon. DMus (Birmingham) 2000, (Kingston) 2002, (Durham) 2007; Radcliffe Award 1975, South Bank Show Award 1998, Evening Standard Classical Music Award 1998, New York Critics' Circle Nat. Public Radio Award 1999, Classical CD Award 1999, Elgar Medal 2011. *Compositions include:* Paraphrases and Cadenzas 1969, Paean for solo piano 1971, Phoenix Mass 1972, The Spirits Harvest for full orchestra 1972, Concerto for Orchestra (Int. Jury Choice for Int. Soc. for Contemporary Music Festival 1976) 1974, The World's Winter for soprano and ensemble 1976, String Quartet 1978, The Stones and Lonely Places Sing (septet) 1979, Song of the Clouds for oboe and orchestra 1980, A Day in the Life of a Mayfly (sextet) 1981, Evening Land for soprano and piano 1981, Spring's Shining Wake for orchestra 1981, Songs and Seascapes for strings 1984, The Song Streams in the Firmament (sextet) 1986, Fanfares and Processional 1986, Half Heard in the Stillness for orchestra 1987, Consort Music for string quintet 1987, Sea Change (septet) 1988, Time's Arrow for orchestra 1990, The Enchantress Plays bassoon and piano 1990, Symphonies of Wind and Rain for chamber ensemble 1991, A Hidden Music 1992, Orchestral Variations: The Seeds Long Hidden 1993, Empty Landscape–Heart's Ease (sextet) 1995, Break, Break, Break for unaccompanied chorus 1996, Elgar's Third Symphony (commissioned by Elgar Trust to complete Elgar's sketches) 1997, Piano Trio 1998, Scenes from The Woodlanders for soprano and ensemble 1999, Of Knots and Skeins for violin and piano 2000, Betwixt Heaven and Charing Cross for unaccompanied chorus 2001, Visions and Journeys for orchestra (British Composers Award 2003) 2001, Poems of Edward Thomas for soprano and piano quartet 2003, Horn Trio 2005, Elgar's Sixth Pomp & Circumstance March (commissioned by Elgar Trust to complete Elgar's sketches) 2006, Windows on Eternity 2007, Piano Quintet 2007, Out of the Depths Comes Song for cello and piano 2008, From a Mouthful of Air for quintet 2009, The Period of Cosmographie for orchestra 2009, Second String Quartet (British Composer Award Chamber category 2011) 2010, Arrangement of Bruckner's Second Symphony for Chamber Ensemble 2012, The Undiscovered Country (octet) 2012, Of Land, Sea and Sky 2016, Third String Quartet 2017. *Recordings include:* The Music of Anthony Payne (Gramophone Critics' Choice) 1977, Time's Arrow 1996, A Day in the Life of a Mayfly 1998, The Stones and Lonely Places Sing 2007, My Own Country (Warlock arrangements) 2008, Elgar/Payne Symphony No. 3 (six recordings), Elgar/Payne Pomp & Circumstance March No. 6 (three recordings), Elgar (orchestrated Payne) Crown of India. *Radio:* frequent talks for BBC Radio 3 (music matters, Proms, etc.). *Television:* appearances, BBC documentaries by John Bridcut on Elgar, Vaughan Williams, Parry and Delius. *Publications include:* Schoenberg 1968, The Music of Frank Bridge 1984, Elgar's Third Symphony: The Story of the Reconstruction 1998; contrib. to Musical Times, Tempo, Music and Musicians, The Listener, Daily Telegraph, The Times, The Independent, Country Life. *Leisure interests:* English countryside, cinema. *Address:* 2 Wilton Square, London, N1 3DL, England (home). *Telephone:* (20) 7359-1593 (home). *E-mail:* paynecomp@gmail.com. *Website:* anthonypayne.org.uk.

PAYNE, Sir David Neil, Kt, CBE, PhD, FRS, FREng; British professor of photonics, academic and entrepreneur; *Professor and Director, Optoelectronics Research Centre, University of Southampton;* b. 13 Aug. 1944; currently Prof. and Dir Optoelectronics Research Centre, Univ. of Southampton, also directs Photonics Hyperhighway research project; f. SPI Lasers PLC (acquired by Trumpf Corpn); Chair. Marconi Soc.; Foreign mem. Russian Acad. of Sciences; Queens Award for Industry 1986, Rank Prize for Optics 1991, Tyndall Award 1991, Japanese Computers and Communications Prize 1993, Benjamin Franklin Medal for Eng 1998, Eduard Rhein Foundation Laureate (Germany), Mountbatten Medal of IEE 2001, Kelvin Medal 2004, IEEE Photonics Award (first time awarded outside USA) 2007, Marconi Prize 2008, Asscn of Laser Users Award 2010. *Publications:* more than 650 papers in professional journals. *Address:* Optoelectronics Research Centre, University of Southampton, Highfield, Southampton, Hants., SO17 1BJ, England (office). *Telephone:* (23) 8059-3583 (office). *Fax:* (23) 8059-3131 (office). *E-mail:* dnp@soton.ac.uk (office). *Website:* www.orc.soton.ac.uk (office).

PAYNE, Julien David, OC, CM, LSM, QC, LLD, FRSC; Canadian/British lawyer; *President, Danreb Incorporated;* b. 4 Feb. 1934, Nottingham, England; s. of Frederick Payne and Kathleen Payne (née Maltby); m. Marilyn Ann Payne; five c.; ed Univ. of London; Asst Lecturer, Queen's Univ., Belfast 1956–60; Prof. of Law in various Canadian univs 1960–2001; Simon Sr Fellowship, Univ. of Manchester 1968; admitted as solicitor and barrister, Prov. of Ont. 1965; served as advocate, mediator and arbitrator of family law disputes across Canada (pioneer of no-fault divorce and Unified Family Courts); adviser to fed. and prov. govts on family and law reform 1966–; Dir Family Law Project, Law Reform Comm. of Canada 1972–75; Prof., Common Law Section, Univ. of Ottawa 1974–99; Chair. Law Foundation of Saskatchewan 1999–2001; Pres. Danreb Inc. 1985–; Founding mem. Int. Soc. on Family Law 1972; visiting univ. fellowships or chairs include Manchester, Santa Clara, Calif., Victoria, British Columbia, Hong Kong Univ., City Univ. of Hong Kong, Saskatchewan; Hon. Life mem. Bd of Dirs, Ont. Asscn of Family Mediation, Ottawa 1992; Hon. Life Fellow, Canadian Inst. for Conflict Resolution, St Paul's Univ., Ottawa; Law Soc. of Upper Canada, Medal for Contribs to Legal Profession 2002. *Publications include:* Power on Divorce 1964, Conceptual Analysis of Unified Family Courts, Law Reform Commission of Canada 1973, Payne on Divorce 1996, Child Support Guidelines in Canada 2015, Canadian Family Law 2015, Divorce Guide for Canadians 2015. *Address:* 1188 Morrison Drive, Ottawa, ON K2H 7L3, Canada (home). *Telephone:* (613) 829-1905 (home). *E-mail:* j_d_payne@sympatico.ca (office); julien.payne@gmail.com (home).

PAYNE, Marise Ann, BA, LLB; Australian politician; *Minister for Foreign Affairs;* b. 29 July 1964, Sydney; partner Stuart Laurence Ayres, MP; ed Univ. of New South Wales; Political Adviser 1987–95; Public Affairs Adviser 1995–97; Senator for NSW 1997–, mem. Senate Privileges Cttee, Jt Standing Cttee on Foreign Affairs and Trade; Shadow Parl. Sec. for Foreign Affairs 2007–08, for Int. Devt Assistance 2008–09, for Indigenous Affairs 2008–09; Minister for Human Services 2013–15, for Defence 2015–18, for Foreign Affairs 2018–; mem. Liberal Party 1982–, Pres. Young Liberal Movement (first female) 1989–91, Liberal Party NSW State Pres. 1987–88, mem. NSW Liberal State Exec. 1991–97. *Address:* Department of Foreign Affairs and Trade, R. G. Casey Bldg, John McEwen Crescent, Barton, ACT 0221, Australia (office). *Telephone:* (2) 6261-1111 (office). *Fax:* (2) 6261-3111 (office). *Website:* www.dfat.gov.au (office).

PAYNE, Nicholas; British opera company director; *Director, Opera Europa;* b. (Geoffrey John Nicholas Payne), 4 Jan. 1945, Bromley, Kent, England; s. of John Laurence Payne and Dorothy Gwendoline Payne (née Attenborough); m. Linda Jane Adamson 1986; two s.; ed Eton Coll. and Trinity Coll., Cambridge; worked for Paterson Concert Management 1967; Arts Council administration course 1967–68; joined finance dept Royal Opera House, Covent Garden 1968–70; Subsidy Officer, Arts Council 1970–76; Financial Controller, Welsh Nat. Opera 1976–82; Gen. Admin. Opera North 1982–93; Dir of Opera, Royal Opera House 1993–98; Gen. Dir ENO 1998–2002; Dir Opera Europa 2003–; Hon. mem. Guildhall School of Music and Drama, Royal Northern Coll. of Music; Dr hc (Leeds Metropolitan Univ.). *Address:* Opera Europa, 23 rue Léopold, 1000 Brussels, Belgium (office). *Telephone:* (2) 217-67-05 (office). *E-mail:* nicholas.payne@opera-europa.org (office). *Website:* www.opera-europa.org (office).

PAZ, George, BS; American business executive; *Chairman, Express Scripts Holding Company;* b. 27 Aug. 1955, St Louis, Mo.; s. of Geronimo Paz and Collen May Hart; m. Georgene Marie Wade 1974; three c.; ed Univ. of Missouri; Jr Accountant, Gen. Am. 1980–82, Sr Accountant 1982–83, Accounting Admin. 1983–85, Tax Planning Analyst 1985–87, Dir of Tax Planning 1987–, mem. Bd of Dirs Gen. Am. Employees Fed. Credit Union 1985–; Partner, Coopers & Lybrand 1988–93, 1996–98; Exec. Vice-Pres. and Chief Financial Officer, Life Partners Group 1993–95; Sr Vice-Pres. and Chief Financial Officer, Express Scripts Holding Co. 1998–2003, Pres. 2003–05, CEO 2005–16, Chair. 2006–; mem. Bd of Dirs, Honeywell, Inc.; mem. Pharmaceutical Care Man. Asscn, American Inst. of Certified Public Accountants; Fellow, Life Office Man. Asscn. *Leisure interests:* golf, running, softball. *Address:* Express Scripts Holding Co., 1 Express Way, St Louis, MO 63121, USA (office). *Telephone:* (314) 996-0900 (office). *E-mail:* info@express-scripts.com (office). *Website:* www.express-scripts.com (office).

PAZ ZAMORA, Jaime; Bolivian politician, academic and fmr head of state; b. 15 April 1939, Cochabamba; ed Colegio Jesuita, Sucre, Seminario Mayor de Villa Allende en Córdoba, Argentina and Catholic Univ. of Louvain, Belgium; fmr Pres. de la Fed. de Estudiantes Latino-Americanos, Belgium; Prof. of Sociology, Univ. Mayor de San Andrés; f. Movimiento de la Izquierda Revolucionaria, currently Leader; cand. for Vice-Pres. of Bolivia 1978 and 1980; first Vice-Pres. of the Andean Parl.; Vice-Pres. of Bolivia and Pres. Nat. Congress 1982–84; Pres. of Bolivia 1989–93; unsuccessful presidential cand. 2002; mem. Exec. Cttee Assoc. Latino-Americana de Derechos Humanos; mem. Movimiento de la Izquierda Revolucionaria. *Address:* Movimiento de la Izquierda Revolucionaria, Avda América 119, 2°, La Paz, Bolivia (office).

PAŽIN, Zoran; Montenegrin judge, mediator and government official; *Deputy Chairman of the Government, responsible for the Political System and Foreign and Internal Affairs, and Minister of Justice;* b. 29 Aug. 1966, Šibenik, Socialist Repub. of Croatia, Socialist Fed. Repub. of Yugoslavia; ed Faculty of Law, Univ. of

Belgrade, Nat. Center for State Courts, Williamsburg, VA, USA; passed bar examination before Comm. of Ministry of Justice; gained legal experience working as a trainee and an assoc. in Municipal Court, Danilovgrad and Basic Court, Pljevlja; elected Judge of Basic Court, Podgorica 2000, Pres. Civil Div. 2002–03, Deputy Pres. Basic Court, Podgorica 2002–03, Pres. 2004–09; mem. Asscn of Judges of Montenegro 2001–03, Sec. 2003–04; mem. Man. Bd, Centre for Mediation in Montenegro 2007–; mediator 2005–, trainer of mediators 2006–; Lecturer, Centre for Judicial Training of Montenegro; Lecturer, School of Human Rights and Democracy School Centre for Civic Educ., Podgorica; Lecturer and Assoc., Centre for Democracy and Human Rights, Podgorica and AIRE Centre, London, UK as well as numerous other nat. and int. orgs; source of law Rep. of Montenegro before European Court of Human Rights 2009–15; Deputy mem. Venice Comm. 2010–; mem. Supervisory Bd for Human Rights of Council of Europe (CDDH) 2012; Minister of Justice 2015–16; Deputy Chair. of the Govt, responsible for the Political System and Foreign and Internal Affairs, and Minister of Justice 2016–; Vice-Pres. Asscn of Lawyers of Montenegro 2008–12. *Address:* Ministry of Justice, 81000 Podgorica, Vuka Karadžica 3, Montenegro (office). *Telephone:* (20) 407501 (office). *Fax:* (20) 407515 (office). *E-mail:* kabinet@mpa.gov.me (office). *Website:* www.pravda.gov.me (office).

PAZNIAK, Zianon Stanislavavich; Belarusian politician; *Chairman, Conservative Christian Party of the Belarusian Popular Front;* b. 24 April 1944, Subotniki; m. 1995; ed Belarusian State Inst. of Theatre and Arts, Inst. of Ethnography, Art and Folklore; fmr anti-Communist dissident; founder mem. Belorussian Popular Front (BPF) Oct. 1988, Leader 1989–99, Chair. Conservative Christian Party of the BPF (breakaway faction) 1999–; elected to Supreme Soviet as mem. Belorussian Democratic Bloc 1990–; cand. in presidential elections 1994; lives in Warsaw. *Address:* c/o Conservative Christian Party of the BPF, PO Box 208, 220040 Minsk, Belarus.

PEACE, Sir John Wilfred, Kt, FRSA; British retail executive; *Chancellor, Nottingham Trent University;* b. 2 March 1949; m. Christine Blakemore; three d.; ed Royal Mil. Acad., Sandhurst; joined Great Universal Stores (now GUS) PLC 1970, held several sr IT man. positions 1970–80, Co-founder CCN (market information services co.) 1980, CEO CCN 1991–2000, mem. Bd GUS PLC 1997–2006, Group CEO 2000–06; Chair. Burberry Group PLC 2002–18; Chair. Experian plc 2006–14; apptd Chair. Midlands Connect 2016, Midlands Engine 2016; Ind. Dir (non-exec.) Standard Chartered PLC, Deputy Chair. Standard Chartered PLC 2007–09, apptd Chair. 2009; served as Chair. Bd of Govs Nottingham Trent Univ. 1999– 2009, Chancellor 2017–; Chair. The Work Foundation, Nottingham Econ. Resilience Forum; East Midlands Amb. for Business in the Community; mem. Bd Companions of the Chartered Man. Inst., Octo Group S.p.A; Trustee, Djanogly City Acad., Nottingham 1999; DL Notts., High Sheriff 2011–; Dr hc (Nottingham) 2015. *Leisure interests:* horse riding, golf, watching Manchester United Football Club. *Address:* Nottingham Trent University, 50 Shakespeare Street, Nottingham, NG1 4FQ, England (office). *Telephone:* (115) 941-8418 (office). *Website:* www.ntu.ac.uk (office).

PEACH, Air Chief Marshall Sir Stuart, GBE, KCB, ADC, DL, BA, MPhil; British military commander; *Chairman of the Military Committee, North Atlantic Treaty Organization;* b. 1956, West Midlands; s. of Clifford Peach and Jean Mary Peach; m. Brigitte Ender 1986; one s. one d.; ed Aldridge Grammar School, Univ. of Sheffield, Univ. of Cambridge, RAF Staff Coll., Jt Services Command and Staff Coll.; commissioned into RAF 1977; qualified as weapons and electronic warfare instructor; commanded IX (Bomber) Squadron, RAF Brüggen, Germany 1994–96, Deputy Sr British Mil. Adviser, US HQ Central Command 2001–02, Commdr, Air Warfare Centre, RAF Waddington 2000–03, Dir-Gen. Intelligence Collection, Ministry of Defence 2003–06, Chief of Defence Intelligence and Deputy Chair., Jt Intelligence Cttee 2006–09, Chief of Jt Operations, Perm. Jt HQ (UK) 2009–11, Commdr, Jt Forces Command 2011–13, Vice-Chief of the Defence Staff 2013–16, Chief of the Defence Staff 2016–18; Chair. Military Cttee NATO 2018–; Deputy Lt, County of Lincs.; Trustee, Imperial War Museum; Pres. Combined Services and RAF Rugby League; Dr hc (Kingston, Sheffield); Hon. Col (Intelligence Corps) of Jt Services Signals Unit (Volunteers), Hon. Fellow, Downing Coll. Cambridge; Queen's Commendation for Valuable Service in the Air 1990. *Leisure interests:* sport, military history, cooking. *Address:* North Atlantic Treaty Organization (NATO), Blvd Léopold III, 1110 Brussels, Belgium (office). *Telephone:* (2) 707-41-11 (office). *Fax:* (2) 707-45-79 (office). *E-mail:* natodoc@hq.nato.int (office). *Website:* www.nato.int (office).

PEACOCK, Hon. Andrew Sharp, AC, GCL, LLB; Australian diplomatist and fmr politician; b. 13 Feb. 1939, Melbourne, Vic.; s. of A. S. Peacock and Iris Peacock; m. 1st Susan Renouf (divorced), three d.; m. 2nd Margaret Ingram 1983 (divorced); m. 3rd Penne Percy North 2002; ed Scotch Coll., Univ. of Melbourne; Pres., Victorian Liberal Party 1965–66; mem. House of Rep. for Kooyong, Vic. 1966–94; fmr Partner, Rigby and Fielding (solicitors); fmr Chair. Peacock & Smith Pty Ltd (engineers); Minister for the Army and Minister Assisting the Prime Minister 1969–71, Assisting the Treas. 1971–72; Minister for External Territories 1972; mem. Opposition Exec. 1973–75, Spokesman on Foreign Affairs 1973–75; Minister for Foreign Affairs 1975–80, for the Environment Nov.–Dec. 1975, for Industrial Relations 1980–81, for Industry and Commerce 1982–83; Leader Parl. Liberal Party 1983–85; Opposition Spokesman on Foreign Affairs 1985–87; Deputy Leader of the Opposition and Shadow Treas. 1987–89; Leader of the Opposition 1989–90; Shadow Attorney-Gen. and Shadow Minister for Justice 1990–92; Shadow Minister for Trade 1992–93, for Foreign Affairs 1993–94; Chair. Parl. Political Strategy Cttee 1994; Amb. to USA 1997–2000; Chair. Int. Democrat Union 1989–92, Australian Horse Council 1996; Pres. Boeing Australia 2002–07; Dir Orbital Engine Corpn Ltd 2001–02; Chief Grand Companion, Order of Logohu (New Guinea) 2006. *Leisure interests:* horse racing, Australian Rules Football, surfing, reading. *Address:* 19 Queens Road, Melbourne, Vic. 3004, Australia.

PEACOCK, John A., BSc, PhD, FRS, FRSE; British astronomer, cosmologist and academic; *Professor of Cosmology, Institute for Astronomy, University of Edinburgh;* b. 27 March 1956, Shaftesbury, Dorset, England; m. Heather Peacock 1982; one s. two d.; ed Jesus Coll., Cambridge; Research Fellow, Royal Observatory, Edinburgh 1981–83, Tenured Research Astronomer 1983–92, Head of Research 1992–98, Prof. of Cosmology, Univ. of Edinburgh 1998–, PPARC Sr Research Fellowship 2002, Head of Inst. for Astronomy 2007–13; Visiting Fellow,

Canadian Inst. for Theoretical Astrophysics, Toronto 1988, 1990, Observatoire de Meudon, Paris 1992, Inst. for Advanced Study, Princeton 1993, California Inst. of Tech. 1997, (Kingsley Visitor) 2009, Inst. for Astronomy, Honolulu 2001, 2005, Sterrewacht Leiden (Sackler Lecturer) 2005, Australian Astronomical Observatory (AAO Distinguished Visitor) 2011; Ed. Annals of Physics 2002–12; mem. Editorial Bd, Astronomy & Astrophysics Reviews 2011–14; Assoc., Canadian Inst. for Advanced Research 1990; Hon. Fellow, Univ. of Edinburgh 1988, Hon. Prof. 1994; Keller Prize 1977, Group Achievement Award for 2dFGRS, Royal Astronomical Soc. 2008, Shaw Prize in Astronomy (co-recipient) 2014. *Publications include:* Cosmological Physics 1999; numerous papers in professional journals. *Leisure interests:* classical music, playing clarinet, hill walking and rock climbing. *Address:* Room C20, Royal Observatory, Institute for Astronomy, University of Edinburgh, Blackford Hill, Edinburgh, EH9 3HJ, Scotland (office). *Telephone:* (131) 668-8390 (office). *Fax:* (131) 668-8416 (office). *E-mail:* jap@roe.ac.uk (office). *Website:* www.ph.ed.ac.uk/people/john-peacock (office); www.roe.ac.uk/~jap (office).

PEACOCK, William James, AC, PhD, FRS, FAA, FAIAS, FTSE; Australian research scientist; *Fellow, Commonwealth Scientific and Industrial Research Organisation (CSIRO);* b. 14 Dec. 1937, Leura, NSW; s. of William Edward Peacock and Evelyn Alison Peacock; m. Margaret Constance Woodward 1961; one s. two d.; ed Univ. of Sydney; Visiting Research Scientist, Genetics, CSIRO, Canberra 1963; Fellow, Dept of Biology, Univ. of Oregon 1963–64, Visiting Assoc. Prof. 1964–65; Research Consultant, Biology Div., Oak Ridge Nat. Lab., USA 1965; Sr Research Scientist, Div. of Plant Industry, CSIRO, Canberra 1965–69, Prin. Research Scientist 1969–73, Sr Prin. Research Scientist 1973–77, Chief Research Scientist 1977–78, Chief 1978–2003, now CSIRO Fellow; Distinguished Prof., Univ. of Technology, Sydney 2012–; Pres. Australian Acad. of Science 2002–06; Chief Scientist of Australia 2006–08; Adjunct Prof. of Biology, Univ. of California, San Diego, USA 1969–70; Visiting Prof. of Biochemistry, Stanford Univ., USA 1970–71; Visiting Distinguished Prof. of Molecular Biology, UCLA, USA 1977; Scientific Adviser, Australian Genetic Eng Ltd; Foreign Assoc., NAS 1990; Fellow, Australian Acad. of Technological Sciences; Foreign Fellow, Indian Nat. Science Acad. 1990; Hon. DSc (Charles Sturt Univ., Wagga Wagga) 1996, (Ghent) 2004, (Sydney) 2008, Hon. DScAg (Sydney) 2002, (Univ. of Technology, Sydney) 2014; Edgeworth David Medal, Royal Soc. of NSW 1967, Lemberg Medal, Australian Biochemical Soc. 1978, N.I. Vavilov Medal 1987, BHP Bicentennial Prize 1988, Burnet Medal, Australian Acad. of Science 1989, CSIRO Medal 1989, Farrer Memorial Medal 1999, Prime Minister's Prize for Science 2000, Rabobank Leadership Award 2012, ACT Sr Australian of the Year 2013. *Publications:* 350 research papers on molecular biology, cytogenetics and evolution; ed. of six books. *Leisure interests:* bush-walking. *Address:* 16 Brassey Street, Deakin, ACT 2600, Australia (home). *Telephone:* (2) 6246-5250 (office); (2) 6281-4485 (home). *Fax:* (2) 6246-4866 (home). *E-mail:* jim.peacock@csiro.au (office).

PEACOCKE, Christopher Arthur Bruce, MA, DPhil, FBA; British academic; *Johnsonian Professor of Philosophy, Columbia University;* b. 22 May 1950, Birmingham; s. of Arthur Peacocke and Rosemary Peacocke; m. Teresa Rosen 1980; one s. one d.; ed Magdalen Coll. School, Exeter Coll., Oxford, Harvard Univ. (Kennedy Scholar), USA; Sr Scholar, Merton Coll., Oxford 1972–73; Jr Research Fellow, Queen's Coll., Oxford 1973–76; Visiting Lecturer, Univ. of California, Berkeley 1975–76; Prize Fellow, All Souls Coll., Oxford 1975–79; Visiting Prof., Univ. of Mich. 1978; Fellow, New Coll., Oxford and Common Univ. Fund Lecturer in Philosophy, Univ. of Oxford 1979–85; Visiting Prof., UCLA 1981; Visiting Fellow, ANU 1981, 1998; Fellow, Center for Advanced Study in Behavioural Sciences, Stanford Univ. 1983–84; Susan Stebbing Prof. of Philosophy, King's Coll. London 1985–88; Pres. Mind Asscn 1986; Waynflete Prof. of Metaphysical Philosophy, Univ. of Oxford and Fellow, Magdalen Coll., Oxford 1989–2000; Leverhulme Research Professorship 1996–2000; Visiting Prof., New York Univ. 1996–2000, Prof. of Philosophy 2000–04; apptd Prof. of Philosophy, Columbia Univ. 2004, Johnsonian Prof. 2013–, Chair. Philosophy Dept 2013–16; Richard Wollheim Chair of Philosophy, Univ. Coll. London 2007–15; Fellow, American Acad. of Arts and Sciences 2010, Inst. of Philosophy, School of Advanced Studies, London 2016–; Hon. Fellow, Exeter Coll., Oxford 2018; Hon. DLitt (Warwick) 2007; Wilde Prize 1971, Webb-Medley Prize 1971, John Locke Prize 1972; Whitehead Lecturer, Harvard Univ. 2001, Immanuel Kant Lecturer, Stanford Univ. 2003, Gareth Evans Memorial Lecturer, Univ. of Oxford 2010, Context and Content Lecturer, Institut Jean Nicod, École Nat. Supérieure, Paris 2010, Kohut Lecturer, Univ. of Chicago 2011. *Publications include:* Holistic Explanation: Action, Space, Interpretation 1979, Sense and Content 1983, Thoughts: An Essay on Content 1986, A Study of Concepts 1992, Being Known 1999, The Realm of Reason 2004, Truly Understood 2008, The Mirror of the World 2014; papers in Mind, Philosophical Review, Journal of Philosophy etc. *Leisure interests:* music, visual arts. *Address:* Department of Philosophy, MC 4971, Columbia University, 1150 Amsterdam Avenue, New York, NY 10027, USA (office). *Telephone:* (212) 854-3384 (office). *Fax:* (212) 854-4986 (office). *E-mail:* cp2161@columbia.edu (office). *Website:* philosophy.columbia.edu (office).

PEAKE, Karolína; Czech lawyer and politician; *Leader, LIDEM—Liberal Democrats;* b. (Karolína Kvačková), 10 Oct. 1975, Prague; m. Charles Peake 1999; two s.; ed Faculty of Law, Charles Univ.; mem. Civic Democratic Party while studying at univ. 1997–98; worked as trainee lawyer in Czech br of Baker & McKenzie; co-f. a maternal centre, along with other mothers from Prague 1; became involved in local politics, including campaigns to save a local park and extend local children's playgrounds 2005; elected to town council of Prague 1 as ind. 2006; mem. Public Affairs (Věci veřejné—VV) party 2007–12 (left with seven other MPs); mem. Chamber of Deputies 2010–, Chair. Constitutional Law Cttee, Chair. VV Parl. Group April–July 2011, Chair. Govt Anti-corruption Cttee 2011, Legis. Council of Govt 2011–12; Deputy Prime Minister 2011–13; Founder and Leader, LIDEM—Liberal Democrats 2012–; Minister of Defence 12–20 Dec. 2012. *Address:* LIDEM—Liberal Democrats, Štěpanská 611/14, 110 00 Prague, Czech Republic (office). *Telephone:* 777756704 (office). *E-mail:* info@lidem.cz (office). *Website:* www.lidem.cz (office); www.karolinapeake.cz.

PEARCE, Sir (Daniel Norton) Idris, Kt, CBE, TD, DL, FRICS; British chartered surveyor; b. 28 Nov. 1933, Neath, W Glam., Wales; s. of Lemeul George Douglas Pearce and Evelyn Mary Pearce; m. Ursula Helene Langley 1963

(divorced 1997); two d.; ed West Buckland School, Coll. of Estate Man.; joined Richard Ellis 1959, Partner 1961–92, Man. Partner 1981–87, Consultant 1992–2000; Chair. English Estates 1989–94; Chair. Higher Educ. Funding Council for Wales 1992–96; mem. Advisory Panel for Institutional Finance in New Towns 1974–80; mem. Property Services Agency Advisory Bd 1981–86; Property Adviser to Nat. Health Service Man. Bd 1985–90; mem. FCO Advisory Panel on Diplomatic Estate 1982–90, Financial Reporting Review Panel 1991–92, UFC 1991–93; Vice-Chair. Greater London TA & VRA 1991–94; mem. Gen. Council The Royal Inst. of Chartered Surveyors 1989–95, mem. Exec. Cttee 1984–91, Pres. 1990–91, Chair. Int. Assets Valuation Standards Cttee 1981–86; mem. Higher Educ. Funding Council for England 1992–96; Deputy Chair. Urban Regeneration Agency 1993–2000; Dir (non-exec.) Swan Hill 1993–2002, Nat. Mortgage Bank 1992–97, Innisfree Man. Ltd 1996–, Redburgh Ltd 1996–98, Millennium and Copthorne Hotels PLC 1996–2006; Gov. Peabody Trust 1992–2003; Pro-Chancellor Univ. of Surrey 1994–2003, Chair. Council 1997–2000, Pro-Chancellor Emer. 2003–; Sr Fellow, RCA 2012; Hon. Fellow, Coll. of Estate Man., Univ. of Wales, Cardiff 1997; Hon. Col, 135 Independent Topographic Squadron Royal Engineers (V); Hon. DSc (City Univ., London, Salford, Oxford Polytechnic); Hon. DTechSc (Univ. of E London); Hon. DEng (Bristol, Univ. of W of England); Hon. DUniv (Surrey), (Glamorgan); Thames Polytechnic, Centenary Fellowship 1991, Companion, De Monfort Univ. *Publications include:* Profession of the Land – A Future; articles on valuation and property matters. *Leisure interests:* reading, opera, ballet, travel.

PEARCE, Reynold, BA, MA; British fashion designer; ed Nottingham Trent Univ., Central St Martin's Coll. of Art and Design; worked for John Galliano (q.v.); design asst for Roland Klein; Co-founder, with Andrew Fionda (q.v.), and Man. Dir Pearce Fionda 1994–, first capsule collection for Spring/Summer 1995 shown in New Generation show during London Fashion Week; also designs PIIF collection for Designers at Debenhams range 1997–, duo now concentrate on eveningwear range and children's bridesmaid creations; with Andrew Fionda received New-comers Award for Export, British Knitwear Clothing Export Council and Fashion Weekly 1994, New Generation Award, Lloyds Bank British Fashion Awards 1995, World Young Designers Award, Int. Apparel Fed. 1996, Glamour Award, Lloyds Bank British Fashion Awards 1997. *Address:* Pearce Fionda, The Loft, 27 Horsell Road, Highbury, London, N5 1XL, England. *Telephone:* (20) 7609-6470. *Fax:* (20) 7609-6470. *E-mail:* info@pearcefionda.com. *Website:* pearcefionda.com.

PEARL, Judea, BS, MS, PhD; Israeli/American computer scientist, philosopher and academic; *Professor of Computer Science and Statistics and Director, Cognitive Systems Laboratory, University of California, Los Angeles;* b. 1936, Tel-Aviv; m. Ruth Pearl; three c. (one s. deceased); ed Technion, Haifa, Israel, Rutgers Univ. and Polytechnic Inst. of Brooklyn, USA; worked at RCA Research Labs, Princeton, NJ –1970; joined UCLA 1970, currently Prof. of Computer Science and Statistics and Dir Cognitive Systems Lab.; Distinguished Visiting Prof. of Computer Science, Inst. of Tech., Technion, Israel 2013; mem. Nat. Acad. of Eng 1995, American Acad. of Arts and Sciences 2012, NAS; Corresp. mem. Spanish Acad. of Eng 2002; mem. Int. Advisory Bd NGO Monitor 2011; Fellow, IEEE 1988, American Asscn of Artificial Intelligence 1990, Cognitive Science Soc. 2011; Hon. DSc (Toronto) 2007; Hon. DHumLitt (Chapman Univ.) 2008; RCA Labs Achievement Award 1965, Nat. Sr Fellowship in Science 1975, UCLA 81st Faculty Research Lecturer 1996, IJCAI Research Excellence Award in Artificial Intelligence 1999, AAAI Classic Paper Award 2000, Lakatos Award 2001, Pekeris Memorial Lecturer 2003, 2003 Allen Newell Award 2004, Purpose Prize 2006, Benjamin Franklin Medal in Computers and Cognitive Science 2008, Festschrift and symposium in honour of Judea Pearl 2010, IEEE AI's Hall-of-Fame Aug. 2011, Rumelhart Prize Symposium 2011, Rumelhart Lecturer, Cognitive Science Soc. 2011, David E. Rumelhart Prize 2011, Harvey Prize 2012, A.M. Turing Award, Asscn for Computing Machinery 2012, Special Issue honouring Judea Pearl, Cognitive Science Journal Aug. 2013, Medallion Lecturer, Inst. of Math. Statistics 2013, Harvey Prize 2012, Sells Award for Distinguished Multivariate Research 2017. *Achievements include:* pioneered use of Bayesian networks and probabilistic approach to artificial intelligence. *Publications:* Heuristics 1984, Probabilistic Reasoning in Intelligent Systems 1988, I Am Jewish: Personal Reflections Inspired by the Last Words of Daniel Pearl 2004, Causality: Models, Reasoning, and Inference (second edn) 2009, Causal Inference in Statistics: A Primer (with Madelyn Glymour and Nicholas Jewell) 2016; numerous papers in professional journals. *Leisure interests:* music: tenor, guitar, choir conducting; early printed books: science, philosophy, Judaica; history of science. *Address:* 4532 Boelter Hall, Computer Science Department, Cognitive Systems Lab, University of California, Los Angeles, CA 90024-1596, USA (office). *Telephone:* (310) 825-3243 (office). *Fax:* (310) 825-2273 (office). *E-mail:* judea@cs.ucla.edu (office). *Website:* bayes.cs.ucla.edu/jp_home.html (office).

PEARLSTEIN, Philip, MA; American artist; b. 24 May 1924, Pittsburgh, Pa; s. of David Pearlstein and Libbie Kalser; m. Dorothy Cantor 1950; one s. two d.; ed Carnegie Inst. of Tech. and New York Univ.; Instructor Pratt Inst. 1959–63; visiting critic, Yale 1962–63; Asst Prof. then Prof., Art Dept Brooklyn Coll. 1963–82, now Distinguished Prof. Emer.; Pres. American Acad. of Arts and Letters 2003–06; work in perm. collections including Whitney Museum and Museum of Modern Art, New York; Fulbright Fellow 1958–59; Guggenheim Fellow 1971–72. *Address:* 361 West 36th Street, Apt 6a, New York, NY 10018, USA.

PEARLSTINE, Norman, LLB; American journalist, editor and publishing executive; *Executive Editor, The Los Angeles Times;* b. 4 Oct. 1942; s. of Raymond Pearlstine and Gladys Pearlstine; m. Jane Boon Pearlstine; ed Haverford Coll., Univ. of Pennsylvania; staff reporter, Wall Street Journal, Dallas, Detroit, LA 1968–73, Tokyo Bureau Chief 1973–76, Man. Ed. Asian Wall Street Journal, Hong Kong 1976–78; Exec. Ed. Forbes Magazine, LA 1978–80; Nat. News Ed. Wall Street Journal, New York 1980–82, Ed. and Publr Wall Street Journal Europe, Brussels 1982–83, Man. Ed. and Vice-Pres. Wall Street Journal, New York 1983–91, Exec. Ed. 1991–92; Pres. and CEO Friday Holdings L.P., New York 1993–94; Ed.-in-Chief Time Inc. 1995–2006, then Sr Advisor to Time Warner; Sr Advisor to global telecommunications and media team, The Carlyle Group 2006–08; Chief Content Officer, Bloomberg L.P. 2008–13; Exec. Ed. The Los Angeles Times 2018–; Pres. and CEO The American Acad. in Berlin 2006–11; mem. Bd Carnegie Corpn, Cttee to Protect Journalists, Tribeca Film Inst., Watson Inst. for Int. Relations; mem. New York Historical Soc., Council on Foreign Relations, American Acad. of Arts and Sciences; mem. advisory bd, Graduate School of Journalism, City Univ. of New York; mem. Bar Asscn, District of Columbia; Ed. of Year Award, Nat. Press Foundation 1989, Loeb Lifetime Achievement Award for Distinguished Business and Financial Journalism 2000, American Soc. of Magazine Editors Lifetime Achievement Award 2005. *Publication:* Off the Record: The Press, The Government, and The War Over Anonymous Sources 2007. *Address:* c/o Lynn Nesbit, Janklow & Nesbit Associates, New York, NY 10022, USA (office). *Telephone:* (212) 421-1700 (office). *E-mail:* lynn@janklow.com (office); norm@normanpearlstine.com. *Website:* www.janklowandnesbit.com (office); www.normanpearlstine.com.

PEARSE, Sir Brian, Kt, FCIB; British banker; *Chairman of Trustees, Centre for the Study of Financial Innovation;* b. 23 Aug. 1933; s. of Francis Pearse and Eileen Pearse; m. Patricia M. Callaghan 1959; one s. two d.; ed St Edward's Coll., Liverpool; joined Martin's Bank Ltd 1950; joined Barclays Bank 1969, Local Dir Birmingham 1972, Gen. Man. 1977, CEO, N America 1983, Finance Dir Barclays Bank PLC 1987–91; Chief Exec. Midland Bank 1991–94; Pres. Chartered Inst. of Bankers 1993–94; Chair. Housing Corpn 1994–97, British Invisibles 1994–97, Lucas Industries PLC 1994–96, LucasVarity PLC 1996–98; mem. and fmr Chair. Governing Council, Centre for the Study of Financial Innovation, currently Chair. of Trustees; Dir British American Chamber of Commerce 1987–98; Dir (non-exec.), Smith & Nephew 1993–; Dir British Overseas Trade Bd 1994–97; Gov. Univ. of Plymouth 1997– (Vice-Chair. 1999–); Deputy Chair. Britannic Assurance PLC 1997–; mem. Bd of Banking Supervision 1998–. *Leisure interests:* rugby, opera. *Address:* Centre for the Study of Financial Innovation, First Floor, 73 Leadenhall Market, London, EC3V 1LT (office); Flat 7, 14 Gloucester Street, London, SW1V 2DN, England (home). *Telephone:* (20) 7621-1056 (office). *E-mail:* info@csfi.org (office). *Website:* www.csfi.org (office).

PEARSON, Ralph Gottfried, PhD; American chemist and academic; *Professor Emeritus of Chemistry, University of California, Santa Barbara;* b. 12 Jan. 1919, Chicago, Ill.; s. of Gottfried Pearson and Kerstin Pearson (née Larson); m. Lenore Johnson 1941 (died 1982); two s. one d.; ed Lewis Inst., Northwestern Univ.; First Lt in USAF 1944–46; Asst Prof., Chem. Dept, Northwestern Univ. 1946–52, Assoc. Prof. 1952–57, Prof. 1957–76; Prof. of Chem., Univ. of Calif., Santa Barbara 1976–89, Prof. Emer. 1989–; mem. NAS 1974–; fmr Guggenheim Fellow; Inorganic Award, ACS, Chemical Pioneer Award, American Inst. of Chemists 1995. *Publications:* Kinetics and Mechanism 1953, Mechanisms of Inorganic Reactions 1958, Hard and Soft Acids and Bases 1974, Symmetry Rules for Chemical Reactions 1976, Chemical Hardness 1997. *Leisure interest:* classical music. *Address:* 4619 Physical Sciences Building North, Chemistry Department, University of California, Santa Barbara, CA 93106 (office); 715 Grove Lane, Santa Barbara, CA 93105, USA (home). *Telephone:* (805) 893-3745 (office); (805) 687-7890 (home). *Fax:* (805) 893-4120 (office). *Website:* www.chem.ucsb.edu (office).

PEARSON WRIGHT, Stuart, BA; British portrait artist; b. 1975, Northampton, England; m. Polly Pearson Wright; one s.; ed Slade School of Fine Art, Univ. Coll. London; grew up in Eastbourne; award-winning portrait painter; noted persons depicted in paintings include six past-Presidents of the British Acad., Charles Saumerez Smith (Dir Nat. Gallery, London), HRH The Duke of Edinburgh, Mike Leigh (film dir), Brenda Blethyn, Richard E. Grant, John Hurt, David Thewlis (actors), J. K. Rowling (author); co-ran a project space on Vyner Street called Five Hundred Dollars 2009; curated a group drawing exhbn called Kunskog which featured the work of Gillian Wearing, Michael Landy, Paul Noble and Ged Quinn, amongst others; has working on a series of set designs: one for an opera, Dido and Aeneas by Jevington Nat. Opera and also for his wife, the singer/songwriter The Tiger's Bride, who performed at the Nat. Portrait Gallery 2012; lives and works in East London; Travel Award, BP Portrait Award 1998, Third Prize, Singer & Friedlander/Sunday Times Watercolour competition 1999, British Finalist, Windsor & Newton Millennium Competition 2000, Grant Award, Elizabeth Greenshield Foundation 2000, Third Prize, Garrick/Milne Prize 2000, Winner, BP Portrait Award 2001, Travel Award, Discerning Eye (Sri Lanka) 2003, Printmaking Award, Joseph Webb Commemorative Fund 2004, Purchase Prize, Univ. of Wales, Aberystwyth 2004, First Prize, Singer & Friedlander/Sunday Times Watercolour competition 2004, First Prize, Garrick/Milne Prize 2005. *Works in public collections:* Aberdeen Art Gallery, Aldo Coronelli Collection, Ashmolean Museum, Oxford, British Academy, British Museum, Daniel Radcliffe Collection, David Roberts Art Foundation, David Thewlis Collection, London, Frank Cohen Collection, Manchester Garrick Club, London, Govt Art collection, House of Commons, London, Graham Fink Collection, Beijing, Index ventures Collection, Geneva, ING Barings Bank, Brussels, Jerwood Foundation, London, J. K. Rowling Collection, Edinburgh, John Hurt Collection, London, Keira Knightley Collection, London, Nat. Portrait Gallery, London, Nick Candy Collection, London, Omer Koç Collection, Istanbul, Philip Mould Collection, London, Rhode Island School of Design Museum, USA, School of Art Gallery & Museum, Aberystwyth, Wales, Singer and Friedlander Bank, Singer and Friedlander PLC, Sir Paul Smith Collection, London, Scheringa Museum, Netherlands, Taylor Thomson Collection, Los Angeles. *Telephone:* 7794-629188 (mobile, Riflemaker). *E-mail:* info@riflemaker.org. *Website:* www.stuartpearsonwright.com.

PÉBEREAU, Michel Jean Denis; French banker; *Honorary Chairman, BNP Paribas SA;* b. 23 Jan. 1942, Paris; s. of Alexandre Pébereau and Yvonne Raybaud; m. Agnès Faure 1962; two s. two d.; ed Lycées Buffon and Louis-le-Grand, Paris, Ecole Polytechnique and Ecole Nat. d'Admin; various appointments in Ministry of Economy and Finance 1970–81; Man. Dir Crédit Commercial de France 1982–87, Chair. and CEO 1987–93; Chair. and CEO Banque Nationale de Paris (BNP) 1993–2000, apptd Chair. Paribas 1999, Chair. and CEO BNP Paribas SA 2000–03, Chair. 2006–11, Hon. Chair. 2011–, mem. Bd of Dirs BNP Paribas SA (Switzerland); Dir SA des Galeries Lafayette (non-voting), Lafarge, Cie de Saint-Gobain, Total, European Aeronautic Defence and Space Co. (EADS) NV, Pargesa Holding SA (Switzerland); Comm. for Selective Aid for Film Distribution 1987–88; Lecturer, Inst. d'Etudes Politiques Paris 1967–78, Prof. 1980–, mem. Man. Cttee 1984–; Lecturer, Ecole Nat. de Statistiques et d'Admin Economique 1968–79; Inspecteur Général des Finances; mem. Supervisory Bd Dresdner Bank 1997–2009, AXA, Banque Marocaine pour le Commerce et l'Industrie (Morocco); mem. Int. Capital Markets Advisory Cttee Fed. Reserve Bank, New York 1998; Pres. Comm. d'exploitation bancaire de l'Asscn française des banques 2000;

Censor, Galeries Lafayette SA; mem. Bd AXA, Lafarge, Cie de Saint-Gobain, Total, BNP Paribas SA (Switzerland), EADS NV (Netherlands), Pargesa Holding SA (Switzerland); Chair. Investment Banking and Financial Markets Cttee, Fédération Bancaire Française, Man. Bd of Institut d'Etudes Politiques de Paris, Supervisory Bd of Institut Aspen, France, Institut de l'Entreprise, European Financial Round Table; mem. Acad. des sciences morales et politiques, Exec. Cttee Mouvement des Entreprises en France, Haut Conseil de l'Educ., European Financial Round Table, Institut Int. d'Etudes Bancaires, Int. Advisory Panel of Monetary Authority of Singapore, Int. Capital Markets Advisory Cttee of Fed. Reserve Bank of New York, Int. Business Leaders' Advisory Council for the Mayor of Shanghai, Supervisory Bd of Banque Marocaine pour le Commerce et l'Industrie (Morocco); Non-voting Dir Soc. Anonyme des Galeries Lafayette; Grand Officier, Légion d'honneur; Commdr, Ordre nat. du Mérite. *Publications:* La politique économique de la France (three vols); science fiction book reviews magazine Le Journal du dimanche. *Leisure interest:* piano. *Address:* BNP Paribas SA, 3 rue d'Antin, 75002 Paris, France (office). *Telephone:* 1-42-98-12-34 (office). *Fax:* 1-40-14-45-46 (office). *Website:* www.bnpparibas.com (office).

PECCERELLI, Fredy, BA; Guatemalan forensic anthropologist; *Executive Director, Guatemalan Forensic Anthropology Foundation;* b. 1971; m.; several c.; ed Brooklyn Coll., City Univ. of New York, USA and Univ. of Bournemouth, UK; went into exile with his family to New York aged nine; led forensic archeological investgations of war crimes in Bosnia and Herzegovina for Int. Criminal Tribunal for the Fmr Yugoslavia; founding mem. Fundación de Antropología Forense de Guatemala (FAFG–Guatemalan Forensic Anthropology Foundation) 1996, responsible for investigating human rights abuses committed during 36-year civil war, now Exec. Dir FAFG; studied for MSc degree in UK; chosen by Time magazine as one of 50 Latin American Leaders for the New Millennium 1999, named by Guatemalan Youth Comm. an Icon for Youth of Guatemala 1999. *Address:* c/o AAAS Science and Human Rights Program, 1200 New York Avenue, NW, Washington, DC 20005, USA (office). *Website:* www.ted.com.

PECINA, Martin, MBA; Czech engineer, business executive and politician; b. 9 July 1968, Ostrava; m.; two c.; ed Mechanical Eng High School, Karviná, Faculty of Mechanical Eng, VSB-Tech. Univ. of Ostrava, Masaryk Inst. of Higher Educ., Prague, Sheffield Business School, UK; sales dir of pvt. co. 1992–96; employee, Hutní projekt Frýdek-Místek 1996–99; CEO Hutní projekt Frýdek-Místek Jt-Stock Co. 1999–2003; Deputy Minister of Industry and Trade 2003–05; Chair. Office for the Protection of Competition 2005–09; Minister of the Interior 2009–10; Deputy Prime Minister and Minister of the Interior 2013–14; mem. Civic Democratic Party (ODS) –1997, Czech Social Democratic Party (ČSSD) 2001–05. *Address:* c/o Ministry of the Interior, Nad Štolou 3, PO Box 21, 170 34 Prague 7, Czech Republic. *E-mail:* public@mvcr.cz.

PECKER, Jean-Claude, (Jean-Claude Pradel); French astronomer; *Honorary Professor, Collège de France;* b. 10 May 1923, Reims, Marne; s. of Victor-Noel Pecker and Nelly Catherine Herrmann; m. 2nd Annie A. Vormser 1974 (died 2002); one s. two d. (by previous m.); ed Lycée de Bordeaux, Univs of Grenoble and Paris (Sorbonne) and Ecole Normale Supérieure; Research Asst, CNRS 1946–52; Assoc. Prof., Univ. of Clermont-Ferrand 1952–55; Assoc. Astronomer, Paris Observatory 1955–62, Astronomer 1962–65; Dir Nice Observatory 1962–69; Dir Inst. of Astrophysics, Paris 1972–79; Prof., Collège de France 1963–89, Hon. Prof. 1989–; Asst Gen. Sec. Int. Astronomical Union 1961–63, Gen. Sec. 1964–67; Pres. Comité Nat. Français d'Astronomie 1970–73; Dir Inst. Astrophysique, Paris 1971–78; Pres. Soc. Astronomique de France 1973–76; Pres. French Asscn for Advancement of Science 1978; Chair. Orientation Cttee, Sciences-Industries Museum, La Villette 1983–85; Chair. Nat. Cttee Scientific and Tech. Culture 1985–87; Vice-Chair. French Comm. for UNESCO 1991–96; Perm. Rep. to UNESCO of Int. Humanist and Ethical Union; Vice-Chair. Scientific Cttee Musées de France 1988–; Pres. Asscn française d'information scientifique 1999–2001; Assoc. Royal Soc. of Science, Liège 1967; Corresp., Bureau des Longitudes 1968; Assoc. Royal Astronomical Soc. 1968; Corresp. mem. Acad. des Sciences, France 1969, mem. 1977; mem. Acad. Nat. Bordeaux 1977, Acad. Royale Belgique 1979, Acad. European of Science, Arts and Letters 1982, Int. Acad. of Humanism 1983 (Sec.), Acad. Europaea 1988 (Council mem., Vice-Pres. 1989–92; Commdr, Légion d'honneur, des Palmes académiques, Grand Croix, Ordre nat. du Mérite; Prix Forthuny, Inst. de France, Prix Stroobant Acad. des Sciences de Belgique 1965, Prix Manley-Bendall de l'Acad. de Bordeaux 1966, Prix des Trois Physiciens 1969, Janssen Medal Astronomical Soc., France 1967, Prix Jean Perrin, Soc. Française de Physique 1973, Medal Univ. de Nice 1972, Adion Medal 1981, Prix Union Rationaliste 1983, Personnalité de l'année 1984, Janssen Medal, Photographic Soc. of France 1989, Lodén Prize, Royal Astronomical Soc. of Sweden 1996. *Radio includes:* many programmes on popular astronomy 1957–. *Television includes:* many programmes on popular science. *Publications include:* L'astronomie au jour le jour (with P. Couderc and E. Schatzman) 1954, Astrophysique générale (with E. Schatzman) 1959, Le ciel 1959, L'astronomie expérimentale 1969, Les laboratoires spatiaux 1969, Papa, dis-moi: L'astronomie, qu'est-ce que c'est? 1971, L'astronomie nouvelle (ed.) 1971, Clefs pour l'astronomie 1981, Sous l'étoile soleil 1984, Astronomie (ed.) 1985, Pour comprendre l'univers (with Delsemme and Reeves) 1988, L'avenir du soleil 1990, Le promeneur du ciel 1992, Le soleil est une étoile 1992, Débat sur les phénomènes paranormaux 1997, Understanding the Universe 2001, L'Univers exploré, peu à peu expliqué 2003, La photographie astronomique 2003, Lalanduana I (with S. Dumont) 2007. *Leisure interests:* painting, poetry, swimming. *Address:* Annexe du Collège de France, 3 rue d'Ulm, 75005 Paris (office); Pusat-Tasek, Les Corbeaux, 85350 L'Île d'Yeu, France (home). *Telephone:* 1-44-27-16-95 (office); (2) 51-58-58-27 (home). *E-mail:* j.c.pecker@wanadoo.fr (home).

PECKHAM, Sir Michael John, Kt, MA, MD, FRCP, FRCPath, FRCR, FRCS, FMedSci; British physician and academic; b. 2 Aug. 1935, Panteg, Wales; s. of William Stuart Peckham and Gladys Mary Peckham (née Harris); m. Catherine Stevenson King 1958; three s.; ed St Catharine's Coll. Cambridge, Univ. Coll. Hosp. Medical School; Sr Lecturer, Inst. of Cancer Research 1972–74, Prof. and Hon. Consultant, Inst. of Cancer Research and Royal Marsden Hosp. 1974–86, Dean Inst. of Cancer Research 1984–86; Dir British Post grad. Medical Fed. 1986–90; Ed.-in-Chief European Journal of Cancer 1990–95; Dir of Research and Devt, Dept of Health 1991–95; Dir School of Public Policy, Univ. Coll. London

1996–2000; Vice-Chair. Imperial Cancer Research Fund 1987–90; Chair. Office of Science and Tech. Healthcare Foresight Programme 1999–2000, Nat. Educational Research Forum 2000, Devt Forum 2000; Founding Pres. British Oncological Asscn 1986–88; Pres. Fed. of European Cancer Socs 1989–91, European Soc. for Therapeutic Radiology and Oncology 1983–85; Foreign Assoc. mem. NAS Inst. of Medicine 1994–; Hon. Fellow, St Catharine's Coll., Cambridge 1998, Univ. Coll. London 1995; Dr hc (Besançon), (Catholic Univ. of Louvain) 1993; Hon. DSc (Loughborough) 1992, (Exeter) 1996, (Inst. of Cancer Research) 2007. *Publications:* Oxford Textbook of Oncology (co-author) 1995, Clinical Futures 1999, A Model for Health: Innovation and the Future of Health Services 2000. *Address:* 6 Crescent Place, London, SW3 2EA, England (home). *E-mail:* michael.peckham@yahoo.com (home).

PECKOVÁ, Dagmar; Czech singer (mezzo-soprano); b. 4 April 1961, Chrudim; m. 1st J. Vejvoda; m. 2nd Aleš Kasprík 1997; one s.; m. 3rd Klaus Schiesser; one d.; ed Prague Conservatory; soloist at Karlín Musical Theatre, Prague 1982–85; soloist with numerous cos including Czech Philharmonic 1985–, with Semper Opera, Dresden 1985–88, with State Opera Berlin 1989–92; guest appearances in Tokyo, Paris 1992, Bregenz Festival, Austria 1992, 1993, Hamburg 1993, Salzburg Festival 1993, 1995, 1996, Basel 1994, Zürich 1994, London 1995, Tel-Aviv 1996, La Corona Festival, Spain 1996, San Sebastien Festival, Spain 1996, Prague Spring Festival 1996, Frankfurt 1996; concert tours Austria, Switzerland, Germany, UK 1993, France, Japan 1990, 1994, USA 1997–99; charity concerts after floods in Czech Repub. 2002; roles include Leonora (Basel), Cherubino in The Marriage of Figaro (London), Rosina in The Barber of Seville (Berlin, Dresden), Carmen (Prague), Varvara in Katya Kabanova (Salzburg, Barcelona); resident performer, Schleswig-Holstein Music Festival 2014; First Prize, Antonín Dvořák Competition 1982, Second Prize, Brno Vocal Competition 1985, Czech Music Fund Award (for role of Eliza Doolittle in My Fair Lady) 1985, First Prize, Prague Spring Vocal Competition 1986, Berlin Critics' Prize (for role of Dorabella in Così fan tutte) 1989, European Foundation for Music Prize 1993, Thalia Prize (for Carmen) 2000. *Recordings include:* Martinů—Nipponari 1991, Mozart—Che Bella 1994, Janáček—Moravian Folk Poetry in Song 1994, Mahler—Adagietto, Kindertotenlieder 1996, Songs of Mahler and Berio 1997, Janáček—Kátá Kabanová 1997, Janáček—Diary of One Who Disappeared 1999, recital of music by Wagner, Schoenberg, Zemlinsky and Brahms 2000, Lieder by Strauss, Schoeck, Berg 2001, Lieder by Dvořák 2001, Arias (live) 2002. *Leisure interests:* reading, driving. *Address:* c/o Franz Tscherne, Tscherne Artists, Führichgasse 8, 1010 Vienna, Austria (office). *E-mail:* franz@tscherneartists.com (office). *Website:* www .tscherneartists.com/peckova_dagmar.html (office); www.dagmarpeckova.com/en.

PÉCRESSE, Valérie; French politician; *President of the Regional Council, Île-de-France;* b. 14 July 1967, Neuilly-sur-Seine (Hauts-de-Seine); d. of Dominique Roux; m.; two s. one d.; ed Haute École de Commerce, École Nat. d'Admin; auditor, Conseil d'État 1992–98; adviser, French Presidency 1998; Deputy for Yvelines, Nat. Ass. 2002–07, 2012–16; mem. Comm. on Cultural, Family and Social Affairs, Rapporteur, Mission of Information on Family and Rights of Children, Pres. Study Group on Applications of Biotechnologies in Genetics and Ethical Problems, Vice-Pres. Study Group on Internet, Information Technologies and of Communication and e-Commerce, mem. Del. on Rights of Women and Gender Equality, Organizer, Union pour un Mouvement Populaire (UMP) Working Group on the Family, fmr UMP Spokeswoman; elected Regional Councillor, Île-de-France 2004, Pres. Regional Council 2015–; Minister of Higher Educ. and Research 2007–11, of the Budget, Public Finances, Civil Service and State Reform 2011–12; Spokeswoman for Govt 2011–12; Deputy Sec.-Gen. UMP 2013–14; Chair. S'engager contre l'échec scolaire (foundation); f. le labo des idées (think-tank) 2010. *Publications:* Etre une femme politique… c'est pas si facile! 2007, Controverses (with Axel Kahn) 2011. *E-mail:* contact@valeriepecresse.fr. *Website:* www.iledefrance.fr (office); www .valeriepecresse.fr.

PEDDER, Anthony P. (Tony), OBE, MSc; British company director and fmr steel industry executive; b. 1949; m.; two. s.; ed Univ. of London; joined steel industry 1972; several sr man. positions in British Steel (now Corus), mem. bd British Steel 1992, mem. bd Corus Group (after merger with British Steel) 1999, CEO 2001–03; Chair. Sheffield Forgemasters International Ltd 2005–17; Dir (non-exec.), Metalysis Ltd 2005–, JSW (India) Ltd 2005–, HCF International Ltd 2006–, EEF Ltd 2008; Chair. Sheffield Teaching Hospitals Trust 2012–, Council of Univ. of Sheffield 2013–; DL, South Yorks. 2007; Master Cutler 2013–14.

PEDERSEN, Helga; Norwegian politician; b. 13 Jan. 1973; d. of Terje Pedersen and Sør Varanger; m. Erik Brenli 2008; two d.; ed Univ. of Tromsø, Univ. of Bergen; teacher, Boftsa School, Tana 1992–93; Civil Servant, Econ. Devt and Transport Dept, Finnmark County 1998–2000, County Council Rep. 1999–2005, Chair. County Council 2003–05; Political Adviser to Minister of Trade and Industry 2001; part-time project worker, UNEP/GRID, Arendal 2001–02; Head of Project to Promote Econ. and Cultural Devt, Tanafjord Area 2002–03; Minister of Fisheries and Coastal Affairs 2005–09; mem. Det norske Arbeiderparti (Norwegian Labour Party), Deputy Leader 2007–15; mem. Parl. (Finnmark) 2009–13 (parl. leader Norwegian Labour Party group), 2013–17, mem. Foreign and Defence and European Affairs Cttees 2009–13, Storting Del. for Relations with European Parl. 2009–13, Del. UN Gen. Ass. 2010–, First Deputy Election Cttee 2013–17, First Deputy Municipal Man. Cttee 2013–17; Hon. Citizen Village Sørvær, Finnmark 2008. *Address:* c/o Norwegian Labour Party, Youngstorget 2a, 5th floor, PO Box 8743, 0028 Oslo, Norway.

PEDERSEN, K(nud) George, OC, OOnt, OBC, PhD, FRSA, FCCT; Canadian university president (retd) and academic; b. 13 June 1931, Peace River, Alberta; s. of Hjalmar Pedersen and Anna Jensen; m. 1st Joan Vanderwarker 1953 (died 1988); m. 2nd Penny Jones 1988; one s. one d.; ed Chilliwack Sr High School and Univs of BC, Washington and Chicago; school teacher, N Vancouver school system 1952–56; Vice-Prin., North Star Elementary School 1956–59; Prin. Carisbrooke Elementary School 1959–61; Vice-Prin., Handsworth Secondary School 1961–63; Prin., Balmoral Secondary School 1963–65; Research Assoc. Univ. of Chicago 1965–68; Asst Prof., Ont. Inst. for Studies in Educ. and Univ. of Toronto 1968–70; Assoc. Dir Midwest Admin. Center, Univ. of Chicago 1970–72; Dean, Faculty of Educ. Univ. of Vic. 1972–75, Vice-Pres. (Academic) 1975–78; Pres. and Vice-Chancellor Simon Fraser Univ. 1979–83, Univ. of British Columbia 1983–85, Univ. of Western Ontario 1985–94, Univ. of Northern British Columbia 1995–2004,

Royal Roads Univ. 1995–96; Chancellor Univ. of Northern British Columbia 1998–2004; Chair. Bd Govs, Emily Carr Univ. of Art and Design 2004–10; Fellow, Canadian Coll. of Teachers; Commemorative Medal 1992, Queen's Golden Jubilee Medal 2002, Queen's Diamond Jubilee Medal 2012; Hon. LLD (McMaster) 1996, (Simon Fraser Univ.) 2003, (Univ. of Northern British Columbia) 2005; Hon. DLitt (Emily Carr Univ. of Art and Design) 2003, (Univ. of the Fraser Valley) 2007; ten major scholarships, including Univ. of Chicago Scholarships 1965–68, Canada Council Scholarships 1966–68, Ford Foundation Fellowship 1967–68. *Publications include:* The Itinerant Schoolmaster 1973; book chapters and numerous articles. *Leisure interests:* fishing, golf, gardening, cooking, carving. *Address:* 2232 Spruce Street, Vancouver, BC V6H 2P3, Canada (home). *Telephone:* (604) 733-2400 (home); (360) 371-7071 (home). *Fax:* (604) 733-2400 (home); (360) 371-7071 (home). *E-mail:* pgpedersen@telus.net (home); pennyandgeorgep@gmail.com (home).

PEDERSEN, Roger A., PhD; American embryologist and academic; *Professor of Regenerative Medicine and Director of Research in Regenerative Medicine, Department of Surgery and the Anne McLaren Laboratory for Regenerative Medicine, University of Cambridge;* Prof., Univ. of California, San Francisco –2001, Prof. Emer. 2001–; Prof. of Regenerative Medicine, Dept of Surgery, Univ. of Cambridge School of Clinical Medicine, UK 2001–, Dir Cambridge Stem Cell Inst. (fmrly Cambridge Centre for Stem Cell Biology and Medicine) 2004–, Prin. Collaborator, Cambridge Inst. of Medical Research 2004–, currently Dir of Research in Regenerative Medicine, Dept of Surgery and the Anne McLaren Lab. for Regenerative Medicine; sabbatical, Inst. for Stem Cell Biology and Regenerative Medicine, Stanford Medical School 2012–13. *Publications:* Experimental Approaches to Mammalian Embryonic Development 1988, Current Topics in Developmental Biology 1998, Embryonic Stem Cells for Medicine: A Scientific American article 2002, Handbook of Stem Cells –Vol. 1: Embryonic Stem Cells, Vol. 2: Adult and Fetal Stem Cells 2004; numerous articles in medical and scientific journals on stem cell research. *Address:* Anne McLaren Laboratory for Regenerative Medicine, Cambridge Stem Cell Institute, University of Cambridge, Cambridge, CB2 2XY, England (office). *Telephone:* (1223) 763236 (office). *E-mail:* ralp2@cam.ac.uk (office). *Website:* www.stemcells.cam.ac.uk/researchers/principal -investigators/rpedersen (office).

PEDERSEN, Thor; Danish politician; b. 14 June 1945, Gentofte; s. of Laurits Pedersen; ed Copenhagen Univ.; fmr mem. staff, Assessments Div.; fmr Man. Dir of a construction co., North Zealand; fmr Mayor of Helsinge; mem. Folketing (Parl.) 1985–2011, Speaker 2007–11; Minister of Housing 1986–87, of the Interior 1987–93, of Nordic Affairs 1988, of Econ. Affairs 1992–93, of Finance 2001–07.

PEDLEY, Timothy John, ScD, FRS; British academic; *G. I. Taylor Professor Emeritus of Fluid Mechanics, University of Cambridge;* b. 23 March 1942, Leicester; s. of Richard Rodman Pedley and Jeanie Mary Mudie Pedley; m. Avril Jennifer Martin Uden 1965; two s.; ed Rugby School, Trinity Coll., Cambridge; Postdoctoral Fellow, Johns Hopkins Univ., USA 1966–68; Research Assoc. and lecturer, Imperial Coll. London 1968–73; Lecturer, Dept of Applied Math. and Theoretical Physics, Univ. of Cambridge 1973–89, Reader in Biological Fluid Dynamics 1989, G. I. Taylor Prof. of Fluid Mechanics 1996–2009, Prof. Emer. 2009–, Head, Dept of Applied Math. and Theoretical Physics 2000–05; Fellow, Gonville & Caius Coll. Cambridge 1973–89, 1996–; Prof. of Applied Math., Univ. of Leeds 1990–96; Ed. Journal of Fluid Mechanics 2000–06; Pres. Inst. of Math. and its Applications (IMA) 2004–05, Int. Union of Theoretical and Applied Mechanics 2008–12; Chair. World Council for Biomechanics 2002–06; mem. Eng and Physical Sciences Research Council 2009–; Fellow, American Inst. of Medical and Biological Eng 2001, American Physical Soc. 2005; Adams Prize, Univ. of Cambridge 1977, IMA Gold Medal 2008. *Publications:* The Mechanics of the Circulation (co-author) 1978, Scale Effects in Animal Locomotion (ed.) 1977, The Fluid Mechanics of Large Blood Vessels 1980, Biological Fluid Dynamics (co-ed.) 1995. *Leisure interests:* bird-watching, running, reading. *Address:* Department of Applied Mathematics and Theoretical Physics (DAMTP), Centre for Mathematical Sciences, University of Cambridge, Wilberforce Road, Cambridge, CB3 0WA (office); Oakhurst Farm, 375 Shadwell Lane, Leeds, LS17 8AH, England (home). *Telephone:* (1223) 339842 (office); (113) 266-2854 (home). *Fax:* (1223) 760497 (office). *E-mail:* t.j.pedley@damtp.cam.ac.uk (office). *Website:* www.damtp.cam.ac.uk (office).

PEDNYCYA, Kazys; Lithuanian lawyer; b. 16 Nov. 1949, Plaskunai, Kaisiadoriai Region, Lithuania; m. Viktorija Pednycienė; two s.; ed Vilnius State Univ.; interrogator, Kedainai Regional Public Prosecutor's Office 1972–76; Asst Public Prosecutor, Panevezys City 1976–84; Supervision Prosecutor, Lithuanian Repub. Reformatories 1984–91; Judge, Lithuanian Repub. Supreme Court 1991–92; Sr Customs Official, Lithuanian Repub. 1992–93; Asst Dir-Gen. Lithuanian Nat. Security Dept 1993–97; Gen. Public Prosecutor 1997–2001.

PEDRAZA RODRÍGUEZ, Lina, BSc; Cuban politician; b. 15 Sept. 1955, Villa Clara prov.; head of Central Bank in Villa Clara prov. in the early 1990s; Deputy, Nat. Ass. of People's Power; elected to Central Cttee, Communist Party of Cuba (Partido Comunista de Cuba—PCC) 1991, Head of Econs Div. 2006–09, mem. CP Secr. 2006–09; Minister of Auditing and Control 2001–06, of Finance and Prices 2009–19. *Address:* c/o Ministry of Finance and Prices, Calle Obispo 211, esq. Cuba, Habana Vieja, Havana; Partido Comunista de Cuba (Communist Party of Cuba), Plaza de la Revolución, Avenida Paseo, Havana, Cuba (office). *Telephone:* (7) 8593000 (office). *E-mail:* siteweb@cc.cu (office). *Website:* www.pcc.cu (office).

PEDROSO, Iván; Cuban fmr track and field athlete; b. 17 Dec. 1972, Havana; long jumper; jumped more than 8m for the first time aged 17 July 1990; winner Pan American Junior Championships, Kingston, Jamaica 1991, Ibero-American Championships, Seville 1992, World Cup, Havana 1992, Pan American Games, Mar del Plata, Argentina 1995, IAAF Grand Prix Final, Monte Carlo 1995, Central American and Caribbean Championships, San Juan, Puerto Rico 1997, Universiade, Catania, Italy 1997, IAAF Grand Prix Final, Fukuoka, Japan 1997, World Cup, Johannesburg 1998, Central American and Caribbean Games, Maracaibo, Venezuela 1998, Goodwill Games, Uniondale, USA 1998, Pan American Games, Winnipeg 1999, IAAF Grand Prix Final, Munich 1999, Goodwill Games, Brisbane 2001, Pan American Games, Santo Domingo, Dominican Repub. 2003; gold medallist, World Indoor Championships, Toronto 1993, Barcelona 1995, Paris 1997, Maebashi 1999, Lisbon 2001; gold medallist, World Championships Gothenburg 1995, Athens 1997, Seville 1999, Edmonton 2001; gold medallist,

Olympic Games, Sydney 2000; best jump officially 8.71m, in Salamanca 1995; announced retirement Sept. 2007; coach of 2013 triple jump world champion, Teddy Tamgho; Flagbearer for Cuba, Olympic Summer Games, Athens 2004, London 2012; voted Best Cuban Sportsman 1998. *Address:* c/o Cubadeportes SA, 710 Calle 20 no. 710 e/ 7ma y 9na, Miramar, Havana, Cuba. *Website:* www.iaaf.org/ athletes/cuba/ivan-pedroso-4205.

PEEBLES, Phillip James Edwin, BS, PhD, FRS, FRSC; American (b. Canadian) cosmologist and academic; *Professor Emeritus of Physics and Albert Einstein Professor Emeritus of Science, Princeton University;* b. 25 April 1935, Winnipeg, Man.; m. Alison Peebles; one s. two d.; ed Univ. of Manitoba, Princeton Univ.; Instructor, Princeton Univ. 1961–62, Research Assoc. 1962–64, Research Staff mem. 1964–65, faculty mem. Physics Dept 1965–, Asst Prof. to Prof. 1965–84, Albert Einstein Prof. of Science 1984–2000, Albert Einstein Prof. Emer. of Science 2000–; mem. NAS (Foreign Assoc.), American Astronomical Soc., AAAS, Int. Astronomical Union; Fellow, American Acad. of Arts and Sciences, American Physical Soc., American Philosophical Soc.; proposed the primordial isocurvature baryon model for the devt of the early universe 1987; Hon. DSc (Toronto) 1986, (Chicago) 1986, (McMaster) 1989, (Manitoba) 1989, (Newcastle-upon-Tyne, Catholic Univ. of Louvain); numerous hon. lectureships, including Henry Norris Russell Lectureship, American Astronomical Soc. 1993, Silliman Lectureship, Yale Univ., de Vaucouleurs Lectureship, Univ. of Texas, Jansky Lectureship, Nat. Radio Astronomy Observatory, Feshbach Lectureship, MIT, McPherson Lectureship, McGill Univ., Klein Lectureship, Univ. of Stockholm, Danz Prof., Univ. of Washington; A.C. Morrison Award in Nat. Science, New York Acad. of Sciences 1977, Eddington Medal, Royal Astronomical Soc. 1981, Gold Medal 1998, Heineman Prize, American Astronomical Soc. 1982, Robinson Prize, Univ. of Newcastle, Henry Norris Russell Lectureship 1993, Bruce Medal, Astronomical Soc. of the Pacific 1995, Oskar Klein Medal 1997, Lemaitre Award, Université catholique de Louvain, Cosmology Prize, Peter Gruber Foundation (co-recipient) 2000, ADION Medal (France) 2003, Shaw Prize in Astronomy (Hong Kong) 2004, Crafoord Prize, Royal Swedish Acad. of Sciences (co-recipient) 2005, Hitchcock Professorship 2006, Asteroid 18242 Peebles named after him. *Publications:* Physical Cosmology 1971; numerous scientific papers in professional journals. *Leisure interest:* gardening. *Address:* Department of Physics, Princeton University, 216 Jadwin Hall, Princeton, NJ 08544-0001, USA (office). *Telephone:* (609) 258-4386 (office). *Fax:* (609) 258-6853 (office). *E-mail:* pjep@princeton.edu (office); pjep@pupgg.princeton.edu (office). *Website:* phy.princeton.edu/people/p-james -peebles (office).

PEERS, Most Rev. Michael Geoffrey, BA, zert.dolm., LTh; Canadian ecclesiastic (retd); b. 31 July 1934, Vancouver, BC; s. of Geoffrey H. Peers and Dorothy E. Mantle; m. Dorothy E. Bradley 1963; two s. one d.; ed Univs of British Columbia, Univ. of Heidelberg, Trinity Coll., Toronto; ordained priest 1960; Curate, Ottawa 1959–65; Univ. Chaplain, Diocese of Ottawa 1961–66; Rector, St Bede's, Winnipeg 1966–72, St Martin's, Winnipeg with St Paul's Middlechurch 1972–74; Archdeacon of Winnipeg 1969–74; Rector, St Paul's Cathedral, Regina 1974–77; Dean of Qu'Appelle 1974–77; Bishop of Qu'Appelle 1977–82; Archbishop of Qu'Appelle and Metropolitan of Rupert's Land 1982–86; Primate, Anglican Church of Canada 1986–2004; Ecumenist-in-Residence, Toronto School of Theology 2004–06; fmr Pres. Metropolitan Council of Cuba; confessor to the monastery, Soc. of St John the Evangelist mem. Cen. Cttee World Council of Churches (WCC) 1991–98, Jt Standing Cttee of Anglican Communion 1994–2003, WCC Special Comm. on relations with Orthodox Churches 1999–2006; Hon. DD (Trinity Coll. Toronto) 1978, (Wycliffe Coll. Toronto) 1981, (St John's Coll. Winnipeg) 1981, (Univ. of Kent) 1988, (Montreal Diocesan Coll.) 1989, (Coll. of Emmanuel and St Chad, Saskatoon) 1990, (Thorneloe Univ. Sudbury) 1993, (Huron Coll., London, Ont.) 1998, (Huron Univ. Coll.) 1998, (Lutheran Theological Seminary Saskatoon) 2001, (Episcopal Divinity School, Cambridge USA) 2004; Hon. DCL (Bishop's Univ., Lennoxville) 1993. *Publications:* Grace Notes: Journeying with the Primate 1995–2004 2005. *Address:* 195 Westminster Avenue, Toronto, Ont., M6R 1N9, Canada. *Telephone:* (416) 531-8958. *E-mail:* mpeers@sympatico.ca.

PEERTHUM, Satteeanund; Mauritian diplomatist; b. 15 March 1941; m.; three c.; ed People's Friendship Univ., Moscow; Sr Research Fellow, Inst. of Oriental Studies, Moscow, USSR 1973–74; Head of History Dept, Bhojoharry Coll., Mauritius several times between 1975 and 1987; Sr Research Fellow, School of Mauritian Asian and African Studies, Mahatma Gandhi Inst. 1985–87; Founding mem. Mouvement Socialiste Militant; mem. Mauritian Parl. and Minister of Labour and Industrial Relations 1982–83; Chair. Sugar Industry Devt Fund Bds of Mauritius 1984–87; Amb. and Perm. Rep. to UN, New York 1987–96; Chair. Nat. Steering Cttee for the Teaching of Mauritian History; mem. Advisory Cttee, African Cultural Centre of Mauritius 1986–87; fmr mem. Court, Nat. Univ. of Mauritius. *Address:* c/o Ministry of Foreign Affairs, Regional Integration and International Trade, Newton Tower, 9th–11th Floors, Sir William Newton Street, Port Louis, Mauritius. *E-mail:* mfa@mail.gov.mu.

PEFANIS, Harry N.; American petroleum industry executive; *President and Chief Operating Officer, Plains All American Pipeline LP;* b. 1957, Buffalo, NY; ed Univ. of Oklahoma; has worked with Plains All American Pipeline LP and its predecessors since 1983, Special Asst for Corp. Planning, Plains Resources 1983–87, Products Marketing Man. 1987–88, Vice-Pres. Products Marketing 1988–96, Sr Vice-Pres. 1996–98, Exec. Vice-Pres., Midstream of Plains Resources 1998–2001, Pres. and COO Plains All American Pipeline LP 1998–, Plains GP Holdings 1998–; mem. Bd of Dirs PAA/Vulcan. *Address:* Plains All American Pipeline LP, 333 Clay Street, Suite 1600, Houston, TX 77002, USA (office). *Telephone:* (713) 646-4100 (office). *Fax:* (713) 646-4572 (office). *E-mail:* info@ plainsallamerican.com (office). *Website:* www.plainsallamerican.com (office); ir .pagp.com/management (office).

PÉGARD, Catherine; French journalist and government official; *President, Public Establishment of the Palace, Museum and National Estate of Versailles;* b. 5 Aug. 1954, Le Havre; began career in journalism at daily J'informe 1977; worked in Political Dept of Quotidien de Paris (Groupe Quotidien) 1978–82; joined weekly Le Point 1982, becoming Asst Ed.-in-Chief, later Ed.-in-Chief; Co-host Les Femmes et les Patrons d'abord, Paris Première 2004–07; adviser to Pres. Sarkozy 2007–08, in charge of 'pôle politique' at Elysée Palace 2008–11; Pres. Public Establishment of the Palace, Museum and Nat. Estate of Versailles 2011–; Chevalier, Légion d'honneur 2012. *Address:* Établissement Public du château, du musée et du domaine national de Versailles, Ministry of Culture and Communication, 3 rue de Valois, 75033 Paris Cedex 01, France (office). *Telephone:* 1-40-15-80-00 (office). *Fax:* 1-40-15-85-30 (office). *E-mail:* point.culture@culture.fr (office). *Website:* www.culturecommunication.gouv.fr (office); www.chateauversailles.fr (office).

PEH, Joanne; Singaporean actress; b. 25 April 1983; m. Qi Yuwu 2014; one s. one d.; ed Nanyang Technological Univ.; won numerous nat. film awards. *Television includes:* Beautiful Connection 2002, To Mum With Love 2004, The Ties That Bind 2004, A Life of Hope 2005, Yours Always 2006, Like Father, Like Daughter 2007, Path of Gold 2007, The Truth 2008, The Little Nyonya (Star Awards Best Actress Award) 2008, Your Hand in Mine 2009, Love in a Cab (film) 2010, C.L.I.F. 2 (series) 2013, Love at Risk 2013, The Journey: A Voyage 2013, C.L.I.F. 3 2014, Mind Game 2015, Dream Coder 2017, Say Cheese 2018, Heart To Heart 2018. *Films:* City Beat 2002, High on Life 2005, Tua Seh Kai 2011. *Address:* c/o Artiste Management Division, MediaCorp Studios Pte Ltd, Caldecott Broadcast Centre, Andrew Road, East Wing Building, Level 3, 29939 Singapore (office). *Telephone:* 63575973 (office). *E-mail:* carolhar@mediacorp.com.sg (office); joannepeh.email@gmail.com (office). *Website:* joannepeh.com (office).

PEI, I(eoh) M(ing), MArch, FAIA, RIBA; American architect; b. 26 April 1917, Canton, China; s. of Tsu Yee Pei and Lien Kwun Chwong; m. Eileen Loo 1942; three s. one d.; ed Shanghai Univ., Massachusetts Inst. of Tech., Harvard Univ.; moved to USA 1935, became naturalized citizen 1954; est. architectural practice 1939; Nat. Defense Research Cttee 1943–45; Asst Prof. Harvard Graduate School of Design 1945–48; Webb and Knapp Inc. 1948–55, Pei, Cobb, Freed & Pnrs (fmrly I. M. Pei & Pnrs) 1955–90; Wheelwright Traveling Fellowship, Harvard Univ. 1951; MIT Traveling Fellowship 1940; Fellow AIA; mem. Nat. Council on the Humanities 1966–70, American Acad. of Arts and Sciences, Nat. Acad. of Design, American Acad. of Arts and Letters (Chancellor 1978–80), Nat. Council on the Arts 1981–84, RIBA, Urban Design Council (New York), Corpn of MIT 1972–77, 1978–83, American Philosophical Soc., Institut de France (Foreign Assoc.); Commdr, Ordre des Arts et des Lettres, Officier, Légion d'honneur 1988; Hon. DFA (Pennsylvania) 1970, (Rensselaer Polytechnic Inst.) 1978, (Northeastern Univ.) 1979, (Univs of Mass., Rochester, Brown) 1982, (New York Univ.) 1983; Hon. LLD (Chinese Univ. of Hong Kong) 1970, Hon. DHL (Columbia Univ., Univs of Colorado, Rochester, Hong Kong, American Univ. of Paris); Hon. Prof. Tonji Univ., Shanghai 1985; Brunner Award, Nat. Inst. of Arts and Letters 1961; Medal of Honor NY Chapter AIA 1963, The Thomas Jefferson Memorial Medal for Architecture 1976, Gold Medal (American Acad. of Arts and Letters) 1979, Gold Medal (American Inst. of Architects) 1979, La Grande Medaille d'Or (Académie d'Architecture) 1981, Pritzker Architecture Prize 1983, Asia Soc. Award 1984, Medal of Liberty 1986, Nat. Medal of Arts 1988, Praemium Imperiale (Japan Art Asscn) 1989, Univ. of Calif. Gold Medal 1990, Calbert Award for Excellence 1991, Presidential Medal of Freedom 1992, Edward MacDowell Medal 1998, BZ Kulturpreis (Germany) 1999, Historic Landmarks Preservation Center, New York Cultural Laureate 1999, Erwin Wickert Foundation Orient und Okzident Preis 2006, Royal Gold Medal for Architecture, RIBA 2010. *Address:* Pei Cobb Freed & Partners, 88 Pine Street, New York, NY 10005, USA (office). *Telephone:* (212) 872-4010 (office). *Fax:* (212) 872-4222 (office). *E-mail:* information@pcf-p.com (office). *Website:* www.pcf-p.com (office).

PEI, Yanling; Chinese opera actress; b. Aug. 1947, Shuning Co., Hebei Prov.; m. 1st Ding Bao Jin 1971 (divorced 1990); two d.; m. 2nd Guo Jing Chun; Vice-Chair. Hebei Fed. of Literary and Art Circles 1993–, China Fed. of Literary and Art Circles 2001–; Chair. Hebei Professional Dramatists' Asscn; currently Dir Pei Yanling Co. of Hebei Prov. Peking Opera Theatre; mem. 7th CPPCC 1987–92, 8th CPPCC 1992–97; Excellent Performing Artist Award, Ministry of Culture 1992, Plum Blossom Award 1986, 1995, Grand Plum Blossom Award 2009, White Magnolia Award for Special Achievement in the Performing Arts 2009. *Performances include:* The Man and the Ghost, Lotus Lantern, Ren gui qing (Woman-Demon-Human) 1987 and numerous others.

PEICHL, Gustav; Austrian architect and caricaturist; b. 18 March 1928, Vienna; Prof., Acad. of Fine Arts, Vienna; major works include Austrian Broadcasting Stations in Salzburg, Linz, Innsbrück, Dornbirn 1970–72, Graz 1979–80, Eisenstadt 1981–83; EFA Radio Satellite Station, Aflenz 1976–79; PEA-Phosphate Elimination Plant, Berlin-Tegel; design for Papal visit to Vienna 1984; art and exhbn centre, Bonn 1986–92; extension to Städel Museum, Frankfurt am Main; ÖMV-Center, Vienna 1991–; rehearsal stage of Burgtheater, Vienna 1991–93; Co-founder Peichl & Partner ZT GmbH 2002; caricaturist under alias Ironimus; Ehrenzeichen für Verdienste um das Land Wien 1993, Verleihung der Grossen Verdienst-Kreuzes des Verdienstordens 1996, Ehrenzeichen für Verdienste um das Bundesland Niederösterreich 2003, Österreichische Ehrenzeichen und Österreichische Ehrenkreuz für Wissenschaft und Kunst 2013; Award of City of Vienna for Architecture 1969, Austrian State Award 1971, Reynolds Memorial Award 1975, Styria Award for Architecture 1984, Mies van der Rohe Award 1986, Berlin Architectural Award 1989, German Architecture Prize 1993, Austrian Grand Golden Medal of Honor 1996, Golden Town Hallman of Vienna 2008, Julius Raab Medal 2012. *Address:* Atelier Peichl, Opernring 4/2/19, 1010 Vienna, Austria (office). *Telephone:* (1) 512-32-48 (office). *Fax:* (1) 512-32-48-71 (office). *E-mail:* g.peichl@cehl.at (office).

PEILLON, Vincent Benoît Camille, PhD; French politician; b. 7 July 1960, Suresnes, Paris; Lecturer in Philosophy 1984–97; Econ. Research Dir CNRS 2002–04; Sec. Socialist Party's (PS—Parti socialiste) group of experts 1993–94, seconded to First Sec. of PS 1995–97, Nat. Research Sec. 1997–2000, PS Nat. Spokesman 2000–02, mem. PS Nat. Bureau 1994–; Deputy to Nat. Ass. 1997–2002, Chair. Nat. Ass.'s inquiry into money laundering 1999–2002; mem. European Parl. for North West France (Group of the Progressive Alliance of Socialists and Democrats in the European Parl.) 2004–, mem. Cttee on Foreign Affairs, Del. for relations with the Maghreb countries and the Arab Maghreb Union, Del. to Parl. Ass. of the Union for the Mediterranean; Minister of Nat. Educ. 2012–14. *Address:* c/o Ministry of National Education, Hôtel de Rochechouart, 110 rue de Grenelle, 75357 Paris SP 07, France (office).

PEIMBERT, Manuel, BS, MA, PhD; Mexican astronomer and academic; *Professor Emeritus, Instituto de Astronomía, Universidad Nacional Autónoma de México;* b. 9 June 1941, Mexico City; s. of Gonzalo Peimbert and Catalina Sierra; m. Silvia Torres-Peimbert 1962; one s. one d.; ed Universidad Nacional Autónoma de México (UNAM) and Univ. of California, Berkeley, USA; Research Asst, Instituto de Astronomía, UNAM 1960–63, Prof., Faculty of Sciences 1968–2006, Prof. Emer. 2006–, Instituto de Astronomía 1970–2006, mem. Academic Bd of Govs 2000–10; Research Asst, Univ. of California, Berkeley 1963–64, Postdoctoral Fellow 1967–68; on sabbatical leave at Kitt Peak Nat. Observatory, USA 1975–76, Univ. Coll., London, UK 1976, Tokyo Astronomical Observatory 1986; Emer. Researcher, Nat. System of Researchers 2007–; Vice-Pres. Int. Astronomical Union 1982–88; mem. Science Advisory Council of the Presidency of the Repub.; Assoc. Ed. Journal of the National Autonomous University of Mexico 1994–2001; Foreign Assoc., NAS 1987; Assoc., Royal Astronomical Soc. 1989; mem. Nat. Coll. (Mexico) 1992; Foreign mem. American Philosophical Soc. 2002; Fellow, Third World Acad. of Sciences (TWAS) 1987 (Vice-Pres. 1998–2003), Acad. of Sciences of Latin America 1996; Investigador ad Honorem, Francisco J. Duarte Centre for Astronomy, Venezuela 1981; Luis G. León Medal, Sociedad Astronómica de México, Science Prize, Academia Mexicana de Ciencias 1971, Guillaume Budé Medal, Coll. de France 1974, Premio Nacional de Ciencias y Artes en el área de Ciencias Físico-Matemáticas y Naturales en 1978, Mexican Nat. Prize in Science and Arts 1981, UNAM Science Prize 1988, Academic Medal, Mexican Soc. of Physics 1991, Medal and Lecture, TWAS 1996. *Publications:* Selected Topics in Astrophysics (ed.) 1984, Frontiers of the Universe (ed.) 2000, The Evolution in Astronomy (ed.) 2006; more than 200 research papers in int. journals of astronomy and astrophysics; more than 50 popular articles and book chapters. *Address:* Instituto de Astronomía, Universidad Nacional Autónoma de México, Apartado Postal 70-264, 04510 México DF, Mexico. *Telephone:* (5) 622-3906. *Fax:* (5) 616-0653. *E-mail:* peimbert@astroscu.unam.mx. *Website:* www.astroscu.unam.mx/~peimbert.

PEIRANO, Miguel Gustavo; Argentine economist and government official; b. 1 Oct. 1966; ed Universidad de Buenos Aires; began career at Banco Sudameris 1989; worked for Techint Group 1990–92; various posts at Argentine Industrial Union (UIA) 1993–2004; Prof. of Political Economy, Colegio Nacional de Buenos Aires 1995–97; served as econ. adviser to Dir-Gen. of Industry of the City of Buenos Aires, Bd of Bank of the Province of Buenos Aires, Nat. Sub-secretariat of Small and Medium Enterprise and Regional Devt; fmr Pres. Econs Dept, Buenos Aires City Industrial Union; Sr Vice-Pres. Bank of Investment and Foreign Trade (BICE) –2007; Minister of Economy and Production July–Dec. 2007.

PEIRIS, Gamini Lakshman, LLB (Hons), DPhil, PhD; Sri Lankan politician and academic; b. 13 Aug. 1946, Colombo; s. of Glanville S. Peiris and Lakshmi C. Salgado; m. Savitri N. Amarasuriya 1971; one d.; ed St Thomas' Coll., Mount Lavinia, Univ. of Ceylon and New Coll., Oxford, UK; Prof. of Law, Univ. of Colombo 1979, Dean, Faculty of Law 1982–88; Vice-Chancellor, Univ. of Colombo 1988–94; Dir Nat. Film Corpn of Sri Lanka 1973–88; Commr Law Comm. of Sri Lanka 1986–; mem. Inc. Soc. of Legal Educ. 1986–; Visiting Fellow, All Souls Coll. Oxford 1980–81; Butterworths Visiting Fellow, Inst. of Advanced Legal Studies, Univ. of London 1984; Distinguished Visiting Fellow, Christ's Coll. Cambridge, UK 1985–86; Smuts Visiting Fellow in Commonwealth Studies, Univ. of Cambridge 1985–86; Chair. Cttee of Vice-Chancellors of the Univs of Sri Lanka; Minister of Justice, Constitutional Affairs, Ethnic Affairs and Nat. Integration and Deputy Minister of Finance 1994–99, of Enterprise Devt, Industrial Policy and Investment Promotion and of Constitutional Affairs 1999–2004, of Export Devt and Int. Trade 2007–10, of External Affairs 2010–15; mem. United People's Freedom Alliance (UPFA) 2007–; Vice-Chair. Janasaviya Trust Fund; mem. Securities Council of Sri Lanka 1987–; mem. Pres. Comm. on Youth Unrest 1989; mem. Nat. Educ. Comm., Exec. Cttee of Asscn of Teachers and Researchers in Intellectual Property Law, Bd Govs Inst. of Fundamental Studies; Assoc. mem. Int. Acad. of Comparative Law; Chair. Sri Lanka Podujana Peramuna 2016–; Presidential Award 1987. *Publications:* Law of Unjust Enrichment in South Africa and Ceylon 1971, General Principles of Criminal Liability in Ceylon 1972, Offences Under the Penal Code of Sri Lanka 1973, The Law of Evidence in Sri Lanka 1974, Criminal Procedure in Sri Lanka 1975, The Law of Property in Sri Lanka 1976, Landlord and Tenant in Sri Lanka 1977; numerous articles on comparative and admin. law and law of evidence. *Leisure interest:* walking. *Address:* No. 37, Kirula Place, Off Kirula Road, Colombo 05, Sri Lanka (home).

PEIRIS, Mohan, PC; Sri Lankan lawyer, judge and government official; m. Priyanthi Peiris; one d.; ed St Joseph's Coll., Colombo, Royal Coll., Colombo, Sri Lanka Law Coll., Nat. Inst. of Trial Advocacy, Harvard Law School, Centre for Police and Criminal Justice Studies, Jesus Coll., England, George Washington Univ., USA; called to the Bar 1975; began legal practice under sr lawyers D. R. P. Gunatilleke and Daya Perera; enrolled as a solicitor, Supreme Court of England and Wales 1978; joined Attorney-Gen.'s Dept as State Counsel 1981, later became Sr State Counsel and served for more than 15 years; est. pvt. practice in Unofficial Bar, specialized in original and appellate courts in areas of admin. law, commercial law, land law, fundamental rights, industrial law, injunctions and criminal law and as arbitrator; Attorney-Gen. 2009–11; Sr Legal Adviser to Cabinet of Ministers 2011–13; Chief Justice of the Supreme Court 2013–15 (appointment deemed illegal by govt 2015); Chair. Inter Agency Comm. to Implement the Interim Recommendations of the Lessons Learnt and Reconciliation Comm. (LLRC); fmr Chair. Bd of Examiners for Intermediate Examination and Examiner of Sri Lanka Law Coll.; fmr Visiting Lecturer, Faculty of Law, Univ. of Colombo; fmr Deputy Pres. Sri Lanka Bar Asscn; mem. Sri Lankan Del. to Universal Periodic review at Eighth Session of the Human Rights Council of the UN.

PEIROTES, Yves Jean-Marie, MSc; French business executive; b. 7 Nov. 1940, Epinal, Vosges; s. of Marcel Georges Peirotes and Germaine Eugénie Schaeffer; m. 1st Victoria Longacre 1968 (divorced 1981); two s.; m. 2nd Viviane France Bastiani 1987; ed Lycée de Belfort, Lycée Kleber, Strasbourg, Ecole Polytechnique, Paris, Ecole Nat. Supérieure du Génie Maritime, Paris, Univ. of Calif., Berkeley; prin. engineer, Maritime Eng, Del. Ministérielle pour l'Armement 1966–70; Head of Logistics, Strafor, Strasbourg 1971–72, Tech. and Industrial Devt Dir 1972–77; Gen. Man. Industrial Equipment Div., Forges de Strasbourg 1977–81; Man. Dir Air Industrie 1981–84; Chair., Man. Dir Sofiltra Poelman 1981–84; Deputy Man. Dir Cie Industrielle et Financière de Pompey 1984–85; Gen. Man. White Goods Div. Electrolux France 1985–90, White Goods & Floor Care Appliances Div. 1990–94, Man. Dir Electrolux France SA 1995–97, apptd Chair. and Man. Dir

1997; Chair. Usines et Fonderies Arthur Martin 1985; Pres. Bureau Départemental d'Industrialisation des Ardennes 1987–91; fmr mem. Advisory Bd Senlis branch, Banque de France 1995; Chevalier, Ordre nat. du Mérite. *Leisure interests:* skiing, jogging, swimming.

PEISACH, Max, PhD, DSc, FRSSA, FRPSL; South African nuclear analytical chemist; b. 3 Aug. 1926, Birzai, Lithuania; s. of Hyman Peisach and Sonia Kantor; m. Eunice Sheila Glick 1950; one s. three d.; ed Boys' High School, Worcester, Univ. of Cape Town; demonstrator, Univ. of Cape Town 1948–49, Jr lecturer 1949–50, lecturer 1950–53; Research Officer, Nat. Chemical Research Lab., S African Council for Scientific and Industrial Research 1953–57, Sr Research Officer 1957–60; Head, Isotope Production, Israel Atomic Energy Comm. 1960–63; Head Chem. Div., Southern Univs Nuclear Inst. 1963–83; Head Nuclear Analytical Chem. Div., Nat. Accelerator Centre 1983–91, Chief Specialist Researcher 1986–91; mem. Int. Cttee on Modern Trends in Activation Analysis 1969–91, Hon. Life mem. 1994–; Nat. Rep., IUPAC Comm. on Radiochemistry 1985–96; Research Consultant, Witwatersrand Chem. Ion-Beam Analysis Group 1992–98; Research Fellow, Solid State and Materials, Nat. Accelerator Centre 1994; Research Adviser, Dept of Materials and Interfaces, Weizmann Inst., Rehovot, Israel 1995–2004; Assoc. Royal Soc. of Chem. (London) 1951–61, Fellow 1962–86; Fellow, Royal Soc. of SA 1984–, Royal Philatelic Soc. London 1966–; mem. S African Chemical Inst. 1952–96, Sr mem. 1996–98, Life mem. 1998–; Hon. Citizen, State of Tenn., USA 1965; Order of the Postal Stone 1988; AE & CI Gold Medal 1965, Roll of Distinguished Philatelists (South Africa) 1966, Int. Hevesy Medal 1981, South Africa Chemical Inst. Gold Medal 1986. *Publications include:* Elemental Analysis by Particle Accelerators; many scientific papers; research papers on nuclear analytical chem.; book chapters on specialized analytical topics; research articles on philately of South Africa and Israel. *Leisure interests:* philately, numismatics, judging philatelic exhbns. *Address:* Sderot Ye'elim 30/4, Beersheba 84739 (home); PO Box 3581, Beersheba 8413502, Israel. *Telephone:* 8-6442232. *E-mail:* mpeisach@bezeqint.net.

PEJANOVIĆ-ĐURIŠIĆ, Milica, BSc, MSc, PhD; Montenegrin electrical engineer, academic, diplomatist and politician; b. 27 April 1959, Nikšić; m. Zoran Djurišić; two s.; ed Univ. of Montenegro, Podgorica, Univ. of Belgrade; Teaching/Research Asst, Dept of Electrical Eng, Univ. of Montenegro 1983–88, Asst Prof. 1988–94, Assoc. Prof. 1994–98, Prof. 1998–; mem. State Presidency of Montenegro 1990–92; mem. Ass. of Repub. of Montenegro 1992–2001; Amb. of State Union of Serbia and Montenegro to Belgium and Luxembourg 2004–06, Amb. of Montenegro to France, Monaco and UNESCO 2007–10; Minister of Defence 2012–16; consultant to Ericsson ETK, Zagreb 2002–04, Telecom Montenegro 2002–05, Ericsson, Stockholm 2002–04, Agency for Telecommunications, Montenegro 2004–07; mem. Democratic Party of Socialists of Montenegro, Vice-Pres. 1992–97, Pres. 1997–98.

PEJČINOVIĆ BURIĆ, Marija, BSc; Croatian politician; *Deputy Prime Minister and Minister of Foreign and European Affairs;* b. 9 April 1963, Mostar, People's Repub. of Bosnia and Herzegovina, Fed. People's Repub. of Yugoslavia; ed Univ. of Zagreb, Coll. d'Europe, Bruges; Expert Assoc. for Foreign Trade, Končar Engineering, Zagreb 1988–91; Sec. Gen., Europe House Zagreb 1991–94, Dir 1995–97; Deputy Sec. Gen., European Movement Croatia 1991–94; Dir of Corp. Communications, PLIVA Inc. (pharmaceutical co.), Zagreb 1997–2000; Asst Minister of European Integration 2000–04, mem. Croatia–EU negotiating team for Stabilisation and Asscn 2000–01, nat. coordinator for ISPA (EU Structural Pre-Accession Instrument) 2004–06, Sec. of State for European Integration 2004–05, Sec. of State for Foreign Affairs and European Integration 2005–08, mem. Croatian negotiating team for EU membership 2006–08, Sec. of State for Foreign and European Affairs 2016–17, Deputy Prime Minister and Minister of Foreign and European Affairs 2017–; mem. Sabor (parl.) (HDZ) for 6th electoral district 2008–11; ind. consultant on European policy (worked with EU and UNDP) 2013–16; mem. Bd of Dirs Centre for European Policy Studies, Brussels 2016–; mem. Hrvatska Demokratska Zajednica (HDZ—Croatian Democratic Union). *Address:* Ministry of Foreign and European Affairs, 10000 Zagreb, trg Nikole Šubića Zrinskog 7–8, Croatia (office). *Telephone:* (1) 4569964 (office). *Fax:* (1) 4551795 (office). *E-mail:* ministarstvo@mvep.hr (office). *Website:* www.mvep.hr (office).

PEKHTIN, Vladimir Alekseyevich, DrTechSci; Russian politician and engineer; b. 9 Dec. 1950, Leningrad; m.; one s.; ed Leningrad Polytech. Inst.; engineer with Kolymagestroi (power co.), then Kolymaenergo 1974–97; Chair. Magadan Regional Duma 1994; Chair. Council of Feds of Russia 1997; mem. State Duma (Parl.) 1999–2013, Head Cttee on Property; Head Yedinstvo Parl. Group in State Duma (Parl.) 2001–07, fmr First Deputy, United Russia Parl. Group; fmr Deputy Chair. of Man. Bd, RusHydro; Order, Friendship of Peoples, Merited Constructor of Russia, Hon. Power Engineer. *Leisure interests:* hunting, shooting (Master of Sports).

PEKKANEN, Raimo Oskari, LLD; Finnish judge; b. 29 July 1927, Kivennapa; m. Eeva Niittyla 1953; two s.; ed Univ. of Helsinki; State Admin. 1950–60; researcher and teacher, Helsinki School of Econ. and Univ. of Tampere 1961–67; Acting Prof. in Labour Law, Univ. of Helsinki 1967–68; Justice, Supreme Admin. Court of Finland 1969–90; Sec.-Gen. Ministry of Justice (on leave of absence from Supreme Admin. Court) 1982–90; Judge, European Court of Human Rights 1990–98; apptd Chair. Sub-Cttee on Medical Research Ethics, Nat. Advisory Bd on Health Care Ethics 2000; Commdr Order of Finnish Lion, Commdr Order of Finnish White Rose; KJ Ståhlberg Medal. *Publications:* Mixed Type Contracts of Employment 1966, On the Commencement and Termination of Employment Relationships 1968, On Participation in Water System Regulation 1968; articles in legal publs. *Leisure interests:* fly-fishing, skiing. *Address:* Nyyrikinte 8, 02100 Espoo, Finland (home). *Telephone:* (9) 4554557 (home). *E-mail:* raimo.pekkanen@ppl.inet.fi (home).

PEKKARINEN, Mauri, MSc; Finnish politician; b. 6 Oct. 1947, Kinnula; m. Raija Kaarina Pekkarinen 1979; four c.; ed Univ. of Jyväskylä; mem. Jyväskylä Town Council 1977–2004, 2008–; mem. Parl. (Finnish Centre Party) 1979–, Vice-Pres. Finnish Centre Party Parl. Group 1987–91, Chair. 1999–2003, Chair. Finance Cttee 1995–99; Political Sec. Ministry of Labour 1976–77, Ministry of the Interior 1978–79; Minister of the Interior 1991–95, of Trade and Industry 2003–07, of Econ. Affairs 2008–11; Chair. Cen. Finland 1999–2002, Cen. Finnish Sports Fed. 1995–2002, Asscn of Finnish Local Councils 1997–2001; Vice-Pres. Biathlon Asscn 2006–; mem. Cen. Finland Regional Planning Asscn of the Fed. Govt 1981–84; mem. Supervisory Bd Export Credit Agency 1982–86; mem. Supervisory Bd State Guarantee Fund 1995–96; mem. Supervisory Bd Finnish Broadcasting Company YLE 1982–91, Chair. 1987–91; Bd mem. Cen. Prov. of Finland 1985–90; Chair. Cen. Finland Centre Party constituency 1987–91; mem. Parliamentary Supervisory Bd, Bank of Finland 1995–2003, Chair. 2003; DSc hc (Lappeenranta) 2008, (Jyväskylä) 2009. *Leisure interests:* music, sport. *Address:* c/o Ministry of Employment and the Economy, Aleksanterinkatu 4, POB 32, 00170 Helsinki, Finland.

PELAELO, Moses Dinekere, BCom, MBA; Botswana central banker; *Governor, Bank of Botswana;* ed Univ. of Swaziland, Univ. of Miami, USA; Lecturer, Accounting and Man. Studies, Botswana Inst. of Admin and Commerce and Univ. of Botswana 1984–90; apptd Sr Bank Examiner, Bank of Botswana 1990, Head of Admin. Services Dept 1996, Dir Banking Supervision Dept 1996, sabbatical leave at Financial Stability Inst., BIS, Basel 2003–06, Deputy Gov. Bank of Botswana 2006–16, Gov. 2016–, mem. Exec. Cttee, High-Level Inter-Agency Cttee for Financial Sector Devt Strategy 2012–16, mem. Currency Design Cttee, Monetary Policy Cttee, Investment Cttee. *Address:* Bank of Botswana, PMB 154, 17938 Khama Crescent, Gaborone, Botswana (office). *Telephone:* 3606000 (office). *Fax:* 3974859 (office). *E-mail:* selwej@bob.bw (office). *Website:* www.bankofbotswana.bw (office).

PELÉ; Brazilian fmr professional footballer; b. (Edson Arantes do Nascimento), 23 Oct. 1940, Três Corações, Minas Gerais State; s. of João Ramos do Nascimento (Fluminense footballer nicknamed Dondinho) and Maria Celeste Arantes; m. 1st Rosemeri dos Reis Cholby 1966 (divorced 1978); one s. two d.; m. 2nd Assiria Lemos Seixas 1994; one s. one d. (twins); ed Santos Univ.; forward; first played football at Baurú, São Paulo 1952–56; mem. Baurú Atlético Clube; played for Santos Football Club 1956–74 (438 appearances, scored 474 goals, won Campeonato Paulista 1958, 1960, 1961, 1962, 1964, 1965, 1967, 1968, 1969, 1973, Torneio Rio-São Paulo 1959, 1963, 1964, Torneio Roberto Gomes Pedrosa (Taça de Prata) 1968, Taça Brasil 1961, 1962, 1963, 1964, 1965, Copa Libertadores 1962, 1963, Intercontinental Cup 1962, 1963, South-American Recopa 1968, Recopa Intercontinental 1968), Dir 1993–; played for Brazil nat. team 1957–71, first int. game vs Argentina, played in World Cup 1958, 1962, 1966, 1970; finished career with New York Cosmos 1975–77 (NASL Champions 1977); Chair. Pelé Soccer Camps 1978–82; Special Minister for Sports, Govt of Brazil 1994–98; Dir Soccer Clinics; three World Cup winners' medals 1958, 1962, 1970; two World Club Championship medals; Roca Cup winner 1957, 1963; 110 int. caps, 97 goals for Brazil; 1,114 appearances for Santos, 1,088 goals; career total 1,282 goals in 1,364 games, most goals in season 53 (1958); Goodwill Amb. for UN Conf. on Environment and Devt, Rio de Janeiro 1992; Hans Christian Andersen Amb. 2003–; UNESCO Goodwill Amb.; appeared at closing ceremony of Summer Olympics, London Aug. 2012; Hon. Pres. New York Cosmos 2010; Hon. KBE 1997; hon. degree (Univ. of Edinburgh, UK) 2012; FIFA World Cup Golden Ball (Best Player) 1970, BBC Sports Personality of the Year Overseas Personality 1970, Int. Peace Award 1978, Athlete of the Century 1980, WHO Medal 1989, Gold Medal for outstanding services to the sport (Brazil) 1995, elected Athlete of the Century by IOC 1999, elected Athlete of the Century by Reuters News Agency 1999, UNICEF Football Player of the Century 1999, FIFA World Footballer of the Century (with Diego Maradona) 2000, elected Football Player of the Century by France Football's Golden Ball Winners 1999, elected Football Player of the Century by Int. Fed. of Football History and Statistics (IFFHS) 1999, elected South America Football Player of the Century by IFFHS 1999, Laureus World Sports Awards Lifetime Achievement Award from Pres. Nelson Mandela 2000, BBC Sports Personality of the Year Lifetime Achievement Award 2005, World Soccer Greatest XI of All Time 2013, FIFA Ballon d'Or Prix d'Honneur 2013. *Films include:* O Barão Otelo no Barato dos Bilhões 1971, A Marcha 1973, Os Trombadinhas 1978, Escape to Victory 1981, A Minor Miracle 1983, Pedro Mico 1985, Os Trapalhões e o Rei do Futebol 1986, Hotshot 1987, Solidão, Uma Linda História de Amor 1990, Mike Bassett: England Manager 2001, ESPN SportsCentury 2004, Pelé Eterno (documentary about Pelé's career) 2004. *Music:* has composed numerous songs in Samba style. *Television includes:* Os Estranhos (series) 1969. *Publications:* Eu Sou Pelé 1962, Jogando com Pelé 1974, My Life and the Beautiful Game 1977, Pelé Soccer Training Program 1982, The World Cup Murders (novel) 1988, Pelé: The Autobiography 2006. *Address:* 75 Rockefeller Plaza, New York, NY 10019, USA.

PELED, Efrat, BA, MBA, CPA; Israeli business executive; *Chairman and CEO, Arison Investments;* b. 1974; ed Tel-Aviv Univ., Kellogg-Recanati (int. programme of Northwestern and Tel-Aviv Univs); began career as Chief Financial Officer, Ted Arison Family Foundation in Israel and USA –2003, CEO SAFO (Shari Arison's Family Office) LLC, Miami, Fla 2003–, CEO Arison Investments 2006–, Chair. 2010–, Vice-Chair. Miya (part of Arison Group); Dir Miya, Bank Hapoalim 2006–, Shikun & Binui (real estate and infrastructure group), Israel Salt Industries. *Address:* Arison Investments, Golda Center, 23 Shaul Hamelech Boulevard, Tel-Aviv 64367, Israel (office). *Telephone:* (3) 6073100 (office). *Fax:* (3) 6073101 (office). *E-mail:* info@arison.co.il (office). *Website:* www.arison.co.il (office).

PELEVIN, Viktor Olegovich; Russian writer; b. 27 Nov. 1962, Moscow; ed Moscow Power Engineering Inst., Gorky Inst. of Literature, Moscow; army service; corresp., Face-to-Face journal 1989–90; journal Science and Religion; author of numerous novels and stories; Wanderer Prize 1995, Nonino Literary Prize 2001, Robert Schönefeld Prize 2000, 2001, Grigoriev Prize 2004. *Publications include:* (most in trans.) Omon Ra (novel) 1996, Vera Pavlovna's Ninth Dream, Reconstructor, Prince of Gosplan, The Yellow Arrow (novella) 1996, Ivan Kublakhanov, Generation, Babylon, The Blue Lantern (short stories) (Russian Booker Prize 1997), The Life of Insects 1998, Crystal World, A Werewolf Problem in Central Russia (short stories) 1998, Chapayev and Pustota (Buddha's Little Finger, aka Babylon) 2000, The Clay Machine-Gun (novel), Generation P 1999, Homo Zapiens (aka Generation P) 2002, Dialectic for the Transitional Phase From Nowhere to Nowhere 2003, The Sacred Book of the Werewolf 2006, The Helmet of Horror 2006, Empire V 2006, t 2009, S.N.U.F.F 2011, Batman Apollo 2013, Lubov k trem cukerbrinam (Love for Three Zuckerbrins) 2014. *Address:* c/o Aragi Inc., 143 West 27th Street, #4F, New York, NY 10001, USA (office).

PELHAM, Sir Hugh Reginald Brentnall, Kt, MA, PhD, FRS; British research scientist; b. 26 Aug. 1954, Shawford, nr Winchester, Hants.; s. of Reginald Arthur Pelham and Pauline Mary Pelham; m. Mariann Bienz; one s. one d.; ed Marlborough Coll. and Christ's Coll., Cambridge; Research Fellow, Christ's Coll., Cambridge 1978–84; Postdoctoral Fellow, Carnegie Inst. of Washington, Baltimore, Md 1979–81; mem. Scientific Staff, MRC Lab. of Molecular Biology, Cambridge 1981–, Head of Cell Biology Div. 1995–2006, Deputy Dir 1996–2006, Dir 2006–18; mem. European Molecular Biology Org. 1985, Academia Europaea 1990, Acad. of Medical Sciences 1998; Hon. Prof. of Molecular Biology, Univ. of Cambridge; Colworth Medal 1988, European Molecular Biology Org. Medal 1989, Louis Jeantet Prize for Medicine 1991, King Faisal Int. Prize for Science 1996, Royal Soc. Croonian Medal 1999. *Publications:* articles on molecular and cell biology in scientific journals.

PELL, HE Cardinal George, AC, STL, MEd, DPhil (Oxon.), DD, FACE; Australian ecclesiastic; b. 8 June 1941, Ballarat, Vic.; s. of George Arthur Pell and Margaret Lillian Burke; ed Loreto Convent and St Patrick's Coll., Ballarat, Corpus Christi Coll., Werribee, Propaganda Fide Coll. and Urban Univ., Rome, Italy, Univ. of Oxford, UK, Monash Univ., Vic.; signed to play professional Australian Rules Football with Richmond Football Club, Melbourne 1959 (currently Vice-Patron), chose to study for priesthood; fmr sports coach in soccer, Aussie Rules and rowing; ordained priest 1966; Asst Priest, Swan Hill 1971–72, Ballarat East 1973–83; Episcopal Vicar for Educ., Diocese of Ballarat 1973–84; Dir Aquinas Campus, Inst. of Catholic Educ. 1974–84, Prin., Inst. of Catholic Educ. (now merged into Australian Catholic Univ.) 1981–84; Rector Corpus Christi Seminary 1985–87; Parish Priest, Mentone and Bishop for the Southern Region of Melbourne 1987–96; Auxiliary Bishop of Melbourne and Titular Bishop of Scala 1987–96; Apostolic Visitor on behalf of the Congregation for Evangelization of Peoples to the seminaries of New Zealand 1994, Papua New Guinea and the Solomon Islands 1995, the Pacific 1996, Irian Jaya and Sulawesi 1998; Metropolitan Archbishop of Melbourne 1996–2001; Metropolitan Archbishop of Sydney 2001–14; cr. Cardinal (Cardinal Priest of Santa Maria Dominica Mazzarello) 2003; participated in Conclave of Cardinal Electors 2005, 2013; Prefect of the Secr. for the Economy 2014–19; mem. Nat. Catholic Educ. Comm. 1988–97; Sec. Bishops' Cttee for Educ. 1994–97, 2000–03 (Chair. 2003–06), Council of Cardinals for the Study of Admin. and Econ. Problems of the Holy See 2007–14; Chair. Caritas Australia 1988–97; Chair. cttee charged with setting up the new Australian Catholic Univ. 1989, served as Univ.'s Foundation Pro-Chancellor 1991–95, Pres. Univ.'s Bd of Owners 1996–; fmrly Chair. Australian Catholic Bishops' Cttee for Doctrine and Morals; mem. Bishops' Cttee for Justice Devt and Peace 1987–97, Pontifical Council for Justice and Peace 1990–95, 2002–, Vatican Congregation for the Doctrine of the Faith 1990–2000, Vatican Council of the Synod of Bishops 2001–05, 2006–08, 2012–18, Supreme Cttee of the Pontifical Missions Socs 2005, Vatican Congregation for Bishops 2012, Advisory Group of Cardinals to Pope Francis 2013–18; Visiting Scholar, Campion Hall, Oxford 1979, St Edmund's Coll., Cambridge, UK 1983; weekly columnist for Sunday Telegraph, Sydney 2001–14; has lectured throughout Australia and in USA, UK, Ireland, New Zealand, Croatia and Italy; convicted of sexual assault offences in Australia and sentenced to six years in prison March 2019; Hon. Fellow, St Edmund's Coll., Cambridge 2003; Grand Prior Equestrian Order of the Holy Sepulchre of Jerusalem, Australian Lieutenancy-Southern 1998–2001, Grand Prior for the Order in NSW 2001, Kt Grand Cross 2003, Grand Cross of Merit, Order of St Lazarus, Nat. Chaplain 2001–07, Ecclesiastic Grand Cross of St Lazarus 2003, Bailiff Grand Cross of Honour and Devotion, Sovereign Mil. Order of Malta 2007, Conventual Chaplain 2007, Thomas Aquinas Medallion, Thomas Aquinas Coll. USA 2008, Bailiff Grand Cross of Justice, Sacred Mil. Constantinian Order of St George 2011, Medal of Gratitude (Poland) 2011; Dr hc (Christendom Coll., USA) 2006, (Univ. of Notre Dame) 2010; Centenary Medal 2003. *Publications include:* The Sisters of St Joseph in Swan Hill 1922–72 1972, Catholicism in Australia 1988, Rerum Novarum – One Hundred Years Later 1992, Issues of Faith and Morals 1996, Catholicism and the Architecture of Freedom 1999, Be Not Afraid 2004, God and Caesar: Selected Essays on Religion, Politics and Society 2007, Free for All: Negotiating Freedom in a World of Individuals 2009, Test Everything: Hold Fast to What is Good 2010, One Christian Perspective on Climate Change 2011, Contemplating Christ with Luke 2012. *Leisure interests:* reading, writing, football.

PELLEGRINI, Federica; Italian swimmer; b. 5 Aug. 1988, Mirano, Venice; Olympic Games, Athens 2004: silver medal, 200m freestyle; Olympic Games, Beijing 2008: gold medal, 200m freestyle; World Championships (long course): gold medal, 200m and 400m freestyle, Rome 2009, 200m and 400m freestyle, Shanghai 2011, silver medal, 200m freestyle, Montreal 2005, Barcelona 2013, silver medal, 200m freestyle, Kazan 2015, silver medal, 4×200m freestyle relay, Kazan 2015, bronze medal, 200m freestyle, Melbourne 2007; World Championships (short course): silver medal, 200m freestyle, Shanghai 2006, bronze medal, 400m freestyle, Shanghai 2006, 400m freestyle, Dubai 2010; European Championships (long course): gold medal, 400m freestyle, Eindhoven 2008, 200m freestyle, Budapest 2010, gold medal, 200m freestyle, London 2016, silver medal, 4×100m freestyle relay, Eindhoven 2008, silver medal, 4×100m freestyle relay, London 2016, silver medal, 4×100m mixed freestyle relay, London 2016, silver medal, 4×100m mixed medley relay, London 2016, bronze medal, 4×200m freestyle relay, Eindhoven 2008, 800m freestyle, Budapest 2010; European Championships (short course): gold medal, 200m freestyle, Trieste 2005, 200m freestyle, Rijeka 2008, 200m freestyle, Istanbul 2009, 800m freestyle, Eindhoven 2010, silver medal, 400m freestyle, Helsinki 2006, 400m freestyle, Debrecen 2007, bronze medal, 400m freestyle, Trieste 2005, 4×50m medley relay, Rijeka 2008, 4×50m medley relay, Eindhoven 2010; Summer Universiade: gold medal, 200m freestyle, Bangkok 2007, 400m freestyle, Bangkok 2007; swims for Circolo Canottieri Aniene club; coaches, Alberto Castagnetti –2009, Philippe Lucas 2009–11, Federico Bonifacenti 2011, Claudio Rossetto 2012, Philippe Lucas 2013; Flag-bearer for Italy, Summer Olympic Games, Rio de Janeiro 2016; World Swimmer of the Year 2009, European Swimmer of the Year 2009, 2010, 2011. *Achievements include:* became first female swimmer to breach the four-minute barrier in 400m freestyle 2009; first female swimmer in history to get a medal in the same event at six consecutive World Championships. *Address:* c/o Circolo Canottieri Aniene a.s.d., Lungotevere dell'Acqua Acetosa 119, Rome, Italy. *Telephone:* (02) 121341008. *E-mail:* info@ccaniene.com. *Website:* www.ccaniene.com.

PELLEGRINI, Peter; Slovak engineer and politician; *Prime Minister;* b. 6 Oct. 1975, Banská Bystrica, Slovak Socialist Repub., Czechoslovak Socialist Repub.; ed Matej Bel Univ., Banská Bystrica, Tech. Univ. of Košice; self-employed 1998–2002; asst to mem. of Národná rada Slovenskej republiky (Nat. Council of Slovak Repub.—Parl.) 2002–06; mem. Smer-Sociálna demokracia (Direction-Social Democracy); mem. Národná rada Slovenskej republiky 2006–, mem. Cttee on Econ. Affairs (Chair. Comm. on Transport, Postal Services, Communications and Informatisation of Soc.) 2006–10, Cttee for Review of Decisions of Nat. Security Authority 2006–10, Mandate and Immunity Cttee 2006–10, Cttee on Finance and Budget 2010–12, Cttee for Review of Decisions of Nat. Security Authority 2010–12, Chair. (Speaker) Národná rada Slovenskej republiky 2014–16; State Sec., Ministry of Finance 2012–14; Digital Leader for Slovak Repub. 2012–; Minister of Educ., Science, Research and Sport July–Nov. 2014; Deputy Prime Minister, responsible for Investment 2016–18, Prime Minister 2018–; Chair. Supervisory Bd, Nat. Nuclear Fund 2012–14, Slovenská konsolidačná, a.s. 2012–14; mem. Supervisory Bd, Social Insurance Agency 2012–14; mem. Scientific Bd, Faculty of Econs, Matej Bel Univ. 2012–14, Econ. and Social Council of Slovak Repub. 2012, Admin. Council of Council of Europe Devt Bank 2012–14. *Address:* Office of the Government, nám. Slobody 1, 813 70 Bratislava, Slovakia (office). *Telephone:* (2) 5729-5111 (office). *Fax:* (2) 5249-7595 (office). *E-mail:* peter_pellegrini@nrsr.sk (office); vicepremier@vlada.gov.sk (office). *Website:* www.vlada.gov.sk (office).

PELLERIN, Fleur; French (b. South Korean) politician; b. (Kim Jong-suk), 29 Aug. 1973, Seoul, South Korea; m. Laurent Olléon; one d.; ed École Supérieure des Sciences Économiques et Commerciales, Cergy-Pontoise, Institut d'École Politiques (Sciences Po), Paris, École Nationale d'Admin, Strasbourg; abandoned on streets of Seoul at three or four days old, sent to an orphanage, adopted six months later by a French family; Magistrate of the Court of Auditors 2001–05, Rapporteur to Standing Cttee on Scrutiny of Companies and Perception of Copyright (SPRD); external audit assignments within statutory auditors of UN in Iraq, New York and Geneva 2001–06; Assoc. Dir Tilder (communication strategy consultancy) 2007–08; Rapporteur, Comm. on Public Ethics 2007–09; Auditor and Counsellor at Court of Auditors 2009–; in charge of societal and digital economy issues in François Hollande's presidential election campaign 2012; Minister Delegate with responsibility for Small and Medium Enterprises, Innovation, and the Digital Economy attached to the Minister for Econ. Regeneration (fmr Ministry of the Economy, Finance, and Industry) 2012–16; fmr mem. Bd and Pres. Club XXIe siècle; fmr mem. Bd and Treas. Entretiens de l'excellence; Dir Unis-Cité asscn; fmr Dir Fondation de Royaumont; fmr mem. Cttee on Sanctions of ARJEL; fmr mem. Bd of Dirs Public Sénat; fmr mem. Diversity Cttee of France Télévisions.

PELLI, César, MArch, FAIA, RIBA, JIA; Argentine/American architect and academic; *Senior Principal, Pelli Clarke Pelli Architects;* b. 12 Oct. 1926, Tucumán, Argentina; s. of Victor Vicente Pelli and Teresa S. Pelli (née Suppa); m. Diana Balmori 1950; two s.; ed Universidad Nacional de Tucumán, Univ. of Illinois-Urbana Champaign; emigrated to USA 1952, naturalized 1964; known for designing some of the world's tallest buildings and other major urban landmarks; Project Designer, Eero Saarinen Offices, Mich., Conn. 1954–64; Dir of Design, Daniel, Mann, Johnson & Medenhall 1964–68; Partner in Charge of Design, Gruen Assocs 1968–76; Prof. of Architecture, Yale Univ. 1977–, Dean Yale School of Architecture 1977–84; Sr Prin., César Pelli & Assocs 1977– (now known as Pelli Clarke Pelli Architects); mem. American Acad. of Arts and Letters; 14 hon. doctorates including Hon. Dr of Arts (Yale) 2008; over 200 awards and prizes, including UN City Competition First Prize, Vienna 1969, Arnold W. Brunner Prize, Nat. Inst. Arts and Letters 1978, AIA Honor Award for Fed. Office Bldg, Lawndale, San Bernardino City Hall, Calif., Arnold M. Brunner Memorial Prize, Nat. Acad. of Design 1991, listed by AIA amongst the ten most influential living American architects 1991, AIA Honor Award 1994, AIA Firm Award 1989, and Gold Medal 1995, The Lynn S. Beedle Lifetime Achievement Award, Council on Tall Buildings and Urban Habitat 2008, Diamond Konex Award for Visual Arts, Konex Foundation 2012. *Buildings completed include:* Worldway Postal Center, Los Angeles Int. Airport 1966, Kukui Gardens housing, Honolulu, Hawaii 1967, San Bernardino City Hall, Calif. 1969, US Embassy, Tokyo 1972, Commons Centre and Mall, Columbus, Ind. 1973, Eaton's Dept Store, Vancouver, BC 1973, Design Center, Los Angeles 1973, 1988 and 2014, Wintergarden Arboretum, Niagara Falls, New York 1977 (demolished 2009), World Financial Center, New York 1981–87, Residential Tower atop Museum of Modern Art, New York 1984, Cleveland Clinic 1984–86, Mattatuck Museum Arts and History Center renovation, Waterbury, Conn. 1984, Carnegie Hall Tower, New York 1987–90, Maryland Residence, Bethesda 1987–89, One Canada Square, Canary Wharf, London, UK 1987–91, Wells Fargo Center (fmrly Norwest Center), Minneapolis 1988, Gaviidae Common, Minneapolis 1989, Nippon Telegraph and Telephone HQ, Tokyo 1990, Roy Nutt Math., Eng & Computer Science Center, Trinity Coll., Hartford, Conn. 1990, 181 West Madison Street, Chicago, Ill. 1990, Key Tower, Cleveland, Ohio 1991, 777 Tower, Los Angeles 1991, Bank of America Corp. Center, Charlotte, North Carolina 1992, Plaza Tower, Costa Mesa, Calif. 1992, Worrell Professional Center, Wake Forest Univ. School of Law 1993, Physics and Astronomy Bldg, Univ. of Washington, Seattle 1994, Aronoff Center for Performing Arts, Cincinnati, Ohio 1995, Edificio República, Buenos Aires 1996, Residencial del Bosque, Mexico City 1996, Owens Corning World HQ, Toledo, Ohio 1996, expansion of Washington Reagan Nat. Airport, Washington, DC (AIA Design Award 1998, Design for Transportation Award 2000) 1997, Overture Center, Madison, Wis. 1998, Petronas Twin Towers, Kuala Lumpur, Malaysia (Aga Khan Award 2004) 1998, Schuster Center, Dayton, Ohio 1998, Cheung Kong Centre, Hong Kong 1999, Zurich tower office bldg in The Hague, Netherlands 1999, Kurayoshi Park Square, Kurayoshi, Japan 2000, Boston Bank Bldg, Buenos Aires 2000, KABC-TV, Los Angeles 2000, Citigroup Centre, 25 Canada Square, Canary Wharf, London 2001, Bucksbaum Center for the Arts, Grinnell Coll. 2001, Athletic and Fitness Center, Grinnell Coll. 2001, The Investment Building, Washington, DC 2001, JP MorganChase Bldg, San Francisco 2002, Enron HQ, 1500 Louisiana Street, Houston, Tex. 2002, Gerald Ratner Athletics Center, Univ. of Chicago 2003, Two Int. Finance Centre, Hong Kong 2003, Center for Drama and Film & the Martel Theater, Vassar Coll. 2003, 25 Bank Street, Canary Wharf, Docklands, London 2003, 40 Bank Street, Canary Wharf, Docklands, London 2003, Benjamin & Mariam Schuster Performing Arts Center, Dayton, Ohio 2003, Goldman Sachs Tower, Jersey City, New Jersey 2004, Malone Engineering Center, Yale Univ.

2005, Theodore Roosevelt Fed. Bldg Eastern Dist Courthouse, Brooklyn, New York 2006, Science and Eng Research and Classroom Complex, Univ. of Houston 2006, Minneapolis Public Library's Central br. 2006, Joe Rosenfield '25 Center, Grinnell Coll. 2006, Renée and Henry Segerstrom Concert Hall, Segerstrom Center for the Arts, Orange County Performing Arts Center, Costa Mesa, Calif. 2006, Thomas E. Golden Jr Center, St Thomas More Catholic Chapel and Center, Yale Univ. 2006, Adrienne Arsht Center for the Performing Arts, Miami, Fla 2006, Torre de Cristal, Madrid, Spain 2008, Repsol-YPF Bldg, Buenos Aires 2008, St Regis Residences and Hotel, Mexico City 2008, Business Instructional Facility, Univ. of Illinois 2008, Co-operative Arts and Humanities High School, New Haven, Conn. 2009, Connecticut Science Center 2009, Aria Resort & Casino, the central feature of CityCenter, Las Vegas, 2009, Shanghai IFC, Pudong, sister project of Two Int. Finance Centre, Hong Kong 2010, New Airport Terminal Bldg (Phase 1), Winnipeg James Armstrong Richardson Int. Airport 2011, Iberdrola Tower, office bldg, Bilbao, Spain 2011, St Katharine Drexel Chapel, Xavier Univ., New Orleans 2012, UniCredit Headquarters, Porta Nuova Garibaldi, Milan, Italy 2013, Ocean Financial Center, Singapore 2013, The Theatre School, DePaul Univ., Chicago 2013, The Landmark, Abu Dhabi, UAE 2013, Torre Mitikah, Mexico City 2014, Utah Performing Arts Center 2016, Chemical Biomolecular Engineering and Chemistry Building, Ohio State Univ. 2015, Lanphier Center for Mathematics, Choate Rosemary Hall 2015, Center for Innovation in Medical Professions Cleveland State Univ. 2015, Yale-NUS Coll., Singapore 2015, Buerger Center for Advanced Pediatric Care, Children's Hospital of Philadelphia 2015, Hancher Auditorium, Iowa City, Iowa 2016, Maral Explanada, Mar del Plata, Argentina 2016, FMC Tower, Cira Centre South, Philadelphia 2016, Riverview Plaza, Wuhan, China 2016, Torre Sevilla, Sevilla, Spain 2016. *Publications include:* Architecture and Urbanism 1985, César Pelli (monograph) 1991, César Pelli, in The Master Architect series 1993, Cesar Pelli: Recent Themes (co-author) 1995, World Architecture Review 1998, Observations for Young Architects 1999; various articles in specialist journals. *Address:* Pelli Clarke Pelli Architects, 1056 Chapel Street, New Haven, CT 06510, USA (office). *Telephone:* (203) 777-2515 (office). *Fax:* (203) 787-2856 (office). *E-mail:* InfoNH@pcparch.com (office). *Website:* pcparch.com (office).

PËLLUMBI, Servet, PhD; Albanian politician; b. 14 Dec. 1936, Korçë; s. of Ismail Pëllumbi and Hazize Pëllumbi; ed State Univ. of St Petersburg; Prof. of Philosophy 1960–74; Univ. Prof. of Philosophy 1974–91; Vice-Chair. Socialist Party of Albania 1991–96; mem. Parl. 1992–2003; Speaker of Parl. of Albania 2002–05; Academic Dir Inst. of Political and Social Studies; Dir Publishing Bd, Policy & Society magazine. *Publications include:* Think Differently, Transition in its Light-Shade, Endeavour in Political Sociology, Sociology Tracing, Dictionary of Philosophy 1974, 1982; univ. text books and numerous articles on policy and society. *Leisure interests:* sports, reading, books, music, community devt activities, writing memories. *Address:* Rruga "Brigada e tetë", Pallati Havari, shk. 2, Apartment 7/1, Tirana, Albania (home). *Telephone:* (5) 4271500 (home).

PELOSI, Nancy Patricia D'Alesandro; American politician; *Speaker, House of Representatives;* b. 26 March 1940, Baltimore, Md; d. of Thomas D'Alesandro, Jr; m. Paul Pelosi 1963; one s. four d.; ed Trinity Coll., Washington, DC; Democratic Nat. Committeewoman 1976–96, Chair. Democratic Nat. Convention Host Cttee 1984, Chief Fundraiser for Nat. Democratic Senatorial Campaign Cttee 1986, State and Northern Chair. Calif. Democratic Party –1987; Rep. (Democrat) 8th Congressional Dist of Calif. 1987–, mem. House Perm. Select Cttee on Intelligence, House Democratic Whip 2001–03, Democratic Minority Leader 2002–07 (first woman to lead a major party in Congress), 2011–19, Speaker (first female speaker) 2007–11, 2019–; sr mem. House Appropriations Cttee, mem. Appropriations Sub-cttee on Labor, Health and Human Services and Educ.; Chair. Congressional Working Group on China; Co-Chair. AIDS Task Force of House Democratic Caucus, Bio-Medical Research Caucus; fmr Ranking Democrat on Appropriations Sub-cttee on Foreign Operations and Export Financing; fmr mem. House Cttee on Standards of Official Conduct (Ethics); Democrat; Knight, Grand Cross of the Order of Merit of the Italian Repub. 2007, Grand Cordon, Order of the Rising Sun (Japan) 2015; Hon. LLD (Mount Holyoke Coll.) 2018; inducted into Nat. Women's Hall of Fame 2013, Foremother Award, Nat. Center for Health Research 2016, John F. Kennedy Profile in Courage Award 2019. *Address:* Office of the Speaker, H-232, The Capitol, Washington, DC 20515, USA (office). *Telephone:* (202) 225-0600 (office). *Fax:* (202) 225-5117 (office). *Website:* www.speaker.gov (office); pelosi.house.gov (office).

PELPOLA, Daya; Sri Lankan lawyer, politician and diplomatist; *Ambassador to Italy;* fmr sports sub-ed., Ceylon Daily News; fmr mem. Parl.; Vice-Chair. United Nat. Party, also legal adviser to party leader Ranil Wickramasinghe; Chair. Sri Lankan Airlines Ltd 2002–08; Ambassador to Italy 2015–. *Leisure interests:* sports, especially hockey and rugby. *Address:* Embassy of Sri Lanka, Via Adige 2, 00198 Rome, Italy (office). *Telephone:* (06) 884801 (office). *Fax:* (06) 84241670 (office). *E-mail:* embassy@srilankaembassyrome.org (office). *Website:* www.srilankaembassyrome.org (office).

PELTIER, Guillaume; French politician and business executive; *Vice-President and National Secretary, Union pour un Mouvement Populaire;* b. 27 Aug. 1976, Paris; m.; four c.; f. a business in Tours, and runs Lettre de l'opinion monthly magazine; also involved with Univ. of Orléans; cand. in local elections in Municipality of Tours South (Febvotte, Prébendes and Sanitas) 2011; fmr mem. Nat. Front and fmr leader of youth section; leader La Droite forte (The Strong Right) faction of Union pour un Mouvement Populaire (UMP) 2012–15, Vice-Pres. and Nat. Sec. UMP 2013–15, Communications Man. UMP Indre-et-Loire; Mayor of Neung-sur-Beuvron 2014–17; mem. Les Républicains 2015–, Spokesperson 2016–17; mem. Assemblée nationale (Parl.) (2nd Dist of Loir-et-Cher) 2017–. *Address:* Les Républicains, 238 rue de Vaugirard, 75015 Paris, France (office). *Telephone:* 1-40-76-60-00 (office). *Website:* www.republicains.fr (office); www.guillaumepeltier.com.

PELTOLA, Timo Veikko, MSc; Finnish petroleum industry executive; b. 19 April 1946, Lieto; m. Katariina Helena Toivonen; three c.; Product Man. Huhtamäki Corpn 1971–75, Marketing Dir 1975–81, Pres. Polarcup Div. 1981–83, Corp. Vice-Pres. 1984–86, Exec. Vice-Pres. 1987–89, CEO 1989–2004; Ind. Chair. Neste Oil Oyj 2005, Chair. Personnel and Remuneration Cttee; Chair. AW-Energy Oy; Chair. Supervisory Bd Ilmarinen Mutual Pension Insurance Co.; Vice-Chair. Nordea AB; mem. Bd of Dirs TeliaSonera AB, SAS AB; mem. Supervisory Bd Finnish Fair Corpn Co-operative; mem. Advisory Bd CVC Capital Partners; Hon. DEcon.

PEMBAYUN, Mangkubumi Gusti Kanjeng Ratu; Indonesian; *Crown Princess of Yogyakarta;* b. (Gusti Raden Ajeng Nurmalita Sari), 24 Feb. 1972, Bogor; d. of Sri Sultan Hamengku Bawono X (Sultan of Yogyakarta) and Tatiek Drajad Supriastuti; m. Kanjeng Pangeran Haryo Wironegoro 2002; one s. one d.; ed Int. School of Singapore, Griffith Univ., Australia; Chair. Karangtaruna Prov. 2002–12; Chair. Indonesian Asscn of Market Traders 2006–11; Dir PT Yogyakarta Indonesian Tobacco, PT Yarsilk Gora Mahottama, PT Madu Baru, PT Mataram Mitra Manunggal, PT Yogyakarta Tembakau Indonesia; mem. Bd of Honor Indonesian Red Cross; named Crown Princess by her father in a sabdaraja (king's proclamation) May 2015 (first nomination of a female to the line of succession). *Address:* Ndalem Wironegaran, Panembahan, Kraton, Yogyakarta City, Special Region of Yogyakarta, Indonesia (office).

PEÑA, Federico, LLB; American lawyer, business executive, fmr politician and fmr government official; *Senior Advisor, Vestar Capital Partners;* b. 15 March 1947, Laredo, Tex.; m.; four c.; ed Univ. of Texas; fmr Partner, Peña & Peña (law firm); mem. Colo Legis. 1979–83; Mayor of Denver, Colo 1983–91; f. Peña Investment Advisors Inc. 1991, Pres. and CEO 1991–92; apptd part-time legal consultant, Brownstein Hyatt Farber & Strickland (law firm), Denver 1992; US Sec. of Transportation 1993–97, of Energy 1997–98; Sr Advisor, Vestar Capital Partners (pvt. equity firm), Denver 1998–2000, Man. Dir 2000–09, Sr Advisor 2009–; Nat. Co-Chair. Presidential campaign of Barack Obama 2008; mem. Bd of Dirs Marsico Capital Man., Prin. Financial Group 1999–2006, Sonic Corpn 2001–, Valor Telecommunications 2005–, Wells Fargo & Co. 2011–; mem. Toyota North American Diversity Advisory Bd; Assoc., Harvard Univ. Centre for Law and Educ.; Advisor, Latino Leadership Inst., Daniels Coll. of Business, Univ. of Denver; mem. Bd of Trustees Univ. of Denver 2015–. *Address:* Vestar Capital Partners, 1555 Blake Street, #200, Denver, CO 80202, USA (office). *Telephone:* (303) 292-6300 (office). *E-mail:* info@vestarcapital.com (office). *Website:* www.vestarcapital.com (office).

PEÑA, Marcos, BA; Argentine politician; *Cabinet Chief;* b. 15 March 1977, Buenos Aires; s. of Félix Peña and Clara Braun; m. Luciana Mantero; two c.; ed Univ. Torcuato Di Tella; began career in politics as mem., Buenos Aires City Legislature (Propuesta Republicana list) 2003–07, Chair. Educ., Science and Tech. Cttee 2005–07; Sec.-Gen., Buenos Aires City Govt 2007–15; Cabinet Chief, Govt of Argentina 2015–; Founding mem. Propuesta Republicana 2005–. *Address:* Office of the Cabinet Chief, Avda Julio Argentino Roca 782, C1067ABP Buenos Aires, Argentina (office). *Telephone:* (11) 4331-1951 (office). *E-mail:* privada@jgm.gov.ar (office). *Website:* www.jgm.gov.ar (office).

PEÑA, Paco; Spanish flamenco guitarist, musical director and professor of flamenco guitar; *Director, Paco Peña Flamenco Company;* b. (Francisco Peña Perez), 1 June 1942, Córdoba; s. of Antonio Peña and Rosario Pérez; m. Karin Vaessen 1982; two d.; int. concert artist since 1968; f. Paco Peña Flamenco Co. 1970, Centro Flamenco Paco Peña, Córdoba 1981; Prof. of Flamenco, Rotterdam Conservatory, Netherlands 1985; composed Misa Flamenca 1991; produced Musa Gitana 1999, Voces y Ecos 2002; composed Flamenco Requiem 2004; produced flamenco dance show A Compas! 2006; devised dance productions Flamenco sin Fronteras 2009, Quimeras 2010, Flamenco Vivo 2011, Quimeras 2012; Oficial de la Cruz de la Orden del Mérito Civil 1997; Ramón Montoya Prize 1983, Arts Gold Medal in the Arts, John F. Kennedy Center for the Performing Arts, Washington, DC 2012. *Publication:* Toques Flamencos. *Address:* Maja Majazaković Arts Management, 9 Gayfere Place, London, SE25 6DY, England (office). *E-mail:* maja@majazarkovic.com (office); MPM@pacopena.com. *Website:* www.pacopena.com.

PEÑA NIETO, Enrique, LicenDer, MBA; Mexican lawyer, politician and fmr head of state; b. 20 July 1966, Atlacomulco, State of Mexico; s. of Enrique Peña del Mazo and Maria del Socorro Nieto Sánchez; m. 1st Mónica Pretelini Sáenz 1993 (died 2007); one s. two d.; m. 2nd Angélica Rivera 2010; ed Universidad Panamericana, Instituto Tecnológico y de Estudios Superiores de Monterrey; taught law at Universidad Panamericana; Sec. Citizen Movt of Zone I of State Directive Cttee of Nat. Confed. of Popular Orgs (CNOP) 1990; del. to Org. and Citizen Front in different municipalities of State of Mexico 1991; also served as instructor at Electoral Training Centre of Partido Revolucionario Institucional (PRI—Institutional Revolutionary Party); held admin. positions in state govt during this time; Chief of Staff for Sec. of Econ. Devt of State of Mexico 1993–98; Deputy Sec. of Govt of State of Mexico 1999–2000; exercised different tasks for state's admin: Govt Admin Sec., Pres. Directive Council for Social Security Inst. of State of Mexico and its municipalities, Pres. Internal Council of Health Inst. of State of Mexico and Vice-Pres. for State of Mexico's Govt Bd for the Integral Family Devt System (DIF) 2000–02; mem. Nat. Inst. of Public Admin, Admin. Council for different decentralized public agencies; mem. PRI's Nat. and State Political Council and del. to PRI's XVIII Gen. Ass. 2001; won election for local rep. for XIII Dist in LV Legis.; Co-ordinator PRI's Parl. group in LV Legis. and Chair. Bd of Political Co-ordination of the local congress 2003–04; PRI cand. for governorship 2005; Gov. of State of Mexico 2005–11; involved in Supreme Court case, along with other politicians, charged with abuse of power in events of civil unrest in San Salvador Atenco 2006, exonerated 2009; Pres. of Mexico 2012–18. *Publication:* México, la gran esperanza: un Estado eficaz para una democracia de resultados (Mexico, The Great Hope: An Efficient State for a Democracy of Results) 2011. *Address:* c/o Office of the President, Los Pinos, Col. San Miguel Chapultepec, 11850 México, DF, Mexico (office).

PEÑA PALACIOS, Santiago, MPA; Paraguayan economist and politician; b. 16 Nov. 1978; ed Univ. Católica de Asunción and Columbia Univ., IMF Inst., USA; began career as analyst with Industrial Devt Fund, Asunción 1999; Asst Prof. of Financial Theory, Univ. Católica de Asunción 2004–05, Prof. of Econ. Theory 2005–; Economist, Central Bank of Paraguay 2000–09, Full Mem. of Bd 2012–15; Economist responsible for Africa Div., IMF, Washington DC 2009–12; Minister of Finance 2015–17.

PEÑALOSA, Antonio; Spanish international organization official; *Special Adviser to President and Management Board, International Organization of*

Employers; ed Univ. of Santiago, Coll. of Europe, Brussels, Belgium; staff mem. Industrial Policy Directorate, EC 1977–78; Asst to Sec.-Gen. of Int. Org. of Employers 1978–1983, Exec. Sec. 1983–94, Deputy Sec.-Gen. 1993–99, Sec.-Gen. 1999–2011, Special Adviser to Pres. and Man. Bd 2011–. *Address:* International Organization of Employers, 26 Chemin de Joinville, Cointrin, 1216 Geneva, Switzerland (office). *Telephone:* (22) 9290000 (office). *Fax:* (22) 9290001 (office). *E-mail:* penalosa@ioe-emp.org (office). *Website:* www.ioe-emp.org (office).

PEÑALOSA LONDOÑO, Enrique, BA, MA, DESS; Colombian politician, international organization official and consultant; *Mayor of Bogotá;* b. 30 Sept. 1954, Washington, DC, USA; s. of Enrique Peñalosa Camargo and Cecilia Londoño; ed Duke Univ., USA, Institut Int. d'Admin Publique and Univ. of Paris II, France; Pres. of the Instituto Colombiano de Ahorro y Vivienda (ICAV); Sec. of Econ. Affairs, Presidency of Colombia 1986–89; mem. Chamber of Reps 1990–91; Mayor of Bogotá 1998–2001, 2015–; Consultant on Urban Strategy, Vision and Policy 2001–; Visiting Scholar, New York Univ. 2007; Pres. Bd of Dirs, Inst. for Transportation and Devt Policy, New York 2009–15; Co-Pres. Colombian Green Party 2010–; Eisenhower Fellowship, Nat. Simon Bolivar Prize for Journalism, Soc. of Economists of Bogotá and Cundinamarca Prize, Göteborg Award for Sustainable Devt 2009. *Publications:* Capitalism: The Better Option 1989, Democracy and Capitalism: The Challenges of the Next Century 1990, Cerros de Bogotá 2003; numerous articles on econ. and urban issues. *Leisure interests:* cycling, reading, going to the movies. *Address:* Secretaría General de la Alcaldía Mayor de Bogotá DC, Avenida Carácas No. 53-80, Bogotá, Colombia. *Website:* portel.bogota.gov.co (office); www.enriquepenalosa.com.

PENCE, Michael (Mike) Richard; American lawyer and politician; *Vice-President;* b. 7 June 1959, Columbus, Ind.; s. of Edward J. Pence, Jr and Nancy Jane Pence (née Cawley); m. Karen Pence 1985; one s. two d.; ed Columbus North High School, Hanover Coll., Indiana Univ. Robert H. McKinney School of Law; early career as attorney in pvt. practice beginning 1986; Pres. Indiana Policy Review Foundation (think-tank) 1991–94; host, The Mike Pence Show (radio programme) 1994–2000, also hosted Sunday morning TV show in Indianapolis 1995–99; mem. US House of Reps for 2nd Congressional Dist of Indiana 2001–03, for 6th Congressional Dist 2003–13, mem. Cttee on Foreign Affairs, Cttee on the Judiciary, mem. Congressional Internet Caucus, Int. Conservation Caucus, Sportsmen's Caucus, Tea Party Caucus, Chair. House Republican Conf., Republican Study Cttee 2009–11; Gov. of Indiana 2013–17; chosen as cand. for Vice-Pres. by Republican presidential nominee Donald Trump July 2016, Vice-Pres. of USA 2017–. *Address:* Office of the Vice-President, Eisenhower Executive Office Building, 1650 Pennsylvania Avenue, NW, Washington, DC 20502, USA (office). *Telephone:* (202) 456-1414 (office). *Fax:* (202) 456-2461 (office). *Website:* www.whitehouse.gov/administration/vice-president-pence (office).

PENCHAS, Shmuel, MD, DIC, MSc; Israeli professor of health administration and physician; *Consultant, Hadassah Medical Organization;* b. 12 Feb. 1939, Romania; s. of Nathan Penchas and Liuba Penchas; four s.; ed Hebrew Univ.-Hadassah Medical School, Jerusalem, Haifa Technion Grad. School, Imperial Coll. and Univ. Coll., London, UK, Harvard Univ., USA; Physician, Hadassah Univ. Hosp., Jerusalem 1967–76, Dir of Computing 1977–78; Lecturer in Medicine, Hebrew Univ.-Hadassah Medical School, Jerusalem 1975, Sr Lecturer 1978, Assoc. Prof. of Internal Medicine 1984, Prof. of Health Care Admin 1993; Research Fellow, Harvard Univ. Medical School 1978; Deputy Dir-Gen. Hadassah Medical Org. 1978, Dir-Gen. 1981–98, now Consultant; Chair. Israel Asscn of Hosp. Dirs 1984–91, Foreign Assoc. Inst. of Medicine of NAS; Consultant to Hadassah (Women's Zionist Org. of America); Advisor to the Prime Minister of Bosnia (Srbska); mem. Romanian Nat. Acad. of Science; Hon. PhD, Hon. DrSc. *Publications include:* articles in professional journals. *Address:* 6 Manger Street, Tel-Aviv 64585, Israel (office). *Telephone:* (3) 5220090 (office). *Fax:* (3) 5220090 (office). *E-mail:* penchas@netvision.net.il (office).

PENDAROVSKI, Stevo, LLB, MA, PhD; Macedonian academic, politician and head of state; *President;* b. 3 April 1963, Skopje; ed SS Cyril and Methodius Univ., Skopje; Asst Minister for Public Relations, Ministry of Internal Affairs and Head of Analytical and Research Dept 1998–2001; Nat. Security and Chief Foreign Policy Adviser to Pres. Boris Trajkovski 2001–04; Head of State Election Comm. 2004–05; Nat. Security and Chief Foreign Policy Adviser to Pres. Branko Crvenkovski 2005–09; Assoc. Prof. in Int. Security, Foreign Policy and Globalization, Univ. American Coll. Skopje 2008–12, Asst Prof. 2012–; second-placed Social Democratic Union of Macedonia cand. in presidential election 2014, 2019; mem. of Parl. 2016–17; Nat. Coordinator for NATO membership 2017–; Pres. of North Macedonia 2019–. *Publications:* International Security 2010, Europe After the Lisbon Treaty, 5th Annual Int. Conf. on European Integration (ed.) 2010, Constructing Europe as a Global Power: From Market to Identity?, 6th Annual Int. Conf. on European Integration (ed.) 2011, Replacing European Union: Eastern Alternatives Awaiting?, 7th Annual Int. Conf. on European Integration 2012, Macedonian Foreign Policy 1991–2011: Aspects of Internal and International legitimacy (book) 2012, Macedonia and the Ohrid Framework Agreement: Framed Past, Elusive Future (in Alternatives: The Turkish Journal of International Relations) 2013, Electoral Authoritarianism at the End of Transition in the Western Balkans (conf., Thucydides vs. Kant in Our Time, Skopje) 2014, On-Line Politics and Voting: Overcoming the Democratic Deficit 2015, The Promise of E-Democracy and the Internet: Myths About Digital Agoras?, UACS Conf. on European Integration 2015. *Address:* Office of the President, 1000 Skopje, Aco Karamanov 33A, North Macedonia (office). *Telephone:* (2) 3253124 (office). *Fax:* (2) 3253124 (office). *E-mail:* president@president.gov.mk (office). *Website:* www.president.gov.mk (office).

PENDERECKI, Krzysztof; Polish composer and conductor; b. 23 Nov. 1933, Dębica, Kraków Prov.; s. of Tadeusz Penderecki and Zofia Penderecka; m. Elżbieta Solecka 1965; one s. two d.; ed Jagiellonian Univ., and State Higher Music School (now Music Acad.), Kraków, studied composition first with Skołyszewski, later with Malawski and Wiechowicz, Kraków; Lecturer in Composition, State Higher Music School, Kraków 1958–66, Prof. Extraordinary 1972–75, Prof. 1975–; Rector Kraków Conservatory 1972–87; Prof. of Composition, Folkwang Hochschule für Musik, Essen 1966–68; Musical Adviser, Vienna Radio 1970–71; Prof. of Composition, Yale Univ., USA 1973–78; Music Dir, Casals Festival, Puerto Rico 1992–2002; Music Man. Sinfonia Varsovia Orchestra 1997–; Guest Conductor

China Philharmonic Orchestra 2000–; mem. Presidential Council of Culture 1992–; Corresp. mem. Arts Acad. of GDR, Berlin 1975, Academia Nacional de Bellas Artes, Buenos Aires 1982; Extraordinary mem. Arts Acad. of W Berlin 1975; mem. Royal Acad. of Music, Stockholm 1976, Acad. Nat. de Sciences, Belles-Lettres et Arts, Bordeaux, American Acad. of Arts and Letters 1999, Hong Kong Acad. for the Performing Arts 2001 etc.; Fellow, Royal Irish Acad. of Music; Hon. RAM, London 1974; Hon. mem. Accad. Nazionale di Santa Cecilia, Rome 1976, Acad. Int. de Philosophie et de l'Art, Berne 1987, Musikkreis der Stadt, Duisburg 1999, Gesellschaft der Musikfreunds, Vienna 2000; Hon. Prof., Moscow Conservatory 1997, Cen. Beijing Conservatory 1998, St Petersburg Conservatory 2003, Komitas State Conservatory, Yerevan 2008; Officier, Ordre de Saint-Georges de Bourgogne (Belgium) 1990, Grand Cross Order of Merit (FRG) 1990, Commdr, Ordre des Arts et des Lettres 1996, Ordine al Merito della Repub. Italiana 2000, Commdr of the Three Star Order, Riga (Latvia) 2006, Order of the White Eagle (Poland) 2006; Dr hc (Univ. of Rochester, NY) 1972, (St Olaf Coll., Northfield, Minn.) 1977, (Katholieke Univ., Leuven) 1979, (Univ. of Bordeaux) 1979, (Georgetown Univ., Washington, DC) 1984, (Univ. of Belgrade) 1985, (Univ. Autónoma, Madrid) 1987; Hon. DMus (Glasgow) 1995, (Jagiellonian Univ., Krakow) 1998, (Ukrainian Nat. Tchaikovsky Acad. of Music) 1999, (Pittsburgh) 1999, (Lucerne) 2000, Univ. of St Petersburg, Yale Univ., Univ. of Leipzig 2003, and many others; Fitelberg Prize for Threnody for the Victims of Hiroshima 1960, also UNESCO award 1959, Polish Minister of Culture and Art Prize 1961, (First Class) 1981, Krakow Composition Prize for Canon 1962, North Rhine-Westphalia Grand Prize for St Luke's Passion 1966, also Pax Prize (Poland) 1966, Alfred Jurzykowski Foundation Award, Polish Inst. of Arts and Sciences in America 1966, Prix Italia 1967/68, State Prize (1st Class) 1968, Gustav Charpentier Prize 1971, Gottfried von Herder Prize 1977, Prix Arthur Honegger for Magnificat 1978, Grand Medal of Paris 1981, Sibelius Prize (Wihouri Foundation, Finland) 1983, Order of Banner of Labour (1st Class) 1983, Premio Lorenzo il Magnifico (Italy) 1985, Wolf Foundation Award 1987, Grammy Award Nat. Acad. of Recording Arts and Sciences (for Best Contemporary Composition) 1988, (for Best Instrumental Soloist Performance with Orchestra) 1999, (for Best Choral Composition) 2001, Grawemeyer Award for Music Composition 1992, City of Strasbourg Medal 1995, Crystal Award, World Econ. Forum, Davos 1997, Business Center Club Special Award, Warsaw 1998, AFIM Indie Award 1999, Köhler-Osbahr-Stiftung Music Award 1999, Best Living Composer Award, Midem Classic Award, Cannes 2000, Príncipe de Asturias Award 2001, Roman Guardini Prize, Catholic Acad. of Music 2002, North Rhine-Westphalia Award 2003, Praemium Imperiale 2004, Gold Medal, Ministry of Culture (Armenia) 2009, Lifetime Achievement Award, Int. Classical Music Awards 2012, Grammy Award for Best Classical Compendium 2013. *Works include:* Psalms of David (for choir and percussion) 1958, Emanations (for two string orchestras) 1958, Strophes (for soprano, speaker and ten instruments) 1959, Anaklasis (for strings and percussion) 1959–60, Dimensions of Time and Silence (for 40-part mixed choir and chamber ensemble) 1959–60, String Quartet no. 1 1960, no. 2 1968, Threnody for the Victims of Hiroshima (for 52 strings) 1960, Polymorphia (for strings) 1961, Psalms (for tape) 1961, Fluorescences (for large orchestra) 1961, Sonata for Cello and Orchestra 1964, St Luke's Passion 1965–66, De natura sonoris (for large orchestra) 1966, Dies irae (for soprano, tenor, bass, chorus and large orchestra) 1967, Violin Concerto 1967–77, The Devils of Loudun (opera) 1968–69, Cosmogony 1970, De natura sonoris II (for wind instruments, percussion and strings) 1970, Canticum Canticorum Salomonis (for 16 voices and chamber orchestra) 1970–73, Partita (for harpsichord, guitars, harp, double bass and chamber orchestra) 1972, Symphony no. 1 1972–73, Magnificat (for bass solo, voice ensemble, double choir, boys' voices and orchestra) 1973–74, When Jacob Awoke (for orchestra) 1974, Paradise Lost (opera) 1976–78, Christmas Symphony No. 2 1979–80, Te Deum 1979–80, Lacrimosa 1980, Cello Concerto No. 2 1982, Viola Concerto 1983, Black Mask (opera) 1984–86, Der unterbrochene Gedanke (for string quartet) 1988, Adagio (for orchestra) 1989, Symphony No. 4 (Adagio for orchestra) 1989, Sinfonietta (for orchestra) 1990–91, Symphony No. 5 (for orchestra) 1991–92, Partita (for orchestra, rev. ed.) 1991, Ubu Rex (opera) 1991, Benedicamus Domine 1992, Benedictus 1992, Flute Concerto 1992–93, Quartet for Clarinet and String Trio 1993, Violin Concerto No. 2 1992–95, Symphony No. 3 1995, Agnus Dei from Versöhnung Messe (a cappella choir) 1995, Seven Gates of Jerusalem (oratorio) 1995–96, Passacaglia (chamber music) 1995–96, Larghetto (chamber music) 1997, Credo 1997–98, Sonata for Violin and Piano 2000, Sextet for Violin, Viola, Cello, Piano, Clarinet and French Horn 2000, Benedictus 2002, Resurrection Piano Concerto 2002, Largo for violoncello and orchestra 2003, Symphony No. 8 2005–07, Concerto per corno 'Winterreise' 2007–08, Quartetto per archi No. 3 2008, Drei chinesische Lieder 2008, Kaddisz 2009, Prelude for Peace 2009, De Natura Sonoris No. 3 2012, The Complete Symphonies (Int. Classical Music Award for Contemporary Music 2014), Clarinet Concerto, Flute Concerto and Concerto grosso (Int. Classical Music Award for Contemporary Music 2016), Polonaise for orchestra 2016. *Leisure interest:* dendrology. *Website:* www.penderecki.de.

PENDEŠ, Marina Zdravko; Bosnia and Herzegovina business executive and politician; *Minister of Defence;* b. 20 Aug. 1964, Travnik, Socialist Repub. of Bosnia and Herzegovina, Socialist Fed. Repub. of Yugoslavia; d. of Zdravko Pendeš and Veronika Pendeš; ed High School, Travnik, Mil.-Tech. Faculty, Zagreb; Technician, Zagreb Electrical, Electronic and Communications Eng Technology 1983–98; Ind. Constructor, TRZ, Travnik 1992–98; Head of Dept, TKC SB, Vitez 1995–2003; mem. Hrvatska Demokratska Zajednica Bosne i Hercegovine (HDZ BiH—Croatian Democratic Union of Bosnia and Herzegovina) Vitez and Cen. Bosnia Canton 1996–98, 2000–06, Del. to HDZ BiH Vitez 1997–2000, 2000–03, Rep. in Ass., Cen. Bosnia Canton 2000–02, 2002–03, Vice-Pres. HDZ BiH Vitez 2000–02, 2002–04, 2011, mem. Cen. Cttee HDZ BiH, mem. Nat. Council, HDZ BiH, mem. Presidency, HDZ BiH; mem. Municipal Council, Vitez 1997–2002; Minister of Physical Planning, Restructuring and Return, Cen. Bosnia Canton 2003–04; Deputy Minister of Defence for Resources Man. 2004–07, 2007–12, for Policy and Planning 2012–15, Minister of Defence 2015–; mem. UO Agency for Privatization, Cen. Bosnia Canton 1998–2000; lay judge, Dist Court of Vitez 1999; For 'National Defence', First Class (Hungary) 2009; Municipal Coat of Arms of Vitez. *Address:* Ministry of Defence, 71000 Sarajevo, Hamdije Kreševljakovića 98, Bosnia and Herzegovina (office). *Telephone:* (33) 285501 (office). *Fax:* (33) 285507 (office). *E-mail:* marina.pendes@mod.gov.ba (office). *Website:* www.mod.gov.ba (office).

PENDLETON, Victoria Louise, CBE, MBE, BSc; British fmr track cyclist; b. 24 Sept. 1980, Stotfold, Beds., England; d. of Max Pendleton and Pauline M. Viney; m. Scott Gardner 2013; ed Northumbria Univ.; began cycling aged six, first race, 400m event on grass track at Fordham aged nine; gold medal, 800m, Nat. Grass Track Championship 1998, 1999, 2005; three silver medals, bronze medal, Nat. Track Championship 2001; gold medal, sprint, bronze medal, 500m, World Cup, Manchester 2004; silver medal, sprint, World Championship, Bordeaux 2006; gold medal, sprint, silver medal, 500m trial, Commonwealth Games, Melbourne 2006; gold medal, Nat. Derny Championship 2006; gold medal, sprint, gold medal, Keirin, gold medal, sprint (team), Union Cycliste Internationale Track Cycling World Championship, Palma de Mallorca 2007; gold medal, sprint, silver medal, Keirin, gold medal, sprint (team), Union Cycliste Internationale Track Cycling World Championship, Manchester 2008; gold medal, sprint, Olympic Games, Beijing 2008; gold medal, sprint, Union Cycliste Internationale Track Cycling World Championship, Pruszków 2009; bronze medal, sprint, silver medal, sprint (team), World Championship 2011; gold medal, sprint (team), European Track Championship 2011; gold medal, Keirin, silver medal, sprint, Olympic Games, London 2012; mem. Sky Track Cycling until her retirement from professional cycling Sept. 2012; Dr hc (Northumbria Univ.) 2008; Sunday Times Sportswoman of the Year 2007, Sportswoman of the Year, Sports Journalists' Asscn of Great Britain 2007. *Television:* contestant, series 10 of Strictly Come Dancing, with professional partner Brendan Cole 2012. *Achievements include:* rode in Foxhunter Chase, Cheltenham Festival 2016 (finished fifth). *Address:* c/o three60 Sports Management, The Studio, Hudson Street, Deddington, OX15 0SW, England. *Website:* victoriapendleton.co.uk.

PENDRY, Sir John Brian, Kt, BA, MA, PhD, FRS, FInstP; British physicist and academic; *Professor of Theoretical Solid State Physics, Imperial College London;* b. 4 July 1943; s. of Frank Johnson Pendry and Kathleen Pendry (née Shaw); m. Patricia Gard; ed Downing Coll., Cambridge; Research Fellowship in Physics, Downing Coll., Cambridge 1969–73, Fellow in Physics and Praelector 1973–75; ICI Post-doctoral Fellow 1969–71; mem. tech. staff, Theoretical Physics Dept, Bell Labs, Murray Hill, NJ, USA 1972–73; Sr Asst in Research, Cavendish Lab., Cambridge 1973–75; Sr Prin. Scientific Officer: Head of Theory Group, Science and Eng Research Council (SERC) Daresbury Lab. 1975–81; Prof. of Theoretical Solid State Physics, Imperial Coll. of Science and Tech. and Head of Condensed Matter Theory Group 1981–, Head of Experimental Solid State Physics Group 1983–85, Assoc. Head of Physics Dept 1984–92, Head of Physics Dept 1998–2001, Prin., Faculty of Physical Sciences 2001–02; mem. SERC Science Bd, SERC Nuclear Physics Bd 1992–93, Council, Royal Soc. 1992–94, Particle Physics and Astronomy Research Council 1998–2002; Dean, Royal Coll. of Science 1993–96; Ed. Proceedings A of the Royal Society 1996–2002; Leverhulme Trust Sr Research Fellowship 1996–97; Eng and Physical Sciences Research Council (EPSRC) Sr Research Five-Year Fellowship 1997–98, (resgnd) 2003; Commonwealth Scholarships Commr 1998–2000; Chair. Physics sub-panel of Research Assessment Exercise (RAE 2008) 2005–08, Inst. of Physics Publishing 2007–11, Cockcroft Inst. BC 2009–12; Visiting Prof., Inst. of Advanced Studies, Hong Kong Univ. of Science and Tech. 2011–; Lorentz Prof., Leiden Univ. 2015; Foreign Assoc., NAS 2013; Foreign mem. Norwegian Acad. of Sciences 2014; Fellow, Optical Soc. of America 2005, AAAS 2009, American Acad. of Arts and Sciences 2012, American Physical Soc. 2015; Hon. Prof., Nanjing South Eastern Univ. 2012, Hon. Fellow, Inst. of Physics 2016; Dr hc (Universität Erlangen, Nürnberg) 2010, (Duke Univ.) 2010; Hon. DSc (Hong Kong Baptist Univ.) 2010, (Hong Kong Univ. of Science and Tech.) 2015; British Vacuum Council Prize and Medal 1994, Dirac Medal and Prize, Inst. of Physics 1996, Int. Surface Structure Prize 1996, Appleton Lecturer 2003, Celsius Lecturer, Univ. of Uppsala, Sweden 2004, Bakerian Lecturer, Royal Soc. 2005, Larmor Lecturer, Queen's Univ. Belfast 2005, Fröhlich Lecturer, Univ. of Liverpool 2005, EU Decartes Prize for "extending electromagnetism through novel artificial materials" 2005, Royal Medal, Royal Soc. 2006, Centenary Kelvin Lecturer, Inst. of Eng and Tech. 2009, UNESCO-Niels Bohr Gold Medal 2009, W.E. Lamb Medal for Laser Science and Quantum Optics 2010, Fred Kavli Distinguished Lectureship in Nanoscience, MRS Fall Meeting 2012, APS McGroddy Prize (co-recipient) 2012, 30th Anniversary Prize, European Materials Research Soc. 2013, Newton Medal, Inst. of Physics 2013, Kavli Prize for Nanotechnology 2014, EPS Quantum Electronics and Optics Prize 2015, Dan David Prize for Nanotechnology 2016, Ugo Fano Gold Medal 2016, Int. Union Of Radio Science Dellinger Gold Medal 2017, SPIE Mozi Award 2019. *Publications:* numerous scientific papers in professional journals on condensed matter theory, optics and metamaterials. *Leisure interests:* music, gardening, photography. *Address:* Room 808 Blackett, Department of Physics, Imperial College London, Prince Consort Road, London, SW7 2AZ, England (office). *Telephone:* (20) 7594-7606 (office). *E-mail:* j.pendry@imperial.ac.uk (office). *Website:* www.imperial.ac.uk/people/j.pendry (office).

PENG, Chun, MA (Econ); Chinese banking executive; *Vice-Chairman and President, Bank of Communications;* b. Jan. 1962; ed Grad. School of People's Bank of China; Deputy Gen. Man. and Gen. Man. Urumqi Br., Bank of Communications, Gen. Man. Nanning Br. and Gen. Man. Guangzhou Br. 1994–2001, Asst Pres. Bank of Communications 2001–04, Asst Pres. and Dir June–Sept. 2004, Exec. Vice-Pres. Sept. 2004–05, Exec. Vice-Pres. and Exec. Dir 2005–10, Deputy Gen. Man. China Investment Corpn 2010–13, Exec. Dir and Gen. Man. Central Huijin Investment Ltd 2010–13, Pres. Bank of Communications Oct. 2013–, Vice-Chair. and Exec. Dir Nov. 2013–. *Address:* Bank of Communications, 188 Yinchengzhong Road, Shanghai 200120, People's Republic of China (office). *Telephone:* (21) 95559 (office). *E-mail:* 95559@bankcomm.com (office). *Website:* www.bankcomm.com (office).

PENG, Liyuan; Chinese singer and actress; *First Lady;* b. 20 Nov. 1962, Yuncheng, Shandong Prov.; d. of Peng Longkun; m. Xi Jinping (Pres. of People's Repub. of China 2013–) 1987; one d.; ed Shandong Acad. of Arts, China Acad. of Music; solo singer, Qianwei Song and Dance Troupe of Ji'nan Mil. Command 1980–84; appeared on China Central TV (CCTV) New Year Gala 1983; solo singer and civilian mem., Song and Dance Troupe, PLA Gen. Political Dept 1984–; nicknamed 'The Peony Fairy'; specializes in traditional Chinese folk music and patriotic songs; frequent appearances on stage and on state TV; has performed overseas in USA, Canada, Japan and Austria; part-time Prof., Central Beijing Conservatory; Ministry of Health Amb. for HIV/AIDS Prevention 2006–; Vice-Chair. China Fed. of Literary and Art Circles 2011–; Amb. Chinese Asscn on Tobacco Control 2009–; WHO Goodwill Amb. for Tuberculosis and HIV 2011–14; UNESCO Amb. for Women's Education 2014–; mem. CCP 1985–, mem. 11th CPPCC Nat. Cttee; Hon. DLit (Massey Univ.) 2014; several awards including Plum Blossom Award 1985, Nat. Cultural Projects Award, China Golden Records Award, Lincoln Center for the Arts Distinguished Artist Award. *Works include:* People from Our Village, Mount Everest, On the Plains of Hope, Mountain Song, I Love You Saibei Snow, High Heaven Clouds, We are the Yellow Tarzan, Folks, Exalted, Sunnyway. *Operas include:* White Haired Girl, The Daughter of the Party, Melancholy Dawn, Poems of Mulan. *Television:* regular appearances on China Central TV (CCTV) New Year Gala. *Address:* China Federation of Literary and Art Circles, On Court North, Chaoyang District, Beijing 100029; Song and Dance Troupe, People's Liberation Army General Political Department, A-16, East Huayuan Road, Haidian District, Beijing 100083, People's Republic of China (office). *Telephone:* (10) 62010693 (office). *Fax:* (10) 62369748 (office).

PENG, Lucy, (Peng Lei); Chinese business executive; *CEO, Alibaba Small and Micro Financial Services Group;* b. 1973; ed Hangzhou Inst. of Commerce, Zhejiang Gongshang Univ.; taught for five years at Zhejiang Univ. of Finance and Econs; co-f. Alibaba Group (business-to-business e-commerce platform) 1999, 10 years as Chief People Officer, becoming CEO, Alibaba Small and Micro Financial Services Group 2013–; CEO, Alipay (online payment service) 2010–13; CEO Ant Financial Services Group 2014–16, Exec. Chair. 2016–18; CEO Lazada 2018–. *Address:* Alibaba.com, 6th Floor Chuangye Mansion, East Software Park, No. 99 Huaxing Road, Hangzhou, Zhejiang Province, 310012 (office); Alibaba.com Technology Corpn Ltd, Room 408, Fanli Building, 22 Chaoyangwai Street, Chaoyang District, Beijing, 100020, People's Republic of China (office). *Telephone:* (571) 85022088 (Hangzhou) (office); (10) 6588-9698 (office). *Fax:* (571) 88157866 (Hangzhou) (office); (10) 6588-9699 (office). *Website:* www.alibaba.com (office).

PENG, Ming-Min; Taiwanese politician; b. 15 Aug. 1923; m. Li Chun 1949; one c.; ed in Japan and Nat. Taiwan Univ.; lost left arm during US bombing raid on Nagasaki; fmr Chair. Political Science Dept, Nat. Taiwan Univ.; arrested for activities supporting self-determination for Taiwan 1964 and sentenced to eight years' imprisonment; sentence commuted to house arrest; escaped into exile in USA; returned home 1992; joined Democratic Progressive Party (DDP) 1995; DDP cand., presidential elections March 1996; Sr Adviser to the Office of the President 2001. *Publication:* A Perfect Escape 2009.

PENG, Peiyun; Chinese administrator; *Honorary President, All-China Women's Federation;* b. 1929, Liuyang Co., Hunan Prov.; ed Tsinghua Univ., Beijing; joined CCP Communist Youth League 1945, CCP 1946; Sec.-Gen. CCP Party Br., Tsinghua Univ. 1949–78 (also Deputy Sec. CCP Party Cttee); Vice-Chair. CCP Revolutionary Cttee, Beijing Chemical Eng Inst., Beijing 1949–78; Head, 1st Bureau, State Science and Tech. Comm., 1978–79; Vice-Minister of Educ. 1982–88, State Educ. Comm. 1982–88; Sec. CCP Party Cttee, Chinese Univ. of Science and Tech., Anhui Prov. 1982–88; mem. Central Comm. for Discipline Inspection, CCP Cen. Cttee 1982–92; Minister of State Family Planning Comm. 1988–98; State Councillor 1988–98; Del., 12th CCP Nat. Congress 1982–87, 13th CCP Nat. Congress 1987–92; mem. 14th CCP Cen. Cttee 1992–97, 15th CCP Cen. Cttee 1997–2002; Chair. Coordination Cttee for the Handicapped (State Council) 1993–; Chair. Nat. Cttee for Patriotic Public Health Campaign 1994–; Women and Children's Work Cttee of the State Council; Vice-Chair. Standing Cttee of 9th NPC 1998–2003; Pres. Chinese Asscn for Promotion of the Population Culture 1993, Soc. of Population 1994, Exec. Cttee All-China Women's Fed. 1998–2003, Hon. Pres. 2003–; Pres. Red Cross Soc. of China 1999–2009. *Website:* www.womenofchina.cn.

PENGO, HE Cardinal Polycarp, DTheol; Tanzanian ecclesiastic; *Archbishop of Dar es Salaam and President of Symposium of Episcopal Conferences of Africa and Madagascar (SECAM);* b. 5 Aug. 1944, Mwazye; ed Kipapala Major Seminary, Tabora, Makerere Univ., Pontifical Lateran Univ.; ordained priest 1971; sec. to Bishop of Sumbawanga 1971–73; Rector Segerea Major Seminary 1977–90; Bishop of Nachingwea 1984–87, of Tunduru-Massai 1987–90; Coadjutor Archbishop of Dar es Salaam 1990–92, Archbishop of Dar es Salaam 1992–; cr. Cardinal (Cardinal-Priest of Nostra Signora de La Salette) 1998; participated in Papal Conclave 2005, 2013; Pres. Symposium of Episcopal Confs of Africa and Madagascar (SECAM) 2007–. *Address:* Archbishop's House, PO Box 167, Dar es Salaam, Tanzania. *Telephone:* (22) 2113223 (office). *Fax:* (22) 2125751 (office). *E-mail:* nyumba@cats-net.com (office).

PENJO, Daw, MA; Bhutanese diplomatist and government official; b. 7 March 1958; m.; three c.; ed Univ. of Delhi, India, Tufts Univ., USA; joined Ministry of Foreign Affairs 1980; assigned to Perm. Mission to UN, Geneva 1986–90; Head of Bilateral and Multilateral Div., Ministry of Foreign Affairs 1990–94; First Sec. and Deputy Chief of Mission, Dhaka, Bangladesh 1994–97; Counsellor and Deputy Chief of Mission, New Delhi 1997–2000; Dir of Bilateral Dept 2000–03; Amb. and Perm. Rep. to UN, New York 2003–08 (also accred as Amb. to Canada) 2004–08; Foreign Sec., Ministry of Foreign Affairs 2008–13; Amb. and Perm. Rep. to UN, Geneva 2013–16; Vice-Pres. ECOSOC 2004.

PENJOR, Rinzin, BCom, LLB, LLM; Bhutanese lawyer and government official; b. Kazhi geog, Wangduephodrang; ed Univ. of Delhi, India, Lord Dalhousie Law Coll., Canada; began career with High Court 1989, served as Drangpoen in Tsirang, Sarpang and Punakha Dist Courts; Militia Officer with Royal Bhutan Army 1990–95; Attorney-Gen. 2008–10; Judge (Drangpon) Supreme Court; Patang. *Address:* c/o Office of the Attorney General, POB 1045, Thori Lam, Lower Motithang, Thimphu, Bhutan.

PENJORE, Dasho, MA; Bhutanese government official and central banker; *Governor and Chairman of the Executive Committee, Royal Monetary Authority;* ed Northeastern Univ., USA; served for 17 years in various capacities at Royal Monetary Authority (RMA—central bank), including as Deputy Man. Dir –2007; Gyalpoi Zimpon (Office for People's Welfare and Wellbeing) 2007–14; CEO Nat. Pension and Provident Fund 2014–15; Gov. and Chair. Exec. Cttee, RMA 2015–; mem. Bd of Dirs Druk Holding and Investments; apptd Adviser to pre-election interim Govt in Ministry of Forests and Agriculture Aug. 2018; fmr mem. Bd of Dirs India Bhutan Foundation; Bura Maap (red scarf) 2008, Druk Thuksey 2017. *Address:* Office of the Governor, Royal Monetary Authority, POB 154, Thimphu,

Bhutan (office). *Telephone:* (2) 323111 (office). *Fax:* (2) 322847 (office). *E-mail:* rmarsd@rma.org.bt (office). *Website:* www.rma.org.bt (office).

PENJORE, Thrizin Namgye, MBA; Bhutanese politician; b. 21 May 1966, Amrimo, Punakha; m. Namgay Lhamo; one s. one d.; elected as mem. Nat. Council (Upper House of bicameral Parl.) from Punakha Dzongkhag (constituency), Chair. Nat. Council 2008–13. *Address:* c/o National Council Secretariat, Langjophakha, PO Box 200, Thimphu, Bhutan. *Telephone:* 17-603532 (mobile).

PENN, Sean; American actor; b. 17 Aug. 1960, Burbank, Calif.; s. of Leo Penn and Eileen Penn (née Ryan); m. 1st Madonna (q.v.) 1985 (divorced); m. 2nd Robin Wright 1996 (divorced 2010); two c.; f. Clyde is Hungry Films (production co.); Chair. Cannes Film Festival jury 2008; named Amb. to Haiti 2012–; Modern Master Award, Santa Barbara Int. Film Festival 2002, Donostia Lifetime Achievement Award, San Sebastian Film Festival 2003, John Steinbeck Award 2004, Christopher Reeve First Amendment Award 2006. *Theatre appearances include:* Heartland (Broadway debut), Slab Boys, Hurlyburly 1988. *Films include:* Taps 1981, Fast Times at Ridgemont High 1982, Bad Boys 1983, Crackers 1984, Racing with the Moon 1984, The Falcon and the Snowman 1985, At Close Range 1986, Shanghai Surprise 1986, Colors 1988, Judgement in Berlin 1988, Casualties of War 1989, We're No Angels 1989, State of Grace 1990, Carlito's Way 1993, Dead Man Walking 1996 (Best Actor Award Berlin Film Festival 1996), U Turn 1997, She's So Lovely 1997, Hurlyburly 1998, As I Lay Dying 1998, Up at the Villa 1998, The Thin Red Line 1998, Sweet and Lowdown 1999, The Pledge 2000, Up at the Villa 2000, Before Night Falls 2000, The Weight of Water 2000, I am Sam 2001, It's All About Love 2003, Mystic River (Golden Globe Award, Best Dramatic Actor 2004, Critics' Choice Award Best Actor 2004, Acad. Award, Best Actor 2004) 2003, 21 Grams (Venice Film Festival Best Actor Award 2003) 2003, The Assassination of Richard Nixon 2005, The Interpreter 2005, All the King's Men 2006, Persepolis 2007, What Just Happened? 2007, Milk 2008 (Acad. Award for Best Actor 2009), Fair Game 2010, The Tree of Life 2011, This Must Be the Place 2011, Gangster Squad 2013, The Secret Life of Walter Mitty 2013, The Gunman 2015, The Angry Birds Movie (voice); dir and writer The Indian Runner 1991, The Crossing Guard 1995, The Pledge 2001, Into the Wild 2007, The Last Face 2016. *Publications:* Bob Honey Who Just Do Stuff: A Novel 2018. *Address:* 2049 Century Park East, Suite 2500, Los Angeles, CA 90067-3101, USA (office).

PENNANEACH, Biova-Soumi, MSc; Togolese diplomatist; b. 5 Oct. 1941, Lomé; m. 1972; two s. four d.; ed State Univ. of Moscow, USSR and Laval Univ., Québec, Canada; active trade unionist from 1966; Head, Soils Analysis Labs 1966–74, 1976–80; Dir Agricultural and Land Legislation Service 1980–82; Prefect of Tchaoudjo and the Lakes and tech. Adviser, Nat. Science Inst. 1982–87; Dir Office of Minister of Rural Devt 1987–90; Under-Sec.-Gen. Nat. Confed. of Workers of Togo 1988–90; Amb. and Perm. Rep. to UN, New York 1990–96, Vice-Pres. 46th session of UN Gen. Ass. 1991. *Publications:* numerous, on conservation and environment protection. *Address:* c/o Ministry of Foreign Affairs and Cooperation, Place du Monument aux Morts, Avenue Georges Pompidou, BP 900, Lomé, Togo. *E-mail:* maeirtgce@yahoo.fr.

PENNANT-REA, Rupert Lascelles, MA; British editor and business executive; *Chairman, Royal London Group;* b. 23 Jan. 1948, Harare, Zimbabwe; s. of Peter A. Pennant-Rea and Pauline E. Pennant-Rea; m. several times; two s. one d.; ed Peterhouse, Zimbabwe, Trinity Coll., Dublin and Univ. of Manchester; with Confed. of Irish Industry 1970–71, Gen. and Municipal Workers' Union 1972–73, Bank of England 1973–77; with The Economist 1977–93, Ed. 1986–93; Deputy Gov. of Bank of England 1993–95; Chair. Henderson Group plc 2005–12, The Economist Group 2009–, Royal London Group (mutual life, pensions and investment firm) 2013–; mem. Bd of Dirs Times Newspapers, PGI Group Ltd; Chair. Bd of Trustees, Shakespeare Schools Festival; Wincott Prize for Journalism 1984. *Publications:* Gold Foil 1979, Who Runs the Economy? (co-author) 1980, The Pocket Economist (co-author) 1983, The Economist Economics (co-author) 1986. *Leisure interests:* music, tennis, fishing, golf, family.

PENNER, Gregory B., BS, MBA; American business executive; *Chairman, Walmart;* b. 1970; s. of Clifford Penner and Joyce Penner; son-in-law of Rob Walton and grandson-in-law of Sam Walton (Founder of Walmart); m. Carrie Walton; four c.; ed Georgetown Univ., Stanford Grad. School of Business; worked as a financial analyst at Goldman, Sachs & Co., Inc. and as a Gen. Partner of Pennisula Capital; Founder and Gen. Partner, Madrone Capital Partners, Menlo Park, Calif.; has worked for Walmart in several capacities 1994–, including as man. trainee, asst buyer, Sr Vice-Pres. and Chief Financial Officer, Japan, and Sr Vice-Pres. of Finance and Strategy for walmart.com, mem. Bd of Dirs 2008–, fmr Chair. Tech. and eCommerce Cttee, Chair. Walmart 2015–; Partner, DT Capital Partners; mem. Bd of Dirs, Baidu, Inc. 2004–, Hyatt Hotels Corpn 2007–14. *Address:* Walmart, 702 SW 8th Street, Bentonville, AR 72716-8611, USA (office). *Telephone:* (479) 273-4000 (office). *Fax:* (479) 277-1830 (office). *Website:* www.walmart.com (office); corporate.walmart.com (office).

PENNIE, Michael William, ARCA; British sculptor and teacher; *Professor Emeritus and Artist-in-Residence, Bath Spa University;* b. 23 Oct. 1936, Wallasey, Cheshire; s. of George A. Pennie and Isabel Duff; m. 1st Norah Kimmit 1959 (divorced 1977); m. 2nd Marlene Stride 1985; two s. one d.; ed Bede Collegiate for Boys, Sunderland, Sunderland Coll. of Art and Royal Coll. of Art; Visiting Lecturer, Bath Acad. of Art, Winchester and Wimbledon Schools of Art, Norwich Coll. of Art and Brighton Polytechnic 1962–82; Sr Sculpture Lecturer, Bath Spa, Univ. Coll. 1985–2001, Prof. Emer. 2001–, Artist-in-Residence, Corsham Court, Bath Spa Univ. 2009–; Co-organizer, Sculpture in the City, Bath 1986; Consultant, Goodwill Art Service 1992–; Chair. Bath Area Network for Artists 2001–03; Consultant, Horniman Museum and Gardens, Bath Spa Sculpture Garden, Bath Spa Univ. 2005–; 12 research trips to W Africa 1994–2000; Rome Scholar 1962, Gregynog Fellow, Univ. of Wales 1971. *Publications:* Where Shall We Put This One? 1987, Smoke of the Savannah 1989, African Assortment: African Art in Museums in England and Scotland 1991, Friday's Rain Takes a Long Time to Stop 1994, Some Sculptors and African Art 1995, Marriage Poles of the Lobi 1996, Adventures with Lobi – an abc 1998, West African Journeys 2001, Lobi Notes 2002, Across the Board and 2 Other Sculptures 2007, Michael Pennie: Sculpture Making and Teaching 2014, Adventures in Wiltshire 2016. *Leisure interests:* crime writers and writing. *Address:* 117 Bradford Road, Atworth, Melksham, Wilts., SN12 8HY,

England (home). *Telephone:* (1225) 705409 (home). *E-mail:* michael_pennie@sky.com (home). *Website:* www.michaelpennie.net; michaelpennie.bathspa.ac.uk.

PENNINGER, Josef, MD; Austrian biologist and academic; *Scientific Director, Institute for Molecular Biotechnology, Austrian Academy of Sciences;* b. 5 Sept. 1964, Gurten; m. Liqun Zhang 1997; one s. two d.; ed Humanistic Gymnasium, Ried, Univ. of Innsbruck; Post-doctoral Fellow, Ont. Cancer Inst., Princess Margaret Hosp., Toronto, Canada 1990–94, Assoc. Scientist, Dept of Molecular and Cellular Biology 1994–; Prin. Investigator, Amgen Inst., Toronto 1994–; Asst Prof., Depts of Immunology and Medical Biophysics, Univ. of Toronto 1994–99, Full mem. School of Grad. Studies 1998–, Assoc. Prof., Depts of Immunology and Medical Biophysics 1999–2002, Full Prof. 2002–, Adjunct Full Prof. of Immunology 2003–; Assoc. Prof. (Dozent), Dept of Experimental and Gen. Pathology, Univ. of Innsbruck 1998–; Scientific Dir Inst. for Molecular Biotechnology of the Austrian Acad. of Sciences (IMBA), Vienna 2002–; Prof. of Genetics, Univ. of Vienna 2004–; Affiliate Scientist, Keenan Research Centre, Li Ka Shing Knowledge Inst., St Michael's Hosp., Toronto 2010–; Guest Prof., Medical Univ., Vienna 2011–; Corresp. mem. Austrian Acad. of Sciences 2002, mem. 2007; mem. Deutsche Akad. der Naturforscher Leopoldina 2004, European Molecular Biology Org. 2008, Academia Europaea 2009, European Research Inst. for Integrated Cellular Pathology (ERI-ICP), Paris 2009 (Vice-Pres. 2011–), European Acad. for Tumor Immunology 2010; Fellow, AAAS 2012; Hon. Prof., Peking Union Medical Coll., Beijing 2005–; Special fellowship from Austrian Ministry for Arts and Science 1987, Scholarship from European Fed. of Immunological Societies 1988, 'Highest Talented' Award, Rotary Club, Innsbruck 1990, Anton von Eiselsberg Prize for best medical related scientific work in Austria 1991, Erwin Schroedinger Fellowship, Austrian Fonds zür Foerderung der Wissenschaftlichen Forschung 1990–92, Austrotransplant-Biotest Prize, Austrian Soc. of Transplantation, Transfusion and Genetics 1993, Talentefoerderpraemie (talent prize for science and culture), Prov. of Upper Austria 1994, The William E. Rawls Prize, Nat. Cancer Inst. of Canada 1999, included in 'Celebration of Canadian Healthcare Research' of leading historical and contemporary medical scientists in Canada during 20th century selected by Asscn of Canadian Medical Colls, Asscn of Canadian Teaching Hosps, Alumni and Friends of the Medical Research Council and Partners in Research 2000, selected as a 'Young Leader in Medicine in Canada' by the Globe and Mail, Univ. of Toronto 2000, CIAR Young Canadian Explorer Award 2002, Culture Prize for Science, Prov. of Upper Austria 2003, Int. Research Prize in Bone Research 2003, Austrian Scientist of the Year Award 2003, Austria04 Award: Austrian of the Year (in science), Die Presse newspaper 2004, Young Global Leader appointed by World Econ. Forum 2004, Descartes Prize for Research, European Comm. 2007, Ernst Jung Prize, Jung-Stiftung für Wissenschaft und Forschung (co-recipient) 2007, Carus Medal, German Academy of Sciences Leopoldina 2007, Wellenreiter Prize, Austrian Man. Club 2007, Carus-Prize, City of Schweinfurt 2008, Karl Landsteiner Prize, Austrian Soc. of Immunology and Allergology 2008, first ERC Advanced Grant 2009, ESCI Award, European Soc. for Clinical Investigation 2009, Medal of the Australian Soc. for Medical Research 2009, Innovator Award, Era of Hope/DOD 2012. *Publications:* more than 400 scientific papers in professional journals. *Leisure interest:* football. *Address:* IMBA, Institute of Molecular Biotechnology of the Austrian Academy of Sciences, Dr Bohrgasse 3, 1030 Vienna, Austria (office). *Fax:* (1) 79044-4702 (office). *E-mail:* josef.penninger@imba.oeaw.ac.at (office). *Website:* www.imba.oeaw.ac.at (office).

PENNINGTON, (Thomas) Hugh, CBE, MB, PhD, FRCPath, FRCP, FRSE, FMedSci; British microbiologist and academic; *Professor Emeritus of Bacteriology, University of Aberdeen;* b. 19 April 1938, Edgware, London; m. Carolyn Beattie 1966; two d.; ed Royal Grammar School, Lancaster, St Thomas's Medical School, Univ. of London; house appointments, St Thomas's Hosp. 1962–63, Asst Lecturer in Medical Microbiology, St Thomas's Hosp. Medical School 1963–67; Postdoctoral Fellow, Univ. of Wisconsin-Madison, USA 1967–68; Lecturer, then Sr Lecturer in Virology, Univ. of Glasgow 1969–79; Prof. of Bacteriology, Univ. of Aberdeen 1979–2003, Prof. Emer. 2003–, Dean of Medicine 1987–92; Gov. Rowett Research Inst. 1980–88, 1996–; Gov. Moredun Research Inst. 2003–; Chair. Expert Group on 1996 E. Coli Outbreak in Cen. Scotland; Vice-Chair. Broadcasting Council for Scotland; Vice-Pres. Chartered Inst. of Environmental Health; mem. Scottish Food Advisory Cttee, Food Standards Agency; Pres. Soc. for Gen. Microbiology 2003–06; mem. Advisory Council, Campaign of Science and Eng; Hon. DSc (Lancaster) 1999, (Strathclyde) 2001, (Aberdeen) 2003; Caroline Walker Trust Consumer Advocate Award 1997, John Kershaw Memorial Prize for Notable Services to Public Health 1998, Royal Scottish Soc. of Arts Silver Medal 1999, Thomas Graham Medal, Royal Glasgow Philosophical Soc. 2001, Burgess of Guild, City of Aberdeen 2002. *Publications:* When Food Kills 2003, Food Poisoning, Policy and Politics: Corned Beef and Typhoid in Britain in the 1960s (co-author) 2005; numerous papers, articles and book chapters on viruses and bacteria and on food safety. *Leisure interest:* collecting old books. *Address:* Department of Medical Microbiology, Medical School, University of Aberdeen, Foresterhill, Aberdeen, AB25 2ZD (office); 13 Carlton Place, Aberdeen, AB15 4BR, Scotland (home). *Telephone:* (1224) 55863 (office); (1224) 645136 (home). *Fax:* (1224) 685604 (office). *E-mail:* t.h.pennington@abdn.ac.uk (office). *Website:* www.abdn.ac.uk (office).

PENNY, Gareth, MA; South African business executive; *Executive Chairman, New World Resources plc;* b. 24 Dec. 1962; m. Kate Penny; two c.; ed Diocesan Coll. (Bishops), Cape Town, Eton Coll., Oxford, UK; joined Anglo American Corpn 1988, becoming Man. Anglo American/De Beers Small Business Initiative, SA, Personal Asst to Chair. of Anglo American/De Beers, Dir of Sales and Marketing, Diamond Trading Co. 2001–04, Dir De Beers 2003–, Group Man. Dir and Chair. Exec. Cttee, De Beers Group 2006–10; Exec. Chair. New World Resources plc 2010–; also mem. Bd Julius Baer Holding Ltd, OKD 2012–; mem. Advisory Bd TowerBrook Capital Partners; Vice-Chair. Botswana Economic Advisory Cttee; Hon. Life mem. London Diamond Bourse & Club. *Address:* New World Resources plc, Jachthavenweg 109h, 1081 KM Amsterdam, Netherlands (office). *E-mail:* info@nwrgroup.eu (office). *Website:* www.newworldresources.eu (office).

PENNY, Sir Nicholas, Kt, PhD; British art historian, gallery director (retd) and academic; b. 21 Dec. 1949; m. Mary Crettier; ed Shrewsbury School, St Catharine's Coll., Cambridge, Courtauld Inst. of Art, London; academic career began with a research fellowship at Clare Hall, Cambridge; taught art history at Univ. of

Manchester 1975–82; Slade Prof. of Fine Art, Univ. of Oxford 1980–81; Sr Research Fellow, King's Coll., Cambridge 1982–84; Keeper of Dept of Western Art, Ashmolean Museum, Oxford 1984–89; Clore Curator of Renaissance Painting, Nat. Gallery, London 1990–2000, identified the Madonna of the Pinks belonging to the Duke of Northumberland as a genuine Raphael, and not a copy of a lost original, as was previously supposed 1991, Keeper 1998–2002, made unsuccessful bid for directorship of Nat. Gallery 2002, Dir 2008–15; Andrew W. Mellon Prof., Center for Advanced Study in the Visual Arts, Nat. Gallery of Art, Washington, DC, USA 2000–07, Sr Curator of Sculpture, Nat. Gallery of Art 2002–07. *Publications include:* Church Monuments in Romantic England 1977, Taste and the Antique (co-author, with Francis Haskell) 1981, Raphael (co-author) 1987, Ruskin's Drawings (Ashmolean Handbooks) 1988, Alfred and Winifred Turner: Exhibition Catalogue 1988, Giotto to Dürer: Early Renaissance Painting in The National Gallery (co-author) 1991, three-volume scholarly catalogue of European sculpture in the Ashmolean Museum 1992, The Materials of Sculpture 1993, Tradition and Revolution in French Art, 1700–1880: Paintings and Drawings from Lille 1993, Making and Meaning: the Young Michelangelo: The Artist in Rome, 1496–1501 (Making & Meaning Series) (co-author) 1994, Frames 1997, Saints (National Gallery Pocket Guides) 2000, Dürer to Veronese: Sixteenth-century Painting in the National Gallery (co-author) 2002, Titian (National Gallery Catalogues) 2003, The Sixteenth-Century Italian Paintings, Vol. 1 2004, Desiderio Da Settignano: Sculpture of Renaissance Florence (co-author) 2007, The Sixteenth-Century Italian Paintings, Vol. 2: Venice 1540–1600 2008; regular contrib. to The Burlington Magazine and London Review of Books.

PENONE, Fabien; French diplomatist; *Ambassador to South Korea;* b. 19 Oct. 1968; ed Business School of Lyon, Ecole nat. d'admin, Institut d'études politiques, Paris; Ed. in North Africa and Middle East 1997–2000; Ed. Service of Common Foreign and Security Policy, Directorate Gen. for Political Affairs and Security, Ministry of Foreign Affairs (MFA) 2000–01, First Sec., Perm. Mission to EU, Brussels 2001–02, Deputy Rep. to Political and Security Cttee, EU, Brussels 2002–05, Second Counsellor, Embassy in London 2005–07, Deputy Dir of Political Affairs, UN Div., Int. Orgs, Human Rights and Francophonie, Directorate Gen. for Political Affairs and Security, MFA 2007–10, Head of External Relations, Dept of EU, EU Div. 2010–12, Americas Adviser, Russia, Balkans, Eastern Europe outside the EU, Caucasus, Cen. Asia and Foreign Policy of EU, Diplomatic Unit of the Presidency of the Repub. 2012–15, Amb. to South Korea 2015–. *Address:* Embassy of France, 30 Hap-dong, Seodaemun-gu, Seoul 120-030, Republic of Korea (office). *Telephone:* (2) 3149-4300 (office). *Fax:* (2) 3149-4310 (office). *E-mail:* ambafrance@hanafos.com (office). *Website:* www.ambafrance-kr.org (office).

PENROSE, Oliver, PhD, FRS, FRSE; British mathematician and academic; *Professor Emeritus, Heriot-Watt University;* b. 6 June 1929, London, England; s. of Lionel S. Penrose and Margaret Leathes; m. Joan L. Dilley 1953 (deceased); three s. (one deceased) one d.; ed Cen. Collegiate Inst., London, Ont., Canada, Univ. Coll., London, King's Coll., Cambridge; Math. Physicist, English Electric Co., Luton 1952–55; Research Asst, Yale Univ., USA 1955–56; Lecturer, then Reader, Imperial Coll. London 1956–69; Prof. of Math., Open Univ. 1969–86; Prof. of Math., Heriot-Watt Univ. 1986–94, Prof. Emer. 1994–. *Publications:* Foundations of Statistical Mechanics 1969 (reprinted 2005); about 85 papers in scientific journals. *Leisure interests:* music, chess. *Address:* Department of Mathematics, Heriot-Watt University, Riccarton, Edinburgh, EH14 4AS (office); 29 Frederick Street, Edinburgh, EH2 2ND, Scotland (home). *Telephone:* (131) 451-3225 (office); (131) 225-5879 (home). *E-mail:* o.penrose@hw.ac.uk (office). *Website:* www.macs.hw.ac.uk/~oliver (office).

PENROSE, Sir Roger, Kt, OM, PhD, FRS; British mathematician, writer and academic; *Rouse Ball Professor Emeritus of Mathematics, University of Oxford;* b. 8 Aug. 1931, Colchester, Essex; s. of Lionel Sharples Penrose; m. 1st Joan Wedge 1959 (divorced 1981), three s.; m. 2nd Vanessa Thomas 1988; one s.; ed Univ. Coll. School, Univ. Coll. London and St John's Coll., Cambridge; Asst Lecturer, Bedford Coll. London 1956–57; Research Fellow, St John's Coll. Cambridge 1957–60; NATO Research Fellow, Princeton and Syracuse Univs 1959–61; Research Assoc., King's Coll. London 1961–63; Visiting Assoc. Prof., Univ. of Texas, Austin 1963–64; Reader, Birkbeck Coll. London 1964–66, Prof. of Applied Math. 1966–73, Fellow 1998–; Rouse Ball Prof. of Math., Univ. of Oxford 1973–98, Prof. Emer. 1998–, Emer. Fellow, Wadham Coll.; Fellow, Univ. Coll. London 1975; Gresham Prof. of Geometry, Gresham Coll. 1998–2001; Visiting Prof. Yeshiva, Princeton and Cornell Univs 1966–67, 1969; Lovett Prof. Rice Univ. Houston 1983–87; Distinguished Prof. of Physics and Math. Syracuse Univ. 1987–93, Francis and Helen Pentz Distinguished Prof. of Physics and Math., Penn State Univ. 1993–; mem. London Math. Soc., Cambridge Philosophical Soc., Inst. for Math. and its Applications, Int. Soc. for Gen. Relativity and Gravitation; Foreign mem. Polish Acad. of Science, Accad. Nazionale dei Lincei; Foreign Assoc. NAS 1998; Fellow, Inst. of Physics 1999; Distinguished Supporter, British Humanist Asscn; a Patron of the Oxford Univ. Scientific Soc.; Hon. Fellow, St John's Coll. Cambridge 1987; Hon. mem. Royal Irish Acad. of Science 2001; Dr hc (New Brunswick) 1992, (Surrey) 1993, (Bath) 1994, (London) 1995, (Glasgow) 1996, (Essex) 1996, (St Andrew's) 1997, (Santiniketon) 1998, (Warsaw) 2005, (Katholieke Universiteit Leuven) 2005; Hon. DUniv (Open Univ.) 1998, (Southampton) 2002, (Waterloo, Ontario) 2003, (Leiden) 2004, (Athens) 2005, (York) 2006, (CINVESTAV-IPN, Mexico) 2016; Adams Prize, Univ. of Cambridge 1966–67, Dannie Heinemann Prize, American Physics Soc. and American Inst. of Physics 1971, Eddington Medal, Royal Astronomical Soc. (with S. W. Hawking) 1975, Royal Medal, Royal Soc. 1985, Wolf Foundation Prize in Physics (with S. W. Hawking) 1988, Dirac Medal and Prize, Inst. of Physics 1989, Einstein Medal 1990, Science Book Prize 1990, Naylor Prize, London Math. Soc. 1991, DeMorgan Medal 2004, Copley Medal, Royal Soc. 2008, Fonseca Prize, Univ. of Santiago de Compostela 2011, Richard R. Ernst Medal, ETH Zurich 2012, Clay Award for Dissemination of Mathematical Knowledge 2018. *Publications include:* Techniques of Differential Topology in Relativity 1973, Spinors and Space-time (with W. Rindler), (Vol. I) 1984, (Vol. II) 1986, The Emperor's New Mind 1989, The Nature of Space and Time (with S. W. Hawking) 1996, The Large, the Small and the Human Mind 1997, White Mars (with B. Aldiss) 1999, The Road to Reality: A Complete Guide to the Laws of the Universe 2004, Cycles of Time: An Extraordinary New View of the Universe 2010, Fashion, Faith, and Fantasy in the New Physics of the Universe 2016; articles in scientific journals. *Leisure interests:* three-dimensional puzzles, doodling at the piano. *Address:* Mathematical Institute, University of Oxford, Andrew Wiles Building, Radcliffe Observatory Quarter, Woodstock Road, Oxford, OX2 6GG, England (office). *Telephone:* (1865) 273525 (office). *E-mail:* roger.penrose@maths.ox.ac.uk (office); roger.penrose@penroseinstitute.com (office). *Website:* www.maths.ox.ac.uk/people/profiles/roger.penrose (office); penroseinstitute.com (office).

PENSKE, Roger S.; American motor racing team owner, business executive and fmr racing driver; *Chairman, Penske Corporation;* b. 20 Feb. 1937, Shaker Heights, Ohio; m.; five c.; ed Lehigh Univ.; early career buying, racing and selling race cars, f. Penske Racing 1958–, launched Team Penske 1966, Founding Chair. Penske Corpn 1969, Chair. Penske Truck Leasing Business 1982–, Chair. and CEO Penske Automotive Group, Inc. 1999–; co-f. Championship Auto Racing Teams (CART); Penske Racing has won 12 Indianapolis 500s and 9 CART points titles; Nat. Sports Car Driving Champion 1964; Chair. Bd United Auto Group 1999–; mem. Bd of Dirs Home Depot, Inc., Universal Technical Inst. Inc., Detroit Renaissance, Inc.; fmr mem. Bd of Dirs General Electric Co., Internet Brands, Inc.; Chair. Detroit Super Bowl XL Host Cttee 2004–06; Chair. Downtown Detroit Partnership 2006–, Business Leaders for Mich.; mem. Business Council; Sports Illustrated Driver of the Year 1960, New York Times Driver of the Year 1962, inducted into Int. Motorsports Hall of Fame 1998. *Address:* Penske Corporation, 2550 Telegraph Road, Bloomfield Hills, MI 48302, USA (office). *Telephone:* (248) 648-2000 (office). *Fax:* (248) 648-2005 (office). *Website:* www.penske.com (office).

PENTUS-ROSIMANNUS, Keit; Estonian politician; b. 3 March 1976, Tallinn; m. Rain Rosimannus 2012; ed Univ. Nord, Tallinn Univ., Univ. of Tartu; mem. Tallinn City Council 1999–2007; Political Adviser in Ministry of Justice 2001–02, Ministry of Social Affairs 2002, Ministry of Foreign Affairs 2002–03; Gov., Kesklinn Dist, Tallinn 2003–05; Head of Prime Minister Andrus Ansip's Office 2005; mem. Riigikogu (Parl.) 2007–; Minister of the Environment 2011–14, of Foreign Affairs 2014–15; mem. Reform Party 1998–. *Address:* Riigikogu, Lossi plats 1a, Tallinn 15165, Estonia (office). *Telephone:* 631-6562 (office). *E-mail:* Keit.Pentus-Rosimannus@riigikogu.ee (office). *Website:* www.riigikogu.ee/en (office).

PENZIAS, Arno Allan, PhD; American astrophysicist; *Venture Partner, New Enterprise Associates;* b. 26 April 1933, Munich, Germany; s. of Karl Penzias and Justine Penzias; m. 1st Anne Barras Penzias 1954; one s. two d.; m. 2nd Sherry Chamovelevit 1996; ed City Coll. of New York, Columbia Univ.; mem. tech. staff Bell Laboratories, Holmdel, NJ 1961–72, Head Radiophysics Research Dept 1972–76, Dir Radio Research Lab. 1976–79, Exec. Dir Research, Communications Sciences Div. 1979–81, Exec. Dir Research, Bell Labs, Murray Hill, NJ 1979–81, Vice-Pres. Research 1981–95, Vice-Pres., Chief Scientist 1995–96; Vice-Pres., Chief Scientist Bell Labs Innovations 1996–98; Venture Partner, New Enterprise Assocs 1998–; Sr Tech Adviser Lucent Technologies 1998–; Lecturer, Princeton Univ. 1967–72, Visiting Prof. Astrophysical Sciences Dept 1972–85; Harvard Coll. Observatory Research Assoc. 1968–80; Adjunct Prof., State Univ. of New York (SUNY) at Stony Brook 1974–84; discovered cosmic microwave background radiation 1965; Assoc. Ed. Astrophysical Journal 1978–82; mem. Editorial Bd Annual Review of Astronomy and Astrophysics 1974–78, AT & TBL Tech. Journal 1978–84 (Chair. 1981–84); mem. Bd of Trustees of Trenton State Coll. 1977–79, Visiting Cttee of Calif. Inst. of Tech. 1977–79; mem. Astronomy Advisory Panel of NSF 1978–79, Industrial Panel on Science and Tech. 1982–, Bd of Overseers, School of Eng and Applied Science, Univ. of Pa 1983–86; mem. Max Planck Inst. Fachbeirat 1978–85 (Chair. 1981–83); mem. Council on Competitiveness 1989–; Vice-Chair. Cttee Concerned Scientists; mem. NAS, Nat. Acad. Eng, American Astronomical Soc., World Acad. Art and Science; Fellow AAAS, American Physical Soc.; numerous hon. degrees; numerous prizes, awards and lectureships including Henry Draper Medal, NAS 1977, Herschel Medal, Royal Astronomical Soc. 1977, Pender Award 1992, Int. Eng Consortium Fellow Award 1997, Nobel Prize in Physics 1978. *Publications:* Ideas and Information 1989, Digital Harmony 1995; over 100 scientific papers in various journals. *Leisure interests:* swimming, jogging, skiing. *Address:* New Enterprise Associates, 2490 Sand Hill Road, Menlo Park, CA 94025, USA (office). *Telephone:* (650) 854-9499 (office). *Fax:* (415) 544-0833. *E-mail:* apenzias@nea.com (office). *Website:* www.nea.com (office).

PEPPER, Sir David Edwin, Kt, KCMG, MA, DPhil; British civil servant; *Chairman, Defence Science and Technology Laboratory;* b. 8 Feb. 1948; m.; two s.; ed St John's Coll., Oxford; joined Govt Communications HQ (GCHQ) 1972, held various positions in operational intelligence work, Dir of Personnel 1995–98, Head Corp. Devt Directorate Home Office 1998–2000, Dir of Finance GCHQ 2000–03, Dir GCHQ 2003–08 (retd); conducted consulting work on cyber risk and national security issues in both public and private sectors 2008–14; Chair. Defence Science and Technology Laboratory 2014–; mem. Bd of Dirs Gloucestershire County Council 2008–10; fmr mem. Bd of Dirs National School of Government; fmr Fellow, Sunningdale Inst.; fmr mem. Advisory Bd Thales UK; fmr adviser to Deloitte LLP. *Leisure interests:* music, reading, walking, cooking. *Address:* Defence Science and Technology Laboratory, Porton Down, Salisbury, Wiltshire, SP4 0JQ, England (office). *E-mail:* centralenquiries@dstl.gov.uk (office). *Website:* www.gov.uk/government/organisations/defence-science-and-technology-laboratory (office).

PEPPER, John Ennis, Jr; American business executive; b. 2 Aug. 1938, Pottsville, Pa; s. of John Ennis Pepper, Sr and Irma O'Connor; m. Frances Graham Garber 1967; three s. one d.; ed Yale Univ.; joined Procter & Gamble Co. 1963, Gen. Man. Italian subsidiary 1974–77, Vice-Pres. and Gen. Man. packaged soap div. 1977–80, Group Vice-Pres. 1980–84, mem. Bd Dirs 1984–2003, Exec. Vice-Pres. 1984–86, Pres. 1986–95, Chair. and CEO 1995–99, Chair. 2000–02, Chair. Exec. Cttee of the Bd 2000–03 (retd); Vice-Pres. for Finance and Admin, Yale Univ. 2004–05; Chair. The Walt Disney Co. 2007–12; mem. Bd of Dirs Boston Scientific Corpn 2003–10; Co-Chair. Gov.'s Educ. Council of State of Ohio; CEO Nat. Underground Railroad Freedom Center 2005–07, apptd Presiding Co-Chair. 2007, now Hon. Co-Chair.; mem. Advisory Council Yale School of Man., Exec. Cttee Cincinnati Youth Collaborative, Bd Nat. Campaign to Prevent Teen Pregnancy, Partnership for a Drug-Free America, Trustee, Xavier Univ.; inducted into Junior Achievement US Business Hall of Fame 2008.

PEPPER, Sir Michael, Kt, BSc, MA, ScD, PhD, FRS, FREng; British physicist, academic and business executive; *Pender Professor of Nanoelectronics, University College, London;* b. 10 Aug. 1942, London, England; s. of Morris Pepper and Ruby

Pepper; m. Dr Jeannette D. Josse 1973; two d.; ed St Marylebone Grammar School, London, Reading Univ.; physicist, Mullard Research Lab. 1967–69; physicist engaged in solid state device research, Allen Clark Research Centre, Plessey Co. 1969–73; Researcher, Cavendish Lab., Cambridge 1973–, Prof. of Physics, Univ. of Cambridge 1987–2009; Pender Prof. of Nanoelectronics, Univ. Coll. London 2009–; Visiting Prof., Univ. of Oxford 2010–; Jt Man. Dir Toshiba Research Europe Ltd 1991–2007; Co-founder and Dir TeraView Ltd 2001–; Warren Research Fellow, Royal Soc. 1978–86; Sr Research Fellow, Trinity Coll., Cambridge 1982–87, Professorial Fellow 1987–; Sr Research Fellow, GEC Hirst Research Centre 1982–87; Visiting Prof., Bar-Ilan Univ., Israel 1984; Fellow, Royal Acad. of Eng, American Physical Soc., Academia Europaea; Hon. Prof., Univ. of Otago, NZ 2005–11; Hon. FInstP 2012; Hon. DSc (Bar-Ilan) 1993, (Linköping) 1997, (New South Wales) 2012; Guthrie Prize and Medal, Inst. of Physics 1985, Hewlett-Packard Prize, European Physical Soc. 1985, Hughes Medal, Royal Soc. 1987, Mott Prize, Inst. of Physics 2000, Bakerian Lecturer, Royal Soc. 2004 and various other named lectures, Royal Medal, Royal Soc. 2005, Gold Medal for Business and Innovation, Inst. of Physics 2010, Faraday Medal, Inst. of Eng and Tech. 2013, Silver Dirac Medal, Univ. of New South Wales/Australian Inst. of Physics 2013. *Publications include:* numerous papers on solid state physics and semiconductors in scientific journals. *Leisure interests:* travel, music, whisky tasting. *Address:* Department of Electronic and Electrical Engineering, University College, Torrington Place, London, WC1E 7JE, England (office). *Telephone:* (20) 7679-3978 (office). *E-mail:* michael.pepper@ucl.ac.uk (office).

PEPY, Guillaume; French transport industry executive; *Chairman, Société Nationale des Chemins de Fer Français (SNCF);* b. 26 May 1958, Neuilly-sur-Seine (Hauts-de-Seine); ed Alsace School, Paris, Inst. of Political Studies, Paris, Ecole Nat. d'Admin; began career as magistrate Conseil d'Etat (French Admin. Court); Chief of Staff to Chair., Soc. Nat. des Chemins de Fer Français (SNCF–French Nat. Railways) 1988–93, Dir of Strategy 1993–98, apptd mem. Exec. Cttee 1998, Vice-Pres. –2003, CEO 2003–08, Chair. 2008–, also Chair., Pres. and CEO Man. Bd, SCNF Mobilités 2014–; Chair. Eurostar Group 2002–10, Asscn pour le Développement du Mécénat Industriel et Commerciel (Admical) 2008; Vice-Chair. Keolis Group, Systra; mem. Bd of Dirs Suez Environment SA 2008–17; Officier, Légion d'honneur. *Address:* Société Nationale des Chemins de Fer Français (SNCF), 34 rue du Commandant Mouchotte, 75699 Paris Cedex 14, France (office). *Telephone:* 1-53-25-62-02 (office). *Fax:* 1-53-25-62-25 (office). *E-mail:* guillaume.pepy@sncf.fr (office). *Website:* www.sncf.fr (office).

PEPYS, Sir Mark Brian, Kt, PhD, MD, FRCP, FRCPath, FMedSci, FRS; British physician and academic; *Principal Clinical Research Associate and Director of the Wolfson Drug Discovery Unit, School of Life and Medical Sciences, University College London;* b. 18 Sept. 1944, Cape Town, South Africa; s. of Jack Pepys and Rhoda Pepys; m. Elizabeth Olga Winternitz 1971; one s. one d.; ed Trinity Coll., Cambridge, Univ. Coll. Hosp. Medical School, London, Harvard Medical School; house officer, Univ. Coll. Hosp., London 1968–69; Sr House Officer, Hammersmith Hosp. 1969–70, Asst Lecturer/Hon. Sr Registrar 1974–76, Head of Immunological Medicine and Hon. Consultant Physician 1977–79, Sr Lecturer 1977–81, Reader 1981–84; Prof. of Immunological Medicine 1984–99; MRC Jr Research Fellowship, Cambridge Univ., Research Scholar 1970–73, Fellow (Title A) Trinity Coll. Cambridge 1973–79, Registrar 1973–74; Sr Lecturer/Hon. Consultant and Head of Immunology Dept, Royal Free Hosp. School of Medicine, London 1976–77, Prof. and Head of Medicine 1999–2011, Prof. Emer. of Medicine 2011–, Prin. Clinical Research Assoc. 2011–, Hon. Consultant Physician 1999–, also Dir Wolfson Drug Discovery Unit, School of Life and Medical Sciences 2011–; Fellow, Univ. Coll., London 2003; Founder Fellow, Acad. of Medical Sciences 1998; Royal Coll. of Surgeons of England Sir Arthur Sims Commonwealth Travelling Professorship 1991; Royal Coll. of Physicians Goulstonian Lecturer 1982, Lumleian Lecturer 1998, Moxon Trust Medal 1999, Royal Coll. of Pathologists Kohn Lecturer, GlaxoSmithKline Prize 2007, Ernst Chain Prize 2008. *Publications:* Samter's Immunologic Diseases (contrib.) 2001, Oxford Textbook of Medicine (contrib.) 2003; numerous research papers in learned journals. *Leisure interests:* tennis, surfing, skiing, wine. *Address:* Centre for Amyloidosis and Acute Phase Proteins, Department of Medicine, Royal Free Campus, Rowland Hill Street, London, NW3 2PF (office); 22 Wildwood Road, London, NW11 6TE, England (home). *Telephone:* (20) 7433-2801 (office). *Fax:* (20) 7433-2803 (office). *E-mail:* m.pepys@ucl.ac.uk (office); m.pepys@rfc.ucl.ac.uk (office). *Website:* www.ucl.ac.uk/medicine/amyloidosis (office).

PERA, Marcello; Italian politician and professor of philosophy; b. 28 Jan. 1943, Lucca, Tuscany; ed Univ. of Pisa; Full Prof. of Theoretical Philosophy, Univ. of Catania 1989–92; Full Prof. of Philosophy of Science, Univ. of Pisa 1992–2005; Visiting Fellow, Univ. of Pittsburgh, USA 1984, Van Leer Foundation, Jerusalem 1987, MIT Dept of Linguistics and Philosophy, Cambridge, Mass 1990, Center for the Philosophy of Natural and Social Sciences, LSE 1995–96, American Enterprise Inst., Washington 2008–09, Hudson Inst., Washington 2009–12; mem. Steering Cttee Forza Italia Party, Deputy Leader Forza Italia Parl. Group 1996–2001; Senator, XIII Legislature, Polo List of Freedoms 1996–2001, XIV Legislature, House of Liberty List 2001–06, XV Legislature, House of Freedom List 2006–08, XVI Legislature, People's Liberty List 2008; Head, Judiciary Dept, Nat. Co-ordinator Convention for Liberal Reform; Senator (Forza Italia) 1996–2006, Pres. of Senate 2001–06, Chair. Bd of Regulations 2001–06; mem. Cttee on Justice, Cttee on Educ. and Culture, Jt Cttee on Constitutional Reforms 1996–2001, Foreign Affairs Cttee 2006–13; Benedict XVI School, Rome 2015–17; Pres. Comitato nazionale per il Referendum Costituzionale Liberi Sì 2016–; mem. Advisory Panel Physis – Rivista internazionale di storia della scienza, Epistemologia, Perspectives on Science, Philosophical, Historical, Social; Fellow, Center for the Study of Science in Soc., Univ. of Virginia, USA; mem. Accademia Lucchese di Lettere, Scienze e Arti, Bd of Dir Società italiana di logica e filosofia delle scienze (SILFS) 1990–93; Hon. Grand Commdr of the Order of the Defender of the Realm (Malaysia) 2003. *Publications include:* The Ambiguous Frog – The Galvani-Volta Controversy on Animal Electricity 1991, The Discourses of Science 1994; Senza radici (with Cardinal Joseph Ratzinger); ed. or co-ed. several books including Rational Changes in Science 1987, Persuading Science – The Art of Scientific Rhetoric 1991, Scientific Controversies 2000, Without Roots (with Pope Benedict XVI) 2006, Perché dobbiamo dirci cristian 2008, Why We Should Call Ourselves

Christians: The Religious Roots of Free Societies 2011; numerous articles and essays in learned journals. *Leisure interests:* reading essays and novels.

PERAHIA, Murray; American pianist and conductor; b. 19 April 1947, New York, NY; s. of David Perahia and Flora Perahia; m. Naomi (Ninette) Shohet 1980; two s.; ed High School of Performing Arts, Mannes Coll. of Music, studied with Jeanette Haien, Arthur Balsam, Mieczyslaw Horszowski; debut, Carnegie Hall 1968; has appeared with many of world's leading orchestras and with Amadeus, Budapest, Guarneri and Galimir string quartets; regular recital tours N America, Europe, Japan; Co-Artistic Dir Aldeburgh Festival 1983–89; numerous recordings including complete Mozart Piano Concertos; Prin. Guest Conductor, Acad. of St Martin-in-the-Fields; Dr hc (Univ. of Leeds), (Duke Univ.); Hon., FRCM, FRAM; Hon. KBE 2004; won Leeds Int. Piano Competition 1972, Kosciusko Chopin Prize 1965, Avery Fisher Award 1975, eight Gramophone Record Awards, three Grammy Awards, Royal Acad. of Music Bach Prize 2013, Wolf Prize in Arts 2015. *Recordings include:* Bach Partitas Nos 2, 3, 4 (Midem Classical Award for Solo Instrument Recording 2009) 2008, Bach Partitas Nos 1, 5, 6 2009, Brahms: Händel Variations 2010, Beethoven: Piano Sonatas Nos. 4, 11, 7 2013, Murray Perahia Plays Chopin 2014, The Art of Murray Perahia 2016. *Address:* c/o Linda Petrikova, IMG Artists, Carnegie Hall Tower, 152 West 57th Street, 5th Floor, New York, NY 10019, USA (office). *Telephone:* (212) 994-3500 (office). *Fax:* (212) 994-3550 (office). *E-mail:* lpetrikova@imgartists.com (office). *Website:* www.imgartists.com (office); www.murrayperahia.com.

PERAK, HRH The Sultan of; Tuanku Nazrin Muizzuddin Shah ibni al-Marhum Sultan Azlan Muhibuddin Shah, MA, MPA, PhD; Malaysian; *Timbalan Yang di-Pertuan Agong (Deputy Supreme Ruler);* b. 27 Nov. 1956, George Town, Penang; s. of Sultan Azlan Muhibbudin Shah ibni Almarhum Sultan Yusuff Izzudin Shah Ghafarullahu-lahu (Sultan of Perak) and Tuanku Bainun Binti Mohd Ali (Raja Permaisuri of Perak); m. Zara Salim Davidson, Raja Puan Besar of Perak 2007; one s. one d.; ed Worcester Coll., Oxford, UK, Kennedy School of Govt, Harvard Univ., USA; proclaimed Raja Muda (Crown Prince) of Perak 15 April 1984; apptd Regent of Perak 1989–94 (while father was ninth Yang di-Pertuan Agong); proclaimed Sultan of Perak (following death of his father) 29 May 2014, installed 6 May 2015; elected Timbalan Yang di-Pertuan Agong (Deputy Supreme Ruler) 14 Oct. 2016, took office 13 Dec. 2016, Acting Yang di-Pertuan Agong (Supreme Ruler) following abdication of Sultan Muhammad V 6–24 Jan. 2019; fmr Financial Amb. of Malaysian Int. Islamic Financial Centre; Pro-Chancellor, Universiti Malaya 1989–; Chair. Bd of Govs Malay Coll., Kuala Kangsar; Eminent Fellow, Inst. of Strategic and Int. Studies Malaysia; Grand Kt, Order of Cura Si Manja Kini (Perak Sword of State) 1986, Kt Grand Commdr, Order of Taming Sari (Perak State Kris) 1989, Second Class, Royal Family Order of Selangor 2003, Royal Family Order of Perak, Superior Class, Perak Family Order of Sultan Azlan Shah 2005, mem. First Class, Azlanii Royal Family Order, Kt Grand Commdr, Order of the Perak State Crown, Kt Grand Commdr, Order of the Crown of Perlis. *Address:* Office of HRH The Sultan of Perak, Istana Cempaka Sari, 25 Jalan Sultan Azlan Shah, 31400 Ipoh, Perak Darul Ridzuan, Malaysia. *Telephone:* (5) 2533524; (5) 2536363. *E-mail:* pejsultan@perak.gov.my (office). *Website:* www.rajanazrin.com (office).

PERBEN, Dominique; French lawyer, fmr politician and civil servant; b. 11 Aug. 1945, Lyon; s. of Jacques Perben and Agnès Berthier; m. 1st Annick Demoustier 1968; m. 2nd Corinne Garnier 1996; one s. two d. from previous m.; ed Univ. of Paris, Inst. of Political Studies, Paris; Pvt. Sec. to Maine-et-Loire Prefect 1972–75, to Norbert Ségard (Sec. of State for Postal Services and Telecommunications) 1977; Sec.-Gen. Territoire de Belfort 1975–76; Head of Mission Del. of Devt of Belfort Region 1977, Pres.'s Office Regional Council at Rhône-Alpes 1983–86; Admin. Télédiffusion de France 1980; with Ministry of the Interior 1981; Mayor of Chalon-sur-Saône 1983–2002, Deputy Mayor 2002–04; Vice-Pres. Regional Council Saône-et-Loire 1985–88; mem. Assemblée Nat. (parl) (RPR) for Saône-et-Loire 1986–93, 1995, 1997–2002, for Rhône 2007–12; mem. Regional Council Bourgogne 1992–93; Vice-Pres. Regional Council Rhône 2004–08; RPR Nat. Sec. of Local Elections 1984–86, of General Elections 1986–88, of Communication 1988–89, Asst Sec.-Gen. 1990–93; Minister of Overseas Territories 1993–95, for the Civil Service, Admin. Reform and Decentralization 1995–97; Keeper of the Seals and Minister of Justice 2002–05, Minister of Transport, Capital Works, Tourism and the Sea 2005–07; Chevalier du Mérite agricole. *Leisure interests:* skiing, tennis.

PERDUE, Beverly (Bev) Eaves, BA, MEd, PhD; American fmr politician; *Senior Advisor, Whiteboard Advisors LLC;* b. (Beverly Marlene Moore), 14 Jan. 1947, Grundy, Va; d. of Alfred P. Moore and Irene Morefield Moore; m. 1st Gary Perdue 1970 (divorced 1994); two s.; m. 2nd Bob Eaves 1997; ed Univ. of Kentucky, Univ. of Florida; Dir of Human Services, Neuse River Council of Governments (now the Eastern Carolina Council) 1975–77; Consultant, Craven Co. Hosp. (now Craven Regional Medical Center) 1982; Pres. The Perdue Co. 1985–; mem. N Carolina State Gen. Ass. Reps 1986–90, N Carolina State Senate 1990–2001; Lt Gov. of N Carolina 2001–09, Gov. of N Carolina (first woman) 2009–13; Distinguished Visiting Fellow, Sanford School of Public Policy, Duke Univ. 2013; Founder and Chair. DigiLEARN: Digital Learning Inst.; mem. Advisory Network, Education Post 2014–; Sr Advisor, Whiteboard Advisors LLC 2015–; Democrat. *Address:* Whiteboard Advisors LLC, 100 M Street, SE, Suite 500, Washington, DC 20003, USA. *E-mail:* Info@whiteboardadvisors.com. *Website:* www.whiteboardadvisors.com; www.digilearn.org.

PERDUE, David Alfred, Jr, BS, MS; American business executive and politician; *Senator from Georgia;* b. 10 Dec. 1949, Macon, Ga; s. of David A. Perdue and Gervaise Perdue (née Wynn); m. Bonnie Dunn Perdue; two c.; ed Georgia Inst. of Tech.; Staff Consultant, Kurt Salmon Associates, New York City 1972–75, Partner 1976–83; Vice-Pres. Professional Planning Associates, Atlanta, Ga 1983–86; Vice-Pres., Paul R. Ray & Co., Atlanta 1986–87; Pres., Westar Holding Co. 1987–92; Sr Vice-Pres. (Operations), Sara Lee Corpn, Hong Kong 1992–94; Sr Vice-Pres., Haggar Inc. 1994–98; Sr Vice-Pres. Global Supply Chain, Reebok International Ltd 1998–99, Exec. Vice-Pres. Global Operations Units 1999–2001, Exec. Vice-Pres. Global Supply Chain 2001–02, Pres. and CEO Reebok Brand 2001–02; Chair. and CEO Pillowtex Corpn 2002–03; Chair. and CEO Dollar General Corpn 2003–07; Sr Consultant, Gujarat Heavy Chemicals Ltd, New Delhi, India 2007–11; Partner, Perdue Partners, Atlanta 2011–; Senator from Georgia 2015–; mem. Bd of Dirs Alliant Energy Corpn, Dollar General Corpn

2003–07, Jo-Ann Stores, Inc. 2008–11, Liquidity Services, Inc., Cardlytics, Inc., BRG Sports Inc.; mem. Georgia Council on Youth 1972, Atlanta Care Advisory Bd 1983–85; mem. Mortgage Banking Asscn, Inst. of Certified Financial Planners, Atlanta Athletic Club; Republican. *Leisure interests:* tennis, golf, sailing, reading. *Address:* B40D Dirksen Senate Office Building, Washington, DC 20510, USA (office). *Telephone:* (202) 224-3521 (office). *Website:* www.perdue.senate.gov (office).

PERDUE, George Ervin (Sonny), III, DVM; American politician and fmr state governor; *Secretary of Agriculture;* b. 20 Dec. 1946, Perry, Ga; s. of Ervin Perdue, Jr and Ophie Perdue; m. Mary Ruff 1972; two s. two d.; ed Warner Robbins High School, Univ. of Georgia Coll. of Veterinary Medicine; Capt., USAF 1971–74; fmr veterinarian, Raleigh, NC; Propr Houston Fertilizer and Grain, Agrowstar Inc.; began public service 1980s serving on Houston County Planning and Zoning Bd; Democratic mem. of State Senate, Ga 1991–98, Chair. Higher Educ. Cttee 1993–94, Majority Leader 1995–96, Pres. Pro Tempore 1997, re-elected as Republican cand. 1998–2002; Gov. of GA 2003–11; Sec. of Agric. 2017–. *Leisure interests:* flying, playing sports. *Address:* Department of Agriculture, Washington, DC 20250, USA (office). *Telephone:* (202) 720-2791 (office). *Website:* www.usda.gov (office).

PEREIRA, Domingos Simões, MEng, PhD; Guinea-Bissau civil engineer and politician; b. 20 Oct. 1963, Farim; ed Odessa Inst. of Eng, USSR, California State Univ.-Fresno, USA; began career as civil engineer with Ministry of Public Works, Cacheu, various roles including Nat. Dir of Roads and Land Transport, Dir-Gen. of Roads and Bridges, Chief de Cabinet to Minister of Public Works, Dir, Civil Eng Lab.; Deputy Gen. Dir Cooperativa Unidade e Progresso (construction cooperative), Cacheu 1990; Technical Asst, Infrastructure Reform and Private Sector Devt Project, World Bank 2000; Minister of Infrastructure 2002–03, of Public Works 2004–05; Sec.-Gen., Caritas Guinea-Bissau (charity) 2006–08; Exec. Sec., Comunidade de Países de Língua Portuguesa 2008–12; Prime Minister 2014–15; mem. Partido Africano da Independência da Guiné e Cabo Verde—PAIGC, mem. Standing Cttee, Pres. PAIGC 2014–; Grand Cruz, Ordem do Infante Don Henrique (Portugal) 2012. *Address:* Partido Africano da Independência da Guiné e Cabo Verde (PAIGC), CP 106, Bissau, Guinea-Bissau (office). *E-mail:* dsimoespereira@gmail.com. *Website:* www.dsimoespereira.com.

PEREIRA, Raimundo; Guinea-Bissau lawyer and politician; b. 1956; mem. Partido Africano da Independência da Guiné e Cabo Verde (PAIGC—African Party for Independence of Guinea and Cabo Verde); mem. Assembléia Nacional Popular (Parl.) 2008–, Speaker 2008–12; Pres. (interim) of Guinea-Bissau March–Sept. 2009, Acting Pres. Jan.–April 2012 (deposed).

PEREIRA DOS SANTOS VAN-DÚNEM, Gen. Cândido; Angolan army officer and politician; fmr Deputy Minister of Nat. Defence, Minister of Nat. Defence 2010–14; mem. Cen. Cttee Movimento Popular de Libertação de Angola. *Address:* c/o Ministry of National Defence, Rua 17 de Setembro, Luanda, Angola (office).

PEREIRA PUCHY, Gonzalo; Chilean lawyer, academic and international organization official; b. 1967; ed Inst. of Int. Studies, Univ. of Chile; participated in numerous courses, seminars and meetings organized or sponsored by Cepal, FAO, Int. Whaling Comm., Int. Fund for Animal Welfare, Inst. of Int. Studies, Univ. of Chile and other Chilean univs on Law of the Sea, fishing legislation and environment; represented Chile at int. meeting of operating countries of ships of fishing and oceanographic investigation, Barcelona, Spain 1997; visited Spain and Portugal to observe insts and examine fishing legislation 2001; mem. Chilean del. to XXV Ordinary Meeting of Comision Permanente del Pacifico Sur Quito, Ecuador 2001, Chilean del. to VIII Ronda de Negociaciones Chile, EU to obtain Agreement on Free Trade, Brussels, Belgium 2002, Chilean del. to X Round of Chile Negotiations EU 2002; Prof. of Environmental Law, Univ. of the Sea, Valparaiso, Chile 2001–02; worked at Legal Div. of Under-Sec.'s Office of Fishing, Ministry of Economy 1995–98; Head of Legal Dept, Nat. Fishing Service, Ministry of Economy 1998–2002; Under-Sec. Comision Permanente del Pacifico Sur (Perm. Comm. of the South Pacific) 2002–06, Sec.-Gen. 2006–10.

PEREK, Luboš, DrSc; Czech astronomer and academic; b. 26 July 1919, Prague; s. of Zdeněk Perek and Vilemina Perek (née Trapp); m. Vlasta Straková 1945 (died 2007); ed Masaryk Univ., Brno and Charles Univ., Prague; Asst Astronomical Inst., Masaryk Univ., Brno 1946, Head 1953; Head, Stellar Dept, Astronomical Inst. of Czechoslovak Acad. of Sciences, Prague 1956, Dir Astronomical Inst. 1968–75; Vice-Pres. Comm. of the Galactic Structure and Dynamics, Int. Astronomical Union 1961–64, Asst Gen. Sec., Int. Astronomical Union 1964–67, Gen. Sec. 1967–70; Chief, Outer Space Affairs Division, UN Secr. 1975–80; Visiting Prof., Dearborn Observatory, Evanston, Ill. 1964; mem. Czechoslovak Astronomical Soc., Exec. Cttee Int. Council of Scientific Unions 1967–70, Vice-Pres. 1968–70; Chair. Int. Astronautical Fed. 1980–82; mem. Leopoldina Acad., Int. Acad. of Astronautics, Int. Inst. of Space Law, Nat. Acad. of the Air and Space, Toulouse, Czech Learned Soc. 1999; Assoc. mem. Royal Astronomical Soc.; Dr hc (Masaryk Univ., Brno) 1999; Silver Plaque for services to science 1969, Gold Plaque 1989, Janssen Medal, Paris 1992. *Publications include:* Catalogue of Galactic Planetary Nebulae (with L. Kohoutek) 1967, about 80 articles on geostationary orbits, definition of space, space debris and environment of space. *Leisure interest:* collecting seashells. *Address:* Astronomical Institute, Bočni II 1401, 141 31 Prague 4 (office); Kouřimská 28, 130 00 Prague 3, Czech Republic (home). *Telephone:* (267) 103068 (office); (272) 744780 (home). *Fax:* (272) 769023 (office). *E-mail:* perek@ig.cas.cz (office). *Website:* www.galaxy.ig.cas.cz (office); www.asu.cas.cz.

PERELLA, Joseph (Joe) Robert, MBA, CPA; American investment banker; *Chairman, Perella Weinberg Partners LP;* b. 20 Sept. 1941, Newark, New Jersey; s. of Dominic Perella and Agnes Perella; m. Amy Gralnick 1974; ed Lehigh Univ., Harvard Business School; public accountant, Haskins & Sells, New York 1964–70; consultant, IBRD, Washington, DC 1971; Assoc. The First Boston Corpn New York 1972–74, Asst Vice-Pres. 1974–75, Vice-Pres. 1975–78, Man. Dir 1978–88; Chair. Wasserstein, Perella & Co. New York 1988–93; head of mergers and acquisitions then Chair. Institutional Securities and Investment Banking Group, mem. operating Cttee Morgan Stanley 1993–2005; co-f. Perella Weinberg Partners LP (investment banking firm), New York, Chair. 2006–, CEO 2006–14. *Address:* Perella Weinberg Partners LP, 767 Fifth Avenue, New York, NY 10153, USA (office). *Telephone:* (212) 287-3200 (office). *Fax:* (212) 287-3201 (office). *Website:* www.pwpartners.com (office).

PERELMAN, Grigori Yakovlevich, CandSci; Russian mathematician; b. 13 June 1966, Leningrad (now St Petersburg); ed Leningrad Secondary School #239, Leningrad State Univ.; worked under Aleksandr Danilovich Aleksandrov and Yuri Dmitrievich Burago at Leningrad Dept of Steklov Math. Inst. of USSR (now Russian) Acad. of Sciences –2003; held posts at several univs in USA late 1980s–early 1990s; invited to spend a semester each at New York Univ. and State Univ. of NY at Stony Brook 1992; held fellowship at Univ. of Calif., Berkeley 1993–95; returned to Steklov Math. Inst. 1995; accepted invitation to visit and give series of talks on his work at MIT, Princeton Univ., State Univ. of NY at Stony Brook, Columbia Univ. and Harvard Univ. 2003; solved affirmatively the famous Poincaré conjecture, posed in 1904, and regarded as one of the most important and difficult open problems in math.; won Gold Medal as mem. USSR team competing in Int. Math. Olympiad 1982, Fields Medal (co-recipient) for "his contributions to geometry and his revolutionary insights into the analytical and geometric structure of the Ricci flow" (declined to accept the award or appear at the congress) 2006, Millennium Prize, Clay Mathematical Inst. 2010. *Publications:* numerous papers in professional journals. *Address:* c/o Steklov Mathematical Institute, Gubkina str. 8, 119991 Moscow, Russia.

PERELMAN, Ronald Owen, MBA; American business executive and philanthropist; *Chairman, Revlon, Inc.;* b. 1 Jan. 1943, Greensboro, NC; s. of Raymond G. Perelman and Ruth Perelman (née Caplan); m. 1st Faith Golding 1965 (divorced 1984); four c.; m. 2nd Claudia Cohen 1985 (divorced 1994); one d.; m. 3rd Patricia Duff 1995 (divorced 1996); one d.; m. 4th Ellen Barkin (q.v.) 2000 (divorced 2006); m. 5th Anna Chapman 2010; two c.; ed The Haverford School, Univ. of Pennsylvania Wharton School of Finance; along with his father and brother, controlled American Paper Products corpn; left co. to buy Belmont Industries Inc. 1966–78; Dir, Chair. and CEO MacAndrews & Forbes Group, Inc., New York City 1978–, MacAndrews & Forbes Holdings, Inc., Andrews Group Inc., New York 1985–; Dir, Chair. and CEO Revlon Group, Inc. (later Revlon, Inc.), New York City 1985–; Chair., CEO and Man. REV Holdings LLC; Chair. Nat. Health Labs, La Jolla, Calif. 1985–; Chair. Technicolor Inc., Hollywood, Calif.; Co-Chair. and CEO Panavision Inc.; Pres. Solomon R. Guggenheim Museum, NY 1995–; Dir Four Star International Inc., Compact Video Inc., M&F Worldwide Corpn, Scientific Games Corpn. *Address:* Revlon, Inc., 237 Park Avenue, New York, NY 10017 (office); Solomark Guggenheim Museum, 1071 5th Avenue, New York, NY 10128, USA. *Telephone:* (212) 527-4000 (office). *Fax:* (212) 527-4995 (office). *E-mail:* investor.relations@revlon.com (office). *Website:* www.revlon.com (office); www.revloninc.com (office).

PERÉNYI, Miklós; Hungarian cellist and composer; b. 5 Jan. 1948, Budapest; ed Ferenc Liszt Music Acad. of. Budapest, Accademia Santa Cecilia, studied with Enrico Meinardi in Rome, Ede Bande in Budapest, Pablo Casals in Zermatt; started playing cello aged five, first public recital aged nine, Budapest; Violoncello Teacher and Lecturer, Ferenc Liszt Acad. of Music, Budapest 1974–, Prof. 1980–; numerous appearances at int. music festivals including Edinburgh, Lucerne, Prague, Salzburg, Vienna, Hohenems, Warsaw, Berlin, also cello festivals in Kronberg, Winterthur and Manchester, Festival Pablo Casals, Prades, France, as well as in Japan, China and USA; collaborates with pianist András Schiff, including concerts at Schubertiade Festival, Austria, Wigmore Hall, London, Edinburgh and Ruhr Festivals; performed Lutoslawski's Cello Concerto with Berlin Philharmonic Orchestra and Sir Simon Rattle, Berlin, Essen and Paris 2013; tour with Israel Philharmonic and András Schiff 2013–14; Prizewinner, Int. Pablo Casals Cello Competition, Budapest 1963, Liszt Prize 1970, Kossuth Prize 1980, Bartók-Pasztory Prize 1987. *Recordings include:* works of Ernö Dohnányi, Ferenc Farkas, Zoltán Kodály, György Ligeti, András Mihály and Sándor Veress (with Dénes Várjon), Hungarian Cello Music, Haydn Cello Concertos 1991, Zoltán Kodály, Sonatas for Cello and Piano 1994, Complete Beethoven Sonatas (with András Schiff) 2004, Beethoven: Complete Music for Piano and Violoncello (with András Schiff) (Cannes Classical Award 2005) 2004, Bach, Brahms, Britten (with Dénes Várjon) 2010, Britten, Bach, Ligeti 2012, Schubert: String Quartet 2013. *Leisure interests:* swimming, cycling. *Address:* c/o Impresariat Simmenauer GmbH, Kurfürstendamm 211, 10719 Berlin, Germany (office). *Telephone:* (30) 414-781-714 (office). *Fax:* (30) 414-781-713 (office). *E-mail:* oda.caspar@impresariat-simmenauer.de (office). *Website:* www.impresariat-simmenauer.de (office).

PERERA, Amrith Rohan; Sri Lankan lawyer and diplomatist; b. 1947; ed Univ. of Ceylon; apptd Advocate Supreme Court 1973; Asst Legal Adviser Ministry of Foreign Affairs 1976, then Additional Legal Adviser and Legal Adviser, working for 30 years in the Ministry; Commr Lessons Learnt and Reconciliation Comm. (LLRC) 2010; Perm. Rep. to UN 2015–; fmr Chair. UN Ad-hoc Cttee on Measures to Eliminate Int. Terrorism, Vice-Pres. UN 72nd Gen. Ass.; Chair. Eminent Persons Group (EPG) Asian African Legal Consultative Org. (AALCO); mem. Int. Law Comm. (ILC) 2007–11. *Publications:* International Terrorism 1997, International Law Changing Horizons 1997. *Address:* Permanent Missions of Sri Lanka, 820 Second Avenue, 2nd Floor, New York, NY 10017, USA (office). *Telephone:* (212) 986-7040 (office). *Fax:* (212) 986-1838 (office). *E-mail:* mail@slmission.com (office). *Website:* www.un.int/srilanka (office).

PERERA, Air Chief Marshal G. Donald; Sri Lankan diplomatist and air force officer; s. of G. Victor Perera and W. Somawathi Perera; ed Nat. Defence Coll., India, Air Command and Staff Coll., Air Univ., Maxwell Air Force Base, Ala, USA; participated in Air Operations in North and East since 1983, Chief of Staff 1998–2002, Commdr Sri Lanka Air Force 2002–06, Chief of Defence Staff 2006–09; Amb. to Israel 2010–13; Vishista Seva Vibhushanaya, Utthama Seva Padakkama, Repub. of Sri Lanka Armed Services Medal, Sri Lanka Air Force 50th Anniversary Medal, Sri Lanka Armed Services Long Service Medal, Presidential Inauguration Medal, 50th Independence Anniversary Commemoration Medal, North and East Operations Medal, Purna Bhumi Padakkama, Vadamarachchi Operations Medal, Riviresa Campaign Service Medal.

PERERA, Joseph Michael; Sri Lankan politician; b. 15 Sept. 1941; m.; mem. Ja-Ela Urban Council 1964–71, Vice-Chair. 1967–70, Chair. 1970–71; Chief Organiser of the Opposition (United National Party—UNP) 1971–76; mem. First Nat.

State Ass. 1976–77, Second Nat. State Ass. 1977–78, mem. First Parl. 1978–88, mem. Parl. for Gampaha Dist 1989–2010, Nat. List 2010–, Speaker 2001–04; Minister of Home Affairs Jan.–Aug. 2015. *Address:* Gamameda Road, Thudella, Ja-Ela, Sri Lanka (home).

PERETSMAN, Nancy B., AB, MPPM; American investment banker; *Executive Vice-President and Managing Director, Allen & Co. LLC;* m. Robert Scully 1988; one d.; ed Woodrow Wilson School, Princeton Univ., Yale School of Man.; joined Salomon Brothers in 1983, Man. Dir 1990–95; Exec. Vice-Pres. and Man. Dir Allen & Co. LLC (fmrly Allen & Co. Inc.) 1995–; mem. Bd Dirs Charter Communications Inc. –2004, Priceline.com 1999–, several privately held cos; mem. Advisory Bd Narad Networks; Vice-Chair. The New School; mem. Bd Teach for America; Trustee Inst. of Advanced Study, Princeton Univ. (Emer.); named by Money magazine one of Smartest Women in the Money Business, Financial Women's Asscn Private Sector Woman of the Year 2001. *Address:* Allen & Co. LLC, 711 5th Avenue, 9th Floor, New York, NY 10022, USA (office). *Telephone:* (212) 832-80000 (office). *Fax:* (212) 832-8023 (office).

PERETZ, Amir; Israeli politician and fmr trade union official; b. (Armand Peretz), 1952, Morocco; m. Ahlama; four c.; emigrated to Israel at age of four; fmr Munitions Officer, Paratroopers Div., Israeli Army; fmr farmer; elected Mayor of Sderot 1983; mem. Knesset 1988–; CEO Histadrut Haovdim Haleumit 1995–2005; founder and Leader Am Ehad (One Nation) 1999–2004 (until merger with Israel Labour Party); Chair. Israel Labour Party 2005–07; Deputy Prime Minister and Minister of Defence 2006–07; Minister of Environmental Protection 2013–14; mem. Labor Party 2004–12, 2015–, Ha'Tnuah Party 2012–15; mem. Peace Now. *Address:* Israel Labour Party, POB 62033, Tel-Aviv 61620, Israel (office). *Telephone:* 3-6899444 (office). *Fax:* 3-6899420 (office). *E-mail:* aperetz@knesset .gov.il (office); mifkad@havoda.org.il (office). *Website:* www.knesset.gov.il (office); www.havoda.org.il (office).

PERETZ, David Lindsay Corbett, CB, MA; British international finance official; b. 29 May 1943; s. of Michael Peretz and April Peretz; m. Jane Wildman 1966; one s. one d.; ed The Leys School Cambridge and Exeter Coll. Oxford; Asst Prin. Ministry of Tech. 1965–69; Head of Public Policy and Institutional Studies, Int. Bank Research Org. 1969–76; Prin. HM Treasury 1976–80, Asst Sec. External Finance 1980–84, Prin. Pvt. Sec. to Chancellor of Exchequer 1984–85, Under-Sec. (Home Finance) 1985–86, (Monetary Group, Public Finance) 1986–90; UK Exec. Dir IMF and IBRD and Econ. Minister, Washington, DC 1990–94; Deputy Dir Int. Finance, HM Treasury 1994–99; UK G7 Financial Sherpa 1994–98; Sr Adviser, World Bank Group 1999–2005, Exec. Sec. World Bank Joint Task Force on Small States 2001; consultant, Ind. Evaluation Office of the IMF, Washington, DC 2007–; Chair. UK Advisory Cttee on Devt Effectiveness 2007–10, Bermuda Fiscal Responsibility Panel 2015–. *Leisure interests:* walking, sailing, listening to music. *E-mail:* dlcperetz@yahoo.co.uk (home).

PEREZ, Antonio M., MBA; American/Spanish business executive; *Special Advisor to the Board, Eastman Kodak Company;* ed Technical Univ. of Madrid, INSEAD, France; fmrly with Hewlett-Packard Co., positions including Corp. Vice-Pres., Pres. Consumer Business, mem. Exec. Council; Pres. and CEO Gemplus Int. 2000–01; COO Eastman Kodak Co. 2003–05, Pres. 2003–06, CEO 2005–14, Chair. 2006–14, Special Advisor to Bd of Dirs 2014–; mem. Bd of Dirs Freescale Semiconductor Inc.; mem. Business Roundtable. *Address:* Eastman Kodak Company, 343 State Street, Rochester, NY 14650, USA (office). *Fax:* (585) 724-1089 (office). *Website:* www.kodak.com (office).

PEREZ, Thomas Edward, BA, JD; American lawyer and government official; b. 7 Oct. 1961, Buffalo, New York; s. of Rafael Perez and Grace Perez (née Brache); m. Ann Marie Staudenmaier; three c.; ed Brown Univ., Harvard Law School, John F. Kennedy School of Govt; law clerk for Judge Zita Weinshienk, US Dist Court, Colo 1987–89; called to the Bar, New York 1988, Washington, DC 1988; Trial Lawyer, Criminal Section, Civil Rights Div., US Dept of Justice, Washington, DC 1989–94, Deputy Chief, Criminal Section 1994–97, Deputy Asst Attorney for Civil Rights 1998–99, Asst Attorney-Gen. for Civil Rights 2009–13; Special Counsel to Senator Edward Kennedy 1995–98; Dir Office of Civil Rights, US Dept of Health and Human Services, Washington, DC 1999–2002; Asst Prof. and Dir Clinical Law Office, Univ. of Maryland School of Law, Baltimore 2001–07; Sec., Dept of Labor, Licensing & Regulation, State of Maryland 2007–09; Sec. of Labor 2013–17; Hon. LLD (Brown Univ.) 2014, (Drexel Univ. School of Law) 2014, Hon. DH (Oberlin Coll.) 2014.

PEREZ, Vincent; Swiss actor; b. 10 June 1964, Lausanne; m. Karine Silla; three c.; ed acting studies in Geneva, Conservatoire Nat. Supérieur d'Art Dramatiqu, Paris, school of the Théâtre Nanterre-Amandiers; best known internationally for playing the title character Ashe Corven in The Crow: City of Angels and for starring in Queen of the Damned, playing Marius de Romanus; Prix Jean Gabin 1992, named one of People magazine's 50 Most Beautiful People in the World 1995. *Films include:* Gardien de la nuit 1986, Hotel de France 1987, La maison de jade 1988, Cyrano de Bergerac 1990, The Voyage of Captain Fracassa 1990, La neige et le feu 1991, Indochine 1992, Cendre d'or (short) 1992, Fanfan 1993, La Reine Margot 1994, Beyond the Clouds 1995, Line of Life 1996, The Crow: City of Angels 1996, Amy Foster 1997, On Guard (Best Actor, Cabourg Romantic Film Festival 1998) 1997, Those Who Love Me Can Take the Train 1998, The Treat 1998, Talk of Angels 1998, Time Regained 1999, Épouse-moi 2000, The Libertine 2000, I Dreamed of Africa 2000, Love Bites 2001, Bride of the Wind 2001, Queen of the Damned 2002, The Pharmacist 2003, Happiness Costs Nothing 2003, Fanfan la Tulipe 2003, I'm Staying! 2003, The Car Keys 2003, Welcome to Switzerland 2004, Battle of the Brave 2004, Kod apokalipsisa (as Vensan Peres) 2007, Arn: The Knight Templar 2007, Tomorrow at Dawn 2009, Bruc, the Manhunt 2010, Inhale 2010, Tempus Fugit (short) 2010, Monsieur Papa 2011, A Butterfly Kiss 2011, Ma première fois 2012, Lines of Wellington 2012, Ce que le jour doit à la nuit 2012, Un prince (presque) charmant 2013, Puppylove 2013, The Price of Desire 2015, Dalida 2016, Everyone's Life 2017, Based on a True Story 2017, At Eternity's Gate 2018, The Summer House 2018, L'intervention 2019; dir: L'échange (short) (also writer) 1992, Rien à dire (short) 1999, Once Upon an Angel (also writer) 2002, The Secret (also producer) 2007. *Television includes:* Série noire (series) 1986, Hamlet (film) 1990, Shot Through the Heart (film) 1998, Frankenstein (film) 2004, Le juge (mini-series) 2005, Avec le temps… (film) 2006, Madame De Pompadour: The King's Favourite (film) 2006, Paris Criminal Inquiries (series) 2007–08, Die Jahrhundertlawine (film) 2008, Lo scandalo della Banca Romana (series) 2010, Trahie! (film) 2010, Arn (mini-series) 2010, Cesare Mori: Il prefetto di ferro (film) 2012, As Linhas de Torres Vedras (mini-series) 2012, Disparus (mini-series) 2014, Riviera (series) 2017. *Address:* c/o Fanny Minvielle, Ubba Agence Artistique. 3, rue de Turbigo, 75001 Paris, France (office). *Telephone:* 1-44-54-26-40 (office). *E-mail:* fm@ubba.eu (office). *Website:* www.ubba.eu (office).

PEREZ, William (Bill) D., BA; American business executive; *Senior Advisor, Greenhill & Co.;* b. 10 Sept. 1947, Akron, Ohio; m. Catherine A. Perez; two c.; ed Cornell Univ., American Grad. School of Int. Man.; joined S.C. Johnson & Son Inc. 1970, fmr positions include Gen. Man. S.C. Johnson Spain, S.C. Johnson Iberia, Vice-Pres. and Regional Dir of Consumer Products, Latin America, Vice-Pres. Home Care business, Exec. Vice-Pres. of Consumer Products, N America, Pres. and COO Worldwide Consumer Products 1993–96, Pres. and CEO S.C. Johnson & Son Inc. 1996–2004; Pres. and CEO Nike Inc. 2004–06 (resgnd), mem. Bd of Dirs –2006; Pres. and CEO Wm. Wrigley Jr. Co., Chicago 2006–08; Sr Advisor, Greenhill & Co. 2010–; mem. Bd of Dirs Campbell Soup Co., Johnson & Johnson, Whirlpool Corpn, Northwest Memorial Hospital, Boys and Girls Clubs of Chicago; Trustee, Cornell Univ. *Leisure interests:* running. *Address:* Greenhill & Co., 155 North Upper Wacker Drive, #4550, Chicago, IL 60606, USA (office). *Telephone:* (312) 846-4994 (office). *Website:* www.greenhill.com (office).

PÉREZ BALLADARES, Ernesto, MBA; Panamanian fmr head of state; b. 29 June 1946, Panama City; s. of Ernesto Pérez Balladares Sr and María Enriqueta González Revilla; m. Dora Boyd; two s. three d.; ed Univs of Notre Dame and Pennsylvania; Dir and Corp. Credit Official for Cen. America and Panama, Citibank 1971–75; Minister of Finance and the Treasury 1976–81, of Planning and Econ. Policy 1981–82; Founding mem. Partido Revolucionario Democrático (PRD) 1979, Sec.-Gen. 1982, 1992; Dir-Gen. Instituto de Recursos Hidráulicos y Electrificación 1983; Pres. of Panama 1994–99; Pres. Golden Fruit, SA, Inversionista el Torreón, SA; mem. Legislation Comm., PRD Political Comm.; under house arrest during investigation by Special Prosecutor of money laundering charges 2010; Order of Sacred Treasure (1st class) (Japan) 1980, Orden Aguila Azteca en Grado de Bando (Mexico) 1981.

SÁNCHEZ PÉREZ-CASTEJÓN, Pedro, PhD; Spanish politician; *President of the Government (Prime Minister);* b. 29 Feb. 1972, Madrid; m. María Begoña Gómez Fernández; two d.; ed Complutense Univ., Univ. of Brussels, IESE Business School, Univ. of Navarra, Camilo José Cela Univ.; apptd Adviser EU 1998; Chief of Staff to High Rep. of UN in Bosnia and Herzegovina 1999; Econ. Adviser of Comisión Ejecutiva Federal, Spanish Socialist Workers' Party (PSOE) 2000–04, mem. Congress of Deputies (PSOE) 2009–11, 2013–16, Gen. Sec. PSOE 2014–16, 2017–18, Leader of Opposition 2014–16, 2017–18; Pres. of the Govt (Prime Minister) 2018–; mem., Madrid City Council 2004–09; Prof. of Econ. Structure and History of Econ. Thought, Camilo José Cela University 2008. *Address:* Office of the President of the Government, Complejo de la Moncloa, Avda de Puerta de Hierro s/n, 28071 Madrid, Spain (office). *Telephone:* (91) 3214000 (office). *E-mail:* secretariapresidente@presidencia.gob.es (office). *Website:* www .lamoncloa.gob.es (office).

PÉREZ DE BRICIO OLARIAGA, Carlos; Spanish oil industry executive; b. 31 Dec. 1927, Madrid; Vice-Pres. Comm. of Basic Industries of Iron and Steel 1968; Chair. Sub-Cttee on Iron and Steel, OECD 1969; Chief of Directorate of Naval and Iron and Steel Industries 1969–74; Minister of Industry 1975–76, 1976–77; Pres. Sodiex 1981–83; Dir Compañía Española de Petróleos SA (CEPSA) 1991–2008, Exec. Vice-Pres. 1996, Chair. and CEO 1996–2008; Head of Ministry of Public Works 1997; Pres. Union of Iron and Steel Cos (UNESID) 1968; Founder and Pres. Spanish Confed. of Metal Cos (CONFEMETAL) 1978–; Vice-Pres. Spanish Confed. of Enterprise Orgs (CEOE) 1981–98, European Org. of Metallurgical Industries 1990; fmr mem. Advisory Bd Macosa, Carburos Metálicos, Acerinox; mem. Bd Dirs Compañía Logistica de Hidrocarburos CLH SA 2004.

PÉREZ DE CUÉLLAR, Javier; Peruvian politician and diplomatist (retd); b. 19 Jan. 1920, Lima; m. Marcela Temple; two c.; ed Catholic Univ., Lima; joined Foreign Ministry 1940, diplomatic service 1944; served as Sec. in embassies in France, UK, Bolivia, Brazil (later Counsellor); Dir Legal and Personnel Dept, Dir of Admin., of Protocol and of Political Affairs, Ministry of External Relations 1961–63; Amb. to Switzerland 1964–66; Perm. Under-Sec. and Sec.-Gen. Foreign Office 1966–69, Amb. to USSR (concurrently to Poland) 1969–71, to Venezuela 1978; Perm. Rep. to UN 1971–75; mem. UN Security Council 1973–74, Pres. 1974; Special Rep. of UN Sec.-Gen. in Cyprus 1975–77; UN Under-Sec.-Gen. for Special Political Affairs 1979–81; apptd Legal Adviser, Ministry of Foreign Affairs 1981; UN Sec.-Gen. 1982–91; Prime Minister of Peru 2000–01; Amb. to France 2001–04; Pres. World Comm. on Culture and Devt UN/UNESCO 1992, Int. Disability Foundation 1992, Fondation de l'Arche de la Fraternité 1993; unsuccessful cand. for Pres. of Peru 1995; fmr Prof. of Diplomatic Law, Acad. Diplomática del Perú and Prof. of Int. Relations, Acad. de Guerra Aérea del Perú; del. to First UN Gen. Ass. 1946–47; Montague Burton Visiting Prof. of Int. Relations, Univ. of Edinburgh 1985; Dir Repub. Nat. Bank of New York 1992; mem. Club de Madrid, Acad. Mexicana de Derecho Int. 1988–; Dr hc (Univ. of Nice) 1983, (Jagiellonian, Charles and Sofia Univs, Univ. of San Marcos and Vrije Univ., Brussels) 1984, (Carleton Univ., Ottawa, Sorbonne Univ., Paris) 1985, (Osnabruck) 1986, (Univs of Mich., Coimbra, Mongolian State, Humbolt, Moscow State) 1987, (Univ. of Leiden) 1988, (Cambridge) 1989, (Univ. of Kuwait) 1993, (Oxford) 1993; Prince of Asturias Prize for Int. Cooperation 1987, Olaf Palme Prize for Public Service 1989, Alexander Onassis Foundation Prize 1990, Presidential Medal of Freedom (US) 1991, Four Freedoms Award (Franklin Delano Roosevelt Inst.) 1992. *Publication:* Manual de Derecho Diplomático 1964, Anarchy or Order 1992, Pilgrimage for Peace 1997.

PÉREZ ESQUIVEL, Adolfo; Argentine human rights leader, architect, painter, writer and sculptor and academic; b. 26 Nov. 1931, Buenos Aires; m. Amanda Pérez 1956; three s.; ed Nat. School of Fine Arts, Buenos Aires; trained as architect and sculptor; Prof. of Art, Manuel Belgrano Nat. School of Fine Arts, Buenos Aires 1956–71; Prof., Faculty of Architecture and Urban Studies, Univ. Nacional de la Plata; gave up teaching to concentrate on non-violent human rights movt; f. Servicio Paz y Justicia en America Latina, Buenos Aires 1973, Sec.-Gen. 1974–86,

Hon. Pres. 1986–; Co-founder Ecumenical Movt for Human Rights, Argentina; Pres. Perm. Ass. for Human Rights; arrested 1977, released May 1978; visited Europe 1980; Pres. Int. League for Human Rights and Liberation of Peoples, Milan 1987; Prof. of Peace and Human Rights Studies, Univ. of Buenos Aires 1998; fmr Rector UN Univ. for Peace; campaigned against practice by Esquel Police Dept of training children into paramilitary squads 2010; criticized Pres. Barack Obama over the killing of Osama Bin Laden 2011; Hon. Citizen of Assisi 1982; Nobel Prize for Peace 1980, Pacem in Terris Award 1999. *Publication:* Caminando Junto al Pueblo (Walking Together with the People) 1995. *Address:* Servicio Paz y Justicia, Piedras 730, CP 1070, Buenos Aires, Argentina.

PÉREZ MOLINA, Gen. (retd) Otto Fernando; Guatemalan fmr army officer, politician and fmr head of state; b. 1 Dec. 1950, Guatemala City; ed School of the Americas (now Western Hemisphere Inst. for Security Cooperation), Fort Benning, Columbus, Ga and Inter-American Defense Coll., Washington, DC, USA; served as Dir of Mil. Intelligence and Insp.-Gen. of the Army, member of group of army officers who backed Defence Minister Óscar Mejía's coup d'état against de facto Pres. Efraín Ríos Montt 1983, also instrumental in restoring normality in aftermath of Pres. Jorge Serrano Elías's abortive 'self-coup' 1993; apptd by incoming Pres. Ramiro de León Carpio as Head of Presidential Gen. Staff (EMP) 1993–95; also represented mil. in negotiations that led to 1996 Peace Accords, ending Guatemala's 30-year-long civil war; represented Guatemala on Inter-American Defense Bd 1998–2000; retd from active mil. duty in Jan. 2000; f. Partido Patriota (Patriotic Party) 2001; elected to Congress 2003; cand. in presidential elections 2007, 2011; Pres. of Guatemala 2012–15 (resgnd). *Address:* c/o Partido Patriota, 11 Calle 11-54, Zona 1, Guatemala City, Guatemala.

PÉREZ-REVERTE, Arturo; Spanish journalist and writer; b. 1951, Cartagena, Murcia; fmr journalist, war corresp., Pueblo; war corresp., Spanish nat. TV; now writes fiction full-time; mem. Royal Spanish Acad. 2003–; Chevalier des Arts et des Lettres 1998, Ordre nat. du Mérite 2008; Gran Cruz del Mérito Naval 2005; Grand Prix for Detective Literature (France) 1993, Asturias Prize for Journalism for his coverage of the war in the fmr Yugoslavia for TV 1993, Ondas Prize for Radio de España's La Ley de la Calle 1993. *Films include:* El Maestro de Esgrima 1992, La Tabla de Flandes 1994, Cachito 1995, Territorio Comanche 1997, La Novena Puerta 1999, Gitano 2000, Alatriste 2006, La Carta Esférica 2007. *Television includes:* Camino de Santiago 1999, Quart. El hombre de Roma 2007, La Reina del Sur 2011, Las aventuras del capitán Alatriste 2015. *Publications include:* El Húsar 1986, El maestro de esgrima (trans. as The Fencing Master) 1988, La tabla de Flandes (trans. as The Flanders Panel) 1990, El club Dumas (trans. as The Dumas Club) 1993, La sombra del águila 1993, Territorio comanche 1994, Un asunto de honor 1995, Obra breve 1995, La piel del tambor (trans. as The Seville Communion; Jean Monnet Prize for European Literature 1997) 1995, El capitán Alatriste (trans. as Captain Alatriste) 1996, Limpieza de sangre (trans. as Purity of Blood) 1997, El sol de Breda (trans. as The Sun Over Breda) 1998, Patente de corso 1998, La carta esférica (trans. as The Nautical Chart) (Prix Beau Livre, Acad. de Marine Française) 2000, El oro del rey (trans. as The King's Gold) 2000, Con ánimo de ofender 2001, La Reina del Sur (translated as The Queen of the South) 2002, El caballero del jubón amarillo (trans. as The Man in the Yellow Doublet) 2003, Cabo Trafalgar 2004, No me cogeréis vivo 2005, El pintor de batallas (trans. as The Painter of Battles) (Premio Vallombrosa-Gregor von Rezzori 2008) 2006, Corsarios de Levante 2006, Un Día de Cólera 2007, Ojos Azules 2009, Cuando éramos honrados mercenarios 2009, El asedio 2010, El puente de los Asesinos 2011, Los barcos se pierden en tierra 2011, El tango de la Guardia Vieja 2012, El francotirador paciente 2013, Perros e hijos de perra 2014, El asedio 2015, Hombres buenos 2015, La Guerra Civil contada a los jóvenes 2015, Falcó 2016, Eva 2017, Los perros duros no bailan 2018, Sabotaje 2018; contrib. to Spanish periodicals, including XL Semanal (weekly article). *Address:* c/o RDC Agencia Literaria, Fernando VI 13–15, 3° derecha, 28004 Madrid, Spain (office). *Telephone:* (91) 3085585 (office); (91) 3912034 (office). *Fax:* (91) 3085600 (office). *E-mail:* rdc@rdclitera.com (office); RDCprom@rdclitera.com (office). *Website:* www.perezreverte.com.

PÉREZ RODRÍGUEZ, Florentino; Spanish civil engineer and construction industry executive; *Chairman and CEO, ACS Group;* b. 1947, Madrid; ed Polytechnic Univ. of Madrid; fmr Lecturer in Physical Foundations of Tech., Higher Tech. School of Civil Eng, Madrid; began career as Dir Spanish Road Asscn 1971; served in various public admin posts 1976–82, including Del. for Sanitation and Environment, Madrid City Council, Gen. Sub-Dir of Promotion, Centre for Devt of Industrial Tech., Ministry of Industry and Energy, Gen. Man. Transport Infrastructures, Ministry for Transport, Chair. Inst. for Agrarian Reform and Devt (IRYDA), Ministry of Agric.; joined Construcciones Padrós SA as CEO 1983; Chair. OCP Construcciones SA 1993–97; mem. Bd Dirs ACS Group (Actividades de Construcción y Servicios SA) 1989–, Chair. and CEO 1993–; Dir and Second Vice-Chair. Abertis Infraestructuras SA 2007–; mem. Bd Dirs, Sanef. *Address:* Actividades de Construcción y Servicios (ACS) SA, Avenida Pío XII 102, Madrid 28036, Spain (office). *Telephone:* (91) 3439200 (office). *Fax:* (91) 3439456 (office). *E-mail:* infogrupoacs@grupoacs.com (office). *Website:* www.grupoacs.com (office).

PEREZ ROQUE, Felipe Ramón; Cuban politician; b. 28 March 1965, Havana; m.; two c.; ed Superior Politécnico José A. Echeverría; head univ. students union 1988; fmr electronics engineer; involved with biotechnology complex 1960; mem. Cen. Cttee CP of Cuba 1991–2009; mem. Nat. Ass. 1986–2009, State Council 1993–2009; Pvt. Sec. to Fidel Castro; Minister of Foreign Affairs 1999–2009; currently works as Engineer; José A. Echeverría Medal.

PÉREZ VERA, Víctor Luis, MSc; Chilean civil engineer, university administrator and academic; b. 8 Jan. 1943, Rancagua; m. Carmen K. Stephens; three c.; ed liceo Manuel Barros Borgoño de Santiago and studies with Prof. Elisa Gayán, Faculty of Physical Sciences and Math., Univ. of Chile, Univ. of Michigan, USA; Dir Polytechnic Inst. of Santiago 1967–69; Investigator and Prof., Dept of Industrial Eng, Universidad de Chile 1969, Titular Prof. 1986, Dir Dept of Industrial Eng 1980–84, 1988–90, Vice-Dean Faculty 1984–85, mem. Comm. of Academic Evaluation 1991–92, Pro-Rector Universidad de Chile 1993, Dean, Faculty of Physical Sciences and Math. 1994–2002, mem. Special Univ. Senate Comm. 2002–05, Rector Universidad de Chile 2006–14; Visiting Prof. at several nat. and Latin American univs; mem. Editorial Cttee Information and Management journal; Coordinator Higher Educ. Comm.; mem. Inst. of Engineers of Chile; Premio 'Profesor Enrique Silva a la Trayectoria Docente', Dept of Industrial Eng, Universidad de Chile 1994, Premio 'Ingeniero Civil Industrial del Año', Especialidad Civil Industrial, Coll. of Engineers of Chile, AG 1994, Premio 'Raúl Devés Julliàn', Inst. of Engineers of Chile 2001, Premio 'Al Ingeniero por Acciones Distinguidas' 2003. *Publications:* author or co-author of seven books; numerous scientific papers in professional journals on information systems and financial analysis; articles on higher educ. in El Mercurio, La Segunda, El Mostrador, La Tercera. *Address:* c/o Office of the Rector, Universidad de Chile, Avda Libertador Bernardo O'Higgins 1058, Casilla 10-D, Santiago, Chile.

PERIGOT, François; French business executive; b. 12 May 1926, Lyon; s. of Jean-Paul Perigot and Marguerite de la Tour; m. 2nd Isabelle Paque 1986; one s. one d. from fmr marriage; ed Lycée de Bastia, Faculté de Droit, Paris and Inst. d'Etudes Politiques, Paris; joined Unilever group (France) 1955, Head of Personnel 1966; Pres.-Dir-Gen. Thibaud Gibbs et Cie 1968–70; Dir Unilever (Spain) 1971–75; Pres.-Dir-Gen. Unilever (France) 1976–86; Pres. Campagnie de Plâtre 1987–98; mem. Bd of Sodexho, OENEO, CDC Ixis Pvt. Equity, Lever, Astra; mem. Exec. Council, Conseil Nat. du Patronat Français (CNPF) 1981–86, Pres. 1986–94; Vice-Pres. Union des confédérations de l'industrie et des employeurs d'Europe (UNICE) 1988–92, Pres. 1994; mem. Social and Econ. Council (CES) 1989–99; Pres. MEDEF Int. (Int. Br. of French Employers' Asscn) 1997–2005, Hon. Pres. 2005–; Pres. Org. Int. des Employeurs (OIE), Geneva 2001–06, Hon. Pres. 2006–; mem. Bd of Dirs Sodexho; mem. World Comm. on the Social Dimension of Globalization; Commdr, Légion d'honneur; Grand Officer, Order of the Republic (Tunisia); Grand Cross of Civil Merit (Spain); Commdr, Nat. Order of Merit (Poland), Order of the Polar Star (Sweden), Order of Orange Nassau (Netherlands), Order of the Aztec Eagle (Mexico), Order of Merit (Germany), Order of Leopold (Belgium), Order of Wissam Alaoui (Morocco). *Leisure interest:* golf. *Address:* Organisation Internationale des Employeurs, Geneva, Switzerland (office); 9 avenue Fréderic le Ploy, 75007 Paris, France (home). *Telephone:* 1-53-59-16-12 (office). *Fax:* 1-45-55-03-77 (office). *E-mail:* ioe@ioe-emp.org (office). *Website:* www.ioe-emp.org (office).

PERINO, Dana Marie, BA; American journalist, consultant and fmr government official; *Chief Issues Counselor, Burson-Marsteller;* b. 9 May 1972, Evanston, Wy.; d. of Leo Perino and Jan Perino; m. Peter McMahon; ed Ponderosa High School, Parker, Colo, Univ. of Southern Colorado, Univ. of Illinois at Springfield; while attending univ. worked with KTSC (Univ. of Southern Colorado radio station), also host Capitol Journal, weekly TV summary of Colo politics and producer Standoff, a weekly TV public affairs program; worked as daily reporter covering Springfield, Ill. for WCIA-TV; early career in Washington, DC as Staff Asst for US Congressman Scott McInnis of Colo 1995, then Press Sec. for US Congressman Dan Schaefer of Colo; worked in high-tech public affairs, San Diego, Calif.; Spokesperson, US Dept of Justice, Washington, DC 2001, then Dir of Communications, White House Council on Environmental Quality; Deputy Asst to Pres. and Deputy White House Press Sec. 2006–07, White House Press Sec. 2007–09; Chief Issues Counselor, Burson-Marsteller, Washington, DC 2009–; co-host The Five (TV show), Fox News. *Address:* Burson-Marsteller, 1110 Vermont Avenue, NW, Suite 1200, Washington, DC 20005-3554, USA (office). *Telephone:* (202) 530-0400 (office). *Fax:* (202) 530-4500 (office). *Website:* www.burson-marsteller.com (office).

PERIŠIC, Zoran; Serbian film director, writer, producer and visual effects supervisor; b. 16 March 1940, Zemun; Dir Sky Bandits/Gunbus (film) 1986; Producer-Dir The Phoenix and the Magic Carpet 1995; Dir-Writer Captain Cook's Travels (TV, animated series), Magic Fountain (TV, animated series), In Search of the Real Dracula (documentary), etc.; cr. visual and/or special effects for 2001: A Space Odyssey 1968, Land of the Minotaur 1976, Superman I 1978, Superman II 1980, Superman III 1983, Return to Oz 1985, Sky Bandits 1986, Cliffhanger and other films; several patents, including ZOPTIC front-projection system and 3D cinematography; Acad. Award (Oscar) for Outstanding Achievement in Visual Effects (for Superman: the Movie), BAFTA Award for Outstanding Contrib. to the Cinema, American Acad. Tech. Achievement Award for the invention and devt of the ZOPTIC dual-zoom front-projection system. *Publications:* Special Optical Effects, The Animation Stand, Photoguide to Shooting Animation, Visual Effects Cinematography 2000. *Leisure interest:* flying (pvt. pilot's licence). *E-mail:* zoptic@hotmail.com (office); zoran@zoptic.force9.co.uk (home). *Website:* www.zoptic.com (office).

PERISSICH, Riccardo; Italian/French international civil servant, business executive, consultant and author; *Senior Fellow, School of European Political Economy, LUISS University, Rome;* b. 24 Jan. 1942, Milan; m. Anne Treca 1989; one s.; writer on foreign policy for Il Punto (Rome weekly) 1962; with Italconsult SpA (consulting engineers) 1962–64; Head of EC Studies, Istituto Affari Internazionali, Rome 1966–70; joined Comm. of EC, Brussels 1970; Chef de Cabinet of Altiero Spinelli 1970–76, Cesidio Guazzaroni 1976; Dir, Directorate A (energy savings and energy forecasts) 1977–81; Chef de Cabinet of Antonio Giolitti (regional policy) 1981–84, of Carlo Ripa di Meana (institutional affairs) 1985–86; Dir, later Deputy Dir-Gen. Directorate-Gen. for Industry 1986, Dir-Gen. 1990–94; Bd mem. and Dir, Public and Econ. Affairs, Pirelli SpA 1994–2001, Co-ordinator of Institutional Affairs 2001–06; Dir, Public and Econ. Affairs, Telecom Italia Group 2001–06, Chair. Telecom Italia Media 2002–06; Chair. Seat Pagine Gialle 2002; Vice-Chair. Assolombarda 1995–2006, Unione Industriali di Roma, ASSONIME (Italian Cos Asscns) 2002–06; Chair. ONI Communications, Lisbon 2008–10; Exec. Vice-Pres. Italian br. of Council for the United States and Italy (CONSIUSA) 2010–17; mem. Bd, European Inst. of Oncology 1996–2001, Fondation Notre Europe, Institut Jaques Delors, Paris; mem. IISS, London, Istituto Affari Internazionali, Rome, Aspen Inst. Italia; Sr Fellow, School of European Political Economy, LUISS Univ., Rome; Chevalier des Arts et des Lettres. *Publications:* Gli eurocrati fra realtà e mitologia 1969, Europa America: materiali per un dibattito (with S. Silvestri) 1970, L'Unione europea, una storia non ufficiale 2008, Le Regole del Gioco (novel) 2012, Il Seminatore (novel) 2014, Insospettabili (novel) 2016; contrib. to Italian and foreign publs on European and int. politics. *Leisure interests:* history, music, arts, cinema, reading, golf.

PERISSINOTTO, Giovanni, BEcons, PhD; Italian insurance executive; b. 6 Dec. 1953, Conselice (Ravenna); m.; three c.; ed Università degli Studi di Trieste; chartered accountant 1978; internship at Generali UK Br. Financial Office, London 1979; joined Generali Assicurazioni SpA, Trieste 1980, Cen. Dept of parent co. 1988–89, Deputy Man. responsible for the Italian and foreign market 1989–92, responsible for Admin. Office 1992–93, responsible for co-ordination of corp. assets at Admin and Finance Dept 1993–95, Jt Man. responsible for Accounting and Finance Dept 1995–96, Deputy Gen. Man. with responsibilities a.i. for Admin and Finance Dept 1996–98, Gen. Man. 1998–2001, Group CEO and Jt Man. Dir 2001–12 (resgnd), also Chair. Banca Generali SpA, Generali Properties SpA, Supervisory Bd Generali Investments SpA, Vice-Chair. Banca della Svizzera Italiana SA (BSI SA); mem. Bd Dirs Participatie Maatschappij Graafscap Holland NV, Transocean Holding Corpn, Generali France Holding, Generali España Holding de Entidades de Seguros, Alleanza Toro Assicurazioni SpA, INA Assitalia SpA, Generali Immobiliare Italia SGR SpA, Generali Business Solutions, Pirelli & Co. SpA 2003–12; mem. Supervisory Bd Participatie Maatschappij Transhol BV, Man. Bd Intesa San Paolo, Man. Council Federazione ABI-ANIA, Presidential Cttee Assonime, Exec. Cttee ANIA; Cavaliere del Lavoro 2007. *Publications include:* articles on econs including The Creation of Value through a Specialized Distribution Network 2003.

PÉRISSOL, Pierre-André Daniel; French engineer and politician; *Mayor of Moulins;* b. 30 April 1947, Nice, Alpes-Maritimes; s. of Louis Périssol and Aline Cardiec; ed Lycée Massena, Nice, Ecole Polytechnique, Ecole Nat. des Ponts et Chaussées; Dir of Planning, Saint-Quentin-en-Yvelines new town 1972–74; Adviser to Sec. of State for Housing 1974–76; Chief Eng Ecole Nat. des Ponts et Chaussées 1986; Dir-Gen. Soc. Centrale de Crédit Immobilier 1977–91, Pres., Dir-Gen. 1991–92, Pres. 1993–95; Founder and Dir-Gen. Groupe Arcade 1980–91, Pres. 1991–95; Pres. Coopérer pour Habiter 1982, Aiguillon Construction 1987, Fed. Nat. (now Chambre Syndicale) des Sociétés de Crédit Immobilier 1988, Caisse Centrale de Crédit Immobilier 1990–93; Regional Councillor, Île-de-France 1983–86; Councillor, Paris 1983–95; Deputy Mayor of Paris responsible for Educ. 1989–93; RPR Deputy to Nat. Ass. 1993–95; Minister of Housing May–Nov. 1995, Deputy Minister 1995–97; Mayor of Moulins, Allier 1995–, Pres. Moulins Communauté; Vice-Pres. Regional Council of Auvergne 1998–; UMP Deputy to Nat. Ass. 2002–07; Pres. Agence Française de Développement 2010–; Officier, Légion d'honneur, Ordre nat. du Mérite. *Publications:* Le défi social 1985, En mal de toit 1995, A bonne école 2002. *Leisure interests:* travel, tennis. *Address:* Mairie de Moulins, 12 place de l'Hôtel de ville, BP 1629, 03016 Moulins cedex, France (office). *Telephone:* (4) 70-48-50-21 (office). *Fax:* (4) 70-48-50-84 (office). *E-mail:* contact@ville-moulins.fr (office). *Website:* www.ville-moulins.fr (office).

PERKINS, Donald Hill, CBE, MA, PhD, FRS; British physicist and academic; *Professor Emeritus of Physics, University of Oxford;* b. 15 Oct. 1925, Hull; s. of G. W. Perkins and G. Perkins; m. Dorothy M. Maloney 1955; two d.; ed Imperial Coll., London; Sr 1851 Scholar, Univ. of Bristol 1949–52, G. A. Wills Research Assoc. 1952–55, Lecturer, then Reader in Physics 1956–65; Visiting Scientist, Univ. of California, USA 1955–56; Prof. of Elementary Particle Physics, Univ. of Oxford 1965–93, Prof. Emer. 1993–, Fellow, St Catherine's Coll. 1965–; mem. Science and Eng Research Council 1985–89; Hon. DSc (Sheffield) 1982, (Bristol) 1995; Guthrie Medal, Inst. of Physics 1979, Holweck Medal, Soc. française de physique 1992, Royal Medal, Royal Soc. of London 1997, High-Energy Physics Prize, European Physical Soc. 2001. *Publications:* Study of Elementary Particles by the Photographic Method (with C. F. Powell and P. H. Fowler) 1959, Introduction to High Energy Physics 1972, Particle Astrophysics 2002. *Leisure interests:* squash, skiing, lepidoptera. *Address:* 37 Redan Street, London, W14 0AB, England (home). *Telephone:* (20) 7348-0028 (home). *E-mail:* d.perkins1@physics.ox.ac.uk (office).

PERKINS, Edward Joseph, DPA; American diplomatist and academic; *Professor Emeritus, University of Oklahoma;* b. 8 June 1928, Sterlington, La; s. of Edward Joseph Perkins, Sr and Tiny Estella Noble Holmes; m. Lucy Cheng-mei Liu; two d.; ed Univ. of Maryland, Univ. of Southern California; Chief of Personnel, Army and Air Force Exchange Service, Taiwan 1958–62; Deputy Chief, Okinawa, Japan 1962–64, Chief of Personnel and Admin. 1964–66; Asst Gen. Services Officer, Far East Bureau, AID 1967–69, Man. Analyst 1969–70; Deputy Dir Man. US Operations, Mission to Thailand 1970–72; Staff Asst Office of Dir-Gen. of Foreign Service 1972; Personnel Officer 1972–74; Admin. Officer, Bureau of Near Eastern and South Asian Affairs 1974–75; Man. Analysis Officer, Office of Man. Operations, Dept of State 1975–78; Counsellor for Political Affairs, Accra 1978–81; Deputy Chief of Mission, Monrovia 1981–83; Dir Office of W African Affairs, Dept of State 1983–85; Amb. to Liberia 1985–86, to S Africa 1986–89; Dir-Gen. Foreign Service, Washington 1989–92; Amb. and Perm. Rep. to UN, New York 1992–93; Amb. to Australia 1993–96; William J. Crowe Chair Prof. of Geopolitics and Exec. Dir Int. Programs Center, Univ. of Oklahoma 1996–2007, Prof. Emer. 2007–; fmr Bd Dir Asscn for Diplomatic Studies and Training 1998; Gov. Jt Center for Political and Econ. Studies 1996–2002; fmr mem. Advisory Council, Univ. Office of Int. Programs Pa State Univ., fmr mem. Advisory Bd, Inst. of Int. Public Policy; fmr mem. Bd of Visitors, Nat. Defense Univ., Pres.'s Advisory Cttee on Trade Policy ad Negotiation; Trustee, Lewis and Clark Coll. 1994–, Asia Soc. 1997–2000, Inst. of Int. Educ. 1997–2000, Woodrow Wilson Fellowship Foundation 1999; Distinguished Alumni Award, Univ. of Southern California 1991, Distinguished Honor Award, Dept of State 1992, Statesman of the Year Award, George Washington Univ. 1992, Dept of State Dir-Gen. Cup 2001, and numerous other awards. *Publications include:* The Seedlings of Hope: U.S. Policy in Africa 1989, Preparing America's Foreign Policy for the 21st Century (co-ed. 1999, Palestinian Refugees: Traditional Positions and New Solutions (co-ed.) 1999, Democracy, Morality and the Search for Peace in America's Foreign Policy (co-ed.) 2002, The Middle East Peace Process: Vision versus Reality (co-ed.) 2002, The Palestinian Refugees: Old Problems – New Solutions (Studies in Peace Politics in the Middle East) 2002, Mr. Ambassador, Warrior for Peace (memoirs) 2006; contribs to specialized journals and reviews. *Leisure interests:* art, jazz.

PERKINS, Frederick J., MSc; British business executive; *Founding Chairman and CEO, Information TV Limited;* b. 2 March 1948, Glasgow, Scotland; ed Univs of Glasgow, Strathclyde, Warwick, Bangor and Sussex; fmr Vice-Pres., Europe, McGraw-Hill; Chief Exec. and COO The Stationery Office (fmrly Her Majesty's Stationery Office) 1996–2003; Group Dir The Financial Times, Citibank; Chair. Electronic Publrs Forum from 1998, Dept for Trade and Industry's Innovation and Growth Task Force for software, digital content and related services, Public Policy Forum from 2001; Founding Chair. and CEO Information TV Ltd 2003–; fmr mem. Exec. of the Broadband Stakeholder Group. *Address:* Information TV Ltd, 64 Newman Street, London, W1T 3EF, England (office). *Telephone:* (20) 3764-0570

(office). *E-mail:* fred.perkins@information.tv (office). *Website:* www.information.tv (office).

PERKINS, (Lawrence) Bradford, Jr, BA, BArch, MBA, FAIA, MRAIC, AICP; American architect; *Chairman, Perkins Eastman;* b. 13 Jan. 1943, Chicago, Ill.; s. of Lawrence B. Perkins and Margery Perkins; m. Phyllis Friedman 1966; three d.; ed Cornell and Stanford Univs and City Coll. of New York; Pres. Omnidata Services 1971–73; Man. Partner, Llewellyn-Davies Assocs 1973–77; Sr Vice-Pres. and Partner, Perkins && Will 1977–81; Partner, Attia & Perkins 1981–83; Chair. Perkins Eastman 1983–; Dir Settlement Housing Fund 1991–, Helen Keller International 1993– (fmr Chair.); fmr Dir, New York City Chapter of AIA, NY Foundation for Architecture; currently Adjunct Faculty mem., Coll. of Architecture, Cornell Univ.; Fellow, Epsilon Asscn (Pres. 1993–96); fmr Pres. New York State Asscn of Consulting Planners; mem. Ontario Asscn of Architects, American Planning Asscn, Royal Architectural Inst. of Canada, American Inst. of Certified Planners; various design awards; Lifetime Achievement Award, New York Soc. of Architects, Platinum Circle Award, Hospitality Design Asscn. *Publications:* several books, including Building Type Basics for Senior Living; Architect's Essentials of Starting, Assessing, and Transitioning a Design Firm; Building Type Basics for Elementary and Secondary Schools; chapters for professional textbooks and more than 80 articles in professional journals. *Address:* Perkins Eastman, 115 Fifth Avenue, New York, NY 10003 (office); 4 Rectory Lane, Scarsdale, NY 10583, USA (home). *Telephone:* (212) 353-7200 (office); (914) 723-8875 (home). *Fax:* (212) 353-7676 (office). *E-mail:* info@perkinseastman.com (office). *Website:* www.perkinseastman.com (office).

PERLE, Richard Norman, BA, MA; American business executive and fmr government official; *Visiting Scholar, American Enterprise Institute;* b. 16 Sept. 1941, New York, NY; s. of Jack Perle and Martha Perle; m. Leslie Barr; one s.; ed Univ. of Southern California, Princeton Univ.; Asst Sec., US Dept of Defense, Int. Security Policy 1981–88; fmr foreign policy adviser; mem. Defense Policy Bd 2001–04, Chair. 2001–03 (resgnd); fmr Dir, GeoBiotics; Dir, Hollinger Int. Inc. 1994–2005; adviser to Libyan dictator Muammar al-Gaddafi 2006; Visiting Scholar, American Enterprise Inst. for Public Policy Research 1987–; Patron, Henry Jackson Soc. *Television:* The Gulf Crisis: The Road to War (producer for PBS) 1992, presenter, The Case for War: In Defense of Freedom (documentary) 2007. *Publications:* Reshaping Western Security (ed.) 1991, Hard Line (novel) 1992, An End to Evil: How to Win the War on Terror (with David Frum) 2004. *Address:* American Enterprise Institute for Public Policy Research, 1150 17th Street NW, Washington, DC 20036, USA (office). *Telephone:* (301) 656-0390 (office). *Fax:* (202) 862-4875 (office). *E-mail:* rperle@aei.org (office). *Website:* www.aei.org (office).

PERLET, Helmut, PhD; German business executive; *Chairman of the Supervisory Board, Allianz SE;* b. 9 April 1947, Planegg, Munich; ed Ludwig Maximilians Univ., Munich, Univ. of Hamburg; worked for tax office in Munich 1971–72; employee, Allianz Versicherungs-AG, Munich 1973–81, involved in establishment and management of Foreign Tax Dept 1981–90, Head of Finance Dept (Nondomestic) 1990–92, Head of Dept of Group Accounting and Dept Group Planning and Control 1992–97, in addition Head of Tax Dept 1994–97, mem. Bd of Man., Allianz SE, Munich 1997–2009, Chair. Supervisory Bd 2012–; mem. Supervisory or Admin. Bd, Commerzbank AG, Frankfurt-am-Main, GEA Group AG, Düsseldorf (Chair.); Hon. Prof., Dr Wolfgang Schieren Inst. of Insurance and Risk Man., Econs Faculty of Humboldt Univ., Berlin. *Publications include:* Rückstellungen für noch nicht abgewickelte Versicherungsfälle in Handels- und Steuerbilanz, Vol. 2 of Veröffentlichungen des Seminars für Versicherungswissenschaft der Universität Hamburg und des Vereins zur Förderung der Versicherungswissenschaft in Hamburg e.V. 1986, Die deutsche Unternehmensbesteuerung im europäischen Binnenmarkt (co-author) 1994 (second edn 2003), Die Hinzurechnungsbesteuerung bei Auslandsbeteiligungen: Mit den neuen Grundsätzen der Finanzverwaltung zur Anwendung des Außensteuergesetzes (co-author) 1996, Solvency II & Risikomanagement: Umbruch in der Versicherungswirtschaft (co-author) 2005. *Address:* Allianz SE, Königinstrasse 28, 80802 Munich, Germany (office). *Telephone:* (89) 3800-5592 (office). *Fax:* (89) 3800-5593 (office). *E-mail:* info@allianz.com (office). *Website:* www.allianz.com (office).

PERLIS, HRH The Raja of; Tuanku Syed Sirajuddin ibni al-Marhum Syed Putra Jamalullail; Malaysian ruler; b. 1943; s. of Tuanku Syed Putra ibni Almarhum Syed Hassan Jamalullail and Tengku Budriah binti Almarhum Tengku Ismail; m.; one s. one d.; ed Sandhurst Mil. Acad., UK; apptd Raja Muda (Crown Prince) of Perlis 1960; fmr army officer; Raja of Perlis 2000–; elected as twelfth Yang di-Pertuan Agong (Supreme Head of State) 13 Dec. 2001–06; fmr Chair. Football Asscn of Perlis; numerous decorations along with, Marshal of the Royal Malaysian Air Force, Colonel-in-Chief, Royal Ranger Regiment.

PERLMAN, Itzhak; Israeli violinist and conductor; b. 31 Aug. 1945, Tel-Aviv; s. of Chaim Perlman and Shoshana Perlman; m. Toby Lynn Friedlander 1967; two s. three d.; ed Shulamit High School, Tel-Aviv, Tel-Aviv Acad. of Music and Juilliard School, USA, studied with Ivan Galamian and Dorothy De Lay; gave recitals on radio at the age of 10; went to USA 1958; first recital at Carnegie Hall 1963; has played with maj. American orchestras 1964–; has toured Europe regularly and played with maj. European orchestras, including Berlin Philharmonic, Concertgebouw Orchestra, London Philharmonic, English Chamber Orchestra; debut in UK with London Symphony Orchestra 1968; toured Poland, Hungary, Far East; played with Israel Philharmonic Orchestra in fmr Soviet Union; appearances at Israel Festival and most European Festivals; Music Advisor, St Louis Symphony 2002–04; Prin. Guest Conductor Detroit Symphony Orchestra 2001–05; Dorothy Richard Starling Foundation Chair, Juilliard School; numerous recordings; Hon. DMus (Univ. of S Carolina) 1982; Dr hc (Yale, Harvard and Yeshivah Univs); several Grammy awards, four Emmy Awards, Medal of Liberty (USA) 1986, EMI Artist of the Year 1995, Royal Philharmonic Soc. Gold Medal 1996, Nat. Medal of Arts (USA) 2000, Kennedy Center Honor, John F. Kennedy Center for the Performing Arts 2003, Grammy Lifetime Achievement Award 2008, Presidential Medal of Freedom 2015, Genesis Prize 2016. *Leisure interest:* cooking. *Address:* IMG Artists, Pleiades House, 7 West 54th Street, New York, NY 10019, USA (office). *Telephone:* (212) 994-3547 (office). *E-mail:* dlai@imgartists.com (office). *Website:* www.itzhakperlman.com.

PERLMUTTER, David H., BA, MD; American paediatrician and university administrator; *Executive Vice-Chancellor for Medical Affairs and Dean, School of Medicine, Washington University, St Louis;* b. 11 May 1952, Brooklyn, New York; s. of Herman Arthur Perlmutter and Ruth Perlmutter (née Jacobs); m. Barbara Ann Cohlan 1981; one s. one d; ed Univ. of Rochester, Washington Univ. School of Medicine; Intern, later Resident in Paediatrics, Univ. of Pennsylvania School of Medicine 1978–81; Fellow in Paediatric Gastroenterology, Harvard Univ. School of Medicine 1981–84, Instructor in Paediatrics 1983–85, Asst Prof. of Paediatrics 1985–86; Donald Strominger Prof. of Paediatrics, Washington Univ. School of Medicine 1986–89, St Louis, Prof. of Cell Biology and Physiology 1989–2001, also Dir Gastroenterology and Nutrition Div., St Louis Children's Hosp. 1992–2001, Exec. Vice-Chancellor for Medical Affairs and Dean, School of Medicine, Washington Univ., St Louis 2015–; Physician-in-Chief and Scientific Dir Children's Hosp. Pittsburgh 2001–15, also Vira I. Heinz Prof. and Chair. of Paediatrics, Univ. of Pittsburgh School of Medicine 2001–15, Prof. of Cell Biology and Physiology 2001–15; mem. Editorial Bd Hepatology, American Journal of Physiology; Consultant Ed. Pediatric Research; mem. Nat. Acad. of Sciences Inst. of Medicine 2008, American Pediatric Soc., Asscn of American Physicians, American Asscn for the Study of Liver Disease, Soc. of Pediatric Research (fmr Pres.), American Soc. of Cell Biology, American Soc. of Clinical Investigation; Research Scholar Award, American Gastroenteritus Asscn 1985, Established Investigator Award, American Heart Asscn 1987, E. Mead Johnson Award for Research in Pediatrics, American Pediatric Soc. 1994, Sass-Kortsak Award for Pediatric Liver Research, Canadian Liver Asscn, Hepatology and Nutrition Shwachman Award for Lifetime Achievement, North American Soc. for Pediatric Gastroenterology. *Publications:* author of nearly 200 scientific publications; holder of nine US patents or patent applications; numerous articles in professional journals. *Address:* Office of the Dean, Washington University School of Medicine, 660 South Euclid Avenue, St Louis, MO 63110, USA (office). *Telephone:* (314) 362-5000 (office). *E-mail:* mpa@wusm.wustl.edu. (office). *Website:* medicine.wustl.edu (office).

PERLMUTTER, Saul, BS, PhD; American physicist and academic; *Professor, University of California, Berkeley;* b. 22 Sept. 1959, Champaign-Urbana, Illinois; m. Laura Nelson; one d.; ed Harvard Univ., Univ. of California, Berkeley; currently astrophysicist, Lawrence Berkeley Nat. Lab. and Leader of Int. Supernova Cosmology Project; Prof., Physics Dept, Univ. of California, Berkeley 2004–; Fellow, Ameican Acad. of Arts and Sciences; Henri Chretien Award, American Astronomical Soc. 1996, Lawrence Award in Physics, US Dept of Energy 2002, Calif. Scientist of Year 2003, John Scott Award 2005, Padua Prize 2005, Feltrinelli International Prize, Lincei Acad., Rome 2006, Shaw Prize in Astronomy (co-recipient) 2006, Gruber Cosmology Prize (co-recipient) 2007, Nobel Prize in Physics (co-recipient) 2011, Breakthrough Prize in Fundamental Physics (co-recipient) 2015. *Achievements include:* discovery through the study of distant supernovae that the expansion of the universe is speeding up rather than slowing down. *Television:* has appeared in Public Broadcasting System and BBC TV documentaries on astronomy and cosmology. *Publications:* numerous scientific papers in professional journals; popular articles for Sky and Telescope magazine. *Address:* 429 Old LeConte Hall, Department of Physics, University of California, Berkeley, CA 94720, USA (office). *Telephone:* (510) 642-3596 (office). *Fax:* (510) 643-8497 (office). *E-mail:* saul@lbl.gov (office). *Website:* physics.berkeley.edu/people/faculty/saul-perlmutter (office); supernova.lbl.gov/saul.html (office).

PERMAN, Finley S.; Micronesian auditor and government official; ed Hawaii Pacific Coll.; previous positions include Devt Specialist, Pohnpei Small Business Guarantee and Finance Corpn, Sr Service Asst, Bank of Hawaii, Pohnpei br.; Dir Pohnpei State Dept of Treasury and Admin 2005–07; Sec. Dept of Finance and Admin 2007–10 (resgnd); Chief Financial Officer, Bank of the FSM Feb.–Dec. 2011, Advisor Man. and Budget 2014–15, Man. Public Financial Man. Reform Program 2015–16; Owner FSM Supply Products 2012–; Agency Man. MoneyGram Int. 2013–.

PERNG, Fai-Nan, MA; Taiwanese central banker and economist; b. 2 Jan. 1939; m.; two s.; ed Nat. Chung Hsing Univ., Univ. of Minnesota, USA and Int. Monetary Fund Inst.; with Bank of Taiwan 1969; Asst Specialist, Cen. Bank of China (CBC), later Deputy Div. Chief, Div. Chief, Econ. Research Dept 1971–78, Asst Dir-Gen. and Div. Chief, Econ. Research Dept 1978–80, Deputy Dir-Gen. 1980–86, Dir-Gen. 1986–89, Dir-Gen. Foreign Exchange Dept 1989–94, Deputy Gov. CBC 1994–95, apptd mem. Bd of Dirs 1995, Gov. 1998–2018, also mem. Exec. Yuan (cabinet); Chair, Cen. Trust of China 1995–97, Int. Commercial Bank of China 1997–98; Gov. for Taiwan, Asian Devt Bank 1998–2014, Cen. American Bank for Econ. Integration 1998–2014; Adjunct Prof., Nat. Chung Hsing Univ. 1986–89; Hon. LLD (Univ. of Minnesota) 2006, (Nat. Taipei Univ.) 2009; Office of the Pres. Best Employee Award 1975, Cen. Bank of China Best Essay Award 1982, Excellence Magazine Outstanding Govt Official 1998, Nat. Chung Hsing Univ. Outstanding Alumnus Award 1999, Univ. of Minn. Outstanding Achievement Award 2000, Global Finance Top Central Banker Award 2000, 2005, 2006, 2007, 2008, 2009, 2010, 2011, 2012, 2013, 2014, Central Banker of the Year (Asia) Award, The Banker magazine 2009. *Publications include:* Possible Methods for the Liberalization of Foreign Exchange Control 1985, Asian Financial Crisis 1998; numerous articles.

PÉROL, François; French civil servant and business executive; *Chairman of the Management Board, Groupe BPCE;* b. 1963; ed Haute École Commerciale School of Man., Institut d'Études Politiques (Sciences Po), École Nationale d'Admin, Paris; began career in Inspection générale des Finances 1990; served as rapporteur and later Asst Sec.-Gen., Comite Interministeriel de Restructuration Industrielle 1994–96; Head, Office of Financial Markets, Treasury Dept 1996–99, Asst Dir of Financial Support and Devt 2001–02; Sec.-Gen. Club de Paris 1999–2001; served as Deputy Chief of Staff to ministers François Mer and Nicolas Sarkozy, Ministry of Economy 2002–05; Gen. Partner, Rothschild Bank 2005–; Deputy Gen. Sec., Office of the Pres. 2007–09; Chair. Man. Bd Caisse Nationale des Caisses d'Epargne (CNCE) and CEO Banque Fédérale des Banques Populaires (BFBP) March–Aug. 2009, Chair. Man. Bd, Groupe BPCE (following merger) Aug. 2009–; Chair. Supervisory Bd, Natixis; Chair. French Banking Fed. 2014–15. *Address:* Groupe BPCE, 50 avenue Pierre Mendès France, 75201 Paris Cedex 13, France

(office). *Telephone:* 1-58-40-41-42 (office). *E-mail:* info@bpce.fr (office). *Website:* www.bpce.fr (office).

PERÓN, María Estela (Isabelita) (see Martínez de Perón, María Estela (Isabelita)).

PEROT, (Henry) Ross; American business executive; b. 27 June 1930, Texarkana, Tex.; s. of Gabriel Ross Perot; m. Margot Birmingham 1956; five c.; ed US Naval Acad.; served in USN 1953–57; with IBM Corpn 1957–62; f. Electronic Data Systems Corpn 1962, Chair. and CEO 1982–86; Dir Perot Group, Dallas 1986; Founder and Chair. Perot Systems Corpn, Washington, DC 1988–2009; Chair. Bd of Visitors US Naval Acad. 1970; unsuccessful cand. for Pres. of USA 1992, 1996, f. Reform Party 1995, Chair. 1995–99. *Publications:* Not For Sale at Any Price 1993, Intensive Care 1995. *Leisure interest:* horses.

PEROVIĆ, Željko; Montenegrin diplomatist; *Ambassador to Austria;* b. 15 Nov. 1954, Kotor; m. Tatjana Perović; two c.; ed Univ. of Belgrade; Adviser to Cabinet, Ministry of Foreign Affairs of Yugoslavia 1981–84, Adviser in Political Admin for Neighbouring Countries 1984–86; Vice-Consul, New York 1986–90, Adviser Office for Research and Documentation, 1990–92, Adviser Fed. Ministry for Foreign Affairs 1992–98; Special Adviser to Minister of Foreign Affairs 1999–2000; Head Montenegrin Mission for Cooperation with UN, New York 2000–03, Deputy Minister Dept for Multilateral Affairs, Ministry of Foreign Affairs of Serbia and Montenegro 2003–06; Amb. of Montenegro to Albania 2008–12; Gen. Dir for Bilateral Affairs, Ministry of Foreign Affairs and European Integration 2012, Amb. (non-residential) to Spain 2013, to Portugal May 2014, to Cuba and Costa Rica May 2015; Perm. Rep. to UN 2015–18; Amb. to Austria 2018–. *Address:* Embassy of Montenegro, Nibelungengasse 13, 1010 Vienna, Austria (office). *Telephone:* (1) 715-31-02 (office). *Fax:* (1) 715-31-02-20 (office). *E-mail:* diplomat-mn@me-austria.eu (office).

PERPIÑA-ROBERT PEYRA, Fernando; Spanish diplomatist; b. 17 April 1937, San Sebastián; s. of Benito Perpiña and Cármen Peyra; m. Alba Navarro Feussier 1964; two s. two d.; ed Univ. of Barcelona; joined Diplomatic Service 1965, Consul-Gen. Boston 1978, Minister Counsellor, Bonn 1982–85, Under-Sec. of State, Ministry of Foreign Affairs 1985–88, Sec.-Gen. 1988–91, Amb. to Germany 1991–96, to Hungary 1996–2001, Special Rep. for Terrorism Affairs, Ministry of Foreign Affairs 2001–03, Consul-Gen. to Paris 2003–07; Sec.-Gen. Club of Madrid 2010; mem. Group of Experts on NATO's Strategic Concept; numerous Spanish and foreign decorations. *Leisure interest:* bridge. *E-mail:* clubmadrid@clubmadrid.org.

PERRAULT, Dominique; French architect and urban planner; *Principal, Dominique Perrault Architecture;* b. 9 April 1953, Clermont-Ferrand; s. of Jean Perrault and Thérèse Souchon; m. Aude Lauriot-dit-Prévost 1986; three c.; ed Ecole Nationale Supérieure des Beaux-Arts de Paris, Ecole Nationale des Ponts et Chaussées, Ecole des Hautes Etudes en Sciences Sociales; f. architectural practice, Paris 1981; opened offices in Berlin 1992, Luxembourg 2000, Madrid 2006; architect-consultant to City of Nantes 1990–92, Bordeaux 1992–97, Barcelona 2000–03; Pres. Institut français d'architecture 1998–2001; Pres. Bd of Clermont-Ferrand ENSA 2010–; mem. Salzburg Urban Cttee 1994–97, Bd of Cité de l'Architecture et du patrimoine 2004–, Bd of Grand Paris Scientific Council 2008–09; Curator of French Pavilion at 12th Architecture Biennale in Venice 2010 (installation Metropolis); mem. Académie des Beaux Arts 2015; Hon. mem. RIBA; Chevalier, Légion d'honneur; numerous architectural awards and prizes, including Grand prix nat. d'architecture 1993, Grande Médaille d'Or d'Architecture, Acad. d'Architecture, Praemium Imperiale Award 2015. *Major works include:* ESIEE – Electronic Engineers Acad., Marne-la-Vallée 1987, Industrial Hotel Berlier, Paris (Equerre d'Argent Award) 1990, Nat. Library of France, Paris (Mies van der Rohe Pavilion Award for European architecture 1997) 1995, Velodrome and Olympic Swimming Pool, Berlin 1999, Town Hall, Innsbruck 1997, Aplix Factory, Le Cellier 1999, EU Court of Justice, Luxembourg 2008, Ewha Womans Univ., Seoul (Seoul Metropolitan Architecture Award) 2008, Olympic Tennis Centre, Madrid 2009, NH Fieramilano Hotel (four star) 2009, Fukoku Tower, Osaka 2010, Arganzuela Footbridge, Madrid 2011, La Liberté Building, Groningen 2011. *Ongoing projects include:* Piazza Garibaldi, Naples, Congress and Exhbn Hall, Leon, DC Towers, Vienna, rehabilitation/extension of fmr mechanical eng halls and central library and construction of Teaching Bridge of Ecole Polytechnique Fédérale, Lausanne, Grand Theatre, Albi, Dobrée Museum, Nantes, renovation of Pavillon Dufour, Château de Versailles, Sports Palace, Rouen, New European neighbourhood and business centre, Sofia, new FSS train station dist, Locarno. *Publications:* An Atmosphere of Falling Meteors, Perrault Architecte (monograph) Italy 2000, 2004, El Croquis 2001, Mesh A+U 2003, Dominique Perrault by Gilles de Bure 2004, Dominique Perrault Architecture (exhbn catalogue) 2008; several articles in professional journals. *Address:* Dominique Perrault Architecture, 6 rue Bouvier, 75011 Paris, France (office). *Telephone:* 1-44-06-00-00 (office). *Fax:* 1-44-06-00-01 (office). *E-mail:* dpa@d-p-a.fr (office). *Website:* www.perraultarchitecte.com (office).

PERRIN, Edouard; French journalist; b. 1971, Belfort; ed Inst. d'etudes politiques, Strasbourg, Univ. of the West of England, Centre de Formation des journalistes, Paris; Reporter, Enquiry team, France 2 (public TV station) 2007–10, Special Investigator 2010–11, Sr Reporter, Cash Investigation series 2012–15; Investigative Reporter, Premières Lignes TV 2011–; uncovered 'LuxLeaks' scandal when he exposed widespread corp. tax avoidance schemes based in Luxembourg 2015; subsequently charged by a court in Luxembourg as an accomplice to theft April 2015, acquitted June 2016 and March 2017 (following appeal); Knight Wallace Fellow, Univ. of Michigan 2015–16; mem. Int. Consortium of Investigative Journalists (ICIJ); Louise Weiss Prize for European Journalism 2012. *Television includes:* Cash Investigation (series) 2012–. *Address:* Premières Lignes Télévision, 10, rue Nicolas Appert, 75011 Paris, France (office). *Telephone:* 1-55-28-93-50 (office). *Website:* www.pltv.fr (office).

PERROTIN, Emmanuel; French art dealer and gallery owner; b. May 1968; opened first gallery in his apartment 1992; represented Damien Hirst, Maurizio Cattelan, Takashi Murakami, Mariko Mori, Xavier Veilhan, Sophie Calle and Bernard Frize; opened gallery in Miami, Fla, USA 2004, then in the rue de Turenne, Paris, then in New York 2013; represented artists including Jeff Koons 2008, Xavier Veilhan 2009, Takashi Murakami 2010; other artists represented include Chiho Aoshima, Daniel Arsham, Hernan Bas, Sophie Calle, Maurizio Cattelan, Peter Coffin, Johan Creten, Matthew Day Jackson, Wim Delvoye, Elmgreen & Dragset, Lionel Esteve, Daniel Firman, Bernard Frize, Giuseppe Gabellone, Gelitin, Duane Hanson, Jesper Just, Bharti Kher, Kolkoz, Klara Kristalova, Guy Limone, Jin Meyerson, Mariko Mori, Mr., Jean-Michel Othoniel, Paola Pivi, Claude Rutault, Michael Sailstorfer, Aya Takano, Tatiana Trouve, Piotr Uklanski and Peter Zimmermann. *Publications:* publishes own magazine, Bing. *Address:* Galerie Perrotin, 76 rue de Turenne, 75003 Paris, France (office); Galerie Perrotin, 909 Madison Avenue & 73rd Street, Upper East Side, New York, NY 10021, USA (office). *Telephone:* 1-42-16-79-79 (Paris) (office); (212) 812-2902 (New York) (office). *Fax:* 1-42-16-79-74 (Paris) (office). *E-mail:* paris@perrotin.com (office); newyork@perrotin.com (office). *Website:* www.perrotin.com (office).

PERRY, Egbert L. J., BS, MS, MBA; American real estate executive; *Non-Executive Chairman, Fannie Mae (Federal National Mortgage Association);* ed The Towne School and The Wharton School at Univ. of Pennsylvania; began working in real estate industry 1979; Founder, Chair. and CEO The Integral Group LLC, Atlanta, Ga 1993–; Dir, Fed. Reserve Bank of Atlanta 2002–08; Dir (non-exec.), Fannie (Fed. Nat. Mortgage Asscn) 2008–, Chair. (non-exec.) 2014–, Chair. Exec. Cttee; Chair. Atlanta Life Financial Group, Central Atlanta Progress; Chair. Advisory Bd The Penn Inst. for Urban Research; Trustee, Univ. of Pennsylvania, Children's Healthcare of Atlanta 2004–14; Gallery of Distinguished Eng Alumni, Univ. of Pennsylvania. *Address:* Fannie Mae, 3900 Wisconsin Avenue, NW, Washington, DC 20016-2892 (office); The Integral Group LLC, 191 Peachtree Street NE, Suite 4100, Atlanta, GA 30303, USA. *Telephone:* (202) 752-7000 (DC) (office); (404) 224-1860 (Atlanta). *E-mail:* egbert_perry@fanniemae.com (office). *Website:* www.fanniemae.com (office).

PERRY, Grayson, CBE, BA, RA; British artist; b. 24 March 1960, Chelmsford, Essex, England; m. Philippa Perry; one d.; ed Portsmouth Polytechnic; known for his ceramic vases and cross-dressing; curated the Tomb of the Unknown Craftsman at the British Museum 2011; Turner Prize 2003, BAFTA Award for Specialist Factual (mem. production team) 2013. *Works include:* Mother of All Battles 1996, Growing Up As a Boy, Strangely Familiar, Golden Ghosts 2001. *Radio includes:* Playing to the Gallery, Reith Lectures (BBC Radio 4 and BBC World Service) 2013. *Television includes:* BBC: Question Time, Hard Talk, Desert Island Discs, Have I Got News for You, subject of a South Bank Show 2006, of an Imagine documentary 2011; Channel 4: All In The Best Possible Taste with Grayson Perry (series) 2012. *Publication:* Portrait of the Artist as a Young Girl (with Wendy Jones) 2006. *Address:* c/o Tate Britain, Millbank, London, SW1P 4RG, England.

PERRY, James Richard (Rick); American rancher and government official; *Secretary of Energy;* b. 4 March 1950, Paint Creek, Tex.; s. of Joseph Ray Perry and Amelia June Perry (née Holt); m. Anita Thigpen 1982; one s. one d.; ed Paint Creek High School, Texas A&M Univ.; served in USAF 1972–77, rank of Capt.; farmer and rancher 1977–90; mem. Tex. House of Reps 1985–91; Tex. Commr of Agric. 1991–99; Lt-Gov. of Tex. 1999–2000; Gov. of Texas 2000–15; cand. for Republican US presidential nomination 2012; Sec. of Energy 2017–; Democrat –1989, Republican 1989–; Border Texan of the Year 2001, Govt Leadership Award, Nat. Comm. Against Drunk Driving 2001, Top Cowboy of the Year Award 2001. *Publications include:* On My Honor: Why the American Values of the Boy Scouts are Worth Fighting For 2008, Fed Up! Our Fight to Save America from Washington 2010. *Address:* Department of Energy, Forrestal Bldg, 1000 Independence Avenue, SW, Washington, DC 20585, USA (office). *Telephone:* (202) 586-5000 (office). *Fax:* (202) 586-4403 (office). *E-mail:* the.secretary@hq.doe.gov (office). *Website:* www.energy.gov (office); www.rickperry.org.

PERRY, John Richard, PhD; American philosopher and academic; *Henry Waldgrave Stuart Professor Emeritus of Philosophy, Stanford University;* b. 16 Jan. 1943, Lincoln, Neb.; s. of Ralph R. Perry and Ann Roscow Perry; m. Louise E. French 1962; two s. one d.; ed Doane Coll., Crete, Neb. and Cornell Univ.; Asst Prof. of Philosophy, UCLA 1968–72, Assoc. Prof. 1972–74; Assoc. Prof. of Philosophy, Stanford Univ. 1974–77, Prof. of Philosophy 1977–85, Henry Waldgrave Stuart Prof. of Philosophy 1985–2011, Prof. Emer. 2011–, Chair. Dept of Philosophy 1976–82, 1990–91, Dir Center for Language and Information 1982–83, 1985–86, 1993–99; Distinguished Prof. of Philosophy (half-time), Univ. of California, Riverside 2008–; Pres. American Philosophical Asscn 1993–94; Hon. DLitt (Doane Coll.) 1982; Dr hc (Univ. of the Basque Country) 2002, (Ruhr-Universität, Bochum) 2013; Woodrow Wilson Fellow 1964, Danforth Fellow 1964–68, Guggenheim Fellow 1975–76, NEH Fellow 1980–81, Dinkelspiel Teaching Award 1989, Humboldt Prize 1998, Nicod Prize 1999, Ig-Nobel Prize (Literature) 2011, Quinn Prize 2013. *Radio includes:* Philosophy Talk 2003–. *Publications include:* A Dialogue on Personal Identity and Immortality 1978, Situations and Attitudes (co-author) 1983, The Problem of the Essential Indexical and Other Essays 1993 (second enlarged edn 2000), A Dialogue on Good, Evil and the Existence of God 1999, Knowledge, Possibility and Consciousness 2000, Reference and Reflexivity 2001 (second revised edn 2011), Identity, Personal Identity and the Self 2002, Critical Pragmatics (co-author) 2011, The Art of Procrastination 2011. *Leisure interests:* reading, walking, grandchildren. *Address:* 127 Cordura Hall, CSLI, Stanford University, 210 Panama Street, Stanford, CA 94305, USA (office). *Telephone:* (650) 796-2798 (office). *Fax:* (650) 723-0985 (office). *E-mail:* john@csli.stanford.edu (office); johnperry43@gmail.com (home). *Website:* john.jperry.net.

PERRY, Katy; American singer; b. (Katheryn Elizabeth Hudson), 25 Oct. 1984, Santa Barbara, Calif.; d. of Maurice Keith Hudson and Mary Perry (née Christine); m. Russell Brand 2010 (divorced 2012); as a child sang in local church, at family functions; moved to Nashville to work with professional songwriters and producers, aged 15; solo artist 2007–; UNICEF Goodwill Amb. 2013–; MTV Europe Music Awards for Best New Act 2008, for Best Female 2013, for Best Video (featuring Juicy J, for Dark Horse) 2014, for Best Look 2014, People's Choice Awards for Favorite Pop Song (for I Kissed a Girl) 2009, for Favorite Female Artist 2011, 2012, 2013, BRIT Award for Best Int. Female Artist 2009, Billboard Music Awards for Top Female Artist 2014, for Top Digital Songs Artist 2014, MTV Video Music Award for Best Female Video (featuring Juicy J, for Dark Horse) 2014, American Music Awards for Favorite Pop/Rock Female Artist 2014, for Favorite Adult Contemporary Artist 2014, for Single of the Year (featuring Juicy J, for Dark Horse) 2014, Audrey Hepburn Humanitarian Award, UNICEF 2016, Inspiration DVF Award 2019. *Recordings include:* albums: Katy Hudson 2001, One of the Boys 2008, Teenage Dream 2010, Prism 2013, Witness 2017. *Address:* c/o Bradford Cobb, Direct Management Group Inc., 8332 Melrose Avenue, Top Floor, Los Angeles, CA 90069, USA (office). *Telephone:* (310) 854-3535 (office). *E-mail:* bradford@directmanagement.com (office). *Website:* www.directmanagement.com (office); www.katyperry.com.

PERRY, Matthew Langford; American/Canadian actor; b. 19 Aug. 1969, Williamstown, Mass; s. of John Bennett Perry and Suzanne Perry; ed Ashbury Coll., Ottawa, Canada; mem. Bd of Dirs Ron Clark Acad. *Films:* A Night in the Life of Jimmy Reardon 1988, She's Out of Control 1989, Getting In 1994, Fools Rush In 1997, Almost Heroes 1998, Three To Tango 1999, Imagining Emily (writer) 1999, The Whole Nine Yards 2000, Serving Sara 2002, The Whole Ten Yards 2004, Numb 2007, Birds of America 2008, 17 Again 2009. *Television includes:* Friends (series) 1994–2004, The West Wing (series) 2003, The Ron Clark Story 2006, Studio 60 on the Sunset Strip (series) 2006, The End of Steve 2008, Mr Sunshine (series) 2011, Go On (series) 2012–13, The Odd Couple (series) 2015–17. *Play:* Sexual Perversity in Chicago, Comedy Theatre, London 2003. *Leisure interests:* ice hockey, softball. *Address:* c/o CAA, 9830 Wilshire Blvd, Beverly Hills, CA 90212-1825, USA (office). *Telephone:* (310) 288-4545. *Fax:* (310) 288-4800.

PERRY, Sir Michael Sydney, Kt, GBE, MA; British business executive; b. 26 Feb. 1934, Eastbourne, East Sussex, England; s. of Sydney Albert Perry and Jessie Kate Perry (née Brooker); m. Joan Mary Stallard 1958; one s. two d.; ed King William's Coll., Isle of Man, St John's Coll., Oxford; Chair. Lever Brothers (Thailand) Ltd 1973–77, Centrica 1997–2004, Nippon Lever (Japan) 1981–83, UAC Int. Ltd 1985–87, Unilever PLC 1992–96, Dunlop Slazenger Group 1996–2002; Pres. Lever y Asociados (Argentina) 1977–81; Dir Unilever NV 1985–96 (Vice-Chair. 1992–96), Bass PLC 1991–2001 (Deputy Chair. 1996–2001); Dir (non-exec.) British Gas 1994–97, Marks & Spencer 1996–2001; Pres. Liverpool School of Tropical Medicine 1997–2002; Pres. Advertising Asscn 1993–96; Chair. Leverhulme Trust 2008–14, Three Choirs Foundation 2015–; Trustee, Shakespeare Globe Trust 1987–2014 (Chair. 1993–2006), Glyndebourne Arts Trust 1996–2004, Dyson Perrins Museum Trust 2000–, Inst. of Public Policy Research 2003–07, Three Choirs Festival Asscn 2007–; Hon. Fellow, St John's Coll., Oxford 2013; Commdr, Order of Oranje Nassau 1996; Hon. LLD (London South Bank) 1995; Hon. DSc (Cranfield) 1995; Hon. DUniv (Brunel) 1995; Hon. DLit (Worcester) 2013; Shakespeare's Globe Sam Wanamaker Award 2013. *Leisure interest:* music. *Address:* Bridges Stone Mill, Alfrick, Worcester, WR6 5HR, England (home).

PERRY OF SOUTHWARK, Baroness (Life Peer), cr. 1991, of Charlbury in the County of Oxfordshire; **Pauline Perry,** MA, FRSA, CIMgt; British fmr university administrator, fmr political party official and author; b. (Pauline Welch), 15 Oct. 1931, Wolverhampton; d. of John Welch and Elizabeth Welch (née Cowan); m. George W. Perry 1952 (died 2008); three s. one d.; ed Wolverhampton Girls' High School, Girton Coll., Cambridge; Univ. Lecturer in Philosophy, Univs of Manitoba, Canada, Massachusetts, USA, Exeter and Oxford 1956–59, 1961–63, 1966–70; HM Insp. 1970, Staff Insp. 1975, HM Chief Insp. of Schools 1981–86; Vice-Chancellor South Bank Univ. (fmrly South Bank Polytechnic) 1987–93; Pres. Lucy Cavendish Coll., Cambridge 1994–2001; Pro-Chancellor Univ. of Surrey 2001–06; Chair. Council of Roehampton Univ. 2001–05; Chair. Dept of Trade and Industry Export Group for Educ. and Training Sector 1993–98; Vice-Pres. City and Guilds of London Inst. 1994–99, Chair. City and Guilds Quality and Standards Cttee 2005–10; Chair. Comm. on Free Schools and Academies, Wandsworth Borough 2012–, Kaplan Coll. Governing Body 2014–15; Co-Chair. All-Party Univs Group 1996–2010; mem. (Conservative) House of Lords 1991–2016, mem. House of Lords Select Cttee on Science and Tech. 1992–95, 1997–2000, 2004–07, 2009–14, on Scrutiny of Delegated Powers 1995–98, on Cen. and Local Govt Relations 1995–96, on Religious Offences 2002–03, Conservative Party Whip 2011–16; mem. Prime Minister's Advisory Group on the Citizen's Charter 1993–97, Jt Select Cttee on Human Rights 2001–03; Chair. Judges Panel on Citizen's Charter 1997–2003, Church of England Review of the Crown Appointments Comm. 1999–2001, Nuffield Council on Bio-Ethics Inquiry into Animals in Scientific Experiments 2003–05; Co-Chair. Conservative Party Policy Comm. on Public Services 2007–08; mem. Bd of Patrons, Royal Soc. Appeal 1995–2001, Governing Body, Abbey Plus Schools 2013–15; Trustee, Cambridge Univ. Foundation 1997–2006; Patron, Nat. Conf. of Univ. Profs 2016–; Liveryman, Worshipful Co. of Bakers; Hon. Freeman, Worshipful Co. of Fishmongers; Freeman of the City of London; Hon. Fellow, Coll. of Preceptors, City and Guilds of London, Girton Coll. Cambridge, Roehampton Univ., Lucy Cavendish Coll. Cambridge, Swedish Acad. of Sciences (Pedagogy); Hon. LLD (Aberdeen, Bath); Hon. DLitt (Sussex, South Bank, City Univ.); Hon. DUniv (Surrey); Hon. DEd (Wolverhampton); Hon. DHL (Mercy Coll., New York). *Publications include:* The Womb in Which I Lay 2003; four earlier books, several chapters in 12 books and numerous articles. *Leisure interests:* music, power walking. *Address:* House of Lords, Westminster, London, SW1A 0PW, England (office). *Website:* www.parliament.uk/biographies/lords/Baroness-Perry-of-Southwark/3157 (office).

PERRY, Simon Frank, CBE, BA; British film producer; *President, ACE Producers;* b. 5 Aug. 1943, Farnham, Surrey; s. of Frank Horace Perry and Brenda Mary Dorothea Perry; ed Eton Coll., King's Coll., Cambridge; worked in theatre production (RSC, Bristol Old Vic, London West End) 1965–69, TV production (Anglia TV, Yorkshire TV) 1969–74; ind. filmmaker 1974–77; entertainment trade journalist (Variety Magazine etc.) 1978–80; Admin. Nat. Film Devt Fund 1980–82; feature film producer 1982–; Chief Exec. British Screen Finance 1991–2000 (taken over by the Film Council); CEO Bord Scannán na hÉireann (Irish Film Bd) 2005–10; currently Pres. ACE Producers; Officier de l'Ordre des Arts et Lettres. *Films include:* Knots 1975, Loose Connections 1983, Another Time, Another Place 1983, Nineteen Eighty-Four 1984, Hôtel du paradis 1986, Nanou 1986, White Mischief 1987, The Favour, the Watch and the Very Big Fish 1991, The Playboys 1992, Innocent Lies 1995. *Leisure interests:* cinema-going, cycling, European travel. *Address:* c/o ACE Producers, W G Plein 508, 1054 SJ Amsterdam, The Netherlands (office). *Telephone:* (62) 2861338 (office). *E-mail:* simonperry@ace-producers.com (office). *Website:* ace-producers.com (office).

PERRY, Tyler; American actor, director, producer and screenwriter, author, playwright and songwriter; b. (Emmitt Perry, Jr), 14 Sept. 1969, New Orleans, La; s. of Emmitt Perry, Sr and Willie Maxine Perry (née Campbell); wrote a series of letters to himself, which became the basis for the musical, I Know I've Been Changed; moved to Atlanta 1990; wrote and produced numerous stage plays during the 1990s and early 2000s; known for creating, and performing in drag, the character Mabel 'Madea' Simmons; f. The Tyler Perry Foundation; lives and works in SW Atlanta where he operates the Tyler Perry movies and TV studios; Helen Hayes Award for Excellence in Theater 2001, Black Business Professionals Entrepreneur of the Year 2004, Brandon Tartikoff Legacy Award, Nat. Asscn of Television Program Execs 2009, honoured by BET at Second Annual BET Honors 2009, NAACP Chair.'s Award 2010, inaugural Visionary Award, CinemaCon 2011. *Films include:* Madea's Family Reunion (video) 2002, Diary of a Mad Black Woman (video) (Outstanding Actor in a Theatrical Film and Outstanding Writing for Theatrical Film, BET Comedy Awards 2005, Outstanding Achievement in Screenwriting, Black Movie Awards 2005, MTV Movie Award for Breakthrough Male 2005) 2002, I Can Do Bad All by Myself (video) 2002, Madea's Class Reunion (video) 2003, Meet the Browns (video) 2004, Madea's Family Reunion 2006, Madea Goes to Jail (video) 2006, Why Did I Get Married? (video) 2006, Daddy's Little Girls 2007, Why Did I Get Married? 2007, What's Done in the Dark (video) 2008, Meet the Browns 2008, The Family That Preys (Movieguild Award for Most Inspirational Film 2008) 2008, Madea Goes to Jail 2009, I Can Do Bad All by Myself 2009, Why Did I Get Married Too? 2010, For Colored Girls (Best Movie BET Award 2011, NAACP Image Awards for Outstanding Motion Picture and for Outstanding Director 2011) 2010, Madea's Big Happy Family (video) 2010, Madea's Big Happy Family 2011, Laugh to Keep from Crying (video) 2011, A Madea Christmas (video) 2011, Good Deeds 2012, Madea's Witness Protection 2012, Aunt Bam's Place 2012, Alex Cross (actor) 2012, The Marriage Counselor 2013, We the Peeples (producer) 2013, Madea Gets a Job 2013, Temptation: Confessions of a Marriage Counselor 2013, The Single Moms Club 2014, Gone Girl (African-American Film Critics Asscn Award for Best Supporting Actor 2014) 2014. *Television includes:* House of Payne (series) (NAACP Image Awards for Outstanding Comedy Series 2009, 2010, 2011, 2012) 2007–12, Meet the Browns (series) 2009, Love Thy Neighbor 2013, For Better or Worse (series) 2013–14, The Tyler Perry Show 2014, If Loving You Is Wrong 2014–16, The Haves and the Have Nots 2013–16. *Publications:* Don't Make a Black Woman Take Off Her Earrings: Madea's Uninhibited Commentaries on Love and Life (novel) (Book of the Year, Best Humor Book, Quill Awards 2006) 2006, Madea's Big Happy Family 2010. *Address:* c/o WME, 1325 Avenue of the Americas, New York, NY 10019, USA (office). *Website:* www.tylerperry.com.

PERRY, William James, BS, MS, PhD; American academic and fmr government official; *Michael and Barbara Berberian Professor Emeritus, Freeman Spogli Institute for International Studies, Center for International Security and Cooperation, Stanford University;* b. 11 Oct. 1927, Vandergift, Pa; s. of Edward Martin Perry and Mabelle Estelle Dunlop; m. Leonilla Mary Green 1947; three s. two d.; ed Stanford Univ., Pennsylvania State Univ.; served in US Army Corps of Engineers 1946–47, Reserve Officer Training Corps 1948–55; laboratory dir General Telephone and Electronics 1954–64; f. and served as Pres. ESL, Inc. 1964–77; Exec. Vice-Pres. Hambrecht & Quist, Inc. 1981–85; f. and served as Chair. Tech. Strategies & Alliances 1985–93; Prof. (half-time) Stanford Univ. 1988–93, also Co-Dir Center for Int. Security and Arms Control; Under-Sec. of Defense for Research and Eng 1976–81; Mil. Tech. Adviser to Pres. Clinton 1993; Deputy Sec. of Defense 1993–94, Sec. of Defense 1994–97; Sr Fellow, Stanford Univ. 1997–, now also Sr Fellow, Freeman Spogli Inst. for Int. Studies (FSI) and Michael and Barbara Berberian Prof. Emer. (FSI and School of Eng), Stanford Univ., also Co-Dir Preventive Defense Project; Chair. Global Tech. Partners; mem. Bd of Dirs, United Technologies Corpn, FMC Corpn, Sylvania/General Telephone's Electronic Defense Labs, Space Foundation, Thomas Jefferson Program in Public Policy, Concord Coalition, Strategic Partnerships LLC, Center for the Study of the Presidency; mem. Pres.'s Foreign Intelligence Advisory Bd, Sec. of State's Arms Control and Nonproliferation Advisory Bd, FBI Dir's Advisory Bd, Iraq Study Group, US Inst. of Peace 2006; fmr Chair. Bd of Visitors, US Naval Acad.; fmr Co-Chair. Pres. Comm. on Intelligence Capabilities of the US Regarding Weapons of Mass Destruction; mem. Nat. Acad. of Eng, NAS Cttee on Int. Security and Arms Control; Fellow, American Acad. of Arts and Sciences; Trustee MITRE Corpn, Carnegie Endowment for Int. Peace; fmr Fellow, Inst. of Politics, Harvard Univ., Marshall Wythe School of Law, Coll. of William and Mary; mem. project team, Hiroshima for Global Peace 2011; f. William J. Perry Project 2013; Hon. KBE 1998; Grand Order of King Dmitar Zvonimir (Croatia) 1998; Grand Cordon, Order of the Rising Sun (Japan) 2002; Chevalier, Ordre nat. du Mérite; several nat. and int. honours, including Outstanding Civilian Service Medals from the Army 1962, 1997, Air Force 1997, Navy 1997, Defense Intelligence Agency 1977, 1997, NASA 1981, Coast Guard 1997; Dept of Defense Distinguished Service Medal 1980, 1981, American Electronic Asscn Medal of Achievement 1980, Forrestal Medal 1994, Henry Stimson Medal 1994, Arthur Bueche Medal 1996, Eisenhower Award 1996, Marshall Award 1997, Presidential Medal of Freedom 1997. *Address:* CISAC, C230 Encina Hall, Stanford University, Stanford, CA 94305-6165, USA (office). *Telephone:* (650) 725-6501 (office). *Fax:* (650) 725-0920 (office). *E-mail:* dcgordon@stanford.edu (office). *Website:* cisac.fsi.stanford.edu (office).

PERSAD-BISSESSAR, Kamla, BA, LLB, MBA; Trinidad and Tobago lawyer, academic and politician; b. 22 April 1952, Penal; m. Dr Gregory Bissessar; one s.; ed Univ. of the West Indies, Norwood Technical Coll., UK, Hugh Wooding Law School, Arthur Lok Jack Grad. School of Business; fmr Social Worker for Church of England Children's Soc., London; taught at St Andrew High School, Jamaica and St Augustine campus of Univ. of the West Indies; fmr Consultant Lecturer, Jamaica Coll. of Insurance; fmr Lecturer, Tertiary Educ. Inst.; Alderman, St Patrick Co. Council 1987–91; mem. Parl. 1995–; Attorney-Gen. and Minister of Legal Affairs 1995–96, Oct.–Dec. 2001; Minister of Legal Affairs 1996–99; Minister of Education 1999–2001; Leader of the Opposition 2006–07, Feb.–May 2010, Prime Minister 2010–15; Commonwealth Chair.-in-Office 2010–11; fmr Sec. and Vice-Chair. Nat. Org. for Women; Hon. Prof., China Agricultural Univ. 2014; Democracy Medal 2013. *Leisure interests:* reading, walking. *Address:* Office of the Parliament, Levels G-8, Tower D, Port of Spain International Waterfront Centre, 1A Wrightson Road, Port of Spain, Trinidad and Tobago (office).

Telephone: 624-7275 (office). *Fax:* 625-4672 (office). *E-mail:* webmaster@ ttparliament.org (office). *Website:* www.ttparliament.org (office).

PERSEKIAN, Jack; Palestinian art foundation director, gallery curator and producer; b. Jerusalem; Founding Dir Anadiel Gallery, Al-Ma'mal Foundation for Contemporary Art, Jerusalem, XEIN Productions; Dir and Producer Millennium Celebrations Bethlehem 2000, Palestinian Cultural Evening, World Economic Forum in the Dead Sea, Jordan 2004); Chief Curator 7th Sharjah Biennial, Sharjah, UAE 2005, Artistic Dir 8th Sharjah Biennial 2007, 9th Sharjah Biennial 2009; Dir Sharjah Art Foundation 2009–11; Dir and Head Curator Palestinian Museum 2012–16. *Films:* several short films and video works.

PERSSON, (Carl) Stefan (Erling); Swedish retail executive; *Chairman, H&M Hennes & Mauritz AB;* b. 4 Oct. 1947, Stockholm; s. of Erling Persson and Margrit Persson; m. Carolyn Denise Persson; three c.; ed Univs of Stockholm and Lund; started working for family-controlled H&M Hennes & Mauritz AB 1967, Country Man. for H&M in UK and responsible for H&M's expansion abroad 1967–82, Man. Dir and CEO 1982–98, Chair. (succeeded on death of his father) 1998–; owns substantial stake in Swedish tech. co., Hexagon AB; owns properties in London, Paris and Stockholm; acquired 21-cottage village of Linkenholt, Hants., UK 2009; Deputy Bd of Dirs Stockholm School of Econs; mem. Bd of Dirs AB Electrolux, Investor AB, Atlas Copco, ABB, Ingha Holding, Mentor Foundation (founder), Stockholm School of Entrepreneurship. *Leisure interests:* downhill skiing, tennis, golf. *Address:* H&M Hennes & Mauritz AB, Mäster Samuelsgatan 46A, 106 38 Stockholm, Sweden (office). *Telephone:* (8) 796-55-00 (office). *Fax:* (8) 796-57-03 (office). *Website:* www.hm.com (office); about.hm.com (office).

PERSSON, Göran; Swedish politician; b. 20 Jan. 1949, Vingaker; m. 1st Gunnel Persson 1978 (divorced 1995); two c.; m. 2nd Annika Barthine 1995 (divorced 2002); m. 3rd Anitra Steen 2003; ed Orebro Univ.; Org. Sec. Swedish Social Democratic Youth League Sörmland 1971; Studies Sec. Workers' Educ. Asscn Sörmland, 1974–76; Chair. Katrineholm Educ. Authority 1977–79; mem. Parl. 1979–84; Councillor, Chair. Municipal Exec. Bd Katrineholm 1985–89; Minister with special responsibility for schools and adult educ., Ministry of Educ. and Cultural Affairs 1989–91, of Finance 1994–96; Prime Minister of Sweden 1996–2006; Chair. Sveriges Socialdemokratiska Arbetareparti (SAP) (Swedish Social Democratic Party) 1996–2007; Vice-Chair. Bd Oppunda Savings Bank 1976–89, Nordic Museum 1983–89; Chair. Sörmland Co-operative Consumers' Asscn 1976–89; Chair. Sörmland Co. Bd of Educ. 1982–89; Nat. Auditor, Swedish Co-operative Wholesale Soc. 1988–89.

PERSSON, Jörgen; Swedish director of photography; b. 10 Sept. 1936, Helsingborg; s. of Erik W. Persson and Thyra Liljeroth; m. Anne von Sydow 1969; two s.; ed High School and Swedish Film School; Dir of Photography (Features) 1965–; Felix Award, Paris 1989, several Swedish and Danish awards. *Films include:* Elvira Madigan 1967, Ådalen-31 1969, My Life as a Dog 1986, Pelle the Conqueror 1988, Best Intentions 1991, Sofi 1991, Young Indy, The House of the Spirits 1993, Jerusalem 1995, Smilla's Sense of Snow 1996, Digging to China 1996, Les Misérables 1997, Faithless 2000, A Song for Martin 2001, Wolf 2008, Underkastelsen (documentary) 2010. *Leisure interests:* off-road sport, classic cars.

PERSSON, Olof Erland, BSc; Swedish business executive; *Chairman, New Wave Group AB;* b. 22 June 1964; m.; three c.; ed Karlstad Univ.; began career at ABB, held several exec. positions at AdTranz and Bombardier, including Pres., Mainline and Metros Div. 2004–06; mem. Group Exec. Cttee AB Volvo and Pres. Volvo Aero 2006–08, Pres. Volvo Construction Equipment 2008–11, Exec. Vice-Pres. AB Volvo and Deputy CEO May–Aug. 2011, mem. Bd of Dirs, Pres. AB Volvo and CEO Volvo Group 2011–15; Chair. New Wave Group AB 2016–; Chair. German-Swedish Chamber of Commerce; mem. Confed. of Swedish Enterprise, Swedish-American Chamber of Commerce. *Address:* New Wave Group AB, Orrekulla Industrigata 61, 425 36 Hisings Kärra, Sweden (office). *Telephone:* (31) 712-89-00 (office). *E-mail:* info@nwg.se (office). *Website:* www.nwg.se (office).

PERT, Geoffrey (Geoff) James, PhD, FRS, FInstP, CPhys; British physicist and academic; *Professor Emeritus, University of York;* b. 15 Aug. 1941, Market Harborough, Leics., England; s. of Norman James Pert and Grace W. Pert; m. Janice Ann Alexander 1967; one d.; ed Norwich School, Imperial Coll., Univ. of London; Asst Prof., Univ. of Alberta 1967–70; Lecturer, Univ. of Hull 1970–76, Sr Lecturer, Reader 1976–82, Prof. 1982–87; Prof. of Physics, Univ. of York 1987–2007, Prof. Emer. 2007–. *Publications:* numerous scientific papers. *Leisure interests:* hill-walking, gardening. *Address:* York Plasma Physics Institute, Department of Physics, University of York, Heslington, York, YO10 5DD, England (office). *Telephone:* (1904) 324910 (office). *Fax:* (1904) 322214 (office). *E-mail:* gjp1@ york.ac.uk (office). *Website:* www.york.ac.uk/depts/phys (office).

PERTHES, Volker; German political scientist and research institute director; *Director, Stiftung Wissenschaft und Politik (German Institute for International and Security Affairs);* b. 16 May 1958, Homberg/Niederrhein; ed Duisburg Univ.; fmr mem. Faculty, Univs of Duisburg, Munich and Münster; fmr Adjunct Prof., Humboldt Univ.; Asst Prof., American Univ. of Beirut 1991–93; Sr Research Assoc., Stiftung Wissenschaft und Politik (German Inst. for Int. and Security Affairs) and Head of Middle East and Africa Div. 1992–2005, Dir and Exec. Chair. 2005; mem. Trilateral Comm., Int. Spectator, Rome; mem. Advisory Bd, Shanghai Inst. for Int. Studies Studies, Finnish Inst. of Int. Affairs (Chair.), Hellenic Foundation for European and Foreign Policy (ELIAMEP); Verdienstkreuz am Bande der Bundesrepublik Deutschland 2011; Hon. Prof., Free Univ. of Berlin, Humboldt Univ., Berlin. *Publications include:* The Political Economy of Syria under Assad 1995, Arab Elites: Negotiating the Politics of Change 2004, Orientalische Promenaden: Der Nahe und Mittlere Osten im Umbruch 2006, Of Trust and Security: The Challenge of Iran, a Report to the Trilateral Commission 2008, Iran: Eine politische Herausforderung 2008, Der Aufstand: Die arabische Revolution und ihre Folgen 2011; numerous research papers and articles. *Address:* Stiftung Wissenschaft und Politik, Ludwigkirchplatz 3–4, 10719 Berlin, Germany (office). *Telephone:* (30) 88007-101 (office); (30) 88007-102 (office). *Fax:* (30) 88007-100 (office). *E-mail:* swp@swp-berlin.org (office); volker.perthes@swp-berlin.org (office). *Website:* www.swp-berlin.org (office).

PERUASHEV, Azat, PhD; Kazakhstani politician; *Leader, Bright Road Democratic Party of Kazakhstan (Ak Jol);* b. 8 Sept. 1967, Rgayty village, Zhambyl (now

Taraz) Oblast, Kazakh SSR, USSR; ed Maxim Gorky Ural State Univ., Higher School of Public Admin, Zhetysu Econ. Inst.; worked in various management positions, including in Panfilov Dist Cttee of the party 1991–92, in Taldy-Kurgan Oblast Admin 1992–95, as a consultant and div. man. in Office of Pres. of Kazakhstan 1996–98; Deputy Gen. Dir JSC Aluminium of Kazakhstan 1998–2000, Vice-Pres. 2001–05; First Sec. Cen. Cttee, Civil Party of Kazakhstan 1999–2006, party merged with Otan party 2006, Deputy Chair. Nur Otan party 2006–07, left the party 2011; Chair. 'Atameken' Union of Entrepreneurs and Employers of Kazakhstan 2006–07, Chair. 'Atameken' Union Nat. Chamber of Economy of Kazakhstan 2007–11; mem. Pres.'s Council of Entrepreneurs 2007–11; also acted as an int. election observer and was a mem. of the State Comm. on Democratization under the Pres. of Kazakhstan; Leader, Bright Road Democratic Party of Kazakhstan (Ak Jol) (Kazakstannyn 'Ak Jol' Demokratiyalyk Partiyasy) 2011–; Deputy of the Majlis (Parl.) 2012–; Hon. Prof., South Kazakhstan State Univ. named after M. Auezova, East Kazakhstan State Univ. named after S. Amanzholov, Taldy-Kurgan Inst. of Economy; 'Dostyk' Medal (II Degree), Russian Medal of Community, 'Barys' Medal (III Degree); Young Researchers' Award of Cultural Initiative, Soviet-American Fund, Moscow 1991. *Address:* Bright Road Democratic Party of Kazakhstan (Ak Jol), 010000 Nur-Sultan, Kazakhstan (office). *Telephone:* (7172) 20-05-85 (office). *Fax:* (7172) 21-37-50 (office). *E-mail:* akzholpress@mail.ru (office). *Website:* www.akzhol.kz (office).

PERVAIZ, Ansar, BSc, MSc, PhD; Pakistani nuclear scientist, educationalist and administrator; b. 1949, Lahore, British India (now in Pakistan); ed Punjab Univ., Quaid-e-Azam Univ., Islamabad, Rensselaer Polytechnic Inst., USA; started career as teacher in training inst. of Pakistan Atomic Energy Comm. (PAEC), put in charge of nuclear tech. labs, promoted to Jr Scientific Prin. Officer 1986, formed nuclear safety group, later transferred to Karachi Nuclear Power Plant (KANUPP) where he worked in different capacities for 18 years, apptd Head of Nuclear Safety Dept, also est. PAEC food processing and agricultural eng labs, served as Gen. Man. of Chashma Nuclear Power Unit-2, Chair. PAEC April 2009–15; Visiting Asst Prof. of both Nuclear Physics and Nuclear Tech., Purdue Univ., USA 1982–84; fmr mem. Bd of Govs IAEA (Chair. 2010–11); Hilal-i-Imtiaz 1998. *Publications:* numerous scientific papers in int. journals and proceedings.

PERVYSHIN, Erlen Kirikovich, CandTechSci; Russian industrial manager; b. 25 June 1932, Rasskazovo, Tambov Oblast; ed Moscow Electrotechnical Inst. of Communications; mem. Int. Engineer Acad.; engineer 1955–, then Head of Ass. Section, Deputy Chief Engineer, Head of Admin., Manager of Design and Ass. Trust, Dir-Gen. All-Union Scientific production Asscn; Deputy USSR Minister of Radio Industry 1970–74, Minister of Communications Equipment Mfg 1974–89, of Communications 1989–91; Chair. Telecom (now Mirtelecom Corpn) 1991–; Pres. ORB & TEL Co., Andrew Int. Corpn 1997–; Pres. Mirtelecom Asscn 1999–; Deputy to ninth and tenth convocations of Supreme Soviet of USSR; Order of Lenin, Order of the October Revolution, Order of the Red Banner of Labour, various medals. *Address:* Mirtelecom, Profsouznaya str. 84/32, 117997 Moscow, Russian Federation. *Telephone:* (495) 710-75-58. *Fax:* (495) 645-92-04. *E-mail:* sanal@cce.ru. *Website:* www.mir-tele.com.

PESÁNTEZ BENÍTEZ, Johana Farina, DJur, PhD; Ecuadorean lawyer, academic and government official; *Partner and President, Tradelex Servicios Legales;* b. 20 Nov. 1975, Quito; m. Jaime Xavier Cazar Valencia; ed Pontificia Universidad Católica del Ecuador, Universidad Pablo de Olavide, Seville, Spain; served in several positions in legal practice, including as Research Asst responsible for monitoring processes in Supreme Court; fmr Legal Co-ordinator, Nat. Court of Justice; fmr Lecturer, Universidad Católica, Universidad de las Americas, Universidad Tecnológica Indoamérica de Ambato, Universidad Técnica Particular de Loja; consultant on issues of justice to Pres. of Ecuador; Minister of Justice, Human Rights and Worship 2011–13; currently Partner and Pres. Tradelex Servicios Legales; Dir-Gen. Universidad Tecnológica Indoamérica 2014–15. *Publications include:* several works of legal analysis. *Address:* Tradelex Servicios Legales, Mariana de Jesús E7-8 y La Pradera, Quito, Ecuador (office). *Telephone:* (2) 290-7322 (office). *Website:* tradelex.com.ec (office).

PESCI, Joe; American film actor; b. 9 Feb. 1943, Newark, NJ; s. of Angelo Pesci and Mary Pesci; m. 1st 1964 (divorced); m. 2nd Claudia Haro 1988 (divorced 1992); one d. *Films include:* Death Collector 1976, Raging Bull 1980, I'm Dancing as Fast as I Can 1982, Easy Money 1983, Dear Mr Wonderful 1983, Eureka 1983, Once Upon a Time in America 1984, Tutti Dentro 1984, Man On Fire 1987, Moonwalker 1988, Backtrack 1988, Lethal Weapon 2 1989, Betsy's Wedding 1990, Goodfellas (Acad. Award for Best Supporting Actor) 1991, Home Alone 1990, The Super 1991, JFK 1991, Lethal Weapon 3 1992, Home Alone II 1992, The Public Eye 1992, My Cousin Vinny (American Comedy Award for Funniest Lead Actor in a Motion Picture) 1992, A Bronx Tale 1993, With Honours 1994, Jimmy Hollywood 1994, Casino 1995, 8 Heads in a Duffel Bag 1997, Gone Fishing 1997, Lethal Weapon 4 1998, The Good Shepherd (Berlin Int. Film Festival Award for Outstanding Artistic Contribution 2007) 2006, Love Ranch 2010, A Warrior's Tail 2015. *Address:* c/o Melissa Prophet Management, Los Angeles, CA, USA (office). *E-mail:* melissamp2000@yahoo.com (office).

PESCUCCI, Gabriella; Italian costume designer; b. 1941, Castiglioncello, Tuscany; ed Accademia di Belle Arti, Florence; worked as Asst to Piero Tosi on set of Luchino Visconti's films Death in Venice and Ludwig; solo debut designing costumes for Charlotte Rampling in Italian film adaptation of 'Tis Pity She's a Whore 1971; designed costumes for Maria Callas in Medea, for Sean Connery in The Name of the Rose, Montserrat Caballé in Norma at La Scala, Milan; two Donatello Davids from Italian Acad. of Cinema and two BAFTA Awards. *Films as costume designer include:* I Sette fratelli Cervi 1967, Uomini contro 1970, Addio, fratello crudele 1971, Fatti di gente per bene 1974, Identikit 1974, Divina creatura 1976, L' Eredità Ferramonti 1976, Prova d'orchestra 1978, La Città delle donne 1980, Tre fratelli 1981, Passione d'amore 1981, La Nuit de Varennes 1982, Once Upon a Time in America 1984, Il Trovatore 1985, Orfeo 1985, The Name of the Rose 1986, La Famiglia 1987, The Adventures of Baron Munchausen 1988, Haunted Summer 1988, Splendor 1989, Che ora è? 1989, Indochine 1992, Per amore, solo per amore 1993, The Age of Innocence (Acad. Award for Best Costume Design 1994) 1993, The Scarlet Letter 1995, Albergo Roma 1996, Dangerous Beauty 1998, Les Misérables 1998, Cousin Bette 1998, Le Temps retrouvé 1999, A Midsummer Night's Dream 1999, Perduto amor 2003, Secret Passage 2004, Van Helsing 2004,

Charlie and the Chocolate Factory 2005, The Brothers Grimm 2005, Beowulf 2007, Agora 2009, The First Beautiful Thing 2010, The Jewel 2011.

PEŠEVSKI, Vladimir, BSc, MBA; Macedonian politician, electrical engineer and business executive; b. 19 June 1970; m.; three c.; ed SS Cyril and Methodius Univ., Skopje, Univ. of Sheffield, UK; served as CEO of publishing co. that publishes Dnevnik newspaper; Research Asst, Macedonian Inst. for Energy and Computer Science 1993–95; worked as consultant providing gen. man. and financial consulting services to medium and large Macedonian cos, Macedonian Business Resource Centre (USAID-funded project) 1995–98; joined Small Enterprise Assistance Funds (SEAF) South Balkan LLC (US-based pvt. equity investment fund) 1998, Deputy Dir Gen. SEAF Macedonia 2000, Dir Gen. SEAF South Balkan LLC 2000–, Dir in first AmCham Bd in Macedonia 2001; mem. bd of dirs of several cos and regional think-tanks, including Nat. Entrepreneurship and Competitiveness Council, First Bd of Dirs American Chamber of Commerce in Macedonia; Lecturer in MA Studies, Univ. of Sheffield (Program on Strategic Man., City Coll., Thessaloníki); advised Pres. of Macedonia on econ. policies for small and medium enterprises in the troubled regions 2001; Deputy Prime Minister, responsible for Econ. Affairs 2009–17; Alt. Gov., EBRD, London. *Address:* c/o Office of the Prime Minister, Ilindenska bb, 1000 Skopje, North Macedonia (office).

PEŠIĆ, Vesna, BA, MA, PhD; Serbian sociologist, lawyer, diplomatist and politician; b. 6 May 1940, Groska; m.; one s.; ed Univ. of Belgrade; mem. staff, Inst. of Social Sciences 1964–72; Sr Researcher, Inst. of Social Policy 1972–78; Prof., Higher School for Social Workers 1978–91; Sr Researcher, Inst. of Philosophy and Social Theory, Belgrade 1991–2001; Sr Scientific Assoc.; Co-f. Union for Yugoslavian Democratic Initiative (IZDI) 1991, Helsinki Cttee for Serbia, Belgrade 1985; Founder and Pres. Center of Peace and Democracy Devt (fmrly Cen. for Antiwar Action); mem. Cttee for Freedom of Speech and Self-Expression; fmr Pres. Civil Alliance of Serbia (now merged into Liberal Democratic Party), currently Pres. Political Council of Liberal Democratic Party; Amb. to Mexico 2001–05; mem. Narodna skupština (Parl.) 1993–97, 2007–12; Int. Policy Fellowship 2006–07; Award for Democracy Nat. Foundation of Democracy, Washington, DC 1993, Andrej Sakharov Freedom Price, Norwegian Sakharov Freedom Fund 1997, W. Averell Harriman Democracy Award, Nat. Democratic Inst. 1997. *Publications include:* Social Traditions and Style of Life 1977, Social Deviations: Criticism of Social Pathology (with I. Jancović) 1981, Ethnomethodology and Sociology 1985, Brief Course of Equality 1988, Theory of Changes and Parsons Concept of Contemporary Soc. 1990, Yugoslavian Military Crisis and World Movement 1992, Nationalism, War and Disintegration of Communist Federation 1993; articles in scientific journals and periodicals.

PESONEN, Jussi, MSc; Finnish paper industry executive; *President and CEO, UPM-Kymmene Corporation;* b. 24 Nov. 1960, Helsinki; ed Univ. of Oulu; joined UPM 1987, various positions including Production Man. Jämsänkoski Mill, Production Unit Dir Kajaani, Kaukas and Shotton Mills, Vice-Pres. Newsprint Product Group, Publ. Papers Div. 2001, Group Sr Exec. Vice-Pres. and COO 2001–04, Pres. and CEO 2004–; Chair. Ilmarinen Mutual Pension Insurance Co. 2012–; mem. Bd of Dirs Outokumpu Ltd 2009–12; mem. Bd, Confed. of European Paper Industries 2004– (Chair. 2012–, mem. Exec. Cttee 2006–), Asscn of European Publ. Paper Producers, Finnish Forest Industries Fed. 2003– (Deputy Chair. 2005, 2009–11, Chair. 2006–08, mem. Exec. Cttee 2004–07), East Office of Finnish Industries Oy; Co-Chair. Forest Solutions Group, World Business Council for Sustainable Devt. *Address:* UPM, Alvar Aallon katu 1, PO Box 380, 00101 Helsinki, Finland (office). *Telephone:* (8) 204-15-111 (office). *Fax:* (8) 204-15-110 (office). *E-mail:* jussi.pesonen@upm.com (office). *Website:* www.upm.com (office).

PESSINA, Stefano; Italian engineer and pharmaceutical industry executive; *Executive Vice-Chairman and CEO, Walgreens Boots Alliance, Inc.;* m.; two c.; ed Univ. of Milan; trained as nuclear engineer; fmr Lecturer, Univ. of Milan; Consultant, AC Nielsen 1973–76; f. Gruppo Alliance Santé 1977 (merged with UniChem PLC to form Alliance UniChem Plc 1997), apptd to Bd 1997, Exec. Deputy Chair. 2004–06 (merged with Boots PLC to form Alliance Boots plc), Exec. Deputy Chair. 2006–07, Exec. Chair. 2007–, Dir (non-exec.), Walgreens 2012–, Exec. Vice-Chair. and CEO Walgreens Boots Alliance, Inc. 2015–; Dir (non-exec.) Galenica, Walgreen Co. 2012–; mem. Council Int. Fed. of Pharmaceutical Wholesalers (IFPW) 1999–, Chair. 2000–02. *Leisure interest:* yachting. *Address:* Walgreens Boots Alliance, Inc., 108 Wilmot Road, Deerfield, IL 60015, USA (office). *Telephone:* (847) 315-3700 (office). *E-mail:* investor.relations@wba.com (office). *Website:* www.walgreensbootsalliance.com (office).

PESSOA PEREIRA DA SILVA PINTO, Ana Maria; Timor-Leste politician and lawyer; *Prosecutor General;* b. 5 Jan. 1956, Bobonaro; m. José Ramos-Horta (divorced); one s.; mem. Nat. Political Comm. of Timorese Resistance 1998–2000; mem. Transitional Cabinet for Internal Admin 2000–01; Minister of Justice 2001–03; Deputy Prime Minister and Minister of State and Minister of the Presidency of the Council of Ministers 2003–05; Minister for State and Internal Admin 2005–07, Sr Minister of State 2006; unsuccessful cand. for Prime Minister 2006; mem. Nat. Parl. 2007–; Prosecutor Gen. 2009–; mem. FRETILIN (Frente Revolucionaria do Timor-Leste Independente). *Address:* Ministry of Justice, Av. Jacinto Candido, Dili, Timor-Leste (office). *Telephone:* 77305734 (office). *E-mail:* gabinete@mj.gov.tl (office). *Website:* www.mj.gov.tl (office).

PESTER, Paul, DPhil; British business executive; ed Univs of Manchester and Oxford; spent 10 years in management consultancy, mostly at McKinsey & Co.; Group CEO Virgin Money 2000–05; Man. Dir Consumer Banking, Lloyds TSB 2005–08; joined Santander UK 2008, led acquisition of Bradford & Bingley and subsequent integration of Abbey, Alliance & Leicester and Bradford & Bingley; Man. Dir of Consumer Banking and Payments, Lloyds Banking Group 2010–11, CEO Verde programme 2011–13, led development and establishment of new TSB Bank within Lloyds Banking Group; CEO TSB Bank plc 2013–18. *Address:* c/o TSB Bank plc, Henry Duncan House, 120 George Street, Edinburgh, EH2 4LH, Scotland (office).

PESTILLO, Peter J., BEcons, LLB; American automotive executive; b. 22 March 1938, Bristol, Conn.; ed Fairfield Univ., Georgetown Univ., Harvard Business School Advanced Management Program; admitted to Bar, Washington, DC; began career in industrial relations, General Electric (GE) Co.; Vice-Pres. Corp. and Employee Relations, B.F. Goodrich –1980; Vice-Pres. Labour Relations Ford Motor

Co. 1980–85, Vice-Pres. Employee Relations 1985–86, Vice-Pres. Employee Relations and External Affairs 1986–90, Vice-Pres. Corp. Relations and Diversified Businesses 1990–93, apptd Exec. Vice-Pres. Corp. Relations 1993, Vice-Chair. and Chief of Staff –1999; Chair. and CEO Visteon (following spin-off from Ford Motor Co.) 2000–04, Chair. 2004–05; mem. Bd of Dirs Rouge Industries, Mich. Mfrs Asscn, Nat. Asscn of Mfrs and Sentry Insurance; Hon. Chair. Motorsports Hall of Fame of America 2001.

PESTON, Robert James Kenneth; British journalist and broadcaster; *Political Editor, ITV News;* b. 24 April 1960, London; s. of Maurice Peston and Helen Peston (née Conroy); m. Siân Busby (died 2012); one s. one step-s.; ed Balliol Coll., Oxford, Université Libre de Bruxelles, Belgium; began career as stockbroker with Williams de Broë; journalist, Investors Chronicle 1983; City Corresp., The Independent 1986–89; Deputy City Ed., Sunday Correspondent 1989–90; City Ed., Independent on Sunday 1990–91; Banking Ed., Financial Times 1991–93, Head of Investigations 1993–95, Political Ed. 1995–2000, Financial Ed. 2000; Editorial Dir, Collins Stewart Quest 2001–02; columnist, Daily Telegraph 2001; Assoc. Ed., The Spectator 2001; Business Columnist, New Statesman and Sunday Times 2002; City Ed. and Asst Ed., Sunday Telegraph 2002–06; Business Ed., BBC News 2006–13, Econs Ed. 2013–15; Political Ed., ITV News 2015–; f. Speakers for Schools (educ. charity); Fellow, Aberystwyth Univ. 2011; Hon. DLitt (Heriot-Watt) 2010; numerous awards including What The Papers Say Investigative Journalist of the Year 1994, Wincott Sr Financial Journalist of the Year 2005, London Press Club Scoop of the Year 2007, Business Journalism Awards Journalist of the Year 2007/08, Royal TV Soc. Journalism Awards TV Journalist of the Year, Specialist Journalist of the Year and Scoop of the Year 2008, Harold Wincott Awards Broadcaster of the Year and Online Media Award 2008, London Press Club Awards Business Journalist of the Year 2009, Political Studies Asscn Political Journalist of the Year 2009, Press Gazette Business Journalist of the Year 2009, Foreign Press Asscn Award Financial/Economic Story of the Year 2012. *Publications include:* Brown's Britain 2005, Who Runs Britain? How the Super-Rich are Changing our Lives 2008, How Do We Fix This Mess? The Economic Price of Having it All and the Route to Lasting Prosperity 2012, WTF 2017. *Address:* ITV News, London Television Centre, Upper Ground, London, SE1 9LT, England (office). *Website:* www.itv.com/news (office).

PETERLE, Lojze; Slovenian politician; b. 5 July 1948, Čužnja Vas, Trebnje; ed Ljubljana Univ.; Researcher, Urban Planning Inst. 1975–84; environmental protection adviser, Social Planning Inst. 1985–89; mem. Nat. Ass. 1990–, Chair. Parl. Cttee on European Affairs 1997–; Pres. Slovenian Christian Democrats (SKD) 1989–2000 (merged to form Slovenian People's Party 2000); Prime Minister of Slovenia 1990–92; Minister of Foreign Affairs 1993–94, June–Nov. 2000; First Vice-Pres. European Union of Christian Democrats 1996–99; Observer, European Parl. 2003–04, mem. European Parl. 2004–, mem. Cttee on Foreign Affairs, Del. to EU-Fmr Yugoslav Repub. of Macedonia Jt Parl. Cttee, Cttee on the Environment, Public Health and Food Safety, Substitute mem. Cttee on the Environment, Public Health and Food Safety, Del. for Relations with India; unsuccessful cand. in presidential elections 2007; mem. Praesidium of Convention on the Future of Europe 2002–03; Vice-Pres. Union of European Federalists 2004–; mem. State Legis. Leaders Foundation 1989; Kt Grand Cross, Papal Order 1993. *Address:* Cankarjeva 11, 1000 Ljubljana, Slovenia; European Parliament, Bâtiment Altiero Spinelli, 09E146, 60 rue Wiertz/Wiertzstraat 60, 1047 Brussels, Belgium (office). *Telephone:* (1) 4223585; (2) 2845638 (Brussels) (office). *Fax:* (1) 4261092; (2) 2849638 (Brussels) (office). *E-mail:* alojz.peterle@ep.europa.eu (office); alojz .peterle-office@ep.europa.eu (office); press@peterle.si. *Website:* www.europarl .europa.eu/meps/en/23693/ALOJZ_PETERLE_home.html (office); www.peterle .eu/kontakt.

PETERS, Gary Charles, BA, MA, MBA, JD; American lawyer and politician; *Senator from Michigan;* b. 1 Dec. 1958, Pontiac, Mich.; s. of Herbert Garrett Peters and Madeleine Peters (née Vignier); m. Colleen Ochoa; one s. two d.; ed Alma Coll., Univ. of Detroit, Wayne State Univ., Michigan State Univ.; various roles with Merrill Lynch, Pierce, Fenner & Smith, Inc., Rochester, Mich. 1980–89, including Financial Consultant and Asst Vice-Pres.; called to the Bar, Mich. 1990; Rochester Hills City Councilman 1991; mem. Michigan State Senate for Dist 14 1994–2002; Commr, Mich. State Lottery 2003–08; Griffin Endowed Chair in American Govt, Central Michigan Univ. 2007–08; mem. House of Reps from 9th Mich. Dist 2009–13, from 14th Michigan Dist 2013–15; Senator from Michigan 2015–; Officer, US Naval Reserve 1993–2000, 2001–05; Democrat; Navy and Marine Corps Achievement Medal, Mil. Outstanding Voluntary Service Medal. *Leisure interests:* hiking, motorcycling, travel, scuba diving. *Address:* SRC-2 Russell Senate Office Building, Washington, DC 20510, USA (office). *Telephone:* (202) 224-6221 (office). *Website:* www.peters.senate.gov (office).

PETERS, Jānis, Latvian writer, poet, essayist, publicist and fmr diplomatist; b. 30 June 1939, Liepāja Region; s. of Janis Peters and Zelma Peters; m. Baiba Kalniņa 1969; one s.; ed Rīga 25 secondary school; started as journalist in Latvian newspapers, later freelance; Chair. Bd of Latvian Writers' Union 1985–89; led historic Latvian Writers' Union conf. against censorship and for freedom of speech 1st and 2nd June 1988; participant democratic movt for independence; Chair. Org. Cttee People's Front of Latvia 1988; signed petition to Pres. of Communist Czechoslovakia to free dissident Vaclav Havel in Copenhagen (with Danish PEN Club members) 1990; USSR People's Deputy 1989–90; Perm. Rep. of Council of Ministers of Latvia to Russia 1990–91, then first Amb. of Repub. of Latvia to Russian Fed. after regaining independence 1992–97; mem. govt del. to negotiations with Russia, negotiations del. to Russian Fed. on withdrawal of Russian Fed. troops from Latvia 1992–94; Hon. mem. Latvian Acad. of Sciences 1990–, Latvian Univ. 1991–; Cavaliere di San Marco 1993, Order of Three Stars (Latvia), Order of the Dannebrog (Denmark), Order of Barricades (Latvia), Cross of Recognition (Latvia), Cross of Merit (Latvia) 2008; Cicero prize 2008. *Publications:* more than 20 books of poetry, prose and essays in Latvian, Russian, English, Ukrainian; poems translated also into Lithuanian, Estonian, Finnish, Georgian, Spanish, Bulgarian, German, Danish, etc. *Leisure interests:* gardening, driving. *Address:* Vesetas Str. 8, Apt 12, 1013 Rīga, Latvia (home). *Telephone:* 6733-9350 (home). *E-mail:* peters@apollo.lv (office).

PETERS, Mary E., BA; American consultant and fmr government official; b. 4 Dec. 1948, Peoria, Ariz.; m. Terry Peters; three c.; ed Univ. of Phoenix; joined Ariz.

Dept of Transportation 1985, served in several positions including Contract Admin., Deputy Dir for Admin, Deputy Dir –1998, Dir 1998–2001; US Fed. Highway Admin. 2001–05; Nat. Dir for Transportation Policy and Consulting, HDR, Inc., Phoenix 2005–06; US Sec. of Transportation 2006–09; f. Mary E Peters Consulting Group LLC 2009; fmr Chair. Standing Cttee on Planning and Asset Man. Task Force, American Asscn of State Highway Officials; Nat. Woman of the Year Award, Women's Transportation Seminar 2004, ARTBA Award, American Road and Transportation Builders Asscn 2005. *Address:* Mary E Peters Consulting Group LLC, 8323 West Via Montoya Drive, Peoria, AZ 85383, USA (office).

PETERS, Rt Hon Winston R., PC, BA, LLB; New Zealand lawyer and politician; *Deputy Prime Minister and Minister of Foreign Affairs;* b. 11 April 1945, Whangarei, Northland; m.; one s. one d.; ed Dargaville High School, Univ. of Auckland; MP (National Party) for Hunua 1978–81, for Tauranga 1984–2005 (1984–93 for National Party, 1993 as Ind. then for New Zealand First), for New Zealand First List 2005–08, 2011–17, for Northland (New Zealand First) 2015–17, Opposition Spokesperson on Maori Affairs, Consumer Affairs and Transport 1984–87, Opposition Front Bench Spokesperson on Maori Affairs, Employment and Race Relations 1987–90; Minister of Maori Affairs, Minister in charge of the Iwi Transition Agency, Chair. Cabinet Cttee on Treaty of Waitangi Issues 1990–91; Leader New Zealand First Party 1993–; Deputy Prime Minister 1996–98, 2017–; Treas. 1996–98; Minister of Foreign Affairs and for Racing 2005–08; Minister of Foreign Affairs 2017–; fmr Capt. Auckland Maori Rugby team and played for Auckland Univ. seniors. *Leisure interests:* sport, fishing, reading. *Address:* New Zealand First Party, Albany, North Shore City, PO Box 301158, Auckland 0752 (office); Department of Prime Minister and Cabinet, Executive Wing, Parliament Buildings, Wellington 6011, New Zealand (office). *Telephone:* (9) 422-2370 (Auckland) (office); (4) 817-9743 (DPMC) (office). *Fax:* (9) 422-2370 (Auckland) (office); (4) 472-3181 (DPMC) (office). *E-mail:* nzfirstparty@ nzfirstparty.org.nz (office); dpmc.information@dpmc.govt.nz (office). *Website:* nzfirst.org.nz (office); www.dpmc.govt.nz (office).

PETERSEN, George Bouet, ONZM, MSc, MA, DPhil, DSc, FRSNZ; New Zealand scientist and academic; *Professor Emeritus of Biochemistry, University of Otago;* b. 5 Sept. 1933, Palmerston North; s. of George C. Petersen and Elizabeth S. Petersen; m. Patricia J.E. Caughey 1960; four d.; ed Univ. of Otago and Univ. of Oxford, England; scientist, Dept of Scientific and Industrial Research Plant Chem. Div., Palmerston North 1959–60, 1963–67; Departmental Demonstrator in Biochemistry, Univ. of Oxford 1961–63; Head of Dept of Biochemistry, Univ. of Otago 1968–91, Prof. of Biochemistry 1968–99, Prof. Emer. 1999–; Deputy Dean, Otago Medical School 1991–95; Pres. Acad. Council Royal Soc. of New Zealand 1997–2000; Visiting Research Fellow, Harvard Univ., USA 1964; Royal Soc. Commonwealth Bursar, MRC Lab. of Molecular Biology, Cambridge, UK 1973–74, 1981; Carnegie Corpn of New York Travel Grantee 1964; Officer, New Zealand Order of Merit 1997; Hon. DSc (Otago) 2000; Marsden Medal, New Zealand Asscn of Scientists 1995, Rutherford Medal, Royal Soc. of New Zealand 2003. *Publications include:* numerous papers on aspects of nucleic acid chemistry and biochemistry in various scientific journals. *Leisure interests:* music, literature, book collecting. *Telephone:* (3) 477-0784 (home). *E-mail:* george.petersen@otago.ac .nz (office).

PETERSEN, Jan, LLB; Norwegian politician and diplomatist; b. 11 June 1946, Oslo; s. of Kaare Petersen and Elsa Olsen; m. Gerda Mollatt Petersen; two c.; with Norwegian Consumers' Asscn 1974, Norwegian Agency for Devt Co-operation (NORAD) 1975–78; Chair. Unge Høyre (Young Conservatives) 1971–73; Mayor of Oppegård 1976–81; mem. Stortinget (Parl.) for Akershus constituency 1981–2009, mem. Standing Cttee on Local Govt and Environment 1981–84, Standing Cttee on Foreign Affairs 1984–2009 (Chair. 1985–86); Leader Akershus Conservative Party 1992–94, Conservative Party (Høyre) 1994–2004; Chair. NATO Political Cttee 1996–2001; Minister of Foreign Affairs 2001–05; Amb. to Austria 2009–14; Commdr with Star, Order of St Olav 2004. *Address:* Ministry of Foreign Affairs, 7 juni-plassen/Victoria Terrasse, PO Box 8114 Dep., 0032 Oslo, Norway (office). *Telephone:* 23-95-00-00 (office). *Fax:* 23-95-00-99 (office). *E-mail:* post@mfa.no (office). *Website:* www.regjeringen.no/ud (office).

PETERSEN, Wolfgang; German film director, producer and screenwriter; b. 14 March 1941, Emden; m. 1st Ursula Sieg (divorced 1978); m. 2nd Maria Borgel-Petersen 1978; ed Gelehrtenschule des Johanneums, Hamburg, German Film and TV Acad., Berlin; actor and Asst Stage Dir, Ernst Deutsch Theatre, Hamburg 1964–69; directed six 100-minute episodes for West German TV series Tatort (Scene of the Crime) 1971–76; first feature film, Einer von uns beiden 1973; German Film Award for Best New Direction. *Films include:* Der Eine – Der Andere (short) 1967, Die rote Fahne (documentary short) 1968, Ich nicht (short) 1969, I Will Kill You, Wolf 1971, One or the Other of Us (German Nat. Film Prize for Best New Director 1973) 1974, For Your Love Only, Scene of the Crime, Die Konsequenz 1977, Das Boot (Bavarian Film Award for Best Dir 1983) 1981, The Neverending Story 1984, Enemy Mine 1985, Shattered 1991, In the Line of Fire 1993, Outbreak 1995, Air Force One, The Red Corner 1997, The Perfect Storm 2000, Troy 2004, Poseidon 2006; exec. producer: Instinct 1999, Chicxulub (short) 2006. *Television includes:* Stadt auf Stelzen (film) 1965, Tatort (series) (Prix Italia and Best Dir, Monte Carlo Television Festival 1977) 1971–77, Anna und Totò (film) 1972, Smog (film) (Prix Futura, Berlin Festival 1975), Van der Valk und die Reichen (film) 1973, Aufs Kreuz gelegt (film) 1974, Die Stadt im Tal (mini-series) 1975, Stellenweise Glatteis (film) 1975, Hans im Glück (film) 1976, Vier gegen die Bank (film) 1976, Planübung (film) 1977, Schwarz und weiß wie Tage und Nächte (film) 1978, Das Boot (mini-series) 1985; exec. producer: The Agency (series) 2001, Avenger (film) 2006. *Address:* c/o Creative Artists Agency, 2000 Avenue of the Stars, Los Angeles, CA 90067, USA (office). *Telephone:* (424) 288-2000 (office). *Fax:* (424) 288-2900 (office). *Website:* www.caa.com (office); wolfgangpetersen.net.

PETERSON, Hon. David Robert, PC, CStJ, LLD, QC; Canadian lawyer, business executive and fmr politician; *Chairman, Cassels Brock & Blackwell LLP;* b. 28 Dec. 1943, Toronto, Ont.; s. of Clarence Peterson; m. Shelley Matthews 1974; two s. one d.; ed Univ. of Western Ontario, Univ. of Toronto; called to the Bar 1969; MP for London Centre 1975, re-elected 1977, 1981; elected Leader of Ont. Liberal Party 1982, won election for Liberal Party 1985; Premier of Ont. 1985–90; currently Chair. Cassels Brock & Blackwell LLP; Chancellor Univ. of Toronto 2006–12; Chair. Toronto 2015 Pan American Games Organizing Cttee 2013–;

numerous directorships; Founding Chair. Toronto Raptors Basketball Club, Chapters Inc.; Dir Young Presidents' Org., Council for Canadian Unity etc.; Adjunct Prof., York Univ.; Liberal; Chevalier, Légion d'honneur 1994, Ordre de la Pléiade, Int. Ass. of French-speaking Parliamentarians 1995, Order of Ontario 2009; several hon. degrees, including Hon. DUniv. *Leisure interests:* theatre, riding, jogging, golf, skiing, tennis, reading, gardening. *Address:* Cassels Brock & Blackwell LLP, 2100 Scotia Plaza, 40 King Street West, Toronto, ON M5H 3C2 (office); 8 Gibson Avenue, Toronto, ON M5R 1T5, Canada (home). *Telephone:* (416) 869-5451 (office); (416) 925-0460 (home). *Fax:* (416) 350-6961 (office). *E-mail:* dpeterson@casselsbrock.com (office). *Website:* www.casselsbrock.com (office).

PETERSON, G. P. (Bud), BS, MS, PhD; American engineer, academic and university administrator; *President, Georgia Institute of Technology;* b. 1 Sept. 1952, San Francisco, Calif.; m. Val Peterson; four c.; ed Kansas State Univ., Texas A&M Univ.; Visiting Research Scientist, NASA Johnson Space Center 1981–82; Lecturer and Researcher, Dept of Mechanical Eng, Texas A&M Univ. 1985–90, Halliburton Prof. of Mechanical Eng Sept. 1990–Aug. 1991, Tenneco Prof., Coll. of Eng 1991–2000, Head of Dept of Mechanical Eng 1993–96, Exec. Assoc. Dean, Coll. of Eng 1996–2000, Assoc. Vice-Chancellor for Eng 1996–2000; Provost Rensselaer Polytechnic Inst. 2000–06; Chancellor Univ. of Colorado, Boulder 2006–09; Pres. Georgia Inst. of Tech. 2009–, Prof. of Mechanical Eng 2009–; Program Dir Thermal Transport and Thermal Processing Div., NSF 1993–94; mem. Nat. Science Bd 2008–14; mem. American Asscn of Colls and Univs, Middle States Comm. on Higher Educ., New England Asscn of Schools and Colls; Fellow, ASME, AIAA; Hon. DEng (Colorado School of Mines) 2013; Ralph James and the O.L. 'Andy Lewis' Awards, ASME, Pi Tau Sigma Gustus L. Larson Memorial Award, ASME, AIAA Thermophysics Award, ASME Memorial Award, AIAA Sustained Service Award, NSF Award for Outstanding Man., Int. Astronautical Fed. Frank J. Malina Astronautics Medal 2005, GEM Academic Leadership Award. *Publications:* author or co-author of 14 books and book chapters, 165 refereed journal articles and more than 140 conf. publs. *Address:* Office of the President, Georgia Institute of Technology, North Avenue, PO Box 0325, Atlanta, GA 30332, USA (office). *Telephone:* (404) 894-5051 (office). *E-mail:* bud.peterson@gatech.edu (office). *Website:* www.president.gatech.edu (office).

PETERSON, James Scott, DCL, LLM; Canadian lawyer and politician; *Counsel, Fasken Martineau DuMoulin LLP;* b. 30 July 1941, Ottawa; m. Heather Peterson; ed McGill Univ., Columbia Univ., USA, Univ. of West Ontario, Acad. de Droit Int., The Hague, The Netherlands, La Sorbonne, Paris, France; mem. Faculty of Law, Univ. of Toronto 1974–79; pvt. practice, int. tax and business law 1970–80; Chair. Cambridge Acceptance Corpn Ltd 1984–87; MP for Willowdale 1980, re-elected 1988, 1993, 1997; fmr Liberal Party Industry Critic, Treasury Bd Critic, Parl. Sec. to Minister of State for Econ. Devt, Science and Tech. and to Minister of Justice; Chair. Parl. Task Force on Regulatory Reform; Chair. Standing Cttee on Finance 1993–97, Sec. of State (Int. Financial Insts) 1997–2002, Minister of Int. Trade Dec. 2003–06; fmr legal counsel and consultant to UN on jt ventures and major devt projects; Sr Resident Massey Coll., Munk Centre for Int. Studies, Univ. of Toronto 2002–; Co-Chair. Canada/US Law Inst.; mem. Canadian Bar Asscn, Ontario Bar Asscn. *Publications:* numerous works on int. taxation and int. jt business ventures. *Address:* Fasken Martineau DuMoulin LLP, 333 Bay Street, Suite 2400, Bay Adelaide Centre, Box 20, Toronto, ON M5H 2T6, Canada (office). *Telephone:* (416) 865-5489 (office). *Fax:* (416) 364-7813 (office). *E-mail:* jpeterson@fasken.com (office). *Website:* www.fasken.com (office).

PETERSON, Paul E., BA, MA, PhD; American political scientist and academic; *Henry Lee Shattuck Professor of Government and Director, Program on Education Policy and Governance, John F. Kennedy School of Government, Harvard University;* b. 16 Sept. 1940, Montevideo, Minn.; ed Concordia Coll., Moorhead, Minn. and Univ. of Chicago; Asst Prof., then Assoc. Prof. and Prof., Depts of Political Science and Educ., Univ. of Chicago 1967–83, Chair. Cttee on Public Policy Studies 1981–83; Dir Governmental Studies, The Brookings Inst., Washington, DC 1983–87; Benjamin H. Griswold III Prof. of Public Policy, Dept of Political Science, Johns Hopkins Univ. 1987–88; Prof. Dept of Govt, Harvard Univ. 1988–89, Henry Lee Shattuck Prof. of Govt 1989–, Dir Centre for American Political Studies 1989–2000, Dir Program on Educ. Policy and Governance 1996–; Acad. Visitor, Dept of Govt, LSE, England 1977–78; John Simon Guggenheim Fellowship, German Marshall Fund of the US Fellowship 1977–78; Fellow, Center for Advanced Study in the Center for the Behavioral and Social Sciences, Stanford 1996–97; Sr Fellow, Hoover Inst., Stanford Univ. 2000–; mem. Title I Ind. Review Cttee, US Dept of Educ. 2003, Educ. Research and Devt Center Grants Peer Review Panel, Inst. of Educ. Sciences, US Dept of Educ. 2005; Ed.-in-Chief, Education Next (journal); apptd Head, Florida Educ. Transition Team by Gov.-Elect Charlie Crist 2006; mem. Nat. Acad. of Educ., American Acad. of Arts and Sciences; Norton Long Career Achievement Award, American Political Science Asscn 1996, Thomas B. Fordham Prize for Distinguished Scholarship 2003, Star Family Prize for Excellence in Advising 2015. *Publications include:* School Politics Chicago Style 1976 (Gladys Kammerer Award, American Political Science Asscn Award), City Limits 1981 (Woodrow Wilson Foundation Award), The Politics of School Reform, 1870–1940 1985, The New Urban Reality (ed.) 1985, The New Direction in American Politics (co-ed. with J. Chubb) 1985, When Federalism Works (with B. Rabe and K. Wong) 1987, Political Institutions and Effective Government, Can the Government Govern? 1989, Welfare Magnets (with Mark Rom) 1991, The Urban Underclass (with C. Jencks) 1991, The President, the Congress and the Making of Foreign Policy 1994, The Price of Federalism 1995 (Aaron Wildavsky Award 1996, Martha Derthick Best Book Award 2010), Classifying by Race 1995, The New American Democracy (with M. Fiorina) 2001, Learning from School Choice (co-ed. with B. Hassel) 1998, Earning and Learning (co-ed. with S. Mayer), Charters, Vouchers and Public Education (co-ed. with David E. Campbell) 2001, The Education Gap: Vouchers and Urban Schools (with William G. Howell) 2002, Saving Schools: From Horace Mann to Virtual Learning 2011, Endangering Prosperity: A Global View of the American School (co-author) 2013, Teachers Versus the Public: What Americans Think About Schools and How to Fix Them (co-author) 2014. *Leisure interests:* tennis, piano. *Address:* Taubman 306, John F. Kennedy School of Government, Harvard University, 79 John F. Kennedy Street, T306, Cambridge, MA 02138, USA (office). *Telephone:* (617) 495-8312 (office). *Fax:* (617) 496-4428 (office). *E-mail:* Paul_Peterson@hks.harvard.edu (office). *Website:* www.hks.harvard.edu/pepg (office); www.educationnext.org; paulepeterson.org.

PETERSON, Sandra E., BA, MPA; American business executive; *CEO, Bayer CropScience;* b. 1959, New York, NY; ed Cornell Univ., Princeton Univ.; received fellowship from Robert Bosch Foundation, Stuttgart, Germany, spent a year serving with Fed. Ministry of Finance and Fed. of German Industries 1984–85; Man. Consultant, McKinsey & Co. 1987–93; held various global exec. positions with Whirlpool Corpn 1993–96; Exec. Vice-Pres. Nabisco 1996–99; Sr Vice-Pres. Merck-Medco's Health Businesses 1999, mem. Exec. Man. team, played role in spin-off of Medco Health from Merck & Co., Inc., latterly serving as Group Pres. Medco Health Solutions, Inc.; mem. Exec. Cttee Bayer HealthCare 2005–, Head of Diabetes Care Div. –2009, Head of Medical Care Div. 2009–10, CEO Bayer CropScience and Chair. Bayer CropScience AG 2010–; mem. Bd of Dirs Dun & Bradstreet; mem. Bd CropLife International; mem. and fmr Chair. Wildlife Trust; mem. Committee of 200, Women's Forum. *Address:* Bayer CropScience AG, Alfred-Nobel-Str. 50, 40789 Monheim am Rhein, Germany (office). *Telephone:* (21) 7338-0 (office). *Website:* www.cropscience.bayer.com (office).

PETERSON, Thage Edvin Gerhard; Swedish politician; *Senior Adviser, Expandum AB;* b. 24 Sept. 1933, Berg, Småland; m. Marion Karlsson 1962; ed Inst. of Social Studies, Lund; Municipal Treas., Community Centre Asscn 1957–59, Head 1967–71; Sec. and Vice-Chair. Social Democratic Youth Union 1964–67; mem. Riksdag (Parl.) 1971–98, Speaker 1988–91; Under-Sec. of State to Cabinet 1971–75; Chair. Stockholm Co. br. of Socialdemokratiska Arbetarepartiet (Social Democratic Labour Party—SDLP) 1974–89; mem. SDLP Exec. Cttee 1975–90; Minister without Portfolio 1975–76; SDLP spokesman for Industrial Policy 1976–82; mem. SDLP Parl. Group Exec. and Head of Research Div.; Minister of Industry 1982–88, of Justice 1988, of Defence 1994–97, Minister in the Prime Minister's Office 1997–98; Chair. Standing Cttee on the Constitution 1991–94; Sr Adviser Expandum AB; an initiator of the petition, Bring Home the Swedish Troops from Afghanistan, against the war, published in Aftonbladet Feb. 2007; Medal Illis Quorum in Gold of the 18th magnitude 1998. *Publications:* Resan mot Mars: anteckningar och minnen (The Journey to Mars: Notes and Memories) 1999, Resan till Berg: ska hela Sverige leva?: en tidsresa (Journey to the Mountains: Should the Whole of Sweden Live?: A Journey Through Time) 2000, Olof Palme som jag minns honom (Olof Palme, as I Remember Him) 2002. *Address:* Expandum AB, Box 840, 982 28 Gällivare, Sweden (office). *Telephone:* (970) 641-60 (office). *Fax:* (970) 641-05 (office). *E-mail:* info@expandum.se (office). *Website:* www .expandum.se (office).

PETERSSON, Lars-Eric Gustav, BSc; Swedish business executive; b. 21 June 1950, Mönsterås; m.; two s.; Exec. Vice-Pres. Sparbanken/Svenska Sparbanksförmingen 1984–90; Pres., later Pres. and Chair. Pronator 1990–93; with Skandia Insurance Co. Ltd as mem. Man. Group, Head Business Control/Business Devt, Exec. Vice-Pres., mem. Exec. Man., Head Int. Direct Insurance and Reinsurance (IDR), Acting Head, Skandia Investment Man., Deputy Chief Exec. 1993–97, Pres. and CEO Skandia Insurance Co. Ltd 1997–2003.

PETHICA, Sir John Bernard, Kt, BA, PhD, FRS, FREng; British physicist and academic; *Principal Investigator, School of Physics, Trinity College, Dublin;* b. 1953; ed St Ambrose Coll., Altrincham, Univ. of Cambridge; Staff Scientist, Brown Boveri Corp. Research Centre, Baden, Switzerland 1980–82; Oppenheimer Fellow, Univ. of Cambridge 1982–84; Guest Scientist, ABB Research Centre, Baden, Switzerland 1983–87; Royal Soc. Univ. Research Fellow, Cavendish Lab., Cambridge 1984–87; Guest Scientist, Oak Ridge Nat. Lab., Tenn., USA 1985–89; Univ. Lecturer in Physics of Materials and Fellow of St Cross Coll., Oxford 1987–96, Prof. of Materials Science 1996–2003; Visiting Prof., Univ. of Konstanz, Germany 1990, Univ. of Nijmegen, Netherlands 1992, Dept of Materials Univ. of Oxford 2013–; Sabbatical Chair., Sony Corpn, Yokohama, Japan 1993–94; Visiting Fellow, Australian Nuclear Science and Tech. Org., Menai, Australia 1994; Science Foundation Ireland Research Prof., Trinity Coll., Dublin, Ireland 2001–, Founding Dir Centre for Research on Adaptive Nanostructures and Nanodevices 2003–05, Prin. Investigator, School of Physics; part-time Chief Scientific Adviser, Nat. Physical Lab. 2007–; Official Guest of Japan Acad. from the Royal Soc. Jan. 2002; IP for SMEs, UK Intellectual Property Conf., Said Business School, Oxford June 2003; Founder and Dir, Nano Instruments Inc., Knoxville, Tenn., USA 1984–98; consultant for several cos.; Physical Sciences Sec. and Vice-Pres. Royal Soc. 2009–; mem. Thin Films & Interfaces Cttee, Inst. of Physics 1987–90 (mem. Tribology Cttee 1991–94), Surface & Interface Science Bd, European Physical Soc. 1988–97, UK-Japan N+N Panels 1990–2003; Fellow, Royal Acad. of Eng 2013; Elegant Work Prize, Inst. of Materials 1994, Rosenhain Medal and Prize, Inst. of Materials 1997, Royal Soc. Hughes Medal 2001, Holweck Medal, Sociéte Française de Physique 2002. *Address:* Department of Materials, University of Oxford, 16 Parks Road, Oxford, OX1 3PH, England (office); Department of Physics, Trinity College, Dublin 2, Ireland (office). *Telephone:* (1865) 273700 (Oxford, switchboard) (office); (1) 8963036 (Dublin) (office). *Fax:* (1865) 273783 (Oxford) (office). *E-mail:* john .pethica@materials.ox.ac.uk (office); jp12@tcd.ie (office); john.pethica@tcd.ie (office). *Website:* www.materials.ox.ac.uk/peoplepages/pethica.html (office); www .crann.tcd.ie/Research/Investigators/School-of-Physics/Prof-John-Pethica.aspx (office); people.tcd.ie/jp12 (office); www.npl.co.uk/people/john-pethica (office).

PETHRICK, Richard Arthur, PhD, CChem, FRSC, FRSE, FIMMM; British physical chemist and academic; *Professor Emeritus of Chemistry, University of Strathclyde;* b. 26 Oct. 1942, Yate, Glos., England; s. of A. T. A. Pethrick and L. M. Pethrick; m. J. Hume 1975; one s.; ed Univs of London and Salford; Lecturer, Dept of Pure and Applied Chem., Univ. of Strathclyde 1970, Sr Lecturer 1978, Reader 1981, Prof. of Chem. 1983–2003, Head of Dept 1992–95, 1999–2005, Burmah Prof. of Physical Chem. 2003–08, Prof. Emer. 2008–; mem. Editorial Bd British Polymer Journal 1979–93, Int. Journal of Polymeric Materials 1990–, Polymer News 1991–, Trends in Polymer Science 1992–, Polymer Int. 1993–; Ed. Polymer Yearbook 1983–; Visiting Prof., Univ. of Punjab 1979; British Council Visiting Lecturer, Australia 1985, 1989; Royal Soc. Visiting Lecturer, UK-China Del., Beijing 1992; mem. Int. Swedish Tech. Review Cttee for Polymer Science 1988, Int. Danish Tech. Review Cttee for Polymer Science 2003, Polymers and Composites Cttee Science and Eng Research Council 1993–, Large Area Displays Cttee Eng and Physical Sciences Research Council 1994–, IRC Review Cttee 1995–; Chair. Science Sector Scottish Vocational Awards Council 1995–2001; mem. RSC Accreditation Cttee

1996–2002, RSC Educ. Cttee 2005–, NSF Polymers Cttee 2009, Materials Panel, Royal Soc. of Edinburgh 2008–; elected mem. Hon. Craft of Weavers of Glasgow 1991; Fellow, Inst. of Materials, Minerals and Mining 1998. *Publications:* Molecular Motion in High Polymers 1979, Modern Methods of Polymer Characterization 1999, Polymer Characterization – Physical Techniques (with D. Campbell, J. R. White) 2000, Techniques for Polymer Organization and Morphological Characterization 2003, Polymer Structure Characterization – From Nano to Macro Organization 2007, Polymer Science and Technology for Engineers and Scientists 2011, Introduction to Molecular Motion in Polymers (with T. Amornsakchai and A. M. North) 2011; more than 460 scientific papers and numerous book chapters and review articles. *Leisure interests:* walking, painting, photography. *Address:* WestCHEM, Department of Pure and Applied Chemistry, University of Strathclyde, Thomas Building, 295 Cathedral Street, Glasgow, G1 1XL, Scotland (office). *Telephone:* (141) 548-4760 (office); (141) 548-2795 (office). *Fax:* (141) 548-4822 (office). *E-mail:* r.a.pethrick@strath.ac.uk (office).

PETIT, Christine, MD, PhD; French geneticist, biochemist and academic; *Director, Laboratory of Genetics and Physiology of Hearing, Institut Pasteur;* b. (Christine Chavance), 4 Feb. 1948, Laignes; ed Univ. Paris VI (Medicine), Univ. Paris XI-Orsay (Sciences), Univ. Paris VII; Post-graduate medicine student, Faculty of Medicine, Creteil 1973–74; Student, Cellular Genetics Lab., Institut Pasteur 1974–75, researcher, Immunochemistry Lab. 1976–81, Staff scientist, Recombination and Genetics Expression Lab. 1985–90, Head, Human Molecular Genetics Lab. 1993–96, Dir, Sensory Deficit Genetics Lab. 1996–2007, Head, Dept of Biotechnology 1998–2001, Dir, Lab. of Genetics and Physiology of Hearing 2008–, also Head, Dept of Neuroscience 2006–10, mem. Bd of Dirs, Institut Pasteur 2003–11; postdoctoral researcher, Basel, Switzerland 1982–83; researcher, CNRS Molecular Genetics Centre, Gif-sur-Yvette 1983–84; Prof. of Genetics and Cellular Physiology, Collège de France, Paris 2002–, also Chair of Genetics and Cellular Physiology; Head of INSERM UMRS 587 Lab., Univ. Pierre & Marie Curie 2003–12; mem. Council for Teaching, Ecole Supérieure de Physique et de Chimie Industrielles de la Ville de Paris 2007–13; Pres. Steering Cttee CTRS/RTRS 'Sensory Handicap' 2007–; mem. Bd of Dirs Institut Carnot 'Seeing and Hearing' 2006–, Minna-James-Heineman Foundation, Germany 2011–; mem. Scientific Council, Université Paris-Descartes 2008–10, Ecole Normale Supérieure, Louis-Jeantet Foundation 2008–10; mem. Commissariat à l'Energie Atomique 2008–15; mem. jury for several awards including IPSEN Awards 1995–2013, L'Oréal-UNESCO Awards For Women in Science 2015, Wellcome Trust Collaborative Awards Cttee 2015–; mem. Acad. des sciences 2002, European Molecular Biology Org. 1996, Academia Europaea 1998, Nat. Acad. of Medicine 2011–; Chevalier, Légion d'honneur 2002, Officier, Ordre Nat. du Mérite 2011, Officier, Légion d'honneur 2014; numerous awards including Prix Janine Courrier de l'Académie des sciences 1992, Charles-Léopold Meyer Award 1999, Ernst Jung Prize für Wissenschaft und Forschung (Medicine) 2001, L'Oréal-UNESCO Award For Women in Science 2004, Research and Medicine Award, Inst. for Health Sciences 2004, Freedom to Discover in Neuroscience Prize, Bristol-Myers Squibb Inst. 2005, Prix Louis-Jeantet de Médecine 2006, Grand Prix, INSERM 2007, Pasarow Medical Research Award (Neuropsychiatry) 2011, Brain Prize 2012, Hugh Knowles Prize for Distinguished Achievement 2015. *Publications:* numerous articles in medical journals on genetic basis of sensory disorders and pathophysiology. *Address:* Institut Pasteur, 25 rue du Dr Roux, 75724 Paris Cedex 15, France (office). *Telephone:* 1-45-68-88-90 (office). *E-mail:* cpetit@pasteur.fr (office). *Website:* www.pasteur.fr (office).

PETKOV, Petko Danev; Bulgarian politician; b. 2 March 1942, Dobrotich; ed Higher Naval School, Varna; joined Dimitrov Young Communist League 1956, Bulgarian Communist Party (BCP) 1973; worked for 1st Coast Artillery Regt, Varna, radio mechanic for Navigation Maritime Bulgare Shipping Co., designer at Resprom Plant, Varna, Deputy Man., then Man. of Radio Navigation Equipment Works, Varna, Man. Dir of Cherno More Research and Industry Combined Works; apptd First Sec., BCP Municipal Cttee, Varna Sept. 1987; Alt. mem., BCP Cen. Cttee; Alt. mem., Political Bureau 1989.

PETKOVSKI, Tito; Macedonian politician; *President, New Social Democratic Party;* b. 23 Jan. 1945, Psacha, Kriva Palanka; m. Tanja Petkovska; two d.; ed Kriva Palanka High School, Skopje Univ.; worked in Municipal court Kriva Palanka, Repub. Bureau on Urban Planning and Communal Issues; political career started as deputy in Karposh Communal Ass., deputy City Ass. Skopje; later Vice-Pres. Exec. Council City Ass. Skopje; Sec. Cen. Cttee League of Communists of Macedonia—Party for Democratic Prosperity; mem. Cttee on Constitutional Problems, Ass. Repub. of Macedonia; Vice-Pres. first multi-party Ass. of Macedonia 1994–96; co-ordinator Parl. Group Social-Democratic Union of Macedonia; mem. Council of Inter-Parl. Union; Pres. Ass. (Sobranje) Repub. of Macedonia 1996–98, Pres. Standing Inquiry Cttee for Protection of Citizens' Freedoms and Rights 1998–; Pres. and Founding mem. New Social Democratic Party 2005–; cand. in presidential elections 1999. *Publications include:* legal articles on housing policy, town planning and land devt. *Address:* New Social Democratic Party, Veljko Vlahović 4, blvd, 1000 Skopje, North Macedonia (office). *Telephone:* (2) 3238775 (office). *Fax:* (2) 3290465 (office). *E-mail:* nsdp@nsdp.org.mk (office). *Website:* nsdp .org.mk (office).

PETO, Sir Richard, Kt, MSc, MA, FRS; British epidemiologist; *Professor of Medical Statistics and Epidemiology, University of Oxford;* b. 14 May 1943, Reading, Berks.; s. of Leonard Huntley Peto and Carrie Clarinda Peto; m. 1st Sallie Messum 1970 (divorced); two s.; partner Gale Mead (deceased); two s.; partner Sasi Phosri; ed Tauntons School, Southampton, Trinity Coll., Cambridge, Imperial Coll., London; Research Officer, MRC 1967–69; with Univ. of Oxford 1969–, Lecturer 1972–75, Reader in Cancer Studies 1975–92, Prof. of Medical Statistics and Epidemiology 1992–; Guy Medal in Silver 1986, Royal Medal, Royal Soc. 2002, Charles S. Mott Prize 2002, King Faisal Int. Prize (co-winner) 2005, Dr A.H. Heineken Prize in Medicine 2008, Lifetime Achievement Prize, Cancer Research UK 2010, Lifetime Achievement Award, BMJ Group 2011, ESMO Lifetime Achievement Award 2016, William L. McGuire Memorial Lecture Award, San Antonio Breast Cancer Symposium (SABCS) 2017. *Publications include:* Natural History of Chronic Bronchitis and Emphysema 1976, Quantification of Occupational Cancer 1981, The Causes of Cancer 1983, Diet, Lifestyle and Mortality in China 1990, Mortality from Smoking in Developed Countries

1950–2000 1994, Emerging Tobacco Hazards in China 1998, Tobacco: The Growing Epidemic 2000, Geographic Study of Mortality, Biochemistry, Diet and Lifestyle in Rural China 2006; more than 500 papers. *Leisure interests:* science, children. *Address:* Clinical Trial Service Unit and Epidemiological Studies Unit (CTSU), Nuffield Department of Population Health, Richard Doll Building, Old Road Campus, Oxford, OX3 7LF (office); 62 Great Clarendon Street, Oxford, OX2 6AX, England (home). *Telephone:* (1865) 743801 (office). *E-mail:* richard.peto@ndph.ox .ac.uk (office). *Website:* www.ctsu.ox.ac.uk/researchers/professor-sir-richard-peto (office); www.cardioscience.ox.ac.uk/bhf-centre-of-research-excellence (office).

PETRAEUS, Gen. (retd) David Howell, BS, MPA, PhD; American government official, academic and fmr army officer; *Visiting Professor of Public Policy, Macaulay Honors College, City University of New York;* b. 7 Nov. 1952, Cornwall-on-Hudson, New York; m. Holly Knowlton 1974; one s. one d.; ed West Point Mil. Acad., Princeton Univ.; commissioned Second-Lt 1974, assigned to 509th Airborne Infantry Bn, Vicenza, Italy, served in various leadership posts in airborne, mechanized and air assault infantry units in Europe and USA including Operations Officer, 3rd Infantry Div. (Mechanized) 1st Bn 1978–79, command of 101st Airborne Div. (Air Assault) 3rd Bn 1991–93, command of 82nd Airborne Div. 1st Brigade 1995–97; staff posts have included Aide to Chief of Staff of the Army, Mil. Asst to Supreme Allied Commdr—Europe, Chief Mil. Operations Officer, UN Mission, Haiti 1995, Exec. Asst to Dir of Jt Staff and subsequently Chair. Jt Chiefs of Staff, Pentagon 1997–99; promoted to Brig.-Gen. 1999; Asst Div. Commdr for Operations, 82nd Airborne Div., Fort Bragg, NC 1999–2000; Chief of Staff, XVIII Airborne Corps 2000–01; promoted to Maj.-Gen. 2001; Asst Chief of Staff for Operations, NATO Stabilization Force and Deputy Commdr, US Jt Interagency Counter-Terrorism Task Force, Bosnia 2001–02; commanded 101st Airborne Div. during Operation Iraqi Freedom, Iraq 2003; promoted to Lt-Gen. 2004; Commdr, Multi-Nat. Security Transition Command and NATO Training Mission, Iraq 2004–05; Commanding Gen. US Army Combined Arms Center and Fort Leavenworth 2005–07; promoted to Gen. 2007; Commdr Multi-Nat. Force-Iraq, overseeing all coalition forces 2007–08; Commdr US Cen. Command 2008–10; Commdr Int. Security Assistance Force (ISAF) and Commdr, US Forces Afghanistan (USFOR-A) 2010–11; Dir CIA 2011–12 (resgnd); Visiting Prof. of Public Policy, Macaulay Honors Coll., CUNY 2013–; Chair. Kohlberg Kravis Roberts (KKR) Global Inst. 2013–; Judge Widney Prof., Univ. of S California 2013–; Sr Fellow, Harvard Univ. 2013–; Sr Vice-Pres., Royal United Services Inst. 2013; Co-Chair. Council on Foreign Relations Task Force on N America 2013–; sentenced to two years of probation and fined for sharing classified material 2015; Hon. Prof., Exeter Univ. 2014; Gold Award of the Iraqi Order of the Date Palm; Gen. George C. Marshall Award 1983, Combat Action Badge, Army Achievement Medal, Defense Distinguished Service Medal, two Distinguished Service Medals, two Defense Superior Service Medals, four Legion of Merit awards, Bronze Star Medal for Valor, State Dept Superior Honor Award, NATO Meritorious Service Medal. *Publication:* US Army Counterinsurgency Field Manual (co-author). *Address:* Macaulay Honors College, City University of New York, 35 West 67th Street, New York, NY 10023, USA (office). *Website:* www.macaulay.cuny.edu (office).

PETRÁŇOVÁ, Ludmila; Czech business executive; *CEO, Lumen Energy a.s.;* ed Faculty of Nuclear and Physical Eng, Czech Tech. Univ., Prague; Chair. and CEO ČEPS a.s. (state-owned transmission grid) 2002–06; mem. Bd Electricity Market Operator (OTE) 2006–09; CEO Lumen Energy a.s. 2009–; mem. energy advisory team, Ernst & Young 2011–. *Address:* Lumen Energy a.s., Tylovická 372/16, 155 21 Prague 5, Czech Republic (office). *Telephone:* (2) 272655855 (office). *Fax:* (office). *E-mail:* ludmila.petranova@lumen-energy.com (office). *Website:* www.lumen -energy.cz (office).

PETRESCU, Ioana Maria, BA, MA, PhD; Romanian economist, academic and government official; b. 1 July 1980, Bucharest; ed Wellesley Coll., Mass and Harvard Univ., USA; lived in Boston and Washington, DC for 14 years; NRI Fellow, American Enterprise Inst., Washington, DC 2008–10, Adjunct Scholar 2010–; Asst Prof., School of Public Policy, Univ. of Maryland, USA 2010– (on leave), Dir Int. Development Specialization 2012–13; Econ. Adviser to Romanian Prime Minister 2013–; Minister of Public Finance March–Dec. 2014, also Gov. of Romania to World Bank, EBRD, EIB, Chief Co-negotiator with IMF, World Bank, EC; Founding mem. Econs of Nat. Security Asscn; mem. American Econ. Asscn. *Address:* Piata Victoriei Nr. 1, Sect. 1, Bucharest 5, Str. Apolodor 17, Romania. *Website:* faculty.publicpolicy.umd.edu/petrescu.

PETRESKI, Dušan; Macedonian association executive; b. 19 Jan. 1948, Mavrovo; m. Liliana Mirchevska 1973; two s.; ed Skopje Univ.; Sec. and mem. Exec. Bd Econ. Chamber of Macedonia 1984–87, Vice-Pres. 1987–90, Pres. 1990–2005; Vice-Pres. Asscn of Balkan Chambers 1997–98, Pres. 1998; many state and other decorations and awards. *Publications:* professional articles in many magazines and journals. *Leisure interests:* social activities, sport, walking.

PETRIASHVILI, Aleksi, BA; Georgian politician; b. 24 Aug. 1970, Tbilisi; ed Tbilisi State Univ., NATO Defence Coll., Rome; Sr Specialist, Foreign Relations Div., State Logistic Service, Staff of the Head of State 1994–95; State Adviser, Foreign Policy Analysis Service, State Chancellery, Staff of Pres. of Georgia 1995–98; Head of Bilateral Relations Div., Politico-Mil. Dept, Ministry of Foreign Affairs May–Sept. 1998, Deputy Dir Politico-Mil. Dept 1998–2001; Sr Counsellor, Embassy in Vienna, Perm. Mission of Georgia to OSCE and other Int. Orgs in Vienna, UN Orgs, UNIDO, UN Office on Drugs and Crime, etc. 2001–02, Sr Counsellor, Embassy in Washington, DC 2002–04, Amb. to Turkmenistan 2004–09; mem. Parl. Oct. 2012; Political Sec., Davisuphali demokratebi (Free Democrats) party 2009–12; Political Bd mem. Qartuli Ocneba (Georgian Dream) coalition 2012–; State Minister, responsible for European and Euro-Atlantic Integration 2012–14. *Address:* c/o Ministry of European and Euro-Atlantic Integration, 0134 Tbilisi, P. Ingorovka 7, Georgia. *E-mail:* office@eu-nato.gov.ge.

PETRIČ, Ernest, PhD; Slovenian judge, diplomatist and academic; *Judge, Constitutional Court;* b. 18 Nov. 1936, Trzic; s. of Joze Petrič and Angela Godnov; m. Silvestra Rogelj; three d.; ed Univ. of Ljubljana, Univ. of Vienna; Research Asst, Inst. for Ethnic Studies, Ljubljana 1961–65; Asst Prof. of Int. Law, Univ. of Ljubljana 1965–67, Prof. 1972–83; mem. Exec. Council of Slovenia, Minister of Science and Tech. 1967–72; Prof., Univ. of Addis Ababa, Ethiopia 1983–86; Dean Faculty of Social Science, Univ. of Ljubljana 1986–89; Amb. of Yugoslavia to India (also accred to Nepal) 1989–91, to USA (also accred to Mexico) 1991–97; State Sec. Ministry of Foreign Affairs 1997–2000; Amb. and Perm. Rep. to UN, New York 2000–02; Amb. to Austria and Perm. Rep. to UN, Vienna and to OSCE 2002–09; Judge, Constitutional Court of the Repub. of Slovenia 2008–, Pres. 2010–13; Prof., European Law Faculty, Ljubljana 2007–; Sr Adviser to the Pres. 2017–; mem., International Law Comm. 2007–; mem. of Strategic Council, Ministry of Foreign Affairs 2008–; Yugoslav Silver Medal for Achievement 1986, Colorado Meritorious Service Medal, USA 1997, Golden Medal for Services 2006, Great Golden Medal of Honour, Austria 2008, Order of Isabella the Catholic, Spain 2013, Order of Merit, Grand Cross Star, Hungary 2014; Kidric Award 1979. *Publications:* International Legal Protection of Minorities 1977, The International Legal Position of the Slovenian Minority in Italy 1981, The Right to Self-Determination 1984, From Emperor to Leader 1987, Foreign Policy: From Concept to Practice 2013. *Leisure interests:* literature, skiing, tennis. *Address:* Constitutional Court of the Republic of Slovenia (Ustavno sodišča Republike Slovenije), 1001 Ljubljana, Beethovnova 10 (office); Na rebri 4a, 4260 Bled, Slovenia (home). *Telephone:* (1) 4776400 (office); (5) 1301630 (home). *Fax:* (1) 2510451 (office). *E-mail:* info@us-rs.si (office); ernest_petric@hotmail.com (home). *Website:* www.us-rs.si (office).

PETRIE, Sir Peter (Charles), 5th Bt, cr. 1918, of Carrowcarden, CMG; British diplomatist; b. 7 March 1932, London; s. of Sir Charles Petrie, Bt, CBE and Lady Petrie; m. Countess Lydwine von Oberndorff 1958; two s. one d.; ed Westminster School and Christ Church, Oxford; Second Sec. UK del. to NATO 1958–62; First Sec. New Delhi 1961–63; Chargé d'affaires, Kathmandu 1963–64; Cabinet Office, London 1965–67; FCO 1967–69; First Sec. later Counsellor, UK Perm. Mission at UN, New York 1969–73; Counsellor, Bonn 1973–76; FCO 1976–79; Minister, Paris 1979–85; Amb. to Belgium 1985–89; Adviser to Gov. of Bank of England on European and Parl. Affairs 1989–2003; mem. Franco-British Council 1995, Chair. British Section 1997–2002; Acad. de Compatibilité (Paris) 1997–; mem. Council, City Univ. 1997–2002. *Leisure interests:* gardening, golf, shooting. *Address:* 16a Cambridge Street, London, SW1V 4QH, England (home); 40 rue Lauriston, 75116 Paris, France (home); 4 Hameau du Jardin, 50310 Lestre, France (home). *Telephone:* (20) 7834-0801 (home). *E-mail:* lydwinepo@aol.fr (home).

PETRIN, Tea, MEconSc, PhD; Slovenian economist, academic, politician and diplomatist; *Professor Emeritus, University of Ljubljana;* b. (Tea Terezija), 9 July 1944, Celje; ed Univ. of Ljubljana, Louisiana State Univ., USA; Visiting Prof., Univ. of Massachusetts at Amherst, USA 1988–89, Haas School of Business, Univ. of Calif., Berkeley 1992; Head, Research Centre and Centre for Continuous Educ., Faculty of Econs, Univ. of Ljubljana 1989–92, Prof., then Prof. Emer., f. Postgraduate Studies in Entrepreneurship Programme 1990; Adviser to Cttee for Small Business Devt, Govt of Slovenia 1987–90, to Agency for Restructuring and Privatization Fund 1990–91, to Govt on Real Sector Structuring 1992–93; Adviser on Devt of Entrepreneurship in Rural Areas, to Foreign Affairs Office (FAO) Regional Office for Europe 1990–93, mem. staff 1994–97; involved in assessment of financial entrepreneurs in Slovenia, World Bank (IBRD) 1993; mem. working group World Bank, UNDP/UNIDO 1988–92, FAO Investment Centre 1996–97, EU Enterprise Enlargement Unit 2000; Minister for Econ. Affairs 1999–2000, of the Economy 2001–04; Amb. to Netherlands 2004–08; mem. Editorial Bd Review of Industrial Org. 1994–97; mem. Int. Small Business Council 1992–, Econ. Council of Govt of Slovenia 1992, European Small Business Council 1994–96, European Asscn for Industrial Econs Research 1998–, Bd of Advisers of The Competitiveness Inst., European Asscn for Industrial Econs Research, UN Cttee for Devt Policy 2013–; Fulbright Scholar, Inst. of Int. Studies, Univ. of California, Berkeley 1993–94, Univ. of Massachusetts, Lowell 1994. *Publications include:* over 200 books, monographs and articles in professional journals in fields of industrial policy, competition policy, restructuring of enterprises and entrepreneurship. *Address:* Department of Economics, University of Ljubljana, 1000, Ljubljana, Kardeljeva ploščad 17, Slovenia (office). *Telephone:* (1) 5892-400 (office). *E-mail:* tea.petrin@ef.uni-lj.si (office). *Website:* www.uni-lj.si (office).

PETRITSCH, Wolfgang, PhD; Austrian diplomatist and writer; *President, Austrian Marshall Plan Foundation;* b. 26 Aug. 1947, Klagenfurt; ed Univ. of Vienna, Univ. of Southern California, USA; Adviser, Press Sec. of Austrian Fed. Chancellor 1977–83; mem. Austrian Mission to OECD, Paris 1983–84; Head Austrian Press and Information Service, New York 1984–92; Acting Head Dept for Multilateral Econ. Co-operation, Ministry of Foreign Affairs 1992–94; Head Dept for Information on European Affairs, Fed. Chancellery 1994; Head Dept for Int. Relations, City of Vienna 1995–97; Amb. to Yugoslavia 1997–99; EU Special Envoy for Kosovo 1998–99, EU Chief Negotiator at Kosovo peace talks, France Feb.–March 1999; High Rep. of the Int. Community in Bosnia and Herzegovina 1999–2002; Amb. and Perm. Rep. to UN, WTO, Geneva 2002–08, to OECD 2008–13; Pres. Austrian Marshall Plan Foundation 2013–; Joseph A. Schumpeter Fellow, Harvard Univ., USA 2013–; Pres. Mine Ban Convention's First Review Conf. (Nairobi Summit) 2004; Chair. Vienna Cluster Munitions Conf. 2007, European Cultural Foundation, Amsterdam, Paul Lazarsfeld Soc. for Social Research, Vienna, Centre for European Integration Strategies, Geneva-Vienna-Sarajevo, Bruno Kreisky Forum for Int. Dialogue, Vienna, Herbert C. Kelman Inst. for Interactive Conflict Transformation, Vienna; Person of the Year, Bosnia and Herzegovina 2002, Friedrich Torberg Medal for Human Rights 2002, Bruno Kreisky Award for Best Political Book 2004, European Award for Human Rights Strasbourg 2006. *Publications include:* Kosovo-Kosova. Mythen, Daten, Fakten, Bosnien und Herzegowina fünf Jahre nach Dayton – Hat der Friede eine Chance? Zielpunkt Europa: Von den Schluchten des Balkan und den Mühen der Ebene, Das Kreisky-Prinzip: Der Mensch im Mittelpunkt 2009, Bruno Kreisky: Die Biografie 2011, Kärnten liegt am Meer: Konfliktgeschichten über Trauma, Macht und Identität 2012. *Address:* Austrian Marshall Plan Foundation, Marshallplan Jubiläumsstiftung, Walcherstraße 11A, 1020 Vienna, Austria (office). *Telephone:* (1) 50175597 (office). *Fax:* (1) 50175900 (office). *E-mail:* office@marshallplan.at (office); wolfgang.petritsch@bka.gv.at (office). *Website:* www.marshallplan.at (office); www.wolfgangpetritsch.com.

PETROV, Andrei Borisovich; Russian ballet dancer and choreographer; *Artistic Director, Kremlin Ballet Theatre;* b. 27 Dec. 1945, Moscow; s. of Boris Kholfin and Olga Petrova; m. Olga Polyanskaya; ed Moscow Higher School of Choreography, Moscow Inst. of Theatre Arts; ballet dancer, Bolshoi Theatre 1965–86, head of ballet troupe 1987–89, choreographer 1989–90; Founder and Artistic Dir Kremlin Ballet Theatre 1990–; Juror and Chair. Organizing Cttee, Moscow Int. Ballet Competition; juror, Maya (St Petersburg), Benoit de la Dance (UNESCO); Chair. Theatre Artists' League Choreography Cttee; Order of the Great Services to the Native Land, Order of Saint Prince Daniyl of Moscow, RSFSR People's Artist 1985. *Ballets include:* Don Quixote, Swan Lake, Fountain of Bakhchisarai, Raimonda, Romeo and Juliet. *Ballets directed include:* Red Snowball-Tree, Wooden Prince, Sketches, Knight of a Sorrowful Look, Ruslan and Ludmila, Swan Lake, Nutcracker, Zeus, Napoleon Bonaparte, Nevsky Prospect, Tom Sawyer, Fantastic Symphony, Coppelia. *Address:* Kremlin Ballet Theatre, Kremlin, Palace of Congresses, 03073 Moscow (office); Academician Zelensky str. 6, 41, Moscow, Russia (home). *Telephone:* (495) 917-23-36 (office); (495) 419-44-49 (home). *Fax:* (495) 928-52-32 (office). *Website:* www.kremlin-gkd.ru (office).

PETROV, Božo; Croatian psychiatrist and politician; *President, Most Nezavisnih Lista (Bridge of Independent Lists);* b. 16 Oct. 1979, Metković; s. of Jakov Petrov and Marija Petrov; m. Maša Petrov; two s. one d.; ed gymnasium in Sinj, Medical Faculty of Univ. of Mostar, Bosnia and Herzegovina; specialized psychiatry at Psychiatric Hosp. Vrapče, Zagreb, then worked as psychiatrist at Univ. Clinical Hosp., Mostar; began political career as ind. cand. on list of conservative HRAST (Croatian Growth) party, wanting to oppose SDP-HDZ political duopoly, ended collaboration with HRAST 2015; Co-founder and first Pres. Most Nezavisnih Lista (Bridge of Independent Lists) 2012–; Mayor of Metković 2013–16; Deputy Prime Minister Jan.–Oct. 2016; Pres. (Speaker) of the Ass. (Sabor) Oct. 2016–May 2017. *Address:* Most Nezavisnih Lista (Most) (Bridge of Independent Lists), 20350 Metković, Splitska 4, Croatia. *Telephone:* (1) 3450819. *E-mail:* office@most-nl.com. *Website:* most-nl.com.

PETROV, Rem Viktorovich, DMedSc; Russian immunologist; b. 22 March 1930, Serafimovitch; s. of Victor Ivanovich Petrov and Kutniak Evdokia Emelianovna; m. 1st Tatiana Kuk 1960 (died 1970); m. 2nd Natalia Yemetz 1978; one s. one d.; ed Voronezh Medical Inst.; mem. CPSU 1956–91; research work at various grades in USSR (now Russian) Ministry of Health Inst. of Bio-Physics 1959–83, Head of Lab. 1983–; Pres. USSR (now Russian) Immunology Soc. 1983–; Dir of USSR (now Russian) Ministry of Health Inst. of Immunology 1983–88; Head of Dept of Immunology of Second Moscow Inst. of Medicine 1974–; Vice-Chair. Molecular Cell Biology Network; mem. Int. Scientific Advisory Bd of UNESCO 1996–, Council of Int. Union of Immunological Soc., Bioethics Cttee; Ed. Sciences in Russia 1989; mem. Acad. of Medical Sciences 1978, USSR (now Russian) Acad. of Sciences 1984 (Vice-Pres. 1988–), World Acad. of Art and Sciences 1989, Acad. of Agric. 1991, New York Acad. of Sciences 1992, Washington Acad. of Sciences 1993, Norwegian Acad. of Sciences 1999; Hero of Labour 1990, Order of Lenin 1990, Achievements for the Fatherland, Third Degree 1999; Dr hc (Bar-Ilan Univ.) 1990, (Madrid Polytechnic Univ.) 1995; L. Mechnikov Gold Medal and Prize, Acad. of Sciences 1987, State Prize in Science and Tech. 2001, Prix Galien Russia. *Publications:* Essays on the New Immunology 1976, Immunology and Immunogenetics 1981, Immunology 1982, Me or Not Me 1983, Suppressor B-lymphocytes 1988, Myelopeptides 1999, Scientific Publicistics 2000; more than 300 scientific publs in professional journals. *Leisure interests:* fishing, hunting, woodwork. *Address:* Russian Academy of Sciences, Leninsky pr. 14, 117901 Moscow (office); 38-8-86 Zelinskogo str., 117334 Moscow, Russian Federation (home). *Telephone:* (495) 954-32-76 (office); (495) 135-10-63 (home). *Fax:* (495) 954-32-26 (office). *E-mail:* petrov@pran.ru (office).

PETROVIĆ, Slobodan; Kosovo lawyer and politician; b. 21 Dec. 1969, Prishtina; m.; one s.; Co-founder and Pres. Ind. Liberal Party (SLS) 2006–; mem. Kosovo Ass. 2008–, signed coalition agreement with Prime Minister Hashim Thaçi Feb. 2011; Dir for Integration in Post and Telecommunications of Kosovo 2007–10; Deputy Prime Minister and Minister of Local Govt 2011–14; mem. Steering Council, Kosovo Privatization Agency 2008–; has participated in numerous int. confs and debates, official visits and meetings around the world; named Politician of the Year by Ass. of Non-governmental Orgs in Kosovo 2008, Amb. of Peace Award, Universal Peace Fed. 2012.

PETRU, Ryszard Jerzy; Polish economist and politician; *President, .Nowoczesna (.Modern);* b. 6 July 1972, Wrocław; m. Małgorzata Petru 1997; two d.; ed Wrocław Univ. of Tech., Warsaw School of Econs; became an asst to Władysław Frasyniuk MP; later worked for Centre for Social and Econ. Research; asst to Deputy Prime Minister and Minister of Finance Leszek Balcerowicz 1995, later his adviser working as consultant in Office of Govt Plenipotentiary for Pension System Reform 1997–2000; teacher, Warsaw School of Econs 1998; mem. Unia Wolności (Freedom Union) and cand. in parl. elections 2001; economist for Polish and Hungarian affairs, World Bank 2001–04; Chief Economist, Bank BPH 2004–08; then Dir of Strategy and Chief Economist, BRE Bank (later mBank); later Man. Dir, PKO BP; informal adviser to Prime Minister Donald Tusk, acting as intermediary with IMF 2008–13; Partner, PricewaterhouseCoopers 2011–14; Chair. Asscn of Polish Economists 2011–; econ. adviser to Marshal of Lower Silesian Voivodship 2013; Chair. Supervisory Bd, Polish State Railways Feb.–March 2014, Solaris Bus & Coach Enterprise 2014; Vice-Chair. Supervisory Bd EUCO SA; f. NowoczesnaPL (Modern PL) foundation in Rzeszów and then asscn with same name May 2015, name changed to .Nowoczesna (.Modern) Aug. 2015, Pres. 2015–; mem. Sejm (Parl.) for Warsaw (19) Dist 2015–. *Television:* appeared as expert in seven episodes of Religia.tv show Morality and Ethics in the Time of Crisis 2013. *Publications:* several books, including The End of the Free Market? The Origins of the Crisis 2014 and two children's books on economics. *Address:* .Nowoczesna (.Modern), Biuro Krajowe, 00-279 Warsaw, ul. Nowy Świat 27, Poland (office). *Telephone:* (22) 5353667 (office). *Fax:* (22) 3797334 (office). *E-mail:* info@nowoczesnapl.org (office). *Website:* nowoczesna.org (office).

PETRUCCIOLI, Claudio; Italian journalist, broadcasting executive, politician, writer and essayist; b. 22 March 1941, Terni, Umbria; obtained degree in political science and moved to Rome to become a professional journalist; mem. Partito Comunista Italiano (Italian Communist Party—PCI) 1960s, Municipal and Regional Sec., Terni and Regional Vice-Sec. in Umbria, Pres. Italian Communist Youth Fed. 1966–69, Nat. Dir PCI 1987; contributed to definition of first major reform of broadcasting system, implemented by Law 103 1975; Dir L'Unità 1980–83; elected to Lower House for Democratici di Sinistra (Democrats of the Left—DS) 1992–94; mem. 8th Perm. Comm. (Public Works, Communications) 1996, 2001–03 (Pres. 1996–2001), 13th Perm. Comm. (Territory, Environment)

2003–05; Pres. Radiotelevisione Italiana SpA (RAI), Parl. Cttee for Supervision of Broadcasting 2005–09. *Publications:* Rendi conto 2001, Quale Futuro per Il Servizio Pubblico Radiotelevisivo: Una [i.E. Un] Dibattito a Partire Dal Documento Per Una Discussione Su Televisione E Servizio Pubblico. Dentro E Fuori La Rai Di Claudio Petruccioli 2006.

PETRUSHEVSKAYA, Liudmila Stefanovna; Russian author, playwright and poet; b. 26 May 1938, Moscow; d. of Stefan Antonovitsh Petrushevskij and Valentina Nikolaevna Jakovleva; m. 1st Evgenij Kharatian; one s.; m. 2nd Boris Pavlov; one s. one d.; ed Moscow Univ.; newspaper and radio journalist 1957–73; started writing short stories 1968, plays and folk tales 1971; stage productions and publ. of works were forbidden for many years; first underground performance 1975, first official performance, Tallinn 1979; mem. Bayerische Akad. der Schönen Kunste 1997; Int. A. Pushkin Prize (Germany) 1991, Triumph Award for Lifetime Achievement 2002, Russian State Prize for Arts 2004, Stanislavsky Award 2005, Triumph Prize 2006; prizes for the best short story of the year from Ogoniok 1988, 1989 and Oktiabr 1993, 1996, Grand Prize for play The Time: Night, Annual All-Russian Theatre Festival of Solo Theatre, Perm 1995, Moscow-Penne Prize (Russia/Italy) 1996. *Plays include:* Two Windows 1971, Music Lessons 1973, Cinzano 1973, Love 1974, The Landing 1974, Andante 1975, The Execution, A Glass of Water, Smirnova's Birthday 1977–78, Three Girls in Blue 1980, Colombina's Flat 1981, Moscow Choir 1984, The Golden Goddess 1986, The Wedding Night 1990, The Men's Quarters 1992; co-author of screenplay Tale of Tales (prize for best animated film of all time, Los Angeles 1980). *Publications include:* Immortal Love 1988, Songs of the 20th Century 1988, On the Way to the God Eros 1993, The Mystery of the House 1993; (children's books) Vasilli's Treatment 1991, Once Upon a Time There Was a Trrrr! 1994, Real Fairy Tales 1997, The Alphabet's Tale 1997; Complete Works (five vols) 1996, The Girl's House 1998, Find Me, My Dream 2000, There Once Lived a Woman Who Tried to Kill Her Neighbor's Baby (World Fantasy Award 2010) 2009, There Once Lived a Mother Who Loved Her Children, Until They Moved Back In: Three Novellas About Family 2014, The Girl from the Metropol Hotel 2017. *Leisure interest:* watercolour painting. *Address:* 107113 Moscow, Staroslobodsky per. 2A, Apt 20, Russia. *Telephone:* (495) 269-74-48. *Fax:* (495) 269-74-48.

PETRY, Frauke, BSc, DrSc; German research chemist, business executive and politician; b. 1 June 1975, Dresden; m. Sven Petry; four c.; ed Univ. of Reading, UK, Univ. of Göttingen; began career as Research Asst, Inst. of Pharmacology and Toxicology, Göttingen; f. PURinvent GmbH (mfr of environmentally friendly polyurethanes), Leipzig 2007, Man. Dir 2007–14; mem. Sächsischer Landtag (Saxony Regional Ass.) 2014–; mem. Alternative für Deutschland (AfD, Alternative for Germany), Co–Spokesperson 2013–15, Leader 2015–17; mem. Gesellschaft Deutscher Chemiker, Royal Soc. of Chemistry; Medal of Merit of FRG 2012. *Address:* Alternative für Deutschland, Frankfurter Landstr. 153–155, 61231 Bad Nauheim, Germany (office). *E-mail:* geschaeftsstelle@alternativefuer.de (office). *Website:* www.alternativefuer.de (office).

PETSALNIKOS, Philippos I.; Greek lawyer and politician; b. 1 Dec. 1950, Mavrochori, Kastoria; m. Mariele Biedehdick; one s. two d.; ed Kastoria High School, Aristotle Univ. of Thessaloniki, Univ. of Bonn, Germany; fmr Scientific Assoc., Univ. of Bonn; Founding mem. Panhellenic Socialist Movt (PASOK), served as Sec. for Sector of Educ. as well as Sec. for PASOK's br. for Greeks living abroad; Gen. Sec., Ministry of Nat. Educ. and Religion (section of People's Educ.) 1984–85; mem. Vouli (Parl.) for Kastoria 1985–2012, Vice-Pres. 2004–09, Pres. (Speaker) 2009–12, Chair. Cttee on Parl. Procedure, Cttee on Public Enterprises, Banks, Public Utilities and Social Security Orgs; Deputy Minister of Educ. and Religious Affairs 1986–87, 1988–89, of Culture (responsible for Youth, for Greeks Living Abroad and for People's Educ.) 1987–88; Alt. Minister of Educ. and Religious Affairs 1994–96; Minister of Macedonia-Thrace 1996–98, of Public Order 1998–99, of Educ. and Religious Affairs 2000–01, of Justice 2001–04. *Address:* Ath. Diakou 2, 521 00 Kastoria, Greece. *E-mail:* petsaln@otenet.gr (office). *Website:* www.petsalnikos.gr.

PETTENGILL, Gordon Hemenway, PhD; American physicist and academic; *Professor Emeritus of Planetary Physics, Department of Earth, Atmospheric and Planetary Sciences, Massachusetts Institute of Technology;* b. 1926, Providence, RI; s. of Rodney G. Pettengill and Frances Pettengill; m. Pamela Wolfenden 1967; one s. one d.; ed Massachusetts Inst. of Tech., Univ. of California, Berkeley; mem. staff, MIT Lincoln Lab. 1954–68, Assoc. Leader, Haystack Observatory 1965–68; Dir Arecibo Observatory, Puerto Rico (operated by Cornell Univ.) 1968–70; Prof. of Planetary Physics, Dept of Earth Atmospheric and Planetary Sciences, MIT 1970–2001, Prof. Emer. 2001–; Dir MIT Center for Space Research 1984–90; Prin. Investigator, Pioneer Venus Radar Mapper 1978–81, Magellan Venus Radar Mapper 1990–93; team mem. Mars Orbiting Laser Altimeter 1996–2001; mem. NAS, American Acad. of Arts and Sciences, AAAS, American Physical Soc., American Astronomical Soc., Int. Radio Science Union; Fellow, American Geophysical Union; Guggenheim Fellow 1980–81, Magellan Premium, American Philosophical Soc. 1994, Charles A. Whitten Medal, American Geophysical Union 1997. *Achievements include:* involved in the study of the solar system using radar and radio techniques; discovered 3/2 spin-orbit resonance of Mercury 1965; pioneered delay-doppler radar mapping of planets; mapped surface of Venus using radar to penetrate the thick cloud layer. *Leisure interests:* ornithology, amateur radio (W1OUN). *Address:* MIT Center for Space Research, Room 37-587, Massachusetts Institute of Technology, 77 Massachusetts Avenue, Cambridge, MA 02139, USA (office). *Telephone:* (617) 253-4281 (office). *Fax:* (617) 253-0861 (office). *E-mail:* ghp@space.mit.edu (office). *Website:* space.mit.edu (office).

PETTIGREW, Hon. Pierre S., PC, BA, MPhil; Canadian politician; b. 18 April 1951; ed Univ. du Québec à Trois-Rivières, Balliol Coll., Oxford, UK; Dir Political Cttee NATO Ass., Brussels 1976–78; Exec. Asst to Leader of Québec Liberal Party 1978–81; Foreign Policy Adviser to Prime Minister, Privy Council Office 1981–84; Vice-Pres. Samson Belair Deloitte and Touche Int. (Montreal) 1985–95, Exec. Adviser (Int.), Deloitte Canada 2006–; MP for Papineau 1996–2006; Minister for Int. Co-operation and Minister with special responsibility for La Francophonie 1996–97, Minister of Human Resources Devt 1997–99, of Int. Trade 1999–2003, of Health, of Intergovernmental Affairs, responsible for Official Languages 2003–04, of Foreign Affairs 2004–06; Co-Chair. First Nat. Forum on Canada's Int. Relations 1994; Hon. LLD (Univ. of Warwick) 2008. *Publication:* The New Politics of Confidence 1999. *Address:* Deloitte Canada, 33 Yonge Street, 2nd floor, Toronto, ON M5E 1G4, Canada (office). *E-mail:* pierre.pettigrew@fondationtrudeau.net (office). *Website:* www.deloitte.com (office); www.trudeaufoundation.ca (office).

PETTIT, Philip Noel, PhD, FAHA, FASSA, FAAAS, FBA, MRIA; Irish/Australian philosopher and academic; *L.S. Rockefeller University Professor of Politics and Human Values, Princeton University;* b. 20 Dec. 1945, Ballinasloe, Co. Galway, Ireland; s. of Michael A. Pettit and Bridget C. Molony; m. Victoria McGeer; two s.; ed Maynooth Coll., Nat. Univ. of Ireland, Queen's Univ. Belfast, Northern Ireland; Lecturer, Univ. Coll. Dublin 1968–72, 1975–77; Research Fellow, Trinity Hall Cambridge, UK 1972–75; Prof. of Philosophy, Univ. of Bradford, UK 1977–83; Professorial Fellow, Research School of Social Sciences, ANU, Canberra, Australia 1983–89, Prof. of Social and Political Theory 1989–2002, Distinguished Prof. of Philosophy 2013–; Visiting Prof. of Philosophy, Columbia Univ., New York, USA 1997–2001; William Nelson Cromwell Prof. of Politics, Princeton Univ., USA 2002, currently L.S. Rockefeller Univ. Prof. of Politics and Human Values; Distinguished Univ. Prof. of Philosophy, ANU; Hon. mem. Italian Soc. for Analytical Philosophy; Hon. MRIA; Hon. DLitt (Nat. Univ. of Ireland) 2000, (Queen's Univ., Belfast) 2007; Hon. PhD (Crete) 2005, (Montreal) 2006, (Athens) 2014; Hon. DPhil (Lund) 2008; Univ. Medal, Univ. of Helsinki 1992. *Publications:* Concept of Structuralism 1975, Judging Justice 1980, Semantics and Social Science (with G. Macdonald) 1981, Not Just Deserts: A Republican Theory of Criminal Justice (with J. Braithwaite) 1990, The Common Mind: An Essay on Psychology, Society and Politics 1992, Republicanism: A Theory of Freedom and Government 1997, A Theory of Freedom: From the Psychology to the Politics of Agency 2001, Rules, Reasons and Norms: Selected Essays 2002, Penser en Société 2003, Mind, Morality, and Explanation: Selected Collaborations (co-author) 2004, The Economy of Esteem (with Geoffrey Brennan) 2004, Made with Words: Hobbes on Language, Thought and Mind 2008, A Political Philosophy in Public Life (with Jose Marti) 2010, Group Agency (with Christian List) 2011, On the People's Terms 2012, Just Freedom 2014, The Robust Demands of the Good 2015. *Leisure interest:* cycling. *Address:* UCHV, 308 Marx Hall, Princeton University, Princeton, NJ 08544-1012 (office); 16 College Road, Princeton, NJ 08540, USA (home). *Telephone:* (609) 258-4759 (office); (609) 924-3664 (home). *E-mail:* ppettit@princeton.edu (office). *Website:* www.princeton.edu/~ppettit (office).

PETTY, Richard; American fmr racing driver and entrepreneur; *Co-Owner, Richard Petty Motorsports;* b. 2 July 1937, Level Cross, NC; s. of Lee Petty Lee; m. Lynda Owens Petty 1959 (died 2014); one s. three d.; stock car racing driver 1958–92; total of 200 Career NASCAR Winston Cup Victories, NASCAR Winston Cup Champion 1964, 1967, 1971, 1972, 1974, 1975, 1979; winner Daytona 500 1964, 1966, 1971, 1973, 1974, 1979, 1981; 27 victories in one season 1967; sport's first million-dollar driver; last race in 1992; f. Petty Enterprises LLC (complete stock car racing operation), now Richard Petty Motorsports; est. Richard Petty Museum 1988; Winston Cup Rookie of the Year 1959, Most Popular Winston Cup Driver 1962, 1964, 1968, 1970, 1974, 1975, 1976, 1977, 1978; Nat. Motorsports Press Asscn (NMPA) Myers Brothers Award 1964, 1967, 1971, 1992, NMPA Driver of the Year 1974, 1975, inducted into Nat. NC Athletic Hall of Fame 1973, Presidential Medal of Freedom 1992, inducted into Int. Motorsports Hall of Fame 1997, named as one of NASCAR's 50 Greatest Drivers 1998, inducted into Automotive Hall of Fame 2002, American Auto Racing Writers & Broadcasters Asscn (AARWBA) Man of the Year 1995, inducted into NASCAR Hall of Fame 2010. *Films:* Speedway 1968, 43: The Richard Petty Story 1972, Stroker Ace 1983, Speed Zone! 1989, Days of Thunder 1990, Swing Vote (as himself) 2008. *Address:* Richard Petty Motorsports, 7065 Zephyr Place, Concord, NC 28027 (office); Richard Petty Museum, 142 West Academy Street, Randleman, NC 27317, USA. *Telephone:* (704) 743-5420 (office); (336) 495-1143. *E-mail:* info@richardpettymotorsports.com (office). *Website:* www.richardpettymotorsports.com (office).

PETZOLD, Christian; German film director; b. 14 Sept. 1960, Hilden; ed Free Univ. of Berlin, German Film and Television Acad.; Film Award of City of Hof (Saale), Internationale Hofer Filmtage 2009. *Films include:* The State I am In (German: Die innere Sicherheit) (Verband der deutschen Filmkritik Award for Best Acting Film 2001, Deutscher Filmpreis Award for Best Movie 2001) 2000, Wolfsburg (FIPRESCI Award in Panorama, Berlin Int. Film Festival 2003, Adolf Grimme Golden Award 2005) 2003, Gespenster (Verband der deutschen Filmkritik Award as Best Acting Film 2006) 2005, Yella (Verband der deutschen Filmkritik Award as Best Acting Film 2008) 2007, Jerichow (Verband der deutschen Filmkritik Award as Best Acting Film 2009) 2008, Barbara (Silver Bear for Best Dir, Berlin Int. Film Festival) 2012, Phoenix 2014, Transit 2018. *Television includes:* Das warme Geld (video) 1992, Pilotinnen (film) 1995, Cuba Libre (film) (Max Ophüls Assistance Award for Best Feature-length Film) 1996, Die Beischlafdiebin (film) 1998, Something to Remind Me (German: Toter Mann) (film) (Acad. of Arts, Berlin Television Award 2002, Deutscher Fernsehpreis 2002, Adolf Grimme Award 2003) 2002, Dreileben – Beats Being Dead (part of Dreileben trilogy, made in collaboration with Dominik Graf and Christoph Hochhäusler) (mini-series) 2011. *Address:* c/o The Match Factory GmbH, Balthasarstr. 79–81, 50670 Cologne, Germany. *Telephone:* (221) 539709-0. *Fax:* (221) 539709-10. *E-mail:* info@matchfactory.de. *Website:* www.the-match-factory.com.

PEUGEOT, Patrick; French insurance executive; b. 3 Aug. 1937, Paris; s. of Jacques Peugeot and Edith Peugeot (née Genoyer); m. Catherine Dupont 1963; three s.; ed Lycée Hoche, Ecole Sainte-Geneviève à Versailles, Ecole polytechnique, Ecole nat. d'admin.; auditor, Cour des comptes 1965, Commissariat au plan (Public Enterprises Cttee) 1966–70; Sec.-Gen. Librairie Hachette 1972–74; Sec.-Gen. Groupe des Assurances générals de France (AGF) 1975–83, Dir-Gen. AGF-Réassurance 1979–83; tech. consultant to Ministry of Economy and Finances 1981–83; Dir-Gen. Caisse centrale de réassurance 1983–84, Pres. Advisory Bd 1984–85, Hon. Pres. 1985–; Pres. Dir-Gen. Société commerciale de réassurance (Scor) 1983–94, Hon. Pres. and Dir. 1994–; Vice-Pres. Dir-Gen. La Mondiale 1995, Chair. and CEO 1996–2005, then Hon. Pres.; Pres. Groupement des assurances des personnes (Gap) 1997–99; Pres. Réunion des organismes d'assurance mutuelle 1999–2005; Chair. Asscn Int. des Socs d'Assurance Mutelle 2004–, Comité Intermouvements auprès des Évacués (CIMADE) 2005–13; apptd Pres. Lille Métropole 2009, Lille-Kortrijk-Tournai Eurometropole 2009; Chevalier, Ordre nat. du Mérite.

PEUGEOT, Thierry; French automotive industry executive; *Vice-Chairman of the Supervisory Board, PSA Peugeot Citroën SA;* b. 19 Aug. 1957; s. of Pierre Peugeot; ed ESSEC Business School; early career as Export Man. for Middle East, Marrel Group, then Dir of American subsidiary; joined Peugeot 1988, fmrly Regional SE Asia Man., Peugeot, Man. Dir Peugeot do Brasil, Man. Dir SLICA, Vice-Pres. Citroën Large Int. Accounts, Citroën Services and Spare Parts, Chair. Peugeot SA 2002–03, Chair. Supervisory Bd, PSA Peugeot Citroën SA 2002–14, Vice-Chair. 2014–, Chair. Compensation Cttee, mem. Appointments and Governance Cttee, Strategy Cttee; Vice-Chair. and COO Établissements Peugeot Frères; Dir, Soc. Foncière, Financière et de Participations, Soc. Anonyme de Participations, Immeubles et Participations de l'Est, Faurecia, Cie Industrielle de Delle (CIS), Air Liquide; Perm. Rep. of CID on Bd of Dirs of LISI Aerospace. *Address:* PSA Peugeot Citroën SA, 75 avenue de la Grande Armée, 75116 Paris, France (office). *Telephone:* 1-40-66-55-11 (office). *Fax:* 1-40-66-54-14 (office). *Website:* www.psa-peugeot-citroen.com (office).

PEVKUR, Hanno, BA; Estonian politician; b. 2 April 1977, Iisaku; m.; one s. one d.; ed Järva-Jaani Secondary School, Tallinn School of Econs, Faculty of Law of Univ. of Tartu; mem. Eesti Reformierakond (ER—Estonian Reform Party), Chair. 2017–18; active in Nõmme City Dist Govt, first as Admin. Sec. and later as Dist Elder 2000–05; mem. Tallinn City Council and Chair. Nõmme Admin. Council 2005–07, mem. Nõmme Admin. Council 2007–09; mem. Riigikogu (Parl.) 2007–09; Minister of Social Affairs 2009–12, of Justice 2012–14, of Regional Affairs 2014–15, of the Interior 2014–16. *Address:* c/o Eesti Reformierakond (Estonian Reform Party), Tõnismägi 9, Tallinn 10119, Estonia (office). *Telephone:* 680-8080 (office). *Fax:* 680-8081 (office). *E-mail:* info@reform.ee (office). *Website:* www.reform.ee (office).

PEVTSOV, Dmitry Anatlyevich; Russian actor; b. 8 July 1963, Moscow; m. Olga Drozdova; ed Moscow State Inst. of Theatre Arts; actor, Taganka Theatre 1985–91; Moscow Theatre of Leninsky Komsomol (LENKOM) 1991–; has taken part in Volkswagen Polo Cup race 2001–; host, Last Hero 2 (TV game show) 2002; European Prize Felix (Glasgow). *Plays include:* The Marriage of Figaro, The Seagull. *Films include:* Podzemelye vedm 1989, Mother 1990, . . .Po prozvishchu 'Zver' 1990, Progulka po eshafotu 1992, Na tebya upovayu 1992, Besy 1992, Alisa i bukinist 1992, Mafiya bessmertna 1993, Line of Life 1996, Notti di paura (as Dmitriv Pevcov) 1997, Kontrakt so smertyu 1998, Tonkaya shtuchka 1999, Lvinaya dolya 2001, Turetskiy gambit 2005, Blind Man's Bluff 2005, Popsa 2005, Den vyborov 2007, Karnavalnaya noch 2, ili 50 let spystya 2007, Artistka 2007, Khranit vechno 2008, Boris Godunov 2012. *Television includes:* Koroleva Margo (series) 1996, Grafinya de Monsoro (series) 1998, Banditskiy Peterburg: Advokat (mini-series) 2000, Ostanovka po trebovaniyu (mini-series) 2000, Ostanovka po trebovaniyu – 2 (mini-series) 2001, Kholostyaki (series) 2004, Rodstvennyy obmen (series) 2005, The Fall of the Empire (mini-series) 2005, The First Circle (mini-series) 2006, Snezhnyy angel (film) 2008, Snayper. Oruzhie vozmezdiya (mini-series) 2009, Lektor (series) 2011, Tochka vzryva (film) 2013. *Address:* Teplichny per. 5, Apt 139, 123298 Moscow, Russian Federation (home). *Telephone:* (495) 198-77-69 (home).

PEYRAT, Jérôme, LenD; French civil servant; *First Vice-President, Communauté de Communes du Périgord Noir;* b. 28 Nov. 1962, Sarlat, Dordogne; m.; three c.; ed Institut d'études politiques de Paris, École nationale d'administration, Institut des Hautes Etudes de la Défense Nationale; served as intern in Embassy in Turkey; joined Dept of Int. Relations, Mayor of Paris 1990; served as foreign press adviser and asst spokesperson to Pres. Jacques Chirac; Dir of Communications to Mayor of Paris 1998–2000; Dir of Communications and Dir of Cabinet to Michèle Alliot-Marie, Pres. Rassemblement pour la République 2000–02; Political Adviser to Minister of Interior, Nicolas Sarkozy 2005–07, to Pres. Nicolas Sarkozy 2007–09; mem. Union pour un Mouvement Populaire (UMP) 2002–09; unsuccessful UMP cand. for parl. elections in Dordogne; Mayor, La Roque-Gageac 2008–14; Dir of Cabinet to Alain Joyandet, Minister of State for Cooperation and Francophony 2009; Special Adviser to Minister of Sustainable Devt, Transport and Housing, Nathalie Kosciusko-Morizet 2010; currently First Vice-Pres. Communauté de Communes du Périgord Noir; Chevalier, Ordre Nat. du Mérite. *Publications:* Les Petits matins: essai sur la pensée politique (with Nathalie Kosciusko-Morizet) 2002. *Leisure interests:* mountaineering, skiing, hiking. *Address:* Communauté de Communes Périgord Noir, Place Marc Busson, 24200 Sarlat La Canéda, France (office). *Telephone:* 5-53-31-90-20 (office). *Website:* www.cc-sarladais.com (office).

PEYRELEVADE, Jean; French business executive; *Partner, Toulouse et Associés;* b. 24 Oct. 1939, Marseille; s. of Paul Peyrelevade and Nadia Benveniste; m. Anne Chavy 1962; three s. one d.; ed Faculté de droit de Paris, Ecole Nat. de l'aviation civile; fmr armaments and aviation engineer; Dir Dept of Foreign Business, Crédit Lyonnais 1973–82; Asst Dir Cabinet of M. Pierre Mauroy 1982; Pres. Cie Financière de Suez 1983–86; Pres. Banque Stern 1986–88; Chair. Union des Assurances de Paris 1988–93; Chair. Crédit Lyonnais 1993–2003 (resgnd after bank's acquistion by Crédit Agricole); Govt Rep. on Bd of Renault 1996–2000; mem. Econ. and Social Council 1994–; Partner Toulouse et Assocs 2004–; fmr Chair. Leonardo Midcap CF; Vice-Chair. Leonardo France; mem. Supervisory Bd CMA-CGM 2005, KLM Royal Dutch Airlines 2007–; mem. Bd of Dirs Suez, Bouygues 1994–, DNCA Finance, GDF SUEZ SA, and Société Monégasque de l'Electricité et du Gaz, Club Méditerranée, MK2, Assurances Générales de France and Power Corporation of Canada; fmr mem. Bd of Dirs Air Liquide Canada Inc., Saipem SA, Clinvest SA, and Credit Agricole SA. *Publications:* La mort du dollar 1974, L'economie de spéculation 1978, Economie de l'entreprise 1989, Pour un capitalisme intelligent 1993, Le gouvernement d'entreprise 1999, Sarkozy: l'erreur historique 2008, France, état critique 2011, Histoire d'une névrose, la France et son économie 2014, Journal d'un sauvetage 2016. *Leisure interests:* skiing, golf.

PFAFF, Judy, BFA, MFA; American artist; b. 22 Sept. 1946, London, England; ed Wayne State Univ., Southern Illinois Univ., Univ. of Washington and Yale Univ.; numerous visiting faculty positions since 1971 including Calif. Inst. of Arts, Yale Univ., Rhode Island School of Design, Oberlin Coll., Princeton Univ.; mem. of Grad. Faculty, School of Visual Arts, New York 1986–91; Prof. of Visual Arts, Columbia Univ. 1992–94; Chair., Art Dept, Bard Coll. 1992–2014; Guggenheim Fellowship for Sculpture, MacArthur Fellow 2004, Barnett and Annalee Newman Foundation Fellowship 2006, Acad. Member Fellowship, American Acad. of Arts and Sciences 2013; mem. American Acad. of Arts and Letters 2009–; Dr hc (Pratt Inst.) 1999; Award of Merit Gold Medal for Sculpture, American Acad. of Arts and Letters 2002, Lifetime Achievement Award, Southern Graphics Council Int. Conf. 2010. *Address:* 83 W. Kerley Corners Road, Tivoli, NY 12583, USA (office). *Telephone:* (845) 757-5440 (office). *E-mail:* info@judypfaffstudio.com (office). *Website:* www.judypfaffstudio.com.

PFEIFFER, Michelle; American actress; b. 29 April 1957, Santa Ana, Calif.; d. of Dick Pfeiffer and Donna Pfeiffer; m. 1st Peter Horton (divorced 1987); one adopted d.; m. 2nd David E. Kelley 1993; one s.; ed Fountain Valley High School, Golden West Coll., Whitley Coll. *Television includes:* The Wizard of Lies (film) 2017. *Films include:* Grease 2, Into the Night, The Witches of Eastwick, Sweet Liberty, Married to the Mob, Tequila Sunrise 1989, Dangerous Liaisons 1989, The Fabulous Baker Boys 1989, The Russia House 1989, Love Field, Frankie and Johnny 1991, Batman Returns 1992, The Age of Innocence 1993, Wolf 1994, My Posse Don't Do Homework 1994, Dangerous Minds, Up Close and Personal, To Gillian on Her 37th Birthday, One Fine Day 1997, A Thousand Acres 1997, Privacy 1997, The Prince of Egypt (voice) 1998, The Story of Us 1999, The Deep End of the Ocean 1999, A Midsummer Night's Dream 1999, Being John Malkovich 1999, What Lies Beneath 2000, I am Sam 2001, White Oleander 2002, Sinbad: Legend of the Seven Seas (voice) 2003, I Could Never Be Your Woman 2007, Hairspray 2007, Stardust 2007, Chéri 2009, Personal Effects 2009, Dark Shadows 2012, People Like Us 2012, The Family 2013, Where is Kyra? 2017. *Address:* ICM, 8492 Wilshire Blvd, Beverly Hills, CA 90211-1934, USA (office). *Telephone:* (310) 550-4000 (office). *Website:* www.icmtalent.com (office).

PFISTER, Bruno, LLM, MBA; Swiss business executive; *Chairman, Wealth, Management & Trust, Rothschild & Co;* b. 1959; ed Univ. of Geneva, Grad. School of Man., Univ. of California, Los Angeles, USA; called to the Bar, Geneva; worked for Chase Manhattan Bank in London and Geneva; Man. Consultant, McKinsey & Co. 1988–96; Chief of Staff of Pvt. Banking Div., Liechtenstein Global Trust 1996–98, Chief Financial Officer LGT Group and LGT Bank, Liechtenstein 1998–99; mem. Credit Suisse Group Exec. Bd, Head of Customer Segment Man. and Product Man., Credit Suisse 1999–2002; Chief Financial Officer Swiss Life Group 2002–06, CEO Swiss Life Group International 2006–08, Group CEO Swiss Life Group 2008–14; Chair. Wealth Man. & Trust, Rothschild & Co 2014–; mem. Bd of Dirs Gottex Fund Man. Holdings Ltd, St Peter Port, Guernsey, Swiss Insurance Asscn; Vice-Chair. Admission Bd and Exec. Cttee of Admission Bd of SIX Swiss Exchange. *Address:* Rothschild Global Advisory, Zollikerstrasse 181, 8034 Zürich, Switzerland (office). *Website:* www.rothschild.com (office).

PFLIMLIN, Etienne Alphonse Marie Georges; French banking executive and fmr civil servant; b. 16 Oct. 1941, Thonon les Bains, Haute Savoie; s. of Pierre Pflimlin and Marie-Odile Pflimlin (née Heinrich); m. Marie-Sophie Nehlil; two s.; ed Ecole Polytechnique, Ecole Nat. d'Admin, Institut d'Etudes Politiques, Paris; fmr teacher, Univ. Paris-IX Dauphine, Institut d'Etudes Politiques de Paris; Commr, Ministry of Finance 1964–67; Dir of Cabinet, Pref. of Finistère 1968; Counsellor, Cour des Comptes (Nat. Audit Office) 1970–84; with Ministry of Culture 1973–78; Counsellor, Ministry of Budget 1978–79; Dir of Cabinet Ministry of Commerce and Handicrafts 1979–81; joined Crédit Mutuel 1984, became Pres. Banque Fédérative du Crédit Mutuel 1985, Pres. Crédit Mutuel Centre Est Europe 1985, Pres. Confédération Nationale du Crédit Mutuel 1987, Pres. Supervisory Bd Banque de l'Economie du Commerce et de la Monetique 1992, Chair. CIC Crédit Industriel et Commercial SA 1998–11; Pres. Groupe L'Alsace 1988–2010, Le Monde Enterprises 1988, European Co-operative Bank Group 2002; Pres. European Cttee Int. Co-operative Banking Asscn; mem. Bd of Dir Fimalac financial group 2014; Chevalier, Order nat. du Mèrite, Officier, Légion d'honneur, des Palmes académiques.

PHAM, Binh Minh, MA; Vietnamese diplomatist and politician; *Deputy Prime Minister and Minister of Foreign Affairs;* b. 26 March 1959, Vu Ban Dist, Nam Dinh Prov.; s. of Nguyen Co Thach (Pham Van Cuong) and Phan Thi Phuc; m. Nguyen Nguyet Nga; two c.; ed Univ. of Foreign Affairs, Fletcher School of Law and Diplomacy, Tufts Univ., USA; Attaché, Embassy in London 1982–86; Officer, Dept of Public Affairs, Ministry of Foreign Affairs (MFA) 1986–91, Deputy Dir, Dept of Int. Orgs 1991, Deputy Perm. Rep., Perm. Mission to UN, New York 1999, Minister and Deputy Amb., Embassy in Washington, DC 2001–03, Dir Dept of Int. Orgs, MFA 2003, Asst Minister of Foreign Affairs 2006, Deputy Minister 2007–11, Minister 2011–; Deputy Prime Minister 2013–; Chair. Vietnam–Cambodia Cooperation Sub-Cttee; mem. Dang Cong San Viet Nam (Communist Party of Viet Nam), alt. mem. Cen. Cttee 1996–2009, official mem. 2009–11, mem. 2011–16, mem. Politburo 2016–; mem. Nat. Ass. 2013, 2016; Medal for Foreign Affairs 2003, 2011, Labor Medal (grade three) 2009, Labor Order (first class) 2015; Prime Minister's Certificate of Merit 2006, Title of Emulation Soldier 2010. *Address:* Ministry of Foreign Affairs, 1 Ton That Dam, Ba Dinh District, Hanoi, Viet Nam (office). *Telephone:* (4) 37992000 (office). *Fax:* (4) 38231872 (office). *E-mail:* banbientap@mofa.gov.vn (office). *Website:* www.mofa.gov.vn (office).

PHAM, Gia Khiem, PhD; Vietnamese politician and government official; b. 6 Aug. 1944, Hanoi; m.; one s. one d.; ed Hanoi Univ. of Tech. and postgraduate studies in Czechoslovakia; Lecturer, Bac Thai Univ. of Mechanical Eng and Electronics 1968–70; worked at Ministry of Investment and Planning 1976–96, positions included Head, Industrial Div. and Dir Dept of Science, Educ. and Environment, then Deputy Minister of Investment and Planning, Minister of Science, Tech. and Planning 1996–97; Deputy Prime Minister 1997–2011; Minister of Foreign Affairs 2006–11; Deputy, Nat. Ass. 1997–2011; mem. Cen. Cttee, CP of Viet Nam 1997–2006, Politburo 2006–11.

PHAM, Gen. Van Tra; Vietnamese army officer and politician; b. 19 Aug. 1935, Que Vo, Bac Ninh, Tonkin; served in army 1953–2006; Chief of the Gen. Staff and Vice-Minister of Defence 1995–97; Minister of Nat. Defence 1997–2006; mem. Politburo, CP of Viet Nam 1996–2006, Vice-Sec. Party Cen. Cttee Mil. Comm.; Deputy, Nat. Ass.; Hero of the People's Armed Forces.

PHAM MINH MÂN, HE Cardinal Jean-Baptiste, MEd; Vietnamese ecclesiastic; *Archbishop Emeritus of Thành-Phô Hô Chí Minh (Hôchiminh Ville);* b. 5 March 1934, Ca Mau; ed Minor Seminary of Cantho, St Joseph's Major Seminary, Saigon (now Ho Chi Minh City, and in USA; ordained priest 1965; Prof., Minor Seminary of Cantho; further studies in USA 1968–71; returned to Viet Nam and again named Prof. at Minor Seminary of Cantho until Communist invasion in 1975; Rector Major Seminary of Can Tho for three dioceses of Can Tho, Vinh Long and Long Xuyen 1989–93; Coadjutor Bishop of My Tho 1993–98; Archbishop of Thành-Phô Hô Chí Minh (Hôchiminh Ville) 1998–2014, Archbishop Emer. 2014–; cr. Cardinal (Cardinal Priest of San Giustino) 2003; attended Xth Ordinary Ass. of World Synod of Bishops, Vatican City 2001. *Address:* Archdiocese of Thanh-Pho Ho Chi Minh, Toa Tong Muc, 180 Nguyen Dink Chieu, Q. 3, Thanh-Pho Ho Chi Minh City, Viet Nam (office). *Telephone:* (8) 930-3828 (office). *Fax:* (8) 930-0598 (office).

PHANSTIEL, Howard (Howie) G., BA, MA; American healthcare industry executive; *Chairman, United Online Inc.;* ed Syracuse Univ., NY and its Maxwell School of Citizenship and Public Affairs; various exec. and man. positions with Prudential Bache Int. Bank, Marine Midland Bank, Student Loan Marketing Asscn (Sallie Mae), US Dept of Health, Educ. and Welfare, Health Care Financing Administration (HCFA), Citibank, Illinois Bureau of Budget, Wisconsin Bureau of Planning and Budget; fmr Exec. Vice-Pres. Finance and Information Services, WellPoint Health Networks Inc., Calif.; Chair. and CEO ARV Assisted Living Inc., Calif. –2000, Exec. Vice-Pres. and Chief Financial Officer, PacifiCare Health Systems July–Oct. 2000, CEO Oct. 2000–05, Chair. 2002–04; Exec. Vice-Pres. UnitedHealth Group Inc. 2006–07; Man. Mem. Phanstiel Enterprises LLC 2007–; mem. Bd of Dirs United Online Inc. 2008–, Chair. 2013–, Dir, Classmates Media Corpn (subsidiary) 2007–10; Partner, HG Phanstiel LP 2009–; Vice-Chair. Bd of Trustees, Syracuse Univ. *Address:* United Online Inc., 21301 Burbank Boulevard, Woodland Hills, CA 91367, USA (office). *Telephone:* (818) 287-3000 (office). *E-mail:* info@unitedonline.com (office). *Website:* www.unitedonline.com (office).

PHARAON, Ghaith Rashad, MBA, PhD; Saudi Arabian business executive and financier; b. 7 Sept. 1940, Riyadh; ed Colorado School of Mines, Stanford and Harvard Univs, USA; Founder Saudi Arabia Research and Devt Corpn (Redec) 1965, now Chair. and Dir-Gen.; Chair. Bd Saudi Arabian Parsons Ltd, Saudi Automotive Industries Ltd, Redec Daelim Ltd, Interstal, Saudi Chemical Processors Ltd, Arabian Maritime Co., Saudi Inland Transport, Attock Petroleum, Nat. Refinery Ltd, Attock Cement Pakistan Ltd, Attock Refinery Ltd –2011; Vice-Chair. Jezirah Bank Ltd, Saudi Light Industries Ltd, Arabian Chemical Industries Ltd; mem. Bd Okaz Publications, Pakistan Oilfields, Attock Refinery Ltd, Attock Cement Pakistan Ltd, Nat. Refinery Ltd, Tihama, Bd of Assocs of Harvard Business School, Int. Devt Council of Colorado School of Mines; int. fugitive, wanted by the FBI following collapse of Bank of Credit and Commerce International (BCCI) on charges of fraud, money laundering and racketeering 1992, has travelled the world aboard luxury yacht Le Pharaon; Commendatore (Italy); King Abdul Aziz Award. *Address:* PO Box 1935, Jeddah (office); Ghaith Pharaon Residence, Ruwais, Jeddah, Saudi Arabia (home).

PHASEE, Sommai; Thai civil servant; b. 26 June 1944; m. Sophang Phasee; one s. one d.; ed Vanderbilt Univ., USA, Thammasat Univ., Nat. Defence Coll. of Thailand; several years' experience at Ministry of Finance, including as Deputy Sec.-Gen. for Finance 1998, fmr Deputy Minister of Finance 2006, Minister of Finance 2014–15; Chair. Gulf Electric PCL 2004–, Asean Potash Mining PCL 2004–, TMB Bank Public Co. Ltd –2006.

PHAYSITH, Sompao; Laotian economist and fmr central banker; Deputy Gov. Bank of the Lao PDR (central bank) 2006–11, Gov. 2011–18; mem. Bd of Govs South East Asian Central Banks 2012–; fmr mem. Lao Securities Exchange Comm. *Address:* c/o Office of the Governor, Bank of the Lao PDR, rue Yonnet, BP 19, Vientiane, Laos (office).

PHELPS, Edmund Strother, PhD; American economist and academic; *McVickar Professor of Political Economics and Director of Center on Capitalism and Society, Columbia University;* b. 26 July 1933, Evanston, Ill.; s. of Edmund S. Phelps and Florence Stone Phelps; m. Viviana Montdor 1974; ed Amherst Coll. and Yale Univ.; Research Economist, RAND Corpn 1959–60; lecturer, Yale Univ. 1960–66; Prof., Univ. of Pennsylvania 1966–71; Prof., Columbia Univ. 1971–78, 1979–82, McVickar Prof. of Political Econs 1982–, also Dir, Center on Capitalism and Soc.; Prof., New York Univ. 1977–78; Sr Adviser Brookings Inst. 1976–; Econ. Adviser EBRD 1991–94; mem. NAS 1982; mem. Econ. Policy Panel, Observatoire Français des Conjonctures Economiques 1991–; Sr Adviser Consiglio Nazionale delle Ricerche 1997–2000; Dean, New Huadu Business School of China and Switzerland 2010–; Full Foreign mem. Russian Acad. of Sciences; Distinguished Fellow, American Econ. Asscn 2000; several hon. professorships; Hon. Patron Univ. Philosophical Soc., Trinity Coll.; Hon. DH (Amherst Coll.) 1985, (Univ. of Mannheim) 2001, (Univ. Tor Vergata, Rome) 2001, (Université Paris-Dauphine) 2004, (Institut d'Etudes Politiques) 2006, (Univ. of Buenos Aires) 2007, (Tsinghua Univ.) 2007, (Université Libre de Bruxelles) 2010, (LUISS, Rome) 2018; Chevalier, Légion d'honneur 2008; Kenan Enterprise Award 1996, Nobel Memorial Prize in Econ. Sciences 2006, Premio Pico della Mirandola for humanism 2008, Kiel Global Economy Prize 2008, Louise Blouin Creative Leadership Award 2011, Mendeleev Medal and Pres.'s Medal, Nat. Univ. of Ireland 2012, Yale Univ. Wilbur Lucius Cross Medal 2014, China Friendship Award 2014, Hon. Academician, Royal European Academy of Doctors 2017, Int. Fed. of Finance Museums Lifetime Contribution Award 2015. *Publications:* Golden Rules of Economic Growth 1966, Microeconomic Foundations of Employment and Inflation Theory (ed.) 1970, Studies in Macroeconomic Theory: Vols 1, 2 1979, 1980, Political Economy: An Introductory Text 1985, The Slump in Europe 1988, Seven Schools of Macroeconomic Thought 1990, Structural Slumps 1994, Rewarding Work 1997, Enterprise and Inclusion in Italy 2002, Designing Inclusion (ed.) 2003, Rethinking Expectations (co-ed.) 2012, Mass Flourishing: How Grassroots Innovation Created Jobs, Challenge, and Change 2013. *Leisure interest:* music. *Address:* Center on Capitalism and Society, Columbia University, 1126 International Affairs Building, 420 West 118th Street, New York, NY 10027, USA (office). *Telephone:* (212) 854-2060 (office). *Fax:* (212) 854-3735 (office). *E-mail:* esp2@columbia.edu (office). *Website:* www.columbia.edu/~esp2.

PHELPS, Michael Fred; American swimmer; b. 30 June 1985, Baltimore, Md; s. of Fred Phelps and Debbie Davisson Phelps; ed Towson High School, Univ. of Michigan; Olympic Games, Sydney 2000: 5th 200m butterfly; World Championships, Fukuoka 2001: gold medal, 200m butterfly (world record); Pan Pacific Championships, Yokohama 2002: gold medal, 200m individual medley, 400m individual medley, 4×100m medley relay (world record), silver medal, 200m butterfly, 4×200m freestyle relay; World Championships, Barcelona 2003: gold medal, 200m butterfly (world record), 200m individual medley (world record), 400m individual medley (world record), 4×100m medley relay (world record), silver medal, 100m butterfly (broke world record in semi-final, subsequently broken by gold-medallist Ian Crocker), 4×200m freestyle relay; youngest male Olympian since 1932, Olympic Games, Sydney 2000; Olympic Games, Athens 2004: gold medal, 100m butterfly, 200m butterfly, 200m individual medley, 400m individual medley (world record), 4×200m freestyle relay, 4×100m medley relay (world record), bronze medal, 200m freestyle, 4×100m freestyle relay; first in 200m freestyle, World Short Course Championships 2004; World Championships, Montreal 2005: gold medal, 200m freestyle, 200m individual medley, 4×100m freestyle relay, 4×200m freestyle relay, 4×100m medley relay, silver medal, 100m butterfly; three gold medals, US Nat. Championships 2005; Pan Pacific Championships, Victoria 2006: gold medal, 200m butterfly (world record), 200m individual medley (world record), 400m individual medley, 4×100m freestyle relay (world record), 4×200m freestyle relay, silver medal, 200m backstroke; six medals, US Nat. Championships 2006; World Championships, Melbourne 2007: gold medal, 100m butterfly, 200m butterfly (world record), 200m freestyle (world record), 200m individual medley (world record), 400m individual medley (world record), 4×100m freestyle relay, 4×200m freestyle relay (world record); Olympic Games, Beijing 2008: gold medal, 100m butterfly, 200m butterfly (world record), 200m freestyle (world record), 200m individual medley (world record), 400m individual medley (world record), 4×100m freestyle relay (world record), 4×200m freestyle relay (world record), 4×100m medley relay (world record) (five gold medals won in individual events, tying record for individual gold medals at a single Games originally set by Eric Heiden in 1980 Winter Olympics and equalled by Vitaly Scherbo at 1992 Summer Games); World Championships, Rome 2009: gold medal, 100m butterfly (world record), 200m butterfly (world record), 4×100m freestyle relay, 4×200m freestyle relay (world record), 4×100m medley relay (world record), silver medal, 200m freestyle; Pan Pacific Games, Irvine 2010: gold medal, 100m butterfly, 200m butterfly, 4×100m freestyle relay, 4×200m freestyle relay, 4×100m medley relay; World Championships, Shanghai 2011: gold medal, 100m butterfly, 200m butterfly, 4×200m freestyle, 4×100m medley, silver medal, 200m freestyle, 200m individual medley, bronze medal, 4×100m freestyle relay; Olympic Games, London 2012: gold medal, 100m butterfly, 200m individual medley, 4×200m freestyle relay, 4×100m medley relay, silver medal, 200m butterfly, 4×100m freestyle relay; Olympic Games, Rio: gold medal, 200m butterfly, 4×200m freestyle relay, 200m medley, 4×100m freestyle relay, 200m individual medley 2016, silver medal 100m butterfly 2016; holds record in total career of Olympic medals, with total of 29 medals (24 gold) (the most by any Olympian); only man to win five US Nat. titles at the same Championships, only swimmer to win US Nat. titles in three different strokes at the same Championships 2003; set seven world records and one Olympic record at Beijing Olympics 2008 (only swimmer to break seven world records at one tournament); coach Bob Bowman; swims for North Baltimore Aquatic Club; est. Michael Phelps Foundation 2008; American Swimmer of the Year Award 2001, 2002, 2003, 2004, 2006, 2007, 2008, 2009, FINA Trophy (Best Swimmer, World Championships 2003) 2003, James E. Sullivan Award 2003, World Swimmer of the Year 2003, 2004, 2006, 2007, 2008, 2009, Golden Goggle Male Performance of the Year 2004, 2006, 2007, 2008, 2009, a street in Baltimore re-named The Michael Phelps Way 2004, Golden Goggle Male Athlete of the Year 2004, 2007, 2008, US Olympic Cttee SportsMan of the Year Award 2004, 2008, Golden Goggle Relay Performance of the Year 2006, 2007, 2008, 2009, Sports Illustrated Sportsman of the Year 2008, invited to appear before Maryland House of Delegates and Maryland Senate to be honoured for his Olympic accomplishments 2009. *Address:* c/o Melissa Gagnon, Octagon, 15 Lund Road, Suite 101, Saco, ME 04072, USA (office); PO Box 1734, Olney, MD 20830-1734, USA. *Telephone:* (207) 775-1500 (office). *E-mail:* melissa.gagnon@octagon.com (office); info@michaelphelpsfoundation.org (office). *Website:* www.octagon.com (office); www.michaelphelpsfoundation.org (office).

PHELPS DE CISNEROS, Patricia, (Patty Cisneros), BA; Venezuelan philanthropist, art collector and museum trustee; *Founder, Fundación Cisneros and Colección Patricia Phelps de Cisneros;* b. Caracas; d. of William Walther Phelps; m. Gustavo A.Cisneros 1970; ed Wheaton Coll., Mass, USA; began collecting art works from 1970, Co-founder (with husband and brother-in-law, Ricardo Cisneros, in asscn with Cisneros Group of Cos) and Chair. Fundación Cisneros (pvt. philanthropic org. based in Caracas, Venezuela); runs four main programmes: Colección Patricia Phelps de Cisneros (CPPC), Piensa en arte/Think Art, Cl@se and AME, Professional Devt for Educators; collaboration with Hunter Coll., New York, Bard Graduate Center, Museum of Modern Art (MoMA); Trustee, MoMa, mem. Architecture and Design Cttee 1992–2014, Chair. 2001–06, mem. Library Council 2011–; exhbn at Museo Reina Sofia in Madrid, La invención concreta: Colección Patricia Phelps de Cisneros, introduced new artists to the European public, including Lygia Clark, Lygia Pape and Hélio Oiticica 2013; mem. Amigos del Museo de Arte Ponce, Puerto Rico 2015–17; mem. Advisory Cttee David Rockefeller Center for Latin American Studies, London Tate Modern Int. Council and Latin American Acquisition Cttee; mem. Bd Fundación Museo Nacional Centro de Arte Reina Sofia, Fundación Amigos del Museo del Prado, Madrid 2014–; mem. Council, Berggruen Museum, Berlin; mem. American Friends of the Beyeler Fondation, New York; Golden Lion of San Marco 2000; Chevalier, Légion d'honneur 2002; Dr hc (Wheaton Coll.) 2003, Hon. DHumLitt (Univ. of New York) 2015; Gertrude Vanderbilt Whitney Award for Patronage of the Arts 2008, Bard Graduate Center Iris Prize 2010. *Address:* 2 East 78th Street, New York, NY 10075, USA (office). *Telephone:* (212) 717-6080 (office). *Fax:* (212) 717-6183 (office). *E-mail:* info@coleccioncisneros.org (office). *Website:* www.coleccioncisneros.org (office); www.fundacion.cisneros.org (office).

PHILARET, (Kyrill Varfolomeyevich Vakhromeyev); Russian/Belarusian ecclesiastic; b. 21 March 1935, Moscow; s. of Varfolomey and Aleksandra V. Vakhromeyev; ed Moscow Theological Seminary and Moscow Theological Acad.; became monk 1959, ordained as a priest 1961; lecturer, Asst Prof., Moscow Theological Acad. 1961–65, Rector 1966–73; Bishop of Tikhvin 1965, of Dmitrov 1966; Vice-Chair. Dept of External Church Relations, Moscow Patriarchate 1968–71, Chair. 1981–; Archbishop 1971; Archbishop of Berlin and Middle Europe 1973–78; Metropolitan 1975, of Minsk and Byelorussia 1978, of Minsk and Grodno (later Minsk and Slutsk 1992), Patriarchal Exarch of All Byelorussia 1989; Perm.

mem. Holy Synod of Russian Orthodox Church 1981–2013, Chair. Foreign Relations Dept 1987–89, Theological Comm. 1993; Dean, Theological Faculty of St Methodius & Cyril, European Humanities Univ. 1993–2005; apptd Rector, Theological Inst. of St Methodius & Cyril, Byelorussian State Univ. 2005; Chair. Editorial Bd Theological Studies 2001; Hon. mem. Moscow and St Petersburg Theological Acads; Order of St Vladimir 1969, Order of St Sergey of Radonezh 1981, Order of Friendship of the Peoples 1985, 2005, Order of Daniil of Moscow 1990, Order of Fatherland 1998, Cross of St Euphrosyne of Polotsk 1998, Order of St Seraphim of Sarov 2005; DTheol hc (St Vladimir Seminary, New York), (St Sergey Orthodox Theological Inst., Paris); Medal of Frantsysk Skorina 1995, Hero of Belarus 2006. *Publications:* Russian Orthodox Church Relations to Western Non-Orthodox Churches, St Cyril and Methodius' Works in the Territory of The Russian State in Russian Historical Literature, Patriotic Character of Patriarch Aleksiy, Theology of Neighbourhood 2002, The Vital Way of Life 2004, The Search for the Kingdom 2005; contrib.: Studies of the Minsk Theological Acad. *Address:* 220004 Minsk, 10 Osvobozdeniya Street, Belarus (home).

PHILBIN, Ann, BA, MA; American museum curator; *Director, Hammer Museum of Art and Cultural Center, University of California, Los Angeles;* b. 21 March 1952, Boston, Mass; ed Univ. of New Hampshire, New York Univ.; Researcher, Frick Art Reference Library, New York 1977–79; Program Coordinator, Artists Space 1979–80; Asst Curatorial Coordinator, The New Musuem 1980–81; Curator The Ian Woodner Family Collection 1981–83; Asst Dir Grace Borgenicht Gallery 1983–85; Dir Curt Marcus Gallery 1985–88; Dir The Drawing Center, New York 1989–98; Dir UCLA Hammer Museum of Art and Cultural Center 1999–; mem. Bd of Dirs several arts and non-profit orgs, including Vera List Center for Art and Politics at The New School for Social Research, Etant Donne (grant-making agency promoting French–American cultural exchange), Streb/Ringside dance co., HIV Law Project, New York. *Address:* The Hammer Museum, 10899 Wilshire Blvd, Los Angeles, CA 90024, USA (office). *Telephone:* (310) 443-7032 (office). *E-mail:* info@hammer.ucla.edu (office). *Website:* hammer.ucla.edu (office).

PHILEMON, Bart; Papua New Guinea politician; b. 1945, Morobe Prov.; mem. Morobe Prov. Ass. 1984–88; mem. Nat. Parl. for Lae constituency 1992–2012; Minister for Transport and Civil Aviation 1999–2000, for Foreign Affairs and Bougainville Affairs Jan.–May 2001; Minister (in Caretaker Gov.) for Treasury, Finance, Privatisation and Agric. 2002; Minister for Finance and Treasury 2002–06, for Public Service and Sport 2011–12; f. New Generation Party 2006. *Address:* c/o New Generation Party, POB 1853, Waigani NCD, Papua New Guinea (office).

PHILIPPE, Édouard; French lawyer and politician; *Prime Minister;* b. 28 Nov. 1970, Rouen; m. Édith Chabre; three c.; ed Univ. Sciences-Po, Paris, École nat. d'admin; began career as legal asst to Mayor of Le Havre 2001; Lawyer, Debevoise & Plimpton LLP (US law firm) 2004–07; Regional Councillor, Haute-Normandie 2004–08; Dir of Public Affairs, Areva Group (multinational nuclear energy group) 2007–10; Gen. Councillor, Seine-Maritime 2008–12; Pres. Communauté de l'agglomération havraise (regional action group) 2010–; Mayor of Le Havre 2010–17; mem. Nat. Ass. for Seine-Maritime (7th Dist) 2012–, mem. Law Cttee; Prime Minister 2017–; mem. Union pour un mouvement populaire (UMP) 2002–15, UMP Dir-Gen. of Services –2004; mem. Les Républicains 2015–. *Publications include:* L'Heure de vérité (with Gilles Boyer) 2007, Dans l'ombre (with Gilles Boyer) 2011. *Address:* Office of the Prime Minister, Hôtel de Matignon, 57 rue de Varenne, 75007 Paris, France (office). *Telephone:* 1-42-75-80-00 (office). *E-mail:* premier-ministre@premier-ministre.gouv.fr (office). *Website:* www.gouvernement.fr (office).

PHILIPPE, Guy; Haitian rebel leader and fmr police chief; *Secretary-General, Front pour la Réconstruction Nationale;* b. 29 Feb. 1968, Pestel, Nippes; m.; two c.; ed Saint-Louis de Gonzague, law degree from Ecuador and studied medicine in Mexico for a year, Escuela Superior de Poilicia General Alberto Enriquez Gallo, Ecuador; fmr mem. FAD'H (Haitian Army); trained by US Special Forces in Ecuador 1991–94; sr security official under Pres. René Preval 1995; when FAD'H was dissolved in early 1995, Philippe incorporated into new Nat. Police Force, served as police chief in Port-au-Prince suburb of Delmas 1997–99, in Cap-Haitien 1999–2000; accused of organizing coup attempt, fled to Ecuador then to Dominican Repub. 2002, remained there until coup d'état that ousted Pres. Jean-Bertrand Aristide Feb. 2004; named commdr of rebel army by Buteur Metayer; Sec.-Gen. Front pour la Réconstruction Nationale 2004–; presidential cand. in general election 2006; wanted by US Govt for drug trafficking. *Address:* Front pour la Réconstruction Nationale, Gonaïves (office); Pestel, Grand'Rue #12, Haiti (home). *Telephone:* 22782174 (office); 34588379 (home). *E-mail:* HotelKaribu25@yahoo.fr (office); guyphilippe68@hotmail.com (home).

PHILIPPE I, HM King of the Belgians Philippe Léopold Louis Marie, MA; Belgian; b. 15 April 1960, Brussels; s. of King Albert II and Queen Paola; m. Mathilde d'Udekem d'Acoz 1999; children: HRH Princess Elisabeth, HRH Prince Gabriel, HRH Prince Emmanuel and HRH Princess Eléonore; ed Royal Mil. Acad., Trinity Coll., Oxford, UK and Stanford Univ., USA; apptd Second Lt Belgian armed forces 1980, subsequently obtained fighter pilot's wings and certificates as parachutist and commando, attended Royal Higher Defence Inst. 1989, apptd Col 1989, apptd Maj.-Gen. and Rear-Adm. 2001; Royal Household est. 1992; Pres. Nat. Sustainable Devt Council 1993–97; apptd Senator 1994; Founder Le Fonds Prince Philippe 1998–; succeeded to the throne 21 July 2013; Hon. Pres. Bd of Dirs, Foreign Trade Office 1993–, Fed. Sustainable Devt Council 1997–; Hon. Chair. Belgian Investment Co. for Developing Countries 2003–, European Chapter of the Club of Rome 2004–, Int. Polar Foundation 2004–; Sovereign Kt Grand Cordon, Order of Leopold, Sovereign Kt, Order of the African Star, Sovereign Kt, Royal Order of the Lion, Sovereign Kt Grand Cross, Order of the Crown, Sovereign Kt, Order of Leopold II; Grand Cross, Order of the Liberator Gen. San Martín (Argentina), Kt, Order of the Golden Fleece (Austrian Imperial and Royal Family), Grand Cross, Order of the Condor of the Andes (Bolivia), Kt Grand Cross, Order of the Elephant (Denmark), Grand Cross with Collar, Order of the White Rose of Finland, Grand Cross, Order of Merit of the FRG, Special Class, Grand Cross, Order of Honour (Greece), Grand Cross with Chain, Order of Merit of the Repub. of Hungary, Kt Grand Cross with Collar, Order of the Holy Sepulchre (Vatican), Kt Grand Cross of Justice, Sovereign Mil. Order of Malta, First Class, Kt Grand Cordon with Collar, Order of the Chrysanthemum (Japan), Kt Grand Cordon with Collar, Order of al-Hussein bin Ali (Jordan), Kt Grand Cross, Order of the Gold Lion of the House of Nassau (Luxembourg), Kt Grand Cross, Order of Orange-Nassau (Netherlands), King Willem-Alexander Inauguration Medal (Netherlands), Kt Grand Cross with Collar, Order of St Olav (Norway), Grand Cross, Order of the White Eagle (Poland), Grand Cross, Order of Merit of the Repub. of Poland, Grand Cross, Order of Christ (Portugal), Grand Cross, Order of Aviz (Portugal), Kt Grand Cross, Order of Isabella the Catholic (Spain), Kt Grand Cross, Royal Order of the Seraphim (Sweden), 70th Birthday Badge Medal of King Carl XVI Gustaf (Sweden), Mem. of the Decoration of the State of Repub. of Turkey, First Class. *Address:* Royal Palace, 16 rue Bréderode, 1000 Brussels, Belgium. *Telephone:* (2) 5512020. *Website:* www.monarchie.be.

PHILIPPOU, Andreas N., BSc, MSc, PhD; Cypriot mathematician, statistician, academic and politician; *Professor Emeritus of Probability and Statistics, University of Patras;* b. 15 July 1944, Katokopia; s. of Nicholas Philippou and Maria G. Protopapa; m. Athina Roustani 1984; three d.; ed Pancyprian Gymnasium, Athens Univ., Greece, Univ. of Wisconsin, USA; Teaching and Research Asst, Univ. of Wisconsin; Asst Prof. of Math., Univ. of Texas, El Paso; Asst then Assoc. Prof. of Math., American Univ. of Beirut, Lebanon; Prof. of Business Admin., Beirut Univ. Coll.; Visiting Prof. of Applied Math., Univ. of Patras, Greece, Prof. of Probability and Statistics 1980–2011, Prof. Emer. 2012–, Vice-Pres. for Academic Affairs 1983–86, Chair. Math. Dept 1984–86; Minister of Educ. 1988–90; Pres. Preparatory Cttee for establishment of Univ. of Cyprus, then first Pres. Interim Governing Bd of Univ. 1988–90; mem. House of Reps 1991–2001, mem. House Cttees on Educ. and the Budget, Council of IPU, Rapporteur for Kosovo 1998, for the Middle East 1991–2001; Founding mem. Cen. Cttee, Social Democratic Movt (EDEK) 2000–12; mem. Tax Tribunal 2004–07, Hellenic Statistical Authority 2010–11; Pres. Council of the Technological Educational Inst. of Lamia (now TEI of Cen. Greece following merger of TEI of Chalkida with TEI of Lamia) 2012–14; fmr Vice-Pres. Hellenic Aerospace Industry; has lectured and presented papers at confs and univs in Europe, India, North America and Russia; initiated int. confs on Fibonacci numbers and their applications 1984, held every two years in a different country, Co-Chair. –2004, 2008; mem. Editorial Bd Fibonacci Quarterly; reviewer of more than 450 papers and books for Mathematical Reviews and/or Zentralblatt für Mathematik; Hon. Pres. Math. Asscn of Cyprus 1988; Grande Ufficiale Repub. of Italy. *Publications:* 75 research papers; co-ed seven books 1986–98. *Leisure interests:* swimming, sailing. *Address:* University of Patras, Section of Statistics, Probability and Operations Research, 265 00 Patras, Greece (office); 26 Atlantis Street, 2107 Nicosia, Cyprus (home). *Telephone:* (2610) 997383 (office); (22) 336360 (also fax) (home). *Fax:* (2610) 997307 (office). *E-mail:* anphilip@math.upatras.gr (office); professoranphilippou@gmail.com (home). *Website:* www.math.upatras.gr/~anphilip (office).

PHILIPS, Dalton, MBA; Irish retail executive; *CEO, daa plc;* b. 18 Feb. 1969, Co. Wicklow; ed Univ. Coll. Dublin, Harvard Univ., USA; began retail career with Jardine Matheson, NZ 1995; with Wal-Mart 1998–2005, held various man. positions in Int. Div. including COO in Germany; CEO Brown Thomas Group Ltd, Dublin 2005–07; COO Loblaw Companies Ltd, Canada 2007–10; CEO William Morrison Supermarkets PLC 2010–15; CEO daa plc 2017–; Chair. (non-Exec.), The Ridgeons Group 2016–, Byron Jan.–Sept. 2017; mem. Bd of Dirs, Dept for Business, Innovation & Skills, UK Govt 2012–15, One51 plc 2016–17, Social and Innovation Fund Ireland 2016–. *Address:* daa plc, Old Central Terminal Building, Dublin Airport, Dublin, Ireland (office). *Telephone:* (1) 8141111 (office). *E-mail:* info@daa.ie (office). *Website:* www.daa.ie (office).

PHILIPS, Luc; Belgian financial services industry executive; b. 1952; ed Coll. of Man. and Commercial Sciences, Brussels; joined KBC Bank 1971, various positions in Credit Dept and Int. Credit Div., with New York Br., 1981–87, Man.-Dir New York Br. 1987–91, Head of Cen. Man.–Multinationals Div. 1991–93, Gen.-Man. Investment Banking Directorate 1993–97, Man.-Dir and mem. Exec. Cttee KBC Bank and KBC Bank and Insurance Holding Co. 1998–2003; Man.-Dir and mem. Exec. Cttee Kredietbank 1997–98; Man.-Dir and mem. Exec. Cttee Almanij NV 2003–05, mem. Bd of Dirs KBC Bank and Insurance Holding Co., KBC Bank, KBC Insurance, then Chair. KBC Insurance, Deputy Chair. KBC Bank and Dir KBC Group NV (following merger of KBC Bank and Insurance Holding Co. with Almanij in 2005), mem. Exec. Cttee and Chief Financial and Risk Officer KBC Groep May–Sept 2009, mem. Exec. Cttee and Chief Financial Officer KBC Groep NV 2009–11.

PHILLIPPE, Ryan; American actor; b. 10 Sept. 1974, New Castle, Del.; m. Reese Witherspoon 1999 (divorced 2007); one s. one d. *Films include:* Crimson Tide 1995, Invader 1996, White Squall 1996, Nowhere 1997, I Know What You Did Last Summer 1997, Little Boy Blue 1997, Homegrown 1998, 54 1998, Playing by Heart 1998, Cruel Intentions 1999, Company Man 2000, The Way of the Gun 2000, Antitrust 2001, Igby Goes Down 2002, Gosford Park 2002, The I Inside 2003, Crash 2004, Five Fingers 2005, Chaos 2005, Flags of Our Fathers 2006, Breach 2007, Stop-Loss 2008, MacGruber 2010, The Bang Bang Club 2010, The Lincoln Lawyer 2011, Setup 2011, Revenge for Jolly! 2012, Straight A's 2013, Reclaim 2014, Catch Hell 2014. *Television includes:* The Secrets of Lake Success (mini-series) 1993, Natural Enemies 1993, Deadly Invasion: The Killer Bee Nightmare 1995, Damages (series) 2012, Secrets and Lies (series) 2015. *E-mail:* ryanphillonline@yahoo.com. *Website:* www.ryan-phillippe.com.

PHILLIPS, Caryl, BA, FRSL, FRSA; British/Saint Kitts and Nevis writer and academic; *Professor of English, Yale University;* b. 13 March 1958, St Kitts, West Indies; ed The Queen's Coll., Oxford; Writer-in-Residence, The Factory Arts Centre, London 1980–82, Univ. of Mysore, India 1987, Univ. of Stockholm 1989; visiting writer, Amherst Coll., Mass., USA 1990–92, Writer-in-Residence and Co-Dir Creative Writing Center 1992–94, Prof. of English 1994–97, Prof. of English and Writer-in-Residence 1997–98; Prof. of English and Henry R. Luce Prof. of Migration and Social Order, Barnard Coll., Columbia Univ., New York 1998–2005, Dir of Initiatives in the Humanities 2003–05; Prof. of English, Yale Univ. 2005–; Visiting Prof. of English, Dartmouth Coll., NH 2008, Univ. of Oxford 2009; Writing Instructor, Arvon Foundation, UK 1983–; Visiting Prof. of Humanities, Univ. of the West Indies, Barbados 1999–2000; Exec. Sec., N American Network of Cities of Asylum 2005–09; Consultant Ed., Faber Inc., Boston 1992–94, Graywolf Press, Minneapolis 1994–; Contributing Ed., Bomb Magazine, New York 1993–; Dir Heartland Productions Ltd 1994–2000; Advisory Ed. Wasifiri Magazine, London

1995–; Series Ed. Faber and Faber, London 1996–2000; mem. Arts Council of GB Drama Panel 1982–85, British Film Inst. Production Bd 1985–88, Bd, The Bush Theatre, London 1985–89; mem. English PEN 1997, Writers' Guild of GB 1997, American PEN (Council mem.) 1998; mem. Advisory Bd, Small Axe, New York 2011–, Brill Publishers, Netherlands 2017–; Fellow, New York Public Library 2002–03; Founding Patron, David Oluwale Memorial Asscn 2012–; Patron, The Leeds Library 2016–, Chapeltown Arts, Leeds 2017–; Hon. Sr mem. Univ. of Kent 1988–; Hon. Fellow The Queen's Coll., Oxford 2006–; Hon. AM (Amherst Coll.) 1995; Hon. DUniv (Leeds Metropolitan) 1997, (York) 2003; Hon. DLett (Leeds) 2003, (Univ. of the West Indies) 2010, (Edinburgh) 2012; Hon. MA (Yale) 2006, Dr hc (Univ. of Liege) 2015; British Council 50th Anniversary Fellowship 1984, Guggenheim Fellowship 1992, Lannan Literary Award 1994, Anthony N Sabga Caribbean Award for Excellence in Arts and Letters 2013. *Films:* Playing Away 1986, The Mystic Masseur 2001. *Plays:* Strange Fruit 1980, Where There is Darkness 1982, The Shelter 1983, Rough Crossings 2007. *Radio:* plays: The Wasted Years (BBC Giles Cooper Award for Best Radio Play of the Year) 1984, Crossing the River 1985, The Prince of Africa 1987, Writing Fiction 1991, A Kind of Home 2004, Hotel Cristobel 2005, Dinner with Friends 2011; several documentaries. *Television:* The Final Passage (Channel 4) 1996. *Publications:* fiction: The Final Passage (Malcolm X Prize for Literature) 1985, A State of Independence 1986, Higher Ground 1989, Cambridge (Sunday Times Young Writer of the Year Award) 1991, Crossing the River (James Tait Black Memorial Prize 1994) 1993, The Nature of Blood 1997, A Distant Shore (Commonwealth Writers Prize 2004) 2003, Dancing in the Dark (PEN/Beyond Margins Award 2006) 2005, In the Falling Snow 2009, The Lost Child 2015, A View of the Empire at Sunset 2018; non-fiction: The European Tribe (Martin Luther King Memorial Prize) 1987, The Atlantic Sound 2000, A New World Order: Selected Essays 2001, Foreigners: Three English Lives 2007, Colour Me English: Selected Essays 2011; ed.: Extravagant Strangers 1997, The Right Set: A Tennis Anthology 1999. *Leisure interests:* golf, running. *Address:* c/o Georgia Garrett, Rogers, Coleridge & White Literary Agency, 20 Powis Mews, London, W11 1JN, England (office); Department of English, Yale University, 63 High Street, New Haven, CT 06511-6642 (office); PO Box 3623, Chapel Hill, NC 27515, USA (home). *Telephone:* (20) 7221-3717 (office); (203) 432-6893 (office). *Fax:* (20) 7229-9084 (office). *E-mail:* georgia@rcwlitagency.co.uk (office); caryl.phillips@yale.edu (office). *Website:* www.rcwlitagency.co.uk (office); www.english.yale.edu (office); www.carylphillips.com.

PHILLIPS, Charles E., Jr, BS, MBA, JD; American business executive; *CEO, Infor;* b. June 1959, Little Rock, Ark.; ed USAF Acad., Hampton Univ., New York Law School; served as Capt. in US Marine Corps 1981–86; Vice Pres. (Software) BNY Mellon 1986–89; Sr Vice Pres. Kidder Peabody 1991–94; Man. Dir Morgan Stanley 1994–2003, fmr mem. Bd of Dirs; joined Oracle in 2003, mem. Bd of Dirs and Pres. Oracle Corpn 2003–10, responsible for global field operations, including consulting, marketing, sales, alliances and channels, and customer programmes; mem. Bd of Dirs Infor (software co.) 2009–, CEO 2010–; mem. Bd of Dirs, New York Law School 2002–17, Viacom Inc. 2006–, Federal Reserve Bank of New York 2018–, Jazz at Lincoln Center, New York City, American Museum of Natural History. *Address:* Infor, 641 Avenue of the Americas, New York, NY 10011, USA (office). *Telephone:* (646) 336-1700 (office). *Website:* www.infor.com (office).

PHILLIPS, David, CBE, OBE, BSc, PhD, FRS, FRSC, FCGI; British chemist and academic; *Professor Emeritus and Senior Research Investigator, Imperial College, London;* b. 3 Dec. 1939, Kendal, Westmorland (now Cumbria), England; s. of Stanley Phillips and Daphne Ivy Phillips (née Harris); m. Caroline L. Scoble 1970; one d.; ed South Shields Grammar Tech. School and Univ. of Birmingham; Postdoctoral Fellow and Fulbright Scholar, Univ. of Texas, USA 1964–66; Visiting Scientist, Acad. of Sciences of USSR 1966–67; Lecturer, Dept of Chem., Univ. of Southampton 1967–73, Sr Lecturer 1973–76, Reader 1976–80; Wolfson Prof. of Natural Philosophy, Royal Inst. of GB 1980–89, Acting Dir 1986, Deputy Dir 1986–89; Prof. of Physical Chem., Imperial Coll. of Science, Tech. and Medicine 1989–2002, Head of Dept of Chem. 1992–2002, Hofmann Prof. of Chem. 1999–2006, Dean of Life Sciences and Physical Sciences Faculties 2002–05, Sr Dean 2005–06, Prof. Emer. and Sr Research Investigator 2006–, Fellow of Imperial Coll. 2010–; Chair. European Photochemistry Asscn, London Gifted and Talented; mem. Council, RSC, Chair. Educ. and Qualification Bd; Vice-Pres. and Gen. Sec. BAAS 1987–89, Hon. Life Fellow 2006; Pres. RSC 2010–12; Hon. Life Fellow, City and Guilds of London Inst., Royal Inst. of GB 2005, British Science Asscn; Hon. DSc (Birmingham) 2011, (Southampton) 2012, (Durham) 2012, (Leicester) 2013, (Westminster) 2013; Hon. LLD (Bath) 2012; Spinks Lecturer, Univ. of Saskatchewan 1979, Wilsmore Fellow, Univ. of Melbourne 1983, 1990, RSC Nyholm Lectureship and Medal 1994, Faraday Award for Public Understanding of Science, Royal Soc. 1997, Premio Internazionale Sebetia Ter, Premio Internazionale Sebetia-Ter, Napoli 1999, B.D. Shaw Medal, Univ. of Nottingham 2005, RSC Award for Service 2008, Porter Medal, European Photochemistry Asscn, Inter-American Photochemistry Soc. and Asian Oceanic Photochemistry Asscn 2010. *Radio:* Desert Island Discs (BBC Radio 4) 2011, Private Passions (BBC Radio 3) 2012. *Television:* BBC TV Christmas Lectures for Young People (with J. M. Thomas) 1987. *Publications:* Time-Correlated Single-Photon Counting 1984, Polymer Photophysics 1985, Time-Resolved Laser Raman Spectroscopy 1987, Jet Spectroscopy and Dynamics 1994, Life and Scientific Legacy of George Porter, Nobel Laureate 2006; 598 publs in refereed literature on photochemistry and related topics. *Leisure interests:* music, theatre, popularization of science, tennis. *Address:* Department of Chemistry, Imperial College London, Exhibition Road, London, SW7 2AZ (office); 195 Barnett Wood Lane, Ashtead, Surrey, KT21 2LP, England (home). *Telephone:* (20) 7594-5716 (office); (1372) 274385 (home). *E-mail:* d.phillips@imperial.ac.uk (office); dclphillips@btinternet.com (home). *Website:* www.ch.imperial.ac.uk (office).

PHILLIPS, Douglas George; Canadian politician; b. 4 Dec. 1946, Toronto; s. of Norm Phillips and Grace Phillips; m. Dale Stokes; five c.; spent several years as small business owner, Yukon Territory; mem. Yukon Legis. Ass. for Riverdale N constituency 1985–2000, becoming Minister of Tourism, Minister of Educ., Minister responsible for the Women's Directorate, Minister of Justice, Minister responsible for the Public Service Comm.; Yukon Admin. 2007–10, Commr of Yukon 2010–18; fmr Dir Yukon Sourdough Rendezvous Cttee; fmr mem. and Pres. Yukon Fish and Game Asscn; mem. Yukon Land Use Planning Council 2004–10 (Chair. 2007–10); fmr Chair. Whitehorse Hosp. Close to Your Heart Fund; Dir Yukon Hosp. Foundation. *Leisure interests:* travelling, gardening, fishing, hunting and trapping. *Address:* c/o Office of the Commissioner, 1098 First Avenue, Closeleigh Manor Building, Whitehorse, YT Y1A 0C1, Canada (office).

PHILLIPS, Dwight; American track and field athlete and business executive; b. 1 Oct. 1977, Decatur, Ga; m. Valerie Phillips 2004; ed Univ. of Kentucky, Arizona State Univ.; started out in triple jump before switching to long jump; gold medal World Indoor and Outdoor Championships 2003; gold medal Athens Olympics 2004; gold medal World Outdoor Championships 2005, 2009, 2011; gold medal Continental Cup, Split 2011; currently Prin., Rebel Star Media (film production co.), Atlanta. *Address:* Rebel Star Media, Suite Ell-2, 500 Bishop Street, Atlanta, GA 30318, USA (office). *Telephone:* (678) 973-0977 (office). *E-mail:* win@rebelstarmedia.com (office). *Website:* www.rebelstarmedia.com (office).

PHILLIPS, John R., BA, JD; American lawyer and diplomatist; b. 1942, Leechburg, Pa; s. of William Phillips (né Filippi) and Hilda Phillips; m. Linda Douglass; ed Univ. of Notre Dame, Univ. of California, Berkeley; co-f. one of the first Ford Foundation-funded Public Interest law firms in Los Angeles; played a role in getting Congress to modernize the dormant Federal False Claim Act 1986; Partner, Phillips & Cohen, LLP 1988–2013; Founder, Center for Law in Public Interest, Taxpayers Against Fraud; mem. Bd Batonga Foundation; Chair. Pres.'s Comm. on White House Fellowships 2009; Amb. to Italy (also accred to San Marino) 2013–17.

PHILLIPS, Leon Francis, MSc, PhD, ScD, FRSNZ, FNZIC; New Zealand physical chemist, academic and novelist; *Professor of Chemistry, University of Canterbury;* b. 14 July 1935, Thames; m. Pamela A. Johnstone 1959; two s.; ed Westport Tech. Coll., Christchurch Boys' High School, Univ. of Canterbury, Univ. of Cambridge, UK; Upper Atmosphere Chem. Group, McGill Univ., Canada 1961; Lecturer, Univ. of Canterbury 1962, Prof. of Chem. 1966–; Pres. NZ Inst. of Chem. 2001; Visiting Prof., Univ. of Washington 1968, Monash Univ. 1969, Univ. of Perugia 2000; Visiting Fellow, Balliol Coll., Oxford 1975, Japan Soc. for Promotion of Science 1984; Visiting Scholar, Rice Univ., Houston, USA 1987; SERC Research Fellow, Univ. Birmingham 1989; Harkness Fellow 1968; Fellow, NZ Inst. of Chem.; RSC Corday-Morgan Medal 1971, Hector Medal, Royal Soc. of NZ 1979, Fulbright Award 1980, Easterfield and ICI prizes, NZ Inst. of Chem., Research Medal, Univ. of Canterbury 2000, JILA Fellowship, Univ. of Colorado, Boulder 2011. *Publications:* Basic Quantum Chemistry, Electronics for Experimenters, Chemistry of the Atmosphere (with M. J. McEwan), First Year Chemistry (with J. M. Coxon and J. E. Fergusson); over 200 scientific papers; novels: Fire in His Hand 1978, The Phoenix Reaction 1979, Ritual Fire Dance 1980. *Leisure interests:* sailing, skiing, reading, writing. *Address:* Department of Chemistry, University of Canterbury, Private Bag 4800, Christchurch 1 (office); Apartment I A, 105 McLean Apartments, 1 Lady Isaac Way Mairehau, Christchurch 8052, New Zealand (home). *Telephone:* (3) 351-9193 (home). *E-mail:* leon.phillips@canterbury.ac.nz (office). *Website:* www.canterbury.ac.nz/science/contact-us/people/leon-phillips.htmll (office).

PHILLIPS, Leslie Samuel, OBE, CBE; British actor, producer and director; b. 20 April 1924, Tottenham, London; m. four c.; ed Chingford School; early career as child actor; fmr army officer; Vice-Pres. Royal Theatrical Fund, Disabled Living Foundation; Evening Standard Lifetime Achievement in Films Award 1997, Dilys Powell Award, London Film Critics' Circle Awards 2007. *Theatre includes:* Falstaff in The Merry Wives of Windsor (RSC), On the Whole Life's Been Jolly Good (Edin. Festival), Love for Love, Naked Justice, For Better or Worse, Ghosts of Albion, Charley's Aunt, Camino Real, Deadly Game, Diary of a Nobody, Man Most Likely To…, Passion Play, Naked Justice. *Films include:* Train of Events 1949, The Woman with No Name 1950, Pool of London 1951, The Sound Barrier 1952, The Fake 1953, The Limping Man 1953, You Know What Sailors Are 1954, Value for Money 1955, As Long as They're Happy 1955, High Flight 1956, The Gamma People 1956, Just My Luck 1957, The Barretts of Wimpole Street 1957, Brothers in Law 1957, Les Girls 1957, The Smallest Show on Earth 1957, I Was Monty's Double 1958, The Big Money 1958, This Other Eden 1959, Please Turn Over 1959, The Night We Dropped a Clanger 1959, The Navy Lark 1959, The Man Who Liked Funerals 1959, The Angry Hills 1959, Carry on Nurse 1959, Carry on Teacher 1959, Ferdinando I. re di Napoli (Ferdinand I: King of Naples) 1959, Watch Your Stern 1960, No Kidding 1960, Inn for Trouble 1960, Carry on Constable 1960, Doctor in Love 1960, Raising the Wind 1961, In the Doghouse 1961, Very Important Person 1961, A Weekend with Lulu 1962, Crooks Anonymous 1962, The Fast Lady 1962, Father Came Too! 1963, You Must Be Joking! 1965, Doctor in Clover 1966, Maroc 7 (also producer) 1967, Some Will, Some Won't 1969, Doctor in Trouble 1970, The Magnificent Seven Deadly Sins 1971, Don't Just Lie There, Say Something 1973, Not Now Darling 1973, Not Now, Comrade 1976, Spanish Fly 1976, Out of Africa 1985, Empire of the Sun 1987, Scandal 1989, Mountains of the Moon 1990, King Ralph 1991, Carry on Columbus 1992, August 1996, Caught in the Act (video) 1997, The Jackal 1997, Gex: Enter the Gecko (video game; voice) 1998, The Orgasm Raygun 1998, Saving Grace 2000, Lara Croft – Tomb Raider 2001, Harry Potter and the Philosopher's Stone (voice) 2001, Arthur's Amazing Things 2002, Thunderpants 2002, Harry Potter and the Chamber of Secrets (voice) 2002, Collusion 2003, Doctor in Trouble, Pool of London, Churchill: The Hollywood Years 2004, Colour Me Kubrick 2005, With Shadows, Venus 2006, Is Anybody There? 2008. *Radio:* numerous plays including Navy Lark, Les Miserables, Tales From the Backbench, Round the World in 80 Days, Wind in the Willows. *Television includes:* Impasse 1963, Our Man at St. Mark's (series) 1963, The Time and Motion Man 1965, Foreign Affairs (series) 1966, The Suit 1969, The Culture Vultures (series) 1970, Casanova '73 (series) 1973, Monte Carlo 1986, Reluctant Debutante, A Very Fine Line, Casanova 74 (series), You'll Never See Me Again, Rumpole, Summer's Lease (mini-series) 1989, Chancer (series) 1990, The Trials of Oz 1991, Royal Celebration 1993, Two Golden Balls 1994, The Changeling 1994, Bermuda Grace 1994, Honey for Tea (series) 1994, Lovejoy, Boon, The House of Windsor (series) 1994, Love on the Branch Line (mini-series) 1994, Vanity Dies Hard 1995, The Canterville Ghost 1996, Die Katze von Kensington 1996, Das Karussell des Todes 1996, Der Blinde 1996, The Pale Horse 1997, Dalziel and Pascoe: Recalled to Life 1999, Cinderella 2000, Take a Girl Like You 2000, Sword of Honour 2001, Ghosts of Abion: Legacy (voice) 2003, Revolver (series) 2004, Into the Void, Tales of the Crypt, Who Bombed Birmingham?, Holby City, Midsomer Murders, Where the Heart Is, Heartbeat, Marple: By the Pricking of My Thumbs 2006, Harley Street

2008. *Publication:* Hello: The Autobiography 2006. *Leisure interests:* restoring property, chess, poker, racing, gardening. *Address:* c/o Jonathan Lloyd, Curtis Brown Ltd, Haymarket House, 28–29 Haymarket, London, SW1Y 4SP, England (office).

PHILLIPS, Lisa, CBE; British civil servant and head of government; *Governor of St Helena, Ascension Island and Tristan da Cunha;* m. Dave Honan 2018; one s.; Programme Man., SA, Namibia, Botswana, Lesotho, Swaziland –1984, Barbados 1988–90, India 1990–93, SE Asia, Indonesia 1993–96; Resources Man., Aid Policy Dept, Dept for Int. Devt 1996–99, Regional Policy Man., EU, Eastern Europe and Central Asia Dept 1999–2002, Deputy Team Leader, then Team Leader, Fragile States, Policy Div. 2004–06, Migration Team Leader, Migration Team, Policy and Research Div. 2006–08, Head of Cabinet, Policy and Research Directorate 2009–11, Head of Dept, Governance and Fragile States Dept 2011–12, Head of Dir's Cabinet, Policy Div. 2012–13, Head of Kenya Office 2013–16; Programme Man. for UNICEF and Commonwealth, UN and Commonwealth Dept 2002–04; Gov. of St Helena, Ascension Island and Tristan da Cunha 2016–. *Address:* The Castle, Jamestown, St Helena Island STHL 1ZZ, St Helena (office). *Telephone:* (290) 22555 (office). *E-mail:* linda.glanville@sainthelena.gov.sh (office); pagovernor@sainthelena.gov.sh (office). *Website:* www.sainthelena.gov.sh (office).

PHILLIPS, Nigel James, MBA, CBE; British diplomatist and fmr military officer; *Governor, Falkland Islands;* b. May 1963; m. Emma Phillips; one d.; ed Durham Univ., King's Coll., London, Defence Acad. Advanced Command and Staff Course; served in Royal Air Force (RAF) 1984–2000, rising to rank of Air Cdre; Sr Staff Officer (Communication Operations Planning), Defence Communications Services Agency 2001–03; Defence Attaché, Embassy in Stockholm 2003–07; Deputy Commdt and Garrison Commdr, Defence Coll. Communications Information Systems 2007–09; Defence Attaché, Embassy in Warsaw 2010–12; mem. Royal Coll. of Defence Studies 2013–14; Head, Russian Strategic Studies/Wider Europe Policy, Ministry of Defence 2014–16; Deputy Mil. Rep., Perm. Mission to EU, Brussels 2016–17; Gov. of the Falkland Islands and HM Commr for South Georgia and South Sandwich Islands 2017–. *Address:* Office of the Governor, Government House, Stanley, FIQQ 1ZZ, Falkland Islands (office). *Telephone:* 28200 (office). *Fax:* 27434 (office). *E-mail:* gov.house@horizon.co.fk (office).

PHILLIPS, Peter David, BSc, MSc, PhD; Jamaican economist, academic and politician; b. 28 Dec. 1949, Kingston; s. of Aubrey Phillips and Thelma Phillips; m. Sandra Minott; two s.; ed Univ. of the West Indies, State Univ. of New York, Binghampton, USA; Lecturer, Univ. of the West Indies 1981–89; Gen. Sec. People's Nat. Party 1991–94, Vice-Pres. 1998–2008; MP (People's Nat. Party) for East Central St Andrew 1994–; Minister without Portfolio, Office of the Prime Minister 1993–94, Minister of Special Projects 1994–95, of Health 1995–97, of Transport and Works 1998–2001, of Nat. Security 2002–07, also Minister of Electoral Matters, of Finance, Planning and the Public Service 2012–16; Leader, House of Reps 1995–2007, Leader of Opposition Business 2007–08; currently Partner, Belleville Consultants Ltd; mem. Electoral Advisory Cttee, Jt Select Cttee on Constitutional Reform. *Publications:* numerous works on Caribbean devt issues. *Address:* Belleville Consultants Ltd, 26 Trafalgar Road, Kingston 10, Jamaica (office). *Telephone:* 926-2345 (Belleville Consultants) (office). *Fax:* 960-1944 (Belleville Consultants) (office). *E-mail:* belleconsults@gmail.com (office).

PHILLIPS, Ronald Lewis, BS, MS, PhD; American geneticist and academic; *Regents Professor Emeritus and McKnight Presidential Chair in Genomics, University of Minnesota;* b. 1 Jan. 1940, Indiana; s. of Philemon Phillips and Louie Phillips; m. Judith Phillips; one s. one d.; ed Purdue Univ., Univ. of Minn., Cornell Univ.; Prof., Univ. of Minn. 1967–, now Regents Prof. Emer. and McKnight Presidential Chair in Genomics, fmr Dir Plant Molecular Genetics Inst. and Center for Microbial and Plant Genomics; specializes in plant biotechnology and genetics related to agric.; Chief Scientist, US Dept of Agric. 1996–98; judge, Beachell-Borlaug Int. Scholars Program; fmr Pres. Crop Science Soc. of America; fmr mem. Scientific Advisory Bd Donald Danforth Plant Science Center; fmr mem. Bd of Trustees, Int. Rice Research Inst. of the Philippines; mem. NAS 1991, fmr Chair. Section on Plant, Soil and Microbial Sciences; fmr Fellow (non-resident), Noble Foundation; Dr hc (Purdue Univ.); Purdue Univ. Agric. Distinguished Alumni Award, Dekalb Genetics Crop Science Distinguished Career Award, Wolf Foundation Prize in Agric. 2007, Medal of Science, Univ. of Bologna, Italy, Presidential Award, Crop Science Soc. of America, Distinguished Service Award, World Food Prize. *Publications:* over 70 chapters, 130 refereed journal articles and 300 abstracts. *Address:* Department of Agronomy and Plant Genetics, University of Minnesota, 411 Borlaug Hall, 1991 Upper Buford Circle, St Paul, MN 55108-6026, USA (office). *Telephone:* (612) 625-1213 (office). *Fax:* (612) 625-1268 (office). *E-mail:* phill005@umn.edu (office). *Website:* www.umn.edu (office).

PHILLIPS, Dame Siân, DBE, CBE, BA (Hons), FRSA; British actress and writer; b. (Jane Elizabeth Ailwen Phillips), 14 May 1933, Betws, Carmarthenshire, Wales; d. of D. Phillips and Sally Phillips; m. 1st D. H. Roy 1954; m. 2nd Peter O'Toole 1960 (divorced 1979); two d.; m. 3rd Robin Sachs 1979 (divorced 1992); ed Pontardawe Grammar School, Univ. of Wales (Cardiff Coll.), Royal Acad. of Dramatic Art, London; child actress at BBC Radio Wales and BBC TV Wales; newsreader and announcer and mem. BBC repertory co. 1953–55; toured for Welsh Arts Council with Nat. Theatre Co. 1953–55; Arts Council Bursary to study drama outside Wales 1955; Royal TV Soc. annual televised lecture 1992; Vice-Pres. Welsh Coll. of Music and Drama; mem. Gorsedd of Bards (for services to drama in Wales) 1960; mem. Arts Council Drama Cttee for five years; Gov. St David's Trust; fmr Gov. Welsh Coll. of Music and Drama; Vice-Pres. Actors Benevolent Fund; Patron Restoration of Appearance and Function Trust; Hon. Fellow, Univ. of Cardiff 1981, Polytechnic of Wales 1988, Univ. of Wales, Swansea 1998, Trinity Coll., Carmarthen; Hon. DLitt (Wales) 1984; numerous awards for work in cinema, theatre and on TV, including BAFTA Wales Lifetime Achievement Award 2001. *Stage appearances include:* Hedda Gabler 1959, Ondine and The Duchess of Malfi 1960–61 (first RSC season at Aldwych), The Lizard on the Rock 1961, Gentle Jack, Maxibules and the Night of the Iguana 1964, Ride a Cock Horse 1965, Man and Superman and Man of Destiny 1966, The Burglar 1967, Epitaph for George Dillon 1972, A Nightingale in Bloomsbury Square 1973, The Gay Lord Quex 1975, Spinechiller 1978, You Never Can Tell, Lyric, Hammersmith 1979, Pal Joey, Half Moon and Albery Theatres 1980 and 1981, Dear Liar 1982, Major Barbara, Nat. Theatre 1982, Peg (musical) 1984, Love Affair 1984, Gigi 1986, Thursday's Ladies

1987, Brel (musical) 1987–88, Paris Match 1989, Vanilla 1990, The Manchurian Candidate 1991, Painting Churches 1992, Ghosts, Cardiff and Wales tour 1993, The Lion in Winter 1994, Marlene, An Inspector Calls, Broadway 1995, A Little Night Music, Royal Nat. Theatre 1995–96, Marlene 1996–97, int. tour 1998, concert tour Middle East 1999, Marlene, Broadway 1999, Lettice and Lovage 2001, Divas at The Donmar Season 2001, My Old Lady, Doolittle Theatre, Los Angeles 2002, Promenade Theatre, New York 2002–03, Nat. Tour The Old Ladies 2003, The Dark, Donmar, London 2004, Falling in Love Again, Cabaret, London, Europe, Israel, New York, continuing UK Tour, The Unexpected Man, UK tour 2004, Quartet, New York 2005, Regrets Only, Broadway 2006, Great Expectations, Royal Shakespeare Co., Stratford 2007, Les Liaisons Dangereuses, Broadway 2008, Calendar Girls, UK tour and West End 2009, Juliet and Her Romeo, Bristol Old Vic 2010, A Little Night Music, St Louis Opera 2010, Lovesong Frantic, Assembly Tour and London, Bitter Sweet (USA), Little Dogs, Nat. Theatre Wales, My Fair Lady, Royal Albert Hall, Cabaret (musical), UK tour and West End, solo cabaret, Crossing Borders, London and UK tour, The Importance of Being Earnest (USA) 2013, 2014, Playing for Time, Crucible Sheffield 2015, The Importance of Being Earnest UK tour 2015, Les Blancs, Royal Nat. Theatre 2016, Driving Miss Daisy 2017. *Films include:* Becket 1963, Goodbye Mr. Chips (Critics' Circle Award, New York Critics' Award and Famous Seven Critics' Award 1969), Laughter in the Dark 1968, Murphy's War 1970, Under Milk Wood 1971, The Clash of the Titans 1979, Dune 1983, Ewok II, The Two Mrs Grenvilles, "Siân" (Cineclaire), Valmont 1988, Dark River 1990, The Age of Innocence 1993, House of America 1997, Coming and Going 2001, The Gigolos 2006, Bella Fleace Gave a Party (short) 2011, Hochelaga City of Souls 2016, Voyageuse 2017, Miss Dalí 2018. *Radio includes:* Phédre, Oedipus, Henry VIII, Antony and Cleopatra, Bequest to a Nation, The Maids, Henry VIII, All's Well That Ends Well, Leopard in Autumn, Bridge of San Luis Rey, Ghosts, Dance to the Music of Time, Private Lives, The Visits, Calendar Girls (BBC) 2015, Doctor Who The Fourth Doctor 2016, Wounded Light (BBC) 2016, Writing the Century – The Trials of St Patrick, Augustine Inst. 2016, Pygmalion 2017, The Things We Never Said 2017. *Television includes:* Shoulder to Shoulder 1974, How Green was my Valley (BAFTA Award) 1975, I, Claudius (Royal Television Soc. Award and BAFTA Award for Best Actress 1978) 1976, Boudicca, Off to Philadelphia in the Morning 1977, The Oresteia of Aeschylus 1978, Crime and Punishment 1979, Tinker, Tailor, Soldier, Spy 1979, Sean O'Casey (RTÉ) 1980, Churchill: The Wilderness Years 1981, How Many Miles to Babylon 1982, Smiley's People 1982, George Borrow 1983, A Painful Case (RTÉ), Beyond All Reason, Murder on the Exchange, The Shadow of the Noose (BBC series) 1988, Snow Spider (HTV serial) 1988, Freddie & Max, Emlyn's Moon, Perfect Scoundrels 1990, Heidi 1992, The Borrowers (series) 1992, 1993, The Chestnut Soldier 1992, Huw Weldon TV Lecture 1993, Summer Silence (HTV musical), The Vacillations of Poppy Carew (BBC), Mind to Kill (film series), Ivanhoe (mini-series) 1997, The Scold's Bridle 1998, Alice Through the Looking Glass (film) 1998, Aristocrats (mini-series) 1999, La Femme Nikita (series) 1999, The Magician's House 1999, 2000, Cinderella 2000, Attila (film) 2001, Ballykissangel (series) 2001, The Last Detective (series) 2003, The Murder Room 2004, Midsomer Murders (series) 2006, Kitchen (film) 2007, Holby City (series) 2007, Agatha Christie's Poirot 2008, Shortland Street (series) 2008, Missing (series) 2010, New Tricks (series) 2010, Lewis (series) 2011, An Audience with Sian Phillips (S4C) 2013, Playhouse Presents (series) – Gifted 2013, Under Milk Wood (film) 2014, Coming Home (BBC) 2015, Aberfan: The Green Hollow 2016, Casualty (BBC) 2016, Cormoran Strike (BBC/HBO series) – The Cuckoo's Calling 2017. *Recordings include:* Bewitched, Bothered and Bewildered, Pal Joey, Peg, I Remember Mama, Gigi, A Little Night Music 1990, A Little Night Music (2) 1995, Marlene 1996, Both Sides Now 2002. *Publications:* Needlepoint 1987, Private Faces (autobiog., Vol. I) 1999, Public Places (autobiog., Vol. II) 2001 (USA) 2003. *Leisure interests:* travelling, drawing. *Address:* c/o Simon Beresford, Dalzell Beresford, The Paddock Suite, The Courtyard, 55 Charterhouse Street, Clerkenwell, London, EC1M 6HA, England (office). *Telephone:* (20) 7336-0351 (office). *E-mail:* vicki@dbltd.co.uk (office).

PHILLIPS, Tom, CBE, MA, NDD, RA, RE; British artist, writer and composer; b. 24 May 1937, London; s. of David John Phillips and Margaret Agnes Arnold; m. 1st Jill Purdy 1961 (divorced 1988); one s. one d.; m. 2nd Fiona Maddocks 1995; two step-d.; ed St Catherine's Coll., Oxford and Camberwell School of Art; solo exhbns: A1A Galleries, Angela Flowers Gallery, Marlborough Fine Art and Waddingtons, London, Galerie Ba Ma, Paris; touring retrospective exhbn, Serpentine Gallery, London, Gemeente Museum, The Hague, Kunsthalle, Basel 1975; 50 years of Tom Phillips, Angela Flowers Gallery, Mappin Art Gallery, Sheffield 1987, British Council Touring Exhbn, Nat. Gallery, Australia 1988; retrospective exhbns: Nat. Portrait Gallery, London 1989, NC Museum of Art, USA 1990, Royal Acad., London 1992, Victoria & Albert Museum, London 1992, Univ. of Pennsylvania 1993, Yale Centre for British Art, USA 1994, Dulwich Picture Gallery 1998, South London Gallery 1998, Modern Art Museum, Forth Worth 2001, Flowers East 2004, Ashmolean Museum Oxford 2006; publ. music scores 1965–; first performance opera IRMA, York Univ. 1973, revival ICA, London 1983 (CD 1986), Irma: The Full Score, new production South London Gallery 2017; collaborations with Jean-Yves Bosseur and John Tilbury on music works/performances 1970–84, Retrospective Concert ICA 1992; Music Works CD 1996, Six of Hearts CD 1997, Libretto to Heart of Darkness, Première at Linbury Theatre, Royal Opera House 2011 (US première, Opera Parallèle, San Francisco 2015); worked with Peter Greenaway on TV version of Dante's Inferno, as published, translated and illustrated by the artist, broadcast 1990 (1st Prize Montreal TV Festival 1990, Italia Prize 1991); Curator of exhbn Africa: The Art of a Continent, Royal Acad., London, Gropius Bau, Berlin, Guggenheim Museum, New York 1995–96; stage design for A Winter's Tale 1997, Otello 1998, The Entertainer 2003, The Magic Flute, Opera Holland Park 2008; Vice-Chair. Copyright Council 1985–89; Chair. Royal Acad. Library, Exhbns, Royal Acad.; Pres. Heatherley's School of Fine Art 2004; Slade Prof. of Fine Art, Univ. of Oxford 2005–06; mem. Royal Soc. of Painter-Etchers and Engravers; Trustee, Nat. Portrait Gallery 1998, British Museum 2000; Judge, Man Booker Prize 2017; Hon. mem. Royal Soc. of Portrait Painters 1999, Pastel Soc. 2001; Hon. Fellow, The London Inst. 1999, St Catherine's Coll., Oxford, Univ. of Leeds (Bretton Hall); John Moores Prize 1969, Frances Williams Memorial Prize, Victoria and Albert Museum 1983. *Opera includes:* Irma 1969, Heart of Darkness (libretto) 2011. *Publications:* Trailer 1971, A Humument 1966–, Works and Texts to 1974 1975, Dante's Inferno 1983, Heart of a Humument 1985, Where are They

Now? The Class of '47 1990, Works and Texts II 1992, Merely Connect (with Salman Rushdie) 1994, Africa: The Art of a Continent 1995, Aspects of Art 1997, Music in Art 1997, The Postcard Century 2000, We Are The People 2004, Merry Meetings 2005. *Leisure interests:* opera, ping pong. *Telephone:* (20) 7701-3978 (home). *Fax:* (20) 7703-2800 (home). *E-mail:* tom@tomphillips.co.uk (home). *Website:* www.tomphillips.co.uk (home).

PHILLIPS, (Mark) Trevor, OBE, BSc, ARCS, FRSA; British journalist, broadcaster and public servant; b. 31 Dec. 1953; s. of George Milton Phillips and Marjorie Eileen Canzius; m. Asha Bhownagary 1981; two d.; ed Queens' Coll., Georgetown, Guyana, Imperial Coll., London; Pres. Nat. Union of Students 1978–80; researcher London Weekend TV 1980–81, producer Black on Black, The Making of Britain 1981–86, Ed. London Programme 1987–92 (presenter 1987–2000), Head of Current Affairs 1992–94; reporter This Week, Thames TV 1986–87; presenter, Crosstalk 1994–2000, The Material World 1998–2000; Dir Pepper Productions 1994–; mem. and Chair. London Ass., GLA 2000–03; columnist, The Independent 1997–99; Chair. Runnymede Trust 1993–98, Hampstead Theatre 1993–97, London Arts Bd 1997–2000; Chair. or Deputy Chair. London Ass. 2000–03; Chair. Comm. for Racial Equality 2003–06, Equality and Human Rights Comm. 2006–09, part-time position 2009–; Chevalier, Légion d'Honneur 2007; Hon. DLitt (Westminster, South Bank, Warwick, York, City Univ., Luton, Open Univ.); Hon. MU (London Metropolitan); Journalism Award, Royal TV Soc. 1988, 1993, 1998. *Television:* several series and productions including The London Programme, Windrush. *Publication:* Windrush: The Irresistible Rise of Multi-Racial Britain 1998, Britain's Slave Trade 1999. *Leisure interests:* music, reading, running, crosswords. *Address:* Equality and Human Rights Commission, Fleetbank House, 2-6 Salisbury Square, London, EC4Y 8JX, England (office). *Telephone:* (20) 7832-7800 (office). *Fax:* (20) 7832-7801 (office). *E-mail:* chair@equalityhumanrights.com (office). *Website:* www.equalityhumanrights.com (office).

PHILLIPS, William D., BS, PhD; American physicist and academic; *Physicist, National Institute of Standards and Technology;* b. 5 Nov. 1948, Wilkes-Barre, Pa; s. of William Cornelius Phillips and Mary Catherine Phillips (née Savine); m. Jane Van Wynen 1970; two d.; ed Juniata Coll., Huntington, Massachusetts Inst. of Tech.; mem. tech. staff, Nat. Inst. of Standards and Tech., Gaithersburg, Md 1978–; Distinguished Univ. Prof., Univ. of Maryland 2001–06, Fellow, Jt Quantum Inst. 2006–; Eastman Prof., Univ. of Oxford, UK 2002–03; mem. NAS; Fellow, American Physical Soc., American Acad. of Arts and Sciences; Fellow and Hon. Mem. Optical Soc. of America; Hon. DSc (Williams Coll.) 1998, (Juniata Coll.) 1999; Dr hc (Universidad de Buenos Aires) 1998; shared Nobel Prize for Physics for developing methods of cooling matter to very low temperatures using lasers 1997, Schawlow Prize in Laser Sciences 1998, Pennsylvania Soc. Gold Medal 1999, Service to America Medal, Career Achievement Award 2006. *Publications:* Laser Cooling and Trapping of Neutral Atoms (Nobel Lecture, published in Reviews of Modern Physics, Vol. 70, pp. 721–741 1998); numerous scientific papers in professional journals. *Address:* National Institute of Standards and Technology, 100 Bureau Drive, Stop 8424, Gaithersburg, MD 20899, USA (office). *Telephone:* (301) 975-6554 (office). *E-mail:* william.phillips@nist.gov (office); william.phillips@physics.umd.edu (office). *Website:* www.physics.umd.edu/amo (office); www.nist.gov (office).

PHILLIPS, Zara Anne Elizabeth, MBE; British professional equestrian; b. 15 May 1981, London; d. of Capt. Mark Phillips and HRH The Princess Anne, Princess Royal; grand-daughter of HRH Queen Elizabeth II; m. Michael Tindall 2011; two d.; ed Gordonstoun, Univ. of Exeter; victories include Individual Gold Medal, European Eventing Championship 2005, Gold Team Medal; Individual Gold Medal, World Equestrian Games 2006, Silver Team Medal, named Eventing World Champion (third rider in history to hold both European and World titles simultaneously); rides horse ToyTown; Pres. Club 16-24, Cheltenham Racetrack 2000–05; mem. Cheltenham Ladies Hockey Club; Eventing European Champion 2005, Sunday Times Sportswoman of the Year Award 2005, Eventing World Champion 2006, BBC Sports Personality of the Year Award 2006, Equestrian Olympic Athlete of the Year 2006, British Equestrian Writers Asscn Personality of the Year 2006. *Address:* The Bothy, Gatcombe Park, Minchinhampton, Stroud, Glos., GL6 9AT, England (home).

PHILLIPS-DAVIES, Alistair, BSc; British chartered accountant and business executive; *Chief Executive, SSE plc;* worked for HSBC and National Westminster Bank in corp. finance and business devt roles in London and New York –1997; joined Southern Electric 1997, apptd to Bd of SSE plc as Energy Supply Dir 2002, Deputy Chief Exec. 2012–13, Chief Exec. SSE plc 2013–. *Address:* SSE plc, Inveralmond House, 200 Dunkeld Road, Perth, PH1 3AQ, Scotland (office). *Telephone:* (1738) 456000 (office). *E-mail:* info@sse.com (office). *Website:* www.sse.com (office); www.hydro.co.uk (office).

PHILLIPS OF WORTH MATRAVERS, Baron (Life Peer), cr. 1999, of Belsize Park in the London Borough of Camden; **Nicholas Addison Phillips,** Kt, PC, MA; British judge; b. 21 Jan. 1938; s. of Michael Pennington Phillips and Dora Hassid; m. Christylle Marie-Therese Rouffiac 1972; two d. one step-s. one step-d.; ed Bryanston School, King's Coll. Cambridge; called to the Bar 1962; in practice 1962–87; Jr Counsel to Ministry of Defence and Treasury 1973–78; QC 1978; Recorder 1982–87; Judge, Queen's Bench Div., High Court of Justice 1987–95; Lord Justice of Appeal 1995–98; Chair. BSE Inquiry 1998–2000; Lord of Appeal in Ordinary 1999–2000; Master of the Rolls 2000–05; Lord Chief Justice of England and Wales 2005–08; Sr Law Lord 2008–09; Pres. The Supreme Court 2009–12; Chair. Law Advisory Cttee, British Council 1991–97; Chair. Council of Legal Educ. 1992–97; Vice-Pres. British Maritime Law Asscn 1993; Gov. Bryanston School 1975–2008, Chair. of Govs 1981–2008; Chancellor Bournemouth Univ. 2009–; Hon. Fellow, Soc. for Advanced Legal Studies 1999, American Coll. of Trial Lawyers 2002–, King's Coll. Cambridge 2003; Hon. LLD (Exeter) 1998, (Birmingham) 2003, (London) 2004; Hon. DCL (City Univ.) 2003. *Leisure interests:* sea, mountains. *Address:* House of Lords, London, SW1A 0PW, England. *Telephone:* (20) 7219-5353. *Fax:* (20) 7219-5979.

PHILO, Phoebe, OBE; British fashion designer; *Creative Director, Céline;* b. 1973, Paris, France; m. Max Wigram; three c.; ed Central St Martin's Fashion Coll.; grew up in London suburb; invited to work at Chloé, Paris (part of Swiss-based Richemont Group) working as Asst to Stella McCartney 1997–2001, Creative Dir 2001–06 (resgnd); presented first collection for Spring/Summer 2002; mem. Bd and Creative Dir, Céline 2008–; Best Dressed Jan. issue of Vogue 2003, British Designer of the Year, British Fashion Council 2005, 2010, Int. Designer of the Year, Council of Fashion Designers of America 2011. *Address:* Céline, 23–25 rue du Pont Neuf, 75001 Paris, France (office). *Telephone:* 1-55-80-12-12 (office). *Website:* www.celine.com (office).

PHILPOTT, Jane, PC, MD, MPH; Canadian physician and politician; b. 23 Nov. 1960, Toronto; d. of Wallace Little; m. Pep Philpott; four c.; ed Univ. of Western Ontario, Univ. of Toronto; practised gen. medicine and helped to develop training programme for village health workers in Niger 1989–98; worked as family doctor, Markham-Stouffville 1998–2015; Chief, Dept of Family Medicine, Markham-Stouffville Hosp. 2008–14; Assoc. Prof., Univ. of Toronto Dept of Family and Community Medicine 2008–; Family Medicine Lead, Toronto–Addis Ababa Academic Collaboration 2008–14; Pres. and Lead Physician, Health for All Family Health Team, Markham, Ont. 2010–15; co-curator, TEDxStouffville 2012; f. Give a Day to World AIDS (charity fundraising campaign) 2004; returned to Niger with Médecins sans Frontières during food crisis 2005; mem. House of Commons (Parl.) for Markham-Stouffville 2015–; mem. Treasury Bd 2015–; Minister of Health 2015–17, Minister of Indigenous Services 2017–19, Pres. of the Treasury Bd Jan.–March 2019; mem. Liberal Party of Canada, Policy Chair., Oak Ridges Markham Electoral Dist Asscn 2012–13; Hon. mem., Fed. of Medical Women of Canada 2009; numerous awards in the field of healthcare. *Address:* House of Commons, Confederation Building, Suite 162, 111 Wellington Street, Ottawa, ON K1A 0A6, Canada (office). *Telephone:* (613) 992-3640 (office). *E-mail:* jane.philpott@parl.gc.ca (office). *Website:* jphilpott.liberal.ca (office).

PHOENIX, Joaquin Rafael; American actor, producer and musician; b. (Joaquín Rafael Bottom), 27 Oct. 1974, Rio Piedras, Puerto Rico; s. of John Lee Bottom and Arlyn Phoenix (née Dunitz Jochebed); brother of River Phoenix; began career by appearing in episodes on TV shows with his brother and sister Summer Phoenix. *Films include:* SpaceCamp 1986, Russkies 1987, Parenthood 1989, Walking the Dog 1991, To Die For 1995, Inventing the Abbotts 1997, U Turn 1997, Return to Paradise 1998, Clay Pigeons 1998, 8MM 1999, The Yards 2000, Gladiator 2000, Quills 2000, Buffalo Soldiers 2001, Signs 2002, It's All About Love 2003, Brother Bear 2003, The Village 2004, Hotel Rwanda 2004, Ladder 49 2004, Walk the Line 2005 (Golden Globe Award for Best Performance by Actor in a Musical or Comedy 2006), We Own the Night 2007, Reservation Road 2007, Two Lovers 2008, I'm Still Here 2010, The Master (Coppa Volpi for Best Actor (shared with Philip Seymour Hoffman), Venice Int. Film Festival) 2012, Back Beyond (video short) 2013, The Immigrant 2013, Her 2013, Inherent Vice 2015, Irrational Man 2015, You Were Never Really Here (Best Actor, Cannes Film Festival 2017) 2017. *Television includes:* Backwards: The Riddle of Dyslexia 1984, Kids Don't Tell 1985, Morningstar/Eveningstar 1986, Secret Witness 1988. *Address:* c/o The Endeavour Agency, 9601 Wilshire Blvd, 10th Floor, Beverly Hills, CA 90210, USA (office). *Telephone:* (310) 248-2000 (office). *Fax:* (310) 248-2020 (office).

PHOSA, Nakedi Mathews, LLB; South African lawyer, business executive and politician; b. 1 Sept. 1952, Mbombela township, Nelspruit; m. Pinkie Phosa; three c.; ed Univ. of the North (Turfloop); articled clerk, Godfrey Rabin Attorneys 1979–81; f. Nelspruit (first black-owned legal firm) 1981, Pnr 1981–85 (went into exile); fmr Nat. Organiser Black Lawyers' Asscn; fmr Head Legal Div., African Nat. Congress (ANC) Dept of Constitutional and Legal Affairs, mem. ANC Nat. Exec. Cttee 1999–2012, Treasurer-Gen. ANC 2007–12; fmr mem. Nat. Negotiations Comm.; Premier Mpumalanga regional govt 1994–99; Chair. (non-exec.) EOH 2003–12; fmr Chair. (non-exec.) Atos KPMG Consulting; Chair. Vuka Alliance (Pty) Ltd, Du Toit-Smuts & Mathews Phosa Inc. (attorneys), Zero Pollution Motors SA (Pty) Ltd, Value Logistics Ltd, Hans Merensky Holdings; Chair. Council Univ. of SA, Special Olympics SA; mem. Bd of trustees Black Tie Ensemble; Hon. Trustee, Die Woordeboek van die Afrikaanse Taal Trust; Hon. PhD (Boston); Afrikaanse Sakekamer 2004, Marketing and Branding Capabilities Award, Cape Chamber of Commerce 2005. *Publication:* Deur die oog van 'n naald 1996.

PHOSIKHAM, Chansy; Laotian politician; fmr Gov. Prov. of Luang Prabang; Gov. State Bank –2003; Minister of Finance 2003–07; apptd Gov. Vientiane Prov. 2007; mem. Seventh Party Cen. Cttee; mem. Lao People's Revolutionary Party, Politburo of Cen. Cttee, Secr. of Cen. Cttee, Head, Cen. Org. Comm. 2017.

PHOUPHET, Khamphounvong; Laotian fmr central banker and politician; Alt. Gov. for Laos, IFAD 2003, Asian Devt Bank –2007; Deputy Gov., then Gov. Bank of the Lao PDR 2006–11; Minister of Finance 2011–14.

PHUNG, Gen. Quang Thanh; Vietnamese army officer and government official; b. 2 Feb. 1949, Thach Da commune, Me Linh, Hanoi; m. Nguyen Thi Loc; one c.; ed School for Infantry Officiers, Acad. of Infantry, Voroshilov Acad., USSR, Mil. Acad. of Viet Nam; joined army 1967 and fought in various battles during the Viet Nam War, served as co. commdr in 9th Bn, 64th Regt, 320th Div., apptd Commdr of 9th Bn, 320th Div., 1st Army Corps 1972, held several positions in 1st Army Corps from Chief of Staff of 64th Regt to Acting Commdr of 312th Div. 1988; promoted to Commdr of 312th Div. 1991, later served in Gen. Staff of Viet Nam People's Army 1993–97, Commdr 1st Mil. Zone 1997–2001, Chief of the Gen. Staff and Deputy Minister of Defence 2001–06, Minister of Nat. Defence 2006–16, mem. Nat. Defence and Security Council; admitted to CP of Viet Nam (fmrly Vietnam Workers' Party) 1968, elected to Politburo 2006; rank of Maj.-Gen. 1994, Lt-Gen. 1999, Col-Gen. 2003, Gen. 2007; Hero of the People's Armed Forces 1971, three Liberation Distinguished Service Medals, 1st Order, three Brave Soldier Titles and other awards.

PHUVANATNARANUBALA, Thirachai, BEcons; Thai economist and politician; b. 21 Dec. 1951, Bangkok; m.; three c.; ed London School of Econs; fmrly worked at Price Waterhouse, London; worked at Bank of Thailand 1977–2003, Deputy Gov. –2003; Sec.-Gen. Securities and Exchange Comm. of Thailand 2003–11; Minister of Finance 2011–12; Chair. ASEAN Capital Markets Forum 2003–11; fmr Bd mem. Experts for Interpretation of Tax Code, Thai Inst. of Dirs, Bank of Thailand Financial Inst. Policy Bd, Nat. Credit Bureau Co. Ltd, Insurance Comm.

PHUYAL, Hari, LLB, LLM; Nepalese lawyer and government official; *Senior Consultant, Law and Policy Forum for Social Justice; b.* 10 Oct. 1970, Rajghat Morang; ed Nat. Law School of India Univ., Bangalore, Univ. of Essex, UK; Advocate, Supreme Court of Nepal, also serves as Sr Legal Adviser to International Commission of Jurists; Exec. Ed., NYAYADOOT, Nepal Bar Asscn journal 1995–98; consultant to FAO, Nepal Office reviewing legislation related to agriculture 2002; Nat. Legal Adviser at OHCHR in Nepal 2005–06; has taught law courses at Tribhuban Univ., Kathmandu; trainer on migrant workers' rights, Diplomacy Training Program, Sydney, Australia; Attorney-Gen. 2016; currently Sr Consultant, Law and Policy Forum for Social Justice; mem. Advisory Bd, Forum for Nation Building. *Publications include:* Refugee Law (course book) 1996; contrib. to other titles including Police and Human Rights, Handbook of International Humanitarian Law in South Asia 2007, Judicial Reform Handbook; numerous articles in professional journals including Nepal Law Journal. *Address:* Law and Policy Forum for Social Justice, Anamnagar-32, POB 44600, Kathmandu, Nepal (office). *Telephone:* 9841428678 (mobile) (office). *E-mail:* info@lapsoj.org (office). *Website:* www.lapsoj.org (office).

PIACENZA, HE Cardinal Mauro, JCD; Italian ecclesiastic and academic; *Major Penitentiary of the Apostolic Penitentiary; b.* 15 Sept. 1944, Genoa; ed Major Archiepiscopal Seminary of Genoa, Pontifical Lateran Univ., Rome; ordained priest, Diocese of Genoa 1969; served as a parochial vicar, as Chaplain and later Apostolic Del. to Univ. of Genoa; taught canon law at Theological Faculty of Northern Italy; held several other curial positions and served as the Archbishop's Press Officer; fmr Diocesan Asst of the ecclesial Movt of Cultural Commitment; fmr Prof. of Contemporary Culture and History of Atheism, Ligurian Higher Inst. of Religious Studies as well as Prof. of Dogmatic Theology, Diocesan Inst. of Theology for the Lay 'Didascaleion'; also taught theology at several state lyceums; made a Canon of the Genoa Cathedral 1986; entered Congregation for the Clergy 1990, Undersecretary 2000–07, Sec. 2007–10, Prefect 2010–13; Major Penitentiary of the Apostolic Penitentiary 2013–; Pres. Pontifical Comm. for the Cultural Heritage of the Church 2003–04; Titular Bishop of Victoriana 2003–07, Titular Archbishop 2007–10; Pres. Pontifical Comm. for Sacred Archeology 2004–07; cr. Cardinal (Cardinal-Deacon of San Paolo alle Tre Fontane) 2010; participated in Papal Conclave 2013. *Address:* Paenitentiaria Apostolica, Palazzo della Cancelleria, Piazza della Cancelleria 1, 00186 Rome, Italy (office). *Telephone:* (06) 69887526 (office). *Fax:* (06) 69887557 (office). *Website:* www.penitenzieria.va (office).

PIANO, Renzo; Italian architect; *b.* 14 Sept. 1937, Genoa; *s.* of Carlo Piano and Rosa Odone; *m.* 1st Magda Ardnino 1962; two s. one d.; *m.* 2nd Emilia Rossato 1992; one c.; ed Milan Polytechnic School of Architecture; worked with Louis I. Kahn, Phila, USA, Z.S. Makowsky, London 1965–70, with Richard Rogers (as Piano & Rogers) 1977–, with Peter Rice (as Atelier Piano & Rice) 1977–; currently has offices in Genoa, Paris, Berlin (Renzo Piano Bldg Workshop); mem. Nat. Acad. of Design 2013; Hon. Fellow Union Int. des Architectes 1978, AIA, 1981, RIBA, 1985, American Acad. of Arts and Letters 1994; Dr hc (Stuttgart) 1990, (Delft) 1992; Compasso d'Oro Award, Milan 1981, RIBA Gold Medal 1989, Kyoto Prize, Japan 1990, Neutra Prize, Pomona, Calif. 1991, Goodwill Amb. of UNESCO for Architecture 1994, Premio Michelangelo 1994, Art Prize of Akademie der Künste, Berlin 1995, Praemium Imperiale, Tokyo 1995, Erasmus Prize, Amsterdam 1995, The Pritzker Architecture Prize, Washington, DC 1998, Médaille d'Or, Int. Union of Architects 2002, Gold Medal, American Inst. of Architects 2008, and other prizes and awards; Commdr des Arts et des Lettres, Légion d'honneur, Cavaliere di Gran Croce, Officer, Ordre Nat. du Mérite, Senator for Life (highest Italian honour) 2013–. *Completed projects include:* office bldg for B&B, Como 1973, Georges Pompidou Centre, Paris (with Richard Rogers) 1977, IRCAM Inst. for Acoustic Research, Paris 1977, housing, Rigo Dist, Perugia 1982, office bldg for Olivetti, Naples 1984, office bldg for Lowara, Vicenza 1985, museum for Menil Collection, Houston, USA 1988, HQ for Light Metals Experimental Inst., Novara 1988, S. Nicola Football Stadium, Bari 1989, Underground stations for Ansaldo, Genoa 1990, Bercy commercial centre, Paris 1990, Thomson factories, Guyancourt, France 1991, HQ for Credito Industriale Sardo, Cagliari 1992, Lingotto congress and concert hall, Turin 1994, Kansai Int. Airport, Osaka, Japan 1994, Meridien Hotel, Lingotto and Business Centre, Turin 1995, Harbour Authorities HQ, Genoa 1995, cinema, offices, contemporary art gallery, conf. centre, landscaping, Cité Int., Lyon 1996, Ushibuka Bridge, Kumamoto, Japan 1996, Museum of Science and Tech., Amsterdam 1997, Museum of Beyeler Foundation, Basel 1997, Debis Bldg HQ, Daimler Benz, Berlin 1997, Cultural Centre J.-M. Tjibao, Nouméa, New Caledonia 1998, Mercedes-Benz Design Centre, Stuttgart 1998, Daimler-Benz Potsdamer Platz project including Imax theatre, offices, housing, shops, Berlin 1998, Lodi Bank HQ, Milan 1998, KPN Telecom office tower, Rotterdam 2000, Aurora Palace office block, Sydney, Australia 2000, Maison Hermès, Tokyo 2001, Rome Auditorium 2003, Padre Pio Basilica Church, Puglia, Italy 2004, Morgan Library extension, NY 2006, NY Times Bldg, Manhattan 2007, Broad Contemporary Art Museum, Los Angeles 2008, California Acad. of Sciences rebuilding, San Francisco 2008, Nichols Bridgeway, Chicago 2009, Modern Wing expansion, Art Inst. of Chicago 2009, Central Saint Giles, London 2010, The Shard, London (tallest skyscraper in Europe) 2000–12, Astrup Fearnley Museum of Modern Art, Tjuvholmen, Oslo 2002–12, HQ newspaper Il Sole/24 Ore, Milan2004, Isabella Stewart Gardner Museum wing, Boston 2005–12, Zentrum Paul Klee, Bern 2005, Harvard Univ. Art Gallery 2014, Whitney Museum of American Art, New York 2015, Stavros Niarchos Cultural Centre, Athens 2016, Centro de Arte Botín, Santander 2017, Float Building, Düsseldorf 2018. *Projects in progress include:* Acad. Museum of Motion Pictures, Los Angeles, Palais de Justice, Paris, 565 Broome SoHo, New York, Südbahnhof, Vienna, Krause Gateway Center, Des Moines, Columbia University Manhattanville Campus, New York, JNBY Headquarters, Hangzhou, China; work shown at exhbns Europe, USA, Australia, Japan 1967–; numerous lectures worldwide. *Leisure interest:* sailing. *Address:* Renzo Piano Building Workshop, Via Rubens 29, 16158 Genoa, Italy; 34, rue des Archives, 75004 Paris, France. *Telephone:* (010) 61711 (Genoa). *Fax:* (010) 6171350 (Genoa). *E-mail:* italy@rpbw.com. *Website:* rpbw.r.ui-pro.com.

PIĄTAS, Gen. Czesław; Polish army officer and politician; *Lecturer, General Tadeusz Kosciuszko Military Academy of Land Forces; b.* 20 March 1946, Hausach, Germany; *m.* Danuta Piątas; two c.; ed Armour Officer's School, Acad. of Gen. Staff, USSR, US Nat. War Coll., Washington, DC, USA; began career in Polish Armed Forces 1968; served in a variety of command and staff positions in armour

units 1970s; Chief of Staff, Deputy Commdr of 10th Armoured Div. and Commdr of tank regt 1980–82; apptd G-3 Dir Silesian Mil. Dist HQ 1982; Commdr 4th Mechanized Div.; Staff Position, Silesian Mil. Dist HQ 1993–94; Chief of Staff, DCG, Warsaw Mil. Dist 1995–96; Chief of Operational and Strategic Div., Gen. Staff 1996–99; Deputy Chief of Gen. Staff of Polish Armed Forces 1999–2000, Chief of Gen. Staff 2000–06; Sec. of State, Ministry of Defence 2008–11; Lecturer, Gen. Tadeusz Kościuszko Mil. Acad. of Land Forces 2012–; rank of Brig. Gen. 1992, Maj. Gen. 1999, Lt Gen. 2000, Gen. 2000. *Leisure interests:* mil. history, tennis. *Address:* General Tadeusz Kosciuszko Military Academy of Land Forces, Czajkowskiego Street 109, 51-150 Wroclaw, Poland (office). *E-mail:* rzecznik@wso.wroc.pl (office). *Website:* www.wso.wroc.pl (office).

PICADO SOTELA, Sonia, LicenD; Costa Rican lawyer, international organization official, academic and fmr politician; *b.* 20 Dec. 1936; *d.* of Antonio de Picado and Odile Sotela; *m.* (divorced); one s. one d.; ed Univ. of Costa Rica; Prof., Faculty of Law, Univ. of Costa Rica 1972–2003, Dean, Faculty of Law 1980–84, Cathedratical Chair. 1984; Co-Chair. Int. Comm. for Central American Recovery and Devt 1987–89; mem. Cttee of Jurists, World Conf. on Refugees, UNHCR, Geneva 1988–89; Prof., Inter-American Inst. of Human Rights 1985–, Exec. Dir 1988–94, fmr Pres., currently Hon. Pres.; Vice-Pres. Inter-American Court of Human Rights 1988–94; Co-Chair. Inter-American Dialogue, Washington, DC 1993–94; Amb. to USA 1994–98; Head of UN Comm. of Inquiry on East Timor 1999–2000; mem. Legislative Ass. for San José 1999–2001; Pres. Nat. Liberation Party 1999–2001; mem. Comm. on Human Security; Pres. UN Voluntary Fund for Victims of Torture; currently Chair. UN Advisory Bd on Human Security; Trustee, Equal Rights Trust; Dr hc (Elmhurst Coll., Chicago) 2000, (Univ. of Miami) 2002, (Colby Coll.) 2003; Max Planck/Humboldt Award (Germany) 1991, Leonidas Proaño Award (Ecuador) 1991, UN Prize in Human Rights 1993, UNDP Award 1995, Gallery of Women, Nat. Women's Inst. 2005. *Publications:* Women and Human Rights 1986, Philosophical Fundamentals of Human Rights in Latin America 1987, Religion, Tolerance and Liberty: A Human Rights Perspective 1989, Peace, Development and Human Rights 1989. *Address:* Inter-American Institute of Human Rights, PO Box 10.081-1000, San José, Costa Rica (office). *Telephone:* 234-0404 (office). *Fax:* 234-0955 (office). *E-mail:* instituto@iidh.ed.cr (office). *Website:* www.iidh.ed.cr (office).

PICARD, Dennis J.; American business executive; *Chairman Emeritus, Raytheon Company; b.* 1932, Rhode Island; *m.* Dolores M. Petit; five c.; ed LaSalle Acad., Providence, RI, RCA Inst., New York, Northeastern Univ.; served in USAF during Korean War early 1950s; joined Raytheon 1955, Sr Vice-Pres., Gen. Man. Missile Systems Div. Raytheon Co., Lexington, Mass 1985–89, Pres. 1989–90, Chair. 1990–99, CEO 1990–99 (also mem. Bd of Dirs), Chair. Emer. 1999–; Pres. AIAA 2001, Hon. Fellow; mem. Defence Policy Advisory Cttee on Trade, Pres.'s Export Council; fmr Dir, State Street Boston Corpn, Discovery Museums, Acton, Mass; fmr mem. Advisory Cttee, American Red Cross, Armed Services YMCA of the US, Business Council, Defense Policy Advisory Cttee on Trade, Pres.'s Nat. Security Telecommunications Advisory Cttee, Pres.'s Export Council; Trustee, Northeastern Univ.; Trustee Emer., Bentley Coll.; mem. Nat. Acad. of Eng; Life Fellow, IEEE; US Army's Order of Santa Barbara 1991; Dr hc (Northeastern Univ.), (Merrimack Coll.), (Bentley Coll.); Environmental Achievement Award, Nat. Security Industrial Asscn 1996, Adm. Chester W. Nimitz Award, Navy League of the US Fleet 1997, Intrepid Salute Award, Intrepid Museum Foundation 1997, John R. Allison Award, USAF Asscn 1997, John W. Dixon Medal, Asscn of the US Army 1997, New Englander of the Year, New England Council 1997, Ralph Lowell Distinguished Citizen Award, Boston Minuteman Council, Boy Scouts of America 1997, Industrial Leadership Award, Nat. Defense Industrial Asscn 1998, Semper Fidelis Award, Marine Corps Scholarship Foundation 1998, Rear Adm. John J. Bergen Leadership Medal for Industry, Navy League (New York Council) 1998, IEEE Dennis J. Picard Medal for Radar Technologies and Applications est. in his honour 1999. *Address:* Raytheon Company, 870 Winter Street, Waltham, MA 02451-1449 (office); 1373 Monument Street, Concord, MA 01742, USA (home). *Telephone:* (781) 522-3000 (office). *E-mail:* info@raytheon.com (office). *Website:* www.raytheon.com (office).

PICARDO, Fabian Raymond, LLB, QC; Gibraltarian lawyer and politician; *Chief Minister; b.* 18 Feb. 1972; *m.* 2nd Justine Olivero 2011; two s. one d.; ed Oriel Coll., Oxford, Inns of Court School of Law, Gray's Inn, London, UK; called to the Bar 1994; joined Hassans Int. Law Firm 1994, currently Pnr; mem. Gibraltar Socialist Labour Party, Leader 2011–; Chief Minister of Gibraltar Dec. 2011–; mem. Hon. Soc. of Middle Temple; mem. Bar in Gibraltar and British Virgin Islands. *Address:* Office of the Chief Minister, 6 Convent Place, Gibraltar (office). *Telephone:* 20070071 (office). *Fax:* 20076396 (office). *E-mail:* cm@gibraltar.gov.gi (office). *Website:* www.gibraltar.gov.gi (office).

PICASSO, Manuel; Peruvian diplomatist and international organization official; held various positions with Ministry of External Relations, including in Cabinet of Minister of External Relations, in Directorate for Econ. Affairs and Under-Secr. of Political Affairs, Sec., Embassy in Ottawa 1979–82, Embassy in The Hague 1982–85, Sec. and Counsellor, Embassy in Brasília 1988–92, Counsellor, Embassy in Paris 1992–93, Consul-Gen. in Barcelona 1997–99, Jt Perm. Rep. to UN, New York 1999–2001, Exec. Dir for Peru, Binational Plan for Devt of Peru-Ecuador Transboundary Region 2001–04, also Chair. Binational Plan Governing Bd, Peru-Ecuador Binational Fund for Peace and Devt, Amb. to Finland (also accred to Latvia, Estonia and Lithuania) 2004–08, to India 2008–09; fmr Dir Pro Tempore Secr., Deputy Pro Tempore Sec., Amazon Co-operation Treaty, Sec.-Gen. Amazon Co-operation Treaty Org. 2009–11; mem. Peru-Ecuador Binational Business Group; Order of Merit for Distinguished Services (Peru) 1976, Officer, Order of Orange Nassau (Netherlands) 1985, Grand Cross, Order of Merit (Ecuador) 2003, Order of Merit for Distinguished Services, Grand Cross of the Order (Peru) 2004, Grand Cross, Order of Lion of Finland 2008.

PICASSO, Paloma; French designer; *b.* 19 April 1949, Paris; *d.* of Pablo Ruiz-Picasso and Françoise Gilot; *m.* 1st Rafael Lopez-Cambil (Lopez-Sanchez) 1978 (divorced 1998); *m.* 2nd Eric Thevennet 1999; ed Univ. of Paris (Sorbonne); studied jewellery design and manufacture; fashion jewellery for Yves St Laurent 1969; jewellery for Zolotas 1971, costumes and sets for Parisian theatre productions, L'Interprétation 1975, Succès 1978; created Paloma Picasso brand, creations designed include jewellery for Tiffany & Co. 1980, fragrances (Paloma Picasso

1984, Minotaure 1992, Tentations 1996) and cosmetics for L'Oréal, eyewear for Metzler Optik Partner AG, bone china, crystal, silverware and tiles for Villeroy & Boch, home linens for KBC, fabrics and wall coverings for Motif; f. Paloma Picasso Foundation, Lausanne, Switzerland; Council of Fashion Design of America Accessory Award 1989. *Film:* Contes immoraux 1974. *Address:* c/o Paloma Picasso Foundation, c/o Piaget & De Mitri SA, Avenue Mon-Repos 14, 1000, Lausanne, Switzerland.

PICCOLI, Michel; French actor; b. 27 Dec. 1925, Paris; s. of Henri Piccoli; m. Éléonore Hirt 1954 (divorced); one d.; m. 2nd Juliette Gréco 1966; m. 3rd Ludivine Clerc 1978; ed Collège d'Annel, Collège Sainte Barbe, Paris; Man. of the Théâtre de Babylone for two years before joining the Madeleine Renaud and Jean-Louis Barrault Theatre Co.; appeared in Phèdre at the Théâtre Nationale Populaire; jury mem. Cannes Film Festival 2007; Chevalier Légion d'honneur, Ordre nationale du Mérite; European Prize, Taormina Theatre, Sicily 2001. *Films include:* Le point du jour 1946, Parfum de la dame en noire 1949, French Cancan 1955, The Witches of Salem 1956, Le mépris 1963, Diary of a Chambermaid 1964, De l'amour 1965, Lady L 1965, La curée 1965, Les demoiselles de Rochefort 1967, Un homme de trop 1967, Belle de jour 1967, Dillinger is Dead 1968, The Milky Way 1969, Topaz 1969, The Discreet Charm of the Bourgeoisie 1972, Themroc 1972, Blow-out 1973, The Infernal Trio 1974, Le fantôme de la liberté 1974, La faille 1975, Léonar 1975, Sept morts sur ordonnance 1976, La dernière femme 1976, Savage State 1978, Le divorcement 1979, Le saut dans le vide 1979, Le mors aux dents 1979, La città delle donne 1980, Salto nel Vuoto (Best Actor, Cannes Film Festival 1980) 1980, La passante du sans-souci 1982, Adieu Bonaparte 1985, The Night is Young 1986, L'homme voilé, Maladie d'amour, La rumba 1987, Y a bon les blancs, Blanc de Chine 1988, Milou en mai 1990, Martha et moi 1991, La belle noiseuse 1991, Les equilibristes, Le voleur d'enfants 1991, Le bal des cassepieds 1992, Archipel 1993, Rupture(s) 1993, L'Ange noir 1994, Les cent et une nuits 1995, 2 × 50 Years of French Cinema 1995, Compagna di Viaggio 1996, Beaumarchais l'insolent 1996, Généalogies d'un crime 1997, Alors voilà (dir) 1997, Rien sur Robert 1999, Compagne de voyage 2000, Les acteurs 2000, Je rentre à la maison 2001, La Plague noire 2001, Ce Jour-là 2003, Belle Toujours 2006, Jardins en Automne 2006, We Have a Pope 2011, Holy Motors 2012. *Publication:* Dialogues égoistes 1976. *Leisure interests:* riding, flying. *Address:* 11 rue des Lions Saint-Paul, 75004 Paris, France.

PICEK, Lt-Gen. Vlastimil; Czech military officer and politician; b. 25 Oct. 1956, Turnov; m. Dagmar Picková (divorced); two c.; ed Mil. Acad., Brno, Czech Tech. Univ.; sr radio operator 1975–78; Deputy Battalion Commdr for Tech. Issues 1983–86, Sr Officer, Nat. Air Defence HQ 1986–89; Chief of Signal Br., Fourth Air Defence Corps HQ 1993–94; Section Chief Signal Br., Armed Forces Gen. Staff 1994–95, Deputy Chief 1995–96, Chief of Signal Br. 1996–97, Chief of Operational-Tactical C2 Systems Dept 1997–2000, Chief of Command and Control Div. 2000–03; Security Dir, Ministry of Defence 2001–03; promoted to Brig. 2001; Chief of Mil. Office of Pres. 2003–07; rank of Maj.-Gen. 2003, Lt Gen. 2006; Chief of Gen. Staff 2007–12; rank of Army Gen. 2009; First Deputy Minister of Defence Sept. 13–Dec. 2012, 21 Dec. 2012–13; Minister of Defence 2013–14; Cross of Merit of the Minister of Defence Third Grade, ACR Medal Third Grade, Nat. Service Medal, Hon. Commemorative Badge for Service in Peace Operation in the Balkans, NATO 50th Anniversary Medal. *Leisure interests:* tennis, skiing. *Address:* c/o Ministry of Defence, Tychonova 1, 160 01 Prague 6, Czech Republic. *E-mail:* info@army.cz.

PICHAI, Sundar, BTech, MS, MBA; American technology industry executive; *CEO, Google Inc.;* b. (Pichai Sundararajan), 12 July 1972, Chennai, Tamil Nadu, India; s. of Regunatha Pichai and Lakshmi Pichai; m. Anjali Pichai; two c.; ed Vana Vani Matriculation Higher Secondary School, Indian Inst. of Tech., Kharagpur, Stanford Univ., Wharton School, Univ. of Pennsylvania; fmrly worked in engineering and product man., Applied Materials; fmr man. consultant, McKinsey & Company; joined Google Inc. (now subsidiary of newly formed holding co. Alphabet Inc.) 2004, Vice-Pres. of Product Man. 2004–11, Sr Vice-Pres. Google Chrome and Apps 2011–13, Sr Vice-Pres. Android, Chrome and Apps 2013–14, Product Chief 2014–15, apptd CEO Google Inc. 2015, mem. Bd of Dirs Alphabet Inc. 2017–; B C Roy Silver Medal, Indian Inst. of Tech. 1993. *Address:* Google Inc., 1600 Amphitheatre Parkway, Mountain View, CA 94043, USA (office). *Telephone:* (650) 253-0000 (office). *Website:* www.google.com (office).

PICHET, Patrice; French entrepreneur and business executive; *CEO, Groupe Pichet;* b. 1959, Bassin d'Arcachon, Bordeaux; four s.; has spent his entire career in construction industry, initially as trading and sales man. 1983–87; Founder and CEO Groupe Pichet (nationwide real-estate business) 1988–, now 20 subsidiaries, covering the construction trades, four regional offices: Bordeaux (HQ in Pessac), Biarritz, Nantes and Paris, also partner of Girondins de Bordeaux and Bayonne rugby team; leads a consulting team within IG2P; interests in wine and vineyards of Bordeaux (Château Haut Brion Carmelite), acquired 17 hectares of vineyards in Martillac; Palm'Elec Nat. Award for Sustainable Devt 2007, Prix Bas Carbone des Trophées Nationaux Habitat Bleu Ciel EDF 2011. *Address:* Pichet Immobilier, Siège social sur Bordeaux, 20–24 avenue de Canteranne, 33600 Pessac, France (office). *Telephone:* 5-56-07-47-00 (office). *Website:* www.pichet.com (office); www.pichet-immobilier.fr (office).

PICHLER, Joseph A., MBA, PhD; American business executive; b. 3 Oct. 1939, St Louis, Mo.; s. of Anton Pichler and Anita Pichler; m. Susan Eyerly 1962; two s. two d.; ed Notre Dame Univ. of Chicago, Univ. of Chicago; Prof., School of Business, Univ. of Kan., Dean 1974–80; Exec. Vice-Pres. Dillon Companies Inc. 1980–82, Pres. 1982–84, Pres. and CEO 1984–86, CEO 1986–88; Exec. Vice-Pres. The Kroger Co. 1985–86, Pres. and COO 1986–90, Pres. and CEO 1990–2003, Chair. 1990–2004; mem. Bd of Dirs Macy's Inc. 1997–2012; Woodrow Wilson Fellow 1961, Ford Foundation Doctoral Fellow 1962–64, Standard Oil Industrial Relations Fellow 1964; 1993, Trustee Xavier University 1993–, Chair. 2004–09; mem. Cincinnati Business Comm. 1991, Chair. 1997–98; Dr hc (Univ. of Cincinnati) 2009; Performance Award, US Dept of Labor Manpower Admin. 1969, William Booth Award, The Salvation Army 1998, Horatio Alger Award 1999, Distinguished Service Award, Nat. Conf. Cttee of Justice 2000, 2003, inducted into Grocery Manufacturer's Asscn Grocery Hall of Fame 2003, Great Living Cincinnatian, Cincinnati Regional Chamber of Commerce 2008, Founders' Day Award, Xavier Univ. 2013. *Publications:* Inequality: The Poor and the Rich in America (with Joseph W. McGuire) 1969, Ethics, Free Enterprise and Public Policy (with Richard T. De George) 1978. *Leisure interests:* fly-fishing, music, reading.

PICKARD, Ann Darlene, BA, MA; American energy industry executive; *Executive Vice-President of Arctic—Upstream Americas, Royal Dutch Shell PLC;* b. Wyo.; m.; two c.; ed Univ. of California, San Diego, Univ. of Pennsylvania; worked for Mobil, left co. upon merger with Exxon; joined Shell 2000, Dir Global Businesses and Strategy and mem. Shell Gas & Power Exec. Cttee with responsibility for Global LNG, Power, and Gas & Power Strategy –2005, Regional Exec. Vice-Pres. for Sub-Sahara Africa, based in Lagos, Nigeria, 2005–10, Exec. Vice-Pres. Upstream Australia within Shell Upstream International org. 2010–13, also Country Chair Shell in Australia, Dir of Shell Energy Holdings Australia Ltd and its subsidiary cos, Exec. Vice-Pres., Arctic—Upstream Americas 2013–; mem. Bd Energy & Minerals Inst. of Int., Univ. of Western Australia. *Address:* Royal Dutch Shell PLC, Carel van Bylandtlaan 30, The Hague 2596 HR, Netherlands (office). *Telephone:* (70) 3779111 (office). *Website:* www.shell.com (office).

PICKARD, Sir (John) Michael, Kt, FCA, CIMgt; British fmr business executive; b. 29 July 1932, Banstead, Surrey, England; s. of John Stanley Pickard and Winifred Joan Pickard; m. Penelope Jane Catterall 1959; one d. three s.; ed Oundle School; Finance Dir British Printing Corpn 1965–68, Man. Dir Trusthouses Ltd 1968–70, Trusthouse Forte Ltd 1970–71; Chair. Happy Eater Ltd 1972–86, Grattan PLC 1978–84, Courage Ltd and Imperial Brewing & Leisure Ltd 1981–86; CEO Sears PLC 1986–92; Chair. Freemans PLC 1988–92, Bullough PLC 1996–2002 (Dir 1995–), London Docklands Devt Corpn 1992–98, Servus Holdings Ltd 1997–2001, Nat. House-Building Council 1998–2002, London First Centre 1998–2001; Past Pres. Surrey Co. Cricket Club; Dir (non-exec) Brown Shipley Holdings PLC 1986–93, Electra Investment Trust PLC 1989–2002, Nationwide Bldg Soc. 1991–94, Pinnacle Clubs Ltd 1992–99, Bentalls PLC 1993–2001, United Racecourses (Holdings) Ltd 1995–02; mem. Bd London First 1992–2002 (Deputy Chair. 1998–03); Epsom Downs Racecourse Ltd (Deputy Chair. 2002–06); mem. Cttee The Automobile Asscn 1994–99; Chair. Roedean School Council 1980–90, The Housing Forum 1999–2002, Freeport PLC 2001–03; Gov. Oundle School 1987–2000, Chair. Bd Govs 2004–07; Hon. LLD (East London) 1997. *Leisure interests:* sport, education. *Address:* Kingsbarn, Tothill, Headley, Surrey, KT18 6PU, England. *Telephone:* (1372) 377331. *Fax:* (1372) 363350.

PICKARD, Vivian R., BS, MS; American automobile industry executive and philanthropist; *President, General Motors Foundation and Director, Corporate Relations, General Motors Company;* b. Sturgis, Miss.; ed Ferris State Univ., Central Michigan Univ.; joined General Motors 1980, has held several key roles, including admin. and man. positions within the Finance, Human Resources and Public Policy functions, Pres. General Motors Foundation and Dir, Corp. Relations, General Motors Company 2010–; mem. Bd Washington, DC Martin Luther King, Jr Nat. Memorial, Friends of African and African American Art (Detroit Inst. of Arts), Detroit Regional Chamber Foundation, The Parade Company, New Detroit The Coalition, Fifth Third Bank – Eastern Michigan, Michigan Women's Foundation, Council of Michigan Foundations, Cultural Alliance of Southeastern Michigan, Sphinx Org.; Past Pres. The Black Women's Agenda, Inc.; fmr Chair. Inforum; mem. The Executive Leadership Council; Exec. Cttee for The Links, Inc.; Lifetime mem. Nat. Asscn for the Advancement of Colored People (NAACP), Nat. Council of Negro Women, Nat. Black MBA Asscn, Leadership Detroit; Women of Excellence Award, Michigan Chronicle 2009, Inforum Inner Circle Honoree 2010, Alpha Award of Honor, Alpha Phi Alpha Fraternity, Inc. 2011, Bridge Builder Award, Rainbow PUSH Coalition 2011. *Address:* General Motors Corporation, 300 Renaissance Center, Detroit, MI 48265-3000, USA (office). *Telephone:* (313) 556-5000 (office). *Website:* www.gm.com (office).

PICKENS, T(homas) Boone, Jr, BS; American business executive; *Chairman and CEO, BP Capital;* b. 22 May 1928, Holdenville, Okla; s. of Thomas Boone Pickens and Grace Pickens (née Molonson); m. 1st Lynn O'Brien 1949 (divorced 1971); two s. two d.; m. 2nd Beatrice (Bea) Carr Stuart 1972 (divorced 1998); one step-d.; m. 3rd Nelda Cain 2000 (divorced 2004); m. 4th Madeleine Paulson 2005 (divorced 2012); m. 5th Toni Chapman Brinker 2014; ed Oklahoma A&M (now Oklahoma State) Univ.; delivered newspapers aged 12; geologist, Phillips Petrol-eum Co. 1951–55; Founder, Pres., Chair. Bd Mesa Petroleum Co., Amarillo, Tex. 1956–96; Gen. Partner, Mesa Inc. 1985–; Founder, Chair. and CEO BP Capital (pvt. investment firm) 1997–; f. Pickens Fuel Corpn (now Clean Energy) 1997; mem. Nat. Petroleum Council 1970–; Founder and Chair. United Shareholders Asscn Washington 1986–93; launched the Pickens Plan (to help reduce US dependence on OPEC oil) 2008; inducted into Oklahoma Hall of Fame 2003, Albert Schweitzer Leadership Award, Hugh O'Brian Youth Leadership Foundation 2012. *Publications:* Boone 1987, The Luckiest Guy in the World 2001, The First Billion is the Hardest: Reflections on a Life of Comebacks and America's Energy Future 2008. *Address:* BP Capital, 8117 Preston Road, Suite 260, Dallas TX 75225, USA (office). *Telephone:* (214) 265-4165 (office). *Fax:* (214) 615-3832 (office). *E-mail:* info@bpcap.net (office). *Website:* www.bpcap.net (office); www.boonepickens.com; www.pickensplan.com.

PICKERING, Thomas Reeve, MA; American diplomatist and business execu-tive; *Vice-Chairman, Hills and Company;* b. 5 Nov. 1931, Orange, NJ; s. of Hamilton Reeve Pickering and Sarah P. Chasteney; m. Alice Jean Stover 1955; one s. one d.; ed Bowdoin Coll., Brunswick, Maine, Fletcher School of Law and Diplomacy, Medford, Mass., Univ. of Melbourne, Australia; Lt Commdr USNR 1956–64; joined Dept of State 1959, Intelligence Research Specialist 1960, Foreign Affairs Officer 1961, Arms Control and Disarmament Agency 1961–62; mem. US Del. to Disarmament Conf., Geneva 1962–64; Prin. Officer, Zanzibar 1965–67; Deputy Chief of Mission, Dar es Salaam 1967–69; Deputy Dir Bureau of Politico-Mil. Affairs 1969–73; Exec. Sec. Dept of State, Special Asst to Sec. of State 1973–74; Amb. to Jordan 1974–78; Asst Sec. of State, Bureau of Oceans, Environment and Science 1978–81; Amb. to Nigeria 1981–83; Amb. to El Salvador 1983–85, to Israel 1985–88; Perm. Rep. to UN 1989–92, Amb. to India 1992–93, to Russia 1993–96; Under-Sec. of State for Political Affairs 1997–2000; named Career Amb.; Pres. Eurasia Foundation 1996–97; fmr Sr Vice-Pres. Int. Relations, The Boeing Co., now consultant; Vice-Chair. Hills and Co. 2006–. *Leisure interests:* archaeology, scuba, photography, carpentry. *Address:* Hills and Company, 901 15th Street, NW, Washington, DC 20006 (office); 2318 Kimbro Street, Alexandria, VA 22307-1822, USA (home). *Telephone:* (202) 822-4912 (office); (903) 660-8929 (home).

PICKETT, John Anthony, CBE, PhD, DSc, CChem, FRS, FRSC, FRES; British research chemist and academic; *Michael Elliott Distinguished Research Fellow, Rothamsted Research;* b. 21 April 1945, Leicester, England; s. of Samuel Victor Pickett and Lilian Frances Hoar; m. Ulla Birgitta Skålén 1970; one s. one d.; ed King Edward VII Grammar School, Coalville, Univ. of Surrey; Postdoctoral Fellowship, UMIST (organic chem.) 1970–72; Sr Scientist, Chem. Dept, Brewing Research Foundation, Surrey 1972–76; Prin. Scientific Officer, Dept of Insecticides and Fungicides, Rothamsted Experimental Station 1976–83, Individual Merit (Grade 2) and Head of Dept of Insecticides and Fungicides (now Biological Chem. Div.), Inst. of Arable Crops Research (now Rothamsted Research) 1984–2010, Michael Elliott Distinguished Research Fellow 2010–, Scientific Leader of Chemical Ecology, Rothamsted Research 2010–14; Pres. Int. Soc. of Chemical Ecology (ISCE) 1995; mem. and Chair. Int. Centre of Insect Physiology and Ecology Governing Council, Nairobi 2005–15; mem. Deutsche Akad. der Naturforscher Leopoldina 2001; Foreign mem. Royal Swedish Acad. of Agric. and Forestry 2005; mem. Bd of Trustees, Int. Inst. of Tropical Agric. 2010–16; mem. NAS 2014; Hon. Prof., Univ. of Nottingham 1991; Hon. mem. Academic Staff, Univ. of Reading 1995, Chemical Soc. of Ethiopia; Hon. Fellow, Royal Entomological Soc. 2010; Hon. Distinguished Prof., Cardiff Univ. 2016; Hon. DSc (Aberdeen) 2008; Rank Prize for Nutrition and Crop Husbandry 1995, ISCE Medal 2002, Wolf Prize in Agric. (co-recipient) 2008, Croonian Prize Lecture, Royal Soc. 2008, Milennium Award, Associated Chambers of Commerce and Industry of India 2011. *Research:* chemical ecology and insect pheromones in particular. *Publications:* more than 530 papers, including patents. *Leisure interest:* jazz trumpet playing. *Address:* Biological Chemistry Department, Rothamsted Research, Harpenden, Herts., AL5 2JQ (office); 53 Parkfield Crescent, Kimpton, nr Hitchin, Herts., SG4 8EQ, England (home). *Telephone:* (1582) 938321 (office); (1438) 832832 (home). *Fax:* (1582) 762595 (office). *E-mail:* john.pickett@rothamsted.ac.uk (office). *Website:* www.rothamsted.ac.uk/people/jpickett (office).

PICKETT-HEAPS, Jeremy David, BA, PhD, FAA, FRS; Australian botanist and academic; *Professorial Fellow of Botany, University of Melbourne;* b. 5 June 1940, Bombay, India; m. 1st Charmian Scott 1964; one s. one d.; m. 2nd Julianne Francis 1978; two s.; ed Univ. of Cambridge; Prof., Dept of Molecular, Cellular and Developmental Biology, Univ. of Colorado, Boulder, USA 1970–88; Prof. of Botany, Univ. of Melbourne 1988–, Professorial Fellow 2003–. *Publications:* Green Algae 1975; 180 research publs in peer-reviewed journals. *Address:* School of Botany, University of Melbourne, Parkville, Vic. 3052 (office); PO Box 247, Mallacoota, Vic. 3892, Australia (home). *Telephone:* (3) 5158-0123 (office); (3) 5158-0123 (home). *E-mail:* jeremyph@unimelb.edu.au (office). *Website:* www.cytographics.com (office).

PICKLES, Rt Hon. Sir Eric Jack, Kt; British politician; *Special Envoy for Post-Holocaust issues;* b. 20 April 1952, Keighley, Yorks., England; s. of Jack Pickles and Constance Joyce Pickles; m. Irene Coates 1976; ed Greenhead Grammar School (later Greenhead High School, now Univ. Acad. Keighley), Leeds Polytechnic; worked as Consultant in Employment Practice; Councillor, Bradford Metropolitan Dist Council 1979–91, Leader, Conservative Group 1988–90; Nat. Chair. Young Conservatives 1980–81; Deputy Leader of Conservative Group, Asscn of Metropolitan Authorities 1989–91; MP for Brentwood and Ongar 1992–2010, for Brentwood and Ongar (revised boundary) 2010–17; Opposition Spokesperson for Social Security 1998–2001; Shadow Minister for Transport 2001–02; Shadow Sec. of State for Local Govt and the Regions 2002–03, for Local Govt 2003–05; Shadow Minister for Local Govt 2005–07; Shadow Sec. of State for Communities and Local Govt 2007–09; Sec. of State for Communities and Local Govt 2010–15; UK Special Envoy for Post-Holocaust issues 2015–; mem. Conservative Party Nat. Union Exec. Cttee 1975–97; mem. Conservative Party Nat. Local Govt Advisory Cttee 1985–, One Nation Forum 1987–91; Local Govt Ed., Conservative Newsline 1990–92; Vice-Chair. Conservative Party 1993–97, Deputy Chair. (Local Govt) 2005–07, Chair. 2009–10; mem. (Select Cttees), Environment, Transport and Regional Affairs 1997–98, Environment, Transport and Regional Affairs (Transport Sub-Cttee) 1997–98; mem. Yorkshire Regional Health Authority 1982–90; Chair. Jt Cttee Against Racism 1982–87, Nat. Local Govt Advisory Cttee 1992–95; Vice-Pres. Local Govt Asscn 1997–2010; Trustee, Brentwood Foyer, Brentwood Theatre. *Radio:* fmr presenter on The Eric and Brandon Show for local community radio station Phoenix FM (together with the then Leader of Brentwood Council Brandon Lewis). *Leisure interests:* bird watching, opera, film. *Address:* Human Rights and Democracy Department, Foreign and Commonwealth Office, King Charles Street, London, SW1A 2AH, England (office). *Website:* www.ericpickles.com.

PICULA, Tonino; Croatian politician and historian; b. 31 Aug. 1961, Mali Losinj; ed Zagreb Univ.; Assoc. Prof. and Sec. Kulturni Radnik (magazine), Cultural and Educ. Ass. 1987–89; mem. Exec. Cttee, Int. Sec. SDP of Croatia 1993–; Counsellor, SDP Co. Ass. of Zagreb, mem. Cttee for Int. Co-operation for Local Self-Govt Devt, Pres. City Org. SDP for Velika Gorica 1997–2000; mem. Croatian Parl. 2000–; Minister of Foreign Affairs 2000–03; Mayor of Velika Gorica 2005–09; Observer of European Parl. for Croatia 2012–13, mem. European Parl. (Group of the Progressive Alliance of Socialists and Democrats) 2013–, Chair. Del. for relations with Bosnia and Herzegovina, and Kosovo, Vice-Chair. Del. for relations with Albania, Bosnia and Herzegovina, Serbia, Montenegro and Kosovo. *Address:* European Parliament, Altiero Spinelli 09G265, 60 rue Wiertz, 1047 Brussels, Belgium (office). *Telephone:* (2) 284-59-48 (office). *Fax:* (2) 284-99-48 (office). *E-mail:* tonino.picula@europarl.europa.eu (office). *Website:* www.europarl.europa.eu/meps/en/112744/TONINO_PICULA_history.html (office).

PIEBALGS, Andris; Latvian politician, diplomatist and fmr EU official; b. 17 Sept. 1957, Valmiera; m.; three c.; ed Univ. of Latvia; teacher, Headmaster, Secondary School No. 1, Valmiera 1980–88; desk officer, Head of Dept, Ministry of Educ. 1988–90; Minister of Educ. 1990–93; mem. Parl. 1993–94, Chair. Budget and Finance Cttee; Minister of Finance 1994–95; Amb. to Estonia 1995–97; Perm. Rep. of Latvia to EU 1998–2003; Deputy Sec. of State, Ministry of Foreign Affairs, responsible for relations with EU 2003–04; Head of Cabinet of Commr Kalniete 2004, Commr for Energy, EC 2004–10, for Devt 2010–14; mem. Lead Group of the Scaling Up Nutrition Movt 2011–; mem. UN High Level Group on Sustainable Energy for All 2011–, UN High Level Panel on the post-Millennium Devt Goals agenda beyond 2015 2012–; mem. CP –1991, Latvian Way 1993–2007, Latvia's First Party/Latvian Way 2007–11, Ind. 2011–16, Vienotība (Unity) 2016– (Chair. 2016–17). *Leisure interests:* tennis, skiing. *Address:* Vienotība (Unity), Zigfrīda Annas Meierovica bulv. 12-3, Rīga 1050, Latvia (office). *Telephone:* 6720-5472 (office). *E-mail:* andris.piebalgs@vienotiba.lv (office). *Website:* vienotiba.lv (office).

PIËCH, Ferdinand Karl; Austrian automotive industry executive; b. 17 April 1937, Vienna; grand-s. of Ferdinand Porsche, founder of Porsche, Stuttgart; m. Ursula Piëch; ed Eidgenössische Technische Hochschule (ETH), Zürich; joined Porsche KG in engine testing 1963, Tech. Man. 1971; joined Audi NSU Auto Union AG 1972, Divisional Man. Gen. Testing 1973, mem. Bd of Man. 1975, Vice-Chair. Bd of Man. 1983, Chair. Bd of Man. Audi AG 1988; Chair. Bd Dirs Volkswagen AG 1993–2002, Dir Head of Research and Devt 1995–2000, responsible for Production Optimisation and Purchasing 1996–2001, Chair. Supervisory Bd 2002–15 (resgnd); Chair. Supervisory Bd MAN SE; Pres. Asscn of European Automobile Mfrs 1999–2000; Chair. Scania 2000–02; Hon. Citizen of Zwickau 1999, Ingolstadt 2001, Wolfsburg 2002; Hon. Prof., Tech. Univ., Vienna 2002; Hon. DTech (Tech. Univ. Vienna) 1984; Dr hc (Ben Gurion Univ.) 1997, (ETH, Zurich) 1999; Distinguished Service Medal (1st Class) 1984, Automobile Business Manager of the Century 1999, Automobile Magazine Man of the Year 2011.

PIECHOCIŃSKI, Janusz; Polish politician; b. 15 March 1960, Pancerne (now Studzianki Pancerne), Mazowieckie Voivodship; m. Halina Piechocińska; one s. two d.; ed Warsaw Univ. of Tech., Warsaw School of Econs; researcher, Dept of Econ. and Social History, Warsaw School of Econs 1987–99; Councillor, Mazowieckie Municipal Ass. 1999–2001, 2006–07; mem. Sejm (Parl.) for Warsaw 20 constituency –2005, 2007–11, 2011–, mem. Parl. Cttee on Finance and Budget 1991–97, Chair. Cttee on Infrastructure 2001–05; Deputy Prime Minister and Minister of the Economy 2012–15; Pres. Regional Fund for Environmental Protection and Water Man., Warsaw 1999–2001, Nat. Social Ecological Movt 2005–07; Vice-Pres. Comm. for Economic Reform 1996; mem. Prime Minister's Nat. Council for European Integration 2000–01; mem. Polskie Stronnictwo Ludowe (PSL—Polish People's Party) 1990–, Pres. 2012–15. *Leisure interests:* football (mem. Sejm football team), ecology, politics, history. *Address:* Polskie Stronnictwo Ludowe (Polish People's Party), 00-924 Warsaw, ul. Kopernika 36/40, Poland (office). *Telephone:* (22) 6206020 (office). *Fax:* (22) 6543583 (office). *E-mail:* biuronkw@psl.org.pl (office). *Website:* www.psl.pl (office); www.piechocinski.pl.

PIEDRABUENA RICHARD, Guillermo; Chilean lawyer; *Advocate Member of the Supreme Court;* b. 18 Jan. 1937, Santiago de Chile; m. Isabel Keymer; six c.; ed St George's Coll., Santiago, School of Law, Universidad de Chile, Santiago; lawyer, Consejo de Defensa del Estado 1963–76, Lawyer Counsellor 1976–96, Pres. 1990–93; Sub-Sec., Justice Dept 1970; mem. Appeal Court, Santiago 1997, Special Tribunal of Industrial Property 1993–2000, Advocate mem. 2007–08; Nat. Public Prosecutor of Chile 1999–2007; Advocate mem. Supreme Court 2012–; Prof. of Procedural Law, Universidad de Chile, Universidad Gabriela Mistral; Pres. Asociación Iberoamericana de Ministerios Públicos 2005–07. *Publications include:* Breves comentarios a la reforma procesal penal 1998, El Recurso de apelación y la consulta 1999, Introducción a la reforma procesal penal 2000, 33 años de Historia del Consejo de Defensa del Estado 2009, Memorias del Primer Fiscal Nacional 2011. *Address:* Corte Suprema, Compañia Nº 1140 - 2º Piso, 60301000-0 Santiago (office); Huérfanos 1117, Ofic. 635, Santiago, Chile. *Telephone:* (2) 873-5000 (office); (2) 698-7212. *E-mail:* gpiedrabuenar@tie.cl (office). *Website:* www.pjud.cl/corte-suprema (office).

PIENAAR, Jacobus François, LLB; South African fmr rugby union player; b. 2 Jan. 1967, Vereeniging; s. of Johan Pienaar and Valerie Du Toit; m. Nerene Winter 1996; two s.; ed Patriot High School and Rand Afrikaans Univ.; flanker; capped for S African Schools 1985, S African Under 20 1987, S African Barbarians 1990; Capt. Transvaal 1989–96, won Super 10, Currie Cup and Lion Cup 1993, retained Currie Cup 1994; Capt. S African Rugby Team 1993–96, World Cup winners 1995; holds record for most tests as Capt. of SA (29); played for Saracens, UK 1997–2000, Coach and CEO 2000–02, won Pilkington Cup, then mem. Bd of Dirs; captained the Barbarians v. Leicester 1999; involved in South Africa's failed bid to host the 2011 Rugby World Cup 2005; subject of book by John Carlin, Playing the Enemy: Nelson Mandela 2008, filmed as Invictus 2009; pundit for ITV Sport, Rugby World Cup 2007, 2011; motivational speaker; Dr hc (Univ. of Hertfordshire) 2000; voted by Rugby Union Writers' Club as Rugby Personality of the Year 1995, Newsmaker of the Year in South Africa 1995, Lifetime Achievement Award, British Rugby Writers 1995, voted 50th in the Top 100 Great South Africans 2004, inducted into Int. Rugby Hall of Fame 2005, inducted into IRB Hall of Fame 2011. *Publication:* Rainbow Warrior (autobiog., with Edward Griffiths) 1999. *Leisure interests:* golf, spending time at home.

PIERANTOZZI, Sandra Sumang, BEd; Palauan politician and business executive; b. 9 Aug. 1953, Koror; d. of Yechadrechemai Sumang Demei and Mitsko Wong Sumang; m. Marcello Pierantozzi; ed Palau Mission Acad., Union Coll., USA, Univ. of Hawaii; teacher, Micronesian Occupational Coll. 1974–79; Journal Clerk, First Palau Constitutional Convention 1979; Office Man. Koror Wholesalers 1980; owner pvt. business including MVP Construction & Realty, Belau Business Services, SPACO Finance 1980–; newscaster WALU-TV 1980–82; Clerk of the Senate 1981–91; Minister of Admin. 1991–92; Special Consultant, Nat. Congress 1992–93; Senator, Floor Leader, Chair. Cttee on Health and Social Welfare 1997–2000; Minister of Health 2001–04, of Finance; Vice-Pres. of Palau 2001–05; Minister of State responsible for foreign and domestic affairs 2009–10; mem. Bd of Dirs Palau Chamber of Commerce; Gov. and Dir Pacific Islands Devt Bank; Senate Rep., Bd of Dirs Asscn Pacific Island Legislatures; Sec. Center for Asia-Pacific Women in Politics; Founding Dir Palau Conservation Soc.; f. Sumang Demei Memorial Scholarship Award 1992. *Leisure interests:* philately, numismatics, environmental conservation, travel.

PIERCE, Dame Karen Elizabeth, DCMG, CMG, MA; British diplomatist; *Permanent Representative to United Nations;* b. 23 Sept. 1959; m. Charles Roxburgh; two s.; ed Girton Coll., Cambridge; joined FCO 1981, Japanese language training followed by first posting to Embassy in Tokyo 1984–87, Security Policy Department, FCO 1987–91, Pvt. Sec. to Amb., Embassy in Washington, DC 1992–95, Team Leader for Ukraine, Belarus and Moldova, Eastern Europe Dept, FCO 1996–97, Eastern Adriatic (Balkans) Dept, later Deputy Head of Dept 1997–99, Head of Newsroom 1999–2000, Head, EU Bilateral Dept 2000–01 and concurrently after 9/11 Head of Afghanistan Political Mil. Unit 2000–03, Balkans Co-ordinator and UK Rep. on Contact Group 2003–06, Amb. and Deputy Perm. Rep. to UN, New York 2006–09, Dir South Asia and Afghanistan, FCO 2009–12, Special Rep. for Afghanistan and Pakistan 2010–11, Perm. Rep. to UN and other Int. Orgs, Geneva 2012–15, Amb. to Afghanistan 2015–16, COO, FCO 2016–17, Dir-Gen. Political 2017–18, Perm. Rep. to UN 2018–. *Address:* UK Mission to UN, One Dag Hammarskjöld Plaza, 885 Second Avenue, New York, NY 10017, USA (office). *Telephone:* (212) 745-9200 (office). *Fax:* (212) 745-9316 (office). *E-mail:* uk@un.int (office).

PIERCE, Mary; French (b. Canadian) fmr professional tennis player; b. 15 Jan. 1975, Montréal, Canada; d. of Jim Pierce and Yannick Pierce; turned professional 1989; moved to France 1990; first career title, Palermo 1991; runner-up French Open 1994; winner Australian Open 1995, Tokyo Nichirei 1995; semi-finalist Italian Open, Canadian Open 1996; finalist Australian Open singles 1997, doubles (with Martina Hingis q.v.), 2000; won singles and doubles (with Martina Hingis) French Open 2000; highest singles ranking No. three; winner of doubles (with Martina Hingis q.v.), Pan Pacific; French Fed. Cup team 1990–92, 1994–97, 2003; French Olympic team 1992, 1996, 2004; 28 WTA Tour singles and doubles titles; singles title Acura Classic 2005; won mixed doubles (with Mahesh Bhupathi) Wimbledon Championship 2005; retd after knee injury 2006; coaching in Mauritius 2009–; Dir Mary Pierce Indian Ocean Series 2015–; Vice-Capt. (with Yannick Noah), French Team for Fed. Cup 2017; commentator, Eurosport UK, France Télévisions; mem. Bd of Dirs, Int. Tennis Federation, Professional Tennis Registry; France's (rising star) Burgeon Award 1992, WTA Tour Comeback Player of the Year 1997, Meridith Inspiration Award 2002, la Racchetta d'Oro Award 2012. *Leisure interests:* hiking, jet skiing, boating, shopping, reading, yoga. *Website:* www.marypierce.com.

PIERCY, Marge, AB, MA; American novelist, poet and essayist; b. 31 March 1936, Detroit, Mich.; d. of Robert Douglas Piercy and Bert Bernice Piercy (née Bunnin); m. Ira Wood 1982; ed Univ. of Michigan and Northwestern Univ.; instructor, Gary Extension, Indiana Univ. 1960–62; Poet-in-Residence, Univ. of Kansas 1971; Distinguished Visiting Lecturer, Thomas Jefferson Coll., Grand Valley State Coll. 1975, 1976, 1978, 1980; mem. staff, Fine Arts Work Center, Provincetown, Mass 1976–77; Visiting Faculty, Women's Writers' Conf., Cazenovia, NY 1976, 1978, 1980; Fiction Writer-in-Residence, Holy Cross Univ., Worcester, Mass 1976; Purdue Univ. Summer Write-In 1977; Butler Chair of Letters, State Univ. of NY at Buffalo 1977; poetry and fiction workshops at Writers' Conf., Indian Univ., Bloomington 1977, 1980; poetry, Writers Conf., Vanderbilt Univ. 1981; Visiting Faculty, Women's Writers' Conf., Hartwick Coll. 1979, 1981, 1984; poetry and fiction, Lake Superior Writers' Conf. 1984; Fiction Writer-in Residence, Ohio State Univ. 1986; Elliston Poetry Fellow, Univ. of Cincinnati 1986; master-class in poetry, Omega Inst. for Holistic Studies 1990, 1991, 1994; DeRoy Distinguished Visiting Prof., Univ. of Michigan 1992; Thunder Bay Writers Conf. 1994; Univ. of North Dakota Writers Conf. 1995; Florida Suncoast Writers Conf. 1996; Hassayampa Summer Inst. for Creative Writing, Prescott, Ariz. 1998, 2000, 2002, 2004, 2006; Washington Library Asscn Conf., Spokane 2001; Bilgray Scholar-in-Residence, Temple Emmanuel Residency, Univ. of Arizona 2001; Residency and Silver Memorial Lecture, Temple Israel, Duluth, Minn. 2002; Writer-in-Residence, World Fellowship Center, Conway, NH 2005, World Fellowship Center 2005; mini-residency, Trinity Coll., San Antonio, Tex. 2003, Rowe Camp and Conf. Center 2007, 2009, 2012, Christopher Newport Univ. 2007, St Louis Community Coll. in connection with Nishmah 2007, Wayne State Univ. 2008, State Univ. of NY (SUNY), Brockport 2009, Vermont Studio Center 2009, Lafayette Coll. 2009, Northhampton Community Coll. 2009, 2010, Kripalu Center 2010–11, Univ. of Tennessee 2010, SUNY, Oswego 2011, Univ. of Michigan 2012, Jewish Community of Amherst 2013; Instructor, Juried Intensive Poetry Workshop, Wellfleet 2009–; judge, Leapfrog Press Fiction Contest 2009; mem. Advisory Bd Eastern Massachusetts Abortion Fund 1999–, Advisory Bd FEMSPEC: An Interdisciplinary Feminist Journal 1998–2004, Advisory Bd The Poetry Center at Passaic Co. Community Coll. 2004–, Advisory Bd Carrie A. Seaman Animal Shelter 2005–, Artists Grants Panel in Poetry 2006; Ed. Leapfrog Press 1997–; Poetry Ed. Lilith 2000–; Fiction Ed. Seattle Review 2003–; fmr James B. Angell Scholar and Lucinda Goodrich Downs Scholar; Hon. DLitt (Lesley Coll.), (Bridgewater State Coll.); Hon. DHumLitt (Hebrew Union Coll.) 2004, (Eastern Connecticut State Univ.) 2005; Hopwood Award 1957, Borestone Mountain Poetry Award 1968, 1974, Rhode Island School of Design Faculty Asscn Medal 1985, Orion Scott Award in Humanities, Literary Award, Gov. of Mass Comm. on Status of Women 1974, Nat. Endowment for the Arts Award 1978, Carolyn Kizer Poetry Prize, Calapooya Coll. 1986, 1990, Sheaffer-PEN/New England Award for Literary Excellence 1989, Golden Rose Poetry Prize 1990, Barbara Bradley Award, New England Poetry Club 1992, Brit ha-Dorot Award, Shalom Center 1992. *Recording:* Louder We Can't Hear You (Yet!): The Political Poems of Marge Piercy 2004. *Publications include:* Breaking Camp 1968, Hard Loving 1969, Going Down Fast 1969, Dance the Eagle to Sleep 1970 (republished with new introduction by Marge Piercy 2012), Small Changes 1973, To Be of Use 1973, Living in the Open 1976, Woman on the Edge of Time 1976, The High Cost of Living 1978, Vida 1980 (republished with new introduction by Marge Piercy 2011), The Moon is Always Female 1980, Braided Lives 1982, Circles on the Water 1982, Stone, Paper, Knife 1983, My Mother's Body 1985, Gone to Soldiers 1988, Available Light (May Sarton Award 1991) 1988, Summer People 1989, He, She, and It (published as Body of Glass in UK), (Arthur C. Clarke Award 1993) 1991, Mars and Her Children 1992, The Longings of Women 1994, Eight Chambers of the Heart 1995, City of Darkness, City of Light 1996, What Are Big Girls Made Of? 1997, Storm Tide 1998, Early Grrrl 1999, The Art of Blessing the Day (Paterson Poetry Prize 2000) 1999, Three Women 1999, So You Want to Write: How to Master the Craft of Writing Fiction and the Personal Narrative (with Ira Wood) 2001, 2005, Sleeping with Cats, A Memoir 2002, The Third Child 2003, Colors Passing Through Us (Paterson Award for Literary Achievement 2004) 2003, Sex Wars 2006, The Crooked Inheritance 2006, Pesach for the Rest of Us 2007, The Hunger Moon, New and Selected Poems, 1980–2010 2011, The Cost of Lunch, Etc., (short stories) 2014, Made in Detroit (poetry) 2015. *Address:* PO Box 1473, Wellfleet, MA 02667, USA (home). *Telephone:* (508) 349-3163 (office). *E-mail:* hagolem@c4.net (office). *Website:* www.margepiercy.com (office).

PIERRE, Most Rev. Christophe Louis Yves Georges, MTheol, DCL; French ecclesiastic and diplomatist; *Apostolic Nuncio to USA;* b. 30 Jan. 1946, Rennes; ed Institut Catholique de Paris, Pontifical Ecclesiastical Acad., Rome; ordained as priest, Archdiocese of Rennes 5 April 1970; Vicar, parish of St-Pierre-Saint-Paul de Colombes, Diocese of Nanterre 1970–73; apptd Archbishop 1995, apptd Titular Archbishop of Gunela 1995; entered diplomatic service of the Holy See 1977, held posts in Wellington, New Zealand, Mozambique, Zimbabwe, Cuba and Brazil, served with Perm. Mission to UN, Geneva –1995, Apostolic Nuncio to Haiti 1995–99, to Uganda 1999–2007, to Mexico 2007–16, to USA 2016–. *Address:* Apostolic Nunciature of the Holy See, 3339 Massachusetts Avenue, NW, Washington, DC 20008, USA (office). *Telephone:* (202) 333-7121 (office). *Fax:* (202) 337-4036 (office). *E-mail:* nuntiususa@nuntiususa.org (office). *Website:* nuntiususa.org (office).

PIERRE, D. B. C. (Dirty But Clean); British novelist; b. (Peter Finlay), 18 June 1961, Australia; s. of Dr Keith W. Finlay and Lilian Mary Tate; allegorist, cartoonist, photographer, designer, filmmaker; James Joyce Award, Literary & Historical Soc., Univ. Coll., Dublin 2005. *Television:* Imagine, with Alan Yentob (biographical; BBC) 2004, The Last Aztec (UK Channel 4 two-hour special on the Spanish conquest of Mexico) 2006. *Publications include:* Vernon God Little (Man Booker Prize 2003, Bollinger Everyman Woodhouse Award for Comic Fiction 2003, Whitbread Prize for First Novel 2003) 2003, Ludmila's Broken English 2006, Lights Out in Wonderland 2010, Petit Mal 2013, Breakfast with the Borgias 2014, Release The Bats 2016. *Leisure interests:* travel, music, cricket. *Address:* c/o Conville & Walsh Ltd, Haymarket House, 28–29 Haymarket, London, SW1Y 4SP, England (office). *Telephone:* (20) 7287-3030 (office). *Fax:* (20) 7287-4545 (office). *E-mail:* info@cwagency.co.uk (office). *Website:* www.cwagency.com (office); www.dbcpierre.com.

PIERRE, Ericq; Haitian economist and politician; ed Univ. d'Etat d'Haiti, Ecole Universelle de Paris; teacher, Lycée Nord Alexis 1964–69; Dir FADAC Agric. Project, Petit Bourg du Borgne 1971–73; Supervisor, Plantation Dauphin, Fort Liberté 1973–75; Asst to Econ. Counsellor, US Embassy in Port-au-Prince 1976–79; Economist, Ministry of Agric., Natural Resources and Rural Devt 1979–80; mem. CARICOM Caribbean Basin sub-regional cttee 1981–83; mem. Exec. Cttee, Asscn Nat. des Agro-Professionels 1986–88; Regional Specialist, Inter-American Devt Bank (IDB), Haiti 1980–91, Technical Asst for Central America and Haiti, IDB, Washington, DC 1991–96, Adviser on Argentina and Haiti 1996–2008.

PIERRE-LOUIS, Michèle Duvivier, MEconSc, DH; Haitian economist and politician; b. 5 Oct. 1947, Jeremie; one s.; ed Queens Coll., City Univ. of New York and St Michael's Coll., USA; Operations and Credit Officer, Bank of Nova Scotia 1976–79; Asst Dir-Gen. Nat. Airport Authority 1979–82; Admin. Dir Soc. Financière Haïtienne de Développement (SOFIHDES) 1983–84; Nat. Trainer, Mission Alpha (nat. literacy program) 1986–88; consultant to Pres. Jean-Bertrand Aristide on land reform 1991; Exec. Dir Knowledge and Freedom Foundation 1995–; Prime Minister of Haiti 2008–09; mem. Sec.-Gen.'s High-Level Advisory Bd on Mediation, UN 2017–; Resident Fellow, Inst. of Politics, Harvard Univ., USA 2010; fmr Dir Karl Leveque Inst., Man. Consultant Haitian Devt Foundation.

PIERRET, Christian; French politician, economist and lawyer; *Partner, August Debouzy;* b. 12 March 1946, Bar-le-Duc; s. of Jean Pierret and Anne Radet; m. Marie-Odile Schibler 1978; one d. (and three d. from previous marriages); ed Faculty of Law and Econs, Paris, Inst. d'Etudes Politiques de Paris, Ecole Nat. d'Administration; civil servant, Ministry for the Economy and Finance, then Cour des Comptes 1972–78; fmr Lorraine regional councillor and mem. Vosges Gen. Council; Nat. Ass. Deputy for Vosges 1978–93, 1997–; Vice Minister attached to Minister for the Economy, Finance and Industry, with responsibility for Industry 1997–2002; Mayor of St-Dié-des-Vosges 1989–97, 2002–14, Deputy Mayor 1997–2002; Chair. Caisse Nat. d'Epargne 1986–93; Vice-Chair. Accor Hotels group 1993–96; Chair. Parl. Study Group on Textile and Clothing industry 1988–, France–Israel Parl. Friendship Group 1988–; Vice-Chair. France–Great Britain Parl. Friendship Group 1988–; Chair. Fédération des Villes Moyennes; Regional councillor of Vosges (Saint Dié Est) 1979–89, of Lorraine 1978–88, 1998–2001; Partner, August Debouzy; Pres. Société d'équipement vosgienne 1990, Festival international de géographie 1990; mem. Comité pour l'union monétaire de l'Europe (CUME); lawyer, Paris Bar 2003–; Chevalier de la Légion d'honneur, Chevalier des Palmes Académiques, Chevalier de l'Ordre des Arts et des Lettres. *Publications:* Plan et autogestion, Socialisme et multinationales, Ministre à gauche 2002, France 2012, refusons le déclin! 2011; many articles in various publs. *Address:* 6–8, Avenue de Messine, 75008 Paris, France (office). *Telephone:* 1-45-61-51-80 (office). *E-mail:* contact@christianpierret.net (home). *Website:* www.august-debouzy.com (office); www.christianpierret.net.

PIETERS, Bruno, BA; Belgian fashion designer; *Founder, Honest By;* b. 17 June 1975, Bruges; ed Royal Acad. of Antwerp; began career as an asst designer for Martin Margiela, Josephus Thimister and Christian Lacroix Haute Couture 1999; also worked as freelance designer for cos such as New York Industry, Milan and Antonio Pernas, Madrid; presented his first couture collection entitled 'Part I: Daywear. The Suit' during the Paris couture week in 2001; launched his first complete ready-to-wear collection March 2002; Creative Dir Delvaux 2005–07; Artistic Dir for Hugo Boss 2007–10; Founder, Honest By 2012–; Andam Award, Pierre Berge and Yves St Laurent Foundation 1997, Swiss Textiles Award 2006, Elle Style Award 2008, The H&M Conscious Designer Award 2014. *Address:* c/o MO Communications, 33 avenue de l'Opera, 75002 Paris, France (office); Honest By, Aalmoezenierstraat 2, 2000 Antwerp, Belgium (office). *Telephone:* 1-44-77-93-60 (office). *Fax:* 1-44-77-93-70 (office). *E-mail:* presse@mocommunications.com (office); contact@honestby.com (office). *Website:* www.mocommunications.com (office); www.honestby.com (office).

PIETERSEN, Kevin Peter, MBE; South African-born professional cricketer; b. 27 June 1980, Pietermaritzburg, Natal; s. of Jannie Pietersen and Penny Pietersen (English); m. Jessica Taylor 2007; ed Maritzburg Coll., Univ. of South Africa; moved to England after protesting at racial quota system in SA 2000; right-handed middle order batsman; occasional right-arm off-spin bowler; plays for Natal B 1997–98, KwaZulu-Natal B 1998–99, KwaZulu-Natal 1999–2000, Notts. 2001–04, MCC 2004, Hants. 2005–10, ICC (Int. Cricket Council) World XI 2005, England

2005– (Capt. Test side 2008–09 (resgnd)), Royal Challengers Bangalore (Capt.) 2009–10, Surrey 2010–, Deccan Chargers 2011, Delhi Daredevils 2012–; First-class debut: for Natal B 1997/98; Test debut: England v Australia, Lord's 21–24 July 2005; One-Day Int. (ODI) debut: Zimbabwe v England, Harare, 28 Nov. 2004; T20I debut: England v Australia, Southampton 13 June 2005; has played in 104 Tests, taken 10 wickets and scored 8,181 runs (23 centuries, 35 fifties), highest score 227, average 47.28, best bowling (innings) 3/52, (match) 4/78; ODIs: 136 matches, scored 4,440 runs, average 40.73, highest score 130, took 7 wickets, average 52.85, best bowling 2/22; First-class: 213 matches, 16,053 runs, average 48.79, highest score 254 not out, took 73 wickets, average 51.39, best bowling (innings) 4/31; mem. England Ashes-winning Test team 2009, 2010–11, England ICC Twenty20 World Cup winning team (against Australia), Barbados, West Indies 2010; first batsman to reach 5,000 Test runs in less than five years (taking four years 242 days in Test against Bangladesh, Mirpur 20 March 2010); fastest batsman to reach both 1,000 and 2,000 runs in ODI cricket and has highest average of any England player to have played more than 20 innings of one-day cricket; has second-highest run total from his first 25 Tests, behind only Donald Bradman; only third English batsman to top ICC ODI rankings March 2007; ICC Emerging Player of the Year 2005, ICC One-Day Player of the Year 2005, Wisden Cricketer of the Year 2006, called by The Times "the most complete batsman in cricket" 2008, Player of the Tournament, ICC Twenty20 World Cup 2010. *Publication:* Kevin Pietersen: Crossing the Boundary (autobiog.) 2007. *Address:* c/o Surrey County Cricket Club, The Kia Oval, Kennington, London, SE11 5SS, England. *Telephone:* (20) 7820-5700. *Fax:* (20) 7735-7769. *E-mail:* enquiries@surreycricket.com. *Website:* www.kiaoval.com.

PIETRUSKI, John Michael, BS; American business executive; b. 12 March 1933, Sayreville, NJ; s. of John M. Pietruski, Sr and Lillian Christensen Pietruski; m. Roberta Jeanne Talbot 1954; two s. one d.; ed Sayreville High School and Rutgers Univ.; First Lt US Army 1955–57; Mfg Man., Industrial Eng Man., Procter & Gamble Co. 1954–63; Pres. Medical Products and Hosp. Divs, C.R. Bard, Inc. 1963–77; Pres. Pharmaceutical Group, Sterling Drug Inc. 1977–81, Corp. Exec. Vice-Pres. 1981–83, Pres. and COO 1983–85, Chair. and CEO 1985–88, mem. Bd of Dirs 1977–88; Pres. Dansara Co. 1988–; Chair. Bd Encysive Pharmaceuticals Inc. (fmrly Texas Biotech Corp.) 1990–2008; mem. Bd of Dirs Irving Bank Corpn 1985–89, Associated Dry Goods Corpn 1985–88, Hershey Foods Corpn 1987–2003, Cytogen Corpn 1989–94, Gen. Public Utilities Corpn 1989–2001, Lincoln Nat. Corpn 1989–2003, McKesson Corpn 1990–99, PDI Inc. 1998–2010, FirstEnergy Corpn 2001–04, Xylos Corpn 2001–12, Trial Card Inc. 2002–10; mem. Pharmaceutical Mfrs Asscn 1985–88; Trustee Rutgers Univ. Foundation 1985–94; Regent, Concordia Coll. 1993–2003, 2005–; Hon. LLD 1993. *Leisure interests:* boating, fishing, travelling, athletics. *Address:* Suite 3408, One Penn Plaza, New York, NY 10119, USA (home). *Telephone:* (212) 268-5510 (office). *Fax:* (212) 268-5765 (office).

PIGEAT, Henri Michel; French civil administrator and publisher; *President and CEO, Editions de l'Ilissos;* b. 13 Nov. 1939, Montluçon; s. of Eugène Pigeat and Odette Micard; m. Passerose Cyprienne Rueff 1976; one d.; ed Inst. des Sciences Politiques, Paris and Ecole Nat. d'Admin; Civil Servant Office of Gen. Admin. and Public Service 1965–69; Head Office of Sec. of State for Public Service 1969–71, Tech. Adviser 1971–72; Head of Information Services, Office of Sec. of State for Public Service and Information 1973; Sec.-Gen. Interministerial Cttee for Information 1973–74; Asst Gen. Dir Information, Gen. Office of Information 1974, Dir 1975–76; Dir Information and Broadcasing Service 1976–; Deputy Man. Dir Agence France-Presse 1976–79, Chair. and Man. Dir 1979–86; Chair. and Man. Dir IBIS SA: Prof. Univ. of Paris II; Prof. Inst. d'Etudes Politiques de Paris 1986–92; Dir Soc. nat. des entreprises de presse 1974–76; Dir Soc. financière de radiodiffusion (Sofirad) 1972–76; fmr Dir E1, RMC, Sud Radio, SNEP, TDF, Europe 1, Radio Monte Carlo; Maître de conférances, Inst. d'études politiques, Paris 1966–73, Ecole nat. d'admin. 1967–69, Inst. int. d'admin publique 1966–73; CEO Burson Marsteller 1987–89; Pres. Quicom SA; mem. Exec. Cttee Int. Inst. of Communications, London, fmr Pres. of French section; Pres. and Dir Gen. L & A Editions 2000; Pres. and CEO Editions de l'Ilissos 2002–; mem. Int. Press Inst.; Chevalier, Ordre nat. du Mérite; Commdr Nat. Order of FRG. *Publications:* La France contemporaine, L'Europe contemporaine (both jointly) 1966–70, Saint Ecran ou la télévision par câbles 1974, Du téléphone à la télématique, La télévision par cable commence demain 1983, Le nouveau désordre mondial de l'information 1987, Les agences de presse 1997, Médias et déontologie 1997, Tendences Economiques Internationales de la Presse 2002. *Leisure interest:* tennis. *Address:* Editions de l'Ilissos, 14 rue de la Sourdière, 75001 Paris (office); 23 quai Antatole France, 75007 Paris, France (home). *Telephone:* 1-42-60-11-03 (office); 1-45-51-70-01 (home). *E-mail:* edesc@wanadoo.fr (home).

PIGGOTT, Arnold A., BBA; Trinidad and Tobago diplomatist, politician and fmr banker; m. Allison Wendy Kitson-Piggott; two s. one d.; ed St Francis Coll., Brooklyn, New York; pvt. consultant in electronic banking –2001; mem. Senate (Parl.) 2007–10; Minister of Works and Transport 2001–02; High Commr to Canada 2003–06; Minister of Foreign Affairs and Govt Senator 2006–07, Minister of Agric., Land and Marine Resources 2007–10; Chair. Bd of Man., Bishop Anstey Jr School 1992–97.

PIGGOTT, Lester Keith; British fmr professional jockey and trainer; b. 5 Nov. 1935, Wantage, Oxon., England; s. of Keith Piggott and Iris Rickaby; m. Susan Armstrong 1960; two d.; one s. with Anna Ludlow; rode over 100 winners per year in UK alone in several seasons since 1955; rode 3,000th winner in UK 27 July 1974; Champion Jockey 11 times (1960, 1964–71); frequently rode in France; equalled record of 21 classic victories 1975; retd Oct. 1985; races won include: 1000 Guineas (twice): Humble Duty 1970, Fairy Footsteps 1981; 2000 Guineas (five times): Crepello 1957, Sir Ivor 1968, Nijinsky 1970, Shadeed 1985, Rodrigo de Triano 1992; the Derby (nine times): Never Say Die 1954, Crepello 1957, St Paddy 1960, Sir Ivor 1968, Nijinsky 1970, Roberto 1972, Empery 1976, The Minstrel 1977, Teenoso 1983; St Leger (eight times): St Paddy 1960, Aurelius 1961, Ribocco 1967, Ribero 1968, Nijinsky 1970, Athens Wood 1971, Boucher 1972, Commanche Run 1984; Prix de l'Arc de Triomphe (three times): Rheingold 1973, Alleged 1977, 1978; Breeders' Cup Mile, USA: Royal Academy 1990; Washington, DC Int. on Sir Ivor 1968 (first time since 1922 an English Derby winner raced in USA), Karabas 1969, Argument 1980; trainer 1985–87; sentenced to three years' imprisonment for tax fraud Oct. 1987, released after 12 months, returned to racing Oct. 1990; retd as jockey 1995; achieved a record of 30 classic wins; 4,493 winners in total; nickname The Long Fellow; OBE (withdrawn); British flat racing Champion Jockey 1960, 1964, 1965, 1966, 1967, 1968, 1969, 1970, 1971, 1981, 1982, annual jockey awards, The Lesters, named in his honour 1990. *Leisure interests:* swimming, water skiing, golf. *Address:* Florizel, Newmarket, Suffolk, CB8 0NY, England. *Telephone:* (1683) 662584.

PIGOTT, Mark C., BA, BS, MS; American business executive; *Executive Chairman, PACCAR Inc.;* b. 1954; s. of Charles McGee Pigott and Yvonne Flood; ed Stanford Univ.; Internal Auditor, PACCAR Inc. 1977–88, Vice-Pres. 1988–90, Sr Vice-Pres. 1990–93, Exec. Vice-Pres. 1993–95, mem. Bd of Dirs 1994–, Vice-Chair. 1995–96, Chair. and CEO 1997–2013, Exec. Chair. 2013–; Chair. PACCAR Foundation Europe; mem. Washington State Roundtable, World Econ. Forum; Hon. OBE 2003, Hon. KBE 2012. *Address:* PACCAR Inc., 777 106th Avenue NE, Bellvue, WA 98004, USA (office). *Telephone:* (425) 468-7400 (office). *Fax:* (425) 468-8216 (office). *Website:* www.paccar.com (office).

PIGOZZI, Jean, BA; Italian photographer and investor; *Owner, Contemporary African Art Collection;* b. 1952, Paris, France; s. of Henry Pigozzi; ed lycée in Paris, Harvard Univ., USA; worked in Accounting Dept at Gaumont Film Co., Paris and at Fox Studios, Los Angeles, USA 1975–80; venture capital investor, mainly in USA and UK 1981–; est. Contemporary African Art Collection 1992, world's largest collection of contemporary African Art; recently est. Liquid Jungle Lab in Panama working on high-tech ecological research with Smithsonian Tropical Research Inst., Woods Hole Oceanographic Inst., Royal Botanical Garden of Madrid, Yale School of Forestry; started JaPigozzi-Collection of contemporary Japanese art 2006; created LimoLand-clothing and accessories line featuring bright colours and prints 2007. *Publications:* Pigozzi's Journal of the Seventies 1979, A Short Visit to Planet Earth: Photographs 1991, Catalogue Déraisonné 2010, Pool Party 2016. *Address:* The Contemporary African Art Collection, Geneva, Switzerland (office). *E-mail:* caacart-contact@cogitel-forum.com (office). *Website:* www.caacart.com (office); www.jeanpigozzi.com.

PIKE, Edward Roy, PhD, CPhys, CMath, FRS, FInstP, FIMA, FRMS; British physicist and academic; *Professor Emeritus of Physics, King's College London;* b. 4 Dec. 1929, Perth, Western Australia; s. of Anthony Pike and Rosalind Irene Davies; m. Pamela Sawtell 1955; one s. two d.; ed Southfield Grammar School, Oxford, Univ. Coll., Cardiff; Royal Corps of Signals 1948–50; Instructor, Physics Faculty, MIT 1958–60; Sr Scientific Officer, Royal Signals and Radar Establishment Physics Group 1960, Prin. Scientific Officer 1967, Deputy Chief Scientific Officer 1973, Chief Scientific Officer 1984–91; Visiting Prof. of Math., Imperial Coll. London 1985–86; Clerk Maxwell Prof. of Theoretical Physics, King's Coll. London 1986–2010, Prof. Emer. 2010–, Head, School of Physical Sciences and Eng 1991–94; fmr Fulbright Scholar; Chair. Oval (114) Ltd 1984–85; Vice-Pres. for Publs, Inst. of Physics 1981–85; Chair. Adam Hilger Ltd 1981–85, Stilo Tech. Ltd 1996–2002; Chair. (non-exec.), Stilo International PLC 2000–02, Dir (non-exec.) 2002–04; Dir (non-exec.), Richard Clay plc 1985–86, Phonologica Ltd 2004–05; Fellow, King's Coll. London; Royal Soc. Charles Parsons Medal and Lecture 1975, MacRobert Award (co-recipient) and Lecture 1977, Worshipful Co. of Scientific Instrument Makers Annual Achievement Award (co-recipient) 1978, Civil Service Award to Inventors 1980, Guthrie Medal and Prize, Inst. of Physics 1996. *Publications:* The Quantum Theory of Radiation (co-author) 1995, Light Scattering and Photon Correlation Spectroscopy (co-author) 1997, Scattering (co-author) 2002; Jt-Ed.: Photon Correlation and Light-Beating Spectroscopy 1974, High Power Gas Lasers 1975, Photon Correlation Spectroscopy and Velocimetry 1977, Frontiers in Quantum Optics 1986, Fractals, Noise and Chaos 1987, Quantum Measurement and Chaos 1987, Squeezed and Non-classical Light 1988, Photons and Quantum Fluctuations 1988, Inverse Problems in Scattering and Imaging 1992, The Limits of Resolution (co-author) 2016; numerous papers in scientific journals. *Leisure interests:* music, languages, woodwork. *Address:* Physics Department, King's College, Strand, London, WC2R 2LS (office); 22 Mathew Close, North Kensington, London, W10 5YJ, England (home). *Telephone:* (20) 7848-2043 (office). *Fax:* (20) 7848-2420 (office). *E-mail:* roy.pike@kcl.ac.uk (office). *Website:* www.kcl.ac.uk/nms/depts/physics/people/emeritus (office).

PIKE, Rosamund Mary, BA; British actress; b. 28 Jan. 1979, London; d. of Julian Pike and Caroline Pike (née Friend); pnr Robie Uniacke; two s.; ed Badminton School, Wadham Coll., Oxford; began acting career with Nat. Youth Theatre. *Theatre includes:* Hitchcock Blonde 2002, Summer and Smoke 2006, Gaslight 2007, Madame de Sade 2009, Hedda Gabler 2010. *Films include:* Die Another Day (Empire Awards Best Newcomer 2003) 2002, Bond Girls Are Forever 2002, Promised Land 2004, The Libertine (British Independent Film Awards Best Supporting Actress 2005) 2004, Pride & Prejudice 2005, Doom 2005, Fracture 2007, Fugitive Pieces 2007, An Education 2009, Surrogates 2009, Yesterday We Were in America 2009, Burning Palms 2010, Jackboots on Whitehall 2010, Barney's Version 2010, Made in Dagenham 2010, The Organ Grinder's Monkey 2011, Johnny English Reborn 2011, The Big Year 2011, The Devil You Know 2012, Wrath of the Titans 2012, Jack Reacher 2012, The World's End 2013, A Long Way Down 2014, Hector and the Search for Happiness 2014, What We Did on Our Holiday 2014, Gone Girl (London Film Critics Circle Awards British Actress of the Year 2014, Palm Springs Int. Film Festival Breakthrough Performance 2014) 2014, Gone Girl 2014, Return To Senders 2015, A United Kingdom 2016, The Man with the Iron Heart 2017, Hostiles 2017, Beirut 2018. *Television includes:* A Rather English Marriage 1998, Wives and Daughters 1999, Love in a Cold Climate 2001, Foyle's War 2002, Freefall 2009, Women in Love 2011. *Address:* United Agents, 12–26 Lexington Street, London, W1F 0LE, England (office). *Telephone:* (20) 3214-0800 (office). *Fax:* (20) 3214-0801 (office). *E-mail:* saustin@unitedagents.co.uk (office). *Website:* unitedagents.co.uk (office).

PIKETTY, Thomas, MSc, PhD; French economist and academic; *Professor of Economics, Paris School of Economics;* b. 7 May 1971, Clichy; ed Ecole normale supérieure (ENS), Econs, Ecole des Hautes Etudes en Sciences Sociales, London School of Econs, UK; Asst Prof., Dept of Econs, MIT, USA 1993–95, Visiting Prof. 2000–01; Research Fellow, CNRS and Centre pour la Recherche Économique et ses applications, Paris 1995–2000; Prof. of Econs, Ecole des Hautes Etudes en Sciences Sociales, Paris 2000–; Dir Paris School of Econs 2005–07, Prof. of Econs 2007–; Centennial Prof., International Inequalities Inst., LSE 2015–; Co-Dir Public Policy Programme, Center for Econ. and Policy Research, London 2002–13; Dir Dept of

Social Sciences, ENS 2004–06; Co-ed. Journal Public Economics 1996–2012; columnist, Libération, Le Monde; CNRS Bronze Medal 2001, Best Young Economist, Le Monde/Le Cercle des économistes 2002, Yrjö Jahnsson Prize, European Econ. Asscn 2013. *Publications include:* World Top Incomes Database (with F. Alvaredo, A. Atkinson and E. Saez) 2011–14, A Theory of Optimal Inheritance Taxation (with E. Saez) 2013, Capital is Back: Wealth-Income Ratios in Rich Countries 1700–2010 (with G. Zucman) 2014, Le capital au 21e siècle (Capital in the 21st Century) (Prix Pétrarque de l'essai France Culture-Le Monde 2014, The Economics of Inequality 2015, Chronicles: On Our Troubled Times 2016; numerous articles published in journals including Quarterly Journal of Economics, Journal of Political Economy, American Economic Review, Review of Economic Studies. *Address:* Paris School of Economics, Campus Paris-jourdan, 48, boulevard Jourdan, Building B, 1st Floor, Office B112, 75014 Paris, France (office). *Telephone:* 1-43-13-62-50 (office). *E-mail:* piketty@psemail.eu (office); thomas .piketty@psemail.eu (office). *Website:* piketty.pse.ens.fr (office); www.lse.ac.uk/ International-Inequalities (office).

PIKHOYA, Rudolf Germanovich, DHistSc; Russian historian; b. 27 Jan. 1947, Polevskoe, Sverdlovsk Region; m.; one s.; ed Ural Univ.; with Ural Univ. 1971–, Pro-Rector 1986–90; Sr Researcher, Ural Scientific Centre, USSR Acad. of Sciences 1981–86; Chair. Cttee on problems of archives, Council of Ministers of Russian Fed. 1990–, Chief, Archive Service of Russia 1992–96; participated in movt for making secret documents of the Communist period public; Vice-Pres. Int. Fund for Democracy, Dir of Research Programmes 1996–98; Prof. and Chair. Acad. of State Service 1998–. *Publications:* The History of Modern Russia – The Crisis of the Communist Regime in the USSR and the Birth of the New Russia End of 1970–1991 2008. *Leisure interest:* music. *Address:* Academy of State Service, Vernadskogo prospekt 84, 117606 Moscow, Russian Federation. *Telephone:* (495) 436-98-14.

PIKIOUNE, Gaetan; Ni-Vanuatu accountant and politician; *Minister of Finance and Economic Management;* b. 6 July 1965, Santo; accountant, Coravi 1983–86; accountant and Man., Nitchiku (agricultural machinery co.) 1986; MP for Banks constituency 2016–; Minister of Finance and Econ. Man. 2016–; mem. Nagriamel. *Address:* Ministry of Finance and Economic Management, PMB 9031, Port Vila, Vanuatu (office). *Telephone:* 23032 (office). *Fax:* 27937 (office). *E-mail:* rdaniel@ vanuatu.gov.vu (office). *Website:* doft.gov.vu (office).

PIKIS, Georghios M., LLB; Cypriot judge; b. 22 Jan. 1939, Larnaca; s. of Michael I. Pikis and Erini M. Pikis; m. Maria G. Pikis (née Papaneophytou); two s. one d.; ed Univ. of London, UK; called to the Bar, Gray's Inn, London 1961; Advocate of the Cyprus Bar 1961–66; Dist Judge 1966–72; Pres. Dist Court 1972–81; Justice of Supreme Court of Cyprus 1981–95, Pres. Supreme Court 1995–2004; Judge, Appeals Div., Int. Criminal Court, The Hague 2003–09, full-time mem. 2004–09; *ad hoc* judge, European Court of Human Rights 1993, 1997; mem. UN Cttee against Torture 1996–98; mem. Bd of Dirs Int. Asscn of Supreme Admin. Jurisdictions 1999–2004; mem. Circle of Pres of Conf. of European Constitutional Courts 1999–2004, Pres. 2002–04. *Publications:* books: Criminal Procedure in Cyprus (in English, co-author) 1975, Sentencing in Cyprus (in English) 1978, The Common Law and Principles of Equity and Their Application in Cyprus (in Greek) 1981, Basic Aspects of Cyprus Law (in Greek) 2003, Constitutionalism – Human Rights – Separation of Powers, The Cyprus Precedent (in English) 2006, Rome Statute for the International Criminal Court 2010; numerous lectures, speeches and reports (including reports to Int., European and Commonwealth Judicial Confs and Asscns) on human rights, constitutional law and the judiciary.

PIKRAMMENOS, Panagiotis; Greek judge and government official; b. 26 July 1945, Athens; s. of Otto Pikrammenou; m. Athina Noutsou; one d.; ed German School of Athens, Law School at Kapodistrian Univ. of Athens, Pantheon-Assas Paris II Univ., France; worked as a lawyer in Athens and London, UK; became rapporteur of Council of State 1976, held several sr positions, then Pres. 2009–12; worked on several legis. cttees for Ministry of Justice; special adviser on judicial affairs to Prime Minister Konstantinos Mitsotakis 1991–93; Gen. Man. Nat. School of Judges 2005–09; Prime Minister of Greece 16 May–20 June 2012; Ind.

PĪKS, Rihards; Latvian politician; b. 31 Dec. 1941, Rīga; m. Sarmīte Pīka; four c.; ed All-Union Cinematography Inst., Moscow, two-year advanced filmmaking course, Moscow; film dir, producer, cameraman, Rīga Film Studio –1987, Studio Dir 1987–1990; Founder-Dir Nat. Cinematography Centre 1991–93, SIA Baltic Cinema 1993–95; Founder-Pres. Baltic Films asscn 1991–93; Founder, lecturer Cinematography Dept, Latvian Acad. of Culture 1993–95; Deputy Chair. Nat. Radio and TV Council 1995–96; Minister for Culture 1996–97; Pres. SIA Audiovizualie Multimediji Baltija 1997–98; mem. Parl. 1998–, Deputy Speaker 1999–2002, Chair. Foreign Affairs Cttee Feb.–March 2004; Minister of Foreign Affairs March–July 2004; mem. European Parl. 2004–09; mem. People's Party; around 20 int. awards at film festivals; Commdr, Order of Merit (Italy). *Films:* as dir: four full length features, five documentaries; as producer: 35 full length features; as cameraman: 20 documentaries; as dir of photography: 11 full length features. *Publications:* numerous articles in newspapers and magazines. *Leisure interests:* basketball, summer, nature, tourism. *Address:* 29 Balozu prosp., 1024 Rīga, Latvia. *Telephone:* 6799-4803. *Fax:* 6799-4803. *E-mail:* rpiks@inbox.lv; piks .rihards@gmail.com.

PILARCZYK, Most Rev. Daniel Edward, MA, PhD, STD; American ecclesiastic; *Archbishop Emeritus of Cincinnati;* b. 12 Aug. 1934, Dayton, Ohio; s. of Daniel J. Pilarczyk and Frieda S. Hilgefort; ed St Gregory Seminary, Ohio, Pontifical Urban Univ. Rome, Xavier Univ. Cincinnati and Univ. of Cincinnati; ordained Roman Catholic priest 1959; Asst Chancellor, Archdiocese of Cincinnati 1961–63; Faculty, Athenaeum of Ohio (St Gregory Seminary) 1963–74, Vice-Pres. 1968–74, Trustee 1974–; Rector, St Gregory Seminary 1968–74; Synodal Judge, Archdiocesan Tribunal 1971–82; Dir of Archdiocesan Educ. Services 1974–82; Auxiliary Bishop of Cincinnati 1974–82, Archbishop 1982–2009, Archbishop Emer. 2009–, pleaded no contest on behalf of the Archdiocese to five misdemeanor counts of failing to report a crime during period 1978–82 2003; Vice-Pres. Nat. Conf. of Catholic Bishops 1986–89, Pres. 1989–92; mem. Episcopal Bd Int. Comm. on English in Liturgy 1987–97; mem. Jt Cttee of Orthodox and Catholic Bishops 2002; numerous professional appintments; Hon. LLD (Xavier Univ.) 1975, (Calumet Coll.) 1982, (Univ. of Dayton) 1990, (Marquette Univ.) 1990, (Thomas More Coll.)

1991, (Coll. of Mount St Joseph) 1994, (Hebrew Union Coll./Jewish Inst. of Religion) 1997, Dr hc (Athenaeum of Ohio, Cincinnati) 2007; Distinguished Alumni Award, Univ. of Cincinnati 2001, Bishop John England Award 2009, Daniel J. Kane Religious Communication Award 2010. *Publications:* Twelve Tough Issues 1988, We Believe 1989, Living in the Lord 1990, The Parish: Where God's People Live 1991, Forgiveness 1992, What Must I Do? 1993, Our Priests: Who They Are and What They Do 1994, Lenten Lunches 1995, Bringing Forth Justice 1996, Thinking Catholic 1997, Practicing Catholic 1998, Believing Catholic 2000, Live Letters 2001, Twelve Tough Issues and More 2002, Being Catholic: How We Believe, Practice and Think 2006, When God Speaks 2006; numerous articles in newspapers and journals. *Address:* 100 East Eighth Street, Cincinnati, OH 45202, USA (office). *Telephone:* (513) 421-3131 (office). *E-mail:* dpilarczyk@ catholiccincinnati.org (office). *Website:* www.catholiccincinnati.org.

PILGER, John Richard; Australian journalist, filmmaker and writer; b. Sydney, NSW; s. of Claude Pilger and Elsie Pilger (née Marheine); m. (divorced); one s. one d.; ed Sydney High School, Journalism Cadet Training, Australian Consolidated Press; journalist, Sydney Daily/Sunday Telegraph 1958–62, Reuters, London 1962; feature writer, columnist and Chief Foreign Corresp., Daily Mirror, London 1963–86; columnist, New Statesman, London 1991–2014; freelance contrib., The Guardian, London, The Independent, London, The New Internationalist, UK, Counterpunch, Consortiumnews.com, Z-Net; documentary filmmaker, Granada TV, UK 1969–71, Associated Television 1972–80, Central/Carlton/Granada Television, UK 1980–; Visiting Fellow, Deakin Univ., Australia 1995; Frank H. T. Rhodes Visiting Prof., Cornell Univ., USA 2003–; Hon. DLitt (Staffordshire Univ.) 1994, (Lincoln) 2008; Hon. PhD (Dublin City Univ.) 1995, (Kingston) 1999, (Open Univ.); Hon. DArts (Oxford Brookes Univ.) 1997; Hon. DrIur (St Andrews) 1999; Hon. DUniv (Open Univ.) 2001; Hon. DrLaw (Rhodes, SA) 2008; Descriptive Writer of the Year, UK 1966, Journalist of the Year, UK 1967, 1979, Int. Reporter of the Year, UK 1970, Reporter of the Year, UK 1974, BAFTA Richard Dimbleby Award 1991, US Acad. Award (Emmy) 1991, Reporteurs sans frontières, France 1993, George Foster Peabody Award, USA 1992, Sophie Prize for Human Rights 2003, Royal TV Soc. Award 2005, One World Award for Best Documentary 2008, Sydney Peace Prize 2009, Grierson Trust Lifetime Award 2011, International Journalism Prize, Mexico, 2017, Order of Timor-Leste 2017. *Feature film:* The Last Day 1983. *Documentary films include:* Cambodia: Year Zero 1979 (and four other films on Cambodia), The Quiet Mutiny 1970, Do You Remember Vietnam 1978 (and four other films on Vietnam), Mexico 1980, The Truth Game 1983, Nicaragua: the Right to Life 1985, Japan Behind the Mask 1986, The Last Dream 1988, Death of a Nation 1994, Flying the Flag: Arming the World 1994, Inside Burma 1996, Breaking The Mirror: The Murdoch Effect 1997, Apartheid Did Not Die 1998, Welcome to Australia 1999, Paying the Price: Killing the Children of Iraq 2000, The New Rulers of the World 2001, Palestine Is Still The Issue 2002, Breaking the Silence: Truth and Lies in the War on Terror 2003, Stealing a Nation 2004, The War on Democracy 2007, The War You Don't See 2010, Utopia 2013, The Coming War on China 2016. *Achievements include:* articles and films credited with alerting much of int. community to horrors of Pol Pot regime in Cambodia, also occupation of Timor-Leste, successful campaign on behalf of Thalidomide children for recognition and compensation, successful campaign to make safe and upgrade maternity services at Hackney General Hospital, London, to save school in Lewisham, London, from closure, successful raising of awareness for the indigenous people of Australia. *Publications include:* The Last Day 1975, Aftermath: The Struggle of Cambodia and Vietnam 1981, The Outsiders 1983, Heroes 1986, A Secret Country 1989, Distant Voices 1992, Hidden Agendas 1998, Reporting the World: John Pilger's Great Eyewitness Photographers 2001, The New Rulers of the World 2002, 2016, Tell Me No Lies: Investigative Journalism and its Triumphs (ed) 2004, Freedom Next Time 2006. *Leisure interests:* swimming, reading, sunning, mulling. *Address:* 57 Hambalt Road, London, SW4 9EQ, England (home). *Telephone:* (20) 8673-2848 (home). *E-mail:* jpilger2003@yahoo.co.uk (home). *Website:* www.johnpilger.com.

PILLAY, Navanethem (Navi), BA, LLB, LLM, SJD; South African judge and UN official; b. 23 Sept. 1941, Durban; m. (deceased); two d.; ed Natal Univ., Harvard Univ., USA; first woman to start a law practice in Natal Prov. 1967, Sr Partner 1967–95; first black woman apptd Acting Judge High Court of SA 1995; Judge, UN Int. Criminal Tribunal for Rwanda 1995–2003, Pres. 1999–2003; Judge, Int. Criminal Court 2003–08; UN High Commr for Human Rights, Geneva 2008–14; Chair. Equality Now 1990–95, Hon. Chair. 1995–; Pres. Advice Desk for Abused Women 1989–99, Women Lawyers' Asscn 1995–98; Vice-Chair. of Council, Univ. of Durban-Westville 1995–98; Lecturer, Dept of Public Law, Natal Univ. 1980; Trustee, Legal Resources Centre 1995–98, Lawyers for Human Rights 1998–2001; mem. Women's Nat. Coalition 1992–93, Black Lawyers' Asscn 1995–98, UN Expert Groups on Refugees and on Gender Persecution 1997, Rules Bd for Courts 1997–98, Expert Group on African Perspectives on Universal Jurisdiction, Cairo and Arusha 2001–02; currently mem. Int. Criminal Law Network, Advisory Bd Journal of Int. Criminal Justice, Bd Harvard-South Africa Scholarship Cttee, Bd Dirs Nozala Investments (women's component of Nat. Econ. Initiative); Hon. mem. American Soc. of Int. Law; Unifem and Noel Foundation Life Award (Los Angeles), Award for Leadership in the Fight for Human Rights, California Legislative Assembly, Dr Edgar Brookes Award, Natal Univ., Award for Outstanding contrib. in Raising Awareness of Women's Rights and Domestic Violence, Advice Desk for Abused Women, Award for Dedication to Human Rights, Equality Now, New York, One Hundred Heroines Award, Washington DC, Human Rights Award, Int. Asscn of Women Judges, Award for High Achievement by a Woman in the Legal Profession, Center for Human Rights and Univ. of Pretoria; further awards from Asscn of Law Soc. of SA, Black Lawyers' Asscn, Feminist Majority Foundation, Int. Bar Asscn, Peter Gruber Foundation. *Publications include:* contrib.: Civilians in War 2001, Essays in Memory of Judge Cassese 2003.

PILLAY, Patrick Georges, MA; Seychelles politician and diplomatist; two s. (one adopted) one d.; fmr Minister of Educ., of Youth and Culture, of Industries and Int. Business; fmr Seychelles Gov. to African Devt Bank; fmr Pres. Seychelles Nat. Comm. for UNESCO; Minister of Health –2005, of Foreign Affairs 2005–10; High Commr to UK 2010–12; cand. in presidential election 2015; Speaker, National Assembly 2016–18 (resgnd); fmr mem. Linyon Demokratik Seselwa (Seychellois Democratic Alliance); currently mem. and Leader, Lalyans Seselwa (Seychellois Alliance). *Address:* Lalyans Seselwa (Seychellois Alliance), Bodco Building,

Victoria, Seychelles (office). *Telephone:* 4410277 (office). *E-mail:* lalyansseselwa@gmail.com.

PILNÝ, Ivan; Czech management consultant and politician; b. 6 July 1944, Prague; m.; four c.; ed Czech Tech. Univ., Prague; Gen. Man., Microsoft, Czech Repub. 1992–98; Chair. Czech Telecom 2000–01; CEO eTEL 2001–02; co-f. Občané.cz political party 2009, Vice-Chair. 2009–12; mem. Chamber of Deputies (Poslanecká Sněmovna) for Hradec Králové Region 2013–17, Chair. Econ. Cttee; Minister of Finance May–Dec. 2017; mem. Ano (YES) 2014–; Pres. Asscn for Information Soc. (SPIS) 1997–98, Tuesday Business Network 2003–. *Address:* c/o Ano (YES), Babická 2329/2, 149 00 Prague 4, Czech Republic (office). *Telephone:* 272192122. *E-mail:* kubovicova@anobudelip.cz.

PILON, Jean-Guy, OC, LLB, CQ; Canadian poet; b. 12 Nov. 1930, Saint-Polycarpe, Quebec; s. of Arthur Pilon and Alida Besner; m. 2nd Denise Viens 1988; two s. from 1st marriage; ed Univ. de Montréal; f. Liberté (review) 1959, Ed. 1959–79; Head of Cultural Programmes and Producer Radio-Canada 1970–88; with Les Ecrits (literary review); mem. Académie des lettres du Québec 1982, Royal Soc. of Canada 1967–; Chevalier, Ordre Nat. du Québec 1987, Officier Ordre des Arts et des Lettres 1992; Prix de Poésie du Québec 1956, Louise Labé (Paris) 1969, France-Canada 1969, van Lerberghe (Paris) 1969, du Gouverneur gén. du Canada 1970, Athanase-David 1984, Prix littéraire int. de la Paix (PEN Club Québec) 1991. *Publications:* poetry: La fiancée du matin 1953, Les cloîtres de l'été 1954, L'homme et le jour 1957, La mouette et le large 1960, Recours au pays 1961, Pour saluer une ville 1963, Comme eau retenue 1969 (enlarged edn 1985), Saisons pour la continuelle 1969, Silences pour une souveraine 1972. *Address:* 5724 Côte St-Antoine, Montréal, PQ H4A 1R9, Canada (home).

PILOT, Sachin, BA, MBA; Indian politician; b. 7 Sept. 1977, Uttar Pradesh; s. of Rajesh Pilot and Rama Pilot; m. Sara Abdullah 2004; two s.; ed St Stephen's Coll., Univ. of Delhi, Inst. of Man. Tech., Ghaziabad, Wharton Business School, Univ. of Pennsylvania, USA; began career with Delhi Bureau of BBC; two years with General Motors; elected to 14th Lok Sabha (lower house of Parl.) for Ajmer constituency 2004, re-elected to 15th Lok Sabha 2009–14, mem. Cttee on Home Affairs; Union Cabinet Minister of State for Communications and Information Tech. 2009–12, for Corp. Affairs 2012–14; mem. Indian Nat. Congress (Congress); fmr Pres. Rajasthan Pradesh Congress Cttee; named as Young Global Leader by World Econ. Forum 2008. *Leisure interests:* flying (private pilot's licence), shooting, squash, cricket. *Address:* Indian Nat. Congress, 24 Akbar Road, New Delhi 110 001, India (office). *Telephone:* (11) 23019080 (office). *Fax:* (11) 23017047 (office). *E-mail:* contact@sachinpilot.com; connect@inc.in (office). *Website:* www.inc.in (office); www.sachinpilot.com.

PILSWORTH, Michael (Mick) John, MA; British media executive; *CEO, Chrysalis Vision Ltd;* b. 1 April 1951, Leeds; s. of Alwyne Pilsworth and Catherine Pilsworth (née Silverwood); m. Stella Frances Pilsworth (née Hore) 1972; one s. one d.; ed King Edward VI Grammar School, Retford, Univ. of Manchester; Research Asst, Inst. of Advanced Studies, Manchester Polytechnic 1972–73; Research Assoc., Univ. of Manchester 1973–75, Lecturer 1973–77; Research Fellow, Centre for TV Research 1977–79, Univ. of Leeds 1979–81; Researcher, London Weekend 1982–83; Head of Programme Devt TV South 1984–86, Controller, Corp. Devt 1987–88; Chief Exec. MGMM Communications Ltd 1988–89; Man. Dir Alomo Productions Ltd 1990–92, Selec TV PLC 1990–93; Chief Exec. Chrysalis TV Group Ltd 1993–2002; Exec. Chair. Motive Television PLC 2005–14, Chair. (non-exec.) 2014–; CEO Chrysalis Vision Ltd (production co.) 2014–; Owner, Michael Pilsworth Media 2013–15; mem. Bd of Dirs Futuremedia Plc 2005–07; fmr mem. Advisory Bd MediaWin & Partners. *Publications include:* co-author Broadcasting in the Third World 1977. *Leisure interests:* reading, cinema, gardening. *Address:* Chrysalis Vision Ltd, First Floor, Suite 181B, Kensington High Street, London, W8 6SH, England (office).

PIMIENTO RODRÍGUEZ, HE Cardinal José de Jesús; Colombian ecclesiastic; *Archbishop Emeritus of Manizales;* b. 18 Feb. 1919, Zapatoca; ordained priest, Archdiocese of Socorro y San Gil 1941; apptd Auxiliary Bishop of Pasto and consecrated Titular Bishop of Apollonis 1955; Bishop of Montería 1959–64; Bishop of Garzón-Neiva 1964–75; Archbishop of Manizales 1975–96, Archbishop Emer. 1996–; resumed work as a parish priest 1996; cr. Cardinal (Cardinal-Priest of San Giovanni Crisostomo a Monte Sacro Alto) 2015. *Address:* Archdiocese of Manizales, Carrera 23 N. 19–22, Manizales, Caldas, Colombia (office). *Telephone:* (968) 840114 (office); (968) 840151 (office). *Fax:* (968) 821853 (office).

PIMM, Stuart Leonard, BA, PhD; American (b. British) ecologist and academic; *Doris Duke Professor of Conservation Ecology, Duke University;* b. 27 Feb. 1949, Derbyshire, England; m. Julia Killeffer 1990; two d.; ed Univ. of Oxford, UK, New Mexico State Univ.; Asst Prof., Clemson Univ. 1974–75; Asst Prof., Texas Tech Univ. 1975–79, Assoc. Prof. 1979–82; Assoc. Prof., Dept of Ecology and Evolutionary Biology, Univ. of Tennessee 1982–86, Prof. 1986–99; Prof., Center for Environmental Research and Conservation, Columbia Univ. 1999–2002; Doris Duke Prof. of Conservation Ecology, Duke Univ. 2002–; Extraordinary Prof., Univ. of Pretoria, SA 2001–; visiting appointments at Griffith Univ., Australia 1983–84, Inst. for Nonlinear Science, Univ. of California, San Diego 1987, School of Ecosystem Man., Univ. of New England, Australia 1987, Centre for Population Biology, Imperial Coll., Silwood Park, UK 1990, Nat. Research Council (Sr Visiting Scholar) 1995, Conservation Ecology Research Unit, Univ. of Pretoria 1996, 2000; Fellow, American Acad. of Arts and Sciences 2004; Pew Scholar in Conservation and the Environment 1993, Sigma Xi Nat. Lecturer 1993–95, Kempe Prize for Distinguished Ecologists 1994, Aldo Leopold Leadership Fellow 1999, Marsh Prize, Zoological Soc. of London 2004, Alumnus of the Year, Coll. of Arts and Sciences, New Mexico State Univ. 2005, Edward T. LaRoe III Memorial Award, Soc. for Conservation Biology 2006, Dr A.H. Heineken Prize for Environmental Sciences, Royal Netherlands Acad. of Arts and Sciences 2006, William Proctor Prize for Scientific Achievement, Sigma Xi, The Scientific Research Soc. 2007, Tyler Prize for Environmental Achievement, Univ. of Southern California 2010. *Films:* contrib. to: The Planet (dir Michael Stenberg) 2006, The 11th Hour 2007, What a Way to Go (dir T. S. Bennett) 2007, Racing Extinction (dir L. Psihoyos) 2015. *Publications include:* Food Webs 1982 (second edn 2003), The Balance of Nature? Ecological Issues in the Conservation of Species and Communities 1991, The Bird Watcher's Handbook: A Field Guide to the Natural History of European Birds (co-author, also of species treatments) 1994, The World According to Pimm: A Scientist Audits the Earth 2001, Sparrow in the Grass 2002, Patterns in Nature (co-author); about 300 papers in professional journals. *Address:* Nicholas School of the Environment and Earth Science, Box 90328, Room A301, LSRC Building, Durham, NC 27708, USA (office). *Telephone:* (919) 613-8141 (office). *Fax:* (919) 684-8741 (office). *E-mail:* stuartpimm@me.com (office). *Website:* nicholas.duke.edu/people/faculty/pimm (office); www.savingspecies.org.

PINA-CABRAL, Prof. João de, BA, DPhil Hab; Portuguese social anthropologist and academic; *Research Coordinator, Institute of Social Sciences, University of Lisbon;* b. 9 May 1954; s. of Daniel de Pina Cabral and Ana A. de Pina Cabral; m. Monica Chan; ed Univ. of Witwatersrand, Johannesburg, Univ. of Oxford, Univ. of Lisbon; Auxiliary Prof., Dept of Social Anthropology, ISCTE, Lisbon 1982–84, Assoc. Prof. 1988–; Gulbenkian Fellow in Portuguese Studies, Univ of Southampton 1984–86; Research Fellow, Inst. of Social Sciences, Univ. of Lisbon 1986–92, Sr Research Fellow 1992–2004, Research Coordinator 2004–, Pres. Scientific Bd 1998–2004; Pres. European Asscn of Social Anthropologists 2003–05; Head School of Anthropology and Conservation, Univ. of Kent 2013–16; mem. Portuguese Acad. of Sciences 2004–, Acad. of Sciences of Lisbon; Corresp. mem. Real Academia de Ciencias Morales y Politicas; Hon. mem. Royal Anthropological Inst.; Malinowski Memorial Lecturer 1992. *Publications:* over 80 papers in refereed journals; books: Death in Portugal (co-ed.) 1983, Sons of Adam, Daughters of Eve 1986, Os Contextos da Antropologia 1991, Europe Observed (co-ed.) 1992, Aromas de Urze e de Lama 1993, Em Terra de Tufões 1993, Elites: Choice, Leadership and Succession (co-ed.) 2000, Between China and Europe 2002, O Homem na Família 2003, A persistência da história: Passado e contemporaneidade em África (co-ed.) 2004, Nomes: Género, Etnicidade e Familia (co-ed.) 2007, On the margins of Religion (co-ed.) 2008, World: An Anthropological Examination 2017. *Address:* Institute of Social Sciences, University of Lisbon, Avenida A. Bettencourt 9, 1600-189 Lisbon, Portugal (office). *Telephone:* (21) 7804700 (office). *Fax:* (21) 7940274 (office). *E-mail:* pina.cabral@ics.ul.pt (office). *Website:* www.ics.ul.pt (office).

PINA TORIBIO, César, PhD; Dominican Republic politician; b. 17 Dec. 1946, Santo Domingo; ed Universidad Autonoma de Santo Domingo; worked as Prof. of criminal sciences in various Univs. of country; Pres. Dominican Coll. of Notaries, Inc. 1977–79; Dir Law Dept Univ. of Agricultural Sciences 1983–86; apptd Chair. Disciplinary Tribunal, Bar Asscn of Dominican Republic 1991; Head, Comisión de Asuntos Jurídicos 1995–98, Secretaría de Asuntos Electorales 1998–99, Juridical Consultant of the Presidency 1996–99, 2004–08; Attorney Gen. 1999–2000; Sec. of State for the Presidency 2008–12; mem. Partido de la Liberación Dominicana (PLD), also PLD del. to Cen. Electoral Bd; mem. Political Cttee, Máximo organismo de dirección, Comisión Nacional de Ejecución de la Reforma Procesal Penal, Governing Counci, Comisión Nacional de Ética y Combate a la Corrupción. *Publication:* Temas Notariales.

PINARD, Hon. Yvon, BA, LLL; Canadian politician, lawyer and judge; b. 10 Oct. 1940, Drummondville, Québec; ed Immaculate Conception School, Drummondville, Nicolet Seminary, Sherbrooke Univ.; Pres. Sherbrooke Univ. Law Faculty 1963; admitted to Québec Bar 1964; mem. Admin. Council Centre Communautaire d'Aide Juridique Mauricie-Bois-Francs region; mem. Commonwealth Parl. Asscn and Canadian Del. Interparl. Union; mem. House of Commons (Liberal) 1974–84, Parl. Sec. to Pres. of Privy Council Oct. 1977; Pres. of HM the Queen's Privy Council for Canada and Govt House Leader 1980–84; Judge, Federal Court of Canada, Trial Div. Judge 1984–2013; mem. ex-officio Fed. Court of Appeal 1984–2013.

PINAULT, François; French business executive; *Honorary Chairman, Kering;* b. 21 Aug. 1936, Champs Géraux (Côtes-du-Nord); s. of François Pinault and Eugénie Gabillard; m. Mary Campbell 1970; two s. (including François-Henri Pinault) two d.; ed Collège Saint-Martin, Rennes; worked in father's timber co. aged 16; f. Société Pinault, Rennes 1963, Président-Directeur Général 1970; Pres. Co. française de l'Afrique occidentale (CFAO) 1990–91; Vice-Pres. Supervisory Bd Groupe Pinault-Printemps-Redoute (renamed PPR SA, now Kering) 1992, led PPR in protracted battle for control of Italian fashion house Gucci against rival co. LVMH and its Chair. Bernard Arnault 1999–2004, currently Hon. Chair.; Founder, Président-Directeur Général Artémis SA (family holding co.) 1992 owns, amongst others, Christie's, London 1998–, Château Latour vineyard, Vail ski resort in Colo, USA, Converse shoes, luggage mfrs Samsonite and majority shareholding in French real estate investment co. Sefimeg, also owns Executive Life (now Aurora Life) in Calif.; leading modern art collector, acquired ownership of Palazzo Grassi in Venice to display his collection 2006, 'Mapping the Studio' exhbn in Punta della Dogana, a second museum in Venice opened by Pinault 2009, includes 300 works from more than 50 leading artists; Officier, Légion d'honneur, Croix de la Valeur Militaire. *Leisure interests:* cinema, theatre, art collecting, cycling, walking. *Address:* Kering, 10 avenue Hoche, 75381 Paris Cedex 08, France (office); Christie's International PLC, 8 King Street, London, SW1Y 6QT, England (office). *Telephone:* 1-45-64-61-00 (Paris) (office). *Fax:* 1-44-90-62-25 (Paris) (office). *E-mail:* info@kering.com (office). *Website:* www.kering.com (office).

PINAULT, François-Henri, BBA; French business executive; *Chairman and CEO, Kering SA;* b. 28 May 1962, Rennes, Brittany; s. of François Pinault and Louise Gautier; m. 1st Dorothée Lepère 1996 (divorced 2004); one s. one d., and one s. with Linda Evangelista; m. 2nd Salma Hayek 2009; one d.; ed HEC (Hautes Etudes Commerciales) business school, Paris; began career as salesman in timber import and retail business at Evreux br. of Pinault Distribution, joined Pinault Group 1987, held positions in several of the Group's operating businesses, established co.'s purchasing group 1988–89, later apptd CEO France Bois Industries and managed co.'s 14 plants, Chair. Pinault Distribution 1990–93, Chair. Co. française de l'Afrique occidentale (CFAO) and mem. Exec. Bd PPR (fmrly Pinault-Printemps-Redoute) 1993–97, Chair. and CEO FNAC 1997–2000, Deputy CEO PPR SA 2000–05, Co-Man. Financière Pinault 2000–, Chair. Artemis Group 2003–05, Chair. and CEO PPR SA 2005– (renamed Kering SA 2013), mem. Bd of Dirs Sapardis SE (subsidiary of Kering SA) 2008–; Chair. Supervisory Bd Puma AG 2011–17; Vice-Chair. Supervisory Bd CFAO; mem. Bd of Dirs Fnac SA 1994–2013, Bouygues 1998–2016, Christie's Int. Plc, UK 2003–14, Stella McCartney Ltd, UK 2011–, Volcom Inc. 2011–, Brioni SpA, Italy 2012–15, Yves Saint Laurent 2013–, Ulysse Nardin le Locle SA, Switzerland 2014–; Zeitz

Foundation Amb. for Commerce 2009–; Chevalier, Légion d'Honneur 2006; Global Carrier Community Award 2015, Anti-Defamation League's Int. Leadership Award 2015, inducted into Vanity Fair Hall of Fame 2016. *Address:* Kering SA, 40, rue de Sèvres, 75007 Paris, France (office). *Telephone:* 1-45-64-61-00 (office). *E-mail:* info@kering.com (office). *Website:* www.kering.com (office).

PINCAY, Laffit Alejandro, Jr; Panamanian fmr professional jockey; b. 29 Dec. 1946, Panama City; m. 1st Linda Pincay 1967 (died 1985); one s. one d.; m. 2nd Jeanine Pincay; one s.; learned to ride by watching his father racing at numerous tracks in Panama and Venezuela; rode first winner 1964, first US winner 1966, 3,000th winner 1975; Winner Belmont Stakes 1982, 1983, 1984, Kentucky Derby 1984; rode 6,000th winner 1985; broke Willie Shoemaker's record with 8,834 wins 1999; first jockey to reach 9,000 wins; seven Breeders' Cup wins; 9,530 wins in total (passed by Russell Baze 2006), retd 2003; lifesize bust of him erected at Santa Anita Park, US Champion Jockey by earnings 1970–74, 1979, 1985, US Champion Jockey by wins 1971, Eclipse Award for Outstanding Jockey 1971, 1973, 1974, 1979, 1985, inducted into Nat. Museum of Racing and Hall of Fame 1975, Eclipse Special Award 1999, Big Sport of Turfdom Award 2000, Pincay Drive (fmrly 90th Street) at Prairie Avenue, Inglewood, Calif. renamed 2003, Laffit Pincay Jr Award cr. in his honour by Hollywood Park Racetrack 2004.

PINCHUK, Victor Mykhaylovych, PhD; Ukrainian business executive and philanthropist; b. 14 Dec. 1960, Kyiv, Ukrainian SSR, USSR; m. 1st Olena Arshava (divorced); m. 2nd Olena Leonidivna Pinchuk (d. of fmr Pres. of Ukraine, Leonid Kuchma); one s. three d.; ed Dnipropetrovsk Metallurgical Inst.; owner of wide range of businesses, including Interpipe Corpn (industrial conglomerate) 1990, Geo Alliance, Starlight Media TV Group (first nat. commercial TV network in Ukraine that includes ICTV, STB, NOVY, M1, M2, QTV Int.), Fakty i Kommentarii newspaper; Founder EastOne Group Ltd (investment and advisory group); mem. Verkhovna Rada (Parl. of Ukraine) 1998–2006; f. Victor Pinchuk Foundation 2006, PinchukArtCentre 2007; Founder, Future Generation Art Prize for artists under the age of 35 and awarded biannually 2009; mem. Bd Peterson Inst. for Int. Econs, Int. Advisory Council of Brookings Inst., Bd of Trustees of the Museum of Contemporary Art; Hon. Citizen of Kiev 2009; Chevalier des Arts et des Lettres 2013; Trebbia European Award 2011, ranked first by Inst. of World Policy amongst promoters of Ukraine abroad, Metropolitan Andrey Sheptytsky Award 2014, Palazzo Strozzi Renaissance Man of the Year Award 2014. *Address:* Victor Pinchuk Foundation, 01601 Kyiv, vul. Mechnykova 2, Ukraine (office). *Telephone:* (44) 490-48-35 (office). *Fax:* (44) 490-48-78 (office). *E-mail:* info@pinchukfund.org (office). *Website:* pinchukfund.org (office).

PINDA, Mizengo Kayanza Peter, LLB; Tanzanian lawyer; b. 12 Aug. 1948, Rukwa Region; ed Univ. of Dar es Salaam; State Attorney, Ministry of Justice and Constitutional Affairs 1974–78; Pres.'s Office 1978–82; Asst Pvt. Sec. to the Pres. 1982–92; State House Clerk to the Cabinet 1996–2000; MP for Mpanda East 2000–05, for Mpanda Mashariki 2005–; Deputy Minister in Prime Minister's Office for Regional Admin and Local Govt 2000–05; Minister of State for Regional Admin and Local Govt 2006–08; Prime Minister 2008–15.

PINDLING, Dame Marguerite, DCMG; Bahamian government official; *Governor-General;* b. 26 June 1932, Long Bay Cay, South Andros; d. of Reuben McKenzie and Viola McKenzie; m. Lynden Pindling (fmr Prime Minister of the Bahamas) 1956 (deceased); four c.; ed Western Sr School; early career as asst with photographers Stanley Toogood and Colyn Rees; involved for many years in charity fund-raising, including as Chair. Bahamas Red Cross fund-raising Cttee; Gov.-Gen. of the Bahamas 2014–. *Address:* Office of the Governor-General, Nassau, Bahamas (office). *Website:* www.bahamas.gov.bs (office).

PINEAU-VALENCIENNE, Didier; French company director; b. 21 March 1931, Paris; s. of Maurice and Madeleine (née Dubigeon) Pineau-Valencienne; m. Guillemette Rident 1964; one s. three d.; ed Lycée Janson-de-Sailly, Paris, Hautes Etudes Commerciales, Paris, Dartmouth Univ. (USA) and Harvard Business School; Man. Asst Banque Parisienne pour l'Industrie 1958, Prin. Man. Asst 1962, Dir 1964–67, Dir-Gen. 1969 and Admin. 1971; Pres. and Dir-Gen. Carbonisation et Charbons Actifs (CECA) 1972–74, Société Resogil 1975–76; Dir-Gen. Société Celogil 1975–76; Admin. Isorel 1976; Dir of Admin. and Strategy and Planning Rhone-Poulenc SA 1976–77, Dir-Gen. (Polymer Div.) 1978; Admin. Quartz et Silice; Admin., Vice-Pres., Dir-Gen. Schneider SA 1980–81, Pres.-Dir-Gen. 1981–98; Pres.-Dir-Gen. Jeumont-Schneider 1987–89, Pres. Schneider Industries Services Int. 1991–92, Schneider Electric SA 1993–98; apptd Asst Admin. Société Electrorail SA 1980; Dir Merlin-Gérin 1981, Pres.-Dir-Gen. 1989; Chair. Empain-Schneider Group 1981–99, Société Parisienne d'Etudes et de Participations 1982; Chair. and Man. Dir Creusot-Loire 1982–84; Vice-Chair. Crédit Suisse First Boston, London 1999; Dir Paribas 1989–98, Whirlpool Corpn 1992; Pres. Admin. Council, Tech. Univ. of Compiègne 1992–96; Pres. Inst. de L'Entreprise 1993–96, Hon. Pres. 1996; Pres. Asscn française des entreprises privées 1999; Vice-Pres. and Pres. Comm. Sociale du Conseil nat. du patronat français (CNPF) 1997; Chair. Advisory Bd Sisie 1997–98; fmr teacher Ecole des Hautes Etudes Commerciales; Officier, Légion d'honneur, Officier Ordre nat. du Mérite; Chair. and Partner SAGARD; Senior Advisor Crédit Suisse First Boston (Europe) Ltd; Manager of the Year (Le Nouvel Economiste) 1991, Falk Award (USA) 1998, Man of the Year (Franco-American Chamber of Commerce). *Leisure interests:* tennis, skiing, collecting books.

PINEL, Sylvia; French politician; b. 28 Sept. 1977, L'Union (Haute-Garonne); d. of Michel Pinel; ed Lycée Michelet, Montauban, Univ. of Toulouse 1 Capitole; began in politics as project man. and Chief of Staff to Pres. of Gen. Council of Tarn-et-Garonne; mem. (PRG—Parti Radical de Gauche) Assemblée nationale for Second Dist of Tarn-et-Garonne 2007–17 (re-elected 2012); Regional Councillor for Midi-Pyrénées 2010–; Chair. Departmental Fed. of PRG of Tarn-et-Garonne and Deputy Del. Gen. of PRG; Vice-Pres. Rights of Citizens, Security and Justice, PRG nat. party 2011–; mem. presidential election campaign team of François Hollande 2012; Minister delegated to Minister of Productive Recovery, responsible for Crafts, Trade and Tourism May–June 2012, Minister for Crafts, Trade and Tourism 2012–14, of Territorial Equality and Housing 2014–16. *Address:* National Assembly, 126 rue de l'Université, 75355 Paris Cedex 07, France (office). *Telephone:* 1-40-63-60-00 (office). *E-mail:* infos@assemblee-nationale.fr (office). *Website:* www.assemblee-nationale.fr (office).

PIÑERA ECHENIQUE, (Miguel Juan) Sebastián, MA, PhD; Chilean engineer, business executive, politician and head of state; *President;* b. 1 Dec. 1949, Santiago; s. of José Piñera Carvallo and Magdalena Echenique Rozas; m. Cecilia Morel Montes 1973; two s. two d.; ed Pontificia Universidad Católica de Chile, Harvard Univ., USA; fmr Prof. of Econs, Pontificia Universidad Católica de Chile and Adolfo Ibáñez Univ.; Prof. of Econ. Political Theory, Univ. of Chile 1971; Prof., Valparaiso Business School 1972; business interests include 100% ownership of Chilevisión (terrestrial TV channel), LAN Airlines stock, Axxion SA (holding co.); mem. Senado (Senate) for East Santiago 1990–98; mem. Renovación Nacional (RN), Pres. 2001–04; presidential cand. 2005, (unsuccessful) 2009 (elected as Coalición por el Cambio cand.); Pres. of Chile 2010–14; Pres. 2018–. *Address:* Office of the President, Palacio de La Moneda, Santiago, Chile (office). *Telephone:* (2) 6904000 (office). *Website:* www.gob.cl (office).

PINES, Alexander, BSc, PhD, FRS; American chemist and academic; *Glenn T. Seaborg Professor of Chemistry, University of California, Berkeley;* b. 1945; m. Ditsa Pines; five c.; ed Hebrew Univ. of Jerusalem, Massachusetts Inst. of Tech.; joined Dept of Physics, Univ. of Calif., Berkeley 1972, becoming Faculty Sr Scientist, Lawrence Berkeley Nat. Lab., also Chancellor's Research Prof. in Chem. 1997, Glenn T. Seaborg Prof. of Chem. 1998–, Faculty Affiliate, Calif. Inst. for Quantitative Biomedical Research 2007–, Core mem. Univ. of Calif., Berkeley, Jt Graduate Group in Bioengineering 2008–; mem. NAS 1988–, American Acad. of Arts and Sciences 1999; Foreign mem. Royal Society (UK); fmr Pres. Int. Soc. of Magnetic Resonance; Einstein Prof., Chinese Acad. of Sciences 2013; numerous hon. lectureships, including Loeb Lecturer, Harvard Univ., Joliot-Curie Prof., Ecole Superieure de Physique et Chemie, Paris 1987, Hinshelwood Prof., Univ. of Oxford 1990, Centenary Lecturer and Medal, Royal Soc. of Chem. 1994, Lord Todd Prof., Cambridge Univ. 1999; Dr hc (Paris VI) 1999, (Universite Paul Cezanne, Marseilles) 2010, (Weizmann Inst. of Science) 2011; ACS Baekeland Award in Pure Chem. 1985, Univ. of Calif. Distinguished Teaching Award 1986, ACS Nobel Signature Award for Grad. Educ., Pittsburgh Spectroscopy Award 1989, ACS Harrison Howe Award 1991, Royal Soc. of Chem. Bourke Medal, ACS Langmuir Award, Wolf Prize in Chem. 1991 (jtly), Baylor Univ. Robert Foster Cherry Great Teacher Award 1995, Dept of Energy Ernest O. Lawrence Award 1997, ACS Irving Langmuir Award in Chemical Physics 1998, F. A. Cotton Medal for Excellence in Chemical Research 1998, ACS Remsen Award 2000, Carnegie Mellon Univ. Dickson Prize in Science, Seaborg Medal 2003, Michael Faraday Medal 2003, Russell Varian Prize, European Magnetic Resonance Soc. 2008. *Address:* Department of Chemistry, Stanley Hall 208B, University of California, Berkeley, CA 94720-3220, USA (office). *Telephone:* (510) 642-1220 (office). *Fax:* (510) 666-3768 (office). *E-mail:* pines@berkeley.edu (office). *Website:* chem.berkeley.edu (office).

PING, Jean, PhD; Gabonese economist, politician, international organization official and business executive; b. 24 Nov. 1942, Omboué; s. of Cheng Zhiping; m. 1st Pascaline Bongo; two c.; m. 2nd; six c.; ed Univ. of Paris I (Panthéon-Sorbonne); began career at Sector for External Relations and Co-operation, UNESCO, Paris 1972, Perm. Rep. to UNESCO 1978–84; Dir Cabinet of the Pres. of Gabon 1984–90; Minister of Information 1990, then Minister of Mines, Energy and Water Resources and Deputy Minister, Ministry of Finance, Economy, Budget and Privatization, then Minister of Planning, Environment and Tourism –1999, Vice-Prime Minister, Minister of Foreign Affairs, Co-operation, Francophonie and Regional Integration 1999–2008; Pres. 59th session of UN Gen. Ass. 2004–05; Chair. Comm. of the African Union 2008–12; co-f., with his two sons, Ping & Ping Consulting 2012–; mem. Gabonese Democratic Party –2014; cand. in presidential election 2016; mem. French Nat. Asscn of Doctors of Econs; Commdr of the Equatorial Star, Grand Officer of the Equatorial Star, Commdr of the Maritime Merit Order, Commdr of the Gabonese Nat. Order of Merit, Commdr Légion d'honneur, Officer of the Order of the Pleiad and the Order of la Francophonie, Grand Cross of the Order of Merit (Portugal); Dr hc (Inst. of Diplomacy of China), (Inst. of African Studies, Russian Acad. of Sciences). *Publication:* Mondialisation, Paix, Démocratie et Développent: l'expérience du Gabon 2002.

PINKAYAN, Subin, MEng, PhD; Thai engineer and business executive; b. 16 June 1934, Chiang Mai; m. Boonsri Pinkayan; one s. one d.; ed Chulalongkorn Univ., Asian Inst. of Tech., Colorado State Univ., USA; civil engineer, Port Authority of Thailand, Bangkok 1958–60; hydrologist, Royal Irrigation Dept 1967–69; Assoc. Prof. Asian Inst. of Tech. 1969–74; mem. Parl. for Chiang Mai 1983–91; Deputy Leader Social Action Party 1986–91, mem. Exec. Cttee 1981–91, Registrar 1981–86, Deputy Sec.-Gen. 1979–80; Deputy Minister of Finance 1986, Minister of Univ. Affairs 1986–88, Minister of Commerce 1988–90, Minister of Foreign Affairs 1990; Pres. SEATEC (Southeast Asia Technology Co. Ltd) Group 1974–85, Chair. 1991, now Chief Hon. Advisor; Hon. Advisor, MDX Group, GMS Power Public Co. Ltd; Chair. Bd of Trustees, Asian Inst. of Tech. 2013–; Commdr (Third Class) of the Most Noble Order of the Crown of Thailand 1983, Commdr (Third Class) of the Most Exalted Order of the White Elephant 1985, Kt Grand Cross (First Class) of the Most Noble Order of the Crown of Thailand 1986, Kt Grand Cross (First Class) of the Most Exalted Order of the White Elephant 1987, Kt Grand Cordon (Special Class) of the Most Exalted Order of the White Elephant 1989; Personal Service Award in 'National and International Prestige,' Colorado State Univ. 1991, Outstanding Alumni Award, Asian Inst. of Tech. Alumni Asscn of Thailand 2003, inducted into Asian Inst. of Tech. Hall of Fame 2010. *Leisure interests:* golf, travel, gardening. *Address:* Seatec Group, 281 Soi Phanit Anan 7, Preedee Phanomyong 42, Sukhumvit 71, Bangkok 10110, Thailand (office). *Telephone:* (2) 7133888 (office). *Fax:* (2) 7133889 (office). *E-mail:* seatec@seatecgroup.com (office). *Website:* www.seatecgroup.com (office).

PINKER, Robert Arthur, CBE, MSc; British academic; *Professor Emeritus of Social Administration, London School of Economics;* b. 27 May 1931; s. of Dora Elizabeth Pinker and Joseph Pinker; m. Jennifer Farrington Boulton 1955 (died 1994); two d.; ed Holloway Co. School, London School of Econs; Head of Sociology Dept, Goldsmiths Coll., London Univ. 1964–72, Lewisham Prof. of Social Admin., Goldsmiths Coll. and Bedford Coll. 1972–74; Prof. of Social Studies, Chelsea Coll. 1974–78; Prof. of Social Work Studies, LSE 1978–93, Pro-Dir LSE 1985–88, Prof. of Social Admin. 1993–96, Prof. Emer. 1996–; Pro-Vice-Chancellor for Social Sciences, Univ. of London 1989–90; Chair. Editorial Bd Journal of Social Policy 1981–86; Chair. British Library Project on Family and Social Research 1983–86; mem. Council, Advertising Standards Authority 1988–95, Press Complaints

Comm. 1991–2014 (Privacy Commr 1994–2004, Acting Chair. 2002–03), Council, Direct Mail Accreditation and Recognition Centre 1995–97 (Int. Consultant 2002–), Bd of Man. London School of Hygiene and Tropical Medicine 1990–94; Chair. Govs Centre for Policy on Ageing 1988–94; Fellow, Soc. of Eds 2004; Hon. Fellow, Goldsmiths Coll., Univ. of London 1999; Hon. LLD (Ulster) 2016. *Publications include:* English Hospital Statistics 1861–1938 1964, Social Theory and Social Policy 1971, The Idea of Welfare 1979, Social Work in an Enterprise Society 1990, Privacy and Personality Rights (with Robert Deacon and Nigel Lipton) 2010, Social Policy and Welfare Pluralism: Selected Writings of Robert Pinker (with John Offer) 2017. *Leisure interests:* reading, writing, relatives and friends. *Address:* 76 Coleraine Road, Blackheath, London, SE3 7PE, England (home). *Telephone:* (20) 8858-5320 (home). *E-mail:* rpinker@freenetname.co.uk (home).

PINKER, Steven, BA, PhD; Canadian/American psychologist, scientist, writer and academic; *Johnstone Family Professor of Psychology, Harvard University;* b. 18 Sept. 1954, Montreal, Canada; s. of Harry Pinker and Roslyn Pinker; m. 1st Nancy Etcoff 1980 (divorced 1992); m. 2nd Ilavenil Subbiah 1995 (divorced); ed McGill Univ., Harvard Univ.; Asst Prof., Harvard Univ. 1980–81, Johnstone Family Prof. of Psychology 2003–, Harvard Coll. Prof. 2008–13; Asst Prof., Stanford Univ. 1981–82; Asst Prof., Dept of Psychology, MIT 1982–85, Assoc. Prof., Dept of Brain and Cognitive Sciences 1985–89, Prof. 1989–2000, Peter de Florez Prof. 2000–03, Co-Dir Center for Cognitive Science 1985–94, Dir McDonnell-Pew Center for Cognitive Neuroscience 1994–99; Chair. Usage Panel, American Heritage Dictionary 2008–; Contributing Ed. The New Republic 2008–, Seed 2006–; Exec. Assoc. Ed. Cognition: International Journal of Cognitive Science 1985–2006; Herbert Simon Fellow, American Acad. of Political and Social Science 2006–; Fellow, AAAS 1987–, American Psychological Soc. 1990–, American Psychological Asscn 1992–, American Acad. of Arts and Sciences 1998–, Linguistics Soc. of America 2007–, Académie Internationale de Philosophie des Sciences 2007–; Distinguished Fellow, New England Inst. for Cognitive Science and Evolutionary Psychology 2001–04; Hon. Pres. Canadian Psychological Asscn 2008; Hon. DSc (McGill) 1999, (Newcastle) 2005; Hon. DPhil (Tel-Aviv) 2003; Hon. DUniv (Surrey) 2003; Dr hc (Albion Coll.) 2007, (Univ. of Tromsø, Norway) 2008; Distinguished Scientific Award for Early Career Contribution to Psychology, American Psychological Asscn 1984, Boyd R. McCandless Young Scientist Award, Div. of Developmental Psychology, American Psychological Asscn 1986, Troland Research Award, NAS 1993, Linguistics, Language and the Public Interest Award, Linguistics Soc. of America 1997, Golden Plate Award, American Acad. of Achievement 1999, Humanist Laureate Int. Acad. of Humanism 2001, Henry Dale Prize 2004, Humanist of the Year 2006, Innovation for Humanity Prize, La Ciudad de las Ideas 2008, George Miller Prize, Cognitive Neuroscience Soc. 2010. *Publications include:* Language Learnability and Language Development 1984, Visual Cognition (ed.) 1985, Connections and Symbols (ed. with J. Mehler) 1988, Learnability and Cognition: The Acquisition of Argument Structure 1989 (new edition 2013), The Language Instinct 1994 (William James Book Prize, American Psychological Asscn 1995), How the Mind Works (William James Book Prize, American Psychological Asscn 1999, Los Angeles Times Book Prize in Science and Technology 1998) 1997, Words and Rules: The Ingredients of Language 1999, The Blank Slate: The Modern Denial of Human Nature (Troland Award 2003, Walter P. Kistler Book Award 2005) 2002, The Stuff of Thought: Language as a Window into Human Nature 2007, The Better Angels of Our Nature 2011, Language, Cognition, and Human Nature: Selected Articles 2013, The Sense of Style: The Thinking Person's Guide to Writing in the 21st Century 2014; numerous articles in scholarly journals, including, Animal Learning and Behavior, Annals of the New York Academy of Sciences, Behavioral and Brain Sciences, Canadian Journal of Psychology, Child Development, Cognition, Cognitive Psychology, Cognitive Science, Communication and Cognition, Journal of Child Language, Journal of Cognitive Neuroscience, Journal of Experimental Psychology, Journal of Mental Imagery, Journal of Psycholinguistic Research, Journal of Verbal Learning and Verbal Behavior, Language and Cognitive Processes, Language, Lingua, Memory and Cognition, Monographs of the Society for Research in Child Development, Nature, New York Times, The New Yorker, Papers and Reports in Child Language, Psychological Science, Science, Slate, Time, Trends in Cognitive Science, Trends in Neurosciences, Visual Cognition. *Leisure interests:* bicycling, photography. *Address:* Department of Psychology, Harvard University, William James Hall 970, 33 Kirkland Street, Cambridge, MA 02138, USA (office). *Website:* pinker.wjh.harvard.edu (office); stevenpinker.com.

PINNOCK, Trevor David, CBE, ARCM, FRAM; British harpsichordist and conductor; b. 16 Dec. 1946, Canterbury, Kent; s. of Kenneth Pinnock and Joyce Pinnock; ed Canterbury Cathedral School, Royal Coll. of Music, London; Co-founder Galliard Harpsichord Trio, debut, London 1966, solo debut, London 1968, Dir The English Concert 1973–2003; Artistic Dir and Prin. Conductor Nat. Arts Centre Orchestra, Ottawa 1991–96, Artistic Adviser 1996–; f. European Brandenburg Ensemble 2006–, numerous tours and recordings; has toured Western Europe, USA, S America, Canada, Australia, Japan with The English Concert, as solo harpsichordist and as orchestral/opera conductor; debut at Metropolitan Opera, New York 1988; has worked with Opera Australia, Freiburg Baroque Orchestra, Salzburg Camerata, Salzburg Mozarteum Orchestra, Deutsche Kammerphilharmonie Bremen, Deutsches Symphonie-Orchester Berlin, Amsterdam Concertgebouw Orchestra; Gramophone Award for Bach Partitas BWV 825–30 2001. *Recordings include:* Rameau, Pièces de Clavecin (with Jonathan Manson, J. S. Bach, Sonatas for viola da gamba and obligato harpsichord, and works by Handel, C. P. E. Bach, Vivaldi, Scarlatti, 16th, 17th and 18th-century harpsichord music and most of the standard baroque orchestral/concerto/choral repertoire, Brandenburg Concertos (with European Brandenburg Ensemble) (Gramophone Award for Best Baroque Instrumental Recording 2008), Scarlatti: Sonatas 2015, The Harmonious Blacksmith 2015, Journey 2016. *Website:* www.askonasholt.co.uk (office); www.trevorpinnock.com.

PINÓS, Carmen; Spanish architect; b. 23 June 1954, Barcelona; ed Escuela Superior de Arquitectura de Barcelona, Int. Lab. of Architecture with Urban Design, Urbino, Columbia Univ., USA; Visiting Prof. at Univs of Illinois at Urbana-Champaign, USA 1994–95, Kunstakademie, Dusseldorf, Germany 1994–98, Columbia Univ. 1999, École Polytechnique Federale de Lausanne, Switzerland 2001–02, Escola Tècnica Superior d'Arquitectura del Vallès, Barcelona 2002, Università degli Studi di Sassari, Alghero, Italy 2002, 2004, Harvard Univ. Grad. School of Design, USA 2003; FAD Prize, La Llauna School, FAD Prize for the Igualada Cemetery, The City of Barcelona Prize for the archery range building for the 1992 Olympic Games, Spanish Nat. Architecture Prize for the boarding school of Morella 1995, Inst. of Architects Award from the Valencia Govt for the public spaces of the Waterfront Juan Aparicio in Torrevieja 2001, Vila de Pedreguer Prize 2004, First Prize, IX Biennal of Spanish Architecture 2007, Premio Nacional de Arquitectura y Espacio Urbano 2008, Berkeley Univ. Berkeley-Rupp Prize 2016. *Major works:* El Croquis 1986, Arte Cemento 1987, Baumeister 1989. *Publications:* Carme Pinós: Some Projects (since 1991) 1998, Carme Pinós: An Architecture of Overlay (Ana Maria Torres) 2004. *Address:* Diagonal 490, 3-2, 08006 Barcelona, Spain (office). *Telephone:* (93) 4160372 (office). *Fax:* (93) 2781473 (office). *E-mail:* info@cpinos.com (office). *Website:* www.cpinos.com (office).

PINOTTI, Roberta; Italian politician; b. 20 May 1961, Genoa; m.; two d.; began career in local govt, including as Dist Councillor for Educ., Youth and Social Policies, Prov. of Genoa 1993–97, Councillor for Educ. Insts, Genoa City Council 1997–99, Councillor, Prov. of Genoa 1999–2011; mem. Chamber of Deputies (Parl.) (Ulivo list) for Genoa 7 constituency 2001–08, Pres. Defence Cttee 2006; mem. Senate for Liguria 2008–18, for Piedmont 2018–, Vice-Chair. Senate Defence Cttee 2010; Shadow Minister of Defence 2008–09, Deputy Minister of Defence 2013–14, Minister of Defence 2014–18; mem. Partito Democratico (PD); Legion d'Honneur 2008, Chancellor and Treasurer, Mil. Order of Italy 2014. *Address:* Partito Democratico, Via Sant'Andrea delle Fratte 16, 00187 Rome, Italy (office). *Website:* www.partitodemocratico.it (office); www.robertapinotti.it.

PINSENT, Sir Matthew Clive, Kt, CBE, BA; British fmr oarsman; b. 10 Oct. 1970, Norfolk; s. of Rev. Ewen Pinsent and Jean Pinsent; m. Demetra Pinsent 2002; three c.; ed Eton Coll. and Univ. of Oxford; first rep. UK at Jr World Championships 1987, 1988, Gold Medal in Coxless Pairs (with Tim Foster) 1988; competed three times in Univ. Boat Race for Oxford 1990, 1991, 1993, winning twice; Gold Medal, Coxless Pairs (with Steve Redgrave q.v.) World Championships 1991, 1993, 1994, 1995, Olympic Games, Barcelona 1992, Atlanta 1996; Gold Medal, Coxless Fours (with Steve Redgrave, Tim Foster and James Cracknell) World Championships 1997, 1998, 1999, Olympic Games, Sydney 2000; Gold Medal, Coxless Pairs (with James Cracknell) World Championships 2001, 2002 (new world record); Gold Medal, Coxless Fours (with Cracknell, Coode and Williams) Olympic Games, Athens 2004; mem. Int. Olympic Cttee 2002–04; announced retirement Nov. 2004; currently working as journalist and broadcaster with BBC; Int. Rowing Fed. Male Rower of the Year, mem. BBC Sports Team of the Year 2004, Thomas Keller Medal, Int. Rowing Fed. 2005. *Publication:* A Lifetime in a Race 2004. *Leisure interests:* golf, flying. *Address:* Professional Sports Group, 7-9 Baker Street, Weybridge, Surrey, KT13 8AF, England (office). *Website:* www.profsports.com (office); www.matthewpinsent.com.

PINSKY, Robert Neal, BA, MA, PhD; American poet and academic; *Professor of Creative Writing, Boston University;* b. 20 Oct. 1940, Long Branch, New Jersey; s. of Milford Simon Pinsky and Sylvia Pinsky (née Eisenberg); m. Ellen Jane Bailey 1961; three d.; ed Rutgers Univ., Stanford Univ.; Asst Prof. of English, Univ. of Chicago 1966–67; Prof. of English, Wellesley Coll. 1967–80; Visiting Lecturer, Harvard Univ. 1980; Prof. of English, Univ. of Calif., Berkeley 1980–89; Prof., Boston Univ. 1980–89, Prof. of Creative Writing 1989–; Hurst Prof., Washington Univ., St Louis 1980; Poet Laureate of USA 1997–2000; Poetry Ed. New Republic magazine 1978–87, Slate Magazine 1996–2013; Guggenheim Fellow 1980; mem. American Acad. of Arts and Letters (Sec. 2003–06), American Acad. of Arts and Sciences; Chancellor, Acad. of American Poets; f. Favorite Poem Project; contrib., The NewsHour with Jim Lehrer 1997–2004; columnist, Washington Post Book World 2005–08; Artist's Award, American Acad. of Arts and Letters 1980, Eunice B. Tietjens Prize 1983, William Carlos Williams Prize 1985, Shelley Memorial Award 1996, Harold Washington Literary Award 1999, Distinguished Service in the Arts Medal, Fine Arts Work Center 2003, PEN/Voelcker Award for Poetry 2004, Manhae Foundation Prize (South Korea) 2006, Jewish Cultural Foundation Achievement Award 2006, Premio Capri 2009, PEN American Center Lifetime Achievement Award 2011. *Publications include:* Landor's Poetry 1968, Sadness and Happiness 1975, The Situation of Poetry 1977, An Explanation of America (Saxifrage Prize 1980) 1980, History of My Heart 1980, Poetry and the World 1988, The Want Bone 1990, The Inferno of Dante (trans.; Howard Morton Landon Trans. Prize 1995, Los Angeles Times Book Award 1995, Acad. of American Poets Translation Award 1994) 1994, The Figured Wheel: New and Collected Poems 1966–96 (Lenore Marshall Award 1997, Amb. Book Award, English Speaking Union 1997) 1996, The Sounds of Poetry 1998, The Handbook of Heartbreak 1998, Americans' Favorite Poems (co-ed.) 1999, Jersey Rain 2000, Democracy, Culture, and the Voice of Poetry 2002, Poems to Read (co-ed.) 2002, Invitation to Poetry (co-ed.) 2004, First Things to Hand 2006, Gulf Music (Theodore Roethke Prize 2008) 2007, The Life of David (Jewish Encounters) 2008, Thousands of Broadways: Dreams and Nightmares of the American Small Town 2009, Essential Pleasures: A New Anthology of Poems to Read Aloud 2009, Death and the Powers (libretto) 2010, Selected Poems 2011, Singing School: Learning to Write (and Read) Poetry by Studying with the Masters 2013, At the Founding Hospital 2016. *Address:* Boston University, Creative Writing Program, 236 Bay State Road, Boston, MA 02215, USA (office); Steven Barclay Agency, 12 Western Avenue, Petaluma, CA 94952, USA (office). *Telephone:* (617) 353-2821 (office). *E-mail:* rpinsky@bu.edu (office). *Website:* www.bu.edu/english (office); www.robertpinskypoet.com; www.barclayagency.com (office); www.favoritepoem.org.

PINTAT SANTOLÀRIA, Albert, Lic en Sc économiques; Andorran diplomatist and politician; b. 23 June 1943, Sant Julià de Lòria; m.; three c.; ed Catholic Univ. of Friburg, Switzerland; Asst Consul, Sant Julià 1982–83; Sec. to Josep Pintat, Head of Govt 1984–85; Counsellor-Gen. 1986–91; Amb. to Benelux countries and EU 1995–97; Minister of Foreign Affairs 1997–2001; Amb. to Switzerland and UK 2001–04; Cap de Govern (Head of Govt) 2005–09; mem. Liberal Party of Andorra (Liberals d'Andorra since 2012). *Address:* c/o Liberals d'Andorra, Carrer Babot Camp 13, 2°, Andorra la Vella AD500, Andorra.

PINTER, Frances Mercedes Judith, PhD; American/British publisher; *CEO, Manchester University Press;* b. 13 June 1949, Venezuela; d. of George Pinter and Vera Hirschenhauser Pinter; m. David Percy 1985; ed Univ. Coll., London;

Research Officer, Centre for Criminological Research, Univ. of Oxford, UK 1976–79; Man. Dir Pinter Publrs 1979–94; Chair. Ind. Publrs Guild 1979–82, Publrs Asscn E European Task Force 1990–; Man. Dir Cen. European Univ. Press 1994–96; Chair. Bd of Trustees, Int. House 2001, CEO Int. House Trust 2002–06; Deputy Chair. Book Devt Council 1985–89; Publr, Bloomsbury Academic 2008–12; Interim CEO Manchester University Press 2013–14, CEO 2014–; mem. Bd UK Publrs Asscn 1987–92, IBIS Information Services 1988–90, Libra Books 1991–; Exec. Dir Centre for Publishing Devt 1994–, Open Soc. Inst. 1994–99, Knowledge Unlatched 2012–; Visiting Fellow, LSE 2000–01, 2006–14; Hon. DLitt (Curtin). *Leisure interests:* reading, travelling, hiking. *Address:* Manchester University Press, Floor J, Renold Building, Altrincham Street, Manchester, M1 7JA (office); 1 Belsize Avenue, London, NW3 4BL, England (home). *Telephone:* (161) 275-2310 (office). *E-mail:* mup@manchester.ac.uk (office); frances@pinter.org.uk (office). *Website:* www.manchesteruniversitypress.co.uk (office); www.pinter.org.uk.

PINTÉR, Sándor; Hungarian politician and police officer (retd); *Deputy Prime Minister and Minister of the Interior;* b. 3 July 1948, Budapest; m.; three d.; ed Budapest Police Acad., Faculty of Law, Eötvös Loránd Univ.; driver, Ministry of the Interior 1972–78; rapporteur, Dept of Test Drafts, Nat. Police HQ 1978–85, Head of Criminal Police Dept of the Castle, then in charge of appointments of police station chiefs 1985–88, Head of Investigation Dept, Pest Co. HQ 1988–90, Deputy Prov. Police Chief of Public Security 1990–91, Chief of Budapest Police March–Sept. 1991, Chief of Nat. Police 1991–96 (retd); Minister of the Interior 1998–2002, 2010–, Deputy Prime Minister 2018–; Security Adviser, Preventive Security Inc. (CEO 2003–10), OTP Bank Rt 1997–98; Man. Dir P&V Consulting 2002; attained rank of Maj. 1991, Lt Gen. 1993. *Address:* Ministry of the Interior, 1903 Budapest, Pf. 314 (office); Ministry of the Interior, 1051 Budapest, József Attila u. 2–4, Hungary (office). *Telephone:* (1) 441-1717 (office). *Fax:* (1) 441-1720 (office). *E-mail:* miniszter@bm.gov.hu (office). *Website:* www.kormany.hu/en/ministry-of-interior (office).

PINTO, Elsa Maria Neto d'Alva Teixeira de Barros; São Tomé and Príncipe politician; *Minister of Foreign Affairs, Cooperation and Communities;* Sec. of State for Reform of the State and Public Admin 2002–03, 2003–04, Minister of Justice 2004–08, of Public Admin and Parl. Affairs 2004–05, of Nat. Defence 2008–10, Minister of Foreign Affairs, Cooperation and Communities 2018–, also Minister of Internal Order, Justice and Parl. Affairs; mem. Movimento de Libertação de São Tomé e Príncipe—Partido Social Democrata (MLSTP—PSD). *Address:* Assembleia Nacional, Palácio dos Congressos, CP 181, São Tomé, São Tomé and Príncipe (office); Ministry of Foreign Affairs and Communities, Av. 12 de Julho, CP 111, São Tomé and Príncipe (office). *Telephone:* 2222309 (office). *Fax:* 2223237 (office). *E-mail:* info@mnec.gov.st (office). *Website:* www.mnec.gov.st (office).

PINTO BALSEMÃO, Francisco José Pereira; Portuguese journalist, lawyer and politician; *Chairman and CEO, Impresa SGPS;* b. 1 Sept. 1937, Lisbon; s. of Henrique Pinto Balsemão and Maria Adelaide C. P. Pinto Balsemão; m. 1st Maria Isabel de Lacerda Pinto da Costa Lobo (divorced); m. 2nd José da Franca de Horta Machado Guedes Leitão Cruz; one s. one d.; m. 3rd Maria Mercedes Aliu Presas 1975; one s. one d.; one s. with Isabel Maria Supico Pinto; Ed.-in-Chief Mais Alto review 1961–63; Sec. to Man. Bd, Diário Popular, later Man. –1971; f. weekly Expresso 1973; mem. Nat. Ass. during govt of Dr Marcello Caetano; f. Popular Democratic Party (PPD), later renamed Social Democratic Party (PSD), with the late Dr Sá Carneiro and Joaquim Magalhães Mota May 1974, Chair. Int. Relations Cttee and mem. Political Cttee PSD, Party Leader 1980–83; Vice-Pres. Constituent Ass. 1975; Opposition Spokesman on Foreign Affairs 1977; mem. Ass. of the Repub. 1979; Minister Without Portfolio and Deputy Prime Minister 1980; Prime Minister of Portugal 1981–83; Pres. Instituto Progresso Social e Democracia, Francisco dá Carneiro 1983–, Sociedad Independente de Comunicação (SIC), European Inst. for the Media 1990; Chair. Sojornal and Controjornal (Media) Groups; Chair. and CEO Impresa SGPS SA; Chair. European Publrs Council; Pres. Companhia de Seguros Allianz Portugal SA; Prof. of Communication Science, New Univ., Lisbon; Rafael Calvo Serer Prize, Spain 2007. *Address:* Impresa SGPS SA, Rua Ribeiro Sanches 65, 1200-787 Lisbon, Portugal (office). *Telephone:* (213) 929780 (office). *Fax:* (213) 929787 (office). *E-mail:* impresa@impresa.pt (office). *Website:* www.impresa.pt (office).

PINTO COELHO SERRA, João António, BEcon; Cabo Verde politician and central banker; *Governor, Banco de Cabo Verde;* b. 25 Jan. 1961, Praia, Santiago; fmr Sec. of State for Finance; fmr Pres. Admin. Council, Instituto Nacional da Previdência Social; fmr Man. Dir Instituto do Emprego e Formação Profissional; fmr Dir Projecto de Promoção de Microempresas; Minister of Finance and Public Admin 2005, of Finance, Planning and Devt 2006; fmr Chair. Tourism Development Corpn of Boa Vista and Maio Islands (SDTIBM); Gov. Banco de Cabo Verde 2014–. *Address:* Banco de Cabo Verde, Av. Amílcar Cabral 117, CP 101, Praia, Santiago, Cabo Verde (office). *Telephone:* 2607000 (office). *Fax:* 2607095 (office). *E-mail:* fevora@bcv.cv (office). *Website:* www.bcv.cv (office).

PINTO DA COSTA, Manuel; São Tomé and Príncipe politician, economist and fmr head of state; b. 5 Aug. 1937, Água Grande; s. of Manuel de Espirito Santo Costa and Maria do Sacramento Pinto; ed Hochschule für Ökonomie, Berlin; co-f. Movt for the Liberation of São Tomé e Príncipe (MLSTP) 1972, Sec.-Gen. MLSTP, based in Gabon 1972–75, Pres. 1978, Leader 1998–2005; Pres. of São Tomé e Príncipe and C-in-C of the Armed Forces 1975–91, 2011–16; Minister of Agric., Land Reform and Defence 1975–78, of Labour and Social Security 1977–78, of Territorial Admin. 1978–82, of Defence and Nat. Security 1982–86, fmr Minister of Planning and Econs; Prime Minister 1978–88; Dr hc (Berlin); José Marti Medal, Cuba. *Address:* c/o Palácio Presidêncial, CP 38, São Tomé, São Tomé e Principe (office).

PINTO MARANHÃO, Rossano, MEconSc; Brazilian banking executive; *President and Director, Group Safra SA;* b. 17 July 1957, São Luís, Maranhão; m.; one s. two d.; ed Univ. of Illinois at Urbana-Champaign, USA, Univ. of Brasília; joined Banco do Brasil 1976, served as Man. Dir for Int. Div., CEO BB Leasing Co., Vice-Pres. for Int. Businesses and Wholesale 2001–04, Vice-Chair., Interim Pres. and CEO 2004–06; mem. Bd of Dirs Telecomunicacões do Rio de Janeiro (Telemar Rio) 1998–99, Tele Norte Leste (Telemar) 1999–2003, Banco Latino Americano de Exportaciones SA (BLADEX) 1999–2000; Ind. Dir Iguatemi Empresa de Shopping Centers SA 2007–; currently Pres. and Dir Group Safra SA; fmr Prof. Instituto Brasileiro de Mercado de Capitais–Ibmec and Universidade Católica de Brasília. *Address:* Iguatemi Empresa de Shopping Centers SA, Avenida Dr Chucri Zaidan 920, São Paulo 04583-110 (office); Group Safra SA, Avenida Paulista 2100, São Paulo 01310-930, Brazil (office). *Telephone:* (11) 3048-7289 (office); (11) 3175-7575 (Safra) (office). *Fax:* (11) 3048-7292 (office); (11) 3175-7211 (Safra) (office). *E-mail:* info@iguatemi.com.br (office). *Website:* www.iguatemi.com.br (office); www.safra.com.br (office).

PINTO MONTEIRO, Fernando José; Portuguese lawyer and judge; b. 5 April 1942, Porto de Ovelha, Almeida; s. of Amílcar Monteiro and Lurdes Monteiro; m.; one s. one d.; ed Univ. of Coimbra; Public Prosecutor, Idanha-a-Nova, Anadia, Porto and Lisbon 1966; Judge, Ponta do Sol, Alcácer do Sal, Loures, Torres Vedras and Lisboa; fmr Asst High Commr Higher Authority Against Corruption; Judge Court of Appeals 1990–98; Judge Supreme Court of Justice 1998–2006; Chief Public Prosecutor 2006–12; Visiting Prof. of Law, Autonomous Univ. of Lisbon 1992–2006; Pres. Disciplinary Council, Portuguese Football Asscn 1995–97; fmr Sec. Gen. Portuguese Asscn of Judges; Grand Cross of Military Order of Christ.

PINTO RUBIANES, Pedro Alfredo; Ecuadorean politician and business executive; b. 31 Jan. 1931, Quito; ed Univ. Cen. del Ecuador, Vanderbilt Univ., USA; Gen. Man. Textile San Pedro SA 1967–82, 1984–97, Pres. 1997; Pres. Asscn of Textile Mfrs 1968–70; Dean Faculty of Admin, Univ. Cen. del Ecuador 1970–72; Pres. Chamber of Mfrs of Pichincha 1971–73, Fed. of Industrialists of Ecuador 1972–73; town councillor, Quito 1973–77; Dir Corporación Financiera Ecuatoriana (COFIEC) 1976–82; Minister of Finance and Public Credit 1982–84; Gov. for Ecuador, Banco Interamericano de Desarrollo (BID), IBRD 1983–84; Dir CORDES 1988, Bank of Pichincha 1993–98, Chamber of Mfrs of Pichincha 1997–98; Deputy for Pichincha 1998; Vice-Pres. of Ecuador 2000–03.

PINZÓN BUENO, Juan Carlos; Colombian economist, politician and diplomatist; b. 22 Dec. 1971; s. of Rafael Pinzón Rincón and Marlene Bueno; m. María del Pilar Lozano; one s. one d.; ed Universidad Javeriana, Bogota, Paul H. Nitze School of Advanced Int. Studies, Washington, DC, Belfer Center for Science and Int. Affairs, Harvard Univ., Woodrow Wilson School of Public and Int. Affairs, Princeton Univ., USA; Researcher, Federación Nacional de Cafeteros 1996; Researcher, Asociación Bancaria y de Entidades Financieras de Colombia 1996–97, Vice-Pres. 2003–04; Head of Econ. Investigation Dept, Citibank-Citigroup, Bogota 1997–2000, Asst Vice-Pres. of Investment Banking 2002; Private Sec., Ministry of Finance and Public Credit 2000–02; Prof. of Macroeconomics, Universidad Javeriana 2000–04; Sr Adviser to Exec. Dir, World Bank, Washington, DC 2004–06; Deputy Minister of Defence for Strategy and Planning 2006–09, Minister of Nat. Defence 2011–15; Dir Admin. Dept of Presidency of Colombia 2010–11; Amb. to USA 2015–17; mem. Partido Social de Unidad Nacional.

PIO DOS SANTOS GOURGEL, Abraão; Angolan economist, politician and fmr central banker; *Minister of the Economy;* b. 11 Nov. 1961; fmr Coordinator, Gabinete Técnico dos Projectos dos Programas de Investimento Públicos, Uíge Prov.; Vice Minister of Industry 2005–09; Gov. Nat. Bank of Angola 2009–10; Minister of the Economy 2010–; Central Bank Gov. of the Year for Africa, Banker Magazine 2009. *Address:* Ministry of the Economy, Luanda, Angola (office). *E-mail:* geral@minec.gov.ao (office). *Website:* www.minec.gov.ao (office).

PIOT, Baron; **Peter,** MD, PhD, FRCP; Belgian physician, international organization official and academic; *Professor of Global Health and Director, London School of Hygiene and Tropical Medicine;* b. 17 Feb. 1949, Leuven; m. 1st Greet Kimzeke 1975; two c.; m. 2nd Heidi Larson; ed Univs of Ghent and Antwerp, Belgium, Univ. of Washington, USA; Asst in Microbiology, Inst. of Tropical Medicine, Antwerp 1974–78, Prof., Head Dept of Microbiology 1981–92; NATO Fellow 1978–79; Sr Fellow, Microbiology and Infectious Diseases, Washington Univ. 1978–79; Researcher, Nairobi Univ., STD/AIDS Project, Kenya 1981–92; Supervisor, Project SIDA, Kinshasa 1985–91; Asst Prof. of Public Health, Free Univ. Brussels 1989–94; Assoc. Dir Global Program AIDS, WHO 1995, Exec. Dir Jt UN Program on HIV/AIDS (UNAIDS), Geneva 1995–2008, Under-Sec.-Gen. UN 1995–2008; Prof. and Dir, Inst. of Global Health, Imperial Coll. London 2009–10; currently Dir London School of Hygiene and Tropical Medicine and Prof. of Global Health; Chair. MRC Global Health Group and mem. MRC Strategy Bd; fmr Dir WHO Collaborating Centre on AIDS, Antwerp; fmr Chair. King Baudouin Foundation, Brussels; mem. Bd of Dirs Global Health Innovative Technology Fund, Japan, Oxford Martin Comm. on Future Generations; mem. Royal Acad. of Medicine (Belgium), Académie Nationale de Médicine (France), Int. AIDS Soc. (fmr Pres.); Foreign mem. Inst. of Medicine, Washington, DC; cr. baron by King Albert II 1995; numerous decorations including Officier, Ordre Nat. du Léopard (Zaïre) 1977, Ordre du Lion (Senegal), Nat. Order, Burkina Faso, Madagascar, Vietnam, Grand Official, Order of the Infante Don Enrique (Portugal) 2005, Commandeur, Ordre Nat., Mali 2008; various hon. doctorates; numerous awards including De Kerkheer Prize for Medicine 1989, Health Research Award (Belgium) 1989, Public Health Award, Flemish Community 1990, AMICOM Award for Medicine 1991, H. Breurs Prize 1992, A. Jaunioux Prize 1992, van Thiel Award 1993, Glaxo award for infectious diseases 1995, Nelson Mandela Award 2001, Royal Acad. of Arts and Sciences Gold Medal, Belgium 2002, E. Calderone Medal, Columbia Univ. 2003, Outstanding Physician AMA Chicago, Vlerick Award, Belgium 2004, Congressional Award of Achievement, Philippines 2005, Mother Theresa Award, New Delhi, 2007, Person of the Year, Knack Magazine, Belgium 2008, Hideyo Noguchi Africa Prize for Medical Research 2013, Prince Mahidol Award for Public Health 2014. *Achievements include:* credited as co-discoverer of Ebola virus in Zaire 1976. *Publications:* author and co-author of 16 books and over 500 scientific papers on women's health, AIDS and other sexually transmitted diseases. *Address:* London School of Hygiene and Tropical Medicine, Room 42, Keppel Street, London, WC1E 7HT, England (office). *Telephone:* (20) 7927-2278 (office). *Fax:* (20) 7636-7679 (office). *E-mail:* director@lshtm.ac.uk (office). *Website:* www.lshtm.ac.uk (office).

PIOTROVSKY, Mikhail Borisovich, DHist; Russian art researcher and museum director; *Director, State Hermitage;* b. 9 Dec. 1944, Yerevan, Armenia; s. of Boris Borisovich Piotrovsky and Hripsime Djanpoladjian; m. Irina Leonidovna Piotrovskaya; one s. one d.; ed Leningrad State Univ., Cairo Univ.; researcher, Leningrad Inst. of Oriental Studies, USSR Acad. of Sciences 1967–91; First Deputy

Dir State Hermitage, St Petersburg 1991–92, Dir 1992–; Prof., St Petersburg State Univ., Chair. Dept of Museology and Dept The History of Ancient Orient, a Dean of Oriental Faculty; mem. Presidium, Cttee on State Prizes of Russian Presidency, Presidium, Russian Cttee of UNESCO, Int. Council of Museums, Pres.'s Council for Culture and Art, Pres.'s Council for Science and Educ.; mem. Group of Consultants for Council of Europe art exhbns, and other nat. and int. and orgs; Chair. First Channel (Russian TV) 2001–; Pres. Union of Museums in Russia, Worldwide Club of St Petersburg; Chair. European Univ. in St Petersburg; Ed.-in-Chief The Christian Orient magazine; Corresp. mem. Russian Acad. of Sciences 1997, German Archeological Inst.; mem. Acad. of Humanitarian Sciences, Acad. of Arts, Acad. of Sciences (Tatarstan); Foreign mem. Acad. of Art (Armenia); Hon. Prof., Kazan Univ., Saratov State Univ.; Honoured Citizen of St Petersburg 2011; Order of Orange-Nassau (Netherlands) 1996, Order of Honour 1997, Chevalier, Légion d'honneur 1998, Officier 2004, Order of the Northern Star (Swedish) 1999, Kt, Order of Merit of Italian Republic 2000, Officer 2004, Order of Saint Mesrop, Armenian Apostle Church 2000, Order of Yaroslav the Wise (Ukraine) 2003, Order of Merit (Poland) 2004, Order of Service to the Fatherland 2004, 2009, Order of Honour Al-Fahr (Council of Muftis of Russia) 2005, Order of the Finish Lion 2005, Order of the Rising Sun (Japan) 2007, Order of the Crown (Belgium) 2011, Medal of Anatoliy Koni, Ministry of Justice 2013; minor planet Piotrovski named by Astronomical Union in joint honour of him and his father 1997, Presidential Prize in the Field of Art and Literature 2003, Silver Medal of Amsterdam 2009, Woodrow Wilson Award (USA) 2009. *Publications:* more than 250 works, including catalogues of Arabic manuscripts, publications of Medieval monuments and ancient inscriptions, works on Islamic political history and Arabic culture, amongst them: series of articles devoted to Muslim mythology in The Encyclopedia of World Mythology, series of articles about the prophet Muhammad, and monographs: The Legend of the Himyarite King As'ad al-Kamil 1977, Fundamentals of Arab-Islamic Art 1984, Southern Arabia in the Early Middle Ages 1985, Islam: An Encyclopaedia 1991, Tales of the Koran 1991, The Hermitage: Essays on the History of the Collection (co-author) 1997, Earthy Art: Heavenly Beauty. Art of Islam (co-ed.) 2000, On Islamic Art 2001, The Hermitage 2003, The Great Collections of the Great Museum: The Hermitage 2003, The Historical Legends of the Koran 2005, The Islamic Art: Between China and Europe 2008, The View from the Hermitage 2009, The Two Holy Sites Regained: Futuh al-Haramayn 2011. *Address:* State Hermitage, Dvortsovaya nab. 34, 191186 St Petersburg, Russian Federation (office). *Telephone:* (812) 710-90-79 (office). *Fax:* (812) 570-57-48 (office). *E-mail:* chancery@hermitage.ru (office). *Website:* hermitagemuseum.org (office).

PIOTROWSKA, Teresa; Polish politician; b. 5 Feb. 1955, Tczew; m.; one s.; ed Maria Skłodowska-Curie Secondary School of Gen. Educ., Tczew, Faculties of Theology and History at Acad. of Catholic Theology; mem. Bydgoszcz Municipal Council 1994–98, later of its Bd; Voivode of Bydgoskie Voivodeship March–Dec. 1998; Deputy Pres. Public Procurement Office 1999–2001; Deputy (Civic Platform) to the Sejm (Parl.) for Bydgoszcz Constituency 2001–, mem. State Audit Cttee; Minister of the Interior 2014–15. *Address:* Kancelaria Sejmu, 00-902 Warsaw, ul. Wiejska 4/6/8, Poland (office). *Telephone:* (22) 6942500 (office). *Fax:* (22) 6941446 (office). *E-mail:* teresa.piotrowska@sejm.pl (office). *Website:* www.sejm.gov.pl/Sejm7.nsf/posel.xsp?id=304 (office).

PIPE, Martin Charles, CBE; British race horse trainer (retd); b. 29 May 1945; s. of D. A. C. Pipe and M. E. R. Pipe; m. Mary Caroline; one s.; ed Queen's Coll., Taunton; first trainer's licence 1977; major wins include: Grand National (with Miinnehoma) 1994, Champion hurdle (twice), Welsh National (six times), Irish National, Scottish National, Midlands National, Hennessy Gold Cup (three times), Mackeson Gold Cup; only British trainer to train 200 winners in a season 1989; 15 times National Hunt champion trainer (1989/90, 1990/91, 1991/92, 1992/93, 1995/96, 1996/97, 1997/98, 1998/99, 1999/2000, 2000/01, 2001/02, 2002/03, 2003/04); four winners at Royal Ascot; 28 winners at Cheltenham Festival including record four winners in consecutive years. *Publications:* Martin Pipe: The Champion Trainer's Story (with Richard Pitman) 1992. *Address:* Pond House, Nicholashayne, Wellington, Somerset, TA21 9QY, England. *Telephone:* (1884) 840715. *E-mail:* Martin@MartinPipe.co.uk. *Website:* www.martinpipe.com.

PIPER, Martha Cook, BSc, MA, PhD, OC, OBC; Canadian/American epidemiologist, academic and university administrator; *Chairman, Board of Trustees, National Institute for Nanotechnology;* b. Lorain, OH; ed Univ. of Michigan, Univ. of Connecticut, McGill Univ.; physical therapist, Sr then Chief Physical Therapist at various US hosps 1967–73; Dir School of Physical and Occupational Therapy, McGill Univ., Montréal 1979–85, Asst Prof. then Assoc. Prof. 1979–84; Dean, Assoc. Prof., then Prof. of Rehabilitation Medicine and Vice Pres. (Research, later Research and External Affairs), Univ. of Alberta, Edmonton 1985–96; Pres. and Vice-Chancellor, Univ. of British Columbia 1997–2006, Interim Pres. 2015–16; Chair. Bd of Trustees Nat. Inst. of Nanotechnology 2008–; fmr Dir Canadian Genetic Diseases Network; mem. Bd of Dirs Bank of Montreal 2006–, Transalta Corpn 2006–, Shoppers Drug Mart Corpn 2007–, Grosvenor Americas Ltd, CARE Canada, Inst. for Research on Public Policy, BC Children's Hosp. Foundation; fmr mem. Bd of Dirs Center for Frontier Engineering Research 1993–97, Telecommunications Research Labs 1993–97, Alberta Research Council 1993–97, Canada Israel Industrial Research Foundation 1994–97, The Conf. Bd of Canada, Pierre Elliot Trudeau Foundation, PrioNet Canada; fmr mem. Advisory Council on Science and Tech. 1996–2004, Protein Eng Network Centre of Excellence (PENCE), Canada Foundation for Innovation, Advisory Bd Vancouver Econ. Devt Comm., Distinguished Profs Selection Cttee, Univ. of Manitoba, Canadian-American Business Council, Nat. Univ. of Singapore Council, Steering Cttee, Asscn of Pacific Rim Univs; fmr Chair. Standing Advisory Cttee on Univ. Research, Asscn of Univs and Colls of Canada; fmr Public Gov., Bd of Canadian Acads of Science; Specially Elected Fellow, Royal Soc. of Canada 2009–; Trustee Dalia Lama Center for Peace and Educ., Vancouver; mem. Trilateral Comm., Canadian Insts of Advanced Research; Hon. Fellow, Merton Coll., Oxford 2007; Hon. DSc (McGill) 1998, (Western Ontario) 2002; Hon. LLD (Dalhousie) 1999, (Toronto) 2001, (Melbourne, Australia) 2003, (Saskatchewan) 2005, (St Francis Xavier) 2006, (Calgary) 2006, (Alberta) 2006, (Victoria) 2006, (Simon Fraser) 2008; Educator of the Year, Learning Partnership 2004. *Address:* c/o Board of Trustees, National Institute for Nanotechnology, 11421 Saskatchewan Drive, Edmonton, AB T6G 2M9, Canada. *E-mail:* nintinfo@nrc.gc.ca. *Website:* nint-innt.nrc-cnrc.gc.ca.

PIQUÉ I CAMPS, Josep, LLB, PhD; Spanish economist, politician and business executive; *CEO and Chairman, OHL Group;* b. 21 Feb. 1955, Barcelona; m. Gloria Lomana; ed Univ. of Barcelona; Lecturer in Econ. Theory, Univ. of Barcelona 1977–86, 1990; Economist, Studies Dept, La Caixa 1984–85; Gen. Dir of Industry, Catalan Autonomous Govt 1986–88; Gen. Man. of Corp. Strategy, Ercros. SA (pvt. chemicals group) 1989–91, Man. Dir 1992, Chair. and CEO 1992–96, various posts in group including Chair. EMESA 1989–91, ERKIMIA SA 1990–96, FERTIBERIA 1993–96, FYSE 1992–93, LISAC 1992, META 1990–94, Sole Admin. FESA 1992–93, mem. Bd Prisma 1991–96, Río Tinto Minera 1991–93, Erkol 1991–96, Rhodiamul 1991–92; Minister of Industry and Energy 1996–2000; Govt Spokesman 1998–2000; Minister of Foreign Affairs 2000–02, of Science and Tech. 2002–04; Chair. Vueling Airlines SA, Barcelona 2007–13; CEO and Vice-Chair. OHL Group 2013–; mem. Bd of Dir European Aeronautics Group, Spain 2012–. *Address:* OHL Group, Torrespacio, Paseo de la Castellana, 259 D, Madrid 28046, Spain (office). *Telephone:* (91) 3484100 (office). *E-mail:* info@ohl.es (office). *Website:* www.ohl.es (office).

PIQUET (SOUTO MAIOR), Nélson; Brazilian fmr racing driver and businessman; b. 17 Aug. 1952, Rio de Janeiro; s. of Estácio Souto Maior and Clotilde Maior; m. 1st Maria Clara 1976 (divorced 1977); one s.; m. 2nd Sylvia Tamsma; one s. (racing driver Nelson Angelo 'Nelsinho' Piquet Jr) two d.; one s. with Katherine Valentin 1987; m. 3rd Viviane de Souza Leão; one s. one d.; brief career in tennis before taking up karting; Brazilian nat. karting champion 1971–72, won Formula Vee championship 1976; went to Europe to further success by taking record number of wins in Formula Three 1978, defeating Jackie Stewart's all-time record; Formula One debut, Germany 1978; mem. Ensign Grand Prix team 1978, BS McLaren team 1978, Brabham team 1978–85, Williams team 1986–87, Lotus team 1988–89, Benetton team 1990; winner of 23 Grand Prix races; Formula One World Champion 1981, 1983, 1987; competed in Indianapolis 500 for two years; also tried his hand at sports car racing during and after Formula One career; currently retired (1991) and runs several businesses in Brazil; f. Autotrac 1994; f. racing team Piquet Sports to help manage his son Nelson Piquet Jr 2000; Procar BMW M1 Champion 1980, Autosport Int. Racing Driver Award 1983, Int. Motorsports Hall of Fame 2000, two racing circuits in Rio de Janeiro (fmrly Jacarepaguá Circuit) and in Brasília named Autódromo Internacional Nelson Piquet. *Leisure interest:* sports. *Website:* www.grandprix.com/gpe/drv-piqnel.html.

PIRES, Maria Helena Lopes de Jesus, BA; Timor-Leste politician and diplomatist; *Permanent Representative to United Nations, New York;* b. 19 June 1966, Dili, Portuguese Timor; m. Zacarias da Costa; one s.; ed Univ. of New England, Australia; mem. UN for East Timor Transitional Admin 2001–02, also Vice-Pres. Nat. Council, Country Programme Coordinator UN Devt Fund for Women (UNIFEM) 2003–07, Expert mem. UN Cttee on Elimination of Discrimination against Women 2011–14; Perm. Rep. to UN, New York 2016–; mem. Nat. Parl. (Partido Social Democrata) 2002, 2007; Coordinator of Justice Sector Report, State of the Nation Report 2007–08; Civil Soc. Strengthening Specialist Asia Foundation, Justice Facility Program 2008–09; Exec. Dir and Founding mem. Centre for Women and Gender 2013–16; Chief Political Adviser to Minister for Commerce, Industry and Environment –2016, also Sr Adviser to Vice-Prime Minister 2008–16. *Publication:* articles published for different journals. *Address:* Permanent Mission of Timor-Leste, 866 Second Avenue, Suite 441, New York, NY 10017, USA (office). *Telephone:* (212) 759-3675 (office). *Fax:* (212) 759-4196 (office). *E-mail:* timor-leste@un.int (office).

PIRES, Maria Madalena Emília; Timor-Leste politician; ed La Trobe Univ., Australia; moved to Australia as refugee with family aged 14 in 1975; fmr Admin. Nat. Council of Timorese Resistance office, Darwin; fmr Pres. Timorese Asscn of Vic.; mem. World Bank jt assessment mission in Timor-Leste 1999; est. East Timor Devt Office, Melbourne; Head, Nat. Planning and Devt Agency, Timor-Leste 2000–01; joined Ministry of Planning and Finances, held several positions including Sec., East Timor Planning Comm. 2002, Advisor on Planning and External Assistance Man. 2003–04; Sr Coordination Adviser to UN Deputy Special Rep. of the Sec.-Gen. for Int. Compact on Timor-Leste –2007; Minister of Finance 2007–15.

PIRES, Gen. Pedro Verona Rodrigues; Cabo Verde politician and fmr head of state; *President, Amílcar Cabral Foundation;* b. 29 April 1934, Sant' Ana, Fogo; s. of Luís Rodrigues Pires and Maria Fidalga Lopes Pires; m. Adélcia Maria da Luz Lima Barreto Pires 1975; two d.; ed Liceu Gil Eanes de São Vicente, Faculty of Science, Lisbon Univ., Portugal; left Portugal to join Partido Africano da Independência da Guiné e Cabo Verde (PAIGC) 1961; mem. PAIGC dels 1961–63; involved in preparation for liberation of Cape Verde 1963–65; mem. Cen. Cttee of PAIGC 1965, of Council of War, PAIGC 1967; re-elected mem. of Commissão Permanente do Comité Executivo da Luta (CEL) and of Council of War 1970; involved in admin. of liberated areas of southern Guinea-Bissau 1971–73; Pres. Nat. Comm. of PAIGC for Cape Verde 1973 (reaffirmed as mem. of Council of War and CEL), appointed an Asst State Commr in first Govt of Repub. of Guinea-Bissau 1973–74; negotiated independence agreements of Cape Verde and Guinea-Bissau 1974; Dir PAIGC policies during transitional govt before independence of Cape Verde 1975; elected Deputy in Nat. Popular Ass. of Cape Verde June 1975–, re-elected 1980; Prime Minister of Cape (now Cabo) Verde 1975–91, with responsibility for Finance, Planning and Co-operation; elected Deputy Gen. Sec. Partido Africano da Independência de Cabo Verde (PAICV) 1981, Sec. Gen. 1990–93, fmr Chair. Gen. 1993; Pres. of Cabo Verde 2001–11; Pres. Fundação Amílcar Cabral, Cabo Verde; mem. Perm. Comm. of CEL 1977; Ordem Amílcar Cabral 1976, Order of the Lion (Senegal), Ordem Infante D. Henrique (Portugal), Orden José Marti (Cuba), Orden de las Islas Canarias (Spain), Nat. Order (Gambia), Grande Colar da Ordem de Timor-Leste 2011, Mo Ibrahim Prize for Achievement in African Leadership 2011; Dr hc (Universidade do Ceará, Brazil), (Universidade Técnica de Lisboa), (ISCSP), (Universidade Lusófona de Humanidades e de Tecnologias, Lisbon). *Leisure interests:* philosophy, sociology, politics. *Address:* Fundação Amílcar Cabral, Praia, Santiago; CP 429, Praia, Santiago; Rua Dr Manuel Duarte, Praia, Santiago, Cabo Verde (home). *Telephone:* (261) 6585 (home). *E-mail:* pvrodriguespires@gmail.com (home).

PIRIE, Madsen Duncan, MA, PhD, MPhil; British research institute director; *President, Adam Smith Institute;* b. 24 Aug. 1940; s. of Douglas G. Pirie and Eva Madsen; ed Univs of Edinburgh, St Andrews and Cambridge; Republican Study

Cttee 1974; Distinguished Visiting Prof. of Philosophy, Hillsdale Coll., Mich. 1975–78; Pres. Adam Smith Inst. 1978–; mem. Citizens' Charter Advisory Panel 1991–95; RC Hoiles Fellow 1975; Sr Visiting Fellow, Dept of Land Economy, Cambridge 2010. *Publications:* Trial and Error 1978, Book of the Fallacy 1985, Privatization 1988, Micropolitics 1988, How to Win Every Argument 2006, 101 Great Philosophers: Makers of Modern Thought 2009, Economics Made Simple 2012, Think Tank 2012. *Leisure interest:* calligraphy. *Address:* 23 Great Smith Street, London, SW1P 3BL, England (home). *Telephone:* (20) 7222-4995 (office). *E-mail:* m.pirie@adamsmith.org (office). *Website:* www.adamsmith.org (office).

PIRINSKI, Georgi Georgiev; Bulgarian politician; b. 10 Sept. 1948, New York, USA; m.; two c.; ed English Language Secondary School No. 114, Sofia, Karl Marx Higher Inst. of Econs, Sofia; moved to Bulgaria 1952; Research Assoc., Int. Relations and Socialist Integration Inst. 1972–74; economist, Int. Orgs Div., Ministry of Foreign Trade 1974–76; Advisor, Council of Ministers 1976–80; fmr Deputy Minister and First Deputy Minister of Foreign Trade 1980–89; Deputy Minister and First Deputy Minister of Foreign Trade 1980–90; Deputy Prime Minister Nov. 1989–Feb. 1990, Aug.–Dec. 1990; Minister of Foreign Affairs 1995–96 (resgnd); mem. Parl. for Blagoevgrad in 7th Grand Nat. Ass. (Parl. Group of Bulgarian Socialist Party—BSP), for Plovdiv in 36th Nat. Ass. (Parl. Union for Social Democracy), for Sofia in 37th, 38th, 39th and 40th Nat. Ass. (Parl. Group of Democratic Left) 1995–2009, Pres. (Speaker) 40th Nat. Ass. 2005–09, Vice-Pres. 41st Nat. Ass. 2009–13; mem. Foreign Policy and Defence Cttee 2009–13, Dels of Nat. Ass. to Parl. Ass of OSCE, Council of Europe, WEU, NATO Parl. Ass. 2009–13; nominated from BSP for Pres. in Oct. 1996 presidential elections but rejected by Constitutional Court on basis of not being a Bulgarian citizen by birth; mem. Bulgarian CP/BSP 1969–2005 (mem. Cen. Cttee Bulgarian 1989–90, Presidency and Deputy Chair. Supreme Council 1990–2005), Coalition for Bulgaria (led by BSP) 2005–. *Address:* c/o Office of the Chairman, Narodno Sobranie, 1169 Sofia, pl. Narodno Sobranie 2, Bulgaria. *Telephone:* (2) 939-39. *E-mail:* infocenter@parliament.bg.

PIRK, Jan, MD, DSc; Czech heart surgeon; *Head, Cardiocentre, IKEM Clinic for Heart Surgery;* b. 20 April 1948, Prague; s. of Otto Pirk and Jitka Pirk; m. Blanka Pirk; two s.; ed Charles Univ., Prague; occupied numerous medical and surgical positions; researcher 1978–90; consultant, Odense Univ. Hosp., Denmark 1990–91, Ochsner Hosp., New Orleans, USA 1983–84; Head, Cardiocentre, Institutu Klinické a Experimentální Medicíny (IKEM) Clinic for Heart Surgery 1991–; Hon. mem. Czech Medical Soc., Czech Cardiology Soc. *Publications include:* The Effect of Antiaggregation Drugs on the Patency of Grafts in the Arterial System 1980, Improved Patency of the Aortocoronary Bypass by Anti-Trombic Drugs (co-author) 1986, Surgery for Ischaemic Heart Disease in Patients Under Forty (co-author) 1989, An Alternative to Cardioplegia (with M. D. Kellovsky) 1995. *Leisure interests:* skiing, biking, long-distance running, theatre, yachting. *Address:* IKEM Clinic for Heart Surgery, Vídeňská 1958, 140 21 Prague 4 (office); V Domově 28, 130 00 Prague 3, Czech Republic (home). *Telephone:* (2) 3605-5014 (office). *Fax:* (2) 3605-2776 (office). *E-mail:* japx@medicon.cz (office). *Website:* www .ikem.cz (office).

PIRUMOV, Rear Adm. (retd) Vladimir Semenovich, DrMilSc; Russian naval officer, politician and scientist; b. 1 Feb. 1926, Kirovakan, Armenia; m.; two d.; ed Caspian Higher Mil. Marine School, Mil. Marine Acad.; artillery officer, Asst to Commdr of cruiser, Commdr of destroyer Baltic Navy 1948–60; Head of Dept Gen. Staff of Mil. Marine forces 1974–85; teacher, Sr teacher, Head of Chair Mil. Marine Acad. 1963–74; Prof. Mil. Acad. of Gen. Staff 1985–; mem. Russian Acad. of Nat. Sciences; Vice-Pres., Head Section of Geopolitics and Security, Russian Acad. of Sciences 1993; Pres. Cen. of Studies of Problems of Geopolitics and Security at Security Council of Russian Fed. 1993–; First Vice-Pres. Acad. of Geopolitics and Security 2000–; mem. Ed. Bd journals Geopolitica i Besopasnost, Vooruzheniye, Politika, Konversia; P. Kapitsa Silver Medal, Piotr the Great Gold Medal, State Prize of Russian Fed. 1977, Merited Worker of Science of Russian Fed., various scientific awards. *Publications:* over 170 publications including Actual Problems of Security, Regions of Russia and the World, Strategy of Socio-Survival. *Address:* Russian Academy of Natural Sciences, Varshawskoye shosse 8, 113105 Moscow, Russia (office). *Telephone:* (495) 252-55-74 (office). *E-mail:* mediterra@yandex.ru (home).

PISAN, Manawapat, BSc, MSc; Thai diplomatist; *Ambassador to USA;* b. 1956; m. Wanchana Manawapat; one d.; ed London School of Econs and Univ. of London, UK, Nat. Defence Coll.; served as American Political Science Asscn Congressional Fellow, working for Congressman Don Peck and Senator Daniel Inouye, Washington, DC 1986, then First Sec., Embassy in Washington, DC 1987–90, Asst to Foreign Minister Arsa Sarasin 1991–92, Minister Counsellor, Embassy in Kuala Lumpur 1993–95, Dir Personnel Div. then Deputy Dir-Gen., Dept of East Asian Affairs 1995–98, Deputy Dir-Gen., East Asia Dept 1995–98, Deputy Chief of Mission, Embassy in Tokyo 1999–2002, Dir-Gen. Dept of Int. Econ. Affairs 2002–04, Chief Negotiator for the Japan-Thailand Economic Partnership Agreement (JTEPA) 2002–06, Amb. to Belgium and Luxembourg, also Head of Mission to EU 2007–11, Amb. to India 2011–13, to Canada 2013–15, to USA 2015–; Most Exalted Order of the White Elephant 2011. *Address:* Embassy of Thailand, 1024 Wisconsin Avenue, NW, Washington, DC 20007, USA (office). *Telephone:* (202) 944-3600 (office). *Fax:* (202) 944-3611 (office). *E-mail:* info@thaiembdc.org (office). *Website:* www.thaiembdc.org (office).

PISANI-FERRY, Jean; French economist; *Commissioner General for Policy Planning, France Stratégie;* b. 28 July 1951, Boulogne-Billancourt; ed Ecole Supérieure d'Electricité, Université Paris V, Centre d'études des programmes économiques; Econ. Adviser with EC 1989–92; Dir of CEPII (Centre d'études prospectives et d'informations internationales—French inst. for int. econs) 1992–97; Sr Econ. Adviser to the Minister of Finance 1997–2000; Exec. Pres. of the Prime Minister's Council of Econ. Analysis 2001–02; Commr Gen. for Policy Planning, France Stratégie 2013–; Prof. of Econs, Université Paris-Dauphine; Dir Bruegel (economic think tank) 2005; current research interests include economic policy in Europe and global macroeconomics; regular columns in Le Monde, Handelsblatt, The FT A-List, Project Syndicate and the Chinese magazine Caixin; Chevalier de la Légion d'honneur. *Publications:* recent publications include Economic Policy (co-author) 2010, Le Réveil des Démons 2011, Démons: la crise de l'euro et comment nous en sortir (in French) 2011 (in English 2012), Global

Currencies for Tomorrow (co-author) 2011, An Ocean Apart?: Comparing Transatlantic Responses to the Financial Crisis (co-ed.) 2011. *Address:* France Stratégie, 18 rue de Martignac, 75700, Paris cedex 07, France (office). *Telephone:* (1) 42-75-60-00 (office). *Fax:* (1) 45-55-53-37 (office). *Website:* www.strategie.gouv.fr (office); www.pisani-ferry.net.

PISANU, Giuseppe (Beppe); Italian politician; b. 2 Jan. 1937, Ittiri, Sassari; m.; three s.; Deputy Man. Dir Soc. of Finance and Industry for the Rebirth of Sardinia (SFIRS); Prov. Sec., Regional Sec. (Sardinia), Exec. Sec. to Pres. Democrazia Cristiana (Christian Democrats) 1975–80; mem. Chamber of Deputies (Christian Democrats) 1972–92; Under-Sec. of State for Treasury 1980–83; Under-Sec. of State for Defence 1986–90; mem. Forza Italia (Sardinia) 1994–2009, Vice-Pres. 1994–96, Pres. of faction 1996–2001; mem. Chamber of Deputies (Forza Italia) 1994–2006, mem. Pres.'s Cttee 1994–96, Deputy-Chair. Parl. Group, then Chair. 1996–2001, mem. Defence Cttee, Del. of Italy to CSCE 1998, to WEU 1999; Italian Minister for the actuation of the govt programme 2001–02; Minister of the Interior 2002–06; Senator 2006–13; mem. Il Popolo della Libertà (PdL—The People of Freedom) 2009–12, Scelta Civica (SC—Civic Choice) 2013–. *E-mail:* info@ sceltacivica.it (office). *Website:* www.sceltacivica.it (office).

PISCHETSRIEDER, Bernd Peter, DipEng; German automotive engineer and business executive; *Chairman of the Supervisory Board, Münchener Rückversicherungsgesellschaft AG (Munich Re);* b. 15 Feb. 1948, Munich, Bavaria; ed Technical Univ. Munich; joined BMW AG, Munich as production planning eng 1973; Production Dir BMW South Africa (Pty) Ltd 1982–85; Dir for Quality Control, BMW AG 1985–87, for Tech. Planning 1987–90; Deputy mem. Admin. Bd in charge of Production 1990, mem. Admin. 1991, Chair. Admin. Bd 1993–99; fmr Chair. Rover; Chair. SEAT SA 2000–02; Chair. Bd of Man., Volkswagen AG 2002–06 (resgnd), Advisor to the Bd; Chair. Scania AB 2002–07; mem. Supervisory Bd Münchener Rückversicherungsgesellschaft AG (Munich Re) 2002–, Chair. 2013–; mem. Jt Advisory Council, Allianz Group of Cos –2012; Dr hc (Birmingham, UK) 1996. *Address:* Münchener Rückversicherungs-Gesellschaft AG, Königinstrasse 107, 80802 Munich, Germany (office). *Telephone:* (89) 38910 (office). *Fax:* (89) 399056 (office). *E-mail:* info@munichre.com (office). *Website:* www.munichre .com (office).

PISCHINGER, Franz Felix, Dr Techn.; Austrian scientist, academic and business executive; *Chairman, FEV GmbH;* b. 18 July 1930, Waidhofen; s. of Franz Pischinger and Karoline Pischinger; m. Elfriede Pischinger 1957 (died 2001); m. Elisabeth Pischinger 2003; four s. one d.; ed Graz Univ. of Tech.; tech. asst, Graz Univ. of Tech. 1953–58; Head of Research Dept, Inst. of Internal Combustion Engines, Prof. List (AVL) 1958–62; leading positions in research and devt with Kloeckner-Humboldt-Deutz AG, Cologne 1962–70; Dir Inst. for Applied Thermodynamics, Aachen Tech. Univ. 1970–97; Founder, Pres. and CEO, FEV Motorentechnik GmbH (now FEV GmbH), Aachen 1978–2003, Chair. 2003–; Vice-Pres. DFG (German Research Soc.) 1984–90, Acatech German Acad. of Science and Eng 2002–05; Foreign Assoc. mem. Nat. Acad. of Eng (USA) 1997–; Fellow, Soc. of Automotive Engineers 1996–; Hon. Prof., Dalian Univ., People's Repub. of China 2005; Österreichischer Ehrenring 1954, Deutsches Bundesverdienstkreuz 1978, Cross of Honour for Science and Art, First Class (Austria) 1998; Dr hc (Graz Univ. of Tech.) 1994; Herbert Akroyd Stuart Award 1962, Carl-Engler-Medaille, Deutsche Wissenschaftliche Gesellschaft für Erdöl, Erdgas und Kohle (DGMK) 1990, Medal of Honour, Verein Deutscher Ingenieure 1993, Soichiro Honda Medal, ASME 2000, FISITA Medal 2012. *Publications:* articles in professional journals. *Address:* FEV GmbH, Neuenhofstrasse 181, 52078 Aachen, Germany (office). *Telephone:* (241) 5689100 (office). *Website:* www.fev.com (office).

PISTOLETTO, Michelangelo; Italian artist; b. 1933, Biella; worked with his father as painting restorer 1947–58; first solo exhbn at Galleria Galatea, Turin 1960; first solo exhbn in USA at Walker Art Center, Minneapolis 1966; f. Zoo Group of performance artists 1968; associated with Arte Povera movt; works include paintings, sculptures with steel, mirrors and everyday objects, films and video work and performance art; launched his Progetto Arte manifesto 1994, f. Cittadellarte—Fondazione Pistoletto for the study and promotion of creative projects 1998; Grand Prize, Bienale of São Paulo 1967, Belgian Art Critics' Award 1967, Wolf Foundation Prize in the Arts (Painting and Sculpture) 2007, Roswitha Haftmann Prize 2018. *Works include:* Autoritratto oro 1960, Il Presente: Uomo di schiena 1960–61, Quadri Specchianti (Mirror Paintings), Oggetti in meno (Minus Objects) 1965–66, Venere degli stracci (Venus of the Rags) 1967, Pietra miliare 1967, Opera Ah (performance work) 1979, Anno uno (performance work) 1981. *Publications:* L'uomo nero, il lato insopportabile 1970. *Address:* Cittadellarte—Fondazione Pistoletto, via Serralunga 27, Biella 13900, Italy (office). *Telephone:* (015) 28400 (office). *Fax:* (015) 2522540 (office). *E-mail:* fondazionepistoletto@ cittadellarte.it (office). *Website:* www.cittadellarte.it (office).

PISTORIO, Pasquale, M.Electronics; Italian business executive; b. 1936, Sicily; ed Polytechnic of Turin; began career as salesman for Motorola Italy 1967, becoming Dir of Int. Marketing, Phoenix, Ariz. 1977, also Vice-Pres. Motorola Corpn 1977, Gen. Man. Int. Semiconductor Div. 1978–80; Pres. and CEO SGS Group 1980–98 (renamed STMicroelectronics 1998), Pres. and CEO STMicroelectronics 1998–2005, Hon. Chair. 2005–; Chair. Telecom Italia SpA April–Dec. 2007; f. Pistorio Foundation (charity) 2005; Vice-Pres. for Innovation and Research, Confindustria (Confed. of Italian Industrialists); mem. numerous bds including FIAT SpA, Telecom Italia, Atos, Brenbo, STATS ChipPAC; Hon. Citizen of Singapore 2003; Commendatore al Merito 1974, Chevalier, Ordre nat. du Mérite 1990, Cavaliere del Lavoro 1997, Ouissam Alaouite (Morocco) 1999, Public Service Star (Singapore) 1999, Chevalier, Légion d'Honneur 1999, Officier, Légion d'Honneur 2005, Commdr, Ordre nat. du Mérite 2009; Dr hc (Genoa), (Malta), (Pavia), (Catania), (Palermo), (Sannio), (Bicocca), (Bristol); Akira Inoue Award for Outstanding Achievement in Environmental Health and Safety in the Semiconductor Industry 2000, Lifetime Achievement Award, Reed Electronics Group 2003, Prix du Manager d'Entreprise, Prix des Technologies de l'information 2003, Green Hero Lifetime Achievement Award, AnalogZONE magazine 2005, ACE Lifetime Achievement Award, EETimes magazine 2010, IEEE Robert N. Noyce Medal Award 2011, Ellis Island Medal of Honor Award 2012. *Address:* Pistorio Foundation, Associazione Amici della Fondazione Pistorio, Via Lecco, 61, 20059 Vimercate MI, Italy. *Website:* www.pistoriofoundation.org.

PITCHER, Sir Desmond Henry, Kt, CEng, FIEE, CIMgt, FRSA; British business executive; b. 23 March 1935, Liverpool; s. of George Charles Pitcher and Alice Marion Pitcher (née Osborne); m. 1st Patricia Ainsworth 1961 (divorced 1973); two d.; m. 2nd Carol Ann Rose 1978 (divorced); two s.; m. 3rd Norma Barbara Niven 1991; ed Liverpool Coll. of Tech. and Commerce; Man. Dir then Vice-Pres. Int. Div. The Sperry Corpn 1961–76; Man. Dir British Leyland Truck and Bus Div. 1976–78, Plessey Telecommunications and Office Systems Ltd 1978–83; Group Chief Exec. The Littlewoods Org. PLC 1983–93, Vice-Chair. 1993–95; Chair. The Mersey Barrage Co. Ltd 1986–96, The Merseyside Devt Corpn 1991–98, The North West Water Group PLC (now United Utilities) 1993–98 (Dir 1990–98), Royal Liverpool Philharmonic Social Devt Trust 1992, Westminster Green Man. Co. Ltd 2010–14; Vice-Pres. Royal Liverpool Children's Hosp. 2004–; Dir Everton Football Club Co. Ltd 1987–90, Deputy Chair. 1990–98; Dir Northern Advisory Bd of Nat. Westminster Bank PLC 1989–92, Dir (non-exec.) Nat. Westminster Bank 1994–98, Liverpool School of Tropical Medicine 1996; Visiting Prof., Univ. of Manchester 1993–98; Hon. Fellow, Liverpool John Moores Univ. 1993. *Publication:* Water Under the Bridge: 30 Years of Industrial Management 2003. *Leisure interests:* football, golf, 19th century history, opera, sailing.

PITCHER, Hon. Frederick W., BA, MBA; Nauruan/Australian politician, diplomatist and environmentalist; b. 5 Feb. 1967, Nauru; s. of Graeme Pitcher and Melody Halstead; m. Juliana Pitcher; three c.; ed educated in Australia, Japan and UK; govt statistician/economist 1992–96; Sec. for Finance 1997; Adviser to Exec. Dir, Asian Devt Bank, Manila, The Philippines 1997–99; Deputy Perm. Rep., UN, New York 2000–04; mem. Parl. 2004–13, mem. Constitutional Review Cttee 2005; served in second Admin of fmr Pres. Ludwig Scotty; Minister for Island Devt and Industry 2004–07, of Finance and Econ. Planning 2007, of Commerce, Industry and Environment and Minister for Utilities 2007–11; Acting Foreign Minister 2007; elected Pres. of Nauru 10 Nov. 2011, but removed by parl. 15 Nov.; Pres. Nauru Island Basketball Asscn. *Leisure interests:* fishing, music, sports.

PITHART, Petr, JUDr; Czech politician and academic; b. 2 Jan. 1941, Kladno; s. of Vilém Pithart and Blažena Pithart (née Krystýnková); m. Drahomíra Hromádková 1964; one s. one d.; ed Charles Univ., Prague (Faculty of Law); Dept of Theory of State and Law, Charles Univ. 1964–70; scholarship Univ. of Oxford, UK 1969–70; labourer 1970–72; co. lawyer 1972–77; signed Charter 77; labourer 1977–79; clerk with Central Warehouses, Prague 1979–89; Spokesman Co-ordination Centre, Civic Forum 1989–90; Prime Minister of Czech Repub. 1990–92; Deputy to Czech Nat. Council 1990–92; mem. and Chair. Senate 1996–98, Vice-Chair. 1998–2000, Chair. 2000, Vice-Pres. 2004–12; mem. Christian and Democratic Union, Czech People's Party (KDÚ-ČSL) 1999–2012, cand. presidential election 2003; Sr Research Fellow, Cen. European Univ., Prague 1992–94; teacher, Faculty of Law, Charles Univ., Prague 1994, Head of Dept of Political Science and Sociology, Faculty of Law 2007; Ed.-in-Chief The New Presence (periodical) 1992–96; Commdr's Cross with Star (Poland) 2004, Great Gold Cross of Merit (Austria) 2004, Officier, Légion d'honneur 2004; Frantisek Kriegel Prize, Foundation of Chart 77, Prague 1991. *Publications:* The Defence of Politics 1974, The Year Sixty-Eight 1978, 1990, History and Politics 1992, Czechs in the History of Modern Times (co-author) 1992, Who We Are After '89 1997, The Reading on the Resettled History (co-author) 1998, The Year Eighty-Nine 2009; numerous articles and essays. *Leisure interests:* politics, history, hiking, fishing. *E-mail:* petr@pithart.cz (home). *Website:* www.pithart.cz.

PITT, Brad; American film actor and producer; b. 18 Dec. 1963, Shawnee, Okla; s. of Bill Pitt and Jane Pitt; m. Jennifer Aniston (q.v.) 2000 (divorced 2005); six c. (with Angelina Jolie), m. 2014; ed Univ. of Missouri; Special Amb. for Nelson Mandela's 46664 campaign against HIV/AIDS 2004. *Films appearances include:* Cutting Glass, Happy Together 1989, Across the Tracks 1990, Contact, Thelma and Louise 1991, The Favor 1992, Johnny Suede 1992, Cool World 1992, A River Runs Through It 1992, Kalifornia 1993, Legend of the Fall 1994, Interview With The Vampire 1994, 12 Monkeys (Golden Globe Award for Best Supporting Actor) 1995, Seven 1996, Sleepers 1996, Tomorrow Never Dies 1996, Seven Years in Tibet 1997, The Devil's Own 1997, Meet Joe Black 1998, Fight Club 1999, Snatch 2000, The Mexican 2001, Spy Game 2001, Ocean's Eleven 2001, Full Frontal 2002, Confessions of a Dangerous Mind 2002, Sinbad: Legend of the Seven Seas (voice) 2003, Troy 2004, Ocean's Twelve 2004, Mr and Mrs Smith 2005, Babel 2006, Ocean's Thirteen 2007, The Assassination of Jesse James by the Coward Robert Ford (Best Actor, Venice Film Festival 2007) 2007, Burn After Reading 2008, The Curious Case of Benjamin Button 2008, Inglourious Basterds 2009, Megamind (voice) 2010, The Tree of Life 2011, Moneyball 2011, Killing Them Softly 2012, World War Z 2013, 12 Years a Slave 2013, The Counsellor 2013, Fury 2014, By the Sea 2015, The Big Short 2015, War Machine (also producer) 2017. *Films produced include:* The Departed 2006, A Mighty Heart 2007, The Assassination of Jesse James by the Coward Robert Ford 2007, The Time Traveller's Wife 2009, Eat Pray Love 2010, The Tree of Life 2011, Moneyball 2011, Killing them Softly 2012, World War Z 2013, 12 Years a Slave (BAFTA Award for Best Picture, Golden Globe Award for Best Motion Picture, Drama, Academy Award for Best Picture 2014) 2013, Vice 2018. *Television appearances include:* Dallas (series), Glory Days (series), Too Young to Die? (film), The Image (film). *Address:* c/o Creative Artists Agency, 2000 Avenue of the Stars, Los Angeles, CA 90067, USA (office).

PITT, Hon. Harvey Lloyd, BA, JD; American lawyer and fmr government official; *CEO and Managing Director, Kalorama Partners LLC;* b. 28 Feb. 1945, Brooklyn, New York; s. of Morris Jacob Pitt and Sara Pitt (née Sapir); m. Saree Ruffin 1984; one s. one d. (and one d. one s. from previous marriage); ed City Univ. of New York (Brooklyn Coll.) and St John's Univ., New York; called to Bar, NY 1969, US Supreme Court 1972, DC 1979; with SEC, Washington, DC 1968–78, Legal Asst to Commr 1969, Ed. Institutional Investor Study 1970–71, Special Counsel, Office of Gen. Counsel 1971–72, Chief Counsel Market Regulation Div. 1972–73, Exec. Asst to Chair. 1973–75, Gen. Counsel 1975–78, Chair. 2001–03; f. Kalorama Partners LLC, CEO and Man. Dir 2003–; Man. Partner, Fried, Frank, Harris, Shriver & Jacobson, Washington, DC 1978–89, Co-Chair. 1998–2001; currently Sr Advisor, Teneo Holdings LLC; Adjunct Prof. of Law, George Washington Univ. Nat. Law Centre 1974–82, Georgetown Univ. Law Center 1975–84, Univ. of Pennsylvania Law School 1983–84, Yale Law School 2007; Founding Trustee and First Pres. SEC Historical Soc.; mem. ABA, Fed. Bar Asscn, Admin. Conf. of US, American Law Inst.; mem. Bd of Dirs Premier Alliance Group, Inc.; Chair. Medical Faculty Assocs, Inc., George Washington Univ.; Hon. LLD (St John's Univ. School of Law) 2002; Outstanding Young Lawyer Award, Fed. Bar Asscn 1975, Learned Hand Award, Inst. for Human Relations 1988, Brooklyn Coll. Pres. Medal of Distinction 2003, William O. Douglas Award 2011. *Address:* Kalorama Partners LLC, 1101 Pennsylvania Avenue, NW, Suite 600, Washington, DC 20004 (office); 2404 Wyoming Avenue, NW, Washington, DC 20008-1643, USA (home). *Telephone:* (202) 721-0000 (office). *Fax:* (202) 721-0007 (office). *E-mail:* Harvey@KaloramaPartners.com (office). *Website:* www.kaloramapartners.com (office).

PITTMAN, Robert (Bob) Warren; American media executive; *Chairman and CEO, iHeartMedia, Inc.;* b. 28 Dec. 1953, Jackson, Miss.; s. of Warren E. Pittman and Lanita Pittman (née Hurdle); m. 1st Sandra Hill 1979 (divorced); one s.; m. 2nd Veronique Choa 1997; one c.; ed Millsaps Coll., Univ. of Pittsburgh, Harvard Univ.; disc jockey, WJDX-FM, Miss. 1970–72, WRIT, Milwaukee 1972; Research Dir WDRQ, Detroit 1972–73; Programme Dir WPEZ, Pittsburgh 1973–74; with WMAQ-WKQZ, New York and NBC Radio 1974–77; with WNBC, New York 1977–79; exec. producer, Album Tracks NBC TV 1977–78; Dir, Vice-Pres., then Sr Vice-Pres. Warner Amex Satellite Entertainment Co. (now MTV Networks Inc.) 1979–82, Pres. and CEO 1985–86, Exec. Vice-Pres. and COO MTV Networks Inc. 1983–85; Pres. and CEO Quantum Media Inc. 1987–89; Exec. Advisor, Warner Communications Inc. 1989–90, Pres. and CEO Time Warner Enterprises 1990–95; CEO Six Flags Entertainment 1991–95; Man. Pnr and CEO Century 21 Real Estate 1995–96; Pres. and CEO America On-Line Networks 1996–97, Pres. and COO America On-Line Inc. 1997–2001, Co-COO 2001–02; currently Chair. and CEO iHeartMedia, Inc.; Co-founder Pilot Group LLC (investment firm), New York 2003; Chair. New York Shakespeare Festival 1987–94; fmr Chair. New York Public Theater; mem. Bd of Dirs Robin Hood Foundation (fmr Chair.), Rock and Roll Hall of Fame, Alliance for Lupus Research; Golden Plate Award, American Acad. of Achievement 1990, Lifetime Achievement Int. Monitor Award, Int. Teleproduction Soc. 1993, inducted into Advertising Hall of Fame, Broadcasting and Cable Hall of Fame, Robert F. Kennedy Ripple of Hope Award, Council of Fashion Designers Award and many others. *Address:* iHeartMedia, Inc., 20880 Stone Oak Pkwy, San Antonio, TX 78258, USA (office). *Telephone:* (210) 822-2828 (office). *Website:* www.iheartmedia.com (office).

PITTS, Simon, BSc (Hons); British engineer and academic; *Professor of Practice in Engineering Leadership and Director, Gordon Engineering Leadership Program, Northeastern University;* b. London, England; ed Loughborough Univ., Institut Européen d'Admin des Affaires (INSEAD), France; began career in advanced powertrain devt and research at Ford Motor Co. 1976, Dir World Wide Powertrain Planning 1994–97, Dir of Manufacturing Operations 1997–99, Vehicle Line Dir 1999–2001, Dir of Product Devt Operations for all Ford, Jaguar, Land Rover, Mazda and Volvo brands globally 2001–04; Exec. Dir Ford-MIT Research Alliance 2004–09; Prof. of Practice in Eng Leadership and Dir, Gordon Eng Leadership Program, Northeastern Univ. 2010–; Fellow, Inst. of Mechanical Engineers; Gordon Prize, Nat. Acad. of Eng (co-recipient) 2015. *Address:* Engineering Office Of the Dean, Northeastern University, 360 Huntington Avenue, Boston, MA 02115, USA (office). *Telephone:* (617) 373-3630 (office). *E-mail:* s.pitts@neu.edu (office). *Website:* www.northeastern.edu/news/faculty-experts/simon-pitts (office).

PIVOT, Bernard; French journalist and writer; *Chairman, Académie Goncourt;* b. 5 May 1935, Lyon; s. of Charles Pivot and Marie-Louise Pivot (née Dumas); m. Monique Dupuis 1959; two d.; ed Centre de formation des Journalistes; on staff of Figaro littéraire, then Literary Ed.; Figaro 1958–74; Chronique pour sourire, on Europe 1 1970–73; columnist, Le Point 1974–77; producer and presenter of Ouvrez les guillemets 1973–74, Apostrophes, France 2 1975–90, Bouillon de culture 1991–2001, Double Je 2002–05; Ed. Lire 1975–93; Dir Sofica Créations 1986–; mem. Conseil supérieur de la langue française 1989–; Pres. Grévin Acad. 2001–; mem. Acad. Goncourt 2004–, Chair. 2014–; Chevalier du Mérite agricole; Hon. OC 2008; Nat. Order of Québec; Grand Prix de la Critique, Acad. française 1983, Prix Louise Weiss, Bibliothèque Nat. 1989, Prix de la langue française décerné à la Foire 2000. *Publications include:* L'Amour en vogue (novel) 1959, La vie oh là là! 1966, Les critiques littéraires 1968, Beaujolaises 1978, Le Football en vert 1980, Le Métier de lire. Réponses à Pierre Nora 1990, Remontrances à la ménagère de moins de cinquante ans (essay) 1998. *Leisure interests:* tennis, football, gastronomy. *Address:* Grévin, 10 boulevard Montmartre, 75009 Paris (office); Les Jonnerys, 69430 Quincié-en-Beaujolais, France (home). *Telephone:* 1-47-70-85-05 (office). *Website:* www.academie-goncourt.fr.

PIVOVAROV, Yuri Sergeyevich, Dr rer. pol; Russian political scientist and research institute director; *Director, Institute of Scientific Information for Social Sciences (INION), Russian Academy of Sciences;* b. 25 April 1950, Moscow; m.; one s. one d.; ed Moscow Inst. of Int. Relations; Jr, then Sr Researcher, Prof., Head of Div., Deputy Dir Inst. of Scientific Information for Social Sciences (INION), USSR (now Russian) Acad. of Sciences 1976–98, Dir 1998–; mem. Exec. Bd Russian Asscn of Political Sciences, Pres. 2001–05, Pres. Emer. 2005–; mem. Council on Politology, Presidium, Russian Acad. of Sciences, Expert Council under the Chair. of the Fed. Council, Scientific Council under Russian Fed. Ministry of Foreign Affairs, Council of the Russian Int. Affairs Council; Ed.-in-Chief Gosudarstvo i Pravo (journal), Politicheskaya Nauka (periodical); Corresp. mem. Russian Acad. of Sciences 1997, Full mem. 2006. *Publications:* Political Culture of Russia after Reforms, Essays on the History of Russian Socio-political Ideas of the 19th and Early 20th Century; six monographs and more than 250 articles on the history of Russian socio-political ideas, history of Russian political culture and statehood, comparative studies of Russian and Western political cultures, etc. *Address:* INION, Nakhimovsky prosp. 51/21, 117997 Moscow, Russian Federation (office). *Telephone:* (495) 128-89-30 (office); (495) 123-88-81 (office). *Fax:* (495) 420-22-61 (office). *E-mail:* info@inion.ru (office). *Website:* www.inion.ru (office).

PIWOWSKI, Marek; Polish/American film director, writer, actor and journalist; b. 24 Oct. 1935, Warsaw; s. of Władysław Piwowski and Jadwiga Piwowska; ed State Acad. of Film, Łódź, Univ. of Warsaw; Visiting Prof., City Univ. of New York; Dir and writer of 17 films which have won 24 int. film festival awards; mem. American Film Inst.; Order of Polonia Restituta. *Films include:* Kirk Douglas 1967, Flybeater 1967, Rejs (The Cruise) 1970, Corkscrew 1971, Psychodrama 1972, Blue Hair 1972, How to Recognize the Vampire 1974, Przepraszam, czy tu biją?

(Foul Play) 1976, Trouble is My Business 1988, Catch 22 1990, Kidnapping Agata 1993, The Parade Step 1998, The Barracuda's Kiss 1998, The Knife in the Head of Dino Baggio 1999, Olympiad in Zakopane 1999, Executioners 2001, Martin's Law 2001, Body Language 2002, Oskar (dir, scriptwriter) 2005. *Leisure interests:* sailing, skiing, gliders, windsurfing. *Address:* ul. Promenada 21 m 7, 00-778 Warsaw, Poland. *Telephone:* (58) 5858858 (office); 50-1011111 (mobile) (office); (22) 841-80-80; 60-6600000 (mobile). *Fax:* (22) 841-80-80. *E-mail:* wujekpiwek@gmail.com (office); piwek@eranet.pl.

PIZA, Arthur Luiz; Brazilian painter and printmaker; b. 1928, São Paulo; painter and exhibitor 1943–; moved to Paris 1952; works in many important museums and pvt. collections; Purchase Prize 1953 and Nat. Prize for Prints São Paulo Biennale 1959, Prizes at biennales at Ljubljana 1961, Santiago 1966, Venice 1966, Grenchen Triennale 1961, biennales of Norway and Mexico 1980, Puerto Rico 1991, Nat. Asscn of Critics Grand Prize, Brazil 1994. *Publications:* Abstract Painting 1962, Larousse of Paintings (Small Larousse of Paintings, Vol. II) 1979, Bénézit Dictionary of Painters, Sculptors and Engravers 1999, Arthur Luiz Piza 2003. *Address:* 16 rue Dauphine, 75006 Paris, France.

PIZARRO MORENO, Manuel, LicenDer; Spanish lawyer, business executive and politician; b. 29 Sept. 1951, Teruel; m. Yolanda Barcina 2016; ed Univ. Complutense de Madrid; Attorney-Gen. (Advocate of the State); apptd mem. Bd of Dirs Endesa SA 1996, mem. Exec. Cttee 1997–98, Vice-Chair. 1998–2002, Chair. 2002–07; mem. Bd of Dirs Telefónica 2007–08; Chair. Ibercaja 1995–2004, Spanish Savings Banks Confed. 1998–2002, World Savings Banks Inst. 2000–02; Pres. Madrid Stock Exchange 1991–92, 1994–95, Vice-Pres. 1995–2008; Pres. Ibero-American Fed. 1995–97, Savings Bank of Zaragoza 1995–04, World Savings Bank Institute 1998–2002; Vice-Pres. Bolsas y Mercados Españoles 2002–08; fmr Vice-Chair., Bolsa de Madrid, Bolsas y Mercados Espaqoles, Sociedad Holding de Mercados y Sistemas Financieros SA, Real Sociedad Económica Aragonesa de Amigos del Pais; mem. Spanish Royal Acad. of Legislation and Jurisprudence, Real Academia de Jurisprudencia y Legislación, Real Academia de Ciencias Económicas y Financieras, Academia Aragonesa de Jurisprudencia y Legislación, Comité Ético de Cáritas, Fundación para el análisis y los estudios sociales; Chair. Bd of Trustees, Nat. Park of Ordesa and Monte Perdido; Vice-Chair. Bd of Trustees, Nat. Museum of Archeology; Chair. Social Council, Universidad Autónoma de Madrid, Spanish Univs; Chair. Advisory Bd, Baker and McKenzie Madrid; mem. Bd Consejero de ECI, Consejero de Sanitas; mem. Bd Fundación para el análisis y los estudios sociales, Advisory Bd Reina Sofía Foundation 2003–07, Bd of Trustees, Univ. Pontificia de Salamanca, Santa María de Albarracín Foundation; joined Partido Popular 2008, Partido Popular spokesman, Constitutional Comm., Congress of Deputies 2008–10; Hon. mem. Real Sociedad Geográfica; Kt Commdr of the Order of St Gregory the Great, Grand Officer of the Order of Congress of Colombia, Silver Cross of the Order of Merit of the Civil Guard Corps, Cross of San Jorge of the Provincial Delegation of Teruel; Medal of the Cortes de Aragón. *Address:* Constitutional Commission, Congress of Deputies, Carrera de San Jerónimo s/n, 28071 Madrid, Spain (office). *Telephone:* (91) 3906000 (office). *Fax:* (91) 4298707 (office). *E-mail:* servicio.informacion@sgral.congreso.es (office). *Website:* www.congreso.es (office).

PIZZO, Philip A., BA, MD; American physician and academic; *David and Susan Heckerman Professor of Pediatrics and of Microbiology and Immunology, School of Medicine, Stanford University;* b. 6 Dec. 1944, New York City; s. of Vito Pizzo; m. Peggy Pizzo; ed Fordham Univ., Univ. of Rochester School of Medicine; intern, Children's Hosp. Medical Center, Boston 1970–71, Jr Asst Resident 1971–72, Sr Asst Resident 1972–73; Clinical Assoc., Nat. Cancer Inst. 1973–75, Investigator 1975–76, Fellow 1976, Sr Investigator 1976–80, Head of Infectious Disease Section, Pediatric Br., Nat. Cancer Inst. 1980–96, Chief of Pediatrics 1982–96; Thomas Morgan Rotch Prof. and Chair., Dept of Pediatrics, Harvard Univ. Medical School, Children's Hosp., Boston 1996–2001, also Faculty Dean for Academic Programs 1996–99; Dean, Stanford Univ. School of Medicine 2001–12, also Carl and Elizabeth Naumann Prof. of Pediatrics 2001–12, currently David and Susan Heckerman Prof. of Pediatrics and of Microbiology and Immunology, Founding Dir Stanford Distinguished Careers Inst. 2013–; Attending Physician, NIH, Bethesda, Md 1976–96; Prof. of Pediatrics, F. Edward Hebert School of Medicine, Bethesda 1987–96; mem. Bd of Dirs Lucile Packard Children's Hosp. 2001–12, Stanford Hosp. and Clinics 2001–12; mem. numerous professional socs including American Soc. for Clinical Investigation 1987, American Pediatric Soc. 1995, NAS Inst. of Medicine 1997, American Asscn of Physicians 1998; mem. Bd of Dirs Ludwig Inst. for Cancer Research 2014; mem. Governing Bd California Inst. of Regenerative Medicine 2004–12; mem. Bd of Trustees Univ. of Rochester 2009; mem. editorial bd numerous journals; Hon. ScD (Fordham Univ.) 1996, Hon. MA (Harvard Univ.) 1996; numerous awards including Commendation Medal 1980, US Public Health Service Meritorious Service Award 1985, Barbara Bohen Pfiefer Award for Scientific Excellence 1991, Outstanding Service Medal 1995, Elizabeth Kubler-Ross Award 2008, Award of Excellence, Ronald McDonald Foundation 2009, John Howland Award 2012, John and Emma Bonica Public Service Award 2013. *Publications include:* over 615 papers in professional journals, 16 books and monographs including Principles and Practice of Pediatric Oncology 2010. *Address:* Stanford University School of Medicine, 291 Campus Drive, Li Ka Shing Building, Stanford, CA 94305-5101, USA (office). *Telephone:* (650) 723-2895 (office). *E-mail:* ppizzo@stanford.edu (office). *Website:* med.stanford.edu (office).

PLACIDO, Michele; Italian actor and director; b. 19 May 1946, Ascoli Satriano, Foggia; m. 1st Simonetta Stefanelli (divorced); three c.; m. 2nd Federica Vincenti; two c. with other pnrs; ed Centro Sperimentale di Cinematografia, Acad. of Dramatic Arts, Rome; made acting debut 1969, has appeared in more than 70 films and numerous tv series; has worked with dirs including Luigi Comencini, Mario Monicelli, Salvatore Samperi, Damiano Damiani, Francesco Rosi, Walerian Borowczyk, Marco Bellocchio, Carlo Lizzani; made directorial debut 1989; jury mem. Venice Film Festival 2006; Bambi Award 1989, Actor's Mission Award, Art Film Festival 1999. *Television:* actor: Il Picciotto 1973, Moses the Lawgiver 1975, Yerma (film) 1978, Volontari per destinazione ignota (film) 1979, Il Passo falso 1983, La Piovra 1983, La Piovra 2 1985, La Piovra 3 1987, La Piovra 4 1989, Scoop 1991, Drug Wars: The Cocaine Cartel (film) 1992, Uomo di rispetto (film) 1993, Racket (also story) 1997, Uno sguardo dal ponte 1997, La Missione (film) (also writer) 1998, Padre Pio - Tra cielo e terra 2000, Il Sequestro Soffiantini (film) 2002, Un Papà quasi perfetto 2003, Soraya (film) 2003, Il Grande Torino (film) 2004, Karol, un Papa rimasto uomo (film) 2006, Assunta Spina (film) 2006, L'Ultimo padrino (film) 2007, Aldo Moro - Il presidente (film), Volare: La grande storia di Domenico Modugno (film) 2013, Trilussa: Storia d'amore e di poesia (film) 2013, Living Legends 2014, Questo è il mio paese 2015, In Treatment (series) 2015–16. *Films:* actor: Teresa la ladra 1972, Il Caso Pisciotta 1972, La Mano nera - prima della mafia, più della mafia 1973, Mia moglie, un corpo per l'amore 1973, Mio Dio come sono caduta in basso! 1974, Processo per direttissima 1974, Romanzo popolare 1974, Peccati in famiglia 1975, Orlando Furioso movie, 1975, L'Agnese va a morire 1976, La Orca 1976, Divina creatura 1976, Marcia trionfale (Acting Award, David di Donatello Awards, Best Actor, Silver Ribbon Awards) 1976, Corleone 1977, Fontamara 1977, Kleinhoff Hotel 1977, La Ragazza dal pigiama giallo 1977, Casotto 1977, Un Uomo in ginocchio 1978, Io sono mia 1978, Letti selvaggi 1979, Il Prato 1979, Sabato, domenica e venerdì 1979, Ernesto (Best Actor, Berlin Int. Film Festival) 1979, Lulu 1980, Salto nel vuoto 1980, Cargo film 1981, Les Ailes de la colombe 1981, Tre fratelli 1981, Sciopèn 1982, Ars amandi 1983, Les Amants terribles 1984, Pizza Connection (Best Actor, Silver Ribbon Awards) 1985, Grandi magazzini 1986, Notte d'estate con profilo greco, occhi a mandorla e odore di basilico 1986, Ti presento un'amica 1987, Via Paradiso 1988, Big Business 1988, Come sono buoni i bianchi 1988, Ya bon les blancs 1988, Mery per sempre 1989, Afganskiy izlom 1990, Le Amiche del cuore 1992, Uomo di rispetto 1992, Quattro bravi ragazzi 1993, Giovanni Falcone 1993, Padre e figlio 1994, Poliziotti 1994, Lamerica 1994, Un Eroe borghese 1995, La Lupa 1996, Le Plaisir (et ses petits tracas) 1998, Del perduto amore (FEDIC Award, Venice Film Festival) 1998, Terra bruciata 1999, Un Uomo perbene 1999, La Balia 1999, Panni sporchi 1999, Liberate i pesci! 2000, Tra due mondi 2001, Searching for Paradise 2002, Il Posto dell'anima 2003, L'Odore del sangue 2004, L'Amore ritorna 2004, Romanzo criminale 2005, Arrivederci amore, ciao 2006, Commediasexi 2006, Le Rose del deserto 2006, La Sconosciuta 2006, Smutek paní Snajdrové 2006, Il Caimano 2006, 2061: Un anno eccezionale 2007, Piano, solo 2007, SoloMetro 2007, Estrenando sueños 2007, Liolà 2007, Smutek paní Snajderové 2008, Il sangue dei vinti 2008, Focaccia blues 2009, Baarìa 2009, Genitori & figli: Agitare bene prima dell'uso 2010, Manuale d'am3re 2011, Amici miei - Come tutto ebbe inizio 2011, Tulpa: Perdizioni mortali 2011, Le guetteur 2012, Viva l'Italia 2012, Razza bastarda 2012, Itaker - Vietato agli italiani 2012, Io che amo solo te 2015, La scelta 2015, Un'avventura romantica 2016, 7 minuti (also dir) 2016, La cena di Natale 2016; director: Pummarò (writer/dir) 1989, Le Amiche del cuore (writer/dir) 1992, Un Eroe borghese (Special Award, David di Donatello Awards) 1995, Del perduto amore (writer/dir) 1998, Un Altro mondo è possibile 2001, Un Viaggio chiamato amore (writer/dir) 2002, Ovunque sei (writer/dir) 2004, Romanzo criminale (co-writer/dir) (Best Screenplay, David di Donatello Awards (jtly) 2006, Best Director, Silver Ribbon Awards 2006) 2005, Il grande sogno 2009, Vallanzasca: Gli angeli del male 2010, Le guetteur 2012, Prima di andar via 2014, La scelta 2015; other: L'Uomo giusto (producer and writer) 2007, Itaker: Vietato agli italiani 2012 (writer), La scelta (screenplay) 2015. *Address:* c/o Cattleya S.p.A., Via della Frezza, 59, 00186 Rome, Italy (office). *E-mail:* info@cattleya.it (office).

PLAHOTNIUC, Vlad, BEng, MBA, MCL; Moldovan economist, politician and business executive; *President, Partidul Democrat din Moldova (PDM—Democratic Party of Moldova);* b. 1 Jan. 1966, Pituşca, Călăraşi Dist, Moldovan SSR, USSR; m. Oxana Plahotniuc; ed Tech. Univ. of Moldova, European Studies Univ. of Moldova; specialist at Minor Centre for prevention and rehabilitation of juvenile offenders (affiliated with Chişinău City Hall) 1991–93; economist at Euro EstHundel Ltd, then worked at Voyage Ltd; f. Angels Moldovan-American Financial Group 1995–98, Man. –2001; Commercial Man., later Gen. Man. Petrom Moldova JSC 2001–10; Vice-Chair. Victoriabank (commercial bank) 2005–06, Chair. 2006–11; mem. Partidul Democrat din Moldova (PDM—Democratic Party of Moldova) 2010–, Deputy Pres. 2010–16, Pres. 2016–; mem. (PDM), Parl., First Deputy Speaker 2010–, mem. Economy, Budget and Finance Comm., mem. Interparliamentary Ass. of CIS Mem. States, Parl. Friendship Group with Switzerland, Greece and Hungary; Vice-Chair. Nat. Council for Judiciary Reform 2011–. *Address:* Partidul Democrat din Moldova, 2001 Chişinău, str. Tighina 32, Moldova (office). *Telephone:* (22) 54-17-22 (office); (22) 80-90-83. *Fax:* (22) 27-70-08 (office). *E-mail:* vp@plahotniuc.md; pdm@mtc.md (office). *Website:* www.pdm.md (office); www.plahotniuc.md.

PLANT OF HIGHFIELD, Baron (Life Peer), cr. 1991, of Weelsby in the County of Humberside; **Raymond Plant,** PhD, DLitt; British academic and politician; *Professor of Jurisprudence, King's College London;* b. 19 March 1945, Grimsby; s. of Stanley Plant and Marjorie Plant; m. Katherine Dixon 1967; three s.; ed Havelock School, Grimsby, King's Coll. London and Univ. of Hull; Lecturer, then Sr Lecturer in Philosophy, Univ. of Manchester 1967–79; Prof. of Politics, Univ. of Southampton 1979–94, Pro-Chancellor 1996–2002, Prof. of European Political Thought 2000–02; Prof. of Jurisprudence, King's Coll. London 2001–10 (retd, now part-time); Prof., Sciences Po, Paris (one semester a year); Prof. of Humanities, Univ. of Winchester; Lay Canon, Winchester Cathedral 2008–; Master, St Catherine's Coll. Oxford 1994–2000; Chair of Trustees, Hansard Trust; Pres. Nat. Council of Voluntary Orgs 1997–2002, Acad. of Learned Socs in the Social Sciences; Gov., Pilgrims' School Winchester; Hon. Fellow, Harris Manchester Coll., Oxford, St Catherine's Coll., Oxford, Univ. of Cardiff; Hon. DLitt (Hull, London Guildhall), Hon. DUniv (York), (Winchester); Stanton Lecturer, Univ. of Cambridge 1989–91, Sarum Lecturer, Univ. of Oxford 1991, Boutwood Lecturer, Univ. of Cambridge 2006, Bampton Lecturer, Univ. of Oxford. *Publications:* Hegel 1973, Community and Ideology 1974, Political Philosophy and Social Welfare 1981, Philosophy, Politics and Citizenship 1984, Conservative Capitalism 1989, Modern Political Thought 1991, Democracy, Representation and Elections 1992, Hegel on Religion 1997, Politics, Theology and History 2000, The Neo-Liberal State 2009. *Leisure interests:* music, opera, politics. *Address:* House of Lords, London, SW1A 0PW; 6 Woodview Close, Bassett, Southampton, SO16 3PZ, England (home). *Telephone:* (20) 7848-2448 (office); (23) 8076-9529 (home). *E-mail:* raymond.plant@kcl.ac.uk (office).

PLANTUREUX, Jean-Henri, (PLANTU); French artist, cartoonist, journalist and editor; *Editorial Cartoonist, Le Monde, L'Express;* b. (Jean-Henri Plantureux), 23 March 1951, Paris; s. of Henri Plantureux and Renée Seignardie; m. Chantal Meyer 1971; four c.; ed Baccalaureate, Lycée Henri IV, Paris, Saint-Luc Art School, Brussels, Belgium; political cartoonist, Le Monde 1972–, L'Express 1991–;

caricaturist, Droit de réponse (TV show) 1981–87; special edition of Le Monde to mark 40 years of collaboration and 19,000 cartoons published, Oct. 2012; Dr hc (Liège) 2013; Mumm Foundation Prize 1988, Black Humour Award 1989, Grand Prix de l'Humour noir Granville 1989, Prix du Festival du Scoop (film on Yasser Arafat) 1991, Int. Gat Perich Caricature Award 1996, UN Political Cartoon Award 2006, Second Prize, UN Best Caricature of the Year 2007, Markiezenaward 2013. *Publications include:* Pauvres chéris 1978, La Démocratie? Parlons-en 1979, Les Cours de caoutchouc sont trop élastiques 1982, C'est le goulag 1983, Pas nette, la planète! 1984, Politic-look 1984, Bonne année pour tous 1985, Ça manque de femmes 1986, Wolfgang, tu feras informatique 1988, Ouverture en bémol 1988, Des fourmis dans les jambes 1989, C'est la lutte finale 1990, Reproche-Orient 1991, Le Président Hip-Hop! 1991, Le Douanier se fait la malle 1992, Ici Maastricht, les Européens parlent aux Européens 1992, Cohabitation à l'Eau de Rose 1993, Le Pire est derrière nous! 1994, Le Petit Mitterrand Illustré 1995, Le Petit Chirac et le Petit Balladur Illustrés 1995, Le Petit Raciste Illustré 1995, Le Petit Communiste Illustré 1995, Le Petit Socialiste Illustré 95, Magic Chirac 1995, Les Années vaches folles 1996, La France dopée 1998, Le Petit Juge Illustré 1999, L'Année PLANTU 1999, Ils pourraient dire merci! 2004, À quoi ça rime 2005, Je ne dois pas dessiner 2006, La Présidentielle 2007, Racaille Le Rouge 2007, Un Boulevard pour Sarko 2008, Parmis de croquer – Un tour du monde du dessin de presse 2008, Petite histoire de la chute du communisme 2008, Sarko Le Best Of 2009, Almaniak 2010, Bas les masques 2009, Tête de Gondole 2010, Les conseils de tonton DSK 2011, On a marché sur les urnes - Présidentielle 2012, Sarko, sors de ce corps !! 2013. *Address:* Le Monde, 80 blvd Auguste Blanqui, 75707 Paris Cedex 13, France (office). *Telephone:* 1-57-28-25-30 (office). *Fax:* 1-57-28-21-69 (office). *E-mail:* plantu@lemonde.fr (office). *Website:* www.plantu.net (home).

PLASSAT, Georges; French business executive; b. 1949; ed Ecole hôtelière, Lausanne, Switzerland, Cornell Univ., USA; with Casino Group 1983–97, Marketing Dir and subsequently Chief Exec. of Restaurant Div. 1988–90, Chief Exec. of Casino France 1990–92, Man. Dir 1992–94, Vice-Pres. Man. Bd 1994–96, Chair. Man. Bd Casino Group 1996–97; Exec. Dir for Spain, Carrefour Group and Chief Exec. Pryca 1997–99, COO Carrefour Group April–May 2012, Chair. and CEO May 2012–17; Chair. Man. Bd Vivarte Group (fmrly Groupe André) 2000–04, Chair. and CEO 2004–12.

PLASTERK, Ronald Hans Anton, PhD; Dutch geneticist and politician; b. 12 April 1957, The Hague; ed RK Sint Janscollege, The Hague, Univ. of Leiden, California Inst. of Tech., USA; MRC Lab. of Molecular Biology, Cambridge, UK 1984–87; Head of Research Group, Netherlands Cancer Inst., Antoni van Leeuwenhoek Hospital, Amsterdam 1987–2000; Chair in Molecular Biology, VU Univ., Amsterdam 1993–97; Prof. of Molecular Genetics, Univ. of Amsterdam 1997–2000; Prof. of Developmental Genetics, Univ. of Utrecht 2000–07; Dir Hubrecht Lab., Netherlands Inst. for Developmental Biology 2000–07; Minister of Educ., Culture and Science 2007–10, Minister of the Interior and Kingdom Relations 2012–17; mem. European Molecular Biology Org., Bd of Govs Wellcome Trust, Standing Cttee on Genetics, Dutch Health Council; mem. Royal Netherlands Acad. of Arts and Sciences, Royal Dutch Soc. of Sciences and Humanities; mem. Labour Party (PvdA); Netherlands Org. for Scientific Research Spinoza Prize 1999, European Molecular Biology Org. Award for Communication in the Life Sciences 2002, Inst. de France Prix Louis D 2005.

PLASTOW, Sir David Arnold Stuart, Kt, CIMgt, FBIM, FRSA; British business executive; b. 9 May 1932, Grimsby, Lincs., England; s. of James Stuart Plastow and Marie Plastow; m. Barbara Ann May 1954; one s. one d.; ed Culford School, Bury St Edmunds; apprenticed to Vauxhall Motors Ltd 1950; joined Rolls-Royce Ltd, Motor Car Div. Crewe 1958, Marketing Dir Motor Car Div. 1967–71, Man. Dir 1971–72; Man. Dir Rolls-Royce Motors Ltd 1972–74, Group Man. Dir 1974–80; Regional Dir Lloyds Bank 1974–76; Dir Vickers Ltd 1975–92, Man. Dir 1980–86, Chief Exec. 1980–92, Chair. 1987–92; Chair. Inchape PLC 1992–95; Dir GKN Ltd 1978–84, Legal & General 1985–87, Guinness PLC 1986–94 (Deputy Chair. 1987–89, Jt Deputy Chair. 1989–94), Tenneco Automotive Inc. 1985–92, 1996–, F.T. Everard & Sons Ltd 1991–2001, Vinters Engineering Ltd 1992, Genome Research Ltd 1993–96, Lloyds Bank Trustee Services Ltd 1995, Kent Messenger Ltd 2000–03, Norman Court School Ltd 2008–11; Deputy Chair. (non-exec.) TSB Group PLC 1991–95; Dir (non-exec.) Cable and Wireless PLC 1991–93, Lloyds TSB 1996–99; Gov. (non-exec.) BUPA 1990–95 (Deputy Chair. 1992–95); Pres. Soc. of Motor Mfrs and Traders Ltd 1976–78, Deputy Pres. 1978–80; Pres. Motor Industry Research Asscn 1978–81; Vice-Pres. Inst. of Motor Industry 1974–82; Chair. Grand Council, Motor and Cycle Trades Benevolent Fund 1976–78; mem. Eng Council 1981–83, Council CBI, Council, Manchester Business School, Court of Manchester Univ., Council, Regular Forces Employment Asscn, Council, Industrial Soc., Chair. 1983–87, British Overseas Trade Bd 1980–83, British North American Cttee; Chair. MRC 1994–98; Chancellor Univ. of Luton (now Univ. of Bedfordshire) from 1993; Chair. of Govs, Culford School, Bury St Edmunds from 1979; Trustee, Royal Opera House Trust 1992–93 (Chair. 1992–93); Patron, Coll. of Aeronautical and Automobile Eng 1972–79; Liveryman, Worshipful Co. of Coachmakers and Coach Harness Makers; Hon. DSc (Cranfield Inst. of Tech.) 1978; Young Businessman of the Year Award (The Guardian) 1976. *Leisure interests:* golf, music. *Address:* c/o Office of the Chancellor, University of Bedfordshire, University Square, Luton, Beds., LU1 3JU, England.

PLATINI, Michel François; French sports administrator, football coach, broadcaster and fmr footballer; b. 21 June 1955, Joeuf; s. of Aldo Platini and Anna Pillenelli; m. Christele Bigoni 1977; one s. one d.; attacking midfielder; youth player, AS Joeuf 1966–72; professional footballer, AS Nancy-Lorraine 1972–79 (Ligue 2 Champions 1975, won Coupe de France 1978), AS St-Etienne 1979–82 (Ligue 1 Champions 1981), Juventus, Turin, Italy 1982–87 (scored 68 goals in 147 games, won Coppa Italia 1983, European Cup Winners' Cup Winner 1984, UEFA Super Cup Winner 1984, Serie A 1984, 1986, European Cup 1985, Intercontinental Cup 1985); player with French nat. team 1976–87 (winners European Championship 1984, Artemio Franqui Trophy 1985), Nat. Team Coach 1988–92; co-presenter, ed. and consultant, French TV 1985–88, consultant 1993–; Founder and Pres. Michel Platini Foundation 1987–; Jt Pres. French 1998 World Cup Organizng Cttee; Vice-Pres. French Football Fed.; fmr Adviser to Pres. of FIFA; mem. Exec. Cttee Union of European Football Asscns (UEFA) 2002–15, Pres. 2007–15; mem. Exec. Cttee FIFA, fmr Chair. Tech. and Devt Cttee, Vice-Pres. FIFA 2007–16, announced candidacy for 2016 FIFA presidential election July 2015, suspended for 90 days from all football-related activity pending an investigation into corruption allegations Oct. 2015, suspension escalated to eight years Dec. 2015, reduced to six years 2016 then reduced to four years, announced he would not be standing in FIFA presidential election Jan. 2016; mem. Laureus World Sports Acad.; Chevalier, Légion d'honneur 1985, Officier 1988, Officier, Ordre nat. du Mérite; France Football French Player of the Year 1976, 1977, L'Équipe French Champion of Champions 1977, selected in FIFA XI to play Argentina 1979, selected in Europe team to face FIFA XI in charity match for UNICEF 1982, Capocannoniere (top scorer) in Italian championship (16 goals) 1983, (20 goals) 1984, (18 goals) 1985, Coppa Super Clubs Payer of the Tounament 1983, Chevron Award (best goal per game ratio in Italian league) 1983, Ballon d'Or (European Footballer of the Year) 1983, 1984, Onze d'Or 1983, 1984, European Championship Payer of the Tournament 1984, European Championship top goal-scorer (nine goals) 1984, Guerin Sportivo magazine's Player of the Italian Championship 1984, L'Équipe French Champion of Champions 1984, World Soccer Player of the Year 1984, 1985, Ballon d'Or (European Footballer of the Year) 1983, 1984, 1985, French Player of the Century 1984, Chevron Award (best goal per game ratio in Italian league) 1985, European Cup top scorer (seven goals) 1985, Intercontinental Cup Man of the Match 1985, Man of the Match, English Football League Centenary Classic Match 1987, El País European Coach of the Year 1991, World Soccer Manager of the Year 1991, lighter of the Olympic Flame with François-Cyrille Grange, Winter Olympics, Albertville, France 1992, Artemio Franchi Prize 2003, named in FIFA 100 2004, inducted into the English Football Hall of Fame and voted All-Time Great European Footballer (only person outside the English game to be honoured by the Museum) 2008, Premio Internazionale Giacinto Facchetti 2011. *Publication:* Ma vie comme un match 1987.

PLATONOV, Vladimir Mikhailovich, CandJurSc; Russian politician, political scientist and academic; *Professor of Political Sciences, Faculty of Humanities and Social Sciences, Peoples' Friendship University of Russia;* b. 24 Dec. 1954, Moscow; m.; one s. one d.; ed Lumumba Univ. of Peoples' Friendship; worked in machine-construction factory 1972–75; investigator Prosecutor's Office, Deputy Prosecutor Moskvoretsky Dist of Moscow 1983–91; pvt. law practice, Exec. Dir Avtum Co. 1991–94; mem. Moscow City Duma 1993, Chair. (Speaker) 1994–; mem. Party Block Choice of Russia; mem. Russian Council of Fed. 1996–, Deputy Chair. 1998; Chair. Cttee on Constitutional Law Feb. 1996–; Prof. of Political Sciences, Faculty of Humanities and Social Sciences, Peoples' Friendship Univ. of Russia; Order of Honour 1998, Order of Merit for the Fatherland, Fourth Degree 2004. *Publications:* Models of Legislative Regulation of Relations Between the federal Centre and Regions 2003, Legislative Activity: Political and Legal Analysis (co-author) 2007, Modern Russia: Peculiarities of Politics and the Political Process (co-author) 2008. *Address:* Peoples' Friendship University of Russia, 117198 Moscow Miklukho-Maklaya str. 6, Russian Federation (office). *Telephone:* (495) 434 5300 (office). *Fax:* (495) 433 1511 (office). *E-mail:* site@rudn.ru (office). *Website:* www.rudn.ru (office); duma.mos.ru.

PLATONOV, Vladimir Petrovich, DSc; Belarusian mathematician and academic; b. 1 Dec. 1939, Staiki, Byelorussian SSR; s. of Petr Platonov and Anna Platonova; m. Valentina Platonova 1974; two d.; ed Byelorussian State University; Asst Prof., Byelorussian State Univ. 1963, Prof. 1968, Head of Algebra Dept 1967–71; Head, Algebra Dept, Inst. of Math. 1971–93, Dir 1977–92, Lecturer; mem. Inst. for Advanced Studies, Princeton, NJ 1991–92; Prof., Univ. of Michigan, USA 1993, Univ. of Bielefeld 1994, Univ. of Waterloo, Canada 1995–2001; Chief Science Officer, Scientific Research Inst. of System Devt; People's Deputy of the USSR 1989–91; Corresp. mem. Acad. of Sciences of Byelorussian SSR (now Belarus) 1969, mem. 1972 (Pres. 1987–92); mem. USSR (now Russian) Acad. of Sciences 1987, Belarus Acad. for Educ. 1995, New York Acad. of Sciences 1995, American Mathematical Soc., Canadian Mathematical Soc.; Foreign mem. Indian Nat. Science Acad.; convicted of assault and given a conditional two-year sentence 1999; Hon. mem. Chinese-Henan Acad. of Sciences; Lenin Komsomol Prize 1968, Lenin Prize 1978, Humboldt Prize 1993. *Publications include:* Algebraic Groups and Number Theory 1991, Finite-dimensional Division Algebras 1992. *Leisure interest:* literature. *Address:* c/o National Academy of Sciences of Belarus, 66 Independence Avenue, Minsk 220072, Belarus. *Telephone:* (17) 284-18-01. *Fax:* (17) 284-28-16. *E-mail:* nasb@presidium.bas-net.by. *Website:* nasb.gov.by.

PLATT, Nicholas, Sr, BA, MA; American diplomatist and educational administrator; *President Emeritus, Asia Society;* b. 10 March 1936, New York, NY; s. of Geoffrey Platt; m. Sheila Maynard; three s.; ed Harvard Coll. and Johns Hopkins Univ. School of Advanced Int. Studies; Chinese language student, Taiwan 1963; Political Officer, Hong Kong 1964–68, Beijing 1973–74, Tokyo 1974–77; staff mem. President Nixon's Del. to China 1972, later mem. US Liaison Office, Beijing; Dir for Japanese Affairs, Dept of State 1977–78; Nat. Security Council staff mem. specializing in Asian Affairs 1978–79; Deputy Asst Sec. for Defense 1980–81; Acting Asst Sec. of State for UN Affairs 1981–82; Amb. to Zambia 1982–84, to the Philippines 1987–91, to Pakistan 1991–92; Pres. Asia Soc. 1992–2004, Pres. Emer. 2004–; Special Asst to Sec. of State and Exec. Sec., Dept of State 1985–87; Chair. US-China Educ. Trust Advisory Bd; Sr Advisor on China programs for Philadelphia Orchestra; mem. New York Council on Foreign Relations, Friends of China Heritage Fund Ltd. *Publication:* China Boys: How U.S. Relations with the PRC Began and Grew. A Personal Memoir 2010. *Address:* 131 East 69th Street, New York, NY 10021, USA (home). *Telephone:* (212) 772-0724 (office). *Fax:* (212) 772-0732 (office). *E-mail:* nickplattsr@gmail.com (home).

PLATT, Trevor, PhD, FRS, FRSC; British/Canadian oceanographer; *Professorial Fellow and Executive Director, Partnership for Observation for the Global Oceans Secretariat, Plymouth Marine Laboratory;* b. 12 Aug. 1942, Salford, England; s. of John Platt and Lily Platt; m. Shubha Sathyendranath 1988; ed Nottingham, Toronto and Dalhousie Univs; research scientist, Bedford Inst. of Oceanography, Canada 1965–72, Head of Biological Oceanography 1972–2008; mem. Professorial Fellow and Exec. Dir Partnership for Observation for the Global Oceans Secr., Plymouth Marine Lab., UK 2008–; Chair. Int. Ocean-Colow Co-ordinating Group 1996–, Jt Global Ocean Flux Study 1991–93; Huntsman Medal 1992, Hutchinson Medal, Rosenstiel Medal, Plymouth Marine Medal 1999, Timothy R. Parsons Award 2006. *Publications:* numerous papers in learned journals. *Leisure interests:* cycling, fly-fishing, languages. *Address:* Plymouth Marine Laboratory, Prospect

Place, The Hoe, Plymouth, PL1 3DH, England (office). *Telephone:* (1752) 633164 (office). *Fax:* (1752) 633101 (office). *E-mail:* treatt@pml.ac.uk (office). *Website:* rsg.pml.ac.uk (office).

PLATTER, Günther; Austrian politician; *Governor of Tyrol;* b. 7 June 1954; m.; two c.; police officer, Landeck and Imst 1976–94; mem. Council, Zams 1986–89, Mayor of Zams 1989–2000; mem. Parl. 1994-2000; Minister for Sport, Culture, School, Employee Promotion and Citizenship, Tyrol Govt 2000–03; Fed. Minister of Defence 2003–07, of the Interior 2007–08; Gov. of Tyrol 2008–; mem. ÖVP (Austrian People's Party). *Address:* Governor of Tyrol, Eduard-Wallnöfer-Platz 3, 6020 Innsbruck, Tyrol, Austria (office). *Telephone:* (5) 125-08-20-02 (office). *Fax:* (5) 125-08-20-05 (office). *E-mail:* buero.lh.platter@tirol.gv.at (office). *Website:* www.tirol.gv.at (office).

PLATTNER, Hasso; German computer industry executive; *Chairman of the Supervisory Board, SAP AG;* b. 21 Jan. 1944, Berlin; m.; two c.; ed Univ. of Karlsruhe; consultant, IBM 1968–72; Co-founder SAP AG 1972, Chair. SAP America, CEO SAP Markets, Co-Chair. and CEO –2003, Chair. Supervisory Bd 2003–; f. HassoPlattnerVentures (HPV), Potsdam 2005, Hasso Plattner Inst. of Design, Stanford Univ., USA 2005, HPV Africa 2009; investor in San Jose Sports & Entertainment Enterprises (owns San Jose Sharks, HP Pavilion at San Jose and other related properties); bought out two of the partners in SJS&E and began serving as the Sharks' Rep. on Nat. Hockey League's Bd Govs 2013; Hon. Prof., Univ. of Saarbrücken. *Leisure interests:* golf, sailing. *Address:* SAP AG, Dietmar-Hopp-Allee 16, 69190 Walldorf, Germany (office). *Telephone:* (6227) 747474 (office). *Fax:* (6227) 757575 (office). *E-mail:* info@sap.com (office). *Website:* www.sap.com (office).

PLAYER, Gary Jim; South African professional golfer (retd); b. 1 Nov. 1935, Johannesburg; s. of Francis Harry Audley Player and Muriel Marie Ferguson; m. Vivienne Verwey 1957; two s. four d.; turned professional 1953; first overseas player for 45 years to win US Open Championship 1965; Winner, British Open Championship 1959, 1968, 1974; Piccadilly World Match Play Champion 1965, 1966, 1968, 1971, 1973; US Open Champion 1965; US Masters Champion 1961, 1974, 1978; US Professional Golf Asscn Champion 1962, 1972; Winner, South African Open 13 times; South African PGA Champion 1959, 1960, 1969, 1979, 1982; Winner, Australian Open 7 times; Quadel Sr Classic Champion 1985; third player ever to win all four major world professional titles; holds world record for lowest 18-hole score in any Open Championship (59 in the Brazilian Open 1974); Sr Tour victories include: Sr British Open 1988, 1990, 1997, Sr PGA Champion 1986, 1988, 1990, Long Island Sr Classic, Sr Skins Game 2000; Capt. Rest of the World Team, Pres.'s Cup 2003, 2005; f. Gary Player Group, Gary Player Foundation (rural educ.); golf course designer (over 200 projects world-wide); breeds thoroughbred racehorses; DMS, Order of Ikhamanga; Dr hc (Ulster) 1997, (Dundee) 1999; South African Sportsman of the Century 1989, Hilton Hotel Lifetime Achievement Award 1995, Laureus Lifetime Achievement Award 2003, Asia Pacific Golf Humanitarian Award 2009, Canada Lifetime Achievement Award 2009, Asia Pacific Hall of Fame 2010, PGA Tour Lifetime Achievement Award. *Publications include:* Gary Player: The Autobiography 1991, The Golfer's Guide to the Meaning of Life 2001. *Leisure interests:* breeding thoroughbred racehorses, farming, educ., family, health, fitness. *Address:* Gary Player Stud, POB 189, Colesberg 9795, South Africa (office); POB 785629, Sandton 2146. *Telephone:* (11) 8833333 (office); (11) 6592800 (home). *Fax:* (11) 8834444 (office). *E-mail:* info@garyplayer.co.za (office).

PLÉAH, Natié; Malian politician; b. 1953, Moutigué, Ké-Macina Circle; m.; seven c.; ed secondary school in Sévaré, Markala Coll., school in Badalabougou, Ecole Nationale d'Admin, Paris, France; began serving Gov.-Gen. Sikasso 1976, held several posts as an admin., including Second Deputy Commdr Ansongo Circle, Deputy Commdr Koulikoro then Yanfolila Circles, Commdr Circle then Koulikoro Timbuktu, Admin. Affairs Advisor to Gov. of Timbuktu, Advisor for Admin. Affairs in Ségou, Chief of Staff to Gov. of Mopti and High Commr of Kayes; Acting High Commr First Econ. Region 2002–04, Gov. of Kayes 2004–05; Gov. Dist of Bamako 2005; Minister of Youth and Sports 2005–07, of the Environment and Sanitation May 2007, of Defence and Veterans 2007–12. *Leisure interests:* reading and agricultural activities.

PLEISTER, Christopher, Dr rer. pol; German banker; b. 15 May 1948, Hamburg; m.; three s.; ed Ludwig-Maximilians Univ., Munich; with Landesgenossenschaftsbank AG, Hanover 1977–81, Hallbaum, Maier & Co. Landkreditbank AG, Hanover 1981–84; Exec. Man. Norddeutsche Genossenschaftsbank AG 1984, mem. Bd of Man. 1985–90; mem. Bd of Man. DG Bank (now DZ Bank), Frankfurt-am-Main 1990–99, Chair. Supervisory Bd DZ Bank 2001–08; Chair. Bundesverband der Deutschen Volksbanken und Raiffeisenbanken (BVR—Fed. Asscn of German Co-operative Banks) 2000–08; Pres. European Asscn of Cooperative Banks (EACB) 2006; mem. Man. Cttee Financial Market Stabilization Fund (SoFFin) 2009; mem. Bd of Dirs DEPFA Bank PLC 2015–. *Address:* c/o DEPFA Bank PLC, 1 Commons Street, Dublin 1, Ireland.

PLENDERLEITH, Ian, CBE, MA, MBA, MSI, FCT; British economist and central bank executive; b. 27 Sept. 1943, York; s. of Raymond William Plenderleith and Louise Helen Plenderleith (née Martin); m. Kristina Mary Bentley; one s. two d.; ed King Edward's School, Birmingham, Christ Church, Oxford, Columbia Business School, USA; joined Bank of England 1965, seconded to IMF, Washington, DC 1972–74, Pvt. Sec. to Gov. Bank of England 1976–79; Alt. Dir EIB 1980–86, Head of Gilt-Edged Div. 1982–90, Asst Dir 1986–90, Sr Broker to Commrs for Reduction of Nat. Debt 1989–2002, Assoc. Dir 1990–94; Dir Bank of England Nominees Ltd 1994–2002, Exec. Dir Bank of England and mem. Monetary Policy Cttee 1994–2002; Deputy Gov. and mem. Monetary Policy Cttee, South African Reserve Bank 2003–05; Chair. BH Macro Ltd 2007–17; Alt. Dir BIS 1994–2002; Dir London Stock Exchange (fmrly mem. Stock Exchange Council) 1989–2001 (Deputy Chair. 1996), Chair. Stock Borrowing and Lending Cttee 1990–95; Chair. G-10 Gold and Foreign Exchange Cttee 1995–2001; Co-Chair. Govt Borrowers' Forum 1991–94; Chair. Sterling Money Markets Liaison Group 1999–2002; Chair. Corpn for Public Deposits 2003; mem. Bd of Dirs (non-exec.) BMCE Bank Int. 2006–16, Sanlam, South Africa 2006–, Bond Exchange of South Africa 2007–09, Europe Arab Bank 2009–12, Morgan Stanley Int. Ltd 2011– (currently Chair.), Morgan Stanley Bank Int. Ltd 2013–; mem. Editorial Cttee OECD Study on Debt Man. 1990–93, Legal Risk Review Cttee 1991–92, Financial Law Panel 1992–94, G-10 Cttee on Global Financial System 1994–2002; mem. Advisory Bd Inst. of Archaeology Devt Trust, Univ. Coll. London 1987–96, Bd of Overseers, Columbia Business School 1991, Fundraising Planning Group, St Bartholomew's Hosp. 1992–94, Council, British Museum Friends 1993–99, 2000–03, Fundraising Planning Cttee St Bartholomew's and The London Hosps 1998–2003, Advisory Bd The Actors Centre 2002, Devt Council Shakespeare's Globe 2002, Advisory Bd London Capital Club 2002; adviser to Asscn of Corp. Treasurers, International Capital Markets Asscn, Central Banking Publications and the Invoice Clearing Bureau South Africa; Dir City Arts Trust 1997–2003; mem. Securities Inst.; Liveryman Innholders' Co.; Sec., Tillington Cricket Club 1983–2003; Chair. Bd of Govs. Reed's School, Surrey 2007–; Beta Gamma Sigma Medal 1971. *Leisure interests:* archaeology, theatre, cricket, long-distance walking.

PLENEL, Edwy; French journalist and writer; *President and Editor-in-Chief, Mediapart;* b. (Hervé Edwy Plenel), 31 Aug. 1952, Nantes; s. of Alain Plenel and Michèle Bertreux; m. Nicole Lapierre; one d.; ed Institut d'études politiques, Paris; journalist, Rouge 1976–78, Matin de Paris 1980; joined Le Monde 1980, Educ. Ed. 1980–82, Legal columnist 1982–90, Reporter 1991, Head Legal Dept 1992–94, Chief Ed. 1994–95, Asst Editorial Dir 1995–96, Ed. 1996–2000, Ed.-in-Chief 2000–04 (resgnd); co-f. Mediapart 2008, currently Pres. and Ed.-in-Chief; Mumm Foundation Prize 1986, 13th Int. Omar Aourtilane Freedom of the Press Award (Algeria) 2012. *Television:* Une affaire d'état (film, writer) 1991. *Publications include:* L'Effet Le Pen (with Alain Rollat) 1984, La République inachevée: l'État et l'école en France 1985, Mourir à Ouvéa: le tournant calédonien 1988, Voyage avec Colomb 1991, La République menacée: dix ans d'effet Le Pen 1992, La Part d'ombre 1992, Un temps de chien 1994, Les Mots volés 1997, L'Epreuve 1999, Secrets de jeunesse (Prix Médicis essai) 2001, La Découverte du monde 2002, Procès 2006, Le Journaliste et le Président 2006, Chroniques marranes 2007, Combat pour une presse libre: Le manifeste de Mediapart (translated into Spanish) 2009, Le Président de trop: Vertus de l'antisarkozysme, vices du présidentialisme 2011, Notre France (conversation with Farouk Mardam Bey and Elias Sanbar) 2011, Le Droit de savoir 2013, Dire non 2014, Pour les musulmans 2014, La Troisième Equipe: Souvenirs de l'affaire Greenpeace 2015, Dire nous: Contre les peurs et les haines, nos causes communes 2016, Voyage en terres d'espoir 2016, Le devoir d'hospitalité 2017, La valeur de l'information 2018. *Website:* www.mediapart.fr (office); blogs.mediapart.fr/blog/edwy-plenel (office).

PLENKOVIĆ, Andrej, LLM; Croatian diplomatist and politician; *Prime Minister;* b. 1970, Zagreb, Socialist Repub. of Croatia, Socialist Fed. Repub. of Yugoslavia; s. of Mario Plenković and Vjekoslav Raos-Plenković; m. Anne Maslać Plenković; one s.; ed Zagreb Faculty of Law, Croatian Ministry of Foreign and European Affairs Diplomatic Acad.; mem. European Asscn of Law Students (ELSA), Pres. ELSA Zagreb 1991, first Pres., ELSA Croatia 1992, Pres. ELSA Int. Cttee, Brussels 1993; Assoc., Dept for European Integration, Ministry of Foreign Affairs 1994, worked in Dept for Analytics 1996–97, Head, Dept for European Integration 1997–99, Adviser to Minister for European Affairs 1999, mem. Advisory Council, Govt Office for European Integration (worked on launch of Stability Pact for SE Europe), Deputy Sec.-Gen., Org. of Zagreb meeting of Heads of State and Govt of EU and countries of SE Europe Nov. 2000, Croatian Nat. Coordinator for Central European Initiative, Deputy Head, Croatian Mission to EU, Brussels 2002–05, Deputy Amb. to France 2005–10, Sec. of State for European Integration 2010–11; mem. Sabor (Parl.) 2011–13; mem. European Parl. (Group of European People's Party) 2013–16, Vice-Pres. Foreign Affairs Cttee 2014–16; Prime Minister of Croatia 2016–; fmr Lecturer at law schools in Zagreb, Split and Osijek, at Diplomatic Acad. of Ministry of Foreign and European Affairs, the European Movt, Pan-European Union and several other colls and insts in Croatia, Belgium, Bosnia and Herzegovina, France, Germany, Hungary, Italy, Monaco, Spain and Sweden; mem. Hrvatska Demokratska Zajednica (Croatian Democratic Union) 2011–, Pres. 2016–; Order of Merit, Third Class (Ukraine). *Address:* Office of the Prime Minister, 10000 Zagreb, trg sv. Marka 2, Croatia (office). *Telephone:* (1) 4569239 (office). *Fax:* (1) 6303022 (office). *E-mail:* press@vlada.hr (office). *Website:* vlada.gov.hr (office); www.andrejplenkovic.hr.

PLEŞCA, Valeriu; Moldovan politician, business executive and economist; b. 8 Nov. 1958, Dumitreni, Floresti Dist; m.; one s. one d.; ed State Univ. of Moldova, Acad. of Econ. Studies; Adviser, Ministry of Social Assistance 1983–86, Office of the Chief Prosecutor 1986–91; Head of Gloria V&A Co. 1990–; mem. Parl. 1998– (ind. 2003–), fmr Deputy Chair. Comm. for Rules and Immunities; Minister of Defence 2004–05, 2005–07; Pres. Foundation for the Promotion of Justice, Security and Defense (PRISA) 2008; Vice-Pres. Nat. Boxing Fed. 2009; Founder and Owner MBC TV (Moldavian Buiness Channel) 2014; Serghei Radonejskii Award 2006. *Publications include:* numerous articles on defence and security policy. *Leisure interests include:* tennis, skiing, hunting.

PLESHAKOVA, Olga Alexandrovna, CandSci (Eng); Russian airline industry executive; *General Director and CEO, Transaero Airlines;* b. 7 Dec. 1966, Moscow; d. of T. G. Anodina; m. Alexander Petrovich Pleshakov; ed Moscow Aviation Inst.; joined Transaero Airlines after graduation 1992, Sr Expert, Tech. Dept 1992–93, Head of in-flight service 1993–96, Deputy Gen. Dir for Service 1996–99, First Deputy Gen. Dir for Commercial Operations and Service 1999–2001, Gen. Dir and CEO 2001–; Order of the Russian Orthodox Church 2011, Officier, Ordre national du Mérite 2014; CIS Business Leader 2011, Award of Imperial Orthodox Palestine Soc. 2011. *Address:* OJSC Transaero Airlines, 119180 Moscow, 47 Bolshaya Polyanka Street, Building 1, Russia (office). *Telephone:* (495) 788-8080 (office). *E-mail:* info@transaero.com (office). *Website:* www.transaero.com (office).

PLEŞU, Andrei Gabriel, PhD; Romanian philosopher, college rector and fmr government official; b. 23 Aug. 1948, Bucharest; s. of Radu Pleşu and Zoe Pleşu; m. Catrinel Maria Lăcrămioara 1972; two s.; ed Acad. of Fine Arts and Univ. of Bucharest; Lecturer, Acad. of Fine Arts, Bucharest 1980–82, Prof. 1991–92; Prof., Univ. of Bucharest 1992–, Prof. of Philosophy of Religion 1999–97; Dir of Dilema (weekly); Founder and Rector New Europe Coll., Bucharest 1994–2001; Minister of Culture 1989–91, of Foreign Affairs 1997–99; mem. Romanian Artists' Union 1975, Romanian Writers' Union 1980, World Acad. of Art and Science, Acad. Internationale de Philosophie de l'Art, Geneva, Scientific Advisory Bd Europe Inst., Budapest, Advisory Group for Social Sciences and Humanities in the European

Research Area (Research Directorate Gen. of the EU Comm.), Bd of Trustees, Collegium Budapest, Bd of Trustees, Maison des Sciences de l'Homme, Paris, Bd of Trustees and Advisory Bd, Centre for Advanced Study, Sofia; Corresp. mem. Consejo Argentino para las Relaciones Internacionales; Perm. Research Fellow, Wissenschaftskollege, Berlin 1992; Commdr des Arts et des Lettres 1990, Gran Cruz, Orden El Sol del Perú (Peru) 1998, Grand Officier, Légion d'honneur 1999, Grand Officer, Order of Diplomatic Merit, Grand Cross, Order of the Faithful Service; Hon. PhD (Albert-Ludwig Univ., Freiburg) 2000, (Humboldt Univ., Berlin) 2001; Humboldt Research Fellowship, Univ. of Bonn 1975–77, Univ. of Heidelberg 1983–84, Prize for Art Criticism, Romanian Artists' Union 1980, Prize for Essay, Writers' Asscn, Bucharest 1980, Prize, Ateneu review 1991, Prize, Flacara weekly 1993, New Europe Prize 1993, Prize of Brandenburg Acad. of Sciences, Berlin 1996, Humboldt Medal (Germany) 1998, Hannah Arendt Prize 1998, Goethe Medal, Goethe Inst., Weimar 1999, Konstantin Jireček Medal, South-Eastern European Soc., Berlin 2000 and numerous other prizes, two volumes published in his honour, both edited by Mihail Neamţu and Bogdan Tătaru-Cazaban: O filozofie a intervalului: In Honorem Andrei Pleşu (A Philosophy of the Interval: In Honor of Andrei Plesu, in Romanian) and an int. Festschrift in honour of his 60th birthday 2009. *Publications:* Călătorie în lumea formelor (Journey to the World of Forms) 1974, Pitoresc şi melancolie (The Picturesque and Melancholy) 1980, Francesco Guardi 1981, Ochiul şi lucrurile (The Eye and Things) 1986, Minima moralia (Moral Minimum) 1988, Dialoguri de seară (Evening Dialogues) 1991, Jurnalul de la Tescani (The Tescany Journal) 1993, Limba păsărilor (The Language of Birds) 1994, Chipuri şi măşti ale tranziţiei (Faces and Masks of Transition) 1996, Despre îngeri (On Angels) 2003, Obscenitatea publică (Public Obscenity) 2004, Comedii la porţile Orientului (Comedies at the Gates of the Orient) 2005, Despre bucurie în Est şi în Vest şi alte eseuri (About Joy in East and West and other essays) 2006, Despre frumuseţea uitată a vieţii (About the Forgotten Beauty of Life) 2011, Parabolele lui Iisus. Adevarul ca poveste (Jesus' Parables. The Truth as Story) 2012, On Angels – Exposition for a Post Modern World (in English) 2012; numerous papers and articles. *Address:* Faculty of Philosophy, University of Bucharest, Splaiul Independentei nr. 204, Sector 6, 060024 Bucharest (office); Str. Paris 14, 71241 Bucharest 1, Romania (home). *Telephone:* (21) 3181556 (office). *E-mail:* filosofie@ub-filosofie.ro (office). *Website:* www.filosofie.unibuc.ro (office); www.humanitas.ro/andrei-plesu.

PLETNEV, Mikhail Vasilievich; Russian pianist, conductor and composer; b. 14 April 1957, Arkhangelsk; ed Moscow State Conservatory with Yakov Flier and Lev Vlasenko (piano), Albert Leman (composition); gave recitals and played with orchestras in major cities of Russia, Europe, Japan and America; gained reputation as Russian music interpreter; Founder and Chief Conductor, Russian Nat. Orchestra 1990–99, Hon. Conductor 1999–, head of Conductor Collegium 2006–; Prin. Guest Conductor, Orchestra della Svizzera Italiana 2008–10; has performed with Haitink, Maazel, Chailly, Tennstedt, Sanderling, Blomstedt, Järvi, Thielemann; has conducted Philharmonia Orchestra, Deutsche Kammerphilharmonie, Norddeutsche Rundfunk Symphony Orchestra, London Symphony Orchestra, Berlin Philharmonic, Bayerische Rundfunk Symphony, Orchestre Nat. de France, Israel Philharmonic, San Francisco Symphony and Pittsburgh Symphony; teacher, Moscow Conservatory 1981–92; f. Mikhail Pletnev Fund for the Support of National Culture 2006; Advisor, Russia Cultural Council; First Prize, Int. Tchaikovsky competition, Moscow 1978, People's Artist of Russia 1990, State Prize of Russia 1982, 1993, Presidential Prize for his contributions to the artistic life of Russia 2007. *Recordings:* numerous recordings, including of Scarlatti's Keyboard Sonatas (Gramophone Award) 1996, Rachmaninov and Prokofiev Piano Concertos No. 3 2003, Schumann Symphonic Etudes 2004, Prokofiev's Cinderella (Grammy Award) 2005, recorded all of Beethoven's piano concertos with Deutsche Grammophon 2007. *Address:* Russian National Orchestra, Moscow 117335, Orchestrion, Garibaldi 19, Russia (office). *Website:* russiannationalorchestra.org (office).

PLEVNELIEV, Rosen Asenov; Bulgarian business executive, politician and fmr head of state; b. 14 May 1964, Gotse Delchev; m. Yuliyana Plevnelieva; three s. (one deceased); ed Blagoevgrad Math. and Natural Sciences High School, Higher Mechanical-Electrotechnical Inst., Sofia, Technical Univ. of Sofia; Fellow, Inst. for Microprocessing Tech., Pravets 1989; f. and managed several businesses including Iris International JSC 1990, Linbalgariya Ltd 1994, Iris Lindner Immobilien Ltd 1998, Business Park Sofia EOOD 1999, Lindner Bulgaria Ltd 2001, Residential Park Sofia Ltd 2003, Lindner Imobilen Management Ltd 2005; Minister of Regional Devt and Public Works 2009–11; Pres. of Bulgaria 2012–17; mem. Citizens for European Devt of Bulgaria –2012; Ind. 2012–; mem. Bd Confed. of Employers and Industrialists in Bulgaria 2007, American Chamber of Commerce, Sofia 2008; mem. Bd of Trustees, 'For Our Children' (non-profit org.) 2008; Honour of Nation Order (Albania), Grand Collar, Order of the Southern Cross (Brazil), Grand Cross (Special Class), Order of Merit of the FRG, Kt Grand Cross with Collar, Order of Merit of the Italian Repub., Order for Exceptional Merits (Slovenia), Companion of Honour, Nat. Order of Merit (Malta). *Address:* c/o Office of the President, 1123 Sofia, bul. Dondukov 2, Bulgaria. *E-mail:* priemna@president.bg.

PLOIX, Hélène Marie Joseph, MA, MBA; French business executive; *Chairman, Pechel Industries;* b. 25 Sept. 1944, Anould; d. of René Ploix and Antoinette Jobert; m. Alexandre Lumbroso 1988; ed Univ. of Paris, Univ. of California, Berkeley; Man. Consultant, McKinsey and Co., Paris 1968–78; Special Asst to Cabinet of Sec. of State for Consumer Affairs 1977–78; Dir Cie Européenne de Publication 1978–82; Chair. Banque Industrielle et Mobilière Privée 1982–84; mem. of Bd Comm. des Opérations de Bourse 1983–84; Adviser to Prime Minister for Econ. and Financial Affairs 1984–86; Exec. Dir IMF and World Bank, representing France 1986–89; Deputy CEO Caisse des dépôts et consignations 1989–95; Chair. Caisse autonome de refinancement 1990–95, CDC Participations 1992–95; Chair. Pechel Industries 1997–, Chair. Investment Cttee 2017–; currently mem. Jt Staff Pension Fund Investments Cttee, UN; mem. Bd of Dirs (non-exec.) BNP Paribas 2003–, Ferring Pharmaceuticals, Publicis Groupe 1998–, Lafarge 1999–, The Boots Co. PLC 2000–, Completel; mem. Strategic Advisory Bd Generis Capital Partners; Chevalier Ordre Nat. du Mérite, Chevalier Légion d'honneur. *Publications:* Le dirigeant et le gouvernement d'entreprise 2003, Gouvernement d'enterprise 2006. *Leisure interest:* golf. *Address:* Pechel Industries, 162 rue du Faubourg Saint-Honoré, 75008 Paris (office); 42 quai des Orfèvres, 75001 Paris, France. *Telephone:* 1-56-59-79-59 (office). *Fax:* 1-56-59-79-56 (office). *E-mail:* helene.ploix@pechel.com (office). *Website:* www.pechel.com (office).

PLOTNITSKII, Igor Venediktovich; Ukrainian army officer and politician; b. 26 June 1964, either in Luhansk or in Kelmentsi, Chernivtsi Oblast, Ukrainian SSR, USSR; s. of Venyamin Plotnitskii and Nina Plotnitskaya; m.; one s. one d.; ed Marshal N.N. Voronov Artillery Eng Inst., Perm, Russian SFSR, Volodymyr Dal East Ukrainian Nat. Univ., Luhansk; served in Soviet Army 1982–91, attained rank of Maj.; reserve officer in Soviet Army; engaged in business activities following break-up of Soviet Union 1991; worked as manager in various commercial orgs; Head of T.F. Skarabei fuel-trading firm 1996; worked in Consumer Protection Dept, Luhansk Oblast Admin 2004, headed quality control section; First Commdr of newly formed 'Zarya' (Dawn) bn of separatists in Luhansk April 2014; Minister of Defence (following declaration of independence of self-proclaimed 'Luhansk People's Republic', LNR) May 2014; Head of 'Luhansk People's Republic' 2014–17 (resgnd), also Chair. Council of Ministers; mem. Mir Luganshchine (Peace for Lugansk Region) movt.

PLOWDEN, David, BA; American photographer, fmr academic, author and teacher; b. 9 Oct. 1932, Boston, Mass; s. of Roger Stanley Plowden and Mary Plowden (née Butler); m. 1st Pleasance Coggeshall (divorced 1976); m. 2nd Sandra Schoellkopf 1977; three s. one d.; ed Yale Univ.; Asst to Trainmaster, Great Northern Railway 1955–56; self-employed photographer/writer 1962–; Assoc. Prof., Illinois Inst. of Tech. Inst. of Design 1978–85; Lecturer, Univ. of Iowa School of Journalism 1985–88; Visiting Prof., Grand Valley State Univ. 1988–2007 (retd); numerous photographic exhbns; John Simon Guggenheim Memorial Fellowship 1968; Smithsonian Inst. Award 1970–71, 1975–76, Iowa Humanities Award and Nat. Endowment for the Humanities Award 1987–88. *Publications:* Lincoln and His America 1970, The Hand of Man on America 1971, Floor of the Sky, The Great Plains 1972, Commonplace 1974, Bridges: The Spans of North America 1974, revised edn 2002, Tugboat 1976, Steel 1981, An American Chronology 1982, Industrial Landscape 1985, A Time of Trains 1987, A Sense of Place 1988, End of an Era 1992, Small Town America 1994, Imprints 1997, David Plowden: The American Barn 2003, A Handful of Dust 2006, Vanishing Point 2007, Requiem for Steam 2010, Heartland: The Plains and the Prairie 2013; co-author of numerous books. *Address:* 609 Cherry Street, Winnetka, IL 60093, USA (home). *Telephone:* (847) 446-2793 (home). *Fax:* (847) 446-2795 (home). *E-mail:* david@davidplowden.com. *Website:* www.davidplowden.com.

PLOWRIGHT, Dame Joan Ann, DBE; British actress; b. 28 Oct. 1929, Brigg, Lancashire; d. of William Plowright and Daisy Plowright (née Burton); m. 1st Roger Gage 1953 (divorced); m. 2nd Sir Laurence (later Lord) Olivier 1961 (died 1989); one s. two d.; ed Scunthorpe Grammar School and Old Vic Theatre School; mem. Old Vic Company, toured South Africa 1952–53; first leading rôle in The Country Wife, London 1956; mem. English Stage Company 1956; at Nat. Theatre 1963–74; Vice-Pres. Nat. Youth Theatre; Vice-Pres. and mem. Council English Stage Co.; mem. Council, Royal Acad. of Dramatic Art (RADA); Best Actress Soc. of West End Theatre (Filumena) 1978, 18th Crystal Award for Women in Film, USA 1994. *Plays include:* The Chairs 1957, The Entertainer 1958, Major Barbara and Roots 1959, A Taste of Honey (Best Actress (Tony) Award 1960) 1960, Uncle Vanya 1962, 1963, 1964, St Joan (Best Actress (Evening Standard) Award 1964) 1963, Hobson's Choice 1964, The Master Builder 1965, Much Ado About Nothing 1967, Tartuffe 1967, Three Sisters 1967, 1969 (film 1969), The Advertisement 1968, 1969, Love's Labour's Lost 1968, 1969, The Merchant of Venice, 1970, 1971–72, Rules of the Game, Woman Killed with Kindness 1971–72, Taming of the Shrew, Doctor's Dilemma 1972, Rosmersholm 1973, Saturday Sunday Monday 1973, Eden's End 1974, The Sea Gull 1975, The Bed Before Yesterday (Variety Club Award 1976) 1975, Filumena 1977, Enjoy 1980, Who's Afraid of Virginia Woolf? 1981, Cavell 1982, The Cherry Orchard 1983, The Way of the World 1984, Mrs Warren's Profession 1985, Revolution 1985, The House of Bernarda Alba 1986, And a Nightingale Sang 1989, Time and the Conways 1991, Absolutely Perhaps 2003. *Films include:* Equus 1976, Britannia Hospital 1981, Richard Wagner 1982, Brimstone and Treacle 1982, Drowning by Numbers (Variety Club Film Actress of the Year Award 1987) 1987, The Dressmaker 1988, Conquest of the South Pole 1989, I Love You to Death 1989, Avalon 1990, Enchanted April (Golden Globe Award 1993) 1991, Stalin (Golden Globe Award 1993) 1991, Dennis the Menace, A Place for Annie 1992, A Pin for the Butterfly 1993, Last Action Hero 1993, Widow's Peak 1994, On Promised Land 1994, Return of the Natives 1994, Hotel Sorrento 1994, A Pyromaniac's Love Story 1994, The Scarlet Letter 1994, Jane Eyre 1994, If We Are Women 1995, Surviving Picasso 1995, Mr. Wrong 1995, 101 Dalmatians 1996, The Assistant 1996, Shut Up and Dance 1997, Tom's Midnight Garden 1997, America Betrayed 1998, Tea with Mussolini 1999, Return to the Secret Garden 2001, Callas Forever 2002, Global Heresy 2002, Bringing Down the House 2003, I Am David 2003, The Great Goose Caper 2003, George and the Dragon 2004, Goose! 2004, Mrs Palfry at the Claremont (AARP Best Actress Award 2006) 2005, Curious George (voice) 2006, The Spiderwick Chronicles 2007. *Television includes:* Merchant of Venice 1973, Daphne Laureola 1977, Saturday Sunday Monday 1977, The Importance of Being Earnest 1988, It May Be the Last Time 1997, Frankie and Hazel 2000, Bailey's Mistake 2001. *Publication:* And That's Not All (autobiog.) 2001. *Leisure interests:* entertaining, music, reading. *Address:* c/o ICM, 76 Oxford Street, London, W1N 0AX, England (office).

PLOWRIGHT, Jonathan Daniel, Dip RAM, ARAM, FRAM; British pianist and academic; *Professor of Piano, Royal Conservatoire of Scotland;* b. 24 Sept. 1959, Doncaster, S Yorks.; s. of Cyril James Plowright and Molly Plowright; m. Diane Rosemary Shaw 1990; ed Stonyhurst Coll., Univ. of Birmingham, Royal Acad. of Music, Peabody Conservatory of Music, USA; debut at Carnegie Recital Hall, New York 1984, Purcell Room, London 1985; has performed with all major UK orchestras and numerous int. orchestras; solo recitals throughout UK and many int. tours; regular BBC broadcasts and commercial recordings; performed world premiere of Constant Lambert's piano concerto, St John's Smith Square 1988; Head of Keyboard, Univ. of Chichester; currently Prof. of Piano, Royal Conservatoire of Scotland (fmrly Royal Scottish Acad. of Music and Drama); RAM McFarren Gold Medal 1983, Fulbright Scholarship 1983, Countess of Munster Scholarship, Commonwealth Musician of the Year 1983, Gold Medal, Royal

Overseas League 1983, winner, Baltimore Symphony Orchestra Awards 1984, winner, European Piano Competition 1989. *Recordings include:* Capital Virtuosi, Brahms Solo Piano, Chopin Solo Piano, Vol. 1, Jonathan Plowright (recital), Paderewski (solo piano), Sigismund Stojowski Piano Concertos, Sigismund Stojowski (solo piano), Constant Lambert Piano Concerto, Rarities of Piano Music at Schloss vor Husum 2003, 2004, 2007, 2010, Paderewski (solo piano), Henryk Melcer Piano Concertos 2008, Hommage à Chopin 2010, Johann Sebastian Bach Piano Transcriptions 2010, Homage to Paderewski 2011, Zelenski & Zarebski Chamber Music 2012, Brahms Works for Solo Piano Vol. 1, 2, 3 2013–16, Zelenski Piano Concertos 2014, Rozycki Piano Concertos 2016. *Film:* pianist Ernest Ziegler in Florence Foster Jenkins 2016. *Leisure interests:* wine, rugby, cricket, fishing. *E-mail:* jonathan@jonathanplowright.com. *Website:* www.jonathanplowright.com.

PLOWRIGHT, Rosalind Anne, OBE, LRAM; British singer (mezzo-soprano); b. 21 May 1949, Worksop, Notts.; d. of Robert Arthur Plowright and Celia Adelaide Plowright; m. James Anthony Kaye 1984; one s. one d.; ed Notre Dame High School, Wigan, Royal Northern Coll. of Music; began career at London Opera Centre 1973–75; Glyndebourne Chorus and Touring Co. 1974–77; debut with ENO as Page in Salome 1975, Miss Jessel in Turn of the Screw 1979 (Soc. of West End Theatre Laurence Olivier Award 1980), at Covent Garden as Ortlinde in Die Walküre 1980; Metropolitan Opera debut 2003; has also sung in Argentina, Austria, Chile, Denmark, France, Germany, Greece, Israel, Italy, Japan, Netherlands, Portugal, Spain, Switzerland, USA; wide repertoire as soprano, but has sung mezzo roles since 1999; principal roles (as soprano) include Ariadne, Alceste, Médée, Norma, Tosca, title role and Elizabeth I in Mary Stuart, Maddalena in Andrea Chénier, Antonia in The Tales of Hoffman, Donna Anna in Don Giovanni, Vitellia in La Clemenza di Tito, Madame Butterfly, Manon Lescaut, Suor Angelica, Giorgetta in Il Tabarro, Aida, Abigaille in Nabucco, Desdemona in Otello, Elena in I Vespri Siciliani, Leonora in Il Trovatore, Amelia in Un Ballo in Maschera, Leonora in La Forza del Destino, Violetta in La Traviata; (as mezzo) Kostelnička in Jenufa, Amneris in Aida, Fricka in Das Rheingold and Die Walküre, Gertrude in Hansel & Gretel, Klytemnestra in Elektra, Madame de Croissy in Dialogues des Carmelites, Herodias in Salome; Mrs. Sedley in Peter Grimes for Opera de Lyon and Theater an der Wien 2015; First Prize, 7th Int. Competition for Opera Singers, Sofia 1979, Prix Fondation Fanny Heldy, Acad. Nat. du Disque Lyrique 1985, Grammy 2009. *Recordings:* numerous recordings, including Mary Stuart, Otello, Aida and Hansel & Gretel (Grammy Award for best recording) for Opera in English series, Elijah, La Vestale, Contes d'Hoffmann, Mahler 2nd Symphony, La Belle Dame sans Merci 2014. *Television:* House of Elliot 1992, The Man Who Made Husbands Jealous 1997. *Address:* Zemsky/Green Artists Management, 104 West 73rd Street, Suite 1, New York, NY 10023, USA (office); 83 St Mark's Avenue, Salisbury, Wilts., SP1 3DW, England (home). *Website:* www.rosalindplowright.com (home); www.ros-sing.co.uk (home).

PLUGCHIEVA, Meglena Ivanova, PhD; Bulgarian diplomatist and politician; *Ambassador to Switzerland;* b. 12 Feb. 1956, Balchik; m.; two c.; ed German Language High School, Varna, Forestry Univ.; worked as an insp. at Regional Environmental Protection Directorate, Varna 1981–84; a Deputy Dir Varna Regional Forestry Directorate 1984–90; Head of Foreign Relations Dept, Nat. Forestry Directorate 1990–95; mem. Parl. (Bulgarian Socialist Party—BSP) 1995–2001, 2009–12; Deputy Minister of Agric. and Forests 2001–04 (resgnd as mem. Supreme Council of BSP to take this position), Deputy Prime Minister, responsible for EU Funds 2008–09; Amb. to Germany 2004–08; to Switzerland 2012–; Rep. of Bulgaria at Rheinland-Pfalz, Germany 1997–2008, mem. Governing Bd Bulgarian-German Forum 1996; Bundesverdienstkreuz. *Address:* Embassy of Bulgaria, Bernastr. 2–4, 3005 Bern, Switzerland (office). *Telephone:* 313511455 (office). *Fax:* 313510064 (office). *E-mail:* bulembassy@bluewin.ch (office). *Website:* www.mfa.bg/embassies/switzerland (office).

PLUMB, Baron (Life Peer), cr. 1987, of Coleshill in the County of Warwickshire; **(Charles) Henry Plumb,** Kt, DL; British politician; b. 27 March 1925; s. of Charles Plumb and Louise Plumb; m. Marjorie Dorothy Dunn 1947; one s. two d.; ed King Edward VI School, Nuneaton; mem. Council Nat. Farmers Union 1959, Vice-Pres. 1964, 1965, Deputy-Pres. 1966–69, Pres. 1970–79; mem. Duke of Northumberland's Cttee of Inquiry on Foot and Mouth Disease 1967–68; Chair. British Agricultural Council 1975–79; Pres. Nat. Fed. of Young Farmers' Clubs 1976–86; Pres. Royal Agricultural Soc. of England 1977, Deputy Pres. 1978; Pres. Int. Fed. of Agricultural Producers 1979–82, Royal Agricultural Benevolent Inst.; MEP (Conservative) 1979–99, Chair. Agricultural Cttee 1979–82, Leader, European Democratic Group (Conservative) 1982–87, 1994–97, Pres. European Parl. 1987–90, Leader British Conservatives in European Parl. 1994–97, Co-Pres. EU/ACP Jt Ass. for Africa/Caribbean/Pacific Countries 1994–99, Hon. Pres. 1999–; Vice-Pres. EPP Group in European Parl. 1994–97; Chancellor Coventry Univ. 1995–2007; Founder EU lobbying law firm Alber & Geiger, The Henry Plumb Foundation; Chair. Agricultural Mortgage Corpn 1994–95; mem. Temporary Cttee of Enquiry into BSE 1996–97; Fellow, Royal Agric. Socs, Duchy; Order of Merit, FRG and decorations from Portugal, Luxembourg, Spain, France, Greece, Italy and others; Hon. DSc (Cranfield) 1983; Hon. DLitt (Warwick Coll.); Royal Agricultural Soc. of England Gold Medal 1983. *Leisure interests:* fishing, shooting, country pursuits. *Address:* House of Lords, Westminster, London, SW1A 0PW (office); The Dairy Farm, Maxstoke, Coleshill, Warwicks., B46 2QJ, England (home). *Telephone:* (20) 7219-1233 (Westminster) (office); (1675) 463133 (Coleshill) (home). *Fax:* (20) 7219-1649 (Westminster) (office); (1675) 464156 (Coleshill) (home). *E-mail:* plumbh@parliament.uk (office). *Website:* www.thehenryplumbfoundation.org.uk.

PLUMBLY, Sir Derek John, KCMG, BA; British diplomatist and UN official; b. 15 May 1948, Lyndhurst, Hants.; s. of John Plumbly and Jean Plumbly (née Baker); m. Nadia Youssef Gohar 1979; one d. two s.; ed Brockenhurst Grammar School, Magdalen Coll., Oxford; with VSO, Pakistan 1970–71; joined FCO 1972, Arabic language training, Middle East Centre for Arab Studies, Lebanon 1973–74, Second Sec., Embassy in Jeddah 1975–77, First Sec., Embassy in Cairo 1977–80, at FCO 1980–84, at Embassy in Washington, DC 1984–88, Counsellor, Embassy in Riyadh 1988–92, with Perm. Mission to UN, New York 1992–96, Dir Drugs and Crime Dept, FCO 1996–97, Dir Middle East and North Africa Dept 1997–2000, Amb. to Saudi Arabia 2000–03, to Egypt 2003–07; Chair. Assessment and Evaluation Comm., est. under Sudan Comprehensive Peace Agreement, Khartoum 2008–11; Special Coordinator of UN Sec.-Gen. for Lebanon 2012–14; Dr hc (Loughborough) 2007. *Leisure interests:* family, reading, travel.

PLUMBRIDGE, Robin Allan, MA; South African business executive (retd); b. 6 April 1935, Cape Town; s. of C. O. Plumbridge and of M. A. Plumbridge; m. Celia Anne Millar 1959; two s. two d.; ed St Andrew's Coll., Grahamstown, Univ. of Cape Town, Univ. of Oxford, UK; joined Gold Fields of South Africa Ltd 1957, Asst Man. 1962–65, Man. 1965–69, Exec. Dir 1969–80, CEO 1980–95, Chair. 1980–97; Chair. World Gold Council 1993–95; Dir Standard Bank Group 1980–2005, Newmont Mining Corpn 1983–2008; Founding Trustee Navarre Farm Trust 2004–; Hon. LLD. *Address:* Navarre Farm, Stellenbosch, South Africa (home). *E-mail:* rplum@mweb.co.za (home).

PLUMMER, (Arthur) Christopher (Orme), CC; Canadian actor; b. 13 Dec. 1929, Toronto, Ont.; m. 1st Tammy Lee Grimes 1956 (divorced 1960); one d.; m. 2nd Patricia Audrey Lewis 1962 (divorced 1967); m. 3rd Elaine Regina Taylor 1970; ed public and pvt. schools in Montréal, Province of Quebec; studied under Iris Warren and C. Herbertcasari; professional debut as Faulkland in The Rivals, Ottawa Repertory Theatre; Broadway debut in Starcross Story 1954; film debut in Stage Struck 1958; numerous appearances in theatres in USA; played many leading Shakespearean roles in productions by the Stratford Canadian Festival Co.; British debut in title role of Richard III, Stratford on Avon 1961 and then in London as Henry II in Anouilh's Becket; a leading actor in the Nat. Theatre Co. of GB 1971–72; has appeared in Nat. Theatre productions of Amphytrion 38, Danton's Death 1971; many TV roles including Hamlet in BBC TV/Danish TV production, Hamlet in Elsinore, Jesus of Nazareth 1977; Hon. DFA (Juilliard School of Performing Arts) 1993, Dr hc (Ryerson Univ., Toronto) 2002, (Univ. of Toronto) 2003, (Univ. of Western Ontario) 2004, (McGill Univ.) 2006; Theatre World Award 1955, Delia Australian Medal 1973, Australian Golden Badge of Honour 1982, Maple Leaf Award 1982, Edwin Booth Lifetime Achievement Award 1997, Maple Leaf Award, LAFCA 1999, Gov. Gen.'s Performing Arts Award 2001, Jason Robards Award for Excellence in Theatre 2002, The Sir John Gielgud Award for Excellence in the Dramatic Arts (aka The Golden Quill) 2006. *Plays include:* Faulkland in The Rivals 1950, Old Mahon in The Playboy of the Western World 1952, Anthony Cavendish in The Royal Family 1952, Ben in The Little Foxes 1952, Duke Manti in The Petrified Forest 1952, Father in George and Margaret 1952, Hector Benbow in Thark 1952, Bernard Kersal in The Constant Wife 1952, George Phillips in The Starcross Story 1954, Manchester Monaghan in Home Is the Hero 1954, Jason in Medea 1955, Earl of Warwick in Anouilh's The Lark 1955, The Dark is Light Enough 1955, Mark Antony in Julius Caesar 1955, Ferdinand in The Tempest 1955, Henry V 1956, 1981, The Narrator in Stravinsky's L'Histoire du Soldat 1956, Hamlet 1957, Twelfth Night 1957, The Winter's Tale 1958, Much Ado About Nothing 1958, Henry IV Part 1 1958, The Devil in J.B. 1958, Romeo and Juliet 1960, King John 1960, Much Ado About Nothing 1961, Becket (London Evening Standard Award for Best Actor 1961) 1961, Richard III 1961, Macbeth 1962, 1988, The Resistible Rise of Arturo Ui 1965–66, The Royal Hunt of the Sun 1965–66, Anthony and Cleopatra 1967, Danton's Death 1971, Cyrano (Tony Award for Best Leading Actor in a Musical 1974) 1973, The Good Doctor 1973, Iago in Othello 1982, Peccadillo 1985, A Christmas Carol 1990, No Man's Land 1994, Barrymore (Tony Award for Best Leading Actor in a Play 1997) 1996, King Lear 2004, A World or Two, Before You Go 2005, Inherit the Wind 2007, Barrymore (Toronto) 2010. *Films include:* Stage Struck 1958, Wind Across the Everglades 1958, The Fall of the Roman Empire 1964, The Sound of Music 1965, Inside Daisy Clover 1965, Triple Cross 1966, The Night of the Generals 1967, Oedipus the King 1968, Nobody Runs Forever 1968, Lock Up Your Daughters! 1969, Battle of Britain 1969, The Royal Hunt of the Sun 1969, Waterloo 1970, The Pyx 1973, The Happy Prince (short, voice) 1974, The Spiral Staircase 1975, The Return of the Pink Panther 1975, Conduct Unbecoming 1975, Sarajevski atentat 1975, The Man Who Would be King 1975, Aces High 1976, The Assignment 1977, The Disappearance 1977, International Velvet 1978, The Silent Partner 1978, Starcrash 1978, Murder by Decree (Genie Award for Best Actor 1980) 1979, Hanover Street 1979, Somewhere in Time 1980, The Janitor 1981, Eyewitness 1981, The Amateur 1981, Highpoint 1982, Dreamscape 1984, Lily in Love 1984, Playing for Keeps 1985, Ordeal by Innocence 1985, The Boy in Blue 1986, The Boss's Wife 1986, An American Tail 1986, The Gnomes' Great Adventure (narrator) 1987, I Love N.Y. 1987, Dragnet 1987, Gandahar (voice, English version) 1988, The Man Who Planted Trees (short) 1988, Nosferatu a Venezia 1988, Shadow Dancing 1988, Kingsgate 1989, Souvenir 1989, Mindfield 1989, Where the Heart Is 1990, Red Blooded American Girl 1990, Firehead 1991, Money 1991, Rock-A-Doodle (voice) 1991, Star Trek VI: The Undiscovered Country 1991, Liar's Edge 1992, Malcolm X 1992, Wolf 1994, Crackerjack 1994, Dolores Claiborne 1995, Twelve Monkeys 1995, Skeletons 1996, Babes in Toyland (voice) 1997, The First Christmas (narrator) 1998, Blackheart 1998, The Clown at Midnight 1999, Hidden Agenda 1999, Madeline: Lost in Paris (narrator) 1999, The Insider (Boston Society of Film Critics Award 1999, Los Angeles Film Critics Association Award 1999) 1999, All the Fine 1999, Dracula 2001, Lucky Break 2001, A Beautiful Mind 2001, Full Disclosure 2001, Ararat 2002, Nicholas Nickleby 2002, Blizzard 2003, The Visual Bible: The Gospel of John (narrator) 2003, Cold Creek Manor 2003, National Treasure 2004, Alexander 2004, Tma 2005, Must Love Dogs 2005, Syriana 2005, Heidi 2005, The New World 2005, Inside Man 2006, The Lake House 2006, Man in the Chair 2007, Closing the Ring 2007, Emotional Arithmetic 2007, Already Dead 2007, Caesar and Cleopatra 2009, Up (voice) 2009, The Imaginarium of Doctor Parnassus 2009, My Dog Tulip 2009, 9 2009, The Last Station 2009, Beginners (Golden Globe Award for Best Supporting Actor 2012, BAFTA Film Award for Best Supporting Actor 2012, Acad. Award for Best Performance by an Actor in a Supporting Role 2012) 2010, Priest 2011, Barrymore 2011, The Girl with the Dragon Tattoo 2011. *Television includes:* Ford Television Theatre (series) 1953, Studio One (series) 1953, Suspense (series) 1953, Broadway Television Theatre (series) 1953, The Web (series) 1954, Kraft Television Theatre (series) 1954, Kraft Television Theatre (series) 1955, Producers' Showcase (series) 1955, General Electric Theater (series) 1956, Appointment with Adventure (series) 1956, The Alcoa Hour (series) 1956, Eye on New York (series) 1956, Omnibus (series) 1957–58, The DuPont Show of the Month (series) 1957–61, Hallmark Hall of Fame (series) 1958–62, The Philadelphia Story (film) 1959, Sunday Showcase (series) 1960, Playdate (series) 1961–62, Hamlet at Elsinore (film) 1964, The Secret of Michelangelo (film) 1968, BBC Play of the Month (series) – Don Juan 1971,

Witness to Yesterday (series) 1974, After the Fall (film) 1974, Arthur Hailey's The Moneychangers (mini-series) (Emmy Award as Outstanding Lead Actor in a Limited Series 1976) 1976, Jesus of Nazareth (mini-series) 1977, Silver Blaze (short) 1977, Riel (film) 1979, The Shadow Box (film) 1980, Desperate Voyage (film) 1980, When the Circus Came to Town (film) 1981, Dial M for Murder (film) 1981, Little Gloria… Happy at Last (film) 1982, The Scarlet and the Black (film) 1983, The Thorn Birds (mini-series) 1983, Parade of Stars (film) 1983, Prototype (film) 1983, The Velveteen Rabbit (film) 1985, Rumpelstiltskin (film) 1985, David el gnomo (series) 1985, Spearfield's Daughter (mini-series) 1986, The Tin Soldier (film) 1986, Crossings (mini-series) 1986, The Nightingale (film) (voice) 1986, The Cosby Show (series) 1987, A Hazard of Hearts (film) 1987, Nabokov on Kafka (short) 1989, Madeline (film) 1989, The Little Crooked Christmas Tree (short) 1990, A Ghost in Monte Carlo (film) 1990, Counterstrike (series) 1990–93, Madeline's Christmas (film, voice) 1990, Madeline's Rescue (film, voice) 1990, Young Catherine (film) 1991, Madeline and the Bad Hat (film, voice) 1991, A Marriage: Georgia O'Keeffe and Alfred Stieglitz (film) 1991, Madeline and the Gypsies (film, voice) 1991, Madeline in London (film, voice) 1991, Berlin Lady (mini-series) 1991, The First Circle (film) 1992, Secrets (film) 1992, A Stranger in the Mirror (film) 1993, Madeline (children's series) (Emmy Award for Outstanding Voice-Over Performance 1994) 1993–94, Harrison Bergeron (film) 1995, The New Adventures of Madeline (series) 1995, We the Jury (film) 1996, The Arrow (film) 1997, The Conspiracy of Fear (film) 1997, Skeletons (film) 1997, Winchell (film) 1998, The Dinosaur Hunter (film) 2000, Possessed (film) 2000, American Tragedy (film) 2000, Leo's Journey (film) 2001, On Golden Pond (film) 2001, Night Flight (film) 2002, Agent of Influence (film) 2002, Odd Job Jack (series) 2003, Our Fathers (film) 2005, Four Minutes (film) 2005, The American Experience (series documentary) 2006, The Summit (mini-series) 2008, The Tempest (film) 2010. *Publication includes:* In Spite of Myself: A Memoir 2008. *Leisure interests:* piano, skiing, tennis, old cars. *Address:* c/o Lou Pitt, The Pitt Group, 9465 Wilshire Boulevard, Suite 480, Beverly Hills, CA 90212, USA (office). *Telephone:* (310) 246-4800 (office). *Fax:* (310) 275-9258 (office).

PLUMMER, Francis (Frank) Allan, OC, OM, MD, FRSC; Canadian medical researcher and academic; *Distinguished Professor of Medicine and Medical Microbiology, University of Manitoba;* b. 2 Dec. 1952, Winnipeg; s. of Donald Malcolm Plummer and Muriel May (Lints) Plummer; m. Carla Sue Goldman 1976; three c.; ed Univ. of Manitoba; Intern, Univ. of Southern California Medical Center, Los Angeles 1976–77; Resident, Univ. of Manitoba Affiliated Teaching Hospitals, Winnipeg 1977–79; Research Fellow, Medical Research Council of Canada, Univ. of Manitoba 1979–80, Consultant in infectious diseases, Misericordia Gen. Hosp., Winnipeg 1982; spent 16 years in Kenya researching sexually transmitted diseases and HIV/AIDS, as Research Assoc., Univ. of Nairobi 1981, Visiting Lecturer 1985–95, Visiting Prof. 1996–2000; Asst Prof., Univ. of Manitoba 1984–89, Assoc. Prof. 1989–94, Prof. of Medicine and Medical Microbiology 1994–, Distinguished Prof. 2002–; Chief Science Officer, Public Health Agency of Canada 2000–; Scientific Dir Gen., Nat. Microbiology Lab., Health Canada 2000–14; Dir Gen., Centre for Infectious Disease Prevention and Control (CIDPC) 2003–07; Founding mem. Network AIDS Researchers East and Southern Africa; mem. Canadian Asscn for HIV Research, AIDS and Reproductive Health Network; Hon. Researcher, Kenya Medical Research Inst. 1986–; Hon. LLD (Calgary) 2005; Hon. DSc (McMaster) 2011; Friends of Hebrew Univ. Scopus Award 2004, Queen Elizabeth II Diamond Jubilee Medal 2012, Royal Soc. of Canada McLaughlin Medal 2012, Prix Galien 2013, Killam Prize 2014, Canada Gairdner Wightman Award 2016. *Achievements include:* considered among world's leading specialists on HIV/AIDS. *Publications include:* more than 375 scientific papers. *Address:* University of Manitoba, 730 William Avenue, Room 514, Winnipeg, MB R3E 0W3, Canada (office). *Telephone:* (204) 789-3312 (office). *Fax:* (204) 789-3310 (office). *E-mail:* frank_plummer@hc-sc.gc.ca (office). *Website:* www.mrsi.ca/plummerlab.htm (office).

PLUMMER, James D., BS, MS, PhD; Canadian electrical engineer and academic; *John M. Fluke Professor of Electrical Engineering, Stanford University;* b. Toronto, Ont.; m. Patti Plummer; two d.; ed Univ. of California, Los Angeles, Stanford Univ.; research staff member, Integrated Circuits Lab, Stanford Univ. 1971–78, Assoc. Prof. 1978–83, Prof. of Electrical Eng 1983–, served as Dir IC Lab., as Sr Assoc. Dean in School of Eng, and as Chair. Electrical Eng Dept, apptd John M. Fluke Prof. of Electrical Eng, Dir Stanford Nanofabrication Facility 1994–2000, Frederick Emmons Terman Dean of the School of Eng 1999–2014; Co-founder T-RAM; mem. Bd of Dirs and Tech. Advisory Bd several public and start-up cos; mem. Nat. Acad. of Eng, American Acad. of Arts and Sciences 2008; Fellow, IEEE; teaching awards, Stanford Univ. 1991, 1992, 1993, Solid State Science and Tech. Award, Electrochemical Soc. 1991, NSF commendation for nat. leadership in building the NNUN (consortium of five univs who opened their nanofabrication facilities as nat. resources for industry and for students from around the nation) 2000, Semiconductor Industry Asscn Univ. Research Award 2001, IEEE Third Millennium Medal 2001, Aviation Week & Space Technology Laurels Award – Electronics 2003, IEEE J.J. Ebers Award 2003, IEEE Aldert Van der Ziel Award 2003, McGraw-Hill/Jacob Millman Award 2004, IEDM Paul Rappaport Award 2006, IEEE Andrew S. Grove Award 2007; eight conf. and student best paper awards, including two at IEDM and three at ISSCC. *Publications:* Silicon VLSI Technology – Fundamentals, Practice and Modeling; more than 400 scientific papers in professional journals on the physics governing device operation in silicon integrated circuits and the technology used to fabricate these circuits. *Address:* Department of Electrical Engineering, Stanford University, 420 Via Palou Mall, CISX Room 330, Stanford, CA 94305, USA (office). *Telephone:* (650) 725-3606 (office). *E-mail:* plummer@stanford.edu (office). *Website:* profiles.stanford.edu (office).

PLUSHENKO, Evgeni Viktorovich; Russian figure skater; b. 3 Nov. 1982, Solnechni, Khabarovsk region in Siberia; s. of Viktor Plushenko and Tatiana Vasilievna; m. Maria Erma 2005; one s.; family moved to Volgograd aged three; began skating aged four; sent to St Petersburg to train under Alexei Mishin aged 11; Nat. Champion 1999–2002, 2004–06, 2010, 2012; gold medal, Grand Prix Final 2000, 2001, 2003, 2005, silver medal, 2002, 2004, bronze medal 1999; gold medal, World Jr Championships 1997; silver medal, European Championships 1998, 1999, 2004, gold medal, 2000, 2001, 2003, 2005, 2006, 2010, 2012; bronze medal, World Championships 1998, silver medal, 1999, gold medal, 2001, 2003, 2004;

silver medal, Winter Olympics, Salt Lake City 2002, Vancouver 2010, gold medal, Winter Olympics, Turin 2006, team competition, Sochi 2014; first skater in the world to perform a 4-3-2 (quadruple toe loop-triple toe loop-double loop) jump combination and later a 4-3-3 (quadruple toe loop-triple toe loop-triple loop) jump combination at Cup of Russia 2002; youngest male skater to receive perfect score of 6.0 aged 16; received total of 70 6.0s before new Code of Points judging system was introduced; retd from competition following Sochi Winter Olympics Feb. 2014; mem. Ybileiny Sport Club, St Petersburg. *Address:* c/o Ari Zakaryan. *Telephone:* 916-968-04-26 (mobile); (917) 434-0424 (USA). *E-mail:* ari.zakaryan@evgeni-plushenko.com. *Website:* evgeni-plushenko.com.

POCAR, Fausto, LLD; Italian judge, international organization executive and academic; *Appeals Judge, International Criminal Tribunal for the former Yugoslavia (ICTY);* b. 21 Feb. 1939, Milan; ed Univ. of Milan; Prof. of Int. Law, Univ. of Milan, fmr Dean, Faculty of Political Sciences, fmr Vice-Rector Univ. of Milan, now Prof. Emer.; Judge, Int. Criminal Tribunal for fmr Yugoslavia (ICTY), The Hague 2000–, Appeals Judge 2000–, also Judge of the Appeals Chamber and mem. Int. Criminal Tribunal for Rwanda (ICTR), Vice-Pres. ICTY 2003–05, Pres. 2005–08; mem. Human Rights Cttee under Int. Covenant on Civil and Political Rights 1984–2000, Rapporteur 1989–90, Chair. 1991–92; Special Rep. of UN High Commr for Human Rights for visits to Chechnya and Russian Fed. 1995–96; has chaired informal working group that drafted declaration on the rights of people belonging to nat. or ethnic, religious or linguistic minorities, Comm. on Human Rights 1992; Italian del. to Cttee on the Peaceful Uses of Outer Space and its Legal Sub-cttee; Rapporteur, Lugano Convention on Jurisdiction and Enforcement of Civil Judgments Between EU and EFTA Countries 2007; Pres. Int. Inst. of Humanitarian Law, San Remo 2012–; mem. Panel of Arbitrators for Outer Space Disputes, Perm. Court of Arbitration 2012–; has lectured at The Hague Acad. of Int. Law; mem. and Treas. Institut de Droit Int.; mem. several other int. law asscns; Grand Ufficiale 2003, Cavaliere di Gran Croce 2014; Dr hc (Antwerp) 2007, (Buenos Aires) 2008. *Publications:* author of numerous publs on int. law, including human rights and humanitarian law, pvt. int. law and European law; Ed.-in-Chief, Rivista di diritto int. privato e processuale. *Address:* International Criminal Tribunal for the Former Yugoslavia, PO Box 13888, 2501 EW The Hague, Netherlands (office). *Telephone:* (70) 512-5362 (office). *Fax:* (70) 512-5307 (office). *E-mail:* pocar.icty@un.org (office). *Website:* www.un.org/icty (office).

POČIATEK, Ján; Slovak economist and politician; *Minister of Transport, Construction and Regional Development;* b. 19 Sept. 1970; m. Ivana Počiatek; one d.; ed Slovak Tech. Univ., Univ. of Econs, Bratislava, Stockholm School of Econs, Sweden, Telenor Corp. Univ., Norway; Project Dir, Satellite Communications Div., Telenor Slovakia 1997–2000, Commercial Dir and Vice-Exec. Dir 2000–01, Exec. Dir 2001–06; mem. Bd Dirs Int. Satellite Communication 2001–06; Minister of Finance 2006–10; mem. Slovak Repub. Council 2010–12; Minister of Transport, Construction and Regional Devt 2012–. *Address:* Ministry of Transport, Construction and Regional Development, nám. Slobody 6, POB 100, 810 05 Bratislava, Slovakia (office). *Telephone:* (2) 5949-4111 (office). *Fax:* (2) 5249-4794 (office). *E-mail:* info@mindop.sk (office). *Website:* www.telecom.gov.sk (office).

PODESTA, John David, BS, JD; American lawyer and government official; *Chairman, Center for American Progress;* b. 1 Aug. 1949, Chicago, Ill.; s. of John David Podesta and Mary Kokoris; m. Mary Spieczny 1978; one s. two d.; ed Knox Coll., Illinois, Georgetown Univ. Law Center; attorney, Dept of Justice 1976–77; Special Asst to Dir, ACTION 1978–79; Counsel, Senate Judiciary Cttee 1979–81; Chief Minority Counsel, Senate Judiciary Sub-Cttee 1981–86; Chief Counsel, Senate Agric. Cttee 1987–88; Pres., Gen. Counsel, Podesta Assocs Inc. 1988–93; Asst to the Pres. (Staff Sec.) 1993–95; Asst to Pres. (Deputy Chief of Staff) 1997–98; Chief of Staff to the Pres. 1998–2001; Pres. and CEO Center for American Progress 2001–13, Chair. 2013–; Sr Advisor to the Pres., The White House, Washington, DC 2014–15; Visiting Prof. of Law, Georgetown Univ. Law Center 1995–98, Adjunct Prof. 1998–. *Publication:* Protecting Electronic Messaging 1990. *Address:* Center for American Progress, 805 15th Street, NW, Suite 400, Washington, DC 20005 (office); 3743 Brandywine Street, Washington, DC 20016, USA (home). *Telephone:* (202) 682-1611 (office). *E-mail:* progress@americanprogress.org (office). *Website:* www.americanprogress.org (office).

PODHORETZ, John, AB; American writer and editor; *Editor, Commentary;* b. 18 April 1961, New York; s. of Norman Podhoretz (q.v.) and Midge Podhoretz (née Rosenthal); m. 1st Elisabeth Hickey 1996 (divorced); m. 2nd Ayala Cohen; two d.; ed Univ. of Chicago; Exec. News Ed. Insight Magazine 1985–87; contrib. US News and World Report 1987–88; speechwriter for US Pres. Ronald Reagan, Pres. George H.W. Bush 1988–89; Asst Man. Ed. Washington Times 1989–91; Sr Fellow, Hudson Inst. 1991–94; Ed. of editorial page, lead political columnist, arts ed., New York Post, TV critic 1994–95, now political columnist; Co-founder and Deputy Ed. The Weekly Standard 1995–97, now movie critic; Editorial Dir Commentary (magazine) 2007–09, Ed. 2009–; J. C. Penney/Mo. Award for Excellence in Feature Sections 1990. *Publication:* Hell of a Ride: Backstage at the White House Follies 1989–93 1993, Bush Country: How Dubya Became a Great President While Driving Liberals Insane 2004, Can She Be Stopped?: Hillary Clinton Will Be the Next President of the United States Unless… 2007. *Address:* Commentary, 165 East 56th Street, New York, NY 10022, USA (office). *E-mail:* letters@commentarymagazine.com. *Website:* www.commentarymagazine.com (office).

PODHORETZ, Norman, BA, MA, BHL; American writer and editor; b. 16 Jan. 1930, Brooklyn, NY; s. of Julius Podhoretz and Helen Podhoretz (née Woliner); m. Midge R. Decter 1956; one s. (John Podhoretz) three d.; ed Columbia Univ., Jewish Theological Seminary and Univ. of Cambridge, UK; Assoc. Ed. Commentary 1956–58, Ed.-in-Chief 1960–95, Ed.-at-Large 1995–2008; Ed.-in-Chief, Looking Glass Library 1959–60; Chair. New Directions Advisory Comm. US Information Agency 1981–87; Sr Fellow, Hudson Inst. 1995–2003; Fulbright Fellow 1950–51; Kellett Fellow 1950–53; Hon. LLD (Jewish Theological Seminary); Hon. LHD (Hamilton Coll.), (Boston) 1995, (Adelphi) 1996; Hon. DHumLitt (Yeshiva) 1991; Presidential Medal of Freedom 2004. *Publications include:* Doings and Undoings: The Fifties and After in American Writing 1964, Making It 1968, Breaking Ranks: A Political Memoir 1979, The Present Danger 1980, Why We Were in Vietnam 1982, The Bloody Crossroads: Where Literature and Politics Meet 1986, Ex-Friends 1999, My Love Affair with America 2000, The Prophets: Who They Were, What They Are 2002, The Norman Podhoretz Reader 2004, World War IV 2007,

Why Are Jews Liberal? 2009. *Leisure interest:* listening to music. *E-mail:* nhp30@hotmail.com (office).

PODNAR, Gregor; Slovenian gallery owner; Artistic Dir Galerija Škuc, Ljubljana 1996–2003; est. Galerija Gregor Podnar in Kranj as part of Asscn DUM 2003, gallery moved to Ljubljana 2005; opened second gallery in Berlin 2007; represents established artists mostly from Eastern European centres, including Slovenian collective IRWIN, Yuri Leiderman, Vadim Fiškin, Dan Perjovschi, Goran Petercol and Attila Csörgő, as well as young emerging artists, including Alexander Gutke, Magnus Larsson, Tobias Putrih and Ariel Schlesinger. *Address:* Galerija Gregor Podnar, Lindenstrasse 35, 10969 Berlin, Germany (office); Galerija Gregor Podnar, Kolodvorska 6, 1000 Ljubljana, Slovenia (office). *Telephone:* (30) 25934651 (Berlin) (office); (1) 4304929 (Ljubljana) (office). *Fax:* (30) 25934652 (Berlin) (office); (1) 4304928 (Ljubljana) (office). *E-mail:* berlin@gregorpodnar.com (office); ljubljana@gregorpodnar.com (office). *Website:* www.gregorpodnar.com (office).

PODOLSKY, Daniel K., BA, MD; American physician and university administrator; *President and Professor, University of Texas Southwestern Medical Centre;* b. 1953; m. Dr. Carol P. Podolsky; three c.; ed Harvard Coll., Harvard Medical School; residency, Massachusetts Gen. Hospital 1978–80; Clinical Fellow in Medicine, Harvard Medical School 1978–80, Research Fellow 1980–81, Asst Prof. of Medicine 1982–86, Assoc. Prof. 1986–96, Prof. 1996–2008, Mallinckrodt Prof. of Medicine 1998–2008; Asst Resident, Mass Gen. Hosp. 1978–80, Clinical Research Fellow 1980–81, Asst in Medicine 1982–86, Assoc. Physician 1988–93, Physician 1993–2008, Chief of Gastroenterology 1989–2008; Pres. and Prof. (Doris and Bryan Wildenthal Distinguished Chair. in Medical Science, Philip O'Bryan Montgomery Jr, MD, Distinguished Presidential Chair. in Academic Admin), Univ. of Texas Southwestern Medical Center 2008–; Chair. and Scientific Co-Founder GI Co., Framingham, Mass; Chief Academic Officer, Partners HealthCare System, Boston 2005–08; mem. Bd of Dirs GlaxoSmithKline plc, Agilent Technologies Inc. 2015–, Southwestern Medical Foundation; mem. Scientific Advisory Bd Antibe Therapeutics, Inc. Pres. American Gastroenterological Asscn 2003–04; fmr Ed.-in-Chief Gastroenterology (journal); mem. NAS; MERIT Award, NIH 1998, Distinguished Achievement Award, American Gastroenterological Asscn 2007, Julius Friedenwald Award 2009. *Publications:* more than 300 original research and review articles. *Address:* Office of the President, University of Texas Southwestern Medical Center, 5323 Harry Hines Blvd, Dallas, TX 75390, USA (office). *Telephone:* (214) 645-0595 (office). *Fax:* (214) 648-8690 (office). *E-mail:* daniel.podolsky@utsouthwestern.edu (office). *Website:* www.utsystem.edu/hea/Presidents.htm (office).

PODSIADŁO, Andrzej; Polish banking executive; b. 2 Dec. 1950; ed Main School of Econs and Planning, Warsaw (now Warsaw School of Econs); fmr teacher, Main School of Planning and Statistics, Warsaw; Dir, Econ. Analysis Team, Planning Comm. of Council of Ministers 1978–88, Under-Sec. and later Sec. of State, Ministry of Finance 1989–92; Pres., Man. Bd, Powszechny Bank Handlowy Gecobank SA 1994; Vice-Pres., Man. Bd, PKO BP 1994–95; Pres., Man. Bd, Powszechny Bank Kredytowy SA 1995–2002; Pres., Man. Bd, PKO Bank 2002–06; Vice-Pres. Supervisory Bd, Bank Pocztowy SA 2004; fmr Chair., Gornoslaski Bank Gospodarczy SA, Powszechne Towarzystwo Emerytalne PBK SA, PTE Ergo Hestia SA, Bank Pekao SA, TUiR Warta; mem. Supervisory Bd, Poskie Koleje Panstwowe, Huta Katowice SA, Fabryka Samochodow Malolitrazowych w Bielsku-Bialej, Bank Wschodni SA, Polska Fundacja Promocji Kadr; fmr Pres., Man. Bd Polish Red Cross; mem. Curriculum Bd, Warsaw Banking School; mem. Council of Banks; Polish Rep., Int. Bank of Econ. Co-operation, Moscow, Int. Investment Bank, Moscow; Vice-Pres., Union of Polish Banks; mem. Bd, Nat. Museum, Warsaw.

POE, Jeff; American gallery owner and art dealer; *Co-Owner, Blum & Poe;* worked as dir of Kim Light Gallery, Los Angeles; co-founded (with Tim Blum) small exhbn space in Santa Monica, Calif. 1994; introduced Japanese artists Takashi Murakami and Yoshito Nara in USA; Co-Owner Blum & Poe gallery, expanded to larger space in 2003, renovated and opened new gallery 2009, regularly exhibits local and internationally recognized artists, including Chiho Aoshima, J. B. Blunk, Slater Bradley, Chuck Close, Nigel Cooke, Carroll Dunham, Sam Durant, Kōji Enokura, Anya Gallaccio, Mark Grotjahn, Tim Hawkinson, Drew Heitzler, Julian Hoeber, Zhang Huan, Zhu Jinshi, Matt Johnson, Susumu Koshimizu, Friedrich Kunath, Shio Kusaka, Linder, Sharon Lockhart, Florian Maier-Aichen, Victor Man, Dave Muller, Takashi Murakami, Yoshitomo Nara, Matt Saunders, Hugh Scott–Douglas, Nobuo Sekine, Jim Shaw, Dirk Skreber, Kishio Suga, Henry Taylor, Keith Tyson, Lee Ufan, Chris Vasell and Michael Wilkinson. *Address:* Blum & Poe, 2727 S La Cienega Blvd, Los Angeles, CA 90034, USA (office). *Telephone:* (310) 836-2062 (office). *Fax:* (310) 836-2104 (office). *E-mail:* info@blumandpoe.com (office). *Website:* www.blumandpoe.com (office).

POFALLA, Ronald; German lawyer and politician; *Chief Representative for Policy and International Relations, Deutsche Bahn;* b. 15 May 1959; ed Fachhochschule, Kleve, Univ. of Cologne; mem. Christlich-Demokratische Union (Christian Democratic Union—CDU) 1975–, initially engaged in Junge Union (JU), Chair. JU, North Rhine-Westphalia 1986–92, Gen. Sec. CDU 2005–; mem. Bundestag (Parl.) 1990–, Deputy Chair. CDU/CSU (Christlich-Soziale Union) Parl. Group in Bundestag 2004–05; passed Staatsexamen (bar examination) 1991, in legal practice 1991–; Chief of Staff, Fed. Chancellery and Minister for Special Affairs 2009–13; Chief Rep. for Policy and Int. Relations, Deutsche Bahn 2015–. *Address:* c/o Deutsche Bahn AG, Potsdamer Platz 2, 10785 Berlin, Germany (office). *Website:* www.deutschebahn.com (office); www.ronald-pofalla.de.

POGEA, Gheorghe, PhD; Romanian business executive and politician; b. 21 Dec. 1955; m.; two c.; ed Bucharest Polytechnic Inst., École Superieure de Commerce Marseille, France; Dir-Gen. S.C Siderurgica SA 1996–2000, S.C Marmosin SA 2001–04, SC Titan Mar SA 2006–08; mem. Democratic Liberal Party (PDL), Pres. PDL Org. for Hunedoara Co. 2000–06, Coordinator PDL Strategy Comm. 2005–06; Minister of State 2005–06; Minister of Economy and Finance 2008–09; apptd to Supervisory Bd Fondului Proprietatea 2010, Bd of Dirs CEC Bank 2010; Gen. Man. Cris-Tim 2013–. *Address:* Chris-Tim, 012 367 Bucharest, Boulevard Bucurestii Noi no. 140, Sector 1, Romania (office). *Website:* en.cristim.ro (office).

POGGIO, Albert Andrew, OBE; British diplomatist; b. 18 Aug. 1946, Ballymena, Co. Antrim, Northern Ireland; m. Sally; one d.; ed Christian Brothers Coll., Gibraltar and City of London Coll.; UK Rep. for HM Govt of Gibraltar 1988–, also Dir Gibraltar House, London; Chair. British Overseas Territories Asscn, Vital Health Group of Cop, Westex Group of Cos; Vice-Chair. Calpe House Trust; Dir Friends of Gibraltar Heritage Soc., SVP Medcruise (Asscn of Mediterranean Ports); Freeman, City of London; Gibraltar Medallion of Honour 2014, Grassroot Diplomat Initiative Award 2015. *Leisure interests:* reading, walking, military memorabilia, sports. *Address:* The Old House, Manor Place, Chislehurst, Kent, BR7 5QJ, England (home).

POHAMBA, Hifikepunye Lucas; Namibian politician and fmr head of state; b. 18 Aug. 1935; Sec. of Finance, SWAPO 1977–89, Sec.-Gen. SWAPO 1997–2002, Vice-Pres. 2002–07, Pres. 2007–; Minister of Home Affairs 1990–95, of Fisheries and Marine Resources 1995–98, without Portfolio 1998–2000, of Lands, Resettlement and Rehabilitation 2001–04; Pres. of Namibia and C-in-C of the Defence Force 2005–15; Chancellor Univ. of Namibia 2011–18; Hon. PhD (Univ. of Namibia) 2011; Swapo Ongulumbashe Medal 1987, Mo Ibrahim Foundation Prize for Achievement in African Leadership 2015. *Address:* c/o Office of the President, State House, Robert Mugabe Avenue, PMB 13339, Windhoek, Namibia (office).

POHIVA, Samuela 'Akilisi, BA; Tongan politician and fmr teacher; *Prime Minister;* b. 7 April 1941; m. Neomai Tu'itupou Pohiva; c.; ed Univ. of the South Pacific, Fiji; worked as a teacher for several years, including as lecturer in History and Sociology, Tongan Campus of Univ. of the South Pacific; became active in Tongan pro-democracy movt late 1970s; contributed to monthly radio programme Matalafo Laukai early 1980s; Asst Ed. Kele'a (democracy movt's monthly newsletter); Co-founder, Friendly Islands Human Rights & Democracy Movt 1987; People's Rep. (MP) for Tongatapu 3 Constituency 1987–89, for Tongatapu 1 Constituency 2010–; Minister for Health 2011, Prime Minister 2014–, also Minister of Internal Affairs 2014–18, also of Foreign Affairs and Trade 2014–17, Minister for Educ. and Training 2015–16, also Minister of Foreign Affairs 2018–19; mem. Human Rights and Democracy Movt –2010; mem. Democratic Party of the Friendly Islands 2010–; Asscn of Parliamentarians For Global Action (PGA) Defender of Democracy Award 2013. *Address:* Office of the Prime Minister, POB 62, Nuku'alofa, Tonga (office). *Telephone:* 24644 (office). *Fax:* 23888 (office). *E-mail:* pressoffice@pmo.gov.to (office). *Website:* www.pmo.gov.to (office).

POHL, Reimund, MBA; German business executive; joined Hageda AG (later part of Phoenix Group), Cologne 1981, mem. Exec. Bd Phoenix Pharmahandel AG & Co. KG 1997–2014, CEO 2005–14 (retd); mem. Bd of Dirs and Chair. Phoenix-Pharma Einkauf GmbH; mem. Supervisory Bd Amedis-Ue AG; Dir, COMIFAR SpA, Tamro Group 2000–. *Address:* c/o Phoenix Pharmahandel AG & Co. KG, Pfingstweidstr. 10–12, 68199 Mannheim, Baden-Württemberg, Germany.

POITIER, Sir Sidney, Kt, KBE; American/Bahamian actor and film director; b. 20 Feb. 1927, Miami, Fla; s. of Reginald James Poitier and Evelyn Poitier (née Outten); m. 1st Juanita Hardy 1950–65; four d.; m. 2nd Joanna Shimkus 1976; two d.; ed Western Senior High School, Nassau, Governors High School, Nassau; grew up in the Bahamas; army service 1941–45; acted with American Negro Theatre 1946; appeared in Anna Lucasta 1948, A Raisin in the Sun 1959; mem. Bd of Dirs, Walt Disney Co. 1994–2003, Pres. 1994–2003; Amb. to Japan from Commonwealth of the Bahamas (non-resident) 1997–2007; Amb. to UNESCO 2002–07; Silver Bear Award, Berlin Film Festival 1958; New York Film Critics' Award 1958; Acad. Award Best Actor of 1963 (for Lilies of the Field); Cecil B. De Mille Award 1982, Life Achievement Award American Film Inst. 1992, Kennedy Center Honors 1995, Hon. Acad. Award for Lifetime Achievement 2002, Lincoln Medal 2009, Presidential Medal of Freedom 2009, BAFTA Fellowship 2016. *Films include:* No Way Out 1950, Cry, the Beloved Country 1951, Red Ball Express 1952, Go, Man, Go! 1954, Blackboard Jungle 1955, Good-bye, My Lady 1956, Edge of the City 1957, Something of Value 1957, Band of Angels 1957, The Mark of the Hawk 1957, Virgin Island 1958, The Defiant Ones 1958, Porgy and Bess 1959, All the Young Men 1960, A Raisin in the Sun 1961, Paris Blues 1961, Pressure Point 1962, The Long Ships 1963, Lilies of the Field 1963, The Bedford Incident 1965, The Greatest Story Ever Told 1965, A Patch of Blue 1965, The Slender Thread 1965, Duel at Diablo 1966), To Sir, with Love 1967, In the Heat of the Night 1967, Guess Who's Coming to Dinner 1967, For Love of Ivy (also writer) 1968, The Lost Man 1969, They Call Me Mister Tibbs! 1970, Brother John 1971, The Organization 1971, Buck and the Preacher (also dir) 1972, A Warm December (also dir) 1973, Uptown Saturday Night (also dir) 1974, The Wilby Conspiracy 1975, Let's Do It Again (also dir) 1975, A Piece of the Action (also dir) 1977, Stir Crazy dir) 1980, Hanky Panky (dir) 1982, Fast Forward (dir) 1985, Shoot to Kill 1988, Little Nikita 1988, Ghost Dad (dir) 1990, Sneakers 1992, The Jackal 1997, Bicentennial Nigger 2006. *Television includes:* Separate But Equal 1991, Children of the Dust 1995, To Sir, with Love II 1996, Mandela and de Klerk 1997, David and Lisa 1998, Free of Eden (also exec. producer) 1999, The Simple Life of Noah Dearborn 1999, The Last Brickmaker in America 2001. *Publications include:* This Life 1981, The Measure of a Man: A Spiritual Autobiography 2000, Life Beyond Measure: Letters to My Great Granddaughter 2009. *Leisure interests:* football, tennis, gardening.

POIVRE D'ARVOR, Patrick, LenD; French journalist and radio and television presenter; b. 20 Sept. 1947, Reims (Marne); s. of Jacques Poivre and Madeleine France Jeuge; m. Véronique Courcoux 1971 (divorced); six c. (two deceased); ed Lycée Georges-Clemenceau, Reims, Instituts d'études politiques, Strasbourg and Paris, Faculties of Law, Strasbourg, Paris and Reims, École des langues orientales vivantes; Special Corresp., France-Inter 1971, journalist 1971–74, Head Political Dept 1975–76, Deputy Chief Ed., Antenne 2 1976–83, Presenter, evening news programme 1976–83, 1987–2008, Deputy Dir News 1989; Leader writer, Paris-Match, Journal du Dimanche 1983–91; Producer and Compère, A nous deux, Antenne 2 1983–86, A la folie, TF1 1986–88; Compère, Tous en Scène, Canal Plus 1984–85; Compère and Producer Ex libris 1988–99; Compère Vol de nuit 1999–; Presenter and Producer magazine programme Le Droit de savoir, TF1 1990–94; presenter La traversée du miroir on France 5 2009–; Vice-Pres. Jeunes Républicains Indépendants 1969–70; Pres. Prix Bretagne 2001–11, Jury du Grand Prix de l'Héroïne; UNICEF Goodwill Amb.; Chevalier, Légion d'honneur; Officier, Ordre nat. du Mérite; Commdr des Arts et des Lettres; Prix Interallié 2000, Prix des Lettres du Livre de Poche 2003, Prix Cyrano 2004. *Television:* led a team in the French TV show Fort Boyard 2010. *Publications include:* Mai 68-Mai 78 1978, Les enfants de l'aube 1982, Deux amants 1984, Le Roman de Virginie 1985, Les derniers trains de rêve 1986, La traversée du miroir 1986, Rencontres 1987, Les femmes de ma vie 1988, L'homme d'images 1992, Lettres à l'absente 1993, Les loups et la bergerie 1994, Elle n'était pas d'ici 1995, Anthologie des plus beaux poèmes d'amour 1995, Un héros de passage 1996, Lettre ouverte aux violeurs de vie privée 1997, Une trahison amoureuse 1997, La fin du monde (collection) 1998, Petit homme 1999, Les rats de garde (collection) 2000, L'Irrésolu 2000 (Prix Interallié), Un enfant 2001, Courriers de nuit (collection) 2002, J'ai aimé une reine 2003, Coureurs des morts (collection) 2003, La mort de Don Juan (Prix Maurice-Genevoix 2005) 2004, Les plus beaux poèmes d'amour 2004, Chasseurs de trésors et autres flibustiers 2005, Pirates et corsaires 2005, Coureurs des mers 2005, Le monde selon Jules Verne 2005, Confessions 2005, Disparaître (co-author) 2006, Age d'or du voyage en train 2006, Rêveurs des mers (co-author) 2007, J'ai tant rêvé de toi 2007, La vie jusqu'à l'excés 2011, Un homme en fuite 2015, Éloge des écrivains maudits 2017.

POK, Fabian, MEcons, PhD; Papua New Guinea politician; *Minister for Petroleum and Energy;* b. 1963, Ambang Village; ed Univ. of Papua New Guinea, Univ. of New England, Australia; Sr Lecturer, Dept of Commerce, Univ. of Papua New Guinea –1997; fmr pvt. consultant to various govt depts and pvt. businesses; mem. Nat. Parl. Ind.) for North Wahgi Open constituency 1997–2002, (United Resources Party) 2012–; Minister for Forests 1997–98, for Public Enterprise and for Communications 1998–91 (resgnd), for Trade and Tourism, Commerce and Industry and Police 1999, for Lands and Physical Planning 1999–2000, for Petroleum and Energy March–Nov. 2000, 2017–, for Labour and Employment 2001, for Defence 2013–17 (resgnd). *Publications include:* three books and numerous papers on accounting issues in developing countries. *Address:* Department of Petroleum and Enegry, POB 1993, Port Moresby, NCD, Papua New Guinea (office). *Telephone:* 3212476 (office). *E-mail:* enquiries@petroleum.gov.pg. *Website:* www.petroleum.gov.pg.

POKHAREL, Bhoj Raj; Nepalese civil servant; has worked for Ministry of Health, of Supply, of Information and Communication as Sec.; associated with Nat. Referendum Comm. 1979; has worked with numerous nat. and int. orgs including Asian Development Bank, UK Dept for Int. Devt, Danish Int. Devt Agency, WHO, UNDP; Chief Election Commr 2006–09; mem. UN panel to monitor Southern Sudan referendum 2010–11; Sr Facilitator 2012–14; Int. Consultant-Sr Adviser for Political and Electoral process, UNDP Sept. 2013–April 2014; mem. Election Integrity Core Group, Kofi Annan 2015–; Sr Fellow, United States Inst. of Peace 2017–. *Address:* United State Institute of Peace, 2301 Constitution Avenue NW, Washington, DC 20037, USA. *Telephone:* (202) 457-1700 (office). *E-mail:* interviews@usip.org (office). *Website:* www.usip.org (office).

POKHAREL, Ishwar; Nepalese politician; *Deputy Prime Minister and Minister of Defence;* b. 4 Feb. 1954, Okhaldhunga; s. of Shivraj Pokharel and Ram Kumari Pokharel; m. Mira Dhonju Pokharel; two s.; ed Tribhuvan Univ., Kathmandu; mem. Communist Party of Nepal—Unified Marxist-Leninist (CPN—UML), Sec.-Gen. 2009–; mem. House of Reps (lower house of parl.) for Kathmandu 5 constituency 2017–; Deputy Prime Minister and Minister of Defence 2018–; Head, Del. to Ministerial Conference on Intellectual Property for the Developing Countries, Korea 2005; mem. High Level Del. to People's Republic of China and Mongolia 1993, Del. for 8th SAARC 1995, Del. to Preparatory Meeting on Conference on Social Summit, UN 1995, Nepalese Parl. Del. to Korea 2000, Nepalese Del. UN Gen. Ass. 2001, Del. 9th São Paulo Forum 2002. *Address:* Ministry of Defence, Singha Durbar, Kathmandu, Nepal (office). *Telephone:* (1) 4211289 (office). *Fax:* (1) 4211294 (office). *E-mail:* info@mod.gov.np (office); ipokhrel8@gmail.com. *Website:* www.mod.gov.np (office); www.ishwarpokhrel.com.

POKHMELKIN, Victor Valeryevich, CandJur; Russian politician and jurist; b. 3 Feb. 1960, Perm; m.; one s.; ed Perm State Univ., Moscow State Univ.; Docent, Lecturer, Higher Courses of USSR Ministry of Internal Affairs, Perm; Founder and Scientific Head, Research Inst. of Legal Policy; mem. State Duma (Parl.) 1993–; mem. Vybor Rosii 1993–99, Union of Rightist Forces 2000–01, Co-Chair. Liberal Russia 2001–04; Deputy Chair. Comm. on Law and Legal Reform; mem. Political Council Demokratichesky Vybor Rossii 1994–; Founder and Chair. Motorists of Russia 2002–. *Publications:* several monographs and scientific publs. *Address:* State Duma, Okhotny Ryad 1, 103265 Moscow, Russian Federation (office). *Telephone:* (495) 692-77-66 (office). *Fax:* (495) 692-32-87 (office). *E-mail:* pokhmelkin@duma.gov.ru (office). *Website:* www.pokhmelkin.ru (office).

POKORNI, Zoltán, AB; Hungarian politician and academic; *Vice-President, FIDESZ Party;* b. 10 Jan. 1962, Budapest; s. of János Pokorni and Klara Vincz; m. Andrea Beck 1992; four s.; ed Loránd Eötvös Univ., Budapest; Lecturer, Toldy Ferenc High School, Budapest 1987–94; Founding mem. 1988, spokesman 1988–93, Ed. Democratic Trades Union of Teachers' paper –1993; joined Fed. of Young Democrats–Hungarian Civic Party (Magyar Polgári Párt–FIDESZ) 1993, Vice-Pres. 1994–2001, 2003–, Leader 2001–02; mem. Parl. 1994–; Deputy Head Parl. Group 1994–97, Head 1997–98, personal rep. of Budapest XIIth Dist 1998–; fmr Head FIDESZ Dept for Educational Politics; (FIDESZ) Minister of Educ. 1998–2001; Vice-Pres. Parl. Cttee for Educ. and Science; Mayor, Budapest XII Dist 2006. *Address:* FIDESZ, Szentkirályi u.18, 1088 Budapest, Hungary. *Telephone:* (1) 327-6100 (office). *Fax:* (1) 441-5414 (office). *E-mail:* sajtoosztaly@fidesz.hu (office). *Website:* www.fidesz.hu (office); www.pokornizoltan.hu.

POKROVSKY, Valentin Ivanovich, DrMed; Russian physician and research institute director; *Director, Central Scientific Research Institute of Epidemiology;* b. 1 April 1929; m. Nina Yakovlevna Pokrovskaya; one s.; ed First Moscow Medical Inst.; mem. CPSU 1959–91; Dir Central Scientific Research Inst. of Epidemiology 1971–; USSR People's Deputy 1989–91; has studied problems of AIDS treatment, meningitis and intestinal diseases; Chair. Scientific Soc. of Microbiologists, Epidemiologists and Parasitologists; mem. Physicians for the Prevention of Nuclear War; mem. WHO Expert Cttee, WHO Global Cttee on AIDS and Diarrhoeal Diseases, Bd Int. Fed. of Infectionists; mem. USSR (now Russian) Acad. of Medical Sciences 1982– (Pres. 1987–2006), Presidium of USSR (now Russian) Fed. of Space Flight; Hon. mem. Soc. of Microbiologists of Czech Repub.; V. Timakov Prize, D. Ivanovsky Prize. *Publications:* Symptoms, Treatment and Diagnostics of Salmonellesis in Adults 1981, Immuno-ferment Analysis 1985, Symptoms, Pathogenesis and Treatment of Cholera 1988, Small Medical Encylopaedia (ed.) 1991, Encyclopaedia of Health 1992, Epidemiology of Viral Diseases 2000, Cholera in the USSR – Period of the VIIth Pandemia 2000, Social Hygiene Monitoring and Epidemiology Surveillance in Moscow 2000, Cholera – Acute Problems 2000, Manual of Infectious Diseases and Epidemiology 2004, Prion Diseases 2004. *Address:* Central Scientific Research Institute of Epidemiology, 111123 109544, Novogireevskaya str. 3A (office); Russian Academy of Medical Sciences, 109544 GSP Moscow, Solyanka str. 14, Russia. *Telephone:* (495) 672-10-69 (office); (495) 298-21-37 (home). *Fax:* (495) 304-22-09 (office); (495) 921-56-15. *E-mail:* ramn@rosmail.ru. *Website:* crie.ru (office); www.russmed.ru/eng/ramn.htm.

POL, Marek; Polish politician and economist; b. 8 Dec. 1953, Słupsk; m.; one s. one d.; ed Poznań Univ. of Technology and Acad. of Economy, Poznań; mem. staff advancing to Deputy Dir for Financial and Commercial Affairs, Agric. Vehicle Factory, Antoninek, Poznań 1977–93; mem. Polish United Workers' Party (PZPR) 1976–90; Co-Founder Union of Labour (UP) 1992–, Chair. 1998–; Minister of Industry and Trade 1993–95; Govt Plenipotentiary responsible for reforming the cen. econ. admins 1995–97; apptd Econ. Expert, Polskie Stronnictwo Ludowe 1992; Deputy Prime Minister and Minister of Infrastructure 2001–04; Deputy to Sjem (Parl.), mem. Social, Health and Family Affairs Cttee, Alternate mem. Cttee on Culture, Science and Educ., fmr Vice-Chair. Extraordinary Cttee (for Econ. reform law); fmr Vice-Pres. Ownership Transformation Cttee; mem. Supervisory Bd Daewoo-FSO 2000–01. *Leisure interests:* walks with family, reading books and journals. *Address:* Sejm, Chancellerie de la Diète, ul. Wiejska 4/6/8, 00-902, Warsaw, Poland (office); Biuro Poselskie Marka Pola, ul. Torowa 2B 62-510 Konin. *Telephone:* (22) 630-1000 (office); (63) 245-3745.

POLANČEC, Damir; Croatian business executive and politician; b. 25 June 1967, Koprivnica; m. Jasmink Polančec; two c.; ed Univ. of Zagreb, Leeds Metropolitan Univ.; Import-Export Dept, Podravka dd (food co.) 1992–94, Commercial Assoc. 1994–97, Sr Assoc. 1997, Dir of Cen. Buying 1997–2000, mem. Bd 2000–; Deputy Prime Minister 2005–09, Minister of Economy, Labour and Entrepreneurship 2008–09; mem. Man. Cttee, Croatian Handball Asscn; Pres. HC Podravka, Koprivnica 2000; mem. Croatian Democratic Union (Hrvatska demokratska zajednica—HDZ) 2003, Head 2004; sentenced to jail on charge of power abuse 2010; released from prison 2012.

POLANCO MORENO, Ignacio, BA (Econ), MBA; Spanish media executive; *Honorary Chairman, Grupo Prisa;* b. 5 Nov. 1954, Madrid; s. of Jesús de Polanco; m. María Jaraíz; two c.; ed Univ. of Madrid (Complutense), Instituto de Empresa; professional positions at Timón SA and Promotora de Informaciones SA; mem. Bd of Dirs Grupo Prisa 1993–, Corp. Asst to Chair. Prisa –2006, Deputy Chair. Prisa 2006–07, Chair. 2007–12, now Hon. Chair.; Chair. Timón SA, Promotora de Publicaciones, SL, Fundación Santillana, Sociedad Española de Radiodifusión SL, Union Radio Servicios Corporativos SA, Union Radio Servicios Corporativos SA, Rucandio SA; Pres. El País newspaper; fmr Chair. Diario EL Pais SL; mem. Bd of Dirs Promotora de Publicaciones SL (also fmr Chair.), Asgard Inversiones SL. *Address:* Grupo Prisa, Gran Vía 32 28013 Madrid. *Fax:* (91) 330-1038 (Prisa) (office). *E-mail:* sugerencias@prisa.es (office). *Website:* www.prisa.es (office).

POLAŃSKI, Roman; French film director, writer and actor; b. 18 Aug. 1933, Paris; s. of Ryszard Polański and Bule Katz-Przedborska; m. 1st Barbara Kwiatkowska-Lass (divorced); m. 2nd Sharon Tate 1968 (died 1969); m. 3rd Emmanuelle Seigner; one s. one d.; ed Polish Film School, Łódź; Acad. française Pris René Clair for Lifetime Achievement 1999, European Film Acad. Lifetime Achievement Award 2006, Federico Fellini Prize for lifetime achievement 2006. *Film roles include:* A Generation, The End of the Night, See You Tomorrow, The Innocent Sorcerers, Two Men and a Wardrobe, The Vampire Killers, What? 1972, Chinatown 1974, The Tenant 1976, Chassé-croisé 1982, Back in the U.S.S.R. 1992, A Pure Formality 1994, Dead Tired 1994, Tribute to Alfred Lepetit 2000, The Revenge 2002. *Films directed include:* Two Men and a Wardrobe 1958, When Angels Fall, Le Gros et Le Maigre, Knife in the Water (prize at Venice Film Festival 1962), The Mammals (prize at Tours Film Festival 1963), Repulsion (prize at Berlin Film Festival 1965), Cul de Sac (prize at Berlin Film Festival 1966), The Vampire Killers 1967, Rosemary's Baby 1968, Macbeth 1971, What? 1972, Lulu (opera), Spoleto Festival 1974, Chinatown (Soc. of Film and TV Arts Best Dir Award) 1974, Le Prix Raoul-Levy 1975) 1974, The Tenant 1976, Rigoletto (opera) 1976, Tess (Golden Globe Award) 1980, Vampires Ball 1980, Amadeus (play) 1981, Pirates 1986, Frantic 1988, Tales of Hoffmann (opera) 1992, Bitter Moon (Dir, produced, written) 1992, Death and the Maiden 1994, Dance of the Vampire (play) 1997, The Ninth Gate 1999, Icons, A Pure Formality, In Stuttgart 2000, The Pianist (Best Film, Cannes Film Festival 2002, Acad. Award for Best Dir 2003, BAFTA Award for Best Film and Best Dir 2003) 2002, Oliver Twist 2005, The Ghost Writer (European Film Awards for Best Dir, Best Film) 2010, Carnage 2011, La Vénus à la fourrure 2013, D'après une histoire vraie 2017. *Publication:* Roman (authobiography) 1984. *Address:* c/o ICM, 8942 Wilshire Boulevard, Beverly Hills, CA 90211-1934, USA (office). *Telephone:* (310) 550-4000 (office). *Website:* www.icmtalent.com (office).

POLANYI, John Charles, CC, PhD, FRS, FRSC, FRSE; Canadian physical chemist and academic; *University Professor of Physical Chemistry, University of Toronto;* b. 23 Jan. 1929, Berlin, Germany; s. of Michael Polanyi and Magda Polanyi (née Kemeny); m. 1st Anne Ferrar Davidson 1958 (died 2013); one s. one d.; m. 2nd Brenda Bury; ed Manchester Grammar School and Univ. of Manchester, UK; Postdoctoral Fellow, Nat. Research Council of Canada 1952–54; Research Assoc., Princeton Univ., USA 1954–56; Lecturer, Univ. of Toronto, Canada 1956–57, Asst Prof. 1957–60, Assoc. Prof. 1960–62, Prof. of Chem. 1962–; numerous visiting lectureships; mem. numerous professional asscns, including American Acad. of Arts and Sciences, Pontifical Acad. of Sciences; Foreign Assoc., NAS; Hon. Foreign mem. AAAS; Hon. FRSC; Hon. FCIC; hon. degrees from over 30 univs; Marlow Medal, Faraday Soc. 1962, British Chemical Soc. Award 1971, Chemical Inst. of Canada Medal 1976, Henry Marshall Tory Medal, Royal Soc. of Canada 1977, Wolf Prize in Chem. (shared with G. Pimentel) 1982, shared Nobel Prize for Chem. 1986, John Charles Polanyi Prizes est. in his honour by Ont. Govt 1986, Izaak Walton Killam Memorial Prize 1988, Royal Medal, Royal Soc. 1989, Gerhard Herzberg Canada Gold Medal for Science and Eng 2007, pictured on Canada Post first class postage stamp issued for the Int. Year of Chem. 2011, John

C. Polanyi Award est. by Natural Sciences and Eng Research Council in his honour, Toronto District School Bd changed name of Sir Sandford Fleming Acad. to the John Polanyi Collegiate Inst. 2011. *Film:* produced Concepts in Reaction Dynamics 1970. *Publications:* The Dangers of Nuclear War (co-ed.) 1979; author of over 250 scientific papers and over 100 articles on policy, the impact of science on society and armament control. *Leisure interests:* walking, skiing. *Address:* Department of Chemistry, University of Toronto, 80 St George Street, Toronto, ON M5S 3H6 (office); 142 Collier Street, Toronto, ON M4W 1M3, Canada (home). *Telephone:* (416) 978-3580 (office); (416) 961-6545 (home). *Fax:* (416) 978-7580 (office). *E-mail:* jpolanyi@chem.utoronto.ca (office). *Website:* www.utoronto.ca/jpolanyi (office); www.chem.utoronto.ca (office).

POLEGATO, Mario Moretti; Italian business executive; *President, Board of Directors, Geox Group;* b. 16 Aug. 1952, Crocetta del Montello; m.; one c.; worked in family wine and agricultural business; f. Geox SpA 1995 (now Geox Group), created and developed a range of 'breathable' footwear, currently Pres. Bd of Dirs and leading shareholder; mem. Bd of Dirs Siparex Italia (pvt. equity fund); mem. arbitration panel Confindustria; Founder ONLUS 'Il Ponte del Sorriso' charitable org. 2004; mem. Aspen Inst. Italia; Hon. Consul-Gen. for Northeastern Italy to Romania 2000, Hon. Affiliate Prof. of Entrepreneurship, ESCP-EAP Business School; Cavaliere al Merito dell'Ordine Nazionale di Romania 2002, Cavaliere del Lavoro 2005; Dr hc (Banatului-Timisoara Univ., Romania) 2003, (Ca' Foscari Univ., Venice); Confindustria Award 1994, Ernst & Young/Il Sole 24 Ore/Borse Italiana Entrepreneur of the Year 2002, Ernst & Young Global Best Italian Entrepreneur in the World 2003, Italian Marketing Asscn Award 2004. *Address:* Geox Group, Via Feltrina Centro 16, Montebelluna, Treviso, Italy (office). *Telephone:* (04) 232822 (office). *Website:* www.geox.biz (office).

POLESE, Kim Karin, BS; American computer industry executive; *Chairman, ClearStreet, Inc.;* b. 13 Nov. 1961; ed Univ. of California, Berkeley, Univ. of Washington, Seattle; started career at IntelliCorp, Inc.; Product Man. Sun Microsystems 1988–95 played a role in definition, direction and launch of Java; Co-founder Marimba Inc. 1996, Pres. and CEO 1996–2000, Chair. 1996–2004; Founder and CEO SpikeSource Inc. 2004–11; currently Chair. ClearStreet, Inc.; mem. Exec. Council TechNet; mem. Bd of Dirs Global Security Inst., Univ of Calif. Pres.'s Bd on Science and Innovation, Silicon Valley Leadership Group; Fellow, Center for Engineered Innovation, Carnegie Mellon Univ; mem. Bd Technorati, Inc. 2004–06, Bd Global Security Inst., Bd Long Now Foundation, Univ. of California Pres.'s Bd on Science and Innovation, Exec. Council of TechNet, Silicon Valley Leadership Group; Hon. DHumLitt (California State Univ.) 2011; named one of Top 25 Most Influential People in America 1997, Symons Innovator Award, Nat. Center for Women & Information Tech. 2010. *Website:* myclearstreet.com (office).

POLET, Robert, MBA; Dutch business executive; b. 25 July 1955, Kuala Lumpur; m.; two d.; ed Nijenrode and Univ. of Oregon, USA; joined Marketing and Sales Dept, Unilever in 1978, worked in Paris for two years, spent one year in Milan, then moved to Hamburg, Chair. Unilever Malaysia 1990–92, Chair. Van den Bergh's (Dutch subsidiary) 1993–96, Vice-Pres. Home and Personal Care, Unilever HPC Europe, Brussels 1996, Exec. Vice-Pres., later Business Group Pres. and mem. Unilever Exec. Council, Ice Cream and Frozen Foods Europe Business Group, Rotterdam 1997–2001, Pres. Global Business, Ice Cream and Frozen Foods (following merger with Bestfoods and re-org. of Unilever's foods business) 2001–04; CEO Gucci Group NV 2004–11; mem. Supervisory Bd Reed Elsevier NV 2007–16. *Leisure interests:* spending time with family, sailing, travelling, playing golf.

POLETTI, Alan Ronald, DPhil, FRSNZ; New Zealand physicist; *Professor Emeritus of Physics, University of Auckland;* b. 19 Oct. 1937, New Plymouth; s. of John Poletti and Pearl Poletti; m. 1st Dorothy M. Martin 1961 (died 1994); three s. one d.; m. 2nd Marcia M. Stenson 1996; ed Univ. of Oxford; Prof. of Physics, Univ. of Auckland 1969–98, Head of Dept of Physics 1986–92, now Prof. Emer. *Publications:* over 100 scientific papers. *Leisure interests:* sailing, public history. *Address:* 11 Tole Street, Ponsonby, Auckland, New Zealand (home). *Telephone:* (9) 373-7599 (home).

POLETTO, HE Cardinal Severino; Italian ecclesiastic; *Archbishop Emeritus of Turin;* b. 18 March 1933, Salgareda, Treviso; ordained priest 1957; parish priest St Mary of the Assumption, Casale 1965; f. Diocesan Centre for Family Ministry 1973; Coadjutant Bishop of Fossano 1980; Bishop of Fossano 1980–89, of Asti 1989–99; Archbishop of Turin 1999–2010, Archbishop Emer. 2010–; cr. Cardinal (Cardinal-Priest of San Giuseppe in via Trionfale) 2001. *Address:* Archdiocese of Torino, Via Val della Torre 3, 10149 Turin, Italy (office). *Telephone:* (011) 5156300 (office). *Website:* www.diocesi.torino.it (office).

POLFER, Lydie; Luxembourg lawyer and politician; *Mayor of Luxembourg City;* b. 22 Nov. 1952; d. of Camille Polfer; m. Hubert Wurth (q.v.); one d.; ed Lycée Robert Schuman, Univ. of Grenoble, France, Univ. Centre for Int. and European Research, Grenoble; admitted to Luxembourg Bar 1977; mem. Chamber of Deputies (Parl.) 1979–99; Mayor of Luxembourg City 1982–99, 2013–; mem. European Parl. 1985–89, 1990–94, 2004–09, mem. Group of the Alliance of Liberals and Democrats for Europe, Chair. Del. to ACP–EU Jt Parl. Ass., mem. Cttee on Foreign Affairs; Chair. Democratic Party 1994–2004; Deputy Prime Minister, Minister of Foreign Affairs and External Trade, Minister of Civil Service and Admin. Reform 1999–2005; Großes Goldenes Ehrenzeichen am Bande für Verdienste um die Republik Österreich 2006. *Address:* Hôtel de Ville, 42 place Guillaume II, 2090 Luxembourg Ville, Luxembourg (office). *Telephone:* 4796-2660 (office). *Fax:* 22-74-99 (office). *E-mail:* admcommunale@vdl.lu (office). *Website:* villedeluxembourg.lu (office).

POLI, HE Cardinal Mario Aurelio, DTheol; Argentine ecclesiastic; *Archbishop of Buenos Aires;* b. 29 Nov. 1947, Buenos Aires; ed Seminario Metropolitano de la Inmaculada Concepción, Villa Devoto, Univ. of Buenos Aires, Pontifical Catholic Univ. of Argentina; ordained priest, Archdiocese of Buenos Aires 1978, Parish Priest of San Cayetano, Liniers for two years; consecrated Titular Bishop of Abidda 2002; Auxiliary Bishop of Buenos Aires 2002–08; Bishop of Santa Rosa 2008–13; Archbishop of Buenos Aires 2013–; Bishop of Argentina, Faithful of the Eastern Rites 2013–; cr. Cardinal (Cardinal-Priest of San Roberto Bellarmino) 2014–. *Address:* Arzobispado, Rivadavia 415, C1002AAC, Buenos Aires, Argentina

(office). *Telephone:* (11) 4343-0812 (office). *Fax:* (11) 4334-8373 (office). *E-mail:* info@arzbaires.org.ar (office). *Website:* www.arzbaires.org.ar (office).

POLI, Roberto; Italian academic and energy industry executive; *President, Poli e Associati SpA;* b. 28 June 1938; Prof. of Corp. Finance, Cattolica di Milano 1966–98; fmr Chair. Rizzoli-Corriere della Sera SpA, Publitania SpA; currently Pres. Poli e Associati SpA (fmrly Poli Morelli & Partners SpA); Chair. Ente Nazionale Idrocarburi (Eni) Group SpA (oil and gas co.) 2002–11; mem. Bd of Dirs Fininvest SpA, Mondadori SpA, Merloni Termosanitari SpA, Coesia SpA, Maire Tecnimont SpA, Perennius Capital Partners SGR SpA. *Address:* Poli e Associati SpA, Via Pontaccio 10, 20121 Milan, Italy (office). *Telephone:* (02) 72011020 (office).

POLIAKOFF, Sir Martyn, Kt, CBE, BA, PhD, FRS, FRSC, FIChemE; British chemist and academic; *Research Professor of Chemistry, Faculty of Science, University of Nottingham;* b. 16 Dec. 1947; s. of Alexander Poliakoff and Ina Poliakoff (née Montagu); brother of Stephen Poliakoff; m. Dr Janet Frances Keene; one s. one d.; ed Westminster School, King's Coll., Cambridge; Research/Sr Research Officer, Dept of Inorganic Chem., Univ. of Newcastle upon Tyne 1972–79; Lecturer, Dept of Chem., Univ. of Nottingham 1979–85, Reader in Inorganic Chem. 1985–91, Prof. of Chem. 1991–, EPSRC/Royal Acad. of Eng Clean Tech. Fellow 1994–99; Foreign Sec. and Vice-Pres. Royal Soc. 2011–16; mem. Council Inst. of Chemical Enginners 2009–13, Advisory Council for Campaign for Science and Eng; Chair. Editorial Bd RSC journal Green Chemistry; Foreign mem. Russian Acad. of Sciences 2011; Fellow, Academia Europaea 2012; Assoc. Fellow, TWAS, the World Acad. of Science 2013; Hon. Prof. of Chem., Moscow State Univ.; Hon. mem. Chemical Soc. of Ethiopia 2008; RSC Meldola Medal and Prize 1976, Leverhulme Medal, Royal Soc. 2010, Nyholm Prize for Educ. 2011. *Videos:* The Periodic Table of Videos (narrator). *Publications:* numerous papers in professional journals on the chemical applications of supercritical fluids, with particular emphasis on Green Chemistry. *Address:* Room B13A, School of Chemistry, University Park, Nottingham, NG7 2RD, England (office). *Telephone:* (115) 951-3520 (office). *Fax:* (115) 951-3058 (office). *E-mail:* martyn.poliakoff@nottingham.ac.uk (office). *Website:* www.nottingham.ac.uk/chemistry/people/martyn.poliakoff (office); www.nottingham.ac.uk/supercritical/beta (office).

POLIAKOFF, Stephen, CBE, FRSL; British playwright and film director; b. 1 Dec. 1952, London; s. of Alexander Poliakoff and Ina Montagu; m. Sandy Welch 1983; one s. one d.; ed Westminster School and Univ. of Cambridge; Co-founder (with wife) and Dir Amor Road Films Ltd (production co.) 2013–; Hon. degree (Tavistock Inst.). *Theatre includes:* Clever Soldiers 1974, The Carnation Gang 1974, Hitting Town 1975, City Sugar 1976, Strawberry Fields (Nat. Theatre) 1978, Shout Across the River (RSC) 1978, The Summer Party 1980, Favourite Nights 1981, Breaking the Silence (RSC) 1984, Coming in to Land (Nat. Theatre) 1987, Playing with Trains (RSC) 1989, Siena Red 1992, Sweet Panic (Hampstead) 1996, Blinded by the Sun (Nat. Theatre) 1996 (Critics' Circle Best Play Award), Talk of the City (RSC) 1998, Remember This (Nat. Theatre) 1999, My City 2011. *Films include:* Runners (original story and screenplay) 1983, Hidden City 1988, Close My Eyes (Best British Film Award, Evening Standard) 1991, Century 1993, Glorious 39 2009. *Television includes:* Stronger Than the Sun 1977, Bloody Kids (aka One Joke Too Many, USA) 1979, Caught on a Train (BAFTA for Best Single Drama) 1980, Soft Targets 1982, She's Been Away (Venice Film Festival Prize) 1989, Frontiers 1996, Food of Love 1998, The Tribe 1998, Shooting the Past (Prix Italia for Best Drama, RTS Award for Best Drama) 1999, Perfect Strangers/Almost Strangers (RTS Award for Best Drama and Best Writer, BAFTA Dennis Potter Award, Peabody Award for Drama) 2001, The Lost Prince (Primetime Emmy for Outstanding Miniseries, Best Costume and Best Production Design) 2004, Friends and Crocodiles 2006, Gideon's Daughter (Peabody Award for Drama) 2007, Joe's Palace 2007, A Real Summer 2007, Capturing Mary 2007, Dancing on the Edge 2013, Close to Enemy 2016. *Publications include:* Plays One 1989, Plays Two 1994, Plays Three 1998, Sweet Panic and Blinded by the Sun, Talk of the City, Shooting the Past, Remember This. *Leisure interests:* watching cricket, going to the cinema. *Address:* Judy Daish Associates, Ltd, 2 St Charles Place, London, W10 6EG, England (office); Amor Road Films Ltd, 37 Warren Street, London, W1T 6AD, England (office).

POLIS, Jared, BA; American, philanthropist, entrepreneur and politician; *Governor of Colorado;* b. 12 May 1975, Boulder, Colo; s. of Stephen Schutz and Susan Polis Schutz; partner Marlon Reis; one s. one d.; ed Princeton Univ.; co-f. BlueMountainArts.com 1996, American Information Systems 1998; founder and owner, ProFlowers (renamed Provide Commerce, Inc. 2003) 1998–2014; founder, Jared Polis Foundation 2000; est. several educational institutions including New America Coll. and New America School 2004; co-f. Acad. of Urban Learning 2005; mem.-at-large, Chair. and Vice-Chair., Colo State Bd of Educ. 2000–07; Co-Chair. Coloradans for Clean Govt Cttee 2006, Building for Our Future campaign 2007; mem. State House of Reps, Colo 2009–19; mem. Red to Blue Program Chair, Democratic Congressional Campaign Cttee 2012; Gov. of Colo 2019–; Co-Chair. United States–Mexico Congressional Caucus; Chair. Lesbian Gay Bisexual Trans-Sexual Caucus, Immigration Task Forces; Chair. Equal Protection Task Force, US House of Reps, Co-Chair. Democratic Coalition Immigration Task Force, Congressional Caucus on Nepal, Vice-Chair. Sustainable Energy and Environment Coalition; mem. Exec. Cttee Democratic Party 2000–07, Boulder County Democrats 2000–07; mem. and Chair. Congressional Progressive Caucus; mem. Bd Latin American Research and Service Agency, Colo Consumer Health Initiative, Colo Conservation Voters, Colo Anti-Defamation League; mem. Bd of Visitors, United States Air Force Acad.; Entrepreneur of the Year, Ernst and Young 2000, Boulder Daily Camera Pacesetter Award in Educ. 2007, Martin Luther King Jr. Colo Humanitarian Award 2018, Kauffman Foundation Community Award, Boulder Community Builder Award. *Leisure interests:* baseball, flowers, fish, chocolate, movie theatres, internet start-ups, e-commerce, dog, kids. *Address:* Office of the Governor, 136 State Capitol Building, Denver, CO 80203, USA (office). *Telephone:* (303) 866-2471 (office). *Website:* www.colorado.gov (office).

POLITI, Mauro; Italian judge and professor of law; b. 13 Sept. 1944, Fabrica di Roma; ed Univ. of Florence; Asst Prof. of Pvt Int. Law, Univ. of Cagliari, Sardinia 1976–79; Asst Prof. of Public Int. Law, Univ. of Urbino 1979–83, Assoc. Prof. of Int. Law 1983–86; Assoc. Prof. of Int. Law, Univ. of Trento 1986–90, Prof. of Int. Law 1990–; began judicial career at Tribunal of Florence 1969; Judge, Tribunal of

Oristano 1972, of Milan 1975–83; Deputy Prosecutor, Juvenile Court, Milan 1972–75; Legal Adviser, Perm. Mission to UN, New York, USA 1992–2001; *ad litem* Judge, Int. Criminal Tribunal for Fmr Yugoslavia (ICTY) 2001; Judge, Int. Criminal Court (ICC), The Hague 2003–09; mem. Del. to UN Security Council 1995–96; mem. Del. to Preparatory Cttee for ICC 1995–97, 1999–2002; Chair. Sixth Legal Cttee of UN Gen. Ass. 2000–01; mem. Nat. Group of Perm. Court of Arbitration 2011; Kt of the Order of Italian Repub. 2005. *Publications include:* The Rome Statute of the International Criminal Court: A Challenge to Impunity (co-ed.) 2001, International Criminal Court and National Jurisdictions (co-ed.) 2008; book chapters and articles in professional law journals. *Address:* Università degli Studi di Trento, Facoltà di Giurisprudenza, Dipartimento di Scienze Giuridiche, Via Giuseppe Verdi 53, 38100 Trento, Italy (office). *Telephone:* (0461) 881818 (office). *Fax:* (0461) 881899 (office). *E-mail:* mauro.politi@jus.unitn.it (office). *Website:* www.jus.unitn.it (office).

POLITZER, H. David, BS, PhD; American physicist and academic; *Richard Chase Tolman Professor of Theoretical Physics, California Institute of Technology;* b. 31 Aug. 1949, New York; ed Univ. of Michigan, Harvard Univ.; Jr Fellow, Harvard Society of Fellows 1974–77; Visiting Assoc., Calif. Inst. of Tech. 1975–76, Assoc. Prof. Theoretical Physics 1976–79, Prof. 1979–2004, Exec. Officer, Dept of Physics 1986–88, Richard Chase Tolman Prof. of Theoretical Physics 2004–; J. J. Sakurai Prize for Theoretical Particle Physics 1986, Nobel Prize in Physics (jt recipient) 2004. *Films:* appeared in minor role in film Fat Man and Little Boy 1989. *Address:* California Institute of Technology, High Energy Physics, 1201 East California Boulevard, Mail Code 452-48, Pasadena, CA 91106-3368, USA (office). *Telephone:* (626) 395-4252 (office). *E-mail:* politzer@theory.caltech.edu. *Website:* www.pma.caltech.edu.

POLKINGHORNE, Rev. John Charlton, Kt, KBE, MA, PhD, ScD, FRS; British fmr physicist and fmr ecclesiastic; b. 16 Oct. 1930, Weston-super-Mare; s. of George B. Polkinghorne and Dorothy E. Charlton; m. Ruth I. Martin 1955 (died 2006); two s. one d.; ed Perse School, Cambridge, Trinity Coll., Cambridge and Westcott House, Cambridge; Commonwealth Fund Fellow Calif. Inst. of Tech. 1955–56; Lecturer, Univ. of Edin. 1956–58; Lecturer, Univ. of Cambridge 1958–65, Reader 1965–68, Prof. of Math. Physics 1968–79, Fellow, Trinity Coll., Cambridge 1954–86, Fellow and Dean, Trinity Hall, Cambridge 1986–89, Hon. Fellow 1989–, Pres. Queens' Coll. Cambridge 1989–96, Hon. Fellow 1996–; ordained deacon 1981, priest 1982; Curate, St Andrew's, Chesterton 1981–82, St Michael & All Angels, Bedminster 1982–84; Vicar of St Cosmus and St Damian in the Blean 1984–86; Canon Theologian, Liverpool Cathedral 1994–2005; Six Preacher, Canterbury Cathedral 1996–2006; Founding Pres. Int. Soc. for Science and Religion; Co-founder Soc. of Ordained Scientists; mem. Church of England Doctrine Comm. 1989–95, General Synod 1990–2000, Human Genetics Advisory Comm. 1996–99, Human Genetics Comm. 2000–02; Hon. Fellow, St Edmund's Coll., Trinity Coll., Cambridge 2002; Hon. Prof. of Theoretical Physics, Univ. of Kent 1984–89; Hon. DD (Kent) 1994, (Durham) 1999, (Gen. Theological Seminary) 2010, (Wycliffe Coll.) 2011; Hon. DSc (Exeter) 1994, (Leicester) 1995, (Marquette) 2003; Hon. DHum (Hong Kong Baptist) 2006; von Humboldt Foundation Award 1999, Templeton Prize 2002. *Publications include:* The Analytic S-Matrix (jointly) 1966, The Particle Play 1979, Models of High Energy Processes 1980, The Way the World Is 1983, The Quantum World 1984, One World 1986, Science and Creation 1988, Science and Providence 1989, Rochester Roundabout 1989, Reason and Reality 1991, Science and Christian Belief 1994, Quarks, Chaos and Christianity 1994, Serious Talk 1995, Scientists as Theologians 1996, Beyond Science 1996, Searching for Truth 1996, Belief in God in an Age of Science 1998, Science and Theology 1998, Faith, Science and Understanding 2000, The End of the World and the Ends of God (ed with M. Welker) 2000, Faith in the Living God (with M. Welker) 2001, The Work of Love (ed.) 2001, The God of Hope and the End of the World 2002, Quantum Theory: A Very Short Introduction 2002, Living with Hope 2003, Science and the Trinity 2004, Exploring Reality 2005, Quantum Physics and Theology 2007, From Physicist to Priest 2007, Theology in the Context of Science 2008, Questions of Truth (with N. Beale) 2009, Encountering Scripture 2010, Science and Religion in Quest of Truth 2011. *Leisure interest:* reading. *Address:* Queens' College, Cambridge, CB3 9ET, England (office).

POLLACK, Ilana, BA; Israeli librarian; b. 13 Aug. 1946, Tel-Aviv; d. of Leon Pinsky and Mala First Pinsky (née Ferszt); m. Joseph Pollack 1977 (died 1994); two s.; ed Re'alit High School, Rishon Le Zion, Tel-Aviv Univ. and Hebrew Univ. Jerusalem; served in Israeli Army 1964–66; joined Weizmann Inst. of Science, Rehovot, Asst Librarian 1966, Librarian in charge of Physics Faculty Library 1975, Chief Librarian, Weizmann Inst. of Science 1983–2009 (retd). *Address:* 22 Shenkin Street, Rishon Le-Zion 75282, Israel. *Telephone:* 3-9692186. *Fax:* 8-9344176.

POLLACK-BEIGHLE, Yildiz; Surinamese government official and politician; *Minister of Foreign Affairs;* b. 21 April 1983, Paramaribo; ed Anton de Kom Univ. of Suriname, FHR Lim A Po Inst. for Social Studies; Youth Amb. Caribbean Community (CARICOM) 2005–08, Policy Officer Secr. CARICOM 2008–13, Deputy Programme Man. Youth Devt 2013–17; Adviser to Minister of Trade and Industry 2007–11; Head CARICOM Dept, Ministry of Foreign Affairs 2011–13; Minister of Foreign Affairs 2017–. *Address:* Ministry of Foreign Affairs, Henck Arronstraat 8, Paramaribo, Suriname (office). *Telephone:* 471209 (office). *Fax:* 410411 (office). *E-mail:* sec.minister@foreignaffairs.gov.sr (office). *Website:* www.gov.sr/sr/ministerie-van-buza/contact.aspx (office).

POLLARD, Catherine, MA; Guyanese UN official; *Under-Secretary-General for General Assembly and Conference Management, United Nations;* b. 1960, Georgetown; ed Univ. of the West Indies, Kingston; Audit Supervisor, Deloitte 1983–89; long career in financial and human resource man. with UN, including as Chief, Nat. Execution Projects Financing Unit, Bureau of Finance and Admin, UNDP 1989–93, Chief, Budget for Africa, Europe and Latin America Sections, Dept of Peacekeeping Operations 1993–95, Chief of Budget, UN Protection Force (UNPROFOR) 1995–96, Chief, Budget and Finance, UNDP (UN Volunteers) 1996–2001, Dir, UN Peacekeeping Finance Div. 2001–07, Chief of Staff, Dept of Peacekeeping Operations 2007–08, Asst Sec.-Gen. for Human Resources 2008–14, Asst Sec.-Gen. for Gen. Ass. Affairs and Conf. Man. 2014–15, Under-Sec.-Gen. for Gen. Ass. Affairs and Conf. Man. 2015–. *Address:* Office of the Secretary-General, United Nations, New York, NY 10017, USA (office). *Telephone:* (212) 963-1234 (office). *Fax:* (212) 963-4879 (office). *Website:* www.un.org (office).

POLLINI, Maurizio; Italian pianist; b. 5 Jan. 1942, Milan; s. of Gino Pollini and Renata Melotti; m. Maria Elisabetta Marzotto 1968; one s.; has played with Berlin and Vienna Philharmonic Orchestras, Bayerischer Rundfunk Orchestra, London Symphony Orchestra, Boston, New York, Philadelphia, LA and San Francisco Orchestras; has played at Salzburg, Vienna, Berlin, Prague Festivals; First Prize, Int. Chopin Competition, Warsaw 1960, Ernst von Siemens Music Prize, Munich 1996, Edison Classical Music Award for Best Instrumental Solo Recital 2007, Grammy Award for Best Instrumental Soloist Performance 2007, Disco d'Oro 2007, Praemium Imperiale 2010, RPS Instrumentalist Award 2012. *Recordings include:* Chopin's Nocturnes (Prix Victoire for Best Classical Recording) 2007, Bach's The Well-Tempered Clavier, Book 1 2010, Chopin Etudes Opp.10 & 25 (Gramophone Award for Best Historic Recording 2012) 2011, Brahms Piano Concerto No. 1 op.15 (ECHO Klassik Award for Concerto Recording of the Year/Piano – 19th Century 2012), Chopin: Late Works opp. 59-64 (Echo Klassik Award for Best Instrumentalist (Piano) 2017) 2017. *Address:* HarrisonParrott, The Ark, 201 Talgarth Road, London, W6 8BJ, England (office). *Telephone:* (20) 7229-9166 (office). *Fax:* (20) 7221-5042 (office). *E-mail:* jasper.parrott@harrisonparrott.co.uk (office). *Website:* www.harrisonparrott.com/artist/profile/maurizio-pollini (office).

POLLO, Genc; Albanian politician; b. 7 April 1963, Tirana; m.; two c.; ed Univ. of Tirana, Univ. of Vienna, Austria; Researcher, Acad. of Sciences 1986–88; adviser to Pres. of Albania 1992–96; Chair. New Democrat Party 2001; Minister of Educ. and Science 2005–07, Deputy Prime Minister 2007–09, Minister of State and Parliamentary Relations 2009–10, Minister for Innovation and Information and Communication Technologies 2010–13; mem. Parl. *Address:* People's Assembly, Bulevardi Dëshmorët e Kombit 4, 1010 Tirana, Albania (office). *Telephone:* (4) 2278261 (office). *E-mail:* albana.shtylla@parlament.al (office). *Website:* www.parlament.al (office).

POLLOCK, Shaun MacLean, BCom; South African fmr professional cricketer; b. 16 July 1973, Port Elizabeth, Cape Prov.; s. of Peter Pollock and Inez Pollock; m. Patricia 'Trish' Lauderdale; two d.; ed Northwood High School, Univ. of Natal, Durban; bowling all-rounder: right-hand batsman, right-arm fast-medium bowler; played for KwaZulu-Natal 1992–2004, S Africa 1995–2008 (Capt. Test side 2000–03, ODI side 2000–05), Warwicks. 1996–2002, Dolphins 2004/05, Africa XI 2007, Durham 2008, Mumbai Indians 2008, Natal, ICC (Int. Cricket Council) World XI; First-class debut: Natal B v Western Prov. B, Pietermaritzburg 1991; Test debut: S Africa v England, Centurion 16–20 Nov. 1995; One-Day Int. (ODI) debut: S Africa v England, Cape Town 9 Jan. 1996; S Africa v NZ, Johannesburg 21 Oct. 2005; played in 108 Tests, scored 3,781 runs (average 32.31, highest score 111, 2 hundreds), bowling figures: 421 wickets at an average of 23.11 runs, best bowling (innings) 7/87, (match) 10/147; ODIs: played in 303 matches, scored 3,519 runs, took 393 wickets; First-class: played in 186 matches, scored 7,023 runs (average 33.12), took 667 wickets at an average of 23.25 runs; announced retirement from all forms of int. cricket 11 Jan. 2008; Wisden Cricketer of the Year 2003. *Leisure interests:* music, golf, reading.

POLMAN, Paul, BBA, BA, MA, MBA, KBE; Dutch business executive; *Chairman, International Chamber of Commerce;* b. 1956, Enschede; m.; three c.; ed Univ. of Groningen, Univ. of Cincinnati, USA; began career with Procter & Gamble in finance 1979, assignments in Belgium, the Netherlands, France, Spain, UK and USA, Assoc. Finance position, Procter & Gamble 1979–86, Category Man. and Marketing Dir Baby, FemPro, Cleanser and Beverages, Procter & Gamble France 1986–89, Vice-Pres. and Gen. Man. Procter & Gamble Iberia 1989–95, Vice-Pres. and Gen. Man. Procter & Gamble UK 1995–98, Pres. Global Fabric Care 1998–2001, Group Pres. Procter & Gamble Europe 2001–06; Chief Financial Officer Nestlé SA 2006–08, Exec. Vice-Pres. and Zone Dir for US, Canada, Latin America and The Caribbean 2008, Chair. and Dir Enterprises Maggi SA, Nestlé Finance SA, Nestlé International Travel Retail SA, Nestlé Capital Advisers; Chair. and Dir Intercona Re AG; Exec. Dir, Unilever PLC and Unilever NV 2008–18, CEO Unilever NV 2008–18, Unilever PLC 2009–18; Chair. ICC 2018–; mem. Bd of Dirs, Alcon Inc. 2006–10; Dir (non-exec.), Dow Chemical Co. 2010–; Chair. Perkins Int. Advisory Bd; Pres. Kilimanjaro Blindtrust; mem. Exec. Cttee World Business Council for Sustainable Devt, European Round Table, Int. Business Council of the World Econ. Forum, Swiss American Chamber of Commerce, Bd of Consumer Goods Forum (Co-Chair. Bd Strategy and Sustainability Cttees), Int. Council of the Global Comm. on the Economy and Climate, High Level Panel on the Post-2015 Development Agenda, Business and Sustainable Devt Comm.; asked by UN Sec.-Gen. to join SDG Advocacy Group, tasked with promoting action on the 2030 Agenda 2016; Trustee, Leverhulme Trust, Asia House; Hon. DCL (Univ. of Northumbria, UK) 2000, Dr hc (Business School Lausanne) 2014, Hon. DHumLitt (George Mason Univ.) 2018; WSJ/CNBC European Business Leader of the Year 2003, Carl Lidner Award, Univ. of Cincinnati 2006, Chief Financial Officer of the Year, Investor Magazine 2007, Atlantic Council Award for Distinguished Business Leadership 2012, CK Prahalad Award for Global Sustainability Leadership 2012, Duke of Edinburgh Gold Conservation Medal, Worldwide Fund for Nature 2013, Commitment to Development Ideas in Action Award, Centre for Global Development 2013, Rainforest Alliance Lifetime Achievement Award 2014, Champion for Global Change Award, UN Foundation 2014, Chevalier de la Légion d'Honneur 2017, Government Public Service Star, Singapore 2017, Treaties of Nijmegen Medal 2018. *Leisure interests:* running marathons, mountaineering, sailing, reading, travelling. *Address:* International Chamber of Commerce, 33-43 avenue du Président Wilson, 75116 Paris, France (office). *Telephone:* 1-49-53-28-28 (ICC) (office). *Fax:* 1-49-53-28-59 (ICC) (office). *E-mail:* icc@iccwbo.org (office). *Website:* www.iccwbo.org (office).

POLOLIKASHVILI, Zurab; Georgian diplomatist, politician and international organizations official; *Secretary-General, World Tourism Organization (UNWTO);* b. 12 Jan. 1977, Tbilisi; m.; three c.; ed Georgian Technical Univ., Instituto de Empresa, Madrid; CEO FC Dinamo Tbilisi 2001–11; Dir Cen. Branch Office, TBC Bank 2001–05, Vice Pres. TBC Group 2010–11; Deputy Minister of Foreign Affairs 2005–06, Minister of Econ. Devt 2009–10; Amb. to Spain 2006–09, 2002–17; Perm. Rep. to World Tourism Org. (UNWTO) –2017, Sec.-Gen. 2018–. *Address:* World Tourism Organization (UNWTO), Capitán Haya 42, 28020 Madrid, Spain (office). *Telephone:* (91) 5678100 (office). *Fax:* (91) 5713733 (office). *E-mail:* omt@unwto.org (office). *Website:* www.unwto.org (office).

POLOZ, Stephen S., BA, MA, PhD; Canadian economist and central banker; *Governor, Bank of Canada;* b. 1955, Oshawa, Ont.; m. Valerie Poloz; one s. one d.; ed Queen's Univ., Univ. of Western Ontario; served 14 years at Bank of Canada (central bank) 1981–94, becoming Chief of Research Dept 1992–94, Gov. 2013–; economist with BCA Research (ind. investment research firm), Montreal 1994–99; Man. Ed. The International Bank Credit Analyst 1996; Vice-Pres. and Chief Economist, Export Devt Canada 1999–2004, Sr Vice-Pres. of Corp. Affairs 2004–08, Sr Vice-Pres. of Financing 2008–10, Pres. and CEO 2011–13; fmr Visiting Scholar, IMF, Washington, DC and Econ. Planning Agency, Tokyo; fmr Pres. Ottawa Econs Asscn. *Address:* Bank of Canada, 234 Wellington Street, Ottawa, ON K1A 0G9, Canada (office). *Telephone:* (800) 303-1282 (office). *Fax:* (613) 782-7713 (office). *E-mail:* info@bankofcanada.ca (office). *Website:* www.bankofcanada.ca (office).

POLTAVCHENKO, Lt-Gen. Georgy Sergeyevich; Russian politician and engineer; b. 24 Feb. 1953, Baku, Azerbaijan SSR, Soviet Union (now Azerbaijan); m.; one s.; ed Leningrad Inst. of Aviation Machinery, Higher KGB Courses, St Petersburg Finance Tech. School; constructor, involved in bldg Kama truck plant 1972, worked in unit Leninets, worked in local Comsomol Cttee St Petersburg; on staff in KGB orgs 1979–, with KGB, Leningrad Region 1980–92; People's Deputy of Leningrad Regional Council 1990–93; Head Dept Fed. Service of Tax Police, St Petersburg 1993–99; unsuccessful cand. in Leningrad City Council elections 1998; Rep. of Russian Pres. to Leningrad Region 1999–2000, to Cen. Fed. Okrug (Dist) 2000–11; Gov. of St Petersburg 2011–18; Pres. St Petersburg Basketball Fed.

POLTORAK, Col-Gen. Stepan Timofeyevich, PhD; Ukrainian army officer and government official; *Minister of Defence;* b. 11 Feb. 1965, Vesela Dolyna, Tarutyne Dist, Odesa Oblast, Ukrainian SSR, USSR; ed Ordzhonikidze Higher Mil. Command School, Kirov Acad. of USSR Ministry and Armed Forces of Ukraine; has served in mil. since 1983, roles include Chief of Directorate for Combat and Special Training of Internal Forces, Ministry of Interior, Chief of Acad. of Internal Forces 2002–14, Commdr Internal Troops of Ukraine Feb.–Oct. 2014, Nat. Guard of Ukraine April–Oct. 2014, rank of Gen. of the Army; Minister of Defence 2014–; Hon. Citizen, Kharkiv City; Order of Bohdan Khmelnytsky (Third Class), Medal 'For Irreproachable Service', Defender of the Motherland Medal, Medal of Zhukov, Medal for Battle Merit, Jubilee Medal '70 Years of the Armed Forces of the USSR', Medal 'For Impeccable Service'. *Address:* Ministry of Defence, 01021 Kyiv, vul. M. Hrushevskoho 30/1, Ukraine (office). *Telephone:* (44) 238-74-85 (office); (44) 253-04-71 (office). *Fax:* (44) 226-20-15 (office). *E-mail:* admou@mil.gov.ua (office). *Website:* www.mil.gov.ua (office).

POLTORANIN, Mikhail Nikiforovich; Russian politician and journalist; b. 22 Nov. 1939, Leninogorsk, E Kazakhstan Region; m.; two s.; ed Kazakh State Univ., Higher CP School; corresp., Ed.-in-Chief local newspapers in Altai 1966–68, Exec. Sec. Kazakhstanskaya Pravda 1970–75, Corresp. Pravda in Kazakhstan 1975–86, Ed.-in-Chief Moskovskaya Pravda 1986–88, Political Corresp. Press Agency Novosti 1988–90; USSR People's Deputy 1989–91; Minister of Press and Mass Media of Russia 1990–92, Deputy-Chair. of Govt (Deputy Prime Minister) of Russia Feb.–Nov. 1992, Dir Fed. Information Agency 1992–93, also Chair. Special Comm. on Archives under the Pres. of Russian Fed.; mem. State Duma (Parl.) 1993–95; Chair. Cttee on Information Policy and Communications 1994–95; Chair. Bd Moment of Truth Corpn 1994; mem. Bd of Dirs TV-3 Russia 1998–, Exec. Dir 1999–.

POLUNIN, Vyacheslav Ivanovich; Russian mime artist and clown; b. 12 June 1950, Novosil, Orlov Region; s. of Pavlovich Polunin and Nikolayevna Polunina; m. Elena Ushakova; two s.; ed Leningrad Inst. of Culture; f. Theatre of Comic Pantomime Actors Litsedei 1968; f. Leningrad Mime Parade 1982; f. All-Union Festival of Street Theatres 1987, All-Union Congress of Fools 1988, Russian Acad. of Fools; took part in European Caravan of Peace 1989; tours around Europe; lives in UK; Golden Angel Prize of Edin. Festival, Golden Nose Prize, Spain, Lawrence Olivier Prize, England, Triumph Prize, Russia 1999. *Plays:* Snowshow 1993. *Films:* Only in Music Hall 1980, Believe It or Not 1983, To Kill a Dragon 1988, Hello, Fools! 1996, Clown 2002, Hoffmaniada 2016. *Leisure interests:* painting, sculpture, architecture, design. *Website:* www.slavasnowshow.com.

POLVINEN, Tuomo Ilmari, PhD; Finnish historian and professor of history; *Professor Emeritus, Academy of Finland;* b. 2 Dec. 1931, Helsinki; s. of Eino Ilmari Polvinen and Ilona Vihersalo; m. Eeva-Liisa Rommi 1965; two d.; ed Univ. of Helsinki; Docent, Univ. of Helsinki 1965; Prof. of Modern History, Tampere Univ. 1968–70; Dir-Gen. Nat. Archives of Finland 1970–74; Prof. of Modern History, Univ. of Helsinki 1974–92; Research Prof., Acad. of Finland 1979–95, now Prof. Emer.; Urho Kekkonen Prize 1981. *Publications include:* Venäjän vallankumous ja Suomi 1917–1920, I–II 1967, 1971, Suomi kansainvälisessä politiikassa 1941–47, I–III 1979, 1980, 1981, Between East and West: Finland in International Politics 1944–47 1986, J. K. Paasikivi, Valtiomiehen elämäntyö Vol. 1, 1870–1918 1989, Vol. 2, 1918–39 1992, Vol. 3, 1939–44 1995, Vol. 4, 1944–48 1999, Vol. 5, 1948–56 2003, Imperial Borderland: Bobrikov and the Attempted Russification of Finland, 1898–1904 1995. *Address:* Purotie 3 A 10, 00380 Helsinki, Finland (home). *Telephone:* (9) 408554 (home). *E-mail:* tuomo.polvinen@elisanet.fi.

POLYAKOV, Alexander Markovich, PhD; Russian theoretical physicist and academic; *Joseph Henry Professor of Physics, Princeton University;* b. 27 Sept. 1945, Moscow; fmrly with Landau Inst. for Theoretical Physics, Moscow; Joseph Henry Prof. of Physics, Princeton Univ., USA 1999–; mem. USSR (now Russian) Acad. of Sciences 1984, NAS 2005; Dirac Medal, Int. Centre for Theoretical Physics 1986, Dannie Heineman Prize for Math. Physics 1986, Lorentz Medal 1994, Oskar Klein Medal 1996, Harvey Prize, Technion, Israel 2010, Lars Onsager Prize (co-recipient) 2011, Breakthrough Prize in Fundamental Physics (co-recipient) 2013. *Publications:* numerous papers in professional journals. *Address:* Department of Physics, Princeton University, 348 Jadwin Hall, Princeton, NJ 08544, USA (office). *Telephone:* (609) 258-4314 (office). *Fax:* (609) 258-1073 (office). *E-mail:* polyakov@princeton.edu (office). *Website:* www.princeton.edu/physics (office).

POLYDORAS, Vyron; Greek lawyer, politician and writer; *President, Union for the Fatherland and People;* b. 27 Jan. 1947, Perivolia, Olympia; m.; one s. twin d.; ed Univ. of Athens, Univ. of Nevada, USA, Acad. of Int. Law, The Hague, Netherlands, Univ. of Strasbourg, France, Univ. of Salzburg, Austria; mem. (New Democracy) of the Vouli (Parl. for Athens B) 1981–2014, mem. Standing Cttee on Public Admin, Public Order and Justice, Cttee for the Revision of the Constitution, mem. Parl. Assemblies of the Council of Europe and WEU 1995–2000, elected Dean of the House June and Nov. 1989, Vice-Pres. of the Vouli (Deputy Speaker) 2009–12, Pres. (Speaker) 6 May 2012; Deputy Minister for the Presidency and Govt Spokesman 1990–91, 1991–92; Deputy Minister for Educ. and Religious Affairs Aug.–Dec. 1992; Deputy Minister for Foreign Affairs (responsible for Greeks Abroad) 1992–93; Minister of Public Order 2006–07; elected onto Admin. Cttee of New Democracy 1979, stood for office of Party Chair. 1997, Head of New Democracy Section on the Interior, Public Admin and Decentralization 2000–01, mem. Cen. Cttee of New Democracy and group co-ordinator for the Standing Cttee on Public Admin, Public Order and Decentralization 2001, Party Officer responsible for trade, medium-sized enterprises and the Cttee for Competition; Pres. Union for the Fatherland and People 2014–; fmr reserve officer in the Greek Army; Makarios III Medal (highest decoration of the Repub. of Cyprus); Ipektsi Award for Greek-Turkish friendship 1995. *Publications include:* (in Greek): Greek Ideology, In the Ideological Trenches, On Meritocracy, Politics and Art, Positive Logos, Bushido, Greek Political Development; trans. into Greek of John Keats' Eve of St Agnes (awarded Prize for Best Trans.), For a New Ideology 2008. *Address:* Union for the Fatherland and People, Hymettus 122 Papagou, 156169 Athens, Greece (office). *Telephone:* (210) 6528000 (office). *E-mail:* vpolydoras@yahoo.gr (office). *Website:* www.enosi-patrida.gr/home (office); www.vyron-polydoras.gr.

POLYE, Don; Papua New Guinea civil engineer and politician; spent several years working in transport infrastructure sector; mem. Nat. Parl. for Kandep Open electorate 2002–09; Minister for Transport and Civil Aviation 2006–09, Deputy Prime Minister July–Dec. 2010, Minister for Foreign Affairs, Trade and Immigration 2010–11 (dismissed), apptd Minister for Finance and Treasury 2011, lost finance portfolio 2012, Minister for Treasury 2012–14; Founding mem. Nat. Alliance Party.

POMERANTS, Marko, MA; Estonian politician; b. 24 Sept. 1964, Tamsalu, Lääne-Viru Co.; m.; two s.; ed Univ. of Tartu; Deputy Head, Rakvere Nature Protection Admin 1989–90; Head of Nature Protection Service, Lääne-Viru Co. Govt 1990–94, Head of Environment Dept 1994–95, Gov. Lääne-Viru Co. 1995–2003; mem. (Union of Pro Patria and Res Publica) 10th Riigikogu (Parl.) 2003, 2005–07, 11th Riigikogu 2007–09; Minister of Social Affairs 2003–05, of the Interior 2009–11, of Environment 2015–17; mem. Union of Pro Patria and Res Publica; Estonian Border Guards Meritorious Service Cross (2nd class) 2000; Memorial Medal for 10 Years of the Re-Established Defence Forces 2001, Golden Cross of the Rescue Service 2002, Border Guards Sword and Lynx Badge 2002. *Leisure interests:* volleyball, nature, family, physical and social environment.

POMEROL, Jean-Charles; French computer scientist, academic and fmr university administrator; *Professor, Collège des Ingénieurs (CDI);* b. 22 May 1943, Mantes-la-Jolie, Yvelines, Île-de-France; s. of Charles Pomerol and Marcelle Legay; m. Marie-Jeanne Danjou 1972; three c.; ed Univ. Pierre et Marie Curie, Paris; began career as teacher, Lycée Saint-Quentin 1966; Lecturer, Centre universitaire Saint-Quentin (Aisne); Sr Lecturer, Univ. Pierre et Marie Curie, Paris (UPMC) later Prof. of Computer Science and Dir Teaching and Research Dept, now Prof. Emer., Project Leader CNRS 1995–2000, Dir CNRS-UPMC Lab. for Artificial Intelligence, Vice-Pres. of Science 2002–06, Pres. UPMC 2006–11; currently Prof. Collège des Ingénieurs (CDI); Pres. Fondation Voir et Entendre, Fondation des Sciences Mathématiques de Paris; fmr Ed. Revue Française d'Intelligence Artificielle; Founder Journal of Decision Systems; Chevalier, Légion d'honneur. *Publications:* numerous books and publs, including Multicriterion Decision Making for Business 2000, Decision-Making and Action 2012. *Leisure interest:* the mountains. *Address:* Collège des Ingénieurs, 215 boulevard Saint, Germain, 75007 Paris (office); Université Pierre et Marie Curie, 4 place Jussieu, 75252 Paris Cedex 05, France (office). *Telephone:* 1-44-27-44-27 (UPMC) (office); 1-49-54-72-60 (CDI) (office). *E-mail:* jean-charles.pomerol@upmc.fr (office); info@cdi.eu (office). *Website:* www.upmc.fr (office); www.cdi.eu/en/mba/professors/prof-jean-charles-pomerol.html (office); jeancharles.pomerol.free.fr.

POMODORO, Arnaldo; Italian sculptor and theatrical designer; b. 23 June 1926, Morciano di Romagna; s. of Antonio Pomodoro and Beatrice Luzzi; has worked as jeweller and goldsmith 1950–; artist-in-residence, Stanford Univ. 1966–67, Univ. of Calif., Berkeley 1968; lecture course, Mills Coll., Oakland, Calif. 1979–82; f. Fondazione Arnaldo Pomodoro, Milan 1999; Grande Ufficiale, Ordine al Merito (Italy) 1986, Cavaliere di Gran Croce dell' Ordine al merito 1996; Hon. DLitt (Dublin) 1992, Hon. DArch (Ancona) 2001; Int. Sculpture Prize, São Paulo Biennale, Brazil 1963, Premio Nazionale di scultura, Venice Biennale 1964, Int. Sculpture Prize (Carnegie Inst., Pittsburgh) 1967, Henry Moore Grand Prize (Hakone Open-Air Museum, Japan) 1981, Praemium Imperiale for Sculpture (Japan Art Asscn) 1990, VII Premio Michelangelo per la Scultura 1998, Ministry of Culture Gold Medal 2005, Premio Lex Spolentina 2006, Guglieelmo Marconi Award 2006, ISC Lifetime Achievement in Contemporary Sculpture Award 2008. *Theatrical designs include:* Semiramide, Rome 1982, Orestea, Gibellina, Sicily 1983–85, Didone 1986, Alceste, Genoa 1987, Oedipus Rex, Siena 1988, Cleopatra, Gibellina, Sicily 1989, I Paraventi at Bologna 1990, Nella solitudine dei campi di cotone by Koltès, Rome 1991, Benevento 1998, More Stately Mansions by O'Neill, Rome 1992, Oreste by Alfieri, Rome 1993, Stabat Mater by Tarantino, Rome 1994–95, Moonlight by Pinter, Brescia, Rome 1995, Antigone by Anouilh, Taormina 1996, Il Caso Fedra by di Martino 1997, The Tempest, Palermo 1998, Capriccio by Strauss, Naples 2002, Madama Butterfly by Puccini, Torre del Lago 2004, Un Ballo in Maschera by Verdi, Lipsia 2005, Teneke 2007. *Publications:* L'arte lunga 1992, Arnaldo Pomodoro 1995, Scritti critici per Arnaldo Pomodoro e opere dell'artista 1955–2000 2000, Arnaldo Pomodoro nei giardini del Palais-Royal di Parigi 2003, Arnaldo Pomodoro e il Museo Poldi Pezzoli, La Sala d'Armi 2004, Corona nella Cattedrale di Milwaukee (with Giuseppe Maraniello) 2004, Catalogo della scultura 2007. *Leisure interests:* photography, theatre, literature. *Address:* Via Vigevano 5, 20144 Milan, Italy. *Telephone:* (02) 58104131. *Fax:* (02) 89401303 (office). *E-mail:* info@arnaldopomodoro.it (office). *Website:* www.fondazionearnaldopomodoro.it (office).

POMPEO, Michael (Mike) Richard, JD; American lawyer, politician and government official; *Secretary of State;* b. 30 Dec. 1963, Orange, Calif.; s. of Wayne Pompeo and Dorothy Pompeo (née Mercer); m. Susan Pompeo; one s.; ed US Mil. Acad., West Point, Harvard Law School; army service 1986–91, served with 2nd

Squadron, 7th Cavalry, Fourth Infantry Div.; fmr Ed. Harvard Law Review; Co-Founder and CEO Thayer Aerospace (later renamed Nex-Tech Aerospace) 1997; Pres. Sentry International (oilfield equipment co.) 2003; mem. House of Reps from Kansas 4th Dist 2011–17, mem. House Energy and Commerce Cttees; Dir, CIA 2017–18; Sec. of State 2018–; mem. Nat. Rifle Asscn; Republican. *Address:* Department of State, 2201 C St, NW, Washington, DC 20520, USA (office). *Telephone:* (202) 647-4000 (office). *Fax:* (202) 647-6738 (office). *Website:* www.state.gov (office).

PONCE CEVALLOS, Javier; Ecuadorean journalist, banker and fmr government official; *President, Banco Nacional de Fomento;* b. 28 April 1948, Quito; ed Escuela de Sociología y Ciencias Políticas, Univ. Central del Ecuador; columnist, El Tiempo newspaper 1966–70; with Ministry of Agric. 1973–77; Dir Artes cultural review 1977–78; Sec. Gen. Ecumenical Cttee of Projects 1986–97, Coordinator 1997; Ed. HOY 1992–99, de investigaciones 1999–2001, columnist 1989–2001; columnist, El Universo 2001–; Ed. Enciclopedia Planeta 2002–03; Personal Sec. to Pres. Rafael Correa 2006–08; Minister of Nat. Defence 2008–12; of Agric. 2012–13; Pres. Banco Nacional de Fomento 2013–. *Address:* Banco Nacional de Fomento, Antonio Ante Oeste 1–15 y Avda 10 de Agosto, Casilla 685, Quito, Ecuador (office). *Telephone:* (2) 294-6500 (office). *Fax:* (2) 257-0286 (office). *E-mail:* sugerencias@bnf.fin.ec (office). *Website:* www.bnf.fin.ec (office).

PONCE ENRILE, Juan, LLM; Philippine lawyer and government official; b. 14 Feb. 1924, Gonzaga, Cagayan; s. of Alfonso Ponce Enrile and Petra Furagganan; m. Cristina Castañer 1957; one s. one d.; ed Ateneo de Manila, Univ. of the Philippines and Harvard Law School; practising corp. lawyer and Prof. of Law 1956–64; Under-Sec. of Finance 1966–68; Acting Sec. of Finance; Acting Insurance Commr; Acting Commr of Customs; Sec. of Justice 1968–70; Sec. of Nat. Defence 1970–71 (resgnd), 1972–78, Minister 1978–86 (reappointed under Aquino Govt 1986); Chair. Cttee on Nat. Security, Defense, Peace and Order; mem. Senate and Opposition Leader (Nacionalista Party) 1987–92, 1995–2001, 2004–16, Senate Pres. 2008–13; mem. House of Reps 1992–95, mem. Finance, Appropriations and Steering Cttees; Chair., Bd of Dirs Philippine Nat. Bank until 1978, Nat. Investment and Devt Co., United Coconut Planters Bank, Nat. Disaster Control Center; Dir Philippine Communications Satellite Corpn; Trustee and Sec., Bd of Trustees, Cultural Centre of the Philippines; Chair. Exec. Cttee, Nat. Security Council; mem. Bd, Nat. Econ. and Devt Authority, Energy Devt, Philippine Nat. Oil Co., Nat. Environmental Protection Council, Philippine Overseas Telecommunications Corpn, Philippine Crop Insurance Corpn; mem. numerous law and commercial asscns; two hon. degrees; Commdr, Philippine Legion of Honour 1986; Mahaputra Adipranada Medal (Indonesia) 1975, People of the Year Award 2010 (Govt Service) 2011. *Publications include:* A Proposal on Capital Gains Tax 1960, Income Tax Treatment of Corporate Merger and Consolidation Revisited 1962, Tax Treatment of Real Estate Transactions 1964, Where There's a Will 1995, Juan Ponce Enrile – A Memoir 2012. *Leisure interests:* reading, golf, tennis, swimming, water-skiing, fishing. *Address:* 2305 Morado Street, Dasmariñas Village, Makati, Metro Manila, Philippines (home). *Website:* www.juanponceenrile.com.

PONCELET, Christian; French politician; b. 24 March 1928, Blaise (now part of Vouziers) in the Ardennes; s. of Raoul Poncelet and Raymonde Poncelet (née Chamillard); m. Yvette Miclot 1949; two d.; ed Coll. Saint-Sulpice, Paris and Nat. Ecole Professionelle des Postes, Télégraphes et Télécommunications; Deputy (Union pour un Mouvement Populaire—UMP) to Nat. Ass. for the Vosges 1962–77; Sec. of State, Ministry of Social Affairs 1972–73, Ministry of Employment, Labour and Population 1973–74; Sec. of State for the Civil Service attached to Prime Minister March–May 1974; Sec. of State for the Budget, Ministry of Econ. Affairs and Finance 1974–77, for Relations with Parl. 1977; Conseiller Général, Remiremont 1963–73; Pres. Conseil Général des Vosges 1976–2015; Sénateur des Vosges 1977–2014, Pres. Comm. for Finance, Budgetary Control and Econ. Accounts of the Nation to the Senate 1986–98, Pres. of Senate 1998–2008; mem. European Parl. 1979–80; Mayor of Remiremont 1983–2001; Pres. groupe France-Viet Nam, Groupe français de l'Union Interparlementaire; mem. French Section Assemblée parlementaire de la francophonie; mem. Institut de France, Acad. des Sciences morales et politiques; Grand Cross of the Royal Norwegian Order of Merit 2000. *Leisure interest:* hunting. *Address:* 17 rue du Etats-Unis, 88200 Remiremont, France (home).

PONDER, Sir Bruce Anthony John, Kt, MB, BChir, PhD, FRS, FRCP, FRCPath, FMedSci; British medical scientist, oncologist and academic; *Professor Emeritus of Oncology, University of Cambridge;* b. 25 April 1944, Haywards Heath, Sussex, England; s. of Anthony West Ponder and Dorothy Mary Ponder (née Peachey); m. Margaret Ann Hickinbotham; four c.; ed Univ. of Cambridge; began career as clinician, St Thomas' Hosp., London; fmr Sr Registrar Oncology Dept, St Bartholomew's Hosp., London; Researcher, Imperial Cancer Research Fund 1973–77; Hamilton Fairley Fellowship, Harvard Medical School, USA 1977–78; Researcher, Inst. of Cancer Research, Sutton 1978, also clinical appointment, Royal Marsden Hosp.; Prof. and Head of Dept of Oncology, Univ. of Cambridge 1996–, also becoming Li Ka-shing Prof. of Oncology 2007–11, Prof. Emer. 2013–; Co-Dir Hutchison/MRC Research Centre; Co-Dir Strangeways Research Labs 1996–2009; Founding Dir, Cancer Research UK Cambridge Inst. 2006–13, Cambridge Cancer Centre 2010–15; Founder-Fellow, Acad. of Medical Sciences; Ed.-in-Chief Breast Cancer Research 1999–2009; Pres. British Asscn for Cancer Research 2010–14; mem. Bd of Dirs, American Asscn for Cancer Research 2007–11; Founder Faculty, Acad. of the American Asscn for Cancer Research 2013; Trustee, Cancer Research UK 2016–; Hamilton Fairley Award, Eur Soc. for Medical Oncology 2004, MD Anderson Cancer Center Bertner Award 2007, NCI Alfred Knudson Award for Cancer Genetics 2008, Ambuj Nath Bose Prize, Royal Coll. of Physicians 2008, Lifetime Achievement Award in Cancer Research, Cancer Research UK 2013. *Publications:* more than 500 peer-reviewed scientific papers on cancer research and genetics. *Leisure interests:* photography, gardening, golf, travel, wine. *Address:* Cancer Research UK, Cambridge Research Institute, Li Ka Shing Centre, Robinson Way, Cambridge, CB2 0RE, England (office). *Telephone:* (1223) 761860 (office). *E-mail:* bruce.ponder@cruk.cam.ac.uk (office). *Website:* www.cambridgecancer.org.uk (office).

PONOMAREV, Aleksander Sergeyevich; Russian journalist and television executive; *Director General, Centre Television Broadcasting Company;* b. 13 Oct. 1956; m. Nadezhda Grigoryevna Ponomareva; one s. one d.; ed Higher Komsomol

(Young Communists' League) School, Saratov State Univ.; engineer, Research Inst. of Mechanics and Physics, Saratov State Univ. 1978; Komsomol work 1979–87; Deputy Ed.-in-Chief Cen. Youth Programme Section, USSR Cen. TV 1987–88, Ed.-in-Chief 1988–91; Dir Creative Union of Experimental TV, Ostankino 1992–93, First Deputy Dir-Gen. Oskankino 1992–93; Co-founder and Vice-Pres. Moscow Ind. Broadcasting Corpn (MNVK), Dir-Gen. 1993–2001, First Vice-Pres. 1997–2001, Deputy Dir-Gen. and Exec. Dir March–April 2001; Dir-Gen. Kultura (Culture) State TV and Radio Broadcasting Co. and Deputy Chair. All-Russian State TV and Radio Broadcasting Co. (VGTRK) 2001–06; Dir-Gen. Centre TV Broadcasting Co. 2006–; Deputy Chair. All-Russian State TV Co.; Dir Cultura Camel 2001–. *Address:* Centre TV Broadcasting Company, 115184 Moscow, Building 1, ul. B. Tatarskaya 33, Russia (office). *Telephone:* (495) 959-39-01 (office). *Fax:* (495) 959-39-03 (office). *E-mail:* ic@centertv.ru (office). *Website:* www.tvc.ru (office).

PONS, Bernard Claude, DenM; French physician and fmr politician; b. 18 July 1926, Béziers, Hérault; s. of Claude Pons and Véronique Vogel; m. Josette Cros 1952; one s. three d.; ed Lycées, Marseilles and Toulouse and Faculté de Médecine, Montpellier; gen. practitioner, Cahors 1954; mem. Union pour la nouvelle République 1967–68, Union des Démocrats pour la République 1968–78, Rassemblement pour la République (RPR) 1978–2002, Union pour un Mouvement Populaire (UMP) 2002–08; Deputy to Nat. Ass. 1967–69, 1973–86, 1988–95, 1997–2002, Pres. RPR Group 1988–95; Conseiller-Gen. Cajarc canton 1967–78; Sec. of State, Ministry of Agric. 1969–73; mem. Conseil-Gen. Ile-de-France 1978; Sec.-Gen. RPR 1979–84; Paris City Councillor 1983–2008; apptd Pres. Admin. Council, Paris Câble 1984; Rep. to Ass. of EC 1984–85; Minister for Overseas Departments and Territories 1986–88; Minister of Town and Country Planning, Equipment and Transport May–Nov. 1995, for Capital Works, Housing, Transport and Tourism 1995–97.

PONSOLLE, Patrick; French business executive; b. 20 July 1944, Toulouse; s. of Jean Ponsolle and Marie-Rose Courthaliac; m. Nathalie Elie Lefebvre 1983; two d.; ed Lycées Janson-de-Sailly and Henry IV, Paris, Ecole normale supérieure de la rue d'Ulm, Ecole Nat. d'Admin; civil servant Ministry of Econs and Finance 1973–77; Financial Attaché Embassy, Washington 1977–79; Head of Mission for Dir of Forecasting, Ministry of Econs and Finance 1980; Sec.-Gen. Nat. Accounts and Budgets Comm. 1980–81; Deputy Chief of Staff to Budget Minister 1981–83; Deputy Dir, Asst Man. Dir Compagnie de Suez 1983–87, Man. Dir 1988, Chief Exec. 1991–93; Vice-Chair., Man. Dir then Chair. and Man. Dir Suez International 1985; Chair. Soc. financière pour la France et les pays d'outre mer (Soffo) 1990–96; Co-Chair. Eurotunnel Group, Chair. Eurotunnel SA 1994–96, Exec. Co-Chair. 1996–2001; Dir Unichem PLC 1998–2006; Dir (non-exec.) Alliance Boots PLC 2006–07; Adviser, Morgan Stanley Dean Witter (now Morgan Stanley) 1999, Chair. Morgan Stanley France 2001–09, also served as Vice-Chair. and Man. Dir; Vice-Chair. Rothschild & Co 2009–14; Dir numerous cos, including France Télécom, Banque Indosuez; chair. numerous bodies; mem. Supervisory Bd PAI Partners; mem. Advisory Cttee Amundi Asset Man. *Address:* c/o PAI Partners,232 rue de Rivoli, 75054 Paris Cedex 01 (office); 3 rue Danton, 75006 Paris, France (home).

PONTA, Victor-Viorel, BA, MA; Romanian lawyer and politician; b. 20 Sept. 1972, Bucharest; m. 1st Roxana Ponta (divorced 2006); one s.; m. 2nd Daciana Sârbu 2008; one d.; ed Neculce High School, Univ. of Bucharest, Univ. of Catania, Italy, Carol I Nat. Defence Univ., Social Democratic Inst., Bucharest; Lecturer in Criminal Law, Romanian-American Univ. 1996–98, 2002–12; worked as Prosecutor, Sector 1 Courthouse 1995–98; Prosecutor, Supreme Court of Justice in anti-corruption div. dealing with econ. and financial crimes 1998–2001; co-ordinated Bureau for Combating Money Laundering 2000–01; held rank of Sec. of State as Head of Govt's Control Dept 2001–04; joined Supervisory Council of Authority for State Assets Recovery 2001, mem. special cttee investigating penal infractions committed by mems of govt 2001; Minister-Del. for Control of Int. Grant Programmes Implementation and for Monitoring the Application of EU Acquis Communautaire 2004; mem. Partidul Social Democrat (PSD—Social Democratic Party) 2002–, Head of Interim Nat. Council of Tineretul Social Democrat (TSD—Social Democratic Youth) July–Nov. 2002, mem. Nat. Council of PSD Oct. 2002–, mem. Exec. Bureau Nov. 2002–, Pres. TSD Nov. 2002–06, Vice-Pres. PSD 2006–10, Pres. 2010–15; mem. Camera Deputaţilor (Chamber of Deputies) for Gorj Co. 2004–, served as Sec. and Vice-Pres. of its Perm. Bureau; Minister-Del. for Relations with Parl. in Office 2008–09; apptd Vice-Pres. European Community Org. of Socialist Youth 2005; Prime Minister of Romania 2012–June 2015, July–Nov. 2015 (resgnd); unsuccessful cand. in presidential election 2014; Jt Leader, Uniunea Social Liberală (LUS—Social Liberal Union) 2012–14; Vice-Pres. Socialist International 2012–; renounced his doctorate in law following allegations of plagiarism Dec. 2014; Kt, Nat. Order for Faithful Service 2002, Ordine della Stella della Solidarietà Italiana 2004. *Achievements include:* won nat. championships in basketball 1989, auto-racing 2008. *Publications:* Scurt istoric al justiţiei penale internaţionale 2001, Drept Penal – Partea generală 2004, Curtea Penală Internaţională 2004, Noi provocări ale secolului XXI – Constituţia europeană. Importanţă, efecte şi natură juridică 2005, Drept penal. Partea generală 2006. *Address:* Partidul Social Democrat (Social Democratic Party), 011346 Bucharest 1, Şos. Kiseleff 10 (office); 210191, jud Gorj, Târgu Jiu, Str. Victoriei 2–4; Birou de avocatură, Bucharest, bl. Dimitrie Cantemir, 2A, bl. P2 sc. 1 et. 1 ap. 3 Sector 4, Romania. *Telephone:* (21) 2222953 (office); (253) 214224. *Fax:* (21) 2223272 (office); (353) 810513 (office). *E-mail:* drp@guv.ro (office), pontavictor@ymail.com (office), info@psd.ro (office). *Website:* www.psd.ro (office); www.victorponta.ro.

PONTAL, Jean-François; French business executive; b. 17 April 1943, Chaton; m. Martine Lorain-Broca 1968; two c.; ed Centres d'Etudes Supérieures des Techniques Industrielles; human resources consultant, Inst. Bossard; Vice-Pres. of Operations, then of Resources and Markets, Carrefour; CEO Pryca (Spanish subsidiary), mem. bd with responsibility for S Europe 1993–96; Head of Consumer Services Div., France Télécom 1996–2001, apptd Pres. Wanadoo 2000, Exec. Vice-Pres. France Télécom –2001, CEO Orange (after merger with France Télécom) 2001–03 (retd); Adviser, Retail Banking Segment ING Direct France 2003; mem. Bd of Dirs Sonaecom 2003–, Southwing S.L. 2004–, Investcom LLC 2005–, OTL 2006–; Chevalier, Ordre nat. du Mérite. *Leisure interests:* sailing, tennis.

PONTI, Michael; German/American concert pianist; b. 29 Oct. 1937, Freiburg, Germany; s. of Joseph Ponti and Zita Wüchner; m. 1st Carmen Wiechmann 1962 (divorced 1971); one s. two d.; m. 2nd Beatrice van Stappen 1984; one s.; ed studied piano in Washington, DC with Gilmour McDonald and in Frankfurt with Erich Flinsch; taken to USA as a child; debut in Vienna performing Bartók's Second Piano Concerto under conductor Wolfgang Sawallisch 1964, New York 1972; has toured extensively world-wide, including visits to Southern Africa 1974, Australia 1977; f. own trio (with violinist Robert Zimansky and cellist Jan Polasek) 1977; suffered a stroke 2000, now performs concerts for left hand only; First Prize, Busoni Piano Competition (Italy) 1964. *Recordings:* more than 80 albums; noted for his wide-ranging recordings of the unknown romantic repertoire; recorded a series of concertos, many of which had never been recorded before, and some of which have been unrecorded since, by composers including Clara Schumann, Ignaz Moscheles, Charles-Valentin Alkan, Sigismond Thalberg, Moritz Moszkowski and Hans Bronsart von Schellendorff; committed to disc the complete piano music of Scriabin, much of which was otherwise unavailable then; also recorded the complete piano music of Tchaikovsky and Rachmaninoff. *Address:* Heubergstrasse 32, 82438 Eschenlohe, Germany. *Telephone:* (8824) 913754.

PONTING, Ricky Thomas, AO; Australian fmr professional cricketer; b. 19 Dec. 1974, Launceston, Tasmania; s. of Graeme Ponting and Lorraine Ponting (née Campbell); m. Rianna Jennifer Cantor 2002; two d.; ed Brooks Sr High School, Launceston; right-handed higher middle-order batsman; occasional right-arm medium-pace and off break bowler; slips and close catching fielder; played for Tasmania 1992–2013 (Capt. 2001–02, 2007–08), Australia 1995–2012 (Vice-Capt. Test side 2000–03, Capt. 2003–11, Capt. ODI side 2002–11), Somerset 2004, Kolkata Knight Riders 2008, Hobart Hurricanes 2011–13, Mumbai Indians (Capt.) 2013, Surrey June–July 2013, Antigua Hawksbills 2013, ICC (Int. Cricket Council) World XI; First-class debut: Nov. 1992; Test debut: Australia v Sri Lanka, Perth 8–11 Dec. 1995; final Test: Australia v South Africa, Perth 30 Nov.–3 Dec. 2012; One-Day Int. (ODI) debut: Australia v S Africa, Wellington, NZ 15 Feb. 1995; T20I debut: NZ v Australia, Auckland, NZ 17 Feb. 2005; played in 168 Tests, took five wickets and scored 13,378 runs (41 centuries, 62 fifties), highest score 257, average 51.85; ODIs: 375 matches, took three wickets and scored 13,704 runs, highest score 164, average 42.03; Capt. of Australia's World Cup winning side 2003 (scored 140 in final against India), 2007; second batsmen ever to score more than 1,500 runs in a calendar year 2003; only fourth batsman to score more than 11,000 career runs in Test cricket 2009; highest Australian run-scorer in history of Test cricket 31 July 2009; only the third player and the first Australian (after Sachin Tendulkar and Rahul Dravid) to pass 13,000 career Test runs 2012; most successful Australian capt. of all time; player with Most World Cup matches as capt.; retd from all forms of the game 2013; commentator, Big Bash League, Network Ten; One-Day Int. Player of the Year 2002, ICC Test Player of the Year 2003, 2004, 2006, Allan Border Medal as Australian Cricketer of the Year 2004, 2006, 2007, 2009 (jtly), Wisden Cricketer of the Year 2006, Compton-Miller Medal (The Ashes Man of the Series) 2006–07, ICC Player of the Year 2006, 2007, voted Cricinfo Player of the Decade 2000–09 2010, inducted into Australian Inst. of Sport 'Best of the Best' 2011, inducted into ICC Cricket Hall of Fame 2018. *Leisure interests:* football, golf. *Address:* c/o DSEG, Level 1, 189 Rouse Street, Port Melbourne, Vic. 3207, Australia (office). *Telephone:* (3) 9645-6911 (office). *Fax:* (3) 9646-8470 (office). *E-mail:* enquiries@dseg.com.au (office). *Website:* dseg.com.au (office).

PONTZIOUS, Richard; American conductor and artistic director; *Artistic Director and Conductor, Asian Youth Orchestra;* ed studied with Lou Harrison, Sergiu Comissiona, Ferdinand Leitner and Josef Krips; has conducted orchestras, bands and choirs in Europe and Asia; first overseas musician to be invited to live for an extended time in China following Cultural Revolution, Conductor-in-Residence at Shanghai Conservatory of Music early 1980s, toured with Conservatory orchestra and conducted orchestras of Nanjing, Hangzhou, Fuzhou and Harbin (revived its Summer Arts Festival), recently returned to the Conservatory to conduct programme including Chinese premiere of Martinu's Rhapsody for Viola and Orchestra with San Francisco Symphony Assoc. Prin. Violist Jay Liu; Co-founder Asian Youth Orchestra 1987, Artistic and Exec. Dir and Conductor 2002–, recent tours have included live TV and radio broadcasts from Hong Kong Cultural Centre Concert Hall as well as performances in Nat. Centre for Performing Arts, Beijing, Shanghai Oriental Arts Centre, Xian Concert Hall, Dewan Petronas Filharmonik, Kuala Lumpur, Esplanade, Singapore, Hanoi Opera House marking its 100th anniversary, Hong Kong Cultural Centre, Hong Kong Coliseum, Nat. Concert Hall, Taipei, Opera City Concert Hall, Tokyo; collaborations with Yehudi Menuhin, Sergiu Comissiona, James Judd, Wang Jian, Yo-Yo Ma, Alisa Weilerstein, Elmar Oliveira, Gidon Kremer, Elly Ameling, Cho-Liang Lin, Gil Shaham, Young Uck Kim, Stefan Jackiw, Jean Luis Steuerman and Alicia de Larrocha; Bronze Bauhina Star, Hong Kong Govt 2000. *Achievements:* gained pvt. pilot's licence 2000, piloted a single engine Piper Archer across USA 2005. *Address:* Suite 15A, One Capital Place, 18 Luard Road, Wanchai, Hong Kong Special Administrative Region, People's Republic of China (office). *Telephone:* (852) 28661623 (office). *Fax:* (852) 28613340 (office). *E-mail:* ayo@asianyouthorchestra.com (office). *Website:* www.asianyouthorchestra.com (office).

POO, Murdaya Widyawimarta; Indonesian business executive and politician; b. (Poo Tjie Gwan), 21 Jan. 1941, Blitar, East Java; m. Siti Hartati Murdaya; four c.; f. Berca Group (now Central Cipta Murdaya—CCM), cos include PT Abdibangun Buana, PT Asea Brown Boveri Sakti, PT Intracawood Manufacturing (Intraca), also owns Nike Shoe factories in Indonesia; Dir Metropolitan Kentjana (real estate co.); Commr PT Dharmala Intiland; fmr mem. Partai Demokrasi Indonesia Perjuangan (expelled Dec. 2009), mem. House of Reps (parl.) for Banten –2009; Pres. Dir Pondok Indah Golf Course. *Address:* c/o Metropolitan Kentjana, Jl Metro Pd Indah Bl III-B Pon., Jakarta 12310, Indonesia (office).

POOLE, David James, PPRP, ARCA; British artist; b. 5 June 1931, London, England; s. of Thomas Herbert Poole and Catherine Poole; m. Iris Mary Toomer 1958; three s.; ed Stoneleigh Secondary School, Wimbledon School of Art, Royal Coll. of Art; Sr Lecturer in Painting and Drawing, Wimbledon School of Art 1961–77; Pres. Royal Soc. of Portrait Painters 1983–91; work in HM The Queen's collection, London and in pvt. collections in Australia, Bermuda, France, Germany, S Africa, Saudi Arabia, Switzerland and USA; solo exhbns in Zurich and London; portraits include: HM Queen Elizabeth II, HRH Prince Philip, HM

Queen Elizabeth the Queen Mother, HRH Prince Charles, HRH Prince Andrew, HRH Prince Edward, HRH The Princess Royal, The Duke of Kent, Earl Mountbatten of Burma, mems of royal staff including Sir Alan Lascelles, Sir Michael Adeane, Sir Martin Charteris, Sir Philip Moore, Sir William Heseltine, Sir Robert Fellowes, Sir Robin Janvrin, mems of govt, industry, commerce, medicine and acad. and legal professions. *Leisure interests:* French travel, food and drink. *Address:* Trinity Flint Barn, Weston Lane, Weston, Petersfield, GU32 3NN, England. *Telephone:* (1730) 265075. *E-mail:* david@trinity04.fsnet.co.uk.

POON, Christine A., MS, MBA; American business executive; *Dean, Fisher College of Business;* b. Cincinnati, Ohio; d. of James Poon and Virginia Poon; m. Mike Tweedle; ed Northwestern, St Louis and Boston Univs; joined Bristol-Myers Squibb in 1985, various man. positions including Pres. and Gen. Man. Squibb Diagnostics' Canadian operation 1994, Sr Vice-Pres. for Canada and Latin America, Pharmaceutical Operations –1997, Pres. Medical Devices 1997–98, Pres. Int. Medicines 1998–2000; Co. Group Chair. Pharmaceuticals Group, Johnson & Johnson 2000–01, mem. Exec. Cttee and Worldwide Chair. Pharmaceuticals Group 2001–03, Worldwide Chair. Medicines and Nutritionals 2003–09, Vice-Chair., mem. Office of the Chair. and mem. Bd Dirs Johnson & Johnson 2005–09; Dir, mem. Finance Cttee and Investment Cttee, Prudential Financial, Inc. 2006–; mem. Advisory Bd Healthcare Businesswomen's Asscn; Dean and John W. Berry, Sr Chair in Business, Ohio State Univ.'s Fisher Coll. of Business 2009–; Dir, mem. Compensation Cttee and Corporate Governance & Compliance Cttee, Regeneron Pharmaceuticals, Inc. 2010–; mem. Bd Dirs Fox Chase Cancer Center, Phila; Healthcare Businesswomen's Asscn Woman of the Year 2004. *Address:* The Fisher College of Business, The Ohio State University, 201 Fisher Hall, 2100 Neil Avenue, Columbus, OH 43210, USA (office). *Telephone:* (614) 292-2666 (office). *Website:* fisher.osu.edu (office).

POON, Chung-Kwong, OBE, BSc, PhD, DSc, CChem, FRSC, JP; Hong Kong chemist, university president and academic; *President Emeritus, The Hong Kong Polytechnic University;* b. 1940, Hong Kong; m.; three c.; ed St Paul's Co-educational Coll., Univ. of Hong Kong, Univ. of London, UK; Post-doctoral Research Fellow, Univ. Coll. London 1967, Calif. Inst. of Tech., USA 1967–68 (Visiting Research Assoc. 1976, 1979); Visiting Research Assoc., Univ. of Southern California 1972; Lecturer in Chem., Univ. of Hong Kong 1968–75, Prof. of Chem. 1982–90, Dean of Faculty of Science 1983–90; Dir Hong Kong Polytechnic 1991–94; Pres. The Hong Kong Polytechnic Univ. 1991–2008, Pres. Emer. 2009–; has chaired or been a mem. of numerous cttees of Hong Kong Govt and of industrial, business and educational sectors, including mem. Legis. Council 1985–91, Preparatory Cttee for Hong Kong Special Admin. Region 1994–97; Founding Chair. Govt's Cttee on Science and Tech. 1988–91; mem. CPPCC Nat. Cttee 1998–; Chair. Radiological Protection Advisory Group 1989–2007; Consultant of Science and Tech. Consulting Cttee, Shenzhen Municipal People's Govt 2000–; mem. Policy Consultative Cttee, Shaanxi Prov. 2000–; mem. Nuclear Safety Consultative Cttee, Guangdong Daya Bay Nuclear Power Station 1986, Huaqiao Univ. Council 1992–, Shantou Univ. Council 2000–07; mem. Bd of Dir K. Wah Int. Holdings Ltd 2009–15; Fellow, Univ. Coll. London 1996; Foreign mem. Russian Acad. of Eng 2004; apptd a non-official JP 1989; Hon. Prof. at several univs on Chinese mainland; Gold Bauhinia Star 2002; recipient of UK Commonwealth Scholarship 1964–67, Fulbright Scholarship 1967–68, honoured as one of "Ten Outstanding Young Persons in Hong Kong" 1979. *Address:* Office of the President Emeritus, The Hong Kong Polytechnic University, Yuk Choi Road, Hung Hom, Kowloon, Hong Kong Special Administrative Region, People's Republic of China (office). *Telephone:* 27665381 (office). *Fax:* 27731447 (office). *E-mail:* pckpoon@polyu.edu.hk (office). *Website:* www.polyu.edu.hk (office).

POON, Sir Dickson, Kt, CBE, SBS; Hong Kong business executive and philanthropist; *Group Executive Chairman, Dickson Concepts (International) Limited;* s. of Poon Kam Kai; m. 1st Marjorie Yang (divorced); one d.; m. 2nd Michelle Yeoh (q.v.) 1988 (divorced 1991); m. 3rd Pearl Yu 1992; ed St Joseph's Coll., Hong Kong, Uppingham School, UK and Occidental Coll., Los Angeles, USA; apprenticeship in watchmaking at Chopard's, Geneva, Switzerland; returned to Hong Kong and opened first Dickson watch and jewellery shop 1980; Co-founder (with Sammo Hung) DMV film co. 1983; Head of Dickson Concepts, Hong Kong, operating more than 240 boutiques and outlets throughout SE Asia and in China; acquired French co. S.T. Dupont label 1987, sold 1997; acquired stake in Harvey Nichols, London 1991, floated co. 1996, pvt. takeover 2002, opened brs in Leeds 1997, Edinburgh 2002, Manchester 2003; bought 85% stake in Hong Kong and Shenzhen brs of Japanese dept store Seibu 1996; sole benefactor of Hong Kong Univ.'s Man. Inst.; Silver Bauhinia Star; The Dickson Poon China Centre, St Hugh's Coll., Oxford named in his honour 2010, The Dickson Poon School of Law, King's Coll., London named in his honour 2012. *Address:* Dickson Concepts (International) Ltd, Fourth Floor, East Ocean Centre, 98 Granville Road, Tsimshatsui East, Kowloon, Hong Kong (office). *Telephone:* 2311-3888 (office). *Fax:* 2311-3323 (office). *E-mail:* info@dickson.com.hk (office). *Website:* www .dickson.com.hk (office).

POOS, Jacques F., Dr.Oec; Luxembourg politician; b. 3 June 1935; m.; three c.; ed Athénée Grand-Ducal, Univ. of Lausanne and Luxembourg Int. Univ.; Ministry of Nat. Economy 1959–62; Service d'Etudes et de Statistiques Economiques (STATEC) 1962–64; Dir Imprimerie Coopérative 1964–76; Pres. SYTRAGAZ 1970–76; MP 1974–76; Minister of Finance, Gov. IBRD, IMF, EIB 1976–79; Dir Banque Continentale du Luxembourg SA 1980–82, Banque Paribas (Luxembourg) SA 1982–84; Vice-Pres. Parti Socialiste 1982; Deputy Prime Minister and Minister of Foreign Affairs, Foreign Trade and Co-operation 1984–99; Pres. EU Council of Ministers 1985, 1991, 1997; mem. European Parl. 1999–2004, mem. Comm. for Foreign Affairs, Human Rights, Public Security and Defence Policy; fmr Pres. Council of European Union; currently mem. Council, Banque Centrale du Luxembourg; mem. various Bds of Dirs in financial sector; Hon. DIur (Athens) 2002. *Publications:* Le Luxembourg dans le Marché Commun 1961, Le Modèle Luxembourgeois 1981, La Crise Economique et Financière: est-elle encore maitrisable? 1984; numerous newspaper and periodical articles. *Address:* 45 Square Mayrisch, 4240 Esch-Alzette, Luxembourg (home). *Telephone:* (352) 556425 (home). *Fax:* (352) 570419 (home). *E-mail:* poosj@pt.lu (home).

POP, Iggy; American singer, musician (guitar) and actor; b. (James Jewel Osterberg), 21 April 1947, Ann Arbor, Mich.; ed Univ. of Michigan; formed high-school band Iguanas 1962, Prime Movers 1966; concerts in Michigan, Detroit and Chicago; formed The Stooges (originally the Pyschedelic Stooges) 1967, re-formed 2007–; solo artist 1976–; collaborations with David Bowie 1972–; numerous tours and TV appearances; inducted into Rock and Roll Hall of Fame 2010; Q Award for Best Track (for Bells and Circles) (with Iggy Pop) 2018. *Film appearances:* Rock & Rule (voice) 1983, Sid and Nancy 1986, The Color of Money 1986, Hardware 1990, Cry-Baby 1990, Atolladero 1995, Tank Girl 1995, Dead Man 1995, The Crow – City of Angels (also known as The Crow II) 1996, The Brave 1997, The Rugrats Movie (voice) 1998, Snow Day 2000, Coffee and Cigarettes 2003, Persepolis (voice) 2007. *Television appearances:* Miami Vice (series), The Adventures of Pete & Pete (series). *Radio:* as regular presenter: BBC 6 Music programme 2014–. *Other appearances include:* Driv3r (video game, voice) 2004. *Compositions include:* China Girl (with David Bowie). *Film songs include:* Repo Man (theme song 'Repo Man') 1984, Sid and Nancy (song 'I Wanna Be Your Dog') 1986, Dogs in Space (songs 'Dog Food' and 'Endless Sea') 1987, Slaves of New York (song 'Fall in Love with Me') 1989, Tales from the Crypt (TV series, songs 'Kill City' and 'Five Foot One' for episode 'For Cryin' Out Loud') 1989, Va mourire 1995, Trainspotting (song 'Nightclubbing') 1996, Space Goofs (series theme song) 1997, Full Blast (song 'Loose') 1997, The Brave 1997, Home to Rent (TV series theme song) 1997, Great Expectations (song) 1998, The Wedding Singer (song 'China Girl') 1998, Velvet Goldmine (song 'T.V. Eye') 1998, Whatever (song 'Gimme Danger') 1998, Lock, Stock and Two Smoking Barrels (song 'I Wanna Be Your Dog', as James Oaterberg, Jr) 1998, Radiofreccia (song 'The Passenger') 1998, Born to Lose (song 'Tight Pants') 1999, The Filth and the Fury (song 'No Fun') 2000, Almost Famous (song 'Search and Destroy') 2000, Dogtown and Z-Boys (song 'I Wanna Be Your Dog') 2001, Intimacy (songs 'Consolation Prizes' and 'Penetration', as J. Osterberg alias I. Pop) 2001, Gran Turismo 3: A-Spec (video game) 2001, Killer Barbys vs. Dracula (song 'Candy') 2002, Pro BMX 2 (video game) (song 'The Passenger') 2002, Rugrats Go Wild! (song 'Lust for Life') 2003, Wonderland (song 'Search and Destroy') 2003, The School of Rock (song 'T.V. Eye', as James Osterberg) 2003, The Life Aquatic with Steve Zissou (song 'Search and Destroy') 2004. *Recordings:* albums: with The Stooges: The Stooges 1969, Fun House 1970, Jesus Loves The Stooges 1977, I'm Sick of You 1977, Raw Stooges 1988, Raw Stooges 2 1988, The Weirdness 2007; solo: Raw Power 1973, Metallic KO 1976, The Idiot 1977, Lust For Life 1977, TV Eye Live 1978, Kill City 1978, New Values 1979, Soldier 1980, Party 1981, I'm Sick of You 1981, Zombie Birdhouse 1982, I Got The Right 1983, Blah Blah Blah 1986, Rubber Legs 1987, Live At The Whiskey A Go Go 1988, Death Trip 1988, Instinct 1988, Brick By Brick 1990, American Caesar 1994, Naughty Little Doggie 1996, Heroin Hates You 1997, King Biscuit Flower Hour 1997, Your Pretty Face is Going to Hell 1998, Sister Midnight 1999, Avenue B 1999, Iggy Pop 1999, Hippodrome Paris '77 (live) 1999, Beat 'Em Up 2001, Skull Ring 2003, Preliminaires 2009, Après 2012, Post Pop Depression 2016. *Publications:* I Need More (autobiog.), Iggy Pop's A–Z (autobiog.) 2005. *Website:* www.iggypop.com.

POP, Ioan-Aurel, DHist; Romanian historian and university administrator; *Rector, Universitatea Babeş-Bolyai;* b. 1 Jan. 1955, Sântioana; m. Amelia Pop; one d.; ed Universitatea Babeş-Bolyai; Prof., Industrial High School no. 6 1979–84; Asst Prof., Faculty of History and Philosophy, Universitatea Babeş-Bolyai 1984–90, Lecturer 1990–92, Assoc. Prof. 1992–96, Prof. 1996–, Rector 2012–; Scientific Researcher and Dir Center for Transylvanian Studies 1993–; Visiting Prof. Univ. of Pittsburgh 1991–92, Institut Nat. des Langues et Civilisations Orientales (INALCO), Paris 1998, Univ. of Trento 2001, Universitatea Ca' Foscari, Venice 2003–05; Chair. Editorial Staff, Articles, Creative Research and Art, Haifa, Israel; Pres. Inst. for the Study of Imperial Policies 2009–; Vice-Pres. Nat. History Cttee of Romania; mem. numerous cttees including Int. Relations History Cttee, Int. Science Cttee 1990; mem. Romanian Acad. 2001–, Pres. 2018–; mem. European Acad. of Sciences and Arts 2013, European Center for Studies in Ethnic Issues, Virginia Accademia Nazionale Virgiliana, Mantua 2015; mem. Editorial Bd, Memoirs of the Dept of History and Archeology, Academica Magazine of Romanian Academy, Zagreb magazine, History Magazine of Moldova, Akademos, Acta Musei Napocensis; Corresp. mem. Acad. of Sciences, Letters and Arts 1999–; Hon. mem. Acad. of Sciences of Moldova 2015–; Order of Cultural Merit, Romania 2010, Order of Honour, Moldova 2010, Commdr, Military Order of Romania 2014, Nat. Order "Star of Romania" 2015, Order "Star of Italy", Commdr of the Italian Repub. 2016, Kt, Ordre des Palmes Academiques 2016; Dr hc (Univ. of Alba Iulia), (West Univ. of Timişoara), (Univ. of Oradea), (Bogdan Petriceicu Haşdeu State Univ.), (Universitatea Danubius din Galati), (Lucian Blaga Univ. of Sibiu), (Petru Maior Univ. of Târgu Mureş), (State Univ. of Chişinău); George Bariţiu Prize, Romanian Acad. 1991, Eudoxiu Hurmuzachi Inst. of Excellence Award for Romanians Abroad 2011, Transylvanian Cross, Metropolitan Church of Cluj, Maramures and Salaj 2014, Nicolae Iorga Historical Shop Cultural Foundation 2017, George Apostu Prize, George Apostu Culture Center 2017. *Publications include:* Instituţii medievale româneşti: Adunările cneziale şi nobiliare (boiereşti) din Transilvania în secolele XIV–XVI 1991, Românii şi maghiarii în secolele IX-XIV. Geneza statului medieval în Transilvania 1996, Istoria României: Transilvania (co-author) 1997, Geneza medievală a naţiunilor moderne (secolele XIII–XVI) 1998, Naţiunea română medievală: Solidarităţi etnice româneşti în secolele XIII–XVI 1998, Românii şi România: O scurtă istorie 1998, Istoria, adevărul şi miturile. Note de lectură 2002, Contribuţii la istoria culturii româneşti (cronicile braşovene din secolele XVII-XVIII) 2003, Istoria românilor 2010, Biserică, societate şi cultură în Transilvania secolului al XVI-lea. Între acceptare şi excludere 2012, De manibus Vallacorum scismaticorum... Romanians and Power in the Mediaeval Kingdom of Hungary (The Thirteenth and Fourteenth Centuries) 2013, Cultural Diffusion and Religious Reformation in Sixteenth-Century Transylvania: How the Jesuits Dealt with the Orthodox and Catholic Ideas 2014, Transilvania, starea noastră de veghe 2016, Identitatea românească: Felul de a fi român de-a lungul timpului 2016, Istoria, adevărul şi miturile 2018. *Address:* Faculty of History and Philosophy, Universitatea Babeş-Bolyai, 400084 Cluj-Napoca, Str. Kogalniceanu nr.1, Romania (office). *Telephone:* (26) 4405300 (office). *Fax:* (26) 4446024 (office). *E-mail:* rector@ubbcluj.ro (office). *Website:* hiphi.ubbcluj.ro.

POP, Mihai; Moldovan economist and government official; b. 31 Oct. 1955, Apşa de Mijloc, Transcarpathian Oblast, Ukraine; m.; two c.; ed Chişinău Polytechnic Inst.; Head, Dept for Econ. Planning, Făleşti tobacco factory 1977–86; Industry Coordinator, Făleşti Dist Agricultural and Industrial Agency 1986–89; instructor, organisational agency of Făleşti Dist CP Cttee 1989–90, Head of Finance Dept, then Deputy Head of Finance and Econs Dept 1990–94; Head, State Fiscal Inspectorate of Bălţi Dist 1994–99; Head, Ministry of Finance Fiscal Inspectorate 1999–2005, Deputy Minister of Finance, May–Oct. 2005, Minister of Finance Oct. 2005–08.

POPAL, Ghulam Jilani Jelani, LLB; Afghan/American politician and international organisation official; b. 9 Jan. 1955, Kabul; ed Kabul Univ.; Programme Officer, Salvation Army Refugee Assistance Programme in Pakistan 1982–89; Founder, Afghan Devt Asscn, Founding Dir, Afghan Health and Devt Services 1990–2000; social worker, UN devt programme in Afghanistan 1995–99; Sr Social Worker for San Joaquin County, California, USA 2000–03; Head, Independent Directorate of Local Governance, Kabul 2008–10; Governance Adviser to Pres. of Afghanistan 2012–15; WHO Rep. for Somalia 2013–; mem. Afghan Social Democratic Party. *Address:* Afghan Social Democratic Party, National Bank Club, 3rd Floor, Nader Pashtoon Jadah, Kabul, Afghanistan (office). *Telephone:* 70224793 (mobile) (office). *E-mail:* afghanmellat2@yahoo.com (office).

POPE, Martin, BS, PhD; American physical chemist and academic; *Professor Emeritus of Physical Chemistry, New York University;* b. 22 Aug. 1918, New York City; ed City Coll. of New York, Brooklyn Polytechnic Inst.; parents immigrated to USA from Poland; Scientist, Radiation Lab., Brooklyn Navy Yard 1942; First Lt, US Armed Forces, Pacific theatre, World War II 1945; Research Scientist, Balco Research Lab. 1947–51, Tech. Dir 1951–56; Sr Research Scientist, Radiation and Solid State Physics Lab., New York Univ. 1956–60, Research Assoc. Prof. 1960–65, Assoc. Prof. of Chem. 1965–68, Prof. of Chem. 1968–88, Co-Dir Radiation and Solid State Physics Lab. 1968–83, Dir 1983–88, Prof. Emer. of Physical Chem. 1988–; Visiting Prof. in Puerto Rico 1969–70; Scientific Guest of State and Visiting Prof., China 1978, USSR 1987; Visiting Prof., Univ. of Alexandria, Egypt 1981; Guest Lecturer in Leningrad, Moscow, Kiev, Riga, Israel, Gdansk, Kraków, Puerto Rico, Japan, Czechoslovakia and Germany 1980s; Founder Gordon Conf. on Electronic Processes in Organic Materials 1990; mem. Editorial Bd, Mol. Cryst. Liq. Cryst. 1965–94; Fellow, American Physics Soc., New York Acad. of Sciences, AAAS; Fulbright Scholar 1981, Citation of Honor, US Dept of Energy 1988, Citation of Honor, Gordon Research Confs 1990, Townsend Harris Medal, CUNY 1996, Royal Society Davy Medal for "his pioneering work in the field of molecular semiconductors" 2006, Distinguished Lecturer, CUNY Center for Advanced Tech. 2006. *Publications:* Electronic Processes in Organic Crystals (co-author) 1982, Electronic Processes in Organic Crystals and Polymers (co-author) 1992; more than 100 scientific papers in professional journals. *Address:* Department of Chemistry, New York University, 100 Washington Square East, Room 1001, New York, NY 10003-6688, USA (office). *Telephone:* (212) 998-8414 (office). *Fax:* (212) 252-6605 (office). *E-mail:* martin.pope@nyu.edu (office). *Website:* chemxserver.chem.nyu.edu/MPope/index.htm (office).

POPESCU, Dan Mircea, DJur; Romanian politician; b. 6 Oct. 1950, Bucharest; m.; one c.; ed Faculty of Law, Bucharest Univ.; legal adviser, then researcher at Inst. of Political Sciences, Bucharest and Lecturer in Int. Relations, Acad. of Socio-Political Studies, Bucharest 1975–89; mem. Council Nat. Salvation Front, then mem. of Provisional Council of Nat. Union; Presidential Adviser for matters of domestic policy Dec. 1990; Minister of State for Living Standards and Social Security 1991; Minister of Labour and Social Protection 1991–92, Minister of State, Minister of Labour and Social Protection 1992–96; Deputy Prime Minister 1992–96; Dir Romanian Inst. of Social-Democratic Studies 1999–2001; Vice-Pres. Partidul Social Democrat (PSD), mem. Exec. Bureau 2001–; Senator for Teleorman constituency 1992–; Pres. Labour Comm. of Senate 1996–2000, Econ. Comm. of Senate 2000–03, Vice-Pres. Senate 2003–08; Minister of Labour, Social Solidarity and Family 2004; mem. Ass. Council of Europe (Socialist Group) 2003; Nat. Order of Faithful Service 2003; Grosser Verdienstkreuz mit Stern (Germany) 2005. *Publications:* books and studies in the field of political sciences. *Address:* Senatul României, Calea 13 Septembre 1–3, Bucharest (office); 42–46 Aurel Vlaicu Street, Bucharest, Romania (home). *Telephone:* (21) 3124198 (office). *Fax:* (21) 3158928 (office). *E-mail:* dmpopescu@senat.ro (office).

POPESCU, Dumitru Radu; Romanian writer and editor; *Director General, Editura Academiei Române;* b. 19 Aug. 1935, Păusa Village, Bihor Co.; ed Colls of Medicine and Philology, Cluj; reporter, literary magazine Steaua 1956–69; Ed.-in-Chief, literary magazine Tribuna 1969–82, Contemporanul 1982; Dir Gen., Editurii Academiei Române 2006–; Alt. mem. Cen. Cttee Romanian CP 1968–89, mem. 1979–90; Chair. Romanian Writers' Union 1980–90; Corresp. mem. Romanian Acad. 1997–; Prize of the Writers' Union 1964, 1969, 1974, 1977, 1980, Prize of the Romanian Acad. 1970, Grand Prize for Balkan Writers 1998, Writers' Union Prize 1994, Writers' Asscn of Bucharest Prize 1997, Grand Prize Camil Petrescu 1995. *Publications include:* collections of short stories: Fuga (Flight) 1958, Fata de la miazăzi (A Girl from the South) 1964, Somnul pământului (The Earth's Sleep) 1965, Dor (Longing) 1966, Umbrela de soare (The Parasol) 1967, Prea mic pentru un război aşa de mare (Too Little for Such a Big War) 1969, Duios Anastasia trecea (Tenderly Anastasia Passed) 1967, Leul albastru (The Blue Lion) 1981, The Ice Bridge 1980, the Lame Hare 1981, God in the Kitchen 1994, Truman Capote and Nicolae 1995; novels: Zilele săptămînii (Weekdays) 1959, Vara oltenilor (The Oltenians' Summer) 1964, F 1964, Vînătoarea regală (Royal Hunt) 1973, O bere pentru calul meu (A Beer for My Horse) 1974, Ploile de dincolo de vreme (Rains beyond Time) 1976, Împăratul norilor (Emperor of the Clouds) 1976; plays: Vara imposibilei iubiri (The Summer of Impossible Love) 1966, Vis (Dream) 1968, Aceşti îngeri trişti (Those Sad Angels) 1969, Pisica în noaptea Anului nou (Cat on the New Year's Eve) 1970, Pasărea Shakespeare (The Shakespeare Bird) 1973, Rezervaţia de pelicani (The Pelican Reservation) 1983, Iepurele şchiop (The Lame Rabbit) 1980, Orasul îngerilor (The Angel's City) 1985, Powder Mill 1989, The Bride with False Eyelashes 1994, Love is like a Scab 1995; poems: Cîinele de fosfor (The Phosphorus Dog) 1981; essays: Virgule (Commas) 1978, Galaxy 1994, Ophelia's Complex 1998. *Address:* Office of the Director, Editura Academiei Române, 050711 Bucharest 5, Calea 13 Septembrie nr. 13, Romania (office). *Telephone:* (21) 3188146 (office). *Fax:* (21) 3182444 (office). *Website:* www.ear.ro (office).

POPESCU, Ioan-Iovitz (Iovitzu), PhD; Romanian academic; b. 1 Oct. 1932, Burila-Mare, Mehedintzi Co.; s. of Dumitru Popescu and Elvira Popescu; m. Georgeta-Denisa Chiru 1963 (died 2003); ed Univ. of Bucharest; Asst Prof. of Optics and Gaseous Electronics, Univ. of Bucharest 1955–60, Prof., Faculty of

Physics 1972–, Dean 1972–77, Rector of Univ. of Bucharest 1981–89; Head of Plasma Physics Lab., Inst. of Physics, Bucharest 1960–67, Scientific Deputy Dir 1970–72; Dir Inst. of Physics and Radiation Tech. 1977–81, Romanian Centre for Induced Gamma Emission 1995–2010; Alexander von Humboldt Dozenten Stipendium, Kiel Univ. 1967–69; Corresp. mem. Romanian Acad. 1974, Full mem. 1990 (Pres. Physics Section 1990–92); Hon. Citizen of Mehedintzi Co. 1997, of Drobeta-Turnu Severin City; Labour Order of Romania 1964, Scientific Merit Order 1981, Commdr Loyal Service Nat. Order 2000; Dr hc (Univ. of Craiova) 1998; Prize for Physics, Romanian Acad. 1966, Romanian Omnia Prize 2009, Medal of Honor, Inst. of Atomic Physics 2010, Grigore Moisil Prize for Exact Sciences, Nat. Grand Lodge of Romania 2012. *Publications include:* Ionized Gases 1965, General Physics 1971–75, Plasma Physics and Applications 1981, Plasma Spectroscopy 1987, Optics 1988, The Nobel Prizes for Physics 1901–1998 1998, Word Frequency Studies 2009, The Lambda – Structure of Texts (Grigore Moisil Award for Exact Sciences) 2012, Quantitative Analysis of Poetic Texts 2015; 165 scientific papers cited in about 3,300 foreign works; numerous articles on gas discharges and pioneering works in optogalvanic and multiphoton spectroscopy. *Leisure interests:* linguistics: word frequency studies, quantitative linguistics. *Address:* Str. Fizicienilor 14, Block M4, Apt 6, 077125 Magurele, Bucharest, Romania (home). *Telephone:* 72-4115865 (mobile) (home). *E-mail:* iovitzu@gmail.com (home). *Website:* www.iipopescu.com.

POPESCU, Sandu, PhD; Romanian/British physicist and academic; *Professor of Physics, University of Bristol;* b. 1956, Oradea, Romania; post-doctoral positions with François Englert, then with Abner Shimony and Bahaa Saleh; Reader, Isaac Newton Inst., Univ. of Cambridge 1996–99; Prof. of Physics, Univ. of Bristol 1999–; Adams Prize, Faculty of Math., Univ. of Cambridge 2001, Clifford Paterson Prize and Lecturer, Royal Soc. 2004, Distinguished Research Chair, Perimeter Inst. 2009–11, The Ambassador's Diploma, Romanian Embassy 2010, Distinguished Research Chair, Chapman Univ. 2011–, ERC Advanced Grant on Nonlocality in Space and Time 2011, John Stewart Bell Prize 2012, Templeton Frontiers Distinguished Visiting Research Chair, Perimeter Inst. 2012–15, Wolfson Research Merit Award, Royal Soc. 2012, Dirac Medal, Inst. of Physics 2016. *Publications:* Introduction in Quantum Information and Computation (co-ed.) 1997, Quantum Effects in Biology (co-author); numerous papers in professional journals. *Address:* Office 3.53, H.H. Wills Physics Laboratory, University of Bristol, Tyndall Avenue, Bristol, BS8 1TL, England (office). *Telephone:* (117) 928-8803 (office). *E-mail:* s.popescu@bristol.ac.uk (office). *Website:* www.bristol.ac.uk/physics (office); www.sandupopescu.com.

POPESCU-TĂRICEANU, Călin Constantin Anton, MSc; Romanian politician; *Chairman, Senatul (The Senate);* b. 14 Jan. 1952; m. 1st Cornelia Tăriceanu (divorced); m. 2nd Livia Tăriceanu (divorced); m. 3rd Ioana Popescu-Tăriceanu; m. 4th Loredana Moise; two s.; ed Inst. of Civil Eng, Univ. of Bucharest; started as engineer, Nat. Water Admin, Argeş Co. 1976–77, Industrial Building Co., Bucharest 1977–79; Prof., Faculty of Hydro-technology, Inst. of Civil Eng, Bucharest 1980–91; f. Radio Contact (Romania's first pvt. radio network) 1990, Gen. Man. 1992–96; Founder-mem. Partidul Naţional Liberal (PNL—Nat. Liberal Party) 1990–2014, Exec. Sec. 1990–92, Deputy Chair. 1993–2004, Pres. 2004–09; mem. Constituent Ass. (Parl.) 1990–92, 1996–2012, Leader of PNL Parl. Group 2008–12; Deputy Prime Minister 1996–97; Minister of Industry and Trade 1996–97; Prime Minister 2005–08; Acting Minister of Foreign Affairs 21 March–5 April 2007; mem. Senatul (The Senate) 2012–, Ind. Senator 2014–, Chair., Senatul 2014–; Founder Partidul Liberal Reformator (Liberal Reformist Party) 2014; Co-founder and Co-Pres. Partidul Alianţa Liberalilor şi Democraţilor (Alliance of Liberals and Democrats Party) 2015–; cand. in presidential election 2014; mem. Economy, Reform and Privatization Comm. 1996–2000; Vice-Pres. Fiscal and Budgetary Policies Comm. 2000–; Assoc. Partner, Automotive Trading Services 1993–; Founding mem. and Chair. Automobile and Importers Asscn 1994–97, 2001–03, Hon. Pres. 2003–. *Publications:* 37 scientific papers and articles on water treatment and distribution. *Address:* Senatul (The Senate), 050711 Bucharest 5, Calea 13 Septembrie 1–3, Romania (office). *Telephone:* (21) 4141111 (office). *Fax:* (21) 3160300 (office). *E-mail:* cabinet.presedinte@senat.ro (office). *Website:* www.senat.ro (office); www.tariceanu.ro.

POPHAM, Stuart; British lawyer, business executive and research institute executive; *Chairman, Chatham House;* ed Univ. of Southampton; joined Clifford Chance LLP (law firm) 1976, elected to Partnership 1984, held various roles including leading the Banking and Finance practice areas 1999–2003, Sr Partner (worldwide) 2003–10, Chair. Partnership Council (Supervisory Bd); Chair. TheCityUK 2009–12; Vice-Chair. EMEA Banking, Citigroup 2012–; Council mem. Royal Inst. of Int. Affairs (now Chatham House), Chair. 2012–; mem. Bd of Dirs Legal & General Insurance, The Barbican Centre Trust, Council of the Royal Nat. Lifeboat Inst. (now Vice-Chair.); mem. Bd of Govs Birkbeck Univ. of London 2011–; mem. Advisory Forum of the Saïd Business School, Univ. of Oxford; mem. CBI, fmr Chair. London Region and fmr mem. Chair.'s and other cttees; Hon. QC 2011; Dr hc (Univ. of South Wales) 2013. *Address:* Chatham House, 10 St James's Square, London, SW1Y 4LE, England (office). *Telephone:* (20) 7957-5700 (office). *Fax:* (20) 7957-5710 (office). *E-mail:* contact@chathamhouse.org (office). *Website:* www.chathamhouse.org.uk (office).

POPOFF, Frank Peter, AB, MBA; Bulgarian/American business executive and academic; b. 27 Oct. 1935, Sofia, Bulgaria; s. of Eftim Popoff and Stoyanka Kossoroff; m. Jean Urse; three s.; ed Indiana Univ.; family emigrated to USA 1941; with Dow Chemical Co. 1959–2000, Exec. Vice-Pres. 1985–87, Pres. 1987–92, CEO 1987–96, Chair. 1992–2000, Dir Emer. 2000–; Exec. Vice-Pres., then Pres. Dow Chemical European subsidiary, Switzerland 1976–85; Dir Dow Corning Corpn 1982–, Chemical Bank & Trust Co. 1985–2006, Chemical Financial Corpn 1989–2006 (Chair. 2004–06), American Express Co. 1990–2008, United Technologies Corpn 1996–2008, US West, Inc. 1998–, The Salk Inst., Shin-Etsu Chemical Co. Ltd, Qwest Communications International Inc.; Dir Emer., Indiana Univ. Foundation; mem. ACS, Société de Chimie Industrielle (American Section), Chemical Mfrs Asscn (Bd of Dirs); fmr mem. The Business Roundtable, Business Council; apptd Harold A. 'Red' Poling Chair of Business and Govt, Kelley School of Business, Indiana Univ. 2001; Kt Commdr, Order of Oranje-Nassau (Netherlands) 1989; Leadership Award, US Council for Int. Business 1992, René Dubos Environmental Award 1993, Palladium Medal 1994. *Address:* c/o Kelley School

of Business, Indiana University, Godfrey Graduate and Executive Education Center, 1275 East 10th Street, Bloomington, IN 47405, USA.

POPOLIZIO BARDALES, Néstor Francisco, LLB; Peruvian lawyer, diplomatist and government official; *Minister of Foreign Affairs;* b. 25 Feb. 1955, Pucallpa; m. Irma E. Ríos Garate; one d.; ed National Univ. of San Marcos, Diplomatic Acad. of Peru, Inst. int. d'admin publique (IIAP), Paris; more than 35 years with Ministry of Foreign Affairs, including postings to embassies in USA and Brazil, Perm. Rep. of Peru to UN in New York 2000–05, fmr Asst Sec. for American Affairs, Amb. to Portugal –2013, to Colombia 2013, Deputy Minister of Foreign Affairs 2016–18, Minister of Foreign Affairs 2018–; Grand Cross, Nat. Order of Merit Don José Falcón, Order Al Mérito por Servicios Distinguidos, Order Al Mérito del Servicio Diplomático del Perú, José Gregorio Paz Soldán, Order Libertador San Martín (Argentina), Grand Officer, Order Al Mérito por Servicios Distinguidos, Order Nacional do Cruzeiro do Sul (Brazil). *Address:* Ministry of Foreign Affairs, Jirón Lampa 535, Lima 1, Peru (office). *Telephone:* (1) 2042401 (office). *E-mail:* npopolizio@rree.gob.pe (office). *Website:* www.gob.pe/rree (office).

POPOSKI, Nikola, BEcons, MA, MA; Macedonian economist and politician; b. 24 Oct. 1977, Skopje; m.; three c.; ed Univ. of Skopje, Univ. of Nice, France, EU Univ. of Rennes, France, College of Europe, Bruges, Belgium; Man.'s Asst, British Royal Engineers Quality 1999–2001; Analysis and Devt Dept, Rouen Port Authorities, France 2003–04; Sec., Embassy of France to the Fmr Yugoslavia Repub. of Macedonia 2001–04; Client Relationship Man., DEPFA Bank plc HQ, Dublin, Ireland 2005–06; Team Leader, Jt Research Centre, EC, Brussels 2006–09; Amb. and Head of Mission to the EU 2010–11; Minister of Foreign Affairs 2011–17; EC-trained internal auditor for implementation of integrated environmental management and health and safety standards; mem. Vnatrešno-Makedonska Revolucionerna Organizacija-Demokratska Partija za Makedonsko Nacionalno Edinstvo (VMRO-DPMNE—Internal Macedonian Revolutionary Org.-Democratic Party for Macedonian Nat. Unity); Grand Officer, Order of the Star of Italian Solidarity 2016. *Leisure interest:* sports. *Address:* Vnatrešno-Makedonska Revolucionerna Organizacija-Demokratska Partija za Makedonsko Nacionalno Edinstvo (Internal Macedonian Revolutionary Organization-Democratic Party for Macedonian National Unity), 1000 Skopje, Makedonija 17A, North Macedonia (office). *Telephone:* (2) 3215550 (office). *Fax:* (2) 3215551 (office). *E-mail:* contact@vmro-dpmne.org.mk (office). *Website:* vmro-dpmne.org.mk (office).

POPOV, Anatolii Aleksandrovich, DEconSci; Russian/Chechen politician; b. 10 July 1960, Sovetskoye village, Volgograd Oblast; m.; one s.; ed Volgograd Agricultural Inst.; fmr researcher, agricultural scientific research inst. and irrigation farming scientific research inst.; Sec. of Gorodishchenskii Raion (dist) Cttee of V.I. Lenin Young Communist League (Komsomol), Volgograd Oblast; Adviser to the Council of Ministers of the USSR; fmr Deputy to Head of Man. MENATEP Bank; Financial Dir Rosoboroneksport (Russian Defence Export) State Corpn April–Sept. 1998; fmr Deputy Leader Dept of Food Resources, Govt of Moscow City; Head Centre for Econ. Strategy, Volgograd Oblast; Dir Centre of School of Investment Man. VAPK, Acad. of Nat. Economy, Govt of Russian Fed.; apptd Gen. Dir Direction for the Works of Construction-Restoration in Chechnya (state firm responsible for rebuilding Chechnya) 2001; Deputy Chair. Comm. for the Reconstruction of Chechnya 2002; Prime Minister of the Govt of Chechnya Feb.–Aug. 2003; Acting Pres. Aug.–Oct. 2003; Presidential Asst in Charge of Domestic Politics Dept from 2004. *Address:* c/o Office of the Government, Krasnopresnenskaya nab. 2, 103274 Moscow, Russia.

POPOV, Gavriil Kharitonovich, DEcon; Russian economist; *Chairman, Board of Trustees, International University, Moscow;* b. 31 Oct. 1936, Moscow; s. of Khariton Popov and Theodora Popova; m. Irina Popova 1968; two s.; ed Moscow State Univ.; mem. CPSU 1959–90; teacher at Moscow Univ. 1960–89, Dean of Econ. Faculty 1977–80; introduced man. and business studies to Moscow Univ., Prof. 1971–; Ed.-in-Chief, Voprosy ekonomiki (Questions of Economics) journal 1988–90; People's Deputy of USSR 1989–91; Co-Chair. Inter-regional Group of Deputies, pressing for radical change; Chair. Moscow City Soviet 1990–91; Mayor of Moscow 1991–92 (resgnd); mem. Consultative Council 1991–2000 (Chair. Foreign Policy Cttee 1996–2000); Pres., Int. Univ., Moscow 1991–2015 (Chair., Bd of Trustees 2015–), Int. Union of Economists 1991–, Free Econ. Soc. of Russia 1991–2016; M. Lomonosov Prize 1996. *Publications include:* The Wolfhound Century Leaps on my Neck (10-vol. series). *Leisure interest:* bees. *Address:* International University, 143085 Moscow Region, Russia. *Telephone:* (495) 534-89-83. *Fax:* (495) 534-81-85. *E-mail:* ghpopov@mail.ru. *Website:* www.interun.ru.

POPOV, Vadim Aleksandrovich; Belarusian politician; b. 1940, Demidov, Smolensk Oblast, Russia; m.; two c.; ed Minsk Higher CPSU School, Belarus State Inst. of Agric. Mechanisation; army service 1961–64; Komsomol functionary 1964–71; Dir Sovkhoz Mogilev region 1972–76; party functionary, instructor, Head of Div. Mogilev Regional CP Cttee, First Sec. 1976–92; instructor, Cen. Cttee CP of Belarus 1976–92; worked in agric. roles in complex of Mogilev region 1992–99; First Deputy Minister of Agric. and Food March–July 1999, Minister July–Nov. 2000; mem. Palata Predstaviteley (House of Reps), Nat. Ass. (Parl.) 2000, Chair. 2000–04, 2007–09; Deputy Prime Minister March–June 2001, Prime Minister June–Nov. 2001; Order, Labour Red Banner, three medals; Hon. Diploma Supreme Soviet Belarus SSR.

POPOV, Yevgeny Anatolyevich; Russian writer; b. 5 Jan. 1946, Krasnoyarsk; m. Svetlana Anatoliyevna Vasilyeva; one s.; ed Moscow Inst. of Geological Survey; worked as geologist in various regions 1968–73; mem. USSR Union of Writers 1978, expelled 1979, readmitted 1988; Assoc. mem. Swedish PEN 1980–; Founder and mem. Bd Russian PEN 1989–; Venets Prize (Corona), Moscow 2000, Triumph Prize, Moscow 2010. *Publications:* The Merriment of Old Russia (short stories) 1981, Awaiting Untreacherous Love (short stories) 1989, Wonderfulness of Life (novel) 1990, A Plane to Cologne (short stories) 1991, On the Eve, On the Eve (novel) 1993, The Soul of a Patriot (novel) 1994, Green Musicians (novel) 1998, Thirteen (essays) 1999, Badly Tempered Piano (play), The Bold Boy (play) 2000, A Quiet Barque Named 'Hope' (short stories) 2001, Master Chaos (novel) 2002, Communists (novel) 2003, The Bold Boy (prose, co-author) 2004, Beggars' Opera (prose) 2006, The Song of a First Love (short stories) 2009, Red-hot Iron (short stories) 2009, A Restaurant 'The Birch' (novel) 2009, Arbeit: A Broad Canvas 2012.

Address: Leningradsky prospect 26, korp. 2, Apt 52, 125040 Moscow, Russia. *Telephone:* (495) 612-33-97. *Fax:* (495) 612-33-97. *E-mail:* popov1984@yandex.ru.

POPOVIČ, Štěpán, CSc; Czech engineer; b. 28 Dec. 1945, Ústí nad Labem; m. Iva Popovič; one s. one d.; ed Mechanical Eng and Textile Coll., Liberec, Econs Univ., Prague; with Sklo Union Teplice 1968–89, Dir-Gen. 1989; Dir-Gen. Glav Union from 1991; Country Man. for Czech Operations and Gen. Man. Russian Operations, Glaverbel (acquired by AGC and renamed AGC Flat Glass Europe 2007, AGC Glass Europe 2009), CEO –2011; Pres. Union of Industry and Transport 1992–2000; Chair. FC Teplice 2000–01; Man. of the Year 1993, 1998. *Leisure interests:* sport, music, playing the piano. *Address:* AGC Glass Europe Headquarters, Avenue Jean Monnet 4, 1348 Louvain-la-Neuve, Belgium (office). *Telephone:* (2) 409-30-00 (office). *Fax:* (2) 672-44-62 (office). *E-mail:* info@agc-glass.eu (office). *Website:* www.agc-glass.eu (office).

POPPEMA, Sibrand, MD, PhD; Dutch pathologist, academic and university administrator; *President, University of Groningen;* b. 24 July 1949, Emmen; ed Gymnasium, Ubbo Emmius Lyceum Stadskanaal, Univ. of Groningen; Resident in Pathology, Univ. of Groningen 1974–79; Research Fellow, Dept of Pathology, Christian Albrechts Univ., Kiel, Germany 1978; Research Fellow, Massachusetts Gen. Hosp., Harvard Medical School, Boston, USA 1979–80; Pathologist (Asst Prof.), Univ. of Groningen 1979–82, Pathologist (Assoc. Prof.) 1982–85, J.K. de Cock Prof. of Immunopathology 1985–87, Prof. of Gen. and Surgical Pathology and Chair. Dept of Pathology 1995–98, Head, Dept of Pathology, Univ. Hosp., Groningen, Prof. and Chair. Dept of Pathology and Lab. Medicine 1998–2002, Head, Dept of Pathology and Lab., Univ. Hosp., Groningen, Dean, Faculty of Medical Sciences 1999–2005, Pro-Rector Univ. of Groningen, Prof. of Pathology 2005–08, Dean, Faculty of Medical Sciences, Vice-Pres. Univ. Medical Centre, Groningen, Prof. of Pathology and Pres. Univ. of Groningen 2008–; Prof. of Pathology, Univ. of Alberta, Canada 1987–95, Prof. of Oncology and Dir of Lab. Medicine, Cross Cancer Inst. (CCI), Edmonton, Dir Tumor Immunobiology Program, CCI 1992–95, Dir Dept of Experimental Oncology, CCI, Assoc. Dir of Research, CCI Jan.–Sept. 1995; Visiting Professorship, McGill Univ. 1998, Université de Montreal 1998; Co-founder IQ Corpn (biotech co.), Groningen 1985, Alimmune, Del., USA 2001; Chair. Energy Academy Europe, Platform Sensor Universe, AOG (Academic Postgraduate Courses); mem. Supervisory Bd BMM (Biomedical Materials), Bd Netherlands Antillean Foundation for Clinical Higher Educ., Supervisory Bd Energy Delta Inst., Supervisory Bd Energy Valley, Supervisory Bd Energy Delta Gas Research, Supervisory Bd LifeLines Biobank, Supervisory Bd INCAS3, Supervisory Bd Leveste, Advisory Bd Healthy Ageing Network Northern Netherlands, THES Univ. Ranking Expert Platform Group; Special Advisor, Skolkovo Univ.; mem. US and Canadian Acad. of Pathologists, American Soc. of Investigative Pathology, Int. Acad. of Pathologists (British Div.), American Soc. of Hematology, Soc. of Hematopathology, European Asscn of Hematopathology, Royal Coll. of Physicians and Surgeons of Canada 1987; Hon. Consul Gen., Repub. of Korea; Hon. Prof., Peking Union Medical Coll. 2003–, Tianjin Medical Univ. 2006–, Peking Univ. 2007–; Kt, Order of the Netherlands Lion 2007. *Publications:* editor of two books on Hodgkin's disease; 231 papers in professional journals; five US and two int. patents. *Address:* Office of the President, University of Groningen, Oude Boteringestraat 44, 9712 GL Groningen, The Netherlands (office). *Telephone:* (6) 29163746 (home). *E-mail:* sibrandes@netscape.net (office). *Website:* www.rug.nl/staff/s.poppema (office).

POPPER, Frank Geoffrey, DèsL; British/French art historian; *Professor Emeritus, University of Paris VIII;* b. (Franz Gottfried Popper), 17 April 1918, Prague, Czech Repub.; s. of Otto Popper and Paula Goldmann; m. 1st Hella Guth 1946; m. 2nd Aline Dallier 1973; ed Univ. of Paris IV (Paris-Sorbonne); voluntary service in RAF 1941–46; Dir of shipping and travel agencies 1947–53; mem. research group Inst. of Aesthetics, Paris 1961–68; Asst Prof. of Aesthetics and the Science of Art, Univ. of Paris VIII (Vincennes à St-Denis) 1969–71, Dir of Art Dept 1970–83, Temp. Reader 1971–73, Reader 1973–75, Prof. 1975–76, Full Prof. 1976–85, Prof. Emer. 1985–; also organizes art exhbns, including Electra at Musée d'art moderne de la ville de Paris 1983; Chevalier, Ordre nat. du Mérite 1998, Commdr, Ordre des Arts et des Lettres 2004, Chevalier, Légion d'honneur 2010. *Publications include:* Kunst-Licht-Kunst (exhbn catalogue) 1966, Lumière et Mouvement (exhbn catalogue) 1967, Naissance de l'Art Cinétique 1967, Origins and Development of Kinetic Art 1968, Art, Action and Participation 1975, Agam 1976, Electra, Electricity and Electronics in the Art of the Twentieth Century (exhbn catalogue) 1983, Art of the Electronic Age 1993, Réflexions sur l'Exil, l'Art et l'Europe 1998, From Technological to Virtual Art 2005, Ecrire sur l'art: de l'art optique à l'art virtuel 2007, Collection Frank Popper (exhbn catalogue) 2009. *Leisure interests:* chess, music, literature. *Address:* 6 rue du Marché Saint-Honoré, 75001 Paris, France (home). *Telephone:* 1-42-61-21-38 (home). *E-mail:* fpopper@club-internet.fr (home). *Website:* www.arpla.univ-paris8.fr (office).

PORAT, Ruth M., BA, MSc (Econ), MBA; American investment banking executive; *Senior Vice-President and Chief Financial Officer, Alphabet Inc.;* b. 1958; d. of Dan I. Porat and Freida Porat; m. Anthony Paduano 1983; three c.; ed Stanford Univ., London School of Econs, UK, Wharton School, Univ. of Pennsylvania; early position as man. consultant, Yankelovich, Skelly & White, New York; with Mergers and Acquisitions, Morgan Stanley, New York 1987–90, Chair. Equity Capital Markets 1996–2006, Co-head Global Tech. Group, Vice-Chair. Investment Banking Div. 2003–09 (Chair. Financial Sponsors Group 2004–06), Global Head Financial Insts Group 2006–09, Exec. Vice-Pres. and Chief Financial Officer 2010–15; with Smith Barney 1993–96; Chief Financial Officer, Google Inc. May 2015–, Sr Vice-Pres. and Chief Financial Officer, Alphabet Inc. (holding co. containing Google and new ventures) Aug. 2015–. *Address:* Alphabet Inc., 1600 Amphitheatre Parkway, Mountain View, CA 94043, USA (office). *Telephone:* (650) 253-0000 (office). *Website:* www.google.com (office).

PORNCHAI, Rujiprapa, BSc, MSc, PhD; Thai business executive and government official; b. 19 April 1952; ed Kasetsart Univ. of Econs, Thammasart Univ., Univ. of Pennsylvania, USA; fmr Deputy Sec.-Gen. Nat. Econ. and Social Devt Bd; fmr Dir Regional Econ. Devt Cooperation Cttee Office (REDCCO); fmr Exec. Dir Office of the E Seaboard Devt Cttee (OESB); fmr Exec. Dir Office of the S Seaboard Devt Cttee (OSSB); Deputy Perm. Sec. of Energy, Ministry of Energy 2003–06, Perm. Sec. of Energy 2006–; Chair. and Dir Electricity Generating Public Co. Ltd (EGCO) 2006–07 (resgnd), 2009; fmr Chair. PTT Public Co. Ltd; Chair. Electricity Generating Authority of Thailand.

POROSHENKO, Petro Oleksiyovych; Ukrainian business executive, politician and head of state; *President;* b. 26 Sept. 1965, Bolhrad, Odesa Oblast, Ukrainian SSR, USSR; m. Maryna Anatoliivna Poroshenko; two s. two d.; ed Taras Shevchenko Univ., Kyiv; Deputy Dir-Gen. Respublika Asscn of Small Businesses and Businessmen 1990–91; Pres. Birzhovy Dim Ukraina (Exchange House Ukraine) 1991–93; Pres. and prin. shareholder PJSC Ukrprominvest 1993–98 (holding co. with control of Roshen confectionery, Mriya bank, Radomysh brewery, Leninsak Kuznia Works, Lutsk automobile plant, Cherkasy bus plant, Channel 5 (5 Kanal) TV station, currently Hon. Pres.; mem. Verkhovna Rada (Parl.) 1998–2005, 2006–07, 2012–14, Chair. Sub-cttee for Securities, Stock and Investment Markets 2000, Budget Cttee 2002–04, later Chair. Finance and Banking Cttee, mem. Cttee for European Integration 2012–14; mem. Sotsial-Demokratychnya Partiya Ukrainy—Obyednana (Social Democratic Party of Ukraine—United) –2000; f. Solidarnist (Solidarity) party 2000, then joined Partiya Rehioniv (Party of Regions), then joined Nasha Ukraina (Our Ukraine) party 2001, Solidarnist renamed Blok Petra Poroshenka (Petro Poroshenko Bloc) 2014, then Blok Petra Poroshenka 'Solidarnist' (Solidarity—Petro Poroshenko Bloc) 2015; apptd mem. Pres.'s Coordinating Council for the Securities Market 1998; Deputy Man. Viktor Yushchenko's presidential campaign 2004; Sec. Nat. Security and Defence Council Feb.–Sept. 2005; Chair. Council of Nat. Bank of Ukraine 2007–12; Minister of Foreign Affairs 2009–10, of Econ. Devt and Trade March–Dec. 2012; Pres. of Ukraine 7 June 2014–; Honoured Economist of Ukraine; Order of Merit; Order of the Republic (Moldova); Order of the White Eagle (Poland); Grand Cross, Order of Civil Merit (Spain); State Prize of Ukraine in Science and Tech., Merited Economist of Ukraine, Pylyp Orlyk Int. Prize. *Address:* Office of the President, 01220 Kyiv, vul. Bankova 11, Ukraine (office). *Telephone:* (44) 255-73-33 (office). *Fax:* (44) 255-65-97 (office). *E-mail:* president@apu.gov.ua (office); vidkrytist@apu.gov.ua (office). *Website:* www.president.gov.ua (office); www.poroshenko.com.ua.

POROZHANOV, Roumen, MA; Bulgarian politician; b. 17 Aug. 1964; ed Univ. of Nat. and World Economy; several positions within Ministry of Finance, including Expert in Financing Special Activities Dept, in charge of financing cos in defence sector 1992–95, Head of Finance, Agric., Trade and Services Dept 1995–2001, Dir, Real Sector Finance Directorate 2001–09, Chief of Staff, Cabinet of Minister of Finance 2009–11, CEO State Agric. Fund 2011–13, Pres. Governing Council, Center for Strategic Analysis, Financing and European Funds Feb.–Aug. 2014, Minister of Finance (in caretaker govt) Aug.–Nov. 2014; Chair. Arsenal JSC, Kazanlak 1993–99, Bulgartabac Holding JSC 2001–05, Project Company Oil Pipeline Burgas-Alexandroupolis 2010–11; mem. Governing Council, Sofia Tobacco Co. 2005–11; mem. Supervisory Council, Bulgarian Bank for Devt 2009–.

PORRITT, Sir Jonathon Espie, 2nd Bt, cr. 1963, CBE, BA; British environmentalist and writer; *Founding Director, Forum for the Future;* b. 6 July 1950, London; s. of Lord Porritt (11th Gov.-Gen. of New Zealand); m. Sarah Staniforth 1986; two d.; ed Eton Coll. and Magdalen Coll. Oxford; trained as solicitor; English teacher, St Clement Danes Grammar School (later Burlington Danes School), Shepherd's Bush, West London 1975–84; Head of English, Burlington Danes School, London 1980–84; Chair. Ecology Party 1979–80, 1982–84; parl. cand. at gen. elections in 1979, 1983; Dir Friends of the Earth 1984–90; Founder Dir Forum for the Future 1996–; Chair. UK Sustainable Devt Comm. 2000–09; Co-Dir Prince of Wales Business and Environment Programme; currently Dir (non-exec.), Willmott Dixon Holdings Ltd; mem. Bd South West Regional Devt Agency 2000–09; adviser to many bodies on environmental matters, as well as to individuals, including Prince Charles and Chief Exec. of Marks & Spencer; Chancellor, Keele Univ. 2012–; mem. Advisory Bd BBC Wildlife magazine; Patron, Population Matters. *Publications include:* Seeing Green: The Politics of Ecology Explained 1984, Friends of the Earth Handbook 1987, The Coming of the Greens 1988, Save the Earth (ed.) 1990, Where on Earth are We Going? 1991, Captain Eco (for children) 1991, The Reader's Digest Good Beach Guide 1994, Liberty and Sustainability: Where One Person's Freedom is Another's Nuisance 1995, Playing Safe: Science and the Environment (Prospects for Tomorrow) 2000, Making the Net Work: Sustainable Development in a Digital Society 2004, Capitalism: As if the World Matters 2005 (revised edn 2007), The World We Made 2013. *Leisure interests:* walking, cooking. *Address:* 9 Imperial Square, Cheltenham, Glos., GL50 1QB; 9 Lypiatt Terrace, Cheltenham, Glos., GL50 2SX, England (home). *Telephone:* (1242) 262737 (office). *Fax:* (1242) 262757 (office). *E-mail:* jpoffice@forumforthefuture.org (office). *Website:* www.jonathonporritt.com.

PORTAS, Paulo Sacadura Cabral, LLD; Portuguese journalist and politician; b. 12 Sept. 1962, Lisbon; s. of Nuno Portas and Helena de Sacadura Cabral; ed Univ. Católica de Lisboa; began career as journalist with O Tempo (newspaper); mem. Grupo de Ofir (reform group) 1986; mem. political comm. for presidential candidacy of Freitas do Amaral 1986; f. O Independente (weekly newspaper) 1988, Dir –1995; Jt Founder Instituto de Estudos Políticos 1995; Deputy, Assembleia da República (Parl.), (CDS/Partido Popular) 1995–2002, Parl. Leader 1999–2001; Municipal Deputy, Oliveira de Azeméis 1997; fmr Pres. CDS/Partido Popular (now Partido Popular); Speaker, Câmara Municipal de Lisboa 2001; Minister of State and of Nat. Defence 2002–05; Minister of Foreign Affairs 2011–13; Deputy Prime Minister 2013–15; Lecturer, Dept of Politics, Univ. Moderna 1995–97; Distinguished Public Service Award, US Defense Dept 2005.

PORTER, Brian Johnston, BCom; Canadian banking executive; *President and CEO, Bank of Nova Scotia (Scotiabank);* b. Calgary, Alberta; m. Megan Porter; three c.; ed Dalhousie Univ.; began career with investment dealer McLeod Young Weir 1981 (co. acquired by Scotiabank 1987), held various sr positions with Scotiabank including exec. roles with Global Banking & Markets Dept, Global Risk Man., Group Treasury and Int. Banking, Chief Risk Officer 2006–08, Group Head of Risk and Treasury 2008–10, Group Head of Int. Banking 2010–12, Pres. 2012–, elected to Bd of Dirs April 2013, CEO Nov. 2013–; Hon. LLD (Dalhousie) 2008. *Address:* The Bank of Nova Scotia (Scotiabank), 44 King Street West, Toronto, ON M5H 1H1, Canada. *Telephone:* (416) 866-6430 (office). *Fax:* (416) 866-3750 (office). *E-mail:* email@scotiabank.com (office). *Website:* www.scotiabank.com (office).

PORTER, Michael Eugene, MBA, PhD; American economist, academic and consultant; *Bishop William Lawrence University Professor and Director, Institute for Strategy and Competitiveness, Harvard Business School;* b. 23 May 1947, Ann Arbor, Mich.; ed Princeton Univ., Harvard Business School, Harvard Univ.; currently Bishop William Lawrence Univ. Prof., Harvard Business School, also Dir Inst. for Strategy and Competitiveness 2001–; advisor to local and nat. govts; mem. Exec. Cttee, Council on Competitiveness; Co-Chair. Global Competitiveness Report; has led studies for Govts of India, NZ, Canada and Portugal; advised on competitive strategy for US and int. cos, including DuPont, Procter & Gamble, Royal Dutch Shell, Taiwan Semiconductor Manufacturing Co.; mem. Bd of Dirs, Parametric Technology Corpn, Thermo Electron Corpn; Co-founder and Sr Advisor, Center for Effective Philanthropy; Hon. FRSE 2005; Creu de St Jordi (Spain), Jose Dolores Estrada Order of Merit (Nicaragua); Dr hc (HHL, Leipzig), (Univ. of Iceland), (Univ. of Los Andres), (Stockholm School of Econs, Sweden), (Erasmus Univ., Netherlands), (Hautes Ecoles Commerciales, France), (Univ. Tech. de Lisboa, Portugal), (Adolfo Ibanez Univ., Chile), (INCAE, Central America), (Johnson and Wales Univ.), (Mount Ida Coll., Universidad del Pacifico, Peru), (Toronto Univ.), (McGill Univ., Canada), (Nyenrode Business Universiteit, Netherlands), (Illinois Inst. of Tech.), (Universidad Popular Autónoma del Estado de Puebla, Mexico), (Universidad Católica Nuestra Senora de la Asunción, Paraguay), (Université Laval, Canada); seven McKinsey Awards (for best Harvard Business Review article of the year), Charles Coolidge Parlin Award, American Marketing Asscn 1991, Richard D. Irwin Outstanding Educator in Business Policy and Strategy, Acad. of Man. 1993, Adam Smith Award, Nat. Asscn of Business Economists 1997, Distinguished Award for contribs in the field of man. 1998, Acad. of Man. Award 2003, John Kenneth Galbraith Medal, American Agricultural Econs Asscn 2005, Lifetime Achievement Award in Economic Devt, US Dept of Commerce 2008, CK Prahalad Distinguished Scholar-Practitioner Award, Strategic Man. Soc. 2015, Sheth Medal 2016. *Publications include:* author of 19 books, including Competitive Strategy: Techniques for Analyzing Industries and Competitors 1980, Competitive Advantage: Creating and Sustaining Superior Performance (George R. Terry Book Award Acad. of Man.) 1985, The Competitive Advantage of Nations 1990, On Competition 1998, 2008, Can Japan Compete? 2000, Redefining Health Care 2006; contrib. of more than 125 essays and articles to magazines, journals and newspapers. *Address:* Institute for Strategy and Competitiveness, Ludcke House, Harvard Business School, Soldiers Field Road, Boston, MA 02163, USA (office). *Telephone:* (617) 495-6309 (office). *Fax:* (617) 547-8543 (office). *E-mail:* mporter@hbs.edu (office). *Website:* www.isc.hbs.edu (office).

PORTER, Robert, AC, MA, DM, DSc, FRACP, FRACMA, FAA; Australian professor of medical research; *Honorary Adjunct Professor, School of Medicine and Dentistry, James Cook University;* b. 10 Sept. 1932, Port Augusta, S Australia; s. of William J. Porter and Amy Porter (née Tottman); m. Anne D. Steell 1961; two s. two d.; ed Univ. of Adelaide and Univ. of Oxford, UK; House Physician and House Surgeon, Radcliffe Infirmary, Oxford 1959–60; Univ. Lecturer in Physiology, Oxford 1961–67; Medical Tutor and Fellow, St Catherine's Coll. Oxford 1963–67; Prof. of Physiology, Monash Univ. 1967–80, Dean 1989–98, Deputy Vice-Chancellor 1992–93; Dir John Curtin School of Medical Research and Howard Florey Prof. of Medical Research, ANU 1980–89; Planning Dean (Medicine), James Cook Univ. of N Queensland, Townsville 1998–99, Dir Research Devt 1999–2008, currently Hon. Adjunct Prof., School of Medicine and Dentistry; Rhodes Scholar 1954; Radcliffe Travelling Fellow in Medical Science 1963–64; Sr Fulbright Fellow, Washington Univ. School of Medicine, St Louis 1973; Fogarty Scholar-in-Residence, NIH, Bethesda, Md, USA 1986–87; Chair. Nat. Expert Advisory Group on Safety and Quality in Australian Health Care 1998–2000; Fellow, Royal Australian Coll. of Medical Admins; Companion of the Order of Australia 2001; Hon. DSc (Univ. of Sydney) 2001, (James Cook Univ.) 2009; Centenary Medal 2003. *Publications:* Corticospinal Neurones: Their Role in Movement (with C. G. Phillips) 1977, Corticospinal Function and Voluntary Movement (with R. N. Lemon) 1993; articles on neurophysiology. *Leisure interests:* sport, reading, photography. *Address:* 21 Tamarind Place, Twin Waters, Queensland 4564, Australia (home). *Telephone:* (7) 5457-0905 (home). *E-mail:* Robert.Porter@jcu.edu.au (office).

PORTES, Richard David, CBE, DPhil, FBA; American/British economist and academic; *Professor of Economics, London Business School;* b. 10 Dec. 1941, Chicago, Ill., USA; s. of Herbert Portes and Abra Halperin Portes; m. 1st Barbara Diana Frank 1963 (divorced); one s. one d.; m. 2nd Helene Mireille Rey 2006; one d.; ed Yale Univ., Balliol and Nuffield Colls, Oxford; Official Fellow and Tutor in Econs, Balliol Coll. Oxford 1965–69, Hon. Fellow 2014–; Asst Prof. of Econs and Int. Affairs, Princeton Univ. 1969–72; Prof. of Econs, Birkbeck Coll., Univ. of London 1972–94, Head Dept 1975–77, 1980–83, 1994; Prof. of Econs, London Business School 1995–; Tommaso Padoa-Schioppa Prof., European Univ. Inst. 2014–; Pres. Centre for Econ. Policy Research, London 1983–2016 (Hon. Pres. 2016–); Directeur d'Etudes, Ecole des Hautes Etudes en Sciences Sociales, Paris 1978–2011; fmr Rhodes Scholar, Woodrow Wilson Fellow, Danforth Fellow; Guggenheim Fellow 1977–78; British Acad. Overseas Visiting Fellow 1977–78; Research Assoc., Nat. Bureau of Econ. Research, Cambridge, Mass 1980–; Visiting Prof., Harvard Univ. 1977–78, Univ. of California, Berkeley 1999–2000, Columbia Univ. Business School 2003–04; Chair. Collegio di Probiviri (Wise Men Cttee), MTS 2001–; Vice-Chair. Econs Cttee Social Science Research Council 1981–84; Sec.-Gen. Royal Econ. Soc. 1992–2008; Co-Chair. Bd of Govs and Sr Ed., Economic Policy 1985–, ESRB Joint Expert Group on Shadow Banking 2015–; Vice-Chair. Advisory Scientific Cttee, European Systemic Risk Bd 2016–; mem. Bd of Dirs, Soc. for Econ. Analysis 1967–69, 1972–80 (Sec. 1974–77); mem. Council on Foreign Relations 1978–, Hon. Degrees Cttee, Univ. of London 1984–89, Council, Royal Econ. Soc. 1986–92, 2008– (mem. Exec. Cttee 1987–2008), Bellagio Group on the Int. Economy 1990–, Council, European Econ. Asscn 1992–96, Franco-British Council 1996–2002, Comm. on the Social Sciences 2000–03; mem. and fmr mem. several editorial bds; Fellow Econometric Soc. 1983; Hon. DSc (Université Libre de Bruxelles) 2000; Hon. PhD (London Metropolitan) 2000, (Paris-Dauphine) 2013. *Publications:* The Polish Crisis 1981, Deficits and Detente 1983, Threats to International Financial Stability (co-author) 1987, Crisis? What Crisis? Orderly Workouts for Sovereign Debtors 1995, Making Sense of Globalization 2002, Crises de la Dette 2003, International Financial Stability 2007; editor: Global Macroeconomics: Policy Conflict and Cooperation 1987, Blueprints for Exchange Rate

Management 1989, Macroeconomic Policies in an Interdependent World 1989, The EMS in Transition: a CEPR Report 1989, External Constraints on Macroeconomic Policy: The European Experience 1991, The Path of Reform in Central and Eastern Europe 1991, Economic Transformation of Central Europe 1993, European Union Trade with Eastern Europe 1995, Macroeconomic Stability and Financial Regulation 2009, The Social Value of the Financial Sector 2013; numerous papers and contribs to learned journals. *Leisure interest:* living beyond my means. *Address:* London Business School, Regent's Park, London, NW1 4SA, England (office). *Telephone:* (20) 7000-8424 (office). *Fax:* (20) 7000-8401 (office). *E-mail:* rportes@london.edu (office). *Website:* faculty.london.edu/rportes (office); www.richardportes.eu.

PORTILLO, Rt Hon. Michael Denzil Xavier, PC, MA; British politician, writer and broadcaster; b. 26 May 1953, London; s. of Luis G. Portillo and Cora W. Blyth; m. Carolyn C. Eadie 1982; ed Harrow Co. Boys' School and Peterhouse, Cambridge; Ocean Transport & Trading Co. 1975–76; Conservative Research Dept 1976–79; Special Adviser to Sec. of State for Energy 1979–81; Kerr McGee Oil (UK) Ltd 1981–83; Special Adviser to Sec. of State for Trade and Industry 1983, to Chancellor of Exchequer 1983–84; MP for Enfield, Southgate 1984–97, for Kensington and Chelsea 1999–2005; Asst Govt Whip 1986–87; Parl. Under-Sec. of State, Dept of Health and Social Security 1987–88; Minister of State, Dept of Transport 1988–90; Minister of State for Local Govt and Inner Cities 1990–92; Chief Sec. to the Treasury 1992–94; Sec. of State for Employment 1994–95, for Defence 1995–97; Shadow Chancellor of the Exchequer 2000–01; freelance writer and broadcaster 1997–2001; Theatre Critic, The New Statesman 2004–06; adviser, Kerr McGee Corpn 1997, mem. Bd of Dirs 2006; currently, Chair. Fed. of British Artists; Chair. of jury, Man Booker Prize for Fiction 2008; columnist, The Sunday Times 2004–; mem. Bd of Dirs (non-exec.) BAE Systems PLC 2002–06; mem. Int. Comm. for Missing Persons in Fmr Yugoslavia 1998–; Pres. DebRA (charity working on behalf of people with Epidermolysis Bullosa—EB); British Chair. British-Spanish Tertulias; Trustee, Parl. Cttee Against Anti-Semitism; fmr weekly columnist, The Scotsman; Hon. Vice-Pres., Canning House, Hispanic and Luso Brazilian Council. *Television includes:* Portillo's Progress (three-part series for Channel 4), BBC 2's Great Railway Journeys series, Art That Shook the World: Richard Wagner's Ring (BBC 2), Portillo in Euroland, Elizabeth I in the series Great Britons (BBC 2), When Michael Portillo Became a Single Mum (BBC 2) 2003, Railways of the Great War with Michael Portillo (BBC) 2014, Portillo's State Secrets (BBC 2) 2015, Great American Railroad Journeys (BBC) 2016. *Radio includes:* Capitalism on Trial, BBC Radio 4 2011, The Things We Forgot to Remember, BBC Radio 4 2011, panel mem. The Moral Maze, BBC Radio 4. *Publications:* Clear Blue Water 1994, Democratic Values and the Currency 1998. *Address:* Office of The Rt Hon Michael Portillo, Suite 99, 34 Buckingham Palace Road, London, SW1W 0RH, England (office). *Telephone:* (20) 7931-9422 (office). *Fax:* (20) 7931-6549 (office). *E-mail:* michael@michaelportillo.co.uk (office). *Website:* www.michaelportillo.co.uk (office).

PORTILLO CABRERA, Alfonso Antonio; Guatemalan politician and fmr head of state; ed Universidad Autónoma de Guerrero, Mexico, Universidad Autónoma de México; fmr columnist, daily newspaper Siglo Veintiuno; mem. Editorial Bd Suplemento Económico Pulso; Prof. of Law, Econs and Politics in univs in Latin America; fmr Leader of Democracia Cristiana (DC) Deputies in Congress, Chair. Comm. of Econ., Foreign Trade and Integration; Asst Gen. Sec. DC, Dir DC's Centro de Estudios Socio-Políticos (IGESP); Pres. of Guatemala 2000–04; fled to Mexico to escape corruption charges 2004, extradited to Guatemala 2008, extradited to USA 2013, pled guilty and fined and sentenced to five years and 10 months for taking bribes from Taiwan and attempting to launder money 2014.

PORTISCH, Lajos; Hungarian chess player and singer; b. 4 April 1937, Zalaegerszeg; s. of Lajos Portisch, Sr and Anna Simon; represented Hungary at World Junior Chess Championships, Antwerp 1955; represented Hungary four times at Student Olympiads 1956, 1957, 1958, 1959; to-ranking player of Hungary's selected team from 1962; Hungarian Chess Champion 1958, 1959, 1961, 1964, 1965, 1971, 1975, 1981; holder of Int. Grandmaster title from 1961; European Team Championships bronze medallist 1961, 1965, 1973, team silver medallist 1970, 1977, 1980; Chess Olympiad team bronze medallist 1956, 1966, silver 1970, 1972, 1980, gold 1978; qualified eight times as cand. for the individual chess world title; holder of Master Coach qualification; bass-baritone singer, gives regular concerts; positional style earned him the nickname of the "Hungarian Botvinnik"; mem. MTK-Sport Club; Labour Order of Merit (Golden Degree); Nemzet Sportoloja (highest nat. sports achievement award) 2004. *Publication:* Six Hundred Endings (with B. Sárközi) 1973. *Leisure interest:* music. *Address:* c/o Hungarian Chess Federation, 1055 Budapest, Falk Miksa u. 10, Hungary. *Telephone:* (1) 473-2360. *E-mail:* chess@chess.hu.

PORTMAN, Natalie; American/Israeli actress; b. 9 June 1981, Jerusalem; m. Benjamin Millepied; ed Harvard Univ.; left Israel with her family aged three and moved to USA; discovered by modelling scout at New York pizza parlour aged 11; Genesis Prize 2017. *Theatre includes:* A Midsummer Night's Dream, Cabaret, Anne of Green Gables (title role), Tapestry, The Seagull 2001. *Films include:* The Professional (also known as Léon) 1994, Developing 1995, Heat 1995, Beautiful Girls 1996, Everyone Says I Love You 1996, Mars Attacks! 1996, The Diary of Anne Frank 1997, Star Wars: Episode I – The Phantom Menace (as Queen Amidala) 1999, Anywhere But Here, Where the Heart Is 2000, The Seagull 2001, Zoolander 2001, Star Wars: Episode II – Attack of the Clones 2002, Cold Mountain 2003, Garden State 2004, True 2004, Closer (Best Supporting Actress, Golden Globe Awards 2005) 2004, Star Wars: Episode III – Revenge of the Sith 2005, V for Vendetta 2006, Paris, je t'aime 2006, Goya's Ghosts 2006, My Blueberry Nights 2007, Hotel Chevalier 2007, The Darjeeling Limited 2007, Mr Magorium's Wonder Emporium 2007, The Other Boleyn Girl 2008, Love and Other Impossible Pursuits 2009, New York, I Love You 2009, Brothers 2009, Hesher 2010, Black Swan (several awards, including Boston Soc. of Film Critics Award for Best Actress, Las Vegas Film Critics Soc. Award for Best Actress, Southeastern Film Critics Asscn Award for Best Actress, Golden Globe Award for Best Actress 2011, BAFTA Award for Leading Actress 2011, Academy Award for Actress in a leading Role 2011) 2010, No Strings Attached 2011, Your Highness 2011, Thor 2011, The Heyday of the Insensitive Bastards 2014, Knight of Cups 2015, A Tale of Love and Darkness

2015, Jane Got a Gun 2016, Jackie 2016. *Address:* c/o CAA, 2000 Avenue of the Stars, Los Angeles, CA 90067, USA. *Website:* www.natalieportman.com.

PORTMAN, Rachel Mary Berkeley, OBE; British composer; b. 11 Dec. 1960, Haslemere, Surrey; m. Uberto Pasolini; three d.; ed Worcester Coll., Oxford; composer of film and TV scores, for US productions 1992–; British Film Inst. Young Composer of the Year Award 1988, Carlton TV/Rank Films Laboratories Award for Creative Originality 1996, Muse Award from New York Women in Film and Television 2000, BMI Richard Kirk Award 2010. *Compositions for film and television include:* Experience Preferred... But Not Essential 1982, The Storyteller (TV series) 1986–88, 1990, Life is Sweet 1990, Oranges Are Not the Only Fruit (TV drama) 1990, Antonia and Jane 1991, Where Angels Fear to Tread 1991, Used People 1992, The Joy Luck Club 1993, Benny and Joon 1993, Friends 1993, Sirens 1994, Only You 1994, War of the Buttons 1994, To Wong Foo – Thanks for Everything! 1995, A Pyromaniac's Love Story 1995, Smoke 1995, The Adventures of Pinocchio 1996, Marvin's Room 1996, Emma (Academy Award for Best Music, Original Music or Comedy Score 1997) 1996, Addicted to Love 1997, The Cider House Rules 1999, Ratcatcher (Georges Delerue Prize, Ghent Int. Film Festival) 1999, Chocolat 2000, The Legend of Bagger Vance (Phoenix Film Critics Soc. Award for Best Original Score) 2000, The Emperor's New Clothes 2001, Hart's War 2002, The Truth About Charlie 2002, Nicholas Nickleby 2002, The Human Stain 2003, Mona Lisa Smile 2003, The Little Prince 2003, Lard 2004, The Manchurian Candidate 2004, Because of Winn-Dixie 2005, Oliver Twist 2006, The Lake House 2006, Miss Potter 2006, Infamous 2006, H2hOpe: The Water Diviner's Tale (BBC Proms) 2007, Little House on the Prairie Musical (theatre) 2008, The Duchess 2008, Grey Gardens (TV) 2009, London Assurance (Royal Nat. Theatre) 2010, Never Let Me Go (San Diego Film Critics Soc. Award for Best Score) 2010, Snowflower and the Secret Fan 2011, One Day 2011, The Vow 2012, Bel Ami 2012, Private Peaceful 2012, The Right Kind of Wrong 2013, Paradise 2013, Still Life 2013, Belle 2013, Dolphin Tale 2 2014, Bessie (Primetime Emmy Award for Outstanding Music Composition for a Limited Series, Movie or a Special (Original Dramatic Score) 2015) 2015, Despite the Falling Snow 2016, A Dog's Purpose 2017. *Recordings include:* Rachel Portman Soundtracks (compilation album), numerous soundtrack recordings. *Address:* c/o Robert Messinger, Fortress Talent Management, 23632 Calabasas Road, Calabasa, CA 91302, USA (office). *E-mail:* rm@fortresstalentmgmt.com (office). *Website:* www.rachelportman.co.uk.

PORTMAN, Robert (Rob) Jones, BA, JD; American lawyer, politician and fmr government official; *Senator from Ohio;* b. 19 Dec. 1955, Cincinnati, Ohio; m. Jane D. Dudley 1986; two s. one d.; ed Dartmouth Coll., Univ. of Michigan Law School; Assoc., Patton Boggs law firm, Washington, DC 1984–86; Partner, Graydon, Head & Ritchey, Cincinnati 1986–89, 1991–93; Assoc. Counsel to the Pres., The White House, Washington, DC 1989–91, then Dir White House Office of Legis. Affairs; mem. US Del. to UN Sub-cttee on Human Rights 1992; mem. US House of Reps, 2nd Dist of Ohio 1993–2005, Vice-Chair. Budget Cttee, mem. Ways and Means Cttee, Chair. House Republican Leadership; US Trade Rep., Exec. Office of the Pres. 2005–06, Dir Office of Man. and Budget 2006–07; Of Counsel, Squire, Sanders & Dempsey LLP (law firm), Cincinnati and Washington, DC 2007–09; Senator from Ohio 2011–; Founding Chair. Coalition for a Drug Free Greater Cincinnati; mem. Advisory Bd, John Glenn School of Public Affairs, Ohio State Univ. 2008–; Vice-Chair. Hamilton Co. George Bush for President Campaign 1988, 1992, active in Hamilton Co. Republican Party Exec. Cttee, Hamilton Co. Republican Party Finance Cttee; Chair. Republican Early Bird Campaign Cttee 1992; del., Republican Nat. Convention 1988, 1992; mem. Bd of Trustees, Springer School, The United Way, Hyde Park Community United Methodist Church; Founding Trustee, Cincinnati-China Sister City Cttee; mem. Cincinnati World Trade Asscn; Excellence in Public Service Award, John Glenn School of Public Affairs, Ohio State Univ. 2008, Nelson A. Rockefeller Distinguished Public Service Award, Nelson A. Rockefeller Center, Dartmouth Coll., PLANSPONSOR magazine Legend Award, Nat. Leadership Award, Community Anti-Drug Coalition of America 2008, Leadership on Alcohol & Other Drug Services Award, Hamilton Co. Mental Health & Recovery Services Bd, Albert Gallatin Award, Swiss-American Chamber of Commerce, Jacob K. Javits Prize for Bipartisan Leadership 2017. *Publication:* Wisdom's Paradise: The Forgotten Shakers of Union Village (with Cheryl Bauer) 2004. *Leisure interests:* biking, kayaking, hunting. *Address:* 448 Russell Senate Office Building, Washington, DC 20510, USA (office). *Telephone:* (202) 224-3353 (office). *Fax:* (513) 361-1201 (office). *E-mail:* Dhruv@robportman.com. *Website:* portman.senate.gov (office); www.robportman.com.

PORTOLANO, Maj.-Gen. Luciano; Italian army officer and UN official; *Chief of Staff, Allied Joint Force Command Naples;* b. 18 Sept. 1960, Agrigento, Sicily; m. Susy Portolano 1986; one s. one d.; ed Univ. of Turin, Army Mil. Acad., US Army Command and Gen. Staff Coll., Fort Leavenworth, Kansas, USA; joined Italian army Sept. 1981, held numerous posts in Italy and as part of Italian mil. missions deployed in Kosovo, Iraq and Afghanistan including UN Iran-Iraq Observers Group 1990–91, UN Iraq-Kuwait Observers Group 1991–92, Operation Jt Endeavour, Fmr Yugoslavian Repub. of Macedonia 1999, Operation Jt Guardian, Kosovo 1999, Operation Antica Babilonia, Iraq 2003; Mil. Attaché, Embassy in London 2007–10; Commdr, Int. Security Assistance Force (ISAF) Regional Command-West, Herat, Afghanistan 2011–12; Deputy Chief of Staff for Jt Operations 2012–14; Commdr, UN Interim Force in Lebanon (UNIFIL) 2014–16; Chief of Staff for Jt Force Command, Naples and Head of EU Command Element 2016–; Kt, Mil. Order of Italy 2003, Kt, Order of Merit of the Italian Repub. 2005, Officer, Mil. Order of Italy 2012; Silver Cross of Merit of the Army 1999, Gold Cross of Merit of the Army 2006. *Address:* Allied Joint Force Command Naples, Via Madonna del Pantano, 80014 Naples, Italy (office). *E-mail:* JFCNPPAOGROUP@jfcnp.nato.int (office). *Website:* jfcnaples.nato.int (office).

PORTOS, Michel; French chef and restaurateur; *Director, Le Saint-James Hotel;* b. 4 April 1963; ed school leaving certificate in accountancy and vocational training certificate in cooking; two-star Michelin chef; began apprenticeship and worked at Le Rouzic, Gauthier's restaurant in Bordeaux, Dominique Toulousy's restaurant, Les Jardins de l'Opéra, Troisgros in Roanne; owned restaurant in Perpignan; currently Relais & Châteaux Grand Chef and Dir Le Saint-James Hotel, Bordeaux; f. Le Malthazar 2012, Le Poulpe 2014; named by Gault & Millau gastronomy guide as Chef of the Year 2012. *Address:* Le Saint-James, 3 place Camille Hostein, 33270 Bouliac, Gironde, France (office). *Telephone:* (5) 57-97-06-00 (office). *Fax:* (5) 56-20-92-58 (office). *E-mail:* stjames@relaischateaux.com (office). *Website:* www.saintjames-bouliac.com (office); www.malthazar.com; www.lepoulpe-marseille.com.

PORTZAMPARC, Christian de; French architect; b. 9 May 1944, Casablanca, Morocco; s. of Maurice Urvay de Portzamparc and Annick de Boutray; m. Elizabeth Jardim Neves 1982; two s.; ed Ecole Supérieure des Beaux Arts; worked with Eugene Baudoin and George Candilis; cr. own agency 1980, now has offices in New York and Rio de Janeiro; retrospective exhbn, Pompidou Centre 1996; Artistic Creation Chair, Collège de France (first occupant) 2006–; Commdr des Arts et des Lettres 1989; Great Prize of Architecture of the City of Paris awarded by the Mayor of Paris 1990, Médaille d'Argent, French Acad. of Architecture 1992, Great Nat. Prize of Architecture, Ministry of Urbanism and Transport 1993, Pritzker Prize for Architecture, Hyatt Foundation 1994, Great Urbanism Prize 2004, Créateurs sans Frontières Trophy, Ministry of Foreign Affairs 2008, Praemium Imperiale 2018. *Publications include:* La Cité de la musique 1986, Scènes d'atelier, Généalogie des formes 1996, Christian de Portzamparc, Le Dantec 1995, Christian de Portzamparc 1996, Généalogie des formes 1996, Disegno e forma dell'architettura per la città 1996, Voir écrire (with Philippe Sollers) 2005, Architecture: figures du monde, figures du temps, Leçons inaugurales au Collège de France 2006, Rêver la ville (exhbn catalogue) 2007. *Address:* 38, rue La Bruyère, 75009 Paris, France (office). *Telephone:* 1-80-05-32-00 (office). *Fax:* 1-43-27-74-79 (office). *E-mail:* contact@2portzamparc.com (office). *Website:* www.christiandeportzamparc.com (office).

POSOKHIN, Mikhail Mikhailovich; Russian architect; b. 10 July 1948, Moscow; s. of Mikhail Vasilyevich Posokhin and Galina Arkadyevna Posokhina; m. 1st (divorced); one s.; m. 2nd Vitalina Kudzyavtseva; two d.; ed Moscow Inst. of Architecture; Chief Architect Dept of Civil and Residential Construction Mosproyekt-1 1976–80; head of workshop, Dept for Designs of Exemplary Perspective residential area Chertanovo 1980–82; head of workshop, Dept for Designs of Public Bldgs and Edifices Mosproyekt-2 1982, Gen. Dir 1983; fmr Vice-Chair. Cttee on Architecture and Town-planning of Moscow 1994; mem. Presidium Russian Acad. of Arts, Int. Acad. of Architecture, Acad. Architectural Heritage; The Honour Order, Sergey Radonezhsky Order (2nd and 3rd Degrees), Moscow Daneel Godly Prince Order (2nd Degree), Golden Order of Labour (Bulgary), Golden Order, Russian Acad. of Arts; Merited Architect of Russia, State Prize of Russia, Public Acknowledgement Prize. *Works include:* numerous residential complexes and public edifices including restoration of Cathedral of Christ the Saviour, the Business Centre on Kudrinskaya Square, trade complex on Manege Square, the Gosinny Dvor, reconstruction of the Kremlin and others; 101 projects.

POSPÍŠIL, Jiří, JUDr; Czech lawyer and politician; b. 24 Nov. 1975, Chomutov; ed Univ. of Western Bohemia, Plzeň; early career as articled clerk in pvt law firm; mem. Civic Democratic Alliance (Občanská demokratická aliance) 1994–98; mem. Civic Democratic Party (Občanská demokratická strana) 1998–2014, Chair. Regional Asscn for Plzeň 2003, mem. Exec. Council 2005; mem. Parl. 2002–14, Shadow Minister of Justice 2003–06, Minister of Justice 2006–09, 2010–12, Vice-Chair. Constitutional-Legal Cttee 2002–06, mem. Sub-Cttee for Penal System 2002–06, Deputy Chair. Chamber of Deputies of Parl. 2012–13; Expert Asst, Admin. Law Dept, Univ. of Western Bohemia 2002–; Dean Faculty of Law, Univ. of Western Bohemia 2009–10; mem. European Parl. 2014–. *Address:* Parlement Européen, 60, rue Wiertz, 1047 Brussels, Belgium (office). *Telephone:* (2) 284-55-86 (office). *Fax:* (2) 284-95-86 (office). *Website:* www.europarl.europa.eu (office).

POSSER DA COSTA, Guilherme; São Tomé and Príncipe politician; b. 1953; Minister of Foreign Affairs and Co-operation 1987–88, 1990–91; Prime Minister 1999–2001; Vice-Pres. Movimento de Libertação de São Tomé e Príncipe–Partido Social Democrata (MLSTP-PSD), Pres. 2005–11. *Address:* c/o Movimento de Libertação de São Tomé e Príncipe–Partido Social Democrata, Riboque Cidade Capital, São Tomé e Príncipe (office).

POST, Herschel, MBE, MA, LLB; American investment banker; b. 9 Oct. 1939; s. of Herschel E. Post and Marie C. Post; m. Peggy Mayne 1963; one s. three d.; ed Yale and Harvard Univs and New Coll., Oxford, UK; Assoc., Davis, Polk & Wordwell (attorneys) 1966–69; Exec. Dir Parks Council of New York City 1969–72; Deputy Admin., Parks, Recreation and Cultural Affairs Admin, New York 1973; Vice-Pres. and Man. Euro-clear Operations, JPMorgan & Co. Brussels 1974–78; Vice-Pres. and Deputy Head, Int. Investment Dept JPMorgan, London 1978–83; Pres. Posthorn Global Asset Man., London 1984–90, Shearson Lehman Global Asset Man., London 1984–90; Deputy Chair. London Stock Exchange 1988–95, Chair. Trading Markets Man. Bd 1990–95, Euroclear Plc 1992–2000, Euroclear UK and Ireland 2002–12, Earthwatch Europe 1988– (Chair. 1997–2011); COO Lehman Brothers Int. Ltd 1990–94, Coutts & Co. 1994–95 (CEO and Deputy Chair. 1995–2000); Int. Man. Dir of Business Devt, Christie's International PLC 2000–05; Chair. Woodcock Foundation 2000–05; Deputy Chair. EFG Private Bank Ltd 2002–05; Dir (non-exec.), Investors Capital Trust 2000–13, Ahli United Bank BSC 2002–, Notting Hill Housing Group 2002–07, Threadneedle Asset Management SARL 2006–. *Address:* Ahli United Bank BSC, PO Box 2424, Bldg 2495, Road 2832, Al Seef District 428, Manama, Bahrain (office). *Telephone:* (17) 585858 (Manama) (office); (20) 7792-9337 (London) (office). *Fax:* (17) 580589 (Manama) (office); (20) 7243-2775 (London) (office). *E-mail:* info@ahliunited.com (office). *Website:* www.ahliunited.com (office).

POST, Mark, MD, PhD; Dutch physiologist and academic; *Professor of Vascular Physiology and Chairman, Physiology Department, Maastricht University;* ed Utrecht Univ.; Instructor in Pharmacology 1984–85; Sr Investigator, Interuniversity Cardiology Inst. of the Netherlands 1989–97; Visiting Scientist, Harvard Medical School, Beth Israel Deaconess Medical Center, USA 1995–97, Instructor in Medicine, Harvard Medical School 1997–98, Asst Prof. of Medicine 1998–2001; Assoc. Prof. of Medicine and of Physiology, Dartmouth Medical School, NH, USA 2001–02, Visiting Prof. in Medicine and in Physiology 2002–10; Prof. of Angiogenesis in Tissue Eng (HL1), Tech. Univ., Eindhoven 2002–10, Vice-Dean BMT 2006-11; Prof. of Vascular Physiology and Tissue Eng (HL2), Maastricht Univ. 2002–, Chair. Physiology Dept (HL2) 2004–11, 2012–, Acting Chair. Biophysics 2005–10, Acting Scientific Dir CARIM, FHML 2011–12; World Technology Award (Environment) 2013. *Publications:* numerous papers in professional journals. *Address:* Physiology Department, Maastricht University, PO Box 616, 6200 MD Maastricht, The Netherlands (office). *Telephone:* (43)

3881085 (office). *E-mail:* m.post@maastrichtuniversity.nl (office). *Website:* www
.maastrichtuniversity.nl (office).

POSTE, George, CBE, BVSC, PhD, FRS, FRCVS, FRCPath; American (b.
British) research scientist, business executive and academic; *Co-Director and
Chief Scientist, Complex Adaptive Systems Network, Arizona State University;* b.
30 April 1944, Polegate, Sussex, England; s. of John H. Poste and Kathleen B.
Poste; m. Linda Suhler 1992; one s. two d.; ed Bristol Univ.; Lecturer, Royal
Postgraduate Medical School, Univ. of London 1969–72, Sr Lecturer 1974; Assoc.
Prof. of Experimental Pathology, State Univ. of New York (SUNY), Buffalo
1972–74, Prin. Cancer Research Scientist and Prof. of Cell and Molecular Biology
1975–80; Vice-Pres. and Dir of Research, Smith Kline & French Labs,
Philadelphia, Pa 1980–83, Vice-Pres. Research and Devt Technologies 1983–86,
Vice-Pres. Worldwide Research and Preclinical Devt 1987–88, Pres. Research and
Devt 1988–89, Exec. Vice-Pres. Research and Devt SmithKline Beecham Pharma-
ceuticals 1989–91, Pres. Research and Devt 1991–97, Chief Science and Tech.
Officer 1997–99; CEO Health Tech. Networks 2000–; Partner, Care Capital,
Princeton, NJ 2000–; Research Prof., Univ. of Pennsylvania 1981–, Univ. of Texas
Medical Center 1986–; Fleming Fellow, Lincoln Coll. Oxford 1995; William Pitt
Fellow, Pembroke Coll. Cambridge 1996–; Distinguished Visiting Fellow, Hoover
Inst., Stanford Univ. 2000–; Del E. Webb Distinguished Prof. of Biology and
Founder and Dir Biodesign Inst., Arizona State Univ. 2003–09, Regents Prof.
2006–, Co-Dir and Chief Scientist, Complex Adaptive Systems Initiative and Del
E. Webb Chair in Health Innovation 2009–; Chair. (non-exec.) Orchid Biosciences,
Princeton NJ; mem. Bd of Dirs Exelixis, Monsanto; mem. Defense Science Bd of US
Dept of Defense 2003–09, Chair. Task Force on Bioterrorism; mem. NAS Working
Group on Defense Against Bioweapons; mem. Human Genetics Advisory Cttee
1996–; mem. Bd of Govs Center for Molecular Medicine and Genetics, Stanford
Univ. 1992–; mem. Alliance for Ageing 1992–97; Jt Ed. Cell Surface Reviews
1976–83, New Horizons in Therapeutics 1984–; mem. Council on Foreign Relations
2004–; Fellow, Royal Coll. of Veterinary Surgeons; Hon. FRCP 1993; Hon. Fellow,
Univ. Coll. London 1993; Hon. DSc 1987, (Sussex) 1999; Hon. LLD (Bristol) 1995,
(Dundee) 1998; R&D Scientist of the Year, R&D Magazine 2004, Albert Einstein
Award, Global Business Leadership Council 2006, SCRIP Lifetime Achievement
Award 2009. *Publications:* numerous reviews and papers in learned journals.
Leisure interests: automobile racing, mil. history, photography, desert exploration.
Address: Complex Adaptive Systems Network, Arizona State University-Skysong
1475 North Scottsdale Road, Ste 361, Scottsdale, AZ 85257, USA (office).
Telephone: (480) 727-8662 (office). *Fax:* (480) 965-2765 (office). *E-mail:* george
.poste@asu.edu (office). *Website:* www.casi.asu.edu (office).

POTANIN, Vladimir Olegovich; Russian politician, banker and business
executive; *President, Mining and Metallurgical Company Norilsk Nickel;* b. 3
Jan. 1961, Moscow; m. Ekaterina Potanina 2014; two s. one d. (from previous m.);
ed Moscow Inst. of Int. Relations; mem. staff, USSR Ministry of Foreign Trade
1983–90; Head Econ. Co. Interros 1991–92; Vice-Pres., Pres. Joint-Stock Commercial Bank International Financial Co. 1992–93; Pres. UNEXIM Bank 1993–98,
InterRos Financial and Industrial Group (now Interros Holding Co.) 1994–2012;
with partners acquired several govt oil and mineral assets including Norilsk
Nickel (world's largest producer of nickel); First Deputy Chair. Govt of Russian
Fed. 1996–97; mem. Civic Chamber of the Russian Fed. 2006–14; CEO Mining and
Metallurgical Co. Norilsk Nickel 2012–15, Pres. 2015–; joined Giving Pledge 2013;
mem. Bd of Trustees, State Hermitage, Solomon R. Guggenheim Foundation, New
York, Moscow State Inst. of Int. Relations, Russian Int. Olympic Univ., St
Petersburg Univ., Moscow Church Construction Foundation, Russian Geograph-
ical Soc.; Officier, Ordre des Arts et des Lettres 2007, Fourth Degree, Order of
Merit for the Motherland 2007, Third and Second Degree, Order of St Prince
Vladimir Equal-to-the-Apostles, Third and Second Degree, Order of St Sergius of
Radonezh, Second Degree, Order of the Holy Prince Daniel of Moscow, First
Degree, Order of the St Seraphim of Sarov 2012. *Leisure interests:* travelling,
soccer, alpine skiing, various water sports, chess. *Address:* Mining and Metallur-
gical Company Norilsk Nickel, 123100 Moscow, 1st Krasnogvardeysky Drive 15,
Russia (office). *Telephone:* (495) 787-76-67 (office). *E-mail:* gmk@nornik.ru (office).
Website: www.nornik.ru (office).

POTAPOV, Alexander Serafimovich, CandPhil; Russian journalist and newspaper publishing executive; *Director, Izvestia TV News Channel;* b. 6 Feb. 1936,
Oktyabry, Kharkov Region, Ukraine; m.; one s.; ed Vilnius State Univ., Lithuania;
contrib. Leninskaya Smena (newspaper) 1958–66; Head of Dept, Deputy Ed.-in-
Chief Belgorodskaya Pravda (newspaper) 1966–73; Head of Dept Belgorod
Regional Exec. CPSU Cttee 1973–75; Ed. Belgorodskaya Pravda 1975–76;
instructor, CPSU Cen. Cttee 1976–78, 1981–85; apptd Ed.-in-Chief Trud (Labour)
newspaper 1985; Ed.-in-Chief Marker (online business newspaper) 2010–12; Ed.-
in-Chief Izvestia 2012–13, also Deputy Editorial Dir Holding News Media, Dir
Izvestia TV News Channel 2013–; People's Deputy of Russian Fed., mem. Cttee of
Supreme Soviet of Russian Fed. on Problems of Glasnost and Human Rights
–1993. *Address:* Izvestia, 127994 Moscow, ul. Tverskaya 18/1, POB 4, Russia
(office). *Telephone:* (495) 209-05-81 (office). *Fax:* (495) 933-64-62 (office). *E-mail:*
a.potapov@izvestia.ru (office). *Website:* www.izvestia.ru (office).

POTAPOV, Leonid Vasilyevich; Russian politician; b. 4 July 1935, Uakit,
Buryatia; m.; two c.; ed Khabarovsk Inst. of Railway Eng, Irkutsk Inst. of Nat.
Econs; various positions from engineer to Chief Engineer, Ulan-Ude train factory
1959–76; Head Div. of Industry, then Sec. Buryat Regional CP Cttee 1976–87;
Chair. Mary Regional Exec. Cttee Turkmenia 1987–89; Chair. Supreme Soviet
Turkmen SSR 1989–90; First Sec. Buryat CPSU Cttee 1990–91; Chair. Supreme
Soviet Buryat Autonomous SSR (now Buryatskaya Repub.) 1991–94; Pres. of
Buryatskaya Repub. 1994–2007; mem. Council of Fed., Russian Fed. 1993–2001;
Hon. Engineer, Buryat Repub., Hon. Prof., Buryat State Univ., Modern Univ. for
the Humanities, Irkutsk State Univ., Irkutsk State Technical Univ., Plekhanov
Russian Economic Univ., Hon. Citizen, City of Ulan-Ude; Order of Merit for the
Fatherland 1997, 2008, Order of the Oct. Revolution, Red Banner of Labour,
Honour Award, Order of Friendship, Order for Excellent Service to the Native
Land (IV degree), Polar Star Order (Mongolia), Order of the Red Banner of Labour,
Order of the Badge of Honour. *Leisure interest:* reading literature on history,
philosophy and economics.

POTERBA, James Michael, AB, MPhil, DPhil; American economist and
academic; *President and CEO, National Bureau of Economic Research;* b. 13
July 1958, New York, NY; m. Nancy Lin Rose 1984; two s. one d.; ed Harvard Coll.,
Univ. of Oxford, UK; Jr Research Fellow, Nuffield Coll. Oxford 1982–83; Asst Prof.
of Econs, MIT 1983–86, Assoc. Prof. of Econs 1986–88, Prof. of Econs 1988–96,
Assoc. Head, Dept of Econs 1994–2000, 2001–06, Mitsui Prof. of Econs 1996–,
Head, Dept of Econs 2006–08, mem. Program Bd MIT Center for Energy and
Environmental Policy Research 1993–, MIT Advisory Cttee on Shareholder
Responsibility 2006–08; CRSP Visiting Prof. of Finance, Univ. of Chicago GSB
1988; Faculty Research Fellow, Nat. Bureau of Econ. Research (NBER) 1982–85,
Research Assoc. 1985, Assoc. Dir Taxation Research Program, NBER 1989–91, Dir
NBER Public Econs Research Program 1991–2008, Pres. and CEO NBER 2008–;
Dir American Finance Asscn 1993–95; Fellow, Center for Advanced Study in
Behavioral Sciences 1993–94; George and Karen McCown Distinguished Visiting
Fellow, Hoover Inst. 2000–01; Distinguished Scholar, American Council on Capital
Formation 2002; CES Distinguished Fellow, Univ. of Munich 2003; TIAA-CREF
Inst. Fellow 2004–06; Int. Research Fellow, Inst. for Fiscal Studies, London, UK
2006; Int. Research Fellow, Centre for Business Taxation, Univ. of Oxford 2007–;
mem. Research Advisory Bd American Council on Capital Formation 1993–,
Advisory Bd Stanford Inst. for Econ. Policy Research 2005–, Econs Advisory Panel
Congressional Budget Office 2006–, Retirement Security Task Force, Investment
Co. Inst. 2007; First Vice-Pres. Nat. Tax Asscn 2008 (Second Vice-Pres. 2007);
mem. Exec. Cttee American Econs Asscn 2001–03, Chair. Honors and Awards
Cttee 2006–; Sr Fellow, Inst. for Policy Reform 1992–93; Assoc. Ed. Journal of
Finance 1988–2000, Review of Economics & Statistics 1993–2002, Regional
Science & Urban Economics 1997–2004; Co-Ed. RAND Journal of Economics
1986–95, Journal of Public Economics 1995–97 (Ed. 1998–2006, Advisory Ed.
2007–); mem. Advisory Bd Journal of Investment Consulting 1998–2005, Journal
of Wealth Management 1998–, Retirement Income Review 2002–; mem. Editorial
Advisory Bd National Tax Journal 2007–; mem. NAS 2015–; Fellow, Econometric
Soc. 1988, Nat. Acad. of Social Insurance 1992, American Acad. of Arts and
Sciences 1996; Trustee, Coll. Retirement Equity Fund (TIAA-CREF) 2006–; John
Williams Prize 1980, Marshall Scholarship 1980–83, George Webb Medley MPhil
Thesis Prize 1982, Batterymarch Financial Fellowship 1986, James L. Barr Award
1986, Alfred P. Sloan Fellowship 1988, MIT Econs Dept Teacher of the Year 1990,
1993, 1995, Certificate of Excellence, Paul Samuelson Prize, TIAA-CREF 1996,
2004, Nat. Acad. of Sciences Award for Scientific Reviewing 1999, Duncan Black
Prize, Public Choice Soc. 2000, Hon. Mention, Culp-Wright Book Award, American
Risk and Insurance Asscn 2003, EFACT Hon. Award, Univ. of Tilburg 2005, Daniel
Holland Medal, Nat. Tax Asscn 2014. *Publications:* Economic Policy Responses to
Global Warming (co-ed.), Tax Policy and the Economy: Vols 6–22 (ed.) 1992–2008,
Public Policies and Household Saving (ed.) 1994, Housing Markets in the United
States and Japan (co-ed.) 1994, International Comparisons of Household Saving
(ed.) 1994), Empirical Foundations of Household Taxation (co-ed.) 1996, Border-
line Case: International Tax Policy, Corporate Research and Development, and
Investment (ed.) 1998, Fiscal Institutions and Fiscal Performance (co-ed.) 1999,
Fiscal Rules and State Borrowing Costs: Evidence from California and Other
States (co-author) 1999, The Role of Annuity Markets in Financing Retirement (co-
author) 2001, Fiscal Reform in Colombia: Problems and Prospects (co-ed.) 2005;
more than 200 book chapters, reviews, articles and papers in professional journals.
Address: Department of Economics, Massachusetts Inst. of Tech., E17-214, 77
Massachusetts Avenu, Cambridge, MA 02139 (office); National Bureau of
Economic Research, Inc., 1050 Massachusetts Avenue, Cambridge, MA 02138-
5398, USA. *Telephone:* (617) 253-6673 (MIT) (office); (617) 868-3900 (NBER)
(office). *Fax:* (617) 868-2742 (NBER) (office). *E-mail:* poterba@mit.edu (office).
Website: econ-www.mit.edu/faculty/poterba (office); www.nber.org (office).

POTIER, Benoît; French business executive; *Chairman and CEO, Air Liquide;* b.
3 Sept. 1957, Mulhouse; m. Claude Menard; ed Ecole Centrale Paris; joined
Research Devt Dept, Air Liquide 1981, positions in Eng and Construction Div.
1993–97, CEO 1997–, mem. Bd 2000–, Chair. 2006–, Chair. and CEO Air Liquide
International, American Air Liquide Inc.; mem. Bd of Dirs Danone Group; mem.
Supervisory Bd Michelin; Vice-Chair. European Round Table of Industrialists
–2014, Chair. 2014–; Admin. École Centrale des Arts et Manufactures; mem.
Conseil de France, Institut Européen d'Admin des Affaires (INSEAD), European
Trilateral Comm.; Chevalier, Légion d'honneur, Officier, Ordre nat. du Mérite.
Address: Air Liquide, 75 quai d'Orsay, 75321 Paris Cedex 07, France (office).
Telephone: 1-40-68-55-55 (office). *Fax:* 1-40-68-58-40 (office). *E-mail:* info@
airliquide.com (office). *Website:* www.airliquide.com (office).

POTOČNIK, Janez, BA, MA, PhD; Slovenian economist, government official and
fmr EU official; b. 22 March 1958, Kropa; m.; two c.; ed Univ. of Ljubljana; Analyst,
SDK 1983–84; Asst Dir Inst. of Econ. Analysis and Devt, Ljubljana 1984–87; Sr
Researcher, Inst. for Econ. Research, Ljubljana 1988–93; part-time Asst Prof. of
Statistics and Economy, Faculty of Law, Univ. of Ljubljana 1991–2004; Dir Inst. of
Macroeconomic Analysis and Devt, Ljubljana 1993–2001; Head of negotiating
team for Slovenian accession to EU 1998–2004; Minister Counsellor in Prime
Minister's Cabinet 2001–02; Minister for European Affairs 2002–04; EC 'Shadow'
Commr for Enlargement, sharing portfolio with Commr Günther Verheugen
May–Nov. 2004, for Science and Research 2004–10, for Environment 2010–14;
mem. Liberalna demokracija Slovenije; Hon. DSc (Imperial Coll. London) 2008; Dr
hc (Ghent Univ., Belgium) 2009; Fray Int. Sustainability Award 2011.

POTRČ, Marjetica; Slovenian artist and architect; b. 1953, Ljubljana; d. of Ivan
Potrč and Branka Jurca; ed Univ. of Ljubljana; Assoc. Prof., Dept of Design, Acad.
of Fine Arts and Design, Ljubljana 1993–2004; taught at MIT, USA 2005,
Städelschule Art Acad., Frankfurt am Main, Germany 2006, Fondazione Antonio
Ratti, Como, Italy 2006, IUAV Faculty of Arts and Design, Venice 2008, 2010; Prof.
of Social Practice, Univ. of Fine Arts/HFBK, Hamburg, Germany 2011–18; Visiting
Prof. at numerous institutions, including MIT 2005, Università Iuav di Venezia
2008, 2010; work has been exhibited extensively throughout Europe and the
Americas, including Venice Biennial 1993, 2003, 2009, São Paulo Biennial 1996,
2006, Skulptur: Projekte in Münster, Germany 1997; her work 'Soweto House with
Prepaid Water Meter' exhibited at Eli and Edythe Broad Art Museum, Michigan
State Univ., East Lansing 2013; Pollock-Krasner Foundation Grants 1993, 1999,
Hugo Boss Prize 2000, Caracas Case Project Fellowship, Federal Cultural
Foundation, Germany and Caracas Urban Think Tank, Venezuela 2002, Vera

List Center for Arts and Politics Fellowship, New School in New York 2007. *Publications include:* Urban Negotiation 2003, Next Stop, Kiosk 2003, Urgent Architecture 2003, Fragment Worlds 2006, Florestania 2009; several essays on contemporary architecture and art. *Address:* c/o Galerie Nordenhake, Berlin/Stockholm Lindenstrasse 34, Berlin 10969, Germany. *Telephone:* (30) 206-1483. *Fax:* (30) 2061-4848. *E-mail:* berlin@nordenhake.com. *Website:* www.nordenhake.com; www.potrc.org.

POTRČ, Miran; Slovenian politician and lawyer; b. 27 March 1938, Maribor, Slovenia; s. of Ivan Potrč and Olga Potrč; m. Zdenka Potrč 1992; one d.; ed Univ. of Ljubljana; with Secr. of Justice and Public Admin Maribor 1962–63; Head, Legal Dept Mariborska Livarna (Maribor Foundry) 1963–68; Sec. Communal Cttee of League of Communists of Maribor 1968–73; mem. Presidency of Cen. Cttee League of Communists of Slovenia and Pres. Comm. for Socio-Economic Matters and Social Policy 1973; mem. Exec. Cttee Presidency of Cen. Cttee of League of Communists of Slovenia 1974–78; Vice-Pres. Repub. Council of Trade Unions of Slovenia 1978–80; mem. Presidency, Trade Unions of Yugoslavia 1980–82, Pres. 1980–81; Head, Del. of Skupshtina (Parl.) of SR of Slovenia in Fed. Chamber of Repubs and Provs 1982–86; Pres. Skupshtina of SR of Slovenia 1986–90; mem. Parl. of Repub. of Slovenia, Head of Parl. Group and mem. Presidium, Party of Democratic Reforms of Slovenia 1990–2011; Head of Parl. Group United List of Social Democrats, Vice-Pres. Social Democrats 2009; fmr Pres. Council, Univ. of Maribor. *Address:* c/o Assembly of the Republic of Slovenia, Tomšičeva 5, 61000 Ljubljana, Slovenia. *E-mail:* miran.potrc@dz-ns.si.

PÖTSCH, Hans Dieter, MSc; Austrian automotive industry executive; *Chairman of the Supervisory Board, Volkswagen AG;* b. 28 March 1951, Traun; ed Tech. Univ. of Darmstadt, Germany; Head of Group Controlling, BMW 1979–87; Man. Dir Finance and Admin, Trumpf GmbH & Co. KG, Ditzingen 1987–91; Chair. Traub AG, Reichenbach 1991–95; moved to Dürr AG, Stuttgart 1995, CEO 2002–03; mem. Supervisory Bd, Volkswagen AG 2003–, mem. Exec. Bd, initially without portfolio, responsible for Finance and Control at Group level, Chief Financial Officer Porsche Automobil Holding SE 2009–15, CEO Porsche SE, Chair. Supervisory Bd, Volkswagen AG 2015–; Chair. Supervisory Bd, LeasePlan Corpn NV –2007; mem. Supervisory Bd, Bertelsmann SE & Co. KGaA 2011, MAN SE 2012–; Ind. Dir Scania AB 2007–. *Address:* Volkswagen AG, PO Box 1849, VHH 11th Floor, 38436 Wolfsburg, Germany (office). *Telephone:* (5361) 9-86622 (office). *Fax:* (5361) 9-30411 (office). *E-mail:* info@volkswagenag.com (office). *Website:* www.volkswagenag.com (office).

POTTAKIS, Yannis A.; Greek politician; b. 1939, Corinth; m. Constantina Alexopoulou; two s. one d.; ed Univs of Athens and Munich, Germany; founding mem. of Pasok; mem. Parl. 1977–; Alt. Minister of Nat. Economy 1982–83, Minister of Finance 1983–84, of Agric. 1985–89, of Justice 1995–96; Alt. Minister of Foreign Affairs; Chair. Council of Budget Ministers of EEC 1983.

POTTER, David Edwin, CBE, PhD, MA, FREng; British business executive; b. 4 July 1943, East London, South Africa; s. of Paul James Potter and Mary Agnes Snape; m. Elaine Goldberg 1969; three s.; ed Trinity Coll. Cambridge, Imperial Coll. London; Lecturer, Blackett Lab., Imperial Coll. London 1970–80; Asst Prof., UCLA 1974; Founder, Chair. and CEO Psion PLC 1980–2009; Dir Press Assoc. Ltd 1994–97 (Vice-Chair. 1995–97), London First Centre 1994–, Finsbury Tech. Trust 1995; Chair. Symbian Ltd 1998–2004; mem. Nat. Cttee of Inquiry into Higher Educ. (Dearing Cttee) 1996–97, Higher Educ. Funding Council for England 1997–2003, Council for Science and Tech., Cabinet Office 1998–2003; fmr mem. CBI London Regional Council; Visiting Fellow, Nuffield Coll. Oxford 1998–; Gov. London Business School 2000; Dir Bank of England 2003–09; Trustee, David and Elaine Potter Foundation; Hon. Fellow, Imperial Coll. 1998, London Business School 1998; Hon. DTech (Kingston) 1998, (Brunel) 1998, Hon. DSc (Sheffield) 2000, (Warwick) 2001, (York) 2002, (Edinburgh) 2002; Mountbatten Medal for Outstanding Services to Electronics Industry, Nat. Electronics Council 1994. *Publications:* Computational Physics 1972, contribs to numerous physics journals. *Leisure interests:* flute, gardening, reading, tennis. *Address:* 8 Hamilton Terrace, St John's Wood, London, NW8 9UG, England (home).

POTTER, John (Jack) E., MA; American business executive; *President and CEO, Metropolitan Washington Airports Authority;* b. 1956, Bronx, New York; m. Maureen Potter; two c.; ed Fordham Univ., Massachusetts Inst. of Tech. (Sloan Fellow); began career as distribution clerk, US Postal Service, Westchester, NY 1977, various exec. and man. positions including Sr Vice-Pres. Labour Relations 1998–99, Sr Vice-Pres. Operations 1999–2000, COO and Exec. Vice-Pres. 2000–01, Postmaster Gen. and CEO 2001–10, mem. Postal Service Bd of Govs; Pres. and CEO Metropolitan Washington Airports Authority 2011–; fmr Vice-Chair. Int. Post Corpn, Chair. Kahala Posts Group; mem. Pres.'s Nat. Hire Veterans Cttee; Republican; American Postal Services Bd of Govs Award 1999, Elmo Zumwalt Legacy Award, Marrow Foundation 2003, J. Edward Day Award, Asscn of Postal Commerce 2003, Tom Tully Award, AM Business Media 2006, Roger W. Jones Award for Executive Leadership, American Univ. 2007. *Address:* Metropolitan Washington Airports Authority, 1 Aviation Circle, Washington, DC 20001-6000, USA (office). *Telephone:* (703) 417-8600 (office). *E-mail:* info@mwaa.com (office). *Website:* www.mwaa.com (office).

PÖTTERING, Hans-Gert, PhD; German politician; b. 15 Sept. 1945, Bersenbrueck; two s.; ed Univs of Bonn and Geneva, Institut des Hautes Études Internationales, Geneva; Reserve Officer, Nat. Service 1966–68; European Policy Spokesman, Young Union of Lower Saxony 1974-80; Research Assistant Univ. of Osnabrueck, 1976–79, Lecturer 1989–95, Hon. Prof. 1995–; mem. European Parl. 1979–, Chair. European Parl. Sub-cttee on Security and Defence 1984–94, Vice-Chair. European People's Party–European Democrats Group (EPP–ED) Group 1994–99, Chair. 1999–2007, Leader EPP EU Enlargement Working Group 1996–99, Pres. European Parl. 2007–09; Chair. Konrad-Adenauer-Stiftung 2010–, Europa-Union Deutschland 1997–99; European Hon. Senator; Grand Order of Merit of the FRG, Grand Decoration of the Repub. of Austria, Grand Cross, Order of St Gregory the Great, Grand Order of Queen Jelena with Sash and Star (Croatia); Dr hc (Babeş-Bolyai-Univ., Cluj-Napoca, Romania); Konsul-Penseler P, Artland-Gymnasium, Quakenbrück, Robert Schuman Medal, EPP-Group, Gold Medal of Mérite Européen, Luxembourg, MEP of the Year 2004 (European Voice), Walter Hallstein Prize (Frankfurt am Main) 2007. *Publications:*

Adenauers Sicherheitspolitik 1955–1963. Ein Beitrag zum deutsch-amerikanischen Verhältnis (Adenauer's Security Policy 1955–1963. A Contribution to the German-American relationship) 1975, Die vergessenen Regionen: Plädoyer für eine solidarische Regionalpolitik in der Europäischen Gemeinschaft (The Forgotten Regions: for a European Community Regional Policy Based on Solidarity) (with Frank Wiehler) 1983, Europas vereinigte Staaten: Annäherungen an Werte und Ziele (Europe's United States: Approaches to Values and Objectives) (with Ludger Kühnhardt) 1993, Kontinent Europa: Kern, Übergänge, Grenzen (The Continent of Europe: Nucleus, Transitions, Borders) (with Ludger Kühnhardt) 1998, Weltpartner Europäische Union (The European Union as a World Partner) (with Ludger Kühnhardt) 2001, Von der Vision zur Wirklichkeit. Auf dem Weg zur Einigung Europas (From Vision to Reality: Towards a United Europe) 2004. *Address:* European Parliament, Rue Wiertz 60, PHS 08B043, 1047 Brussels, Belgium (office). *E-mail:* hans-gert.poettering@europarl.europa.eu (office). *Website:* www.poettering.eu (office).

POUDEL, Ram Chandra, MA; Nepalese politician; ed Tribhuvan Univ., Kathmandu; mem. Parl. for Tanahu Dist 1994–99, 2013–; Minister for Local Devt and Agriculture 1991–94, Speaker, House of Reps (lower house) 1994–98, fmr Deputy Prime Minister and Minister of Home 1999–2002, Minister for Peace and Reconstruction 2007–08; apptd Gen. Sec. Cen. Cttee Nepali Congress 2006, Vice-Pres. 2007; mem. Nepali Nat. Congress party. *Publications:* What Nepali Congress Says 1976, Satyagraha: Why and How 1984, Democratic Socialism: A Study 1990, Journey of Faith 1996, Abhisapta Ethihas 2004, Socialism: In New Context 2012, Agricultural Revolution and Socialism 2013. *Address:* Nepali Congress Party, Bhansar Tole, Teku, Kathmandu, Nepal (office). *Website:* www.nepalicongress.org (office).

POUGATCHEV, Sergueï, DTechSc; Russian politician and banker; b. 4 Feb. 1963, Kostroma; s. of Viktor Fyodorovich Pugachev; m. 1st Galina Pugacheva (divorced); two s.; m. 2nd Alexandra Tolstoy (divorced); five c.; f. Mejprombank 1992, Dir and later Pres. –2001; mem. (Senator) Council of the Fed. for Tver Oblast 2001–11; acquired numerous properties and cos including Luxe TV, Poljot (watches), Hédiard (French luxury grocer) 2007, France-Soir (French newspaper) 2010; co-f. Almazi Yakoutil co.; full mem. Int. Eng. Acad.; Order of Holy Prince Daniel of Moscow 1996, Order of St Serafim of Sarov, 3rd degree 2010.

POUND, Richard (Dick) William Duncan, CC, OQ, QC, BCom, BA, BCL, LLD, FCPA; Canadian fmr Olympic swimmer, lawyer, chartered accountant and university administrator; *Of Counsel, Stikeman Elliott LLP;* b. 22 March 1942, St Catharines, Ont.; s. of William Thomas Pound and Jessie Edith Duncan Thom; m. Julie Houghton Keith; ed McGill Univ. and Sir George Williams Univ. (now Concordia Univ.), Montreal; competitor in Olympics Games, Rome 1960, double finalist in 100m freestyle (6th) and 4×100m medley relay (4th); Gold Medal in 110-yard freestyle event, two Silver Medals in 440- and 880-yard freestyle relay, and Bronze Medal in 440-yard medley relay, Commonwealth Games 1962; Canadian Champion in freestyle 1958, 1960–62, butterfly 1961; Sec. Canadian Olympic Asscn 1968–76, Pres. 1977–82; Deputy Chef de Mission, Canadian Olympic Del., Munich 1972; joined IOC in 1978, served on Exec. Bd 1983–91, 1992–2000, Vice-Pres. IOC 1987–91, 1996–2000, Chair. Coordination Comm. for Olympic Games in Atlanta 1996; his investigation of Salt Lake City Winter Olympics scandal led to creation of new ethics watchdog to monitor future interaction between bidding cities and IOC mems; Chair. World Anti-Doping Agency (WADA), Lausanne, Switzerland 1999–2007, Chair. WADA Ind. Comm. to investigate doping in athletics in Russia; Chair. Olympic Broadcasting Services; currently Of Counsel, Stikeman Elliott LLP, Montreal; lectured in taxation matters at Faculty of Law, McGill Univ., Montreal and at McGill Centre for Continuing Educ. in Chartered Accountancy program, Past Pres. Grads' Soc. (now McGill Alumni Asscn), fmr Chair. Alma Mater Fund and McGill's Fund Council, mem. Bd Govs 1986 (Chair. 1994–99), Chancellor, McGill Univ. 1999–2009, Chancellor Emer. 2009–; apptd to Fed. Court Bench and Bar Liaison Cttee; Ed. Canada Tax Cases, Stikeman Annotated Income Tax Act, Pound's Tax Case Notes; fmr Ed. Legal Notes, CGA Magazine; mem. Int. Council Arbitration for Sport 2007–18 (currently Arbitrator), Canadian Tax Foundation, Asscn de planification fiscale et financière, Canadian Bar Asscn, Int. Fiscal Asscn, American Bar Asscn, IOC; Chubb Fellow, Timothy Dwight Coll., Yale Univ. 2004; mem. Quebec and Ontario Bars; Hon. Consul Gen. of Norway in Montreal 1991–2011; Hon. Col, Canadian Grenadier Guards; several Canadian and foreign decorations; Hon. PhD (United Sports Acad.) 1989; Hon. LLD (Univ. of Windsor) 1997, (Univ. of Western Ontario) 2004, (McGill Univ.), (Concordia Univ.), (Univ. of Toronto), (Law Soc. of Upper Canada); Dr hc (Laurentian Univ.) 2005, (Beijing Sport Univ.) 2006, (Université de Québec), (Loughborough Univ.), (Univ. of Bristol), (Lakehead Univ.); Carswell Company Prize, McGill Univ. 1967, Laureus Spirit of Sport Prize 2008, inducted into Canada Sports Hall of Fame 2011. *Publications:* Five Rings Over Korea 1994, Chief Justice W. R. Jackett: By the Law of the Land 1999, Stikeman Elliott: The Firts Fifty Years 2002, Inside the Olympics 2004, High Impact Quotations 2004, Canadian Facts and Dates 2004, Inside Dope 2006, Unlucky to the End: The Story of Janise Gamble 2007, Rocke Robertson, Surgeon and Shepherd of Change 2008, Stikeman Elliott: New Millennium, New Paradigms 2012, Quotations for the Fast Lane 2013, Made in Court: Supreme Court Cases That Shaped Canada 2014; Ed.-in-Chief: Annotated Stikeman Income Tax Act (Carswell), Canada Tax Cases (Carswell), Doing Business in Canada; ed. and author of Pound's Tax Case Notes (Carswell). *Address:* Stikeman Elliott LLP, 1155 René-Lévesque Blvd West, 41st Floor, Montreal, QC H3B 3V2 (office); 87 Arlington Avenue, Westmount, QC H3Y 2W5, Canada (home). *Telephone:* (514) 397-3037 (office). *Fax:* (514) 397-3063 (office). *E-mail:* rpound@stikeman.com (office). *Website:* www.stikeman.com (office).

POUNDS, Kenneth (Ken) Alwyne, CBE, BSc, PhD, FRS; British astrophysicist and academic; *Professor Emeritus of Space Physics, University of Leicester;* b. 17 Nov. 1934, Leeds, Yorks., England; s. of Harry Pounds and Dorothy Pounds (née Hunt); m. 1st Margaret Connell 1961; two s. one d.; m. 2nd Joan Mary Millit 1982; one s. one d.; ed Salt High School, Shipley, Yorks., Univ. Coll., London; Prof. of Space Physics, Univ. of Leicester 1973–2002, Prof. Emer. 2002–, Dir X-ray Astronomy Group 1973–94, Head of Dept of Physics and Astronomy 1986–2002 (on leave of absence 1994–98); Chief Exec. Particle Physics and Astronomy Research Council 1994–98; Pres. Royal Astronomical Soc. 1990–92; mem. Academia Europaea, Int. Acad. of Astronautics; Fellow, University Coll. London 1993,

Hon. Distinguished Fellow; Leverhulme Research Fellow 2003–05; Founding Trustee, Nat. Space Centre 2001–16; Hon. DUniv (York), Hon. DSc (Loughborough, Sheffield Hallam, Warwick, Leicester); Gold Medal, Royal Astronomical Soc. 1990, Planetary Scientist of the Year 2007, COSPAR Space Science Award 2008. *Publications:* more than 375 scientific publs. *Leisure interests:* sport, music. *Address:* Department of Physics and Astronomy, University of Leicester, University Road, Leicester, LE1 7RH (office); 12 Swale Close, Oadby, Leics., LE2 4GF, England (home). *Telephone:* (116) 252-3509 (office); (116) 271-9370 (home). *E-mail:* kap@le.ac.uk (office). *Website:* www2.le.ac.uk/departments/physics/research/xroa (office).

POUNGUI, Ange-Edouard; Republic of the Congo politician, economist and banker; b. 1942; began career in school, student unions; apptd mem. Nat. Council for Revolution 1968, then mem. Political Bureau, Minister for Finance 1971–73, Vice-Pres. Council of State and Minister for Planning 1973–76; Prime Minister of The Congo 1984–89; fmr Pres. Union pour le Renouveau Démocratique (URD); worked for IMF and African Devt Bank, then Dir-Gen. Cen. African Bank 1976–79, then CEO Congolese Commercial Bank; Dir Cen. Bank of the Congo 1994–2001; apptd one of 25 Vice-Presidents of Union panafricaine pour la démocratie sociale (UPADS); selected as UPADS cand. for 2009 presidential election, but ruled ineligible to stand; mem. Senate for Bouenza Dept 2011–. *Address:* c/o Union panafricaine pour la démocratie sociale, BP 1370, Brazzaville, Republic of the Congo (office). *E-mail:* courrier@upads.org (office). *Website:* www.upads.org (office).

POUNTNEY, David Willoughby, CBE, MA; British opera director; b. 10 Sept. 1947, Oxford; s. of E. W. Pountney and D. L. Byrt; m. 1st Jane R. Henderson 1980; one s. one d.; m. 2nd Nicola Raab 2007; ed St John's Coll. Choir School, Cambridge, Radley Coll. and St John's Coll., Cambridge; first opera production, Scarlatti's Trionfo dell'Onore, Cambridge 1967; Katya Kabanova at Wexford Festival 1972; Dir of Productions, Scottish Opera 1975–80; Australian debut in Die Meistersinger 1978; world premiere of Philip Glass's Satyagraha, Netherlands Opera 1980; Prin. Prod. and Dir of Productions, ENO 1982–93; US debut with Houston Opera, Verdi's Macbeth, returning for world premiere of Bilby's Doll by Carlisle Floyd, Katya Kabanova and Jenůfa; produced Weill's Street Scene for Scottish Opera 1989; Independent and Artistic Dir Bregenzer Festspiele 2003–13; Chief Exec. and Artistic Dir Welsh Nat. Opera 2011–15, Artistic Dir 2015–19; Janáček Medal, SWET Award, Martinu Medal, Olivier Award; Chevalier des Arts et des Lettres, Knight's Cross, Order of Merit of the Repub. of Poland, Ehrenkreuz des Bundes Osterreich 2014. *Publications include:* Powerhouse; The Doctor of Mydffai (libretto for Peter Maxwell Davies), Mr Emmett Takes a Walk (libretto for Peter Maxwell Davies), Kommilitonen (libretto for Peter Maxwell Davies); several trans. from German, Italian, Russian and Czech. *Leisure interests:* gardening, cooking, croquet. *Address:* IMG Artists, Capital Tower, 91 Waterloo Road, London, SE1 8RT, England (office). *Telephone:* (20) 7957-5800 (office). *Fax:* (20) 7957-5801 (office). *E-mail:* bsegal@imgartists.com (office). *Website:* imgartists.com/artist/david_pountney (office).

POUPARD, HE Cardinal Paul; French ecclesiastic; b. 30 Aug. 1930, Bouzillé; s. of Joseph Poupard and Celestine Guéry; ed Catholic Univ., Angers, Ecole Pratique des Hautes Etudes Sorbonne Univ.; ordained priest 1954; Parochial Minister, Paris and attaché to CNRS 1958; attaché to Sec. of State 1959–71; Rector Institut Catholique de Paris 1971–81; Titular Bishop of Usula 1979, Archbishop 1980; cr. Cardinal 1985; Priest of S. Prassede; Pres. Pontifical Council for Culture 1982–2007, for Inter-Religious Dialogue 2006–07; Commdr, Légion d'honneur, Grand Cross Order of Merit (Germany), Grand Prix Cardinal Crente, Acad. Française, Prix Robert Schuman, Prix Empedocle. *Publications include:* Les Religions 1987, L'Eglise au Défi des Cultures 1989, The Church and Culture 1989, Dieu et la Liberté 1992, Après Galilée, Science et Foi, Nouveau Dialogue 1994, What Will Give Us Happiness 1992, Dictionnaire des Religions 1993, Le Christianisme à l'aube du troisième millénaire 1999, Where is Your God? Responding to the Challenge of Unbelief and Religious Intolerance Today 2004, Que sais-je: Les Religions 2004, Foi et cultures au tournant du nouveau millénaire 2005, Chant Grégorien: Art et Prière de l'Eglise 2005, Foi Catholique 2005, L'affaire Galilée 2005, Le christianisme, ferment de nouveauté en Europe 2005, Lumières de Terre Sainte 2005, Le catholicisme au défi des cultures 2006, Des femmes prêtres? 2006, Paul de Tarse : Navigateur de l'espérance 2006, La Voie de la Beauté: Assemblée plénière de 2006, Voyage apostolique de Benoît XVI à Munich, Altötting et Ratisbonne 2006, Le concile Vatican II 2007. *Address:* Piazza San Calisto, 00120 Vatican City (home).

POUSSOT, Bernard; French business executive; ed Ecole Supérieure de Commerce de Paris; Chair. Students' Council, Ecole Supérieure de Commerce de Paris 1975; mil. service as civil servant in Casablanca, Morocco 1976–77; began career with Merck and Searle in marketing positions in Europe and USA; joined Wyeth Gen. Man. France 1986–91, Head of Europe 1991–93, Exec. Vice-Pres. 1993–96, Pres. Wyeth International 1996–97, Pres. Wyeth Pharmaceuticals (global pharmaceutical div. of Wyeth) 1997–2006, Pres. and Vice-Chair. Wyeth 2006–, mem. Bd of Dirs, Vice-Chair., Pres. and COO 2007–08, Vice-Chair., Pres. and CEO Jan.–June 2008, Chair., Pres. and CEO June 2008–09; mem. Bd Univ. of Pennsylvania School of Dental Medicine, Eisenhower Fellowships, French American Chamber of Commerce, Opera Co. of Philadelphia, World Affairs Council; mem. Bd of Dirs Cargill Inc. 2010–, Roche Holding 2015–, Pharmaceutical Research and Manufacturers of America; mem. Bd of Trustees Lankenau Hospital Foundation 2011–15; Fellow, New York Acad. of Medicine 2009; Légion d'Honneur 2007; Sabin Lifetime Award 2003, Union League Founders Award for Business Leadership 2006. *Website:* www.roche.com.

POUYANNÉ, Patrick; French engineer and energy industry executive; *Chairman and CEO, Total SA;* b. 24 June 1963, Petit-Quevilly (Seine-Maritime); m.; four c.; ed École Polytechnique, Paris; fmr Chief Engineer, Corps des Mines eng school; held various admin. positions in Ministry of Industry 1989–93; tech. adviser to Prime Minister Edouard Balladur on environment and industry 1993–95; Cabinet Dir, Minister for Information and Aerospace Technologies 1995–96; joined Total's Exploration and Production Div. 1997, Chief Admin. Officer in Angola 1997–99, Group Rep. in Qatar and Pres. of Exploration and Production subsidiary there 1999–2002, Pres., Finance, Economy and IT, Exploration and Production Div. 2002–06, Pres., Strategy, Growth and Research

2006–11, mem. Man. Cttee 2006–, Vice-Pres., Chemicals and Vice-Pres., Petrochemicals 2011–12, Pres., Refining and Chemicals and mem. Exec. Cttee 2012–14, CEO Total SA and Pres. Exec. Cttee 2014–, mem. Bd of Dirs May 2015–, Chair. Dec. 2015–. *Address:* Total SA, 2 place Jean Millier, La Défense 6, 92078 Paris La Défense Cedex, France (office). *Telephone:* 1-47-44-22-44 (office); 1-47-44-22-33 (office). *Fax:* 1-47-44-49-53 (office). *E-mail:* info@total.com (office). *Website:* www.total.com (office).

POUZIN, Louis; French computer scientist; b. 20 April 1931, Chantenay-Saint-Imbert (Nièvre); ed École Polytechnique, Paris; on staff, MIT Computer Center 1960s; Dir Cyclades project at Institut de Recherche d'Informatique et d'Automatique, France 1970s; Lecturer, Asscn for Computing Machinery (ACM); Dean of Information Tech., THESEUS (France Telecom inst.) early 1990s; Project Dir, Eurolinc France; apptd Chair. Native Language Internet Consortium 2006; Chevalier, Légion d'honneur 2003; Silver Core Award, Int. Fed. for Information Processing, IEEE Internet Award, ACM SIGCOMM Award 1997, inducted into Internet Hall of Fame, Internet Soc. 2012, Queen Elizabeth Prize for Eng (corecipient) 2013, Global IT Award 2016. *Achievements include:* best known as inventor and advocate of datagram, designed the first packet communications network, Cyclades; also created first forms of command-line interface; his work was broadly used by Vinton Cerf in his development of Internet and TCP/IP. *Publications:* one book and 82 articles on computer networks.

POWATHIL, Most Rev. Joseph, MA, DD; Indian ecclesiastic; *Archbishop Emeritus of Changanacherry;* b. 14 Aug. 1930, Kurumpanadom; s. of Ulahannan Joseph Powathil and Mariyam Joseph Powathil; ed St Berchmans' Coll., Changanacherry, Loyola Coll., Madras, St Thomas Minor Seminary, Parel and Papal Seminary, Pune; ordained RC priest 1962; Lecturer in Econs, St Berchmans's Coll., Changanacherry 1963–72; Auxiliary Bishop of Changanacherry 1972–77, Titular Bishop of Caesarea Philipi, 1972, consecrated Bishop 1972; 1st Bishop of Kanjirappally Diocese, Kerala 1977–85; Archbishop of Changanacherry 1985–2007, Archbishop Emer. 2007–; Chair. Kerala Catholic Bishops' Conf. (KCBC) and Chair. Educational Comm. 1993–96; Pres. Catholic Bishops' Conf. of India (CBCI) 1993–98; Perm. mem. Syro Malabar Bishops' Synod 1993; Chair. CBCI Comm. for Educ. and Clergy, KCBC Comm. for Vigilance 1998–; mem. Comm. for Devt, Justice and Peace; Chair. SMBC Comm. for Ecumenism 1993–; Chair. Inter-Church Council for Educ. 1990–; mem. Asian Synod of Bishops, Post Synodal Council (for Asia) 1998–; mem. Pontifical Comm. for Dialogue with the Orthodox Syrian Church; Chair. Religious Fellowship Foundation 1994; Hon. mem. Pro-Oriente, Vienna 1994. *Address:* Metropolitan Archbishop's House, PO Box 20, Changanacherry, Kottayam 686 101, India (office). *Telephone:* (481) 2420040 (office). *Fax:* (481) 2422540 (office). *E-mail:* abchry@sancharnet.in (office). *Website:* www.archdiocesechanganacherry.org.

POWELL, Gen. Colin Luther, MBA; American business executive, academic, fmr army officer and fmr government official; *Strategic Advisor, Kleiner Perkins Caufield and Byers;* b. 5 April 1937, New York, NY; s. of Luther Powell and Maud A. McKoy; m. Alma V. Johnson 1962; one s. (Michael K. Powell) two d.; ed City Coll. of New York and George Washington Univ.; commissioned, US Army 1958, Commdr 2nd Brigade, 101st Airborne Div. 1976–77, rank of Lt Gen. 1986; Exec. Asst to Sec. of Dept of Energy 1979; Sr Mil. Asst to Sec. of Dept of Defense 1979–81; Asst Div. Commdr 4th Infantry Div., Fort Carson, Colo 1981–83; Mil. Asst to Sec. of Defense 1983–86; assigned to US V Corps, Europe 1986–87; Nat. Security Adviser, White House, Washington, DC 1987–88; C-in-C US Forces, Fort McPherson, Ga April–Sept. 1989; Chair. Jt Chiefs of Staff 1989–93; Sec. of State for Defense 2001–05 (resgnd); public speaker 1993–2000; Strategic Advisor, Kleiner Perkins Caufield & Byers (venture capital firm) 2005–; investor and mem. Bd, Revolution Health Group LLC 2005–; Founder, Advisory Council Chair, Distinguished Scholar, Colin Powell Center for Policy Studies, City Coll. of New York 1997–; Chair. Pres.'s Summit for America's Future 1997–; Founding Chair. America's Promise: The Alliance for Youth 1997–2001; Fellow, American Acad. of Arts and Sciences 2009–; Legion of Merit, Bronze Star, Air Medal, Purple Heart, Presidential Medal of Freedom, Presidential Citizen's Medal; Hon. KCB 1993; Order of Jamaica; Hon. LLD (Univ. of West Indies) 1994. *Publication:* My American Journey (autobiog., with Joseph E. Persico) 1995. *Address:* Kleiner Perkins Caufield & Byers, 2750 Sand Hill Road, Menlo Park, CA 94025, USA (office). *Telephone:* (650) 233-2750 (office). *Fax:* (650) 233-0300 (office). *E-mail:* plans@kpcb.com (office). *Website:* www.kpcb.com (office).

POWELL, Dina Habib; American (b. Egyptian) business executive and fmr government official; b. 12 June 1973, Cairo, Egypt; d. of Onsi Habib and Hoda Soliman; m. Richard C. Powell; two d.; ed Univ. of Texas; began career as intern for US Senator Kay Bailey Hutchinson and US Rep. Dick Armey, Washington, DC; Dir of Congressional Affairs and Sr Advisor to Chair., Republican Nat. Cttee 1999–2001; Special Asst to Pres. George W. Bush 2001–03, Asst to Pres. for Presidential Personnel 2003–05, Asst Sec. of State for Educational and Cultural Affairs, US State Dept 2005–07; joined Goldman Sachs as Man. Dir 2007, Partner 2010–, Dir of Global Corp. Engagement, Goldman Sachs Group 2007–, also Pres. Goldman Sachs Foundation; Sr Counselor to Pres. for Econ. Initiatives 2017; US Deputy Nat. Security Advisor for Strategy 2017–18; mem. Bd of Dirs Center for Global Development; mem. Bd of Trustees American Univ. in Cairo, Vital Voices Global Partnership, Nightingale-Bamford School; mem. Council on Foreign Relations; named Young Global Leader by World Econ. Forum.

POWELL, Earl Alexander, III, AB, AM, PhD; American art museum director; *Director, National Gallery of Art;* b. 24 Oct. 1943, Spartanburg, SC; s. of Earl Alexander Powell, II and Elizabeth Duckworth; m. Nancy Landry 1971; three d.; ed Williams Coll. and Harvard Univ.; served in USN 1966–69, Naval Reserve 1969–80; Teaching Fellow, Harvard Univ. 1970–74; Curator, Michener Collection, Univ. of Texas, Austin 1974–76, also Asst Prof. of Art History; Museum Curator, Sr Staff Asst to Asst Dir and Chief Curator, Nat. Gallery of Art, Washington, DC 1976–78, Exec. Curator 1979–80, Dir 1992–; Dir LA Co. Museum of Art 1980–92; Trustee, American Fed. of Arts, Morris and Gwendolyn Cafritz Foundation, Nat. Trust for Historic Preservation, White House Historical Asscn, John F. Kennedy Center for Performing Arts, Norton Simon Museum, The Mariner's Museum; mem. Comm. of Fine Arts 2003–, Vice-Chair. 2004–05, Chair. 2005–; mem. Asscn of Art Museum Dirs, Cttee for the Preservation of the White House, Pres.'s Cttee on the Arts and Humanities, American Philosophical Soc., American Acad. of Arts and Sciences, Fed. Council on the Arts and the Humanities, Nat. Portrait Gallery Comm., Friends of Art and Preservation in Embassies; Grand Official, Order of the Infante D. Henrique 1995, Commendatore, Ordine al Merito (Italy) 1998, Chevalier Légion d'honneur 2000, Officier Ordre des Arts et des Lettres 2004, Order of the Aztec Eagle (Mexico) 2007, Officer's Cross of the Order of Merit (Hungary); Dr hc (Williams Coll.) 1993, (Otis Parsons Art Inst.); King Olav Medal 1978, Williams Bicentennial Medal 1995, Mexican Cultural Inst. Award 1996, Centennial Medal, Harvard Graduate School of Arts and Sciences 2008. *Publications:* American Art at Harvard 1973, Selections from the James Michener Collection 1975, Abstract Expressionists and Imagists: A Retrospective View 1976, Milton Avery 1976, The James A. Michener Collection (catalogue) 1978, Thomas Cole monograph 1990. *Address:* National Gallery of Art, Sixth Street and Constitution Avenue, NW, Washington, DC 20565, USA (office). *Website:* www.nga.gov (office).

POWELL, Jerome (Jay) Hayden, AB, JD; American lawyer and central banker; *Chairman, Board of Governors, Federal Reserve System;* b. 4 Feb. 1953, Washington, DC; s. of Jerome Powell and Patricia Powell (née Hayden); m. Elissa Leonard 1985; three c.; ed Princeton Univ., Georgetown Univ. Law Center; Legis. Asst to Senator Richard Schweiker 1975–76; clerk to Judge Ellsworth Van Graafeiland, US Court of Appeals for the Second Circuit 1979–81; Lawyer, Davis Polk & Wardwell 1981–83; Lawyer, Werbel & McMillen 1983–84; with Dillon, Read & Co. (investment bank) 1984–90, 1995–97; worked at US Dept of the Treasury 1990–93, UnderSec. of the Treasury for Domestic Finance 1992–93; Man. Dir Bankers Trust 1993–95; Partner, The Carlyle Group 1997–2005; f. Severn Capital Partners (private investment firm) 2005; Man. Partner, Global Environment Fund (private equity and venture capital firm) 2008; Visiting Scholar, Bipartisan Policy Center (think tank), Washington, DC 2010–12; mem. Bd of Govs, Fed. Reserve System 2012–, Chair. 2018–; Republican. *Address:* Board of Governors of the Federal Reserve System, 20th Street and Constitution Avenue, NW, Washington, DC 20551, USA (office). *Telephone:* (202) 452-3000 (office). *Fax:* (202) 452-3819 (office). *Website:* www.federalreserve.gov (office).

POWELL, Jonathan Leslie; British television producer and academic; b. 25 April 1947, Faversham, Kent; s. of James Dawson Powell and Phyllis N. Sylvester (née Doubleday); m. Sally Brampton 1990 (divorced 2000); one d.; ed Sherborne School and Univ. of East Anglia; script and producer of drama, Granada TV 1970–77; producer, drama serials, BBC TV 1977–83, Head of Drama Series and Serials 1983–87; Controller BBC 1 1987–92; Dir Drama and Co-Production, Carlton TV 1993–2004; apptd Prof. of Media, Royal Holloway Coll., Univ. of London 2007, Head, Dept of Media Arts 2013–; Royal TV Soc. Silver Award 1979–80. *Television includes:* Testament of Youth 1979 (BAFTA award), Tinker, Tailor, Soldier, Spy 1979, Pride and Prejudice 1980, The Bell 1982, Smiley's People 1982 (Peabody Medal, USA), The Old Men at the Zoo 1983, Bleak House 1985, Tender is the Night 1985, A Perfect Spy 1987, The Woman in White 1997, Noah's Ark 1997, The Unknown Soldier 1998, Frenchman's Creek 1998, Big Bad World 1999, Dirty Tricks 2000, Bertie and Elizabeth 2002, Lloyd & Hill 2003, Fortysomething 2003, Doctors and Nurses 2004, Blue Dove 2004. *Leisure interest:* fly-fishing. *Address:* 1 First Avenue, Acton, London, W3 7JP, England (home). *Telephone:* (20) 8740-7853 (home).

POWELL, Jonathan Nicholas, MA; British political adviser and diplomatist; *Special Envoy to Libya;* b. 14 Aug. 1956, Fulbeck; s. of Air Vice-Marshal John Frederick Powell and Geraldine Ysolda Powell; m. Karen Drayne (divorced 1997); two s.; pnr Sarah Helm; two d.; ed Univ. Coll. Oxford, Univ. of Pennsylvania, USA; with BBC 1978, Granada TV 1978–79; joined FCO 1979, served in Lisbon 1980–83, FCO, London 1983–85, CSCE, Vienna 1985–89, FCO, London 1989–91, Washington 1991–95, UK Special Envoy to Libya 2014–; Chief of Staff to Leader of the Opposition 1995–97, to Prime Minister 1997–2007; Man. Dir of European Investment Banking, Morgan Stanley and Co. 2008–09; f. Inter Mediate (charity) 2011; mem. Bd of Dirs Save the Children Int. 2013–. *Publications:* Great Hatred, Little Room: Making Peace in Northern Ireland 2008, The New Machiavelli 2010, The Public Sector: Managing the Unmanageable, Kogan Page 2013, Talking to Terrorists: How to End Armed Conflicts, The Bodley Head 2014. *Leisure interests:* walking, skiing. *Address:* Foreign and Commonwealth Office, King Charles Street, London SW1A 2AH, England (office).

POWELL, Kendall (Ken) J., BA, MBA; American business executive; *Chairman and CEO, General Mills, Inc.;* b. 1954, Denver, Colo; ed Harvard Univ., Stanford Univ.; joined General Mills, Minneapolis, Minn. 1979, held various positions, helped launch Cereal Partners Worldwide (CPW) joint venture with Nestlé 1990, Pres. Yoplait USA 1996–97, Pres. General Mills Big G cereal div. 1997–99, CEO CPW 1999–2006, Pres. and COO General Mills 2006–07, CEO 2007–, Chair. 2008–; mem. Bd of Dirs Medtronic, Inc. *Address:* General Mills, Inc., PO Box 9452, Minneapolis, MN 55440, USA (office). *Telephone:* (800) 248-7310 (office). *Fax:* (763) 764-8330 (office). *E-mail:* info@generalmills.com (office). *Website:* www.generalmills.com (office).

POWELL, Michael K., JD; American lawyer and fmr government official; *President and CEO, National Cable and Telecommunications Association;* s. of Gen. Colin L. Powell (q.v.) and Alma V. Powell; m. Jane Knott Powell; two s.; ed Coll. of William and Mary, Georgetown Univ. Law Center; US Army service as Cavalry Platoon Leader and Troop Exec. Officer, 3/2 Armored Cavalry Regt, Amberg, Germany; fmr Policy Advisor to US Sec. of Defense; fmr Judicial Clerk to Chief Judge of Court of Appeals for DC Circuit; fmr Assoc., O'Melveny & Myers LLP, Washington, DC; fmr Chief of Staff, Antitrust Div., Dept of Justice; apptd mem. US Fed. Communications Comm. 1997, Chair. 2001–05; apptd Advisor, Providence Equity Pnrs Inc. 2005; fmr Co-Chair. Broadband for America; Pres. and CEO Nat. Cable and Telecommunications Asscn 2011–; fmr Rector, Bd of Visitors, Coll. of William and Mary; mem. Bd of Visitors, Georgetown Univ. Law Center; Henry Crown Fellow, Aspen Inst. 1999–, Sr Fellow, Communications and Society Program 2005–; mem. Bd of Dirs AOL 2009–, America's Promise Alliance (Co-Chair. Grad Nation); Henry Crown Leadership Award, Aspen Inst. 2004. *Address:* National Cable & Telecommunications Association, 25 Massachusetts Avenue, NW, Suite 100, Washington, DC 20001, USA (office). *Telephone:* (202) 222-2300 (office). *Fax:* (202) 222-2514 (office). *E-mail:* info@ncta.com (office). *Website:* www.ncta.com (office).

POWELL, Robert; British actor; b. 1 June 1944, Salford, Lancs., England; s. of John Wilson Powell and Kathleen C. Powell (née Davis); m. Barbara Lord 1975; one s. one d.; ed Manchester Grammar School, Univ. of Manchester; first job, Victoria Theatre, Stoke On Trent 1964; best known for the title role in Jesus of Nazareth 1977 and as the fictional secret agent Richard Hannay; also known for his role as Mark Williams in the medical drama, Holby City (BBC 1), and as David Briggs in the sitcom The Detectives; Hon. MA (Salford) 1990; Hon. DLitt (Salford) 2000. *Theatre includes:* has appeared in repertory seasons at Stoke, Scarborough and Bolton, A Smashing Day at the Arts Theatre, Ubu Roi and Pirates at The Royal Court Theatre, Hamlet at The Leeds Playhouse 1971, The Lady from the Sea (Greenwich Theatre), Glasstown (Prospect Theatre Co.), Travesties by Tom Stoppard for RSC 1975, Terra Nova at the Watford Palace Theatre 1982, Private Dick at the Whitehall Theatre 1982, Tovarich at the Chichester Festival Theatre 1991, and a season in the West End at the Piccadilly Theatre; starred in Sherlock Holmes – The Musical at the Bristol Old Vic 1992 and then on a nat. tour and played Louis Mazzini in Kind Hearts and Coronets and starred with Susannah York in Double Double on nat. tours; played Guy Burgess and Anthony Blunt in a tour of Alan Bennett's Single Spies 2002; toured The Picture of Dorian Gray playing Lord Henry 2003, Jeffrey Bernard is Unwell 2013, Doctor in the House (nat. tour) 2013, Singin' in the Rain (Palace Theatre) 2014. *Films include:* Robbery (uncredited) 1967, Walk a Crooked Path 1969, The Italian Job 1969, Secrets 1971, Running Scared 1972, Asylum 1972, The Asphyx 1973, Mahler 1974, Tommy 1975, Al di là del bene e del male 1977, The Thirty-Nine Steps 1978, Harlequin (Best Actor Award, Paris Film Festival) 1980, Jane Austen in Manhattan 1980, The Survivor 1981, La chanson du mal aimé 1981, Imperativ (Best Actor, Venice Film Festival) 1982, The Jigsaw Man 1984, What Waits Below 1984, D'Annunzio 1985, Laggiù nella giungla 1986, Love SIns 1987, Romeo.Juliet (voice) 1990, Chunuk Bair 1992, The Mystery of Edwin Drood 1993, Hey Mr DJ 2003, Colour Me Kubrick: A True…ish Story 2005. *Television includes:* The Hunchback of Notre Dame (series) 1966, City 68' (series) 1968, Z Cars (series) 1969, Tower of London: The Innocent (film) 1969, ITV Sunday Night Theatre (series) – Nora 1969, Diddled 1969, The Wednesday Play (series) – Bam! Pow! Zapp! 1969, – The Season of the Witch 1970, – The Hunting of Lionel Crane 1970, Thirty-Minute Theatre (series) – Roses, Roses, All the Way 1969, – Is Nellie Dead? 1973, Doomwatch (series) 1970, Sentimental Education (mini-series) 1970, Jude the Obscure (mini-series) 1971, Masterpiece Classic (series) 1971, ITV Playhouse (series) – Seventeen Percent Said Push Off 1972, Shelley (film) 1972, Stage 2 (series) 1972, The Edwardians (mini-series) 1972, Mr. Rolls and Mr. Royce (film) 1972, The Wide World of Mystery (series) 1973, BBC Play of the Month (series) – Caucasian Chalk Circle 1973, – You Never Can Tell 1977, Crown Court (series) 1974, Thriller (series) 1973–74, Zodiac (series) 1974, Looking for Clancy (series) 1975, Jesus of Nazareth (mini-series) (Best Actor Awards from TV Times and Italian TV Times, Int. Arts Prize, Fiuggi Film Festival, Grand Prize, Saint-Vincent Film Festival) 1977, The Four Feathers (film) 1978, Pygmalion (film) 1981, The Hunchback of Notre Dame (film) 1982, Frankenstein (film) 1984, Shaka Zulu (mini-series) 1986, Hannay (series) 1988–89, Pasternak (film) 1990, Canned Carrott (series) 1990, Merlin of the Crystal Cave (series) 1991, The Golden Years (film) 1992, The First Circle (film) 1992, Il segno del comando (film) 1992, Das lange Gespräch mit dem Vogel (film) 1992, The Legends of Treasure Island (series) 1993, Kings and Queens of England Volume I (video; voice) 1993, Volume II 1994, The Detectives (series) 1993–97, Fantomcat (series) 1995, Treasure Island (video) 1997, Pride of Africa (film) 1997, Kind Hearts and Coronets 1998, Escape (series, voice) 1998, Mudan Ting: The Peony Pavilion – A Kunju Opera (video) 2001, Agatha Christie's Marple – The Murder at the Vicarage 2004, The Alchemist of Happiness (documentary; voice) 2004, Dalziel and Pascoe (series) 2005, Holby City (series) 2005–11, B-Mail (short animation; voice) 2006, The Bible (mini-series) 2013. *Leisure interests:* golf, tennis, cricket, computers. *Address:* c/o Diamond Management, 31 Percy Street, London, W1T 2DD, England (office). *Telephone:* (20) 7631-0400 (office). *Fax:* (20) 7631-0500 (office). *E-mail:* agents@diman.co.uk (office). *Website:* diamondmanagement.co.uk (office).

POWELL, Sandy, OBE; British costume and set designer; b. 7 April 1960, London; m.; ed St Martin's Coll. of Art and Design, Cen. School of Art, London. *Designs:* costume designer for most shows by The Cholmondoleys and The Featherstonehaughs; stage sets include: Edward II (RSC), Rigoletto (Netherlands Opera) and Dr. Ox's Experiment (ENO); costumes for films include: The Last of England 1988, Stormy Monday 1988, Caravaggio 1986, Venus Peter 1989, The Pope Must Die (Best Tech. Achievement Award, Evening Standard Award 1992) 1991, Edward II (Best Tech. Achievement Award, Evening Standard Award 1992) 1991, The Miracle (Best Tech. Achievement Award, Evening Standard Award 1992) 1991, The Crying Game 1992, Orlando (Evening Standard Award 1994) 1992, Being Human 1994, Interview with a Vampire (Saturn Award 1995) 1994, Rob Roy 1995, Michael Collins 1996, The Butcher Boy 1997, The Wings of the Dove 1997, Shakespeare in Love (Academy Award 1999) 1998, Velvet Goldmine (BAFTA Award 1999) 1998, Hilary and Jackie 1998, The End of the Affair 1999, Felicia's Journey 1999, Miss Julie 1999, Gangs of New York 2002, Far From Heaven (OFCS Award 2003) 2002, Sylvia 2003, The Aviator (Academy Award, Sierra Award 2005) 2004, Mrs Henderson Presents (Golden Capital Award 2006) 2005, The Departed 2006, The Young Victoria (PFCS Award 2009, Academy Award, BAFTA Award, CDG Award 2010) 2009, The Tempest 2010, Shutter Island 2010, Hugo 2011, The Wolf of Wall Street 2013, Cinderella 2015, Carol 2015, How to Talk to Girls at Parties 2017, Wonderstruck 2017, The Favourite (BAFTA Award 2019) 2018, Mary Poppins Returns 2018, The Irishman 2019.

POWELL JOBS, Laurene, BA, BSc, MBA; American business executive and philanthropist; *Founder and Chairwoman, Emerson Collective;* b. 6 Nov. 1963, NJ; m. Steve Jobs 1991 (died 2011); one s. two d. one step-d.; ed Univ. of Pennsylvania, Univ. of Pennsylvania Wharton School, Stanford Grad. School of Business; spent several years working in investment banking and later co-f. Terravera (natural foods co.); worked for Merrill Lynch Asset Management and spent three years at Goldman Sachs as a fixed-income trading strategist; fmr angel investor in SocialCam (mobile video sharing start-up); inherited estate of the late Steve Jobs Oct. 2011, maintains control of living trusts under her late husband's name, including the Steven P. Jobs Trust (largest shareholder of Walt Disney Co.); Co-founder, with Carlos Watson, and Pres. of the Bd, College Track 1997–; Founder and Chair. Emerson Collective (works with entrepreneurs to advance education, immigration reform, social justice and conservation); mem. or fmr mem. Bd of Dirs Achieva, Teach for America, Global Fund for Women, KQED (PBS), EdVoice, Stanford Schools Corpn, New Schools Venture Fund, New America Foundation –2012; mem. Advisory Bd Stanford Grad. School of Business; mem. Bd of Trustees, Stanford Univ. 2012–; apptd mem. of White House Council for Community Solutions by Pres. Obama 2010. *Address:* College Track, 111 Broadway Avenue, Suite 101, Oakland, CA 94607, USA (office). *Telephone:* (510) 834-3295 (office). *Fax:* (510) 834-3312 (office). *E-mail:* info@collegetrack.org (office). *Website:* www.collegetrack.org (office).

POWELL OF BAYSWATER, Baron (Life Peer), cr. 2000, of Bayswater; **Charles David Powell,** Kt, KCMG, BA; British company director, policy adviser and fmr diplomatist; b. 6 July 1941, Sussex; s. of Air Vice-Marshal John Frederick Powell OBE; m. Carla Bonardi 1964; two s.; ed King's School, Canterbury, New Coll., Oxford; Diplomatic Service 1963–83; Pvt. Sec. and Foreign Affairs Adviser to the Prime Minister 1983–91; mem. (Crossbench), House of Lords 2000–; mem. Bd of Dirs, National Westminster Bank 1991–2000 (also Chair. Int. Advisory Bd), Matheson & Co. 1991–, Jardine Matheson Holdings 1992–2000, Jardine Strategic Holdings 1992–2000, 2017–, Hong Kong Land Holdings 1992–2000, 2006–, Mandarin Oriental Hotel Group 1992–2017, J. Rothschild Name Co. 1993–2003, LVMH Louis Vuitton-Moet Hennessy 1995– (Chair. LVMH UK), British Mediterranean Airways 1997–2007, Sagitta 2000–06, Caterpillar Inc. 2001–14, Textron Corpn 2001–16, Schindler Corpn 2003–14, Northern Trust Global Services 2005–14, Northern Trust Corpn 2014–; mem. Advisory Bd, Rolls-Royce (Chair.), Bowmark (Chair.), GEMS (Chair.), Barrick Gold, Chubb, Council on Foreign Relations, New York; Co-Chair. Asia Task Force 2005–14; Chair. Said Business School Foundation, Oxford; Pres. Singapore–British Business Council 1994–2001, China–Britain Business Council 1995–2007; Trustee, British Museum Trust (also Chair.), Aspen Inst., Said Foundation, IISS; Foundation Fellow, Somerville Coll. Oxford; Hon. Fellow, King's Coll., London, Ashmolean Museum, Oxford; Singapore Public Service Medal. *Leisure interests:* walking, reading. *Address:* LVMH House, 15 St George Street, London, W1S 1FH, England (office); House of Lords, Westminster, London, SW1A 0PW, England (home). *Telephone:* (20) 7399-1609 (office); (20) 7222-2423 (home); (78) 4306-4177 (home). *E-mail:* lordpowell@charlespowell.com (office). *Website:* www.parliament.uk/biographies/lords/lord-powell-of-bayswater/2527 (office).

POWER, Samantha, BA, JD; American academic, journalist and diplomatist; b. 21 Sept. 1970, Dungarvan, Co. Waterford, Ireland; m. Cass Sunstein 2008; one s. one d.; ed Lakeside High School, Atlanta, Ga, Yale Univ. and Harvard Law School; emigrated to USA aged nine; early career as staff mem. CBS Sports and Atlanta affiliate; covered wars in fmr Yugoslavia as reporter for US News and World Report, Boston Globe, and the Economist 1993–96; joined International Crisis Group (ICG) as political analyst and helped launch ICG in Bosnia 1996; also worked for Carnegie Endowment for Peace, Washington, DC; adviser to fmr Democratic presidential cand. Wesley Clark 2004; Founding Exec. Dir Carr Center for Human Rights Policy, John F. Kennedy School of Govt, Harvard Univ. 1998–2002, Lecturer in Public Policy 2002–05, Anna Lindh Prof. of Practice of Global Leadership and Public Policy 2005–09, took leave of absence to advise US Senator Barack Obama (Democrat from Ill.) on issues of foreign policy 2005–06; Dir for Multilateral Affairs, Nat. Security Council, The White House 2009–13; Amb. and Perm. Rep. to UN, New York 2013–17; columnist, Time magazine 2007–. *Publications:* Realizing Human Rights: Moving from Inspiration to Impact (co-ed.) 2000, A Problem from Hell: America and the Age of Genocide (Pulitzer Prize for Gen. Nonfiction 2003, Award for Gen. Nonfiction, Nat. Book Critics' Circle 2003, Arthur Ross Prize, Council on Foreign Relations 2003) 2002, Chasing the Flame: Sergio Vieira de Mello and the Fight to Save the World 2008; new introduction to Hannah Arendt's Origins of Totalitarianism; numerous articles on human rights and public policy.

POWER, Simon, BA, LLB; New Zealand lawyer, business executive and fmr politician; *General Manager, Consumer Banking and Wealth, Westpac New Zealand Ltd;* b. 5 Dec. 1969; m.; ed St Peter's Coll., Victoria Univ., Harvard Business School, USA; Assoc. Pnr and Solicitor, Fitzherbert Rowe 1993–97; Solicitor, Kensington Swan 1997; MP for Rangitikei 1999–, mem. Select Cttees on Transport and Industrial Relations 1999–2002, Justice 2002, Educ. and Science 2002–03, Foreign affairs, Defence and Trade 2003–04, Business 2004, Standing Orders 2004–05, Law and Order 2005–08, Chair. Privileges Cttee 2006–08, Sr Whip 2004–05; mem. New Zealand Nat. Party 2003–, Party Spokesman for Labour and Industrial Relations 1999–2002, for Youth Affairs 1999–2004, for Justice 2002–03, for Tertiary Educ. 2002–03, for Defence 2003–04, Veterans' Affairs 2003–04, for Conservation 2004–05, for Law and Order 2005–06, Assoc. Spokesman for Foreign Affairs 2003–04, for Educ. 2004–05; Minister of Justice, of State Owned Enterprises, of Commerce, Minister Responsible for the Law Comm., Assoc. Minister of Finance and Deputy Leader of the House 2008–11; joined Westpac New Zealand Ltd 2012, held several exec. positions, including Head of Private Bank, Gen. Man., Business Bank, Private Bank, Wealth and Insurance and Man. Dir Private, Wealth and Insurance, Gen. Man. Consumer Banking and Wealth 2015–; Chair. NZUS Council; Fellow, Inst. of Finance Professionals New Zealand; mem. Bd of Dirs New Zealand Stock Exchange 2012–15; Trustee Asia NZ Foundation. *Address:* Westpac New Zealand Ltd, PO Box 934, Shortland Street, Auckland 1140, New Zealand (office). *Website:* www.westpac.co.nz (office).

POWERS, Richard; American writer and academic; *Emeritus Professor of English, University of Illinois;* b. 18 June 1957, Evanston, Ill.; m. Jane Powers; spent much of his early life with family in Bangkok, Thailand; worked as a computer programmer in Boston; apptd Swanlund Prof. of English, Univ. of Illinois 1996, Fellow, Center for Advanced Study 2000, now Prof. Emer.; Samuel Fischer Guest Prof., Free Univ., Berlin 2009; Stein Visiting Writer, Stanford Univ. 2010, 2013, Phil and Penny Knight Prof. of Creative Writing 2013; Hurst Visiting Prof., Washington Univ. in St Louis 2012; Fellow, American Acad. of Arts and Sciences 1998, American Acad. of Arts and Letters 2010–; Pushcart Prize 2003, 2009, John D. and Catherine T. MacArthur Foundation grant 1989, Lannan Literary Award 1999, Corrington Award for Literary Excellence 2001, John Dos Passos Prize For Literature 2003. *Publications include:* Three Farmers on Their Way to a Dance (Richard and Hinda Rosenthal Foundation Award, American Acad. and Inst. of Arts and Letters 1985, PEN/Hemingway Foundation special citation) 1985, Prisoner's Dilemma 1988, The Gold Bug Variations 1991, Operation Wandering Soul 1993, Galatea 2.2 1995, Gain (American Soc. of Historians James Fenimore Cooper Prize 1999) 1998, Plowing the Dark (American Acad. and Inst. of Arts and Letters Vursell Prize) 2000, The Time of Our Singing (WH Smith Literary Award 2004) 2003, The Echo Maker (Nat. Book Award for Fiction) 2006, Generosity: An Enhancement 2009, Orfeo (California Book Awards Silver Medal for Fiction 2015) 2014, The Overstory (Pulitzer Prize For Fiction 2019) 2018; contrib. to journals and magazines. *Address:* 2515BI, Department of English, University of Illinois, 608 South Wright Street, Urbana, IL 61801, USA (office). *Telephone:* (217) 244-4958 (office). *E-mail:* rpowers@illinois.edu (office). *Website:* www.english.illinois.edu (office); www.richardpowers.net.

POYNTER, John Riddoch, AO, OBE, PhD, FAHA, FASSA; Australian historian, academic and university administrator; *Professor Emeritus and Professorial Fellow, University of Melbourne;* b. 13 Nov. 1929, Coleraine, Vic.; s. of Robert Poynter and Valetta Riddoch; m. 1st Rosslyn M. Rowell 1954 (divorced 1983); two d.; m. 2nd Marion Davidson 1984; ed Trinity Grammar School, Kew, Victoria, Trinity Coll. Univ. of Melbourne and Magdalen Coll. Oxford; Dean, Trinity Coll., Univ. of Melbourne 1953–64, Ernest Scott Prof. of History 1966–75, Dean, Faculty of Arts 1971–73, Pro-Vice-Chancellor 1972–75, Deputy Vice-Chancellor (Research) 1975–82, Deputy Vice-Chancellor 1982–89, Deputy Vice-Chancellor (Academic) 1989–90, Dean, Faculty of Music, Visual and Performing Arts 1991–93, Asst Vice-Chancellor (Cultural Affairs) 1991–94, Prof. Emer. and Prof. Fellow 1995–; Nuffield Dominion Travelling Fellow, London and Oxford 1959; Visiting Fellow, ANU 1968, Carnegie Fellow, Fulbright Grant, USA 1968; Section Ed. Australian Dictionary of Biography 1972–90; Australian Sec. Rhodes Trust 1974–97; Chair. Melbourne Univ. Press 1976–88; mem. Bd Australian-American Educ. Foundation 1977–84; Rhodes Scholar 1951; Chevalier, Ordre des Palmes Académiques 1981, Centenary Medal 2001; Australian Dictionary of Biography Medal 2004, Distinguished Friend of Oxford Award 2012, Univ. of Melbourne Award 2017. *Publications:* Russell Grimwade 1967, Society and Pauperism 1969, A Place Apart 1996, Doubts and Certainties 1997, Mr Felton's Bequests 2003, The Tarnished Swan 2009, The Audacious Adventures of Louis Laurence Smith 2014, Miegunyah 2015. *Leisure interest:* music. *Address:* 38 Brougham Street, North Melbourne, Vic. 3051, Australia (home). *Telephone:* (3) 9329-8163 (home). *E-mail:* j.poynter@unimelb.edu.au (office); johnpoynter@fastmail.com (home).

POZNER, Vladimir Gerald Dmitri Vladimirovich; Russian/French/American broadcaster; b. 1 April 1934, Paris, France; s. of Vladimir Aleksandrovich Pozner and Géraldine Lutten; m. 1st Valentina Tchemberdji 1957 (divorced 1967); one d.; m. 2nd Yekaterina Orlova 1969–2005; one step-s.; m. 3rd Nadezhda Solovieva 2005; ed Stuyvesant High School, Manhattan, USA, Moscow State Univ.; moved with his mother to New York City aged three months, parents reunited and family returned to Paris 1939, fled Paris, travelling via Marseilles, Madrid, Barcelona and Lisbon, before sailing back to USA 1940, family moved to Soviet sector of Berlin 1948, then to Moscow 1952; worked as trans. of medical biological literature, literary sec. of poet Samuel Marshak 1959–61; Sr Ed., Exec. Sec. Soviet Life 1961–67, Sputnik 1967–70; commentator, USA and Britain Broadcasting Service of USSR TV and Radio Cttee 1970–86; political observer, Central TV 1986–91; returned to Moscow to continue working an ind. TV journalist 1997; Pres. Russian TV Acad. 1996–2008; mem. Fed. Tenders Comm. 2004–; mem. Bd of Dirs Transatlantic Partners Against AIDS (TPAA); Co-owner, with brother Pavel, French brasserie (Chez Géraldine) in Moscow 2004–; best known in the West for appearing on TV to represent and explain the views of the Soviet Union during the Cold War; Communicator of the Year Prize, Soviet Journalists' Union 1986, Communicator of the Year Medal, Better World Soc. (with Phil Donahue). *Television shows:* regular appearances in Pozner-Donahue show, Multimedia Entertainment Inc. (USA) 1991–95; Meetings with Vladimir Pozner (Moscow Channel, Russia) 1991–94, If 1995, We 1995–2000, Man in a Mask 1996–99, Time and US 1998–2000, Times 2000–. *Publications:* Remembering War: A U.S.-Soviet Dialogue (co-author) 1990, Parting with Illusions: The Extraordinary Life and Controversial Views of the Soviet Union's Leading Commentator 1991, Eyewitness: A Personal Account of the Unraveling of the Soviet Union 1992, The Communist Manifesto (contrib.) 1992, Odnoétazhnaia Amerika (co-author) 2008; film scripts and numerous articles in Russian and American newspapers and magazines. *Address:* Pozner School for Television Excellence, 127006 Moscow, Russia (office). *Telephone:* (495) 785-77-87 (office). *E-mail:* study@poznerschool.ru (office). *Website:* www.poznerschool.ru (office); pozneronline.ru.

POZO CRESPO, Mauricio, MEconSci; Ecuadorean banker, economist and government official; ed Pontificia Universidad Católica del Ecuador, Univ. of Colorado and Univ. of Notre Dame, USA; Dir Stock Exchange, Quito; Dir Chamber of Commerce, Quito; Dir Seguros Equinoccial; Tech. Co-ordinator, Ecuadorean Sub-cttee, Pacific Econ. Co-operation Council (PECC); Pres. Investments Tech. Cttee, Inst. Ecuatoriano de Seguridad Social (IESS); Dir Tech. Div., Cen. Bank of Ecuador; Pres. Monetary Council 1981–91; Prof. of Econs, Pontificia Univ. Católica del Ecuador 1987–2003, Monterrey Tech. Inst. 1997–; Dir Masters Program in Man. Business, Univ. of the Americas, Quito 2004–; Pres. Magna Credit Card 1991–93; Vice-Pres. Produbanco 1993–2000; Analyst, Economist Intelligence Unit, London, UK 1998–2001; Pres. Multienlace 2001–02; Minister of Economy and Finance 2003–04 (resgnd); Exec. Chair. and Gen. Man. Conjunto Clinico Nacional Conclina CA (Metropolitan Hosp.), Quito 2006–; columnist for Diario Hoy and for several print media; Order of Isabella the Catholic (Spain) 2004, Decoration 'Consular Excellence', Hon. Consular Corps of Quito 2005. *Publications:* co-author of books and numerous articles in professional journals on economics and finance.

PRABHU, Suresh Prabhakar, BCom, LLB, FCA; Indian chartered accountant and politician; *Minister of Commerce and Industry;* b. 11 July 1953, Mumbai; s. of Prabhakar Prabhu; m. Uma Prabhu; one s.; ed M.L. Dahanukar Coll., New Law Coll., Inst. of Chartered Accountants of India; practising CA 1996; MP from Rajapur, Maharashtra 1996–2009, currently mem. Rajya Sabha for Haryana; mem. Shiv Sena party 1996–2014, joined Bharatiya Janata Party—BJP 2014; Minister for Industries 1996, for Environment and Forests 1998–99, for Fertilizers and Chemicals 1999–2000, of Power 2000–02, of Heavy Industry and Public Enterprises 2002, of Railways 2014–17, of Commerce and Industry 2017–; Chair. Maharashtra State Finance Comm. 1995–96, Manav Sadhan Vikas Sansthan (NGO), Konkan Kala Acad., Adult Education Inst., Maharastra State Table Tennis

Acad.; fmr Chair. (now Dir) Saraswat Bank, Maharashtra State Finance Comm.; Vice-Pres. Table Tennis Fed. of India; Trustee, Khar Residents Asscn, Manavendra Charitable Hosp., IFFCO (Indian Farmers Fertiliser Cooperative) Foundation. *Publications include:* numerous papers on econs, sociology and taxation. *Leisure interests:* reading, travelling, sports, collecting stamps, music and drama. *Address:* Ministry of Commerce and Industry, Udyog Bhawan, New Delhi 110 007 (office); B-21, Sadhana, 16th Road Khar-West, Mumbai 400 052, India (home). *Telephone:* (11) 23062261 (office). *Fax:* (11) 23063418 (office). *E-mail:* wio-commerce@nic.in (office). *Website:* commerce.gov.in (office); www.sureshprabhu.in.

PRADA, Michel André Jean Edmond; French fmr civil servant; *Chairman, Public Sector Accounting Standards Council;* b. 2 April 1940, Bordeaux; s. of Robert Prada and Suzanne Prada (née Bouffard); m. Annick Saudubray 1963; two s. three d.; ed Lycée Montesquieu Bordeaux, Faculté de Droit et Inst. d'Etudes Politiques de Bordeaux, Ecole Nat. d'Admin; Inspecteur des Finances with Ministry of Econ. and Finance 1966–; Chargé de Mission, Inspection Générale des Finances 1969; Chargé de Mission, Direction de la Comptabilité Publique 1970, Asst Dir 1974, Head of Service 1977, Dir de la Comptabilité Publique 1978–85; Dir of Budget, Ministry of the Economy, Finance and the Budget 1986–88; Chair. Bd Dirs Credit d'équipement des petites et moyennes entreprises (CEPME) 1988–95; Chair. Comm. des Opérations de Bourse 1995–2002; Chair. French Financial Markets Authority 2003–09, Orchestre de Paris 1989–2001, Inst. d'Etudes Politiques de Bordeaux 1989–2005, Exec. Cttee Int. Org. of Securities Comms (IOSCO) 1996–98, Tech. Cttee of IOSCO 1998–2001, 2005–08; fmr mem. Econ. and Social Council, Nat. Credit Council; Chair. Public Sector Accounting Standards Council, Ministry of the Budget 2009–; Chair. Bd of Trustees, Int. Valuation Standards Council 2009–11; Chair. Bd of Trustees, Int. Financial Reporting Standards Foundation 2012–18; mem. Bd ICE Benchmark Admin 2014–; Chevalier des Arts et Lettres 1995, Commdr, Légion d'honneur 2002, Grand Officier, Ordre nat. du Mérite 2005, Grand Croix, Ordre nat. du Mérite 2012. *Address:* 139 rue de Bercy Batiment Vauban, 75572 Paris Cedex 12 (office); 2 rue Cart, 94160 Saint-Mandé, France (home). *Telephone:* 1-53-18-29-23 (office); 1-43-74-95-33 (home). *Fax:* 1-53-44-22-97 (office). *E-mail:* michel.prada@finances.gouv.fr (office).

PRADA, Miuccia, PhD; Italian fashion designer; b. (Miuccia Prada Bianchi), 10 May 1949, Milan; d. of Luisa Prada; youngest granddaughter of Prada founder Mario Prada; m. Patrizio Bertelli; two c.; ed Univ. of Milan, Teatro Piccolo, Milan; inherited Prada SpA business from her mother, designer for Prada since 1979, with her husband led co.'s expansion into haute couture, launched collection of women's clothing 1988, Miu Miu collection 1992, men's collection 1994; currently has about 250 stores in 65 countries; opened a contemporary art space, Fondazione Prada 2002; Council of Fashion Designers of America Int. Award 1993, British Fashion Awards Int. Designer of the Year 2013. *Leisure interest:* collecting contemporary art, including several works by Young British Artists (YBAs) such as Damien Hirst. *Address:* Prada SpA, via Andrea Maffei 2, 20135 Milan, Italy (office). *Telephone:* (02) 76001426 (office). *Website:* www.prada.com (office).

PRADA BORDENAVE, Emmanuelle; French government official; *President, l'Institut national de l'information géographique et forestière (IGN);* ed Institut d'Etudes Politiques de Paris, Ecole Nationale d'Admin, Strasbourg; began career at Admin. Tribunal of Paris 1984–97, now Rapporteur and Govt Commr; Head of Legal Dept, CNRS 1990–92; Master of Requests, Conseil d'État –2008; also served as Rapporteur Général, State Comm. of Public Ethics 2001–04, as Head of Mission of Legal Council of State from Social Ministries 2004–07, as Deputy Rapporteur to Constitutional Council and Govt Commr to Tribunal of Conflicts 2007–08; participated in Gen. Review of Public Policies (RGPP) in the field of justice 2008; apptd Dir Gen. Agence de la Biomédecine 2008; Chair. Ethics and Independence Cttee High Authority of Health 2015–; Pres. l'Institut national de l'information géographique et forestière (IGN) 2016–, Chair. Ethics Cttee 2016–. *Address:* IGN, 73 avenue de Paris, 94165 Saint Mande Cedex, France (office). *Telephone:* 1-43-98-80-00 (office). *Website:* www.ign.fr (office).

PRADHAN, Mukti Narayan, LLM; Nepalese lawyer and fmr government official; mem. Law and Human Rights Dept, Maoist Party; Attorney-Gen. 2011–13. *Address:* c/o Office of the Attorney-General, Ramshah Path, Kathmandu, Nepal. *E-mail:* info@attorneygeneral.gov.np.

PRADHAN, Lyonpo Om, BA; Bhutanese diplomatist, politician and business executive; b. 6 Oct. 1946; m.; three c.; ed Delhi Univ., India; various posts in Ministry of Trade, Industry and Forests 1969–80; Perm. Rep. to the UN 1980–84, 1998–2004; Amb. to India (also accred to Nepal and Maldives) 1984–85, Head of Bhutanese Del. to first and second rounds of boundary talks with China; Deputy Minister, Ministry of Trade and Industry 1985–89, Head of Del. to fifth round of boundary talks with China; Minister for Trade and Industry 1989–98; fmr Chief, Policy Devt and Coordination Monitoring and Reporting Unit, UN Office of High Rep. for the Least Developed Countries, Landlocked Countries and Small Island Developing Sites (UN-OHRLLS); Chair. Druk Holding and Investments Ltd 2007–14; mem. Nat. Ass., Council of Ministers; Chair. State Trading Corpn, Chhukha Hydroelectric Project Corpn and Tala Hydroelectric Project Authority; mem. Planning Comm., Nat. Environment Comm.; apptd an adviser to interim govt 2013. *Publication:* Bhutan, The Roar of The Thunder Dragon 2012.

PRADHAN, Trilochan, MSc, PhD; Indian physicist and academic; *Professor Emeritus, Institute of Physics, Bhubaneshwar;* b. 3 Jan. 1929, Ghanashalia, Orissa; s. of Ramachandra and Ahalya Dakshinaray; m. Sanjukta Pradhan 1959; one s. one d.; ed Utkal Univ., Benares Hindu Univ. and Univ. of Chicago; Research Assoc., Univ. of Chicago 1956–57, Niels Bohr Inst., Copenhagen 1957–58; Lecturer in Physics, Ravenshaw Coll., Cuttack 1951–62; Assoc. Prof., Saha Inst. of Nuclear Physics, Calcutta 1962–67, Prof. and Head, Div. of Theoretical Nuclear Physics 1967–74; Founder Dir, Inst. of Physics, Bhubaneshwar 1974–89, Prof. Emer. 1989–; Visiting Prof., Univ. of Virginia 1985; Vice-Chancellor, Utkal Univ. 1989–91; Visiting Scientist, Int. Centre for Theoretical Physics, Trieste 1966–97, Univ. of Syracuse 1967, Univ. of Texas, Austin 1970, Inst. of Theoretical Physics, Gothenberg 1973, KEK, Japan 1985; Meghnad Saha Award, Univ. Grants Comm. of India 1980, Pres. of India's Padma Bhusan Award 1990, Kalinga Prize 2014. *Publications:* The Photon 2001, Quantum Mechanics 2008; about 60 papers on theoretical physics in the areas of elementary particles, atomic physics, plasma physics. *Leisure interests:* gardening, indoor games. *Address:* Institute of Physics, Sachivalaya Marg, Bhubaneswar 751 005 (office); 71 Gajapatinagar, Bhubaneswar 751 005, India (home). *Telephone:* (674) 2300637 (office); (674) 2300962. *Fax:* (674) 2300142 (office). *E-mail:* pradhan@iopb.res.in (office). *Website:* www.iopb.res.in (office).

PRAK, Sokhonn; Cambodian politician, fmr army officer and fmr diplomatist; *Deputy Prime Minister and Minister of Foreign Affairs and International Co-operation;* b. 3 May 1954, Phnom Penh; m.; three c.; ed International Inst. for the Training of Journalists, Budapest, International Inst. of Public Administration, Paris; joined Royal Cambodian Army 1979, served as journalist with army newspaper 1979–86, Deputy Ed.-in-Chief 1986–92, becoming Chief of Army Information Service, Spokesman of Royal Cambodian Armed Forces (RCAF) 1993, attained rank of four-star Gen. 2010; Adviser to Prime Minister 1993–98; Amb. to France, Belgium, Netherlands, Austria, Denmark, Sweden, Finland, EU and Office of UN in Geneva 1999–2002; Deputy Sec.-Gen., Royal Govt of Cambodia, also Adviser to Prime Minister 2003; Sec. of State, Council of Ministers 2004; Minister attached to Prime Minister 2009–13; Minister of Posts and Telecommunications 2013–16; Minister of Foreign Affairs and Int. Co-operation 2016–; Deputy Prime Minister 2018–; Chair. Nat. Coordination Cttee for UN-Peace Keeping Operations 2004, 2009–; Chair. Information Research and Analysis Group, Council of Ministers 2013–16; Vice-Pres. Cambodian Mine Action and Victim Assistance Authority (CMAA) 2013–18; Pres. 11th Meeting of State Parties to Anti-Personnel Mine Ban Convention (11MSP) 2011–12; Mohasereiwaddh Medal of Nat. Merit, Medal of Nat. Defence and Protection of Homeland, Grand Cross, Royal Order of Cambodia, Officier, Ordre Nat. de la Légion d'Honneur (France). *Address:* Ministry of Foreign Affairs and International Co-operation, 3 rue Samdech Hun Sen, Sangkat Tonle Bassac, Khan Chamkarmon, Phnom Penh, Cambodia (office). *Telephone:* (23) 214441 (office). *Fax:* (23) 216144 (office). *E-mail:* mfaic@mfa.gov.kh (office). *Website:* www.mfaic.gov.kh (office).

PRAKKE, Lucas, LLD; Dutch academic; *Professor Emeritus of Law, University of Amsterdam;* b. 20 Feb. 1938, Groningen; m. Margaretha M. O. de Bruijn Kops 1965; two s.; ed Gemeentelijk Lyceum, Doetinchem, Univ. of Amsterdam and Columbia Univ. Law School, New York; Asst Prof. of Law, Univ. of Amsterdam 1963–72, Prof. of Dutch and Comparative Constitutional Law 1972–2003, Dean, Faculty of Law 1981–83, Prof. Emer. 2003–; Judge, Civil Service Appeal Tribunal 1977–89; mem. Royal Comm. on Constitution 1982–85; mem. Royal Netherlands Acad. *Publications:* Principles of Constitutional Interpretation in the Netherlands 1970, Toetsing in het publiekrecht 1972, Pluralisme en staatsrecht 1974, Het bestuursrecht van de landen der Europese Gemeenschappen 1986, Bedenkingen tegen het toetsingsrecht (Report of Netherlands Lawyers' Asscn) 1992, Swamping the Lords, Packing the Court, Sacking the King: Address on 'dies natalis' of University of Amsterdam 1994, Handboek van het Nederlandse staatsrecht 1995, Het staatsrecht van de landen van de Europese Unie (fifth edn, co-ed.) 1998 (trans. as Constitution Law of 15 EU Member States 2005), Pluralisme van Staatsrecht 2003. *Leisure interests:* history, music, walking. *Address:* Faculteit der Rechtsgeleerdheid, Universiteit van Amsterdam, Postbus 1030, 1000 BA Amsterdam (office); Koedijklaan 15, 1406 KW Bussum, Netherlands (home). *Telephone:* (20) 5253966 (office); (35) 6989520 (home). *Fax:* (35) 6989501 (home).

PRANCE, Sir Ghillean Tolmie, Kt, DPhil, FRS; British botanist; b. 13 July 1937, Brandeston, Suffolk; s. of Basil Camden Prance and Margaret Hope Prance (née Tolmie); m. Anne Elizabeth Hay 1961; two d.; ed Malvern Coll., Keble Coll. Oxford; Research Asst, The New York Botanical Garden 1963–66, Assoc. Curator 1966–68, Krukoff Curator of Amazonian Botany 1968–75, Dir of Botanical Research 1975–81, Vice-Pres. 1977–81, Sr Vice-Pres. 1981–88, Dir Inst. of Econ. Botany 1981–88; Dir Royal Botanic Gardens, Kew 1988–99; Dir of Research, The Eden Project 1999–2016, apptd Trustee 2016; McBryde Prof. Nat. Tropical Botanical Garden 2000–02; Adjunct Prof., CUNY, USA 1968–99; Dir of Grad. Studies, Instituto Nacional de Pesquisas da Amazônia, Brazil 1973–75; Exec. Dir Org. for Flora Neotropica 1975–88; Visiting Prof. in Tropical Studies, Yale Univ., USA 1983–88; Visiting Prof., Univ. of Reading 1988–; Chair. Bentham-Moxon Trust 1988–99, Brazilian Atlantic Rainforest Trust 1999–2017, Pres. 2017–, Global Diversity Foundation 1999–2008; Pres. Linnean Soc. of London 1997–2000; Trustee, Au Sable Inst. of Environmental Studies 1984–91, Margaret Mee Amazon Trust 1988–96, Worldwide Fund for Nature International 1989–93, Horniman Museum 1990–99; Pres. Asscn of Tropical Biology 1979–80, American Asscn of Plant Taxonomists 1984–85, Systematics Asscn 1988–91, Inst. of Biology 2000–02; mem. Bd of Govs, Lovaine Trust Co. Ltd 1989–99; Council mem. Royal Horticultural Soc. 1990–2000; Corresp. mem. Botanical Soc. of America 1994; Hon. mem. British Ecological Soc. 1996–; Commendador da Ordem Nacional do Cruzeiro do Sul (Brazil) 2000, Order of the Rising Sun (Japan) 2012; Hon. FilDr (Göteborg) 1983; Hon. DSc (Univ. of Kent at Canterbury) 1994, (Portsmouth) 1994, (Kingston) 1994, (St Andrews) 1995, (CUNY) 1998, Dr hc (Bergen) 1996, (Sheffield) 1997, (Florida) 1997, (Liverpool) 1998, (Glasgow) 1999, (Plymouth) 1999, (Keele) 2000, (Exeter) 2000, (Gloucester) 2006; Henry Shaw Medal, Missouri Botanical Garden 1988, Linnean Medal 1990, Int. Cosmos Prize 1993, Patron's Medal (Royal Geographical Soc.) 1994, Asa Gray Award (American Soc. of Plant Taxonomists) 1998, Int. Award of Excellence (Botanical Research Inst. of Tex.) 1998, Lifetime Discovery Award 1999, Victoria Medal of Honour, Royal Horticultural Soc. 1999, Fairchild Medal for Botanical Exploration 2000, Soc. for Econ. Botany Award 2002, Graziela Barroso Prize Brazilian Botanic Garden Network 2004, Allerton Award, Nat. Tropical Botanical Garden 2005. *Television:* Superteacher (NHK, Japan) 2002. *Publications:* Arvores de Manaus 1975, Extinction is Forever 1977, Biological Diversification in the Tropics 1981, Amazonia–Key Environments 1985, Tropical Forests and World Climate 1986, Leaves 1986, White Gold 1989, Wildflowers for All Seasons 1989, Out of the Amazon 1992, Bark 1993, Rainforests of the World 1998, Rainforest Light and Spirit 2009, Go to the Ant 2013, That Glorious Forest 2014; Ed. 14 books; numerous scientific and gen. articles. *Leisure interests:* bird watching, stamp collecting. *Address:* The Old Vicarage, Silver Street, Lyme Regis, Dorset, DT7 3HS, England (home). *Telephone:* (1297) 444991 (home). *E-mail:* gprance@edenproject.com (office); siriain01@yahoo.co.uk (home).

PRANCKIETIS, Viktoras, PhD; Lithuanian agronomist, politician and academic; *Chairman (Speaker), Seimas (Parliament);* b. 26 July 1958, Ruteliai, Kelmė dist, Lithuanian SSR, USSR; m. Irena Pranckietienė; one s. two d.; ed Tytuvėnai

Agricultural Coll., Lithuanian Acad. of Agric. (now Aleksandras Stulginskis Univ., Akademija, Kaunas Co.); worked briefly as an agronomist at a local farm in Tytuvėnai 1973; spent most of his career at Lithuanian Acad. of Agric., initially as a Jr Researcher, then Asst Vice-Dean, Faculty of Agronomy, Horticulture, Lithuanian Acad. of Agric., Head of Dept 2008–16, Dean, Faculty of Agronomy, Prof. 2016–; mem. Lietuvos valstiečių ir žaliųjų sąjunga (LVZS—Lithuanian Farmers and Greens' Union) 2014–, Deputy Chair. 2014–; unsuccessful cand. in parl. elections 2012; elected to Kaunas Dist Council 2015; mem. Seimas (Parl.) for Raudondvaris constituency 2016–, Chair. (Speaker) of the Seimas Nov. 2016–. *Television:* gardening consultant on numerous Lithuanian TV shows. *Publications:* numerous books, textbooks and scientific papers, specializing in gardening. *Address:* Seimas (Parliament), Kab, I-306, Gedimino pr. 53, Vilnius 01109 (office); Constituency Office, Klaipėdos g. 7-43, 20130 Ukmergė m., Lithuania. *Telephone:* (5) 239-6001 (office); (5) 239-6060 (office). *Fax:* (5) 239-6289 (office). *E-mail:* viktoras.pranckietis@lrs.lt (office); priim@lrs.lt (office). *Website:* www.lrs.lt (office).

PRASAD, Alok, BA, MA; Indian diplomatist (retd); *Senior Advisor, India/South Asia, BowerGroupAsia;* m. Nandini Prasad; two c.; ed Delhi Univ.; joined Indian Foreign Service 1974, has represented India in various capacities in Germany, UN (New York), the Netherlands, Nepal, Burma and Botswana; also worked in Prime Minister's Office; Jt Sec. for Americas Div., Ministry of External Affairs, New Delhi 1995–2000; Deputy Chief of Mission, Washington, DC 2000–04; High Commr to Singapore 2004–06, to Sri Lanka 2006–09; Deputy Nat. Security Adviser 2009–11; Amb. to Japan 2011–12; currently Sr Advisor, India/South Asia, BowerGroupAsia; Fellow, Center for Int. Affairs, Harvard Univ., USA. *Address:* BowerGroupAsia, 10533 Main Street, Fairfax, VA 22030, USA (office). *Telephone:* (202) 747-2893 (office). *E-mail:* aprasad@bowergroupasia.com (office). *Website:* www.bowergroupasia.com (office).

PRASAD, Ashoka, MD, FRHistS; Indian psychiatrist, medical anthropologist, academic, author and newspaper columnist; b. 10 May 1955, Patna; s. of Judge Jahnavi Prasad and Usha Prasad; ed Colvin Taluqdar's Coll., Lucknow, GSVM Medical Coll., Kanpur, Univs of Oxford and St Andrews, UK, Univ. of North Carolina at Chapel Hill, Harvard Univ. and Brandeis Univ., USA; Resident in Paediatrics and Psychiatry, Castlebar Gen. Hosp., Ireland, Resident in Psychiatry, Royal Edinburgh Hosp., UK 1980–83; Research Fellow, Depts of Biochemistry and Psychiatry, Univ. of Leeds, UK 1983–85; Kate Stillman Lecturer in Psychiatry, Univ. Coll. Hosp. and Queen Charlotte's Hosp., London, UK 1984–86; Consultant Psychiatrist, Whipps Cross Hosp., Claybury Hosp. and Thorpe Coombe Hosp., London 1986–87; Prof., Dalhousie Univ., Canada 1987, Columbia Univ., USA 1989, Univ. of British Columbia, Canada 1990, Univ. of Pennsylvania, USA 1992, Drexel Univ., USA; in charge of Psychopharmacology and Hon. Sr Lecturer, Mental Health Research Inst. and Monash Univ., Melbourne, Australia, Assoc. Dept of Psychiatry, Univ. of Melbourne 1987; Visiting Specialist, Kingseat Hosp., NZ 1988; Consultant Psychiatrist, Claybury Hosp., London and St Margaret's Hosp., Essex 1988–89; at Dept of Psychiatry, Dalhousie Univ., Canada, Dept of Psychology, St Mary's Univ., Canada 1989; J. Ernest Runions Fellow, Dept of Psychiatry, Univ. of British Columbia, Vancouver 1989–90; Prof. of Psychiatry, Hahnemann Univ., Phila, USA 1990–91; Adjunct Prof. of Medical Anthropology, Columbia Univ., USA 1990–91, of Anthropology, Univ. of Pa 1991; Medical Dir Phila Consultation Center 1990–92; currently hon. consultant to several bodies; freelance newspaper columnist for Daily Pioneer, Newslaundry, Hoot, Different Truths, Hindustan Times, The Indian Practitioner, India Medical Times; several visiting professorships, including Harvard Univ. 1986, 1991; Visiting Psychiatrist, Sahlgrenska Univ. Hosp., Gothenberg, Sweden 2009; Hon. DrMed (Natal, South Africa) 2000; Murphy Award 1987, Blueler Award 1987, delivered Annual Mil. Medicine Oration in Bombay 2012, Maati Samman 2018. *Achievement:* first person to describe medical condition Hashimoto's thyroditis (presented) as mania which was eponymously named Prasad's syndrome. *Publications:* more than 200 books, including Biological Basis and Therapy of Neuroses and A Psychoanalytical Journey; more than 125 publs in various journals; more than 500 newspaper column contribs. *Leisure interests:* bird-watching, unravelling Greek myths, cricket, history of science and medicine, naturopathy, medical anthropology, aviation medicine, Jalaluddin Rumi's works, reading, light classical music, collecting cookery books. *Address:* 1 Avas Vikas, Betia Hata, Gorakhpur 273 001, India (home). *Telephone:* (551) 334020 (home). *Fax:* (551) 332845 (home). *E-mail:* praashok@gmail.com (home).

PRASAD, Ganga, BCom; Indian business executive and politician; *Governor of Sikkim;* b. 8 July 1937, Patna; four s. one d.; mem. Bharatiya Jana Sangh 1967; mem. Bihar Vidhan Parishad (Bihar Legis. Council) 1994–2012, Leader of Opposition 1997–2005, Leader, Legis. Council 2005–12; Gov. of Meghalaya 2017–18, of Sikkim 2018–; Chair., Bihar Food Grain Dealers' Asscn; mem. Bharatiya Janata Party (BJP), Gen. Sec. Bihar BJP. *Address:* Raj Bhavan, Gangtok 737 103, India (office). *Telephone:* (3592) 222400 (office). *Fax:* (3592) 222742 (office). *Website:* www.rajbhavansikkim.gov.in (office).

PRASAD, H. Rajesh, BCom, MBA, MPM; Indian civil servant and government official; *Member Secretary, Delhi Dialogue and Development Commission;* b. 1 June 1967; fmr Collector and Dist Magistrate, South Goa; fmr Deputy Commr and Dist Magistrate, West Kamang Dist, Arunachal Pradesh, East and South Delhi; fmr Commr (Lands), Delhi Devt Authority; Admin. of Union Territory of Lakshadweep 2012–15; Mem. Sec., Delhi Dialogue and Devt Comm. 2016–; VAT Commr, NCT of Delhi 2016–. *Address:* Delhi Dialogue and Development Commission, 33, Shamnath Marg, Civil Lines, Delhi 110 054, (office); Department of Trade & Taxes, Govt of NCT of Delhi, Vyapar Bhawan, IP Estate, New Delhi 110 002, India. *Telephone:* (11) 23815541 (office); (11) 23318568 (Department of Trade & Taxes) (office). *Fax:* (11) 23319474 (Department of Trade & Taxes) (office). *E-mail:* ddc.delhi@gov.in (office). *Website:* delhi.gov.in/wps/wcm/connect/DOIT_DDC/ddc/homenew (office); dvat.gov.in.

PRASAD, Siddheshwar, DLitt; Indian politician, author and journalist; b. 19 June 1929, Bind; s. of Bhikari Mahton; m. Rajkumari Prasad; six c.; Lecturer, Nalanda Coll., Biharsharif 1953–61; mem. Lok Sabha 1962–77; Deputy Minister for Irrigation and Power 1967–71, for Industrial Devt 1971–73, for Heavy Industry Feb.–Nov. 1973, for Irrigation 1973–74, for Energy 1974–77; Minister, Govt of Bihar 1985–88; Gov. of Tripura 1995–99; Chair. Gandhi-Marx Research Inst.; Exec. Chair. Rashtra Bhasha Prachar Samiti; Sec.-Gen. Third World Hindi Conf. *Publications:* Chhayavadottar Kavya, Satyagraha Aur Vigyan, Sahitya Ka Muyankan, Upanishad Chintan Aur Adhunik Jiwan, Ekalavyon Aur Abimanyuon Se, Multi-Dimensional Transformation, Vichar Pravah, New Economic Policy, The Vedic Vision, Kamayni: Vishwa Kavya Ka Abhinava Sarga.

PRASAD, Sunand, MA, PhD; British (b. Indian) architect; *Senior Partner, Penoyre & Prasad LLP;* b. 22 May 1950, Dehra Dun, India; m. Susan Francis; three c.; ed Cambridge School of Architecture, Architectural Asscn, Royal Coll. of Art; Partner, Edward Cullinan Architects 1976–85; Leverhulme Research Fellow, RCA 1985–88; Co-founder and Partner, Penoyre & Prasad LLP 1988, now Sr Partner; Vice-Pres. Architectural Asscn 1999–2001; apptd Commr, Comm. for Architecture and the Built Environment 1999; Pres. RIBA 2007–09, Pres. Architects Benevolent Soc. 2011; Chair. Advisory Bd, Journal of Architecture; mem. Advisory Bd and Trustee, Article 25 2007–; mem. London Mayor's Design Advisory Panel 2009–, Green Construction Bd, UK Govt; Trustee, Cycle to Cannes 2007–, Centre for Cities 2009–, Cape Farewell 2010–; Hon. Fellow, Royal Town Planning Inst., Royal Architectural Inst. of Canada, Hon. Fellow, Royal Incorporation of Architects, Scotland, Hon. mem. American Inst. of Architects, Hon. mem. Royal Town Planning Inst.; Dr hc (Univ. of East London); Eternit Award for Architecture 1989, RIBA Regional Award 1991, 1992, RIBA Award 1997, 1999, 2000, 2001, 2003, American Inst. of Architects/UK Excellence in Design Award 1998, Design Sense 1999, numerous other architectural awards. *Radio:* 'The Essay': Architecture the 4th R (BBC Radio 3) 2010. *Publications include:* Accommodating Diversity: Housing Design in a Multi-Cultural Society 1998, Paradigms of Indian Architecture 1998, Designing Better Buildings 2003, Contemporary Hospital Design (ed) 2005, Transformations: The Architecture of Penoyre & Prasad 2007, Changing Hospital Architecture (ed) 2008; chapters in Le Corbusier: Architect of the Century 1987. *Leisure interests:* music, cycling. *Address:* Penoyre & Prasad LLP, 28–42 Banner Street, London, EC1Y 8QE, England (office). *Telephone:* (20) 7250-3477 (office). *Fax:* (20) 7250-0844 (office). *E-mail:* mail@penoyreprasad.com (office). *Website:* www.penoyreprasad.com (office); www.sunandprasad.com.

PRASAD SINGH, Balmiki, MA; Indian politician; b. 1 Jan. 1942, Begusarai, Bihar; m. Karuna Singh; three c.; ed Patna Univ., Oxford Univ.; fmr Lecturer in Political Sciences, Patna Univ.; joined Indian Administrative Service 1964; Deputy Sec., Ministry of Defence 1975–79; Sec. for all d epts under the Chief Sec. and Home Sec., Govt of Assam 1980–82, mem. Assam Planning Bd 1982–84, Agricultural Production Commr, Special Commr and Special Sec., Sec. 1990–92; Jt Sec. Ministry of Steel and Mines 1984–89; Jt Sec., then Additional Sec., Ministry of Home Affairs 1992–93; Additional Sec., Ministry of Environment and Forests 1993–95, Chair. Nat. Cttee on Bio-diversity Conservation, Asia Rep. on Ramar Convention on Wetlands, Gland, Switzerland; Union Culture Sec., Govt of India 1995–97, Union Home Sec. 1997–99; Exec. Dir World Bank, representing India, Bangladesh, Bhutan and Sri Lanka 1999–2002; Gov. of Sikkim 2008–13; Jawaharlal Nehru Fellow 1982–84; Queen Elizabeth Fellow, Univ. of Oxford 1989–90; fmr Mahatma Gandhi Nat. Fellow; fmr Chancellor Cen. Inst. of Higher Tibetan Studies, Sarnath; Chancellor Sikkim Manipal Univ. 2008–; fmr Chair. Nat. Comm. for Economically Backward Classes; mem. Indian Nat. Trust for Arts and Cultural Heritage 1995–; Patna Univ. Gold Medals 1960, Gov. of Assam Gold Medal 1991, Gulzarilal Nanda Award 1998, Man of Letters Award from Dalai Lama 2003. *Publications include:* Threads Woven: Ideals, Principles & Administration 1975, The Indian National Congress and Cultural Renaissance, The Problem of Change: A Study of North-East India 1987, India's Culture: the State, the Arts and Beyond 1998, Bahudha and the post-9/11 World 2008, Our India 2011; numerous articles and monographs on culture, poverty, ecology and public admin in India and abroad. *Website:* www.balmikiprasadsingh.com.

PRASETIO, John A.; Indonesian business executive and diplomatist; *President Commissioner, Indonesia Stock Exchange;* Asia Pacific CEO/Area Man. Partner, Andersen Worldwide, Singapore; fmr Regional Sr Adviser, Ernst & Young Global, fmr Exec. Chair. Ernst & Young Indonesia; Founder and Chair. CBA Consulting; mem. Bd, PT Bank Permata Tbk, PT Sarana Menara Nusantara Tbk; mem. Advisory Panel, P&G Indonesia, Crowe Horwath Indonesia, Mitsui Indonesia; Special Staff to Minister of Industry; mem. Pres.'s Nat. Econ. Council, Nat. Cttee on Good Governance, Investment Cttee of the Investment Coordinating Bd; mem. Advisory Bd, Asscn of Publicly Listed Companies, Indonesian Chamber of Commerce and Industry; fmr Deputy Pres. Indonesian Chamber of Commerce and Industry, fmr Chair. Int. Econ. Co-operation Dept; mem. or fmr mem. Bd, APEC Business Advisory Council, UNESCAP Business Advisory Council, East Asia Business Council, Global Practice Council of Ernst & Young, London, Global Exec. Bd of Andersen Worldwide, New York, Bd of Partners of Andersen Worldwide SC, Geneva, Exec. Bd of SGV Group, Manila, Int. Business Leader Advisory Council of Tianjin Municipality Govt, China, Exec. Centre for Global Leadership, Pres.'s Nat. Business Devt Council, Nat. Foster Parents Movt, World Wide Fund for Nature, Red Cross Indonesia; fmr Commr, PT Tri Polyta Indonesia, PT Asuransi CIGNA, PT Kalbe Farma Tbk, PT Global Mediacom Tbk, Energy Devt Corpn, Manila; represented Indonesia at G-20 Business Summits in London and Toronto; Amb. to South Korea 2015–17; Pres. Commr Indonesia Stock Exchange 2017–. *Address:* Indonesia Stock Exchange Building, 1st Tower, 6th Floor, Jl. Jend. Sudirman Kav 52-53, Jakarta 12190, Indonesia (office). *Website:* www.idx.co.id (office).

PRASHAR, Baroness (Life Peer), cr. 1999, of Runnymede in the County of Surrey; **Rt Hon Usha Kumari Prashar,** CBE, PC, BA, FRSA; British public policy specialist; b. 29 June 1948, Nairobi, Kenya; d. of Nauhria Lal Prashar and Durga Devi Prashar; m. Vijay Kumar Sharma 1973; ed Duchess of Gloucester School, Nairobi, Wakefield Girls' High School, Univs of Leeds and Glasgow; Conciliation Officer, Race Relations Bd 1971–75; Asst Dir Runnymede Trust 1975–77, Dir 1977–84; Sr Fellow, Policy Studies Inst. 1984–86 (mem. Council 1992–97); Dir Nat. Council for Voluntary Orgs 1986–91; Vice-Chair. British Refugee Council 1987–89; Civil Service Commr (part-time) 1990–96, First Civil Service Commr 2000–05; Deputy Chair. Nat. Literacy Trust 1992–2000, Chair. 2001–05; Chair. Parole Bd of England and Wales 1997–2000, Judicial Appointments Comm. 2006–10; Dir (non-exec.) Channel 4 1992–99, Unite PLC 2001–04, ITV 2005–; mem. Bd Salzburg Seminar 2000–04, Arts Council of GB 1979–81, Arts Council of England 1994–97, Study Comm. on the Family 1980–83, Social Security Advisory Cttee 1980–83, Exec. Cttee, Child Poverty Action Group 1984–85, Greater London Arts Asscn

1984–86, London Food Comm. 1984–90, BBC Educational Broadcasting Council 1987–89, Advisory Council, Open Coll. 1987–89, Solicitors' Complaints Bureau 1989–90, Royal Comm. on Criminal Justice 1991–93, Lord Chancellor's Advisory Cttee on Legal Educ. and Conduct 1991–97, Bd Energy Saving Trust 1992–98; mem. (Crossbench), House of Lords 1999–; Cttee mem., The Iraq Inquiry 2009–16; Chair. English Advisory Cttee, Nat. AIDS Trust 1988–89; Deputy Chair. British Council 2012–18; currently Chair and Non-Exec. Dir Nationwide Building Soc., Cumberland Lodge; Chancellor De Montfort Univ. 2000–06 (Gov. 1996–2006); Trustee, King's Fund 1998–2002, Jt Cttee on Human Rights 2001–04, 2008–, Thames Help Trust 1984–86, Charities Aid Foundation 1986–91, Ind. Broadcasting Telethon Trust 1987–92, Acad. of Indian Dance 1987–91, Camelot Foundation 1996–, Ethnic Minority Foundation 2000–; Patron Sickle Cell Soc. 1986–, Elfrida Rathbone Soc. 1988–; Hon. Pres. Community Foundation Network, Nat. Literacy Trust; Hon. Fellow, Goldsmiths' Coll., Univ. of London 1992; Hon. LLD (De Montfort) 1994, (South Bank) 1994, (Greenwich) 1999, (Leeds Metropolitan) 1999, (Ulster) 2000, (Oxford Brookes) 2000, (Leeds), (Exeter), (Glasgow); Dr hc (London), (Kalinga); Asian Women of Achievement Award 2002. *Publications include:* contribs to Britain's Black Population 1980, The System: A Study of Lambeth Borough Council's Race Relations Unit 1981, Scarman and After 1984, Sickle Cell Anaemia, Who Cares? A Survey of Screen, Counselling, Training and Educational Facilities in England 1985, Routes or Road Blocks, A Study of Consultation Arrangements Between Local Authorities and Local Communities 1985, Acheson and After: Primary Health Care in the Inner City 1986. *Leisure interests:* reading, music, golf, current affairs. *Address:* House of Lords, Westminster, London, SW1A 0PW, England (office). *Telephone:* (20) 7219-6792 (office). *Fax:* (20) 7219-5979 (office). *E-mail:* prasharu@parliament.uk (office). *Website:* www.parliament.uk/biographies/lords/baroness-prashar/2476 (office).

PRASOLOV, Ihor Nikolayevych; Ukrainian political economist, academic and politician; b. 4 Feb. 1962, Peschanyi, Murmansk Oblast, Russian SFSR, USSR; m. Natalia Prasolova; one s. one d.; ed Rostov State Univ., Donetsk State Univ.; electrical fitter trainee and electrical fitter, Novocherkassk power plant 1979–80; mil. service in Soviet Army, discharged with rank of Staff Sergeant 1980–82; Asst Prof. of Political Economy, Donetsk State Univ. 1987–93; Gen. Dir CJSC Investment Co. Keramet Invest 1993–2000, JSC System Capital Man. 2000–05; mem. Verkhovna Rada (Parl.) (Party of Regions) 2006–, Chair. Cttee on Finance, Banking, Tax and Customs Policy, Subcommittee on Securities and Stock Market, mem. Group for Interparliamentary Relations with Russian Fed., with Repub. of Belarus, with Czech Repub.; Minister of Econ. Devt and Trade 2012–14 (dismissed by Parl.).

PRAT-GAY, Alfonso; Argentine economist, business executive, politician and fmr central banker; ed Univ. of Pennsylvania, USA; worked for macro-econ. consultancy, Buenos Aires –1991; country economist (Argentina), JP Morgan, New York 1994, Head of Emerging Market Proprietary Trading Desk, London –1999, Chief of Currency Strategy (cr. Liquidity and Credit Premia Index), London 1999–2001; Prof., Univ. of Buenos Aires 2001–02; Gov. Cen. Bank of Argentina 2002–04; Chair. Tilton Capital (asset man. firm); mem. Cámara de Diputados (Coalición Cívica Afirmación para una República Igualitaria) 2009–; Minister of Economy and Public Finance 2015–16; Pres. Fundación Andares para el desarrollo de las Microfinanzas. *Address:* Coalición Cívica Afirmación para una República Igualitaria, Rivadavia 1475, C1022AAB Buenos Aires, Argentina. *Telephone:* (11) 4384-1268. *E-mail:* ccariprovincia@gmail.com. *Website:* www.ccaribuenosaires.org.ar.

PRATS MONNÉ, Xavier; Spanish politician and EU official; *Director-General for Health and Food Safety, European Commission;* b. 30 April , Tarragona; m.; two c.; ed Univ. of Madrid, Centre int. de hautes études agronomiques méditerranéennes, paris, Coll. of Europe, Bruges, Belgium; Asst Prof., Dept of Public Admin, Coll. of Europe 1982–83; Deputy Del., EC Representation in Spain 1983–86, EC Rep. in Spain 1986–89, Desk Officer for relations with Caribbean region, Directorate Gen. for Devt Cooperation 1990–91, Asst to EC Spokesperson 1991–94, mem., Cabinet of the EC Vice-Pres. responsible for foreign affairs 1995–99, Deputy Head 1998–99, Adviser, Cabinet of Commr responsible for regional policy 1999–2001, Head of Unit, European Social Fund (ESF) Policy Coordination 2001–03, Dir ESF country programming and implementation 2004–06, Dir for Employment Policy, Lisbon Strategy and Int. Relations, Directorate Gen. for Employment, Social Affairs and Inclusion 2006–10, Deputy Dir-Gen., Directorate-Gen. for Educ. and Culture 2011–14, Dir-Gen. 2014–15, Dir-Gen. for Health and Food Safety 2015–; Orden Civil de Alfonso X el Sabio. *Address:* Directorate-General for Health and Food Safety, rue Breydel 4, 1049 Brussels, Belgium (office). *Telephone:* (2) 296-12-30 (office). *E-mail:* sante-dg@ec.europa.eu (office). *Website:* ec.europa.eu/dgs/health_food-safety (office).

PRATT, (John) Christopher, OC, CC, RCA, BFA; Canadian painter and printmaker; b. 9 Dec. 1935, St John's, Newfoundland; s. of John Kerr Pratt and Christine Emily Pratt (née Dawe); m. 1st Mary Frances West 1957 (divorced 2004); two s. two d.; m. 2nd Jeanette Meehan 2007; ed Prince of Wales Coll., St John's, Newfoundland, Memorial Univ. of Newfoundland, Mount Allison Univ., Sackville, NB and the Glasgow School of Art, Scotland; taught as specialist in art, Memorial Univ. 1961–63; freelance artist 1963–; mem. Mount Carmel Town Council 1969–73, Postage Stamp Design Cttee, Ottawa 1970–73, The Canada Council 1976–82, Memorial Univ. Bd of Regents 1972–75; designed prov. flag for Newfoundland and Labrador 1980; Hon. Chair. Bay Roberts Heritage Soc. 1999–; Hon. Fellow, Royal Architectural Inst. of Canada 2012; Hon. DLitt (Memorial) 1972; Hon. LLD (Mount Allison) 1973, (Dalhousie) 1986. *Publications:* Christopher Pratt 1982, The Prints of Christopher Pratt (with Mira Godard) 1991, Christopher Pratt: Personal Reflections on a Life in Art 1995, Christopher Pratt: All My Own Work 2005, A Painter's Poems 2005, Ordinary Things: A Different Kind of Voyage 2009, Christopher Pratt: Six Decades 2013. *Leisure interests:* offshore sailing, walking/hiking and fly-fishing. *Address:* PO Box 87, Mount Carmel, St Mary's Bay, Newfoundland, A0B 2M0, Canada. *Telephone:* (709) 521-2048. *Fax:* (709) 521-2707.

PREBBLE, Mark, CNZM, PhD; New Zealand civil servant (retd) and academic; *Adjunct Professor, School of Government, Victoria University of Wellington;* b. 12 May 1951, Auckland; s. of Archdeacon K. R. Prebble and Mary Prebble; brother of Richard William Prebble (q.v.); m. 1st Fenella Druce 1974 (died 1977); m. 2nd Lesley Bagnall 1978; two s. two d.; ed Auckland Grammar School, Auckland Univ. and Victoria Univ. of Wellington; with Treasury, Govt of NZ 1977–82, Dept of Labour 1982–85; Seconded to Prime Minister and Cabinet as Man. Change Team on Targeting Social Assistance 1991–92; Minister (Econ.) NZ High Comm., London 1992–93; Deputy Sec. of Treasury 1993–98; Chief Exec. Dept of Prime Minister and Cabinet 1998–2004; State Services Commr 2004–08 (retd); Adjunct Prof., School of Govt, Victoria Univ. of Wellington 2012–; Hon. Fellow, School of Govt, Victoria Univ. of Wellington; Companion of the NZ Order of Merit 2009. *Publications:* Smart Cards: Is it Smart to Use a Smart Card? 1990, Information, Privacy and the Welfare State 1990, Incentives and Labour Supply: Modelling Taxes and Benefits (ed. with P. Rebstock) 1992, New Zealand: The Turnaround Economy 1993, With Respect: Parliamentarians, Officials and Judges Too 2010; articles in econ., public policy and educational journals. *Leisure interests:* walking, family and gardening. *Address:* School of Government, Victoria University of Wellington, PO Box 600, Wellington 6140, New Zealand (office). *Telephone:* (4) 472-1000 (office). *E-mail:* info@victoria.ac.nz (office). *Website:* www.victoria.ac.nz (office).

PREBBLE, Hon. Richard William, CBE, BA, LLB; New Zealand fmr politician and lawyer; b. 7 Feb. 1948, UK; s. of Archdeacon K.R. Prebble; brother of Mark Prebble (q.v.); m. 1st Nancy Prebble 1970; m. 2nd Doreen Prebble 1991; ed Auckland Boys' Grammar School, Auckland Technical Inst. and Auckland Univ.; admitted as barrister and solicitor, NZ Supreme Court 1971; admitted to Bar, Fiji Supreme Court 1973; MP for Auckland Cen. 1975–93, 1996–2005; Jr Opposition Whip 1978–79; Minister of Transport, of Railways, of Civil Aviation and Meteorological Services, of Pacific Island Affairs, Assoc. Minister of Finance 1984–87; Minister of State-Owned Enterprises, Postmaster-Gen., Minister of Works and Devt and Minister of Pacific Island Affairs 1987–88, of Railways, Police, State-Owned Enterprises and Pacific Island Affairs Jan.–Oct. 1990; Leader ACT New Zealand 1996–2004. *Publications:* I've Been Thinking 1996, What Happens Next 1997, I've Been Writing 1999, Now it's time to act 2006, Out of the Red 2006. *Leisure interests:* Polynesian and Melanesian culture, opera, drama. *Website:* www.richardprebble.com.

PREBBLE, Stuart, BA (Hons); British media executive; *Director, Storyvault Films;* b. (Stuart Colin Prebble), 15 April 1951, London; s. of Dennis Stanley Prebble and Jean McIntosh; m.; one d.; ed Beckenham and Penge Grammar School for Boys, Newcastle Univ.; joined BBC as grad. trainee, worked as regional reporter for BBC TV in Newcastle; presenter for Granada TV; Deputy Ed. of World in Action (ITV) 1987, Ed. 1988 (fmr presenter and producer); Head of Granada's Regional Programmes 1990, Head of Factual Programmes 1992; Controller of Network Factual Programmes, ITV Network Centre 1993; CEO Granada Sky Broadcasting and Man. Dir of Channels and Interactive Media, Granada Media Group; CEO ONdigital PLC 1999–2002, ITV 2001–02; Co-founder and Man. Dir Liberty Bell Productions 2002–11; Founder www.storyvault.com (social history and genealogy networking website) 2009; Co-founder and Dir Storyvault Films 2010–; RTS Award for Best Factual Series 1995. *Television productions include:* as Exec. Producer: Stars Reunited (BBC 1) 2003–04, Grumpy Old Men (BBC 2) 2003–04, Grumpy Old Women (BBC 2) 2004–07, Three Men in a Boat (BBC 2) 2006, Why We Went To War 2006, The Alastair Campbell Diaries, the Widow's Tale, Portrait Artist of the Year 2013–, Landscape Artist of the Year 2013–. *Publications include:* A Power in the Land 1988, The Lazarus File 1989, Grumpy Old Men – The Official Handbook 2004, Grumpy Old Men – The Secret Diary 2005, Grumpy Old Christmas 2007, Grumpy Old Workers 2007, Grumpy Old Drivers 2008, Secrets of The Conqueror 2012, The Insect Farm 2015, The Bridge 2017. *Leisure interests:* politics, cinema. *Address:* Storyvault Films, Bridge Studios, 107A Hammersmith Bridge Road, London, W6 9DA, England (office). *Telephone:* (20) 8741-3929 (office). *E-mail:* stuart.prebble@storyvault.tv (office). *Website:* www.storyvault.tv (office).

PREDOIU, Cătălin Marian, PhD; Romanian lawyer and government official; b. 27 Aug. 1968, Buzău; ed Univ. of Bucharest; commercial and corp. governance lawyer; completed a training programme in commercial law at Caen Bar, France 1994; Lecturer in Commercial Law, Univ. of Bucharest 1994–2007; Assoc. Lawyer, ZRP law partnership 2005–; mem. Council of Bucharest Bar Asscn 2003–; Minister of Justice (ind.) Feb.–Dec. 2008, of Justice Dec. 2008–12, also Acting Minister of Foreign Affairs Oct.–Nov. 2009, Interim Prime Minister Feb. 2012; Prize of Romanian Acad. as a co-author of a law treatise. *Publications:* has published several articles and studies about commercial law.

PREM, Gen. Tinsulanonda; Thai politician, army officer, government official and head of state; *President, Privy Council;* b. 26 Aug. 1920, Songkhla, Songkhla; ed Suan Kularb School and Chulachomklao Royal Mil. Acad., Bangkok, US Army Armor School, Fort Knox, USA; started mil. career as Sub-Lt 1941; Commdr Cavalry HQ 1968; Commdr-Gen. 2nd Army Area 1974; Asst C-in-C Royal Thai Army 1977, C-in-C 1978–81; Deputy Minister of Interior, Govt of Gen. Kriangsak Chomanan 1977; Minister of Defence 1979–86; Prime Minister of Thailand 1980–88; Chair. Petroleum Authority of Thailand 1981; Pres., Privy Council 1998–; Regent of Thailand (apptd following death of King Bhumibol Adulyadej) Oct.–Dec. 2016; named as a leading figure in the Thailand political crisis of 2005–06; Chair. Hon. Bd of Govs and Hon. Chair. Bd of Govs, Prem Tinsulanonda Int. School; Kt Grand Cordon (Special Class) of the Most Noble Order of the Crown of Thailand 1975, Kt Grand Cordon (Special Class) of the Most Exalted Order of the White Elephant 1978, Kt Grand Cross (First Class) of the Most Illustrious Order of Chula Chom Klao 1982, Seri Maharajah Mangku Negara (Malaysia) 1984, Order of Symbolic Propitiousness Ramkeerati Boy Scout Citation Medal (Special Class) 1988, Kt of the Ancient and Auspicious Order of the Nine Gems 1988, Kt Grand Commdr (First Class) of the Hon. Order of Rama 1990, Kt Grand Cross (First Class) of the Most Admirable Order of the Direkgunabhorn 1996; Victory Medal – Indochina, Victory Medal – World War II, Freemen Safeguarding Medal (First Class), Safeguarding the Constitution Medal, Chakra Mala Medal (15 years military/police service), King Rama IX Royal Cypher Medal, 1st Class 1982, Red Cross Medal of Appreciation. *Address:* HM Privy Council, Grand Palace, Thanon Na Phra Lan, Bangkok 10200 (office); 279 Sri Ayutthaya Road, Sisao Theves, Bangkok 10300, Thailand. *Website:* www.generalprem.com; ptis.threegeneration.org.

PREMAJAYANTHA, A. D. Susil, LLB, MPA; Sri Lankan politician and lawyer; b. 10 Jan. 1955, Gangodawila village, Nugegoda; m.; ed St John's Coll., Nugegoda, Univ. of Colombo (external student), Postgraduate Inst. of Man., Univ. of Sri Jayawardanepura; joined Bank of Ceylon while a student; enrolled as an attorney-at-law 1985; resigned from bank and began practice as a defence counsel in Colombo High Courts; Deputy Chair. Urban Council, Sri Jayawardanepura, Kotte 1991–93; mem. Prov. Council, Western Prov. 1993–94, Minister of Western Prov. 1994–95, Chief Minister of Western Prov. 1995–98, 1999–2000; Minister of Educ. 2000–01, 2005–10; mem. Parl. (for Dist of Colombo) 2001–; Gen. Sec. United People's Freedom Alliance 2004–15; Minister of Power and Energy 2004–05, of Petroleum Industries 2010–13, of the Environment and Renewable Energy 2013–15, of Tech. and Research 2015–18; mem. Sri Lanka Freedom Party. *Address:* Parliament of Sri Lanka, Parliamentary Complex, Sri Jayawardenapura (office); No. 123/1, Station Road, Gangodawila, Nugegoda, Sri Lanka. *Telephone:* (11) 2199119 (office); (11) 2812181. *E-mail:* premajayantha_s@parliament.lk. *Website:* hwww.parliament.lk.

PREMJI, Azim Hashim, BS, BEng; Indian engineer, business executive and philanthropist; *Chairman, Wipro Ltd;* b. 24 July 1945, Bombay (now Mumbai); s. of Mohamed Husain Premji and G. M. H. Premji; m. Yasmeen Premji; two s.; ed Stanford Univ., USA; took over his father's Western India Vegetable Products Ltd (WIPRO) vegetable oil business upon his death 1966; apptd Chair., CEO and Man. Dir Wipro Ltd (IT and software co.), Bangalore 1983, currently Chair.; mem. Prime Minister's Cttee for Trade and Industry, Prime Minister's Advisory Cttee for Information Tech. in India; f. Azim Premji Foundation 2001; Hon. Fellowship, Inst. of Electronics and Telecommunication Engineers 2000; Chevalier de la Legion d'Honneur 2018; Dr hc (Indian Inst. of Tech.), (Manipal Acad. of Higher Educ.) 2000, (Wesleyan Univ.) 2009, (Visveswaraya Technological Univ.); Hon. DLitt (Aligarh Muslim Univ.) 2008; Sir M. Visvesvaraya Memorial Award 2000, Businessman of the Year, Business India magazine 2000, Business Leader of the Year, Econ. Times 2004, Padma Bhushan, Govt of India 2005, Faraday Medal 2005, Global Vision Award, US-India Business Council, Sir Jehangir Ghandy Medal, XLRI, Jamshedpur, Lakshya Business Visionary, Nat. Inst. of Industrial Eng 2006, Padma Vibhushan, Govt of India 2011, Ernst & Young Lifetime Achievement Award 2019. *Leisure interests:* jogging, spending time at hillside resorts. *Address:* Wipro Ltd, Doddakannelli, Sarjapur Road, Bangalore 560 035 (office); Bakhtawar, 229, Nariman Point, Mumbai 400 021, India (home). *Telephone:* (80) 28440011 (office); (80) 5569991 (home). *Fax:* (80) 28440256 (office). *E-mail:* azim.premji@corp.wipro.co.in (office); info@azimpremjifoundation.org. *Website:* www.wipro.com (office); www.wiprocorporate.com (office); www .azimpremjifoundation.org.

PRENDERGAST, Patrick J., BA, BAI, PhD, ScD, MRIA, FREng; Irish engineer, academic and university administrator; *Provost and President, Trinity College Dublin;* b. 23 June 1966, Enniscorthy, Ireland; s. of John Prendergast and Mary Prendergast (née Goodall); three c.; ed Trinity Coll. Dublin (Univ. of Dublin); post-doctoral positions in Bologna, Italy and Nijmegen, The Netherlands; apptd to Faculty of Eng, Trinity Coll. Dublin 1995, later Prof. of Bioengineering and Dir Trinity Centre for Bioengineering, Dean of Grad. Studies 2004–07, Vice-Provost and Chief Academic Officer 2008–11, Provost and Pres. 2011–; Visiting Prof., Inst. of Fundamental Technological Research, Poland, Erasmus Univ. Rotterdam, Tech. Univ. of Delft, Univ. Politicnic of Catalonia, Barcelona 2008; fmr mem. Bd of Dirs ClearStream Technologies plc; apptd by EC to Governing Bd of European Inst. of Innovation and Tech. 2012–; mem. Bd Tallaght Hosp.; Fellow, Irish Acad. of Eng; Int. Fellow, Royal Acad. of Eng (UK). *Publications:* several hundred articles related to implant design and tissue mechanobiology. *Address:* Office of the Provost, House 1, Trinity College, Dublin, 2, Ireland (office). *Telephone:* (1) 8964362 (office). *Fax:* (1) 8962303 (office). *E-mail:* provost@tcd.ie (office). *Website:* www.tcd.ie/provost (office).

PRENTICE, Christopher Norman Russell, CMG, MA, LitHum; British diplomatist; b. 5 Sept. 1954, London; m. Marie-Josephine (Nina) King 1978; two s. two d.; ed Christ Church Coll., Oxford; joined FCO 1977, Desk Officer (Arab-Israel, Near East N Africa Dept/NENAD) 1977–78, Arabic language training 1978–79, Third, later Second Sec., Kuwait 1980–83, Middle East Analyst, Cabinet Office, London 1983–85, First Sec. (Near East and S Asia), Embassy in Washington, DC 1985–89, Asst Head of EC Dept (External), FCO 1989–90, Asst Pvt. Sec. to Foreign Sec. Douglas Hurd (covering Middle East, EU, W and E Europe) 1990–93, Hungarian language training 1993–94, Deputy Head of Mission, Embassy in Budapest 1994–98, Head of NENAD 1998, Amb. to Jordan 2002–06, UK Special Rep., later FCO Co-ordinator for the Sudan Peace Process 2006–07, Amb. to Iraq 2007–09, to Italy 2011–16.

PRESCOTT, Edward Christian, MS, PhD; American economist and academic; *W.P. Carey Chaired Professor, Arizona State University;* b. 26 Dec. 1940, Glens Falls, NY; s. of William Clyde Prescott and Mathilde Helwig Prescott; ed Swarthmore Coll., Pa, Case-Western Reserve Univ., Cleveland, Carnegie-Mellon Univ., Pittsburgh; Lecturer, Econs Dept, Univ. of Pennsylvania 1966–67, Asst Prof. 1967–71; Asst Prof. of Econs, Grad. School of Industrial Admin, Carnegie-Mellon Univ. 1971–72, Assoc. Prof. 1972–75, Prof. 1975–80; Prof., Dept of Econs, Univ. of Minnesota 1980–98, 1999–2003, McKnight Presidential Chair in Econs 2003; Prof. of Econs, Univ. of Chicago 1998–99; Prof., Dept of Econs, Ariz. State Univ. 2003–, W.P. Carey Chaired Prof. 2003–; Sr Advisor, Research Dept, Fed. Reserve Bank of Minneapolis 1980–2003, Sr Monetary Advisor 2003–; Visiting Prof. of Econs, Norwegian School of Business and Econs 1974–75; Ford Visiting Research Prof., Univ. of Chicago 1978–79; Visiting Prof. of Econs, Northwestern Univ. 1979–80, Visiting Prof. of Finance, Kellogg Grad. School of Man. 1980–82; Regents' Prof., Univ. of Minnesota 1996, 2006; Maxwell Pellish Distinguished Visiting Prof. of Econs, Univ. of California, Santa Barbara 2004; Shinsei Bank Visiting Prof. of Political Economy, Stern School of Business, New York Univ. 2005–07; Dir Center for the Advanced Study in Economic Efficiency, Arizona State Univ. 2009–; Leader Nat. Bureau of Econ. Research/NSF Workshop in Industrial Org. 1977–84; Research Assoc., Nat. Bureau of Econ. Research 1988–; Pres. Soc. for the Advancement of Econ. Theory 1992–94, Soc. of Econ. Dynamics and Control 1992–95; Assoc. Ed. Journal of Econometrics 1976–82, International Economic Review 1980–90, Journal of Economic Theory 1990–92; Co-Ed. Economic Theory 1991; Brookings Econ. Policy Fellow 1969–70; mem. NAS 2008; Fellow, Econometric Soc. 1980, American Acad. of Arts and Sciences 1992; Hon. Prof., Gumilyov Eurasian Nat. Univ. 2012; Hon. mem. Omega Rho Int. Honor Soc. 2012; Laurea hc in Economica (Univ. of Rome 'Tor Vergata') 2002; Hon. Dr of Math. (Univ. of Athens) 2007; Alexander Henderson Award, Carnegie Mellon Univ. 1967, Guggenheim Fellow 1974–75, First Lionel McKenzie Lecturer 1990, Walras-Pareto Lecturer 1994, First Lawrence R. Klein Lecturer 1997, Sidrauski Lecturer, Latin America Econometric Soc. 1999, Plenary Lecturer, Soc. for Econ. Dynamics 2001, Richard T. Ely Lecturer, American Econ. Asscn Meetings 2002, Erwin Plein Nemmers Prize in Econs, Northwestern Univ. 2002, Bank of Sweden Prize in Econ. Sciences in Memory of Alfred Nobel (Nobel Prize) (with Finn E. Kydland) 2004. *Publications:* Contractual Arrangements for Intertemporal Trade (co-ed.) 1987, Recursive Methods in Economic Dynamics (collaborator) 1989, Applied General Equilibrium Symposium (co-ed.) 1995, Great Depressions of the 20th Century (co-ed.) 2002, Barriers to Riches (co-author) 2000, Contributions in Economic Theory: Symposium in the honor of C. D. Aliprantis (co-ed.) 2008; numerous articles in econs journals. *Address:* Department of Economics, W.P. Carey School of Business, Arizona State University, PO Box 879801, Tempe, AZ 85287-9801 (office); Research Department, Federal Reserve Bank of Minneapolis, 90 Hennepin Avenue, Minneapolis, MN 55400-0291, USA (office). *Telephone:* (480) 965-3531 (Tempe) (office); (612) 204-5520 (Minneapolis) (office). *Fax:* (480) 965-0748 (Tempe) (office); (612) 204-5515 (Minneapolis) (office). *E-mail:* edward.prescott@asu.edu (office); prescott@minneapolisfed.org (office). *Website:* wpcarey.asu.edu (office); www.minneapolisfed.org (office).

PRESCOTT, John Barry, AC, BComm, FAICD, FAIM, FTSE; Australian business executive; b. 22 Oct. 1940, Sydney, NSW; s. of John Norman Prescott and Margaret Ellen Brownie; m. Jennifer Mary Louise Cahill; one s. three d. (one deceased); ed North Sydney Boys' High School, Univ. of New South Wales, Northwestern Univ. USA; Gen. Man. Transport, Broken Hill Pty Co. Ltd (BHP) 1982–87, Exec. Gen. Man. and CEO BHP Steel 1987–91, Dir BHP 1988–98, Man. Dir and CEO BHP 1991–98; Chair. Horizon Pvt. Equity 1998–2005, ASC Pty Ltd 2000–09, Aurizon Holdings Ltd (fmrly QR National Ltd, fmrly QR Ltd) 2006–15; Dir Tubemakers 1988–92, Normandy Mining 1999–2001, Newmont Mining Corpn 2002–13; mem. Advisory Bd Booz Allen 1991–2003; mem. Defence Industry Cttee 1988–93, Bd, Business Council of Australia 1995–97; Chair. Mfg Council 1990–95, Sunshine Coast Business Council, Queensland 2004–07 (Patron 2007–09); mem. Int. Council of JP Morgan 1994–2003, Asia Pacific Advisory Cttee of New York Stock Exchange 1995–2005, Council of World Econ. Forum 1996–98, Bd of The Walter and Eliza Hall Inst. of Medical Research 1994–98; Trustee, The Conf. Bd 1993–2001, mem. Global Advisory Council 2013–16; Patron Australian Quality Council 1990–2000; Fellow, Australian Inst. of Co. Dirs, Australian Acad. of Technological Sciences; Hon. LLD (Monash) 1994, Hon. DSc (Univ. of New South Wales) 1995; Centenary Medal 2003. *Leisure interests:* tennis, golf. *Address:* Suite 1.02, Level 1, 11 Queens Road, Melbourne, Vic. 3004, Australia (office). *Telephone:* (3) 8547-1500 (office). *E-mail:* jbp@jbprescott.com (home).

PRESCOTT, Baron (Life Peer), cr. 2010, of Kingston-upon-Hull in the County of East Yorkshire; **John Leslie Prescott,** DipEconPol; British trade union official and politician; b. 31 May 1938, Prestatyn, Denbighshire, North Wales; s. of John Herbert Prescott and Phyllis Prescott; m. Pauline Tilston 1961; two s.; ed WEA correspondence courses, Ruskin Coll. Oxford, Univ. of Hull; trainee chef 1953–55; steward in Merchant Navy 1955–63; Recruitment Officer, Gen. & Municipal Workers Union 1965; contested Southport for Labour 1966; full-time official Nat. Union of Seamen 1968–70; MP for Kingston-upon-Hull East 1970–83, for Hull East 1983–2010; mem. Select Cttee Nationalized Industries 1973–79, Council of Europe 1972–75, European Parl. 1975–79; Parl. Pvt. Sec. to Sec. of State for Trade 1974–76; Opposition Spokesman on Transport 1979–81, Regional Affairs and Devolution 1981–83, on Transport 1983–84, on Employment 1984–87, on Energy 1987–89, on Transport 1988–93, on Employment 1993–94; Deputy Prime Minister and Sec. of State for the Environment, Transport and the Regions 1997–2001, Deputy Prime Minister and First Sec. of State, Head of Office of the Deputy Prime Minister 1997–2006, Deputy Prime Minister 2006–07; British Rep. to Parl. Ass., Council of Europe, Strasbourg, France 2007–, also sits on Ass. of Western European Union; mem. Labour Party Nat. Exec. Cttee 1989–, Deputy Leader 1994–2007, contested Labour Party Treas. 2010; mem. Shadow Cabinet 1983–97; mem. Bd Hull Kingston Rovers Rugby League Club; resgnd from Privy Council in protest over its role in the debate surrounding press regulation July 2013; North of England Zoological Soc. Gold Medal 1999, Priyadarshni Award 2002. *Publications:* Not Wanted on Voyage: A Report of the 1966 Seamen's Strike 1966, Alternative Regional Strategy: A Framework for Discussion 1982, Planning for Full Employment 1985, Real Needs–Local Jobs 1987, Moving Britain into the 1990s 1989, Moving Britain into Europe 1991, Full Steam Ahead 1993, Financing Infrastructure Investment 1994, Jobs and Social Justice 1994, Prezza: My Story: Pulling No Punches 2008. *Address:* House of Lords, Westminster, London, SW1A 0PW, England (office). *Telephone:* (20) 7219-5353 (office).

PRESS, Frank, PhD; American geophysicist and academic; *Professor Emeritus of Geophysics, Massachusetts Institute of Technology;* b. 4 Dec. 1924, Brooklyn, New York; s. of Solomon Press and Dora Press (née Steinholz); m. Billie Kallick 1946; one s. one d.; ed Coll. of City of New York and Columbia Univ.; Research Associate, Columbia Univ. 1946–49, Instructor, Geology 1949–51, Asst Prof. of Geology 1951–52, Assoc. Prof. 1952–55; Prof. of Geophysics, Calif. Inst. of Tech. 1955–65, Dir Seismological Lab. 1957–65; Co-Ed. Physics and Chemistry of the Earth 1957–; Chair. Dept of Earth and Planetary Sciences, MIT 1965–77, Prof. Emer. 1981–; Dir Office of Science and Tech. Policy, Exec. Office of Pres. and Science and Tech. Adviser to Pres. 1977–81; Consultant to USN 1956–57, US Dept of Defense 1958–62, NASA 1960–62, 1965–70; mem. US del. to Nuclear Test Ban Conf. Geneva 1959–61, Moscow 1963; Pres. Science Advisory Comm. 1961–64; Chair. Bd of Advisors Nat. Center for Earthquake Research of the US Geological Survey 1966–76; Planetology Subcomm. NASA 1966–70; Chair. Earthquake Prediction Panel Office of Science and Tech. 1965–66; Fellow, American Acad. of Arts and Sciences 1966, Royal Astronomical Soc.; mem. Nat. Science Bd 1970–77, NAS 1958, Pres. 1981–93; Cecil & Ida Green Sr Fellow, Carnegie Inst. of Washington 1993–97; Co-founder Washington Advisory Group 1996; fmr Pres. American Geophysical Union; Chair. Cttee on Scholarly Communication with People's Repub. of China 1975–77; mem. French Acad. of Science, Japan Acad. of Eng, Royal Soc., London; Hon. LLD (City Univ. of NY) 1972, Hon. DSc (Notre Dame

Univ.) 1973, (Univ. of Rhode Island, of Arizona, Rutgers Univ., City Univ. of New York) 1979; Townsend Harris Medal Coll. of the City of New York, Royal Astronomical Soc. Gold Medal (UK) 1971, Day Medal Geological Soc. of America, Interior 1972, NASA Award 1973, Killian Faculty Achievement Award, MIT 1975, Japan Prize 1993, Nat. Medal of Science 1994, Philip Hauge Abelson Prize, AAAS 1995, Lomonosov Gold Medal, Russian Acad. of Sciences 1998. *Publications:* Earth (with R. Siever) 1986, Understanding Earth 2000. *Leisure interests:* skiing, sailing. *Address:* Suite 616 South, 2500 Virginia Avenue, Washington, DC 20037, USA.

PRESS, James (Jim) E., BS; American automotive industry executive; *President, McLarty Global Transportation LLC;* b. 4 Oct. 1946, Los Angeles, Calif.; ed Kansas State Coll. (now Pittsburgh State Univ.); with Ford Motor Co. until 1970; with Toyota Motor Sales, USA Inc., in various positions, since 1970, Sr Vice-Pres. and Gen. Man. Lexus 1995–98, Sr Vice-Pres. Toyota Motor USA Inc. 1998–99, Exec. Vice-Pres. 1999–2001, COO 2001–03, Man. Officer Toyota Motor Corpn 2003–06, Pres. and COO (first non-Japanese) Toyota Motor North America Inc. 2006–07, Bd of Dirs Toyota Motor Corpn (first non-Japanese mem.) 2006–07, mem. Bd of Dirs Toyota Motor Credit Corpn 1999–2007; mem. Bd of Dirs, Vice-Chair. and Pres. Chrysler LLC, Detroit 2007–09, Deputy CEO and Special Advisor June–Dec. 2009, mem. Bd Mans and Vice-Chair. Cerberus Operations and Advisory Co. (COAC) LLC; Pres. McLarty Global Transportation LLC 2011–; mem. Bd of Dirs and mem. Nominating, Corp. Governance and Public Policy Cttee, Best Buy Co. Inc. 2006–07; fmr Chair. Asscn of Automotive Mfrs; mem. Pittsburgh State Univ., Pittsburgh, Kan., Advisory Bd and Switzer Center School, Torrance, Calif.; Gold Medallion, Int. Swimming Hall of Fame, Distinguished Service Citation Award, Automotive Hall of Fame, named an industry All-Star by both Automotive News and Automobile Magazine.

PRESSLER, Larry, MA, JD; American politician and lawyer; *President and CEO, Pressler Group LLC;* b. 29 March 1942, Humboldt, SDak; s. of Antone Pressler and Loretta Claussen; m. Harriet Dent 1982; one d.; ed Univ. of South Dakota, Univ. of Oxford, UK (Rhodes Scholar), Harvard Kennedy School of Govt and Harvard Law School; Lt in US Army, Viet Nam 1966–68; mem. House of Reps 1975–79; Senator from South Dakota 1979–97, mem. Cttee on Foreign Relations 1981–95, Cttee on Finance 1995–97, Chair. Commerce, Science and Transport Cttees 1995–96; Congressional Del. to 47th UN Gen. Ass. 1992; mem. US Comm. on Improving the Effectiveness of the UN 1993; Sec. US Del. to Inter-Parl. Union 1981; Dir USAF Bd of Visitory 1987–; Founder, Pres., CEO Pressler and Assocs (now Pressler Group LLC), Washington 1997–; fmr Visiting Prof. of Govt, Univ. of S Dakota; mem. Adjunct Faculty, Native American Oglala Lakota Coll., S Dakota; Sr Fellow, UCLA 2001; taught American Govt at Fudan Univ., Shanghai, People's Repub. of China 2005; mem. Bd of Advisors, Chrys Capital 2002–05; Dir Spectramind 1999–2003; mem. seven Corp. Bds, including Infosys Technologies, Bangalore, India; mem. Council on Foreign Relations, Vietnam Veterans Memorial Educ. Center Advisory Council; mem. US Comm. for the Preservation of America's Heritage Abroad 2009, Jericho Project Veterans Advisory Council 2010; decorations for service as Lt in US Army in Viet Nam. *Publications:* US Senators from the Prairie 1982, Star Wars: The SDI Debates in Congress 1986. *Leisure interests:* running, tennis. *Address:* 800 25th Street, NW, The Plaza, Suite 504, Washington, DC 20037, USA (office). *Telephone:* (202) 210-5330 (office); (202) 546-5959 (home). *Fax:* (202) 333-5854 (office); (202) 333-5854 (home). *E-mail:* lpressler@larrypressler.com (home). *Website:* www.larrypressler.com (office); www.senatorlarrypressler.com.

PRESSLER, Paul S., BS; American business executive; *Partner, Clayton, Dubilier & Rice LLC;* b. 1956, New York; ed State Univ. of New York at Oneonta; various positions in branding and marketing, Remco Toys, Mego Toys and Kenner-Parker –1987; Sr Vice-Pres. Product Licensing, The Walt Disney Co. 1987–90, Sr Vice-Pres. Consumer Products 1990–93, Pres. The Disney Stores 1993–96, Pres. Disneyland Resort, Anaheim, Calif. 1996–99, Chair. Global Theme Park and Resorts Div. 1999–2002; Pres. and CEO Gap Inc. 2002–07; Partner, Clayton, Dubilier & Rice LLC, (pvt. equity firm), New York 2009–; Chair. AssuraMed 2010–13; currently Chair. David's Bridal, Inc., SiteOne Inc.; mem. Bd of Dirs The DryBar, Inc., eBay Inc. 2015–; fmr mem. Bd of Dirs Avon Products Inc., Oveture Acquisition Corporate, OpenTable Inc. *Address:* Clayton, Dubilier & Rice LLC, 375 Park Avenue, 18th Floor, New York, NY 10152, USA (office). *Telephone:* (212) 407-5200 (office). *Fax:* (212) 407-5252 (office). *Website:* www.cdr-inc.com (office).

PRESTON, Sir Paul, Kt, CBE, MA, DPhil, FRHistS, FBA; British historian, author and academic; *Prince of Asturias Professor of Contemporary Spanish History, London School of Economics;* b. 21 July 1946, Liverpool; s. of Charles R. Preston and Alice Hoskisson; m. Gabrielle P. Ashford-Hodges 1983; two s.; ed St Edward's Coll. Liverpool, Oriel Coll. Oxford and Univ. of Reading; Research Fellow, Centre for Mediterranean Studies, Rome 1973–74; Lecturer in History, Univ. of Reading 1974–75; Lecturer in Modern History, Queen Mary Coll. London 1975–79, Reader 1979–85, Prof. of History 1985–91; Prof. of Int. History, LSE 1991–94, Prince of Asturias Prof. of Contemporary Spanish History 1994–; regular contrib. to Times Literary Supplement; columnist in ABC, Diario 16 and El País, Madrid; Comendador, Orden del Mérito Civil (Spain) 1987, Caballero Gran Cruz de la Orden de Isabel la Católica (Spain) 2006; Yorkshire Post Book of the Year 1994, Así fue – La Historia rescatada Prize 1998, Premi Internacional Ramon Llull, Catalan Govt 2005, Trias Fargas Non-Fiction Prize 2006, Marcel Proust Chair of European Acad. 2006. *Publications:* The Coming of the Spanish Civil War 1978, The Triumph of Democracy in Spain 1986, The Spanish Civil War 1986, The Politics of Revenge 1990, Franco: A Biography 1993, Comrades: Portraits from the Spanish Civil War 1999, Doves of War: Four Women of Spain 2003, Juan Carlos: A People's King 2004, We Saw Spain Die 2008, The Spanish Holocaust: Inquisition and Extermination in Twentieth-Century Spain 2011, The Last Stalinist: The Life of Santiago Carrillo 2014, The Last Days of the Spanish Republic 2016. *Leisure interests:* classical music, especially opera, modern fiction, supporting Everton Football Club. *Address:* Cañada Blanch Centre for Contemporary Spanish Studies, London School of Economics, Houghton Street, London, WC2A 2AE, England (office). *Telephone:* (20) 7955-6508 (office). *Fax:* (20) 7955-6757 (office). *E-mail:* p.preston@lse.ac.uk (office). *Website:* www.lse.ac.uk/internationalHistory/home.aspx.

PRESTON, Simon John, CBE, MusB, MA, FRAM, FRCM, FRCO, FRCCO, FRSA; British organist and conductor; b. 4 Aug. 1938, Bournemouth, Dorset, England; m. Elizabeth Hays; ed Canford School, King's Coll., Cambridge; Sub-Organist, Westminster Abbey 1962–67; Acting Organist, St Albans Abbey 1967–68; Organist and Lecturer in Music, Christ Church, Oxford 1970–81; Organist and Master of the Choristers, Westminster Abbey 1981–87; Conductor, Oxford Bach Choir 1971–74; Artistic Dir, Calgary Int. Organ Festival; Patron, Univ. of Buckingham; mem. Royal Soc. of Musicians, Council of Friends of St John's Smith Square; over 30 recordings; Edison Award 1971, Grand Prix du Disque 1979, Performer of the Year Award, American Guild of Organists 1987, Medal of the Royal Coll. of Organists 2014. *Leisure interests:* croquet, theatre, opera. *Address:* 15 St Margaret's Road, Oxford, OX2 6RU, England. *Telephone:* (1865) 512276.

PRESTON, Steven C., BA, MBA; American business executive and fmr government official; *CEO, Livingston International;* b. 4 Aug. 1960; m. Molly Preston; five c.; ed Northwestern Univ., Univ. of Chicago, Ludwig-Maximilians Univ., Germany; Sr Vice-Pres. and Treas., First Data Corpn 1993–97; Chief Financial Officer, then Exec. Vice-Pres. Service Master 1997–2006; Admin., US Small Business Admin, Washington, DC 2006–08; US Sec. of Housing and Urban Devt 2008–09; Pres. and CEO Oakleaf Waste Management 2009–11, Exec. Vice-Pres. for Finance, Recycling and Energy Services, Waste Management (after acquisition of Oakleaf) 2011–12; advisor to Republican Presidential nominee Mitt Romney 2012; CEO Livingston International 2013–; mem. Bd of Dirs Habitat for Humanity, Wheaton Coll.; mem. Bd of Visitors, Weinberg Coll. of Arts and Sciences, Northwestern Univ. *Address:* Livingston International, 150 Pierce Road, Suite 500, Itasca, IL 60143-1222, USA (office). *E-mail:* info@livingstonintl.com (office). *Website:* www.livingstonintl.com (office).

PRETTEJOHN, Nicholas Edward Tucker, BA; British business executive; *Chairman, Scottish Widows Group Ltd;* b. 22 July 1960; s. of Edward Joseph Tucker Prettejohn and Diana Sally Prettejohn; m. 1st Elizabeth Esch 1986 (divorced 1997); m. 2nd Claire Helen McKenna 1997; two d.; ed Taunton School, Somerset and Balliol Coll., Oxford; Research Assoc., Bain & Co. 1982–91, Partner 1988–91; Dir Apax Partners 1991–94; Dir Corp. Strategy, Nat. Freight Corpn PLC 1994–95; Head of Strategy, Lloyd's of London 1995–97, Man. Dir Business Devt Unit 1997–99, N America Business Unit 1998–99, CEO 1999–2006, Dir (non-exec.) 2014–; CEO, Prudential UK and Europe 2006–09, also mem. Bd of Dirs; Chair. Brit Insurance 2011–14; Chair. Scottish Widows Group Ltd 2014–, Reach PLC 2018–; Dir (non-exec.) Anglo & Overseas Trust PLC 1998–2004, Legal & General 2010–, Bank of England 2013–, HBOS PLC 2014–; Chair. Financial Services Practitioner Panel 2007–09; Chair. Britten-Pears Foundation 2009–; mem. Bd of Trustees, Royal Opera House 2005–13 (Chair. Finance and Audit Cttee 2008–); Chair. Bd Govs, Royal Northern Coll. of Music 2012–; mem. Advisory Bd Chartered Insurance Inst.; Trustee BBC Trust; Hon. Fellow, Chartered Insurance Inst. 2004. *Leisure interests:* opera, music, theatre, horse racing, golf, cricket, rugby, current affairs. *Address:* Scottish Widows Ltd, 25 Gresham Street, London, EC2V 7HN, England (office). *Telephone:* (11) 7929-0290 (office). *Website:* www.scottishwidows.co.uk (office).

PREUSS, Daphne, BS, PhD; American geneticist, business executive and academic; *President and CEO, Chromatin, Inc;* m.; ed Univ. of Denver, Massachusetts Inst. of Tech.; performed postdoctoral research at Stanford Univ. 1990–95; joined Dept of Molecular Genetics, Univ. of Chicago 1995, Asst Prof. then Prof., Albert D. Lasker Prof. in Molecular Genetics and Cell Biology 1995–2006, Investigator, Howard Hughes Medical Inst. 2001–06; Co-founder Chromatin, Inc., Chicago 2002, Sr Vice-Pres. then Pres. and Chief Scientific Officer 2007–08, Pres. and CEO 2006–; fmr mem. Bd of Govs Argonne Nat. Lab.; David and Lucile Packard Fellow; Searle Scholar; Lifetime Nat. Assoc., NAS. *Address:* Chromatin, Inc., 10 South LaSalle Street, Suite 2100, Chicago, IL 60603, USA (office). *Telephone:* (312) 292-5400 (office). *Website:* www.chromatininc.com (office).

PRIA OLAVARRIETA, Melba Maria; Mexican government official and diplomatist; *Ambassador to India;* ed Nat. Univ. of Mexico, Technological Inst. of Superior Studies, Kennedy School of Govt, Harvard Univ., USA; fmr Ed. (Publs Dept) and Chief of Cultural Promotion, Mexican Social Security Inst.; fmr Vice-Pres. for Devt and Communication, Mexicana de Aviación; fmr Head of Special Del. of Ministry of Public Educ. in Chiapas for five years; fmr Head (State Minister) of Nat. Indigenous Inst.; fmr Vice-Pres. Latin American and Caribbean Indigenous People's Devt Fund; served in Foreign Service in Israel and China, Ministry of Foreign Affairs; fmr Dir-Gen. State and Fed. Liaison Office; fmr Dir-Gen. Mexican Communities Abroad; fmr Dir-Gen. Public Diplomacy; Amb. to Indonesia 2007–15, to India 2015–. *Publications:* several books and lectures. *Address:* Embassy of Mexico, C-8 Anand Niketan, New Delhi 110 021, India (office). *Telephone:* (11) 24107182 (office). *Fax:* (11) 24117193 (office). *E-mail:* contact@embmexin.com (office). *Website:* embamex.sre.gob.mx/india (office).

PRICE, Antony, MA; British fashion designer; b. 5 March 1945, Keighley, Yorks., England; s. of Peter Price and Joan Price; ed Eshton Hall School for Boys, Gargrave, Yorks., Bradford Coll. of Art and Royal Coll. of Art, London; designer for Sterling Cooper 1968–72, for Plaza 1972–79; Chair. of own fashion co. 1979–; has collaborated with several musicians, including David Bowie, Steve Strange and Duran Duran, but especially Bryan Ferry and Roxy Music; more recently, noted for dressing celebrities including Tara Palmer-Tomkinson, Patsy Kensit, Anjelica Huston, Jerry Hall, Camilla Parker Bowles, Diana Ross, Melanie Griffith, Yasmin Le Bon and Dita Von Teese; opened own shop in Chelsea 2000; British Glamour Award 1989. *Leisure interests:* tropical plants, tropical ornithology, modern and classical music. *Telephone:* (1895) 833415. *E-mail:* ap@antonyprice.com.

PRICE, Frank; American television and cinema producer; b. 17 May 1930, Decatur, Ill.; s. of William Price and Winifred Price (née Moran); m. Katherine Huggins 1965; four s.; ed Michigan State Univ.; served with USN 1948–49; Writer and Story Ed., CBS-TV, New York 1951–53; with Columbia Pictures, Hollywood 1953–57, NBC-TV 1957–58; Producer, Writer, Universal Television, Calif. 1959–64, Vice-Pres. 1964–71, Sr Vice-Pres. 1971–73, Exec. Vice-Pres. 1973–74, Pres. 1974–78; Pres. Columbia Pictures 1978–79, Chair. and CEO 1979–83; Chair. and CEO MCA Motion Picture Group 1983–86, Price Entertainment 1991, Chair. Columbia Pictures 1990–91; Dir Sony Pictures Entertainment, Savoy Pictures; mem. Writers Guild of America; Peabody Award 1996, NAACP Image Award 1996. *Films produced include:* Gladiator 1992, Circle of Friends 1995, The Walking Dead

1995, Mariette in Ecstasy 1996, Getting Away with Murder 1996, Zeus and Roxanne 1997, Texas Rangers 2001. *Television includes:* Rich Man, Poor Man (mini-series) (producer) 1976, The Tuskegee Airmen (film) (exec. producer) 1995.

PRICE, Leontyne; American singer (soprano); b. (Mary Violet Leontine Price), 10 Feb. 1927, Laurel, Miss.; d. of James A. Price and Kate Price (née Baker); m. William Warfield 1952 (divorced 1973); ed Central State Coll., Wilberforce, Ohio, Juilliard School of Music; appeared as Bess (Porgy and Bess), Vienna, Berlin, Paris, London, New York 1952–54; recitalist, soloist 1954–; soloist, Hollywood Bowl 1955–59, 1966; opera singer, NBC-TV 1955–58, San Francisco Opera Co. 1957–59, 1960–61, Vienna Staatsoper 1958, 1959–60, 1961; recording artist RCA-Victor 1958–; appeared at Covent Garden 1958–59, 1970, Chicago 1959, 1960, 1965, Milan 1960–61, 1963, 1967, Metropolitan Opera, New York 1961–62, 1963–70, 1972, Paris Opéra as Aida 1968, Metropolitan Opera as Aida 1985 (retd); Fellow, American Acad. of Arts and Sciences; Trustee, International House; Hon. Vice-Chair. US Cttee of UNESCO; Order of Merit (Italy), Ordre des Arts et des Lettres; Hon. DMus (Howard Univ., Cen. State Coll., Ohio); Hon. DHL (Dartmouth); Hon. DH (Rust Coll., Miss.); Hon. DHumLitt (Fordham); Presidential Medal of Freedom 1964, Kennedy Center Honor 1980, Nat. Medal of Arts 1985, Essence Award 1991, 20 Grammy Awards including for Lifetime Achievement 1989, Nat. Asscn of Black Broadcasters Award 2002, Gramophone Lifetime Achievement Award 2003, Nat. Endowment for the Arts Opera Award 2008, and numerous other awards.

PRICE, Michael F., BBA; American financial industry executive; *Managing Partner, MFP Investors LLC;* b. 1952; m. (divorced); three s.; ed Univ. of Oklahoma; joined Heine Securities Corpn as Research Asst 1975, Owner and CEO 1988–96; sold co. to Franklin Resources 1996 and f. advisory co. Franklin Mutual Advisers Inc., Pres., CEO 1996–2001, later Chair.; Founder and Man. Partner, MFP Investors LLC (investment fund) 2001–; Founder and Pres. Michael F. Price Foundation; Founder and CEO Mobile Briefs; currently Chair. Franklin Mutual Series Fund Inc.; mem. Bd of Dirs Liquidnet Holdings, Albert Einstein College of Medicine, Univ. of Okla Foundation, Jazz at Lincoln Center; Sr Advisor, Michael F. Price School of Business, Univ. of Okla, also mem. Bd of Visitors Int. Programs Center; Hon. DHumLitt (Univ. of Okla) 1999; Fund Action Lifetime Achievement Award 2005. *Address:* MFP Investors LLC, 51 JFK Parkway, Short Hills, NJ 07078, USA. *Telephone:* (973) 921-2201. *Fax:* (973) 921-2236. *E-mail:* mprice@mfpllc.com.

PRICE, Nicholas Raymond Leige (Nick); Zimbabwean (b. South African) professional golfer; b. 28 Jan. 1957, Durban, Natal Prov.; m. Sue Price; one s. two d.; turned professional 1977; won Asseng Invitational 1979, Canon European Masters 1980, Italian Open, S African Masters 1981, Vaals Reef Open 1982, World Series of Golf 1983, Trophée Lancôme, ICI Int. 1985, West End S Australian Open 1989, GTE Byron Nelson Classic, Canadian Open 1991, Air New Zealand/Shell Open, PGA Championships, H-E-B Texas Open 1992, The Players' Championship, Canon Greater Hartford Open, Sprint Western Open, Federal Express St Jude Classic, ICL Int., Sun City Million Dollar Challenge 1993, The Open Championship, ICL Int. Honda Classic, Southwestern Bell Colonial, Motorola Western Open, PGA Championship, Bell Canadian Open 1994, Alfred Dunhill Challenge, Hassan II Golf Trophy, Morocco, Zimbabwe Open 1995, MCI Classic 1997, Suntory Open 1999, CVS Charity Classic 2001, MasterCard Colonial 2002, CVS/pharmacy Charity Classic (unofficial event) 2006, CVS Caremark Charity Classic (unofficial event) 2009; reached No. 1 in Official World Golf Ranking mid-1990s; f. Nick Price Golf Course Design 2001, has designed courses in Fla, Dominican Repub., Ireland, South Africa and Mexico; named Amb. of Golf by Northern Ohio Golf Charities 2011; lives in Fla, USA; Sunshine Tour Order of Merit Winner 1982–83, PGA Player of the Year 1993, 1994, PGA Tour Player of the Year 1993, 1994, PGA Tour leading money winner 1993, 1994, Vardon Trophy 1993, 1997, Byron Nelson Award 1997, Payne Stewart Award 2002, inducted into World Golf Hall of Fame 2003, Bob Jones Award, USGA 2005, Old Tom Morris Award, Golf Course Supts Asscn of America 2011. *Publication:* The Swing 1997. *Leisure interests:* water skiing, tennis, fishing, flying. *Address:* 900 S US Highway 1, Suite 204, Jupiter, FL 33477, USA; c/o PGA Tour, 100 PGA TOUR Boulevard, Ponte Vedra Beach, FL 32082, USA. *Telephone:* (561) 575-6588. *E-mail:* wayne@nickprice.com. *Website:* www.pgatour.com/players/player.01968.html; www.nickprice.com.

PRICE, Paul Buford, Jr, BS, PhD; American physicist and academic; *Professor, Graduate School, University of California, Berkeley;* b. 8 Nov. 1932, Memphis, Tenn.; s. of Paul Buford Price, Sr and Eva Price (née Dupuy); m. Jo Ann Baum 1958; one s. three d.; ed Davidson Coll., Univ. of Virginia, Univ. of Bristol, Univ. of Cambridge, UK; Physicist, Gen. Electric Research Lab., New York 1960–69; Visiting Prof., Tata Inst. of Fundamental Research, Bombay, India 1965–66; Adjunct Prof. of Physics, Rensselaer Polytechnic Inst. 1967–68; Prof. of Physics, Univ. of Calif., Berkeley 1969–2001, Chair. Dept of Physics 1987–91, William H. McAdams Prof. of Physics 1990–92, Dean, Physical Sciences, Coll. of Letters and Science 1992–2001, Prof., Grad. School 2001–; Dir Space Science Lab. 1979–85; NASA Consultant on Lunar Sample Analysis Planning Team; mem. Bd of Dirs Terradex Corpn 1978–86; mem. Visiting Cttee, Bartol Research Inst. 1991–94, Advisory Cttee, Indian Inst. of Astrophysics 1993–95; Fellow and Chair, Cosmic Physics Div., American Physical Soc.; mem. NAS 1975–, mem. Space Science Bd, Sec. Physical and Math. Sciences Class of NAS 1985–88, Chair. 1988–91, mem. Steering Group on Future of Space Science (NAS) 1994–95, Polar Research Bd (NAS) 1999–2002; Regional Dir Calif. Alliance for Minority Participation 1994–2004; US Ice Core Working Group 2001–03; led a 20-person review of Uppsala Univ., Sweden 2001–02; Chair. Scientific Advisory Bd, Univ. of Vienna, Austria 2006–, Workshop on Antarctic Science Symposium 2011; Co-organizer Conf. and Proceedings of Workshop on Methane on Mars, Frascati, Italy 2009–10; Fellow, American Geophysical Union, American Astronomical Soc.; Hon. Fellow, Indian Inst. of Astrophysics 2000; Hon. mem. Int. Nuclear Track Soc.; Hon. ScD (Davidson Coll.) 1973; Distinguished Service Award, (American Nuclear Soc.) 1964, Ernest O. Lawrence Memorial Award of Atomic Energy Comm. 1971, NASA Medal for Exceptional Scientific Achievement 1973, Scientific Symposium in Honor of P.B. Price's 65th Birthday 1997, Berkeley Citation for outstanding research and leadership 2002, Price Terrace, located at 77°19'40"S, 161°18'00"E, a region of Antarctica named for P. B. Price by US Bd on Geographic Names, Berkeley Citation, IR-100 Awards for invention of Nuclepore Filter, radon detector and radiation dosimeter). *Achievements include:* scientific inventions: nuclepore filter, fission track dating, radon detector, optical dust logger, Berkeley fluorescent spectrometer. *Publications:* Nuclear Tracks in Solids (co-author); more than 550 research papers in specialized journals. *Leisure interests:* skiing, travel, walking, reading. *Address:* Physics Department, University of California, Berkeley, 335 LeConte Hall, Berkeley, CA 94720 (office); 1056 Overlook Road, Berkeley, CA 94708, USA (home). *Telephone:* (510) 642-4982 (office); (510) 548-5206 (home). *Fax:* (510) 643-8497 (office); (510) 548-5206 (home). *E-mail:* bprice@berkeley.edu (office). *Website:* www.physics.berkeley.edu (office).

PRICE, Thomas (Tom) Edmunds, BA, MD; American politician, government official and fmr surgeon; b. 8 Oct. 1954, Lansing, Mich.; m. Elizabeth Clark; one s.; ed Univ. of Michigan; fmr Resident in orthopaedic surgery, Emory Univ. School of Medicine, also fmr Asst Prof. of Orthopaedic Surgery; fmr Medical Dir, Orthopaedic Clinic, Grady Memorial Hosp., Atlanta; Founder, Compass Orthopedics (fmrly North Fulton Orthopedic Clinic); mem. Georgia State Senate 1997–2004, Majority Leader 2002–03; mem. US House of Reps from Georgia's 6th Dist 2005–, Chair. Republican Study Cttee 2009–11, House Republican Policy Cttee 2011–13, House Budget Cttee 2015–17; US Sec. of Health and Human Services Feb.–Sept. 2017; mem. Bd of Dirs North Metro YMCA; Republican. *Address:* US House of Representatives, Washington, DC 20515, USA (office). *Telephone:* (202) 224-3121 (office). *Website:* www.house.gov (office).

PRIEBUS, (Reinhold) Reince (Richard), BA, JD; American lawyer, politician and fmr government official; b. 18 March 1972, Dover, NJ; s. of Richard Priebus and Dimitra Priebus; m. Sally Sherrow 1999; one s. one d.; ed Univ. of Wisconsin, Whitewater, Univ. of Miami; fmr clerk, Wisconsin State Ass. Educ. Cttee; fmr clerk, Wisconsin Court of Appeals, Wisconsin Supreme Court, US Dist Court for Florida Southern Dist; fmr intern, Nat. Asscn for the Advancement of Colored People (NAACP) Legal Defense Fund, California; joined Michael Best & Friedrich LLP (law firm), Wisconsin, becoming Partner, Litigation and Corp. Practice Groups 2006–17; Chair. Republican Party of Wisconsin 2007–11; Gen. Counsel, Republican Nat. Cttee 2009–10, Chair. 2011–17; Chief of Staff, The White House Jan.–July 2017; mem. ABA, Milwaukee, Kenosha, Racine, Wisconsin Bar Asscns; mem. Advisory Bd Kenosha Symphony Orchestra (fmr Pres.).

PRIESTMAN, Jane, OBE, FCSD; British design management consultant; b. 7 April 1930; d. of Reuben Stanley Herbert and Mary Elizabeth Herbert (née Ramply); m. Arthur Martin Priestman 1954 (divorced 1986); two s.; ed Northwood Coll., Liverpool Coll. of Art; design practice 1954–75; Design Man., Gen. Man. Architecture and Design British Airports Authority 1975–86; Dir Architecture and Design British Railways Bd 1986–91; Visiting Prof., De Montfort Univ. 1997–2001; mem. London Regional Transport Design Panel 1985–88, Jaguar Styling Panel 1988–91, Percentage for Art Steering Group, Arts Council 1989–91; mem. Council of Design Council 1996–2000; Gov. Commonwealth Inst. 1987–98, Kingston Univ. 1988–96; Enabler Comm. for Architecture and the Built Environment; Hon. FRIBA, Hon. FRSA; Dr hc (De Montfort) 1994, (Sheffield Hallam) 1998; Ada Louise Huxtable Prize 2015. *Leisure interests:* textiles, city architecture, opera, travel. *Address:* 30 Duncan Terrace, London, N1 8BS, England (home). *Telephone:* (20) 7837-4525 (home). *Fax:* (20) 7837-4525 (home). *E-mail:* janepriestman30@gmail.com (home).

PRIETO JIMÉNEZ, Abel Enrique; Cuban writer, academic and politician; b. 11 Nov. 1950, Pinar del Rio; ed Univ. of Havana; joined Communist Party of Cuba 1978, mem. Cen. Cttee 1991–; Deputy, Nat. Ass. of People's Power 1993–; Minister of Culture 1997–2012, 2016–18; Advisor to Pres. Councils of State and Ministers, Raul Castro 2012–16; fmr Prof. of Literature, Univ. of Havana, Ed.-in-Chief and Dir Letras Cubanas, Dir Arte y Literatura, Dir Juan Marinello Cultural Centre; fmr Pres. Unión de Escritores y Artistas de Cuba; Chevalier, Ordre des Arts et des Lettres; Premio Nacional de Literatura. *Publications include:* Los bitongos y los guapos 1980, Noche de sábado 1989, El vuelo del gato (Critics Award 2001) 1999.

PRIFTI, Dritan V., BA, MPA; Albanian politician; b. 27 Aug. 1968; m. 1995; three s. one d.; ed Univ. of Tirana, Univ. of New Mexico, John F. Kennedy School of Govt, Harvard Univ., USA; Foreign Relations specialist, INSIG (insurance company) Tirana 1990–93; Chief of Staff to Minister of Labour and Social Affairs 1997–98; Chief of Staff to Minister of Finance 1998–99; Dir of Cabinet (Chief of Staff) to Prime Minister July–Oct. 2000; CEO Albanian Electro-Energy Corpn 2000–01; Minister of State for Energy 2001–02; Minister of the Economy, Trade and Energy 2009–10; mem. Socialist Movt for Integration (SMI), currently Deputy Chair.; mem. Kuvendi Popullor (Parl.) for Fier Region (Socialist Party) 2001–05, (SMI) 2005–13; Partner, Premiere Services Ltd (consultancy), Tirana 2013–; Chair. Albanian Devt Council 1998; named Citizen of Honor by Libofsha Municipality. *Address:* Rr. Dervish Hima, Kulla 1, Ap 3, Tirana, Albania. *E-mail:* dritanprifti2768@yahoo.com.

PRIKHODKO, Sergey Eduardovich; Russian diplomatist and government official; b. 12 Jan. 1957, Moscow, Russian SFSR, USSR; m.; two d.; ed Moscow State Inst. of Int. Relations; mem. of staff, Ministry of Foreign Affairs 1980–93, including as diplomat at Soviet Embassy in Prague, Attaché and Third Sec., Office of European Socialist Countries, Soviet Foreign Ministry 1986–87, Second Sec., later First Sec., Embassy of Russia in Prague 1992–93; Head Div. of Baltic Countries, Deputy Dir Second European Dept 1993–97; Asst to Russian Pres. on Int. Problems 1997–98, Deputy Head of Admin, Russian Presidency 1998–99, concurrently Head, Dept of Admin on Int. Policy 1998; Adviser to the Pres. 2004–12; Head of the Govt Admin 2012–18, Deputy Chair. of the Govt 2013–18; Public Recognition Award 1999. *Leisure interests:* literature, fishing, hunting. *Address:* c/o Office of the Government, 103274 Moscow, Krasnopresnenskaya nab. 2, Russia (office).

PRINCE, Charles (Chuck) O., III, BA, MA, LLM, JD; American banker; b. 13 Jan. 1950, Lynwood, Calif.; s. of Charles Owen Prince, II and Mrs Charles Prince (née Doyle); m. Margaret L. Wolff 2003; ed Univ. of Southern California, Georgetown Univ. Law Center; began career as attorney US Steel Corpn 1975–79; joined Commercial Credit Co. (later renamed Citigroup Inc.) 1979, Sr Vice-Pres. and Gen. Counsel 1983–86, Exec. Vice-Pres. 1996–2000, Chief Admin. Officer 2000–01, COO 2001–02, CEO and Dir Citigroup Inc. 2003–07, Chair. and CEO 2006–07 (resgnd); Chair. and CEO Global Corp. and Investment Bank 2002–03; later a Sr Counsellor, Albright Stonebridge Group; mem. Financial

Services Forum, Council on Foreign Relations, Business Roundtable; mem. Bd of Dirs United Negro Coll. Fund, Teachers' Coll., Columbia Univ., New York; fmr mem. Bd of Dirs New York Urban League; Trustee, Weill Medical Coll., Teachers Coll., The Juilliard School; mem. various bar asscns and professional asscns.

PRINCE, Harold (Hal) Smith, LittD; American theatre director; b. 30 Jan. 1928, New York; s. of Milton A. Prince and Blanche Prince (née Stern); m. Judith Chaplin 1962; one s. one d.; ed Emerson Coll.; mem. Council, Nat. Endowment of the Arts, League of New York Theatres; Critics Circle awards, Best Music Award, Evening Standard; Commonwealth Award 1982; John F. Kennedy Center Awards 1994, Tony Award for Lifetime Achievement 2006. *Productions include:* co-produced Pajama Game 1954–56 (Antoinette Perry Award for Best Musical 1955), Damn Yankees 1955–57 (Antoinette Perry Award), New Girl in Town 1957–58, West Side Story 1957–59, Fiorello! 1959–61 (Antoinette Perry Award for best musical 1960, Pulitzer Prize), Tenderloin 1960–61, A Call on Kuprin 1961, They Might Be Giants 1961, Side by Side by Sondheim 1976; produced Take Her, She's Mine 1961–62, A Funny thing Happened on the Way to the Forum 1962–64 (Antoinette Perry Award), Fiddler on the Roof 1964–72 (Antoinette Perry Award), Poor Bitos 1964, Flora the Red Menace 1965; dir, producer She Loves Me! 1963–64, London 1964, Superman 1966, Cabaret 1966–69 (Antoinette Perry Award for best musical 1966), London 1968, Zorba 1968–69, Company 1970–72 (Antoinette Perry Award), London 1972, A Little Night Music 1973–74 (Antoinette Perry Award) (London 1975), Pacific Overtures 1976; co-dir, producer Follies 1971–72; co-producer, dir Candide 1974–75, Merrily We Roll Along 1981; dir A Family Affair 1962, Baker Street 1965, Great God Brown 1972–73, The Visit 1973–74, Love for Love 1974–75, On the Twentieth Century 1978, Evita, London 1978, Broadway 1979, Los Angeles 1980, Chicago 1980, Australia 1980, Vienna 1981, Mexico City 1981, Sweeney Todd, the Demon Barber of Fleet Street 1979–80, London 1980, A Doll's Life 1982, Diamonds 1984, Grind 1985, The Phantom of the Opera (Antoinette Perry Award for Best Dir 1988) 1986, Play Memory, End of the World, Rosa 1987, Grandchild of Kings (The O'Casey Project) (author and dir) 1992, Kiss of the Spider Woman (Toronto, London) 1992, (New York, Vienna) 1993, Show Boat (Toronto) 1993, (New York) 1994, (nat. tour) 1996, Candide 1997, Parade 1998. *Films include:* (co-producer) The Pajama Game 1957, Damn Yankees 1958; (dir) Something for Everyone 1970, A Little Night Music 1978. *Operas:* Ashmedai 1976, Silverlake 1980, Don Giovanni 1989 (New York City Opera); Madame Butterfly 1982; Candide 1982; Willie Stark 1982 (Houston Opera Co.); Turandot 1983 (Vienna Staatsoper); Faust 1990, 1991 (Metropolitan Opera), La Fanciulla del West 1991 (Chicago Lyric Opera, San Francisco Opera). *Publication:* Contradictions: Notes on Twenty-Six Years in the Theatre (autobiography) 1974. *Address:* Suite 1009, 10 Rockefeller Plaza, New York, NY 10020, USA.

PRINCE, Richard; American painter and photographer; b. 6 Aug. 1949, Panama Canal Zone; m. 2nd Noel Grunwald; two c.; began career at Time-Life magazine; trained as a figure painter, began creating collages containing photographs 1975; lives and works in New York City and Upstate NY. *Works include:* Untitled (Cigarettes) 1978–79, Untitled (Cowboy) 1980–84, Entertainers 1982–83, Spiritual America 1983, Jokes 1986, My Usual Procedure 1988, The Wrong Joke 1989, Untitled (Hoods) 1989, Girlfriends 1992, Second House, Debutante Nurse 2004, Untitled (Covering Pollock) (series of 27 works) 2009–11. *Publications:* numerous articles and reviews in art magazines. *Address:* c/o Gagosian Gallery, Rockefeller Center, 45 Rockefeller Plaza, New York, NY 10111, USA. *Telephone:* (212) 744-2313. *E-mail:* info@richardprince.com; newyork@gagosian.com. *Website:* www.richardprince.com.

PRINCIPI, Anthony J., BS, JD; American business executive, fmr government official and fmr naval officer; b. 16 April 1944, New York City; m. Elizabeth Ann Ahlering 1971; three s.; ed US Naval Acad., Seton Hall Univ.; service with USN in Viet Nam, Chief Defense Counsel, Judge Advocate Gen. Corps, San Diego, Staff Counsel, Commdr US Pacific Fleet; Legis. Counsel, Dept of the Navy 1980; Deputy Sec. of Veterans' Affairs, 1989, Acting Sec. 1992, Sec. of Veterans' Affairs 2001–04; Chair. Fed. Quality Inst. 1991; Chief Counsel and Staff Dir, US Senate Cttee on Armed Services 1993; Chair. Comm. on Service Mems and Veterans Transition Assistance; COO Lockheed Martin Integrated Solutions 1995–2001; Principal, Principi Group, LLC; Co-Founder, Pres. and Chair. Fed. Network; Pres. QTC Medical Services (now QTC Management Inc.) 1999–2001, then Exec. Chair.; Sr Vice-Pres. for Government Relations, Pfizer, Inc. 2005–10; Chair. 2005 Defense Base Closure and Realignment Comm. 2005; mem. Bd of Dirs Engility Holdings, Inc., Mutual of Omaha, A.T. Kearney PSDS, Cleveland BioLabs, Lung Cancer Alliance, Wounded Warrior Project; Bronze Star, Vietnamese Cross of Gallantry, Navy Combat Action Medal and other decorations. *Address:* Principi Group, 1850 M Street, NW, Suite 840, Washington, DC 20036, USA (office).

PRINGLE, Dame Anne Fyfe, DCMG, CMG, MA, FRSA; British diplomatist; b. 13 Jan. 1955, Glasgow, Scotland; d. of George Grant Pringle and Margaret Fyfe; m. Bleddyn Glynne Phillips 1987; ed Univ. of St Andrews; joined FCO 1977, Third Sec., Moscow 1980–83, Vice-Consul, San Francisco 1983–85, Brussels 1986–87, First Sec., FCO 1987–91, Brussels 1991–94, African Security Coordination Dept, FCO 1994–96, Head of Common Foreign and Security Policy Dept 1996–98, Head of Eastern Dept 1998–2001, Amb. to Czech Repub. 2001–04, Dir Directorate for Strategy and Information 2004–07, Amb. to Russian Fed. 2008–11; Public Appointments Assessor 2012–; mem. Bd of Dirs Ashmore Group PLC 2013–, VSO 1996–97, Czech/Slovak Asscn, Court of Univ. of St Andrews 2012–; mem. Foreign Secretary's advisory Locarno Group; Trustee Shakespeare's Globe Theatre; Dr hc (Heriot-Watt Univ.) 2010. *Address:* Commissioner for Public Appointments, 1 Horse Guards Road, London, SW1A 2HQ, England (office). *Website:* publicappointmentscommissioner.independent.gov.uk (office).

PRINGLE, James Robert Henry, MA; British economist and journalist; *Managing Director, Central Banking Publications Ltd;* b. 27 Aug. 1939, Surrey; s. of John Pringle and Jacqueline Pringle (née Berry); m. 1st Rita Schuchard 1966 (divorced 1998); m. 2nd Ikuko Hiroe 2003; ed King's School, Canterbury, King's Coll., Cambridge and London School of Econs; Asst to Ed., then Asst Ed. The Banker, London 1963–67, Ed. 1972–79; mem. editorial staff The Economist, London 1968; Asst Dir, later Deputy Dir Cttee on Invisible Exports 1969–72; Exec. Dir Group of Thirty, Consultative Group on Int. Econ. and Monetary Affairs, New York 1979–86; Sr Fellow, World Inst. for Devt Econs Research of the UN Univ. 1986–89; Sr Research Fellow, David Hume Inst., Edinburgh 1989–91; Dir Graham Bannock and Pnrs 1989–97; apptd Ed.-in-Chief, Central Banking Publications Ltd 1990, now Man. Dir; fmr Man. Dir Public Policy, The World Gold Council. *Publications:* Banking in Britain 1973, The Growth Merchants 1977, The Central Banks (co-author) 1994, International Financial Institutions 1998. *Leisure interests:* classical music, the theatre. *Address:* 9 Northwood Lodge, Oakhill Park, London, NW3 7LL (home); Central Banking Publications, Tavistock House, Tavistock Square, London, WC1H 9JZ, England (office). *Telephone:* (20) 7388-0006 (office). *Fax:* (20) 7388-9040 (office). *E-mail:* info@centralbanking.co.uk (office). *Website:* www.centralbanking.co.uk (office).

PRINGUET, Pierre; French business executive and fmr government official; *Vice-Chairman and Senior Independant Director, Vallourec SA;* b. 31 Jan. 1950, Paris; m.; two d.; ed École Polytechnique and École des Mines, Paris; began career with French civil service 1975, held various positions including Tech. Adviser to Govt Minister Michel Rocard 1983–85 Dir for Agriculture and food Industries (DIAA) at Ministry of Agric. 1985–87; joined Pernod Ricard as Devt Dir 1987, Dir-Gen. of Soc. pour l'Exportation des Grandes Marques 1987–96, Pres. and Dir-Gen. Pernod Ricard Europe 1997–2000, together with Richard Burrows at corp. HQ served as one of Pernod Ricard's two jt Man. Dirs 2000–05, mem. Bd of Dirs 2004–, led acquisition of Allied Domecq 2005, Man. Dir 2005–08, led acquisition of Vin & Sprit and its vodka brand Absolut 2008, CEO Pernod Ricard 2008–15, Vice-Pres. 2012–15; Chair. Comité Sully (French food-processing industry asscn) 1990–2015, Scotch Whisky Asscn 2014–; Vice-Chair. and Sr Independant Dir Vallourec SA 2015–; mem. Bd of Dirs, Iliad (Free) 2007–, Capgemini 2008–, Groupe Avril 2015–; mem. Asscn française des entreprises privées 2012–, Amicale du Corps de Mines 2015–; Kt de la Légion d'honneur, Chevalier, Ordre nat. du Mérite, Officier du Mérite agricole. *Leisure interests:* skiing, golf, opera. *Address:* Vallourec SA, 27 avenue du Général Leclerc, 92100 Boulogne Billancourt, France (office). *Telephone:* 1-49-09-38-00 (office). *E-mail:* info@vallourec.com (office). *Website:* www.vallourec.com (office).

PRIORY, Richard B., MSc; American energy executive; b. 1946, Lakehurst, NJ; m. Joan Priory; one s. one d.; ed West Virginia Univ. Inst. of Tech., Princeton Univ., Univ. of Michigan; registered professional engineer in NC and SC; design and product engineer, Union Carbide Corpn 1969–72; Asst Prof. of Structural Eng, Univ. of NC at Charlotte 1973–76; joined Duke Power Corpn as design engineer 1976, various positions including Vice-Pres. Design Eng 1984–91, Exec. Vice-Pres. Power Generation Group 1991–94, Pres. and COO 1994–97, Chair. and CEO 1997–2003 (retd); fmr Dir Dana Corpn, US Airways Group, Inc.; mem. Bd Edison Electric Inst., Asscn of Edison Illuminating Cos; mem. NC Govs Business Council of Man. and Devt, Conf. Bd, Business Roundtable, Pres's Advisory Group, US Chamber of Commerce, Business Council; fmr Chair. Inst. of Nuclear Power Operations, Charlotte Research Inst. and Foundation; Dir Univ. of NC at Charlotte; mem. Nat. Acad. of Eng 1993–; Hon. DSc (West Virginia Univ. Inst. of Tech.); Distinguished Service Award, Charlotte Engineers Club 1998, Alumnus of the Year Award, WV Univ. Inst. of Tech. 1998, Ellis Island Medal of Honor 1999.

PRITCHARD, David E., BS, PhD; American physicist, academic and education consultant; *Cecil and Ida Green Professor of Physics, Massachusetts Institute of Technology;* b. 15 Oct. 1941, New York, NY; s. of Edward M. Pritchard and Blanche M. Allen Pritchard; m. Andrea Hasler Pritchard; two s.; ed California Inst. of Tech., Harvard Univ.; Postdoctoral Fellow, MIT 1968, Instructor 1968–70, Asst Prof. 1970–75, Assoc. Prof. 1975–80, Cecil and Ida Green Prof. of Physics 1980–, also Assoc. Dir Research Lab. of Electronics; Div. Assoc. Ed. Physics Review Letters 1983–88; Distinguished Traveling Lecturer, LSTG/American Physical Soc. 1991–93; Distinguished Visitor, Joint Inst. for Laboratory Astrophysics, Univ. of Colorado; f. Effective Educational Technologies (online educ. co.); mem. NAS, Nat. Research Cttee on Undergraduate Physics Educ.; Fellow, AAAS, American Physical Soc., Optical Soc. of America (mem. Bd of Dirs 1996–2000), American Acad. of Arts and Sciences; Broida Prize, American Physical Soc. 1991, Arthur L. Schawlow Prize, American Physical Soc. 2003, Max Born Award Optical Soc. of America 2004, IUPAP Precision Measurements Medal 2008, Earll M. Murman Award for Excellence in Undergraduate Advising 2010, MIT Dean's Award and numerous other awards and honours. *Achievements include:* mentored four Nobel Prize winners and four Nat. Thesis Award winners. *Publications:* over 200 scientific papers, articles and contribs to books. *Leisure interests:* piano playing, sailing. *Address:* Department of Physics, Bldg 26-241, Massachusetts Institute of Technology, 77 Massachusetts Avenue, Cambridge, MA 02139-4307 (office); 88 Washington Avenue, Cambridge, MA 02140, USA (home). *Telephone:* (617) 253-6812 (office). *Fax:* (617) 253-4876 (office). *E-mail:* dpritch@mit.edu (office). *Website:* web.mit.edu/physics/people/faculty/pritchard_david.html (office); www.relate.mit.edu.

PRITZKER, Penny S., BA, MBA, JD; American lawyer and business executive; b. 2 May 1959, Chicago, Ill.; d. of Donald N. Pritzker and Sue Ann Pritzker (neé Sandel); m. Bryan Traubert 1988; one s. one d.; ed Harvard and Stanford Univs; fmr Chair. Superior Bank (now defunct); Chair. Classic Residence by Hyatt 1987–, TransUnion LLC (credit reporting firm) 2005–; Pres. Pritzker Realty Group 1990–; Partner, Pritzker & Pritzker 1987–; Sec. of Commerce 2013–17; mem. Bd of Dirs William Wrigley Jr Co.; fmr Chair. Chicago Museum of Contemporary Art; mem. Women's Issues Network 1991–, The Chicago Network 1992–, Int. Women's Forum, Council on Foreign Relations, Econ. Recovery Advisory Bd 2009–; mem. Harvard Bd of Overseers 2002–; served as Nat. Finance Chair for Barack Obama's presidential campaign 2008. *Leisure interests:* competing in marathons and recreational ski races. *Address:* Department of Commerce, 1401 Constitution Avenue, NW, Washington, DC 20230 (office); Trans Union LLC, 555 West Adams Street, 6th Floor, Chicago, IL 60661-3614, USA (office). *Telephone:* (202) 482-2000 (Washington) (office); (312) 258-1717 (Chicago) (office). *E-mail:* thesec@doc.gov (office). *Website:* www.commerce.gov (office); www.transunion.com (office).

PRITZKER, Thomas J., MBA, JD; American business executive; *Executive Chairman, Hyatt Hotels Corporation;* b. 6 June 1950; s. of Jay A. Pritzker and Marian Pritzker; m.; four c.; ed Claremont McKenna Coll., Univ. of Chicago; Exec. Chair. Hyatt Hotels Corpn, Chair. and CEO The Pritzker Organization; Chair. Marmon Group; Chair., Man. Dir and Co-founder Bay City Capital; Co-founder First Health Group Corpn, Chair. 1990–2001, mem. Bd of Dirs 1985–86, 1990–2002; Founder Triton Container; Founding Gen. Pnr, GKH; Dir Pritzker Philanthropic Fund, Royal Caribbean Cruise Lines; mem. Bd of Trustees, Univ. of

Chicago; mem. Interdisciplinary Biosciences Advisory Cttee (Bio-X program), Stanford Univ. *Address:* Hyatt Hotels Corporation, 71 South Wacker Drive, Suite 4700, Chicago, IL 60606, USA (office). *Telephone:* (312) 750-1234 (office). *Fax:* (312) 750-8550 (office). *Website:* www.hyatt.com (office).

PRIX, Wolf D.; Austrian architect and academic; *Design Principal and CEO, Coop Himmelb(l)au;* b. 13 Dec. 1942, Vienna; ed Tech. Univ., Vienna, Architectural Asscn, London, UK, Southern California Inst. of Architecture, USA; Co-founder (with Helmut Swiczinsky and Michael Holzer) Coop Himmelb(l)au 1968, now Design Prin. and CEO; Prof. of Architecture, Univ. of Applied Arts, Vienna 1993–, Head, Inst. for Architecture, Head, Studio Prix and Vice-Rector, Univ. of Applied Arts 2003–; Visiting Prof., Architectural Asscn, London 1984, Harvard Univ., USA 1990; Adjunct Prof., Southern Calif. Inst. of Architecture, LA 1985–95; Faculty mem. Columbia Univ., New York 1998–; Harvey Perloff Prof., UCLA 1999, Adjunct Prof. 2001; mem. Architectural Council, Fed. Ministry of Science, Research and the Arts 1995–97; mem. Austrian Art Senate, European Acad. of Sciences and Arts, Advisory Cttee for Building Culture, Architectural Asscn of Austria, Architectural Union Santa Clara, Cuba, Architectural Asscn of Italy, Union of German Architects (BDA); Int. FRIBA 2006, AIA; Hon. mem. League of German Architects 1989, Hon. FAIA 2006; Officier des Arts et des Lettres 2002, Austrian Decoration for Science and Art 2009, Silbernes Komturkreuz des Landes Niederösterreich 2011; Dr hc (Universidad de Palermo, Buenos Aires) 2001, (Ion Mincu Univ., Bucharest) 2004; numerous awards including Berlin Prize for Building Art 1982, Austrian Architectural Asscn (AAA) Award 1985, PA Award 1991, European Industrial Architecture Award 1992, Erich-Schelling-Architecture Prize 1992, Tau Sigma Delta Award 1993, Grosser Österreichischer Staatspreis 1999, Gold Medal for Merits to the Fed. State of Vienna 2002, Annie Spink Award for Excellence in Architectural Education 2004, Jencks Award: Visions Built 2008. *Architectural works include:* Rooftop Remodelling Falkestrasse (City of Vienna Award for Architecture 1989) 1983–88, Funder Factory 3 (State of Carinthia Award for Superior Architecture 1989, AAA Award 1990) 1988–89, Los Angeles Art Park (PA Award 1989), Open House (PA Award 1990), Groninger Museum (Dutch Nat. Steel Prize 1992) 1993–94, Seibersdorf Office and Research Centre (AAA Prize 1996) 1993–95, UFA Cinema Centre, Dresden (Neuer Sächsicher Kunstverein Prize 1996, German Architecture Prize 1999, Concrete Architectural Prize 1999, European Steel Design Award 2001) 1993–98, SEG Apt Tower (AAA Award 1999) 1994–98, SEG Remise (Austrian Cement Industry Award 2001) 1994–2000, Wassertum Hainburg (Anerkennungspreis für Architektur des Landes Niederösterreich 2002) 1999, Akron Art Museum (American Architecture Award 2005) 2001–07, Busan Cinema Complex, S Korea 2005–11, Acad. of Fine Arts, Munich 1992, 2002–05, Space of Contemporary Artistic Creation, Cordoba, Spain 2005, The Great Egyptian Museum, Cairo, Egypt (Int. Architecture Award 2007) 2002, BMW Welt (RIBA European Award 2008, Preis des Deutschen Stahlbaues 2008, World Architecture Festival Award: Production, Wallpaper Design Award 2009: Best New Public Building, Detail Prize 2009 – Innovation Steel) 2001–07, Busan Cinema Center, S. Korea 2011, Musée des Confluences, Lyon, France 2014, House of Music, Aalborg, Denmark 2014, European Central Bank, Frankfurt, Germany 2014, Museum of Contemporary Art & Planning Exhbn, Shenzhen, China 2007–10, Dalian Int. Conf. Centre, China 2008–12, Cloud Roof, Riva del Garda, Italy 2014. *Publications include:* Coop Himmelb(l)au – Sie leben in Wien 1975, Coop Himmelb(l)au: Architecture is Now 1983; The Vienna Trilogy and One Cinema 1999, Blue Universe: Architectural Manifestos by Coop Himmelb(l)au 2002, Get Off of My Cloud 2005, Dynamic Forces 2007, Coop Himmelb(l)au: Beyond the Blue 2007, I Maestri dell'Architettura: Coop Himmelb(l)au 2011, Coop Himmelb(l)au Complete Works 1968–2010 (ed. Peter Gössel) 2010, Himmelblau no es ningún color – Wolf D. Prix, Coop Jimmelb(l)au (ed. Thomas Kramer) 2010, Coop Himmelb(l)au: Pavillon 21 MINI Opera Space 2010, Coop Himmelb(l)au: HS#9, Central Los Angeles Area High School #9 for the Visual and Performing Arts 2010. *Address:* Coop Himmelb(l)au, Wolf D. Prix & Partner ZT GmbH, Spengergasse 37, 1050 Vienna, Austria (office). *Telephone:* (1) 546-60-0 (office). *Fax:* (1) 546-60-600 (office). *E-mail:* office@coop-himmelblau.at (office). *Website:* www.coop-himmelblau.at (office).

PRLIĆ, Jadranko, DSc; Bosnia and Herzegovina politician and academic; b. 10 June 1959, Djakovo; m. Ankica Prlić; two d.; ed Univs of Mostar and Sarajevo; worked as a journalist; joined teaching staff, Univ. of Mostar 1987, Prof. Emer. 1999–; Mayor of Mostar 1987–88; fmr Gen. Man. Apro-Mostar agricultural enterprise; Vice-Pres. Govt of Bosnia and Herzegovina 1989–91; Deputy Prime Minister and Minister of Defence following signing of Washington (1994) and Dayton (1995) Agreements; mem. Parl. of Bosnia and Herzegovina and Minister of Foreign Affairs 1996–2001; mem. Council of Ministers 2001–03; Deputy Minister of Foreign Trade and Econ. Relations 2001–03; Founder and Pres. European Movt in Bosnia and Herzegovina; fmr IMF Gov. for Bosnia and Herzegovina; Pres. Pro-European People's Party; indicted by Int. Criminal Tribunal for the Fmr Yugoslavia for crimes against humanity and war crimes against the non-Croat population 2005, surrendered voluntarily to Tribunal. *Publications:* Policy of Fluctuating Foreign Exchange Rates 1990, Imperfect Peace 1998, Fuga Della Storia 2000, Return to Europe 2002, Unfinished Game 2002; numerous articles in field of int. economy, particularly finance and political issues. *Leisure interests:* tennis, soccer, econ. and political literature, etc. *Telephone:* (33) 213001 (home). *Website:* www.jprlic.ba (home).

PROCHÁZKA, Radoslav, LLM, JUDr, PhD; Slovak lawyer, academic and politician; b. 31 March 1972, Bratislava; m. Katarína Procházková; one s. one d.; ed Gymnázium Laca Novomeského, Bratislava, Comenius Univ., Yale Univ. Law School, USA, Univ. of Trnava; lawyer in Prague br of Hogan & Hartson law firm 1998–99; adviser and consultant, Constitutional Court of Slovak Repub. 2001–04; also served as legal counsel, Slovak del. to EC, Brussels 2001–04; rep. of Slovakia to EU 2004, then rep. to European Court of Justice 2004–06 (resgnd from Ministry of Justice); Assoc. Prof., Univ. of Trnava 2005–; mem. Krestanskodemokratické Hnutie (KDH—Christian Democratic Movt) 2010–13; mem. (KDH) Nat. Council of Slovakia 2010–14; Co-founder and Leader, Siet' (Network) political party 2014–16; unsuccessful ind. cand. in presidential election 2014. *Address:* c/o Siet' (Network), Röntgenova 28, 851 01 Bratislava, Slovakia (office). *E-mail:* siet@siet.sk (office). *Website:* siet.sk (office).

PRODI, Romano, LLB; Italian academic, politician and fmr UN official; b. 9 Aug. 1939, Scandiano; s. of Mario Prodi and Enrica Prodi; m. Flavia Franzoni; two s.; ed Catholic Univ. of Milan, London School of Econs; Prof. of Econs and Industrial Policy, Univ. of Bologna 1971–99, Prof. of Industrial Org. and Policy, 1990–93; Minister of Industry 1978–79; Chair. Scientific Cttee Econ. Research Inst. Nomisma, Bologna 1981–95; Chair. Istituto per le Ricostruzione Industriale (IRI) 1982–89, 1993–94; Founder l'Ulivo (The Olive Tree coalition of centre-left parties) 1995–2007 (evolved into Partito Democratico 2007), Pres. Partito Democratico 2007–08; Pres. Council of Ministers (Prime Minister) 1996–98; Pres. European Comm. 1999–2004; Prime Minister of Italy 2006–08; apptd Jt Chair. UN–African Union Peacekeeping Panel 2008; Special Envoy of the Sec.-Gen. for the Sahel, UN 2012–14; unsuccessful cand. in Italian presidential election 2013; Pres. Int. Advisory Bd Unicredit 2014–; mem. Club de Madrid; mem. Asscn di cultura e politica, Il Mulino, Bologna, Asscn Italiana degli Economisti, Rome; Hon. mem. Real Academia de Ciencias Morales y Políticas, Madrid, Hon. Fellow, LSE; Knight Grand Cross, Order of Merit (Italy), 1993, Knight Grand Cross, Order of Merit (Poland) 1997, Knight Grand Cross, Order of the Star of Romania, Order of the Rising Sun, Grand Cordon 2012, Chevalier, Légion d'Honneur 2014; numerous hon. degrees. *Publications include:* author of numerous scientific publs with particular reference to questions of European industrial policies, public enterprises in Italy and comparative analysis of econ. systems. *Address:* Ministry of Foreign Affairs, Piazzale della Farnesina 1, 00194 Roma, Italy (office). *Telephone:* (06) 36911 (office). *Fax:* (06) 3236210 (office). *E-mail:* ministero .affariesteri@cert.esteri.it (office). *Website:* www.esteri.it (office).

PROFUMO, Alessandro; Italian banking executive; *CEO, Leonardo SpA;* b. 17 Feb. 1957, Genoa; m. Sabina Ratti; ed Luigi Bocconi Univ., Milan; various commercial and exec. positions, Banco Lariano 1977–87; financial consultant, McKinsey & Co. 1987; marketing consultant, Bain, Cuneao & Associati 1988–91; Gen. Man. Banking and Parabanking, Riunione Adriatica di Sicurtà (RAS) 1991–94; Deputy Gen. Man. Planning and Group Control, Credito Italiano SpA 1994–95, Chief Gen. Man. 1995–96, CEO 1997–99, Man. Dir and CEO UniCredit Group 1997–2010 (resgnd); Chair. Supervisory Bd Bank Pekao SA –2005, Unicredit Bank AG (Bayerische Hypo- und Vereinsbank AG) 2005–09, UniCredit Bank Austria AG (Bank Austria Creditanstalt AG) 2006–11; Deputy Chair. UniCredit Banca Mobiliare (UBM); Chair. Banca Monte dei Paschi di Siena SpA 2012–15; Chair. Equita SIM SpA 2015–17, also mem. Bd; CEO Leonardo SpA 2017–; Chair. Fondazione Ricerca & Impreditorialità 2018–; Pres. European Banking Fed., Brussels; mem. Supervisory Bd Deutsche Börse AG 2004–07, Sberbank 2011; mem. Bd of Dirs and Exec. Cttee Asscn Bancaria Italiana; mem. Bd of Dirs Together To Go Foundation; mem. European Financial Services Round Table, London, Steering Cttee of The Group of Thirty, New York, Italian Group of the Trilateral Comm., Investment Advisory Council for Turkey, Istanbul, Man. Cttee Harvard Business School European Advisory Bd, Boston, Asscn for the Devt and Study of Banks and the Stock Exchange, Exec. Bd of AIRC (Italian Asscn for Cancer Research), Bd of Arnaldo Pomodoro Foundation, Bd Teatro alla Scala Foundation; Hon. Chair., Italian Industries Fed. for Aerospace, Defence and Security (AIAD) 2017–; Cavaliere al Merito del Lavoro 2004. *Publications include:* Plus Valori (with Giovanni Moro) (co-eds Baldini & Castoldi) 2003; numerous articles and studies. *Address:* Leonardo SpA, Piazza Monte Grappa North 4, 00195 Rome, Italy (office). *Telephone:* (63) 24731 (office). *Fax:* (63) 208621 (office).

PROGLIO, Henri; French business executive; b. 29 June 1949, Antibes; ed École des Hautes Études Commerciales, Paris; began career with Compagnie Générale des Eaux 1972, Chair. and CEO of waste man. and transportation subsidiary 1990–91, Sr Exec. 1991–90, CEO Vivendi Water, Chair. Générale des Eaux and Sr Exec. Vice-Pres. Vivendi 1999–2000, Chair. (non-exec.) Veolia Environnement (fmrly Vivendi Environnement) 2000–10, CEO 2003–09; Dir (non-exec.), EDF Group 2004–14, Chair. and CEO 2009–14; Chair. Thales Group 2014–15; Dir (non-exec.), CNP Assurances, Dassault Aviation, Natixis; mem. Exec. Cttee Vinci, Elior, Fomento de Construcciones y Contratas, Madrid; Commdr, Ordre nat. du Mérite, Légion d'honneur. *Address:* c/o EDF Group, 22–30 avenue de Wagram, 75382 Paris, Cedex 8, France. *E-mail:* info@edf.fr.

PROKEŠ, Jozef, DSc; Slovak politician; b. 12 June 1950, Nitra; s. of Jozef Prokeš and Elena Manicová; m. 1979; one s. one d.; ed Komenský Univ., Bratislava; research student with Inst. of Physics, Slovak Acad. of Sciences, Bratislava 1973–82; worked for Heavy Current Electrotechnical Works, Čab 1982–85; research worker Inst. of Measurements, Slovak Acad. of Sciences, Bratislava 1985–89; co-f. Forum of Co-ordinating Cttees of Workers in Slovakia 1989; Chair. Independent Trade Unions 1990; Chair. Trade Union of Research Workers of Slovak Acad. of Sciences 1990; Deputy to Slovak Nat. Council 1990–92; Chair. Slovak Nat. Party (SNP) 1991–92, Hon. Chair. 1992–; Vice-Pres. Slovak Nat. Council 1992–93; Deputy Premier of Slovak Govt 1993–94; Deputy to Nat. Council 1994–2003; Vice-Chair. Foreign Cttee of Nat. Council 1994–98; Mayor of Nitra 1998–2002, unsuccessful cand. 2006; Head, Slovak Del. to CSCE 1993–94; mem. Slovak del. to WEU 1995.

PROKHOROV, Mikhail Dmitriyevich; Russian business executive and politician; *Founder, ONEXIM Group;* b. 3 May 1965, Moscow; s. of Dmitry Prokhorov and Tamara Prokhorova; brother of Irina Prokhorova; ed Moscow Finance Inst. (now the Finance Acad. under the Govt of the Russian Fed.); Head of Man. Bd Dept, Int. Bank for Econ. Co-operation 1989–92; Chair. International Finance Co. (jt stock commercial bank) 1992–93; Chair. ONEXIM Bank 1993–, Chair. and Pres. 1998–2000, Pres. ONEXIM Group 2007–11; Pres. Rosbank (jt stock commercial bank) 2000–01; Gen. Dir and Chair. MMC Norilsk Nickel 2001–07, mem. Bd of Dirs June–Dec. 2008; Chair. OJSC Polyus Gold 2006, CEO 2010–11; Chair. JSCB IFC Bank 2010, Soglasiye Insurance Co. LLC 2010–; Prin. Owner, New Jersey Nets (professional basketball team) and shareholder of Barclays Center (team's arena in Brooklyn, NY) 2010–; mem. Bd of Dirs JSC Int. Airport Sheremetyevo 2009; f. Cultural Initiatives Charitable Foundation (Mikhail Prokhorov Foundation) 2004; Pres. Russian Biathlon Union 2008–; Amb. for Peace and Sport (Monaco-based int. org.) 2011–; Leader of Right Cause party June–Sept. 2011 (forced to resign); Leader Platform (Grazhdanskaya Platforma) 2012–13; ind. cand. in presidential election 2012; Order of Friendship 2006, Chevalier, Légion d'honneur 2011. *Leisure interest:* martial arts. *Address:* ONEXIM Group, 123104 Moscow, Tverskoi bulv. 13/1, Russia (office). *Telephone:* (495) 229-29-39 (office).

E-mail: info@onexim.org (office). *Website:* www.onexim.org (office); www.polyusgold.com (office); md-prokhorov.livejournal.com; mprokhorov.com.

PROKHOROVA, Irina, PhD; Russian editor, literary critic, cultural historian and politician; *Editor-in-Chief, New Literary Observer;* b. 3 March 1956, Moscow; d. of Dmitry Prokhorov and Tamara Prokhorova; sister of Mikhail Prokhorov; one d.; ed Moscow State Univ.; fmr Ed., Literaturnoe Obozrenie (Literary Review) magazine; Founder, Novoe Literaturnoe Obozrenie (New Literary Observer) magazine and publishing house 1992, currently Ed.-in-Chief; Leader Civic Platform (Grazhdanskaya Platforma) 2013–14; Co-founder, Mikhail Prokhorov Fund 2004; Chevalier, Ordre des Arts et des Lettres, France 2005, Chevalier, Légion d'Honneur 2012; honoured by Govt of Russian Fed. (for New Literary Observer Magazine) 2002, Liberty Award 2003, Laureate of Andrey Bely Prize for Literature 2006. *Publication:* 1990: Russians Remember a Turning Point (ed.) 2013. *Address:* New Literary Observer, 129626 Moscow, PO Box 55, Russia (office). *Telephone:* (495) 229-91-03 (office). *Fax:* (495) 229-91-03 (office). *Website:* www.nlobooks.ru (office).

PROKOPOVICH, Petr Petrovich; Belarusian engineer, politician and fmr central banker; b. 3 Nov. 1942, Rovno, Brest Region; s. of Petr Prokopovich and Evgeniya Prokopovich; m. Ludmila Prokopovich; one s. one d.; ed Dnepropetrovsk Eng and Construction Inst.; Dir-Gen. Brest Regional Planning and Construction Asscn 1976–96; mem. Supreme Soviet 1990–95; Deputy Head of Admin. of Pres. of Belarus 1996; First Deputy Prime Minister of Belarus 1996–98; Chair. Nat. Bank of the Repub. of Belarus 1998–2011; apptd Econ. Adviser to Pres. 2011; Order of Labour Red Banner, Order of Honour; Honoured Constructor of the USSR Award, Diploma of the Supreme Soviet of Belarus. *Publications:* various articles in Belarusian and foreign edns. *Leisure interests:* billiards, tennis.

PROKUDIN, Pavel; Moldovan accountant, business executive and politician; b. 17 Aug. 1966, Smolenskii, Novosibirsk dist (now Moshkovskii dist), Novosibirsk Oblast, USSR; m.; two c.; ed Odesa Nat. Maritime Acad., Ukrainian SSR; worked in Soviet Danube Shipping Co. 1988–92; worked at Jt LLC Molodezhnyi fond 'Miloserdiye' (Youth Benevolent Foundation) as Head of Youth, Dept for External Econ. Relations 1992–94, Dir 1994–96; dir of a commercial org. 1997–2000; Chief Accountant, Akvarel 2000–06; Gen. Dir JSC Fabrika Suvenirov Luchafer 2006–; Gen. Dir CJSC Bender (Tighina) River Port 2010–11; apptd Dir, Bender Fortress Historic-Mil. Memorial Complex 2011; Chair. public org. to promote restoration and conservation of Bender Fortress 2014–; Chair. of Govt of 'Transnistrian Moldovan Republic' 2015–16; Ind.; Order of St Michael the Archangel, 'Protection of the Virgin' Medal, Medal 'For Distinguished Labour'. *Address:* c/o Office of the Chairman of the Government, 3300 Tiraspol, ul. 25 Oktyabrya 45, Moldova. *Telephone:* (533) 6-24-43 (office). *E-mail:* office@gov-pmr.org (office). *Website:* gov-pmr.org (office).

PRONK, Johannes (Jan) Pieter; Dutch international organization official, academic and fmr politician; *Professor Emeritus of Theory and Practice of International Development, Institute of Social Studies, The Hague;* b. 16 March 1940, The Hague; m.; one s. one d.; ed Erasmus Univ., Rotterdam; Lecturer, Devt Programming Centre, School of Econs and Netherlands Econ. Inst. 1965–71; mem. Second Chamber (Parl.) 1971–73, 1978–80, 1986–89; Minister for Devt Co-operation 1973–77, 1989–98; Treas., Brandt Comm. 1978–81; Prof. of Int. Devt Policy, Inst. of Social Studies, The Hague 1979–80; Deputy Sec.-Gen. UNCTAD 1980–85, Asst Sec.-Gen. UN 1985–86; Deputy Chair. Dutch Labour Party 1986–89; Den Uyl Chair, Univ. of Amsterdam 1989; Minister of Housing, Spatial Planning and the Environment 1998–2002; Pres. UN Conf. of Parties of the Convention on Climate Change, The Hague 2000, Bonn 2001, Special Envoy of the Sec.-Gen. for the World Summit on Sustainable Devt, Johannesburg 2002; Chair. Water Supply and Sanitation Collaborative Council 2002–04, Int. Inst. for Environment and Devt, London 2002–04, Netherlands Interpeace Council 2008–11; Prof. of Theory and Practice of Int. Devt, Inst. of Social Studies, The Hague 2003–16, Prof. Emer. 2016–; Visiting Prof., UN Univ. for Peace, Costa Rica 2009–17, Univ. of Amsterdam 2012–17; Assoc. Fellow Nijmegen 2012–17; Special Rep. of the UN Sec.-Gen. for Sudan 2004–06; Pres. Soc. for Int. Devt 2008–11; Grootlint Orde Palm (Suriname) 1977, Ridder Orde Nederlandse Leeuw (Netherlands) 1978, Gran Cruz Orden Bernardo O'Higgins (Chile) 1993, 26th September Medal (Yemen) 1996, Officier, Légion d'honneur 2001, Officier, Orde Oranje Nassau (Netherlands) 2002; Dr hc (San Marcos Univ., Lima) 1974, (Inst. of Social Studies, The Hague) 2002, (Victoria Univ., Neuchatel) 2015; US Business Council for Sustainable Energy Climate e-Award 2001. *Publications:* De Kritische Grens 1994, Catalysing Development? 2004, Willens en Wetens 2005, Het Pantser Afleggen 2007, Op Zoek naar een Nieuwe Kaart 2015, Strijd rond de Grote Meren 2018. *Leisure interests:* fitness. *Address:* Institute of Social Studies, PO Box 29776, 2502 LT The Hague, The Netherlands (office). *Telephone:* (70) 4260460 (office). *Fax:* (70) 4260799 (office). *E-mail:* pronk@iss.nl (office); pronk333@gmail.com (home). *Website:* www.iss.nl (office); www.janpronk.nl.

PROPPER, Carol, CBE, PhD, FBA; British economist and academic; *Professor of Economics, Imperial College London;* ed Univs of Bristol, Oxford and York, Univ. of Toronto, Canada; Community Worker, Islington, London 1977–79; Research Officer, Nuffield Coll., Oxford 1981–82; Research Economist, New Zealand Inst. of Econ. Research 1983–84; Research Fellow, Centre for Health Econs, Univ. of York 1986–87, Visiting Fellow 1987–96; Lecturer in Econs, Brunel Univ. 1987–88; Lecturer, Univ. of Bristol 1988–93, Reader 1993–94, Prof. of Econs of Public Policy 1995–2007, Deputy Dir Centre for Market and Public Organisation 1998–2002, Dir 2002–04 (part-time 2007–15); Prof. of Econs, Imperial Coll. Business School, London 2007–, Head, Healthcare Man. Group 2007–10; Visiting Prof., La Follette Inst. for Public Affairs, Univ. of Wisconsin, USA 1993; Research Assoc., Welfare State Programme, LSE 1987–94; Sr Econ. Adviser to NHS Exec. on Regulation of NHS Internal Market 1993–94, Incentives Sanction Group, Dept of Health 1999–, Adding It Up Implementation Group, HM Treasury 2000–; Research Fellow, CEPR 1998–; Co-Dir Centre for Social Exclusion, LSE 1997–2007; EC Expert on Social Protection in Europe (DGV) 1991–93; Research Team mem. ECuity Project on Health Care Reform 1992–, COMAC-HSR Project on Equity in Healthcare Finance and Delivery 1992–94; Chair. Cttee on Women in Econs, Royal Econ. Soc. 1998–2001, mem. Council 2000–05, Chair. Conf. Programme 2001; Ed. Economic Journal Conference Supplement 2002; mem. Editorial Bd Journal of Health Economics, Health Economics, Fiscal Studies. *Publications include:* The Economics of Social Policy (co-author) 1992, Quasi-Markets: The Emerging Findings (co-ed.) 1994, Who Pays For, Who Gets Health Care: Equity in the Finance and Delivery of Health Care in the UK 1998, Private Welfare and Public Policy (co-ed.) 1999; numerous chapters in books, articles in professional journals and reports. *Address:* Imperial College London, 276 Business School Building, South Kensington Campus, London, SW7 2AZ, England (office). *Telephone:* (20) 7594-9291 (office). *E-mail:* c.propper@imperial.ac.uk (office). *Website:* www.imperial.ac.uk (office).

PROSOR, Ron; Israeli diplomatist; *Head, Abba Eban Institute of International Diplomacy, Interdisciplinary Center Herzliya;* m. Hadas Prosor; served in USA and in major European capitals, served as spokesman in London and Bonn, as Minister-Counsellor for Political Affairs, Embassy in Washington, DC; mem. Israeli del. to Wye River Plantation talks, Md 1998; Sr Deputy Dir-Gen., Ministry of Foreign Affairs and Chief of Policy Staff to the Minister –2004, Dir-Gen., Ministry of Foreign Affairs 2004–06, Amb. to UK 2007–11, Perm. Rep. to UN, New York 2011–15; Head, Abba Eban Inst. of Int. Diplomacy, Interdisciplinary Center Herzliya (IDC) 2015–; Scholar-Statesman Award, Washington Inst. of Near East Policy 2017. *Address:* The Raphael Recanati International School, Interdisciplinary Center, PO Box 167, 1 Kanfei Nesharim Street, Herzliya 4610101, Israel (office). *Telephone:* 9-9527272 (office). *Fax:* 9-9567392 (office). *E-mail:* ron.prosor@idc.ac.il (office). *Website:* www.idc.ac.il/en/research/aei/pages/main.aspx (office).

PROSPER, Pierre-Richard, BA, JD; American lawyer and fmr government official; *Partner, Arent Fox LLP;* b. 1963, Denver, Colo; ed Boston Coll., Pepperdine Univ.; Deputy Dist Attorney, Los Angeles County 1989–94; Asst US Attorney for Cen. Dist of California 1994–96; war crimes prosecutor, UN Int. Criminal Tribunal for Rwanda 1996–98; Special Asst to Asst Attorney Gen. for Criminal Div., US Dept of Justice, seconded to US Dept of State as Special Counsel and Policy Advisor on War Crimes Issues 1999–2001, Amb.-at-Large, War Crimes Issues, US Dept of State 2001–05; joined Arent Fox LLP (law firm), Los Angeles 2007, currently Partner; fmr Amb.-in-Residence and Adjunct Prof., S.J. Quinney College of Law, Univ. of Utah; mem. UN Cttee on the Elimination of Racial Discrimination, Geneva 2008–, US Holocaust Memorial Council 2008–2014, Int. Centre for Settlement of Investment Disputes 2013–; Trustee, Boston Coll. *Address:* Arent Fox LLP, Gas Company Tower, 555 West Fifth Street, 48th Floor, Los Angeles, CA 90013, USA (office). *Telephone:* (213) 443-7511 (office). *Fax:* (213) 629-7401 (office). *E-mail:* pierre.prosper@arentfox.com (office). *Website:* www.arentfox.com (office).

PROSSER, Sir David J., Kt, BSc, FIA; British fmr insurance executive; b. 26 March 1944, Wales; s. of Ronald Prosser and Dorothy Prosser; m. Rosemary Snuggs 1971; two d.; ed Ogmore Grammar School, Univ. of Wales, Aberystwyth; with Sun Alliance and London Assurance Co. 1965–69; Hoare Govett & Co. 1969–73; joined Superannuation Investments Dept, Nat. Coal Bd as Head of Stock Market Activities 1973; Man. Dir Venture Capital CIN Industrial Investments 1981–85, CEO 1985–88; Group Dir Investments, Legal & Gen. PLC 1988–91, Deputy CEO Jan.–Sept. 1991, Group CEO Sept. 1991–2006 (retd); Dir (non-exec.) InterContinental Hotels Group 2003–08, Epsom Downs Racecourse 2003–, Investec 2006–14; Chair. Royal Automobile Club 2007–12. *Address:* 206 Gilbert House, The Barbican, London, EC2Y 8BD, England (office). *Telephone:* (1306) 731113 (office). *E-mail:* sirdavid.prosser@btconnect.com (office).

PROSSER, Sir Ian Maurice Gray, Kt, BComm, FCA; British business executive; *Chairman of the Board of Trustees, BP Pension Fund;* b. 5 July 1943, Bath, Avon; s. of Maurice Prosser and Freda Prosser; m. 1st Elizabeth Herman 1964 (divorced 2003); two d.; m. 2nd Hilary Prewer 2003; ed King Edward's School, Bath, Watford Grammar School, Univ. of Birmingham; with Cooper Bros (chartered accountants) 1964–69; with Bass Charrington Ltd 1969–82, Financial Dir 1978; Vice-Chair. and Financial Dir Bass PLC 1982–84, Vice-Chair. and Group Man. Dir 1984–87, Chair. and CEO 1987–2000, Exec. Chair. 2000, co. then demerged into Intercontinental Hotels Group PLC, Chair. 2000–03 (retd); Chair. The Brewers' Soc. 1992–94; Chair. Exec., World Travel and Tourism Council 2001–04; Chair. Navy, Army and Air Force Insts 2008–, Aviva Staff Pension Fund 2013–; Dir (non-exec.) BP (later BP Amoco now BP PLC) 1997–2010, Deputy Chair. 1999–2010, Dir BP Pension Fund 2010–, currently Chair. Bd of Trustees; Dir (non-exec.) The Boots Co. 1984–96, Lloyds TSB Group PLC 1988–99, Glaxo SmithKline PLC 1999–2009, Sara Lee Inc. 2004–12, Hillshire Brands 2012–14; Hon. DUniv. *Leisure interests:* bridge, gardening, golf. *Address:* BP Pensions Ltd, 1 St James's Square, London, SW1Y 4PD, England (office). *Telephone:* (20) 7496-4000 (office). *Fax:* (20) 7496-4630 (office). *E-mail:* ian.prosser@imgp.co.uk (office).

PROST, Alain Marie Pascal; French motor racing team owner and fmr racing driver; b. 24 Feb. 1955, Saint-Chamond; s. of André Prost and Marie-Rose Karatchian; m. Anne-Marie Prost 1955 (divorced); two s. one d.; ed Coll. Sainte-Marie, Saint-Chamond; joined Marlboro MacLaren Group 1980, Renault team 1981–83, McLaren TAG team 1984–87, McLaren Honda 1988–89, Ferrari 1990–91, Williams Renault 1993; winner Formula 1 Grand Prix races in France 1981, 1983, 1988, 1989, 1990, 1993, Netherlands 1981, 1984, Italy 1981, 1985, 1989, Brazil 1982, 1984, 1985, 1987, 1988, 1990, South Africa 1982, 1993, Austria 1983, 1985, 1986, Britain 1983, 1985, 1989, 1990, 1993, Belgium 1983, 1987, Europe 1984, Monte Carlo 1984, 1985, 1986, 1988, San Marino 1984, 1986, 1993, Portugal 1984, 1987, 1988, Germany 1984, 1993, Australia 1986, 1988, Mexico 1988, 1990, Spain 1988, 1990, 1993, USA 1989, Canada 1993; Formula 1 World Champion 1985, 1986, 1989, 1993; total 51 Grand Prix wins, 106 podium finishes; technical consultant to McLaren Mercedes 1995; founder and Pres. Prost Grand Prix Team 1997–2002; races for e.dams Renault 2017; Hon. OBE 1994; Officier, Légion d'honneur; Trophée du champion automobile du siécle en Autriche 1999. *Publications:* Vive ma vie 1993.

PROT, Baudouin Daniel Claude; French banker; b. 24 May 1951, Paris; s. of André Prot and Marguerite Le Febvre; m. Viviane Abel 1981; one s. one d.; ed Inst. de Sainte-Croix, Neuilly, Ecole Saint-Louis des hautes études commerciales, Ecole nat. d'admin.; Inspecteur, Inspection générale des finances, Paris 1976; Deputy Dir-Gen. Energy and Raw Materials, Ministry of Industry 1982–83; joined Banque Nat. de Paris (BNP) 1983, managerial positions depts for Europe 1985–87, metropolitan networks 1987–92, France 1992–96, Deputy Dir-Gen. BNP 1992–96, apptd Dir-Gen. 1996, mem. Bd of Dirs, BNP Paribas SA 2000–14, CEO 2005–11, Chair. 2011–14; Chair. Carte bleue group 1991–97; Dir Pinault-Printemps-

Redoute, Veolia Environnement 2003–, Erbé SA (Belgium), Pargesa Holding SA (Switzerland) 2004–14; mem. Exec. Bd, Fédération Bancaire Française; Inspecteur générale des finances 1993; Chevalier, Légion d'honneur 2010, Ordre nat. du Mérite; Financier of the Year 2006, Social and Corporate Responsibility Award, Foreign Policy Asscn 2007, named by Invester magazine as Best European Banking CEO 2010. *Publications:* Armée-Nation, le Rendez-vous manqué 1975, Nationalisations 1977, Réduire l'impôt 1985, Dénationalisation 1986, La Jeunesse inégale 1987, Le Retour de capital 1990. *Leisure interests:* tennis, skiing, sailing. *Address:* Veolia Environnement, 36–38 Avenue Kléber, 75116 Paris, Cedex 8 (office); 21 rue Monsieur, 75007 Paris, France (home). *Telephone:* 1-71-75-00-00 (office). *Fax:* 1-71-71-15-45 (office). *E-mail:* info@veoliaenvironnement.com (office). *Website:* www.veoliaenvironnement.com (office).

PROULX, (Edna) Annie, MA; American writer; b. 22 Aug. 1935, Norwich, Conn.; d. of George Napoleon Proulx and Lois Nellie Gill; m. 1st H. Ridgeley Bullock 1955 (divorced); one d.; m. 2nd James Hamilton Lang 1969 (divorced 1990); three s.; ed Univ. of Vermont and Sir George Williams (now Concordia) Univ., Montréal; freelance journalist, Vt 1975–87; f. Vershire Behind the Times newspaper, Vershire, Vt; short stories appeared in Blair & Ketchums Country Journal, Esquire, etc.; Vt Council Arts Fellowship 1989, Ucross Foundation Residency, Wyo. 1990, 1992; mem. PEN; Guggenheim Fellow 1993; active anti-illiteracy campaigner; Hon. DHumLitt (Maine) 1994; Alumni Achievement Award, Univ. of Vt 1994, New York Public Library Literary Lion 1994, John Dos Passos Prize for Literature 1997, American Acad. of Achievement Award 1998, Nat. Book Foundation Medal for Distinguished Contribution to American Letters 2017. *Publications:* Heart Songs and Other Stories 1988, Postcards (novel) (PEN/Faulkner Award for Fiction 1993) 1992, The Shipping News (Chicago Tribune Heartland Prize for Fiction, Irish Times Int. Fiction Prize, Nat. Book Award for Fiction, Pulitzer Prize for Fiction 1994) 1993, Accordion Crimes 1996, Best American Short Stories (ed.) 1997, Brokeback Mountain (short story, Nat. Magazine Award 1998, O. Henry Awards Prize 1998) 1998, Close Range: Wyoming Stories (New Yorker Book Award Best Fiction 1999, English-Speaking Union's Amb. Book Award 2000, Borders Original Voices Award in Fiction 2000) 1998, That Old Ace in the Hole (Best Foreign Language Novels of 2002/Best American Novel Award, Chinese Publishing Asscn and Peoples' Literature Publishing House 2002) 2002, Bad Dirt: Wyoming Stories 2 2004, Fine Just the Way It Is: Wyoming Stories 3 2008, Bird Cloud: A Memoir 2011, Barkskins: A Novel 2016. *Leisure interests:* fly-fishing, canoeing, playing the fiddle. *Address:* PO Box 230, Centennial, WY 82055; c/o Simon & Schuster Inc., 1230 Avenue of the Americas, New York, NY 10020, USA (office). *Fax:* (307) 742-6159. *Website:* authors.simonandschuster.com/Annie-Proulx/8544.

PROVOPOULOS, Georgios A., BA, MA, PhD; Greek economist, academic and fmr central banker; *Chairman of the Supervisory Board, Eurobank EFG Bulgaria AD (Postbank);* b. 20 April 1950, Pireaus; m.; three c.; ed Univ. of Athens, Univ. of Essex, UK; Assoc. Prof., Dept of Econs, Univ. of Athens 1979–2007; Chair. Centre for Planning and Econ. Research (KEPE) 1989–90; Chair. Council of Econ. Experts, Ministry of Economy and Finance July–Nov. 1989, April–Oct. 1990, mem. –1992; Deputy Gov. Bank of Greece and Alt. Gov. for Greece in IMF 1990–93; Gen. Man. Foundation of Econ. and Industrial Research (IOBE) 1993–97; Chair. and CEO Emporiki Bank 2004–06; Vice-Chair. and Man. Dir Piraeus Bank 2006–08, Chair. Piraeus Bank's subsidiaries in Romania, Albania, Bulgaria, Serbia and Egypt 2007–08; Gov. Bank of Greece 2008–14; Chair. Supervisory Bd Eurobank EFG Bulgaria AD (Postbank), Sofia 2015–; Econ. Adviser, Alpha Bank 1994–2004; Vice-Chair. Hellenic Banks' Asscn 2007–08; mem. EU Monetary Cttee 1990–93; Chair. Cttee for reform of Greek tax system 1989; Chair. Piraeus AEEAP 2006–08, Piraeus Real Estate 2006–08, Marathon Banking Corpn 2007–08, Marathon Nat. Bank of New York 2007–08, Alpha Investment Portfolio 2000–03, Alpha Mutual Fund Man. Co. 2000–04, ICAP 2000–05; Vice-Chair. Hellenic Postbank 1992–93, Hellenic Banks' Asscn (Rep. of Asscn at European Banking Fed.) 2004–06; mem. Bd of Dirs TITAN Cement Co. 1996–2004, Foundation of Econ. and Industrial Research 1998–2006, Hellenic Centre for Investment (ELKE) 1999–2004, European Cen. Bank Governing Council; mem. Co-ordination Cttee, Ministry of Finance for reform of taxation system 2001; Greek State Scholarship's Foundation (IKY). *Publication:* The Dynamics of the Financial System (with P. Kapopoulos) (Award of the Class of Ethical and Political Sciences, Acad. of Athens 2003). *Address:* Eurobank EFG Bulgaria AD (Postbank), 260, Okolovrasten pat, str., 1766 Sofia, Bulgaria (office). *Website:* www.postbank.bg/en (office).

PRUAITCH, Patrick; Papua New Guinea politician; mem. Parl. for Aitape-Lumi; Minister of Finance and the Treasury 2007–10 (suspended by Supreme Court May 2010), 2011; Minister of Forestry and Climate Change 2012–14, of Treasury 2014–17 (removed); Leader and mem. Nat. Alliance Party.

PRUEHER, Adm. (retd) Joseph Wilson, MS; American naval officer (retd), diplomatist and academic; *Consulting Professor, Center for International Security and Co-operation, Stanford University;* b. 25 Nov. 1942, Nashville, Tenn.; m. Suzanne Prueher; one s. one d.; ed Montgomery Bell Acad., US Naval Acad., Annapolis, Md, Naval War Coll., Newport, RI and George Washington Univ.; started naval career as Command Ensign, USN, advanced through grades to Adm., C-in-C US Pacific Command, Camp HM Smith, Hawaii 1996–99; Amb. to People's Repub. of China 1999–2001; Consulting Prof., Center for Int. Security and Co-operation, Stanford Univ. 2001–, also Sr Adviser, Preventive Defense Project; mem. Bd of Dirs, Merrill Lynch from 2001, Fluor Corpn, Emerson Electric Co., Amerigroup Corpn; Hon. AO; decorations from govts of Singapore, Thailand, Japan, Korea, Philippines and Indonesia; Distinguished Grad. Leadership Award, Naval War Coll. 1997, Distinguished Alumni Achievement Award, George Washington Univ. 2001; multiple awards for combat flying as well as naval and jt service. *Publications include:* numerous articles on leadership, mil. readiness and Pacific region security issues. *Address:* Center for International Security and Co-operation, Stanford University, 616 Serra Street, E200, Stanford, CA 94305-6165, USA (office). *Telephone:* (650) 723-9625 (office). *Fax:* (650) 724-5683 (office). *E-mail:* dcgordon@stanford.edu (office). *Website:* cisac.fsi.stanford.edu (office).

PRUITT, E(dward) Scott, BA, JD; American lawyer, politician and government official; b. 9 May 1968, Danville, Ky; m. Marlyn Loyd; one s. one d.; ed Georgetown Coll., Univ. of Tulsa; called to the Bar, Okla 1993; mem. Okla State Senate for Dist 54, Dist 36 1998–2006, Republican whip 2000–02, Asst Republican floor leader 2002–06; served as Counsel, Latham Stall Wagner Steele & Lehman PC (law firm), Tulsa; Attorney Gen. of Oklahoma 2011–17; Admin., US Environmental Protection Agency 2017–18 (resgnd); Co-owner and Man. Gen. Partner, Oklahoma City Redhawks (Triple A professional baseball team) 2002–10; fmr Pres. Republican Attorneys Gen. Asscn; Republican. *Website:* www.scottpruitt.com.

PRUNĂ, Raluca Alexandra, PhD; Romanian lawyer, political scientist, academic and politician; b. 24 Sept. 1969; ed Univ. of Bucharest, Al. I. Cuza Univ., Nanterre Univ. of Paris VII, France, Cen. European Univ., Budapest, Hungary; Asst Prof., Faculty of Philosophy and Nat. School of Political Science and Public Admin, Faculty of Political Science, Univ. of Bucharest 1996–2001; lawyer, Bucharest Bar 1996–2000; legal adviser and founding mem., Romanian Asscn for Transparency/Transparency International Romania 1999–2000, Pres. and mem. Ethics Cttee 2005–08; collaboration with USAID, World Bank, European Centre for Constitutional Law 2000–01; Justice Portfolio Man., Business and Internal Anti-corruption, EC Del. in Romania 2000–04; lawyer and linguist, Legal Service, Gen. Secr., Council of Ministers 2005–07; lawyer and programme co-ordinator, Unity Man. of Migration Flows, Directorate Gen. for Justice, Freedom and Security, EC, Brussels 2007–08, official responsible for policies on combating organized crime, Directorate Gen. for Home Affairs 2009–10, official responsible for policies on combating organized crime Sept.–Nov. 2010, Head of Internal Market and Acquisitions Unit, Directorate Gen. for Enterprise and Industry 2010–12, Head of Unit for Free Movt of Goods Sectors Harmonized (Articles 34–36 of Treaty for the Functioning of the EU), entrepreneurship, Industry and SMEs, Directorate Gen. for the Internal Market 2012–15, Advisor-Co-ordinator, Policy Unit for the Single Market Mutual Recognition and Market Surveillance June–Nov. 2015; Parl. Asst, European Parl. June–Sept. 2010; Minister of Justice 2015–17.

PRUNARIU, Lt-Gen. (retd) Dumitru-Dorin, PhD; Romanian airspace engineer, cosmonaut and diplomatist; *President, Romanian Association for Space Technology and Industry;* b. 27 Sept. 1952, Brasov; s. of Simion Prunariu and Elena Prunariu; m. Crina Prunariu; two s.; ed Airspace Eng Faculty at Polytechnic Univ., Bucharest, Cosmonaut Training Course, Star City, Russia, Int. Aviation Man. Training Inst. (IAMTI/IIFGA), Montreal, Canada, Nat. Defence Coll., Bucharest, course on applied diplomacy within Ministry of Foreign Affairs; engineer at IAR-BRASOV (aircraft co.) 1976–77; Romanian Air Force 1977–2007; crew member, Soyuz 40 space mission 1981, Chief Inspector for Airspace Activities 1981–89; Deputy Minister to Ministry of Transportation and Chief of Romanian Civil Aviation Dept 1990–91; Co-leader World Bank Project on reorganization of the higher educ. and research system in Romania 1992–93; Sec. Romanian Space Agency 1992–95, mem. Admin. Council 1995–98, Pres. 1998–2004, Pres. Bd 2005–, Pres. Scientific Bd 2008–; Amb. to Russian Fed. 2004–05; Dir Romanian Office for Science and Tech. to the EC, Nat. Authority for Scientific Research 2006–08; Vice-Pres. European Inst. for Risk Man., Security and Communication (EURISC) Foundation 1995–; Chair. S&T Sub-cttee, UN COPUOS 2004–06, Chair. UN COPUOS 2010–12, Vice-Chair. Working Group on Space Agenda 2030 2018–; Pres. Romanian Asscn for Space Tech. and Industry 2013–, Aeronautic and Astronautic Comm., Romanian Acad. 2016–; Assoc. Prof. of Geopolitics, Faculty of Int. Business and Econs, Acad. of Econ. Studies, Bucharest 1995–2004; Founder-mem. Asscn of Space Explorers, Paris 1985, mem. Exec. Cttee 1995–2001, Pres. 2011–14; mem. Romanian Nat. COSPAR Cttee 1994–, Group of Govt Experts on outer space transparency and confidence-building measures, in accordance with UN Gen. Ass. Resolution 65/68 2012–13, 2018–19; mem. Bd, TAROM air co. 2012–13; Vice-Chair. ESA Int. Relations Cttee 2014–17; mem. Task Force for EU Inst. for Security Studies Report on Space Security for Europe 2015–16, European Academy of Sciences and Arts (EASA) 2015; Trustee Int. Astronautic Acad. 1992; Pres. First Rotary Club of Bucharest 2009–10; hon. citizen of several cities; Hon. mem. American Romanian Acad. of Arts and Sciences, registered in Calif., USA 2002, Romanian Acad. 2011; Hero of Romania 1981, Golden Star and Hero of the Soviet Union 1981, Grand Officer of the Order Steaua României (Star of Romania) 2000, mil. orders; several hon. degress; Yuri Gagarin Medal, Int. Astronautic Fed. 1982, Hermann Oberth Gold Medal, German Rocket Soc. Hermann Oberth-Wernher von Braun, Germany 1984, Medal for Merits in Space Exploration, Pres. of Russian Fed. 2011 and others. *Publications:* author or co-author of several books and numerous scientific papers on space tech. and space flight; studies on security, risk and communication man., geopolitics accomplished within the EURISC Foundation; articles on scientific topics published in Romanian and foreign publs. *Leisure interest:* photography. *Address:* Romanian Space Agency, Mendeleev Str. 21–25, 010632 Bucharest, Romania (office). *Telephone:* (21) 3168722 (office). *Fax:* (21) 3128804 (office). *E-mail:* dorin52@yahoo.com (home). *Website:* www.rosa.ro (office).

PRUNSKIENĖ, Kazimiera Danutė, DEconSci; Lithuanian politician; b. 26 Feb. 1943, Švenčionėliai Region; d. of Ona Stankevičienė and Pranas Stankevičius; m. 1st Povilas Prunskus 1961 (divorced); m. 2nd Algimantas Tarvydas 1990 (divorced); one s. two d.; ed Vilnius State Univ.; teacher, then Dean of Faculty, Vilnius State Univ. 1965–85; Deputy Dir Inst. of Econ. Agric. 1986–88; People's Deputy of the USSR 1989–90, mem. USSR Supreme Soviet 1989–90; Deputy Chair. Council of Ministers of Lithuania 1989–90, Chair. 1990–91; mem. Lithuanian Parl. 1990–92, 1996–; Prime Minister March 1990–Jan. 1991; Minister of Agric. 2005–08; Pres. Lithuanian-European Inst. 1991; Pres. pvt. consulting firm K. Prunskienė-Consulting 1993–96; Prof. of Econs, Vilnius Gediminas Tech. Univ. 1996–2000; Founder and Pres. Lithuanian Women's Party (later New Democracy Party) 1995; Chair. Lithuanian Peasant Nationalists' Union (fmrly Peasants' and New Democracy Union 2001–06) 2001–09; mem. CEPS Int. Advisory Council 1992, Int. Cttee for Econ. Reform and Co-operation 1994; Pres. Baltic Women's Basketball League 1994; mem. Communist Party –1990, Lithuanian People's Party 2003–; mem. Council of Women World Leaders 1997–; Order of Grand Duke of Lithuania Gediminas (2nd Degree) and Medal of the Order of Gediminas 2000, Medal of the Independence of Lithuania 2000, Medal of the FRG, Order of Merit 2000, Grand Cross of Merit with Star 2001; Minerva Prize, Italy 1991, Alexander von Humboldt Foundation Scholarship. *Publications:* Amber Lady's Confession 1991, Leben für Litauen 1992, Behind the Scenes 1992, Challenge to Dragon 1992, Price of Liberation 1993, Markt Balticum 1994, Transformation, Co-operation and Conversion 1996, Science and Technology Policy of the Baltic States and International Co-operation 1997, Intellectual

Property Rights in Central and Eastern Europe: the Creation of Favourable Legal and Market Preconditions 1998. *Leisure interests:* sports, music, literature, knitting, cooking, walking in the forest. *Address:* Lithuanian Peasant Nationalists' Union (Lietuvos Valstiečių Liaudininkų Sajunga), Pamėnkalnio g. 28, Vilnius 01114 (office); Krivių g. 53a-13, Vilnius 02007, Lithuania (home). *E-mail:* k.prunskiene@gmail.com (office).

PRUSAK, Mikhail Mikhailovich, DEcon; Russian politician and economist; b. 23 Feb. 1960, Ivano-Frankovskaya region, Ukraine; m.; one s. one d.; ed Higher Komsomol School, Acad. of National Econs; Sec. Novgorod regional Komsomol Cttee –1988; Dir Sovkhoz Trudovik Novgorod region 1988–91; People's Deputy, mem. USSR Supreme Soviet, mem. Interregional Deputies' Group 1989–91; Gov. of Novgorod Region 1991–2007 (resgnd); mem. Council of Federal Ass. of Russian Fed. 1996–2001; Chair. Democratic Party of Russia; Vice-Pres. Parl. Ass. Council of Europe 1999–2001; author of numerous works; Corresp. mem. St Petersburg Acad. of Eng; recipient of awards. *Leisure interest:* hunting.

PRUSINER, Stanley B., AB, MD; American neuroscientist, neurologist and academic; *Professor of Neurology, University of California, San Francisco;* b. 28 May 1942, Des Moines, Ia; ed Walnut Hills High School, Cincinnati, Ohio, Univ. of Pennsylvania, Univ. of California, San Francisco; with US Public Health Service, NIH 1968–71; Internship in Medicine, Univ. of California, San Francisco 1968–69, Residency in Neurology 1972–74, Asst Prof. of Neurology in Residence 1974–80, Lecturer, Dept of Biochemistry and Biophysics 1976–78, Assoc. Prof. of Neurology in Residence 1980–81, Assoc. Prof. of Neurology 1981–84, Prof. of Neurology 1984–, Prof. of Biochemistry 1988–, also Dir Inst. for Neurodegenerative Diseases 1999–; Asst Prof. of Virology in Residence, Univ. of California, Berkeley 1979–83, Prof. of Virology in Residence 1984–; Visiting Prof., Coll. de France, Paris 1994, Garvin Inst., Sydney 1999; Leverhulme Visiting Prof., Imperial Coll., London 2007–08; mem. American Neurological Asscn (currently Pres.-elect), American Soc. of Biochemistry and Molecular Biology, American Soc. for Clinical Investigation (Emer.), ACS, AAAS, American Soc. for Neurochemistry, American Soc. for Microbiology, International Soc. for Neurochemistry, American Soc. for Cell Biology, California Medical Asscn, San Francisco Neurological Soc., Soc. for Neuroscience, American Soc. of Virology, American Soc. of Human Genetics, Asscn of American Physicians, Asscn of California Neurologists; Hon. mem. American Acad. of Neurology, American Asscn of Anatomists; Hon. DPhil (Hebrew Univ.) 1995, (Université René Descartes–Paris V) 1996, (Claremont Coll.) 2007, (Rosalind Franklin Univ.) 2010; Hon. DrSci (Univ. of Pennsylvania) 1998, (Dartmouth Coll.) 1999, (Pennsylvania State Univ.) 2001; Dr hc (Liège) 2000, (Universidad Cardenal Herrera-CEU, Moncada) 2005; Potamkin Prize for Alzheimer's Disease Research, American Acad. of Neurology 1991, NIH Christopher Columbus Quincentennial Discovery Award in Biomedical Research 1992, Metropolitan Life Foundation Award for Medical Research 1992, Dickson Prize for Distinguished Scientific Accomplishments, Univ. of Pittsburgh 1992, Charles A. Dana Award for Pioneering Achievements in Health 1992, NAS Richard Lounsbery Award for Extraordinary Scientific Research 1993, Gairdner Foundation Award for Outstanding Achievement in Medical Science 1993, Bristol-Myers Squibb Award for Distinguished Achievement in Neuroscience Research 1994, Albert Lasker Award for Basic Medical Research 1994, Paul Ehrlich Prize, Paul Ehrlich Foundation and FRG 1995, Wolf Prize in Medicine, Wolf Foundation and State of Israel 1996, Keio Int. Award for Medical Science, Keio Univ., Tokyo 1996, Nobel Laureate in Physiology or Medicine (for his discovery of prions) 1997, Nat. Medal of Science 2009. *Publications include:* The Molecular and Genetic Basis of Neurological Disease, Prions Prions Prions (Current Topics in Microbiology and Immunology, Vol. 207), Prions – Novel Infectious Pathogens Causing Scrapie and Creutzfeldt-Jakob Disease, Prion Diseases of Humans and Animals, Slow Transmissible Diseases of the Nervous System, Clinical Companion to the Molecular and Genetic Basis of Neurological Disease 1998, Prion Biology and Diseases 2003, The Molecular and Genetic Basis of Neurologic and Psychiatric Disease 2003, Madness and Memory (memoir) 2014. *Address:* University of California, San Francisco, 675 Nelson Rising Lane, Box 0518, San Francisco, CA 94158, USA (office). *Telephone:* (415) 476-4482 (office). *Fax:* (415) 476-8386 (office). *E-mail:* stanley.prusiner@ucsf.edu (office). *Website:* ind.ucsf.edu (office).

PRYCE, Jonathan, CBE; British actor; b. 1 June 1947, Holywell, North Wales; s. of Isaac Price and Margaret Ellen Price (née Williams); partner Kate Fahy; two s. one d.; ed Royal Acad. of Dramatic Art; Patron Friends Works, Saving Faces; Dr hc (Liverpool); Tony and Drama Desk Awards, Best Actor, Cannes Film Festival 1995. *Stage appearances include:* Comedians (Tony Award 1976), Nottingham Old Vic 1975, New York 1976, Hamlet (Olivier Award 1980), Royal Court Theatre, London 1980, The Caretaker, Nat. Theatre 1981, Accidental Death of an Anarchist, Broadway 1984, The Seagull, Queen's Theatre 1985, Macbeth, RSC 1986, Uncle Vanya 1988, Miss Saigon (Olivier and Variety Club Awards 1991), Drury Lane 1989, New York 1991, Nine – The Concert 1992, Under Milk Wood 1992, Cabaret 1994, Oliver!, London Palladium 1995, Hey! Mr Producer 1998, My Fair Lady, Nat. Theatre and Drury Lane, London 2001, A Reckoning, Soho Theatre 2003, The Goat, Almeida Theatre 2004, Dirty Rotten Scoundrels, New York 2005, Glengarry Glen Ross, Apollo Theatre 2007–08, Dimetos, Donmar Warehouse 2009, The Caretaker, Liverpool Everyman, Theatre Royal Bath, Trafalgar Studios, London 2011, The Caretaker, World Tour 2012, King Lear, Almeida Theatre 2012, Merchant of Venice, The Globe 2015 (World Tour 2016). *Films include:* Something Wicked This Way Comes 1982, The Ploughman's Lunch 1983, Brazil 1985, The Doctor and the Devils 1986, Haunted Honeymoon 1986, Jumpin' Jack Flash 1987, Consuming Passions 1988, The Adventures of Baron Munchausen 1988, The Rachel Papers 1989, Glengarry Glen Ross 1992, Barbarians at the Gate 1992, Great Moments in Aviation 1993, The Age of Innocence 1993, A Business Affair 1993, Deadly Advice 1994, Carrington (Best Actor, Evening Standard Film Awards 1996) 1995, Evita 1996, Tomorrow Never Dies 1997, Regeneration 1997, Ronin 1998, Stigmata 1999, Taliesin Jones 2000, The Suicide Club 2000, Very Annie Mary 2001, The Affair of the Necklace 2001, Bride of the Wind 2001, Unconditional Love 2002, Mad Dogs 2002, What a Girl Wants 2003, Pirates of the Caribbean: The Curse of the Black Pearl 2003, De-Lovely 2004, The Brothers Grimm 2005, The New World 2005, Pirates of the Caribbean 2: Dead Man's Chest 2006, Brothers of the Head 2006, The Moon and the Stars 2007, Pirates of the Caribbean: At the World's End 2007, Leatherheads 2007, Bedtime Stories 2008, G.I. Joe: The Rise of Cobra 2009, Hysteria 2011, City State 2011,

Dark Blood 2012, GI Joe: Retaliation 2013, Listen Up Philip 2014, Dough 2014, The Salvation 2014, Narcopolis 2014, The Ghost and the Whale 2015, Woman in Gold 2015, The White King 2016, One Last Dance 2016, The Healer 2016, The Ghost and the Whale 2017. *Radio:* HR (BBC Radio 4) 2007–. *Television includes:* Roger Doesn't Live Here Anymore (series) 1981, Timon of Athens 1981, Martin Luther 1983, Praying Mantis 1983, Whose Line Is It Anyway? 1988, The Man from the Pru 1990, Selling Hitler 1991, Mr Wroe's Virgins 1993, Barbarians at the Gate 1993, Thicker than Water 1993, Great Moments in Aviation 1993, David 1997, Hey, Mr Producer! The Musical World of Cameron Mackintosh 1998, The Union Game: A Rugby History (series) (voice) 1999, Victoria & Albert 2001, Confessions of an Ugly Stepsister 2002, HR (film) 2007, Sherlock Holmes and the Baker Street Irregulars (film) 2007, My Zinc Bed (film) 2008, Clone (series) 2008, Cranford (series) 2009, Under Milk Wood (film) 2014, Wolf Hall (mini-series) 2015, Game of Thrones (series) 2015-16, Taboo (series) 2016. *Recordings include:* Miss Saigon 1989, Nine – The Concert 1992, Under Milk Wood 1992, Cabaret 1994, Oliver! 1995, Hey! Mr Producer 1998, My Fair Lady 2001. *Leisure interests:* painting, drawing. *Address:* c/o Julian Belfrage Associates, 3rd Floor, 9 Argyll Street, London, W1F 7TG, England (office).

PRYOR, David Hampton, LLB; American lawyer, politician and academic; b. 29 Aug. 1934, Camden, Ark.; s. of Edgar Pryor and Susan Pryor (née Newton); m. Barbara Jean Lunsford 1957; three s. including Mark Pryor (q.v.); ed Henderson State Univ., Univ. of Arkansas; admitted to Ark. Bar 1964; mem. Ark. House of Reps 1961–66; mem. US House of Reps 1966–73; Gov. of Ark. 1974–79; Senator from Ark. 1979–97, Chair. Senate Special Cttee on Aging 1989–95, Democratic Conf. Sec. of the US Senate 1989–95; Chair. Arkansas Democratic Party 2008–09; mem. ABA, Ark. Bar Asscn; Fellow, Inst. of Politics, School of Govt, Harvard Univ. 1999; Dir Inst. of Politics, Kennedy School of Govt, Harvard Univ. 2000–02; Dean, Clinton School of Public Service, Univ. of Arkansas 2004–06, taught a political science course at Univ. of Arkansas, Fayetteville 2008, apptd to Bd of Trustees 2009; mem. Bd Corpn for Public Broadcasting 2006–12; Democrat. *Publications:* A Pryor Commitment (co-author) (autobiography) 2008. *Address:* 2701 Kavanaugh Boulevard, Suite 300, Little Rock, AR 72205, USA (office). *E-mail:* info@clintonschool.uasys.edu.

PRYOR, Mark, BA, LLB; American lawyer and fmr politician; *Partner, Venable LLP;* b. 10 Jan. 1963, Fayetteville, Ark.; s. of David Hampton Pryor; m. Jill Pryor (divorced); one s. one d.; ed Univ. of Arkansas; practised law with Wright, Lindsey & Jennings, Little Rock 1982–90; elected to Ark. State House of Reps (Democrat) for two terms 1990; Attorney-Gen. for Ark. 1999–2003; Senator from Arkansas 2003–Jan. 2015; Partner, Venable LLP, Washington, DC 2015–; served as campaign chair. in Ark. for Vice-Pres. Al Gore 2000; Democrat. *Address:* Venable LLP, 575 7th Street, NW, Washington, DC 20004, USA (office). *Telephone:* (202) 344-4572. *E-mail:* mlpryor@Venable.com.

BENAKI-PSAROUDA, Anna, PhD; Greek politician, lawyer and academic; *Professor Emeritus of Criminal Law, University of Athens;* b. 12 Dec. 1934, Athens; m. Linos Benakis 1957; ed Pierce Coll. of Athens, Univ. of Athens, Univ. of Bonn, Germany; attorney-at-law 1962–; Researcher, Max Planck Inst. for Int. Criminal Law, Freiburg 1962–78; Asst Prof., Prof. of Criminal Law, Univ. of Athens 1978–2002, now Prof. Emer.; mem. Vouli (Parl.) 1981–2009, Alt. Minister of Education 1989, of Culture 1990–92, of Justice 1992–93; Vice-Pres. Vouli 2002–04, Pres. (Speaker) 2004–07; mem. Council of Europe Parliamentary Ass. 2007–09; mem. Acad. of Athens 2010– (Vice-Pres. 2019–); Grand Cross, Royal Norwegian Order of Merit 2004, Grand Cross, Order of Honour of Hellenic Repub. 2005, Grand Cross, Order of the Dannebrog (Denmark) 2006, Grand Decoration of Honour for Services (Austria) 2007. *Publications include:* five books and several articles on criminal matters; political articles. *Leisure interests include:* swimming, classical music, literature. *Address:* National and Kapodistrian University of Athens, Faculty of Law, Akadimias 45, 10672 Athens; Sina 58, 106 72 Athens, Greece (home). *Telephone:* (210) 3636818 (home); (210) 3688646 (office). *Fax:* (210) 3636681 (home); (210) 3688640 (office). *Website:* www.en.law.uoa.gr (office).

PSZONIAK, Wojciech Zygmunt; Polish actor; b. 2 May 1942, Lvov, Poland (now Lviv, Ukraine); m.; ed State High Theatre School, Kraków; Asst State High Theatre School, Kraków 1967–72, lecturer 1972–; prin. theatrical roles at Stary Theatre, Kraków 1968–72, Narodowy Theatre, Warsaw 1972–74, Powszechny Theatre, Warsaw 1974–80; presenter TV show Wojtek Pszoniak – pytania do siebie (Pszoniak – Questions to Himself) 1995–96; Gold Cross of Merit 1975, Kt's Cross, Order of Polonia Restituta 1997, Commdr Cross of the Order of Polonia Restituta 2011; Prize of Ministry of Culture (2nd Class) 1975, Masters Award, Montréal Film Festival 1982, Gold Medal of Merit for Culture Gloria Artis 2007, Nat. Merit Order 2008. *Films:* Wesele (The Wedding) 1973, Ziemia obiecana (The Promised Land) 1975, Austeria 1981, Danton 1982, Je hais les acteurs 1986, Les années-sandwiches 1987, Czerwona Wenecja (Red Venice) 1988, Korczak 1990, Gawin 1991, Le Bal des Casse-Pieds 1992, Coupable d'innocence 1992, Le Vent d'Est 1993, La Chica 1995, Wielki Tydzien 1996, Our God's Brother 1997, Deuxième vie 2000, Bajland 2000, Chaos 2001, Le Pacte du silence 2003, Là-haut, un roi au-dessus des nuages (Above the Clouds) 2003, Vipère au poing 2004, Hope 2007, Mniejsze zlo 2009, Nie ten czlowiek 2009, Mystification 2010, Mala matura 1947 2010, Robert Mitchum est mort 2010, Czarny czwartek. Janek Wisniewski padl 2011, Wygrany 2011, Le chat du rabbin 2011, Cassos 2012, À la vie 2014, Carte Blanche 2015, Excentrycy, czyli po slonecznej stronie ulicy 2015, If You Saw His Heart 2017. *Television:* J'aime pas qu'on m'aime 1993, Fall from Grace 1994, Natalia (TV Mini-Series) 1995, Anne Le Guen 1997, L'Atelier (TV) 1999, Oficerowie (Mini-series) 2006, Teraz albo nigdy! 2008, L'arche de Babel 2010, Rosemary's Baby (Mini-Series) 2014. *Plays:* Poskromienie złośnicy (The Taming of the Shrew) 1969, Sen nocy letniej (A Midsummer Night's Dream) 1970, Wszystko dobre, co się dobrze kończy (All's Well That Ends Well) 1971, Biesy 1971, Makbet (Macbeth) 1973, Les gens déraisonnables sont en voie de disparition, Théâtre des Amandiers, Nanterre 1978, Zemsta (Revenge) 1980, Czekając na Godota (Waiting for Godot) 1989, Król Ubu (King Ubu) 1992, The Deep Blue Sea, Apollo Theatre, London 1993, Atelier, Théâtre Hébertot, Paris 1999, Pracownia krawiecka (Tailor's Shop – actor and dir) 2000, Kolacja dla głupca (Supper for Fools) 2001, La boutique au coin de la rue, Théâtre Montparnasse, Paris 2001. *Publication:* Pszoniak & Co. czyli Towarzystwo Dobrego Stołu 1993. *Leisure interests:* classical music, jazz, cooking.

PTASHNE, Mark Stephen, BA, PhD; American biochemist and academic; *Ludwig Chair of Molecular Biology, Sloan-Kettering Cancer Center;* b. 5 June 1940, Chicago, Ill.; s. of Fred Ptashne and Mildred Ptashne; ed Reed Coll. and Harvard Univ.; Jr Fellow, Harvard Soc. of Fellows 1965–68; Lecturer, Dept of Biochemistry and Molecular Biology, Harvard Univ. 1968–71, apptd Prof. 1971, Chair. Dept of Biochemistry and Molecular Biology 1980–83, apptd Herchel Smith Prof. of Molecular Biology 1993; joined Faculty, Molecular Biology Program, Memorial Sloan-Kettering Cancer Center, Ludwig Chair of Molecular Biology 1997–; Guggenheim Fellow 1973–74; Fellow, American Acad. of Arts and Sciences 1977, New York Acad. of Arts and Sciences 1977; mem. NAS 1979; Ledlie Award, Harvard Univ. (with W. Gilbert) 1968, Eli Lilly Award in Biological Chemistry 1975, le Prix Charles-Léopold Mayer, Acad. des Sciences, Inst. de France (with W. Gilbert and E. Witkin) 1977, US Steel Foundation Award in Molecular Biology 1979, Louisa Gross Horwitz Prize (with D. Brown) 1985, Gairdner Foundation Int. Award (with Charles Yanofsky) 1985, Feodor Lynen Lecturer 1988, Cancer Research Foundation Award 1990, Lasker Award 1997. *Publications:* A Genetic Switch 1986, A Genetic Switch: Phage (Lambda) and Higher Organisms 1992, Genes and Signals 2002, Genetic Switch: Phage Lambda Revisited 2004; 122 papers in scientific journals 1950–89. *Leisure interests:* playing violin, classical music, opera. *Address:* Molecular Biology Program, Memorial Sloan-Kettering Cancer Center, 1275 York Avenue, New York, NY 10021, USA. *Telephone:* (212) 639-2297 (office); (212) 639-5183 (office). *Fax:* (212) 717-3627 (office). *E-mail:* m-ptashne@mskcc.org (office). *Website:* www.mskcc.org/research-areas/labs/mark-ptashne (office); www.markptashne.com.

PRITZKER, Jay Robert (J.B.), AB, JD; American philanthropist and politician; *Governor of Illinois;* b. 19 Jan. 1965, Atherton, Calif.; s. of Donald Pritzker and Sue Pritzker (née Sandel); m. Mary Kathryn Muenster 1993; one s. one d.; ed Duke Univ., Pritzker School of Law, Northwestern Univ.; Founder and Managing Partner, New World Ventures 1996–, renamed Pritzker Group Venture Capital; f. 1871 2012; Chair. Pritzker Family Foundation 2002–07; fmr Chair. ChicagoNEXT, now Chair. Emer.; Gov. of Ill. 2019–; founder and mem. Democratic Leadership; fmr Chair. Bd of Trustees, Ill. Holocaust Museum & Educ. Center; mem. Ill. State Bar Assn, Chicago Bar Assn, Economic Club of Chicago, Commercial Club of Chicago; Trustee, Northwestern Univ. 2011–19, Duke Univ. 2017–; Spirit of Erikson Inst. Award 2007, Entrepreneurial Champion Award, Chicagoland Entrepreneurial Center 2008, Survivors' Legacy Award 2013, Moxie Award for Tech Investor of the Year, EY Entrepreneur of the Year Award, ACG Lifetime Achievement Award, numerous awards from Young Pres.s' Org. *Leisure interest:* hockey. *Address:* Office of the Governor, James R. Thompson Center, 100 W Randolph, 16-100, Chicago, IL 60601, USA (office). *Telephone:* (312) 814-2121 (office). *Website:* www2.illinois.gov (office); www.pritzkergroup.com (office).

PU, Haiqing; Chinese politician; b. 1941, Nanbu, Sichuan Prov.; ed Chongqing Univ.; joined CCP 1973; Man. Chongqing Iron and Steel Co.; Vice-Gov. Sichuan Prov.; Acting Mayor of Chongqing Municipality 1996–97, Mayor 1997–99, Deputy Sec. CCP Chongqing Municipal Cttee 1997–99; Dir Nat. Metallurgical Industry Bureau 1999–2001 (Sec. CCP Leading Party Group); Deputy Dir Three Gorges Project Construction Cttee, Office of the State Council 2001–03 (Deputy Sec. CCP Leading Party Group), apptd Dir 2003 (Sec. CCP Leading Party Group); Del., 14th CCP Cen. Cttee 1992–97, mem. 15th CCP Cen. Cttee 1997–2002, 16th CCP Cen. Cttee 2002–07.

PUAPUA, Rt Hon. Sir Tomasi, Kt, GCMG, KBE, PC; Tuvaluan physician and politician; b. 10 Sept. 1938; s. of Fitilau Puapua and Olive Puapua; m. Riana Tabokai 1971; two s. two d.; ed Fiji School of Medicine and Univ. of Otago, NZ; Prime Minister of Tuvalu 1981–90, also Minister for Civil Service Admin., Local Govt and Minister for Foreign Affairs; Speaker of Parl. 1993–98; Gov. Gen. of Tuvalu 1998–2005. *Leisure interests:* athletics, rugby, tennis, volleyball, cricket, soccer, fishing, pig and poultry farming, gardening.

PUCCIO HUIDOBRO, Osvaldo, LLB, PhD; Chilean fmr diplomatist; b. 21 Dec. 1952; three c.; ed Univ. of Chile, Humboldt Univ., Berlin; consultant, Latin-American Faculty of Social Sciences (FLASCO) 1984–86; Assoc. Researcher, Centre for Devt Studies (CED) 1986–88; consultant, UNDP 1987–88, 2000–03; Founder mem. Chilean Assn of Political Sciences 1988; Dir Centro de Estudios Sociales AVANCE 1988–94; political advisor to Minister Sec.-Gen. of the Presidency 1990–94, 2000–03; Amb. to Austria 1994–2000, to Brazil 2003–05, to Spain 2006–08; Vice-Chair. Int. Cooperation Agency of Chile (AGCI) 2000–03; Minister Sec.-Gen. of the Presidency 2005–06; mem. Bd of Dirs Victoria de Lebu- Carville (coal co.) 1990–92, SACOR-CORFO (agric. co.) 1992–93; mem. Academic Cttee, Santo Tomás Univ. 1992–94; Dir for Latin America, Acciona SA 2008–. *Address:* Acciona SA, Avenida Apoquindo, n° 4499-piso 14, Las Condes, 7580575 Santiago, Chile (office).

PUCHETA, Alicia, PhD; Paraguayan lawyer and politician; *Vice-President;* b. (Alicia Beatriz Pucheta de Correa), 14 Jan. 1950, Asunción; d. of Justo Pucheta Ortega and Beatriz Valoriani; m. Carlos Alberto Correa Vera (died 2016); two s.; ed Columbia Univ., Universidad Nacional de Asunción; started as Practitioner 1971, more than 35 years of court career; Head of Chair for Exercise, Catholic Univ. 2002; Full Prof. of Child and Adolescent Law, Faculty of Law and Social Sciences, Universidad Nacional de Asunción 2005, mem. Bd of Dirs; Minister of Supreme Court of Justice 2004, Vice-First Pres. Supreme Court of Justice 2005–06, Pres. 2007–08, 2016–17, Pres. Criminal Chamber 2018–(19); Vice-Pres. 2018–; mem. Colorado Party. *Address:* Office of the President, Palacio Gobierno, El Paraguayo Independiente, entre O'Leary y Ayolas, Asunción, Paraguay (office). *Telephone:* (21) 414-0200 (office). *Website:* www.presidencia.gov.py (office).

PÚCIK, Brig.-Gen. Vladimir; Slovak air force officer; b. 20 June 1952, Lazisko; m. Viera Púciková; two c.; ed Mil. Acad., Liptovský Mikuláš, Air Defence Mil. Acad., Tver, Royal Coll. Defence Studies, London; promoted to Lt 1976; Deputy Commdr, 52nd Air Surveillance Unit, Stod 1976–77, Commdr 1977–79; promoted to First Lt 1979; Chief of Staff, 54th Air Surveillance Battalion, Nepolisy 1979–81, Commdr 1981–83; promoted to Capt. 1982, to Maj. 1985; Sr Officer, Air Surveillance Branch 3rd AD Div., Žatec 1986–87; Sr Officer, Air Surveillance Dept, HQ of AF and Air Defences, Stará Boleslav 1987–91; promoted to Lt Col 1989; Chief Air Surveillance Branch 1st AD Div., Zvolen 1991–93; Deputy Chief of AD Dept, HQ AF and Air Defence of SR, Trencín 1993–94; promoted to Col 1994; Deputy Commdr in Chief, 3rd AF and Air Defence Corps, Zvolen 1994–98; promoted to Col of Gen. Staff 2000; Deputy Commdr in Chief, Slovak AFs, Zvolen 2000-02; promoted to Brig.-Gen. 2002; Mil. Rep. of Slovakia to NATO and EU 2002–06; Medal for Homeland Service, Medal for Merit of Homeland Defence, Medal for Merit of Czechoslovak Armed Forces, Memorial Medal of Ministry of Defence of Slovak Repub., Mil. Badge of Honour, Slovak Armed Forces. *Leisure interests:* downhill skiing, hiking.

PUDDEPHATT, Andrew Charles, OBE, BA; British company director; *Founder Director, Adapt;* b. Luton, Beds.; s. of Andrew Ross Puddephatt and Margaret Deboo; two c.; ed Kingsbury School, Dunstable and Sidney Sussex Coll., Cambridge; Dir Global Partners and Associates Ltd 2004–13, Exec. Chair. Global Partners Digital 2016–; Chair. Int. Media Support, Denmark 2011–; Deputy Chair. Sigrid Rausing Trust; Exec. Cttee mem., European Council on Foreign Relations 2007–; Exec. Dir Article 19 1999–2004; Dir Nat. Council for Civil Liberties 1989–95; Founder Dir Adapt 2017–; Chair. Internet Watch Foundation 2018–. *Publications include:* Freedom of Expression, Association and Assembly 2003, Post Conflict Intervention 2003, A Guide to Measuring the Impact of Right to Information (for UNDP) 2004, Media Development Indicators: A Framework for Assessing Media Development (for UNESCO) 2008, Implementing EU Democracy Support-Political Economy Analysis 2014 and numerous other. *Leisure interests:* music, literature, cinema, walking. *Address:* Global Partners Digital, Second Home, 68 Hanbury Street, London, E1 5JL, England (office). *Telephone:* (20) 3818-3258 (office). *E-mail:* andrew@gp-digital.org (office). *Website:* www.gp-digital.org (office).

PUDDEPHATT, Richard John, OC, PhD, FRS, FRSC; British/Canadian chemist and academic; *Professor of Chemistry, University of Western Ontario;* b. 12 Oct. 1943, Aylesbury; s. of Harry Puddephatt and Ena Puddephatt; m. Alice Poulton 1969; one s. one d.; ed Univ. Coll. London; Teaching Postdoctoral Fellow, Univ. of Western Ontario 1968–70, Prof. of Chem. 1978–; Lecturer, Univ. of Liverpool 1970–77, Sr Lecturer 1977–78; Nyholm Award 1997, CIC Medal 1998, Montréal Medal, Queen's Diamond Jubilee Medal 2012. *Publications include:* The Chemistry of Gold 1978, The Periodic Table of the Elements 1986. *Leisure interest:* gardening. *Address:* Department of Chemistry, Chemistry Building, University of Western Ontario, London, ON N6A 5B7, Canada (office). *Telephone:* (519) 679-2111 (office). *Fax:* (519) 661-3022 (office). *E-mail:* pudd@uwo.ca (office). *Website:* www.uwo.ca/chem/Tpuddr (office).

PUDJIASTUTI, Susi; Indonesian entrepreneur and government official; *Minister of Maritime Affairs and Fisheries;* b. 15 Jan. 1965, Pangandaran, West Java; d. of Haji Ahmad Karlan and Hajjah Suwuh Lasminah; divorced; three c.; began career as seafood distributor, Fish Auction Facility, Pangandaran 1983; Founder and Pres. PT ASI Pudjiastuti Marine Product (seafood export business); f. PT ASI Pudjiastuti Aviation (operates Susi Air charter airline) 2004; Minister of Maritime Affairs and Fisheries 2014–; Ernst & Young Indonesia Young Entrepreneur of the Year 2005, Ministry of Maritime Affairs and Fisheries Sofyan Ilyas Award 2009, Institut Teknologi Bandung Ganesha Widyajasa Aditama Award 2011, Keraton Surakarta Sultanate Kanjeng Ratu Ayu (Kray) Award 2015. *Address:* Ministry of Marine Affairs and Fisheries, Gedung Humpus, Jalan Medan Merdeka Timur 16, Jakarta 10110, Indonesia (office). *Telephone:* (21) 3500023 (office). *Fax:* (21) 3519133 (office). *E-mail:* mail@kkp.go.id (office). *Website:* www.kkp.go.id (office).

PUENZO, Luis Adalberto; Argentine film director, producer and screenplay writer; b. 19 Feb. 1946, Buenos Aires; began career producing TV advertising spots in Argentina 1965; worked as storyboard designer in advertising, becoming advertising dir; co-f. Luis Puenzo Cinema production co. (name changed to Cinemanía SA 1974). *Films include:* Luces de mis zapatos (Lights of My Shoes) 1973, Las Sorpresas (segment Cinco años de vida) 1975, The Official Story (Palme d'Or, Cannes, Acad. Award for Best Foreign Film 1986 and 47 other int. awards) 1985, Gringo viejo (Old Gringo) 1989, With Open Arms 1990, La Peste (The Plague) 1992, La Puta y la Ballena (The Whore and the Whale) 2004. *Television:* Broken Silence (segment Some Who Lived) (mini-series) 2002. *Address:* c/o Instituto Nacional de Cinematografía, Lima 319, 1073 Buenos Aires, Argentina.

PUGACHEV, Sergey Victorovich; Russian politician and business executive; b. 4 Feb. 1963, Kostoma; m. Galina Pugacheva; two c.; partner Alexandra Tolstoy; two s. one d.; ed Leningrad State Univ.; credit inspector, Head of Div., mem. Bd of Dirs USSR Promstroibank 1985–90; mem. Bd of Dirs N Trade Bank 1990–92; made fortune through shipyards and property deals; Chair. Int. Industrial Bank (Mezhprombank) 1992–2002, bank became insolvent 2010; purchased Luxe.tv (transmitted in western Europe, Asia and Russia) 2006, co. wound up in Luxembourg 2010; his investment holding co., Obyedinyonnaya Promyshlennaya Korporatsia, lost rights to major construction project for Red Square, Moscow 2009; mem. Bureau Russian Union of Businessmen and Entrepreneurs 2002–; mem. Council of Feds, Rep. of Govt, Tuva Repub. 2001–11 (dismissed); French courts ordered seizure of Gairaut Castle, nr Nice, France 2012; mem. Cttee on Problems of Fed. and Regional Policy Council of Feds; mem. Russian Acad. of Eng. *Publications include:* Commercial Bank in Conditions of Free Market Relations Formation: Economic and Financial Analysis 1998.

PUGACHEVA, Alla Borisovna; Russian singer; b. 15 April 1949, Moscow; m. 1st Mykolas Orbakas 1969 (divorced 1973); m. 2nd Alexander Stefanovich 1976 (divorced 1980); m. 3rd Yevgeniy Boldin 1985 (divorced 1993); m. 4th Filipp Kirkorov 1994 (divorced 2005); one d.; ed M. Ippolitov-Ivanov Music High School, A. Lunacharsky State Inst. of Theatre Art; debut as soloist of Lipetsk vocal-instrumental group 1970; with O Lundstrem Jazz orchestra 1971; soloist, Veselye Rebyata Ensemble 1973–78; f. Song Theatre 1988; numerous prizes and awards including 3rd prize All-Union Contest Moscow, 1974; Grand Prix Int. Competition Golden Orpheus Bulgaria 1975, Int. Festival Sopot 1978; tours in USA, Germany, Switzerland, India, France, Italy and other countries; f. Theatre of Songs 1988, Alla Co. 1993, Alla Magazine 1993; toured Russia and other countries in honour of her 60th birthday 2009; Head Judge, Faktor A (TV programme) 2011–13; Order of Merit for the Fatherland, 2nd degree 1999, 3rd degree 2009, Order of Dostlugn (Friendship) (Azerbaijan) 2009, Order of St Mesrop Mashtots (Armenia) 2009; USSR People's Artist 1991, Ovation Prize 1994, State Prize of Russia 1995. *Repertoire includes:* numerous songs by popular Soviet composers such as R. Pauls, A. Muromtsev, A. Zatsepin and others, also songs of her own; albums: Alla

1990, Yes! 1998, River Tram 2001, Was There a Boy? 2002, Live Peacefully, My Country! 2003, Invitation to a Sunset 2008. *Address:* Tverskaya-Yamskaya str., Apt 57, Moscow, Russia (home). *Telephone:* (495) 250-95-78 (home).

PUGIN, Nikolai Andreyevich; Russian industrialist; b. 30 June 1940; ed Gorky Polytechnic Inst.; worker, foreman at car factory 1958–75; chief engineer at gearbox factory 1975–81; Tech. Dir 1981–83, Gen. Dir of Gorky Automobile Works 1983–86; Minister of Automobile Industry 1986–88, of Automobile and Agricultural Machines Industry 1988–91; Pres. ASM Holding Inc. (mfrs of motor vehicles and farm machinery in CIS) 1992–; Chair. GAZ Co., Nizhny Novgorod; Pres. Ind. Financial Group Nizhegorodskiye Automobili 1994–; Chair. Autobank 1996–2002; mem. Nizhny Novgorod Regional Ass. 2002–; mem. Russian Eng Acad. 1991, Russian Acad. of Natural Science 1992. *Address:* ASM Holding, 21/5 Kuznetsky Most, 103895 Moscow; GAZ, Lenina prosp. 9, 603046 Nizhny Novgorod; Oblastnaya Duma, Kremlin, korp. 2, 603082 Nizhny Novgorod, Russian Federation. *Telephone:* (495) 921-68-21 (Moscow); (495) 924-53-85 (Moscow); (8312) 56-10-70 (Nizhny Novgorod). *Fax:* (495) 924-39-00 (Moscow). *Website:* www.asm-holding.ru.

PUIGDEMONT I CASAMAJÓ, Carles; Spanish journalist and politician; b. 29 Dec. 1962, Amer, La Selva; s. of Xavier Puigdemont and Nuria Casamajó; m. Marcela Topor; two d.; ed Univ. Coll. of Girona; began professional career as journalist with El Punt (Catalan daily newspaper), Girona, later becoming Ed.-in-Chief; fmr Dir Agència Catalana de Notícies (news agency); fmr Dir Catalonia Today (English-language newspaper); elected mem. Parl. of Catalonia 2006; Mayor of Girona 2011–16; Pres., Generalitat (Govt) of Catalonia 2016–17 (removed from office by Prime Minister Mariano Rajoy 28 Oct. 2017); Chair. Asscn of Municipalities for Independence 2015–16; Dir Casa de Cultura, Girona 2002–04; mem. Convergència Democràtica de Catalunya 1983–2016; mem. Partit Demòcrata Europeu Català 2016–17; in exile in Belgium 2017–18; Founder and Pres. Crida Nacional 2018–. *Publications:* Cata… què? 1994; several essays on communication and new technologies. *Website:* www.cridanacional.cat (office).

PUISSOCHET, Jean-Pierre, LLD, PhD; French lawyer and international judge; b. 3 May 1936, Clermont-Ferrand; s. of René Puissochet and Hélène Puissochet (née Brengues); m. Eliane Millet 1973; one d.; ed Lycée du Parc, Lyon, Inst. for Political Studies, Lyon, School of Law, Lyon, Ecole Nat. d'Admin., Paris; Auditeur, Conseil d'Etat 1962, Maître des Requêtes 1968, Conseiller 1985; Dir Legal Service, Council of EC 1968–70, Dir-Gen. 1970–73; Dir-Gen. Agence Nat. pour l'Emploi 1973–75; Dir Ministry of Industry and Research 1977–79; Dir of Legal Affairs, OECD 1979–85; Dir Int. Inst. of Public Admin. 1985–87; Legal Adviser, Dir of Legal Affairs, Ministry of Foreign Affairs 1987–94; Judge, Court of Justice of the European Communities (now EU) 1994–2006; mem. Perm. Court of Arbitration, The Hague 1990–; Officier, Légion d'honneur, Grand Officier Ordre nat. du Mérite, Officier du Mérite agricole, Grand'Uffiziale dell Ordine al Merito (Italy). *Publications:* The Enlargement of the EC 1974; numerous articles on Community and int. law. *Address:* 15 rue Jean-Pierre Brasseur, 1258, Luxembourg (home).

PUJATS, HE Cardinal Jānis; Latvian ecclesiastic; *Archbishop Emeritus of Rīga;* b. 14 Nov. 1930, Nautrani, Rezekne Dist; ed Catholic Seminary, Riga; ordained priest 1951; taught art history and liturgy at Catholic Theological Seminary, Rīga; Vicar-Gen., Metropolitan Curia in Rīga 1979–84; KGB declared him persona non grata 1984; consecrated Bishop 1991; Archbishop of Rīga 1991–2001, Emer. 2001–; cr. Cardinal (in pectore—secretly) 1998, (openly) 2001; Pres. Latvian Bishops' Conf.; mem. Congregation for the Causes of Saints. *Address:* Metropolijas Kurija, Pils iela 5–9, 1050 Rīga, Latvia (office). *Telephone:* 2910-3393 (home). *E-mail:* sacerdos@inbox.lv (home).

PUJOL I SOLEY, Rt Hon. Jordi, MD; Spanish politician, pharmacologist and business executive; b. 9 June 1930, Barcelona; s. of Florenci Pujol i Brugat and Maria Soley i Mas; m. Marta Ferrusola 1956; seven s.; ed Faculty of Medicine, Univ. of Barcelona; worked in pharmaceutical industry 1953–60; f. Banca Catalana group 1959, Man. Dir 1959–76; f. Convergència Democratica de Catalunya 1974; Councillor, provisional Generalitat 1977–80; mem. Congress, Madrid 1977, 1979; Head Convergència i Unió Parl. Group in Congress 1977–80; mem. Catalan Parl. 1980; Pres. Generalitat de Catalunya 1980–2003; Vice-Pres. Ass. of European Regions 1988–92, Pres. 1992–96; Pres. Centre Estudis Jordi Pujol 2005–14; Dr hc (Brussels, Toulouse, Lyon, Rosario, Argentina, Barcelona). *Publications include:* Una política per Catalunya 1976, Construir Catalunya 1980, Als joves de Catalunya 1988, La Força serena i constructiva de Catalunya 1991, Pensar Europa 1993, Passió per Catalunya 1999, El Libre Roig de Jordi Pujol 2003, Sobre Europa (i altres coses) 2004, Una reflexió necessària 2006, Memòries Història d'una convicció (1930–1980) 2007, Memòries Temps de construir (1980–2003) 2009. *Leisure interests:* reading, walking, cycling.

PUJOLS ALCÁNTARA, (José Alberto) Albert; American (b. Dominican Repub.) professional baseball player; b. 16 Jan. 1980, Santo Domingo; s. of Bienvenido Pujols; m. Deidre Pujols 2000; three c.; ed Fort Osage High School, Independence, Mo., Maple Woods Community Coll., Kansas City, Mo.; emigrated to USA 1996; played in Jayhawk League, Kan. 1999; signed with St Louis Cardinals professional baseball team 1999, assigned to minor leagues 1999–2000; played for Peroia Chiefs 2000, then Potomac Cannons, Memphis Redbirds, first baseman St Louis Cardinals 2001–11; signed as free agent with Los Angeles Angels of Anaheim 2011–; Co-f. Pujols Family Foundation 2005; Nat. League Batting Champion (average .359) 2003, Nat. League Rookie of the Year 2001, Sporting News Player of the Year 2003, 2008, Gold Glove Award 2006, Roberto Clemente Award 2008, Nat. League Most Nat. League Valuable Player 2005, 2008, 2009, Hank Aaron Award 2003, 2009, nine times All-star selection 2001, 2003–10. *Address:* Angels Baseball LP, 2000 Gene Autry Way, Anaheim, CA 92806, USA (office). *Telephone:* (714) 940-2000 (office). *Website:* losangeles.angels.mlb.com (office).

PUKHAYEV, Erik Georgiyevich, BSc; Georgian mathematician, academic and government official; *Prime Minister of 'Republic of South Ossetia';* b. 5 May 1957, Skhlit, Znaur Dist, South Ossetian Autonomous Oblast, Georgian SSR, USSR; m.; three c.; ed South Ossetian State Pedagogical Inst.; worked in cannery in Tskhinvali; fmr Lab. Asst, Dept of Physics, South Ossetian State Pedagogical Inst., later Lecturer, then Sr Lecturer, Chair of Math.; Head of Dept of State Statistics; Deputy Prime Minister of 'Republic of South Ossetia' –2017; Prime Minister of 'Republic of South Ossetia' 2017–; 'For Labour Distinction' Medal; 'For Strengthening International Cooperation' Medal of 'Transnistrian Moldovan Republic'. *Address:* Office of the Government of the 'Republic of South Ossetia', 100001 South Ossetia, Tskhinvali, Government House, ul. Stalina 18, Georgia (office). *Telephone:* (9974) 45-65-55 (office). *Fax:* (9974) 45-65-55 (office). *E-mail:* ospress@mail.ru (office). *Website:* rso-government.org (office).

PULAT, Abdurakhim; Uzbekistani politician; Chair. Unity People's Movt Party ('Birlik' Xalq Harakati Partiyasi—Birlik) founded in 1988; leading opposition group, banned in 1992; registered as social movt; refused registration as political party 2004), living in self-imposed exile in USA *c.* 2003.

PULATOV, Timur Iskhakovich; Uzbekistani writer; b. 1939, Bukhara; ed Bukhara Pedagogical Inst., High School of Scriptwriters and Film Directors; freelance writer 1974–; First Sec., Co-ordinator Exec. Bd Int. Soc. of Writers' Unions 1992; Ed. Literary Eurasia; Order, Friendship of Peoples for devt of lit. and art and strengthening of int. relations 1994. *Publications:* Life Story of a Naughty Boy from Bukhara 1984, Other Populated Points, Properties, Passions of the Bukhara House, Tortoise Tarasi, Swimming Eurasia.

PULIKOVSKY, Lt-Gen. Konstantin Borisovich; Russian army officer and politician; b. 9 Feb. 1948, Ussuriysk, Primorsk Territory; ed M. Frunze Mil. Acad., Mil. Acad. of Gen. Staff; mil. posts to rank of Army Commdr 1972; took part in conflict in Chechnya 1994–96; Commdr group of Fed. forces in Chechen Repub. 1996, Deputy Commdr., N Caucasus Mil. District 1997; leader Krasnodar Org. All-Russian Movt of veterans of local wars and mil. conflicts Boyevoye Bratstvo; Rep. of Russian Pres. to Far Eastern Fed. Dist 2000–04; head of Rostekhnadzor (Fed. Service for Environmental, Tech. and Nuclear Supervision) 2005–08. *Publications include:* The Eastern Express: Through Russia With Kim Jong Il 2002.

PULJIĆ, HE Cardinal Vinko; Bosnia and Herzegovina ecclesiastic; *Archbishop of Vrhbosna;* b. 8 Sept. 1945, Prijećani, Banja Luka; s. of Ivan Puljić and Kaja Puljić (née Pletikosa); ed seminary of Šalata, Zagreb and at Đakovo; ordained priest of Đakovo 1970; Parish Vicar, Banja Luka, Parish Priest Sasina, then Ravska; Pedagogue, Zmajević seminary, Zadar 1978–87; Parish Priest, Bosanska Gradiška 1987–90; Vice-Rector Catholic Theological Seminary of Vrhbosna, Sarajevo 1990; Archbishop of Vrhbosna 1990–; cr. Cardinal (Cardinal Priest of Santa Chiara a Vigna Clara) 1994; participated in Papal Conclave 2005, 2013; travelled to many countries in Europe and N America to publicise the suffering caused by the war in Bosnia and Herzegovina and discuss possible solutions; Hon. Dr of Humanitarian Science (Grand Valley State Univ., Mich., USA) 1995; Hon. Dr of Pastoral Theology (Catholic Univ. Santa Maria in Apartade, Peru) 2001; Humanist of the Decade and Golden Diploma of Humanism, Int. League of Humanists, Sarajevo 1995. *Publications:* Suffering With Hope: Appeals, Addresses, Interviews 1995, Non cancellato l'uomo – Un grido di speranza da Sarajevo 1997, Per amore dell'uomo–Testimone di pace a Sarajevo 1999. *Address:* Nadbiskupski Ordinarijat, Kaptol 7, BiH 71000 Sarajevo, Bosnia and Herzegovina (office). *Telephone:* (33) 225501 (office); (33) 218823 (office). *Fax:* (33) 218824 (office). *E-mail:* kartolka@bih.nct.ba (office).

PULLEN, Roderick (Rod) Allen, BA, DPhil; British diplomatist; b. 11 April 1949; m. Karen Sketchley; four s. one d.; ed Mansfield Coll. and Univs of Oxford and Sussex; with Ministry of Defence 1975–78, 1980–81; Second Sec. UK Del. to NATO 1978–80, First Sec., Del. to CSCE 1981–82, FCO 1982–84, 1988–90, Deputy High Commr, Suva 1984–88, Nairobi 1994–97, Abuja 1997–2000, High Commr to Ghana 2000–04, Amb. to Zimbabwe 2004–06, UK Special Rep. at Inter-Sudanese Peace Talks on Darfur 2006; Junior Bursar, Trinity Coll., Cambridge 2006–16; mem. Bd of Dirs Eureka Man. Co. Ltd 2006–.

PULLEN PARENTE, Pedro; Brazilian engineer, business executive and politician; *Chairman, BRF SA;* b. 21 Feb. 1953, Rio de Janeiro; m.; began career at Banco do Brasil 1971, transferred to Cen. Bank 1973; consultant to IMF and to public insts in Brazil, including Depts of State and of Nat. Constituent Ass. 1988, served in various positions in govt's econ. area; Pres. Serpro 1990–91; Deputy Minister of Planning 1998; Minister of Planning, Budget and Man. May–July 1999; Chief of Staff of the Presidency 1999–2003; Exec. Sec., Ministry of Finance and Minister of Mines and Energy 2002; fmr Exec. Vice-Pres. (COO) RBS Group; Pres. and CEO Bunge Brazil 2010–14; mem. Bd of Dirs and CEO Petróleo Brasileiro SA (Petrobras) 2016–18; Chair., BM&F Bovespa SA 2015–17, BRF SA 2018–. *Address:* BRF SA, R. Viradouro, 63-Itaim Bibi, São Paulo, 04538-110, Brazil (office). *Telephone:* (11) 3071-2785 (office). *Website:* www.brf-global.com (office).

PULLMAN, Bill; American actor; b. 17 Dec. 1953, Hornell, NY; m. Tamara Pullman; three c.; ed Univ. of Massachusetts; fmr drama teacher, bldg contractor, dir of a theatre group; started acting in fringe theatres, New York; f. Big Town Productions (film production co.). *Films include:* Ruthless People, A League of Their Own, Sommersby, Sleepless in Seattle, While You Were Sleeping, Caspar, Independence Day, Lost Highway 1997, The End of Violence 1997, The Thin Red Line 1998, Zero Effect 1998, A Man is Mostly Water 1999, History is Made at Night 1999, The Guilt 1999, Brokedown Place 1999, Lake Placid 1999, Coming To Light: Edward S. Curtis and the North American Indians (voice) 2000, Titan A.E. 2000, Lucky Numbers 2000, Ignition 2001, A Man Is Mostly Water 2001, Igby Goes Down 2002, 29 Palms 2002, Rick 2003, The Grudge 2004, The Orphan King 2005, Dear Wendy 2005, Scary Movie 4 2006, You Kill Me 2007, Nobel Son 2007, Bottle Shock 2008, Phoebe in Wonderland 2008, Surveillance 2008, Your Name Here 2008, The Killer Inside Me 2010, Peacock 2010, Rio Sex Comedy 2010, Bringing Up Bobby 2011, Lola Versus 2012, May in the Summer 2013, Cymbeline 2014, The Equalizer 2014, American Ultra 2015. *Television includes:* Revelations (mini-series) 2005, Nathan vs. Nurture (film) 2010, Torchwood (series) 2011, Innocent (film) 2011, Too Big to Fail (film) 2011, 1600 Penn (series) 2012–13. *Address:* c/o One Talent Management, 9220 Sunset Blvd, Los Angeles, CA 90069, USA (office). *E-mail:* billpullman.org@gmail.com (office); ceres21@juno.com (office). *Website:* www.billpullman.org (office).

PULLMAN, Sir Philip, CBE, BA, FRSL; British writer; b. 19 Oct. 1946, Norwich, Norfolk; m. Jude Speller 1970; two s.; ed Exeter Coll., Oxford; teacher in Oxford 1972–86; part-time Lecturer, Westminster Coll., Oxford 1986–96; Hon. Fellow, Univ. of Wales, Bangor; Hon. DLitt (Univ. of East Anglia), (Oxford Brookes Univ.), (Oxford Univ.) 2009, (Exeter Univ.) 2010, Hon. DUniv (Univ. of Surrey

Roehampton); Booksellers' Asscn/Book Data Author of the Year Award 2001, Booksellers' Asscn Author of the Year 2001, 2002, British Book Awards Author of the Year Award 2002, Whitbread Book of the Year Award 2002, Astrid Lindgren Memorial Award 2005, JM Barrie Award 2019. *Publications include:* Count Karlstein 1982, The Ruby in the Smoke (Sally Lockhart series) 1985, The Shadow in the Plate 1986, The Shadow in the North (Sally Lockhart series) 1987, Spring-Heeled Jack 1989, The Tiger in the Well (Sally Lockhart series) 1990, The Broken Bridge 1990, The White Mercedes 1992, The Tin Princess (Sally Lockhart series) 1994, The New Cut Gang: Thunderbolt's Waxwork 1994, The New Cut Gang: The Gas-fitter's Ball 1995, The Wonderful Story of Aladdin and the Enchanted Lamp 1995, The Firework-Maker's Daughter 1995, Northern Lights (aka The Golden Compass, Vol. I, His Dark Materials trilogy) (Carnegie Medal 1996, Guardian Children's Fiction Prize 1996, British Book Awards Children's Book of the Year 1996, CILIP Carnegie Medal 2007) 1995, Clockwork 1996, The Subtle Knife (Vol. II, His Dark Materials trilogy) 1997, The Butterfly Tattoo 1998, Mossycoat 1998, Detective Stories (ed.) 1998, I Was a Rat! 1999, The Amber Spyglass (Vol. III, His Dark Materials trilogy) (British Book Awards WH Smith Children's Book of the Year, Whitbread Children's Book of the Year Prize 2001, Whitbread Book of the Year Award 2001) 2000, Puss-in-Boots 2000, Sherlock Holmes and the Limehouse Horror 2001, Lyra's Oxford 2003, The Scarecrow and his Servant 2004, A Word or Two About Myths 2005, The Good Man Jesus and the Scoundrel Christ 2010, Grimm Tales for Young and Old 2012, The Book of Dust 2017, La Belle Sauvage 2017, Daemon Voices: Essays on Storytelling 2017, The Adventures of John Blake 2018, The Secret Commonwealth 2019; *contrib.* reviews to Times Educational Supplement, The Guardian. *Address:* c/o Caradoc King, United Agents LLP, 12–26 Lexington Street, London, W1F 0LE, England (office). *Telephone:* (20) 3214-0800 (office). *Fax:* (20) 3214-0801 (office). *E-mail:* info@unitedagents.co.uk (office). *Website:* www.unitedagents.co.uk (office); www.philip-pullman.com.

FERNÁNDEZ-CID DE LAS ALAS PUMARIÑO, Luis; Spanish diplomatist; *Ambassador to Mexico;* b. 19 Dec. 1959, Madrid; ed Complutense Univ. of Madrid; Programme Dir, Office of Cooperation with Equatorial Guinea 1985; Consul-Gen. in Bata, Nigeria 1986–89, in Strasbourg 1998–2003, in Rabat 2003–07; Sec. Embassy of Spain in Bonn, Fed. Repub. of Germany 1989–90, Counsellor 1990–94, Sr Officer 1994–98; Adviser on Nationality Law, Directorate-Gen. of Consular Affairs and Assistance, Ministry of Foreign Affairs 2007–08, Deputy Dir-Gen. Consular Legal Affairs 2008–11, Dir-Gen. for Spaniards Abroad and of Consular and Migratory Affairs 2012–14, Amb. to Mexico 2014–. *Address:* Embassy of Spain, Galileo 114, esq. Horacio, Col. Polanco, Del. Miguel Hidalgo, 11550 México, DF, Mexico (office). *Telephone:* (55) 5282-2271 (office). *Fax:* (55) 5282-1520 (office). *E-mail:* emb.mexico@maec.es (office). *Website:* www.maec.es/embajadas/mexico (office).

PUN, Barsha Man (Ananta); Nepalese politician; fmr Deputy Commdr Maoist People's Liberation Army (PLA); mem. Unified Communist Party of Nepal (Maoist), mem. Cen. Secr.; mem. Constituent Ass. for Lalitpur No 1 constituency; Minister for Peace and Reconstruction March–Aug. 2011, Minister of Finance 2011–13; fmr Chair. Indigenous Peoples' Caucus; Chair. Nat. Council of Nepal Scouts.

PUN, Nanda Bahadur, (Comrade Pasang); Nepalese politician and fmr rebel military commander; *Vice-President;* b. 23 Oct. 1965, Rangsi Village, Rolpa Dist; s. of Ramsur Pun and Mansura Pun; taught at local Rangsi Lower Secondary School 1986–94; joined CP of Nepal (Unity Centre) 1990, becoming district central cttee mem., then district pres. of student cadre; apptd one of four Commdrs of People's Liberation Army (PLA) 2001, apptd Chief Commdr 2008 and served until end of conflict; mem. Standing Cttee, Unified CP of Nepal (Maoist) (UCPN—M) 2013–; unsuccessful cand. for Constituent Ass. from Kathmandu constituency-4 2013; Vice-Pres. of Nepal 2015–. *Address:* Office of the Vice-President of Nepal, Kathmandu, Nepal (office). *Telephone:* (1) 4212040 (office). *Fax:* (1) 4228284 (office). *Website:* www.vpn.gov.np (office).

PUNA, Henry; Cook Islands lawyer and politician; *Prime Minister;* s. of Tupuariki Puna; m. Akaiti Puna; ed Univ. of Auckland, New Zealand, Univ. of Tasmania, Australia; fmr pearl farmer; pvt. practise as lawyer; MP for Manihiki 2005–06, 2010–, Prime Minister 2010–, also Attorney-Gen., Minister of Energy and Renewable Energy, the Outer Islands, Marine Resources, the Public Service Comm., Tourism, Parl. Services, Transport and Foreign Affairs and Immigration; mem. Cook Islands Party, Leader 2006–. *Address:* Office of the Prime Minister, Government of the Cook Islands, Private Bag, Avarua, Rarotonga, Cook Islands (office). *Telephone:* 25494 (office). *Fax:* 20856 (office). *E-mail:* coso@pmoffice.gov.ck (office). *Website:* www.pmoffice.gov.ck (office).

PURCELL, James (Jim) Nelson, Jr, MPA; American international official and international consultant; *Chairman, US Association for International Migration;* b. 16 July 1938, Nashville, Tenn.; s. of James Nelson Purcell, Sr; m. Walda Primm 1961; two d.; ed Furman Univ., Syracuse Univ.; Budget Analyst, US Atomic Energy Comm. 1962–66; Man. Analyst, Agency for Int. Devt 1966–68; Deputy Dir Budget Preparation Staff, Office of Man. and Budget (OMB) 1968–72, Sr Examiner, Int. Affairs Div. OMB 1972–74, Chief Justice, Treasury Br. OMB 1974–76; Chief Resources Programming and Man. Div., Bureau for Educ. and Cultural Affairs, Dept of State 1976–77; Deputy Budget Dir Dept of State 1977–78; Exec. Dir Bureau of Admin., Dept of State 1978–79; Deputy Asst Sec., Programmes and Budget, Bureau for Refugee Programs, Dept of State 1979–82, Dir, Asst Sec., Bureau for Refugee Programmes 1982–87; Dir-Gen. Int. Org. for Migration 1988–98; int. consultant 1998–; Chair. US Asscn for Int. Migration 2009–; mem. Council for Community of Democracies, Columbia Housing Corpn; mem. American Soc. of Public Admin.; Order of the Phoenix (Greece) 1993; Distinguished Honor Award, State Dept 1987, Meritorious Executive Award, US Sr Exec. Service 1985, Golden Medal of Pres. of Hungary 1995, Immigration and Refugee Policy Award, Centre for Migration Studies 1998, Wings of Hope Award, US Asscn for Int. Migration 1992, Helping Hands Award, World Relief 1987, Special Commendation Award, Inst. for Int. Humanitarian Law, San Remo, Italy 1998, Appreciation Award, Pres. of Armenia 1994. *Publication:* The Perils of Unresolved Humanitarian Problems: A Region of Crisis-the Middle East 2001. *Address:* 5113 West Running Brook Road, Columbia, MD 21044, USA (home). *Telephone:* (443) 745-1004 (office). *Fax:* (410) 730-1353 (office). *E-mail:* jpurcell7@verizon.net (office). *Website:* www.iom.int (office).

PURCELL, Philip James, MSc, MBA; American business executive; *President, Continental Investors, LLC;* b. 5 Sept. 1943, Salt Lake City, Utah; m. Anne Marie McNamara 1964; seven s.; ed Univ. of Notre Dame, London School of Econs, UK, Univ. of Chicago; Man. Dir McKinsey & Co. Inc., Chicago 1967–78; Vice-Pres. Planning and Admin., Sears, Roebuck & Co., Chicago 1978–82; Pres., CEO then Chair., CEO Dean Witter Discover & Co., New York 1982–97, Chair. and CEO Morgan Stanley, Dean Witter & Co. (after merger with Morgan Stanley), New York 1997–2005 (co. name changed to Morgan Stanley 2001); Pres. Continental Investors, LLC 2006–; Dir New York Stock Exchange 1991–96 (Vice-Chair. 1995, 1996, later mem. Exec. Bd), AMR Corpn –2013, American Airlines –2013; Founder and Chair. Financial Services Forum; Trustee, Univ. of Notre Dame, Chair. Athletic Affairs Cttee. *Address:* Continental Investors, LLC, 227 West Monroe Street, Suite 5045, Chicago, IL 60606, USA (office). *Telephone:* (312) 628-2451 (office). *E-mail:* ellie@continv.com (office). *Website:* www.continentalinvestors.com (office).

PURCHEKOV, Charymyrat Hyvaliyevich; Turkmenistani politician; *Minister of Energy;* fmr Deputy Chair. Turkmenenergo State Power Corpn; Minister of Energy 2017–; For Love of the Fatherland Medal (Turkmenistan) 2016. *Address:* Ministry of Energy, 744000 Aşgabat, 2022 köç. 55, Turkmenistan (office). *Telephone:* (12) 37-94-59 (office). *Fax:* (12) 92-52-73 (office). *E-mail:* minenergo@minenergo.gov.tm (office). *Website:* www.minenergo.gov.tm (office).

PUREVSUREN, Lundeg, MA; Mongolian politician and diplomatist; *Permanent Representative of Mongolia to United Nations Office, Geneva;* b. 24 Dec. 1964; m.; two c.; ed Moscow State Inst. of Int. Relations, USSR; Attaché, Dept of Public Admin, Ministry of Foreign Affairs (MFA) 1989–91; Interpreter, Embassy of FRG to Mongolia 1991–93; Attaché and Third Sec., Europe and America Dept, MFA 1993–95; Second, later First Sec., Embassy in Germany 1995–2000; First Sec. and Counsellor, European Dept, Ministry of Foreign Affairs and Trade 2001–09; Adviser on Nat. Security and Foreign Policy to Pres. of Mongolia 2009–14, 2016–18; Minister of Foreign Affairs 2014–16; Perm. Rep. of Mongolia to the UN Office, Geneva 2018–; mem. Democratic Party. *Address:* Chemin des Mollies 4, 1293 Bellevue, Switzerland (office). *Telephone:* 227741974 (office). *Fax:* 227743201 (office). *E-mail:* mongolie@bluewin.ch (office). *Website:* www.missionmongolia.ch (office).

PURI, Manjeev Singh, BA (Hons), MA; Indian diplomatist; *Ambassador to Nepal;* b. 3 Dec. 1959, Meerut, Uttar Pradesh; s. of Surjit Singh Puri; m. Namrita Puri; two c.; ed St Stephen's Coll., Univ. of Delhi; worked for Hindustan Unilever –1982; joined Foreign Service 1982, served at Embassy in Bonn 1984–86, then in Berlin 1991–94, Co-ordinator of Festival of India in Germany 1991–92, est. Indian Cultural Centre in Berlin, other postings have included Embassies in Bangkok 1986–89, Caracas 1989–91, Cape Town 1998–2002, Muscat 2002–05 and as Deputy Chief of Protocol in charge of High Level Visits, Ministry of External Affairs, New Delhi 1994–98, Head of UN Div. 2005–09, led Indian del. to first meeting of Global Forum on Migration and Devt, Brussels July 2007, Amb. and Deputy Perm. Rep. to UN, New York 2009–13 (sr mem. of India's Security Council team 2011–12, lead negotiator on India's del. to UN Conf. on Sustainable Devt, Rio de Janeiro June 2012, mem. of Indian dels at various climate change negotiations, including Major Economies Forum and Conf. of Parties of UNFCCC, Copenhagen Dec. 2009, Amb. to Belgium (also accred to Luxembourg and the EU, Brussels) 2014–17, Amb. to Nepal 2017–; mem. Bd, Asia-Pacific Partnership on Clean Devt and Climate, Advisory Bd, The Energy and Resources Inst., New Delhi. *Address:* Embassy of India, 336 Kapurdhara Marg, PO Box 292, Kathmandu, Nepal (office). *Telephone:* (1) 4410900 (office). *Fax:* (1) 4428279 (office). *E-mail:* amb.kathmandu@mea.gov.in (office). *Website:* www.indianembassy.org.np (office).

PURICELLI, Arturo Antonio; Argentine politician; b. 1947, Río Gallegos, Santa Cruz Prov.; Gov. Santa Cruz Prov. 1983–87; mem. Partido Justicialista, Pres. Santa Cruz chapter 1987; elected to Cámara de Diputados (Parl.) 1989; Head of Encotesa (state postal service) 1996; elected to Prov. Lower House, Santa Cruz 1997; Vice-Pres. Nat. Airports Regulatory Agency –1999; Sec. of Provincial Affairs 2001–03; Head of Fabricaciones Militares (state-owned defence contractor) 2006–10; Minister of Defence 2010–13, of Security June–Dec. 2013.

PURISIMA, Cesar V., BSc, MBA; Philippine financial services executive and government official; b. 3 April 1960; m. Corrie Purisima; ed De la Salle Univ., Kellogg Grad. School of Man., Northwestern Univ., USA; Regional Managing Partner and Head of Asean operation, Andersen Worldwide 2000–01, Area Man. Partner and Head of Asia Pacific Assurance Practice 2001–02, mem. Global Bd 1999–2002; Chair. and Man. Pnr, SGV & Co. –2004; mem. Global Exec. Bd and Global Practice Council, Ernst & Young 2002–04; Chair. Exec. Cttee, Ciba Capital 2006; Sec., Dept of Trade and Industry 2004–05, Sec., Dept of Finance Feb.–July 2005, Sec. of Finance 2010–16; fmr Chair. National Power Corpn, Land Bank of the Philippines; Ind. Dir Energy Devt Corpn 2009–10; fmr mem. Monetary Bd Bangko Sentral ng Pilipinas; mem. Management Asscn of the Philippines, Philippine Inst. of Certified Public Accountants, Philippine-France Business Council, Philippine-Thailand Business Council, Makati Business Club; Finance Minister of the Year Award for Asia, Emerging Markets 2011, Finance Minister of the Year, Euromoney magazine 2012.

PURNELL, James Mark Dakin, BA; British broadcasting executive and fmr politician; *Director, Radio and Education, British Broadcasting Corporation;* b. 2 March 1970; s. of John Purnell and Janet Purnell; ed Royal Grammar School, Guildford, Balliol Coll., Oxford; researcher for Shadow Employment Sec. Tony Blair 1989–92; researcher, Hydra Assocs (media consultants), London 1992–94; Research Fellow, Inst. for Public Policy Research 1994–95; Head of Corp. Planning, BBC 1995–97, Dir, Strategy and Digital 2013–16, Radio and Educ. 2016–; Special Adviser to Prime Minister Tony Blair 1997–2001; Labour MP for Stalybridge and Hyde 2001–10, Parl. Pvt. Sec. to Ruth Kelly 2003–04, Asst Govt Whip 2004–05, Parl. Under-Sec. of State, Dept for Culture, Media and Sport 2005–06, Minister of State for Pensions Dept for Work and Pensions 2006–07, Sec. of State for Culture, Media and Sport 2007–08, Sec. of State for Work and Pensions 2008–09 (resgnd); mem. Bd of Dirs Open Left Project, Demos (think-tank), London 2009, Royal Nat. Theatre, British Film Inst.; Chair. of Trustees, Inst. for Public Policy Research (think-tank) 2010. *Leisure interests:* film, music, theatre and football. *Address:* BBC Broadcasting House, Portland Place, London, W1A 1AA, England (office). *Website:* www.bbc.co.uk (office).

PUROHIT, Banwarilal, BCom; Indian politician and fmr journalist; *Governor of Tamil Nadu;* b. 16 April 1940; s. of Dasji Purohit; m. Pushpa Devi Purohit 1959; two s. one d; ed Nagpur Univ.; Man. Ed. The Hitavada (Nagpur daily newspaper) 1978–; mem. Maharashtra Legis. Ass. from Nagpur East seat 1978–80, from Nagpur South 1980, Maharashtra Minister of State for Urban Devt, Slum Improvement and Housing 1982–83; mem. Lok Sabha (lower house of parl.) from Nagpur constituency (Congress) 1984, 1989, (BJP) 1996–2009, mem. Parl. Defence Consultative Cttee 1989–91, mem. Parl. Consultative Home Affairs and Railways Cttees, mem. Public Sector Undertaking Cttee; Gov. of Assam 2016–17, of Meghalaya Jan.–Sept. 2017, of Tamil Nadu 2017–; Chair. Ramdeobaba Coll. of Engineering, Subhash Mandal (sports org.); Dir regional unit of Bharatiya Vidya Bhavan (cultural org.); Life mem., Vidarbha Cricket Asscn. *Leisure interests:* reading, travelling and games. *Address:* Office of the Governor, Raj Bhavan, Chennai, Tamil Nadu, India (office). *Telephone:* (44) 22351313 (office). *Fax:* (44) 22350570 (office). *E-mail:* govtam@nic.in (office). *Website:* www.tnrajbhavan.gov .in (office).

PURPURA, Dominick Paul, AB, MD; American neuroscientist and academic; *Distinguished Professor Emeritus and Dean Emeritus, Albert Einstein College of Medicine, Yeshiva University;* b. 2 April 1927, New York, NY; s. of John R. Purpura and Rose Ruffino; m. Florence Williams 1948; three s. one d.; ed Columbia Univ. and Harvard Medical School; mem. Faculty, Coll. of Physicians and Surgeon, Columbia Univ. 1957–67; Chair. and Prof., Dept of Anatomy, Albert Einstein Coll. of Medicine, Yeshiva Univ. 1967–74, Dept of Neuroscience 1974–82, Prof. and Chair. of Neuroscience 1974–82, Dean, Albert Einstein Coll. of Medicine and Vice-Pres. for Medical Affairs 1984–2006, Distinguished Prof. Emer. and Dean Emer. 2006–; Dir Rose F. Kennedy Center for Research in Mental Retardation and Human Devt 1972–82; Dean, Stanford Univ. School of Medicine 1982–84; Pres. Soc. for Neuroscience 1982–83, Int. Brain Research Org. 1987–98, Vice-Pres. for Medical Affairs UNESCO from 1961; Chief Ed. Brain Research for 25 years; mem. NAS, Inst. of Medicine; Fellow, New York Acad. of Sciences; first annual Nat. Medical Research Award, Nat. Health Council (co-recipient) 1983, Lifetime Achievement Award for Research, American Epilepsy Society 1993, Presidential Award, Soc. of Neuroscience 1996, New York City Mayor's Lifetime Achievement Award for Excellence in the Medical and Biological Sciences 2001. *Publications:* about 200 scientific papers. *Address:* Albert Einstein College of Medicine, Yeshiva University, Room 912D, Rose F. Kennedy Center, 1410 Pelham Parkway South, Bronx, NY 10461, USA (office). *Telephone:* (718) 430-3617 (office). *E-mail:* dominick.purpura@einstein.yu.edu (office). *Website:* www.einstein.yu.edu/ departments/neuroscience/dominick-purpura.aspx (office).

PURRYAG, Rajkeswur (Kailash); Mauritian attorney and fmr head of state; b. 12 Dec. 1947, Camp Fouquereaux; m. Aneetah Purryag; one d.; ed Mauritius Coll., Curepipe; has worked as attorney since 1973; mem. Vacoas/Phoenix Municipal Comm. 1974–76; elected mem. Nat. Ass. (Parl.) 1976, Speaker 2005–12; Minister of Social Security 1980–82, of Health 1984–86, of Econ. Planning, Information and Telecommunications 1995–97, Deputy Prime Minister and Minister of Foreign Affairs and Int. Trade 1997–2000; Pres. of Mauritius 2012–15 (resgnd); mem. Mauritius Labour Party, Sec.-Gen. 1987–91, Pres. 1991–96; Hon. Freedom of the City of Port Louis 2007; Grand Officer, Order of the Star and Key of the Indian Ocean 1998, Grand Commdr, Order of the Star and Key of the Indian Ocean 2009, Pravasi Bharatiya Samman Award 2013. *Address:* c/o Office of the President, State House, Le Réduit, Port Louis, Mauritius (office).

PURUSHOTHAMAN, Vakkom B.; Indian politician; b. 12 April 1928, Vakkom, Kerala; s. of Bhanu Panicker and Smt Bhavani; m. Lilly Purushothaman; two s. one d.; mem. Indian Nat. Congress Party, fmr Pres. Thiruvananthapuram Dist Congress Cttee, Gen. Sec. and Vice-Pres., Kerala Pradesh Congress Cttee, mem. All-India Congress Cttee for 25 years; elected to Kerala Legis. Ass. from Attingal constituency 1970, 1977, 1980, 1982, Speaker 1982–84, 2001–04, State Minister of Agric. and Labour 1971–77, for Health and Tourism 1980–81, Minister of Finance and Excise 2004; mem. Lok Sabha (lower house of nat. parl.) 1984–89, 1989–91; Lt-Gov. of Andaman and Nicobar Islands 1993–96; Gov. of Mizoram 2011–14, of Nagaland July 2014. *Address:* Indian National Congress, 24 Akbar Road, New Delhi 110 011, India (office). *Telephone:* (11) 23019080 (office). *Fax:* (11) 23017047 (office). *E-mail:* connect@inc.in (office). *Website:* www.inc.in (office).

PURVES, Sir William, Kt, KStJ, CBE, DSO; British banker (retd); b. 27 Dec. 1931, Kelso, Roxburghshire, Scotland; s. of Andrew Purves and Ida Purves; m. 1st Diana T. Richardson 1958 (divorced 1988); two s. two d.; m. 2nd Rebecca Jane Lewellen 1989; ed Kelso High School; with Nat. Bank of Scotland, Kelso 1948–54; joined the Hongkong and Shanghai Banking Corpn 1954, Chief Accountant 1970–74, Man., Tokyo 1974–76, Sr Man. Overseas Operations 1976–78, Asst Gen. Man. Overseas Operations 1978–79, Gen. Man. Int. 1979–82, Exec. Dir 1982–84, Deputy Chair. 1984–86, Chair. and CEO 1986–92, Exec. Chair. HSBC Holdings PLC 1992–98; Pres. Int. Monetary Conf. 1992, mem. Exec. Council Hong Kong 1987–93; Chair. British Bank of the Middle East 1979–98, Midland Bank PLC 1994–97 (Dir 1987–98); Dir HBSC Americas Inc. 1984–88; Deputy Chair. (non-exec.) Alstom SA 1998–2003; Dir (non-exec.) Shell Transport and Trading Co. PLC 1993–2002, Trident Safeguards Ltd 1999–2003, World Shipping and Investment Ltd 1998–2004, Reuters Founders Share Co. Ltd 1998–2009, Scottish Medicine Ltd 1999–2003, Interpacific Holding Ltd 2000–08, Aquarius Platinum 2004–12, BW Group Ltd 2004–12; Chair. Hakluyt & Co. 2000–09; Chair. Royal Hong Kong Jockey Club 1992–93; Fellow, Chartered Inst. of Bankers; Trustee, Gurkha Welfare Trust 1993–2006; Gov. Queenswood School 1997–2007; Pres. Penguin Rugby Football Club 2006–08; Hon. DUniv (Stirling) 1987; Hon. DLaws (Sheffield) 1993; Hon. LLD (Nottingham) 1997; Hon. Dr Business Admin. (Hong Kong Polytechnic) 1993, (Strathclyde) 1996; Dr hc (Hong Kong) 1997, (Napier) 1998, (Hong Kong Open) 1998, (Manchester Science and Tech.) 2000; Grand Bauhinia Medal (Hong Kong). *Leisure interests:* golf, rugby. *Address:* One Ebury House, 39 Elizabeth Street, London, SW1W 9RP, England (home). *Telephone:* (20) 7823-6775 (home). *Fax:* (20) 7824-8351.

PURVIS, Stewart Peter, CBE, BA, FRTS; British media executive, journalist and academic; *Professor of Television Journalism, City University;* b. 28 Oct. 1947,

Isleworth; s. of Peter Purvis and Lydia Purvis; m. Mary Presnail 1972 (divorced 1993); one d.; two s. with Jacqui Marson; ed Dulwich Coll., Univ. of Exeter; fmr presenter Harlech TV; news trainee BBC 1969; Ind. TV News producer 1972, Programme Ed. News at Ten 1980, Ed. Channel 4 News 1983; Deputy Ed. Ind. TV News 1986, Ed. 1989, Ed.-in-Chief 1991, CEO 1995–2003; Pres. EuroNews 1997; Dir Travel News Ltd 1995, London News Radio 1996; Prof. of TV Journalism, City Univ. London 2003–; fmr Deputy Chair . King's Cross Partnership (Dir 1996); Dir (non-exec), Royal Marsden Nat. Health Service Trust, Channel 4 Corpn 2013–; Specialist Adviser, House of Lords Select Cttee on Communications 2011; mem. council, European Journalism Centre 1996–; Trustee, Services Sound and Vision Corpn 2013–; Fellow, Royal TV Soc., Vice-Pres. 2013–; Hon. LLD (Univ. of Exeter) 2005; two Royal TV Soc. Awards, BAFTA Award for Best News or Outside Broadcast 1987, 1988, Broadcasting Press Guild Award for Best News or Current Affairs Programme 1988, RTS Gold Medal for Outstanding Contrib. to TV 2009. *Leisure interests:* being at home, keeping fit, yoga. *Address:* Department of Journalism, City University, Northampton Square, London, EC1V 0HB, England (office). *Telephone:* (20) 7040-8783 (office). *Fax:* (20) 7040-8562 (office). *Website:* www.city.ac.uk (office).

PURWAR, A(run) K(umar), MCom; Indian banker; ed Allahabad Univ.; fmr Man. Dir State Bank of Patiala; fmr Lecturer in Commerce, Business Admin Dept, Allahabad Univ.; joined State Bank of India 1968, held numerous positions including CEO Tokyo Br. 1995–98, Chair. State Bank of India 2002–06 (retd); Exec. Chair. India Venture Advisors; fmr Chair. Fed. of Indian Chambers of Commerce and Industry (FICCI) Banking and Financial Insts, later Chair. FICCI Diaspora Div.; Dir (non-exec.) Caparo Group 2007; apptd Ind. Dir India Infoline Investment Services Ltd 2009; mem. Bd of Dirs Apollo Tyres Ltd; CEO of the Year Award, Inst. for Tech. & Man. 2004, Outstanding Achiever of the Year Award, Indian Banks Asscn 2004, Finance Man of the Year Award, Bombay Man. Asscn 2006.

PUSIĆ, Vesna, DSc; Croatian sociologist, academic and politician; b. 25 March 1953, Zagreb; d. of Eugen Pusić and Višnja Pusić; m.; one d.; ed Univ. of Zagreb; Faculty mem. Dept of Sociology, Univ. of Zagreb 1978–, Prof. 1988–; Founding mem. Hrvatska Narodna Stranka (HNS—Croatian People's Party) 1990–2017, Pres. 2000–08, 2013–16; Co-founder and Dir Erasmus Guild (think-tank) 1993–98; mem. Sabor (Parl.) 2000–11, Deputy Speaker 2003–07, 2016, Chair. HNS parl. group 2008–11; fmr Vice-Pres. European Liberal Democrat and Reform Party; Minister of Foreign and European Affairs 2011–16; First Deputy Prime Minister 2012–16; Croatian cand. for UN Sec.-Gen. 2016, withdrew candidacy; Co-founder Građansko-liberalni savez 2017–. *Publications include:* Industrial Democracy and Civil Society 1986, Rulers and Administrators 1992, Democracies and Dictatorships 1998; more than 50 scientific articles in Croatian and int. journals. *Address:* Građansko-liberalni savez, 10000 Zagreb, Pasarićeva ulica 12, Croatia (office). *Telephone:* (1) 2342685 (office). *E-mail:* ured@glas.com.hr (office). *Website:* glas .com.hr (office); vesna-pusic.hns.hr.

PUSKA, Pekka, MD, PhD, MPolSci; Finnish epidemiologist, public health official and academic; *Director General Emeritus, National Institute for Health and Welfare;* b. 18 Dec. 1945, Vaasa; m. Arja Puska; one s. one d.; ed Univ. of Turku, Univ. of Kuopio; Prin. Investigator, N Karelia Project, Univ. of Kuopio 1972–78; Visiting Prof., Stanford Univ., USA 1983; Research Prof. and Dir Dept of Epidemiology and Health Promotion, Nat. Public Health Inst. 1978–, Dir Div. of Health and Chronic Diseases 1992–2000, Deputy to Dir-Gen. 1995–2000, Dir Gen. Nat. Public Health Inst. 2000–01, 2004–08; Dir Dept of Noncommunicable Disease Prevention and Health Promotion WHO, Geneva, Switzerland 2001–03; Dir-Gen. Nat. Inst. for Health and Welfare (THL) 2009–13, Dir-Gen. Emer. 2013–; mem. Parl. (Eduskunta) 1987–91, 2017–; Elector of Presidents of Repub. 1988; Pres. Centre for Health Educ. 1989–95; mem. City Council, Joensuu 1993–97; mem. WHO panel of experts on cardiovascular diseases 1978–2001; Dir Int. Quit and Win 1994–2006; Vice-Chair. ALKO Ltd (nat. alcohol monopoly) 2007–13; chair. several organizing cttees of int. confs on tobacco and health 1996–; Pres. Finnish Heart Asscn 2004–09; Chair. Nat. Nutrition Council 2005–11, UKK Inst. 2005–10 (Pres.-Elect 2007–08, Pres. 2009–10), World Heart Fed. (Vice-Pres. 2006–12, Pres. 2013–14), Int. Asscn of Nat. Public Health Insts, Governing Council WHO IARC (Lyon) (Vice-Chair. 2008–10, Chair. 2010–13), Ind. Expert Group on Impact Assessment of Framework Convention on Tobacco Control, WHO 2015–16; Chancellor Univ. of Turku 2010–13; mem. Russian Acad. of Natural Sciences 1997; Hon. DSc (St Andrews, Scotland) 1999, Hon. DMed (Turku) 2009, Hon. DPhil l (Kuopio) 2010, Academician (Russian Academy of Natural Sciences) 1997; WHO Annual Health Educ. Award 1990, Int. Union for Health Educ. AMIE Award 1991, WHO Tobacco Free World Award 1999, Nordic Public Health Award 2005, Rank Prize 2008. *Publications:* 10 books on public health; contrib. of numerous articles to journals. *Address:* Parliament of Finland (Eduskunta), 00102 (office); National Institute for Health and Welfare (THL), Mannerheimintie 166, 00300 Helsinki, Finland (office). *Telephone:* 40-7715571 (office). *Fax:* (2) 95246020 (office). *E-mail:* pekka.puska@eduskunta.fi; pekka.puska@thl.fi (office). *Website:* www.eduskunta.fi (office); www.thl.fi (office).

PUSTOVOITENKO, Valery Pavlovich, CandTechSc; Ukrainian politician; b. 23 Feb. 1947, Adamivka, Nikolayev Region; m.; two c.; ed Dnipropetrovsk Inst. of Construction Eng; worked as mechanical eng.; head of trusts in Odessa and Dnipropetrovsk 1965–87; People's Deputy of Ukraine; Chair. Dnipropetrovsk City Soviet 1987–93; mem. Higher Econ. Council, Security Council 1997; Head election campaign of Pres. Kuchma 1994; mem. Ukrainian Cabinet of Ministers 1994–97; apptd Head of Ukrainian Football Fed. 1996; mem. People's Democratic Party of Ukraine (Chair. 1999–2006), fmr Leader; mem. Parl.; mem. Political Exec. Council 1996; Prime Minister of Ukraine 1997–99; Minister of Transport 2000–02.

PUTILIN, Nikolai Georgiyevich; Russian singer (baritone); b. 1954, Saratov region; ed Krasnoyarsk Inst. of Arts, lessons with Nikola Nikolov in Bulgaria; started career as singer of Variety Theatre; soloist, Syktyvkar Musical Theatre, Komi Repub. 1983–85; soloist, Musa Dzhalil Academic Theatre of Opera and Ballet (Kazan) 1985–92; soloist, Kirov (Mariinsky) Theatre, St Petersburg 1992–; has toured with Mariinsky Opera Company and independently to Germany, France, Spain, Italy, the Netherlands, Belgium, Finland, Great Britain, Japan, USA, Hungary, Czech Republic, Bulgaria, Korea, Israel and Luxembourg; has performed at Metropolitan Opera, New York, Chicago Lyric Opera, Royal Opera

House, Covent Garden, London, La Scala, Milan, Accademia Santa Cecilia, Rome; has performed at Salzburg Festival; winner, Int. Vocalists' Competition, Sofia 1988, Int. Chaliapin Competition 1989, State Prize of Russia, People's Artist of Tatarstan, People's Artist of Russia. *Repertoire includes:* over 40 leading roles with Metropolitan Opera, La Scala, Teatro Comunale di Firenze, Covent Garden, Bolshoi Theatre and others. *Address:* James Fox Artist Management, LLC, 1 Riverplace Drive, Suite 420, La Crosse, WI 54601, USA (office); Mariinsky Theatre, 190000 St Petersburg, 1 Theatre Square, Russia (office). *E-mail:* peter@jfartists.com (office). *Telephone:* (812) 326-41-41 (office). *Website:* www.mariinsky.ru/en (office).

PUTIN, Col Vladimir Vladimirovich, PhD; Russian politician and head of state; *President;* b. 7 Oct. 1952, Leningrad (now St Petersburg), Russian SFSR, USSR; s. of Vladimir Spiridonovich Putin and Mariya Ivanovna Putin; m. Lyudmila Aleksandrovna Shkrebneva 1983 (divorced 2014); two d.; ed Law Dept, Leningrad State Univ.; assigned to work on staff of KGB, USSR 1975–91, with First Chief Dept of KGB and in GDR 1985–90; asst to Pro-Rector, Leningrad State Univ. 1990; adviser to Chair. of Leningrad City Exec. Cttee 1990–91; Chair. Cttee on Foreign Relations, St Petersburg City Council 1991–96, then also First Deputy Chair. St Petersburg City Govt (First Deputy Mayor) 1994–96; Deputy Head, Admin. of Russian Presidency, Property Man. Directorate 1996–98, then also Deputy Head, Exec. Office of Pres. (Presidential Admin) and Head, Cen. Supervision and Inspections Directorate 1997–98; First Deputy Head, Presidential Admin May–July 1998; Dir Fed. Security Service of Russian Fed. 1998–99; Sec. Security Council of Russia March–Aug. 1999; Chair. of Govt (Prime Minister) 1999–2000, 2008–12; Acting Pres. of Russian Fed. 1999–2000, Pres. of Russian Fed. 2000–08, 2012–; Chair. Group of 8 (G8) 2006, Russia excluded from the G8 group as a result of Russian invasion and annexation of Crimea 2014; Chair. Yedinaya Rossiya (United Russia) party 2008–12; Grand Cross Bundesverdienstkreuz (Germany) 2001, Grand Croix, Légion d'honneur 2006, King Abdul Aziz Award (Saudi Arabia) 2007, Order of Zayed (UAE) 2007, Order of Manas (Kyrgyzstan) 2017; Dr hc (Univ. of Belgrade) 2011; named Person of the Year by TIME magazine 2007, named Person of the Year by Expert magazine 2007, Confucius Peace Prize, China Int. Peace Research Centre 2011, Hugo Chavez Prize for Peace and Sovereignty 2016. *Leisure interests:* judo, biking, supports FC Zenit Saint Petersburg. *Address:* Office of the President, 103132 Moscow, Staraya pl. 4, Russia (office). *Telephone:* (495) 625-35-81 (office). *Fax:* (495) 606-07-66 (office). *E-mail:* president@gov.ru (office). *Website:* putin.kremlin.ru (office); kremlin.ru (office).

PUTS, Kevin, MMus; American composer, pianist and academic; *Member of the Composition Faculty, Peabody Institute;* b. 1972, St Louis, Mo.; ed Eastman School of Music, Yale Univ.; works commissioned and performed throughout North America, Europe and the Far East; commissions from New York Philharmonic, Nat. Symphony Orchestra, Tonhalle Orchester Zurich, symphony orchestras of Baltimore, Cincinnati, Detroit, Atlanta, Colorado, Houston, Fort Worth, Utah, St Louis, Boston Pops, Minnesota Orchestra and chamber ensembles including Mirò Quartet, Eroica Trio, eighth blackbird, Pittsburgh New Music Ensemble and Chamber Music Soc. of Lincoln Center; Concerto for Everyone premiered at Carnegie Hall 1999; premieres performed by artists including Evelyn Glennie, Yo-Yo Ma, Bill Jackson and Makoto Nakura; Composer-in-Residence, Young Concert Artists and California Symphony 1996, Fort Worth Symphony and Bravo! Vail Valley Music Festival 2007; Assoc. Prof. of Composition, Univ. of Texas at Austin 1999–2005; mem. Composition Faculty, Peabody Inst., Johns Hopkins Univ., Baltimore 2006–; John Simon Guggenheim Memorial Foundation Fellowship 2001; Dir Minnesota Orchestra Composer's Inst.; William Schuman Prize 1998, Charles Ives Scholarship, Barlow Int. Prize for Orchestral Music 1999, Rome Prize, American Acad. in Rome 2001–02, Benjamin H. Danks Award for Excellence in Orchestral Composition, American Acad. of Arts and Letters 2003, Eddie Medora King Award for Composition, Butler School of Music, Univ. of Texas 2013, Arts and Letters Award, American Acad. of Arts and Letters 2015, Alfred I. duPont Composer's Award, Delaware Symphony Orchestra 2015; numerous grants and awards from ASCAP, BMI. *Compositions include:* numerous orchestral, chamber and ensemble works including Night 2008, How Wild The Sea (chamber music) 2013, The City 2016, four symphonies and several concertos; works for solo instruments with and without orchestra; other: Silent Night (opera, Pulitzer Prize for Music 2012), The Trial of Elizabeth Cree (chamber opera) 2017. *Recordings:* works included on CDs including Violinguistics: American Voices, Alternating Current 2010, Playing the Edge: Music for Violin and Percussion 2010, River of Light 2011, Sound the Bells! 2011, American Portraits 2011. *E-mail:* bgoldstein@gginternationalllc.com (office). *Address:* Peabody Institute, Johns Hopkins University, 1 East Mount Vernon Place, Baltimore, MD 21202, USA (office). *Website:* www.peabody.jhu.edu/conservatory/faculty/puts (office); www.kevinputs.com.

PUTTNAM, Baron (Life Peer), cr. 1997, of Queensgate in the Royal Borough of Kensington and Chelsea; **David Terence Puttnam,** Kt, CBE, FRGS, FRSA; British film producer and educationalist; b. 25 Feb. 1941, London; s. of Leonard Arthur Puttnam and Marie Beatrix Puttnam; m. Patricia Mary Jones 1961; one s. one d.; ed Minchenden Grammar School, London; in advertising 1958–66, photography 1966–68, film production 1968–2000; Chair. Enigma Productions Ltd 1978–, Spectrum Strategy Consultants 1999–2006; Dir Nat. Film Finance Corpn 1980–85, Anglia TV Group 1982–98, Village Roadshow Corpn 1989–99, Survival Anglia 1982–99, Chrysalis Group 1993–96; Chair., CEO Columbia Pictures, USA 1986–88; Pres. Council for Protection of Rural England 1986–92; Visiting Prof., Univ. of Bristol 1984–96; Gov. and Lecturer, LSE 1997–2002; Gov. Nat. Film and TV School 1974–87, Chair. 1988–96, Life Pres. 2017–; Chair. Gen. Teaching Council 1998–2001; Trustee Tate Gallery 1985–92, Nat. Museum of Science and Tech. 1996–2003, IPPR, Royal Acad. of Arts 1998–2003; Chancellor Univ. of Sunderland 1998–2007; Chair. Nat. Endowment for Science, Tech. and the Arts 1998–2003, Nat. Museum of Photography, Film and Television 1994–2003; Chair. of Trustees, Nat. Teaching Awards 1998–2008; Vice-Pres. BAFTA 1995–2002, Chair. BAFTA Trustees 2002–04; mem. Advisory Committee/Council, Tate Gallery Liverpool 1988–94, Educ. Standards Task Force 1997–2001, Arts Council Lottery Panel 1995–98; Pres. UNICEF, UK 2002–09; Chair. QCA 2000–03; Lay Canon Durham Cathedral 2002–08; Chancellor Open Univ. 2006–14; Fellowship, Sam Spiegel Film School, Jerusalem 2012; BAFTA Acad. Fellowship 2006, Fellow, British Film Inst. 1997, RTS Fellowship 2002, Hon.

Fellow, British Inst. of Educ., Univ. of London 2007, Royal Photographic Soc., Bd Landscape Foundation, Royal Inst. of Chartered Designers, British Inst. of Professional Photographers, Hon. life mem. BECTU, Royal Dublin Soc. 2018; Hon. FCSD, Commander des Arts et des Lettres 2006; Hon. degrees (Bristol, Keele, Leicester, Manchester, Leeds, Birmingham, Southampton, Bradford, Heriot-Watt Edin., Westminster, Humberside, Sunderland, Cheltenham and Glos., Kent, Queens Belfast, London Guildhall Univs, North London, London (City), Royal Scottish Acad., Imperial Coll. London, Sheffield Hallam, American Int. Univ., Richmond, Nottingham, Winchester, Surrey, Navarra, Abertay, Leicester, Middlesex, Brunel, Greenwich, Bath Spa, Gateshead, Edinburgh, Griffin Brisbane, Queen Margaret Thames Valley, Hertzen St Petersberg, Durham Cathedral); Special Jury Prize for The Duellists, Cannes 1977, two Acad. Awards and three BAFTA Awards for Midnight Express 1978, four Acad. Awards (including Best Film), three BAFTA Awards (including Best Film) for Chariots of Fire 1981, three Acad. Awards and eight BAFTA Awards for The Killing Fields 1985; Michael Balcon Award for outstanding contrib. to the British Film Industry, BAFTA 1982; Palme d'Or (Cannes), one Acad. Award and three BAFTA Awards for The Mission 1987. *Films:* producer of around 50 feature films including Bugsy Malone 1976, The Duellists 1977, Midnight Express 1978, Chariots of Fire 1981, Local Hero 1983, The Killing Fields 1984, Cal 1984, The Mission 1986, Memphis Belle 1990, Meeting Venus 1991. *Television:* 15 films including Lawrence: A Dangerous Man, Josephine Baker (Emmy Awards), P'tang, Yang, Kipperbang 1982, Without Warning (Golden Globe Award) 1991. *Publications:* Rural England: Our Countryside at the Crossroads 1988, Undeclared War: The Struggle to Control the World's Film Industry 1997; contrib.: The Third Age of Broadcasting 1982, A Submission to the EC Think Tank on Audio-Visual Policy 1994, The Creative Imagination in 'What Needs to Change' 1996, Movies and Money 1998, Members Only? Parliament in the Public Eye: Report of the Hansard Society Commission on the Communication of Parliamentary Democracy 2005, Parliament in the Public Eye 2006: Coming into Focus? 2006. *Address:* Enigma Productions, PO Box 54828, London, SW1A 0WZ, England (office). *Telephone:* (20) 7219-6822 (office). *E-mail:* puttnamd@parliament.uk (office).

PUYOL ANTOLIN, Rafael; Spanish professor of geography and university rector; *Executive Vice-President, IE University;* b. 26 Feb. 1945, Gijón, Asturias; m. Dolores Martínez-Ferrando; four c.; ed Colegio de la Inmaculada, Gijón, Universidad Complutense de Madrid; Asst Prof. of Human Geography, Faculty of Geography and History, Universidad Complutense de Madrid 1975–78, Assoc. Prof. 1978–82, Prof. 1982–, Chair. Dept of Geography 1981–82, Dean, Faculty of Geography and History 1986–87, Vice-Chancellor for Academic Affairs 1988–95, Rector of Univ. 1995–2003; currently Exec. Vice-Pres., IE Univ., Vice-Pres. of Institutional Relations, IE Business School, Chair. IE Univ.; mem. editorial bds of various journals; fmr mem. Pres. and current mem. Population Group, Asociación de Geógrafos Españoles 1986–; Vice-Pres. Exec. Cttee Real Sociedad Geográfica; fmr Vice-Pres. Gen. Foundation of the UCM; mem. Exec. Cttee and Bd of Dirs Portal Universia; mem. Jury, Prince of Asturias Award for scientific and technical research 1996–2006; Vice-Pres. Conf. of Rectors of Spanish Universities 1997–; fmr Pres. Instituto Universitario Ortega y Gasset 1996–98, Inst. of Musical Studies 1999–2003; mem. Bd Spanish Chapter of the Club of Rome, Club of the Hague; Trustee, five foundations; Academician, Royal Acad. of Physicians, Acad. of Social Sciences at the European Acad. of Sciences and Arts, Salzburg; Hon. mem. UNICEF; Commdr's Cross, Order of Merit (FRG), Grand Cross of Aeronautical Merit and Naval Merit with White Distinctive, Order of Honour Nuñez de Balboa (Panama), Order Grand Duke Gediminas (Lithuania); Dr hc (Universidad Anáhuac, Mexico), (Universidad del Norte, Paraguay), (Nat. Univ. of Cuzco, Peru), (Universidad Ricardo Palma, Peru), (Inter American Univ. of Puerto Rico), (Univ. Rodríguez Ureña, Dominican Repub.), (Univ. of Panama); UNICEF Commemorative Medal, Gold Medal, Universidad Complutense de Madrid. *Publications include:* Emigración y desigualdades regionales en España 1979, Población y Espacio 1982, Población y recursos 1984, Población española 1988, Los grandes problemas demográficos 1993, La Unión Europea 1995, Estructura demográfica de la población española. Un ejercicio de prospectiva 2006, Aspectos demográficos de la inmigración 2006, Población y Dinámica demográfica 2006, El futuro de la población española 2007, Demografía y sanidad 2008, El reto demográfico. El verdadero sentido de la emigración 2008, El envejecimiento de la población y sus repercusiones sobre el mercado de trabajo 2008, Población e inmigración en España 2009, Las consecuencias demográficas de la crisis económica 2011, Crecemos, pero menos 2011, Demografía y políticas demográficas para una nueva década 2011; more than 200 articles in professional journals on migration and demographic aging; regular columnist for several national newspapers. *Leisure interests:* music, reading. *Address:* IE University, María de Molina 11, 28006 madrid (office); C/ Marbella 50, 28034 Madrid, Spain (home). *Telephone:* (91) 5689600 (office); (91) 3720480 (home). *Fax:* (91) 3943472 (home). *E-mail:* university@ie.edu (office). *Website:* www.ie.edu (office).

PUZANOV, Col Gen. Igor Yevgenyevich; Russian army officer; b. 31 Jan. 1947, Tyumen; ed Omsk Gen. Army Command School, M. V. Frunze Mil. Acad., Mil. Acad. of Gen. Staff; Commdr platoon Siberian Mil. Command –1976, Deputy Div. Commdr, then Commdr 1981–88; Deputy Regt Commdr, then Commdr Karpaty Mil. Command 1976–79; served in Afghanistan 1979–81; Head of Gen. Staff Baltic Mil. Command 1988–90; Army Commdr N Caucasian Mil. Command 1990–92; First Deputy Commdr Moscow Mil. Command 1992–2001, Statistics-Sec.; apptd Deputy Minister of Defence 2001; Merited Mil. Specialist. *Address:* Ministry of Defence, 105175 Moscow, ul. Myasnitskaya 37, Russia (office). *Telephone:* (495) 293-38-54 (office). *Fax:* (495) 296-84-36 (office). *Website:* www.mil.ru (office).

PUZDER, Andrew (Andy) Franklin, BA, JD; American lawyer and business executive; b. 11 July 1950, Cleveland, Ohio; s. of Andrew F. Puzder and Winifried M. Puzder; m. 1st Lisa Henning; m. 2nd Deanna L. Descher; six c.; ed Cleveland State Univ., Washington Univ. School of Law, St Louis; private law practice, Offices of Morris A. Shenker 1978–84; Attorney, Stolar Partnership 1984–91; Partner, Lewis, D'Amato, Brisbois, & Bisgaard 1991–94; Partner, Stradling, Yocca, Carlson & Rauth 1994–95; Exec. Vice-Pres. and Gen. Counsel, Fidelity National Financial, Inc. 1995–97; CEO, Santa Barbara Restaurant Group 1997–2000; Gen. Counsel and Exec. Vice-Pres., Carls Jr (subsidiary of CKE Restaurants, Inc.) 1997–98, Pres. CKE Restaurants, Inc. 2000–09, CEO 2000–17, also CEO and Pres., Hardee's Food Systems, Inc. (subsidiary of CKE Restaurants,

Inc.) 2000; nominated as US Sec. of Labor Dec. 2016 (withdrew nomination Feb. 2017); mem. State Bar of Nevada, Missouri Bar, State Bar of California. *Address:* c/o CKE Restaurants Inc., 6307 Carpinteria Avenue, Suite A, Carpinteria, CA 93013, USA (office).

PYAVKO, Vladislav Ivanovich; Russian singer (tenor); b. 4 Feb. 1941, Krasnoyarsk; s. of Nina Piavko and step-s. of Nikolai Bakhin; m. Irina Arkhipova (died 2010); four s. two d.; ed State Inst. of Theatrical Art, Moscow, studied under S. Rebrikov, Moscow, R. Pastorino, La Scala, Milan; mem. CPSU 1978–89; soloist with Bolshoi Opera 1965–89, Berliner Staatsoper 1989–96; teacher of singing and dramatic art, State Inst. of Theatrical Art 1980–89, Dean of School 1983–89; producer at Mosfilm 1980–83; Prof., Moscow State Conservatory 2000–; Pres. Int. Union of Musicians 2010–, Arkhipova Foundation 2010–; has also sung at Teatro Colón, Buenos Aires, Teatro Comunale, Florence, Opéra Bastille, Paris, Nat. and Smetana Operas, Prague, Metropolitan, New York, Kirov, St Petersburg and in many other houses and at numerous int. festivals; mem. Acad. of the Arts 1992; Hon. Prof., Lomonosov Moscow State Univ. 2004–; Gold Medal in tenor section, Vervier Int. Competition 1969, Silver Medal, Tchaikovsky Int. Competition 1970, Gold Medal and Pietro Mascagni Silver Medal, Livorno 1984, Gold Plank of Cisternino, Italy 1993; People's Artist of USSR 1983, of Kyrgyzstan 1993, Prize of Moscow 2004 and other awards. *Major roles include:* Hermann in Queen of Spades, Andrei in Mazeppa, Dmitry and Shuisky in Boris Godunov, Andrei and Golitsin in Khovanshchina, Radames, Otello, Manrico in Il Trovatore, Cavaradossi in Tosca, Pinkerton in Madam Butterfly, Don José in Carmen, Turiddu in Cavalleria Rusticana, Guglielmo Ratcliff, Sergei in Katerina Izmailova, Canio in Pagliacci and many other roles. *Film:* You're My Delight My Suffering... (Mosfilm) 1983. *Recordings include:* numerous recordings for leading int. labels including EMI, HMV, Philips, Chant du Monde, Columbia. *Publication:* Tenor, Vladislav Pyavko. *Leisure interests:* poetry, photography, cars. *Address:* Bryusov, per. 2/14, stroenie 2, Apt 26, 125009 Moscow, Russia. *Telephone:* (495) 629-43-07 (home); (495) 629-60-29 (office). *Fax:* (495) 629-60-29 (office). *E-mail:* amguem@gmail.com (home).

PYE, William Burns, ARCA, FRBS; British sculptor; *President, Hampshire Sculpture Trust;* b. 16 July 1938, London, England; s. of Sir David Pye and Virginia Pye; m. Susan Marsh 1963; one s. two d.; ed Charterhouse School, Wimbledon School of Art, Royal Coll. of Art; Visiting Prof., California State Univ. 1975–76; kinetic sculpture Revolving Tower 1970; sculpture 'Zemran' on South Bank, London 1971 (Grade II listed 2016); currently Pres. Hampshire Sculpture Trust; introduction of tensioned cables with less emphasis on volume 1972; combined working on comms with smaller work and installations 1972–75; water an integral element of sculptures since mid-1970s in public, private and corporate comms internationally; works include: Slipstream and Jetstream (water sculptures) for Gatwick Airport 1988, Balla Frois (30m long water sculpture) comm. for Glasgow Garden Festival 1988, Chalice water sculpture for 123 Buckingham Palace Road, London 1990, cr. Water Wall and Portico for British Pavilion, Expo '92, Seville, Spain, Cristos at St Christopher's Place, London, Downpour at British Embassy, Oman, Cascade at Market Square, Derby 1994, Water Cone at Antony House, Cornwall for Nat. Trust 1996, bronze of Lord Hurd for Nat. Portrait Gallery 1996, Cader Idris at Cen. Square, Cardiff 1998, Prism for Cathay Pacific at Hong Kong Airport 1999, Aquarena Millennium Square, Bristol 2000, Cornucopia at Millfield School; St John's Innovation Park, Cambridge, Millennium Fountain for Wilton House and Sunderland Winter Garden 2001, Jubilee Fountain, Lincoln's Inn, London 2003, eight Water Sculptures for Serpent Garden, Alnwick Castle 2004, three sculptures at Mariinsky Concert Hall, St Petersburg, 8m high water piece nr Athens 2006, stone and bronze font for Salisbury Cathedral 2008, Sakirin Mosque fountain, Istanbul, 2009, Hypanthium for British Columbia Botanical Gardens, Vancouver 2010, Water Pavilion in Drammen nr Oslo 2011, Vortex water sculptures in Campinas, Brazil & Muscat, Oman, 2012, two fountains for Dumfries House, Scotland 2014, Antwerp Zoo 2015, water sculpture for Wimbledon Tennis 2016; Hon. FRIBA 1993; Prix de Sculpture, Budapest 1981, Vauxhall Mural Prize 1983, Peace Sculpture Prize 1984, ABSA award for best commission of new art in any medium 1988, Art at Work award for best site-specific comm. 1988, Royal Ueno Museum Award (Japan) 1989. *Film:* Reflections

1972. *Publication:* William Pye – His Work and His Words 2010. *Leisure interest:* playing the flute. *Address:* The Studio, Rear of 31 Bellevue Road, London, SW17 7EF (office); 43 Hambalt Road, London, SW4 9EQ, England (home); The Hampshire Sculpture Trust, St Thomas Centre, Southgate Street, Winchester, SO23 9EF, England (office). *Telephone:* (20) 8682-2727 (Studio) (office). *Fax:* (20) 8682-3218 (office). *E-mail:* william.pye@btconnect.com (office); hst@soton.ac.uk (office). *Website:* www.williampye.com (office); www.hampshiresculpturetrust.co.uk (office).

PYETSUKH, Vyacheslav Alekseyevich; Russian author and essayist; b. 18 Nov. 1946, Moscow; m. Irina Pyetsukha; ed Moscow State Pedagogical Inst.; history teacher, Moscow Pedagogical Inst.; work first published in Selskaya Molodezh magazine; freelance writer 1970s–; Pushkin Prize 2007, Nat. Ecological Award 2009, Triumph Award for excellence in the arts and literature 2010. *Publications:* Alphabet 1983, New Times 1988, History of the Town of Glupov in New and Newest Times, The New Moscow Philosophy 1989, Rommat, I and Others 1990, Cycles 1991, State Child 1997; short story: Me and the Sea (Emily Clark Balach Prize, Virginia Quarterly Review 1999); work has appeared in The Penguin Book of New Russian Writing and several journals. *Address:* c/o Vagrius Publishers, Troitskaya str. 7/1, Building 2, 129090 Moscow, Russian Federation. *Telephone:* (495) 785-09-03.

PYNCHON, Thomas Ruggles, Jr, BA; American novelist; b. 8 May 1937, Glen Cove, New York; s. of Thomas R. Pynchon and Katherine Frances Bennett; m. Melanie Jackson; one s.; ed Cornell Univ.; fmr editorial writer, Boeing Aircraft Co.; Fellow, American Acad. of Arts and Sciences 2009; John D. and Catherine T. MacArthur Foundation Fellowship 1988; American Acad. of Arts and Letters Howells Medal 1975. *Publications include:* V (Faulkner Prize for Best First Novel) 1963, The Crying of Lot 49 (Rosenthal Foundation Award 1967) 1965, Gravity's Rainbow (Nat. Book Award) 1973, Mortality and Mercy in Vienna 1976, Low-Lands 1978, Slow Learner (short stories) 1984, In the Rocket's Red Glare 1986, Vineland 1989, Deadly Sins 1994, Mason & Dixon 1996, Against the Day 2006, Inherent Vice 2009, Bleeding Edge 2013; contrib. short stories to various publs, including Saturday Evening Post.

PYNE, Christopher, LLB; Australian lawyer and politician; *Minister for Defence;* b. 13 Aug. 1967, Adelaide; m. Carolyn Pyne; four c.; ed Univ. of Adelaide, Univ. of South Australia; Research Asst to Senator Amanda Vanstone 1987–90; practised as Solicitor 1991–93; MP (Liberal) for Sturt 1993–, Leader of the House 2013–; Minister for Ageing March–Dec. 2007, for Educ. 2013–14, for Educ. and Training 2014–15, for Industry, Innovation and Science 2015–16, for Defence Industry 2016–18, Minister for Defence 2018–; mem. Liberal Party of Australia, mem. Liberal Party Federal Exec. 1990–91. *Publication:* A Letter to my Children 2015. *Address:* Department of Defence, Russell Offices, Russell Dr., Campbell, Canberra, ACT 2600, Australia (office). *Telephone:* (2) 6265-9111 (office). *E-mail:* mediaops@defence.gov.au (office). *Website:* www.defence.gov.au (office).

PYNZENYK, Viktor Mikhailovich, DEcon; Ukrainian politician and economist; b. 15 April 1954, Smologovitsa; s. of Mikailo Vasilyevich Pynzenyk and Maria Ivanovna Pynzenyk; m. 1st; two d.; m. 2nd Mariya Romanivna Pynzenyk; two s.; ed Lviv State Univ.; Asst, then Docent, Sr Researcher, Prof., Chair. Lviv State Univ. 1975–92; mem. Vakhovna Rada (Parl.) 1991–2001, 2012–; Deputy Chair. Bd on Problems of Econ. Policy 1992; Minister of Economy 1992–93, Deputy Prime Minister 1992–97; Pres. Foundation of Support to Reforms 1993; Chair. Council on Econ. Reforms 1994; Chair. Nat. Council on Statistics 1995; Head, State Comm. on Admin. Reform 1997–99; Head, Partiya 'Reformy i poryadok' (Reforms and Order Party) 1998–2010; Minister of Finance 2005–06, 2007–09 (resgnd); apptd Deputy Chair. Supervisory Bd UkrSibbank 2011; Dir Inst. of Reforms; Hon. Prof., Mohyla Acad., Nat. Univ. of Kyiv 1996, Econs Inst. of Ternopil; named an Honoured Economist of Ukraine 2004. *Publications:* more than 400 papers in professional journals. *Leisure interests:* tourism, music, playing the preferans card game. *Address:* 01008 Kyiv, vul. M. Hrushevskoho 5, Ukraine. *E-mail:* umz@rada.gov.ua.

Q

QABOOS BIN SAID AS-SAID, Sultan of Oman; *Prime Minister and Minister of Foreign Affairs, Defence and Finance;* b. 18 Nov. 1940, Salalah; s. of HH Said bin Taimur; m. Sayyidah Nawwal bint Tariq 1976 (divorced 1977); ed privately in UK, Royal Mil. Acad. Sandhurst; 14th descendant of the ruling dynasty of Albusaid Family; Sultan of Oman (following deposition of his father) 23 July 1970–, also Prime Minister, Minister of Foreign Affairs, Defence and Finance; Hon. KCMG. *Leisure interests:* reading, horse-riding, classical music. *Address:* Diwan of the Royal Court, PO Box 632, Muscat 113, Sultanate of Oman. *Telephone:* 738711. *Fax:* 739427.

QADIR, Irfan; Pakistani lawyer and government official; served in numerous govt legal positions including Prosecutor-Gen. Nat. Accountability Bureau, Consultant (Legal Affairs), Pres.'s Secr., Sec. of Law, Justice and Parl. Affairs; Attorney-Gen. 2012–13; licence to practise law suspended by Supreme Court 2015; joined Pakistan Tehreek-e-Insaf (PTI) (Pakistan Movement for Justice) 2016.

QADRI, Muhammad Tahir-ul-, MA, LLB, PhD; Pakistani politician, scholar and fmr academic; *Founder and Chairman, Minhaj-ul-Quran International;* b. 19 Feb. 1951, Jhang; s. of Farida'd-Din al-Qadri; m. 1976; two c.; ed Univ. of the Punjab; started legal practice as advocate in dist courts of Jhang; Lecturer in Law, Univ. of the Punjab 1978–83, later Prof. of Int. Constitutional Law and Islamic Law; Founder-Chair., Minhaj-ul-Quran Int. 1981–; f. Pakistan Awami Tehreek (PAT) 1989; Opposition Leader 1989–93; mem. Nat. Ass. –2004 (resgnd); Founder and Chair., Bd of Govs, Minhaj Univ.; Founder, Minhaj Educ. Soc., Minhaj Welfare Foundation (also Chair.), Minhaj-ul-Qur'an Ullama Council, Minhaj-ul-Qur'an Women League, Minhaj Youth League, Mustafavi Students Movts, Muslim Christian Dialogue Forum; instrumental in Islamabad Long March Declaration 2013; Quaid-e-Azam Gold Medal 1971, Pakistan Cultural Gold Medal 1972, Qarshi Gold Medal 1984. *Publications include:* around 400 books. *Address:* Minhaj-ul-Quran International, 365 M, Model Town, Lahore, Pakistan (office). *Telephone:* (11) 1140140 (office). *E-mail:* tehreek@minhaj.org (office). *Website:* www.minhaj.org (office).

QAHTAN, Maj.-Gen. Abd al-Qader, MA, PhD; Yemeni academic and politician; b. 13 Dec. 1952, Taiz; Prof. of Public Law, Sana'a Univ. 1992–2011; Gen. Man. for security, Taiz 1992–96; Pres. Interpol – Sana'a 1996–2011; Minister of the Interior 2011–14.

QAHTANI, Sheikh; **Tareq Abdel Hadi Al-;** Saudi Arabian business executive; *Chairman, Abdel Hadi Abdullah Al-Qahtani Group of Companies;* Chair. Abdel Hadi Abdullah Al-Qahtani Group of Cos, activities involve petrochemicals, oil and gas sectors, manufacturing, contracting and services, insurance, travel, tourism, transportation and custom clearance, est. an office in Texas, USA 1970s, subsequently est. offices in Europe and elsewhere. *Address:* Abdel Hadi Abdullah Al-Qahtani & Sons Co., Al Qahtani Building, Street 9, Al Adami Area, PO Box 20, Dammam 31411, Saudi Arabia (office). *Telephone:* (3) 8261477 (office). *Fax:* (3) 8269894 (office). *E-mail:* info@ahqsons.com (office). *Website:* www.ahqsons.com (office).

QAISER, Asad, BA; Pakistani politician; *Speaker of National Assembly;* b. 15 Nov. 1968, Swabi Dist, Khyber Pakhtunkhwa; m.; two s., two d.; ed Univ. of Peshawar, Govt Post-Grad. Coll.; Coordinator, Kotha Coll. (as a Cand. of Islami Jamiat-e-Talaba) 1984–86; mem. Jamaat-e-Islami Pakistan (JI) –1996, Divisional Pres. Pasban (youth wing of JI) 1995–96; mem. Pakistan Tehreek-e-Insaf (PTI) 1996–, Pres. PTI Khyber Pakhtunkhwa 2008–13; mem. Prov. Ass. (Khyber Pakhtunkhwa constituency) 2013–18, Speaker of Prov. Ass. 2013–18; mem. Nat. Ass. (Swabi-I constituency) 2018–, Speaker 2018–. *Address:* National Assembly of Pakistan, Parliament House, Islamabad, Pakistan (office). *Telephone:* (51) 9221082 (office). *Fax:* (51) 9221106 (office). *E-mail:* speaker@na.gov.pk (office). *Website:* www.na.gov.pk.

QAMAR, Syed Naveed, BSc, MS, MBA; Pakistani politician; b. 22 Sept. 1955, Karachi; m.; one s. three d.; ed Univ. of Manchester, UK, California State Univ., USA; mem. Computer Science faculty, FAST-NU (then called FAST-ICS) 1988–89; sr mem. Pakistan People's Party, currently mem. Cen. Exec. Cttee; elected mem. Prov. Ass., Sindh 1988–90, mem. Nat. Ass. 1990–93, 1993–96, 1997–99, elected from NA-222 (Tando Muhammad Khan-cum-Hyderabad-cum-Badin) constituency in gen. elections 2008; Prov. Minister (Sindh) for Information 1990; Chair. Privatization Comm. 1993; apptd Fed. Minister for Finance and Privatization 1996, for Privatization and Investment (with additional charge of Finance, Revenue, Econ. Affairs and Statistics) 2008, for Petroleum and Natural Resources (with additional charge of Ministry of Privatization) 2009–11, for Privatization (with additional charge of Ministry of Water and Power) 2011, of Defence 2012–13. *Address:* National Assembly of Pakistan, A-305, Parliament Lodges, Islamabad (office); 14-F, Block 4, Kehkashan Clifton, Karachi, Pakistan (home). *Telephone:* (21) 5874751. *Fax:* (51) 9222118.

QÄMBÄR, İsa Yunis oğlu; Azerbaijani politician and historian; b. 24 Feb. 1957, Baku, Azerbaijan SSR, USSR; s. of Yunis Qämbärov and Tahira Qämbärov; m. Prof. Aida Bağırova 1986; two s.; ed Baku High School No. 62, Baku State Univ.; researcher, Azerbaijan Acad. of Sciences 1979–82, Inst. of Oriental Studies 1982–90; active participant in democratic movt in late 1980s, head of organizational div. of Popular Front 1990–, Deputy Chair. 1990–91; mem. Supreme Soviet of Azerbaijan 1990–95, Chair. Nat. Ass. (Milli Mäclis—Parl.) and Acting Pres. of Azerbaijan 1992–93 (resgnd); Chair. Comm. on Foreign Affairs 1991–92; Chair. Müsavat Partiyası (Equality Party) 1992–2015; Co-founder and Chair. Democratic Congress 1999, 2001–03; joined United Opposition Alliance 2002; presidential cand. 2003; played a major part in organizing demonstrations inspired by other protests throughout the Middle East, Spring 2011; 'A Friend of Journalists' Prize 2000. *Address:* Müsavat Partiyası (Equality Party), 1025 Baku, Därnagül qasabasi 30/97, Azerbaijan (office). *Telephone:* (12) 448-23-82 (office); (12) 461-15-00 (home). *Fax:* (12) 448-23-81 (office); (12) 498-31-66 (home). *E-mail:* info@musavat.org (office); isa.gambar@gmail.com (home). *Website:* isagambar.blogspot.com (office).

QANDIL, Hisham Mohamed, BEng, PhD; Egyptian water resources engineer and politician; b. 17 Sept. 1962, Beni Suef; m.; five d.; ed Univ. of Cairo, Utah State Univ., North Carolina State Univ., USA; began career with Nat. Water Research Centre, Ministry of Water Resources and Irrigation, becoming Chief of Staff for Minister of Water Resources 1999–2005; worked for ADB, Tunisia, becoming Chief Water Resources Engineer; Minister of Water Resources and Irrigation 2011–12; Prime Minister 2012–13 (dismissed); fmr Pres. African Ministers Council on Water; fmr Observer, Jt Egyptian–Sudanese Nile Water Authority; mem. Nile Basin Initiative Council of Ministers; Egyptian Order of the Repub., Second Class 1995; Presidential Award 1995.

QANUNI, Yunus; Afghan politician; *Leader, Hizb-i Afghanistan-i Naweem (New Afghanistan Party);* b. 1957, Panjshir Valley; ed Kabul Univ.; joined mujahidin troops fighting against Soviet occupation forces 1979–89; apptd Jt Minister of Defence 1993; co-f. Defence of the Motherland and United Nat. Islamic Front for the Salvation of Afghanistan (Unifsa–Northern Alliance) 1996; political head of NA's main Jamiat-i Islami party 2001; Leader, NA Del. to Future of Afghanistan Govt Talks, Bonn Nov. 2001; Minister of the Interior, Afghan Interim Authority Dec. 2001–02; Minister of Educ. 2002–04 (resgnd); apptd Head of Nizzat-i-Milli Party 2002; unsuccessful presidential cand. 2004; Founder and Leader Hizb-i Afghanistan-i Naween (New Afghanistan Party) 2005–; Chair. Nat. Understanding Front (opposition coalition) 2005; Speaker of Wolasi Jirga (House of Reps.) –2011; Vice-Pres. of Afghanistan March–Sept. 2014. *Address:* Hizb-i Afghanistan-i Naween (New Afghanistan Party), 1st Road, Khair Khana Phase One, Parwan Hotel Road, District 11, Kabul, Afghanistan (office). *Telephone:* 799342942 (mobile) (office).

QARABALİN, Uzaqbay Süleymenulı; Kazakhstani politician and government official; b. 14 Oct. 1947, Qosşağil village, Embi dist, Guriyev (now Atiraw) Oblast; ed Moscow Gubkin Inst. of Oil and Gas; tech. engineer in exploration of South Embi gas and oil fields 1973–74, head of labs of drilling technologies, Kazakh Research Inst. of Oil Geology and Prospecting 1974–81; Deputy Dir for Academic Work 1981–88; Head of Dept for Devt of Technological Progress and Deep Drilling, 'Prikaspiigeologiya' territorial management, Oral 1988–90; Chair. Guriyev br. of Kazakh Lenin Polytechnical Inst. 1990; Sr Officer, Dept of Industry in apparatus of Pres. and Cabinet of Ministers of Kazakhstan 1991–92; Head of Oil and Gas Dept, Ministry of Energy and Fuel Reserves 1992–94; Deputy Man. of Energy and Fuel Resources, Deputy Man. of the Oil and Gas Industry 1994–95; secondment to Agip, Italy 1995–97; Vice-Pres. for Corp. Devt, Dir for Devt of Prospecting, Vice-Pres. of Dept, first Vice-Pres. 'Kazakhoil' Oil & Gas Co. 1997–2000, Acting Pres. 'Kazakhoil' Aug.–Oct. 1999; Pres. 'KazTransGaz' Co. 2000–01; Deputy Minister of Energy and Mineral Resources 2001–03; Pres. 'KazMunaiGaz' Nat. Co. 2003–08; Pres. 'Mangistaumunaigaz' 2008–, Acting Gen. Dir 2008–09, Gen. Dir 2010–13; Minister of Oil and Gas 2013–14, First Deputy Minister of Energy 2014–16; Badge for excellence in exploring natural resources of the USSR 1998, Qurmet 2000, Leader of the Russian Economy 2005, Baris, Third Degree 2005; '10 Years of Constitution of Kazakhstan' 2005, '10 years of Parl. of Repub. of Kazakhstan' 2006, Award for Honoured Explorer of Natural Resources of Repub. of Kazakhstan 2003, Honoured Sportsman of Repub. of Kazakhstan 2007, awarded titles of 'Person of the Year' and 'Golden Prometheus', KazEnergy Eurasian Energy Forum 2009, 'Kazakstanyn Enbek Eri' Award 2011. *Publications:* more than 40 academic and literary works and publs, articles and books.

QARADAWI, Ilham Yousef al-, PhD, CPhys, FInstP; Qatari physicist and academic; *Professor of Nuclear Physics, Qatar University;* ed Univ. of London, UK; Teaching Asst, Physics Dept, Qatar Univ. 1981–84, Lecturer 1984–91, Assoc. Prof. 2003–08, Prof. of Physics 2009–; Asst Prof., Physics Dept, Univ. of Qatar 1991–2002; Research Fellow, Dept of Physics and Astronomy, Univ. Coll. London 1998–99; Adjunct Prof. of Physics, Texas A&M Univ. Qatar, Doha 2011–; Pres. Qatar Physics Soc.; Chevening Scholarship (UK) 1998, Merit Award for Excellence in Research, Univ. of Qatar 2004, honoured by Arab World Inst. (Institut du Monde Arabe), Paris 2005, Fellowship of the World Nuclear Univ. 2007, Ahmad Badeeb Prize for Arab Women in Science (Paris) 2008, Women Innovation in Science and Eng Leadership Program, US Dept of State 2011, Outstanding Contrib. to Science Award, CEO Middle East 2012. *Achievements include:* est. a positron lab and successfully built the first variable energy slow positron beam in the Middle East; has also est. a radiation measurement lab carrying out research in the area of environmental radiation physics. *Publications:* numerous papers in professional journals on positron physics and its applications, environmental nuclear and radiation physics, and recent trends in physics education. *Address:* Physics Department, Qatar University, PO Box 2713, Doha, Qatar (office). *Telephone:* 44034634 (office). *E-mail:* ilham@qu.edu.qa (office); ilham@ilhamalqaradawi.com. *Website:* www.ilhamalqaradawi.com.

QARASE, Laisenia, BCom; Fijian politician; b. 4 Feb. 1941; m.; four s. one d.; ed Ratu Kadavulevu School, Queen Victoria School, Suva Boys' Grammar School, Univ. of Auckland, NZ, British Co-operative Coll., UK, Auckland Tech. Inst.; exec. cadet, Fijian Affairs Bd 1959–66, financial adviser 1979–99; joined Civil Service 1967, Co-operative Officer 1, Co-operatives Dept 1967–68, Asst Registrar of Co-operatives 1969–70, Sr Asst Registrar 1971–72, Chief Asst Registrar 1973–75, Registrar 1976–78; Deputy Sec. of Finance 1978–79; Perm. Sec. for Commerce and Industry 1979–80; Sec. of the Public Service Comm. 1980–83; Prime Minister and Minister for Nat. Reconciliation and Unity July 2000–06 (resigned following Court of Appeal ruling that his Govt was illegal March 7th 2001, reappointed March 15th 2001, dismissed by Acting Pres. Commodore Voreqe Bainimarama in mil. takeover of Govt Dec. 2006), also fmrly Minister for Fijian Affairs, Culture and Heritage, Multi-Ethnic Affairs and Reform of the Sugar Industry; Founder and Leader, Social Democratic Liberal Party (fmrly Soqosoqo Duavata ni Lewenivanua) 2001–14; Man. Dir Fiji Devt Bank 1983–97, Merchant Bank of Fiji 1997–2000; Chair. South Pacific Fertilizers Ltd 1985–86, Fiji Post & Telecommunications Ltd 1990–91, Fiji TV Ltd 1994–98; Dir Fiji Int. Telecommunication Ltd (FINTEL) 1978–79, Foods Pacific Ltd 1985–86, Fiji Forest Industries Ltd 1988–97, Carlton Brewery (Fiji) Ltd 1989–99, Unit Trust of Fiji 1990–99, Voko Industries Ltd

1993–97, Air Pacific Ltd 1996–98, Colonial Advisory Council 1996–99; Chair. Mavanu Investments Ltd, Qalitu Enterprises Ltd; Dir Mualevu Tikina Holdings Ltd, Yatu Lau Co. Ltd; imprisoned following trial for abuse of office Aug. 2012 (served eight months in prison).

QASEM, Subhi, PhD; Jordanian agriculturalist, politician and academic; *Professor Emeritus, University of Jordan;* b. 9 May 1934, Palestine; ed Kansas State Univ., Univ. of Minnesota, USA; worked in Ministry of Agric.; Prof. of Agric., Univ. of Jordan, Dean Faculty of Grad. Studies 1986, Founding Dean Faculties of Sciences, Agric. and Grad. Studies, now Prof. Emer.; Minister of Agric. 1991; consultant in scientific and tech. educ., research and devt, agric. policy and the environment; Fellow Islamic Acad. of Sciences; Medal of the Kawkab (Star) Award, Istiqlal (Independence) Medal. *Address:* Villa No. 7, University District, Abdul Rahim Omar Street, Amman, Jordan (home). *Telephone:* (6) 5155200 (home).

QASIMI, Sheikha Lubna bint Khalid bin Sultan al-, BSc, MBA; United Arab Emirates information technology manager, business executive and government official; *President, Zayed University;* ed Al Zahra Secondary School, Sharjah, California State Univ., Chico, USA, American Univ. of Sharjah; computer programmer with Datamation 1981; fmr Dubai br. man. for Gen. Information Authority; Sr Man. Information Systems Dept, Dubai Ports Authority 1993–2000; apptd CEO Tejari.com (online business-to-business marketplace) 2000; headed Dubai e-Govt Exec. team responsible for instituting e-govt initiatives throughout public sector 2001; Minister of Economy and Planning (first woman minister) 2004, of Foreign Trade 2004–13, of Devt and Int. Co-operation 2013–16, Minister of State for Tolerance 2016–17; Pres. Zayed Univ. 2014–; mem. Bd of Dirs Dubai Chamber of Commerce and Industry, Dubai Autism Centre, Simsari.com; mem. Bd of Trustees Dubai Univ. Coll., Electronic-Total Quality Man. Coll., Thunderbird, American Grad. School of Int. Man., Phoenix, Ariz., Zayed Univ., UAE; volunteer for Friends of Cancer Patients' Soc.; Hon. Kentucky Col, Commonwealth of Kentucky 2003; Hon. mem. Bd of Dirs Nat. US-Arab Chamber of Commerce; Hon. DSc (California State Univ.); Distinguished Govt Employee Award 1999, Dubai Quality Group Award For Support to Leadership, Quality, and Change 2000, ITP Best Personal Achievement Award 2000, Datamatix IT Woman of the Year 2001, Business.com Personal Contribution Award 2001, Datamatix Outstanding Contrib. 2002, World Summit Award for .com 2003, UK House of Lords Special Entrepreneurship Award 2004. *Address:* Zayed University, PO Box 4783, Abu Dhabi, United Arab Emirates (office). *Telephone:* (2) 4434847 (office). *Website:* www.zu.ac.ae (office).

QASIMI, HH Sheikh Saud ibn Saqr al-, BSc; United Arab Emirates ruler; *Ruler of Ras al-Khaimah;* b. 10 Feb. 1956, Dubai; s. of Sheikh Saqr bin Mohammad al-Qasimi (fmr Ruler of Ras al-Khaimah); ed American Univ. of Beirut, Lebanon, Univ. of Michigan, USA; Chief of the Ruler's Court, Ras al-Khaimah 1979, named Crown Prince 14 June 2003, mem. Supreme Council and Ruler of Ras al-Khaimah 27 Oct. 2010–; Chair. Ras al-Khaimah Municipal Council 1986; f. Ras al-Khaimah Investment Authority 2005; Chancellor Ras al-Khaimah Medical and Health Sciences Univ.; Dr hc (Univ. of Bolton–Ras al-Khaimah) 2010. *Address:* The Ruler's Palace, Ras al-Khaimah, United Arab Emirates (office).

QASIMI, HH Sheikh Sultan bin Muhammad al-, (Ruler of Sharjah), PhD; United Arab Emirates; b. 1 July 1939, Sharjah, Trucial States; m. Sheikha Jawaher bint Mohammed al-Qasimi; two s. (one deceased) several d.; ed Cairo Univ., Univ. of Exeter and Durham Univ., UK; Minister of Educ., UAE 1972; Ruler of Sharjah 1972–; Pres. American Univ. of Sharjah 1997–, Univ. of Sharjah 1997–, Prof. of Modern History of the Gulf 1999–; Visiting Prof., Univ. of Exeter 1998, Cairo Univ. 2008; Chair. Sharjah Human Soc., Arab/African Symposium; mem. Arab Historians Union; Fellow, Durham Univ.; Hon. Fellow, Centre for Middle Eastern and Islamic Studies 1992, Royal Coll. of Surgeons of England 2009; Hon. Pres. Egyptian Asscn for the Study of History 2001, Islamic Int. Org. for the History of Sciences 2008, Soc. of Arab Astronomy and Space Sciences 2008, Arab Theatre Inst. 2008, Union of Arab Univs 2009; Hon. DSc (Univ. of Agric., Faisalabad) 1983; Hon. LLD (Khartoum) 1986, (South Bank Univ., London) 2003, (McMaster Univ., Canada) 2004; Hon. PhD (Int. Islamic Univ. of Malaysia) 2001, (Univ. of Tübingen, Germany) 2006; Hon. Dr in Admin (Univ. of Jordan) 2008; Hon. Dr in Arts (Univ. of Sheffield) 2008; Hon. DHumLitt (American Univ. in Cairo) 2009, (Univ. of Paris Diderot) 2012; Hon. DPolSci (Hanyang Univ., Seoul) 2011; Dr hc (Univ. of Exeter) 1993, (Acad. of Russian Studies, Moscow) 1995, (Univ. of Edinburgh) 2001, (Armenian Acad. of Science) 2005, (Kanazawa Univ., Japan) 2010; Distinguished Personality Prize, Univ. of Exeter 1993, Zaid Medal for The President Merit Award for Culture, Arts and Literature (Abu Dhabi) 2012, and numerous awards. *Publications include:* The Myth of Arab Piracy in the Gulf 1986, The Division of the Omani Empire (1856–1862) 1989, The British Occupation of Aden 1990, Arab Omani Documents in the French Archives Centre 1993, Omani–French Relations (1715–1905) 1994, The White Shaikh 1996, The Rebel Prince 1998, The Return of Holako (play) 1998, Power Struggles and Trade in the Gulf (1620–1820) 1999, The Gulf in Historic Maps (1478–1861) 1999, Theatre International Day Message 2007, The Correspondence of the Sultans of Zanzibar 2012, Al Qwasim Wal Al Udwan Al Britani 2012. *Leisure interest:* reading. *Address:* Ruler's Palace, Sharjah, United Arab Emirates.

QASIMOV, Gen. Qalmuxanbet Nurmuxanbetulı; Kazakhstani army officer and government official; b. 18 May 1957, Dmitrievka, Ili Dist, Almatı Oblast, Kazakh SSR, USSR; m.; three c.; ed Kazakh State Univ.; Investigator, Sr Investigator, Head of Investigation Dept, Deputy Chief ATC, ATS Ili Dist, Almatı 1979–88, Deputy Head of Public Order ATC, Almatı Oblast 1988–89; Head of Police Dept, Kapchagai, Almatı Oblast 1989–92, Head of Criminal Police, Deputy Chief of Police, Almatı Oblast 1992–97; Head of Criminal Police, Ministry of Internal Affairs March–July 1997, Head of Main Dept of Internal Affairs of Almatı 1997–2003, Head of Main Dept of Internal Affairs, Dept of Internal Affairs, Almatı Oblast 2003–05; First Deputy Minister, Deputy Minister of Internal Affairs 2005–09; Head of Dept of Internal Affairs, Eastern Kazakhstan Oblast 2009–11; Minister of Internal Affairs 2011–19; Maj.-Gen. of the Militia; several state decorations and medals, including 'Dank' Order of Second Degree, Astana Medal, Honoured Worker of Internal Affairs Badge. *Address:* c/o Ministry of Internal Affairs, 010000 Nur-Sultan, Tauelsizdik d-ly 1, Kazakhstan.

QASSEM, Sheikh Naim; Lebanese politician; *Deputy Secretary-General, Hezbollah;* b. 1953, Kfar-Fila; fmr Prof. of Chem.; Head, Asscn for Islamic Religious Educ. 1974–88; Founding mem. Hezbollah (Party of God) 1982, Deputy Sec.-Gen. 1991–. *Publication:* Hizbullah: The Story from Within 2005. *E-mail:* info@moqawama.net. *Website:* www.moqawama.org.

QASSEMI, HH Sheikh Sultan Sooud al-, BSc, MA; United Arab Emirates business executive and political commentator; ed European Business School, London, American Univ. of Paris; Founder and Chair. Barjeel Geojit Securities 2001–; Man. Dir Al-Saud Co. Ltd 1998–; Lecturer in Middle Eastern History and Entrepreneurship, Dubai Men's Coll.; non-resident Fellow, Dubai School of Govt 2009–; Columnist The National (English language newspaper, Abu Dhabi) 2008–; widely recognised for posts on Twitter; columns have appeared in The New York Times, Financial Times, Foreign Policy, Open Democracy, the Independent, the Guardian and Gulf News; Founder Barjeel Art Foundation 2010; Sheikh Rashid Award for Academic Excellence 2006, Patrons of the Arts Award, Dubai Culture 2010. *Address:* Barjeel Geojit Securities LLC, PO Box 32313, Suite No #403, United Bank Ltd Building, Bank Street, Bur Dubai, Dubai, United Arab Emirates (office). *Telephone:* (4) 3555900 (office). *Fax:* (4) 3555903 (office). *E-mail:* dubai@barjeel.ae (office). *Website:* www.barjeel.ae (office); sultanalqassemi.com/Sultan_Sooud_Al_Qassemi.

QASSIS, Nabil, PhD; Palestinian physicist, academic and politician; b. 1945; ed Mainz Univ., Germany, American Univ. of Beirut; worked in France and Italy 1972–80, returned to Palestine 1980; Prof. of Theoretical Physics, Birzeit Univ., Ramallah 1982–, Chair. Dept of Physics 1982–84, Univ. Vice-Pres. for Academic Affairs 1984–89; sr mem. of Palestinian dels to several sets of negotiations, including Madrid Conf. 1991–93, Deputy Head of del. to Washington talks 1993–94, mem. perm. status negotiating team 1999; frequent participant in unofficial negotiations with Israeli leaders, including at Harvard Univ. Jt Working Group on the right of return 1998, in South Africa 2002, Stafford, UK 2002; Co-founder Palestine Econ. Research and Policy Inst. 1996, Dir 1996–98; Minister and Coordinator-Gen., Bethlehem 2000 project 1998–; Chair. Yasser Arafat Foundation –2012; Minister of Finance 2012–13 (resgnd).

QAYYUM, Malik Muhammad; Pakistani lawyer, judge and government official; b. 18 Dec. 1944; s. of Justice Muhammad Akram; Sr Advocate, Supreme Court; began career as legal practitioner 1964; elected Sec., Bar Asscn, Lahore 1970, Pres. Dist Bar Asscn, Lahore 1980; mem. Punjab Bar Council 1984–88; Deputy Attorney-Gen. of Pakistan 1984–88; Judge, Lahore High Court 1988–2001 (resgnd); Attorney-Gen. of Pakistan 2007–08; mem. Pakistan Law Comm.; Chief Ed. Pakistan Supreme Court Cases.

QAZIXANOV, Erjan, PhD; Kazakhstani diplomatist and politician; *Ambassador to USA;* b. 21 Aug. 1964; m.; two c.; ed St Petersburg State Univ.; Second Sec., later First Sec., Protocol-Political Div., Ministry of Foreign Affairs 1989–92, Head of Div., Deputy Chief of State Protocol Service 1992–95; First Sec. and Counsellor, Perm. Mission of Kazakhstan to UN, New York 1995–2000; Dir Dept of Multilateral Cooperation, Ministry of Foreign Affairs 2000–03; Amb. and Perm. Rep. to UN 2003–07 (also accred as Amb. to Cuba); Asst to Pres. of Kazakhstan Feb.–Dec. 2008; Amb. to Austria and Perm. Rep. to the Int. Orgs, Vienna 2009–11; Deputy Minister of Foreign Affairs Feb.–April 2011; Minister of Foreign Affairs 2011–12; Asst to Pres. 2012–14; Amb. to UK 2014–17, to USA 2017–; Chair. OIC Conf. 2011; Medals 'For Valorous Work' 2005, '10 Years of Independence of the Repub. of Kazakhstan' 2001, '10 Years of the Constitution of Kazakhstan' 2005, '10 Years of the Parl. of the Repub. of Kazakhstan' 2006, '10 Years of Astana' 2008. *Publications:* numerous articles and publs in Kazakh and foreign periodicals on multilateral diplomacy issues and the UN. *Address:* Embassy of Kazakhstan, 1401 16th Street, NW, Washington, DC 20036, USA. *E-mail:* washington@mfa.kz. *Website:* www.kazakhembus.com.

QI, Huaiyuan; Chinese diplomatist and state official; b. 1930, Ezhou City, Hubei Prov.; ed North China People's Univ., Harbin Foreign Languages Coll.; joined CCP 1948; Counsellor, Chinese Embassy, Bonn, FRG 1974–77; Dir-Gen. Information Dept, Ministry of Foreign Affairs –1984 Asst to Minister of Foreign Affairs 1984–86, Vice-Minister of Foreign Affairs 1986–91, Dir Foreign Affairs Office of State Council 1991–94; Alt. mem. 13th CCP Cen. Cttee 1987–92, mem. 14th CCP Cen. Cttee 1992–97; Del., 15th CCP Nat. Congress 1997–2002; Pres. Chinese People's Asscn for Friendship with Foreign Countries (CPAFFC) 1994–2000; mem. Standing Cttee, 9th Nat. Cttee of CPPCC 1998–2003, Vice-Chair. Foreign Affairs Sub-cttee 1998–2003. *Address:* c/oMinistry of Foreign Affairs, 2 Chaoyangmen Nandajie, Chaoyang Qu, Beijing 100701, People's Republic of China.

QI, Zhala, (Che Dalha); Chinese (Tibetan) government official; *Governor, Tibet Autonomous Region;* b. Aug. 1958, Zhongdian County (Shangri-La), Yunnan Prov.; ed CCP Central Party School; joined CCP 1982; served in different positions in Yunnan Prov. including Deputy Sec., Zhongdian County Communist Youth League, CCP Chief, mem. Standing Cttee and Gov., People's Govt, Diqing Tibetan Autonomous Prefecture; relocated to Lhasa, becoming Head, CCP United Front Works Dept, Tibet Autonomous Region 2010, Sec.-Gen, Tibet Autonomous Region CCP 2010, CCP Party Sec., Lhasa municipality 2011, Deputy Sec., Tibet Autonomous Region CCP 2016–17; Gov., Tibet Autonomous Region 2017–. *Address:* Tibet Autonomous Region People's Congress, 85000 Lhasa, Tibet, People's Republic of China (office).

QIAN, Guanlin; Chinese politician; b. Oct. 1946, Funing, Jiangsu Prov.; ed Shanghai Foreign Trade Inst.; joined CCP 1973; Deputy Head, Customs Dept, Guangzhou City, Guangdong Prov. 1984–86; Deputy Dir, later Dir Prov. Br., Gen. Admin of Customs, Guangdong Prov. 1987–90; Deputy Dir-Gen. Admin of Customs 1990–93, Dir 1993–2001; Deputy Dir Nat. Narcotics Control Comm. 1993–2001; Deputy Dir State Admin of Taxation 2001–12 (Deputy Sec. CCP Leading Party Group); mem. CCP 14th Cen. Cttee for Discipline Inspection 1992–97, Alt. mem. CCP 15th Cen. Cttee 1997–2002.

QIAN, Gen. Guoliang; Chinese army officer; b. 1940, Wujiang, Jiangsu Prov.; ed Mil. Acad. of the Chinese PLA; joined PLA 1958, CCP 1960; Squad Leader, Combat Training Section, Army (or Ground Force), PLA Services and Arms, Staff Officer and Deputy Section Chief 1966, Div. Commdr, PLA 1979–83, Chief of Staff, Army (or Ground Force) 1983–85, Commdr Group Army 1985; rank of Maj.-Gen.

1988–95, Lt-Gen. 1995–2002, Gen. 2002–; Chief of Staff, PLA Jinan Mil. Region 1993–96; Deputy Mil. Region C-in-C 1996, C-in-C 1996–99 (Deputy Sec. CCP Party Cttee); C-in-C PLA Shenyang Mil. Region 1999–2004; Alt. mem. 13th CCP Cen. Cttee 1987–92, 14th CCP Cen. Cttee 1992–97, mem. 15th CCP Cen. Cttee 1997–2002, 16th CCP Cen. Cttee 2002–07.

QIAN, Gen. Shugen; Chinese army officer; b. Feb. 1939, Wuxi City, Jiangsu Prov.; ed Chongqing Artillery School, PLA Mil. Acad. and Univ. of Nat. Defence; mem. CCP 1956–; entered army 1954; Deputy Div. Commdr 47th Army 1981; Div. Commdr 139th Div. 1983; Deputy Army Commdr 47th Army 1984; Army Commdr 47th Group Army 1985; Chief of Staff, Lanzhou Mil. Region 1992; Deputy Political Commissar, Lanzhou Mil. Region 1993; rank of Lt-Gen. 1993; Asst to Chief of Gen. Staff 1994; Deputy Chief, PLA Gen. Staff 1995; rank of Gen. 2000; Alt. mem. 13th CCP Cen. Cttee 1987–92, 14th CCP Cen. Cttee 1992–97, mem. 15th CCP Cen. Cttee 1997–2002, 16th CCP Cen. Cttee 2002–07.

QIAN, Yi, BS, MS; Chinese environmental scientist and academic; *Professor, Department of Environmental Science and Engineering, Tsinghua University;* b. 1936, Suzhou, Jiangsu Prov.; d. of Qian Mu; ed Tongji Univ., Shanghai, Tsinghua Univ., Beijing; Teaching Asst, Dept of Civil Eng, Tsinghua Univ. 1959–65, Lecturer, Dept of Environmental Eng 1965–79, Assoc. Prof., Dept of Environmental Science and Eng 1979–87, Prof. 1987–; Visiting Prof., Dept of Civil Eng, Cornell Univ. 1981–83, Delft Univ. of Tech. 1988–89, Hong Kong Univ. of Science and Tech. 1996; Distinguished Lecturer of US-China of Fulbright Program at various educational Insts. including Yale and Harvard University May–June 2000; Dir State Key Jt Lab. of Environmental Simulation and Pollution Control; science consultant, Environmental Protection Comm. of State Council; Vice-Chair. Gen. Cttee of ICSU; Vice-Chair. Eng and Environment Cttee of the World Fed. of Eng Orgs; Deputy, 7th NPC 1988–93, mem. Standing Cttee 8th NPC 1993–98, 9th NPC 1998–2003, Vice-Chair. Cttee of Environment and Resource Protection; mem. Exec. Cttee All-China Women's Fed. 1993; mem. Chinese Acad. of Eng 1994–; Nat. Science and Tech. Advancement Award (2nd Class), State Educ. Comm. Science and Tech. Advancement Award (1st Class) 1987, 2nd Award of Nat. Science and Tech. Progress 2003. *Publications:* Modern Wastewater Treatment Technology; The Prevention and Control of Industrial Environmental Pollution; Water Pollution Volume of Environmental Engineering Handbook; more than 100 research papers. *Address:* Department of Environmental Science and Engineering, Tsinghua University, Beijing 100084, People's Republic of China (office). *Telephone:* (10) 62784453 (office). *E-mail:* qiany@tsinghua.edu.cn (office). *Website:* www.tsinghua.edu.cn (office).

QIAN, Yongchang; Chinese politician; *President, China Communication & Transportation Association;* b. 1933, Shanghai City; joined CCP 1953; Vice-Minister of Communications 1982–84, Minister 1984–91; Chair. Bd of Dirs, Hong Kong China Merchants Group 1985–; fmr Chair. China Ocean Shipping Co. (COSCO); Pres. China Communications and Transportation Asscn; Alt. mem. 12th Cen. Cttee CCP 1982–87, mem. 13th Cen. Cttee 1987–92. *Address:* China Communication & Transportation Association, Beijing, People's Republic of China (office).

QIAN, Yunlu; Chinese politician (retd); b. Oct. 1944, Dawu Co., Hubei Prov.; ed Hubei Univ.; joined CCP 1965; sent to do manual labour, Sanli Commune 1968–70; Sec. Publicity Dept, CCP Dawu Co. Cttee, Hubei Prov. 1970–73, later Deputy Sec. Co. Cttee; Sec. Org. Dept CCP Xiaogan Prefectural Cttee, Hubei Prov. 1970–73; fmr Sec. CCP Party Cttee, Xinhe People's Commune, Hanchuan Co., Hubei Prov., later Deputy Sec. CCP Co. Cttee; fmr Magistrate, Dawu Co. (Dist) People's Court; Sec. CCP Communist Youth League Hubei Prov. Cttee 1973–83; Deputy Sec. CCP Hubei Prov. Cttee and mem. Standing Cttee 1983–91; Sec. CCP Wuhan City Cttee 1991–95; Chair. Hubei Prov. Cttee CPPCC 1995–98; Vice-Gov. Guizhou Prov. 1998–99, Gov. 1999–2001; Deputy Sec. CCP Guizhou Prov. Cttee 1998–2000, Sec. 2000–05; Chair. Standing Cttee Guizhou Prov. People's Congress 2003–05; Sec., CCP Heilongjiang Prov. Cttee 2005–08; Alt. mem. 14th CCP Cen. Cttee 1992–97, 15th CCP Cen. Cttee 1992–97, mem. 16th CCP Cen. Cttee 2002–07, 17th CCP Cen. Cttee 2007–12; Sec.-Gen. 11th CPPCC Nat. Cttee 2008–13 (retd). *Address:* c/o Guizhou Provincial People's Congress, Guiyang, Guizhou Province, People's Republic of China.

QIAN, Zhengying; Chinese engineer and government official; b. 1923, Jiaxing Co., Zhejiang Prov.; m. Huang Xinbai; ed Dadong Univ., Shanghai; joined CCP 1941; Section Chief, Water Conservancy Bureau (Jiangsu-Anhui Border Regional Govt) 1945–48; Dir Front Eng Div., Dept of Army Service Station (E China Mil. Command) 1945–48; Sec. and Deputy Dir Yellow River Man. Bureau, Shandong Prov. 1948–50; Deputy Head, E China Mil. Admin. Cttee, Dept of Water Conservancy 1949; Deputy Head, Cttee for Harnessing Huaihe River 1950–52; Vice-Minister of Water Conservancy 1952–67, Minister of Water Conservancy and Electrical Power 1970–88; Adviser to State Council 1981–82, mem. 1982–; Vice-Chair. CCP Nat. Comm., Chair. Women, Youth and Legal Affairs Cttee; Adviser to State Flood Control HQ 1988–; mem. 10th Cen. Cttee of CCP 1972–77, 11th Cen. Cttee of CCP 1977–82, 12th Cen. Cttee 1982–87, 13th Cen. Cttee 1987–92, 14th Cen. Cttee 1992–97; Vice-Chair. 7th CPPCC Nat. Cttee 1988–93, 8th CPPCC Nat. Cttee 1993–98, 9th CPPCC Nat. Cttee 1998–2003; Pres. Red Cross Soc. of China 1994–, China-India Friendship Asscn, China Award Foundation for Teachers of Middle and Primary Schools and Kindergartens; Dr hc (Univ. of Hong Kong) 2004; Gold Medal (Somalia), China Eng Science and Tech. Prize 2000.

QIAO, Baoping, BA; Chinese economist and business executive; *Chairman, China Guodian Corporation;* ed Nankai Univ., Party School of CCP Cen. Cttee; fmr Deputy Sec.-Gen. All-China Students Fed. and Deputy Dir of Gen. Office of All-China Students Fed.; Man. Dir Standing Cttee and Org. Dept at Cen. Cttee of Communist Youth League 1998–2000; Man. Dir Mass Work Dept of Cen. Work for Cen. Govt-led Enterprises 2000–03, Sec. of Cttee of Communist Youth League for Cen. Govt-led Enterprises; Man. Dir Mass Work Bureau and United Front Work Dept of SASAC 2003–05; Disciplinary Officer/Chief of Discipline Inspection Group, China Power Investment Corpn 2005–08; fmr Deputy Gen. Man. and Party Sec., China Guodian Group, Exec. Vice-Pres. China Guodian Corpn –2013, Chair. 2013–; Supervisor, China Longyuan Power Group Corpn Ltd 2011–13, Chief Supervisor of 2012–13, Chair. Bd of Supervisors 2013–; Chair. Bd of Supervisors, Guodian Technology and Environment Group Corpn Ltd 2011–13; fmr mem. Exec. Cttee China Power Investment Corpn. *Address:* China Guodian Corporation, 6–8 Fuchengmen Bei Street, Beijing 100034, People's Republic of China (office). *Telephone:* (10) 58682000 (office). *Fax:* (10) 58553900 (office). *E-mail:* cgdcb@cgdc.com.cn (office). *Website:* www.cgdc.com.cn (office).

QIAO, Shibo, BA; Chinese business executive; ed Jilin Univ.; worked as section dir in Ministry of Foreign Trade and Econ. Co-operation (MOFTEC, now the Ministry of Commerce); joined China Resources (Holdings) Co. Ltd 1992, Man. Dir and also Pres. China Resources Nat. Corpn –2016, also Chair. and Exec. Dir China Resources Enterprise Ltd, CEO China Resources Medications Group Ltd; Vice-Chair. China Vanke Co. Ltd. *Address:* c/o China Resources (Holdings) Co. Ltd, Floor 49, CRC Building, 26 Harbour Road, Wanchai, Hong Kong Special Administrative Region, People's Republic of China. *E-mail:* crc@crc.com.hk.

QIAO, Shiguang; Chinese artist; b. 5 Feb. 1937, Guantao Co., Hebei Prov.; s. of Qiao Lu De and Wang Hao Ling; m. Luo Zhen Ru 1961; two d.; Prof., Cen. Acad. of Arts and Design; Founder-Chair. Chinese Soc. of Lacquer Painting 1990 (group exhbn, Beijing 1990); Dir Chinese Artists Asscn; Dir Int. Culture of Lacquer 1992–; Founder Korea-China Lacquer Art Exchange Exhbn, Seoul 1994. *Publications:* Selected Lacquer Paintings of Qiao Shiguang 1993, The Skill and Artistic Expression of Lacquer Painting 1995, Collection of Qiao Shiguang's Lacquer Paintings 1996. *Leisure interests:* calligraphy, writing poetry. *Address:* QIAO Gallery, Seven Star Street, 798 Art Zone Jiuxianqiao Rd.4, Chaoyang District, Beijing 100015 (office); 3 602 Building, 6 Hong Miao Bei Li, Chao Yang District, Beijing 100025, People's Republic of China (home).

QIN, Jiaming; Chinese railway executive; b. 1945, Guilin, Guangxi Prov.; ed Changsha Railway Univ.; fmr Dir-Gen. China Railway Construction Soc. and Vice-Pres. China Construction Enterprise Man. Asscn; Second Sec., Eng Bureau, Ministry of Railways 1975–78, Deputy Chief, Electrification Eng Bureau 1978–84; Commdr, China Railway Eng Corpn 1995–96, apptd Pres. 2006; Ministry of Railways Educ. Medal 1989, Henan Provincial Award for Excellent Constructors 1990, Ministry of Railways Excellent Zhigong-Zhi-You 1997, Ministry of Railways Huo-Che-Tou (Locomotive) Medal 1998, State Award for Excellent Constructors 1999.

QIN, Wencai; Chinese energy industry executive; b. Feb. 1925, Shanxi; s. of Qin Wanrong and Qin Wangshi; m. Zhang Huang 1950; one s. three d.; Vice-Minister, Minister of Petroleum Industry 1979–82; Pres. China Nat. Offshore Oil Corpn 1982–87; apptd Chair. Consultative Cttee 1987; Chair. Capital Entrepreneurs Club 1991–2001, now consultant; Consultant and Vice-Chair. China Entreprises Man. Asscn 1991–2003. *Publications include:* Facts About China National Offshore Oil Corporation, Oil People in the Chinese Petroleum Industry, A Century's Journey in the China Sea, Oil People in CNOOC, Oil People in Yumen. *Leisure interests:* reading, sports.

QIN, Xiao, PhD; Chinese business executive and banker (retd); *Chairman, Boyuan Foundation;* b. 25 April 1947; ed Shanxi Mining Inst., China Univ. of Mining and Tech., Univ. of Cambridge, UK; joined China Int. Trust and Investment Corpn (CITIC) 1986, becoming Vice-Pres. 1994–95, Pres. 1995, Vice-Chair., fmr Deputy Party Sec. and Chair. CITIC Industrial Bank; Chair. China Merchants Group 2001–10, China Merchants Bank Co. Ltd 2001–10 (retd); Chair. Boyuan Foundation 2010–; Chair. Hong Kong Chinese Enterprises Asscn; mem. Toyota Int. Advisory Bd, Asia Business Council; Adviser and Sr Research Fellow, Hong Kong and Macao Research Inst. of State Council Devt and Research Centre; Guest Prof., School of Econs and Man., Tsinghua Univ. and Grad. School of the People's Bank of China; mem. 10th CPPCC; Deputy, 16th Nat. Congress of CCP 2002–07; Rep. 9th NPC 1998–2003; mem. 10th Nat. Cttee CPPCC, 11th Nat. Cttee CPPCC; adviser on Foreign Currency Policy of State Admin of Foreign Exchange. *Publications:* several papers and books in the fields of economics and management. *Address:* Boyuan Foundation, Hong Kong Special Administrative Region, People's Republic of China (office). *E-mail:* info@boyuan.hk (office). *Website:* www.boyuan.hk (office).

QIRBI, Abu Bakr Abdallah al-, BSc, MB, ChB, FRCP, FRCPath, FRCP (C); Yemeni medical consultant and politician; b. 6 June 1941, Aden; s. of Abdulla al-Qirbi and Fatoom al-Qirbi; m.; two s.; ed Aden Coll.; Edinburgh Univ. and Univ. of London, UK; Prof. of Clinical Pathology, San'a Univ., Dean Faculty of Science 1979–83, Faculty of Medicine 1982–87, Univ. Vice-Rector 1982–83; Minister of Educ. 1993–94; mem. Consultative Council 1997–2001; Minister of Foreign Affairs 2001–14, 2016 (in the al-Houthi Govt of Abd al-Aziz bin Habtour), of Immigrants' Affairs 2006–07; Chair. People's Charitable Soc. 1995; has made several radio and TV programmes on educ., scientific research, non-governmental work, charity and medical topics; Yemen Unification Medal; WHO Scholarship for Postgraduate Study. *Publications:* author of book on political and devt issues in Yemen; more than 40 papers on the biological effects of clinical chemistry, renal disease, gastro-intestinal diseases and numerous papers on politics and social affairs. *Leisure interests:* tennis, billiards, swimming.

QIU, Bojun; Chinese business executive; b. 1964, Hebei Prov.; ed Univ. of Science and Tech. for Nat. Defence; developed Chinese word-processing system WPS; f. Kingsoft Corpn 1988, Dir 1988–, est. Zhuhai Kingsoft Computer Co. Ltd 1993; designed and developed Pangu Office System 1994, WPS97 Chinese processing system 1997; received funds from Legend and reconstructed Kingsoft 1998, establishing two e-commerce websites www.joyo.com and www.xoyow.myrice.com 2000; fmr Chair. Zhuhai Jinshan Computer Co. Ltd. *Publications:* A WPS Course, WPS User Guide.

QIU, Guohong; Chinese diplomatist; *Ambassador to Republic of Korea;* b. Dec. 1957, Shanghai; ed Shanghai Int. Studies Univ.; assigned to Ministry of Foreign Affairs (MFA), stationed in Embassy in Tokyo for 20 years, Deputy Dir of Asian Affairs, MFA, Amb. to Nepal 2008–11, Dir of Security Affairs, MFA 2011–14 Amb. to Repub. of Korea 2014–. *Address:* Embassy of the People's Republic of China, 54 Hyoja-dong, Jongno-gu, Seoul 110-033, Republic of Korea (office). *Telephone:* (2) 738-1038 (office). *Fax:* (2) 738-1046 (office). *E-mail:* chinaemb_kr@mfa.gov.cn (office). *Website:* www.chinaemb.or.kr (office).

QIU, Xiaoqi; Chinese diplomatist; *Ambassador to Mexico;* m.; one s.; Officer, Dept of American and Oceanian Affairs, Ministry of Foreign Affairs (MFA) 1979–82, Officer, Attaché and Third Sec., Embassy in Havana 1982–86, Third Sec. and

Deputy Dir, Dept of Directorate Gen. of American and Oceanian Affairs, MFA 1986–89, Second Sec., then Sec., Embassy in Lima 1989–91, First Sec. and Deputy Head of Dept of Directorate Gen. for Latin America and the Caribbean, MFA 1991–93, Counsellor, Embassy in Santiago, Chile 1993–96, Amb. to Bolivia 1996–98, Deputy Dir-Gen. for Latin America and the Caribbean, MFA 1998–2000, Dir-Gen. for Latin America and the Caribbean 2000–02, Amb. to Spain (also accred to Andorra) 2002–08, to Brazil 2008–11, Amb. of MFA 2011–13, Amb. to Mexico 2013–. *Address:* Embassy of China, Avenida Rio Magdalena 172, Col. Tizapan San, Angel, Mexico City, DF 01090, Mexico (office). *Telephone:* (55) 5616-0609 (office). *Fax:* (55) 5616-5849 (office). *E-mail:* chinaemb_mx@mfa.gov.cn (office). *Website:* mx.china-embassy.org (office).

QU, Xing, BA, MA, PhD; Chinese political scientist and diplomatist; *President, China Institute of International Studies;* b. May 1956; ed Beijing Foreign Studies Univ., China Foreign Affairs Univ., Inst. of Political Studies, Paris, France; teacher at China Foreign Affairs Univ. 1985–, Vice-Pres. 1995–2006; fmr Dir Teaching and Research Section, Dept of Diplomacy, fmr Deputy Dean; Minister, Embassy in Paris 2006–09; Pres. China Inst. of Int. Studies 2010–. *Publications include:* A Diplomatic History of China 1979–1994 1995, Diplomacy of the Contemporary China 1997, New Dimensions of China's Diplomacy 1998, The Art of Diplomacy of Deng Xiaoping 1999, 50 Years of China's Diplomacy 2000, Le temps de soupecon, relations franco-chinoises 1949–1955 2006, China's Diplomacy in Decades of Reform and Opening to the Outside World 1978–2008 2008; numerous articles. *Address:* China Institute of International Studies, 3 Toutiao, Taijichang, Beijing 100005, People's Republic of China (office). *Telephone:* (10) 85119547 (office). *Fax:* (10) 65123744 (office). *E-mail:* info@ciis.org.cn (office). *Website:* www.ciis.org.cn (office).

QUADEN, Baron; Guy, PhD; Belgian economist and banker; b. 5 Aug. 1945, Liège; ed Univ. of Liège, Univ. of Paris (Sorbonne), France; Prof. of Econs, Univ. of Liège 1978–; Pres. High Council for Econ. Affairs 1984–88; Exec. Dir Nat. Bank of Belgium 1988–99, Gov. 1999–2011, now Hon. Gov.; Belgian Govt Gen. Commr for the Euro 1996–99; mem. Governing Council, European Cen. Bank 1999–2011; Officier, Légion d'honneur 2001. *Publications include:* Le budget de l'état belge 1980, La crise des finances publiques 1984, L'économie belge dans la crise 1987, Politique économique 1991. *Leisure interests:* soccer, modern art. *E-mail:* pressoffice@nbb.be (office).

QUADRIO CURZIO, Alberto, PhD; Italian economist and professor of political economy; *Professor Emeritus of Political Economy of Institutions, Università Cattolica del Sacro Cuore, Milan;* b. 25 Dec. 1937, Tirano-Valtellina; ed Faculty of Political Sciences, Catholic Univ., Milan, St John's Coll., Cambridge, UK; Assoc. Prof. of Econs, Univ. of Cagliari 1965–68; Assoc. Prof. of Econs, Univ. of Bologna 1968–72, Prof. 1972–75, Chair., Faculty of Political Sciences 1974–75; Prof. of Econs, Università Cattolica del Sacro Cuore, Milan 1976–2010, apptd Prof. of Political Economy of Insts 2010, now Prof. Emer., Dir Centre of Econ. Analysis 1977–2010, Chair. Faculty of Political Sciences 1989–2010, Pres. Scientific Bd, Centre of Econ. Analysis 2010–; Distinguished Academic Visitor, Queens' Coll., Cambridge and Visiting Research Fellow, Centre for Financial Analysis and Policy, Judge Business School, Cambridge, UK 2010–11; Dir Economia Politica – Journal of Analytical and Institutional Economics (quarterly review) 1984–; mem. Italian Nat. Research Council 1977–88; Pres. Italian Econs Asscn 1995–98, Bd for Donato Menichella scholarships, Bank of Italy 2004–07, Scientific Bd for Paolo Baffi Lectures, Bank of Italy 2003–07, Centesimus Annus Foundation 2003–17; Pres. Accad. Naz. dei Lincei 2015–18, now Pres. Emer.; mem. Reflection Group on Spiritual and Cultural Dimension of Europe est. by Pres. of EC 2002–04, Bd for European Investment Bank Prize 1995–2000; has delivered lectures at many Italian and foreign univs; speaker at many confs and seminars in Italy and abroad; mem. Istituto Lombardo-Accad. di Scienze e Lettere; Kt Grand Cross of the First Class of the Order of St Gregory the Great 2014, Kt of the Order of Pope Pius XI 2017; St Vincent Award 1984, W. Tobagi Award 1996, Cortina Ulisse Int. Award 1997, Gold Medal for contribs to Science and Culture, Pres. of Italian Repub. 2000, Capri-San Michele for Econs 2003, Targa alla coerenza Zoli Foundation 2004, Cardano-Beccaria Int. Prize Rotary Pavia 2004, Associazione Nuova Spoleto Award for Economy 2005, Economia Internazionale Chamber of Commerce and Univ. of Genoa 2009, Canova Award 2010, Gozzo d'Argento Int. Prize (with R. Prodi) 2011, Scanno Prize for Economy 2011, Gold Medal "Ambrogino d'Oro" City of Milan 2011, Guido Carli Award 2012, Basilicata Award 2012. *Publications:* published more than 400 works, including Reddito e Saggio di Interesse nelle Decisioni di Consumo e Risparmio nell'ipotesi di comportamento razionale 1965, Rendita e distribuzione in un modello economico plurisettoriale 1967, Investimenti in istruzione e sviluppo economico 1973, Protagonisti del pensiero economico 1977, Rent, Income Distribution, Order of Efficiency and Rentability 1980, The Gold Problem: Economic Perspectives 1982, Planning Manpower Education and Economic Growth 1983, Sui Momenti costitutivi della Economia Politica (co-author) 1983–84, The Exchange-Production Duality and the Dynamics of Economic Knowledge (co-author) 1986, Industrial Raw Materials: A Multi-Country, Multi-Commodity Analysis (co-author) 1986, The Agro-Technological System towards 2000: A European perspective (co-ed.) 1988, Rent, Distribution and Economic Structure 1990, Structural Rigidities and Dynamic Choice of Technologies (co-author) 1991, Issues on International Development and Solidarity 1992, On Economic Science: Its Tools and Economic Reality 1993, Innovation, Resources and Economic Growth (co-ed.) 1994, Risorse, Tecnologie, Rendita (co-author) 1996, Noi, l'Economia e l'Europa 1996, Production and Efficiency with Global Technologies 1996, Rent Resources, Technology (co-author) 1999, Il Made in Italy oltre il 2000 2000, La Società Italiana degli Economisti 2000, Profili della Costituzione Europea 2001, Complexity and industrial clusters (co-ed.) 2002, Il Gruppo Edison: 1993–2003 (co-ed) 2003, Technological Scarcity: An Essay on Production and Structural Change 2003, La globalizzazione e i rapporti Nord-Est-Sud 2004, Rent, Technology, and the Environment (co-author) 2004, Research and Technological innovation (co-ed.) 2005, Research and Technological Innovation: The Challenge for a New Europe (co-ed.) 2006, Industria e Distretti. Un Paradigma di perdurante competitività italiana (co-ed.) 2006, Economisti ed Economia. Per un'Italia europea: paradigmi tra il XVIII e il XX secolo 2007, Intrapresa, sussidiarietà, sviluppo (co-ed.) 2007, Valorizzare un'economia forte. L'Italia e il ruolo della sussidiarietà (co-ed.) 2007, The EU and the Economies of the Eastern European Enlargement (co-ed.) 2008, Democracy, Institutions and Social Justice

(co-ed.) 2008, Historical Stylizations and Monetary Theory (co-author) 2008, Fondazioni, enti e reti nello spazio europeo della ricerca. La sussidiarietà in atto (co-ed.) 2009, I fondi sovrani (co-author) 2009, Social Capital and Human Development (co-ed.) 2009, Nuove polarità nella geo-economia. Globalizzazione, crisi ed Italia (co-ed.) 2010, Values and Rules for a New Model of Development (co-ed.) 2010, Sovereign Wealth Funds: A Complete Guide to State-Owned Investment Funds (co-author) 2010, La Facoltà di Scienze Politiche della Università Cattolica 1989–2010, Profili istituzionali e internazionali nella interdisciplinarietà 2011, Economia oltre la crisi 2012, L'industria nei 150 anni dell'Unità d'Italia. Paradigmi e Protagonisti (co-ed.), Debito e crescita. L'equazione della crisi (co-ed.) 2013, Un economista eclettico. Distribuzione, tecnologie e sviluppo nel pensiero di Nino Andreatta (co-ed.) 2013, L'economia reale nel Mezzogiorno (co-ed.) 2014, L'Europa tra ripresa e squilibri (co-ed.) 2014, Solidarity as a "Social Value". Paradigms for a Good Society (co-ed.) 2015, Il ruolo strategico del sistema metalmeccanico italiano. Dai metalli alla meccatronica (co-ed.) 2015, Riforme, Ripresa, Rilancio. Europa e Italia (co ed.) 2016, Eurobonds for EMU stability and structural growth (co-ed.) 2017. *Leisure interest:* skiing. *Address:* CRANEC, Università Cattolica del Sacro Cuore, Largo Gemelli, 20123 Milan (office); Via A. Saffi 31, 20123 Milan, Italy (home). *Telephone:* (02) 72342474 (office). *Fax:* (02) 72342475 (office). *E-mail:* alberto.quadriocurzio@unicatt.it (office). *Website:* www.unicatt.it (office); docenti .unicatt.it/ita/alberto_quadrio_curzio (office).

QUAH, Danny, AB, PhD; British (b. Malaysian) economist and academic; *Dean and Li Ka Shing Professor in Economics, Lee Kuan Yew School of Public Policy, National University of Singapore;* b. (Danny Quah Lim Seng Hin), 26 July 1958, Penang; m. 1st Kathleen Tyson; two s.; m. 2nd Aileen Lim; ed Princeton Univ., Harvard Univ., USA; Asst Prof. of Econs, MIT 1985–91; Prof. of Econs and Int. Devt, LSE 1996–2016, Head of Dept of Econs 2006–09, Sr Adviser to Dir 2015–16; Visiting Prof. of Econs, Tsinghua Univ. School of Econs and Man., Beijing May–June 2010, Nanyang Technological Univ., Singapore 2011; Tan Chin Tuan Visiting Prof. of Econs, Nat. Univ. of Singapore 2010–16, Li Ka Shing Prof. in Econs, Lee Kuan Yew School of Public Policy 2016–, Vice Dean 2017–18, Dean 2018–; fmr consultant to World Bank, Bank of England, Monetary Authority of Singapore; Gov. Nat. Inst. of Econ. and Social Research 2002–16; mem. Editorial Bd, Journal of Global Policy 2009–, Asia Pacific Business Review 2014–; mem. European Advisory Bd, Princeton Univ. Press 2011–; mem. Advisory Bd, Journal of Global Analysis 2013–; Fellow, European Econ. Asscn 2004; Sr Fellow, Khazanah Research Inst., Kuala Lumpur 2016–. *Leisure interest:* Taekwon-do. *Address:* Lee Kuan Yew School of Public Policy, National University of Singapore, 469C Bukit Timah Road, Oei Tiong Ham Building, Singapore 259772 (office). *Telephone:* 65166875 (office). *E-mail:* d.quah@nus.edu.sg (office). *Website:* lkyspp.nus.edu.sg (office); www.dannyquah.com.

QUAID, Dennis; American actor; b. 9 April 1954, Houston, Tex.; s. of William Rudy Quaid and Juanita B. Quaid; m. 2nd Meg Ryan (q.v.) 1991 (divorced); one s.; m. 3rd Kimberly Buffington 2004; one s. one d.; ed Univ. of Houston; appeared on stage in Houston before moving to Hollywood; appeared on stage in New York with brother, Randy Quaid, in True West; performs with rock band The Electrics; wrote songs for films The Night the Lights Went Out in Georgia, Tough Enough, The Big Easy; Lifetime Achievement Award by Houston Film Critics Soc. 2016. *Films:* September 30 1955, 1978, Crazy Mama, Our Winning Season, Seniors, Breaking Away, I Never Promised You a Rose Garden, Gorp, The Long Riders, All Night Long, Caveman, The Night the Lights Went Out in Georgia, Tough Enough, Jaws 3-D, The Right Stuff, Dreamscape, Enemy Mine, The Big Easy, Innerspace, Suspect, D.O.A., Everyone's All-American, Great Balls of Fire, Lie Down With Lions, Postcards From the Edge, Come See the Paradise, A 22 Cent Romance, Wilder Napalu, Flesh and Bone, Wyatt Earp, Something To Talk About 1995, Dragonheart 1996, Criminal Element 1997, Going West 1997, Gang Related 1997, Savior 1997, Switchback 1997, The Parent Trap 1998, Any Given Sunday 1999, Frequency 2000, Traffic 2000, The Rookie 2002, Far From Heaven 2002, Cold Creek Manor 2003, The Alamo 2004, The Day After Tomorrow 2004, Flight of the Phoenix 2004, Synergy 2004, In Good Company 2004, Yours, Mine and Ours 2005, American Dreamz 2006, Smart People 2007, Vantage Point 2008, The Express 2008, Playing for Keeps 2012, Beneath the Darkness 2012, What to Expect When You're Expecting 2012, At Any Price 2012, Playing for Keeps 2012, Truth 2015, A Dog's Purpose 2017, I Can Only Imagine 2018, Kin 2018. *Television includes:* Amateur Night at the Dixie Bar and Grill 1979, Johnny Belinda 1982, Bill: On His Own 1983, Everything That Rises 1998, Dinner with Friends 2001, Vegas (series) 2012–13, The Art of More (series) 2015, Fortitude (series) 2016. *Address:* c/o William Morris Endeavor Entertainment, LLC, 9601 Wilshire Blvd, Beverly Hills, CA 90210, USA.

QUAITI, Monasser al-; Yemeni economist and central banker; b. 1955; m.; three c.; ed Univ. of Economy, Aden; Econ. Researcher, IMF; mem. Bd of Dirs, Cen. Bank of Yemen 2002–15, Gov. 2016–18; Minister of Finance 2015–16; fmr Dir Cooperative and Agricultural Credit Bank YSC.

QUAKE, Stephen R., BS, MS, DPhil; American biophysicist and academic; *Professor of Bioengineering, Stanford University;* ed Stanford Univ., Univ. of Oxford, UK; Postdoctoral Assoc., Steven Chu group, Stanford Univ. 1994–96, Prof. of Bioengineering 2004–; Asst Prof. of Applied Physics, California Inst. of Tech. 1996–99, Assoc. Prof. 1999–2002, Assoc. Prof. of Applied Physics and Physics 2002–03, Prof. 2003–04, Thomas E. and Doris Everhard Prof. of Applied Physics and Physics 2004–05; Investigator, Howard Hughes Medical Inst. 2006–; Visiting Scholar, Univ. of Minnesota 1996; mem. Quake Group, California Inst. of Tech., Pasadena, CSULA-California Inst. of Tech. partnerships for Research and Educ. in Materials (PREM) Collaborative 2004–, Inst. of Medicine 2012–, Nat. Acad. of Inventors, NAS 2013–, Nat. Acad. of Eng 2013–, American Acad. of Arts and Sciences 2014–; Co-founder, fmr Dir and Chair. Scientific Advisory Bd Fluidigm Corpn 1999–, Helicos, Inc. 2003–; consultant, Pharma Genomix 2000–, Axon Instruments 2003, Intel Corpn 2003, Molecular Technologies, Inc. 2004–05; participant in Nat. Acad. of Eng Symposium for Frontiers in Eng 1999; Fellow, American Inst. for Medical and Biological Eng 2007, American Physical Soc. 2010; Firestone Prize, Stanford Univ. 1991, Apker Award, American Physical Soc. 1991, Marshall Scholar 1991, NSF Grad. Fellow 1993, NIH R29 'FIRST' Award 1997, NSF Career Award 1997, Packard Fellow 1999, NIH Dir's Pioneer Award 2004, Lemelson-MIT Prize for outstanding mid-career inventors 2012, Nakasone Human Frontier Science Program Award 2014. *Publications:* numerous papers in professional journals on fundamental and applied topics in biophysics, especially single molecule science. *Address:* Department of Bioengineering, Stanford University, James H Clark Center, Room E300, 318 Campus Drive, Stanford, CA 94305, USA (office). *Telephone:* (650) 736-7890 (office). *E-mail:* quake@stanford.edu (office). *Website:* thebigone.stanford.edu (office).

QUALTROUGH, Carla, PC, LLB; Canadian lawyer and politician; *Minister of Public Services, Procurement and Accessibility;* b. 15 Oct. 1971, Calgary; m. Eron Main; four c.; ed Univ. of Ottawa, Univ. of Victoria; legal practice, including as counsel to BC Human Rights Tribunal and Canadian Human Rights Comm.; fmr Vice-Chair. BC Workers' Compensation Appeal Tribunal; mem. House of Commons (Liberal Party) for Delta 2015–; Minister of Sport, and Persons with Disabilities 2015–17, Minister of Public Services and Procurement 2017–18, Minister of Public Services, Procurement and Accessibility 2018–; Pres. (acting) of the Treasury Bd 2018–19; Dir of Inclusion and Dir of Sport Initiatives, 2010 Legacies Now Soc.; fmr Sr Adviser to Parl. Sec. (Sport) to Prime Minister, also to Sec. of State (Physical Activity and Sport); fmr Special Adviser to Dir-Gen., Sport Canada; Vice-Chair. Delta Gymnastics Soc.; Vice-Pres. Americas Paralympic Cttee; Dir Canadian Centre for Ethics in Sport; fmr Pres. Canadian Paralympic Cttee; Queen Elizabeth II Diamond Jubilee Medal 2012. *Achievements include:* represented Canada in swimming at Paralympic Games, Barcelona 1992 and Seoul 1998 (won three medals). *Address:* Office of the Minister of Public Works and Government Services Canada, 11 rue Laurier, Place du Portage, PDP III, Room 18A1, Gatineau, PQ K1A 0S5, Canada (office). *Telephone:* (819) 956-3115 (office). *Fax:* (819) 956-9062 (office). *E-mail:* minister@tpsgc-pwgsc.gc.ca (office). *Website:* www.tpsgc-pwgsc.gc.ca (office).

QUAM, Lois E., BA, MA, MHCA; American business executive and government official; *President and CEO, Pathfinder International;* b. 21 June 1961; m. 1st Matt Entenza (divorced); two s.; m. 2nd Arshad Mohammed; ed Macalaster Coll., Univ. of Oxford, UK; Pres. and CEO Penrose-St Francis Health System, Colo –1989; Dir Research and Evaluation, UnitedHealth Group 1989–93, Vice-Pres. Public Sector Services and Dir Research and Evaluation 1993, Corp. Vice-Pres. Man. Process 1996, CEO American Asscn of Retired Persons (AARP) Health Care Options Div. 1996–98, CEO Ovations, UnitedHealth Group 2002–06, Exec. Vice-Pres. Public and Sr Markets Group 2006–07; Man. Dir of Alternative Investments, Piper Jaffray and Co., Minneapolis 2007–09; Founder Tysvar, LLC 2009–; Sr Fellow, Center for American Progress, Washington, DC 2009; Exec. Dir Global Health Initiative, US Dept of State, Washington, DC 2011–12; CEO The Nature Conservancy (charitable environmental org.) 2014–16; CEO and Pres. Pathfinder Int. (nonprofit org. focusing on women's reproductive health) 2017–; Sr Advisor to White House Task Force on Nat. Health Care Reform 1993–96; Chair. Minn. Health Care Access Comm. 1989–91; mem. Bd of Dirs General Mills, Inc. 2007–11, The Commonwealth Fund 2016–; mem. Council on Foreign Relations; Trustee, Macalaster Coll.; fmr Trustee, George C. Marshall Foundation, National Wildlife Federation; Dr hc (Augsburg Coll., Minneapolis); Rhodes Scholar. *Publication:* Wills, Trusts & Estate Planning (co-author) 2001. *Address:* Pathfinder International, 9 Galen Street, Suite 217, Watertown, MA 02472, USA (office). *Telephone:* (617) 924-7200 (office). *Fax:* (617) 924-3833 (office). *E-mail:* communications@pathfinder.org (office). *Website:* www.pathfinder.org (office).

QUAN, Zhenghuan; Chinese muralist, painter and academic; b. 16 June 1932, Beijing; d. of Quan Liang-Su and Qin Xiao-Qing; m. Li Hua-Ji 1959; two d.; ed Cen. Acad. of Fine Arts, Beijing; Asst Lecturer, Cen. Acad. of Fine Arts 1955–56, Cen. Acad. of Applied Arts 1956–59, Lecturer 1959–78, Asst Prof. 1978–87, Prof. and mem. Academic Cttee 1987–; mem. Standing Cttee Artists' Asscn of China. *Murals include:* The Story of the White Snake (Beijing Int. Airport) 1979, Jin Wei filled the Ocean (Beijing Yian Jing Hotel), Dances of China (Beijing Opera House) 1984. *Leisure interests:* Beijing Opera, old movies of 1930–1940s, football. *Address:* Central Academy of Applied Arts, Beijing (office); 3-601, 6/F Hongmiao Beili, 100025, Beijing, People's Republic of China. *Telephone:* (1) 5963912 (office); (1) 5015522.

QUANT, Dame Mary, (Barbara Mary Plunkett Greene), DBE, FCSD, RDI, FSIA; British fashion, cosmetic and textile designer; *Joint Chairperson, Mary Quant Ltd;* b. 11 Feb. 1934, Blackheath, London, England; d. of Jack Quant and Mildred Quant (née Jones); m. Alexander Plunket Greene 1957 (died 1990); one s.; ed Blackheath High School, Goldsmiths Coll. of Art, London; began apprenticeship at Erik (high-end Mayfair milliner on Brook Street, nr Claridge's hotel); began career opening first shop Bazaar with photographer and fmr solicitor, Archie McNair on the King's Road, Chelsea 1955, opened second Bazaar store in Knightsbridge 1957, est. Ginger Group 1963, launched Mary Quant Cosmetics 1964; Dir Mary Quant Group of cos 1955–2000, currently Jt Chair. Mary Quant Ltd; apptd Dir (non-exec.), House of Fraser 1997; mem. Design Council 1971–74, UK-USA Bicentennial Liaison Cttee 1973, Advisory Council Victoria and Albert Museum 1976–78; instrumental figure in 1960s London-based Mod and youth fashion movts; retrospective exhbn of 1960s fashion, London Museum 1973; apptd mem. 200th Anniversary of Diplomatic Relations between UK and US Cttee 1973; Fellow, Soc. of Industrial Artists 1967; Hon. mem. Royal Coll. of Art 1991; Hon. Fellow, Goldsmiths Coll., London 1993; Hon. FRSA 1995; Dr hc (Winchester Coll. of Art) 2000; Dress of the Year Award 1963, Sunday Times Int. Fashion Award 1963, Maison Branch Rex Award (USA) 1964, Annual Design Medal, Soc. of Industrial Artists and Designers, Piavolo d'Oro (Italy) 1966, Design Award, Soc. of Industrial Artists 1967, Royal Designer for Industry 1969, inducted into British Fashion Council Hall of Fame 1969, Pret-à-porter Fashion Fed. Award (France) 1985, British Fashion Council (for outstanding contrib. to British fashion) 1990. *Video:* Mary Quant's Style File 1989. *Publications include:* Quant by Quant 1966, Colour by Quant 1984, Quant on Make-up 1986, Mary Quant Classic Make-up and Beauty Book 1996, Mary Quant: Autobiography 2011. *Address:* Mary Quant Ltd, 37 Duke of York Square, Chelsea, London, SW3 4LY, England (office). *Telephone:* (20) 7881-9833 (office). *E-mail:* mq.shop@maryquant.co.uk (office); mqoverseas@maryquant.co.jp (office). *Website:* www.maryquant.co.uk (office); mq.maryquant.co.uk (office).

QUARREY, David, CMG; British diplomatist; *Ambassador to Israel;* m. Aldo Oliver Henriquez 2011; joined FCO 1994, served in missions to UN, New York and Embassies New Delhi and Harare, served as Dir for Near East and Africa; Pvt. Sec. to Prime Minister Tony Blair 2004–06; fmr Dir for Foreign Policy, Nat. Security Secr.; Amb. to Israel 2015–. *Address:* British Embassy, 192 Hayarkon Street,

6340502, Tel-Aviv, Israel (office). *Telephone:* 3-7251222 (office). *Fax:* 3-5278574 (office). *E-mail:* webmaster.telaviv@fco.gov.uk (office). *Website:* www.gov.uk/government/world/organisations/british-embassy-tel-aviv (office); www.gov.uk/government/world/israel (office).

QUARRIE, Donald (Don), CD; Jamaican athletic coach and fmr athlete; b. 25 Feb. 1951, Kingston; m. Yulanda Quarrie; two d.; ed Univ. of Southern California, USA; competed at Olympic Games, Munich 1972, reaching semifinal of 200m; Montreal 1976, won gold medal at 200m and silver medal at 100m; Moscow 1980, won bronze medal at 200m; Los Angeles 1984, won silver medal 4×100m relay; competed at Commonwealth Games, Edinburgh 1970, won gold medals at 100m, 200m and 4×100m relay; Christchurch, NZ 1974 won gold medals at 100m and 200m; Edmonton 1978, won gold medal at 100m; coach in Calif.; fmr mem. Exec. Bd Jamaica Amateur Athletic Asscn (now Jamaica Athletics Administrative Asscn); Technical Leader for Jamaican National Team at IAAF World Championships 2005, 2007, 2009; contracted with Chinese Athletics Asscn as consultant in preparations for Beijing 2008 Summer Olympics 2006; fmr IAAF Advertising Commr for int. track meets; inducted into California Sports Hall of Fame 2008.

QUARTA, Roberto; American (b. Italian) business executive; *Partner and Chairman, Clayton, Dubilier & Rice Europe;* b. 10 May 1949; ed Coll. of the Holy Cross, Mass; served for six years in US Army; Pnr, Clayton, Dubilier & Rice (CD&R), Inc. (pvt. equity group) 2001–, Chair. CD&R Europe, London; CEO BBA Group 1993–2001 (renamed BBA Aviation following demerger of Fiberweb 2006), Chair. –2007, Chair. Supervisory Bd Rexel SA (owned by CD&R) 2007, Chair., Pres., Man. Dir and mem. Exec. Cttee ItalTel SpA (owned by CD&R); Chair. IMI plc 2011–15, Smith & Nephew PLC 2014–; Chair. (non-Exec.) WPP plc 2015–18, Exec. Chair. (acting) April 2018–; mem. Bd of Dirs Foster Wheeler AG; mem. Country Advisory Bd Institut Européen d'Admin des Affaires (INSEAD); mem. Bd of Trustees Coll. of the Holy Cross. *Address:* Clayton, Dubilier & Rice Ltd, Cleveland House, 33 King Street, London, SW1Y 6RJ, England (office). *Telephone:* (20) 7747-3800 (office). *Fax:* (20) 7747-3801 (office). *E-mail:* info@cdr-inc.com (office). *Website:* www.cdr-inc.com (office).

QUAYLE, James Danforth (Dan), BS, JD; American international business consultant and fmr politician; *Chairman, Cerberus Global Investments LLC;* b. 4 Feb. 1947, Indianapolis, Ind.; s. of James C. Quayle and Corinne Quayle (née Pulliam); m. Marilyn Tucker 1972; two s. one d.; ed DePauw Univ., Indiana Univ.; served in Indiana Nat. Guard 1969–75; court reporter, Huntington Herald Press, Ind. 1965–69, Assoc. Publr and Gen. Man. 1974–76; mem. Consumer Protection Div., Office of Ind. Attorney-Gen. 1970–71; Admin. Asst to Gov. of Ind. 1971–73; Dir Ind. Inheritance Tax Div. 1973–74; admitted to Indiana bar 1974; teacher of business law, Huntington Coll. 1975; mem. US House of Reps 1977–79; Senator from Ind. 1981–88; Vice-Pres. of USA 1989–93; with Circle Investors 1993; currently Chair. Cerberus Global Investments, LLC; Distinguished Visiting Prof., American Grad. School of Int. Man. 1997–99; f. J. D. Quayle & Co. 2000; Dir and Sr Advisor, Senex Financial Corp. 2004–; Dir Heckmann Corp. 2007–; mem. Huntington Bar Asscn; mem. Hoosier State Press Asscn; Chair. Council on Competitiveness; Republican. *Publications include:* Standing Firm 1994, The American Family 1995, Worth Fighting For 1999. *Address:* Cerberus Capital Management, L.P., 875 Third Avenue, New York, NY 10022; c/o Kathleen Murphy, 7001 N. Scottsdale Road, Suite 2010, Scottsdale, AZ 85253, USA (office). *Telephone:* (212) 891-2100 (office); (480) 922-5700 (office). *E-mail:* info@cerberuscapital.com (office). *Website:* www.cerberuscapital.com (office); www.vicepresidentdanquayle.com.

QUAYLE, Quinton Mark; British diplomatist (retd); b. 5 June 1955; m. Alison Quayle; two s.; ed Bromsgrove School, Univ. of Bristol, School of Oriental and African Studies, London, École Nationale d'Admin, Paris, Chiang Mai Univ.; joined FCO 1977, Cen. and Southern African Dept 1977–78, full-time language training 1979–80, Second Sec., Chancery, Bangkok 1980–83, S America Dept, FCO 1983–84, Trade Relations and Exports Dept 1984–85, First Sec., Chancery, Paris 1987–91, Deputy Head, EC Dept (External), FCO 1991–93, Dir Jt Export Promotion Directorate 1994–96, Deputy Head of Mission, Jakarta 1996–99, Int. Group Dir British Trade Int., Trade Partners UK 1999–2002, language training in Iasi 2002, Amb. to Romania 2002–07, to Thailand (also accred to Laos) 2007–10; Hon. Chair. Int. Beverage Holdings Ltd (int. arm of ThaiBev) 2011–; mem. Governing Council, Inst. of Chartered Accountants of Scotland 2011–15; mem. Regulatory Bd, Royal Inst. of Chartered Surveyors 2012–15; Sr Adviser, Sindicatum 2011–, Salamander Energy 2011–15, De La Rue 2011–15, Prudential Assurance 2013–; mem. Governing Council, Nursing and Midwifery Council; mem. Queen's Counsel Selection Panel 2013–; Sr Consultant, Price Waterhouse 1993–94. *Leisure interests:* book collecting, especially first edns of detective fiction, West Bromwich Albion Football Club. *Address:* c/o International Beverage Holdings Ltd, Moffat Distillery, Airdrie, Lanarkshire, ML6 8PL, Scotland.

QUBAISI, Amal Abdullah Juma Karam al-, BArch, MArch, PhD; United Arab Emirates politician and academic; *President and Speaker, Federal National Council;* b. Abu Dhabi; ed United Arab Emirates Univ., Univ. of Sheffield, UK; Prof. of Architecture, Emirates Univ. 2000–06; Pres., Cultural Heritage Unit, Al Ain Tourism and Econ. Devt Authority 2001–03; mem. Fed. Nat. Council (first woman) 2006–, mem. Health, Labour and Social Affairs Cttee 2007–09, Pres. Educ., Youth, Media and Culture Cttee (first woman to head a council's panel) 2007–09, Deputy Speaker, then Pres. and Speaker, Fed. Nat. Council (first woman) 2015–; Dir-Gen. Abu Dhabi Education Council; mem. Nat. Bd for the Conservation of Antiquities and Archeological Sites 2002–07; Founding mem. Soc. of Conservation of the Architectural Heritage 2003–07; mem. Architects Asscn 2006–07; Hon. PhD (Univ. of Sheffield) 2016, (Dublin City Univ., Ireland) 2018; Abu Dhabi Award 2008, Middle East Excellence Award of Women Leadership 2008, Abu Dhabi Medal of Honor 2009, Emirati Pioneers Award 2014, Parliamentarian Excellence Award 2017. *Address:* Federal National Council, PO Box 836, Abu Dhabi, United Arab Emirates (office). *Telephone:* (2) 6199500 (office). *Fax:* (2) 6812846 (office). *E-mail:* a.alqubaisi@almajles.gov.ae (office). *Website:* www.almajles.gov.ae (office).

QUBAISI, Khadem Abdulla al-, BEcons; United Arab Emirates business executive; b. 27 Sept. 1971, Abu Dhabi; Sr Financial Analyst, N America Equities Dept, Abu Dhabi Investment Authority 1994–99; Investment Man. Div. Man., Int.

Petroleum Investment Co. 2000–07, Man. Dir –2015; Chair. Aabar Investments PJSC 2008–15, Borealis 2010–15, Nat. Central Cooling Co. (Tabreed) 2008–11, Abu Dhabi Nat. Takaful Co. (Takaful) 2008–14, I-Media Newspaper (Alrroya Aleqtisadiya) 2009–, First Energy Bank 2011–, Hyundai Oilbank Co. Ltd, S Korea, Gulf Energy Maritime PJSC 2004–10, Arabtec Holding PJSC; Dir, Compañía Española de Petróleos SA (CEPSA) 2009 (Chair. 2011–15), First Gulf Bank, Emirates Investment Authority, Aldar Properties PJSC –2010; voted Arabian Businessman of the Year 2009, ICIS Power Player of the Year 2009. *Website:* www.khadem.com.

QUBAYSI, Sheikha Munira al-; Syrian educator; *Founder and Director, Al-Qubaysiat;* b. 1933, Damascus; Founder of Al-Qubaysiat (female-only quasi-Sufi movt, largest women-only Islamic movt in the world), offers Islamic educ. exclusively to girls and women, banned by Syrian Govt until 2006; directs approx. 80 schools in Damascus with 75,000 students.

QUDAH, Adel, BA, MA; Jordanian government official; b. Al-Salt; m.; four c.; ed Cairo Univ., Egypt, Univ. of Southern Calif., USA; Gen. Dir Customs Dept, Ministry of Finance 1982–91, Income Tax Dept 1990–91; Pres. Audit Bureau 1991–94; Minister of Supply 1996–2005; Chair. Exec. Privatization Comm. 1996–2005; Minister of Finance July–Nov. 2005; convicted of bribery by mil. court July 2010, sentenced to three years' imprisonment; Order of the Jordan Star of the First Order, Order of the Repub. of Egypt of the First Order.

QUE AZCONA, Vivian; Philippine business executive; b. 1 Sept. 1955; d. of Mariano and Estelita Que; m. Eduardo Azcona; ed Univ. of Santo Tomas; Pres. Mercury Drug Corpn (f. by father 1945) 1998–; Vice-Pres. Philippine Retailers Asscn 2016–; mem. Philippine Pharmacists Asscn, Inc.; Asia Pacific Entrepreneurship Awards Woman Entrepreneur of the Year 2015. *Address:* Mercury Drug Corporation, 7 Mercury Avenue, corner C.P. Garcia Avenue, Bagumbayan, Quezon City 1110, The Philippines (office). *Telephone:* (2) 9115071 (office). *Fax:* (2) 9116673 (office). *E-mail:* info@mercurydrug.com (office). *Website:* www.mercurydrug.com (office).

QUEEN LATIFAH; American rap artist and actress; b. (Dana Owens), 18 March 1970, East Orange, NJ; d. of Lance Owens and Rita Bray; worked with female rap act, Ladies Fresh; recorded with producers Dady-O, KRS-1, DJ Mark the 45 King and mems of De La Soul; moved to Motown Records; began acting career with sitcom Living Single; est. man. co., Flavor Unit Entertainment and label, Flavor Unit Records 1993–; guest appearance on Shabba Ranks' single, Watcha Gonna Do; other recording collaborations with De La Soul and Monie Love; Grammy Award for Best Rap Solo Performance 1994, Grace Award 2016. *Films include:* Living Single, Jungle Fever 1991, House Party 2 1991, Juice 1992, My Life 1993, Set It Off 1996, Hoodlum 1997, Sphere 1998, Living Out Loud 1998, The Bone Collector 1999, Bringing Out the Dead 1999, The Country Bears 2002, Brown Sugar 2002, Chicago 2002, Bringing Down the House (also exec. producer) 2003, Scary Movie 3 2003, Barbershop 2: Back in Business 2004, The Cookout (also writer and producer) 2004, Beauty Shop (also producer) 2005, Last Holiday 2006, Ice Age: The Meltdown (voice) 2006, Stranger Than Fiction 2006, Hairspray 2007, The Perfect Holiday 2007, Mad Money 2008, What Happens in Vegas 2008, The Secret Life of Bees 2008, Joyful Noise 2012, House of Bodies 2013, 22 Jump Street 2014, Miracles from Heaven 2016. *Television includes:* Living Single (series) 1993, Mama Flora's Family 1998, Queen Latifah Show 1999–2001, 2013–15, Single Ladies (series) 2011–12, Living with the Dead (mini series) 2002, The Muppets' Wizard of Oz 2005, Life Support (Golden Globe Award for Outstanding Performance by a Female Actor in a Television Movie or Miniseries 2008) 2007, Steel Magnolias 2012, Bessie (also exec. producer), The Wiz Live! 2015, Ice Age: The Great Egg-Scapade (film) 2016. *Recordings include:* albums: All Hail The Queen 1989, Latifah's Had It Up 2 Here 1989, Nature Of A Sista 1991, Black Reign 1993, Queen Latifah and Original Flava Unit 1996, Order In The Court 1998, The Dana Owens Album 2004, Trav'lin' Light 2008, Persona 2009. *Publications include:* Ladies First 2000, Queen of the Scene 2006, Put On Your Crown 2010. *Website:* www.queenlatifah.com.

QUEFFÉLEC, Anne; French concert pianist; b. 17 Jan. 1948, Paris; d. of Henri Queffélec and Yvonne Pénau; m. Luc Dehaene 1983; ed Conservatoire Nat., Paris; since 1968 has played in tours of Europe, Japan, Israel, Africa, Canada and USA; has played with BBC Symphony, London Symphony, Royal Philharmonic, Bournemouth Symphony, Hallé, Scottish Chamber, City of Birmingham Symphony, Miami Symphony, NHK Tokyo, Tokyo Symphony orchestras, Nouvel orchestre philharmonique de Radio-France, Orchestre nat. de Radio-France, Orchestre de Strasbourg, Ensemble Intercontemporain, etc., under conductors including Zinman, Groves, Leppard, Marriner, Boulez, Semkow, Skrowaczewski, Eschenbach, Gardiner, Pritchard, Atherton, etc.; has played at numerous festivals including Strasbourg, Dijon, Besançon, La Roque d'Anthéron, La Grange de Meslay, Bordeaux, Paris, King's Lynn, Bath, Cheltenham, London Proms; judge in several int. piano competitions; master-classes in France (including Ecole normale de musique, Paris), England and Japan; Pres. Asscn des amis d'Henri Queffélec, Asscn musicale 'Ballades'; Chevalier, Légion d'honneur 1998, Officier, Ordre nat. du Mérite 2001; First Prize for Piano 1965, for Chamber Music 1966, Conservatoire Nat., Paris; First Prize, Munich Int. Piano Competition 1968, Prizewinner, Leeds Int. Piano Competition 1969, Best Classical Artist of the Year, Victoires de la Musique 1990. *Recordings include:* more than 30 records of music by Scarlatti, Handel, Chopin, Schubert, Fauré, Ravel (complete piano works), Debussy, Liszt, Hummel, Beethoven, Mendelssohn, Bach, Satie, complete piano works of Henri Dutilleux 1996 and Mozart and Haydn recitals. *Radio includes:* numerous appearances on BBC Radio 3, France Musique and Japanese radio. *Television includes:* numerous appearances on musical, but also literary and religious, programmes. *Leisure interests:* children, literature, cycling, theatre, friends, humour, art. *Address:* c/o Christine Talbot-Cooper, International Artists, Stoneville Cottage, Gretton Fields, Cheltenham, Glos., GL54 5HH, England (office); 15 avenue Corneille, 78600 Maisons-Laffitte, France (home). *Telephone:* (1242) 620736 (office); 1-39-62-25-64 (home). *Fax:* (1242) 620736 (office); 1-39-62-25-64 (home). *E-mail:* talbotcooper@onetel.com (office). *Website:* www.ctcinternationalartists.com (office).

QUEK, Tan Sri Leng Chan; Malaysian barrister and business executive; *Executive Chairman and CEO, Hong Leong Group Malaysia;* b. 1941; m.; three c.; called to Bar, Middle Temple, UK; has extensive business experience in financial services, manufacturing and real estate; Co-founder, Exec. Chair. and CEO Hong Leong Group Malaysia (includes semiconductor cos, automotive assembly, materials, newsprint, furniture); Exec. Chair. Guoco Group Ltd 1990–2016, Tasek Corp. Bhd –2004, OYL Group –2006, BIL Int. Ltd 2007–16 (Dir 1997–2016), GuocoLand Berhad 2016– (Chair. of Bd 2012–13, mem. Bd of Dirs 2013–16); Chair. HL Holdings Sdn Bhd. *Address:* Hong Leong Group Malaysia, Wisma Hong Leong, 18 Jalan Perak, 50450 Kuala Lumpur, Malaysia (office). *Telephone:* (3) 2164-1818 (office). *Fax:* (3) 2164-2477 (office). *E-mail:* info@hongleong.com (office). *Website:* www.hongleong.com (office).

QUELCH, John Anthony, CBE, MA, MBA, MS, DBA, CIMgt, FRGS; British/American academic; *Vice-Provost for Executive Education, University of Miami;* b. 8 Aug. 1951, London, UK; s. of Norman Quelch and Laura Sally Quelch (née Jones); m. Joyce Ann Huntley 1978; ed Exeter Coll., Oxford, Wharton School, Univ. of Pennsylvania, Harvard Univ., USA; Asst Prof., Univ. of Western Ontario, Canada 1977–79; Asst Prof., then Assoc. Prof., then Prof., then Sebastian S. Kresge Prof. of Marketing, Harvard Univ., USA 1979–98, Sr Assoc. Dean and Lincoln Filene Prof. of Business Admin., Harvard Business School 2001–11; Dean of London Business School 1998–2001; Dean, Vice-Pres. and Distinguished Prof. of Int. Man., China Europe Int. Business School, Shanghai 2011–13; Charles Edward Wilson Prof. of Business Admin and Prof. in Health Policy and Man., Harvard Univ. 2013–17, now Emer.; Chair. Massachusetts Port Authority 2002–11; Dir (non-exec.), Aramark, Inc., Alere, Inc., Americans For Oxford 2002–11; Vice-Provost for Exec. Educ., Univ. of Miami 2017–, Dean, School of Business Admin 2017–, also Prof. of Marketing; Fellow, Int. Acad. of Man. 2000, American Acad. of Arts and Sciences 2017; Hon. Fellow, Exeter Coll. Oxford 2002, London Business School 2009; Hon. Consul-Gen., Kingdom of Morocco; Hon. Chair. British American Business Council of New England 2010; Dr hc (Vietnam Nat. Univ.) 2011; Leadership Award, British American Business Council of New England 2008, World Boston Int. Citizens Award 2010. *Publications:* How to Market to Consumers 1989, Sales Promotion Management 1989, Cases in Advertising and Promotion Management 1995, Marketing Management 2004, Global Marketing Management 2004, The Global Market 2004, The New Global Brands 2005, Business Solutions for the Global Poor 2007, Greater Good: How Good Marketing Makes for Better Democracy 2009, All Business Is Local 2011, Consumers, Corporations and Public Health 2016, Building a Culture of Health 2016. *Leisure interests:* squash, tennis. *Address:* Miami Business School, University of Miami, 5250 University Drive, Coral Gables, FL 33124-6520 (office); 57 Baker Bridge Road, Lincoln, MA 01773, USA (home). *Telephone:* (781) 259-0594 (home). *E-mail:* jaquelch@yahoo.com (home). *Website:* www.bus.miami.edu (office).

QUESTROM, Allen I., BA; American retail executive; *Senior Advisor, Lee Equity Partners LLC;* m. Kelli Questrom; ed Boston Univ.; began career with Federated Dept Stores, Inc. 1964, apptd Chair. and CEO Rich Div. 1980, Chair. and CEO fmr Bullock Div. 1984–88, Exec. Vice-Pres. 1988, Chair. and CEO 1990–97; Pres. and CEO Neiman Marcus 1988–90; joined Barneys New York Inc. 1997, Chair., Pres. and CEO 1999–2000; Chair. and CEO J. C. Penney Co. Inc. 2000–04; Prin. AEA Investors Inc.; Partner Mellon Ventures; Sr Advisor, Lee Equity Partners LLC 2006–; mem. Bd of Dirs Barneys New York Inc., Foot Locker, Inc., Glazer Family of Cos; fmr Dir Nat. Retail Fed.; fmr mem. Bd of Dirs Wal-Mart Stores, Inc., AEA Investors LLC; mem. Nat. Cttee Whitney Museum of American Art, New York; mem. Nat. Council, Aspen Art Museum; Trustee, Boston Univ., Aspen Music Festival and School. *Address:* Lee Equity Partners, 650 Madison Avenue, 21st Floor, New York, NY 10022, USA (office). *Telephone:* (212) 888-1500 (office).

QUEVEDO, HE Cardinal Orlando Beltrán, STB, MA, OMI; Philippine ecclesiastic; *Archbishop Emeritus of Cotabato;* b. 11 March 1939, Laoag, Ilocos Norte; ed Notre Dame High School, Marbel, San Jose Seminary, St Peter's Novitiate, Mission, Tex., USA, Oblate Coll. (Catholic Univ. of America), Washington, DC; ordained priest of Missionary Oblates of Mary Immaculate 1964; assigned Asst Parish Priest of Cotabato Cathedral 1964; Prelate of Kidapawan 1980–82, Bishop of Kidapawan 1982–86; Archbishop of Nueva Segovia 1986–98; Archbishop of Cotabato 1998–2018, Archbishop Emer. 2018–; cr. Cardinal (Cardinal-Priest of Santa Maria 'Regina Mundi' a Torre Spaccata) 2014–; fmr Sec.-Gen. Fed. of Asian Bishops' Confs; fmr Pres. Catholic Bishops' Conf. of the Philippines. *Address:* c/o Archbishop's Residence, PO Box 186, 158 Sinsuat Avenue, 9600 Cotobato City, Philippines (office).

QUEYRANNE, Jean-Jack; French politician; b. 2 Nov. 1945, Lyon; s. of Maurice Queyranne and Jeanne Bonavent; First Deputy Mayor of Villeurbanne (Rhône) 1977–88; Parti Socialiste (PS) mem. Rhône Gen. Council 1979–90, Regional Council Rhône-Alps 1986–2002, Pres. Regional Council 2004–16; Nat. Ass. Deputy (alt.) for Rhone 1981–93, re-elected 1986, 1988, 1997, 2002, 2007; Minister of State attached to Minister of the Interior, with responsibility for Overseas Depts and Territories 1997–2000; Minister of Relations with Parliament 2000–02; Mayor of Bron (Rhône) 1989–97, Deputy Mayor 1997–2004; mem. PS Steering Cttee, Deputy Nat. Sec. responsible for cultural policy 1983, for press and culture 1985, Party Spokesman 1985, Nat. Del. and Spokesman 1987, Nat. Sec. responsible for audiovisual policy 1988, mem. Nat. Council 1993–94. *Leisure interests:* theatre, music, cinema. *Address:* 1 rue Roger Salengro, 69500 Bron, France (office).

QUIGLEY, Michael (Mike), BSc, BEE; British/Australian business executive; b. 1953; m.; three d.; ed Univ. of New South Wales; joined ITT Australia (now Alcatel Australia) 1971, positions including research and devt, manufacturing, sales and marketing, Gen. Man. for Australia and NZ 1996–99, COO Alcatel USA 1999, later CEO Alcatel USA, Pres. Alcatel N America, mem. Exec. Cttee, Pres. Fixed Communications Activities 2003, Pres. and COO Alcatel 2005–06, COO joint Alcatel-Lucent techs co. after Alcatel acquisition of Lucent 2006–07 (resgnd), also fmr mem. Exec. Bd; CEO NBN (National Broadband Network) Co Ltd 2009–13; mem. Bd Alliance for Telecommunications Industry Solutions; Charles Todd Medal for outstanding services to telecommunications in Australia 2013.

QUIGNARD, Pascal Charles Edmond, LicenFil; French writer; b. 23 April 1948, Verneuil-sur-Avre, Eure; s. of Jacques Quignard and Anne Quignard (née Bruneau); one s.; ed Lycée de Havre, Lycée de Sèvres and Faculté des Lettres de Nanterre; Lecturer 1969–77; mem. Cttee of Lecturing 1977–94; Sec.-Gen. for Editorial Devt, Editions Gallimard; Pres. Int. Festival of Opera and Baroque

Theatre, Château de Versailles 1990–94; Pres. Concert des Nations 1990–93; Chevalier, Légion d'honneur; Prix de la Soc. des gens de lettres for his collected works 1998, Grand prix du roman de la Ville de Paris 1998, Prix de la fondation Prince Pierre de Monaco for his collected works 2000. *Publications include:* L'être du balbutiement 1969, Alexandra de Lycophron 1971, La parole de la Délie 1974, Michel Deguy 1975, Echo 1975, Sang 1976, Le lecteur 1976, Hiems 1977, Sarx 1977, Inter aerias fagos 1977, Sur le défaut de terre 1979, Carus 1979, Le secret du domaine 1980, Les tablettes de buis d'Apronenia Avitia 1984, Le vœu de silence (essay) 1985, Une gêne technique à l'égard des fragments 1986, Ethelrude et Wolframm 1986, Le salon de Wurtemberg 1986, La leçon de musique 1987, Les escaliers de Chambord 1989, Petits traités (tome I à VIII) 1990, La raison 1990, Albucius 1990, Tous les matins du monde 1991, Georges de La Tour 1991, La Frontière 1992, Le nom sur le bout de la langue 1993, Le sexe et l'effroi 1994, L'occupation américaine 1994, Rhétorique spéculative 1995, L'amour conjugal 1995, Les septante 1995, La haine de la musique 1996, Vie secrète 1998, Terrasse à Rome (Grand Prix du roman de l'Acad. française 2000) 2000, Albucius 2001, Les ombres errantes (Prix Goncourt 2002) 2002, Sur le jadis 2002, Abîmes 2002, Les Paradisiaques 2005, Sordidissimes 2005, Écrits de l'éphémère 2005, Pour trouver les Enfers 2005, Villa Amalia 2006, L'Enfant au visage couleur de la mort 2006, Triomphe du temps 2006, Ethelrude et Wolframm 2006, Le Petit Cupidon 2006, Requiem 2006, La Nuit sexuelle 2007, Boutès 2008, La Barque Silencieuse 2009, Assises du roman 2009. *Address:* c/o Éditions du Seuil, 25 boulevard Romain Rolland, 75993 Paris, France (office). *Website:* www.seuil.com (office).

QUIJANO CAPURRO, José Manuel; Uruguayan economist and international organization official; b. 20 April 1944; Dir Consultora Alianza Cooperativa Internacional, ACI, Uruguay; Advisor, Perm. Secr., Sistema Economico Latinoamericana (SELA) *c.* 2001; fmr consultant with Integración AFAP, Montevideo; mem. Mercosur Sectoral Comm., Exec. Dir Mercosur Secr. 2008–09.

QUILÈS, Paul; French politician; *Mayor of Cordes-sur-Ciel (Tarn);* b. 27 Jan. 1942, St Denis du Sig, Algeria; s. of René Quilès and Odette Tyrode; m. Josephe-Marie Bureau 1964; three d.; ed Ecole Polytechnique, Paris; engineer, Shell Française 1964–78; Socialist Deputy to Nat. Ass. 1978–83, 1986–88, 1993–2007; Minister of Town Planning and Housing 1983–85, of Transport 1984–85, of Defence 1985–86, of Posts, Telecommunications and Space 1988–91, of Public Works, Housing, Transportation and Space Research 1991–92, of the Interior and Public Security 1992–93; Chair. Nat. Defence and Armed Forces Comm. 1997–2002; Mayor of Cordes-sur-Ciel (Tarn) 1995–; mem. Econ. and Social Council 1974–75; mem. Parl. Foreign Affairs Comm. 2002, Vice-Pres. 2004–07. *Publications:* La Politique n'est pas ce que vous croyez 1985, Nous vivons une époque intéressante 1992, Les 577, Un parlement pour quoi faire 2001, Face aux désordres du monde 2005, 18 mois chrono 2010, On a repris la Bastille 2011, Nucléaire: un mensonge français 2012, Arrêtez la bombe 2013. *Address:* Mairie, 34 Grande Rue Raymond VII, 81170 Cordes-sur-Ciel, (Tarn) France (office). *Website:* paul.quiles.over-blog.com.

QUINLAN, Gary Francis, BA (Hons); Australian civil servant and diplomatist; *Ambassador to Indonesia;* ed Univ. of Newcastle; joined the then Dept of Foreign Affairs 1973, Third Sec., later Second Sec., Embassy in Dublin 1974–77, Policy Officer, UN Social and Tech. Section, Dept of Foreign Affairs 1977–79, Deputy Perm. Del. to UNESCO, Paris 1979–81, Policy Officer, International Comm. for the Conservation of Antarctic Marine Living Resources (CCAMLR) 1981, First Sec., Perm. Mission to UN, New York 1981–85, attached to Econ. Devt Inst., World Bank, Washington, DC 1984, Dir Maritime Resources Section, Dept of Foreign Affairs 1985–87, Head of Australian Del., later Head of Del. to the Law of the Sea Preparatory Comm. 1986–87, Dir SEA Law and Oceans Policy 1987–88; Pvt. Sec. to Minister for Resources 1988–89, Chief of Staff to Minister for Resources 1989–90, to Minister for Industrial Relations, Public Service and Shipping and Aviation Support 1990–93, to Minister for Trade 1993–94, to Minister for Industry, Science and Regional Devt (later known as Industry, Science and Tech.) 1994–96; Asst Sec., East Asia Br., Dept of Foreign Affairs 1996–98, First Asst Sec., Diplomatic Security, Property and Information Man. Div. 1999, First Asst Sec., Americas and Europe Div., Dept of Foreign Affairs and Trade 2000–01, High Commr to Singapore 2001–05, First Asst Sec., Consular, Public Diplomacy and Parl. Affairs Div. 2007, Minister (Deputy Head of Mission), Embassy in Washington, DC 2005–07, Sr Adviser to Prime Minister on Foreign Affairs, Defence and Nat. Security 2007–09, Amb. and Perm. Rep. to UN, New York 2009–15; Amb. to Indonesia 2018–; Hon. DLitt (Newcastle) 2007. *Address:* Australian Embassy in Indonesia, Jalan Patra Kuningan Raya Kav. 1-4, Jakarta Selatan, 12950, Indonesia (office). *Telephone:* (21) 25505555 (office). *Fax:* (21) 29226775 (office). *E-mail:* public-affairs-jakt@dfat.gov.au (office). *Website:* indonesia.embassy.gov.au (office).

QUINLAN, Michael (Mike) R., BS, MBA; American business executive; *Chairman Emeritus, McDonald's Corporation;* b. 9 Dec. 1944, Chicago, Ill.; s. of Robert Joseph Quinlan and Kathryn Quinlan (née Koerner); m. Marilyn DeLashmutt 1966; two s.; ed Loyola Univ., Chicago; started career as part-time mailroom worker, McDonald's Corpn 1963, Asst Buyer 1966, Pres. (USA) 1980–82, CEO 1987–98, Chair. 1989–97, Dir 1979–2002 (retd), now Chair. Emer.; mem. Bd of Trustees Loyola Univ., Chicago 1999– (fmr Chair.); mem. Bd of Dirs Dun & Bradstreet Corpn 1989–2012, May Dept Stores Co. 1993–2005, Warren Resources, Inc. 2002–12; Sword of Loyola, Loyola Univ., Chicago 2005. *Leisure interest:* racquetball.

QUINN, Aidan; American actor; b. 8 March 1959, Chicago, Ill.; s. of Michael Quinn and Teresa Quinn; m. Elizabeth Bracco 1987; two d.; worked with various theatre groups in Chicago before moving to New York; off-Broadway appearances in Sam Shepard's plays Fool for Love and A Lie of the Mind; appeared in Hamlet, Wisdom Bridge Theater, Chicago, numerous other plays. *Films include:* Reckless 1984, Desperately Seeking Susan 1985, The Mission 1986, Stakeout 1987, Crusoe 1989, The Handmaid's Tale 1990, The Lemon Sisters 1990, Avalon 1990, At Play in the Fields of the Lord 1991, The Playboys 1992, Benny & Joon 1993, Blink 1994, Legends of the Fall 1994, Mary Shelley's Frankenstein 1994, The Stars Fell on Henrietta 1995, Haunted 1995, Michael Collins 1996, Looking For Richard 1996, Commandments 1997, The Assignment 1997, This is My Father 1998 (also exec. producer), Practical Magic 1998, In Dreams 1999, Music of the Heart 1999, Songcatcher 2000, Stolen Summer 2002, Evelyn 2002, Song for a Raggy Boy 2003, Cavedweller 2004, Shadow of Fear 2004, Bobby Jones, Stroke of Genius 2004, Plainsong 2004, Return to Sender 2004, Proud 2004, Nine Lives 2005, Dark Matter 2007, Wild Child 2008, The Eclipse 2009, The 5th Quarter 2009, Flipped 2010, Jonah Hex 2010, Unknown 2011, The Stand Up 2011, The Greening of Whitney Brown 2011, If I Were You 2012, Allegiance 2012, Christmas Rescue 2012, The Last Keepers 2013, Rushlights 2013, Stay 2013. *Stage appearances include:* Fool for Love 1983, A Streetcar Named Desire (Theatre World Award) 1988. *Television includes:* An Early Frost 1985, Perfect Witness 1989, Lies of the Twins 1991, A Private Matter 1992, Forbidden Territory: Stanley's Search for Livingstone 1997, The Prince and the Pauper 2000, See You in My Dreams 2000, Two of Us 2000, Benedict Arnold: A Question of Honor 2003, Plainsong 2004, Cavedweller 2004, Miracle Run 2004, Third Watch (series) 2004–05, The Exonerated 2005, Empire Falls 2005, Mayday 2005, The Book of Daniel (series) 2006, Bury My Heart at Wounded Knee 2007, Canterbury's Law 2008, White Collar 2010, Weeds 2011, Prime Suspect USA 2011–12, Elementary 2012–16. *Address:* Framework Entertainment, 9057 Nemo Street, Suite C, West Hollywood, CA 90069; c/o ICM, 8942 Wilshire Boulevard, Beverly Hills, CA 90211, USA.

QUINN, Brian, CBE, MA (Hons), MA (Econ), PhD; British banker, economist and consultant; *Chairman, Bvalco Ltd;* b. 18 Nov. 1936, Glasgow, Scotland; s. of Thomas Quinn and Margaret Cairns; m. Mary Bradley 1961; two s. one d.; ed Univs of Glasgow and Manchester, Cornell Univ., USA; economist, African Dept, IMF, Washington, DC 1964–70; Rep. of IMF in Sierra Leone 1966–68; joined Bank of England 1970, Econ. Div. 1970–74, Chief Cashier's Dept 1974–77, Head of Information Div. 1977–82, Asst Dir 1982–88, Head of Banking Supervision 1986–88, Exec. Dir 1988–96, Acting Deputy Gov. 1995; Chair. Nomura Bank Int. PLC 1996–99; Vice-Chair. Celtic PLC 1996–2000, Chair. 2000–07; Chair. Bvalco Ltd 2010–; mem. Club Financial Control Body, Union of European Football Asscns (UEFA) 2009–; Dir (non-exec.) Bankgesellschaft Berlin UK PLC 1996–2001, Britannic Asset Man. 1998–2004, Nomura Holdings Europe 1998–99; Man. Dir Brian Quinn Consultancy 1997–; Chair. Financial Markets Group, LSE 1996–2001; consultant, World Bank 1997–; Fellow, Chartered Inst. of Bankers in Scotland; Hon. Prof. of Econs and Finance, Univ. of Glasgow 2006–. *Publications:* contribs to various books and journals. *Leisure interests:* fishing, watching football, reading, walking. *Address:* Bvalco Ltd, Munro House, Portsmouth Road, Cobham, Surrey, KT11 1PP (office); 14 Homewood Road, St Albans, Herts., AL1 4BH, England (home). *Telephone:* (1727) 853900. *Fax:* (1727) 866646. *E-mail:* bqconns@aol.com. *Website:* www.bvalco.com (office).

QUINN, Marc, BA; British artist; b. 8 Jan. 1964, London; ed Univ. of Cambridge; contemporary visual artist working with organic and degradable materials including bread, lead, flowers and blood; known for portrayal of issues such as corporeality, decay and preservation; based in London. *Solo exhibitions include:* Tate Britain, London 1995, Kunstverein Hannover 1999, Fondazione Prada, Milan 2000, Tate Liverpool 2002, Irish Museum of Modern Art, Dublin 2004, DHC/ART Foundation for Contemporary Art, Montréal 2007, Fondation Beyeler, Basel 2009, White Cube Bermondsey, London 2015, Galerie Thomas, Munich 2015, Anima Gallery, Doha 2016, Galerie LeRoyer, Montréal 2018. *Group exhibitions include:* Royal Acad. of Arts, London 1997, Victoria and Albert Museum, London 2001, Henry Moore Inst., Leeds 2002, Louisiana Museum, Humblebaek 2004, Guangdong Museum of Art, Guangzhou 2007, Chatsworth House, Derbyshire 2008, 2011, Gloucester Cathedral, Gloucester 2010, Nat. Gallery, Helsinki 2010, Inst. of Contemporary Art, London 2012, Opera Gallery, London 2013, Osborne Samuel, London 2015, Tanya Baxter Contemporary, London 2016, Corridor Contemporary, Tel-Aviv 2017, New Gallery of Modern Art, Charlotte 2018. *E-mail:* mail@marcquinn.com. *Website:* www.marcquinn.com.

QUINN, Patrick (Pat) Joseph, III, BA, JD; American lawyer and fmr politician; b. 16 Dec. 1948, Hinsdale, Ill.; m. (divorced); two s.; ed Georgetown Univ., Northwestern Univ. School of Law; Commr, Cook Co. Bd of (Property) Tax Appeals 1982–86; Revenue Dir, City of Chicago 1986; Treas. State of Illinois 1991–95; Lt Gov. of Illinois 2003–09, Gov. of Illinois 2009–15; Chair. Blackout Solutions Task Force, Mississippi River Coordinating Council, Illinois Green Govts Coordinating Council, Illinois Biofuels Investment and Infrastructure Working Group, Broadband Deployment Council; Democrat; Commdr's Cross, Order of Merit (Poland) 2012. *Publication:* How to Appeal Your Property Taxes ... Without a Lawyer.

QUINN, Ruairi, BArch, RIBA; Irish politician, architect and town planner; b. 2 April 1946, Dublin; s. of Malachi Quinn and Julia Quinn; m. 1st Nicola Underwood 1969 (divorced); one s. one d.; m. 2nd Liz Allman 1990; one s.; ed Blackrock Coll. and Univ. Coll., Dublin, Athens Center of Ekistics, Greece; Athens Center of Ekistics, Greece 1970–71; Architects' Dept, Dublin Corpn 1971–73; Pnr, Burke-Kennedy Doyle and Pnr 1973–82; mem. Dublin Corpn 1974–77, 1981–82; mem. Seanad Éireann 1976–77, 1981–82; mem. Dáil Éireann for Dublin SE constituency 1977–81, 1982–; Minister of State, Dept of Environment 1982–83; Minister for Labour and Minister for Public Service 1983–87; Deputy Leader, Irish Labour Party 1989, Leader 1997–2002; Treas. Party of European Socialists 2000, also Vice-Pres.; Dir of Elections for Pres. Mary Robinson; Labour Spokesperson on Finance and Econ. Affairs 1990, on European Affairs, on Enterprise, Trade and Employment 2006; Minister for Enterprise and Employment 1993–94, for Finance 1994–97, for Educ. and Skills 2011–14; mem. Royal Inst. of Architects of Ireland. *Publication:* Straight Left: A Journey in Politics 2005. *Leisure interests:* athletics, reading, hill walking. *Address:* Dáil Éireann, Leinster House, Kildare Street, Dublin 2 (office); 23 Strand Road, Sandymount, Dublin 4, Ireland (home). *Telephone:* (1) 6183434 (office). *Fax:* (1) 6184153 (office). *E-mail:* ruairi.quinn@oireachtas.ie (office). *Website:* www.ruairiquinn.ie (office).

QUIÑONES AMEZQUITA, Mario Rafael; Guatemalan lawyer and diplomatist; b. 4 June 1933, Quezaltenango; s. of Hector Quiñones and Elisa de Quiñones; m. Yolanda de Quiñones 1963; two s. two d.; ed Univ. of San Carlos and Univ. of Rio Grande do Sul, Brazil; lawyer and notary with law firm of Viteri, Falla, Quiñones, Umaña, Orellana y Cáceres 1959–; Prof. of Law, Rafael Landívar Univ. 1962, Dean Dept of Legal and Social Sciences 1974–82; Vice-Pres. of Landívar Univ. 1978–82, Pres. March–Oct. 1982; Amb. and Perm. Rep. to UN 1982–84; Minister of Foreign Affairs 1986–87; Vice-Pres. N and Cen. American Region, Union of Latin Notaries 1978; Pres. Asscn of Lawyers and Notaries of Guatemala 1977; mem. Guatemalan Del. UN Comm. on Int. Trade Law 1974; Orden de Malta, Orden dell Quetzal, Orden de los Cinco Volcanes and decorations from govts of Spain, Peru, Germany,

Argentina and Mexico; Dr hc (Univ. Rafael Landivar) 1998. *Leisure interests:* reading, music. *Address:* 6A Calle 5-47, Zona 9 –3er. Nivel, Guatemala City 01009 (office); 8 Avenida 5-55, Zona 14, Condominio Villalbosque Torre Norte, Apartamento 1501, Guatemala (office). *Telephone:* (2) 2331-1721 (office); (2) 2368-1449 (home). *Fax:* (2) 2337-0186 (home). *E-mail:* mrqamz20@gmail.com (office).

QUIÑÓNEZ, Alfonso, MA; Guatemalan lawyer, diplomatist and international organization executive; ed Francisco Marroquín Univ. of Guatemala, Georgetown Univ., Washington, DC, Univ. of Maryland, Inter-American Defense Coll., Washington, DC; mem. Guatemalan Foreign Service for 10 years, held positions of Counsellor in Spain, Minister Counsellor in USA, Amb. and Perm. Rep. to OAS 1998–2000; Exec. Dir Alvaro Arzú Foundation for Peace, Guatemala and Adviser to Mayor of Guatemala City –2001; Dir Dept of Co-operation Policies, OAS 2001, later Dir Office of Policies and Programs for Devt, OAS Exec. Secr. for Integral Devt, later Chief of Staff to Asst Sec.-Gen., Acting Exec. Sec. for Integral Devt and Acting Dir-Gen. Inter-American Agency for Integral Devt 2004–05, Exec. Sec. for Integral Devt and Dir-Gen. Inter-American Agency for Co-operation and Devt 2005, fmr Sec. for External Relations, OAS; Prof., Schools of Law and Int. Relations, Francisco Marroquín Univ. 2001–02; currently Int. Relations Man. Grupo Progreso; mem. Bd of Trustees UN Inst. for Training and Research (UNITAR); mem. Advisory Council ADF Int. *Address:* c/o ADF International, PO Box 0001, 1082, Vienna, Austria. *Website:* www.adfinternational.org.

QUINTANILLA SCHMIDT, Carlos, BSc; Salvadorean lawyer and politician; b. 5 Aug. 1953, San Miguel; m. Alexandra Rodríguez; two s.; ed José Matías Delgado Univ., San Salvador, American Univ., Washington, DC, USA; Pnr, Guandique-Segovia-Quintanilla, San Salvador (law firm) 1981–; Prof. of Commercial Law, José Matías Delgado Univ. 1985–, Dean, School of Law 1986–92, Deputy Dean of Univ. 1992; Legal Counsel to Alianza Republicana Nacionalista (ARENA) party 1988–97, mem. Exec. Body 1997–; Vice-Pres. of El Salvador 1999–2004; Vice-Pres. Canadian Chamber of Commerce of El Salvador; mem. Bd of Dirs Fundación Salvadoreña para el Desarrollo Económico y Social (think tank) 2005; Dr hc (Univ. Dr José Matías Delgado) 2014. *Address:* Guandique-Segovia-Quintanilla, Pasaje Senda Florida Norte #124, Colonia Escalón, San Salvador, El Salvador (office). *Telephone:* 2245-3444 (office). *Fax:* 2298-6613 (office). *E-mail:* cquintanilla@gsqlaw.com (office). *Website:* www.gsqlaw.com (office).

QUIRK, James Patrick, AO, PhD, DSc, FAA; Australian agricultural scientist and academic; *Professor Emeritus, Faculty of Natural and Agricultural Sciences, University of Western Australia;* b. 17 Dec. 1924, Sydney; s. of J. P. Quirk; m. Helen M. Sykes 1950; one s. one d.; ed Christian Brothers High School, Lewisham, St John's Coll., Univ. of Sydney and Univ. of London; Research Scientist, CSIRO Div. of Soils, Soil Physics Section 1947; CSIRO Sr Postgraduate Studentship, Physics Dept, Rothamsted Experimental Station, England 1950; Research Scientist, Sr Research Scientist, CSIRO 1952–56; Reader in Soil Science, Dept of Agricultural Chem., Waite Agricultural Research Inst., Univ. of Adelaide 1956–62; Carnegie Travelling Fellow, USA 1960; Foundation Prof. and Head, Dept of Soil Science and Plant Nutrition, Univ. of WA 1963–74, Emer. Prof. 1974–, Dir Inst. of Agric. 1971–74, Dir, Waite Agricultural Research Inst. and Prof. 1974–89, Emer. Prof. and Hon. Research Fellow, Univ. of WA 1990–; Prof. Fellow, Dept Applied Math., ANU 1990–96, Hon. Prof. Fellow 1996–; Commonwealth Visiting Prof., Oxford Univ. 1967; Fellow, Australian Acad. of Science (Sec. Biological Sciences 1990–94), Australian Inst. of Agricultural Science, Australian Acad. of Technological Sciences and Eng (mem. Council 1996–), American Soc. of Agronomy, Australian and NZ Asscn for Advancement of Science; Hon. mem. Int. Union of Soil Science 1998; Hon. DSc Agric. (Louvain, Belgium) 1978, (Melbourne) 1990, (Western Australia) 1991, (Sydney) 1997; Prescott Medal for Soil Science 1975, Medal of Australian Inst. of Agricultural Science 1980, Farrer Memorial Medal 1982, Mueller Medal 1988, Brindley Lecturer (USA) 1992, Distinguished Service Award (Soil Science Soc. of America) 1996. *Publications:* about 200 scientific publs. *Leisure interests:* reading, tennis. *Address:* 70 Archdeacon Street, Nedlands, WA 6009, Australia (home). *Telephone:* (8) 9386-5948 (home).

QUIROGA RAMÍREZ, Jorge Fernando, BEng, MBA; Bolivian engineer and politician; b. 5 May 1960, Cochabamba; m. Virginia Gillum 1989; four c.; ed La Salle Coll., Santa Cruz de la Sierra, Texas A&M Univ. and St Edward's Univ., Austin, Tex.; with IBM, Austin, Tex. 1981–88; returned to Bolivia 1988; Econometrician, Mintec 1988; Vice-Pres. Banco Mercantil de Bolivia 1988; mem. Acción Democrática Nacionalista (ADN) 1988–, apptd Deputy Leader 1995, Leader 2001–04; Under-Sec. for Public Investment and Int. Co-operation, Ministry of Planning 1989–90; Minister of Finance 1990–93; Gov. Cooperación Financiera de Inversiones –1993; Dir Andean Devt Corpn –1993; Nat. Sec. Política Social –1993; led electoral campaign of ADN 1993 then worked in pvt. sector; Vice-Pres. of Bolivia 1997–2001, Acting Pres. July–Aug. 2001, Pres. of Bolivia 2001–02; Leader, Poder Democrático Social (PODEMOS) 2005; cand. in presidential election (Partido Demócrata Cristiano) 2014; fmr Gov. IBRD and IMF. *Leisure interests:* football, basketball, mountain-climbing. *Address:* Acción Democrática Nacionalista (ADN), La Paz, Bolivia (office). *Website:* www.bolivian.com/adn.

QUJAUKITSOQ, Vittus; Greenlandic politician; *Minister of Finance and Nordic Cooperation;* b. 5 Oct. 1971, Qaanaaq; m. Naja Kreutzmann Qujaukitsoq 2011; one d.; ed Nuuk Trade and Business School; Head of Secr. of Trade and Industrial Council, Sisimiut 1997; Pvt. Asst to Minister of Social Affairs, Labour and Public Works 1997–99, to Minister of Fisheries, Hunting, Agric. and Industry 2000–01; Corp. Sec., Royal Greenland A/S (fishing co.) 2001–05; Corp. Sec. and Communications Officer, Nukissiorfiit (state-owned energy co.) 2005; Communication Dir KNI A/S (trading group) 2005–06; Pvt. Asst to MP Lars-Emil Johansen 2007–10, to Minister of Culture, Educ., Church and Research 2008, to Minister of Housing, Transportation and Infrastructure 2009; Mineral Resources Adviser, SIK (trade union) 2010–13; mem. Inatsisartut (parl.) 2013–; Minister for Finance and Domestic Affairs 2013–14, for Foreign Affairs 2014–16, Minister of Commerce, Employment, Trade, Energy and Foreign Affairs 2016–17, Minister of Minerals, Labour, Interior and Nordic Cooperation 2018, Minister of Finance and Nordic Cooperation 2018–; mem. Siumut party, Organizational Sec. 1994–95, Organizational Vice-Chair. 2011–14. *Address:* Grønlands Selvstyre (Naalakkersuisut), Imaneq 4, POB 1015, 3900 Nuuk, Greenland (office). *Telephone:* 345000 (office). *Fax:* 325002 (office). *E-mail:* info@nanoq.gl (office). *Website:* naalakkersuisut.gl (office).

QURAISHI, Abdul Aziz Bin Said al-, MBA, FIBA; Saudi Arabian government official and business executive; *CEO, Ali Zaid Al-Quraishi & Brothers Company Ltd;* b. 1930, Hail; s. of Zaid al-Quraishi and Sheikhah Abdul Aziz; m. Amal Abdul Aziz al-Turki 1965; one s. two d.; ed Univ. of Southern California, USA; Gen. Man. State Railways 1961–68; Pres. Gen. Personnel Bureau 1968–74; Minister of State 1971–74; Gov. Saudi Arabian Monetary Agency 1974–83; fmr Gov. for Saudi Arabia, IMF, Arab Monetary Fund; fmr Alt. Gov. for Saudi Arabia, Islamic Devt Bank; fmr mem. Bd of Dirs Supreme Council for Petroleum and Mineral Affairs, Gen. Petroleum and Mineral Org., Public Investment Fund, Pension Fund; CEO Ali Zaid Al-Quraishi & Brothers Co. Ltd, Riyadh 1983–; Co-Chair. US-Saudi Arabian Business Council 1993–; fmr Chair. Nat. Saudi Shipping Co., Riyadh 1983; Vice-Chair. Saudi Int. Bank, London 1983–; mem. Int. Advisory Bd, Security Pacific Nat. Bank of LA 1983–; King Abdul Aziz Medal (Second Class), Order of Brilliant Star with Grand Cordon (Taiwan), Order of Diplomatic Merit, Gwan Ghwa Medal (Repub. of Korea), King Leopold Medal, Commdr Class (Belgium), Emperor of Japan Award, Order of Sacred Treasure (First Class) 1980. *Address:* Ali Zaid Al-Quraishi & Brothers Co. Ltd, PO Box 339, Dammam 31411 (office); PO Box 1848, Riyadh 11441, Saudi Arabia (home). *Telephone:* (3) 833-3339 (office). *Fax:* (3) 834-3402 (office). *E-mail:* info@alquraishi.com (office). *Website:* www.alquraishi.com (office).

QURAISHI, Shahabuddin Yaqoob, PhD; Indian fmr government official and author; b. 11 July 1947; m. Huma Quraishi (separated); ed St Stephen's Coll., Delhi; joined Indian Admin. Services 1971, has held numerous positions including Special Sec. (Health), Sec., Sports and Youth Affairs –2006; Chief Election Commr 2010–12; served as consultant to UNICEF, Dir-Gen. Nat. AIDS Control Org., Doordarshan, Nehru Yuva Kendra Sangathan; Founder-Dir Rajiv Gandhi Nat. Inst. of Youth Devt, Sriperumbudur, Dir 1993–97; fmr Dir Women and Child Devt; nominated as Specialist and Resource Person for Int. Conf. on Islam and Family Planning, Ankara 1995; Hon. Fellowship of Nat. Indian Students 2016, Alumni Union UK 2016. *Publication:* Social Marketing for Social Change 1996, Old Delhi: Living Traditions 2011, An Undocumented Wonder: The Great Indian Election 2014.

QURAY, Ahmad, (Abu Ala); Palestinian diplomatist and politician; b. 1937, Abu Dis; joined Fatah 1968, currently mem. Revolutionary Council Cen. Cttee; fmr Minister of Economy and Trade and Minister of Industry, Palestinian Authority; Chief Palestinian Negotiator, Oslo Agreement 1993 and all subsequent Israeli–Palestinian talks including Taba, Cairo, Wye River, and talks in 2007; Founder and Dir Palestinian Econ. Council for Devt and Reconstruction 1993; Deputy and Speaker Palestinian Legis. Council 1996–2003; Prime Minister, Palestinian Authority (PA) 2003–05 (resgnd), Head Nat. Security Council 2004–05; mem. Palestinian Nat. Council; mem. Bd Palestinian Econ. Policy Research Inst., Peres Center for Peace; mem. Bd of Advisers Gleitsman Foundation; Norwegian Royal Order of Merit 1994; Seeds of Peace Foundation Award 1996, Gleitsman Foundation Int. Activist Award 1999. *Publications include:* Hanging Peace; numerous economic essays.

QURBONOV, Abdusalom; Tajikistani politician; Head, Construction Dept of Presidential Admin –2013; Minister of Finance 2013–17.

QURBONOV, Maj.-Gen. Bahodir; Uzbekistani army officer and politician; *Minister of Defence;* Deputy Minister of Internal Affairs 2015; Commdr, Tashkent Mil. Dist 2018–19; Minister of Defence 2019–. *Address:* Ministry of Defence, 100000 Tashkent, Mirzo Ulug'bek ko'ch. 100, Uzbekistan (office). *Telephone:* (71) 269-82-00 (office). *Fax:* (71) 262-82-28 (office). *E-mail:* mudofaa@umail.uz (office). *Website:* www.mudofaa.uz (office).

QURESHI, Ashraf; Pakistani diplomatist and public servant; ed Fletcher School of Law and Diplomacy, Tufts Univ., USA, Quaid-e-Azam Univ.; joined Foreign Service 1977, served in numerous positions including Section Officer 1978–80, Dir 1985–87, 1995–97, Dir-Gen. 1997–98, 2003–04, Additional Sec., Prime Minister's Secr. 2004–05; diplomatic assignments include postings in Tunis 1980–85, New York 1988–93, Kuala Lumpur 1993–95, Brussels 1998–2001, High Commr to Sri Lanka 2001–03, to South Africa 2006–10, to Bangladesh 2010–11, Amb., Ministry of Foreign Affairs 2011–12 (retd); Advisor, ABWA Knowledge Village 2017–; mem. Punjab Public Service Comm., Govt of Punjab 2012–. *Address:* Punjab Public Service Commission, LDA Plaza (Edgerton Road), Lahore 54000, Pakistan (office). *Telephone:* (42) 99202752 (office). *E-mail:* ppsc@punjab.gov.pk (office).

QURESHI, Aziz, MA, LLB; Indian lawyer and politician; b. 24 April 1940, Bhopal; ed Govt Hamidia Coll., Bhopal, Agra Univ., Vikram Univ., Ujjain, Bhopal Univ.; nine years as Head of Dept of Political Science, one year as Prin., Aurobindo Arts and Law Coll., Bhopal; mem. Madhya Pradesh Legis. Ass. (state Parl.) 1972–77; served as minister in several Madhya Pradesh state govts, including as Minister for Irrigation and Power 1972–75, for Educ. and Endowments 1976–77; mem. Lok Sabha (lower house of Parl.) from Satna, Madhya Pradesh (Congress) 1984–89; Gov. of Uttarakhand 2012–14, also of Uttar Pradesh June–July 2014, of Mizoram 2014–15. *Leisure interests:* reading, music, travelling, angling.

QURESHI, Makhdoom Shah Mehmood, BA, MA; Pakistani politician; *Minister of Foreign Affairs;* b. 22 June 1956, Murree; s. of Makhdoom Muhammad Sajjad Hussain Qureshi; m.; one s. two d.; ed Aitchison Coll., Lahore, Forman Christian Coll., Lahore, Corpus Christi Coll., Cambridge, UK; grew up in Multan; returned to Pakistan following law studies in UK 1983; mem. Punjab Ass. 1985–93; Chair. Dist Council, Multan 1987–91; served as Minister for Planning and Devt, Punjab; Minister of Finance, Punjab 1990–93; Fed. Minister for Parl. Affairs 1994–96; Dist Nazim (Mayor) of Multan 2001–02; mem. Nat. Ass. (Pakistan People's Party, PPP) from Multan 2002–11 (resigned); Minister of Foreign Affairs 2008–11, 2018–; resigned from PPP and joined Pakistan Tehreek-e-Insaf (PTI) party 2011, Vice-Chair. 2011–; mem. Nat. Ass. (PTI) from NA-150 (Multan-III) 2013–; Chair. Farmers Asscn of Pakistan 1991; Co-Chair. SOS Children's Village, Multan 1997; mem. Bd of Govs Aitchison Coll.; Life Patron Al-Shifa Trust. *Leisure interests:* reading, watching television. *Address:* Ministry of Foreign Affairs, Constitution Avenue, Islamabad (office); Bab E Alquresh, Doulat Gate, Circular Road, House No. 445/W-6M, Multan, Pakistan (home). *Telephone:* (51) 9210335 (office). *Fax:* (51) 9207600 (office). *E-mail:* info@mofa.gov.pk (office). *Website:* www.mofa.gov.pk (office).

R

RA, Jong-yil, BA, MA, PhD; South Korean academic, university administrator and fmr diplomatist; *University Distinguished Professor of Political Science, Gachon University;* b. 5 Dec. 1940, Seoul; s. of Ra Ionggwyn and Park Gwinye; m. Hong Jae-ja; one s. three d.; ed Seoul Nat. Univ., Trinity Coll., Cambridge, UK; held teaching posts at several univs, including Kyunghee, Southern California, Michigan and Stanford, USA, Cambridge and Sussex, UK; Chief of Admin of Presidential Transition Cttee 1997–98; First and Second Dir Nat. Intelligence Service 1998–99; Special Asst to Pres. for Foreign and Security Affairs 1999–2001; Amb. to UK 2001–03; Sr Adviser to Pres. for Nat. Security 2003; Amb. to Japan 2004–07; Pres. Woosuk Univ. 2007–11; currently Univ. Distinguished Prof. of Political Science, Gachon Univ.; mem. Presidential Cttee for Preparation of Unification; Chair. Prof., Nat. Defence Coll.; Grand Cordon, Order of the Rising Sun (Japan); Hon. Medal of Sahak Metrey with rank of Moha Sena (Cambodia). *Publications include:* Politics of Western Europe 1982, Cooperation and Conflict 1986, The New Right 1990, Perestroika and its Impacts 1991, Points of Departure 1992, Unfinished War 1994, Man and Politics 1995, In Preparation for the New Millennium 1999, Advantage of Hindsight 2001, Conflict and Resolution in the Korean Church 2002, The Perspectives on the Community of Nations in East Asia, Beijing 2004, Cultural Perspective of East Asian Regional Community 2006, The Discovery of the World: A Korean Perspective 2009 (Korean trans. 2009, subsequently translated into 12 languages), On the Idea of America 2010, Wizard of Naktong River (co-author) 2010, Poreuthentes 2011, Aristotle's Politics (revised edn) 2012, Forgotten Terrorist 2013, Democracy or Alternative Political Systems in Asia 2014, Most Trivial Salvation 2015, The Way of Jang 2016. *Leisure interest:* playing tennis. *Address:* Gachon University, 1342 Seongnam-daero, Bokjeong-dong, Sujeong-gu, Seongnam-si, Gyeonggi-do, Republic of Korea (office). *Telephone:* (31) 750-8904 (office). *E-mail:* froggi1970@naver.com (office).

RAAB, Dominic, LLM, JD; British lawyer and politician; b. 25 Feb. 1974, Buckinghamshire; m. Erika Rey-Raab; two c.; ed Lady Margaret Hall, Oxford, Jesus Coll., Cambridge; began career as solicitor, Linklaters, London; worked at Foreign & Commonwealth Office 2000–06, including as Legal Advisor, Embassy in The Hague 2003; Chief of Staff to Shadow Home Sec. David Davis 2006–08, to Shadow Sec. of State for Justice Dominic Grieve 2008–10; mem. House of Commons (Conservative) for Esher and Walton 2010–; Parl. UnderSec. of State for Civil Liberties 2015–16; Minister of State for Housing, Ministry of Housing, Communities and Local Govt Jan.–July 2018; Sec. of State for Exiting the EU July–Nov. 2018 (resgnd); mem. Conservative Party. *Address:* c/o Department for Exiting the European Union, 9 Downing St, London, SW1A 2AS, England (office).

RAAD, Walid, BFA, MA, PhD; Lebanese artist and academic; *Associate Professor of Art, Cooper Union School of Art;* b. (Walid Ra'ad), 1967, Chbanieh; ed Boston Univ., Rochester Inst. of Tech. and Univ. of Rochester, USA; works include mixed media, installations, performance, video and photography, and literary essays; f. The Atlas Group (imaginary foundation whose objective is to research and document Lebanon's contemporary history, especially the Lebanese wars 1975–91) 1999, with work presented through films, photography exhbns, videos and documents; has co-curated, with Akram Zaatari, the exhbn Mapping Sitting: On Portraiture and Photography, an investigation in Arab photography and its relationship to questions of identity; Instructor, Dept of Art and Art History, Univ. of Rochester 1991–95, Instructor, Dept of Film Studies 1994–95; Asst Prof., School of Humanities, Cultural Studies and Arts, Hampshire Coll. 1995–98; Asst Prof., Dept of Media Studies, Queen's Coll., CUNY 1998–2002; Asst Prof. of Art, Cooper Union School of Art, New York 2002–05, Assoc. Prof. of Art 2005–; Fellow, Vera List Center for Art and Politics, New School 2004–05; mem. Arab Image Foundation; Best Conceptual Innovation Award, New England Film and Video Festival, Boston 1997, Award of Accomplishment Experimental, Missouri Video Festival, St Louis, Mo. 1998, Director's Citation, Black Maria Film and Video Festival, NJ 1999, Best Short Film and Best Scenario for a Short Film, Beirut Film Festival 1999, Grand Prize, 8th Biennial of the Moving Image, Switzerland 1999, First Prize, VideoEx, Zurich 2000, 2001, Special Jury Prize, 5th Biennial of Arab Cinemas, Institut du Monde Arabe, Paris 2000, Certificate of Merit, San Francisco Int. Film Festival 2000, Rhineland Award, Oberhausen Film and VideoFest, Oberhausen, Germany 2001, Juror Citation Award, Black Maria Festival 2002, Special Prize, Media Arts Awards, ZKM, Karlsruhe, Germany 2002, First Prize, Oneiras Film and Video Festival, Lisbon 2002, First Prize, Vidarte Festival, Mexico City 2002, First Prize, Onion City Experimental Film and Video Festival 2002, Rockefeller Fellowship, NYSCA 2003, Rockefeller Fellowship 2003, Camera Austria Award 2005, Lauréat d'Aide au projet, Rencontres d'Arles, Arles, France 2006, First Prize, Deutsche Börse Photography Prize, London 2007, Alpert Award for Visual Arts, Herb Alpert Foundation 2007, Hasselblad Prize 2011. *Video works include:* Talaeen a Junuub (Up to the South) 1993, I Think It Would Be Better If I Could Weep, a collection of video shorts titled The Dead Weight of a Quarrel Hangs 1996–99, Hostage: The Bachar Tapes 2000; mixed-media projects include The Atlas Group: Documents from The Atlas Group Archive (1999–), The Loudest Muttering Is Over: Documents from The Atlas Group Archive (2001–), My Neck Is Thinner Than A Hair 2004. *Publications:* The Truth Will be Known When the Last Witness is Dead, My Neck is Thinner than a Hair, Scratching on Things I Could Disavow, Let's Be Honest, The Weather Helped. *Address:* The Cooper Union School of Art, Room 236, 7 East 7th Street, New York, NY 10003, USA (office). *Telephone:* (212) 353-4214 (office); (917) 345-0065 (office). *E-mail:* wraad@earthlink.net; info@walidraad.com. *Website:* www.walidraad.com; www .theatlasgroup.org; cooper.edu/art/people/walid-raad (office).

RÄÄTS, Jaan; Estonian composer and teacher; *Professor Emeritus of Composition, Estonian Academy of Music;* b. 15 Oct. 1932, Tartu; s. of Peeter Rääts and Linda Rääts; m. 1st Marianne Rääts 1958; m. 2nd Ebba Rääts 1983; three c.; ed Tartu Music School with Aleksandra Sarv, Tallinn Conservatory with Mart Saar, Heino Eller; mem. CPSU 1964–90; recording engineer, Estonian Radio 1955–66, Chief Dir Music Programmes, Estonian TV 1966–74; teacher of composition, Tallinn Conservatory (later Estonian Acad. of Music) 1968–70, 1974, Prof. 1990–2003, Prof. Emer. 2003–; initiated Estonian Music Days 1979; mem. Estonian Composers Union 1957–, Vice-Chair. 1964–74, Chair. 1974–93; Order

of the White Star (3rd Class) 2002; Merited Art Worker of Estonian SSR 1965, Literature and Art Award of Estonian Soviet Communist Youth Organisation 1970, Annual Music Award, Estonian SSR 1974, People's Artist of Estonian SSR 1977, Estonian State Cultural Award 1995, Annual Prize of Endowment for Music of Culture Endowment of Estonia 2002, Annual Award of Cultural Endowment of Estonia 2007, Lifetime Achievement Award, Estonian National Culture Foundation 2011, Lifetime Achievement Award of Repub. of Estonia 2011. *Compositions include:* Symphony No. 1 1957, Symphony No. 2 1958, Symphony No. 3 1959, Symphony No. 4 Cosmic 1959, Concerto for chamber orchestra No. 1 1961, Violin Concerto No. 1 1963, Symphony No. 5 1966, Symphony No. 6 1967, Piano Concerto No. 1 1968, 24 Preludes 1968, Toccata 1970, Symphony No. 7 1973, 24 Estonian Preludes 1977, Violin Concerto No. 2 1979, 24 Marginalia 1979, 24 Marginalia for two pianos 1982, Piano Concerto No. 2 1983, Symphony No. 8 1985, Concerto for two pianos and symphony orchestra 1986, Concerto for chamber orchestra No. 2 1987, Piano Concerto No. 3 1990, Concerto for guitar and orchestra 1992, Concerto for trumpet and piano 1994, Concerto for violin and chamber orchestra 1995, Violin Concerto No. 3 1995, Five Sketches for Requiem for symphony orchestra 1999, Concerto for flute, guitar and symphony orchestra 2001, Symphony No. 9, Symphony No. 10, 10 piano sonatas, seven piano trios –2004, six string quartets. *Film scores:* Roosa kübar 1963, Null kolm 1965, Tütarlaps mustas 1966, Supernova 1966, Viini postmark 1967, Gladiaator 1969, Tuulevaikus 1971, Väike reekviem suupillile 1972, Ohtlikud mängud 1974, Aeg elada, aeg armastada 1976, Pihlakaväravad 1982. *Leisure interests:* technology, science. *Address:* c/o Estonian Composers' Union, A. Lauteri Street 7c, 10145 Tallinn, Estonia. *Telephone:* 646-6536 (office); 648-5744 (home). *E-mail:* heliloojate.liit@gmail.com (office); emie@emie.ee; ebba@hot.ee. *Website:* www.jaanraats.com.

RABAN, Jonathan Mark Hamilton Priaulx, BA, FRSL; British author and critic; b. 14 June 1942, Fakenham, Norfolk, England; s. of Rev. Peter J. C. P. Raban and Monica Sandison; m. 1st Bridget Johnson (divorced 1970s); m. 2nd Caroline Cuthbert 1985 (divorced 1992); m. 3rd Jean Cara Lenihan 1992 (divorced 1997); one d.; ed King's School, Worcester, Peter Symonds School, Winchester, Brockenhurst Grammar, Univ. of Hull; Asst Lecturer, Univ. Coll. of Wales, Aberystwyth 1965–67; Lecturer in English and American Literature, Univ. of East Anglia 1967–69; professional writer 1969–; emigrated to USA 1990; Hon. DLitt (Univ. of Hull); Pacific Northwest Booksellers Asscn Award, Murray Morgan Prize, Gov.'s Award of State of Washington. *Publications include:* The Technique of Modern Fiction 1969, Mark Twain: Huckleberry Finn 1969, The Society of the Poem 1971, Soft City 1973, Robert Lowell's Poems (ed.) 1974, Arabia Through the Looking Glass 1979, Old Glory (RSL Heinemann Award 1982, Thomas Cook Award 1982) 1981, Foreign Land (novel) 1985, Coasting 1986, For Love and Money 1987, God, Man & Mrs Thatcher 1989, Hunting Mister Heartbreak (Thomas Cook Award 1991) 1990, The Oxford Book of the Sea (ed.) 1992, Bad Land: An American Romance (Nat. Book Critics Circle Award 1996, PEN/West Creative Nonfiction Award 1997) 1996, Passage to Juneau 1999, Waxwings (novel) 2003, My Holy War: Dispatches from the Home Front 2005, Surveillance (novel) 2006, Driving Home: An American Journey 2011; contribs to Harper's, Esquire, New Republic, Atlantic Monthly, New York Review of Books, London Review of Books, Outside, Granta, New York Times Book Review, Vogue, The Guardian, Independent, Financial Times, Wall Street Journal. *Leisure interest:* sailing. *Address:* c/o Aitken Alexander Associates Ltd, 18–21 Cavaye Place, London, SW10 9PT, England (office). *Telephone:* (20) 7373-8672 (office). *Fax:* (20) 7373-6002 (office). *E-mail:* reception@aitkenalexander.co.uk (office). *Website:* www.jonathanraban.com (office).

RABARY-NJAKA, Henry; Malagasy lawyer and politician; b. 14 Sept. 1965, Antananarivo; s. of Henri Rabary-Njaka and Julienne Rasamoelina; m. Dominique Rabearivelo 1992; two s.; ed Coll. St Antoine, Antananarivo, Univ. Panthéon Assas, Paris, Univ. Panthéon Sorbonne, Paris; began career with Malagasy Civil Service 1982–83; Lawyer, Kaba & Assocs, Abidjan 1988–90, Trainee Attorney 1990–91, Fellow Attorney 1991–93; Int. Trainee, Conference Int. des Barreaux francophones 1990–91; moved to France 1993; mem. Barreau (Bar) de Paris; Lawyer, Bochet & Assocs, Paris 1995–98; fmr Dir, Cabinet of the Presidency; fmr Chair., Air Madagascar; Minister of Foreign Affairs 2017–18. *Publication:* Le crédit documentaire à Madagascar 1987. *Address:* c/o Ministry of Foreign Affairs, rue Andriamifidy, Anosy, BP 836, 101 Antananarivo, Madagascar (office).

RABBAGLIETTI AMOR, Linda; Uruguayan accountant and international organization official; ed Univ. de La República, Montevideo; more than 20 years as Technical Adviser, Ministry of Economy and Finance; Alt Rep. of Uruguay to Asociación Latinoamericana de Integración (ALADI) and MERCOSUR 2006–15; Dir, MERCOSUR Secr. (first female) 2017–18. *Address:* c/o MERCOSUR, Edif. Mercosur, Luis Piera 1992, 1°, 11200 Montevideo, Uruguay (office).

RABBANI, Raza, BA, LLB; Pakistani lawyer and politician; b. 23 July 1953, Lahore; s. of Mian Ata Rabbani; ed Univ. of Karachi; Founder-Chair. Nat. Org. of Progressive Students 1971–74, jailed during Gen. Zia regime; held several local positions in Pakistan Peoples Party (PPP), including Information Sec., East Karachi Dist, Deputy Sec.-Gen. Karachi Div., mem. PPP Sindh Exec. Cttee, Pres. Peoples Lawyers Forum Sindh; Adviser to Chief Minister for Cooperatives, Sindh 1989–90; mem. Senate for Sindh 1994–2018, Deputy Leader of the Opposition 1996–99, Leader of the Opposition 2005–06, Leader Parl. Party PPP-Senate 2006–09, Leader of the House 2008–09, Chair. Parl. Cttee on Nat. Security, Parl. Cttee on Constitutional Reform, Chair. of the Senate 2015–18; Fed. Minister for Inter-provincial Coordination 2008 (resgnd), 2011 (resgnd), Fed. Minister of State for Law and Justice 1994–96; apptd Deputy Sec.-Gen. PPP 1997, Acting Sec.-Gen. PPP 2001–03; Adviser to Prime Minister 2010–11; Chair. Implementation Comm. on 18th Constitutional Amendment 2010–11; jt cand. (PPP, Awami Nat. Party, Balochistan Nat. Party) for Pres. of Pakistan 2013 (boycotted election); mem. High Court Bar Asscn; Nishan-i-Imtiaz, Human Rights Award of the Lawyers Cttee for Human Rights 1986, Bacha Khan Award for Defence of Prov. Rights 2011. *Publications:* A Biography of Pakistani Federalism, LFO: A Fraud on the Constitution. *Address:* House No:16, Minister Enclave, F-5, Islamabad (home);

14/II, Street 31, Phase-V, DHA, Opp. Khayaban-e-Shamshir, Karachi, Pakistan (home). *Telephone:* (51) 9223854 (home). *E-mail:* rrabbani@cyber.net.pk (office).

RABBANI, Salahuddin, BSc, MBA, MIA; Afghan politician and diplomatist; *Minister of Foreign Affairs;* b. 10 May 1971, Kabul; s. of Burhanuddin Rabbani (fmr Pres. of Afghanistan); m.; four c.; ed King Fahd Univ. of Petroleum and Minerals, Saudi Arabia, Kingston Univ., UK, Columbia Univ., USA; started career in Financial Accounting Dept, Aramco, Saudi Arabia; apptd interpreter and adviser, Presidential Palace 1998; joined Ministry of Foreign Affairs 2002, Political Consular, Perm. Mission to UN, New York 2003–06; Deputy Head for Political Affairs, Jamiat-i-Islami Party 2008, apptd Chair. (acting) 2012 (after assassination of his father), also Man. Noor TV (party's TV channel); Amb. to Turkey 2011–12; apptd Chair. High Peace Council 2012; Minister of Foreign Affairs 2015–. *Address:* Ministry of Foreign Affairs, Malek Asghar Street, Kabul, Afghanistan (office). *Telephone:* (20) 2100372 (office). *Fax:* (20) 2100360 (office). *E-mail:* contact@mfa.gov.af (office). *Website:* mfa.gov.af (office).

RABBATTS, Dame Heather Victoria, DBE, BA, MSc; British lawyer and business executive; *Managing Director, Smuggler Entertainment;* b. 6 Dec. 1955, Kingston, Jamaica; d. of Thomas Rabbatts and Hyacinth Rabbatts; m. 2nd Mike Lee; one s. from previous m.; ed Univ. of London, London School of Econs; called to the Bar 1981; Policy and Parl. Adviser to Local Govt Information Unit 1985–87; Deputy Chief Exec., London Borough of Hammersmith & Fulham 1987–92; Chief Exec., London Borough of Merton 1992–95, London Borough of Lambeth 1995–2000; Founder and CEO iMpower Group PLC 2000; joined Channel 4 2002, Man. Dir 4Learning (Head of Educ.) 2002–06; currently Man. Dir Smuggler Entertainment, Cove Pictures; Gov., BBC 1999–2001; Chair. (non-exec.) Shed Media PLC 2009; Dir Millwall Holdings PLC 2006–10, Exec. Deputy Chair. May–Oct. 2006, Exec. Chair. 2006; Dir (non-exec.) Grosvenor (property co.), Bank of England 2003–07, Crossrail Ltd 2008–14, Royal Opera House 2009–, The Football Asscn 2011–17; fmr Dir (non-exec.) UK Film Council. *Address:* Smuggler Entertainment, 6–10 Great Portland Street, London, W1W 8QL, England (office). *Telephone:* (20) 7636-7665 (office). *Fax:* (20) 7637-4667 (office). *E-mail:* rabbatts@smugglersite.com (office). *Website:* smugglersite.com (office).

RABE, Thomas, BA, MBA, Dr rer. pol; Luxembourg business executive; *Chairman and CEO, Bertelsmann SE & Co. KGaA;* b. 6 Aug. 1965; ed École Européenne, Brussels, Belgium, Rheinisch-Westfaelische Technische Hochschule Aachen and Univ. of Cologne, Germany; with Directorate-Gen. for Financial Insts and Corp. Law, EC, Brussels 1989–90; Assoc., Forrester Norall & Sutton law firm (now White & Case), Brussels 1990–91; joined Treuhandanstalt, Berlin 1991, Dir Controlling 1993; Head of Acquisitions, Beteiligungsgesellschaft New Länder, Berlin 1993–98; Chief Financial Officer (CFO) Clearstream Int. 1996–98, mem. Bd of Dirs 1998–2000; CFO RTL Group, Luxembourg 2000–06, Head of Corp. Centre 2003–06; CFO and Head of Corp. Centre, Bertelsmann AG, Gütersloh 2006–12, Head of Bertelsmann Music Group 2006–08, Chair. and CEO Bertelsmann SE & Co. KGaA 2012–. *Address:* Bertelsmann SE & Co. KGaA, Carl-Bertelsmann-Str. 270, 33311 Gütersloh, Germany (office). *Telephone:* (5241) 80-0 (office). *Fax:* (5241) 80-62321 (office). *E-mail:* info@bertelsmann.com (office). *Website:* www.bertelsmann.com (office).

RABEA, Abdullah ibn Abd al-Aziz al-, MD, FRCS; Saudi Arabian surgeon and politician; m. Huda al-Ghunaim; eight c.; ed King Saud Univ., Riyadh, Univ. of Alberta, Canada, Dalhousie Univ. Faculty of Medicine; began training in surgery in Riyadh, moved to Edmonton, Canada 1981 for residency in gen. surgery, then paediatric surgery in Edmonton and at Dalhousie 1987; started as Asst Lecturer, King Saud Univ.; spent 14 years with Nat. Guard Health Affairs (medical complex) becoming Exec. Dir, later CEO and also Pres. King Saud Univ. for Medical Sciences; Minister of Health 2009–14; mem. several nat. cttees; Dir King Faisal Specialist Hosp. and Research Center, King Saud bin Abdulaziz Univ., also Pres. Faculty of Nursing and Allied Health Sciences; King Abdul Aziz Medal of the First Order. *Achievements include:* as head of surgical team at Abdulaziz Medical City, Riyadh, became world renowned for surgery separating conjoined twins.

RABEE, Hayder K. Gafar, BA; Iraqi teacher of calligraphy; *Head, Calligraphy Department, Institute of Fine Arts;* b. 22 Feb. 1962, Najaf; m. Ahalam A. al-Zahawi 1986; two s. one d.; ed Coll. of Fine Arts; calligrapher, Baghdad TV 1982–88; worked as designer, newspapers and magazines 1989–91; teacher, Inst. of Fine Arts, Baghdad 1992–, Head, Calligraphy Dept (evening classes) 1995–; teacher of Arabic Calligraphy, Jordanian Calligraphers' Soc. 1998; Gen. Sec. Iraqi Calligraphers' Soc. 1998–99; mem. Iraqi Plastic Arts Soc. 1996–2002, Iraqi Union of Artists, Iraqi Soc. for Calligraphy Jordanian Calligraphers' Soc., Egyptian Calligraphers' Soc.; State Trophy for Plastic Arts and Calligraphy 1989, 1999, Gold Medal, 2nd World Festival 1992, Third World Festival 1993, Gold Medal for Creativity, Dar Es-Salaam 1st Nat. Festival 1993, Appreciation Prize, 4th Baghdad Nat. Festival 1998, Appreciation Prize in 5th Int. Competition for Calligraphy, Turkey 2001, a main prizewinner, Int. Meeting for Calligraphy of the Islam World, Tehran 2002, Certificate in first contest of the miniatures and decoration, Algeria 2008, Certificate in Festival of the Holy Quran, Dubai 2009/2011, Certificate, Second Int. Festival of Culture and Arts, Greece 2010, Certificate in Calligraphy, Sharjah Biennial 2012. *Publication:* Proposed Alphabetic Study for Arabic Calligraphy in Printing 1989. *Leisure interest:* chess. *Address:* al-Waziria, Sector 301, Street 13 Ho. 50, Baghdad (home); Department of Calligraphy, Institute of Fine Arts, al-Mansur, Baghdad, Iraq (office).

RABEE, Mohammed al-; Yemeni economist and international organization official; Asst Sec.-Gen. Council of Arab Econ. Unity (CAEU) 2005–10, Sec.-Gen. CAEU 2010–. *Address:* Council of Arab Economic Unity, 1113 Corniche en-Nil, 4th Floor, PO Box 1, 11518 Cairo, Egypt (office). *Telephone:* (2) 25755045 (office). *Fax:* (2) 25754090 (office). *E-mail:* caeu@idsc.net.eg (office).

RABEMANANJARA, Gen. Charles; Malagasy politician; b. 9 June 1947, Antananarivo; fmr sr police officer, later Head of Gen. Armoured Corps; Dir Presidential Security Cabinet 2004–05; Minister of the Interior and Admin. Reform 2005–09, Prime Minister 2007–09.

RABINOVICH, Itamar, PhD; Israeli university administrator, historian, academic and fmr diplomatist; *Senior Research Fellow, Moshe Dayan Center for Middle Eastern and African Studies, Tel-Aviv University;* b. 1942, Jerusalem; ed UCLA; joined faculty Tel-Aviv Univ. 1971, Dir Moshe Dayan Center for Middle Eastern and African Studies 1980–88, now Sr Research Fellow and Ettinger Prof. of Contemporary Middle Eastern History, Dean of Humanities, Tel-Aviv Univ. 1989–90, Rector 1990–92, Pres. 1999–2007, now Prof. Emer. of Middle Eastern History; Israel's Chief Negotiator with Syria and Amb. to USA 1992–96; A.D. White Prof. at Large, Cornell Univ. 1997–2002; fmr Visiting Prof. Univ. of Pa, Univ. of Toronto, Woodrow Wilson Int. Center for Scholars, Inst. of Advanced Studies, Princeton; Distinguished Global Prof. New York Univ.; currently Founding Pres. Israel Inst.; mem. Trilateral Comm.; Chair. Advisory Council, Wexner Israel Program, Dan David Foundation; Chair. Heseg Project; Vice-Chair. Inst. of Nat. Security Studies; Foreign Hon. Fellow, American Acad. of Arts and Sciences 2009. *Publications:* Syria Under the Ba'th 1972, The War for Lebanon, 1970–1985 1985, The Road Not Taken: Early Arab–Israeli Negotiations 1991, The Brink of Peace: Israel and Syria 1999, Waging Peace: Israel and the Arabs at the End of the Century 2004, Israel in the Middle East 2008, The View from Damascus 2008, The Lingering Conflict: Israel, The Arabs, and the Middle East, 1948–2012 2012; numerous articles, essays and chapters in books and journals. *Address:* Moshe Dayan Center for Middle Eastern and African Studies, Tel-Aviv University, Ramat Aviv, Tel-Aviv 69978, Israel (office); Israel Institute, 1250 Eye Street, NW, Suite 710, Washington, DC 20005, USA (office). *Telephone:* (3) 6409646 (office); (202) 289-1431 (Israel Institute) (office). *Fax:* (3) 6415802 (office). *E-mail:* efratal@post.tau.ac.il (office); info@israelinstitute.org (office). *Website:* www.dayan.org (office); www.israelinstitute.org (office).

RABINOVITCH, Robert, BComm MA, PhD; Canadian broadcasting executive; b. 1943, Montréal; m.; one s. one d.; ed McGill Univ., Univ. of Pennsylvania, USA; held various positions with Fed. Govt, including Deputy Minister of Communications 1982–85, Under-Sec. of State 1985–86, also held several positions within Privy Council Office, including Deputy Sec. to the Cabinet and Sr Asst Sec. to the Cabinet for Priorities and Planning; Exec. Vice-Pres. and COO Claridge Inc. 1987–99; Pres. and CEO CBC/Radio Canada 1999–2007, Acting Chair. March–Sept. 2005, Sept. 2006; fmr mem. Bd of Dirs Cineplex Odeon, NetStar Communications; Special Advisor, MaxLink Communications, Loews Cineplex; fmr mem. Govt of Canada Direct-to-Home Satellite Broadcasting Policy Review Panel; fmr mem. Canadian Exec. Service Org., CRB Foundation, Samuel and Saidye Bronfman Family Foundation, Canadian Film Centre; Chair. Exec. Cttee Canadian Jewish Congress (Québec) –1999; mem. Bd of Govs McGill Univ. 1997, Chair. 1999–2009, mem. Bd of Dirs McGill Univ. Health Centre 2007–; mem. Advisory Bd Sauvé Scholars Foundation, McGill Univ., Nunavut Trust Investment Advisory Cttee 1991– (Chair. 2008–); Hon. LLD (York Univ.) 2003, (McGill Univ.) 2010. *Website:* muhc.ca.

RABINOWITZ, Cay Sophie, MA, PhD; American curator, editor and arts executive; *Artistic Director, Art Basel;* b. 1965, Norfolk, Va; d. of Ralph Rabinowitz and Jeanne Rabinowitz; m. Christian Rattemeyer; ed Tufts Univ., Reed Coll., Univ. of California, Berkeley, Emory Univ.; DAAD Fellow, Hochschule der Künste, Berlin 1995–96; curator or co-curator for numerous exhbns including Lauretta Rix's Paint and Graphic, Atlanta 1996, Splendid Isolation, Berlin 1997, Patterns of Intention, OSMOS, Berlin 1998, Thinking Loud/Cutting Through, Space 1181, Atlanta 1999, Tonal Bliss, Marietta/Cobb Museum of Art, Atlanta 2001, Scarlett Hooft-Graafland and Jeff Feld, Mary Goldman Gallery, Los Angeles 2003, Erik Schmidt, Henry Urbach Gallery, New York 2004, APEX Summer show, New York 2004; curatorial asst, Venice Biennial 1999; Sr Ed., USA, Parkett Publishers 1999–2008; mem. Faculty, Parsons School of Fine Art, New York 1999–; fmr mem. Faculty, Emory Univ., Calif. Inst. of the Arts; Artistic Dir Art Basel and Art Basel Miami Beach 2008–; Contributing Ed., Art Papers Magazine 1998. *Publications include:* Escape 1994, Thomas Schutte (co-author) 2001, Julie Mehretu: Black City (co-author) 2007, Fiona Banner's work as work-in-progress 2007; contribs to Financial Times, Artforum, Grand Street, Afterall, Boiler, Self Service; other: numerous exhbn catalogues. *Address:* Art Basel, MCH Swiss Exhibition (Basel) Ltd, 4005 Basel, Switzerland (office). *Telephone:* 582062703 (office). *Fax:* 582063130 (office). *E-mail:* info@artbasel.com (office). *Website:* www.artbasel.com (office).

RABIU, Abdulsamad, CON; Nigerian business executive; *Chairman and CEO, BUA Group;* b. 4 Aug. 1960; s. of Isyaku Rabiu; m.; four c.; ed Govt Coll., Kano, Capital Univ., Columbus; started career by importing basic commodities such as rice, sugar, cement during 1980s; est. BUA Int. Ltd (now BUA Group) 1988, currently Chair. and CEO; Chair. Nigeria's Bank of Industry 2010–, Cement Co. of Northern Nigeria Plc. *Leisure interests:* squash, polo. *Address:* BUA Group, 35 Saka Tinubu Street, Victoria Island, Lagos, Nigeria (office). *Telephone:* (1) 4610669 (office). *Fax:* (1) 2623535 (office). *E-mail:* info@buagroup.com (office). *Website:* www.buagroup.com (office).

RABKIN, Mitchell T., MD; American physician, academic and hospital administrator; *Professor of Medicine, Harvard Medical School;* b. 27 Nov. 1930, Boston, Mass; s. of Morris A. Rabkin and Esther Quint Rabkin; m. Adrienne M. Najarian 1956; one s. one d.; ed Harvard Coll. and Harvard Medical School, Massachusetts Gen. Hosp., Boston; US Public Health Service, NIH, Bethesda, Md 1957–59; Chief Resident in Medicine, Massachusetts Gen. Hosp. 1962, medical staff 1963–66, Bd Consultation 1972–80, Hon. Physician 1981–; Gen. Dir Beth Israel Hosp., Boston 1966–80, Pres. 1980–96, now CEO Emer.; Prof. of Medicine, Harvard Medical School 1983–, Pres. Harvard Medical Alumni Council 2000–01; CEO CareGroup, Boston 1996–98; Distinguished Inst. Scholar, Inst. for Educ. and Research, Beth Israel Deaconess Medical Center, Boston 1998–; mem. Bd of Dirs Duke Univ. Health System 1998–2003; Dir Washington Advisory Group, LECG; mem. Bd of Trustees, New York Univ. School of Medicine Foundation 2000–07, Vice-Chair. 2006–07; mem. NAS Inst. of Medicine; Fellow, AAAS, ACP; Hon. DSc (Brandeis), (Curry Coll., Milton, Mass.), (Mass. Coll. of Pharmacy) 1983, (Northeastern Univ.) 1994; Distinguished Service Award, American Hosp. Asscn 1999, Distinguished Service Medal, Asscn of American Medical Colls 1999. *Publications:* numerous articles in academic journals. *Leisure interests:* sailing, gardening, travel. *Address:* Carl J. Shapiro Institute for Education and Research at Harvard Medical School and Beth Israel Deaconess Medical Center, 330 Brookline Avenue, Boston, MA 02215, USA (office); 124 Canton Avenue, Milton, MA 02186, USA (home). *Telephone:* (617) 667-9400 (office); (617) 696-6614 (home). *Fax:* (617) 667-9122 (office); (617) 696-1008 (home). *E-mail:* mtrabkin@caregroup.harvard.edu (office); mtrabkin@mindspring.com (home). *Website:* www.bidmc.org (office).

RABUKA, Maj.-Gen. Sitiveni Ligamamada, OBE, MSc; Fijian politician and army officer; *Leader, Social Democratic Liberal Party (SODELPA);* b. 13 Sept. 1948, Nakobo; s. of Kolinio E. V. Rabuka and Salote Lomaloma; m. Suluweti Camamaivuna Tuiloma 1975; two s. two d.; ed Prov. School Northern, Queen Victoria School, NZ Army schools, Indian Defence Services Staff Coll. and Australian Jt Services Staff Coll.; Sr Operational Plans Officer, UN Interim Force in Lebanon (UNIFIL) 1980; Commdr Fiji Bn UNIFL Lebanon 1980–81; Chief of Staff, Fiji July–Dec. 1981; SO 1 Operations and Training, Fiji Army 1982–83, 1985–87; Chief of Mil. Personnel MFO, Sinai, Egypt 1983–84; Commdr Fiji Bn MFO, Sinai, Egypt 1984–85; staged coup 14 May 1987; Adviser on Home Affairs and Head of Security May–Sept. 1987; staged second coup 25 Sept. 1987; declared Fiji a Repub. 7 Oct. 1987; Commdr and Head of Interim Mil. Govt of Fiji Sept.–Dec. 1987; Commdr Fiji Security Forces 1987–91; Minister for Home Affairs, Nat. Youth Service and Army Auxiliary Services 1987–90; Commdr Republic of Fiji Military Forces 1991; Deputy Prime Minister 1991, Minister for Home Affairs 1991; elected Founding Pres. Fijian Political Party 1991; Prime Minister of Fiji 1992–99, fmrly Minister for Home Affairs, Immigration, Fijian Affairs and Rural Devt and Foreign Affairs, fmrly with special responsibility for the Constitutional Review and the Agricultural, Landlords and Tenants Act; Commonwealth Rep. to Solomon Islands 1999–2000; Chair. Cakaudrove Prov. Council 2001–08; Pres. Fijian Political Party (SVT); Leader, Social Democratic Liberal Party (SODELPA) 2016–; Commdr, Légion d'honneur 1980, Grand Officier 1997, Meritorious Service Decoration 1987, Officer, Order of St John of Jerusalem 1987, Companion of the Order of Fiji 1998, Order of Tahiti Nui 1998; Dr hc (Cen. Queensland Univ.) 1997. *Film:* Operation Surprise (documentary on Fiji coup d'etat) 1987. *Publications:* No Other Way 1988, Rabuka of Fiji 2000. *Leisure interests:* golf, rugby, weightlifting. *Address:* Social Democratic Liberal Party (SODELPA), 66 McGregor Street, POB 17889, Suva, Fiji (office). *Telephone:* 3303544 (office). *E-mail:* piotab8@gmail.com (office). *Website:* www.sodelpa.org (office).

RABY, Geoffrey William, BEc, MEc, PhD; Australian fmr diplomatist; b. Sept. 1953, Melbourne; ed La Trobe Univ.; fmr Sr Tutor in Econs, La Trobe Univ.; trade policy adviser, Office of Nat. Assessments 1984–86, to Minister for Trade 1993; served twice as Head, Econ. Section, Embassy in Beijing 1986–91; est. Northeast Asia Analytical Unit, Dept of Foreign Affairs and Trade (DFAT) 1991, Head of Unit 1991–93; other sr positions at DFAT include First Asst Sec., Trade Negotiations Div. 1995–98, First Asst Sec., Int. Orgs and Legal Div. 2001–02, Deputy Sec. DFAT 2002–06; Head, Trade Policy Issues Div., OECD, Paris 1993–95, Perm. Rep. to WTO, Geneva 1998–2001; Amb. to APEC, Singapore 2002–04; Amb. to People's Repub. of China (also accred to Mongolia and North Korea) 2007–11; Chair. and CEO Geoff Raby and Associates, Beijing; Sr Advisor Kreab Gavin Anderson. *Address:* Geoff Raby and Associates, Room 303, Sunjoy Mansion, No.6 Ri Tan Road, Jian Guo Men Wai Street, Chaoyang District, Beijing 100020, People's Republic of China (office). *E-mail:* info@geoffraby.com (office). *Website:* www .geoffraby.com.

RACHDI, Allal; Moroccan civil servant and international organization executive; b. 17 June 1951; ed Grande Ecole of Public Admin, Faculty of Law (Political Sciences), Certificate of Trade Policy, GATT, Geneva; sr civil servant at Ministry of Foreign Trade since 1978, participated in devt and implementation of Structural Adjustment programmes, also took part in bilateral and multilateral trade negotiations, particularly in negotiations for accession of Morocco to GATT, co-operation and asscn agreements of Morocco with EU, Uruguay Round negotiations as well as negotiations of several free trade agreements, Dir Foreign Trade Policy, Ministry of Foreign Trade 1994–2000, Co-ordinator at Gen. Secr., Acting Sec.-Gen. 1996–2000; Chair. Nat. Comm. of Foreign Trade Facilitation 1986–2000, Nat. Imports Consultative Comm. 1992–2000; Admin., Common Fund for Commodities, Amsterdam 1998–2000, Moroccan Exports Asscn; mem. Jt Cttee of Pvt./Public Sector; Dir-Gen. Islamic Centre for the Devt of Trade, OIC 2000–11; Dir-Gen. AS3M (investment co.) 2011–.

RACHMAT, Theodore (Teddy) Permadi; Indonesian business executive; b. 15 Dec. 1943; m.; ed Bandung Inst. of Tech.; Pres. Dir PT Astra Int. Tbk (Indonesian car mfr) 1984–98, 2000–02, Commr 1998–2000, Pres. Commr 2002–05; f. Triputra Group 1998, has interests in agribusiness, manufacturing, mining, trading and services; Pres. Commr Adira Finance 2004–; Vice-Pres. PT Adaro Energy Tbk; fmr Commr PT Unilever Indonesia Tbk; fmr Chair. Indonesian Business Execs Asscn (Apindo); Adviser, Protocol One; mem. Nat. Econs Bd. *Address:* Triputra Group, Menara Kadin 23rd Floor, H.R. Rasuna Said Kav. 2&3, Jakarta 12950, Indonesia (office). *Telephone:* (21) 5274323 (office). *E-mail:* info@triputra-group.com (office). *Website:* www.triputra-group.com (office).

RACICOT, Marc F., BA, JD; American lawyer, association executive and fmr politician; b. 24 July 1948, Thompson Falls, Mont.; s. of William E. Racicot and Patricia E. Racicot (née Bentley); m. Theresa J. Barber 1970; two s. three d.; ed Carroll Coll., Univ. of Montana; called to Bar, Mont. 1973; served US Army 1973–76, Chief Trial Counsel, Kaiserslautern, FRG 1975–76 (resgnd); Deputy Co. Attorney, Missoula Co., Mont. 1976–77; Asst Attorney-Gen., State of Mont. 1977–88, Attorney-Gen. 1988–93; Gov. of Montana 1993–2001; Pnr, Bracewell & Patterson LLP (now Bracewell & Giuliani, LLP), Washington, DC 2001–05; Chair. Republican Nat. Cttee 2002–04; Chair. Bush-Cheney re-election campaign 2004; Pres. American Insurance Asscn 2005–09; mem. Bd of Dirs Avista Corpn 2009–, Massachusetts Mutual Life Insurance Co., The Washington Companies, Weyerhaeuser Co. 2016–, Plum Creek Timber Co. 2010–16.

RACZKO, Andrzej, DEcons; Polish economist; b. 27 Feb. 1953, Kutno; m.; two c.; ed Univ. of Łódź; early career as Asst, then Asst Prof., Inst. of Econs, Univ. of Łódź 1977–86; Chief Specialist on Foreign Cooperation, Łódźkie Towarzystwo Kredytowe Bank SA 1992–93; Econ. Dir Petrobank SA 1993–97, mem. Man. Bd LG Petro Bank SA 1995–97, Dir 1997–99; Man. Mortgage Team, PKO Bank Polski SA 1999–2001; Under-Sec. of State, Ministry of Finance 2001–02, Minister of Finance 2003–04; mem. Bd of Dirs Bank Gospodarki Żywnościowej SA 2002–03; fmr mem. EU negotiating team; fmr Vice-Gov. IMF, Alt. Exec. Dir (Poland) 2004; fmr Chief Economist and Dir of Research Dept, Polish Financial Supervision Authority; mem. Bd of Man. Nat. Bank of Poland 2010–; fmr Co-Chair. Public Debt Cttee.

Address: National Bank of Poland, 00-919 Warsaw, ul. Świętokrzyska 11/21, Poland (office). *Website:* www.nbp.pl (office).

RADAVIDSON, Benjamin Andriamparany, MBA, MA; Malagasy politician and religious leader; b. 5 Oct. 1961, Antananarivo; ed J.J. Rabearivelo School, Institut Nat. des Sciences Comptables et de l'Admin d'Entreprises, Columbia Univ., USA; fmr Admin. and Financial Man. of a mining co. in Andasibe; Chief Financial Officer, Omnibranche 2000–02; Chief of Staff of Deputy Prime Minister in charge of Finance and Budget March–June 2002; Minister of Economy and Planning June–Oct. 2002, of Economy, Finance and Budget Oct. 2002–07, of Nat. Educ. and Scientific Research 2007–08; mem. Parl. for 4th Dist of Antananarivo 2007–; fmr mem. Bd of Govs, IMF, World Bank, African Devt Bank, Nat. Authorizing European Devt Fund; Nat. Pres. Laics FJKM Reformed Church of Madagascar. *Address:* FJKM Reformed Church of Madagascar, BP 623, Antananarivo, Madagascar (office). *E-mail:* fjkm@fjkm.mg (office). *Website:* www.fjkm.mg (office).

RADCLIFFE, Daniel Jacob; British actor; b. 23 July 1989, London; s. of Alan Radcliffe and Marcia Gresham; ed Sussex House School, London, City of London School. *Films include:* The Tailor of Panama 2001, Harry Potter and the Philosopher's Stone 2001, Harry Potter and the Chamber of Secrets 2002, Harry Potter and the Prisoner of Azkaban 2004, Harry Potter and the Goblet of Fire 2005, Harry Potter and the Order of the Phoenix 2007, December Boys 2007, Harry Potter and the Half-Blood Prince 2009, Harry Potter and the Deathly Hallows: Part 1 2010, Harry Potter and the Deathly Hallows: Part 2 2011, The Woman in Black 2012, Kill Your Darlings 2013, Horns 2013, What If 2013, Trainwreck 2015, Victor Frankenstein 2015, Swiss Army Man 2016, Imperium 2016, Jungle 2017, Beast of Burden 2018, Guns Akimbo 2019. *Television appearances include:* David Copperfield 1999, My Boy Jack 2007, The Simpsons (voice) 2010, 2014, A Young Doctor's Notebook (series) 2012–13, The Gamechangers (film) 2015, Miracle Workers (series) 2019. *Theatre appearances include:* The Play What I Wrote 2002, Equus (London and Broadway) 2007, The Cripple of Inishmaan (WhatsOnStage Award for Best Actor in a Play) 2014. *Address:* Artists Rights Group, 4 Great Portland Street, London, W1W 8PA, England (office). *Telephone:* (20) 7436-6400 (office). *E-mail:* Vanessa.Davies@organic-marketing.co.uk (office). *Website:* argtalent.com (office).

RADCLIFFE, Paula Jane, MBE, BA; British athlete; b. 17 Dec. 1973, Northwich, Cheshire, England; d. of Peter Radcliffe and Pat Radcliffe; m. Gary Lough; one s. one d.; ed Loughborough Univ.; distance runner; World Jr Cross Country Champion 1992; started sr career 1993; fifth place, 5,000m, Olympic Games 1996; won Fifth Avenue Mile, New York 1996, 1997; third place, Int. Asscn of Athletics Feds (IAAF) World Cross Challenge series 1997; fourth place, 5,000m, World Championships 1997; European Cross Country Champion 1998; second place, 10,000m, European Challenge 1998; silver medal, 10,000m World Championships, 1999; fourth place, 10,000m Olympic Games 2000; World Half Marathon Champion 2000, 2001; World Cross Country Champion 2002; gold medallist, 5,000m, Commonwealth Games 2002; gold medallist, 10,000m, European Championships 2002; won London Marathon 2002, 2003, 2005, Chicago Marathon 2002, New York City Marathon 2004, 2007, 2008; set world best time for 5,000m in Flora Light 5km 2003; won Great North Run Half Marathon in world best time 2003; won World Championship's marathon 2005; world record holder for 10,000m, 20,000m and marathon; Capt. GB's Women's Athletic Team 1998–; Hon. DLitt (De Montfort, Loughborough); British Female Athlete of the Year 1999, 2001, 2002, IAAF World Female Athlete of the Year 2002, BBC Sports Personality of the Year 2002, Sunday Times Sportswoman of the Year 2002, Laureus World Comeback of the Year 2008. *Publication:* Paula: My Story So Far 2004. *Leisure interests:* dining out, languages, reading, music, cinema, travel, spending time with family and friends. *Address:* c/o Octagon, Octagon House, 2 Waterhouse Square, 140 Holborn, London, EC1N 2AE, England (office). *Telephone:* (20) 7862-0000 (office). *Website:* europe.octagon.com (office); www.paularadcliffe.com.

RADCLIFFE, Timothy Peter Joseph, OP, MA; British RC ecclesiastic and Dominican friar; b. 22 Aug. 1945, London; s. of Hugh Radcliffe and Marie-Therese Pereira; ed Downside School, Le Saulchoir, Paris and St John's Coll., Oxford; joined Dominican Order 1965, Chaplain to Imperial Coll., Prior of Blackfriars, Oxford 1982–88, Chair. New Blackfriars 1983–88, Provincial of Prov. of England 1988–92, Master of the Dominican Order 1992–2001; Pres. Conf. of Major Religious Superiors of England and Wales 1991–; Grand Chancellor, Pontifical Univ. of St Thomas (The Angelicum), Rome 1992–2001, Univ. of Santo Tomas, Manila 1992–2001, Ecole Biblique, Jerusalem 1992–2001; mem. Faculty of Theology, Fribourg 1992–2001; Consultor, Pontifical Council for Justice and Peace 2015–; mem. Bd, Las Casas Inst., Blackfriars, Oxford; Hon. Citizen of Augusta (Italy) and Sepahua (Peru); Hon. Fellow, St John's Coll., Oxford, Sarum Canon of Salisbury Cathedral, Freedom of the City of London; Hon. DD (Oxford), (Pontifical Univ. of St Thomas), (Fribourg) 2016; Hon. STD (Providence Coll. RI); Hon. LLD (Barry Univ., Fla) 1996; Hon. DHumLitt (Ohio Dominican Coll.) 1996 (Dominican Univ., Chicago) 2007, (Aquinas Inst., St Louis); Dr hc (Université Catholique de l'Ouest, Angers) 2007; Prix de Littérature Religieuse 2001, Prix Spiritualités d'aujourd'hui 2001, Premio Ecumenico San Nicola 2004, Prix des lecteurs du Procure 2005, Michael Ramsey Award for Theological Writing 2007. *Publications include:* El Manantial de la Esperanza 1998, Sing a New Song: The Christian Vocation 1999, I Call You Friends 2001, Seven Last Words of Christ 2004, What is the Point of Being a Christian? (Michael Ramsey Prize 2007) 2005, Just One Year – A Global Treasury of Prayer and Worship 2007, Why Go to Church? The Drama of the Eucharist 2008, Take the Plunge 2012, The Way of the Cross 2015. *Leisure interests:* walking, reading long novels. *Address:* Blackfriars, St Giles, Oxford, OX1 3LY, England (home). *Telephone:* (1865) 278422 (home). *Fax:* (1865) 278403 (home). *E-mail:* timothy.radcliffe@english.op.org (office). *Website:* english.op.org/profiles/timothy-radcliffe.htm (office).

RADDA, Sir George Karoly, Kt, CBE, MA, DPhil, FRS; British medical research director and academic; *Chairman, Singapore A* Biomedical Research Council;* b. 9 June 1936, Gyor, Hungary; s. of Gyula Radda and Anna Bernolak; m. 1st Mary O'Brien 1961 (divorced 1995), two s. one d.; m. 2nd Sue Bailey 1995; ed Pannonhalma and Eötvös Univ., Budapest and Merton Coll. Oxford; Research Assoc., Univ. of Calif., USA 1962–63; Lecturer in Organic Chem., St John's Coll., Oxford Univ. 1963–64, Fellow and Tutor in Organic Chem., Merton Coll. 1964–84,

Lecturer in Biochem, Oxford Univ. 1966–84, British Heart Foundation Prof. of Molecular Cardiology 1984–2003, Prof. Emer. 2003, Prof. and Head, Dept of Physiology, Anatomy and Genetics 2006–08; Professorial Fellow, Merton Coll. 1984–2008, Head Dept of Biochem. 1991–96; Chair. MRC Cell. Bd 1988–92; mem. MRC Council 1988–92, Chief Exec. MRC (on leave from Oxford Univ.) 1996–2003; Chair. Nat. Cancer Research Inst. 2001–03, Singapore Bioimaging Consortium 2005–10, Singapore A* Biomedical Research Council 2008–; mem. Council, Royal Soc. 1990–92, ICRF 1991–96; Ed. Biochemical and Biophysical Research Communications 1977–84; Man. Ed. Biochimica et Biophysica Acta 1977–, Chair. 1989–95; Founder mem. Oxford Enzyme Group 1970–87, Acad. of Medical Sciences 1998; Pres. Soc. for Magnetic Resonance in Medicine 1985–86, Fellow 1994–; Fellow, Int. Soc. of Magnetic Resonance in Medicine 1995–; mem. European Molecular Biology Org. 1997– (Fellow 2008–), Academia Europaea 1999–; Hon. Dir MRC Biochemical and Clinical Magnetic Resonance Unit 1988–96; Hon. FRCR 1985; Hon. Fellow, American Heart Asscn and Citation for Int. Achievement 1987; Hon. FRCP 1997; Hon. mem., European Soc. of Magnetic Resonance in Medicine and Biology 2007, Hungarian Acad. of Sciences 2010, Hungarian Soc. of Cardiology 2013; Hon. Citizen, Repub. of Singapore 2015; Hon. DrMed (Berne) 1985, (London) 1991; Hon. DSc (Stirling) 1997, (Sheffield) 1999, (Debrecen, Hungary) 2001, (Birmingham) 2003, (Univ. de la Mediterranée) 2003, (Aberdeen) 2004, (Heinrich Heine Univ., Düsseldorf) 2004, (Semmelweis, Hungary) 2004, (Hull) 2005, (Leicester) 2006; Colworth Medal, Biochemical Soc. 1969, CIBA Medal and Prize 1983, Feldberg Prize 1982, British Heart Foundation Prize and Gold Medal for cardiovascular research 1982, Gold Medal, Soc. for Magnetic Resonance in Medicine 1984, Buchanan Medal, Royal Soc. 1987, Rank Prize in Nutrition 1990, Medal of Merit, Int. Acad. of Cardiovascular Sciences 2006, Public Service Medal, Friends of Singapore 2008, Budapest Semmelweis Award 2011, BioSpectrum Life Time Achievement Award 2013. *Publications:* articles in books and scientific journals. *Leisure interests:* opera, jazz, swimming. *Address:* Agency for Science Technology and Research, Singapore Bioimaging Consortium, 11 Biopolis Way, #02-02 Helios, Singapore, 138667, Singapore (office). *Telephone:* 64788721 (office). *E-mail:* george.radda@sbic.a-star.edu.sg (office).

RADEBE, Bridgette, BA; South African mining industry executive; *Executive Chairman, Mmakau Mining (Pty) Ltd;* b. 26 Feb. 1960, Johannesburg; sister of Patrice Motsepe; m. Jeffrey Radebe; ed Univ. of Botswana; Founder and Exec. Chair. Mmakau Mining (Pty) Ltd 1995–; Pres. South African Mining Devt Asscn; fmr Vice-Chair. Minerals and Mining Devt Bd; Co-founder and Trustee, New Africa Mining Fund; participated in design of SA Mining Charter; mem. Bd of Dirs Sappi Ltd 2004–, Nat. Research Foundation, Leadership Foundation, Int. Women's Forum Washington, DC; mem. ANC; Business Person of the Year Award, Global Foundation for Democracy 2008. *Address:* Mmakau Mining (Pty) Ltd, PO Box 2236, Houghton, 2041, South Africa (office). *Telephone:* (11) 268 6780 (office). *Fax:* (11) 268 0186 (office). *E-mail:* info@mmakau.co.za (office). *Website:* www.mmakaumining.co.za (office).

RADEBE, Jeffrey (Jeff) Thamsanqa, LLB; South African politician; *Minister of Energy;* b. 18 Feb. 1953, Cato Manor; m. Bridgette Radebe; three c.; ed Isibonelo High School, Univ. of Zululand, Leipzig Univ., Germany, Lenin Int. School, Moscow; joined Black Consciousness Movt 1970; Co-founder Kwamashu Youth Org. 1972; articled clerk with A. J. Gumede & Phyllis Naidoo, E. S. Mchunu & Co. 1976–77; with Radio Freedom 1977–78; Deputy Chief African Nat. Congress (ANC) Rep., Tanzania 1981; headed clandestine political movt of ANC and South African Communist Party (SACP) 1986, Head of Political Dept and Co-ordinator of 12 day hunger strike on Robben Island; arrested and sentenced to ten years on Robben Island 1986, sentence reduced to six years, released 1990; Sec. interim leadership group of SACP 1990–91; Deputy Chair. ANC Southern Natal Region 1990–91, Chair. 1991–94, also mem. ANC Nat. Exec. Cttee (NEC) and Nat. Working Cttee, Head ANC Policy Unit and NEC Convener in North West Prov.; Minister of Public Works, Govt of Nat. Unity 1994–99, of Public Enterprises 1999–2004, of Transport 2004–09, of Justice and Constitutional Devt 2009–14, Minister of Planning, Monitoring and Evaluation in the Presidency 2014–18, Minister of Energy 2018–; Chair. Nat. Planning Comm. 2015–; mem. Nat. Ass. 2009–; Hon. Col, South Africa Air Force Hon. LLM (Leipzig), Hon. DHumLitt (Chicago State Univ.) 1996. *Address:* Ministry of Energy, 192 Visagie St, cnr Paul Kruger St, Pretoria, South Africa (office). *Telephone:* (12) 4068000 (office). *Fax:* (12) 3223416 (office). *E-mail:* info@energy.gov.za (office). *Website:* www.energy.gov.za (office).

RADER, Paul Alexander, BA, BD, MTh, DMiss; American religious leader and fmr university administrator; b. 14 March 1934, New York; s. of Lyell M. Rader and Gladys Mina Damon; m. Frances Kay Fuller 1956; one s. two d.; ed Asbury Theological Seminary, Southern Baptist Theological Seminary, Salvation Army's School for Officers' Training, New York, Fuller Theological Seminary; mem. staff, Salvation Army Training School, Seoul, S Korea 1962–67, Vice-Prin. 1967–71, Training Prin., then Educ. Officer, then Asst Chief Sec. Salvation Army in S Korea 1973–77, Chief Sec. with rank of Lt-Col 1977–84, Prin., School for Officers' Training, Suffern, NY 1984–87, Div. Leader 1987–89, Chief Sec. USA Eastern Territory 1989, attained rank of Commr 1989, Commdr USA Western Territory 1989–94, Pres. The Salvation Army Calif. Corps 1989–94, Gen. The Salvation Army 1994–99 (retd); Pres. Asbury Coll. 2000–06 (retd); Hon. DD (Asbury Theological Seminary, Roberts Wesleyan Coll.), Hon. LHD (Asbury Coll.); Order of Diplomatic Service Merit; Gwanghwa Medal "for distinguished service in the field of mission to the Repub. of Korea and the world" 1998. *Publications:* To Seize This Day of Salvation (co-author with Commr Kay F. Rader) 2015. *Address:* 3953 Rock Ledge Lane, Lexington, KY 40513, USA (home). *E-mail:* paularader@aol.com (home).

RADEV, Dimitar; Bulgarian banking executive, international organization official and central banker; *Governor, Bulgarian National Bank;* b. 12 July 1956; ed Univ. of Nat. and World Economy, Int. Relations Inst., Georgetown Univ., USA; held various govt positions including Head of Dept at Ministry of Finance, Council of Ministers and Ministry of Economy and Planning 1980–92, Deputy Minister of Finance 1992–2001, Alt. Gov. for Bulgaria at IMF and Co-Chair. of Bulgaria-EU Economic Sub-Cttee 1997–2001; Co-Chair. Ministry of Finance-BNB Coordination Council 1998–2001; Asst to Exec. Dir, IMF 2001–03, Advisor 2003–06, Sr Economist, Head of Mission for Tech. Asst, Eastern Europe, Cen. Asia, Middle East and Africa 2006–15; Gov. Bulgarian Nat. Bank 2015–, mem. Gen. Council, European Cen. Bank 2015–, Gen. Bd, European Systemic Risk Bd 2015–; mem. Admin. Council, Council of Europe Devt Bank 1995–2002; mem. Supervisory Bd ExpressBank 1996–99, Nat. Social Security Inst. 1996–2001. *Address:* Bulgarian National Bank, 1000 Sofia, pl. Knyaz Aleksandar I 1, Bulgaria (office). *Telephone:* (2) 914-59 (office). *Fax:* (2) 980-24-25 (office). *E-mail:* press_office@bnbank.org (office). *Website:* www.bnb.bg (office).

RADEV, Maj.-Gen. Rumen Georgiev, DMilSci; Bulgarian air force officer and head of state; *President;* b. 18 June 1963, Dimitrovgrad; s. of George Radev and Stanka Radeva; m. 1st Ginka Radeva (divorced 2011); one s. one d.; m. 2nd Desislava Gencheva; one step-s.; ed Mathèmatical School, Haskovo (Gold Medal), Georgi Benkovski Bulgarian Air Force Univ., US Air Force Squadron Officer School, Maxwell Air Force Base, Ala, USA, Rakovski Defence and Staff Coll., Air War Coll., Maxwell Air Force Base; joined Bulgarian Air Force 1987, jr pilot, 15th Fighter Aviation Regt (Ravnets) 1987–88, Unit Deputy Commdr 1989–90, Unit Commdr 1990–94, MiG-29 Squadron Commdr, Fifth Fighter Airbase, Ravnets 1996–98, Deputy Commdr for Flight Preparation 1998–99, Deputy Commdr for Flight Training, Third Fighter Airbase, Graf Ignatievo 1999–2000, Study of the Air Defence of Bulgaria, NATO HQ, Brussels 2000, Chief of Staff of Third Fighter Airbase, Graf Ignatievo 2000–02, 2003–05, Commdr of Third Fighter Airbase, Graf Ignatievo 2005–09, Deputy Commdr of Bulgarian Air Force 2009–14, Commdr Bulgarian Air Force 2014–16; promoted to rank of Lt 1987, Sr Lt 1990, Capt. 1994, Maj. 1997, Lt Col 2000, Col 2003, Brig.-Gen. 2007, Maj.-Gen. 2014; Pres. of Bulgaria 22 Jan. 2017– (ind. cand. supported by Balgarska Sotsialisticheska Partiya—Bulgarian Socialist Party); numerous mil. medals and awards, including the badge 'For Loyal Service Under the Flags' (Third Degree); Hon. Badge of the Ministry of Defence 'Saint George' (Second Degree). *Address:* Office of the President, 1123 Sofia, bul. Dondukov 2, Bulgaria (office). *Telephone:* (2) 923-93-33 (office). *E-mail:* priemna@president.bg (office). *Website:* www.president.bg (office).

RADEV, Valentin, MA (Econ), PhD; Bulgarian munitions expert, fmr army officer and politician; b. 6 Feb. 1958, Elin Pelin; ed Artillery Acad., Shumen, Univ. of Nat. and World Economy, Sofia, Defence Research Inst., Sofia; specialized courses in Russian Fed., Canada, Czech Repub. and Germany and at George C. Marshal European Center for Security Studies, Garmisch-Partenkirchen, Germany; graduated as Armament Mil. Officer and Ammunition and Chem. of Explosives Engineer; began career as Head of Artillery Weapon Office in a mil. unit; Research Scientist, Defence Research Inst., Sofia 1983–96, Research Scientist (Second Degree) from 1996, later Head of Ammunition Dept, Dir of Inst. 2000–02; Deputy Dir Defence Advanced Research Inst., Sofia 1999–2000; fmr Assoc. Prof., Univ. of Nat. and World Economy and New Bulgarian Univ.; fmr Chair. NITI Ltd, Kazanlak; fmr Scientific Sec. Specialised Scientific Council on Defence Eng Sciences, Supreme Attestation Cttee; Chair. Asscn of Ammunition Specialists in Bulgaria 2005–; mem. Defence Expert Committee, Grazhdani za Evropeysko Razvitie na Balgariya (Citizens for European Devt of Bulgaria); Deputy Minister of Defence 2009–13; mem. Nat. Ass. (Narodno Sobraniye) 2009–; Minister of the Interior 2017–18; mem. Union of Scientists in Bulgaria 2006. *Publications:* more than 130 scientific articles and reports, standards, etc.; author of 17 products for mil. use; nine patents, three industrial designs and two trademarks. *Address:* National Assembly (Narodno Sobranie), 1169 Sofia, pl. Narodno Sobranie 2, Bulgaria (office). *Fax:* (2) 981-31-31 (office). *E-mail:* infocenter@parliament.bg (office). *Website:* www.parliament.bg (office).

RADHAKRISHNAN, Koppillil, BSc, MBA, PhD; Indian scientist; *Chairman, Indian Institute of Engineering Science and Technology;* b. 29 Aug. 1949, Irinjalkuda, Kerala; m. Padmini Radhakrishnan; ed Univ. of Kerala, Indian Inst. of Man., Bangalore, Indian Inst. of Tech.; started career as Avionics Engineer, Vikram Sarabhai Space Centre 1971, Dir 2007–09; Dir, Budget and Economic Analysis, Indian Space Research Org. (ISRO) 1987–97, Chair. 2009–14; Dir Nat. Natural Resources Man. System-Regional Remote Sensing Service Centres 1989–97; Mission Dir Integrated Mission for Sustainable Devt 1997–2000; Deputy Dir Nat. Remote Sensing Agency, Hyderabad 1997–2000, Dir 2005–08; Founder-Dir Indian Nat. Centre for Ocean Information Services 2000–05; Vice-Chair. Intergovernmental Oceanographic Comm. 2001–05; Founder-Dir Regional Alliance in Indian Ocean for Global Ocean Observing System (IOGOOS) 2002–06; Pres. Indian Soc. of Remote Sensing 2005–07; Vice-Pres. Indian Geophysical Union 2007–09; mem. Space Comm. 2008–09, apptd Chair. 2009; apptd Sec., Dept of Space, Govt of India 2009; Chair. Indian Inst. of Eng Science and Technology 2014–; Pres. Astronautical Soc. of India; Chair. Scientific Advisory Bd, B M Birla Science Centre, Hyderabad; mem. Int. Acad. of Astronautics; leads Indian del. to UN Cttee on Peaceful Use of Outer Space; Fellow, Indian Nat. Acad. of Eng, Andhra Pradesh Acad. of Sciences, Indian Soc. of Remote Sensing, Systems Soc. of India, Indian Geophysical Union, Indian Nat. Acad. of Science; Hon. Life Fellow, Inst. of Engineers, Hon. Fellow, Inst. of Electrical and Telecommunication Engineers; Dr hc (Sri Venkateswara Univ.), (Rajasthan Technical Univ.), (GITAM Univ.), (Tumkur Univ.), (SRM Univ.) 2010, (KIIT Univ.) 2010; K. R. Ramanathan Memorial Gold Medal of Indian Geophysical Union 2003, VASVIK Industrial Research Award in Electrical and Electronics Sciences and Technology 2005, Silver Jubilee Honour, Ministry of Earth Sciences 2006, BHASKARA Award, Indian Soc. of Remote Sensing 2008, Dr. Y. Nayudamma Memorial Award, Andhra Pradesh Acad. of Sciences 2009, Padma Bhushan 2014. *Leisure interest:* Kathakali dance. *Address:* Indian Inst. of Eng Science and Technology, Botanic Garden, Howrah 711103, West Bengal, India (office). *Telephone:* (033) 26684561 (office). *Fax:* (033) 26682916 (office). *Website:* www.iiests.ac.in (office).

RADHAKRISHNAN, S., BTech (Mech), MBA; Indian mechanical engineer and business executive; ed Univ., Indian Inst. of Tech., Chennai, Indian Inst. of Man., Bangalore; Man. Dir Bharat Shell Ltd –1977; joined Bharat Petroleum 1977, Dir (Marketing), Bharat Petroleum Corpn Ltd 2002–11, Chair. and Man. Dir Aug.–Dec. 2010; Ind. Dir (non-exec.) Indraprastha Gas Ltd –2005, apptd Additional Dir 2007, Chair. 2009; fmrly Dir, Numaligarh Refinery Ltd 2002, Kochi Refineries Ltd, Sabarmati Gas Ltd, Bharat Stars Services Pvt. Ltd, Petronet India Ltd.

RADICE, Vittorio; Italian retail executive; *CEO, La Rinascente;* b. 29 April 1957, Como; m. Gemma Radice; two s.; ed Univ. of Milan; fmrly served in Italian Army;

home furnishings buyer, Associated Merchandising Corpn; Buying Dir Habitat Int., then Man. Dir Habitat UK 1990–96; Man. Dir Selfridges PLC 1996–98, CEO 1998–2003; Exec. Dir and Head of Home Furnishings, Marks and Spencer PLC 2003–04; CEO La Rinascente, Milan 2005–; Dir (non-exec.) Shoppers Stop India 2000–06, McArthurGlen 2005–, Ishaan plc 2006–, YOOX Net-A-Porter Group SpA 2015–18. *Leisure interests:* travel, India, art, music. *Address:* la Rinascente s.r.l., Via Washington 70, 20146 Milan (office); Strada 8, Palazzo N, 20089 Rozzano-Milano, Italy (office). *Telephone:* (2) 46771 (office). *Fax:* (2) 4677187 (office). *E-mail:* vittorio.radice@lu.centralretail.com (office). *Website:* www.rinascente.it (office).

RADIČOVÁ, Iveta, PhDr, PhD; Slovak politician, political scientist and academic; b. 7 Dec. 1956, Bratislava; m. Stano Radič (died 2005); one d.; ed Comenius Univ., Bratislava, Slovak Acad. of Sciences, Bratislava, Univ. of Oxford, UK; Research Team Coordinator for Family Policy, Inst. for Sociology 1979–83, Dir of Inst. 2005; Univ. Lecturer, Dept of Sociology, Comenius Univ. 1990–93, Reader 1997, Univ. Lecturer, Dept of Political Science 1997–2005, Prof. 2005–, Univ. Lecturer, Dept of Social Work 2007–; Exec. Dir SPACE Foundation – Centre for Social Policy Analysis, Bratislava 1992–2005; Deputy Dir Academia Istropolitana, Bratislava 1993–97; Sociology Dept Supervisor, Dept of Sociology, Univ. of Constantine the Philosopher, Nitra 2005–07; Visiting Prof. at univs in USA, UK, Sweden, Finland, Austria while EC's expert on social policy; Minister of Labour, Social and Family Affairs 2005–06; Prime Minister (first female) 2010–12, Minister of Defence 2011–12; mem. Slovak Democratic and Christian Union-Democratic Party (Slovenská demokratická a kresťanská únia-Demokratická strana—SDKÚ-DS); mem. Parl. (SDKÚ-DS) 2006–09, Chair. Parl. Cttee for Social Affairs and Housing; led SDKÚ-DS party list in 2010 parl. elections. *Publications:* For People and People: Issues Shaping Social Policy in Slovakia 1995, Cross-Roads of Social Knowledge 1996, We Reject What We Know and What We Want? Environmental Strategy of Slovak Citizens 1998, Social Policy in Slovakia 1998, Social Policy in Bohemia and Slovakia after ROCE 1989 (co-ed.) 1998, Health, Work, Retirement (with H. Woleková and J. Nemec) 1999, Hic Sunt Romales 2001, S.O.S.: Social Protection in Slovakia 2003. *E-mail:* iveta.radicova@sdkuonline.sk.

RADIŠIĆ, Živko; Bosnia and Herzegovina politician; b. 15 Aug. 1937, Prijedor; m.; two c.; ed Univ. of Sarajevo; Mayor of Banja Luka 1977–82; Minister of Defence of the Fmr Socialist Repub. of Bosnia and Herzegovina 1982–85; Man. Cajavec Holding Co., Banja Luka 1985–92; Chair. Ass., Banja Luka; Pres. and Chair. of the Presidency of Bosnia and Herzegovina 1998–99, 2000–01, Co-Pres. 1999–2001, Mem. of the Presidency 2002; Founding mem. Socialist Party (fmrly Socialist Party of Republika Srpska) 1996, fmr Chair.; apptd Senator Republike Srpska 2009; Order of Honor of the Republike Srpska with golden eyes 2010.

RADMANOVIĆ, Nebojša; Bosnia and Herzegovina politician; b. 1 Oct. 1949, Gračanica; m.; two c.; ed high school in Banja Luka, Faculty of Philosophy, Univ. of Belgrade; has held numerous positions in culture and state admin including Dir Bosanska Krajina Archives and Archives of Republika Srpska, Dir Nat. Theatre of Republika Srpska, Banja Luka, Dir and Ed.-in-Chief GLAS, Pres. Exec. Bd Banja Luka Urban Municipality, Rep. Nat. Ass., Republika Srpska and Minister of Admin and Local Self-Man.; Serb mem. State Presidency 2006–14, Chair. (Pres. of Bosnia and Herzegovina) 2006–07, 2008–09, 2010–11, 2012–13; mem. Alliance of Ind. Social Democrats. *Publications include:* several books and scientific papers.

RADNER, Roy, PhB, BS, MS, PhD; American economist, applied mathematician and academic; *Leonard N. Stern Professor Emeritus of Business, New York University;* b. 29 June 1927, Chicago, Ill.; s. of Samuel Radner and Ella Radner; m. 1st Virginia Honoski (died 1976); one s. three d. (one d. deceased); m. 2nd Charlotte V. Kuh 1978; ed Hyde Park High School, Chicago and Univ. of Chicago; served in US Army 1945–48; Research Assoc., Cowles Comm., Univ. of Chicago 1951–54, Asst Prof. 1954–55; Asst Prof. of Econs, Yale Univ. 1955–57; Assoc. Prof. of Econs and Statistics, Univ. of Calif., Berkeley 1957–61, Prof. 1961–79, Chair. Dept of Econs 1965–69; Distinguished mem. tech. staff, AT&T Bell Labs 1979–95; Research Prof. of Econs, New York Univ. 1983–95, Prof. of Econs and Information Systems 1995–96, apptd Leonard N. Stern Prof. of Business 1995, now Prof. Emer.; Guggenheim Fellow 1961–62 and 1965–66; Overseas Fellow, Churchill Coll. Cambridge, UK 1969–70, 1989; Assoc. Ed. Journal of Econ. Theory 1968–, Games and Economic Behavior 1989–, Review of Economic Design 1994–, Information Systems Frontiers, 1999–; mem. NAS; Fellow, American Acad. of Arts and Sciences, Econometric Soc. (Pres. 1973); Distinguished Fellow, American Econ. Assen, AAAS; Woytinsky Award, Univ. of Mich. 1998. *Publications:* Notes on the Theory of Economic Planning 1963, Optimal Replacement Policy (with others) 1967, Decision and Organization (co-ed.) 1972, Economic Theory of Teams (with J. Marschak) 1972, Demand and Supply in U.S. Higher Education (with L. S. Miller) 1975, Education as an Industry (co-ed.) 1976, Mathematicians in Academia (with C. V. Kuh) 1980, Information, Incentives and Economic Mechanisms (co-ed.) 1987, Perspectives on Deterrence 1989 (co-ed.), Bargaining with Incomplete Information (co-ed.) 1992; and many articles. *Leisure interests:* music, hiking, cross-country skiing. *Address:* Stern School of Business, Kaufmann Management Center, Room 8–87, New York University, 44 West Fourth Street, New York, NY 10012 (office); 3203 Davenport Street, NW, Washington, DC 20008, USA (home). *Telephone:* (212) 998-0813 (office). *Fax:* (212) 995-4228 (office). *E-mail:* rradner@stern.nyu.edu (office). *Website:* www.stern.nyu.edu/~rradner (office).

RADOJIČIĆ, Igor, MEng; Bosnia and Herzegovina (Republika Srpska) engineer, politician and academic; b. 13 Sept. 1966, Banja Luka; m. Ranja Radojičić; one s. one d.; ed Faculty of Electrical Eng, Banja Luka; mem. staff, Faculty of Electrical Eng, Banja Luka 1991–2002; mem. Savez nezavisnih socijaldemokrata (Alliance of Ind. Social Democrats), apptd Sec.-Gen. 2003; Deputy in Nat. Ass., Pres. Nat. Ass. 2006–14; Acting Pres. of Republika Srpska Oct.–Dec. 2007; fmr Chair. City Council of Banja Luka. *Publications:* 14 scientific works on signal processing.

RADOŠ, Jozo, MSc; Croatian academic, engineer and politician; b. 3 Nov. 1956, Seonica, Tomislavgrad, Bosnia-Herzegovina; m.; one s. two d.; ed Zagreb Univ.; Prof. of History and Electrical Eng, Osijek and Dakovo 1983–86; Devt Planner, Rade Kondar Co., Zagreb 1986–90; engineer, Zagreb Electric Bulb factory 1990–92; mem. House of Reps 1992–2000, 2002–08, 2011–; Observer in European Parl. 2012–13, MEP 2014–; mem. Zagreb City Ass. 1995–97, 2005; mem. Croatian Parl. Del. to Parl. Ass. of Council of Europe 1998–2000, to Parl. Ass. of WEU 2004–08; Minister of Defence 2000–02; Acting Chair. Croatian Social Liberal Party (HSLS) 2001–02; Chair. Party of Liberal Democrats (Libra) 2002–05 (merged with Croatian People's Party to form Croatian People's Party—Liberal Democrats 2005), Vice-Pres. 2005–12; Homeland War Memorial Certificate. *Leisure interests:* mountaineering, bowling. *Address:* Hrvatska narodna stranka—Liberalni demokrati, 10000 Zagreb, Kneza Mislava 8, Croatia (office). *Telephone:* (1) 4629111 (office). *Fax:* (1) 4629110 (office). *E-mail:* hns@hns.hr (office). *Website:* www.hns.hr (office).

RADOVANOVIĆ, Nikola; Bosnia and Herzegovina government official; ed Ground Forces Acad., GHQ School, King's Coll. London and Univ. of Oxford, UK; Head of Office for Peace and Stability, Ministry of Foreign Affairs –2004; Minister of Defence 2004–07; apptd Co-Chair. Defence Reform Comm. 2004.

RĂDUCU, Aura Carmen; Romanian chemical engineer and politician; *Minister of European Funds;* b. 9 March 1956; Chemical Engineer, Faculty of Eng, Polytechnic Inst. of Bucharest 1975–80; Head Chemist, FIROS (nat. co. for production of glass fibre yarns) 1980–91; Counsellor and Deputy Gen. Man., Commercial, Ministry of Industry and Directorate-Gen. for Programmes and Int. Orgs 1991–99; Dir Nat. Agency for Regional Devt, Bucharest April–July 1999; Program Man., European Policies European Comm. Gen. Directorate for Regional Policy, Brussels, Belgium 1999–2007; Co-ordinator of urban devt projects, urban mobility plans and for developing sustainable models of public service contracts under European law 2007–12; Co-ordinator of Regional Operational Program 2007–13; Prin. Man., European Programmes, EBRD, Bucharest 2014–15; Minister of European Funds 2015–. *Address:* Ministry of European Funds, 011171 Bucharest 1, Bd Ion Mihalache 15–17, Romania (office). *Telephone:* (37) 2838500 (office). *Fax:* (37) 2838501 (office). *E-mail:* contact.minister@fonduri-ue.ro (office). *Website:* www.fonduri-ue.ro (office).

RADULOVIĆ, Saša; Serbian electronics engineer, tax adviser and politician; *President, Dosta je bilo (DjB—Enough is Enough!);* b. 7 June 1965, Bihać; s. of Budimir Radulović; m.; two c.; ed Univ. of Sarajevo; was part of Neo-primitivism cultural movt formed in Sarajevo, together with film dir Emir Kusturica and mems of Zabranjeno Pušenje rock band; moved to Germany 1990 and worked at Siemens AG on system monitoring for nuclear plants located in Germany, USA and Russia; moved to Toronto, Canada for Antares Alliance (subsidiary of Amdahl/EDS) 1994; switched to Interpro Medical Network as Vice-Pres. of Devt and then as mem. Bd of Dirs, Gen. Man. of the co. dealing with servers for TrueSpectre pictures 1997–2001; tax adviser to several investment cos 2002–06; returned to Serbia 2005 and became a pioneer blogger, writing on economics, business and tax reforms; owned a co. and worked as a bankruptcy trustee for several other cos; licensed as a bankruptcy trustee and portfolio manager; fmr Advisor to Council of Europe, OSCE, US Embassy, Deutsche Gesellschaft für Internationale Zusammenarbeit (GIZ) GmbH, Nacionalna Alijansa Lokalni Ekonomski Razvoj, Asscn of Small and Medium Enterprises; provided training to Serbian police and prosecutors on prosecution of financial crimes; non-partisan Minister of Economy 2013–14 (resgnd); mem. and Pres. Dosta je bilo (DjB—Enough is Enough!) 2014–; mem. Nat. Ass. (Parl.) 2016–; cand. in presidential election 2017. *Address:* Dosta je bilo (Enough is Enough!), 11000 Belgrade, Brankova 21, Serbia (office). *Telephone:* (11) 3282600 (office). *E-mail:* kontakt@dostajebilo.rs (office). *Website:* dostajebilo.rs (office).

RADUNOVIČ, Darko; Montenegrin politician and fmr banker; *Minister of Finance;* b. 31 March 1960, Podgorica; m.; two c.; ed Faculty of Law, Titograd; fmr CEO Montenegro Euromarket Bank-Bank AD Podgorica; CEO Prva Banka 2014–16; Minister of Finance 2016–; Pres. Managing Bd, Asscn of Montenegrin Banks 2014–15; fmr mem. Bd of Dirs Montenegro Airlines, Jugobanci AD Podgorica 1988–98; mem. Democratic Party of Socialists (DPS); mem. Bd of Govs., EBRD. *Address:* Ministry of Finance, 81000 Podgorica, Stanka Dragojevića 2, Montenegro (office). *Telephone:* (20) 242835 (office). *Fax:* (20) 224450 (office). *E-mail:* mf@mif.gov.me (office). *Website:* www.mf.gov.me (office).

RADWAN, Samir, BSc, MSc, PhD; Egyptian economist, international organization official and government official; *Senior Associate, Economic Research Forum;* ed Cairo Univ., School of Oriental and African Studies, Univ. of London, UK; Research Officer, Inst. of Nat. Planning, Cairo and Aswan Regional Planning Project, Cairo and Aswan 1963–64; Asst Lecturer, Faculty of Econs, Cairo Univ. 1963–65; Lecturer, Inst. of Econs and Statistics and Sr Assoc. Member, St Anthony's Coll., Oxford, UK 1972–76; with ILO 1976–2003, positions included Dir Devt Policies Dept 1996–99, Sr Policy Adviser, Employment Sector 1999–2001, Adviser to Dir-Gen. on Devt Policies and Counsellor on Arab Countries 2001–03; Man. Dir Econ. Research Forum, Egypt 2003–06, now Sr Assoc.; Adviser and mem. Bd of Trustees, Gen. Authority for Investment, Egypt 2006–11; fmr Exec. Dir Egyptian Nat. Competitiveness Council; Minister of Finance Feb.–July 2011. *Publications:* several publications on labour markets, industrialization, development and agrarian systems and poverty. *Address:* Economic Research Forum, 21 Al-Sad Al-Aaly Street, Dokki, Cairo, Egypt (office). *E-mail:* Liloradwan@hotmail .com. *Website:* www.erf.org.eg (office).

RADZIKHOVSKY, Leonid; Russian journalist and political analyst; fmr sr columnist for liberal daily newspaper, Segodnya (now defunct); currently with Rossiyskaya Gazeta, Vzglyad, Evreisky Mir; mem., RIA Novosti Expert Council, Moscow Writers' Union; Russia's Golden Pen Prize. *Publications:* numerous articles in newspapers and journals. *Address:* c/o Rossiiskaya Gazeta, PO Box 40, ul. Pravdy 24, 125993 Moscow, Russia. *Telephone:* (495) 257-52-52. *Fax:* (495) 973-22-56. *E-mail:* sekretar@rg.ru. *Website:* www.rg.ru.

RADZINSKY, Edvard Stanislavovich; Russian dramatist; b. 23 Sept. 1936, Moscow; s. of Stanislav Radzinsky and Sofia Radzinsky; m. 2nd Yelena Timofeyevna Denisova; ed Inst. of History and Archival Science. *Plays include:* My Dream is India 1960, You're All of Twenty-Two, you Old Men! 1962, One Hundred and Four Pages on Love 1964, Kolobashkin the Seducer 1967, Socrates 1977, Lunin 1980, I Stand at the Restaurant 1982, Theatre of the Time of Nero and Seneca 1984, Elderly Actress in the Role of Dostoevsky's Wife 1986, Sporting Scenes 1987, Our Decameron 1989. *Television:* author and narrator of TV series Mysteries of History 1997–. *Publications include:* novels: The Last of the Romanovs 1989, Our Decameron 1990; non-fiction: The Last Tsar: The Life and Death of Nicholas II 1992, God Save and Restrain Russia 1993, Stalin 1996, Mysteries of History 1997, Mysteries of Love 1998, Fall of Gallant Century 1998,

Collected Works (7 Vols) 1998–99, Rasputin 1999, The Theatrical Novel (memoirs) 1999, Alexander II, The Last Great Tsar 2005. *Address:* Usiyevicha Street 8, Apartment 96, 125319 Moscow, Russia (home). *E-mail:* edvard@radzinski.ru (office). *Website:* www.radzinski.ru (office).

RADZIWILL, John S. A., MA; British lawyer and business executive; *Chairman, INTL FCStone Inc.;* ed Univ. of Oxford; mem. Bar of England and Wales; with Markman Securities (British investment banking firm) 1973–74; Pres. Radix Org. Inc. 1976–97, Radix Ventures Inc. 1979–95; mem. Bd of Dirs Int. Assets Holding Corpn (INTL) 2002– (merged with FCStone Sept. 2009), Chair. 2012–; Chair. New York Holdings Ltd, Co-founder and Chair. (non-exec.) Acquisitor PLC, fmr Chair. Acquisitor Holdings (Bermuda) Ltd; mem. Bd of Dirs Baltimore PLC 2006–, Oryx Int. Growth Fund Ltd 2007–, Lionheart Group, Inc., USA Micro Cap Value Co. Ltd, Goldcrown Group Ltd (and subsidiaries), New York Holdings Ltd (parent of Lionheart Advisors, Inc.); fmr mem. Bd of Dirs Interequity Capital Corpn, GP, Air Express Int. Corpn 1995–2000; registered rep. associated with Cohmad Securities Corpn –1997. *Address:* INTL FCStone Inc., 708 Third Avenue, 15th Floor, New York, NY 10017, USA (office). *Telephone:* (212) 485-3500 (office). *Fax:* (212) 485-3505 (office). *E-mail:* info@intlfcstone.com (office). *Website:* www.intlfcstone.com (office).

RAE, Barbara, CBE, RA, RE, RSA, RSW, RGI, FRSE; Scottish painter and printmaker; b. 10 Dec. 1943, Falkirk, Scotland; d. of James Rae and Mary Young; one s.; ed Morrison's Acad., Crieff, Perthshire, Edinburgh Coll. of Art; Lecturer, Glasgow School of Art 1975–96; mem. Bd, Royal Fine Art Comm. 1995–2004; solo exhbns annually in Edinburgh, London, Bath, Dublin, Belfast and selected European and US cities; numerous group exhbns UK, USA, Germany, Norway, Netherlands, Spain, Ireland; artwork in numerous public and pvt. collections, including Scottish Nat. Gallery of Modern Art, Univs of Edinburgh, Glasgow, Aberdeen, St Andrews and York, Royal Bank of Scotland, Bank of England, Lloyds TSB Group, Robert Fleming Holdings, HRH the Duke of Edinburgh; mem. Royal Scottish Soc. of Painters and Watercolour (RSW), Royal Glasgow Inst. of Fine Arts, Soc. of Scottish Artists, Royal Soc. of Painter-Printmakers (RE); Trustee, British School, Rome 1997–2000; Hon. Fellow, RCA, London, Royal Inst. of Architects, Scotland; Hon. DArts (Napier Univ., Edinburgh) 2000; Hon. DLitt (Aberdeen) 2003, (St Andrews) 2008; awards include Guthrie Award, RSA 1977, May Marshall Brown Award, RSW Centenary Exhbn 1979, Sir William Gillies Travel Award 1983, Calouste Gulbenkian Printmaking Award 1983, Alexander Graham Munro Award, RSW 1989. *Publications:* Barbara Rae – Paintings 2008, Barbara Rae – Prints 2010, Barbara Rae – Sketchbooks 2011, Barbara Rae – The Northwest Passage 2018, Barbara Rae – Arctic Sketchbooks 2018. *Leisure interest:* travel. *Address:* Royal Academy of Arts, Burlington House, Piccadilly, London, W1J 0BD, England. *Telephone:* (0131) 339-8000 (office); (20) 7300-8000. *E-mail:* garethwardell@hotmail.com (office). *Website:* www.barbararae.com (home).

RAE, Hon. Robert (Bob) Keith, CC, O.Ont., PC, QC, BA, BPhil, LLB; Canadian lawyer, arbitrator and fmr politician; *Partner, Olthuis Kleer Townshend LLP;* b. 2 Aug. 1948, Ottawa; s. of Saul Rae and Lois George; m. Arlene Perly 1980; three d.; ed public school in Washington, DC, Int. School of Geneva, Univ. of Toronto and Balliol Coll., Oxford; fmr volunteer, legal aid clinics in Toronto and Asst counsel for United Steelworkers of America and Union of Injured Workers; mem. Canadian Fed. Parl. 1978–82; Prov. Leader, New Democratic Party (NDP), Ont. 1982–96; mem. Ont. Prov. Legis. 1982–95; Premier of Ontario 1990–95; Partner Goodman Phillips & Vineberg (now Goodmans LLP) 1996–2007; MP for Toronto Centre 2008–13, mem. Security Intelligence Review Cttee; Interim Leader, Liberal Party of Canada 2011–13; Distinguished Sr Fellow, Univ. of Toronto School of Public Policy and Governance 2013–; Partner, Olthuis Kleer Townshend LLP 2014–; mem. Bd of Dirs Hydro One Inc., Niigon Technologies Ltd, Iter Canada Inc., Tembec Ltd, Trojan Technologies; Chair. Forum of Federations, Toronto Symphony Orchestra, Ivesprint, Inc., Inst. for Research on Public Policy; Chancellor Wilfrid Laurier Univ.; Dr hc (Law Soc. of Upper Canada), (Univ. of Toronto), (Assumption Univ.). *Publications include:* From Protest to Power 1996, The Three Questions: Prosperity and the Public Good 1998, Ontario, A Leader in Learning 2005, Air India, Lessons to be Learned 2005. *Leisure interests:* tennis, golf, fishing, reading, music. *Address:* Olthuis Kleer Townshend LLP, 250 University Avenue, 8th Floor, Toronto, ON M5H 3E5, Canada (office). *Telephone:* (416) 981-9441 (office). *E-mail:* brae@oktlaw.com (office). *Website:* www.oktlaw.com (office); www.bobrae.ca.

RAFELSON, Robert (Bob) Jay; American film director and producer; b. 21 Feb. 1933, New York; m. 1st Toby Carr Rafelson 1995 (divorced 1977); one s.; m. 2nd Gabrielle Taurek; ed Dartmouth Coll.; Co-founder (with Bert Schneider and Steve Blauner) Raybert/BBS Productions (later acquired by Columbia Pictures); Dartmouth Film Soc. Film Award 1997. *Films directed include:* Head 1968, Five Easy Pieces 1970 (New York Film Critics Award), The King of Marvin Gardens 1972, Stay Hungry 1976, The Postman Always Rings Twice (also co-producer) 1981, Black Widow 1987, Mountains of the Moon 1990, Man Trouble 1992, Wet 1993, Armed Response 1994, Blood and Wine 1996, Poodle Springs 1998, Erotic Tales-Porn.com 2002, House on Turk Street 2002, No Good Deed 2002. *Television:* The Monkees (producer, also directed six episodes) 1966–68.

RAFFARIN, Jean-Pierre; French politician; b. 3 Aug. 1948, Poitiers (Vienne); s. of Jean Raffarin and Renée Michaud; m. Anne-Marie Perrier 1980; one d.; ed Lycée Henri IV, Poitiers, Faculté de Droit, Paris-Assas, Ecole Supérieure de Commerce, Paris; Marketing Dept Cafés Jacques Vabre 1973–76; Adviser, Office of Minister of Labour 1976–81; Pres. Crédit Immobilier Rural de la Vienne 1978–95; Lecturer, Inst. d'Etudes Politiques, Paris 1979–88; Dir-Gen. Bernard Krief Communication 1981–88; Gen. Del. Inst. Euro-92 1988–89; Nat. Del., Deputy Sec.-Gen. and mem. Political Bureau, Parti Républicain 1977–2002; City Councillor, Poitiers 1977–95; Conseiller Régional 1986–88; Pres. Conseil Régional, Poitou-Charentes 1988–2002; mem. European Parl. 1989–95; Deputy Sec.-Gen. and Spokesman for Union pour la Démocratie Française 1993, Sec.-Gen. 1995–2002; Pres. Comm. Arc Atlantique 1994–98; Minister of Small and Medium-Sized Businesses, of Commerce and Craft Industry 1995–97; mem. Senate (for Vienne) 1995, 1997–2002, 2005–; Vice-Mayor of Chasseneuil-du-Poitou 1995–2001; Vice-Pres. Démocratie Libérale 1997–2002 (merged with Union pour un Mouvement Populaire, UMP 2002), First Vice-Pres. UMP 2002–; Pres. Asscn des régions de France 1998–2002; Prime Minister of France 2002–05; Grand Croix, Ordre nat. du Mérite 2002, Officier, Ordre nat. du Québec 2003, Grand Cross, Order of the Star of Romania 2004, Grand Officier, Légion d'honneur 2008. *Publications:* La vie en jaune 1977, La publicité nerf de la communication 1983, L'avenir a ses racines 1986, Nous sommes tous les régionaux 1988, Pour une morale de l'action 1992, Le livre de l'Atlantique 1994, Notre Contrat pour l'Alternance 2001, La Nouvelle Gouvernance 2002, La France de Mai 2003, La dernière marche 2007, Je marcherai toujours à l'affectif 2012. *Leisure interests:* contemporary painting, regional literature. *Address:* Senat, 15 rue de Vaugirard, 75291 Paris Cedex 06; Union pour un Mouvement Populaire, 55 rue La Boétie 75384 Paris Cedex 08 (office); 7 route de Saint-Georges, 86360 Chasseneuil-du-Poitou, France (home). *Telephone:* 1-42-34-20-00 (Senat) (office); 1-40-76-60-00 (UMP) (office). *Fax:* 1-42-34-26-77 (office). *E-mail:* jpr@carnetjpr.com (office). *Website:* www.senat.fr (office); www.carnetjpr.com.

RAFFENNE, Gen. Jean-Paul; French army officer (retd); b. 1944; Liaison Officer, Fort Leavenworth, USA 1990–92; Deputy Defence Attaché, Embassy in Washington, DC 1994–96; Head, French Del. to EU Mil. Cttee 2001; Chief French Liaison Officer in unit directing Operation Enduring Freedom (mil. campaign in Afghanistan), Tampa, Fla, USA 2001; Head, Direction du renseignement militaire (mil. intelligence agency) 2002; fmr Prof. and Dir, Sr Exec. Seminar, George C. Marshall European Center for Security Studies, Germany; currently with Ministry of Defence. *Address:* Ministry of Defence, 14 rue Saint Dominique, 75007 Paris, France (office). *Telephone:* 1-80-50-14-00 (office). *Fax:* 1-47-05-40-91 (office). *E-mail:* sdbc.courrier-ministre.fct@intradef.gouv.fr (office). *Website:* www.defense.gouv.fr (office).

RAFINI, Brigi; Niger politician; *Prime Minister;* b. 7 April 1953, Iférouane, Agadez Dist; ed École nat. d'admin, Niamey, Inst. Int. d'admin publique and École nat. d'admin, France; mem. Mouvement nat. pour la société de développement—Nassara 1989–91, left to join Alliance nigérienne pour la démocratie et le progrès social—Zaman Lahiya (breakaway faction) 1993–96, Co-founder Rassemblement pour la démocratie et le progrès—Djamaa; currently mem. Parti nigérien pour la démocratie et le socialisme—Tarayya; spent several years as civil servant; served several terms as mayor of Iferouane Dist; Minister of Agriculture in late 1980s; elected mem. Assemblée Nat. (Parl.) for Agadez region 2004, Fourth Vice-Pres., Assemblée Nat. 2004–09, Prime Minister 2011–. *Address:* Office of the Prime Minister, BP 893, Niamey, Niger (office). *Telephone:* 20-72-26-99 (office). *Fax:* 20-73-58-59 (office).

RAFIQUE, Muhammad; Pakistani trade union official; b. 3 Oct. 1942, Delhi, India; s. of Muhammad Umer; m.; three s. two d.; technician Karachi Water and Sewerage Bd 1971; currently man. of tech. affairs, water treatment plant; joined local union 1972; Treas. Nat. Trade Union Fed. (NTUF), apptd Pres. 1999; Pres. KMC United Workers Housing Soc.; Best Trade Unionist Award, NTUF-SINDH. *Leisure interest:* singing.

RAFSANJANI, Faezeh (see HASHEMI BAHREMANI (Rafsanjani), Faezeh).

RAFTER, Patrick Michael; Australian fmr professional tennis player; b. 28 Dec. 1972, Mount Isa, Queensland; s. of Jim Rafter and Jocelyn Rafter; partner Lara Feltham; one s.; turned professional 1991; won first career singles title in Manchester 1994; Grand Slam highlights: semi-finalist French Open 1997; winner US Open 1997, 1998; winner Canadian Open and Cincinnati Masters 1998; semi-finalist Wimbledon 1999, finalist 2000, 2001; semi-finalist Australian Open 2001; winner Australia Open Doubles title (with Jonas Bjorkman) 1999; sustained serious shoulder injury and took extended break from tennis following Australia's Davis Cup defeat in Dec. 2001; winner of 11 singles titles, 10 doubles titles; announced retirement Jan. 2003; brief comeback (doubles only) 2004; f. Patrick Rafter Cherish the Children Foundation 1999; Captain, Australia Davis Cup 2010–15; ATP Newcomer of the Year 1993, Awarded Diploma of Honor Int. Cttee for Fair Play by Int. Olympic Cttee 1997, ATP Tour Stefan Edberg Sportsmanship Award 1997, Australian Sports Personality of the Year Award 1997, Media Sports Personality of the Year Award 1997, ATP Arthur Ash Humanitarian Award 1998, Australian People's Choice Award - Male Sports Star 1998, Awarded Honorary Ambassador for Queensland (presented with the keys to city of Brisbane) 1998, Queensland Young Achiever Award 1998, ATP Tour Stefan Edberg Sportsmanship Award 1998, ATP Tour's Web site Star of the Year Award 1999, Australian People's Choice Award - Male Sports Star 1999, ATP Tour Stefan Edberg Sportsmanship Award 2000, ANSVAR The Bill Brown Community Award 2000, ATP Tour Stefan Edberg Sportsmanship Award 2001, Australian Of The Year 2002, inducted into Sport Australia Hall of Fame 2006, inducted into Australian Open Hall of Fame 2008. *Leisure interests:* golf, fishing. *Address:* c/o Patrick Rafter Cherish the Children Foundation, POB 1855, Noosa Heads, Queensland 4567, Australia (office). *Fax:* (7) 5455 4433 (office). *Website:* www.cherishthechildren.com.au (office).

RAGAGLINI, Cesare Maria; Italian diplomatist; b. 6 Feb. 1953, Massa; ed Free Univ. of Brussels, Belgium, Cesare Alfieri Faculty, Univ. of Florence; joined Foreign Service 1978, served with Directorate-Gen. for Personnel 1979–81, Consul, Embassy in Teheran 1981–84, First Sec., Embassy in Ottawa 1984–87, assigned to Minister's Cabinet, Office of Parl. Relations, Ministry of Foreign Affairs 1987–89, assigned to create Foreign Ministry's Intelligence Unit 1989, Dir 1989–92, Deputy Head of Mission, Embassy in New Delhi 1992–95, Deputy Acting Head of Service, Press and Information Service, Ministry of Foreign Affairs 1995–96, assigned to reopen Italian Diplomatic Mission in Baghdad 1996, Head of Mission 1996–99, Deputy Diplomatic Adviser to the Prime Minister 1999–2002, Prime Minister's Rep. for Balkan Reconstruction Effort 2001–02, Chef de Cabinet to Minister of Foreign Affairs 2002–04, Prime Minister's Rep. to G8 Summit (Sherpa) and in charge of preparations for the Gleneagles and St Petersburg Summits 2004–05, Head of Italian Del. to jt inquiry with US Authorities into the case of Nicola Calipari (MOVM), killed in Baghdad 2005–06, Dir-Gen. for the Countries of the Mediterranean and Middle East 2006–08, Amb. 2008, Amb. and Perm. Rep. to UN, New York 2009–13, Amb. to Russian Fed. 2013–18; rank of Second Lt in Carabinieri Corps Reserves 1979; Grand Officer, Order of Merit of the Italian Repub. 2006.

RAGGI, Virginia Elena; Italian lawyer and politician; *Mayor of Rome;* b. 18 July 1978, Rome; m. Andrea Severini; one c.; ed Univ. Rome III; legal training with law firm specializing in civil law 2003–07; registered as lawyer with Bar Council of

Rome 2006; worked as lawyer with Sammarco and Assocs in the areas of civil, commercial and industrial law 2007; mem. Rome City Council 2013–15, mem. Culture, Employment and Youth Policies Cttee, Social Policies and Health Cttee, apptd spokesperson for Capitoline Council 2013; Mayor of Rome 2016–; mem. MoVimento 5 Stelle (M5S, Five Star Movt) 2010–. *Publications:* articles in Diritto dell'Informazione e dell'Informatica. *Leisure interests:* skiing, swimming. *Address:* Office of the Mayor, Palazzo Senatorio, Piazza del Campidoglio, 00186 Rome, Italy (office). *Telephone:* (06) 67081 (office). *Website:* www.comune.roma.it (office).

RAGHEB, Ali Abu, BSc; Jordanian politician; b. 1946, Amman; ed Univ. of Tennessee, USA; Pnr and Man. Dir National Engineering and Contracting Co. 1971–91; Minister of Industry and Trade 1991, 1995, Minister of Energy and Mineral Resources 1991–93; elected mem. Nat. Ass. 1993; Prime Minister of Jordan and Minister of Defence 2000–03 (resgnd); Grand Cordon of the Order of Al-Kawkab Al-Urduni, Grand Cordon of the Order of Al-Nahda, Kt Grand Cross (Italy), GCMG (UK).

RAGNEMALM, Hans Olof, LLD; Swedish judge; b. 30 March 1940, Laholm; m. Vivi Ragnemalm 1961; Assoc. Prof. of Public Law, Univ. of Lund 1970–75; Prof. of Public Law, Univ. of Stockholm 1975–87, Dean, Faculty of Law 1984–87; Parl. Ombudsman 1987–92; Judge, Supreme Admin. Court 1992–94, Justice 1999, Pres. 2000–05; Judge, European Court of Justice 1995–99; currently Juris Ombudsmen; Alt. Mem. Court of Conciliation and Arbitration, OSCE; HM The King's Medal of the 12th Size with Chain 2008. *Publications:* Appealability of Administrative Decisions 1970, Extraordinary Remedies in Administrative Procedure Law 1973, Elements of Administrative Procedure Law 1977, The Constitution of Sweden 1980, Administrative Justice in Sweden 1991; numerous other books and articles. *Address:* c/o Regeringsrätten, PO Box 2293, 103 17 Stockholm, Sweden. *Telephone:* (8) 6176212 (office). *Fax:* (8) 6176234 (office).

RAGON, Michel, Dr d'Etat-ès-Lettres; French writer and lecturer; b. 24 June 1924, Marseille; s. of Aristide Ragon and Camille Sourisseau; m. Françoise Antoine 1968; worked in manual jobs from the age of 14; lived in Paris 1945–, bookseller on the Seine embankments 1954–64; art critic, architectural historian, novelist; Lecturer, l'Ecole Nat. Supérieure des Arts Décoratifs, Paris 1972–85; Chevalier, Ordre du Mérite, Légion d'honneur, Commdr des Arts et des Lettres; Prix de l'Acad. Française et de l'Acad. d'Architecture. *Publications:* 25 ans d'art vivant 1969, Histoire mondiale de l'architecture et de l'urbanisme modernes 1971–78, L'art pour quoi faire? 1971, L'art abstrait 1973–74, Histoire de la littérature prolétarienne en France 1974, L'homme et les villes 1975, L'accent de ma mère 1980, L'espace de la mort 1981, Ma soeur aux yeux d'Asie 1982, Les mouchoirs rouges de Cholet 1984, La louve de Mervent 1985, Le marin des sables 1988, La mémoire des vaincus 1990, Le Cocher du Boiroux 1992, Journal de l'Art Abstrait 1992, Le roman de Rabelais 1994, Les Coquelicots sont revenus 1996, Un si bel espoir 1999, Georges et Louise 2000, Un rossignol chantait 2001, Cinquante ans d'art vivant 2001, Un amour de Jeanne 2003, La ferme d'en haut 2005, Le prisonnier 2007, Dictionnaire de l'Anarchie 2009, Ils se croyaient illustres et immortels 2011, Journal d'un critique d'art désabusé 2013. *Address:* 4 rue du Faubourg Poissonnière, 75010 Paris, France. *Telephone:* 1-48-24-66-47. *Website:* www.michelragon.fr.

RAGOUSSIS, Yiannis; Greek politician; b. 11 Dec. 1965, Athens; m. Katerina Roussou; one s. two d.; ed Aristotle Univ. of Thessaloniki, Univ. of Sussex, UK; joined Panhellenic Socialist Movt (PASOK) 1983, mem. Cen. Cttee 1994–96, Spokesman 2007–08, Gen. Sec. Political Council of PASOK 2008–09; Gen. Dir Research Centre for Equality Issues (KETHI) 1994–95, Special Adviser to European Commr Christos Papoutsis 1995–98; elected Mayor of Paros Island 2002 (re-elected) 2006, mem. Bd in Cyclades Pref.'s Local Union of Municipalities and Communities; mem. Parl. (PASOK) 2007–; Minister of the Interior, Decentralization and e-Governance 2009–11, of Infrastructures June–Nov. 2011, Alt. Minister for Nat. Defence in govt of nat. unity of Lucas Papademos 2011–12. *Address:* 37 Harilaou Trikoupi Street, 106 80 Athens, Greece. *Telephone:* (210) 3665401. *Fax:* (210) 3665409. *E-mail:* ragousis@pasok.gr (office). *Website:* www.hellenicparliament.gr (office); www.yme.gr (office).

RAHA, Air Chief Marshall Arup; Indian air force officer; b. 26 Dec. 1954, Baidyabati, West Bengal; m. Lily Raha; two c.; ed Sainik School, Purulia, Defence Services Staff Coll., Nat. Defence Acad., Air Force Acad.; Cat A Qualified Flying Instructor and Fighter Combat Leader, commissioned into Indian Air Force (IAF) 1974, CO, No: 47 Squadron, Black Archers 1992–94, has also served as Directing Staff, Flying Instructors' School, Chennai, Tactics and Combat Devt Establishment, Staff Officer to Chief of Air Staff, Inspector, Directorate of Air Staff Inspection, Air HQ, Deputy Commdt, Air Force Acad., Hyderabad, Sr Air Staff Officer, Western Air Command HQ, operational assignments include CO MiG-29 Squadron, Station Commdr of Air Force Station Bhatinda, Punjab during 'Op Parakram', Air Officer Commdg, Air Force Station Adampur and Western Air Command Advance HQ, Chandimandir; Mil. and Air Attache, Embassy in Kiev 1999–2001; Sr Air Staff Officer, Western Air Command –2011, Air Officer Commdg-in-Chief, Central Air Command 2011–12, Air Officer Commdg-in-Chief, Western Air Command, 2012–13, Vice-Chief of Air Staff July–Dec. 2013, Chief of Air Staff 2014–16; Hon. Aide De Camp (Air) to Pres. of India 2012–; Pres.'s Gold Medal for Best Cadet, Nat. Defence Acad. 1973, Param Vishisht Seva Medal, Ati Vishisht Seva Medal, Vayusena Medal. *Leisure interests:* reading, golf, travelling.

RAHARDJO, Soegeng, BEcons; Indonesian diplomatist; b. 18 Sept. 1954, Bandung; m. Aslida N. Rahardjo; one c.; ed Catholic Univ. of Buenos Aires, Argentina, School of Advanced Int. Studies, Johns Hopkins Univ., Washington, DC; served as Attaché to Third Cttee, UN, New York, and in Embassy in Washington, DC 1991, participated in treaty negotiations between ASEAN, People's Repub. of China and EU, Head of Investment Guarantee Agreements Div., Directorate-Gen. for Int. Econ. Relations, Ministry of Foreign Affairs 1995–98, Chair. Asian Group in negotiating Declaration of UNCTAD X 2000, played role in organizing ASEAN Summit IX 2003 2002–05, 37th ASEAN Ministerial Meeting 2004, and in establishment of ASEAN Leaders' Special Meeting on Aftermath of Earthquake and Tsunami Jan. 2005, Asian-African Summit 2005, Amb. to South Africa 2005–09, Insp.-Gen., Ministry of Foreign Affairs 2009–13, Amb. to People's Repub. of China 2013–17.

RAHBANI, Ziad; Lebanese composer, singer and playwright; b. 1956, Antelias; s. of Assi Rahbani and Nuhad Haddad (née Fairuz); m. Dalal Karam (divorced); composer of numerous songs for mother Fairuz (successful Lebanese singer); contributor to several political radio shows including Bazdna Taybeen Oulou Allah and El Akl Zeeneh; columnist, Al-Akhbar (daily newspaper) 2006–; well known as satirist of Lebanese politics. *Recordings include:* solo albums: Belly Dance 1972, Bil Afrah 1972, Sahrieh - Songs 1973, Abou Ali 1979, Ana Mosh Kafer 1985, Hodou' Nisbi 1985, Bema Enno 1996, Amrak Seedna 2000, Bnisba la boukra shou Monodose 2001, Live at Damascus Citadel 2009; with Music for Fairuz: Wahdon 1979, Maarefti Fik 1987, Kifak Inta 1991, Ila Assi 1995, Mich Kayen Hayk Tkoun 1999, Wala Kif 2002, Eh, Fi Amal 2010. *Plays:* Sahriyyeh 1973, Nazl el Sourour 1974, Bennesbe La Boukra Shou? 1978, Film Ameriki Taweel 1980, Shi fashel 1983, Bikhsous el Karameh wel Shaab el aaneed 1993, Lawla Fos'hat el Amali 1994. *Address:* c/o Al-Akhbar, POB 5963-113, 6th Floor, Concorde Centre, rue Verdun, Beirut, Lebanon (office).

RAHEEN, Sayed Makhdoom, MA, PhD; Afghan diplomatist, politician and writer; b. 1946, Kabul; ed Tehran Univ., Iran; apptd Lecturer, Kabul Univ. 1973; fmr Head of Bureau of Afghan Culture and Art, Ministry of Information, Culture and Tourism; fmr mem. Drafting Cttee of Constitution of Afghanistan; mem. Grand Nat. Ass. (Loya Jirga) 1976; put under house arrest following Communist coup d'etat April 1978; moved to Pakistan after Soviet invasion; apptd mem. High Council and Chair. Cttee of Culture and Publicity, Islamic Unity of Afghanistan Mujahedeen 1982; selected as Head of Radio Free Kabul by Mujahidin parties; served as adviser with rank of Minister to Pres. of Afghan Interim Govt; co-f. Nat. Islamic Movt of Afghanistan in Peshawar, Pakistan 1988; abandoned Afghan resistance and left for USA following disagreements with Jihad leaders 1991; Co-founder and first Chair. Asscn for Peace and Democracy for Afghanistan 1996; mem. Exec. Cttee Loya Jirga, Rome 1998; selected as Minister of Information, Culture and Tourism of Interim Admin, Bonn Conf. 2002; Chair. Kabul City Council 2003; Amb. to India 2007–09; Minister of Information and Culture 2009–15; Medal for serving the freedom of speech and promoting cultural activities, presented by HM Zahir Shah 2004. *Publications include:* Tears of Khorasan, The Mourners, Reply to Khalili (poetry), Today's Muslims (in Pashto); several books and articles on culture, literature, history and Islamic Sufism, the works of Sayed Jamaludeen Afghani, Daqiqi Nama, research on Amir Khosrow, and the relations of Afghanistan and the subcontinent; f. and published resistance magazines and papers, in Dari, Pashto, Urdu, Arabic and English.

RAHIM, Arbab Ghulam, MB BS; Pakistani physician and politician; b. 15 Sept. 1956, Mirpurkhas Dist, Sindh Prov.; s. of Arbab Taj Muhammad; m.; ed Cadet Coll. Petaro, Sind Medical Coll., Karachi; Chair. Dist Council, Mirpurkhas 1984–87; Public Health Eng and Rural Devt Adviser to Chief Minister of Sindh 1988; elected to Nat. Ass. 1993, 1996, 1999, Chair. Steering Cttee for Ind. Mems, Standing Cttee on Commerce, Parl. Sec. for Water and Power; Prov. Minister of Sindh for Local Govt, Katchi Abadis and Public Health Eng 2000, for Works and Services 2003–04; Chief Minister of Sindh and Leader of the House 2004–07; Founding Pres. Sindh Democratic Alliance 1999–2000; apptd Pres. Pakistan Muslim League 2011; beaten with shoes by mob of political activists and fmr servants 7 April 2008. *Address:* Khetlari, Tehsil Diplo, District Tharparkar, Sindh, Pakistan (home). *Telephone:* (21) 5383114 (home).

RAHIMOV, Saidahmad Borievich, PhD; Uzbekistani politician and banker; *Chairman, National Bank for Foreign Economic Activity;* b. 1960; m.; three c.; ed Tashkent Inst. of Agric.; Asst Sr Teacher, Tashkent Econ. Inst. 1989–93; fmr Presidential Adviser for Socioeconomic Affairs; fmr Chair., Auditing Comm.; fmr Man. Asaka Bank; Minister of Finance 2004–05; currently Chair. Nat. Bank for Foreign Economic Activity; Dustlik Medal 2010. *Address:* National Bank for Foreign Economic Activity, 100047 Tashkent, Uzbekistan (office). *Telephone:* (71) 133-62-87 (office). *Fax:* (71) 132-01-72 (office). *E-mail:* webmaster@central.nbu .com (office); info@central.nbu.com (office). *Website:* www.nbu.com/en (office).

RAHIMZODA, Lt Gen. Ramazon Hamro, CandLegalSci; Tajikistani lawyer and government official; *Minister of Internal Affairs;* b. 25 April 1960, Dangar Dist, Kulob Viloyat (now Khatlon Viloyat), Tajik SSR, USSR; m.; three s. two d.; ed Agrarian Univ. of the Tajik SSR, Dushanbe, Higher School of Ministry of Internal Affairs Militia of the Repub. of Tajikistan, Acad. of Ministry of Internal Affairs of the Russian Fed.; joined Ministry of Internal Affairs 1983, Chief of Div. of Combat of Econ. Crimes, Kulob Dist 1992, Chief of Dept of Internal Affairs, Dangara Dist 1992–94, Chief of Dept of Internal Affairs, Khovaling Dist 1994–95, Chief of Dept of Internal Affairs, Norak Dist 1995, Deputy to Chief of Dept on Combat of Econ. Criminality 1995–2001, Rep. to Agency on Co-ordination of Combat of Organized Criminality and Other Dangerous Crimes in Territory of CIS 2001–04, First Deputy Dir of Agency 2004–05, Deputy Minister of Internal Affairs 2005–07, Chief of Migration Services 2007–08; Head of Exec. Office of Pres. 2008–11; First Deputy Minister of Internal Affairs 2009–11, Minister of Internal Affairs 2012–; attained special rank of Militia Lt Gen. 2011; state and departmental awards. *Publications:* more than 100 academic works on legal commentary, the combat of corruption, terrorism, extremism and economic crimes. *Leisure interest:* chess (Master). *Address:* Ministry of Internal Affairs, 734025 Dushanbe, Kuchai Texron 29, Tajikistan (office). *Telephone:* (372) 21-21-21 (office). *Fax:* (372) 21-18-97 (office). *Website:* mvd.tj (office).

RAHMAN, A. S. F.; Bangladeshi business executive; *Chairman, Beximco Group;* Chair. Beximco Group, including Beximco Pharmaceutical Ltd, Beximco Holdings Ltd, Beximco Agro-Chemicals Ltd, Beximco Foods Ltd, Beximco Synthetics Ltd, Comtrade Beximco Apparels Ltd, Sonali Ansh., Beximco Infusions Ltd; Dir IPDC; mem. Bd of Govs Bangladesh Enterprise Inst. *Address:* Beximco Pharmaceuticals Ltd, 17 Dhanmondi R/A, Road 2, Dhaka 1205, Bangladesh (office). *Telephone:* (2) 9127721 (office). *Fax:* (2) 8613470 (office). *Website:* www.beximco.net (office).

RAHMAN, A(llah) R(akha); Indian musician (keyboards), singer and composer; b. (A. S. Dileep Kumar), 6 Jan. 1967, Chennai; s. of R. K. Sekhar and Kareema Begum; m. Saira Banu; three c.; ed Padma Seshadri Bal Bhavan, Madras Christian Coll. and Trinity Coll. of Music, London; studied piano aged four; began musical career aged 11 as keyboard player, performing with Illaiyaraja's troupe, later with orchestras of M. S. Vishwanathan and Ramesh Naidu; mem. local rock bands, including Roots, Magic and Nemesis Avenue; began composing 1987–; f.

Panchathan Record Inn studio 1989; performances and recordings with many artists, including Nusrat Fateh Ali Khan, Apache Indian, Zakir Hussein, Dr L. Shankar, Talvin Singh, Dominic Miller, David Byrne and Michael Jackson (Friends of the World, Munich 2002); has created music for many TV and radio advertisements as well as scores for corp. videos and documentaries; fuses music of different traditions (Western classical, reggae, rock and Karnatic music); apptd Global Amb. of WHO Stop TB Partnership project 2004; UN Amb. for 2015 Millennium Devt Goals; f. A R Rahman Foundation, KM Music Conservatory, Chennai; Dr hc (Aligarh Muslim Univ.), (Middlesex Univ.); SuMu Music Award 1993, R. D. Burman Awards 1993, 1995, Telega Purashkar Award 1992, 1993, 1994, Filmfare Awards 1992–2002, Padma Shree 2000, Awadh Sammaan UP govt 2001, Al-Ameen Educ. Soc. Community Award 2001, Amir Khusro Sangeet Nawaz Award 2002, Lata Mangeshkar Samman, MP govt 2005, Mahavir Mahatma Award, Oneness Foundation 2005, Stanford Univ. Award for contrib. to Global Music 2006, Bommai Nagi Reddy Award, Rajiv Gandhi Award, Padma Bhushan 2010; several other nat. and int. awards. Selected film soundtracks include: Roja (Nat. Film Award 1993, Cinema Express Award 1993) 1992, Gentleman (Cinema Express Award 1994) 1993, Kadhalan (Cinema Express Award 1995) 1994, Kadhal Desam (Screen-Videocon Awards 1997, Cinema Express Award 1997) 1996, Minsaara Kanavu (Nat. Film Award for Best Music Direction 1998, Screen-Videocon Award 1998) 1997, Dil Se… (Zee Sangeet Award, MTV-VMA Award 1999) 1998 Jeans (Cinema Express Award 1999) 1998, Taal (Screen-Videocon Award 2000, Zee Cine Award 2000, Zee Gold Bollywood Award 2000, Int. India Film Award 2000) 1999, Lagaan (Nat. Film Award) 2001, Elizabeth – The Golden Age 2007, Slumdog Millionaire (Golden Globe Award for Best Musical Score 2009, BAFTA Award for Best Film Music 2009, Academy Award for Best Original Score 2009, Academy Award for Best Original Song (music) 2009, Grammy Awards for Best Compilation Soundtrack Album for Motion Picture 2010, Best Song Written for Motion Picture 2010) 2008, Vinnaithaandi Varuvaayaa (Filmfare Best Music Dir Award (Tamil), Vijay Best Music Dir Award) 2010, Ye Maaya Chesave (CineMAA Award for Best Music Dir, Filmfare Best Music Dir Award (Telugu) 2010, 127 Hours (Denver Film Critics Soc. Award) 2010, Rockstar (Filmfare Best Music Dir Award, Zee Cine Best Music Dir Award, Screen Best Music Dir Award) 2011, Ekk Deewana Tha 2012. TV soundtracks include: Vande Mataram (Screen-Videocon Award 1998) 1997. Musicals include: Bombay Dreams (with Don Black) 2001, The Lord of the Rings (with Varttina) (Princess of Wales Theatre, Toronto) 2006. Recordings include: Deen Isai Malai (Muslim devotional songs) 1988, Set Me Free (launch album of Malgudi Subha) 1992, Vande Mataram 1997, Jana Gana Mana 2000, Pray For Me Brother 2007, Thenvandhu Paayedhu, Connections, Andhi Maalai, Gurus of Peace, Harem, Indian Mantra. Leisure interest: singing. Address: c/o The Really Useful Group, 22 Tower Street, London, WC2H 9TW, England. E-mail: info@arrahman.com. Website: www.arrahman.com.

RAHMAN, Atiur, BA (Hons), MA, PhD; Bangladeshi economist, academic and fmr central banker; b. 3 Aug. 1951, Jamalpur; m. Prof. Shahana Rahman; three d.; ed Mirzapur Cadet Coll., Univ. of Dhaka, School of Oriental and African Studies, Univ. of London, UK (Commonwealth Scholarship); Chair. Bd of Trustees Shamunnay (centre for devt research); also served as Chair. Unnayan Shamannay (non-profit org. for research, devt and cultural learning); fmr Sr Research Fellow, Bangladesh Inst. of Devt Studies; Commonwealth Devt Fellowship, Univ. of Manitoba, Canada 1989, Ford Foundation Post-doctoral Fellowship, Univ. of London 1991–92, Visiting Research Fellowship, Inst. of South-East Asian Studies, Singapore 1998–99; Prof. of Econs, Dept of Devt, Univ. of Dhaka 2006–09; Gov. and Chair. Bangladesh Bank (Cen. Bank of Bangladesh) 2009–16 (resgnd); fmr visiting/adjunct prof. at several univs; fmr Dir several socio-cultural orgs, including Biswa Sahitya Kendra and Monajatuddin Smriti Sangsad; Project Dir/ Team Leader on 22 int. and 58 nat. socio-econ. devt projects; participated in 75 int. and more than 250 nat. workshops; fmr Chair. Janata Bank, Credit Devt Forum; fmr mem. Bd of Dirs Sonali Bank; fmr Gen. Sec. Bangladesh Econ. Asscn; Life mem. Asiatic Soc. (Bangladesh), Bangla Acad.; Atish Dipankar Gold Medal 2000, Chandrabati Gold Medal 2008, Cen. Bank Gov. of the Year (Asia), Emerging Markets newspaper 2015, Bangla Acad. Award 2015. Publications include: 45 books (16 in English and 29 in Bangla); numerous papers in nat. and int. journals.

RAHMAN, Atta-Ur, BSc, MSc, PhD, FRS, FRSC; Pakistani politician, chemist and academic; Professor Emeritus, University of Karachi; b. 20 Sept. 1942, Delhi, India; s. of Jameel-Ur-Rahman and Amtul Subhan; m. Nargis Begum; ed Coventry Univ. and Univs of Cambridge and Bradford, UK, Karachi Univ.; Lecturer in Chem., Karachi Univ. 1964–69, Asst Prof. 1969–74, Assoc. Prof. 1974–81, Prof. 1981–2011, Prof. Emer. 2011–; Fellow, King's Coll. Cambridge 1969–73, Hon. Life Fellow 2007–; Co-Dir Husein Ebrahim Jamal Research Inst. of Chem. 1977–81, apptd Dir 1990; Co-ordinator-Gen., Org. of Islamic Conf. (OIC) Standing Cttee on Scientific and Technological Co-operation (COMSTECH) 1996–2012; Fed. Minister for Science and Tech. 1999–2002, for Educ. 2002; Chair. Higher Educ. Comm. (rank of Fed. Minister) 2002–08; Adviser to Prime Minister and Minister, Ministry of Science and Tech. 2003–04; Adviser to Prime Minister on Science and Tech. 2002–08; Pres. Chem. Soc. of Pakistan 1992, Network of Acads of Science in the Countries of the Org. of Islamic Conf. (NASIC) 2007–; Vice-Pres. Pakistan Acad. of Sciences 1997–2001, Pres. 2003–06, 2011–14; Chair. Working Group on Science and Tech. (Pakistan) 1998–2003, Cttee on Science, Tech. and Innovation, UN Econ. and Social Comm. for Asia; Scientific Adviser to CIBA Foundation, London 1995; mem. Nat. Comm. for Science and Tech. 1985, Steering Cttee for Establishment of Chem. Centre in Trieste, Italy; mem. editorial bds of several int. journals, Advisory Bd Journal of Pharmacy of Istanbul Univ., Turkey 1998; mem. ACS, American Soc. of Pharmacognosy, Swiss Chemical Soc., New York Acad. of Sciences, Russian Acad. of Sciences, Repub. of Uzbekistan Acad. of Natural Sciences; Fellow, Third World Acad. of Sciences 1985 (Vice-Pres. (Cen. and S Asia) Council), Islamic Acad. of Sciences 1988; Foreign mem. Chinese Acad. of Sciences; Foreign Fellow, Korean Acad. of Science and Tech. 2004; Hon. Fellow, Chinese Chemical Soc. 2012; Tamgha-I-Imtiaz 1983, Sitara-I-Imtiaz 1991, Hilal-I-Imtiaz 1998, Nishan-I-Imtiaz 2002, Grand Decoration of Honour in Gold with Sash (Austria); Hon. ScD (Cambridge) 1987; Hon. DEduc (Coventry) 2007; several awards, including Pakistan Acad. of Sciences Gold Medal 1977, 1984, 1996, Gold Medal, Govt of Kuwait 1980, Commonwealth Scholar 1985–86, Best Scientist of the Year Award, Govt of Pakistan 1986, FPCCI Prize for Technological Innovation (Pakistan) 1985, Scientist of the Year (Pakistan) 1987, Islamic Org. Prize for

Science (Kuwait) 1988, First Prize at Sixth Khwrazmi Festival, Pres. of Iran 1993, Baba-I-Urdu Award (Pakistan) 1994, Salimuzzaman Siddiqui Gold Medal, Pakistan Intellectuals Forum 1995, Prime Minister's Gold Medal 1995, Pakistan Acad. of Sciences-INFAQ Foundation Prize in Science 1995, Fed. of Asian Chemical Socs Award (Japan) 1997, Third World Acad. of Sciences Award 1999, UNESCO Science Prize (first Muslim scientist) 1999, ECO Prize 2000, ISESCO Chem. Award 2001, Gold Medal of the Scientific Partnership Charitable Foundation, Inter Bio Screen Ltd, Russia 2004, Int. Scientific Co-operation Award, Chinese Acad. of Sciences 2013, Friendship Award, Govt of China 2016, inducted into Chinese Acad. of Sciences 2018. Achievements include: 27 patents. Publications include: has written or edited 116 books, 65 book chapters, 30 different book series, 701 research papers in leading int. scientific journals. Leisure interests: reading, cricket, table tennis. Address: International Centre for Chemical and Biological Sciences, University of Karachi, Karachi 75270 (office); 37, S/6, PECHS, Karachi, Pakistan (home). Telephone: (21) 8543084 (home). E-mail: aurahman786@gmail.com (home); ibne_sina@hotmail.com (office). Website: www .atta-ur-rahman.com.

RAHMAN, Hafiz Hafizur; Pakistani politician; Chief Minister of Gilgit-Baltistan; b. Kashrote village, Gilgit; served for several years as chief organizer for Northern Areas (now Gilgit-Baltistan), Pakistan Muslim League—Nawaz (PML–N), then Pres. PML–N Gilgit-Baltistan; mem. Gilgit-Baltistan Legis. Ass. for Gilgit GBLA-II constituency 2015–; Chief Minister of Gilgit-Baltistan 2015–. Address: Gilgit-Baltistan Secretariat, Gilgit, Gilgit-Baltistan, Pakistan (office). Telephone: (58) 11920573 (office). E-mail: info@gilgitbaltistan.gov.pk (office). Website: www.gilgitbaltistan.gov.pk (office).

RAHMAN, Mir Shakil-ur-; Pakistani media executive and philanthropist; CEO, Jang Group; s. of Mir Khalil-ur-Rahman; Founder and CEO GEO TV (24-hour news network), CEO Jang Group (part-owner of Independent Media Corpn which publishes several newspapers and magazines in Urdu and English and also owns GEO TV); Pres. Council of Pakistan Newspapers Eds 1995–96, 2003–04, All Pakistan Newspapers Soc., Pakistan Broadcasters' Asscn. Address: Jang Group of Newspapers, Printing House, I.I. Chundrigar Road, Karachi 74200, Pakistan (office). E-mail: groupeditor@janggroup.com.pk (office). Website: www.jang.com.pk (office).

RAHMAN, Air Marshal (retd) Shah Mohammad Ziaur; Bangladeshi fmr air force officer; b. 1955, Gopalgonj; m. Shameema Parveen; one s. one d.; ed Univ. Defence Services Command & Staff Coll., Dhaka, Pakistan Air Force Air War Coll., Nat. Defence Coll., Pakistan, Exec. Course seminars, USA Asia Pacific Centre for Security Studies, Mil. and Peace Keeping Operations in Accordance with Rule of Law course, RI, USA; guerrilla fighter in Dhaka area during Liberation War of Bangladesh 1971; joined Bangladesh Air Force (BAF) as flight cadet 1975, commissioned in Gen. Duties (Pilot) br. 1976; qualified fighter pilot and Qualified Flying Instructor of BAF with more than 2,400 flying hours; has flown almost all types of fighter aircraft in BAF, including MiG-21MF, A-5IIIA, F-6, F-7MB, L-39ZA, FT-5, FT-6, FT-7B as well as Bell Helicopters; has held command positions with most of the air squadrons of BAF; commanded BAF's two fighter squadrons, 25 Squadron and 35 Squadron; Directing Staff and Sr Instructor in Defence Services, Command and Staff Coll., Mirpur 1994–98; commanded Flying Wing of BAF Base Bashar, Dhaka 1999; Deputy Commdt BAF Acad. 2000; also held several staff command positions, including Air Officer Commdg, Paharkanchanpur, Air Officer Commdg, Bashar and Air Officer Commdg, Jahurul Huq 2001–05; Asst Chief of Air Staff (Operations and Training) at Air HQ 2005–07; promoted from Air Cdre to Air Vice-Marshal and apptd Chief of Air Staff 2007–12; promoted to Air Marshal (first ever) 2007; Pres. Nat. Hockey Fed. Leisure interest: golf.

RAHMANI, Chérif, PhD; Algerian politician; b. 16 Jan. 1945, Aïn Oussera; s. of Caïd Bouamama; m.; four c.; ed Ecole Nat. d'Admin; fmr Prof., Univ. of Poitiers; fmr Prof., Ecole Nat. d'Admin; fmr Sub-Man. Local Communities, Ministry of the Interior, also Dir Admin and Local Finances and Gen. Man. Local Communities; fmr Inspector Gen., Presidency of the Repub.; fmr Wali de Tébessa; fmr Wali of Algiers; fmr Sec.-Gen. to Ministry of the Interior; Minister of Youth and Sport 1988–89, of Equipment 1989–90, for Equipment and Regional Planning, Minister Gov. of Greater Algiers, on Mission Extraordinary in Charge of Admin of Wilaya of Algiers; fmr Minister of Territorial Planning and the Environment, fmr Minister of Industry, Small and Medium-sized Enterprises and Investment Promotion; UNEP Champion of the Earth Laureate 2007.

RAHMON, Emomali, BEcons; Tajikistani politician and head of state; President and Chairman of the Government; b. (Imamali Rahmonov), 5 Oct. 1952, Dangar, Kulob Viloyat (now Khatlon Viloyat), Tajik SSR, USSR; m. Azizmo Asadullayeva; two s. seven d.; ed Lenin Tajikistan State Univ.; served in USSR army; early jobs as electrician, salesman, as trade union sec. and on various CP cttees; Dir Dangarin Sovkhoz (Soviet farm), Kulob Oblast 1982–92, Chair. Union Cttee 1976–88; Chair. Kulob Oblast Exec. Cttee 1992; Chair. Supreme Ass. (Majlisi Oli) 1992–94; Pres. of Tajikistan and Chair. of the Govt 1994–; Leader, Hizbi halki-demokratii Tojikiston (People's Democratic Party of Tajikistan); Order of the Repub. of Serbia 2013, Order of Alexander Nevsky 2017; Dr hc (Taras Shevchenko Kyiv Univ.) 2008, (Inst. of Oriental Studies, Russian Acad. of Sciences) 2009; Hon. Dr of Leadership (Limkokwing University of Creative Tech.) 2014; World Peace Corps Acad. Gold Medal 2000, Anniversary Award '10 Year Old Astana', Olympic Award of Asia 2009, Golden Medal of FIAS 2009, Golden Medal of UNESCO by Jalolidinni Rumi 2009. Address: Office of the President, 734023 Dushanbe, Xiyoboni Rudaki 80, Tajikistan (office). Telephone: (372) 21-25-20 (office). Fax: (372) 21-25-20 (office). E-mail: mail@president.tj (office). Website: www.president .tj (office).

RAHMOUNI, Hassan, LLM, PhD; Moroccan lawyer, academic and politician; b. 10 Dec. 1949; m.; four c.; ed Fairfax High School, Va, USA, Mohammed V Univ., Rabat, Univ. of Paris (Sorbonne), France; Chief of Legal Service, Office for Industrial Devt, Ministry of Industry 1975–77; Asst Prof., Lecturer and Chair Prof., School of Law and Econs, Mohammed V Univ., Rabat 1977–98; Prof. of Admin. Law, Moroccan Royal Mil. Acad. 1977–80, Prof. of English Terminology in Law 1983–85; Prof. and Staff Coordinator, US Peace Corps, Michigan State Univ. 1981; Prof. of Law, Institut Nat. d'Aménagement et d'Urbanisme, Ministry of Urban Devt 1981–82; Counsellor to Cabinet of Minister of Admin. Affairs 1987–88;

Dir of Gen. Matters, Ministry of Communication 1989–92; Gov. of Mohammedia, apptd by King Hassan II 1992–93; Gov. of Mohammedia (Casablanca) 1994–98; Prof. of Constitutional Law, Political Science and Local Admin, Hassan II Univ. 1998–2005, Vice-Pres. of Hassan II Univ. 2002–03; currently attorney and legal consultant, Casablanca; Visiting Prof., Indiana State Univ. 2000–04, Wayne State Univ. 2000, Purdue Univ. 2001; Program Dir Indiana State Univ., funded by USAID 2003; consultant to Govt of Equatorial Guinea 1992, Govt of Congo 1992; Vice-Pres. Moroccan Nat. Asscn for Governance; mem. Casablanca Order of Lawyers, Moroccan Fulbright Asscn, Nat. Union of Univ. Profs, Nat. Asscn of Civil Service; Trustee, Mohammedia School of Law and Social Sciences; Chevalier, Order of the Throne 1994; Green March Medal 1975, Fulbright Scholar, George Washington Univ. 1985, Fulbright Visiting Specialist, Harvard Univ. 2004. *Publications:* English for Economists (co-author) 1985, Droit Administratif et Sciences Administratives (co-author) 1990; numerous book chapters, scholarly articles and conf. papers. *Address:* Quartier Alsace Lorraine, Mers Sultan, Casablanca, Morocco. *Telephone:* (522) 541515. *Fax:* (522) 541717. *E-mail:* hr@hassanrahmouni.com. *Website:* www.hassanrahmouni.com.

RAÏ, HE Cardinal Béchara Boutros, OMM, PhD; Lebanese ecclesiastic; *Patriarch of Antioch (Maronite);* b. (Bechara al-Rahi), 25 Feb. 1940, Himlaya, Matn Dist; ed Collège Notre Dame de Jamhour, Lateran Univ., Rome; ordained priest, Archdiocese of Ar-Rouhbanyat Al-Marounyat Liltoubawyat Mariam Al-Azra 1967; responsible for Arabic transmissions of Vatican Radio 1967–75; Titular Bishop of Caesarea Philippi 1986–; Auxiliary Bishop of Antioch (Maronite) 1986–90; Bishop of Jbeil (Maronite) 1990–2011; Patriarch of Antioch (Maronite) 2011–; cr. Cardinal 2012; participated in Papal Conclave (one of four cardinal-electors from outside the Latin Church) 2013; Sec. Maronite Synod 2003–09; Pres. Lebanese Episcopal Comm. for the Media 2009–11; mem. Congregation for Oriental Churches 2012–, Supreme Tribunal of Apostolic Signatura 2013–, Pontifical Council for Pastoral Care of Migrants and Itinerants 2013–, Pontifical Council for Social Communications 2013–; Nat. Order of the Cedar 2007; Grand Croix, Légion d'honneur 2011. *Address:* See of the Maronite Catholic Patriarchate, Bkerké, Lebanon (office).

RAI, Max Hufanen, BA; Papua New Guinea government official and diplomatist; *Permanent Representative to United Nations;* b. 15 Jan. 1954; m.; six c.; ed Australian Nat. Univ., Canberra, Univ. of Papua New Guinea; Roving Amb. to Federated States of Micronesia and Marshall Islands 1997–2003, Amb. to China 2003–07; Perm. Rep. to UN 2016–; First Sec. and Adviser to Minister for Mining and Statutory Body 2013; Dir-Gen. Trade Div., Dept of Trade, Commerce and Industry 2014–16. *Address:* Permanent Mission of Papua New Guinea, 201 E 42nd Street, Suite 2411, New York, NY 10017, USA (office). *Telephone:* (212) 557-5001 (office). *Fax:* (212) 557-5009 (office). *E-mail:* pngun@pngmission.org (office).

RAI BACHCHAN, Aishwarya (Aish); Indian actress and model; b. 1 Nov. 1973, Mangalore, Karnataka; d. of Krishnaraj Rai and Vrinda Rai; m. Abhishek Bachchan 2007; one d.; studied architecture in Bombay (now Mumbai); worked as model for advertising campaigns and major fashion shows; won Miss Catwalk, Miss Photogenic and Miss Perfect 10 competitions; runner-up in Miss India Contest 1994; winner Miss World Contest 1994; Int. Goodwill Amb., Joint UN Programme on HIV/AIDS (UNAIDS) 2012–; Ordre des Arts et des Lettres 2012; Discovery of the Year (Screen) 1998, Rajiv Gandhi Award 2002, GR8! Women Award 2004, 2010, Next Step World Diversity Champion Award, UK Govt 2005, Padma Shri 2009, India Today Women Award 2010; several nat. and int. awards. *Films include:* Mamagaru 1991, Iruvar (also known as Duo, Iddaru) 1997, Aur Pyar Ho Gaya 1997, Jeans 1998, Aa Ab Laut Chalen 1999, Hum Dil De Chuke Sanam 1999, Taal 1999, Mela – The Great Entertainer 2000, Kandukondain Kandukondain 2000, Josh 2000, Mohabbatein 2000, Dhai Akshar Prem Ke 2000, Hamare Dil Aapke Paas Hai 2000, Sanam Tere Hain Hum 2000, Albela 2001, Devdas (Filmfare Awards, Best Actress 2003) 2002, Hum Tumhare Hain Sanam 2002, Hum Kisi Se Kum Nahin 2002, 23rd March 1931: Shaheed (song) 2002, Shakthi: The Power 2002, Dil Ka Rishta 2003, Kyon Ho Gaya Na 2003, Khakee 2003, Chokher Bali 2003, Kuch Naa Kaho 2003, Khakee 2004, Bride and Prejudice 2004, The Mistress of Spices 2005, Provoked 2006, Umrao Jaan 2006, Guru 2007, The Last Legion 2007, Jodhaa Akbar 2007, The Pink Panther 2009, Raavan 2010, Enthiran 2010, Action Replay 2010, Guzaarish 2010. *Address:* Pratiksha, 10th Road, JVPD Scheme, Mumbai 400 049 (home); 402 Ramlaxmi Niwas, 16th Road, Khar (West), Mumbai 400 054, India. *Telephone:* (22) 6207579 (home); (22) 6206162 (home).

RAIDI; Chinese politician; b. 1938, Biru Co., northern Tibet; ed Cen. Nationalities Inst., Cen. Political Science and Law Cadre School, Beijing, CCP Cen. Cttee Cen. Party School; Sec. Public Security Div., Nagqu Prefectural Admin. Office, Tibet Autonomous Region 1962–66; worker, Mil. Control Comm., Nagqu Prefecture, PLA Tibet Mil. Region 1966–68, CCP Revolutionary Cttee 1968–72; Sec. CCP Nagqu Autonomous Prefectural Cttee 1972–75; Sec. CCP Tibet Autonomous Regional Cttee 1977–85, Deputy Sec. 1985–2002, Sec. Comm. for Discipline Inspection 1979–85; Chair. Peasants' Fed. of Tibet 1975; Vice-Chair. Revolutionary Cttee, Tibet Autonomous Region 1977–79; Vice-Chair. Standing Cttee Tibet Autonomous Regional People's Congress 1979–83, Chair. 1986–93; apptd Chair. Standing Cttee Tibet Autonomous Regional 6th People's Congress 1993; Deputy, 8th NPC, Tibet Autonomous Region; Alt. mem. 11th CCP Cen. Cttee 1977–82, mem. 12th CCP Cen. Cttee 1982–87, 13th CCP Cen. Cttee 1987–92, 14th CCP Cen. Cttee 1992–97, 15th CCP Cen. Cttee 1997–2002, 16th CCP Cen. Cttee 2002–07; Vice-Chair. 10th Standing Cttee of NPC 2003–08. *Address:* Chinese Communist Party, Tibet Autonomous Region, Lhasa, Tibet, People's Republic of China.

RAIDL, Claus J.; Austrian economist, business executive and central banker; *President, Oesterreichische Nationalbank;* b. 6 Nov. 1942, Kapfenberg, Styria; m.; three c.; ed Vienna Univ. of Int. Trade; Asst, Inst. for Applied Social and Econ. Research, Vienna 1970–71; worked at bank and accounting firm, also consultant to OECD on issues of int. taxation on multinational enterprises 1971–74; with Österreichische Volksfürsorge Allgemeine Versicherung AG (insurance co.) 1974–81; mem. Bd of Man. Wiener Holding GmbH 1981–82; mem. Bd of Man. ÖIAG (Österreichische Industrieverwaltungs AG) 1982–86; Deputy Chair. Voest Alpine AG 1986–88, mem. Bd of Man. 2007–10; Deputy Chair. Voest Alpine Stahl AG 1988–92; Chair. Boehler-Uddeholm AG 1991–2010; mem. Bd of Man. Austrian Industries AG 1993–94; Pres. Oesterreichische Nationalbank 2008–; Chair. Bd of Trustees IST Austria (Inst. of Science and Tech.); Vice-Pres. European Forum Alpbach; mem. Bd Technical Museum Vienna. *Publications:* Mehrwertsteuer und Preisniveau 1971; numerous contribs to specialist publs on econ., tax, business and budgetary issues. *Address:* Office of the President, Oesterreichische Nationalbank, Otto-Wagner-Pl. 3, 1090 Vienna, Austria (office). *Telephone:* (1) 404-20 (office). *Fax:* (1) 404-23-99 (office). *E-mail:* oenb.info@oenb.at (office). *Website:* www.oenb.at (office).

RAIGETAL, Larry; Micronesian civil servant and business executive; *President, Waa'gey Inc.;* b. 4 July 1968, Lamotrek Atoll; two d.; ed Univ. of Oxford, UK, Univ. of San Francisco, USA; Dean of Students, Xavier High School, Chuuk 1992–93; diplomatic functions 1993–2001; Chair. FSM Banking Bd 1998; Chief of Manpower, Yap State Govt 2001–04; Dir, Dept of Youth and Civic Affairs, Yap State Govt 2007–; currently Pres. Waa'gey Inc. *Leisure interest:* fishing. *Address:* Waa'gey Inc., PO Box 254, Colonia Yap, FM 96943 (office); Box 254, Colonia Yap, 96943, Micronesia (home). *Telephone:* 952-6346 (office). *Fax:* 950-1151 (office). *E-mail:* larry@waagey.org (home); contact@waagey.org (office). *Website:* www.waagey.org (office).

RAIKIN, Konstantin Arkadyevich; Russian actor and theatre director; *Artistic Director, Theatre Satirikon;* b. 8 July 1950, Leningrad; s. of Arkady Raikin and Roma M. Joffe; m. Elena Butenko; one d.; ed M. Shchukin Theatre High School, Moscow; theatre Sovremennik 1971–81, debut in Valentin and Valentina; 38 roles including 15 leading, acted in plays of Shakespeare and Russian classics; actor State Theatre of Miniatures (renamed Theatre Satirikon 1987) under Arkady Raikin 1981–87, actor and Artistic Dir 1988–; Prize for Best Acting, Belgrade Festival 1990, People's Artist of Russia 1992, State Prize 1996, Gold Mask Prize 1996, Stanislavsky Prize 1998, Order of the Fatherland 2000. *Films:* Sensation is Anything 1971, Friends Among Strangers, Strangers Among Friends 1972. *TV Films:* Truffaldino from Bergamo 1976, The Island of Dead Ships 1988, Shadow 1990, Failure Puaro 2002. *Stage appearances include:* Cyrano de Bergerac (Cyrano) 1992, The Magnanimous Cuckold (Bruno) 1994, Metamorphosis (Gregor Zamza) 1995, The Threepenny Opera (Mack the Knife) 1996, Jacques and His Master (Jacques) 1998, Hamlet (Hamlet) 1998, Double Bass 2000. *Plays directed include:* Mowgli 1990, Butterflies Are Free 1993, Romeo and Juliet 1995, The Chioggian Squabbles 1997, Quartet 1999, Chanticleer 2001. *Address:* Theatre Satirikon, Sheremetyevskaya str. 8, 129594 Moscow, Russia. *Telephone:* (495) 289-87-07 (office). *Fax:* (495) 284-49-37 (office). *E-mail:* theatre@satirikon.msk.ru (office). *Website:* www.satirikon.ru (office).

RAIMI, Samuel (Sam) Marshall; American film director, producer and screenwriter; b. 23 Oct. 1959, Franklin, Mich.; ed Michigan State Univ. *Films include:* The Evil Dead (also producer/writer) 1981, Evil Dead II (also producer/writer) 1987, Darkman 1990, Army of Darkness (also producer/writer) 1993, The Quick and the Dead 1995, A Simple Plan 1998, For Love of the Game 1999, The Gift 2000, Spider-Man 2002, Spider-Man 2 (Empire Award for Best Director 2005) 2004, Spider-Man 3 (also writer) 2007, Oz the Great and Powerful 2013; as producer: Hard Target 1993, Timecop 1994, The Hudsucker Proxy (writer) 1994, The Grudge 2004, Boogeyman 2005, Rise 2007, 30 Days of Night 2007, Drag Me to Hell 2009, Oz the Great and Powerful 2013, Poltergeist (producer) 2015, Don't Breathe (producer) 2016, The Jungle Book (voice) 2016. *Television series:* as producer: M.A.N.T.I.S. 1994, Hercules: The Legendary Journeys 1994, American Gothic 1995, Xena: Warrior Princess 1995, Spy Game 1997, Young Hercules 1998, Jack of All Trades 2000, Cleopatra 2525 2000, Legend of the Seeker 2008–09, 2013: Fear is Real 2009, Spartacus (Exec. producer) 2010–13, Ash vs Evil Dead (Exec. producer) 2015–18.

RAIMONDI, Ruggero; Monegasque singer (bass) and director; b. 3 Oct. 1941, Bologna, Italy; m. Isabel Maier 1987; operatic debut in La Bohème, Spoleto Festival 1964; debut at Metropolitan Opera, New York in Ernani 1970; engagements include Don Giovanni, Le Nozze di Figaro, Faust, Attila, Nabucco, Don Carlos, Boris Godunov, Don Quichotte, Don Pasquale, Otello, Contes d'Hoffmann, Carmen, Il Viaggio a Rheims, Falstaff, I Vespri Siciliani, I Lombardi, L'Italiana in Algieri, Il Turco in Italia, Tosca, Assassinio nella Cattedrale, Così fan tutte and others; played role of Pagano in Verdi's I Lombardi alla prima crociata, anniversary concert on roof of Milan cathedral 2011; Commdr des Arts et des Lettres, Officier, Légion d'honneur, Kt, Order of Malta, Grand Ufficiale della Repubblica Italiana 1996, Citizen of Honour, Athens, Commdr du Mérite Culturel (Monaco) 1999. *Opera productions include:* Don Giovanni, The Barber of Seville, Don Carlos. *Films include:* Don Giovanni 1979, Six Characters in Search of a Singer 1981, La Truite 1982, Life is a Bed of Roses 1983, Carmen 1984, Boris Godunov 1989, Tosca 2001, Assassinio nella cattedrale (opera) 2007, Rigoletto a Mantova 2010. *Television includes:* Boris Godunov staged by Joseph Losey at Opéra Nat. de Paris 1980, Six personnages en quête d'un chanteur by Maurice Béjart 1981, Verdi's Requiem 1982, Ernani directed by Kirk Browning (with Milnes and Pavarotti) 1983, Le nozze di Figaro directed by Jonathan Miller 1992, Tosca: In the Settings and at the Times of Tosca, directed by Brian Large (with Malfitano and Domingo) 1992, Il Turco in Italia with Cecilia Bartoli at Zurich Opera House 2001, Così fan tutte staged by Patrice Chéreau 2005. *Recordings include:* Verdi: Aida 1983, 2005, Rossini: L'Italiana in Algeri 1989, Puccini: Turandot 1990, Rossini: Il Viaggio a Reims 1990, Verdi: Don Carlos 1990, Rossini: Il barbiere di Siviglia 1993, Verdi: Un Ballo in Maschera 1998, Mozart: Le Nozze di Figaro 2003, Rossini: La Cenerentola 2003, Rossini: Il Barbiere di Siviglia (DVD) 2005, Verdi: Attila 2005. *Address:* 140 bis rue Lecourbe, 75015 Paris, France (office).

RAIMONDO, Gina Marie, BS, JD; American lawyer and politician; *Governor of Rhode Island;* b. 17 May 1971, Smithfield, RI; d. of Joseph Raimondo and Josephine Raimondo; m. Andrew Kind Moffit 2001; one s. one d.; ed Harvard Univ., Univ. of Oxford, UK, Yale Univ. Law School; law clerk to Kimba Wood, US Dist Court (Southern Dist), New York City 1998–99; Sr Vice-Pres. for Fund Devt, Village Ventures (venture capital firm) 1999–2001; Co-Founder and Gen. Partner, Point Judith Capital, RI 2001–10; Gen. Treas., State of Rhode Island 2011–15; Gov. of Rhode Island (first woman) 2015–; Chair. Democratic Govs. Asscn 2018–; mem. Council on Foreign Relations; Democrat; Dr hc (Bryant Univ. 2012), Yale Alumni Fellow 2014. *Address:* Office of the Governor, 82 Smith Street, Providence, RI 02903, USA (office). *Telephone:* (401) 222-2080 (office). *Fax:* (401) 222-8096 (office). *E-mail:* governor@governor.ri.gov (office). *Website:* www.governor.ri.gov (office); ginaraimondo.com.

RAINE, Craig Anthony, BA, BPhil; British writer; b. 3 Dec. 1944, Shildon, Co. Durham; s. of Norman Edward and Olive Marie Raine; m. Ann Pasternak Slater 1972; three s. one d.; ed Exeter Coll., Oxford; Lecturer, Exeter Coll., Oxford 1971–72, 1975–76, Lincoln Coll. 1974–75, Christ Church 1976–79; Books Ed. New Review 1977–78; Ed. Quarto 1979–80; Poetry Ed. New Statesman 1981; Poetry Ed. Faber and Faber Ltd 1981–91; Fellow in English, New Coll., Oxford 1991–2010, then Emer. Prof.; Ed. Areté 1999–; Kelus Prize 1979, Southern Arts Literature Award 1979, Cholmondeley Poetry Award 1983, Sunday Times Award for Literary Excellence 1998. *Publications include:* The Onion, Memory 1978, A Martian Sends a Postcard Home 1979, A Free Translation 1981, Rich 1984, The Electrification of the Soviet Union (opera) 1986, A Choice of Kipling's Prose (ed.) 1987, The Prophetic Book 1988, '1953' (play) 1990, Haydn and the Valve Trumpet: Literary Essays 1990, Rudyard Kipling: Selected Poetry (ed.) 1992, History: The Home Movie 1994, Clay. Whereabouts Unknown 1996, New Writing 7 1998, A la recherche du temps perdu 1999, In Defence of T.S. Eliot: Literary Essays (Vol. 2) 2000, Collected Poems 1978–1999 2000, Rudyard Kipling: The Wish House and Other Stories (ed.) 2002, T.S. Eliot 2006, Heartbreak (novel) 2010, How Snow Falls (poems) 2010, The Divine Comedy (novel) 2012, More Dynamite (essays) 2012. *Leisure interests:* music, skiing. *Address:* New College, Oxford, OX1 3BN, England (office).

RAIS, Abdul Qader al-; United Arab Emirates artist; b. 1951, Dubai; ed United Arab Emirates Univ.; began career as legal adviser, Ministry of Labour; became full-time painter in mid-1990s; works often include Arabic writing; co-f. Emirates Fine Arts Soc.; works held in numerous public collections; several awards including First Prize, Arab Painters' Exhbn, Kuwait, Gold Medal, Abu Dhabi Spring Exhbn, Golden Palm Leaf, GCC Exhbn 1999, Sheikh Khalifa Emirates Appreciation Award for Science, Arts and Literature 2006, First Prize, Emirates in the Eyes of its People Exhbn 2016. *Publication:* The Colours of My Life 2008. *Address:* c/o Majlis Gallery, Al Musalla Roundabout, Al Fahidi Street, Bastakiya, Bur Dubai, POB 42885, Dubai, United Arab Emirates. *Telephone:* (4) 3536233. *Fax:* (4) 3535550. *E-mail:* majlisgallery@gmail.com. *Website:* www.themajlisgallery.com.

RAIS, Amien; Indonesian politician; b. 26 April 1944, Solo, Java; m. Kusnariyati Sri Rahayu; three s. two d.; ed Gadjah Mada Univ., Al Azhar Univ., Egypt, Univ. of Notre Dame and Univ. of Chicago, USA; joined Muhammadiyah (Muslim group) 1985, Vice-Chair 1990–95, 1995–98; Chair. People's Consultative Ass. (MPR) 1999–2004; Co-founder Partai Amanat Nasional (PAN) (National Mandate Party), Gen. Chair. 1998–2004, currently Chair. Advisory Bd; helped found Asscn of Indonesian Muslim Intellectuals (ICMI); Chair. Bd of Trustees Gadjah Mada Univ. 2007–12. *Address:* Partai Amanat Nasional, Rumah PAN, Jalan Raya Warung Buncit 17, Jakarta Selatan, Indonesia (office). *Telephone:* (21) 7975588 (office). *Fax:* (21) 7975632 (office). *Website:* www.pan.or.id (office).

RAISANI, Nawab Muhammad Aslam Khan, MA; Pakistani politician and farmer; b. 5 July 1955, Sarawan, Balochistan; s. of Nawab Ghaus Bakhsh Khan Raisani (fmr Gov. of Balochistan and fed. minister); ed Univ. of Balochistan; Tumandar of Raisani Tribe; became Chief of Sarawan and Raisani tribe following his father's assassination; fmr Deputy Man., BDA; fmr Purchase Officer, PASCO, Jacobabad; apptd as DSP in Balochistan police force following graduation; Minister for Agric., Cooperative, Labour and Manpower in caretaker Prov. Govt Cabinet 1988; Minister for Food and Fisheries in caretaker Prov. Cabinet; elected mem. Prov. Ass. from PB-27 Mastung; mem. Prov. Ass. of Balochistan 1988, 1990, 1993, 2002; joined Pakistan Nat. Party (PNP) 1989, elected Parl. Leader of PNP in Prov. Ass.; apptd Pres. PNP of Balochistan 1990; Minister for Finance in Prov.; joined Pakistan People's Party 1999, mem. Cen. Exec. Cttee; Chief Minister of Balochistan 2008–13 (dismissed); Pres. Chamber of Agric., Balochistan; Founder and fmr Pres. Fed. of Chambers of Agric. Pakistan. *Leisure interests:* farming, angling, hiking. *Address:* Pakistan Peoples Party (PPP), 8, Street 19, F-8/2, Islamabad, Pakistan (office). *Telephone:* (51) 2255264 (office). *Fax:* (51) 2282741 (office). *E-mail:* ppp@comsats.net.pk (office). *Website:* www.ppp.org.pk (office).

RAISER, Konrad; German theologian, academic and fmr organization official; b. 25 Jan. 1938, Magdeburg; m. Bertha Elisabeth von Weizsaecker 1967; ed Univ. of Tübingen, Ruprecht-Karls-Univ. of Heidelberg, Univ. of Zurich Protestant theology, Harvard Univ.; Protestant Faculty of Theology, Tübingen 1967–69; Study Sec., Comm. on Faith and Order, WCC 1969–73, Deputy Gen. Sec. WCC, Gen. Sec. 1992–2004 (retd); Prof. of Systematic Theology and Ecumenics, Univ. of the Ruhr, Bochum 1983–93; currently Visiting Prof., Ecumenical Inst., Château de Bossey, Switzerland; mem. Evangelical Church in Germany (EKD), editorial Cttees European Ecumenical Ass., Basel, Switzerland 1989, WCC World Ass. for Justice, Peace and the Protection of Creation, Seoul, Korea 1990; investor in Oikocredit (microfinance and microcredit org.); Dr hc (Theological Acad., Budapest) 1992, (Univ. of Geneva) 1996, (Univ. of Hamburg) 2010. *Publications:* Identität und Sozialität 1971, Ökumene im Übergang (Ecumenism in Transition) 1989, Wir stehen noch am Anfang 1994, To Be the Church 1997, For a Culture of Life 2002; more than 200 articles and essays on theological and ecumenical subjects. *Address:* Ecumenical Institute, Château de Bossey, PO Box 1000, 1299 Crans-près-Céligny, Switzerland (office). *Telephone:* (22) 960-7300 (office). *Fax:* (22) 960-7367 (office). *Website:* www.oikoumene.org (office).

RAISI, Hojatoleslam Val-Moslemin Sayyed Ebrahim, PhD; Iranian politician and religious leader; *Chief Justice;* b. 14 Dec. 1960, Mashhad; s. of Seyed Haji; m. Jamileh Alamolhoda; two d.; ed Qom Seminary, Shahid Motahari Univ.; Chair., Gen. Inspection Office 1994–2004; mem. Ass. of Experts 2007–; First Vice Chief Justice of Iran 2004–14; Attorney-Gen. of Iran 2014–16; Custodian and Chair. Supervisory Bd, Astan Quds Razavi 2016–; Chief Justice of Iran 2019–; mem. Islamic Republican Party –1987, currently Combatant Clergy Asscn. *Address:* Office of the Head of the Judiciary, Tehran, Iran (office). *Website:* dadiran.ir (office); raisi.ir.

RAISMAN, John Michael, CBE, CBIM, MA; British business executive; b. 12 Feb. 1929, Lahore, India; s. of Sir Jeremy Raisman and Renee Mary Raisman (née Kelly); m. Evelyn Anne Muirhead 1953; one s. three d. (one deceased); ed Rugby School, Queen's Coll., Oxford; joined Shell Int. Petroleum Co. Ltd 1953, served in Brazil 1953–60; Gen. Man., Shell Panama 1960–62; Asst to Exploration and Production Co-ordinator, Shell Int. Petroleum, Maatschappij 1963–65; Gen. Man., Shell Co. of Turkey Ltd 1965–69; Pres. Shell Sekiyu KK 1970–73; Head of European Supply and Marketing, Shell Int. Petroleum 1974–77; Man. Dir, Shell UK Oil 1977–78; Deputy Chair. and CEO Shell UK Ltd 1978–79, Chair. and CEO 1979–85; Chair. Shell Chemicals UK Ltd 1979–85; Dir Vickers 1981–90, Glaxo Holdings PLC 1982–90, Lloyds Bank 1985–95, Lloyds TSB 1996–98, Lloyds Merchant Bank Holdings 1985–87, Candover 1990–98, Tandem Computers 1991–97, British Biotech. 1993–98 (Chair. 1995–98); Deputy Chair. British Telecom 1987–91; mem. Pres.'s Cttee of Confed. of British Industry (CBI), Chair. Europe Cttee of CBI 1980–88, Council of Industry for Man. Educ. 1981–85, Oil Industry Emergency Cttee (OIEC) 1981–85, Advisory Council, London Enterprise Agency 1979–85, Investment Bd Electra Candover Pnrs 1985–95, Electronics Industry EDC 1986–88, Business Forum of European Movt, Council for Industry and Higher Educ. 1991–98; Deputy Chair. Nat. Comm. on Educ. 1991–95; Gov. Nat. Inst. of Econ. and Social Research 1981–; mem. Governing Council of Business in the Community 1982–85; mem. Council, Inst. for Fiscal Studies 1982–; mem. Royal Comm. on Environmental Pollution 1986–87; Chair. Bd of Trustees RA 1986–96; Pro-Chancellor Univ. of Aston 1987–93; Chair. British Empire and Commonwealth Museum Trust 2002–06; Hon. DUniv (Stirling) 1983; Hon. LLD (Aberdeen) 1985, (Manchester) 1986, (UWE) 1994; Hon. DSc (Aston) 1992. *Leisure interests:* golf, travel, opera, theatre.

RAISS, Sid Ahmed Ould; Mauritanian politician and central banker; *Governor, Banque Centrale de Mauritanie;* b. 9 Sept. 1964, Atar; ed Univ. de Nouakchott, Univ. de Tunis, Ecole Nat. d'Admin., Paris, France; Asst Lecturer, Dept of Law, Univ. de Nouakchott 1991–95; lawyer, Comm. for Food Security 1993–94; Auditor, Court of Auditors 1994–2002; Minister of Trade and Industry 2007–08, of Finance 2008–09; Gov. Banque Centrale de Mauritanie 2009–. *Address:* Banque Centrale de Mauritanie, ave de l'Indépendance, BP 623, Nouakchott, Mauritania (office). *Telephone:* 45-25-22-06 (office). *Fax:* 45-25-27-59 (office). *E-mail:* info@bcm.mr (office). *Website:* www.bcm.mr (office).

RAITT, Bonnie Lynn; American blues singer and musician (guitar, piano); b. 8 Nov. 1949, Burbank, Calif.; d. of John Raitt; m. Michael O'Keefe 1991 (divorced 1999); ed Radcliffe Coll.; performer in blues clubs on American E Coast; numerous concert tours and live appearances. *Recordings include:* albums: Bonnie Raitt 1971, Give It Up 1972, Takin' My Time 1973, Streetlights 1974, Home Plate 1975, Sweet Forgiveness 1977, The Glow 1979, Green Light 1982, Nine Lives 1986, Nick of Time (Grammy Awards for Best Female Rock Vocal Performance, Best Female Pop Vocal Performance, Album of the Year 1990) 1989, I'm in the Mood (with John Lee Hooker) (Grammy Award for Best Blues Traditional Record 1990), The Bonnie Raitt Collection 1990, Luck of the Draw (Grammy Award for Best Female Rock Vocal Performance, Best Duet 1992) 1991, Longing in Their Hearts (Grammy Award for Best Pop Album) 1994, Road Tested (Grammy Award for Best Rock Instrumental Performance 1997) 1995, Fundamental 1998, Silver Lining 2002, Souls Alike 2005, Bonnie Raitt and Friends 2006, SlipStream (Grammy Award for Best Americana Album 2013) 2012, Dig in Deep 2016. *Address:* PO Box 626, Los Angeles, CA 90078, USA. *Website:* www.bonnieraitt.com.

RAITT, Lisa, PC, BSc, MSc, LLB; Canadian politician; b. 7 May 1968, Nova Scotia; m.; two s.; ed St Francis Xavier Univ., Univ. of Guelph, Osgoode Hall Law School; Corp. Sec., Toronto Port Authority 2001, becoming Gen. Counsel, Harbourmaster 2001–04, Pres. and CEO 2002; MP (Conservative) for Halton 2008–15, for Milton 2015–; Minister of Natural Resources 2008–10, of Labour 2010–13, of Transport 2013–15. *Address:* 218 Justice Building, House of Commons, Ottawa, ON K1A 0A6, Canada (office). *Telephone:* (613) 996-7046 (office). *Fax:* (613) 992-0851 (office). *E-mail:* lisa.raitt@parl.gc.ca (office). *Website:* lisaraittmp.ca (office).

RAJ, Mithali Dorai; Indian cricketer; *Captain, Indian Women's Cricket Team;* b. 3 Dec. 1982, Jodhpur; d. of Dorai Raj and Leela Raj; ed Kasturba Gandhi Jr Coll. for Women, Secunderabad; right-handed batswoman; right-arm legbreak bowler; plays for Railways Cricket Team, Indian Women's Cricket Team; ODI debut: India vs Ireland, Milton Keynes 26 June 1999; Test debut: India vs England, Lucknow 14 Jan. 2002; T20I debut: India vs England, Derby 5 August 2006; played 10 tests (to Nov. 2014), scored 663 runs (average 51.00) with one century and four fifties, best score of 214 against England in Taunton 2002; played 203 ODIs (to 28 Feb. 2019), scored 6,720 runs (average 51.29) with seven centuries and 52 fifties, best score of 125; played 86 T20Is (to 9 March 2019), scored 2,307 runs (average 37.81) with 17 fifties, best score of 97; Captain, Indian Women's Cricket Team (Tests 2005–, ODI 2003–, T20I 2006–16); Arjuna Award 2003, Padma Shri 2015, Youth Sports Icon of Excellence Award 2017, Vogue Sportsperson of the Year 2017. *Address:* Board of Control for Cricket in India, 4th Floor, Cricket Centre, Wankhede Stadium, 'D' Road, Churchgate, Mumbai 400 020, Maharashtra, India (office). *Telephone:* (22) 22898800 (office). *Fax:* (22) 22898801 (office). *E-mail:* office@bcci.tv (office); mithalirajofficial@gmail.com. *Website:* www.bcci.tv (office).

RAJAN, Raghuram G., BTech, MBA, PhD; Indian academic, fmr central banker and fmr international organization official; b. 3 Feb. 1963, Bhopal; m. Radhika Puri Rajan; one s. one d.; ed Indian Inst. of Tech., Delhi, Indian Inst. of Man., Ahmedabad, Massachusetts Inst. of Tech., USA; Officer, Tata Admin. Service 1987; fmr consultant to US Fed. Reserve Bd, World Bank, IMF, Swedish Parl. Comm., Indian Finance Ministry; Asst Prof. of Finance, Booth School of Business, Univ. of Chicago 1991–95, 2016–, Prof. of Finance 1995–96, Joseph L. Gidwitz Prof. of Finance 1997–2003, Eric J. Gleacher Distinguished Service Prof. of Finance 2006–13 (on leave of absence); Gov. Reserve Bank of India 2013–16, apptd Vice-Chair. BIS 2015; Visiting Prof. of Finance, Kellogg School, Northwestern Univ. 1996–97; Bertil Daniellson Visiting Prof. of Banking, Stockholm School of Econs 1996–97; Fischer Black Visiting Prof., MIT 2000–01; Econ. Counselor and Dir of Research, IMF 2003–07; Program Dir for Corp. Finance, Nat. Bureau of Econ. Research; Dir Int. School of Business, Hyderabad; Dir American Finance Asscn 2001–04, then Vice-Pres.; Dir Chicago Council on Global Affairs; Program Dir (Corp. Finance) Nat. Bureau of Econ. Research 1998; mem. Advisory Bd US Comptroller Gen.; mem. Int. Advisory Bd Indian Inst. of Man., Ahmedabad; Adviser Securities and Exchange Bd of India; Founding mem. Academic Council, Indian School of Business; mem. Academic Advisory Council, Moodys Investor Services; mem. Int. Advisory Bd Itau-Unibanco Bank; Assoc. Ed. American

Economic Review, Journal of Financial Intermediation, Review of Financial Studies, Journal of Finance, Quarterly Journal of Economics, Financial Management (various times); Fellow, American Acad. of Arts and Sciences 2009–; fmr Sr Advisor, Booz and Co.; Hon. Econ. Advisor to Indian Prime Minister 2008–; Dr hc (London Business School) 2012, (Hong Kong Univ. of Science and Tech.) 2015; Western Finance Asscn Treffstz Prize for Outstanding Academic Achievement 1991, Smith Breeden Prize 1992, 1994, Fifth Annual Small Firm Research Symposium Best Paper Award 1993, Michael Brennan Award 1997, Brattle Prize 2000, 2001, 2002, Fischer Black Prize, American Finance Asscn 2003, Fama/DFA Prize 2003, Jensen Prize 2006, Infosys Prize for the Econ. Sciences 2012, Deutsche Bank Prize for Financial Econs 2013, Euromoney Central Banker of the Year 2014, Central Banker of the Year, The Banker Magazine 2016. *Publications include:* Saving Capitalism from the Capitalists (co-author) 2003, Fault Lines: How Hidden Fractures Still Threaten the World Economy (Financial Times/Goldman Sachs Business Book of the Year) 2010. *Leisure interests:* tennis, squash, history, Indian politics.

RAJAONARIMAMPIANINA, Hery Martial, CPA; Malagasy accountant, politician and fmr head of state; b. 6 Nov. 1958; ed Université des Trois Rivières, Canada; fmr Prof., Institut Nat. des Sciences Comptables et de l'Admin d'Entreprises, Antananarivo; Chair. Ordre des Experts Comptables et Financiers de Madagascar (Chartered Accountants and Financial Experts Asscn) –2009; Minister of Finance 2009–11 (resgnd), of Finance and the Budget 2011–13; cand. in presidential election 2013; Pres. 2014–18; Founder Cabinet Auditeurs Associés (Accounting Expertise and Auditing); Commdr, Ordre Nat. Malagasy 2010. *Address:* c/o Office of the President, BP 955, 101 Antananarivo, Madagascar (office).

RAJAPAKSA, Basil Rohana; Sri Lankan politician; s. of D. A. Rajapaksa; brother of Mahinda Rajapaksa; m. Pushpa Rajapaksa; three c.; ed Ananda Coll.; apptd MP 2007, elected MP for Gampaha 2010; fmr Sr Adviser to Pres. of Sri Lanka; Minister of Econ. Devt 2010–15; mem. Sri Lanka Freedom Party; fmr mem. United Nat. Party; arrested for misappropriation of state funds April 2015, released on bail March 2016.

RAJAPAKSA, Chamal Jayantha; Sri Lankan politician; b. 30 Oct. 1942; s. of D. A. Rajapaksa, fmr Minister of Agric. and Land; elder brother of Mahinda Rajapaksa, Pres. of Sri Lanka; m. Chandra Malini Wijewardena Rajapaksa 1975; two s.; ed Police Training Acad.; MP for Hambantota 1989–, Speaker of the Parl. 2010–15; Minister of Ports, Aviation, Irrigation and Water Man. –2010; mem. Sri Lanka Freedom Party (now part of United People's Freedom Alliance). *Address:* Parliament of Sri Lanka, Sri Jayewardenepura Kotte, Colombo (office); No. C 79, Gregory's Avenue, Colombo 07, Sri Lanka. *Telephone:* (11) 2777100 (office). *Fax:* (11) 2777564 (office). *E-mail:* rajapaksa_c@parliament.lk (office). *Website:* www.parliament.lk (office); www.chamalrajapaksa.lk.

RAJAPAKSA, Lt-Col (retd) Gotabhaya; Sri Lankan government official and fmr army officer; b. 20 June 1949, Palatuwa, Matara Dist; s. of D. A. Rajapaksa; brother of Mahinda Rajapaksa (Pres. of Sri Lanka); m. Ioma Rajapaksa; one s.; ed Ananda Coll., Colombo; joined Sri Lanka Army as Cadet Officer 1971, rank of Second Lt 1972, becoming Officer, Ceylon Signals Corps, served with Sri Lanka Sinha Regt and Rajarata Rifles, transferred to Gajaba Regt 1983, Second-in-Command, 1st Gajaba Regt, Commdr 1983–90, promoted to Lt-Col, Commdt, Kotelawala Defence Acad. –1992 (retd); worked as Unix System Admin., Loyola Law School, Los Angeles, USA –2005; Perm. Sec., Ministry of Defence 2005–15; Hon. DLitt (Colombo) 2009; several awards for gallantry including Rana Wickrama Padakkama (Combat Gallantry Medal), Rana Sura Padakkama (Combat Excellence Medal).

RAJAPAKSA, Mahinda; Sri Lankan politician, lawyer and fmr head of state; *Leader of the Opposition;* b. (Percy Mahendra Rajapaksa), 18 Nov. 1945, Weerakatiya, Hambantota, British Ceylon; s. of D. A. Rajapaksa; m. Shiranthi Wickramasinghe; three s.; ed Richmond Coll., Galle, Nalanda and Thurstan Colls, Colombo, Sri Lanka Law Coll.; fmr lawyer, Tangalle; mem. Parl. for Beliatta 1970; fmr Minister of Labour, of Fisheries, of Ports and Shipping; Leader of the Opposition 2002–04; Prime Minister of Sri Lanka 2004–05; Pres. of Sri Lanka 2005–15; Minister of Defence and of Finance and Planning 2005–07, of Defence, Public Security, Law and Order, Religious Affairs, Nation Building and Finance and Planning 2007–10, of Defence and Urban Devt, of Finance and Planning, of Ports and Highways, of Law and Order 2010–15, Prime Minister and Minister of Finance Oct.–Dec. 2018; Leader of the Opposition 2018–; mem. United People's Freedom Alliance 2004–; Pres. Sri Lankan Cttee for Solidarity with Palestine; Chair. Sri Lanka Freedom Party 2006–15, now Patron; mem. Sri Lanka Podujana Peramuna 2018–; Sri Rohana Janaranjana 2000. *Address:* Carlton House, Tangalle, Sri Lanka (home). *Telephone:* (47) 2240344 (home). *Fax:* (47) 2241113 (home). *E-mail:* mahinda.rajapaksa@mahindarajapaksa.lk. *Website:* www.mahindarajapaksa.lk.

RAJAPAKSA, Wijedasa; Sri Lankan lawyer and politician; *Minister of Higher Education and Cultural Affairs;* b. 16 March 1959, Walasmulla, Hambantota dist; Mala Rajapakshe; ed Univ. of Colombo; early career in banking, subsequently became lawyer; fmr Examiner, Faculty of Law, Univ. of Colombo; mem. Parl. (Sri Lanka Freedom Party Nat. List) 2004–10, for Colombo 2010–, Chair. parl. Cttee on Public Enterprise (COPE) 2006–07; joined United National Party—UNP 2007, apptd UNP party organiser for Maharagama electorate; apptd mem. President's Counsel 2001; Minister of Banking Devt 2005–06 (resgnd), Minister of Justice and Labour Relations 2015–17, of Higher Education and Cultural Affairs 2018–; fmr Chair. Sri Lanka Press Council; fmr Vice-Pres. World Association of Press Councils; mem. Bar Asscn of Sri Lanka (Pres. 2012); one of Ten Outstanding Young Persons in the field of law 1988, Sri Lankan of the Year, LMD 2007, Nat. APEX Award 2013. *Publications:* has written 17 seventeen books, nine on matters of law. *Address:* Ministry of Higher Education & Cultural Affairs, #18, Ward Place, Colombo 7, Sri Lanka (office); No.17, Wijayaba Mawatha, Nawala Road, Nugegoda, Sri Lanka (home). *Telephone:* (11) 2868710 (office). *Fax:* (11) 2884197 (office). *E-mail:* info@mohe.gov.lk (office); rajapakshew@gmail.com. *Website:* www.mohe.gov.lk; www.facebook.com/wijeyadasarajapakshe.

RAJARAM, Sanjaya, BSc, MSc, PhD; Mexican (b. Indian) plant scientist and entrepreneur; *Owner and Director of Research and Development, Resource Seed Mexicana;* b. 1943, Uttar Pradesh; ed Coll. of Jaunpur at Univ. of Gorakhpur, Indian Agricultural Research Inst., Univ. of Sydney, Australia; worked with Norman Borlaug at Int. Maize and Wheat Improvement Center (Centro Internacional de Mejoramiento de Maíz y Trigo—CIMMYT), Dir Global Wheat Program 1969–2002, Leader, Bread Wheat Breeding Team 1973–95; Dir Biodiversity and Integrated Gene Man. (BIGM) Program, Int. Center for Agricultural Research in the Dry Areas, Aleppo, Syria 2005–08, Consultant 2008–; Owner and Dir of Research and Devt, Resource Seed Mexicana; Fellow, American Soc. of Agronomy, Crop Science Soc. of America; Padma Shri; more than 80 nat. and int. awards, Rotary Club of Narrabri scholarship, including Rank Prize Award, Friendship Award, M.S. Swaminathan Award, Trust for Advancement of Agricultural Sciences, World Food Prize 2014. *Achievements include:* successfully cross bred winter and spring wheat varieties, with distinct gene pools, that had been isolated from one another for hundreds of years, which led to his developing as many as 480 new wheat varieties that have higher yields and a broad genetic base. *Publications:* more than 400 papers in professional journals. *Address:* Resource Seed Mexicana, Juan Aldama 10, Col. San Miguel, Chapultepec, Mexicaltzingo, México, DF, Mexico (office). *Telephone:* (722) 263-0732 (office).

RAJAVI, Maryam, BSc; Iranian politician; b. (Maryam Qajar-Azedanllo), 3 Dec. 1953, Tehran; m. Massoud Rajavi 1985; one s. one d.; ed Sharif Univ. of Tech., Tehran; leader anti-Shah student movt; joined Mojahedin-e Khalq Org. (People's Mojahedin of Iran, leading Iranian opposition group) 1970s, parl. cand. for Tehran in first post-revolution parl. elections 1979; official in social dept 1980–81, organized demonstrations against Khomeini Govt 1980–81; left Iran for Paris 1982; elected jt-leader of Mojahedin 1985, Sec.-Gen. 1989–93; Deputy C-in-C Nat. Liberation Army of Iran (NLA) 1987–93, launched programme for introduction of women in front-line combat and combat pilots 1987, transformed NLA from infantry to armoured force 1989–93; Pres.-Elect, Nat. Council of Resistance of Iran (540-mem. Parl. in exile) 1993–; Int. Human Rights Conf., Paris 2004, Int. Conf. of Jurists, Paris 2004, Parls of Norway and UK 1995–96; awards include Medal of Honour for contrib. to emancipation of women, Nat. Comm. for Gender Equality, Italy 1993, one of The Times 100 Most Powerful Women, UK 1996. *Publications include:* Charter of Fundamental Freedoms in Post-dictatorship Iran 1995, Message to Fourth Int. Women's Conf., Beijing 1995, A Message of Tolerance 1995, Women, Islam and Fundamentalism 1996, Women, Voice of the Oppressed 1996, United Against Fundamentalism 1996, Message to Women in Frontline (conf.) 1997, Misogyny, Pillar of Religious Fascism 2003, Message to Int. Federation of Women against Fundamentalism and for Equality (conf.) 2004, Women and Islamic Fundamentalism 2004, Women Empowerment 2005, Women in Leadership 2006, Ten-Point Platform for Future Iran 2006; contrib.: Le Monde, De Welt, Le Figaro, International Herald Tribune. *Leisure interest:* reading. *Website:* www.ncr-iran.org; www.maryam-rajavi.com/en.

RAJE SCINDIA, Vasundhara, BA; Indian politician; b. 8 March 1953, Bombay (now Mumbai); d. of Jivaji Rao Scindia and Rajmata Vijya Raje Scindia; m. Raja Hemant Singh 1972; one s.; ed Presentation Convent, Kodaikanal, Sophia Coll., Mumbai Univ.; MLA for Dholpur 1984–89; Vice-Pres. Bharatiya Janata Party (BJP) Yuva Morcha 1984–89; Vice-Pres. Rajasthan State BJP 1985–89, Pres. 2002–; mem. Lok Sabha 1989–2003; Jt Sec. BJP Parl. Cttee 1997; Union Minister for Foreign Affairs 1998–99; Minister for Small Scale Industries and Agric. and Rural Industries (Ind. charge) 1999–2003; State Minister for Personnel and Training, Pensions and Welfare, Personnel, Public Grievance and Pension Ministry, Atomic Energy and Space Dept 1999–2003; Chief Minister of Rajasthan 2003–08, 2013–18; mem. Rajasthan Legis. Ass. 2008–, Leader of Opposition 2009–10, 2011–13; UN Women Together Award 2007. *Leisure interests:* reading, music, horse riding, gardening. *Address:* 13, Civil Lines, Jaipur 302 006, India (home). *Telephone:* (141) 2229900 (home). *Fax:* (141) 2222521 (home).

RAJHI, Ahmed bin Suleiman al-; Saudi Arabian politician and businessman; *Minister of Labour and Social Development;* b. 1967; s. of Sulaiman al-Rajhi; ed King Fahd Univ. of Petroleum and Minerals; CEO Nat. Industries Group 1997–2010; Minister of Labour and Social Devt 2018–; Chair. Saudi Chambers, Riyadh Chamber of Commerce and Industry, also Chair. Industrial Cttee 2008–12; Vice-Chair., Al Rajhi Holding Group, Al Rajhi Takaful Co. and Humanitarian Foundation; Chair. of Exec. Cttee, of Industrial Sector and Risk Man. Cttee, Hail Cement Co.; First Deputy Chair., Fed. of GCC Chambers; Chair. Bd of Dirs, Al-Arab Contracting Co. 2003–11, Triomada Plastic Int. Co., Mattex, Saudi Manufacturing Industries Holding Co., Vision Green, AEP; mem. Bd of Dirs, Advanced Petrochemical Manufacturing Co. 2005–13, Industrial City Authority 2011–14, Farabi Petrochemical Co., Econ. Cities Authority, Saudi Export Devt Authority, Supreme Comm. for the Devt of Riyadh City; mem. Bd of Supervisory Cttee, Nat. Centre for Palm and Dates; mem. Bd, Coordinating Cttee for Labor Market Policies, King Sa'ud Univ. Fund for Scientific Research Support. *Address:* Ministry of Labour and Social Development, PO Box 21110, King Abd al-Aziz Rd, al-Mursalat District, Riyadh 11475, Saudi Arabia (office). *Telephone:* (11) 200-6666 (office). *Fax:* (11) 210-4600 (office). *Website:* mlsd.gov.sa (office).

RAJHI, Sheikh; **Sulaiman bin Abdul Aziz Al-,** BA; Saudi Arabian banking executive and philanthropist; *Chairman, Al Rajhi Bank;* b. 1920; m.; at least 23 c.; ed King Abdulaziz Univ.; grew up in Nejd desert; began business with late brother Saleh changing money for pilgrims in camel caravans crossing the desert to Mecca and Medina; Co-founder (with Saleh) and Chair. Al Rajhi Bank; diversified family investments into gypsum, agriculture, steel and other industrial sectors; opened office in Kuwait 2010, opened branches in Jordan 2011; holds stakes in several Saudi firms, including Yanbu Cement Co. and National Agricultural Development Co. (Nadec) (Chair. 2015–); f. SAAR Foundation; launched Sulaiman Al Rajhi Univ.; King Faisal Int. Prize 2012. *Address:* Al Rajhi Bank, Riyadh, Saudi Arabia (office). *Telephone:* (1) 8282562 (office). *Fax:* (1) 2795860 (office). *E-mail:* shareholders@alrajhibank.com.sa (office). *Website:* www.alrajhibank.com.sa (office).

RAJINIKANTH; Indian actor and producer; b. (Shivaji Rao Gaekwad), 12 Dec. 1950, Bangalore; s. of Ramoji Rao Gaekwad and Rambhai Gaekwad; m. Latha Rajinikanth 1981; two d.; ed Acharya Patasala, Ramakrishna Mission, Bangalore; worked with Bangalore Transport Service; moved to Chennai, joined Madras Film Inst. 1973; Kalaimamani Award, Tamil Nadu Govt 1984, MGR Award, Tamil Nadu Govt 1989, Kalaichelvam Award, Nadigar Sangam 1995, Oshobismit Award,

Rajinish Ashram Award 1995, Padma Bhushan 2000, Raj Kapoor Award 2007, Vijay Award 2010. *Films include:* Apoorva Raagangal (Nat. Award, Filmfare Award, Arima Sangam Award, Filmfans Award) 1975, Moondru Mudichu 1976, Tholireyi Gadichindi 1977, Bhuvana Oru Kelvikkuri (Tamil Nadu Govt Award, Filmfans Award) 1977, 16 Vayathinile (Filmfans Award, ThiraiKadhir, Arima Sangam Award) 1977, Vayasu Pilichindi 1978, Ilamai Oonjal Aadukirathu (Tamil Nadu Govt Award) 1978, Mullum Malarum (Tamil Nadu Govt Award, Filmfans Award, Filmfare Award, Cinema Express Award) 1978, Tiger 1979, Thayillamal Nannilai 1979, Dharma Yuddham 1979, Ram Robert Rahim 1980, Mr. Rajanikant 1980, Anbukku Naan Adimai 1980, Ranuva Veeran 1981, Netri Kann 1981, Thanikkattu Raja 1982, Pudhu Kavithai 1982, Agni Sakshi 1982, Engeyo Ketta Kural (Tamil Nadu Govt Award, Filmfans Award) 1982, Thudikkum Karangal 1983, Thanga Magan 1983, Tiger Rajani 1984, Takkaridonga 1984, Naan Mahaan Alla 1984, Bhooka Sher 1984, Unn Kannil Neer Vazhindal 1985, Nyayam Meere Cheppali 1985, Mera Inteqam 1985, Viduthalai 1986, Maaveran 1986, Dosti Dushmani 1986, Uttar Dakshin 1987, Bloodstone 1988, Siva 1989, Raajadhi Raaja 1989, Adisaya Piravi 1990, Hum 1991, Shanti Kranti 1991, Pandian 1992, Chor Ke Ghar Chorni 1992, Valli 1993, Badsha 1995, Peda Rayudu (Filmfans Award, Cinema Express), Arunachalam (Tamil Nadu Govt Award) 1997, Padaiyappa (Tamil Nadu Govt Award) 1999, Bulandi 2000, Baba (writer, producer) 2002, Chandramukhi 2005, Sivaji 2007, Kuselan 2008, Endhiran 2010, Kochadaiiyaan 2014, Lingaa 2014, Kabali 2016. *Address:* 18, Raghava Veera Avenue, Poes Garden, Chennai 600 086, India. *Fax:* (44) 24838890. *Website:* www.rajinikanth.com.

RAJKHOWA, J(yoti) P(rasad); Indian civil servant and government official; b. 1 Nov. 1944, Jorhat; s. of Bhoba Rajkhowa and Annada Rajkhowa; m. Rita Rajkhowa; one s. two d.; ed Gauhati Univ., Delhi School of Econs, Delhi Univ.; long career in Indian Admin. Service (IAS), beginning as Asst Commr, Tezpur, later Asst Commr, Demagiri Mizo Hills, Under-Sec., Shillong; various roles in Govt of Assam including Additional Chief Sec. of Home and Political Depts, Additional Chief Sec. and Agricultural Production Commr, Prin. Sec. of Educ., Dir of Vigilance and Chief Vigilance Officer, NTPC (energy conglomerate), Commr and Sec. to Govt of Assam in several depts including Public Enterprises, Labour and Employment, Health and Family Welfare, Industries; fmr Chair. Assam State Electricity Bd; fmr Divisional Commr, Lower Assam Div.; fmr Deputy Commr and Dist Magistrate, Undivided Kamrup Dist, Commr of Transport, Jt Sec. of Finance, Industries; Chief Sec. of Assam 2003–04; Gov. of Arunachal Pradesh 2015–16. *Leisure interests:* reading, writing, farming, cooking, billiards, angling.

RAJNA, Thomas, DMus, ARCM; British composer, pianist and teacher (retd); b. 21 Dec. 1928, Budapest, Hungary; s. of Nandor Rajna and Hella Eisen; m. Anthea Valentine Campion 1967; one s. two d.; ed Nat. Musical School, Budapest, Franz Liszt Acad. of Music, Budapest and Royal Coll. of Music, London; freelance composer, pianist and teacher, London 1951–63; Prof. of Piano, Guildhall School of Music 1963–70; Lecturer, Univ. of Surrey 1967–70; Sr Lecturer in Piano, Faculty of Music, Univ. of Cape Town 1970–89, Assoc. Prof. 1989–93; launched own record label Amarantha Records 2001; Fellow, Univ. of Cape Town 1981; DMus (Cape Town) 1985; Liszt Prize, Budapest 1947, Artes Award (SABC) 1981, UCT Book Award 1996, Cape Tercentenary Foundation Merit Award 1997. *Compositions include:* film and ballet music, orchestral and chamber music, two piano concertos, Harp Concerto 1990, Amarantha (opera in 11 scenes) 1991–94, Video Games (for orchestra) 1994, Rhapsody for clarinet and orchestra 1995, Fantasy for violin and orchestra 1996, Suite for violin and harp 1997, Stop All the Clocks (four songs on poems by W. H. Auden) 1998, The Creation – A Negro Sermon for unaccompanied choir 2000, Valley Song (opera) 2002–04, Tarantulla for violin and piano 2001, Violin Concerto 2007. *Recordings include:* works by Stravinsky (complete piano works), Messiaen: Vingt regards sur l'Enfant-Jesus; Scriabin, Granados (complete piano works), Liszt (Transcendental Studies), Schumann (A minor Piano Concerto and Piano Quintet and Quartet), Dohnanyi (Nursery Variations), The Hungarian Connection: Instrumental Works by Dohnányi and Rajna, Bach Harpsichord Concertos, Bartok 2nd and 3rd Piano Concertos, Stravinsky Capriccio, Prokofiev 3rd Piano Concerto, Barber Piano Concerto, A Garland of Spanish Songs; own compositions: Amarantha (opera), Valley Song (opera), Suite for violin and harp, Rhapsody for clarinet and orchestra, 1st Piano Concerto, Piano Preludes and Capriccio, 2nd Piano Concerto and Harp Concerto, Video Games and other orchestral works, The Creation – A Negro Sermon for chorus and orchestra, Violin Concerto. *Publications:* Dialogues for Clarinet and Piano 1970, Piano Preludes 1988, Music for Violin and Piano 1990, Concerto for Harp and Orchestra 1990; publs by Amarantha Music: Video Games for Orchestra 1994, Rhapsody for Clarinet and Orchestra 1995, Amarantha (opera) 1995, Fantasy for Violin and Orchestra 1996, Suite for Violin and Harp 1998, Stop All the Clocks – Four Songs on Poems by W. H. Auden 1998, Tarantulla for Violin and Piano 2001, Valley Song (opera) 2004, The Creation – A Negro Sermon for Chorus and Orchestra 2006, Violin Concerto 2007. *Leisure interests:* chess, swimming. *Address:* 10 Wyndover Road, Claremont, Cape Town, West Cape 7708, South Africa (home). *Telephone:* (21) 6713937 (home). *Fax:* (21) 6713937 (home). *E-mail:* trajna@telkomsa.net (home).

RAJOELINA, Andry Nirina; Malagasy politician, broadcasting and media executive and head of state; *President;* b. 30 May 1974, Antananarivo; m. Mialy Rajoelina; two s. one d.; worked as disc jockey around Antananarivo early 1990s; gained prominence after establishing own radio station, Viva Radio, and a successful advertising co.; Mayor of Antananarivo 2007–09; owner, Viva TV and Viva FM (TV and radio stations); led protest movement against Pres. Marc Ravalomanana; installed by mil. as head of state (following resignation of Pres. Ravalomanana) 19 March 2009; Head of the High Authority of Transition 21 March 2009–25 Jan. 2014 (presidency not recognised by Southern African Devt Community); Pres. of Madagascar 2019–; Leader, Miaraka amin'ny Prezidà Andry Rajoelina (MAPAR). *Address:* Office of the President, BP 955, 101 Antananarivo, Madagascar (office). *Telephone:* (20) 2254703 (office). *Fax:* (20) 2256252 (office). *E-mail:* communication@presidence.gov.mg (office). *Website:* www.presidence.gov.mg (office).

RAJOUB, Jibril; Palestinian government official; b. 1953, Dura; m.; three c.; spent 17 years in Israeli prison 1968–85; exiled to Lebanon 1988, returned to West Bank 1994; Chief West Bank Preventive Security Service 1994–2002; Nat.

Security Adviser to Yasser Arafat and Head of Nat. Palestinian Security Council 2003–04; Pres. Palestinian Football Asscn 2006–, Palestine Olympic Cttee; Deputy-Sec., Fatah Central Cttee 2009–17, Sec.-Gen. 2017–; Head, PLO Supreme Council for Sport and Youth Affairs; Chair. Palestinian Scout Asscn; mem. Fatah-Revolutionary Council. *Telephone:* (2) 2348691 (office). *Fax:* (2) 2348690 (office). *E-mail:* international.dept.pfa@gmail.com (office); fateh@fateh.org. *Website:* www.pfa.ps (office).

RAJOY BREY, Mariano; Spanish politician and property registrar; b. 27 March 1955, Santiago de Compostela (La Coruña); m.; two s.; ed Universidad de Santiago de Compostela; fmr Prof. of Law, Univ. of Santiago de Compostela; Vice-Chair. Governing Council Alianza Popular (People's Alliance) in Galicia, Chair. Local and Prov. Council of Alianza Popular in Pontevedra, mem. Perm. Cttee of Alianza Popular; mem. Regional Parl. of Galicia 1981, fmr Dir-Gen. for Institutional Relations of Regional of Galicia; Pres. Prov. Council of Pontevedra 1983–86; Vice-Pres. Regional Govt of Galicia 1986–87; mem. Nat. Exec. Cttee Partido Popular (People's Party—PP) 1989–, Deputy Gen. Sec. PP 1990–2003, Gen. Sec. PP 2003–04, Pres. 2004–18; mem. Congress of Deputies (Parl.) July–Dec. 1986, 1989–; Minister for Public Admin Services 1996–99, for Educ. and Culture 1999–2000; First Vice-Pres. of the Govt and Minister for Home Affairs 2001–02; First Vice-Pres. of the Govt, Govt Spokesperson and Minister for the Presidency 2002–03; cand. for presidency of the govt 2004, 2008; Prime Minister and Pres. of the Govt 2011–18 (resigned following vote of no confidence); Vice-Pres. Int. Democratic Union 2005–, Centrist Democrat International 2006–; Trustee, Foundation for Social Studies and Analysis (FAES); Order of Charles III 2003, Order of the Aztec Eagle (Mexico) 2012, Knight Grand Cross, Order of Merit of Chile; Dr hc (Sergio Arboleda Univ., Bogotá, Colombia) 2012. *Address:* c/o Partido Popular, Génova 13, 28004 Madrid, Spain (office). *Telephone:* (91) 5577200 (office). *Fax:* (91) 3122322 (office). *E-mail:* secretariapresidente@presidencia.gob.es (office); presidencia@pp.es (office). *Website:* www.pp.es (office).

RAJU, B(yrraju) Ramalinga, BCom, MBA; Indian business executive; b. 16 Sept. 1954, Bhimavaram, Andhra Pradesh; m. Nandini Raju; two s.; ed Loyola Coll., Vijayawada, Ohio Univ., USA; Co-founder and Chair. Satyam Computer Services Ltd, Satyam Infoway Ltd and VisionCompass, Inc. 1987–2009 (resgnd), jt ventures include Satyam–GE Software Services Ltd, Satyam Venture Eng Services Pvt. Ltd, Satyam Manufacturing Technologies Ltd, Satyam ideaEdge Technologies Pvt. Ltd, CA Satyam ASP Pvt. Ltd; f. several trusts and charities including Alambana, Naandi and the Byyrajyu Foundation; Chair. Nat. Asscn of Software and Service Cos 2006–07; held in Hyderabad's Chanchalguda jail on criminal charges of corp. fraud July 2009, granted bail 2010; Dr hc (Andhra Univ.) 2007; Ernst & Young Entrepreneur of the Year Award 2000, 2007, Dataquest IT Man. of the Year Award 2001, Asia Business Leader Award for Corp. Citizen of the Year, Hong Kong 2002. *Leisure interests:* reading, snooker.

RAJU, M. Mangapati Pallam, BE, MBA; Indian business executive and politician; b. 31 Aug. 1962, Pithapuram, East Godavari Dist, Andhra Pradesh; s. of M. S. Sanjeevi Rao and Rama Rajeshwari; m. Mamatha Raju 1989; one s. one d.; ed Andhra Univ., Visakhapatnam, Temple Univ., Philadelphia, USA; Research Asst Temple Univ., USA 1985–86; Research Assoc. Federal Group Inc. (man. consulting firm), South Natick, Mass, USA 1986–87; Dir Air India & Indian Airlines 1994–97; Man. Dir TTM (India) Pvt. Ltd (ASIC Design Services), Secunderabad 1999–; mem. Lok Sabha (lower house of Parl.) for Kakinada constituency (youngest MP when first elected) 1989–91, 2004–14; Gen. Sec. Andhra Pradesh Congress Cttee 1995–2000; mem. All India Congress Cttee 1997–2000; Union Cabinet Minister of State for Defence 2006–12, Minister of Human Resource Devt 2012–14; Life mem. Equestrian Fed. of India; Fellow, Inst. of Electronics & Telecommunications Engineers, New Delhi. *Leisure interests:* athletics, football, swimming, horse riding, music, photography and travelling. *Address:* Bharatiya Janata Party (BJP), 11 Ashok Road, New Delhi 110 001, India (office). *Telephone:* (11)-23005700 (office). *Fax:* (11)-23005787 (office). *E-mail:* webmaster@bjp.org (office). *Website:* www.bjp.org (office).

RAJWANA, Rafique, LLB, LLM, GDL; Pakistani lawyer, judge and politician; b. 20 Feb. 1949, Multan; s. of Malik Ameer Bukhsh; ed Emerson Coll., Multan, Forman Christian Coll. Univ., Gilani Law Coll.; joined judiciary in 1987, served as Additional Dist and Session Judge, also served as Pres. Lahore High Court Bar Asscn, Multan 1996–97; resgnd judiciary to start law firm Rajwana & Rajwana, Multan; mem. Pakistan Muslim League Nawaz (PML-N), has served as Sr Vice-Pres. PML-N Punjab and Vice-Pres. PML-N Lawyers Wing; mem. Senate 1997–99, 2012–15; Gov. of Punjab 2015–18 (resgnd). *Address:* 65/A Rajwana Road, Ameerabad, Multan, Pakistan (home).

RAKE, Sir Michael Derek Vaughan, Kt, FCA; British accountant and business executive; *Chairman, BT Group plc;* b. 17 Jan. 1948; s. of Derek Shannon Vaughan Rake and Rosamund Rake (née Barrett); m. 1st Julia Rake Cook 1970; three s.; m. 2nd Caroline Thomas 1986; one s.; ed Wellington Coll.; with Turquands Barton Mayhew, London and Brussels 1968–74; accountant, KPMG (Peat Marwick Mitchell Continental Europe), Brussels 1974, apptd Pnr 1979, Pnr in charge of Audit, Belgium and Luxembourg 1983–86, Sr Resident Partner, ME 1986–89, Pnr, London office 1989, mem. UK Bd 1991, Regional Man. Partner, SE Region 1992–94, Chief Exec. London and SE Region 1994–96, COO, UK 1996–98, Sr Partner, UK and Chair. UK Bd 1998, Chair. KPMG Europe 1999–2002, Chair. KPMG Int. 2002–07; Chair. BT Group plc 2007–, Majid Al Futtaim Holding LLC 2009–, Worldpay 2015–; Deputy Chair. EasyJet June–Dec. 2009, Chair. 2010–13; Chair. Business in the Community 2004–07, Guidelines Monitoring Cttee (pvt. equity oversight group), UK Comm. for Employment and Skills 2007–10; Pres. CBI 2013–; mem. Bd of Dirs McGraw Hill Inc., Financial Reporting Council 2008–11, Barclays PLC 2008–15 (fmr Deputy Chair.); mem. Bd Prince of Wales Int. Business Leaders' Forum 1998–2007, Britain in Europe Business Leaders' Group 2000–, TransAtlantic Business Dialogue, Chartered Man. Inst., DTI's US/UK Regulatory Taskforce, Advisory Council for Business for New Europe, Ethnic Minority Employment Taskforce, SOAS Advisory Bd, Advisory Bd of Judge Inst. at Univ. of Cambridge 2004, Nat. Security Forum 2009–10, Prime Minister's Business Advisory Group 2010–12; Vice-Pres. Royal Nat. Inst. of Blind People 2003–, Reviseur d'Entreprise (Luxembourg); Assoc. mem. BUPA; Sr Adviser, Chatham House, Global Advisory Bd of Univ. of Oxford Centre for Corp. Reputation; Vice-Pres. and Chair. of Govs of Wellington Coll.; mem. Bd Guards

Polo Club; Trustee, Prince of Wales' Charitable Foundation; William Pitt Fellow, Pembroke Coll., Cambridge; British American Business UK Transatlantic Business Award 2011, Channing Award for Corporate Citizenship 2013, ICAEW Outstanding Achievement Award 2013. *Leisure interests:* polo, skiing. *Address:* BT Group plc, BT Centre, 81 Newgate Street, London, EC1A 7AJ, England (office). *Telephone:* (20) 7356-5000 (office). *Fax:* (20) 7356-5520 (office). *E-mail:* btgroup@bt .com (office). *Website:* www.btplc.com (office).

RAKHIMOV, Murtaza Gubaidullovich; Russian politician; b. 7 Feb. 1934, Tavakanovo, Bashkiria; s. of Gubaidulla Zufarovich Rakhimov and Galima Abdullovna Rakhimova; m. Luiza Galimovna Rakhimova; one s.; ed Ufa Oil Inst.; operator, then Chief of Oil Rig, Chief Chemist, Chief Engineer, Dir Ufa Oil Processing Plant 1956–90; USSR People's Deputy 1990–92; Chair. Supreme Soviet Repub. of Bashkortostan 1990–93, Pres. 1993–2010; mem. Russian Council of Fed. (Parl.) 1993–2001; Public Services to Repub. of Bashkortostan, Order of Peter the Great, Labour Red Banner, People's Friendship Order, Honour Symbol, Order of Salavat Yulayev. *Leisure interests:* sports, music, literature.

RAKIĆ, Goran; Kosovo economist and politician; *Leader, Srpska Lista (Serb List);* Mayor, Mitrovica e Veriut/Severna Kosovska Mitrovica (North Mitrovicë) 2014–; Leader Srpska Lista (Serb List) 2017–. *Address:* Srpska Lista, 38220 Mitrovica e Veriut/Severna Kosovska Mitrovica, Lagja e Boshjnakëve, Kosovo (office); Mitrovica e Veriut/Severna Kosovska Mitrovica (North Mitrovicë) Municipal Administration 38220 Mitrovica e Veriut/Severna Kosovska Mitrovica, Lagja e Boshjnakëve, Kosovo (office). *Telephone:* (65) 4119873 (office). *E-mail:* info@ srpskalista.net (office); contact.mnao@rks-gov.net (office). *Website:* srpskalista.net (office); kk.rks-gov.net/mitroviceeveriut.

RAKOTOARIMANANA, François Marie Maurice Gervais; Malagasy accountant and politician; ed Univ. du Québec à Trois-Rivières, Canada; fmr Prof., Accountancy Dept, Inst. Nat. des Sciences Comptables et de l'Admin d'Entreprises, Antananarivo; fmr auditor, Rindra (auditing and consulting firm), Antananarivo; worked for Canada Revenue Agency as specialist on tax auditing; Sr Financial Man. Specialist with World Bank, based in Madagascar, Mauritius, Comoros, Seychelles and Djibouti 1998–2010; worked for Direction Generale des entreprises Trois-Rivières, Québec 2010–12; Minister of Finance and the Budget 2015–17. *Address:* c/o Ministry of Finance and the Budget, BP 61, Antaninarenina, Antananarivo, Madagascar (office).

RAKOTOARIMASY, Lt-Gen. André Lucien; Malagasy army officer and politician; b. 12 Feb. 1953, Ambohimanga Rova, Antananarivo; s. of Alphonse Rakotofiringa and Marie Jeanne Raveloharimanana; m.; four c.; ed Univ. of Antananarivo, Mil. Acad., Antsirabe, Malagasy Inst. for Planning Techniques, Antananarivo, Collège Interarmées de Défense, Paris, France, Centre for Strategic and Diplomatic Studies, Antananarivo; Dir of Human Resources, Ministry of Defence 2004–06, Gen. Man. of Operations and Planning 2007–08; Chief of the Gen. Staff of the Malagasy Army 2008–09; Dir of Mil. Cabinet at the Presidency of the High Authority of the Transition 2009–10; Minister of the Armed Forces 2010–14; Kt of the Malagasy Nat. Order 1994, Officer 1999; Kt of the Madagascar Order of Merit 1996, Officer; Commdr, Malagasy Nat. Order, Grand Officer. *Leisure interest:* tennis practice. *E-mail:* rakotoarimasyal@yahoo.fr (office).

RAKOTONANDRASANA, Gen. Noël; Malagasy army officer and government official; fmrly with Parachute Regt; Commdr, Corps d'Armée du Personnel et des Services Administratif et Technique (Capsat) 2009; led army faction during coup d'état of March 2009; Minister of the Armed Forces 2009–10 (dismissed).

RAKOTONIRINA, Gen. Léon Jean Richard; Malagasy politician and fmr army officer; *Minister of National Defence;* b. 9 April 1963, Farafangana; s. of Alfred Rakotonirina and Elise Ravaoarisoa; widower; four c.; ed Univ. d'Antananarivo, Antsirabe Mil. Acad. (ACMIL), US Army War Coll.; long career in army, roles include Head of PT-76 Tank Platoon, Imerintsiatosika 1985–87, Deputy Officer, PT-76 Tank Co. 1986–89, Section Head of BA1 Infantry trainees, Ecole Nat. des Sous-Officier d'Active 1988–89, Chief of Staff, Gen. Inspectorate of the Army 1991–93, Lecturer, Army Staff Coll. 1995–98, Head of Documentation Dept, Directorate of Presidential Security, Army Gen. Staff 1994–96, Head of Cultural Heritage Dept, Ministry of the Armed Forces 1997–99, Technical Adviser 1999–2000, Deputy Dir, Ministry of Nat. Defence 2003–07, Dir, Nat. Office for Veterans Affairs 2008–10, Dir of Cabinet of Minister of Armed Forces 2010–11, Commdr, Antsirabe Mil. Acad. 2012–15, Dir Gen. of Defence Orgs, Ministry of Nat. Defence 2015–17, Perm. Sec. of Defence and Nat. Security 2017–19, Minister of Nat. Defence 2019–; Chevalier, Ordre du Mérite 2005, Chevalier, Ordre Nat. 2009, Officier, Ordre Nat. 2014, Chevalier, Ordre du Mérite (France) 2016, Commdr, Ordre du Mérite de Madagascar 2017; Médaille d'Argent de la Défense de la République Française. *Address:* Ministry of National Defence, BP 08, Ampahibe, 101 Antananarivo, Madagascar (office). *Telephone:* (20) 2222211 (office). *Fax:* (20) 2235420 (home). *E-mail:* mdn@wanadoo.fr (office). *Website:* www.defense.gov.mg (office).

RAKOTOVAHINY, Emmanuel; Malagasy politician; *Vice-President;* b. Aug. 1938, Toliara; fmr Chair. Union nat. pour la démocratie et le développement; fmr Minister of State for Rural Devt and Land Reform; Prime Minister of Madagascar 1995–96; Pres. Comité pour la Réconciliation Nationale 2009; Vice-Pres. of Madagascar 2009–. *Address:* Comité pour la Réconciliation Nationale, Villa la Franchise, Lot II-I 160 A, Alarobia, Antananarivo, Madagascar (office). *Telephone:* (20) 2242022 (office).

RAKOTOZAFY, Gen. Dominique Jean Olivier; Malagasy army officer and politician; b. 10 Aug. 1959, Andapa; m.; three c.; ed Acad. Mil. Antsirabe, Centre d'Etudes Diplomatiques et Stratégiques, Antananarivo, Defense Language Inst., USA; Officer attached to Deputy Co. Commdr, Fianarantsoa 1981–84, attached to Head of Training Bureau, Support Regt 1984–90, Co. Commdr, Support Regt 1990–94; Head of Div., Language Training, Ministry of Armed Forces 1995–2001; Commdr, Ecole Militaire Préparatoire (mil. acad.) 2002–05; Head of Mil. Training, EMGAM (mil. acad.) 2005–07, Commdr, Acad. Militaire 2007–09; Tech. Adviser to Minister of Armed Forces 2009–11; Head of Mil. Cabinet in the Presidency 2011–14; Minister of Nat. Defence 2014–16; attained rank of Sub-Lt 1981, Lt 1983, Capt. 1989, Commdr 1994, Lt-Col 1998, Col 2003, Brig.-Gen. 2010, Gen.

2012; Officier, Ordre du Mérite de Madagascar, Officier, Ordre Nat. Malagasy, Médaille d'or de la Défense (Terre) de la République Française.

RALDA MORENO, Gen. Luis Miguel; Guatemalan army officer and politician; *Minister of National Defence;* b. 17 Jan. 1963, Guatemala City; ed Polytechnic School; 31 years of military service, fmr Col 5th Battalion, Brigade of Infantry, Commdr Engineering Battalion, Third Commdr, Second Commdr, Commdr Army Corps of Engineers –2017; Minister of Nat. Defence 2017–; Instructor, Polytechnic School, Adolfo V. Hall Inst., Superior Command of Educ. of Army; Legal Adviser Stabilization Mission of UN in Haiti (MINUSTAH); numerous awards received. *Address:* Ministry of National Defence, Antiguas Escuela Politécnica, Avda La Reforma 1-45, Zona 10, Guatemala City, Guatemala (office). *Telephone:* 2360-9966 (office). *Fax:* 2360-9919 (office). *E-mail:* dip@mindef.mil.gt (office). *Website:* www .mindef.mil.gt (office).

RALPH, Richard Peter, CMG, CVO, MSc (Hons); British diplomatist (retd) and consultant; *Director, Foro Consulting Ltd;* b. 27 April 1946, London, England; s. of Peter Ralph and Evelyn Marion Ralph; m. 1st Margaret Elisabeth Coulthurst 1970 (divorced 2001); one s. one d.; m. 2nd Jemma Victoria Elizabeth Marlor 2002; one d.; ed The King's School, Canterbury, Univ. of Edinburgh; served at Embassy in Vientiane, Laos 1970–73, Lisbon 1974–77, at FCO, London 1977–81, High Comm. to Zimbabwe 1981–84, Councillor, Embassy in Washington, DC 1989–93, Amb. to Latvia 1993–95, Gov. Falkland Islands 1996–99, concurrently Commr S Georgia and S Sandwich Islands, Amb. to Romania (also accred to Moldova) 1999–2002, to Peru 2003–06 (retd); Chair. Monterrico Metals plc 2006–08; Dir, British-Peruvian Infrastructure Devt Co. plc 2009–; Co-founder and Dir, Foro Consulting Ltd (Latin American business consultancy) 2010–; fmr Chair. Anglo-Peruvian Soc., South Georgia Asscn. *Leisure interests:* reading, int. relations, theatre, music, art, travel, tennis. *Address:* 29 Surrey Lane, Battersea, London, SW11 4PA, England (home). *Telephone:* (20) 7924-4188 (office). *E-mail:* r.ralph@foroconsulting.com (office); richardralph87@hotmail.com (home). *Website:* www.foroconsulting.com (office).

RALSTON, Gen. Joseph W.; American air force officer (retd); *Vice-Chairman, Cohen Group;* b. 4 Nov. 1943, Hopkinsville, Ky; m. Diane Dougherty; two s. two d.; ed Miami Univ., Ohio, Cen. Michigan Univ., Army Command and Gen. Staff Coll., Nat. War Coll., Harvard Univ.; mem. reserve officer training program USAF 1965; Vice-Chair. of Jt Chiefs of Staff 1996–2000; concurrently Chair. Jt Requirements Oversight Council, Planning, Programming and Budgeting Systems; Vice-Chair. Defense Acquisition Bd; mem. Nat. Security Council Deputies Comm., Nuclear Weapons Council; Supreme Allied Commdr, Europe 2000–03; C-in-C, US European Command 2000–03; Vice-Chair. Cohen Group 2003–; Dir Timken Co., URS Corpn; mem. Bd of Dirs Lockheed Martin; numerous mil. decorations including Defense Distinguished Service Medal (two awards), Distinguished Service Medal. *Address:* Cohen Group, 500 Eighth Street, NW, Suite 200, Washington, DC 20004, USA (office). *Telephone:* (202) 863-7200 (office). *E-mail:* jralston@cohengroup.net (office). *Website:* www.cohengroup.net (office).

RAMA, Edi Kristaq; Albanian politician and artist; *Prime Minister;* b. 4 July 1964, Tirana; s. of Kristaq Rama (sculptor) and Aneta Rama (née Koleka); m. 1st Matilda Makoci; one s.; m. 2nd Lindita Basha (aka Lindita Xhillari) 2010; two c.; ed Albanian Acad. of Arts, Tirana; player for Dinamo (basketball team) and Albanian nat. basketball team in early 1980s; Prof., Albanian Acad. of Arts; emigrated to France and lived as an artist 1994, returned to Albania 1998; Founding mem. Movt for Democracy 1996; Minister of Culture, Youth and Sports 1998–2000; Mayor of Tirana 2000–11; Prime Minister 2013–, also acting Minister of Foreign Affairs 2019–; mem. Partia Socialiste e Shqipërisë (Socialist Party of Albania) 2003–, Chair. 2005–; Robert C. Wood Visiting Prof. of Public and Urban Affairs, Univ. of Massachusetts, USA 2003; mem. Kuvendi Popullor (People's Ass.) for Vlorë 2017–; mem. Regional Advisory Bd of UNDP; Pres. Albanian Municipalities Asscn; fmr Bd mem. Open Society Foundation; Hon. Citizen of Ulcinj 2015; Commdr, Légion d'honneur 2017; UN Poverty Eradication Award 2002, World Mayor 2004, included in TIME magazine's European Heroes list 2005, Prize for Cultural Pluralism 2018. *Publications include:* Refleksione (with Ardian Klosi) 1991, Edi Rama 2009, Kurban 2011; numerous articles in Albanian and int. magazines and newspapers. *Address:* Office of the Prime Minister, Bulevardi Dëshmorët e Kombit 1, 1000 Tirana (office); Partia Socialiste e Shqipërisë (Socialist Party of Albania), Tirana, Albania (office). *Telephone:* (4) 2227409 (office). *Fax:* (4) 2227417 (office). *E-mail:* info@kryeministria.al (office); info@ps.al (office). *Website:* www .kryeministria.al (office); www.ps.al (office); www.facebook.com/edirama.al.

RAMACHANDRAN, Dato C(herubala) P(athayapurayil), MSc, DrMedSc, DAP&E, FIBiol; Malaysian medical scientist and academic; *Professor Emeritus, Universiti Sains Malaysia;* b. 3 June 1936, Kuala Lumpur; s. of KK Madhavan Nair and Kamalam M. Nair; m. Githa Priya Darshini 1966; one s. one d.; ed St John's Inst., Kuala Lumpur, Christian Coll., Madras, India, Univ. of London, UK, Univ. of Liverpool, UK, Tulane Univ., USA, Univ. of Tokyo, Japan; Wellcome Trust Research Scholar and Demonstrator in Medical Parasitology, Liverpool School of Tropical Medicine 1959–62, Research Fellow in Tropical Medicine, Inst. for Medical Research, Kuala Lumpur 1962–63, Head Filariasis Research Div. 1967–70; Asst Prof. in Medical Parasitology Faculty of Medicine, Univ. of Malaya, Kuala Lumpur 1963–67; Assoc. Prof. in Medical Parasitology and Head, School of Biological Sciences, Universiti Sains Malaysia, Penang 1970–72, Prof. and Dean 1972–79, now Prof. Emer.; Sr Scientist Human Resource Devt Tropical Disease Research WHO, Geneva, Switzerland 1979–87, Man. Research and Devt Filariasis Research Programme, Tropical Disease Research, WHO, Switzerland 1987–92; Chief Filariasis Research and Control, WHO, Geneva 1992–96, Chair., Programme Review Group, Pacific Island Countries, Global Programme to Eliminate Lymphatic Filariasis; Prof. of Clinical Parasitology, Universiti Putra, Malaysia 1996–2005; Adjunct Prof., Faculty of Medicine, Universiti Technologi MARA, Malaysia; Adjunct Prof., MAHSA Univ.; Visiting Prof., Faculty of Tropical Medicine, Mahidol Univ., Bangkok, Thailand; Pres. Int. Civil Service Asscn of Malaysia-Singapore and Brunei Darasalam; fmr Pres. Malaysian Soc. of Parasitology and Tropical Medicine, mem. Council, World Fed. of Parasitologists, Council; mem. Council and Vice-Pres. UN Asscn Malaysia; Fellow, Liverpool School of Tropical Medicine, UK, Malaysian Scientific Asscn, Acad. of Medicine (Malaysia), Australian Coll. of Tropical Medicine; Academician, Acad. of Sciences, Malaysia; Sandosham Medal (Malaysia) 1974, Mary Kingsley Medal for Tropical Medicine (UK) 1998, Darjah Setia Pangkuan Negeri (Malaysia) 1999, Johan Setia

Mahota (Malaysia), Gold Medal, Rotary Int., Life Time Achievement Award, Indian Council for Medical Research. *Publications:* numerous scientific papers in learned journals. *Leisure interests:* squash, photography, music. *Address:* Universiti Sains Malaysia, 11800 Gelugor, Penang (office); Apt-8A-4-4, Belvedere, off Jalan Tunku, Bukit Tunku, 50480 Kuala Lumpur, Malaysia (home). *Telephone:* 26987275 (home). *Fax:* 26986152 (home). *E-mail:* ramacp@hotmail.com (home). *Website:* www.usm.my (office).

RAMACHANDRAN, Vilayanur Subramanian, MD, PhD; Indian neuroscientist, psychologist, physician and academic; *Director, Center for Brain and Cognition and Professor Psychology Department and Neurosciences Program, University of California, San Diego;* b. 10 Aug. 1951, Madras; ed Stanley Medical Coll., Trinity Coll., Cambridge; currently Dir Center for Brain and Cognition, Prof. of Psychology, Dept and Neurosciences Program, Univ. of Calif., San Diego; Adjunct Prof. of Biology, Salk Inst.; Ed.-in-Chief Encyclopedia of Human Behavior; Fellow, Neurosciences Inst., La Jolla, Inst. for Advanced Studies in Behavioral Sciences, Stanford; lectures worldwide including BBC Reith Lectures 2003; Trustee, San Diego Museum of Art; mem. Nat. Acad. of Sciences (India); Visiting Prof., Stanford Univ., Harvard Univ. 2008, Columbia Univ.; Fellow, Stanford Univ., Neurosciences Inst., Calif., Athenaeum Club, London; Hon. Fellow, Royal Inst. of GB; Dr hc (Conn. Coll.); Gold Medal, ANU, Ariens Kappers Medal, Royal Netherlands Acad. of Sciences, Presidential Lecture Award, American Acad. of Neurology, Chancellor's Award for excellence in research, Univ. of Calif., Henry Dale Medal 2005, Padma Bhushan 2007, Ramony Cajal Award, Int. Neuropsychiatry Soc. *Publications:* Phantoms in the Brain (co-author) 1998, The Emerging Mind 2003, A Brief Tour of Human Consciousness: From Impostor Poodles to Purple Numbers 2005, The Tell-Tale Brain: A Neuroscientist's Quest for What Makes Us Human 2010; over 180 papers in scientific journals. *Address:* Center for Brain and Cognition, University of California, 9500 Gilman Drive, #0109, La Jolla, CA 92093-0109, USA (office). *Telephone:* (858) 534-6240 (office). *Fax:* (858) 534-7190 (office). *E-mail:* vramachandran@ucsd.edu (office). *Website:* www.ucsd.edu (office).

RAMADAN, Tariq, MA, PhD; Swiss academic; b. 26 Aug. 1962, Geneva; s. of Said Ramadan and Wafa al-Banna; m. Iman Ramadan 1986; ed Univ. of Geneva; fmr Prof. of Islamic Studies and Philosophy, Freiburg Univ.; Prof. of Islamic Studies and Luce Prof. of Religion, Conflict and Peacebuilding, Kroc Inst., Univ. of Notre Dame, USA Aug.–Dec. 2004 (visa revoked); Sr Research Fellow, Lokahi Foundation 2004–, Doshisha Univ., Kyoto 2007–; apptd Prof. of Contemporary Islamic Studies, St Antony's Coll., Oxford, UK 2004–17 (leave of absence post sexual misconduct allegations); Dir Research Center for Islamic Legislation and Ethics 2012–; arrested on charges of rape Feb. 2018; Visiting Prof., Mundiapolis Univ., Morocco, Univ. of Malaysia Perlis, Hamad Bin Khalifa Univ., Qatar; Guest Prof. of Citizenship and Identity, Erasmus Univ., Rotterdam, Netherlands 2007–09; mem. Int. Union of Muslim Scholars (IUMS) 2014–; Pres. Bd of Trustees, European Muslim Network, Brussels; One of the Seven Innovators of the 21st Century, Time magazine 2000, One of the 100 People of the Year 2004, European of the Year, European Voice 2006, The Muslim News Special Award for Excellence (Faith and Action) for academic and intellectual contrib. to Islamic thought 2007. *Publications:* Les Musulmans dans la Laïcité, responsabilités et droits des musulmans dans les sociétés occidentales 1994, Islam, le face à face des civilisations, Quel projet pour quelle modernité? 1995, To be a European Muslim 1999, Muslims in France: The Way Towards Coexistence 1999, Islam, the West, and the Challenges of Modernity 2001, Jihad, Violence, War and Peace in Islam (in French) 2002, Western Muslims and the Future of Islam 2004, Globalisation: Muslim Resistances 2004, Radical Reform, In the Footsteps of the Prophet 2007, Radical Ijtihad 2008, The Quest for Meaning: Developing a Philosophy of Pluralism 2010, Islam and the Arab Awakening 2012, De l'islam et des musulmans 2014, Introduction à l'éthique islamique 2015, Être occidental et musulman aujourd'hui 2015, Le génie de l'islam 2016, Islam: The Essentials 2017, Introduction to Islam 2017; contrib. of more than 850 articles, reviews and chapters in books and magazines. *Leisure interest:* literature. *Address:* St Antony's College, 62 Woodstock Road, Oxford, OX2 6JF, England (office); 39 rue de la boulangerie, 93200 Saint Denis, France (home). *Telephone:* (1865) 612302 (Oxford) (office); 1-49-22-01-12 (home). *Fax:* (1865) 612844 (office); 1-49-22-00-39 (home). *E-mail:* office@tariqramadan.com; tariq.ramadan@sant.ox.ac.uk (office). *Website:* www.tariqramadan.com.

RAMADHANI, Rt Rev. John Acland, BA; Tanzanian ecclesiastic (retd); b. 1 Aug. 1932, Zanzibar; s. of Augustine Ramadhani and Mary Majaliwa; ed Dar es Salaam Univ., Queen's Coll., Birmingham and Univ. of Birmingham, UK; Prin. St Andrew's Teacher Training Coll., Korogwe 1967–69; Warden, St Mark's Theological Coll., Dar es Salaam 1977–79; Bishop of Zanzibar and Tanga 1980–2000; Archbishop of the Prov. of Tanzania 1984–97; Bishop of Zanzibar 2001–02; Chair. Christian Council of Tanzania –2002; Patron Misufini Leprosy Centre. *Leisure interest:* reading. *Address:* c/o Anglican Church of Tanzania, Diocese of Zanzibar, PO Box 5, Mkunazini, Zanzibar, Tanzania. *Telephone:* 68-71131829 (mobile); (24) 2231510. *E-mail:* zanjohnramadhani@gmail.com.

RAMADORAI, Subramaniam, CBE, BSc, BEng, MSc; Indian business executive; b. 6 Oct. 1944, Nagpur; m. Mala Ramadorai; ed Univ. of Delhi, Indian Inst. of Science, Bangalore, Univ. of California and Massachusetts Inst. of Tech., USA; jr engineer, Tata Consultancy Services (TCS) 1972, later set up TCS's operations in New York 1979, CEO and Man. Dir TCS 1996–2009, Vice-Chair. –2014; apptd Adviser to Prime Minister for the Nat. Skill Devt Council 2011; Chair. Tata Technologies Ltd, TATA Elxsi (India) Ltd, Computational Research Laboratories Ltd, CMC Ltd; Ind. Dir (non-exec.) Hindustan Lever Ltd 2002–; mem. Bd of Dirs Nicholas Piramal, TATA Ltd (India), TATA Infotech Ltd (India), TATA Internet Services Ltd, Nelito Systems Ltd; IT Adviser to Qingdao City and Hangzhou City, People's Repub. of China; Fellow, Inst. of Electrical and Electronics Engineers, Indian Nat. Acad. of Engineers; Vice-Chair. Nat. Asscn of Software Cos; apptd Chair. AirAsia India 2013; mem. Nat. Council of the Confed. of Indian Industry, Corp. Advisory Bd, Marshall School of Business; Dr hc (Anna Univ., Tamil Nadu) 2004, Hon. DrSc (Sastra Univ.) 2006; Asia Business Leader of the Year Award, Hong Kong 2002, Business India Businessman of the Year 2004, UK Trade and Investment Special Recognition Award 2005, Padma Bhushan 2006, Int. CEO of the Year, LT Bravo Business Awards 2008, Nayudamma Award 2008.

RAMADOSS, Anbumani, MD; Indian physician and politician; b. 9 Oct. 1968, Puducherry; s. of S. Ramadoss and Shrimati R. Saraswathi; m. Sowmiya Anbumani 1991; three d.; ed Madras Medical Coll., London School of Econs, UK; fmr medical practitioner, Tamil Nadu; Leader, Pattali Makkal Katchi; mem. Rajya Sabha (Parl.) 2004–10, Lok Sabha 2014–; Minister of Health and Family Welfare 2004–09 (resgnd); Co-f. Nat. Rural Health Mission 2005; Pres. Pasumai Thayagam (Green Mother Land); unsuccessful cand. for Tamil Nadu Legis. Ass. 2016; Luther L. Terry Award, American Cancer Soc. 2006. *Address:* 30/34, 4th Cross St, Kasturibai Nagar, Raja Anamalai Puram, Chennai 600 028, India (home).

RAMAHATRA, Maj.-Gen. (retd) Victor; Malagasy international business strategy consultant, fmr politician and fmr army officer; b. 6 Sept. 1945, Antananarivo; s. of Pierre Longin Ramahatra and Marie Lucile Ratsimandresy; m. Nivonirina Rajoelson 1971 (deceased); two s. one d.; ed Saint-Cyr Mil. Acad. and Ecole Supérieure du Génie Militaire, France; officer in Corps of Engineers 1967; mil. engineer 1972; Minister of Public Work 1982–87; Prime Minister of Malagasy Repub. 1987–91; man. locust plague control campaign 1998–2000; Special Adviser to Pres. of Malagasy Repub. in econs and int. affairs 1997–2001; Int. Business Consultant and mem. Bd Vision Madagascar (VIMA) Group 2009, HFF Group; Adviser, UBP Group (Mauritius), Bd Adviser 2005; mem. Supervisory Bd Henri Fraise Fils Group 2010; mem. Asscn des Ingénieurs Diplômés de l'Ecole Supérieure du Génie Militaire d'Angers, Asscn des Anciens Elèves de Saint-Cyr (Madagascar), Asscn des Anciens de Saint-Cyr dans la Vie Civile (France); mem. Supervisory Bd Henri fraise Holding (Madagascar), Bd mem., Vision Madagascar Group; Adviser, United basalt Products group of Mauritius; Grand-Croix, Ordre nat. du Mérite 1990, Officier, Légion d'honneur 2000, Grand Officier de l'Ordre nat. (Madagascar) 2000. *Leisure interests:* reading, march/walking, swimming. *Address:* VR. 104P, Fenomanana, 101 Antananarivo (home); PO Box 6004, 101 Antananarivo, Madagascar. *Telephone:* (202) 223767 (home); 33-18147 (mobile). *Fax:* (202) 2453088 (office). *E-mail:* ramfan@moov.mg (home).

RAMAKRISHNAN, T. V., BSc, MSc, PhD; Indian physicist and academic; *Distinguished Associate, Centre for Condensed Matter Theory, Department of Physics,, Indian Institute of Science;* b. 14 Aug. 1941, Madras (now Chennai); s. of T. R. Venkatachala Murti and Jayalakshmi Murti; m. Meera Rao; one s. one d.; ed Banaras Hindu Univ., Columbia Univ., USA; CSIR Junior Research Fellow, Banaras Hindu Univ., Varanasi 1961–62; Lecturer in Physics, Indian Inst. of Tech. (IIT), Kanpur 1966–67, Asst Prof. 1967, 1970–77, Prof., 1977–80; Asst Research Physicist, Univ. of California, San Diego, USA 1968–70; Consultant, Bell Laboratories, Murray Hill, NJ 1980–81, 1990–91; Coordinator, Research Programme on Disorder, Inst. for Theoretical Physics, Univ. of Calif., Santa Barbara 1983; Prof. of Physics, Banaras Hindu Univ., Varanasi 1984–86, DAE Homi Bhabha Prof. 2003–08, Prof. Emer. 2006–; TIFR-NCBS Distinguished Research Prof. 2012–13; Visiting Prof., Dept of Physics, Indian Inst. of Science, Bangalore 1981–84, Prof. of Physics 1986–2003, Distinguished Assoc., Centre for Condensed Matter Theory 2003–; INSA Srinivasa Ramanujan Research Prof. 1997–2002; Visiting Fellow, Princeton Univ., USA 1978–81, Visiting Prof. and Visiting Research Physicist 1990–91; Rothschild Visiting Prof., Isaac Newton Inst. for Math. Sciences, Univ. of Cambridge, UK 2000, Visiting Fellow Commoner, Trinity Coll. and Visiting Prof. 2004; Pres. Indian Acad. of Sciences 2004–06; Vice-Pres. Indian Nat. Science Acad. 2000–03; Distinguished Lifetime Prof., Univ. of Mysore 2013–; Fellow, Indian Acad. of Sciences (Bangalore) 1980, Indian Nat. Science Acad. (New Delhi) 1984, American Physical Soc. 1984, Third World Acad. of Sciences (Trieste, Italy) 1991, Nat. Acad. of Sciences, Allahabad 1993, Royal Soc., London 2000, Inst. of Physics (UK) 2000; Foreign Assoc., Acad. of Sciences, Paris 2005; mem. Indian Asscn for Cultivation of Science, Kolkata 2004–, Science Advisory Council to the Prime Minister 2005–; mem. Union of Concerned Scientists (USA) 1994–; Hon. Prof., Jawaharlal Nehru Centre for Advanced Scientific Research, Bangalore 1993–, Hon. Fellow, TIFR, Mumbai 2004–, Hon. Distinguished Prof., IIT Kanpur 2004–; Hon. Assoc., Tata Inst. of Fundamental Research, Mumbai; Padma Shri 2001; Dr hc (Banaras Hindu Univ.) 2004; numerous awards including Devasthale Prize in Physics 1959, Shanti Swarup Bhatnagar Award for Physical Sciences, CSIR 1982, Third World Acad. of Sciences Award in Physics 1990, Jawaharlal Nehru Award for Science, MP Council for Science and Technology 1999, C.V. Raman Centenary Medal, Indian Science Congress 2001, Meghnad Saha Medal, Asiatic Soc. 2002, Distinguished Materials Scientist of the Year, Materials Research Soc. of India 2004, Goyal Prize in Physics, Kurukshetra 2004, Trieste Science Prize 2005, G.M. Modi Award 2008, H.K. Firodia Award 2012, Hari Om Ashram Prerit Senior Scientist Award 2014, G N Ramachandran Award in Physics 2016. *Address:* Department of Physics, Indian Institute of Science, Bangalore 560 012, India (office). *Telephone:* (80) 23600228 (office). *Fax:* (80) 23602602 (office). *E-mail:* tvrama@physics.iisc.ernet.in (office); tvrama2002@yahoo.co.in (office). *Website:* www.physics.iisc.ernet.in (office).

RAMAKRISHNAN, Sir Venkatraman, Kt, BSc, PhD, FRS; American/British (b. Indian) biologist and academic; *Deputy Director, MRC Laboratory of Molecular Biology, University of Cambridge;* b. 1952, Chidambaram, Tamil Nadu, India; ed Maharaja Sayajirao Univ., Baroda, India, Ohio Univ., Univ. of California, San Diego; Postdoctoral Fellow, Dept of Chem., Yale Univ. 1978–82; mem. Research Staff, Oak Ridge Nat. Lab. 1982–83; Asst Biophysicist, Biology Dept, Brookhaven Nat. Lab. 1983–85, Assoc. Biophysicist 1985–88, Biophysicist 1988–90, Biophysicist with tenure 1990–94, Sr Biophysicist 1994–95; Visiting Scientist, MRC Lab. of Molecular Biology, Cambridge, UK 1991–92, Sr Scientist and Group Leader, Structural Studies Div. 1999–, Deputy Dir 2013–, Sr Research Fellow, Trinity Coll., Cambridge 2008–, Fellow, Trinity Coll. 2008–; Prof., Biochemistry Dept, Univ. of Utah, also Faculty mem., Grad. Programs in Biological Chem. and Molecular Biology 1995–99; Pres. Royal Soc. 2015–; mem. Scientific Advisory Cttee, EMBL 2002–06, IMP, Vienna 2008–; mem. Scientific Advisory Bd Rib-X Pharmaceuticals, New Haven, Conn., USA; mem. European Molecular Biology Org. 2002, European Molecular Biology Org. (EMBO) 2002, NAS 2004, Leopoldina 2010; Foreign mem., Indian Nat. Science Acad. 2008; Rolf-Sammet Professorship, Univ. of Frankfurt 2009; Guggenheim Fellowship 1991–92, Datta Medal and Lecture, FEBS annual meeting, Vienna 2007, Louis Jeantet Prize for Medicine 2007, Heatley Medal, British Biochemical Soc. 2008, Nobel Prize in Chem. (with Thomas A. Steitz and Ada E. Yonath) 2009, Sir Hans Krebs Medal 2012, Jimenez Díaz Prize Lecturer 2014. *Address:* Structural Studies Division, MRC Laboratory of Molecular Biology, Hills Road, Cambridge, CB2 0QH, England (office).

Telephone: (1223) 402213 (office); (1223) 248011 (office). *Fax:* (1223) 213556 (office). *E-mail:* ramak@mrc-lmb.cam.ac.uk (office). *Website:* www.mrc-lmb.cam.ac.uk/ribo/homepage/ramak/index.html (office); royalsociety.org.

RAMALHO, Ivan, PhD; Brazilian economist and international organization official; *Executive Secretary, Ministry of Development, Industry and Foreign Trade;* Head of Dept, Banco do Brasil (Cacex) 1973–2003; Sec. of Foreign Trade, Ministry of Devt, Industry and Foreign Trade 2003–06, Exec. Sec. 2006–10, 2015–; Pres. Brazilian Foreign Trade Asscn 2011–12; High Rep. Mercosur 2012–15; mem. Bd of Dirs BNDES Participações SA (BNDESPar); mem. Brazilian Foreign Trade Chamber, Foundation Council, Centre for the Study of Foreign Trade (Funcex); served as Pres. Exports Guarantee and Finance Cttee, Orientation Council of Devt Nat. Fund; fmr Dir Dept of Foreign Trade Operations (Decex), served as coordinator of technical group responsible for devt and implementation of Integrated Foreign Trade System (Siscomex). *Address:* Ministry of Development, Industry and Foreign Trade, Esplanada dos Ministérios, Bloco J, Brasília, DF, 70053-900, Brazil (office). *Telephone:* (61) 2027-7000 (office). *Website:* www.mdic.gov.br (office).

RAMANATHAN, Veerabhadran (Ram), BE, MSc, PhD; American (b. Indian) scientist and academic; *Victor Alderson Professor of Applied Ocean Sciences and Distinguished Professor of Climate and Atmospheric Sciences, University of California, San Diego;* b. 24 Nov. 1944, Madras, India; m. Girija (Giri) Ramanathan; one s. two d.; ed Annamalai Univ., Indian Inst. of Science, State Univ. of New York (SUNY) at Stony Brook (Planetary Atmospheres); engineer, Shri Ram Refrigeration Industries, Secunderabad, India 1965–67; Nat. Research Council Post Doctoral Fellow, NASA Langley Research Center and George Washington Univ., Hampton, Va 1975–76; Scientist, Nat. Center for Atmospheric Research (NCAR), Boulder, Colo 1976–82; Prin. Investigator, NASA Earth Radiation Budget Experiment 1979–; Sr Scientist, Nat. Center for Atmospheric Research (NCAR), Boulder, Colo 1982–86; Affiliate Prof., Colorado State Univ., Fort Collins 1985–88; Visiting Prof., Université Catholique de Louvain, Belgium 1985–88; Prof., Dept of Geophysical Sciences, Univ. of Chicago, Ill. 1986–90; Victor C. Alderson Prof. of Applied Ocean Sciences, and Prof. of Climate and Atmospheric Sciences, Scripps Inst. of Oceanography, Univ. of California, San Diego 1990–, Dir Center for Clouds, Chem. and Climate 1991–, Dir Center for Atmospheric Sciences 1996–, Distinguished Prof. of Atmospheric and Climate Sciences 2004–; mem. Bd of Dirs Tata Energy Research Inst., Arlington, Va 1992–; Chief Scientist, Cen. Equatorial Pacific Experiment (CEPEX) 1993; Co-Chief Scientist, Indian Ocean Experiment (INDOEX) 1996–2002, Chair. Int. Steering Cttee 1996–2002; First K.R. Ramanathan Visiting Prof., Physical Research Lab., India 1998; Chair. US Climate Change Science Program 2006–; mem. Science Editorial Bd NASA Earth Observatory 1999–, Atmospheric Brown Cloud Project (ABC) 2002– (Chair. 2005–), Geophysical Inst. Review Panel for Atmospheric Sciences 2002–, Advisory Bd World Clean Air Congress 2005–, NCAR Earth Observing Lab. External Advisory Cttee 2005–, Strategic Advisory Bd, Inst. for Advanced Sustainability Studies, Potsdam, Germany, US Climate Change Science Program 2011–; mem. Royal Swedish Acad. of Sciences 2011; numerous awards, including NASA Special Achievement Award 1975, NCAR Outstanding Publication Award 1981, Distinguished Alumnus Award, SUNY 1984, NASA Medal for Exceptional Scientific Achievement 1989, Buys Ballot Medal, Royal Netherlands Acad. of Sciences 1995, Volvo Environment Prize (co-recipient) 1997, elected to Stonybrook 40, SUNY 1998, W.S. Jardetzky Lecturer, Lamont Doherty Observatory, Columbia Univ. 2000, Rossby Medal, American Meteorological Soc. 2002, NSF Pioneer Award 2003, Johannes Gutenberg Lecturer 2004, Cozzarelli Prize 2007, Zayed Int. Prize for the Environment, Category II: Scientific/Technological Achievements in Environment, H.H. Sheikh Mohammad Bin Rashid Al Maktoum (co-recipient) 2007, Henry W. Kendall Memorial Lecturer, MIT 2008, Tyler Prize for Environmental Achievement, Univ. of Southern California (co-recipient) 2009, Tang Prize in Sustainable Devt (co-recipient) 2018. *Publications:* numerous scientific papers in professional journals on mitigation of climate change, climate dynamics, the greenhouse effect, air pollution, clouds, aerosols, satellite radiation measurements and global climate models. *Address:* Center for Clouds, Chemistry and Climate, Scripps Institution of Oceanography, University of California, San Diego, 9500 Gilman Drive, MC 0221, La Jolla, CA 92093-0221, USA (office). *Telephone:* (858) 534-8815 (office). *Fax:* (858) 822-5607 (office). *E-mail:* vram@ucsd.edu (office). *Website:* www-ramanathan.ucsd.edu (office).

RAMANDIMBIARISON, Zaza Manitranja; Malagasy politician and engineer; b. 12 Dec. 1953, Ambatosoratra; s. of André Ramandimbiarison and Delphine Razanamanarivo; m.; one s. two d.; ed France and USA; Sr Engineer, Africa Transport Dept, World Bank 1998–2002; Deputy Prime Minister in charge of Econ. Programmes, Minister of Transport, Public Works and Regional Planning 2002–07; fmr Chief of Staff, High Transitional Authority of Madagascar; Program Manager, Sub-Saharan African Transport Policy Program 2006–08; self-employed devt consultant 2009–. *Leisure interests:* tennis, football, reading. *Address:* Villa Manarivo, Lot MC, 1209 Mandrosoa, Ivato, 105 Antananarivo, Madagascar (home). *Telephone:* (20) 22-455-77 (home).

RAMAPHOSA, (Matamela) Cyril, BProc; South African business executive, politician and head of state; *President;* b. 17 Nov. 1952, Johannesburg; s. of Samuel Ramaphosa and Erdmuth Ramaphosa; m. Tshepo Motsepe; two s. two d.; ed Sekano-Ntoane High School, Soweto, Univ. of Turfloop and Univ. of S Africa; Chair. Univ. br. S African Students' Org. 1974; imprisoned under Section Six of Terrorism Act for 11 months, then for 6 months in 1976; returned to law studies and qualified 1981; apptd legal adviser, Council of Unions of S Africa; Gen. Sec. Nat. Union of Mineworkers 1982–91; Sec.-Gen. African National Congress (ANC) 1991–96, Deputy Pres. 2012–17, Pres. 2017–; Deputy Pres. of S Africa 2014–18, Pres. 2018–; apptd Leader of Govt Business in Nat. Ass. 2014; Chair. Nat. Planning Comm. 2014–15; Deputy Visiting Prof. of Law, Stanford Univ. 1991; mem. Parl. 1994–96; Chair. of Constitutional Ass. 1994–96; Weapons Inspector N Ireland 2000; Exec. Chair. New Africa Investments Ltd 1996–99; with Nat. Empowerment Consortium 1996–; Chair. and CEO Molope Group 1999–2000; Chair. Rebserve Ltd 2000–03; Chair. Millennium Consolidated Investments (MCI) 2003; currently Exec. Chair. Shanduka Group; Dr hc (Univs of Natal, Port Elizabeth, Mass., Cape Town, Lesotho, Galway, Ireland); Olaf Palme Prize (Sweden) 1987. *Address:* The Presidency, Union Bldgs, West Wing, Government Ave, Pretoria 0001, South Africa (office). *Telephone:* (12) 3005200 (office). *Fax:* (12) 3238246 (office). *E-mail:* president@presidency.gov.za. *Website:* www.thepresidency.gov.za (office).

RAMAROSON, Vice-Adm. Hyppolite Rarison; Malagasy naval officer and politician; b. 28 Sept. 1951, Antananarivo; m.; three c.; ed Collège Saint Michel, Institution Sainte Famille, Académie Militaire, Antsirabe, Ecole Navale de Brest, France, Ecole supérieure de guerre navale, Paris, France; naval officer, responsibilities include fmr Coast Guard Officer, Fanantenana, Commdr, Antsiranana Naval Base, Head of Int. Relations, Ministry of Nat. Defence, Dir of Cabinet, Ministry of Nat. Defence; took part in NATO jt operations; apptd Pres. of Madagascar for one day 17 March 2009; Deputy Prime Minister and Minister of Foreign Affairs 2010–11 (resgnd).

RAMATHLODI, Ngoako, LLB, MSc; South African politician; b. 21 Aug. 1955, Potgietersrus (Tauatswala); m. Mathuding Ouma Ramatlhodi; one s. one d.; fmr Chair. African Nat. Congress (ANC), Northern Prov.; Deputy Registrar (student affairs), Exec. Asst to Vice-Chancellor Univ. of the N; in exile 1979, Commdr Unkhonto weSizwe; Head Political and Mil. ANC Council, Zimbabwe 1986; Political Sec., Asst to Oliver Tambo and Nelson Mandela 1988–91; Premier of Northern Prov. 1994–2002, of Limpopo Prov. 2002–04; Deputy Minister of Correctional Services 2010–14; Minister of Public Service and Admin 2015–17; mem. ANC Nat. Exec. Cttee 2007–; Hon. LLD (Univ. of the North, Limpopo). *Publications:* History of the ANC, Charade of Social Emanicipation and National Liberation, Ethnicity: How The ANC Must Govern. *Leisure interests:* music, reading, writing. *Address:* c/o National Executive Committee, African National Congress, PO Box 61884, Marshalltown 2107, South Africa (office). *Website:* www.anc.org.za (office).

RAMATOV, Achilbay; Uzbekistani railway engineer and government official; *First Deputy Prime Minister, responsible for Integrated Regional Development, Municipal Services, Transport, Capital Works and the Construction Industry;* b. 1962, Shavat Dist, Xorazm Violyat, Uzbek SSR, USSR; m.; three d.; ed Tashkent Inst. of Railway Transport Engineers; began career as asst locomotive driver, Urgench city locomotive depot 1980; graduated 1988; worked as a foreman, Deputy Chief of Locomotive Div. and Chief of Repair Shop, Tashkent locomotive repair plant 1988–95; Dir Gen. UE UzJelDorRemMash 1995–2001; Gen. Man. and Chief Engineer, O'zbekiston Temir Yo'llari (Uzbekistan State Railway Co.) 2001–02, Chair. 2002–; First Deputy Prime Minister, responsible for Integrated Regional Devt, Municipal Services, Transport, Capital Works and the Construction Industry 2016–; Honoured Industry Worker of Repub. of Uzbekistan 2000, Order Fidorkorona Hizmatlari Uchun (For Selfless Service) 2007, Order El-yurt Hurmati (Respect of Motherland) 2011, O'zbekiston Kahramoni (Hero of Uzbekistan) 2013. *Address:* Office of the Cabinet of Ministers, 100078 Tashkent, Mustaqillik maydoni 5, Uzbekistan (office). *Telephone:* (71) 239-86-76 (office). *Fax:* (71) 239-84-63 (office). *Website:* www.gov.uz (office).

RAMBARRAN, Jwala, BSc; Trinidad and Tobago economist and fmr central banker; b. 1967; ed Univ. of the West Indies, Univ. of London, UK, Kennedy School of Govt, Harvard Univ., USA, IMF Inst., Washington, DC, Fed. Reserve Bank of New York; Research Asst, Dept of Econs, Univ. of the West Indies 1989–90; Economist, Research Dept, Cen. Bank of Trinidad and Tobago 1990–98, Economist/Man., Money and Finance Unit, Research Dept 1998–2001, Sr Economist, Monetary and Financial Policy 2003–04, Gov. and Chair. Bd of Dirs 2012–15; Asst to Exec. Dir, IMF 2001–03; Chief Economist, Caribbean Money Market Brokers 2004–07; f. own business, Cap-M Research; CEO Infinity Financial Eng 2010; Chair. Bd of Govs Nat. Inst. of Higher Educ., Research, Science and Tech., Trinidad 2010–12; apptd mem. Bd of Dirs NOVO Technology 2010; apptd mem. Latin American and Caribbean Econs Asscn 2010, Nat. Comm. for Higher Educ. 2011, mem. World Future Soc., McKinsey Online Quarterly Panel.

RAMBAUD, Patrick; French writer; b. 21 April 1946, Paris; s. of François Rambaud and Madeleine de Magondeau; m. Pham-thi Tieu Hong 1988; mil. service with French AF 1968–69; co-f. Actual magazine 1970–84; mem. Acad. Goncourt 2008–. *Plays:* Fregoli (with Bernard Haller) (Théâtre nat. de Chaillot 1991. *Publications include:* La Saignée 1970, Les Aventures communautaires de Wao-le-Laid (with Michel-Antoine Burnier) 1973, Les Complots de la liberté: 1832 (with Michel-Antoine Burnier) (Prix Alexandre Dumas 1976) 1976, Parodies (with Michel-Antoine Burnier) 1977, 1848 (with Michel-Antoine Burnier) (Prix Lamartine 1981) 1977, Le Roland Barthes sans peine (with Michel-Antoine Burnier) 1978, Comme des rats 1980, La Farce des choses et autres parodies (with Michel-Antoine Burnier) 1982, Fric-Frac 1984, La Mort d'un ministre 1985, Frontière suisse (with Jean-Marie Stoerkel) 1986, Comment se tuer sans en avoir l'air 1987, Virginie Q (Prix de l'Insolent 1988) 1988, Le Visage parle (with Bernard Haller) 1988, Bernard Pivot reçoit... 1989, Le Dernier voyage de San Marco 1990, Ubu Président ou L'Imposteur 1990, Les Carnets secrets d'Elena Ceaucescu (with Francis Szpiner) 1990, Les Mirobolantes aventures de Frégoli 1991, Mururoa mon amour 1996, Le Gros secret 1996, Oraisons funèbres des dignitaires politiques qui ont fait leur temps et feignent de l'ignorer (with André Balland) 1996, La Bataille (Grand Prix du Roman de l'Acad. française 1997, Prix Goncourt 1997, Napoleonic Soc. of America Literary Award 2000) 1997, Le Journalisme sans peine (with Michel-Antoine Burnier) 1997, Les Aventures de Mai 1998, Il neigeait (Prix Ciné-Roman 2001) 2000, L'Absent 2003, L'Idiot du village (Prix de la dédicace sonore 2005, Prix Rabelais 2005) 2004, Le Chat botté 2006, La Grammaire en s'amusant 2007, Chronique du règne de Nicolas I 2008, Deuxième Chronique du règne de Nicolas I 2009, Troisième Chronique du règne de Nicolas I 2010, Quatrième Chronique du règne de Nicolas I 2011, Cinquième Chronique du règne de Nicolas I 2012, Tombeau de Nicolas I et avènement de François IV 2013, Le Maître (Grand Prix Palatine du roman historique 2015, Prix Montblanc du Salon du livre de Genève 2015) 2015, François, le Petit, chronique du règne 2016. *Leisure interests:* writing, cooking, walking. *Address:* c/o Editions Grasset, 61 rue des Saints-Pères, 75006 Paris, France. *Telephone:* (06) 03-97-72-52 (home).

RAMDEV, Baba; Indian yoga teacher; b. (Ram Krishna Yadav), 25 Dec. 1965, Ali Saiyad Pur, Mahendragarh dist, Haryana; s. of Ram Nivas Yadav and Gulabo Devi; ed Aarsh (Arya) Gurukul, Gurukul Kangri Vishwavidyalaya; f. Patanjali Yogpeeth 2006, Divya Yog Mandir Trust, Patanjali Ayurved Coll., Patanjali Chikitsalaya, Yog Gram, Go-Shala, Patanjali Herbal Botanical Garden, Organic

Agriculture Farm, Patanjali Food and Herbal Park Ltd; conducts yoga training camps in India and abroad; Host, Divya Yog on Aastha TV; Dr hc (Kalinga Inst. of Industrial Tech., Bhubaneswar) 2007, (Amity Univ.) 2010, (Dr D. Y. Patil Deemed Univ.) 2010; Sri Chandrashekharendra Saraswati Nat. Eminence Award 2011. *Address:* Patanjali Yogpeeth, Maharshi Dayanand Gram, Delhi-Haridwar National Highway, Near Bahadarbad, Haridwar 249 405, India (office). *Telephone:* (13) 34240008 (office). *Fax:* (13) 34244805 (office). *E-mail:* divyayoga@divyayoga .com (office). *Website:* www.divyayoga.com (office).

RAMDIN, Albert R.; Suriname diplomatist and international organization executive; *Assistant Secretary-General, Organization of American States (OAS);* b. 27 Feb. 1958; m. Charmaine Baksh; one s. one d.; ed schools in Paramaribo and the Netherlands, Univ. of Amsterdam and Free Univ.; career diplomat in public service at nat. and int. level, served as Sr Adviser to Minister of Trade and Industry; worked for two years in pvt. sector before returning to public service; apptd Adviser to Minister of Foreign Affairs and Minister of Finance; Amb. and Perm. Rep. to OAS, Washington, DC 1997, Chair. Perm. Council Jan.–March 1998, Inter-American Council for Integral Devt 1999, co-ordinated Caribbean Community (CARICOM) Ambs' Caucus during Suriname's chairmanship of sub-regional group; apptd to serve concurrently as non-resident Amb. to Costa Rica 1999; Asst Sec.-Gen. for Foreign and Community Relations, CARICOM Secr. 1999; served as Amb. at Large and Special Adviser to Govt of Suriname on Western Hemispheric Affairs –2005; Adviser to OAS Sec.-Gen. with special attention to the Caribbean 2001–05, Asst Sec.-Gen. OAS 2005–. *Address:* Organization of American States, 17th Street and Constitution Avenue NW, Washington, DC 20006-4499, USA (office). *Telephone:* (202) 370-5000 (switchboard) (office). *Fax:* (202) 458-3967 (office). *E-mail:* pi@oas.org (office); oasweb@oas.org (office). *Website:* www.oas.org (office).

RAMDORAI, Sujatha, BSc, MSc, PhD; Indian mathematician and academic; *Canada Research Chair, University of British Columbia;* b. 23 May 1962, Bangalore; d. of Parthasarathy Rangarajan and Shrimati Rangarajan; m. Srinivasan Ramdorai; one d.; ed St Joseph's Coll., Bangalore, Annamalai Univ. and Tata Inst. of Fundamental Research; Research Fellow, Univ. of Regensburg, Germany 1992–93, Ohio State Univ., USA 1993–95; Assoc. Prof., Indian Acad. of Sciences 1994–97; Assoc. Prof. of Math., Tata Inst. of Fundamental Research 2000–06, apptd Prof. of Math. 2006; Vaidyanathaswamy Visiting Chair Prof., Chennai Mathematical Inst. 2008–11; Canada Research Chair, Univ. of British Columbia, Vancouver 2010–; Adjunct Prof., Indian Inst. of Science Education and Research, Pune; mem. Nat. Knowledge Comm. 2007–09, Prime Minister's Scientific Advisory Council 2009–; Alexander von Humboldt Fellow 1997–98; Man. Ed. International Journal of Number Theory; Ed. Journal of Ramanujan Mathematical Soc.; Assoc. Ed. Expositiones Mathematicae; mem. Nat. Innovation Council; Fellow, Indian Acad. of Sciences 2003; Young Scientist Award 1993, Shanti Swarup Bhatnagar Prize, Council of Scientific & Industrial Research 2004, Ramanujan Prize, Int. Centre for Theoretical Physics 2006. *Leisure interests:* education, research. *Address:* Mathematics Department, 1984 Mathematics Road, University of British Columbia, Vancouver, BC V6T 1Z2, Canada (office). *Telephone:* (604) 822-3627 (office). *E-mail:* sujatha@math.ubc.ca (office). *Website:* www.math.ubc.ca/~sujatha (office).

RAMESH, Shri Jairam; Indian politician; b. 9 April 1954, Chikmagalur, Karnataka; s. of C. K. Ramesh and Shrimati Sridevi Rameshat; m. K. R. Jayashree; two s.; ed Indian Inst. of Tech., Mumbai, Carnegie Mellon Univ., Massachusetts Inst. of Tech., USA; Adviser to Prime Minister 1991, to Deputy Chair., Planning Comm. 1992–94, to Finance Minister 1996–98; mem. Rajasthan Devt Council 1999–2003; Deputy Chair. Karnataka Planning Bd 2000–02; Econ. Adviser to govt of Chattisgarh 2001–03; elected mem. Rajya Sabha (Council of States) for Andhra Pradesh constituency 2004, for Karnataka constituency 2016–; Minister of State for Commerce and Industry 2006–09, for Power 2008–09, for Environment and Forests 2009–11; Minister of Rural Devt and of Panchayati Raj 2011–14; chief negotiator for India at UN Climate Change Conf., Copenhagen, Denmark 2009; mem. Nat. Advisory Council; Founding mem. Indian School of Business, Hyderabad; mem. Indian Nat. Congress party; Hon. Fellow, Inst. of Chinese Studies, New Delhi 2002–; Distinguished Alumnus Award, Indian Inst. of Tech., Mumbai 2001. *Publications:* Kautilya Today 2002, Making Sense of Chindia 2006. *Address:* Rajya Sabha, Parliament House Annexe, New Delhi 110 001 (office); H.No.6-3-862/3, Khairatabad, Hyderabad, India (home). *Telephone:* (11) 24635888 (office). *E-mail:* jairam@sansad.nic.in (office); jairam@jairam-ramesh .com. *Website:* rajyasabha.nic.in (office); www.jairamramesh.in.

RAMGOOLAM, Hon. Navinchandra, LLB, LRCP; Mauritian physician, barrister and politician; b. 14 July 1947, Mauritius; s. of Sir Seewoosagur Ramgoolam (first Prime Minister of Mauritius) and Lady Sushil Ramgoolam; m. Veena Ramgoolam 1979; ed Royal Coll. of Surgeons, Dublin, Ireland, London School of Econs and Inns of Court School of Law, London, UK; called to the Bar, Inner Temple 1993; Leader, Mauritius Labour Party (MLP) 1991–, Pres. 1991–92; Leader of Opposition and mem. Nat. Ass. 1991–95, 2000–05; Prime Minister 1995–2000, also Minister of Defence and Home Affairs, External Communications; Prime Minister 2005–14, also Minister of Defence and Home Affairs, of Defence, Home Affairs and External Communications 2010–14; acting Minister of Foreign Affairs 2008; mem. Int. Advisory Bd Center for Int. Devt, Harvard Univ. 1999–; Licentiate, Royal Coll. of Surgeons in Ireland; Hon. Fellow, London School of Econs 1998; Dr hc (Mauritius) 1998, (Aligarh Muslim Univ.) 1998, (Jawaharlal Nehru Univ.) 2005. *Leisure interests:* reading, music, water skiing, chess.

RAMÍREZ ACUÑA, Francisco Javier; Mexican politician; b. 22 April 1952, Jamay, Jalisco; m. María de la Paz Verduzco; two s. two d.; ed Universidad de Guadalajara; joined Partido Accíon Nacional (PAN) 1969; Congressional Deputy for Jalisco State 1974–77, 1980–83; Local Rep. to Municipal Pres. of Zapopan 1983–85; Dir-Gen. Sistecozome (public transport system of Jalisco) 1995–97; Mayor of Guadalajara 1998–2000; Gov. of Jalisco 2001–06; Sec. of the Interior 2006–08 (resgnd). *Address:* Partido Accíon Nacional, Avda Coyoacán 1546, Col. del Valle, Juárez 03100, Mexico (office). *Telephone:* (55) 5200-4000 (office). *E-mail:* correo@cen.pan.org.mx (office). *Website:* www.pan.org.mx (office).

RAMÍREZ CARREÑO, Rafael Dario; Venezuelan engineer and politician; b. 4 Aug. 1963, Pampán; m. Beatrice Sansó de Ramírez; ed Universidad de los Andes, Universidad Central de Venezuela; Founding Pres. Ente Nacional del Gas (gas watchdog and regulatory agency) 2000–02; mem. Bd of Dirs Petróleos de Venezuela, SA (state-owned petroleum co.) 2002, Pres. 2004–14; Minister of Petroleum and Mining 2002–14, Minister Plenipotentiary of Economy for E Region 2014, Minister of Foreign Affairs Sept.–Dec. 2014, also Vice-Pres., Council of Ministers 2014; Perm. Rep. to UN, Geneva 2014–17; Sr Coordinator, Nat. Authority for Housing and Habitat 2011–12; Chair. Simón Bolívar Fund 2012; mem. Exec. Bd, Nat. Devt Fund (Fonden); Chair. Ministerial Council, Petrocaribe 2005; mem. Partido Socialista Unido de Venezuela.

RAMÍREZ CORZO, Luis, MSc; Mexican petroleum industry executive; *President, Integracion de Servicios Petroleros Oro Negro;* ed Nat. Univ. of Mexico, Univ. of Louisiana, USA Instituto Tecnológico Autónomo de México; fmr teacher Eng Dept, Nat. Univ. of Mexico; Dir-Gen. PEMEX Exploration and Production 2001–04, Dir-Gen. PEMEX 2004–06; currently Pres. Integracion de Servicios Petroleros Oro Negro; mem. Academia de Ingeniería, Asociación de Ingenieros Petroleros de México, Soc. of Petroleum Engineers of American Inst. of Mechanical Engineers; Nat. Petroleum Eng Prize 2000. *E-mail:* contact@oronegro.com (office). *Website:* www.oronegro.com.mx (office).

RAMÍREZ DE RINCÓN, Marta Lucía, PhD; Colombian politician and lawyer; b. Bogotá; m.; ed Javeriana Pontifical Univ., Univ. of the Andes, Harvard Univ., USA; fmr Prof., Univ. of the Andes; fmr Prof. of Foreign Trade, Faculty of Law, Javeriana Pontifical Univ.; Exec. Pres. Inversiones de Gases de Colombia SA, Federación Colombiana de Compañías Leasing, Nat. Asscn of Finance Insts, Financiera Mazda Crédito SA; fmr Vice-Minister of External Trade, Minister of External Trade 1998–2002; Amb. to France Feb.–Oct. 2002; Minister of Nat. Defence 2002–03; Gen. Man. and Pnr Ramirez and Orozco Int. Strategy Consultants 2004–06; Senator (Partido Social de Unidad Nacional) 2006–; Dir-Gen. Instituto de Comercio Exterior; Fellow, Center for Int. Affairs, Harvard Univ. *Publications include:* El Contrato de Descuento y la Apertura de Crédito Antecedentes y Perspectivas del Negocio Fiduciario en Colombia, Régimen Legal de las Compañías de Financiamiento Comercial, Los Avances del Proceso de Interación Andina entre 1990 y 1991, El Programa Especial de Cooperación de la CEE para los Países Andines. *Address:* Senado, Bogotá DC, Colombia (office). *E-mail:* martha.ramirez.derincon@senado.gov.co (office). *Website:* martaluciaramirez.com.

RAMÍREZ LEZCANO, Rubén, MA, MBA; Paraguayan economist, diplomatist and government official; b. 11 Jan. 1966; m. Adriana Cabelluzzi; two s.; ed Univ. of Buenos Aires, Argentina, Univ. of Paris, Sorbonne, France, Univ. of California, Los Angeles, USA; with Int. Econ. Affairs Counselling Dept, Pres.'s Office 1989; Sec., Embassy in Buenos Aires, in charge of Commercial Dept 1989–92; Dir Dept of Foreign Trade, Ministry of Foreign Affairs (MFA) 1994–96; Exec. Sec. Nat. Council for Foreign Trade 1994–96; Counsellor, Embassy in Paris and Standing Rep. at UNESCO 1996–98; Consul-Gen. in Los Angeles 1998–99; Gen. Dir Export and Promotion Dept, MFA 1999–2000; Embassy Minister and Standing Rep., Latin American Integration Asscn, Montevideo, Uruguay 2000; Standing Rep., UN Int. Orgs, Geneva 2001–04; Vice-Minister for Econ. Relations and Integration 2004–06; Minister of Foreign Affairs 2006–08; mem. Asoc. Nacional Republicana-Partido Colorado (Nat. Republican Asscn-Colorado Party). *Address:* Asociación Nacional Republicana-Partido Colorado, Casa de los Colorados, 25 de Mayo 842, Asunción, Paraguay (office). *Telephone:* (21) 45-2543 (office). *Fax:* (21) 45-4136 (office). *E-mail:* contacto@anr.gov.py (office). *Website:* www.anr.org.py (office).

RAMÍREZ MARTIARENA, Gonzalo; Argentine business executive; *CEO, Louis Dreyfus Commodities Holdings Group;* Dir, Nidera 1986–2000; COO Louis Dreyfus Commodities (LDC) Argentina SA 2009–11, CEO, South and West Latin America, LDC 2012–14, CEO LDC Argentina 2012–14, CEO LDC Asia Pte Ltd Jan.–Dec. 2015, CEO Louis Dreyfus Commodities Holdings Group 2016–. *Address:* Louis Dreyfus Commodities Holdings BV, Westblaak 92, 3012 Rotterdam, The Netherlands (office). *E-mail:* DRH-Paris@louisdreyfus.fr (office). *Website:* www .ldcom.com (office); www.louisdreyfus.com (office).

RAMÍREZ MERCADO, Sergio; Nicaraguan author and politician (retd); b. 5 Aug. 1942, Masatepe, Masaya; s. of Pedro Ramírez Gutiérrez and Luisa Mercado Gutiérrez; m. Gertrudis Guerrero Mayorga 1964; one s. two d.; ed Univ. Autónoma de Nicaragua, León; f. Ventana 1960; was active in revolutionary student movt and founding mem. of Frente Estudiantil Revolucionario 1962; mem. Cen. American Univ. Supreme Council (CSUCA), Costa Rica 1964, Pres. 1968, 1976; mem. Int. Comm. of FSLN (Sandinista Liberation Front) 1975, undertook tasks on diplomatic front, propaganda and int. work on behalf of FSLN leading to overthrow of regime 1979; mem. Junta of Nat. Reconstruction Govt 1979; Vice-Pres. of Nicaragua 1984–90; minority leader, Speaker, Nat. Ass. 1990–94; Pres. Movimiento de Renovación Sandinista (MRS) 1994, MRS pre-cand. for presidency 1996; Co-founder literary journal Ventana; Pres. Int. Jury, Festival de Cine de Cartagena de Indias 1993, Jury, Festival Iberoamericano – de Cine de Huelva 2002, Premio Internacional de Novela Alfaguara 2008; Chair. Mario Vargas Llosa, Spanish Univ. 2014, Univ. of Peru 2015; mem. Jury, Premio Internacional de Periodismo Rey de España 1995, Premio Ulises de relato periodístico, Letra Internacional, Berlin 2005, 2006, Manuel Rojas Novel Prize, Santiago, Chile 2015, Clarín Novel Award, Buenos Aires 2015; mem. Governing Council, Fundación Nuevo Periodismo, Steering Cttee, Julio Cortazar Chair, Univ. of Guadalajara; Perm. mem. Iberoamerican Forum; columnist for numerous newspapers and journals; mem. Nicaraguan Acad. of Language; Corresp. mem. Royal Spanish Acad.; mem. Bd of Trustees Instituto Cervantes, Madrid; Hon. Prof., Faculty of Humanities, Universidad Pedagógica Francisco Morazán, Honduras 2007; Chevalier des Arts et des Lettres 1993, Orden Mariano Fiallos Gil del Consejo Nacional de Universidades de Nicaragua 1994, Medalla Presidencial del centenario de Pablo Neruda, otorgada por el gobierno de Chile 2004, Order of Merit, First Class (Germany) 2007, Orden de Oficial de las Artes y las Letras de Francia 2013, Orden Isabel la Católica de España, Encomienda de Número 2015; Dr hc (Universidad Central del Ecuador) 1984, (Université Blaise Pascal de Clermont-Ferrand, France) 2000, (Universidad der Catamarca, Argentina) 2007, (Universidad Latina, Panamá) 2011; De Tropeles y Tropelías 1971, La Fugitiva 2011, Premio Iberoamericano de Letras José Donoso 2011, Premio Carlos Fuentes 2014, Miguel de Cervantes Prize 2017. *Publications include:* Cuentos 1963, El cuento centroamericano 1974, Charles Atlas también muere 1976, El cuento nicaragüense 1976, ¿Te dio miedo la sangre? (Premio Latinoamericano de Cuento, revista Imagen, Caracas) 1978, Castigo divino (Premio Dashiel Hammett 1990) 1988, Confesión de amor 1991, Clave de sol 1992, Cuentos 1994, Oficios compartidos 1994, Un baile de máscaras (Premio Laure Bataillon for Best Foreign Book translated in France 1998) 1995, Margarita, Está Linda la Mar (Premio Internacional de Novela Alfaguara 1998, Premio Latinoamericano de Novela José María Arguedas 2000) 1998, Adiós muchachos 1999, Mentiras Verdaderas 2001, Catalina y Catalina 2001, Sombras nada más 2002, El viajo arte de menir 2004, Mil y una muertes 2004, El reino animal 2006, Tambor Olvidado 2007, Juego perfecto 2008, El cielo llora por mi 2008, Cuando todos hablamos 2008, Perdón y olvido: Antología de cuentos (1960–2009) 2009, Casa de las Américas (Premio Iberoamericano de Letras José Donoso) 2011, La Fugitiva 2011, Abiertos/Puertas Abiertas 2011, La manzana de oro 2012, La viuda Carlota y otros cuentos 2012, Por qué cantan los pájaros y otros cuentos 2012, Historias para ser contadas 2012, La jirafa embarazada 2013, Flores oscuras 2013, Sara 2015. *Leisure interests:* classical music, reading. *Address:* Apdo Postal LM-280, Managua, Nicaragua (office). *Telephone:* (22) 771718 (office). *Fax:* (22) 660548 (office). *E-mail:* srm@ibw.com.ni (office); sergioramirezm@gmail.com (office). *Website:* www.sergioramirez.org.ni (office); www.sergioramirez.com (office).

RAMÍREZ VALDIVIA, Avil; Nicaraguan fmr lawyer and government official; b. 19 Feb. 1964, El Jicaral, León; m.; three c.; ed Universidad Nacional Autónoma de Nicaragua; joined Juventud Democrática Nicaragüense, Movimiento Democrático Nicaragüense 1979; moved to USA 1982, with AmeriFirst Bank, Miami 1983–89; returned to Nicaragua 1989; with USAID 1989; Sub-Dir for Europe, Ministry of Foreign Affairs 1994; mem. of Foreign Service of Nicaragua since 2000; Sec. to the Presidency 2001–03; Deputy Minister of the Interior, Dir of Immigration and Foreign Services 2004; Minister of Nat. Defence 2005–06; Exec. Dir American Chamber of Commerce of Nicaragua 2007–; Order of Isabel La Catolica, Spain, Order of Great Cross to Merit, Germany, Order of St Gregory the Great, Rome, Order of Glowing Flag", China, Order of Merit, Org. of American States, Order to the Military Merit, Guatemala, Order of Monja Blanca. *Address:* American Chamber of Commerce in Nicaragua, Apartado Postal 202, Managua, Nicaragua (office). *Telephone:* (5052) 67-30-99. *Fax:* (5052) 67-30-98. *E-mail:* avil.ramirez@amcham.org.ni. *Website:* www.amcham.org.ni.

RAMKALAWAN, Rev. Wavel John Charles, BTheol; Seychelles theologian and politician; *Leader, Seychelles National Party;* b. 15 March 1961, Mahé; m.; three s.; ed Seychelles Coll., St Paul's Theological Coll., Univ. of Birmingham, UK; Founder and Leader of Parti Seselwa 1991–94; mem. Nat. Ass. 1993–97; Leader of Seychelles Nat. Party; Leader of the Opposition 1998–; cand. in presidential election 2006, 2015. *Address:* Seychelles National Party, Arpent Vert, Mant Fleuri, PO Box 81, Victoria (office); St Louis, Mahé, Seychelles (home). *Telephone:* (248) 224124 (office); (248) 516465 (home). *Fax:* (248) 225151 (office). *E-mail:* wavel24@hotmail.com (office).

RAMLI, Rizal, MA, PhD; Indonesian economist, business executive and fmr government official; *Independent Commissioner, PT First Media Tbk;* b. 10 May 1953, Padang, West Sumatra; ed Bandung Inst. of Tech., Sophia Univ., Tokyo, Boston Univ., USA; econ. analyst; imprisoned for one year for writing white paper exposing failings of 'trickle-down' econs 1980s; ran ind. consultancy, Jakarta 1990s; Chair. Nat. Logistics Agency (Bulog) 2000; Chief Econs Minister –2001; Coordinating Minister for Economy, Finance and Industry 2000–01; Maritime Affairs 2015–16; Minister of Finance June–July 2001; fmr Sr Consultant Van Zorge, Heffernan and Assocs., Jakarta; Pres. Bd of Comms. PT Semen Gresik (Persero) Tbk 2006–08; Ind. Commr PT First Media Tbk 2008–15. *Address:* PT First Media Tbk, Berita Satu Plaza 5th Floor, Suite 401, Jl. Jendral Gatot Subroto Kav, 35–36 Jakarta 12950, Indonesia (office). *Telephone:* (21) 5278811 (office). *Fax:* (21) 5278833 (office). *Website:* www.firstmedia.com (office).

RAMMENSEE, Hans-Georg, Dr rer. nat (Habil.); German immunologist and academic; *Professor of Immunology and Director, Interfaculty Institute for Cell Biology, University of Tübingen;* b. 12 April 1953, Tübingen; s. of Hermann Rammensee and Irmgard Rammensee; m. Gabriele Teufel; four s.; ed Eberhard Karls Univ. of Tübingen, Max Planck Inst. for Biology, Tübingen; postdoctoral studies, Scripps Inst., La Jolla, Calif., USA 1982–85; Scientific Mem., Basel Inst. for Immunology, Switzerland 1985–87; Group Leader, Dept of Immunogenetics, Max Planck Inst. for Biology 1987–93; academic teaching duties at Univs of Tübingen and Heidelberg 1988–93; Head of Dept of Tumor-Virus Immunology, German Cancer Research Centre, Heidelberg and Prof., Univ. of Tübingen 1993–96, Chair. Dept of Immunology (Full Prof., C4), Interfaculty Inst. for Cell Biology 1996–, Dir Interfaculty Inst. for Cell Biology 2008–; Co-Ed. of several journals including Immunogenetics, Cellular and Molecular Life Science, European Journal of Immunology, and others; Co-founder immatics GmbH 2000 (now Head of Scientific Advisory Bd and mem. Scientific Advisory Bd, Immatics US, Inc.), CureVac GmbH 2000, Synimmune GmbH 2010; Gottfried Wilhelm Leibniz Prize, Deutsche Forschungsgemeinschaft 1992, Robert Koch Prize 1993, Paul Ehrlich and Ludwig Darmstaedter Prize 1996, German Cancer Aid Prize 2013, Hansen Family Award 2013, Ernst Jung Prize for Medicine 2016. *Publications:* more than 250 articles in professional journals. *Address:* Department of Immunology, Interfaculty Institute for Cell Biology, Auf der Morgenstelle 15, 72076 Tübingen, Germany (office). *Telephone:* (7071) 2987628 (office). *Fax:* (7071) 295653 (office). *E-mail:* lynne.yakes@uni-tuebingen.de (office). *Website:* www.immunology-tuebingen.de (office).

RAMON, Haim, BA; Israeli politician and lawyer; b. 10 April 1950, Jaffa; s. of Asher Vishnia and Bina Vishnia; m. 1st Prina Tenenbaum (divorced); one s. one d.; m. 2nd Vered Ramon Rivlin; ed Tel-Aviv Univ.; fmr Capt. in Israeli Air Force; Chair. Public Council for Youth Exchanges; Nat. Sec. Labour Party's Young Guard 1978–84; co-ordinator Finance Cttee, Labour Party 1984–88, Chair. Labour Party 1988–92; Minister of Health 1992–94, of the Interior 1995–96, 2000–01; apptd mem. Foreign Affairs and Defence Cttee 2001; Minister responsible for Jerusalem Affairs, Prime Minister's Office –2001; Minister without Portfolio 2005–06, of Justice 2006 (resgnd); Vice-Premier of Israel and Minister in Prime Minister's Office 2007; mem. Knesset 1983–2009; served on numerous cttees 1983–92 (Labour); fmr Sec.-Gen. Histadrut (Gen. Fed. of Labour in Israel); joined Kadima

Party 2005; Chair. Int. Inst.—Histadrut; convicted of indecent assault 2007, sentenced to community service.

RAMOS, Arlindo; São Tomé and Príncipe politician; ed Liceu Nacional de São Tomé e Príncipe; Minister of Internal Admin 2014–16, of Defence and Internal Admin 2016–18. *Address:* c/o Ministry of Defence and Internal Administration, Av. 12 de Julho, CP 427, São Tomé, São Tomé and Príncipe (office).

RAMOS, Gen. Fidel Valdez; Philippine fmr head of state and army officer; *Chairman, Ramos Peace and Development Foundation;* b. 18 March 1928, Lingayen, Pangasinan; s. of Narciso Ramos and Angela Valdez; m. Amelita Martinez; five d.; ed Nat. Univ. Manila, US Mil. Acad., West Point and Univ. of Illinois; active service in Korea and Viet Nam; Deputy Chief of Staff 1981–84; Acting Chief of Staff, Philippines Armed Forces 1984–86, Chief of Staff 1986–88; Sec. of Nat. Defence 1988–91, cand. for Pres. May 1992; Pres. of the Philippines 1992–98; Special Envoy to People's Repub. of China July–Nov. 2016; Chair. Emer. Lakas-Christian Muslim Democrats Party (CMD); Chair. Bd of Advisors Boao Forum for Asia; mem. ASEAN Eminent Persons Group 2005–; f. and Chair. Ramos Peace and Devt Foundation; Légion d'honneur 1987; numerous hon. degrees; Peace Prize Award, UNESCO 1997 and numerous other awards. *Address:* c/o Ramos Peace and Development Foundation, 26th Floor, Export Bank Plaza, Corner Senator Gil Puyat and Chino Roces Avenues, 1200 Makati City (office); 120 Maria Cristina Street, Ayala Alabang Village, Muntinlupa City, Philippines (home). *Telephone:* (2) 8878964 (office). *Fax:* (2) 8878966 (office). *E-mail:* fvr@rpdev.org (office); rpdev@skyinet.net (home). *Website:* www.rpdev.org; www.boaoforum.org.

RAMOS, Maria Da Conceiçao Das Neves Calha, BCom, MSc; South African business executive; *Group Chief Executive, Absa Group Ltd;* b. 22 Feb. 1959, Lisbon, Portugal; m. Trevor Andrew Manuel; ed Univ. of the Witwatersrand, Univ. of London, UK, Inst. of Bankers Diploma (CAIB); emigrated to S Africa as a child; various positions, First Nat. Bank 1978–89; Lecturer in Econs, Univ. of South Africa 1989–91; Co-ordinator Econ. Study Cttee, Centre for Devt Studies 1989–90; mem. Transitional Exec. Council, Sub-Council on Finance 1989–95; Economist, Dept of Econ. Planning, African Nat. Congress (ANC) 1990–94, Project Leader, Inflation Project, Macro Econ. Research Group 1992–93; Research Assoc., Centre for Study of South African Econs and Int. Finance, LSE 1990–94, Research Officer, Centre for Research into Econs and Finance 1994–95; Lecturer in Econs, Univ. of the Witwatersrand 1991–94; Deputy Dir-Gen., Financial Planning, Dept of Finance 1995–96; joined Nat. Treasury, Pretoria as jr 1992, Dir-Gen. 1996–2003; Group Chief Exec. Transnet Ltd (state-owned transport group) 2004–09; Group Chief Exec. Absa Group 2009–, mem. Barclays Group Exec. Cttee; Dir (non-exec.) South African Airways (Pty) Ltd, Sanlam Ltd 2004–; Ind. Dir (non-exec.) Remgro 2007–; mem. World Bank Chief Economist Advisory Panel; Global Leader for Tomorrow, World Econ. Forum, British Council Scholarship (Helen Suzman Award) 1991, 1992, Santambank Marketing Prize, Inst. of Bankers Marketing Prize, Barclays Bank Grad. Scholarship, Senbank Prize for Honours Dissertation, Econ. Soc., Nedbank/Old Mutual Budget Competition, Business Women of the Year, Leader of the Year, Sunday Times Business Times, South Africa's Businesswoman of the Year 2001. *Address:* Absa Group Banks, Absa Towers West, 15 Troye Street, Johannesburg 2001 (office); Absa Group Banks, PO Box 7735, Johannesburg 2000, South Africa (office). *Telephone:* (11) 350-0304 (office). *Fax:* (86) 584-9760 (office). *E-mail:* Michelle.Buthelezi@absa.co.za (office). *Website:* www.absa.co.za (office).

RAMOS-HORTA, José, MA; Timor-Leste politician, UN official and fmr head of state; b. 26 Dec. 1949, Dili; s. of Francisco Horta and Natalina Ramos Filipe Horta; m. Ana Pessoa Pinto 1978 (divorced); one s.; ed Hague Acad. of International Law, The Netherlands, Int. Inst. of Human Rights, Strasbourg, France, Columbia Univ., Antioch Univ., USA; journalist and broadcaster 1969–74; Minister for External Affairs and Information, Timor-Leste 1975; Perm. Rep. of Fretilin to UN, New York 1976–89; Public Affairs and Media Dir Mozambican Embassy, Washington, DC 1987–88; Exec.-Dir Lecturer Diplomacy Training Programme, Univ. of New South Wales 1990–, Visiting Prof. 1996–; Special Rep. Nat. Council of Maubere Resistance 1991–; returned to Timor-Leste Dec. 1999; Vice-Pres. Nat. Council of Resistance 1999–; Sr Minister for Foreign Affairs and Co-operation 2000–06 (resgnd), apptd Acting Defence Minister June 2006; Prime Minister of Timor-Leste 2006–07, also Minister of Defence; Pres. of Timor-Leste 2007–12; served in Timor-Leste Transitional Admin. 2000–02; Special Rep. of the Sec.-Gen. and Head of Integrated Peacebuilding Office in Guinea-Bissau (UNIOGBIS), UN 2013–14; Chair. UN High-Level Ind. Panel on Peace Operations 2014–15; Bd mem. Timor-Leste Human Rights Centre, Melbourne; Sr Assoc. Mem. St Antony's Coll., Oxford 1987–; mem. Sec.-Gen.'s High-Level Advisory Bd on Mediation, UN 2017–; Order of Freedom (Portugal) 1996, Hon. Companion, Order of Australia 2013; Prof. Thorolf Rafto Human Rights Prize 1993, Gleitzman Foundation Award 1995, received Unrepresented Nations and People's Org. Award 1996, shared Nobel Peace Prize 1996 (with Mgr Carlos Ximenes Belo q.v.) 1996. *Publications include:* Funu: The Unfinished Saga of East Timor 1987, Timor Amanha em Dili, Dom Quixote 1994; articles in numerous publs worldwide. *Leisure interest:* tennis. *Address:* High-Level Independent Panel on Peace Operations, Room S-3727B, United Nations, New York, NY 10017, USA (home).

RAMOTAR, Donald; Guyanese politician and fmr head of state; b. 22 Oct. 1950, Caria Caria, Essequibo Islands, West Demerara region; ed Govt Tech. Inst., Univ. of Guyana, sent to USSR to study political science; worked for Guyana Import Export Co. (Gimpex) 1966–75; joined People's Progressive Party (PPP) 1967, numerous party positions including Man. of Freedom House (party HQ) 1975–79, elected to PPP Cen. Cttee 1979, Exec. Cttee 1983, Exec. Sec. of PPP 1993–97, Gen. Sec. 1997–2013, mem. Editorial Bd Thunder (PPP newspaper) 2008–; Deputy, Nat. Ass. 1992–2011; Political Adviser to Pres. Bharrat Jagdeo April–Dec. 2011; Pres. of Guyana 2011–15; mem. Editorial Council, Problems of Peace and Socialism magazine 1983–88; represented Guyana as mem. of ACP (African, Caribbean and Pacific States)–EU Jt Parl. Ass.

RAMPHAL, Sir Shridath Surendranath (Sonny), GCMG, OE, OM, ONZ, AC, QC, SC, LLM, FRSA; Guyanese barrister, politician and international organization official; b. 3 Oct. 1928, New Amsterdam, British Guiana; s. of James I. Ramphal and Grace Ramphal (née Abdool); m. Lois Winifred King 1951; two s. two d.; ed Queen's Coll., Georgetown, King's Coll., London, Harvard Law School; Crown Counsel, British Guiana 1953–54; Asst to Attorney-Gen. 1954–56; Legal Draftsman 1956–58; Solicitor-Gen. 1959–61; Legal Draftsman, West Indies 1958–59; Asst Attorney-Gen., West Indies 1961–62; Attorney-Gen., Guyana 1965–73; mem. Nat. Ass. 1965–75; Minister of State for External Affairs 1967–72, Minister of Foreign Affairs 1972–75, of Justice 1973–75; Commonwealth Sec.-Gen. 1975–90; Chancellor, Univ. of Guyana 1988–92, Univ. of Warwick 1989–2001, Univ. of West Indies 1989–; Queen's Counsel 1965 and Sr Counsel, Guyana 1966; mem. Int. Comm. of Jurists, Ind. Comm. on Int. Devt Issues, Ind. Comm. on Disarmament and Security Issues, Ind. Comm. on Int. Humanitarian Issues, World Comm. on Environment and Devt, South Comm., Carnegie Comm. on Deadly Conflict, Bd of Govs Int. Devt Research Center, Canada, Exec. Cttee of Int. Inst. for Environment and Devt, Council of Int. Negotiation Network Carter Center, Georgia, USA 1991–97; Patron One World Broadcasting Trust; Chair. UN Cttee for Devt Planning 1984–87, West Indian Comm. 1990–92, Bd Int. Inst. for Democracy and Electoral Assistance (IDEA) 1995–2001, Advisory Cttee Future Generations Alliance Foundation 1995–97; Pres. World Conservation Union—IUCN 1990–93; Int. Steering Cttee Leadership for Environment and Devt Program Rockefeller Foundation 1991–98; Co-Chair. Comm. on Global Governance 1992–2000; Adviser to Sec.-Gen. of UNCED 1992; Chief Negotiator on Int. Econ. Issues for the Caribbean Region 1997–2001; Facilitator Belize–Guatemala Dispute 2000–02; John Simon Guggenheim Fellowship 1962; Hon. Bencher of Gray's Inn 1981; Fellow, King's Coll., London 1975, LSE 1979, RSA 1981, Magdalen Coll., Oxford 1982; Order of the Repub. (Egypt) 1973; Grand Cross, Order of the Sun (Peru) 1974; Grand Cross, Order of Merit (Ecuador) 1974, Order of Nishaan Izzuddeen (Maldives) 1989, Grand Commdr, Order of Niger 1990, Grand Commdr, Order of the Companion of Freedom (Zambia) 1990, Nishan-e-Quaid-i-Azam (Pakistan) 1990, Order of the Caribbean Community 1991, Commdr Order of the Golden Ark 1994; Hon. LLD (Panjab Univ.) 1975, (Southampton) 1976, (Univ. of the West Indies) 1978, (St Francis Xavier Univ., Halifax, Canada) 1978, (Aberdeen) 1979, (Cape Coast, Ghana) 1980, (London) 1981, (Benin, Nigeria) 1982, (Hull) 1983, (Yale) 1985, (Cambridge) 1985, (Warwick) 1988, (York Univ., Ont., Canada) 1988, (Malta) 1989, (Otago, NZ) 1990; Hon. DHL (Simmons Coll., Boston) 1982; Hon. DCL (Oxon.) 1982, (East Anglia) 1983, (Durham) 1985; Dr hc (Surrey) 1979, (Essex) 1980; Hon. DHumLitt (Duke Univ., USA) 1985; Hon. DLitt (Bradford) 1985, (Indira Gandhi Nat. Open Univ.) 1989; Hon. DSc (Cranfield Inst. of Tech.) 1987; Arden and Atkin Prize, Gray's Inn 1952, Int. Educ. Award (Richmond Coll., London) 1988, RSA Albert Medal 1988, Medal of Friendship, Cuba 2001, Pravasi Bharata Samman Award 2003. *Publications:* One World to Share: Selected Speeches of the Commonwealth Secretary-General 1975–79, Nkrumah and the Eighties (1980 Kwame Nkrumah Memorial Lectures), Sovereignty and Solidarity (1981 Callander Memorial Lectures), Some in Light and Some in Darkness: The Long Shadow of Slavery (Wilberforce Lecture) 1983, The Message not the Messenger (STC Communication Lecture) 1985, The Trampling of the Grass (Econ. Comm. for Africa Silver Jubilee Lecture) 1985, For the South, a Time to Think 1986, Making Human Society a Civilized State (Corbishley Memorial Lecture) 1987, Inseparable Humanity: An Anthology of Reflections of Shridath Ramphal 1988, An End to Otherness (six speeches) 1990, Our Country, The Planet 1992, No Island is an Island and contribs to journals of legal, political and int. affairs, including International and Comparative Law Quarterly, Caribbean Quarterly, Public Law, Guyana Journal, The Round Table, Royal Society of Arts Journal, Foreign Policy, Third World Quarterly, International Affairs. *Leisure interests:* photography, cooking. *Address:* 31 St Mathew's Lodge, 50 Oakley Square, London, NW1 1NB (home); 1 The Sutherlands, 188 Sutherland Avenue, London, W9 1HR, England. *Telephone:* (20) 7266-3409. *Fax:* (20) 7286-2302. *E-mail:* ssramphal@msn.com (office).

RAMPHELE, Mamphela Aletta, MB, ChB, BCom, DPH, PhD; South African physician, anthropologist, business executive and fmr international organization official; *Co-founder and Global Brand Ambassador, Reimagine SA;* b. 28 Dec. 1947, Pietersburg; d. of Pitsi Eliphaz Ramphele and Rangoato Rahab Ramphele (née Mahlaela); two s.; ed Setotolwane High School, Pietersburg, Univ. of Natal, Univ. of Capetown; community health worker Black Community Programmes, Ktown 1975–77, Ithuseng Community Health Programme, Tzaneen 1978–84; Sr Researcher Dept Social Anthropology, Univ. of Cape Town 1986, Deputy Vice-Chancellor 1991–95, Vice-Chancellor 1996–2000; Researcher and Consultant to Western Cape Hostel Dwellers' Asscn 1986–92; Man. Dir World Bank 2000–05; Chair. Ind. Devt Trust, Circle Capital Ventures 2005–13; Co-Chair. Global Comm. on Int. Migration 2004–05; Chair. Gold Fields Ltd 2010–13; Leader, Agang South Africa 2013–14; Co-founder and Global Brand Amb. Reimagine SA 2016–; mem. Bd of Dirs (non-exec.) Anglo-American Corpn of SA 1992–95, Old Mutual 1993–, Anglo American 2006–; played key role in formation of Black Consciousness Movt 1969; Patron, Cape Town Opera 2006–; mem. NAMDA 1985–; Carnegie Distinguished Int. Fellow, Harvard Coll. 1988–89; Hon. DHumLitt (Hunter Coll., New York), 1984, New York Univ.) 2007; Hon. MD (Natal) 1989, (Sheffield) 1998; Dr hc for Distinguished Career (Tufts Univ., Mass.) 1991; Hon. DSc (Univ. Coll., London) 1997; Hon. LLD (Princeton) 1997, (Brown Univ.) 1998, (Mich.) 1998; Dr hc (Inst. of Social Studies, Netherlands) 1997; Hon. DPhil (Univ. of Orange Free State); Barnard Medal of Distinction, Barnard Coll., New York 1991. *Publications:* Children on Frontline (UNICEF report) 1987, Uprooting Poverty: The South African Challenge (with David Philip) 1989 (Noma Award for publishing in Africa 1991), A Bed Called Home: Life in Migrant Labour Hostels of Cape Town (with David Philip) 1993, Mamphela Ramphele: A Life (with David Philip) 1995, Across Boundaries: The Journey of a South African Woman Leader 1996. *Leisure interests:* reading, walking. *Address:* Reimagine SA, 1st Floor, Equity House, Cnr 5th Avenue and Rivonia Blvd, Rivonia 2128, South Africa (office). *E-mail:* info@reimaginesa.com (office). *Website:* reimaginesa.com (office).

RAMPL, Dieter; German/Austrian banking executive; b. 5 Sept. 1947, Munich; m.; one s.; ed studies in econs in Munich; traineeship with Bayerischen Vereinsbank AG, Munich –1966, positions in Düsseldorf, Frankfurt and NY, 1968–83, mem. Exec. Cttee 1968–87, 1994–98, 1998–2006, Head of Regional Office, Munich 1995–97, Man. Dir Bayerische HypoVereinsbank Aktiengesellschaft (HVB group, cr. through merger between Vereinsbank and Bayerischen Hypotheken und Wechselbank 1998) 1998, Spokesman Group Bd of Man. Dirs 2003–05; Chair. UniCredit SpA 2006–07, Unicredit Group (following merger of

Unicredit and Capitalia) 2007–10, Oct. 2010–12, Chair. and Interim CEO Sept. 2010, Chair. Perm. Strategic Cttee, Corp. Governance, HR and Nominations Cttee, Remuneration Cttee, mem. Internal Control and Risks Cttee; with Société de Banque Suisse, Geneva 1966–68; with N American Div., BHF-Bank AG 1983–94; Chair. Supervisory Bd Koenig & Bauer AG, Bayerische Börse AG –2010; Chair. Man. Bd Hypo-Kulturstiftung; Vice-Chair. Mediobanca SpA; mem. Supervisory Bd FC Bayern München AG 2003–14; mem. Bd of Dirs Bode Hewitt Beteiligungs AG –2009, ABI (Italian Banking Asscn), ICC; mem. Bd of Dirs KKR Man. LLC (New York), mem. Audit Cttee and mem. Conflicts Cttee –2011; Ind. Dir and Chair. Audit Cttee KKR Guernsey GP Ltd –2010; Dir (non-exec.) Babcock and Brown; Vice-Chair. Inst. for Int. Political Studies; mem. Bd of Dirs AIRC (Italian Asscn for Cancer Research), Gen. Council of Aspen Inst. Italia, Trilateral Comm.– Gruppo Italia; Trustee, European School of Man. and Tech. –2009.

RAMPLING, Anne (see RICE, Anne).

RAMPLING, Charlotte, OBE; British actress; b. (Tessa Charlotte Rampling), 5 Feb. 1946, Sturmer, Essex; d. of Godfrey Rampling and Isabel Anne Gurteen; m. 1st Bryan Southcombe 1972 (divorced 1976); one s.; m. 2nd Jean-Michel Jarre 1978 (divorced 1998); one s.; one step-d.; fiancé Jean-Noël Tassez 1998; ed St Hilda's School, Bushey, Jeanne d'Arc Acad. pour Jeunes Filles; film debut 1963; Chevalier des arts et des lettres 1986; César d'honneur 2001; Chevalier, Légion d'honneur 2002. *Films include:* The Knack 1963, Rotten to the Core, Georgy Girl, The Long Duel, Kidnapping, Three, The Damned 1969, Skibum, Corky 1970, 'Tis Pity She's a Whore, Henry VIII and His Six Wives 1971, Asylum 1972, The Night Porter, Giordano Bruno, Zardoz, Caravan to Vaccares 1973, The Flesh of the Orchid, Yuppi Du 1974–75, Farewell My Lovely, Foxtrot 1975, Sherlock Holmes in New York, Orca The Killer Whale, The Purple Taxi 1976, Stardust Memories 1980, The Verdict 1983, Viva la vie 1983, Beauty and Sadness 1984, He Died with His Eyes Open 1985, Max mon Amour, Max My Love 1985, Angel Heart 1987, Paris by Night 1988, Dead on Arrival 1989, Helmut Newton, Frames from the Edge, Hammers Over the Anvil 1991, Time is Money 1992, La marche de Radetzky (TV film) 1994, Asphalt Tango 1995, The Wings of the Dove 1997, The Cherry Orchard 1999, Signs and Wonders 2000, Hommage à Alfred Lepetit 2000, Aberdeen 2000, The Fourth Angel 2001, Under the Sand 2001, Superstition 2001, Spy Game 2001, See How They Run 2002, Summer Things 2003, I'll Sleep When I'm Dead 2003, Swimming Pool 2003, The Statement 2003, Jerusalem 2003, Vers le sud 2004, Lemming 2005, Basic Instinct 2 2006, Angel 2006, Deception 2007, The Duchess 2008, Babylon AD 2008, Never Let Me Go 2010, The Eye of the Storm 2011, I, Anna 2010, Cleanskin 2012, Tutto parla di te 2012, Night Train to Lisbon 2013, Young & Beautiful 2013, The Sea 2013, The Blueblack Hussar (documentary) 2013, Portrait of the Artist 2014, The Forbidden Room 2015, 45 Years (Silver Bear for Best Actress, Berlin Int. Film Festival) 2015, Seances 2015, The Sense of an Ending 2017, Hannah (Volpi Cup for Best Actress, Venice Film Festival 2017) 2017, Euphoria 2017. *Television includes:* La Femme abandonnée 1992, Murder In Mind 1994, Radetzkymarsch (mini-series) 1995, Samson le magnifique 1995, La Dernière fête 1996, Great Expectations 1999, My Uncle Silas (series) 2000, Imperium: Augustus (film) 2003, Le grand restaurant 2010, Restless 2012, Dexter (series) 2013, Broadchurch (series) 2015, London Spy (mini-series) 2015. *Address:* c/o Artmédia, 20 avenue Rapp, 75007 Paris, France (office). *Telephone:* 1-43-17-33-00 (office). *Fax:* 1-44-18-34-60 (office). *E-mail:* b.delabbey@artmedia.fr (office). *Website:* www.artmedia.fr (office).

RAMQVIST, Lars Henry, PhD; Swedish business executive; *Honorary Chairman, Telefonaktiebolaget L. M. Ericsson;* b. 2 Nov. 1938, Grängesberg; s. of Henry Ramqvist and Alice Ramqvist; m. Barbro Pettersson 1962; one s. one d.; ed Univ. of Uppsala; Section Head, Stora Kopparberg AB 1962–65; with Axel Johnson Inst. 1965–80, Pres. 1975–80; joined Telefonaktiebolaget L. M. Ericsson as Vice-Pres. and Head of Information Systems Div. 1980, Pres. and CEO 1990–98, Chair. 1998–2002, Hon. Chair. 2002–, Pres. subsidiary RIFA AB 1984–86, Ericsson Radio AB 1988–90; Vice-Chair. AB Volvo 1998, Chair. 1999–2004 (resgnd); Chair. Skandia Insurance Co. Ltd 1999–2003; mem. Bd of Dirs Svenska Cellulosa Aktiebolaget SCA (publ) 1994–2004, Astra Zeneca; mem. Bd Swedish Eng Employers' Asscn, Asscn of Swedish Eng Industries and Fed. of Swedish Industries (Chair. 1999), European Round Table of Industrialists 1994–2002; mem. Prime Minister's Special Industry Advisory Cttee 1994–; mem. Royal Swedish Acad. of Science, Royal Swedish Acad. of Eng Sciences; Hon. mem. IEEE; Dr hc (Technical Univ. Beijing), (Technical Univ. Moscow).

RAMS, Dieter; German industrial designer; b. 20 May 1932, Wiesbaden; m. Ingeborg Rams; ed Wiesbaden Werkkunstschule (School of Art); worked for Otto Apel (architect), Frankfurt 1953–55; joined Braun AG as architect and interior designer 1955, Chief of Design 1962–95, Exec. Dir, Corp. Identity Affairs 1995–97 (retd after designing, co-designing and overseeing designs of more than 400 products, including audiovisual equipment, coffee makers, calculators, radios and office products as well as a shelving system for Vitsœ); mem. Supervisory Bd German Design Council (Rat für Formgebung) 1976, Chair. 1988–98, Hon. Chair. 1998–; Prof., Acad. of Fine Arts, Hamburg 1980; Hon. Royal Designer for Industry, RSA, UK 1968, Hon. Foreign mem. Academia Mexicana de Diseno, Mexico 1985, Hon. Int. Faculty mem., Ontario Coll. of Art, Toronto, Canada 1986; Hessian Order of Merit 1997, Verdienstkreuz des Verdienstordens der Bundesrepublik Deutschland 2002; Dr hc (RCA, UK) 1989; UK Soc. of Industrial Artists and Designers Medal 1978, Industrial Designers Soc. of America World Design Medal 1996, ONDI Design Award, Havana, Cuba 2003, Design Prize of FRG 2007, Raymond Loewy Foundation Lucky Strike Designer Award 2007, Lifetime Achievement Medal, London Design Festival 2013. *Address:* c/o Vitsœ, Centric Close, London, NW1 7EP, England (office). *Website:* www.vitsoe.com/en/gb/about/dieterrams (office).

RAMSAMY, Pakereesamy (Prega), BA, MBA, PhD; Mauritian economist and international organization official; b. 1950, Rose Hill; m. Novia Ramsamy; two d.; with Preferential Trade Area for Eastern and Southern Africa, then Common Market for Eastern and Southern Africa for 14 years; Chief Economist, Southern African Devt Community 1997–98, Deputy Exec. Sec. 1998–2000, Acting Exec. Sec. 2000, Exec. Sec. 2001–05; Dir-Gen. Econ. Devt Bd of Madagascar 2006–14. *Leisure interests:* reading, indoor games, swimming, fishing.

RAMSAUER, Peter, Dr.oec.publ; German politician; b. 10 Feb. 1954, Traunwalchen, Bavaria; m.; four d.; ed Ludwig-Maximilians-Universität, Munich; Propr, Ramsauer Talmühle eK (milling co.), Traunwalchen; mem. Junge Union (JU) 1972, Chair., JU Traunwalchen 1973–75, JU Traunreut 1977–79, Deputy Dist Chair., JU Upper Bavaria 1979–81, Dist Chair., JU Dist Div., Traunstein 1983–87, Deputy State Chair., JU Bavaria 1983–89; mem. CSU 1973–, Local Chair., CSU Traunreut 1985–91, Deputy Party Leader 2008–15; mem. Traunreut City Council 1978–91, Traunstein Dist Council 1984; mem. Bundestag (parl.) for Traunstein/Berchtesgadener Land constituency 1990–, Parl. Sec., CSU Regional Group 1998–2005, Chair. 2005–09; Fed. Minister of Transport, Building and Urban Affairs 2009–13, Chair. Cttee on Econ. and Energy Affairs 2014–17, Cttee for Econ. Cooperation and Devt 2018–; mem. Supervisory Bd Deutsche Energie-Agentur GmbH –2012; mem. Bd of Dir Kreditanstalt für Wiederaufbau; Hon. mem., Traunstein Dist, Hon. Bd of Trustees Bürgerstiftung Berchtesgadener Land, Hon. Chair., Ensemble Amphion München-Wien eV. *Leisure interests:* playing piano, jogging. *Address:* Deutscher Bundestag, Platz der Republik 1, 11011 Berlin, Germany (office). *E-mail:* peter.ramsauer@wk.bundestag.de (office). *Website:* www.peter-ramsauer.de (office).

RAMSAY, Lynne; British film director and writer; b. 5 Dec. 1969, Glasgow, Scotland; m. Rory Kinnear 2010; ed Nat. Film and Television School; trained as camera operator; directed promotional video for Manchester-based indie-rock band Doves' single Black and White Town 2005; Carl Foreman Award for Newcomer in British Film, BAFTA Awards 2000, Sutherland Trophy, London Film Festival, Silver Hugo for Best Dir, Chicago Int. Film Festival, ranked No. 12 in the Guardian Unlimited's list of the world's 40 best directors working today 2007. *Films include:* Small Deaths (short) (Prix de Jury, Cannes Film Festival 1996), Kill the Day (short) (Clemont Ferrand Prix du Jury) 1996, Gasman (short) (Prix de Jury, Cannes Film Festival, Scottish BAFTA for Best Short Film) 1998, Ratcatcher (debut feature) (numerous awards, including the Guardian New Dirs Prize, Edinburgh Int. Film Festival) 1999, Morvern Callar (Award of Confédération Internationnale des Cinémas d'Art et d'Essai, Award of The Youth, Cannes Film Festival) 2002, We Need to Talk about Kevin (Kermode Award 2011) 2011, You Were Never Really Here 2017. *Address:* 16 West Central Street, London, WC1A 1JJ, England (office). *Telephone:* (20) 7395-4155 (office). *E-mail:* reception@academyfilms.com (office). *Website:* www.academyfilms.com (office).

RAMSEY, Paul Glenn, AB, MD; American physician and academic; *CEO of UW Medicine, Executive Vice-President for Medical Affairs and Dean of the School of Medicine, University of Washington;* b. 1949, Pittsburgh, Pa; m. Bonnie Ramsey; ed Harvard Coll., Harvard Medical School; Residency in Internal Medicine, Mass Gen. Hosp., Boston 1975–78; Acting Instructor, Dept of Medicine, Univ. of Washington 1980–81, Acting Asst Prof. 1981–82, Asst Prof. 1982–86, Assoc. Prof. 1986–91, Prof. 1991–, Assoc. Chair. Dept of Medicine 1988–90, Chair. 1992–97, Robert G. Petersdorf Endowed Chair. in Medicine 1995, Exec. Vice-Pres. for Medical Affairs and Dean, School of Medicine 1997–, Acting Chair., then Chair. UW Medicine 1990–97, CEO UW Medicine 2006–; Teaching and Research Scholar, American Coll. of Physicians 1982–85; Henry J. Kaiser Family Foundation Faculty Scholar in Gen. Internal Medicine 1987–92; mem. Asscn of American Physicians, NAS Inst. of Medicine; Univ. of Washington School of Medicine Distinguished Teacher Award 1984, 1986, 1987, Margaret Anderson Award 1989, Nat. Bd of Medical Examiners John P. Hubbard Award 1999. *Address:* Office of the Dean, UW School of Medicine, University of Washington, 1959 NE Pacific Street, Seattle, WA 98195, USA (office). *Telephone:* (206) 543-7718 (office). *E-mail:* pramsey@u.washington.edu. *Website:* www.uwmedicine.org (office).

RAMZI, Rashid; Bahraini (b. Moroccan) athlete; b. 17 July 1980, Morocco; middle-distance runner; competes internationally for Bahrain in 800m, 1,500m and 5,000m; only Bahraini Olympic medallist; raised in Safi, Morocco; competed internationally for Morocco until he joined Bahraini armed forces and gained citizenship in 2002; gold medal, Asian Athletics Championships, 2002 Asian Games; Silver Medal, 800m, World Indoor Championships 2004; became first athlete in history to win gold medals in 800m and 1,500m at same World Championships and first man to perform this feat in a global championship (World Championships or Olympic Games) since Peter Snell in 1964, World Championships, Helsinki 2005; Silver Medal, 1,500m, World Championships, Osaka 2007; Gold Medal, 1,500m, Olympic Games, Beijing 2008. *Address:* c/o Bahrain Amateur Athletics Federation, PO Box 29269, 12344 Manama, Bahrain. *Telephone:* 684905. *Fax:* 687506. *E-mail:* athletic@batelco.com.bh.

RANA, Gen. Gaurav Shamsher Jung Bahadur, BA, MA; Nepalese army officer (retd); b. 12 Dec. 1955; s. of Maj.-Gen. Aditya S. J. B. Rana and Rani Sunita Rana; m. Rohini Rana; two d.; ed Tribhuvan Univ., Quaid-E-Azam Univ. of Pakistan, Royal Mil. Acad. Sandhurst, UK, US Army Command and Gen. Staff Coll., Fort Leavenworth, USA, Nat. Defence Univ., Pakistan; commissioned into Purano Gorakh Bn 1974, commanded Shree Taradal Gulma (Ind. Infantry Co.) and Shree Purano Gorakh Bn, led bn in active operational duty in UNIFIL, Lebanon 1994, served as Commdt of Nepalese Mil. Acad., Kharipati, active operational commands include Brigade Commdr in 5th and 9th Infantry Brigades in counter-insurgency environment in far western and cen. Nepal, respectively, commanded Western Div., headquartered in Pokhara, major staff appointments at the Army HQs include Chief of Gen. Staff, Chief of Staff, Dir of Recruitment, Dir of Logistics, Dir of Army Research and Devt, Insp. Gen. of the Army and Dir-Gen. of Mil. Operations, as the latter during the Koshi floods of 2008, represented the Nepalese Army in the Cen. Natural Disaster Relief Cttee and was the gen. officer in charge of rescue and relief operations, attained rank of Gen. 2012, Chief of the Army Staff 2012–15, Col Commdt Purano Gorakh Bn; Suprabal Jana Sewa Shree; awards include Tri Shakti Patta, Disaster Rescue Award, UN Medal with Bar, Remote Area Service Medal (Mountain Warfare) and Parachutist Wings. *Leisure interests:* military history, golfer, bird watching, mountain biking.

RANA, Kipkorir Aly Azad, MPolSci, PhD; Kenyan international civil servant and trade consultant; *Managing Director, Mabwa Enterprise Ltd;* b. 11 March 1948, Kericho; ed Univ. of Nairobi, Univ. of California, Los Angeles, USA; Deputy Head of Mission, Tokyo 1993–96; Deputy Perm. Rep. and Alt. Del./ Co-ordinator to Security Council, UN, New York 1997; Perm. Sec. (Devt Co-ordination), Office of the Pres. of Kenya 1998; Amb. and Perm. Rep. UN, Geneva 1998–2000; Co-ordinator of African Dels to WTO and Sr Trade Policy Adviser, Minister for Trade and Industry 1999–2001; Deputy Dir-Gen. WTO 2002–05; Fulbright Hays Fellow 1973–79; Man. Dir Mabwa Enterprise Ltd (agro-business) 2006–. *Address:* Mabwa Enterprise Ltd, POB 1979-40100, Kisumu, Kenya (office). *E-mail:* info@mabwa-ent.com (office). *Website:* www.mabwa-ent.com (office).

RANA, Madhukar Shumshere J. B., BA, MA; Nepalese economist, academic and fmr government official; *Professor, South Asian Institute of Management;* b. 1941, Jawalakhel, Lalitpur; ed McMaster Univ., Canada, Univ. of Manchester, UK, Univ. of Geneva, Switzerland, Delhi Univ., India; Manpower Economist, Govt of Canada 1967; fmr Lecturer in Econs, Nippising Univ.; fmr Assoc. Teaching Master, Cambrian Coll. of Applied Arts and Tech.; Assoc. Prof., Centre for Econ. Devt and Admin, Tribhuvan Univ. 1971, then became Exec. Dir; Chief Econ. Adviser to Ministry of Finance 1983–84; Sr Regional Programme Man. for South Asia, UNDP 1994–95; Special Adviser to Ministry of Foreign Affairs 1996–98; Minister of Finance Jan.–Dec. 2005; Prof., South Asian Inst. of Man., Kathmandu 2006–; Commr SAARC Ind. Comm.; Pres. Shaligram Apartment-Hotel; fmr Pres. Rotary Jawalakhel, Man. Asscn of Nepal; mem. South Asian Ind. Comm. on Poverty Allevation 1991–2001. *Address:* South Asian Institute of Management, Lagankhel, Lalitpur, Kathmandu, Nepal (office). *Telephone:* (1) 5522044 (office). *Fax:* (1) 5522044 (office). *E-mail:* info@saim.edu.np (office). *Website:* www.saim.edu.np (office).

RANA, Pashupati S. J. B. R., BA; Nepalese politician; b. 7 May 1941, Laxmi Niwas, Kathmandu; s. of Gen. Bijaya Shumsher Jung Bahadur Rana and Rani Sarla Devi Rana; m. Rani Usha Rajya Laxmi Devi Rana (Princess of Gwailor); two d.; ed Haileybury, ISC and New Coll., Oxford, UK; mem. Parl. 1973–; Minister of Educ., Transport, Civil Aviation and Tourism 1979, Minister of Water Resources 1983–86, 1995–98, Minister of Panchayat and Local Devt 1986–88, Minister of Foreign Affairs, Finance, Water Resources and Communications 1990, Gen. Sec. Rashtriya Prajatantra Party (Nat. Democratic Party) 1991–97, Chair. 2003–14, 2014–16; mem. India-Int. Centre, Int. Council Asia Soc.; Pres. Alliance française. *Publications:* Bikas Tatha Yojana 1971, Nepal's Forth Plan: A Critique 1971, Kathmandu: A Living Heritage 1989, Contemporary Nepal 1998, The Ranas of Nepal 2002. *Leisure Interests:* reading, European classical music, writing, shooting, trekking. *Address:* Bijaya Bas, PO Box 271, Maharaj Gunj, Kathmandu, Nepal (home). *Telephone:* (1) 4437902 (home). *Fax:* (1) 4423384 (home). *E-mail:* p-rana@ntc.net.np (home).

RANA, Rukma Shumsher, MA; Nepalese business executive and diplomatist; b. 12 March 1936, Kolkata, India; s. of Suvarna Shumsher Rana; ed St Xavier's Coll., Darjeeling, India, Univ. of Kolkata; fmr Pres. Nepal Taekwondo Asscn, Pres. Nepal Olympic Cttee 1998–2006; fmr Man. Dir Dabur Nepal Pvt. Ltd; fmr Pres. Nepal-India Chamber of Commerce and Industry; Amb. to India 2009–11.

RANATUNGE, Prasanna; Sri Lankan politician; *Chief Minister of Western Province;* b. 1 Jan. 1967, Colombo; fmr Leader, United People's Freedom Alliance, Gampaha Dist; Chief Minister of Western Prov. 2009– (Educ., Finance and Planning, Law and Order, Land, Prov. Admin, Human Resources and Employment, and Econ. Devt portfolios). *Address:* Office of the Chief Minister of Western Province, 'Srawasthi Mandiraya', No 32 Sri Marcus Fernando Mawatha, Colombo 07, Sri Lanka (office). *Telephone:* (11) 2698410 (office). *E-mail:* chiefminister@wpc.gov.lk (office); chiefminist@sltnet.lk (office). *Website:* en.wpc.gov.lk (office).

RANCHOD, Bhadra, BA, LLB, LLM, LLD; South African diplomatist, lawyer and academic; b. 11 May 1944, Port Elizabeth; s. of Ghalloo Ranchod and Parvaty Ranchod; m. Vibha M. Desai 1980; two d.; ed Univs of Cape Town, Oslo, Norway and Leiden, The Netherlands; Sr Lecturer, Dept of Pvt. Law, Univ. of Durban-Westville 1972, Prof. of Pvt. Law 1974, Dean, Faculty of Law 1976–79; Advocate of Supreme Court 1973–; mem. Bd of Govs S African Broadcasting Corpn; mem. S African Law Comm.; mem. Human Sciences Research Council, numerous cttees and public bodies etc.; Visiting Scholar, Columbia Univ., New York, USA 1980–81; Amb. and Head of S African Mission to European Communities 1986–92; Minister of Tourism 1993–94; Chair. Minister's Council in House of Dels 1993–94; MP 1994–96; Deputy Speaker, Nat. Ass. 1994–96; High Commr in Australia (also accred to NZ and Fiji Islands) 1996–2001; apptd Faculty of Dept of Pvt. and Roman Law 2001, now retd; Vice-Chair. Bd Christel House Cape Town; Dir Maritime Mutual Insurance Co. (NZ); mem. Advisory Cttee Children's Rights Int. *Publications:* Foundations of the South African Law of Defamation (thesis) 1972, Law and Justice in South Africa 1986; about 100 papers on human rights issues. *Leisure interests:* jogging, reading, travel.

RANCIÈRE, Jacques; French social historian, philosopher, literary critic, author and academic; *Professor of Philosophy, European Graduate School;* b. 10 June 1940, Algiers, Algeria; ed École Normale Supérieure; currently Prof. of Philosophy, European Grad. School, Saas-Fee, Switzerland; Prof., Univ. de Paris St Denis, now Prof. Emer. *Publications include:* in trans.: Reading Capital (co-author) 1968, The Nights of Labor: The Workers' Dream in Nineteenth-Century France 1989, The Ignorant Schoolmaster 1991, Five Lessons in Intellectual Emancipation 1991, The Names of History 1994, On the Poetics of Knowledge 1994, On the Shores of Politics 1995, Disagreement: Politics and Philosophy 1998, The Politics of Aesthetics: The Distribution of the Sensible 2004, The Future of the Image 2007, Hatred of Democracy 2007, The Aesthetic Unconscious 2009, The Emancipated Spectator 2009, Chronicles of Consensual Times 2010, The Politics of Literature 2011, Aisthesis: Scenes from the Aesthetic Regime of Art 2013, Modern Times 2017. *Address:* European Graduate School, Philosophy, Art & Critical Thought, Alter Kehr 20, 3953 Leuk-Stadt, Switzerland (office). *Telephone:* 274749917 (office). *Fax:* 274749918 (office). *E-mail:* public@egs.edu (office). *Website:* egs.edu (office).

RANDALL, Jeff William, BA; British business executive and fmr journalist; b. 3 Oct. 1954, London; s. of Jeffrey Charles Randall and Grace Annie Randall (née Hawkridge); m. Susan Diane Fidler 1986; one d.; ed Royal Liberty Grammar School, Romford, Univ. of Nottingham, Univ. of Florida, USA; with Hawkins Publrs 1982–85; Asst Ed. Financial Weekly 1985–86; City Corresp. Sunday Telegraph 1986–88; Deputy City Ed. The Sunday Times 1988–89, City Ed. 1989–94, City and Business Ed. 1994–95, Asst Ed. and Sports Ed. 1996–97; Ed. Sunday Business 1997–2001; Business Ed. BBC 2001–05; Ed.-at-Large and columnist, The Daily Telegraph 2005–13; host, Jeff Randall Live (Sky News) 2007–14; Dir Times Newspapers 1994–95; Deputy Chair. Financial Dynamics Ltd

1995–96; Sr Adviser to Group CEO Prudential PLC 2014–; Visiting Fellow, Said Business School, Univ. of Oxford; mem. Bd of Dirs Babcock Int. Group (Chair. Remuneration Cttee) 2014–, Sandown Park Racecourse 2014–; mem. Univ. Council, Univ. of Nottingham 2013–; Hon. Prof., Univ. of Nottingham Business School; Dr hc (Anglia Ruskin Univ.) 2001, (Univ. of Nottingham) 2006, (BPP Univ. Coll.) 2011; Financial Journalist of the Year, FT-Analysis 1991, Business Journalist of the Year, London Press Club 2000, Sony Gold Award 2003, Communicator of the Year 2004, Business Broadcaster of the Year, Wincott Awards 2004. *Publications:* The Day That Shook the World (co-author). *Leisure interests:* golf, horse racing, football.

RANDALL, William James, BBus; American business executive; *Executive Director and Co-CEO, Noble Group;* b. 1974; ed Australian Catholic Univ.; began career with Noble Group in Australia 1997, transferred to Asia where he established Noble's coal operations, mining and supply chain man. businesses 1999, Dir of Noble Energy Inc. before being apptd Global Head of Coal & Coke 2006, mem. Noble Group Internal Man. Bd 2008, Head of Energy Coal & Carbon Complex –2012, Exec. Dir and Head of Hard Commodities 2012–14, Pres. 2014–16, Exec. Dir and Co-CEO Noble Group 2016–; Vice-Pres. Commr PT Atlas Resources Tbk 2013–16, Commr 2013–; Chair. (non-exec.), Blackwood Corpn Ltd 2010–14; mem. Bd of Dirs, Territory Resources Ltd 2011–, Osendo, East Energy Resources Ltd –2013, Gloucester Coal Ltd 2009–, Yancoal Australia Ltd 2012–. *Address:* Noble Group Ltd, 18th Floor, Mass Mutual Tower, 38 Gloucester Road, Hong Kong Special Administrative Region, People's Republic of China (office). *Telephone:* 2861-3511 (office). *Fax:* 2527-0282 (office). *E-mail:* noble@thisisnoble.com (office). *Website:* www.thisisnoble.com (office).

RANDEL, Don Michael, AB, MFA, PhD; American musicologist, foundation executive and fmr university administrator; *President Emeritus, Andrew W. Mellon Foundation;* b. Panama; m. Carol Randel; four d.; ed Princeton Univ.; Asst Prof., Dept of Fine Arts, Syracuse Univ. 1966–68; Asst Prof. of Music, Cornell Univ. 1968–71, Assoc. Prof. 1971–75, Chair. Dept of Music 1971–76, Prof. of Music 1975–2000, Vice-Provost 1978–79, Assoc. Dean, Coll. of Arts and Sciences 1989–91, Harold Tanner Dean 1991–95, Provost 1995–2000; Pres. Univ. of Chicago 2000–06, now Pres. Emer., mem. Faculty, Dept of Music, now Prof. Emer.; Pres. Andrew W. Mellon Foundation 2006–13, now Pres. Emer.; Vice-Pres. American Musicological Soc. 1977–78 (Ed.-in-Chief Journal of the American Musicological Society 1972–74); Fellow, American Acad. of Arts and Sciences 2001– (currently Chair.); mem., AAAS, Modern Language Asscn, American Philosophical Soc. 2002–; mem. Bd of Trustees Carnegie Corporation of New York, Chicago Symphony Orchestra Asscn 2001–, Music and Dance Theater, Chicago 2001; mem., Bd of Govs Partnership for Public Service 2001–; mem., Bd of Dirs Chicago Council on Foreign Relations 2001–, CNA Financial Corpn 2002–. *Publications include:* Index to the Chant of the Mozarabic Rite 1973, New Harvard Dictionary of Music (Ed.) 1986, Harvard Biographical Dictionary of Music (Ed.) 1996, Harvard Concise Dictionary of Music and Musicians (Ed.) 1999, Harvard Dictionary of Music, 4th edition 2003, The Responsorial Psalm Tones for the Mozarabic Office 2015; various publications on Mozarabic chant, Arabic music theory, and Latin American popular music, author of numerous articles in musical journals. *Telephone:* (212) 500-2550 (office). *E-mail:* dr@mellon.org (office).

RANDERSON, Baroness (Life Peer), cr. 2011, of Roath Park in the City of Cardiff; **Jenny Randerson;** British politician; m.; several c.; began career in politics in Cardiff late 1970s; Cyncoed Councillor 1983–99; Leader of Opposition, Cardiff Co. Council 1994–99; contested Cardiff Cen. seat 1997; MLA (Liberal Democrat) for Cardiff Cen. in newly est. Welsh Ass. 1999–; Minister for Culture, Sport and the Welsh Language 2003–07; Welsh Liberal Democrat Spokesperson for Health, Social Care, Finance and Local Govt 2007–08; Welsh Liberal Democrat Shadow Minister for the Economy, Educ. and Transport 2008–; introduced into law first ever Pvt. Mems Bill in Wales. *Address:* National Assembly for Wales, Cardiff Bay, Cardiff, CF99 1NA, Wales (office); House of Lords, Westminster, London, SW1A 0PW, England. *Telephone:* (29) 2089-8355 (office); (20) 7219-5353; (29) 2089-8356 (office). *Fax:* (20) 7219-5979. *E-mail:* jenny@jennyranderson.com (office). *Website:* www.jennyranderson.com (office).

RANDRIAMANDRATO, Richard J.; Malagasy economist and politician; *Minister of the Economy and Finance;* two c.; ed Inst. of Political Studies, Aix-en-Provence, Univ. Libre de Bruxelles Centre for Int. and Strategic Relations, American Univ., Washington, DC, Georgetown Univ. School of Business; started his career at ILO; fmr Expert for Private Sector Devt in Madagascar with World Bank; Chief of Staff, Ministry of Foreign Affairs 1998; Dir of Strategic Planning and Research, Common Market for Eastern and Southern Africa (COMESA) 2001–09; Programme Coordinator, UNDP 2012–13; fmr Special Adviser to Prime Minister, in charge of relations with technical and financial partners and cooperation; Special Adviser to Pres. of the Senate 2016; Minister of the Economy and Finance 2019–; Chair. Africa Strategic Regional Assistance 2018–; Dir Centre de Politiques Alternatives. *Address:* Ministry of the Economy and Finance, 101 Antananarivo, Madagascar (office). *Website:* www.mefb.gov.mg (office).

RANDT, Clark Thorp, Jr, BA, JD; American lawyer and diplomatist; *President, Randt & Company LLC;* b. 1 Jan. 1945, Conn.; m. Sarah A. Talcott; two s. one d.; ed Hotchkiss School, Yale Univ., Univ. of Michigan Law School; served with USAF Security Service 1968–72; China Rep., Nat. Council for US-China Trade 1974; First Sec. and Commercial Attaché, US Embassy in Beijing 1982–84; pvt. law practice as Partner, Shearman & Sterling, Hong Kong; Amb. to People's Repub. of China 2001–09; Special Advisor, Hopu Investment Man. Co., Beijing 2009–; currently Pres. Randt & Co. LLC; mem. Bd of Dirs Valmont Industries 2009–, United Parcel Service 2010–, Qualcomm Inc. 2013–; mem. ABA, American Soc. of Int. Law, Hong Kong Law Soc.; fmr Gov. and First Vice-Pres. American Chamber of Commerce, Hong Kong; mem. Council on Foreign Relations.

RANE, Pratapsingh Raoji, BSc, BBA; Indian politician; b. 28 Jan. 1939; s. of Raoji Rane; m.; Chief Minister of Goa 1980–85, 1985–89, 1990, 1994–99, Feb.–March 2005, June 2005–07; Speaker, Goa Legis. Ass. Speaker 2007–12; mem. Indian Nat. Congress, fmr Leader of the Opposition, Chair. Public Accounts Cttee, Business Advisory Cttee 2002–03. *Leisure interests:* outing, camping, nature study, listening to classical music, reading, drama, reading, watching TV. *Address:* Golden Acres, Kulan, Sanquelim 403 505, India (home). *Telephone:* (832) 2362229 (home). *E-mail:* mla-pori.goa@nic.in.

RANGARAJAN, Chakravarthi, PhD; Indian economist, academic and politician; *Chairman, Madras School of Economics;* b. 5 Jan. 1932, Ariyalur; s. of B. R. Chakravarty and Rangam Chakravarty; m. Haripriya Chakravarty; one s. one d.; ed Madras Univ., Univ. of Pennsylvania, USA; Lecturer, Loyola Coll. Chennai 1954–58, Wharton School of Finance and Commerce, Univ. of Pennsylvania 1963–64; Reader, Raj Univ. 1964–65; Prof., Indian Statistical Inst., New Delhi 1965–66; Visiting Assoc. Prof., New York Univ. 1966–68, Visiting Prof. 1972–73; Prof., Indian Inst. of Managaement, Ahmedabad 1968–81; Deputy Gov. Reserve Bank of India 1982–91, Gov. 1992–97; mem. Econ. Advisory Council for the Prime Minister 1985–91, Chair. 2005–08; Gov. of Andhra Pradesh 1997–2003; Chair. Tenth Finance Comm., Ministry of Finance 2003, Twelfth Finance Comm. 2005, Prime Minister's Econ. Advisory Council 2005–08; mem. Rajya Sabha 2008–09; currently Chair. Madras School of Econs; mem. Planning Comm., Indian Govt 1991–92; Chair. Task Force on Jammu and Kashmir; Pres. Indian Econ. Asscn 1988, Indian Econometric Soc. 1994; Hon. Fellow, Indian Inst. of Man., Ahmedabad 1997; Businessman of the Year, Madras Man. Asscn 1997, Bank of India Award of Excellence 1998, Finance Man of the Decade, Bombay Man. Asscn 1998, Financial Express Award for Economics 1998, Padma Vibhushan 2002, Wharton India Econ. Forum Alumni Award 2002. *Publications include:* author or co-author: Short-Term Investment Forecasting 1974, Principles of Macro-Economics 1979, Strategy for Industrial Development in the 80s 1982, Innovations in Banking 1982, Agricultural Growth and Industrial Performance in India 1982, Structural Reforms in Industry Banking and Finance 2000; contrib.: Indian Economy: Essays on Money and Finance 1998, Perspectives on Indian Economy 2000, Select Essays on Indian Economy; and more than 40 papers. *Address:* Madras School of Economics, Behind Anna Centenary Library, Gandhi Mandapam Road, Kottur, Chennai 600 025, India (office). *Telephone:* (44) 22300301 (office). *Fax:* (44) 22352155 (office). *E-mail:* c.rangarajan@mse.ac.in (office). *Website:* www.mse.ac.in/faculty/Rangarajan.asp (office).

RANGASAMY, N.; Indian politician; b. 4 Aug. 1950, Puducherry; has held several positions in Puducherry govt including Minister of Agric. 1991, of Public Works Dept 1996, of Educ. 2000; Chief Minister of Puducherry 2001–08, 2011–16; mem. Indian Nat. Congress party 1990–2011, left to found new party All India N.R. Congress 2011, then Pres.

RANGBA, Samuel; Central African Republic diplomatist and politician; b. 1973; ed Univ. de Bangui, Ecole Nat. d'Admin; long career within Ministry of Foreign Affairs including as Dir-Gen. of State Protocol 2010–13, Dir-Gen. of Political Affairs 13–14, Head of Cttees 2014–15, Minister of Foreign Affairs, African Integration and Francophony 2015–16.

RANGEL SILVA, Gen.-in-Chief Henry de Jesús; Venezuelan army officer and government official; *Governor of Trujillo;* b. 28 Aug. 1961, Santiago, Trujillo State; ed Bolivarian Military Acad., Caracas; took part in military coup with the late Hugo Chávez 1992; fmr Head of Nat. Housing Council; Dir Directorate of Intelligence and Prevention Services 2005–09; Dir CANTV (public telecommunications co.) 2009; attained rank of Maj.-Gen. 2008, of Gen.-in-Chief 2010; Strategic Operational Commdr of the Armed Forces 2010; Minister of Defence Jan.–Oct. 2012; Gov. of Trujillo 2012–. *E-mail:* contacto@psuv.org.ve (office); webmaster@psuv.org.ve (office). *Website:* www.psuv.org.ve (office).

RANGEL VALE, José Vicente; Venezuelan politician; b. 10 July 1929, Caracas; s. of José Vicente Rangel Cárdenas and Leonor Vale de Rangel; m. Ana Avalos; one s.; ed Colegio La Salle, Barquisimeto, Universidad de los Andes, Cen. Univ. of Venezuela, Univ. of Chile, Univs of Salamanca and Santiago de Compostela, Spain; joined Unión Republicana Democrática aged 16; fmr TV Presenter, Televen, Canal 10; fmr columnist, El Universal, El Informadro, La Tarde, El Regional and Bohemia; cand. in presidential elections 1973, 1978, 1983; elected Deputy to Congress for Estado Miranda; fmr Co-ordinator Movimento Independientes (with Hugo Chávez); Minister of Foreign Affairs 1999–2001, of Defence 2001–02; Vice-Pres. of Venezuela 2002–07. *Publications include:* Tiempo de Verdades, Socialismo y Democracia, Expediente Negro, La Administración de La Justica en Venezuela.

RANJEVA, Gen. Marcel Razanakombana; Malagasy army officer (retd) and politician; b. 15 Jan. 1944, Antananarivo; s. of Rene Ranjeva Raolosoa and Eugenie Raolosoa; m. Michele Rajaonera; two c.; ed Univ. of Paris I (Sorbonne), France; mem. Christian Students Youth 1960–64; assigned to Army Staff Tech. Bd 1975, then to Dept of Econ. Affairs, Ministry of Defence 1976; apptd Dir of Mil. Operations, Office of Mil. Agricultural Production 1982; Commdr Mil. Acad. 1986; Sec.-Gen. Office Malagasy des Tabacs 1992; Chief of Staff, Office of the Pres. 1995–96; Minister of Defence 1996–2002 (resgnd), of Foreign Affairs 2002–09; mem. Asscn des Anciens Elèves de Coëtquidan; Grand Croix de 2ème Classe de la République Malgache; Grand Officier, Légion d'honneur, Commdr; Officier, Ordre nat. du Mérite.

RANJEVA, Raymond, BA, LLD; Malagasy lawyer, judge, academic and international official; b. 31 Aug. 1942, Antananarivo; m. Yvette Madeleine R. Rabetafika 1967; five c.; ed Univ. of Madagascar, Madagascar Nat. School of Admin., Univ. of Paris, France; trainee, Judicial Div., Conseil d'Etat, Paris; Civil Admin., Univ. of Madagascar 1966, Asst Lecturer 1966–72, Lecturer 1972, Dir Dept of Legal and Political Science 1973–82, Prof. 1981–91, Dean of Faculty of Law, Econs, Man. and Social Sciences 1982–88; Lecturer, Hague Acad. of Int. Law 1987–97; Prof., Madagascar Mil. Acad., Madagascar School of Admin.; Dir Public Law and Political Science Study Centre; First Rector, Univ. of Antananarivo 1988–90; Man. Dir Jureco (econ., financial and legal databank for advisory and research bodies) 1986–90, Ed. Lettre mensuelle de Jureco 1986–88; Conciliator, IBRD Int. Centre for Settlement of Investment Disputes 1970; Attorney to Mali, Border Dispute (Burkina Faso/Mali); Consultant on transfer to the State of activities of Eau-Electricité de Madagascar and Electricité de France 1973; Judge, Int. Court of Justice, The Hague 1991–2009, Vice-Pres. 2003–06; Founder-mem. Malagasy Human Rights Cttee 1971; mem. and Vice-Pres. Malagasy Acad. 1974, Pres. Ethics and Political Science section 1975–91; mem. Nat. Constitutional Cttee 1975; mem. Court of Arbitration for Sport 1995; legal adviser to Catholic Bishops' Conf., Madagascar; mem. Governing Body of African Soc. of Int. and Comparative Law, French Soc. of Int. Law, Québec Soc. (Canada); Sec.-Gen. Malagasy Legal

Studies Soc.; mem. Pontifical Comm. 'Justice et Paix' 2002, Curatorium de l'Acad. de Droit Int. 2002; Commdr, Ordre Nat. Malgache of Madagascar, Chevalier, Ordre de Mérite of Madagascar, Officier, Ordre Nat. of Mali, Grand-Croix nat. malgache 2003 Dr hc (Univs of Strasbourg and Limoges).

RANQUE, Denis; French business executive; *Chairman, Airbus Group SE;* b. 7 Jan. 1952, Marseille; m. Monique Ranque; ed École Polytechnique, École des Mines, Paris; began career at Ministry for Industry, various positions in the energy sector; joined Thomson group as Dir of Planning 1983, CEO Thomson Tubes Electroniques 1989–92, Chair. and CEO Thomson Sintra ASM 1992–96, CEO Thomson Marconi Sonar 1996–98, Chair. and CEO Thomson-CSF group (now called Thales) 1998–2009; Chair. École Nationale Supérieure des Mines de Paris 2001–12, Cercle de l'Industrie (French Industrial Asscn) 2002–12; Chair. (non-exec.), Technicolor 2010–12, Airbus Group SE 2013–; Dir, CGG VERITAS 2010–12, Fonds Strategique d'Investissement 2011–12, CMA-CGM, Saint Gobain SA, Scilab; Chair. Fondation École polytechnique 2014–; Chair. Fondation Paristech 2010–15, Haut Comité de Gouvernement d'Entreprise 2013–17; Co-Chair. La Fabrique de l'industrie 2014–17; mem. Academie des Technologies 2015–; Chevalier, Légion d'honneur 1999, Officier 2009; Officier, Ordre nat. du Mérite 2003, Commandeur 2016; Hon. CBE 2004; Verdienstkreuz am Bande 2010. *Leisure interest:* music, sailing. *Address:* Airbus Group, 12 rue Pasteur, BP 76, 92152 Suresnes Cedex, France (office). *E-mail:* chairman@airbus.com (office). *Website:* www.airbus.com (office).

RANTALA, Pekka, MSc; Finnish business executive; *Chief Marketing Officer, HMD Global;* b. 21 Sept. 1966; m. Pirjo Rantala; two c.; ed Helsingin Kauppakorkeakoulu (Helsinki School of Econs); Export Man., Nokia Mobile Phones EMEA 1994–96, Man. Dir Nokia Mobile Phones Alps 1996–98, Nokia Mobile Phones Italia 1998–2000, Vice-Pres. Marketing EMEA 2000–03, Sr Vice-Pres. Marketing Multimedia Business Group Nokia 2004–05, Sr Vice-Pres. Customer and Market Operations 2006–07, Sr Vice-Pres. Global Marketing 2008–11; Man. Dir Fazer Bakeries and Confectionery, Fazer Group 2011–12, Man. Dir Fazer Brands 2012–13; CEO Oy Hartwall Ab 2013–14; CEO Rovio Entertainment Ltd 2014–15; Chair. JOT Automation 2014–16; Chief Marketing Officer, HMD Global (global licensee of Nokia brand) 2016–. *Leisure interests:* running, basketball, cross country skiing, photography, playing the drums. *Address:* HMD Global, Karaportti 2, 02610 Espoo, Finland (office). *E-mail:* info@hmdglobal.com (office). *Website:* www.hmdglobal.com (office).

RANTANEN, Juha Ilari, MSc, MBA; Finnish business executive; b. 25 Jan. 1952, Helsinki; m. Eija Jaaskelainen 1975; three s. one d.; ed Helsinki School of Econs, Int. Man. Inst., Geneva; Man., Internal Accounting, Neste Oy 1977–78, Planning Man. 1979–81, Exec. Vice-Pres., Gas 1986–89, Chemicals 1989–92, Chief Financial Officer 1992–94; Product Line Man., Covering Materials, Partek Oy 1981–84, Vice-Pres., Insulations 1984–86; CEO Borealis A/S 1994–97; Exec. Vice-Pres. Ahlstrom Corpn 1997–98, Pres., CEO 1998–2004; CEO Outokumpu Oyj 2004–11; mem. Bd of Dirs Yara Int. 2012–; Vice-Chair. Moventas Group 2007; Chair. Finpro 2005–09; Vice-Pres. European Confed. of Iron and Steel Industries (Eurofer); fmr Chair. Forest Industries Fed.; Vice-Chair. Confed. of Finnish Industry and Employers; Pres. Asscn of Plastics Manufacturers in Europe 1994–96; mem. Supervisory Bd Varma-Sampo Mutual Pension Insurance Co. *Address:* c/o Board of Directors, Yara International ASA, PO Box 2464, Solli Bygdøy allé 2, 0202, Oslo, Norway.

RANTZEN, Dame Esther Louise, DBE, MA, FRTS; British journalist, television presenter, producer and writer; b. 22 June 1940, Berkhamsted, Herts., England; d. of Harry Barnato Rantzen and Katherine Flora Rantzen (née Leverson); m. Desmond Wilcox 1977 (died 2000); one s. two d.; ed North London Collegiate School and Somerville Coll., Oxford; studio man. making dramatic sound effects, BBC Radio 1963; presenter and producer, That's Life, BBC TV 1973–94, scriptwriter 1976–94; producer, The Big Time (documentary series) 1976–80; regular contrib., Daily Mail, Daily Telegraph, Sunday Times; mem. Nat. Consumer Council 1981–90, Health Educ. Authority 1989–95; Founder and Chair. ChildLine (charity) 1986–2006, Pres. (following merger with Nat. Soc. for the Prevention of Cruelty to Children—NSPCC) 2006–; unsuccessful parl. cand. for Luton South in Gen. Election 2010; f. The Silver Line 2012, now Pres. and Trustee; Pres. Asscn of Youth with ME (AYME) 1996–, Meet-a-Mum Asscn, Anti-Bullying Alliance; Vice-Pres. ASBAH; Chair. Commission4Children 2009; mem. Nat. Consumer Council 1981–90, Health Educ. Authority 1989–95, Campaign for Quality Television; Trustee, NSPCC, Ben Hardwick Memorial Fund; Patron Red Balloon (charity for bullied children), Iain Rennie Hospice at Home, Hillingdon Manor School for Autistic Children, Princess Diana's School, The New School at West Heath, North London Hospice, Campaign for Courtesy; Fellow, Liverpool John Moores Univ.; Hon. Fellow, Somerville Coll., Oxford; six hon. doctorates, including Hon. DLitt (South Bank Univ.) 2000, (Southampton Inst., Univ. of Portsmouth) 2003, (Univ. of Staffordshire) 2009, (Univ. of Wolverhampton) 2009; Special Judges' Award, Royal TV Soc. (RTS) 1974, 1986, BBC TV Personality of 1975, Variety Club of GB, European Soc. for Organ Transplant Award 1985, Richard Dimbleby Award, BAFTA 1988, Snowdon Award for Services to Disabled People 1996, RTS Hall of Fame Award 1997, Champion Community Legal Service 2000, Lifetime Achievement Award, Women in Film and TV. *Television includes:* presenter: That's Life 1973–94, Esther Interviews... 1988, Hearts of Gold 1988–96, Drugwatch (BBC 1), Childwatch (BBC 1), The Lost Babies (also producer), Esther (talk show) 1994–, The Rantzen Report 1996–, That's Esther (ITV) 1999–, Children in Need (BBC 1), Hearts of Gold (BBC 1), Loose Women (guest presenter), Winton's Children (ITV 1), Excuse My French (BBC 2), Old Dogs, New Tricks (BBC 2), How to Have a Good Death (BBC) 2006; other: All Star Family Fortunes (contestant; ITV 1), Would Like To Meet – Celebrity Episode, Prostitute (mini-series) 1998, Grumpy Old Women (guest; BBC 2), Strictly Come Dancing (contestant; BBC 1), Celebrity Stars in Their Eyes (contestant, as Edith Piaf; ITV 1) 2002), Celebrity Cash in the Attic (contestant; BBC 1), Who Do You Think You Are (BBC 1) 2008, I'm a Celebrity Get Me Out of Here (contestant; ITV 1) 2008, Pointless Celebrities (contestant; BBC 1) 2012, Piers Morgan's Life Stories (ITV 1) 2013, Pointless: Children in Need Special (contestant with Terry Wogan; BBC 1) 2013, Celebrity Antiques Road Trip (BBC 1) 2014, The Chase: Celebrity Special (contestant; ITV 1) 2014. *Publications:* Kill the Chocolate Biscuit (with D. Wilcox) 1981, Baby Love 1985, The Story of Ben Hardwick (with S. Woodward) 1985, Once Upon a Christmas 1996, Esther: The Autobiography 2001, A Secret Life (novel) 2003, Running Out of Tears (25 Years of Childline) 2011; writes regularly on social issues for the Daily Mail, Mail on Sunday, Daily Telegraph and Daily Express. *Leisure interests:* work and fantasy. *Address:* c/o Billy Marsh Associates, 4th Floor, 158–160 North Gower Street, London, NW1 2ND, England (office). *Telephone:* (20) 7383-9979 (office). *Fax:* (20) 7388-2296 (office). *E-mail:* talent@billymarsh.co.uk (office). *Website:* www.billymarsh.co.uk/female-clients/esther-rantzen (office).

RAO, A. Janardhana; Indian government official; *Managing Director, Indian Ports Association;* fmr Financial Advisor and Chief Accounts Officer, Kandla Port Trust, apptd Chair. 2004; currently Man. Dir Indian Ports Asscn. *Address:* Indian Ports Association, First Floor, South Tower, NBCC Place, Bhisham Pitamah Marg, Lodi Road, New Delhi 110 003, India (office). *Telephone:* (11) 24365632 (office). *Fax:* (11) 24365866 (office). *E-mail:* md.ipa@nic.in (office). *Website:* www.ipa.nic.in (office).

RAO, Calyampudi Radhakrishna, MA, ScD, FRS; American/Indian statistician; *Professor Emeritus of Statistics, Pennsylvania State University;* b. 10 Sept. 1920, Hadagali, Karnataka State; s. of C. D. Naidu and A. Laxmikanthamma; m. Bhargavi Rao 1948; one s. one d.; ed Andhra and Calcutta Univs; Research at Indian Statistical Inst. 1943–46, Univ. of Cambridge, UK 1946–48; Prof. and Head of Div. of Theoretical Research and Training 1949–64; Dir Research and Training School, Indian Statistical Inst. 1964–71, Sec. and Dir 1972–76, Jawaharlal Nehru Prof. 1976–84; Univ. Prof., Univ. of Pittsburgh 1979–88; Nat. Prof., India 1987–92; Eberly Prof. of Statistics, Pennsylvania State Univ. 1988–91, Dir Center for Multivariate Analysis 1988–2009, Prof. Emer. 2009–; Ed. Sankhya 1964–80, Journal of Multivariate Analysis 1988–92; Fellow, Inst. of Mathematical Statistics, USA, Pres. 1976–77; Treas. Int. Statistical Inst. 1961–65, Pres. 1977–79; Pres. Int. Biometric Soc. 1973–75, Forum for Interdisciplinary Math.; mem. NAS; Foreign mem. Lithuanian Acad. of Sciences; Fellow, American Statistical Asscn, Econometric Soc., Nat. Acad., Third World Acad. of Sciences; Hon. Life Fellow, King's Coll. Cambridge, Hon. Fellow, Royal Statistical Soc., European Acad. of Sciences, Hon. mem. Int. Statistical Inst., Inst. of Combinatorics and Applications, Finnish Statistical Soc., Portuguese Statistical Soc., Hon. Foreign mem. American Acad. Arts and Sciences, Hon. Life mem. Biometric Soc.; Hon. DSc (31 univs), Hon. DLitt (Delhi); Emanuel and Carol Parzen Prize for Statistical Innovation; Bhatnagar Memorial Award for Scientific Research 1963, Guy Silver Medal Royal Statistical Soc. 1965, Meghnad Saha Medal 1969, Nat. Science Acad., J.C. Bose Gold Medal, Wilks Memorial Medal 1989, Calcutta Univ. Gold Medal, Mahalanobis Birth Centenary Gold Medal, Army Wilks Medal, Padma Vibhushan 2001, Nat. Science Acad. Ramanujan Medal 2003, Int. Statistics Inst. Mahalanobis Prize 2003, Sankhyiki Bhushan, Pres.'s Nat. Medal for Science, USA 2002, India Science Award 2010, Guyn Medal in Gold, Royal Statistical Soc. 2011. *Publications include:* Advanced Statistical Methods in Biometric Research, Linear Statistical Inference and its Application, Generalized Inverse of Matrices and its Applications, Linear Statistical Inference, Characterization Problems of Mathematical Statistics (with A. Kagan and V. Linmik) 1973, Estimation of Variance Components and its Applications (with J. Kleffe) 1988, Statistics and Truth 1989, Choquet Deny Type Functional Equations with Applications to Stochastic Models (with D. N. Shanbhaq) 1994, Linear Models: Least Squares and Alternatives (with H. Toutenburg) 1995, Matrix Algebra and Its Applications to Statistics and Econometrics (with M. B. Rao) 1998; more than 350 research papers in math. statistics. *Leisure interest:* writing humorous essays. *Address:* 29 Old Orchard Street, Williamsville, NY 14229, USA (home). *Telephone:* (716) 639-0902 (home). *E-mail:* crr1@psu.edu (office). *Website:* www.stat.psu.edu/~crrao (office).

RAO, Chennamaneni Vidyasagar, BSc, LLB; Indian lawyer and politician; *Governor of Maharashtra and of Tamil Nadu;* b. 12 Feb. 1942, Nagaram, Karimnagar, Hyderabad State; s. of C. Srinivasa Rao and Chandramma Rao; m. Vinoda Rao; two s. one d.; ed Osmania Univ.; pvt. law practice, Karimnagar 1973–; mem. Andhra Pradesh Legis. Ass. from Metpalli 1985–98; mem. Lok Sabha (lower house of parl.) from Karimnagar 1998–2004; Union Minister of State for Home Affairs, Commerce and Industry 1999–2004; Gov. of Maharashtra 2014–, also of Tamil Nadu 2016–; mem. Bharatiya Jana Sangh (party dissolved 1977), re-est. as Bharatiya Janata Party, Pres. Maharashtra State Unit 1999; fmr Pres. Janata Party, Karimnagar Dist. *Address:* Office of the Governor, Raj Bhavan, Walkeshwar Rd, Malabar Hills, Mumbai, 400 035, India (office). *Telephone:* (22) 23632660 (office). *Fax:* (22) 23680505 (office). *E-mail:* governor-mh@nic.in (office). *Website:* rajbhavan.maharashtra.gov.in (office).

RAO, Chintamani Nagesa Ramachandra, PhD, DSc, FRS, FNA; Indian chemist and academic; *National Research Professor, Linus Pauling Research Professor and Honorary President, Jawaharlal Nehru Centre for Advanced Scientific Research;* b. 30 June 1934, Bangalore; s. of H. Nagesa Rao; m. Indumati Rao 1960; one s. one d.; ed Banaras Univ., Purdue Univ., USA, Mysore Univ.; Lecturer, Indian Inst. of Science, Bangalore 1959–63, Chair. Solid State and Structural Chem. Unit and Materials Research Lab. 1977–84, Dir Indian Inst. of Science 1984–94; Prof., later Sr Prof., Indian Inst. of Tech., Kanpur 1963–77, Dean of Research and Devt 1969–72; Albert Einstein Research Prof. and Pres. Jawaharlal Nehru Centre for Advanced Scientific Research 1995–99, Linus Pauling Research Prof. and Hon. Pres. 1999–; Visiting Prof., Purdue Univ. 1967–68, Univ. of Oxford, UK 1974–75; Prof., Indian Inst. of Science, Bangalore; Fellow, King's Coll., Cambridge, UK 1983–84; Chair. Science Advisory Council to Prime Minister of India 1985–89, Indo-Japan Science Council, Scientific Advisory Cttee to Union Cabinet 1997–98; fmr Chair. Advisory Bd of Council of Scientific and Industrial Research (India); mem. Atomic Energy Comm. of India; Pres. St Catherine's Coll. Oxford 1974–75, Indian Nat. Science Acad. 1985–86, IUPAC 1985–87, Indian Science Congress Asscn 1987–88, Indian Acad. of Sciences 1988–91, Materials Research Soc. of India 1989–91; Nehru Visiting Prof., Univ. of Cambridge, Linnett Visiting Prof. 1998; Gauss Professorship, Acad. of Sciences, Göttingen, Germany 2003; Distinguished Visiting Prof., Univ. of California, USA, Univ. of Cambridge, UK; Albert Einstein Prof., Chinese Acad. of Sciences 2012; mem. Editorial Bd of 15 leading scientific journals; Founding mem. and Pres. Third World Acad. of Sciences; mem. Pontifical Acad. of Sciences; Titular mem. European Acad. of Arts, Sciences and Humanities; Corresp. mem. Brazilian Acad. of Sciences; Foreign mem. Academia Europaea, Serbian and Slovenian Acads of Science, Yugoslavia, Russian, Czech and Polish Acads of Sciences, American Acad.

of Arts and Sciences, Royal Spanish Acad. of Sciences, French Acad. of Sciences, American Philosophical Soc., African Acad., Materials Socs of Japan and Korea, Int. Acad. of Ceramics; Foreign Assoc. NAS; Foreign Fellow, RSC; Hon. Foreign mem. Korean Acad. of Science and Tech., Hon. mem. Japan Acad., Hon. FRSC 1989, Hon. Fellow, Inst. of Physics, London 2006, St Catherine's Coll. Oxford 2007; Albert Einstein Prof., Chinese Acad. of Sciences 2012; Commdr, Nat. Order of Lion (Senegal) 1999, Karnataka Ratna 2001, Officier des Palmes académiques 2002, Grand-Cross, Order of Scientific Merit (Brazil) 2002, Commdr, Order of Rio Branco (Brazil) 2002, Chevalier, Légion d'honneur 2005, Order of Friendship, Pres. of Russia 2009, Bharat Ratna 2014, Order of the Rising Sun 2015; Dr hc from 60 univs, including Purdue, Bordeaux, Banaras, Mysore, Indian Inst. of Tech., Bombay, Indian Inst. of Tech., Kharagpur, Notre Dame, Novosibirsk, Université Joseph Fourier, Uppsala, Wales, Wrocław, Caen, Khartoum, Calcutta and Sri Venkateswara Univ.; numerous awards including Marlow Medal, Faraday Soc. 1967, Bhatnagar Award 1968, Jawaharlal Nehru Fellowship, Indian Inst. of Tech. 1973, Padma Shri 1974, Sir C. V. Raman Award 1975, ACS Centennial Foreign Fellowship 1976, Fed. of Indian Chamber of Commerce and Industry Award for Physical Sciences 1977, S.N. Bose Medal, Indian Nat. Science Acad. 1980, Royal Soc. of Chem. (London) Medal 1981, Padma Vibhushan 1985, Jawaharlal Nehru Award 1988, Saha Medal, Indian Nat. Science Acad. 1990, Blackett Lecturer, Royal Soc. 1991, NAS Int. Science Lecture, USA 1993, Sahabdeen Int. Award of Science, Sri Lanka 1994, Third World Acad. of Sciences Medal in Chem. 1995, Albert Einstein Gold Medal, UNESCO 1996, Asutosh Mookerjee Medal 1996, Centenary Lectureship and Medal, Royal Soc. of Chem. 2000, Hughes Medal, Royal Soc. 2000, Millennium Plaque of Honour, Indian Science Congress 2001, Chemical Pioneer, American Inst. of Chemists 2005, India Science Award, Govt of India 2005, Nat. Research Professorship, Govt of India 2006, Nikkei Asia Prize for Science, Tech. and Innovation from Japan 2008, Royal Medal (Queen's Medal), Royal Soc., London 2009, August Wilhelm von Hoffmann Medal for outstanding contribs to chem., German Chemical Soc. 2010, Ernesto Illy Trieste Science Prize for materials research 2011, Award for Int. Science Co-operation, Chinese Acad. of Sciences 2012, Sheikh Saud International Prize for Materials Research 2019. *Publications include:* 45 books, including Ultraviolet Visible Spectroscopy 1960, Chemical Applications of Infra-red Spectroscopy 1963, Spectroscopy in Inorganic Chemistry 1970, Modern Aspects of Solid State Chemistry 1970, Solid State Chemistry 1974, Educational Technology in Teaching of Chemistry 1975, Phase Transitions in Solids 1978, Preparation and Characterization of Materials 1981, The Metallic and Non-Metallic States of Matter 1985, New Directions in Solid State Chemistry 1986, Chemistry of Oxide Superconductors 1988, Chemical and Structural Aspects of High Temperature Oxide Superconductors 1988, Bismuth and Thallium Superconductors 1989, Chemistry of Advanced Materials 1992, Chemical Approaches to the Synthesis of Inorganic Materials 1994, Transition Metal Oxides 1995, Colossal Magnetoresistance 1998, Understanding Chemistry 1999; more than 1,500 original research papers. *Leisure interests:* gourmet cooking, general reading, music. *Address:* Jawaharlal Nehru Centre for Advanced Scientific Research, Jakkur PO, Bangalore 560 064 (office); JNC President's House, Indian Institute of Science Campus, Bangalore 560 012, India (home). *Telephone:* (80) 23653075 (office); (80) 23601410 (home). *Fax:* (80) 22082760 (office); (80) 23602468 (office). *E-mail:* cnrrao@jncasr.ac.in (office). *Website:* www.jncasr.ac.in/cnrrao (office).

RAO, G. M. (Grandhi Mallikarjuna), BE; Indian mechanical engineer and business executive; *Group Chairman, GMR Group;* b. 14 July 1950, Rajam, Andhra Pradesh; m. Varalakshmi Rao; three c.; ed Vizag Eng Coll.; began career with single jute mill, Rajam 1978; Founder GMR Group, Chair. and Man. Dir 1978–2007, Group Chair. 2007–; infrastructure interests in India and abroad including power plants, airports (Hyderabad, Delhi and Istanbul); Chair. Emer. ING Vysya Bank; f. GMR Varalakshmi Foundation; mem. Central Bd of Dirs Reserve Bank of India 2011–; Dr hc (Jawaharlal Nehru Technological Univ.) 2005, (York Univ., Canada) 2011; Hon. DLitt (Andhra Univ.) 2010; Economic Times Awards for Corp. Excellence Entrepreneur of theYear 2006/07, Indian Business Leader Award, CNBC TV 18 2007, Sir M. Visveswaraiah Award, Fed. of Karnataka Chamber Of Commerce and Industry 2008, Most Inspiring Entrepreneur of the Year Award, Nat. Inst. of Industrial Eng Mumbai 2008, Infrastructure Person of the Year Award 2009, First Generation Entrepreneur of the Year Award, CNBC TV18 2009. *Address:* GMR Group, Skip House, 25/1, Museum Road, Bangalore 560 025, India (office). *Telephone:* (80) 22070100 (office). *Fax:* (80) 22213091 (office). *E-mail:* info@gmrgroup.in (office). *Website:* www.gmrgroup.co.in (office).

RAO, Kalvakuntla Chandrasekhar, MA; Indian politician; *Chief Minister of Telangana;* b. 17 Feb. 1954, Chintamadaka; m. Kalvakuntla Shobha 1969; one s. one d.; ed Osmania Univ., Hyderabad; mem. AP Legis. Ass. 1985–2004, Chair. Cttee on Public Undertakings 1992–93, Deputy Speaker 1999–2001; Minister of State, Govt of AP 1987–88, Cabinet Minister 1997–99; mem. Lok Sabha from Karimnagar, AP constituency 2004–09, for Mahbubnagar 2009–14; Minister without Portfolio May–Nov. 2004, Minister of Labour and Employment 2004–06; Founder and Pres. Telangana Rashtra Samithi 2001–09; mem. Telangana Legis. Ass. from Gajwel constituency 2014–; Chief Minister of Telengana (first, following creation of new state 2 June 2014) 2014–. *Address:* Office of the Chief Minister, Hyderabad, Telangana (office); Telangana Rashtra Samithi, Karimnagar, India (office). *Telephone:* (40) 23555798 (office). *Website:* www.aponline.gov.in (office).

RAO, Kamini A., MCh, FRCOG; Indian gynaecologist; *Medical Director, BACC Healthcare Private Ltd;* b. 2 July 1953, Hyderabad, Andhra Pradesh; m. Dr Arvind Rao; one s. one d.; ed St John's Medical Coll., Bangalore Univ., Royal Coll. of Physicians, Ireland, Univ. of Liverpool, UK; worked at King's Coll. School of Medicine, St Bartholomew's Hospital, UK; est. Bangalore Assisted Conception Centre (now BACC Healthcare Private Ltd), currently Medical Dir; Sr Vice-Pres. Fed. of Obstetric and Gynaecological Societies (FOGSI) 1997–98, Pres. 2000–01; Sec., Bangalore Soc. of Obstetricians and Gynecologists 1992–94, Pres. 1998–99; mem. Exec. Cttee Indian Soc. for Assisted Reproduction; Chair. Cttee for Genetics and Fetal Medicine 1991–96; Vice-Pres. Karnataka Asscn for Sexual and Reproductive Medicine 1997–, Soc. for Fetal Medicine and Genetics 1998–; Co-Chair. Int. Fed. of Obstetrics and Gynecology (FIGO) Women's Sexual and Reproductive Rights (WSRR) Cttee and Coordinator for WSRR project; FOGSI Rep. to Asia Oceania Fed. of Obstetrics and Gynecology 2003; FOGSI Rep. to FIGO 2004; Fellow, Indian Coll. of Obstetricians and Gynecologists, Bangalore, Royal Coll. of Obstetricians and Gynecologists, UK; mem. Royal Coll. of Physicians, Ireland, Royal Coll. of Surgeons, Ireland, Indian Soc. of Prenatal Diagnosis and Therapy, Indian Asscn of Gynaecological Endoscopists, Indian Menopause Soc., Indian Soc. of Health Admins, Indian Asscn of Human Reproduction, Medical Ultrasound Soc., Karnataka, Tech. Advisory Cttee, Nat. Abortion Assessment Project, Task Force for Health and Family Welfare, Govt of Karnataka; Rajyotsava Award, Govt of Karnataka 1997, Vidya Ratan Award 1998, Lifetime Achievement Honours Tribute Award, Vivekananda Inst. of Human Excellence, Padma Shri 2014. *Publications include:* An Introduction to Genetics and Fetal Medicine, Chorionic Villus Sampling (co-author), Reproductive Medicine and Prenatal Diagnosis, Diagnosis and Management of Infertility, Amniotic Fluid (co-author), The Infertility Manual (co-author), Current Concepts in Perinatology, A Handbook on Obstetric Emergencies. *Address:* BACC Healthcare Private Limited, No 6/7, Kumarakrupa Road, High Grounds, Bangalore 560 001, India (office). *Telephone:* (80) 22260880 (office); (80) 41138255 (office). *Fax:* (80) 2250465 (office). *E-mail:* kambacc@vsnl.com (office); drkaminirao@gmail.com (office). *Website:* www.baccweb.com (office).

RAO, Nirupama Menon, MA; Indian diplomatist (retd) and civil servant; b. 6 Dec. 1950, Malappuram, Kerala; m. Shri Sudhakar Rao; two s.; ed Univ. of Mysore, Marathwada Univ., Maharashtra; joined Indian Foreign Service 1973, First Sec. (Agreement), Mission in Colombo 1981–83, Desk Officer, Southern Africa and Nepal Desks, Ministry of External Affairs, then with East Asia Div. 1984–92, Minister for Press Affairs, Embassy in Washington, DC 1993–95, Amb. to Peru 1995–98, Deputy Chief of Mission, Embassy in Moscow 1998–99, Head of Div. in charge of Multilateral Econ. Relations, Ministry of External Affairs 2000–01, Jt Sec. for External Publicity and Official Spokesperson 2001–02, Additional Sec. Human Resources Div. 2002–04, Foreign Service Inspector 2004, High Commr to Sri Lanka 2004–06, Amb. to People's Repub. of China (first woman) 2006–09, Foreign Sec. (second woman) 2009–11, Amb. to USA 2011–13; Meera and Vikram Gandhi Fellow, Brown-India Initiative, Watson Inst. for Int. Studies, Brown Univ. 2014–; Jawaharlal Nehru Fellow, Jawaharlal Nehru Memorial Fund, New Delhi 2014; fmr Fellow specializing in Asia-Pacific Security, Center for Int. Affairs (now Weatherhead Center), Harvard Univ., USA; Distinguished Int. Exec. in Residence, Univ. of Maryland, USA 1999–2000; Hon. DLitt (Pondicherry Univ.). *Publication:* Rain Rising (book of poetry; translated into Chinese and Russian) 2004. *Leisure interests:* fine arts, classical music, literature. *Website:* www.nirupamamenonrao.net.

RAO, Yi, PhD; Chinese neuroscientist and academic; *Founding Director, IDG/McGovern Institute for Brain Research, Peking University;* b. 1962, Jiangxi; ed Shanghai Medical Univ., Univ. of California, San Francisco; mem. Faculty, Washington Univ., St Louis, USA –2000; apptd first Elsa A. Swanson Research Prof., Feinberg School of Medicine, Northwestern Univ., USA 2000; Chair Prof. Peking Univ. School of Life Sciences 2007–, Dean 2007–13, Founding Dir, IDG/McGovern Inst. for Brain Research 2013–; Investigator, Nat. Inst. of Biological Sciences, Beijing; mem. Editorial Bd The Journal of Neuroscience, Developmental Brain Research, NeuroSignals, Neuroscience Research; ad hoc referee for Biochemical Journal, Journal of Molecular Biology, Journal of Cell Biology and other publs; Esther A. and Joseph Lingenstein Fellowship in Neuroscience 2000, Charles B. Wilson Brain Tumor Research Excellence Award in Neuroscience. *Publications:* numerous papers in professional journals on molecular studies of neuronal polarity and genetic analysis of social behaviour. *Address:* IDG/McGovern Institute for Brain Research, Peking University, 5 Yiheyuan Road, Beijing 100871, People's Republic of China (office). *Telephone:* (10) 80726672 (office). *Fax:* (10) 80726673 (office). *E-mail:* raolab@126.com (office); yrao@pku.edu.cn (office). *Website:* mgv.pku.edu.cn (office); www.bio.pku.edu.cn (office); raolab.org.

RAO, Zihe, BSc, MSc, PhD; Chinese biologist, biophysicist, virologist and academic; *Associate Professor, Nankai University;* b. 6 Sept. 1950, Nanjing, Jiangsu Prov.; ed Univ. of Science and Tech. of China, Inst. of Biophysics, Chinese Acad. of Sciences, Melbourne Univ., Australia; Postdoctoral Fellow, Lab. of Molecular Biophysics, Univ. of Oxford, UK 1989–92, Researcher with Prof. David Stuart FRS 1992–96; returned to China to found Lab. of Structural Biology, Tsinghua Univ., Beijing 1996–; Dir-Gen. Inst. of Biophysics (IBP), Chinese Acad. of Sciences, Beijing 2003–07; apptd Pres. Nankai Univ., Tianjin 2006, now Assoc. Prof.; Prof. and Head, Tsinghua-Nankai-IBP Jt Lab. for Structural Biology 2006–; mem. Chinese Acad. of Sciences 2003–, Third World Acad. of Sciences 2004–; Fellow, Hertford Coll. 2011; Qiushi Outstanding Scientist Prize in Life Sciences, Hong Kong 1999, Yangtze River Distinguished Scholar, Ministry of Educ. 2000, He Liang Heli Foundation Science and Tech. Prize 2003. *Publications:* more than 130 papers in int. scientific journals, including Cell, Nature, PNAS, Journal of Molecular Biology, Journal of the American Chemistry Society, on proteins related to human health and disease. *Address:* Biochemistry and Molecular Biology, A201, New Life Sciences Building, College of Life Sciences, Nankai University, Tianjin 300071 (office); Laboratory of Structural Biology, Rooms 201–218, Life Science Building, Tsinghua University, Beijing 100084, People's Republic of China (office). *Telephone:* (22) 23502351 (office); (10) 62771493 (office). *Fax:* (10) 62773145 (office). *E-mail:* raozh@nankai.edu.cn (office); raozh@xtal.tsinghua.edu.cn (office). *Website:* sky.nankai.edu.cn (office); xtal.tsinghua.edu.cn (office).

RAOUIA, Abderrahmane; Algerian economist and politician; b. 7 Nov. 1960, Mostaganem; m.; two c.; ed Univ. of Algiers, Ecole Nat. des Impôts, Clermont-Ferrand, France; Dir, Tax Studies and Legislation Dept, Ministry of Finance 1985–87, Head of Int. Tax Conventions Bureau 1990–93, Deputy Dir of Int. Tax Conventions 1993–2000, Dir of Tax Legislation 2000–03, Study and Synthesis Officer in Cabinet of Minister of Finance 2005–06, Dir-Gen. of Taxation 2006–17, Minister of Finance 2017–19; worked for IMF in Democratic Repub. of the Congo 2003–05. *Address:* c/o Ministry of Finance, Immeuble Ahmed Francis, Ben Aknoun, Algiers, Algeria.

RAOULT, Éric, LèsScEcon; French politician; b. 19 June 1955, Paris; m. Corinne Sapet 2002; ed Inst. d'Etudes Politiques, Paris and Inst. Français de Presse; Parl. Asst to Claude Labbé; Town Councillor, Raincy 1977; Deputy Mayor of Raincy 1983–95, Mayor 1995–14; mem. Cen. Cttee of RPR 1982; Deputy to Nat. Ass. 1986–1995, 2002–12, Vice-Pres. 1993–95, 2002–07; mem. Comm. on Foreign

Affairs; Regional Councillor, Île de France 1992–2004; Minister of Integration and the Fight against Exclusion May–Nov. 1995, Deputy Minister with responsibility for Urban Affairs and Integration 1995–97; Nat. Sec. with responsibility for elections 1998–99, with responsibility for Feds and Dom-Tom (RPR) 1999–2002, Union pour un Mouvement Populaire 2007–12, now Political Adviser; French mem. OSCE Parliamentary Ass. 2011–; Chevalier de la Légion d'honneur. *Publication:* S.O.S Banlieues 1994.

RAPACZYNSKI, Wanda, MPPM, PhD; Polish/American business executive; b. 1947; m.; one d.; ed Yale Univ. and City Univ. of New York, USA; began career as a prof. of psychology, lectured at several univs in New York and Conn.; Post-doctoral Fellow, Educational Testing Service, Princeton, NJ –1980; Researcher and Project Dir, Yale Univ. Family TV Research and Consultation Center 1980–82; fmr Exec., Vice-Pres. and Head of Project Devt Citibank (NY) –1992; apptd Pres. and CEO Agora SA (media corpn) 1992, Pres. Man. Bd, Head of Finance and Radio Divs, Pres. Supervisory Bd AMS SA (subsidiary) 2002–07, currently mem. Bd Agora Foundation and Supervisory Bd; Pres. Supervisory Bd of Polish Union of Pvt. Employers in Media and Advertising 2003–; mem. Advisory Bd of Centre for European Reform, Polish Group in Trilateral Comm. 2002; mem. Bd of Dirs Adecco SA 2008–; Trustee Cen. European Univ., Hungary; Media Trend Person of the Year statuette 2002, Person of the Year 2002 in the Advertising Industry, Impactor Awards 2003, ranked first by IR Magazine in the Best IR by a CEO/CFO in CEE region category 2003. *Address:* Agora SA, Czerska 8/10, 00-732 Warsaw, Poland (office). *Telephone:* (22) 5554002 (office). *Fax:* (22) 5554850 (office). *Website:* www .agora.pl (office).

RAPANOS, Vassilis, PhD; Greek economist, politician and fmr central banker; b. 1947, Kos; ed Athens Univ. of Econs and Business, Queen's Univ., Kingston, Canada; imprisoned for more than four years for participating in resistance against mil. regime ruling Greece 1969; fmr Assoc. Prof., Athens Univ. of Econs and Business; financial adviser to Prime Minister Costas Simitis 2000–04, to Perm. Greek Del. to EU, Brussels; fmr Deputy Head of Greek Del. to OECD, Paris; Chair. Hellenic Telecommunications Org. (OTE) 1998–2000; fmr Gov. Nat. Mortgage Bank of Greece (merged with Nat. Bank of Greece 1998), Chair. Nat. Bank of Greece 2009–12, Hellenic Bank Asscn 2009–12; Minister of Finance (designate) following formation of coalition govt with Panhellenic Socialist Movt (PASOK) and Democratic Left (Dimokratiki Aristera) 20–25 June 2012 (resgnd due to ill health); Research Assoc., Inst. of Econ. and Industrial Research (IOBE) 2007–09.

RAPHAEL; Spanish singer; b. (Rafael Martos), 5 May 1942, Linares, Jaén; m. Natalia Figueroa 1972; two s. one d.; first prize winner at Salzburg Festival children's singing competition aged nine; subsequently won numerous other competitions; began professional career in Madrid nightclub 1960; rep. of Spain, Eurovision Song Contest 1966, 1967; US debut 1967; toured USSR 1968, Japan 1970, Australia 1971; Broadway debut 1974; celebrated 25th anniversary as professional singer with open-air concert at Bernabé Stadium, Madrid 1985. *Films include:* Las gemelas 1963, Cuando tú no estás 1966, Al ponerse el sol 1967, Digan lo que digan 1968, El Ángel 1969, El golfo 1969, Sin un adiós 1970, Volveré a nacer 1973, Ritmo, amor y primavera 1981. *Television include:* Donde termina el camino (series) 1978, Horas doradas (series) 1980. *Recordings include:* Los hombres lloran también 1964, Sigo siendo aquel 1985, Toda una vida 1985, Las apariencias engañan 1988, Maravilloso corazón 1989, El monstruo de la canción 1990, Andaluz 1990, Fantasia 1994, Brillantes 1994, Monstruo 1995, Desde el fondo de mi alma 1995, Raphael 1998, Dama Dama 1999, Sentado a la vera del camino 1999, Hotel de l'universe 2001, Yo soy aquel 2001, Maldito Raphael 2001, Realite 2003, De vuelta 2003, Vuelve Por Navidad 2004, A Que No Te Vas 2006, Cerca de tí 2006, 50 Años Despues 2008, Viva Raphael! 2009, Te Llevo En El Corazón 2010, El Reencuentro 2012, Mi gran noche 2013, 50 Éxitos de Mi Vida 2013, De Amor y Desamor 2014, Ven a mi casa esta navidad 2015, Infinitos Bailes 2016. *Website:* www.raphaelnet.com.

RAPHAEL, Frederic Michael, MA, FRSL; American writer; b. 14 Aug. 1931, Chicago, Ill.; s. of Cedric Michael Raphael and Irene Rose Mauser; m. Sylvia Betty Glatt 1955; two s. one d.; ed Charterhouse, St John's Coll., Cambridge (major scholar in Classics); Lippincott Prize 1961, Prix Simone Genevois 2000. *Films:* screenplays: Nothing But the Best 1964 (Writers' Guild Best Comedy), Darling (Acad. Award for Best Original Screenplay, Writer's Guild Best Screenplay, British Film Acad. Award) 1965, Far from the Madding Crowd 1967, Two for the Road 1968, Daisy Miller 1974, Rogue Male 1976, School Play 1978, Richard's Things 1980, The Man in the Brooks Brothers Shirt (ACE Award 1991), Armed Response 1995, Eyes Wide Shut 1998, Coast to Coast 2002. *Radio plays:* The Daedalus Dimension 1982, The Thought of Lydia 1988, The Empty Jew 1993, Final Demands 2010, Couples 2010. *Television plays:* The Glittering Prizes (Royal TV Soc. Writer of the Year Award) 1976, From the Greek 1979, Oxbridge Blues 1984, After the War 1989, A Thousand Kisses 2011, Jake Liebowitz, A Life in Film 2013. *Publications include:* novels: Obbligato 1956, The Earlsdon Way 1958, The Limits of Love 1960, A Wild Sunrise 1961, The Graduate's Wife 1962, The Trouble with England 1962, Lindmann 1963, Orchestra and Beginners 1967, Like Men Betrayed 1970, April, June and November 1972, The Glittering Prizes 1976, Heaven and Earth 1985, After the War 1988, A Wild Surmise 1991, A Double Life 1993, Old Scores 1995, All His Sons 1999, Fame and Fortune 2007, Final Demands 2010, Private Views 2014; short stories: Sleeps Six 1979, Oxbridge Blues 1980, Think of England 1986, The Hidden I (illustrated by Sarah Raphael) 1990, The Latin Lover and Other Stories 1994; biography: Somerset Maugham and his World 1977, Byron 1982, A Jew among the Romans, Flavius Josephus and His Legacy 2013; essays: Cracks in the Ice 1979, Of Gods and Men (illustrated by Sarah Raphael) 1992, The Necessity of Anti-Semitism 1997, Historicism and its Poverty 1998, Karl Popper 1998, Eyes Wide Open 1999, Personal Terms 2001, The Benefits of Doubt 2002, Rough Copy (Personal Terms II) 2004, Cuts and Bruises (Personal Terms III) 2006, Ticks and Crosses (Personal Terms IV) 2008, Ifs and Buts (Personal Terms V) 2011, There and Then (Personal Terms VI) 2013, J. R. Oppenheimer, for example (e-book essay) 2013; translations: Catullus (with K. McLeish) 1976, The Oresteia of Aeschylus 1978, Aeschylus (complete plays, with K. McLeish) 1991, Euripides' Medea (with K. McLeish) 1994, Euripides: Hippolytus, Bacchae (with K. McLeish) 1997, Sophocles Aias (with K. McLeish) 1998, Bacchae 1999, The Satyrica of Petronius 2009. *Leisure interests:* tennis,

bridge, having gardened. *Address:* Ed Victor Ltd, 6 Bayley Street, Bedford Square, London, WC1B 3HE, England (office).

RAPLEY, Christopher G., CBE, PhD; British museum director, earth system scientist and academic; *Professor of Climate Science, University College London;* b. 8 April 1947, West Bromwich, West Midlands; s. of Ronald Rapley and Barbara Helen Rapley (née Stubbs); m. Norma Rapley; two d. (twins); ed King Edward's School, Bath, Jesus Coll. Oxford, Victoria Univ. of Manchester, Univ. Coll., London; Head of Remote Sensing, Mullard Space Science Lab., Univ. Coll. London 1982–94, Prof. of Remote Sensing 1991–97, Hon. Prof. 1998–, currently Prof. of Climate Science 2010–; Exec. Dir Int. Geosphere-Biosphere Programme, Stockholm 1994–97; Dir British Antarctic Survey 1998–2007 (retd); Dir Science Museum, London 2007–10; Chair. Policy Comm. on Communicating Climate Science, Univ. Coll., London 2012–; Chair. London Climate Change Partnership 2013–, Dir-Gen.'s High-Level Science Policy Advisory Cttee, European Space Agency 2014–16; Chair. Int. Polar Year 2007–08, Planning Group 2003–04; mem. American Geophysical Union 1984–; Fellow, St Edmund's Coll., Cambridge 1999–; Hon. Prof., Univ. of East Anglia 1999–, Univ. Coll. London 1999–; Hon. DrSc (Bristol) 2009, (East Anglia) 2010; Edinburgh Science Medal 2008. *Play:* 2071 (co-author). *Publications:* more than 200 articles and papers in professional scientific literature. *Leisure interests:* digital photography. *Address:* University College London, Gower Street, London, WC1E 6BT, England (office). *Telephone:* (20) 3108-6320 (office). *E-mail:* christopher.rapley@ucl.ac.uk (office). *Website:* www.ucl.ac.uk/earth-sciences (office).

RAPOTA, Lt-Gen. Grigory Alekseyevich; Russian government official and fmr intelligence officer; b. 5 Feb. 1944, Moscow; m.; three c.; ed Moscow Bauman Higher School of Tech., Inst. of Intelligence Service; mem. First Chief Dept of KGB; worked in USA and Finland; Deputy Dir Intelligence Service Russian Fed. 1994–98; Deputy Sec., Security Council April–Nov. 1998; Dir-Gen. Rosvooruzheniye state co. 1998–99; First Deputy Minister of Econ. Devt and Trade 1999–2000; First Deputy Minister of Industry, Science and Tech. 2000–01; Sec.-Gen. Eurasian Econ. Community—EurAsEC 2002–07; Presidential Rep. to Southern Fed. Okrug (Dist) 2007–08, to Volga Fed. Okrug 2008–11.

RAPPENEAU, Jean-Paul; French film director and screenwriter; b. 8 April 1932, Auxerre, Yonne; s. of Jean Rappeneau and Anne-Marie Rappeneau (née Bornhauser); m. Claude-Lise Cornély 1971; two s.; ed Lycée Jacques-Amyot, Auxerre, Faculté de droit, Paris; asst dir 1953–57; dir and screenwriter 1958–; Officier, Légion d'honneur, Officier, Ordre Nat. du Mérite, Commdr des Arts et Lettres; 10 César Awards 1990 (including Best Dir, Best Picture), Golden Globe Award for best foreign film 1990, US Nat. Review Bd Best Foreign Film 1990, Grand Prix Nat. du Cinéma 1994. *Films include:* as director: La Maison sur la place, Chronique provinciale 1958; wrote and directed La Vie de château 1966 (Prix Louis-Delluc), Les Mariés de l'An Deux 1970, Le Sauvage 1975, Tout feu, tout flamme 1982; as dir and jt adaptor Cyrano de Bergerac 1990, Le Hussard sur le toit 1995, Bon Voyage (Best Dir Cabourg Romantic Film Festival) 2002; as screenwriter: Signé Arsène Lupin 1959, Le Mariage (in La Française et l'Amour) 1959, Zazie dans le métro 1960, Vie privée 1961, Le Combat dans l'île 1961, L'Homme de Rio 1962, La Fabuleuse aventure de Marco Polo 1965, Les Survivants (TV) 1965, Le Magnifique 1973, Le Sauvage 1975, All Fired Up 1982, Cyrano de Bergerac (César Award for Best Film, César Award for Best Director, David di Donatello for Best Foreign Film, Golden Globe Award for Best Foreign Language Film, London Film Critics' Circle Award for Foreign Language Film of the Year, Nat. Bd of Review Award for Best Foreign Language Film, People's Choice Award, Toronto Int. Film Festival) 1990, Le hussard sur le toit 1995, Bon voyage (Swann d'Or for Best Dir) 2003, Belles familles 2015. *Address:* c/o Artmédia, 20 avenue Rapp, 75007 Paris (office); 24 rue Henri Barbusse, 75005 Paris, France (home). *E-mail:* info@artmedia.fr (office).

RARAWA, Denton, MSc; Solomon Islands central banker; *Governor, Central Bank of Solomon Islands;* ed Australian Nat. Univ., Cardiff Business School, Univ. of Wales, UK; joined Cen. Bank of Solomon Islands as Research Officer, Econs Dept 1983, Asst Man., Econs Dept 1988–92, Man. 1992–98, Deputy Gov., Cen. Bank of Solomon Islands 1998–2008, Gov. 2008–. *Address:* Office of the Governor, Central Bank of Solomon Islands, POB 634, Honiara, Solomon Islands (office). *Telephone:* 21791 (office). *Fax:* 23513 (office). *E-mail:* info@cbsi.com.sb (office). *Website:* www.cbsi.com.sb (office).

RASHEED, Mohamed; Maldivian politician; fmr Dir, Ministry of Health; Minister of Econ. Devt 2008–10 (resgnd); mem. Nat. Planning Council 2009.

RASHEEDI, Bakheet Shibeeb al-, BSc; Kuwaiti chemical engineer and politician; *Minister of Oil and of Electricity and Water;* b. April 1957; ed Kuwait Univ., Alexandria Univ., Egypt; Chair. and Man. Dir Kuwait Aromatics (KARO, jt venture pvt.-sector petrochemicals co.) 2009–12; mem. Bd of Dirs Kuwait Oil Co. (KOC, upstream arm of Kuwait Petroleum Corpn, KPC) 2011–12; Deputy Chair. and Deputy Man. Dir for Planning and Local Marketing, Kuwait Nat. Petroleum Co. (KNPC, downstream domestic refining co.) 2012–13; CEO, KPC Holdings-Aruba 2013–17; Pres., Kuwait Petroleum Int. (Q8) 2013–17; headed several major Kuwaiti local and int. oil sector projects, including Nghi Son Refinery and Petrochemicals Project in Vietnam and the proposed expansion of KPI refining capacity in Oman; Minister of Oil 2017–, also Minister of Electricity and Water 2017–, also Chair., Kuwait Petroleum Corpn 2017–; co-f. Gulf Downstream Asscn (GDA, non-profit org. fostering cooperation between oil cos); Chair. Gulf Refining Fed. 2016–. *Address:* Ministry of Oil, POB 5077, 13051 Safat, Kuwait City, Kuwait (office). *Telephone:* 22406990 (office). *E-mail:* alnaft@moo.gov.kw (office). *Website:* www.moo.gov.kw (office).

RASHID, Shaikh Ahmed, MA, LLB; Pakistani politician; b. 6 Nov. 1950, Balra Bazar, Rawalpindi; ed Polytech. Coll., Rawalpindi, Gordon Coll., Punjab Univ.; mem. (Ind.) Nat. Ass. 1985–2008; fmr Minister of Labour and Manpower, of Industries and Production, of Culture and Sports, of Tourism and Investment; Fed. Minister of Information and Broadcasting 2002, for Railways 2006–08; participated in Geneva Accords, Moscow Conf.; Head of Gulf War Monitoring Programme; Rep. of Pakistan to UN and numerous int. confs. *Publications include:* Farzand-I -Pakistan, Suboatta Hai.

RASHID, Ahmed; Pakistani journalist and author; b. 1948, Rawalpindi; m.; two c.; ed Malvern Coll., UK, Government Coll., Lahore, Fitzwilliam Coll., Univ. of Cambridge, UK; fmr Pakistan, Afghanistan and Cen. Asia Corresp. Far Eastern Economic Review; now writes regularly for Daily Telegraph, London, New York Review of Books, BBC Online, The Nation, Lahore and other academic and foreign affairs journals as well as several Pakistani newspapers and magazines; appears on TV and radio including BBC World Service, ABC Australia, Radio France Int. and German Radio; mem. Advisory Bd Eurasia Net of Soros Foundation; Scholar, World Economic Forum; mem. Int. Advisory Bd Central Asia Survey; consultant for Human Rights Watch; mem. Bd of Advisers ICRC, Geneva 2004–08; f. Open Media Fund for Afghanistan (charity) 2002; Nisar Osmani Award for Courage in Journalism, Human Rights Soc. of Pakistan 2001. *Publications include:* The Resurgence of Central Asia: Islam or Nationalism, Fundamentalism Reborn: Afghanistan and the Taliban, Jihad: The Rise of Militant Islam in Central Asia, Taliban: Islam, Oil and the New Great Game in Central Asia 2000, Descent into Chaos 2008, Pakistan on the Brink: The Future of America, Pakistan, and Afghanistan 2012, Afghanistan Revealed (jtly) 2012; contrib. numerous essays to other books. *Website:* www.ahmedrashid.com.

RASHID, Tan Sri Hussain; Malaysian business executive and banker; fmrly with London Stock Exchange; worked with Bumiputra Merchant Bankers Bhd 1976–83; est. brokerage house 1983; est. Rashid Hussain Berhard group of financial services companies 1996, ceded control 1998; Chair. Exec. Cttee Khazanah Govt holding co. 1994–98, Putrajaya Holdings Sdn Bhd 1995–2000. *Website:* rhbgroup.com.

RASHID, Muhammad ibn Ahmad ar-, PhD; Saudi Arabian politician and academic; b. 1944, Al-Majma'a; m.; five s. two d.; ed Imam Mohammed Bin Saud Islamic Univ., Riyadh, Univ. of Indiana, Univ. of Oklahoma; teacher Inst. of Religious Studies, Riyadh 1964–65; Grad. Asst Coll. of Shari'a and Islamic Studies, Makkah 1965–66; sent on mission to USA by King Abdulaziz Univ. 1966–72; Asst Prof. King Saud Univ. 1972–79, Assoc. Prof. 1979–89, Vice-Dean Coll. of Educ. 1974–76, Dean 1976–79; Dir-Gen. Arab Bureau of Educ. for Gulf States 1979–88; Founder of Arab Gulf States Univ. and Vice-Pres. of Founding Cttee 1979–88; Prof. of Educ. King Saud Univ. 1989–94; mem. Saudi Nat. Council 1994–95; Minister of Educ. 1995–2004; Distinguished Fulbright Fellow 1988–89, Distinguished Fellow, World Council for Teacher Training 1989; Gold Medal of Merit (Arab League Educ. Cultural and Scientific Org.). *Publications:* numerous articles and research papers in professional journals. *Leisure interests:* walking, swimming, reading.

RASIZADÄ, Artur Tahir oğlu; Azerbaijani politician and engineer; b. 26 Feb. 1935, Gäncä, Transcaucasian SFSR (now Azerbaijan), USSR; m.; one d.; ed Azerbaijan Inst. of Industry; engineer, Deputy Dir Azerbaijan Inst. of Oil Machine Construction 1957–73, Dir 1977–78; Chief Engineer, Trust Soyuzneftemash 1973–77; Deputy Head Azerbaijan State Planning Cttee 1978–81; Head of Section, Cen. Cttee of Azerbaijan CP 1981–86; First Deputy Prime Minister 1986–92; adviser, Foundation of Econ. Reforms 1992–96; Asst to Pres. Heydär Äliyev Feb.–May 1996; First Deputy Prime Minister May–July 1996, Acting Prime Minister July–Nov. 1996, Prime Minister Nov. 1996–Aug. 2003, Nov. 2003–2018; İstiqlal Order 2005, Shohrat Order 2015.

RASMUSSEN, Anders Fogh, MSc; Danish politician and international organization official; b. 26 Jan. 1953, Ginnerup, Jutland; s. of Knud Rasmussen and Martha Rasmussen (née Fogh); m. Anne-Mette Rasmussen; three c.; ed Viborg Cathedral School, Univ. of Århus; consultant to Danish Fed. of Crafts and Small Industries 1978–87; mem. Folketing (Parl.) 1978–2009, mem. Econ. and Political Affairs Cttee 1982–87, Vice-Chair. 1993–98; Vice-Chair. Housing Cttee 1981–86; Minister for Taxation 1987–92, also for Econ. Affairs 1990–92; Vice-Chair. Econ. and Political Affairs Cttee 1993–98; Prime Minister of Denmark 2001–09; Sec.-Gen. NATO 2009–14; mem. Venstre (Liberal Party), Vice-Chair. Nat. Org. Venstre 1985–98, mem. Man. Cttee Parl. Party 1984–87, 1992–2001, Spokesman for Venstre 1992–98, Vice-Chair. Foreign Policy Bd 1998–2001, Chair. Venstre 1998–2009; Grand Cross of the Portuguese Order of Merit 1992, Commdr (First Degree) of the Order of the Dannebrog 2002, Danish Gold Medal of Merit 2002, Grand Cross of the German Order of Merit 2002, Grand Cross of the Order of Merit of Poland 2003, Grand Cross of the Order of the Oak Crown of Luxembourg 2003, Grand Cross of the Order of Nicaragua 2003, Great Cross of the Pedro Joaquín Chamorro Order 2003, Ordinul Steaua României Mare Cruce 2004, Grand Cross of the Order of the Lithuanian Grand Duke Gediminas 2004, Three Star Order of Latvia 2005, Order of Stara Planina, First Class (Bulgaria) 2006, Grand Cross of the Nordstjärneorden (Sweden) 2007, Grand Cross of the Order of the South Cross (Brazil) 2007, Grand Cross of Order of Dannebrog 2009, Estonian Order of Cross of Terra Mañana 2009, Hon. KCMG 2015; Dr hc (George Washington Univ.) 2002, Hon. DIur (Hampden-Sydney Coll., Virginia) 2003, Hon. Alumni (Århus) 2009; Adam Smith Award 1993, Politician of the Year (Dansk Markedsfuringsforbund) 1998, Netherlands Youth Org. for Freedom and Democracy Liberal of the Year 2002, European Leader Award, Polish Leaders Forum 2003, Danish European Movt European of the Year 2003, Robert Schumann Medal 2003, Pedro Joaquin Chamorro Medal, Nicaragua 2003, Best Leader in Denmark 2005, Politician of the Year 2005, Chevalier du St-Chinian 2007. *Publications include:* Oprør med skattesystemet 1979, Den truede velstand (co-author) 1980, Kampen om boligen 1982, Fra Socialstat til Minimalstat 1993, I Godvejr og storm (interviews) 2001. *Leisure interests:* cycling, kayaking. *Address:* c/o Venstre, Danmarks Liberale Parti, Søllerødvej 30, 2840 Holte, Denmark.

RASMUSSEN, Lars Løkke; Danish politician; *Prime Minister;* b. 15 May 1964, Vejle; m. Sólrun Løkke Rasmussen; three c.; ed Copenhagen Univ.; Nat. Chair. Young Liberals 1986–89, Vice-Chair. Liberal Party (Venstre) 1998; mem. Folketing (Parl.) for Frederiksborg Co. Constituency 1994; mem. Græsted-Gilleleje Municipal Council 1986–97; Co. Mayor of Frederiksborg Co. 1998–2001; Minister of the Interior and Health 2001–07, of Finance 2007–09; Prime Minister of Denmark 2009–11, 2015–; Commdr, Order of the Dannebrog 2003, Commdr (First Class), Order of the Dannebrog 2009, Grand Cross, Order of the Phoenix (Greece) 2009. *Address:* Prime Minister's Office, Christiansborg, Prins Jørgens Gård 11, 1218 Copenhagen K, Denmark (office). *Telephone:* 33-92-33-00 (office). *E-mail:* stm@stm.dk (office). *Website:* www.stm.dk (office).

RASMUSSEN, Michael Pram, LLB; Danish business executive; *Chairman, The Mærsk Group;* b. 14 Jan. 1955; m. Anne Pram Kjølbye; ed Univ. of Copenhagen; began career with Nye Danske Lloyd 1979; Asst Man. Dir Baltica Forsikring A/S 1982–84, Man. Dir 1984–86, Vice-Pres. 1986–88, Pres. 1988–95; Pres. Tryg Forsikring A/S (later renamed Tryg-Baltica Forskring A/S) 1995–96; CEO Topdanmark A/S (insurance co.) 1996–2006, Chair. 2006–15; Chair. Mærsk Olie & Gas A/S; Vice-Chair. Forsikring & Pension 2000–03; mem. Bd of Dirs, A.P. Møller-Mærsk A/S (now The Maersk Group) 1999–, Vice-Chair. June–Dec. 2002–03, Chair. 2003–; Chair. Semler Holding A/S, Henning Larsen Architects A/S, Arp-Hansen Hotel Group; mem. JPMorgan Chase Int. Council; mem. Bd of Dirs Coloplast A/S, 2005– (now Chair.), Louisiana Museum of Modern Art; fmr mem. Bd of Dirs Baltica Forsikring A/S, William Demant Holdings A/S, Oticon A/S, Danmark-Amerika Fondet, Øresundsbro Konsortiet. *Address:* The Mærsk Group, Esplanaden 50, 1098 Copenhagen K, Denmark (office). *Telephone:* 33-63-33-63 (office). *Fax:* 33-63-30-03 (office). *E-mail:* info@maersk.com (office). *Website:* www.maersk.com (office).

RASMUSSEN, Stephen S. (Steve), BBA; American insurance company executive; *CEO, Nationwide Mutual Insurance Company;* ed Univ. of Iowa; joined Allied Insurance 1974, later Exec. Vice-Pres. for Product Man., Vice-Pres. for Underwriting and Regional Vice-Pres. for the Pacific Coast Region, Pres. and COO Allied Insurance –2003, held same positions with CalFarm Insurance (affiliated co.) –2003; Pres. and COO Property and Casualty Operations, Nationwide Mutual Insurance Co. 2003–09, CEO 2009–; mem. Bd, Nat. Urban League, Insurance Inst. for Highway Safety, OhioHealth Bd of Dirs, Columbus Metropolitan Library; mem. Columbus Partnership; fmr Trustee Grand View Coll., Des Moines, Ia; fmr Co-Chair. United Way of Cen. Ohio Alexis de Tocqueville Vingt-Cinq Soc. campaign; holds the Chartered Property Casualty Underwriter designation; Co-Chair. 2012 United Way of Central Ohio campaign. *Address:* Nationwide Mutual Insurance Co., One Nationwide Plaza, Columbus, OH 43215-2220, USA (office). *Telephone:* (614) 249-7111 (office). *Fax:* (614) 249-7705 (office). *E-mail:* info@nationwide.com (office). *Website:* www.nationwide.com (office).

RASMUSSEN, Hon. Wilkie Olaf Patua, BA, LLB, MA (Hons); Cook Islands lawyer, politician, writer and artist; b. (Wilkie Olaf Patua Rakoroa Matara), 21 March 1958, Omoka, Penrhyn; s. of Rakoroa Matara (birth father) and Christmas Matara (née Gifford) (birth mother), raised by Dane Isidor Wilkie Rasmussen and Anna Rasmussen (née Pange); m. Tungane Rasmussen (née Woonton); one s. one d.; ed Univ. of Auckland, NZ; odd jobs as labourer, steel worker, freezing worker, kitchen hand; artist/painter 1980–87; journalist for New Zealand Herald 1988–89; practised as sole barrister/solicitor 1996–99, 2011–; fmr Man. Dir Northern Traders Ltd; Cabinet Sec. 1999–2000; High Commr to NZ 2000–02; mem. Parl. for Penrhyn 2002–, Chair. Media Select Cttee 2007, mem. Property Law Select Cttee 2007, Parl. Privileges Select Cttee 2007, 2011, CPA Cook Islands Cttee, Employment Relations Bill Select Cttee 2011, Family Law Bill Select Cttee 2011; Minister of Foreign Affairs and Immigration, Tourism, Cultural Devt, Marine Resources and Natural Environment Resources 2005–09, Minister of Finance and Econ. Man., Financial Intelligence Unit, Public Expenditure and Review Cttee, Business, Trade and Investment Bd, Commerce Comm., Nat. Superannuation, Pearl Authority and Attorney-Gen. 2009–10; Panellist, Pacific Ministers for Post-Forum Dialogue 2006–; fmr Acting Prime Minister; Deputy Leader Democratic Party 2007–09, 2010–12, Leader 2012–15; Pres. African Caribbean Pacific Parl. (ACP); Co-Pres. ACP-EU Jt Parl. Ass. 2007–09; Chair. Media Select Cttee 2007, Pacific Forum Trade Ministers Meeting 2008; Pres. Tongareva (Penrhyn) Island Cttee, Cook Islands Law Soc.; Deacon of Avarua CICC (Cook Islands Christian Church); Maori and Pacific Islands Univ. Scholarship, Univ. of Auckland Scholarship. *Achievements include:* Cook Islands Bantamweight Boxing Champion. *Publications:* poetry published in Diplomats Journal, Wellington. *Leisure interests:* golden oldies rugby, golf, cricket, reading, photography, compiling genealogies, staying fit and healthy. *Address:* Tongareva (Penrhyn) MP's Office, PO Box 534, Punanga Nui Market, Ruatonga, Avarua, Rarotonga, Cook Islands (office). *Telephone:* 21726 (office). *Fax:* 21725 (office). *E-mail:* mpwilkie@tongareva.net.ck (office); wilkie@oyster.net.ck (home). *Website:* www.wilkierasmussen.com.

RASOLOFONIRINA, Gen. Béni Xavier; Malagasy army officer and politician; fmr Commdr, Académie mil. d'Antsirabe; fmr Second Deputy Chief of Staff of Armed Forces, becoming First Deputy Chief of Staff of Armed Forces 2012–14, Chief of Staff of Armed Forces 2014–16; Deputy Dir of Study, Centre d'étude diplomatique et stratégique (CEDS) 2014; Minister of Nat. Defence 2016–19. *Address:* c/o Ministry of National Defence, BP 08, 101 Antananarivo, Madagascar (office).

RASOOL, Ali Mahmoud Abd al-; Sudanese politician; b. Rahid al-Bardi, Southern Darfur Prov.; ed Univ. of Khartoum; worked on agricultural projects with World Bank; served within Ministry of Finance of Southern Darfur Prov., becoming state Minister of Finance; Gov. Southern Darfur Prov. 2008; Minister of Finance and Nat. Economy 2010–13; mem. Nat. Congress Party.

RASSOUL, Zalmai, MD; Afghan physician and government official; b. 1943, Kabul; s. of Abdu'l Qayyum Khan Sarkar and Farukh Begum; ed Estiqlal High School, Univ. of Paris, France; worked at Research Inst. of Cardiac Diseases, Paris, Mil. Hosp. of Saudi Arabia; served as Chief of Staff of HM King Mohammad Zahir Shah, Rome; worked for Haqiqat e Afghan publ. regarding Jihad in Afghanistan, Paris; Minister of Civil Aviation and Tourism and Nat. Security Adviser, Interim Govt of Afghanistan; Nat. Security Adviser, Govt of Afghanistan –2010; Minister of Foreign Affairs 2010–13; cand. in presidential election 2014; mem. American Soc. of Nephrology. *Publications:* more than 30 medical books and booklets published in Europe and USA.

RASULZODA, Qohir; Tajikistani politician and fmr engineer; *Prime Minister;* b. (Abdulqohir Nazirov), 8 March 1961, Khujand Dist, Leninabad Viloyat (now Ghafurov Dist, Sughd Viloyat), Tajik SSR, USSR; m.; three c.; ed Agricultural Inst. of Tajik SSR (now Tajikistan Agrarian Univ.), Acad. of State Service at the Presidency of the Russian Fed.; began career as technician supervisor, Tajikirsovkhozstroi Asscn Building Lab., Bobojonghafurov Dist 1982; fmr engineer, Production Dept, later chief engineer and Head, Tajikirsovkhozstroi, Khujand; Minister of Land Reclamation and Water Resources 2000–06; Chair. Sughd Viloyat 2006–13; Prime Minister of Tajikistan 2013–; mem. Majlisi Milliy (Nat.

Ass.), First Vice-Chair. 2007–13; Honoured Worker of Repub. of Tajikistan. *Address:* Secretariat of the Prime Minister, 734023 Dushanbe, Xiyoboni Rudaki 80, Tajikistan (office). *Telephone:* (372) 21-18-71 (office). *Fax:* (372) 21-51-10 (office).

RATANARAK, Krit; Thai business executive; *Chairman, Bangkok Broadcasting & Television Company;* b. 19 April 1946; s. of Chuan Ratanarak and Sasithorn Ratanarak; divorced; one s.; ed Husson Univ., USA; joined Bank of Ayudhya 1972, becoming Pres. 1982, CEO 1990, Chair. and CEO 1993; Chair. Bangkok Broadcasting & Television Co. (BBTV) 1993–; Chair. Siam City Cement 1993–, Ayudhya Insurance 1993–; Owner Tonson Property; mem. Woothi Sapha (Senate) 1981–2005. *Address:* Bangkok Broadcasting & Television Company, 998/1 Soi Sirimitr, Phaholyothin, Talad Mawchid, POB 456, Bangkok 10900, Thailand (office). *Telephone:* (2) 272-0201 (office). *Fax:* (2) 272-0010 (office). *E-mail:* prdept@ch7.com (office). *Website:* www.ch7.com (office).

RATAS, Jüri, MEconSci, LLB; Estonian politician; *Prime Minister;* b. 2 July 1978, Tallinn, Estonian SSR, USSR; s. of Rein Ratas; m. Karin Ratas; two s. one d.; ed Tallinn Univ. of Tech., Tartu Univ. School of Law; Market Researcher, ANR Amer Nielsen Eesti OÜ (market research consultancy) 1996–98; Analyst, Estonian Building Research Inst. 1997–99; Sales Rep., Sampo Eesti Kindlustus (insurance co.) 1999–2000; Chair. Värvilised OÜ (car maintenance agency) 1999–2002; Econ. Adviser to Tallinn City Office 2002–03, mem. Tallinn City Council 2005–, Deputy Mayor of Tallinn 2003–04, 2005, Mayor of Tallinn 2005–07; mem. Riigikogu (Parl.) 2007–, Vice-Pres. 2007–16; Prime Minister of Estonia 2016–; Head of Youth Basketball, Estonian Basketball Asscn 2001–02, Pres. 2012–; mem. Eesti Keskerakond (EK—Estonian Centre Party) 2000–, Chair. 2016–. *Address:* Office of the Prime Minister, Stenbocki maja, Rahukohtu 3, Tallinn, 15161, Estonia (office). *Telephone:* 693-5710 (office). *Fax:* 693-5554 (office). *E-mail:* riigikantselei@riigikantselei.ee (office). *Website:* valitsus.ee (office).

RATCLIFFE, Sir James A., Kt, BSc (ChemEng), MBA; British business executive; *Chairman and CEO, Ineos Group Holdings PLC;* ed Univ. of Birmingham, London Business School; qualified as an accountant; began career with Exxon Chemicals before moving to Courtaulds; joined Advent Int. 1989, led successful buyout of Inspec Group plc 1992, floated co. 1994, left Inspec to lead acquisition of Ineos PLC (now Ineos Oxide) from Inspec 1998; Dir and Chair. Ineos Group Holdings PLC and Chair. CEO Ineos Capital 1998–; Hon. FIChemE 2009. *Leisure interests:* skiing, sailing. *Address:* Ineos Group Holdings PLC, Hawkslease, Chapel Lane, Lyndhurst, SO43 7FG, Hants., England (office); 58 Rue Charles Martel, Luxembourg Ville 2134, Luxembourg (office). *Telephone:* (23) 8028-7067 (Lyndhurst) (office). *Fax:* (23) 8028-7054 (Lyndhurst) (office). *E-mail:* info@ineos.com (office). *Website:* www.ineos.com (office).

RATCLIFFE, Sir Peter John, Kt, MD, FRS, FMedSci; British molecular biologist, physician and academic; b. 14 May 1954, N Lancs.; m.; four c.; ed Lancaster Royal Grammar School, Gonville and Caius Coll., Cambridge, St Bartholomew's Hosp., London; trained in renal medicine at Univ. of Oxford 1978; changed fields to found a new lab. and gained Sr Fellowship from The Wellcome Trust 1990; clinician at John Radcliffe Hosp., Oxford, Nuffield Prof. and Head of Nuffield Dept of Clinical Medicine, Univ. of Oxford 2003–16; Dir Target Discovery Inst.; Supernumerary Fellow, Magdalen Coll.; Dir of Clinical Research, Francis Crick Inst. 2016–; Foreign Hon. mem. American Acad. of Arts and Sciences 2007; Milne-Muerke Foundation Award 1991, Graham Bull Prize 1998, Int. Soc. for Blood Purification Award 2002, EMBO Fellowship 2006, Louis-Jeantet Prize for Medicine 2009, Canada Gairdner Int. Award 2010, Robert J. and Claire Pasarow Foundation Award in Cardiovascular Research 2011, Baly Medal, Royal Coll. of Physicians 2011, Scientific Grand Prix, Foundation Lefoulon-Delalande, Inst. of France 2012, Annual Review Prize, The Physiological Soc.'s 2012, Jakob Herz Prize, Friedrich Alexander Univ., Erlangen-Nürnberg, Germany 2013, Wiley Prize for Biomedical Science 2014, Albert Lasker Basic Medical Research Award, Lasker Foundation (co-recipient) 2016. *Publications:* numerous papers in professional journals. *Address:* Target Discovery Institute, University of Oxford, NDM Research Building, Old Road Campus, Headington, Oxford, OX3 7FZ, England (office). *Telephone:* (1865) 612680 (office). *E-mail:* peter.ratcliffe@ndm.ox.ac.uk (office). *Website:* www.ndm.ox.ac.uk (office); www.magd.ox.ac.uk/member-of-staff/peter-ratcliffe (office).

RATHER, Dan, BA; American broadcast journalist; b. 31 Oct. 1931, Wharton, Tex.; m. Jean Goebel; one s. one d.; ed Sam Houston State Teachers Coll., Univ. of Houston, South Texas School of Law; writer and sports commentator with KSAM-TV; taught journalism for one year at Houston Chronicle; with CBS 1962; with radio station KTRH, Houston for about four years; News and Current Affairs Dir CBS Houston TV affiliate KHOU-TV late 1950s, joined CBS News 1962, Chief London Bureau 1965–66, covered Viet Nam, White House, anchor, CBS Reports 1974–75, co-anchor 60 Minutes 1975–81, anchor, Dan Rather Reporting CBS Radio Network 1977–2006, co-ed. Who's Who 1977, CBS Nat. Political Consultant 1964–2006, anchor and Man. Ed. CBS Evening News with Dan Rather 1981–2005, co-anchor 1993–2005; f. News and Guts 2006, currently Pres. and CEO; anchor and Man. Ed. Dan Rather Reports, HDNet (now AXS TV) 2006–13; anchored numerous CBS News Special Programmes, including coverage of presidential campaigns in 1982 and 1984; numerous acad. honours; 10 Emmy awards; Distinguished Achievement for Broadcasting Award, Univ. of Southern Calif. Journalism Alumni Asscn, Bob Considine Award 1983, Peabody Award (for 60 Minutes II report about prisoner abuse at Abu Ghraib prison in Baghdad) 2005, CPJ Burton Benjamin Memorial Award 2011, Lifetime Achievement Award, Banff World Media Festival 2014. *Publications include:* The Palace Guard 1974 (with Gary Gates), The Camera Never Blinks Twice (with Mickey Herskowitz) 1977, I Remember (with Peter Wyden) 1991, The Camera Never Blinks Twice: The Further Adventures of a Television Journalist 1994, The American Dream: Stories from the Heart of Our Nation 2001, Rather Outspoken: My Life in the News (with Digby Diehl) 2012, What Unites Us: Reflections on Patriotism (with Elliot Kirschner) 2017. *Address:* News and Guts, 1180 Avenue of the Americas, Suite 1802, New York, NY 10036 USA (office). *E-mail:* info@newsandgutsmedia.com (office). *Website:* www.danrather.com; www.danratherjournalist.org.

RATHKE, Most Rev. Heinrich Karl Martin Hans, DTheol; German ecclesiastic; *Bishop and Pastor Emeritus, Evangelical-Lutheran Church of Mecklenburg;*

b. 12 Dec. 1928, Mölln, Kreis Malchin; s. of Paul Rathke and Hedwig Rathke (née Steding); m. Marianne Rusam 1955; six s. one d.; ed Univs of Kiel, Erlangen, Tübingen and Rostock; parish priest, Althof bei Bad Doberan 1954–55, Warnkenhagen, Mecklenburg 1955–62, Rostock Südstadt 1962–70; Priest in charge of community service and people's mission, Mecklenburg 1970–71; Bishop of the Evangelical-Lutheran Church of Mecklenburg 1971–84; Presiding Bishop of the United Evangelical Lutheran Church of the GDR 1977–81; Pastor in Crivitz/Mecklenburg 1984–91; Bishop and Pastor Emer. 1991–; Asst Bishop, Evangelical-Lutheran Church of Kazakhstan 1991–93; Hon. DTheol (Rostock) 1999. *Publications:* Ignatius von Antiochien und die Paulusbriefe 1967, Gemeinde heute und morgen 1979, Einstehen für Gemeinschaft in Christus 1980, Kirche unterwegs 1995, Predigthilfen (three vols) 1998–2000, Märtyrer, Vorbilder für das Widerstehen 2002, Mitmenschlichkeit, Zivilcourage, Gottvertrauen – Opfer des Stalinismus 2003. *Address:* Vitanas Senioren Centrum, Pfaffenstrasse 3, 19055 Schwerin, Germany. *Telephone:* (385) 562887.

RATIANI, Sergo, CandPhilSci; Georgian philosopher, academic and politician; *Acting Secretary-General, Ertiani Natsionaluri Modzraoba (ENM—United National Movement);* b. 27 Nov. 1967; ed Tbilisi State Univ., Ilia Chavchavadze Foreign Languages Inst., Tbilisi; mil. service 1986–88; Chair in Scientific Research of Religions, Pedagogues' Retraining Inst. 1991–93; Pedagogue, Tbilisi Spiritual Acad. 1993–96; Deputy Dir Caucasus LLC 1995–97; Dir Arili LLC 1997–2002; Pedagogue, Tbilisi State Univ. 2001–02, Acting Head of the Chair, Ilia Chavchavadze Foreign Languages Inst. 2002–06; Assoc. Prof., Ilia Chavchavadze State Univ. 2006–08, Head of Admin 2006–12, Prof. 2008–; mem. Ertiani Natsionaluri Modzraoba (ENM—United Nat. Movt), Acting Sec.-Gen. 2015–; mem. Sakartvelos Parlamenti (Parl.), Deputy Chair. Educ., Science and Culture Cttee, mem. Cttee on European Integration. *Publications include:* chapters in Identity Studies Vols 1 and 2 (ed. Giga Zedania) 2009, 2013. *Address:* Ertiani Natsionaluri Modzraoba (United National Movement), 0118 Tbilisi, Kakheti 45A, Georgia (office). *Telephone:* (32) 292-30-84 (office); (32) 228-12-33 (Parl.). *Fax:* (32) 292-30-91 (office). *E-mail:* info@unm.ge (office). *Website:* www.unm.ge (office); www.parliament.ge/en/mp/1992.

RATMANSKY, Alexei; Russian ballet dancer and choreographer; *Artist-in-Residence, American Ballet Theatre;* b. 27 Aug. 1968, St Petersburg; ed Ballet School of the Bolshoi Theatre, Moscow; has danced with Ukrainian Nat. Ballet, Kiev Ballet, Royal Winnipeg Ballet; joined Royal Danish Ballet as soloist 1997–2000, Prin. Dancer 2000–04; Artistic Dir Bolshoi Ballet 2004–08; Resident Choreographer, New York City Ballet 2009; Artist-in-Residence American Ballet Theatre 2014–; has performed leading roles, including Basil in Don Quixote, Prince Siegfried in Swan Lake, Albrecht in Giselle, James in La Sylphide, and Copain in Gaité Parisienne; has also danced soloist roles in Grass, Mahler's 5th Symphony, A Folk Tale and Suite en Blanc; cr. first ballet, Betwix, as participant in Choreographer Workshop at Royal Danish Ballet 1999; other works include Turandot's Dream, performed as part of the Shaken – Not Stirred program at Old Stage of the Royal Theatre, The Nutcracker and Anna Karenina for The Royal Danish Ballet, Poem of Ecstasy, The Fairy's Kiss, Middle Duo and Cinderella for The Maryinsky Ballet, as well as Capriccio, Dreams About Japan, The Bright Stream, Leah, Bolt for the Bolshoi Ballet, The Russian Seasons, Le Corsaire, Bizet Variations, Flames of Paris, The Little Humpbacked Horse, Lost Illusions, Souvenir d'un lieu cher 2012, 24 Preludes, Tanzsuite 2014, Serenade After Plato's Symposium 2016, Whipped Cream; First Prize, Ukrainian Ballet Competition 1998, Gold Medal, Moscow Diaghilev Competition 1992, Nijinsky Prize 1992, Prix Benois de la Danse 2005, Golden Mask Award for Best Choreographer 2007, MacArthur Fellow 2013. *Address:* American Ballet Theatre, 890 Broadway, 3rd Floor, New York, NY 10003, USA (office). *Telephone:* (212) 477-3030 (office). *Fax:* (212) 254-5938 (office). *Website:* www.abt.org (office).

RATNAM, Anita, MA; Indian dancer and choreographer; *Director, Arangham Trust;* b. 21 May 1954, Madurai, Tamil Nadu; m.; two c.; ed Univ. of New Orleans, USA; trained in Bharatanatyam 1969–78, Mohiniattam 1968–78, Kathakali 1968–78; Founder-Dir Arangham Trust 1992–; f. Arangham Dance Theatre 1993; co-f. The Other Festival 1998–2007; f. Narthaki.com 2000, now Consulting Ed.; Observer, Post Modern Dance Festival Germany 2002; columnist, New Indian Express; mem. Int. Advisory Bd Pangea World Theatre USA, Preaksha Dance Canada; Hon. mem. The Duchess Club; Nritya Choodamani, Sri Krishna Gana Sabha 1996, Chennai Kalaimamani, Govt of Tamil Nadu 1998, Media Achievement Award 1991, Mahatma Gandhi Award for Cultural Harmony 1986, Lalithakalaratna, Lalithakala Acad. Foundation Trust 2003, Natya Ratna, Sri Shanmukhananda Sangeeta Sabha 2003, Price Award, Shakespeare Millennium Club Chennai 2004, Natya Kireeta Ratnam Award 2005. *Achievements include:* created unique dance style called Neo Bharat Natyam. *Dance:* 7 Graces New York 2007 (solo). *Films include:* Kandukondain Kandukondain 2000, Boys 2003. *Address:* Arangham Trust, #10, Cenotaph 2nd Lane, Chennai 600 018, India (office). *Telephone:* (44) 28522224 (office); 9841026123 (mobile). *Fax:* (44) 28522224 (office). *E-mail:* anita@arangham.com (office); aratnam@vsnl.com. *Website:* www.arangham.com (office); www.anitaratnam.com.

RATNAM, Mani, BCom, MBA; Indian film director and screenwriter; b. (Gopala Ratnam Subramaniam), 1956, Madurai; s. of Gopal Ratnam Iyer; m. Suhasini Hassan 1988; one s.; ed Univ. of Madras, Jamnalal Bajaj Inst., Mumbai; fmr man. consultant; worked for TVS Sudaram; f. Madras Talkies film production co.; six Nat. Film Awards, three Bollywood Filmfare Awards; Padma Shri 2002, Jaeger-Lecoultre Glory to the Filmmaker, Venice Int. Film Festival) 2010, Sun Mark Lifetime Achievement Award, London Film Festival 2015. *Films include:* Pallavi Anu Palavi 1983, Mauna Ragam 1986, Nayakan 1987, Agni Nakshatram 1988, Gitanjali (Golden Lotus Award for Best Popular Film) 1989, Anjali 1990, Roja (Nargis Dutt Award for Best Feature Film on Nat. Integration) 1992, Thiruda Thiruda 1993, Bombay (Nargis Dutt Award for Best Feature Film on Nat. Integration) 1994, Dalpati 1995, Chor Chor 1996, Iruvar 1996, Dil Se 1998, Alay Payuthe 2000, Kannathil Muthamittal (A Peck on the Cheek) 2002, Saathiya 2002, Yuva (The Youth) 2004, Ayitha Ezhuthu 2004, Guru 2007, Raavan 2010, Kadal 2013, OK Kanmani 2015, OK Jaanu 2017, Kaatru Veliyidai 2017. *Address:* 1 Murrey Gate Road, Alwarpet, Chennai 600 018, India (office). *Telephone:* (44) 456998.

RATNAYAKE, Susantha Chaminda; Sri Lankan business executive; *Chairman, John Keells Holdings PLC;* ed Trinity Coll., Kandy, Royal Coll., Colombo; joined Mackinnons Travel as a trainee exec. working under mentorship of Tyrell Mutthiah, rose rapidly within the John Keells Group, apptd a Dir of main group 1992, Deputy Chair. John Keells Holdings PLC 2004–05, Chair. 2006–, Chair. of all subsidiary cos of the Group; mem. Council of Employers Fed. of Ceylon, Cttee of Ceylon Chamber of Commerce, Tourism, Sovereign Rating and Investment Promotion Clusters of Nat. Council of Econ. Devt. *Address:* John Keells Holdings PLC, 130 Glennie Street, Colombo 2, Sri Lanka (office). *Telephone:* (11) 2306000 (office). *E-mail:* jkh@keells.com (office). *Website:* www.keells.com (office).

RATNER, Gerald Irving; British business executive and motivational speaker; *Chief Executive, GeraldOnLine;* b. 1 Nov. 1949, Richmond, Surrey; s. of Leslie Ratner and Rachelle Ratner; m. 1st (divorced 1989); two d.; m. 2nd Moira Ratner; one s. one d.; ed Hendon County Grammar School, London; Man. Dir Ratners Group 1984, Chair. 1986–91, CEO 1986–92, Dir –1992; Chief Exec. GeraldOnline (online jewellery retailer) 2003–; Dir (non-exec.) Norweb 1991; consultant, Tobacco Dock 1993–; Dir Workshop Health and Fitness Club 1997–2001. *Radio:* On the Ropes (Stephen Nolan). *Television:* Celebrity Apprentice, Trouble at the Top. *Publication:* Gerald Ratner-The Rise and Fall… and Rise Again (illustrated) 2007. *Leisure interests:* cycling, music. *Telephone:* 7710-032619 (mobile) (home). *E-mail:* gerald@geraldonline.com (office); gerald.ratner@btinternet.com (home). *Website:* www.geraldratner.co.uk (home).

RATNER, Mark A., BA, PhD; American chemist and academic; *Professor of Chemistry and Lawrence B. Dumas Distinguished University Professor, Northwestern University;* b. 8 Dec. 1942, Cleveland, Ohio; s. of Max Ratner and Betty Ratner; ed Harvard and Northwestern Univs; postdoctoral work in Aarhus, Denmark and Munich, Germany; taught Chem. at New York Univ. 1970–74; fmr Visiting Prof., Nat. Sciences Research Council, Odense Univ., Denmark; Chair. Dept of Chem., Northwestern Univ. 1988–91, Assoc. Dean, Coll. of Arts and Sciences 1980–84, now Prof. of Chem. and Lawrence B. Dumas Distinguished Univ. Prof.; mem. American Acad. of Arts and Sciences 2001, NAS 2002, Int. Acad. of Quantum Molecular Science 2003; Fellow, AAAS; Hon. ScD (Hebrew Univ. of Jerusalem) 2005, (Copenhagen) 2010; ACS Langmuir Award 2004, John Stauffer Lecturer, Stanford Univ. 2009, Willard Gibbs Medal Award, ACS Chicago Local Section 2012, Peter Debye Aeward, ACS 2016. *Achievements include:* proposed, with Arieh Aviram, the first unimolecular electronic rectifier 1974. *Publications include:* Molecular Electronics II (Annals of the New York Academy of Sciences) 1998, Same (co-ed.) 2002, Introduction to Quantum Mechanics in Chemistry (co-author) 2000, Quantum Mechanics in Chemistry (co-author) 2002, Nanotechnology: A Gentle Introduction to the Next Big Idea (co-author) 2002, Nanotechnology and Homeland Security: New Weapons for New Wars (co-author) 2003; numerous papers in professional journals. *Leisure interests:* fishing, hiking and architecture. *Address:* Ryan 4015, Department of Chemistry, Northwestern University, 2145 Sheridan Road, Evanston, IL 60208-3113, USA (office). *Telephone:* (847) 491-5652 (office). *Fax:* (847) 491-7713 (office). *E-mail:* ratner@northwestern.edu (office). *Website:* www.chemistry.northwestern.edu (office); chemgroups.northwestern .edu/ratner/ratner.html (office).

RATO Y FIGAREDO, Rodrigo, JD, MBA, PhD; Spanish international banker and fmr government official; b. 18 March 1949, Madrid; s. of Ramón Rato; m.; two d.; ed Complutense Univ. Madrid, Univ. of California, Berkeley, USA; mem. Exec. Cttee Partido Popular party 1979–, mem. Parl. for Cádiz 1982–89, for Madrid 1989–2004; co-f. party's Econ. Comm., Parl. Sec.-Gen., 1982–84, Econ. Spokesman 1984–86, Sec.-Gen. for Electoral Action 1988, apptd Vice-Sec. 1996; Second Deputy Prime Minister and Minister of Economy and Finance 1996–2000, First Deputy Prime Minister for Econ. Affairs and Minister of Economy 2000–04, including posts as Gov. for Spain on Bds IMF, World Bank, IDB, EIB and EBRD, also in charge of foreign trade relations for Spain; Man. Dir IMF 2004–07 (resgnd); Sr Man. Dir of Investment Banking, Lazard Ltd 2008; apptd Vice-Chair. and Dir Iberia Lineas Aereas de Espana SA 2010; Pres. Caja Madrid 2010–12, Bankia 2010–12 (Dir 2011–); Dir Mapfre SA 2010–12, Int. Consolidated Airlines Group SA –2012; mem. Bd of Govs Asian Devt Bank; Trustee, Royal Theatre, Madrid.

RATSIRAHONANA, Norbert; Malagasy lawyer and politician; *Leader, Ny asa vita no ifampitsara (AVI) Party;* b. 18 Nov. 1938, Antsiranana; Pres. Constitutional High Court –1996; Prime Minister of Madagascar 1996–97; Leader Ny asa vita no ifampitsara (AVI—People are judged by the work they do) Party 1997–; ambassadeur itinérant of the Pres. –2006; apptd Special Adviser, High Authority of Transition 2009.

RATTLE, Sir Simon Dennis, Kt, OM, CBE; British conductor; *Artistic Director and Chief Conductor, Berlin Philharmonic Orchestra;* b. 19 Jan. 1955, Liverpool; s. of Denis Guttridge Rattle and Pauline Lila Violet Rattle (née Greening); m. 1st Elise Ross 1980 (divorced 1995); two s.; m. 2nd Candace Allen 1996 (divorced 2004); m. 3rd Magdalena Kožená 2008; two s. one d.; ed Royal Acad. of Music; has conducted Bournemouth Symphony, Northern Sinfonia, London Philharmonic, London Sinfonietta, Berlin Philharmonic, LA Philharmonic, Stockholm Philharmonic, Vienna Philharmonic, Philadelphia Orchestra, Boston Symphony orchestras, etc.; debut at Queen Elizabeth Hall, London 1974, Royal Festival Hall, London 1976, Royal Albert Hall, London 1976; Asst Conductor, BBC Symphony Orchestra 1977–80; Assoc. Conductor, Royal Liverpool Philharmonic Soc. 1977–80; Glyndebourne debut 1977, Royal Opera, Covent Garden debut 1990; Artistic Dir, London Choral Soc. 1979–84; Prin. Conductor and Artistic Adviser, City of Birmingham Symphony Orchestra (CBSO) 1980–90, Music Dir 1990–98; Artistic Dir South Bank Summer Music 1981–83; Jt Artistic Dir Aldeburgh Festival 1982–93; Prin. Guest Conductor, LA Philharmonic 1981–94, Rotterdam Philharmonic 1981–84; Prin. Guest Conductor Orchestra of the Age of Enlightenment 1992–; Artistic Dir and Chief Conductor Berlin Philharmonic Orchestra 2002– (announced in 2013 that he would step down in 2018); Music Dir, London Symphony Orchestra Sept. 2017–; conducted LSO at Opening Ceremony of London Olympics 2012; UNICEF Goodwill Amb. 2007–; Patron Elton John AIDS Foundation; Hon. Fellow, St Anne's Coll. Oxford 1991; Hon. Fellow, Soc. of Arts 2006; Officier, Ordre des Arts et des Lettres 1995; Order of Merit of the FRG; Chevalier, Légion d'honneur 2010; Hon. DMus (Liverpool) 1991, (Leeds) 1993, (RAM) 2011; won John Player Int. Conducting Competition 1973, Edison Award (for recording of Shostakovich's Symphony No. 10) 1987, Grand Prix du Disque (Turangalîla Symphony) 1988, Grand Prix Caecilia (Turangalîla Symphony, Jazz Album) 1988, Gramophone Record of the Year Award (Mahler's Symphony No. 2) 1988, Gramophone Opera Award (Porgy and Bess) 1989, Int. Record Critics' Award (Porgy and Bess) 1990, Grand Prix de l'Acad. Charles Cros 1990, Gramophone Artist of the Year 1993, Montblanc de la Culture Award 1993, Shakespeare Prize, Toepfer Foundation, Hamburg 1996, Gramophone Award for Best Concerto recording (Szymanowski Violin Concertos Nos 1 and 2), RSA Albert Medal 1997, Choc de l'Année Award (for recording of Brahms Piano Concerto Op. 15) 1998, Outstanding Achievement Award, South Bank Show 1999, Diapason Recording of the Year Award (complete Beethoven Piano Concertos) 1999, Gramophone Award for Best Opera Recording (Szymanowski's King Roger) 2000, Gramophone Awards for Best Orchestral Recording and Record of the Year (Mahler's Symphony No. 10) 2000, Comenius Prize (Germany) 2004, Classical BRIT Award (for Beethoven Symphonies) 2004, Schiller Special Prize, City of Mannheim 2005, Classical BRIT Award for Classical Recording of the Year (Holst's The Planets) 2007, Gramophone Award for Best Choral Recording (Brahms' Ein deutsches Requiem) 2007, Gold Medal 'Gloria Artis', Premio Don Juan de Borbón de la Música 2009, Wolf Prize in Music (shared with Plácido Domingo) 2012, ECHO Klassik Award for Symphonic Recording of the Year – 20th/21st Century (for Schönberg CD) 2012, voted into the inaugural Gramophone Hall of Fame 2012, Léonie Sonning Music Prize 2013, Int. Classical Music Award for Symphonic Music (for Sibelius Symphonies Nos. 1–7) 2016. *Address:* Berlin Philharmonic Orchestra, Herbert-von-Karajan-Str. 1, 10785 Berlin, Germany (office). *Telephone:* (30) 25488999 (office). *Website:* www.berliner -philharmoniker.de (office); www.askonasholt.co.uk/artists/conductors/simon -rattle (office).

RATTNER, Steven (Steve) Lawrence, BA; American journalist, financial industry executive and fmr government official; *Chairman, Willett Advisors LLC;* b. 5 July 1952, New York; s. of George Seymour Rattner and Selma Ann Silberman; m. P. Maureen White 1986; three s. one d.; ed Brown Univ.; Asst to James Reston, New York Times Corresp., Washington, DC New York and London 1974–82; Assoc. Vice-Pres. Lehman Brothers Kuhn Loeb, New York 1982–84; Assoc. Vice-Pres., Prin., Man. Dir then Head communications group Morgan Stanley and Co., New York 1984–89; Man. Dir then Head communications group Lazard Frères and Co. 1989–97, Deputy CEO and Deputy Chair. 1997–99; Man. Prin. Quadrangle Group LLC 2000–09; Counselor to the Sec. of the Treasury, US Dept of the Treasury, Washington, DC 2009 (resgnd); currently Chair. Willett Advisors LLC; Dir Falcon Cable Holding Group 1993–98; mem. Bd of Dirs Cablevision, ProSiebenSat.1 Media AG, InterActiveCorp; mem. Man. Cttee Access Spectrum LLC, Global Energy Decisions, GT Brands; Dir New York Outward Bound Center 1990–2001, mem. Advisory Council 2001–; Harvey Baker Fellow, Brown Univ. 1974; Poynter Fellow, Yale Univ. 1979; mem. Council on Foreign Relations; Assoc. mem. Royal Inst. for Int. Affairs; Trustee, Brown Univ. 1987–93, 1994–2000 (Fellow 2000–), Educational Broadcasting Corpn 1990– (Vice-Chair. 1994–98, Chair. 1998–), Metropolitan Museum of Art 1996–, Brookings Inst. 1998–, New America Foundation, 2003–; Chair. Mayor's Fund to Advance NYC 2003–; Contributing Writer for Op-Ed page, New York Times; Econ. Analyst, MSNBC's Morning Joe (TV show). *Publications:* Overhaul: An Insider's Account of the Obama Administration's Emergency Rescue of the Auto Industry 2010; contrib. to various news publs including Wall Street Journal, Los Angeles Times, Newsweek and Financial Times. *Address:* Willett Advisors LLC, 25 East 78th Street, New York, NY 10075, USA (office). *Website:* willettadvisors.com (office); stevenrattner.com.

RATZINGER, Joseph Alois (see BENEDICT XVI).

RAUBER, HE Cardinal Karl-Josef, DCL; German ecclesiastic and diplomatist (retd); *Apostolic Nuncio Emeritus to Belgium;* b. 11 April 1934, Nürnberg; ed St Michael's High School of the Benedictines, Metten, Univ. of Mainz, Pontifical Gregorian Univ. and Pontifical Ecclesiastical Acad., Rome; ordained priest, Archdiocese of Mainz 1959; chaplain in Nidda; one of four secs of Substitute of Secr. of State, Archbishop Giovanni Benelli 1966; Nuntiaturrat in Belgium and Luxembourg 1977–81, in Greece 1981–82; consecrated Titular Archbishop of Iubaltiana 1983; Apostolic Pro-Nuncio to Uganda 1982–90; Pres. Pontifical Ecclesiastical Acad. 1990–93; assigned to investigate issues encountered in Diocese of Chur by Bishop Wolfgang Haas 1991–93; Apostolic Nuncio to Switzerland (also accred to Liectenstein) 1993–97, to Hungary (also accred to Moldova) 1997–2003, to Belgium (also accred to Luxembourg) 2003–09, Apostolic Nuncio Emer. to Belgium 2009–; cr. Cardinal (Cardinal-Deacon of Sant'Antonio di Padova a Circonvallazione Appia) 2015; Hon. Prelate of His Holiness 1976. *Address:* Roman Curia, 00120 Città del Vaticano, Rome, Italy (office). *Website:* www.vatican.va (office).

RAUCH, Neo; German artist; b. 18 April 1960, Leipzig; ed Hochschule für Grafik und Buchkunst, Leipzig; Asst Lecturer, Hochschule für Grafik und Buchkunst, Leipzig 1993–98, Prof. 2005–09, Hon. Prof. 2009–14; Vincent Award 2002. *Works include:* Das geht alles von ihrer Zeit ab, Stereo, Falle, Schwieriges Gelände 1997, Handel 1999, Weiche 1999, Quiz 2002, Hatz 2002, Haus des Lehrers 2003, Scheune 2003, Gold 2003, Schmerz 2004. *Address:* Wächterstrasse 11, 04107 Leipzig, Germany (office). *Telephone:* (3) 412135–0 (office). *Website:* www.hgb -leipzig.de (office).

RAUH, Markus, DrScTech; Swiss telecommunications industry executive; b. 1939, St Gallen; ed Swiss Fed. Inst. of Tech. (ETH), Zürich; began career as Sales Man., Sperry Univac 1971–78; Head of Data Systems Dept, Philips AG 1978–83; apptd mem. Corp. Exec. Cttee, Philips Kommunikations Industrie AG 1983, Chair. 1985–88; Pres. Wild Leitz 1988–90; CEO Leica Group 1990–98; apptd Dir Leica Geosystems 1998, Vice-Chair. 2000; Chair. Swisscom AG 1998–2006 (retd); Chair. Synthes Chur AG, Anova Holding AG; Chair. Bd of Dirs AO Foundation; Vice-Chair. Dietiker AG; mem. Bd of Dirs Unaxis Holding AG, The Generics Group AG, Madison Man. AG, Cantonal Bank of St Gallen AG, Sagentia Group 2000, Madison Pvt Equity Holding Ltd 2002; mem. Exec. Bd Economiesuisse; Chair. AO ASIF Foundation; Pres. Bd of Trustees, Inst. of Tech. Man., Univ. of St Gallen; Hon. Senator, Univ. of St Gallen 2005. *Address:* c/o AO Foundation, Clavadelerstrasse 8, 7270 Davos Platz, Switzerland. *Telephone:* 814142801. *Fax:* 814142280. *E-mail:* foundation@aofoundation.org. *Website:* www.aofoundation.org.

RAÚL; Spanish professional footballer (retd); b. (Raúl González Blanco), 27 June 1977, Madrid; m. María del Carmen 'Mamen' Redondo Sanz; four s. one d.; centre forward; youth player, San Cristóbal de los Ángeles 1987–90, Atlético Madrid 1990–92, Real Madrid 1992–94; sr player, Real Madrid C 1994, Real Madrid B 1994, Real Madrid 1994–2010 (won La Liga 1994/95, 1996/97, 2000/01, 2002/03, 2006/07, 2007/08, Spanish Super Cup 1997, 2001, 2003, 2008, UEFA Champions League 1997/98, 1999/2000, 2001/02, UEFA Super Cup 2002, Intercontinental Cup 1998, 2002, All-time top scorer with 321 official goals, All-time highest with 726 official matches, Capt. 2003–10), Schalke 04 2010–12, Al Sadd 2012–14, New York Cosmos 2014–15; mem. Spain U-18 team 1994, Spain U-20 team 1995, Spain U-21 team 1995–96, Spain U-23 team 1996–97, Spain 1996–2006 (102 appearances, 44 goals (Capt. 2002–06); Royal Order Gold Medal for Sports Merit 2006; Don Balón Award for Breakthrough Player in La Liga 1995, IFFHS World Goalgetter 1999, Euro 2000 Team of the Tournament 2000, ESM Team of the Year 1996/97, 1998/99, 1999/2000, Pichichi Trophy 1999, 2001, UEFA Champions League Top Scorer 1999/2000, 2000/01, FIFA World Player of the Year Bronze Award 2001, European Footballer of the Year Silver Award 2001, UEFA Club Forward of the Year 1999/2000, 2000/01, 2001/02, Premio Don Balón for Best Spanish Player in La Liga 1996/97, 1998/99, 1999/2000, 2000/01, 2001/02, named in FIFA 100 2004, Trofeo Alfredo Di Stéfano 2008, Madrid Gold Medal 2009, Second Place, Golden Foot 2009. *Leisure interests:* reading (especially the books of Arturo Pérez Reverte), listening to Spanish music.

RAUNER, Bruce Vincent, MBA; American business executive, politician and fmr state governor; b. 18 Feb. 1957, Chicago, Ill.; s. of Vincent Joseph Rauner and Ann E. Rauner (née Erickson); m. 1st Beth Konker Wessel 1980 (divorced 1993), one s. two d.; m. 2nd Diana Mendley 1994, one s. two d.; ed Dartmouth Coll., Harvard Univ.; Chair. GTCR (private equity firm) 1981–2012; f. R8 Capital Partners 2012; fmr Advisor to Mayor of Chicago Rahm Emanuel; Gov. of Illinois 2015–19; Chair. Educ. Cttee, Commercial Club of Chicago; Co-Chair. Chicago-China Initiative; Chair. ACT Charter School, Choose Chicago –2013, Chicago Public Educ. Fund; Republican. *Leisure interests:* fishing, hunting. *Address:* c/o Office of the Governor, 207 State House, Springfield, IL 62706, USA. *E-mail:* info@brucerauner.com. *Website:* brucerauner.com.

RAUSCH, Jean-Marie Victor Alphonse; French politician; b. 24 Sept. 1929, Sarreguemines, Moselle; s. of Victor Rausch and Claire Hessemann; m. 2nd Nadine Haven 1980; two s. by first m.; ed Lycée de Sarreguemines and Ecole française de meunerie, Paris; Dir Moulin Rausch, Woippy 1953–76; Admin. Soc. Anonyme des Moulins Rausch, Woippy 1976–77; Pres. departmental milling syndicate 1967–81; Pres. Moselle section, Centre des jeunes dirigeants d'entreprise 1967–69, Millers' Union of Moselle 1974–80; Conseiller-Gen. Metz III 1971, 1976, 1982–88, Pres. of Council 1979–82; Mayor of Metz 1971–2008; Senator of Moselle 1974–88, 1992–2001; Pres. Dist of the agglomeration Messina 1975–79, 1984–2002, Vice-Pres. 1979–83; Pres. Urban Planning Agency of the agglomeration of Messina 1975–89, 1999–2001, Communauté d'agglomération de Metz Métropole 2002–08; Pres. Crédit Immobilier de Moselle 1977–88, Fédération des associations de maires de la Moselle 1977–2005, l'Institut lorrain de participation 1984–88, l'association Arsenal 1992–2001 (Vice-Pres. 2001), Metz Interactive 1995–2000, Communauté numérique interactive de l'Est 2000–02, mem. Lorraine Regional Council 1974–92, Pres. 1982–92; mem. Nat. Statistical Council 1979, Conseil Nat. du Crédit 1984; numerous other civic, public and professional appointments; Minister of Foreign Trade 1988–91, of Foreign Trade and Tourism 1990–91, of Posts and Telecommunications 1991–92; Deputy Minister attached to Minister of Econ. and Finance in charge of Commerce and Labour April–Oct. 1992; Senator (Moselle) 1974–83, 1983–88, 1992–2001; Pres. Fed. des Asscns de maires de la Moselle 1977–2005, Institut Lorrain de Participation 1984–88, Médiaville 1995–, Metz-interactive 1995–2000, Communauté Numérique Interactive de l'Est 2000–02; Hon. mem. Metz Rotary Club, Acad. de Metz; Chevalier, Légion d'honneur, Commdr, Ordine della Stella della Solidarietà Italiana. *Publication:* Le laminoir et la puce: la troisième génération industrielle 1987 (Grand Prix de la littérature micro-informatique). *Leisure interests:* photography, skiing. *Address:* Médiaville, 42 rue Notre Dame des Champs, 75006 Paris (office); 4 rue Chanoine Collin, 57000 Metz, France (home). *Telephone:* 1-44-39-34-56 (office); 3-87-55-50-00 (home). *E-mail:* hotline@si.mairie-metz.fr (office).

RAUSING, Hans Anders; Swedish business executive; *Honorary Chairman, Ecolean AB;* b. 26 March 1926; s. of Ruben Rausing and Elisabeth Rausing; m. Märit Norrby; one s. two d.; ed Univ. of Lund; Man. Dir Tetra Pak 1954–83, moved to UK 1983, Chair. and CEO Tetra Pak 1983–91, Chair. Bd of Dirs 1985–91, Chair. and CEO Tetra Laval 1991–93, Hon. Chair. 1993–95; Hon. Chair. and majority investor Ecolean AB, Helsingborg, Sweden 2001–; f. Märit and Hans Rausing Charitable Foundation 1996, Hans and Märit Rausing Charitable Trust 2002; mem. Russian Council on Business Devt 1995; Hon. mem. Royal Swedish Acad. of Eng Sciences, Russian Acad. of Natural Sciences; Hon. Fellow, Isaac Newton Inst., Univ. of Cambridge; Order of People's Friendship 1994; Hon. KBE 2006; Dr hc (Univ. of Lund) 1979, (Royal Inst. of Tech., Stockholm) 1985, (Stockholm School of Econs) 1987, (American Univ. in London) 1991, (Imperial Coll. London) 2005, (Mälardalens Högskola) 2004, (Dubna, Russia). *Address:* Wadhurst Park, Wadhurst, East Sussex, TN5 6NT, England (office). *Website:* www.ecolean.com.

RAUSING, Sigrid, BA, MSc, PhD; Swedish anthropologist, philanthropist and publisher; *Publisher, Granta;* b. 1962, Lund; d. of Hans Anders Rausing and Märit Rausing; m. 1st Dennis Hotz; one s.; m. 2nd Eric Abraham 2003; ed Univ. of York, Univ. Coll. London, UK; family-owned co. Tetra-Pak (manufacturer of drink cartons); f. Ruben and Elisabeth Rausing Trust 1995 (changed name to Sigrid Rausing Trust 2003); co-f. Portobello Books 2005; acquired Granta (magazine and publishing house) 2005, now Publr; mem. Bd of Dirs, Human Rights Watch, now Emer. Mem.; mem. Advisory Bd, Coalition for the Int. Criminal Court; fmr Trustee, Charleston (museum), Sussex; Hon. Fellow, LSE 2010–, St Anthony's Coll., Oxford; Dr hc (York) 2014; Int. Service Human Rights Award, Global Human Rights Defender Category 2004, Beacon Special Award for Philanthropy 2005, Changing Face of Philanthropy Award, Women's Funding Network 2006. *Publications include:* History, Memory, and Identity in Post-Soviet Estonia 2004, Everything is Wonderful 2014, Mayhem 2017; articles in newspapers and academic journals.

RAVALOMANANA, Marc; Malagasy business executive, politician and fmr head of state; b. 12 Dec. 1949, Imerikasina; m. Lalao Rakotonirainy; three s. one d.; ed in Imerikasina and in Sweden; f. TIKO (dairy and oil producing co.); owns Malagasy

Broadcasting System (TV and radio stations), MAGRO (supermarket chain), FANAMBY (rice-producing co.); elected Mayor of Antananarivo 1999; following disputed victory in presidential elections Dec. 2001, declared himself Pres. of Madagascar Feb. 2002, High Constitutional Court ruled that he had won by an overall majority May 2002, Pres. of Madagascar 2002–09 (resgnd); Vice-Pres. Protestant Church of Madagascar; in exile in South Africa; sentenced in absentia to four years in jail for alleged abuse of office June 2009; Dr hc (Univ. of Antananarivo) 2007 Grand Commdr, Order of the Star and Key of the Indian Ocean (Mauritius), Sonderstufe des Großkreuzes (Germany) 2006; Prix Louise Michel 2005.

RAVASI, HE Cardinal Gianfranco; Italian ecclesiastic and academic; *President of the Pontifical Council for Culture;* b. 18 Oct. 1942, Merate, Prov. of Lecco; ed seminary of Milan, Pontifical Gregorian Univ. and Pontifical Biblical Inst., Rome; ordained priest, Diocese of Milan 1966; spent summers in Syria, Jordan, Iraq and Turkey working as an archaeologist with Kathleen Kenyon and Roland de Vaux; later served as Prof. of Exegesis of the Old Testament at Theological Faculty of Northern Italy, Milan; Prefect of the Ambrosian Library 1989–2007; collaborated with Cardinal Carlo Maria Martini, SJ; Titular Archbishop of Villamagna in Proconsulari 2007–; Pres. Pontifical Council for Culture 2007–, Pontifical Comm. for the Cultural Heritage of the Church 2007–, Pontifical Comm. for Sacred Archeology 2007–; cr. Cardinal (Cardinal-Deacon of San Giorgio in Velabro) 2010; participated in Papal Conclave 2013; Laurea hc specialistica in Antropologia ed Epistemologia delle Religioni (Urbino Univ.); Socio onorario dell' Accad. delle Belle Arti, Brera and Diploma di Secondo Livello in Comunicazione e Didattica dell'Arte hc 2010; Dr hc (Bucharest) 2011, (Lublin) 2012, (Pontifical Lateran Univ.) 2012. *Address:* Pontifical Council for Culture, 00120 Città del Vaticano, Rome, Italy (office). *Telephone:* (06) 69893811 (office). *Fax:* (06) 69887368 (office). *E-mail:* cultura@cultura.va (office). *Website:* www.cultura.va (office).

RAVELONARIVO, Gen. (retd) Jean; Malagasy politician, construction industry executive and fmr air force officer; b. 17 April 1959, Berevo, Menabe Region; m.; three c.; ed Univ. d'Antananarivo; began career as pilot, Ivato Aeronavale Base 1985, becoming Station Man. 1991–97; Gen. Man. J.J. Entreprise (real estate co.) 1995–2010; Dir-Gen., Société d'Equipement Immobilier de Madagascar (SEIMad) (construction agency) 1997–2002; Dir, Habitat & Francophonie (social housing agency) 2000–05; Tech. Adviser to Pres. of Senate 2001–02; Air Force Adviser to Gen. Chief of Staff of Malagasy Army 2012–15; Prime Minister 2015–16; Sec.-Gen. Building Trade Asscn 2001–03.

RAVEN, Abbe, BA, MA; American television executive; *President and CEO, A&E Television Networks;* b. New York; m.; one s.; ed Univ. of Buffalo, Hunter Coll. (Brookdale Fellow); currently Pres. and CEO A&E Television Networks (jt venture of The Hearst Corpn, The Walt Disney Co.'s Disney-ABC Television Group and General Electric's NBCUniversal), oversees History Channel and A&E; fmr Fellow, Center for Theater Research, Univ. of Buffalo; inducted into Hunter Coll. Hall of Fame 1997, Distinguished Alumnus Award, Univ. of Buffalo 2001. *Address:* A&E Television Networks, 235 East 45th Street, Suite 2, New York, NY 10017-3379, USA (office). *Telephone:* (212) 210-1400 (office). *E-mail:* info@aetv.com (office). *Website:* www.aetv.com (office).

RAVEN, Peter Hamilton, BS, PhD; American botanist, administrator and academic; *President Emeritus, Missouri Botanical Garden;* b. 13 June 1936, Shanghai, China; s. of Walter Raven and Isabelle Raven (née Breen); m. 1st Tamra Engelhorn 1968; one s. three d.; m. 2nd Patricia Duncan 2001; ed Univ. of California, Berkeley, Univ. of California, Los Angeles; Nat. Science Foundation Postdoctoral Fellow, British Museum, London 1960–61; Taxonomist, Rancho Santa Ana Botanical Garden, Claremont, Calif. 1961–62; Asst Prof., then Assoc. Prof. of Biological Sciences, Stanford Univ. 1962–71; Pres. Mo. Botanical Garden 1971–2011, Pres. Emer. 2011–, Engelmann Prof. of Botany, Washington Univ., St Louis, Mo. 1973–, now Prof. Emer.; Adjunct Prof. of Biology, Univ. of Missouri, St Louis 1973–; John D. and Catherine T. MacArthur Foundation Fellow, Univ. of Missouri 1985–90; Chair. Nat. Museum Services Bd 1984–88; mem. Nat. Geographic Soc. Comm. on Research and Exploration 1981, Governing Bd Nat. Research Council 1983–86, 1987–88, Bd World Wildlife Fund (USA) 1983–88, NAS Comm. on Human Rights 1984–87, Smithsonian Council 1985–90; Home Sec. NAS 1987–99; Pres. Org. for Tropical Studies 1985–88; apptd Pres.'s Cttee on the Nat. Medal of Science 2004; mem. Bd of Trustees Nat. Geographic Soc.; Foreign mem. Royal Danish Acad. of Sciences and Letters, Royal Swedish Acad. of Sciences; Fellow, American Acad. of Arts and Sciences, Calif. Acad. of Sciences, AAAS (fmr Pres.), Linnean Soc. of London; Hon. mem. American Soc. of Landscape Architects; several hon. degrees; Distinguished Service Award, American Inst. of Biological Sciences 1981, Int. Environmental Leadership Medal of UNEP 1982, Int. Prize in Biology, Japanese Govt, Pres.'s Conservation Achievement Award 1993, inducted into St Louis Walk of Fame 1995, Field Museum of Natural History Centennial Merit Award 1994, Nat. Medal of Science 2000, Tyler Prize for Environmental Achievement, Int. Cosmos Prize 2003, Gold Veitch Memorial Medal, RHS 2004, Botanical Soc. of America Centennial Award 2006, World Ecology Award 2007, BBVA Foundation Award for Scientific Research in Ecology and Conservation 2008, Arthur Hoyt Scott Medal 2009, William L. Brown Award for Excellence in Genetic Resource Conservation 2010, American Soc. of Plant Biologists Leadership in Science Public Service Award 2012. *Publications:* Papers on Evolution (with Ehrlich and Holm) 1969, Biology of Plants 1970, Principles of Tzeltal Plant Classification 1974, Modern Aspects of Species (with K. Iwatsuki and W. J. Bock) 1986, Understanding Biology (with G. Johnson) 1988; more than 400 professional papers; Ed.: Coevolution of Animals and Plants 1975, Topics in Plant Population Biology 1979, Advances in Legume Systematics 1981, Biology (with G. B. Johnson) 1986, Understanding Biology 1988; contrib. to many other publs. *Leisure interests:* reading, collecting plants. *Address:* Missouri Botanical Garden, PO Box 299, St Louis, MO 63166-0299, USA (office). *Telephone:* (314) 577-5111 (office). *Fax:* (314) 577-9595 (office). *E-mail:* peter.raven@mobot.org (office). *Website:* www.mobot.org (office).

RAVETCH, Jeffrey Victor, BS, PhD, MD; American geneticist, physician and academic; *Theresa and Eugene M. Lang Professor and Head of Leonard Wagner Laboratory of Molecular Genetics and Immunology, The Rockefeller University;* m. Wendy Evans Joseph 2001; ed Yale Univ., The Rockefeller Univ., Cornell Univ. Medical School; postdoctoral studies, NIH; mem. Faculty, Memorial Sloan-

Kettering Cancer Center and Cornell Medical Coll. 1982–96; Guest Investigator, Lab. of Cellular Physiology and Immunology, The Rockefeller Univ. 1984, Prof. 1996–, Theresa and Eugene M. Lang Prof. 1997–, Head of Leonard Wagner Lab. of Molecular Genetics and Immunology, Faculty mem. David Rockefeller Grad. Program, Tri-Institutional MD-PhD Program; Co-founder Macrogenics, Inc. 2000; Founder Virdante Pharmaceuticals, Inc. 2007; mem. Bd of Dirs MabVax Therapeutics; has served as mem. Scientific Advisory Bd Cancer Research Inst., Irvington Inst. for Medical Research, Damon Runyon Foundation, Xencor, Inc., SuppreMol GmbH, Millennium Pharmaceuticals, Exelexis Pharmaceuticals, Regeneron Pharmaceuticals, Medimmune, Genentech, Novartis, Micromet, Inc; mem. NAS 2006, Inst. of Medicine 2007; Fellow, American Acad. of Arts and Sciences, AAAS; Dr hc (Friedrich Alexander Univ., Erlangen-Neurenberg, Germany) 2013; Burroughs Wellcome Fund Award in Molecular Parasitology 1986, Lee C. Howley Sr Prize for Arthritis Research 2004, Huang Foundation Meritorious Career Award, American Asscn of Immunologists 2005, William B. Coley Award, Cancer Research Inst. 2007, Canada Gairdner Int. Award 2012, Sanofi-Pasteur Award 2012, Wolf Prize in Medicine (co-recipient) 2015. *Publications:* more than 150 papers in professional journals. *Address:* Leonard Wagner Laboratory of Molecular Genetics and Immunology, The Rockefeller University, 1230 York Avenue, New York, NY 10065, USA (office). *Telephone:* (212) 327-7323 (office). *Fax:* (212) 327-7319 (office). *E-mail:* jeffrey.ravetch@rockefeller.edu (office). *Website:* www.rockefeller.edu/research/faculty/labheads/JeffreyRavetch (office).

RAVI, Vayalar, BA, BL, MA; Indian politician; b. 4 June 1937, Vayalar, Alappuzha Dist, Kerala; s. of M. K. Krishnan and Devaky Krishnan; m. Mercy Ravi (died 2009); one s. two d.; ed Sanatana Dharma Coll., Alappuzha, Maharajas Coll., Ernakulam, Kerala, Ernakulam Law Coll.; elected to Fifth Lok Sabha (lower house of Parl.) for Chirayinkil constituency 1971–77, Sixth Lok Sabha 1977–79; mem. Kerala Legis. Ass. 1982–91, Minister of Home Affairs, Govt of Kerala 1982–86; elected to Rajya Sabha (upper house of Parl.) 1994, re-elected 2003, mem. Cttee on Transport, Tourism and Culture 2003–04, Cttee on Petitions 2003–04, Chair. Parl. Standing Cttee on Human Resource Devt 2004–06; mem. Rubber Bd 2003–06; mem. Consultative Cttee, Ministry of Civil Aviation 2004–06; Union Cabinet Minister of Overseas Indian Affairs 2006–14, also Minister of Civil Aviation 2011, of Micro, Small and Medium Enterprises Aug.–Oct. 2012, of Science and Tech. and Earth Sciences Aug.–Oct. 2012; fmr Pres. Kerala Pradesh Congress Cttee; attended UN Gen. Ass., New York as mem. Indian Parl. Del. 1986, 1988, 1994, 2004. *Address:* Kumarapuram, Medical College, Thiruvananthapuram 110 021, India.

RAVIER, Paul-Henri, LenD; French international organization official and civil servant; *Senior Counsellor, French Court of Audit;* b. 9 Sept. 1948, Lyon; s. of Philibert André Ravier and Roselyne Marie Bellon; m. Martine Caffin; one s.; ed Inst. d'Etudes Politiques, Ecole Nat. d'Admin.; joined Trade Dept, Ministry of the Economy and Finance, in charge of bilateral trade relations with SE Asia and Middle East, later Head of Trade Finance Policy Unit, Asst Dir responsible for man. of bilateral trade relations with Eastern Europe, Asia, the Pacific and the Middle East 1985–90, Deputy Sec. 1991–99; adviser on int. econ. issues to Prime Minister Raymond Barre 1980; Jt Deputy Head World Trade Org. 1999–2002; Sr Counsellor, French Court of Audit (Cour des Comptes) 2006–; mem. Bd Agence Française de Développement 1993–99, SNECMA 1994–99, Pechiney 1993–97; Chevalier, Ordre nat. du Mérite 1993, Légion d'honneur 1998. *Leisure interests:* golf, skiing, mountain climbing, cooking, wine tasting. *Address:* Cour des Comptes, 13 rue Cambon, 75001 Paris (office); 16 rue Théodore de Banville, 75017 Paris, France (home). *Telephone:* 1-42-98-95-00 (office); 1-45-55-42-46 (home). *Fax:* 1-45-56-10-15 (home). *E-mail:* phravier@ccomptes.fr (office); phravier@noos.fr (home). *Website:* www.ccomptes.fr (office).

RAVINET DE LA FUENTE, Jaime; Chilean politician; b. 17 Oct. 1946, Abogado; ed Univ. of Chile; Pres. Fed. of Students of Univ. of Chile 1968–69, Univ. Council 1967–72; Exec. Sec. Presidential Command of Pres. Patricio Azócar 1989; Mayor of Santiago 1990–2000; Pres. Union of Municipalities and Local Govts 1995–97, Union of Latin American Capital Cities 1995–96, World Asscn of Cities and Local Authorities Coordination 1996–97, Latin American Centre of Urban Strategic Devt 1995–97; Vice-Pres. Latin American Org. of Inter-municipal Co-operation; Minister of Housing and Urban Planning 2000–04; Minister of Nat. Defence 2004–06, 2010–11 (resgnd); mem. Exec. Bureau Worldwide Fed. of United Cities 1992–95; apptd mem. Bd of Dirs Universidad Mayor 2006; mem. Partido Demócrata Cristiano (PDC) –2010 (resgnd).

RAVITCH, Diane Silvers, PhD; American education scholar and academic; *Research Professor of Education, New York University;* b. (Diane Silvers), 1 July 1938, Houston, Tex.; d. of Walter Cracker and Ann Celia Silvers (née Katz); m. Richard Ravitch 1960 (divorced 1986); three s. (one deceased); partner, Mary Butz; ed Wellesley Coll., Mass, Columbia Univ., New York; Adjunct Asst Prof. of History and Educ., Teachers Coll., Columbia Univ. 1975–78, Assoc. Prof. 1978–83, Adjunct Prof. 1983–91; Dir Woodrow Wilson Nat. Fellowship Foundation 1987–91; Chair. Educational Excellence Network 1988–91; Asst Sec. Office of Research and Improvement, US Dept of Educ., Washington, DC 1991–93, also Counsellor to Sec. of Educ.; Visiting Fellow, Brookings Inst. 1993–94, Brown Chair in Educ. Policy 1997–2012; Sr Research Scholar, New York Univ. 1994–98, Research Prof. in Educ. 1998–; Sr Fellow, Progressive Policy Inst. 1998–2002, Hoover Inst. 1999–2009; Adjunct Fellow, Manhattan Inst. 1996–99; Pres. Network for Public Educ. 2013–; Trustee, New York Historical Soc. 1995–98, New York Council on the Humanities 1996–2004; Hon. DHumLitt (Williams Coll.) 1984, (Reed Coll.) 1985, (Amherst Coll.) 1986, (State Univ. of NY) 1988, (Ramopo Coll.) 1990, (St Joseph's Coll., NY) 1991; Hon. LHD (Middlebury Coll.) 1997, (Union Coll.) 1998, (Siena Coll.) 2012, (Columbia Coll.) 2014, (Friend of Texas Public Schools) 2015; Leadership Award, Klingenstein Inst., Teachers Coll. 1994, Horace Kidger Award, New England History Teachers Asscn 1998, Leadership Award, New York City Council of Supervisors and Admins 2004, John Dewey Award, United Fed. of Teachers of New York City 2005, Gaudium Award, Breukelein Inst. 2005, Uncommon Book Award, Hoover Inst. 2005, Kenneth J. Bialkin/Citigroup Public Service Award 2006, Friend of Educ., Nat. Educ. Asscn 2010, Distinguished Service Award, Nat. Asscn of Secondary School Prins 2010, Charles W. Eliot Award, New England Asscn of Schools and Colls 2010, American Educ. Award, American Asscn of School Admins 2011, Outstanding Friend of Educ. Award, Horace Mann League 2011, Distinguished Alumni Award, Teachers Coll., Columbia Univ. 2011, Daniel Patrick Moynihan Prize, American Acad. of Political and Social Science 2011. *Publications include:* The Great School Wars: New York City 1805–1973 1974, The Revisionists Revised 1977, Educating an Urban People (co-author) 1981, The Troubled Crusade: American Education 1945–1980 1983, The School and the City (co-author) 1983, Against Mediocrity (co-author) 1984, The Schools We Deserve 1985, Challenges to the Humanities (co-author) 1985, What Do Our 17-Year-Olds Know? (with Chester E. Finn Jr) 1987, The American Reader (co-ed.) 1990, The Democracy Reader (ed. with Abigail Thernstrom) 1992, National Standards in American Education 1995, Debating the Future of American Education (ed.) 1995, Learning from the Past (ed. with Maris Vinovskis) 1995, New Schools for a New Century (ed. with Joseph Viteretti) 1997, Left Back 2000, City Schools (ed.) 2000, The Language Police 2003, Forgotten Heroes of American Education (co-ed.) 2006, The English Reader (co-ed.) 2006, Edspeak 2007, The Death and Life of the Great American School System 2010, Reign of Error 2013; contrib. of articles and reviews to scholarly books and professional journals. *Leisure interest:* blogging. *Address:* New York University, 82 Washington Square East, New York, NY 10003, USA (office). *E-mail:* dr19@nyu.edu (office); gardendr@gmail.com (home). *Website:* dianeravitch.com; dianeravitch.net.

RAVKOV, Lt-Gen. Andrei; Belarusian army officer and government official; *Minister of Defence;* b. 25 June 1967, Revyaki village, Vitebsk Region; ed Moscow Higher Combined Arms Command School, Belarusian Mil. Acad., Russian Fed. Armed Forces Gen. Staff Acad.; long career in army including positions as platoon leader, bn commdr, Chief of Staff and Chief Commdr of weapons and equipment storage base 1999, Commdr, 103rd Guards Ind. Mobile Brigade 2005, Chief of Operations and Deputy Chief of Staff, W Operational Command, also Chief of Staff and First Deputy Commdr, NW Operational Command 2006–12, Commdr, NW Operational Command 2012–14; Minister of Defence 2014–; Order For Service to Motherland, 3rd grade; numerous Belarus state awards. *Address:* Ministry of Defence, 220034 Minsk, vul. Kamunistychnaya 1, Belarus (office). *Telephone:* (17) 297-11-19 (office). *Fax:* (17) 297-15-55 (office). *E-mail:* milcoop@mod.mil.by (office); modmail@mod.mil.by (office). *Website:* mod.mil.by (office).

RAWABDEH, Abd ar-Raouf ar-, BSc; Jordanian politician; *President of the Senate;* b. 13 Feb. 1939, Es-Sarih, Irbid; m. Fandieh Rawabdeh; 11 c.; ed American Univ. of Beirut, Univ. of Jordan; Inspector of Pharmacies, Ministry of Health 1962–64, Head, Pharmacy Section 1964–68, Dir Dept of Pharmacy and Supplies 1968–75, Dept of Planning and Foreign Relations 1975–76; Dir Dept of Admin and Services, Univ. of Yarmouk April–July 1976; Minister of Communications 1976–77, of Communications and Health 1977–78, of Health 1978–79, of Public Works and Housing 1989–91, of Educ. 1994–95, 1995–96, Deputy Prime Minister 1995–96, Prime Minister and Minister of Defence 1999–2000; mem. Nat. Consultative Council 1978–83 (Vice-Pres. 1978–83); mem. House of Reps (Lower House of Parl.) 1989–2001, 2003–10; mem. Senate (Upper House of Parl.) 2001–03, 2010–, Vice-Pres. 2011–13, Pres. 2013–; Chair. Bd of Dirs, Jordan Phosphate Mining Co. 1982–85; Vice-Chair., Jordan Fertilizer Co. 1982–85, Zetuna Co. 1982–92; Lecturer, School of Pharmacy, Univ. of Jordan 1982–89; Mayor of Amman 1983–86, of Greater Amman 1987–89; Chair. Amman Devt Corpn 1983–89; Sec.-Gen. Awakening Party (Al-Yakza) 1993–96; Vice-Chair., Bd of Trustees, Jordan Univ. of Science and Tech. 1998–99, Jadara Univ. 2006–; Deputy Sec.-Gen. Nat. Constitutional Party 1996–97; mem. Bd of Dirs Al-Aqsa Schools 1964– (Vice-Chair. 1992–94); mem. Jordan Pharmaceutical Asscn 1962–, Royal Soc. for the Conservation of Nature 1994–; Pres., Bd of Trustees, King Abdallah II Prize for Innovation 2001–; Pres. Jordan Football Asscn 1984–85; mem. Jordan Olympic Cttee 1984–85; Great Cross, Spanish Order of Isabella the Catholic 1999, Royal Norwegian Order of Merit 2000; Jordan Al-Kawkab Medal (First Degree) 1976, Italian Medal of Honour (Sr Officer) 1983, German Medal of Merit 1984, Austrian Grand Silver Medal of Honour 1987, Jordan Education Medal (Excellent Degree) 1997, Al-Nahda Medal (First Degree) 1999, French Medal of Merit (First Degree) 2000. *Publications include:* An Outline of Pharmacology 1965, Pharmacy 1965, Microbiology 1965, Physiology 1965, Democracy, Theory and Application 1992, Parliamentary Elections 1992, Education and the Future 1996, Tribes of Jordan 2010. *Leisure interests:* reading. *Address:* Office of the President of the Senate, PO Box 72, Amman 11101 (office); El-Sarih Street, Abu-Nusair, Amman, Jordan (home). *Telephone:* (6) 5664121 (office); (6) 523855 (home). *Fax:* (6) 5676981 (office); (6) 523877 (home). *E-mail:* info@senate.jo (office); alizy_67@yahoo.com. *Website:* www.senate.jo (office).

RAWAL, Bhim Bahadur, MA; Nepalese lawyer and politician; *Vice-President, Communist Party of Nepal (Unified Marxist-Leninist) (UML);* b. 14 Dec. 1956, Achham; m.; two s.; ed Tribhuvan Univ.; several years' legal practise (worked on legal literacy and assistance issues for Nepal Bar Asscn) late 1980s; Adviser to Jhala Nath Khanal (minister in interim govt) 1990–91; served on UN's Cambodian elections panel 1992–93; mem. Parl. for Achham 1 1994; Minister for Commerce, Tourism and Civil Aviation 1994–95, 1998–99, also Minister of Science and Tech. 1998–99, Minister of Home Affairs 2009–15, Deputy Prime Minister and Minister of Defence 2015–16; Proportional Rep., 2nd Nepalese Constituent Ass. April 2008–, (renamed Legislature-Parl. 2015); mem. Communist Party of Nepal (Unified Marxist-Leninist) (UML), mem. Cen. Cttee, currently Vice-Pres. *Address:* Communist Party of Nepal (Unified Marxist-Leninist) (UML), Dhumbarahi, Kathmandu, Nepal (office). *Telephone:* (1) 4015979 (office). *Website:* www.cpnuml.org (office).

RAWAL, Tilak, MA, MS, PhD; Nepalese economist, banker and academic; b. 6 Dec. 1950; ed Trihhuvan Univ., Univ. of the Philippines, Dhaka Univ.; Deputy Exec. Dir Agric. Projects Services Centre (APROSC) 1990–91; CEO Agricultural Devt Bank of Nepal 1991–94; Exec. Chair. Rastriya Banijjya Bank 1995–99; Gov. Nepal Rastra Bank 2000–05; consultant for several int. orgs, including World Bank, ADB, OECD, FAO, UN, ESCAP; mem. Faculty of Econs, Global Coll. of Man., Kathmandu; mem. Nepal Econ. Asscn. *Publications include:* Corporate Governance and Financial Sector Reform in Nepal 2006; numerous articles.

RAWASHDEH, Mazen, BS; American internet industry executive; *Vice-President, Infrastructure Operations Engineering, Twitter, Inc.;* ed Chapman Univ.; began career in various technical roles at Oracle and OPSWARE; Vice-Pres. of Technical Operations, eBay, Inc. 2004–11; Vice-Pres. Infrastructure Operations

Eng, Twitter, Inc. 2011–. *Address:* Twitter, Inc., 1355 Market Street, Suite 900, San Francisco, CA 94103, USA (office). *Telephone:* (415) 222-9670 (office). *Website:* twitter.com (office).

RAWAT, Lt-Gen. Bipin, PhD, M. Phil; Indian army officer; *Chief of Army Staff;* b. Pauri Garhwal Dist, Uttarakhand; ed Nat. Defence Acad., Khadakwasla, Defence Services Staff Coll., Madras Univ., Chaudhary Charan Singh Univ., Meerut; commissioned into 5th Bn, 11th Gorkha Rifles, Indian Army 1978; commanded infantry bn, along the Line of Actual Control in the Eastern Sector, a Rashtriya Rifles sector; an infantry division in the Kashmir Valley, corps in the north-east, multinational brigade, Chapter VII mission in the Democratic Republic of Congo, theatre of operations along the western front; served as instructor, Indian Military Acad., Dehradun, Gen. Staff Officer, Military Operations Directorate, logistics staff officer, division in Central India, Col Military Sec. and Deputy Military Sec., Military Sec.'s Branch; Sr Instructor, Junior Command Wing; fmr Major-Gen., Gen. Staff of the Eastern Theatre, then Vice Chief of the Army Staff; Chief of Army Staff 2016–; Uttam Yudh Seva Medal, Ati Vishisht Seva Medal, Wound Medal, Sainya Seva Medal, Yudh Seva Medal, Samanya Seva Medal, High Altitude Service Medal, Sena Medal, Special Service Medal, Videsh Seva Medal, Vishisht Seva Medal, Operation Parakram Medal, 9 Years Long Service Medal, 20 Years Long Service Medal, 30 Years Long Service Medal. *Address:* Indian Army, South Block, Integrated Headquarters of MoD (Army), New Delhi 110011, India (office). *E-mail:* webmaster.indianarmy@nic.in (office). *Website:* indianarmy.nic.in (office).

RAWAT, Harish, BA, LLB; Indian trade unionist and politician; b. 27 April 1948, Mohanari, Almora Dist, Uttarakhand; s. of Rajendra Singh Rawat and Devaki Devi; m. Renuka Rawat; ed Lucknow Univ.; held various posts in Indian Youth Congress including Nat. Jt Sec. and Gen. Sec.; elected to 7th Lok Sabha (lower house of Parl.) for Almora constituency 1980–84, 8th Lok Sabha 1984–89, 9th Lok Sabha 1989, 15th Lok Sabha for Hardwar constituency 2009–14; mem. Rajya Sabha (upper house of Parl.) for Uttarakhand 2002–08; Pres. Uttarakhand Pradesh Congress Cttee 2001–07; Union Cabinet Minister of State for Labour and Employment 2009–11, for Agric. and Food Processing Industries Jan.–June 2011, for Parl. Affairs 2011–12, Minister of Water Resources 2012–14; Chief Minister of Uttarakhand 2014–17 (suspended 18 March 2016 and President's rule imposed, reinstated 11 May 2016); mem. All India Congress Cttee 1980–; apptd mem. House Cttee 1989, Cttee on Official Language 1990, Consultative Cttee, Ministry of Communications 1990; fmr mem. Consultative Cttee of Law and Company Affairs, Public Account Cttee.

RAWAT, Om Prakash, MSc; Indian government official; b. 2 Dec. 1953; ed Banaras Hindu Univ., Varanasi; Collector, Madhya Pradesh 1983–88; apptd Dir and Jt Sec. Ministry of Defence 1993; Prin. Sec. to Chief Minister 2004–06; Additional Chief Sec. then Vice-Chair., Narmada Valley Devt Dept 2009–12; fmr Prin. Sec., SC/ST Welfare Dept, Govt of Madhya Pradesh; Sec. Dept of Public Enterprises, Ministry of Heavy Industries 2012–13; Election Commr, Election Comm. of India 2015–18, Chief Election Commr Jan.–Dec. 2018; other past positions held include Commissioner, Women and Child Devt, Registrar,Co-operative Socs., Sec., Cooperation, Agriculture, State Excise Commr in Madhya Pradesh; Prime Minister's Award 2010. *Address:* c/o Election Commission Office, Nirvachan Sadan, Ashoka Rd, New Delhi 110 001, India (office). *Telephone:* (11) 23717391 (office). *Fax:* (11) 23717075. *E-mail:* feedbackeci@gmail.com. *Website:* eci .nic.in.

RAWI, Najih Mohamed Khalil ar-, MSc, PhD; Iraqi civil engineer, educationalist and fmr government official; b. 4 April 1935, Rawa; m.; one s. two d.; ed Univ. of Wales, Purdue Univ., Oklahoma State Univ.; instructor, Univ. of Baghdad 1967, Asst Prof. of Civil Eng 1971, Prof. 1980; Prof. Emer. 1990–; Dean Higher Inst. of Industrial Eng, Univ. of Baghdad 1968–69; Dean Coll. of Industry (now Tech. Univ.) 1969–70; mem. Bureau of Educ. Affairs, Revolutionary Command Council 1973–74, Council of Higher Educ. 1970–74, 1980–85; Deputy Minister of Municipalities 1974, of Public Works and Housing 1974–77; Minister of Industry and Minerals 1977–78; Vice-Pres. Iraqi Engineers Syndicate 1969–71; Pres. Iraqi Teachers Syndicate 1970–74, Iraqi–Soviet Friendship Soc. 1979–88, Nat. Cttee Tech. and Transfer 1984–89, Man and the Biosphere 1980–89, Int. Geological Correlation Programme 1980–89, Geophysics and Geodesy 1982–89, Council of Scientific Research 1980–89, Iraqi Acad. of Sciences 1996–2001 (mem. 1996–); Head Union of Arab Educators 1983–86; mem. Bd of Trustees, Al-Mustansiryah Univ. 1970–74, Arabian Gulf Univ. 1986–89, Teachers' Union Univ. Coll. 1990–96; mem. Iraq Eng Soc. 1959, American Soc. of Civil Engineers 1967, Council of the World Fed. of Educators 1973–74, 1979–82; Founding Fellow, Islamic Acad. of Sciences 1986; Corresp. mem. Syrian Acad. of Language, Damascus 2001. *Publications:* On Science and Technology (in Arabic) 2003; 65 papers in scientific journals 1960–2003. *Address:* Iraqi Academy of Sciences, Waziriya, A'Adamiah, Baghdad (office); 2/40/635 Hai Al-Jamea, Baghdad, Iraq (home). *Telephone:* (1) 4224202 (office); (1) 5559635 (home). *E-mail:* aos@uruklink.net (office); ahmedelrawi@yahoo.com (home).

RAWLINGS, Hunter R., III, PhD; American academic and fmr university administrator; *Professor Emeritus and University President Emeritus, Cornell University;* b. Norfolk, Va; m. Elizabeth Trapnell Rawlings; four c.; ed Haverford Coll., Princeton Univ.; Asst Prof. Univ. of Colo 1970–80, Dept Chair. 1978–88, Prof. 1980–88, Assoc. Vice Chancellor for Instruction 1980–84, Vice-Pres. for Academic Affairs and Research Dean of the System Grad. School 1984–88; Pres. and Prof. of Classics Univ. of Iowa 1988–95, Chair. Gov's Comm. on Foreign Languages Studies and Int. Educ. 1988–91; Pres. Cornell Univ. 1995–2003, Pres. Emer. 2003–, Interim Pres. 2005–06, Prof. of Classics 1995, now Prof. Emer.; fmr Chair. Ivy Council of Pres.; mem. Bd of Dirs American Council on Educ., Exec. Cttee Asscn of American Univs (Pres. 2011), Nat. Cttee for Selection of Mellon Fellows in Humanities; mem. American Acad. of Arts and Sciences, American School of Classical Studies in Athens, Haverford Coll., Nat. Acad. Foundation; Woodrow Wilson Fellow, Nat. Defense Educ. Act Fellow, Univ. of Colo Teaching Excellence Award 1979. *Publications:* The Structure of Thucydides' History 1981, The Classical Journal (Ed.); numerous monographs and articles. *Address:* c/o Department of Classics, Cornell University, 120 Goldwin Smith Hall, Ithaca, NY 14853-3201, USA (office).

RAWLINGS, Flight-Lt Jerry John; Ghanaian fmr head of state and fmr air force officer; b. 22 June 1947, Accra; s. of John Rawlings and Victoria Agbotui; m. Nana Konadu Agyeman; one s. three d.; ed Achimota School and Ghana Mil. Acad., Teshie; commissioned as Pilot Officer 1969, Flight-Lt 1978; arrested for leading mutiny of jr officers May 1979; leader mil. coup which overthrew Govt of Supreme Mil. Council June 1979; Chair. Armed Forces Revolutionary Council (Head of State) June–Sept. 1979; retd from armed forces Nov. 1979, from air force Sept. 1992; leader mil. coup which overthrew Govt of Dr Hilla Limann Dec. 1981; Head of State 1982–2001; Chief of Defence Staff 1982–2001; Chair. Provisional Nat. Defence Council 1981–93; Pres. of Ghana 1993–2001; named African Union Envoy to Somalia 2010; Hon. DLit (Univ. for Devt Studies, Northern Ghana) 2013; Africa Prize for the Sustainable End of Hunger, Hunger Project 1993, Global Champion for People's Freedom, Mkiva Humanitarian Foundation 2013. *Leisure interests:* boxing, deep-sea diving, swimming, horse riding, carpentry. *Address:* c/o PO Box 1627, Osu, Accra, Ghana. *Website:* www.jjrawlings.info.

RAWLINGS, Menna Frances, CMG; British diplomatist; *High Commissioner to Australia;* m.; three c.; joined FCO 1989, postings include to Washington, DC, Ghana, Israel, Kenya and Brussels, served as Pvt. Sec. to Perm. Under-Sec. as well as in Press Office and Africa and EU Directorates, Human Resources Dir, FCO Man. Bd –2015, High Commr to Australia 2015–. *Address:* British High Commission, Commonwealth Avenue, Yarralumla, Canberra, ACT 2600, Australia (office). *Telephone:* (2) 6270-6666 (office). *Fax:* (2) 6273-3236 (office). *E-mail:* canberra.enquiries@fconet.fco.gov.uk (office). *Website:* www.gov.uk/government/world/organisations/british-high-commission-canberra (office); www.gov.uk/government/world/australia (office).

RAWLINS, Peter Jonathan, MA, FCA, FRSA; British business executive and management consultant; b. 30 April 1951, London; s. of Kenneth Raymond Ivan Rawlins and Constance Amande Malzy; m. 1st Louise Langton 1973 (divorced 1999); one s. one d.; m. 2nd Christina Conway 2000; two s. one d.; ed St Edward's School and Keble Coll. Oxford; with Arthur Andersen & Co., Chartered Accountants, London 1972–85, Partner 1983–85; seconded as Personal Asst to CEO and Deputy Chair. Lloyd's of London 1983–84; Dir Sturge Holdings PLC 1985–89, Man. Dir R. W. Sturge & Co. 1985–89, Dir Sturge Lloyd's Agencies Ltd 1986–89; Dir Wise Speke Holdings Ltd 1987–89; CEO The London Stock Exchange 1989–93 (resgnd); consultant, Rawlins Strategy Consulting 1994–; FSI Portfolio Dir, Accenture 1995; Man. Dir (Europe, Middle East and Africa) Siegel & Gale Ltd 1996–97; Dir Scala Business Solutions NV 1998–2000, Oyster Partners Ltd 2001–02; Chair. (non-exec.) Higham Group 2004–05; Assoc., Bale Crocker; fmr Chair. Asscn for Research into Stammering in Childhood; Chair. Spitalfields Festival 1998–2003. *Leisure interests:* the performing arts, tennis, shooting, travelling, national heritage, rugby. *Address:* Rawlins Strategy Consulting, The White House, Hadlow Road East, Tonbridge, TN11 0AE (office); Ramley House, Ramley Road, Lymington, Hants., SO41 8LH, England (home). *Telephone:* (1732) 852248 (office); (1590) 689661 (home). *Fax:* (1590) 689662 (home). *E-mail:* peter@rawlinsp.fsnet.co.uk (home).

RAWNSLEY, Andrew Nicholas James, MA, FRSA; British journalist, broadcaster and author; *Associate Editor and Chief Political Commentator, The Observer;* b. 5 Jan. 1962, Leeds, Yorks., England; s. of Eric Rawnsley and Barbara Rawnsley (née Butler); m. Jane Leslie Hall 1990; three d.; ed Lawrence Sheriff Grammar School, Rugby, Rugby School, Sidney Sussex Coll., Cambridge; with BBC 1983–85, The Guardian 1985–93 (political columnist 1987–93); Assoc. Ed. and Chief Political Commentator, The Observer 1993–; Ed.-in-Chief, politicshome.com (political website) 2008–09; Presenter Channel 4 TV series A Week in Politics 1989–97, ITV series The Agenda 1996, Channel 4 series Bye Bye Blues 1997, Blair's Year 1998, BBC 2 series What The Papers Say and Review of the Year 2002–07, ITV series The Sunday Edition 2006–08, BBC Radio 4 series The Westminster Hour 1998–2006, The Unauthorised Biography of the United Kingdom 1999, Channel 4 series The Rise and Fall of Tony Blair 2007, Gordon Brown: Where Did it All Go Wrong? 2008, Crash Gordon: The Inside Story of the Financial Crisis 2009, Cameron Uncovered 2010, BBC Radio 4 series Leader Conference 2011–; Fellow, Royal Soc. of Arts & Sciences 2011; Trustee, The Speakers Trust 2018–; Hon. Fellow, Sidney Sussex Coll. 2018; Student Journalist of the Year, Guardian/NUS Media Awards 1983, Young Journalist of the Year, British Press Awards 1987, Columnist of the Year, What the Papers Say Award 2000, Book of the Year Award, Channel 4 Political Awards 2001, Political Journalist of the Year, Channel 4 Political Awards 2003, Commentator of the Year, Public Affairs Awards 2005, Commentator of the Year, House Magazine Awards 2008, Comment Awards Chair's Prize for Editorial Intelligence 2015. *Publications include:* Servants of the People: The Inside Story of New Labour (Channel 4 Book of the Year 2001) 2000 (revised edn 2001), The End of the Party: The Rise and Fall of New Labour 2010. *Leisure interests:* skiing, scuba diving, mah jong, books, cinema, food and wine. *Address:* The Observer, Kings Place, 90 York Way, London, N1 9GU, England (office). *Telephone:* (20) 7278-2332 (office). *E-mail:* a.rawnsley@observer.co.uk (office). *Website:* www.theguardian.com/profile/andrewrawnsley (office).

RAWSON, Dame Jessica Mary, DBE, MA, DLitt, FBA; British archaeologist, college warden and writer; *Professor of Chinese Art and Archaeology, Institute of Archaeology, University of Oxford;* b. 20 Jan. 1943; d. of Roger Quirk and Paula Quirk; m. John Rawson 1968; one d.; ed New Hall, Cambridge and Univ. of London; Asst Prin. Ministry of Health 1965–67; Asst Keeper II, Dept of Oriental Antiquities, British Museum 1967–71, Asst Keeper I 1971–76, Deputy Keeper 1976–87, Keeper 1987–94; Warden, Merton Coll. Oxford 1994–2011, currently Prof. of Chinese Art and Archaeology, Inst. of Archaeology, Univ. of Oxford; Visiting Prof., Kunsthistorisches Inst. Heidelberg 1989, Univ. of Chicago 1994; Chair. Oriental Ceramic Soc. 1993–96; Vice-Chair. Bd of Govs, SOAS, Univ. of London 1999–2003; mem. British Library Bd 1999–2003; Gov. St Paul's Girls' School 2009–, Compton Verney House Trust; Hon. DSc (St Andrews) 1997, Hon. DLitt (Sussex) 1998, (Royal Holloway, London) 1998, (Newcastle) 1999. *Publications:* Chinese Jade Throughout the Ages (with J. Ayers) 1975, Animals in Art 1977, Ancient China, Art and Archaeology 1980, Chinese Ornament: The Lotus and the Dragon 1984, Chinese Bronzes: Art and Ritual 1987, The Bella and P.P. Chiu Collection of Ancient Chinese Bronzes 1988, Western Zhou Ritual Bronzes from the Arthur M. Sackler Collections 1990, Ancient Chinese and Ordos Bronzes (with E. Bunker) 1990, The British Museum Book of Chinese Art (ed.) 1992, Chinese Jade from the Neolithic to the Qing 1995, The Mysteries of Ancient China (ed.) 1996, Cosmological Systems and Sources of Art, Ornament and Design 2002, China: The Three Emperors, 1662–1795 (co-ed. with Evelyn Rawski) 2005, Treasure from Shanghai 2009. *Leisure interest:* gardening. *Address:* Institute of Archaeology, University of Oxford, 36 Beaumont Street, Oxford, OX1 2PG, England (office). *Telephone:* (1865) 278240 (office). *Website:* www.arch.ox.ac.uk/institute.html (home).

RAY, Pratibha, BSc, MEd, PhD; Indian academic and writer; b. 21 Jan. 1943, Alabol, Cuttack Dist, Orissa; d. of Parashuram Das and Manorama Devi; m. Akshaya Chandra Ray; two s. one d.; ed Balikuda High School, Ravenshaw Coll., Cuttack; Oriya writer; school teacher at various Orissa State Govt colls for 30 years; mem. Public Service Comm., Orissa State 1998–2004; f. Bhashyan Literary Foundation 2004; mem. Exec. Bd Sahitya Akademi; mem. Bd of Dirs Tata Refractories Ltd; mem. General Ass., Indian Council of Cultural Relations, Central Bd of Film Certification, Indian Red Cross Soc., Nat. Book Trust of India, Central Acad. of Letters, Odia Bhasa Pratisthan, Academic Council, Culture Univ., Govt of Odisha; Life mem. IIPA, INTACH; DLit (Utkal Univ. of Bhubaneswar) 2011; Jhankara Award 1989, Saptarshi Award, Sambalpur Univ. 1989, Katha Prize 1994, 1999, Bisuva Award for Lifetime Achievement 1995, Rastriya Ekta Puruskar 1999, Kapilash Award 2000, Katha Bharati Title 2000, Rajiv Gandhi Sacbhawana Nat. Puraskar 2002, Chitrapuri Samman 2006, Amrita Keerti Award 2006, Padma Shri 2007, Gopichand Nat. Award for Literature 2008, Guru Pranam Samman 2009, Pathaka Sammana 2010, Jnanpith Award 2011, Utkal Pragyan, Bhubaneswar Doordarshan Kendra 2012, Odisha Living Legend Award 2013. *Publications include:* novels: Barsha Basanta Baishakha 1974, Aranya 1977, Nishidha Prithivi 1978, Parichaya 1979, Aparichita 1979, Punyatoya 1979, Meghamedura 1980, Ashabari 1980, Ayamarambha 1981, Nilatrishna 1981, Samudrara Swara 1982, Shilapadma (trans. as Stone Lotus, Orissa Sahitya Akademi Award 1985) 1983, Yajnaseni (Sarla Award 1990, Moorti Devi Bharatiya Jnanpath Award 1991) 1984, Dehatit 1986, Uttarmarg 1988, Aadibhoomi (trans. as Primal Land) 1993, Maha Moha 1998, Magnamati (trans. as The Tranced Earth) 2004, Citadel of Love (Odisha Sahitya Akademi Award) 2016; short stories: Samanya Kathana 1978, Gangashiuli 1979, Asamapta 1980, Aikatana 1981, Anabana 1983, Hatabaksa 1983, Ghasa o Akasha 1984, Chandrabhaga o Chadrakala 1984, Shrestha Galpa 1984, Abyakta 1986, Itibut 1987, Haritpatra 1989, Prithak Ishwar 1991, Bhagabanara Desha (trans. as Land of God) 1991, Manushya Swara 1992, Sasthasati 1996, Moksha 1996, Ullanghana (Sahitya Akademi Award 2000) 1998, Nivedanamidam 2000, Gandhinka 2002, Jhoti paka Kantha 2006. *Leisure interest:* philanthrophy. *Website:* www.pratibharay.org.

RAY, Rachael Domenica; American television presenter, author and chef; b. 25 Aug. 1968, Glens Falls, NY; d. of James Ray and Elsa Scuderi; m. John Cusimano (lawyer and lead singer of rock band The Cringe) 2005; raised in Cape Cod, Mass where family owned four restaurants; family moved to Lake George, NY 1976, then moved to New York City 1995; first job at candy counter at Macy's, later managed fresh foods dept; later helped open a New York City market; moved back to upstate NY and managed Mister Brown's Pub at The Sagamore (hotel), Lake George; became a buyer at Cowan & Lobel (gourmet market in Albany); cr. concept of 30 Minute Meals for people who were reluctant to cook, taught course showing how to make meals in less than 30 minutes; asked by WRGB (local CBS TV affiliate) to appear in weekly segment on their newscasts; led to Today show spot and her first Food Network contract 2001; signed deal with Oprah Winfrey and King World Productions to host syndicated daytime TV talk show, Rachael Ray 2006; f. Rachael's Rescue (charity to help at-risk animals); launched Yum-O! charity to help children eat more healthily 2006; hosts syndicated talk and lifestyle programme Rachael Ray and three Food Network series, 30 Minute Meals, Rachael Ray's Tasty Travels and $40 a Day; wrote cookbooks based on the 30 Minute Meals concept, and launched a magazine, Every Day with Rachael Ray 2006. *Television includes:* 30 Minute Meals (Daytime Emmy Award for Outstanding Service Show 2006), The Rachael Ray Show (Daytime Emmy Award for Outstanding Talk Show/Entertainment 2008, 2009) 2002–, Rachael's Vacation (series) premiered on the Food Network 2008, Rachael Ray's Week In a Day on the Cooking Channel 2010. *Publications include:* 30 Minute Meals 1999, Rachael Ray's Open House Cookbook 2000, Comfort Foods 2001, Veggie Meals 2001, 30-Minute Meals 2 2003, Get Togethers: Rachael Ray 30 Minute Meals 2003, Cooking Rocks!: Rachael Ray 30-Minute Meals for Kids 2004, $40 a Day: Best Eats in Town 2004, Rachael Ray's 30-Minute Meals: Cooking 'Round the Clock 2004, Rachael Ray's 30-Minute Meals for Kids: Cooking Rocks! 2004, Rachael Ray's 30-Minute Get Real Meals: Eat Healthy Without Going to Extremes 2005, Rachael Ray 365: No Repeats: A Year of Deliciously Different Dinners 2005, Rachael Ray 2, 4, 6, 8: Great Meals for Couples or Crowds 2006, Rachael Ray's Express Lane Meals 2006, Rachael Ray: Just In Time 2007, Yum-O! The Family Cookbook 2008, Rachael Ray's Big Orange Book 2008, Rachael Ray's Book Of 10: More Than 300 Recipes To Cook Every Day 2009; Reader's Digest Association launched eponymous magazine, Every Day with Rachael Ray 2005, seven issues 2006, ten issues 2007. *Website:* www.rachaelrayshow.com (office); www.foodnetwork.com/rachael-ray (office); www.rachaelray.com.

RAY, Robert Francis, BA; Australian fmr politician; b. 8 April 1947, Melbourne; m. Jane Ray; ed Rusden State Coll., Monash Univ.; fmr tech. school teacher; Senator for Victoria 1981–2008, Parl. Rep. on Australian Council for Union Training 1983–85, Minister for Home Affairs and Deputy Man. of Govt Business in the Senate 1987–88 (Man. 1988–91, Deputy Leader 1993–96), for Transport and Communications Jan.–Sept. 1988, for Immigration, Local Govt and Ethnic Affairs and Minister assisting Prime Minister for Multicultural Affairs 1988–90, for Defence 1990–96, fmr mem. Finance and Admin. Estimates Cttee, Deputy Leader of Govt in Senate 1993–96; Parl. Adviser, Gen. Ass., UNA, New York, Sept.–Dec. 1999, Sept.–Dec. 2005; mem. Australian Labor Party (ALP) Nat. Exec. 1983–98; mem. Parl. Del. to Sri Lanka and Bangladesh Sept.–Oct. 2003, Parl. Del. to Indonesia and Papua New Guinea Dec. 2003, Parl. Del. to South Africa Sept.–Oct. 2006; retd 2008. *Leisure interests:* films, billiards, tennis, watching Australian Rules football, golf and cricket.

RAYAMAJHI, Rt Hon. Min Bahadur; Nepalese judge; b. 1944, Helaunchha, Bhojpur dist; joined the judiciary as section officer, Supreme Court 1970; served as Dist Judge in Khotang, Parbat, Kapilvastu, Mugu, has also served in Janakpur and Bagmati Zonal Courts; served in Hetauda, Janakpur and Patan Appellate Courts 1991–2001; Justice of the Supreme Court of Nepal 2001–10, Chief Justice April 2001, 2009–10 (retd); Chair. Nat. Judicial Acad.

RAYKHELHAUS, Iosif Leonidovich; Russian theatre director; b. 2 June 1947, Odessa, Ukraine; m. Maria Khazina; two d.; ed Moscow Inst. of Theatre Arts; stage Dir Moscow Stanislavsky Theatre 1973; founder and Artistic Dir School of Contemporary Play theatre 1989–; teacher All-Union Inst. of Cinematography 1997–; Prize of Moscow Festival of Chamber Productions Martenitsa 1991, Merited Worker of Arts 1993. *Productions include:* Salute, Don Juan!, A Man Came to a Woman, The Seagull. *Address:* Moscow Theatre School of Contemporary Play, Neglinnaya str. 29/14, 103031 Moscow, Russia (office). *Telephone:* (495) 200-09-00 (office). *Fax:* (495) 200-30-87 (office).

RAYKOV, Marin; Bulgarian government official, politician and diplomatist; b. 17 Dec. 1960, Washington, DC, USA; s. of Rayko Nikolov and Lydia Nikolova; m.; two c.; ed Univ. for Nat. and World Economy; joined Ministry of Foreign Affairs 1987, served as Intern Attaché, then Attaché, later Third Sec., Balkan Countries Dept 1987–92, Third, then Second, then First Sec., Embassy in Belgrade 1992–95, Political and Social Issues Expert, Dept for Human Rights, Humanitarian and Social Cooperation, Council of Europe 1995–97; Deputy Perm. Rep., Council of Europe, Strasbourg 1997–98, Deputy Minister of Foreign Affairs 1998–2001, Amb. to France and Perm. Rep. to UNESCO 2001–05, also personal envoy of Head of State to Org. Internationale de la Francophonie; Head of Common European Foreign Policy and Strategic Issues Sections, Foreign Policy Coordination and Planning Directorate 2005–08, Sr Diplomatic Official, Political Issues Directorate 2008–09, Deputy Minister of Foreign Affairs 2009–10, Amb. to France 2010–13; Prime Minister and Minister of Foreign Affairs in caretaker govt March–May 2013; mem. Union of Bulgarian Journalists, Bulgarian Asscn of Int. Law, Bd of Govs, Bulgarian Foreign Policy Asscn; teaches at New Bulgarian Univ.; Grand Officer, Ordre nat. du Mérite; Grand Commdr, Order of Phoenix (Greece).

RAYMOND, Lee R., PhD; American oil industry executive (retd); b. 13 Aug. 1938, Watertown, South Dakota; m. Charlene Raymond 1960; ed Univ. of Wisconsin, Univ. of Minnesota; various eng positions in Exxon Corpn (now Exxon Mobil Corpn), Tulsa, Houston, New York and Caracas, Venezuela 1963–72, Man. Planning, Int. Co. Div., New York 1972–75, Pres. Exxon Nuclear Co. Div. 1979–81, Exec. Vice-Pres. Exxon Enterprises Inc. Div. 1981–83, Sr Vice-Pres. and Dir Exxon Corpn 1984–86, Pres. and Dir 1987–93, Chair. and CEO 1993–99, Chair. and CEO Exxon Mobil Corpn 1999–2005 (retd), Pres. 1999–2003; Vice-Pres. Lago Oil, Netherlands Antilles 1975–76, Pres. and Dir 1976–79; Pres. and Dir Esso Inter-American Inc., Coral Gables, Fla 1983–84, Sr Vice-Pres. and Dir 1984; mem. Bd of Dirs J. P. Morgan & Co. Inc., New York, Morgan Guaranty Trust Co. of New York, American Petroleum Inst.; mem. Bd of Dirs Nat. Action Council for Minorities in Eng Inc., New York 1985, New American Schools Devt Corpn 1991, Project Shelter PRO-AM 1991; mem. American Petroleum Inst. (mem. Bd of Dirs 1987), The Business Roundtable, American Council on Germany 1986, British-N American Cttee 1985, Singapore-US Business Council, Visitors' Cttee Univ. of Wis. Dept of Chem. Eng 1987, Dallas Cttee on Foreign Relations 1988, The Conf. Bd 1991, Bd of Govs, Dallas Symphony Asscn; Trustee, American Enterprise Inst.; Public Service Star (Distinguished Friends of Singapore Award) 2004, Hon. Citizen of Singapore 2006.

RAYMOND, Réal, MBA; Canadian banker; ed Univ. of Quebec, Montreal; joined Nat. Bank 1970, Sr Vice-Pres. Treasury and Financial Markets 1992–99, Sr Exec. Vice-Pres. Corporate Financing Lévesque Beaubien Geoffrion (now National Bank Financial) 1997–99, Pres. Personal and Commercial Bank 1999–2001, Pres. and COO Nat. Bank of Canada 2001–02, Pres. and CEO 2002–07 (retd), apptd Special Adviser 2007; Pres. Montreal Museum of Fine Arts Foundation; mem. Bd of Dirs Fondation de l'Univ. du Québec à Montréal, St Mary's Hosp. Foundation, Montreal Symphony Orchestra; Dir Metro Inc. 2010–15, Chair. Bd of Corpn 2015–.

RAYMUND, Steven A., BS, MA; American computer industry executive; *Chairman, Tech Data Corporation;* b. 16 Nov. 1955, Van Nuys, Calif.; s. of Edward C. Raymund and Annette Leah Raymund; ed Univ. of Oregon, Georgetown Univ. School of Foreign Service; early position with Manufacturers Hanover Corpn, New York 1980–81; Operations Man. Tech Data Corpn (distributor of computer products f. by Edward Raymund 1974) 1981–84, COO 1984–86, mem. Bd of Dirs 1986–, CEO 1986–2006, Chair. 1991–2006, Chair. (non-exec.) 2006–; mem. Bd of Dirs Jabil Circuit Inc. 1996–, WESCO Int., Inc. 2006–, PopCap Games, Inc. 2010–11; Chair. St Petersburg Area Chamber of Commerce 2009; named to Industry Hall of Fame, Computer Reseller News (CRN) 1999. *Address:* Tech Data Corporation, 5350 Tech Data Drive, Clearwater, FL 33760-3122, USA (office). *Telephone:* (727) 539-7429 (office). *Fax:* (727) 538-7803 (office). *E-mail:* info@techdata.com (office). *Website:* www.techdata.com (office).

RAYNAUD, Jean-Pierre; French sculptor; b. 20 April 1939, Courbevoie; s. of André Raynaud and Madeleine Dumay; ed Ecole d'Horticulture du Chesnay; first one-man exhbn Galerie Larcade, Paris 1965; numerous other one-man shows in France, Europe, USA, Japan, Israel; retrospective exhbns The Menil Collection, Houston, Museum of Contemporary Art, Chicago and Int. Centre of Contemporary Art, Montreal 1991, CAPC, Bordeaux 1993, Paume 1998, Jérôme de Noirmont Gallery, Paris 2001; Grand Prix Nat. de Sculpture 1983, Prix Robert Giron, Palais des Beaux Arts, Brussels 1985, Grand Prix de Sculpture de la Ville de Paris 1986, Prix d'honneur de la Biennale de Venise 1993; Officier des Arts et des Lettres, Chevalier du Mérite, Légion d'honneur. *Work includes:* windows at Cistercian Abbey at Noirlac, Cher 1976–77, large sculpture in gardens of Fondation Cartier pour l'Art Contemporain, Jouy-en-Josas 1985, Autoportrait for City of Québec 1987, Container Zero, Pompidou Centre, Paris 1988, Carte du Ciel, Grande Arche, Paris La Défense 1989. *Address:* 26 Rue Des Plantes, 75014 Paris, France. *Telephone:* 1-45-44-47-17. *E-mail:* daphne.raynaud@sfr.fr.

RAYNER, Steve, BA, PhD, FRSA; British social scientist and academic; *James Martin Professor of Science and Civilization, Saïd Business School, University of Oxford;* ed Univ. of Kent at Canterbury, Univ. Coll. London; began career as Sr Research Assoc., Centre for Occupational and Community Research, Middx Polytechnic; Deputy Dir, Global Environmental Studies Center, Oak Ridge Nat. Lab., USA –1991; Chief Scientist, Pacific NW Nat. Lab., Richland, Wash. 1991–96;

Prof. of Environment and Public Affairs and Prof. of Sociology, Columbia Univ. –2002, also Chief Social Scientist, Int. Research Inst. for Climate Prediction; James Martin Prof. of Science and Civilization, Saïd Business School, Univ. of Oxford 2002–, also Dir Inst. for Science, Innovation and Soc.; Professorial Fellow, Keble College, Oxford; fmr Visiting Scholar, Columbia Univ., Boston Univ. School of Public Health; Fellow, Royal Anthropological Inst., Soc. for Applied Anthropology, AAAS 2003; mem. Royal Comm. on Environmental Pollution; Hon. Prof. of Climate Change and Soc., Univ. of Copenhagen, Denmark. *Publications:* co-author or ed. of seven books, three special issues of journals, more than 50 articles and papers, and 20 technical reports. *Address:* Institute of Science, Innovation and Society, University of Oxford, 64 Banbury Road, Oxford, OX2 6PN, England (office). *Telephone:* (1865) 288938 (office). *E-mail:* Steve.Rayner@insis.ox.ac.uk (office). *Website:* www.insis.ox.ac.uk (office).

RAYNES, Edward Peter, MA, PhD, DSc, FRS; British physicist and academic; b. 4 July 1945, York, Yorks.; s. of Edward Gordon Raynes and Ethel Mary Raynes; m. Madeline Ord 1970; two s.; ed St Peter's School, York, Gonville & Caius Coll. and the Cavendish Lab., Cambridge; with Royal Signals and Radar Establishment, Malvern 1971–92, Deputy Chief Scientific Officer 1988–92; Chief Scientist Sharp Laboratories of Europe Ltd 1992–98, Dir of Research 1995–98; Visiting Prof., Dept of Eng Science, Univ. of Oxford 1996–98, Prof. of Optoelectronic Eng 1998–2010; Leverhulme Emer. Research Fellow, Dept of Chem., Univ. of York 2010–12; Hon. FInstP; Rank Opto-Electronic Prize 1980, Paterson Medal, Inst. of Physics 1986, Special Recognition Award, Soc. of Information Display 1987, G.W. Gray Medal, British Liquid Crystal Soc. 2001, Jan Rajchman Prize, Soc. of Information Display 2009. *Publications:* numerous scientific publs and patents; The Physics, Chemistry and Applications of Liquid Crystals (co-ed.). *Address:* Department of Chemistry, University of York, York, YO10 5DD, England (office). *Telephone:* (1904) 322527 (office). *E-mail:* peter.raynes@york.ac.uk (office). *Website:* www.york.ac.uk/chemistry (office).

RAYNSFORD, Wyvill Richard Nicolls (Nick), MA; British politician; b. 28 Jan. 1945, Northampton, Northants., England; s. of Wyvill Raynsford and Patricia Raynsford (née Dunn); m. Anne Jelley 1968; three d.; ed Repton School, Sidney Sussex Coll. Cambridge, Chelsea School of Art and Design; mem. staff, Soc. of Co-operative Dwellings, AC Nielen, Market Research; Dir SHAC, The London Housing Aid Centre 1976–86, Raynsford & Morris, Housing Consultants 1987–92; Councillor, London Borough of Hammersmith and Fulham 1971–75; MP for Fulham 1986–87, for Greenwich 1992–97, for Greenwich and Woolwich 1997–2015, mem. House of Commons Environment Select Cttee 1992–93; Front Bench Spokesperson for London 1993–94; Shadow Minister for Housing and Construction, Spokesperson for London 1994–97; Parl. Under-Sec. of State, Minister for London and Construction 1997–99; Minister of State for Housing, Planning and London July–Sept. 1999, for Housing and Planning 1999–2001, for Local Govt and the Regions 2001–04; mem. Nat. Energy Foundation 1989–93. *Publications:* A Guide to Housing Benefits 1982, Making Sense of Localism 2004, Choice Cuts 2004. *Leisure interests:* walking, photography.

RAZ, Joseph, MA, MJr, DPhil, FBA; British (b. Israeli) philosopher and academic; *Thomas M. Macioce Professor of Law, Columbia University;* b. 21 March 1939, Haifa; ed Hebrew Univ., Jerusalem and Univ. of Oxford, UK; Lecturer, Faculty of Law and Dept of Philosophy, Hebrew Univ. 1967–71, Sr Lecturer 1971–72; Research Fellow, Nuffield Coll., Oxford 1970–72; Fellow and Tutor in Law, Balliol Coll., Oxford 1972–85, also mem. Sub-faculty of Philosophy 1977–2009, Prof. of Philosophy of Law and Fellow, Balliol Coll. 1985–2006, Research Prof., Univ. of Oxford 2006–09, Fellow Emer., Balliol Coll. 2006–; Visiting Prof., School of Law, Columbia Univ., New York 1995–2002, Thomas M. Macioce Prof. of Law 2002–; Research Prof. (part-time), King's Coll., London 2011–; Visiting Prof., Rockefeller Univ. 1974, ANU 1979, Univ. of California, Berkeley 1984, Univ. of Toronto 1987, Yale Law School 1988, Univ. of Southern California 1989; British-Hispanic Prof., Complutensa Univ., Madrid 2007; Philosopher-in-Residence, Univ. of Michigan 2001; Fellow, Humanities Research Inst., Univ. of California, Irvine 1989; Visiting Mellon Fellow, Princeton Univ. 1993; Foreign Hon. mem. American Acad. of Arts and Sciences; Dr hc (Katholieke Univ. Brussels) 1993, (Hebrew Univ. Jerusalem) 2014, Hon. DJur (King's Coll., London) 2009; first Hector Fix-Zamudio Int. Prize for Legal Research (Univ. Nacional Autonoma de Mexico) 2005, Tang Prize in Rule of Law 2018. *Publications include:* The Concept of a Legal System 1970, Practical Reason and Norms 1975, The Authority of Law 1979 (second edn 2009), The Morality of Freedom (W.J.M. Mackenzie Book Prize, Political Studies Asscn of the UK, Elaine and David Spitz Book Prize, Conf. for the Study of Political Thought, New York) 1986, Ethics in the Public Domain 1994, Engaging Reason 2000, Value, Respect and Attachment 2001, The Practice of Value 2003, Between Authority and Interpretation 2009, From Normativity to Responsibility 2011; Co-Ed. (with Prof. A. M. Honoré), The Clarendon Law Series 1984–92. *Address:* School of Law, Columbia Universuty, 435 West 116th Street, JGH, Room 518, New York, NY 10027, USA (office). *Telephone:* (212) 854-5191 (office). *Fax:* (212) 854-7946 (office). *E-mail:* jr159@columbia.edu (office). *Website:* sites.google.com/site/josephnraz (home).

RAZA, Syed Salim, MA; Pakistani banking executive; b. 16 Feb. 1946, Lucknow, Uttar Pradesh, India; s. of Syed Hashim Raza; ed Univ. of Oxford, UK; has worked in int. banking since 1973; Country Head for Citibank in Pakistan 1983–87, various positions with Citibank, N.A. (Nat. Asscn), including Country and Regional Man. across the Middle East, Africa and UK, Cen. and Eastern Europe, based in London 1989–2006; CEO Pakistan Business Council 2006–09; Gov. State Bank of Pakistan 2009–10; Ind. Consultant 2010–.

RAZAFINDRAVONONA, Jean; Malagasy economist and politician; b. 26 March 1964, Fianarantsoa; m.; three c.; ed Univ. of Antananarivo, Ecole Nat. de la Statistique et de l'Admin Economique, Univ. de Paris I Panthéon-Sorbonne, France, World Bank Econ. Devt Inst.; mem. Technical Unit, World Bank Document de stratégie pour la réduction de la pauvreté (DSRP, poverty reduction programme) 1999–2005; several positions with Institut Nat. de la Statistique (INS) including Tech. Dir, Perm. Household Survey 1991–96, Dir of Household Statistics 1996–2002, Dir-Gen., INS 2002–07; Dir of Budget Office, Ministry of Finance 2007–14, Minister of Finance and the Budget 2014–15; Chair. Public Markets Regulatory Authority 2012–; Lecturer in Econs, Univ. of Antananarivo 2007–11; Vice-Pres. Higher Bd of Accounting; Authorizing Officer for Madagascar, Euro-

pean Devt Fund 2008–11; Dir Banque Centrale de Madagascar 2007–11, Madagascar Airport 2011–; mem. African Econ. Research Consortium (AERC), Nairobi 1999–, Int. Asscn of Survey Statisticians 1999–, Institut des Relations Internationales et Stratégiques (IRIS), Paris 2005–. *Publications:* numerous publs on econs and devt. *Leisure interests:* basketball, hunting, fishing. *Address:* c/o Ministry of Finance and the Budget, BP 61, Antaninarenina, Antananarivo, Madagascar.

RAZAFITRIMO, Arisoa Lala; Malagasy diplomatist and politician; *Permanent Representative to UN;* b. 26 April 1954, Tamatave; ed Univ. of Antananarivo, Inst. d'Admin Publique, France; early career as French teacher at Lycée Galliéni, Antananarivo and Coll. d'enseignement général, Avaradoha, becoming Prof. of Philosophy and Malagasy, Ministry of Educ. and Coll. des Jésuites St-Michel 1973–76; joined Ministry of Foreign Affairs as Head of Africa and Asia Div. 1976–79, of E Europe Div. 1979–82, of W Europe Div. 1982–84, Head of European Div., Bilateral Relations Dept 1984–87, Head, UN Special Insts Dept 1987–91, Cultural Counsellor, Embassy in Paris 1991–94, Dir of Multilateral Co-operation 1994–96, Dir-Gen. and Acting Sec.-Gen. 1996–99; Special Adviser on Diplomatic Affairs to fmr Pres. Didier Ratsiraka 1999–2002, Perm. Tech. Advisor for Diplomatic Affairs to Pres. of Madagascar 2015–18, Amb. and Perm. Rep. to UN 2018–; Sr Expert, Newton 21 Int. (int. consultancy co.), Belgium 2004–07; teacher, Inst. Réussit-School, Brussels 2006–08; Deputy Dir of Advertising, DIFCOM/Groupe Jeune Afrique, France April–Sept. 2008; Special Adviser to Pres. of African Union, Addis Ababa, Ethiopia 2008–12; Special Adviser and Dir of Int. Relations to Presidency (during transition period), Antananarivo 2013–14, Dir of Int. Relations to Presidency Jan.–April 2014; Minister of Foreign Affairs 2014–15. *Leisure interests:* reading, learning languages, music (including singing and piano), cooking and travelling, table tennis, volleyball. *Address:* Permanent Mission of Madagascar, 820 Second Avenue, Suite 800, New York, NY 10017, USA (office). *Telephone:* (212) 986-9491 (office). *Fax:* (212) 986-6271 (office). *E-mail:* repermad@verizon.net (office). *Website:* www.un.int/madagascar (office).

RAZAK, Dato' Seri Mohamad Najib bin tun Haj Abdul, BA; Malaysian politician; b. 23 July 1953, Kuala Lipis, Pahang; m. 2nd Toh Puan Indera Datin Sri Rosmah Mansor; five c.; ed Univ. of Nottingham; Exec. Patronas 1974–76; Pengerusi Majuternak 1977–78; mem. Parl. 1976–; Deputy Minister of Energy, Telecommunications and Posts 1978–80, of Educ. 1980–81, of Finance 1981–82; mem. State Ass. for Pakan constituency 1982–86; Menteri Besar Pahang 1982–86; Minister of Culture, Youth and Sports 1986–87, of Youth and Sports 1987–90, of Defence 1990–95, 1999–2008, of Educ. 1995–99, of Finance 2008–18; Deputy Prime Minister 2004–09, Prime Minister 2009–18; mem. United Malays Nat. Org. (UMNO) Supreme Council 1981–; Vice-Pres. UMNO Youth 1982–2018; Pres. UMNO 2009–18; Chair. Pahang Foundation 1982–86; Chair. Bd Khazanah Nasional Bhd –2018; Grand Order of Youth (Korea) 1988, Kt Grand Cross, First Class (Thailand), Bintang Yudha Dharma Utama (Indonesia) 1994, Distinguished Service Order (Singapore) 1994, DUBC (Thailand) 1995; Hon. PhD (US Acad. of Sports) 1992, (Nottingham) 2004; Orang Kaya Indera Shahbandar 1976, Darjah Sultan Ahmad Shah 1978, Seri Indera Mahkota Pahang 1983, Darjah Kebesaran Seri Sultan Ahmad Shah 1985, Man of the Year Award, New Straits Times 1990, Panglima Bintang Sarawak 1990, Dato Paduka Mahkota Selangor 1992, Seri Panglima Darjah Kinabalu (SPDK) 2002. *Website:* www.umno-online.my (office).

RAZALEIGH, Tan Sri Tengku Hamzah, PSM, SPMK; Malaysian politician and fmr company executive; b. 13 April 1936; s. of Tengku Mohamed Hamzah bin Zainal Abidin (fmr Chief Minister of Kelantan); m. Puan Sri Noor Yvonne Abdullah (died 2015); ed Queen's Univ., Belfast and Lincoln's Inn, London; Chair. of Kelantan Div. of United Malays' Nat. Org. (UMNO) in early 1960s; mem. Kelantan State Ass. for some years; Exec. Dir Bank Bumiputra 1963, Chair., Man. Dir 1970; MP for Gua Musang 1969–; Exec. Dir PERNAS 1971–74; Chair. Malaysian Nat. Insurance; led trade mission to Beijing 1971; Vice-Pres. UMNO 1975; Pres. Assoc. Malay Chambers of Commerce until Oct. 1976; Chair. PETRONAS (Nat. Oil Co.) 1974–76; Minister of Finance 1976–84, of Trade and Industry 1984–87; Chair. IMF Meetings 1978, Asram Devt Bank 1977, Islamic Devt Bank 1977; f. Angkatan Amanah Merdeka (Amanah) 2011; mem. United Malays Nat. Org. (Pertubuhan Kebangsaan Melayu Bersatu) (UMNO Baru) (New UMNO); Hon. LLD (Queen's Univ. Belfast, Northern Ireland) 1982. *Address:* United Malays National Organization (Pertubuhan Kebangsaan Melayu Bersatu) (UMNO Baru) (New UMNO), Menara Dato' Onn, 38th Floor, Jalan Tun Ismail, 50480 Kuala Lumpur, Malaysia (office). *Telephone:* (3) 40429511 (office). *Fax:* (3) 40412358 (office). *E-mail:* email@umno.net.my (office). *Website:* www.umno-online.com (office).

RAZBOROV, Alexander A., DPhysMathSci; Russian mathematician, computational theorist and academic; *Andrew MacLeish Distinguished Service Professor, University of Chicago;* b. 16 Feb. 1963; Researcher, Dept of Math. Logic, Steklov Math. Inst., Russian Acad. of Sciences, Moscow 1987–91, Leading Researcher 1991–2000, Principal Researcher 2000–08, Principal Researcher (part-time) 2008–; Andrew MacLeish Distinguished Service Prof., Univ. of Chicago 2008–; Prof. (part-time), Toyota Technological Inst., Chicago 2008–; Visiting Researcher, Dept of Computer Science, Princeton Univ. 1999–2000; Visiting Prof., Inst. for Advanced Study, Princeton 2003–08; mem. Inst. for Advanced Study, Princeton 1993–94, 2002–03, Academia Europea 1993; Corresp. mem. Russian Acad. of Sciences; Nevanlinna Prize, Univ. of Helsinki 1990, Tarski Lecturer, Univ. of Calif., Berkeley 2000, Gödel Prize, Asscn for Computing Machinery (with Steven Rudich) 2007. *Publications:* numerous articles in math. journals. *Address:* Dept of Computer Science, Univ. of Chicago, 1100 E 58th Street, Ryerson Physical Lab., Chicago, IL 60637, USA (office). *Telephone:* (773) 702-6614 (office). *Fax:* (773)702-8487 (office). *E-mail:* razborov@cs.uchicago.edu (office). *Website:* www.cs.uchicago.edu (office).

RAZEE, Mahmoud; Maldivian politician; fmr Chair. Privatization Cttee; fmr Exec. Dir Civil Aviation Dept; Minister of State, Ministry of Civil Aviation and Communication –2009, Minister 2009–10; Minister of Econ. Devt and of Transport and Communication 2010–12; mem. Maldivian Democratic Party; Owner Lintel Investment Maldives.

RAZI, Syed Sibtey, BCom, LLB; Indian politician; b. 7 March 1939, Jais, Rai Bareli Dist, UP; s. of Syed Wirasat Husain and Razia Begum; m. Chand Farhana

1973; two s. two d.; ed Husainabad Higher Secondary School, Shia Coll., Lucknow Univ.; began political career as student leader, elected Pres. Commerce Asscn, Lucknow Univ.; Pres. Shia Coll. Student Union 1958–59; joined Congress Party 1969, Gen. Sec. UP Youth Congress 1971–73; Vice-Pres. Youth Welfare Bd, UP Govt 1975–77; mem. Parl. (Rajya Sabha) 1980–85, 1988–98, Vice-Chair. Rajya Sabha (Panel of Presiding Officers) 1993–95; Gen. Sec. UP Congress Cttee 1980–84, Vice-Pres. 2000–02; mem. UP Legis. Council 1985–88; Minister of Educ. and Muslim Waqf, UP Govt 1985–88; mem. All India Congress Cttee 1985–2004, Jt Sec. 1984–85, Spokesperson 2002–04; mem. Indian Del. led by Prime Minister Indira Gandhi to 9th Non-Aligned Movt Summit, New Delhi 1983, Indian Del. to 42nd UN Gen. Ass. 1986; Vice-Chair. UP Institutional Finance Corpn, UP Govt July–Dec. 1988; Deputy Leader Parl. Congress Party 1993–95; Union Minister of State for Home Affairs 1995–96; Gov. of Jharkhand 2004–09, of Assam July–Nov. 2009; mem. Exec. Cttee CPP 1992–94; Chair. Sarvodaya Degree Coll., Salon, Rai Bareli 1999–2004; mem., NGO del. to Human Rights Comm., Geneva 2000–01, Aligarh Muslim Univ. Court 2002–04, Exec. Council Maulana Azad Urdu Univ., Hyderabad 2002–04; Repertoire of Social Justice Cttee, All India Congress Cttee, Simla Camp 2003. *Leisure interests* reading, philanthrophy. *Telephone:* 98-10864830 (mobile).

RAZIN, Aharon, PhD; Israeli biochemist and academic; *Dr Jacob Grunbaum Professor Emeritus of Medical Science, The Hebrew University of Jerusalem;* b. Tel-Aviv; ed The Hebrew Univ. of Jerusalem; Lecturer, The Hebrew Univ. of Jerusalem 1967–71, Sr Lecturer 1971–76, Assoc. Prof. 1976–82, Head, Dept of Cellular Biochemistry, School of Medicine 1980–84, Head, Genetic Engineering Centre 1981–84, Chair. School of Medicine 1985–89, Dr Jacob Grunbaum Prof. of Medical Science 1982–2003, Prof. Emer. 2003–; Visiting Scientist, Univ. of Cambridge, UK 1971, City of Hope Medical Center, Calif., USA 1977; Fogarty Scholar, Fogarty Int. Center, NIH, USA 1984–86; mem. Israel Acad. of Sciences and Humanities, Human Genome Org. (HUGO), European Molecular Biology Org.; Israel Prize 2004, Wolf Prize in Medicine (with Howard Cedar) 2008, EMET Prize in Life Sciences 2009, Canada Gairdner Award (with Howard Cedar), Gairdner Foundation 2011, Louisa Gross Horwitz Prize (co-recipient with Howard Cedar and Gary Felsenfeld) 2016. *Publications:* numerous papers in professional journals. *Address:* Department of Developmental Biology and Cancer Research, Faculty of Medicine, The Hebrew University of Jerusalem, Ein Kerem, PO Box 12272, 91120 Jerusalem, Israel (office). *Telephone:* 2-6758172 (office). *Fax:* 2-6415848 (office). *E-mail:* aharonr@ekmd.huji.ac.il (office). *Website:* research.ekmd .huji.ac.il (office).

RAZOV, Sergey Sergeyevich, PhD; Russian diplomatist and economist; *Ambassador to Italy;* b. 28 Jan. 1953, Sochi, Krasnodar Territory; m.; one s. one d.; ed Moscow Inst. of Int. Relations; Economist, Sr Economist, USSR Trade Mission to Repub. of China 1975–79; Head of Div., Head of Group, Cen. CPSU Cttee 1979–90; Head Dept of Far East Countries and Indochina, USSR Ministry of Foreign Affairs 1990–92; Amb. of the Russian Fed. to Mongolia 1992–96, Dir Third Dept of CIS Countries, Ministry of Foreign Affairs 1996–99, Amb. to Poland 1999–2002, Deputy Minister of Foreign Affairs 2002–05, Amb. to People's Repub. of China 2005–13, to Italy (also accred to San Marino) 2013–; state awards. *Publications:* Foreign Policy of Open Doors of People's Republic of China 1985, The People's Republic of China 1991; articles and other publs. *Address:* Embassy of the Russian Federation, Via Gaeta 5, 00185 Rome, People's Republic of China (office). *Telephone:* (06) 4941680 (office). *Fax:* (06) 491031 (office). *E-mail:* rusembassy@ libero.it (office). *Website:* roma.mid.ru (office).

RAZZAZ, Omar Ahmad Munif al-, PhD; Jordanian politician and academic; *Prime Minister;* b. 1 Jan. 1961, Al-Salt; s. of Munif Razzaz and Lam'a Bseiso; ed Mass Inst. of Tech., Cambridge, Harvard Univ., Cambridge; fmr Dir Gen. Social Security Inst. Jordan; Asst Prof., Mass Inst. of Tech. 1995–97; worked for World Bank, Washington DC 1997–2002, Dir World Bank, Lebanon 2002–06; Dir Jordan's Social Security Corpn 2006–10; fmr Dir Jordan Strategy Forum; Head Jordan Nat. Employment Strategy Team 2011–12, Chair. Privatization Assessment Cttee 2013–14, Ahli Bank 2014–17; Minister of Educ. 2017–18, Prime Minister 2018–. *Address:* Prime Ministry of Jordan, POB 80, Fourth Circle, Fas Street, Bldg 1, Amman 11180, Jordan (office). *Telephone:* (6) 4641211 (office). *Fax:* (6) 4642520 (office). *E-mail:* info@pm.gov.jo (office). *Website:* www.pm.gov.jo (office).

RE, HE Cardinal Giovanni Battista; Italian ecclesiastic; *Prefect Emeritus of the Congregation for Bishops;* b. 30 Jan. 1934, Borno, Brescia; ordained priest 1957; consecrated Bishop 1987; Titular Archbishop of Vescovio; Asst Sec. of State, General Affairs; Prefect of the Congregation for Bishops 2000–05, 2005–10, currently Prefect Emer.; Pres. Pontifical Comm. for Latin America 2000–05, 2005–10; cr. Cardinal (Cardinal-Priest of Santi XII Apostoli) 2001, (Cardinal Bishop of Sabina-Poggio Mirteto) 2002; participated in Papal Conclave 2005, 2013. *Address:* Palazzina dell'Arciprete, 00120 Vatican City. *Telephone:* (06) 69883942. *Fax:* (06) 69885303 (office). *Website:* www.vatican.va/roman_curia/congregations/ cbishops/index.htm (office).

REA, Stephen James; Irish actor; b. 1949, Belfast, Northern Ireland; s. of James Rea and Jane Rea (née Logue); m. Dolours Price 1983; two s.; ed Queen's Univ., Belfast; formed (with Brian Friel) Field Day Theatre Co. 1980; Hon. DLitt (Univ. of Staffs.) 1999, (Univ. of Ulster) 2004, Hon. DUniv (Queen's Univ., Belfast) 2004. *Stage appearances include:* The Shadow of a Gunman, The Cherry Orchard, Miss Julie, High Society, Endgame, The Freedom of the City, Translations, Communication Card, St Oscar, Boesman and Lena, Hightime and Riot Act, Double Cross, Pentecost, Making History, Someone Who'll Watch Over Me 1992 (Broadway, New York), Uncle Vanya 1995; at Nat. Theatre: Ashes to Ashes 1997, Playboy of the Western World, Comedians, The Shaughraun, Cyrano de Bergerac (Nat. Theatre) 2004. *Directed:* Three Sisters, The Cure at Troy, Northern Star 1998. *Films include:* Angel 1982, Company of Wolves 1985, The Doctor and the Devils 1985, Loose Connections 1988, Life is Sweet 1991, The Crying Game 1992, Bad Behaviour 1993, Princess Caraboo 1993, Angie 1994, Interview with the Vampire 1994, Prêt-à-Porter 1994, All Men are Mortal 1994, Citizen X 1994, The Devil and the Deep Blue Sea 1994, Michael Collins 1995, Trojan Eddie 1995, A Further Gesture 1995, The Butcher Boy 1998, Guinevere 1999, The End of the Affair 2000, I Could Read the Sky 2000, Fear Dot Com 2002, Proud 2003, Bloom 2003, The Halo Effect 2004, Romeo and Me 2004, The Good Shepherd 2004, Fluent Dysphasia

2004, Proud 2004, Breakfast on Pluto 2005, River Queen 2005, V for Vendetta 2006, Sixty Six 2006, Until Death 2007, The Reaping 2007, Stuck 2007, The Devil's Mercy 2008, The Heavy 2009, Espion(s) 2009, Ondine 2009, The Heavy 2010, Blackthorn 2011, Stella Days 2011, Underworld: Awakening 2012, Tasting Menu 2013, Asylum 2014, Styria 2014, Out of the Dark 2014, Ruby Strangelove Young Witch 2015. *TV appearances include:* Four Days in July, Lost Belongings, Scout, St Oscar, Not with a Bang, Hedda Gabler, Crime of the Century, Copenhagen 2002, I Didn't Know You Cared, Father & Son (mini-series) 2009, Single-Handed (series) 2010, The Shadow Line (mini-series) 2011, Utopia (series) 2013, The Honourable Woman (mini-series) 2014, Dickensian (series) 2015–16, War & Peace (mini-series) 2016. *Address:* c/o ICM, 76 Oxford Street, London, W1N 0AX, England (office). *Telephone:* (20) 7636-6565 (office).

READ, Desmond (see MOORCOCK, Michael John).

READ, Ian C., BSc, CA; British/American chartered accountant and pharmaceutical industry executive; *Executive Chairman, Pfizer Inc.;* b. 1953, Scotland; ed Imperial Coll., London; earned certification from Inst. of Chartered Accountants of England and Wales 1978; began career with Pfizer as operational auditor 1978, worked in Latin America until 1995, held numerous positions including Chief Financial Officer, Pfizer Mexico and Country Man., Pfizer Brazil, Pres. Int. Pharmaceuticals Group, with responsibility for Latin America and Canada 1996–2000, Exec. Vice-Pres., Europe 2000–06, Corp. Vice-Pres. 2001–06, assumed additional responsibility for Canada 2002, later responsible for Africa/Middle East region and Latin America, Sr Vice-Pres., Pfizer Inc. 2006–10, Pres. Worldwide Pharmaceutical Operations 2006–09, Group Pres. Worldwide Biopharmaceutical Businesses 2009–10, oversaw Primary Care, Specialty Care, Oncology, Established Products and Emerging Markets global business units, mem. Bd of Dirs, Pres. and CEO Pfizer Inc. 2010–11, Chair. and CEO 2011–19, Exec. Chair. 2019–, mem. Exec. Compliance Exec.; Pfizer's Rep. on Int. Section Exec. Cttee of PhRMA and fmr Chair. Europe Cttee; mem. Bd of Dirs Kimberly-Clark Corpn 2007– (Lead Dir 2017–), Pharmaceutical Research and Mfrs of America, US Council for Int. Business, European Fed. of Pharmaceutical Industries and Asscns; fmr Dir Brazilian Anglo American Pharmaceutical Asscn (CIFAB), Brazilian Asscn of the Pharmaceutical Industry (ABIFARMA); fmr Chair. PhRMA's Latin America Regional Cttee; fmr Vice-Chair. Intellectual Property Coordination Cttee section of Int. Fed. of Pharmaceutical Mfrs and Asscns. *Address:* Pfizer Inc., 235 East 42nd Street, New York, NY 10017-5755, USA (office). *Telephone:* (212) 733-2323 (office). *E-mail:* info@pfizer.com (office). *Website:* www.pfizer.com (office).

READ, Nicholas (Nick) Jonathan, BA, CMA; British business executive; *Chief Executive Officer, Vodafone PLC;* b. Sept. 1964; ed Manchester Metropolitan Univ.; senior global finance positions with United Business Media PLC and Federal Express Worldwide (FedEx); joined Vodafone PLC 2001, held a variety of senior roles including CEO, Africa Middle East and Asia Pacific Region 2010–14, mem. Bd of Dirs 2014–, Group Chief Financial Officer 2014–18, CEO 2018–; mem. Bd of Dirs Talkland Communications Ltd 2003–08, Uniquear Ltd 2003–08, Ternhill Communications Ltd 2003–08, Isis Telecommunications Man. Ltd 2006–08, China Mobile Ltd 2009–10, Safaricom Ltd 2011–13, Booking Holdings Inc. 2018– (also, mem. Nominating and Corp. Governance Cttee). *Address:* Vodafone House, The Connection, Newbury, Berks. RG14 2FN, England (office). *Telephone:* (1635) 33251 (office). *Fax:* (1635) 238080 (office). *E-mail:* nick.read@vodafone.com (office). *Website:* www.vodafone.com (office).

READ, Piers Paul, MA, FRSL; British author; b. 7 March 1941, Beaconsfield, Bucks., England; s. of Herbert Edward Read and Margaret Ludwig; m. Emily Albertine Boothby 1967; two s. two d.; ed Ampleforth Coll., York and St John's Coll., Cambridge; Artist-in-Residence, Ford Foundation, West Berlin, Germany 1964; Sub-Ed. Times Literary Supplement, London 1965; Harkness Fellow, Commonwealth Fund, New York 1967–68; Council mem. Inst. of Contemporary Arts (ICA), London 1971–75; Cttee of Man. Soc. of Authors, London 1973–76; mem. Literature Panel Arts Council, London 1975–77; Adjunct Prof. of Writing, Columbia Univ., New York 1980; Chair. Catholic Writers' Guild 1992–97; mem. Bd Aid to the Church in Need 1991–2012; Trustee, Catholic Library 1997–2011; mem. Council RSL 2001–07; Sir Geoffrey Faber Memorial Prize 1968, Somerset Maugham Award 1969, Hawthornden Prize 1969, Thomas More Award (USA) 1976, James Tait Black Memorial Prize 1988. *Publications include:* Game in Heaven with Tussy Marx 1966, The Junkers 1968, Monk Dawson 1969, The Professor's Daughter 1971, The Upstart 1973, Alive: The Story of the Andes Survivors 1974, Polonaise 1976, The Train Robbers 1978, A Married Man 1979, The Villa Golitsyn 1981, The Free Frenchman 1986, A Season in the West 1988, On the Third Day 1990, Quo Vadis? The Subversion of the Catholic Church 1991, Ablaze: The Story of Chernobyl 1993, A Patriot in Berlin 1995, Knights of The Cross 1997, The Templars 1999, Alice in Exile 2001, Alec Guinness: The Authorised Biography 2003, Hell and Other Destinations (essays) 2006, The Death of a Pope 2009, The Misogynist 2010, The Dreyfus Affair 2012, Scarpia 2015. *Leisure interest:* family life. *Address:* c/o Aitken Alexander Associates, 291 Gray's Inn Road, London, WC1X 8QJ, England (office); 23 Ashchurch Park Villas, London, W12 9SP, England (home). *Telephone:* (20) 7373-8672 (office); (20) 8740-9148 (home). *Fax:* (20) 7373-6002 (office). *Website:* www.aitkenalexander.co.uk (office); www.pierspaulread.co.uk. *E-mail:* piersread@gmail.com (office).

REARDON, Raymond (Ray), MBE; British professional snooker player (retd); b. 8 Oct. 1932, Tredegar, Monmouthshire, Wales; s. of Benjamin Reardon and Cynthia Jenkins; m. 1st Susan Carter (divorced); one s. one d.; m. 2nd Carol Lovington 1987; ed Georgeton Secondary Modern School, Tredegar; fmr coal miner and police officer; Welsh Amateur Champion 1950–55; English Amateur Champion 1964; invited to tour South Africa; turned professional 1967; Pot Black Champion 1969, 1979; World Snooker Champion 1970, 1973, 1974, 1975, 1976, 1978; Benson & Hedges Masters Champion 1976; Welsh Champion 1981, 1983; Professional Players Tournament Champion 1982; Yamaha International Masters Champion 1983; team wins: World Cup (with Wales) 1979, 1980; ranked World No. 1 for six years; retd 1992; advised Ronnie O'Sullivan on his way to World Championship victory 2004; active in running World Professional Billiards and Snooker Asscn; occasional appearances on BBC TV's Big Break show; Pres. Churston golf club, Devon; lives in Torquay, Devon. *Publications:* Classic Snooker 1974, Ray Reardon (autobiog.) 1982. *Leisure interest:* golf.

REBEK, Julius, Jr, BA, PhD; American chemist and academic; *Director, Skaggs Institute for Chemical Biology and Professor of Chemistry, Scripps Research Institute;* b. (Gyula Rebek), 11 April 1944, Beregszasz, Hungary; s. of Julius Rebek, Sr and Eva Racz; m. (divorced); two d.; ed Univ. of Kansas and Massachusetts Inst. of Tech.; lived in Austria 1945–49; Asst Prof., UCLA 1970–76; Assoc. Prof., Univ. of Pittsburgh 1976–80, Prof. 1980–89; Prof., Dept of Chem., MIT 1989–96, Camille Dreyfus Prof. of Chem. (Thousand Talents Program) 1991–96; Dir Skaggs Inst. for Chemical Biology and Prof. of Chem., Scripps Research Inst. 1996–; faculty mem. Fudan Univ., Shanghai 2013–16; mem. ACS, NAS; Fellow, American Acad. of Arts and Sciences; Dr hc (Bonn) 2010, (Jaume I) 2015; NSF Fellow 1967–70, Sloan Fellow 1977, von Humboldt Fellow 1981, Guggenheim Fellow 1986, Cope Scholar Award 1991, James Flack Norris Award in Physical Organic Chem. 1997, Chemical Pioneer Award, American Inst. of Chemists 2002, Ronald Breslow Award for Achievement in Biomimetic Chem., ACS 2004, Medal of the Acad. of Sciences (Czech Repub.) 2005, Medal of the Nat. Acad. of Sciences, Letters and Arts (Italy) 2005, Distinguished Scientist Award, ACS 2006, Evans Award, Ohio State Univ. 2006, Univ. of Oregon Creativity Award in Chem., Dance and Music 2007, Humboldt Sr Scientist Award (Germany) 2008, Tau-Shue Chou Award, Academia Sinica 2008, Nichols Medal, ACS 2011, Prelog Medal, ETH 2012. *Publications:* 500 publs in scientific journals. *Leisure interest:* tennis. *Address:* Rebek Laboratory, Skaggs Institute for Chemical Biology, Scripps Research Institute, 10550 North Torrey Pines Road, La Jolla, CA 92037 (office); 2330 Calle del Oro, La Jolla, CA 92037, USA (home). *Telephone:* (858) 784-2250 (office). *Fax:* (858) 784-2802 (office). *E-mail:* jrebek@scripps.edu (office). *Website:* www.scripps .edu/skaggs/rebek (office).

REBELO DE SOUSA, Marcelo Nuno Duarte, LLD, PhD; Portuguese journalist, professor of law, politician and head of state; *President;* b. 12 Dec. 1948, Lisbon; s. of Baltasar Rebelo de Sousa and Maria das Neves Fernandes Duarte; m. Ana Cristina da Gama Caeiro da Mota Veiga 1972; two c.; partner Rita Maria Lagos do Amaral Cabral; ed Univ. of Lisbon; Founding Ed., Expresso (weekly newspaper) 1972, Dir and Admin. 1975–79; mem. Constituent Ass. 1975–76; Pres., Municipal Ass. of Cascais 1979–82; fmr Deputy, Ass. of the Republic (Parl.); Sec. of State to Prime Minister 1981–82; Minister of Parl. Affairs 1982–83; co-f. Semanário (weekly journal) 1983, Dir 1983–87; Vereador (City Councillor), Lisbon 1989, mem. Lisbon Metropolitan Ass. 1993–97; apptd Prof., Faculty of Law, Univ. of Lisbon 1990, Chair., Inst. for Legal and Political Science 2005; presented weekly programme of political analysis on TSF (radio news station) 1993–96, also on TV1 2000–04 and on public TV station RTP –2010; Pres., Municipal Ass. of Celorico de Basto 1997; mem. Council of State 2000–01, 2006–15; Pres. of Portugal 2016–; mem. Bd of Dirs Fundação da Casa de Bragança (historical and cultural fund) 1994–; mem. Social Democratic Party (Pres. 1996–99); Commdr, Order of Santiago da Espada, Grand Cross, Ordem do Infante Dom Henrique; Dr hc (Porto) 2005; Gold Medal, City of Cascais 2000. *Leisure interest:* surfing. *Address:* Office of the President, Presidência da República, Palácio de Belém, Calçada da Ajuda 11, 1349-022 Lisbon, Portugal (office). *Telephone:* (21) 3614600 (office). *Fax:* (21) 3636603 (office). *E-mail:* belem@presidencia.pt (office). *Website:* www.presidencia .pt (office).

REBELO FIGUEIREDO, Aldo; Brazilian politician; b. 23 Feb. 1956, Viçosa, Alagoas; s. of José Figueiredo Lima and Maria Cila Rebelo Figueiredo; ed Colégio Agrícola Floriano Peixoto, Universidade Federal de Alagoas; mem. Partido Comunista do Brasil (PCdoB) 1977–2017, Partido Socialista Brasileiro (PSB) 2017–18, Solidariedade (SD) 2018–; Pres. Nat. Union of Students 1980, Continental Latin American and Caribbean Students Org. 1980; mem. city council, São Paulo 1989–90; mem. Chamber of Deputies 1989–, Leader, PCdoB parl. group 1992–, Pres. Cttee on Foreign Relations and Nat. Defence 2002, Leader of the Govt in the Chamber of Deputies 2003, Speaker 2005–07; Minister, Secr. of Political Coordination and Institutional Relations 2004–05, Minister of Sport 2011–15, of Science, Tech. and Innovation Jan.–Oct. 2015, of Defence Oct. 2015–May 2016; mem. Council, Brazilian Center for Int. Relations 2005; Grand Cross, Defence Order of Merit, Grand Officer, Order of Naval Merit, Mil. Order of Merit, Order of Aeronautical Merit, Grand Cross, Order of Rio Branco, Grand Officier, Légion d'honneur (France). *Address:* Solidariedade (SD), Edif. Multiempresarial, Sala 278, SRTVS, Quadra 701, Bloco O, 04015-011 Brasília, DF Brazil (office). *Telephone:* (61) 3548-2215 (office). *Fax:* (61) 3548-2214 (office). *E-mail:* falecom@ solidariedade.org.br (office). *Website:* www.solidariedade.org.br (office); aldorebelobrasil.com.br.

REBELO PINTO CHICOTI, George; Angolan academic and politician; b. 15 June 1955, Dondi, Huambo Prov.; s. of Mateus Pinto Chikoti and Catarina Chikoti Kanjila; m. Elisabeth Apoque Chikoti; four c.; ed Univ. of Abidjan, Côte d'Ivoire, Univ. de Paris XII, France, Univ. of Ottawa, Canada; in exile with family in Zambia 1964–75; Prof. of English, Escola Industrial do Huambo 1975–76; Asst Prof., Univ. of Abidjan, Côte d'Ivoire 1983–85; with Credit and Int. Investment Dept, Canadian Imperial Bank of Commerce, Toronto, Canada 1987–89; Asst Prof., Univ. of Ottawa 1989–90; mem. Conselho da República de Angola 1992–; Deputy Minister, Ministry of Foreign Affairs 1992, rank of Amb. 1994, Minister of Foreign Affairs 2010–17; Pres. Fórum Democrático Angolano 1990–.

REBUCK, Baroness (Life Peer), cr. 2014, of Bloomsbury in the London Borough of Camden; **Gail Ruth Rebuck,** DBE, BA, FRSA; British publishing executive; *Chairman, Penguin Random House UK;* b. 10 Feb. 1952, London; d. of Gordon Rebuck and Mavis Rebuck; m. Philip Gould 1985 (died 2011); two d.; ed Lycée Français de Londres, Univ. of Sussex, Wharton Business School; Production Asst, Grisewood & Dempsey (children's book packager) 1975–76; Ed., later Publr Robert Nicholson Publs London Guidebooks 1976–79; Publr Hamlyn Paperbacks 1979–82; Founder Partner Century Publishing Co. Ltd, Publishing Dir Non-Fiction 1982–85; Publr Century Hutchinson 1985–89, Chair. Random House Div., Random Century 1989–91, Chair. and Chief Exec. Random House UK Ltd (now The Random House Group Ltd) 1991–2013, Chair. Penguin Random House UK 2013–; mem. House of Lords (Labour) 2014–; mem. Group Man. Cttee, Bertelsmann 2012–; mem. COPUS 1995–97, Creative Industries Task Force 1997–2000, Court of Univ. of Sussex 1997–, Advisory Bd Cambridge Judge Inst. 2004–08, Govt Fair Access to the Professions panel 2010; mem. Council of RCA 1999–, Pro-Provost and Chair of RCA Council 2015–; Dir (non-exec.) Work Foundation 2001–09, BSkyB 2002–, Skillset 2009–11; Trustee, Inst. for Public

Policy Research 1993–2003, Nat. Literacy Trust 2007–; Chair. Quick Reads Charity 2006–. *Leisure interests:* reading, travel. *Address:* Penguin Random House UK, 20 Vauxhall Bridge Road, London, SW1V 2SA, England (office). *Telephone:* (20) 7840-8400 (office). *Fax:* (20) 7233-6120 (office). *E-mail:* grebuck@ penguinrandomhouse.co.uk (office). *Website:* www.penguinrandomhouse.com (office).

RECCHI, Giuseppe; Italian business executive; *Chairman, Telecom Italia SpA;* b. 1964; ed Polytechnic of Turin; began career at Recchi SpA (construction co.) 1989, Exec. Chair. Recchi America Inc. 1994–99; joined General Electric (GE) 1999, held several managerial positions in Europe and USA, served as Dir of GE Capital Structure Finance Group, Gen. Man. for Industrial M&A and Business Devt for GE EMEA, Pres. and CEO GE Italy, Pres. and CEO GE South Europe –2011, Vice-Chair. GE Capital SpA; Chair. Eni SpA 2011–14; Chair. Telecom Italia SpA 2014–; mem. Bd of Dirs, Compensation and Audit Cttees, Exor SpA; mem. European Advisory Bd, Blackstone; mem. Exec. Cttee, Confindustria (Italian Corp. Asscn); mem. Hon. Cttee for the Rome Candidacy for the 2020 Olympic Games, Bd of Permasteelisa SpA; Visiting Prof. in Structured Finance, Turin Univ.; occasional editorial commentator for financial papers, national dailies and Harvard Business Review. *Address:* Telecom Italia SpA, Corso d'Italia 41, 00198 Rome, Italy (office). *E-mail:* info@telecomitalia.com (office). *Website:* www .telecomitalia.com (office).

REDDY, Jaipal Sudini, BJ, MA; Indian agriculturalist and politician; b. 16 Jan. 1942, Madgul, Mahbubnagar Dist, Andhra Pradesh; s. of Durga Reddy and Yashodamma Reddy; m. Lakshmi Reddy; two s. one d.; ed Osmania Univ., Hyderabad; Pres. AP Youth Congress 1965–71; Gen. Sec. AP Congress Cttee 1969–72; mem. AP Legis. Ass. 1969–84; mem. Nat. Exec. Janata Party 1979–88, Gen. Sec. 1985–88; elected to 8th Lok Sabha (lower house of Parl.) (in alliance with Telugu Desam Party, TDP) 1984, 12th Lok Sabha 1998, 13th Lok Sabha for Miryalaguda constituency (Congress Party) 1999, 14th Lok Sabha 2004, 15th Lok Sabha for Chelvella constituency 2009–14, mem. Cttee on Finance 1998–99, Chair. Cttee of Privileges 1999–2000; mem. Rajya Sabha (upper house of Parl.) 1990–96, 1997–98, Leader of Opposition 1991–92; Union Cabinet Minister of Information and Broadcasting 1997–98, of Information and Broadcasting and Culture 2004–05, of Urban Devt and Culture 2005–06, of Urban Devt 2006, 2009–11, of Petroleum and Natural Gas 2011–12, of Science and Tech. and of Earth Sciences 2012–14; Indian Parl. Group Outstanding Parliamentarian Award 1998. *Address:* c/o Ministry of Science and Technology, Technology Bhavan, New Mehrauli Road, New Delhi 110 016, India. *Website:* www.sjaipalreddy.com.

REDDY, K. Srinath, MSc, MD; Indian cardiologist, epidemiologist and academic; *President, Public Health Foundation of India;* ed Osmania Medical Coll., Hyderabad, All India Inst. of Medical Sciences, New Delhi, McMaster Univ., Canada; Prof. of Cardiology, All India Inst. of Medical Sciences, New Delhi, also fmr Head, Dept of Cardiology; coordinator Cardiovascular Health Research Initiative in Developing Countries; Pres. Public Health Foundation of India, Nat. Bd of Examinations; apptd Bernard Lown Visiting Prof. of Cardiovascular Health, Harvard School of Public Health 2009; Adjunct Prof., Rollins School of Public Health, Emory Univ.; Chair. Scientific Council on Epidemiology and Prevention, World Heart Fed. 2003–06, mem. Advisory Bd 2007–10, Pres. World Heart Fed. 2013–14; Adviser on Health and Cabinet Minister, Govt of Odisha 2017; Chair. Advisory Group on Health and Human Rights, Nat. Human Rights Comm. of India, High Level Expert Group on Universal Health Coverage, Planning Comm. of India, Thematic Group on Health, Sustainable Devt Solutions Network; Co-Chair. WHO Scientific Advisory Cttee on Tobacco Product Regulation; Foreign Assoc. NAS Inst. of Medicine 2004; mem. Nat. Science and Engineering Research Bd, Govt of India, Leadership Council Sustainable Devt Solutions Network, Global Panel, Agriculture and Food Systems for Nutrition; Ed. National Medical Journal of India; Fellow, Nat. Acad. of Medical Sciences 2000, London School of Hygiene and Tropical Medicine 2009, Faculty of Public Health, UK 2009; Hon. Fellow, London School of Hygiene and Tropical Medicine 2009, Hon. Prof., Univ. of Sydney; Hon. DrSc (Univ. of Aberdeen, Scotland) 2011, (Dr. NTR Medical Sciences Univ.) 2011, (Univ. of Lausanne, Switzerland) 2012, (Univ. of Glasgow, Scotland) 2013, (Univ. of London, UK) 2014, Hon. DLit (Jodhpur National Univ.) 2013; WHO Dir-Gen.'s Award for Outstanding Contrib. to Global Tobacco Control 2003, Queen Elizabeth Medal Royal Soc. for Promotion of Health 2005, Padma Bhushan 2005, Queen Elizabeth Medal, Royal Soc. for Health Promotion, UK 2005, Luther L Terry Award, American Cancer Society 2009. *Publications:* contrib. over 200 papers and articles in scientific journals; more than 480 scientific publications. *Address:* Public Health Foundation of India, Plot No. 47, Sector 44, Institutional Area, Gurgaon, Haryana 122002, India (office). *Telephone:* (12) 44781400 (office). *Fax:* (12) 44781600 (office). *E-mail:* contact@phfi.org (office); ksrinath.reddy@phfi .org (office). *Website:* www.phfi.org (office).

REDDY, Nallari Kiran Kumar, LLB; Indian lawyer and politician; b. 13 Sept. 1960, Hyderabad; s. of Amarnatha Reddy and Sarojamma Reddy; m. Radhika Reddy; one s. one d.; ed Nizam Coll., Hyderabad, Osmania Univ.; mem. Andhra Pradesh Legis. Ass. for Vayalpadu constituency, Chittoor Dist 1989–94, 1999–2009, for Pileru constituency 2009; Govt Chief Whip 2004–09; Speaker, 13th AP Ass. 2009; Chief Minister of Andhra Pradesh 2010–14 (resgnd); fmr mem. Indian Nat. Congress party; f. Jai Samaikyandhra party 2014. *Achievements include:* represented Hyderabad in cricket in Ranji Trophy. *E-mail:* info@ jaisamaikyandhraparty.net. *Website:* www.jaisamaikyandhraparty.net.

REDDY, Dame Patricia (Patsy) Lee, LLB, LLM; New Zealand lawyer and government official; *Governor-General;* b. Matamata; d. of Neil Reddy and Kay Reddy; m. 2nd Sir David Gascoigne; ed Victoria Univ. of Wellington; Jr Lecturer, later Lecturer, Victoria Univ. Faculty of Law; Partner, Watts and Patterson (law firm, now Minter Ellison Rudd Watts) 1982–87; joined Brierley Investments Ltd as Group Legal Counsel 1987, becoming Group Man. for Special Projects –1998; Chair. New Zealand Film Comm., Educ. Payroll Ltd; Deputy Chair. New Zealand Transport Agency, Sky City Entertainment Group Ltd –2008; Chief Crown Negotiator for Treaty of Waitangi settlements; Gov.-Gen. of New Zealand 2016–; Co-founder Active Equities Ltd (pvt. investment co.) 1999; Dir Payments NZ Ltd; fmr Dir Telecom Corpn of New Zealand Ltd, New Zealand Post, Air New Zealand Ltd; Founder-mem. Global Women New Zealand 2009; Dame Companion, NZ Order of Merit 2014. *Address:* Office of the Governor–General, Government House,

Private Bag 39995, Wellington Mail Centre, Lower Hutt 5045, New Zealand (office). *Telephone:* (4) 389-8055 (office). *Fax:* (4) 389-5536 (office). *Website:* www.gg.govt.nz (office).

REDDY, Preetha, MD; Indian hospital administrator and business executive; *Executive Vice-Chairperson, Apollo Hospitals;* d. of Prathap C. Reddy; m.; two c.; ed Stella Maris Coll. Chennai, Madras Univ., Annamalai Univ.; joined Apollo Group as Jt Man. Dir 1989, Man. Dir Apollo Hospitals, Chennai (largest pvt. healthcare provider in Asia and third—largest in the world) 1994–2014, Exec. Vice-Chair. 2014–; Sr Vice-Chair. All India Man. Asscn (fmr Pres.); mem. Bd of Dirs Superbrand India Council, Medtronic plc 2012–15; Founding mem. Nat. Quality Council; mem. Wipro Business Leadership Council; mem. Governing Bd XLRI Jamshedpur; Dr hc (Tamilnadu Dr. MGR Medical Univ.); Outstanding Personality Award, Indian Medical Asscn 1999, Good Samaritan Award, Rotary Club 1999. *Address:* Apollo Hospitals, 21 Greams Lane, off Greams Road, Chennai 600 006, Tamil Nadu, India (office). *Telephone:* (44) 28290200 (office). *Fax:* (44) 28293524 (office). *E-mail:* enquiry@apollohospitals.com (office). *Website:* www.apollohospitals.com (office).

REDDY, Y(aga) Venugopal, MA, PhD; Indian central banker and academic; b. 17 Aug. 1941, Kadapa, Andhra Pradesh; ed Madras Univ., Osmania Univ., Hyderabad, Inst. of Social Studies, Netherlands; joined Indian Admin. Service in 1964, has held several key positions including Sec. (Banking), Ministry of Finance, Additional Sec., Ministry of Commerce, Jt Sec., Ministry of Finance, Prin. Sec., Govt of Andhra Pradesh; Deputy Gov. Reserve Bank of India 1996–2002, Gov. 2003–08; Exec. Dir for India, Sri Lanka, Bangladesh and Bhutan, IMF 2002; Visiting Prof., Osmania Univ.; Visiting Faculty in Admin. Staff, Coll. of India; fmr Visiting Fellow, LSE, London, UK; now Prof. Emer., Univ. of Hyderabad; Chair. Bank for Int. Settlements 2007–09, Asian Consultative Council 2007–09; fmr Chair. of South Asian Association for Regional Cooperation (SAARC) SAARCFINANCE; Founder mem. and mem. Bd of Govs Centre for Econ. and Social Studies; mem. Advisory Bd, Inst. for New Economic Thinking; Conf. Pres. 97th Annual Conf. of Indian Econ. Asscn 2014; Hon. Sr Fellow, Centre for Econ. and Social Studies, Hyderabad, Hon. Fellow, LSE 2008; Hon. DLitt (Sri Venkateswara Univ.), Hon. DCL (Univ. of Mauritius); Padma Vibhushan 2010. *Publications include:* India and the Global Financial Crisis: Managing Money and Finance 2008, Global Crisis, Recession and Uneven Recovery 2011; numerous publs on finance, planning and public enterprises. *Address:* Plot No. 297, Road No. 25, Jubilee Hills, Hyderabad 500 033, India (home). *Telephone:* (40) 23553292 (home). *E-mail:* yvenureddy@yahoo.com. *Website:* www.yvreddy.com.

REDFORD, Alison, QC, MLA; Canadian lawyer and politician; b. 7 March 1965, Kitimat, BC; m. Glen Jermyn; one d.; ed Bishop Carroll High School, Calgary, Univ. of Saskatchewan Coll. of Law; worked as tech. adviser on constitutional and legal reform issues in various parts of Africa for EU, Commonwealth Secr., Canadian Govt and Govt of Australia 1990s; employed by Govt of Alberta as Communications Officer on Cttee for Justice Reform 1999; apptd by Sec.-Gen. of UN as one of four Int. Election Commrs to administer Afghanistan's first parl. elections held Sept. 2005; also assignments in Bosnia and Herzegovina, Serbia, Namibia, Uganda, Zimbabwe, Mozambique and the Philippines; managed a judicial training and legal reform project for Ministry of Justice and Supreme People's Court in Viet Nam; served as Sr Policy Advisor to Rt Hon. Joe Clark, Sec. of State for External Affairs and in Office of Prime Minister 1988–90; organized series of nat. foreign policy consultations facilitating public input on Govt of Canada's White Papers on Foreign Affairs and Defence; MLA for Calgary-Elbow 2008–, mem. Cabinet Policy Cttee on Public Safety and Services and Standing Cttee for Private Bills; Minister of Justice and Attorney Gen. 2008–11; led Govt of Alberta's Safe Communities Secr. (SafeComm); Leader of Progressive Conservative Asscn of Alberta Oct. 2011–; Premier of Alberta 2011–14 (resgnd); mem. Lycee Louis Pasteur Soc., Heritage Park Foundation, Calgary Winter Club; Progressive Conservative.

REDFORD, (Charles) Robert, Jr; American actor and director; *President, Sundance Group;* b. 18 Aug. 1936, Santa Monica, Calif.; s. of Charles Robert Redford, Sr and Martha W. Redford (née Hart); m. 1st Lola Van Wegenen 1958 (divorced 1985); two s. (one s. died 1959) two d.; m. 2nd Sibylle Szaggars 2009; ed Van Nuys High School, Univ. of Colorado, Pratt Inst. of Design, American Acad. of Dramatic Arts; Founder and Pres. The Sundance Group 1981–, includes Sundance Channel, Sundance Ski Resort, Utah, Sundance Catalog, Sundance Cinemas, North Fork Preservation Alliance, and Sundance Inst., sponsor of Sundance Film Festival; Légion d'Honneur 2010; Hon. DHumLitt (Bard Coll.) 1995; hon. degrees from Univ. of Colorado, Boulder 1983, Brown Univ. 2008; Audubon Medal 1989, Dartmouth Film Soc. Award 1990, Screen Actors' Guild Award for Lifetime Achievement 1996, Hon. Acad. Award 2002, Kennedy Center Honor 2005, Americans for the Arts Lifetime Achievement Award 2009, Presidential Medal of Freedom 2016. *Films include:* Tall Story 1960, War Hunt 1961, Situation Hopeless But Not Serious 1965, Inside Daisy Clover 1965, The Chase 1965, This Property is Condemned 1966, Barefoot in the Park 1967, Tell Them Willie Boy is Here 1969, Butch Cassidy and the Sundance Kid 1969, Downhill Racer 1969, Little Fauss and Big Halsy 1970, Jeremiah Johnson 1972, The Candidate 1972, How to Steal a Diamond in Four Uneasy Lessons 1972, The Way We Were 1973, The Sting 1973, The Great Gatsby 1974, The Great Waldo Pepper 1974, Three Days of the Condor 1975, All the President's Men 1976, A Bridge Too Far 1977, Ordinary People (dir; Acad. Award and Golden Globe Award for Best Dir 1981) 1980, The Electric Horseman 1980, Brubaker 1980, The Natural 1984, Out of Africa 1985, Legal Eagles 1986, Milagro Beanfield War 1988 (also producer), Promised Land (exec. producer) 1988, Havana 1991, Sneakers 1992, A River Runs Through It (also dir) 1992, Quiz Show (dir) 1994, The River Wild 1995, Up Close and Personal 1996, The Horse Whisperer (also dir and producer) 1997, The Legend of Bagger Vance (also dir and producer) 2000, How to Kill Your Neighbour's Dog (exec. producer) 2000, The Last Castle 2001, Spy Game 2001, The Motorcycle Diaries (exec. producer) 2004, The Clearing 2004, Sacred Planet (narrator) 2004, An Unfinished Life 2005, Charlotte's Web (voice) 2006, The Unforeseen (exec. producer) 2006, Lions for Lambs (also dir) 2007, The Conspirator (dir) 2010, The Company You Keep (also producer and dir) 2012, All is Lost (Best Actor Award, New York Film Critics Circle) 2013, Captain America: The Winter Soldier 2014, A Walk in the Woods 2015, Truth 2015, Pete's Dragon 2016. *Television includes:* Skinwalkers (exec. producer) 2002, Coyote Waits (exec. producer) 2003, A Thief of Time (exec. producer) 2004, Iconoclasts (documentary series) 2005–07, One More Chance (film) 2016. *Address:* c/o Sundance Institute, PO Box 684429, Park City, UT 84068 (office); c/o Sundance Institute, 8530 Wilshire Blvd, 3rd Floor, Beverly Hills, CA 90211-3114 (office); c/o David O'Conner, Creative Artists Agency, 9830 Wilshire Boulevard, Beverly Hills, CA 90212, USA (office). *Telephone:* (801) 328-3456 (Sundance) (office). *Fax:* (801) 575-5175 (Sundance) (office). *E-mail:* institute@sundance.org (office); la@sundance.org (office). *Website:* institute.sundance.org (office).

REDGRAVE, Sir Steven Geoffrey (Steve), Kt, CBE; British fmr oarsman; b. 23 March 1962, Marlow, Bucks., England; m. Elizabeth Ann Redgrave; one s. two d.; ed Marlow Comprehensive School; rep. UK at Jr World Championships 1979, 1980, silver medal (with Clift) rep. Marlow Rowing Club 1976–2000, Leander 1987–2000; stroke, British coxed four, gold medal winners, Los Angeles Olympic Games 1984; gold medals, single scull, coxless pair (with Andy Holmes) and coxed four, Commonwealth Games 1986, coxed pair (with Holmes), World Championships 1986; coxless pair gold medal and coxed pair silver medal (with Holmes), World Championships 1987; gold medal (with Holmes), coxless pair and bronze medal, coxed pair, Olympic Games, Seoul 1988; silver medal (with Simon Berrisford), coxless pairs, World Championships 1989; bronze medal, coxless pair (with Matthew Pinsent q.v.) World Championships, Tasmania 1990; gold medal, coxless pair (with Pinsent), World Championships, Vienna 1991; gold medal, Olympic Games, Barcelona 1992; gold medal, World Championships, Czech Repub. 1993; gold medal, Indianapolis, 1994; gold medal, Finland 1995; gold medal, Olympic Games, Atlanta 1996; gold medal, coxless four (with Pinsent, Foster, Cracknell), Aiguebelette 1997; gold medal, coxless four, Cologne 1998; gold medal, coxless four (with Pinsent, Coode, Cracknell), St Catherines 1999; gold medal, Olympic Games, Sydney 2000; holds record for most consecutive Olympic gold medals won in an endurance event (five); f. Sir Steve Redgrave Charitable Trust, Steve Redgrave Fund (with Comic Relief); Vice-Pres. SPARKS, Steward Henley Royal Regatta; active in raising money for children's charities; launched own Fairtrade Cotton Brand of Clothing, FiveG; Hon. Pres. Amateur Rowing Asscn, Hon. Vice-Pres. British Olympic Asscn, Diabetes UK; Hon. DCL (Durham) 1996, Hon. DSc 2001, (Buckingham) 2001, (Hull), Hon. DLitt (Reading, Nottingham), Hon. DUniv (Buckingham Chiltern, Heriot-Watt, Oxford Brookes, Open Univ.), Hon. DTech (Loughborough), Hon. LLD (Aberdeen) 2007; BBC Sports Personality of the Year 2000, British Sports Writers' Asscn Sportsman of the Year 2000, Laureus Lifetime Achievement Award 2001, BBC Golden Sports Personality 2003, BBC Sports Personality of the Year Lifetime Achievement Award 2011. *Publications:* Steven Redgrave's Complete Book of Rowing 1992, A Golden Age (autobiog., with Nick Townsend) 2000, You Can Win at Life! (with Nick Townsend) 2005. *Leisure interest:* golf, skiing. *Address:* c/o IMG, McCormack House, Hogarth Business Park, Burlington Lane, London, W4 2TH, England (office). *Telephone:* (20) 8233-5300 (office). *Fax:* (20) 8233-5301 (office). *E-mail:* katie.leggate@img.com (office). *Website:* www.img.com (office); www.steveredgrave.com.

REDGRAVE, Vanessa, CBE; British actress; b. 30 Jan. 1937; d. of Sir Michael Redgrave and Rachel Kempson; sister of the late Lynn Redgrave; m. Tony Richardson 1962 (divorced 1967, died 1991); two d.; one s. by Franco Nero; ed Queensgate School, London and Cen. School of Speech and Drama; actress 1957–; co-f. Moving Theatre 1974; mem. Workers' Revolutionary Party (Cand. for Moss Side 1979); Fellow, BFI 1988, BAFTA 2010; Chevalier, Légion d'Honneur; Dr hc (Mass.) 1990; Ibsen Centennial Award 2006. *Stage appearances include:* A Midsummer Night's Dream 1959, The Tiger and the Horse 1960, The Taming of the Shrew 1961, As You Like It 1961, Cymbeline 1962, The Seagull 1964, 1985, The Prime of Miss Jean Brodie 1966, Daniel Deronda 1969, Cato Street 1971, Threepenny Opera 1972, Twelfth Night 1972, Antony and Cleopatra 1973, 1986, Design for Living 1973, Macbeth 1975, Lady from the Sea 1976 and 1979 (Manchester), The Aspern Papers (Laurence Olivier Award 1984) 1984, Ghosts 1986, A Touch of the Poet 1988, Orpheus Descending 1988, A Madhouse in Goa 1989, The Three Sisters 1990, Lettice and Lovage 1991, When She Danced 1991, Isadora 1991, Heartbreak House 1992, The Master Builder 1992, Maybe 1993, The Liberation of Skopje 1995, John Gabriel Borkman 1996, The Cherry Orchard 2000, The Tempest 2000, Long Day's Journey into Night 2003; Dir and acted in Antony and Cleopatra, Houston, Tex. 1996, John Gabriel Borkman 1996, Song at Twilight 1999, Lady Windermere's Fan 2002, Long Day's Journey Into Night (Tony Award for Best Actress in a Play) 2003, The Year of Magical Thinking 2007, Driving Miss Daisy 2010. *Television includes:* Second Serve 1986, A Man for All Seasons 1988, Orpheus Descending 1990, Young Catherine 1991, What Ever Happened to Baby Jane? 1991, Great Moments in Aviation 1993, They 1993, Down Came a Blackbird 1995, The Wind in the Willows 1995, Two Mothers for Zachary 1996, The Willows in Winter 1996, Bella Mafia 1997, If These Walls Could Talk 2 (Emmy Award for Outstanding Lead Actress, Golden Globe Award for Best Supporting Actress) 2000, Jack and the Beanstalk: The Real Story 2001, The Gathering Storm (Broadcasting Press Guild Award for Best Actress) 2002, The Locket 2002, Byron 2003, Nip/Tuck (series) 2004–05, The Shell Seekers 2006, The Day of the Triffids (mini-series) 2009, Call the Midwife (voice) (series) 2012–. *Films include:* Morgan—A Suitable Case for Treatment (Cannes Film Festival Award, Best Actress 1966) 1965, Sailor from Gibraltar 1965, Camelot 1967, Blow Up 1967, Charge of the Light Brigade 1968, Isadora (US Nat. Soc. of Film Critics Award) 1968, The Seagull 1968, A Quiet Place in the Country 1968, Dropout, The Trojan Women 1970, The Devils 1970, The Holiday 1971, Mary Queen of Scots 1971, Katherine Mansfield (BBC TV) 1973, Murder on the Orient Express 1974, Winter Rates 1974, 7% Solution 1975, Julia (Academy Award for Best Supporting Actress 1978) 1977, Agatha 1978, Yanks 1978, Bear Island 1979, Playing for Time (CBS TV) 1979, Playing for Time 1980, My Body My Child (ABC TV) 1981, Wagner 1982, The Bostonians 1983, Wetherby 1984, Prick Up Your Ears (New York Film Critics Circle Award for Best Supporting Actress) 1987, Comrades 1987, Consuming Passions 1988, King of the Wind 1989, Diceria dell'intore 1989, The Ballad of the Sad Cafe 1990, Howards End 1992, Breath of Life, The Wall, Sparrow, They, The House of the Spirits, Crime and Punishment, Mother's Boys, Little Odessa, A Month by the Lake 1996, Mission Impossible 1996, Looking for Richard 1997, Wilde 1997, Mrs Dalloway 1997, Bella Mafia (TV) 1997, Deep Impact 1998, Cradle Will Rock 2000, The Pledge 2001, The Gathering Storm (TV) 2002, Crime and Punishment 2002, The Fever 2004, The Keeper 2005, Short Order 2005, The White

Countess 2005, Thief Lord 2006, Venus 2006, How About You 2007, The Riddle 2007, Atonement (London Film Critics Circle Award for British Supporting Actress of the Year) 2007, Evening 2007, Gud, lukt och henne 2008, Letters to Juliet 2010, The Whistleblower 2010, Coriolanus 2011, Anonymous 2011, Song for Marion 2012, The Last Will and Testament of Rosalind Leigh 2012, The Butler 2013; produced and narrated documentary film The Palestinians 1977. *Publications:* Pussies and Tigers 1963, An Autobiography 1991. *Leisure interest:* changing the status quo. *Address:* c/o Gavin Barker Associates, 2d Wimpole Street, London, W1M 7AA, England (office).

REDHEAD, Michael Logan Gonne, PhD, FBA; British professor of philosophy; *Co-Director, Centre for Philosophy of Natural and Social Science, London School of Economics;* b. 30 Dec. 1929, London; s. of Robert Arthur Redhead and Christabel Lucy Gonne Browning; m. Jennifer Anne Hill 1964 (died 2010); three s.; ed Westminster School, Univ. Coll. London; Prof. of Philosophy of Physics, Chelsea Coll., London 1984–85, King's Coll. London 1985–87; Prof. of History and Philosophy of Science, Univ. of Cambridge 1987–97, Fellow, Wolfson Coll. Cambridge 1988–, Vice-Pres. 1992–96, acting Pres. 1992, 1993; Co-Dir Centre for Philosophy of Natural and Social Science, LSE 1998–, Centennial Prof. 1999–2002; Fellow, King's Coll. London 2000; Tarner Lecturer, Trinity Coll. Cambridge 1991–94; Visiting Fellow, All Souls Coll. Oxford 1995; Pres. British Soc. for Philosophy of Science 1989–91; Lakatos Award for Philosophy of Science 1988. *Publications:* Incompleteness, Nonlocality and Realism 1987, From Physics to Metaphysics 1995. *Leisure interests:* poetry, music, tennis. *Address:* Centre for Philosophy of Natural and Social Science, Lakatos Building, Room T111, London School of Economics, Houghton Street, London, WC2A 2AE (office); 119 Rivermead Court, London, SW6 3SD, England (home). *Telephone:* (20) 7955-7330 (office); (20) 7736-6767 (home). *Fax:* (20) 7955-6869 (office); (20) 7731-7627 (home). *E-mail:* mlr1000@cam.ac.uk (office). *Website:* www.lse.ac.uk/collections/CPNSS (office).

REDING, Viviane, PhD; Luxembourg journalist, politician and fmr EU official; b. 27 April 1951, Esch-sur Alzette; ed Univ. of Paris (Sorbonne), France; journalist, Luxemburger Wort 1978–99; mem. Parl. 1979–89; communal councillor, City of Esch 1981–99; Pres. Luxembourg Union of Journalists 1986–98; Nat. Pres. Christian-Social Women 1988–93; mem. European Parl. 1989–99, 2014– (Group of the European People's Party–Christian Democrats); Pres. Cultural Affairs Cttee 1992–99; Vice-Pres. Parti Chrétien-Social 1995–99; Vice-Pres. Civil Liberties and Internal Affairs Cttee 1997–99; EU Commr for Educ. and Culture 1999–2004, for Information Soc. and Media 2004–10, Vice-Pres. EC and Commr for Justice, Fundamental Rights and Citizenship 2010–14; mem. Benelux Parl., N Atlantic Ass. (Leader Christian Democrat/Conservative Group); Officier, Légion d'honneur 2005; Dr hc (Hu Chen Univ. of Taiwan) 2004, (Genoa) 2004, (Turin) 2004, (Sacred Heart Univ., Luxembourg) 2009, (Glasgow) 2012; St George's Cross, Generalitat of Catalunya 1992, Gold Medal of European Merit 2001, Robert Schuman Medal 2004, Prince of Asturias Int. Co-operation Prize 2004, Gloria Artins Medal of Honour (Poland) 2005, Internet Villain Award, UK Internet Service Providers Asscn Awards 2007, Deutscher Mittelstandspreis 2007, BeNeLux Europa Award 2010. *Address:* European Parliament, Bâtiment Altiero Spinelli 11E202, 60 Rue Wiertz/Wiertzstraat 60, 1047 Brussels, Belgium (office). *Telephone:* (2) 284-54-60 (office). *Fax:* (2) 284-94-60 (office). *Website:* www.europarl.europa.eu/meps/en/1185/VIVIANE_REDING_home.html (office).

REDMAYNE, Edward (Eddie) John David, OBE, BA; British actor; b. 6 Jan. 1982, London; s. of Richard Redmayne and Patricia Redmayne (née Burke); m. Hannah Bagshawe 2014; ed Eton Coll., Trinity Coll., Cambridge; performed with Nat. Youth Music Theatre; early stage appearance aged 12 in Oliver! in London's West End. *Theatre includes:* Twelfth Night 2002, The Goat, or Who Is Sylvia? 2004, Hecuba 2004, Now or Later 2007, Red (Laurence Olivier Award for Best Actor in a Supporting Role 2010, Tony Award for Best Featured Actor in a Play 2010) 2009–10, Richard II (Critics' Circle Theatre Award for Best Shakespearean Performance 2011) 2011–12. *Films include:* Like Minds 2006, The Good Shepherd 2006, Elizabeth: The Golden Age 2007, The Other Boleyn Girl 2008, Glorious 39 2009, Hick 2011, My Week with Marilyn 2011, Les Misérables 2012, The Theory of Everything (Screen Actors Guild Award for Outstanding Performance by a Male Actor in a Leading Role 2015, Golden Globe Awards Best Actor – Drama 2015, Acad. Award for Best Actor 2015) 2014, Jupiter Ascending 2015, Thomas & Friends: Sodor's Legend of the Lost Treasure (voice) 2015, The Danish Girl 2015, Fantastic Beasts and Where to Find Them 2016. *Television includes:* Animal Ark (series) 1998, Doctors (series) 2003, Elizabeth I (mini-series) 2005, Tess of the d'Urbervilles (mini-series) 2008, The Pillars of the Earth (mini-series) 2010, The Miraculous Year (film) 2011, Birdsong (mini-series) 2012. *Address:* c/o United Agents, 12–26 Lexington Street, London, W1F 0LE, England (office). *Telephone:* (20) 3214-0800 (office). *Fax:* (20) 3214-0801 (office). *E-mail:* saustin@unitedagents .co.uk (office). *Website:* unitedagents.co.uk/eddie-redmayne (office).

REDRADO, Martín; Argentine economist and fmr central banker; b. 10 Sept. 1961; m. Ivana Pagés; ed Harvard Univ., USA; fmrly with Salomon Brothers, USA; fmr Man. Dir Security Pacific Bank; Pres. Nat. Securities Comm. 1991; fmr Chair. Emerging Markets Cttee, Int. Org. of Securities Comms (IOSCO); est. Fundación Capital 1994, Chief Economist –2001; Sec. of State, Technological Educ. Section, Ministry of Educ. 1996; Sec. for Trade and Int. Econ. Relations 2002–04; Gov. Banco Central de la República Argentina 2004–10. *Publications include:* Cómo sobrevivir a la Globalización (How to Survive Globalization) 2002, Exportar para crecer (Exports for Growth) 2003.

REDSTONE, Sumner Murray, BA, LLB; American lawyer and business executive; *Chairman Emeritus, Viacom Inc. and CBS Corporation;* b. (Sumner Murray Rothstein), 27 May 1923, Boston, Mass; s. of Michael Redstone and Belle Redstone (neé Ostrovsky); m. Phyllis Redstone (divorced 2002); one s. one d.; ed Harvard Univ.; served as 1st Lt, US Army 1943–45; called to Bar of Mass 1947; Special Asst to US Attorney-Gen., Washington, DC 1948–51; Partner, Ford, Bergson, Adams, Borkland & Redstone (law firm), Washington, DC 1951–54; Pres. and CEO Nat. Amusements Inc., Dedham, Mass 1967, Chair. 1986–87, Chair. Viacom Inc., New York 1987–2006, CEO 1996–2006, Exec. Chair. Viacom 2006–16, Exec. Chair. CBS Corpn 2006–16, Chair. Emer. 2016–; Prof., Boston Univ. Law School 1982, 1985–86; Chair. Corp. Comm. on Educ. Tech. 1996–; mem. Corpn, New England Medical Center 1967–, Massachusetts Gen. Hosp.; Sponsor, Boston Museum of Science; mem. Bd of Dirs, Boston Arts Festival, John F. Kennedy Library Foundation; mem. Nat. Asscn of Theatre Owners, Theatre Owners of America, Motion Picture Pioneers (mem. Bd of Dirs), Boston Bar Asscn, Massachusetts Bar Asscn; mem. Exec. Cttee, Will Rogers Fund; mem. Bd of Overseers, Boston Museum of Fine Arts; mem. Exec. Bd, Combined Jewish Philanthropies; Hon. LLD (Boston) 1994; Hon. LHD (New York Inst. of Tech.) 1996; Army Commendation Medal, Legends in Leadership Award, Emory Univ. 1995, Lifetime Achievement Award American Cancer Soc. 1995, Trustees Award Nat. Acad. of TV Arts and Sciences 1997, Robert F. Kennedy Memorial Ripple of Hope Award 1998, Int. Radio and TV Gold Medal Award 1998, Nat. Conf. of Christians and Jews Humanitarian Award 1998, numerous other awards. *Publication:* A Passion to Win (autobiog.) 2001. *Address:* Viacom Inc., 1515 Broadway, New York, NY 10036 (office); National Amusements Inc., 200 Elm Street, Dedham, MA 02026 (office); 98 Baldpate Hill Road, Newton, MA 02159, USA (home); CBS Corporation, 51 West 52nd Street, New York, NY 10019-6188 (office). *Telephone:* (212) 258-6000 (Viacom) (office); (212) 975-4321 (CBS) (office). *Fax:* (212) 258-6464 (Viacom) (office); (212) 975-4516 (CBS) (office). *Website:* www .viacom.com (office); www.national-amusements.com (office); www.cbscorporation .com (office).

REDWOOD, Rt Hon. John Alan, PC, MA, DPhil, CISI, IFA; British politician; b. 15 June 1951, Dover, Kent, England; s. of William Charles Redwood and Amy Emma Champion; m. Gail Felicity Chippington 1974 (divorced 2004); one s. one d.; ed Kent Coll., Canterbury and Magdalen and St Antony's Colls, Oxford; Fellow, All Souls Coll., Oxford 1972–85, 2003–05; Investment Adviser, Robert Fleming & Co. 1973–77; Dir (fmrly Man.) N.M. Rothschild & Sons 1977–87; Dir Norcros PLC 1985–89, Jt Deputy Chair. 1986–87, Chair. (non-exec.) 1987–89; Head, Prime Minister's Policy Unit 1983–85; MP for Wokingham 1987–; Parl. Under-Sec. of State, Dept of Trade and Industry 1989–90, Minister of State 1990–92, Minister of State, Dept of Environment 1992–93; Sec. of State for Wales 1993–95; unsuccessful cand. for leadership of Conservative Party 1995; Opposition Front Bench Spokesman on Trade and Industry 1997–99, on the Environment 1999–2000; Shadow Sec. of State for Deregulation 2004–05; Chair. Econ. Policy Review, Conservative Party 2005–10; Chair. Concentric PLC 2002–07, Investment Cttee Evercore Pan Asset 2007–, Conservative Econ. Affairs Cttee 2010–; Visiting Prof., Univ. of Middlesex Business School; Parliamentarian of the Year Awards 1987, 1995, 1997, 2013. *Publications:* Reason, Ridicule and Religion 1976, Public Enterprise in Crisis 1980, Value for Money Audits (with J. Hatch) 1981, Controlling Public Industries (with J. Hatch) 1982, Going for Broke 1984, Equity for Everyman 1986, Popular Capitalism 1989, The Global Marketplace 1994, The Single European Currency (with others) 1996, Our Currency, Our Country 1997, The Death of Britain? 1999, Stars and Strife 2001, Just Say No 2001, Third Way – Which Way? 2002, Singing the Blues 2004, I Want to Make a Difference – But I Don't Like Politics 2006, After the Credit Crunch – No More Boom and Bust? 2008. *Leisure interests:* water sports, village cricket. *Address:* House of Commons, Westminster, London, SW1A 0AA, England (office). *Telephone:* (20) 7219-4205 (office). *Fax:* (20) 7219-0377 (office). *E-mail:* redwoodj@parliament.uk (office); john .redwood.mp@parliament.uk (office); office@wokinghamconservatives.org.uk. *Website:* www.parliament.uk/biographies/commons/mr-john-redwood/14 (office); wwww.johnredwoodsdiary.com (office).

REED, Bruce; American fmr government official; *President, Eli and Edythe Broad Foundation;* b. Coeur d'Alene, Ida; ed Princeton Univ., Univ. of Oxford, UK; served as chief speechwriter for US Senator Al Gore 1985–89; Policy Dir Democratic Leadership Council, Washington, DC 1990–91; Deputy Campaign Man. for Policy, Clinton-Gore Presidential Campaign 1992, then Asst to Pres. and Head of Domestic Policy Council 1997–2001; Pres. Democratic Leadership Council, Washington, DC 2001–11, also Ed.-in-Chief Blueprint (journal); Exec. Dir Nat. Comm. on Fiscal Responsibility and Reform (Bowles-Simpson Comm.) 2010; Chief of Staff to Vice-Pres. of USA, Washington, DC 2011–13; Pres. Eli and Edythe Broad Foundation 2013–. *Publication:* The Plan: Big Ideas for Change in America (with Rahm Emanuel) 2009. *Address:* Eli and Edythe Broad Foundation, 2121 Avenue of the Stars, 30th Floor, Los Angeles, CA 90067, USA (office). *Telephone:* (310) 954-5000 (office). *Website:* www.broadfoundation.org (office).

REED, David Patrick, BS, MS, PhD; American computer scientist and academic; *Chief Scientist, TidalScale Inc.;* b. 30 Jan. 1952, Portsmouth, Va; ed Massachusetts Inst. of Tech.; mem. Summer Research Staff, IBM San Jose Research Lab. 1975; Asst Prof. of Computer Science and Eng, MIT Lab. for Computer Science 1978–84; Vice-Pres. Research and Exploratory Devt and Chief Scientist, Software Arts (creator of VisiCalc, the first electronic spreadsheet) 1983–85; Chief Scientist, Lotus Development Corpn 1989–92, Vice-Pres. 1985–92; with Interval Research Corpn 1992–96; with Viewpoints Research Inst. 2001–; Visiting Scientist, MIT Media Lab., Adjunct Prof. of Media Arts and Sciences 2002–10; HP Fellow, Hewlett-Packard Labs 2003–09; apptd Sr Vice-Pres., Chief Scientist Group, SAP Labs 2010; currently Chief Scientist, TidalScale Inc.; Fellow, Diamond Technology Pnrs Diamond Exchange Program; World Tech. Award in Communication Tech., The World Tech. Network 2004, IP3 Award 2005. *Achievements include:* pioneer in design and construction of internet protocols, distributed data storage and PC software systems and applications; co-inventor of the end-to-end argument, often called the fundamental architectural principle of the internet; discovered Reed's Law, a scaling law for group-forming network architectures; along with Metcalfe's Law, Reed's Law has significant implications for large-scale network business models. *Publications:* numerous scientific papers in professional journals on densely scalable, mobile and robust RF network architectures and highly decentralized systems architectures. *Address:* TidalScale Inc., 4555 Great America Parkway, Suite 301, Santa Clara, CA 95054 (office); 8 Old Greendale Avenue, Needham, MA 02492, USA. *Telephone:* (408) 638-4540 (office); (781) 449-0372. *E-mail:* info@tidalscale.com (office); dpreed@reed.com. *Website:* www .tidalscale.com (office). www.reed.com.

REED, Debra L., BEng; American business executive; *CEO, Sempra Energy;* ed Univ. of Southern California; Pres. San Diego Gas & Electric (SDG&E) and Chief Financial Officer SDG&E and Southern California Gas Co. (SoCalGas) –2004, Pres. and COO SDG&E and SoCalGas 2004–06, Pres. and CEO 2006–10, Exec. Vice-Pres. Sempra Energy –2011, Pres. and CEO 2011–; mem. Bd of Dirs Halliburton Co.; Chair. San Diego Regional Econ. Devt Corpn; mem. Advisory Council, Jacobs School of Eng., Univ. of California, San Diego, Precourt Energy

Efficiency Center, Stanford; mem. The Trusteeship (affiliate of Int. Women's Forum); fmr mem. Bd of Dirs Genentech, Dominguez Services Corpn, Avery Dennison Corpn; fmr mem. Bd of Councilors, Univ. of Southern California. *Address:* Sempra Energy, 101 Ash Street, San Diego, CA 92101-3017, USA (office). *Telephone:* (619) 696-2000 (office). *E-mail:* info@www.sempra.com (office). *Website:* www.sempra.com (office).

REED, Ishmael Scott; American writer, poet and publisher; b. 22 Feb. 1938, Chattanooga, Tenn.; s. of Bennie S. Reed and Thelma Coleman; m. 1st Priscilla Rose 1960 (divorced 1970); two s.; m. 2nd Carla Blank; one d.; ed Univ. of Buffalo; Co-founder and Dir Reed, Cannon & Johnson Co. 1973–; Assoc. Fellow, Calhoun House, Yale Univ. 1982–; Founder (with Al Young) and Ed., Quilt magazine 1981; Guest Lecturer, Univ. of Calif., Berkeley 1968, then Sr Lecturer, now Lecturer Emer.; Founder and Publr Konch Magazine 1998–; mem. usage panel, American Heritage Dictionary; Assoc. Ed. American Book Review; Exec. Producer, Personal Problems (video soap opera); collaborator in multimedia Bicentennial mystery, The Lost State of Franklin (winner Poetry in Public Places contest 1975); Chair. Berkeley Arts Comm.; Advisory Chair. Co-ordinating Council of Literary Magazines; Pres. Before Columbus Foundation 1976–; currently Distinguished Prof. California Coll. of Arts; Nat. Endowment for Arts Writing Fellow 1974; Guggenheim Fellow 1975, MacArthur Fellowship (genius award) 1998; mem. Authors Guild of America, PEN; Nat. Inst. of Arts and Letters Award 1975, Rosenthal Foundation Award 1975, Michaux Award 1978, ACLU Award 1978, Lila Wallace-Reader's Digest Award 1997, Robert Kirsch Lifetime Achievement Award, Los Angeles Times 2003. *Publications include:* fiction: The Free-Lance Pallbearers 1967, Yellow Back Radio Broke Down 1969, Mumbo Jumbo 1972, The Last Days of Louisiana Red 1974, Flight to Canada 1976, The Terrible Twos 1982, Reckless Eyeballing 1986, Cab Calloway Stands in for the Moon 1986, The Terrible Threes 1989, Japanese By Spring 1993, Juice! 2011; poetry: Catechism of a Neoamerican Hoodoo Church 1970, Conjure: Selected Poems 1963–1970 1972, Chattanooga 1973, A Secretary to the Spirits 1978, Calafia: The California Poetry (ed.) 1979, New and Collected Poems 1988, New and Collected Poems 1964–2006 2006; non-fiction: The Rise, Fall and...? of Adam Clayton Powell (with others) 1967, 19 Necromancers from Now (ed.) 1970, Yardbird Reader (five vols, ed.) 1971–77, Yardbird Lives! (ed., with Al Young) 1978, Shrovetide in Old New Orleans 1978, Quilt 2–3 (ed., with Al Young, two vols) 1981–82, God Made Alaska for the Indians 1982, Writin' is Fightin': Thirty-Seven Years of Boxing on Paper (ed.) 1988, Ishmael Reed: An Interview 1990, The Before Columbus Foundation Fiction Anthology: Selections from the American Book Awards 1980–1990 (ed., with Kathryn Trueblood and Shawn Wong) 1992, Airin' Dirty Laundry 1993, Multi-America 1996, The Reed Reader (ed.) 2000, New and Collected Poems, 1964–2006 2006; non fiction: Shrovetide in Old New Orleans: Essays 19787, God Made Alaska for the Indians: Selected Essays 1982, Oakland Rhapsody, The Secret Soul Of An American Downtown 1995, Blues City: A Walk in Oakland 2003, Mixing It Up: Taking on the Media Bullies and Other Reflections 2008, Barack Obama and the Jim Crow Media 2010, Going Too Far: Essays About America's Nervous Breakdown 2012, The Complete Muhammad Ali 2015; contrib. to anthologies. *Address:* Lowenstein Associates, 115 East 23rd Street, 4th Floor, New York, NY 10011, USA (office). *Telephone:* (212) 206-1630 (office). *E-mail:* uncleish@aol.com. *Website:* www.ishmaelreed.org; www.ishmaelreedpub.com.

REED, John C., MD, PhD; American clinical scientist; *Executive Vice President and Global Head of Research and Development, Sanofi;* b. 11 Oct. 1958, New York; ed Univ. of Virginia, Univ. of Pennsylvania School of Medicine; Postdoctoral Fellow in Molecular Biology, Wistar Inst. of Anatomy and Biology, Philadelphia 1986–88; Resident in Clinical Pathology, Dept of Pathology and Lab. Medicine, Univ. of Pennsylvania Hosp. 1986–89, Research Assoc., Dept of Pathology and Laboratory Medicine, Univ. of Pennsylvania 1988–89, Asst Prof. 1989–92, Asst Dir Lab. of Molecular Diagnosis, Univ. of Pennsylvania Hosp. 1989–92; Dir Oncogene and Tumor Suppressor Gene Program, The Burnham Inst. for Medical Research, La Jolla, Calif. 1992–95, then Assoc. Prof. and Leader Apoptosis and Cell Death Research Program, Scientific Dir Burnham Inst. 1995–2003, Deputy Dir NCI Cancer Center 1994–2003, Pres. and CEO The Burnham Inst. 2003–13, also Prof. and Donald Bren Presidential Chair; Assoc. mem. Univ. of California, San Diego Cancer Center 1993–2013; Adjunct Prof., Dept of Biology, San Diego State Univ. 1996–2013; Adjunct Prof., Dept of Molecular Pathology, Univ. of California, San Diego School of Medicine 1997–2011; Global Head Roche Pharma Research & Early Devt 2013–18; Exec. Vice Pres. and Global Head of Research and Devt, Sanofi 2018–; Adjunct Prof., Univ. of Central Florida 2007–13, Univ. of Florida 2007–13, ETH Zurich 2015–; Chair. Translational Apoptosis Research Cttee for Prostate Cancer, CaP-CURE 1999–; mem. Advisory Cttee, Specialized Center of Research on Leukemia and Lymphoma, Univ. of California, San Diego 2001–; mem. Editorial Bd Antisense Research and Development 1993–96, Oncology Reports 1993–99, Cell Death and Differentiation 1994–99, Clinical Cancer Research 1994–99, Molecular Carcinogenesis 1994–, Cancer Gene Therapy 1994–, Advances in Leukemia and Lymphoma 1995–, Cancer Research 1995–, Journal of Inflammation 1996–97, Receptors and Signal Transduction 1996–98, Molecular and Cellular Differentiation 1996–98, Journal of Immunology 1996–98, Journal of Clinical Investigation 1996–, Antisense and Nucleic Acid Drug Development 1996–, Frontiers in Bioscience 1996–, Journal of Biological Chemistry 1996–, BLOOD 1997–, Current Opinion in Oncologic and Endocrine and Metabolic Drugs 1998–2000, Neoplasia 1998–, International Journal of Oncology 1998–, Tumor Targeting 1999–, Nature Reviews 2000–, Current Opinion in Investigational Drugs 2000–, Expert Opinion on Therapeutic Targets 2001–, Cell Cycle 2001–; William R. Drell Chair in Molecular Biology 1995; mem. AAAS 1981, (Fellow 2011), American Soc. for Microbiology 1986, American Asscn for Cancer Research 1990, American Asscn of Univ. Pathologists 1991, Acad. of Clinical Lab. Physicians and Scientists 1991–93, Eastern Cooperative Oncology Group 1991, Clinical Cancer Research 1992, American Hematology Soc. 1992, CALGB 1994, American Soc. for Investigative Pathology 1995, Fed. of American Socs for Experimental Biology 1996, Int. Forum for Corp. Dir 1998; Presidential Award, Reticuloendothelial Soc. 1985, Sheard Stanford Award, American Soc. of Clinical Pathologists 1985, Upjohn Achievement Award 1986, Stohlman Memorial Scholar Award, Leukemic Soc. of America 1994, Local Hero in the Fight Against Breast Cancer Award, Susan G. Komen Foundation 1998, 1st Inaugural D. Wayne Calloway Memorial Lecturer, Memorial Sloan-Kettering Cancer Center 1999, 35th

Annual Harold G. Pritzker Memorial Lecture Presenter, Mount Sinai Hosp., Univ. of Toronto 1999, ranked No. 1 Hottest Researcher in Life Sciences WorldWide Inst. for Scientific Information 1999, 2000, 2000 Decade of the Brain Award, American Acad. of Neurology 2000, Warner-Lambert/Parke Davis Award, American Soc. for Investigative Pathology 2000, Harry B. Van Dyke Award, Columbia Univ. 2001. *Publications:* more than 750 articles in scientific journals. *Address:* Sanofi, 54, Rue La Boétie, 75008, Paris, France (office). *Telephone:* 1-53-77-40-00 (office).

REED, John Francis (Jack), BS, MPA, JD; American politician; *Senator from Rhode Island;* b. 12 Nov. 1949, Cranston, RI; s. of Joseph Reed and Mary Monahan; m. Julia Hart; one d.; ed LaSalle Acad., Providence, RI, US Mil. Acad., Kennedy School of Govt, Harvard Univ., Harvard Law School; commissioned, 2nd Lt US Army 1971, served with 82nd Airborne Div. 1973–77, Assoc. Prof., US Mil. Acad., West Point, NY 1977–79, resgnd from Army 1979 with rank of Capt., with US Army Reserve 1979–91, resgnd with rank of Maj.; called to the Bar, DC 1982, Rhode Island 1983; Assoc., Sutherland, Asbill & Brennan, Washington, DC 1982–83, Edwards & Angelli, Providence 1983–89; mem. RI State Senate 1984–90; mem. US House of Reps 1990–96; Senator from Rhode Island 1996–, mem. Appropriations Cttee, Armed Services Cttee, Banking, Housing and Urban Affairs Cttee; Vice-Chair. NE-Midwest Congressional Coalition; Democrat; Army Commendation Medal. *Leisure interests:* reading, hiking. *Address:* 728 Hart Senate Office Building, Washington, DC 20510, USA (office). *Telephone:* (202) 224-4642 (office). *Fax:* (202) 224-4680 (office). *Website:* reed.senate.gov (office).

REED, John Shepard, MS; American business executive; b. 7 Feb. 1939, Chicago, Ill.; m. 1st (divorced), four c.; m. 2nd Cindy McCarthy 1994; ed Washington and Jefferson Coll., Mass Inst. of Tech., Alfred P. Sloan School of Man. (MIT); served with US Army Eng Corps, Korea; fmr Trainee Goodyear Tire & Rubber; joined Citicorp/Citibank 1965, fmrly responsible for operating group, consumer business, fmr Sr Vice-Pres., Chair. and Chief Exec. 1984–98; Jt Chair. and CEO Citigroup (merger between Citicorp and Travelers Group) 1998–2000; Interim Chair. NY Stock Exchange (NYSE) 2003 then Chair. 2004–05; Chair. Coalition of Service Industries, Services Policy Advisory Cttee to the US Trade Rep.; mem. Bd of Dirs Altria Group Inc. (fmrly Philip Morris Inc.) 1979–2003, 2004–, Manpower Demonstration Research Corpn; fmr mem. Bd of Dirs Monsanto Co.; mem. Advisory Bd Sandbox Industries, Morgan Street Document Systems LLC, Bling Nation; mem. Bd of Overseers, Boston Symphony Orchestra Inc.; mem. Business Council, Business Roundtable Policy Cttee; mem. Corpn of MIT; fmr mem. Bd Memorial Sloan-Kettering Cancer Center, Rand Corpn, Spencer Foundation, American Museum of Natural History; Trustee Center for Advanced Studies in Social and Behavioral Sciences.

REEDER, Franklin S., BA; American consultant and fmr government official; *President, The Reeder Group;* b. 25 Oct. 1940, Philadelphia, Pa; s. of Simon Reeder and Hertha Strauss; m. Anna Marie Seroski 1962; one s. two d.; ed Univ. of Pennsylvania, George Washington Univ.; with US Treasury Dept 1961–64, Defense Dept 1964–70; with US Office of Man. and Budget 1970–71, 1980–97, Dir 1995–97; Deputy Dir House Information System, US House of Reps 1977–80; currently Pres. The Reeder Group; Chair. Computer Systems Security and Privacy Advisory Bd (now Information Security and Privacy Advisory Bd), Nat. Inst. of Standards and Tech. (NIST) 2000–06; Chair. Nat. Bd of Information Security Examiners; Co-founder and fmr Chair. Center for Internet Security, now mem. Bd of Dirs; columnist and Contributing Ed. Govt Executive magazine; Fellow, Nat. Acad. of Public Admin; mem. Center for Strategic and Int. Studies Comm. on Cybersecurity; Hon. Certified Information Security Man. (CISM) 2003; numerous awards including Presidential Rank Award as Meritorious Sr Exec., inducted into Govt Computer News Information Resources Man. Hall of Fame. *Leisure interests:* running, swimming, bicycling, watching baseball. *Address:* The Reeder Group, 3200 N Nottingham Street, Arlington, VA 22207, USA (office). *Telephone:* (703) 536-6635 (office).

REES, Sir Dai (David Allan), Kt, PhD, DSc, FIBiol, FRSC, FRS; British scientist and academic (retd); b. 28 April 1936, Silloth, Cumbria; s. of James A. Rees and Elsie Bolam; m. Myfanwy Owen 1959; two s. one d.; ed Hawarden Grammar School, Clwyd and Univ. Coll. of North Wales, Bangor; joined staff at Univ. of Edin. 1960, Asst Lecturer in Chem. 1961, Lecturer 1962–70, Section Man. 1970–72; Prin. Scientist, Unilever Research, Colworth Lab. 1972–82; Assoc. Dir (part-time) MRC Unit for Cell Biophysics Kings Coll., London 1980–82; Dir Nat. Inst. for Medical Research 1982–87; Sec., then Chief Exec. MRC 1987–96, MRC scientist 1996; Chair. European Medical Research Councils 1989, Pres. European Science Foundation 1994–2001; Visiting Professorial Fellow, Univ. Coll., Cardiff 1972–77; mem. Royal Soc. Council 1985–87; Hon. FRCP 1986, Hon. FRCPE 1998, Hon. Fellow, King's Coll., London 1989, Univ. Coll. of N Wales 1988; Hon. DSc (Edin.) 1989, (Wales) 1991, (Stirling) 1995, (Leicester) 1997, (York) 2007; Colworth Medal, Biochemical Soc. 1970, Carbohydrate Award, Chemical Soc. 1970, Philips Lecturer, Royal Soc. 1984. *Publications include:* articles on carbohydrate biochemistry and cell biology. *Leisure interests:* river cruising, reading, listening to music. *Address:* Ford Cottage, 1 High Street, Denford, Kettering, Northants.. NN14 4EQ, England (home). *E-mail:* drees@nimr.mrc.ac .uk (home).

REES, Madeleine Selina, OBE, BA; British lawyer and international organization official; *Secretary-General, Women's International League for Peace and Freedom;* b. 1957; ed Univ. of Wales; began career as teacher in various countries, mainly in Latin America and UK; re-qualified as lawyer 1989, practising lawyer in Britain 1989–97; worked as human rights lawyer for over 20 years, specializing in discrimination law and public and admin. law; worked for int. orgs including UN, Comm. for Racial Equality and Equal Opportunities Comm.; worked at office of the Ombudsman, Bosnia 1997; Head of Office and gender expert, Office of the High Commr for Human Rights, Bosnia and Herzegovina 1998–2006, Head of Women's Rights and Gender Unit 2006–10; Sec.-Gen., Women's Int. League for Peace and Freedom 2010–; worked with British Foreign Sec. William Hague and Angelina Jolie-Pitt at End Sexual Violence in Conflict conf., London 2014; apptd Visiting Prof. in Practice, Centre for Women, Peace and Security, LSE 2016; Hon. DSc in Social Science (Edinburgh) 2015. *Address:* Women's International League for Peace and Freedom, Rue de Varembé 1, Case Postale 28, 1211 Geneva 20, Switzerland (office). *Telephone:* (22) 9197080 (office). *Fax:* (22) 9197081 (office). *E-mail:* secretariat@wilpf.org (office). *Website:* wilpf.org (office).

REES OF LUDLOW, Baron (Life Peer), cr. 2005, of Ludlow in the County of Shropshire; **Martin John Rees,** OM, MA, PhD, FRS; British astronomer and academic; *Astronomer Royal;* b. 23 June 1942, York, Yorks., England; s. of Reginald J. Rees and Joan Rees; m. Caroline Humphrey 1986; ed Shrewsbury School and Trinity Coll., Cambridge; Fellow, Jesus Coll., Cambridge 1967–69; Research Assoc. Calif. Inst. of Tech. 1967–68, 1971; mem. Inst. for Advanced Study, Princeton 1969–70, Prof. 1982–96; Visiting Prof., Harvard Univ. 1972, 1986–87; Prof., Univ. of Sussex 1972–73; Plumian Prof. of Astronomy and Experimental Philosophy, Univ. of Cambridge 1973–91, Royal Soc. Research Prof. 1992–2002, Prof. of Cosmology and Astrophysics 2004–09, now Prof. Emer.; Astronomer Royal 1995–; Master, Trinity Coll., Cambridge 2004–12; Fellow, King's Coll., Cambridge 1969–72, 1973–2003; Visiting Prof., Imperial Coll., London 2001–, Univ. of Leicester 2001–; Dir Inst. of Astronomy 1977–82, 1987–91; Regents Fellow, Smithsonian Inst., Washington, DC 1984–88; mem. Council of Royal Soc. 1983–85, 1993–95, Pres. 2005–10; mem. Council of Royal Inst. of GB –2010; Pres. Royal Astronomical Soc. 1992–94, BAAS 1994–95, Asscn for Science Educ. 2012–; Trustee, British Museum 1996–2002, Inst. for Advanced Study, Princeton, USA 1998–, Nat. Endowment for Sciences, Tech. and Arts 1998–2001, Kennedy Memorial Trust 1999–2004, Inst. for Public Policy Research 2001; Foreign Assoc. NAS; mem. Academia Europaea 1989, Pontifical Acad. of Sciences 1990; Foreign mem. American Philosophical Soc., Royal Swedish Acad. of Science, Russian Acad. of Sciences, Norwegian Acad. of Arts and Science, Accad. Lincei (Rome), Royal Netherlands Acad., Finnish Acad. of Arts and Sciences, Japan Acad.; mem. (Crossbench) House of Lords 2005–; Hon. Fellow, King's Coll., Darwin Coll. and Jesus Coll., Cambridge, Indian Acad. of Sciences, Univ. of Wales, Cardiff 1998, Inst. of Physics 2001, British Acad.; Foreign Hon. mem. American Acad. of Arts and Sciences; Officier, Ordre des Arts et des Lettres, Order of Rising Sun (Gold and Silver Star) (Japan); Hon. DSc (Sussex) 1990, (Leicester) 1993, (Copenhagen, Keele, Uppsala, Newcastle) 1995, (Toronto) 1997, (Durham) 1999, (Oxford) 2000, (Yale) 2008, (McMaster) 2009; Heinemann Prize, American Inst. of Physics 1984, Gold Medal (Royal Astronomical Soc.) 1987, Guthrie Medal, Inst. of Physics 1989, Balzan Prize 1989, Robinson Prize for Cosmology 1990, Bruce Medal, Astronomical Soc. of Pacific 1993, Science Writing Award, American Inst. of Physics 1996, Bower Award, Franklin Inst. 1998, Rossi Prize, American Astronomical Soc. 2000, Cosmology Prize of Peter Gruber Foundation 2001, Einstein Award, World Cultural Congress 2003, Michael Faraday Prize 2004, Crafoord Prize, Royal Swedish Acad. (jtly) 2005, Niels Bohr Medal, UNESCO 2005, Caird Medal, Nat. Maritime Museum 2007, BBC Reith Lecturer 2010, Templeton Prize 2011, Newton Prize, Inst. of Physics 2012. *Achievements include:* various contribs to astrophysics and cosmology and to science policy, Asteroid 4587 Rees named after him. *Television:* What We Still Don't Know (documentary series, Channel 4) 2004. *Publications include:* Perspectives in Astrophysical Cosmology 1995, Gravity's Fatal Attraction (with M. Begelman) 1995, Before the Beginning 1997, Just Six Numbers 1999, Our Cosmic Habitat 2001, Our Final Century? 2003, From Here to Infinity: Scientific Horizons 2011; edited books; more than 500 articles and reviews in scientific journals on the origin of the cosmic microwave background radiation, as well as on galaxy clustering and formation, and numerous gen. articles. *Address:* Trinity College, Cambridge, CB2 1TQ (office); Institute of Astronomy, Madingley Road, Cambridge, CB3 0HA, England (office). *Telephone:* (1223) 338412 (office). *E-mail:* mjr@ast.cam.ac.uk (office). *Website:* www.ast.cam.ac.uk/IoA/staff/mjr (office).

REESE, Colin Bernard, MA, PhD, ScD, FRS; British chemist and academic; *Professor Emeritus of Chemistry, King's College London;* b. 29 July 1930, Plymouth, Devon, England; s. of Joseph Reese and Emily Reese; m. Susanne L. Bird 1968; one s. one d.; ed Dartington Hall School and Clare Coll., Cambridge; Research Fellow, Clare Coll. 1956–59, Harvard Univ., USA 1957–58; Official Fellow and Dir of Studies in Chem., Clare Coll. 1959–73; Univ. Demonstrator in Chem., Univ. of Cambridge 1959–63, Asst Dir of Research 1963–64, Univ. Lecturer in Chem. 1964–73; Daniell Prof. of Chem., King's Coll. London 1973–98, Fellow 1989–, Prof. of Organic Chem. 1999–2003, Prof. Emer. 2003–. *Publications:* scientific papers mainly in chem. journals. *Address:* 21 Rozel Road, London, SW4 0EY, England (home). *Telephone:* (20) 7498-0230 (home). *E-mail:* colin.reese@kcl.ac.uk (office); reese157@btinternet.com (home).

REESE, Stuart Harry, BA, MBA; American fmr business executive; b. 3 May 1955, Richmond, Va; s. of Allison Reese and Virginia Saul; m. Elizabeth Garr 1976; three d. one s.; ed Gettysburg Coll., Dartmouth Coll.; Securities Analyst Aetna 1979–81, Sr Securities Analyst 1981–82, Dir Treas. Investment Planning 1982–83, Sr Investment Officer 1983–84, Asst Vice-Pres. 1984–85, Man. Dir 1985–89, Vice-Pres., Man. Dir Capital Markets 1989–93; Chair. and CEO Babson Capital Man., Massachusetts Mutual Life Insurance Co. (MassMutual) 1993–99, Exec. Vice-Pres. and Chief Investment Officer Massachusetts Mutual Life Insurance Co. (MassMutual) 1999–2005, Pres. 2005–08, CEO 2005–09, Chair. 2007–09, Chair. Exec. Cttee, mem. Corp. Governance Cttee, Investment and Operations Cttee, Chair. (non-exec.) MassMutual Jan.–Dec. 2010, fmr Chair. and CEO C.M. Life Insurance Co. (subsidiary); fmr Chair. Advisory Bd LRN-RAND Center for Corp. Ethics, Law and Governance; mem. Bd of Trustees Gettysburg Coll.; fmr mem. Bd American Council of Life Insurers, Fed. Reserve Bank of Boston, Massachusetts Gov.'s Council of Econ. Advisors; mem. Bd of Dirs Leucadia Nat. Corpn, Lahey Clinic Foundation.

REETZ, Manfred T., BA, MS, PhD; German chemist and academic; *Hans Meerwein Research Professor, Philipps-Universität Marburg;* b. 13 Aug. 1943, Hirschberg; ed Washington Univ., St Louis, Mo., Univ. of Michigan, Ann Arbor, USA, Göttingen Univ.; Postdoctoral Fellow, Univ. Marburg 1971–72, Asst Prof. 1973–78, Prof. 1980–91; Guest Prof., Univ. of Wisconsin, Madison, USA 1978; Assoc. Prof., Univ. of Bonn 1978–80; Guest Prof., Florida State Univ. 1989–90; Dir Max-Planck-Institut für Kohlenforschung 1991–2002, Man. Dir 1993–2002, External (Emer.) Group Leader 2011–, Chair. Studiengesellschaft Kohle mbH 1993–2011; Hans Meerwein Research Prof., Philipps-Universität Marburg 2011–; mem. Advisory Bd, Inst. für Organische Katalyseforschung, Rostock 1993–, Catalysis Nat. Research School Combination (NRSC), Leeuwenhorst, Netherlands 1999–2000; mem. Int. Advisory Bd, Chem. Dept, Nagoya Univ. 2006–07; Senator, Chem. Section, Deutsche Akad. der Naturforscher Leopoldina 2007–11; Associate Ed. Chemistry and Biology 2009–; mem. Editorial Advisory Bd Nachrichten aus Chemie, Technik und Laboratorium 1994–99, Topics in Organometallic Chemistry 1997–, Advanced Synthesis and Catalysis 2000–05, Russian Journal of Organic Chemistry 2000–, Bulletin of the Chemical Society of Japan 2005–; mem. Advisory Bd, Topics in Stereochemistry 2006–, Karl-Ziegler-Foundation 2010–; mem. German Chemical Soc. (Dir 1990–95, Vice-Pres. 1995); mem. Deutsche Akad. der Naturforscher Leopoldina 1997, Nordrheinwestfälischen Akad. der Wissenschaften 2001; Foreign mem. Royal Netherlands Acad. of Arts and Sciences 2005; Hon. Prof., Ruhr-Univ. Bochum 1992–2010, Shanghai Inst. of Organic Chem. 2007, Distinguished Scientist, Chinese Acad. of Sciences 2018–; Chemical Industries Prize 1976, Jacobus van't Hoff Prize 1977, Chem. Prize, Göttingen Acad. of Sciences 1978, Otto-Bayer Prize 1986, Leibniz Prize, Deutsche Forschungsgemeinschaft 1989, Nagoya Gold Medal of Organic Chem. 2000, Hans Herloff Inhoffen Medal 2003, Cliff S. Hamilton Award in Organic Chem. (USA) 2005, Karl-Ziegler-Prize, German Chemical Soc. 2005, Ernst Hellmut Vits-Prize 2006, Prelog Medal (Switzerland) 2006, Ruhr-Prize for Arts and Science 2007, Lilly Distinguished Lectureship Award 2009, ACS Arthur C. Cope Award 2009, Yamada-Koga Prize (Japan) 2009, Tetrahedron Prize for Creativity in Organic Chem. 2011, Otto-Hahn-Prize 2011, IKCOC Prize 2012, Chirality Medal 2014, BioTrans Senior Award 2017. *Publications:* numerous scientific papers in professional journals. *Address:* Room E 5238, Chemistry Building, Philipps-Universität Marburg, Hans-Meerwein-Straße 4, 35032 Marburg, Germany (office). *Telephone:* (6421) 2825500 (office). *E-mail:* reetz@mpi-muelheim.mpg.de (office). *Website:* www.kofo.mpg.de/en/research/organic-synthesis (office).

REEVE, Michael David, MA, FBA; British academic; b. 11 Jan. 1943, Bolton, Lancs.; s. of Arthur Reeve and Edith Mary Barrett; m. Elizabeth Klingaman 1970 (divorced 1999); two s. one d.; one s. with Emma Gee; ed King Edward's School, Birmingham, Balliol Coll., Oxford; Harmsworth Sr Scholar, Merton Coll., Oxford 1964–65; Woodhouse Research Fellow, St John's Coll., Oxford 1965–66; Tutorial Fellow, Exeter Coll., Oxford 1966–84, Emer. Fellow 1984–; Kennedy Prof. of Latin, Univ. of Cambridge 1984–2006, now Prof. Emer., Dir of Research, Faculty of Classics 2006–07, Fellow, Pembroke Coll. 1984–2007, Fellow Emer. 2008–; Visiting Prof., Univ. of Hamburg 1976, McMaster Univ. 1979, Univ. of Toronto 1982–83; Ed. Classical Quarterly 1981–86; Ed.-in-Chief Cambridge Classical Studies –2007, Cambridge Classical Texts and Commentaries 1984–; Chair. Advisory Council, Warburg Inst. 2008–13; Sandars Reader in Bibliography 2012; Corresp. mem. Akad. der Wissenschaften, Göttingen 1990–; Foreign mem. Istituto Lombardo, Milan 1993–; Foreign mem. Accademia dei Lincei, Rome 2017–. *Publications include:* Longus, Daphnis and Chloe 1982; contribs to Texts and Transmission 1983, Cicero, Pro Quinctio 1992, Vegetius 2004, Geoffrey of Monmouth 2007, Manuscripts and Methods 2011; articles in European and American journals. *Leisure interests:* chess, music, gardening, mountain walking. *Address:* Pembroke College, Cambridge, CB2 1RF, England (office). *Fax:* (1223) 335409 (office). *E-mail:* mdr1000@cam.ac.uk (office).

REEVES, Keanu; Canadian actor; b. 2 Sept. 1964, Beirut, Lebanon; s. of Samuel Nowin Reeves and Patricia Reeves; ed Toronto High School for Performing Arts; training at Second City Workshop, Toronto; Toronto stage debut in Wolf Boy; other stage appearances in For Adults Only, Romeo and Juliet; bass guitarist, rock band Dogstar 1996–2002. *Television films:* Letting Go 1985, Act of Vengeance 1986, Babes in Toyland 1986, Under the Influence 1986, Brotherhood of Justice 1986, Save the Planet (TV special) 1990. *Films:* Prodigal, Flying 1986, Youngblood 1986, River's Edge 1987, Permanent Record 1988, The Night Before 1988, The Prince of Pennsylvania 1988, Dangerous Liaisons 1988, 18 Again 1988, Bill and Ted's Excellent Adventure 1988, Parenthood 1989, I Love You to Death 1990, Tune In Tomorrow 1990, Bill and Ted's Bogus Journey 1991, Point Break 1991, My Own Private Idaho 1991, Bram Stoker's Dracula 1992, Much Ado About Nothing 1993, Even Cowgirls Get the Blues, Little Buddha 1993, Speed 1994, Johnny Mnemonic 1995, A Walk in the Clouds 1995, Chain Reaction, Feeling Minnesota, The Devil's Advocate 1996, The Last Time I Committed Suicide 1997, The Matrix 1999, The Replacements 2000, The Watcher 2000, The Gift 2000, Sweet November 2001, The Matrix Reloaded 2003, The Matrix Revolutions 2003, Something's Gotta Give 2003, Thumbsucker 2005, Constantine 2005, A Scanner Darkly 2006, The Lake House 2006, Street Kings 2008, The Day the Earth Stood Still 2008, The Private Lives of Pippa Lee 2009, Henry's Crime 2010, Generation Um 2012, Man of Tai Chi 2013, 47 Ronin 2013, John Wick 2014, Knock Knock 2015, Exposed 2016, The Neon Demon 2016, The Bad Batch 2016, The Whole Truth 2016, To the Bone 2017, John Wick: Chapter 2 2017, A Happening of Monumental Proportions 2017, Siberia 2018, Destination Wedding 2018, Replicas 2018. *Address:* c/o Kevin Houvane, CAA, 9830 Wilshire Boulevard, Beverly Hills, CA 90212-1825; 581 North Crescent Heights Boulevard, Los Angeles, CA 90048, USA.

REFINETTI GUARDIA, Eduardo, BEcon, MA (Econ), PhD; Brazilian economist, academic, government official and banking executive; *Minister of Finance;* b. 19 Jan. 1966; m.; ed Pontifical Catholic Univ. of São Paulo, Inst. of Econs of the Univ. of Campinas, Econ. Research Inst. of the São Paulo Univ. Econs and Business Admin School; held several positions in Fed. and State Govts from 1989; Prof., Pontifícia Universidade Católica de São Paulo 1990–97; Sec., Brazilian Treasury 2002–03; São Paulo State Sec. of Finance 2003–06; Investor Relations Officer, GP Investimentos 2006–07, Chief Financial Officer, GP Investments SA 2006–07; Partner, Pragma Gestão de Patrimônio Ltda 2007–10; Chief Financial Officer, BM & F Bovespa (securities, commodities and futures exchange) 2010–13, mem. Exec. Bd and Chief Product Officer, BM&F Bovespa SA 2013–16; Exec. Sec., Ministry of Finance 2016–18, Minister of Finance 2018–; Dir, Companhia de Saneamento Basico do Estado de São Paulo 2003–, Vale SA 2016–. *Address:* Ministry of Finance, Esplanada dos Ministérios, Bloco P, 5° andar, 70048-900 Brasília, DF, Brazil (office). *Telephone:* (61) 3412-2000 (office). *Fax:* (61) 3412-1721 (office). *E-mail:* gabinete.df.gmf@fazenda.gov.br (office). *Website:* www.fazenda.gov.br (office).

REGAN, Geoff, PC BA; Canadian politician; *Speaker of House of Commons;* b. 22 Nov. 1959, Windsor, Nova Scotia; s. of Gerald Regan and Carole Regan (née Harrison); m. Kelly Regan 1993; three c.; ed St. Francis Xavier Univ.; MP (Halifax West, Liberal) 1993; Minister of Fisheries and Oceans 2003–06; Parl. Sec. to the Govt House Leader 2001–03; Regional Minister Nova Scotia 2003; Minister of Justice and Attorney-Gen. 2004; Speaker of the House of Commons 2015–; mem. of the Queens's Privy Council 2003; Metro Food Bank Society Community Leadership Award 1992, Halifax Board of Trade Certificate of Merit 1992, Queen

Elizabeth II Golden Jubilee Medal 2002, Elisabeth Mann Borgese Medal 2005, Lebanese Community Recognition Award 2008, Queen Elizabeth II Diamond Jubilee Medal 2012;. *Address:* 1496 Bedford Highway (Main Office), Suite 222, Bedford, NS B4A 1E5 (office); House of Commons, Room 339-S, Ottawa, ON K1A 0A6, Canada (office). *Telephone:* (902) 426-2217 (office); (613) 996-3085 (office). *Fax:* (902) 426-8339 (office); (613) 996-6988 (office). *E-mail:* geoff.regan@parl.gc.ca (office). *Website:* www.parl.gc.ca (office); www.ourcommons.ca (office); geoffregan .ca.

REGENVANU, Ralph John, BA; Ni-Vanuatu anthropologist, artist and politician; *Minister of Foreign Affairs, International Co-operation and External Trade;* b. 20 Sept. 1970, Suva, Fiji; s. of Sethy Regenvanu and Dorothy Regenvanu; ed Australian Nat. Univ., Univ. of the South Pacific, Montrueuil Univ., France; fmr Curator, Nat. Museum of Vanuatu; founding mem. Pacific Islands Museums Asscn 1994, mem. Exec. Bd 1997–2009; Dir Vanuatu Cultural Centre 1995–2006; co-f. Fest'Napuan (annual musical festival) 1996; Del. of Vanuatu and Pacific Islands to UNESCO 1998, mem. Advisory Cttee of Experts for UNESCO World Report on Cultural Diversity 2007; also active as painter and illustrator; Artist-in-Residence, British Museum 2006; mem. ni-Vanuatu Parl. for Port Vila (Ind.) 2008–12, (GJP) 2012–; Minister of Cooperatives and ni-Vanuatu Business Devt 2010–11, of Lands Feb.–March 2011, of Justice and Social Affairs 2011–12, of Lands and Natural Resources 2013–15, 2016–18, of Foreign Affairs, Int. Co-operation and External Trade 2017–; Founder and Pres. Land and Justice Party (Graon mo Jastis Pati, GJP) 2010; Chevalier, Ordre des Arts et des Lettres 2006, Libehkamel Tah Tomat (Caretaker of the Sacred Nakamal) 2006. *Address:* Ministry of Foreign Affairs, International Co-operation and External Trade, PMB 9051, Port Vila, Vanuatu (office). *Telephone:* 27045 (office). *Fax:* 27832 (office). *Website:* www.graonmojastis .org/ol-mp/ralph-regenvanu (office).

REGESTER, Michael; British crisis management consultant; *Director, Regester Larkin Ltd;* b. 8 April 1947, Godalming, Surrey, England; s. of Hugh Regester and Monique Levrey; m. 1st Christine Regester 1969 (divorced 1993); two d.; m. 2nd Leanne Moscardi 1994 (divorced 2003); one s. one d.; ed St Peter's School, Guildford; Man. Public Affairs, Gulf Oil Corpn, Europe, W Africa and Middle East 1975–80; Co-founder and Jt Man. Dir Traverse-Healy and Regester Ltd 1980–87; Man. Dir Charles Barker Traverse-Healy Ltd 1987–89; Man. Dir Regester PLC 1990–94; Dir Regester Larkin Ltd 1994–. *Publications:* Crisis Management 1987, Investor Relations (with N. Ryder) 1990, Issues and Crisis Management (with J. Larkin) 2008. *Leisure interests:* sailing, golf, tennis, opera, cooking. *Address:* Regester Larkin Ltd, 16 St Martin's le Grand, London, EC1A 4EN, England (office). *Telephone:* (20) 3179-6000 (office). *Fax:* (20) 3179-6001 (office). *E-mail:* mregester@regesterlarkin.com (office). *Website:* www.regesterlarkin.com (office).

REGIS, John, MBE; British fmr athlete; b. 13 Oct. 1966, Lewisham; s. of Antony Regis and Agnes Regis; winner, UK 200m 1985 (tie), 100m 1988, Amateur Athletics Asscn 200m 1986–87; UK record for 200m, World Championships 1987; World Championships bronze medallist 200m, silver medal, Olympic Games Seoul 1988, 300m indoor record holder Commonwealth Games 1990; silver medal, 200m 1991, gold meda,l 4×100m relay 1991; gold medal, 200m, 4×100m relay, 4×400m relay 1993; gold medal, World Cup 1994, mem. British team Olympic Games, Atlanta 1996; retd 2000; mem. GB bobsleigh training team 2000; Head Athletics Div., Stellar Group Ltd (athletics man. team) 2000–; coach UK Athletics sprint-relay team 2001–. *Leisure interests:* golf, tennis, martial arts.

REGMI, Drona Raj, BL; Nepalese lawyer and government official; b. 30 Dec. 1958, Parbat; s. of Punya Prasad Regmi and Resham Kumari Regmi; ed Bhawani Vidyapeeth School, Parbat, Tribhuwan Univ.; Law Practitioner Certificate; Chair. four Judicial Inquiry Comms; submitted reports to the Govt as Chair. of four Probe Commissions on the causes of air accidents in Nepal; Chair. Nepal Bar Council, Nepal Notary Public Council; mem. Judicial Service Comm.; Returning Officer in elections of 1990; Chair. of monitoring team in elections to Constituent Ass. 2008; Attorney-Gen. –2014; Suprabal Gorkha Dakshin Bahu III from HM the King 2003. *Publications:* articles and papers in law journals, periodic publs and other law and justice magazines and newspapers in Nepal. *Leisure interests:* gardening, playing harmonica, study, travelling. *Address:* Kirtipur-2, Maitrinagar, Kathmandu, Nepal.

REGMI, Khil Raj, BA, BL, MA; Nepalese judge and politician; b. 31 May 1949, Palpa; m.; three c.; ed Tribhuvan Univ.; Kathmandu Section Officer, Supreme Court of Nepal 1972–74; Judge, Dist Court 1974–85; Kathmandu Deputy Registrar 1985–91; Judge, Appellate Court 1991–96, Chief Judge 1996–2003; Justice, Supreme Court 2003–11, Chief Justice 2011–14; Chair. Council of Ministers, and Minister of Defence, and of Co-operatives and Poverty Alleviation (in interim govt) 2013–14.

REGO, Paula, DBE; British (b. Portuguese) artist; b. 26 Jan. 1935, Lisbon, Portugal; d. of José Figueiroa Rego and Maria de San José Paiva Figueiroa Rego; m. Victor Willing (died 1988); one s. two d.; ed St Julian's School, Carcavelos, Portugal, Slade School of Fine Art, Univ. Coll., London; Assoc. Artist to Nat. Gallery 1990; Sr Fellow, RCA 1989; Dr hc (St Andrews), Univ. of E Anglia), (Rhode Island School of Design) 2000, (London Inst.) 2002, (Univ. Coll. London) 2004, (Oxford) 2005, (Univ. of Roehampton) 2005, (Royal Coll. of Art) 2008. *Television:* The South Bank Show 1992, Artsworld 'The Passion of Paula Rego' 2001, Paula Rego (BBC Four) 2002. *Publications:* Monograph Phaidon 1992, 1997, Peter Pan (etchings) 1992, Nursery Rhymes (etchings) 1994, Pendle Witches (etchings) 1996, Children's Crusade (etchings) 1999, Monograph 2002, Complete Graphic Work 2003, Jane Eyre 2003. *Address:* c/o Marlborough Fine Art, 6 Albemarle Street, London, W1X 4BY, England.

REGY, Claude, LLB; French theatre director; b. 1 May 1923, Nîmes; s. of Marcel Régy and Suzanne Picheral; ed Univs of Algiers, Lyon and Paris; dir of plays by Marguerite Duras, Harold Pinter, James Saunders, Tom Stoppard, Edward Bond, David Storey 1960–70, by Nathalie Sarraute, Peter Handke, Botho Strauss 1970–80, by Maurice Maeterlinck, Wallace Stevens, Leslie Kaplan, Victor Slavkine 1980–90, by Gregory Motton, Henri Meschonnic, Charles Reznifoff, Jon Fosse, David Harrower 1990–2000; dir Ivanov (Chekhov) 1985, Huis-Clos (J. P. Sartre) 1990 (both at Comédie Française), Melancholia Théâtre (J. Fosse) 2001, 4.48 Psychose (S. Kane) 2002, Variations sur la mort (J. Fosse) 2003, Comme un chant de David (H. Meschonnic) 2005, Homme sans but (A. Lygre) 2007, Ode maritime (F. Pessoa) 2009, Brume de Dieu (T. Vesaas) 2010, La Barque le soir (T. Vesaas) 2012, Intérieur (M. Maeterlinck) 2013–14, Rêve et Folie (G. Trakl) 2016; dir operas, Die Meistersinger von Nürnberg (Wagner), Théâtre du Chatelet 1990, Jeanne d'Arc au Bûcher (Honegger), Opéra Bastille 1992, Carnet d'un Disparu (Janacek), Kunsten Festival des Arts, Festival d'Aix-en-Provence 2001; Artistic Dir Les Ateliers Contemporains 1976–2018 (retd); Officier des Arts et des Lettres; Kongelige Norske Fortjenstorden; Grand Prix Nat. du Théâtre 1992, Grand Prix des Arts de la Scène de la Ville de Paris 1994. *Film:* Conversation avec Nathalie Sarraute 1989. *Publications:* Espaces Perdus 1991, L'Ordre des Morts 1999, L'Etat d'Incertitude 2002, Au-delà des larmes 2007, La Brulure du monde 2011, Dans le désordre 2011, Du régal pour les vautours 2016. *Address:* Les Ateliers Contemporains, 68 rue J.J. Rousseau, 75001 Paris, France (office). *Telephone:* 1-48-87-95-10 (office). *E-mail:* atelierscontemporains@gmail.com (office). *Website:* claude-regy-theatre.fr (office).

REHMAN, Maulana Fazlur, MA; Pakistani politician; *Leader, Jamiat-e-Ulema-e-Islam—Fazlur;* b. 1 Dec. 1950, Abdulkhel Banyala area in Dera Ismail Khan dist, North-West Frontier Prov.; s. of Mufti Mehmood; ed Dar-al-Ulum Haqania, Akura, Khatak, Univ. of Peshawar, Al-Azhar Univ.; Sec.-Gen. Jamiat-e-Ulema-e-Islam 1974–2007, Leader, Jamiat-e-Ulema-e-Islam—Fazlur (JUI—F) 2007–, fmr Sec.-Gen. Muttahida Majlis-e-Amal political coalition, Head 2018–; mem. Nat. Ass. (Dera Ismail Khan Constituency) 1988–90, 2008–13, (Bannu Consistuency) 1993–96, 2002–07, 2013–18, fmr Leader of the Opposition. *Address:* Jamiat-e-Ulema-e-Islam—Fazlur, Jamia Madnia, Kareem Park, Ravi Road, Lahore, Pakistan (office).

REHMAN, Shehrbano (Sherry), BA, MA; Pakistani journalist, politician and diplomatist; b. 21 Dec. 1960, Karachi; d. of Hassanally A. Rahman Zubedi; m. Nadeem Hussain; one c.; ed Smith Coll., Mass, USA, Univ. of Sussex, UK; journalist for nat. and int. newspapers and journals, including fmr Ed.-in-Chief The Herald (monthly news magazine); mem. Nat. Ass. (Parl.) 2002–07, 2008; Minister for Information and Broadcasting 2008–09; Amb. to USA 2012–13; Guest Lecturer, School of Advanced Int. Studies, Johns Hopkins Univ., USA Nov. 2004; mem. Pakistan Peoples Party (PPP), currently Vice-Pres.; mem. Senate of Pakistan for Sindh 2015–, Leader of Opposition 2018–; mem. Council of Pakistan Newspaper Editors 1988–98; Chair. Lady Dufferin Foundation Trust; Founding Chair. Jinnah Inst. (think-tank), also Pres.; fmr mem. Parliamentarians Network for Conflict Prevention at East West Inst., Brussels, Parliamentarians for Global Action, New York; awarded title of Democracy's Hero, Int. Republican Inst. 2009, Nishan-i-Imtiaz 2013. *Publication:* The Kashmiri Shawl: From Jamawar to Paisley (co-author) 2006. *Address:* Pakistan Peoples Party (PPP), 8, St 19, F-8/2, Islamabad, Pakistan (office). *Telephone:* (51) 2255264 (office). *Fax:* (51) 2282741 (office). *E-mail:* ppp@comsats.net.pk (office). *Website:* www.sherryrehman.com.

REHME, Robert; American film producer; b. 5 May 1935, Cincinnati, Ohio; s. of Gordon W. Rehme and Helen Rehme (neé Henkel); m. Kay Yazell 1964; two d.; ed Univ. of Cincinnati; Pres. and CEO Avco Embassy Pictures 1978–81; Pres. Worldwide Distribution and Marketing, Universal Pictures, then Pres. Theatrical Motion Picture Group 1981–83; Co-Chair. and CEO New World Entertainment Inc. 1983–89; Co-Founder and Pnr Neufeld/Rehme Productions 1989; currently Head Rehme Productions, Los Angeles; Pres. Acad. of Motion Picture Arts and Sciences 1992–93, 1997–2001; mem. Bd of Trustees American Film Inst., Chair Center for Advanced Film and TV Studies (CAFTS–AFI Conservatory) 2000–; mem. BAFTA. *Films:* An Eye for an Eye 1981, Vice Squad 1982, Flight of the Intruder 1991, Necessary Roughness 1991, Patriot Games 1992, Beverly Hills Cop 3 1994, Clear and Present Danger 1994, Blind Faith 1998, Lost in Space 1998, Black Dog 1998, Bless the Child 2000, Gods and Generals 2003, Asylum 2005. *Television:* Lightning Force (series) 1991, Woman Undone 1996, Gridlock 1996, For the Future: The Irvine Fertility Scandal 1996, Escape: Human Cargo 1998, Love and Treason 2001, Conviction 2002, Deacons for Defense 2003. *Address:* Rehme Productions, 10956 Weyburn Avenue, Los Angeles, CA 90024, USA (office).

REHN, Elisabeth, BSc, DSc; Finnish politician and international organization official; b. (Elisabeth Carlberg), 6 April 1935, Helsinki; m. Ove Rehn 1955 (deceased); two s. two d.; ed Grankulla Samskola Swedish School of Econs, Helsinki; mem. Parl. 1979–95; Minister of Defence 1990–95, Minister for Equality 1991–95; cand. in Finnish Presidential election 1994, 2000; mem. European Parl. 1995–96; UN Special Rapporteur for Human Rights in Fmr Yugoslavia 1995–98; UN Under-Sec.-Gen., Special Rep. of UN Sec.-Gen. in Bosnia and Herzegovina 1998–99; UNIFEM Ind. Expert on impact of war on women 2001–02; Chair. Working Table I (Human Rights and Democratisation), Stability Pact for SE Europe, Brussels 2003–04; Chair. Finnish Asscn for Educ. and Training of Women in Crisis Prevention 1997; mem. UN Dept of Peacekeeping Review Bd, Court of Conciliation and Arbitration, OSCE 1994, Int. Steering Cttee of Engendering The Peace Process; mem. UNICEF Finnish Cttee 1982–94, Chair. 1988–93; Vice-Chair. Finnish Red Cross 1984–88; Chair. Bd of Trustees, WWF Finland 2000–06; Vice-Chair. Suomen Unifem ry 2003–05; mem. Bd of Dirs Trust Fund for Victims, Int. Criminal Court, The Hague; mem. Advisory Bd Femmes Africa Solidarité 2005–, Global Leadership Foundation (Switzerland) 2006–, Advisory Bds of European Leadership Network, Women In Int. Security, Women's Regional Lobby (Balkans); Patron United World Coll. project in Bosnia and Herzegovina 2005–; Hon. mem. UNICEF Finland 1994, Zonta Int. 1996; Commdr, Order of the White Rose of Finland 1992, Cross of Liberty, First Class with Grand Star (Finland) 2002, First Class Order, Cross of Terra Mariana (Estonia) 2003, Vuoden Lotta 2011; Hon. DSc (Swedish School of Econs and Business Admin) 1994, Hon. DEcon, Dr hc (Nat. Defence Univ.) 2013. *Publication:* Women, War, Peace (with Ellen Johnson-Sirleaf) 2002. *Leisure interests:* int. politics, sports, nature. *Address:* Saarentie 22, 02400 Kirkkonummi, Finland (home). *Telephone:* 40-5149369 (mobile); (9) 2952842 (home). *E-mail:* elisabeth.rehn@kolumbus.fi (home). *Website:* www .elisabethrehn.com.

REHN, Olli, DPhil; Finnish politician and international organization official; *Governor and Chairman, Bank of Finland;* b. 31 March 1962, Mikkeli; m. Merja Rehn; one c.; ed Macalester Coll., USA, Univ. of Helsinki, Univ. of Oxford, UK; Chair. Centre Youth of Finland 1987–89; Deputy Chair. Centre Party of Finland 1988–94; mem. Helsinki City Council 1988–94; mem. Parl. 1991–95; Special Adviser to Prime Minister 1992–93, Econ. Policy Adviser 2003–04; mem. European Parl. 1995–96; Head of Cabinet, EC 1998–2002, Commr for Enterprise and the

Information Soc. July–Nov. 2004, for Enlargement 2004–10, Vice-Pres. for Econ. and Monetary Affairs and the Euro 2010–14; Prof. and Dir of Research, Dept of Political Science and Centre for European Studies, Univ. of Helsinki 2002–03; Minister of Econ. Affairs 2015–16; mem. Bd Bank of Finland 2016– (Gov. and Chair. 2018–); columnist in several newspapers and magazines; Commissioner of Year, European Voice 2006, Alumnus of Year, Univ. of Helsinki 2011. *Publications:* Europe's Next Frontiers 2006, Suomen eurooppaiainen valinta ei ole suhdannepolitiikkaa 2006. *Leisure interests:* football, reading, rock and jazz. *Address:* Bank of Finland, PO Box 160, 00101 Helsinki, Finland (office). *Telephone:* (9) 1832626 (office). *Fax:* (9) 658424 (office). *E-mail:* info@bof.fi (office). *Website:* www.suomenpankki.fi (office).

REICH, Otto Juan; Cuban/American consultant and fmr government official; *President, Otto Reich Associates LLC;* b. 1945, Cuba; ed Univ. of N Carolina, Georgetown Univ.; Lt, 3rd Civil Affairs Detachment, Panama Canal Zone, US Army 1967–69; Asst Admin. Econ. Assistance to Latin America and the Caribbean, USAID 1981–83; Special Adviser to Sec. of State 1983–86; Founder and Man. Office of Public Diplomacy for Latin America, the Caribbean and US Dept of State 1983–86; Amb. to Venezuela 1986–89; Alt. Rep. to UN Human Rights Comm., Geneva 1991–92; Asst Sec. of State for Western Hemisphere Affairs 2001–02, Special Envoy Nov. 2002–Jan. 2003; Presidential Special Envoy for Latin America, Nat. Security Council 2003–04; Partner, later Pres. Brock Group (consulting firm) 1989–2001; currently Pres. Otto Reich Assocs LLC (consulting firm), Washington, DC; co-host CNN Int.'s Choque de Opiniones public affairs programme 1998–2001; Dir Center for a Free Cuba, Washington, DC; lobbyist for numerous cos including Bacardi and Lockheed Martin; fmr Washington Dir Council of the Americas; fmr Community Devt Co-ordinator for City of Miami, FL; fmr Int. Rep. of FL Dept of Commerce; fmr staff asst, US House of Reps; Meritorious Honour Award, Dept of State. *Address:* Otto Reich Associates LLC, 1101 30th Street, NW, Suite 200, Washington, DC 20007, USA (office). *Telephone:* (202) 333-1360 (office). *E-mail:* ora@ottoreichassociates.com (office). *Website:* www.ottoreichassociates.net (office).

REICH, Robert Bernard, BA, MA, JD; American political economist, academic and fmr government official; *Chancellor's Professor of Public Policy, University of California, Berkeley;* b. 24 June 1946, Scranton, Pa; s. of Edwin Saul Reich and Mildred Dorf Reich (née Freshman); m. Clare Dalton 1973; two s.; ed Dartmouth Coll., Univ. of Oxford, UK (Rhodes Scholar), Yale Univ.; Asst Solicitor-Gen., Dept of Justice, Washington, DC 1974–76; Dir of Policy Planning Fed. Trade Comm., Washington 1976–81; mem. Faculty, John F. Kennedy School of Govt, Harvard Univ. 1981–92; fmr Econ. Adviser to Pres. Bill Clinton (q.v.); Sec. of Labor 1993–97; Univ. Prof., Maurice B. Hexter Prof. of Social and Econ. Policy, Brandeis Univ. Grad. School for Advanced Studies in Social Welfare 1997–2006; Prof. of Public Policy, Goldman School of Public Policy, Univ. of California, Berkeley 2006, now Chancellor's Prof. of Public Policy, Sr Fellow, Blum Center for Developing Economies; Chair. Biotechnology Section, US Office Tech. Assessment, Washington, DC 1990–91; Co-founder and Chair. Editorial Bd The American Prospect 2002–03; mem. Nat. Governing Bd, Common Cause 1982–88; mem. Mass Comm. on Mature Industries 1985–87; mem. Bd of Dirs Business Enterprise Trust 1986–93, Econ. Policy Inst. 1988–93, 2002–03; Trustee, Dartmouth Coll. 1988–93; Contributing Ed. The New Republic 1982–93; Dr hc (Dartmouth Coll.) 1994, (Univ. of New Hampshire) 1997, (Wheaton Coll.) 1998, (Emory Univ.) 1999, (Bates Coll.) 2001, (Grinnell Coll.) 2002, (Pacific Lutheran Univ.) 2008, (California State Fullerton) 2008; Mass Teachers Asscn Award for Excellence 1997, Lifetime Achievement Award, Nat. Ass. of Voluntary Health and Social Welfare Orgs 1997, Eleanor Roosevelt Award for Public Service, Americans for Democratic Action 2001, Nelson Rockefeller Distinguished Public Service Award, Dartmouth Coll. 2002, Vaclev Havel Humanitarian Prize 2003, Galbraith-Schlesigner Award for Lifetime Achievement, Americans for Democratic Action 2009. *Films:* Inequality for All (documentary) 2013. *Publications include:* The Next American Frontier 1983, Tales of a New America 1987, The Power of Public Ideas (co-author) 1987, The Work of Nations 1991, Putting People First 1997, Locked in the Cabinet 1997, The Future of Success 2001, Reason: Why Liberals Will Win the Battle for America 2004, Supercapitalism: The Transformation of Business, Democracy and Everyday Life (Bruno-Kreisky Award 2009) 2007, Aftershock: The Next Economy and America's Future 2010, Beyond Outrage 2012. *Address:* Richard & Rhoda Goldman School of Public Policy, University of California Berkeley, 2607 Hearst Avenue, mail code 7320, Berkeley, CA 94720-7320, USA (office). *Telephone:* (510) 642-0551 (office). *E-mail:* rreich@berkeley.edu (office); bob@RobertReich.org. *Website:* gspp.berkeley.edu/directories/faculty/robert-reich (office); www.robertreich.org.

REICH, Steve, MA; American composer; b. 3 Oct. 1936, New York; s. of Leonard Reich and June Carroll; m. Beryl Korot 1976; two s.; ed Cornell Univ., Juilliard School of Music, Mills Coll., studied composition with Berio and Milhaud, also studied at American Soc. for Eastern Arts and in Accra and Jerusalem; f. own ensemble 1966; Steve Reich and Musicians have completed numerous tours worldwide 1971–; his music performed by maj. orchestras and ensembles in United States and Europe; Montgomery Fellowship, Dartmouth Coll.; Chubb Fellowship, Yale Univ. 2007; mem. American Acad. of Arts and Letters 1994–, Bavarian Acad. of Fine Arts 1995–, Royal Swedish Acad. of Music 2008–; Commdr des Arts et Lettres 1999; Dr hc (Calif. Inst. of the Arts) 2000, (Royal Coll. of Music) 2016; recipient of three Rockefeller Foundation Grants 1975–81 and a Guggenheim Fellowship, Koussevitzky Foundation Award 1981, Schumann Prize, Columbia Univ. 2000, Regent Lectureship, Univ. of Calif., Berkeley 2000, Praemium Imperiale Music Laureate, Japan 2006, Polar Prize, Royal Swedish Acad. of Music 2007, awarded membership in Franz Liszt Acad., Budapest 2006. *Works include:* Electric Guitar Phase for electric guitar and pre-recorded tape (arrangement of Violin Phase 1967) 2000, Tokyo/Vermont Counterpoint for KAT MIDI mallet and pre-recorded tape (arrangement of Vermont Counterpoint 1981) 2000, Three Tales (video opera, video by Beryl Korot) 2002, Dance Patterns for 2 xylophones, 2 vibraphones, 2 pianofortes 2002, Cello Counterpoint for amplified cello and multi-channel tape 2003, You Are (Variations) (text by Rabbi Nachman of Breslov (English), Psalms (Hebrew), Wittgenstein (English) and Pirke Avot (Hebrew) for amplified ensemble and voices, no brass, 2 marimbas, 2 vibraphones, 4 pianofortes, strings, and voices 2004, The Daniel Variations 2006, Double Sextet (Pulitzer Prize in Music 2009) 2008, Finishing the Hat (for two pianos) 2011, Runner (for large ensemble) 2015, Pulse (for winds, strings, piano and electric bass) 2016. *Recordings include:* Come Out, Violin Phase, It's Gonna Rain, Four Organs, Drumming, Six Pianos, Music for Mallet Instruments, Voices and Organ, Music for a Large Ensemble, Octet and Variations for Winds, Strings and Keyboards, Music for 18 Musicians, The Desert Music, Electric Counterpoint, Different Trains, The Four Sections, Nagoya Marimbas, City Life, Proverb, Hindenburg (in collaboration with Beryl Korot), Double Sextet. *Address:* Howard Stokar Management, 870 West End Avenue, New York, NY 10025-4918, USA (office). *Telephone:* (212) 866-5798 (office). *E-mail:* hstokar@stokar.com (office). *Website:* www.stevereich.com.

REICHS, Kathleen (Kathy) J., BA, MA, PhD; American writer and forensic anthropologist; *Professor Emeritus, University of North Carolina;* b. 7 July 1948, Chicago, Ill.; m. Paul Reichs; two d. one s.; ed American Univ., Northwestern Univ.; Asst Prof., Northern Illinois Univ. 1974–78; Instructor, Stateville Correctional Facility, Joliet, Ill. 1975–78; Asst Prof., Davidson Coll. 1981–83; Lecturer, Univ. of North Carolina at Charlotte 1978–81, 1983–87, Asst Prof. 1987–88, Assoc. Prof. 1988–96, then Prof., now Prof. Emer.; works as forensic anthropologist at Office of the Chief Medical Examiner, State of North Carolina and Laboratoires des Sciences Judiciaires et de Médecine Légale, Canada; Visiting Prof., Univ. of Pittsburgh 1987, Visiting Assoc. Prof., Concordia Univ. 1988–89, McGill Univ. 1988–97 (summers); mem. American Acad. of Forensic Sciences (fmr Vice-Pres. mem. Bd of Dirs); mem. Bd of Dirs American Bd of Forensic Anthropology 1986–93, Vice-Pres. 1989–93; mem. Canadian Nat. Police Services Advisory Council; Premio Piemonte Grinzane Noir, Vincitore Sezione Giallo Internazionale Award (Italy) 2007. *Television:* producer of series Bones 2005–14. *Publications include:* Déjà Dead (Ellis Award for Best First Novel) 1997, Death du Jour 1999, Deadly Decisions 2000, Fatal Voyage 2001, Grave Secrets 2002, Bare Bones 2003, Monday Mourning 2004, Cross Bones 2005, Bones to Ashes 2007, Devil Bones 2008, 206 Bones 2009, Spider Bones 2010, Mortal Remains 2010, Flash and Bones 2011, Virals 2011, Seizure 2011, Bones Are Forever 2012, Bones In Her Pocket 2013, Bones Of The Lost 2013, Swamp Bones 2014, Bones Never Lie 2014, Speaking in Bones 2015. *E-mail:* kjreichs@aol.com. *Website:* www.kathyreichs.com.

REICHSTUL, Henri Philippe; Brazilian business executive; *CEO, Brenco (Brazilian Renewable Energy Company);* b. 12 April 1949; Deputy Minister of Planning 1985–88; Partner and Vice-Pres. Banco Interamerican Express 1998–99; Pres. Petrobras 1999–2002; CEO Globopar SA 2002–03; Founding Partner, G&R Gestao Empresarial (consulting firm); fmr Economist, Int. Coffee Org., London, Gazeta Mercantil newspaper, Sao Paulo; Controller, State Enterprises, Sao Paulo Revenue Dept; Sec., Budget Office, State Companies; fmr Sec., Secretaria de Controle de Empresas Estatais, office of the Secretariat of Planning, Office of the Pres.; Exec. Sec., Inter-Ministry Council, Conselho Interministerial de Salários de Empresas Estatais; currently CEO Brenco (Brazilian Renewable Energy Co.); mem. Bd of Dirs Net Serviços de Comunicação, SA 2002–, Refineria La Pampilla S.A.A, AEI Services LLC 2003–, Vivo Participações, SA 2005–, Companhia Brasileira de Distribuicao 2005–, REPSOL-YPF, PSA-Peugeot Citroen (also Supervisory Bd 2007–), Tam SA 2004–07, Repsol, SA 2005–17, Gafisa SA 2011–, Foster Wheeler AG 2011–14, LATAM Airlines Group SA 2014–, BRF SA 2015–17, Brazilian Foundation for Sustainable Devt (also Vice-Chair.); fmr mem. Bd of Dirs, YPF SA, Ashmore Energy Internacional; mem. Consulting Bd, Lhoist Brazil; mem. Admin. Council, Grupo Pão de Açúcar 2003–. *Address:* Brenco, Avenida Brigadeira Faria Lima, 1309 4° andar, São Paulo CEP 01452-002, Brazil (office). *Telephone:* (11) 3095-2250 (office). *E-mail:* brenco@brenco.com.br (office). *Website:* www.brenco.com.br (office).

REID, Sir David Edward, Kt, CA; British business executive and chartered accountant; *Chairman, Intertek Group plc;* b. 5 Feb. 1947, Zambia; two d.; ed Fettes Coll., Univ. of Aberdeen; qualified as chartered accountant; worked for Peat Marwick Mitchell 1970, Philips Industries and BAT Industries –1985; fmr Chief Accountant, Philips Video, then for Int. Stores –1985; Dir of Finance, Tesco plc 1985–97, Deputy Chair. 1997–2004, Chair. (non-exec.) 2004–11; Chair. Kwik-Fit Group Ltd 2006–11; Chair. Intertek Group PLC 2012–; fmr Dir (non-exec.) Legal & General Group PLC, Westbury PLC, De Vere Group, Reed Elsevier Group PLC; Chair. Whizz-Kidz (charity), London Scottish Rugby Club; apptd one of Prime Minister David Cameron's Business Ambs 2010; Founder and Trustee, The Fettes Foundation; mem. Inst. of Chartered Accountants (Scotland); mem. Global Sr Advisory Bd, Jefferies Int. Ltd 2012–; Patron, Restless Devt. *Leisure interests:* golf. *Address:* Intertek Group PLC, 25 Savile Row, London, W1S 2ES, England (office). *Telephone:* (20) 7396-3400 (office). *Fax:* (20) 7396-3480 (office). *Website:* www.intertek.com (office).

REID, Harry Mason, BS JD; American lawyer and politician; b. 2 Dec. 1939, Searchlight, Nev.; s. of Harry Reid, Sr and Inez Reid; m. Landra Joy Gould 1959; four s. one d.; ed Utah State Univ., George Washington Univ.; City Attorney, Henderson, Nev. 1964–66; Trustee, Southern Nev. Memorial Hosp. Bd 1967–69, Chair. Bd of Trustees 1968–69; mem. Nev. Ass. 1968–70; Lt-Gov. of Nev. 1970–74; Chair. Nev. Gaming Comm. 1977–82; mem. US House of Reps, Washington, DC 1982–87; Senator from Nevada 1986–2017, Minority Whip 1999–2001, Jan.–June 2001, 2003–05, Majority Whip Jan. 2001, June 2001–03, Minority Leader 2005–07, 2015–17, Majority Leader 2007–15; mem. Bd of Dirs American Cancer Soc., Legal Aid Soc., YMCA; Democrat; Hon. LLD (Southern Utah State Coll.) 1984; Humanitarian Award, Nat. Jewish Hosp. 1984. *Website:* www.harryreid.com.

REID, Sir Robert Paul (Bob), Kt, MA; British business executive; b. 1 May 1934, Cupar, Fife, Scotland; m. Joan Mary Reid 1958; three s.; ed St Andrews Univ.; joined Shell 1956, Sarawak Oilfields 1956–59, Head of Personnel Nigeria 1959–67; Africa and S. Asia Regional Org. 1967–68, Personal Asst and Planning Adviser to Chair. Shell & BP Services, Kenya 1968–70, Man. Dir Nigeria 1970–74, Man. Dir Thailand 1974–78; Vice-Pres. Int. Aviation and Products Training 1978–80, Exec. Dir Downstream Oil, Shell Co. of Australia Int. Petroleum Co. 1984–90, Chair. and Chief Exec. Shell UK 1985–90; Chair. Foundation for Man. Educ. 1986–2003; Chair. British Railways Bd 1990–95, London Electricity PLC 1994–97, Sears PLC 1995–99, Rosyth 2000 1995–, ICE Futures Europe (fmrly Int. Petroleum Exchange of London) 1999–2016, Milton Keynes Partnership Cttee 2004–08, ICE Clear Europe –2017; Deputy Gov. Bank of Scotland 1997–2004; mem. Bd of Dirs The Merchants Trust 1995–2008, Avis 1997–2004, Sun Life Assurance Co. of Canada 1997–2004, Siemens plc 1998–2006, Intercontinental Exchange Inc. 2001, HBOS 2001–04, CHC Helicopter Corpn 2004–08, Benalla Ltd 2004–, Diligenta Ltd 2005–,

EEA Helicopter Operations 2008–, Belltree 2017–, Liffe Admin and Man.; Chancellor Robert Gordon Univ. 1993–2004; Hon. LLD (St Andrews) 1987, (Aberdeen) 1988, (Sheffield Hallam) 1995, (South Bank) 1995, (Kent) 2003; Hon. DLitt (Heriot-Watt) 2018. *Leisure interests:* golf, opera. *Address:* Belltree Ltd, 14-16 Jackson's Entry, The Tun, Holyrood Road, Edinburgh, EH8 8PJ, Scotland (office); 24 Ashley Gardens, London, SW1P 1QD, England (home). *Telephone:* (131) 225-4428 (office). *Fax:* (131) 225-3796 (office). *E-mail:* info@belltreegroup.co.uk (office). *Website:* www.belltreegroup.co.uk (office).

REID, Timothy (Tim) Escott Herriot, MA, MLitt; Canadian economist, public servant and university administrator; b. 21 Feb. 1936, Toronto, Ont.; s. of Escott Meredith Reid and Ruth Reid (née Herriot); m. Julyan Fancott 1962 (deceased); one s. one d.; ed Univ. of Toronto, Yale Univ., USA, Univ. of Oxford (Rhodes Scholar), UK, Harvard Grad. School of Business; Halfback, Hamilton Tigercats Football Club 1962; Exec. Sec. Canadian Inst. of Public Affairs 1962–63; Asst to Pres., Asst Prof. of Econs, Research Assoc. for Public Policy, York Univ. 1963–72; mem. Ont. Legis. Ass. 1967–71; Prin. Admin., Manpower and Social Affairs, OECD, Paris 1972–74; joined Public Service of Canada 1974, subsequently Deputy Sec. Treasury Bd, Office of Comptroller-Gen. of Canada, Asst Deputy Minister, Dept of Regional Econ. Expansion, Exec. Dir Regional and Industrial Program Affairs, Dept of Regional Industrial Expansion, Asst Deputy Minister responsible for Tourism Canada 1984–85; Referee, NSF (USA) 1979–82; Chair. Research Cttee, Inst. of Public Admin of Canada 1985–87; Dir and mem. exec. Cttee Canada Mortgage and Housing Corpn 1980–82, Canadian Labour Market and Productivity Centre 1989 (Co-Chair. Bd of Dirs 1993–97); Chair. Working Party on Regional Devel, OECD 1982–84, headed 18-nation OECD study visit to Japan 1984; Prof. of Business Man. and Dean, Faculty of Business, Ryerson Polytechnical Inst. 1985–89; Commr Ont. Securities Comm. 1987–89; Prime Minister's Business Rep., Pacific Business Forum APEC 1994, 1995; Pres. Canadian Chamber of Commerce 1989–98; Chair. Advisory Cttee, Faculty of Admin. Studies, Univ. of Ottawa 1992–94, Trade and Security Advisory Cttee, Toronto Bd of Trade 2001–03; Founding mem. and Venture Investor XPV Capital Corpn 2001–05; Chair. Bd of Dirs Ontario Lottery and Gaming Corpn 2004–06; mem. Bd of Dirs Canadian Exec. Service Org. 1991–95, Inst. of Corp. Dirs 1999–2003, VIA Rail Canada Corpn 2000–07; mem. Provisional Council, Co. of Young Canadians 1966–70, Int. Trade Advisory Cttee, Govt of Canada 1991–97; Gov., Univ. of Toronto Governing Council 2002–11 (Exec. Cttee 2006–11); mem. Laurier Club, Liberal Party of Canada; Patron, Canadian Inst. of Int. Affairs 1999–2003; 125 Anniversary Commemorative Medal for Community Contribution, Canada 1992, Queen's Golden Jubilee Medal 2002, inducted into Univ. of Toronto Sports Hall of Fame, Arbour Award for Outstanding Voluntary Service, Univ. of Toronto. *Publications include:* Contemporary Canada: Reading in Economics 1969, Student Power and the Canadian Campus (with Julyan Reid) 1969. *Leisure interests:* tennis, swimming, pilates, weight training. *Address:* 25 Scrivener Square, Suite 904, Toronto, ON M4W 3Y6, Canada (home).

REID OF CARDOWAN, Baron (Life Peer), cr. 2010, of Stepps in Lanarkshire; **John Reid,** PC, PhD; British politician and sports administrator; b. 8 May 1947, Bellshill, Lanarkshire; s. of Thomas Reid and Mary Reid; m. 1st Catherine McGowan (died 1998); two s.; m. 2nd Carine Adler 2002; ed St Patrick's Sr Secondary School, Coatbridge and Stirling Univ.; Research Officer, Labour Party 1979–83; Political Adviser to Neil Kinnock 1983–85; Organizer, Scottish Trade Unionists for Labour 1985–87; MP for Motherwell N 1987–97, for Hamilton N and Bellshill 1997–2005, for Airdrie and Shotts 2005–10; Opposition Spokesman on Children 1989–90, on Defence 1990–97; Minister of State for Defence 1997–98; Minister for Transport 1998–99; Sec. of State for Scotland 1999–2000; Sec. of State for NI 2000–02; Chair. of the Labour Party and Minister without Portfolio 2002–03; Leader of the House of Commons and Pres. of the Privy Council April–June 2003; Sec. of State for Health 2003–05, for Defence 2005–06, for the Home Department 2006–07 (resgnd); Chair. Celtic Football Club, Glasgow 2007–11; f. John Reid Advisory Ltd 2007; Sr Advisor, The Chertoff Group; Hon. Prof. and Chair. Inst. for Security and Resilience Studies, Univ. Coll., London; mem. Armed Forces Cttee and Reserved Forces Cttee 1996–97. *Leisure interests:* football, reading history, crossword puzzles. *Address:* House of Lords, London, SW1A 0PW, England. *Telephone:* (20) 7219-5353. *Fax:* (20) 7219- 2771.

REIDY, Carolyn Kroll, AB, MA, PhD; American publishing executive; *President and CEO, Simon and Schuster, Inc.;* b. (Carolyn Judith Kroll), 2 May 1949, Washington, DC; d. of Henry Kroll and Mildred Kroll; m. Stephen K. Reidy 1974; ed Middlebury Coll., Indiana Univ.; held various positions, Random House, New York 1975–83; Dir of Subsidiary Rights, William Morrow & Co., New York 1983–85; Vice-Pres. Assoc. Publr, Vintage Books, Random House, New York 1985–87; Assoc. Publr, Random House (concurrent with Assoc. Publr and Publr of Vintage Books) 1987–88; Publr, Vintage Books 1987–88, Anchor Books, Doubleday, New York 1988; Pres. and Publr, Avon Books, New York 1988–92; Pres. and Publr, Simon and Schuster Trade Div. 1992–2001, Pres. Adult Publishing Div., Simon and Schuster 2001–08, Pres. and CEO 2008–; Dir NAMES Project 1994–98, New York Univ. Center for Publishing 1997–2008, Literacy Partners, Inc. 1999–2011, Nat. Book Foundation 2000–; Matrix Award 2002, Distinguished Alumna, Indiana Univ. 2011. *Address:* Simon and Schuster, Inc., 1230 Avenue of the Americas, New York, NY 10020, USA (office). *Telephone:* (212) 698-7323 (office). *Fax:* (212) 698-1258 (office). *E-mail:* carolyn.reidy@simonandschuster.com (office). *Website:* simonandschuster.com (office).

REIF, Rafael, PhD; American/ Venezuela computer scientist, academic and university administrator; *President, Massachusetts Institute of Technology;* b. 21 Aug. 1950, Maracaibo, Venezuela; ed Stanford Univ.; mem. Faculty, MIT 1980–, held the Analog Devices Career Devt Professorship in Electrical Eng and Computer Science (EECS) Dept and an IBM Faculty Fellowship from MIT's Center for Materials Science and Eng, served as Dir MIT's Microsystems Tech. Labs, as Assoc. Dept Head for Electrical Eng, EECS Dept and as EECS Dept Head, named Fariborz Maseeh Prof. of Emerging Tech. 2004, Provost of MIT 2005–12, Pres. 2012–; Asst Prof., Universidad Simón Bolívar, Caracas for four years; fmr Visiting Asst Prof., Stanford Univ.; mem. American Acad. of Arts and Sciences, Electrochemical Soc.; Trustee, Carnegie Endowment for Int. Peace; Fellow, IEEE 1993; Hon. LLD (Chinese Univ. of Hong Kong) 2015, Dr hc, (Tsinghua Univ.) 2016, (Technion) 2017, (Arizona State Univ.) 2018, Ingeniero Eléctrico (Universidad de Carabobo, Valencia, Venezuela); US Presidential Young Investigator Award 1984, Aristotle Award, Semiconductor Research Corpn 2000, Tribeca Disruptive Innovation Award 2012, named "Engineer of the Year" by Great Minds in STEM 2018. *Publications:* numerous papers in professional journals on three-dimensional integrated circuit technologies and on environmentally benign microelectronics fabrication; inventor or co-inventor on 15 patents; has edited or co-edited five books. *Address:* Office of the President, Massachusetts Institute of Technology, 77 Massachusetts Avenue, Building 3-208, Cambridge, MA 02139-4307, USA (office). *Telephone:* (617) 253-0148 (office). *Fax:* (617) 253-3124 (office). *E-mail:* president@mit.edu (office). *Website:* president.mit.edu (office).

REIJNDERS, Lucas, PhD; Dutch scientist and academic; *Professor of Environmental Science, University of Amsterdam;* b. 4 Feb. 1946, Amsterdam; s. of C. Reijnders and C. M. Reijnders-Spillekom; one c.; ed Univ. of Amsterdam; Dir Environmental Inst. Univ. of Groningen 1974–80, mem. staff Nat. Environmental Office 1980–, Prof. of Environmental Science Univ. of Amsterdam 1988–; Prof. of Environmental Science, Open Univ., Heerlen 1999–; Winner, Gouden Ganzeveer 1990, Erewimpel ONRI 1992. *Publications:* Food in the Netherlands 1974, A Consumer Guide to Dutch Medicines 1980, Plea for a Sustainable Relation with the Environment 1984, Help the Environment 1991, Environmentally Improved Production and Products 1995, Agriculture in the Low Countries 1997, Travel Through the Ages 2000, Eating Patterns 2005, Energy 2006, Principles of Environmental Science 2008, Biofuels for Road Transport 2009, Design Issues for Improved Performance of Dye-sensitized and Organic Nanoparticulate Cells 2010, Recycling of Elastomeric Nanocomposites 2011, Human Health Hazards of Persistent Inorganic and Carbon Nanoparticles 2012, The Production of Algal Biofuels 2013. *Leisure interest:* 19th-century literature. *Address:* Science Park 904, PO Box 94248, 1090 GE Amsterdam, Netherlands. *Telephone:* (20) 525-62-69. *Fax:* (20) 525-74-31. *E-mail:* l.reijnders@uva.nl. *Website:* www.uva.nl.

REILLY, (David) Nicholas (Nick), CBE, MA, FIMI; British automotive executive; b. 17 Dec. 1949, Anglesey, N Wales; s. of John Reilly and Mona Reilly (née Glynne Jones); m. Susan Haig 1976; one s. two d.; ed Harrow School, St Catharine's Coll., Cambridge; investment analyst 1971–74; joined Gen. Motors 1975, Finance Dir Moto Diesel Mexicana 1980–83, Supply Dir Vauxhall Motors 1984–87, Mfg Dir Vauxhall Ellesmere Port 1990–94, Vice-Pres. Quality Gen. Motors Europe 1994–96, Chair., Man. Dir Vauxhall Motors 1996–2001, Chair. (non-exec.) 2001, Vice-Pres. European Sales and Marketing, Gen. Motors Europe 2001, Pres. and CEO GM Daewoo Auto and Technology Co. 2002–06, Pres. GM Asia Pacific and GM Group Vice-Pres. 2006–09, also Chair. GM Daewoo Auto and Technology Co. Bd of Dirs, Pres. GM Int. Operations July–Dec. 2009, Pres. GM Europe Dec. 2009–12 (retd); Vice-Pres. IBC 1987–90, Chair. IBC Vehicles 1996; mem. Bd Saab GB 1996; Chair. Chester, Ellesmere, Wirral Training and Enterprise Council 1990–94, Training Standards Council 1997–2001, Adult Learning Inspectorate 2001; Pres. Soc. of Motor Mfrs and Traders 2001–02; Global CEO Grand Prize, Korean Acad. of Int. Business 2006. *Leisure interests:* skiing, swimming, sailing, golf, watching sports, music, opera, theatre.

REILLY, Kevin P., BA, MA, PhD; American academic and fmr university administrator; *President Emeritus and Regent Professor, University of Wisconsin;* m. Kate Reilly; three c.; ed Univ. of Notre Dame, Univ. of Minnesota; teaching assoc., Dept of English, Univ. of Minn. 1974–79; various posts NY State Bd of Regents 1979–92; Assoc. Provost for Acad. Programs State Univ. of NY System 1992–95, Sec. 1995–96; Provost and Vice-Chancellor, Univ. of Wis. (UW)-Extension 1996–2000, Chancellor 2000–04, Pres. UW System 2004–13, now Pres. Emer. and Regent Prof.; Sr Consultant, AGB (Asscn of Governing Bds) Consulting; Presidential Advisor for Leadership, American Council on Educ. 2014–; fmr Chair. American Council of Educ.'s Comm. on Adult Learning and Educational Credentials; Signature of Excellence Award, Univ. Continuing Educ. Asscn 2009. *Publications:* has written and edited books and articles on higher education policy, accreditation, biography and Irish studies. *Website:* celticstudies.wisc.edu.

REIMAN, Leonid Dododjonovich; Russian engineer, government official and business executive; *Chairman, Supervisory Board, Mandriva SA;* b. 12 July 1957, Leningrad (now St Petersburg); m.; one s. one d.; ed Leningrad Inst. of Electro-Tech. Communications; engineer, head of workshop Leningrad Telephone Exchange 1979–85; posts at Leningrad City Telephone Network 1985–88, later Deputy Head, Chief Eng, Dir of Int. Relations, Dir of Investments, First Deputy Dir-Gen. Jt Stock Co. Peterburgskaya Telefonnaya Set 1988–99; First Deputy Chair. State Cttee on Telecommunications Russian Fed. July–Aug. 1999; Chair. 1999–2000; Minister of Communications and Information Tech. 1999–2004; Deputy Minister for Transport and Communications April 2004; Minister of Information and Communications Tech. April 2004–08; Adviser to Pres. and Sec., Presidential Council of Information Soc. Devt 2008–10; Chair. Supervisory Bd Mandriva SA 2011–; Honoured Worker of Russian Telecommunications; Order of Merit for the Fatherland, Fourth Class 2005, Third Class 2007; Govt Prize in Educ., Science and Tech., Themis Legal Prize 2003, Person of the Year 2005. *Address:* Mandriva SA, 12 rue Vivienne, 75002 Paris, France (office). *Telephone:* 1-76-64-16-60 (office). *Fax:* 1-40-41-92-00 (office). *E-mail:* sales@mandriva.com (office). *Website:* www.mandriva.com (office).

REIN, Jeffrey A., BS; American retail executive; b. 28 Feb. 1952, New Orleans, La; ed Univ. of Arizona; joined Walgreens as Asst Man., Tucson 1982–84, Store Man., Tex. 1984–90, Dist Man., New Mexico 1990–96, Divisional Vice-Pres. and Treas. 1996–2000, Vice-Pres., Marketing Systems and Services 2000–01, Exec. Vice-Pres., Marketing 2001–03, Pres. and COO 2003–06, Pres. 2003–07, CEO 2006–08, Chair. 2007–08 (retd); mem. Bd of Dirs Stat Health Services 2012–, Nat. Asscn of Chain Drug Stores, Midwest Young Artists, Midtown Educational Foundation, Retail Industry Leaders Asscn, Medworth Acquisition Corpn 2013–; Chair. American Cancer Soc., Illinois Div. of CEOs Against Cancer.

REINEMUND, Steven S., MBA; American business executive; b. 1949; ed US Naval Acad., Univ. of Va; served as officer US Marine Corps 1970–75, achieved rank of Capt. 1975; joined PepsiCo 1984, Pres. and CEO Pizza Hut Div. 1986–91, Pres. and CEO Pizza Hut Worldwide 1991–92, Pres. and CEO Frito-Lay N America 1992–96, Chair. and CEO Frito-Lay Inc. 1996–99, Pres. and COO PepsiCo Inc. 1999–2001, Chair. and CEO PepsiCo Inc. 2001–06 (retd); mem. Bd of Dirs Johnson & Johnson 2003–, Exxon Mobil Corpn 2007–, Marriott Int. Inc. 2007–, American

Express Co., Business Council of New York State Inc.; fmr Chair. Nat. Minority Supplier Devt Council; mem. Nat. Advisory Bd The Salvation Army 1990–99, Chair. 1996–99; fmr mem. Nat. Council of La Raza; Trustee US Naval Acad. Foundation; Exec. Fellow, The Exec. Program, Darden School of Business, Univ. of Virginia 2007; Pres.'s Award, Nat. Council of La Raza 1997, Excellence in Bd Leadership Award, Nat. Ass. of Nat. Voluntary Health and Social Welfare Orgs 1998, Order of Auxiliary Service Medal, Salvation Army 1998, William Booth Award 1999.

REINER, Rob; American actor, writer, director and producer; b. 6 March 1947, New York; s. of Carl Reiner and Estelle Reiner (née Lebost); m. 1st Penny Marshall 1971–79 (divorced); m. 2nd Michele Singer 1989; three c.; ed Univ. of California, Los Angeles; co-f. Castle Rock Entertainment (now subsidiary of Warner Bros. Entertainment); has appeared with comic improvisation groups The Session and The Committee; Chair. First 5 Calif. Children and Families Comm. 1995–2006 (resgnd). *Films include:* Enter Laughing 1967, Halls of Anger 1970, Where's Poppa 1970, Summertree 1971, How Come Nobody's on Our Side? 1975, Fire Sale 1977, This is Spinal Tap (also dir and writer) 1984, The Sure Thing (dir) 1985, Stand By Me (dir) 1986, Throw Momma from the Train 1987, The Princess Bride (dir and producer) 1987, When Harry Met Sally (dir and producer) 1989, Postcards from the Edge 1990, The Spirit of '76 1990, Misery (also dir and producer) 1990, A Few Good Men (dir and producer) 1992, Sleepless in Seattle 1993, Bullets Over Broadway 1994, Mixed Nuts 1994, North (dir and producer) 1994, Bye Bye Love 1995, The American President (dir and producer) 1995, For Better or Worse 1996, The First Wives Club 1996, Mad Dog Time 1996, Ghosts of Mississippi (dir and producer) 1996, Primary Colors 1998, Spinal Tap: The Final Tour (dir, writer and producer) 1998, EdTV 1999, The Story of Us (also dir and producer) 1999, The Majestic 2001, Alex & Emma (also dir and producer) 2003, Rumor Has It (dir) 2005, Everyone's Hero (voice) 2006, The Bucket List (dir and producer) 2007, Flipped (writer, dir and producer) 2010, The Wolf of Wall Street 2013, And So It Goes (also dir) 2014, Being Charlie (dir) 2015. *Television includes:* The Glen Campbell Goodtime Hour (writer, series) 1969, All in the Family (series) (Emmy Award for Best Supporting Actor in a Comedy 1974, Outstanding Continuing Performance by a Supporting Actor in a Comedy Series 1978) 1971–78, The Super (producer) 1972, Thursday's Game 1974, Free Country (series, also producer) 1978, More Than Friends (also writer and producer) 1978, The T.V. Show (also writer and producer) 1979, Million Dollar Infield (also writer and producer) 1982, Morton & Hayes (series, writer and producer) 1991, But Seriously (exec. producer) 1994, I Am Your Child (dir, writer) 1997, Everyday Life 2004. *Address:* c/o Creative Artists Agency, 2000 Avenue of the Stars, Los Angeles, CA 90067; c/o Castle Rock Entertainment, 335 N Maple Drive, Suite 350, Beverly Hills, CA 90210, USA.

REINER, Željko, MD, MSc, PhD; Croatian medical scientist, academic and politician; b. 28 May 1953, Zagreb; ed Zagreb Univ. School of Medicine; specialized in internal medicine at Univ. Hosp. Centre Sestre milosrdnice, Zagreb and at Univ. Hosp. Eppendorf, Hamburg, Germany –1983; postdoctoral training in Oklahoma City, USA –1985; Assoc. Prof., Zagreb Univ. School of Medicine 1986–88, Full Prof. 1988–97, tenured Full Prof. of Internal Medicine 1997–, Chair. Dept of Internal Medicine 2000–06, Head of Dept of Clinical Research, Inst. of Pathophysiology, Univ. Hosp. Centre –1995, 2011–, Head of Dept for Metabolic Diseases 2003, Dir Univ. Hosp. Centre 2004–12, mem. Univ. of Zagreb Council 2010–; Full Prof., Rijeka Univ. Faculty of Medicine 1990–; Deputy Minister of Health 1993–98, Minister of Health 1998–2000; Pres. Nat. Health Council 2010; mem. (Croatian Democratic Union), Ass. (Sabor, Parl.) 2011–, Deputy Speaker and mem. Health and Social Policy Cttee, Educ., Science and Culture Cttee, Interparliamentary Co-operation Cttee, Deputy mem. Del. to Cen. European Initiative Parl. Dimension, Speaker of the Ass. (Sabor) 2015–16; European mem. Exec. Bd, Int. Atherosclerosis Soc. 2012–; mem. Editorial Bd, Nature – Reviews Cardiology, Atherosclerosis, Nutrition, Metabolism and Cardiovascular Diseases, Liječnički vjesnik; volunteer in Homeland War as mem. of Croatian Army Medical Corps HQ; Reserve Col, Croatian Armed Forces; Assoc. mem. Croatian Acad. of Sciences and Arts 1992–2006, Fellow 2006, Chair. Atherosclerosis Cttee 2006; Fellow, Croatian Acad. of Medical Sciences 1990 (Pres. 2004–12); Hon. Fellow, Acad. of Medical Sciences of Bosnia and Herzegovina 2011; Order of Duke Trpimir with Ribbon and Star; Order of Ban Jelaèiæ; Order of the Croatian Star with the effigy of Katarina Zrinska; Order of the Croatian Trefoil; Order of the Croatian Wattle; Homeland War Memorial Medal; Medal for participation in Operation Flash; Medal for participation in Operation Storm; Medal for participation in Operation Summer 95; Vukovar Memorial Medal; Award for Young Scientists, Int. Soc. of Endocrinology 1984, Ladislav Rakovac Award, Croatian Medical Asscn 1999, City of Zagreb Award 2010. *Publications include:* European Guidelines for the Management of Dyslipidaemia (lead author) 2011, Joint European Guidelines on Cardiovascular Disease Prevention in Clinical Practice (co-author) 2007, 2012; co-author of around 30 books and textbooks and editor of 26 books and manuals in medicine; 543 scientific and professional papers; reviewer for European Commission's scientific projects; poetry: Žejni sred zvirajnka 1984, Vrijeme sna i vrijeme jave 2003 and others. *Address:* Assembly (Sabor), 10000 Zagreb, trg sv. Marka 6–7, Croatia (office). *Telephone:* (1) 4569444 (office). *Fax:* (1) 1 6303010 (office). *E-mail:* gradjani@sabor.hr (office). *Website:* www.sabor.hr (office).

REINESCH, Gaston, MSc(Econ); Luxembourg central banker; *Governor, Luxembourg Central Bank;* b. 17 May 1958; ed London School of Econs, UK; fmr Pres. Société Nationale de Crédit et d'Investissement, Nat. Post and Telecommunication Co., Luxembourg Econ. and Social Council; fmr Chair. BGL BNP Paribas SA, Dir 2008–; Prof. of Econs, Legal and Econs Dept, Univ. of Luxembourg; Dir Gen., Ministry of Finance 1995–2012; Gov. Luxembourg Cen. Bank 2012–; fmr Vice-Chair. Banque et Caisse d'Epargne de l'Etat; mem. Bd Nat. State and Savings Bank; mem. Bd of Dirs Cargolux Airlines Int. SA, Entreprise des Postes et Télécommunications, SES SA 1998–, Cegedel SA, European Investment Bank; fmr Dir, Paul Wurth SA; fmr Alt. Bd mem. European Investment Fund. *Address:* Banque Centrale du Luxembourg, 2 boulevard Royal, 2983 Luxembourg (office). *Telephone:* 4774-1 (office). *Fax:* 4774-4901 (office). *E-mail:* info@bcl.lu (office). *Website:* www.bcl.lu (office).

REINFELDT, (John) Fredrik, BS; Swedish politician; b. 4 Aug. 1965, Stockholm; m. Filippa Holmberg 1992 (divorced 2013); two s. one d.; ed Stockholm Univ.; Deputy Chair. Swedish Central Conscripts Council, Swedish Defence Staff 1985–86, Chair. 1986; with Skandinaviska Enskilda Banken, Täby 1986–87; Deputy Chair. Regional Section, Young Moderates, Stockholm 1988–90, Chair. 1990–92, Chair. Exec. Cttee 1992–95; mem. Regional Section, Moderate Party, Stockholm 1992–2003, mem. Bd 1995–2002, mem. Exec. Cttee Moderate Party Group in Riksdag (Parl.) 1999–2003, Group Leader and First Deputy Chair. 2002–03, Chair. 2003–, mem. Bd Moderate Party 2002–, Party Chair. 2003–15; Deputy Sec., Stockholm City Commr 1990–91, Sec. 1991; mem. Riksdag (Parl.) 1991–, Alt. Riksdag Cttee on Taxation 1991–94, mem. Cttee on Finance 1994–2001, Alt. Cttee on EU Affairs 2001–02, Chair. Cttee on Justice 2001–02, Alt. Advisory Council on Foreign Affairs 2002–03; Deputy Chair. Cttee on Finance 2002–03, mem. Advisory Council on Foreign Affairs 2003–06; Prime Minister of Sweden 2006–14; Pres. European Council July–Dec. 2009; Chair. Democratic Youth Community of Europe 1995–97; mem. Bd Swedish Nat. Union of Students 1989–90; Pres. Youth of European People's Party 1997–99. *Publications:* Det sovande folket 1993, Projekt Europa: sex unga européer om Europasamarbetet 1993, Stenen i handen på den starke 1995, Nostalgitrippen (co-author) 1995, Väljarkryss: Personvalshandbok 2002, Framåt tillsammans: Min berättelse om föregångslandet Sverige (co-author) 2010. *Address:* Moderata Samlingspartiet (Moderate Party), Stord Nygatan 30, PO Box 2080, 103 12 Stockholm, Sweden (office). *Telephone:* (8) 676-80-00 (office). *Fax:* (8) 21-61-23 (office). *E-mail:* info@moderat.se (office). *Website:* www.moderat.se (office).

REINHARD, Keith Leon; American advertising executive; *Chairman Emeritus, DDB Worldwide Communications Group Inc.;* b. 20 Jan. 1935, Berne, Ind.; s. of Herman Reinhard and Agnes Reinhard; m. Rose-Lee Simons 1976; two d.; four s. one d. by previous m.; ed public schools in Berne; commercial artist, Kling Studios, Chicago 1954–56; man. tech. communications Dept Magnavox Co., Fort Wayne, Ind. 1957–60; creative/account exec., Biddle Co., Bloomington, Ill. 1961–63; Exec. Vice-Pres., Dir Creative Services and Pres. Needham, Harper & Steers Inc., Chicago 1964; then Chair. and CEO Needham, Harper & Steers/USA, Chicago; also Dir Needham, Harper & Steers Inc.; Chair. and CEO DDB Needham Worldwide Inc. (later DDB Worldwide Communications Group Inc.) New York 1986–2001, Chair. 2001-06, Chair. Emer. 2006–. *Address:* c/o DDB Worldwide Communications Group Inc., 437 Madison Avenue, New York, NY 10022, USA.

REINHARDT, Jörg, PhD; German pharmaceutical industry executive; *Chairman, Novartis AG;* ed Saarland Univ.; joined Sandoz Pharma Ltd 1982, held various positions, including Head of Devt, Head of Preclinical Devt and Project Man. (following merger that created Novartis) 1996–99, Head of Pharmaceutical Devt 1999–2000, Chair. Genomics Inst., Novartis Research Foundation, USA 2000–10, Head of Vaccines and Diagnostics Div. 2006–08, COO Novartis AG 2008–10, Chair. 2013–; Chair. Bd of Man. and Exec. Cttee Bayer HealthCare 2010–13; mem. Supervisory Bd, MorphoSys AG, Germany 2001–04; mem. Bd of Dirs, Lonza Group AG, Switzerland 2012–13; mem. Council, Int. Fed. of Pharmaceutical Mfrs and Asscns. *Address:* Novartis AG, Lichtstrasse 35, 4056 Basel, Switzerland (office). *Telephone:* (61) 324-11-11 (office). *Fax:* (61) 324-80-01 (office). *E-mail:* info@novartis.com (office). *Website:* www.novartis.com (office).

REINHARDT, Klaus, DrPhil; German army officer (retd); b. 15 Jan. 1941, Berlin; m. Heide-Ursula Reinhardt (née Bando) 1966; two s.; ed Univ. of Freiburg; joined army as officer cadet, Mountain Infantry; Commdr Mountain Infantry 1986–88; Commdr Army Führungsakademie 1990–93; Commdg Gen. III Corps 1993–94; Lt Gen., Commdr German Army, Koblenz 1994–96; Commdg Gen. of NATO Peace-keeping Unit in Kosovo (KFOR) 1999–2000; Commdr NATO Forces, Heidelberg 2000; retd 2001; currently Lecturer, Univs of Augsburg and Munich; fmr Vice-Pres. Clausewitz Soc., now Pres.; mem. Int. Advisory Bd World Security Network Foundation. *Publication:* Wende vor Moskau 1998. *Leisure interests:* classical music, skiing, mountaineering, travel. *Address:* Karthäuserhofweg 10, 56075 Koblenz, Germany. *Telephone:* (261) 55690.

REINHOUDT, David N.; Dutch chemist and academic; *Professor of Chemistry, University of Twente;* b. 18 Sept. 1942, Wolfaartsdijk; ed Delft Univ. of Tech.; Researcher, Shell NV 1970–75; part-time Prof. (extraordinarius), Univ. Twente 1975–78, Full Prof. 1978–2012, Prof. Emer. 2012–, Scientific Dir, MESA+ Research Inst., Enschede 1999–2007; Chair. NanoNed (Dutch network for nanotechnology) 2002–11; Prof. of Applied Chem., Radboud Univ., Nijmegen 2012–16; Prof. of Chem., Univ. of Twente 2012–; Chair. Nat. Foundation for Supramolecular Chemistry, European Supramolecular Science and Tech. Foundation; Vice-Chair. Nat. Org. for Applied Science (STW) 1996–; mem. Editorial Bd several journals, including European Journal of Organic Chemistry, Journal of Supramolecular Chemistry, New Journal of Chemistry; mem. Royal Dutch Acad. of Sciences (KNAW), ACS, Royal Dutch Chemical Soc.; Fellow, AAAS 1997–, Inst. of Physics; Kt, Order of the Dutch Lion 2002; Dr hc (Parma), (Pecs); Izatt-Christensen Award 1995, Simon Stevin Meesterschap 1998. *Publications:* more than 1,000 scientific publs, patents, review articles, and books. *Address:* Faculty of Science and Technology/SMCT, Universiteit Twente, Postbus 217, 7500 AE Enschede, Netherlands (office). *Telephone:* (53) 4892980 (office). *Fax:* (53) 4894645 (office). *E-mail:* d.n.reinhoudt@utwente.nl (office). *Website:* www.utwente.nl/en/tnw/mnf/People/Former_members/Academic-staff/prof_reinhoudt (office).

REINICHE, Dominique, MBA; French business executive; b. 13 July 1955; one d. two step-d.; ed ESSEC Business School, Cergy-Pontoise; Marketing Man. Procter & Gamble 1978–83, Assoc. Advertising Man. 1983–86; Dir of Marketing and Strategy, Kraft Jacobs Suchard 1986–92; Marketing and Sales Man., Coca-Cola Enterprises 1992–98, Gen. Man. (France) 1998–2003, Pres. Europe 2003–05, Pres. Europe Group 2005–12, Chair. Europe 2013–14; Vice-Chair. FoodDrinkEurope; mem. Bd of Dirs The AXA Group 2005–, Chr. Hansen 2013–, PayPal Luxembourg; mem. Supervisory Bd Peugeot SA; fmr Pres. Union des annonceurs (French advertiser asscn), UNESDA (European Soft Drink Asscn); fmr mem. Bd ECR (Efficient Consumer Response) Europe; fmr mem. Advisory Bd ING Direct; fmr mem. Exec. Bd Medef (French employers' org.); Chevalier, Legion d'honneur 2002.

REINIG, Gen. Gaston Charles-Marie; Luxembourg military officer; *Military Adviser, Security Council, United Nations;* b. 17 Nov. 1956, Diekirch; two d.; ed Ecole Royale Militaire, Brussels, Ecole d'Application d'Infanterie, Montpellier, Ecole d'Etat-major, Compiègne, Ecole Supérieure de Guerre Interarmées, Paris,

Institut des Hautes Etudes de Défense Nationale, Strasbourg, JF Kennedy School, Harvard Univ., USA; rifle peloton Commdr, Rifle and Recce Co. Commdr, Commdr Luxembourg contingent, NATO Allied Command Europe Mobile Force Land (AMF (L)) 1981–89; Logistics Staff Officer, Personnel 1989–94; Deputy Commdr Mil. Centre, Diekirch (Armed Forces Operational Centre) 1994–98, Commdr 2002–08; Perm. Mil. Rep. to NATO, Brussels 1998–2002, Mil. Del. to WEU 2000–02; Chief of Defence of Luxembourg 2008–13; currently Mil. Adviser, UN Nations Security Council; numerous decorations including Grand Officier, Ordre du Mérite, Commdr, Ordre de la Couronne de Chêne, Croix d'Honneur et de Mérite militaire, Commdr, Ordre du Mérite, Commdr, Ordre de Mérite civil et militaire Adolphe de Nassau, Commdr, Ordre de Mérite civil et militaire de la Couronne de Chêne, Verdienstkreuz am Bande des Verdienstordens der Bundesrepublik Deutschland, ECMM Medal for Service with EC Monitor Mission, Army Commendation Medal, Commandant, Ordre du Lion de Finlande, Grande Ufficiale, Ordine Al Merito della Repubblica Italiana, Commdr, Légion d'Honneur. *Leisure interests:* military history, mountain trekking, swimming, biking; plays the clarinet (several prizes). *Address:* United Nations Security Council, 777 44th Street, New York, NY 10017, USA (office). *Website:* www.un.org/en/sc (office).

REINSALU, Urmas; Estonian politician; *Minister of Foreign Affairs;* b. 22 June 1975, Tallinn, Estonian SSR, USSR; m.; two d.; ed 37th High School, Univ. Law Faculty; Chair. Univ. Student Body Foundation 1994–95; public law specialist, Ministry of Justice 1996–97; legal expert, Assessment Cttee, Constitution of the Govt of Estonia 1996–97; domestic policy adviser to the Pres. 1997–98; Dir Office of the Pres. 1998–2001; Political Sec., Res Publica 2001–02, Chair. 2002–06, Chair. Isamaa ja Res Publica Liit (Union of Pro Patria and Res Publica) 2012–15; Lecturer, Service Acad. 2002–03; mem. Riigikogu (Parl.) 2003–13, 2014–15; Minister of Defence 2012–14, of Justice 2015–19, of Foreign Affairs 2019–; Order of Merit (Second Class), Union of Former Forest Brothers 2013. *Address:* Ministry of Foreign Affairs, Islandi Väljak 1, Tallinn 15049, Estonia (office). *Telephone:* 637-7000 (office). *Fax:* 637-7099 (office). *E-mail:* vminfo@vm.ee (office). *Website:* www.vm.ee (office).

REIRS, Jānis, MA; Latvian politician and business executive; *Minister of Finance;* b. 23 Sept. 1961; ed Univ. of Latvia; Head of Credit Div., Latvian-German Bank 1993–96; mem. Bd, Trasta komercbanka PLC, Vice-Pres. and Head of Admin. Unit 1996–99; Dir and Partner, Prudentia Ltd 1999–2002; Chair. Spodrība PLC chemical plant 2001–02; mem. Standing Cttee, Baltic Sea Parl. Conf. 2004; mem. Saeima (Parl.), Sec. 2002–04, mem. Standing Comm. on Public Expenditure and Audit, State Admin and Municipal Cttee 2002–06, Sec. Legal Affairs Comm., Standing Cttee– Public Expenditure and Audit Comm. 2006–10, Chair. Budget and Finance (Taxation) Comm. 2010–14; Minister for Special Assignments – Electronic Govt Affairs 2004–06; Parl. Sec., Ministry of Health 2010; Pres. Baltic Ass., Head of Latvian Del. and Presidium mem. Baltic Ass. 2002–; Deputy Head of Control Cttee, Nordic Investment Bank 2013–14, Head of Control Cttee 2014–; Minister of Finance 2014–16, 2019–, of Welfare 2016–19. *Address:* Ministry of Finance, Smilšu iela 1, Rīga 1919, Latvia (office). *Telephone:* 6709-5405 (office). *Fax:* 6709-5410 (office). *E-mail:* info@fm.gov.lv (office). *Website:* www.fm.gov.lv (office).

REISMAN, Heather; Canadian publishing executive; *CEO, Indigo Books & Music Inc.;* b. Montreal; m. Gerald Schwartz; four c.; ed McGill Univ.; Co-founder and Man. Dir Paradigm Consulting 1979–92; Pres. Cott Corpn 1992–96; Founder, Pres. and CEO Indigo Books, Music and Café, Inc. 1996–2001, Pres. and CEO Indigo Books & Music Inc. (following merger with Chapters Inc. 2001) 2001–; mem. Bd of Dirs Onex Corpn, Right to Play; fmr mem. Bd of Dirs Magna Int., Suncor, Rogers Communications, Inc., Williams-Sonoma Inc.; Dir and Officer, Mount Sinai Hosp.; fmr Gov. McGill Univ., Toronto Stock Exchange; mem. Bilderberg Steering Cttee; Dr hc (Ryerson Univ.) 2006, (St Francis Xavier Univ.) 2013; Int. Distinguished Entrepreneur Award, Univ. of Manitoba, John Molson School of Business Award of Distinction, Concordia Univ.; inducted into Waterloo Entrepreneur Hall of Fame, Univ. of Waterloo. *Publications include:* numerous articles on media, communications, manufacturing and retailing. *Address:* Indigo Books & Music Inc., 468 King Street West, Suite 500, Toronto, ON M5V 1L8, Canada (office). *Telephone:* (416) 364-4499 (office). *Fax:* (416) 364-0355 (office). *Website:* www.chapters.indigo.ca (office).

REISS, Timothy James, BA, MA, PhD, FRSC; British/Canadian/American academic; *Professor Emeritus of Comparative Literature and Distinguished Scholar-in-Residence, New York University;* b. 14 May 1942, Stanmore, Middx, England; s. of James Martin Reiss and Margaret Joan Ping; m. 2nd Patricia J. Hilden 1988; two s. one d. from previous m.; ed Hardye's School, Dorchester, Univ. of Manchester, Univ. of Paris (Sorbonne), France, Univ. of Illinois, USA; Instructor to Asst Prof., Yale Univ. 1968–73; Assoc. Prof., Univ. de Montréal 1973–79, Prof. and Chair. of Comparative Literature 1979–84; Prof. of Comparative Literature, Modern Languages and Philosophy, Emory Univ. 1983–86, Samuel C. Dobbs Prof. of Comparative Literature and French 1986–87; Prof. and Chair. of Comparative Literature New York Univ. 1987–94, 2005–06, Prof. 1994–2005, Prof. Emer. and Distinguished Scholar in Residence 2007–; Visiting Prof., Univ. of Toronto 1976–77, Univ. of British Columbia 1979, New York Univ. 1982, Univ. of Montreal 1984–87, Grad. Center, CUNY 1985, State Univ. of NY, Binghamton 1990, Univ. of California, Berkeley 1996–97, Univ. of Oregon 1999–2000, Stanford Univ. 2001, 2002–03, 2004; Visiting Scholar, Univ. of Arizona, 2007–12; Visiting Scholar, Univ. of California, Davis 2012; Visiting Prof., Stanford Univ. 2014; mem. Acad. of Literary Studies 1986; Morse Fellowship, Paris 1971–72, Canada Council Sr Fellowship, Oxford 1977–78, Social Sciences Research Council of Canada Sr Fellowship, Oxford 1983–84, ACLS Sr Fellowship 1986–87, Guggenheim Fellowship, Cambridge 1990–91, Outstanding Academic Book 1983, 1993, Forkosch Prize in Intellectual History 1992, various other fellowships and awards. *Publications:* Toward Dramatic Illusion 1971, Science, Language and the Perspective Mind (ed.) 1973, Tragedy and Truth 1980, De l'ouverture des disciplines (ed.) 1981, The Discourse of Modernism (Choice Best Academic Book Award) 1982, Tragique et tragédie dans la tradition occidentale (ed.) 1983, The Uncertainty of Analysis 1988, The Meaning of Literature (Forkosch Prize, Choice Best Academic Book Award) 1992, Knowledge, Discovery and Imagination in Early Modern Europe 1997, For the Geography of a Soul (ed.) 2001, Against Autonomy: Global Dialectics of Cultural Exchange 2002, Sisyphus and Eldorado (ed.) (second revised edn) 2002, Mirages of the Selfe 2003, Music, Writing and Cultural Unity in the Caribbean (ed.) 2005, Topographies of Race and Gender: Mapping Cultural Representations, two vols (co-ed.) 2008–09; more than 160 essays and book chapters. *Address:* Department of French and Italian, Stanford University, Piggott Hall, 450 Serra Mall, Stanford, CA 94305 (office); 1139 Shevlin Drive, El Cerrito, CA 94530, USA (home). *Telephone:* (510) 847-9570 (home). *Fax:* (650) 723-0482 (office). *E-mail:* timothy.reiss@nyu.edu (office). *Website:* complit.as.nyu.edu (office).

REITEN, Eivind Kristofer; Norwegian energy and light metal industry executive and fmr politician; b. 2 April 1953, Midsund; m.; two c.; ed Univ. of Oslo; jr exec. officer, Ministry of Fisheries 1979–82; Sec. to Centre Party's Parl. Group 1982–83; State Sec. Ministry of Finance 1983–; Minister of Fisheries 1985–86, of Petroleum and Energy 1989–90; Man. Hydro Agri Div., Norsk Hydro 1986–88, Asst Gen. Man. Hydro Agri 1988, Pres. Energy Div. 1988, Dir Special Projects 1991–92, Pres. Refining and Marketing Div. 1992–96, Pres. Hydro Aluminium Metal Products 1996–98, Exec. Vice-Pres. and mem. Corp. Man. Bd, Norsk Hydro ASA 1999–2001, Pres. and CEO 2001–10 (resgnd), Chair. StatoilHydro (after acquisition of Norsk Hydro by Statoil) 1–4 Oct. 2007 (resgnd); Chair. Bd Norwegian Postal Service 1995–99, Int. Primary Aluminium Inst. 1998–2000, Telenor 2000–01; mem. Bd Cen. Bank of Norway 1988–94, Norske Skog 1995–2000; mem. Green Tax Comm. 1994–95; Fellow, Norwegian Acad. of Technological Sciences.

REITER, Janusz; Polish diplomatist and international affairs scholar; *Chairman, Centre for International Relations, Warsaw;* b. 6 Aug. 1952, Kościerzyna; s. of Stanisław Reiter and Hilda Reiter; m. Hanna Reiter 1975; two d.; ed Warsaw Univ.; foreign affairs commentator, Życie Warszawy (daily) 1977–81 (dismissed during martial law); Co-founder Foundation for Int. Ventures and Centre for Int. Studies in Warsaw; mem. Dziekania Club of Political Thought; staff writer, Przegląd Katolicki (weekly) 1984–89, Gazeta Wyborcza (daily) and Polish TV 1989–90, Rzeczpospolita (daily); Amb. to FRG 1990–95; f. Centre for Int. Relations, Warsaw 1996, Pres. 2010–13, Chair. 2013–; Amb. to USA 2005–07; Co-founder Council for Foreign Policy; mem. Council on European Integration; Great Cross of Merit with the Star and Ribbon (Germany); Hon. Award, European Univ., Viadrina, Germany; hon. degree from Coll. of the Atlantic, USA. *Publications:* several books, policy papers, and articles on Europe, the transatlantic relations, European security policy and other international topics, including Roads to Europe. *Leisure interests:* music, travelling, literature. *Address:* Office Janusz Reiter, Al. Wyzwolenia 14 m. 71, 00-570 Warsaw, Poland (office). *Telephone:* (22) 252-86-79 (office). *E-mail:* biuro-reiter@csm.org.pl (office). *Website:* csm.org.pl/pl (office).

REITH, Gen. Sir John, Kt, KCB, CBE; British army officer (retd); ed Royal Mil. Acad., Sandhurst; commissioned into Parachute Regiment 1969; fmr Chief of Staff, 20 Armoured Brigade, Detmold, W Germany; fmr co. commdr, 3rd Battalion, Parachute Regiment, fmr Commdr, 1st Battalion; Chief of Staff, 1 (UK) Armoured Div., Verden, W Germany 1988; deployed to Gulf for Operation Granby 1990–91; Commdr 4th Armoured Brigade, Munster and Osnabruck 1992; fmr Commdr, British Forces, fmr Commdr, UN Sector SW; Supervisor, Washington Agreement –1994; Dir Int. Orgs, Ministry of Defence, London 1994–95, Dir of Mil. Operations 1995–97; Commdr, Allied Command Europe Mobile Force (Land) 1997–2000; Asst Chief of Defence Staff (Policy), Cen. Staff, Ministry of Defence 2000–01; Chief of Jt Operations, Perm. Jt HQ, Northwood 2001–04; Deputy Supreme Allied Command Europe (DSACEUR), NATO 2004–07 (retd); Chair. Bd of Govs Millfield School 2008–. *Leisure interests:* walking, gardening, cooking.

REITH, Peter Keaston, BEcons, LLB; Australian company director, consultant, international organization official and fmr politician; b. 15 July 1950, Melbourne, Vic.; s. of A. C. Reith and E. V. Reith (née Sambell); m. Julie Treganowan 1971; four s.; ed Monash Univ.; Supreme Court 1975; worked as solicitor 1976–82; mem. Westernport Waterworks Trust and Cowes Sewerage Authority 1977–82; Councillor, Shire of Phillip Island 1976–81, Pres. 1980–81; mem. various cttees and authorities; MP for Flinders 1982–83, 1984–2001; Deputy Leader of the Opposition 1990–93; Shadow Special Minister of State 1993, responsible for Mabo 1994; Shadow Minister for Defence Jan.–Sept. 1994, Shadow Minister with responsibility for Mabo Jan.–May 1994; Shadow Minister for Defence May–Sept. 1994, for Foreign Affairs 1994–95, for Industrial Relations and Man. of Opposition Business in the House 1995–96; Minister for Industrial Relations and Leader of the House of Reps and Minister Assisting the Prime Minister for the Public Service 1996–97, for Workplace Relations and Small Business and Leader of the House of Reps 1997–98, for Employment, Workplace Relations and Small Business and Leader of the House of Reps 1998–2001, for Defence 2001; Dir representing Australia, South Korea, NZ and Egypt, EBRD 2003–06, Alt. Dir 2006–09; mem. Asscn of Christian Community Colls; Co-ordinator Free Legal Aid Services; Founding Sec. and mem. Newhaven Coll. *Publication:* The Reith Papers. *Leisure interests:* golf, reading. *Address:* 1A Camperdown Street, Brighton East, Vic. 3187, Australia (home). *E-mail:* peterreith@bigpond.com.au (home).

REITHOFER, Norbert, Dr-Ing; German automotive industry executive; *Chairman of the Supervisory Board, BMW AG;* b. 29 May 1956, Penzberg; ed Technische Universität München; joined BMW 1987, has served in numerous sr man. positions including Dir Body-in-White Production Div. 1991–94, Tech. Dir BMW South Africa 1994–97, Pres. BMW Manufacturing Corpn, USA, SC 1997–2000, mem. Bd of Man. with responsibility for production 2000–06, Chair. Bd of Man. BMW AG 2006–15, Chair. Supervisory Bd 2015–; Grand Decoration of Honour in Gold (Grosses Goldenes Ehrenzeichen) for Services to the Repub. of Austria 2005, Bayerischen Verdienstorden 2010; Hon. Dr-Ing. *Address:* BMW AG, 130 Petuelring, Munich 80788, Germany (office). *Telephone:* (89) 382-0 (office). *Fax:* (89) 382-258-58 (office). *E-mail:* info@bmwgroup.com (office). *Website:* www.bmwgroup.com (office); www.bmw.com (office).

REITMAN, Ivan, MusB; Canadian film director and producer; b. 27 Oct. 1946, Komarmo, Czechoslovakia; s. of Leslie Reitman and Clara R. Reitman; m. Genevieve Robert 1976; one s. two d.; ed McMaster Univ.; moved to Canada 1951; Hon. LLD (Toronto); Dir of the Year, Nat. Asscn of Theater Owners 1984, Canadian Genie Special Achievement Award 1985, Star on Hollywood Walk of Fame 1997. *Stage shows produced:* The Magic Show 1974, The National Lampoon Show 1975, Merlin 1983 (also Dir). *Films include:* Foxy Lady 1971, Cannibal Girls

1973, They Came From Within 1975, Shivers 1975, Rabid 1976, The House by the Lake 1976, Death Weekend 1977, Blackout 1978, National Lampoon's Animal House 1978 (People's Choice Award 1979), Meatballs (Golden Reel Award) 1979, Heavy Metal 1981, Stripes 1981, Spacehunter: Adventures in the Forbidden Zone 1983, The Magic Show 1983, Ghostbusters (Saturn Award for Best Fantasy Film) 1984, Legal Eagles 1986, Big Shots 1987, Twins 1988, Casual Sex? 1988, Feds 1988, Ghostbusters II 1989, Kindergarten Cop 1990, Beethoven 1992, Stop! Or My Mom Will Shoot 1992, Dave 1993, Beethoven's 2nd 1993, Junior 1994, Space Jam 1996, Private Parts 1996, Commandments 1996, Father's Day 1996, Six Days/Seven Nights 1998, Doomsday Man 1999, Road Trip 2000, Evolution 2001, Killing Me Softly 2002, Old School 2003, Eurotrip 2004, Trailer Park Boys: The Movie 2006, Disturbia 2007, Post Grad 2009, Hotel for Dogs 2009, The Uninvited 2009, No Strings Attached 2011, Draft Day 2014, Ghostbusters 2016, Baywatch 2017. *TV series:* (producer and dir) Delta House 1978, Alienators: Evolution Continues (exec. producer) 2001, Beethoven (exec. producer) 1994, Mummies Alive! (exec. producer) 1997. *TV films:* (exec. producer) The Late Shift 1996, The First Gentleman 1999; mem. Dirs Guild of America.

REITMAN, Jason; Canadian film director and producer; b. 19 Oct. 1977, Montreal; s. of Ivan Reitman and Geneviève Robert; m. Michele Lee 2004; one c.; ed Univ. of Southern California; began career as production asst on father's films; co-f. Hard C Productions (production co.) 2006; named best debut dir by Nat. Bd of Review and US Comedy Arts 2006. *Films include:* Operation 1998, In God We Trust 2000, Gulp 2001, Consent 2004, Thank You for Smoking 2006, Juno 2007, Jennifer's Body 2008, Up in the Air (also producer and screenplay) 2009, Chloe 2009, Ceremony 2010, Jeff, Who Lives at Home 2011, Young Adult 2011, Labor Day 2013, Whiplash 2014, Men, Women & Children 2014, Demolition 2015. *Television includes:* Casual 2015–17. *Address:* c/o Fox Searchlight Pictures, 10201 W. Pico Blvd, Bldg. 38, Los Angeles, CA 90035, USA (office). *Telephone:* (310) 369-4402 (office).

REITZ, Edgar; German film director; b. 1 Nov. 1932, Morbach; m. Salome Kammer 1995; one s.; co-f. Institut für Filmgestaltung 1963; co-f. (with son Christian Reitz) Reitz & Reitz Media, Munich; f. Edgar Reitz Filmproduktion GmbH; Prof. of Film, Staatliche Hochschule für Gestaltung (State Univ. of Design), Karlsruhe; Bundesverdienstkreuz 1993, Großes Verdienstkreuz des Verdienstordens der Bundesrepublik Deutschland 2006, Officier, Ordre des arts et des lettres 2010; numerous awards including Konrad-Wolf Prize and Hans Abich Prize (for Heimat Trilogy) 2007. *Films include:* Mahlzeiten (appeared in UK as Lust for Love) 1966–67, Die Reise nach Wien 1973, Picnic 1975, Stunde Null 1976, Deutschland im Herbst (with others) 1977–78, Der Schneider von Ulm 1978, Heimat 1980–84, Die zweite Heimat 1991, Die Nacht der Regisseure 1995, Heimat 3: Chronik einer Zeitenwende (TV) 2004, Heimat-Fragmente: Die Frauen 2006. *Address:* Reitz & Reitz Medien, Rottmannstraße 11, 80333 Munich (office); Edgar Reitz Filmproduktion GmbH, Studio, Rottmannstraße 11, 80333 Munich, Germany. *Telephone:* (89) 2724524 (office); (89) 2723276. *Fax:* (89) 2719760 (office). *E-mail:* kontakt@reitz-medien.de (office); mail@erfilm.de. *Website:* www.edgar-reitz.de.

REIZNIECE-OZOLA, Dana; Latvian chess player and politician; b. 6 Nov. 1981, Kuldīga, Latvian SSR, USSR; m. Andris Ozols; won Latvian Chess Championship for women 1998, 1999, 2000, 2001; won European Girls Under-18 Chess Championship 1998, 1999; played for Latvia in Chess Olympiads 1998, 2000, 2004, 2006, 2010, 2012, 2014, in European Team Chess Championship (women) 1999, 2001, 2011; holds title of Woman Grandmaster 2001; mem. Zaļo un Zemnieku Savienība (ZZS—Greens' and Farmers' Union); mem. Saeima (Parl.) 2011–; Minister of the Economy 2014–16, of Finance 2016–19. *Address:* c/o Ministry of Finance, Smilšu iela 1, Rīga 1919, Latvia (office).

RELL, M(ary) Jodi; American fmr politician; b. (Mary Carolyn Reavis), 16 June 1946, Norfolk, Va; m. Lou Rell (died 2014); one s. one d.; ed Old Dominion Univ., Western Connecticut State Univ.; served in Conn. House of Reps for ten years, fmr Asst Minority Leader and Deputy Minority Leader; Lt-Gov. of Conn. 1994–2004, presided over Senate, mem. Prison and Jail Overcrowding Comm., Gov.'s Law Enforcement Council, State Finance Advisory Cttee; est. Lt-Gov.'s Comm. on State Mandate Reform 1995; Gov. of Conn. 2004–11; apptd Chair. Hartford Econ. Devt Advisory Group 1998; fmr Vice-Chair. Brookfield Rep. Town Cttee; mem. Women Execs in State Govt, Nat. Order Women Legislators (fmr Vice-Pres. and Nat. Pres.), Brookfield Business and Professional Women's Club, Brookfield Rep. Women's Club (fmr Pres.); fmr mem. Nat. Conf. of Lt-Govs; mem. Bd of Trustees, Regional YMCA of Western Conn., Candlewood Lions Club; Republican; Hon. LLD (Hartford) 2001, (New Haven) 2004; honoured by Uniformed Professional Fire Fighters, AmeriCares, Arthritis Foundation, CT Race for the Cure, Conn. Library Asscn, Conn. Chapter of American Coll. of Health Care Admins, Conn. Preservation Council, Conn. Fed. of Business and Professional Women, Arnold Markle Public Service Award, Connecticut Voices for Children, First Kids Policy Leadership Award 2001, Impact Award, Connecticut Tech. Council 2001, named a Melvin Jones Fellow, Lions Club Int. Foundation 2003, Nathan Davis Award for outstanding govt service, American Medical Asscn 2008, Leadership Award, Nat. Order of Women Legislators, among others.

RELYVELD, Steven S.; Suriname lawyer and politician; b. 12 July 1964, Paramaribo; ed Anton de Kom Univ., Paramaribo; civil servant, Ministry of Labour 1990–95, later becoming Dir and Perm. Sec., Ministry of Labour, Tech. Devt and the Environment 2011; Minister of Physical Planning, Land and Forestry June–Nov. 2013, Minister of Spatial Planning, Land Management and Forest Policy 2013–17; mem. Megacombinatie.

REMENGESAU, Tommy Esang, Jr, BS; Palauan politician and head of state; *President;* b. 28 Feb. 1956, Koror; s. of Thomas O. Remengesau, Sr and Ferista Esang Remengesau; m. Debbie Mineich; two s. two d.; ed Grand Valley State Univ., Mich., Michigan State Univ., USA; Admin./Planner, Palau Bureau of Health Services 1980–81; Public Information Officer, Palau Legislature 1981–84; Senator, Nat. Congress 1984–92; Vice-Pres. and Minister of Admin. 1993–2001, Pres. of Palau 2001–09, 2013–; Senator 2009–; rep. to IMF 1997; led several official dels to Taiwan (Repub. of China); hosted first Taiwan-Pacific Allies Summit 2006; named by Time magazine a Hero of the Environment 2007. *Leisure interests:* fishing (twice Grand Champion All-Micronesia Fishing Derby). *Address:* Office of the President, POB 6051, Koror, PW 96940, Palau (office). *Telephone:* 488-2403 (office). *Fax:* 488-1662 (office). *E-mail:* pres@palaunet.com (office). *Website:* www.kotedlbelau.com.

REMNICK, David J., AB; American journalist, editor and writer; *Editor, The New Yorker;* b. 29 Oct. 1958, Hackensack, NJ; s. of Edward C. Remnick and Barbara Remnick (née Seigel); m. Esther B. Fein; two s. one d.; ed Princeton Univ.; reporter, The Washington Post 1982–91; staff writer, The New Yorker 1992–, Ed. 1998–; Livingston Award 1991, George Polk Award 1994, Helen Bernstein Award 1994, Editor of the Year, Advertising Age 2000, 2016. *Publications include:* Lenin's Tomb: The Last Days of the Soviet Empire (Pulitzer Prize for General Non-fiction 1994) 1993, The Devil Problem (and other true stories) 1996, Resurrection: The Struggle for a New Russia 1997, King of the World: Muhammad Ali and the Rise of an American Hero 1998, Life Stories: Profiles from The New Yorker (ed.) 1999, Wonderful Town: Stories from The New Yorker (ed.) 1999, Reporting: Writings from The New Yorker 2006, The Bridge: The Life and Rise of Barack Obama 2010; contrib. to newspapers and periodicals. *Address:* The New Yorker, 1 World Trade Center, 38th Floor, New York, NY 10007, USA (office). *E-mail:* themail@newyorker.com (office). *Website:* www.newyorker.com/contributors/david-remnick (office).

REN, Fuyao; Chinese business executive; b. Dec. 1953, Shanxi Xiaxian; joined CCP 1983; with Huozhou Mining bureau 1996–2000, Sec. of Party Cttee and Chair. Huozhou Coal Group Co. 2000–01, Gen. Man. Shanxi Coking Coal Group 2001–05; Deputy Dir State-owned Assets Supervision and Admin Comm., Shanxi Prov. 2005–07; Sec. of Party Cttee and Chair. Yangquan Coal Industry Group 2007–11; joined as Sec. of Party Cttee and Chair. Shanxi Coking Coal Refco Group Ltd 2011; awarded title of 'model worker' by Govt of Shanxi Prov. 1998. *Address:* c/o Shanxi Coking Coal Group, 1 Xinjinci Road, Taiyuan 30024, People's Republic of China.

REN, Hongbin; Chinese business executive; *Chairman, China National Machinery Industry Corporation (Sinomach);* Pres. China Nat. Construction & Agricultural Machinery Import & Export Corpn 1991–2001; Chair. China Nat. Machinery Industry Corpn (Sinomach) 2013–; Vice-Chair. China Enterprise Confed. (CEC); Alt. mem. 18th CCP Cen. Cttee 2012–17, 19th CCP Cen. Cttee 2017–. *Address:* China National Machinery Industry Corporation, 3 Danling Street, Haidian District, Beijing, 100080, People's Republic of China (office). *Telephone:* (10) 82688888 (office). *Fax:* (10) 82688811 (office). *E-mail:* office@sinomach.com.cn (office). *Website:* www.sinomach.com.cn (office).

REN, Jianxin, BA, MA; Chinese business executive; *Chairman, China National Chemical Corporation (ChemChina);* b. Jan. 1958; ed Lanzhou Univ.; worked as farmer in Dunhuang Co., Gansu Prov. during China's Cultural Revolution; with seven colleagues, co-f. China BlueStar Chemical Cleaning (China's first industrial-cleaning co.) 1984, has acquired more than 100 state-owned enterprises, brokered merger between BlueStar and other cos affiliated to fmr Ministry of Chemical Industry to create China Nat. Chemical Corpn (ChemChina) 2004, currently Chair. and Sec. Party Cttee; Communist Youth League Sec., Chemical Machinery Research Inst. of original Chemical Industry Ministry 1984; Del. to NPC; Chevalier, Légion d'honneur 2011; China Annual Businessman of 2008, Annual Best China Overseas Investor 2012. *Address:* China National Chemical Corporation (ChemChina), 62 Beisihuan West Road, Haidian District, Beijing 100080, People's Republic of China (office). *Telephone:* (10) 82677234 (office). *Fax:* (10) 82677088 (office). *E-mail:* zghg@chemchina.com (office). *Website:* www.chemchina.com (office); www.chemchina.com.cn (office).

REN, Jianxin; Chinese judge; b. Aug. 1925, Fencheng (now Xiangfen) Co., Shanxi Prov.; m. Niu Lizhi; ed Eng Coll., Beijing Univ.; joined CCP 1948; Sec., Secr. N China People's Govt 1948–49; Sec.-Gen. Office, Cen. Comm. for Political Science and Law, Sec. Cen. Comm. for Legis. Affairs 1949–54; Sec. Legis. Affairs Bureau, State Council 1954–59; Section Leader, Div. Chief, China Council for the Promotion of Int. Trade (CCPIT) 1959–71, Dir Legal Dept, CCPIT, lawyer 1971–81, Vice-Chair. CCPIT 1981–83; Vice-Pres. Supreme People's Court 1983–88, Pres. 1988–98; Sec.-Gen. Leading Group of Cen. Cttee for Political Science and Law 1989, Deputy Sec. and Sec.-Gen. Cen. Cttee 1990; apptd Chair. Soc. of Chinese Judges 1994; Hon. Chair China Law Soc. (fmr Vice-Pres.), China Foreign Econ. Trade and Arbitration Cttee, China Maritime Arbitration Cttee (fmr Chair.); Hon. Pres. China Int. Law Soc. (fmr Vice-Pres.); Dir China Training Centre for Sr Judges; Prof. (part-time) Beijing Univ.; mem. 13th CCP Cen. Cttee 1987–92, 14th CCP Cen. Cttee 1992–97, Sec. Secr. 14th CCP Cen. Cttee 1992–97; Del., 15th CCP Nat. Congress 1997–2002; Sec. CCP Cen. Comm. for Political Science and Law 1992–98; Vice-Chair. 9th Nat. Cttee CPPCC 1998–2003.

REN, Zhengfei; Chinese business executive; *Deputy Chairman and CEO, Huawei Investment & Holding Company Ltd;* b. 1944, Jiangsu; ed Chongqing Inst. of Civil Eng and Architecture; employed in civil eng industry until 1974, joined military's Eng Corps as a soldier tasked to establish the Liao Yang Chemical Fibre Factory 1974, took positions as technician, engineer, promoted as a Deputy Dir (equivalent to a Deputy Regimental Chief but without mil. rank), invited to attend Nat. Science Conf. 1978 and 12th Nat. Congress of CCP 1982, retd from army 1983; worked in logistics service base of Shenzhen South Sea Oil Corpn; left job to co-f. Huawei Technologies Co. Ltd (now Huawei Investment & Holding Co. Ltd) 1987, Deputy Chair. and CEO 1988–; joined CCP 1978, mem. 12th Nat. Congress of CCP. *Address:* Huawei Investment & Holding Co. Ltd, Huawei Industrial Base, Shenzhen 518129, People's Republic of China (office). *Telephone:* (755) 28780808 (office). *E-mail:* hwtech@huawei.com (office). *Website:* www.huawei.com (office).

RENARD, Ian Andrew, AM, BA, LLM; Australian lawyer, company director and fmr university chancellor; *Director, Hillview Quarries Pty Ltd;* b. 8 Aug. 1946, Melbourne, Vic.; s. of Roy Renard and Dorothy Renard; m. Diana Renard; four d.; ed Univ. of Melbourne; Partner, Arthur Robinson & Hedderwicks 1979–2001, Man. Partner 1989–91; Deputy Chancellor Univ. of Melbourne 2001–05, Chancellor 2005–09, Chair. Univ. of Melbourne Archives 2009–15; fmr Chair. Melbourne Theatre Co.; fmr Pres. Library Bd of Vic.; fmr Treas. Free Kindergarten Asscn; Dir Hillview Quarries Pty Ltd; fmr Dir CSL Ltd, AMP Ltd, Ausnet Services Ltd, Newcrest Mining Ltd, Nth Broken Hill Ltd, Royal Children's Hosp.; Trustee, R.E. Ross Trust; fmr Trustee, The Queen's Fund; Hon. LLD; Supreme Court Prize 1969, Australian Library and Information Asscn Redmond Barry Award. *Publication:* Takeovers and Reconstructions in Australia (co-author). *Address:* Allens

Linklaters, GPO Box 1776, Melbourne, Vic. 3001, Australia (office). *Telephone:* (3) 9613-8917 (office). *Fax:* (3) 9614-4661 (office). *E-mail:* ian.renard@allens.com.au (office). *Website:* www.allens.com.au (office).

RENAULD, Maj. (retd) Lener; Haitian politician and fmr army officer; b. 22 March 1956, Port-au-Prince; ed Univ. d'Etat d'Haiti; several years' army service, including as Service Officer, Gen. HQ of Haiti Armed Forces, Dist Commdr, Aquin, Croix des Bourquets and Delmas districts, Chief of Police of Cap Haitien; left army with rank of Maj. 1994; fmr Instructor, académie militaire d'Haïti; fmr adviser to Pres.; Minister of Nat. Defence 2014–16, also acting Minister of Foreign Affairs 2015–16.

RENDELL, Edward (Ed) Gene, BA, JD; American lawyer and fmr politician; *Partner, Ballard Spahr LLP;* b. 5 Jan. 1944, New York; s. of Jesse T. Rendell and Emma Rendell (née Sloat); m. Marjorie Osterlund 1971; one s.; ed Univ. of Pennsylvania, Villanova Univ. School of Law; 2nd Lt, US Army Reserve 1968–74; called to Bar of Pennsylvania 1968, US Supreme Court 1981; Asst Dist Attorney, Chief Homicide Unit, Phila 1968–74, Deputy Special Prosecutor, Phila 1976, Dist Attorney 1978–86; Partner, Ballard Spahr Andrews & Ingersoll LLP 2000–03, Ballard Spahr LLP 2011–; Mayor of Phila 1992–2000; Gen. Chair. Democratic Nat. Cttee 1999–2000; Gov. Commonwealth of Pa 2003–11; Chair. Nat. Govs Asscn 2008–09; Founder and Co-Chair Building America's Future; Lecturer in Law, Univ. of Pennsylvania; political analyst, NBC News 2011–; mem. Bd of Dirs OwnEnergy Inc. 2011–; mem. Advisory Bd ThinkEco Inc. 2011–; Distinguished Sr Fellow, Brookings Inst. 2011–; mem. ABA, Phila Bar Asscn, Pennsylvania Dist Attorneys Asscn, B'nai B'rith, United Jewish Org., Jewish War Vets, Nat. Constitution Center; Democrat; Man of the Year Award, VFW 1980, American Cancer League 1981, Distinguished Public Service Award, Pa Co. Detectives Asscn 1981, March of Dimes Shining Star Lifetime Achievement Award 2012. *Publication:* A Nation of Wusses: How America's Leaders Lost the Guts to Make Us Great 2012. *Leisure interest:* sports. *Address:* Ballard Spahr LLP, 1735 Market Street, 51st Floor, Philadelphia, PA 19103, USA (office). *Telephone:* (215) 864-8401 (office). *Fax:* (215) 864-8999 (office). *E-mail:* rendell@ballardspahr.com (office). *Website:* www.ballardspahr.com (office); www.edwardrendell.com.

RENFREW, Magnus Archibald, MA (Hons); British exhibition organiser; *Founder and Managing Director, ARTHQ Group;* b. 5 Nov. 1975, Winchester, Hants.; s. of Colin Renfrew, Lord Renfrew of Kaimsthorn and Jane Renfrew; m. Emma Louise Renfrew; three s.; ed Univ. of St Andrews; specialist in contemporary art, Bonhams 1999–2006, Deputy Chair. Asia, Bonhams 2014–16; Head of Exhbns, Pearl Lam's Contrasts Gallery, Shanghai 2006; Founding Fair Dir ART HK 2007–12 (acquired by Art Basel), Dir, Asia and mem. Exec. Cttee, Art Basel 2012–14; Founder and Man. Dir ARTHQ Group 2016–; Co-founder and Fair Dir, Taipei Dangdai 2018–; Chair. Advisory Council, Para Site Art Space 2014–; mem. Hong Kong Arts Devt Council 2014–16; OE Saunders Class Prize for Art History, Univ. of St Andrews, honoured as Young Global Leader, World Economic Forum 2013. *Publication:* Uncharted Territory – Culture and Commerce in Hong Kong's Art World 2017. *Address:* ARTHQ Ltd, Ninth Floor, 33 Des Voeux Road Central, Hong Kong Special Administrative Region, People's Republic of China (office). *Telephone:* 3952-7288 (office). *E-mail:* info@magnusrenfrew.com (home). *Website:* www.arthqgroup.com (office); www.magnusrenfrew.com.

RENFREW OF KAIMSTHORN, Baron (Life Peer), cr. 1991, of Hurlet in the District of Renfrew; **Andrew Colin Renfrew,** PhD, ScD, FBA, FSA; British archaeologist and academic; *Senior Fellow, McDonald Institute for Archaeological Research, University of Cambridge;* b. 25 July 1937, Stockton-on-Tees, Co. Durham, England; s. of Archibald Renfrew and Helena D. Renfrew; m. Jane M. Ewbank 1965; two s. one d.; ed St Albans School, St John's Coll., Cambridge and British School of Archaeology, Athens; Lecturer in Prehistory and Archaeology, Univ. of Sheffield 1965–70, Sr Lecturer 1970–72, Reader in Prehistory and Archaeology 1972; Prof. of Archaeology and Head of Dept, Univ. of Southampton 1972–81; Disney Prof. of Archaeology, Univ. of Cambridge 1981–2004, Dir McDonald Inst. for Archaeological Research 1990–2004, Fellow 2004–, currently Sr Fellow, Fellow, St John's Coll. 1981–86, Hon. Fellow 2004–, Master of Jesus Coll., Cambridge 1986–97, Professorial Fellow 1997–2004, Fellow Emer. 2004–; Visiting Lecturer, UCLA 1967; mem. Ancient Monuments Bd for England 1974–84, Royal Comm. on Historical Monuments 1977–87, Historic Buildings and Monuments Comm. for England 1984–86, Ancient Monuments Advisory Cttee 1984–2002, British Nat. Comm. for UNESCO 1984–86; Trustee, British Museum 1991–2001; Foreign mem. American Philosophical Asscn 2006; Foreign Assoc. NAS; Hon. FSA (Scotland); Hon. FRSE 2001; Hon. LittD (Sheffield) 1990, (Southampton) 1995, (Edinburgh) 2004, (Liverpool) 2004, (St Andrews) 2006, (Kent) 2007, (London) 2008; Dr hc (Faculty of Letters, Univ. of Athens) 1991; Rivers Memorial Medal, British Anthropological Inst. 1979, Sir Joseph Larmor Award 1961, Huxley Memorial Medal, Royal Anthropological Inst. 1991, Prix Int. Fyssen, Fondation Fyssen, Paris 1997, Language and Culture Prize, Univ. of Umeå, Sweden 1998, Rivers Memorial Medal, European Science Foundation Latsis Prize 2003, Balzan Prize 2004. *Publications:* The Emergence of Civilization 1972, Before Civilization 1973, The Explanation of Culture Change (ed.) 1973, British Prehistory (ed.) 1974, Transformations: Mathematical Approaches to Culture Change 1979, Problems in European Prehistory 1979, An Island Polity 1982, Theory and Explanation in Archaeology (ed.) 1982, Approaches to Social Archaeology 1984, The Archaeology of Cult 1985, Peer, Polity Interaction and Socio-Political Change (ed.) 1986, Archaeology and Language: The Puzzle of Indo-European Origins 1987, The Idea of Prehistory (co-author) 1988, Archaeology: Theories, Methods and Practice (co-author) 1991, The Cycladic Spirit 1991, The Archaeology of Mind (co-ed. with E. Zubrow) 1994, Loot, Legitimacy and Ownership 2000, Archaeogenetics (ed.) 2000, Figuring It Out 2003, Archaeology, The Key Concepts (co-ed.) 2005, Phylogenetic Methods and the Prehistory of Languages (co-ed.) 2006, Prehistory: the Making of the Human Mind 2007, Early Cycladic Sculpture in Context (co-ed.) 2017, The Sanctuary on Keros (co-ed.) 2017; contribs to Archaeology, Scientific American. *Leisure interests:* contemporary arts, coins, travel. *Address:* c/o Curtis Brown Ltd, Haymarket House, 28–29 Haymarket, London, SW1Y 4SP, England (office); Room 3.2, West Building, McDonald Institute for Archaeological Research, Downing Street, Cambridge, CB2 3ER, England (office). *Telephone:* (20) 7393-4400 (office); (1223) 333521 (office). *Fax:* (20)

7393-4401 (office); (1223) 333536 (office). *E-mail:* acr10@cam.ac.uk (office). *Website:* www.mcdonald.cam.ac.uk (office).

RENGIFO RUIZ, Marciano; Peruvian government official and fmr army general; b. 25 Sept. 1934, Bellavista, San Martin; ed Escuela Militar de Chorrillos, Lima, Ecole Militaire St Cyr, France, Univ. de Piura, Centro de Altos Estudios Nacionales; numerous sr positions in Peruvian Army 1973–91; Mil. Rep. at OAS 1991; co-founder and mem. Perú Posible political party, mem. Manifesto Cttee 1999–2001; mem. Congress for San Martin 2000–05, Pres. Defence Cttee 2000–02; First Vice-Pres. of Congress 2003–04; Minister of Defence 2005–06.

RENHŌ; Japanese/Taiwanese politician, fmr journalist and fmr model; b. (Hsieh Lien-fang), 28 Nov. 1967, Tokyo, Japan; m. Murata Nobuyuki 1993; one s. one d. (twins); ed Faculty of Law, Aoyama Gakuin Univ., Tokyo, Beijing Univ., People's Repub. of China; born a Taiwanese citizen, also became Japanese citizen when Nationality Law amended 1985; adopted her mother's surname, Saitō; debut as a Clarion Girl 1988, appeared on several TV and radio programmes as commentator; newscaster on TBS and TV Asahi 1993, returned to television, anchoring and reporting on several TBS programmes 2000; Councillor for Tokyo's At-large dist 2004–; mem. (Democratic Party of Japan—DPJ) for Tokyo, House of Councillors 2004–, Chair. Cttee on Educ., Culture and Science 2006, Cttee on Health, Welfare and Labour 2007, Cttee on Educ., Culture and Science 2009, Leader of the Opposition 2016–; Vice-Minister of State for Pensions in the Next Cabinet, DPJ 2009; apptd Minister of State for Govt Revitalization (Kan Cabinet) 2010, Minister for Civil Service Reform (reshuffled Kan Cabinet) 2010–11, apptd Minister of State for Govt Revitalization 2010, Minister of State for Consumer Affairs and Food Safety 2011, Minister for Electricity Conservation Promotion 2011. *Address:* House of Councillors, 1-7-1 Nagatacho, Chiyoda-ku, Tokyo 100-0014, Japan (office). *Telephone:* (3) 3581-3111 (office). *E-mail:* webmaster@sangiin.go.jp (office). *Website:* www.sangiin.go.jp (office); www.renho.jp; ameblo.jp/renho-blog.

RENNEMO, Svein; Norwegian economist and business executive; *Chairman, Statoil ASA;* b. 1947; ed Univ. of Oslo; analyst and monetary policy and econs adviser with Norges Bank (Norwegian cen. bank), OECD Secr., Paris and Ministry of Finance 1972–82; held various man. positions in Statoil 1982–94, latterly as Head of Petrochemical Div., mem. Bd of Dirs and Chair. StatoilHydro ASA (formed from merger of Statoil and Norsk Hydro 2007) 2008–, Chair. Statoil ASA 2008–, mem. Compensation Cttee; Deputy CEO and Chief Financial Officer Borealis 1994–97, CEO 1997–2001; CEO Petroleum Geo Services ASA 2002–08; Chair. Tomra Systems ASA, Pharmaq AS; mem. Bd of Dirs, Norske Skogindustrier ASA. *Address:* Statoil ASA, Forusbeen 50, 4035 Stavanger, Norway (office). *Telephone:* 51-99-00-00 (office). *Fax:* 51-99-00-50 (office). *E-mail:* statoil@statoil.com (office). *Website:* www.statoil.com (office).

RENNER, Jeremy; American actor and musician; b. 7 Jan. 1971, Modesto, Calif.; s. of Lee Renner and Valerie Cearley; UN Goodwill Peace Amb. *Television includes:* Deadly Games 1995, A Nightmare Come True 1997, Time of Your Life 1999, CSI: Crime Scene Investigation 2001, House 2007, The Unusuals 2009. *Films include:* National Lampoon's Senior Trip 1995, Fish in a Barrel 2001, Dahmer 2002, A Little Trip to Heaven 2005, Neo Ned 2005, The Assassination of Jesse James by the Coward Robert Ford 2007, 28 Weeks Later 2007, Taken 2007, The Hurt Locker (Boston Soc. of Film Critics Award for Best Actor, Chicago Film Critics Asscn Award for Best Actor, Las Vegas Film Critics Soc. Award for Best Actor, Nat. Bd of Review Award for Best Breakthrough Performance – Male, Nat. Soc. of Film Critics Award for Best Actor, Online Film Critics Soc. Award for Best Actor) 2009, The Town 2010, Mission: Impossible - Ghost Protocol 2011, Avengers Assemble 2012, The Bourne Legacy 2012, American Hustle 2013, Kill the Messenger 2014, Avengers: Age of Ultron 2015. *Address:* c/o Untitled Entertainment, 1801 Century Park East, Suite 700, Los Angeles, CA 90067, USA (office).

RENNIE, Heughan Bassett (Hugh), CBE, BA, LLB, QC; New Zealand barrister, company director and arbitrator; b. 7 April 1945, Whanganui; s. of W. S. N. Rennie and Reta Rennie; m. 1st Caroline Jane Harding 1967 (died 1992); three s.; m. 2nd Penelope Jane Ryder-Lewis 1998; ed Wanganui Collegiate School and Victoria Univ., Wellington; part-time law clerk, Wanganui 1960–67, legal officer, NZ Electricity, Wellington 1967–70; barrister and solicitor, Macalister Mazengarb Parkin and Rose, Wellington 1970–91, Partner 1972–91, Sr Litigation Partner 1982–91, Chair. 1989–91; sole barrister, Wellington 1991–95; QC 1995–; Chair. Fourth Estate Group 1970–88, Broadcasting Corpn of NZ (BCNZ) 1984–88, Govt Cttee on Restructuring BCNZ 1988, Chatham Is. Enterprise Trust 1990–2001, Policy Cttee, Dictionary of NZ Biography 1991–2001, Ministerial Inquiry into Auckland Power Supply Failure 1998, Royal NZ Ballet 1999–2003, The Marketplace Co. Ltd 1999–2009, M-co Int. Ltd 2001–10; Deputy Chair. Rugby World Cup Authority (NZ) 2010–11; Dir Fletcher Challenge Ltd 1992–99, BNZ Finance Ltd 1993–97, Bank of NZ 1997–2010, Fisher & Paykel Finance 2010–17; Ed. Wellington Dist Law Soc. newspaper 1973–84; mem. NZ Law Soc. Cttees on Professional Advertising and Public Affairs 1981–84, NZ Council for Law Reporting 1983–87, Govt Advisory Cttee to statutory mans of Equiticorp 1989–, Sir David Beattie Chair of Communications Trust Bd (VUW) 1986–90, Scientific Cttee, Nat. Heart Foundation 1988–94, Bd NZ Inst. of Chartered Accountants 2009–14, Chartered Accountants Australia NZ 2015–17; NZ Medal 1990. *Leisure interests:* history, travel, writing, cycling, reading. *Address:* Harbour Chambers, 10th Floor, Equinox House, 111 The Terrace, PO Box 10-242, Wellington 6143, New Zealand (office). *Telephone:* (4) 499-2684 (office); (4) 472-9053 (home). *Fax:* (4) 499-2705 (office). *E-mail:* hughrennie@legalchambers.co.nz (office). *Website:* www.harbourchambers.co.nz (office).

RENO, Jean; French actor; b. (Juan Moreno Jederique y Jimenez), 30 July 1948, Casablanca, Morocco; four c.; m. 3rd Zofia Borucka 2006; Nat. Order of Merit 2003. *Films include:* L'Hypothèse du tableau volé 1979, Claire de femme 1979, Voulez-vous un bébé Nobel? 1980, L'Avant dernier 1981, Les bidasses aux grandes manoeuvres 1981, La passante du Sans-Souci 1982, Ballade sanglante 1983, Le dernier combat 1983, Subway 1985, Signes Extérieurs de Richesse 1983, Ne quittez pas 1984, Alea 1984, Notre Histoire 1984, Le téléphone sonne toujours deux fois 1985, Subway 1985, Strictement personnel 1985, Zone rouge 1986, I Love You 1986, The Big Blue 1988, La Femme Nikita 1990, L'homme au Masque d'Or 1990, L'Opération Corned Beef 1991, Loulou Graffiti (also wrote screenplay) 1991, Kurenai no buta (aka Porco rosso) 1992, La vis (The Screw) 1993, Paranoïa 1993,

Les Visiteurs (The Visitors) 1993, The Professional (Léon) 1994, Les truffes 1995, French Kiss 1995, Beyond the Clouds 1995, Mission: Impossible 1996, Le jaguar 1996, For Roseanna 1997, Un amour de sorcière (Witch Way Love) 1997, Le soeurs soleil 1997, Couloirs du temps: Les visiteurs 2 1998, Godzilla 1998, Ronin 1998, Tripwire 1999, The Crimson Rivers (Les Rivières pourpres) 2000, Just Visiting 2001, Wasabi 2001, Rollerball 2002, The Quiet American 2002, Jet Lag (Décalage horaire) 2002, Ruby & Quentin (Tais-toi!) 2003, Crimson Rivers 2: Angels of the Apocalypse 2004, L'Enquête corse 2004, Hotel Rwanda 2004, L'Empire des loups 2005, La tigre e la neve (The Tiger and the Snow) 2005, The Pink Panther 2006, The Da Vinci Code 2006, Flyboys 2006, Flushed Away (voice) 2006, Ca$h 2008, The Pink Panther 2 2009, Inside Ring 2009, Couples Retreat 2009, Armoured 2009, The Round Up 2010, 22 Bullets 2010, Margaret 2011, You Don't Choose Your Family 2011, The Chef 2012, Les seigneurs 2012 The Day of the Crows 2012, Days and Nights 2014, The Sweeney: Paris 2015, The Visitors: Bastille Day 2016, Family Heist 2017, La ragazza nella nebbia 2017. *Television includes:* L'Aéropostale, courrier du ciel (mini-series) 1980, Quelques hommes de bonne volonté (mini-series) 1983, Et demain viendra le jour 1984, Un homme comblé 1985, Tender Is the Night (mini-series) 1985, Pour venger Pépère 1986, Monsieur Benjamin 1987, Flight from Justice 1993, Les grandes occasions (film) 2006, Jo (series) 2013. *Address:* Chez les Films du Dauphin, 25 rue Yves-Toudic, 75010 Paris, France.

RENSCHLER, Andreas; German automotive industry executive; b. 29 March 1958, Stuttgart; joined Daimler-Benz 1988, held several exec. positions including Head of Project Team Corp. Planning 1991–92, Asst to Chair. of Bd of Man. 1992–93, M-Class Project Man. 1993–96, Man. Dir and CEO Mercedes-Benz U.S.I, Tuscaloosa, Ala, USA 1996–98, Sr Vice-Pres. Personnel Devt 1999, Man. Dir smart GmbH, Sindelfingen and mem. Mercedes-Benz Divisional Bd 1999–2004, assigned to Mitsubishi Motors in Japan 2004, mem. Bd of Man. Daimler Trucks 2004–13, Bd of Man. Production and Purchasing, Passenger Cars and Mercedes-Benz Vans 2013–14; mem. Bd of Man. Volkswagen Aktiengesellschaft (with responsibility for commercial vehicles) 2015–; mem. Deutsche Messe AG; Pres. Commercial Vehicle Bd of Dirs, European Automobile Mfrs Asscn 2008; mem. Bd of Dirs Unaxis Holding AG 2005. *Address:* Board of Management, Volkswagen Aktiengesellschaft VHH, 2nd Floor, PO Box 1849, Wolfsburg 38436, Germany (office). *Website:* www.volkswagenag.com (office).

RENTON OF MOUNT HARRY, Baron (Life Peer), cr. 1997, of Offham in the County of East Sussex; **(Ronald) Tim(othy) Renton,** PC, MA, DL; British politician, business executive and author; b. 28 May 1932, London, England; s. of R. K. D. Renton CBE and Mrs Renton MBE; m. Alice Fergusson 1960; two s. three d.; ed Eton Coll., Magdalen Coll., Oxford; joined C. Tennant Sons & Co. Ltd 1954, with Tennants subsidiaries in Canada 1957–62, Dir 1964–73, Man. Dir Tennant Trading Ltd 1964–73; Dir Silvermines Ltd 1967–84, Australia and New Zealand Banking Group 1967–76, J. H. Vavasseur & Co. Ltd 1971–74; mem. BBC Gen. Advisory Council 1982–84; contested (Conservative) Sheffield Park 1970; MP for Mid-Sussex 1974–97; Parl. Pvt. Sec. to Rt Hon. John Biffen, MP 1979–81, to Rt Hon Geoffrey Howe, MP 1983–84; Parl. UnderSec. of State FCO 1984–85, Minister of State FCO 1985–87; Parl. Sec. to HM Treasury and Govt Chief Whip 1989–90, Minister for the Arts and for the Civil Service 1990–92; mem. Select Cttee on Nationalized Industries 1974–79, Vice-Chair. Conservative Parl. Trade Cttee 1974–79, Chair. Conservative Foreign and Commonwealth Council 1982–84; mem. Select Cttee on Nat. Heritage 1995–97; mem. House of Lords European Communities Cttee 1997–; Chair. House of Lords European Cttee on Agric. and Environment 2004–; Vice-Pres. Conservative Trade Unionists 1978–80, Pres. 1980–84; Chair. Outsider Art Archive 1995–2000, Sussex Downs Conservation Bd 1997–2005, South Downs Jt Cttee 2005–; Vice-Chair. British Council 1992–98; Dir (non-exec.) Fleming Continental European Investment Trust PLC, Chair. 1999–2002; Parl. Consultant Robert Fleming Holdings 1992–97; mem. Council Sussex Univ. 2000–; Fellow, Industry and Parl. Trust 1977–79; mem. Advisory Bd, Know-How Fund for Cen. and Eastern Europe 1992–99; mem. APEX, Council Roedean School 1982–2005 (Pres. 1998–2005), Devt Council, Parnham Trust, Criterion Theatre Trust; Trustee, Mental Health Foundation 1985–89; Founding Pres. (with Mick Jagger) of Nat. Music Day 1992–97; Green Ribbon Political Award for Environmental Campaigning 2000, Bowland Award, Asscn of Areas of Outstanding Natural Beauty 2000. *Publications:* The Dangerous Edge 1994, Hostage to Fortune 1997, Chief Whip 2004. *Leisure interests:* writing, mucking about in boats, listening to opera, growing vines. *Address:* House of Lords, Westminster, London, SW1A 0PW (office); Mount Harry House, Offham, Lewes, East Sussex, BN7 3QW, England (office). *Telephone:* (1273) 473404 (Lewes) (office); (20) 7219-3308 (Westminster) (office); 7787-153082 (mobile). *Fax:* (1273) 471450 (Lewes) (office). *E-mail:* rentont@parliament.uk (office).

RENTZEPIS, Peter M., PhD; American chemist, electrical engineer and academic; *Distinguished TEES Professor of Electrical and Computer Engineering, Texas A&M University;* b. 11 Dec. 1934, Kalamata, Greece; s. of Michael Rentzepis and Leuci Rentzepis; m. Alma Elizabeth Keenan; two s.; ed Denison, Syracuse and Univ. of Cambridge, UK; mem. Tech. Staff Research Labs Gen. Electric Co., New York, then mem. Tech. Staff, Bell Labs, New Jersey, Head, Physical and Inorganic Chem. Research Dept; Presidential Chair. and Prof. of Chem. and Electrical and Computer Eng, Univ. of California, Irvine 1986–2016, Dir CX (IT) 2; Distinguished TEES Prof. of Electrical and Computer Eng, Texas A&M Univ. 2016–; Adjunct Prof. of Chem., Univ. of Pennsylvania, of Chem. and Biophysics, Yale Univ. 1980–; Visiting Prof., Rockefeller Univ. 1971, MIT –1975, of Chem. Univ. of Tel Aviv; mem. numerous academic cttees and editorial bds, including US Army Cttee on Energetic Materials Research and Tech. 1982–83; Dir NATO Advanced Study Inst. 1984–; Co-founder and Chair. Call/Recall Inc. 1996–; mem. Bd of Dirs, KRIKOS—Science and Tech. for Greece, The Quanex Corpn 1984; mem. Advisory Bd, Uniloc Corpn, Physical Chem. Div. of Nat. Inst. of Science and Tech.; mem. US AmCCOM Advisory Cttee, US Army ARRACOM Exec. Science Advisory Cttee, NATO Advanced Study Insts (Dir), Int. Science Foundation; mem. NAS 1978, AAAS, Nat. Acad. of Greece 1980; Fellow, New York Acad. of Sciences, American Physical Soc.; Hon. ScD (Denison) 1981, (Carnegie-Mellon) 1983; Hon. DPhil (Syracuse) 1980; Hon. DSc (Nat. Tech. Univ., Greece) 1990; ACS Peter Debye Prize in Physical Chem., Irving Lungmuize Prize in Chemical Physics, American Physical Soc., Scientist of the Year 1978, New York Acad. of Sciences, Cressy Morison Award in Natural Sciences, Scientist of the Year 1988, ACS Tolman Award 1995, ISCO Award for Biological Research 1999, Richard C. Tolman Award and Medal, Univ. of California, Irvine 2002, and other awards. *Publications include:* more than 400 papers on lasers, photochemistry, picosecond spectroscopy; 68 patents. *Address:* ECE Department, Texas A&M University, 325C WEBTAMU, College Station, TX 77843 (office); Call/Recall, Inc. Sytems Division, 6160 Lusk Blvd, Suite C-206, San Diego, CA 92121, USA (office). *Telephone:* (979) 845-7250 (College Station) (office). *Fax:* (979) 845-6259 (College Station) (office). *E-mail:* prentzepis@tamu.edu (office). *Website:* engineering.tamu.edu/electrical/people/rentzepis-peter (office).

RENWICK, Glenn M., BS, MEng; American insurance industry executive; *President and CEO, The Progressive Corporation;* b. 22 May 1955; m. Deborah Renwick; ed Univ. of Canterbury, NZ, Univ. of Florida; joined The Progressive Corpn (automobile insurance co.) 1986, Auto Product Man. for Fla then Auto Product Man. for Ga 1986–88, Pres. of Mid-Atlantic States 1988–90, Pres. Calif. Div. 1991–93, Pres. Program Operations Consumer Marketing Div. 1993–98, Business Tech. Process Leader and Chief Information Officer 1998–2000, apptd mem. Bd of Dirs 1999, CEO Insurance Operations 2000–01, Pres. and CEO 2001–; mem. Bd of Dirs Fiserv, Inc. 2001–. *Address:* The Progressive Corporation, 6300 Wilson Mills Road, Mayfield Village, OH 44143, USA (office). *Telephone:* (440) 461-5000 (office). *Fax:* (440) 603-4420 (office). *Website:* www.progressive.com (office).

RENWICK OF CLIFTON, Baron (Life Peer), cr. 1997, of Chelsea in the Royal Borough of Kensington and Chelsea; **Robin William Renwick,** KCMG, MA; British diplomatist and business executive; *Vice-Chairman, Investment Banking, JP Morgan;* b. 13 Dec. 1937; s. of Richard Renwick and Clarice Renwick; m. Annie Colette Gidicelli 1965; one s. one d.; ed St Paul's School, Jesus Coll., Cambridge and Univ. of Paris (Sorbonne), France; served in army 1956–58; entered Foreign Service 1963, served in Dakar 1963–64, at Foreign Office 1964–66, Embassy in New Delhi 1966–69, Pvt. Sec. to Minister of State, FCO 1970–72, First Sec., Embassy in Paris 1972–76, Counsellor, Cabinet Office 1976–78, Head of Rhodesia Dept, FCO 1978–80; Political Adviser to Gov. of Rhodesia 1980; Visiting Fellow, Center for Int. Affairs, Harvard Univ. 1980–81; Head of Chancery, Washington, DC 1981–84, Asst Under-Sec. of State, FCO 1984–87, Amb. to S Africa 1987–91, to USA 1991–95; Chair. Save and Prosper 1996–98, Fluor Ltd 1996–2010; Dir British Airways 1996–2006, Robert Fleming (Deputy Chair. Robert Fleming Holdings Ltd 1999–2001), BHP Billiton plc 1997–2005, Fluor Corpn 1997–2010, SAB Miller 1999–2009, Compagnie Financière Richemont AG 1995–, Kazakhmys plc 2005–; Vice-Chair. (Investment Banking) JPMorgan, Vice-Chair. JPMorgan Cazenove 2004–; Deputy Chair. Fleming Family and Partners 2000–; Trustee, The Economist 1996–2011; Hon. LLD (Witwatersrand) 1991, (American Univ. in London) 1993; Hon. DLitt (Coll. of William and Mary) 1993. *Publications:* Economic Sanctions 1981, Fighting with Allies 1996, Unconventional Diplomacy 1997, A Journey with Margaret Thatcher 2013. *Leisure interests:* tennis, fly fishing, islands. *Address:* House of Lords, London, SW1A 0PW; JPMorgan Cazenove, 10 Aldermanbury, London, EC2V 7RF, England (office). *Telephone:* (20) 7219-5353 (House of Lords); (20) 7325-6375 (office). *Website:* www.jpmorgancazenove.com (office).

RENYI, Thomas A., BA, MBA; American banking executive; b. 1946; m. Elizabeth Renyi; two s. one d.; ed Rutgers Univ.; joined Bank of New York Co. Inc. 1971, Pres. 1992–98, Vice-Chair. 1992–98, CEO 1997–2007, Chair. 1998–2007, Exec. Chair. Bank of New York Mellon Corpn (after merger with Mellon Financial Corpn) 2007–08; fmr Chair. New York Bankers Asscn; Advisor, CVC Capital Partners Inc. 2009–; mem. Bd of Dirs Public Service Enterprise Group Inc., Hartford Financial Services Co. 2010–, The Clearing House, World Trade Center Memorial Foundation, Lincoln Center for the Performing Arts, Royal Bank of Canada 2013–; fmr Chair. Financial Services Roundtable; fmr mem. Bd of Execs, New York Stock Exchange; mem. Bd of Mans New York Botanical Garden; mem. Bd of Trustees Bates Coll., Healthcare Chaplaincy, Catholic Charities of the Archdiocese of New York; mem. Bd of Overseers Rutgers Univ. Foundation.

RENZI, Matteo; Italian politician; b. 11 Jan. 1975, Florence; s. of Tiziano Renzi and Laura Bovoli; m. Agnese Landini; three c.; ed Univ. degli Studi, Florence; began career with CHIL Srl (family-owned communications and marketing co.); Pres., Prov. of Florence 2004–09; Mayor of Florence 2009–14; Pres., Council of Ministers (Prime Minister) 2014–16; mem. Partito Popolare Italiano 1996–2002, Democrazia è Libertà - La Margherita 2002–07, Partito Democratico (PD) 2007– (Sec. 2013–17 (resgnd Feb.), May 2017–March 2018). *Publications include:* Fuori! 2011, Stilnovo 2012, Oltre la rottamazione 2013. *Address:* Partito Democratico, Via Sant' Andrea delle Fratte 16, 00187 Roma, Italy (office). *Telephone:* (06) 695321 (office). *E-mail:* redazione@partitodemocratico.it (office). *Website:* www.partitodemocratico.it (office).

RENZI, Nicola, PhD; San Marino politician; *Secretary of State for Foreign Affairs, Political Affairs and Justice;* b. 18 Aug. 1979; m.; one s.; ed Univ. of Bologna; began career as high-school teacher of Latin and Greek 2003; mem. Alleanza Popolare 2009–; mem. Consiglio Grande e Generale (Parl.) 2012–, mem. Justice Cttee, Territorial Policies Cttee; Co-Capt.-Regent (jt head of state) Oct. 2015–April 2016; Sec. of State for Foreign Affairs, Political Affairs and Justice 2016–; mem. San Marino IPU Nat. Group; mem. Dante Alighieri Soc., Rotary Club San Marino. *Leisure interests:* antiques, reading. *Address:* Palazzo pubblico, Piazza della Libertà, 47890 San Marino (office). *Telephone:* (549) 882286 (office). *Website:* www.reggenzadellarepubblica.sm (office).

REPIN, Vadim Viktorovich; Russian violinist; *Artistic Director, Trans-Siberian Arts Festival;* b. 31 Aug. 1971, Novosibirsk, Siberia; s. of Viktor Antonovich Repin and Galina Georgievna Repina; ed Novosibirsk Music School, Hochschule für Musik, Lübeck with Zakhar Bron; began playing violin aged five; first stage performance six months later; won gold medal in all age categories in Wienawski Competition, Poznań aged 11; debut recitals in Moscow and St Petersburg; debuts in Tokyo, Munich, Berlin, Helsinki 1985, Carnegie Hall 1986; has performed with all major orchestras and greatest conductors; regularly collaborates with Nikolai Lugansky and Itamar Golan in recital; other chamber music partners include Martha Argerich, Evgeny Kissin and Mischa Maisky; season 2009–10: concerts with Muti in New York, with Thielemann in Tokyo, with Chailly in Leipzig, tour of Australia with London Philharmonic Orchestra and Vladimir Jurowski, and première of a violin concerto written for him by James MacMillan, performed with London Symphony Orchestra and Valery Gergiev; Founder and Artistic Dir Trans-

Siberian Arts Festival 2013–; Season 14/15: concerts in Vilnius, Prague, Vienna, Paris and Ankara and a Vadim Repin Festival in Tokyo; performances in USA, concerts with Philharmonia Orchestra and Vladimir Ashkenazy in London and Cardiff, German premiere of Yussupov concerto at Berlin Philharmonie, a return to Japan for concerts with Tchaikovsky Symphony Orchestra to celebrate the Tchaikovsky centenary; Season 15/16: concerts in Yerevan, Barcelona, Madrid, Bangkok, Shanghai, Seoul, a tour of European cities with Tokyo Metropolitan Orchestra and Kazushi Ono; London premiere of Aphrodite Raickopoulou's music for the silent film Love (1927) starring Greta Garbo; 70th anniversary of Univ. of Mexico's orchestra; joined Israel Symphony and James Judd with Trans-Siberian Art Festival in Israel; concert with Martha Argerich at her festival in Japan; concerts in Taiwan and performances of Pas de Deux with Svetlana Zakharova in Korea and Japan; concerts with Orchestre Philharmonique de Radio France and Mikko Franck, Monte Carlo Philharmonic, Orchestre du Capitole de Toulouse with Tugan Sokhiev, with Kent Nagano in Elbphilharmonie, Hamburg, with Philadelphia Orchestra and Stéphane Denève, with Andreï Korobeinikov and German Radio Orchestra in Korea, China and Japan; Hon. Prof., Beijing Cen. Conservatory of Music 2014, Shanghai Conservatory 2015; Victoire d'honneur; Chevalier des Arts et des Lettres 2010; Tibor Varga competition winner, Sion 1985, winner, Reine Elisabeth Concours, Brussels 1990, Victoire d'honneur (France) 2010. *Television:* Vadim Repin: A Magician of Sound (film documentary by Claudia Willke) 2010. *Recordings include:* Shostakovich No. 1 and Prokofiev No. 2 with the Hallé Orchestra under Nagano 1995, Prokofiev Violin Sonatas and Five Melodies with Berezovsky 1995, Tchaikovsky and Sibelius Concertos with the London Symphony under Krivine 1996, Tchaikovsky and Shostakovich piano trios with Berezovsky and Yablonsky 1997, Lalo Symphonie Espagnole with the London Symphony Orchestra under Nagano 1998, Tutta Bravura (with Markovich) 1999, Vadim Repin au Louvre (with Berezovsky, Barachovsky, Lakatos, Gothoni) 1999, Tchaikovsky and Myaskovsky violin concertos with the Kirov Orchestra under Gergiev 2002, A Night of Encores (recorded live with the Berlin Philharmonic under Jansons) 2004, Taneyev Piano Quintet and Trio (Gramophone Award for Best Chamber Recording 2006), Beethoven Violin Concerto (with Vienna Philharmonic and Riccardo Muti, coupled with Beethoven's Kreutzer Sonata with Martha Argerich) 2008, Brahms Violin Concerto and Brahms Double Concerto (Truls Mørk, cello, with Gewandhaus Orchester Leipzig and Riccardo Chailly) 2009, Tchaikovsky and Rachmaninov trios with Mischa Maisky and Lang Lang (Echo Award) 2009, recital recording with Nikolai Lugansky 2010, James MacMillan violin concerto with BBC Scottish Symphony under Donald Runnicles 2016. *Leisure interests:* chess, swimming, skiing. *Address:* c/o Interclassica Music Management, Schönburgstrasse 4, 1040 Vienna, Austria (office). *Telephone:* (1) 585-3980 (office). *E-mail:* eleanorhope@interclassica.com (office). *Website:* www.interclassica.com (office); www.vadimrepin.com; www.transsiberianfestival.com.

REPŠE, Einars, MS; Latvian politician, computer scientist, investor and fmr central banker; b. 9 Dec. 1961, Jelgava; s. of Aivars-Rihards Repše and Aldona Repše (née Krasauska); m. Ruta Raginska Repse 1985; three s. one d.; ed Latvia State Univ.; engineer, Latvian Acad. of Sciences 1986–90; entered politics as Co-founder of Latvian Nat. Independence Movt (LNNK) 1988; mem. Parl. 1990–91, re-elected 2002; Gov. Bank of Latvia 1991–2001; Founder and Chair. New Era (Jaunais laiks) 2002; Prime Minister of Latvia 2002–04; Minister of Defence 2004–05 (resgnd), of Finance 2009–10; Chair. Artificial Intelligence Foundation 2010–14, Latvijas Nakotnes Forums 2012–14; Founder and Chair. Latvijas Attistibai 2013–15; Commdr, Order of the Three Stars 1997. *Leisure interest:* aviation, art, alpine skiing, mountaineering, music, natural horsemanship.

RESCHER, Nicholas, PhD, FRSC, FRAS; American philosopher and author; *Distinguished University Professor of Philosophy, University of Pittsburgh;* b. 15 July 1928, Hagen, Germany; s. of Erwin Hans Rescher and Meta Anna Rescher; m. 1st Frances Short 1951 (divorced 1965); one d.; m. 2nd Dorothy Henle 1968; two s. one d.; ed Queens Coll., New York, Princeton Univ.; Assoc. Prof. of Philosophy, Lehigh Univ. 1957–61; Distinguished Univ. Prof. of Philosophy, Univ. of Pittsburgh 1961–, Dir Center for Philosophy of Science 1982–89, Chair. 1989–; consultant, RAND Corpn 1954–66, Encyclopaedia Britannica 1963–64, North American Philosophical Publs 1980–; Ed. American Philosophical Quarterly 1964–94; Sec.-Gen. Int. Union of History and Philosophy of Science 1969–75; visiting lectureships at Univs of Oxford, Munich, Konstanz, Western Ontario and others; Pres. American Philosophical Asscn (Eastern Div.) 1989–90, American Catholic Philosophical Asscn 2003–04, American Metaphysical Soc. 2004–05; mem. Academia Europea, Institut Int. de Philosophie, Acad. Int. de Philosophie des Sciences; Fellow, American Acad. of Arts and Sciences 2009; Hon. mem. Corpus Christi Coll., Oxford; Bundesverdienstkreuz; eight hon. degrees; Guggenheim Fellow 1970–71, Alexander von Humboldt Prize 1983, Aquinas Medal, Cardinal Mercier Prize. *Publications include:* more than 100 books, including The Coherence Theory of Truth 1973, Methodological Pragmatism 1977, Scientific Progress 1978, The Limits of Science 1984, Ethical Idealism 1987, Rationality 1988, A System of Pragmatic Idealism (three vols) 1992–94, Pluralism 1993, Predicting the Future 1997, Paradoxes 2001, Philosophical Reasoning 2001, Metaphysics 2005, Epistemetrics 2006, Free Will 2009, Aporetics 2009; numerous articles in many areas of philosophy. *Leisure interests:* reading history and biography. *Address:* 1012 Cathedral of Learning, University of Pittsburgh, Pittsburgh, PA 15260 (office); 1033 Milton Avenue, Pittsburgh, PA 15218, USA (home). *Telephone:* (412) 624-5950 (office); (412) 243-1290 (home). *Fax:* (412) 383-7506 (office). *E-mail:* rescher@pitt.edu (office). *Website:* www.pitt.edu/~rescher (office).

RESIN, Vladimir Iosifovich, PhD; Russian politician and civil engineer; b. 21 Feb. 1936, Minsk, Byelorussian SSR, USSR; s. of Josif Gilimovich Resin and Roza Volfovna Sheydlina; m. Marta Yakovlevna Chadaeva 1958; one d.; ed Moscow Mining Inst.; began working as mining engineer in Ukraine 1958, then worked at construction sites in Murmansk, Kaluga and Smolensk, transferred to the building orgs of Moscow 1965, held various positions up to Man. of the Trust Tunnelling Works, worked in orgs of USSR Ministry of Coal Industry and Ministry of Ass. and Special Construction; Deputy, First Deputy, then Head, Moscow Dept of Eng and Construction 1974 (apptd); Head, Moscow Industrial Construction Dept 1985; Chair. Moscow Construction Cttee 1989–91; Deputy Chair. Exec. Cttee, Moscow City Council 1989–91; Deputy Premier, Moscow City Govt 1991–92, First Vice-Premier 1992; Head, Dept of Moscow Architecture, Construction, Prospective Devt Complex and Reconstruction 1992–2000, Head of Complex of Architecture, Construction, Devt and Reconstruction of City (CACDR) 2000–02, Head of Dept, City-Planning Policy, Devt and Reconstruction of City 2002; First Deputy Mayor of Moscow 2000–02, Acting Mayor of Moscow Sept.–Oct. 2010, Adviser to the Mayor of Moscow 2011; Deputy (Yedinaya Rossiya) of State Duma, Fed. Ass. of Russian Fed. 2011, mem. Cttee for Land and Construction; Advisor for Construction to the Patriarch of Moscow and All Russia 2012; Prof. G.V. Plekhanov Russian Univ. of Econs 1996, Moscow Int. Univ.; Corresp. mem. and mem. Presidium, Russian Acad. of Architecture and Construction Sciences, Russian Eng Acad.; mem. Russian Union of Architects, and of 21 int. and Russian acads; Sr Fellow, Inst. of Civil Engineers 2000; Hon. Citizen of Yerevan and Gyumri (Armenia), Balakhna (Russia), Honoured Builder of the USSR, Honoured Engineer of Russia, Distinguished Constructor of Russian Fed., Honoured Constructor of Moscow, Hon. Prof., Moscow State Lomonosov Univ., Moscow Int. Univ. 2000, Russian Acad. of Sciences 2005; 60 USSR and Russian State Awards (17 orders, 33 medals, insignias), including Order for Services to the Fatherland of the II, III and IV Ranks 1995, 2005, 2008, Order of Honour 2000, Order of Friendship 2011, Order 'The Symbol of Honor' 1971, Order of Nations' Friendship 1984, Insignia for Services to the City of Moscow; Hon. PhD of leading univs in Russia; six times Laureate of the Pres. of Russian Fed. 1993, 1995, 1996, 1997, 2003, 2006, Hon. Letter of the Pres. of Russian Fed. 2009, 14 awards from Russian Orthodox Church, 250 departmental, public and non-governmental orgs awards. *Publications include:* 26 monographs and books, including Managing the Development of a Large City: A Systems Approach, Development of Large Cities in the Conditions of a Transitional Economy (System Approach), Probabilistic Technologies in Development Management of the City, Vladimir Resin – Moscow's Foreman-in-Chief 1999, Vladimir Resin – Roads of Moscow-Builder 2006, The Working Foreman of Moscow – Roads of Vladimir Resin 2010; 116 scientific publs in the fields of economy and construction (many translated) and 34 inventions. *Leisure interest:* work. *Address:* 121609 Moscow, Osennyaya Street 4/2-6, Russia (home). *Telephone:* (495) 956-80-98. *Fax:* (495) 956-64-90. *E-mail:* alexandro.khomenko@gmail.com.

RESTAD, Gudmund; Norwegian politician; b. 19 Dec. 1937, Smøla; s. of Ola Restad and Olga Marie Dalen; m. Britt Jorun Wollum 1959; three c.; ed officers' training school (anti-aircraft artillery), business school, Nat. Police Acad.; sergeant at Ørland airport 1959–61, country police Ørland and Orkdal 1961–67; detective constable/inspector Crime Police Centre 1967–73; training in police investigation in Denmark and Germany 1967; Lecturer, Nat. Police Training School 1973–75; sergeant in Smøla 1975–85; mem. Parl. 1985–2001; Chair. Local Council, Smøla 1980–85, mem., Chair., Deputy Chair. Nordmøre Interkommunale Kraftlag (Nordmøre Electricity Bd) 1982–91; mem. Bd Central Police Org. 1969–73, Møre og Romsdal Centre Party 1982–83, The Centre Party 1983–89; mem. Judiciary Cttee Storting (Parl.) 1985–89; Deputy Chair. Finance Cttee 1989–97; Minister of Finance and Customs 1997–2000; Deputy Chair. Defence Cttee 2000–01; Deputy mem. Norwegian Parl. Del. to EFTA 1989–93. *Address:* c/o Stortinget, 0026 Oslo, Norway.

RESTON, James Barrett, Jr, BA; American academic and writer; *Senior Scholar, Woodrow Wilson International Center for Scholars;* b. 8 March 1941, New York; m. Denise Brender Leary 1971; ed Univ. of Oxford, UK, Univ. of North Carolina; reporter, Chicago Daily News 1964–65; Lecturer in Creative Writing, Univ. of North Carolina at Chapel Hill 1971–81; Watergate adviser and strategist for David Frost in Nixon interviews 1977; Sr Scholar, Woodrow Wilson Int. Center for Scholars, Washington, DC; mem. Authors Guild, Dramatists Guild, PEN; US Tennis Asscn Capt. 2001–05; Dupont-Columbia Award 1982, Prix Italia, Venice 1982, Nat. Endowment for the Arts grant 1982, Valley Forge Award 1985. *Plays:* Sherman the Peacemaker 1979, Jonestown Express 1983, Galileo's Torch 2014; adviser to playwright Peter Morgan for play Frost/Nixon 2007; also radio and TV documentaries and plays. *Film:* adviser to dir Ron Howard for film Frost/Nixon 2008. *Publications include:* fiction: To Defend, To Destroy 1971, The Knock at Midnight 1975, The Nineteenth Hijacker 2014; non-fiction: The Amnesty of John David Herndon 1973, Perfectly Clear: Nixon from Whittier to Watergate (with Frank Mankiewicz) 1973, The Innocence of Joan Little: A Southern Mystery 1977, Our Father Who Art in Hell: The Life and Death of Jim Jones 1981, The Lone Star: The Life of John Connally 1989, Collision at Home Plate: The Lives of Peter Rose and Bart Giamatti 1991, The Last Apocalypse: Europe at the Year 1000 AD 1998, Warriors of God: Richard the Lionheart and Saladin in the Third Crusade 2001, Dogs of God: Columbus, the Inquisition and the Defeat of the Moors 2005, Fragile Innocence: A Father's Memoir of his Daughter's Courageous Journey 2006, The Conviction of Richard Nixon: The Untold Story 2007, Defenders of the Faith: Charles V, Suleyman the Magnificent, and the Battle for Europe, 1520–1536 2009, Accidental Victim: JFK, Lee Harvey Oswald, and the Real Target in Dallas 2013, Luther's Fortress: Martin Luther and His Reformation Under Siege 2015; contrib. to various periodicals. *Leisure interest:* tennis. *Address:* 4714 Hunt Avenue, Chevy Chase, MD 20815, USA. *E-mail:* james.reston@veizon.net. *Website:* www.jrobsessions.com; www.restonbooks.com.

REUS GONZÁLEZ, María Esther, LLB; Cuban lawyer and politician; *Minister of Justice;* b. 23 May 1962; fmr Pres. Nat. Electoral Comm.; Vice-Minister of Justice –2007, Minister 2007–. *Address:* Ministry of Justice, Calle O, No 216, entre 23 y 25, Plaza de la Revolución, Apdo 10400, Havana 4, Cuba (office). *Telephone:* (7) 838-3450 (office). *E-mail:* apoblacion@oc.minjus.cu (office). *Website:* www.minjus.cu (office).

REVIGLIO, Franco; Italian economist, academic and fmr politician; *Professor Emeritus, University of Turin;* b. 3 Feb. 1935, Turin; m.; one s. two d.; ed Univ. of Turin; asst in Faculty of Law, Univ. of Turin 1959–64, Prof. of Financial Science 1968–2002, Dir Departimento di Scienze Economiche e Finanziarie G. Prato 1995–2000, mem. Bd of Dirs 1971–72, currently Prof. Emer.; economist, IMF, Washington, DC 1964–66; Prof., Univ. of Urbino 1966–68; Consultant, Ministry of Budget and Econ. Planning 1974–79; mem. Cen. Tax Comm. and Tech. Cttee for Tax Reform, Ministry of Finance 1976–79, Minister of Finance 1979–81; Councillor, Municipal Council of Turin 1981–83; Chair. Tech. Comm. on Public Expenditure Ministry of Treasury 1981–83; mem. Tech. Cttee for Econ. Programming, Ministry of the Budget 1981–89, Minister of the Budget 1992–93; Chair. Ente Nazionale Idrocarburi 1983–89; Sr Adviser, Wasserstein Perella 1990–92;

Senator 1992–94; Chair. and Man. Dir Azienda Energetica Metropolitana Torino 2000–06; Pres. AES Corpn 2001–06; Sr Adviser, Lehman Brothers 2002–07; Councillor, Edipower 2002–11; Dir and mem. of Strategic Cttee, Finmeccanica 2003–05; apptd Prof. of Public Econ., ESCP Europe Business School 2005; Gen. Councillor, Fondazione di Venezia 2006; fmr Pres. NNOICOM; Pres. Fondazione per gli Alti Studi sull'Arte 2008–09; Columnist Il Corriere della Sera, La Stampa, L'Espresso, Il Sole 24 Ore, Il Messaggero 1978–2010; mem. Exec. Cttee, Istituto Internazionale di Finanza Pubblica 1967–69; mem. Council of Foreign Relations, Middle-East Econ. Strategy Group (Meesg) 1994–95; Bd mem. Umberto Allemandi & C. SpA 2010; Visiting Fellow, IMF, Washington, DC Sept.–Dec. 1999; St Vincent Prize for Econs 1998, Walter Tobagi Prize 1998. *Publications:* La finanza della sicurezza sociale (co-author) 1969, Spesa pubblica e stagnazione dell'economia italiana 1975, Le chiavi del 2000 1990, Meno Stato più mercato: Come ridurre lo Stato per risanare il Paese 1994, Lo Stato imperfetto 1996, Come siama entrati in Europa 1998, Principi di scienza delle finanze 1998, Sanità senza vincoli di spesa? 1999, PIstituzioni di economia pubblica 2005, Per restare in Europa. Ridurre l'evasione e riformare la spesa pubblica, Utet, Torino 2006, La spesa pubblica. Conoscerla e riformarla, Marsilio 2007, Goodbye Keynes-Meno debito più lavoro-Le riforme per tornare a crescere 2010; contrib. of numerous essays and articles to journals and newspapers. *Address:* Departimento di Scienze Economiche e Finanziarie G. Prato, Facoltà di Economia – Università di Torino, Corso Unione Sovietica 218bis, 10134 Turin, Italy (office). *Telephone:* (011) 6706080 (office); (02) 645750 (home). *Fax:* (011) 6706062 (office). *E-mail:* franco.reviglio@unito.it (home). *Website:* www.econ.unito.it (office).

REY, Rafael; Peruvian business executive, diplomatist and politician; b. 26 Feb. 1954, Lima; ed Univ. Católica del Perú, INCAE, Costa Rica, Univ. de Piura; Man. RANSA Comercial SA 1979–82; Man. Dir Crowley Peru SA (fmrly Crowley Caribbean Transport Inc.) 1982–90; Deputy, Congreso de la Republica (parl.) 1990–2006; Minister of State for Production 2006–08; Amb. to Italy 2008–09; Minister of Defence 2009–10; Dir Crowley Perú SA, Diario La Prensa Perú, S.A.M Trading SA, Corporación ACME; mem. Consultative Cttee, Ministry of Foreign Affairs; mem. Partido Renovación Nacional, Pres. 1992–; unsuccessful cand. for Deputy of Keiko Fujimori in general election 2011; mem. Exec. Council, Instituto de Formación para la Acción Política, Instituto Peruano de Economía de Mercado. *Leisure interests:* swimming, jogging. *Address:* Renovación Nacional, Avda Camino Real 1206, 2°, San Isidro, Lima 1, Peru (office). *Telephone:* (1) 5673798 (office).

REYES-HEROLES GONZÁLEZ GARZA, Jesús, BEcons, PhD; Mexican civil servant and petroleum industry executive; *President, StructurA;* b. 1950, Mexico City; ed Instituto Autónomo de México (ITAM), Massachusetts Inst. of Tech., USA; began career as Research Asst, Banco de México; served in various civil service roles including Dir-Gen. Treas. Planning 1983–88, Gen. Coordinator of Foreign Affairs Secr. Advisers 1989–90; Dir-Gen. GEA Grupo de Economistas y Asociados (consultancy firm) 1991–94; Mexican mem. Asia-Pacific Econ. Cooperation (APEC) Group of Eminent Persons 1993–94; Dir-Gen. Banco Nacional de Obras y Servicios Públicos (Banobras) 1994–95; Mexican Sec. of Energy 1995–97; Amb. to USA 1997–2000; Exec. Pres. GEA StructurA (consultancy) 2001–06, currently Pres. StructurA; Dir-Gen. Petróleos Mexicanos (PEMEX) 2006–09; mem. PRI (Institutional Revolutionary Party) 1972–, Pres. PRI Nat. Comm. on Ideology 1994; fmr mem. Bd of Dirs Banamex, Citigroup, Wal-Mart Mexico; fmr Trustee Gonzalo Río Arronte Foundation, Universidad Iberoamericana (FICSAC). *Publications:* several articles in academic journals. *Address:* StructurA, Av. Del Parque 10, Col. Campestre, CP 01040, México, DF, Mexico (office). *Telephone:* (55) 6237-9894 (office). *Fax:* (55) 5550-0655 (office). *E-mail:* contact@energea.structura.com.mx (office). *Website:* www.energea.structura.com.mx (office).

REYES RAMÍREZ, Leonardo Ovidio, Lic.Econ., MEcons; Nicaraguan economist and central banker; *President, Banco Central de Nicaragua;* ed Univ. Nacional Autónoma de Nicaragua, Pontificia Universidad Católica de Chile, Pennsylvania State Univ., USA; Prof. of Math., School of Agricultural Econs, Univ. Nacional Autónoma de Nicaragua 1990; worked with IMF as Technical Man. of several econ. programmes; Deputy Man., Gen. Econ. Studies and Head of Monetary Program Dept, Banco Central de Nicaragua (BCN) 1995, Gen. Man., BCN 2012–14, Pres. 2014–; Chief Economist and Econ. Adviser, Ministry of Finance and Public Credit 2004–12. *Address:* Banco Central de Nicaragua, Km 7 Carretera Sur, 100 metros al Este, Pista Juan Pablo II, Managua, Nicaragua (office). *Telephone:* (2255) 7171 (office). *Website:* www.bcn.gob.ni (office).

REYES RENDÓN, Samuel Armando; Honduran engineer and politician; *Minister of National Defence;* b. Lempira; fmr Presidential Appointee in Congreso Nacional (Parl.); Second Vice-Pres. of Honduras 2010–14; Minister of Nat. Defence 2014–; mem. Partido Nacional. *Address:* Ministry of National Defence, Boulevard Suyapa, Col. Florencia Sur, frente a Iglesia Colegio Episcopal, Tegucigalpa, Honduras (office). *Telephone:* 2239-2330 (office). *E-mail:* transparencia@sedena .gob.hn (office). *Website:* www.sedena.gob.hn (office).

REYGADAS, Carlos; Mexican filmmaker; b. (Carlos Reygadas Castillo), 10 Oct. 1971, Mexico City; ed Mount St Mary's Coll., UK, law studies in Mexico; played rugby for Mexican nat. team; worked for Mexican foreign service in Brussels. *Films directed include:* Adulte (short, also writer and producer) 1988, Prisionniers (short, also writer and producer) 1999, Max (short, also writer and producer) 1999, Oiseaux 1999 (short, also writer and producer), Japón (also producer and writer) (Special Mention, Cannes Film Festival) 2002, Filmando: Batalla en el cielo (documentary) 2004, Batalla en el Cielo (Battle in Heaven) (also producer, writer and ed.) 2005, Luz Silenciosa (Silent Light) (also producer and writer) 2007, 42 One Dream Rush (short, also writer and producer) 2009, Revolución (segment 'Este es mi reino') 2010, Post Tenebras Lux (Light After Darkness) (also producer and screenwriter) (Best Dir, Cannes Film Festival) 2012, Short Plays (segment 'Mexico') 2014. *Films produced include:* Sangre 2005, La influencia (co-producer) 2007, Los bastardos (assoc. producer) 2008, El árbol (producer and ed.) 2009, Heli (assoc. producer) 2013. *Film edited:* De paseo (short) 2004. *Address:* Tabasco #330, Colonia Roma Norte, Ciudad de México, 06700 Mexico, CDMX (office). *Telephone:* (21) 5273-0230. *E-mail:* coordinacion@mantarraya.com (home). *Website:* mantarraya.com (home).

REYN, Evgeny Borisovich; Russian poet and writer; *Professor, M. Gorky State Literature Institute;* b. 29 Dec. 1935, Leningrad; m. Nadejda Reyn 1989; one s.; ed Leningrad Tech. Inst.; freelance poet published in samizdat magazine Sintaksis and émigré press abroad in magazines Grani, Kovcheg; participated in publ. of almanac Metropol; literary debut in Russia 1984; currently Prof., M. Gorky Inst. of Literature, Moscow; mem. Writers' Union, Union of Moscow Writers, Russian PEN Centre; Peterburg Prize of Arts 'Tsarskoye Selo' 1995, State Prize of Russia in Literature and Art 1996, Ind. Alexander Block Literature Award 1999, Alfred Tepfer Foundation Pushkin Prize (Hamburg, Germany) 2003, State Pushkin Prize in Literature and Art 2004, Grinzane Cavour Prize (Turin, Italy) 2004, Petropol Prize in Literature and Arts, St Peterburg 2005, Kiev Laura 2010, Prize Anton Delvig 2010, Nord South Prize 2011, The Poet Prize 2012. *Television:* Kuprin 1967, The Thcukokkala 1969, The Tenth Chapter 1970, Journeys with Josef Brodsky 1993, Josef Brodsky: The Hatchings to Portrait 1996. *Publications:* The Names of Bridges 1984, Shore Line 1989, The Darkness of Mirrors 1989, Irretrievable Day 1991, Counter-Clockwise 1992, Nezhnosmo 1993, Selected Poems 1993, The Prognostication 1994, Breda 1995, The Top-booty 1995, The Others 1996, The News Stages of the Life of The Moscow Beau Monde 1997, Balkony 1998, Arch over Water 2000, The Remarks of Marathon Man: Inconclusive Memoirs 2003, The Overground Transition 2004, After Our Age 2005, My Best Addressman… 2005, The Poems, Prose, Essays 2006, Balcone e altri poesie 2008, The Memory of the Journey 2011, Labyrinth 2013. *Address:* Leningradsky Prospect, 75, Apt 167, 125057 Moscow, Russia (home). *Telephone:* (499) 157-20-14 (home); (7985) 9976858 (cell) (home). *E-mail:* NADIA_REYNE@mail.ru (home).

REYNDERS, Didier, LLB; Belgian politician; *Deputy Prime Minister and Minister of Foreign and European Affairs and of Defence, in charge of Beliris and Federal Cultural Institutions;* b. 6 Aug. 1958, Liège; m.; four c.; ed Inst. St Jean Berchmans, Liège, Univ. of Liège; lawyer 1981–85; Gen. Man. Ministry of Wallonia Region 1985–88; Chair. Belgian Nat. Railway Co. (SNCB) 1986–91; Chef de Cabinet of Deputy Prime Minister, Minister of Justice and Inst. Reform 1987–88; Chair. Nat. Airways Co. 1991–93; Vice-Chair. Parti Réformateur Libéral (PRL) 1992; Deputy, House of Reps 1992; Head of PRL Group in Liège Council 1995, Chair. PRL-FDF (Front Démocratique des Francophones) Group 1995; Chair. Fed. Provinciale et d'Arrondissement de Liège of PRL 1995–; Lecturer, Hautes Ecoles Commerciales, Liège; Minister of Finance 1999–2007 (resgnd); Deputy Prime Minister 2004–; reappointed Minister of Finance and of Institutional Reform 2008–11, Minister of Foreign Affairs, Foreign Trade and European Affairs 2011–14, Minister of Foreign Affairs and European Affairs, in charge of Beliris and Fed. Cultural Insts 2014–, also Minister of Defence 2018–; Chair. Mouvement Réformateur (MR) (Reformist Movt) 2004–11, Councillor and Leader of MR Group of Uccle Town Council 2012–, Chair. Brussels Regional MR 2013–; Chevalier, Ordre de Léopold 2000. *Leisure interest:* golf. *Address:* Office of the Deputy Prime Minister, Minister of Foreign Affairs and European Affairs, 15 rue des Petits Carmes, 1000 Brussels, Belgium (office). *Telephone:* (2) 501-85-91 (office). *Fax:* (2) 513-25-97 (office). *E-mail:* contact.reynders@diplobel.fed.be (office); president@mr-bruxelles.be; druccle@gmail.com (home). *Website:* www .diplomatie.be (office); www.didierreynders.be.

REYNOLDS, Francis Martin Baillie, QC, DCL, FBA; British barrister, legal scholar, academic and consultant; *Professor Emeritus of Law, University of Oxford;* b. 11 Nov. 1932, St Albans, Herts., England; s. of Eustace Baillie Reynolds and Emma Holmes; m. Susan Shillito 1965; two s. one d.; ed Winchester Coll. and Worcester Coll., Oxford; Bigelow Teaching Fellow, Univ. of Chicago, USA 1957–58; Lecturer, Worcester Coll. Oxford 1958–60, Fellow 1960–2000, Fellow Emer. 2000–; Barrister, Inner Temple 1960, Hon. Bencher 1979; Reader in Law, Univ. of Oxford 1977, Prof. of Law 1992–2000, Prof. Emer. 2000–; Visiting Lecturer, Univ. of Auckland, NZ 1971, 1977, 1995; Visiting Prof., Nat. Univ. of Singapore 1984, 1986; 1988, 1990–92, 1994, 1996, 1997, 2000, 2003, 2005, 2007, 2009, Univ. Coll. London 1987–89, Univ. of Melbourne, Australia 1989, Monash Univ., Australia 1989, Univ. of Otago, NZ 1993, Univ. of Sydney, Australia 1993, Univ. of Hong Kong 2002, 2009, 2011–18; Titular mem. Comité Maritime Int.; Ed. Law Quarterly Review 1988–2014; Hon. QC; Hon. Prof., Int. Maritime Law Inst., Malta. *Publications:* Bowstead and Reynolds on Agency, 13th–18th edns 1968–2006, Benjamin's Sale of Goods, 1st–9th edns (co-author) 1974–2014, English Private Law (co-author) 2000 (revised edn 2006), Carver on Bills of Lading (with Sir G. Treitel) 1st–4th edn 2001–17. *Leisure interests:* music, walking. *Address:* 61 Charlbury Road, Oxford, OX2 6UX, England (home). *Telephone:* (1865) 559323 (home). *E-mail:* francis.reynolds@law.ox.ac.uk (home).

REYNOLDS, Kimberly (Kim) Kay; American politician; *Governor of Iowa;* b. 4 Aug. 1959, Truro, Iowa; m. Kevin Reynolds; three d.; ed NW Missouri State Univ., Iowa State Univ.; began career as Asst Pharmacist; mem. Bd Iowa Public Employees Retirement System 1996–2001; Clarke County Treas. 1998–2006; mem. Iowa Senate from 48th Dist 2009–10; Lt Gov. of Iowa 2011–17; Gov. of Iowa 2017–; Republican. *Address:* Office of the Governor, 1007 East Grand Ave., Des Moines, IA 50319, USA (office). *Telephone:* (515) 281-5211 (office). *Website:* governor.iowa.gov (office).

REYNOLDS, Paula Rosput, BA; American business executive; *President and CEO, PreferWest, LLC;* b. Newport, RI; m. Stephen P. Reynolds; ed Wellesley Coll.; Chair., Pres. and CEO AGL Resources, Atlanta, Ga 2000–05; Pres., CEO and mem. Bd of Dirs Safeco Corpn 2006–08, Chair. 2008; Vice-Chair. and Chief Restructuring Officer, American Int. Group Inc. (AIG) 2008–09; Pres. and CEO PreferWest, LLC, Seattle (business advisory group) 2009–; Chair. Bd of Trustees Fred Hutchinson Cancer Research Center 2013–; Chair. KCTS-9 public television, Seattle; mem. Bd of Dirs Delta Airlines, Inc, TransCanada Corpn, BAE Systems 2011–, BP plc 2015–. *Address:* PreferWest, LLC, 605 Hillside Drive East, Seattle, WA 98112-5055, USA (office).

REZA, (Evelyne Agnès) Yasmina; French novelist, dramatist, screenwriter and actress; b. 1 May 1959, Paris; d. of Jean Reza and of Nora Reza (née Heltaï); one s. one d.; ed Lycée de St-Cloud, Paris Univ. X, Nanterre, Ecole Jacques Lecoq; Chevalier, Ordre des Arts et des Lettres; Prix du jeune théâtre Beatrix Dussane-André Roussin de l'Acad. française 1991. *Stage appearances include:* Le Malade imaginaire 1977, Antigone 1977, Un Sang fort 1977, La Mort de Gaspard Hauser 1978, L'An mil 1980, Le Piège de Méduse 1983, Le Veilleur de nuit 1986, Enorme changement de dernière minute 1989, La Fausse suivante 1990. *Plays directed include:* Birds in the Night 1979, Marie la louve 1981. *Plays written include:* Conversations après un enterrement (Molière Award for Best Author, Prix des

Talents nouveaux de la Soc. des auteurs et compositeurs dramatiques, Johnson Foundation prize) 1987, La Traversée de l'hiver 1989, La Métamorphose (adaptation) 1988, 'Art' 1994, L'Homme du hasard 1995, Trois versions de la vie 2000, Une pièce espagnole 2004, Le Dieu du carnage 2007, Comment Vous Racontez la Partie 2011. *Screenplays written include:* Jusqu'à la nuit (also dir) 1984, Le Goûter chez Niels 1986, A demain 1992, Le Pique-nique de Lulu Kreutz 2000. *Publications:* novels: Hammerklavier 1997, Une Désolation (trans. as Desolation) 1999, Adam Haberberg 2003, Nulle part 2005, Dans la luge d'Arthur Schopenhauer 2005, Heureux les heureux 2013; non-fiction: L'aube le soir ou la nuit (trans. as Dawn, Dusk or Night) 2007. *Address:* c/o Marta Andras (Marton Play), 14 rue des Sablons, 75116 Paris, France.

REZAZADEH, Hossein; Iranian weightlifter (retd); b. 12 May 1978, Ardabil; m.; competes in 105 kilogrammes and over (heaviest category); won snatch (world record of 212.5 kilogrammes) and clean and jerk (world record of 260.5 kilogrammes, combined world record of 472.5 kilogrammes) for gold medal Olympic Games, Sydney 2000; gold medals in snatch, clean and jerk, combined (world record of 472.5 kilogrammes) World Weightlifting Championships, 2002; gold medals in snatch and combined, bronze medal in clean and jerk World Weight Lifting Championships, Canada 2003; won snatch and clean and jerk (world record of 262.5 kilogrammes) for gold medal Olympic Games, Athens, 2004; Man. and head coach, National weightlifting team 2008; mem. City Council of Tehran 2013–17; mem. Saipa club; Iranian Badge of Courage in 2000; Int. Weightlifting Fed. World's Best Weightlifter 2000, 2002, voted Champion of Champions of Iran 2002. *Leisure interests:* cooking.

REZEK, Francisco, LLD, JSD; Brazilian lawyer, fmr judge and fmr politician; *Counsel, Francisco Rezek Sociedade de Advogados;* b. 18 Jan. 1944, Cristina, Minas Gerais; s. of Elias Rezek and Baget Baracat Rezek; ed Fed. Univ. of Minas Gerais, Univ. of Paris (Sorbonne), France, Univ. of Oxford, UK, Harvard Univ., USA, The Hague Acad. of Int. Law, The Netherlands; Attorney of the Repub., Supreme Court 1972–79; Prof. of Int. and Constitutional Law Univ. of Brasília 1971–, Chair. Law Dept 1974–76, Dean, Faculty of Social Studies 1978–79; Prof. of Int., Law Rio Branco Inst. 1976–; Justice of Supreme Court 1983–90, 1992–97; Foreign Minister 1990–92; mem. Perm. Court of Arbitration 1987–2004; Judge, Int. Court of Justice, The Hague 1997–2006; currently lawyer and Counsel, Francisco Rezek Sociedade de Advogados (law firm), São Paulo. *Publications:* Droit des traités: particularités des actes constitutifs d'organisations internationales 1968, La conduite des relations internationales dans le droit constitutionnel latinoaméricain 1970, Reciprocity as a Basis of Extradition 1980, Direito dos Tratados 1984, Public International Law 1989 (16th edn 2016). *Address:* Francisco Rezek Sociedade de Advogados, Avenida Paulista 2200, São Paulo SP, 01310-300, Brazil (office). *Telephone:* (11) 3500-0001 (office). *Fax:* (11) 3500-0002 (office). *E-mail:* contato@franciscorezek.adv.br (office). *Website:* www.franciscorezek.com.br (office).

REZNIK, Genry Markovich, Cand.Jur.; Russian barrister; *Senior Partner, Reznik, Gagarin and Partners;* b. 11 May 1938, Leningrad; m. Larissa Yulianovna Reznik; one s.; ed Kazakhstan Univ., Moscow Inst. of Law; various positions at Acad. of Ministry of Internal Affairs 1975–82, including Internal Investigator, Investigation Dept, Kazakh Repub.; Lecturer in Law, All-Union Legal Acad. 1982–98; admitted to Moscow Bar 1985, Chair. 1997; f. Reznik, Gagarin and Partners, Moscow (law firm), also Sr Partner; Vice-Pres. Inst. of Bar Int. Union of Advocates; currently Prof. Dept on Advocacy and Notary Services, Kutafin Moscow State Law Acad.; mem. Moscow Helsinki Group 1989–, Public Chamber of Russian Fed., of Council, Fed. Chamber of Lawyers 2004, Improvement of Justice at Pres. of the Russian Fed. *Achievements include:* mem. USSR volleyball youth team. *Publications:* over 100 articles on criminal law. *Address:* Reznik, Gagarin and Partners, Schmidtovskiy pr. 3, 123100 Moscow, Russia (office). *Telephone:* (495) 205-27-09 (office). *Fax:* (495) 256-72-52 (office); (499) 256-7252. *E-mail:* main@rgp-law.ru. *Website:* www.abrgp.ru.

RHEINGOLD, Arnold Lange, BS, MS, PhD; American chemist and academic; *Professor, Department of Chemistry and Biochemistry, University of California, San Diego;* b. 6 Oct. 1940, Chicago, Ill.; s. of Joseph Cyrus Rheingold and Harriet Lange Rheingold; m. Janice F. Rheingold; ed Case Western Reserve Univ., Univ. of Maryland; Project Man., Glidden Co., Cleveland 1963–65; Research Assoc., Virginia Polytechnic Inst. and State Univ., Blacksburg, Va 1969–70; Prof. of Chem., State Univ. of NY (SUNY), Plattsburgh 1970–82, Visiting Scholar, SUNY, Buffalo 1980–81; Visiting Prof. and Sr Scientist, Univ. of Delaware, Newark 1981–84, Assoc. Prof. 1984–87, Prof. 1987–2003; Prof., Univ. of California, San Diego 2003–; Councillor, ACS 1998–2001, Chair.-elect Inorganic Div. 2001, Chair. 2002; mem. Editorial Bd ACS Journal – Organometallics 1990–, Journal of Cluster Science 1993–95, ACS Journal – Inorganic Chemistry 1994–96, 2001–, Organometallic Synthesis 1995–, Inorganica Chimica Acta 2003–; mem. Jt Bd-Council, Chemical Abstracts 1998–2001; mem. American Crystallographic Asscn, Int. Council on Main Group Chem.; Fellow, AAAS, ACS 2011; ACS Nat. Award of Distinguished Service in the Advancement of Inorganic Chem. *Publications:* more than 2,000 articles in peer-reviewed scientific journals. *Address:* Department of Chemistry and Biochemistry, University of California, San Diego, 9500 Gilman Drive, La Jolla, CA 92093-0358, USA (office). *Telephone:* (858) 822-3870 (office). *Fax:* (858) 822-3872 (office). *E-mail:* arheingold@ucsd.edu (office). *Website:* www-chem.ucsd.edu (office).

RHINES, Peter Broomell, PhD; American scientist and academic; *Professor of Oceanography and Atmospheric Sciences, University of Washington, Seattle;* b. 23 July 1942, Hartford, Conn.; s. of Thomas B. Rhines and Olive S. Rhines; m. 1st Marie Lenos 1968 (divorced 1983); m. 2nd Linda Mattson Semtner 1984; one s.; ed Loomis School, Massachusetts Inst. of Tech., Trinity Coll., Cambridge, UK; Sloan Scholar, MIT 1960–63, NSF Fellow 1963–64, Asst Prof. of Oceanography 1967–71; Marshall Scholar, Univ. of Cambridge 1964–67, Research Scientist 1971–72, Guggenheim Fellow, Christ's Coll. Cambridge 1979–80; mem. Scientific Staff, Woods Hole Oceanographic Inst. 1972–84, Dir Center for Analysis of Marine Systems 1979–82, oceanographic research cruises 1968–2009; Prof. of Oceanography and Atmospheric Sciences, Univ. of Washington, Seattle 1984–; mem. NAS; Fellow, American Geophysical Union, American Meteorological Soc., American Acad. of Arts and Sciences, Queen's Fellow in Marine Sciences, Australia; Founding mem. Washington State Acad. of Sciences; Fulbright Arctic Chair

2014–15; De Florez Award, MIT 1963, Creativity Award, NSF 1996, Ogura Lecturer, Univ. of Illinois 1996, Stommel Research Award, American Meteorological Soc. 1998, Haurwitz Lecturer, American Meteorological Soc. 2005, Gledden Fellow, Univ. of Western Australia 2005, Fulbright Scholar, Univ. of Concepción, Chile 2011, Albatross Award, American Miscellaneous Soc. 2012, Flint Lecturer, Yale Univ. 2013, 2, Nobel Lecturer, Univ. of Toronto 2014. *Television:* contribs to climate programmes on BBC, PBS, History Channel, Discovery Channel, National Geographic Channel. *Publications:* research papers and edited vols on general circulation of the oceans and atmosphere, waves and climate. *Leisure interests:* classical guitar, conversations about the global environment, wandering the out-of-doors. *Address:* School of Oceanography, University of Washington, Box 357940, Seattle, WA 98195 (office); 5753 61st Avenue NE, Seattle, WA 98105, USA (home). *Telephone:* (206) 543-0593 (office); (206) 522-5753 (home). *E-mail:* rhines@uw.edu (office). *Website:* www.ocean.washington.edu/people/faculty/rhines/rhines.html (office).

RHODES, Frank Harold Trevor, DSc, PhD; American geologist, academic and fmr university president; *President Emeritus, Cornell University;* b. 29 Oct. 1926, Warwickshire, England; s. of Harold C. Rhodes and Gladys Rhodes (née Ford); m. Rosa Carlson 1952; four d.; ed Univ. of Birmingham; Post-doctoral Fellow, Fulbright Scholar, Univ. of Illinois 1950–51, Visiting Lecturer in Geology during summers of 1951–52, Asst Prof., Univ. of Illinois 1954–55, Assoc. Prof. 1955–56, Dir Univ. of Illinois Field Station, Wyoming 1956; Lecturer in Geology, Durham Univ. 1951–54; Prof. of Geology and Head Dept of Geology, Univ. of Wales, Swansea 1956–68, Dean Faculty of Science 1967–68; Prof. of Geology and Mineralogy, Coll. of Literature, Science and Arts, Univ. of Michigan 1968–77, Dean 1971–74, Vice-Pres. for Academic Affairs 1974–77; Pres. Cornell Univ. 1977–94, Prof. of Geology 1977–95, Pres. Emer. 1995–; Dir John Heinz III Center for Science, Econs and the Environment 1996–98; Vice-Pres. Dyson Charitable Trust 1996–98; Prin. Washington Advisory Group 1997–; mem. Atlantic Philanthropics 1995 (Chair. 2000–05); mem. Nat. Science Bd 1987–98 (Chair. 1994–96), American Philosophical Soc. 1991– (Pres. 1999–), Johnson Foundation Bd 2000–, Goldman Sachs Foundation Bd 2000–; mem. Int. Advisory Panel King Abdullah Univ. of Science and Tech.; Trustee, Andrew W. Mellon 1984–99; 36 hon. degrees; Bigsby Medal, Geological Soc. 1967, Higher Educ. Leadership Award, Comm. on Ind. Colls and Univs 1987, Justin Smith Morrill Award 1987, Clark Kerr Medal, Univ. of Calif., Berkeley 1995, Jefferson Lecturer, Univ. of Calif., Berkeley 1999. *Publications include:* The Evolution of Life 1962, Fossils 1963, Geology 1972, Evolution 1974, Language of the Earth 1981, (Ed.) Successful Fund Raising for Higher Education: The Advancement of Learning 1997, The Creation of the Future: The Role of the American University 2001; over 70 maj. scientific articles and monographs and some 60 articles on educ. *Address:* 603 Cayuga Heights Road, Ithaca, NY, 14850 (home); Cornell University, 3104 Snee Hall, Ithaca, NY 14853, USA. *E-mail:* mjw11@cornell.edu.

RHODES, Richard Lee, BA; American writer; b. 4 July 1937, Kansas City, Kan.; s. of Arthur Rhodes and Georgia Collier Rhodes; m. Ginger Untrif 1993; two c. by previous m.; ed East High School, Kansas City, Yale Univ.; Trustee, Atomic Heritage Foundation 2004–; fmr Assoc., Center for Int. Security and Cooperation, Stanford Univ.; Hon. mem. American Nuclear Soc. 2001; Hon. DHumLitt (Westminster Coll., Fulton, Mo.) 1988; Hon. DLitt (Colby Coll., Me) 2010; Fellowships: John Simon Guggenheim Memorial Foundation 1974–75, Nat. Endowment for the Arts 1978, Ford Foundation 1981–83, Alfred P. Sloan Foundation 1985, 1993, 1995, 2001, 2010, 2012, 2014, 2015, 2017, MacArthur Foundation Program on Peace and Int. Co-operation 1990–91, 2008–09. *Play:* Reykjavik 2010. *Publications include:* non-fiction: The Inland Ground: An Evocation of the American Middle West 1970, The Ozarks 1974, Looking for America: A Writer's Odyssey 1979, The Making of the Atomic Bomb (Nat. Book Critics' Circle Award for Gen. Non-fiction, Nat. Book Award for Non-fiction 1987, Pulitzer Prize for Non-fiction 1988) 1987, Farm: A Year in the Life of an American Farmer 1989, A Hole in the World: An American Boyhood 1990, Making Love: An Erotic Odyssey 1992, Nuclear Renewal: Common Sense about Energy 1993, Dark Sun: The Making of the Hydrogen Bomb 1995, How To Write 1995, Trying To Get Some Dignity: Stories of Triumph Over Childhood Abuse (with Ginger Rhodes) 1996, Deadly Feasts: Tracking the Secrets of a Terrifying New Plague 1997, Visions of Technology (ed) 1999, Why They Kill 1999, Masters of Death 2001, John James Audubon: The Making of an American (biog.) 2004, The Audubon Reader (ed) 2006, Arsenals of Folly: Nuclear Weapons in the Cold War 2007, The Twilight of the Bombs 2010, Hedy's Folly 2011, Hell and Good Company: The Spanish Civil War and the World It Made 2015, Energy: A Human History 2018; fiction: The Ungodly 1973, Holy Secrets 1978, The Last Safari 1980, Sons of Earth 1981, Where Do We Come From? What Are We? Where Are We Going? 2015. *Address:* c/o Janklow & Nesbit Assocs, 455 Park Avenue, New York, NY 10021, USA (office). *Telephone:* (212) 421-1700 (office). *E-mail:* rhodes.today@comcast.net (office). *Website:* www.richardrhodes.com.

RHODES, William (Bill) Reginald, BA; American banking executive; *Senior Advisor, Citigroup;* b. 15 Aug. 1935, New York; s. of Edward R. Rhodes and Elsie Rhodes; ed Brown Univ.; joined Citibank 1957, served in various sr positions, Latin America and Caribbean 1957–77, Head, Latin American corp. business and Sr Exec., Int. Citibank NA, New York 1977–91, Vice-Chair. 1991–2001, apptd mem. Bd of Dirs 1991, Sr Vice-Chair. 2001–03, apptd Chair. 2003, apptd Pres. and CEO 2005, Sr Vice-Chair. Citigroup, Inc. 1999–2010, apptd Chair. and CEO Citicorp Holdings, Inc. 2003, apptd Pres. 2005, later Sr Int. Officer, currently Sr Advisor; Founder, Pres. and CEO William R. Rhodes Global Advisors, LLC; fmr chair. several advisory cttees which negotiated debt-restructuring agreements for Argentina, Brazil, Jamaica, Mexico, Peru and Uruguay during 1980s, and S Korea 1998; Dir, Banamex, Private Export Funding Corpn, US-Russia Business Council, US-Hong Kong Business Council, Foreign Policy Asscn; First Vice-Chair. Inst. of Int. Finance; Chair. Emer. Americas Soc., Council of the Americas; Chair. US-Korea Business Council; Vice-Chair. Nat. Cttee on US-China Relations; mem. Inter-American Devt Bank's Pvt. Sector Advisory Bd, Int. Policy Cttee of US Chamber of Commerce, Council on Foreign Relations, Group of Thirty Consultative Group on Int. Econ. and Monetary Affairs, Inc. (G-30), Washington, DC, Econ. Club of New York; Founding mem. US Nat. Advisory Council to the Int. Man. Centre, Budapest, Hungary; Gov. and Trustee, New York Presbyterian Hosp.; mem. Lincoln Center Consolidated Corp. Fund Leadership Cttee; Vice-Chair.

Metropolitan Museum of Art Business Cttee and Chair.'s Cttee; Prof.-at-Large, Watson Inst. for Int. Studies, Brown Univ. 2010–; mem. Bd of Overseers Watson Inst. for Int. Studies, Rhodes Center for Int. Econs and Finance, Brown Univ.; Chair. Emer. Bd of Trustees, Northfield Mount Hermon School; Chevalier and Officier, Légion d'honneur; decorations from South Korea, Brazil, Mexico, Argentina, Panama, Columbia, Venezuela, Jamaica and Poland; Hon. DHumLitt (Brown Univ.); numerous awards. *Address:* Citigroup Inc., 399 Park Avenue, New York, NY 10022, USA (office). *Telephone:* (212) 559-1000 (office). *Website:* www.citibank.com (office).

RHUGGENAATH, Eugene, BBA; Curaçao politician; *Prime Minister;* b. 4 Feb. 1970; ed Univ. of Miami School of Business Admin, Rotterdam School of Man., Erasmus Univ.; mem. Island Council of Curaçao (territorial governing body as part of Netherlands Antilles) 2003–09; Sr Operations Adviser, Matrix Man. Solutions NV 2009–10; Dir of Operations, Int. Finance Centre NV 2010–11; Man. Dir, Citco Banking Corpn NV 2011–15; Minister for Econ. Devt 2015–17; Prime Minister 2017–; mem. States (parl.) of Curaçao May 2017; mem. Partido Alternativa Real (Real Alternative Party). *Address:* Office of the Prime Minister, Fort Amsterdam 17, Willemstad, Curaçao (office). *Telephone:* (9) 463-0495 (office). *Fax:* (9) 461-7199 (office).

RHYS-JAMES, Shani, MBE, BA; Australian artist and painter; b. 2 May 1953, Melbourne, Vic.; d. of Harold Marcus Rhys-James and Jeannie James-Money Vine; m. Stephen West 1977; two s.; ed Parliament Hill Girls School, Loughborough Coll. of Art and Cen. St Martin's Coll. of Art and Design; came to London from Australia aged nine, lived in London 1963–84, moved to mid-Wales with family 1984; regular exhbns with Martin Tinney Gallery, Cardiff 1991–2013, Stephen Lacey Gallery, London, Connaught Brown, Mayfair 2007–13, J. Cacciola Gallery, New York, Hillsboro Fine Art, Dublin; work in art collections of Arts Council of England, Nat. Museum of Wales, Newport Museum and Art Gallery, Cyfartha Castle, Merthyr Tydfil, Usher Gallery, Lincoln, Gallery of Modern Art, Glasgow, Wolverhampton Art Gallery, Birmingham Museum and Art Gallery, Nat. Library of Wales, London Borough of Tower Hamlets, BBC Wales, Glyn Vivian Museum and Art Gallery, Murray Edwards Coll. (fmrly New Hall), Cambridge, Jerwood Foundation; featured artist, Carlow Festival 2000, and at Visual 2010, Royal Cambrian Acad. three-person show 2001; invited artist, Discerning Eye 2004; Artist Advisor, Derek Williams Trust 2007–12; Creative Council mem. for Design and Artists Copyright Soc. 2007–10; frequent radio and TV appearances; mem. Royal Cambrian Acad. 1994; Hon. Fellow, Hereford Coll. of Art 2008, Univ. of Wales Inst., Cardiff 2007; numerous prizes, including First Prize, Mostyn Open, Llandudno 1991, Gold Medal for Fine Art, Royal Nat. Eisteddfod, Ceredigion 1992, First Prize, Hunting/Observer Art Prizes 1993, BBC Wales Visual Artist Award 1994, Second Prize, BP Nat. Portrait Award 1994, Jerwood Painting Prize 2003, Welsh Woman of the Year in Culture 2003, Creative Wales Award, Arts Council of Wales to develop concept of making automata – Cassandra's Rant 2006, Glyndwr Award, MOMA 2007, production grant from the Arts Council of Wales to make an installation collaborating with poets: Florilingua 2012. *Radio:* Relative Values, BBC Wales 2008. *Television includes:* The Slate: Blood Ties 1993, Painting the Dragon 2000, The Little Picture 2000, Paintings from Paradise 2000, Shani Rhys-James: A Conversation 2004, Framing Wales (interviewer Kim Howells) 2011, featured artist on Rolf on Welsh Art 2011, What Do Artists Do All Day? (BBC 4) 2013. *Publications:* Art Today – Edward Lucie-Smith 1997, Facing the Self (essay Andrew Patrizzio), Imagine Wales – Hugh Adams 2003, The Black Cot 2004, Edward Lucie-Smith (monograph essay) 2005, Imaging the Imagination 2005, Shani Rhys-James Pixel Foundry (DVD), Cassandra's Rant Artists book 2006, Azart 10 ans 2002–12, The Life History of Five Contemporary Welsh Woman Artists 2012, The Rivalry of Flowers (essays by William Packer, Francesca Rhydderch and Edward Lucie-Smith), Florilingua artists book collaboration with four poets (monograph to accompany the exhbn) 2013. *Leisure interests:* music, films, plays, books, writing, restoring our Welsh farm and French house and studio. *Address:* Dolpebyll, Llangadfan, Welshpool, Powys, SY21 0PU, Wales. *Telephone:* (1938) 820469. *Fax:* (1938) 820469. *E-mail:* shanirhysjames@btinternet.com. *Website:* www.artwales.com; www.connaught-brown.com.

RI, Kwang-gun; North Korean government official and fmr central banker; *Chairman, Joint Venture and Investment Commission;* began career at Ministry of Foreign Affairs 1977, Chief Econ. Counsellor, Embassy in Berlin mid-1990s; Minister of Foreign Trade 2000–04; Deputy Dir KWP United Front Dept; Pres. Cen. Bank of the DPRK 2009–11; Chair. Joint Venture and Investment Comm. 2012–; fmr Chair. North Korean Football Asscn. *Address:* Joint Venture and Investment Commission (JVIC), Pyongyang, Democratic People's Republic of Korea (office).

RI, Su-yong; North Korean government official and fmr diplomatist; ed Kim il-Sung Univ., Pyongyang Univ. of Foreign Study; Bureau Dir, Ministry of Foreign Affairs 1972, Dir-Gen., Bureau of Protocol and Bureau of Int. Orgs 1974, Amb. to Switzerland 1998–2010; mem. Supreme People's Ass. (Parl.) 2003–; Chair. DPRK Investment Cttee Jt Venture 2011–12; Minister of Foreign Affairs 2014–16; mem. Korean Workers' Party (KWP), Alt. mem. Cen. Cttee 2010–16, Cen. Cttee Vice Chair. and Dept Dir 2016–, Deputy Dir, KWP Org. Guidance Dept, mem. KWP Exec. Policy Bureau 2016–; Order of Kim Jong-il 2012. *Address:* Korean Workers' Party, Pyongyang, Democratic People's Republic of Korea (office). *Website:* www.rodong.rep.kp (office).

RI, Yong-ho; North Korean diplomatist and politician; *Minister of Foreign Affairs;* b. 10 July 1954, Pyongyang; s. of Ri Myong-je; m. Ri Son-yong; ed Pyongyang Univ. of Foreign Languages; began career at Ministry of Foreign Affairs (MFA) 1978, Sec., Embassy in Harare 1979–84, Sec., Embassy in Stockholm 1985–88, Man., MFA Int. Orgs. Bureau 1988–95, Counsellor, MFA 1995–2003, Amb. to UK 2003–07; led North Korean del. to six-nation talks with USA, South Korea, Japan, Russia and China aimed at ending North Korea's nuclear weapons program –2008; took part in North Korean del. to ASEAN forum in Hanoi, July 2010; elected deputy to 13th Supreme People's Ass. 2014; Vice Minister of Foreign Affairs 2010–16, Minister of Foreign Affairs 2016–; mem. Korean Workers' Party (KWP), Alt. mem. Cen. Cttee 2010–16, Full mem. 2016–, Alt. mem. Political Bureau 2016–17, Full mem. 2017–. *Address:* Ministry of Foreign Affairs, Jungsong-dong, Central District, Pyongyang, Democratic People's Republic of Korea (office). *Website:* www.mfa.gov.kp/en/ (office).

RIAZUDDIN, Riaz, BA, MSc, MAS; Pakistani academic and central banker; *Acting Governor, State Bank of Pakistan;* ed Boston Univ., USA, Univ. of Karachi, Applied Econs Research Centre; Computer Programmer, Pakistan Medical Research Centre 1982; Staff Economist/Lecturer, Applied Econs Research Centre, Univ. of Karachi 1982–91, Research Economist/Asst Prof. 1991–94; Additional Dir-Gen. Econ. Research Dept, State Bank of Pakistan 1994–97, Dir/Additional Dir Securities Dept 1997–2000, Dir Research 2000–05, Econ. Adviser 2000–09, Chief Econ. Adviser 2009–15, Deputy Gov. 2015–17, Acting Gov. May–July 2017; fmr Chair. Working Group on Monetary Policy; Dir Bd of Nat. Inst. of Banking and Finance (NIBAF—subsidiary of State Bank of Pakistan); mem. Monetary Policy Cttee, State Bank of Pakistan; mem. Panel of Economists constituted by Govt of Pakistan. *Address:* c/o State Bank of Pakistan, Central Directorate, I. I. Chundrigar Road, POB 4456, Karachi 2, Pakistan (office). *Telephone:* (21) 111727111 (office). *Fax:* (21) 9212433 (office). *E-mail:* info@sbp.org.pk (office). *Website:* www.sbp.org.pk (office).

RIADY, Mochtar, (Lie Mo Tie); Indonesian business executive; *Chairman, Lippo Group;* b. 12 May 1929, Malang, East Java; m.; six c.; f. Lippo Group (conglomerate) 1950s, currently Chair.; Pres. Commr Lippo Bank 1997–2008; fmr Chair. Asian Bankers Asscn; Sr Adviser Ma Chung Univ.; fmr Chair. Bd of Trustees, Univ. of Indonesia; f. Mochtar Riady Inst. for Nanotechnology (centre for cancer research), Karawaci, Banten 2008. *Publications:* Searching For Opportunities Amid Crisis 1999, Nanotechnology Management Style: How to Heal a Company from Old Illnesses and Save a Family Company 2004, Ancient Philosophy and Modern Management 2006. *Address:* Lippo Group, 78 Shenton Way, #17-01/02, 079120 Singapore, Singapore (office). *Telephone:* 62273613 (office). *Fax:* 62273106 (office). *Website:* www.lipporealty.com (office).

RIBAR, Monika; Swiss business executive; b. 1959; m.; ed Univ. of St Gallen, Exec. Program of Grad. School of Business at Stanford Univ., USA; Financial Controller, BASF Vienna, Austria 1984–86; Head of Strategic Planning, Fides Group (KPMG), Zürich 1986–90; Controlling and IT Dept, Panalpina Group (freight forwarding and logistics services provider) 1991–92, SAP Global Project Man. 1992–95, Corp. Controller 1995–2000, mem. Exec. Bd 2000–, Chief Information Officer 2000–05, Chief Financial Officer 2005–06, Pres. and CEO 2006–13; mem. Bd of Dirs Sika AG 2011–, Swiss Int. Air Lines Ltd 2012–, Swiss Federal Railways 2014–, Julius Bär Group, Zurich 2001–10, Logitech Int. SA 2004–15; mem. Supervisory Bd Deutsche Lufthansa AG 2014–.

RIBEIRO, Baron (Life Peer), cr. 2010, of Achimota in the Republic of Ghana and of Ovington in the County of Hampshire; **Bernard Ribeiro,** Kt, CBE, FRCS, FRCSE, FRCP; British surgeon; m. Elisabeth Ribeiro; ed Dean Close School, Cheltenham, Glos., Middlesex Hosp. Medical School, London; began career in surgery 1967; Consultant Gen. Surgeon, Basildon Hosp. (now Basildon Univ. Hosp.) 1979–2008 (retd), helped establish Basildon & Thurrock Univ. Hosps NHS Foundation Trust's advanced laparoscopic unit; examiner in surgery for three univ. medical schools; elected to Council of Royal Coll. of Surgeons 1988, Pres. 2005–08, Patron 2011–; Chair. Ind. Reconfiguration Panel, Research Review Panel of Pelican Cancer Foundation, CORESS (charity); mem. Health Policy Research Advisory Bd of American Coll. of Surgeons; Gov., Dean Close School, Cheltenham; Patron Achimota Trust; Fellow, Acad. of Medicine of Malaysia 2006; Hon. Fellow, Coll. of Physicians and Surgeons of Ghana 2006, Caribbean Coll. of Surgeons 2007; Hon. mem. Académie Chirurgie de Paris 2008; Hon. FACS 2008; Deputy Master, Worshipful Co. of Barbers; Hon. DSc (Anglia Ruskin Univ.) 2008, Hon. DEng (Univ. of Bath) 2012; Officer of Order of the Volta (Ghana) 2008. *Achievements include:* special interest in urology, colorectal and laparoscopic surgery. *Publications:* scientific papers on colorectal cancer. *Address:* House of Lords, Westminster, London, SW1A 0PW, England (office). *Telephone:* (20) 7219-5353 (office). *Fax:* (20) 7219-5979 (office). *E-mail:* ribeirob@parliament.uk (office).

RIBEIRO, Inacio; Brazilian fashion designer; m. Suzanne Clements 1992; one s.; ed Cen. St Martin's Coll. of Art and Design, London; fmrly designer, Brazil; design consultant in Brazil (with wife) 1991–93; f. Clements Ribeiro (with wife), London 1993; first collection launched Oct. 1993, numerous collections since; first solo show London Fashion Week March 1995; Creative Dir (with wife) Cacharel, Paris 2000–07; fashion shows since in London, Paris, Brazil, Japan; consultant to cos in UK and Italy; winners, Designer of the Year New Generation Category 1996. *Address:* BCPR, Unit 18, Archer Street Studios, 10–11 Archer Street, London, W1D 7AZ (office); Clements Ribeiro Trading Ltd, 17 Alexander Street, London, W2 5NT, England. *Telephone:* (20) 7229-9680 (office). *E-mail:* inacioribeiro@hotmail.com (office). *Website:* www.clementsribeiro.com.

RIBEIRO BUTIAM CÓ, João; Guinea-Bissau sociologist and politician; *Minister of Foreign Affairs, International Co-operation and Communities;* b. 15 Oct. 1975; ed Évora Univ., Portugal, Inst. of Economy and Tech. Man., Univ. of Lisbon; Researcher, Centro de Intervenção Para o Desenvolvimento Amílcar Cabral (non-govt org.), Lisbon 2003–04; Asst and Consultant, Int. Org. for Migration 2004; Dir of Research, Ministry of Social Solidarity, Family and the Fight against Poverty 2004–05; joined Instituto Nacional de Estudos e Pesquisa (INEP, Nat. Inst. of Studies and Research) as Researcher 2004, later becoming Dir-Gen.; Lecturer, Dept of Sociology, Amílcar Cabral Univ., Bissau 2005–, Co-ordinator, Sociology Teaching and mem. Scientific Teaching Cttee 2006–; Sec. of State for Educ. and Scientific Research 2015; Minister of Foreign Affairs, Int. Co-operation and Communities 2018–; mem. Partido para a Renovação Social (PRS). *Address:* Ministry of Foreign Affairs, International Co-operation and Communities, Av. dos Combatentes da Liberdade da Pátria, Bissau, Guinea-Bissau (office). *Telephone:* 443204301 (office). *Fax:* 443202378 (office).

RIBEIRO CONSTÂNCIO, Vítor Manuel, BEcons; Portuguese economist, academic, politician and central banker; *Vice-President, European Central Bank;* b. 12 Oct. 1943, Lisbon; ed Instituto Superior de Ciencias Económicas e Financeiras (later Instituto Superior de Economia e Gestao—ISEG), Universidade Técnica de Lisboa, Univ. of Bristol, UK; Asst Prof. of Econs, ISEG 1965–73, Guest Prof. of Econs 1989–94, 1995–99, 2000–09; Head of Dept, Econ. Models and Global Programming, Centre of Planning Studies 1972–73; Prof., Instituto Superior do Serviço Social 1972–73; Sec. of State, Planning in I and II Provisional Govts 1974–75; Head of Research Dept, Banco de Portugal 1975, Deputy Gov. 1977, 1979, 1981–84, Gov. 1985–86, 2000–10, Sr Adviser 1989–94; Sec. of State, Budget and

Planning 1976; Pres., Comm. for European Integration 1977, 1979; Minister of Finance 1978; Prof., Universidade Católica Portuguesa 1980–81; Pres., Portuguese section of European Movt 1980–81; mem. Parl. 1980–81, 1987–88; Pres., Parl. Comm. on European Affairs 1980–81; Guest Prof., Universidade Nova de Lisboa 1982–84; mem. Conselho de Estado 1995–99; Bd mem. and Exec. Dir Banco Portugues de Investimento 1995–99; mem. Governing Council and Gen. Council, European Cen. Bank (ECB) 2000–09, Vice-Pres. 2010–; Order of Christ, Ordem do Infante Dom Henrique. *Address:* European Central Bank, Eurotower (Main Building), Kaiserstrasse 29, 60311 Frankfurt am Main, Germany (office). *Telephone:* (69) 13447455 (office). *Fax:* (69) 13447404 (office). *E-mail:* info@ecb.europa.eu (office). *Website:* www.ecb.europa.eu (office).

RIBEIRO PEREIRA, Lt Gen. (retd) Augusto Heleno; Brazilian military officer; b. 29 Oct. 1947, Curitiba; served in Brazilian mil. mission, Paraguay 1981–83; Mil. Attaché to France 1996–98; Head, Centro de Comunicação do Exército 2002–04; C-in-C UN Stabilization Mission in Haiti (MINUSTAH) 2004–05; Head of Cabinet for Mil. Command 2006; retd 2011; currently security consultant to Grupo Bandeirantes de Comunicação. *Address:* c/o Quartel General do Exército, Bloco B Térreo, Setor Militário Urbano, 70630-901 Brasília, DF, Brazil. *Website:* www.band.uol.com.br/grupo/grupo.asp.

RIBOUD, Franck; Swiss food industry executive; *Chairman, Groupe Danone;* b. 7 Nov. 1955; ed École Polytechnique Fédérale de Lausanne; joined BSN Group (renamed Groupe Danone 1994) 1981, various positions in man. control div., sales and marketing div. and business div. including Brand Man., Sales Rep., Regional Sales Force Trainer, Regional Man., Sales Man., Key Account Sales Man., Dept Man., involved in acquisition of Nabisco's European activities 1989, Gen. Man. Evian Water 1990–92, Gen. Man. Devt BSN 1992–94, Vice-Pres. and Gen. Man. Groupe Danone 1994–96, Chair. and CEO 1996–2014, Chair. 2014–, Chair. danone.communities mutual fund (SICAV) 2007–, Chair. Steering Cttee of Fonds Danone pour l'Écosystème 2009–, Chair. Bd of Dirs, Strategy Cttee 2015–; Chair. Livelihoods Fund for Family Farming SAS 2015–, mem. Steering Cttee 2015–; mem. Bd of Dirs Fiat SpA –2000, Scottish & Newcastle PLC 2000–03, Accor 2001, Lacoste France (Chair. 2006–), L'Oréal SA 2002–, Renault SAS 2000–, Bagley Latinoamerica SA, Rolex SA, Rolex Holding SA, Global Alliance for Improved Nutrition; mem. Supervisory Bd Fondation Ela; mem. representing Danone, Conseil Nat. du Développement Durable; Dir, Asscn Nationale des Industries Agroalimentaires, Int. Advisory Bd HEC business school. *Address:* Groupe Danone, 17 boulevard Haussmann, 75009 Paris, France (office). *Telephone:* 1-44-35-20-20 (office). *Fax:* 1-42-25-67-16 (office). *E-mail:* info@danone.com (office). *Website:* www.danone.com (office).

RICARD, Alexandre, MA, MBA; French business executive; *Chairman and CEO, Pernod Ricard SA;* b. 12 May 1972, Boulogne-Billancourt; joined Pernod Ricard SA (distiller) in Audit & Business Devt Dept 2003, Finance and Admin Dir of Irish Distillers div. 2004–06, CEO Pernod Ricard Asia Duty Free 2006–08, Chair. and CEO Irish Distillers 2008–11, Man. Dir Distribution Network 2011–12, Deputy CEO and COO Pernod Ricard SA 2012–15, Chair. and CEO 2015–, mem. Exec. Cttee 2011–; Consultant, Accenture 1996–99, Morgan Stanley 2001–03. *Address:* Pernod Ricard SA, 12 place des États-Unis, 75783 Paris Cedex 16, France (office). *Telephone:* 1-41-00-41-00 (office). *E-mail:* media.relations@pernod-ricard.com (office). *Website:* pernod-ricard.com (office).

RICARD, François, BA, MA, DLit, FRSC; Canadian author and professor of literature; *James McGill Research Chair in Quebec Literature, McGill University;* b. 4 June 1947, Shawinigan, Quebec; ed Laval Univ., McGill Univ., Univ. of Aix-Marseille, France; apptd Prof., Dept of French Language and Literature, McGill Univ., Montréal 1971, Prof. Emer. 2009–, James McGill Research Chair in Quebec Literature 2002–; Dir Liberté (literary journal) 1980–86; Founder Papiers collés; columnist, L'Atelier du Roman (journal), Paris, L'Inconvénient, Montréal; Hon. DèsL (Manitoba) 2009; awards include Grande Médaille de la Francophonie 2001, Prix André-Laurendeau 2005, Canada Council for the Arts Killam Prize 2009; Kt, Nat. Order of Quebec. *Publications include:* Histoire du Québec contemporain 1986, La génération lyrique 1992, Gabrielle Roy, Une Vie (Prix Jean-Éthier-Blais 1997, Prix Maxime-Raymond, Drainie-Taylor Biog. Prize) 1996, Le dernier après-midi d'Agnès 2003, La littérature contre elle-même (Gov.-Gen.'s Literary Award 1985) 2002, Chroniques d'un temps loufoque 2005. *Address:* McGill University, Department of French Language and Literature, 853 rue Sherbrooke ouest, Bureau Arts W130A, Montréal, PQ H3A 0G5, Canada (office). *E-mail:* francois.ricard@mcgill.ca (office). *Website:* litterature.mcgill.ca/ricard.html (office).

RICARD, HE Cardinal Jean-Pierre Bernard, BA, PhD; French ecclesiastic; *Archbishop of Bordeaux (-Bazas);* b. 25 Sept. 1944, Marseille; s. of Georges Ricard and Jeanine Ricard; ed Lycée de Saint-Charles, Lycée Périer, Marseille, and Thiers, Major Seminary of Marseille, Séminare des Carmes and Institut Catholique de Paris; spent one year of Nat. Service of Co-operation in Bamako, Mali; ordained priest, Archdiocese of Marseille 1968; asst pastor of Parish of Sainte-Émilie de Vialoar 1970–78; responsible for Mistral Centre of Religious Culture 1975–81, diocesan del. for seminarians 1975–85; Pastor of Parish of Sainte-Marguerite 1981–88, assoc. del. for ecumenism and episcopal vicar for zone of South Marseille 1984–88; regional theologian for pastoral affairs 1986–93; Gen. Sec. Diocesan Synod of Marseille 1988–91; Vicar Gen. to Cardinal Robert Coffy, Archbishop of Marseille 1988–93; Titular Bishop of Pulcheriopolis 1993–; Auxiliary Bishop of Grenoble 1993–96; Coadjutor Bishop of Montpellier (-Lodève-Béziers-Agde-Saint-Pons-de-Thomières) July–Sept. 1996, Bishop of Montpellier (-Lodève-Béziers-Agde-Saint-Pons-de-Thomières) 1996–2001; Archbishop of Bordeaux (-Bazas) 2001–; cr. Cardinal (Cardinal-Priest of Sant'Agostino) 2006; Vice-Pres. French Episcopal Conf. 1999–2001, Pres. 2001–07; participated in Tenth Ordinary Ass. of World Synod of Bishops, Vatican City, Sept.–Oct. 2001; attended 11th Gen. Ordinary Ass. of the World Synod of Bishops, Vatican City, Oct. 2005; mem. Pontifical Comm. Ecclesia Dei (deals with issue of Tridentine rite) 2006–, Pontifical Council for Culture 2009–, Pontifical Council for Promoting Christian Unity 2010–, Congregation for Divine Worship and the Discipline of the Sacraments 2010–, Congregation for Catholic Educ. 2012–, Secr. for the Economy 2014–. *Address:* Archevêché, 183 cours de la Somme, 33077 Bordeaux Cedex, France (office). *Telephone:* (5) 56-91-81-82 (office). *Fax:* (5) 56-92-12-98 (office). *E-mail:* accueil@catholique-bordeaux.cef.fr (office). *Website:* catholique-bordeaux.cef.fr (office).

RICCI, Christina; American actress; b. 12 Feb. 1980, Santa Monica, Calif.; d. of Ralph Ricci and Sarah Ricci; began acting career in commercials. *Films include:* Mermaids 1990, The Hard Way 1991, The Addams Family 1991, The Cemetery Club 1993, Addams Family Values 1993, Casper 1995, Now and Then 1995, Gold Diggers: The Secret of Bear Mountain 1995, That Darn Cat 1996, Last of the High Kings 1996, Bastard Out of Carolina 1996, Ice Storm 1997, Little Red Riding Hood 1997, Fear and Loathing in Las Vegas 1998, Desert Blue 1998, Buffalo 66 1998, The Opposite of Sex 1998, Small Soldiers 1998, Pecker 1999, 200 Cigarettes 1999, Sleepy Hollow 1999, The Man Who Cried 2001, All Over the Guy 2001, Prozac Nation 2001, Pumpkin 2002, Miranda 2002, The Laramie Project 2002, Anything Else 2003, Monster 2003, I Love Your Work 2003, Cursed 2005, Penelope 2006, Home of the Brave 2006, Black Snake Moan 2006, Speed Racer 2008, New York, I Love You 209, All's Faire in Love 2009, After Life 2009, Alpha and Omega (voice) 2010, Bucky Larson: Born to Be a Star 2011, Bel Ami 2012, War Flowers 2012, Around the Block 2013, Mothers and Daughters 2016. *Television includes:* Pan Am (series) 2011–12, Lizzie Borden Chronicles (mini-series) 2015, Z: The Beginning of Everything 2017. *Address:* c/o Toni Howard, ICM, 8942 Wilshire Boulevard, Beverly Hills, CA 90211, USA.

RICCIARDONE, Francis Joseph, Jr; American diplomatist and university administrator; *President, American University in Cairo;* b. 1951, Boston, Mass; m. Marie Ricciardone; two d.; ed Dartmouth Coll.; taught in int. schools Italy 1973–76, Iran 1976–78; entered Foreign Service 1978, served in Turkey 1979–81, Research Analyst for Turkey, Greece and Cyprus US Dept of State, Washington, DC 1981–82, Country Officer for Iraq 1982–85, Political Officer, Cairo 1986–89, led Civilian Observer Unit, Multinational Force and Observers, Sinai Desert 1989–91, Deputy Chief of Mission, Baghdad Embassy 1991–93, Political Adviser to Multinational relief operation, Northern Iraq 1993, Office of Dir-Gen., Dept of State, Washington, DC 1993–95, Deputy Chief of Mission and Chargé d'affaires a.i., Ankara 1995–99, Sec. of State's Special Rep. for Transition in Iraq 1999–2001, Dir Task Force on the Coalition Against Terrorism 2001, Amb. to the Philippines (also accred to Palau) 2002–05, to Egypt 2005–08, Jennings Randolph Guest Scholar, US Inst. of Peace 2008, Deputy Amb., Embassy in Kabul 2009–10, Amb. to Turkey 2011–14, also served in Bureau of Intelligence and Research, Bureau of Near Eastern Affairs; Vice-Pres. Atlantic Council and Dir Rafik Hariri Center for the Middle East 2014–16; Pres. American Univ. in Cairo 2016–; Meritorious Honor Award 1984, Dir-Gen.'s Award for Political Reporting 1988. *Address:* Office of the President, American University in Cairo, Tahrir Square Campus, BP 2511, 113 Sharia Kasr el Aini, Cairo, 11511, Egypt (office). *Website:* www.aucegypt.edu (office); www.francisricciardone.com.

RICCIOTTI, Rudy; French architect; b. 1952, Algiers, Algeria; ed School of Engineers, Geneva, UPAM, Marseille; freelance architect in Bandol 1980; Prof., Inst. of Art, Marseille-Luminy 1995–; Visiting Prof., Ecole Spécial d'Architecture Paris 1997–98; Scientific Adviser, Ecole d'architecture de Grenoble 2000–; has participated in numerous publs, confs and exhbns; mem. Acad. des Technologies; Officier des Arts et des Lettres; Chevalier, Légion d'honneur; Officier, Ordre nat. du Mérite; competition entries for remodelling for arte TV station in Strasbourg and Quai de Brainly Museum of Early History in Paris were both awarded prizes, won competitions, including Salle de Musique Actuelle et Contemporaine, Boulogne-Billancourt 2007, Siège d'ITER, Cadarache 2007, Stade Jean Bouin, Paris 2007, École Internationale ITER, Manosque 2007, Grand prix nat. d'architecture. *Works include:* Bibliothèque de prêt de Draguignan 1986, Centre des loisirs de jeunes, Bandol 1986, Ecole Jean de Florette, St Cyr 1991, city centre pedestrian redevelopment, Bandol 1991, highway information and control centre, Marseille 1992, Salle de spectacles et de cinéma, Pierrelatte (prize winner) 1993, Salle des Fêtes, Port Saint Louis du Rhône 1994, Base nautique, Bandol 1995, Aire ludique, Lyon-Gerland 1996, Villa Gros, Gémenos 1997, Collège 600, Saint Ouen 1997, beach redevelopment, Lecques, St Cyr-sur-Mer 1998, Great Hall, Faculty of Science, Marseille 1998, Foyer restaurant of CREPS, Boulouris 1998, Villa Lyprendi, Toulon 1998, Salle de spectacles, Manosque (prize winner) 1999, Musée des Arts Premiers, Quai Branly, Paris (competition) 1999, Cinéma-casino, St Cyr-sur-Mer 1999, urban redevelopment of Celle Ligure, Italy 1999, Villa and Marmonier swimming pool, La Garde 1999, Villa and Le Goff swimming pool, Marseille 1999, Salle de musique actuelle, Nîmes (prize winner) 2000, project for seaside railway station, Marseille (competition) 2000, Concert Room, Potsdam, Germany 2000, Collection Yvon Lambert, Avignon (with A. Putman) 2000, Nat. Photographic Centre, Paris 2001, Pôle santé Hosp., Carpentras (with J.-P. Cassulo) 2001, concert and event halls of Les Tanzmatten, Selesteatt (with G. Heintz) 2001, Nat. Choreographic Centre, Aix-en-Provence 2004, Social Centre Consolat-Mirabeau, Marseille 2004, underground car park, Brussels 2004, reuse and redevelopment of Grands moulins, Université Paris VII 2005, Rive Gauche, Paris 13ème 2005, Navy Testing and Survey Centre at Le Mourillon, Toulon 2005, Pavillon Noir, Aix-en-Provence 2006, Palais du cinéma, Venice 2011, Pavillon Blanc Médiathèque and Centre d'art contemporain, Colomiers 2011, Site of Int. Thermonuclear Experimental Reactor, Cadarache 2012, Museum of European and Mediterranean Civilisations, Marseilles 2013, Educational Complex, La Bouilladisse, Stade Jean Bouin, Paris 2013, Centre des Arts et de la Culture, Douchy-les-Mines 2013. *Leisure interest:* collecting contemporary art. *Address:* Rudy Ricciotti Architecte, 17 blvd Victor Hugo, 83150 Bandol, France (office). *Telephone:* (4) 94-29-52-61 (office). *Fax:* (4) 94-32-45-25 (office). *E-mail:* rudy.ricciotti@wanadoo.fr (office). *Website:* www.rudyricciotti.com (office).

RICE, Anne, (Anne Rampling, A. N. Roquelaure), BA, MA; American writer; b. 4 Oct. 1941, New Orleans, La; m. Stan Rice 1961; one s. one d. (deceased); ed Texas Women's Univ., San Francisco State Coll., Univ. of California, Berkeley; mem. Authors' Guild. *Publications include:* Interview with the Vampire 1976, The Feast of All Saints 1979, Cry to Heaven 1982, The Claiming of Sleeping Beauty (as A. N. Roquelaure) 1983, Beauty"s Punishment (as A. N. Roquelaure) 1984, The Vampire Lestat 1985, Exit to Eden (as Anne Rampling) 1985, Beauty's Release (as A. N. Roquelaure) 1985, Belinda (as Anne Rampling) 1986, The Queen of the Damned 1988, The Mummy, or Ramses the Damned 1989, The Witching Hour 1990, The Tale of the Body Thief 1992, Lasher 1993, Taltos 1994, Memnoch the Devil 1995, Servant of the Bones 1996, Violin 1997, Pandora 1998, Armand 1998, Vittorio the Vampire 1999, Merrick 2000, Blood and Gold 2001, The Master of Rampling Gate (short story) 2002, Blackwood Farm 2002, Blood Canticle 2003, Christ the Lord: Out of Egypt 2005, Christ the Lord: The Road to Cana 2008, Called out of

Darkness: A Spiritual Confession (auto-biog.) 2008, Angel Time: The Songs of the Seraphim 2009, The Wolf Gift 2012, The Wolves of Midwinter 2013, Prince Lestat 2014, Prince Lestat and the Realms of Atlantis 2016, Ramses the Damned: The Passion of Cleopatra 2017, Blood Communion: A Tale of Prince Lestat 2018. *Address:* c/o Alfred A. Knopf Inc., 1745 Broadway, Suite B1, New York, NY 10019-4305, USA (office). *E-mail:* anneobrienrice@gmail.com (office). *Website:* www.annerice.com (office).

RICE, Charles Moen, III, BS, PhD; American virologist and academic; *Maurice R. and Corinne P. Greenberg Professor in Virology, Laboratory of Virology and Infectious Disease, The Rockefeller University;* b. 25 Aug. 1952, Sacramento, Calif.; ed Univ. of California, Davis, California Inst. of Tech.; Postdoctoral Researcher, California Inst. of Tech. 1981–85; Asst Prof., Washington Univ. School of Medicine, St Louis 1986–90, Assoc. Prof. 1991–95, Prof. 1995–2000; Prof., The Rockefeller Univ. 2000–, currently Maurice R. and Corinne P. Greenberg Prof. in Virology, Scientific and Exec. Dir, Center for the Study of Hepatitis C 2000–, Faculty mem. David Rockefeller Grad. Program and Tri-Institutional MD-PhD Program; Ed., Journal of Virology; past Pres. American Soc. for Virology; mem. NAS, American Acad. of Arts and Sciences; Fellow, AAAS; Pew Biomedical Scholar 1986, M.W. Beijerinck Virology Prize 2007, Robert Koch Award 2015, InBev-Baillet Latour Health Prize (Belgium) 2016, Lasker–DeBakey Clinical Medical Research Award, Lasker Foundation (co-recipient) 2016. *Publications:* more than 250 papers in professional journals. *Address:* Laboratory of Virology and Infectious Disease, Box 64, The Rockefeller University, 1230 York Avenue, New York, NY 10065, USA (office). *Telephone:* (212) 327-7009 (office). *E-mail:* charles.rice@rockefeller.edu (office); ricec@rockefeller.edu (office). *Website:* www.rockefeller.edu/research/faculty/labheads/CharlesRice/#content (office).

RICE, Condoleezza, PhD; American academic and fmr government official; *Thomas and Barbara Stephenson Senior Fellow on Public Policy, Hoover Institution, Stanford University;* b. 14 Nov. 1954, Birmingham, Ala; ed Univ. of Denver, Univ. of Notre Dame; teacher at Stanford Univ., Calif. 1981–2001, Provost 1993–99, Thomas and Barbara Stephenson Sr Fellow on Public Policy, Hoover Inst. and Prof. of Political Science 2009–, currently Denning Prof. in Global Business and the Economy, Grad. School of Business, Sr Fellow, Inst. for Int. Studies; Special Asst to Dir of Jt Chiefs of Staff 1986; Dir, then Sr Dir of Soviet and East European Affairs, Nat. Security Council 1989–91; Special Asst to Pres. for Nat. Security Affairs 1989–91; primary foreign policy adviser to presidential cand. George W. Bush 1999–2000; Asst to Pres. for Nat. Security Affairs and Nat. Security Advisor 2001–04; Sec. of State 2005–09; mem. or fmr mem. Bd of Dirs Chevron Corpn, Charles Schwab Corpn, William and Flora Hewlett Foundation, KiOR Inc. 2011–, Dropbox 2014–, and numerous other bds; mem. College Football Playoff, Playoff, Postseason, Selection Cttee 2013–; joined Ban Bossy campaign as a spokesperson advocating leadership roles for girls 2014; Trustee, John F. Kennedy Center for the Performing Arts, Washington, DC; Fellow, American Acad. of Arts and Sciences; Dr hc (Morehouse Coll.) 1991, (Univ. of Alabama) 1994, (Univ. of Notre Dame) 1995, (Mississippi Coll. School of Law) 2003, (Univ. of Louisville) 2004. *Publications:* Uncertain Allegiance: The Soviet Union and the Czechoslovak Army 1984, The Gorbachev Era (co-author) 1986, Germany Unified and Europe Transformed (co-author) 1995, Extraordinary, Ordinary People: A Memoir of Family 2010, No Higher Honor (autobiog.) 2011, Democracy: Stories from the Long Road to Freedom 2017; numerous articles on Soviet and East European foreign and defence policy. *Address:* Hoover Institution, 434 Galvez Mall, Stanford University, Stanford, CA 94305-6010, USA (office). *Telephone:* (650) 723-1754 (office). *Fax:* (650) 723-1687 (office). *Website:* www.hoover.org/profiles/condoleezza-rice (office).

RICE, Sir (Charles) Duncan, Kt, BA, PhD, FRSE, FRSA, FRHistS; British historian, academic and fmr university vice-chancellor; *Principal Emeritus, University of Aberdeen;* b. 20 Oct. 1942, Aberdeen, Scotland; m. Susan Rice; three c.; ed Univ. of Aberdeen, Univ. of Edinburgh; Lecturer, Univ. of Aberdeen 1966–69, Prin. 1996–2010, Prin. Emer. 2010–; Asst Prof. of History, Yale Univ., USA 1975–79, Assoc. Prof. 1970–75; Prof. of History and Dean of Coll., Hamilton Coll., Clinton, NY, USA 1979–85; Vice-Chancellor, New York Univ., USA 1985–96; mem. Bd, Trust for Scotland –2003, BT Scotland –2003, Scottish Ballet –2004, Scottish Opera –2005, Rowett Research Inst. –2006, Scottish Enterprise Grampian –2006, Nat., Univs and Colls Employers Asscn –2006; Chair. Circumpolar Univs Asscn 1997–99, UK Socrates–Erasmus Council –2007, Council for the Advancement and Support of Educ. 2009–16; mem. Heritage Lottery Fund Cttee for Scotland –2009; Burgess, Guild of City of Aberdeen; Hon. Fellow, UHI Millennium Inst.; Hon. Vice-Pres. Scottish Opera; hon. degrees from New York Univ., Robert Gordon Univ., Univ. of Aberdeen, Univ. of Edinburgh; Fellowships at Harvard and Yale Univs. *Publications:* The Rise and Fall of Black Slavery 1975, The Scots Abolitionists 1831–1961 1982; numerous papers in professional journals. *Leisure interests:* hill walking, contemporary literature, opera, studio ceramics. *Address:* c/o Principal's Office, King's College, University of Aberdeen, Aberdeen, AB24 3FX, Scotland (office).

RICE, Jerry Lee; American fmr professional football player; b. 13 Oct. 1962, Starkville, Miss.; s. of Joe Nathan; m. Jacqui Rice; four c.; ed Mississippi Valley State Coll.; wide receiver; played receiver for Miss. Valley State Coll. 1980–84; drafted in first round by San Francisco 49ers, Nat. Football League (NFL) 1985, played with 49ers 1985–2000, Oakland Raiders 2001–03, Seattle Seahawks 2004, Denver Broncos 2005 (retd in pre-season); holds 38 NFL records including most touchdowns receiving (197), most passes received (1,549) and most yards receiving (22,895); only player in NFL history to catch three touchdown passes in two Super Bowl games; currently broadcast commentator and radio talk show host; co-host, Sports Sunday (prime time sports show shown in San Francisco Bay Area); selected to Pro Bowl 1986–96, 1998, 2002, named All-Pro 10 times in 20 NFL seasons, Sporting News NFL Player of the Year 1987, 1990, Sports Illustrated NFL Player of the Year 1986, 1987, 1990, 1993, inducted into SWAC Athletic Hall of Fame 2005, College Football Hall of Fame 2006, Bay Area Sports Hall of Fame 2007, Mississippi Sports Hall of Fame 2007, Pro Football Hall of Fame 2010. *Television includes:* competed in reality show Dancing with the Stars 2005–06, appeared as backup dancer in season two episode of Fox's Don't Forget the Lyrics!, appeared in first episode of Spike TV's Pros vs Joes challenge show, portrayed Hal Gore in film Without a Paddle: Nature's Calling 2009. *Publications:* Rice 1996, Go

Long!: My Journey Beyond the Game and the Fame (autobiography) 2007. *Leisure interest:* golf. *Website:* www.jerryricefootball.com.

RICE, Keren D., OC, PhD; Canadian professor of linguistics; *Professor in Linguistics and Founding Director, Centre for Aboriginal Initiatives, University of Toronto;* b. 1949; apptd Asst Prof., Faculty of Arts and Science, Univ. of Toronto 1984, Prof. in Linguistics 1990–, Canada Research Chair in Linguistics and Aboriginal Studies 2003–, also Founding Dir Centre for Aboriginal Initiatives; Ed. International Journal of American Linguistics, has also served on editorial bds of several journals; Pres. Canadian Linguistics Asscn 1998–2000; mem. Bd Social Sciences and Humanities Research Council (mem. Standing Cttee, Standing Cttee on Ethics and Integrity); Fellow, Linguistic Soc. of America 2008 (Pres., first from univ. outside of USA), AAAS 2005; Bloomfield Book Award, Linguistic Soc. of America, Killam Research Fellowship for the study of Athapaskan languages 1993–94, Faculty of Arts and Science Outstanding Teacher Award 1998, Connaught Research Leave Fellowship 2001–02, recognized in an Honours Ceremony at First Nations House 2005, Killam Prize in Humanities, Canada Council for the Arts 2011, Canadian Linguistics Asscn Nat. Achievement Award 2013, Pierre Chauveau Award, RSC 2015. *Publications include:* Hare Noun Dictionary, Current Issues in Athapaskan Linguistics: Current Perspectives on a Language Family, Morpheme Order and Semantic Scope: Word Formation in the Athapaskan Verb, Athabaskan Prosody (co-ed.) 2005, Featural Markedness, A Grammar of Slave; numerous articles in linguistics and Aboriginal studies. *Address:* Department of Linguistics, Sidney Smith Hall, 4th Floor, University of Toronto, 100 St George Street, Toronto, ON M5S 3G3, Canada (office). *Telephone:* (416) 978-4029 (office). *Fax:* (416) 971-2688 (office). *E-mail:* rice@chass.utoronto.ca (office). *Website:* linguistics.utoronto.ca (office).

RICE, Stuart Alan, SB, AM, PhD; American chemist and academic; *Frank P. Hixon Distinguished Service Professor Emeritus, James Franck Institute, University of Chicago;* b. 6 Jan. 1932, New York; s. of Laurence Harlan Rice and Helen Rayfield; m. 1st Marian Coopersmith 1952 (died 1994); two d.; m. 2nd Ruth O'Brien 1997; one s.; ed Brooklyn Coll. and Harvard Univ.; Asst Prof., Dept of Chem. and Inst. for the Study of Metals, Univ. of Chicago 1957–59, Assoc. Prof., Inst. for the Study of Metals (later James Franck Inst.) 1959–60, 1960–69, Louis Block Prof. of Chem. 1969, Louis Block Prof. of Physical Sciences 1969–71, Chair. Dept of Chem. 1971–77, Frank P. Hixon Distinguished Service Prof. 1977–81, now Emer., Dean, Div. of Physical Sciences, Univ. of Chicago 1981–95; NSF Sr Postdoctoral Fellow and Visiting Prof., Univ. Libre de Bruxelles 1965–66; NIH Special Research Fellow and Visiting Prof., H. C. Orsted Inst., Univ. of Copenhagen 1970–71; Fairchild Distinguished Scholar, California Inst. of Tech. 1979; Newton-Abraham Prof., Univ. of Oxford, UK 1999–2000; lecturer, numerous univs in USA and abroad; mem. Nat. Science Bd 1980–; Jr Fellow, Soc. of Fellows 1955–57; Fellow, American Acad. of Arts and Sciences, NAS, American Philosophical Soc.; Foreign mem. Royal Danish Acad. of Science and Letters 1976; Hon. DSc (Brooklyn Coll., Notre Dame Coll.) 1982; A. Cressy Morrison Prize in Natural Sciences, New York Acad. of Sciences 1955, Alfred P. Sloan Fellow 1958–62, Guggenheim Fellow 1960–61, ACS Award in Pure Chem. 1962, Marlow Medal, Faraday Soc. 1963, Bourke Lecturer, Faraday Soc. 1964, Llewellyn John and Harriet Manchester Quantrell Award 1970, Leo Hendrik Baekeland Award 1971, Peter Debye ACS Prize 1985, Baker Lecturer, Cornell Univ. 1985–86, Centenary Lecturer, Royal Soc. of Chem. 1986–87, John Howard Appleton Lecturer, Brown Univ. 1995, Joel Henry Hildebrand Award, ACS, Centennial Medal, Harvard Univ. 1997, Nat. Medal of Science 1999, Hirschfelder Prize in Theoretical Chem. 2002, Wolf Prize in Chem. (jtly) 2011. *Publications:* Poly-electrolyte Solutions (with Mitsuru Nagasawa) 1961, Statistical Mechanics of Simple Liquids (with Peter Gray) 1965, Physical Chemistry (with R. S. Berry and John Ross) 1980, Optical Control of Molecular Dynamics (with Meishan Zhao) 2000; and 650 papers on chemical physics in scientific journals. *Leisure interests:* reading, carpentry, collecting antique scientific instruments. *Address:* The James Franck Institute, University of Chicago, GCIS E 235, 929 East 57th Street, Chicago, IL 60637 (office); 5517 South Kimbark Avenue, Chicago, IL 60637, USA (home). *Telephone:* (773) 702-7199 (office); (773) 667-2679 (home). *Fax:* (773) 702-5863 (office); (773) 667-0454 (home). *E-mail:* sarice@harper.uchicago.edu (office); s-rice@uchicago.edu (office). *Website:* jfi.uchicago.edu (office).

RICE, Susan Elizabeth, BA, MPhil, DPhil; American government official and diplomatist; b. 17 Nov. 1964, Washington, DC; m.; two c.; ed Stanford Univ. (Truman Scholar), New Coll., Oxford, UK (Rhodes Scholar); Man. Consultant, McKinsey and Co., Toronto, Canada 1991–93; Dir for Int. Orgs and Peacekeeping, Nat. Security Council, Washington, DC 1993–95, Special Asst to the Pres. and Sr Dir for African Affairs 1995–97; Asst Sec. of State for African Affairs, US State Dept 1997–2001; Sr Fellow, Foreign Policy and Global Economy and Devt Program, Brookings Inst., Washington, DC 2002–09; Sr Advisor for Nat. Security Affairs on Kerry-Edwards presidential campaign 2004, on Obama for America Campaign 2007–08, Sr Foreign Policy Advisor on Obama presidential campaign 2008; served on Advisory Bd of Obama-Biden Transition and as Co-Chair. of its Policy Working Group on Nat. Security 2009; Amb. and Perm. Rep. to UN, New York 2009–13; Nat. Security Advisor, The White House 2013–17; Chatham House-British Int. Studies Asscn Prize for the most distinguished doctoral dissertation in the UK in the field of Int. Relations. *Address:* c/o Office of the National Security Advisor, The White House, 1600 Pennsylvania Avenue, NW, Washington, DC 20500, USA (office).

RICE, Thomas Maurice, PhD, FRS; American/Irish scientist and academic; b. 26 Jan. 1939, Dundalk, Ireland; s. of James Rice and Maureen Rice; m. Helen D. Spreiter 1966; one s. two d.; ed Univ. Coll. Dublin and Univ. of Cambridge; asst lecturer, Dept of Mathematical Physics, Univ. of Birmingham 1963–64; Research Assoc. Dept of Physics, Univ. of Calif. at San Diego, La Jolla 1964–66; mem. Technical staff, Bell Laboratories, Murray Hill, NJ 1966–75, Head, Theoretical Dept of Physics 1975–78, Head, Surface Dept of Physics 1978–81; Prof. Simon Fraser Univ. 1974–75; Prof. of Theoretical Physics, ETH, Zürich 1981–2004 (retd); mem. NAS; Fellow, Royal Soc.; Hon. MRIA, Hon. mem. Royal Irish Acad.; Hewlett-Packard Europhysics Prize 1998, John Bardeen Prize 2000. *Address:* Theoretische Physik, ETH-Hönggerberg, 8093 Zürich, Switzerland. *E-mail:* rice@itp.phys.ethz.ch (office). *Website:* www.itp.phys.ethz.ch/staff/rice (office).

RICE, Sir Timothy (Tim) Miles Bindon, Kt; British songwriter; b. 10 Nov. 1944, Amersham; s. of Hugh Gordon Rice and Joan Odette Rice; m. Jane Artereta McIntosh 1974, one s. one d.; pnr Nell Sully, one d.; ed Lancing Coll.; with EMI Records 1966–68, Norrie Paramor Org. 1968–69; Founder and fmr Dir GRRR Books Ltd 1978, Pavilion Books Ltd 1981; Chair. Foundation for Sport and the Arts 1991–; mem. Main Cttee MCC 1992–94, 1995– (Pres. 2002–03); Pres. Lord Taverners 1988–90, 2000; Dr hc (Univ. of Sunderland) 2006; 12 Ivor Novello Awards, three Tony Awards, six Grammy Awards, British Acad. of Songwriters, Composers and Authors Fellowship 2010. *Lyrics for musicals:* (music by Andrew Lloyd Webber q.v. unless otherwise specified): The Likes of Us 1965, Joseph and the Amazing Technicolor Dreamcoat 1968, Jesus Christ Superstar 1970, Evita 1976, Blondel (music by Stephen Oliver) 1983, Chess (music by Benny Andersson and Bjorn Ulvaeus) 1984, Cricket 1986, Starmania/Tycoon (with music by Michael Berger) 1989–90, Aladdin (film musical, music by Alan Menken) 1992, The Lion King (film musical, music by Elton John) 1993 (theatre version 1997), Beauty and the Beast (music by Alan Menken) 1994 (some lyrics for stage version), Heathcliff (music by John Farrar) 1995, King David (music by Alan Menken) 1997, Aida (music by Elton John) 1998, The Road to El Dorado (music by Elton John) 1999, The Wizard of Oz (music by Andrew Lloyd Webber, and Harold Arlen and E.Y. Harburg) 2011, From Here to Eternity (music by Stuart Bryson) 2013; songs include: Don't Cry For Me Argentina, I Know Him So Well, Can You Feel The Love Tonight? (Acad. Award, Golden Globe, with Elton John 1994), I Don't Know How To Love Him, A Winter's Tale, Circle Of Life, Any Dream Will Do, A Whole New World (Acad. Award, Golden Globe, with Alan Menken 1992), All Time High (from film Octopussy), You Must Love Me (Acad. Award, Golden Globe, with Andrew Lloyd Webber 1996), One Night In Bangkok; lyrics for songs with composers, including Paul McCartney, Mike Batt, Freddie Mercury, Graham Gouldman, Marvin Hamlisch, Rick Wakeman, John Barry. *Publications:* Evita (with Andrew Lloyd Webber) 1978, Joseph and the Amazing Technicolor Dreamcoat 1982, Treasures of Lords 1989, Oh, What a Circus (autobiog.) 1995, The Complete Eurovision Song Contest Companion (jtly) 1998, founder and original author, with Paul Gambaccini, Jonathan Rice and Mike Read, of the Guinness Book of Hit Singles and related titles. *Leisure interests:* cricket, history of popular music, chickens. *Address:* Lewis & Golden LLP, 40 Queen Anne Street, London, W1G 9EL, England. *Telephone:* (20) 7580-7313. *Website:* www.timrice.co.uk.

RICH, Frank Hart, Jr, BA; American journalist, critic and writer; b. 2 June 1949, Washington, DC; s. of Frank Hart Rich and Helene Aaronson; m. 1st Gail Winston 1976; two s.; m. 2nd Alexandra Rachelle Witchel 1991; ed Harvard Univ.; Film Critic and Sr Ed. New Times Magazine 1973–75; Film Critic, New York Post 1975–77; Film and TV Critic, Time Magazine 1977–80; Chief Drama Critic, New York Times 1980–93, Op-Ed Columnist 1994–2011, also Sr Adviser to Culture Ed.; Writer-at-Large, New York Magazine 2011–; Assoc. Fellow, Jonathan Edwards Coll., Yale Univ. 1998; George Polk Award 2005. *Television:* Exec. Producer, Veep (series) 2012–. *Publications include:* Hot Seat: Theater Criticism for the New York Times 1980–93 1998, Ghost Light 2000, The Greatest Story Ever Sold 2006. *Address:* New York Media, 75 Varick Street, New York, NY 10013, USA (office). *Website:* nymag.com/frank-rich (office).

RICH, Michael David, BA, JD; American lawyer and research institute director; *President and CEO, RAND Corporation;* b. 23 Jan. 1953, Los Angeles, Calif.; m. Debra Rich 1980; two s.; ed Univ. of California, Berkeley, Univ. of California, Los Angeles; joined RAND Corpn as researcher 1976, Dir Resource Man. 1980–85, Vice-Pres. Nat. Security Research and Dir Nat. Defense Research Inst. 1986–93, Sr Vice-Pres. 1993–95, Exec. Vice-Pres. 1995–2011, Pres. and CEO 2011–; Founding Chair. Communications Inst. 2003–09, now Trustee; mem. Governing Council, IISS 2009–; mem. Bd of Councillors, UCLA Foundation 2000–; mem. Dean's Advisory Council, UCLA Samueli School Engineering 2013–; mem. Bd of Advisors, Santa Monica-UCLA Medical Center, Everychild Foundation; mem. Council on Foreign Relations, California Bar. *Address:* Office of the President, RAND Corporation, 1776 Main Street, Santa Monica, CA 90401-3208, USA (office). *Telephone:* (310) 393-0411, ext. 6934 (office). *E-mail:* Michael_Rich@rand.org (office). *Website:* www.rand.org (office).

RICH, Patrick Jean Jacques; French/Swiss/Canadian business executive (retd); b. 28 March 1931, Strasbourg, France; s. of Henri Rich and Marguerite Rich; m. Louise Dionne 1961; two s. one d.; ed Univ. of Strasbourg and Harvard Univ., USA; worked for Alcan Aluminium Ltd in Guinea, France, UK, Argentina, Spain and Italy 1959–70, Area Gen. Man. for Latin America 1971–75, Exec. Vice-Pres. Europe, Latin America and Africa 1976–77, mem. Bd 1978–86; Exec. Vice-Pres. Alcan Aluminium Ltd and CEO Aluminium Co. of Canada 1978–81; Exec. Vice-Pres. Europe, Africa, Middle East and Chair. Alcan Aluminium SA 1978–86; CEO Société Générale de Surveillance Holding SA, Geneva 1987–89; Deputy Chair. BOC Group PLC 1990–91, Chief Exec. 1991–92, Chair. 1992–94 (non-exec. 1994) and Chief Exec. 1992–94; Chair. Royal Packaging Industries Van Leer, Netherlands 1988–95, IMEC Research Project 1995–; Gov. Van Leer Group Foundation 1982–99, Van Leer Jerusalem Inst. 1995–99; mem. (non-exec.) Bd, La Farge Cement (Canada) 1977–81, Bekaert 1978–87, IMI Geneva 1977–81; Trustee, Bernard van Leer Foundation 1982–99; Croix de la Valeur Militaire, Army Corps citation, Médaille Commémorative Combattants d'Algérie. *Leisure interests:* opera, walking, skiing, piano playing, reading, sailing. *Address:* Terrazas de Marbella 4C, Los Sueños, Playa Herradura Canton Garabito, Pcia, Puntarenas, Costa Rica (home). *Telephone:* (22) 3466643 (Switzerland) (office); 8545-8937 (home). *E-mail:* pjj.rich@gmail.com.

RICHARD, Alain; French politician; *Mayor of Saint-Ouen-l'Aumône;* b. 29 Aug. 1945, Paris; m. Elisabeth Couffignal 1988; one s. one d. and one s. by previous m.; ed Lycée Henri IV, Paris, Institut d'Etudes Politiques, Ecole Nat. d'Admin; Auditor, Conseil d'Etat 1971, Maître des requêtes 1978, Conseiller d'Etat 1993–95; Mayor, Saint-Ouen-l'Aumône 1977–97, 2001–; Deputy, Val d'Oise 1978–93, Senator 1995–97, 2011–; Vice-Pres. Commission des lois 1981–86, Nat. Ass. 1987–88; Minister of Defence 1997–2001; Founder and Vice-Pres. Forum for Man. of Towns 1985–97; mem. Nat. Office, Parti Socialiste Unifié 1972–74; mem. Cttee Parti Socialiste 1979, Exec. Bd 1988; mem. Bd Inst. for Int. Relations 1991–97. *Address:* Hôtel de Ville, 2 place Pierre Mendès-France, Saint-Ouen l'Aumône, 95318 Cergy-Pontoise Cedex (office); 28 rue René Clair, 95310 Saint-Ouen-l'Aumône, France (home). *Telephone:* 1-34-21-25-00 (office). *Fax:* 1-34-64-35-65

(office). *E-mail:* courrier@ville-saintouenlaumone.fr (office). *Website:* www.ville-saintouenlaumone.fr (office).

RICHARD, Dame Alison Fettes, DBE, MA, PhD; British/American university administrator and professor of anthropology and environmental studies; *Senior Research Scientist and Crosby Professor Emerita, Yale University;* b. 1 March 1948, Kent, England; d. of Gavin Sharp Richard and Joyce Napier Matthews; m. Robert E. Dewar; one s. (deceased) two d.; ed Newnham Coll., Cambridge and King's Coll., London; joined Faculty of Yale Univ., USA 1972, Dir of Grad. Studies 1980–86, Prof. of Anthropology 1986–2003, Chair. Dept of Anthropology 1986–90, Prof. of Environmental Studies, Yale School of Forestry and Environmental Studies 1990–2003, Dir Peabody Museum of Natural History 1991–94, Provost, Yale Univ. 1994–2002, Franklin Muzzy Crosby Prof. of Human Environment 1998, Sr Research Scientist and Prof. Emer. 2003–; Vice-Chancellor Univ. of Cambridge 2003–10, Vice-Chancellor Emer. 2010–; Trustee, Liz Claiborne/Art Ortenberg Foundation, Howard Hughes Medical Inst.; Officier, Ordre Nat. (Madagascar) 2005; Dr hc (Peking Univ.) 2004, (Univ. of Antananarivo, Madagascar) 2005, (York Univ., Toronto) 2006, (Univ. of Edinburgh) 2006, (Queen's Univ., Belfast) 2008, (Anglia Ruskin Univ.) 2008, (Yale Univ.) 2009, (Ehwa Woman's Univ., S Korea) 2009, (Chinese Univ. of Hong Kong) 2009, (Univ. of Exeter) 2010, (Univ. of Cambridge) 2011, (Univ. of London) 2011 (Hong Kong Polytechnic Univ.) 2015. *Publications include:* Primates in Nature 1985, Behavioral Variation: Case Study of a Malagasy Lemur 1978; numerous articles in scientific journals. *Address:* PO Box 201, Middle Haddam, CT 06456, USA (home). *Telephone:* (203) 432-3691 (office).

RICHARD, Sir Cliff, Kt, OBE; British singer, musician (guitar) and actor; b. (Harry Rodger Webb), 14 Oct. 1940, India; s. of Rodger Webb and Dorothy Webb; ed Riversmead School, Cheshunt, Herts.; Leader, Cliff Richard and The Shadows; later, solo artist; regular int. concert tours, various repertory and variety seasons; own TV series on BBC and ITV; numerous radio and TV interviews and performances since 1958; mem. Equity; Hon. DUniv (Middlesex) 2003; numerous awards. *Films include:* Serious Charge 1959, Expresso Bongo 1960, The Young Ones 1961, Summer Holiday 1962, Wonderful Life 1964, Finders Keepers 1966, Two a Penny 1968, His Land, Take Me High 1973. *Stage appearances include:* musicals Time, Dominion Theatre, London 1986–87, Heathcliff, UK tour and Hammersmith Apollo, London 1996–97. *Recordings include:* albums: Cliff 1959, Cliff Sings 1959, Me And My Shadows 1960, Listen To Cliff 1961, 21 Today 1961, The Young Ones 1961, 32 Minutes And 17 Seconds With Cliff Richard 1962, Summer Holiday 1963, Cliff's Hit Album 1963, When In Spain 1963, Wonderful Life 1964, Aladdin And His Wonderful Lamp 1964, Cliff Richard 1965, More Hits By Cliff 1965, When In Rome 1965, Love Is Forever 1965, Kinda Latin 1966, Finders Keepers 1966, Cinderella 1967, Don't Stop Me Now 1967, Good News 1967, Cliff In Japan 1968, Two A Penny 1968, Established 1968, The Best Of Cliff 1969, Sincerely 1969, It'll Be Me 1969, Cliff Live At The Talk of The Town 1970, About That Man 1970, His Land 1970, Tracks 'n' Grooves 1970, The Best Of Cliff Vol. Two 1972, Take Me High 1973, Help It Along 1974, The 31st February Street 1974, I'm Nearly Famous 1976, Every Face Tells A Story 1977, 40 Golden Greats 1977, Small Corners 1978, Green Light 1978, Thank You Very Much (Cliff & The Shadows) 1979, Rock 'n' Roll Juvenile 1979, I'm No Hero 1980, Love Songs 1981, Wired For Sound 1981, Now You See Me... Now You Don't 1982, Dressed For The Occasion 1983, Silver 1983, Rock 'n' Roll Silver 1983, Cliff & The Shadows 1984, Always Guaranteed 1987, Private Collection 1988, Stronger 1989, From A Distance – The Event 1990, Together 1991, Cliff Richard: The Album 1993, The Hit List 1994, Songs From Heathcliff 1995, Heathcliff Live 1996, Cliff Richard At The Movies 1996, The Rock 'n' Roll Years 1997, Real As I Wanna Be 1998, The Whole Story 2001, Wanted 2001, The Singles Collection 2002, Cliff At Christmas 2003, Something's Goin' On 2004, Two's Company: The Duets 2006, Love: The Album 2007, 50th Anniversary Album 2008, Reunited (with The Shadows) 2009, Bold As Brass 2010, Soulicious 2011, The Fabulous Rock 'N' Roll Songbook 2013, Cliff Richard 75 at 75 2015, Just... Fabulous Rock 'N' Roll Songbook 2016, Rise Up 2018. *Publications include:* Questions 1970, The Way I See It 1972, The Way I See It Now 1975, Which One's Cliff? 1977, Happy Christmas from Cliff 1980, You, Me and Jesus 1983, Mine to Share 1984, Jesus, Me and You 1985, Single-Minded 1988, Mine Forever 1989, My Story: A Celebration of 40 Years in Showbusiness 1998, My Life, My Way (with Penny Junor) 2008. *Leisure interest:* tennis. *Address:* Cliff Richard Organisation, PO Box 423, Leatherhead, Surrey, KT22 2HJ, England (office). *Telephone:* (1372) 467752 (office). *E-mail:* general@cliffrichard.org (office). *Website:* www.cliffrichard.org (home).

RICHARD, Jean Barthélemy, DèsL; French historian and academic; b. 7 Feb. 1921, Kremlin-Bicêtre; s. of Pierre Richard and Amélie Grandchamp; m. Monique Rivoire 1944; three s. two d.; ed Ecole des Chartes, Ecole Française de Rome and Sorbonne, Paris; Asst Archivist, Dijon 1943–55; Prof., Univ. of Dijon 1955–88, Dean, Faculté des Lettres 1968–71; mem. Acad. des Inscriptions, Inst. de France and other learned socs; Commdr, Légion d'honneur, Grand Officier, Ordre du Mérite, Commdr des Palmes académiques; Dr hc (Cyprus Univ.) 2006; Gold Medal for Altaic Studies, Indiana Univ. *Publications:* The Latin Kingdom of Jerusalem 1953, Les ducs de Bourgogne 1954, L'Esprit de la Croisade 1969, La papauté et les missions d'Orient 1977, Histoire de la Bourgogne 1978, St Louis 1983, Le livre des remembrances de la secrète du royaume de Chypre 1983, Histoire des Croisades 1996, Au-delà de la Perse et de l'Arménie 2005, Lettres papales relatives à Chypre 1314–1378 2013; five vols in Variorum Reprints on Crusades and Oriental History 1976–2003. *Leisure interests:* garden and forest activities. *Address:* 12 rue Pelletier de Chambure, 21000 Dijon (home); Les Billaudots, 71540 Igornay, France. *Telephone:* (3) 80-66-10-28 (home); (3) 85-82-82-98 (home).

RICHARD, Pierre, BEng; French business executive; b. 9 March 1941, Dijon; s. of Henri Richard and Marguerite Richard (née Genty); m. Aleth Sachot 1966; three c.; ed Univ. of Dijon and Univ. of Pennsylvania, USA; teacher, Inst. of Urbanism, Paris 1967–68; Asst Dir-Gen. Public Devt Corpn, new town of Cergy-Pontoise 1967–72; Tech. Adviser to Sec. of State for Housing 1972–74, to Gen. Secr. for the Pres. of Rep. 1974–78; Dir-Gen. for Local Communities, Ministry of the Interior 1978–82; Asst Dir-Gen. of Treasury, Dept of Local Devt 1983–93; Man. Dir Crédit Local de France (CLF) 1993–, Co-Chair. Dexia Group (after merger between CLF and Crédit Communal de Belgique) 1996–99, Deputy Dir 1999, Pres. Supervisory Bd Dexia Crédit Local de France 2000, Group CEO and Chair. Exec. Bd Dexia

Group 2000–05, Chair. Bd of Dirs 2006–08; Pres. Group of Specialized Financial Insts 1991–93; Pres. Inst. of Decentralization 1993–95; Pres. Admin. Bd, Ecole Nat. des Ponts et Chaussées 1994–; Dir Municipal Bond Investors Assurance 1990–, Air France 1995–, Banque européenne d'investissement 1994–, Le Monde 1995–; Chevalier, Légion d'honneur, Officier, Ordre nat. du Mérite, Commdr, Order of Léopold II. *Publications include:* Les Communes françaises d'aujourd'hui, Le Temps des citoyens pour une démocratie décentralisée 1995. *Leisure interest:* horseriding.

RICHARD, Stéphane; French business executive; *Chairman and CEO, Orange;* b. 24 Aug. 1961, Caudéran (Gironde); ed École des Hautes Etudes Commerciales, Paris, Ecole Nationale d'Admin, Strasbourg; assigned to French Inspectorate of Public Finances 1987–91; apptd as tech. adviser for the electronics and IT industries in cabinet of Dominique Strauss-Kahn, Minister for Industry and Foreign Trade 1991–92; joined Compagnie Générale des Eaux 1992, first as Deputy to group's Chief Financial Officer, before being appointed CEO Compagnie Immobilière Phénix 1994–97, Chair. Compagnie Générale d'Immobilier et de Services (now Nexity) 1997–2003, Exec. Vice-Pres. Veolia Environnement and Chief CEO Veolia Transport 2003–07; Chief of Staff to French Minister for the Economy, Industry and Employment 2007–09; mem. Bd of Dirs, France Télécom SA, UGC SA, Nexity SA, all until 2007, mem. Exec. Bd and Deputy CEO in-charge of operations in France, France Télécom-Orange (now called Orange) 2009–10, CEO Del. Jan.–March 2010, CEO March 2010–11, Chair. and CEO Orange 2011–; Chevalier, Légion d'honneur 2007, Ordre nat. du Mérite. *Address:* Orange, 6 place d'Alleray, 75505 Paris Cedex 15, France (office). *Telephone:* 1-44-44-22-22 (office). *Fax:* 1-44-44-95-95 (office). *E-mail:* info@orange.com (office). *Website:* www.orange .com (office); www.orange-business.com (office).

RICHARDS, Ed; British government official; began career as researcher with Diverse Production Ltd; worked with London Economics Ltd (consultancy firm); fmr adviser to Gordon Brown MP; served as Controller of Corporate Strategy at BBC; fmr Sr Policy Adviser to Prime Minister Tony Blair for media, telecoms, internet and e-govt; Sr Pnr, Strategy and Market Devts, Ofcom 2003–05, COO 2005–06, CEO 2006–14; mem. Bd of Dirs Donmar Warehouse Ltd.

RICHARDS, Emma, MBE, BSc; British yachtswoman; b. 10 Oct. 1974; winner Mobil North Sea Race, Banff–Stavanger, Sigma 400 1998, Fastnet Open 60 Team Group Four, Class One; Round Isle of Wight Race, 60 ft Trimaran Fujicolor 1999, Transat Jacques Vabre, double-handed Transatlantic, Open 50 Pindar, Class 2 Monohull 1999, Europe One New Man Star, single-handed Transatlantic race, Open 50 Pindar, Class Two Monohull 2000, RORC 75th Anniversary Round Britain and Ireland Race, Open 50 Pindar, double-handed 2000, OOPS! Cup eight-race series, Scandinavia, 60 ft Trimaran Toshiba 2001; joined Nautor Challenge Amer Sports Too for start of leg four of Volvo Ocean Race 2002; became first woman to sail single-handed across the Atlantic from west to east in a monohull boat 2002; first British woman and youngest competitor to complete Around Alone race May 2003. *Publication:* Around Alone 2004.

RICHARDS, Sir Francis Neville, Kt, KCMG, CVO, DL, MA; British fmr diplomatist and intelligence chief; b. 18 Nov. 1945; s. of Sir Francis Brooks Richards; m. Gillian Bruce Nevill 1971; one s. one d.; ed Eton Coll. and King's Coll., Cambridge; with Royal Green Jackets 1967, served with UN Force in Cyprus (invalided 1969); joined FCO 1969, served in Moscow 1971; UK Del. to Mutual and Balanced Force Reducations negotiations, Vienna 1973; FCO 1976–85 (Asst Pvt. Sec. to Sec. of State 1981–82); Econ. and Commercial Counsellor, New Delhi 1985–88; FCO 1988–90 (Head S Asian Dept); High Commr to Namibia 1990–92; Minister, Moscow 1992–95; Dir (Europe) FCO 1995–97, Deputy Under-Sec. of State 1997–98; Dir Govt Communications HQ (GCHQ) 1998–2003; Gov. and C-in-C of Gibraltar 2003–06; Chair. Insight Certification Ltd 2007–13, Int. Advisory Bd Altimo SA 2007–13; Chair. Bletchley Park Trust 2007–12; Trustee, Imperial War Museum, London 2007–16 (Deputy Chair. 2009–11, Chair. 2011–16); Glos. Co. Pres., SSAFA Forces Help 2011–; Pres. Friends of Gloucester Cathedral 2007–17; mem. Advisory Bd, School of Man., Univ. of Bath 2013, Chair. 2018–; DL for Glos. 2007–; Hon. Prof., School of Social Sciences and Dir Centre for Studies in Security and Diplomacy, Univ. of Birmingham 2007–10; KStJ 2003; Hon. DUniv (Birmingham) 2012, Hon. LLD (Bath) 2017. *Leisure interests:* walking, travelling, riding. *Telephone:* 7969-020177 (mobile) (home). *E-mail:* king.millers@btinternet .com (office).

RICHARDS, Sir Isaac Vivian (Viv) Alexander, KGN, OBE; Antigua and Barbuda fmr cricketer; b. 7 March 1952, St John's; s. of Malcolm Richards; m. Miriam Lewis; one s. one d.; one d. with Neena Gupta; ed Antigua Grammar School; right-hand batsman, off-break bowler, cover-point fielder; played for Leeward Islands 1971–91 (Capt. 1981–91), Somerset 1974–86, Queensland 1976–77, Glamorgan 1990–93; Test debut: India v West Indies, Bangalore 22–27 Nov. 1974; One-Day Int. (ODI) debut: Sri Lanka v West Indies, Manchester 7 June 1975; played in 121 Tests for W Indies 1974–91, 50 as Capt., scoring 8,540 runs (average 50.23, highest score 291) including 24 hundreds and holding 122 catches; scored record 1,710 runs in a calendar year (11 Tests in 1976); played in 187 ODIs, scoring 6,721 runs (average 47.00, highest score 189 not out) including 11 hundreds; scored 36,212 First-class runs (average 49.40, highest score 322) including 114 hundreds, only W Indian to score 100 hundreds); toured England 1976, 1979 (World Cup), 1980, 1983 (World Cup), 1984, 1988 (as Capt.), 1991 (as Capt.); one of only four non-English cricketers to have scored 100 first-class centuries; only West Indies capt. never to lose a Test series; Chair. Selectors, W Indies Cricket Bd 2002–04; frequently heard on BBC's Test Match Special; Kt of the Order of the Nat. Hero (Antigua) 1999; Dr hc (Exeter) 1986; Wisden Cricketer of the Year 1977, one of Wisden's Five Cricketers of the Century 2000, inducted into Cricket Hall of Fame 2001. *Publications:* (with David Foot) Viv Richards (autobiography) 1982, Cricket Masterclass 1988, Hitting Across The Line (auto-biography) 1991, (with Bob Harris) Sir Vivian (autobiography) 2000. *Leisure interests:* music, football, golf, tennis. *Address:* c/o West Indies Cricket Board, PO Box 616 W, St John's, Antigua. *Telephone:* 481-2450. *Fax:* 481-2498. *E-mail:* wicb@ windiescricket.com. *Website:* www.windiescricket.com.

RICHARDS, Keith; British musician (guitar), singer and songwriter; b. (Keith Richard), 18 Dec. 1943, Dartford, Kent; s. of Bert Richards and Doris Richards; m. 1st Anita Pallenberg; two s. (one deceased) one d.; m. 2nd Patti Hansen 1983; two

d.; ed Sidcup Art School; Founder mem., The Rolling Stones 1962–; composer (with Mick Jagger) of numerous songs 1964–; Nordoff-Robbins Silver Clef 1982, Grammy Lifetime Achievement Award 1986, Ivor Novello Award for Outstanding Contribution to British Music 1991. *Films:* Sympathy for the Devil 1970, Gimme Shelter 1970, Ladies and Gentlemen, the Rolling Stones 1974, Let's Spend the Night Together 1983, Hail Hail Rock 'n' Roll 1987 (with Chuck Berry, Eric Clapton and Friends), Flashpoint 1991, Voodoo Lounge 1994, Pirates of the Caribbean: At World's End (actor) 2007, Shine a Light 2007. *Recordings include:* albums: with The Rolling Stones: The Rolling Stones 1964, The Rolling Stones No. 2 1965, Out Of Our Heads 1965, Aftermath 1966, Between The Buttons 1967, Their Satanic Majesties Request 1967, Beggar's Banquet 1968, Let It Bleed 1969, Get Yer Ya-Ya's Out 1969, Sticky Fingers 1971, Exile On Main Street 1972, Goat's Head Soup 1973, It's Only Rock And Roll 1974, Black And Blue 1976, Some Girls 1978, Emotional Rescue 1980, Tattoo You 1981, Still Life 1982, Undercover 1983, Dirty Work 1986, Steel Wheels 1989, Flashpoint 1991, Voodoo Lounge 1994, Stripped 1995, Bridges to Babylon 1997, Forty Licks 2002, Live Licks 2004, A Bigger Bang 2005, Blue & Lonesome (Grammy Award for Best Traditional Blues Album 2018) 2016; solo: Hail Hail Rock 'n' Roll (with Chuck Berry) 1987, Talk Is Cheap 1988, Live At The Hollywood Palladium 1991, Main Offender 1992, Crosseyed Heart 2015. *Publications:* According to the Rolling Stones (jt autobiography) 2003, Life (autobiography) 2010. *Address:* Munro Sounds, 5 Wandsworth Plain, London, SW18 1ES, England (office). *Telephone:* (20) 8877-3111 (office). *Fax:* (20) 8877-3033 (office). *Website:* www.rollingstones.com; www.keithrichards.com.

RICHARDS, Sir Rex Edward, Kt, DSc, FRS, FRSC; British chemist and university administrator (retd); b. 28 Oct. 1922, Colyton, Devon, England; s. of H. W. Richards and E. N. Richards; m. Eva Edith Vago 1948; two d.; ed Colyton Grammar School, Devon, St John's Coll., Oxford; Fellow, Lincoln Coll., Oxford 1947–64; Dr Lee's Prof. of Chem., Oxford 1964–70; Fellow, Exeter Coll., Oxford 1964–69; Warden Merton Coll., Oxford 1969–84; Vice-Chancellor Univ. of Oxford 1977–81; Chancellor Univ. of Exeter 1982–98; Tilden Lecturer 1962; Research Fellow, Harvard Univ., USA 1955; Assoc. Fellow, Morse Coll., Yale, USA 1974–79; Chair. Oxford Enzyme Group 1969–83; Dir Oxford Instruments Group 1982–91; Dir Leverhulme Trust 1985–93; Pres. Royal Soc. of Chem. 1990–92; mem. Chem. Soc. Council 1957, 1988, Faraday Soc. Council 1963, Royal Soc. Council 1973–75, Advisory Bd for Research Councils 1980–82, Advisory Council for Applied Research and Devt 1984–87; Dir IBM United Kingdom Holdings, IBM (UK) 1978–82; Chair. British Postgraduate Medical Fed. 1986–93, Nat. Gallery Trust 1995–99; Commr Royal Comm. for Exhbn of 1851 1984–97; Foreign Assoc. Acad. des Sciences, Inst. de France 1995–; Trustee, CiBA Foundation 1978–97, Nat. Heritage Memorial Fund 1979–84, Tate Gallery 1982–88, 1991–93, Nat. Gallery 1982–93, Henry Moore Foundation 1989–2002 (Vice-Chair. 1993–94, Chair. 1994–2001); Hon. Fellow, St John's Coll., Lincoln Coll., Oxford 1968, Merton Coll., Oxford 1984, Thames Polytechnic 1991; Hon. FRCP 1987; Hon. FBA 1990; Hon. FRAM 1991; Hon. DSc (East Anglia) 1971, (Exeter) 1975, (Leicester) 1978, (Salford) 1979, (Edin.) 1981, (Leeds) 1984, (Birmingham) 1993, (London) 1994, (Oxford Brookes) 1998, (Warwick) 1999; Hon. DLitt (Dundee) 1977, (Kent) 1987; Hon. ScD (Cambridge) 1987; Corday-Morgan Medal, Chemical Soc. 1954, Davy Medal, Royal Soc. 1976, Award in Theoretical Chem. and Spectroscopy, Chemical Soc. 1977, Epic Award 1982, Medal of Honour, Bonn Univ. 1983, Royal Medal, Royal Soc. 1986, Pres.'s Medal, Soc. of Chemical Industry 1991. *Publications:* numerous contribs to scientific journals. *Leisure interests:* painting and sculpture. *Address:* Suite 4, West Heanton, Buckland Filleigh, Beaworthy, Devon, EX21 5PJ, England (home). *Telephone:* (1409) 821985 (home). *E-mail:* rex.richards@merton .ox.ac.uk.

RICHARDS OF HERSTMONCEUX, Baron (Life Peer), cr. 2014; **Gen. (retd) David Julian Richards,** GCB, CBE, DSO, ADC Gen., BA; British army officer; b. 1952; m. Caroline Richards; two d.; ed Eastbourne Coll., Univ. Coll., Cardiff; commissioned into Royal Artillery as Second Lt 1971, served as Capt. 1977–89, Lt-Col 1989–94; Col Army Plans, Ministry of Defence 1994–95, Commdr 4th Armoured Brigade, Germany 1995–98, Chief of Jt Force Operations, Perm. Jt HQ 1998–2000, Chief of Staff, Allied Rapid Reaction Corps, NATO 2001–06, Commdr Int. Stabilisation and Assistance Force in southern Afghanistan 2006–07, C-in-C of Land Forces 2008, Chief of the Gen. Staff 2009–10, Chief of the Defence Staff 2010–13; Chair. Palliser Assocs Ltd (consultancy co-owned with wife) 2013–, Equilibrium Gulf Ltd (majority owner), Arturius Int. Ltd; Adm. Army Sailing Asscn, British Kiel Yacht Club; Pres. Army Tennis; Chair. Gurkha Welfare Trust; Gov. Ditchley Foundation; Deputy Grand Pres., Royal Commonwealth Ex-Services League; Hon. Col of the Royal Rifle Volunteers 2003, Hon. Col Commdt of the Royal Artillery 2005, Col Commdt of the Brigade of Gurkhas 2007; campaign medals for NI, East Timor (Int. Force for East Timor—INTERFET) and Operational Service Medals for Sierra Leone and Afghanistan, Golden Jubilee Medal 2002; Dr Jean Mayer Global Citizenship Award, Tufts Univ. 2016. *Address:* House of Lords, London, SW1A 0PW (office); Palliser Associates Ltd, 3 Ferry Road, Shoreham By Sea, West Sussex, BN43 5RA, England. *Telephone:* (20) 7219-5353 (office).

RICHARDSON, Annette; American consultant and UN official; *Senior Advisor, Office for Partnerships, United Nations;* ed Université Jussieu Paris VII, France; Exec. Asst to Chair. and CEO of Sithe Energies 1996–2000; Chief of Staff to Chair. and CEO of Vivendi Universal 2000–02; Dir of Int. Relations for the New York City 2012 Olympic Bid Cttee in charge of African Affairs and the UN 2002–05; ind. consultant 2005–09; Founder and Man. Partner, Richardson Rogers & Assocs LLC, Washington, DC 2005–; Sr Advisor, UN Office for Partnerships 2011–; Vice-Pres. UN Women for Peace; mem. Bd of Dirs UN Women for Peace, Health and Climate Foundation; mem. Bd of Advisors, Powered By Professionals; mem. PTTOW!, Nat. Asscn of Professional Women; Hon. Amb., Univ. for Peace (UPeace); Global Citizen Award 2010, Professional Woman of the Year Award, Nat. Asscn of Professional Women 2010. *Address:* United Nations Office for Partnerships, 1 United Nations Plaza, Room DC1-1330, New York, NY 10017, USA (office). *Telephone:* (212) 963-1000 (office). *Fax:* (212) 963-1486 (office). *E-mail:* partner@un .org (office). *Website:* www.un.org/partnerships (office).

RICHARDSON, Cosmos; Saint Lucia civil servant and diplomatist; *Permanent Representative to United Nations;* ed Univ. of West Indies; worked for Ministry of Agric., of Fisheries, of Physical Planning, of Natural Resources, of Co-operatives 1986–97; Perm. Sec., Dept of Commerce, Int. Trade, Investment, Enterprise Devt and Consumer Affairs 1997–2002; Perm. Sec. Ministry of External Affairs, Int. Trade and Civil Aviation 2002–07; Cabinet Sec., Office of Prime Minister 2007–12; consultant for various orgs in areas of public policy, policy analysis and strategic planning 2012–17; Amb. to Caribbean Community (CARICOM) and Org. of Eastern Caribbean States (OECS) July. 2016–Feb. 2017; Perm. Rep. to UN 2017–. *Address:* Permanent Mission of Saint Lucia, 800 Second Avenue, 5th Floor, New York, NY 10017, USA (office). *Telephone:* (212) 697-9360 (office). *Fax:* (212) 697-4993 (office). *E-mail:* info@stluciamission.org (office). *Website:* saintluciamissionun.org (office).

RICHARDSON, David John; South African lawyer, sports administrator and fmr professional cricketer; b. 16 Sept. 1959, Johannesburg, Transvaal; m.; several s.; right-hand batsman, fmr South African Test wicket-keeper, also represented Eastern Prov. and Northern Transvaal in various domestic competitions; played 42 Test matches and 122 One Day Ints (ODIs), taking 152 dismissals, scored a maiden and only Test century (109) against New Zealand at Cape Town 1994–95, 1,359 Test runs, batting average 24.26, retd from int. cricket 1998; Business Dir with Octagon SA (co. responsible for negotiating player employment contracts with United Cricket Bd of South Africa); first Gen. Man. of Cricket, Int. Cricket Council (ICC) 2002–12, relocated with ICC to Dubai 2005, CEO ICC 2012–19. *Address:* c/o International Cricket Council, Street 69, Dubai Sports City, Emirates Road, PO Box 500 070, Dubai, United Arab Emirates (office). *Telephone:* (4) 382-8800 (office). *Fax:* (4) 382-8600 (office). *E-mail:* enquiry@icc-cricket.com (office). *Website:* www.icc-cricket.com (office).

RICHARDSON, George Barclay, CBE, MA; British economist and fmr publisher; b. 19 Sept. 1924, London, England; s. of George Richardson and Christina Richardson; m. Isabel A. Chalk 1957 (divorced 1999); two s.; ed Aberdeen Cen. Secondary School and other schools in Scotland, Univ. of Aberdeen and Corpus Christi Coll., Oxford; Admiralty Scientific Research Dept 1944; Lt RNVR 1945; Intelligence Officer, HQ Intelligence Div., British Army of the Rhine 1946–47; Third Sec. HM Foreign Service 1949; student, Nuffield Coll., Oxford 1950; Fellow, St John's Coll. Oxford 1951–88; Univ. Reader in Economics, Univ. of Oxford 1969–73; Warden, Keble Coll. Oxford 1989–94; Pro-Vice-Chancellor, Univ. of Oxford 1988–94; Del. Oxford Univ. Pres. 1971–74, Chief Exec. 1974–88; mem. Econ. Devt Cttee for Electrical Eng Industry 1964–73, Monopolies Comm. 1969–74, Royal Comm. on Environmental Pollution 1973–74; Econ. Adviser, UKAEA 1968–74; mem. Council, Publishers' Asscn 1981–87; Hon. DCL (Oxford), Hon. LLD (Aberdeen). *Publications include:* Information and Investment 1960, 1991, Economic Theory 1964, The Economics of Imperfect Knowledge 1998; articles in academic journals. *Leisure interests:* reading, music. *Address:* 33 Belsyre Court, Observatory Street, Oxford, OX2 6HU, England (home). *Telephone:* (1865) 510113 (home). *Fax:* (1865) 510113 (home). *E-mail:* george.richardson@keble.ox.ac.uk (home).

RICHARDSON, Graham; Australian politician, broadcaster and journalist; b. 27 Sept. 1949, Kogarah, Sydney; s. of Frederick James Richardson and Catherine Maud Richardson; m. Cheryl Gardener 1973; one s. one d.; ed Marist Brothers Coll., Kogarah; state organizer Australian Labor Party, NSW 1971–76, Gen. Sec. 1976–94, State Campaign Dir 1976; Vice-Pres. Nat. Labor Party 1976, Del. to Nat. Conf. 1977–94, convenor Nat. Industrial Platform Cttee; Senator for NSW 1983–94; Minister for Environment and Arts 1987–90, for Sports, Tourism and Territories 1988–90, for Social Security 1990, of Transport and Communications 1991–92, of Health 1993–94; political commentator on election coverage and journalist, The Nine Network 1994, Seven Network, Sky News Live 2011–16; journalist, The Bulletin 1994; Broadcaster, 2GB; fmr Chair. Senate Estimates Cttee 1986, Senate Select Cttee on TV Equalization; mem. several senate cttees and three ministerial cttees; fmr mem. Bd Sydney Organizing Cttee for the Olympic Games. *Leisure interests:* golf, reading, skiing, tennis. *Address:* Macquarie Media Limited, Radio 2GB, Level G, Building C, 33–35 Saunders Street, Pyrmont, NSW 2009, Australia (office). *Telephone:* (02) 8570-0000 (office). *Fax:* (02) 8570 0219 (office). *Website:* www.2gb.com (office).

RICHARDSON, Joely; British actress; b. 9 Jan. 1965, London; d. of Tony Richardson and Vanessa Redgrave (q.v.); m. Tim Bevan 1992 (divorced); one d.; ed Lycée Français de Londres, St Paul's Girls' School, London, Pinellas Park High School, Fla, The Thacher School, Calif. and Royal Acad. of Dramatic Art. *Plays include:* Steel Magnolias 1989, Lady Windermere's Fan 2002. *Films include:* Wetherby 1985, Drowning by Numbers 1988, A proposito di quella strana ragazza (About That Foreign Girl) 1989, King Ralph 1991, Shining Through 1992, Rebecca's Daughters 1992, I'll Do Anything 1994, Sister, My Sister 1995, Believe Me 1995, Loch Ness 1996, Hollow Reed 1996, 101 Dalmatians 1996, Event Horizon 1997, Wrestling with Alligators 1998, Under Heaven 1998, Toy Boys 1999, Return to Me 2000, Maybe Baby 2000, The Patriot 2000, The Affair of the Necklace 2001, Shoreditch 2003, The Fever 2004, The Last Mimzy 2007, The Christmas Miracle of Jonathan Toomey 2007, Anonymous 2011, The Girl with the Dragon Tattoo 2011, Red Lights 2012, Thanks for Sharing 2012, The Devil's Violinist 2013, Vampire Academy 2014, Endless Love 2014, Maggie 2015. *Television appearances include:* Behaving Badly (mini-series) 1989, Lady Chatterley's Lover (mini-series) 1993, The Echo (series) 1998, Nip/Tuck (series) 2003–10, Fallen Angel (film) 2003, Lies My Mother Told Me (film) 2005, Wallis & Edward (film) 2005, Fatal Contact: Bird Flu in America (film) 2006, Day of the Triffids (mini-series) 2009, The Tudors (series) 2010. *Address:* c/o Finch and Partners, First Floor, 6 Heddon Street, London, W1B 4BR (office); c/o ICM London, 4-6 Soho Square, London, W1D 3PZ, England (office). *Telephone:* (20) 7851-7140 (office); (20) 7432-0800 (ICM) (office). *Fax:* (20) 7287-6420 (office). *Website:* www.finchandpartners.com (office); www.icmtalent.com (office).

RICHARDSON, Louise, BA, MA, PhD, FRSE; Irish/American political scientist, academic and university vice-chancellor; *Vice-Chancellor, University of Oxford;* b. Dublin, Ireland; d. of Arthur Richardson and Julie Richardson; m. Thomas Jevon, MD; one s. two d.; ed Trinity Coll., Dublin, Univ. of California, Los Angeles and Harvard Univ., USA; Asst Prof. of Govt, Harvard Univ. 1989–94, Assoc. Prof. 1994–2001, Exec. Dean Radcliffe Inst. for Advanced Study 2001–08, concurrently Lecturer on Law, Harvard Law School, Sr Lecturer in Govt, Faculty of Arts and Sciences; Prin. and Vice-Chancellor Univ. of St Andrews, UK 2009–15; Vice-Chancellor Univ. of Oxford 2016–; mem. Scottish Govt's Council of Econ. Advisers 2011–; Hon. Fellow, Waterford Inst. of Tech. 2010; Sumner Prize for best doctoral dissertation, Harvard Univ. 1989, Levenson Prize, awarded by undergraduate student body to best faculty at Harvard Univ., teaching awards from American Political Science Asscn and Pi Sigma Alpha for outstanding teaching in political science, Abramson Award, numerous awards for teaching excellence from Bok Center, Harvard Univ., awards from orgs including Ford Foundation, Milton Fund, Sloan Foundation, Center for European Studies, Weatherhead Center for Int. Affairs, US Inst. of Peace, Alumni Award, Trinity Coll. Dublin 2009. *Publications:* When Allies Differ: Anglo-American Relations in the Suez and Falkland Crises 1996, What Terrorists Want: Understanding the Enemy, Containing the Threat 2006, The Roots of Terrorism (ed.) 2006, Democracy and Counterterrorism: Lessons from the Past (co-ed.) 2007; several book chapters, reviews and journal articles on the study of terrorism and political violence. *Address:* Office of the Vice-Chancellor, University of Oxford, University Offices, Wellington Square, Oxford, OX1 2JD, England (office). *Website:* www.ox.ac.uk/about/organisation/university-officers/vice-chancellor (office).

RICHARDSON, Miranda; British actress; b. 3 March 1958, Southport, Lancs.; d. of William Alan Richardson and Marian Georgina Richardson (née Townsend); ed Old Vic Theatre School, Bristol; numerous appearances in theatre, film and television; Chair., Women's Prize for Fiction 2013; Dilys Powell Award for Excellence in Film, London Critics' Circle 2015. *Theatre appearances include:* Moving 1980–81, All My Sons, Who's Afraid of Virginia Woolf?, The Life of Einstein, A Lie of the Mind 1987, The Changeling, Mountain Language 1988, Etta Jenks, The Designated Mourner 1996, Orlando 1996, Aunt Dan and Lemon 1999, Grasses of a Thousand Colours 2009. *Film appearances:* Dance with a Stranger (debut; Best Actress Award, Evening Standard) 1985, The Innocent 1985, Empire of the Sun 1987, Eat the Rich 1987, Twisted Obsession (aka The Mad Monkey) 1989, The Bachelor 1992, Enchanted April (Golden Globe Award for Best Comedy Actress 1993) 1992, The Crying Game 1992, Damage (BAFTA Award for Best Supporting Actress 1993) 1992, Tom and Viv 1994, La Nuit et Le Moment 1994, Swann 1995, Kansas City 1996, Evening Star 1996, The Designated Mourner 1996, The Apostle 1996, All For Love 1998, Jacob Two Two and the Hooded Fang 1998, The Big Brass Ring 1998, Sleepy Hollow 1999, Blackadder Back and Forth 1999, Chicken Run (voice) 2000, Get Carter 2000, The Hours 2001, Spider 2002, The Hours 2002, The Actors 2003, The Rage in Placid Lake 2003, Falling Angels 2003, The Prince and Me 2004, Churchill: The Hollywood Years 2004, The Phantom of the Opera 2004, Wah-Wah 2005, Harry Potter and the Goblet of Fire 2005, Merlin's Apprentice 2005, Starry Night 2005, Provoked 2006, Paris, je t'aime 2006, Southland Tales 2006, Spinning into Butter 2007, Puffball 2007, Fred Claus 2007, Young Victoria 2009, Made in Dagenham 2010, Harry Potter and the Deathly Hallows: Part 1 2010, Belle 2014, iBoy 2017, Churchill 2017. *Television appearances include:* The Hard Word 1983, Sorrel and Son 1984, A Woman of Substance 1985, Blackadder II 1985, Death of a Heart 1985, Underworld 1985, After Pilkington 1987, Blackadder the Third 1987, Sweet as You Are (Royal TV Soc.'s Best Actress Award) 1988, Blackadder Goes Forth 1989, Die Kinder (mini-series) 1990, Fatherland (Golden Globe Award) 1994, Saint X 1995, Magic Animals 1995, Dance to the Music of Time 1997, Merlin 1997, The Scold's Bridle 1998, Alice 1998, Ted and Ralph 1998, The Miracle Maker (voice) 2000, Snow White 2001, The Lost Prince 2003, Gideon's Daughter 2006, Final Chance to Save 2006, The Life and Times of Vivienne Vyle 2007, Dagenham Girls 2009, World Without End 2011, Parade's End 2012, Dead Boss 2012, Mapp & Lucia 2014, An Inspector Calls 2015, And Then There Were None 2015. *Leisure interests:* gardening, junkshops, music, occasional art, reading, softball, walking. *Address:* c/o Independent Talent Group Ltd, Oxford House, 76 Oxford Street, London, W1D 1BS, England (office). *Telephone:* (20) 7636-6565 (office). *Fax:* (20) 7323-0101 (office).

RICHARDSON, Peter Damian, BSc, DSc, PhD, FRS, FCGI, DIC; British mechanical engineer, physiologist and academic; *Professor Emeritus of Engineering and Physiology, Brown University;* b. 22 Aug. 1935, West Wickham; s. of Reginald W. Richardson and Marie S. Richardson; one d.; ed Imperial Coll. London, Brown Univ., USA; demonstrator Dept of Mechanical Eng, Imperial Coll. 1955–58; went to USA 1958; Visiting Lecturer, Brown Univ. 1958–59, Research Assoc. 1959–60, Asst Prof. of Eng 1960–65, Assoc. Prof. 1965–68, Prof. 1968–84, apptd Prof. of Eng and Physiology 1984, Chair. Univ. Faculty 1987, now Prof. Emer.; Chair. Exec. Cttee Center Biomedical Eng 1972–; Consultant to Industry US Govt Agencies; mem. American Soc. of Artificial Internal Organs, American Soc. for Eng Educ.; Fellow, ASME, Life Fellow 2001; Founding Fellow, American Inst. of Medical and Biological Eng 1991; Fellow of the City and Guilds of London Inst. 2003, American Soc. of Mechanical Engineers; Inaugural Fellow, Biomedical Eng Soc. 2005; Hon. FRCP 2010, Hon. mem. British Atherosclerosis Soc.; Sr Scientist Award, Alexander Von Humboldt Foundation 1976, Laureate in Medicine, Ernst Jung Foundation 1987, President's Award for Excellence in Faculty Governance 2010. *Publications:* Principles of Cell Adhesion (with M. Steiner) 1995; contrib. to numerous professional journals. *Leisure interests:* country life. *Address:* Division of Engineering and Department of Molecular Pharmacology, Physiology and Biotechnology, Box D, Brown University, Providence, RI 02912-9104, USA (office). *Telephone:* (401) 863-2687 (office). *Fax:* (401) 863-9120 (office). *E-mail:* Peter_Richardson@brown.edu (office). *Website:* www.brown.edu/academics/molecular-pharmacology-physiology-and-biotechnology (office).

RICHARDSON, Sir Thomas Legh, Kt, KCMG, MA; British diplomatist; b. 6 Feb. 1941, Manchester, England; s. of Arthur Legh Turnour Richardson and Penelope Margaret Richardson (née Waithman); m. Alexandra Frazier Wlasiqullah (née Ratcliff) 1979; ed Westminster School, Christ Church, Oxford; postings in Ghana, Tanzania, Milan, New York, mem. Cen. Policy Review Staff 1980–81, Counsellor, Embassy in Rome 1982–86, Head of Econ. Relations Dept, FCO 1986–89, Deputy Perm. Rep. to UN, New York 1989–94, Deputy Political Dir FCO 1994–96, Amb. to Italy 1996–2000; Chair. Governing Body, British Inst. of Florence 2003–08; Pres. British-Italian Soc. 2007–18; mem. Council, British School of Rome 2002–06; Trustee, Monte San Martino Trust 2003–15; Patron, Venice in Peril. *Leisure interests:* reading, music, walking, Italy.

RICHARDSON, William (Bill) Blaine, BA, MA; American business executive, fmr politician, fmr diplomatist and fmr government official; *Chairman, Global Political Strategies Group, APCO Worldwide;* b. 15 Nov. 1947, Pasadena, Calif.; s. of William Blaine Richardson, Jr and María Luisa López-Collada Márquez; m. Barbara Flavin 1972; ed Fletcher School of Law and Diplomacy, Tufts Univ.; mem.

staff, US House of Reps 1971–72, US Dept of State 1973–75, US Senate Foreign Relations Cttee 1975–78; Exec. Dir New Mexico State Democratic Cttee 1978, Bernalillo Co. Democratic Cttee 1978; business exec. in Santa Fe 1978–82; consultant, Salomon Smith Barney; mem. US House of Reps from 3rd Dist of New Mexico 1982–97; Perm. Rep. to UN, New York 1997–98; US Sec. of Energy 1998–2001; Sr Man. Dir Kissinger McLarty Assocs 2001; Adjunct Prof. of Public Policy, Harvard Univ. 2001; Gov. of New Mexico 2003–11; unsuccessful cand. for Democratic party nomination for US Pres. 2007; nominated as US Sec. of Commerce 2008, requested that nomination be withdrawn Jan. 2009; apptd Special Envoy, OAS, Washington, DC 2011; Chair. Global Political Strategies (advisory service), APCO Worldwide 2011–; f. Richardson Center for Global Engagement, Foundation to Preserve New Mexico Wildlife; Chair. Democratic Nat. Convention 2004, Chair. Democratic Gov.'s Assoc. 2005, 2006; mem. Council Foreign Relations, Santa Fe Chamber of Commerce, Santa Fe Hispanic Chamber of Commerce, Big Brothers-Big Sisters, Presidential Consolidate-Dew Party 2008; fmr mem. NATO 2000 Bd; numerous awards, named by TIME magazine as one of 25 Most Influential Hispanics 2005, National Hispanic Hero Award 2015. *Publications:* Between Worlds: The Making of an American Life (autobiography, with Mike Ruby) 2005, Leading by Example: How We Can Inspire an Energy and Security Revolution 2007, How to Sweet-Talk a Shark: Strategies and Stories from a Master Negotiator (co-author) 2013. *Address:* The Richardson Center, 216 Washington Avenue, Suite 5, Santa Fe, NM 87501, USA (office). *Telephone:* (505) 989-7955 (office). *E-mail:* info@richardsondiplomacy.org. *Website:* www.richardsondiplomacy.org; www.billrichardson.com.

RICHARDSON, William Chase, MBA, PhD; American university administrator and foundation executive; b. 11 May 1940, Passaic, NJ; s. of Henry B. Richardson and Frances Richardson (née Chase); m. Nancy Freeland 1966; two d.; ed Trinity Coll., Hartford, Conn. and Univ. of Chicago; Research Assoc. and Instructor, Univ. of Chicago 1967–70; Asst Prof., School of Public Health and Community Medicine, Univ. of Washington 1971–73, Assoc. Prof. 1973–76, Prof. of Health Services 1976–84, Chair. Dept of Health Services 1973–76, Graduate Dean, Vice-Provost for Research 1981–84; Exec. Vice-Pres., Provost and Prof., Dept of Family and Community Medicine, Pennsylvania State Univ. 1984–90; Pres. Johns Hopkins Univ. 1990–95, Pres. Emer. 1995–, Prof., Dept of Health Policy Man. 1990–95, Prof. Emer. 1995–; Pres. and CEO W.K. Kellogg Foundation 1995–2005, Pres. Emer. 2005–, Chair. Kellogg Foundation Trust 1996–2007; mem. Inst. of Medicine, NAS 1980–, American Acad. of Arts and Sciences 1999–; Fellow, American Public Health Asscn; mem. Bd of Dirs CSX Corpn 1992–2008, Kellogg Co. 1996–2007, Bank of New York (now Bank of New York Mellon Corpn) 1998–, Exelon Corpn 2005–; Hon. Fellow, American Coll. of Healthcare Execs 2014; Dr hc (Univ. of Michigan) 2006; Trinity Whitlock Award, Mary H. Bachmeyer Award, Univ. of Chicago. *Publications:* numerous articles in professional journals.

RICHIE, Laurel J., BA; American advertising executive and sports administrator; *President, Women's National Basketball Association;* ed Dartmouth Coll.; worked at Leo Burnett Worldwide (advertising agency), Chicago 1981–83, worked on several Procter & Gamble campaigns; Sr Partner, Exec. Group Dir Ogilvy and Mather 1984–2008; Sr Vice-Pres. and Chief Marketing Officer for Girl Scouts of the USA 2008–11; Pres. Women's Nat. Basketball Asscn 2011–; YMCA Black Achiever's Award, Ebony magazine's Outstanding Women in Marketing and Communications, named by The Network Journal as one of the 25 Influential Black Women in Business 2011. *Address:* Women's National Basketball Association, Olympic Tower, 645 Fifth Avenue, New York, NY 10022, USA (office). *Telephone:* (212) 688-9622 (office). *Fax:* (212) 750-9622 (office). *E-mail:* info@wnba.com (office). *Website:* www.wnba.com (office).

RICHIE, Lionel, BS (Econs); American singer, songwriter and musician; b. 20 June 1949, Tuskegee, Ala; m. Diane Alexander 1996; ed Tuskegee Univ.; mem. The Commodores 1968–82; various tours, concerts; solo artist 1982–; Dr hc Tuskegee Inst.; ASCAP Songwriter Awards 1979, 1984–96, numerous American Music Awards 1979–, Grammy Awards include: Best Pop Vocal Performance 1982, Album of the Year 1985, Producer of the Year (shared) 1986; Lionel Richie Day, Los Angeles 1983, two Nat. Asscn for the Advancement of Colored People (NAACP) Image Awards 1983, NAACP Entertainer of the Year 1987, Acad. Award for Best Song 1986, Golden Globe Award for Best Song 1986, MusiCares Person of the Year 2016, PRS for Music Special Int. Award, Ivor Novello Award 2018, inducted into Songwriters Hall of Fame, Ala Music Hall of Fame, ASCAP Lifetime Achievement Award, United Negro College Fund Achievement Award, Goldene Kamera Award, ECHO Award for Lifetime Achievement, TV Land Icon Award, Hong Kong's Rojo Award, San Remo Festival Lifetime Achievement Award, World Music Awards Lifetime Achievement Award, Nat. Acad. of Recording Arts & Sciences Governors Award. *Compositions include:* with The Commodores: Sweet Love 1975, Just To Be Close To You 1976, Easy 1977, Three Times A Lady 1979, Sail On 1980, Still 1980, Oh No 1981; for Kenny Rogers: Lady 1981; for Diana Ross: Missing You 1984; solo hits: Endless Love, film theme duet with Diana Ross 1981, Truly 1982, All Night Long 1983, Running With The Night 1984, Hello 1984, Stuck On You 1984, Penny Lover (with Brenda Harvey) 1984, Say You Say Me 1986, Dancing On The Ceiling 1987, Love Will Conquer All 1987, Ballerina Girl 1987, My Destiny 1992, Don't Wanna Lose You 1996; contrib. We are the World (with Michael Jackson), USA for Africa 1985. *Recordings include:* albums: with The Commodores: Machine Gun 1974, Caught In The Act 1975, Movin' On 1975, Hot On The Tracks 1976, Commodores 1977, Commodores Live! 1977, Natural High 1978, Greatest Hits 1978, Midnight Magic 1979, Heroes 1980, In The Pocket 1981; solo: Lionel Richie 1982, Can't Slow Down 1983, Dancing On The Ceiling 1986, Back To Front 1992, Louder Than Words 1996, Time 1998, Encore 2002, Coming Home 2006, Just Go 2009, Tuskegee 2012. *Address:* c/o Bruce Eskowitz, Red Light Management, 8439 West Sunset Boulevard, 2nd Floor, Los Angeles, CA 90069, USA (office). *Telephone:* (310) 273-2266 (office). *E-mail:* lionelrichie@redlightmanagement.com (office); web@lionelrichie.com. *Website:* redlightmanagement.com (office); www.lionelrichie.com.

RICHIER, François, LenD; French diplomatist; b. 11 Aug. 1963, Paris; ed Institut d'etudes politiques, Ecole nat. d'admin; trained at Embassy in Addis Ababa 1989, Under-Sec., Asia-Pacific Dept, Ministry of Foreign Affairs 1991–93, Tech. Adviser to Minister of Foreign Affairs (Asian and US Affairs) 1993–95, First Sec., in charge of strategic issues, Perm. Mission to UN, New York 1995–99, Second Counsellor, Embassy in Berlin 1999–2002, Dir, later Deputy Under-Sec., Non-Proliferation and Disarmament Div., Dept for Political and Security Affairs, Ministry of Foreign Affairs 2002–05, Adviser for Strategic and Security Affairs to the Pres. 2007–11, Amb. to India 2011–16, to Afghanistan 2016–18; Grosses Verdienstkreuz der Bundesrepublik Deutschland. *Address:* Ministry of Europe and Foreign Affairs, 37 quai d'Orsay, 75351 Paris Cedex 07, France (office). *Telephone:* 1-43-17-53-53 (office); 1-43-17-47-53 (office). *E-mail:* consul@ambafrance-af.org (office). *Website:* www.diplomatie.gouv.fr (office).

RICHMOND, Sir Mark Henry, Kt, ScD, FRS; British academic and scientist; b. 1 Feb. 1931, Sydney, Australia; s. of Harold Sylvester Richmond and Dorothy Plaistowe Tegg; m. 1st Shirley Jean Townrow 1958 (divorced); one s. one d. (and one d. deceased); m. 2nd Sheila Travers 2000; ed Epsom Coll., Clare Coll., Cambridge; mem. scientific staff, Medical Research Council 1958–65; Reader in Molecular Biology, Univ. of Edin. 1965–68; Prof. of Bacteriology, Univ. of Bristol 1968–81; Vice-Chancellor and Prof. of Molecular Bacteriology, Victoria Univ. of Manchester 1981–90; mem. Public Health Laboratory Service Bd 1976–85; Chair. Cttee of Vice-Chancellors and Prins of the UK 1987–89, Microbiological Food Safety Cttee 1989–90, Science and Eng Research Council 1990–94; Group Head of Research, Glaxo (now GlaxoSmithKline plc) 1993–95, Science Adviser 1995–96; mem. staff, School of Public Policy, Univ. Coll. London 1996–2002, now Emer. Sr Fellow; mem. Int. Science Advisory Cttee, UNESCO 1996–2001; mem. Bd of Dirs AmpliPhi Biosciences Corpn 1996–2005, Genentech Inc. 1999–2005, Cytos Biotechnology AG 1999–2011 (consultant 2011–), OSI Pharmaceuticals Inc., 2000–07, Sosei Group Corpn 2003–07, ARK Therapeutics Group PLC 2004–10; mem. Scientific Advisory Cttee, Inst. for Biotechnology, ETH, Zurich; consultant at Bioscience Managers Pty Ltd, F. Hoffmann La Roche; Robert Koch Award 1977. *Publications:* numerous scientific articles. *Leisure interests:* gardening, hill walking, opera.

RICHTER, Gerhard; German artist; b. 9 Feb. 1932, Dresden; s. of Horst Richter and Hildegard Richter; m. 1st Marianne Richter (née Eufinger); m. 2nd Isa Richter (née Genzken) 1982; m. 3rd Sabine Richter (née Moritz) 1995; one s. two d.; ed Hochschule für Bildende Künste, Dresden, Kunstakademie Düsseldorf; emigrated to West Germany 1961; Visiting Prof., Kunstakademie Hamburg 1967, Coll. of Art, Halifax, Canada 1978; Prof., Staatliche Kunstakademie Düsseldorf 1971–; mem. Akad. der Künste, Berlin; solo exhbns in galleries and museums all over world 1964–; paintings in public collections in Berlin, Cologne, Basle, Paris, New York, Chicago, Toronto, London, etc.; retrospective exhbn at Museum of Modern Art, New York 2002; designed a stained-glass window in Cologne Cathedral that was unveiled in 2007; painting Abstraktes Bild sold for £30.4 million at Sotheby's, London Feb. 2015; mem. Acad. of Arts, Berlin; Dr hc (Université catholique de Louvain-la-Neuve, Belgium) 2001; Kunstpreis Junger Westen 1966, Arnold Bode Preis 1981, Oskar Kokoschka Prize (Austria) 1985, Wolf Prize 1994–95, Venice Biennial Art Festival Jury Prize 1997, Praemium Imperiale, Japan 1997, Wexner Prize 1998, Nordrhein-Westfalen State Prize 2000. *Address:* Osterrietweg 22, 50996 Cologne, Germany; c/o Marian Goodman, 24 West 57th Street, New York, NY 10019, USA. *Website:* www.gerhard-richter.com.

RICHTHOFEN, Hermann Freiherr von, DJur; German diplomatist (retd); b. 20 Nov. 1933, Breslau; s. of Herbert Freiherr von Richthofen and Gisela Freifrau von Richthofen (née Schoeller); m. Christa Gräfin von Schwerin 1966; one s. two d.; joined diplomatic service 1963, served in Saigon and Djakarta, Head of Dept of Perm. Rep. Office of FRG for GDR 1975–78, Dir German and Berlin Dept Ministry of Foreign Affairs 1978–80; Dir Working Party on German Policy, Fed. Chancellery 1980–86; Dir-Gen. Legal Dept Ministry of Foreign Affairs 1986, Political Dept 1986–88, Amb. to UK 1988–93, Amb. and Perm. Rep. to NATO, Brussels 1993–98; Gov. Ditchley Foundation; Hon. Prof., Cen. Connecticut State Univ., Hon. mem. Deutsch-Britische Gesellschaft, Berlin; Officer's Cross Order of Kts of Malta, Commdr's Cross Order of Merit (Italy), Commdr, Légion d'honneur, Grand Officer's Cross Order of Infante D. Henrique (Portugal), Grand Cross Order of Merit (Luxemburg), Kt Commdr's Cross 2nd Class (Austria), Hon. GCVO, Grand Cross Order of Merit (Germany), Commdr's Cross Order of Merit (Poland) 2003; Hon. LLD (Birmingham). *Leisure interests:* literature, history, arts, music. *Address:* Beckerstrasse 6a, 12157 Berlin, Germany (home).

RICKE, Kai-Uwe; German business executive; *Partner and Chairman, Delta Partners Group;* b. Oct. 1961, Krefeld; ed European Business School; began career as asst to Bd of Bertelsmann, Guetersloh, later Head of Sales and Marketing, Scandinavian Club (subsidiary); CEO Talkline and Talkline PS Phone Service, Elmshorn 1990–95, Chair. and CEO 1995–98; Chair. Bd Man. DeTeMobil Deutsche Telekom Mobilnet (now T-Mobile Deutschland) 1998–2000, Chair. T-Mobile Int. 2000–01, COO and mem. Bd of Man. Deutsche Telekom AG 2001, Chair. Bd of Man. and CEO 2002–06 (resgnd); Partner and Chair. Delta Partners 2009–; mem. Supervisory Bd Kabel Baden-Württemberg GmbH & Co. KG, Heidelberg 2007; mem. Bd of Dirs Zalando, United Internet, euNetworks. *Address:* Delta Partners Group, Media One, Level 29, PO Box 502428, Dubai Media City, United Arab Emirates (office). *Telephone:* (4) 3692999 (office). *E-mail:* info@deltapartnersgroup.com (office). *Website:* www.deltapartnersgroup.com (office).

RICKETTS, John Peter (Pete), BS, MBA; American business executive and politician; *Governor of Nebraska;* b. 19 Aug. 1964; m. Susanne Ricketts; three c.; ed Univ. of Chicago; early career with Union Pacific Railroad; various leadership positions at TD Ameritrade Holding Corpn, including COO, Exec. Vice-Pres., Corp. Sec., Pres., Private Client Div. 1993–2005, also Vice-Chair., Bd of Dirs 1999–2006, 2007; Founder, Drakon, LLC, Omaha; Gov. of Nebraska 2015–; Chair. Republican Govs. Asscn 2018–; mem. Bd of Dirs Knights of Columbus, Fund for Omaha Cttee, Community Health Charities of Nebraska, Gambling with the Good Life; Trustee American Enterprise Inst.; Bd Advisor, Alumni Capital Network, Republican Forum, Nebraska Coalition for Ethical Research, Univ. of Chicago School of Business; Chair. Children's Scholarship Fund, Omaha; Pres., Bd of Dirs Platte Inst. for Econ. Research, Inc. 2007; Republican. *Address:* Office of the Governor, State Capitol, POB 94848, Lincoln NE 68509-4848, USA (office). *Telephone:* (402) 471-2244 (office). *Fax:* (402) 471-6031 (office). *Website:* www.governor.nebraska.gov (office).

RICKETTS, Baron (Life Peer), cr. 2016, of Shortlands in the County of Kent; **Peter Forbes Ricketts,** Kt, GCMG, GCVO, MA; British diplomatist; b. 30 Sept.

1952; m.; two c.; ed Univ. of Oxford; joined FCO 1974, with Mission in New York 1974–75, Desk Officer, Cen. and Southern Africa Dept 1975–76, Third, then Second Sec., Embassy in Singapore 1976–78, Second, then First Sec., Del. to NATO, Brussels 1978–81, Desk Officer, Near East and N Africa Dept 1982–83, Asst Pvt. Sec., Office of Sec. of State 1983–86, First Sec., Chancery, Embassy in Washington, DC 1986–89, Deputy Head of Security Policy Dept 1989–91, Head of Hong Kong Dept 1991–94, Counsellor, EC and Finance, Embassy in Paris 1994–97, Deputy Political Dir 1997–99, Dir for Int. Security 1999–2000; Chair. Jt Intelligence Cttee and Intelligence Coordinator, Cabinet Office 2000–01; Dir-Gen. (Political) FCO 2001–03, Perm. Rep. to NATO, Brussels 2003–06, Perm. Under-Sec. and Head of Diplomatic Service 2006–10; Nat. Security Adviser to HM Govt 2010–11; HM's Amb. to France (also accred to Monaco) 2012–16; Strategic Adviser to Lockheed Martin UK 2016–; Dir (non-exec.) Engie 2016–; Hon. Fellow, Pembroke Coll., Oxford; Hon. LLD (Univ. of Bath); Hon. DCL (Univ. of Kent).

RICKS, Sir Christopher Bruce, Kt, BA, BLitt, MA, FBA; British academic and writer; *William M. and Sara B. Warren Professor of the Humanities and Co-Director, Editorial Institute, Boston University;* b. 18 Sept. 1933, London; s. of James Bruce Ricks and Gabrielle Roszak; m. 1st Kirsten Jensen 1956 (divorced 1975); two s. two d.; m. 2nd Judith Aronson 1977; one s. two d.; ed King Alfred's School, Wantage, Oxon., Balliol Coll., Oxford; 2nd Lt, Green Howards 1952; Andrew Bradley Jr Research Fellow, Balliol Coll. Univ. of Oxford 1957, Fellow, Worcester Coll. 1958–68; Prof. of English, Bristol Univ. 1968–75; Fellow, Christ's Coll., Cambridge 1975–86, Prof. of English, Univ. of Cambridge 1975–86, King Edward VII Prof. of English Literature 1982–86; Prof. of English, Boston Univ. 1986–98, William M. and Sara B. Warren Prof. of the Humanities 1998–, Co-Dir Editorial Inst. 1999–; Prof. of Poetry, Univ. of Oxford 2004–09; Visiting Prof., Univ. of California, Berkeley and Stanford Univ. 1965, Smith Coll. 1967, Harvard Univ. 1971, Wesleyan 1974, Brandeis 1977, 1981, 1984, New Coll. of the Humanities 2011–; Distinguished Visiting Fellow in Residence, Columbia Univ. 2006; Pres. The Housman Soc.; Vice-Pres. Tennyson Soc.; mem. Asscn of Literary Scholars, Critics, and Writers (Pres. 2007–08); Fellow, American Acad. of Arts and Sciences 1991; Hon. Fellow, Balliol Coll. 1989, Worcester Coll. 1990, Christ's Coll. Cambridge 1993; Hon. DLitt (Oxford) 1998, (Bristol) 2003; George Orwell Memorial Prize 1979; Beefeater Club Prize for Literature 1980, Distinguished Achievement Award, Andrew W. Mellon Foundation 2004. *Publications include:* Milton's Grand Style 1963, Tennyson 1972, Keats and Embarrassment 1974, The Force of Poetry 1984, T. S. Eliot and Prejudice 1988, Beckett's Dying Words 1993, Essays in Appreciation 1996, Reviewery 2002, Allusion to the Poets 2002, Decisions and Revisions in T. S. Eliot 2003, Dylan's Visions of Sin 2003, True Friendship: Geoffrey Hill, Anthony Hecht and Robert Lowell under the Sign of Eliot and Pound 2010; editor: Poems and Critics: An Anthology of Poetry and Criticism from Shakespeare to Hardy 1966, A. E. Housman: A Collection of Critical Essays 1968, Alfred Tennyson: Poems 1842 1968, John Milton: Paradise Lost and Paradise Regained 1968, The Poems of Tennyson 1969, The Brownings: Letters and Poetry 1970, English Poetry and Prose 1540–1674 1970, English Drama to 1710 1971, Selected Criticism of Matthew Arnold 1972, The State of the Language (with Leonard Michaels) 1980, The New Oxford Book of Victorian Verse 1987, Collected Poems and Selected Prose of A. E. Housman 1988, The Faber Book of America (with William Vance) 1992, Inventions of the March Hare: Poems 1909–1917 by T. S. Eliot 1996, The Oxford Book of English Verse 1999, Selected Poems of James Henry 2002, Samuel Menashe: New and Selected Poems (ed.) 2006, Allusion to the Poets 2002, Reviewery 2002, Decisions and Revisions in T. S. Eliot 2003, Dylan's Visions of Sin 2004, True Friendship: Geoffrey Hill, Anthony Hecht, and Robert Lowell under the Sign of Eliot and Pound 2010, Joining Music with Reason: 34 Poets, British and American, Oxford 2004–2009 (anthology) 2010, Samuel Rogers: Table Talk & Recollections (ed.) 2011; contribs to professional journals. *Address:* Editorial Institute, Boston University, 143 Bay State Road, Boston, MA 02215 (office); 39 Martin Street, Cambridge, MA 02138, USA (home); Lasborough Cottage, Lasborough Park, Tetbury, Glos., GL8 8UF, England (home). *Telephone:* (617) 358-2895 (USA) (office); (617) 354-7887 (USA) (home); (1666) 890252 (England) (home). *E-mail:* cricks@bu.edu (office). *Website:* www.bu.edu/editinst (office).

RICKSON, Ian, BA, PGTC; British theatre and film director; ed Essex Univ., Goldsmiths' Coll., London Univ.; freelance Dir King's Head, The Gate, Chichester Festival Theatre; Special Projects Dir Young People's Theatre 1991–92; Assoc. Dir Royal Court Theatre 1993–98, Artistic Dir 1998–2006. *Plays:* Royal Court Theatre productions: Killers 1992, SAB 1992, Wildfire 1992, Ashes and Sand 1994, Some Voices 1994, Pale Horse 1995, Mojo 1995, The Lights 1996, The Weir 1997, Dublin Carol 2000, Mouth to Mouth 2001, Boy Gets Girl 2001, The Night Heron 2002, Fallout 2003, The Sweetest Swing in Baseball 2004, Alice Trilogy 2005, The Winterling 2006, Krapp's Last Tape 2006, The Seagull 2006; other productions: Rinty (Group Theatre, Belfast) 1990, Who's Breaking (Battersea Arts Centre) 1990, First Strike (Soho Poly) 1990, Queer Fish (Battersea Arts Centre) 1991, Me and My Friend (Chichester Festival Theatre) 1992, The House of Yes (Gate Theatre) 1993, La Serva Padrona (Broomhill) 1993, Mojo (Chicago) 1996, The Day I Stood Still (Cottesloe Theatre) 1997, The Hothouse (Lyttelton) 2007, The Seagull (New York) 2008, Hedda Gabler (Broadway) 2009, Parlour Song (Almeida) 2009, Jerusalem (Royal Court Theatre) 2009, (Apollo Theatre, West End and Broadway) 2010, (Apollo Theatre) 2011, The Children's Hour (West End) 2011, Betrayal (West End) 2011, Hamlet (Young Vic) 2011, The River (Royal Court, Broadway) 2012, Old Times (West End) 2013, Mojo (West End) 2013, Electra (Old Vic) 2014, The Red Lion and Evening at the Talk House (National Theatre) 2015. *Films:* Krapp's Last Tape (BBC Four) 2007, Fallout (Channel 4) 2008, The Clear Road Ahead (FilmFour) 2010. *Address:* c/o Judy Daish Associates Ltd, 2 St Charles Place, London, W10 6EG, England (office).

RICO, Francisco, PhD; Spanish academic; *Professor Emeritus of Medieval Hispanic Literature, Universidad Autónoma de Barcelona;* b. 28 April 1942, Barcelona; s. of Cipriano Rico and María Manrique; m. Victoria Camps 1966; three s.; ed Univ. of Barcelona; Prof. of Medieval Hispanic Literature, Universidad Autónoma de Barcelona 1971–2012, Prof. Emer. 2012–; Visiting Prof., The Johns Hopkins Univ., USA 1966–67, Princeton Univ., USA 1981, Scuola Normale Superiore di Pisa, Italy 1987; Gen. Dir Centre of Spanish Letters, Ministry of Culture 1985–86; Ed. Book Series: Letras e ideas, Filología, Biblioteca clásica; mem. Royal Spanish Acad. 1986–; Foreign mem. British Acad. 1992, Accad. dei

Lincei 2000, Accad. della Crusca 2003, Acads des Inscriptions et belles Lettres 2010; Commdr, Ordre des Palmes académiques 1994, Medalla de Oro al mérito en las Bellas Artes 2015; Dr hc (Università di Napoli) 1992, (Université de Bordeaux) 1994, (Universidad de Valladolid) 1996, (Università di Bologna) 2016; Premio Internacional Menéndez Pelayo 1998, Premio Nacional de Investigación 2004, Premio Natalino Sapegno 2005, Premio Alfonso Reyes del Colegio De México 2013, Premio Internacional de Ensayo Caballero Bonald 2013, Premio Francesco De Sanctis alla filologia. *Publications:* El pequeño mundo del hombre 1970, The Spanish Picaresque Novel and the Point of View 1970, Vida u obra de Petrarca (Vol. 1) 1974, Historia y crítica de la literatura española (eight vols) 1980–84, Breve biblioteca de autores españoles 1990, El sueño del humanismo (De Petrarca a Erasmo) 1993, Critical Edition of Cervantes' Don Quixote 1998, El texto del Quijote 2005, Gabbiani 2008, Mil años de poesía europea 2009, Lazarillo de Tormes (ed. crit.) 2012, Ritratti allo specchio (Boccaccio, Petrarca) 2012, I venerdì del Petrarca 2016. *Leisure interest:* contemporary literature. *Address:* Santa Teresa 38, 08172 St Cugat del Vallès, Barcelona, Spain (home). *Telephone:* (93) 674-07-08 (home); 6-49960695 (mobile) (home). *E-mail:* ilfhf@telefonica.net (office); francisco.rico@rae.es (office). *Website:* bib.cervantesvirtual.com/bib_autor/franciscorico (office).

RICÚPERO, Rubens, LLB; Brazilian international organization official, fmr diplomatist and politician; b. 1 March 1937, São Paulo; m. Marisa Parolari; four c.; ed Univ. of São Paulo and Rio Branco Inst.; Prof. of Theory of Int. Relations, Univ. of Brasília 1979–95; Prof. of History of Brazilian Diplomatic Relations, Rio Branco Inst. 1980–95; with Ministry of Foreign Relations 1981–93, Minister of Environment and Amazonian Affairs 1993–94, of Finance March–Sept. 1994; Perm. Rep. to UN, Geneva 1987–91; Chair. GATT Council of Reps 1989–91, Contracting Parties 1989–91, GATT Cttee on Trade and Devt 1989–91, GATT Informal Group of Developing Countries 1989–91 (also Spokesman); Amb. to USA 1991–93, to Italy 1995; led Brazilian dels to UN Comm. on Human Rights and Conf. on Disarmament, Geneva; Chair. Finance Cttee, UN Conf. on Environment and Devt, Rio de Janeiro 1992; Sec.-Gen. UNCTAD 1995–2004; Dir Fundação Armando Alvares Penteado 2005–; Pres. Consultative Comm. Conversando com as Nações Unidas (CNU)-Brasil 2006–; Lifetime Achievement Award, World Summit of Young Entrepreneurs of the World Trade Univ. 2004. *Publications:* several books on int. relations, econ. devt problems, int. trade and diplomatic history. *Address:* c/o CNU-Brasil, Rua Plínio Barreto, 285, São Paulo, Brazil (office). *Telephone:* (11) 3254-1677. *Fax:* (11) 3254-1675. *Website:* www.cnu-brasil.org.br.

RIDGE, Thomas (Tom) Joseph, BA, JD; American consultant and fmr politician; *President and CEO, Ridge Global LLC;* b. 26 Aug. 1945, Munhall, Pa; m. Michele Moore 1979; one s. one d.; ed Harvard Univ., Dickinson School of Law, Pennsylvania State Univ.; drafted into US Army, served as infantry staff sergeant in Viet Nam; admitted to Pa Bar 1972, practising lawyer, Erie, Pa 1972–82; Asst Dist Attorney, Erie, Pa 1979–82; mem. US House of Reps, Washington, DC 1983–95; Gov. of Pa 1995–2001; Dir US Office of Homeland Security 2001–03, Sec., Dept of Homeland Security 2003–05 (resgnd); Founder, Pres. and CEO Ridge Global LLC (consulting firm), Washington, DC 2006–; Partner, Ridge Policy Group 2010–, Ridge Schmidt Cyber (cybersecurity firm founded with former White House Cybersecurity Advisor Howard A. Schmidt); Sr Advisor, Deloitte & Touche USA LLP 2006–, TechRadium Inc. 2008–; mem. Bd of Dirs Home Depot Inc. 2005–, Exelon Corpn 2005–, Hershey Co. 2007–, Inst. for Defense Analyses, Center for the Study of the Presidency and Congress, Nat. Org. on Disability 2005–; mem. Advisory Bd PURE Bioscience 2009–; mem. Int. Advisory Bd, Center for Int. Relations and Politics, Carnegie Mellon Univ.; Nat. Co-Chair. Flight 93 Memorial Fundraising Campaign; Republican; several hon. degrees; numerous awards while serving in US ARMY, including Bronze Star for Valor, Combat Infantry Badge, Vietnamese Cross of Gallantry, other awards include Woodrow Wilson Award, Veterans of Foreign Wars Dwight D. Eisenhower Award, John F. Kennedy Nat. Award, Ellis Island Medal of Honor, ABA John Marshall Award, US Nat. Guard Harry S. Truman Award, Pennsylvania Wildlife Fed. Conservationist of the Year Award, US-Mexico Chamber of Commerce Good Neighbor Award, American Cancer Soc. Nat. Medal of Honor, Mister Rogers Award, Champion of Public TV Award, Intrepid Freedom Award, Esperanza Leadership Award. *Publications:* The Test of Our Times: America Under Siege...And How We Can Be Safe Again (co-author) 2009. *Address:* Ridge Global LLC, 1140 Connecticut Avenue, NW, Suite 510, Washington, DC 20036, USA (office). *Telephone:* (202) 833-2008 (office). *Fax:* (202) 833-2009 (office). *Website:* www.ridgeglobal.com (office).

RIDHA, Yasser; Egyptian diplomatist; joined Ministry of Foreign Affairs, postings abroad include to People's Repub. of China, Cyprus, Iraq, Germany, Italy; Deputy Dir-Gen. Office of the Minister of Foreign Affairs –2008; Amb. to Israel 2008–12.

RIDI, Rashika Ahmed Fathi, DSc, PhD; Egyptian immunologist and academic; *Professor of Immunology, Cairo University;* b. (Rashika El Ridi), 23 June 1943, Ismailieh; one c.; ed Cairo Univ., Inst. of Molecular Genetics, Czech Acad. of Science, Prague; Lecturer, Zoology Dept, Faculty of Science, Cairo Univ. 1976–81, Assoc. Prof. of Immunology 1981–86, Prof. of Immunology 1986–; Dir of Schistosomiasis Research, Biomedical Research Center, Egyptian Org. for Sera and Vaccines 1990–2000; Visiting Scientist, Dept of Infectious Diseases, Harvard School of Public Health, USA 1995; Egyptian State Award of Excellence in High Tech. Sciences 2002, Cairo Univ. Award for Recognition in Applied Sciences 2002, Egyptian State Award of Merit in High Tech. Sciences 2010, Laureate for Africa and Arab States, L'Oréal-UNESCO Awards for Women in Science 2010. *Publications:* numerous publs in professional journals. *Leisure interest:* reading. *Address:* Department of Zoology, Faculty of Science, Cairo University, Giza, Egypt (office). *Telephone:* (202) 35676708 (office). *E-mail:* rashika_elridi@yahoo.com (office); rashika@sci.cu.edu.eg (office). *Website:* www.cu.edu.eg (office).

RIDLEY, Brian Kidd, PhD, FRS, FInstP, CPhys; British physicist and academic; *Professor Emeritus of Physics, University of Essex;* b. 2 March 1931, Newcastle upon Tyne; s. of Oliver Archbold Ridley and Lillian Beatrice Ridley; m. Sylvia Jean Ridley; one s. one d.; ed Yorebridge (Askrigg) and Gateshead Grammar Schools, Durham Univ.; Research Physicist, Mullard Research Labs 1956–64; Lecturer to Reader, Dept of Physics, Univ. of Essex 1964–86, Prof. of Physics 1986–91, Research Prof. 1991–2007, Prof. Emer. 2007–; several visiting professorial appointments including Cornell, Stanford and Princeton Univs, USA; Paul Dirac

Medal and Prize, Inst. of Physics 2001. *Publications:* Time, Space and Things 1976 (revised edn 1994), The Physical Environment 1979, Quantum Process in Semiconductors 1982 (revised edn 1999), Electrons and Phonons in Semiconductor Multilayers 1997 (revised edn 2009), On Science 2001, Reforming Science: Beyond Belief 2010, Hybrid Phonons in Nanostructures 2017. *Leisure interests:* piano, writing. *Address:* School of Computing Science and Electronic Engineering, University of Essex, Colchester, CO4 3SQ, England (office). *Telephone:* (1206) 872873 (office). *Fax:* (1206) 872900 (office). *E-mail:* bkr@essex.ac.uk (office). *Website:* www.essex.ac.uk/csee (office).

RIEBER-MOHN, Georg Fredrik; Norwegian lawyer; *Chairman, Fritt Ord Foundation;* b. 13 Aug. 1945, Lillehammer; m. Kari Nergaard 1967; two s. one d.; ed Univ. of Oslo; apptd Prof. Univ. of Oslo 1969; Deputy Gov. Western Prison Dist 1971–74; Asst Judge, Magistrates' Court of Stavanger 1975–76; Dist Attorney (Regional Head of Prosecutions) 1976–80; Gen. Dir Prison and Probation Service 1980–85; Judge, Appeal Court 1985–86; Gen. Dir of Public Prosecutions 1986–97 (resgnd); Justice, Supreme Court of Norway 1997–2007; Chair. Fritt Ord Foundation 2011– (fmr deputy leader); also Chair. Cttee investigating the rules on criminal lawlessness, psychiatry and special reactions to dangerous inadmissible offenders; Head, Academic Council, Oslo Catholic diocese 2013–; retd 2012; Commdr, Order of St Olav. *Publications:* numerous articles on law issues and wild salmon conservation efforts. *Leisure interests:* fly fishing, hunting, literature. *Address:* Fritt Ord Foundation, Uranienborgveien 2, 0258 Oslo (office); Tørrhardsveien 39, 3525 Hallingby, Norway (home). *Telephone:* 23-01-46-46 (office); 32-13-00-08 (home). *Fax:* 23-01-46-47 (office). *E-mail:* georg.fr.rieber.mohn@hoyesterett.no (office). *Website:* www.frittord.no (office).

RIEKSTIŅŠ, Māris; Latvian lawyer, diplomatist and politician; *Ambassador to Russia;* b. 8 April 1963, Rīga; m.; two c.; ed Univ. of Latvia; teacher, Faculty of Pedagogy, Latvian Sports Inst. 1982–85; Deputy Chair. and Desk Officer, Cttee of Latvian Youth Orgs 1987–91; lawyer, Faculty of Law, Univ. of Latvia 1989–93; Chair. Control Cttee of Strategic Goods of Repub. of Latvia 1995–2004, Diplomatic Service Agency's Shareholders' Council 1996–2004, Advisory Council for Membership of Latvia in WTO 1999–2004, Supervisory Cttee on Org. of NATO Aspirant Countries Summit in Rīga Jan.–July 2002; several positions within Ministry of Foreign Affairs, including Desk Officer, Political Dept of Europe Div. and Dir Western Europe and Europe Divs Jan.–Nov. 1992, Under-Sec. of State 1992–93, Sec. of State 1993–2004, Head of Latvian del. for accession negotiations with NATO 2002–04; Amb. to USA 2004–07 (also accred to Mexico 2006–07), to Russia 2017–; Chief of Staff to Prime Minister Jan.–Nov. 2007; Minister of Foreign Affairs Nov. 2007–10 (resgnd), Inspector-Gen. for Ministry of Foreign Affairs 2015–17; Amb. and Perm. Rep. to NATO, Brussels 2011–15; Commdr, Royal Norwegian Order of Merit 1998, Grand Officer, Royal Norwegian Order of Merit 2000, Grand Officier, Ordre nat. du Mérite 2001, Order of the Lithuanian Grand Duke Gediminas (Fourth Class) 2001, Order of the Cross of Terra Mariana (Third Class, Estonia) 2003, Ordem do Infante D. Henrique Grande Oficial (Portugal) 2003, Commdr, Three Star Order of Latvia 2003, Grand Official, Order of Merit of the Italian Repub. 2004. *Address:* Embassy of Latvia, 1110 Moscow, Chaplygina 3, Russian Federation (office). *Telephone:* (495) 232-97-60 (office). *Fax:* (495) 232-97-50 (office). *E-mail:* embassy.russia@mfa.gov.lv (office). *Website:* www.mfa.gov.lv/moscow (office).

RIEMSCHNEIDER, Burkhard; German art critic and gallery curator; *Co-Director, Neugerriemschneider Kunstgalerie;* Co-founder and Co-dir (with Tim Neuger) Neugerriemschneider Kunstgalerie, Berlin, represents artists including Franz Ackermann, Ai Weiwei, Pawel Althamer, James Benning, Billy Childish, Keith Edmier, Olafur Eliasson, Andreas Eriksson, Noa Eshkol, Mario García Torres, Isa Genzken, Sharon Lockhart, Renata Lucas, the late Michel Majerus, Antje Majewski, Mike Nelson, Jorge Pardo, Elizabeth Peyton, Tobias Rehberger, Simon Starling, Thaddeus Strode, Wolfgang Tillmans, Rirkrit Tiravanija, Pae White and Jorge Pardo. *Publications include:* Albert Oehlen (co-author) 1995, Twentieth-Century Erotic Art (co-ed.) 1996, Art at the Turn of the Millennium (co-ed.) 1999, Art Now: 137 Artists at the Rise of the New Millennium 2002, 1000 Tattoos (25th Edn) (co-ed.) 2005, Art Now: Artists at the Rise of the New Millennium (25th Edn) (co-ed.) 2005, Studio Olafur Eliasson: An Encyclopedia (ed.) 2008. *Address:* Neugerriemschneider Kunstgalerie, Linienstraße 155, 10115 Berlin, Germany (office). *Telephone:* (30) 288772-77 (office). *E-mail:* mail@neugerriemschneider.com (office). *Website:* www.neugerriemschneider.com (office).

RIES, Col Nico; Luxembourg army officer (retd); b. 30 July 1953, Luxembourg City; m.; two c.; ed Royal Mil. Acad., Belgium, Staff Coll., Compiegne and Ecole Supérieure de Guerre Interarmées, France; joined Luxembourg Army 1973, apptd to Mil. Instruction Centre 1978–94, held positions successively as Infantry Platoon Leader, Co. Commdr, Personnel Officer, Deputy Commdr, Logistics Officer, Army Staff 1994–98, Asst Chief of Staff 1998–2002, Chief of Staff 2002–08; Chargé de la planification, Ministry of Defence 2008–11, Nat. Armament Dir 2014–15; participated in EC Monitor Mission in Fmr Yugoslavia 1991, 1997; Verdienstkreuz, 1st Class 1988; Croix d'honneur et de Mérite militaire en bronze 1998; Meritorious Service Medal (USA) 1998; Grand Officier, Ordre du Mérite du Grand-Duché de Luxembourg 2004; Commdr, Légion d'honneur 2005; Grande Oficial da Ordem Militar de Avis (Portugal) 2005; Grand Officier, Ordre de Viesturs (Latvia) 2006; Commdr, Ordre de Mérite civil et militaire d'Adolphe de Nassau 2007, Grand Officier, Ordre Grand-Ducal de la Couronne de Chêne 2015. *E-mail:* nicories@pt.lu (home).

RIESENHUBER, Heinz Friedrich, Dr rer. nat; German politician; *President, German Parliamentary Society;* b. 1 Dec. 1935, Frankfurt; s. of Karl Riesenhuber and Elisabeth Riesenhuber (née Birkner); m. Beatrix Walter 1968; two s. two d.; ed Gymnasium in Frankfurt and Univs of Frankfurt and Munich; with Erzgesellschaft mbH, c/o Metallgesellschaft, Frankfurt 1966–71; Tech. Man. Synthomer-Chemie GmbH, Frankfurt 1971–82; joined CDU 1961, mem. CDU Hesse Presidium 1968–, Chair. Frankfurt Br. 1973–78, Untermain Br. 1978–; mem. Bundestag 1976–, mem. Cttee on Econ and Tech. 1993– (Chair. 2001–02), Alterspräsident (Father of the House) 2009–; Fed. Minister for Research and Tech. 1982–93; Pres. Deutsche Parlamentarische Gesellschaft (German Parl. Soc.) 2006–; Chair. and mem. of numerous supervisory bds and advisory panels; Hon. Prof., Univ of Frankfurt; Fed. Great Cross of Merit with Star, Commdr, Légion d'honneur and numerous other decorations; Dr hc (Weizmann Inst., Israel, Berg Acad., Poland, Univ. of Surrey, UK), (Göttingen) 1997; Cicero Speaker's Award 1995, Golden Ring of Honour, Deutsches Museum, Munich. *Publications:* Japan ist offen; articles in specialist journals. *Leisure interests:* reading, golf. *Address:* Bundestag, Platz der Republik 1, 11011 Berlin, Germany (office). *Telephone:* (30) 22777381 (office). *Fax:* (30) 22776381 (office). *E-mail:* heinz.riesenhuber@bundestag.de (office). *Website:* www.bundestag.de (office).

RIESS, Adam Guy, BS, AM, PhD; American astrophysicist and academic; *Professor of Astronomy and Physics, Johns Hopkins University;* b. 1969, Washington, DC; ed Massachusetts Inst. of Tech., Harvard Univ.; Miller Fellow, Univ. of California, Berkeley 1996–99; mem. Sr Science Science Staff, Space Telescope Science Inst., Baltimore, Md 1999–2005; Prof. of Physics and Astronomy, Johns Hopkins Univ., Baltimore 2006–; led study for High-z Team which provided first direct and published evidence that expansion of Universe was accelerating and filled with Dark Energy 1998; Prin. Investigator of Higher-z SN Team that found and measured 20 most distant type Ia supernovae known through competitive awarding of more than 800 orbits of Hubble Space Telescope Time in five cycles and $2million in grants 2002–; mem. Jt Dark Energy Mission Science Definition Team 2004, Jt Dark Energy Mission Science Working Group 2008; Founding mem. science team for four active dark energy programmes: ESSENCE, ADEPT, SDSS II SN Survey and Pan-STARRS; Fellow, American Acad. of Arts and Sciences 2008; Margaret Weyerhaeuser Jewett Memorial Fellowship 1993, Distinction in Teaching Award, Harvard Univ. 1994, GSAS Merit Fellow, Harvard Univ. 1995, Science Magazine's Research 'Breakthrough of the Year' 1998, Trumpler Award, Astronomical Soc. of the Pacific 1999, Time Magazine Innovator Award 2000, AURA Science Award 2000, STScI Science Merit Award 2000, 2001, Bok Prize, Harvard Univ. 2001 Time Magazine 'Six Who Probed Cosmos', Esquire Magazine 'Best and Brightest' Award 2003, Helen B. Warner Prize, American Astronomical Soc. 2003, Raymond and Beverly Sackler Prize, Tel-Aviv Univ. 2004, Laurels for Achievement Award, Int. Acad. of Astronautics 2004, Townes Prize in Cosmology, Univ. of California, Berkeley 2005, ISI Most Highly Cited 2006, Shaw Prize in Astronomy (co-recipient) 2006, Kavli Frontier of Science Fellow 2007, Gruber Prize in Cosmology (co-recipient) 2007, MacArthur Fellow 2008, Discover Magazine Twenty Under 40 2008, Nobel Prize in Physics (co-recipient) 2011, Albert Einstein Medal 2011, Breakthrough Prize in Fundamental Physics (co-recipient) 2015. *Publications:* more than 80 scientific papers in professional journals on measurements of the cosmological framework with supernovae (exploding stars) and Cepheids (pulsating stars); more than 20 tech. reports. *Address:* Department of Physics and Astronomy, 207 Bloomberg Center, The Johns Hopkins University, 3400 North Charles Street, Baltimore, MD 21218-2686, USA (office). *Telephone:* (410) 516-4474 (office). *Fax:* (410) 516-7239 (office). *E-mail:* ariess@stsci.edu (office); ariess@pha.jhu.edu (office). *Website:* physics-astronomy.jhu.edu/directory/adam-riess (office); www.stsci.edu/~ariess (office).

RIESS-PASSER, Susanne; Austrian lawyer, business executive and fmr politician; *General Director, Bausparkasse Wüstenrot AG;* b. 3 Jan. 1961, Braunau; ed Univ. of Innsbruck; joined Freedom Party as Assoc. Press Officer 1987, Federal Press Officer 1988–92, Deputy Chair. Freedom Party 1995–96, Chair. 1996–2000, Leader 2000–02; MEP 1995–96; Vice-Chancellor and Minister for Public Affairs and Sports 2000–03; Gen. Dir Bausparkasse Wüstenrot AG 2004–; Deputy Chair. Bundestheater Holding 2004–; mem. Supervisory Bd IHAG Privatbank, Österreichischen Industrieholding AG 2014–; mem. Advisory Bd Signa Holding. *Address:* Bausparkasse Wüstenrot AG, Alpenstraße 70, 5033 Salzburg, Austria (office). *Telephone:* 57070-110 (office). *Fax:* 57070-109 (office). *Website:* www.wuestenrot.at (office).

RIESTER, Walter; German politician and trade union official; b. 27 Sept. 1943, Kaufbeuren; m.; two c.; ed Labour Acad. Frankfurt; apprentice tiler 1957–60; tiler 1960–68; mem. Sozialdemokratischen Partei Deutschlands (SPD) 1966–, Landesvorstandes und Präsidiums 1989–95, Bundesparteivorstandes 1988–2005; youth training officer German TU Fed. Baden-Württemberg Region 1970, Departmental Gen. Sec. for Youth Questions Stuttgart Region 1970–77; Admin. Sec. IG Metall Geislingen 1977–78, Second Deputy 1978–79, Sec. Dist HQ IG Metall Stuttgart 1980–88, Dist Man. 1988–93, Second Chair. IG Metall Germany 1993–98; Fed. Minister of Labour and Social Affairs 1998–2002; mem. (SPD) Bundestag (Parl.) 2002–09 (retd); Merit Medal, State of Baden-Württemberg 2005, Hans Böckler Prize, City of Cologne 2005, Merit Cross 1st Class, Germany 2009, Politikaward 2009. *Address:* Sozialdemokratische Partei Deutschlands (SPD), Willi-Bleicher-Straße 3, Schillerbau II, 73033 Göppingen, Germany. *Telephone:* (30) 25991500 (office). *Fax:* (30) 25991507 (office). *E-mail:* parteivorstand@spd.de (office). *Website:* www.spd.de (office).

RIFAI, Samir Zaid ar-, MA; Jordanian politician; b. 1 July 1966; s. of Zaid ar-Rifai; ed Harvard Univ., USA, Univ. of Cambridge, UK; Sec.-Gen. Royal Hashemite Court and Head, Royal Press Office 1999–2003; Minister of the Royal Court 2003–05; Adviser to King Abdullah 2005; CEO Jordan Dubai Capital (financial group) 2005–09, also Chair. Energy Arabia (Enara); Prime Minister 2009–11, also Minister of Defence Jan. 2010; Grand Cordon, Order of Al-Kawkab Al Urduni, Grand Cordon, Order of Al-Istiqlal.

RIFAI, Taleb, BSc, MSc, PhD; Jordanian architect, academic, government official and international organization official; b. 1949; m.; five c.; ed Univ. of Cairo, Illinois Inst. of Tech. and Univ. of Pennsylvania, USA; Prof. of Architecture, Planning and Urban Design, Univ. of Jordan 1973–93; Head of Jordan's first Econ. Mission to USA, Washington, DC 1993–95; Dir-Gen. Investment Promotion Corpn 1995–97; CEO Jordan Cement Co. 1997–99; held several sr govt portfolios, as Minister of Tourism and Antiquities (Chair. Exec. Council World Tourism Org. (UNWTO) 2002–03) 1999–2003, Minister of Information and Minister of Planning and Int. Co-operation; Asst to Dir-Gen. and Regional Dir for Arab States, ILO 2003–06; Deputy Sec.-Gen. UNWTO 2006–09, Sec.-Gen. 2009–17; fmr Chair. Jordan Tourism Bd; fmr Pres. Ammon School for Tourism and Hospitality. *Achievements include:* responsible for founding Jordan's first Archaeological Park in ancient city of Petra in collaboration with UNESCO and World Bank, along with other projects in Jerash, the Dead Sea and Wadi Rum. *Address:* c/o World Tourism Organization, Capitán Haya 42, 28020 Madrid, Spain (office).

RIFKIND, Sir Malcolm Leslie, Kt, KCMG, QC, LLB, MSc; British politician and business executive; b. 21 June 1946, Edinburgh, Scotland; s. of E. Rifkind; m. Edith Steinberg 1970; one s. one d.; ed George Watson's Coll. and Univ. of Edinburgh; Lecturer, Univ. of Rhodesia 1967–68; called to Scottish Bar 1970; MP for Edin., Pentlands 1974–97; Parl. Under-Sec. of State, Scottish Office 1979–82, FCO 1982–83; Minister of State, FCO 1983–86; Sec. of State for Scotland 1986–90, for Transport 1990–92, for Defence 1992–95, for Foreign and Commonwealth Affairs 1995–97; Pres. Scottish Conservative and Unionist Party 1998–; MP for Kensington and Chelsea 2005–10, for Kensington 2010–15, Shadow Work and Pensions Sec. 2005, mem. Jt Cttee on Conventions 2006, Cttee on Issue of Privilege (Police Searches on Parl. Estate) 2009–10, Chair. Cttee on Standards and Privileges 2009–10, Chair. Intelligence and Security Cttee 2010–15 (resgnd); UK Rep., Eminent Persons Group 2010–11; mem. Queen's Bodyguard for Scotland, Royal Co. of Archers; Patron, Tory Reform Club; Hon. Col 162 Movt Control Regt, Royal Logistic Corps (V); Commdr, Order of Merit (Poland); Hon. LLD (Napier) 1998. *Leisure interests:* walking, field sports, reading. *Website:* www.malcolmrifkind.com.

RIGALI, HE Cardinal Justin Francis, BSacTheol, DCL; American ecclesiastic and diplomatist; *Archbishop Emeritus of Philadelphia;* b. 19 April 1935, Los Angeles, Calif.; s. of Henry Alphonsus Rigali and Frances Irene Rigali (née White); ed Holy Cross School, preparatory seminary in Hancock Park, Los Angeles Coll., Our Lady Queen of Angels Seminary, San Fernando, St John's Seminary, Camarillo, Catholic Univ. of America, Pontifical North American Coll. and Pontifical Gregorian Univ., Rome; ordained priest, Archdiocese of Los Angeles 1961; asst during first two sessions of Second Vatican Council 1962–63; returned to USA summer 1964, served as assoc. pastor in Pomona; returned to Rome to study at Pontifical Ecclesiastical Acad. in preparation for diplomatic work for the Vatican 1964–66; began service in English section of Secr. of State 1964, Sec. of Apostolic Nunciature to Madagascar (also served as apostolic delegation for Réunion and Mauritius) 1966–70; named a Papal Chamberlain 1967; Dir English section of Secr. of State and English trans. to Servant of God Pope Paul VI 1970, subsequently accompanied Pope Paul on several int. trips; also chaplain at a Carmelite monastery and Prof. at Pontifical Ecclesiastical Acad.; apptd Titular Archbishop of Volsinium 1985; Pres. Pontifical Ecclesiastical Acad. 1985–89; serving in Council for Public Affairs of the Church and Pontifical Council for the Laity 1985–90; mem. Order of the Holy Sepulchre 1986–; Sec., Congregation for Bishops 1989–90, Coll. of Cardinals 1990–94; served on Perm. Interdicasterial Comm., Pontifical Comm. for Latin America, Congregation for Doctrine of the Faith; also engaged in pastoral service to several parishes and seminaries in Rome; Archbishop of Saint Louis, Mo. 1994–2003; Archbishop of Philadelphia, Pa 2003–11, Archbishop Emer. 2011–; cr. Cardinal (Cardinal-Priest of Santa Prisca) 2003; mem. Congregation for Bishops 2007–13; apptd Pope Benedict XVI's special envoy to celebrations at Prachatice in Czech Repub. for 200th anniversary of the birth of St John Neumann 2011; Apostolic Admin. (sede vacante) to Diocese of Scranton 2009–10; mem. Kts of Columbus 1994; Hon. Council mem. Wings of Hope; Prelate of Honour of His Holiness 1980; Magistral Chaplain, Order of Kts of Malta 1984. *Address:* 805 S. NorthShore Drive, Knoxville, TN 37919, USA (office). *Telephone:* (865) 862-5748 (office). *Fax:* (865) 583-3836 (office).

RIGBY, Peter William Jack, MA, PhD FRS, FMedSci; British medical research scientist and academic; *Professor Emeritus of Developmental Biology and Chief Executive, Institute of Cancer Research, University of London;* b. 7 July 1947, Savernake; s. of Jack Rigby and Lorna Rigby; m. 1st Paula Webb 1971 (divorced 1983); m. 2nd Julia Maidment 1985; one s.; ed Lower School of John Lyon, Harrow and Jesus Coll. Cambridge; mem. scientific staff, MRC Lab. of Molecular Biology, Cambridge 1971–73; Helen Hay Whitney Foundation Research Fellow, Stanford Univ. Medical School 1973–76; Lecturer, Sr Lecturer in Biochemistry, Imperial Coll. London 1976–83; Reader in Tumour Virology, Univ. of London 1983–86; Head, Genes and Cellular Controls Group and Div. of Eukaryotic Molecular Genetics, MRC Nat. Inst. for Medical Research 1986–2000; Chief Exec. Inst. of Cancer Research, Univ. of London 1999–2011, also Dir of Research, Prof. of Developmental Biology 2001–, now Prof. Emer.; mem. Science Council, Celltech Therapeutics 1982–2003; European Ed. Cell 1984–97; mem. Scientific Advisory Bd Somatix Therapy Corpn 1989–97, KuDos Pharmaceuticals 1999–; Scientific Cttee Cancer Research Campaign 1983–88, 1996–99; Dir (non-exec.), Royal Marsden NHS Foundation Trust 2001–; mem. of Council, Acad. of Medical Sciences 2002–04, St George's Hospital Medical School 2003–; mem. Bd of Govs, Beatson Inst. for Cancer Research, Glasgow 2003–; mem. Nat. Council and Chair. of Medical Research Cttee, Muscular Dystrophy Campaign 2003–; Chair. Principal Research Fellowship Interviewing Cttee, Wellcome Trust 2004–, mem. Bd of Govs 2008– (Deputy Chair. Bd of Govs 2010–13); mem. Strategy Bd, Biotechnology and Biological Sciences Research Council 2005–, Council of Marie Curie Cancer Care; Chair. Hexagen Tech. Ltd 1996–99, Babraham Inst. 2014–, European Molecular Biology Org.; Chair. Scientific Advisory Bd Proflix 1996–2004; Carter Medal, Clinical Genetics Soc. 1994. *Publications:* papers on molecular biology in scientific journals. *Leisure interests:* narrow boats, listening to music, sport. *Address:* Chester Beatty Laboratories, Institute of Cancer Research, 237 Fulham Road, London, SW3 6JB, England (office). *Telephone:* (20) 7153-5125 (office). *Fax:* (20) 7352-0272 (office). *E-mail:* peter.rigby@icr.ac.uk (office). *Website:* www.icr.ac.uk (office).

RIGDZIN, Dasho Chogyal Dago; Bhutanese civil servant; *Chief Election Commissioner;* started civil service career as trainee officer in Home Ministry 1990, Sr Section Officer 1991–98, Under-Sec. 1998–2002, Sarpang Dungpa 2002–06; Commr, Election Comm. 2006–15, oversaw several nat. and local govt elections 2008–13, Chief Election Commr 2015–. *Address:* Election Commission of Bhutan, Democracy House, POB 2008, Kawang jangsa, Thimphu, Bhutan (office). *Telephone:* (2) 334852 (office). *Fax:* (2) 334763 (office). *E-mail:* cec@election-bhutan.org.bt (office). *Website:* www.election-bhutan.org.bt (office).

RIGG, Dame (Enid) Diana Elizabeth, DBE; British actress; b. 20 July 1938, Doncaster, Yorks.; d. of Louis Rigg and Beryl Rigg (née Helliwell); m. 1st Menahem Gueffen 1973 (divorced 1976); m. 2nd Archibald Hugh Stirling 1982 (divorced 1993); one d.; ed Fulneck Girls School, Pudsey, Yorks., Royal Acad. of Dramatic Art; professional début as Natella Abashwilli (The Caucasian Chalk Circle), York Festival 1957; repertory Chesterfield and Scarborough 1958; Chair. MacRobert Arts Centre, Univ. of Stirling, Chancellor Univ. of Stirling 1997–2008; Prof. of Theatre Studies, Univ. of Oxford 1998, Visiting Prof. of Contemporary Theatre 1999; Dir United British Artists 1982–; a Vice-Pres. Baby Life Support Systems (BLISS) 1984–; mem. Arts Council Cttee 1986; mem. British Museum Devt Fund, Asscn for Business Sponsorship of the Arts; Assoc. Artist of RSC, Stratford and Aldwych 1962–79; mem. Nat. Theatre 1972; Dr hc (Stirling Univ.) 1988; Hon. DLitt (Leeds) 1992, (South Bank) 1996; Plays and Players Award for Best Actress (Phaedra Britannica 1975, Night and Day 1978), BAFTA Award for Best Actress in Mother Love 1990, Evening Standard Award for Best Actress (Medea 1993, Mother Courage and Her Children 1996, Who's Afraid of Virginia Woolf?, 1996), Tony Award for Best Actress in Medea 1994, Special Award for The Avengers, BAFTA 2000. *Roles with RSC include:* Andromache (Troilus and Cressida), 2nd Ondine, Violanta and Princess Bertha (Ondine), Philippe Trincant (The Devils), Gwendolen (Becket), Bianca (The Taming of the Shrew), Madame de Tourvel (The Art of Seduction), Helena (A Midsummer Night's Dream), Adriana (Comedy of Errors), Cordelia (King Lear), Nurse Monika Stettler (The Physicists), Lady Macduff (Macbeth); toured Eastern Europe, USSR, USA in King Lear, Comedy of Errors 1964; Viola (Twelfth Night), Stratford 1966. *National Theatre roles include:* Dottie Moore (Jumpers) 1972, Hippolita ('Tis Pity She's A Whore) 1972, Lady Macbeth (Macbeth) 1972, Célimène (The Misanthrope), Washington and New York 1973, 1975, The Governor's Wife (Phaedra Britannica) 1975; rejoined Nat. Theatre at the Lyttelton to play Ilona in The Guardsman 1978. *Other stage appearances include:* Abelard and Heloise (London) 1970, (LA, New York) 1971, Pygmalion (London) 1974, Night and Day (London) 1978, Colette (Seattle and Denver) 1982, Heartbreak House (London) 1983, Rita in Little Eyolf (London) 1985, Antony and Cleopatra (Chichester) 1985, Wildfire (London) 1986, Follies 1987, Love Letters (San Francisco) 1990, All for Love (London) 1991, Berlin Bertie 1992, Medea 1993 (London and Broadway), Mother Courage and Her Children (London) 1995, Who's Afraid of Virginia Woolf? (London) 1996–97, Phèdre 1998, Britannicus 1998, Humble Boy 2001, Suddenly Last Summer (Theatregoers' Award for Best Actress 2005) (Sheffield) 2004, Honour (London) 2006, All About My Mother (London) 2007, The Cherry Orchard (Chichester Festival Theatre) 2008, Hay Fever (Chichester Festival Theatre) 2009. *Films include:* A Midsummer Night's Dream 1969, The Assassination Bureau 1969, On Her Majesty's Secret Service 1969, Julius Caesar 1970, The Hospital 1971, Theatre of Blood 1973, A Little Night Music 1977, The Great Muppet Caper 1981, Evil under the Sun 1982, Snow White 1988, Cannon Movie Tales: Cinderella 1988, A Good Man in Africa 1994, Parting Shots 1999, Heidi 2005, The Painted Veil 2006. *Television appearances include:* The Avengers (series) 1965–67, Women Beware Women 1965, Married Alive 1970, Diana (series) 1973, In This House of Brede 1975, Three Piece Suite (series) 1977, Oresteia (mini-series) 1979, The Marquise 1980, Hedda Gabler 1981, Rita Allmers in Little Eyolf 1982, Regan in King Lear 1983, Witness for the Prosecution 1983, Bleak House (mini-series) 1984, Host, Held in Trust, A Hazard of Hearts 1987, Worst Witch 1987, Unexplained Laughter 1989, Mother Love (mini-series) (BAFTA Award for Best actress) 1989, Host, Masterpiece Mystery (USA) 1989–2004, Running Delilah 1994, Zoya 1995, The Haunting of Helen Walker 1995, The Fortunes and Misfortunes of Moll Flanders 1996, Samson and Delilah 1996, Rebecca 1997 (Emmy Award for Best Supporting Actress 1997), Mrs Bradley Mysteries (series) 1998–2000, In the Beginning (film) 2000, The American (film) 2001, Victoria & Albert (film) 2001, Charles II: The Power and the Passion (mini-series) 2003, Doctor Who 2013, Game of Thrones (series) 2013–17, Detectorist 2015, Victoria 2017. *Publications:* No Turn Unstoned 1982, So To The Land 1994. *Leisure interests:* reading, writing, cooking, travel. *Address:* c/o ARG, 4 Great Portland Street, London, W1W 8PA, England.

RIGGIO, Leonard S.; American business executive; *Chairman, Barnes & Noble, Inc.;* b. 28 Feb. 1941, New York; s. of Stephen Riggio; m. 1st (divorced); two d.; m. 2nd Louise Riggio; one d.; ed Brooklyn Tech. High School, New York Univ.; fmrly with New York Univ. campus bookstore; opened Waverly Student Book Exchange 1965; f. Barnes & Noble Bookstores 1971, Chair. Barnes & Noble Inc. 1986–, CEO 1986–2002, also Chair. barnesandnoble.com inc.; Chair. and, Prin. Beneficial Owner Software Etc. Stores, Mpls, MBS Textbook Exchange, Inc.; Chair. Dia Art Foundation; mem. Bd of Dirs New York Fund for Public Schools, Children's Defense Fund, Black Children's Community Crusade, Brooklyn Tech Foundation, Italian American Foundation; Ellis Island Medal of Honor, Frederick Douglas Medallion, Anti-Defamation League Americanism Award 2002, inducted into Texas A&M Retail Hall of Fame, Acad. of Distinguished Entrepreneurs, Babson Coll.; Dr hc (Baruch Coll.), (Bentley Coll.), (Adelphi Univ.), (Tusculum Coll.), (Long Island Univ.). *Leisure interests include:* collects art and wine, golf. *Address:* Barnes & Noble, Inc., 122 5th Avenue, New York, NY 10011, USA (office). *Telephone:* (212) 633-3300 (office). *Fax:* (212) 675-0413 (office). *Website:* www.barnesandnobleinc.com (office).

RIGILLO, Maurizio; Italian gallery director; *Co-Director and Partner, Galleria Continua;* co-f. (with Mario Cristiani and Lorenzo Fiaschi) Galleria Continua in San Gimignano, Tuscany 1990, other locations include Beijing 2004 and Boissy-le-Châtel, France 2007–; represents several major artists, including Daniel Buren, Kendell Geers, Anish Kapoor and Hans Op de Beeck. *Address:* Galleria Continua, Via del Castello 11, 53037 San Gimignano, Italy (office). *Telephone:* (0577) 943134 (office). *E-mail:* info@galleriacontinua.com (office). *Website:* www.galleriacontinua.com (office).

RIIS-JØRGENSEN, Birger, MA; Danish diplomatist; *CEO, Riis International;* b. 13 Jan. 1949, Odense; m. Karin Riis-Jørgensen; ed Univ. of Copenhagen; Grad. Fellow, Center for Latin American Studies, Univ. of New Mexico, USA 1974–75; Research Librarian, Royal Library, Copenhagen 1975–76; Lecturer in Int. Politics, Univ. of Copenhagen 1975–76; joined Danish Foreign Service 1976, posted to Danish del. to NATO 1979, served as Denmark's Rep. on Political Cttee and subsequently on NATO's Defence Review Cttee and Exec. Working Group, Head of Western Hemisphere and Nordic Countries Section, Political Dept, Ministry of Foreign Affairs and Sec. to Foreign Affairs Cttee of Parl. 1983–87, mem. team of officials who est. Secr. for European Political Co-operation, Brussels 1987–89; with DANIDA (Danish DfID) 1989–91; Head of Africa Dept, Ministry of Foreign Affairs 1991–94, Head of Middle East Dept 1994–96, Under-Sec., responsible for Africa, Asia and Latin America and all Danish bilateral devt assistance 1996–2000, State Sec. (Foreign Trade) and given task of merging trade promotion orgs of four ministries into one (Trade Council of Denmark) in the Foreign Service 2000–06, also joined Four Member Sr Man. Group, Amb. to UK 2006–11, to Italy (also accred to Malta and San Marino) 2011–16; Founder and Co-Owner, Riis Int. 2016–, currently CEO; Strategy/Sr adviser to CBS Executive and other pvt. cos 2017–; Commdr (First Degree), Order of the Dannebrog, Grand Cross, Order of Merit (Italy). *Leisure interests:* tennis, swimming, classical music, reading contemporary history and fiction. *Address:* Riis International, Lille Strandstraede 12 02, 1254 Copenhagen K, Denmark (office). *Telephone:* 61-42-72-32 (office). *E-mail:* b.riis@riisint.dk (office).

RIJKENBERG, Neal; Swazi business executive and politician; *Minister of Finance;* s. of Koos Rijkenberg; m. Barbara Rijkenberg; ed Cedara Agricultural Coll., South Africa; f. Montigny Investments Ltd (diversified timber co.) 1997, CEO –2018; Man. Dir NHR Investments; mem. Bd of Dirs Silulu (farm leasing bd), Swaziland Water and Agricultural Devt Enterprise; Co-Founder and Chair. Bulembu (non-profit community project); apptd to House of Ass. (parl.) 2018; Minister of Finance 2018–. *Address:* Ministry of Finance, Mhlambanyatsi Rd, POB 443, Mbabane, Eswatini (office). *Telephone:* 24048148 (office). *Fax:* 24043187 (office). *E-mail:* ps@finance.gov.sz (office).

RIKABI, Lt-Gen. Mohamed Osman Suleiman; Sudanese politician and fmr army officer; began career with Ministry of Finance; several years in army; fmr Chair. Shiekan Insurance and Reinsurance Co. Ltd; Minister of Finance and Econ. Planning 2017–18. *Address:* c/o Ministry of Finance and Economic Planning, POB 735, Khartoum, Sudan (office).

RILEY, Bridget Louise, CH, CBE, ARCA; British artist; b. 24 April 1931, London; d. of John Fisher and Bessie Louise Riley (née Gladstone); ed Cheltenham Ladies' Coll., Goldsmiths Coll. of Art and Royal Coll. of Art, London; first one-woman exhbn in London at Gallery One 1962, followed by others in England, USA, Italy, Germany, Ireland, Switzerland, Australia and Japan; has exhibited in group shows in Australia, Italy, France, Netherlands, Germany, Israel, USA, Japan and Argentina; represented GB at Biennale des Jeunes, Paris 1965, at Venice Biennale 1968; retrospective exhbn Europe and UK 1970–72; second retrospective exhbn touring America, Australia and Japan 1978–80; Arts Council Touring Exhbn 1984–85; retrospective exhbn Tate Britain 2003; solo exhbn Museum of Contemporary Art, Sydney 2004–05; paintings, drawings and prints in public collections in England, Ireland, Switzerland, Netherlands, Austria, Germany, Japan, Israel, USA, Australia and NZ; Founder-mem. and fmr Dir SPACE Ltd; mem. RSA; Trustee, Nat. Gallery 1981–88; Dr hc (Manchester) 1976, (Exeter) 1997, (Ulster) 1986, (Oxford) 1993, (Cambridge) 1995, (De Montfort) 1996; Hon. DLitt (Cambridge) 1995; AICA Critics Prize 1963, Prize in Open Section, John Moores Liverpool Exhbn 1963, Peter Stuyvesant Foundation Travel Bursary to USA 1964, Maj. Painting Prize, Venice Biennale 1968, Prize at Tokyo Print Biennale 1971, Gold Medal at Grafikk-bienniale, Fredrikstad, Norway 1980, Praemium Imperiale 2003. *Address:* c/o Karsten Schubert, 47 Lexington Street, London, W1R 3LG, England (office). *Telephone:* (20) 7734-9002 (office). *Fax:* (20) 7734-9008 (office). *E-mail:* mail@karstenschubert.com (office). *Website:* www.karstenschubert.com (office).

RILEY, Richard Wilson, LLB; American lawyer and fmr politician; *Partner, Nelson Mullins Riley & Scarborough LLP;* b. 2 Jan. 1933, Greenville, South Carolina; s. of E. P. Riley and Martha Dixon Riley; m. Ann Yarborough 1957; three s. one d.; ed Greenville Sr High School, Furman Univ. and SC School of Law; Lt in USN Legal Counsel to US Senate Cttee of Olin D. Johnston 1960; with family law firm 1961–62; mem. S Carolina State House of Reps 1962–66, S Carolina Senate 1966–76; S Carolina State Chair. for Jimmy Carter's Presidential Election Campaign 1976; Gov. of S Carolina 1979–87; Personnel Dir for Pres. Bill Clinton's Transition Team 1991–92; US Sec. of Educ. 1993–2001; Pnr, Nelson, Mullins, Riley & Scarborough LLP (law firm) 1987–93, 2001–; mem. Bd of Trustees, Carnegie Corpn of NY; mem. Bd ACT Inc., Knowledge Works Foundation, Furman Univ.; Distinguished Visiting Prof., Univ. of S Carolina 2001–, Distinguished Prof. of Govt, Politics, and Public Leadership, Richard W. Riley Inst., Furman Univ. *Address:* Nelson, Mullins, Riley & Scarborough LLP, Suite 900, Poinsett Plaza, 104 South Main Street, Greenville, SC 29601-2122, USA (office). *Telephone:* (864) 250-2290 (office). *Fax:* (864) 232-2925 (office). *Website:* www.nelsonmullins.com (office).

RILEY, Robert (Bob) Renfroe, BBA; American real estate executive and fmr politician; b. 3 Oct. 1944, Ashland, Clay Co., Ala; m. Patsy Adams; one s. three d. (one deceased); ed Clay Co. High School, Univ. of Alabama; fmr propr of poultry and egg business, automobile dealership, trucking co. grocery story and pharmacy; mem. Ashland City Council 1972–76; mem. US House of Reps from 3rd Alabama Dist, Washington, DC 1997–2002; Gov. of Ala 2003–11; fmr Chair. Finance Cttee, Clay Co. Hosp.; Pres. Alabama State Bd of Educ.; men's Sunday school teacher, First Baptist Church; Republican; named Public Official of Year by Governing magazine 2003, Eagle Award, US Distance Learning Asscn 2010.

RILEY, Terence, BArch MS; American architect, author and museum curator; ed Univ. of Notre Dame, Columbia Univ.; f. architectural practice Keenen/Riley Architects (with John Keenen) 1984; curator of 'Paul Nelson Filter of Reason' inaugural exhbn at Arthur Ross Architectural Galleries, Columbia Univ. 1989, Dir –1991; directed exhbns on work of Iacov Chernikhov and restaging of Museum of Modern Art's (MoMA) first exhbn on architecture: 'Exhibition 15: The Int. Style and The Museum of Modern Art', New York; joined MoMA 1991, Philip Johnson Chief Curator of Architecture and Design, MoMA 1992–2006, Instructor, Harvard Design School 2001–; Dir Miami Art Museum 2006–10; Chief Curator, Shenzhen and Hong Kong Biennale of Urbanism/Architecture 2011. *Publications include:* The Un-Private House (jtly with Glenn D. Lowry) 2002, MoMA QNS Box Set 2002; The Changing of the Avant-garde (Ed.) 2002. *Address:* Keenen/Riley Architects, 508 West 26th Street, 9A, New York, NY 10001, USA (office). *Telephone:* (212) 645-9210 (office). *Fax:* (212) 645-9211 (office). *E-mail:* jk@krnyc.com (office). *Website:* www.krnyc.com (office).

RIM, Choe-yong, BE; North Korean politician; b. 20 Nov. 1930, Ryanggang; one s. one d.; ed Kim Il-sung Univ., Univ. Lomonosov and Moscow State Univ.; served in various positions in Cen. Cttee of the Workers' Party of Korea including Instructor, Section Chief, Vice-Dept Dir and Dept Dir; Dir Chief Public Prosecutor's Office 1998–2003; mem. Kim Jong-il's Special Operations Command Group 2004; Sec.-Gen. Presidium of Supreme People's Ass. 2005–10; Chief Sec., Pyongyang City Cttee of the Workers' Party of Korea 2010–10; Premier of North Korea 2010–13; Chair. Gen. Defence Comm.

RIMAWI, Fahid Nimer ar-, BA; Jordanian journalist; *Publisher and Editor-in-Chief, Al Majd;* b. 1942, Palestine; m.; two s. five d.; ed Cairo Univ., Egypt; Ed. Difa (newspaper) 1965–67; Ed.-in-Chief, Jordan News Agency 1968–70; Sec., Editorial Bd, Afkar (magazine) 1970–73; Dir Investigating Dept, Al-Raiue (newspaper) 1975–76, Political Writer 1981–85; writer, Al-Destour (newspaper) 1978–81; Corresp., al Talie'ah (magazine) Paris 1982–85; political writer 1985–94; currently Publr and Ed.-in-Chief, Al Majd (weekly). *Publications include:* Mawaweel Fi al Layl Al Taweel, short stories in Arabic 1982. *Address:* Al Majd, PO Box 926856, Amman 11190 (office); Dahiyat al-Rashid, Amman, Jordan. *Telephone:* (6) 5530553 (office). *Fax:* (6) 553 0352 (office). *E-mail:* almajd@almajd.net (office). *Website:* almajd.net (office).

RIMINGTON, Dame Stella, DCB, MA; British author and fmr civil servant; b. (Stella Whitehouse), 13 May 1935, London; m. John Rimington 1963; two d.; ed Nottingham High School for Girls, Univs of Edinburgh and Liverpool (Diploma Archive Admin); joined Security Service (MI5) 1969 after working part-time in New Delhi office, numerous positions and responsibilities including recruitment 1986–88, Dir counter espionage 1988–91, Dir counter terrorism 1991–92, Deputy Dir-Gen. 1992–96, Dir-Gen. 1992–96; Dir (non-exec.) Marks and Spencer 1997–2004, BG PLC 1997–2000, BG Group 2000–05, GKR Group (now Whitehead Mann) 1997–2001; Chair. Inst. of Cancer Research 1997–2001; Trustee, Royal Marsden Hosp. 1997–2001, Refuge (charity), Int. Spy Museum, Washington, DC, USA; Gov. St Felix School, Southwold 1998–2002, Town Close House Preparatory School, Norwich 1999–2005; Hon. Air Cdre 7006 (VR) Squadron Royal Auxiliary Air Force 1997–2001; Dame Commdr of the Bath 1996; Hon. LLD (Nottingham) 1995, (Exeter) 1996, (London Metropolitan) 2004, (Liverpool) 2006, Hon. DSocS (Nottingham Trent) 2009; Spirit of Everywoman Award 2007. *Publications include:* Intelligence, Security and the Law (non-fiction) 1994, Open Secret (autobiog.) 2001; novels: At Risk 2004, Secret Asset 2006, Illegal Action 2007, Dead Line 2008, Present Danger 2009, Geneva Trap 2012, Close Call 2014, Breaking Cover 2016, The Moscow Sleepers 2018. *Address:* PO Box 1604, London, SW1P 1XB, England.

RIMŠĒVIČS, Ilmārs, BA, MBA; Latvian economist and central banker; *Governor, Bank of Latvia;* b. 30 April 1965, Rīga; ed Rīga High School No. 6, Rīga Tech. Univ., St Lawrence Univ. and Clarkson Univ., USA; Deputy Chair. Econs Cttee, Popular Front of Latvia 1989–90; Man. Foreign Operations Dept and Head of Securities Dept, Latvijas Zemes banka 1990–92; Deputy Gov. Bank of Latvia 1992–2001, Chair. Bd 1992–2001, Gov. 2001–; mem. Governing Council of the European Cen. Bank 2014–. *Address:* Bank of Latvia (Latvijas Banka), K. Valdemāra iela 2A, Rīga 1050, Latvia (office). *Telephone:* 6702-2300 (office). *Fax:* 6702-2420 (office). *E-mail:* info@bank.lv (office). *Website:* www.bank.lv (office).

RINEHART, Georgina (Gina) Hope; Australian business executive; *Chairman, Hancock Prospecting Pty Ltd;* b. 9 Feb. 1954, Perth, WA; d. of Lang Hancock; m. 1st (divorced), two c.; m. 2nd Francis Rinehart (deceased), two c.; ed Univ. of Sydney; joined Hancock Group as personal asst to her father 1973, Exec. Chair. Hancock Prospecting Pty Ltd and Hancock Prospecting Pty Ltd Group 1992–. *Address:* Hancock Prospecting Pty Ltd, 28–42 Ventnor Avenue, West Perth, WA 6005, Australia (office). *Telephone:* (8) 9429-8222 (office). *Fax:* (8) 9429-8268 (office). *E-mail:* mail@hancockprospecting.com.au (office). *Website:* www.hancockprospecting.com.au (office).

RINGHOLM, Bosse; Swedish politician; b. 18 Aug. 1942, Falköping; m. Kerstin Pehrsson; three c.; Chair. Social Democratic Youth 1967–72; Political Adviser, Ministries of Interior and Labour 1973–76; mem. Stockholm Co. Council 1973–97; Alt. mem./mem. Riksdag 1976, 1982; Dir Ministry of Educ. and Science 1976–82; Lead Co. Councillor for Transport 1983–85, for Finance 1989–91, 1994–97, Opposition Lead Co. Councillor 1986–88, 1991–94; Dir-Gen. Nat. Labour Market Bd 1997–99; Minister for Finance 1999–2004; Deputy Prime Minister 2004–06, temp. Minister of Foreign Affairs March 2006; mem. Exec. Cttee Social Democratic Party (Sveriges Socialdemokratiska Arbetareparti—SAP), Chair. Stockholm Br., Social Democratic Party 2001. *Address:* c/o Sveriges Socialdemokratiska Arbetareparti, Sveavägen 68, 105 60 Stockholm (office); Källv. 33, 122 62, Enskede, Sweden (home).

RINGIER, Michael; Swiss publishing and media executive; *Chairman, Ringier AG;* b. 30 March 1949, Zofingen; s. of Hans Ringier and Eva Ringier (née Landolt); m. Ellen Ringier; two d.; ed Hochschule St Gallen; est. himself professionally outside of family-owned firm Ringier (largest media corpn in Switzerland) working as a journalist with Münchner Abendzeitung 1973–76, travelled to Germany to work for Grüner + Jahr and H. Bauer; joined man. of Ringier 1983, CEO 1985–89, Chair., Ringier Holding AG 1990–97, Del. of Bd of Dirs 1997–2003, Chair., Bd of Dirs, Ringier Holding AG 2003–. *Address:* Ringier AG, Dufourstrasse 23, 8008 Zürich, Switzerland (office). *Telephone:* (44) 259-61-11 (office). *Fax:* (44) 259-86-35 (office). *E-mail:* info@ringier.ch (office). *Website:* www.ringier.com (office).

RINI, Snyder; Solomon Islands politician; *Minister for Fisheries and Marine Resources;* b. 27 July 1948; ed Univ. of Papua New Guinea, Univ. of Technology, Lae, Papua New Guinea; Financial Controller, Brewer Solomons Agriculture Ltd. 1975–80; Perm. Sec. for Ministry of Natural Resources 1989, for Ministry of Nat. Planning and Devt 1994–95, for Ministry of Agric. and Fisheries 1997; mem. Parl. for Marovo, Western Prov. 1997–; Minister for Finance and Treasury 2000–01, Deputy Prime Minister for Nat. Planning and Devt 2001–02, Deputy Prime Minister and Minister for Finance and Treasury 2002–03, Deputy Prime Minister and Minister for Educ. and Human Resources Devt 2003–06, Prime Minister April–May 2006 (resgnd), Minister of Finance and Treasury 2007–10 (resgnd), 2014–17, Minister for Fisheries and Marine Resources 2017–; mem. Bd of Dirs Devt Bank of Solomon Islands 1976–84, Cen. Bank of Solomon Islands 1982–84, 1990–96, Solomon Islands Port Authority 1982–84, Nat. Provident Fund 1976–86 (Chair. 1990–96), Solomon Islands Electricity Authority 1988–89. *Address:* Ministry of Fisheries and Marine Resources, POB G13, Honiara, Solomon Islands (office). *Telephone:* 39143 (office). *E-mail:* psfisheries@pmc.gov.sb (office).

RINKĒVIČS, Edgars, BA, MSc; Latvian politician; *Minister of Foreign Affairs;* b. 21 Sept. 1973, Jūrmala; ed Univ. of Latvia, Univ. of Groningen, Industrial Coll. of the Armed Forces/Nat. Defense Univ., Washington, DC, USA; early career as journalist covering foreign policy and int. relations for Latvian Radio 1993–94; Sr Desk Officer, Defence Policy Dept, Ministry of Defence 1995–96, Dir March–Sept. 1996, Acting Sec. of State 2005–08, Sec. of State 1997–2008, Head of Chancery of Pres. 2008–11; Deputy Head, Latvian Del. to negotiations on accession to NATO 2002–03; Minister of Foreign Affairs 2011–; mem. Latvijas Ceļš (Latvian Way) 1998–2004, Reformu Partija (Reform Party) 2012–14, Vienotība (Unity) 2014–; Commdr, Great Cross of the Order of Viesturs 2004, Commdr, Order of Merit of the Repub. of Poland 2005, Order of Merit of the Italian Repub. 2005, Order of Merit of Estonia 2005, Kt, Order of Orange-Nassau (Netherlands) 2006, Grand Officer, Order of Three Stars 2007; Minister of Defence Award—Medal of Hon. Merit for Contrib. to Armed Forces Devt 2000, Minister of Defence Award—Commemorative Medal for Advancing Latvia's Accession to NATO 2004, NATO Award for Meritorious Service 2007. *Address:* Ministry of Foreign Affairs, K. Valdemāra iela 3, Rīga 1395, Latvia (office). *Telephone:* 6701-6201 (office). *Fax:* 6782-8121 (office). *E-mail:* mfa.cha@mfa.gov.lv (office). *Website:* www.mfa.gov.lv (office).

RINNE, Risto, MEng; Finnish petroleum industry executive; b. 1949; with Fortum Corpn (later Neste Oil Oyj) 1975, Pres. Neste Oyj Finland 1999–2004, Pres. Oil Sector Finland 2004, Pres., CEO and Chair. Exec. Team Neste Oil Oyj 2004–08; Chair. Bd of Dirs Chemicals Industry Fed. Finland, Finnish Oil and Gas Fed.; mem. Bd of Dirs European Petroleum Industry Asscn (EUROPIA).

RINNERT, Jan; German business executive; *Chairman of the Board of Management, Heraeus Holding GmbH;* b. 30 Aug. 1968, Oldenburg/Holstein; m.; three c.; worked for State Govt of Bremen as Sr Political Advisor to Senator of Econ. Affairs; moved to pvt. sector, gaining professional experience as man. consultant at leading int. man. consulting firm; Man. Dir Titan-Aluminium-Feinguß GmbH, Bestwig 2002–04; Man. Dir Heraeus Kulzer GmbH 2004–07, mem. Bd of Man., Heraeus Holding GmbH 2007–, Chief Financial Officer 2007–10, Vice-Chair. Bd of Man. 2010–13, Chair. 2013–, Labour Dir 2013–. *Address:* Heraeus Holding GmbH, Postfach 1561, 63405 Hanau (office); Heraeus Holding GmbH, Heraeusstrasse 12–14, 63450 Hanau, Germany (office). *Telephone:* (6181) 35-0 (office). *Fax:* (6181) 35-35-50 (office). *E-mail:* pr@heraeus.com (office). *Website:* www.heraeus.com (office).

RINPOCHE, Samdhong; Tibetan academic and politician; b. (Lobsang Tenzin), 5 Nov. 1939, Nagdug, Tibet; ed monastic studies, Univ. of Drepung, Tibet, Monastery of Gyuto, Dalhousie, India; various positions in Tibetan colls in Simla, Darjeeling and Dalhousie, India; Vice-Pres. Congress of Tibetan Youth 1970–73; Prof. Cen. Inst. of Higher Tibetan Studies, Benares (now Varanasi), India 1971–2001, apptd Dir 1988; mem. Standing Cttee Asscn of Indian Univs 1994–, Pres. 1998–; fmr Pres. Tibetan Parl. in Exile; Kalon Tripa (Chief Minister) of Tibetan Govt in Exile 2001–11; Vice-Pres. Library of Tibetan Works and Files, Dharamsala, India; Chancellor Sanchi Univ. of Buddhist-Indic Studies, Madhya Pradesh 2013–; Adviser, World Peace Univ., USA; mem. Cttee for Charter of Tibetans in Exile and Future Constitution of Tibet; mem. Bd of Dirs Tibetan Schools, New Delhi, India; mem. Bd of Dirs Asiatic Soc., Calcutta; mem. Bd of Dirs Foundation for Universal Responsibility, New Delhi; mem. Directorate of Indian Council for Philosophical Research; mem. Directorate Krishnamurti Foundation, India; Advisory mem. Inst. of Asian Democracy, USA. *Publications include:* numerous academic essays and newspaper articles. *Address:* Kashag Secretariat, Central Tibetan Administration, Dharamsala 176215, Dist Kangra, H.P., India (office). *Telephone:* (18) 92222218 (office). *Fax:* (18) 92224914 (office). *E-mail:* kadrung@gov.tibet.net (home). *Website:* www.tibet.net (office).

RIO, Neiphiu, BA; Indian politician; *Chief Minister of Nagaland;* b. 11 Nov. 1950, Tuophema village, Kohima Dist; s. of Guolhoulie Rio; m. Kaisa Rio; one s. five d.; ed St Joseph's Coll., Darjeeling and Kohima Arts Coll.; apptd Pres. Youth Wing of United Democratic Front 1974, Acting Pres. 1976–77; elected Area Council Chair. Northern Angami 1984; mem. Nagaland Legis. Ass. 1989–2002, 2004–14; State Minister of Sports and School Educ. 1989–91, of Higher and Tech. Educ., Arts and Culture 1991–93, of Works and Housing 1993–98, of Home Affairs 1998–2002; mem. All India Congress Cttee 1993–2002; joined Naga People's Front (NPF) 2002, Leader Democratic Alliance of Nagaland (coalition of NPF and other regional parties) 2004–; Chair. Nagaland Industrial Devt Corpn (NIDC), Nat. Khadi and Village Industries Bd (NKVIB), Devt Authority of Nagaland; Chief Minister of Nagaland 2003–14, 2018–; mem. Lok Sahba (lower house of Nat. Parl.) 2014–18; Hon. Vice-Pres. Indian Red Cross Soc. *Leisure interests* games, sports, reading, music. *Address:* Chief Minister's Secretariat, Nagaland Civil Secretariat, Thizama Road, Kohima 797001, India (office). *E-mail:* cm_nagaland@yahoo.com (office). *Website:* chiefminister.nagaland.gov.in (office).

RIORDAN, Richard Joseph, AB, JD; American business executive, lawyer and fmr politician; *Counsel, Morgan, Lewis & Bockius LLP;* b. 1 May 1930, Flushing, NY; m. 1st Eugenia Riordan; six c. (two deceased); m. 2nd Jill Riordan; m. 3rd Nancy Daly; ed Univ. of California, Santa Clara, Princeton Univ., Univ. of Michigan Law School; served in US Army during Korean War; Attorney, O'Melveny and Myers 1956–59; Co-founder Thompson, Moss, Scott & Riordan (accounting and tax law firm), then Partner, Nossaman, Thompson, Moss, Scott & Riordan (after merger with Brady & Nossaman); Co-founder and Partner, Riordan and McKinzie (law firm) 1975–2003; Co-founder and Partner, Riordan Freeman & Spogli (leveraged buyout firm) 1983–88; Co-founder Riordan Lewis & Hayden (investment firm) 1988; fmr majority Owner, Original Pantry and Seventh Street Bistro restaurants; Mayor of LA 1993–2001; unsuccessful cand. for Gov. of Calif. 2002; Sec. of Educ. for State of Calif. 2003–05; Of Counsel, Bingham, McCutchen LLP 2005–2014; currently Counsel, Morgan, Lewis & Bockius LLP; f. Riordan Foundation 1981; Founding mem. LEARN (school reform initiative) 1991; Co-founder The Riordan Programs, Anderson School, UCLA; mem. Bd of Dirs Alliance for Coll. Ready Public Schools, Inner City Education Foundation; Republica; Business Person of the Year, Los Angeles Business Journal 2005; Dr hc (Claremont Grad. Univ.) 2003. *Publications:* The Mayor: How I Turned Around Los Angeles After Riots, an Earthquake and the O.J. Simpson Murder Trial (autobiography with Patrick Range McDonald) 2014. *Leisure interests:* reading, bicycling. *Address:* Morgan, Lewis & Bockius LLP, 355 South Grand Avenue, Suite 4500, Los Angeles, CA 90071-3107, USA (office). *Telephone:* (213) 229-8444 (office). *Fax:* (213) 830-8640 (office). *E-mail:* richard.riordan@morganlewis.com (office). *Website:* www.morganlewis.com (office); www.riordanfoundation.org.

RIPERT, Jean-Maurice; French diplomatist and UN official; *Ambassador to China;* b. 22 June 1953; m.; one c.; ed Institut d'Etudes Politiques, Paris, Ecole Nationale d'Admin; with Directorate for Legal Affairs, Ministry of Foreign Affairs 1980–82, Directorate for Econ. and Financial Affairs 1982–83; Tech. Adviser to Minister for Co-operation and Devt 1983–84, to Minister for European Affairs 1984, to Minister for Foreign Affairs 1984–86; Second Counsellor, Embassy in Washington, DC 1986–88; Tech. Adviser to Prime Minister of France 1988–90, Diplomatic Adviser 1991; Chief of Staff to Sec. of State for Humanitarian Action 1991, Adviser to Minister for Health and Humanitarian Action 1992–93; Consul-Gen. in Los Angeles 1993–96, Deputy Dir UN and Int. Org. Desk, Ministry of Foreign Affairs 1996–97, Diplomatic Adviser to the Prime Minister 1997–2000, Amb. to Greece 2000–03, Dir UN and Int. Org. Desk, Ministry of Foreign Affairs 2003–05, Amb. and Perm. Rep. to UN, Geneva 2005–07, to UN, New York 2007–09; Deputy Sec.-Gen. of UN Sec.-Gen.'s Special Envoy for Assistance to Pakistan 2009–10, Directorate-Gen. of Admin, Ministry of Foreign Affairs 2011, Amb. and Head of Del. of EU to Turkey, European External Action Service 2012–13, Amb. to the Russian Fed. 2013–17; Amb. to China 2017–; Kt of Nat. Order of Merit 1994, Chevalier of the Legion of Honor 2003. *Address:* Embassy of France in China, 3 Dong San Jie, San Li Tun, Chaoyang Qu, Beijing 100600, The People's Republic of China (office). *Telephone:* (10) 85312000 (office). *Fax:* (10) 85312090 (office). *E-mail:* presse@ambafrance-cn.org (office). *Website:* www.ambafrance-cn.org (office).

RIPKEN, Calvin (Cal) Edward, Jr; American business executive and fmr professional baseball player; b. 24 Aug. 1960, Havre de Grace, Md; s. of Cal Ripken Sr; m. Kelly Ripken; one s. one d.; ed Aberdeen High School, Md; player minor league teams in Bluefield, Miami, Charlotte, Rochester 1978–81; shortstop Baltimore Orioles 1978–2001; highest single season fielding percentage 1990; maj. league record for consecutive games played (breaking Lou Gehrig's record of 2,130 in 1995), 2,632 ending in 1998; 4,000 home runs, 3,000 hits (2000); retd 2001; purchased Utica Blue Sox Class A minor league team 2002, renamed to Aberdeen IronBirds (affiliate of Baltimore Orioles); f. The Kelly and Cal Ripken, Jr Foundation (now Cal Ripkin Sr Foundation) 1992; currently Pres. and CEO Ripken Baseball Inc., also Pres. and CEO Ripken Baseball Group; mem. Bd of Dirs ZeniMax Media Inc.; Dr hc (Delaware) 2008, (Maryland) 2013; Rookie of the Year, Int. League 1981, Rookie of the Year, Baseball Writers Asscn, American League 1982, Silver Slugger Award 1983–86, 1989, 1991, 1993–94, Golden Glove Award 1991–92, Sportsman of the Year, Sports Illustrated 1995; elected to Baseball Hall of Fame 2007. *Publications:* Play Baseball The Ripken Way (with Bill Ripken) 2004, Parenting Young Athletes the Ripken Way 2006. *Address:* Ripken Baseball, 1427 Clarkview Road, Suite 100, Baltimore, MD 21209, USA (office). *Telephone:* (410) 823-0808 (office). *Fax:* (410) 823-0850 (office). *Website:* www.ripkenbaseball.com (office).

RIPPON, Angela, CBE, OBE; British broadcaster and journalist; b. 12 Oct. 1944, Plymouth, Devon, England; d. of John Rippon and Edna Rippon; m. Christopher Dare 1967 (divorced); ed Plymouth Selective School for Girls; Presenter and Reporter, BBC TV Plymouth 1966–69; Ed., Producer, Dir and Presenter, Westward TV (ITV) 1969–73; Reporter, BBC TV Nat. News 1973–75, Newsreader 1975–81; Founder and Presenter TV-am Feb.–April 1983; Arts Corresp. for WNEV (CBS), Boston, 1983; Reporter and Presenter, BBC and ITV 1984–, including co-presenter, Rip Off Britain (BBC) 2009–, Holiday Hit Squad (BBC) 2013–, Amazing Greys (ITV) 2014–; Vice-Pres. Int. Club for Women in TV 1979–, British Red Cross, NCH Action for Children, Riding for the Disabled Asscn; Dir Nirex 1986–89; Chair. English Nat. Ballet 2000–04; Amb. Altzheimer's Soc.; Dr hc (American Int. Univ.) 1994; Hon. Dr of Arts (Plymouth) 2012; New York Film Festival Silver Medal 1973, Newsreader of the Year (TV and Radio Industries Club) 1975, 1976, 1977, TV Personality of the Year 1977, Emmy Award 1984 (Channel 7 Boston), Sony Radio Award 1990, New York Radio Silver Medal 1992, Royal TV Soc. Hall of Fame 1996, European Woman of Achievement 2002 and other awards. *Dance:* National Tour 'Anything Goes' 2007. *Musical:* Side by Side with Sondheim 2008. *Radio series include:* Angela Rippon's Morning Report for LBC 1992, Angela Rippon's Drive Time Show, LBC 1993, The Health Show (BBC Radio 4), Friday Night with Angela Rippon (BBC Radio 2), LBC Arts Programme 2003–05. *Television includes:* Angela Rippon Meets (documentary), Antiques Roadshow, In the Country, Compere, Eurovision Song Contest 1976, The Morecambe and Wise Christmas Show 1976, 1977, Top Gear 1977–79, Royal Wedding 1981, Masterteam (BBC) 1985, 1986, 1987, Come Dancing 1988–91, What's My Line? 1988–90, Healthcheck, Holiday Programme, Simply Money (Family Finance Channel) 2001–02, Channel 5 News 2003–04, Live with Angela Rippon (ITV) 2004–06, Sun, Sea & Bargain Spotting, Cash in the Attic, Rip Off Britain 2009–, Holiday Hit Squad 2013–, Amazing Greys 2014–. *Publications:* Riding 1980, In the Country 1980, Mark Phillips – The Man and his Horses 1982, Victoria Plum (eight children's books) 1983, Angela Rippon's West Country 1982, Badminton: A Celebration 1987, Fabulous at 50 – And Beyond 2005. *Leisure interests:* cooking, tennis, reading, theatre. *Address:* c/o Knight Ayton Management, 35 Great James Street, London, WC1N 3HB, England (office). *Telephone:* (20) 7836-5333 (office). *Fax:* (20) 7836-8333 (office). *E-mail:* info@knightayton.co.uk (office). *Website:* www.knightayton.co.uk (office).

RISBY, Baron (Life Peer), cr. 2010, of Haverhill in the County of Suffolk; **Richard John Grenville Spring,** MA; British politician and business executive; b. 24 Sept. 1946, Cape Town, South Africa; m. Hon. Jane Henniker-Major 1979 (divorced 1993); two c.; ed Rondebosch Boys' High School, Cape, Univ. of Cape Town, Magdalene Coll., Cambridge; began career at Merrill Lynch and spent 15 years before becoming a Vice-Pres.; joined E.F. Hutton Int. Assocs as Jt Man. Dir 1986 (taken over by Lehman Brothers), Exec. Dir, ran US equities Div.; Man. Dir Furman Selz (Xerox subsidiary), with responsibility for European operations –1992; fmr Chair. Westminster Conservative Political Centre; unsuccessful Parl. cand. for Ashton-under-Lyne in Gen. Election 1983; MP (Conservative) for Bury St Edmunds 1992–97, for West Suffolk 1997–2010; Parl. Pvt. Sec. to Sir Patrick Mayhew 1994–95, to defence ministers 1996–97, to Tim Eggar 1996–2005; Opposition Spokesman on Culture, Media and Sport 1998–2000, for Foreign and Commonwealth Affairs, with responsibility for Europe and the Middle East 2000–04; Shadow Minister for the Treasury 2004–05; Vice-Chair. Conservative Party 2005–10, responsible for business links in the City of London and Co-Chair. Conservative City Circle; mem. (Conservative), House of Lords 2010–; Vice-Chair. All-Party Parl. Group for East Asian Business 2011–; Prime Ministerial Trade

Envoy to Algeria 2012–; Chair. British Ukrainian Soc. 2007–; Dir British Syrian Soc. 2003–11; Patron City Future. *Address:* House of Lords, Westminster, London, SW1A 0PW, England (office). *Telephone:* (20) 7219-8996 (office). *E-mail:* risbyr@parliament.uk (office).

RISCH, James (Jim) Elroy, BS, JD; American rancher, lawyer and politician; *Senator from Idaho;* b. 3 May 1943, Milwaukee, Wis.; s. of Elroy A. Risch and Helen B. Risch (née Levi); m. Vicki Risch 1968; three s.; ed Univ. of Wisconsin-Milwaukee, Univ. of Idaho and Univ. of Idaho Coll. of Law; Prosecuting Attorney, Ada Co. 1970–74; Pres. Idaho Prosecuting Attorneys Asscn –1975; taught criminal law at Boise State Univ.; mem. Idaho State Senate 1975–88, 1995–2002, Majority Leader 1976–82, Pres. pro tempore 1982–88; Lt Gov. of Idaho 2003–06, 2007–09; Gov. of Idaho 2006–07; Sr Partner, Risch Goss Insinger Gustavel (law firm) 2008; Senator from Idaho 2009–; mem. Senate Cttee on Small Business and Entrepreneurship (Chair. 2017–19), on Foreign Relations, on Energy and Natural Resources, Select Cttee on Intelligence, Select Cttee on Ethics; Republican; Hon. mem. Idaho Snowmobile Asscn 2013; Presidential Order of Excellence of Georgia 2013; Distinguished Community Health Defender Award, Nat. Asscn of Community Health Centers 2010, Thomas Jefferson Award, Int. Foodservice Distributors Asscn 2010, Award of Legal Merit, Univ. of Idaho Coll. of Law 2012, Micron Legislator of the Year Award 2013. *Address:* SR-483, Russell Senate Office Building, Washington, DC 20510, USA (office). *Telephone:* (202) 224-2752 (office). *Fax:* (202) 224-2573 (office). *Website:* risch.senate.gov (office).

RISDAHL JENSEN, Tom; Danish diplomatist; b. 28 Sept. 1947, Hjørring; m. Helle Bundgaard; Amb. to UK 2001–06, to Sweden 2006–10, to Russia 2010–13; Commdr, Order of the Dannebrog 2005. *Address:* c/o Royal Danish Embassy, 119034 Moscow, Prechistensky Per. 9, Russian Federation (office).

RISHTON, John, FCMA; British business executive; b. 21 Feb. 1958; ed Univ. of Nottingham; worked for Ford Motor Co. in various exec. positions, qualified as an accountant and later became Finance Dir of co.'s Portuguese and Spanish operations; joined British Airways Plc as Head of Finance for US Div. 1994, Operations Controller 1998–99, Commercial Controller 1999–2001, Chief Financial Officer 2001–05; Exec. Vice-Pres. and Chief Financial Officer Royal Ahold NV 2006–07, mem. Corp. Exec. Bd 2006–11, Acting Pres. and CEO July–Nov. 2007, Pres. and CEO Nov. 2007–11; Dir (non-exec.) Rolls Royce Group Plc 2007–15, Chief Exec. 2011–15; Dir (non-exec.) Allied Domecq 2003–05, Unilever 2013–.

RITBLAT, Sir John Henry, Kt, FSVA, FRICS, FRSA; British business executive; *Chairman, Alpha Plus Group Ltd;* b. 3 Oct. 1935; m. 1st Isabel Paja 1960 (died 1979); two s. one d.; m. 2nd Jill Rosemary Zilkha (née Slotover) 1986; ed Dulwich Coll., Coll. of Estate Man., Univ. of London; Founder and Chair. Conrad Ritblat & Co., Consultant Surveyors and Valuers 1958, Man. Dir 1970, Chair. Conrad Ritblat Group PLC 1993, Chair. Colliers Conrad Ritblat Erdman 2000; Chair. The British Land Co. PLC 1970 (Man. Dir 1971–2004), Chair. and Chief Exec. The British Land Corpn 1991–2006, Hon. Pres. 2006–; apptd Chair. European Real Estate Pvt. Equity Advisory Council, Lehman Brothers 2006; Chair. Colliers CRE (now Colliers Int.) 2001–12; Chair. Alpha Plus Group Ltd 2012–; Chair. Delancey's Real Estate Advisory Bd; Man. Dir Union Property Holdings (London) Ltd 1969, Crown Estates Paving Comm. 1969; mem. Bd of Govs London Business School 1991–2014, Chair. 2004–14, Hon. Fellow 2000–, mem. Estates Cttee; mem. Bd of Govs Weizmann Inst. 1991–2008; apptd mem. Council, Business in the Community 1987, Prince of Wales' Royal Parks Tree Appeal Cttee 1987, Patrons of British Art (Tate Gallery), Nat. Art Collections Fund 1995; Dir British Library 1995–2003, 2015–; apptd Dir and Gov. RAM 1998, Deputy Chair. 1999, Hon. Fellow and Hon. Trustee 2000–; Pres. British Ski and Snowboard Fed. 1994–; Vice-Pres. Int. Students' House, Tennis & Racquets Asscn; Trustee, The Wallace Collection 2003–, Chair. 2005–; Life mem. Royal Inst. of GB; Fellow, Dulwich Coll.; Hon. FRIBA 2006; Hon. DLitt (London Metropolitan Univ.) 2005, (Univ. of Buckingham); Hon. DrSci (London Business School). *Leisure interests:* golf, skiing, real tennis, books, architecture. *Address:* Alpha Plus Group Ltd, 50 Queen Anne Street, Marylebone, London, W1G 8HJ (office); 10 Cornwall Terrace, Regent's Park, London, NW1 4QP, England. *Telephone:* (20) 7487-6000 (office). *Fax:* (20) 7487-6001 (office). *E-mail:* enquiries@alphaplusgroup.co.uk (office). *Website:* www.alphaplusgroup.co.uk (office).

RITCHIE, Guy; British film director; b. 10 Sept. 1968, Hatfield, Herts.; s. of John Ritchie and Amber Mary Ritchie; m. 1st Madonna Ciccone 2000 (divorced 2008); one s. one step-d.; m. 2nd Jacqui Ainsley 2015; two s. one d.; ed Standbridge Earls School; directed numerous pop videos 1980s. *Films include:* The Hard Case 1995, Lock, Stock and Two Smoking Barrels 1998, Snatch 2000, What it Feels Like For a Girl (video) 2001, The Hire: Star 2001, Swept Away 2002, Mean Machine (supervising producer) 2002, Revolver 2005, RocknRolla (also producer) 2008, Sherlock Holmes 2009, Sherlock Holmes: A Game of Shadows 2011, The Man from U.N.C.L.E. (also producer) 2015. *Television includes:* The Hard Case 1995, Lock, Stock and Two Smoking Barrels (series exec. producer) 2000, Suspect (also exec. producer) 2007. *Leisure interests:* karate, judo.

RITCHIE, Ian C., CBE, DipArch (Dist), RIBA, RIAI, FRSA, MSIAD, FSFE; British architect; *Principal, Ian Ritchie Architects Ltd;* b. 24 June 1947, Hove, Sussex, England; s. of Christopher Ritchie and Mabel Long; pnr Jocelyne van den Bossche; one s.; ed Polytechnic of Central London (now Univ. of Westminster); project architect, Foster Assocs 1972–76; in pvt. practice, France 1976–78; Founder-Partner Arup Lightweight Structures Group 1978–81; ind. consultant 1979–81; Founder-Partner Chrysalis Architects 1979–81; Co-founder Rice Francis Ritchie 1981, Dir 1981–87, Consultant 1987–89; Prin., Ian Ritchie Architects Ltd 1981–; mem. Royal Inst. of the Architects of Ireland, Soc. of Industrial Artists and Designers; Hon. Prof. of Architecture, Univ. of Liverpool; Hon. FAIA; Hon. mem. Royal Incorporation of Architects in Scotland; Hon. DLitt (Westminster); numerous awards, including Architectural Design Silver Medal 1983, Iritecna Prize for Europe (Italy) 1991, Eric Lyons Memorial Award for Housing in Europe 1992, Robert Matthews Award, Commonwealth Asscn of Architects 1994, AIA Awards 1997, 2003, 2008, Civic Trust Award 1997, RIBA Awards 1998 (two), 2000, 2003, 2004, 2007, RIBA Stephen Lawrence Award 1998, Arts Building of the Year, Royal Fine Arts Comm. (RFAC) 1998, Sports Building of the Year, RFAC 2000, Building of the Year, RFAC 2003, two Design Council Millennium Product Awards 1999, Int. Outstanding Structure Award, IABSE 2000, Regeneration of Scotland

Supreme Award 2000, British Construction Industry Special Award 2000, Copper Building of the Year 2000, Innovation in Copper Award, Copper Devt Asscn 2000, 2003, Abercrombie Awards: Best New Building and Overall Abercrombie Architectural Design Award 2004, West Midlands Architects of the Year 2006, Rail Station of the Year, Nat. Transport Awards 2009, Nat. Winner, 3R Awards Listed Buildings/Structures 2011, British Council of Offices Award 2011, RIAI Award 2011, Major Building Project of the Year, BCI Awards 2016, Overall Winner, LEAF Awards 2016, Best Façade Design and Eng, LEAF Awards 2016, LABC Building Excellence Award 2017, German Design Award 2018, UK Property Award 2019, Civic Trust Award 2019. *Commissions include:* Eagle Rock House, Sussex, several projects for the Louvre, Paris, including work on the Louvre Pyramids and Sculpture Courts, Nat. Museum of Science, Tech. and Industry, La Villette, Pharmacy Boves, France, Jeu de Paume cultural centre, Albert, France, Ecology Gallery, Natural History Museum, London, Stockley Business Park offices, Oxford Science Park offices, Glass Towers, Reina Sofía Museum of Modern Art, Madrid, Glass Hall, Leipzig Int. Exhbn Centre, Bermondsey and Wood Lane Stations for London Underground, EdF HV electricity pylons, France, Royal Opera House Theatre, Tower Bridge, London, Crystal Palace Concert Platform, White City redevelopment, Theatre Royal Production Centre, Plymouth, Scotland's Home of Tomorrow, Glasgow, Spire of Dublin Nat. Monument, 3rd Millennium Light Monument, Milan, Hayward Gallery Exhbns, London, British Museum masterplan, RSC Courtyard Theatre, Stratford upon Avon, King Solomon Acad., London, Wood Lane Station, London, Central Line Underground Sidings, Laureate Nat. Grid Pylon competition, Sainsbury Wellcome Centre at University Coll., London, Mercers Walk, Covent Garden, London, Mriehel masterplan Malta, Farsons Business Park, Malta, RAM musical theatre and recital hall, London. *Films:* La cité en lumière (co-scripted/dir) 1986, The Spire of Dublin 2003, Sainsbury Wellcome Centre (Squintopera) 2016. *Television:* (scripted, directed or produced): Sandcastles (BBC) 1990, Architect and Engineer 1995, Skyscrapers 1999, Surveillance (Channel 4) 2001. *Publications:* (Well) Connected Architecture 1994, The Biggest Glass Palace in the World 1997, Ian Ritchie: Technoecology 1999, Plymouth Theatre Royal Production Centre 2003, The Spire 2004, RSC Courtyard Theatre 2006, Leipzig Glass Hall (construction drawings) 2007, Lines (poetry) 2010, Being: An Architect 2013. *Leisure interests:* art (etchings, inkings and monoprints), swimming, reading, writing, poetry, theatre, wild places. *Address:* Ian Ritchie Architects Ltd, 110 Three Colt Street, London, E14 8AZ, England (office). *Telephone:* (20) 7338-1100 (office). *Fax:* (20) 7338-1199 (office). *E-mail:* mail@ianritchiearchitects.co.uk (office). *Website:* www.ianritchiearchitects.co.uk (office).

RITCHIE, Ian Russell, MA; British barrister, business executive and sports administrator; *CEO, Rugby Football Union;* b. 27 Nov. 1953, Leeds; s. of Hugh Ritchie and Sheelah Ritchie; m. Jill Middleton-Walker 1982; two s.; ed Leeds Grammar School, Trinity Coll. Oxford; Barrister (Middle Temple) 1976–77; Industrial Relations Adviser, Eng Employers' Fed. 1978–79; joined Granada TV 1980, Head Production Services 1987–88; Dir of Resources, Tyne-Tees TV 1988–91, Man. Dir 1991–93, Group Deputy Chief Exec. Yorkshire Tyne-Tees TV PLC 1993; Man. Dir Nottingham Studios, Cen. TV 1993–94; Man. Dir London News Network 1994–96; CEO, subsequently COO Channel 5 Broadcasting 1996–97; Man. Dir Russell Reynolds Assocs 1997–98; Chief Exec. Middle East Broadcasting Centre 1998–2000; CEO Assoc. Press (AP) TV News 2000–04, Vice-Pres. Global Business and Man. Dir AP Int. 2003; CEO All England Lawn Tennis Club 2005–11; CEO Rugby Football Union 2012–; mem. Bd of Dirs Football League 2004–12, Wembley Nat. Stadium Ltd 2008–11. *Leisure interests:* golf, tennis, theatre. *Address:* Rugby Football Union, Rugby House, Twickenham Stadium, 200 Whitton Road, Twickenham, Middx, TW2 7BA, England (office). *Fax:* (20) 8892-9816 (office). *Website:* www.rfu.com (office).

RITHAUDDEEN AL-HAJ BIN TENGKU ISMAIL, Y.M. Tengku Ahmad, PMN, SPMP, SSAP, PMK, LLB; Malaysian politician and barrister; b. 24 Jan. 1932, Kota Bharu; s. of Y. M. Tengku Ismail and Y. M. Besar Zabidah Tengku abd Kadir; m. Y. M. Tengku Puan Sri Datin Noor Aini 1957; three s. two d.; ed Nottingham Univ. and Lincoln's Inn, UK; mem. of royal family of Kelantan; Circuit Magistrate in Ipoh 1956–58, Pres. of Sessions Court 1958–60; Deputy Public Prosecutor and Fed. Counsel 1960–62; mem. Council of Advisers to Ruler of State of Kelantan (MPR), resgnd to enter pvt. practice; Chair. East Coast Bar Cttee of Malaya; Chair. Sri Nilam Co-operative Soc., Malaysia; mem. Malayan Council 1967, 1968, 1969, 1970; Sponsor, Adabi Foundation, Kelantan Youth; Adviser, Kesatria; Chair. Farmers' Org. Authority; apptd Deputy Defense Minister 1970; Minister with Special Functions Assisting Prime Minister on Foreign Affairs 1973–75; mem. Supreme Council, United Malays' Nat. Org. 1975–, Vice-Pres. 1981, Head, Div. of Kota Bharu 1990–93, Lifelong Hon. Attendant, Kota Bharu Div. 1993, Chair. Disciplinary Bd 2001; Minister for Foreign Affairs 1975–81, 1984–86, for Trade and Industry 1981–83, for Information 1986, of Defence 1986–90; Jt Chair. Malaysia-Thailand Devt Authority (Gas and Oil); Chair. Kinta Kellas Investments PLC 1990–, Idris Hydraulic (Malaysia) Berhad 1991–, Concrete Eng Products Berhad, Road Builder (Malaysia) Holdings Berhad; Pres. UN Asscn of Malaysia (UNAM); Adviser, KPMG Peat Marwick Malaysia; Legal Advisor to Lee & Kee Securities; Hon. Adviser Old Frees Asscn 1999–2001; Pro-Chancellor Nat. Univ. of Malaysia –2004; Chair. Univ. of Nottingham Malaysia Campus; Deputy Pres. Football Asscn of Malaysia; mem. Second National Econ. Consultative Council 1999; Perlis Mahkota Perlis Award 1976, Prime Minister's Award Medal, Farmers' Organization Authority 1993, Peace Ambassador Award 2005. *Leisure interest:* golf.

RITOÓK, Zsigmond, PhD; Hungarian professor of Latin; *Professor Emeritus, University of Budapest;* b. 28 Sept. 1929, Budapest; s. of Zsigmond Ritoók and Ilona Ritoók (née Gaylhoffer); m. Agnes Ritoók (née Szalay); one s. two d.; ed Univ. of Budapest; teacher 1958–1970; Research Fellow, Centre of Classical Studies of Hungarian Acad. of Sciences 1970–86; Prof. of Latin, Univ. of Budapest 1986–99, Prof. Emer. 2000–; Corresp. mem. Acad. of Sciences 1990–93, mem. 1993–; Vice-Pres. Section of Linguistics and Literary Scholarship 1990–96, Pres. 1996–99; mem. Academia Latinitati Fovendae, Rome 1984–, Academia Europaea 1991–; Corresp. mem. Österreichische Akad. der Wissenschaften 1998–; Gen. Sec. Hungarian Soc. of Classical Studies 1980–85, Co-Pres. 1985–91, Pres. 1991–97; Dr hc (Miskolc), (Eötvös Loránd Univ., Budapest); Hungarian Order of Merit Cross of the Star 2008; Albert Szent-Gyorgyi Prize (1992, Pázmány Péter Award 1997,

Széchenyi Prize 2001, Bolyai Prize 2009, Prima Prize 2012. *Publications:* Everyday Life in Ancient Greece 1960, The Golden Age of Greek Culture (co-author) 1968, (revised and enlarged) 1984, 2006, Theatre and Stadium 1968, Greek Singer of Tales 1973, Sources for the History of Greek Musical Aesthetics 1982, Desire, Poetry, Cognition, Selected Papers 2010 (all in Hungarian); Griechische Musikästhetik (in German) 2004; more than 130 papers in Hungarian and foreign periodicals. *Address:* ELTE Latin Tanszék, Múzeum Körut, 1088 Budapest (office); Mátyás u. 20, 1093 Budapest, Hungary (home). *Telephone:* (1) 217-4033 (home). *E-mail:* latintanszek@freemail.hu (office).

RITTENMEYER, Ronald (Ron) Allen, BS, MBA; American business executive; *Chairman and CEO, Turnberry Associates Inc.;* b. 22 May 1947, Wilkes-Barre, Pa; Harold E. Rittenmeyer and Shirley A. Rittenmeyer (neé Hitchner); m. Hedy Rittenmeyer; two c.; ed Wilkes Univ., Rockhurst Univ.; Vice-Pres. of Operations, Frito-Lay Inc. 1974–76; fmr Vice-Pres. Middle East and Worldwide Operations, PepsiCo Food Int.; fmr Pres. and COO Merisel; COO Burlington Northern Railroad 1994; Pres. and COO Ryder TRS Inc. 1997–98; Chair., CEO and Pres. RailTex Inc. 1998–2000; CEO and Pres. AmeriServe 2000; Chair., CEO and Pres. Safety-Kleen Inc. 2001–04; Man. Dir The Cypress Group, NY 2004–05; Co-COO and Exec. Vice-Pres. Global Service Delivery Div., Electronic Data Systems Corpn (EDS) 2005, Pres. and COO EDS 2006–07, Pres. and CEO 2007–09, Chair. 2007–08 (following acquisition of EDS by Hewlett-Packard 2008); apptd Pres. and CEO NCO Group Inc. (now Expert Global Solutions) 2011, Chair., CEO and Pres. 2011–14; CEO and Pres. Jennifer Loomis & Assocs Inc. 2011–, Perimeter Credit, LLC; Founder, Chair. and CEO Turnberry Assocs Inc. (real estate devt and property man. co.) 2014–; mem. Bd of Dirs Tenet Healthcare Corpn, American Int. Group, Inc., IMS Health Holdings, Inc.; fmr Chair. ExcellerateHRO; mem. Exec. Bd Southern Methodist Univ. Cox School of Business; mem. Business Council, Gov.'s Business Council; mem. Bd of Visitors US Army War Coll. *Address:* Turnberry Associates Inc., 19501 Biscayne Blvd, Suite 400, Aventura, FL 33180, USA (office). *Telephone:* (305) 937-6262 (office). *Website:* www.turnberry.com (office).

RITTER, August William (Bill), Jr, BA, JD; American lawyer, academic and fmr politician; *Director, Center for the New Energy Economy and Senior Scholar, School of Global Environmental Sustainability, Colorado State University;* b. 6 Sept. 1956, Denver, Colo; s. of August William Ritter and Ethel Ritter; m. Jeannie L. Ritter 1983; three s. one d.; ed Colorado State Univ., Univ. of Colorado School of Law; Deputy Dist Attorney for City and Co. of Denver 1981–87, 1992–93, Dist Attorney 1993–2006; moved with wife to Zambia as missionaries for RC Church 1987–89, opened food distribution and educ. centre; held post in US Attorney's office 1990–92; advised US Attorney Gen. John Ashcroft following attack on World Trade Center, New York 2001; Gov. of Colo 2007–11; Founding Dir Center for the New Energy Economy and Sr Scholar, School of Global Environmental Sustainability, Colorado State Univ., Fort Collins 2011–; Pres. Colorado Dist Attorneys Council 1999–2000, 2003–04; Vice-Pres. Nat. Asscn of Dist Attorneys 1995–2004; Chair. Promoting Alternatives to Violence through Educ. 1992–2003, American Prosecutors Research Inst. 1998–2003; mem. Bd of Dirs Energy Foundation 2011–, Nat. Asscn of Drug Court Professionals 1995–2002, Mile High United Way 1999–2004; fmr mem. Denver Foundation's Human Services Cttee, Mile High United Way Bd, Denver Public Schools Comm. on Secondary School Reform; Democrat. *Address:* School of Global Environmental Sustainability, Mail-Stop 1036, 108 Johnson Hall, Colorado State University, Fort Collins, CO 80523-1036, USA (office). *Telephone:* (970) 491-2903 (office). *Fax:* (970) 492-4130 (office). *E-mail:* linda.wardlow@colostate.edu (office). *Website:* cnee.colostate.edu (office).

RITTER, Jorge Eduardo, PhD; Panamanian lawyer, politician and diplomatist; b. 1950, Panama City; s. of Eduardo Ritter Aislán; m.; two c.; ed Pontificia Univ. Javeriana, Colombia; Clerk to Legis. Comm. 1973–77; Lecturer in Constitutional and Civil Law, Univ. of Panama; fmr mem. Governing Council, Inst. for Human Resources Training and Devt; Vice-Minister of Labour and Social Welfare 1977–78; Pvt. Sec. and Adviser to Pres. of Panama 1978–81; Minister of Foreign Affairs (desig.) 1981; teacher, Nat. Political Training Coll. of the Guardia Nacional 1981; Minister of Interior and Justice 1981–82; Amb. to Colombia 1982–86; Perm. Rep. to UN 1986–88; Minister of Foreign Affairs 1988–89, 1998–99; Minister for Canal Affairs 1998–99; Vice-Chair. Bd Panama Canal Comm. 1998–99; Chair. Exec. Council Nat. Telecommunications Inst. 1981; Chair. Bd Civil Aviation Authority 1981–82, Panama Canal Authority 1998–99; mem. Bd Banco Ganadero 1980–90; Pnr Ritter, Díaz y Ahumada 1982–; Excanciller of Panama; mem. Academia Panameña de la Lengua 2007–. *Publication:* Los Secretos de la Nunciatura 1990. *Address:* Calle José Gabriel Duque, La Cresta, Las Torres (C-6), PO Box 0819-08253, Panamá, Panama (office). *Telephone:* (507) 264-0521 (office). *Fax:* (507) 264-0524 (office). *E-mail:* jritter@cwpanama.net (home).

RITTERMAN, Dame Janet Elizabeth, DBE, MMus, PhD; British/Australian music college director (retd); *Chancellor, Middlesex University;* b. (Janet Elizabeth Palmer), 1 Dec. 1941, Sydney, NSW, Australia; d. of Charles Eric Palmer and Laurie Helen Palmer; m. Gerrard Peter Ritterman 1970; ed North Sydney Girls' High School and New South Wales State Conservatorium of Music, Australia, Univ. of Durham and King's Coll. London, UK; pianist, accompanist, chamber music player, music educator; Sr Lecturer in Music, Middx Polytechnic 1975–79, Goldsmiths, Univ. of London 1980–87; Head of Music, Dartington Coll. of Arts 1987–90, Dean Academic Affairs 1988–90, Acting Prin. 1990–91, Prin. 1991–93; Visiting Prof. of Music Educ., Univ. of Plymouth 1993–2005; Dir Royal Coll. of Music 1993–2005; Chair. Assoc. Bd Royal Schools of Music (Publishing) Ltd 1993–2005, The Mendelssohn and Boise Foundations 1996–98, 2002–04, Advisory Council, Arts Research Ltd 1997–2005, Fed. of British Conservatoires 1998–2003; Vice-Pres. Nat. Asscn of Youth Orchestras 1993–, Royal Coll. of Music 2005–; mem. Music Panel, Arts Council of England 1992–98, Council Royal Musical Asscn 1994–2004 (Vice-Pres. 1998–2004), Bd ENO 1996–2004, Exec. Cttee Inc. Soc. of Musicians 1996–99, Arts and Humanities Research Bd 1998–2004 (Postgraduate Panel 1998–2002, Chair. Postgraduate Cttee 2002–04), Nominating Cttee Arts and Humanities Research Council 2005–07, Bd Nat. Youth Orchestra 1999–2007, Steering Cttee, London Higher Educ. Consortium 1999–2005, Arts Council of England 2000–02, Dept for Educ. and Skills Advisory Group, Music and Dance Scheme 2000–05, Council of Goldsmiths, Univ. of London 2002–07, Bd Anglo-Austrian Soc. 2005–11, Bd The Voices Foundation 2005–11, Advisory Bd Inst. for Advanced Studies in the Humanities, Univ. of Edinburgh 2005–, Advisory Council Inst. of Germanic and Romance Studies 2005–10 and Inst. of Musical Research, Univ. of London 2006–12, Educ. Advisory Group Nuffield Foundation 2007–09; Chancellor, Middlesex Univ. 2013–; Trustee, Countess of Munster Musical Trust 1993–, Prince Consort Foundation 1993–2005, Plymouth Chamber Music Trust 2006–10; Gov. Associated Bd Royal Schools of Music 1993–2005, Purcell School 1996–2000, Heythrop Coll., Univ. of London 1996–2006, Dartington Coll. of Arts 2005–08, Middlesex Univ. 2005–, Univ. Coll. Falmouth 2008–, Royal Welsh Coll. of Music and Drama 2010–; mem. Österreichischer Wissenschaftsrat 2002–12; mem. Court, Worshipful Co. of Musicians 2005–11; Fellow, Royal Northern Coll. of Music 1996, Dartington Coll. of Arts 1997, Univ. Coll., Northampton 1997, Guildhall School of Music and Drama 2000, Higher Educ. Acad. 2007, Heythrop Coll. 2008, Goldsmiths, Univ. of London 2009; Sr Fellow, RCA 2004; Assoc. Fellow, Inst. of Musical Research, Univ. of London 2006–; Chair. Int. Advisory Bd, Programme for Arts-based Research, Austrian Science Fund 2009–; mem. Conseil de fondation, Haute École de Musique de Genève, Switzerland 2009–; Hon. RAM 1995; Hon. FGSM 2000; Hon. DUniv (Birmingham City) 1996, (Middlesex) 2005; Hon. DLitt (Ulster) 2004; Hon. DMus (Sydney) 2010. *Publications:* articles in learned journals in France, Germany, Australia and UK. *Leisure interests:* reading, theatre-going, country walking.

RITTNER, Luke Philip Hardwick, CBE; British arts administrator; *Chief Executive, Royal Academy of Dance;* b. 24 May 1947, Bath, England; s. of Stephen Rittner and Joane Rittner; m. Corinna Frances Edholm 1974; one d.; ed Blackfriars School, Laxton, City of Bath Tech. Coll., Dartington Coll. of Arts and London Acad. of Music and Dramatic Art; Asst Admin., Bath Festival 1968–71, Jt Admin. 1971–74, Admin. Dir 1974–76; Founder and Dir Asscn for Business Sponsorship of the Arts (now Arts & Business) 1976–83; Sec.-Gen. Arts Council of Great Britain 1983–90; UK Cultural Dir Expo '92 1990–92; Chair. English Shakespeare Co. 1990–94; Dir Marketing and Communications, Sotheby's Europe 1992–98; Chief Exec. Royal Acad. of Dance 1999–; Chair. London Chorus (fmrly The London Choral Soc.) 1994–, Exec. Bd London Acad. of Music and Dramatic Art 1994–; mem. Bd of Dirs Carlton Television 1991–93; Artistic Adviser to Spanish Arts Festival, London 1991–94; mem. Music Panel, British Council 1979–83, Council Victoria and Albert Museum 1980–83, J. Sainsbury Arts Sponsorship Panel 1990–96, Olivier Awards Theatre Panel 1992, Council Almeida Theatre 1997–2001; Gov. Urchfont Manor, Wiltshire Adult Educ. Centre 1982–83; Trustee, Bath Preservation Trust 1968–73, Theatre Royal, Bath 1979–82, Hanover Band 1998–2002; Foundation Trustee, Holburne Museum, Bath 1981–83; Patron, New London Orchestra; mem. Dance Panel, Olivier Awards 2003; Dr hc (Bath) 2004; Hon. DCL (Durham) 2006. *Leisure interest:* the arts. *Address:* Royal Academy of Dance, 36 Battersea Square, London, SW11 3RA, England (office). *Telephone:* (20) 7326-8000 (office). *E-mail:* info@rad.org.uk (office). *Website:* www.rad.org.uk (office).

RITZ, Gerry, PC; Canadian politician; b. 19 Aug. 1951, Delisle, Sask.; m. Judy Ritz; two s.; fmr farmer, owner/operator of gen. contracting firm, co-owner of weekly newspaper; mem. Reform Party of Canada 1997–2000, Canadian Alliance 2000–03, Conservative Party of Canada 2003–; MP for Battlefords-Lloydminster 1997–, Vice-Chair. Canada-China Legis. Asscn; Sec. of State for Small Business and Tourism 2007; Minister of Agric. and Agri-Food 2007–15, also Minister for the Canadian Wheat Bd. *Address:* House of Commons, Ottawa, ON K1A 0A6, Canada (office). *Telephone:* (613) 995-7080 (office). *Fax:* (613) 996-8472 (office). *E-mail:* gerry.ritz@parl.gc.ca (office). *Website:* www.parl.gc.ca (office); gerryritz.ca.

RITZEN, Jozef (Jo) Maria Mathias, MSc, PhD; Dutch politician, economist and university administrator; *Professor, Maastricht University;* b. 3 Oct. 1945, Heerlen, Limburg Prov.; m. Hanneke Smulders; four c.; ed Univ. of Tech., Delft, Erasmus Univ., Rotterdam; Project Asst, The Ford Foundation, Dacca 1970; Lecturer, Univ. of California, Berkeley 1971–75, Section Leader, Social and Cultural Planning Office 1975–81; Prof. of Educ. Econs, Nijmegen Univ. 1981–83; Prof. of Public Sector Econs, Erasmus Univ., Rotterdam 1983–89; sometime adviser to Minister of Social Affair, to Minister of Health, Welfare and Sports 1975; Minister of Educ., Culture and Science 1989–99; Special Adviser to the Human Devt Network, IBRD (World Bank) 1998, Vice-Pres. for Devt Policy 1999–2003; Pres. Maastricht Univ. 2003–11, Prof. 2011–; Sr Policy Adviser, Inst. for Study of Labour (IZA), Bonn 2011–; Chair. Empower European Univs 2011–; mem. Int. Advisory Bd, King Abdul Aziz Univ., Jeddah 2011–, Russian Acad. for Nat. Economy and Public Admin 2011–, Univ. Siegen 2011–; Kt, Order of Orange-Nassau, High Merit Cross (Germany), Kt, Order of Leopold (Belgium); Dr hc (Chinese Acad. of Social Sciences); Winkler Prins Prize for best dissertation 1977. *Publications:* 13 books; numerous articles in peer-reviewed and other journals on education, policy, economics, public sector and finance. *Address:* Kloosterweg 54, 6241 GB Bunde, Netherlands (home). *Telephone:* (43) 3261113 (office). *E-mail:* j.ritzen@maastrichtuniversity.nl (office). *Website:* www.empowereu.org (office).

RIVALDO; Brazilian professional footballer (retd); b. (Rivaldo Vitor Borba Ferreira), 19 April 1972, Paulista, Pernambuco; s. of Romildo Borreira; one s. one d.; played with Paulista, Santa Cruz 1989–91, Magi-Mirin 1992–93, Corinthians 1993–94, Palmeiras 1994–96 (won Brazilian Série A 1994, São Paulo State Championship 1994, 1996, Euro-America Cup 1996), Deportivo La Coruña, Spain (21 goals in 41 matches) 1996–97, FC Barcelona, Spain 1997–2002 (won La Liga 1998, 1999, Copa del Rey 1998, European Super Cup 1997), AC Milan, Italy 2002–03 (won UEFA Champions League 2003, Coppa Italia 2003, European Super Cup 2003), signed for Cruzeiro Jan. 2004 but left team 90 days later, with Olympiakos 2004–07 (won Greek League 2005, 2006, 2007, Greek Cup 2005, 2006), AEK Athens 2007–08, Bunyodkor, Uzbekistan 2008–10 (won Uzbek League 2008, 2009, Uzbekistani Cup 2008), Mogi Mirim, Brazil 2010–14; played for Brazil nat. team 1993–2003, scored eight goals in 14 World Cup finals games, runner-up 1998, winner 2002, winner Confederations Cup 1997, Copa América 1999; Pres. Mogi Mirim Esporte Clube 2014–; took retirement from Football 2014; Brazilian Bola de Prata 1993, 1994, named in FIFA World Cup All-Star Team 1998, 2002, FIFA World Player of the Year 1999, Ballon d'Or (European Footballer of the Year) 1999, World Soccer Player of the Year 1999, Onze d'Or 1999, Copa América Top Scorer 1999, Copa América MVP 1999, Spanish League Footballer of the Year 1999, UEFA Champions League Top Scorer 2000, named by Pelé as one of 125 Greatest Living Footballers, FIFA Awards Ceremony 2004, named in FIFA 100 2004, Greek

Championship Best Foreign Player 2006, 2007, Uzbek League Top Scorer 2009. *Address:* c/o Mogi Miram, Rua Dr. Ferreira Lima, 150, Centro Mogi Mirim /SP, Brazil. *Website:* www.mogimirim.com.br.

RIVAS FRANCHINI, Eda Adriana; Peruvian lawyer and politician; b. 23 March 1952, Lima; ed Pontificia Universidad Católica del Perú, Univ. of Las Palmas Gran Canaria, Spain, Univ. of Castilla La Mancha, Toledo; several years' experience in public sector bodies including Comm. for Promotion of Private Investment, Private Investment Promotion Agency, Empresa Nacional de Puertos SA, Organismo Supervisor de la Inversión en Infraestructura de Transporte de Uso Público; worked in Presidency of Council of Ministers; fmr mem. Cabinet of Advisers, Ministry of Justice, fmr Deputy Minister of Justice, Minister of Justice and Human Rights 2012–13, of Foreign Affairs 2013–14.

RIVERA, Chita; American actress, singer and dancer; b. (Dolores Conchita Figueroa del Rivero), 23 Jan. 1933, Washington, DC; d. of Pedro Julio Figuerva del Rivero and Katherine Anderson del Rivero; m. Anthony Mordente (divorced); one d.; ed American School of Ballet, New York; Kennedy Center Honor 2002, Presidential Medal of Freedom 2009, League of Professional Theatre Women's Lifetime Achievement Award 2010. *Stage appearances include:* Father's Day, Threepenny Opera, Born Yesterday, Jacques is Alive and Well and Living in Paris, Ivanhoe, Call Me Madam 1951, Guys and Dolls 1951, Can-Can 1953, Seventh Heaven 1955, Mister Wohderful 1956, West Side Story 1957, Bye Bye Birdie 1960, Flower Drum Song 1966, Sweet Charity 1967, Zorba 1969, Sondheim–A Musical Tribute 1973, Kiss Me Kate 1974, Chicago 1975, Bring Back Birdie 1981, Merlin 1983, The Rink (Tony Award 1984) 1984, Jerry's Girls 1985, Kiss of the Spider Woman (Tony Award for Best Actress in a Musical 1993) 1992, Chita Rivera: The Dancer's Life 2005, Chita Rivera: My Broadway 2010, The Mystery of Edwin Drood 2012, The Visit 2015. *Films:* Chicago 2002, Kalamazoo? 2006. *Television includes:* Kojak and the Marcus Nelson Murders 1973, The New Dick Van Dyke Show 1973–74, Kennedy Center Tonight–Broadway to Washington!, Pippin 1982, The Mayflower Madam 1987. *Recordings include:* And Now I Swing 2009. *Address:* c/o Ken DiCamillo, William Morris Endeavor Entertainment, 1325 Avenue of the Americas, New York, NY 10019, USA (office). *Telephone:* (212) 586-5100 (office). *Fax:* (212) 246-3583 (office). *E-mail:* kdicamillo@wmeentertainment.com (office). *Website:* wmeentertainment.com (office); www.chitarivera.com.

RIVERA, Geraldo, BS, JD; American broadcaster and journalist; b. 4 July 1943, New York; s. of Cruz Allen Rivera and Lillian Friedman; m. 1st Linda Coblentz 1965 (divorced 1969); m. 2nd Edith Vonnegut 1971 (divorced 1975); m. 3rd Sheri Rivera (divorced 1984); m. 4th C.. Dyer 1987 (divorced 2000); m. Erica Michelle Levy 2003; five c.; ed Univ. of Arizona, Brooklyn Law School; with Eyewitness News WABC-TV, New York 1970–75, reporter, Good Morning America, American Broadcasting Co. (ABC) 1973–76, corresp. and host, Good Night America 1975–77, corresp. and Sr Producer, 20/20 Newsmagazine 1978–85, host, syndicated talk show The Geraldo Rivera Show 1987–98; joined CNBC, host, Rivera Life 1994–2001; joined Fox News Channel 2001, war reporter in Afghanistan, Somalia, Lebanon, Israel and Sudan, host, Geraldo at Large (now Geraldo Rivera Reports); ten Emmy Awards, three Peabody Awards, Kennedy Journalism Award 1973, 1975, 2000, two Columbia DuPont Award, two Scripps Howard Journalism Awards and numerous other awards. *Publications:* Willowbrook 1972, Miguel 1972, Puerto Rico: Island of Contrasts 1973, A Special Kind of Courage 1976, Exposing Myself 1991, His Panic: Why Americans Fear Hispanics in the US 2008, The Great Progression: How Hispanics Will Lead America to a New Era of Prosperity 2010. *Leisure interest:* sailing. *Address:* Geraldo Rivera Reports, FOX News Network, LLC, 1211 Avenue of the Americas, New York, NY 10036, USA (office). *Website:* www.foxnews.com/on-air/geraldo/index.html (office); www.geraldo.com.

RIVERA CARRERA, HE Cardinal Norberto, DD; Mexican ecclesiastic; *Archbishop of México, Federal District and Archbishop Primate of Mexico;* b. 6 June 1942, La Purísima, Durango; s. of Ramón Rivera Cháidez and Soledad Carrera de Rivera; ed Conciliary Seminary, Durango, Gregorian Univ., Rome; ordained priest 1966; Prof. of Dogmatic Theology Seminario Mayor, Durango 1967–85; Prof. of Ecclesiology, Pontificia Universidad de México 1982–85, mem. sr council 1993–95, vice-grand councillor 1995–; Bishop of Tehuacán 1985; Archbishop of México, DF and Archbishop Primate of Mexico 1995–; cr. Cardinal (Cardinal-Priest of San Francesco d'Assisi a Ripa Grande) 1998; participated in Papal Conclave 2005, 2013; mem. Secr. for the Economy 2014–; Pres. Episcopal Comm. for Culture, Inter-religion Council of Mexico, Ecumenical Council of Mexico, Exec. Council of Mexico City Historic Centre; mem. numerous cttees and councils, including the perm. Sinod of Bishops. *Address:* Curia Arzobispal, Aptdo Postal 24-433, Durango 90, 5°, Col Roma, CP 06700 México, DF, Mexico (office). *Telephone:* (5) 208-3200 (office). *Fax:* (5) 208-5350 (office). *E-mail:* arzobisp@arquidiocesismexico.org.mx (office). *Website:* www.arzobispadomexico.org.mx (office).

RIVERA DÍAZ, Albert; Spanish lawyer and politician; *President, Ciudadanos;* b. 15 Nov. 1979, Barcelona; s. of Agustín Rivera and María Jesús Díaz; ed Universidad Ramon Llull, Barcelona; began career as lawyer with Caja de Ahorros y Pensiones de Barcelona (savings bank) 2002–06; mem. Parl. of Catalonia 2006–15; Founding mem. and Pres. Ciudadanos (Citizens) 2006–. *Achievements include:* fmr competitive swimmer, won Catalan championship whilst at school. *Publications:* Juntos Podemos, el futuro está en nuestras manos 2014, El cambio sensato 2015. *Address:* Ciudadanos, Gran Vía 751a, 1°, 08013 Barcelona, Spain (office). *Telephone:* (93) 3429436 (office). *E-mail:* info@ciudadanos-cs.org (office). *Website:* www.ciudadanos-cs.org (office).

RIVKIN, Charles H.; American business executive and diplomatist; s. of William R. Rivkin; m. Susan Tolson; two c.; ed Yale Univ., Harvard Univ.; internships with Renault and Columbia Pictures; financial analyst, Salomon Brothers 1984–86; Dir of Planning, Jim Henson Co. 1988–90, mem. Bd of Dirs 1990–2005, Vice-Pres. 1990–91, Sr Vice-Pres. and COO 1991–94, Exec. Vice-Pres. and COO 1994–95, Pres. and COO 1995–2000, Pres. and CEO 2000–03; Pres. and CEO Wildbrain entertainment co. 2005–09; Amb. to France (also accred to Monaco) 2009–13; mem. Young Pres' Org. 1996–2009, Pacific Council on Int. Policy 2007–, Homeland Security Advisory Council, Business Execs for Nat. Security 2008–09; Chair. Bel-Air 2004–05; Dir Chrysalis-Changing Lives through Jobs 1996–2002, Save the Children 1997–2003; served as an at-large California del. to Democratic Nat. Convention for Senator John Kerry 2004, for Senator Barack Obama 2008; BAFTA Award for Best Int. Children's Television Show, Spirit of Chrysalis Award. *Address:* US Department of State, 2201 C Street NW, Washington, DC 20520, USA (office). *Telephone:* (202) 647-4000 (office). *Fax:* (202) 647-6738 (office). *Website:* www.state.gov (office).

RIVLIN, Alice Mitchell, MA, PhD; American economist and fmr government official; *Director, Greater Washington Research Program, Brookings Institution;* b. 4 March 1931, Philadelphia, Pa; d. of Allan Mitchell and Georgianna Fales; m. 1st Lewis A. Rivlin 1955 (divorced 1977); two s. one d.; m. 2nd Sidney G. Winter 1989; ed Bryn Mawr Coll. and Radcliffe Coll.; mem. staff, Brookings Inst. Washington, DC 1957–66, 1969–75, 1983–93, Dir of Econ. Studies 1983–87, apptd Sr Fellow, Johnson Chair. 1999, currently Dir Greater Washington Research Program; Dir Congressional Budget Office 1975–83; Prof. of Public Policy, George Mason Univ. 1992; Deputy Dir US Office of Man. and Budget 1993–94, Dir 1994–96; Vice-Chair Fed. Reserve Bd 1996–99; Chair. Dist of Columbia Financial Control Bd 1998–2001; Visiting Prof., Public Policy Inst., Georgetown Univ.; mem. Bd of Dirs BearingPoint, Washington Post Co.; mem. American Econ. Asscn (Nat. Pres. 1986); MacArthur Fellow 1983–88. *Publications include:* The Role of the Federal Government in Financing Higher Education 1961, Microanalysis of Socioeconomic Systems (jtly) 1961, Systematic Thinking for Social Action 1971, Economic Choices (jtly) 1986, The Swedish Economy (jtly) 1987, Caring for the Disabled Elderly: Who Will Pay? 1988, Reviving the American Dream 1992, The Economic Payoff from the Internet Revolutioin 2001, Beyond the Dot.coms 2001, Restoring Fiscal Sanity 2004. *Address:* Brookings Institution, Center on Urban and Metropolitan Policy, 1755 Massachusetts Avenue, NW, Washington, DC 20036-2188, USA (office). *Telephone:* (202) 797-6026 (office). *Fax:* (202) 797-2965 (office). *E-mail:* ARivlin@brookings.edu (office). *Website:* www.brookings.edu (office).

RIVLIN, Reuven, LLB; Israeli lawyer, politician and head of state; *President;* b. 9 Sept. 1939, Jerusalem; s. of Yosef Yoel Rivlin; m. Nechama Rivlin; four c.; ed Hebrew Univ. of Jerusalem; fmr intelligence officer, Israel Defense Forces; early career as lawyer; mem. Jerusalem City Council 1978–88, leader of Herut party in Jerusalem City Council 1986–93; mem. Knesset (Parl.) 1988–92, 1996–2014, Speaker 2003–06, 2009–13; Minister of Communications 2001–03; Likud cand. in presidential election 2007; Pres. of Israel June 2014–; mem. Exec. Council, El Al 1981–86; mem. Bd of Trustees, Khan Theater, Israel Museum, Jerusalem; fmr team man., legal adviser and Chair., Beitar Jerusalem football team; mem. Likud. *Leisure interest:* football. *Address:* Office of the President, 3 Hanassi Street, Jerusalem 92188, Israel (office). *Telephone:* 2-6707211 (office). *Fax:* 2-5887225 (office). *E-mail:* public@president.gov.il (office). *Website:* www.president.gov.il (office).

RIZA, Iqbal, MA; Pakistani UN official; *Special Adviser to the Secretary-General, United Nations;* b. 20 May 1934, Lonavla, India; s. of Sharif Alijan; m. 1959; two s.; ed Univ. of Punjab, Lahore, Fletcher School of Int. Law, Boston; Pakistan Foreign Service 1958–77; served in Madrid 1959–61, Bonn 1962–64, Khartoum 1964–66, London 1966–68; Dir Foreign Service Acad., Lahore 1968–71; Deputy Chief of Mission, Paris and Deputy Perm. Rep. to UNESCO 1972–76; joined UN 1978, Sec. Cttee on the Exercise of the Inalienable Rights of the Palestinian People 1978–80, Prin. Officer, UN Dept of Public Information 1980–82; assigned to negotiations in Iran–Iraq war 1981–87; Dir Office for Special Political Affairs 1983–88, Div. for Political and Gen. Ass. Affairs 1988–89; Chief, UN Observer Mission for verification of the electoral process in Nicaragua (ONUVEN) 1989–90; Chief of Mission of UN Transition Team in El Salvador March–Aug. 1990; Special Rep. of UN Sec.-Gen. and Chief of UN Observer Mission in El Salvador (ONUSAL) 1991–93; Asst Sec.-Gen. for Peace-keeping Operations 1993–96, Coordinator of UN operations in Bosnia-Herzegovina Feb.–Dec. 1996, Under-Sec.-Gen., Chef de Cabinet in Exec. Office of Sec.-Gen. Kofi Annan 1997–2005 (retd); currently Special Adviser to UN Sec.-Gen.; mem. UN Advisory Bd on Human Security. *Leisure interests:* reading, music, riding. *Address:* c/o Executive Office of the UN Secretary-General, United Nations Plaza, New York, NY 10017, USA (office).

RIZAYEV, Ramiz Gasangulu oglu, DrChemSc; Azerbaijani chemist and diplomatist; b. 2 Nov. 1939, Nakhichevan; m.; one s. one d.; ed Azerbaijan State Univ.; corresp. mem. Azerbaijan Acad. of Sciences 1983, mem. 2001–; Dir Inst. of Inorganic and Physical Chem. Azerbaijan Acad. of Sciences 1985–93; Plenipotentiary Rep., then Amb. of Azerbaijan to Russian Fed. 1993–2006; numerous inventions in the field of oil extraction and oil processing, 36 patents in various cos; mem. Scientific Council on Catalysis, Russian Acad. of Sciences; mem. Int. Acad. of Eng Sciences 2000–; mem. Ed. Bd Neftekhimiya (journal); Honoured Engineer of Russian Fed. 2000. *Publications:* 250 scientific articles on problems of oil chem. and chemical catalysis.

RIZHVADZE, Tornike, LLB, LLM, PhD, MBA; Georgian politician; *Chairman of the Government, Autonomous Republic of Ajara;* b. 25 March 1989, Khulo, Ajaran ASSR, Georgia SSR, USSR; m.; two c.; ed Tbilisi State Univ., Batumi Shota Rustaveli State Univ., Univ. of London, Taras Shevchenko Nat. Univ., Kyiv; Intern, CHF International (USAID program) 2008–09; Intern, Financial Innovation Center (CSFI), London 2012–13; Enterprise and Consulting Activities, Donor Funded Project Management (EBRD Small and Medium Business Support Program) 2007–13; Business Consultant and Employer Relations Coordinator, Int. Org. for Migration 2010–11; Ajara Regional Man., SC Open Revolution Georgia 2011–12; Advisor on Investment and Econ. Issues, Govt of Autonomous Repub. of Ajara Econ. Council 2014–16; Legal Advisor, Ajaristskali Georgia Ltd (energy jt venture) 2013–15, Legal Dir 2015–17; Deputy Minister of Energy July–Dec. 2017; Dir, Georgian Energy Devt Fund 2017–; Chair. of the Govt, Autonomous Repub. of Ajara 2018–. *Address:* Office of the Chairman of the Government, Autonomous Republic of Ajara, 6010 Ajara, Batumi, Gamsakhurdia 109, Georgia (office). *Telephone:* (22) 227-20-06 (office). *E-mail:* info@ajara.gov.ge (office). *Website:* ajara.gov.ge (office).

RIZO CASTELLÓN, José; Nicaraguan lawyer and politician; b. 27 Sept. 1944, Jinotega; ed Univ. Central of Managua, Univ. of Grenoble, France, International Univ. and London School of Economics, UK; held several positions with Ministry of Foreign Affairs, including Deputy Chief of Protocol, Deputy Nat. Dir of Tourism, Head of Mission, Embassy in London, served as Rep. of Nicaragua to Coffee, Sugar and Cocoa Exchange, London and Geneva; fmr Sec. of Mayor of Managua; Vice-Pres. of Nicaragua 2002–05 (resgnd); unsuccessful cand. for Pres. of Nicaragua 2006; Co-founder Partido Liberal Constitucionalista (PLC), has held several party positions including Nat. Treasurer, Sec. Nat., First Vice-Pres., Nat. Chair., now Hon. Pres.; fmr Vice-Pres. Liberal International; currently coffee farmer, Jinotega; Order of the Five Volcanoes (Maximum Gran Cruz) (Guatemala), Order of the Star (China), Order Don Henry the Navigator (Portugal), Order of Civil Merit (Spain); Dr hc (Nicaraguan Univ. of Science and Technology), (Nanhua Univ., China); Jubilee Medal (UK), Champion Award Democracy, US Republican Party, ia). *Address:* c/o Partido Liberal Constitucionalista (PLC), Semáforos Country Club 100 m al este, Apdo 4569, Managua, Nicaragua.

RIZZOLI, Angelo, Jr; Italian film producer and publisher; b. 12 Nov. 1943, Como; s. of Andrea Rizzoli and Lucia Rizzoli (née Solmi); m. Eleonora Giorgi 1979; one c.; fmr Pres. and Man. Ed. Rizzoli Editore, Pres. Cineriz Distributori Associati; Pres. Rizzoli Film 1978–. *Films produced include:* Per grazia ricevuta 1971, Paura e amore 1988, Acque di primavera 1989, Stanno tutti bene 1990, Pore aperte 1990, La Settimana della sfinge 1990, In nome del popolo sovrano 1990, The Comfort of Strangers 1990, To Meteoro vima tou pelargou 1991, Paris s'eveille 1991, Il Ladro di bambini 1992, Un Altra vita 1992, Padre e figlio 1994, Anche i commercialisti hanno un'anima 1994. *Television productions include:* Le Ragazze di Piazza di Spagna (TV series) 1998, Le Ali della vita 2000, Padre Pio 2000, Gioco di specchi 2000, Piccolo mondo antico 2001, Le Ali della vita 2 2001, Cuccioli 2002, Tutti i sogni del mondo 2003, Ferrari 2003, I Ragazzi della via Pal 2003, Al di la delle frontiere (miniseries) 2004, Il Bell'Antonio (miniseries) 2005, 48 ore (series) 2006, La Provinciale 2006, La Freccia nera (miniseries) 2006, Capri (series) 2006, Mafalda di Savoia (miniseries) 2006, Le Ragazze di San Frediano 2007, Il Giudice Mastrangelo (series) 2005–07. *Address:* Via Angelo Rizzoli 2, 20132 Milan, Italy (office). *Telephone:* (02) 25841.

RO, Tu-chol; North Korean politician; *Vice-Premier and Chairman of the State Planning Commission;* Deputy, Supreme People's Ass.; Vice-Chair. State Planning Comm. –2003, Chair. 2009–; Vice-Premier 2003–. *Address:* Office of the Vice-Premier of the Cabinet, Pyongyang, Democratic People's Republic of Korea.

ROBB, Andrew, FCMA; British business executive; *Chairman, Tata Steel Europe Ltd;* m.; two c.; earlier career with Unilever Ltd; various financial positions at P&O Steam Navigation Co. 1971–89, Finance Dir 1983–89; Finance Dir Pilkington plc 1989–2001, Exec. Dir 1989–2003; mem. Bd of Dirs Corus Group plc and Chair. Audit Cttee 2003– (Corus taken over by Tata Steel March 2007), Dir (non-exec.) Tata Steel Ltd 2007– (remained Chair. Audit Cttee and certain other bd cttees of Tata Steel Europe), Chair. Tata Steel Europe Ltd 2009–; Chair. Kesa Electricals plc, Laird plc; mem. Bd of Dirs Paypoint plc, Jaguar Land Rover Automotive plc 2011–; Fellow, Chartered Inst. of Cost and Man. Accountants, Inst. of Corp. Treas; mem. Urgent Issues Task Force of the Accounting Standards Bd 1991–97. *Address:* Tata Steel Europe Limited, 30 Millbank, London, SW1P 4WY, England (office). *Telephone:* (20) 7717-4444 (office). *Fax:* (20) 7717-4455 (office). *E-mail:* feedback@tatasteel.com (office). *Website:* www.tatasteeleurope.com (office).

ROBB, Charles Spittal, BBA, JD; American lawyer, academic and fmr politician; *Distinguished Professor of Law and Public Policy, George Mason University;* b. 26 June 1939, Phoenix, Ariz.; s. of James Spittal Robb and Frances Howard Robb (née Woolley); m. Lynda Johnson (d. of the late Pres. Lyndon B. Johnson) 1967; three d.; ed Cornell Univ., Univ. of Wisconsin, Univ. of Virginia; served on active duty with US Marine Corps during 1960s, including service in 1st and 2nd Marine Divs, assignments included duty as military social aide at White House and command of an infantry co. in combat in Viet Nam, retd from Marine Corps Reserve 1991; admitted to Va Bar 1973; law clerk to John D. Butzner, Jr, US Court of Appeals 1973–74; admitted to US Supreme Court Bar 1976; Attorney, Williams, Connolly and Califano 1974–77; Lt-Gov. of Va 1978–82, Gov. of Va 1982–86; Partner, Hunton and Williams 1986–89; Senator from Virginia 1989–2001; Distinguished Prof. of Law and Public Policy, George Mason Univ. 2001–; Co-Chair. Iraq Intelligence Comm. 2004–05; Co-Chair. Aspen Inst./Rockefeller Comm. to Reform the Presidential Appointments Process, Iranian Nuclear Development Taskforce at Bipartisan Policy Center, Pew/Peterson Foundation's Cttee for a Responsible Federal Budget; Vice-Chair. Concord Coalition; Chair. Democratic Govs Asscn 1984–85, Southern Govs Asscn 1984–85; Chair. Democratic Leadership Council 1986–88; Pres. Council of State Govts 1985–86; Co-Chair. Pres.'s Comm. on Intelligence Capabilities 2004; mem. Bd of Dirs Invacare Corpn 2010–, Nat. Museum for Americans in Wartime, Research Strategies Network; mem. Bd of Trustees, The MITRE Corpn 2001–, Vice-Chair. 2006–14, Chair. 2014–; mem. Advisory Bd Center for Infrastructure Protection, Center for the Study of the Presidency and Congress, Robertson Foundation, Univ. of Virginia Batten School of Leadership and Public Policy, George Washington Univ. Homeland Security Policy Inst.; fmr mem. Iraq Study Group, Pres.'s Foreign Intelligence Advisory Bd, Sec. of State's Arms Control and Nonproliferation Advisory Bd, FBI Dir's Advisory Bd; fmr Chair. Bd of Visitors, US Naval Acad.; fmr mem. Bd of Dirs Space Foundation, Thomas Jefferson Program in Public Policy; Fellow, Inst. of Politics, Harvard Univ., Marshall Wythe School of Law, Coll. of William & Mary; mem. ABA, Va Bar Asscn, Va Trial Lawyers Asscn; mem. Bd of Regents Uniformed Services Univ. of the Health Sciences; Democrat; Bronze Star, Viet Nam Service Medal with four stars, Vietnamese Cross of Gallantry with Silver Star; Raven Award 1973; Seven Socs Org. Award, Univ. of Va. *Address:* School of Law, George Mason University, Room 415, 3301 North Fairfax Drive, Arlington, VA 22201, USA (office). *Telephone:* (703) 993-8000 (office). *Fax:* (703) 993-8088 (office). *Website:* www.law.gmu.edu (office).

ROBB, Graham Macdonald, PhD, FRSL; British writer and historian; b. 2 June 1958, Manchester, England; m. Margaret Hambrick 1986; ed Univ. of Oxford, Goldsmiths Coll., London and Vanderbilt Univ., USA; British Acad. Fellowship 1987–90; Chevalier des Arts et des Lettres; Grande Médaille de la Ville de Paris 2012; New York Times Book of the Year 1994, 1999 and 2001, Whitbread Biography of the Year Award 1997, R.S.L. Heinemann Award 1998. *Publications include:* Le Corsaire – Satan en Silhouette 1985, Baudelaire Lecteur de Balzac 1988, Scènes de la Vie de Bohème (ed.) 1988, Baudelaire (trans.) 1989, La Poésie de Baudelaire et la Poésie Française 1993, Balzac 1994, Unlocking Mallarmé 1996, Victor Hugo: A Biography 1998, Rimbaud 2000, Strangers: Homosexual Love in

the 19th Century, The Discovery of France (Duff Cooper Prize, Ondaatje Prize, Royal Soc. of Literature 2008) 2007, Parisians: An Adventure History of Paris 2010, The Discovery of Middle Earth: Mapping the Lost World of the Celts 2013, Cols and Passes of the British Isles 2016; contribs to Times Literary Supplement, Daily Telegraph, London Review of Books, Sunday Times, New York Times. *Leisure interest:* cycling. *Address:* c/o Rogers, Coleridge & White Ltd, 20 Powis Mews, London, W11 1JN, England (office).

ROBB, J. D. (see ROBERTS, Nora).

RÖBBELEN, Gerhard Paul Karl, Dr rer. nat; German professor of plant breeding; *Professor Emeritus, University of Göttingen;* b. 10 May 1929, Bremen; s. of Ernst Röbbelen and Henny Röbbelen; m. Christa Scherz 1957; two s. one d.; ed Univs of Göttingen and Freiburg; Asst Prof. Inst. of Agronomy and Plant Breeding, Univ. of Göttingen 1957–67, Prof. and Head Div. of Cytogenetics 1967–70, Dir of Inst. 1970–94, Dean Faculty of Agric. 1971–72, Prof. Emer. 1994–; Visiting Prof. Univ. of Mo., USA 1966–67; Ed. Plant Breeding 1976–2000; mem. German Soc. for Genetics (Pres. 1969–70, 1977–79), European Asscn for Research in Plant Breeding–EUCARPIA (Chair. Section for Oil and Protein Crops 1978–86, Pres. 1986–89), German Botanical Soc., Asscn for Applied Botany, Genetics Soc. of Canada, German Soc. Fat Research (Pres. 1989–92), German Soc. of Plant Breeding (Pres. 1991–96), Acad. of Sciences, Göttingen 1981, Acad. Leopoldina 1990; Order of Merit 1st Class (Germany) 2001; Hon. DAgric. (Kiel) 1976, (Halle/Saale) 1997, (Brno Czech Repub.) 2001; Norman Medal, German Soc. of Fat Science 1984, Chevreul Medal, Asscn Française pour l'Etude des Corps Gras 1989, Eminent Scientist Award, Paris 1999. *Publications:* more than 300 articles on research into plant genetics and breeding. *Leisure interests:* music, mountain climbing, gardening. *Address:* University of Göttingen, Stift am Klausberg, App. 534, Habichtsweg 55, 37075 Göttingen, Germany (office). *Website:* www.uni -goettingen.de (office).

ROBBINS, Charles H. (Chuck), BS; American business executive; *CEO, Cisco Systems, Inc.;* b. 1965; m.; four c.; ed Univ. of North Carolina; joined Cisco Systems Inc. as an Account Man. 1997, held several managerial positions within sales organization 1997–2002, Vice-Pres. 2002, assumed leadership of US channel sales org. 2002–07 and of Canadian channel sales org. 2005–07, Sr Vice-Pres., US Commercial 2007–09, Sr Vice-Pres., US Enterprise, Commercial and Canada 2009–11, Sr Vice-Pres., Americas 2011–12, Sr Vice-Pres., Worldwide Field Operations 2012–15, mem. Bd of Dirs and CEO Cisco Systems, Inc. 2015–; mem. Bd, MS Soc. of Northern California, Georgia Tech Advisory Bd for the Pres. of Georgia Tech. *Address:* Cisco Systems, Inc., Building 10, 170 West Tasman Drive, San Jose, CA 95134-1706, USA (office). *Telephone:* (408) 526-4000 (office). *Fax:* (408) 526-4100 (office). *E-mail:* jochambe@cisco.com (office). *Website:* www.cisco .com (office).

ROBBINS, John B., MD; American immunologist and academic; *Head, Laboratory of Developmental and Molecular Immunity, National Institute of Child Health and Human Development;* b. 1 Dec. 1932, Brooklyn, New York; ed New York Univ.; Chief, Lab. of Developmental and Molecular Immunity, Nat. Inst. of Child Health and Human Devt, NIH 1983–; fmr Chair. WHO Ad Hoc Cttee; mem. American Asscn of Immunologists 1965–, NAS, Inst. of Medicine; Assoc. Ed. The Journal of Immunology 1974–78; Albert Lasker Award for Clinical Research (jtly) 1996, Pasteur Award, WHO 2001, Albert B. Sabin Gold Medal Award 2001. *Publications include:* Bacterial Vaccines (ed.) 1987, The Awakened Heart 1997, Diet for a New America: How Your Food Choices Affect Your Health, Happiness, and the Future of Life on Earth 1998, Internal Medicine on Call (co-author) 2002, Reclaiming Our Health – Exploding the Medical Myth and Embracing the Sources of True Healing 2004. *Address:* Office of the Chief, Laboratory of Developmental and Molecular Immunity, National Institute of Child Health and Human Development, 6A/2A06, 31 Center Drive, Bethesda, MD 20892, USA (office). *Telephone:* (301) 496-0850 (office). *E-mail:* robbinsj@nichd.nih.gov (office). *Website:* www.nichd.nih.gov (office).

ROBBINS, Keith Gilbert, DPhil, DLitt, FRSE, FLSW; British historian, academic and fmr university vice-chancellor; b. 9 April 1940, Bristol; s. of Gilbert Henry John Robbins and Edith Mary Robbins; m. Janet Carey Thomson 1963; three s. one d.; ed Bristol Grammar School, Magdalen Coll. Oxford, St Antony's Coll. Oxford; Lecturer, Univ. of York 1963–71; Prof. of History, Univ. Coll. of N Wales, Bangor 1971–79; Prof. of Modern History, Univ. of Glasgow 1980–91; Vice-Chancellor Univ. of Wales, Lampeter 1992–2003; Sr Vice-Chancellor Univ. of Wales 1995–2001; Pres. Historical Asscn 1988–91; Winston Churchill Travelling Fellow 1990; Fellow, Learned Soc. of Wales. *Publications:* Munich 1938, 1968, Sir Edward Grey 1971, The Abolition of War 1976, John Bright 1979, The Eclipse of a Great Power: Modern Britain 1870–1975 1983, 1870–1992 (second edn) 1994, The First World War 1984, Nineteenth-Century Britain: Integration and Diversity 1988, Appeasement 1988, Blackwell Dictionary of Twentieth-Century British Political Life (ed.) 1990, Churchill 1992, History, Religion and Identity in Modern Britain 1993, Politicians, Diplomacy and War in Modern British History 1994, Bibliography of British History 1914–1989 1996, Great Britain: Identities, Institutions and the Idea of Britishness 1997, The World Since 1945: a Concise History 1998, The British Isles 1901–1951 2002, Britain and Europe 1789–2005 2005, England, Ireland, Scotland, Wales: The Christian Church 1900–2000 (ed.) 2008, The Dynamics of Religious Reform in Northern Europe 1780–1920, Political and Legal Perspectives (ed.) 2010; Religion and Diplomacy: Religion and British Foreign Policy 1815 to 1941 2010, Pride of Place: A Modern History of Bristol Grammar School 2010, Transforming the World: Global Political History since World War II 2013. *Leisure interests:* walking, music. *Address:* Gothic House, 48 Bridge Street, Pershore, Worcestershire, WR10 1AT, England (home). *Telephone:* (1386) 555709 (home). *E-mail:* profkgr@clara.co.uk (home).

ROBBINS, Tim, BA; American actor, director and screenwriter; b. 16 Oct. 1958, West Covina, Calif.; s. of folk singer Gil Robbins; fmr pnr Susan Sarandon (q.v.); three c.; ed Univ. of California, Los Angeles; began career as mem. Theater for the New City; Founding Artistic Dir The Actors' Gang 1981–; Founder Havoc Inc. (production co.); Crystal Globe For Outstanding Artistic Contrib. To World Cinema, Karlovy Vary Int. Film Festival 2018. *Theatre includes:* as actor: Ubu Roi 1981; as dir: A Midsummer Night's Dream 1984, The Good Woman of Setzuan 1990; as writer, with Adam Simon: Alagazam, After the Dog Wars, Violence: The

Misadventures of Spike Spangle, Farmer, Carnage – A Comedy (rep. USA at Edin. Int. Festival, Scotland); as writer: Embedded 2004. *Films include:* No Small Affair 1984, Toy Soldiers 1984, The Sure Thing 1985, Fraternity Vacation 1985, Top Gun 1986, Howard the Duck 1986, Five Corners 1987, Bull Durham 1988, Tapeheads 1988, Miss Firecracker 1989, Eric the Viking 1989, Cadillac Man 1990, Twister 1990, Jacob's Ladder 1990, Jungle Fever 1991, The Player 1992, Bob Roberts (also writer and dir) 1992, Amazing Stories: Book Four 1992, Short Cuts 1993, The Hudsucker Proxy 1994, The Shawshank Redemption 1994, Prêt-à-Porter 1994, I.Q. 1994, Dead Man Walking (writer and dir) 1995, Nothing to Lose 1997, Arlington Road 1999, Cradle Will Rock (also writer and dir) 1999, Austin Powers: The Spy Who Shagged Me 1999, Mission to Mars 2000, High Fidelity 2000, Antitrust 2001, Human Nature 2001, The Truth About Charlie 2002, The Day My God Died 2003, Mystic River (Golden Globe for Best Supporting Actor 2004, Critics' Choice Award for Best Supporting Actor 2004, Screen Actors Guild Best Supporting Actor Award 2004, Acad. Award for Best Supporting Actor 2004) 2003, Code 46 2003, The Secret Life of Words 2005, War of the Worlds 2005, La Vida secreta de las palabras 2005, Zathura: A Space Adventure 2005, Catch a Fire 2006, Tenacious D: The Pick of Destiny 2006, Noise 2007, The Lucky Ones 2008, City of Ember 2008, Green Lantern 2011. *Television:* Queens Supreme (pilot episode and series dir) 2003, Cinema Verite (movie) 2011. *Address:* c/o Elaine Goldsmith Thomas, ICM, 40 West 57th Street, New York, NY 10019 (office); Havoc Inc., 16 West 19th Street, 12th Floor, New York, NY 10011; The Actors' Gang at The Ivy Substation, 9070 Venice Blvd., Culver City, CA 90232, USA. *Website:* www.theactorsgang.com.

ROBBINS, Thomas (Tom) Eugene, BA; American writer; b. 22 July 1932, Blowing Rock, NC; s. of George T. Robbins and Katherine Robinson Robbins; m. 1st Terrie Lunden 1967 (divorced 1972); three s.; m. 2nd Alexa d'Avalon 1987; ed Virginia Commonwealth Univ. and Univ. of Washington; U.S. Air Force 1953–57; mem. staff, Times-Dispatch, Richmond, Va 1959–62; Art Critic, The Seattle Times and contrib. to Artforum and Art in America etc. 1962–65; Art Critic, Seattle Magazine 1965–67; Bumbershoot Golden Umbrella for Lifetime Achievement 1998, Writers' Digest 100 Best Writers of the 20th Century 2000, Willamette Writers' Distinguished Northwest Writer Award 2001, Literary Lifetime Achievement Award, Library of Virginia 2012. *Films:* Even Cowgirls Get the Blues 1994. *Plays:* Even Cowgirls Get the Blues 2012, Still Life with Woodpecker 2015–16. *Publications include:* novels: Another Roadside Attraction 1971, Even Cowgirls Get the Blues 1976, Still Life With Woodpecker 1980, Jitterbug Perfume 1984, Skinny Legs and All 1990, Half Asleep in Frog Pajamas 1994, Fierce Invalids Home from Hot Climates 2000, Villa Incognito 2003, Wild Ducks Flying Backward 2005, B is for Beer 2009, Tibetan Peach Pie 2014. *Leisure interests:* volleyball, white magick, psychedelic plants, art, pop culture and religions. *Address:* PO Box 338, La Conner, WA 98257, USA (home).

ROBBINS, Trevor William, CBE, BA (Hons), MA, PhD, FRS, FMedSci; British neuroscientist and academic; *Professor of Cognitive Neuroscience and Director, Behavioural and Clinical Neuroscience Institute, University of Cambridge;* b. 26 Nov. 1949, London, England; s. of William Robbins and Eileen Robbins; m. Barbara Jacquelyn Sahakian; ed Battersea Grammar School, London, Jesus Coll., Cambridge; Prof. of Cognitive Neuroscience, Univ. of Cambridge 1997–, elected to Chair of Experimental Psychology and Head of Dept of Experimental Psychology 2002–, Dir Behavioural and Clinical Neuroscience Inst. 2011–, Fellow of Downing Coll.; Pres. European Behavioural Pharmacology Soc. 1992–94, British Asscn of Psychopharmacology 1996–97, British Neuroscience Asscn 2009–11; Man. Ed. Psychopharmacology 1980–; Advisory Ed., Science 2003–; mem. MRC, Chair. Neuroscience and Mental Health Bd 1995–99; Fellow, British Psychological Soc.; an ISI Most-cited Neuroscientist; Spearman Medal 1982, DM Marquis Award for the Best Paper in Behavioural Neuroscience, British Psychological Soc. 1996, inaugural Distinguished Scientist Award, European Behavioural Pharmacology Soc. 2001, IPSEN Neuronal Plasticity Prize 2005, Distinguished Scientific Contrib., American Psychological Asscn 2011, Grete Lundbeck Brain Prize 2014, Lifetime Achievement Award, British Asscn for Psychopharmacology 2015, Goldman-Rakic Prize 2017. *Publications:* Psychology for Medicine: The Prefrontal Cortex (co-ed.), Executive and Cognitive Function (co-ed.), Disorders of Brain and Mind (co-ed.), Translational Neuroscience (co-ed.); more than 750 papers in professional journals. *Leisure interests:* chess, cricket, cinema, art, theatre, opera, literature. *Address:* Behavioural and Clinical Neurosciences Institute, Department of Experimental Psychology, University of Cambridge, Downing Site, Cambridge, CB2 3EB, England (office). *Telephone:* (1223) 333551 (home). *Fax:* (1223) 333564 (office). *E-mail:* t.robbins@psychol.cam.ac.uk (office); twr2@cam.ac.uk (office). *Website:* research.psychol.cam.ac.uk/~bcni (office); www.psychol.cam.ac.uk (office); www.neuroscience.cam.ac.uk (office).

ROBERT, Jacques Frédéric, DenD; French professor of law; b. 29 Sept. 1928, Algiers, Algeria; s. of Frédéric Robert and Fanny Robert; m. Marie-Caroline de Bary 1958; two s. two d.; ed Lycée E. F. Gautier, Algiers, Univs. of Algiers and Paris, CNRS; Prof. of Law, Univs of Algiers 1956–60, Rabat, Morocco 1960–62, Grenoble 1962–65; Dir Maison franco-japonaise, Tokyo 1965–68; Prof. of Law, Univ. of Nanterre 1968–69, Univ. of Paris II 1969–; Contributor, Le Monde and La Croix 1970; Dir Revue de droit public 1977; Pres. Univ. of Paris II (Panthéon) 1979–85; apptd Pres. of Centre français de Droit comparé 1985; mem. Conseil Constitutionnel 1989–98; mem. Japan Acad. 1997; Commdr Légion d'honneur, Ordre nat. du Mérite, Order of Honour Austria; Order of the Sacred Treasure (Japan), Officier, Ordre des Palmes académiques; Prix Paul Deschanel 1954. *Publications:* Les violations de la liberté individuelle 1954, La monarchie marocaine 1963, Le Japon 1970, Introduction à l'Esprit des Lois 1973, Libertés publiques 1988, L'Esprit de défense 1988, Libertés et droits fondamentaux (5th edn) 2002, Droits de l'homme et Libertés fondamentales (7th edn) 1999, Le juge constitutionnel, juge des libertés 1999, La Garde de la République 2000, Enjeux du siècle: nos libertés 2002, La fin de la Laicité 2004, Les richesses du droit 2005. *Leisure interests:* music, photography, swimming.

ROBERT, Lorin S.; Micronesian diplomatist; *Secretary of Foreign Affairs;* ed American Univ. School of Int. Service, Washington, DC, Univ. of Oxford, UK; Officer, Dept of Foreign Affairs 1984–85, Deputy Chief of Mission for Embassy in Tokyo 1985–90, Deputy Asst Sec. for Asian Affairs 1990–96, Chief, Curriculum & Instruction, Educational Services Devt 1991–2000, Asst Sec. Asia Pacific and Multilateral Affairs Div. 1996–2000, Deputy Sec. for the Dept 2001–07, Sec. of Foreign Affairs 2007–; Chair. Bd of Trustees Micronesian Fisheries Authority; fmr Alt. Gov. IBRD and Asian Devt Bank; has represented Micronesia on various UN panels. *Address:* Department of Foreign Affairs, PS123, Palikir, Pohnpei State, 96941, Federated States of Micronesia (office). *Telephone:* 320-2641 (office). *Fax:* 320-2933 (office). *E-mail:* foreignaffairs@mail.fm (office).

ROBERTO CARLOS; Brazilian professional footballer; b. (Roberto Carlos da Silva Rocha), 10 April 1973, Garça, São Paulo; s. of Oscar and Vera Lúcia; m. 1st Alexandra; three d.; m. 2nd Mariana Luccon; ed Colonel José Levy School, São Paulo; left wing-back; played for União São João 1990–92 (professional debut 1992), Atlético Mineiro 1992, Palmeiras 1993–95 (45 matches, four goals, won Brazilian League 1993, 1994, Rio-São Paulo Tournament 1993, São Paulo State Championship 1993, 1994), Internazionale, Italy 1995–96 (30 matches, five goals), Real Madrid, Spain 1996–2007 (370 matches, 47 goals, won La Liga 1996/97, 2000/01, 2002/03, 2006/07, Spanish Super Cup 1997, 2001, 2003, UEFA Champions League 1997/98, 1999/2000, 2001/02, UEFA Super Cup 2002, UEFA Super Cup, Intercontinental Cup 1998, 2002), Fenerbahçe, Turkey 2007–10 (101 matches 12 goals, won Turkish Super Cup 2007, 2009), Corinthians, São Paulo 2010–11, Anzhi Makhachkala, Dagestan (caretaker man. 2011) 2011–12; played for Brazil nat. team (debut vs USA), 125 int. caps, 11 goals 1992–2006, bronze medal, Olympic Games, Atlanta 1996; Winner, Copa America 1997, 1999, World Cup 2002 (runner-up 1998); apptd Man. Akhisar Belediyespor 2015; Head Coach, Delhi Dynamos, Indian Super League 2015; UEFA Team of the Year 2002, 2003. *Website:* www.robertocarlos.com.br.

ROBERTS, Brian L., BS; American business executive; *Chairman and CEO, Comcast Corporation;* b. 28 June 1959, Philadelphia, Pa; s. of Ralph J. Roberts and Suzanne F. Roberts; m. Aileen Kennedy 1985; one s. two d.; ed Wharton School of Finance Univ. of Pennsylvania; Vice-Pres. Operations, Comcast Cable Communications Inc. 1985–86, Exec. Vice-Pres. Comcast Corpn 1986–90, Pres. 1990, CEO 2001–, Chair. 2004–, also mem. Bd of Dirs (acquired AT&T Broadband 2002); mem. Bd of Dirs Nat. Cable & Telecommunications Asscn, Chair. 1995–96, 2005–07; Chair. CableLabs 1999–2001, 2003–05, 2009–11, Dir Emer. 2011–; Vice-Chair. Walter Katz Foundation; mem. Bd of Dirs Turner Broadcasting System, QVC Network, Bank of NY, Simon Wiesenthal Center, Viewer's Choice; Co-Chair. Resource Devt Campaign for United Way of Southeastern Pennsylvania 2003; Founding Co-Chair. Philadelphia 2000 (nonpartisan host cttee for Republican Nat. Convention) 2000; mem. Business Roundtable, Washington, DC; honoured by The Police Athletic League of Philadelphia 2002, Steven J. Ross Humanitarian Award, UJA Fed. of New York 2003, Humanitarian Award, Simon Wiesenthal Center 2004, named by Institutional Investor magazine as one of America's top CEOs 2004–09, honoured by Nat. Asscn for Multi-ethnicity in Communications 2005, honoured by Partnership for a Drug-Free America 2005, inducted into Cable Television Hall of Fame 2006, Distinguished Vanguard Award for Leadership 2007, recognized by Big Brothers and Big Sisters for outstanding leadership in the community and for serving as a role model to youth 2008, Amb. for Humanity Award, Univ. of Southern California Shoah Foundation Inst. 2011, Fred Dressler Achievement Award, S.I. Newhouse School of Public Communications at Syracuse Univ. 2011 inducted into Babson Coll.'s Acad. of Distinguished Entrepreneurs Hall of Fame 2011, recognized by Fortune magazine as a Businessperson of the Year 2012, Joseph Wharton Award for Leadership 2012. *Achievements include:* earned Silver Medals with US squash team at Maccabiah Games, Israel 1981, 1985, 1997, Gold Medal 2005. *Address:* Comcast Corporation, One Comcast Center, 1701 JFK Blvd, Philadelphia, PA 19103, USA (office). *Telephone:* (215) 286-1700 (office). *Website:* corporate.comcast.com (office).

ROBERTS, Sir Derek Harry, Kt, CBE, BSc, FRS, FEng; British physicist, business executive and fmr university administrator; b. 28 March 1932, Manchester; s. of Harry Roberts and Alice Roberts (née Storey); m. Winifred Short 1958; one s. one d.; ed Manchester Cen. High School and Manchester Univ.; Research Scientist, Plessey Co. 1953–67; Gen. Man. Plessey Semiconductors 1967–69; Dir Plessey Allen Clark Research Centre 1969–73; Man. Dir Plessey Microsystems Div. 1973–79; Dir of Research, The General Electric Co. PLC 1979–83, Tech. Dir 1983–85, Jt Deputy Man. Dir (Tech.) 1985–88, Dir 1988–; Visiting Prof., Univ. Coll., London 1979, Provost and Pres. 1989–99, 2002–03; Pres. BAAS 1996–97, Sr Research Fellow, School of Public Policy 1999; mem. Bd of Dirs Ludwig Inst. for Cancer Research; Hon. Fellow, Univ. Coll. London, British Asscn for the Advancement of Science; Hon. DSc (Bath) 1982, (Loughborough) 1984, (City) 1985, (Lancaster) 1986, (Manchester) 1987, (Queens Univ., Belfast) 1990; Hon. DUniv (Open) 1984, (Salford), (Essex), (London) 1988. *Publications:* about 30 tech. papers in learned soc. journals. *Leisure interests:* gardening, reading. *Address:* The Old Rectory, Maids Moreton, Buckingham, England (home). *Telephone:* (1280) 813470 (home).

ROBERTS, Sir Ivor Anthony, Kt, KCMG, CMG, MA, FCIL; British diplomatist (retd) and college principal (retd); b. 24 Sept. 1946, Liverpool; s. of Leonard Moore Roberts and Rosa Maria Roberts (née Fusco); m. Elizabeth Bray Bernard Smith 1974; two s. one d.; ed St Mary's Coll., Crosby, Keble Coll., Oxford; entered diplomatic service 1968, with Middle East Centre for Arab Studies 1969, Third, then Second Sec. Paris 1970–73, Second, then First Sec. FCO 1973–78, First Sec. Canberra 1978–82, Deputy Head of News Dept FCO 1982–86, Head Security Co-ordination Dept, FCO 1986–88, Minister and Deputy Head of Mission, Madrid 1989–93, Chargé d'affaires Belgrade 1994–96; Amb. to Yugoslavia 1996–97, to Ireland 1999–2003, to Italy 2003–06 (retd); Chair. Council of British School, Rome 2007–12, Keats-Shelley Memorial Asscn 2018–; Sr Assoc. mem. St Antony's Coll., Oxford 1998–99; Pres., Trinity Coll. Oxford 2006–17, Rugby Football Club, Univ. of Oxford; mem. Advisory Bd MacKinder Forum; Fellow, Chartered Inst. of Linguists 1991–; Patron Venice in Peril Fund; Hon. Fellow, Keble Coll. Oxford 2001, Trinity Coll., Oxford 2017; Freeman, City of London 2009. *Publications include:* Conversations with Milošević 2016, Satow's Diplomatic Practice (ed., sixth edn) 2009, (seventh centenary edn) 2017. *Leisure interests:* opera, theatre, skiing, golf, photography. *E-mail:* ivor.roberts@trinity.ox.ac.uk (office).

ROBERTS, John G., Jr, AB, JD; American lawyer and judge; *Chief Justice of the United States;* b. 27 Jan. 1955, Buffalo, NY; m. Jane Marie Sullivan 1996; one s. one d.; ed Harvard Coll., Harvard Law School; served as a law clerk for Judge Henry J. Friendly, US Court of Appeals for the Second Circuit 1979–80, to then-

Assoc. Justice William H. Rehnquist, US Supreme Court 1980–81; Special Asst to the Attorney Gen., US Dept of Justice 1981–82; Assoc. Counsel to Pres. Ronald Reagan, White House Counsel's Office 1982–86; practised law in Washington, DC 1986–89, 1993–2003; Prin. Deputy Solicitor Gen., US Dept of Justice 1989–93; Judge, US Court of Appeals for DC Circuit 2003–05; Chief Justice, Supreme Court of the US 2005–. *Address:* Supreme Court of the United States, 1 First Street NE, Washington, DC 20543, USA (office). *Telephone:* (202) 479-3000 (office). *Website:* www.supremecourt.gov (office).

ROBERTS, Julia; American actress; b. (Julie Fiona Roberts), 28 Oct. 1967, Smyrna, Ga; m. 1st Lyle Lovett 1993 (divorced 1995); m. 2nd Daniel Moder 2002; two s. one d.; ed Campbell High School, Atlanta, Ga; UNICEF Goodwill Amb. 1995; f. film production co. Red Om Films Inc. (fmrly Shoelace Productions); American Cinematheque Award 2007. *Films include:* Satisfaction 1988, Mystic Pizza 1988, Blood Red 1989, Steel Magnolias (Golden Globe Award 1990) 1989, Flatliners 1990, Pretty Woman 1990, Sleeping with the Enemy 1991, Dying Young 1991, Hook 1991, The Player 1992, The Pelican Brief 1993, I Love Trouble 1994, Prêt à Porter 1994, Something to Talk About 1995, Mary Reilly 1996, Michael Collins 1996, Everyone Says I Love You 1996, My Best Friend's Wedding 1997, Conspiracy Theory 1997, Stepmom 1998, Notting Hill 1999, Runaway Bride 1999, Erin Brockovich (Acad. Award for Best Actress 2001) 2000, The Mexican 2001, America's Sweethearts 2001, Ocean's Eleven 2001, Grand Champion 2002, Full Frontal 2002, Confessions of a Dangerous Mind 2002, Mona Lisa Smile 2003, Closer 2004, Ocean's Twelve 2004, The Ant Bully (voice) 2006, Charlotte's Web (voice) 2006, Charlie Wilson's War 2007, Fireflies in the Garden 2008, Duplicity 2009, Valentine's Day 2010, Eat Pray Love 2010, Love, Wedding, Marriage (voice) 2011, Larry Crowne 2011, Mirror Mirror: The Untold Adventures of Snow White 2012, August: Osage County 2013, Secret in Their Eyes 2015, Mother's Day 2016, Money Monster 2016, Wonder 2017, Ben is Back 2018. *Television:* Crime Story (series) 1987, Baja Oklahoma (film) 1988, Miami Vice (series) 1988, Friends (series) 1996, Law & Order (series) 1999, Freedom: A History of Us (series documentary) 2003, The Normal Heart (film) 2014, Homecoming (series) 2018. *Address:* c/o Red Om Films Inc., 145 West 57th Street, 19th Floor, New York, NY 10019 (office); c/o Creative Artists Agency, 2000 Avenue of the Stars, Los Angeles, CA 90067, USA (office). *Telephone:* (212) 243-2900 (Red Om) (office); (310) 288-2000 (CAA) (office). *Fax:* (212) 243-2973 (Red Om) (office); (310) 288-2900 (CAA) (office). *Website:* www.caa.com (office).

ROBERTS, Julian V. F., BA, FCA, MCT; British accountant and business executive; m. Marion Roberts; three s. one d.; ed Univ. of Stirling; qualified as accountant at PricewaterhouseCoopers 1983; with C E Heath 1987–93; mem. Bd of Dirs and Chief Financial Officer Aon UK Holdings Ltd 1993–98; Group Finance Dir Sun Life & Provincial Holdings plc 1998–2006; Group Finance Dir Old Mutual plc 2000–06, Chief Exec. Skandia 2006–08, Group Chief Exec. Old Mutual plc 2008–15. *Leisure interests:* watching sports, playing golf, supporting his children at their rugby, football and hockey fixtures. *Address:* c/o Old Mutual plc, 5th Floor, Old Mutual Place, 2 Lambeth Hill, London, EC4V 4GG, England.

ROBERTS, Kevin John, CNZM; British advertising executive; b. 20 Oct. 1949, Lancaster; s. of John Roberts and Jean Roberts (née Lambert); m. 1st Barbara Beckett; one d.; m. 2nd Rowena Joan Honeywill 1974; two s. one d.; Brand Man. Gillette Co., London 1972–74; Group Marketing Man., Procter & Gamble, Geneva 1975–82; Vice-Pres. Pepsico, Nicosia 1982–86; Pres. and CEO Pepsi Cola Canada, Toronto 1987–89; COO Lion Nathan, Auckland 1990–96; CEO Saatchi & Saatchi Worldwide Inc., New York City 1997–2014, Exec. Chair. 2015–16; Founder Red Rose Consulting 2016; Prof. of Sustainable Enterprise and Sr Fellow, Waikato Man. School, Univ. of Waikato, New Zealand 2003–07; inaugural CEO in Residence, Judge Inst. of Man., Cambridge Univ. UK 2001–09; Chair. USA Rugby Bd 2006–14; Dir Telecom New Zealand 2008–14; Chair. My Food Bag 2015–; Hon. Prof., Peruvian Univ. of Applied Sciences 2007; Dr hc (Univ. of Waikato) 1998; Hon. DLit (Int. Univ. in Geneva) 2009; New Yorker for New York Award 2004. *Publications:* Peak Performing Organisations (co-author) 2000, Lovemarks: The Future Beyond Brands 2004, sisomo: The Future on Screen 2005, Lovemarks Effect: Winning in the Consumer Revolution 2006; Diesel: XXX Years of Diesel Communication 2008. *Leisure interests:* rugby, tennis, art, travel, music.

ROBERTS, Matthew Vernon, MA, MPhil, DipMassComm; Saint Lucia journalist, educator and fmr politician; *Resident Tutor and Head, School of Continuing Studies, University of the West Indies;* b. 29 July 1954, Castries; m. Catherine (Kate) Regis 1980; one s. three d.; ed Univ. of the West Indies, Jamaica, City Univ., London, UK; primary school teacher 1969–72; Asst Ed. The Voice newspaper 1972–80; fmr Public Relations Officer, Saint Lucia Tourist Bd; fmr Regional Communications Consultant, Caribbean Family Planning Affiliation; fmr Chief Information Officer Govt Information Service; currently Resident Tutor and Head, School of Continuing Studies, Univ. of West Indies; Speaker of House of Ass. –2003. *Leisure interests:* reading, swimming, gardening. *Address:* University of the West Indies, School of Continuing Studies, The Morne, Castries (office); Clavier Ridgeway, Entrepot Summit, PO Box 927, Castries, Saint Lucia (home). *Telephone:* 452-7282 (home). *E-mail:* cpe.office@open.uwi.edu (office). *Website:* www.uwi.edu (office).

ROBERTS, Michèle Brigitte, MA (Oxon.), ALA, FRSL; British novelist, poet and academic; *Professor Emeritus of Creative Writing, University of East Anglia;* b. 20 May 1949, Herts.; d. of Reginald Roberts and Monique Caulle; m. 1st Howard Burns 1984 (divorced 1987); m. 2nd Jim Latter 1991 (divorced 2004); two step-s.; ed Convent Grammar School, Somerville Coll., Oxford and Univ. Coll. London; British Council Librarian, Bangkok 1973–74; Poetry Ed. Spare Rib 1974, City Limits 1981–83; Visiting Fellow, Univ. of East Anglia 1992, Univ. of Nottingham Trent 1994; Visiting Prof., Univ. of Nottingham Trent 1996–2001; Prof. of Creative Writing, Univ. of East Anglia 2002–07, Prof. Emer. 2008–; Chair. Literary Cttee British Council 1998–2002; judge, Booker Prize 2001; mem. Soc. of Authors; Chevalier, Ordre des Arts et des Lettres 2001; Hon. MA (Nene) 1999; WHSmith Literary Award 1993. *Plays:* The Journeywoman 1988, Child-Lover 1995. *Television film:* The Heavenly Twins (Channel 4) 1993. *Publications include:* novels: A Piece of the Night 1978, The Visitation 1983, The Wild Girl 1984, The Book of Mrs Noah 1987, In the Red Kitchen 1990, Daughters of the House 1992, Flesh and Blood 1994, Impossible Saints 1997, Fair Exchange 1999, The Looking-Glass 2000, The Mistressclass 2003, Reader, I Married Him 2005, Ignorance 2012, The Walworth Beauty 2017; Paper Houses (auto-biog.) 2007; Mind Readings (co-ed.) 1996; short stories: During Mother's Absence 1993, Playing Sardines 2001, Mud: Stories of Sex and Love 2010, Wooing Mr Wickham: Stories Inspired by Jane Austen and Chawton House 2011; essays: Food, Sex and God 1998; poetry: The Mirror of the Mother 1986, Psyche and the Hurricane 1991, All the Selves I Was 1995; plays: The Journeywoman 1987, Child Lover 1993. *Leisure interests:* reading, talking with friends, cooking, gardening, looking at art. *Address:* Aitken Alexander Associates Ltd, 18–21 Cavaye Place, London, SW10 9PT, England (office). *Telephone:* (20) 7373-8672 (office). *Fax:* (20) 7373-6002 (office). *E-mail:* reception@aitkenalexander.co.uk (office). *Website:* www.aitkenalexander.co.uk (office); www.micheleroberts.co.uk.

ROBERTS, Nora, (J. D. Robb); American writer; b. 10 Oct. 1950, Silver Spring, Md; m. 2nd Bruce Wilder 1985; f. Nora Roberts Foundation; Co-owner, Inn BoonsBoro, Boonsboro, Md; mem. Romance Writers of America, Novelists Inc.; various Romance Writers of America Awards, named as one of 100 People Who Shape Our World, Time magazine 2007. *Publications:* Irish Thoroughbred 1981, Blithe Images 1982, Song of the West 1982, Search for Love 1982, Island of Flowers 1982, The Heart's Victory 1982, From This Day 1983, Her Mother's Keeper 1983, Reflections 1983, Once More with Feeling 1983, Untamed 1983, Dance of Dreams 1983, Tonight and Always 1983, This Magic Moment 1983, Endings and Beginnings 1984, Storm Warning 1984, Sullivan's Woman 1984, Rules of the Game 1984, Less of a Stranger 1984, A Matter of Choice 1984, The Law is a Lady 1984, First Impressions 1984, Opposites Attract 1984, Promise Me Tomorrow 1984, Partners 1985, The Right Path 1985, Boundary Lines 1985, Summer Desserts 1985, Dual Images 1985, Night Moves 1985, Playing the Odds 1985, Tempting Fate 1985, All the Possibilities 1985, One Man's Art 1985, The Art of Deception 1986, One Summer 1986, Treasures Lost, Treasures Found 1986, Risky Business 1986, Lessons Learned 1986, Second Nature 1986, A Will and a Way 1986, Home for Christmas 1986, Affaire Royale 1986, Mind Over Matter 1987, Temptation 1987, Hot Ice 1987, Sacred Sins 1987, For Now, Forever 1987, Command Performance 1987, The Playboy Prince 1987, Brazen Virtue 1988, Local Hero 1988, Irish Rose 1988, The Name of the Game 1988, Rebellion 1988, The Last Honest Woman 1988, Dance to the Piper 1988, Skin Deep 1988, Sweet Revenge 1989, Loving Jack 1989, Best Laid Plans 1989, Gabriel's Angel 1989, Lawless 1989, Public Secrets 1990, Taming Natasha 1990, Night Shadow 1991, Genuine Lies 1991, With This Ring 1991, Night Shift 1991, Without a Trace 1991, Luring a Lady 1991, Courting Catherine 1991, A Man for Amanda 1991, For the Love of Lilah 1991, Suzannah's Surrender 1991, Carnal Innocence 1992, Unfinished Business 1992, The Welcoming 1992, Honest Illusions 1992, Divine Evil 1992, Captivated 1992, Entranced 1992, Charmed 1992, Second Nature 1993, Private Scandals 1993, Falling for Rachel 1993, Time Was 1993, Times Change 1993, Boundary Lines 1994, Hidden Riches 1994, Nightshade 1994, The Best Mistake 1994, Night Smoke 1994, Born in Fire 1994, Born in Ice 1995, True Betrayals 1995, Born in Shame 1996, Montana Sky 1996, From the Heart 1997, Sanctuary 1997, Holding the Dream 1997, Daring to Dream 1997, Finding the Dream 1997, The Reef 1998, The Winning Hand 1998, Sea Swept 1998, Homeport 1999, The Perfect Neighbor 1999, Megan's Mate 1999, Enchanted 1999, Rising Tides 1999, Inner Harbor 1999, Carolina Moon 2000, The Villa 2001, Heaven and Earth 2001, Three Fates 2002, Chesapeake Blue 2002, Key of Knowledge 2003, Key of Light 2003, Once Upon a Midnight 2003, Birthright 2003, Remember When 2003, Blue Dahlia 2004, Key of Valor 2004, Northern Lights 2005, Blue Smoke (Quill Award for Romance) 2006, Angels Fall (Quill Award for Book of the Year and for Romance 2007) 2006, Heart of the Sea 2007, Divine Evil 2007, The Hollow 2008, High Noon 2008, Tribute 2008, The Pagan Stone 2008, Black Hills 2009, Vision in White 2009, Bed of Roses 2009, Hot Rocks 2010, The Search 2010, Savour the Moment 2010, Happy Ever After 2010, The Next Always 2011, Perfect Hope 2012, Dark Witch 2013, Whiskey Beach 2013, The Collector 2014, Shadow Spell 2014, Blood Magick 2014, The Liar 2015, Morrigan's Cross 2016, Year One 2017, Come Sundown 2018, Shelter in Place 2018; as J. D. Robb: Only Survivors Tell Tales 1990, Naked in Death 1995, Glory in Death 1995, Rapture in Death 1996, Ceremony in Death 1997, Vengeance in Death 1997, Holiday in Death 1998, Immortal in Death 1998, Silent Night 1998, Loyalty in Death 1999, Conspiracy in Death 1999, Witness in Death 2000, Judgment in Death 2000, Seduction in Death 2001, Out of this World 2001, Betrayal in Death 2001, Reunion in Death 2002, Purity in Death 2002, Imitation in Death 2003, Remember When 2003, Portrait in Death 2003, Once Upon a Midnight 2003, Divided in Death 2004, Visions in Death 2004, Memory in Death 2006, Born in Death 2006, Innocent in Death 2007, Strangers in Death 2008, Creation in Death 2008, Salvation in Death 2008, Kindred in Death 2009, Fantasy in Death 2010, Savor the Moment 2010, The Search 2010, Indulgence in Death 2010, Happy Ever After 2010, Treachery in Death 2011, Chasing Fire 2011, New York to Dallas 2011, The Next Always 2011, Celebrity in Death 2012, The Witness 2012, The Last Boyfriend 2012, Delusion in Death 2012, Thankless in Death 2013, Calculated In Death 2013, Festive in Death 2014, Concealed in Death 2014, Obsession in Death 2015, Devoted in Death 2015, Devoted in Death 2016, Brotherhood in Death 2016, Apprentice in Death 2017, Echoes in Death 2017, Secrets in Death 2017, Dark in Death 2018, Leverage in Death 2018. *Address:* Inn BoonsBoro, 1 North Main Street, Boonsboro, MD 21713 (office); Writers' House Inc., 21 West 26th Street, New York, NY 10010, USA (office); c/o Matthew Fountainm, Nora Roberts Foundation, 100 Campus Drive, Suite 350, Florham Park, NJ 07932, USA. *Telephone:* (212) 685-2400 (office). *Fax:* (212) 685-1781 (office). *E-mail:* write2nora@msn.com. *Website:* www.noraroberts.com; www.innboonsboro.com.

ROBERTS, (Charles Patrick) Pat; American politician; *Senator from Kansas;* b. 20 April 1936, Topeka, Kan.; s. of Wes Roberts and Ruth Roberts (née Patrick); m. Franki Fann 1970; one s. two d.; ed Holton High School, Kansas State Univ.; served with US Marine Corps 1958–62; Publr Litchfield Park, Ariz. 1962–67; Admin. Asst to US Senator F. Carlson 1967–68, to US Congressman Keith Sebelius 1968–70; mem. 97th–104th US Congresses 1980–97; Senator from Kansas 1997–, fmr Chair. Select Cttee on Intelligence, mem. Cttee on Agric., Nutrition, and Forestry, Cttee on Ethics, Cttee on Finance, Cttee on Health, Educ., Labor, and Pensions, Cttee on Rules and Admin; Republican. *Address:* 109 Hart Senate Office Building, Washington, DC 20510-1605, USA (office). *Telephone:* (202) 224-4774 (office). *Fax:* (202) 224-3514 (office). *Website:* roberts.senate.gov (office).

ROBERTS, Sir Richard John, Kt, BSc, PhD, FRS; British scientist; *Chief Scientific Officer, New England Biolabs;* b. 6 Sept. 1943, Derby, England; s. of John

Walter Roberts and Edna Wilhelmina Roberts; m. 1st Elizabeth Dyson 1965 (deceased); one s. one d.; m. 2nd Jean Tagliabue 1986; one s. one d.; ed Univ. of Sheffield; Research Fellow, Harvard Univ. 1969–70, Research Assoc. in Biochemistry 1971–72; Sr Staff Investigator, Cold Spring Harbor Lab. Research Inst., Long Island 1972–86, Asst Dir for Research 1986–92; Research Dir New England Biolabs 1992–2005, Chief Scientific Officer 2005–; Adviser to Dir NASA Astrobiology Program 2000–; Vice-Chair. Int. Science Advisory Bd, JDW Inst. of Genome Sciences, Hangzhou, China 2003–; Distinguished Scientist, Research Scholar, Boston Univ. 2003–; Distinguished Univ. Prof., Northeastern Univ. 2013–; Chair. NCI Bd of Scientific Counselors 1996–2000; Chair. Scientific Advisory Bd Celera 1998–2002; Chair. Steering Cttee on Genetics and Biotechnology, Int. Council for Science 1998–2001; mem. Editorial Bd Bioinformatics 1985–2002, Current Opinions in Chemical Biology 1997–2001; mem. Scientific Advisory Bd Genex Corpn 1977–85, Molecular Tool 1994–2000, Oxford Molecular Group 1996–99, Conservation Law Foundation 1998–, PubMed Central 2000–03, Orchid Biosciences 2000–03, Center for Functional Genomics, State Univ. of NY, Albany 2002–, Diversa Corpn 2003–05, PubChem 2004–, Rain Dance Techs 2004–, Int. Centre for Genetic Eng and Biotechnology 2005–, InVivo Therapeutics 2007–, Empiriko Corpn 2013–; mem. Bd Albert Schweitzer Acad. of Medicine 1998–2003, Vice-Pres. 2003–; Exec. Ed. Nucleic Acids Research 1987–; Patron Oxford Int. Biomedical Centre 1994–; mem. Advisory Bd Grantham Inst., Sheffield Univ. 2015–; Trustee, Gaddafi Int. Charity and Devt Foundation 2009–11; Fellow, American Soc. of Arts and Sciences 1997, American Acad. of Microbiology 1997, Science Museum, London 2009; Hon. Prof., Chinese Univ. of Hong Kong 2006–, Nankai Univ. 2006–, Astana Medical Univ., Kazakhstan 2012, Eurasian Econ. Club of Scientists 2012, Wuhan Univ., China 2012, Jiang-Nan Univ., Wuxi, China 2012, Pyongyang Univ. of Science & Tech. 2016, Universidad Católica of Valencia 2016, Hon. Citizen of Wuxi, China 2012, Hon. Pres. Richard J. Roberts Inst. of Biotechnology, Yixing, China 2012–; Hon. MD (Uppsala) 1992, (Bath) 1994, (Sheffield) 1994, (Derby) 1995, (Chinese Univ. of Hong Kong) 2005; Dr hc (Athens) 2009, (Univ. of Lisbon) 2012, (Universidad Andrés Bello, Santiago, Chile) 2014, (Univ. of Ljubljana, Slovenia) 2015; Hon. DS (KIIT Univ., Bhubaneswar) 2016, (Amity Univ.) 2017; Nobel Prize in Physiology or Medicine (for the discovery of 'split genes') 1993, American Acad. of Achievement Golden Plate Award 1994, Univ. of Sheffield Convocation Award 1994, Gabor Medal of the Royal Soc. 2007. *Publications include:* Nucleases (co-ed.) 1982, The Applications of Computers to Research on Nucleic Acids (co-ed.) 1982. *Leisure interest:* croquet. *Address:* New England Biolabs, 240 County Road, Ipswich, MA 01938, USA (office). *Telephone:* (978) 380-7405 (office). *Fax:* (978) 412-9910 (office). *E-mail:* roberts@neb.com (office). *Website:* www.neb.com (office).

ROBERTSON, Dawn, BA; American retail executive; *CEO, Stein Mart Inc.;* b. Birmingham, Ala; m. Tom Robertson; two c.; ed Auburn Univ.; Buyer, Macy's-Davison's 1997–83; Divisional Merchandise Man./Vice-Pres. G. Fox Div., May Department Stores 1983–85, Sr Vice-Pres./Gen. Merchandise Man. 1985–96; Pres. and CEO McRae's (div. of Saks Inc.) Jackson, Miss. 1996–98; Exec. Vice-Pres. Federated Merchandising Group 1998–2000, Pres. and Chief Merchandising Officer, Federated Direct (online and catalog business div. for Macy's and Bloomingdale's) 2000–02; Man. Dir Myer (fmrly Myer Grace Bros), Melbourne, Australia 2002–06; Pres. Old Navy Div., Gap Inc., San Francisco 2006–08; Pres. Sean John 2008–10; CEO Avenue (div. of Redcats/PPR) 2010–12; Pres. NYGÅRD International 2012–13; CEO Deb Shops, Inc. 2013–15; CEO UNKNWN 2015–16; CEO Stein Mart Inc. 2016–; mem. Bd of Trustees, The Harvey School, Katonah, NY 2013–. *Address:* Stein Mart Inc., 1200 Riverplace Blvd, Jacksonville, FL 32207, USA (office). *Website:* www.steinmart.com (office).

ROBERTSON, Elizabeth, BSc, MSc, PhD, FRS; British biologist and academic; *Professor of Developmental Biology, Sir William Dunn School of Pathology, University of Oxford;* b. 3 July 1957; ed Univs of Oxford and Cambridge; Postdoctoral Research Asst, then Research Assoc., Dept of Genetics, Univ. of Cambridge; Asst, then Assoc. Prof., Dept of Genetics and Devt, Columbia Univ., New York, USA; Prof., Dept of Molecular and Cellular Biology, Harvard Univ., USA for 12 years, including two years as Herchel Smith Prof. of Molecular Genetics; currently Prof. of Developmental Biology, Sir William Dunn School of Pathology, Univ. of Oxford, Wellcome Trust Prin. Research Fellow; mem. several scientific advisory bds, including for School of Biological Sciences of Univ. of Cambridge, Temasek Life Sciences Lab., Nat. Univ. of Singapore, Skirball Inst. for Biomedical Research of New York Univ.; Trustee, Babraham Inst., Cambridge; Ed.-in-Chief, Current Opinions in Genetics and Development; Ed., Development; mem. Editorial Bd, Developmental Biology, Developmental Cell; Chair. British Soc. for Developmental Biology –2014; mem., Chair. General Motors Cancer Research Foundation, Sloan Prize Cttee; mem. General Motors Cancer Research Foundation Ass.; mem. European Molecular Biology Org. 2002, Academia Europaea; fmr Fellow, David and Lucile Packard Foundation; March of Dimes Basil O'Connor Starter Scholar Award 1989, Irma T. Hirschl Career Devt Award 1990, Stohlman Scholar, Leukemia Soc. of America 1990–95, Cornelius P. Rhoads Award, American Asscn for Cancer Research 1992, Pearl Meister Greengard Prize, Rockefeller Univ. 2007, Edwin G. Conklin Medal, Soc. for Developmental Biology 2008, Waddington Medal 2009, Royal Medal, Royal Soc. 2016. *Publications:* numerous papers in professional journals. *Address:* Sir William Dunn School of Pathology, University of Oxford, South Parks Road, Oxford, OX1 3RE, England (office). *Telephone:* (1865) 275500 (office). *Fax:* (1865) 275515 (office). *E-mail:* elizabeth.robertson@path.ox.ac.uk (office). *Website:* www.path.ox.ac.uk (office).

ROBERTSON, Geoffrey Ronald, QC, BA, LLB, BCL; Australian/British judge and barrister; *Head, Doughty Street Chambers;* b. 30 Sept. 1946, Sydney, NSW; s. of Francis Robertson and Bernice Beattie; m. Kathy Lette (q.v.) 1990; one s. one d.; ed Epping Boys' High School and Univs of Sydney and Oxford; Rhodes scholar; solicitor, Allen, Allen & Hemsley 1970; called to the Bar, Middle Temple, London 1973; QC 1988; Visiting Prof., Univ. of New South Wales 1979, Univ. of Warwick 1981, Univ. of London 2008, New Coll. of Humanities 2014, Regent's Univ. 2016; leader, Amnesty missions to S Africa 1983–90; consultant on Human Rights to Govt of Australia 1984; Founding mem. and Head, Doughty Street Chambers 1990–; Counsel to Royal Comm. on gun-running to Colombian drug cartels 1991; Asst Recorder 1993–99, a Recorder 1999–2012; Master of Bench, Middle Temple 1997–; Chief Counsel Comm. on Admin. of Justice in Trinidad and Tobago 2000; Appeal Judge, UN Special Court for War Crimes in Sierra Leone 2002–07; Chair.

Staff Panel on Reform of UN Justice 2006; mem. Exec. Council Justice; Jurist mem. UN Internal Justice Council 2008–12, Bar Council inquiry into impeachment of the Chief Justice of Sri Lanka 2013, Govt of Mauritius inquiry into Media Law Reform 2013; Trustee, Capital Class Trust 2004–, School of Oriental and African Studies 2016–; Hon. LLD (Sydney) 2006, (Bucharest) 2009, (Brunel) 2010; Freedom of Information Award 1992, Award for Distinction in Int. Law and Affairs, New York Bar Asscn 2011. *Radio:* Chair. You the Jury (BBC Radio 4). *Plays:* The Trials of Oz (BBC) 1992. *Television series:* Hypotheticals, Granada TV, ABC and Channel 7 (Australia). *Publications:* Reluctant Judas 1976, Obscenity 1979, People Against the Press 1983, Geoffrey Robertson's Hypotheticals 1986, Does Dracula Have AIDS? 1987, Freedom, The Individual and The Law 1989, The Justice Game 1998, Crimes Against Humanity 1999 (fourth edn 2012), Media Law (with A. Nicol) 2002 (fifth edn 2006), The Tyrannicide Brief 2006, The Levellers – The Putney Debates 2007, Statute of Liberty 2009, The Case of the Pope 2010, Mullahs without Mercy: Human Rights and Nuclear Weapons 2012, Dreaming Too Loud 2013, Stephen Ward Was Innocent, OK 2013, An Inconvenient Genocide: Who Now Remembers the Armenians? 2014. *Leisure interests:* tennis, opera, fishing. *Address:* Doughty Street Chambers, 11 Doughty Street, London, WC1N 2PL, England (office). *Telephone:* (20) 7404-1313 (office). *Fax:* (20) 7404-2283 (office). *E-mail:* g.robertson@doughtystreet.co.uk (office). *Website:* www.doughtystreet.co.uk (office).

ROBERTSON, Grant Murray, BA; New Zealand politician; *Minister of Finance and for Sport and Recreation;* b. 30 Oct. 1971, Palmerston North; s. of Doug Robertson; civil pnr Alf Kaiwai; ed Univ. of Otago; with Ministry of Foreign Affairs and Trade 1997–2001 (including posting to UN in New York); Advisor to Minister of Environment 2001–02, to Prime Minister 2002–07; Sr Research Marketing Man., Univ. of Otago 2005–08; MP for Wellington Central 2008–, Deputy Leader of the Opposition 2011–13; Minister of Finance 2017–, for Sport and Recreation 2017–, also Assoc. Minister for Arts, Culture, and Heritage; mem. NZ Labour Party, Deputy Leader 2011–13. *Address:* Treasury, Level 5, 1 The Terrace, POB 3724, Wellington, 6011, New Zealand (office). *Telephone:* (4) 472-2733 (office). *Fax:* (4) 473-0982 (office). *E-mail:* info@treasury.govt.nz (office). *Website:* www.treasury.govt.nz (office); grantrobertson.co.nz.

ROBERTSON, Lloyd, OC; Canadian broadcast journalist; b. 19 Jan. 1934, Stratford, Ont.; m. Nancy; four d.; with CJCS radio, Stratford 1952, CJOY, Guelph 1953; with CBC 1954, positions in Winnipeg, Ottawa, Anchor Nat. News 1970–76; joined CTV 1976, Chief Anchor and Sr Ed. CTV News 1983–2011, co-host weekly magazine series W5 2011–; Hon. Chair. Terry Fox Run 1992; Hon. LLD (Royal Roads Univ.) 2006; Gemini Award 1992, 1994, 1997, Cen. Canadian Broadcasters Asscn Broadcaster of the Year 1992, Radio TV News Dirs' Asscn Pres.'s Award 1993, Toronto Sun Reader's Voice Award for Favourite TV Anchor 1994, Canadian Asscn of Broadcasters (CAB) Gold Ribbon Award for Broadcast Excellence 1995–96, CAB Hall of Fame 1998, Canada's Favourite News Anchor, TV Times Readers' Choice Awards 1998, 1999. *Address:* CTV News, CTV Television Network, PO Box 9, Station O, Scarborough, ON M4A 2M9, Canada (office). *Telephone:* (416) 332-5000 (office). *Website:* www.ctv.ca (office).

ROBERTSON, (Marion Gordon) Pat, BA, MDiv; American minister and broadcasting executive; *Chairman and CEO, Christian Broadcasting Network;* b. 22 March 1930, Lexington, Va; s. of A. Willis Robertson and Gladys Churchill; m. Adelia Elmer; two s. two d.; ed Washington and Lee Univ., Yale Univ., New York Theology Seminary; founder and CEO Christian Broadcasting Network, Va Beach, Va 1960–; ordained Minister Southern Baptist Convention 1961–87; founder and Chancellor Regent Univ. (fmrly CBN Univ.) 1977–; founder and Chair. Operation Blessing Int. Relief and Devt Inc. 1978–, Int. Family Entertainment Inc. 1990–97, Asia Pacific Media Corpn 1993–; Chair. Starguide Digital Networks Inc. 1995–, Porchlight Entertainment Inc. 1995–; founder and Pres. Christian Coalition 1989–, American Center for Law and Justice 1990–; cand. for Republican nomination for Pres. 1988; Dir United Va Bank, Norfolk; mem. Nat. Broadcasters (Dir 1973–); Knesset Medallion, Israel Pilgrimage Cttee, Faith and Freedom Award, Religious Heritage America, Bronze Halo Award, Southern Calif. Motion Picture Council, George Washington Honor Medal, Freedom Foundation at Valley Forge 1983. *Publications:* Shout it from the Housetops: The Story of the Founder of the Christian Broadcasting Network (jtly) 1972, My Prayer for You 1977, The Secret Kingdom 1982, Answers to 200 of Life's Most Probing Questions 1984, Beyond Reason 1984, America's Dates with Destiny 1986, The Plan 1989, The New Millennium 1990, The New World Order 1991, The End of the Age 1995. *Address:* The Christian Broadcasting Network, 977 Centreville Turnpike, Virginia Beach, VA 23463, USA (office). *Telephone:* (757) 226-7000 (office). *Website:* www.patrobertson.com; www.cbn.com (office).

ROBERTSON, Paul Douglas, BSc (Econ.), MA, PhD; Jamaican politician; b. 7 July 1946, St Andrew; m.; two d.; ed Univ. of the West Indies (UWI), Univ. of Michigan, USA; teacher, Oberlin High School 1965–68; teaching asst, Dept of Govt, UWI 1968–69, Lecturer 1976; Research Fellow, Inst. of Social and Econ. Research 1973–74; Research Assoc., Inst. of Urban Affairs, Asst Prof., Dept of Political Science, Howard Univ. 1974–76; Chair. JAMAL Foundation 1977–78; Special Adviser, Ministry of Justice 1977; Special Asst to Prime Minister 1978, 1980; Deputy Gen. Sec. for Admin, People's Nat. Party 1978–80, Gen. Sec. 1983–91, nat. campaign dir 2007; Deputy Leader of Govt Business in Senate 1989–93; MP for SE St Catherine 1993–2007; Minister without Portfolio 1989, of Information and Culture 1989, of Public Services and Information 1991, of Foreign Affairs 1992–93, of Foreign Affairs and Foreign Trade 1993–95, of Industry, Investment and Commerce 1995–97, of Industry and Investment 1997–2000, of Foreign Affairs 2000–01, Minister of Devt 2001.

ROBERTSON, Shirley, OBE; British sailor; b. 15 July 1968, Dundee, Scotland; m. Jamie Boag 2001; ed Heriot-Watt Univ.; sailed in Yngling class 2001–, previously sailed in Europe class; position: helm; Olympic results include ninth Barcelona 1992, fourth Atlanta 1996, gold medal, Sydney 2000, gold medal, Athens 2004; results in other competitions include silver medal, Europe World Championships 1998, bronze medal, Europe World Championships 1999, silver medal, Europe European Championships 1999, bronze medal, Pre-Olympic Regatta 1999, silver medal, Europe World Championships 2000, 14th Yngling World Championships 2001, 16th Yngling World Championships, bronze medal, Olympic Test Event 2002, gold medal, Olympic Class Week 2003, gold medal, Princess Sophia

Trophy 2003, fourth Olympic Class Week 2003, bronze medal, SPA Olympic Class Regatta 2003, gold medal, Pre-Olympic regatta 2003; took one year break from sailing 2005; host Mainsail (monthly CNN TV show); mem. London Organising Cttee of the Olympic Games (LOCOG) Sport Advisory Group; BBC South Sports Personality of the Year 2000, Int. Sailing Fed. World Sailor of the Year 2000, Sailor of the Year 2002, Yachtsman of the Year 2004, Spirit of Scotland Top Scot award 2004. *Leisure interests:* cycling, films, dancing, socializing with friends. *Telephone:* (1983) 299202. *E-mail:* jo.grindley@intotheblue.biz. *Website:* www.shirleyrobertson.com.

ROBERTSON, Thomas S., PhD; British academic; *Joshua J. Harris Professor of Marketing, Wharton School and Executive Director, Wharton-INSEAD Alliance, University of Pennsylvania;* b. 16 Nov. 1942, Gourock, Scotland; m. Diana Robertson; three c.; ed Wayne State Univ., Northwestern Univ.; Asst Prof., Anderson School, UCLA 1966–68; Asst Prof., Harvard Business School 1968–70; Assoc. Prof., Wharton School, Univ. of Pennsylvania 1971–76, Prof. 1976–94, Chair. of Marketing Dept 1978–84, 1988–94, Assoc. Dean for Exec. Educ. 1984–88, Pomerantz Prof. of Marketing 1987–94, Reliance Prof. of Man. and Pvt. Enterprise 2007–14, Dean, Wharton School 2007–14, Joshua J. Harris Prof. of Marketing, Wharton School 2014–, Exec. Dir, Wharton-INSEAD Alliance 2014–; Deputy Dean, London Business School 1994–98; Dean, Goizueta Business School, Emory Univ. 1998–2004, Exec. Faculty Dir Inst. for Developing Nations 2006–07; Maynard Award 1987, Wharton School Outstanding Service Award 1987, Planning Forum Award 1993, Best Paper Award, European Marketing Acad. 1995, Best Paper Award, Winter Conf., American Marketing Asscn 1996, Newcomen Soc. Award 2002. *Publications include:* Handbook of Consumer Behavior (co-ed.) 1991, Perspectives on Consumer Behavior (co-ed.) 1991. *Address:* Wharton School, University of Pennsylvania, 769 Jon M. Huntsman Hall, Philadelphia, PA 19104, USA (office). *Telephone:* (215) 898-5405 (office). *Fax:* (215) 573-5001 (office). *E-mail:* robertson@wharton.upenn.edu (office). *Website:* wharton.upenn.edu (office).

ROBERTSON OF PORT ELLEN, Baron (Life Peer), cr. 1999, of Islay in Argyll and Bute; **George Islay MacNeill Robertson,** PC, KT, GCMG, FRSA, LRPS; British business executive; b. 12 April 1946, Port Ellen, Isle of Islay, Argyll, Scotland; s. of George P. Robertson and Marion Robertson; m. Sandra Wallace 1970; two s. one d.; ed Dunoon Grammar School and Univ. of Dundee; Scottish Organizer, Gen. & Municipal Workers' Union 1968–78; MP for Hamilton 1978–97, for Hamilton South 1997–99; Parl. Pvt. Sec. to Sec. of State for Social Services 1979; Opposition Spokesman on Scottish Affairs 1979–80, on Defence 1980–81, on Foreign and Commonwealth Affairs 1981–93; Prin. Spokesman on European Affairs 1984–94; Shadow Spokesman for Scotland 1994–97; Sec. of State for Defence 1997–99; Sec.-Gen. of NATO 1999–2003; Chair. Scottish Labour Party 1977–78; Vice-Chair. Bd British Council 1985–94; Exec. Deputy Chair. Cable & Wireless (C&W) 2003–06, Chair. Cable & Wireless International 2006–07, Sr Int. Adviser Cable and Wireless PLC 2007–; mem. Bd of Dirs Smiths Group 2004–06, Weir 2004–, Western Ferries (Clyde) Ltd 2004–, Scottish Devt Agency 1975–78, Scottish Tourist Bd 1974–76; Sr Counsellor, The Cohen Group, Washington, DC 2004–; Chair. Comm. on Global Road Safety 2004–; mem. Steering Cttee Königswinter Conf. 1983–92; mem. Council, Royal Inst. of Int. Affairs 1984–91, Jt Pres. 2001–11; Deputy Chair. TNK-BP 2006–13, Chair. Audit Cttee 2006–13; Jt Pres. Chatham House 2002–12; Chair. Comm. on Global Road Safety 2004–, Council of Man., Ditchley Foundation 2011–; Elder Brother, Trinity House 2001–; Pres. Hamilton Burns Club 2002; Chancellor, Order of St Michael and St George 2011–; Trustee, Queen Elizabeth Diamond Jubilee Trust 2012–, Advisory Bd, World War One Commemoration 2014; Licentiate, Royal Photographic Soc.; Hon. Regimental Col London Scottish (Volunteers) 2001; Hon. FRSE; Hon. Academician, Nat. Acad. of Sciences, Kyrgyz Repub.; Hon. Prof. of Politics, Univ. of Stirling 2009–; Grand Cross, Order of Merit (Germany, Italy, Poland, Hungary, Luxembourg), Grand Cross, Order of Star of Romania, Order of Jesus (Portugal), Order of Isabel the Catholic (Spain), Order of Leopold (Belgium), Order of Oranje-Nassau (Netherlands), Order of the Cross of Terra Mariana (First Class) 2004; Hon. LLD (Dundee, Bradford, St Andrews, Baku State Univ., Azerbaijan, Glasgow Caledonian, Stirling, West of Scotland), Hon. DSc (Cranfield – Royal Mil. Coll. of Science); Dr hc (European Univ., Armenia), (Acad. of Sciences, Azerbaijan), (School of Political and Admin. Studies, Bucharest); Winston Churchill Medal of Honour (English Speaking Union) 2003, Transatlantic Leadership Award (European Inst., Washington, DC) 2003, Award for Distinguished Int. Leadership (Atlantic Council of USA) 2003, Presidential Medal of Freedom (USA) 2003, Distinguished Service Medal, US Dept of Defense 2003, Wallace Award, American-Scottish Foundation 2009, Hanno R. Ellenbogen Citizenship Award. *Publications:* Islay and Jura: Photographs by George Robertson 2006, Dunblane – Its People in a Century of Change (with John Fraser) 2012. *Leisure interests:* photography, golf, walking, family, reading. *Address:* House of Lords, Westminster, London, SW1A 0PW (office); BP plc, 1 St James's Square, London, SW1Y, England (office). *Telephone:* (20) 7219-3000 (office). *E-mail:* robertsong@parliament.uk (office). *Website:* www.bp.com (office).

ROBINS, Sir Ralph Harry, Kt, DL, BSc, FREng; British business executive; b. 16 June 1932, Heanor, Derbyshire, England; s. of Leonard Haddon and Maud Lillian Robins; m. Patricia Maureen Grimes 1962; two d.; ed Imperial Coll., Univ. of London; Devt Engineer, Rolls-Royce 1955–66, Exec. Vice-Pres. Rolls-Royce Inc. 1971, Man. Dir Rolls-Royce Industrial and Marine Div. 1973, Commercial Dir Rolls-Royce Ltd 1978, Man. Dir Rolls-Royce PLC 1984–89, Deputy Chair. 1989–92 and Chief Exec. 1990–92, Chair. Rolls Royce 1992–2003; Chair. Defence Industries Council 1986–, Alter Technology Group; Deputy Lt Derbyshire 2002–; Pres. Soc. of British Aerospace Cos 1986–87, Deputy Pres. 1987–88; Dir (non-exec.) Standard Chartered 1988–2004, Schroders 1990–2002, Marks & Spencer 1992–2001, Cable & Wireless 1994– (Chair. (non-exec.) 1998–2003), Marshall Holdings; mem. Council for Science and Tech. 1993–98; Fellow, Imperial Coll.; Hon. FRAeS, Hon. FIMechE 1996; Commdr Order of Merit (Germany) 1996; Hon. DSc (Cranfield) 1994, (Cambridge) 2008, Hon. DBA (Strathclyde) 1996, Hon. DEng (Sheffield) 2001, (Nottingham) 2003. *Leisure interests:* tennis, golf, music, classic cars. *Address:* 33 Godfrey Street, Chelsea, London, SW3 3SX, England (home). *Telephone:* (20) 7352-9858 (home). *E-mail:* ralphrobins@mac.com.

ROBINSON, (Francis) Alastair Lavie; British banker; b. 19 Sept. 1937, London; s. of Stephen Robinson; m. Lavinia Napier 1961; two d.; ed Eton Coll.; Gen. Man. Mercantile Credit Co. 1971–78; Chair. Exec. Cttee then CEO and Pres. Barclays America Corpn, USA 1981–83; Regional Gen. Man. Barclays Bank Int. 1983–87; Dir Personnel, Barclays Bank PLC 1987–90, Exec. Dir 1990–96, Group Vice-Chair. 1992–96; Dir RMC PLC 1996–2005; Dir Marshall of Cambridge (Holdings) Ltd 1996–2006, Portman Bldg Soc. 1998–2006; apptd Chair. St Nicholas Hospice (Suffolk). *Leisure interests:* music, country pursuits, golf.

ROBINSON, Anne Josephine; British journalist and broadcaster; b. 26 Sept. 1944; m. 1st Charles Wilson (divorced); one d.; m. 2nd John Penrose (divorced 2008); ed Farnborough Hill Convent, Les Ambassadrices, France; reporter, Daily Mail 1967–68, Sunday Times 1968–77; Women's Ed. Daily Mirror 1979–80, Asst Ed. 1980–93, columnist 1983–93; columnist, Today 1993–95, The Times 1993–95, 1998–2001, The Sun 1995–97, Daily Express 1997–98, The Daily Telegraph 2003; Hon. Fellow, John Moores Univ. 1996. *Radio work includes:* Anne Robinson Show (BBC Radio 2) 1988–93. *Television includes:* presenter and writer (BBC) Points of View 1988–98, Watchdog 1993–2001, 2009–15, Going for a Song 1999–2000, The Weakest Link 2000–12 (also US version 2001–02), Great Britons 2002, Test the Nation 2002–07, Guess Who's Coming to Dinner? 2003, Outtake TV 2004–09, Travels with My Unfit Mother 2004, What's the Problem? 2005, Anne Robinson's Britain 2016. *Publication:* Memoirs of an Unfit Mother (autobiog.) 2001. *Leisure interests:* walking her dogs.

ROBINSON, Sir Anthony (Tony), Kt; British actor, comedian, amateur historian and television presenter; b. 15 Aug. 1946, Homerton, London, England; m. 1st Mary Shepherd (divorced); m. 2nd Louise Hobbs 2011; two c.; ed Wanstead High School, Cen. School of Speech and Drama, London; performed in first professional acting role as mem. of Fagin's gang in original production of musical Oliver! aged 12, including a stint as Artful Dodger; appeared in several West End shows, in film and on TV 1958–63; spent four years in repertory theatre, most notably at West Yorkshire Playhouse, Leeds; won an Arts Council bursary to work as a dir at Midland Arts Centre, Birmingham; f. Avon Touring Co. (Bristol-based community theatre co.) with writer David Illingworth; also wrote and narrated several Jackanory-style children's programmes; presenter, Codex (TV quiz for Channel 4) 2006–; mem. Labour Party, mem. Nat. Exec. Cttee 2000–04; Vice-Pres. actors' union Equity 1996–2000; Patron Street Child Africa charity; Hon. Pres. Young Archaeologists' Club of the Council for British Archaeology; Hon. MA (Bristol) 1999, (East London) 2002; Hon. LLD (Exeter) 2005; Dr hc (Open Univ.) 2005, (Oxford Brookes) 2006, (Chester) 2011; James Joyce Award, Literary and Historical Soc. of Univ. Coll. Dublin 2008. *Films include:* Brannigan 1975, Neverending Story III: Return to Fantasia 1994, Faeries (voice) 1999, Blackadder Back & Forth (short) 1999, Mrs Caldicot's Cabbage War 2002. *Radio includes:* presented Classic FM's Friendly Guide to Classical Music (series). *Television includes:* as actor: Doctor in Charge (series) 1972–73, Soap Opera in Stockwell (film) 1973, Horizon (series documentary) 1974, Lieutenant Kije (film) 1979, Follow the Star (film) 1979, Chronicle (series documentary) – The Crime of Captain Colthurst 1981, The Black Adder (series) 1983, Who Dares Wins (series) 1983–88, Jackanory (series) 1985–91, Black-Adder II (series) 1986, Black Adder the Third (series) 1987, Blackadder: The Cavalier Years (short) 1988, Blackadder's Christmas Carol (film) 1988, Blackadder Goes Forth (series) 1989, Maid Marian and Her Merry Men (series) 1989–94, Blood and Honey (film) 1991, Licence to Live (film) (also assoc. producer) 1994, My Wonderful Life (series) 1997–99, Tales from the Madhouse (mini-series) – The Best Friend 2000, Hogfather (film) 2006, Tony Robinson's Time Walks (series) 2012; as assoc. producer: Time Team (series documentary) 1994–2014, Time Team Digs (series documentary) 2002, Tony Robinson and… (series documentary) 2008; as writer: Jackanory (series) – Theseus the Hero 1985, – Odysseus: The Greatest Hero of Them All 1986, Tales from Fat Tulip's Garden (series) 1985–87, Blood and Honey (film) 1991, Maid Marian and Her Merry Men (series) 1993–94, Tales from the Madhouse (mini-series) – The Best Friend 2000, The Real Macbeth (documentary) 2001, Behind the Scenes at 'Time Team' (documentary) 2001, Time Team (series documentary) – Coventry's Lost Cathedral 2001, Fact or Fiction: Braveheart (special) 2001, Fact or Fiction: Boudica (special) 2002, The Worst Jobs in History (series documentary) 2004, Tony Robinson's Cunning Night Out (video) (also dir) 2007. *Publications:* has written 16 children's books; No Cunning Plan (autobiography) 2016. *Leisure interests:* supports Bristol City and Valencia football clubs, fan of the rock band Genesis. *Address:* Time Team, Channel 4, 124 Horseferry Road, London, SW1P 2TX, England (office). *Telephone:* (20) 7396-4444 (office). *E-mail:* info@channel4.com (office). *Website:* www.channel4.com/programmes/time-team (office).

ROBINSON, Dame Carol Vivien, DBE, MSc, PhD, FRS; British chemist and academic; *Dr Lee's Professor of Physical and Theoretical Chemistry, University of Oxford;* b. (Carol Vivien Bradley), 10 April 1956, Kent; m.; two s. one d.; ed Canterbury Coll. of Tech., Medway Coll. of Tech. Grad. of the Royal Soc. of Chem., Univ. of Wales, Swansea, Univ. of Cambridge, Univ. of Keele; began as Research Technician, Pfizer 1972–79; MRC Training Fellowship, Univ. of Bristol Medical School 1982–83; career break, birth of three children 1983–91; Postdoctoral Research Fellow, Univ. of Oxford 1991–95, Royal Soc. Univ. Research Fellow 1995–2001, Research Fellow, Wolfson Coll., Oxford 1998–2001, Titular Prof., Univ. of Oxford 1999–2001, Royal Soc. Research Prof. 2006–16, Dr Lee's Prof. of Physical and Theoretical Chem. 2009–, Professorial Fellow, Exeter Coll. 2009–, Assoc. Head, Math., Physics and Life Sciences Div., Univ. of Oxford 2012–13; Prof. of Mass Spectrometry, Dept of Chem., Univ. of Cambridge 2001–09, Sr Research Fellow, Churchill Coll. 2003–09; Assoc. Ed. Journal of the American Society for Mass Spectrometry 2000–13; Pres. Royal Soc. of Chemistry 2018–; mem. Editorial Bd Journal of Molecular and Cellular Proteomics 2002–17, Current Opinion in Structural Biology 2012–; mem. Nomination Cttee of Royal Soc. 2011–14, ERC Synergy Grant Panel responsible for selection and evaluation of grants 2012–13, Govt Blackett Review Panel for Biosecurity 2012–13, Council of Royal Soc. 2016–18; Fellow, Acad. of Medical Sciences 2009; Hon. Fellow, Churchill Coll., Cambridge 2012, Royal Soc. of Chemistry 2016, Wolfson Coll., Oxford; Dr hc (Kent) 2009, (York) 2010, (Bristol) 2013, (Liverpool) 2016, (Huddersfield) 2017, (South Denmark) 2017, (Ben-Gurion) 2018; RSC Silver Medal 2002, Biemann Medal, American Soc. for Mass Spectrometry 2003, Rosalind Franklin Award, Royal Soc. 2004, Christian B. Anfinsen Award, Protein Soc. 2007, Prelog Medal, ETH Zurich 2010, Davy Medal, Royal Soc. 2010, Women in Science Award, European

Molecular Biology Org./Fed. of European Biochemical Socs 2011, RSC Interdisciplinary Prize 2011, Aston Medal from the British Mass Spectrometry Soc. 2011, HUPO Award for Distinguished Achievement in Proteomic Sciences 2012, Anatrace Award for Membrane Proteins, American Biophysical Soc. 2013, Laureate, L'Oréal-UNESCO Awards for Women in Science (Europe) 2015, Havinga Medal, Havinga Foundation 2015, Torbern Bergmann Award, Swedish Chemical Soc. 2016, Astra Zeneca Award, Biochemical Soc. 2016, Hans Krebs Medal 2017, Frank H. Field & Joe L. Franklin Award for Outstanding Achievement in Mass Spectrometry, American Chemical Soc. 2018, Novozymes Prize, Novo Nordisk Fonden 2019. *Achievements include:* pioneering work in the devt of mass spectrometry as a tool for investigating structure and dynamics of protein complexes. *Publications:* more than 450 articles in scientific journals. *Leisure interests:* sport, gardening. *Address:* Department of Physical and Theoretical Chemistry Laboratory, University of Oxford, South Parks Road, Oxford, OX1 3QZ (office); Exeter College, Oxford, OX1 3DP, England (home). *Telephone:* (1865) 275473 (office). *E-mail:* carol.robinson@chem.ox.ac.uk (office). *Website:* research .chem.ox.ac.uk/carol-robinson.aspx (office); robinsonweb.chem.ox.ac.uk (office).

ROBINSON, Gene Ezia, BSc, PhD; American entomologist; *Director, Carl R. Woese Institute for Genomic Biology, University of Illinois;* b. 9 Jan. 1955; ed Cornell Univ.; faculty mem., Univ. of Illinois 1989–, becoming Swanlund Chair in Entomology, Prof. of Entomology and Neuroscience, Center for Advanced Study, fmr Dir, Campus Neuroscience Program, Dir, Bee Research Facility, Dir Carl R. Woese Inst. for Genomic Biology 2011–; fmr mem. Advisory Council, Nat. Inst. of Mental Health; Fellow, American Acad. of Arts & Sciences, Entomological Soc. of America; mem. NAS; Dr hc (Hebrew Univ.); Entomological Soc. of America Founders' Memorial Award, Wolf Prize in Agric. 2018. *Publications:* author or co-author of over 250 publications. *Address:* Carl R. Woese Institute for Genomic Biology, University of Illinois at Urbana-Champaign, 1206 West Gregory Drive, MC-195, Urbana, IL 61801, USA (office). *Telephone:* (217) 244–2999 (office). *Fax:* (217) 265-6800 (office). *E-mail:* info-igb@illinois.edu (office). *Website:* www.igb .illinois.edu (office).

ROBINSON, Geoffrey; British politician; b. 25 May 1938; s. of Robert Norman Robinson and Dorothy Jane Robinson (née Skelly); m. Marie Elena Giorgio 1967; one s. one d.; ed Emanuel School, Univ. of Cambridge, Yale Univ.; Research Asst, Labour Party 1965–68; Sr Exec., Industrial Reorganization Corpn 1968–70; Financial Controller, British Leyland 1971–72; Man. Dir Leyland Innocenti, Milan 1972–73; Chief Exec. Jaguar Cars 1973–75, Meriden Motor Cycle Workers' Co-operative 1978–80 (Dir 1980–82); MP (Labour) for Coventry NW 1976–; HM Paymaster Gen. 1997–98; Opposition Spokesman on Science 1982–83, on Regional Affairs and Industry 1983–86. Chair. TransTec PLC 1986–97; Dir West Midlands Enterprise Bd 1980–84; mem. Bd of Dirs, Coventry City Football Club 1996, 2002–, Acting Chair. 2005–07. *Publications:* The Unconventional Minister (autobiog.) 2000. *Leisure interests:* reading, architecture, gardens. *Address:* House of Commons, Westminster, London, SW1A 0AA (office); Constituency Office, Transport House, Short Street, Coventry, CV1 2LS, England. *Telephone:* (20) 7219-4083 (office). *Fax:* (20) 7219-0984 (office). *E-mail:* robinsong@parliament.uk (office); geoffrey@newstatesman.co.uk (office). *Website:* www.parliament.uk/biographies/ commons/mr-geoffrey-robinson/307 (office); www.labourincoventry.org.uk.

ROBINSON, Sir Gerrard Jude, Kt, FCMA; British business executive; b. 23 Oct. 1948; s. of Antony Robinson and Elizabeth Ann Robinson; m. 1st Maria Ann Borg 1970 (divorced 1990); one s. one d.; m. 2nd Heather Peta Leaman 1990; one s. one d.; ed St Mary's Coll., Castlehead; started work as cost clerk in Matchbox toy factory aged 16; Works Accountant, Lesney Products 1970–74; Financial Controller Lex Industrial Distribution and Hire 1974–80; Finance Dir Coca-Cola 1980–81, Sales and Marketing Dir 1981–83, Man. Dir 1983–84; Man. Dir Grand Metropolitan (GrandMet) Contract Services 1984–87; led a man. buy-out of GrandMet catering div. 1987; Chief Exec. Compass GP PLC 1987–91, Granada Group PLC 1991–95, Chair. 1995–2001; Chair. London Weekend Television 1994–96, ITN 1995–97, BSkyB 1995–98, Arts Council 1998–2004, Allied Domecq 2002–05, Moto Hospitality Ltd 2006–15; Hon. DLitt (Ulster), Hon. DSc (Econs) (Queen's) 1999. *Television:* I'll Show Them Who's Boss (series), Can Gerry Robinson Fix the NHS?, Can Gerry Robinson Fix Dementia?. *Publication:* I'll Show Them Who's Boss 2004. *Leisure interests:* golf, opera, chess, skiing, reading, music.

ROBINSON, Sir Ian, Kt, BSc, FREng, FIChemE, FRSE; British business executive; b. 3 May 1942, East Boldon, Durham; s. of Thomas Robinson and Eva Robinson; m. Kathleen Crawford Robinson (née Leay) 1967; one s. one d.; ed Leeds Univ., Harvard Business School, MA, USA; chartered engineer; fmr Chair. and Man. Dir of Eng Div., Trafalgar House PLC; Chair. Amey PLC 2001–03; CEO Scottish Power 1995–2001; Chair. Hilton Group PLC 2001–06, Chair. Ladbrokes PLC (after restructuring of Hilton Group) 2006–09; Chair. Scottish Advisory Task Force for Welfare to Work 1997–2000; Chair. Scottish Enterprise 2001–03; Dir (non-exec.) Scottish & Newcastle PLC 2004–08, Compass Group PLC 2006–; mem. Advisory Bd Siemens UK; mem. Dept of Trade and Industry Overseas Project Bd 1993–97, Offshore Industry Advisory Bd 1993–95, CBI Scottish Business Council 1995–98, Take Over Panel 2004–; Scottish Businessman of the Year, Business Insider's Corp. Elite Awards 1996, George E. Davis Medal for Outstanding Contribution to Chemical Eng 1998. *Leisure interests:* golf, gardening.

ROBINSON, James D., III, BS, MBA; American business executive; *Co-founder and General Partner, RRE Ventures LLC;* b. 19 Nov. 1935, Atlanta, Ga; s. of James D. Robinson, Jr and Josephine Crawford; m. 1st Bettye Bradley (divorced); one s. one d.; m. 2nd Linda Gosden 1984; two s. two d.; ed Georgia Inst. of Tech., Harvard Graduate School of Business Admin.; Officer, US Naval Supply Corps 1957–59; various depts of Morgan Guaranty Trust Co. 1961–66, Asst Vice-Pres. and Staff Asst to Chair. and Pres. 1967–68; Gen. Partner, White, Weld & Co. 1968–70; Pres., CEO American Express Int. Banking Corpn 1970–73; Exec. Vice-Pres. American Express Co. 1970–75, Pres. 1975–77, Dir 1975–93, Chair. Bd 1977–93; Chair. American Express Credit Corpn 1973–75; Pres. J. D. Robinson Inc. 1993–; Chair. and CEO RRE Investors 1994, Gen. Partner, RRE Ventures LLC 1999–; Chair. Bristol-Meyers Squibb Co. 2005–08; mem. Bd of Dirs The Coca-Cola Co. 1995–2015, Novell Inc. 2001–09; fmr mem. Bd of Dirs Concur, Business Insider; Chair. Emer. New York City Partnership, Chamber of Commerce Inc.; Hon. Chair. Memorial Sloan-Kettering Cancer Center; mem. Council on Foreign Relations, US Japan Business Council, Comm. for Econ. Devt; Hon. mem. Bd of Trustees, The

Brookings Inst. *Address:* RRE Ventures, 130 East 59th Street, 17th Floor, New York, NY 10022, USA (office). *Telephone:* (212) 418-5100 (office). *Fax:* (212) 688-0289 (office). *Website:* www.rre.com (office).

ROBINSON, Janet L., BA; American newspaper executive; b. 11 June 1950, Fall River, Mass; ed Salve Regina Coll., Exec. Educ. Program at Amos Tuck School, Dartmouth; public school teacher 1972–83; joined The New York Times in 1983, served in various sr advertising positions for the newspaper as well as for The New York Times Co. Women's Magazine Group and Sports Magazine Group, Sr Vice-Pres. Advertising of The Times 1995–96, Pres. and Gen. Man. The New York Times newspaper 1996–2004, Sr Vice-Pres. Newspaper Operations 2001–04, Exec. Vice-Pres. and COO The New York Times Co. 2004, Pres. and CEO 2004–11; mem. Bd The Advertising Council 1997, Vice-Chair. 2001–04, 2004–05, now mem. Advisory Cttee; mem. Bd of Dirs Steward Partners Holdings LLC 2014–, Ocean Point Financial Partners; mem. Int. Advisory Bd Fleishman Hillard; Chair. Bd of Trustees, Salve Regina Univ.; Trustee, Carnegie Corporation of New York, Univ. of Rhode Island Oceanography Grad. School, Preservation Soc. of Newport County; mem. Council of Foreign Relations; mem. Leadership Cttee, Lincoln Center Consolidated Corporate Fund; Hon. DBA (Salve Regina Univ.) 1998; Dr hc (Pace Univ.), (Univ. of Massachusetts Dartmouth), (Wheaton Coll.).

ROBINSON, John Harris, CBE, BSc, CEng, FREng, CIMgt, FIChemE, FRSA; British business executive; *Chairman, The Abbeyfield Society;* b. 22 Dec. 1940; s. of Thomas Robinson and Florence Robinson; m. Doreen Alice Gardner 1963; one s. one d.; ed Woodhouse Grove School, Univ. of Birmingham; with ICI PLC 1962–65, Fisons PLC 1965–70; Sr Consultant, PA Consulting Group 1970–75; Chief Exec. Woodhouse & Rixson (Holdings)) 1975–79; Man. Dir Healthcare Div., Smith & Nephew PLC 1979–82, Dir 1982–89, Deputy CEO 1989–90, CEO 1990–97, Chair. 1997–99; Chair. Low & Bonar PLC 1997–2001, UK Coal (fmrly RJB Mining) 1997–2003, George Wimpey PLC 1999–2007 (Dir (non-exec.) 1999–2007), Railtrack June–Nov. 2001, Paragon Healthcare Group 2002–06, Consort Medical plc (fmrly Bespak plc) 2004–08, Affinity Healthcare 2005–10, Oasis Healthcare 2007–10, The Abbeyfield Soc. 2009–; Operating Partner, Duke Street Capital 2000–10; Dir (non-exec.) Delta PLC 1993–2001, Esporta Group Ltd 2006–07; Chair. Healthcare Sector Group, Dept of Trade and Industry 1996–2001, mem. Industrial Devt Advisory Bd 1998–2001; mem. Council CBI 1991– (Chair. Tech. and Innovation Cttee 1998–2001), mem. Pres.'s Cttee 2001–; Chair. Council and Pro-Chancellor Univ. of Hull 1998–2006; mem. Cttee of Univ. Chairmen 1998–2006; Pres. Inst. of Chemical Engineers 1999–2000, Chartered Inst. of Man. 2002–03; Chair. McRobert Award, Royal Acad. of Eng 2010–; Trustee, Methodist Ind. Schools Trust 2011–; Gov., Hymers Coll., Hull 1984–2012, Woodhouse Grove School 2004–13; mem. Court of Assts, Worshipful Co. of Engineers 2006, Master 2010; Hon. DEng (Birmingham) 2000; Hon. DUniv (Bradford) 2000; Hon. DBA (Lincoln) 2002, Hon. DrSc (Hull) 2006. *Leisure interests:* theatre, cricket, golf. *Address:* The Abbeyfield Society, Saint Peter's House, 2 Bricket Road, Saint Albans, Herts., AL1 3JW, England (office). *Telephone:* (1727) 857536 (office). *Website:* www.abbeyfield.com (office).

ROBINSON, Mary, LLM, DCL, SC, MRIA; Irish academic, international civil servant, UN official and fmr head of state; *Special Envoy of the Secretary-General for Climate Change, United Nations;* b. 21 May 1944, Ballina, Co. Mayo; d. of Aubrey Bourke and Tessa O'Donnell; m. Nicholas Robinson 1970; two s. one d.; ed Mount Anville, Trinity Coll. Dublin, King's Inns, Dublin, Harvard Univ., USA; Barrister 1967, Sr Counsel 1980; called to English Bar (Middle Temple) 1973; Reid Prof. of Constitutional and Criminal Law, Trinity Coll. Dublin 1969–75, Lecturer in European Community Law 1975–90; Founder-Dir Irish Centre for European Law 1988–90; Senator 1969–89; Pres. of Ireland 1990–97; UN High Commr for Human Rights and Under-Sec.-Gen. 1997–2002; Chancellor, Univ. of Dublin 1998–; mem. Dublin City Council 1979–83; mem. New Ireland Forum 1983–84; mem. Irish Parl. Jt Cttee on EC Secondary Legislation 1973–89; mem. Vedel Cttee on Enlargement of European Parl., EC 1971–72, Saint-Geours Cttee on Energy Efficiency, EC 1978–79, Advisory Bd of Common Market Law Review 1976–90, Irish Parl. Jt Cttee on Marital Breakdown 1983–85, Editorial Bd of Irish Current Law Statutes Annotated 1984–90, Advisory Cttee of Interights, London 1984–90, Int. Comm. of Jurists, Geneva 1987–90, Cttee of Man., European Air Law Asscn 1989–90, Scientific Council of European Review of Public Law 1989–90, Euro Avocats, Brussels 1989–90; Gen. Rapporteur, Human Rights at the Dawn of the 21st Century, Council of Europe, Strasbourg 1993; Prof. of Practice, School of Int. and Public Affairs, Columbia Univ., New York 2004–; Pres. Cherish (Irish Asscn of Single Parents) 1973–90; Founding mem. and Chair. Council of Women World Leaders 2002–; mem. Club of Madrid (fmr Vice-Pres.); Special Envoy of the UN Sec.-Gen. for the Great Lakes Region of Africa 2013–14, for Climate Change 2014–; Pres. and Chair. Bd of Trustees Mary Robinson Foundation - Climate Justice; Founder and Pres. Realizing Rights: The Ethical Globalization Initiative 2002–10; mem. American Philosophical Soc.; mem. Bd of Dirs Vaccine Fund; mem. Leadership Council UN Global Coalition on Women and AIDS; mem. Advisory Bd Earth Inst.; Hon. mem. New York Bar Asscn, American Soc. of Int. Lawyers, Bar of Tanzania, Hon. Fellow, Trinity Coll. Dublin, Inst. of Engineers of Ireland, Royal Coll. of Physicians in Ireland, Hertford Coll. Oxford, LSE, Royal Coll. of Psychiatrists, London, Royal Coll. of Surgeons, Ireland, Royal Coll. of Obstetricians and Gynaecologists, London, Hon. Bencher King's Inns, Dublin, Middle Temple, London; Kt, Military and Hospitaller Order of St Lazarus of Jerusalem 2010; Dr hc (Nat. Univ. of Ireland, Cambridge, Brown, Liverpool, Dublin, Montpellier, St Andrews, Melbourne, Columbia, Nat. Univ. of Wales, Poznań, Toronto, Fordham, Queens Univ. Belfast, Northeastern Univ., Rennes, Coventry, Dublin City, Essex, Harvard, Leuven, London, Seoul, Univ. of Peace, Costa Rica, Uppsala, Yale, Basle, Nat. Univ. of Mongolia, A. Schweitzer Univ. Berne); Berkeley Medal, Univ. of California, Medal of Honour, Univ. of Coimbra, Medal of Honour, Ordem dos Advogados (Portugal), Gold Medal of Honour, Univ. of Salamanca, Andrés Bello Medal, Univ. of Chile, New Zealand Suffrage Centennial Medal, Freedom Prize, Max Schmidheiny Foundation (Switzerland), UNIFEM Award, Noel Foundation (USA), Marisa Bellisario Prize (Italy) 1991, European Media Prize (Netherlands) 1991, CARE Humanitarian Award (USA) 1993, Int. Human Rights Award, Int. League of Human Rights 1993, Liberal Int. Prize for Freedom 1993, Stephen P. Duggan Award (USA) 1994, Council of Europe North South Prize (Portugal) 1997, Collar of Hussein Bin Ali (Jordan) 1997, F. D. Roosevelt Four Freedoms Medal 1998, Erasmus Prize (Netherlands) 1999,

Fulbright Prize (USA) 1999, Garrigues Walker Prize (Spain) 2000, William Butler Prize (USA) 2000, Indira Gandhi Peace Prize (India) 2000, Sydney Peace Prize, Amnesty International Amb. of Conscience Award 2004, Presidential Medal of Freedom 2009. *Publication:* Everybody Matters (memoir) 2012. *Address:* Office of the Secretary-General, United Nations, New York, NY 10017, USA (office). *Telephone:* (212) 963-1234 (office). *Fax:* (212) 963-4879 (office). *Website:* www.un.org/sg (office); www.mrfcj.org.

ROBINSON, Nick; British journalist; b. 5 Oct. 1963, Macclesfield, Cheshire; ed Cheadle Hulme School, Univ. Coll., Oxford; trainee producer on programmes, including Brass Tacks, Newsround, Crimewatch 1986, then Deputy Ed. On the Record, Panorama; fmr presenter Late Night Live and Weekend Breakfast (both on BBC Radio Five Live), Westminster Live (BBC 2); fmr Chief Political Corresp., BBC News 24, presenting Straight Talk and One to One –2002; Political Ed. ITV News 2002–05; columnist of political 'Notebook' in The Times 2003–; Political Ed., BBC 2005–15; Presenter, Today, BBC Radio 4 2015–. *Publications:* Live from Downing Street 2012, Election Notebook: The Inside Story Of The Battle Over Britain's Future And My Personal Battle To Report It 2015. *Leisure interest:* sailing. *Address:* BBC News Centre, Broadcasting House, London, W1A 1AA, England. *Telephone:* (20) 8624-9644. *Website:* www.bbc.co.uk/radio4/today.

ROBINSON, Rt Hon. Peter David, MLA; British politician; b. 29 Dec. 1948, Belfast, NI; s. of David McCrea Robinson and Sheila Robinson; m. Iris Collins 1970; two s. one d.; ed Annadale Grammar School, Castlereagh Coll. of Further Educ.; fmr estate agent; Founding mem. Ulster Democratic Unionist Party (DUP) and mem. Cen. Exec. Cttee 1973– (Sec. 1974–79), Gen. Sec. DUP 1975–79, Deputy Leader 1980–, Spokesman on Constitutional Affairs; MP for Belfast E, House of Commons 1979–2010 (resgnd seat Dec. 1985 in protest against Anglo-Irish Agreement; re-elected Jan. 1986); mem. for Belfast E, NI Ass. 1982–86 (Chair. Environment Cttee 1982–86), mem. NI Select Cttee 1994, Shipbuilding Group 1997, MLA for Belfast E 1998– (Ass. suspended 11 Feb. 2000, restored 30 May 2000); Minister for Regional Devt 1999–2000, 2001–02, for Finance and Personnel 2007–08; First Minister of NI 2008–16 (suspended active role 11 Jan.–3 Feb. 2010, 10 Sept.–20 Oct. 2015); Leader DUP 2008–15; mem. Castlereagh Borough Council 1977–2008, Alderman 1978–2008, Deputy Mayor 1978, Mayor 1986; mem. NI Forum 1996–98, NI Sports Council; Democratic Unionist; Hon. Dir Voice Newspaper Ltd, Crown Publications; Freedom of Borough of Castlereagh. *Publications:* Ulster – The Facts 1982 (co-author); booklets: Give Me Liberty, Hands Off the UDR, IRA/Sinn Fein, The North Answers Back 1970, Capital Punishment for Capital Crime 1978, Ulster the Prey, Carson Man of Action, A War to Be Won, It's Londonderry, Self-inflicted 1981, Ulster in Peril 1981, Savagery and Suffering 1981, Their Cry Was "No Surrender" 1989, The Union Under Fire 1995, Victims. *Leisure interests:* breeding Japanese Koi, bowling, golf. *Address:* Democratic Unionist Party (DUP), 91 Dundela Avenue, Belfast, BT4 3BU (office); 51 Gransha Road, Dundonald, BT16 2HB, Northern Ireland (home). *Telephone:* (28) 9047-1155 (office). *Fax:* (28) 9052-1289 (office). *E-mail:* peter.robinson.mp@btconnect.com (office); info@mydup.com (office). *Website:* www.mydup.com (office); www.peterrobinson.org (office).

ROBINSON, William (Smokey), Jr; American R&B and soul singer, songwriter and producer; b. 19 Feb. 1940, Detroit, Mich.; m. 1st Claudette Robinson 1959; two c.; m. 2nd Frances Robinson; fmr singer with The Matadors; singer with The Miracles 1954–72, also billed as Smokey Robinson and The Miracles 1967–72; solo artist 1973–; Vice-Pres. Motown 1961–88; Exec. Producer and composer on film, Big Time 1977; numerous TV appearances; f. SFGL Foods, Inc.; Dr hc (Howard Univ.) 2006, (Berklee Coll. of Music) 2009; Grammy Award for Best R&B Vocal Performance 1988, Grammy Living Legend Award 1989, Soul Train Heritage Award 1991, Motor City Music Award for Lifetime Achievement 1992, Grammy Lifetime Achievement Award 1999, Kennedy Center Honor 2006, Q Award for Outstanding Contribution to Music 2006, Ivor Novello Special Int. Award 2009. *Compositions include:* most recordings with The Miracles –1968; also The Way You Do The Things You Do (recorded by The Temptations) 1964, My Guy (co-writer, recorded by Mary Wells) 1964, My Girl (recorded by The Temptations) 1965. *Recordings include:* albums: with The Miracles: The Fabulous Miracles 1963, The Miracles On Stage 1963, Doin' Mickey's Monkey 1964, Going To A Go-Go 1966, Make It Happen 1967, Special Occasion 1968, Time Out For... 1969, What Love Has Joined Together 1970, A Pocketful Of Miracles 1970, One Dozen Roses 1971, Flying High Together 1972; solo: Smokey 1973, Pure Smokey 1974, A Quiet Storm 1975, Smokey's Family Robinson 1976, Deep In My Soul 1977, Big Time (OST) 1977, Love Breeze 1978, Smokin' Motown 1979, Where There's Smoke 1979, Warm Thoughts 1980, Being With You 1981, Yes It's You Lady 1982, Touch The Sky 1983, Essar 1984, Smoke Signals 1986, One Heartbeat 1987, Love Songs 1988, Love, Smokey 1990, Double Good Everything 1991, Ballads 1995, Our Very Best Christmas 1999, Intimate 1999, Food For The Spirit 2004, Timeless Love 2006, Time Flies When You're Having Fun 2009, Smokey & Friends 2014. *Address:* c/o WME, 9601 Wilshire Blvd, Beverly Hills, CA 90201, USA (office). *Website:* www.smokeyrobinson.com.

ROBLES, Dayron; Cuban athlete; b. 19 Nov. 1986, Guantánamo; sprinter and hurdler; world record holder in 110m hurdles of 12.87 seconds, set at Golden Spike Ostrava meet 12 June 2008; finished sixth in 110m hurdles at World Youth Championships, Sherbrooke, Canada 2003; gold medal, 110m hurdles, Pan American Junior Championships, Windsor 2005, Cen. American and Caribbean Games, Cartagena, Colombia 2006, Havana, Cuba 2009, Pan American Games, Rio de Janeiro 2007, Int. Asscn of Athletics Feds (IAAF) World Athletics Final, Stuttgart 2007, Olympic Games, Beijing 2008 (12.93 seconds), Pan American Games, Guadalajara, Mexico 2011; gold medal, 60m hurdles, World Indoor Championships, Doha 2010; silver medal, World Jr Championships, Grosseto, Italy 2004, Cen. American and Caribbean Championships, Nassau, Bahamas, 60m hurdles, World Indoor Championships, Moscow 2006 (personal best time of 7.46 seconds); finished fourth in 110m hurdles, World Championships, Osaka 2007.

ROBLES, Josue (Joe), Jr, BBA, MBA; Puerto Rican/American business executive; b. 24 Jan. 1946, Rio Piedras, Puerto Rico; m. Patty Robles; three c.; ed Kent State Univ., Indiana State Univ.; joined US Army 1966, served in a variety of command and staff positions, including active duty posts in Korea, Viet Nam, Germany and Operations Desert Shield/Desert Storm in the Middle East 1966–94, served as Dir of Army Budget and as Commdg Gen. of 1st Infantry Div.; mem. Bd of Dirs United Services Automobile Association (USAA) while on active duty 1990–94, joined USAA as Special Asst to the Chair. after retiring from US Army as Maj.-Gen. 1994, Chief Financial Officer and Controller 1994–2007, Corp. Treas. 1995–2007, Pres. and CEO 2007–15 (retd), includes USAA's Property and Casualty Insurance Group, Fed. Savings Bank, Life Insurance Co. of New York, Investment Man. Co., Alliance Services Co., Financial Planning Services; apptd Chair. MyVA Advisory Cttee 2015; mem. Bd of Dirs DTE Energy, CHRISTUS Santa Rosa Hosp., CHRISTUS Santa Rosa Children's Hosp. Foundation, P16Plus Council of Greater Bexar Co. Foundation; mem. Advisory Bd FM Global, Texas Gov.'s Business Council; Distinguished Service Medal with Oak Leaf Cluster, Legion of Merit with two Oak Leaf Clusters, Bronze Star with Oak Leaf Cluster, Meritorious Service Medal with Oak Leaf Cluster; named by Christian Science Monitor as No. 1 Veteran in Business 2009, named by American Banker as Innovator of the Year 2009.

ROBLES FERNÁNDEZ, Margarita; Spanish judge and politician; *Minister of Defence;* b. 10 Nov. 1956, León; ed Univ. of Barcelona; Pres., Provincial Court of Barcelona 1991–93; Under-Sec., Ministry of Justice 1993–94; Sec. of State for the Interior, Ministry of Justice and Interior 1994–96; Justice of the Supreme Court 2004–16; mem. Gen. Council of the Judiciary 2008–13; mem. Gen. Congress of Deputies (Parl.) (PSOE) for Madrid 2016–18, PSOE Leader in Congress 2017–18; Minister of Defence 2018–; mem. Partido Socialista Obrero Español (PSOE, Spanish Socialist Workers' Party); Grand Cross, Order of St Raymond of Peñafort 2013. *Address:* Ministry of Defence, Paseo de la Castellana 109, 28046 Madrid, Spain (office). *Telephone:* (91) 3955000 (office). *E-mail:* infodefensa@mde.es (office). *Website:* www.defensa.gob.es (office).

ROBLES ORTEGA, HE Cardinal Francisco; Mexican ecclesiastic; *Archbishop of Guadalajara, Jalisco;* b. 2 March 1949, Mascota, Jalisco; ed studies in Mexico and at Pontifical Gregorian Univ., Rome; ordained priest of Autlán, Jalisco 1976; Parish Priest in Menor de Autlan 1979–91; Auxiliary Bishop of Toluca and Titular Bishop of Bossa 1991–96; Bishop of Toluca 1996–2003; Archbishop of Monterrey, Nuevo León 2003–11; cr. Cardinal (Cardinal-Priest of Santa Maria della Presentazione) 2007; Archbishop of Guadalajara, Jalisco 2011–; participated in Papal Conclave 2013; represented Mexico at Special Ass. of the Synod of Bishops for America 1997; Pres. Conferencia del Episcopado Mexicano; Moderator, Caribeña de Líderes Religiosos - Religiones por la Paz; mem. Comisión Pontificia para América Latina 2008–, Pontificio Consejo para la Promoción de la Nueva Evangelización 2011–. *Address:* Arzobispado, Apartado 1-331, Calle Liceo 17, 44100 Guadalajara, Jalisco, Mexico (office). *Telephone:* (33) 3614-5504 (office). *Fax:* (33) 3658-2300 (office). *E-mail:* info@arquidiocesisgdl.org.mx (office). *Website:* www.arquidiocesisgdl.org.mx (office).

ROBSON, Alan David, AM, BAgrSc, PhD, FTSE, FACE, FACEL, FAIAS; Australian professor of agriculture and fmr university administrator; *Professor Emeritus of Agriculture, University of Western Australia;* ed Univ. of Melbourne, Univ. of Western Australia; several positions at Univ. of Western Australia, including Dean of Faculty of Agric., Head of School of Agric., Prof. of Agric. (Soil Science), now Emer., Foundation Dir Co-operative Research Centre for Legumes in Mediterranean Agric. (CLIMA), Deputy Vice-Chancellor and Provost 1993–2004, Vice-Chancellor 2004–12, also currently Hackett Prof. of Agric.; mem. Premier's Science Council; Chair. Group of Eight 2007–10; Deputy Chair. Council of the Nat. Library 1998–2005, Universities Australia 2009–11; mem. Western Australian Science Council 2003–09, CSIRO Bd 2003–08; Foundation Chair. Grain Legumes Research Council; Deputy Chair. Research Grants Cttee of the Australian Research Council; mem. Cttee for Univ. Training and Staff Devt 1998–99, Australian Teaching and Learning Cttee 2000–04, Bd of Dirs Australian Univs Quality Agency; Fellow, Acad. of Tech. Sciences and Eng (Australia) 1987; Citizen of Western Australia 2009; Australian Medal of Agric. Science 1987, Centenary Medal 2003. *Address:* Adjunct and Honorary Staff (Earth and Environment), The University of Western Australia (M087), 35 Stirling Highway, Crawley, WA 6009, Australia (office). *Telephone:* (8) 6488-3466 (office). *E-mail:* alan.robson@uwa.edu (office). *Website:* www.uwa.edu.au/people/alan.robson (office).

ROBSON, Bryan, OBE; British professional football manager and fmr professional footballer; b. 11 Jan. 1957, Chester-le-Street, County Durham; s. of Brian Robson and Maureen Lowther; m. Denise Brindley 1979; one s. two d.; ed Birtley Lord Lawson Comprehensive; midfielder; youth player, West Bromwich Albion 1972–74, sr team 1974–81; played for Manchester United 1981–94 (Capt. 1982–94, won Premier League 1992/93, 1993/94, FA Cup 1983, 1985, 1990, 1994, Football League Cup 1992, FA Charity Shield 1983, 1990, 1993, UEFA Cup Winners' Cup 1991, UEFA Super Cup 1991); only British capt. to lead a side to four FA Cup wins; longest serving capt. in club history; mem. England U-21 team 1979–80, England B team 1979–80, England nat. team (90 int. caps (65 as capt. 1982–91), scoring 26 goals) 1980–91, Asst Man. 1994–96; player/Man. Middlesbrough Football Club 1994–2001 (won Football League First Div. 1994/95), Man. 1996–2000, Jt Man. with Terry Venables 2000–01; Man. Bradford City 2003–04, West Bromwich Albion 2004–06, Sheffield United FC 2007–08; Global Amb. for Manchester United 2008–09, 2011–; Man. Thailand nat. team 2009–11 (resgnd); formed Robson Lloyd Consultancy Ltd (specialist sports co.) (dissolved) 2007–18; Hon. BA (Salford) 1992, (Manchester) 1992; named in list of Football League 100 Legends, an Inaugural Inductee of English Football Hall of Fame 2002, named as one of West Bromwich Albion's 16 greatest players in poll organized as part of club's 125th anniversary celebrations 2004. *Publications:* United I Stand 1983, Robbo: My Autobiography 2006. *Leisure interests:* golf, horse racing. *Telephone:* (16) 1868-8000 (office). *E-mail:* enquiries@manutd.co.uk (office).

ROCCA, Costantino; Italian professional golfer; b. 4 Dec. 1956, Bergamo; m. Antonella Rocca 1981; one s. one d.; fmr factory worker and caddie; turned professional 1981; won Nazionale Open 1984, Enichem Open 1985, Pinetina Open 1986, Index Open 1987, Rolex Pro-Am (Switzerland) 1988, Open V33 Da Grand Lyon 1993, Peugeot Open de France 1993, Volvo PGA Championship 1996, Canon European Masters 1997, West of Ireland Golf Classic 1999; qualified for PGA European Tour through 1989 Challenge Tour; first Italian golfer to be mem. European Ryder Cup team 1993; mem. European Ryder Cup team 1995, 1997; plays on European Seniors Tour 2007–; owner Rocca Golf Acad. *Leisure interests:* fishing, football. *Website:* www.costantinorocca.it.

ROCCA, Francesco; Italian lawyer and international organizations official; *President, International Federation of Red Cross and Red Crescent Societies (IFRC);* b. 1 Sept. 1965; two s.; ed La Sapienza Univ., Public Admin Superior School; worked as volunteer, then as Head, Dormitory of San Saba 1988–93; Volunteer, Caritas 1988–90, Piccola Casa della Divina Provvidenza Cottolengo 1988–91; fought organized crime as a lawyer and volunteer 1990–2003; Gen. Dir Sant'Andrea Hospital, Rome 2003–07; apptd Head of Emergency Operations, Italian Red Cross 2007, Extraordinary Commr 2009–13, Nat. Pres. 2013–17, 2017–; Vice-Pres. Int. Fed. of Red Cross and Red Crescent Socs 2013–17, Pres. 2017– (mem. Bd of Dirs 2009); Gen. Dir IDI Inst. of Dermatology, Rome 2015; mem., Nat. Cancer Inst.-IRCSS Fondazione Pascale di Napoli 2005–09, Nat. Inst. for Infectious Diseases "Lazzaro Spallanzani" of Rome. *Address:* International Federation of Red Cross and Red Crescent Societies (IFRC), POB 303, 1211 Geneva 19, Switzerland (office). *Telephone:* 227304222 (office). *Fax:* 227304200 (office). *E-mail:* secretariat@ifrc.org (office). *Website:* www.ifrc.org (office).

ROĆEN, Milan; Montenegrin diplomatist and politician; *Chief Political Adviser to the Prime Minister;* b. 23 Nov. 1950, Žabljak; m. Stana Roćen; one s.; ed Faculty of Political Science, Univ. of Belgrade; journalist, Ekonomska Politika magazine 1976–79; worked in Information and Propaganda Dept of Pres. of Cen. Cttee of League of Communists of Montenegro 1979–82, Political Chief of Staff 1982–88; Deputy Minister of Foreign Affairs 1988–92; Minister-Counsellor for Political Affairs, Fed. Repub. of Yugoslavia Embassy, Moscow, Russia 1992–97; Foreign Policy Adviser to Prime Minister of Repub. of Montenegro 1997–98, to Pres. 1998–2003; Chief Political Adviser to Prime Minister of Montenegro 2003, Feb.–Sept. 2006, 2012–16; Amb. of Serbia and Montenegro to Russian Fed. (also accred to Kazakhstan, Uzbekistan, Turkmenistan, Tajikistan, Kyrgyzstan and Georgia) 2003–06; Co-ordinator Pro-independence Bloc and Gen. Man. of campaign for referendum on independence Feb.–May 2006; Minister of Foreign Affairs 2006–12, also of European Integration 2010–12; mem. Presidium of Democratic Party of Socialists of Montenegro. *Address:* c/o Demokratska partija socijalista, 81000 Podgorica, Ul. Jovana Tomaševića BB, Montenegro (office). *Telephone:* (20) 482812 (office). *Fax:* (20) 224076 (office). *E-mail:* milan.rocen@gsv.gov.me (office). *Website:* www.dps.me (office).

ROCHA, John, CBE; British fashion designer; b. 1953, Hong Kong; m. Odette Rocha; three c.; ed Croydon Coll. of Design and Technology, London Coll. of Fashion; moved to London 1970; opened a design business in Kilkenny, Ireland 1977, later moved to Dublin; worked briefly in Milan 1987–89 then returned to Ireland; menswear line 1993, jeans line 1997; regular collections at all major int. fashion shows; 13-year collaboration with Debenhams.department store chain; has also designed interiors for hotels and office blocks including The Morrison Hotel, Dublin, Oriaon Building, Birmingham; launched John Rocha at Waterford Crystal collection 1997; f. Three Moon Design Studio, Dublin; retd from British Fashion Week 2014; Dr hc (Univ. of Ulster at Queens), (Univ. College for the Creative Arts, Epsom); British Designer of the Year 1994, Special Award, Ernst and Young Irish Entrepreneur of the Year Awards 2008, Outstanding Achievement in Art and Design, Asian Awards 2015, Gold Award, Asscn of Colleges 2015. *Address:* Three Moon Design Studio, 10 Ely Place, Dublin 2, Ireland (office). *Telephone:* (1) 662-9225 (office). *Fax:* (1) 662-9226 (office). *E-mail:* info@johnrocha.ie (office). *Website:* www.johnrocha.ie (office).

ROCHA, José Luis Fialho; Cabo Verde diplomatist and government official; *Permanent Representative, United Nations;* b. 6 Aug. 1956, São Vicente; m. Yamile Luque Tamayo Saco Rocha; two s. one d.; ed Univ. of Pittsburgh, USA, Univ. of Louvain, Belgium; joined Ministry of Planning and Co-operation 1981, Head of Div. of Bilateral Co-operation (DGCI) 1985–88, Dir of Services, DGCI, mem. Installation Cttee and Recruiting PROMEX (Centre for the promotion of exports and investment) 1988–90, Dir-Gen. for Int. Co-operation, Deputy Nat. Authorizing Officer of European Devt Fund, mem. Gen. Council of PROMEX 1991–95, Amb. to Belgium and Luxembourg and Head of Mission to EU and ACP Group 1995–99, Amb. and Rep. of Org. Int. de la Francophonie to EU 1999–2006, Dir-Gen. of Foreign Policy, Ministry of Foreign Affairs, Co-operation and Communities 2007–09, Nat. Dir for Political Affairs and Co-operation 2010–11, Sec. of State (Deputy Minister) for Foreign Affairs 2011–14, Amb. to USA (also accred to Canada and Mexico) 2014–16, Amb. and Perm. Rep. to UN, New York 2016–; Medal of Merit, Cabo Verde 2017. *Address:* Permanent Mission of Cabo Verde to the United Nations, 27 East 69th Street, New York, NY 10021, USA (office). *Telephone:* (212) 472-0333 (office). *Fax:* (212) 794-1398 (office). *E-mail:* jose.l.rocha@mnec.gov.cv (office); capeverde@un.int (office).

ROCHA VIEIRA, Lt-Gen. Vasco Joaquim, MA; Portuguese administrator and army officer (retd); b. 16 Aug. 1939, Lagoa; s. of João da Silva Vieira and Maria Vieira Rocha e Vieira; m. Maria Leonor de Andrada Soares de Albergaria 1976; three s.; ed Tech. Univ. of Lisbon; Prof., Mil. Acad. Lisbon 1968–69; Army Staff course 1969–72; engineer, Urbanization Dept, Urban Council, Lisbon 1969–73; Sec. for Public Works and Communications, Govt of Macao 1974–75; Dir Engineers Branch, Portuguese Army 1975–76; Army Chief-of-Staff 1976–78; Mil. Rep. of Portugal, SHAPE, Mons, Belgium 1978–82; Army War Coll. course 1982–83; Nat. Defence course 1983–84; Prof., Army War Coll., Lisbon 1983–84; Deputy Dir Nat. Defence Inst., Lisbon 1984–86; Minister for Portuguese Autonomous Region of the Azores 1986–91; Gov. of Macao 1991–99; Chancellor Portuguese Chancery for Honours 2006; Grand Cross, Mil. Order of Christ 1996; Grand Cross, Order of Prince Henry; Kt Commdr, Mil. Order of Aviz; Grand Cross, Order of Infante D. Henrique; service medals; decorations from Brazil, France, Belgium, USA and Japan. *Leisure interests:* tennis, golf. *Address:* c/o Chancelaria das Ordens Honoríficas Portuguesas, Presidência da República, Palácio Nacional de Belém, Calçada da Ajuda, 1340-022 Lisbon (office); Quinta Patino Lote 52, Alcoitão, 2645-143 Alcabideche, Portugal (home). *Telephone:* (21) 3614695 (office); (21) 4693232 (home). *Fax:* (21) 4607258 (home). *E-mail:* vascojrv@yahoo.com (home). *Website:* www.ordens.presidencia.pt (office).

ROCHER, Guy, CC, OQ, PhD, FRSC; Canadian sociologist and academic; *Professor Emeritus of Sociology, University of Montreal;* b. 20 April 1924, Berthierville, PQ; s. of Barthélemy Rocher and Jeanne Magnan; m. 1st Suzanne Cloutier 1949; m. 2nd Claire-Emmanuèle Depocas 1985; four d.; ed Univ. of Montréal, Univ. Laval and Harvard Univ.; Asst Prof. Univ. Laval 1952–57, Assoc. Prof. 1957–60; Prof. of Sociology, Univ. of Montreal 1960–2010, Prof. Emer. 2010–;

Deputy Minister of Cultural Devt Govt of Québec 1977–79, of Social Devt 1981–82; mem. Royal Comm. on Educ. in Québec 1961–66; Vice-Pres. Canada Council of Arts 1969–74, Cttee on Univ. Research, Royal Soc. of Canada 1989–90; Pres. Radio-Québec 1979–81; mem. American Acad. of Arts and Sciences; Hon. LLD (Laval) 1996; Dr hc Sociology (Moncton) 1997, (Univ. of Québec at Montreal) 2002; Prix Marcel-Vincent, ACFAS 1989, Prix Léon-Gérin, Québec Govt 1995, Prix Molson 1997, Prix Esdras-Minville 1998; Outstanding Contrib. Award, Canadian Asscn for Sociology and Anthropology 1988, RSC Médaille Pierre Chauveau 1991, RSC Prix William Dawson 1999. *Films:* subject of film by Anne-Marie Rocher: Guy Rocher, Sociologist as Protagonist. *Publications:* Introduction à la sociologie générale 1969, Talcott Parsons et la sociologie américaine, Le Québec en mutation 1973, Ecole et société au Québec 1975, Entre les rêves et l'histoire 1989, Le Québec en jeu 1992, Entre droit et technique 1994, Etudes de sociologie du droit et de l'éthique 1996, Théories et emergence du droit 1998, May Weber, Rudolf Stammler et le matérialisme historique 2001, Le Droit à l'égalité 2001; and numerous articles on sociology, on sociology of law, of education and of health and on the evolution of Québec society. *Leisure interests:* tai-chi, skiing, swimming, concerts, reading. *Address:* Faculté de Droit, Université de Montréal, CP 6128, Succursale Centre-Ville, Montréal, PQ H3C 3J7 (office); 50 Berlioz, Apt 205, Vedun, PQ H3E 1M2, Canada (home). *Telephone:* (514) 343-5993 (office); (514) 344-0882 (home). *E-mail:* guy.rocher@umontreal.ca (office).

ROCK, Allan, BA, LLB, QC; Canadian lawyer, fmr politician, fmr diplomatist and academic; *Professor, Faculty of Law, Univ. of Ottawa;* b. 30 Aug. 1947, Ottawa; m. Deborah Hanscom; three s. one d.; ed Univ. of Ottawa; Assoc. Fasken and Calvin (now Fasken Martineau Dumoulin) 1973–93, partner 1979–93; pvt. practice –1993; MP for Etobicoke Centre 1993–2004; Minister of Justice and Attorney-Gen. 1993–97, Minister of Health 1997–2002, Minister of Industry 2002–03; Perm. Rep. to UN Jan. 2004–06; apptd attorney, Sutts Strosberg LLP, Windsor, Ont. 2006; Pres. and Vice-Chancellor Univ. of Ottawa 2008–16, Emer. Pres. and Full Prof., Faculty of Law 2016–; Special Advisor on Sri Lanka to UN on subject of Children and Armed Conflict; Chair. Trust Fund for War-Affected Children in Northern Uganda; mem. Security Council Report's Int. Advisory Group; Fellow, American Coll. of Trial Lawyers; fmr Treas. (CEO) Law Soc. of Upper Canada; currently, Univ. Ottawa. *Address:* University of Ottawa, 75 Laurier Avenue, East Ottawa, ON K1N 6N5, Canada (office). *Telephone:* (613) 562-5700 (office). *Fax:* (613) 562-5323 (office). *E-mail:* Allan.Rock@uOttawa.ca (office); uOttawainfo@uOttawa.ca (office). *Website:* www.uottawa.ca.

ROCKBURNE, Dorothea; American/Canadian artist; b. 18 Oct. 1932, Montreal, Canada; m. 1951 (divorced); one d.; ed Ecole des Beaux-Arts, Montreal, Montreal Museum School, Black Mountain Coll., NC; work in many public collections, including Whitney Museum, Museum of Modern Art, Metropolitan Museum of Art, Guggenheim Museum, Nat. Museum of Women in Art, Corcoran Gallery, MoCA LA, Philadelphia Museum of Art, Brooklyn Museum of Art, Nat. Galleries - Washington, Houston Museum of Fine Arts, Carnegie Museum, Museum of Fine Arts - Boston, Cranbrook Art Museum, LACMA, Nat. Acad. of Design Museum, Parrish Art Museum, Queensland Art Gallery-Australia, Nat. Gallery of Canada, Montreal Museum of Fine Arts, Ludwig Museum, Aachen, Germany, Museum of New Zealand; Artist-in-Residence, American Acad. in Rome 1991, Bellagio Study Centre, Italy 1997; Secco frescoes at Hilton Hotel, San Jose, Calif. 1992, Sony HQ, New York 1993, Edward T. Grignoux US Courthouse, Portland, Me 1996, Univ. of Michigan 1997, secco frescoes at US Embassy in Kingston, Jamaica 2012; Visiting Artist, Skowhegan School of Painting and Sculpture 1984; Avery Distinguished Prof., Bard Coll. Annandale-on-Hudson, NY 1986; mem. Dept of Art, American Acad. of Arts and Letters 2001; Vice-Pres. for Art, American Acad. of Arts and Letters 2015–(18); Hon. DFA (Coll. for Creative Studies) 2002; Guggenheim Fellow 1972, Art Inst. of Chicago Witowsky Painting Award 1972, Nat. Endowment for the Arts 1974, Creative Arts Award, Brandeis Univ. 1985, Lifetime Achievement Award, American Acad. of Arts and Letters 1999, American Acad. of Arts and Letters, Dept of Art 2001, Pollock-Krasner Foundation Grant 2002, Nat. Acad. of Design, Pike Award for Watercolour 2002, Art Omi Int., Francis J. Greenberger Award 2003, Pollock-Krasner Foundation Lee Krasner Award 2003 and 2007. *Leisure interests:* astronomy, music, mathematics, theatre, poetry, friends. *Address:* 136 Grand Street, 2WF, New York, NY 10013, USA (home). *Telephone:* (212) 226-4471 (home). *Fax:* (866) 351-4234 (home). *E-mail:* drockburne@gmail.com (office). *Website:* www.dorothearockburne.com (office).

ROCKEFELLER, John (Jay) Davison, IV, BA; American fmr politician; *Distinguished Fellow, Council on Foreign Relations;* b. 18 June 1937, New York; s. of John Davison Rockefeller, III and Blanchette F. Rockefeller (née Hooker); m. Sharon Percy 1967; three s. one d.; ed Harvard and Yale Univs and Int. Christian Univ., Japan; mem. Nat. Advisory Council, Peace Corps 1961, Special Adviser to Dir 1962, Operations Officer in Charge of work in Philippines until 1963; Bureau of Far Eastern Affairs, US State Dept 1963, later Asst to Asst Sec. of State for Far Eastern Affairs; consultant, President's Comm. on Juvenile Delinquency and Youth Crime 1964, White House Conf. on Balanced Growth and Econ. Devt 1978, Pres.'s Comm. on Coal 1978–80; field worker, Action for Appalachian Youth Program 1964; mem. W Virginia House of Dels 1966–68; Sec. of State, W Va 1968–72; Pres. West Virginia Wesleyan Coll., Buckhannon 1973–75; Gov. of W Va 1977–85, Senator from West Virginia 1984–Jan. 2015 (retd), Chair. Senate Select Cttee on Intelligence, Cttee on Commerce, Science, and Transportation, Co-Chair. Senate Steel Caucus, US Trade Advisor; Distinguished Fellow, Council on Foreign Relations 2015–; mem. Asia Soc., Japan Soc., US-Japan Friendship Comm.; Democrat; Order of the Rising Sun (Japan). *Publications:* articles in magazines. *Address:* Council on Foreign Relations, Harold Pratt House, 58 East 68th Street, New York, NY 10065, USA.

ROCKWELL, Sam; American actor; b. 5 Nov. 1968, Daly City, Calif. *Films include:* Clownhouse 1989, Last Exit to Brooklyn 1989, Teenage Mutant Ninja Turtles 1990, Strictly Business 1991, In the Soup 1992, Light Sleeper 1992, Jack and His Friends 1992, Happy Hell Night 1992, Dead Drunk 1992, Somebody to Love 1994, The Search for One-eye Jimmy 1994, Drunks 1995, Basquiat 1996, Box of Moon Light 1996, Glory Daze 1996, Mercy 1996, Bad Liver and a Broken Heart 1996, Lawn Dogs 1997, Arresting Gena 1997, Jerry and Tom 1998, Louis & Frank 1998, Safe Men 1998, Celebrity 1998, The Call Back 1998, A Midsummer Night's Dream 1999, The Green Mile 1999, Galaxy Quest 1999, Charlie's Angels 2000,

BigLove 2001, Heist 2001, Pretzel 2001, D.C. Smalls 2001, 13 Moons 2002, Running Time 2002, Welcome to Collinwood 2002, Confessions of a Dangerous Mind 2002, Matchstick Men 2003, Piccadilly Jim 2004, The Hitchhiker's Guide to the Galaxy 2005, The F Word 2005, Robin's Big Date 2005, Snow Angels 2007, Joshua 2007, The Assassination of Jesse James by the Coward Robert Ford 2007, Woman in Burka 2008, Choke 2008, Frost/Nixon 2008, The Winning Season 2009, Moon 2009, G-Force 2009, Gentlemen Broncos 2009, Everybody's Fine 2009, Iron Man 2 2010, Conviction 2010, Cowboys & Aliens 2011, The Sitter 2011, Seven Psychopaths 2012, The Way Way Back 2013, A Single Shot 2013, Trust Me 2013, A Case of You 2013, Say When 2014, Better Living Through Chemistry 2014, Loitering with Intent 2014, Digging for Fire 2015, Don Verdean 2015, Poltergeist 2015, Mr. Right 2015, Three Billboards Outside Ebbing, Missouri (Golden Globe Award for Best Performance by an Actor in a Supporting Role in any Motion Picture 2018, Academy Award for Best Actor in a Supporting Role 2018) 2017. *Television includes:* F is for Family (series) 2015. *Address:* c/o The Gersh Agency, 130 West 42nd Street, New York, NY 10036, USA (office).

RODAS MELGAR, (Róger) Haroldo; Guatemalan economist, civil servant and politician; ed Universidad de San Carlos de Guatemala, Grad. Inst. of Int. Studies, Switzerland; fmr Adviser, Ministry of Economy; Sec.-Gen. Secretaría de Integración Económica Centroamericana (SIECA) 1997–2007; Minister of Foreign Affairs 2008–12. *Publications:* articles in professional journals.

RODAT, Robert, MBA MFA; American screenwriter; b. 30 Nov. 1953, Keene, NH; m. Mollie Miller; ed Colgate Univ., Harvard Business School, Univ. of Southern California Film School. *Film screenplays include:* Tall Tale (co-writer) 1995, Fly Away Home (co-writer) 1996, Saving Private Ryan 1998, The Patriot 2000, Thor: The Dark World (story) 2013. *Television includes:* TV screenplays include The Comrades of Summer 1992, The Ripper 1997, 36 Hours to Die 1999; Falling Skies (series) 2010–14 (also exec. producer).

RODDICK, Andrew (Andy) Stephen; American fmr professional tennis player; b. 30 Aug. 1982, Omaha, Neb.; s. of Jerry Roddick and Blanche Roddick; m. Brooklyn Decker; number one US jr 1999–2000 and number one world jr 2000, won six world jr singles and seven doubles titles, including US and Australian Open jr singles titles; turned professional 2000; singles titles: Atlanta 2001, Houston 2001, 2002, 2005, Washington, DC 2001, 2005, 2007, Memphis 2002, 2009, Montreal TMS 2003, Indianapolis 2003, 2004, Queen's Club, London 2003, 2004, 2005, 2007, Cincinnati TMS 2003, 2006, St Poelten 2003, US Open 2003, Miami 2004, 2010, San José 2004, 2005, 2008, Lyon 2005, Dubai 2008, Beijing 2008, Eastbourne 2012; singles finalist: Wimbledon 2004, 2005, 2009, US Open 2006; doubles titles: Delray Beach (with Jan-Michael Gambill) 2001, Houston (with Mardy Fish) 2002, Indianapolis (with Bobby Reynolds) 2006, Indian Wells (with Mardy Fish) 2009; 612 career singles wins, 212 defeats, 32 singles titles, highest ranking No. 1 3 Nov. 2003; 67 career doubles wins, 50 defeats, four doubles titles, highest ranking No. 50 11 Jan. 2010; mem. winning US Davis Cup team 2007; fmrly coached by Brad Gilbert; announced retirement from tennis during US Open 2012; currently sports broadcaster for Fox Sports 1; commentator, BBC broadcast of The Championships, Wimbleton 2015; f. Andy Roddick Foundation charity for children 2001. *Leisure interests:* music, films, skydiving. *Address:* c/o Andrew S. Roddick Foundation, Inc., Helping Children Today For Tomorrow, 2901 Clint Moore Road, #109, Boca Raton, FL 33496, USA. *Telephone:* (561) 392-2652; (954) 340-7471. *Fax:* (561) 392-6883. *Website:* www.arfoundation.org; www.foxsports.com/tag/roddick-and-reiter (office).

RODÉ, HE Cardinal Franc, CM, DTheol; Slovenian ecclesiastic, academic and diplomatist; *Prefect Emeritus of the Congregation for Institutes of Consecrated Life and Societies of Apostolic Life;* b. 23 Sept. 1934, Rodica, nr Ljubljana, Yugoslavia (now Slovenia); ed Pontifical Gregorian Univ., Rome, Catholic Inst. of Paris; family fled to Austria 1945, to Argentina 1948; ordained priest of the Congregation of the Mission (Lazarists) 1960; returned to Yugoslavia to work as vice-pastor, director of studies and prov. visitor of the Lazarists and Prof. of Fundamental Theology and Missionology, Theological Faculty of Ljubljana 1965; consultor of Secr. for Non-Believers in Roman Curia 1978, transferred to that dicastery 1981, Under-sec. 1982–87, Sec. 1987–93; Sec., Pontifical Council for Culture 1993–97; Archbishop of Ljubljana 1997–2004; Prefect of Congregation for Insts of Consecrated Life and Socs of Apostolic Life 2004–05, 2005–11, Prefect Emer. 2011–; cr. Cardinal (Cardinal-Deacon of San Francesco Saverio alla Garbatella) 2006, Cardinal Priest, San Francesco Saverio alla Garbatella 2016–; mem. Congregation of Divine Worship and Discipline of the Sacraments, Congregation for Bishops, Congregation for Evangelization of Peoples, Congregation for Catholic Educ., Pontifical Council for Culture, Pontifical Comm. Ecclesia Dei. *Address:* Congregation for Institutes of Consecrated Life and Societies of Apostolic Life, Palazzo della Congregazioni, Piazza Pio XII 3, 00193 Rome, Italy (office). *Telephone:* (06) 69892511 (office); (06) 69884128 (office). *Fax:* (06) 69884526 (office). *Website:* www .vatican.va/roman_curia/congregations/ccscrlife (office).

RODGERS, Jimmie, MD; Solomon Islands physician and international organization executive; holds degree in health admin; Under-Sec., later Perm. Sec. for Health, Ministry of Health and Medical Services, Solomon Islands 1990–96; joined Secr. of the Pacific Community (SPC) as Dir of Programmes in 1996, later re-designated as Deputy Dir-Gen. based in Noumea, Head of SPC Suva Regional Office 1998, later Sr Deputy Dir-Gen., Dir-Gen. SPC 2005–14. *Address:* c/o Secretariat of the Pacific Community Headquarters, BP D5, 98848 Noumea Cédex, New Caledonia. *E-mail:* drjimmier@gmail.com.

RODGERS, Joan, CBE, BA, FRNCM; British singer (soprano); b. 4 Nov. 1956, Whitehaven, Cumbria; d. of Thomas Rodgers and Julia Rodgers; m. Paul Daniel 1988 (divorced); two d.; ed Whitehaven Grammar School, Univ. of Liverpool and Royal Northern Coll. of Music; first maj. professional engagement as Pamina in The Magic Flute, Aix-en-Provence Festival 1982; début at Metropolitan Opera House, New York, in same role 1995; other appearances include title role of Theodora at Glyndebourne, The Governess in Turn of the Screw for Royal Opera House, Blanche in Dialogues des Carmélites for ENO and in Amsterdam, Marschallin in Der Rosenkavalier for Scottish Opera and title role of Alcina for English Nat. Opera; regular appearances at Royal Opera House, English Nat. Opera, Glyndebourne, Promenade Concerts and with leading British and European cos; concert engagements in London, Europe and USA with conductors including Solti, Barenboim, Mehta, Rattle, Harnoncourt and Salonen; Kathleen Ferrier Memorial Scholarship 1981; Teacher (voice), Trinity Laban Conservatoire of Music and Dance; Int. Chair of Singing, RNCM 2010–; Dr hc (Liverpool) 2005; Royal Philharmonic Soc. Award as Singer of the Year 1997, Evening Standard Award for Outstanding Individual Performance in Opera 1997. *Recordings:* numerous recordings, including albums of songs by Tchaikovsky, Rachmaninov, Wolf, Fauré and Mozart, three Mozart Da Ponte operas with Daniel Barenboim and Berlin Philharmonic. *Leisure interests:* walking, cooking, horse riding. *Address:* c/o Jonathan Groves, Groves Artists, 7 St George's Court, 131 Putney Bridge Road, London, SW15 2PA, England (office). *Telephone:* (20) 8874-3222 (office). *E-mail:* jg@grovesartists.com (office). *Website:* www.grovesartists.com/ artist/joan-rodgers-cbe (office).

RODGERS, Patricia Elaine Joan, MA, DPolSc; Bahamian diplomatist; b. Nassau; ed School of St Helen & St Catherine, Abingdon, Univ. of Aberdeen, Graduate Inst. of Int. Relations, St Augustine, Trinidad, Inst. Universitaire des Hautes Etudes Int., Univ. of Geneva; Counsellor and Consul, Washington, DC 1978–83; Alt. Rep. to OAS 1982–83; Deputy High Commr (Acting High Commr) to Canada 1983–86, High Commr 1986–88; High Commr to UK (also Accred to France, Belgium and Germany) 1988–92; mem. Bahamas Del. to UN Conf. on Law of the Sea 1974, 1975, OAS Gen. Ass. 1982, Caribbean Co-ordinating Meeting (Head of Del.), OAS 1983, Canada/Commonwealth Caribbean Heads of Govt Meeting 1985, Commonwealth Heads of Govt Meeting Nassau 1985, Vancouver 1987; Adviser to Bahamas Del., Annual Gen. Meetings of World Bank and IMF 1978–82; mem. Commonwealth Observer Group, Gen. Elections Lesotho 1993; apptd. Perm. Sec., Ministry of Tourism 1995; Perm. Sec., Ministry of Foreign Affairs. *Publications:* Mid-Ocean Archipelagos and International Law: A Study of the Progressive Development of International Law 1981. *Leisure interests:* folk art, theatre, gourmet cooking, gardening.

RODGERS OF QUARRY BANK, Baron (Life Peer), cr. 1992, of Kentish Town in the London Borough of Camden; **William Thomas Rodgers,** PC, MA; British politician and administrator; b. 28 Oct. 1928, Liverpool; s. of William Arthur Rodgers and Gertrude Helen Rodgers; m. Silvia Szulman 1955 (died 2006); three d.; ed Sudley Road Council School, Quarry Bank High School, Liverpool and Magdalen Coll., Oxford; Gen. Sec. Fabian Soc. 1953–60; Labour Cand. for Bristol West 1957; Borough Councillor, St Marylebone 1958–62; MP for Stockton-on-Tees 1962–74, for Stockton Div. of Teesside 1974–83; Parl. Under-Sec. of State, Dept of Econ. Affairs 1964–67, Foreign Office 1967–68; Leader, UK del. to Council of Europe and Ass. of WEU 1967–68; Minister of State, Bd of Trade 1968–69, Treasury 1969–70; Chair. Expenditure Cttee on Trade and Industry 1971–74; Minister of State, Ministry of Defence 1974–76; Sec. of State for Transport 1976–79; Opposition Spokesman for Defence 1979–80; left Labour Party March 1981; Co-founder Social Democratic Party March 1981, mem. Nat. Cttee 1982–87, Vice-Pres. 1982–87; Dir-Gen. RIBA 1987–94; Chair. Advertising Standards Authority 1995–2000; Leader Liberal Democratic Peers 1998–2001; Liberal Democrat; Hon. Fellow, Liverpool John Moores Univ. 2008; Hon. DLL (Liverpool Univ.) 2008. *Publications:* Hugh Gaitskell 1906–1963 (Ed.) 1964, The People Into Parliament (co-author) 1966, The Politics of Change 1982, Government and Industry (Ed. and co-author) 1986, Fourth Among Equals 2000. *Leisure interests:* reading, walking, cinema. *Address:* House of Lords, London, SW1A 0PW (office); 43 North Road, London, N6 4BE, England (home). *Telephone:* (20) 7219-3607 (office); (20) 8341-2434 (home).

RODHE, (Knut) Henning, BSc, PhD; Swedish meteorologist and academic; *Professor Emeritus of Chemical Meteorology, Stockholm University;* b. 15 Feb. 1941, Uppsala; m. Karin Rodhe; four c.; ed Univ. of Lund, Stockholm Univ.; Asst Lecturer in Math., Univ. of Lund 1964–65; Research Asst, Dept of Meteorology, Stockholm Univ. 1965–69, part-time Sr Lecturer, then part-time Research Scientist, Dept of Meteorology 1969–72, Assoc. Prof. of Meteorology 1975–79, Prof. of Chemical Meteorology 1980–2008, Dean, Faculty of Sciences and mem. Bd of the Univ. 2000–05, Vice-Pres. of the Univ. 2003–04, Sr Prof., Dept of Meteorology 2008–13, Prof. Emer. 2013–; Sr Lecturer, Dept of Meteorology, Univ. of Nairobi, Kenya 1972–75; Guest Scientist, Nat. Center for Atmospheric Research, Boulder, Colo, USA 1978; Visiting Prof., Inst. of Environmental Studies and Dept of Atmospheric Sciences, Univ. of Washington, Seattle, USA 1984; Guest Scientist, Div. of Atmospheric Research, CSIRO, Mordialloc, Australia 1990–91; Visiting Prof., Dept of Meteorology, Florida State Univ., Tallahassee, USA 1997, Dept of Oceanography, Univ. of Hawaii, Honolulu, USA 1997; Vice-Chair. Int. Atmospheric Brown Cloud Project 2005–09; Ed., Tellus B 1982–2013; mem. Int. Cttee, Royal Swedish Acad. of Sciences 2005–09, Scientific Advisory Council of Stockholm Environment Inst. 2013–; mem. Academia Europaea 1998; Björkén Prize, Uppsala Univ. 2004, Environmental Protection Medal (in gold), Royal Swedish Acad. of Sciences 2008, Rossby Prize, Swedish Geophysical Soc. 2010, Volvo Environment Prize 2015. *Publications:* author or ed. of five books; more than 130 papers in professional journals. *Address:* Room C648, Department of Meteorology, Stockholm University, 106 91 Stockholm, Sweden (office). *Telephone:* (8) 16-43-42 (office). *E-mail:* rodhe@misu.su.se (office). *Website:* www.misu.su.se (office).

RODIĆ, Nebojša; Serbian lawyer and politician; b. 1953, Šabac; Sec., Electoral Comm. of the Repub. of Serbia 1996, 1997; Sec., Referendum Comm. on foreign mediation in settlement of Kosovo crisis 1998; fmr Deputy Sec. People's Ass. (Parl.); fmr Asst Sec.-Gen., Ministry of the Interior; fmr Amb.; Sec.-Gen. to Pres. of Serbia Tomislav Nikolić May–Aug. 2012; Dir BIA (Security Information Agency) 2012–13; Minister of Defence 2013–14.

RODIER, Jean-Pierre; French business executive and mining engineer; *Chairman, Supervisory Board, HIME (holding company of group SAUR);* b. 4 May 1947, Reims; s. of Pierre Rodier and Gabrielle Sayen; m. Michèle Foz 1969; ed Lycée de Saumur, Lycée de Pamiers, Lycée de Pierre-en-Fermat, Toulouse; Asst Sec.-Gen. Mines Directorate, Ministry of Industry 1975–78, Sec.-Gen. 1978; Head of Econs and Budget mission of Dir-Gen. of Energy and Raw Materials 1979; Head of Raw Material and Subsoil Dept 1981–83; tech. adviser to Prime Minister's Office 1983–84; Dir of Gen. Man. Penarroya mining and metallurgy Co. 1984–85, Asst Dir-Gen. 1985–86, Pres. and Dir-Gen. 1986–88; Pres. Bd of Dirs Metaleurop 1988–91; Deputy Admin. Mining Union 1991–94; Pres. Asscn of Enterprise and Personnel 2001–; Pres. and Dir-Gen. Pechiney 1994–2003; apptd Advisor, CVC

Capital Pnrs (France) SA 2004; Partner Mediobanca 2007–10; Chair. Supervisory Bd, HIME (holding co. of group SAUR) 2013–; mem. Bd of Dirs Vedanta Resources 2004–, Rexam PLC 2006– (also Chair. Remuneration Cttee); Pres. Bd of Dirs Ecole nat. supérieure des techniques industrielles et des mines d'Alès 1992–95; Chevalier de la Légion d'Honneur. *Address:* Group SAUR, 11, Chemin de Bretagne, 92130 Issy-les-Moulineaux, Paris, France (office). *Telephone:* 1-30-60-84-00 (office). *Website:* www.saur.com (office).

RODIN, Judith, PhD; American psychologist, foundation executive and fmr university president; *President, The Rockefeller Foundation;* b. 9 Sept. 1944, Philadelphia, Pa; d. of Morris and Sally (Winson) Seitz; m. 1st 1966; m. 2nd 1978, one s.; m. 3rd Paul Verkuil 1994; ed Univ. of Pennsylvania and Columbia Univ.; NSF Postdoctoral Fellow, Univ. of California 1971; Asst Prof. of Psychology, New York Univ. 1970–72; Asst Prof., Yale Univ. 1972–75, Assoc. Prof. 1975–79, Prof. of Psychology 1979–83, Dir of Grad. Studies 1982–89, Philip R. Allen Prof. of Psychology 1984–94, Prof. of Medicine and Psychiatry 1985–94, Chair. Dept of Psychology 1989–91, Dean Grad. School of Arts and Sciences 1991–92, Provost 1992–94; Prof. of Psychology, Medicine and Psychiatry, Univ. of Pennsylvania 1994–2004, Pres. Univ. of Pennsylvania 1994–2004; Pres. Rockefeller Foundation 2005–; Chair. John D. & Catherine T. MacArthur Foundation Research Network on Determinants and Consequences of Health-Promoting and Health-Damaging Behavior 1983–93; Chair. Council of Pres.'s, Univs Research Asscn 1995–96; Co-Chair., NYS 2100 Cttee 2012–13, White House Council for Community Solutions 2010–12; has served on numerous Bds of Dirs, including Carnegie Hall, Aetna Life & Casualty Co. 1995–, AMR Corpn, Comcast Corpn, Citigroup; has served as mem. of numerous professional cttees, including Pres. Clinton's Cttee of Advisors on Science and Tech.; has served on numerous editorial bds; mem. Bd of Trustees, Brookings Inst. 1995–2006; Fellow, AAAS, American Acad. of Arts and Sciences; 19 hon. doctorates, including Dartmouth (Science), Brown Univ. (Laws), Medical Coll. of Pennsylvania (DHumLitt); numerous awards and prizes, including 21st Century Award, Int. Alliance, Glass Ceiling Award, American Red Cross, American Psychological Asscn Distinguished Outstanding Lifetime Contribution to Psychology 2005, Jacqueline Kennedy Onassis Medal 2013, Yale School of Public Health Winslow Award 2015, Global Conservation Leadership Award, Conservation International 2015, Edmund N. Bacon Prize 2015. *Publications include:* author or co-author of 12 books on the relationship between psychological and biological processes in human health and behaviour, including The University & Urban Renewal: Out of the Ivory Tower and Into the Streets 2007, The Resilience Dividend 2014, The Power of Impact Investing 2014; more than 250 articles in academic journals. *Leisure interests:* tennis, travel, reading. *Address:* The Rockefeller Foundation, 420 Fifth Avenue, New York, NY 10018-2702, USA (office). *Telephone:* (212) 869-8500 (office). *Fax:* (212) 764-3468 (office). *Website:* www.rockfound.org (office).

RODIONOV, Petr Ivanovich; Russian politician; b. 26 Jan. 1951, Przhevalsk, Kyrgyz SSR; m.; three c.; ed Leningrad Inst. of Vessel Construction, Leningrad Inst. of Finance and Econs, Higher School of Commerce, Acad. of Nat. Econs; with USSR Ministry of Gas Industry; Chief Technologist, Head of Div., with Lentransgas 1984–88; Dir-Gen. Lentransgas 1989–96; mem. Bd of Dirs Russian Jt Gazprom 1996–2006, First Deputy Chair. 2001–06; currently investor Severneftegazdobyca (oil and natural gas co.); rep. of Russian Govt to Gazprom 1996, to United Energy System of Russia 1996; Minister of Oil and Gas Industry 1996–97; mem. Govt Comm. for Operational Problems 1996–97; Chair. Bd of Dirs Menatep St Petersburg Bank 1998; Hon. Worker of Gas Industry.

RODKIN, Gary M., BEcons, MBA; American food industry executive; b. 6 April 1952; m. Barbara Rodkin; one s. one d.; ed Rutgers Univ., Harvard Business School; held marketing and man. positions at General Mills 1979–95 including Pres. Yoplait-Colombo 1992–95; Pres. Tropicana N America 1995–98; Pres. and CEO Pepsi Cola N America 1999–2002, Pres. PepsiCo Beverages and Foods 2002–03, Chair. CEO 2002–05; Pres. and CEO ConAgra Foods Inc., Omaha 2005–15; fmr Chair. Boys Town (charity); mem. Bd of Dirs Avon Products, Inc. 2007–, Simon Property Group 2015–; fmr mem. Bd of Dirs Food Marketing Inst., Grocery Manufacturers Asscn (fmr Chair.) United Industries Corpn; mem. Bd of Overseers, Rutgers Univ.; William H. Albers Business Collaboration Award, Food Marketing Inst. 2015.

RODRIGO, Nihal; Sri Lankan diplomatist and international organization official; *Adviser to the President on Foreign Affairs;* b. Kandy; ed Trinity Coll., Kandy; Asst Lecturer, Univ. of Ceylon; with Foreign Service, including diplomatic missions in Australia, Germany, India, Switzerland and USA; Deputy Perm. Rep. to UN, New York, Amb. and Perm. Rep., Geneva; Dir-Gen. for S Asia, SAARC, Sec.-Gen. 1999–2002; co-ordinated activities of Non-Aligned Movt under Sri Lanka's chairmanship 1976–79, del. to summit confs 1976–, Chair. Political Cttee 1995; mem. Advisory Bd on Disarmament of UN Sec.-Gen.; mem. several presidential cttees, including Acquisition of Art Works for State Collections, Foreign Affairs, Human Rights and Information Strategy; mem. Man. Bd Bandaranaike Centre for Int. Studies; Amb. to People's Repub. of China (also accred to Mongolia) 2004–07; Adviser to Pres. of Sri Lanka on Foreign Affairs 2007–. *Address:* President's Secretariat, Republic Square, Colombo 1, Sri Lanka (office). *Telephone:* (11) 2324801 (office). *Fax:* (11) 2430590 (office). *E-mail:* priu@presidentsoffice.lk (office).

RODRIGUE, Antonio, BA; Haitian diplomatist and politician; b. 1954; m. Martha Sajous Rodrigue; one c.; ed Univ. d'Etat d'Haiti, Univ. of Ottawa, School of Diplomacy, Rio Blanco, Brazil, Academic Inst., Princeton Univ.; began career with Ministry of Foreign Affairs, Port-au-Prince, later becoming Consul-Gen. in Geneva, Minister Counsellor and Chargé d'Affaires, Embassy in Paris 1980s, 10 years at Perm. Mission of Haiti to UN, New York, Minister Counsellor and Chargé d'Affaires, Embassy of Haiti in Venezuela 1999, Amb. to Spain 2001–10, 2016–17, Amb. to Bahamas, also Perm. Rep. to OAS, Washington 2010–15, Amb. to EU and Belgium (also accred to Netherlands) 2015–16; Minister of Foreign Affairs and Religious Affairs 2017–18. *Address:* c/o Ministry of Foreign Affairs and Religious Affairs, blvd Harry S Truman, Cité de l'Exposition, Port-au-Prince, Haiti (office).

RODRIGUES, Christopher John, CBE, MA, MBA, FRSA; British business executive and government official; *Chairman, VisitBritain;* b. 24 Oct. 1949; s. of Alfred John Rodrigues and Joyce Margaret Rodrigues (née Farron-Smith); m.

Priscilla Purcell Young 1976; one s. one d.; ed Univ. of Cambridge, Harvard Univ., USA; fmr man. trainee Spillers; fmrly with McKinsey, American Express; fmr COO, fmr Chief Exec. Thomas Cook; Chief Exec. Bradford & Bingley Bldg Soc. (now Bradford & Bingley PLC) 1996–2004; Pres. and CEO Visa Int. 2004–06; Chair. VisitBritain 2007–, Int. Personal Finance 2007–15, Windsor Leadership Trust 2007–15, Almeida Theatre 2008, Openwork LLP 2014–, Port of London Authority 2016–; Founder-Dir Financial Services Authority 1997–2003; mem. Bd of Dirs (non-exec.) Energis PLC 1997–2003, Ladbrokes plc (fmrly Hilton Group) 2003–13; Chair. British Bobsleigh & Skeleton Asscn 2013–; mem. Exec. Cttee and Vice-Chair., World Travel and Tourism Council; mem. Council and Trustee, National Trust; Hon. DUniv (Surrey) 2013. *Leisure interests:* cooking, rowing, opera. *Address:* VisitBritain, Sanctuary Buildings, 20 Great Smith Street, London, SW1P 3BT, England (office). *Telephone:* (20) 7578-1298 (office). *Website:* www.visitbritain.com (office).

RODRIGUES, Eduardo Ferro, BEcons; Portuguese politician, economist and academic; *President, Assembleia da República;* b. 3 Nov. 1949, Lisbon; m. Maria Filomena Lopes Peixoto de Aguiar; one s. one d.; ed Tech. Univ. of Lisbon; Founder Socialist Left Movement; Asst Prof. ISCTE-Univ. Inst. of Lisbon; Sr Prin. Technician, GEBEI; Minister of Public Works, Transport and Communications 2001–02; mem. Socialist Party, Sec.-Gen. 2002–04 (resgnd); Amb., Permanent Rep. of Portugal to OECD; Pres. Assembleia da República (Assembly of the Republic) 2015–; Grand Cross of the Order of May, Merit Class (Argentina) 2003, Grand Cross of the Order of Freedom 2016. *Address:* Assembleia da República (Assembly of the Republic), Palácio de São Bento, 1249-068, Lisbon, Portugal (office). *Telephone:* (21) 3919000 (office). *Fax:* (21) 3917440 (office). *E-mail:* correio.geral@ar.parlamento.pt (office). *Website:* www.parlamento.pt.

RODRIGUES, Gen. (retd) Sunith Francis, MA; Indian fmr army officer and government official; b. 19 Sept. 1933, Bombay (now Mumbai); m. Jean Rodrigues; two s. one d.; ed St Xavier's High School, Bombay, Defence Services Staff Coll., Royal Coll. of Defence Studies, UK; joined Jt Services Wing, Indian Mil. Acad. 1949, commissioned into Regt of Artillery 1952, commanded mountain artillery regt 1970–71, served as Gen. Staff Officer during Indo-Pak War at a Corps HQ 1971, of a Div. 1973–75, commanded mountain brigade at high altitude 1975–77, Chief Instructor (Army) at Defence Services Staff Coll. (DSSC) 1978–81, commanded div. deployed at high altitude on becoming Maj.-Gen. 1981, Chief of Staff of a corps 1983–85, Dir-Gen. Mil. Training and promoted to rank of Lt-Gen. 1985–86, commanded corps in northern sector 1986–89, apptd Hon. ADC to Pres. 1987, served as Vice-Chief of Army Staff 1987–89, GOC-in-C Cen. Command April–Oct. 1989, GOC-in-C Western Command 1989–90, Chief of Army Staff 1990–93; Dir Int. Centre, Goa 1993–99; served two terms on Nat. Security Advisory Bd; mem. Exec. Council Goa Univ. for seven years, Man. Cttee Goa Chamber of Commerce and Industry; Gov. of Punjab and Admin. of Union Territory of Chandigarh 2004–10; mem. Goa Planning Bd, Bd Govs Goa Inst. of Man.; Vishisht Seva Medal (VSM) for distinguished service 1972, Param Vishisht Seva Medal (PVSM) 1988; Hon. DLitt (Goa Univ.); Mother Teresa's Lifetime Achievement Award 2009. *Leisure interests:* social and literary pursuits.

RODRIGUES-BIRKETT, Carolyn; Guyanese politician; b. 16 Sept. 1973, Santa Rosa, Region One; m.; two c.; ed Saskatchewan Federated Coll., Canada, Univ. of Guyana; began career as teacher, Santa Rosa Primary School; Asst Co-ordinator, later Co-ordinator for Amerindian Projects, Social Impact Amelioration Program 1993–2001; Minister of Amerindian Affairs 2001–08, of Foreign Affairs 2008–15.

RODRIGUEZ, Alexander (Alex) Emmanuel; American professional baseball player (retd); b. 27 July 1975, New York; m. Cynthia Scurtis 2002; one d.; ed Westminster Christian High School, Miami, Fla; shortstop and third baseman; Maj. League teams: Seattle Mariners 1994–2000, Texas Rangers 2001–03, NY Yankees 2004–16 (now special advisor); first high school player to trial for Team USA 1993; represented US Junior Nat. Squad 1993; Maj. League debut 8 July 1994 (third 18-year-old shortstop to play Maj. Leagues since 1900); est. Seattle record for average, runs, hits, doubles and total bases 1996; traded to NY Yankees 2004; led American League (AL) in home runs 2001, 2002 (with 57 home runs, sixth highest in AL history), 2003, 2005, 2007; youngest player ever to hit 500 home runs; f. Alex Rodriguez Foundation 1998; currently broadcaster and analyst, Fox Sports; USA Baseball Junior Player of the Year 1993, Nat. Baseball Student Athlete of the Year 1993, finalist for USA Baseball Golden Spikes Award for top amateur player 1993 (while still at school), AL batting champion 1996, Sporting News Maj. League Player of the Year 1996, 2002 2007, Associated Press Maj. League Player of the Year 1996, All-Star 1996–98, 2000–08, 2010, 2011, Silver Slugger 1996, 1998–2003, 2005, 2007, 2008, AL hits leader 1998, Baseball America Maj. League Player of the Year 2000, 2002, AL Hank Aaron Award winner 2001–03, 2007, Rawlings Gold Glove 2002, 2003 for shortstop, AL RBI leader 2002, 2007, American League Most Valuable Player 2003, 2005, 2007, Babe Ruth Award 2009. *Leisure interests:* basketball, golf, boating. *Address:* New York Yankees, Yankee Stadium, 1 East 161st Street, Bronx, New York, NY 10451, USA (office). *Website:* newyork.yankees.mlb.com (office).

RODRIGUEZ, Narciso; American fashion designer; b. 27 Jan. 1961, Newark, New Jersey; Narciso Rodriguez, Sr and Rawedia Maria Rodriguez; m. Thomas Tolan 2013; ed Parsons School of Design, New York; Women's Designer Asst, Anne Klein under Donna Karan 1985–91, Women's Ready-to-Wear, Calvin Klein 1991–95; Women's and Men's Design Dir TSE, New York, Women's Creative Dir Cerruti, Paris 1995–97; Women's Design Dir Loewe, Spain 1997–2001; est. his atelier in New York in 2001; introduced women's frangrance 2003, men's fragrance 2007; Best New Designer, VH1 Fashion Awards 1997, Perry Ellis Award, Council of Fashion Designers of America (CFDA) 1997, Hispanic Designers Moda Award 1997, New York Magazine Award 1997, Womenswear Designer of the Year, CFDA 2002, 2003, Special Achievement in Fashion, American Latino Media Arts Awards 2008, named among Cultural Leaders of 2010 selected by USA Network and Vanity Fair magazine. *Dance:* has designed costumes for several productions and performances, including with Christopher Wheeldon, Founder and Dir of Morphoses 2008, collaboration with choreographer Jonah Bokaer 2010, also performances curated by Cecilia Dean and writer David Coleman. *Address:* Narciso Rodriguez LLC, 30 Irving Place, 9th Floor, New York, NY 10003, USA (office); 22–32 ave. Victor Hugo, 75116 Paris, France. *Telephone:* (212) 677-2989 (office). *Fax:* (212) 677-2475 (office). *Website:* www.narcisorodriguez.com.

RODRÍGUEZ ECHEVERRÍA, Miguel Ángel, PhD; Costa Rican economist, lawyer, business executive, international organization official and fmr head of state; b. 9 Jan. 1940, San José; m.; ed Univ. de Costa Rica, Univ. of California, Berkeley; Lecturer and Economist, Univ. of Costa Rica 1963; Research Asst, Univ. of Calif., Berkeley 1965–66; Dir of Planning Office and Presidential Adviser on Political Econs and Planning 1966–68; Dir Cen. Bank 1967–70; columnist for La Nación 1967–68; with Ministry of Planning 1968–69; Visiting Economist, Univ. of Calif.; with Ministry of the Presidency 1970; exec. with Empacadora de Carne de Cartago and Abonos Superior SA 1970–71; Pres. Agrodinámica Int. SA and subsidiaries 1974–87; Lecturer in Econs, Univ. of Costa Rica and Univ. Autónoma de Centro América 1978; mem. of Counsel (legal and econ. advisers) 1982; mem. nat. political directorate Partido Unidad Social Cristiano 1984, mem. Exec. 1994; Dir Banco Agro Industrial y de Exportaciones SA 1986–87; gen. adviser Grupo Ganadero Int. de Costa Rica SA 1989–90; Deputy Legis. Ass. 1991–92; Vice-Pres. (for Cen. America), Christian Democratic Org. of Latin America 1991, Pres. 1995; Pres. of Costa Rica 1998–2002; Sec.-Gen. OAS Sec.-Oct. 2004 (resgnd and returned to Costa Rica to face allegations of financial wrongdoing during his presidency); sentenced to 5 years imprisonment 2011. *Publications:* El mito de la Racionalidad del Socialismo 1963, El Orden Jurídico de la Libertad 1967, Contributions to Economic Analysis. Production Economics: A Dual Approach to Theory and Applications 1978, Nuestra Crisis Financiera: Causas y Soluciones 1979, De las Ideas a la Acción 1988, Al Progreso por la Libertad 1989, Libertad y Solidaridad: Una Política Social para el Desarrollo Humano 1992, Una Revolución Moral: Democracia, Mercado y Bien Común 1992, Por una Vida Buena, Justa y Solidaria 1993; numerous articles and contribs on econs.

RODRÍGUEZ GARCÍA, José Luis, PhD; Cuban politician; b. 18 March 1946, Havana; mem. Cen. Cttee, CP of Cuba 1997–; Deputy, Nat. Ass. of People's Power 1998–; Minister of Economy and Planning 1998–2009; fmr Vice-Pres. Council of Ministers; mem. Scientific Council, Inst. of Int. Relations, Cuban Acad. of Sciences.

RODRÍGUEZ GIAVARINI, Adalberto; Argentine economist and politician; *Chairman, Argentine Council for International Relations;* b. 18 Oct. 1943, Prov. of Buenos Aires; ed Univ. of Buenos Aires; fmr Comptroller Gen. Trust of State Cos; Pres. and Owner macroeconomics analysis co.; Chair of Microeconomics, Univ. of Buenos Aires 1972–78; Co-ordinator Postgraduate Studies in Econs, Univ. of Salvador 1980–83; Sec. of State for Budget, Ministry of Economy 1983–85, for Planning, Ministry of Defence 1986–89; elected mem. Chamber of Deputies 1995; Minister of Foreign Affairs, Int. Trade and Religion 1999–2001; mem. Bd of Dirs and Exec. Cttee, Fundación Carolina de Argentina, fmr Pres.; Visiting Prof., Univ. of Belgrano 1994; Prof. of Econs, School of Econs and Business Admin. 1995; Chair. Argentine Council for Int. Relations 2007–; mem. various academic insts and advisory bds; guest columnist, major daily newspapers in Argentina and abroad; Fellow, Nat. Acad. of Educ., Academia del Plata, Nat. Acad. of Moral and Political Science; Grand Cross, Order of Isabella the Catholic (Spain); Commdr, Légion d'honneur; Cavalieri di Gran Croce, Ordine al Merito della Repubblica Italiana; Grand Cross, Order of the Polar Star (Sweden); Grand Cross, Ordem do Imfante Dom Henrique (Portugal); Grand Cross, Ordem Nacional do Cruzeiro do Sul (Brazil); Grand Cross, Order of the Aztec Eagle (Mexico); Grand Cross, Nat. Order of Merit (Ecuador); Grand Cross, Order of the Sun of Peru; Grand Cross, Nat. Order of Juan Mora Fernández (Costa Rica); Grand Cross, Order of Merit of Duarte, Sanchez and Mella (Domican Republic); Grand Cross Special, Nat. Order of Merit (Paraguay); Grand Cross, Order of Merit (Chile); Grand Officer, Medal of the Oriental Repub. of Uruguay (Uruguay); Grand Cross, Order of the Condor (Bolivia). *Address:* Argentine Council for International Relations, Uruguay 1037, piso 1° C1016ACA, Buenos Aires, Argentina (office). *Telephone:* (11) 4811-0071 (office). *Fax:* (11) 4815-4742 (office). *E-mail:* cari@cari.org.ar (office). *Website:* www.cari.org.ar/miembros/arg.html (office).

RODRÍGUEZ GÓMEZ, Delcy Eloina; Venezuelan lawyer and politician; *Executive Vice-President;* b. 29 April 1970, Caracas; d. of Jorge Antonio Rodríguez (Co-founder of Liga Socialista); ed Univ. Central de Venezuela; held various public offices during admin of the late Hugo Rafael Chávez including Dir of Int. Affairs, Ministry of Energy and Mines 2003, Deputy Foreign Minister of Relations for Europe 2005–06, Minister in Office of the Presidency 2006, Gen. Coordinator of Vice Presidency 2007; Minister for Communication and Information 2013–14, Minister of Foreign Affairs (first woman) 2014–17; Pres. Constitutional Ass. of Venezuela 2017–18; Exec. Vice-Pres. of Venezuela 2018–; mem. Venezuelan Asscn of Labour Lawyers. *Address:* Office of the Vice-President, Esq. Carmelitas, Avenida Urdaneta, Caracas 1010, Distrito Capital, Venezuela (office). *Telephone:* (212) 801-0500 (office). *Website:* www.vicepresidencia.gob.ve (office); delcy.patria.org.ve.

RODRIGUEZ GÓMEZ, Jorge, PhD; Venezuelan psychologist and politician; *Mayor of Libertador Bolivarian Municipality;* b. 9 Nov. 1965, Caracas; s. of Jorge Rodríguez; ed Luis Razetti School of Medicine, Central Univ. of Venezuela and Andrés Bello Catholic Univ.; Pres. Student Union, Luis Razetti School of Medicine 1987–88; Pres. Venezuelan Fed. of Univs. 1988–92; Resident Doctor, Venezuelan Inst. of Social Security 1995; joined Movimiento Quinto República (MVR) (now Partido Socialista Unido de Venezuela-PSUV) 2000; in pvt. medical practice 2002–03; Pres. Nat. Electoral Team 2003–05; Pres. Nat. Electoral Council 2005–06; Vice–Pres. of Venezuela 2007–08; Mayor, Libertador Bolivarian Municipality, Caracas 2008–. *Address:* Partido Socialista Unido de Venezuela, Calle Lima, cruce con Avda Libertador, Los Cabos, Caracas, Venezuela (office). *Telephone:* (212) 782-3808 (office). *Fax:* (212) 782-9720 (office). *E-mail:* contacto@psuv.org.ve (office). *Website:* www.psuv.org.ve (office).

RODRÍGUEZ HERRER, Elvira; Spanish politician and government official; b. 15 May 1949; m.; four c.; ed Universidad Complutense de Madrid; lawyer; Inspector and State Auditor 1972–74; Head of Fiscal Section, Seville Property Del. 1974–75; Chief of Finance Unit, Directorate of the Treasury 1975–78; Asst Dir-Gen. Social Security 1978–84; Asst Dir-Gen. Nat. Audit Office 1984–96; Dir-Gen. of Budgets 1996–2000; Sec. of State for Budgets and Expenditure, Ministry of Property 2000–03; Minister of the Environment 2003–04; Deputy for Murcia, Congress of Deputies 2004–06, Deputy for Jaén 2011–12; Minister of Transport, Community of Madrid 2006–07; Pres. Ass. of Madrid 2007–11, apptd Senator 2011; Pres. Comisión Nacional del Mercado de Valores (nat. comm. for stock markets) 2012–16; mem. Comms preparing first Gen. Plan of Public Accounts 1981, 1983; Nat. Audit Office Rep. on Comm. of Principles and Public Norms 1991–94.

RODRÍGUEZ IGLESIAS, Gil Carlos, PhD; Spanish judge and professor of law; b. 26 May 1946, Gijón; m. Teresa Diez Gutiérrez 1972; two d.; ed Univ. of Oviedo and Univ. Autónoma de Madrid; Asst, Univs of Oviedo, Freiburg, Autónoma of Madrid and Complutense of Madrid 1969–77; Lecturer, Univ. Complutense of Madrid 1977–82, Prof. 1982–83, Prof. of Int. Law 2003–; Prof., Univ. of Granada 1983–2003, Dir Dept of Int. Law 1983–86, on special leave 1986–; Judge, Court of Justice of European Communities 1986–2003, Pres. 1994–2003; Jean Monnet Chair of European Community Law, Dir Dept of European Studies, Instituto Universitario Ortega y Gasset 2004–05; Arbitrator, 20 Essex Street Chambers, London; Ed. Revista de Derecho Comunitario Europeo; mem. Bd of Dirs Fundación Real Instituto Elcano; mem. Supervisory Bd Max-Planck Inst. of Int. Public Law and Comparative Law, Heidelberg 1990–; Hon. Bencher Gray's Inn 1995, King's Inns, Dublin; Hon. Fellow, Soc. of Advanced Legal Studies, London; Hon. mem. Academia Asturiana de Jurisprudencia; Orden de Isabel la Católica, Orden de San Raimundo de Peñafort; Dr hc (Turin) 1996, (Babeș-Bolyai Cluj-Napoca, Romania) 1996, (Sarre Univ.), (Univ. of Ohrid, Bulgaria); Walter-Hallstein Prize 2003. *Publications:* El régimen jurídico de los monopolios de Estado en la Comunidad Económica Europea 1976; numerous articles and studies on EC law and int. law. *Address:* 20 Essex Street, London, WC2R 3AL, England. *E-mail:* clerks@20essexst.com. *Website:* www.20essexst.com.

RODRÍGUEZ MARADIAGA, HE Cardinal Oscar Andrés, SDB; Honduran ecclesiastic; *Archbishop of Tegucigalpa;* b. 29 Dec. 1942, Tegucigalpa; ordained priest of Salesians of Saint John Bosco 1970; Auxiliary Bishop of Tegucigalpa, Honduras 1978; Titular Bishop of Pudentiana 1978; Sec.-Gen. Latin American Episcopal Conf. 1987–91, Pres. Econ. Cttee 1991–95; Archbishop of Tegucigalpa 1993–; Pres. Conf. of Latin American Bishops 1995–99; cr. Cardinal (Cardinal-Priest of Santa Maria della Speranza) 2001; participated in Papal Conclave 2005, 2013; served as Vatican spokesperson to IMF and World Bank on Third World debt; mem. Congregation for Catholic Educ. 2012; Pres. Caritas Internationalis, Caritas Confed. (network of Catholic relief and devt orgs) 2007–. *Address:* Conferencia Episcopal de Honduras, Los Lavreles, Comayagüela, Apdo 3121, Tegucigalpa, Honduras (office). *Telephone:* 2370353 (office); 2372366 (home). *Fax:* 2222337 (office). *Website:* www.cardinalrodriguez.info; www.caritas.org.

RODRÍGUEZ MENDOZA, Miguel; Venezuelan lawyer, diplomatist and international organization official; *Senior Associate, International Centre for Trade and Sustainable Development;* ed Cen. Univ. of Venezuela, Univ. of Manchester, UK, Ecole des Hautes Etudes en Sciences Sociales, France; First Sec., Perm. Mission to UN, New York 1978–81; Dir for Consultation and Co-ordination, Latin American Econ. System 1982–88; Special Adviser to Pres. on int. econ. affairs 1989–91; Minister of State, Pres. Inst. of Foreign Trade 1991–94; Pres. Comm. of Cartagena Agreement 1993; Chief Trade Adviser, OAS –1998; Visiting Scholar, Georgetown Univ., Washington, DC 1998–; Jt Deputy Dir-Gen. WTO 1999–2002; Of Counsel, Van Bael & Bellis, Geneva 2002–04; Transatlantic Fellow, German Marshall Fund of the US 2005–; Sr Assoc., Int. Centre for Trade and Sustainable Devt, Geneva; apptd Chair. WTO panel to decide US challenge on EU system of protecting products with geographical names 2004. *Publications:* numerous articles in books and journals; has edited numerous books. *Address:* International Centre for Trade and Sustainable Development, International Environment House 2, Chemin de Balexert 7, 1219 Châtelaine, Geneva, Switzerland (office). *Telephone:* (22) 9178492 (office). *Fax:* (22) 9178093 (office). *E-mail:* ictsd@ictsd.ch (office). *Website:* www.ictsd.org/about-us/miguel-rodriguez-mendoza (office).

RODRÍGUEZ PARRILLA, Bruno, LLB; Cuban diplomatist and government official; *Minister of Foreign Relations;* b. 22 Jan. 1958, Mexico City, Mexico; m.; one s.; mem. Cen. Cttee, CP of Cuba 1990–, Head of Cultural Policy Matters 1992–; Deputy Perm. Rep. to UN, New York 1993–95, Perm. Rep. 1995–2003; Deputy Minister for Foreign Relations in charge of Latin America and the Caribbean and for information and communication 2003–04, First Deputy Minister for Foreign Relations 2004–09, Minister of Foreign Relations 2009–. *Address:* Ministry of Foreign Relations, Calzada 360, esq. G, Vedado, Havana, Cuba (office). *Telephone:* (7) 55-3537 (office). *Fax:* (7) 33-3460 (office). *E-mail:* cubaminrex@minrex.gov.cu (office). *Website:* www.cubaminrex.cu (office).

RODRÍGUEZ SAÁ, Adolfo; Argentine lawyer and politician; b. 25 July 1947, San Luis; s. of Juan Rodríguez Saá and Lilia Ester Paez Montero; m.; six c.; ed Nat. Univ. of Cuyo, Univ. of Buenos Aires; Rep. of Partido Justicialista (PJ—Justice Party) 1971–83; Prov. Deputy and Pres. Justicialista Block 1973–76; Prov. Congressman 1976–85; Nat. Congressman (PJ) 1983–91; Nat. Councillor 1987–94; Pres. Partido Justicialista (San Luis Dist) 1985–95, Third Vice-Pres. Nat. Partido Justicialista 1996–2000; Gov. of San Luis Prov. 1983–2001; Interim Pres. of Argentina 23 Dec.–30 Dec. 2001; Nat. Deputy 2003–05; Senator for San Luis 2005–, Chair. Grupo de Parlamentarios Argentinos de Amistad con la República Oriental del Uruguay 2006–, Pres. Grupo Parlamentario Argentino de Amistad con Turquía 2008–, mem. Delegación Externa del Parlamento del Mercosur ante el EUROLAT 2008–; parliamentarian, MERCOSUR 2006–; f. Fundación de Investigación Social Argentino Latinoamericana (FISAL) 1999; unsuccessful cand. for Pres. 2003, 2015; Commdr, Order of Merit (Chile) 1998, Caballero de la Orden del Ejército de los Andes 2000; Gov. of the Year 1987, Medalla Honorífica – ASUR, Asociación de Entidades Oficiales de Control Público del MERCOSUR 2000, Medalla Sanmartiniana 2001. *Address:* National Senate, Buenos Aires, Argentina (office). *Telephone:* (11) 4010-3000 (office). *E-mail:* adolfo.rodriguezsaa@senado.gov.ar (office). *Website:* www.senado.gov.ar (office).

RODRÍGUEZ VELTZÉ, Eduardo, MPA; Bolivian lawyer, judge and fmr head of state; b. 2 March 1956, Cochabamba; m. Fanny Elena Arguedas Calle; four c.; ed Universidad Mayor de San Simón, Harvard Univ., USA; worked as Curriculum Expert, Legal Services to the State, Gen. Adviser, Ministry of Foreign Relations and Worship, Subcontractor of Legal Services, Contraloría General de la República; fmr Resident Co-ordinator, UN Latin American Inst. for the Prevention of Crime and the Treatment of Offenders (ILANUD); fmr Lecturer, Universidad Andina Simón Bolívar, Universidad Mayor de San Andrés, Posgrado de Ciencias de Desarrollo; fmr Chief Justice, Supreme Court; Pres. of the Supreme Court 2004–05; Interim Pres. of Bolivia 2005–06; apptd Plenipotentiary Amb. to Int.

Court of Justice, Hague 2013; Dean, Faculty of Law and Political Sciences, Bolivian Catholic Univ.

RODRÍGUEZ ZAPATERO, José Luis; Spanish lawyer and politician; b. 4 Aug. 1960, Valladolid; m. Sónsoles Espinosa 1990; two d.; ed Univ. of León; worked as a teacher of law; joined Partido Socialista Obrero Español (PSOE) 1978, Leader, Socialist Youth Org., León 1982, mem. Parl. for León and Madrid 1986–2011, Leader, PSOE Regional Chapter for León 1988, mem. PSOE Fed. Exec. Cttee 1997, Sec.-Gen. PSOE 2000–12; Prime Minister of Spain and Pres. of the Council 2004–11; mem. Council of State 2012–. *Leisure interests:* jogging, trout fishing. *Address:* Fundación IDEAS, Gobelas 31, 28023, Madrid, Spain (office). *Telephone:* (91) 5820091 (office). *Fax:* (91) 5820090 (office). *Website:* www.fundacionideas.es (office).

RODRIQUEZ, Julián Isaias, PhD; Venezuelan lawyer, poet and politician; b. 16 Dec. 1942; ed Univs of Santa Maria and Zulia and Cen. Univ. of Venezuela; legal adviser to Ministry of Agric. 1969; fmr Attorney-Gen.; Chief Attorney of Aragua 1990–91; Senator for Aragua 1998; First Vice-Pres. Nat. Constituency Ass. 1999–2000; Vice-Pres. of Venezuela 2000; Attorney-Gen. 2001–07; Prof., Univ. of Carabobo; regular columnist for El Siglo; consultant to Veterinary Asscn 1971; mem. Movimiento Quinta República. *Publications:* legal: New Labour Procedures 1987, Legal Stability in Labour Laws 1993; poetry: Pozo de cabrillas, Con las aspas de todos los molinos, Los tiempos de la sed; contrib. numerous articles.

ROED-LARSEN, Terje, PhD; Norwegian diplomatist, politician and UN official; *President, International Peace Institute;* b. 22 Nov. 1947, Bergen; m. Mona Juul; taught sociology and philosophy at Univs of Bergen and Oslo –1981; Founder and Exec. Dir Inst. of Applied Social Sciences (FAFO) 1991, Hon. Chair. Programme for Int. Co-operation and Conflict Resolution; fmr Deputy Foreign Minister; facilitated negotiations between reps of Israel's Labour Govt and Palestine Liberation Org. (PLO) leading to signing of Declaration of Principles, Washington, DC 13 Sept. 1993; Amb. and Special Adviser to Norwegian Foreign Minister for the Middle East Peace Process 1993, 1998; UN Deputy Sec.-Gen. and Special Co-ordinator in the Occupied Territories, Gaza 1994–96; Minister of Planning 1996–98; Special Co-ordinator for the Middle East Peace Process and Personal Rep. of the UN Sec.-Gen. to the PLO and Palestinian Authority 1999–2005; Under-Sec.-Gen. and Special Envoy for the Implementation of UN Security Council Resolution 1559 (calling for Syrian withdrawal from Lebanon and disarmament of Hezbollah) 2005; Pres. Int. Peace Inst. (fmrly Int. Peace Acad.), New York 2005–; Commdr, Légion d'Honneur 2017, Officer, Légion d'Honneur, Commdr, Nat. Order of the Cedar (Lebanon). *Address:* International Peace Institute, 777 United Nations Plaza, New York, NY 10017-3521, USA (office). *Telephone:* (212) 687-4300 (office). *Fax:* (212) 983-8246 (office). *E-mail:* ipi@ipinst.org (office). *Website:* www.ipinst.org (office).

ROEDER, Robert Gayle, BA, MS, PhD; American biologist and academic; *Arnold O. and Mabel S. Beckman Professor and Head, Laboratory of Biochemistry and Molecular Biology, The Rockefeller University;* b. 3 June 1942, Boonville, Ind.; s. of Frederick Roeder and Helene Roeder (née Bredenkamp); m. 1st Suzanne Himsel 1964 (divorced 1980); one s. one d.; m. 2nd Cun Jing Hong 1990; one d.; ed Wabash Coll., Univ. of Illinois, Urbana, Univ. of Washington, Seattle; Postdoctoral Fellow, Dept of Embryology, Carnegie Inst. of Washington, Baltimore, Md 1971; Asst Prof. of Biological Chem., Washington Univ. School of Medicine, St Louis, Mo. 1971–75, Assoc. Prof. 1975–76, Prof. 1976–82, James S. McDonnell Prof. of Biochemical Genetics 1979–82; Prof. and Head, Lab. of Biochemistry and Molecular Biology, The Rockefeller Univ., New York 1982–, Arnold O. and Mabel S. Beckman Prof. 1985–; Chair. Gordon Research Conf. on Nucleic Acids 1982; mem. Research Grant Review, NIH Molecular Biology Study Section 1975–79; mem. Scientific Advisory Bd Roche Inst. of Molecular Biology 1992–95, Second Int. Review, Karolinska Inst. Center for Biotechnology 1993, Scientific Review Bd, Howard Hughes Medical Inst. 1994–99, Nat. Inst. of Child Health and Human Devt 1995–2000; mem. Editorial Bd Journal of Biological Chemistry 1979–84, Nucleic Acids Research 1980–82, Molecular and Cellular Biology 1980–85, Cell 1990–93, Biological Chemistry Hoppe-Seyler 1994–99, Molecular Cell 1999–; mem. NAS 1988, ACS, American Soc. for Biochemistry and Molecular Biology, American Soc. for Microbiology, American Soc. for Virology, Soc. for Developmental Biology, The Harvey Soc. of New York (Pres. 1994–95), The New York Acad. of Sciences, The Protein Soc.; Fellow, AAAS 1992, American Acad. of Microbiology 1992, American Acad. of Arts and Sciences 1995; Assoc. mem. European Molecular Biology Org. 2003; Hon. DSc (Wabash Coll.) 1990, (Washington Univ.) 2005; Gilbert Scholar, Wabash Coll., US Public Health Service Predoctoral Fellowship 1965–69, Outstanding Biochemistry Grad. Student Award, Univ. of Washington 1967, American Cancer Soc. Postdoctoral Fellow 1969–71, NIH Research Career Devt Award 1973–78, Dreyfus Foundation Teacher-Scholar Award 1976–81, ACS Eli Lilly Award in Biological Chem. 1977, US Steel Award in Molecular Biology, NAS 1986, Outstanding Investigator Award, Nat. Cancer Inst. 1986–2000, Harvey Soc. Lecturer 1988, Passano Award 1995, Lewis S. Rosenstiel Award for Distinguished Work in Basic Medical Sciences 1995, Louisa Gross Horwitz Prize 1999, Alfred P. Sloan Prize, General Motors Cancer Research Foundation 1999, Gairdner Foundation Int. Award 2000, Dickson Prize in Medicine, Univ. of Pittsburgh 2001, ASBMB-Merck Award 2002, Albert Lasker Award for Basic Medical Research 2003, Salk Inst. Medal for Scientific Excellence 2010, Prize in Medicine and Biomedical Research, Albany Medical Center 2012, Award in Basic Science, Hope Funds for Cancer Research 2015, ASBMB Herbert Tabor Research Award 2016. *Publications:* more than 500 papers in scientific journals. *Address:* Laboratory of Biochemistry and Molecular Biology, The Rockefeller University, 1230 York Avenue, New York, NY 10021, USA (office). *Telephone:* (212) 327-7600 (office). *Fax:* (212) 327-7949 (office). *E-mail:* roeder@rockefeller.edu (office); robert.roeder@rockefeller.edu (office). *Website:* www.rockefeller.edu/research/faculty/abstract.php?id=144#content (office).

ROELL, Stephen (Steve) A., BSc; American business executive; ed St Ambrose Univ., Northeastern Univ.; began career as accountant, Arthur Young & Co. 1971; Div. Controller, FMC Corpn 1975–82; joined Johnson Controls Inc. 1982, Operations Controller, Systems and Services Div. 1982, becoming Div. Controller, later Treas. and Corp. Controller, Sr Vice-Pres. and Chief Financial Officer 1991–2004, Exec. Vice-Pres. 2004, Vice-Chair. 2005–07, CEO 2007–08, Chair. and CEO 2008–09, Chair., Pres. and CEO 2009–13; mem. Bd of Dirs Wheaton Franciscan Services Inc.; fmr Chair. United Way of Greater Milwaukee 2013–14; fmr Pres. Bd of Trustees, Medical Coll. of Wisconsin; fmr Trustee, Boys & Girls Club of Greater Milwaukee; mem. Business Roundtable, Financial Execs Inst.

ROELS, Harry J. M.; Dutch energy industry executive; b. 26 July 1948; ed Univ. of Leiden; began career as oil engineer, Royal Dutch/Shell 1972, various eng and man. positions including Head Exploration and Production Offices, Chief Engineer in Turkey, Tech. Man. Norske Shell, Norway, Dir Enterprise Devt, Shell Int. Petroleum Inst., The Hague, Dir Offshore Bureau then Gen. Man. Aardolie Maatschappij, The Netherlands, Office Coordinator for Latin America, Shell Int. Petroleum Co., London, UK, Regional Business Dir for Middle E and Africa, sr man. positions in Malaysia and Brunei, apptd Man. Dir Royal Dutch Petroleum Co. 1999; Pres. and CEO RWE AG 2003–07, Chair. RWE Energy, RWE Thames Water –2006.

ROEMER, John E., AB, PhD; American economist and academic; *Elizabeth S. and A. Varick Stout Professor of Political Science and Economics, Yale University;* b. 1 Feb. 1945, Washington, DC; s. of Milton I. Roemer and Ruth Rosenbaum Roemer; m. Carla Natasha Muldavin 1968; two c.; ed Harvard Univ., Univ. of California, Berkeley; math. teacher, Lowell High School and Pelton Jr High School, San Francisco 1969–74; consultant, UNCTAD, Geneva 1978; Asst Prof. of Econs, Univ. of Calif., Davis 1974–78, Assoc. Prof. 1978–81, Prof. of Econs 1981–2000; Elizabeth S. and A. Varick Stout Prof. of Political Science and Econs, Yale Univ. 2000–, affiliations with Cowles Foundation for Research in Econs, Inst. for Social and Policy Studies, Program in Ethics, Politics, and Econs, MacMillan Center for Int. Studies, Yale Climate and Energy Inst.; Visiting Prof., UCLA 1987, Harvard Univ. 1994, Univ. de Cergy-Pontoise 1995, New York Univ. 1999, Ecole Polytechnique, Paris 2004, EHESS, Marseilles 2005, Univ. de Paris I 2006; Research Prof., Toulouse School of Econs May–June 2013; Dir Program on Economy, Justice and Society 1988–2000; Pres. Soc. for Social Choice and Welfare 2010–11; mem. Editorial Bd, Economics and Philosophy 1983–, Social Choice and Welfare 1990–, Mathematical Social Sciences, 1993–, Journal of Economic Inequality 2001–; Assoc. Ed. Journal of Economic Perspectives 1988–96, Economics and Politics 1988–90, Journal of Economic Literature 1988–97, Review of Economic Design 1992–, Journal of Ethics 1997–, Journal of Economics 2004–, Journal of Institutional and Theoretical Economics 2012–; mem. Advisory Bd Journal of Economic Perspectives 2013–; John Simon Guggenheim Fellow 1980–81; Fellow, Econometric Soc. 1986, American Acad. of Arts and Sciences 2006; Russell Sage Fellow 1998–99; Corresp. Fellow, British Acad. 2005; Dr hc (Univ. of Athens) 2008; German Bernacer Lecturer, Univ. of Alicante, Spain 1993, Graz-Schumpeter Lecturer, Univ. of Graz 2003, Oscar Van Leer Lecturer, Jerusalem 2005, Parthemos Lecturer, Univ. of Georgia 2006, Bernard Correy Lecturer, Queen Mary Coll., London 2006, GINI Lecturer, Milan, Italy 2011. *Publications include:* A General Theory of Exploitation and Class 1982, Free to Lose 1988, Egalitarian Perspectives 1994, A Future for Socialism 1994, Theories of Distributive Justice 1996, Equality of Opportunity 1998, Political Competition 2001, Democracy, Education and Equality 2006; Co-editor (with E.O. Wright and G. A. Cohen) Studies in Marxism and Social Theory (series) 1984–2008. *Address:* Department of Political Science, 115 Prospect Street, Room 313, PO Box 208301, Yale University, 124 Prospect Street, New Haven, CT 06520, USA (office). *Telephone:* (203) 432-5249 (office). *Fax:* (203) 432-6196 (office). *E-mail:* john.roemer@yale.edu (office). *Website:* politicalscience.yale.edu (office); campuspress.yale.edu/johnroemer.

ROESKY, Herbert Walter, DrSc; German chemist and academic; *Professor Emeritus, Institute of Inorganic Chemistry, Georg-August University of Göttingen;* b. 6 Nov. 1935, Laukischken; s. of Otto Roesky and Lina Roesky; m. Christel Roesky 1964; two s.; ed Univ. of Göttingen; Lecturer 1970, Univ. of Frankfurt, Prof. of Inorganic Chem. 1970–80; Dir Inst. of Inorganic Chem., Georg-August Univ. of Göttingen 1980, now Prof. Emer., Dean Dept of Chem. 1985–87; Visiting Prof., Auburn Univ., USA 1984, Tokyo Inst. of Tech. 1987; mem. Gesellschaft Deutscher Chemiker (Vice-Pres. 1995), ACS, Chemical Soc., London, Gesellschaft Deutscher Naturforscher und Ärzte, Deutsche Bunsen-Gesellschaft für Physikalische Chemie, Göttinger Akad., Akad. Leopoldina, Austrian Acad. of Sciences, Russian Acad. of Sciences 1999; Foreign Assoc., Acad. des Sciences, France, Romanian Acad. of Sciences, Indian Acad.; mem. Selection Bd, Alexander von Humboldt-Stiftung 1973–84, numerous editorial bds; Hon. FRSC 2007; Wöhler Prize 1960, French Alexander von Humboldt Prize 1986, Leibniz Prize 1987, Alfred-Stock-Gedächtnispreis 1990, Georg Ernst Stahl Medal 1990; Manfred and Wolfgang Flad Prize 1994, Grand Prix Fondation de la maison de la chimie, Carus Prize 1998, Wilkinson Award 1999, ACS Inorganic Award 2004, Wittig-Grignard Prize 2005, Moissan Award 2009, Rössler Prize 2012. *Publications:* eight books and more than 1,200 learned papers and articles. *Leisure interest:* antique collecting. *Address:* Institute of Inorganic Chemistry, University of Göttingen, Tammannstrasse 4, 37077 Göttingen, Germany (office). *Telephone:* (551) 3933001 (office). *Fax:* (551) 3933373 (office). *E-mail:* hroesky@gwdg.de (office). *Website:* www.roesky.chemie.uni-goettingen.de (office).

ROGEL, Steven R., BS; American business executive; ed Univ. of Washington, Seattle, Dartmouth Coll., Massachusetts Inst. of Tech.; began career with Regis Paper Co. 1966–70; Asst Man., St Anne-Nackawic Pulp and Paper, Nackawic, NB, Canada 1970–72; Tech. Dir Wilamette Industries, Inc., Albany, Ore. 1972, Pres. and COO 1991–95, Pres. and CEO 1995–97; Pres. and CEO Weyerhaeuser Co. 1997–2008, Chair. 1999–2008, Chair. (non-exec.) 2008–09; mem. Bd of Dirs Union Pacific Corpn 2000–, Kroger Co. 2000–14, EnergySolutions Inc. 2009–13 (Chair. 2010–13); fmr Chair. American Forest & Paper Asscn, Nat. Council for Air and Stream Improvement, Inc.; fmr Co-Chair. Wood Promotion Network; fmr Vice-Pres. Admin Western Region Boy Scouts of America, mem. Nat. Exec. Bd Boy Scouts of America; Trustee, Pacific Univ.

ROGER, Bruno; French banking executive; *Chairman and CEO, Lazard Frères Banque SA;* ed Institut d'Études Politiques, Paris; fmr CEO Compagnie Financière Lazard Frères SAS, now Chair., Chair. Lazard Frères SAS, currently Chair. and CEO Lazard Frères Banque SA; fmr CEO Azeo; mem. Bd of Dirs, Euroazeo SA 1969–, Chair. Emer., fmr Chair. Supervisory Bd Eurazeo (non-voting Bd mem.), now Hon. Chair.; fmr Dir of Finance, Cap Gemini SA; fmr CEO and Vice-Chair. EuraFrance; fmr Chair. Global Investment Banking, Lazard Ltd; fmr Co-Chair. European Advisory Bd; Dir, Saint-Gobain 1987–2005, Sidel SA 1987–, Cap Gemini SA 2000–, Paris Europlace, Ernst & Young, Thalès; fmr Dir, Sofina SA (Belgium);

mem. Pinault-Printemps-Redoute SA (PPR SA) 1994–, Supervisory Bd AXA 1997–2005; Admin. and Treas., Les Arts Décoratifs 1999–2013, Chair. 2013–; Chair. Festival d'art lyrique d'Aix-en-Provence 2005–, Fondation Martine Aublet (univ. scholarships and the Atelier Martine Aublet at Musée du Quai Branly); mem. Acquisitions Comm., Musée du Quai Branly. *Address:* Lazard Frères SAS, 121 boulevard Haussmann, 75382 Paris Cedex 08, France (office). *Telephone:* 1-44-13-01-11 (office). *Fax:* 1-44-13-01-00 (office). *E-mail:* info@lazard.com (office). *Website:* www.lazard.com (office).

ROGER, Michel; French lawyer; b. 9 March 1949, Poitiers; called to the Bar, Poitiers; several ministerial roles in France including Keeper of the Seals 1975–76, with Ministry of Planning and Works 1976–77; Regional Councillor, Poitiers 1983–2001; Adviser to cabinet of Prime Minister Jean-Pierre Raffarin 2002; fmr Insp. Gen., French nat. educ. system; Judge, Tribunal suprême, Monaco 2007–10; Minister of State, Monaco Council of Govt 2010–15. *Address:* Ministry of State, place de la Visitation, 98000 Monte Carlo, Monaco (office). *Telephone:* 98-98-80-00 (office). *Fax:* 98-98-82-17 (office). *E-mail:* sgme@gouv.mc (office). *Website:* www.gouv.mc (office).

ROGERS, George Ernest, AO, PhD, DSc, FAA; Australian biochemist and academic; *Professor Emeritus and Honorary Visiting Research Fellow, School of Molecular and Biomedical Science, University of Adelaide;* b. 27 Oct. 1927, Melbourne, Vic.; s. of Percy Rogers and Bertha Beatrice Rogers (née Baxter); m. 2nd Racheline Aladjem 1972; two d.; ed Caulfield Grammar School, Univ. of Melbourne and Trinity Coll., Cambridge, England; Scientist, Wool Research, CSIRO 1951–53, Research Scientist, Div. of Protein Chem. 1957–62; Research Scientist, Univ. of Cambridge, England 1954–56; Reader in Biochem., Univ. of Adelaide 1963–77, Prof. of Biochem. 1978–92 and Chair. Dept of Biochem. 1988–92, now Prof. Emer., Hon. Visiting Research Fellow 1993–; Visiting Fellow, Clare Hall Cambridge 1970; Program Man., Premium Quality Wool CRC 1995–2000; Visiting Scientist, Univ. de Grenoble, France 1977; Guest Scientist, NIH, Bethesda, USA 1985; CSIRO studentship 1954–56; Bourse Scientifique de Haut Niveau 1977; mem. Australian Soc. of Biochemistry and Molecular Biology, New York Acad. of Sciences; Eleanor Roosevelt Int. Cancer Research Fellow 1985; Fellow, Australian Acad. of Science 1977; Hon. Prof., Dept of Medicine, Univ. of Melbourne; Centenary Fed. Medal 2003; Lemberg Medal, Australian Biochemical Soc. 1976. *Publications include:* The Keratins (co-author) 1972, The Biology of Wool and Hair (co-author) 1989; 170 publs in scientific journals on wool and hair growth, hair structure and sheep transgenesis. *Leisure interests:* family activities, swimming, golf, gardening. *Address:* School of Molecular and Biomedical Science, University of Adelaide, Adelaide, SA 5005 (office); 1 Gandys Gully Road, Stonyfell, SA 5066, Australia (home). *Telephone:* (8) 8303-4624 (office); (8) 8332-4143 (home). *Fax:* (8) 8303-7532 (office). *E-mail:* george.rogers@adelaide.edu.au (office). *Website:* www.mbs.adelaide.edu.au/people/biochem/grogers (office).

ROGERS, Grant Simon, BA; British artist, art historian and lecturer; b. 4 March 1964, Singapore; s. of Keith Rogers and Diane Rogers; ed Crofton School, Price's Coll., and Portsmouth Coll. of Art, Hampshire, England; Founder-mem. Cubit Street Artists 1986–92; lecturer at Nat. Gallery, Nat. Portrait Gallery, Wallace Collection, Victoria and Albert Museum, British Museum, Imperial War Museum. *Television:* BBC television and radio, Channel 4 TV. *Films:* animated: TVC cartoons; Father Christmas; Grandpa; When the Wind Blows. *Publications:* numerous articles in UK press. *Leisure interests:* hedonism and futile introspection. *Address:* 66–68 Camberwell Road, London, SE5 0EG, England (home). *Telephone:* (20) 7416-5329 (office). *E-mail:* grogers@iwm.org. *Website:* www.iwm.org.uk (office).

ROGERS, Sir Ivan, Kt, KCMG; British civil servant, business executive and diplomatist; worked as Head of UK Public Sector at Citigroup; later Head of UK Public Sector Business at Barclays Capital; civil service roles include as Prin. Pvt. Sec. to Prime Minister, Dir of Budget and Tax Policy at HM Treasury, Dir of EU Strategy and Policy at HM Treasury, Chef de Cabinet to Vice-Pres. of EC, Pvt. Sec. to Chancellor of Exchequer; Prime Minister's Adviser on Europe and Global Issues, Head of European and Global Issues Secr. –2013; Perm. Rep. to EU 2013–16 (resgnd). *Address:* Foreign and Commonwealth Office, King Charles Street, London, SW1A 2AH, England (office). *Telephone:* (20) 7008-1500 (office). *E-mail:* ivan.rogers@fco.gov.uk (office). *Website:* www.gov.uk/government/organisations/foreign-commonwealth-office (office).

ROGERS OF RIVERSIDE, Baron (Life Peer), cr. 1996, of Chelsea in the Royal Borough of Kensington and Chelsea; **Richard George Rogers,** Kt, CH, AADipl, MArch, RA; British architect; *Chairman, Rogers Stirk Harbour + Partners;* b. 23 July 1933, Florence, Italy; s. of Nino Rogers and Dada Geiringer; m. 1st Su Brumwell 1961; three s.; m. 2nd Ruth Elias 1973; two s.; ed Architectural Asscn, London, Yale Univ., USA; Fulbright, Edward D. Stone and Yale Scholar; worked with Italian architect Renzo Piano; Chair. Rogers Stirk Harbour + Partners (fmrly Richard Rogers Partnership); Pres. Nat. Communities Resource Centre; Chief Advisor to the Mayor on Architecture and Urbanism; Dir River Café Ltd; Saarinen Prof., Yale Univ. 1985; has also taught at Architectural Asscn, London, at Cambridge, Princeton, Columbia, Harvard, Cornell, McGill and Aachen Univs and at UCLA; Vice-Chair. Arts Council of England 1994–97; mem. (Labour) House of Lords 1996–, Hon. Chair. Architecture and Planning Group 2006–; mem. UN Architects' Cttee, Barcelona Urban Strategy Council; Trustee, Tate Gallery 1981–89 (Chair. 1984–88); London First 1993–98, UK Bd Médecins du Monde; Hon. FRIBA, FAIA 1986; Chevalier, Légion d'honneur 1986; Hon. DSc (Bath) 1994; Hon. DLitt (Univ. Coll., London) 1997; Dr hc (Westminster) 1993, (RCA) 1994, (South Bank) 1996, (Alfonso X El Sabio Univ., Madrid), (Oxford Brookes), (Kent), (Czech Tech. Univ., Prague), (Open Univ.); 38 RIBA Awards since 1969, RIBA Royal Gold Medal 1985, 12 Civic Trust Awards 1986–2010, Constructa Prize 1986, 1992, Eternit Int. Prize 1988, Reith Lecturer 1995, Thomas Jefferson Memorial Foundation Medal in Architecture 1999, Praemium Imperiale Award 2000, Golden Lion for Lifetime Achievement, 10th Mostra di Architettura di Venezia 2006, Laureate of the Pritzker Architecture Prize (architecture's highest honour) 2007, Minerva Medal, Chartered Soc. of Designers 2007, Freedom of the City of London 2014 and numerous other awards. *Works include:* major int. work: Pompidou Centre, Paris, France (with Renzo Piano) 1971–77, masterplanning: Royal Docks, London 1984–86, Potsdamer Platz, Berlin 1991, Shanghai Pu Dong Financial Dist 1992, Greenwich Peninsula Masterplan 1997–98; airports and HQ bldgs: PA Tech.,

Cambridge 1975–83, PA Tech., Princeton, NJ, USA 1984, European Court of Human Rights, Strasbourg 1990–95, Marseille Airport 1992, Law Courts, Bordeaux, France 1992–98, VR Techno offices and lab., Gifu, Japan 1993–98, Channel 4 HQ 1991–94; recent projects: masterplanning and design of Heathrow Airport Terminal 5 1989–2008, Montevetro Housing, Battersea, London 1994–2000, ParcBIT Devt, Majorca 1994–, Lloyd's Register of Shipping HQ, London 1995–99, 88 Wood Street, London 1995–99, Minami Yamashiro Primary School 1995–2003, Millennium Dome, London 1996–99, masterplanning of Piana di Castello, Florence 1997–, New Area Terminal, Barajas Airport, Madrid (RIBA Stirling Prize 2006) 1997–2005, Nat. Ass. for Wales 1998–2006, Senedd (Nat. Assembly for Wales), Cardiff 1999–2005, Law Courts, Antwerp 1999–2006, Maggie's Centre, London (RIBA Stirling Prize 2009) 2001–08, Mossbourne Community Acad. 2002–04, 122 Leadenhall Street 2002–, Cen. Park Station (R9), Kaohsiung Mass Rapid Transit system, Kaohsiung City, Taiwan 2003–07, 300 New Jersey Avenue, Washington, DC, USA 2004–09, Ching Fu Group HQ, Kaohsiung City 2005–07, Campus Palmas Altas, Seville, Spain (Abengoa HQ) 2005–09, 175 Greenwich Street, New York 2006–, Capodichino Underground Station, Naples, Italy 2006–, Santa Maria del Pianto Underground Station, Naples 2006–, One Hyde Park, London 2007–10, new city centre and tram station, Scandicci, Italy 2007–, British Museum, Northwest Devt, London 2007–, 360-London 2007–, Bodegas Protos, Peñafiel, Valladolid, Spain 2008, Greater Paris/Grand Paris 2008–, Barangaroo, Sydney, Australia 2009–, Oxley Woods, Milton Keynes, UK (Govt-sponsored 'Design for Manufacture (DfM)') 2010, Las Arenas, Barcelona, remodelling of the bullring into a shopping mall 2011, Neo Bankside, London 2012, Leadenhall bldg ('The Cheesegrater'), London 2014. *Publications:* Richard Rogers and Architects 1985, A+U: Richard Rogers 1978–88 1988, Architecture: A Modern View 1990, A New London (with Mark Fisher) 1992, Reith Lecturer 1995, Cities for a Small Planet 1997, Richard Rogers The Complete Works (Vols I–III) 1999, Cities for a Small Country 2000, Richard Rogers: Architecture of the Future 2006, Richard Rogers 2006, Richard Rogers Architects: From the House to the City 2009. *Leisure interests:* friends, food, travel, art, architecture. *Address:* Rogers Stirk Harbour + Partners, Thames Wharf, Rainville Road, London, W6 9HA (office); House of Lords, Westminster, London, SW1A 0PW, England (office). *Telephone:* (20) 7385-1235 (office); (20) 7219-5353 (House of Lords) (office). *Fax:* (20) 7385-8409 (office). *E-mail:* enquiries@rsh-p.com (office). *Website:* www.rsh-p.com (office).

ROGERS, Thomas (Tom) Sydney, BA, JD; American lawyer and media executive; *Chairman, Tivo, Inc.;* b. 19 Aug. 1954, New Rochelle, NY; s. of Sydney Michael Rogers Jr and Alice Steinhardt; m. Sylvia Texon 1983; two s. one d.; ed Wesleyan Univ., Columbia Univ.; attorney with Wall Street law firm 1979–81; called to New York Bar 1980; Sr Counsel, US House of Reps Sub cttee on Telecommunications, Consumer Protection and Finance 1981–86; Vice-Pres. Policy Planning and Business Devt, NBC 1987–88, Pres. NBC Cable 1988–89, NBC Cable and Business Devt 1989–99, Exec. Vice-Pres. NBC 1992–99, Vice-Chair. NBC Internet 1999; Chair. and CEO Primedia Inc. 1999–2003; Sr Operating Exec. for media and entertainment, Cerberus Capital Man. (pvt. equity firm) 2004–05; mem. Bd of Dirs Tivo, Inc. 2003–, Vice-Chair. 2004–05, Pres. and CEO 2005–2016, Chair. 2016–; Chair. TRget Media LLC 2003–05, Teleglobe Int. Holdings Ltd, 2004–06; mem. Bd of Dirs Dex Media, Inc. 2013–; mem. Advisory Bd for Media and Business, LifeMed Media, Inc; Pres. and CEO Int. Council, Nat. Acad. of TV Arts and Sciences 1994–97, Chair. 1998–99; mem. New York State Bar Asscn, Int. Radio and TV Soc. *Address:* Tivo, Inc., 2160 Gold Street, Alviso, CA 95002-2160, USA (office). *Telephone:* (408) 519-9100 (office). *Website:* www.tivo.com (office).

ROGERSON, Philip Graham, FCA, FCT; British business executive; *Chairman, De La Rue plc;* b. 1 Jan. 1945, Manchester; s. of Henry Rogerson and Florence Rogerson; m. Susan Janet Kershaw 1968; one s. two d.; ed William Hulme's Grammar School, Manchester; with Dearden Harper, Miller & Co. Chartered Accountants 1962–67; with Hill Samuel & Co. Ltd 1967–69; with Thomas Tilling Ltd 1969–71; with Steetley Ltd 1971–72; with J.W. Chafer Ltd 1972–78; joined ICI 1978, Gen. Man. Finance 1989–92; Man. Dir Finance British Gas PLC 1992–94, Exec. Dir 1994–96, Deputy Chair. 1996–98; Deputy Chair. (non-exec.) Aggreko PLC 1997–2002, Chair. 2002–12; Chair. Pipeline Integrity Int. 1998–2002, Bertram Group Ltd 1999–2001, British Biotech 1999–2003, Octopus Capital PLC 2000–01, Copper Eye Ltd 2001–03; Chair. Project Telecom PLC 2000–03, Thus Group plc 2004–08, Carillion plc 2004–13, Davis Service Group PLC 2004–10, Bunzl PLC 2010–, KBC Advanced Technologies PLC, De La Rue plc 2012–; Deputy Chair. Viridian Group PLC 1998, Chair. 1999–2005; mem. Bd of Dirs Halifax Building Society (now Halifax PLC) 1995–98, LIMIT PLC 1997, Int. Public Relations 1997–98, Wates City of London Properties 1998–2001; Blancco Tech. Group PLC 2017–; Chair. Central YMCA 2011–17; Trustee, Changing Faces 1997–2011. *Leisure interests:* golf, tennis, theatre. *Address:* De La Rue plc, Jays Close, Basingstoke, RG22 4BS (office); Bunzl plc, York House, 45 Seymour Street, London, W1H 7JT, England (office). *E-mail:* webcontact@delarue.com (office). *Website:* www.delarue.com (office); www.bunzl.com (office).

ROGGE, Count; Jacques; Belgian surgeon, international organization official and fmr sports administrator; *Special Envoy for Youth Refugees and Sport, United Nations;* b. 2 May 1942, Ghent; m. Anne Rogge; two c.; ed Univ. of Ghent; fmr orthopaedic surgeon and sports medicine lecturer; participated as sailing competitor at Summer Olympics in Mexico City, 1968, Munich 1972, Montreal (team gold medal) 1976; also played on Belgian nat. rugby union team; gold medal, Finn-class World Championships, silver medal twice, Belgian champion 16 times; also won Yachting World Cadet Trophy and took part in the regatta Ton Cup; Pres. Belgian Olympic Cttee 1989–92, European Olympic Cttee 1989–2001, Chef de mission, two winter and three summer Olympic Games (Chief Co-ordinator, Olympic Games 2000, 2004), mem. IOC 1991–, mem. Exec. Bd 1998–2013, Pres. 2001–13, Hon. Pres. 2013–; UN Special Envoy for Youth Refugees and Sport 2014–; knighted in 1992, made a Count in the Belgian nobility by King Albert II 2002, Officier, Légion d'honneur 2011, Hon. KCMG 2014; UNEP Champion of the Earth Laureate 2007, FIFA Presidential Award 2013. *Leisure interests:* modern art, historical and scientific literature. *Address:* United Nations High Commissioner for Refugees, Case Postale 2500, 2 Dépôt, 1211, Geneva, Switzerland (office). *Telephone:* 227398111 (office). *Fax:* 227397377 (office). *Website:* www.unhcr.org (office).

ROGOFF, Ilan; Israeli/Spanish concert pianist and conductor; b. 26 July 1943, Tel-Aviv; s. of Boris Rogoff and Sofija Rogoff; m. Vesna Zorka Mimiça 1985; two d.; ed Tel-Aviv Acad. of Music, Royal Conservatoire, Belgium, Mannes Coll. and Juilliard School, USA; has performed all over Israel, Europe, N America, Latin America, S Africa, Japan and Far East with Israel Philharmonic Orchestra and many other orchestras; recognized for his interpretation of the Romantic composers, including Beethoven, Schumann, Brahms, Chopin, Liszt, César Franck, Rachmaninov, Tchaikovsky, Piazzolla; has performed twentieth-century and contemporary works including world premiere of concerti by John McCabe and by Ivan Erod; performs with various chamber music groups, including Enesco Quartet, Orpheus Quartet, Amati Trio, Festival Ensemble, Matrix Quintet, Sharon Trio and Quartet, soloists of Vienna Chamber Orchestra and Vienna Philharmonic Orchestra; conducting debut 1985, with Israel Philharmonic 1988; radio performances and TV appearances in UK, Spain, Austria, Germany, Israel, Canada, USA, SA, Colombia, Ecuador, Venezuela and Argentina; lectures and recital/lectures, master classes; juror at various int. music competitions; various int. awards. *Recordings include:* Chopin Concerti (version for piano and string quintet edited by him), transcriptions for piano solo of 12 works by Astor Piazzolla; 'Portraits' by Schumann; complete works by Chopin while in Mallorca; numerous works by Bach-Busoni, Beethoven, Schumann, Schubert, Beethoven, Liszt, Schubert/Liszt and César Franck. *Publications:* Transcriptions for Piano Solo of Works by Astor Piazzolla, edited both Chopin Concerti for Piano and String Quintet; articles on music published in Scherzo magazine, Madrid, Piano magazine, London. *Leisure interests:* water sports, reading, visual arts, theatre, cinema and music research. *Address:* Estudio/Taller, Calle Bartomeu Fons 13, 07015 Palma de Mallorca, Spain (office). *Telephone:* (971) 707016 (home); 6-10980906 (mobile). *E-mail:* rogoffilan@gmail.com (home). *Website:* www.ilanrogoff.com.

ROGOFF, Kenneth S., BA, MA, PhD; American economist, academic and international finance official; *Thomas D. Cabot Professor of Public Policy, Harvard University;* b. 22 March 1953, Rochester, NY; s. of Stanley Miron Rogoff and June Beatrice Rogoff; m. Natasha Lance; one s. one d.; ed Yale Univ., Massachusetts Inst. of Tech.; Economist, Int. Finance Div., Fed. Reserve Bd of Govs 1980–83; economist, Research Dept, IMF 1982–83, Chief Economist and Dir of Research 2001–03; Assoc. Prof. of Econs, Univ. of Wisconsin 1985–88; Prof. of Econs, Univ. of California, Berkeley 1989–92; Prof. of Econs and Int. Affairs, Princeton Univ. 1992–94, Charles and Marie Robertson Prof. of Int. Affairs 1995–99; Prof. of Econs, Harvard Univ. 1999–, Thomas D. Cabot Prof. of Public Policy 2004–, Dir Harvard Center for Int. Devt 2003–04; Vice-Pres. American Econ. Asscn 2007; Research Assoc., Nat. Bureau of Econ. Research 1985–; mem. Econ. Advisory Panel, Fed. Reserve Bank of New York 2004–, Academic Advisory Panel, Cen. Bank of Sweden 2005–11, Advisory Cttee, Peterson Inst. for Int. Econs 2001–; Assoc. Ed. Review of Economics and Statistics 1993–, Economics Letters 1993–96, Journal of International Economics 1995–, Quarterly Journal of Economics 1984–95, Journal of Economic Perspectives 1987–90; Councillor, Global Strategy Comm., World Chess Foundation (FIDE) 2018–; mem. Trilateral Comm. 2003–, Council on Foreign Relations 2004–, Group of Thirty Consultative Group on Int. Econ. and Monetary Affairs (G-30) 2008–; Nat. Science Fellowship, MIT 1975–78; Alfred P. Sloan Research Fellow 1986; Nat. Fellow, The Hoover Inst. 1986; German Marshall Foundation Fellow 1991; Econometric Soc. Fellow 1991; Fellow, American Acad. of Arts and Sciences 2001, World Econ. Forum 2003, NAS 2010; Hon. Advisor, Inst. for Monetary and Econ. Studies, Bank of Japan 2001; Guggenheim Fellow 1998, TIAA-CREF Paul A. Samuelson Award, 2010, Adam Smith Award, 2011, Deutsche Bank Prize in Financial Economics, 2011. *Achievements include:* Int. Grandmaster of Chess, World Chess Fed. 1978– (inactive). *Publications include:* Foundations of International Macroeconomics (with Maurice Obstfeld) 1996, Workbook for Foundations of International Macroeconomics 1998, This Time is Different: Eight Centuries of Financial Folly (with Carmen M. Reinhart) (Arthur Ross Book Award 2011) 2009; numerous contribs to learned journals and newspapers. *Leisure interests:* swimming, chess, cinema. *Address:* Harvard University, Department of Economics, Littauer Center 216, Cambridge, MA 02138-3001, USA (office). *Telephone:* (617) 495-4022 (office). *Fax:* (617) 495-7730 (office). *E-mail:* krogoff@harvard.edu (office). *Website:* www.scholar.harvard.edu/rogoff/home (home); www.kenrogoff.com.

ROGOV, Sergey Mikhailovich, Dr. Hist.; Russian political scientist and academic; *Director, Institute for USA and Canadian Studies, Russian Academy of Sciences;* b. 22 Oct. 1948, Moscow; m.; one s. one d.; ed Moscow State Inst. of Int. Relations; jr researcher, sr researcher, then head of sector, Inst. for USA and Canadian Studies, USSR Acad. of Sciences 1976–84, Rep. of Inst. for USA and Canadian Studies to USSR Embassy in Washington, DC 1984–87, Leading Research Fellow, Moscow 1987–89, Chief, Dept of Mil. and Political Studies 1989–91, Deputy Dir 1991–95, Dir 1995–; Dean, School of World Politics and Int. Security, State Academic Univ. for Humanitarian Studies 2010–; mem. Advisory Council, Foreign Ministry; Advisor to Cttee on Foreign Affairs, State Duma; Chair. Int. Security Comm. of Scientific Advisory Bd of Security Council of Russian Fed.; mem. Scientific Council, Federal Council of the Russian Federation; Vice-Chair. Russian Pugwash Cttee; mem. Bd of Dirs Russian Foreign Policy Asscn, New Economic Asscn; Pres. Russian Asscn for Canadian Studies; mem. Presidium of the Russian Asscn for Int. Studies; mem. Scientific Council of Ministry of Foreign Affairs; Corresp. mem. Russian Acad. of Sciences 2002–; Order of Merit 2010. *Publications:* 16 books on foreign policy of USSR and Russian Fed., Russian-American relationship, mil. aspects of foreign policy, problems of nat. security and over 400 scientific publs and articles. *Address:* Institute for USA and Canadian Studies, Russian Academy of Sciences, 123995 Moscow, Khlebny per 2/3, Russia (office). *Telephone:* (495) 290-58-75 (office). *Fax:* (495) 200-12-07 (office). *E-mail:* srogov@rambler.ru (office). *Website:* www.iskran.ru (office).

ROGOZHKIN, Aleksandr Vladimirovich; Russian scriptwriter and film director; b. 3 Oct. 1950, Leningrad; m. Yulia Rumyantseva (died 2011); ed Leningrad State Univ., All-Union Inst. of Cinematography; worked in TV cos in Leningrad; cinema debut in 1980s. *Films directed include:* Ryzhaya, ryzhaya 1981, Radi neskolkikh strochek 1985, Miss millionersha 1988, Karaul (FIPRESCI Prize for Best Film Moscow Int. Film Festival, Alfred Bauer Prize, Berlin Festival 1989) 1989, The Guard 1990, Tretya planeta (also writer) 1991, Chekist 1992, Akt (also writer) 1993, Zhizn s idiotom (also writer) 1993, Osobennosti natsionalnoy okhoty (also writer, Nika Award for Best Dir) 1995, Blokpost (story, Silver Dolphin for Best Dir Tróia Int. Film Festival 1998, Best Dir Karlovy Vary Int. Film Festival 1998) 1998, Osobennosti natsionalnoy rybalki (also writer) 1998, Boldino Fall 1999, Osobennosti natsionalnoy okhoty v zimniy period 2000, Kukushka (also writer, Grand Prix Honfleur Festival of Russian Cinema, Dialog Prize 2002, Silver Dolphin for Best Dir Tróia Int. Film Festival 2002, FIPRESCI Prize for Best Film Moscow Int. Film Festival, Nika Award for Best Film and Best Dir) 2002, Sapiens (also writer) 2004, Peregon (also writer) 2006, Igra 2008, Vopros chesti 2010, Afrodity 2012, Oruzhiye 2012. *Television:* films: Sklyuchenie bez pravil 1986, Operatsiya 'S novym godom' 1996, Svoya chuzhaya zhizn 2005. *Address:* Gertsena str. 21, apt 8, 191065 St Petersburg, Russia (home). *Telephone:* (812) 311-76-81 (home).

ROGOZIN, Dmitrii Olegovich, DrPhil; Russian politician and diplomatist; *General Director, ROSCOSMOS;* b. 21 Dec. 1963, Moscow, Russian SFSR, USSR; s. of Oleg Konstantinovich Rogozin and Tamara Vasilevna Rogozina (née Prokofiyeva); m. Tatyana Gennadyevna Serebryakova; two s.; ed Moscow State Univ.; worked in USSR Cttee of Youth Orgs and as a journalist; Co-founder Research and Educ. Co. RAU Corp. 1986–90; one of Party of People's Freedom 1990; Pres. Asscn of Young Political Leaders of Russia Forum-90; f. Kongress Russkikh Obshchin (Congress of Russian Communities) 1993; active in nat. movt; took part in re-establishment of numerous churches; mem. State Duma (Regiony Rossii—Regions of Russia, Rodina—Motherland) 1997–; Co-founder and Leader Rodina pre-election bloc 2003, Leader Rodina—Narodno-patrioticheskii Soyuz (Motherland—People's Patriotic Union) faction 2004–06; Chair. Cttee on Int. Affairs 2000–03, Deputy Chair. 2003–04; Chief Negotiator with EU on relations with Kaliningrad Oblast 2002–04; Deputy Chair. Cttee on Nationalities, State Duma 2007–08; Amb. to NATO and Head of Perm. Mission 2008–11; Special Rep. of the Pres. of Russian Fed. for Interaction with NATO in Missile Defence Feb.–Dec. 2011; Deputy Chair. of the Govt in charge of Defence Industry 2011–18, Presidential Rep. to the 'Transnistrian Moldovan Republic' 2012; Head of Govt's Mil.-Industrial Comm. 2012; Chair. Marine Bd of the Govt 2012; First Deputy Chair. 'Victory' Organizing Cttee 2012; placed under exec. sanction by US following Crimean status referendum, freezing his assets in USA and banning him from entering USA March 2014; Gen. Dir ROSCOSMOS 2018–. *Publications include:* Russian Answer 1996, War and Peace in Terms and Definitions – Glossary of Military Terminology (Ed.-in-Chief) 2004, 2011, Enemy of the People 2007, Hawks of Peace 2009; numerous articles in the western and Russian press. *Leisure interests:* master of sports, handball. *Address:* State Space Corporation ROSCOSMOS, 107996 Moscow, 42, Schepkina street, Russia (office). *Telephone:* (495) 660-23-23 (office). *Fax:* (495) 631-99-00 (office). *Website:* www.en.roscosmos.ru (office).

ROHATGI, Mukul, LLB; Indian lawyer and government official; s. of Justice Awadh Behari Rohatgi; m. Vasudha Sanghi; ed Univ. of Mumbai; started legal practice in High Court of Bombay; later started own legal practice; Sr Advocate, Supreme Court 1994–, Additional Solicitor-Gen. 1999–2004, Attorney-Gen. 2014–17. *Leisure interests:* travelling, luxury cars. *Address:* No. 217, Greater Kailash-1, New Delhi 110048 (home); Supreme Court of India, Tilak Marg, New Delhi 110201, India (office). *Telephone:* (11) 6485615 (home).

ROHATYN, Felix George, BS; American investment banker and diplomatist; *Special Advisor to the Chairman and CEO, Lazard Ltd;* b. 29 May 1928, Vienna, Austria; s. of Alexander Rohatyn and Edith Rohatyn (née Knoll); m. 1st Jeannette Streit 1956; three s.; m. 2nd Elizabeth Fly 1979; ed Middlebury Coll.; moved to USA 1942, served in US Army 1951–53; joined Lazard Freres & Co. (investment bankers, now Lazard Ltd) 1948, Gen. Pnr 1961–97, Special Advisor to Chair. and CEO 2006–; Amb. to France 1997–2000; Founder and Pres. Rohatyn Assocs LLC 2001–; Sr Advisor, Lehman Brothers Holdings Inc. 2006–09; mem. Bd of Govs New York Stock Exchange 1968–72; Chair. Municipal Assistance Corpn 1975–93; mem. Bd of Dirs LVMH (Moet Hennessy Louis Vuitton), Publicis Groupe SA, Rothschild Continuation Holdings AG, Lagardere; Trustee, Center for Strategic and Int. Studies, now Trustee Emer.; Hon. Trustee, Carnegie Hall, Trustee Emer. Middlebury Coll.; mem. Council on Foreign Relations, Council of American Ambassadors, American Acad. of Arts and Sciences; eight hon. degrees; Commdr, Légion d'honneur. *Publications:* The Twenty-Year Century: Essays on Economics and Public Finance 1983, Money Games: My Journey Through American Capitalism 1950–2000 2003, Bold Endeavors: How our Government Built America, and Why it Must Rebuild Now 2009, Dealings: A Political and Financial Life 2010. *Address:* Rohatyn Associates LLC, 280 Park Avenue, 27th Floor, New York, NY 10017 (office); Lazard Ltd, 30 Rockefeller Plaza, New York, NY 10112-5900, USA (office). *Telephone:* (212) 984-2975 (office); (212) 632-5540 (Lazard) (office). *Fax:* (212) 984-2976 (office). *E-mail:* felix.rohatyn@rohatyn.com (office). *Website:* www.lazard.com (office).

ROHDE, Bruce C., BBA, JD; American lawyer and food industry executive; *Chairman and CEO Emeritus, ConAgra Foods Inc.;* b. 17 Dec. 1948, Sidney, Neb.; ed Creighton Univ., Creighton Univ. School of Law; with McGrath, North, Mullin and Kratz (law firm) 1973–96; Pres. and Vice-Chair. ConAgra Foods Inc. 1996–97, CEO 1997–98, Chair. and CEO 1998–2005, now Chair. and CEO Emer.; Chair. Romar Capital Group; mem. Bd of Dirs Gleacher and Co. 2009–13, H&R Block 2010–, Preventive Medicine Research Inst.; Chair. Bd of Trustees, Creighton Univ. 2001–15; fmr Chair. Strategic Air and Space Museum; mem. Pvt. and Public, Scientific, Academic and Consumer Food Policy Cttee (PAPSAC), Harvard Univ.; mem. STRATCOM (US Strategic Command) Consultation Cttee; mem. Nat. Infrastructure Advisory Council, US Dept of Homeland Security; Business Information Professional of the Year Award 2000, Frost & Sullivan Food and Beverage CEO of the Year 2004.

ROHINI, Hon. G.; Indian lawyer and judge; *Chief Justice, Delhi High Court;* b. 14 April 1955, Visakhapatnam, Andhra Pradesh; ed Osmania Univ., Andhra Univ. Coll. of Law; fmr reporter then Exec. Ed. Andhra Pradesh Law Journals; enrolled as Advocate 1980 and joined office of advocate Koka Raghava Rao, practised primarily in Andhra Pradesh High Court, Hyderabad; Govt Pleader, High Court of Andhra Pradesh 1995–2001, Additional Judge 2001–02, Perm. Judge 2002–14; Chief Justice, Delhi High Court 2014–; Chair. Andhra Pradesh Judicial Acad. *Address:* High Court of Delhi, Sher Shah Road, New Delhi 110 503, India (office). *Telephone:* (11) 43010101 (office). *Website:* delhihighcourt.nic.in (office).

ROHNER, Marcel, PhD; Swiss banker; b. 4 Sept. 1964; m.; two c.; ed Univ. of Zurich; research and teaching asst, Inst. for Empirical Research in Econs, Univ. of Zurich 1990–92; Asst to the Global Head of Derivatives, Union Bank of Switzerland 1992–93; Int. Finance Div. Controlling, Market Risk Control, SBC Zürich 1993–95; Head, Market Risk Control Europe, Warburg Dillon Read 1995–98; Head, Market Risk Control UBS AG 1998–99, Group Chief Risk Officer 1999–2001, COO and Deputy CEO Pvt. Banking unit of UBS Switzerland 2001–02, mem. Group Exec. Bd 2002–, CEO Wealth Man. and Business Banking 2002–04, Chair. and CEO Wealth Man. and Business Banking 2004–05, Deputy Group CEO 2006–07, Group CEO 2007–09 (resgnd), Chair. and CEO Investment Bank 2007–08; Vice-Chair. Swiss Bankers Asscn –2008, Bd of Trustees, Swiss Finance Inst.

ROHNER, Urs; Swiss lawyer and business executive; *Chairman, Credit Suisse Group AG;* b. 1959; ed Univ. of Zurich; lawyer, Lenz & Staehelin, Attorneys at Law, Zurich 1983–88, Partner 1990–99; admitted to Bar of Canton of Zurich 1986, Bar of State of NY, USA 1990; lawyer, Sullivan & Cromwell LLP, New York 1988–89; CEO ProSieben Media AG Jan.–Sept. 2000, Chair. Exec. Bd and CEO 2000–04; mem. Exec. Bd, Credit Suisse Group AG and Credit Suisse AG 2004–09, Gen. Counsel of Credit Suisse Group AG 2004–09, COO and Gen. Counsel of Credit Suisse AG 2006–09, Vice-Chair. Credit Suisse Group AG 2009–11, Chair. 2011–, mem. Chair.'s and Governance Cttee and Risk Cttee; mem. Bd of Dirs, Inst. for Int. Finance, Institut Int. d'Etudes Bancaires, Zurich Opera House; mem. Bd of Trustees, Lucerne Festival; mem. Exec. Bd, Zurich Chamber of Commerce. *Address:* Office of the Chairman, Credit Suisse Group AG, PO Box 1, 8070 Zurich (office); Credit Suisse Group, Paradeplatz 8, 8001 Zurich, Switzerland (office). *Telephone:* (44) 212-16-16 (office). *Fax:* (44) 333-25-87 (office). *E-mail:* info@credit-suisse.com (office). *Website:* www.credit-suisse.com (office).

ROHOVIY, Vasyl Vasylyovich, CandEcons; Ukrainian politician and economist; b. 2 March 1953, Mirivka, Kiev region; s. of Vasyl Loginovich and Zinaida Mikhailivna Rohoviy; m. Svetlana Mikhailivna Rogovaya; one s.; ed Kiev Inst. of National Econs, Ukrainian Acad. of Sciences; engineer and economist, Kiev Artem Production co. 1974–75, 1976–77; Sr Mechanic, Odessa Mil. Command 1975–76; Jr Researcher, Inst. of Econs, then Scientific Sec., Dept of Econs, Ukrainian Acad. of Sciences 1980–88; Chief Expert, Head of Sector, then Head of Div. Ukrainian Council of Ministers 1988–94; First Deputy Minister of Econs 1994–98, Minister 1998–99, 2000–01; First Deputy Head of Admin., Office of the Pres. 2000; Deputy Prime Minister for Econ. Policy 2001–02; Presidential Adviser 2002; fmr Deputy Sec. of Econ., Social and Environmental Security Council, Nat. Security and Defence Council of Ukraine; apptd mem. Supervisory Council UkrExImBank JSC—State Export-Import Bank of Ukraine 2003.

ROHR, Hans Christoph von, Dr jur.; German lawyer and business executive; b. 1 July 1938, Stettin; s. of Hansjoachim von Rohr; m.; two c.; ed Univs of Heidelberg, Vienna, Bonn, Princeton Univ.; joined Klöckner-Werke AG, Bremen; subsequently held leading position with Klöckner subsidiary in Argentina; worked for Fisser & van Doornum, Emden; Partner, TaylorWessing Lawyers, Düsseldorf; mem. Bd Klöckner & Co. Duisburg 1984; Chair. Exec. Bd Klöckner-Werke AG 1991–96; Man. Chair. Industrial Investment Council GmbH 1997–2002; Chair. (non-exec.) ING Barings (Germany) 1996–2001; Chair. Supervisory Bd, Balfour Beatty GmbH, Munich, mem. Bd Balfour Beatty plc, London 2002–09; Chair. Research Inst. of Economy Constitution and Competition –2008, Hon. Chair. 2010–; mem. Supervisory Bd SWB AG –2001; Co-founder Community Foundation Mülheim an der Ruhr, CEO 2002–; mem. Bd Underwriters Laboratories Inc., Chicago 2002–13, Advisory Bd UL Int. GmbH, Frankfurt; Hon. Chair. German Inst. for Competition and Market Economy (FIW), Cologne, Hon. Mem., Econ. Council CDU, Berlin; German Order of Merit 2002. *Publications:* Ein Konservativer Kämpfer: Der NS-Gegner und Agrarpolitker Hansjoachim von Rohr 2010, Paritätische Mitbestimmung: Deutschland einsam auf seinem Sonderweg 2010. *Address:* Orsoyer Strasse 15, 40474 Duesseldorf, Germany.

ROHR, James E., BA, MBA; American business executive; ed Univ. of Notre Dame, Ohio State Univ.; joined PNC Financial Services Group through its man. devt programme 1972, proceeded through various marketing and man. responsibilities in several Corp. Banking areas, Vice-Chair. PNC 1989, apptd mem. Bd of Dirs 1990, Pres. 1992–98, COO 1998–2000, CEO 2000–13, Chair. 2001–14; Chair. Bd of Trustees, Carnegie Mellon Univ. 2015–; mem. Bd of Dirs Allegheny Technologies Inc., EQT Corp. 1996–, Marathon Petroleum Corp., Gen. Electric Co. 2013–; fmr mem. Bd of Dirs BlackRock, Inc.; Fourth Federal Reserve Dist's rep. on Federal Advisory Council, Federal Reserve Bank of Cleveland; mem. RAND Bd of Trustees; fmr Chair. Pennsylvania Business Roundtable, Allegheny Conf. on Community Devt, Pittsburgh Cultural Trust, Greater Pittsburgh Council of the Boy Scouts of America; mem. Financial Services Roundtable, Dir and fmr Chair. BITS (tech. group for Financial Services Roundtable); mem. Bd of Trustees Univ. of Notre Dame, mem. Notre Dame's Coll. of Business Advisory Council; Woodrow Wilson Award for Corp. Citizenship 2006, Sesame Workshop Corp. Honoree Award 2007, Women's Inst. for a Secure Retirement (WISER) Hero Award, Heinz Family Philanthropies 2008, named American Banker's Banker of the Year 2007, Pittsburgh Magazine's Pittsburgher of the Year 2011, Gold Medal for Distinguished Achievement, Pennsylvania Soc. 2014.

ROHRWACHER, Alba Caterina; Italian actress; b. 27 Feb. 1979, Florence; sister of Alice Rohrwacher; ed Centro Sperimentale di Cinematografia, Rome; Shooting Stars Award, Berlin Int. Film Festival 2008. *Theatre includes:* La casa degli spiriti 2003, Bric à brac 2004, Il mondo salvato dai ragazzini 2005, Lisa 2006, Noccioline 2007. *Films include:* An Italian Romance 2004, Kiss Me Lorena 2005, Melissa P. 2005, The Wedding Director 2006, 4-4-2 – Il gioco più bello del mondo 2006, Non c'è più niente da fare 2007, My Brother is an Only Child 2007, Voce del verbo amore 2007, Piano, solo 2007, Days and Clouds (David di Donatello for Best Supporting Actress 2008) 2007, Nelle tue mani 2007, Good Morning Heartache 2008, Quiet Chaos 2008, Giovanna's Father (David di Donatello for Best Actress 2009) 2008, In carne e ossa 2009, Due partite 2009, I Am Love 2009, The Man Who Will Come 2009, Come Undone 2010, Sorelle Mai 2010, The Solitude of Prime Numbers (Ciak d'oro 2011, Nastro d'argento 2011) 2010, Missione di pace 2011, Tormenti – Film disegnato 2011, Bliss 2012, Dormant Beauty 2012, Garibaldi's Lovers 2012, Via Castellana Bandiera (Pasinetti Award for Best Actress) 2013, A Street in Palermo 2013, The Wonders 2014, Hungry Hearts (Volpi Cup for Best Actress, Venice Film Festival, Pasinetti Award for Best Actress) 2014, Virgin 2015, Taj Mahal 2015, L'ultimo vampiro 2015, The Tale of Tales 2015. *Television includes:* Angela (film) 2005, Il vizio dell'amore (series) 2006, Il pirata: Marco Pantani (film) 2007, Maria Montessori: una vita per i bambini (film) 2007. *Address:* Frédérique Moidon, Artmédia, 20 avenue Rapp, 75007 Paris, France (office). *Telephone:* 1-43-17-33-73 (office). *Fax:* 1-44-18-34-60 (office). *E-mail:* f.moidon@artmedia.fr (office); m.delamarre@artmedia.fr (office). *Website:* www.artmedia.fr (office).

ROISS, Gerhard; Austrian business executive; b. 2 April 1952, Linz; m.; three c.; ed Univ. of Vienna, Univ. of Linz, Stanford Univ., USA; Head of OMV Marketing, OMV Group 1990, apptd to Man. Bd of PCD Polymere GmbH 1990–97, transferred to Bd of OMV Group and was responsible for Plastics and Chemicals 1997–2000, also assumed responsibility for the Exploration and Production business 2000–02, Deputy CEO OMV Group responsible for Refining and Marketing including Petrochemicals 2002–11, Chair. Exec. Bd and CEO OMV AG 2011–15 (resgnd), Pres. Supervisory Bd, OMV Petrom SA 2011–15; Chair. Nova Chemicals Corpn 2009–11.

RÕIVAS, Taavi; Estonian politician; b. 26 Sept. 1979, Tallinn; m. Luisa Värk; one d.; ed Univ. of Tartu; mem. Eesti Reformierakond (ER—Estonian Reform Party) 1998–, Chair. 2014–17; adviser to Minister of Justice 1999–2002; Mayor of Haabersti dist of Tallinn 2004–05; adviser to Minister of Population Affairs 2003–04, to the Prime Minister 2005; mem. Tallinn City Council 2005–07; mem. State Ass. (Riigikogu) 2007–; Minister of Social Affairs 2012–14; Prime Minister 2014–16 (resgnd); Commdr Grand Cross, Order of the White Rose of Finland 2016. *Address:* State Assembly (Riigikogu), Lossi plats 1A, Tallinn 15165, Estonia (office). *Telephone:* 631-6331 (office). *Fax:* 631-6334 (office). *E-mail:* riigikogu@riigikogu.ee (office). *Website:* www.riigikogu.ee (office).

ROIZMAN, Bernard, ScD; American scientist and academic; *Joseph Regenstein Distinguished Service Professor of Virology, Departments of Microbiology, Molecular Genetics and Cell Biology and Biochemistry and Molecular Biology, University of Chicago;* b. 17 April 1929, Romania; m. Betty Cohen 1950; two s.; ed Temple Univ., Johns Hopkins Univ.; Instructor of Microbiology, Johns Hopkins Univ. 1956–57, Research Assoc. 1957–58, Asst Prof. 1958–65; Assoc. Prof. of Microbiology, Univ. of Chicago 1965–69, Prof. 1969–84, Prof. of Biophysics 1970–, Chair. Interdepartmental Cttee on Virology 1969–85, 1988–, Joseph Regenstein Prof. of Virology 1981–83, Joseph Regenstein Distinguished Service Prof. of Virology 1984–; Chair. Dept of Molecular Genetics and Cell Biology 1985–88; fmr Ed. of numerous specialist scientific publs and mem. Editorial Bd Journal of Virology 1970–, Intervirology 1972–85, Virology 1976–78, 1983–; Ed.-in-Chief Infectious Agents and Diseases 1992–96; mem. or fmr mem. numerous grant review panels, int. panels, including Chair. Herpes Virus Study Group, Int. Cttee for Taxonomy of Viruses 1971–94 (Chair. 1991–), Scientific Advisory Bd, Showa Univs Center 1983–; mem. Int. Microbial Genetics Comm., Int. Asscn of Microbiological Sciences 1979–86; numerous nat. panels on vaccines, cancers; Scholar in Cancer Research at American Cancer Soc., Inst. Pasteur (with Andre Lwoff), Paris 1961–62; Travelling Fellow, Int. Agency for Research Against Cancer (with Dr Klein), Stockholm, Sweden 1970; mem. NAS, Inst. of Medicine, Nat. Acad. of Inventors, American Asscn of Immunologists, Soc. for Experimental Biology and Medicine, American Soc. for Microbiology (ASM), for Biological Chemists, Soc. for Gen. Microbiology (UK), American Soc. for Virology, Foreign Assoc., Chinese Acad. of Eng, Hon. mem. Hungarian Acad. of Science; Fellow, Japanese Soc. for Promotion of Science, American Acad. of Arts and Sciences, American Acad. of Microbiology; Hon. DHumLitt (Govs State Univ., Ill.) 1984, Hon. MD (Ferrara) 1991, Hon. DSc (Paris) 1997, (Valladolid, Spain) 2001; J. Allyn Taylor Int. Prize in Medicine 1997, Bristol-Myers Squibb Award for Distinguished Achievement in Infectious Disease Research 1998, ICN Int. Prize in Virology 1988, NIH Outstanding Investigator Award 1988–2001, NIH-NCI Merit Award 2003, ASM Lifetime Achievement Award 2008, Brilliant Achievement Award, Chinese Biopharmaceutical Asscn 2012. *Publications include:* author or co-author of more than 600 papers in scientific journals and books; ed. or co-ed. of 20 books. *Address:* Marjorie B. Kohler Viral Oncology Laboratories, University of Chicago, 910 East 58th Street, Chicago, IL 60637 (office); 5555 South Everett Avenue, Chicago, IL 60637, USA (home). *Telephone:* (773) 702-1898 (office); (773) 493-2986 (home). *Fax:* (773) 493-9042 (home). *E-mail:* bernard.roizman@bsd.uchicago.edu (office). *Website:* microbiology.uchicago.edu/page/bernard-roizman (office).

ROJAS ARAVENA, Francisco, MS, PhD; Chilean academic and university administrator; *Rector, University for Peace;* b. 21 March 1949, Santiago; ed Univ. of Utrecht, Netherlands, Facultad Latinoamericana de Ciencias Sociales (FLACSO); Prof., School of Int. Relations, Nat. Univ. of Costa Rica 1980–90; Dir, FLACSO Chile 1996–2004, Sec.-Gen., FLACSO 2004–12; Rector, Univ. for Peace 2013–; fmr Fulbright Prof., Latin American and Caribbean Centre (LACC), Florida Int. Univ., Miami; mem. bd, Spanish edn of Foreign Affairs magazine, Mexico; mem. advisory bd, Pensamiento Iberoamericano magazine, Spain; mem. editorial cttee, Ciencia Política magazine (Nat. Univ. of Colombia); Orden del Mérito José Falcón (Paraguay) 2012, Commdr, Orden Heráldica de Cristobal Colón (Dominican Repub.) 2012, Grand Cross, Orden Nacional Juan Mora Fernández (Costa Rica) 2012; Malinalli Prize 2016. *Publications include:* author, co-author or ed. of more than 80 books, including Iberoamérica: distintas miradas, diferentes caminos para metas compartidas. El bienestar y el desarrollo 2011, América Latina y el Caribe: Relaciones Internacionales en el siglo XXI. Diplomacia de Cumbre y espacios de concertación regional y global (ed.) 2012, Seguridad Humana: Nuevos Enfoques (ed.) 2012. *Address:* University for Peace, Ciudad Colón, San Jose, Costa Rica (office). *Telephone:* 2205-9000 (office). *Fax:* 2249-1929 (office). *E-mail:* frojas@upeace.org (office). *Website:* www.upeace.org/about-upeace/leadership/rector (office).

ROJAS GUTIERREZ, Francisco José; Mexican accountant, politician and business executive; b. 15 Sept. 1944, Mexico City; ed Nat. Autonomous Univ. of Mexico (UNAM); mem. Institutional Revolutionary Party (PRI) since early 1960s, Nat. Pres. of Colosio Foundation, AC 2007–10, mem. Nat. Political Council and Perm. Political Cttee, held various positions, including Sec. of Finance of Nat. Exec. Cttee, Co-ordinator of Nat. Priorities Political Campaign for Presidency of Miguel de la Madrid, Co-ordinator of PRI in LXI Legislature; fmr Deputy Dir-Gen. of Expenditures and Chief of Staff, Ministry of Finance; fmr Gen. Co-ordinator of

Man. Control, Ministry of Planning and Budget; first Holder of Gen. Secr. of Fed. 1983–87; Dir-Gen. Petroleos Mexicanos 1987–94; retd from politics but returned as Deputy (PRI) in LIX Legislature 2003–, Chair. Cttee on Budget and Public Accounts 2003–06, Co-ordinator of PRI Parl. Group 2009; Dir-Gen. Comisión Federal de Electricidad (Fed. Electricity Comm.) 2012–14; Pres. Alumni Asscn, School of Accounting and Admin, UNAM 1992–2003, Pres. UNAM 1995–2003, Chair. UNAM Philharmonic Orchestra 1994–2005, Hon. Pres. Foundation UNAM; Exec. Chair. Mexican Industry Consumer Products, AC 1996–2003; Pres. Corp. Council of Mexican American Solidarity Foundation, AC; Chair. Mexico-Israel Cultural Inst., AC; columnist, El Universal and El Sol de Mexico newspapers 2003–; Nat. Political Council mem. and Chair. Bd of Trustees, Luis Donaldo Colosio; mem. Advisory Bd, Inst. of Political, Econ. and Social IEPES; mem. Nat. Inst. of Public Admin, Mexican Inst. of Public Accountants, Mexican Acad. of Comprehensive Audit, Inst. of Chartered Accountants of Mexico, Forum of Sr Man., Cultural Inst. Mexico-Israel; several awards from professional and social insts and awards from various countries. *Publications include:* political essays in various publs. *Address:* PRI, Edif. 2, Insurgentes Norte 59, Col. Buenavista, Del. Cuauhtémoc 06359, Mexico (office). *Telephone:* (55) 5729-9600 (office). *E-mail:* pri .org.mx (office).

ROJAS IRIGOYEN, Germán Hugo, MBA; Paraguayan banker and government official; b. 1958; m.; three c.; ed Universidad Católica Nuestra Señora de la Asunción; served several years with Central Bank of Paraguay, becoming Man., Int. Operations, Pres. 2007; fmr Project Dir UNDP; various man. positions with Bank of Parana SA, including Head of Financial Man.; Pres. Banco Nacional de Fomento, Asuncion 2003–07; Minister of Finance 2013–Jan. 2015.

ROJO GARCÍA, Francisco Javier; Spanish politician; b. 2 March 1949, Pamplona; m.; two d.; early political work with Gen. Workers Union 1976–79; Prov. Councillor, Álava 1979–83, City Councillor for Vitoria-Gasteiz (Álava) 1983–84; mem. Gen. Ass. of Álava 1983–87; Councillor of the Presidency of Álava 1987–93, Deputy Mayor of Vitoria-Gasteiz 1991–96; Senator for Álava 1993–2004, Pres. of the Senate 2004–11; mem. Basque Parl. 2001–02, mem. Human Rights Cttee and Basque Radio and TV Control Cttee; Sec.-Gen. Basque Socialist Party-Basque Left (PSE-EE), Álava 2000–05, Pres. 2005–; Sec. of Institutional Relations, Spanish Socialist Workers' Party (PSOE) Fed. Exec. Comm. 2002–04; Grand Cross, Order of Civil Merit, Grand Cross, Isabel la Católica; Dr hc (Piura Public Univ., Peru) 2006.

ROKITA, Jan, LLM; Polish politician and lawyer; b. 18 June 1959, Kraków; s. of Tadeusz Rokita and Adela Rokita (née Wajdowicz); m. Nelli Arnold 1994; one d.; ed Jagiellonian Univ., Pontifical Acad. of Theology, Kraków; fmr active mem. Ind. Students' Union (NZS) 1980–82; interned under Martial Law 1982; banned by Communist authorities from practising law 1983–89; Co-founder and participant Freedom and Peace Movt 1985–88; Founder and mem. Intervention and Law-abidingness Comm. of Solidarity Trade Union 1986–89; mem. Civic Cttee attached to Lech Wałęsa (q.v.) 1988–90; organizer and Chair. Int. Conf. on Human Rights, Kraków 1988; participant Round Table negotiations 1989; Chair. Special Parl. Comm. of Inquiry in respect of archives of the former Communist Security Service (Rokita Comm.) 1989–90; Deputy Chair. Civic Parl. Caucus 1989–90, Deputy Chair. Democratic Union Parl. Caucus 1991–96, Deputy Chair. Freedom Union Parl. Caucus 1996–97, mem. Solidarity Election Action Parl. Caucus 1997–2001; Deputy Chair. Civic Platform Parl. Caucus 2001–03, Chair. 2003–05; Chair. Parl. Comm. for Admin. and Internal Affairs 1997–2000; Minister-Chief of Office of Council of Ministers 1992–93; Chair. Conservative People's Party (SKL) 1998–2001; mem. Special Parl. Comm. of Inquiry into the Rywin Affair 2003–04; mem. Civic Platform (PO) (Platforma Obywatelska); Commdr, Order of Polonia Restituta 2008; POLCUL Foundation Award (Australia) 1988, Stefan Kisielewski Award 2003, Edward J. Wende Award 2003, Man of the Year (Wprost weekly magazine, Poland) 2003, Top Parliamentarian (Polityka weekly magazine, Poland) 2003. *Publications:* political and historical journalism; Alfabet Rokity 2004. *Leisure interests:* classical music, jazz, ancient Greek philosophy, bicycle riding. *Address:* Biuro Posła Jana Rokity, 31-143 Kraków, ul. Basztowa 15/10, Poland. *Telephone:* (12) 4300186. *Fax:* (12) 4263560.

ROLANDIS, Nikos A.; Cypriot politician, business executive and barrister; b. 10 Dec. 1934, Limassol; m. Lelia Aivaliotis; one s. two d.; ed Pancyprian Gymnasium Nicosia, Middle Temple, London; called to the bar, Middle Temple 1956; practised law in Cyprus for short time before entering business; owner of industrial and commercial cos; Founding mem. Democratic Group (now Democratic Party); f. Liberal Party 1986, Pres. 1986–98; Minister of Foreign Affairs 1978–83; mem. House of Reps 1991–96; Vice-Pres. Liberal Int. 1994–99; Minister of Commerce, Industry and Tourism 1998–2003. *Publications include:* numerous articles. *Address:* 13 Ayias Agapis, Strovolos, Nicosia, Cyprus (home). *Telephone:* 22591900 (office); 22353811/2 (home). *Fax:* 22591700 (office); 22353100 (home). *E-mail:* nicos@rolandis.com (home).

ROLDÓS AGUILERA, Leon; Ecuadorean lawyer, university administrator and politician; b. 21 July 1942, Guayaquil; s. of Santiago Roldós Soria and Victoria Aguilera Mouton; ed Vicente Rocafuerte High School, Univ. of Guayaquil; practised as lawyer in Guayaquil; Lecturer, Prof. Vicente Rocafuerte Lay Univ. Law School 1967, later Dean; Chair. Monetary Bd 1979–81; Vice-Pres. of Ecuador 1981–83; presidential cand. (Partido Socialista Ecuatoriano (PSE) 1992; Rector, Univ. of Guayaquil 1994–2004; presidential cand. (ind.) 2002, (Red Ética y Democratica-Izquierda Democrática coalition) 2006; mem. Partido Roldosista Ecuatoriano (PRE).

ROLET, Xavier, MBA; French financial services industry executive; b. 12 Nov. 1959, Aix-les-Bains; ed Columbia Univ., New York, Hautes Etudes de Defense Nationale, Paris; Second Lt and Instructor, French Air Force Acad. 1981; joined Goldman Sachs & Co., New York 1984, becoming Co-Head, European Equity Sales and Trading, Goldman Sachs Int. Ltd, London 1990–94; Global Head of European Equities, Credit Suisse First Boston 1994–97; Global Head of Risk and Trading and Deputy Head of Global Equities, Dresdner Kleinwort Benson 1997; Deputy Co-Head of Global Equity Trading, Lehman Brothers, New York 2000, Co-Head Global Equity Trading 2000–01, Head of European and Asian Cash Equities and mem. Global Investment Banking Operating Cttee, Lehman Brothers, London 2001–03, Head of Sr Relationship Man. for Europe 2003–07, CEO Lehman Brothers, France 2007–09; Dir London Stock Exchange Group PLC 2009–17, CEO London Stock Exchange 2009–17, fmr Chair., London Stock Exchange Strategic Advisory Group; fmr mem., Conseil d'Orientation, Euronext Paris; fmr mem. EC European Securities Markets Expert Group. *Leisure interests:* cars, skiing, scuba-diving, fly-fishing.

ROLLE, John A.; Bahamian economist and central banker; *Governor and Chairman, Central Bank of the Bahamas;* ed Coll. of The Bahamas, American Univ., USA, Carleton Univ. and Univ. of Western Ontario, Canada; held several positions at Cen. Bank of the Bahamas, including Man. of Research Dept 1990–2012; Adjunct Lecturer in Econs, American Univ., Washington, DC 2008; fmr part-time Lecturer in Econs and Statistics, Coll. of The Bahamas; Sr Advisor to Exec. Dir for Canada, Ireland and the Caribbean Constituency, Exec. Bd of IMF 2009–12; Financial Sec., Ministry of Finance 2013–16; Gov. and Chair. Cen. Bank of the Bahamas 2016–, mem. IMF Bd of Govs; fmr mem. Bd of Dirs Caribbean Devt Bank. *Publications include:* numerous articles on monetary, fiscal and exchange rate policies. *Address:* Central Bank of the Bahamas, Frederick Street, POB N-4868, Nassau, Bahamas (office). *Telephone:* 302-2600 (office). *Fax:* 322-4321 (office). *E-mail:* cbob@centralbankbahamas.com (office). *Website:* www .centralbankbahamas.com (office).

RÖLLER, Lars-Hendrik, BS, MSc, MA, PhD; German economist and academic; *Head of Economic and Financial Department, Federal Chancellery.;* b. 19 July 1958, Frankfurt; m.; three c.; ed Texas A&M Univ. and Univ. of Pennsylvania, Phila, USA; Research Asst, Dept of Econs, Univ. of Pennsylvania 1983–86, Inst. for Law and Econs 1986–87, Lecturer, Dept of Econs 1986; Asst Prof. of Econs, Institut Européen d'Admin des Affaires (INSEAD), Paris, France 1987–91, Assoc. Prof. 1991–95, Prof. 1995–99; Prof. of Econs and Chair. Inst. of Industrial Econs, Humboldt Univ., Berlin 1995–; Dir Centre for Econ. Policy Research, London 1992, Co-Dir Industrial Org. Programme 1995–2003; Dir Inst. for Competitiveness and Industrial Change Wissenschaftszentrum Berlin für Sozialforschung 1994–2007, now Research Prof.; Research Fellow, Forschungsinstitut zur Zukunft der Arbeit (IZA), Bonn 1999–2006; Prof. (part-time), Norwegian School of Econs and Business Admin 2003; Chief Competition Economist, EC 2003–06; Pres. European School of Man. and Tech., Berlin 2006–11; Head, Economic and Financial Dept, Federal Chancellery 2011–; Visiting Prof., Dept of Applied Econs, Univ. Autonoma, Barcelona, Spain 1989; Visiting Scholar, Starr Center for Applied Econs, New York Univ., USA 1992, Grad. School of Business, Stanford Univ. 1993; apptd mem. Exec. Bd European Asscn for Research in Industrial Econs 1999 (Pres. 2005–07), Scientific Cttee of INSEAD Foundation 1999, Advisory Bd Centre for Competition Policy, Univ. of East Anglia, Norwich 2004, Conselho Consultativo, Universidade Nova de Lisboa, Portugal 2005, Alexander von Humboldt Foundation, Scientific Council for Transatlantic Cooperation (TransCoop) 2003, American Econ. Asscn; mem. Exec. Bd Vereins für Socialpolitik 2001–03, German-French Council of Econ. Advisers, 2003–06; Ed. Managerial and Decision Economics 1993–98, International Journal of Industrial Organization 1999–2004; mem. editorial bds of several int. journals; Fellow, European Econ. Asscn 2004; Best Teacher Award, INSEAD 1998, Gossen Award Verein für Socialpolitik 2002. *Publications:* Situation und Perspektiven der deutschen Raumfahrtindustrie 1998, The Corporate Structure of UK and German Manufacturing Firms 1999, Europas Nätverksindustrier: Telekommunikationer Avregleringen i Europa 1999, The Political Economy of Industrial Policy: Does Europe Have an Industrial Policy? 2000, Die Soziale Marktwirtschaft in der neuen Weltwirtschaft 2001; contrib. of numerous articles to professional journals. *Address:* Federal Chancellery, Bundeskanzler-Amt, Willy-Brandt Str. 1, 10557 Berlin, Germany (office). *Telephone:* (80) 2720000 (office). *E-mail:* poststelle@bundeskanzlerin.de-mail.de (office). *Website:* www.bundeskanzlerin.de (office).

ROLLIER, Michel, MA; French business executive; *Chairman of the Supervisory Board, Michelin;* b. 19 Sept. 1944, Annecy, Haute Savoie; s. of François Rollier; m.; three c.; ed Institut d'Etudes Politiques, Université de Droit, Paris; with Aussedat-Rey (int. paper group) 1971–96, Controller, facilities, divs and group 1973–82, Unit Operational Man. 1982–87, Chief Financial Officer 1987–94, Deputy Man. Dir 1994–96; Chief Legal Officer and Dir for Financial Operations, Compagnie Générale des Établissements Michelin 1976, mem. Michelin Group Exec. Council and Chief Financial and Legal Officer 1999–, Co-Man. Partner 2005–06, Sole Man. Partner 2006–07, Man. Gen. Partner and CEO 2007–12 (retd), Chair. Supervisory Bd 2012–; Chair. Siparex Associés 2013–; Chair. Supervisory Bd Somfy SA 2013–, Chair. Remunerations Cttee 2016–; Chair. Supervisory Bd Asscn Nationale des Sociétés par Actions (ANSA); Chair. Plateforme de la Filière Automobile 2016–; mem. AFEP High Cttee on Corp. Governance 2013–; mem. Bd of Dirs Lafarge SA 2008–; Officier, Légion d'honneur 2009. *Address:* Compagnie Générale des Établissements Michelin, 12 cours Sablon, 63000 Clermont-Ferrand, France (office). *Telephone:* 4-73-32-20-00 (office). *E-mail:* info@michelin.com (office). *Website:* www.michelin.com (office).

ROLLINS, Kevin B., BA, MBA; American business executive; *Senior Advisor, TPG Capital LP;* b. 15 Nov. 1952; ed Brigham Young Univ.; Vice-Pres. and Partner, Bain & Co. (man. consultants) –1996; joined Dell Inc. and held positions successively as Pres. Dell Americas, Vice-Chair. Dell Inc., Pres. and COO, Pres., CEO and Dir 2004–07 (resgnd); Sr Advisor, TPG Capital LP 2007–; Chair. American Enterprise Inst.; mem. Bd of Dirs Avaya, Inc., Deseret Man. Corpn; mem. US Pres.'s Advisory Cttee for Trade Policy and Negotiation, US Business Council, Computer Systems Policy Project; mem. Pres.'s Leadership Council, Brigham Young Univ., Marriott School Nat. Advisory Council; inducted into Hall of Fame, Utah Information Tech. Asscn (UITA) 2004. *Address:* TPG Capital LP, 301 Commerce Street, Suite 3300, Fort Worth, TX 76102, USA (office). *Telephone:* (817) 871-4000 (office). *Fax:* (817) 871-4010 (office). *Website:* www .texaspacificgroup.com (office).

ROLLINS, Theodore Walter (Sonny); American jazz musician (tenor saxophone); b. 7 Sept. 1930, New York; s. of Walter Rollins and Valborg Solomon; m. 1st Dawn Finney 1956 (divorced); m. 2nd Lucille Pearson 1959 (died 2004); ed High School, New York; began rehearsing while in high school, with Thelonious Monk; recorded with Bud Powell 1949; wrote standards 'Airegin' and 'Oleo' recorded with Miles Davis 1953; played and recorded with Clifford Brown/Max Roach 1955; took sabbatical playing on Williamsburg Bridge, New York 1959–61; scored and played music for film Alfie 1966; has appeared in Jazz Heritage series, Smithsonian Inst.

and at Newport Jazz Festival; numerous concert tours in Europe and Far East; annual concert tours of Europe, Japan, USA with Concert Orchestra 1973–; mem. American Acad. of Arts and Sciences 2010–; Dr hc (Bard Coll.) 1993, Hon. DMus (Long Island Univ.) 1998, (New England Conservatory of Music) 2002, (Juilliard School) 2013, Hon. DArts (Wesleyan Univ.) 1998, Hon. DFA (Duke Univ.) 1999; Guggenheim Fellow 1972, Lifetime Achievement Award, Tufts Univ. 1996, Lifetime Achievement Award, Nat. Asscn of Recording Arts and Science 2005, Grammy Award for Best Jazz Instrumental Solo (for Why Was I Born?) 2006, Edward MacDowell Medal 2010, Kennedy Center Honor 2011, Jazz Journalists Asscn Award 2011. *Recordings include:* albums: Sonny Rollins with the Modern Jazz Quartet 1953, Moving Out 1954, Work Time 1955, Sonny Rollins Plus 4 1956, Tenor Madness 1956, Saxophone Colossus 1956, Rollins Plays for Bird 1956, Tour de Force 1956, Sonny Boy 1956, Sonny Rollins, Vol. 1 1957, Way Out West 1957, Sonny Rollins, Vol. 2 1957, The Sound of Sonny 1957, Newk's Time 1957, A Night at the Village 1957, Sonny Rollins Plays/Thad Jones Plays 1957, Freedom Suite 1958, Brass/Trio 1958, Sonny Rollins and the Big Brass 1958, Sonny Rollins and the Contemporary Leaders 1958, Sonny Rollins 'At Music Inn' (split LP with Teddy Edwards At Falcon Lair with Joe Castro) 1959, The Bridge 1962, What's New? 1962, Our Man in Jazz 1962, Sonny Meets Hawk! 1963, Now's the Time 1964, The Standard Sonny Rollins 1964, There Will Never Be Another You 1965, Sonny Rollins on Impulse! 1965, Alfie 1966, East Broadway Run Down 1966, Next Album 1972, Horn Culture 1973, Sonny Rollins in Japan 1973, The Cutting Edge 1974, Nucleus 1975, The Way I Feel 1976, Easy Living 1977, Don't Stop the Carnival 1978, Don't Ask 1979, Love at First Sight 1980, No Problem 1981, Reel Life 1982, Sunny Days, Starry Nights 1984, The Solo Album 1985, G-Man 1986, Dancing in the Dark 1987, Falling in Love with Jazz 1989, Here's to the People 1991, Old Flames 1993, Sonny Rollins + 3 1996, Global Warming 1998, This Is What I Do 2000, Without a Song: The 9/11 Concert 2001, Sonny, Please 2006, Road Shows 2008, Road Shows Vol. 2 2011, Road Shows Vol. 3 2014, Vol. 4 2016. *Address:* c/o Ted Kurland, The Kurland Agency, 173 Brighton Avenue, Boston, MA 02134-2003, USA (office); Route 9G, Germantown, NY 12526, USA. *Telephone:* (617) 254-0007 (office); (518) 537-6112 (office). *E-mail:* ted@thekurlandagency.com (office). *Website:* www.thekurlandagency.com (office); www.sonnyrollins.com. *Fax:* (518) 537-4342 (office).

ROMAHI, Seif al-Wady, PhD; Jordanian diplomacy expert and human resources development consultant; b. 28 Dec. 1938, Muzera, Palestine; s. of Ahmed al-Hajj Abdul-Nabi; m. Zaka al-Masri 1971; one s. two d.; ed Lebanese State Univ., Univ. Coll. London, Southern Illinois Univ., USA and Univ. of Birmingham, UK; Admin. Adviser to Cabinet of Prime Minister of Jordan Wasfi al-Tall; Area Educ. Supt, Ministry of Educ., Qatar 1960–64; seconded to Office of the Ruler of Abu Dhabi, Pres. UAE 1968–73; Rep. League of Arab States in USA 1970–72; Assoc. Prof. of Middle East Studies and Political Science, Southern Ill. Univ., USA 1971–72; Minister Plenipotentiary, Foreign Ministry, UAE 1973–91, set up UAE Embassies in Beijing, Tripoli, Tokyo and Seoul; Founder and Prof., Diplomatic Training Centre, UAE 1980–82; Co-founder and Chief Rep. Nat. Bank of Abu Dhabi in Japan 1982–86; Prof. of Int. Law, Diplomacy and Islamic Civilization, Int. Univ. of Japan, Sophia Univ., Tokyo 1977–80; Founder, Gen. Man. Arab Int. Co. for Investment and Educ. 1988–91, Chair. 1990–94; founder Applied Science Univ., Amman, Jordan, Prof. of Diplomacy and Int. Law 1990–95, American Univ. of the Middle East in Jordan, House of Euro-Arab Experts in Jordan 1992 (also Chair.); Co-Founder Islamic-American Univ. Coll., Chicago; planner Jordan Women's Univ. (now Petra Univ.), Zaitouneh Jordanian Univ., Graduate Studies Univ. in Jordan, Middle East Acad. for Aviation; contrib. (with HE Dr Abdul-Razzaq al-Sanhouri) to writing the Constitution of UAE; co-author Abu Dhabi Public Service Code; Co-Chair. Planning Cttee for British Univ. of Dubai; consultant for establishment of RAK British Univ., UAE 2002; mem. Acad. of Islamic Research (India), Japanese Acad. of Middle East Studies, Middle East Studies Asscn of USA and Canada, Middle East Inst., Washington, DC, British Soc. for Middle East Studies, Japanese Assoc. for Middle Eastern Studies; Fellow, Acad. of Islamic Research, India, Japanese Acad. of Oriental Studies, British Soc. for Middle Eastern Studies, Middle E Inst., Wash., Japan Middle E Studies Asscn; Order of Independence (Jordan) 1979; Hon. PhD (World Univ.) 1985. *Publications:* Economics and Political Evolution in Arabian Gulf States 1973, The Palestinian Question and International Law 1979, Studies in International Law and Diplomatic Practice 1980, Arab Customs and Manners 1984; contribs to professional and scientific journals. *Leisure interests:* calligraphy, art, travel, poetry, listening to music, painting and drawing, reading, research. *Address:* PO Box 35087, Hotel Jordan, Amman 11185, Jordan. *Telephone:* (6) 5537028 (home). *Fax:* (6) 5528328 (home). *E-mail:* seif-romahi@yahoo.co.uk.

ROMAN, Martin, LLB; Czech business executive; b. 1969, Havířov; ed Faculty of Law, Charles Univ., Prague, St Gallen Univ., Switzerland, Karl-Ruprechtsuniversität, Heidelberg, Germany; Sales Dir Wolf Bergstrasse ČR s.r.o. 1992–94; CEO Janka Radotín a.s. 1994–99, Chair. 1998–99; Chair. and Gen. Dir ŠKODA a.s., Pilsen 1999–2000, Chair. and CEO ŠKODA Holding 2000–04; Dir, Chair. and CEO, ČEZ a.s. 2004–13.

ROMAN, Petre, PhD, DTech; Romanian academic and politician; b. 22 July 1946, Bucharest; s. of Valter Roman and Hortensia Roman; m. Mioara Georgescu; two d.; ed Petru Groza High School, Bucharest, Bucharest Polytechnic Inst. and Nat. Polytechnic Inst. of Toulouse, France; fmrly Prof. and Head of Dept Hydraulics Dept, Faculty of Hydroenergy, Bucharest Polytechnic Inst.; Founding mem. Nat. Salvation Front 1989, Pres. 1992–93, renamed Democratic Party (PD) 1993–2003, Pres. 1993–2001; Prime Minister 1989–91; mem. Parl. 1992–, Chair. Defence, Public Order and Nat. Security Cttee, Chamber of Deputies 1992–96; Special Rapporteur of North Atlantic Ass. 1993–96; Co-Pres. Union of Social Democrats (USD=PD+PSDR—Party of Social Democracy in Romania) 1995–97; Senator for Bucharest (USD), Chair. of Senate 1996–97, Senator for Bucharest (PD), Chair. of Senate 1997–99, Senator 2000–04; cand. in presidential elections 1996; Acting Pres. Parl. Ass. of the Black Sea Econ. Cooperation 1997–98; Deputy Prime Minister, Minister of Foreign Affairs 1999–2000; Founder and Chair. Democratic Force of Romania (Forţa Democrâta din România) (FDR) 2004; mem. Partidul Naţional Liberal (PNL); apptd mem. Chamber of Deputies 2012; Grand Cross of Merit (France), Grand Cross of Nat. Order of Repub. of Ecuador, High Award of Repub. of Colombia; Traian Vuia Award, Romanian Acad. 1990. *Publications:* The Nuclear Energy File: Risk and Security (co-author) 1978, Water and Pollution (co-author) 1978, Introduction to the Physics of Fluid Pollution 1981, The Movement of the Compressible Fluids with Heat Transfer 1982, Special Problems in Hydromechanics (co-author) 1985, Hydrology and the Protection of Water Quality 1989, Fluid Mechanics 1989, Dynamic Hydrology (co-author) 1990, Le devoir de liberté 1992, Freedom as Duty 1994, Romania incotro? 1995, Political Notebook: A Political Vision on Romania's Development Strategy at the Threshold of Centuries 1999. *Leisure interests:* sports, hunting, reading, hiking. *Address:* Senatul României, Piata Revolutiei nr. 1, sector 1, Bucharest, Romania (office). *Telephone:* (21) 3150200 (office). *E-mail:* webmaster@senat.ro (office).

ROMANEK, Mark; American music video director and film director; b. 18 Sept. 1959, Chicago, Ill.; ed Ithaca Coll.; early directing experience as second Asst Dir for Brian De Palma on Home Movies 1980; worked on numerous music videos with Satellite Films; music videos Closer (Nine Inch Nails) and Bedtime Story (Madonna) now held in perm. collection of Museum of Modern Art, New York; also dir of numerous TV commercials; Dir Anonymous Content (production co.); 20 MTV Video Music Awards, three Grammy Awards for Best Short Form Music Video. *Music videos include:* Free Your Mind (En Vogue) 1992, Are You Gonna Go My Way (Lenny Kravitz) 1993, Rain (Madonna) 1993, Closer (Nine Inch Nails) 1994, Scream (Michael and Janet Jackson) (Grammy Award for Best Short Form Video 1996) 1995, Got 'Til It's Gone (Janet Jackson) (Grammy Award for Best Short Form Video 1998) 1997, Hurt (Johnny Cash) 2002, 99 Problems (Jay-Z) 2004, Speed of Sound (Coldplay) 2005, Picasso Baby (Jay-Z) 2013, Shake It Off (Taylor Swift) 2014, Summer Nights (U2) 2014, Sandcastles (Beyoncé) 2016, Can't Stop the Feeling! (Justin Timberlake) 2016. *Films:* Static 1985, One Hour Photo 2002, Never Let Me Go 2010. *Address:* Anonymous Content, 3532 Hayden Avenue, Culver City, CA 90232, USA (office). *Telephone:* (310) 558-3667 (office). *E-mail:* mark@markromanek.com (office). *Website:* www.anonymouscontent.com (office); www.markromanek.com (office).

ROMANI, Roger; French politician; b. 25 Aug. 1934, Tunis, Tunisia; s. of Dominique Romani and Madeleine Santelli; m. Joelle Fortier 1971; began career as an asst dir with ORTF; various positions in pvt. offices of Govt Ministers of Posts and Telecommunications, of Information, of State, of the Prime Minister 1967–71; Conseiller de Paris (Paris-Majorité-2ème secteur, then UDP-3ème, then RPR-5ème secteur) 1971–2001; adviser, Office of Jacques Chirac (Minister of Agric. and of Devt 1973, of Interior 1974, Prime Minister 1974–76); Deputy to Mayor of Paris 1977–2001; mem. Conseil Régional, Ile-de-France 1977; Senator of Paris (Ile-de-France) 1977–93, 2002–11, Vice-Pres. RPR Group in Senate 1983–86, Pres. 1986–88, Vice-Pres. Group of RPR, later of Union pour un Mouvement Populaire 2002, mem. Comm. of Foreign Affaires, of Defence and the Armed Forces, Titular mem. Higher Council of the Mil. Reserve 2004–; Vice-Pres. Conseil général de Paris (Departmental Ass.) 1982–2001; Pres. Group 'Rassemblement pour Paris' 1983–2001; Nat. Sec. RPR 1984–86, mem. Political Cttee 1998–2000; adviser to fmr Prime Minister Chirac 1986–88; Minister-Del. for Relations with the Senate 1993–95; Minister for Relations with Parl. 1995–97; adviser to Pres. Chirac 1997–2002; Hon. Pres. Mouvement nat. des élus locaux. *Address:* Sénat, Palais du Luxembourg, 15, rue de Vaugirard, 75291 Paris Cedex 06, France (office). *Telephone:* 1-42-34-20-00 (office). *Fax:* 1-42-34-26-77 (office). *E-mail:* r.romani@senat.fr (office). *Website:* www.senat.fr/senfic/romani_roger59312e.html (office).

ROMANO, Sergio, (Carlo Maurizi), LLD; Italian diplomatist and historian; b. 7 July 1929, Vicenza; s. of Romano Romano and Egle Bazzolo; m. Mary Anne Heinze 1954; two s. one d.; ed Liceo C. Beccaria, Milan, Univ. of Milan, Univ. of Chicago; foreign corresp. and film critic for Italian radio and newspapers, Paris, London and Vienna 1948–52; entered Italian Foreign Service 1954, Vice-Consul, Innsbruck, Austria 1955, Sec., Embassy in London 1958–64, Pvt. Sec. to Minister of Foreign Affairs 1964; mem. Diplomatic Staff of the Pres. of the Repub. 1965–68; Counsellor (later Minister), Embassy in Paris 1968–77, Dir-Gen. of Cultural Relations, Ministry of Foreign Affairs 1977–83; Guest Prof., Faculty of Political Sciences, Univ. of Florence 1981–83; Perm. Rep. to Atlantic Council, Brussels 1983–85, Amb. to USSR 1985–89 (resgnd); currently columnist for Corriere della Sera (newspaper) and Corriere del Ticino (newspaper), also contributes opinion articles to Aspenia, Il Politico; fmr Visiting Prof., Harvard Univ., Univ. of California, Berkeley; Prof. of History of Int. Relations, Bocconi Univ. 1992–98; mem. Ateneo Veneto, Venice, Accad. Olimpica, Vicenza; Corresp. mem. Royal Acad. of Brussels; Pres. Balzan Foundation Prize Cttee –2009; Cavaliere di Gran Croce, Commdr Légion d'honneur, other European and Latin-American honours; Dr hc (Inst. d'Etudes Politiques, Paris, Univ. of Macerat, Inst. of World History, Russian Acad. of Sciences). *Publications include:* Crispi, Progetto per una Dittatura 1973, 1986, La Quarta Sponda 1977, Histoire de l'Italie du Risorgimento à nos jours 1977, Italie 1979, Giuseppe Volpi, Industria e Finanza tra Giolitti e Mussolini 1979, La Francia dal 1870 ai nostri giorni 1981, Benedetto Croce, La Philosophie comme histoire de la Liberté (ed.) 1983, La Lingua e il Tempo 1983, Giovanni Gentile, La Filosofia al Potere 1984, Florence, Toscane 1988, Giolitti, Lo Stile del Potere 1989, Disegni per una Esposizione 1989, L'Italia scappata di mano 1993, Cinquant'anni di storia mondiale: La pace e le guerre da Yalta ai nostri giorni 1995 (Romanian edn 1999), Lo scambio ineguale: Italia e Stati Uniti da Wilson a Clinton 1995, Le Italie parallele 1996, Lettera ad un amico ebreo 1997 (Lithuanian edn 2001, German edn 2007), Storia d'Italia dal Risorgimento ai nostri giorni 1998 (Serbian edn 2007), Confessioni di un revisionista 1998, I luoghi della storia 2000, La pace perduta 2001, Un'amicizia difficile, conversazioni con Gilles Martinet su due secoli di relazioni italo-francesi 2001, I volti della storia 2001, Memorie di un conservatore 2002, Il rischio americano 2003, Giovanni Gentile. Un filosofo al potere negli anni del Regime 2004, Anatomia del terrore. Colloquio con Guido Olimpio 2004, Europa, storia di un'idea (Serbian edn 2009), Dall'impero all'unione 2004 (Serbian edn 2009), La quarta sponda: La guerra di Libia 1911–1912 2005, Libera Chiesa. Libero Stato? 2005 (French edn 2007), Saremo moderni? Diario di un anno 2007 (French edn 2007), Con gli occhi dell'Islam 2007, Vademecum di storia dell'Italia, 2009 unita 2009. *Address:* via P. Verri 6, 20121 Milan, Italy. *Telephone:* (02) 76000870. *Fax:* (02) 76014719. *E-mail:* romanoser@gmail.com.

ROMANOV, Piotr Vasilyevich, DTechSc; Russian politician; b. 21 July 1943, Kansk, Krasnoyarsk territory; m.; three c.; ed Siberia Inst. of Tech.; engineer, then chief of workshop, Chief Engineer, Dir-Gen. Krasnoyarsky Production Unit of Mil. Chemical Enterprise Enisey 1967–96; mem. Russian Council of Fed. 1993; Co-Chair. Russian Nat. Sobor 1992–93, mem. Org. Cttee All-Russia Congress of

Russian Communists, Co-Chair. Co-ordination Council All-Russia Congress of Russian Communists 1994–; mem. State Duma 1995–, First Deputy Chair. of State Cttee on Ecology, mem. Comm. on Problems of North Caucasus; Sec. Cen. Cttee CP of Russian Fed. 1997–; mem. Russian Acad. of Eng Sciences; Hero of Socialist Labour, Distinguished Chemist of Russian Fed., Order of Lenin; Sergei Radonezhsky Medal. *Publications:* I Am Piotr Romanov: About the Times and Myself 1995, With a Son's Care about Russia 1995, The Sovereign Cross 1997. *Leisure interests:* winter sports, gathering mushrooms and berries, gardening. *Address:* State Duma, Okhotny Ryad 1, 103265 Moscow (office); pr. Mira 108, 660017 Krasnoyarsk, Russia. *Telephone:* (495) 292-18-10 (office). *Fax:* (495) 292-40-58 (office). *E-mail:* priemnaya.parliament.gov.ru. *Website:* www.duma.gov.ru (office).

ROMEO, Hon. Donaldson; Montserratian journalist and politician; *Premier and Minister of Finance, Economic Development and Tourism;* b. 1962, Salem; ed Montserrat Secondary School, George School and Temple Univ., USA; returned to Montserrat from USA after a year to help his father with his hardware business; moved to UK where he became an artist 1984; served with a deportation order that was later overturned after gaining support from Ken Livingstone MP and John Carlisle MP and Nat. Portrait Gallery; eventually returned to Montserrat and continued working as an artist before rejoining his family's hardware business; became a journalist following the eruption of the Soufrière Hills volcano mid-1990s; cand. for Montserrat Democratic Party in gen. elections 2006; MP 2009–, Leader of the Opposition 2011–14; est. People's Democratic Movt 2014; Premier and Minister of Finance, Econ. Devt and Tourism 2014–. *Address:* Office of the Premier, Government HQ, PO Box 292, Brades, Montserrat (office). *Telephone:* 491-3378 (office). *Fax:* 491-6780 (office). *E-mail:* op@gov.ms (office). *Website:* www.gov.ms (office).

ROMEO, HE Cardinal Paolo, STL, JCD; Italian ecclesiastic and diplomatist; *Archbishop of Palermo;* b. 20 Feb. 1938, Acireale, Prov. of Catania, Sicily; ed Pontifical Gregorian Univ. and Pontifical Lateran Univ., Rome; ordained priest, Diocese of Acireale 1961; carried out pastoral ministry as Asst to the Scouts Group 'Roma IX' in Collegio San Giuseppe in Piazza di Spagna and Diocesan Asst of Silenziosi Operai della Croce asscn; called to Pontifical Ecclesiastical Acad. 1964, entered diplomatic service of the Holy See 1967, worked in nunciatures in the Philippines, Belgium and Luxemburg and EC, Venezuela, and Rwanda and Burundi, called to Council for Public Affairs of the Church in Secr. of State 1967; worked as dir of Casa Internazionale del Clero and was Regional Asst for the Lazio of the Associazione Genitori Scuole Cattoliche (AGESC); recalled to Vatican Secr. of State to monitor the life of the Catholic community in countries of Latin America and activities of Latin American Episcopal Conf. 1976–83; Titular Archbishop of Vulturia 1983–; Apostolic Nuncio to Haiti 1983–90, to Colombia 1990–99, to Canada 1999–2001, to Italy and San Marino 2001–06; Archbishop of Palermo, Sicily 2006–; Pres. Sicilian Episcopal Conf. 2007–; cr. Cardinal (Cardinal-Priest of Santa Maria Odigitria dei Siciliani) 2010; participated in Papal Conclave 2005, 2013. *Address:* Archdiocese of Palermo, Corso Vittorio Emanuele 461, 90134 Palermo, Italy (office). *Telephone:* (091) 6077111 (office). *Fax:* (091) 6113642 (office). *E-mail:* info@diocesipa.it (office). *Website:* www.diocesipa.it (office).

ROMER, Christina Duckworth, BA, PhD; American economist, academic and fmr government official; *Class of 1957 – Garff B. Wilson Professor of Economics, University of California, Berkeley;* b. 25 Dec. 1958, Alton, Ill.; m. David Romer; three c.; ed Glen Oak High School, Canton, Ohio, Coll. of William and Mary, Massachusetts Inst. of Tech.; Asst Prof. of Econs, Woodrow Wilson School, Princeton Univ. 1985–88; Acting Assoc. Prof. of Econs, Univ. of California, Berkeley 1988–90, Assoc. Prof. of Econs 1990–93, Class of 1957 Prof. of Econs 1997–2009, Class of 1957—Garff B. Wilson Prof. of Econs 2010–; Chair., Council of Econ. Advisors, The White House 2009–10; Fellow, American Acad. of Arts and Sciences 2004; Research Assoc., Program in Monetary Econs, Nat. Bureau of Econ. Research 1990–, Co-Dir 2003–08, 2010–; Mary Louise Smith Chair in Women and Politics, Iowa State Univ. 2011; Dan and Maggie Inouye Distinguished Chair in Democratic Ideals, Univ. of Hawaii at Manoa 2012; mem. Cttee on Honors and Awards, American Econ. Asscn 2004–08, Vice-Pres. 2006; Contributing Ed. Bloomberg Television 2010–12; contrib. New York Times 2010–13; Dr hc (Coll. of William and Mary) 2010; Alfred P. Sloan Doctoral Fellowship 1984–85, Nat. Bureau of Econ. Research Olin Fellowship 1987–88, Alfred P. Sloan Research Fellowship 1989–91, Presidential Young Investigator Award 1989–94, John Simon Guggenheim Memorial Foundation Fellowship 1998–99, Faculty Award for Women Scientists and Engineers 1991–96, Distinguished Teaching Award, Univ. of California, Berkeley 1994, Zale Award for Outstanding Achievement in Policy Research and Public Service, Stanford Univ. 2011. *Publications:* Reducing Inflation: Motivation and Strategy (co-ed.) 1997; numerous articles in professional journals. *Address:* Department of Economics, University of California, 681 Evans Hall #3880, Berkeley, CA 94720-3880, USA (office). *Telephone:* (510) 642-4317 (office). *Fax:* (510) 642-6615 (office). *E-mail:* cromer@econ.berkeley.edu (office). *Website:* www.econ.berkeley.edu/econ (office).

ROMER, Paul Michael, BS, PhD; American economist and academic; *Professor of Economics, Stern School of Business, New York University;* b. 7 Nov. 1955, Denver, Colo; s. of Roy Romer and Beatrice Romer (née Miller); m. Virginia Langmuir; one s. one d.; ed Univ. of Chicago; Asst Prof. of Econs, Univ. of Rochester 1982–88; Prof. of Econs, Univ. of Chicago 1988–90; Fellow, Center for Advanced Study in Behavioral Sciences, Stanford Univ. 1989–90, Prof., Stanford Univ. Grad. School of Business 1996–2007, Ralph Landau Sr Fellow, Stanford Inst. for Econ. Policy Research 1997–, Sr Fellow, Hoover Inst. 1995–; Prof. of Econs, Univ. of California, Berkeley 1990–96; Henry Kaufman Visiting Prof., Stern School of Business, New York Univ. 2010–, Prof. of Econs 2011–, Dir Marron Inst. of Urban Man.; Founder, Aplia Inc. 2000–; Research Assoc., Nat. Bureau of Econ. Research 1987; Chief Economist World Bank 2016–18; Fellow, Econometric Soc. 1990, American Acad. of Arts and Sciences 2000, Center for Global Devt 2010; non-resident scholar, Macdonald Laurier Inst., Ottawa; mem. Bd of Trustees Carnegie Endowment for the Advancement of Teaching; mem. Bd of Dirs Community Solutions; mem. American Econs Asscn 1996–; Distinguished Teaching Award, Stanford Business School 1999, Horst Claus Recktenwald Prize in Econs 2002, Sveriges Riksbank Prize in Econ Sciences in Memory of Alfred Nobel 2018, Nobel Prize in Econ. Sciences (Jtly with William Nordhaus) 2018. *Address:* NYU Stern School of Business, Henry Kaufman Management Center, 44 West Fourth Street, New York, NY 10012, USA (office). *Telephone:* (212) 998-0100 (office). *E-mail:* promer@stern.nyu.edu (office). *Website:* www.stern.nyu.edu (office).

ROMER, Roy R., BS, LLB; American education administrator and fmr politician; *Special Advisor, College Board Advocacy and Policy Center;* b. 31 Oct. 1928, Garden City, Kan.; s. of Irving Rudolph Romer and Margaret Elizabeth Romer (née Snyder); m. Beatrice Miller 1952; five s. two d.; ed Colorado State Univ., Univ. of Colorado, Yale Univ.; farmed in Colo 1942–52; admitted to Colo Bar 1952; ind. practice, Denver 1955–66; mem. Colo House of Reps 1958–62, Colo Senate 1962–66; Commr for Agric. for Colo 1975; State Treas. 1977–86; Gov. of Colo 1987–98; Supt of Schools, LA Unified School Dist 2001–06; Chair. Strong American Schools (non-profit) 2007–09; Special Advisor, Coll. Bd Advocacy and Policy Center 2009–; Owner, Arapahoe Aviation Co., Colo Flying Acad., Geneva Basin Ski Area, Chain Farm Implement and Industrial Equipment Stores in Colo, Fla and Va; Gov. Small Business Council; fmr mem. Agric. Advisory Cttee, Colo Bd of Agric.; mem. Colo Bar Asscn; Chair. Nat. Educ. Goals Panel, Democratic Govs Asscn 1991, Democratic Nat. Cttee 1997–2000. *Address:* College Board Advocacy and Policy Center, 45 Columbus Avenue, New York, NY 10023, USA (office). *E-mail:* cbadvocacy@collegeboard.org (office). *Website:* www.advocacy.collegeboard.org (office).

ROMERO, Pepe; American classical guitarist; b. 3 Aug. 1944, Málaga, Spain; s. of Celedonio Romero and Angelita Romero (née Gallego); m. 1st Kristine Eddy 1965; m. 2nd Carissa Sugg 1987; one s. three d.; ed various music acads in USA, including Music Acad. of the West; began career in Seville, Spain, as part of Romero Quartet 1951, reformed in USA 1960; solo recordings plus others with Romero Quartet and various orchestras; Artist-in-Residence, Univ. of Southern California 1972, Distinguished Artist-in-Residence, Thornton School of Music, Univ. of Southern California 2004; taught at Univ. of California, San Diego 1984, Southern Methodist Univ. and Univ. of San Diego; Order of Isabel la Católica (Spain); Dr hc (San Francisco Conservatory of Music), (Univ. of Victoria); Premio Andalucía de la Música 1996, President's Merit Award, Recording Acad. 2007. *Publications include:* Guitar Method, Guitar Transcriptions for 1, 2 and 4 guitars. *Leisure interests:* photography, chess. *Address:* Columbia Artists Management, Inc., 1790 Broadway, New York, NY 10019, USA (office). *E-mail:* tfox@cami.com (office). *Website:* www.peperomero.com.

ROMERO-BARCELÓ, Carlos Antonio, BA, LLB, JD; American lawyer and fmr politician; b. 4 Sept. 1932, San Juan, Puerto Rico; s. of Antonio Romero-Moreno and Josefina Barceló-Bird; m. 1st; two s.; m. 2nd Kathleen Donnelly 1966; one s. one d.; ed Phillips Exeter Acad., NH, Yale Univ., Univ. of Puerto Rico; admitted to the Bar, San Juan, Puerto Rico 1956; Pres. Citizens for State 51 1965–67; Mayor of San Juan 1968–76; Co-founder New Progressive Party (with Luis Ferré) 1967, Pres. 1974–86, 1989–90, Chair. 1989; Gov. of Puerto Rico 1977–85; Pres. Nat. League of Cities 1976–75; Chair. Southern Govs Conf. 1980–81; Resident Commr in Washington, DC (serving in US Congress) 1993–2001; in pvt. law practice 2001–; mem. Council on Foreign Affairs 1985–, Int. Platform Asscn 1985–, League of United Latin American Citizens (LULAC); Hon. LLD (Univ. of Bridgeport, Conn.) 1977; James J. and Jane Hoey Award for Interracial Justice, Catholic Interracial Council of NY 1977; Special Gold Medal Award, Spanish Inst., New York 1979; US Attorney-Gen.'s Medal 1981. *Publications:* Statehood is for the Poor 1973, Statehood for Puerto Rico, Vital Speeches of the Day 1979, Puerto Rico, USA: The Case for Statehood, Foreign Affairs 1980, The Soviet Threat to the Americas, Vital Speeches of the Day 1981. *Leisure interests:* reading, horse riding, tennis, swimming, water sports, golf. *Address:* Centro de Seguros, Building 701, Ponce de León Avenue # 412, Miramar, PR 00907 (office); PO Box 364351, San Juan, PR 00936, Puerto Rico. *Telephone:* (787) 724-0526; (787) 724-0511. *Fax:* (787) 724-0959 (office). *E-mail:* rbarcelo@prtc.net (office).

ROMERO ORELLANA, Gen. Otto Alejandro; Salvadorean politician and army officer; b. 4 April 1955, Chalatenango; ed Escuele Militar Capt. Gen. Gerardo Barrios; fmr Section Commdr, First Bn, Oscar Osorio Artillery Brigade; Exec. Sec., Ministry of Nat. Defence 1994; Commdr, Third Mil. Zone, Infantry Brigade, Domingo Monterrosa 2002; Gen. Inspector of Armed Forces 2002, Minister of Nat. Defence 2004–07; several nat. and int. decorations.

ROMETTY, Virginia (Ginni) Marie, BSc; American business executive; *Chairman, President and CEO, International Business Machines Corporation (IBM);* b. 29 July 1957, Chicago, Ill.; m. Mark Anthony Rometty; ed Robert R. McCormick School of Eng and Applied Science, Northwestern Univ.; began career with General Motors Corpn; joined Int. Business Machines Corpn (IBM), becoming Gen. Man. Global Insurance and Financial Services Sector, Gen. Man. IBM Global Services, Americas, later becoming Man. Partner, Business Consulting Services –2005, Sr Vice-Pres. Enterprise Business Services 2005–10, Group Exec., IBM Sales, Marketing and Strategy 2010–11, Pres. and CEO Jan. 2012–, Chair. Oct. 2012–; mem. Pres.'s Strategic and Policy Forum Jan.–Aug. 2017; mem. Bd of Dirs American Int. Group (AIG); mem. Council on Foreign Relations, Bd of Trustees Northwestern Univ., Bd of Overseers Memorial Sloan-Kettering Cancer Center, Bd of Dirs, APQC (not-for-profit business research organization), Columbia Business School's Deming Cup Cttee; Dr hc (Rensselaer Polytechnic Inst.) 2014, Northwestern Univ. 2015; Carl Sloane Award, Asscn of Man. Consulting Firms 2006. *Television:* featured in the PBS documentary The Boomer List 2014. *Leisure interest:* scuba diving. *Address:* International Business Machines Corporation (IBM), Somers, NY 10589, USA (office). *Telephone:* (914) 766-2100 (office). *E-mail:* grometty@ibm.com (office). *Website:* www.ibm.com (office).

ROMNEY, (Willard) Mitt, BA, JD, MBA; American business executive and fmr politician; *Senator from Utah;* b. 12 March 1947, Detroit, Mich.; s. of George W. Romney (fmr Gov. of Mich.) and Lenore Romney; m. Ann Romney 1969; five s.; ed Cranbrook School, Bloomfield Hills, Mich., Stanford Univ., Brigham Young Univ., Harvard Univ. Business School, Harvard Law School; served as a Mormon missionary in France; Vice-Pres. Bain & Co. (man. consulting firm) 1978–84, Co-founder Bain Capital (investment firm) 1984–99, CEO (interim) Bain & Co. 1990–92; CEO Salt Lake City Organizing Cttee for 2002 Winter Olympics 1999–2002; Gov. of Mass. 2003–07; unsuccessful cand. for Republican Party presidential nomination 2007–08, unsuccessful cand. (Republican) for Pres. of US 2012; Chair. Exec. Cttee Solamere Capital LLC, Boston 2013–; Senator from Utah

2019–; f. Free and Strong America PAC, Inc. 2008; mem. Bd of Dirs Marriott Int. 1992–2002, 2009–11, 2012–18; Hon. Dr of Business (Univ. of Utah) 1999, Hon. LLD (Bentley Coll.) 2002, Hon. Dr of Public Admin (Suffolk Univ. Law School) 2004, Hon. Dr of Public Service (Hillsdale Coll.) 2007; inaugural Truce Ideal Award for his role in the 2002 Winter Olympics 2004, Canterbury Medal, The Becket Fund for Religious Liberty (shared with his wife) 2008. *Publications:* Turnaround: Crisis, Leadership, and the Olympic Games (with Timothy Robinson) 2004, No Apology: The Case for American Greatness 2010. *Address:* Utah Senate, 320 State Capitol, PO Box 145115, Salt Lake City, UT 84114, USA (office). *Telephone:* (801) 538-1035 (office). *Website:* senate.utah.gov (office); www.mittromney.com.

ROMULO, Alberto (Bert) Gatmaitan, BSc, BL; Philippine politician and business executive; b. 7 Aug. 1933, Camiling, Tarlac Prov. province; s. of Carlos P. Romulo; m. Rosie Lovely Tecson; five c.; ed De La Salle Univ., Universidad de Madrid, Spain; fmr Senator, Majority Leader 1991–96; Sec., Dept of Finance Jan.-June 2001, Exec. Sec. of Philippines 2001–04; Sec. of Foreign Affairs 2004–11; Chair. ASEAN 2007; Vice-Chair. Manila Bulletin Publishing Corpn 2011–; Bd Advisor, Metro Pacific Investments Corpn 2011–; Gintong Ama Award, Philippines Free Press Most Outstanding Senator. *Address:* Manila Bulletin Publishing Corporation, Muralla cor Recolletos Streets., Intramuros, PO Box 769, Manila 1002, Philippines. *Website:* www.mb.com.ph.

RONALD, Mark H., BA, BS, MS; American aerospace and defence industry executive; ed Bucknell Univ., Polytechnic Inst. of New York; served as Vice-Pres., Program Man. Litton Industries, Amecon Div.; fmr mem. Bd of Dirs, Pres. and COO AEL Industries; Pres. and CEO GEC-Marconi Hazeltine 1993–98, later head, GEC's North American businesses; mem. Bd of Dirs and COO BAE Systems plc, Pres. and CEO BAE Systems, Inc., USA 2003–06, Chair. 2007; Special Advisor, Veritas Capital Partners 2007–; mem. Bd of Dirs Cobham plc, Alliant Tech Systems (ATK), DynCorp Int. LLC 2007–10; mem. Exec. Cttee and Bd of Govs, Aerospace Industries Asscn; mem. Bd of Govs Electronic Industries Alliance; Hon. CBE 2005; Distinguished Engineering Alumni Awards (Bucknell Univ., Polytechnic Inst. of New York), Marine Corps Scholarship Foundation Semper Fidelis Award 2005, John Curtis Sword Award 2006, Maryland Int. Business Leadership Award 2007.

RONALDINHO GAÚCHO, (Ronaldinho); Brazilian/Spanish professional footballer (retd); b. (Ronaldo de Assis Moreira), 21 March 1980, Pôrto Alegre, Rio Grande do Sul; s. of João de Assis Moreira and Miguelina de Assis Moreira; m. Janaína Mendes; one s.; winger/attacking midfielder; youth player, Grêmio de Pôrto Alegre 1987–98; won World Youth Cup with Brazil Under-17 team (voted Player of the Tournament), Egypt 1997; sr career with Grêmio de Pôrto Alegre (44 appearances, 21 goals) 1998–2001, Paris Saint-Germain, France (55 appearances, 17 goals) 2001–03, FC Barcelona, Spain (145 appearances, 70 goals) 2003–08 (won La Liga 2005, 2006, Supercopa de España 2005, 2006, UEFA Champions League 2006), AC Milan, Italy 2008–11 (43 appearances, 11 goals), Clube de Regatas do Flamengo 2011–12, Atlético Mineiro 2012–14, Querétaro 2014–15, Fluminense 2015; 98 caps and 33 goals for Brazil 1999–2013, won Copa America 1999 (scoring six goals), World Cup 2002, FIFA Confederations Cup 2005, bronze medal, Olympic Games, Beijing 2008; mem. Bronze Medal-winning team, Men's Football, Olympic Games, Beijing 2008; wore No. 80 shirt; became Spanish citizen Jan. 2007; FIFA Confederations Cup Top Scorer 1999, FIFA Confederations Cup Golden Ball 1999, Rio Grande do Sul State Championship Top Scorer 1999, FIFA World Cup All-Star team 2002, named in FIFA 100 2004, EFE Trophy (best South American player in Spanish leagues) 2004, Don Balón Award (Best Foreign Player in La Liga) 2004, 2006, FIFA World Footballer of the Year 2004, 2005, UEFA Team of the Year 2004, 2005, 2006, Ballon d'Or (European Footballer of the Year) 2005, FIFPro (int. professional football players' union) World Player of the Year 2005, 2006, UEFA Club Footballer of the Year 2005–06, FIFPro World XI 2005, 2006, 2007, FIFA Club World Cup Bronze Ball Award 2006. *Address:* c/o Rua Álvaro Chaves 41, Laranjeiras, Rio de Janeiro, RJ 22231-220, Brazil (office). *Telephone:* (21) 3179-7400 (office). *Website:* www.ronaldinhogaucho.com (home).

RONALDO; Brazilian/Spanish professional footballer (retd); b. (Ronaldo Luiz Nazário de Lima), 18 Sept. 1976, Bento Ribeiro, Rio de Janeiro; s. of Nelio Nazário de Lima and Sonia Nazário de Lima; m. Milene Domingues 1999 (separated 2005); one s.; striker; youth player, Tennis Club Valqueire 1986–89, Social Ramos Club (12 games, eight goals) 1989–90, São Cristóvão, Rio Second Div. (54 games, 36 goals) 1990–93; sr player, Cruzeiro (14 games, 12 goals) 1993–94 (won Campeonato Mineiro 1994, Brazil Cup 1993), PSV Eindhoven, Netherlands (46 games, 42 goals) 1994–96 (won Dutch Cup 1996), Barcelona, Spain (37 games, 34 goals) 1996–97 (won Copa del Rey 1997, UEFA Cup Winners' Cup 1997, Supercopa de España 1996), Inter Milan (68 games, 49 goals) 1997–2002 (won UEFA Cup 1998), Real Madrid (127 games, 83 goals) 2002–07 (won La Liga 2003, 2007, Intercontinental Cup 2002, Supercopa de España 2003), AC Milan (20 games, nine goals) 2007–08, Corinthians (31 games, 18 goals) 2009–11 (won Campeonato Paulista 2009, Copa do Brasil 2009), retd 2011; mem. Brazilian nat. team (97 int. caps, 62 goals) 1994–2006, won World Cup (aged 17) 1994, 2002 (winner Golden Boot), Bronze medal, Summer Olympics, Atlanta 1996, won Copa America 1997, 1999, FIFA Confederations Cup 1997; Supercopa Libertadores Top Scorer 1993/94, Campeonato Mineiro Top Scorer 1993/94, Campeonato Mineiro Team of The Year 1994, Eredivisie Top Scorer 1994/95, La Liga Top Scorer 1996/97, 2003/04, European Golden Boot 1996/97, Don Balón Award (La Liga Foreign Player of the Year) 1996/97, Copa América Final Most Valuable Player (MVP) 1997, Copa América MVP 1997, Confederations Cup All-Star Team 1997, Cup Winners' Cup Final MVP 1997, Cup Winners' Cup Top Goal Scorer 1996/97, IFFHS World's Top Goal Scorer of the Year 1997, UEFA MVP 1997/98, Serie A Player of the Year 1997/98, Serie A Foreign Player of the Year 1997/98, UEFA Best Forward 1997/98, Bravo Award 1995, 1997, 1998, FIFA World Cup Golden Ball 1998, UEFA Cup Final MVP 1998, Copa América Top Scorer 1999, Copa América All-Star Team 1997, 1999, FIFA World Player of the Year 1996, 1997, 2002, Ballon d'Or 1997, 2002, World Soccer Magazine World Player of The Year 1996, 1997, 2002, Onze d'Or 1997, 2002, FIFA World Cup Silver Ball 2002, named in FIFA 100 2002, FIFA World Cup All-Star Team 1998, 2002, FIFA World Cup Final MVP 2002, FIFA World Cup Top Scorer 2002, Intercontinental Cup MVP 2002, UEFA Team of The Year 2002, Laureus Comeback of the Year 2002, Strogaldo De Legendary Award 2002, BBC Sports Personality of the Year Overseas Personality 2002, La Liga South American Player of the Year 1996/97, 2002/03, Golden Foot 2006, inducted into Brazilian Nat. Hall of Fame Class of 2006, Serie A Player of the Decade 1997–2007, France Football Magazine Starting in 11 of all time 2007, FIFA World Cup All-Time Scoring Leader 2008, Campeonato Paulista Best Player 2009, Goal.com Player of the Decade 2000–09 2010. *Address:* c/o Sport Club Corinthians Paulista, Estádio do Pacaembu, São Paulo, Brazil. *E-mail:* ronaldo@fobazo.com. *Website:* www.ronaldo.com.

RONALDO DOS SANTOS AVEIRO, Cristiano; Portuguese professional footballer; b. 5 Feb. 1985, Funchal, Madeira; s. of José Dinis Aveiro and Maria Dolores dos Santos Aveiro; winger/striker; began career as youth player with Andorinha 1993–95, CD Nacional, Madeira 1995–97, Sporting Clube de Portugal 1997–2001; sr career with Sporting Clube de Portugal 2001–03, Manchester United (196 appearances, 84 goals) 2003–09 (won Premier League 2006/07, 2007/08, 2008/09, FA Cup 2003/04, League Cup 2005/06, 2008/09, FA Community Shield 2007, UEFA Champions League 2007/08, FIFA Club World Cup 2008), Real Madrid (La Liga 2011–12, Copa del Rey 2010/11, 2013/14, Supercopa de España 2012, UEFA Champions League 2013/14, 2015/16, 2016/17, 2017/18) 2009–18, Juventus 2018–; mem. Portugal nat. team (68 appearances, 22 goals) 2003– (won Euro Cup 2016); represented Portugal at Summer Olympics, Athens 2004, World Cup, Germany 2006, UEFA European Championship, Portugal (runners-up) 2004, Poland-Ukraine (third place) 2012, France (winners and Team Capt.) 2016; opened fashion boutique with one of his sisters under the name CR7 (his initials and shirt number), one in Lisbon and other in Madeira; took over from David Beckham as spokesmodel for Emporio Armani men's underwear and jeans 2010–; Officer, Order of Infante Dom Henrique, Medal of Merit, Order of the Immaculate Conception of Vila Viçosa (House of Bragança), Grand Officer, Order of Prince Henry; UEFA Team of the Year 2004, 2007, 2008, 2009, 2010, 2011, 2012, 2013, 2014, 2015, UEFA Euro 2004 Team of the Tournament, FIFPro Special Young Player of the Year 2004–05, 2005–06, PFA Premier League Team of the Year 2005–06, 2006–07, 2007–08, 2008–09, Portuguese Footballer of the Year 2006–07, FIFA FIFPro World XI 2007, 2008, 2009, 2010, 2011, 2012, 2013, 2014, 2015, Professional Footballers' Asscn (PFA) Young Player of the Year 2006–07, PFA Players' Player of the Year 2006–07, 2007–08, PFA Fans' Player of the Year 2006–07, 2007–08, ESM Team of the Year 2006–07, 2007–08, 2010–11, 2011–12, 2012–13, Football Writers' Asscn Footballer of the Year 2006–07, 2007–08, Premier League Player of the Season 2006–07, 2007–08, Premier League Player of the Month Nov. 2006, Dec. 2006, Jan. 2008, March 2008, Premier League Golden Boot 2007–08, UEFA Champions League top scorer 2007–08, 2012–13, 2013–14, 2014–15, 2015–16, Barclays Merit Award 2007–08, European Golden Shoe 2007–08, 2010–11, 2013–14, 2014–15, UEFA Club Forward of the Year 2007–08, UEFA Club Footballer of the Year 2007–08, FIFPro World Player of the Year 2007–08, FIFA Ballon d'Or 2008, 2013, 2014, 2016, FIFA Team of the Year 2008, World Soccer Player of the Year 2008, 2013, La Liga top scorer 2010–11, 2013–14, 2014–15, Copa del Rey top scorer 2010–11, Trofeo Alfredo Di Stéfano 2011–12, 2012–13, UEFA Euro Top scorer 2012, La Liga Player of the Month Nov. 2013, May 2015, LFP Most Valuable Player 2012–13, IFFHS World's Best Top Goal Scorer 2013, 2014, La Liga Team of the Season 2013–14, 2014–15, 2015–16, UEFA Best Player in Europe Award 2014, 2016, 2017, BBC Overseas Sports Personality of the Year 2014, Silver Boot as joint second-highest goal-scorer of UEFA European Championships 2016, Best FIFA Men's Player 2016, 2017, Ballon d'Or Award 2017, Best European Sportsperson 2017, Best Footballer, Globe Soccer 2017. *Publication:* Moments (autobiog.) 2007. *Address:* c/o FC Real Madrid, Estadio Santiago Bernabeu, Paseo de la Castellana 104, Madrid, Spain. *E-mail:* info@realmadrid.com. *Website:* www.cristianoronaldo.com; www.realmadrid.com.

RONCAGLIOLO ORBEGOSO, Rafael, MA, PhD; Peruvian political scientist, academic and politician; b. 14 Nov. 1944, Lima; s. of Nicolás Roncagliolo Aste and Susana Orbegoso; three c.; ed Pontifical Catholic Univ. of Peru; fmr Prof., Academia Diplomática del Perú; Dir Communication Studies Div., Latin American Inst. for Transnational Studies, Mexico City 1976–82; Pres. Inst. for Latin America, Lima 1982–94; Sr Policy Adviser for Andean Countries and Head of Mission to Peru, Intergovernmental Inst. for Democracy and Electoral Assistance (Int. IDEA) 2009–11; Minister of Foreign Affairs 2011–13 (resgnd); fmr consultant to numerous int. bodies including UNESCO, UNDP, IDB, Sistema Económico Latinoamericano y del Caribe, OAS and govts of USA, Italy and Germany. *Publications include:* numerous books and articles on communication, political systems and electoral analysis.

RONG, Zhijian, (Larry Yung Chi Kin); Chinese business executive; b. 31 Jan. 1942, Shanghai; s. of Rong Yiren and Yang Jianqing; m. Catherine Yung; three c.; ed Tianjin Univ.; began career as intern in hydraulic power plant near Changbai Mountain, Jilin Prov.; co-founded Elcap Electronics Plant, Hong Kong 1978; co-founded Automation Design Co. Ltd, Calif., USA 1982; joined CITIC Pacific Ltd as Vice-Pres., Hong Kong 1986, Dir 1990, Chair., Pres. and Man. Dir, also Chair. Audit Cttee, Exec. Dir CITIC Group 1990–2009 (resgnd); est. Yung's Enterprise Holdings Ltd 2009; mem. CPPCC; Steward, Hong Kong Jockey Club; mem. Gov.'s Business Council 1994–97; Dr hc (Hong Kong Univ. of Science and Tech.) 1998. *Address:* Yung's Enterprise Holdings Ltd, 25 Westlands Road, 25/F Quarry Bay, Hong Kong, People's Republic of China (office).

RONTÓ, Györgyi, DSc; Hungarian biophysicist and academic; *Professor Emeritus of Biophysics, Semmelweis University;* b. 13 July 1934, Budapest; d. of György Rontó and Erzsébet Lanczkor; m. Dr Dezső Holnapy 1961; two s.; ed Semmelweis Univ. of Medicine, Budapest; Prof. of Biophysics, Semmelweis Univ. 1980, now Prof. Emer., Dir Semmelweis Univ. Inst. of Biophysics 1982–99; Head of Research Group for Biophysics of the Hungarian Acad. of Sciences 1982–2004; Gen. Sec. Hungarian Biophysical Soc. 1969–90, Vice-Pres. 1990–98, Hon. Pres. 2002–; Vice-Pres. Asscn Int. de Photobiologie 1988–92; officer, European Soc. for Photobiology; mem. Nat. Cttee of COSPAR (Cttee on Space Research); specialises in effects of environmental physical and chemical agents on nucleo-proteins; special interest in biological dosimetry of environmental and artificial UV radiations and in exo/astrobiology; Medal of the Hungarian Biophysical Soc. 1990, 2004, Apáczai Csere János Award 1994, Environment Award 1996, Gold Ring, Semmelweis Univ. 1999. *Publications:* A biofizika alapjai (An Introduction to Biophysics With Medical Orientation) (co-author) 1981 (also English and German edns), Light in Biology and Medicine (Vol. 2) 1991; more than 140 articles. *Leisure interests:* arts, architecture, gardening. *Address:* 1094 Budapest, Tűzoltó-u. 34–47 (home); PO Box 263, 1444 Budapest, Hungary (home). *Telephone:* (1) 267-6261 (home); (1) 252-0895 (home). *Fax:* (1) 266-6656 (home). *E-mail:* ronto.gyorgyi@med.semmelweis-univ.hu (office).

ROOS, John Victor, JD; American lawyer, diplomatist and consultant; *Global Adviser, Mitsubishi UFJ Financial Group, Inc.;* b. 14 Feb. 1955, San Francisco, Calif.; m. Susan Roos; one s. one d.; ed Lowell High School, Stanford Univ., Stanford Law School; f. Stanford Speech and Debate Inst., also developed and taught speech and debate course to Stanford undergraduate students; admitted to practise law in Calif. 1980; litigation assoc., O'Melveny & Myers, Los Angeles 1980–84; joined Wilson Sonsini Goodrich & Rosati, Palo Alto, Calif. 1985, Partner 1988–, mem. Bd of Dirs and Man. Dir of Professional Services 2000–05, CEO Wilson Sonsini Goodrich & Rosati 2005–09; Amb. to Japan 2009–13; Global Adviser, Mitsubishi UFJ Financial Group, Inc. 2013–; Special Asst to Nat. Co-Chair. for Walter Mondale's presidential campaign 1984; Sr Advisor to nat. campaign and Chair. Calif. campaign for Bill Bradley's presidential bid 2000, also Treas. Time Future, Inc., Senator Bradley's multi-cand. cttee 2000; Chair. Northern Calif. Finance Cttee for Senator John Kerry's presidential campaign 2004; fmr mem. Nat. Finance Cttee; fmr Co-Chair. Calif. Finance Cttee for the Obama for America presidential campaign and mem. campaign's tech. cttee; mem. San Mateo/Foster City Elementary School Bd 1991–98, Pres. 1995; mem. Stanford Law School Dean's Advisory Council, Stanford School of Educ. Dean's Advisory Bd. *Address:* Mitsubishi UFJ Financial Group, Inc., 7-1, Marunouchi 2-chome, Chiyoda-ku, Tokyo 100-8330, Japan (office). *Telephone:* (3) 3240-8111 (office). *Fax:* (3) 3240-8203 (office). *E-mail:* info@mufg.jp (office). *Website:* www.mufg.jp (office).

ROOSEN, Gustavo; Venezuelan politician and business executive; *Executive President, Instituto de Estudios Superiores de Administración;* ed Andrés Bello Catholic Univ., Caracas, New York Univ., USA; Vice-Pres. Venezuelan Banking Asscn 1981–83; Pres. Caracas Chamber of Commerce 1986–88; Minister of Educ. 1989–92; Pres. Petróleos de Venezuela 1992–95; apptd Pres. CANTV (CA Nacional Teléfonos de Venezuela) 1995, CEO 2002–07 (resgnd); currently Exec. Pres. Instituto de Estudios Superiores de Administración.

ROOT, Joe; English cricketer; *Captain, Test Side, England Cricket Team;* b. (Joseph Edward Root), 30 Dec. 1990, Sheffield, S Yorks.; s. of Matt Root and Helen Root; right-handed batsman; right-arm off break bowler; played for Yorkshire 2009–, England Cricket Team 2012–; First-class debut: Yorkshire vs Loughborough, Leeds 10–12 May 2010; Test debut: England vs India, Nagpur 13–17 Dec. 2012; T20 Int. debut: India vs England, Mumbai 22 Dec. 2012; One Day Int. (ODI): England vs India, Rajkot 11 Jan. 2013; Capt. England Test side 2017–; Wisden Cricketer of the Year 2014, England Test Cricketer of the Year 2015, England Limited-Overs Cricketer of the Year 2015. *Address:* c/o Cherry Tree Lane, Rostherne, Cheshire, WA14 3RZ, England (office). *Telephone:* (1565) 832100 (office). *Fax:* (1565) 83222 (office). *E-mail:* ism@sportism.net (office). *Website:* www.ism.golf (office).

ROOTS, Ott, PhD; Estonian environmental scientist; *Director and Leading Research Scientist, Estonian Environmental Research Institute, Estonian Environmental Research Centre;* b. 9 May 1946, Tallinn; s. of Otto Roots and Ida Roots (née Lass); m. Marika Voit; one s.; ed Tallinn Technological Univ., Inst. of Chem., Estonian Acad. of Sciences; Engineer-Lt, Co. Vice-Commdr, 537 Soviet Army Bldg Bn 1969–71; scientist, Inst. of Zoology and Botany, Estonian Acad. of Sciences 1971–74, Baltic Sea Dept, Inst. of Thermo- and Electrophysics 1974–84; Chief Researcher Baltic Br., Inst. of Applied Geophysics 1984–90; Chief Researcher Water Protection Lab., Tallinn Tech. Univ. 1990–92; Sr Scientist Dept of Environmental Carcinogenesis, Inst. of Experimental and Clinical Medicine 1992–94; Monitoring Counsellor, Environment Information Centre, Ministry of the Environment 1993–2000, Councillor, Dept of Environmental Man. and Tech., Ministry of the Environment 2000–02; Monitoring Co-ordinator, Estonian Environmental Research Centre (EERC) 2002–05, Dir and Leading Research Scientist, Estonian Environmental Research Inst. (under EERC) 2005–, mem. Scientific Council of EERC; Sr Researcher, Estonian Marine Inst., Univ. of Tartu 2007–09, 2010–12, Extraordinary Sr Researcher 2012–14; Del. Helsinki Comm. (HELCOM) (expert on persistent organic contaminants) 1974–, UN ECE ICP (expert on monitoring) 1994–; Co-ordinator Finnish-Estonian Training Project (environmental monitoring) 1996–2002; mem. Estonian Chem. Soc. 1995–, Nat. Geographic Soc., Washington 1996–, New York Acad. of Sciences 1997–, Estonian Nature Fund 1998–2002, Estonia Chemicals Safety Comm. 2000–02, Estonian Toxicological Comm., Ministry of Educ. 2001–, Steering Cttee on the Support Project of Chemicals Control in Estonia 2002–05, Estonian Science Soc. 2004–, American Scientist Soc. 2006–, European Lysimeter Research Group, Estonian Co-ordinator –2007, Advisory Bd Scientific Journal Ecological Chemistry (St Petersburg Univ. and Thesa), Estonian Soc. of Toxicology 2009–; Estonian EERC Focal Point – EFSA Article 36; Amb. Int. HCH and Pesticides Asscn 2003–; Second Prize, Tallinn Tech. Univ. students' scientific works competition 1969, Bronze Medal, Environmental Protection Exhbn (Russia) 1982, honoured by Ministry of the Environment, Estonia, for work in environmental protection 1996, by Ministry of Social Affairs for work on Govt Chemical Safety Comm. 2003, by Ministry of the Environment (Honour Certificate) for great and long-term contrib. to Estonian environmental protection 2006, Cen. European Univ. Foundation Individual Research Support Scheme Grant 1993, 1997–99, Estonian Science Foundation Grant 1994–96, 1997–2000, John D. and Catherine T. Mac Arthur Foundation Grant (USA) 2001–02, Honour Certificate for ten years conscientious and successful work in EERC Scientific Grants 2012. *Publications include:* Polychlorinated Biphenyls and Chlororganic Pesticides in the Ecosystem of the Baltic Sea 1992, Toxic Chlororganic Compounds in the Ecosystem of the Baltic Sea 1996, The Effect of Environmental Pollution on Human Health in the Baltic States 1999, UNEP Persistent Bioaccumulative and Toxic Chemicals in Central and Eastern European Countries (co-author) 2000, UNEP Regionally Based Assessment of Persistent Toxic Substances (co-author) 2003, Persistent Organic Pollutants in our Environment, Ministry of the Environment, Estonian Environmental Research Center 2006; more than 230 scientific articles in learned journals. *Leisure interests:* environmental protection, sport (especially basketball), music. *Address:* Estonian Environmental Research Centre, Marja Str. 4D, Tallinn 10617 (office); Karulaugu tee 9–10, 74001 Tallinn, Estonia (home). *Telephone:* (2) 611-2964 (office). *Fax:* (2) 611-2901 (office). *E-mail:* ott.roots@klab.ee (office); ott.roots@ut.ee (office); ottroots66@gmail.com (home). *Website:* www.klab.ee (office); www.sea.ee (office).

ROP, Anton, MA; Slovenian economist and politician; *Vice-President, European Investment Bank;* b. 27 Dec. 1960, Ljubljana; ed Univ. of Ljubljana; Asst Dir Slovene Inst. for Macroeconomic Analysis and Devt 1985–92; State Sec. Ministry of Econ. Relations and Devt 1993; Minister of Labour, Family and Social Affairs 1996–2000, of Finance 2002; Prime Minister 2002–04; Pres. Liberal Democratic Party (Liberalna Demokracija Slovenije—LDS) 2002–05, Leader, Parl. Group 2004–07; Vice-Pres. European Investment Bank 2010–. *Leisure interests:* reading, sport. *Address:* European Investment Bank, 98–100, boulevard Konrad Adenauer, 2950 Luxembourg, Luxembourg (office). *Telephone:* 43-79-1 (office). *Fax:* 43-77-04 (office). *Website:* www.eib.org (office).

ROPAC, Thaddaeus; Austrian gallery owner; b. 1960, Klagenfurt; served first internship with Joseph Beuys 1982; became acquainted with young artists including Jean-Michel Basquiat, Keith Haring and Robert Mapplethorpe in New York; organized exhbns of their work in opening his first gallery in Salzburg 1983; owns Galerie Thaddaeus Ropac, Salzburg, Austria and Paris, France; opened space in Halle, represents more than 50 major artists, ranging from Rosenquist, Baselitz, Kiefer and the Kabakovs to Fleury, Gormley, Violette, Slominski and Erwin Wurm; Pres. Bd of Trustees, Salzburg Foundation 2009–; mem. Advisory Bd Museum of Contemporary Art, Vienna, Museum of Applied Arts (MAK), Vienna, European Univ. of Science & Art, Salzburg, Salzburg Int. Festival; Officier, Ordre des Arts et des Lettres 2005, Verleihung Goldenes Verdienstkreuz der Republik Österreich im Bundeskanzleramt 2006, Kt of Legion of Honour; Kunst und Kulturpreis der Salzburger Wirtschaft 2007. *Address:* Galerie Thaddaeus Ropac, Mirabelle Platz 2, 5020 Salzburg, Austria (office). *Telephone:* (662) 881393 (office). *Fax:* (662) 8813939 (office). *E-mail:* thaddaeus.ropac@ropac.at (office). *Website:* www.ropac.net (office).

ROPER, Warren Richard, MSc, PhD, FRS, FRSNZ; New Zealand chemist and academic; b. 27 Nov. 1938, Nelson; s. of Robert J. Roper and Nancy L. Robinson; m. Judith D. C. Miller 1961; two s. one d.; ed Nelson Coll., Univ. of Canterbury, Univ. of North Carolina, USA; Lecturer, Univ. of Auckland 1966, Prof. of Chem. 1984–2007; Visiting Lecturer, Univ. of Bristol, UK 1972; Visiting Prof., Univ. of Leeds, UK 1983, Univ. of Rennes, France 1984, 1985, Stanford Univ., USA 1988; Visiting Prof., Univ. of Sydney 2001; Fellow, New Zealand Inst. of Chem., Japan Soc. for Promotion of Science 1992; Hon. DSc (Canterbury) 1999; RSC Award in Organometallic Chem. 1983, ICI Medal, NZ Inst. of Chem., 1984, RSC Centenary Lecturer 1988, Hector Medal, Royal Soc. of NZ 1991, Inorganic Chem. Award, Royal Australian Chemical Inst. 1992, G.T. Seaborg Lecturer, Univ. of California, Berkeley 1995, Dwyer Medal, Univ. of NSW 2000, Stone Lecturer, Univ. of Bristol 2003, Arthur D. Little Lecturer, MIT 2005. *Publications:* more than 200 original papers and reviews in scientific journals. *Leisure interests:* listening to music (especially opera), walking. *Address:* 26 Beulah Avenue, Auckland 0630, New Zealand (home). *Telephone:* (9) 478-6940 (home). *E-mail:* w.roper@auckland.ac.nz (office).

ROQUELAURE, A. N. (see RICE, Anne).

RØRSTED, Kasper; Danish business executive; *CEO, adidas;* b. 24 Feb. 1962, Århus; m.; four c.; ed Int. Business School, Copenhagen, Exec. Summer Program, Harvard Business School, USA; various man. positions in marketing and distribution with Oracle and Digital Equipment Corpn –1995; various man. positions at Compaq, including Head of Compaq Enterprise Business Group in Europe, Middle East & Africa (EMEA) 1995–2001, Vice-Pres. and Gen. Man. Compaq, EMEA Region 2001–02, Sr Vice-Pres. and Gen. Man. Hewlett Packard, EMEA Region 2002–04; Exec. Vice-Pres., Human Resources, Purchasing, Information Technologies, Infrastructure Services, Henkel KGaA 2005–07, Vice-Chair. Man. Bd Henkel KGaA and Exec. Vice-Pres. Human Resources and Infrastructure Services 2007–08, CEO Henkel Group AG, responsible for Human Resources, Infrastructure Services 2008–16, mem. Man. Bd Henkel Group and Chair. 2005–07, apptd Exec. Vice-Pres. Human Resources and Infrastructure Services 2005, CEO Henkel Group 2008–16, Exec. Vice-Pres. Human Resources, Purchasing, Information Technologies and Infrastructure Services, Henkel KGaA (subsidiary of Henkel Group) 2005–07, Vice-Chair. Man. Bd Henkel KGaA 2007–08, apptd Chair. Henkel KGaA 2008; CEO adidas AG 2016–; mem. Bd of Dirs Cable & Wireless Plc (UK), Henkel Norden AB (Sweden), Danfoss A/S (Denmark). *Address:* adidas AG, Adi-Dassler-Strasse 1, 91074 Herzogenaurach, Germany. *Telephone:* 9132840 (office). *Fax:* 9132842241 (office). *Website:* www.adidas-group.com (office).

ROSA BAUTISTA, Leonidas; Honduran lawyer, politician and diplomatist; *Ambassador and Permanent Representative, Organization of American States;* b. 4 Feb. 1947, Lepaera; s. of Leonidas Rosa and Alejandrina Vda. de Rosa; m. Abogada Irma Violeta Suazo de Rosa; three c.; ed Instituto Ramón Rosa, Gracias, Lempira, Universidad Nacional Autónoma de Honduras; fmr legal adviser to Main Directorate of Transport; Vice-Minister of the Interior and of Justice 1978–80; Deputy to Constituent Nat. Ass. 1980–82; fmr Prof., Universidad Nacional Autónoma de Honduras; Minister of Foreign Affairs 2003–05; Attorney-Gen. 2005–09; Amb. and Perm. Rep. to OAS, Washington, DC 2011–; Sr Partner and Dir, Bufete Rosa y Asociados, SA de CV (law firm), Tegucigalpa; Pres. Honduran Bar Asscn 1990–92; Prof., Universidad Nacional Autónoma de Honduras. *Address:* Permanent Mission of Honduras to the Organization of American States, 3007 Tilden Street NW, Suite 4M-400, Washington, DC 20008, USA (office); Bufete Rosa y Asociados, SA de CV, Edificio Rosa y Asociados, Colonia San Rafael Retorno Kobe n. 29, Tegucigalpa, Honduras (office). *Telephone:* (202) 244-5653 (Washington, DC) (office); (202) 244-5430 (Washington, DC) (office); 239-2688 (Bufete Rosa) (office). *Fax:* 239-2718 (Bufete Rosa) (office). *E-mail:* honduras@oas.org (office); lrosab@bufeterosa.com (office). *Website:* www.oas.org (office); www.bufeterosa.com (office).

ROSADILLA, Luis; Uruguayan politician; b. 21 Dec. 1953, Montevideo; m.; six c.; spent nine years in prison for guerrilla activity with Tupamaros Movimiento de Liberación Nacional 1973–82; f. own bakery business 1992; Sec. to Senator Eleuterio Fernández Huidobro 1999–2004; mem. Cámara de Representantes (Parl.) for Montevideo constituency 2005–09, Chair. Defence Cttee, currently

Senator; Minister of Nat. Defence 2010–11; mem. Frente Amplio./Movimiento de Participación Popular. *Website:* www.parlamento.gub.uy.

ROSAIAH, Konijeti, BCom; Indian politician; b. 4 July 1933, Vemuru, Guntur Dist; s. of Subbaiah Rosaiah; m. Sivalaxmi Garu; three s. one d.; ed Guntur Hindu Coll., Andhra Univ.; elected as mem. Andhra Pradesh Legis. Council 1968, 1974, 1980; State Minister for Transportation, Roads and Building 1979, for Transportation and Housing 1980, for Home Affairs 1982, for Finance, Transportation and Electricity 1989, for Finance, Health and Educ. and Electricity 1990, 1992, for Finance 2004–09; MP for Narasaraopeta 1998; Chief Minister of Andhra Pradesh 2009–10 (resgnd); Gov. of Tamil Nadu 2011–16, of Karnataka June–Aug. 2014; mem. Indian Nat. Congress party, Pres. Pradesh Congress Cttee 1995–97; Dr hc (Andhra Univ.) 2007.

ROSALES BOLAÑOS, Antenor; Nicaraguan lawyer, banking executive and fmr central banker; b. 1955, Leon; s. of Rodolfo Rosales and Angela Bolaños; ed Central American Univ., Managua; joined Sandinista Nat. Liberation Front 1970, Pres. Nat. Asscn of Students of Eng and Allied Careers and Coordinator Exec. Cttee Revolutionary Student Front, joined Sandinista People's Army and served as commdr during insurrection of Esteli, retd with rank of Col 1999; fmr mem. Bd of Dirs Superintendency of Banks and Other Financial Institutions; Co-founder and fmr Dir ProCredit Bank; fmr Dir Intercontinental Bank; Gov. Banco Central de Nicaragua (Cen. Bank of Nicaragua) 2007–12; Alternate Gov., Inter-American Devt Bank.

ROSANVALLON, Pierre, PhD; French historian and academic; *Professor of Modern and Contemporary Political History, Collège de France;* b. 1 Jan. 1948, Blois; ed École des Hautes Études Commerciales de Paris; econ. adviser, Confédération française démocratique du travail 1969–72, political adviser to Edmond Maire and Ed. CFDT-Aujourd'hui 1973–77; mem. staff, Univ. of Paris-Dauphine 1978, Dir of Research 1978–82; Univ. Lecturer, École des hautes études en sciences sociales 1983–89, Dir of Studies 1989–92, Head of Raymond Aron Centre of Political Research 1992–2005; Prof. of Modern and Contemporary Political History, Collège de France 2001–; co-f. (with François Furet) Fondation Saint-Simon (think-tank) 1982–99 (now disbanded); mem. Scientific Counsel of French Nat. Library 2002–, Scientific Counsel of École Normale Supérieure de Paris 2004–; Founder and Pres. La République des Idées 2002–; Knight Legion of Honor 1998, Officer Legion of Honor 2010. *Publications include:* L'Âge de l'autogestion 1976, La Crise de l'État-providence 1981 (trans. as The New Social Question: Rethinking the Welfare State 2000), Le Moment Guizot 1985, L'État en France de 1789 à nos jours 1990, La Monarchie impossible 1994, La Nouvelle Question sociale 1995, Le Nouvel Âge des inégalités (with Jean-Paul Fitoussi) 1996, Le Peuple introuvable: Histoire de la représentation démocratique en France 1998, La Démocratie inachevée. Histoire de la souveraineté du peuple en France 2000, Le Sacre du citoyen. Histoire du suffrage universel en France 2001, Pour une histoire conceptuelle du politique 2003, Le Modèle politique français. La société civile contre le jacobinisme de 1789 à nos jours 2004, La contre-démocratie. La politique à l'âge de la défiance 2006 (trans. as Counter-Democracy: Politics in an Age of Distrust 2008), Democracy Past and Future (ed. Samuel Moyn) (excerpts) 2006, The Demands of Liberty – Civil Society in France since the Revolution 2007, La légitimité démocratique. Impartialité, réflexivité, proximité 2008 (trans. by Arthur Goldhammer as Democratic Legitimacy: Impartiality, Reflexivity, Proximity 2011), La Société des égaux 2011, Le Parlement des invisibles 2014, Le Bon Gouvernement 2015. *Address:* Collège de France, 11 place Marcelin Berthelot, 75231 Paris Cedex 05, France (office). *Telephone:* 1-44-27-12-11 (office). *Fax:* 1-44-27-11-47 (office). *E-mail:* message@college-de-france.fr (office). *Website:* www.college-de-france.fr (office).

ROSÁRIO, Carlos Agostinho do, BA, MSc; Mozambican economist, diplomatist and politician; *Prime Minister;* b. 26 Oct. 1954, Maxixe, Inhambane Prov.; s. of Agostinho Juisse and Rosa Sechene; ed Univ. Eduardo Mondlane, Imperial Coll. at Wye, Univ. of London, UK; began career in econ. and financial div., Ministry of Public Works and Housing 1977–83; Prof. of Math., Industrial Inst. of Maputo 1980–82; Economist with Citrus Agricultural Co., Manica 1983–87; Gov., Zambezia Prov. and First Sec., Zambezia Provincial Cttee 1987–94; mem. Assembleia da República (Parl.) 1994–; Minister of Agric. and Fisheries 1995–2000; High Commr to India and Sri Lanka 2002–08; Amb. to Indonesia 2009–15; Prime Minister 2015–; mem. Frente de Libertação de Moçambique (Frelimo), mem. Cen. Cttee 1989–. *Leisure interests:* reading, music and sports (gymnastics, football and swimming). *Address:* Office of the Prime Minister, Praça da Marinha Popular, Maputo, Mozambique (office). *Telephone:* 21426861 (office). *Fax:* 21426881 (office). *Website:* www.portaldogoverno.gov.mz (office).

ROSATI, Dariusz Kajetan, DEcon; Polish economist and politician; b. 8 Aug. 1946, Radom; s. of Angelo Rosati and Wanda Pleszczyńska; m. Teresa Nowińska 1971; one s. one d.; ed Main School of Planning and Statistics, Warsaw; scientific researcher, Main School of Planning and Statistics (now Cen. School of Commerce), Warsaw 1969, Asst Prof. 1978, Prof. 1990–; with Citibank, New York 1978–79; Visiting Prof., Princeton Univ., NJ 1986–87; Founder and first Dir Inst. of World Economy, Warsaw School of Econs 1985; Dir Foreign Trade Research Inst., Warsaw 1988–91; Partner, TKD-Ernst & Young Poland 1989–92; Head UN Section for Cen. and E Europe, Geneva 1991–95; Minister of Foreign Affairs 1995–97; mem. Council of Monetary Policy of Nat. Bank of Poland 1998–2004; mem. Bd of Dirs Int. Exchange Program (IREX), Washington, DC 1998–2001; mem. Polish United Workers' Party (PZPR) 1966–90; mem. Cttee on Econ. Reform 1987–90, team of econ. advisers to Prime Minister 1988–89, Econ. Strategy Cttee to the Cabinet 1994–97; Adviser to Pres. of EC 2001–; Rector Richard Łazarski Univ. of Commerce and Law, Warsaw 2003–; mem. European Parl. (Socialist Group) 2004–09, 2014–, mem. Cttee on Econ. and Monetary Affairs 2004–07, 2014–, mem. Del. to ACP-EU Jt Parl. Ass. 2004–09, 2014–; mem. Sejm (Parl.) for Warsaw 2011–; mem. Polish Econ. Soc. 1969–, Econ. Studies Cttee Polish Acad. of Sciences 1999–, European Econ. Asscn, European Asscn of Comparative Econ. Studies; mem. Civic Platform (PO) (Platforma Obywatelska) 2011–; Silver Cross of Merit 1981; Kt's Cross, Order of Poland Restituta 1989; Orders of Merit from France, Italy, Greece, Ukraine and Lithuania. *Publications:* Decision-Making 1977, Inflation 1989, Export Policies 1990, Polish Way to Market 1998, An Agenda for a Growing Europe: The Sapir Report 2004, Facing the Challenge: Lisbon Strategy for growth and employment 2004, New Europe: Report from Transformation 2005; more than 250 scientific articles. *Leisure interests:* sports, reading. *Address:* European Parliament, Bât. Altiero Spinelli 12E218, 60 rue Wiertz, Brussels, Belgium (office); 00-539 Warsaw, ul. Piękna 3A, lok. 3, Poland (office). *Telephone:* (2) 284-54-82 (Brussels) (office); (22) 502 447 457 (Warsaw) (office). *Fax:* (2) 284-94-82 (Brussels) (office). *E-mail:* dariusz.rosati@europarl.europa.eu (office); dariusz@rosati.pl (office); piotr.kolomycki@rosati.pl (office). *Website:* www.europarl.europa.eu/meps/en/28394/DARIUSZ_ROSATI_history.html (office); www.rosati.pl.

ROSATTI, Horacio Daniel, PhD; Argentine lawyer, academic and fmr government official; *Minister, Supreme Court;* b. 1956, Santa Fe; ed Universidad Nacional del Litoral, Universidad Católica de Santa Fe; apptd Municipal Attorney, City of Santa Fe 1989; Sec. of Govt, Culture and Social Action, Municipality of Santa Fe 1991; Sec.-Gen., Governorate of Santa Fe 1993; elected mem. Constituent Ass. 1994; Mayor of Santa Fe 1995–99; Co-Judge, Supreme Court 2002–03; Attorney-Gen. of the Treasury 2003–04; Minister of Justice, Security and Human Rights 2004–05; Dean of Faculty of Law, Catholic Univ. of Santa Fe 1999–2002; fmr Dean Universidad del Litoral, Pres. Inst. of Legislative Studies, Argentine Fed. of Bar Asscn 2010–11, Argentine Asscn of Constitutional Law 2013–15 (also Dir); Judge, Corte Suprema (Supreme Court) 2015–, Minister 2016–; Corresp. mem. Instituto de Federalismo; mem. Partido Justicialista (PJ). *Address:* Corte Suprema, Talcahuano 550, 4°, C1013AAL Buenos Aires, Argentina (office). *Telephone:* (11) 4370-4600 (office). *Fax:* (11) 4340-2270 (office). *E-mail:* consultas@cjsn.gov.ar (office). *Website:* www.csjn.gov.ar (office).

ROSBASH, Michael, PhD; American geneticist, biologist and academic; *Professor of Biology and Inaugural Peter Gruber Endowed Chair in Neuroscience, Brandeis University;* b. 7 March 1944, Kansas City, Mo.; m. Nadja Abovich; one d. one step-d.; ed California Inst. of Tech., Institut de Biologie Physico-Chimique, Paris (Fulbright Scholar), Massachusetts Inst. of Tech., Univ. of Edinburgh, UK; joined Faculty of Brandeis Univ. 1974, Dir Brandeis Nat. Center for Behavioral Genomics, Prof. of Biology and Inaugural Peter Gruber Endowed Chair in Neuroscience; Investigator, Howard Hughes Medical Inst. 1989–; Co-founder and mem. Scientific Advisory Bd, Hypnion, Inc.; mem. Nat. Center for Sleep Disorders Advisory Panel, NIH, Center for Biological Timing, NSF; mem. American Acad. of Arts and Sciences 1997, NAS 2003; Fellow, AAAS 2007; Helen Hay Whitney Fellow 1971–74, NIH Research Career Devt Award 1976–80, Guggenheim Fellow 1989–90, California Inst. of Tech. Distinguished Alumni Award 2001, Aschoff's Rule Winner, Soc. for Research on Biological Rhythms 2008, Gruber Prize in Neuroscience 2009, Louisa Gross Horwitz Prize, Columbia Univ. 2011, Gairdner Int. Award (co-recipient) 2012, Shaw Prize in Life Science and Medicine (co-recipient) 2013, Nobel Prize in Physiology or Medicine (co-recipient with Michael W. Young and Jeffrey C. Hall) 2017. *Achievements include:* cloned, with Michael Rosbash, the Period gene in *Drosophila melanogaster* controlling its biological rhythms 1984; also discovered that the mRNA and protein encoded by this gene show circadian oscillations. *Publications:* numerous papers in professional journals. *Address:* Carl J. Shapiro Science Center, Room 2-24B, Brandeis University, 415 South Street, Waltham, MA 02453, USA (office). *Telephone:* (781) 736-3160 (office). *Fax:* (781) 736-3164 (office). *E-mail:* rosbash@brandeis.edu (office). *Website:* www.bio.brandeis.edu (office).

ROŞCA, Iurie; Moldovan journalist and politician; b. 31 Oct. 1961, Teleneşti; m. 1st Larisa Roşca (divorced 2011); three c.; m. 2nd Cristina Guţu (divorced 2014); ed Moldova State Univ.; active in pro-democracy movement in 1980s; Ed., Teleradio-Moldova Co.; mem. Parl. 1994–, Deputy Chair. of Parl. 1998–2000, 2005–09, mem. Standing Bureau of Parl.; Chair. People's Christian Democratic Party 1994; Deputy Prime Minister June–Sept. 2009. *Publications:* Escape from the Darkness 1995, Exercises of Lucidity 2000. *Address:* c/o People's Christian Democratic Party (Partidul Popular Creştin Democrat—PPCD), 2009 Chişinău, str. Nicolae Iorga 5, Moldova (office).

ROSCITT, Richard R. (Rick), BEng, MBA; American business executive; *Chairman, Sapien LLC;* ed Stevens Inst. of Tech., Sloan School of Man., Massachusetts Inst. of Tech.; joined AT&T 1973, fmr Pres. AT&T Business Services, then Pres. and CEO AT&T Solutions, fmr mem. Operations Group, AT&T; Chair. and CEO ADC Telecommunications, Inc. 2001–03; Pres. and COO MCI Group 2003–04; Chair. Sapien LLC 2005–; Chair. Orion Telecommunications, SMOBILE Systems 2006, later Chair. and CEO 2007–10; Partner, Core Value Partners Investments; mem. Bd of Dirs ICT Group 2008–, Force 10 Networks, Calif., Inc.; mem. Bd of Trustees Stevens Inst. of Tech. New Jersey. *Address:* Sapien Corporate Headquarters, 36 Cattano Avenue, Morristown, NJ 07960, USA (office). *Telephone:* (866) 372-7436 (office). *Fax:* (973) 944-7558 (home). *E-mail:* info@sapiensoftware.com (office). *Website:* www.sapiensoftware.com (office).

ROSE, Charles (Charlie) Peete, Jr, BA, JD; American broadcaster and journalist; b. 5 Jan. 1942, Henderson, NC; s. of Charles Peete Rose, Sr and Margaret Rose (née Frazier); m. Mary King (divorced); pnr Amanda Burden; ed Duke Univ.; began career with Bankers Trust; first broadcasts as weekend reporter for WPIX-TV, New York 1972; Man. Ed. Bill Moyers' International Report (PBS) 1974–75, Exec. Producer Bill Moyers Journal 1975–76; Political Correspondent, NBC News 1976–77; Program Man. and host, The Charlie Rose Show, KXAS-TV, Dallas-Fort Worth 1979–81; Anchor, CBS News Nightwatch 1984–90; presented Personalities (syndicated programme produced by Fox Broadcasting Co.) 1990; Exec. Producer, Exec. Ed. and host The Charlie Rose Show (interview show) PBS station Thirteen/WNET 1991–2017; Correspondent for 60 Minutes 1999–2005; Co-Presenter CBS This Morning 2012–17; Dir Citadel Broadcasting Corpn 2003–09; Dr hc (C.W. Post Coll., Univ. of North Carolina, Pembroke); George Foster Peabody Award 1976, Emmy Award 1987, 1992, Cable ACE Award 1992, Futrell Award 2005, Lifetime Achievement Award in Entertainment Journalism, Savannah Film Festival 2007. *Address:* Charlie Rose Inc., 731 Lexington Avenue, New York, NY 10022, USA (office). *Website:* www.charlierose.com (office).

ROSE, Harald, PhD; German physicist and academic; *Carl Zeiss Senior Guest Professor for Electron Optics, University of Ulm;* b. 14 Feb. 1935, Bremen; ed Darmstadt Univ. of Tech.; Visiting Researcher, Enrico Fermi Inst., Univ. of Chicago, USA 1973–74; Prin. Research Scientist, New York State Dept of Health 1976–80; Prof., Dept of Physics, Darmstadt Univ. of Tech. 1980–2000, now Prof.

Emer.; Visiting Researcher, Cornell Univ., Univ. of Maryland 1995–96; Research Fellow, Dept of Materials Science, Oak Ridge Nat. Lab., Tenn. 2000–01, Dept of Materials Science, Argonne Nat. Lab., Ill. 2001–02, Advanced Light Source, Lawrence Berkeley Nat. Lab., Calif. 2003–05; Carl Zeiss Sr Guest Prof. for Electron Optics, Univ. of Ulm 2010–, Guest Scientist, Sub-Angstrom Low-Voltage Electron Microscopy I-II Project (SALVE); Visiting Lecturer, Univ. of Illinois, Urbana-Champaign 2011; Hon. mem. Microscopy Soc. of America, German Soc. of Electron Microscopy, 141 Cttee of Japanese Soc. for the Promotion of Sciences; Hon. Prof., Jiaotong Univ., Xian, China 1987; Hon. FRS; Distinguished Scientist Award, Microscopy Soc. of America 2003, Karl Heinz Beckurts Prize (jtly) 2006, Honda Prize (jtly) 2008, Wolf Prize in Physics (jtly) 2011, Frontiers of Knowledge Award in Basic Sciences, BBVA Foundation 2013. *Achievements include:* inventor of the practical realisable aberration correction and considered leading expert in theoretical electron optics; holder of 105 patents on scientific instruments and electron optical components. *Publications:* numerous publications including Geometrical Charged-Particle Optics 2009; 105 patents of scientific instruments and electro-optical components. *Address:* Room N27/2.005, Electron Microscopy Group of Materials Science, University of Ulm, Albert-Einstein-Allee 11, 89081 Ulm, Germany (office). *Telephone:* (731) 50-22941 (office). *E-mail:* harald.rose@uni-ulm.de (office). *Website:* www.uni-ulm.de/en/einrichtungen/electron-microscopy-group-of-materials-science.html (office); www.salve-project.de (office).

ROSE, Gen. Sir (Hugh) Michael, KCB, CBE, DSO, QGM, DL; British army officer (retd); b. 5 Jan. 1940, India; s. of Lt-Col Hugh Rose and Barbara Allcard; m. Angela Shaw 1968; two s.; ed Cheltenham Coll., St Edmund Hall, Oxford and Royal Coll. of Defence Studies; commissioned, Gloucestershire Regt Territorial Army Volunteer Reserve 1959, RAF Volunteer Reserve 1962; with Coldstream Guards 1964, served in Germany, Aden, Malaysia, Gulf States, Dhofar, NI, Falkland Islands, Brigade Maj., 16 Para. Brigade 1973–75, CO 22 SAS Regt 1979–82, Command, 39 Infantry Brigade 1983–85, Commdt School of Infantry 1987–88, Dir Special Forces 1988–89, GOC NE Dist and Commdr 2nd Infantry Div. 1989–91, Commdt Staff Coll. 1991–93, Commdr UK Field Army and Insp.-Gen. of Territorial Army 1993–94, Commdr UN Forces in Bosnia-Herzegovina 1994–95, Adjutant Gen. 1995–97, Aide de Camp Gen. to the Queen 1995–97, Col Coldstream Guards 1999–2010; mem. Bd of Dirs Eurocontrol Technics, Skarbek Associates; fmr mem. Bd of Dirs Control Risks Group; Hon. DLitt (Nottingham) 1999. *Television:* presenter Power House 2000. *Publications:* Fighting for Peace 1998, Washington's War: The American War of Independence to the Iraqi Insurgency 2007. *Leisure interests:* sailing, skiing. *Address:* Skarbek Associates, Central Court, 25 Southampton Buildings, London, WC2A 1AL, England.

ROSE, Sir John E. V., Kt, MA, FRAeS; British business executive; *Deputy Chairman, Rothschild Group;* b. 1953, Blantyre, Malawi; m. Felicity Rose; two s. one d.; ed Univ. of St Andrews, Scotland; fmrly with First Nat. Bank of Chicago and Security Pacific; joined Rolls-Royce 1984, Dir of Corp. Devt 1989–94, mem. Bd 1992–2011, Pres. and Chief Exec. Rolls-Royce plc 1993–96, Man. Dir Aerospace Group 1995–2011, Chief Exec. 1996–2011 (retd); joined Bd of Dirs Holdingham Group Ltd 2012, now Chair.; Deputy Chair. Rothschild Group 2011–; mem. Bd of Dirs (non-exec.) Eli Lilly & Co. 2003–05, BW Group 2012–; Strategic Adviser, Ombu Ltd; Adviser, Greenbriar Equity Group, Abu Dhabi Exec. Affairs Authority; mem. Advisory Bd Econ. Devt Bd of Singapore, CBI Int., Englefield Capital LLP, Bregal Capital LLP; mem. JP Morgan Int. Council, British-American Business Council, European Round Table of Industrialists; Trustee, Eden Project, Baker Dearing Trust; fmr Pres. European Asscn of Aerospace Industries, Soc. of British Aerospace Cos; fmr Chair. The Prince's Trust; Commdr, Légion d'honneur 2008; Hon. DSc (Univ. of St Andrews) 1999, Hon. DEng (Univ. of Exeter) 2010; Singapore Public Service Star 2008. *Leisure interests:* scuba diving, skiing, the arts. *Address:* Rothschild, New Court, St Swithin's Lane, London, EC4N 8AL (office); Holdingham Group, 34 Upper Brook Street, London, W1K 7QS, England (office). *Website:* www.rothschild.com (office); holdingham.com (office).

ROSE, Justin Peter, MBE; British (b. South African) professional golfer; b. 30 July 1980, Johannesburg, South Africa; m. Kate Rose 2006; one s. one d.; moved to UK aged five and began playing golf at Hartley Wintney Golf Club, Hants.; played in the Walker Cup 1997; turned professional 1998; European Tour wins include Dunhill Championship 2002, Victor Chandler British Masters 2002, MasterCard Masters 2006/07, Volvo Masters 2007, Aberdeen Asset Management Scottish Open 2014, UBS Hong Kong Open 2015; PGA Tour wins include Memorial Tournament 2010, AT&T National 2010, BMW Championship 2011, WGC-Cadillac Championship 2012, US Open 2013, Quicken Loans National 2014, Zurich Classic of New Orleans 2015, WGC-HSBC Champions 2017, Fort Worth Invitational 2018, Fedex Cup Champion 2018, Farmers Insurance Open 2019; Japan Golf Tour wins include The Crowns 2002; Sunshine Tour wins include Nashua Masters 2002; other wins include Bilt Skins (India) 2004, Turkish Airlines World Golf Final 2012, Tyco Golf Skills Challenge (USA) 2012, Turkish Airlines Open 2017, 2018; has played most of his golf on the PGA Tour since 2003, whilst keeping his membership on the European Tour since 1999; best results in major championships: runner-up, Masters Tournament 2015, 2017, won US Open 2013, fourth, The Open Championship 1998, third, PGA Championship 2012; gold medal, Olympic Games, Rio 2016; professional team appearances include World Cup (representing England) 2002, 2003, 2007, 2011, Seve Trophy (representing GB & Ireland) 2003 (winners), 2007 (winners), Ryder Cup (representing Europe) 2008, 2012 (winners), 2014 (winners), 2016; Co-founder Kate and Justin Rose Foundation; Order of Merit on European Tour 2007. *Address:* c/o Excel Sports Management, 1700 Broadway, 29th Floor, New York, NY 10019, USA (office); Kate and Justin Rose Foundation, 10524 Moss Park Road, Suite 204-712, Orlando, FL 32832, USA (office). *Telephone:* (646) 454-5900 (office). *Fax:* (646) 366-8480 (office). *Website:* www.excelsm.com (office); kjrosefoundation.org (office); www.justinrose.com. *E-mail:* kate@kjrosefoundation.org (office).

ROSE, Matthew K., BS; American transport industry executive; *Executive Chairman, Burlington Northern Santa Fe Corporation;* b. 1960; ed Univ. of Missouri; began career as Man. Trainee Missouri Pacific Railroad 1981; various positions Schneider Nat., Int. Utilities; Vice-Pres. Triple Crown Services –1993; joined Burlington Northern 1993, Vice-Pres. Vehicles and Machinery 1994–95, Vice-Pres. Chemicals 1995–96 (following merger with Santa Fe 1995), Sr Vice-Pres. Merchandise Business Unit 1996–97, Sr Vice-Pres. and COO 1997–99, Pres. and COO 1999–2000, Pres. and CEO 2000–13, also Chair. 2002–13, Exec. Chair. 2013–; Chair. Asscn of American Railroads; mem. Bd of Dirs AMR Corpn, Centex Building Community, Center for Energy & Econ. Devt; mem. Gov. of Tex. Business Council, Business Roundtable; mem. Bd of Trustees Texas Christian Univ.; mem. NW Univ. Transportation Center Business Advisory Cttee; American Soc. Transportation and Logistics Distinguished Logistics Professional Award 2007. *Address:* Burlington Northern Santa Fe Corpn, 2650 Lou Menk Drive, Fort Worth, TX 76131-2830, USA (office). *Telephone:* (800) 795-2673 (office). *Fax:* (817) 352-7171 (office). *Website:* www.bnsf.com (office).

ROSE, Richard, BA, DPhil, FBA; American writer, professor of public policy and consultant; *Director, Centre for the Study of Public Policy, University of Strathclyde, Scotland;* b. 9 April 1933, St Louis, Mo.; s. of Charles Imse Rose and Mary C. Rose; m. Rosemary J. Kenny 1956; two s. one d.; ed Clayton High School, Mo., Johns Hopkins Univ., London School of Econs and Univ. of Oxford, UK; worked in political public relations, Miss. Valley 1954–55; reporter, St Louis Post-Dispatch 1955–57; Lecturer in Govt, Univ. of Manchester 1961–66; Prof. of Politics, Univ. of Strathclyde, Scotland 1966–82, Prof. of Public Policy and Dir Centre for the Study of Public Policy 1976–2005, 2012–; Prof. of Public Policy, Univ. of Aberdeen 2005–11; Visiting Prof., European Univ. Inst., Florence 1975–77, 2011–; Visiting Prof., Wissenschaftszentrum Berlin 1988–90, 2015–; Specialist Adviser, House of Commons Public Admin Cttee 2002–03; Consultant Psephologist, The Times, ITV, Daily Telegraph, etc. 1964–; Sec., Cttee on Political Sociology, Int. Sociology Asscn 1970–85; Founding mem. European Consortium for Political Research 1970; mem. US/UK Fulbright Comm. 1971–75; Guggenheim Fellow 1974; Visiting scholar at various insts, Europe, USA, Hong Kong; mem. Home Office Working Party on Electoral Register 1975–77; Co-founder British Politics Group 1974–; Convenor Work Group on UK Politics, Political Studies Asscn 1976–88; mem. Council Int. Political Science Asscn 1976–82; Tech. Consultant OECD, UNDP, World Bank, Council of Europe, Int. IDEA; Dir SSRC Research Programme, Growth of Govt 1982–86, Scotland in the World Forum 2008–11; Ed. Journal of Public Policy 1985–2011, Chair. 1981–85; Scientific Adviser, New Democracies Barometer, Paul Lazarsfeld Soc., Vienna 1991–; Fellow, British Acad.; Sr Fellow in Governance, Oxford Internet Inst. 2003–05; Hon. Vice-Pres. UK Political Studies Asscn, Hon. Fellow American Acad. of Arts and Sciences, Finnish Acad. of Science and Letters; Dr hc (Örebro Univ., Sweden), (European Univ. Inst., Florence) 2010; AMEX Prize in Int. Econs 1992, Lasswell Prize for Lifetime Achievement, Policy Studies Org. 1999; Lifetime Achievement Award, UK Political Studies Asscn 2000, Lifetime Achievement, Int. Council on Comparative Study of Electoral Systems 2008, Prize for European Political Sociology, ECPR Dogan Foundation 2009, Sir Isaiah Berlin Award 2009. *Publications include:* numerous books on politics and public policy including Politics in England 1964, People in Politics: Observations Across the Atlantic 1970, Governing Without Consensus: An Irish Perspective 1971, International Almanack of Electoral History (co-author) 1974, The Problem of Party Government 1974, Northern Ireland: A Time of Choice 1976, Managing Presidential Objectives 1976, What is Governing?: Purpose and Policy in Washington 1978, Can Government Go Bankrupt? (co-author) 1978, Do Parties Make A Difference 1984, Understanding Big Government 1984, Public Employment in Western Nations (co-author) 1985, Taxation by Political Inertia (co-author) 1987, Ministers and Ministries 1987, Presidents and Prime Ministers, The Postmodern President 1988, Ordinary People in Public Policy 1989, Training With Trainers? How Germany Avoids Britain's Supply-side Bottleneck (co-author) 1990, The Loyalties of Voters (co-author) 1990, Lesson-Drawing in Public Policy 1993, Inheritance in Public Policy (co-author) 1994, What is Europe? 1996, How Russia Votes (co-author) 1997, Democracy and Its Alternatives, Understanding Post-Communist Societies (co-author) 1998, A Society Transformed: Hungary in Time-Space Perspective, International Encyclopedia of Elections (co-author) 2000, The Prime Minister in a Shrinking World 2001, Elections without Order: Russia's Challenge to Vladimir Putin (co-author) 2002, Elections and Parties in New European Democracies 2003, Learning from Comparative Public Policy 2005, Russia Transformed (co-author) 2006, Parites and Elections in New European Democracies 2009, Understanding Post-Communist Transformation 2009, Popular Support for an Undemocratic Regime 2011, Representing Europeans: A Pragmatic Approach 2013, Learning about Politics in Time and Space 2014, Paying Bribes for Public Services: A Global Guide (co-author) 2015, Bad Governance and Corruption (co-author) 2018; hundreds of papers in academic journals. *Leisure interests:* architecture, music, writing. *Address:* Centre for the Study of Public Policy, University of Strathclyde, Glasgow, G1 1XQ (office); 1 East Abercromby Street, Helensburgh, G84 7SP, Scotland (home). *Telephone:* (1436) 672164 (office). *Fax:* (1436) 673125 (home). *E-mail:* richard.rose@strath.ac.uk (office); prof_r_rose@yahoo.co.uk. *Website:* www.cspp.strath.ac.uk (office); www.profrose.eu (office).

ROSE OF MONEWDEN, Baron (Life Peer), cr. 2014, of Monewden in the County of Suffolk; **Stuart Alan Ransom Rose,** Kt; British retail industry executive; b. 17 March 1949, Gosport, Hants.; s. of Harry Ransom Rose and Margaret Ransom Rose; m. Jennifer Cook 1973 (divorced 2010); one s. one d.; ed St Joseph's Convent, Dar-es-Salaam, Tanzania, Bootham School, York; various exec. positions with Marks & Spencer PLC 1972–89, Commercial Exec. (Europe), CEO Marks & Spencer Group PLC 2004–10, Exec. Chair. 2008–10, Chair. (non-exec.) 2010–11; joined Burton Group 1989, Chief Exec. Multiples Div. 1994–97; CEO Argos PLC 1998, Booker PLC 1998–2000, Iceland Group PLC (after merger with Booker) 2000, Arcadia PLC 2000–02; Ind. Dir (non-exec.) and Chair. (non-exec.) Ocado Group Plc (internet-only grocery retailer) 2013–; mem. Bd of Dirs (non-exec.) Fat Face Ltd, Oasis Healthcare Group Ltd, RM2 Int., Woolworths Holdings South Africa, Majid Al Futtaim, Time Out Mercado; f. Fulton Management (pvt. man. firm); Sr Adviser, HSBC European; mem. Advisory Bd, Bridgepoint Capital 2010–, Li & Fung; Adviser, Aldo Shoes, Canada; fmr Chair. British Fashion Council, Business in the Community; Trustee, Royal Acad. of Arts; Chair.'Britain Stronger in Europe' campaign 2015–; Hon. LLD (Leeds) 2010; 2006 Business Leader of the Year, World Leadership Forum 2007. *Address:* House of Lords, London, SW1A 0PW; Ocado Group Plc, Titan Court, 3 Bishop Square, Hatfield Business Park, Hatfield, Herts., AL10 9NE, England (office). *Telephone:* (20) 7219-5353 (House of Lords); (1707) 227800 (office). *Fax:* (1707) 227999 (office). *E-mail:* company.secretary@ocado.com (office). *Website:* www.ocado.com (office); www.strongerin.co.uk.

ROSEANNE; American comedienne and actress; b. (Roseanne Cherrie Barr), 3 Nov. 1952, Salt Lake City; d. of Jerry Barr and Helen Barr; m. 1st Bill Pentland 1974 (divorced 1989); m. 2nd Tom Arnold 1990 (divorced 1994); three c. (from previous m.); m. 3rd Ben Thomas 1994; one s.; fmr window dresser, cocktail waitress; worked as comic in bars and church coffeehouse, Denver; produced forum for women performers Take Back the Mike, Univ. of Colo; performer, The Comedy Store, LA; featured on TV special Funny and The Tonight Show; TV special, On Location: The Roseanne Barr Show 1987; star of TV series, Roseanne (ABC) 1988–97; Host Search for America's Funniest Mom 2007; Emmy Award (Outstanding Leading Actress in a Comedy Series) 1993. *Films:* She Devil 1989, Look Who's Talking Too (voice) 1990, Freddy's Dead: The Final Nightmare 1991, Even Cowgirls Get the Blues 1993, Blue in the Face 1995, Unzipped 1995, Meet Wally Sparks 1997, Home on the Range (voice) 2004, A Dairy Tale (voice) 2004. *Television includes:* Little Rosie (series) (voice) 1990, Backfield in Motion 1991, Rosey and Buddy Show (series) (voice) 1992, The Woman Who Loved Elvis 1993, General Hospital (series) 1993, Saturday Night Special (series) 1996, The Roseanne Show (host) 1998–2000, Get Bruce 1999. *Publications:* My Life as a Woman 1989, Roseanne: My Lives 1994. *E-mail:* askroseanne@roseanneworld.com. *Website:* www.roseanneworld.com.

ROSELLE, David, PhD; American mathematician and university administrator; *Executive Director, Winterthur Museum and Country Estate;* b. 30 May 1939, Vandergrift, Pennsylvania; s. of William Roselle and Suzanne Clever; m. Louise H. Dowling 1967; one s. one d.; ed West Chester State Coll., Duke Univ.; Asst Prof., Univ. of Maryland 1965–68; Assoc. Prof. later Prof., Los Angeles State Univ. 1968–74; Prof. Virginia Polytechnic Inst. and State Univ. 1974–87; Dean, Grad. School 1979–81, Dean of Research and Grad. Studies 1981–83, Univ. Provost 1983–87; Pres. Univ. of Kentucky 1987–90, Univ. of Delaware 1990–2007, Pres. Emer. 2007–; Exec. Dir Winterthur Museum and Country Estate, Wilmington 2008–; several hon. degrees; numerous grants and honours. *Publications:* numerous mathematics articles in graph theory and combinatorics. *Leisure interests:* golf, reading, walking. *Address:* Office of the Executive Director, Winterthur Museum and Country Estate, Route 52, Wilmington, DE 19735 (office); 14 Laurel Ridge Lane, Wilmington, DE 19807, USA (home). *Telephone:* (302) 888-4770 (office); (302) 421-3603 (home). *E-mail:* roselle@udel.edu (office). *Website:* www.winterthur.org (office).

ROSEN, Hilary B.; American music industry executive and public relations consultant; *Managing Director, SKDKnickerbocker;* b. 22 Oct. 1958, West Orange, New Jersey; one s. one d. with Elizabeth Birch; ed George Washington Univ.; worked for NJ Gov. Brendan Byrne and US Senator Bill Bradley; worked on transition team of US Senator Dianne Feinstein 1992; government affairs specialist with Liz Robbins Assocs and later with her own firm; joined Recording Industry Asscn of America 1987, Chair. and CEO 1998–2003; involved in establishing Secure Digital Music Initiative, passage of Digital Performance Rights Act, US ratification of World Intellectual Property Org. treaties regarding copyright laws, adoption of Digital Millennium Copyright Act; Founding Partner, Berman Rosen Global Strategies LLC (intellectual property consultant), Washington, DC 2006; Man. Dir Brunswick Group, Washington, DC 2008–10, SKDKnickerbocker, Washington, DC 2010–; Political Commentator, CNN 2008–; fmr Political Dir Huffington Post; Founding Bd mem. Rock the Vote; Bd mem. Ford's Theater, Human Rights Campaign Foundation, Kaiser Family Foundation, LifeBeat, Meridian Int. Center, Nat. Cancer Foundation, Nat. Music Council, Y.E.S. to Jobs; American Civil Liberties Union Torch of Liberty.

ROSEN, Jacky, BA; American politician; *Senator from Nevada;* b. (Jacklyn Sheryl Spektor), 2 Aug. 1957, Chicago, Ill.; d. of Leonard Spektor and Carol Spektor; m. Larry Rosen; one d.; ed Univ. of Minnesota; fmr programmer, designer and software developer, Summa Corpn, Southwest Gas, Citibank; mem. US House of Reps 2016–19; Senator from Nevada 2019–; mem. Cttees on Health, Educ., Labor and Pensions, Commerce, Science, and Transportation, Homeland Security and Governmental Affairs, Small Business; mem. Special Cttee on Aging; Democrat. *Address:* United States Senate, G12 Dirksen Senate Office Building, Washington, DC 20510, USA (office). *Telephone:* (202) 224-6244 (office). *Website:* www.rosen.senate.gov (office).

ROSENBERG, Pamela, BA, MA; German (b. American) music administrator and academic; *Chairman, Barenboim Musikkindergarten Berlin;* b. (Pamela Lyn Henry), 24 April 1945, Los Angeles, Calif.; m. Wolf Rosenberg (deceased); two c.; ed Univ. of California, Berkeley, Ohio State Univ., Guildhall School of Music and London Opera Centre, UK; previous positions at Netherlands Opera, Amsterdam, Deutsches Schauspielhaus, Hamburg; Scenic Supervisor, subsequently Artistic Admin., Frankfurt Opera; Co-Dir (Co-Intendant) Stuttgart Opera 1991–2000; Gen. Dir San Francisco Opera 2001–06; Intendant (Gen. Man.) Berlin Philharmonic Orchestra 2006–10; Dean of Fellows and Programs, American Acad. in Berlin 2010–14; currently Chair. Man. Bd, Barenboim Musikkindergarten Berlin, Musiktheater im Revier Foundation; Vice-Chair. Senate of Berlin-Brandenburgische Akad. der Wissenschaften; mem. Univ. Council (Hochschulrat) of Hochschule für Musik, Freiburg; mem. Bd of Advisors, Cogut Center for the Humanities, Brown Univ., Man. Bd, Liz Mohn Foundation; Trustee, Univ. of California, Berkeley Foundation. *Address:* Barenboim Musikkindergarten Berlin, Leipziger Str. 41, 10117 Berlin, Germany (office). *Website:* www.musikkindergarten-berlin.de (office).

ROSENBERG, Pierre Max; French curator; b. 13 April 1936, Paris; s. of Charles Rosenberg and Gertrude Rosenberg; m. 2nd Béatrice de Rothschild 1981; one d.; ed Lycée Charlemagne, Faculté de droit de Paris and Ecole du Louvre; Chief Curator Dept des Peintures, Musée du Louvre 1983, Inspecteur gén. des musées 1988, Conservateur gén. du Patrimoine 1990–94, Pres. and Dir 1994–2001; Curator Musée Nat. de l'Amitié et des Relations franco-américaines de Blérancourt 1981–93; mem. Acad. Française 1995; Foreign mem. American Acad. Arts and Sciences, American Philosophical Soc., Accad. Naz. dei Lincei, Accad. Naz. di San Luca, Accad. del Disegno, Florence, Accad. Pietro Vanucci, Accad. Clementina, Ateneo Veneto, Istituto Veneto di Scienze, Lettere ed Arti; Hon. Fellow, Royal Academy, London; Chevalier Ordre des Arts et des Lettres, Ordre nat. du Mérite, Officier Légion d'honneur, Grand officier de l'ordre du Mérite (Italy), Commdr de l'ordre du Mérite (Germany). *Publications include:* Il Seicento francese 1970, Georges de La Tour 1973, Chardin. Tout l'œuvre peint 1983, Peyron 1983, Saint-Non. Fragonard. Panopticon italiano. Un diario di viaggio ritrovato. 1759–1761 1986, Fragonard. Tout l'œuvre peint 1989, Les frères Le Nain. Tout l'œuvre peint 1993, Nicolas Poussin. 1594–1665 1994, Antoine Watteau 1996, Georges de La Tour 1998, Julien de Parme, 1736–1799 1998, La pittura in Europa 1999, From Drawing to Painting 2000, Michel-François Dandré-Bardon: 1700-1783 2001, Jacques-Louis David: 1748–1825 2002, De Raphaël à la Révolution. Les relations artistiques entre la France et l'Italie 2005, Gesamverzeichnis Französische Gemälde des 17. und 18. Jahrhunderts in deutschen Sammlungen 2005, En Amérique seulement 2006, Dictionnaire amoureux du Louvre 2007. *Address:* 35 rue de Vaugirard, 75006 Paris (home); Institut de France, 23 quai Conti, 75006 Paris, France (office). *Telephone:* 1-45-48-78-13 (home). *E-mail:* pierre.rosenberg@wanadoo.fr (home).

ROSENBERG, Richard Morris, BA, MBA, LLB; American banker (retd); b. 21 April 1930, Fall River, Mass; s. of Charles Rosenberg and Betty Peck; m. Barbara K. Cohen 1956; two s.; ed Suffolk and Golden Gate Univs; Publicity Asst, Crocker-Anglo Bank, San Francisco 1959–62; Banking Services Officer, Wells Fargo Bank 1962–65, Asst Vice-Pres. 1965–68, Vice-Pres. Marketing Dept 1968, Vice-Pres. Dir of Marketing 1969, Sr Vice-Pres. Marketing and Advertising Div. 1970–75, Exec. Vice-Pres. 1975, Vice-Chair. 1980–83; Vice-Chair. Crocker Nat. Corpn 1983–85; Pres. and COO Seafirst Corpn 1986–87; Dir, Pres. and COO Seattle-First Nat. Bank 1985–87; Vice-Chair. Bd Bank America Corpn San Francisco 1987–90; Chair. and CEO BankAmerica Corpn/Bank of America 1990–96 (retd); mem. Bd of Dirs Buck Inst. for Age Research, Health Care Property Investors, Inc., San Francisco Symphony, Naval War Coll. Foundation; mem. Advisory Bd Shorenstein Properties LLC; fmr mem. Bd of Dirs Airborne Express, Northrop Grumman Corpn, Pacific Mutual Life Insurance Co., United Way; Chair. Exec. Council Univ. of Calif. Medical Center; mem. State Bar of Calif.; Trustee, Calif. Inst. of Tech.; Horatio Alger Award, American Acad. of Arts and Science. *Leisure interests:* tennis, avid reader, history.

ROSENBERG, Steven A., BA, MD, PhD; American physician and immunologist; *Chief of Surgery, National Cancer Institute;* b. 2 Aug. 1940, New York; s. of Abraham Rosenberg and Harriet Wendroff; m. Alice R. O'Connell 1968; three d.; ed Johns Hopkins Univ., Harvard Univ.; Intern, Peter Bent Brigham Hosp. Boston 1963–64, Surgical Resident 1968–69, 1972–74; Fellow in Immunology, Harvard Medical School 1969–70; Clinical Assoc., Nat. Cancer Inst., Bethesda, Md 1970–72, Chief of Surgery, 1974–; Prof. of Surgery, Uniformed Services Univ. of Health Sciences Bethesda, Md 1979–, George Washington Univ. School of Medicine and Health Sciences, Washington, DC 1988–; Assoc. Ed. Journal of the National Cancer Institute 1974–80; Ed. Journal of Immunotherapy 1982–85, Ed.-in-Chief 1990–1995, 2000–; Ed. The Cancer Journal 1995–; mem. Immunotherapy Program Scientific Review Group 1971–78, US–USSR Cooperative Cancer Immunotherapy Program 1974–79; mem. Advisory Bd Int. Registry of Tumor Immunotherapy, Nat. Cancer Inst. 1978; mem. Editorial Bd American Journal of Clinical Oncology 1978–86, Surgery 1981–84, Journal of Clinical Oncology 1982–86, Cytokine 1989–; mem. American Surgical Asscn, Soc. of University Surgeons, Soc. of Surgical Oncology Surgical Biology Club II, Halsted Soc., Transplantation Soc., American Asscn of Immunologists, American Asscn for Cancer Research, American Coll. of Surgeons, American Soc. of Clinical Oncology, Inst. of Medicine, NAS; Dr hc (Ben Gurion Univ.) 1986; Meritorious Service Medal, US Public Health Service 1981, 1986, Friedrich Sasse Prize, Univ. of West Berlin, Germany 1986, Nils Alwell Prize 1987, Distinguished Alumnus Award, Johns Hopkins Univ. 1987, Simon M. Shubitz Prize, Univ. of Chicago Cancer Research Center 1988, Griffuel Prize for Research, French Asscn for Research on Cancer 1988, Milken Family Foundation Cancer Award 1988, Armand Hammer Cancer Prize 1985, 1988, Karnofsky Prize 1991, Ellis Island Medal of Honor 1998, John Wayne Award for Clinical Research 1996, Heath Memorial Award 2002, Flance-Karl Award 2002, American-Italian Cancer Foundation Prize 2003, Richard V. Smalley, MD, Memorial Award 2002, Keio Medical Science Prize 2012, Giants of Cancer Care, OncologyLive 2013, Jacobson Innovation Award, American College of Surgeons 2018, Albany Medical Center Prize in Medicine and Biomedical Research 2018, Szent-Györgyi Prize for Progress in Cancer Research 2019. *Publications:* eight books and more than 800 articles in medical journals. *Address:* Center for Cancer Research, Building 10-CRC, Room 3-3940, 10 Center Drive, MSC 1201, Bethesda, MD 20892-1201 (office); National Cancer Institute, 9000 Rockville Pike, Building 10, Room 3-3940, Bethesda, MD 20892, USA (office). *Telephone:* (301) 496-4164 (office). *E-mail:* sar@nih.gov (office). *Website:* ccr.cancer.gov (office).

ROSENFELD, Irene B., BA/BS, MS, PhD; American business executive; *Chairman and CEO, Mondelēz International Inc.;* m.; two c.; ed Cornell Univ.; joined Kraft Foods in 1981, worked in market research and product man., later Exec. Vice-Pres. Kraft and Gen. Man. Desserts and Snacks, Exec. Vice-Pres. Beverages and Marketing Dir Beverages 1991–96, Exec. Vice-Pres. Kraft and Pres. Kraft Canada 1996–2000, Group Vice-Pres. Kraft Foods N American Operations, Tech., Procurement and Information Systems for Canada, Puerto Rico and Mexico 2000–02, Group Vice-Pres. Kraft Foods N America 2002–03 (resgnd), CEO Kraft Foods Inc. 2006–12, Chair. 2007–12, Chair. and CEO Mondelēz International (following spin off of two ind. public cos, Kraft Foods Group and Mondelēz Int. (global snacks business)) Oct. 2012–; Chair. and CEO Frito-Lay Inc. (div. of PepsiCo Inc.) 2004–06; mem. Bd of Dirs AutoNation Inc.; Chair. Grocery Mfrs of America Industry Affairs Council 2001; Co-Chair. Jt GMA/Food Marketers Inst. Trading Pnr Alliance, Food and Health Strategy Group; fmr Chair. Food and Consumer Products Mfrs of Canada; mem. The Economic Club of Chicago; Trustee, Cornell Univ.; elected to YWCA Acad. of Women Achievers, Masters of Excellence Award Center for Jewish Living 2005. *Leisure interests:* playing the piano, rollerblading. *Address:* Mondelēz International, Inc., Three Parkway, North Deerfield, IL 60015, USA (office). *Telephone:* (847) 943-4000 (office). *E-mail:* info@mondelezinternational.com (office). *Website:* www.mondelezinternational.com (office).

ROSENSHINE, Allen Gilbert, BA; American advertising executive (retd); *Chairman Emeritus, BBDO Worldwide;* b. 14 March 1939; s. of Aaron Rosenshine and Anna Zuckerman; m. Suzan Weston-Webb 1979; four c.; ed Columbia Coll.; copywriter, J.B. Rundle, New York 1962–65; copywriter, Batten, Barton, Durstine & Osborn, New York 1965, copy supervisor 1967, Vice-Pres. 1968, Assoc. Creative Dir 1970, Sr Vice-Pres. and Creative Dir 1975–77, Exec. Vice-Pres. 1977–80, Pres.

1980–82, CEO 1981–86, Chair. 1983–86; Pres. and CEO BBDO Int. New York 1984–86; Pres. and COO Omnicom Group, New York 1986–88, CEO BBDO Worldwide (subsidiary), New York 1989–2004, Chair. 1989–2006, now Chair. Emer.; Founding mem. Partnership for a Drug-Free America, currently Vice-Chair. and Exec. Creative Dir; mem. Exec. Cttee and Creative Review Cttee, Advertising Council; mem. Bd of Dirs Business for Diplomatic Action, Int. Advertising Assoc.; Trustee, Connecticut Chapter, The Nature Conservancy; consultant, Democratic Nat. Cttee. *Publications:* Funny Business: Moguls, Mobsters, Megastars and the Mad, Mad World of the Ad Game 2006. *Website:* www.allenrosenshine.com.

ROSENTHAL, Gert, MA; Guatemalan economist and diplomatist; b. 11 Sept. 1935, Amsterdam, Netherlands; s. of Ludwig Rosenthal and Florence Rosenthal (née Koenigsberger); m. Margit Uhlmann; four d.; ed American School of Guatemala, Univ. of California, Berkeley, USA, Universidad de San Carlos de Guatemala; worked in pvt. sector 1959–67; economist, Nat. Planning Secr. 1960–64, Head Econ. Devt Div. 1965, Sec.-Gen. (rank of Minister) 1969–70, 1973–74; Officer in charge of external financing, Ministry of Finance 1966–67; Asst to Sec.-Gen., Secr. of Cen. American Common Market (SIECA) 1968, Project Dir UNCTAD project to promote SIECA, Guatemala City 1972–73; Prof. of Econ. Devt and Public Finance, Universidad Rafael Landivar, Guatemala 1969–74; Dir Sub-regional Office UN ECLA, Mexico 1974–85, Deputy Exec. Sec. UN ECLA, Santiago, Chile 1985–87, Exec. Sec. (rank of Under-Sec.-Gen. of UN) 1988–97; mem. Oversight Comm. of Guatemalan Peace Accords 1998; Amb. and Perm. Rep. to UN, New York 1999–2004, 2008–14; Pres. UN ECOSOC 2003–04; Minister of Foreign Affairs 2006–08; mem. Sec.-Gen.'s High-Level Advisory Bd on Mediation, UN 2017–; Dr hc (Universidad del Valle) 1996. *Publications:* Inside the United Nations: Multilateral Diplomacy Up Close 2017; more than 120 articles on various topics related to devt in Latin America, with emphasis on Cen. America. *Address:* Calle de los Duelos #6, Antigua, Guatemala (home). *Telephone:* 832-3659 (home). *Fax:* 832-3666 (home).

ROSENTHAL, Sir Norman Leon, Kt, BA; British art curator; b. 8 Nov. 1944, Cambridge; s. of Paul Rosenthal and Kate Zucker; m. Manuela Beatriz Mena Marques 1989; two d.; ed Westminster City Grammar School, Univ. of Leicester; Librarian, Thomas Agnew & Sons 1966–68; Exhbns Officer, Brighton Museum and Art Gallery 1970–71; Exhbn Organizer, Inst. Contemporary Arts 1974–76, Exhbns Sec., RA 1977–2008; freelance curator 2008–; TV and radio broadcasts on contemporary art; mem. Opera Bd, Royal Opera House 1994–98; mem. Bd of Dirs ENO 2012–; Trustee, Thyssen Bornemisza Foundation 2002–2012 (resgnd); Hon. Fellow, RCA 1987; Cross, Order of Merit (Germany) 1991, Cavaliere Ufficiale, Order of Merit (Italy) 1992, Officier, ordre des Arts et des Lettres 2003, German British Forum Award 2003; Hon. DLitt (Southampton) 2003; German/British Forum Award 2003. *Television and radio:* undertakes many TV and radio broadcasts and frequently addresses int. confs. *Publications:* contributes numerous articles and essays to catalogues and journals throughout the world. *Leisure interest:* music, especially opera. *Address:* c/o Artuner, 25 Savile Row, London, W1S 2ER, England.

ROSENTHAL, Uri; Dutch political scientist, academic and politician; b. 19 July 1945, Montreux, Switzerland; m. Dinah Rosenthal 1973; two c.; ed Univ. of Amsterdam, Erasmus Univ., Rotterdam; Lecturer, Univ. of Amsterdam 1970–73; Lecturer, Erasmus Univ. 1973–79, Prof. of Political Science 1980–; Prof. of Public Admin, Leiden Univ. 1987–; Chair., Inst. for Safety, Security and Crisis Man., The Hague –2010; mem. Senate (People's Party for Freedom and Democracy—VVD) 1999–2010, Leader VVD Group in Senate 2005–10; Minister of Foreign Affairs 2010–12; Chair. Editorial Bd Liberaal Reveil 1998–2005; Deputy Chair. Netherlands Org. for Scientific Research 1997–2002; Consultant, Centre for Risk and Crisis Man., Nanjing Univ., People's Repub. of China; mem. bd Centre for Parl. History, Int. Inst. for Social History, Urban Regeneration Forum; mem. Social and Econ. Council, Dutch Transport Safety Bd; Officer, Order of Orange-Nassau 1985.

ROSHAL, Leonid Mikhailovich, MD, DSc; Russian paediatrician; *Executive Director, Research Institute of Emergency Children's Surgery and Traumatology;* b. 27 April 1933, Livnya, Orel Region; s. of Mikhail Filippovich Roshal and Emilia Lazarevna Roshal; m. 1st; one s.; m. 2nd Veda Zuponcic; ed Moscow Medical Inst.; paediatrician and specialist, paediatric surgeon Moscow hosp. 1957–61; jr then sr researcher, then sr research paediatric surgeon MONIKI Inst. 1961–81; Dir Emergency Surgery and Children's Trauma Dept, Moscow Pediatric Scientific Research Inst. 1981–, Exec. Dir Research Inst. of Emergency Children's Surgery and Traumatology, Moscow 2003–; Chair. Int. Task Force Cttee on Paediatric Disaster Medicine; Pres. Nat. Medical Chamber, Int. Charity Foundation (providing medical care for children in disasters and wars); founder Foundation of Children's; mem. Exec. Cttee World Asscn for Emergency and Disaster Medicine, Exec. Cttee Russian Union of Paediatrics; Pres. Int. Charitable Fund for Children in Disasters and Wars; mem. Bd of Dirs Russian Asscn of Paediatric Surgery, British Asscn of Paediatric Surgeons, Georgian Acad. of Medical Sciences; organized and carried out rescue operations and rendered medical assistance following earthquakes and wars in many countries in Europe, Asia and America; took part in negotiations with terrorists taking hostages in Moscow theatre Sept. 2002, provided medical assistance to hostages and negotiated release of some children; acted as intermediary during Beslan school siege; elected Children's Doctor of the World by Moscow Journalists Community 1995; mem. Public Chamber of Russia 2005–, Presidential Comm. on Human Rights; Order of Courage 2002; awarded title of National Hero 2002, Person of the Year (chosen by several Russian periodicals) 2002; numerous other awards. *Publications:* 7 books and more than 200 scientific articles on surgery and problems of children in catastrophes and wars. *Leisure interest:* music. *Address:* Research Institute of Emergency Children's Surgery and Traumatology, ul. Bolshaya Polyanka, 22, 119180, Moscow, Russia (office). *Telephone:* (495) 959-27-79 (office). *E-mail:* roshal@lamport.ru. *Website:* www.doctor-roshal.ru (office).

ROSHCHEVSKY, Mikhail Pavlovich; Russian physiologist; b. 5 March 1933; m.; two d.; ed Ural State Univ.; jr then sr researcher, scientific sec. Ural Research Inst. of Agric. 1958–60; Sr Researcher, Inst. of Biology Komi ASSR 1960–70; Deputy Chair. Presidium Scientific Cen. Komi ASSR 1970–83, Chair. 1983–2006; Dir Inst. of Physiology Komi Scientific Cen. Ural br. USSR Acad. of Sciences 1988–2004; Corresp. mem. USSR (now Russian) Acad. of Sciences 1987, mem.

1990; studies of ecological-physiological aspects of blood circulation, electrophysiology of heart, electrocardiology; mem. Dept of Physiology Russian Acad. of Sciences. *Publications:* books and scientific works.

RÖSLER, Philipp, MD; German physician and politician; b. 24 Feb. 1973, Khanh Hung, Ba Xuyen Prov., fmr South Viet Nam (now Soc Trang Prov., Viet Nam); adopted from a RC orphanage near Saigon by a German couple 1973; m. Wiebke Rösler; twin d.; ed Medizinische Hochschule, Hanover, Fed. Armed Forces Hosp., Hamburg; joined Bundeswehr (army) as medical officer cadet 1992; qualified as doctor 2001; mem. FDP 1992–, mem. Lower Saxony FDP Exec. Cttee 1996, Gen. Sec. Lower Saxony FDP 2000–04, Chair. 2006, Chair. FDP 2011–13; mem. Lower Saxony Landtag (prov. parl.) 2003–09, Chair. FDP Parl. Group 2003; Prov. Minister for Econs and Deputy Minister-Pres. of Lower Saxony Feb.–Oct. 2009; Fed. Minister of Health 2009–11, of Econs and Tech. 2011–13; Vice-Chancellor of Germany 2011–13; Chair. Bd of Supervisory Dirs KfW Bankengruppe 2012–. *Address:* Federal Ministry of Economics and Technology, 11019 Berlin (office); Federal Ministry of Economics and Technology, Scharnhorststr. 34–37, 10115 Berlin, Germany (office). *Telephone:* (30) 18615-9 (office). *Fax:* (30) 18615-7010 (office). *E-mail:* info@bmwi.de (office). *Website:* www.bmwi.de (office); www.philipp-roesler.de.

ROSNER, Robert, PhD; American physicist, astronomer and astrophysicist; *William Wrather Distinguished Service Professor in Astronomy and Astrophysics and Physics Director, Energy Policy Institute of Chicago, University of Chicago;* b. 26 June 1947, Garmisch-Partenkirchen, Germany; s. of Heinz Rosner and Faina Rosner; m. Marsha R. Rosner 1971; two d.; ed Brandeis Univ., Harvard Univ.; Asst Prof., later Assoc. Prof. of Astronomy, Harvard Univ. 1978–86; Prof. of Astronomy and Astrophysics, Univ. of Chicago, 1987, Chair. Dept of Astronomy and Astrophysics 1991–97, William E. Wrather Distinguished Service Prof. 1998–, Prof. of Physics 2000–, Co-Dir Energy Policy Inst. of Chicago 2010–, Prof., Harris School of Public Policy Studies 2011–; Assoc. Lab. Dir and Chief Scientist, Argonne Nat. Lab. 2002–05, Dir 2005–09; Rothschild Visiting Prof., Newton Inst. for Math. Sciences, Univ. of Cambridge, UK 2004; mem. American Acad. of Arts and Sciences 2001; Foreign mem. Norwegian Acad. of Science and Letters 2004; Fellow, American Physical Soc. 1988; Visiting Prof., Center for Int. Security and Conflict, Stanford Univ. 2009–10; Life mem. Clare Hall, Cambridge 2005–; Hon. PhD (Illinois Inst. of Tech.) 2007, (Northern Illinois Univ.) 2008; Woodrow Wilson Fellow 1969, Gordon Bell Prize (Supercomputing) 2000, Thompson Lecturer, Nat. Center for Atmospheric Research 2001, Rosseland Lecturer, Univ. of Oslo 1998, Parker Lecturer, American Astronomical Soc./Solar Physics Div. 1995. *Publications include:* more than 200 publs in scientific journals. *Leisure interests:* sailing, skiing, hiking, reading. *Address:* Eckhardt Research Center, University of Chicago, 5640 South Ellis Avenue, Chicago, IL 60637, USA (office). *Telephone:* (773) 702-0560 (office). *E-mail:* r-rosner@uchicago.edu (office).

ROSS, Christopher W. S., BA, MA; American diplomatist and UN official; b. 3 March 1943, Quito, Ecuador; one s.; ed Princeton Univ., Johns Hopkins Univ.; Editorial Asst, Middle East Journal 1965–68; teacher of Arabic, Columbia Univ. 1966, Princeton Univ. 1967; Jr Officer Trainee, US Information Agency (USIA), Washington, DC 1968–69, served in Tripoli 1969–70, Br. Public Affairs Officer and Dir American Cultural Center, Fez, Morocco 1970–73, Information Officer, Beirut 1973–76, Public Affairs Officer, Algiers 1976–79; held several positions at US Dept of State, including Deputy Chief of Mission, Embassy in Algiers 1979–81, Public Affairs Adviser to Asst Sec. for Near Eastern and S Asian Affairs 1981–82, Special Asst to Special Presidential Envoys to Lebanon and Middle East 1982–84, Dir of Regional Affairs, Bureau of Near Eastern and S Asian Affairs 1984–85, Exec. Asst to Under-Sec. for Political Affairs 1985–88, Amb. to Algeria 1988–91, to Syria 1991–98, Coordinator for Counterterrorism 1998–99, Sr Adviser to Under-Sec. of State for Public Diplomacy and Public Affairs 2001–03, Sr Adviser, Coalition Provisional Authority and Embassy in Baghdad 2004, Special Adviser (on Iraq), Bureau of Near Eastern Affairs 2004–09, Sr Adviser for Middle East and N Africa 2006–09, Exec. Dir Search for Common Ground Middle East and N Africa Program 1999–2001, Personal Envoy of UN Sec.-Gen. for Western Sahara 2009–16; Dr hc (Lewis and Clark Coll.) 2002; USIA Superior Honor Awards 1976, 1984, Presidential Meritorious Service Awards 1983, 1985, 1989, 1993, Dept of State's Superior Honor Award 1988 and Distinguished Honor Award 1997, Dept of Defense's Distinguished Public Service Medal 2005.

ROSS, Dennis B., PhD; American academic, diplomatist and fmr government official; *Counselor and William Davidson Distinguished Fellow, Washington Institute for Near East Policy;* b. 26 Nov. 1948, San Francisco, Calif.; m. Deborah Ross; one s. two d.; ed Univ. of California, Los Angeles; Deputy Dir Office of Net Assessment, US Defense Dept, Washington, DC 1982–84, 1989–92; Exec. Dir of program on Soviet Int. Behavior sponsored by Univ. of California, Berkeley and Stanford Univ. 1984–86; Dir Near East and S Asian Affairs, Nat. Security Council (during Reagan Admin); Dir Policy Planning Office, US State Dept 1988–92, Special Middle East Co-ordinator 1992–2001, helped achieve the 1995 Interim Agreement and brokered the Hebron Accord 1997; Counsellor and Ziegler Distinguished Fellow, Washington Inst. for Near East Policy 2001–08, Counsellor (part-time) 2008–09, Counselor 2011–, also William Davidson Distinguished Fellow; Special US Envoy to Middle East, US State Dept 2009; Special Asst to the Pres. and Sr Dir for Cen. Region, Nat. Security Council 2009–10; Adjunct Lecturer, Kennedy School of Govt, Harvard Univ. 2002–04; Fred and Rita Richman Distinguished Visiting Prof., Brandeis Univ. 2003, 2005; Allis-Chalmers Distinguished Prof. of Int. Affairs, Marquette Univ. 2004–05; Adjunct Prof., Georgetown Univ. School of Foreign Service 2006–07, also Adjunct Prof. of Govt, Georgetown Univ. 2007; Bartels World Affairs Fellow, Cornell Univ. 2005; Chair. Inst. for Jewish People Policy Planning, Jerusalem; has served as Foreign Affairs Analyst for Fox News Channel; Hon. DHumLitt (Amherst Coll.) 2002; Dr hc (Jewish Theological Seminary, Syracuse Univ.); UCLA Alumnus of the Year; Presidential Medal for Distinguished Fed. Civilian Service, Truman Peace Prize, Harry S. Truman Research Inst. for the Advancement of Peace, Hebrew Univ. of Jerusalem 2008. *Publications include:* The Missing Peace: The Inside Story of the Fight for Middle East Peace 2004, Statecraft: And How to Restore America's Standing in the World 2007, Myths, Illusions and Peace: Finding a New Direction for America in the Middle East (with David Makovsky) 2009; numerous articles in learned journals and newspapers. *Address:* Washington Institute for Near East Policy,

1828 L Street, NW, Suite 1050, Washington, DC 20036, USA (office). *Telephone:* (202) 452-0650 (office). *Fax:* (202) 223-5364 (office). *Website:* www.washingtoninstitute.org (office).

ROSS, Diana; American singer and actress; b. 26 March 1944, Detroit, Mich.; d. of Fred Ross and Ernestine Ross; m. 1st Robert Ellis Silberstein 1971 (divorced 1976); three d.; m. 2nd Arne Naess 1985 (divorced, died 2004); one s.; fmr lead singer, The Supremes (later Diana Ross and the Supremes), solo singer 1970–; citation from US Vice-Pres. Hubert Humphrey for efforts on behalf of Pres. Lyndon Johnson's Youth Opportunity Programme, from Mrs. Martin Luther King and Rev. Abernathy for contrib. to Southern Christian Leadership Conf., Billboard, Cash Box and Record World magazine awards as world's outstanding female singer, Grammy Award 1970, Female Entertainer of the Year, Nat. Asscn for the Advancement of Colored People 1970, Cue Award as Entertainer of the Year 1972, Golden Apple Award 1972, Gold Medal Award, Photoplay 1972, Antoinette Perry Award 1977, Golden Globe Award 1972, Kennedy Center Honor 2007, BET Lifetime Achievement Award 2007, Grammy Lifetime Achievement Award 2012, Ella Fitzgerald Award, Festival International de Jazz de Montréal 2014, Presidential Medal of Freedom 2016, American Music Award For Lifetime Achievement 2017. *Films include:* Lady Sings the Blues 1972, Mahogany 1975, The Wiz 1978. *Television includes:* Out of Darkness (film) 1993, Double Platinum, (film) 1999. *Recordings include:* albums: Everything Is Everything 1970, I'm Still Waiting 1971, Touch Me In The Morning 1973, Diana 1980, Why Do Fools Fall in Love? 1981, Eaten Alive 1984, Chain Reaction 1986, Workin' Overtime 1989, Surrender 1989, Ain't No Mountain High Enough 1989, The Forces Behind the Power 1991, The Remixes 1994, Take me Higher 1995, Gift of Love 1996, The Real Thing 1998, Every Day is a New Day 1999, Voice of Love 2000, Gift of Love 2000, Blue 2006, I Love You 2006. *Publications include:* Secrets of a Sparrow (autobiography) 1993.

ROSS, Rt Hon. Lord Donald MacArthur, PC, MA, LLB, FRSE; British judge (retd); b. 29 March 1927, Dundee, Scotland; s. of John Ross and Jessie MacArthur Thomson; m. Dorothy M. Annand 1958 (died 2004); two d.; ed High School of Dundee, Univ. of Edinburgh; nat. service with Black Watch 1947–49; TA rank of Capt. 1949–58; Advocate 1952; QC (Scotland) 1964; Vice-Dean, Faculty of Advocates 1967–73, Dean 1973–76; Sheriff Prin. of Ayr and Bute 1972–73; Senator, Coll. of Justice, Scotland and Lord of Session 1977–97; Lord Justice Clerk of Scotland and Pres. of Second Div. of the Court of Session 1985–97; Chair. Judicial Studies Cttee for Scotland 1997–2001; mem. Parole Bd for Scotland 1997–2002; Deputy Chair. Boundary Comm. for Scotland 1977–85; mem. Scottish Cttee of Council on Tribunals 1970–76, Cttee on Privacy 1970; mem. Court of Heriot Watt Univ. 1978–90 (Chair. 1984–90); mem. Council Royal Soc. of Edin. 1997–99, Vice-Pres. 1999–2002; Lord High Commr to Gen. Ass. of Church of Scotland 1990, 1991; Hon. LLD (Edin.) 1987, (Dundee) 1991, (Abertay, Dundee) 1994, (Aberdeen) 1998; Hon. DUniv (Heriot Watt) 1988; Royal Soc. of Edinburgh Bicentenary Medal 2004. *Publication:* contrib. to Stair Memorial Encyclopaedia of Scots Law. *Leisure interests:* gardening, walking, travelling. *Address:* 7/1 Tipperlinn Road, Edinburgh, EH10 5ET, Scotland. *Telephone:* (131) 447-6771. *Fax:* (131) 446-3813. *E-mail:* rosd33@aol.com.

ROSS, James Hood, OBE, BA; British business executive; b. 13 Sept. 1938, London; s. of Capt. T. D. Ross RN and Lettice Ferrier Hood; m. Sara B. V. Purcell 1964; one s. two d.; ed Sherborne School, Jesus Coll., Oxford and Manchester Business School; British Petroleum Co. PLC 1959–92, Gen. Man. BP Zaïre, Burundi and Rwanda, Gen. Man. BP Tanker Co., Gen. Man. Stolt-Nielsen (USA), Gen. Man. Corp. Planning BP, Chief Exec. BP Oil Int., Chair. and Chief Exec. BP America; Chief Exec. Cable & Wireless PLC 1992–95; Chair. Littlewoods Org. 1996–2002, Nat. Grid Group PLC (later) 1999–2002, Co-Chair. Nat. Grid Transco (after Nat. Grid merger with Lattice) 2002–04; Chair. Leadership Foundation for Higher Education 2003–10, Bd of Trustees, Liverpool School of Tropical Medicine 2007–, Liverpool Assocs In Tropical Health Ltd 2009–; mem. Bd of Dirs (non-exec.) McGraw Hill Inc. 1988–2009, Schneider Electric 1996, Datacard Inc. 1997–, Prudential PLC 2004–11; Trustee, The Cleveland Orchestra 1988–. *Leisure interests:* music, gardening, sailing. *Address:* Liverpool Associates in Tropical Health, Liverpool School of Tropical Medicine, Pembroke Place, Liverpool, L3 5QA, England.

ROSS, Wilbur Louis, AB, MBA; American business executive and fmr banker; *US Secretary of Commerce;* b. 28 Nov. 1937, Weehawken, New Jersey; s. of Wilbur Louis Ross and Agnes Ross (née O'Neill); m. 1st Judith Nodine 1961 (divorced 1995), two d.; m. 2nd Betsy McCaughey 1995 (divorced 2000); m. 3rd Hilary Geary 2004; ed Yale Univ., Harvard Business School; served in US Army 1961–63; Assoc., Wood, Struthers and Winthrop, New York 1963–64; Pres., Faulkner, Dawkins and Sullivan Securities Corpn, New York 1964–76; Sr Man. Dir, Rothschild, Inc. 1976–2000; CEO, News Communications Inc. 1996–98; Chair. and Chief Investment Officer, Rothschild Recovery Fund 1997–2000; f. W.L. Ross & Co. LLC 1997, served as Chair. and CEO, co. acquired by Invesco 2006, Chair. and Chief Strategist –2017; US Sec. of Commerce 2017–; apptd mem. Bd of Dirs Casella Waste Systems Inc. 1999–2003, Int. Steel Group, Inc. 2002–04, Ohizumi Manufacturing Co., Japan 2003–, Burlington Industries 2003–, Marquis Who's Who Inc. 2004–06, Mittal Steel Co. 2004–06, Int. Coal Group 2005–11, Int. Textile Group 2005, Arcelor Mittal Steel Co. 2005–, Montpelier Re Holdings, Ltd 2006–10, Wagon, PLC, 2006–08, BankUnited Inc. 2009, The Greenbrier Cos Inc. 2009–13, Sun Bancorp Inc. 2010, Talmer Bancorp, Inc. 2010, Air Lease Corpn 2010–13, Ocluen Finance Corpn 2013; Chair. Nat. Acad. of Design 1985–89, American Art Forum, Smithsonian Inst. 1987; Vice Chair. Brooklyn Museum 1981–95; Treas., American Fed. of Arts 1993–95, The New Museum 1993–95; Order of the Rising Sun, Gold, and Silver Star (Japan) 2015; Yale School of Man. Legend in Leadership Award 2005. *Address:* Department of Commerce, 1401 Constitution Avenue, NW, Washington, DC 20230, USA (office). *Telephone:* (202) 482-2000 (office). *E-mail:* thesec@doc.gov (office). *Website:* www.commerce.gov (office).

ROSSANT, Janet, CC, PhD, FRS, FRSC; British/Canadian geneticist; *President and Scientific Director, Gairdner Foundation;* b. 13 July 1950, Chatham, Kent, England, UK; d. of Leslie Rossant and Doris Rossant; m. Alex Bain 1977; one s.; ed St Hugh's Coll., Oxford, Darwin Coll., Cambridge; Research Fellow in Zoology, Univ. of Oxford 1975–77; Asst Prof. of Biological Sciences, Brock Univ., Canada 1977–82, Assoc. Prof. 1982–85; Assoc. Prof. of Molecular and Medical Genetics, Univ. of Toronto 1985–88, Prof. 1988–, Univ. Prof. 2001–, Sr Investigator,

Programme in Devt and Foetal Health, Samuel Lunenfeld Research Inst. 1985–2005; apptd Sr Scientist in the Developmental and Stem Cell Biology Program and Chief of Research, Hospital for Sick Children, Toronto 2005, now Sr Scientist Emer.; Pres. and Scientific Dir Gairdner Foundation 2016–; Chair. Science Leadership Council, Canadian Stem Cell Foundation; Pres. Soc. for Developmental Biology; mem. American and Canadian Socs for Cell Biology; Foreign Assoc., NAS; Gibb's Prize for Zoology, Oxford 1972, Beit Memorial Fellowship 1975, E.W.R. Steacie Memorial Fellowship 1983, Howard Hughes Int. Scholar 1991, MRC Distinguished Scientist 1996, McLaughlin Medal (Royal Soc. of Canada) 1998, NCIC/Eli Lilly Robert L. Noble Prize 2000, Killam Prize for Health Sciences 2004, Michael Smith Prize for Health Research 2005, Ross G. Harrison Medal (lifetime achievement award), Int. Soc. of Developmental Biologists 2013, ISTT Prize, Int. Soc. for Transgenic Technologies 2014, Gairdner Wightman Award 2015. *Publications include:* Experimental Approaches to Mammalian Embryonic Development (co-author) 1986, Mouse Development (co-author) 2001; over 200 articles in scientific journals. *Leisure interests:* running, cooking, theatre. *Address:* Gairdner Foundation, MaRS Centre, South Tower, 101 College Street, Suite 407, Toronto, ON M5G 1L7, Canada (office). *Telephone:* (416) 596-9996 (office). *E-mail:* thegairdner@gairdner.org (office). *Website:* www.gairdner.org (office).

ROSSEINSKY, Matthew (Matt) Jonathan, BSc, DPhil, FRS, FRSC; British chemist and academic; *Professor of Inorganic Chemistry, University of Liverpool;* m.; three c.; ed St John's Coll. and Merton Coll., Oxford; spent two years at Bell Labs, NJ, USA 1990–92; Univ. Lecturer, Dept of Chem., Univ. of Oxford 1992–99; Prof. of Inorganic Chem., Univ. of Liverpool 1999–; Royal Soc. Research Prof. 2013–; Wolfson Merit Award, Royal Soc. 2002, RSC Tilden Lectureship 2005, Distinguished Summer Lecturer in Inorganic Chem., Northwestern Univ., USA 2006, inaugural de Gennes Prize, RSC 2009, C.N.R. Rao Award, Chemical Research Soc. of India 2010, Hughes Medal, Royal Soc. 2011, Davy Medal, Royal Soc. 2017. *Publications:* numerous papers in professional journals. *Address:* Department of Chemistry, University of Liverpool, Crown Street, Liverpool, L69 7ZD, England (office). *Telephone:* (151) 794-3499 (office). *Fax:* (151) 794-3587 (office). *E-mail:* m.j.rosseinsky@liv.ac.uk (office). *Website:* www.liv.ac.uk/chemistry/research/rosseinsky-group (office).

ROSSEL, Eduard Ergartovich, CandTechSc; Russian politician; b. 8 Oct. 1937, Bor, Gorki region; m.; one d.; ed Sverdlovsk Ore Inst.; master construction site, head of construction trust Sreduralstroi; supervised construction of Krasnouralsk superphosphate factory, Nevyansk cement factory, Nizhny Tagil metallurgy plant; head Sverdlovsk regional exec. cttee, then Gov. Sverdlovsk Region 1991–93, tried to proclaim Ural Repub., discharged by Pres. Yeltsin, re-elected Head of Admin. and Gov. Sverdlovsk Region 1995–2009; mem. Russian Council of Fed. 1993–94, 1995–2001; Chair. Sverdlovsk regional Duma 1994–95; Founder and Chair. Org. Preobrazhenie Otechestva; Pres. Asscn for Econ. Co-operation of Ural Region 1995; mem. Bd Union of Russian Govs 1996; mem. Int. Acad. of Regional Devt and Co-operation; mem. United Russia (UR) (Yedinaya Rossiya); Order 'Decoration of Honour' 1975, 1980, Order for Achievement to Fatherland Fourth Degree 1996, Third Degree 2000 and numerous other decorations; Lenin Centenary Anniversary Medal 'For Valiant Labour' 1970, Honoured Constructor of Russian Soviet Federal Socialist Repub. 1983. *Website:* www.rossel.ru.

ROSSELLI FRIERI, Elbio Oscar, MA, PhD; Uruguayan diplomatist; *Permanent Representative to United Nations;* b. 30 March 1946; m.; three c.; ed Fletcher School of Law and Diplomacy, Tufts Univ., Univ. of Uruguay, Montevideo; Dir-Gen., MERCOSUR Affairs and Nat. Coordinator 1998–2003, Int. Econ. Affairs for Southern Common Market and Integration May–Dec. 2008; Perm. Rep. to Latin American Integration Asscn 2000–03; Amb. to Belgium and Luxembourg 2003–06, also Head of Mission to European Communities 2003–06; Perm. Rep. to UN 2006–08, 2015–; Dir-Gen. Political Affairs 2008–10, Adviser to Minister of Foreign Affairs Aug.–Oct. 2010; Amb. to Canada 2010–15. *Address:* Permanent Mission of Uruguay, 866 United Nations Plaza, Suite 322, New York, NY 10017, USA (office). *Telephone:* (212) 752-8240 (office). *Fax:* (212) 593-0935 (office). *E-mail:* uruguay@un.int (office). *Website:* www.un.int/uruguay (office).

ROSSELLINI, Isabella; American actress and model; b. 18 June 1952, Rome, Italy; d. of Roberto Rossellini and Ingrid Bergman; m. 1st Martin Scorsese (q.v.) 1979 (divorced 1982); m. 2nd Jonathan Wiedemann (divorced); one d.; ed Acad. of Fashion and Costume, Rome and New School for Social Research, New York; worked briefly as costume designer for father's films; went to New York 1972; worked as journalist for Italian TV; cover-girl for Vogue 1980; contract to model Lancôme cosmetics 1982–95; Vice-Pres. Lancaster Cosmetics GPs Marketing Dept 1995–. *Films include:* A Matter of Time 1976, White Nights 1985, Blue Velvet 1986, Tough Guys Don't Dance 1987, Siesta 1987, Zelly and Me, Cousins 1989, Wild at Heart 1990, The Siege of Venice 1991, Death Becomes Her, The Pickle, The Innocent, Fearless 1994, Wyatt Earp 1994, Immortal Beloved 1994, The Innocent 1995, The Funeral 1996, Big Night 1996, Left Luggage 1998, The Imposters, The Real Blonde 1998, Rodger Dodger 2002, Empire 2002, The Tulse Luper Suitcases, Part 1: The Moab Story 2003, The Saddest Music in the World 2003, The Tulse Luper Suitcases, Part 2: Vaux to the Sea 2004, King of the Corner 2004, Heights 2005, La Fiesta del chivo 2005, The Architect 2006, Infamous 2006, The Accidental Husband 2008, Two Lovers 2008, Flat Love 2009, My Dog Tulip 2009, The Solitude of Prime Numbers 2010, Keyhole 2011, The Dandelions 2012, The Zigzag Kid 2012, Enemy 2013, Joy 2015. *Television includes:* Ivory Hunters 1990, Lies of the Twins 1991, The Gift 1994, Crime of the Century 1996, The Odyssey 1997, Don Quixote 2000, Napoleon 2002, Monte Walsh 2003, Legend of Earthsea 2004, Green Porno 2008, The Phantom 2009, Shut-Eye 2016–17. *Publications:* In the Name of the Father, the Daughter and the Holy Spirits: Remembering Roberto Rossellini 2006. *Address:* c/o United Talent Agency, 9560 Wilshire Blvd., Suite 500, Beverly Hills, CA 90212, USA.

ROSSELLÓ, Hon. Pedro, BS, MD, MPH; American surgeon and politician; b. 5 April 1944, San Juan, Puerto Rico; m. Irma Margarita Nevares; three s.; ed Notre Dame Univ., Yale Univ. School of Medical Sciences, Univ. of Puerto Rico; entered pvt. practice as pediatric surgeon and began teaching at Univ. of Puerto Rico 1976; Dir of Health, City of San Juan 1985–87; cand. elections to Congress 1988; Chair. New Progressive Party 1991–99; Gov. of Puerto Rico 1993–2001, unsuccessful cand. for Gov. 2004; mem. Senate 2005–09; Pres. Council of State Govts 1998; fmr

Chair. Democratic Govs Asscn, Southern Govs Asscn 1998–2001, Southern Int. Trade Council 1998–99, Southern Tech. Council 1998–99, Southern Growth Policies Bd 1999–2000; mem. Advisory Council Welfare to Work Partnership; fmr mem. Democratic Nat. Cttee, Nat. Advisory Bd of Initiative and Referendum Inst.; fmr mem. Bd of Dirs US-Spain Council and other bodies; Hon. LLD (Notre Dame) 1995, (Mass.) 1995; Pres.'s Award, US Hispanic Chamber of Commerce 1996, Pres.'s Award, LULAC 1998, Rolex Achievement Award 1999, Woodrow Wilson Public Service Award 2005. *Achievements include:* five times Puerto Rico men's singles tennis champion.

ROSSELLÓ NEVARES, Ricardo (Ricky) Antonio, PhD; Puerto Rican neuroscientist and politician; *Governor of Puerto Rico;* b. 7 March 1979, San Juan; s. of Pedro Rosselló (fmr Gov. of Puerto Rico) and Maga Nevares; m. Beatriz Isabel Areizaga Garcia; one d.; ed Massachusetts Inst. of Tech., Univ. of Michigan; worked as stem cell researcher, Duke Univ.; Co-founder, Beijing Prosperous Biopharm (drug devt co.), Beijing 2010; fmr political commentator, El Vocero (daily newspaper); f. Boricua ¡Ahora Es! (political advocacy group) 2012; Gov. of Puerto Rico 2017–; mem. Partido Nuevo Progresista. *Achievements include:* fmr Puerto Rico jr tennis champion; represented Puerto Rico at Int. Mathematical Olympiad 1997. *Publications:* La Obra de Rosselló 2004, Un Mejor Puerto Rico Es Posible 2012. *Address:* Office of the Governor, La Fortaleza, POB 9020082, San Juan, PR 00902-0082, Puerto Rico (office). *Telephone:* (787) 721-7000 (office). *Fax:* (787) 724-1472 (office). *E-mail:* mensajes@fortaleza.pr.gov (office). *Website:* www .fortaleza.gobierno.pr (office).

ROSSI, Agustín Oscar; Argentine civil engineer and politician; b. 18 Oct. 1959, Vera, Santa Fe Prov.; m. María Raquel Pezzelato; four c.; ed Universidad Nacional de Rosario; joined Peronist Youth movt 1980, participated in Peronist Renewal group; mem. Rosario city council 1987–91, 2002–05, Pres. 1991, 2004–05; Pvt. practice as engineer in 1990s; mem. Cámara de Diputados (lower house of parl.) for Santa Fe Prov. (Frente para la Victoria—FPV) 2005–13, also Pres. FPV parl. group; unsuccessful cand. for governorship of Santa Fe 2007; Minister of Defence 2013–15. *Address:* Partido Justicialista (PJ), Domingo Matheu 128/130, C1082ABD Buenos Aires, Argentina (office). *Telephone:* (11) 4954-2450 (office). *E-mail:* contacto@pj.org.ar (office). *Website:* www.pj.org.ar (office); www .agustinrossi.com.ar.

ROSSI, Derrick, BSc, MSc, PhD; Canadian biologist and academic; *Assistant Professor of Stem Cell and Regenerative Biology, Pathology Department, Harvard Medical School and Harvard University;* b. 1965, Toronto; ed Univ. of Toronto, Univ. of Helsinki; Post-doctoral Fellow, Stanford Univ. 2003–07; Asst Prof. of Stem Cell and Regenerative Biology, Pathology Dept, Harvard Univ. 2007–, Faculty mem. Immune Disease Inst., Harvard Medical School 2007–; Researcher Children's Hosp., Boston; Pathways to Independence (PI) Award, NIH, Robertson Investigator Award, New York Stem Cell Foundation. *Address:* Harvard University Immune Disease Institute, Warren Alpert 253, 200 Longwood Avenue, Boston, MA 02115, USA (office). *Telephone:* (617) 713-8900 (office). *Fax:* (617) 713-8910 (office). *E-mail:* rossi@idi.harvard.edu (office). *Website:* www.hsci.harvard.edu/ people/derrick-j-rossi-phd (office).

ROSSI, José Lucien André, DenD; French politician and lawyer; b. 18 June 1944, Ajaccio, Corsica; s. of Pierre Rossi and Emilie Leca; m. Denise Ferri 1968; two d.; ed Ecoles Sainte-Lucie and Castelvecchio, Lycée Fesch, Ajaccio, Faculté de Droit and Inst. d'Etudes Politiques, Paris; Asst Faculté de Droit, Paris 1969–73; served in pvt. office of Minister of Labour 1972, Minister of Educ. 1972–74; Press Officer to Minister of Health 1974–75; Parl. Relations Officer to Minister of Labour 1975–78, to Minister of Educ. 1978; pvt. office of Pres. of Senate 1981–82; mem. Conseil Général, Corsica 1973, Pres. 1985–98; Conseiller Régional, Corsica 1975–85; Deputy Mayor of Ajaccio 1983–90, 1995; Pres. Corsica Tourism and Leisure Agency 1983–84; Pres. Regional Information Centre 1979–85; Deputy to Nat. Ass. 1988–94; Sec.-Gen. Parti Républicain 1989–91; Mayor of Grosseto-Prugna 1990–95; Vice-Pres. Union pour la Démocratie Française (UDF) group in Nat. Ass. 1993–94; Minister of Industry, Posts and Telecommunications and Foreign Trade 1994–95; Deputy to Nat. Ass. 1995–2002; Deputy Sec.-Gen. UDF 1996–97; Titular Judge Higher Court of Justice 1997–; Pres. Démocratie Liberale Group, Nat. Ass. 1998–2000, Assemblée de Corse 1998–2004, Vice-Pres. Démocratie Libérale 2000–02; fmr Pres. Agence de Développement Economique de la Corse. *Publication:* Les Maires de grandes villes en France 1972.

ROSSI, Valentino; Italian motorcycle racer; b. 16 Feb. 1979, Urbino; s. of Graziano Rossi and Stefania Rossi; began in go-karts, then minimoto before progressing to motorcycles; won first World Championship Grand Prix at Brno, Czech Repub. 1996; by 2004 68 Grand Prix victories; World Champion 125cc class 1997, 250cc class 1999, 500cc class 2001, MotoGP class 2002, 2003, 2004, 2005, 2014; currently races for Yamaha team. *Leisure interests:* football, skiing. *E-mail:* info@yamahamotogp.com. *Website:* www.valentinorossi.com.

ROSSIER, William; Swiss economist and international organization official; b. 25 Oct. 1942; ed Univ. of Lausanne; joined Foreign Econ. Service 1970; Head of Secr., Conf. on Security and Co-operation in Europe, Geneva 1972–73; Deputy Head Div. for Gen. Foreign Econ. Questions, Berne 1973–76; Counsellor, Mission to the EC, Brussels 1976–80; with Fed. Office for External Econ. Affairs 1981–88, apptd Head Div. in charge of Relations with Countries of Eastern Europe and the People's Repub. of China 1981, later Head Div. in Charge of Relations with Western Europe; fmrly involved in negotiations with GATT, OECD, UNCTAD; Amb. to Int. Econ. Orgs in Geneva (GATT/WTO, UNCTAD, UN-ECE, EFTA); Chair. EFTA 2000–06; fmr Chair. ECE, UNCTAD Trade and Devt Bd; Chair. WTO Gen. Council 1996; Perm. Rep. to EFTA, Sec.-Gen. 2000–06. *Address:* c/o Federal Department of Foreign Affairs, Bundeshaus West, 3003 Berne 7, Switzerland (office). *Telephone:* (31) 322-21-11 (office). *Fax:* (31) 323-40-01 (office). *E-mail:* info@eda.admin.ch (office). *Website:* www.eda.admin.ch (office).

ROSSINI MIÑÁN, Renzo Guillermo, BEcons, MSc (Econ); Peruvian central banker; *General Manager, Banco Central de Reserva del Perú;* ed Univ. of the Pacific, London School of Econs, UK, courses with CAF, FMI, BID, The British Council, JICA and Studienzentrum Gerzensee-Suiza, Univ. of Piura; joined Banco Cen. de Reserva del Perú 1982, worked in Dept of Analysis and Financial Planning, Dept of Global Analysis and Dept of Conjunctural Research 1982–91, Head of Dept of External Sector Analysis 1988–90, Deputy Man. of Research and Global Analysis 1990–91, Chief Economist, Banco Cen. de Reserva del Perú 1991–2003, Gen. Man. 2003–; Prof. of Political Economy, Univ. of the Pacific 1997–; Dir Fondo Consolidado de Reservas Previsionales; mem. American Econ. Asscn, Latin American and Caribbean Econ. Asscn, Comité Editorial de la Revista Economía Chilena; Assoc. Asociación Civil Pro Universidad del Pacífico. *Publications include:* El Sesgo Anti-Exportador de la Política Comercial en el Perú (with Adrian Armas and Luis Palacios) 1990, Liberalización del Comercio Exterior en el Perú 1991, Estabilización y Dolarización en el Perú: Comentarios 1993; numerous book chapters and articles in professional journals. *Address:* Banco Central de Reserva del Perú, Jirón Antonio Miró Quesada 441–445, Lima 1, Peru (office). *Telephone:* (1) 6132000 (office). *E-mail:* renzo.rossini@bcrp.gob.pe (office). *Website:* www.bcrp.gob.pe (office).

ROSSINOT, André, DenM; French politician and physician; *President, La métropole du Grand Nancy;* b. 22 May 1939, Briey, Meurthe-et-Moselle; s. of Lucien Rossinot and Jeanne Fondeur; m. 3rd Françoise Cordelier 1985; one s. one d.; three c. from previous marriages; ed Lycée Poincaré and Faculty of Medicine, Nancy; early career as ear, nose and throat specialist in pvt. practice; Town Councillor, Nancy 1969–71; Mayor of Nancy 1983–2014; Vice-Pres. Greater Nancy Urban Council 1996–2001, Pres. 2001–; Deputy to Nat. Ass. (UDF) 1978–86, 1988–93, 1995–97, Vice-Pres. 1988–89; Pres. Parti Radical 1983–88, 1994–97, Hon. Pres. 1997–, Co-Pres. 2005–07, Nat. Vice-Pres. UDF 1983–90, 1994–; mem. Political Bureau Union pour la France 1990–, UDF 1991–2000, Exec. Cttee Union pour un mouvement populaire 2003–; Minister for Relations with Parl. 1986–88, of Civil Service 1993–95; Pres. Conf. Permanente des caisses de crédit municipal 1987–93; Pres. Nouveau Contrat Social 1992, TGV 1994–99, Fed. nat. des agences d'urbanisme 1995–2010, Inst. nat. du génie urbain 1996–98, Asscn Seine-Moselle-Rhône 1999; Founder and Pres. Agence des villes 1998; Vice-Pres. Asscn des Eco Maires 1990; Sec-Gen. l'Association des maires des grandes villes de France (AMGVF) 2001–; Pres. La métropole du Grand Nancy 2014–; Chair. comité d'orientation du Certu 2007–; Chevalier, Légion d'honneur, Commdr Order of Merit (Germany). *Publication:* Stanislas, Le Roi philosophe 1999. *Leisure interests:* walking, tennis, fishing.

ROSSWALL, (Per) Thomas; Swedish scientist, ecologist and academic; b. 20 Dec. 1941, Stockholm; s. of Axel Rosswall and Britta Rosswall; m. Mats Edlund; Science Sec. Swedish Council fo Planning and Co-ordination of Research 1975–77; Dir SCOPE/UNEP Int. Nitrogen Unit, Royal Swedish Acad. of Sciences (RSAS) 1977–80, Exec. Dir Geosphere-Biosphere Programme: A Study of Global Change 1987–94; Asst Prof. in Microbiology and Assoc. Prof. in Soil Ecology, Univ. of Agric. Sciences, Uppsala 1980–84, Rector 1994–2000, Prof. of Water and Environmental Studies 2000–09; Prof., Dept of Water and Environmental Studies, Linköping Univ. 1984–92; Dir Int. START Secr., Washington, DC 1992–93; Prof. of Water and Environmental Studies, Univ. of Stockholm 1992–94; Sec.-Gen. SCOPE 1986–88; Chair. Int. Cttee on Microbial Ecology 1980–83; Dir Int. Foundation for Science 2000–01; Exec. Dir Int. Council for Science 2002–09; Chair. CGIAR Programme on Climate Change, Agric. and Food Security 2009–14, Mistra Council for Evidence-based Environmental Man., RSAS 2011–15; Mistra Urban Futures, Chalmers Univ. of Tech. 2014–, Remote Sensing Cttee, Swedish Nat. Space Bd 2015–, Research Council, Swedish Int. Devt Co-operation Agency 2016–; Vice-Chair. Swedish InfrasTructure for Ecosystem Science (SITES) 2014–; mem. Bd for Polar Research, Ministry of Educ. 1993–96, Scientific Council Foundation for Strategic Environmental Research 1994–97, Cttee on Global Biogeochemical Cycles, Natural Science Research Council 1994–99, Environmental Advisory Council Ministry of the Environment 1995–2001, Bd of Inst. for Ecological Sustainability 1999–2001, Bd of Foundation for Int. Co-operation in Research and Higher Educ. 2000–04, Bd Beijer Inst. of Ecological Econs 2001–06, Council of Int. Cell Research Org. 1987–91, European Environmental Research Org. 1990–2004, Exec. Cttee Int. Soc. for Tropical Ecology 1995–2005, Int. Scientific Advisory Bd UNESCO 1996–2004, Bd Millennium Ecosystem Assessment 2003–05, Bd and Exec. Cttee Stockholm Resilience Centre 2008–13, Prize and Awards Cttee, Royal Swedish Acad. of Agric. and Forestry (RSAAF) 2012–, Cttee on a Green Economy, RSAAF 2013; Ed.-in-Chief Ecological Bulletins 1975–85; mem. or fmr mem. Editorial Bd Advances in Microbial Ecology, Biogeochemistry, Global Biogeochemical Cycles, Soil Biology and Biochemistry, Biology and Fertility of Soils, FEMS Microbial Ecology Journal, Landscape Ecology, MIRCEN Journal of Applied Microbiology and Biotechnology, European Journal of Soil Biology, Revista Estudos Avançados (USP), Brazil; Fellow, Academia Europaea 1989, RSAS 1989, RSAAF 1995, Swedish Royal Patriotic Soc. 1996, Royal Acad. of Arts and Sciences, Uppsala 1999, World Acad. of Arts and Science 2006; Assoc. Fellow, Third World Acad. of Sciences (renamed TWAS, The World Acad. of Sciences in 2012) 2002; Royal Order of Merit 12th Grade with Serafim Ribbon (Sweden) 2000; Second Prof. John Roger Porter Memorial Lecturer, Univ. of Bombay, India 1981, First Industrial Memorial Lecturer, Haarlem, the Netherlands 1989, Fourth Hendrik De Waard Lecturer, Univ. of Groningen, the Netherlands 1990, Award of Excellence in Ecosystem Science, Natural Resources Ecology Lab., Colorado State Univ. 2002, Carl Gustaf Bernhard Lecturer, RSAS 2003, ISI Highly Cited Researcher 2003, Beijer Fellow, The Beijer Inst. of Ecological Econs 2007, Medal of Finnish Acad. of Science and Letters 2008. *Publications:* more than 10 edited books; more than 100 papers in scientific journals. *Address:* 57 chemin du Belvédère, 06530 Le Tignet, France. *Telephone:* 6-30-48-77-98 (mobile). *E-mail:* thomas.rosswall@gmail.org.

ROST, Andrea; Hungarian singer (soprano); b. 15 June 1962, Budapest; d. of Ferenc Rost and Erzsébet Privoda; ed Ferenc Liszt Acad. of Music, Budapest, studied with Zsolt Bende; operatic debut as Juliette in Gounod's Romeo et Juliette, Budapest 1989; solo artist at Wiener Staatsoper 1991; La Scala debut as Gilda in Rigoletto 1994; debut, Metropolitan Opera, New York as Adina in L'Elisir d'amore 1996; took part in Superconcert with José Carreras and Plácido Domingo, Budapest 1996; appeared as Elisabeth in Donizetti's opera, London 1997; debut, Tokyo Opera, as Violetta 1998; took part in concert in memory of Lehár with José Carreras and Plácido Domingo, Bad Ischl, Austria 1998; has also appeared at Staatsoper, Vienna, Salzburg Festival, Opéra Bastille, Paris, Royal Opera House, Covent Garden and Chicago Opera; 2002 roles included debut in Lucia di Lammermoor, Munich, Wigmore Hall recital, London, Valencia recital; debut in La Traviata, Deutsche Oper, Berlin 2003, also Desdemona, Otello, Tokyo; Lucia di Lammermoor premier, Covent Garden, London 2003; Gilda, Rigoletto, Metropolitan Opera, New York 2004; numerous roles with Hungarian State Opera including Desdemona 2012, 2017, Mimi 2012, 2017, Konstanze 2013, Nedda 2014, 2016, Cio Cio San 2015, Girl (in Szekely Fono) 2016–17; First Prize, Helsinki Competition 1989, Bartók Béla – Pásztory Ditta Award, Ferenc Liszt Artistic Merit of Honour 1997, Nat. Artistic Merit of Honour 1999, Medal Obersovszky, Prima Primissima Award 2003, Kossuth Prize 2004, Béla Bartók Memorial Award 2006, Mihály Székely Plaque 2011. *Recordings include:* Mozart – Le nozze di Figaro (Susanna) 1994, Mahler – Symphony No. 8 1995, Verdi – Rigoletto (Gilda) 1995, Mendelssohn – Elias (die Witwe/ein Engel) 1996, Andrea Rost – Le delizie dell'amor 1997, Gaetano Donizetti – Lucia Di Lammermoor (Lucia) 1998, A Tribute to Operetta 1999, Amore II 2000, Escape Through Opera 2001, Erkel: Bánk bán (Melinda) 2003, ...che cosa è amor... (Mozart Arias) 2004, Hungarian Songs – Bartók, Kodály, Ligeti 2008, Colours 2013, Opera Tales 2014, Andersen: The Little Mermaid 2014. *DVD videos include:* Johann Strauss Gala 2000, Wolfgang Amadeus Mozart: Don Giovanni (Zerlina) 2000, A Verdi Gala from Berlin 2002, Erkel: Bánk bán (Melinda) (opera film) 2003. *Address:* c/o Vera Meczner, Gradus Artist Management, 1061 Budapest, Dalszínház utca 10, Hungary (office); Nefelejes u. 27, 2040 Budaörs, Hungary (home). *E-mail:* vera.meczner@gradusartist.com (office); info@andrearost.com (home). *Website:* www.gradusartist.com (office); www.andrearost.com (home). *Fax:* (23) 416-583.

ROST, Yuri Mikhailovich; Russian journalist and photographer; b. 1 Feb. 1939, Kiev, Ukraine; s. of Arkadyevich Rost and Georgiyevna Rost; m. (divorced); columnist Komsomolskaya Pravda (newspaper) 1966–79; reviewer Literaturnaya Gazeta (newspaper) 1979–94; author TV programme Stables of Rost 1994–97; reviewer Obshchaya Gazeta (newspaper) 1993–; currently serves on Editorial Bd of Novaya Gazeta; mem. Russian PEN Centre; Prizes of Acad. of Free Press 1998, 1999, Tsarskoye Selo Artistic Prize 1999, Gilyarovsky Medal 1990, State Prize of Russia 2000, Triumph Prize 2000. *Publications include:* People 1980, 10 Short Stories about Leningrad 1976, Everest 1983, My View 1988, Armenian Tragedy 1990, Group Portrait on the Background of the Century (Nat. Book of the Year Award, XXI Moscow Int. Book Fair 2008) 2007; Birds (jtly); numerous essays. *Leisure interest:* collecting smoking pipes. *Address:* Makarenko str. 1/19, Apt. 21, 103062 Moscow, Russia (home).

ROSTOWSKI, Jacek, (Jan Anthony Vincent-Rostowski), BSc, MSc, MA; Polish/British economist, politician and academic; b. (Jan Rostowski), 30 April 1951, London, England; s. of Roman Rostowski; m.; two c.; ed Westminster School, London, Univ. Coll., London, School of Slavonic and East European Studies, Univ. of London, London School of Econs; born into Polish immigrant family in London, spent much of his childhood in Kenya, Mauritius and the Seychelles where his father was posted, grew up and educated in UK; Lecturer, Kingston Polytechnic –1988; Lecturer, School of Slavonic and East European Studies 1988–95; Adviser to Deputy Prime Minister and Minister of Finance of Poland 1989–91; worked at Centre for Econ. Performance, LSE 1992–95; Prof. of Economy, Cen. European Univ., Budapest 1995–2007, Dean of Faculty of Economy 1995–2000, 2005–06; Chair. Macro-econ. Policy Cttee, Ministry of Finance 1997–2001; Adviser to Pres. Nat. Bank of Poland 2002–04, to Bd of Bank PEKAO SA 2004–; Minister of Finance 2007–13; mem. Sejm (Parl.) (Platforma Obywatelska) 2011–15, Deputy Prime Minister 25 Feb.–27 Nov. 2013; mem. Econ. Council to the Prime Minister 2014–15; currently mem. European Shadow Financial Regulatory Committee; fmr Adviser to Govt of Russian Fed. on macro-econ. policy; Co-founder Centre for Social and Econ. Analysis (CASE), Warsaw, mem. Supervisory Council 1991–2007, Trustee, CASE Foundation; mem. Supervisory Bd Polish Privatization Soc.-Kleinwort Benson, Polski Bank Rozwoju SA 1994–95; named European Finance Minister of the Year by The Banker magazine 2009, cited by the Financial Times as the third best Finance Minister in Europe 2012. *Publications include:* author or ed. of several books, book chapters and numerous articles in professional journals on an enlarged EU, monetary policy, exchange rate policy and transformations of post-communist economies. *Website:* www.esfrc.eu.

ROTELLA, Stephen J., BEcons, MBA; American banking executive; *President, StoneCastle Partners, LLC;* m.; one d.; ed State Univ. of New York, Stony Brook and Albany; held various positions with JP Morgan Chase 1987–2005, including COO Chase Home Finance 1998–2001, mem. Exec. Cttee and CEO 2001–04, fmr Chair. Housing Advisory Bd, mem. Bd of Dirs –2005; mem. Exec. Cttee, Pres. and COO Washington Mutual, Inc. 2004–08, Pres. Retail Banking 2008; currently Pres. StoneCastle Partners, LLC, CEO StoneCastle Cash Man., LLC; Chair. Lift Communities 2015–; mem. Bd of Dirs Mortgage Bankers Asscn, St Barnabas Medical Center, NJ; mem. Exec. Cttee Financial Services Roundtable's Housing Policy Council; mem. Advisory Bd SUNY Stony Brook School of Business. *Address:* StoneCastle Partners, LLC, 152 W 57th Street, 35th Floor, New York, NY 10019, USA (office). *Telephone:* (212) 354-6500 (office). *Fax:* (212) 354-6565 (office). *Website:* www.stonecastlepartners.com (office).

ROTFELD, Adam Daniel, PhD; Polish academic, researcher and fmr politician; *Professor, University of Warsaw;* b. 4 March 1938, Przemyślany; one d.; ed Diplomatic-Consular Faculty, Main School of Foreign Service and Faculty of Journalism, Univ. of Warsaw, Faculty of Law and Admin, Jagiellonian Univ.; Researcher in Int. Law and Int. Relations, Polish Inst. of Int. Affairs 1961–89; Fellow, Inst. of East-West Security Studies, New York, USA 1984–85; Assoc. Prof. and Prof. in Humanities, Univ. of Warsaw 2001, now Prof.; Leader, Project on Building a Co-operative Security System in and for Europe, Stockholm Int. Peace Research Inst. (SIPRI) 1989, Dir SIPRI 1991–2002, apptd Personal Rep. OSCE Chairman-in-Office to settle conflicts in Trans-Dniester region of Moldova 1992; Ed. SIPRI Yearbook: Armaments, Disarmament and International Security 1991–; mem. Nat. Security Council 2001–05; apptd Under-Sec. of State, Ministry of Foreign Affairs 2001, Sec. of State 2003–04; Minister of Foreign Affairs Jan.–Oct. 2005; mem. UN Sec. Gen.'s Advisory Bd on Disarmament Matters 2006–11 (Chair. 2008); Co-Chair. Polish-Russian Group on Difficult Matters 2008–15; Commr of Euro-Atlantic Security Initiative Comm. 2010–14; mem. Royal Swedish Acad. of War Studies 1996, Governing Bd of Hamburg Inst. for Peace Research and Security Policy at Univ. of Hamburg 1995–2007, Advisory Bd of Geneva Centre for Democratic Control of Armed Forces 2001–11, NATO Group of Experts for the New Strategic Concept 2009–10, Scientific Council of Inst. of Political Studies, Polish Acad. of Sciences 2006–15; mem. Bd Bronislaw Geremek Center; mem. Panel of Eminent Persons on European Security as a Common Project 2014–15; mem. Bd European Leadership Network 2011–; mem. Aspen Ministers Forum; Commandoria of the Polar Star 2001 (Sweden), Great Cross of Germany 2005, Great Cross of Polonia Restituta 2010 and many others. *Publications:* has published and edited more than 20 books, including Where is the World Headed? 2008, White Spots – Black Spots. Difficult Matters in Polish–Russian Relations 1918–2008 (co-ed. with Anatoly W. Torkunov) 2010, In Shadow 2012, White Spots–Black Spots: Difficult Matters in Polish-Russian Relations 1918–2008 2015; more than 400 articles on legal and political aspects of relations between Germany and Cen. and Eastern Europe after World War II, human rights, cooperative security, CSBMs, multilateral security structures, and political and legal aspects of security system in Europe. *Address:* Polish Institute of International Affairs, 1A Warecka Street, PO Box 1010, 00-950 Warsaw, Poland (office). *Telephone:* (22) 5568033 (office); (22) 6201706 (home). *Fax:* (22) 5568099 (office). *E-mail:* rotfeld@pism.pl (office). *Website:* www.pism.pl (office).

ROTH, Alvin Elliot, BS, MS, PhD; American economist and academic; *Professor Emeritus, Harvard Business School;* b. 18 Dec. 1951; m.; two c.; ed Columbia Univ., Stanford Univ.; Asst Prof., Dept of Business Admin and Dept of Econs, Univ. of Illinois 1974–77, Assoc. Prof. 1977–79, Prof. 1979–81, Beckman Assoc., Center for Advanced Study 1981–82; A.W. Mellon Prof. of Econs, Univ. of Pittsburgh 1982–98, also Fellow, Center for Philosophy of Science 1983 Prof. of Business Admin, Graduate School of Business 1985; George Gund Prof. of Econs and Business Admin, Dept of Econs, Harvard Business School 1998–2012, Prof. Emer. 2013–; Craig and Susan McCaw Prof. of Economics, Stanford Univ. 2012–, also Prof., Man. Science and Eng, Sr Fellow, Economic Policy Research; Visiting Prof., Dept of Econs, Univ. of Tel-Aviv, Israel 1995; Bogen Visiting Prof., Dept of Econs, Hebrew Univ. of Jerusalem, Israel 1995; Mendes-France Visiting Prof. of Econs, Technion, Haifa, Israel 1986; Research Assoc., Nat. Bureau of Econ. Research 1998–; Founder, New England Program for Kidney Exchange; Pres. elect, Economic Science Asscn 2009–11, Pres. (also mem. Bd of Dirs) 2011–13, Past Pres. 2013–15; Pres. 2017, Past Pres. 2018–, American Economic Asscn; mem. NAS 2013–; mem. Strategic Planning Team, OPTN/UNOS Kidney Paired Donation Pilot Program 2011–, Mathematics of Operations Research 2012–, Inst. for Operations Research and Man. Science; mem. Advisory Bd Nat. Living Donor Assistance Center (NLDAC) 2016–; Corresponding mem., Real Academia de Ciencias Económicas y Financieras, Barcelona 2017; Fellow, Econometric Soc. 1983, American Acad. of Arts and Sciences 1998, AAAS 2012, Soc. for the Advancement of Econ. Theory (SAET) 2013, Game Theory Soc. 2017 (also mem. of Journal Advisory Bd 2000–); Charter Fellow, Soc. for Economic Measurement (SEM) 2014; Hon. Ed., Journal of Behavioural and Experimental Economics 2017–; Dr hc (Technion-Israel Inst. of Tech.) 2013, (Univ. of Amsterdam) 2014, (Lund Univ.) 2014; Hon. DHumLitt (Univ. of Pittsburgh) 2014, DrIur (Exeter Univ.) 2015; "College Educator of the Year" teaching award 1979, Lanchester Prize, Operations Research Soc. of America 1991, Chancellor's Distinguished Research Award, Univ. of Pittsburgh 1992, T.W. Schultz Prize, Dept of Econs, Univ. of Chicago 2006, Wyss Award for Excellence in Mentoring 2008, Charles M. Williams Award for Teaching, Harvard Business 2010–11, Excellence in Mentoring Doctoral Students Award, Harvard Business School, 2011, Sveriges Riksbank Prize in Econ. Sciences in Memory of Alfred Nobel (Nobel Prize) (jtly with Lloyd S. Shapley) 2012, John van Neumann Award 2016. *Publications include:* Game-Theoretic Models of Bargaining 1985, Laboratory Experimentation in Economics: Six Points of View 1987, The Shapley Value: Essays in Honor of Lloyd S. Shapley (Ed.) 1988, Two-Sided Matching: A Study in Game-Theoretic Modeling and Analysis (co-author) 1990, The Handbook of Experimental Economics (co-Ed.) 1995, Game Theory in the Tradition of Bob Wilson (co-Ed.) 2001, Who Gets What and Why 2015. *Address:* Harvard Business School, 441 Baker Library, Boston, MA 02163, USA (office). *E-mail:* al_roth@harvard.edu (office). *Website:* www.hbs.edu; kuznets.fas.harvard.edu/~aroth/alroth.html (office).

ROTH, Jean-Pierre, DEcon; Swiss fmr central banker; b. 28 April 1946, Saxon, Canton of Valais; m. Floriane Tognetti; three c.; ed Univ. of Geneva, Institut Universitaire des Hautes Etudes Internationales, Geneva and MIT, USA; fmr Lecturer, Univ. of Geneva and Institut Universitaire de Hautes Etudes Internationales; Scientific Collaborator, Swiss Nat. Bank (Schweizerische Nationalbank/Banque nationale suisse) 1979, mem. Bd of Dirs, Vice-Chair. and Head of Dept II (capital market, banknotes, business relations with the Confed., admin of gold holdings), Berne 1996, Chair. of Governing Bd and Head of Dept I (Int. Affairs Div., Econ. Div., Legal and Admin. Econ.) 2006–09; Chair. BIS, Basel 2006–09; Gov. IMF for Switzerland, Washington, DC; Switzerland's Rep. in Financial Stability Forum 2007–09; Dir Nestlé, Swatch Group 2010–. *Address:* The Swatch Group Ltd, Seevorstadt 6, P.O. Box 2501 Biel/Bienne Switzerland (office). *Telephone:* 323436811 (office). *Fax:* 323436911 (office). *Website:* www.swatchgroup.com.

ROTH, Joe; American film executive and producer; b. 13 June 1948; m. Donna Roth; three c.; fmrly production asst for various commercials and films; fmrly lighting dir Pitched Players, also producer; co-f. Morgan Creek Productions 1987–89; Chair. Twentieth Century Fox Film Corpn 1989–92; f. Caravan Pictures 1992–94; Chair. Walt Disney Motion Pictures Group 1994–97, Walt Disney Studios, Burbank 1997–2000; f. Revolution Studios 2000–07; Producer, Sony Pictures Entertainment, Inc. 2007–; mem. Bd of Dirs Pixar Studios 2000–06; Majority Owner, Seattle Sounders FC (Major League Soccer team) 2007–; numerous awards, including Variety Clubs Man of the Year Award 1991, Humanitarian Award, Nat. Conf. for Community and Justice 1996, American Museum of Moving Image Award 1997, Dorothy and Sherrill C. Corwin Human Relations Award, American Jewish Cttee 2004. *Films produced include:* Tunnelvision, Cracking Up, Americathon, Our Winning Season, The Final Terror, The Stone Boy, Where the River Runs Black, Bachelor Party, Off Beat, Streets of Gold (also Dir), Revenge of the Nerds (also Dir), Young Guns, Dead Ringers, Skin Deep, Major League, Renegades, Coupe de Ville (also Dir), Enemies: A Love Story; films for Caravan Pictures include Walt Disney's The Three Musketeers, Angie, Angels in the Outfield, I Love Trouble, A Low Down Dirty Shame, Houseguest, The Jerky Boys, Heavyweights, Tall Tale, While You Were Sleeping 1995, Before and After 1996, Tears of the Sun 2003, Daddy Day Care 2003, Hollywood Homicide 2003, Mona Lisa Smile 2003, The Forgotten 2004, An Unfinished Life 2005, The Great Debaters 2007, Demons 2007, Hellboy II: The Golden Army 2008, Alice in Wonderland 2010, Knight and Day 2010, Snow White and the Huntsman 2012, Oz the Great and Powerful 2013, Sabotage, Heaven Is for Real, Million Dollar Arm,

Maleficent 2014, In the Heart of the Sea 2015. *Films directed include:* Christmas with the Kranks 2004, Freedomland 2006. *Address:* c/o Sony Pictures Entertainment Inc., 10202 West Washington Blvd, Culver City, CA 90232, USA. *Telephone:* (310) 244-7737. *Website:* www.sonypictures.com; www.mlsinseattle.com.

ROTH, Tim; British actor; b. 14 May 1961, Dulwich, London; m. Nikki Butler; two s.; ed Dick Sheppard Comprehensive School, Brixton and Camberwell Coll. of Art; began acting career with fringe groups including Glasgow Citizens Theatre, The Oval House and the Royal Court; appeared on London stage in Metamorphosis. *Films include:* The Hit 1984, A World Apart 1988, The Cook The Thief His Wife and Her Lover 1989, Vincent & Theo 1990, Rosencrantz and Guildenstern are Dead 1990, Jumpin' at the Boneyard 1992, Reservoir Dogs 1992, Bodies Rest and Motion, Pulp Fiction 1994, Little Odessa 1994, Captives 1994, Rob Roy 1995, Four Rooms 1995, Everyone Says I Love You 1996, Hoodlum 1997, Deceiver 1997, Animals 1997, The Legend of the Pianist on the Ocean 1998, The War Zone (dir) 1999, Vatel 2000, Lucky Numbers 2000, Planet of the Apes 2001, Invincible 2001, The Musketeer 2001, The Beautiful Country 2004, Silver City 2004, Don't Come Knockin' 2005, Dark Water 2005, Jump Shot 2005, Youth Without Youth 2007, Funny Games 2008, The Incredible Hulk 2008, King Conqueror 2009, Pete Smalls Is Dead 2010, Arbitrage 2012, The Liability 2012, Möbius 2013, Grace of Monaco 2014, United Passions 2014, October Gale 2014, Selma 2014, 600 Millas 2015, Chronic 2015, Mr. Right 2015, The Hateful Eight 2015. *Television:* Made in Britain 1982, Skellig 2009, Lie to Me (series) 2009–11, Klondike (mini-series) 2014, Rillington Place 2016, Twin Peaks 2017, Tin Star 2017–. *Address:* c/o Ilene Feldman Agency, 8730 West Sunset Boulevard, Suite 490, Los Angeles, CA 90069, USA (office).

ROTH, Urs Philipp, DrIur; Swiss lawyer; b. 1947; Deputy Sec.-Gen. Liberal Democratic Party of the Canton of Zurich 1972–75; Judicial Clerk, District Court, Uster/Zurich 1975–76; Legal Counsel, UBS 1976–78, Head of Legal Services, branch offices German part of Switzerland, Zurich 1978–86, Gen. Counsel USA, New York 1978, Headquarter and German part of Switzerland, Zurich 1988–92, Gen. Counsel, Europe 1991–92, worked as Group Gen. Counsel 1992–2001; CEO Swiss Bankers Asscn and Del. of Bd of Dirs 2001–10; Chair. Exec. Cttee Int. Financial Centre Switzerland (LAIF); Chair. Financial Market Authority Liechtenstein 2012–19 (retd); mem. Foundation Bd Swiss Finance Inst.; teaches at Univ. of Zurich. *Publications:* contrib. of numerous papers on banking and stock exchange law.

ROTHBLATT, Martine, PhD, JD, MBA; American laywer and business executive; *Chairman and CEO, United Therapeutics;* b. (Martin Rothblatt), 1954; four c.; ed Univ. of Southern Calif., Queen Mary, Univ. of London; began career with Covington & Burlington, Washington, DC –1983; f. PanAmSat, CD Radio, WorldSpace 1980s; co-f. Sirius Satellite Radio; opened The Law Offices of Martine Rothblatt specializing in satellite communications law; Pres. Geostar 1985–89; opened a second law firm 1989; Pnr Makon & Patusky (law firm), Washington, DC 1990–; endowed the PPH (Primary Pulmonary Hypertension) Cure Foundation to find a treatment for her daughter Jenesis' condition 1994–; f. United Therapeutics (pharmaceutical co.); Founding mem. and Co-Chair. Bioethics Sub cttee, Int. Bar Asscn 1993–; Pres. William Harvey Medical Research Foundation. *Publications include:* The Apartheid of Sex: A Manifesto on the Freedom of Gender 1995, Unzipped Genes: Taking Charge of Baby-Making in the New Millennium 1997. *Address:* United Therapeutics Corporate Headquarters, 1110 Spring Street, Silver Spring, MD 20910, USA (office). *Telephone:* (301) 608-9292 (office). *Fax:* (301) 608-9291 (office). *Website:* www.unither.com (office).

ROTHENBERG, Alan I., BA, JD; American lawyer and business executive; *Chairman and CEO, 1st Century Bank, N.A.;* b. 10 April 1939, Detroit, Mich.; m. Georgina Rothenberg; three c.; ed Univ. of Michigan; admitted to Calif. Bar 1964; Assoc., O'Melveny & Myers (law firm), LA 1963–66; Founder and Man. Pnr, Manatt Phelps Rothenberg & Phillips (law firm), LA 1968–90, Pnr, Latham & Watkins, LA 1990–2000 (retd); Instructor in Sports Law, Univ. of Southern Calif. 1969, 1976, 1984, Whittier Coll. of Law 1980, 1984; Pres. and Gen. Counsel LA Lakers (professional basketball team) and LA Kings (professional ice hockey team) 1967–79, LA Clippers (professional basketball team) 1982–89; Pres. US Soccer Fed., Chicago 1990–98, now Hon. Pres. and Life Mem.; Founder and fmr Chair. Major League Soccer 1993, now mem. Bd of Dirs; Chair. Goal Media 1993–; Organizer and Bd Mem. First Los Angeles Bank 1973–84; Founder, Chair. and CEO First Century Bank NA, LA 2004–; Chair. Premier Partnerships (sports and entertainment marketing firm); mem. Bd of Dirs Arden Realty Inc., Zenith National Corpn, California Pizza Kitchen Inc. 2006–; Full Time Neutral, ADR Services (dispute resolution service) 2001–; mem. Soccer Comm. 1984 Olympic Games; mem. Equal Educ. Opportunities Comm. State of Calif. Bd of Educ. 1972–75; mem. Bd of Govs Nat. Basketball Asscn 1971–79; Pres. Constitutional Rights Foundation 1987–90; Chair. Pres. CEO 1994 World Cup Organizing Cttee 1990–94; fmr Vice-Pres. Confed. of North, Central America and Caribbean Asscn Football (CONCACAF); inducted into US Nat. Soccer Hall of Fame 2007. *Address:* 1st Century Bank, NA, 1875 Century Park East, Suite 1400, Los Angeles, CA 90067, USA (office). *Telephone:* (310) 270-9500 (home). *E-mail:* jdinapoli@1stcenturybank.com (home). *Website:* www.1stcenturybank.com (office).

ROTHERMERE, 4th Viscount, cr. 1919, of Hemsted; **Jonathan Harold Esmond Vere Harmsworth,** BA; British newspaper publisher; *Chairman, Daily Mail and General Trust PLC;* b. 3 Dec. 1967, London, England; s. of 3rd Viscount Rothermere and Patricia Evelyn Beverley Brooks; m. Claudia Clemence 1993; two s. three d.; ed Gordonstoun School, Scotland, Kent School, Conn., USA, Duke Univ., USA; joined Mirror Group 1993; joined Northcliffe Newspapers Group Ltd 1995; Deputy Man. Dir, then Man. Dir Evening Standard 1997; Chair. Assoc. Newspapers Ltd 1998–; Chair. Assoc. New Media 1998, Daily Mail and Gen. Trust PLC 1998–; Pres. Newspaper Press Fund 1999–. *Leisure interests:* family, tennis, golf, polo, skiing, riding. *Address:* Daily Mail and General Trust PLC, Room 602, Northcliffe House, 2 Derry Street, London, W8 5TT, England (office). *Telephone:* (20) 7938-6613. *Fax:* (20) 7937-0043. *E-mail:* chairman@chairman.dmgt.com (office). *Website:* www.dmgt.com (office).

ROTHMAN, James Edward, PhD; American biochemist/biophysicist and academic; *Professor of Chemistry, Professor and Chairman of Cell Biology and Fergus F. Wallace Professor of Biomedical Sciences, Yale University;* b. 3 Nov. 1950, Haverhill, Mass; m.; one s. one d.; ed Yale Univ. and Harvard Medical School; post-doctoral work at MIT; Asst Prof., Dept of Biochemistry, Stanford Univ. 1978–81, Assoc. Prof. 1981–84, Prof. 1984–88; E. R. Squibb Prof. of Molecular Biology, Princeton Univ. 1988-91; Chairman, Cellular Biochemistry and Biophysics Program, Sloan-Kettering Inst., New York 1991–2003, Paul A. Marks Chair, Memorial Sloan-Kettering Cancer Center, Chair. Cellular Biochemistry and Biophysics Program, Rockefeller Research Lab. 1991–2004, Vice-Chair. Sloan-Kettering Inst. 1994–2003; Prof., Dept Physiology and Cellular Biophysics, Columbia Univ. 2004–05, Clyde '56 and Helen Wu Prof. of Chemical Biology 2005–08, Dir Chemical Biology Center 2004–08, Dir Columbia Genome Center 2005–08, mem. Columbia Cancer Center 2004–08; Prof. of Chem., Prof. and Chair. of Cell Biology and Fergus F. Wallace Prof. of Biomedical Sciences, Chair., Dept of Cell Biology, Yale Univ. 2008–; Dir Nanobiology Inst.; fmr Chief Science Advisor, GE Healthcare; mem. Bd of Sr Eds, Journal of Clinical Investigation 2002–; Assoc. Ed., Annual Review of Biochemistry 2003–; mem. NAS, Inst. of Medicine 1995; Fellow, American Acad. of Arts and Sciences 1994, European Molecular Biology Asscn; Hon. mem. Japanese Biochemical Soc. 2005; Dr hc (Regensburg) 1995, (Geneva) 1997; Eli Lilly Award for Fundamental Research in Biological Chem. 1986, Passano Young Scientist Award 1986, Alexander Von Humboldt Award 1989, Heinrich Wieland Prize 1990, Rosenstiel Award in Biomedical Sciences (with R. Schekman) 1994, V.D. Mattia Award 1994, Fritz Lipmann Award 1995, Gairdner Foundation Int. Award 1996, King Faisal Int. Prize in Science 1996, Felix Hoppe-Seyler Lecturer 1996, Harden Medal 1997, NAS Lounsbery Award 1997, Feodor Lynen Award (with G. Blobel and G. Schatz) 1997, Jacobæus Prize 1999, Dr H.P. Heineken Prize for Biochemistry 2000, Otto-Warburg Medal 2001, Louisa Gross Horwitz Prize (with R. Schekman) 2002, Albert Lasker Basic Medical Research Award (with R. Schekman) 2002, Nobel Prize in Medicine (with Randy W. Schekman and Thomas C. Sudhof) 2013. *Publications:* more than 200 articles in scientific journals. *Address:* Rothman Laboratory, Sterling Hall of Medicine, C-207 or C-434 (lab), PO Box 208002, New Haven, CT 06520-8002, USA (office). *Telephone:* (203) 737-5293 (office). *Fax:* (203) 737-3585 (office). *E-mail:* james.rothman@yale.edu (office). *Website:* www.chem.yale.edu/faculty/rothman.html (office); medicine.yale.edu/lab/rothman/index.aspx (office).

ROTHSCHILD, Baron David René James de; French banker; *Chairman, N.M. Rothschild & Sons Ltd;* b. 15 Dec. 1942, New York City, USA; s. of Baron Guy de Rothschild and Baroness Alix Schey de Koromla; m. Princess Olimpia Anna Aldobrandini 1974; four c.; ed Lycée Carnot, Paris and Inst. d'Etudes Politiques, Paris; Dir Société Le Nickel 1970–73; Dir-Gen. Cie du Nord 1973–78; Chair. Man. Bd Banque Rothschild 1978–82; Pres.-Dir-Gen. Paris-Orléans Man. 1982–84, Paris-Orléans Banque 1984–86; Chair. Rothschild & Cie Banque 1986–, Rothschild NA Inc. 1986–, Rothschild Canada 1990–; Chair. Man. Bd Saint-Honoré-Matignon (investment co.) 1986–94; Pres.-Dir-Gen. Francarep; Pres. Financière Viticole SA, Rothschild Europe; Vice-Pres. Incolder 1990; Deputy Chair. N.M. Rothschild & Sons Ltd, London 1992–2003, Chair. 2003–, Chair. N.M. Rothschild Corporate Finance 1996–; mem. Bd of Dirs De Beers, Casino, La Compagnie Financière Saint-Honoré, Compagnie Financière Martin Maurel; Pres. Fondation Rothschild, Entente Cordiale Scholarship Trust, Fondation pour la Mémoire de la Shoah; Chair. Governing Bd World Jewish Congress 2013–. *Leisure interests:* golf, skiing, tennis. *Address:* N.M. Rothschild & Sons Ltd, New Court, St Swithin's Lane, London, EC4P 4DU, England (office); 6 rue de Tournon, 75006 Paris, France (home). *Telephone:* (20) 7280-5000 (office). *Fax:* (20) 7929-1643 (office). *Website:* www.rothschild.com (office).

ROTHSCHILD, Sir Evelyn de, Kt; British fmr banker; b. 29 Aug. 1931, London; s. of Anthony Gustav de Rothschild; m. 1st Victoria Schott 1972 (divorced 2000); two s. one d.; m. 2nd Lynn Forester 2000; ed Harrow, Trinity Coll., Cambridge; Chair. N.M. Rothschild & Sons Ltd 1976–2004, Co-founder E.L. Rothschild Holding 2003; Princess Royal Trust for Carers; Chair. Economist Newspaper 1972–89, United Racecourses Ltd 1977–94, British Merchant Banking and Securities Houses Asscn (fmrly Accepting Houses Cttee) 1985–89; fmr Trustee Shakespeare Globe Trust; fmr mem. Council for Royal Acad. of Dramatic Art. *Leisure interests:* art, racing. *Address:* N.M. Rothschild & Sons Ltd, New Court, St Swithin's Lane, London, EC4P 4DU, England (office). *Telephone:* (20) 7280-5302 (office). *Fax:* (20) 7220-7108 (office). *Website:* www.rothschild.com (office).

ROTHSCHILD, 4th Baron, cr. 1885; **(Nathaniel Charles) Jacob Rothschild,** OM, GBE, BA; British banker and business executive; *Chairman, RIT Capital Partners plc;* b. 29 April 1936; eldest s. of Nathaniel Mayer Victor Rothschild, 3rd Baron Rothschild GBE, GM, FRS and Barbara Hutchinson, Baroness Rothschild; succeeded his father 1990; m. Serena Mary Dunn 1961; one s. three d.; ed Eton Coll. and Christ Church, Oxford; Chair. St James's Place Capital PLC (fmrly J. Rothschild Holdings) 1971–96, RIT Capital Partners plc 1980–, Five Arrows Ltd 1980–; Deputy Chair. BSkyB Group plc 2003–; Chair. Bd of Trustees, Nat. Gallery 1985–91, Bd of Trustees Nat. Heritage Memorial Fund 1992–98 (administering Heritage Lottery Fund 1995–98), Yad Hanadiv Foundation; Pres. Inst. of Jewish Affairs 1992–; mem. Council, RCA 1986–92 (Sr Fellow 1992); co-f. Butrint Foundation to record and conserve the archaeological site of Butrint in Albania 1993; Trustee Open Russia Foundation 2001–; Hon. Fellow, City of Jerusalem 1992; Hon. FBA 1998; Hon. FRIBA 1998; Hon. FRAM 2002; Hon. Fellow, King's Coll. London 2002; Commdr, Order of Henry the Navigator (Portugal) 1985; Hon. PhD (Hebrew Univ of Jerusalem) 1992; Hon. DLitt (Newcastle) 1998, (Warwick) 2003; Hon. LLD (Exeter) 1998; Hon. DUniv (Keele) 2000; Hon. DCL (Oxon.) 2002; Hon. DSc (Econs) (London) 2004; Weizmann Award for Humanities and Sciences 1997. *Address:* The Pavilion, Eythrope, Aylesbury, Bucks., HP18 0HS, England (home). *Telephone:* (1296) 653235 (office). *E-mail:* fsinclair@ritcap.co.uk (office).

ROTHWELL, Dame Nancy, DBE, PhD, DSc, FRS, FMedSci, FRSB, FRSA; British neuroscientist, academic and university administrator; *President, Vice-Chancellor and Professor of Psychology, University of Manchester;* b. 1955, Tarleton, nr Preston, Lancs., England; ed Penwortham Girls' Grammar School, Queen Elizabeth Coll. and King's Coll., Univ. of London; Prof. of Physiology, Univ. of Manchester 1994–98, Chair. Div. of Neuroscience 1998–2000, MRC Research Prof. 1998–, Deputy Pres. and Deputy Vice-Chancellor 2007–10, Pres. and Vice-Chancellor 2010–; fmr mem. MRC Council, Biotechnology and Biological Sciences Research Council, Research Chair in Physiology 1998, Chair. MRC Neuroscience Bd; mem. Council Acad. of Medical Sciences; Chair. Biosciences Fed. Animal

Science group, Research Defence Soc., Wellcome Trust Public Engagement Strategy Cttee; fmr Pres. British Neuroscience Asscn 2000, Biosciences Fed.; columnist, Times Higher Educ. Supplement; currently Vice-Pres. and Council mem. Royal Soc., Chair. Royal Soc. Educ. Comm.; Dir (non-exec.) Astrazeneca; Trustee, Cancer Research UK, the Campaign for Medical Progress, NESTA 2002– (mem. Fellowship Cttee); DL; Fellow, Royal Soc. of Biology; Hon. FRCP; Hon. Fellow, British Pharmacological Soc.; Royal Soc. Research Fellowship 1984, Royal Inst. Christmas Lecturer 1998. *Television:* several TV appearances, including Superhuman. *Publications:* more than 300 research publs. *Address:* Office of the President and Vice-Chancellor, John Owens Building, University of Manchester, Oxford Road, Manchester, M13 9PL, England (office). *Telephone:* (161) 306-6010 (office). *E-mail:* president@manchester.ac.uk (office). *Website:* www.manchester.ac.uk/aboutus/governance (office); www.manchester.ac.uk/research/Nancy.rothwell (office).

ROTICH, Henry K., BA, MA, MPA; Kenyan economist and politician; *Secretary for the National Treasury;* b. 1969, Kerio Valley, Rift Valley Prov.; s. of Kimatui Rotich and Pauline Rotich; m.; two s.; ed Univ. of Nairobi, Harvard Univ. Kennedy School of Govt, USA; began career as economist with Central Bank of Kenya 1996, Asst Dir 2004–06; economist with IMF, Nairobi 2001–04; joined Ministry of Finance 2006, Head of Macroeconomics at Treasury 2006–13, Sec. for the Nat. Treasury (Minister of Finance) 2013–; mem. Bd of Dirs Insurance Regulatory Bd, Industrial Devt Bank, Communication Comm. of Kenya, Kenya Nat. Bureau of Statistics. *Address:* National Treasury, Treasury Bldg, Harambee Avenue, POB 30007, Nairobi, Kenya (office). *Telephone:* (20) 228411 (office). *Website:* www.treasury.go.ke (office).

ROTTERMUND, Andrzej; Polish curator and art historian; b. 11 May 1941, Warsaw; s. of Julian Rottermund and Zofia Lenart; m. Maria Reklewska 1963; one d.; ed Warsaw Univ.; Prof. Inst. of Art, Polish Acad. of Sciences, Warsaw 1990; Dept Dir Nat. Museum, Warsaw 1975–83, The Royal Castle, Warsaw 1987–90 (Dir 1991–2015); Deputy Minister of Culture and Arts 1991; mem. Polish Acad. of Sciences, Polish Art Historians' Asscn 1987–91, Polish ICOM Cttee 1990–96; organized exhbns in Poland and abroad including Treasures of a Polish King, Dulwich Picture Gallery London 1992, Land of the Winged Horsemen: Art in Poland 1572–1764, USA 1999–2000, Thesauri Poloniae, Austria 2002, Treasures of Poland, Japan 2010; Ordre de la Couronne (Belgium) 2002, Officier, Légion d'honneur 2002, Commdr's Cross of Merit (Germany) 2003, Golden Gloria Artis 2009, Great Cross, Order of Polonia Restituta 2011, Commdr's Cross of Order of Art and Literature 2015. *Publications:* 130 books, articles and essays including Katalog rysunków architektonicznych ze zbiorów Muzeum Narodowego w Warszawie (The Catalogue of Architectural Drawings of the Nat. Museum in Warsaw) 1970, Klasycyzm w Polsce (Neoclassicism in Poland) 1984, Zamek Królewski – funkcje i treści rezydencji monarszej wieku Oświecenia (The Royal Castle in the Age of the Enlightenment – the Functions and Symbolic Meaning of the Monarch's Residence) 1988, J.N.L. Durand a polska architektura I połowy XIX wieku (J.N.L. Durand and the Polish Architecture of the First Half of the 19th Century) 1990, Warsaw 2000, The Royal Castle in Warsaw 2003. *Leisure interests:* music, cinema. *Address:* 00-277 Warsaw, The Royal Castle, pl. Zamkowy 4, Poland (office). *Telephone:* (22) 6350808 (office). *Fax:* (22) 6357260 (office). *E-mail:* a.rottermund@zamek-krolewski.pl (office). *Website:* www.zamek-krolewski.art.pl (office).

RÖTTGEN, Norbert, DrIur; German lawyer and politician; b. 2 July 1965, Meckenheim; m.; two s. one d.; ed Univ. of Bonn; mem. CDU 1982–, Chair. CDU Junge Union (youth org.), N Rhine-Westphalia 1992–96, 2009–, Vice-Chair. CDU 2009–; practiced as lawyer at regional court, Cologne 1993–99, at higher regional court 1999–; mem. Bundestag (Parl.) for Rhein-Sieg-Kreis II constituency 1994–, legal policy spokesman for CDU/CSU parl. group 2002–05, Chief Parl. Sec. (chief whip) 2005–09, Chair. Foreign Relations Cttee 2014–; Fed. Minister of Environment, Nature Conservation and Nuclear Safety 2009–12; Chair. Christian Lawyers Asscn 2001–09. *Address:* Bundestag, Platz der Republik 1, 11011 Berlin, Germany (office). *Telephone:* (30) 22771081 (office). *Fax:* (30) 22776981 (office). *E-mail:* norbert.roettgen@bundestag.de (office). *Website:* www.bundestag.de (office); www.norbert-roettgen.de.

ROUCO VARELA, HE Cardinal Antonio María, LicenDer, DCL; Spanish ecclesiastic; *Archbishop Emeritus of Madrid;* b. 20 Aug. 1936, Villalba; s. of Vicente Rouco and María Eugenia Varela; ordained priest of Mondoñedo-Ferrol 1959; taught at Mondoñedo Seminary, Lugo 1964–66, Univ. of Munich 1966–69, Univ. Pontificia de Salamanca 1969–76 (Vice-Rector 1972–76); Titular Bishop of Gergis 1976; Auxiliary Bishop of Santiago de Compostela 1976–84, Archbishop of Santiago de Compostela 1984–94, of Madrid 1994–14, Archbishop Emer. of Madrid 2014–; cr. Cardinal (Cardinal-Priest of San Lorenzo in Damaso) 1998; participated in Papal Conclave 2005, 2013; Pres. Spanish Bishops Conf. 1999–2005, 2008–14; elected Pres. Bishops' Comm. for Seminaries and Univs 1990; Rep. mem. Bishops' Comm. of Teaching and of Catechesis 1981–89, Perm. Comm. of the Spanish Episcopal Conf. 1984, Congregation for Catholic Education 2013–, Royal Acad. of Doctors of Spain (also Prof. of Canon Law), Congregation of Bishops –2013, Council of Cardinals for the Study of Organizational and Econ. Affairs of the Holy See, Supreme Court of the Apostolic Signatura, Pontifical Council for Culture, Congregation; Gran. Canciller San Dámaso Faculty of Theology; Dr hc (Universidad Catolica San Antonio) 2016. *Publications:* Staat und Kirche im Spanien des XVI Jahrhunderts 1965, Sacramento e diritto: antinomia nella Chiesa (with E. Corecco) 1972. *Leisure interests:* music, reading. *Address:* Arzobispado de Madrid, C/ Bailen 8, 28071 Madrid, Spain (office); Conferencia Episcopal Española, Calle Añastro 1, 28033 Madrid, Spain (office). *Telephone:* (91) 4546100 (office); (91) 3439600 (office). *Fax:* (91) 5427906 (office); (91) 3439602 (office). *E-mail:* infomadrid@planalfa.es (home); conferenciaepiscopal@planalfa.es (office). *Website:* www.archimadrid.es (office); www.conferenciaepiscopal.es (office).

ROUHANI, Hassan, DJur, PhD, MPhil; Iranian cleric, lawyer, government official and head of state; *President;* b. (Hassan Feridon), 12 Nov. 1948, Sorkheh; m.; one s. three d.; ed Univ. of Tehran, Semnan Seminary, Qom Seminary, Glasgow Caledonian Univ., UK; mem. Majlis (Parl.) 1980–2000, Deputy Speaker 1992–2000, Chair. Defence Cttee, Foreign Policy Cttee; mem. Supreme Defence Council 1982–88; Commdr Iran Air Defence Force 1986–91, as Deputy to Second-in-Command of Iranian Jt Chiefs of Staff 1988–89; Nat. Security Adviser to President 1989–97; mem. and rep. of Ayatollah Khamenei, Supreme Leader of Iran on Supreme Nat. Security Council 1989–, Sec. 1989–2005; mem. Expediency Council 1991–; Dir Centre for Strategic Research 1992–; Chief Nuclear Negotiator 2003–05; mem. Ass. of Experts 1999–; Pres. of Iran 2013–. *Publications include:* Islamic Revolution, the Roots and Challenges 1999, Rohani's Memories (Vol. 1) 2008, Islamic Political Thought (Vols 1–3) 2009, National Security and Economic System: The Case of Iran 2010, National Security and Nuclear Diplomacy 2011; numerous articles in Iranian journals and magazines on domestic and foreign affairs related to Iran's nat. security interests. *Leisure interests:* hiking, swimming. *Address:* Office of the President, PO Box 1423-13185, Pasteur Avenue, Tehran 13168-43311, Iran (office). *Telephone:* (21) 64451 (office). *E-mail:* webmaster@president.ir (office). *Website:* www.president.ir (office).

ROUILLY, Jean, LenD; French television executive and senior media adviser; *Chairman and CEO, International Media Partners;* b. 21 Dec. 1943, Villennes-sur-Seine; s. of Roger Rouilly and Nicole Antigna; m. Annyck Gratton 1987; one s.; ed Lycées Jules Verne and Georges Clémenceau, Nantes, Faculté de Droit, Bordeaux and Inst. d'Etudes Politiques, Bordeaux; Asst to the Dir, Office de Radiodiffusion-Télévision Francaise, 1966–70, Admin. Documentary Programmes 1970–72, Gen. Man. to Del. Gen. of TV Production 1972–74; Sec.-Gen. Production, Antenne 2 1975–81, Asst Dir Finance 1981–85, Production Man. 1985–87, Dir-Gen. Programme Production 1987–90; Asst Dir-Gen. Antenne 2 1987–90; Dir Films A2 1981–87, Dir-Gen. 1987–90; Sec.-Gen. TV5 1983–85; Dir-Gen. Hachette Int. TV (now Europe Images Int.) 1990–2003, CEO 1999–2003; CEO Lagardère Images Int. and Lagardère Networks Int. 2001– (merged in 2007 to form Lagardère TV Int.); currently Chair. and CEO, Int. Media Partners; Chair. Bonjour China Formation; Chevaler Ordre National du Mérite. *Address:* International Media Partners, 17 rue Vasco de Gama, 75015 Paris, France (office). *Telephone:* 6-86-18-55-34. *E-mail:* jean.rouilly@imcpartners.fr (office).

ROULEAU, Joseph-Alfred, CC; Canadian singer (bass); *Honorary President, Jeunesses Musicales du Canada;* b. 28 Feb. 1929, Matane, Québec; s. of Joseph-Alfred Rouleau and Florence Bouchard; m. 1st Barbara Whittaker 1952; one d.; m. 2nd Renée Morreau; one s. one d.; ed Coll. Jean de Brebeuf, Montréal, Univ. of Montréal, Conservatoire of Music, Province of Québec; debut at Montréal Opera Guild in Un Ballo in Maschera 1951; Royal Opera House, Covent Garden 1957–87, singing 48 roles; guest artist at prin. opera houses all over the world; tours of Canada 1960, Australia (with Joan Sutherland) 1965, Russia 1966, 1969, Romania, S Africa 1974, 1975, 1976; Paris Opera 1975, Metropolitan Opera, New York 1984, 1985, 1986, San Francisco 1986, 1987; roles include title role in Boris Godunov, Philip II and Inquisitore in Don Carlos, Basilio in Barber of Seville, Mephistopheles in Faust, Dosifei in Khovanshchina, title role in Don Quixote, Ramfis in Aida, Prince Gremin in Onegin, Father Lawrence in Roméo et Juliette, Colline in La Bohème, Raimondo in Lucia di Lammermoor, Titurel in Parsifal, Abimelech in Samson et Dalila, Crespel in Contes d'Hoffmann, Arkel in Pelléas et Mélisande, Sarastro, Osmin in Die Entführung, Daland in Der fliegende Holländer, Oroveso in Norma, Don Marco in The Saint of Bleecker Street, Trulove in The Rake's Progress, The Prince in Adriana Lecouvreur, Bartolo; Prof. of Voice, Univ. of Québec 1980–98, mem. Admin. Bd, Prof. Emer. 2004–; mem. Bd Corpn, Montréal Opera Co. 1980–; Pres., Jeunesses Musicales du Canada 1989–2014 (Prix Joseph Rouleau for Vocal Art named after him 1995), Hon. Pres. 2014–; Co-Founder and mem. Bd Concours Musical Int. de Montréal 2002–; Grand Officier, Ordre Nat. du Québec 2004; Dr hc (Université de Québec à Rimouski, McGill Univ.); Prix Archambault 1967, La Société St Jean Baptiste Prix Calixa-Lavallée, Montréal 1967, Royal Opera House, Covent Garden Silver Medal 1983, Felix Award for Best Classical Artist of the Year 1989, Prix du Québec pour les Arts d'interprétation 1990, Panthéon de l'art lyrique du Canada 1992, Jeunesses Musicales du Canada Médaille du mérite exceptionnel 1995, Conseil québecois de la musique Prix Opus Hommage 2003, Prix du Gov. Gen. de Canada (Performing Arts Award) 2004, Opéra Canada Prix Ruby 2004, Médaille de la Ville de Marseille 2007, Gov. Gen.'s Mentorship Prize 2014. *Recordings include:* scenes from Anna Bolena, Ruddigore, Roméo et Juliette (Gounod), L'Enfance du Christ (Berlioz), Semiramide, Lucia di Lammermoor, Don Carlos, Aida, Il Trovatore, Renard (Stravinsky), F. Leclerc's Songs, Les abîmes du rêve de Jacques Hêtu (song cycle), French operatic arias (with Royal Opera House Orchestra), Boris Godunov (Prix Félix 2000), Don Carlos/Lucia di Lammermoor, L'Africaine (Meyerbeer), with Domingo & Verrett, San Francisco Opera; Don Carlo, Royal Opera House Covent Garden. *Leisure interests:* tennis, golf, reading. *Address:* c/o Jeunesses Musicales, 305 avenue du Mont-Royal Est, Montréal, PQ H2T 1P8 (office); 7 Roosevelt, Suite 20, Ville Mont-Royal, PQ H3R 1Z3, Canada (home). *Telephone:* (514) 739-3238 (home); (819) 688-3676 (home); (514) 845-4108 (ext. 232) (office). *Fax:* (514) 739-9135 (home); (514) 845-8241 (office). *E-mail:* joseph.alfred.rouleau@gmail.com (office); renee_rouleau@hotmail.com (home). *Website:* www.jmcanada.ca (office).

ROUNDS, Marion Michael (Mike), BS; American business executive and politician; *Senator from South Dakota;* b. 24 Oct. 1954, Huron, SDak; s. of Don Rounds; m. Jean Vedvei 1978; three s. two d.; ed South Dakota State Univ., Brookings; Pres. and CEO, Fischer, Rounds & Assocs Inc. (insurance and real estate agency), Pierre; mem. from Dist 24, SDak State Senate 1991–2000, Minority Whip 1993–94, Senate Majority Leader 1995–2002; Gov. of SDak 2003–11; Senator from SDak 2015–; Pres. Bd Oahe YMCA, Pierre-Ft. Pierre Exchange Club; Vice-Pres. St Joseph School Home & School Asscn; mem. Midwestern Govs' Asscn (Chair.), Govs' Council, Health Project, Bipartisan Policy Center, Washington, DC 2011–, Elks, Ducks Unlimited, Kts of Columbus, Pierre Elks Lodge; Republican; Guardian of Small Business, Nat. Fed. of Ind. Business 1992, 1998, Agent of the Year, SDak Ind. Insurance Agents 1999, Special Award, SDak Horsemen 2000. *Leisure interests:* flying, hunting, racquetball, camping, boating, family. *Address:* Russell Senate Office Building, Courtyard 4, Washington, DC 20510, USA (office). *Telephone:* (202) 224-5842 (office). *Website:* www.rounds.senate.gov (office).

ROURKE, (Philip Andre) Mickey; American actor and fmr boxer; b. 16 Sept. 1956, Schenectady, NY; s. of Philip Andre Rourke, Sr and Annette Rourke; m. 1st Debra Feuer (divorced); m. 2nd Carre Otis 1992 (divorced 1998); ed Actors Studio, New York; film debut in Steven Spielberg's film 1941; appeared in numerous TV movies; left acting and became professional boxer 1991–95; returned to acting 1995. *Film appearances include:* Fade to Black, 1941 1979, Heaven's Gate 1980,

Body Heat 1981, Diner (Boston Soc. of Film Critics Best Actor Award 1983, Nat. Soc. of Film Critics Best Supporting Actor Award) 1982, Eureka 1983, Rumblefish 1983, Rusty James 1983, The Pope of Greenwich Village 1984, 9½ Weeks 1984, Year of the Dragon 1985, Angel Heart 1986, A Prayer for the Dying 1986, Barfly 1987, Johnny Handsome 1989, Homeboy 1989, Francesco 1989, The Crew 1989, The Desperate Hours 1990, Wild Orchid 1990, On the Sport 1990, Harley Davidson and the Marlboro Man 1991, White Sands 1992, F.T.W., Fall Time, Double Time, Another 9½ Weeks, The Rainmaker 1997, Love in Paris 1997, Double Team 1997, Buffalo '66 1997, Thursday 1998, Shergar 1999, Shades 1999, Out in Fifty 1999, The Animal Factory 2000, Get Carter 2000, The Pledge 2001, The Hire: Follow 2001, Picture Claire 2001, They Crawl 2001, Spun 2002, Once Upon a Time in Mexico 2003, Man on Fire 2004, Domino 2005, Sin City (Chicago Film Critics Assn Best Supporting Actor Award, Irish Film and Television Awards Best Int. Actor Award) 2005, Stormbreaker 2006, The Wrestler (Golden Globe for Best Actor 2009, BAFTA Award for Leading Actor 2009) 2008, The Informers 2008, Killshot 2008, Iron Man 2 2010, The Expendables 2010, Passion Play 2010, Immortals 2011, The Courier 2012, Black November 2012, Java Heat 2013, Sin City: A Dame to Kill For 2014, A Hitman in London 2015, Ashby 2015, War Pigs 2015, Blunt Force Trauma 2015. *Address:* c/o Creative Artists Agency, 2000 Avenue of the Stars, Los Angeles, CA 90067, USA (office).

ROUSE, Cecilia Elena, BA, PhD; American economist and academic; *Lawrence and Shirley Katzman and Lewis and Anna Ernst Professor in the Economics of Education and Dean, Woodrow Wilson School of Public and International Affairs, Princeton University;* m.; two d.; ed Harvard Univ.; fmrly Theodore A. Wells '29 Prof. of Econs and Public Affairs and Prof. of Econs and Public Affairs, Woodrow Wilson School of Public and Int. Affairs, Princeton Univ., Founding Dir Princeton Univ. Educ. Research Section, Dir Industrial Relations Section, currently Lawrence and Shirley Katzman and Lewis and Anna Ernst Prof. in the Econs of Education and Prof. of Econs and Public Affairs, Dean, Woodrow Wilson School 2012–; fmr Sr Ed. The Future of Children, Journal of Labor Economics; fmr mem. MacArthur Foundation's Research Network on the Transition to Adulthood; served in Nat. Econ. Council, The White House 1998–99, mem. Council of Econ. Advisers 2009–11; mem. Bd of Dirs MDRC, T. Rowe Price Equity Mutual Funds; mem. Advisory Bd T. Rowe Price Fixed Income Mutual Funds; Research Assoc., Nat. Bueau of Econ. Research 1992–. *Publications:* numerous articles on labour econs and the econs of educ. *Address:* 424 Robertson Hall, Woodrow Wilson School, Princeton University, Princeton, NJ 08544-1013, USA (office). *Telephone:* (609) 258-4800 (office). *Fax:* (609) 258-1418 (office). *E-mail:* rouse@princeton.edu (office). *Website:* wws.princeton.edu (office).

ROUSSEFF, Dilma Vana, BEcons, MA; Brazilian politician and fmr head of state; b. 14 Dec. 1947, Belo Horizonte, Minas Gerais; d. of Pedro Rousseff (born Pétar Rusév, Bulgarian) and Dilma Jane Silva; m. 1st Cláudio Galeno de Magalhães Linhares 1968 (divorced 1981); one d. with common-law husband Carlos Franklin Paixão de Araújo 1976 (divorced 2000); ed Fed. Univ. of Rio Grande do Sul, Univ. of Campinas, São Paulo; mem. of Política Operária (Polop) 1967; mem. Comando de Libertação Nacional (Colina) 1968–70; arrested 1970 and imprisoned 1970–73; mem. Partido Democrático Trabalhista (PDT) from 1982; Planning and Budget Sec., Porto Alegre 1986–88; Communications, Mines and Energy Sec., Rio Grande do Sul 1991–94, 1999–2002; joined Partido dos Trabalhadores (PT) 2001; Mines and Energy Minister 2003–05; Chief-of-Staff, Presidency 2005–10; PT cand. in presidential election Oct. 2010, Pres.-Elect (first woman) Oct.–Dec. 2010, Pres. 2011–16 (suspended by Senate 12 May 2016 pending impeachment trial, removed from office following impeachment by Senate 31 Aug. 2016); Chair. Petrobras and Petrobras Distribuidora SA 2003–10. *Leisure interests:* history, opera, Greek mythology, embroidery, reading. *Address:* c/o Palácio do Planalto, 4° andar, Praça dos Três Poderes, 70150-900 Brasilia, DF, Brazil (office). *Website:* www.dilma13.com.br.

ROUSSELY, François, MEcon; French industrial executive; *Managing Partner, Messier Maris et Associés;* b. 9 Jan. 1945, Belvès, Dordogne; ed Paris Inst. of Political Science, French Nat. School of Admin, Univ. of Paris; auditor, State Accounting Office 1978; sr civil servant, Ministry of Interior, Prin. Pvt. Sec. 1981–86; assigned to chair. of a parl. cttee, Assemblée Nat. 1986–88; Dir-Gen. Nat. Police (Ministry of Interior) 1989–91; Gen. Sec. for Admin. of Ministry of Defence 1991–97; Sec.-Gen. and mem. Exec. Cttee Soc. Nat. des Chemins de Fer (SNCF) 1997; Prin. Pvt. Sec. Ministry of Defence 1997–98; Chair. and CEO Electricité de France (EDF) 1998–2004; Chair. Crédit Suisse France 2005–, Vice-Chair. Crédit Suisse Europe 2005–15; Man. Partner, Messier Maris et Associés 2015–; mem. Comité de l'Energie Atomique; mem. Bd Usinor, Framatome, Aérospatiale-Matra 1998; currently mem. Bd, Imagine Inst.; mem. Advisory Bd of La Banque de France; Advisor, Int. Business Leaders Advisory Council of Mayor of Beijing, Int. Business Leaders Advisory Council of Gov. of Guangdong 1998; Pres. Bd of Dirs Ecole Nationale de Ponts et Chaussées; mem. Supervisory Bd DALKIA Holding 2000; Chair. EDF Foundation 2001; Admin. AFII (French Agency for Int. Investments) 2002; Commdr, Légion d'honneur 1998, 2013; Officier, Ordre nat. du Mérite, des Arts et des Lettres 2003; Prix 2004 de l'Asscn France-Chine 2000. *Leisure interests:* jogging, classical music, rugby. *Address:* Messier Maris et Associés, 73 rue de Miromesnil, 75008 Paris, France (office). *Telephone:* (1) 53-05-85-99 (office). *E-mail:* fr@messiermaris.com (office).

ROUTS, Robert J.; Dutch business executive; *Chairman of the Supervisory Board, AEGON NV;* b. 1946; fmr Exec. Dir Downstream, Royal Dutch Shell; mem. Supervisory Bd AEGON NV 2008–, Chair. 2010–, Chair. Nominating Cttee and mem. Compensation Cttee; Chair. Supervisory Bd Royal DSM NV; mem. Supervisory Bd Royal KPN NV; mem. Bd of Dirs, ATCO Ltd, A.P. Møller – Mærsk A/S, AECOM Technology Corpn. *Address:* Supervisory Board, AEGON NV, PO Box 202, 2501 The Hague, Netherlands (office). *Telephone:* (70) 344-3210 (office). *E-mail:* info@aegon.com (office). *Website:* www.aegon.com (office).

ROUVOET, André; Dutch fmr politician; *President, Zorgverzekeraars Nederland (Health Insurers Netherlands);* b. 4 Jan. 1962, Hilversum; ed VU Univ. Amsterdam; mem. Reformed Political Fed. 1985–2001; mem. Christian Union 2001, Leader 2002–11; mem. House of Reps 1994–2007; Deputy Prime Minister and Minister for Youth and Families 2007–10, also Acting Minister of Educ., Culture and Science Feb.–Oct. 2010; Pres. Zorgverzekeraars Nederland (Health Insurers Netherlands) 2012–; fmr Chair. Dutch Reformed Churches' Youth Welfare Asscn; mem. Bd Protestant Children's Homes Foundation, Foundation for the New South Africa; Officier in de Orde van Oranje-Nassau 2010. *Address:* Zorgverzekeraars Nederland (Health Insurers Netherlands), POB 520, 3700 AM, Zeist, Netherlands (office). *Telephone:* (30) 6988911 (office). *Fax:* (30) 6988333 (office). *E-mail:* Info@zn.nl (office). *Website:* www.zn.nl (office).

ROUX, Albert Henri, OBE; French chef and restaurateur; b. 8 Oct. 1935, Semur-en-Brionnais; s. of Henri Roux and Germaine Roux (née Triger); brother of Michel André Roux (q.v.); m. 1st Monique Merle 1959; one s. one d.; m. 2nd Cheryl Deborah 2006; ed Ecole Primaire, St Mandé; mil. service, Algeria; founder (with brother Michel Roux), Le Gavroche Restaurant, London 1967 (now owned jtly with his son Michel Jr), The Waterside Inn, Bray 1972 (now owned solely by Michel Roux); opened 47 Park Street Hotel 1981; opened Le Poulbot, Le Gamin, Gavvers, Les Trois Plats and Rouxl Britannia (all as part of Roux Restaurants Ltd) 1969–87; commenced consultancy practice 1989; f. House of Albert Roux (retail catering co.) 1994; Founder-mem. Acad. Culinaire de Grande Bretagne (now renamed Acad. of Culinary Arts) 1980; Hon. Prof. of Hospitality Man., Bournemouth Univ. 1995–; est. Chez Roux Ltd (with brother Michel); Maître Cuisinier de France 1968, Officier du Mérite Agricole 1987, Chevalier de la Légion d'Honneur 2005; Hon. DSc (Council for Nat. Academic Awards) 1987, Hon. PhD (Bournemouth Univ.) 1987; Catey Lifetime Achievement Award (with Michel Roux) 1995, Watreford Wegdwood Hospitality Award 1999, AA Lifetime Achievement Award for Hospitality 2007. *Publications:* with Michel Roux: New Classic Cuisine 1983, The Roux Brothers on Pâtisserie 1986, The Roux Brothers on French Country Cooking 1989, Cooking for Two 1991. *Leisure interests:* fishing, racing. *Address:* Chez Roux Ltd., 539 Wandsworth Road, London, SW8 3JD, England (office). *Telephone:* (20) 7720-6148 (office). *Fax:* (20) 7627-0267 (office). *E-mail:* albertroux@le-gavroche.com; contact@chezroux.com. *Website:* www.albertroux.co.uk.

ROUX, Michel André; French chef and restaurateur; b. 19 April 1941, Charolles, Saône-et-Loire, Burgundy; s. of Henri Roux and Germaine Roux (née Triger); brother of Albert Henri Roux (q.v.); m. 1st Françoise Marcelle Becquet (divorced 1979); one s. two d.; m. 2nd Robyn Margaret Joyce 1984; ed Ecole Primaire St Mandé, Brevet de Collège; commis pâtissier and cuisinier, British Embassy, Paris 1955–57; commis cook to Cécile de Rothschild 1957–59, Chef 1962–67; mil. service 1960–62; Propr Le Gavroche 1967, The Waterside Inn 1972, Le Gavroche (Mayfair) 1981; mem. Acad. Culinaire de France (UK Br.), Asscn Relais et Desserts, Asscn Relais et Châteaux; Chevalier, Ordre nat. du Mérite 1987, Ordre des Arts et des Lettres 1990, Légion d'honneur 2004; Hon. OBE 2002; numerous other decorations; numerous culinary awards including Gold Medal Cuisiniers Français (Paris) 1972, Meilleur Ouvrier de France en Pâtissier 1976, Laureate Restaurateur of the Year 1985. *Publications:* New Classic Cuisine 1983, Roux Brothers on Pâtisserie 1986, At Home with the Roux Brothers 1987, French Country Cooking 1989, Cooking for Two 1991, Desserts, a Lifelong Passion 1994, Sauces 1996 (revised edn) 2009, Life is a Menu (autobiography) 2000, Only the Best 2002, Eggs 2005, Pastry Savoury and Sweet 2008, Sauces Savoury and sweet (revised) 2009, French Country Cooking (revised) 2010, Desserts 2011, Michel Roux: The Collection 2012, The Essence of French Cooking 2014. *Leisure interests:* shooting, skiing, walking, golf. *Website:* www.waterside-inn.co.uk (office).

ROVE, Karl Christian; American political consultant, fmr government official, author, broadcaster and columnist; b. 25 Dec. 1950, Denver; ed Univ. of Utah, Univ. of Maryland-Coll. Park, George Mason Univ., Univ. of Texas, Austin; Founder and Pres. Karl Rove & Co. (public affairs firm), Austin Tex. 1981–99; political adviser to George W. Bush campaigns for Gov. of Texas and US presidency 1993–2001; Sr Advisor and Chief Policy Aide to George W. Bush 2000–07, Deputy Chief of Staff for Policy 2004–07, oversaw Offices of Strategic Initiatives, Political Affairs, Public Liaison, and Intergovernmental Affairs, became known as "The Architect" of Pres. Bush's 2000 and 2004 campaigns; Political Commentator, Fox News Channel 2008–; weekly opinion columnist, Wall Street Journal 2008–. *Publications:* Courage and Consequence: My Life as a Conservative in the Fight 2010; articles for The Daily Beast, Financial Times, Forbes, FoxNews.com, HumanEvents.com, Newsweek, The Times, Washington Post, The Weekly Standard, amongst others. *Address:* 919 Congress Avenue, Suite 1400, Austin, TX 78701, USA (office). *Telephone:* (512) 615-5061. *E-mail:* karl@rove.com. *Website:* www.rove.com.

ROVERATO, Jean-François; French business executive; *Vice Chairman, Eiffage SA;* ed Lycée Carnot, Dijon, Ecole Polytechnique, Ecole Nationale des Ponts et Chaussées; engineer, Roads and Bridges, Directorate of Ministry of Construction Equipment 1969–72, Tech. Adviser to Cabinet of Robert Andrew Vivien (Sec. of State for Housing) 1971–72; Dir Public Office of HLM du Val-de-Marne 1972–74; Dir, Guiraudie et Auffève 1975; joined Fougerolle group (became Eiffage 1993), Dir 1975, Man. Dir Fougerolle Construction 1980, Man. Dir Fougerolle France 1982, Man. Dir Fougerolle International 1984, Man. Dir Eiffage SA 1985–2007, Chair. and Man. Dir 2007–12, Vice Chair. 2016–; Chair. and Man. Dir Autoroutes Paris Rhin Rhône 2006–08; Pres. AREA 2006–; Chair. Ecole Nationale des Ponts et Chaussées 2006, Etablissement public de la porte Dorée–Cité nationale de l'histoire de l'immigration 2007; Officier, Légion d'honneur 2003, Commdr 2009. *Address:* Eiffage SA, 163 Quai du Dr Dervaux, 92601 Asnières-sur-Seine, France (office). *Telephone:* 1-41-32-80-00 (office). *Fax:* 1-41-32-81-13 (office). *E-mail:* info@eiffage.fr (office). *Website:* www.eiffage.fr (office); www.aprr.com (office).

ROVERSI, Paolo; Italian photographer; b. 25 Sept. 1947, Ravenna; fashion photographer since 1973, working for numerous magazines including British and Italian Vogue, Uomo Vogue, W Magazine and others; advertising for Georgio Armani, Cerruti 1881, Comme des Garçons, Christian Dior, Alberta Ferretti, Romeo Gigli and Yohji Yamamoto; dir commercials; worked with Associated Press; Reporter, Huppert Agency. *Publications:* Una Donna 1989, Angeli 1993, Nudi 1999, Libretto 2000, Studio 2006, Studio (French edn) 2009. *Address:* 9 rue Paul Fort, 75014 Paris, France (office). *Telephone:* 1-45-40-40-49 (office). *Fax:* 1-45-40-72-98 (office). *E-mail:* info@paoloroversi.com (office). *Website:* www.paoloroversi.com (office).

ROWE, John W., BS, JD; American lawyer and energy industry executive; *Chairman Emeritus, Exelon Corporation;* b. 1946, Wis.; m. Jeanne M. Rowe; one s.; ed Univ. of Wisconsin; joined Isham, Lincoln & Beale (law firm), Chicago 1970,

Partner 1978–80, served as Gen. Counsel to Trustees of Chicago, Milwaukee, St Paul & Pacific Railroad Co. 1978–80; Sr Vice-Pres. of Law, Consolidated Rail Corpn (Conrail) 1980–84; Pres. and CEO Cen. Maine Power Co. 1984–89; Pres. and CEO New England Electric System (NEES) 1989–98; Chair., Pres. and CEO Unicom Corpn and Commonwealth Edison 1998–2000; Chair. and CEO Exelon Corpn (following merger of Unicom Corpn and PECO Energy 2000) 2000–12, Chair. Emer. 2012–; fmr Commr Nat. Comm. on Energy Policy; Chair. Illinois Inst. of Tech.; fmr Chair. Edison Electric Inst., Mass Business Roundtable, The Commercial Club of Chicago, Chicago History Museum; mem. Bd of Dirs Northern Trust Corpn 2002–, Allstate Corpn, Illinois Holocaust Museum, Morgridge Inst. for Research, SunCoke Energy; mem. Bd of Govs Argonne Nat. Lab., Chicago Urban League, Field Museum, Art Inst. of Chicago, Northwestern Univ., Edison Electric Inst., Chicago Club; mem. Econ. Club of Chicago, Blue Ribbon Comm. on America's Nuclear Future, Secretary of Energy; mem. Bd of Trustees, Bryant Coll. 1994–98, Chicago Council on Foreign Relations, Chicago Historical Soc., Wisconsin Alumni Research Foundation, American Enterprise Inst., The Nature Conservancy (Ill. Chapter); mem. Advisory Bd Opower 2013–; fmr Pres. USS Constitution Museum; Fellow, American Acad. of Arts and Sciences 2009; Hon. DHumLitt (Bryant Coll.), Hon. DBA (Univ. of Massachusetts at Dartmouth) 2002, Hon. PhD (Illinois Inst. of Tech., Drexel Univ., DePaul Univ., Thomas Coll.); Distinguished Alumni Award, Univ. of Wisconsin, World of Difference Award, Anti-Defamation League 2000, Citizen of the Year Award, City Club of Chicago 2002, Corp. Leadership Award, Spanish Coalition for Jobs 2002, City Club of Chicago's Citizen of the Year Award 2002, Civic Leadership Award, American Jewish Cttee 2004, Founder's Award for Business Leadership, Union League of Philadelphia 2005, Univ. of Arizona Exec. of the Year 2007, Illinois Holocaust Museum's Humanitarian Award 2008, named by Institutional Investor magazine as Best Electric Utilities CEO in America 2008, 2009, Daniel H. Burnham Award for Business and Civic Leadership, Chicagoland Chamber of Commerce 2008, inducted into Jr Achievement's Chicago Business Hall of Fame 2008, Humanitarian Award, Illinois Holocaust Museum 2008, Lyman Gage Award for Outstanding Civic Leadership, Civic Fed. of Chicago 2008, Corp. Leadership Award, Nat. Latino Educ. Inst. 2008, Distinguished Leadership Award, Edison Electric Inst. 2009, Chicago Council on Global Affairs Global Leadership Award 2009, Misericordia Heart of Mercy Award 2010, United States Energy Award 2012. *Address:* c/o Exelon Corpn, PO Box 805398, 48th Floor, 10 South Dearborn Street, Chicago, IL 60680-5398, USA.

ROWE, John W., BS, MD; American physician, academic and business executive (retd); *Professor, Joseph Mailman School of Public Health, Columbia University;* b. 20 June 1944, Jersey City, New Jersey; s. of Albert Wallis Rowe and Elizabeth Rowe (née Lynch); m. Valerie Ann DelTufo 1968; three c.; ed Canisius College, Buffalo, Univ. of Rochester; began career with residency in internal medicine, Beth Israel Hosp., Boston, later becoming Chief of Gerontology; Clinical and Research Fellow, Mass. Gen. Hosp.; Research Fellow and later Prof. of Medicine, Harvard Medical School, Founding Dir Div. on Aging; Pres. Mount Sinai School of Medicine 1988–99, Pres. and CEO Mount Sinai Medical Center 1988–2000, CEO Mount Sinai-New York Univ. Health 1988–2000 (renamed Mount Sinai/NYU Medical Center and Health System 1999), also Prof. of Medicine and Geriatrics;, Pres. and CEO Aetna Inc. 2001–06, Chair. 2000–01, Exec. Chair. Feb.–Oct. 2006; Prof. Joseph Mailman School of Public Health, Columbia Univ. 2006–, mem. Faculty, Columbia Aging Center; Chair. Bd of Trustees Univ. of Conn. 2003–09; mem. NAS Inst. of Medicine; Fellow, American Acad. of Arts and Sciences; fmr Dir MacArthur Foundation on Successful Aging; mem. Bd of Govs American Bd of Internal Medicine; fmr Pres. Gerontological Soc. of America, Medicare Payment Advisory Comm.; Hon. DSc (Univ. of Rochester) 2002, Dr hc (Canisius Coll.) 2002; numerous honours and awards. *Publications:* over 200 scientific publs on the aging process; Successful Aging (jt author) 1998. *Address:* Columbia University, Department of Health Policy and Management, 600 West 168th Street, 6th Floor, New York, NY 10032, USA (office). *Telephone:* (212) 305-3505 (office). *E-mail:* jwr2108@columbia .edu (office). *Website:* www.mailman.columbia.edu (office).

ROWE, R. Kerry, BSc, PhD, DEng, FRS, FREng, FRSC, FCAE, FEIC, FIE (Aust), FASCE, FCSCE; Canadian (b. Australian) engineer and academic; *Professor and Canada Research Chair in Geotechnical and Geoenvironmental Engineering, Queen's University;* ed Univ. of Sydney; worked as geotechnical engineer with Australian Govt Dept of Construction; emigrated to Canada 1978; served 22 years as Prof., Dept of Civil and Environmental Eng, Univ. of Western Ont.; Vice-Prin. (Research), Queen's Univ., Kingston 2000–10, Prof. and Canada Research Chair in Geotechnical and Geoenvironmental Eng 2011–; Pres. Int. Geosynthetics Soc. 1990–94, Canadian Geotechnical Soc. 2001–02; Vice-Pres. N American Geosynthetics Soc. 1987–91; Chair. Standards Council of Canada Int. Subcommittee on Geotextiles and Geomembranes 1989–2000, NSERC Civil Eng Grant Selection Cttee 1998–99; Founding Chair. London Dist Section, Canadian Soc. for Civil Eng and Canadian Geotechnical Soc. 1993–96; Tech. Chair. 6th Int. Conf. on Geosynthetics, Atlanta, Ga 1998, 6th Canadian Environmental Eng Conf. 2000; mem. Bd of Dirs High Performance Computing Virtual Lab. (Chair. 2000–10), Canadian Microelectronics Corpn 2000–08, PARTEQ Innovations Inc. (Chair.) 2000–10, CANARIE Inc. 2003–08; mem. Editorial Bd Canadian Geotechnical Journal (Assoc. Ed. 1983–), International Journal for Geotextiles & Geomembranes (Ed. 1997–), International Journal on Computers and Geotechnics, International Journal for Numerical and Analytical Methods in Geomechanics, Geosynthetics International, Journal of Japanese Geotechnical Soc., Italian Geotechnical Journal, Lowland Technology International, Geotechnique, Geotechnical Engineering, Transport in Porous Media, International Journal of Geomechanics (Co-Ed. 2001–12), Journal of Environmental Engineering and Science, Waste Management; Foreign mem. US Nat. Acad. of Eng; Fellow, Royal Acad. of Eng, Eng Inst. of Canada, American Soc. of Civil Engineers, Canadian Soc. for Civil Eng; Hon. mem. Int. Geosynthetics Soc. 2006; Hon. DSc; Edward G. Pleva Award, Univ. of Western Ont. 1996, Ont. Confed. of Univ. Faculty Asscns Excellence in Teaching Award 1997, Professional Engineers Ont. Eng Medal 1997, Ont. Ministry of the Environment Award of Excellence 1999, Keefer Medal 2001, Legget Medal 2003, K. Y. Lo Medal 2003, Killam Prize 2004, Int. Geosynthetics Soc. Award 2004, 45th Rankine Lecturer 2005, XXIII Manuel Rocha Lecturer 2006, Thomas C. Keefer Medal 2007, Casimir Gzowski Medal 2011, 7th Authur Casagrande Lecturer 2011, Third Terzaghi-Ferroco Oration 2012, Queen's Diamond Jubilee Medal 2012, Sir John Kennedy Medal 2012, Donald R. Stanley Award 2014, ICE Thomas Telford Gold Medal 2015, RSC Miroslaw Romanowski Medal 2015, Karl Terzaghi Lecture Award 2017, Arrigo Croce Lecturer 2017. *Publications include:* Barrier Systems for Waste Disposal Facilities (co-author), Geotechnical and Geoenvironmental Engineering Handbook (ed.); more than 600 articles, papers and chapters in journals, confs and books. *Address:* Department of Civil Engineering, Ellis Hall, Queen's University, Kingston, ON K7L 3N6, Canada (office). *Telephone:* (613) 533-3113 (office). *Fax:* (613) 533-2128 (office). *E-mail:* kerry.rowe@queensu.ca (office). *Website:* www.civil.queensu.ca (office).

ROWE, Stephen (Steve) Joseph; British retail executive; *CEO, Marks and Spencer Group plc;* b. July 1967; s. of Joe Rowe; m.; three c.; began retail career aged 15 as Saturday sales asst, Marks and Spencer, Croydon, S London; joined Topshop as trainee 1985, becoming Store Man. –1989; joined Marks & Spencer 1989, becoming Chief Menswear Buyer 1992, various roles in homewares div. including Category Man., Furniture 1998, Head of Home Categories 2003, Dir of Home 2004, Head, Beauty and New Business Devt 2004–08, Dir of Retail and mem. Marks and Spencer Exec. Cttee 2008–12, Exec. Dir, Food 2012–15, Exec. Dir, Gen. Merchandise 2015–16, CEO Marks and Spencer Group plc 2016–; Dir New West End Co.; Liveryman, Worshipful Co. of Furniture Makers. *Leisure interests:* Millwall Football Club, golf, diving. *Address:* Marks and Spencer Group plc, Waterside House, 35 North Wharf Road, London, W2 1NW, England (office). *Telephone:* (20) 7935-4422 (office). *Website:* corporate.marksandspencer.com (office).

ROWLANDS, Christopher John, MA, FCA, FRSA; British fmr business executive; b. 29 Aug. 1951, Leeds, Yorks.; s. of Wilfred John Rowlands and Margaretta Rowlands (née Roberts); m. Alison Mary Kelly 1978; two d.; ed Roundhay School, Leeds, Gonville and Caius Coll., Cambridge; articled clerk Peat Marwick Mitchell 1973–75, Man. 1981, seconded as partner, Zambia 1981–83, Sr Man., London 1983–85; Controller Business Planning Asda Group PLC 1985–86, Div. Dir Group Finance 1986–88, Deputy Man. Dir and Finance Dir Property Devt and Investment 1988–92; Group Finance Dir HTV 1992–93, Chief Exec. 1993–97; Chief Exec. The TV Corpn 1998–2001; Dir (non-exec.), ITouch PLC 2002–05; Deputy Chair. and COO Apace Media PLC 2005–09; mem. Bd of Dirs Standard Life Equity Income Trust PLC 2003–12; mem. Council, Ind. TV Asscn Co. 1993–97. *Leisure interests:* family, theatre, church, reading, skiing, tennis, travel, cycling. *Telephone:* (7813) 919452 (mobile).

ROWLANDS, Gena; American actress; b. (Virginia Cathryn Rowlands), 19 June 1930, Madison, Wis.; m. John Cassavetes 1958 (died 1989); three c.; ed Univ. of Wisconsin, American Acad. of Dramatic Arts; Nat. Bd of Review Career Achievement Award 1996, Lifetime Achievement Award, Los Angeles Film Critics Asscn 2015, Gov.'s Award (Hon. Oscar), Acad. of Motion Picture Arts and Sciences 2015. *Play:* Middle of the Night 1955. *Films include:* The High Cost of Loving 1958, Lonely Are the Brave 1962, The Spiral Road 1962, A Child is Waiting 1963, Tony Rome 1967, Faces 1968, Minnie and Moskowitz 1971, A Woman Under the Influence (Golden Globe Award for Best Actress in a Drama, Nat. Bd of Review Award for Best Actress) 1974, Opening Night (Silver Bear for Best Actress, Berlin Int. Film Festival) 1977, The Brink's Job 1978, Gloria 1980, Tempest 1982, Love Streams 1984, Light of Day 1987, Another Woman 1988, Once Around 1991, Night on Earth 1991, Ted and Venus 1991, Something to Talk About 1995, The Neon Bible 1995, Anything for John 1995, Unhook the Stars 1996, She's So Lovely 1997, Paulie 1998, Hope Floats 1998, The Mighty 1998, Playing by Heart 1998, Taking Lives 2004, The Notebook 2004, The Skeleton Key 2005, Paris, je t'aime 2006, Broken English 2007, Persepolis (voice) 2007, Olive 2011, Yellow 2012, Parts Per Billion 2014, Six Dance Lessons in Six Weeks 2014. *Television includes:* Peyton Place 1967, The Betty Ford Story (Emmy Award) 1987, Face of a Stranger (Emmy Award) 1991, Crazy in Love 1992, Parallel Lives 1994, Grace and Glorie 1998, Hysterical Blindness 2002, Charms for the Easy Life 2002, The Incredible Mrs Ritchie 2003, What If God Were the Sun? 2007. *Address:* c/o ICM, 10250 Constellation Blvd, Los Angeles, CA 90067, USA.

ROWLEY, Keith Christopher, BSc, MSc; Trinidad and Tobago geologist and politician; *Prime Minister;* b. 24 Oct. 1949, Mason Hall, Tobago; m. Sharon Rowley; two s. two d.; ed Univ. of the West Indies, Mona; began career as Research Scientist, Research Fellow and later Head of Seismic Research Unit, Univ. of the West Indies, St Augustine; fmr Gen. Man., Nat. Quarries Co. Ltd; Opposition Senator 1987–90; mem. House of Reps for Diego Martin West constituency 1991–; Minister of Agric., Land and Marine Resources 1992–95, of Planning and Devt 2001–03, of Housing 2003–07, of Trade and Industry 2007–08; Leader of the Opposition 2010–15; Prime Minister 2015–, also Minister of Housing and Urban Devt April–Aug. 2018; mem. People's Nat. Movement, Leader 2010–. *Address:* Office of the Prime Minister, Whitehall, 13–15 St Clair Avenue, St Clair, Port of Spain, Trinidad and Tobago (office). *Telephone:* 622-1625 (office). *Fax:* 622-0048 (office). *E-mail:* permsec@opm.gov.tt (office). *Website:* www.opm.gov.tt (office).

ROWLING, J(oanne) K(athleen), (Robert Galbraith), CH, OBE, BA, FRSL; British writer; b. 31 July 1965, Yate, Glos.; d. of Peter James Rowling and Anne Rowling (née Volant); m. 1st Jorge Arantes 1992 (divorced 1995); one d.; m. 2nd Neil Murray 2001; one s. one d.; ed Wyedean Comprehensive School, Univ. of Exeter, Moray House Teacher Training Coll.; Pres. Gingerbread (single parents charity); Founder Volant (charitable trust); Founder and Pres. Lumos (charity for disadvantaged children); Freedom of the City of London 2012; Chevalier, Légion d'honneur 2009; Dr hc (Univ. of Edinburgh, Edinburgh Napier Univ., Univ. of Exeter, Univ. of St Andrews, Dartmouth Coll., Harvard Univ.); Hon. DJur (Univ. of Aberdeen) 2006; Author of the Year, British Book Awards 2000, Premio Príncipe de Asturias 2003, British Ind. Film Awards 2004, Blue Peter Badge (Gold) 2007, Lifetime Achievement, British Book Awards 2008, The Edinburgh Award 2008, James Joyce Award, Univ. Coll. Dublin 2008, Outstanding Achievement Award, South Bank Show Awards 2008, inaugural winner, Hans Christian Andersen Literature Award 2010, Outstanding British Contrib. to Cinema for the Harry Potter film series, British Acad. Film Awards (shared with David Heyman, cast and crew) 2011, PEN America Literary Service Award 2016. *Films:* script: Fantastic Beasts and Where to Find Them 2016, Fantastic Beasts: The Crimes of Grindelwald 2018. *Play:* Harry Potter and the Cursed Child (story) 2016. *Publications include:* Harry Potter and the Philosopher's Stone (aka Harry Potter and the Sorcerer's Stone) (Smarties Book Prize 1997, British Book Awards

Children's Book of the Year 1998) 1997, Harry Potter and the Chamber of Secrets (Smarties Book Prize 1998, British Book Awards Children's Book of the Year 1999) 1998, Harry Potter and the Prisoner of Azkaban (Smarties Book Prize 1999, Whitbread Children's Book of the Year 1999) 1999, Harry Potter and the Goblet of Fire (Hugo Award for Best Novel 2001) 2000, Quidditch Through the Ages by Kennilworthy Whisp 2001, Fantastic Beasts and Where to Find Them by Newt Scamander 2001, Harry Potter and the Order of the Phoenix (Bram Stoker Award for Best Work for Young Readers 2003, WH Smith People's Choice Fiction Prize 2004) 2003, Harry Potter and the Half-Blood Prince (Quill Book Award for Book of the Year, Best Children's Book, British Book Awards, WH Smith Book of the Year 2006, Royal Mail Award for Scottish Children's Books) 2005, Harry Potter and the Deathly Hallows 2007, The Tales of Beedle the Bard 2008, The Casual Vacancy 2012; as Robert Galbraith: The Cuckoo's Calling 2013, The Silkworm 2014, Career of Evil 2015, Lethal White 2018. *Address:* c/o The Blair Partnership, POB 7828, London, W1A 4GE, England (office); c/o Bloomsbury Publishing PLC, 31 Bedford Avenue, London, WC1B 3AT, England (home). *Telephone:* (207) 504-2520 (office); (20) 7631-5600 (office). *E-mail:* info@theblairpartnership.com (office); contact@bloomsbury.com (office); info@jkrowling.com (office). *Website:* www.theblairpartnership.com (office); www.bloomsbury.com (office); www.jkrowling.com (office); www.pottermore.com (office). *Fax:* (20) 7631-5800 (office).

ROXAS, Manuel (Mar) II, BEcons; Philippine politician; b. 13 May 1957; grandson of Manuel Roxas, fmr Pres. of Philippines; s. of Senator Gerry Roxas; ed Ateneo de Manila Univ., Wharton Business School, Univ. of Pennsylvania, Kennedy School of Govt, Harvard Univ., USA; fmr Dir Kauswagan Devt Corpn, Myapo Prawn Farm Corpn; fmr Vice-Pres. Progressive Devt Corpn; fmr Dir/Pres. Northstar Capital Inc., Atok Big Wedge Mining Co.; fmr banker, Wall Street, New York, USA; mem. House of Reps, First Dist, Capiz 1992–2001; fmr leader admin.-aligned parties in Lower House of Legislature; Co-Chair. Philippines IT Devt; Sec., Dept Trade and Industry 2001–03, Dept of Transportation and Communications 2011–12, Dept of the Interior and Local Govt 2012–15; Senator 2004–10; Co-founder Books for the Barangay Foundation Inc., Capiz Alliance for Ecological Devt Inc.; mem. Liberal Party, Exec. Vice-Pres. *E-mail:* mar@marroxas.com (office). *Website:* marroxas.com (office).

ROY, Aruna, MA; Indian social activist and fmr government official; *Head, Mazdoor Kisan Shakti Sangathana;* b. 26 May 1946, Chennai; d. of Elupai Doraiswami Jayaram and Hema Roy; m. Sanjit Roy (divorced); ed Indraprastha Coll. for Women, Univ. of Delhi; fmr Lecturer, Indraprastha Coll. for Women; worked for Admin. Services 1968–74; worked with Social Work and Research Centre –1983; Founder and Head of Mazdoor Kisan Shakti Sangathana 1990–; mem. Nat. Campaign for People's Right to Information; mem. Nat. Advisory Council –2013; mem. Nat. Employment Guarantee Council, People's Union for Civil Liberties, Concerned Citizens Tribunal; Ramon Magsaysay Award for Community Leadership 2000, Lal Bahadur Shastri National Award for Excellence in Public Admin, Academia and Man. 2010. *Publications:* Education of Out-of-School Children: Case Studies of Selected Non-formal Learning Programmes in South Asia (ed) 1984. *Address:* Mazdoor Kisan Shakti Sangathana, Village Devdungri, Post Brar, District Rajsamand, Rajasthan, India (office). *E-mail:* mkssrajasthan@gmail.com (office). *Website:* www.mkssindia.org (office).

ROY, Arundhati; Indian writer, artist, actress and activist; b. 24 Nov. 1960, Shillong, Meghalaya; d. of Rajib Roy and Mary Roy; m. 1st Gerard Da Cunha (divorced); m. 2nd Pradeep Krishen (divorced); ed School of Planning and Architecture, New Delhi; fmrly with Nat. Inst. of Urban Affairs; judge, Cannes Film Festival 2000–; Lannan Prize for Cultural Freedom 2002, Sydney Peace Prize 2004, Norman Mailer Prize for Distinguished Writing 2011. *Screenplays:* In Which Annie Gives It Those Ones (TV) 1988, Electric Moon 1992, DAM/AGE 2002. *Publications:* The God of Small Things (novel) (Booker Prize 1997) 1997, The End of Imagination (essay) 1998, The Cost of Living (essays) 1998, The Great Common Good (essay) 1999, War is Peace 2000, The Algebra of Infinite Justice (essays) 2001, Power Politics 2002, The Ordinary Person's Guide to Empire (essays) 2004, Public Power in the Age of Empire Seven Stories 2004, Introduction to 13 December, a Reader: The Strange Case of the Attack on the Indian Parliament 2006, The Shape of the Beast: Conversations with Arundhati Roy 2008, Listening to Grasshoppers (essays) 2009, Broken Republic: Three Essays 2011, Walking with the Comrades 2011, Kashmir: The Case for Freedom 2011, The Hanging of Afzal Guru and the Strange Case of the Attack on the Indian Parliament 2013, Capitalism: A Ghost Story 2014, The Ministry of Utmost Happiness (novel) 2017; contribs to periodicals. *Address:* c/o India Ink Publishing Co. Pvt. Ltd, C-1, Soami Nagar, New Delhi 110 017, India (office).

ROY, Donkupar, PhD; Indian politician; *President, United Democratic Party;* b. 10 Nov. 1954; ed North Eastern Hill Univ., Shillong; worked as Prof. before entering politics; first won Shella Ass. seat in Meghalaya Legis. Ass. as ind. cand. 1987, re-elected 1993–, Leader of the Opposition 2013–; joined United Democratic Party (UDP) 1998, currently Pres.; held several portfolios under Chief Minister of Meghalaya, including Health, Educ., Finance and Planning Implementation, before becoming Deputy Chief Minister, formed alliance with other parties to form govt under banner of Meghalaya Progressive Alliance, Chief Minister of Meghalaya 2008–09, state govt dismissed and UDP left Progressive Alliance March 2009. *Leisure interests:* reading, chess, fishing. *Address:* Meghalaya Legislative Assembly, M.G. Road, Shillong 793 001, Meghalaya; Boyce Road Laitumkhrah, Shillong 3, Meghalaya, India. *Website:* megassembly.gov.in.

ROY, Prannoy, CA, PhD; Indian broadcasting executive, political analyst and economist; *Executive Chairman, New Delhi Television Ltd;* b. 15 Oct. 1949, Kolkata; s. of Hurricane Roy; m. Radhika Roy 1972; one d.; ed Doon School, Dehradun, Haileybury School, Queen Mary Coll. and Univ. of London, UK, Delhi School of Econs; Chartered Accountant, PriceWaterhouse India 1979–83; Election Analyst 1980–85; Assoc. Prof., Delhi School of Econs 1985–86; Econ. Adviser, Ministry of Finance 1985–87; Anchor and Ed.-in-Chief for several TV news, budget and election programmes 1998–; Founder and Exec. Chair. New Delhi TV Ltd (NDTV) 1988–; Leverhulme Fellow; mem. Int. Advisory Bd Council On Foreign Relations; Priyadarshini Acad. Bombay Felicitations Award, Dynasty Culture Club Hall of Fame Award for Best Anchor Person 1991, TV and Video Award for Best Anchor Person 1993, B. D. Goenka Award for Excellence in Journalism 1994, 1995, Maharana Mewar Foundation Award for Contrib. to Journalism 1996,

Indian Dance Theatre Best Personality of the Year Award 1998, Screen Videocon Award for Lifetime Achievement 1998, Ernst & Young Entrepreneur of the Year Award (Media) 2003, Lal Bahadur Shastri Nat. Award 2015. *Publications:* A Compendium of Indian Elections 1984, India Decides: Elections 1952–1991 (co-author with David Butler) 1989. *Address:* New Delhi Television Convergence Ltd, 207, Okhla Industrial Estate, Phase 3, New Delhi 110 020, India (office). *Telephone:* (11) 26446666 (office). *Fax:* (11) 41735110 (office). *E-mail:* prannoy@ndtv.com (office). *Website:* www.ndtv.com (office).

ROY, Tathagata; Indian engineer and politician; *Governor of Meghalaya;* b. 14 Sept. 1945, Kolkata; s. of Debesh Chandra Roy; m.; two d.; ed Bengal Eng Coll. (now Indian Inst. of Eng Science and Tech., Shibpur); began career as Engineer and Gen. Man., RITES Ltd (public-sector eng consultancy) 1989–90, also Chief Engineer (Design), Metro Railways, Kolkata –1990 (retd); Founding Head, Dept of Construction Eng, Jadavpur Univ. 1990–; Chair. Bd of Govs, Nat. Inst. of Technical Teachers Training and Research, Kolkata 2000–05; Gov of Tripura May 2015–18, of Meghalaya 2018–; Fellow, Inst. of Engineers; Life mem. Indian Council of Arbitration; mem. Bhartiya Janata Party (BJP) 1990–, Pres. W Bengal BJP State Unit 2002–06, mem. BJP Nat. Exec. 2002–. *Publications include:* several books including Engineering Contracts in Indian Law, Practice and Management, Democracy in Peril: A Quarter Century of CPI(M)s Fraud and Terror-Raj in West Bengal 2003, My People, Uprooted: A Saga of the Hindus of Eastern Bengal 2007, The Life and Times of Dr Syama Prasad Mookerjee 2012. *Address:* Office of the Governor, Raj Bhavan, Shillong 793 001, Meghalaya, India (office). *Telephone:* (364) 2223001 (office). *Fax:* (381) 2224350 (office). *Website:* meggovernor.gov.in (office).

ROY SAHARA, Subrata; Indian business executive; *Managing Worker and Chairman, Sahara India Pariwar;* b. 10 June 1946, Araria, Bihar; m. Swapna Roy 1974; two s.; f. Sahara Group 1978, currently Man. Worker and Chair. Sahara India Pariwar, cos include Sahara India Financial Corpn Ltd, Sahara Care House, Sahara Infrastructure and Housing; Hon. DLitt (Lalit Narayan Mithila Univ.); Noble Citizen Award 1986, Baba-E-Rozgar 1992, Karmaveer Samman 1995, Nat. Citizen Award 2001, Best Industrialist Award 2002, Businessman of the Year Award 2002, Global Leadership Award 2004, Lifetime Achievement Award 2004, Mother Teresa Millennium Award for Renowned Industrialist 2005, ITA ICON 2007, Vishisht Rashtriya Udaan Samman 2010, Vocational Award for Excellence 2010. *Publications:* Shanti Sukh: Santushti, Maan-Samman: Atmasamman. *Address:* Sahara India Pariwar, Sahara Information and Contact Point, POB 2, Gomti Nagar, Lucknow 10, India (office). *Fax:* (522) 2303818 (office). *E-mail:* info@saharaindiapariwar.org (office). *Website:* www.sahara.in (office); www.sahara.in/saharasri.

ROYAL, HRH The Princess; (Princess Anne Elizabeth Alice Louise), LG, GCVO; British; b. 15 Aug. 1950; d. of Queen Elizabeth II (q.v.) and Prince Philip, Duke of Edinburgh (q.v.); m. 1st Capt. Mark Anthony Peter Phillips 1973 (divorced 1992); one s., Peter Mark Andrew, b. 15 Nov. 1977, one d., Zara Anne Elizabeth, b. 15 May 1981; m. 2nd Rear Adm. Timothy Laurence MVO, ADC 1992; ed Benenden School, Kent; Col-in-Chief, 14th/20th King's Hussars, Worcs. and Sherwood Foresters Regt (29th/45th Foot), Royal Regina Rifles, 8th Canadian Hussars (Princess Louise's), Royal Corps of Signals, The Canadian Armed Forces Communications and Electronics Br., The Royal Australian Corps of Signals, The Royal Scots, Royal NZ Corps of Signals, King's Royal Hussars, Royal Logistics Corps; Royal NZ Nursing Corps, The Grey and Simcoe Foresters Militia; Chief Commdt, WRNS; Hon. Air Commodore, RAF Lyneham; Pres. WRNS Benevolent Trust, British Acad. of Film and TV Arts, Hunters' Improvement and Light Horse Breeding Soc., Save the Children Fund, Windsor Horse Trials, The Royal School for Daughters of Officers of the RN and Royal Marines (Haslemere), British Olympic Asscn, Council for Nat. Acad. Awards; Patron, Asscn of Wrens, Riding for the Disabled Asscn, Jersey Wildlife Preservation Fund, The Royal Corps of Signals Asscn, The Royal Corps of Signals Inst., Missions to Seamen, British Knitting and Clothing Export Council, The Army and Royal Artillery Hunter Trials, Glos. and North Avon Fed. of Young Farmers' Clubs, Royal Lymington Yacht Club, Royal Port Moresby Soc. for the Prevention of Cruelty to Animals, Horse of the Year Ball, Benenden Ball, British School of Osteopathy, Communications and Electronics Branch Inst., All England Women's Lacrosse Asscn, Home Farm Trust; Vice-Patron, British Show Jumping Asscn; Commdt-in-Chief, St John Ambulance and Nursing Cadets, Women's Transport Service; Life mem. Royal British Legion Women's Section, Royal Naval Saddle Club; mem. Island Sailing Club; Visitor, Felixstowe Coll.; official visits abroad to the 14th/20th King's Hussars in FRG 1969, 1975, to see the work of the Save the Children Fund in Kenya 1971, to the 2,500th anniversary celebrations of the Iranian monarchy 1971, to 14th/20th King's Hussars and to see the work of the Save the Children Fund, Hong Kong 1971, to SE Asia 1972, Munich 1972, Yugoslavia 1972, Ethiopia and the Sudan 1973, to visit Worcs. and Sherwood Foresters Regt in Berlin 1973, in Hereford, FRG 1974, to Canada 1974, to Australia 1975, to USA 1977, to FRG and Norway 1978, to Portugal, FRG, Thailand, Gilbert Islands, NZ, Australia and the Bahamas, Canada 1979, to Royal Corps of Signals in Cyprus, France, Belgium and Fiji 1980, Royal Corps of Signals in Berlin, Nepal, Worcs. and 14th/20th King's Hussars in FRG; USA, Canada and tour of Africa, North Yemen and Lebanon 1982, to France, Japan, Hong Kong, Singapore, Pakistan, Australia, Netherlands and BAOR 1983, USA, Africa, India, Bangladesh, FRG, UAE 1984; Chancellor, Univ. of London 1981–, Univ. of Edinburgh 2011–; has accompanied the Queen and the Duke of Edinburgh on several State Visits; has taken part in numerous equestrian competitions including Montreal Olympics 1976, Horse of the Year Show, Wembley and Badminton Horse Trials; winner of Raleigh Trophy 1971 and Silver Medal in 1975 in Individual European Three Day Event; Freeman of the City of London, of the Fishmongers' Co., Master Warden Farriers' Co., Master and Hon. Liveryman, Carmen's Co., Hon. Liveryman Farriers' Co., Yeoman, Saddlers' Co., Hon. Freeman, Farmers' Co., Loriners' Co.; Hon. mem. British Equine Veterinary Asscn, Royal Yacht Squadron, Royal Thames Yacht Club, Minchinhampton Golf Club, Lloyds of London; Hon. Life mem. RNVR Officers' Asscn; Sportswoman of the Year, Sports Writers' Asscn, Daily Express, World of Sport, BBC Sports Personality 1971, Special BAFTA Award 1993. *Publication:* Riding Through My Life 1991. *Address:* Buckingham Palace, London, SW1, England. *Website:* www.royal.gov.uk.

ROYAL, Ségolène; French politician; b. 22 Sept. 1953, Dakar, Senegal; d. of Jacques Royal and Hélène Dehaye; fmr pnr Francois Hollande; two s. two d.; ed Univ. of Nancy, Institut d'Etudes Politiques, Paris, Ecole Nationale d'Admin; Conseillère Gen., La Mothe Saint Héray (Deux-Sèvres) 1992–98; adviser on environment, town planning and social affairs to Pres. of Repub. 1982–88; Deputy to Nat. Ass. (Parti socialiste) from Deux-Sèvres 1988–92, 1993–97, 2002–07; Minister of the Environment 1992–93, Deputy Minister of Educ. 1997–2000, of Family and Childhood 2000–01, of Family Childhood and Disabled Persons 2001–02, Minister of Ecology, Sustainable Devt and Energy 2014–17; Pres. region Poitou-Charentes 2004–14; Pres. Nat. Council of Socialist Group 1994–95; unsuccessful Parti socialiste cand. in 2007 presidential elections. *Publications include:* Le Printemps des Grands Parents 1987, Le Ras-le-bol des Bébés Zappeurs 1989, Pays, Paysans, Paysages 1993, La Vérité d'une femme 1996, Désirs d'avenir 2006, Maintenant 2007, Les Droits de l'Enfant 2007, Ma plus belle histoire, c'est vous 2007, Cette belle idée du courage 2013. *Address:* Parti Socialiste, 10 rue de Solférino, 75333 Paris Cedex 07, France (office). *Telephone:* 1-45-56-77-00 (office). *Fax:* 1-47-05-15-78 (office). *E-mail:* interps@parti-socialiste.fr (office). *Website:* www.parti-socialiste.fr (office).

ROYALL OF BLAISDON, Baroness (Life Peer), cr. 2004, of Blaisdon in the County of Gloucestershire; **Janet Anne Royall,** PC, BA (Hons); British politician; b. 20 Aug. 1955, Glos., England; d. of Basil Royall and Myra Royall; m. Stuart Hercock (died 2010); two s. one d.; ed Royal Forest of Dean Grammar School, Westfield Coll., London; Sec.-Gen. British Labour Group, European Parl. 1979–85; policy adviser to Neil Kinnock, Leader of Opposition 1986–92; mem. of Kinnock Cabinet, EC 1995–2001; Parl. Co-ordinator, Directorate-Gen. of Communications, EC 2001; Head, European Comm. Office in Wales 2003–04; Govt Spokesperson for Health, for Int. Devt and for FCO 2005–08; Capt., Hon. Corps of Gentlemen at Arms (Chief Whip, House of Lords) 2007–08, mem. Select Cttees on Admin and Works, Privleges and Procedure 2008–, Leader of the House of Lords 2008–10, Lord Pres. of the Council 2008–09, Chancellor of the Duchy of Lancaster 2009–10; Govt Spokesperson for Equality 2008–10, for NI 2008–10, for the Cabinet Office 2009–10, Leader of the Opposition 2010–, Opposition Spokesperson for the Cabinet Office 2010–12, for Educ. 2010, for NI 2010–11, for Work and Pensions 2010, for Equalities Office 2010–12; Vice-Pres. European Socialist Party 2012–; Prin., Somerville Coll., Univ. of Oxford 2017–; Chair. Centre for Opposition Studies 2017–; mem. USDAW (trade union) 2018, European Council of Foreign Relations; Chair. of Trustees, People's History Museum 2016–. *Leisure interests:* reading, travel, gardening, swimming. *Address:* House of Lords, Westminster, London, SW1A 0PW, England (office). *Telephone:* (20) 7219-6370 (office). *E-mail:* royallj@parliament.uk (office).

ROYE, Marcia, BSc, PhD; Jamaican biotechnologist and academic; *Lecturer in Biotechnology, University of the West Indies;* b. Newforest, Manchester; ed Hampton High School for Girls, St Elizabeth, Univ. of the West Indies; Fulbright Fellow, Int. Lab. for Agricultural Biotechnology, Danforth Plant Science Center, St Louis, Mo., USA 2003; currently Lecturer in Biotechnology, Univ. of the West Indies, also Assoc. Dean of Grad. Studies, Faculty of Pure and Applied Sciences and Leader, Gemini Virus Research Team (research into crop-destroying insect-borne virus); fmr Visiting Researcher, Univ. of Wisconsin; Scientific Research Council Young Scientist Award 2000, L'Oréal Fellowship for Young Women in Science 2000, L'Oréal-UNESCO Special Fellowship 2011. *Achievements include:* co-f. research programme into detection of anti-retroviral drug resistance of HIV in Jamaican patients at Inst. of Human Virology, Univ. of Maryland School of Medicine 2008. *Address:* Biotechnology Centre, The University of the West Indies, Mona, Jamaica (office). *Telephone:* 977-1828 (office). *Fax:* 977-3331 (office). *E-mail:* marcia.roye@uwimona.edu.jm (office). *Website:* www.mona.uwi.edu/biotech (office).

ROYO SÁNCHEZ, Arístides, LLB, JD; Panamanian politician, diplomatist and lawyer; *Partner, Morgan & Morgan;* b. 14 Aug. 1940, La Chorrera; s. of Roberto Royas and Gilma Sánchez; m. Adele Ruíz 1963; one s. two d.; ed Nat. Inst., Panama City, Univs of Salamanca and Bologna; Gen. Sec. of Gen. Solicitorship of Repub. of Panama 1965–68; Prof. of Consular, Notarial and Mercantile Law, Univ. of Panama 1968–74; mem. Law Codification Comm. 1969; mem. drafting comms for Penal Code 1970, Constitution 1972; mem. Legis. Comm. of Nat. Council of Legislation 1972–73; Gen. Sec. School of Lawyers of Panama 1973; Partner, Morgan & Morgan (law firm) 1968–; a negotiator of Torrijos-Carter Canal Treaties between Panama and USA 1977; mem. Org. Comm. of Democratic Revolutionary Party; Minister of Educ. 1973–78; Pres. of Panama 1978–82; Amb. to Spain 1982–84, 1994–96, to France 1996–99, Perm. Amb. to OAS 2004–09; mem. Nat. Bar Asscn of Panama, Union Iberoamericana de Abogados, Instituto Hispano-Luso-Americano de Derecho Internacional, Instituto de Derecho Comparado de la Universidad Complutense de Madrid, Sociedad Bolivariana de Panamá, Fuji-Baru Asscn, Bd of Dirs Univ. of Peace, UN(O) 2013–17; hon. mem. Spanish Law Soc. 1979; Grand Cross, Alfonso X the Wise (Spain) 1977, Extraordinary Grand Cross, Vasco Núñez de Balboa (Panama) 1978; Grand Collar, Order of Manuel Amador Guerrero (Panama) 1978; Grand Collar, Order of Isabel la Católica (Spain) 1979; Grand Cross, Légion d'honneur 1979; Extraordinary Grand Cross, Order of Boyaca (Colombia) 1979; Dr hc (Univ. San Martín de Porres, Lima, Peru) 1979. *Publications:* Philosophy of Law in Cathrein and Del Vecchio 1963, History of Spanish Commercial Code 1964, The Responsibility of the Carrier in Sea Shipping 1965, Extraterritoriality of the Panamanian Criminal Law 1967, Draft Criminal Code of Panama, The Participation of Labourers in the Utilities of Enterprises, Revolution or De Facto Government, Manager in the Enterprise 1970, Commentaries to the Law on Retiring Funds for Journalists 1971, The Technician and the Politician in Public Administration 1973, Popular Consultation of the Law 1972, Las relaciones entre Panamá y los Estados Unidos 1979, Mensajes del Presidente a su pueblo 1981, El canal de Panamá, pasado, presente y futuro 1996, Estrategias para la negociación de los Tratados del Canal de Panamá 1997, Laberinto de ausencias 2000, La frustrada derogatoria de la ley 96–70 2002, El Instituto Nacional de Panama: Memories and Experiences of an Epoch 2009. *Leisure interests:* reading, writing, skiing, jogging. *Address:* Morgan & Morgan, MMG Tower, 23rd Floor Ave., Paseo del Mar, Costa del Este, Panama City, Panama (office). *Telephone:* (507) 265-7777 (office). *Fax:* (507) 265-7700 (office). *E-mail:* aroyo@morimor.com (office). *Website:* www.morimor.com (office).

ROZANOV, Yevgeny Grigoryevich, PhD; Russian architect; b. 8 Nov. 1925, Moscow; s. of Grigory Alexandrovich Rozanov and Anastasiya Nikolaevna Rozanova; m. Aida Ilyenkova 1952; one s.; ed Moscow Inst. of Architecture; mem. CPSU 1964–91; Dir of Mezentsev Inst. of Standard and Experimental Design of Culture and Sports Activities 1970–85; major bldgs designed in Essentuki, Vladivostok, Tashkent, Moscow (notably Dinamo Sports Centre); teacher of architecture at Moscow Architectural Inst. 1960–85, Prof. 1953–85; Chair. State Cttee on Architecture and Town Planning 1987–91; Sec. USSR Union of Architects 1981–92; People's Deputy of the USSR 1989–91; mem. USSR (now Russian) Acad. of Arts 1979; Pres. Int. Acad. of Architecture (Moscow br.) 1991; Vice-Pres. Russian Acad. of Arts 1998–; mem. Russian Acad. of Architecture and Construction Sciences 1997, Acad. of Architecture, Paris 1998; Hon. mem. Acad. of Architecture of Ukraine 1995; Dr hc (Moscow Architectural Inst.) 2001; Khamza Uzbek State Prize 1969, 1970, Navoi Uzbek State Prize 1975, USSR State Prize 1975, 1980, First Prize in Borovitskaya Square Competition, Moscow 1997, People's Architect of USSR 1983. *Publication:* The Works of E. G. Rozanov 1995. *Leisure interests:* painting, drawing, sculpture, music. *Address:* Kosygina Street 9, Apt. 74, Moscow, Russia (home). *Telephone:* (495) 137-56-09 (home).

ROZARIO, Patricia, OBE, BA, FRCM; Indian singer (soprano) and academic; b. 1960, Bombay; m. Mark Troop; one d.; ed Bombay Univ., Guildhall School of Music and Nat. Opera Studio, UK, studied with Jeffrey Talbot; has performed with numerous conductors, including Sir John Pritchard, Solti, Ashkenazy, Jurowski, Belohlavek, Gardiner, Pinnock, Ivan Fischer, Hickox and Andrew Davis; sung opera at Aix-en-Provence, Amsterdam, Lyon, Lille, Bremen, Antwerp, Wexford, English Nat. Opera, Glyndebourne and Opera North; performed regularly with Graham Johnson in The Songmakers' Almanac programmes; solo recitals, South Bank, London and elsewhere; frequent performances of Bach, Handel, Mozart; Vaughan Williams' Serenade to Music, BBC Proms 1988; Schumann's Paradies und der Peri, Madrid with Gerd Albrecht; appearances at Bath and Edin. Festivals; world premiere of Taverner's Apocalypse, BBC Proms, also premiered John Casken's Farness with Northern Sinfonia and Chansons de Verlaine at Wigmore Hall, Jonathan Dove's Minterne; collaboration with Sir John Tavener wrote over thirty works for her; Prof., Royal Coll. of Music; teaches singing course at British Isles Music Festival summer music festival, Ardingly; Assoc., Guildhall School of Music; British Song Prize, Barcelona, Maggie Teyte Prize, Sängerforderungspreis, Salzburg Mozarteum, Guildhall School of Music Gold Medal, Asian Women of Achievement Arts and Culture Award 2002, Global Goan Award 2007, Pravasi Bharatiya Samman Award 2013. *Operatic roles include:* Giulietta (Jommelli's La schiava liberata) for Netherlands Opera, Gluck's Euridice for Opera North, Mozart's Bastienne and Pamina for Kent Opera, Ilia on Glyndebourne tour, Ismene in Lyon production of Mithridate and Zerlina at Aix, Statue in Rameau's Pygmalion and Purcell's Belinda for Kent Opera; Florinda in Handel's Rodrigo at Innsbruck, Nero in L'incoronazione di Poppea and Massenet's Sophie; concert performance of Il re pastore, Queen Elizabeth Hall, London, world premiere of John Casken's Golem, as Miriam, Almeida Festival, London, Ismene at Wexford Festival 1989, cr. title role in premiere of Taverner's Mary of Egypt, Aldeburgh Festival 1992, season 1992–93 in Monteverdi's Il combattimento, ENO and Haydn's L'infedeltà delusa, Garsington Opera, Romilda in Serse, Brussels 1996. *Recordings include:* Mahler Symphony No. 4, London Symphony Orchestra, Songs of the Auvergne with John Pritchard (conductor), Haydn Stabat Mater with Trevor Pinnock (conductor), Golem (Gramophone Award 1991), Taverner: We Shall See Him As He Is, Mary of Egypt, To a Child Dancing in the Wind; Spanish Songs, Britten's Rape of Lucretia. *Address:* Vocal Faculty, Royal College of Music, Prince Consort Road, London, SW7 2BS, England (office). *Website:* www.rcm.ac.uk/vocal (office); www.patriciarozario.com.

ROZENTAL, Andrés, AM, MEconSc; Mexican diplomatist and consultant; *President, Rozental & Asociados;* b. 27 April 1945, Mexico City; s. of Leonid Rozental Wurhaft and Neoma Gutman Rudnicki; m. Vivian Holzer; two d.; ed Universidad de las Américas, Mexico, Univ. of Pennsylvania, USA, Univ. of Bordeaux, France; Amb. to OAS 1971–74; Perm. Rep. to UN, Geneva 1982–83; Amb. to Sweden 1983–88; Deputy Foreign Minister 1988–94; Amb. to UK 1995–97; Amb.-at-Large and Special Presidential Envoy for Pres. Fox 2000–02; Founder and Pres. Rozental & Asociados (consultancy), Mexico City 1997–; Pres. Mexican Council on Foreign Relations 2002–06; Chair. Bd ArcelorMittal Mexico 2000–16, Grupo Industrial Omega; mem. Bd of Dirs Ocean Wilson Holdings, HSBC Mexico; mem. Bd of Govs Int. Devt Research Centre 2007–12; mem. Bd of Advisors, Latin America Advisor, Inter-American Dialogue 2005–, Panel of Sr Advisors, Chatham House, Operating Bd Centre for Int. Governance Innovation, Int. Advisory Bd APCO Worldwide, Washington, DC; fmr mem. Editorial Bd Reforma (newspaper); Sr Nonresident Fellow, The Brookings Inst., Washington, DC 2007–14; mem. Trilateral Comm.; mem. Council of Int. Inst. of Strategic Studies, London; Grand Cross of the Polar Star (Sweden), Grand Cross, Civil Merit Order (Spain), Officier, Ordre nat. du Mérite, Ordre Nat. du Québec, Eminent Amb. of Mexico 1994. *Publications include:* five books on Mexican foreign policy and numerous articles on int. affairs. *Address:* Rozental & Asociados, Campos Elíseos no 345, Edif. Omega, piso 6, México DF, Mexico (office). *Telephone:* (55) 5279-6090 (office). *Fax:* (55) 5279-6089 (office). *E-mail:* mexconsult@gmail.com (office).

ROZES, Simone, LenD, DèsSc, DES; French lawyer; *Honorary President, Cour de Cassation;* b. 29 March 1920, Paris; d. of Léon Ludwig and Marcelle Cetre; m. Gabriel Rozes 1942; one s. one d.; ed Lycée de Sèvres, Lycée de St-Germain-en-Laye, Univ. of Paris, Ecole Libre des Sciences Politiques; trainee lawyer, Paris 1947–49; Surrogate Judge, Bourges 1949–50; Judge 1951–; attaché, Justice Dept 1951–58; Admin. Chief, Cabinet of the Minister of Justice 1958–62, Vice-Pres. Tribunal de Grande Instance de Paris 1969–73, Pres. 1975–81; Dir Reformatory Educ. 1973–76; mem. UN Crime Prevention and Control Cttee 1977; Advocate-Gen. European Court of Justice 1981–84; First Advocate Gen. 1982–84; Pres. Cour de Cassation (Chief Justice) 1984–88, Hon. Pres. 1989–; Int. and Nat. Arbitrator 1989–; Pres. Int. Soc. of Social Defence, fmr Pres. Soc. of Comparative Law; Hon. Vice-Pres. Int. Asscn of Penal Law; Inst. Frederik R. Bull; mem. Bd Alliance Française, Vice-Pres. 1994–; Grand Croix, Légion d'honneur; Officier, Ordre nat. du Mérite; Médaille de l'Educ. Surveillée, Médaille de Admin. Pénitentiaire, Commdr Cross, Order of Merit (FRG); Hon. LLD (Edin.). *Publication:* Le Juge et l'avocat (jtly) 1992. *Leisure interest:* travelling. *Address:* c/o Cour de Cassation, 5 quai de l'Horloge, 75055 Paris Cedex 01 (office); 34 rue Bayen, 75017 Paris, France.

Telephone: 1-43-80-16-67 (office). *Fax:* 1-47-63-42-90 (office). *E-mail:* simone .rozes@neuf.fr (office). *Website:* www.courdecassation.fr (office).

ROZHKOV, Pavel Alekseyevich; Russian politician and fmr wrestler; *First Vice-President and Chairman, Executive Committee, Russian Paralympic Committee;* b. 30 June 1957, Ramenskoye, Moscow region; m. Larisa Viktorovna Rozhkova; ed Moscow Inst. of Physical Culture; metal worker Radipribor plant 1974–75; coach Urozhai classical wrestling team Moscow 1977–78; jr researcher All-Union Research Inst. of Physical Culture, Moscow 1979–82; coach State Sports Cttee 1982–87; docent Cen. State Inst. of Physical Culture, Moscow 1992; Sr coach Olympic Greek-Roman wrestling team 1992–96; Dir-Gen. Olymp-Tour co., Moscow 1997–99; Deputy Minister of Physical Culture, Sports and Tourism 1999, First Deputy Minister 1999–2000; Chair. State Cttee on Physical Culture, Sports and Tourism 2000–02, First Deputy Chair. 2002; Chair. Trade Union of Physical Culture, Sport and Tourism Workers of Russian Fed. 2005–; First Vice-Pres. and Chair. Exec. Cttee, Russian Paralympic Cttee 2006–, Chief of Staff 2009–; mem. Int. Wheelchair and Amputee Sport Fed. 2013–, Vice-Pres. 2015–; Order of Friendship 2010; Badge of Honor 2014, Medal of Petr Lesgaft "For Merit to the Sport Science and education" 2016 including others. *Address:* Russian Paralympic Committee, 101000 Moscow, Turgenevskaya square 2, Russia (office). *Telephone:* (499) 922-11-90 (office). *E-mail:* paralympru@gmail.com (office). *Website:* www .paralymp.ru (office).

ROZOVSKY, Mark Grigorievich; Russian theatre director and scriptwriter; b. 3 April 1937, Petropavlovsk; ed Moscow Univ. Higher Scriptwriters' School; f. and managed 'Our Home' (amateur studio theatre) with fellow students of Moscow Univ. 1958–70; theatre officially disbanded 1970, revived in 1987 as professional co. U Nikitskikh Vorot; wrote 3 books on theatre, dir versions of Karamzin, Kafka, Dostoevsky and others in Leningrad, Moscow and Riga 1970–87; Chief Dir Moscow State Music Hall 1974–79; Dir Orpheus and Eurydice (rock-opera) 1975 and a musical adaptation of 'Strider' jtly with Georgii Tovstonogov, by L. N. Tolstoy for Gorky Theatre, Leningrad; Theatre of Nations Prize Hamburg and Avignon 1979. *Other productions include:* Amadeus (P. Shaffer) for Moscow Arts Theatre; libretto for opera about Mayakovsky; work for TV including documentary on Meyerhold, Triumphal Square 1984; works for Gorky Theatre, Leningrad and Theatre of Russian Drama, Riga, Latvia and his own Studio Theatre, Moscow; Romances with Oblomov, Alexandrinsky Theatre, St Petersburg 1992.

ROZWADOWSKI, Jean F., MBA; French business executive and international organization official; b. 1947, Netherlands; s. of a Polish father and French mother; m.; two c.; ed Ecole Supérieure de Commerce de Paris, Amos Tuck School of Business Admin, Dartmouth Coll., NH, USA; grew up in S Africa; spent 20 years with American Express, including Head of SE Asia, Middle East and Brazil Divs; fmr Pres. American Chamber of Commerce, Sao Paulo, Brazil; Exec. Vice-Pres. for Europe, Middle East and Africa, MasterCard –1999, Pres. Latin American and Caribbean Div. 1999–2004; Sec.-Gen. ICC 2009–11; mem. UN Global Compact Bd 2009–11.

RUAN, Chongwu; Chinese politician; b. May 1933, Huai'an Co., Hebei Prov.; ed Moscow Auto-Eng Inst.; Deputy Dir Shanghai Materials Research Inst.; joined CCP 1952; Deputy Sec. Shanghai Municipal Scientific Workers' Asscn; Science and Tech. Counsellor, Embassy in Bonn 1978; Vice-Mayor Shanghai 1983–85; Sec. CCP, Shanghai Municipality 1983–85; Minister of Public Security 1985–87; Vice-Minister Science and Tech. Comm., State Council 1987–89, of Labour 1989–93; Sec. CCP 2nd Hainan Prov. Cttee 1993; Gov. of Hainan Prov. 1993–98; mem. 12th CCP Cen. Cttee 1982–87, 13th Cen. Cttee 1987–92, 14th Cen. Cttee 1992–97; Del., 15th CCP Nat. Congress 1997–2002; mem. 9th Standing Cttee of NPC 1998–2003. *Address:* c/o National People's Congress, Beijing, People's Republic of China (office).

RUBALCABA, Alfredo Pérez, PhD; Spanish chemist, academic and politician; b. 28 July 1951, Solares, Cantabria; s. of Alfredo Pérez Vega and Maria Dolores Rubalcaba Cabarga; m. Pilar Goya 1979; ed Complutense Univ.; worked at Univ. of Constance, Germany, Univ. of Montpellier, France; Dir Technical Office, Sec. of State for Univs and Research 1982–85; Dir-Gen. of Univ. Educ. 1985–86; Sec.-Gen. of Educ. 1986; Sec. of State for Educ. 1988–92; mem. Congreso de los Diputados (Congress of Deputies), Deputy for Toledo prov. 1993–96, for Madrid prov. 1996–2004, for Cantabria prov. 2004–08, Cádiz prov. 2008–; Acting Minister of Defence May–June 2008, Minister of Educ. and Science 1992–93, of the Presidency 1993–96, of Interior 2006–11 (resgnd); Deputy Prime Minister 2010–11 (resgnd), also Govt Spokesman; Gen. Sec. Spanish Socialist Workers' Party 2012–14; Prof. of Organic Chem., Complutense Univ.; fmr spokesman Parl. Group Socialists, Cttee on Science and Tech.; mem. Fed. Exec. Cttee of Socialist Party.

RUBBIA, Carlo; Italian physicist and academic; *Professor of Physics, Università degli Studi di Pavia;* b. 31 March 1934, Gorizia; s. of Silvio Rubbia and Bice Rubbia; m. Marisa Rubbia; one s. one d.; ed high school, Pisa and Rome Univs and Columbia Univ., USA; joined CERN as Sr Physicist 1961, mem. Cttee CERN 1985–89, Dir-Gen. 1989–93; Higgins Prof. of Physics, Harvard Univ. 1970–88; currently Full Prof. of Physics, Pavia Univ.; Pres. Ente per le Nuove tecnologie, l'Energia e l'Ambiente (ENEA) 1999–2005; Adviser, EC Commr for Research and Educ. Policies 2002; mem. Papal Acad. of Science 1986–; mem. American Acad. of Arts and Sciences, Accad. dei Lincei, European Acad. of Sciences, Accademia dei XL, Pontifical Acad. of Sciences, Polish Acad. of Sciences (Foreign Mem.), Croatian Acad. of Sciences and Arts, Royal Soc., UK, (Foreign Mem.), NAS (Foreign Mem.), Russian Acad. of Sciences (Foreign Mem.), Third World Acad. of Sciences, European Acad. of Sciences, Société Européenne de Culture, Ateneo Veneto, Société Française de Physique, Istituto Lombardo, Austrian Acad. of Sciences; Cavaliere di Gran Croce (Knight Grand Cross) 1985, Officier de la Légion d'Honneur 1989, Polish Order of Merit 1993, Senator for Life (highest Italian honour) 2013; Dr hc (Geneva) 1983, (Carnegie Mellon) 1985, (Genoa) 1985, (Udine) 1985, (La Plata, Argentina) 1986, (Northwestern) 1986, (Camerino) 1987, (Chicago) 1987, (Loyola) 1987, (Boston) 1988, (Sofia, Bulgaria) 1990, (Moscow)1991, (Chile) 1991, (Polytechnic Univ. of Madrid) 1992, (Padova) 1992, (Tech. Univ. of Rio de Janeiro) 1993, (Trieste) 1994, (Oxford) 1994, (Catholic Univ. of Lima, Peru) 1994, (Nat. Univ. of St Antonio Abad of Cusco, Peru) 1994, (Bordeaux) 1998, (Haute Savoie) 1999, (St John's Univ.) 2003, (Università di Torino) 2004; Nobel Prize for Physics 1984, Leslie Prize for Exceptional Achieve-

ments 1985, Jesolo d'Oro 1986. *Address:* Physics Department, Università degli Studi di Pavia, Corso Strada Nuova 65, 27100 Pavia, Italy (office). *Telephone:* 0382-504217 (office). *Fax:* 0382-504529 (office). *Website:* www.unipv.it (office).

RUBENSTEIN, David M., BA, JD; American lawyer and business executive; b. 1949, Baltimore, Md; m. Alice Rogoff; three c.; ed Duke Univ., Univ. of Chicago; with Paul, Weiss, Rifkind, Wharton & Garrison (law firm), New York 1973–75; Chief Counsel, US Senate Judiciary Cttee Sub-Cttee on constitutional amendments, Washington, DC 1975–76; Deputy Asst to Pres. Jimmy Carter for domestic policy 1977–81; admitted to DC Bar Asscn 1981; with Shaw, Pittman, Potts & Trowbridge (now Pillsbury, Winthrop, Shaw Pittman), Washington, DC 1982–87; Co-founder and Man. Dir The Carlyle Group 1987, fmr Co-CEO; mem. Int. Business Council, World Econ. Forum; mem. Nat. Advisory Cttee, JPMorgan Chase; Vice-Chair. Lincoln Center for Performing Arts, Council on Foreign Relations; Co-Chair. Brookings Inst.; Pres. Econ. Club of Washington; mem. Bd of Trustees, Hoover Inst., Duke Univ., Johns Hopkins Univ., Memorial Sloan Kettering Cancer Center, Nat. Gallery of Art, Young Global Leaders Foundation, Univ. of Chicago, Inst. for Advanced Study, John F. Kennedy Center for the Performing Arts; mem. Visiting Cttee, Kennedy School of Govt, Harvard Univ.; mem. Advisory Bd School of Econs and Man., Tsinghua Univ., People's Repub. of China, Stanford Inst. for Econ. Policy Research, Madison Council of Library of Congress, Harvard Business School; mem. Council Nat. Trust for Historic Preservation, American Acad. of Arts and Sciences.

RUBENSTEIN, Howard Joseph, LLB; American lawyer and public relations executive; *President, Rubenstein Associates Inc.;* b. 3 Feb. 1932, New York; s. of Samuel Rubenstein and Ada Sall; m. Amy Forman 1959; three s.; ed Univ. of Pennsylvania, Harvard Univ., St John's Univ. School of Law; admitted New York State Bar 1960; Pres. Rubenstein Assocs Inc. (public relations consultants), New York 1954–, also Chair. Rubenstein Communications, Inc.; Co-Chair. Holocaust Comm. 1993; mem. Exec. Cttee Real Estate Bd of New York, NYC & Co., Asscn for a Better New York; mem. Bd of Dirs Albert Einstein Coll. of Medicine 1997–; mem. Mayor's Business Advisory Council, New York 1996–, communications adviser Gov.'s Jerusalem 3000 Cttee 1996–; mem. Bd of Govs Jewish County Relations Council 1999–; Trustee, Police Athletic League, Inner City Scholarship Fund of the Archdiocese of New York, Foundation for Nat. Archives; mem. City Univ. of New York Business Leadership Council; fmr consultant, US Foreign Claims Settlement Comm.; Hon. LLD (St John's Univ. School of Law) 1990; inducted into PR People Hall of Fame 2013. *Address:* Rubenstein Associates Inc., 1345 Avenue of the Americas, New York, NY 10105 (office); 993 Fifth Avenue, New York, NY 10028, USA (home). *Telephone:* (212) 843-8000 (office). *E-mail:* info@rubenstein.com (office). *Website:* www.rubenstein.com (office).

RUBIANO SÁENZ, HE Cardinal Pedro; Colombian ecclesiastic; *Archbishop Emeritus of Santafé de Bogotá;* b. 13 Sept. 1932, Cartago; ordained priest 1956; Bishop of Cúcuta 1971–83; Coadjutor Archbishop of Cali 1983–85, Bishop of Cali 1985–94; Archbishop of Santafé de Bogotá 1994–2010, Archbishop Emer. 2010–; cr. Cardinal 2001, Cardinal Priest of Trasfigurazione di Nostro Signore Gesù Cristo 2001–; mem. Congregation for Catholic Educ., Pontifical Council for the Pastoral Care of Migrants and Itinerant People; Apostolic Admin. of Popayán 1990–91. *Address:* Arzobispado, Carrera 7 N. 10–20, Bogotá, DC1, Colombia (office). *Telephone:* (1) 3505511 (office). *Fax:* (1) 3347867 (office). *E-mail:* bogotaarq@cec.org.co (office). *Website:* www.arquibogota.org.co (office); www.cec .org.co (office).

RUBIK, Ernő, BA; Hungarian inventor, architect and designer; b. 13 July 1944, Budapest; s. of Ernő Rubik, Sr and Magdolna Szántó; m. Ágnes Hégely; one s. two d.; ed Univ. of Tech. Educ., Budapest, Hungarian Acad. of Applied Arts and Design, Budapest, Budapest School of Commercial Art; consecutively Asst Prof., then Assoc. Prof., Acad. of Applied Arts, Dir of Postgraduate Studies 1983–86; Hon. Prof. Acad. of Crafts and Design, Budapest 1987; inventor of Rubik's Cube 1974, and other games and puzzles; Pres. Rubik Studio; Pres. Hungarian Acad. of Eng 1990–96; Hon. Citizen of Budapest 2014; Labour Order of Merit Gold Medal of the Hungarian People's Repub., Grand Cross of the Order of Saint Stephen 2014; Toy of the Year Award 1981–82 of UK, FRG, Italy, Sweden, Finland, France, USA, State Prize 1983, Juvenile Prize, State Office of Youth and Sport 1988, Dénes Gabor Prize, Novofer Foundation 1995, Ányos Jedlik Prize, Hungarian Patent Office 1996, Prize for the Reputation of Hungary 1997, Kossuth Prize 2007, Moholy-Nagy Prize, Moholy-Nagy Univ. of Arts and Design 2008, Amb. of the Year of Creativity and Innovation, EU 2009, USA Science and Engineering Festival Award 2010, Prima Primissima Prize 2010. *Publications:* co-author and ed. of A bűvös kocka (The Magic Cube) 1981, Rubik's Magic 1986, Rubik's Cubic Compendium 1987. *Leisure interests:* swimming, skiing, sailing. *Address:* Rubik Studio, Városmajor u. 74, 1122 Budapest, Hungary (office). *Telephone:* (1) 356-9533 (office). *Website:* www.rubiks.com (office).

RUBIKS, Alfrēds; Latvian politician; b. 24 Sept. 1935, Daugavpils, Latvia; m.; two s.; ed Rīga Tech. Higher School and Leningrad Higher Party School; mem. CPSU 1958–91; engineer and foreman, Riga Electrotechnical Plant 1957–61; Komsomol and party work; Sec. Latvian Komsomol Cen. Cttee; First Sec. of Leningradsky Region of Rīga Regional CP Cttee 1976–82; Minister of Local Industry for Latvian SSR 1982–84; Chair. Exec. Cttee Rīga City Council of People's Deputies 1984–90; First Sec. Cen. Cttee Latvian CP 1990–91; USSR People's Deputy 1989–91; mem. CPSU Cen. Cttee 1990–91; mem. CPSU Politburo July 1990–91; arrested by Latvian authorities Aug. 1991, accused of high treason; elected to Saeima (Parl.) 1993; sentenced to eight years' imprisonment 1995; released 1997; mem. Saeima 1998; Chair. Latvian Socialist Party 1998–2015; mem. European Parl. 2009–14. *Address:* c/o Latvian Socialist Party, Burtnieku iela 23, Rīga, Latvia.

RUBIN, Hon. James P., BA, MIA; American academic, broadcast journalist and fmr government official; b. 1960, New York; m. Christiane Amanpour; one s.; ed Columbia Univ.; Research Dir Arms Control Asscn, Washington, DC 1985–89, also consultant to US Senate Foreign Relations Cttee on nuclear arms control issues; fmr staff mem., US Senate Foreign Relations Cttee, Sr Foreign Policy Adviser to Joseph R. Biden, Jr; Sr Adviser and spokesman for US Rep. to UN Madeleine Albright 1993–96; Dir of Foreign Policy and Spokesman Clinton/Gore presidential campaign Aug.–Nov. 1996; Sr Adviser to Sec. of State 1996–97; Asst Sec. of State for Public Affairs 1997–2000; Pnr, Brunswick 2001–04; Visiting Prof. of Int. Relations, LSE 2001–04; foreign policy adviser John Kerry US presidential campaign 2004; Anchor, World News Tonight, Sky News (UK) 2005–06, World Affairs Commentator 2006–07; mem. Bd of Dirs Columbia Univ. School of Int. Affairs, then Adjunct Prof. of Int. and Public Affairs; Visiting Fellow and Scholar-in-Residence, Rothermere American Inst., Univ. of Oxford 2013–14; Vice-Chair. Atlantic Partnership; mem. Bd of Dirs Int. Rescue Cttee, UK; mem. Council on Foreign Relations; John Jay Award for Distinguished Professional Achievement (Columbia Univ.) 1998, Distinguished Service Award, Sec. of State 2000. *Address:* c/o Rothermere American Institute, University of Oxford, 1a South Parks Road, Oxford, OX1 3UB, England (office). *Website:* www.rai.ox.ac.uk (office).

RUBIN, Robert, BA, LLB; American financial services industry executive, lawyer and fmr government official; b. 29 Aug. 1938, New York; s. of Alexander Rubin and Sylvia Rubin (née Seiderman); m. Judith L. Oxenberg 1963; two s.; ed Harvard Univ., London School of Econs, Yale Univ. Law School; lawyer, Cleary, Gottlieb, Steen & Hamilton, New York 1964–66; joined Goldman, Sachs 1966, Vice-Chair. & Co-COO 1987–90, Co-Chair. 1990–92; Chair. New York Host Cttee 1992 Democratic Convention; Asst to Pres. Clinton for Econ. Policy 1993–95; Sec. of Treasury 1995–99; Chair. Exec. Cttee and mem. Office of the Chair. Citigroup Inc. 1999–2007, Chair. Nov.–Dec. 2007, Sr Advisor 2007–09 (resgnd); Advisor, Taconic Capital Advisors LP, New York Farallon Capital Man. LLC, San Francisco 2009–10; Counsellor, Centerview Partners, New York 2010–; mem. Bd of Trustees Mount Sinai-New York Univ. Health; fmr mem. Advisory Bd Insight Venture Partners, Gen. Atlantic LLC; fmr Special Advisor Tinicum Capital Partners, LP; mem. Harvard Corpn 2002–; Vice-Chair. Council on Foreign Relations 2003–07, Co-Chair. 2007–; fmr mem. Bd of Dirs Ford Motor Co., Harvard Man. Co., New York Stock Exchange, New York Futures Exchange, New York City Partnership, Center for Nat. Policy; Chair. Local Initiatives Support Corpn (LISC); launched Hamilton Project 2006; mem. Africa Progress Panel 2007–; Hon. DHumLitt (Yeshiva Univ.) 1996; Hon. LLD (Univ. of Miami) 2008; Nat. Asscn of Christians and Jews Award 1977, Columbia Business School Award 1996, Euromoney Magazine's Finance Minister of the Year Award 1996, Medal for High Civic Service, Citizens' Budget Comm. 1997, Foreign Policy Asscn Medal 1998, Jefferson Award, American Inst. for Public Service 1998, Award of Merit, Yale Univ. 1998, Paul Tsongas Award 1998, Global Leadership Award, UN Asscn 1998. *Publication:* In an Uncertain World: Tough Choices from Wall Street to Washington 2003 (with Jacob Weisberg). *Leisure interest:* fly fishing. *Address:* Centerview Partners LLC, 31 West 52nd Street, 22nd Floor, New York, NY 10019, USA (office). *Telephone:* (212) 380-2650 (office). *Fax:* (212) 380-2651 (office). *Website:* www.centerviewpartners.com (office).

RUBINA, Dina Ilyinichna; Israeli writer; b. 19 Sept. 1953, Tashkent, Uzbekistan; ed Tashkent State Conservatory; music teacher, Tashkent Inst. of Culture 1977–90; literary debut in Yunost magazine 1971; emigrated to Israel 1990; edited newspaper (Pyatnitza and others); Head, Dept of Public and Cultural Relations, The Jewish Agency in Russia 1999–2003; Ministry of Culture Award 1982, Arye Dulchin Award (Israel) 1991, Israel Writers' Union Award 1995, Best Book of literary season, France 1996. *Films:* Zavtra, kak obychno 1984, Na Verhney Maslovke 2004. *Publications include:* The Double-Barrelled Name (short stories) 1990, In Thy Gates 1994, An Intellectual Sat Down on the Road 1995, Here Comes the Messiah 1997, The Escort Angel 1998, The Last Wild Boar from Pontevedra Forest 1998, High Water in Venice 1999, Several Hurried Words of Love (short stories) 2003, Syndicate 2009, Platanthera 2009, Adam and Miriam 2010, Window 2012, Zheltukhin 2014, Voice 2014, Prodigal Son 2014. *Leisure interest:* travelling. *Address:* Et Ha'zmir, 11/8, 98491 Maale-Adumim, Israel (home). *Telephone:* 2-5352435 (home). *Fax:* 2-5352435 (home). *E-mail:* contacts@dinarubina.com (home). *Website:* www.dinarubina.com (home).

RUBINSTEIN, Amnon, BA, LLM, PhD; Israeli author, academic and fmr politician; *Professor of Law, Radzyner School of Law, Interdisciplinary Center (IDC), Herzliya;* b. 5 Sept. 1931, Tel-Aviv; s. of Aaron Rubinstein and Rachel Rubinstein (née Vilozny); m. Ronny Havatzeleth 1959; one s. one d.; ed Hebrew Univ. of Jerusalem, London School of Econs; mil. service in Israeli Defence Forces; fmr Dean, Faculty of Law and Prof. of Law, Tel-Aviv Univ.; mem. Knesset (Parl.) 1977–2001 (resgnd), mem. Constitution and Justice Cttee (Chair. 1999–2001), State Audit Cttee; Minister of Communications 1984–87, of Energy and Infrastructure and Science and Tech. 1992–93, of Educ. and Culture 1993–96; currently Prof. of Law, Radzyner School of Law, Interdisciplinary Center (IDC), Herzliya, fmr Dean; Dr hc (Bradford) 1968, (Hewbrew Union Coll., Jerusalem) 1969. *Publications:* Jurisdiction and Illegality 1965, The Zionist Dream Revisited 1985 (French trans. Le Rêve et l'histoire), The Constitutional Law of Israel (5th edn) 1997, From Herzl to Rabin 1999. *Leisure interests:* music, drama, swimming. *Address:* Radzyner School of Law, Interdisciplinary Center Herzliya, Kanfei Nesharim Street, PO Box 167, Herzliya 46150, Israel. *Telephone:* 9-9527325 (office). *Fax:* 9-9513075 (office). *E-mail:* amnon_r@idc.ac.il (office). *Website:* portal.idc.ac.il/en/main/academics/law/Pages/General.aspx (office).

RUBINSTEIN, Ariel, BSc, MA, MSc, PhD; Israeli economist and academic; *Professor of Economics and Salzberg Chair, Tel-Aviv University;* b. 13 April 1951, Jerusalem; s. of Yehuda Rubinstein and Leah Rubinstein; m. Yael Rubinstein; one s. one d.; ed The Hebrew Univ.; Sr Lecturer, Dept of Econs, The Hebrew Univ. 1981–84, Assoc. Prof. 1984–86, Prof. 1986–90; Prof. of Econs and Salzberg Chair, Tel-Aviv Univ. 1990–, Chair. Dept of Econs 1991–93; Lecturer in rank of Prof. Princeton Univ., USA 1991–2004; Prof. of Econs, New York Univ. 2004–; fmr Visiting Prof., Nuffield Coll. Oxford 1979–80, LSE 1986–89, Univ. of Chicago 1988, Univ. of Pennsylvania 1989, Columbia Univ., New York 1990, Russell-Sage Foundation 1996–97; Assoc. Ed. Econometrica 1984–92, Journal of Econ. Theory 1986–94, Games and Economic Behavior 1988–2002, Mathematics of Social Sciences 1993–2001; mem. Editorial Bd Review of Economic Studies 1987–88 (Foreign Ed. 1988–92), Review of Economic Design 1993–, Economics and Philosophy 1994–, International Journal of Game Theory 1995–2000, NAJ Economics 2001–; mem. Advisory Cttee Journal of European Economic Asscn 2003–; mem. Exec. Bd Theoretical Economics 2005–; Fellow, Econometric Soc. 1985– (Pres. 2004), Israeli Acad. of Sciences 1995–, European Econ. Asscn 2004–; mem. European Acad. of Sciences and Arts; Foreign Hon. mem. American Acad. of Arts and Sciences 1994–, American Econ. Asscn 1995–, Hon. Fellow, Nuffield Coll. 2002–; Dr hc (Tilburg) 2002; Michael Bruno Memorial Award 2000, Pras Israel 2002, Nemmers Prize, Northwestern Univ. 2004, EMET Prize 2006. *Publications:* Bargaining and Markets (with M. Osborne) 1990, A Course in Game Theory (with M. Osborne) 1994, Modeling Bounded Rationality 1998, Economics and Language 2000, Lecture Notes in Microeconomic Theory: The Economic Agent 2005, Economic Tales 2009, more than 80 articles in academic journals. *Address:* School of Economics, Tel-Aviv University, Tel-Aviv 69978, Israel (office). *Telephone:* (3) 6409601 (office); (3) 6421111 (home). *Fax:* (3) 6409908 (office). *E-mail:* rariel@post.tau.ac.il (office). *Website:* arielrubinstein.tau.ac.il (office).

RUBIO, Juan Carlos; Spanish writer, director, actor and academic; b. 1967, Montilla, Córdoba; ed School of Theatre de Alcorcón, Royal School of Drama and Dance, Madrid; Prof., Colectivo de Lesbianas, Gays, Transexuales y Bisexuales de Madrid 1999–2000; Prof., TB/IGUELDO 2000; Prof., Antena 3 TV 2000; Prof., Massart 2008; Prof., El Ejido (Almería) 2008; Prof., Leganés (Madrid) 2008; Prof., Lucena (Córdoba) 2008; served as Dir SC Productions. *Films:* writer: Fin de curso 2005, El Calentito 2005, Dolly 2007, Lola, la película 2007, Bon appétit (Best Screenplay Biznaga Málaga Spanish Film Festival) 2010; film writer: El idiota 2000, Slam 2002, El calentito 2005, Fin de curso 2005, Retorno a Hansala 2008; actor: Las trampas del azar 1995, Los padres terribles 1996–97, El cerco de Numancia 1998; playwright: Esta noche no estoy para nadie (City Theatre Prize Alcorcón) 1997, Las heridas del viento (Premio Hermanos Machado 2000, Iberoamerican Film Festival of Huelva Best Filmmaker 2017) 1999, Tres 2000, El bosque es mío 2001, 10 2001, ¿Dónde se esconden los sueños? (Premio teatro infantil Escuela Navarra de Teatro) 2004, Epitafio (Premio Animasur 2005) 2004, Humo (also dir) (Premio SGAE 2005, Premio telón Chivas 2008) 2005, Arizona (also dir) (Premio Raúl Moreno-Fatex, Mención Especial del Premio Lope de Vega) 2006, No quemes la vida 2007, 100 metros cuadrados 2007; dir: The Big Kahuna 2009, Windermere Club 2015, Sensitive 2017. *Publications:* No mires a los ojos de la diosa (City of Alcorcón) 1982, Mama ¿qué es un wellspringt? (Colmenar Viejo) 1982. *E-mail:* carlosrubio06@yahoo.es. *Website:* www.juancarlosrubio.com.

RUBIO, Marco Antonio, BS, JD; American lawyer and politician; *Senator from Florida;* b. 28 May 1971, Miami, Fla; s. of Mario Rubio and Oria Garcia (Cuban exiles); m. Jeanette Dousdebes 1997; two s. two d.; ed South Miami Sr High School, Tarkio Coll. (football scholarship), Santa Fe Coll., Univs of Florida and Miami; interned for Congresswoman Ileana Ros-Lehtinen while studying law; served as City Commr for West Miami –2000; mem. Florida House of Reps for 111th Dist 2000–08, Majority Leader 2003–06, Speaker of the House 2006–08; Senator from Fla 2011–, mem. Commerce, Science and Transportation Cttee, Select Cttee on Intelligence, Cttee on Foreign Relations; Political Analyst, Univision 2008; mem. Bd Alafit Int., Latin Builders Asscn, Miami Performing Arts Center; Florida Chair. Grand Old Party Action Cttee; Visiting Prof., Florida Int. Univ. Metropolitan Center 2008; unsuccessful cand. for Republican Party nomination in 2016 presidential election 2015–16; Republican; Freshman Legislator of the Year, Florida Petroleum Marketers Asscn. *Publications:* 100 Innovative Ideas for Florida's Future: A Plan of Action 2006. *Address:* 317 Hart Senate Office Building, Washington, DC 20510, USA (office). *Telephone:* (202) 224-3041 (office). *Website:* rubio.senate.gov (office).

RUÇI, Gramoz; Albanian politician; *Speaker, People's Assembly;* b. 6 Dec. 1951, Salari village, Tepelenë Dist; m.; one s. one d.; ed Shkodër Pedagogical Inst. (now Univ. of Shkodër), Eqerem Çabej Univ., Gjirokastër; began career as teacher, Progonat, Gjirokastër Dist 1971–78; mem. Partia e Punës e Shqipërisë (Party of Labour) –1991, Partia Socialiste e Shqipërisë (PSSh, Albanian Socialist Party) 1991–, Sec.-Gen. 1991–96, 1999–2005; Minister of the Interior Feb.–June 1991; mem., Kuvendi Popullor (People's Ass., parl.) for Vlora, Gjirokastra, Fier constituencies (PSSh) 1997–, Leader, PSSh Parl. Group 2000–05, 2009, Speaker, People's Ass. 2017–. *Address:* Kuvendi Popullor, Bulevardi Dëshmorët e Kombit 4, 1010 Tirana, Albania (office). *Telephone:* (4) 2278261 (office). *E-mail:* albana.shtylla@parlament.al (office). *Website:* www.parlament.al (office).

RUCKAUF, Carlos Federico; Argentine politician; b. 10 July 1944; m.; three c.; ed Nat. Univ. of Buenos Aires; Asst Sec. Insurance Union 1969–72; Labour Judge 1973–75; Sec. Trabajo de la Nación (Labour of the Nation) 1975–76; Pres. Partido Justicialista de Capital Federal (Fed. Justice Party) 1983, Vice-Pres. 1993, Pres. 1994; Senatorial Cand. 1983; Nat. Deputy 1987–89, 1991–93; Amb. to Italy, Malta and FAO 1989–91; Pres. Foreign Affairs Comm. 1991–93; Minister of the Interior 1993; apptd Vice-Pres. of Argentina 1995; Gov. Buenos Aires Prov. 1999–2002; Minister of Foreign Affairs 2002–03; mem. Parl. (Partido Justicialista—PJ) 2003–07; Knight of the Grand Cross, Order of Merit (Italy) 1995, Grand Cross, Order Bernardo O'Higgins (Chile) 1996, Medal of the Congress of Deputies (Spain) 1997, Commdr, Légion d'honneur (France) 1997, Alaoui Order (Morocco) 1998, Grand Cross, Ordem Nacional do Cruzeiro do Sul (Brazil) 1998, Special Grand Cross, Nat. Order of Merit (Paraguay) 1999.

RUCKELSHAUS, William Doyle; American business executive and fmr government official; *Strategic Director, Madrona Venture Group LLC;* b. 24 July 1932, Indianapolis, Ind.; s. of John K. Ruckelshaus and Marion Covington Ruckelshaus (née Doyle); m. Jill E. Strickland 1962; one s. four d.; ed Portsmouth Priory School, RI and Princeton Univ., Harvard Univ. Law School; served with US Army 1953–55; admitted to Ind. Bar 1960; attorney with Ruckelshaus, Bobbit & O'Connor 1960–68; Partner, Ruckelshaus, Beveridge, Fairbanks & Diamond (fmrly Ruckelshaus, Beveridge & Fairbanks), Sr Partner 1974–76; Deputy Attorney-Gen. Ind. 1960–65; Minority Attorney, Ind. State Senate 1965–67; mem. Ind. House of Reps 1967–69; Asst Attorney-Gen., US Civil Div., Dept of Justice 1969–70; Dir Environmental Protection Agency 1970–73, 1983–84; Acting Dir FBI 1973 and Deputy Attorney-Gen. 1973 (resgnd); Sr Vice-Pres. Weyerhaeuser Co. 1976–83; mem. Perkins Coie (law firm), Seattle 1985–88; Chair. CEO Browning-Ferris Industries Inc., Houston 1988–95; Founder and Prin. Madrona Investment Group (now Madrona Venture Group LLC) 1996, now Strategic Dir; Chair. World Resources Inst., Washington, DC 1999–2006, William D. Ruckelshaus Center, Univ of Washington and Washington State Univ; mem. Bd of Dirs Bullitt Foundation, Energy Foundation, Meridian Inst., Long Live the Kings; mem. Bd of Dirs Weyerhaeuser Co., Nordstrom, Inc., Cummins Engine Co., Solutia, Pharmacia Corpn, Monsanto; fmr Dir Peabody Int. Corpn, Church and Dwight Co. Inc.; fmr Chair. Bd Geothermal Kinetics Inc.; mem. Public Interest Advisory Cttee Harvard Univ. Medical Project, Bd of Overseers, Kennedy School of

Govt, Harvard Univ., Bd of Regents, Seattle Univ., World Resource Inst. (Chair. 1998, now Chair. Emer.), Comm. on Ocean Policy 2001–04, Science Advisory Bd, Nat. Oceanic and Atmospheric Admin 2003; Chair. Salmon Recovery Funding Bd for State of Washington, Puget Sound Cleanup, Univ. of Washington and Washington State Univ. Policy Consensus Center, Seattle Aquarium Soc.; Co-Chair. Joint Ocean Comm. Initiative, Puget Sound Partnership 2005–; Trustee, Pacific Science Center Foundation, Seattle Chamber of Commerce, The Conservation Foundation, Seattle Art Museum; numerous awards and distinctions, including Presidential Medal of Freedom 2015. *Publication:* Reapportionment: A Continuing Problem 1963. *Leisure interests:* tennis, fishing, reading. *Address:* Madrona Investment Group LLC, 1000 2nd Avenue, Suite 3700, Seattle, WA 98104, USA (office). *Telephone:* (206) 674-3009 (office). *Fax:* (206) 674-3013 (office). *E-mail:* bill@madrona.com (office). *Website:* www.madrona.com (office).

RÜCKER, Joachim; German diplomatist and UN official; b. 30 May 1951; one s.; two d.; has served in several positions within Ministry of Foreign Affairs (MFA) including Head, Budget and Finance Div. 2002–05; Mayor of Sindelfingen, Germany 1993–2001; Deputy High Rep. for Admin and Finance, Office of the UN High Rep., Sarajevo, Bosnia and Herzegovina 2001–02, Deputy Special Rep. of Sec.-Gen. in charge of EU Pillar for Econ. Reconstruction, UN Interim Admin Mission in Kosovo (UNMIK) 2005–06, Special Rep. of Sec.-Gen. and Head of UNMIK 2006–08, Amb. to Sweden 2008–11, Inspector-Gen., MFA 2011–14, Perm. Rep. to UN, Geneva 2014–16, Pres. OHCHR 2015, Special Rep. for the Middle East Stability Partnership –2017. *Address:* Federal Foreign Office, Werderscher Markt 1, 10117 Berlin, Germany (office). *Telephone:* (30) 18170 (office). *Fax:* (30) 18173402 (office). *E-mail:* poststelle@auswaertiges-amt.de (office). *Website:* www.diplo.de (office); www.joachim-ruecker.def (home).

RÜCKL, Jiří; Czech business executive and fmr politician; *President, Rückl Crystal a.s.;* b. 20 Oct. 1940, Prague; s. of Jiří Rückl and Věra Rückl; m. Jana Hrabánková; two d.; ed Econ. Univ., Prague; specialist positions in glassware 1961–90; Pres. Rückl Crystal 1992–; Dir Ministry of Industry 1990–92; Councillor for Nibor 1994–; Senator 1996–2004. *Publications include:* specialist papers about glass production. *Address:* Rückl Crystal a.s., 26705 Nižbor 141, Czech Republic (office). *Telephone:* (3) 11696232 (office). *Fax:* (3) 11693510 (office). *E-mail:* ruckl@ruckl.cz (office). *Website:* www.ruckl.eu (office); www.ruckl.cz (office).

RUDD, Rt Hon. Amber; British politician; *Secretary of State for Work and Pensions;* b. 1 Aug. 1963; d. of Tony Rudd and Ethne Fitzgerald; m. A. A. Gill 1990 (divorced 1995); one s. one d.; ed Cheltenham Ladies' Coll., Univ. of Edinburgh; began career with J.P. Morgan & Co., London and New York; worked as financial journalist; f. Lawnstone Ltd (recruitment consultancy) 1981; MP (Conservative) for Hastings and Rye 2010–, mem. Environment, Food and Rural Affairs Cttee 2010–12; Parl. Private Sec. to Chancellor of the Exchequer George Osborne 2012; Asst Whip (HM Treasury) 2013–14, Parl. Under-Sec. (Dept of Energy and Climate Change) 2014–15, Sec. of State for Energy and Climate Change 2015–16, Sec. of State for the Home Dept 2016–18 (resgnd), also Minister for Women and Equalities Jan.–April 2018, Sec. of State for Work and Pensions Nov. 2018–; Trustee, Snowdon Trust; Dir Susan Smith Blackburn Prize 2003–. *Address:* Department for Work and Pensions, Caxton House, Tothill St, London, SW1H 9NA (office); House of Commons, London, SW1A 0AA, England (office). *Telephone:* (20) 3267-5144 (office). *E-mail:* ministers@dwp.gsi.gov.uk (office); amber.rudd.mp@parliament.uk (office). *Website:* www.gov.uk/government/organisations/department-for-work-pensions (office); www.amberrudd.co.uk.

RUDD, Kevin, BA; Australian fmr politician; *President, Asia Society Policy Institute;* b. 21 Sept. 1957, Nambour, Queensland; m. Therese Rudd; two s. one d.; ed Australian Nat. Univ.; joined Dept of Foreign Affairs and Trade 1981, worked in Embassies in Stockholm and Beijing; Chief of Staff to Queensland State Opposition Leader 1988–92; Premier, Queensland State Govt 1989–92, Dir-Gen. of Cabinet 1992–95; China Consultant, KPMG 1996–98; Adjunct Prof. of Asian Languages, Univ. of Queensland 1997–; mem. Parl. (Labor Party) for Griffith 1998–2013, Chair. Fed. Parl. Labor Party's Cttee on Foreign Affairs, Defence and Trade 1998–2001, Shadow Minister for Foreign Affairs 2001–04, Shadow Minister for Foreign Affairs and Int. Security 2004–05, Shadow Minister for Foreign Affairs, Trade and Int. Security 2005–07; Leader, Australian Labor Party 2006–10, June–Sept. 2013; Prime Minister 2007–10, June–Sept. 2013; Minister for Foreign Affairs and Trade 2010–12 (resgnd); Sr Fellow, John F. Kennedy School of Govt, Harvard Univ. 2014; Sr Adviser, Eurasia Group 2014–; Distinguished Fellow, Paulson Inst., Univ. of Chicago 2014–, Distinguished Fellow, Chatham House, Distinguished Statesman, Center for Strategic and Int. Studies; inaugural Pres. Asia Soc. Policy Inst. 2015–; f. Australian Nat. Apology Foundation (to promote reconciliation between indigenous and non-indigenous Australians), Asia Pacific Community Foundation; mem. Australian-American Leadership Dialogue; mem. Advisory Council, Australia-Asia Centre, Korea-Australia Centre. *Publications include:* numerous articles on Chinese politics. *Address:* Asia Society Policy Institute, 725 Park Avenue, New York, NY 10021, USA (office). *Telephone:* (212) 288-6400 (office). *E-mail:* policyinstitute@asiasociety.org (office). *Website:* asiasociety.org/policy-institute (office).

RUDD, Sir (Anthony) Nigel (Russell), Kt, DL, FCA; British business executive; *Chairman, Invensys plc;* b. 31 Dec. 1946; m. Lesley Elizabeth Rudd (née Hodgkinson) 1969; two s. one d.; ed Bemrose Grammar School, Derby; chartered accountant 1968; Div. Finance Dir London & Northern Group 1970–77; Chair. C. Price & Son Ltd 1977–82; Chair. Williams Holdings (later Williams PLC) 1982–2000; Deputy Chair. Raine Industries 1992–94 (Chair. (non-exec.) 1986–92); Dir Pilkington PLC 1994, Chair. 1995–2006; Deputy Chair. Boots PLC 2002, Chair. 2003–06, Chair. Alliance Boots PLC (after merger with Alliance Unichem) 2006–07; Chair. (non-exec.) Pendragon PLC 1989–2010, East Midlands Electricity 1994–97 (Dir 1990–97), Kidde 2000–03, BAA plc 2007–; Deputy Chair. Invensys plc Jan.–July 2009, Chair. July 2009–; Dir (non-exec.) Williams Man. Services 1985–96, Westminster Securities 1987–96, Gartmore Value Investment 1989–93, Gartmore 1993–96, Derby Pride 1993–98, Mithras Investment Trust 1994–98, Barclays Bank 1996–2009 (Deputy Chair. 2004–09), BAE Systems 2006–, Sappi Ltd 2006–; mem. European Round Table of Industrialists –2001, Council CBI 1999–; mem. Chartered Accountants' Co.; DL Derbyshire 1996; Freeman, City of London; Hon. DTech (Loughborough) 1998; Hon. DUniv (Derby) 1998. *Leisure interests:* golf, skiing, theatre, field sports. *Address:* Invensys plc, 3rd Floor, 40 Grosvenor Place, London, SW1X 7AW, England (office). *Telephone:* (20) 3155-1200 (office). *Fax:* (20) 3155-1201 (office). *Website:* www.invensys.com (office).

RUDD, Paul; American actor; b. 6 April 1969, Passaic, New Jersey; m. Julie Yaeger; one s. one d.; ed Univ. of Kansas, American Acad. of Dramatic Arts-West, Los Angeles. *Television includes:* Sisters 1992–95, Friends 2002–04, Cheap Seats 2006, Little Britain USA 2008. *Films include:* Clueless 1995, The Locusts 1997, The Object of My Affection 1998, Wet Hot American Summer 2001, The Shape of Things 2003, Anchorman: The Legend of Ron Burgundy 2004, P.S. 2004, The 40-Year-Old Virgin 2005, Tennis, Anyone? 2005, Night at the Museum 2006, Knocked Up 2007, Forgetting Sarah Marshall 2008, I Love You, Man 2009, Monsters vs Aliens (voice) 2009, Dinner for Schmucks 2010, How Do You Know 2010, Wanderlust 2011, The Perks of Being a Wallflower 2012, This Is 40 2012, Admission 2013, Anchorman 2: The Legend Continues 2014, Ant-Man 2015, Captain America: Civil War 2016. *Address:* c/o Brillstein-Grey Entertainment, 9150 Wilshire Blvd, Suite 350, Beverly Hills, CA 90212, USA (office).

RUDDOCK, Dame Joan Mary, DBE, BSc, ARCS; British politician; b. 28 Dec. 1943, Abergavenny; d. of Ken Anthony and Eileen Anthony; m. 1st Keith Ruddock 1963 (died 1996); m. 2nd Frank Doran 2010; ed Pontypool Grammar School for Girls, Imperial Coll., London; worked for Shelter (nat. campaign for the homeless) 1968–73; Dir Oxford Housing Aid Centre 1973–77; Special Programmes Officer with unemployed young people, Manpower Services Comm. 1977–79; Man., Reading Citizens Advice Bureau 1979–87; Chair. Campaign for Nuclear Disarmament (CND) 1981–85, Vice-Chair. 1985–86; MP for Lewisham Deptford 1987–2015, mem. Select Cttee on Televising House of Commons, mem. British Del., Council of Europe 1988–89, Shadow Spokesperson on Transport 1989–92, on Home Affairs 1992–94, on Environmental Protection 1994–97, Select Cttee on Modernization 2001–05, Select Cttee on Environment, Food and Rural Affairs 2003–05, Select Cttee of Int. Devt 2005–07; Parl. UnderSec. of State for Women 1997–98; Co-founder Women Say No to GMOs 1999; Founder and Co-ordinator UK Women's Link with Afghan Women 2001; Labour Parl. Under-Sec. of State Dept of Environment, Food and Rural Affairs 2007–08; Parl. Under-Sec. of State, Dept of Energy and Climate Change 2008–09; Minister of State for Energy and Climate Change 2009–10; mem. Bd Trinity Laban; mem. Privy Council 2010; Hon. Assoc., Nat. Secular Soc.; Hon. Fellow, Goldsmith's Coll., Univ. of London 1996, Laban Centre, London; Frank Cousins Peace Award 1984. *Publications:* The CND Story (contrib.) 1983, CND Scrapbook 1987, Voices for One World (contrib.) 1988. *Leisure interests:* gardening, music, art. *Website:* www.joanruddock.org.

RUDDOCK, Hon. Philip M., BA, LLB; Australian solicitor and politician (retd); b. 12 March 1943, Canberra; s. of the Hon. Max S. Ruddock; m. Heather Ruddock 1971; two d.; ed Barker Coll., Hornsby, Sydney Univ.; mem. House of Reps 1973–2016; Shadow Minister for ACT and Shadow Minister Assisting Opposition Leader on Public Service Matters 1983–84, Immigration and Ethnic Affairs 1984–85, 1989–93, Shadow Minister for Social Security and Sr Citizens 1993, mem. Shadow Cabinet 1996; Minister for Immigration and Multicultural Affairs 1996–2001, also Minister Assisting Prime Minister for Reconciliation 1998–2001, 2002–03, Minister for Immigration and Multicultural and Indigenous Affairs 2001–02; Attorney-Gen. 2003–07; Shadow Cabinet Sec. 2009–13; Mayor of Hornsby Shire 2017–. *Leisure interests:* jogging, bushwalking, gardening, opera, reading. *Address:* Administration Centre, 296 Peats Ferry Road, Hornsby, NSW 2077, Australia (office). *Telephone:* (2) 9847-6666 (office). *Fax:* (2) 9847-6999. *E-mail:* hsc@hornsby.nsw.gov.au (office). *Website:* www.hornsby.nsw.gov.au.

RUDENSTINE, Neil Leon, PhD; American university administrator and academic; b. 21 Jan. 1935, Ossining, NY; s. of Harry Rudenstine and Mae Rudenstine; m. Angelica Zander 1960; one s. two d.; ed Princeton Univ., Oxford Univ., UK, Harvard Univ.; instructor, English Dept, Harvard Univ. 1964–66, Asst Prof. 1966–68, Prof. of English and Pres., Harvard Univ. 1991–2001, now Pres. Emer.; Assoc. Prof. of English, Princeton Univ. 1968–73, Dean of Students 1968–72, Prof. of English 1973–88, Dean of Coll. 1972–77, Provost 1977–88, now Provost Emer.; Exec. Vice-Pres. Andrew W. Mellon Foundation, New York 1988–91; Chair. Bd of Trustees ARTstor Inc. 2001–; Chair. Bd of Trustees Rockefeller Archive Center; mem. Council on Foreign Relations, American Philosophical Soc., Cttee for Econ. Devt, American Acad. of Arts and Sciences; Trustee, Princeton Univ. 2002–06, New York Public Library, Courtauld Inst. of Art, Barnes Foundation, Getty Trust; Hon. Fellow, New Coll., Oxford, Emmanuel Coll., Cambridge, Courtauld Inst. of Art; Dr hc (Harvard, Oxford, Princeton, Yale). *Publications:* Sidney's Poetic Development 1967, English Poetic Satire: Wyatt to Byron (with George Rousseau) 1972, In Pursuit of the PhD (with William G. Bowen) 1992, Pointing Our Thoughts 2001, The House of Barnes 2012, Ideas of Order 2014. *Address:* ARTstor, 6 East 32nd Street, New York, NY 10016 (office); 41 Armour Road, Princeton, NJ 08540, USA (home). *Telephone:* (212) 500-2419 (office); (609) 683-7516 (home). *Fax:* (212) 500-2418 (office). *Website:* www.artstor.org (office).

RUDIN, Alexander Izraliyevich; Russian cellist, pianist and conductor; *Artistic Director and Chief Conductor, Musica Viva Moscow Chamber Orchestra;* b. 25 Nov. 1960, Moscow; m. Rudina Olga Ryurikovna; two s.; ed Gnessin Music Inst., Moscow State Conservatory; has appeared as a soloist with numerous orchestras including Royal Philharmonic, Danish Radio, St Petersburg Philharmonic, Moscow Philharmonic, Austrian Symphony, Bolshoi Theatre; has worked as conductor with orchestras in Finland, Germany, Italy, Norway, Russia; has participated in festivals in Edin., Istanbul, Kuhmo, Vaasa; Artistic Dir and Chief Conductor Musica Viva Chamber Orchestra 1988–; apptd Artistic Dir Int. Festival Music Ensembles 1988; Prof., Moscow State Conservatory; Visiting Prof. Sibelius Acad., Helsinki 1991–92; partner in chamber music performances with Yuri Bashmet, Alexei Lubimov, B. Davidovich, Dmitry Sitkovetsky, Vladimir Spivakov, Natalia Gutman, and V. Krainev; mem. Jury of many Int. music competitions including 10th and 11th Tchaikovsky competitions (Chair. Jury of 12th Tchaikovsky Competition), Bach Competition; has given numerous master classes; winner of Concertino Prague 1973, J. S. Bach Competition, Leipzig 1976, Nat. Competition, Vilnius 1977, Tchaikovsky Competition, Moscow 1978, 1982, Gaspar Cassado Competition, Florence 1979. *Recording include:* over 30 albums including Symphony-Concerto for Cello 1997, Orchestral Works Vol 11 Cello and Orchestra 1999, Cello Concertos No.1&2 2000, Don Quixote 2000, Bach Cello Suites 2002, Romantic Music for Cello and Orchestra 2002, Cello Sonatas 2015, Hasse, C.P.E

Bach, Hertel Cello Concertos 2016, Mansurian Songs and Music 2017. *Performances:* with Musica Viva Chamber Orchestra: works by Bach, A. Salieri, I. Pleyel, J. Dussek, C. Dittersdorf, O. Kozlovsky, V. Pashkevich and A. Alyabiev. *Address:* ploshad Zhuravleva, 1-1, 107023, Moscow (office); Malaya Ostroumovskaya str. 1/10, Apt. 46, 107014 Moscow, Russia (home). *Telephone:* (495) 964-1965 (office); (499) 268-15-77 (home). *Fax:* (495) 964-1965 (office). *E-mail:* musica-viva@mail.ru (office). *Website:* musicaviva.ru (office).

RUDIN, Scott; American film and theatre producer; b. 14 July 1958, New York; partner John Barlow; production asst, asst to theatre producers Kermit Bloomgarden and Robert Whitehead; Casting Dir, Producer with Edgar Scherick; Exec. Vice-Pres. Production 20th Century Fox 1984–86, Pres. Production 1986–87; f. Scott Rudin Productions 1990–. *Films produced include:* He Makes Me Feel Like Dancing 1982 (Outstanding Children's Program Emmy Award 1982, Feature Documentary Acad. Award 1982), Mrs Soffel 1984, Flatliners 1990, Pacific Heights 1990, Regarding Henry 1991, Little Man Tate 1991, The Addams Family 1991, Sister Act 1992, Jennifer Eight 1992, Life With Mikey 1993, The Firm 1993, Searching for Bobby Fischer 1993, Sister Act 2 1993, Addams Family Values 1993, I.Q. 1994, Nobody's Fool 1994, Sabrina 1995, Clueless 1995, Up Close and Personal 1996, Ransom 1996, Marvin's Room 1996, The First Wives' Club 1996, In and Out 1997, Twilight 1998, The Truman Show 1998, A Civil Action 1998, Wonder Boys 1999, Rules of Engagement 1999, Brokeback Mountain 1999, Angela's Ashes 1999, Bringing Out the Dead 1999, Sleepy Hollow 1999, Shaft 2000, Rules of Engagement 2000, Zoolander 2001, The Royal Tenenbaums 2001, Iris: A Memoir of Iris Murdoch 2001, Orange County 2002, The Hours 2002, Changing Lanes 2002, Marci X 2003, The School of Rock 2003, The Stepford Wives 2004, The Manchurian Candidate 2004, The Village 2004, I Heart Huckabees 2004, Team America: World Police 2004, The Life Aquatic with Steve Zissou 2004, Closer 2004, Lemony Snicket's A Series of Unfortunate Events 2004, Freedomland 2005, Failure to Launch 2006, The Queen 2006, Venus 2006, Notes on a Scandal 2006, No Country for Old Men 2007, Margot at the Wedding 2007, The Darjeeling Limited 2007, Nothing Is Private 2007, There Will Be Blood 2007, The Other Boleyn Girl 2008, Stop Loss 2008, Extremely Loud & Incredibly Close 2011, The Dictator 2012, Captain Phillips 2013, The Grand Budapest Hotel (Golden Globe Award for Best Motion Picture – Comedy or Musical 2015) 2014, Aloha 2015, Steve Jobs 2016. *Theatre includes:* Passion 1994 (Tony Award Best Musical 1994), Indiscretions 1995, Hamlet 1995, Seven Guitars 1995, A Funny Thing Happened on the Way to the Forum 1996, Skylight 1997, On the Town (New York Shakespeare Festival) 1997, The Chairs 1998, The Judas Kiss 1998, Closer (London) 1998, Amy's View 1999, Wide Guys 1999, Copenhagen 1999 (Tony Award), The Book of Mormon 2011. *Recordings include:* as producer: The Book of Mormon (Grammy Award for Best Musical Theater Album 2012) 2011. *Address:* Scott Rudin Productions, 10th Floor, 120 West 45th Street, New York, NY 10036, USA.

RUDINI, Gen.; Indonesian army officer; b. 15 Dec. 1929, Malang, E. Java; s. of R. I. Poespohandojo and R. A. Koesbandijah; m. Oddyana Rudini 1959; one s. two d.; ed Breda Mil. Acad., Netherlands, reaching rank of Second Lt; Commdr Kostrad Infantry/Airborne Brigade 1972–73; Commdr Indonesian contingent of UN Peace-keeping Force in Middle East 1973–76; Commdr Kostrad Airborne Combat 1976–81; Commdr N. and Cen. Sulawesi Mil. Region, Manado 1981, later Commdr of Kostrad; Chief of Staff, Indonesian Army 1983–88; Minister of Home Affairs 1988–93, concurrently Chair. of the Election Cttee. *Leisure interests:* sport, music.

RUDISHA, David Lekuta; Kenyan track and field athlete; b. 17 Dec. 1988, Trans Mara; s. of Daniel Rudisha and Naomi Rudisha; m. Lizzy Naanyu; two d.; ed St Patrick's, Kimuron Secondary School; initially 400m. runner; gold medal, 800m., World Junior Championships, Beijing 2006; gold medal, 800m., African Junior Championships, Ouagadougou 2007; gold medal, 800m., African Championships, Addis Ababa 2008; won Int. Asscn of Athletics Feds. (IAAF) Grand Prix, (set new African record of 1:42.01) Rieti 2009, Ostrava 2009; gold medal, 800m., World Athletics Final, Thessaloniki 2009; winner 800m., Golden League, Brussels 2009, Zurich 2009; gold medal, 800m., Continental Cup, Split 2010; gold medal, 800m., African Championships, Nairobi 2010; won 800m., Diamond League, Doha 2010, Oslo 2010, Lausanne 2010, 2011, Brussels 2010, 2011, Monaco 2011, New York 2012, Paris Saint-Denis 2012; also won 800m., World Challenge, Melbourne 2010, 2011, 2012, Ostrava 2010, Berlin 2010, Rieti 2010, 2011; gold medal, 800m., World Championships, Daegu 2011; gold medal, 800m. (1:40:91, world record), Olympic Games, London 2012; IAAF World Athlete of the Year Award 2010, Kenyan Sportsman of the Year Award 2010, Best Male Athlete of London Award 2012.

RUELLE, David Pierre, PhD; French research mathematician and physicist; *Professor Emeritus, Institut des Hautes Etudes Scientifiques;* b. 20 Aug. 1935, Ghent, Belgium; s. of Pierre Ruelle and Marguerite de Jonge; m. Janine Lardinois 1960; one s. two d.; ed high school at Mons and Free Univ. of Brussels; Research Asst and Privatdozent, ETH, Zurich 1960–62; mem. Inst. for Advanced Study, Princeton, NJ, USA 1962–64; mem. Acad. des Sciences 1985, Academia Europaea 1993; Foreign Assoc. NAS 2002–; Foreign mem. Accad. Nazionale dei Lincei 2003–; Foreign Hon. mem. American Acad. of Arts and Sciences 1992; Hon. Prof., Institut des Hautes Etudes Scientifiques, Bures-sur-Yvette 1964–2000; Chevalier, Légion d'honneur; Dannie Heineman Prize 1985, Boltzmann Medal 1986, Matteuci Medal 2004, Henri Poincaré Prize 2006, Max Planck Medal, Deutsche Physikalische Gesellschaft 2014. *Publications:* Statistical Mechanics: Rigorous Results 1969, Thermodynamic Formalism 1978, Elements of Differentiable Dynamics and Bifurcation Theory 1989, Chance and Chaos 1991, The Mathematician's Brain 2007. *Address:* I.H.E.S., 91440 Bures-sur-Yvette (office); 1 avenue Charles-Comar, 91440 Bures-sur-Yvette, France (home). *Telephone:* 1-60-92-66-52 (office); 1-69-07-61-52 (home). *Website:* www.ihes.fr/~ruelle (office).

RUEMMLER, Kathryn, BA, JD; American lawyer and government official; *Partner, Latham & Watkins LLP;* b. Wash.; ed Univ. of Washington, Seattle, Georgetown Univ. Law Center; fmr Ed.-in-Chief Georgetown Law Journal; clerked for the Hon. Timothy K. Lewis on US Court of Appeals for the Third Circuit; Assoc. Counsel to Pres. Bill Clinton 2000–01; served as a Fed. Prosecutor 2001–07, Co-Lead Prosecutor in successful prosecution of fmr CEOs of Enron; Litigation Partner, Latham & Watkins, Washington, DC 2007–09; Prin. Assoc. Deputy Attorney-Gen., Dept of Justice 2009–10; Prin. Deputy Counsel to the Pres. 2010–11, White House Counsel 2011–14; Partner, Latham & Watkins LLP 2014–; Attorney-Gen.'s Award for Exceptional Service for work on Enron investigation, Lawyer of the Year, Bar Asscn of the Dist of Columbia 2011, Nat. Asscn of Women Lawyers' Public Service Award 2014. *Address:* Latham & Watkins LLP, 555 Eleventh Street, NW, Suite 1000, Washington, DC 20004-1304, USA (office). *Telephone:* (202) 637-2179 (office). *E-mail:* kathryn.ruemmler@lw.com (office). *Website:* www.lw.com (office).

RUF, Beatrix; German/Swiss art gallery curator; b. 1960; ed studied in Vienna, New York and Zurich; Curator Canton of Thurgau Kunstmuseum 1994–98; Curator Ringier Collection 1995–; Dir/Curator Kunsthaus Glarus 1998–2001; apptd Dir/Curator Kunsthalle Zürich 2001; mem. Bd Schweizerische Graphische Gesellschaft 1999–, Art Comm., Swiss Re, Cultural Advisory Bd for CERN; Assoc. Ed. JRP/Ringier (publr) 2003–; Curator Tate Triennial 2006; Player/Co-Curator Lyon Biennale 2007; Co-Curator Yokohama Triennale 2008; Dir Stedelijk Museum, Amsterdam 2014–17; mem. Jury, Deutsche Börse Photography Prize 2012, Artissima Illy Present Future Prize 2012. *Publications include:* Jenny Holzer: Xenon 2001, The Tate Triennial Exhibition of Contemporary British Art 2006, The Metaphor Problem Again: A Conversation Between John Baldessari, Lawrence Weiner, and Liam Gillick 2006, Terence Koh (co-author) 2007, Blasted Allegories (ed.) 2008, Liam Gillick 2009, Mark Morrisroe 2010 and many others.

RUFFALO, Mark; American actor and director; b. 22 Nov. 1967, Kenosha, Wis.; s. of Frank Lawrence Ruffalo, Jr and Marie Rose Ruffalo (née Hebert); m. Sunrise Coigney; one s. two d.; ed Stella Adler Conservatory, Los Angeles; co-f. Orpheus Theatre Co., Los Angeles. *Television includes:* Due South 1994, The Bear 2000, The Normal Heart (Outstanding Performance by a Male Actor in a Television Movie or Mini-Series, Screen Actors Guild 2015) 2014. *Films include:* The Last Big Thing 1996, Ride with the Devil 1999, You Can Count on Me (Montreal World Film Festival Award for Best Actor) 2000, Windtalkers 2002, My Life Without Me 2003, Eternal Sunshine of the Spotless Mind 2004, 13 Going on 30 2004, Collateral 2004, Just Like Heaven 2005, Rumor Has It 2005, All the King's Men 2006, Reservation Road 2007, Zodiac 2007, Blindness 2008, What Doesn't Kill You 2008, The Brothers Bloom 2008, Sympathy for Delicious 2009, Where the Wild Things Are 2009, Shutter Island 2010, The Kids Are All Right (New York Film Critics Circle Award for Best Supporting Actor, Comedy Film Award for Best Supporting Actor) 2010, Date Night 2010, Avengers Assemble 2012, Now You See Me 2013, Foxcatcher 2014, Avengers: Age of Ultron 2015, Spotlight 2015, Avengers: Infinity War 2018. *Address:* c/o Robert Stein Management, 1180 South Beverly Drive, Suite 304, Los Angeles, CA 90035, USA (office).

RUFIN, Jean-Christophe, MD; French writer, physician and diplomatist; b. 28 June 1952, Bourges; s. of Marcel Rufin and Denise Bonneau; one s. two d.; ed Lycées Janson-de-Sailly and Claude Bernard, Paris, Pitié-Salpêtrière School of Medicine, Paris, Institut d'études politiques, Paris; Hosp. Intern, Paris 1975–81, Dir of Clinic and Asst Hôpitaux de Paris 1981–83, attaché Hôpitaux de Paris 1983–86; Chief of Mission of Sec. of State for Human Rights 1986–88; Cultural Attaché French Embassy in Brazil 1989–90; Vice-Pres. Médécins sans Frontières 1991–93; Adviser to Minister of Defence 1993–95; doctor, Nanterre Hosp. 1994–95; Practitioner, St Antoine Hosp., Paris 1995–98; Dir French Red Cross 1994–96, Inst. Pasteur, Groupe France Télévisions, Office français de protection des réfugiés et apatrides 2005–; Medical Dir, then Pres. Action contre la faim 2002–07; Amb. to Senegal (also accred to Gambia) 2007–10; mem. Acad. Française 2008–; Chevalier, Légion d'honneur 2003, Officier 2013, Commdr, Ordre nat. du Lion (Sénégal) 2012, Chevalier des Arts et des Lettres; Dr hc (Laval Univ., Catholic Univ. of Louvain). *Publications include:* Le Piège humanitaire 1986, L'Empire et les nouveaux barbares 1992, La Dictature libérale (Prix Jean-Jacques Rousseau) 1994, L'Aventure humanitaire 1994, L'Abyssin (Prix Goncourt du Premier Roman, Prix Méditerranée) 1997, Sauver Ispahan 1998, Les Causes perdues (Prix Interallié) 1999, Rouge Brésil (Prix Goncourt) 2001, Globalia 2004, La Salamandre 2005, Le Parfum d'Adam 2006, Un léopard sur le garrot 2008, 100 Stunden 2009, Katiba 2010, Sept histoires qui reviennent de loin 2011, Le grand Coeur 2012, Immortelle randonnée 2013, Le collier rouge 2014, Checkpoint (Prix Grand Témoin 2015) 2015, Le Tour du monde du roi Zibeline 2017, Le Suspendu de Conakry 2017, Les Sept Mariages d'Edgar et de Ludmilla 2019. *Leisure interest:* mountain climbing. *Address:* c/o Les Editions Gallimard, 5 rue Gaston-Gallimard, 75328 Paris cedex 07, France (office). *Website:* www.gallimard.fr (office).

RUGAR, Daniel, BA PhD; American scientist; *Manager, Nanoscale Studies, IBM Almaden Research Center;* ed Stanford Univ.; joined IBM in 1984, currently Man. Nanoscale Studies, IBM Almaden Research Center, San Jose, Calif.; currently also Consulting Prof. in Applied Physics, Stanford Univ.; Fellow, American Physical Soc., AAAS, IEEE; received IBM internal awards for contribs to scanning probe microscopy, near field optical data storage and single spin detection 1999–2000, Distinguished Lecturer, IEEE Magnetic Soc. 1999, Scientific American 50 Award for research leadership in the field of imaging 2004, World Tech. Award in Materials, World Tech. Network (co-recipient) 2005, Cozzarelli Prize, NAS 2009, Gunther Laukien Prize 2010. *Achievements include:* co-inventor of thermo-mechanical recording technique that is basis of IBM 'Millipede' AFM storage device; pioneered mechanical detection of ultrasmall forces, achieving current record of 800 zeptonewtons in a 1 Hertz bandwidth; made first demonstrations of magnetic resonance force microscopy (MRFM) 1992, work reached key milestone with manipulation and detection of individual electron spin 2004. *Publications:* more than 120 scientific papers in professional journals on scanning microscopy; 20 patents. *Address:* IBM Almaden Research Center, Mailstop K13/D1, 650 Harry Road, San Jose, CA 95120-6099, USA (office). *Telephone:* (408) 927-2027 (office). *Fax:* (408) 927-2100 (office). *E-mail:* rugar@us.ibm.com (office). *Website:* almaden.ibm.com (office).

RUGE, Boris, MA; German diplomatist; *Minister and Deputy Chief of Mission, Embassy of Germany in USA;* b. 18 April 1962, Cologne; m.; four c.; ed Univ. of Cologne, Univ. of North Carolina, USA, Bologna Centre, School of Advanced Int. Studies, Johns Hopkins Univ., Italy, Royal Coll. of Defence Studies, UK; mil. service, German Air Force 1982–83; undergraduate studies 1983–85, postgraduate studies 1985–88; Political Officer, Fed. Foreign Office, Bonn 1989–92, Political Officer, Perm. Mission to UN, New York 1992–95, Head of Public Affairs Div. and Head of Consular Div., Embassy in Copenhagen 1996–99, German Liaison Officer with Media Operations Centre, NATO HQ, Brussels, supporting NATO Spokesman Jamie Shea and later with HQ Kosovo Force Press Centre, Pristina 1999, Officer, Personnel Div., Fed. Foreign Office 1999–2001, Chief Political Adviser to two successive Commdrs of Kosovo Force, HQ KFOR, Pristina 2001–02, Deputy Head of Div. for European Security and Defence Policy, Fed. Foreign Office 2002–05, Course Participant, Royal Coll. of Defence Studies, London 2005, Head of Political Dept, Office of High Rep. and EU Special Rep. in Bosnia and Herzegovina, Sarajevo 2006–08, Head of Near East Div., Fed. Foreign Office 2008–11, Regional Dir for Near and Middle East and Maghreb 2011–14, Amb. to Saudi Arabia (also Special Envoy to Org. of Islamic Cooperation) 2014–16, Minister and Deputy Chief of Mission, Embassy of Germany in USA 2016–. *Address:* Embassy of Germany, 4645 Reservoir Road, NW, Washington, DC 20007, USA (office). *Telephone:* (202) 298-4000 (office). *Fax:* (202) 298-4249 (office). *Website:* www.germany.info (office).

RUGGIERO, Riccardo; Italian telecommunications industry executive; *CEO, Tiscali SpA;* b. 26 Aug. 1960, Naples; s. of Renato Ruggiero; Sales Man. Fininvest SpA 1986–88; Sales and Marketing Man. AT&T Italia 1988–90; Asst to CEO, Olivetti Group 1990, Vice-Pres. Int. Customers and Communications Sales Devt 1992–94, Vice-Pres. Telemedia Sales and Marketing Devt 1994–96, CEO Infostrada (subsidiary co.) 1996–2001, also CEO Italia On Line 1996–99; joined Telecom Italia Group 2001, Head, Telecom France Business Unit 2001, CEO Telecom Italia Domestic Wireline Business Unit 2001–02, CEO Telecom Italia SpA 2002–07, CEO of Operations 2005, fmr Man. Dir, Exec. Dir and mem. of Strategy Cttee; CEO Aria SpA 2010–, Tiscali SpA 2016–; mem. Bd of Dirs Societa Azionaria Fabbrica Italiana Lavorazione Occhiali SpA 2005–. *Address:* TiscaliGiacomo Robustelli loc. Sa Illetta SS 195, Km 2300, 09123 Cagliari, Italy (office). *Telephone:* (070) 46011 (office). *E-mail:* info@tiscali.com (office). *Website:* investors.tiscali.it (office).

RUGOFF, Ralph; American art critic and gallery director; *Director, Hayward Gallery;* b. 1957, New York; ed Brown Univ.; fmr Research Fellow, Goldsmiths Coll., London; fmr Pew Arts Journalism Fellow, Columbia Univ., New York; started curating career after presenting lecture on "the pathetic in art", followed by Just Pathetic exhbn, Los Angeles 1990; Dir CCA Wattis Inst., San Francisco 2000–06; Curatorial Adviser to Sydney Biennale 2002; Dir Hayward Gallery, London 2006–; Ordway Prize 2005. *Publications include:* numerous monographs; Art of Susan Rios 1988, Circus Americanus 1995, Transformers 1995, Gallaccio Anya: Chasing Rainbows 1999, Great Illusions 1999, The Greenhouse Effect 2000, Baja to Vancouver: The West Coast and Contemporary Art (with Douglas Coupland) 2003, Monuments for the USA 2005, Scene of the Crime 1997, At the Threshold of the Visible, The Painting of Modern Life: 1960s to Now 2008, Amateurs 2008. *Address:* The Hayward Gallery, Southbank Centre, Belvedere Road, London, SE1 8XX, England (office). *Telephone:* (20) 7960-4200 (office). *Website:* www.southbankcentre.co.uk/venues/hayward-gallery (office).

RUGUNDA, Ruhakana, MB, ChB, MSc; Ugandan physician, politician and diplomatist; *Prime Minister;* b. 7 Nov. 1947, Kabale Dist; s. of Surumani Rugunda; m. Jocelyn Rugunda; ed Kigezi High School, Busoga Coll. (Head Prefect), Makerere Univ. Medical School, Univ. of Zambia, Univ. of California, Berkeley, USA; worked as Medical Officer in Zambia, as a physician at DC Gen. Hosp., Washington, DC and at Kenyatta Nat. Hosp., Nairobi, Kenya; served as Pres. Nat. Union of Students of Uganda; mem. Uganda People's Congress; involved with Ugandan Nat. Resistance Movt (NRM) mid-1980s; fmr Minister of Internal Affairs, of Foreign Affairs, of Information, of Works, Transport and Communication; elevated to cabinet ministerial level and apptd Amb. and Perm. Rep. to UN, New York 2009–11, Pres. UN Security Council July 2009; Minister of Information and Communication Tech. 2011–13, of Health 2013–14; Prime Minister of Uganda 2014–; fmr Commr for Animal Industry, Game and Fisheries; fmr Chair. NRM Electoral Comm.; fmr mem. of Parl. for Kabale Municipality; fmr Pres. Governing Council UNEP; led Ugandan Govt negotiating team to Juba, Sudan to hold peace talks with Lord's Resistance Army July 2006. *Leisure interests:* reading, playing tennis, chess. *Address:* Office of the Prime Minister, Plot 9-11, Apollo Kagwa Road, PO Box 341, Kampala, Uganda (office). *Telephone:* (41) 7770500 (office). *Fax:* (41) 4341139 (office). *E-mail:* ps@opm.go.ug (office). *Website:* www.opm.go.ug (office).

RÜHE, Volker; German politician; b. 25 Sept. 1942, Hamburg; m. Anne Rühe 1968; two s. one d.; ed Univ. of Hamburg; fmr teacher; mem. Hamburg City Council 1970–76; mem. Bundestag 1976–2005, Chair. Foreign Policy Cttee 2002; Deputy Chair. CDU/CSU Parl. Group 1982–89, 1998; Sec.-Gen. CDU 1989–92, Deputy Party Leader 1998–2002; Minister of Defence 1992–98; now retd from active politics; Adviser, Cerberus Deutschland Beteiligungsberatung GmbH (pvt. equity co.); mem. Exec. Bd, European Leadership Network. *Address:* European Leadership Network, Suite 7, Southbank House, Black Prince Road, London, SE1 7SJ, England (office); Cerberus Deutschland Beteiligungsberatung GmbH, Bockenheimer Landstrasse 2–4, 60323 Frankfurt am Main, Germany. *Telephone:* (20) 3176-2552 (office). *E-mail:* info@europeanleadershipnetwork.org (office). *Website:* www.europeanleadershipnetwork.org (office).

RUI, Xiaowu, BA, MA; Chinese business executive; *Chairman, China Electronics Corporation;* b. May 1959; ed Nat. Univ. of Defence Tech., 710 Inst. of Ministry of Space Industry; qualified in computer-aided design as researcher from 710 Inst. of Ministry of Space Industry 1985; held several posts, including Deputy Dir and Dir 710 Inst. of China Aerospace Science and Tech. Corpn (CASC) 2002–04, Business Asst of Pres. and Dir of Planning and Operation Dept 2000, mem. Party Leadership Group, Pres. Asst and Vice-Pres. of CASC, also Pres. and Sec. Party Cttee of China Satellite Communications Co. Ltd; Chair. China Electronic Information Industry Group Co., Ltd (now China Electronics Corpn) 2011–, Sec. Party Leadership Group 2011–, mem. Bd of Dirs 2011–16; fmr Chair., China Spacesat Co. Ltd, Beijing NavInfo Science and Technology Co. Ltd, China Aerospace Int. Holdings Ltd, CASIL Telecommunications Holdings Ltd, APT Satellite Holdings Ltd; winner Special Govt Allowance from the State Council 1986. *Address:* China Electronics Corporation, 27 Wanshou Road, Haidian District, Beijing 100846, People's Republic of China (office). *Telephone:* (10) 68207014 (office). *Website:* www.cec.com.cn (office).

RUIA, Shashi; Indian business executive; *Chairman, Essar Group;* b. 1931, Mumbai; s. of Nand Kishore Ruia; m.; two c.; Co-founder (with brother Ravi), Essar Group, currently Chair.; fmr Pres. Indian Nat. Shipowners Asscn; fmr Chair. Indo-US Jt Business Council; fmr mem. Man. Cttee, Fed. of Indian Chambers of Commerce and Industry; Business India Businessman of the Year Award 2010. *Address:* Essar Group, Essar House, 11 Keshavrao Khadye Marg, Mahalaxmi,

Mumbai, 400 034, Maharashtra, India (office). *Telephone:* (22) 50011100 (office); (22) 66601100 (office). *Fax:* (22) 66601809 (office). *E-mail:* corporatecommunications@essar.com (office). *Website:* www.essar.com (office).

RUINI, HE Cardinal Camillo; Italian ecclesiastic; *Vicar General Emeritus of Rome;* b. 19 Feb. 1931, Sassuolo; ed Pontifical Gregorian Univ. and Almo Collegio Capranica, Rome, Italy; ordained priest 1954; returned to Reggio Emilia and taught philosophy at diocesan seminary until 1968; taught dogmatic theology at Studio Teologico Interdiocesano di Modena-Reggio-Emilia-Carpi-Guastalla 1968–86, Headmaster 1968–77; taught dogmatic theology at Studio Teologico Accademico Bolognese 1977–83; Chaplain to Catholic Univ. grads 1958–66; Del. for Catholic Action 1966–70; Pres. John XXIII Diocesan Cultural Centre 1968; Auxiliary Bishop of Reggio Emilia and Guastalla and Titular Bishop of Nepte 1983; Vice-Pres. Preparatory Cttee, Ecclesial Convention of Lorreto 1985; elected mem. Bishops' Comm. for Catholic Educ., Culture and School 1985; Sec.-Gen. Italian Episcopal Conf. 1986, Pres. 1991–2007; currently Vicar Gen. Emer. of Rome; mem. Cen. Cttee for Marian Year 1987–88; Consultor, Congregation for Bishops 1988–2011; elected mem. Council of Gen. Secr., 8th Gen. Ass. of Synod of Bishops 1990; Archbishop and Pro-Vicar Gen. of Pope for Diocese of Rome 1991, Vicar Gen. and Archpriest of Patriarchal Lateran Basilica, Grand Chancellor Pontifical Lateran Univ. and Pres. Emer. Peregrinatio ad Petri Sedem 1991–; Relator for Special Ass. for Europe of Synod of Bishops, Vatican City 1991; cr. Cardinal (Cardinal Priest of S. Agnese fuori le mura) 1991; Pres. Scientific Cttee Vatican Foundation Joseph Ratzinger-Benedict XVI 2010–15; mem. Cttee of the Great Jubilee of the Year 2000. *Publications:* has published many essays and research work since 1971. *Address:* Viale Vaticano 42, 00165 Roma, Italy (office). *Telephone:* (06) 6988-2509 (office). *Fax:* (06) 6988-2153 (office). *E-mail:* camillo.ruini@vicariatusurbis.org (office). *Website:* www.vatican.va (office).

RUITENBERG, Elis Joost, DVM, PhD; Dutch professor of immunology; *Chairman, Aglaia Oncology Fund B.V.;* b. 24 May 1937, Amersfoort; s. of E J. Ruitenberg and D. H. van Mechelen; m. Christiane Friederike Ambagtsheer 1963; three d.; ed Univ. of Utrecht; veterinarian, Lab. Zoonoses, Nat. Inst. of Public Health, Bilthoven 1964, Head Pathology Lab. 1970–86, Dir Div. of Immunology 1979, Vaccine Production 1980–86, Dir Div. of Microbiology and Immunology, Nat. Inst. of Public and Environmental Protection, Bilthoven 1984, Deputy Dir-Gen. –1986; Prof. of Veterinary Immunology, Univ. of Utrecht 1984, now Prof. Emer.; Gen. and Scientific Dir Sanquin Blood Supply Foundation (CLB) 1989–2001; Prof. of Int. Public Healthcare, Vrije Universiteit, Amsterdam 2001–; Chair. Netherlands-Vietnam Medical Cttee 1998–, Council Cttee Nat. Vaccination Programme 2001–; Chair. Aglaia Oncology Fund B.V., Aglaia Oncology Seed Fund B.V., mem. non-exec. bd AGLAIA BioMedical Ventures B.V; Visiting Prof., Nat. School of Public Health, Madrid, Spain 1987; retd; mem. numerous advisory cttees including Advisory Council for Devt Research, Advisory Bd Royal Numico N.V.; mem. Royal Netherlands Acad. of Arts and Sciences, Netherlands Health Council 1982–, Supervisory Bd Danone Baby and Medical Nutrition B.V. 1996–2004; Schimmel Viruly Award 1976, Annual Award, Nat. Journal of Veterinary Medicine 1977, Award Medical Acad., Poznan, Poland, Kt, Order of Netherlands Lion 1988, Schornagel Award 1996. *Publications include:* Anisakiasis, Pathogenesis, Diagnosis and Prevention 1970, Preventive Screening of Adults (with D.A.T. Griffiths) 1987, Statistical Analysis and Mathematical Modelling of AIDS (with J.C. Jager) 1988, AIDS Impact Assessment Modelling and Scenario Analysis (with J.C. Jager) 1992; numerous articles on immunology, vaccinology, pathology and parasitology. *Leisure interests:* European languages, history, cycling. *Address:* AGLAIA BioMedical Ventures B.V., Businesspark Berg & Bosch, Professor Bronkhorstlaan 10-XI, Building 92, 3723 MB, Bilthoven, Netherlands. *Telephone:* (30) 2296090. *Fax:* (30) 2296099. *E-mail:* info@aglaia-biomedical.com. *Website:* www.aglaia-biomedical.com.

RUIZ, Gisel, BS; American business executive; *Executive Vice-President and Chief Operating Officer, Walmart US;* ed Santa Clara Univ.; began career at Walmart as store man. trainee 1992, held a variety of leadership positions in store operations, labour relations and human resources, Vice-Pres. and Regional Gen. Man. in Field Operations Div. 2006–08, responsible for 150 Walmart stores in western Texas and New Mexico, Sr Vice-Pres., Walmart People 2008–10, Exec. Vice-Pres., People, Walmart US 2010–12, Exec. Vice-Pres. and COO Walmart US 2012–; Walmart Leadership Award 2008, honoured by Latina Style as 2010 Latina Exec. of the Year 2011, Woman of the Year Distinguished Service Award, USO of Metropolitan New York 2013. *Address:* Walmart, 702 SW 8th Street, Bentonville, AR 72716-8611, USA (office). *Telephone:* (479) 273-4000 (office). *Fax:* (479) 277-1830 (office). *E-mail:* info@walmartstores.com (office). *Website:* walmartstores.com (office).

RUIZ, Hector de Jesus, BEng, MEng, DEng, PhD; Mexican business executive; b. 25 Dec. 1945, Piedras Negras, Coahuila; m. 1st (deceased); one s.; m. 2nd Judy Ruiz; two step-c.; ed Univ. of Texas, Rice Univ., USA; held various positions with Texas Instruments; fmr Pres. Semiconductor Products Sector, Motorola; COO and Pres. Advanced Micro Devices (AMD), Inc. 2000–02, CEO 2002–08, Chair. 2004–08; Chair. Spansion Inc.; Chair. GlobalFoundries 2009–10; currently Chair. and CEO Advanced Nanotechnology Solutions, Inc.; Co-founder and CEO Bull Ventures (consultancy) 2011–; Board Advisor, EDCO Ventures 2010–; mem. Bd of Dirs, Eastman Kodak Co., Semiconductor Industry Asscn; mem. Bd of Trustees Rice Univ., RAND Corpn; fmr mem. Pres.'s Council of Advisors for Science and Tech.; mem. Hispanic Professional Engineers; Fellow, Int. Eng Consortium 2002–; Hispanic Engineer Nat. Awards Conference Hall of Fame 2000, CEO of the Year, Electronic Business 2005, Exec. of the Year, EE Times 2005, Semico Bellwether Award 2009. *Address:* Bull Ventures, LLC, 601 Van Ness Avenue, Suite E603, San Francisco, CA 94102, USA (office). *Telephone:* (415) 373-0197 (office). *E-mail:* info@bullventuresllc.com (office). *Website:* bullventuresllc.com (office).

ARROCHA RUÍZ, Melitón Alejandro, LLM; Panamanian politician and diplomatist; *Permanent Representative to United Nations;* b. 1968; m.; two c.; ed Santa María La Antigua Univ., American Univ., Georgetown Univ., Washington; taught at Santa María La Antigua Univ.; mem. of Parl.; Vice-Minister of Presidency –2018; Perm. Rep. to UN 2018–; fmr Vice-Minister of Foreign Trade, of Foreign Affairs, of Trade and Industries; Head Panama Antitrust Agency. *Address:* Permanent Mission of Panama, 708 Third Avenue, 26th Floor, New York,

NY 10017, USA (office). *Telephone:* (212) 421-5420 (office). *E-mail:* emb@panama-un.org (office). *Website:* www.panama-un.org (office).

RUIZ-GALLARDÓN JÍMENEZ, Alberto; Spanish lawyer and politician; b. 11 Dec. 1958, Madrid; s. of José María Ruiz-Gallardón; m. María del Mar Utrera; four s.; ed Complutense Univ., Madrid, San Pablo CEU Univ.; began career in prov. courts in Málaga; elected to Madrid City Council 1983; mem. Partido Popular Exec. 1986; elected as mem. Regional Parl. for Autonomous Community of Madrid 1987, spokesperson in Senate for Partido Popular parl. group 1987–95; Pres. Comunidad de Madrid (Community of Madrid) 1995–2003; Mayor of Madrid 2003–11; Minister of Justice 2011–14 (resgnd); Perm. Advisor, Advisory Council of Comunidad de Madrid 2014–. *Website:* www.madrid.org (office).

RUIZ GUINAZU, Magdalena; Argentine journalist; b. 13 Feb. 1935, Buenos Aires; four c.; fmr mem. Comision Nacional por la desaparicion de Personas (Nat. Comm. on the Disappearance of People); currently host, Magdalena Tempranisimo, Radio Continental and La vuelta con Magdalena (Back with Magadalena) 2002–; columnist, La Nación and Pagina 12 newspapers; Co-founder and fmr Pres. Asociación para la Defensa del Periodismo Independiente (Asociación Periodistas) (press freedom org.); Officer, Legion d'Honneur, Order of Merit (Italy); Martin Fierro de Oro (Gold Martin Fierro Award) for Lifetime Achievement 1994, Int. Women's Media Foundation Lifetime Achievement Award 2003, Diamond Konex, Communication-Journalism 2007. *Publications include:* Huésped de un verano 1994, Había una vez... la vida 1995, Qué mundo nos ha tocado! (with Father Rafael Braun) 2001, Historias de hombres, mujeres y jazmines 2002. *Address:* c/o Asociación Periodistas, Piedras 1675 Oficina B, Secretaría de Derechos, 1140 Buenos Aires, Argentina. *E-mail:* magdalena@continental.com.ar (office). *Website:* www.continental.com.ar; www.magdalenatempranisimo.blogspot.com.

RUIZ-MADURO, Xiomara Jeanira; Aruban politician; *Minister of Finance, Economic Affairs and Culture;* b. 24 Dec. 1974; mem. Staten (Parl.) 2009–; Minister of Finance, Econ. Affairs and Culture 2017–; mem. Movimiento Electoral di Pueblo (MEP). *Address:* Ministry of Finance, Economic Affairs and Culture, L. G. Smith Blvd 76, Oranjestad, Aruba (office). *Telephone:* 528-4900 (office). *Fax:* 528-7518 (office). *E-mail:* info@deaci.aw (office). *Website:* www.deaci.aw (office).

RUIZ MATEOS, Gerardo; Mexican business executive and politician; b. Mexico City; ed Instituto Tecnológico de Estudios Superiores de Monterrey; Dir-Gen. Automotive Moulding Mexico (now Linde Pullman Mexico) 1989–; Pres. Mexican Foundation for Rural Devt 1995; mem. Nat. Action Party 1995–, Exec. Sec. Nat. Exec. Cttee 1996–98, mem. Cttee 2002–05; Pres. Surveillance Comm., Nat. Council 2001–02; Admin and Finance Co-ordinator, Felipe Calderón's Presidential Campaign 2005–06; Co-ordinator of Cabinets and Special Projects of the Pres.'s Office 2006–08; Sec. of the Economy 2008–10; Head of Office of the Presidency of the Repub. 2010–12; mem. Council of the Social Union of Mexican Businessmen 1996–2000, Pres. 2000.

RUIZ SEVILLA, Martha Elena, LLM; Nicaraguan lawyer and politician; *Minister of Defence;* m. Brig.-Gen. Bayardo Ramón Rodríguez Ruiz; ed Charles Univ., Prague; worked for Nat. Authority OPCW, Ministry of Environment and Natural Resources; Gen. Sec. Ministry of Defence 2013–14, Minister of Defence 2014–. *Address:* Ministry of Defence, De los semáforos el Redentor, 4 c. arriba, donde fue la casa 6 'Ricardo Morales Aviles', Managua, Nicaragua (office). *Telephone:* 2222-2201 (office). *Fax:* 2222-5439 (office). *E-mail:* prensa.midef@midef.gob.ni (office). *Website:* www.midef.gob.ni (office).

RUKAVISHNIKOV, Aleksander Yulianovich; Russian sculptor; b. 2 July 1950, Moscow; s. of Yulian Rukavishnikov and of Anagelina Filippova; m. Olga Mikhailovna Rukavishnikova; one s.; ed Surikov Moscow State Inst. of Arts; freelance artist; Prof., Surikov Inst.; apptd Head, Dept of Sculpture, Moscow State Art Inst. 1995; mem. Presidium, Russian Acad. of Fine Arts; mem. Union of Artists (Sec. 1986–88); Order "Badge of Honor" 1986, Order of Friendship 2000; Lenin Komsomol Prize 1976, Silver Medal, Russian Acad. of Fine Arts 1982, People's Artist of the Russian Fed. *Major works include:* portraits: Feofan Grek 1977, Sergey of Radonezh 1981, Dmitry Donskoy 1982, Aleksander Peresvet 1983, John Lennon 1982, Tamara Bykova 1983, Vladimir Vysotsky memorial, installation Intrusion 1988, Tatishchev monument, Togliatti 1997, Dostoyevsky statue 1997, Nikulin monument 2000. *Address:* Granatny per. 11, Apt 30, 103001 Moscow, Russia (home). *Telephone:* (495) 291-05-52 (home). *Fax:* (495) 291-01-52 (home).

RUKINGAMA, Luc, PhD; Burundian academic, UNESCO official and fmr politician; b. 23 Dec. 1952, Kiremba; m. Thérèse Niyonzima; two s. two d.; ed Univ. of the Sorbonne, Paris; mem. Parl.; fmr Minister for Higher Educ., for Cooperation, for Foreign Affairs and Cooperation; Minister of Communication and Govt Spokesman 2000–01; stakeholder in Burundian peace process 1994–2004; fmr Co-Pres. Union pour le Progrès National (UPRONA); Sr Programme Specialist and Chief of Higher Educ. Unit, UNESCO/BREDA (Regional Bureau for Educ. in Africa) –2008; UNESCO Dir and Rep. to Ethiopia 2008–10, UNESCO Rep. to Zimbabwe, Malawi, Botswana, Zambia and to SADC 2010–13, apptd Dir UNESCO Office, Harare 2010, later Regional Dir to Southern Africa Region and to SADC Secr. 2013; Chevalier, Ordre des Palmes académiques, Medaille de l'Unité Nationale; UNESCO Medal. *Publications:* Voyage au Congo d'André Gide ou la steréotype au cœur de l'image 1995, Intahe et la gestion de la cité, Société colonisée et écriture romanesque, Migration et diversité: le cas de l'Afrique (conf., Univ. of Sherbrooke 2011); numerous articles. *Leisure interests:* reading, sport, music. *Address:* Avenue de Juillet 4, Kiriri, PO Box 704, Bujumbura, Burundi (home).

RULI, Genc, DEcon; Albanian economist, academic and politician; b. 4 Nov. 1958; m.; ed Univ. of Tirana; Lecturer in Econs, Univ. of Tirana 1982–90, Prof. of Finance and Accounting 1996–; Minister of Finance June-Dec. 1991, of Finance and the Economy 1992–93, of Economy, Trade and Energy 2007–09, of Agriculture, Food and Consumer Protection 2009–13; Deputy, People's Ass. for Tirana 1991, for Gjirokaster 1992–96, Chair. Perm. Parl. Comm. for Finance and Economy 1994–96; Chair. Bd of Govs Albanian Inst. of Insurance 1992–2005; Chair. Inst. for Contemporary Science 1996–2005; mem. Democratic Party of Albania.

RUMAS, Syarhey (Sergei) Mikalayevich, CSc; Belarusian politician and economist; *Prime Minister;* b. 1 Dec. 1969, Gomel; m.; four s.; ed Yaroslavl Higher Military Financial School, Yaroslavl, Academy of Public Administration; served in the Soviet Armed Forces 1990–92; Head of Accounting & Operating, Nat. Bank of the Repub. of Belarus 1992–94; Deputy Chair. Severo-Zapad Commercial Bank May–Aug. 1994, Sodruzhestvo joint-stock bank 1994–95; Regional Dir Belarusbank 1995–2002, Deputy Chair. Bd of Dirs 2002–05; Chair. Belagroprombank 2005–10; Deputy Prime Minister 2010–12; Chair. Devt Bank of the Repub. of Belarus 2012–18; Prime Minister 2018–; Chair. Belarusian Football Fed. (BFF) 2011–; Certificate of Honour of the Cabinet of Ministers of Belarus 2009, Certificate of Honour of the Nat. Ass. of Belarus 2009. *Address:* Office of the Council of Ministers, 220010 Minsk, vul. Savetskaya 11, Belarus (office). *Telephone:* (17) 222-41-73 (office). *Fax:* (17) 222-66-65 (office). *E-mail:* contact@government.by (office). *Website:* www.government.by (office).

RUMHY, Muhammad bin Hamad bin Saif al-; Omani petroleum engineer and government official; *Minister of Oil and Gas;* fmr Prof. of Petroleum Eng, Sultan Qaboos Univ.; Minister of Oil and Gas 1997–; Chair. Petroleum Devt Oman 2003–; mem. Bd of Dirs Oman LNG L.L.C (also Chair.). *Address:* Ministry of Oil and Gas, POB 551, Muscat 113 (office); Petroleum Development Oman (PDO), Bait Saih Maleh Building, Mina Al Sahel Street, PO Box 81, 113 Muscat, Oman (office). *Telephone:* 24603333 (Ministry) (office); 24678111 (PDO) (office). *Fax:* 2469672 (Ministry) (office); 24677106 (PDO) (office). *E-mail:* external-affairs@pdo.co.om (office). *Website:* www.mog.gov.om (office); www.pdo.co.om (home).

RUML, Jan; Czech journalist and fmr politician; b. 5 March 1953, Prague; s. of Jiří Ruml; m. Marie Ruml; two s.; ed grammar school, Prague, Faculty of Law, Univ. of Plzeň; stoker, woodcutter, hosp. technician, mechanic, bookseller, cattle-minder; signed Charter 77, Feb. 1977; freelance journalist 1977–79; mem. Cttee for Protection of the Unjustly Persecuted 1979–89; in custody, indicted for subversive activities 1981–82; co-founder Lidové noviny (monthly samizdat) 1988–90; spokesman of Charter 77 1990; First Deputy Minister of Interior of CSFR 1990–91; Deputy Minister of Interior 1991–92; mem. Civic Democratic Party (ODS) 1992–97; Deputy to House of Nations, Fed. Ass. June–Dec. 1992; Minister of Interior of Czech Repub. 1992–97; mem. Interdepartmental Anti-drug Comm. 1993–97, Comm. for Prevention of Crime 1994–97; mem. of Parl. 1996–98, Senator 1998–2004, Vice-Pres. of Senate (Parl.) 2000–04; Gen Man Secar Bohemia 2010–; Founder Freedom Union (US), Chair. 1998–99; Chair. Olympic Watch; Hon. Medal of the French Nat. Police 1992. *Films:* Hledání Pevného Bodu (Looking for a Stable Point). *Publication:* (with Jana Klusáková) What Was, Is and Will Be (in Czech). *Address:* Secar Bohemia, Londýnská 48, 12000 Prague 2, Czech Republic (office). *Telephone:* 513-111 (office). *Website:* www.janruml.cz.

RUMMEL, Reinhard Franz, DrIng; German scientist and academic; *Carl von Linde Senior Fellow, Institute for Advanced Study, Technical University of Munich;* b. 3 Dec. 1945, Landshut; m. Renate Schophaus 1970; one s. one d.; ed Hans Leinberger Gymnasium, Technical Univ. of Munich, Technische Hochschule, Darmstadt; Research Asst Technical Univ., Darmstadt 1970–74; Research Assoc. Dept of Geodetic Science, Ohio State Univ., Columbus, Ohio 1974–76; scientist, German Geodetic Research Inst. and Bavarian Acad. of Science, Munich 1976–80; Prof. of Physical Geodesy, Faculty of Geodetic Eng, Delft Univ. of Tech. 1980–93; Prof., Institut für Astronomische und Physikalische Geodäsie, Technical Univ. of Munich 1993–2011, Carl von Linde Sr Fellow, Inst. for Advanced Study 2011–; mem. Netherlands Acad. of Science, Bavarian Acad. of Sciences and Humanities, German Acad. of Sciences Leopoldina; Fellow, American Geophysical Union; Bavarian Order of Merit 2008, Bavarian Maximilian Order for Science and Art 2010; Dr hc (Bonn) 2005, (Tech. Univ. of Graz) 2005, (Ohio State Univ., USA) 2013, (Aristotle Univ. of Thessaloniki, Greece) 2014; Heiskanen Award 1977, Speuerwerkpreis, KIVI, Netherlands 1987, Vening Meinesz Medal, European Geophysical Union 1998, Hon. Award of German Asscn for Surveying 2013, Gauβmedaille of the Braunschweigische Wissenschaftschafts Gesellschaft 2016. *Publications:* Zur Behandlung von Zufallsfunktionen und -folgen in der physikalischen Geodäsie 1975, Geodesy's Contribution to Geophysics 1984, Satellite Gradiometry 1986, Encyclopedia of Earth System Science, Vol. II (on geodesy) 1992; articles in professional journals. *Address:* TUM Emeriti of Excellence, Technical University of Munich, Arcisstrasse 21, 80333 Munich, Germany (office). *Telephone:* (89) 28922092 (office). *Fax:* (89) 28925245 (office). *E-mail:* eoe@zv.tum.de (office). *Website:* www.emeriti-of-excellence.tum.de.

RUMSFELD, Donald H., BA; American business executive, fmr politician and fmr government official; b. 9 July 1932, Chicago, Ill.; s. of George Rumsfield and Jeannette Rumsfeld (née Husted); m. Joyce Pierson 1954; one s. two d.; ed New Trier High School, Ill., Princeton Univ.; aviator, USN 1954–57; Admin. Asst, House of Reps 1957–59; investment broker, A. G. Becker & Co., Chicago 1960–62; mem. US House of Reps from Ill. 13th Dist 1962–69; Asst to Pres. and Dir Office of Econ. Opportunity 1969–70; Dir Econ. Stabilization Program, Counsellor to Pres. 1971–72; Amb. to NATO, Brussels 1973–74; White House Chief of Staff 1974–75; Sec. of Defense 1975–77, 2001–06; Pres., CEO then Chair. G. D. Searle and Co., Skokie, Ill. 1977–85; Sr Advisor, William Blair and Co. 1985–90; Chair. and CEO General Instrument Corpn 1990–93; Chair. Gilead Sciences, Inc. 1997–2000; Pres.'s Special Middle East Envoy 1983–84; Chair. Eisenhower Exchange Fellowships 1986–93, US Ballistic Missile Threat Comm. 1998–99; mem. Presidential Advisory Cttee on Arms Control 1982–86, Nat. Econ. Comm. 1988–89, Trade Deficit Review Cttee, US Comm. to Assess Nat. Security, Space Man. and Org. 2000–01; Distinguished Visiting Fellow, Hoover Inst., Stanford Univ. 2007–08; f. Rumsfeld Foundation 2007; Grand Cordon of the Order of the Rising Sun 2015; 11 hon. degrees; Presidential Medal of Freedom 1977, Woodrow Wilson Award 1985, Outstanding Pharmaceutical CEO 1980, George C. Marshall Medal 1984, Eisenhower Medal 1993, Lone Sailor Award, US Navy Memorial Foundation 2002, James H. Doolittle Award, Hudson Inst. 2003, Statesmanship Award, Claremont Inst. 2007, Victory of Freedom Award, Richard Nixon Foundation 2010. *Publication:* Known and Unknown (memoirs) 2011, Rumsfeld's Rules: Leadership Lessons in Business, Politics, War, and Life 2013. *Leisure interests:* skiing, squash, ranching, reading. *Address:* Rumsfeld Foundation, 1718 M Street, NW, #366, Washington, DC 20036, USA. *E-mail:* contact@rumsfeldfoundation.org. *Website:* rumsfeldfoundation.org.

RUMYANTSEV, Aleksandr Yu., DrPhysMathSci; Russian physicist and diplomatist; b. 26 July 1945, Kushka, Turkmenistan; m. Galina F. Rumyantseva; one d.; ed Moscow Inst. of Physics and Eng; trained as engineer; Jr, then Sr Researcher, Head of Div., Dir of Scientific Devt, Russian Scientific Centre, Kurchatov Inst. of Atomic Energy 1969–94, Dir 1994–2001; Minister of Atomic

Energy of the Russian Fed. 2001–04; Head of Fed. Agency for Atomic Energy 2004–05; Amb. to Finland 2006–17; Prof., Moscow Inst. of Physics and Eng; Chair. Bd of Trustees, Global Energy Int. Prize 2005–; mem. Bd of Dirs Nuclear Soc. of the Russian Fed.; Corresp. mem. Russian Acad. of Sciences 1997, Academician 2000; Order of Honour 2001; USSR State Prize 1986. *Publications:* more than 100 scientific papers in professional journals on new methods of solid-state physics studies by means of stationary nuclear reactors.

RUNDGREN, Todd; American singer, songwriter, musician (guitar) and record producer; b. 22 June 1948, Philadelphia, Pa; m. Michele Gray 1998; mem. Woody's Truck Stop; Founder-mem. The Nazz 1967–70; solo recording artist 1970–; formed progressive rock group Utopia 1974–. *Recordings include:* albums: with The Nazz: Nazz 1968, Nazz Nazz 1969, Nazz III 1970; with Utopia: Todd Rundgren's Utopia 1974, Another Live 1975, Ra 1977, Oops! Wrong Planet 1977, Adventures In Utopia 1980, Deface The Music 1980, Swing To The Right 1982, Utopia 1982, Oblivion 1984; solo: Runt 1970, The Ballad of Todd Rundgren 1971, Something / Anything? 1972, A Wizard, A True Star 1973, Todd 1974, Initiation 1975, Faithful 1976, Hermit of Mink Hollow 1978, Back To The Bars 1978, Healing 1981, The Ever Popular Tortured Artist Effect 1983, A Cappella 1985, POV 1985, Anthology – Todd Rundgren 1988, Nearly Human 1989, Second Wind 1991, No World Order 1993, No World Order Lite 1994, The Individualist 1995, With a Twist 1997, Up Against It 1998, Live in Chicago 1991 1999, One Long Year 2000, Liars 2004, Arena 2008, (re)Production 2011, State 2013, Global 2015, Runddans (with Emil Nikolaisen and Hans Peter Lindstrom) 2015; record producer, Bat Out of Hell, Meat Loaf 1977; also producer/engineer, recordings by New York Dolls, Grand Funk Railroad, Hall and Oates, XTC, The Band. *Website:* www.todd-rundgren .com.

RUNDQUIST, Dmitri Vasilyevich; Russian geologist and mineralogist; b. 10 Aug. 1930; m.; two d.; ed Leningrad Inst. of Mines; jr, then sr researcher, Deputy Dir All-Union Research Inst. of Geology 1954–84; Dir Inst. of Geology and Geochronology Russian Acad. of Sciences 1984–90, Head of Lab. 1990; Corresp. mem. USSR (now Russian) Acad. of Sciences 1984, mem. 1990, Acad.-Sec. Dept of Geology, Geophysics, Geochemistry and Mining Sciences 1996–2002; research in mineralogy, petrography, developed theory on laws of mineral deposit location; USSR State Prize, Merited Geologist of Russian Fed., Demidov's Prize 2010. *Publications include:* Greisen Deposits 1971, Zones of Endogenic Mineral Deposits 1975, Precambrian Geology 1988, Largest Mineral Deposits of the World 2006.

RUOSLAHTI, Erkki, MD, PhD; Finnish medical scientist and academic; *Distinguished Professor, Sanford Burnham Prebys Medical Discovery Institute;* b. 16 Feb. 1940, Puumala; ed Univ. of Helsinki, California Inst. of Tech.; various appts at Univ. of Helsinki, Univ. of Turku, City of Hope Nat. Medical Center, Duarte, Calif., USA; joined Burnham Inst. for Medical Research (now Sanford Burnham Prebys MedicalDiscovery Inst.) 1979, Pres. and CEO 1989–2002, Distinguished Prof. 2002–; Adjunct Distinguished Prof., Dept of Molecular, Cellular and Developmental Biology, Univ. of California, San Diego 2006– (after establishment of programme affiliation with Burnham); mem. NAS, Inst. of Medicine, American Acad. of Arts and Sciences, European Molecular Biology Org., Finnish Acad. of Sciences; Nobel Fellow, Karolinska Inst., Stockholm; title of Academician granted by the Pres. of Finland 2009; Kt, Order of the White Rose of Finland; Commdr, Order of the Lion of Finland 2010; Hon. MD (Lund, Sweden); Gairdner Foundation Int. Award, G.H.A. Clowes Award, American Asscn for Cancer Research, Robert J. and Claire Pasarow Foundation Award, Jacobaeus Int. Prize, Jubilee Award British Biochemical Soc., Japan Prize in Cell Biology (jtly), Science and Tech. Foundation of Japan 2005. *Publications include:* numerous articles and essays in professional journals. *Address:* Sanford Burnham Prebys Medical Discovery Institute, 10901 North Torrey Pines Road, La Jolla, CA 92037, USA (office). *Telephone:* (858) 646-3100 (office). *Fax:* (858) 795-5323 (home). *E-mail:* ruoslahti@sbpdiscovery.org (office). *Website:* www.sbpdiscovery.org (office).

RUOZI, Roberto; Italian economist, academic and business executive; *Professor Emeritus, Bocconi University;* Dean of L. Bocconi Univ. 1995–2000, Prof. of Econs of Financial Intermediaries –2002, Prof. Emer. 2003–; Prof. at Univs of Ancona, Siena, Parma, Paris (Sorbonne) and Milan Politecnico; Chair. Gruppo Mediolanum SpA –2012, Palladio Finanziaria SpA, Touring Club Italiano, Retelit SpA; Chair. Bd of Statutory Auditors, Borsa Italiana SpA; Pres. Banca Intermobiliare; mem. Bd of Dirs Gewiss SpA, Cerruti Tessile SpA. *Publications:* numerous publs on banking and finance. *Address:* Bocconi University, Via Roentgen 1, Room 2-D1-09, 20136 Milan, Italy (office). *Telephone:* (02) 58365903 (office). *Fax:* (02) 58366893 (office). *E-mail:* roberto.ruozi@unibocconi.it (office). *Website:* www.sdabocconi.it (office).

RUPANI, Shri Vijay R., BA, LLB; Indian politician; *Chief Minister of Gujarat;* b. 2 Aug. 1956, Rangoon (now Yangon), Myanmar; s. of Ramniklal Rupani and Mayaben Rupani; m. Anjali Rupani; one s.; moved to Rajkot, Gujarat with parents aged four; started political career as activist of Rashtriya Swayamsevak Sangh (RSS)-backed Akhil Bhartiya Vidyarthi Parishad student org. 1971; elected Councillor, Rajkot Municipal Corpn 1987, then Chair. Standing Cttee 1988–96, Mayor of Rajkot 1996–97; Chair. Tourism Corpn of Gujarat 2006–12; mem. Rajya Sabha 2006–12; Chair. Gujarat Municipal Finance Bd 2013–14; mem. Gujarat Legis. Ass. from Rajkot West 2014–; Chief Minister of Gujarat 2016–; mem. Bharatiya Janata Party (BJP) (Indian People's Party), served as Pres. BJP Rajkot Dist unit, then several years as Gen. Sec. Gujarat BJP, also served as party spokesperson at state level, Leader, Gujarat BJP 2016–; Partner Rasiklal & Sons. *Address:* Office of the Chief Minister, 3rd Floor, Swarnim Sankul-1, New Sachivalaya, Gandhinagar 382 010, India (office). *Telephone:* (79) 23232611 (office). *Website:* www.gujaratindia.com (office).

RUPARELIA, Sudhir; Ugandan business executive; *Chairman, Ruparelia Group of Companies;* b. 1 Jan. 1956, Mengo, Kampala; m. Jyostna Ruparelia; three c.; ed Jinja Secondary School, Kololo Secondary School; moved to UK 1972; initially worked in a factory making test tubes, also drove taxis; returned to Uganda 1985; began importing commodities such as salt, sugar, cigarettes, alcoholic beverages to Kampala; started Uganda's first foreign exchange bureau; Founder-Chair. Ruparelia Group of Cos; owns Crane Bank, Goldstar Insurance, Speke Resort, Conference Centre Ltd, Premier Finance Ltd, Kabira Leisure Centre, Crane Man. Services Ltd, Crane Financial Services Ltd, Munyonyo Commonwealth Resort Ltd, Speke Hotel, Kabira Country Club, Tourist Hotel, Speke Apartments, Equator Rafts, Speke Resort, Bujagali, Sanyu FM, Sunrise Radio, Kampala Parents School (acquired in 2004), Kampala Int. School, Kabira Forex Bureau Ltd; Dr hc (Uganda Pentecostal Univ.) 2007. *Address:* Ruparelia Group of Companies, PO Box 3673, Kampala, Uganda (office). *Telephone:* (41) 4343500 (office). *Fax:* (41) 4231578 (office). *E-mail:* info@rupareliagroup.com (office). *Website:* www.rupareliagroup.com (office).

RUPEL, Dimitrij, PhD; Slovenian politician, diplomatist and writer; b. 7 April 1946, Ljubljana; m. Marjetica-Ana Rudolf-Rupel; ed Univ. of Ljubljana, Brandeis Univ., Mass, USA; worked as journalist in Yugoslav newspapers and magazines; was considered as dissident for criticism of Yugoslav Communist regime; Asst Prof., Ljubljana Univ. 1980–89, Prof. 1989–; Lecturer, Queen's Univ. (Canada) 1977–78, New School for Social Research, NY (USA) 1985, Cleveland State Univ. (USA) 1989; Co-founder Cultural-Political journal Nova Revija 1984–87; Founder and first Pres. Opposition Slovenian Democratic Alliance Party 1989–90; Minister of Foreign Affairs 1990–93, mem. first elected Govt of Slovenia 1990, Chair. Cttee for Culture, Educ. and Sports; mem. State Ass. 1992–95; Mayor of Ljubljana 1994–97; Amb. to USA 1997–2000; Minister of Foreign Affairs 2000–08; Pres. Council of the EU 2008; Prime Ministerial Special Envoy for Foreign Affairs 2008; Boris Kidrič Prize 1986, Golden Medal of Honour of the Repub. of Slovenia 1992. *Publications include:* novels: Half Way to the Horizon 1968, White Rooms 1970, Secretary of the Sixth International 1971, Tea and Guns at Four 1972, Fifth Floor of the Three-Floor House 1972, Time in It the Cruel Hangman 1974, Chi Square 1975, The Family Connection 1977, Cold Storms, Mad Homes 1978, Pleasant Life 1979, Max 1983, Follow the Addressee, Job 1984, Forgotten Invited 1985, Why is the World Upside Down? 1987, Lion's Share 1989, Story About Time 1989; non-fiction: Reading 1973, Free Words 1976, Words and Acts 1981, Reality Tests 1982, Sociology of Literature 1982, Sociology of Culture and Art 1986, Words of God and Words Divine 1987, Slovenian Intellectuals 1989, Slovenian Holidays and Everydays 1990, Slovenian Faith 1992, Slovenian Path to Independence and Recognition 1992, Secret of the State (memoirs) 1992, Disenchanted Slovenia 1993, Time of Politics 1994, Unity, Happiness, Reconciliation 1996, Freedom Against State 1998, Meetings and Partings 2001, Taking Over the Success Story 2004; plays: Less Terrible Night 1981, Job 1982, PDFS (Follow the Addressee) 1984; film screenplay: Oxygen 1971.

RUPÉREZ, Francisco Javier, LLB; Spanish diplomatist, politician and author; *President, Ruperez International;* b. 24 April 1941, Madrid; m. Rakela Cerovic; two d.; ed El Pilar Coll., Univ. of Madrid; joined Diplomatic Service 1965, posts in Addis Ababa 1967–69, Warsaw 1969–72, Helsinki 1972–73; mem. Del. to CSCE, Helsinki 1972–73, to Int. Orgs, Geneva 1973–75; Chief of Staff of Under-Sec. of Foreign Affairs 1976; Chief of Staff of Ministry of Foreign Affairs 1976–77; mem. Exec. Cttee, Union of Democratic Centre (UCD) 1977–82; mem. Parl. for Cuenca 1979–82, 1986–89, for Madrid 1989–93, for Ciudad Real 1993–2000; Amb. and Head of Del. to Madrid Session of CSCE 1980–82; First Spanish Amb. to NATO 1982–83; Senator and mem. Regional Parl. of Castilla La Mancha 1983–86; Vice-Pres. Democratic People's Party (PDP) 1983–87; Pres. Christian Democratic Party 1987–89; Vice-Pres. People's Party (PP) 1989–90, Spokesman in Parl. Defence Cttee 1989–91, Spokesman in Parl. Foreign Affairs Cttee 1991–96; Vice-Pres. NATO Parl. Ass. 1994–96, Pres. Parl. Ass. 1998–2000; Pres. Parl. Ass. of OSCE 1996–98, Spanish Atlantic Asscn (AAE) 1996–2000; Pres. Foreign Affairs Cttee, House of Deputies 1996–2000, Cttee on Defence 2000; Pres. Christian-Democratic Int. (CDI) 1998–2000; Amb. to USA 2000–04; Asst Sec.-Gen. and Exec. Dir UN Counter-Terrorism Exec. Directorate 2004–07; Consul-Gen. to Chicago 2007–11; currently Pres. Ruperez Int.; Pres. Foundation for Humanism and Democracy 1989–2000; Co-founder Cuadernos para el Diálogo (monthly political magazine) 1963–77; lectures regularly and directs courses at Int. Univ. Menéndez Pelayo, Univ. of Madrid and the Diplomatic School; Gran Cruz de la Orden de Isabel la Católica, Comendador de la Orden de Carlos III, Oficial de Isabel la Católica, Oficial de la Orden del Mérito Civil, Orden Bernardo O'Higgins (Chile), Gran Cruz de Vasco Núñez de Balboa (Panama), Grand Ordre de Léopold II (Belgium), Comendador con Placa de la Orden del Infante Don Enrique (Portugal), Kt Commdr of the Order of Alistical (Jordan), Kt Commdr, Order of the Arab Repub. of Egypt, Officier, Légion d'honneur (France). *Publications include:* Confessional State and Religious Liberty 1970, Europe Between Fear and Hope 1976, Spain in NATO 1986, First Book of Short Stories 1987, Kidnapped by ETA: Memoirs 1990, The Price of a Shadow (novel) 2005, El espejismo multilateral 2009, Memoria de Washington 2011; contribs to co-authored books and numerous articles in the Spanish press and specialized publs. *Leisure interests:* music, cinema, theatre, literature. *E-mail:* info@ruperezinternational.com (office). *Website:* www .ruperezinternational.com (office).

RUPERT, Johann; South African business executive; *Chairman, Compagnie Financiere Richemont SA;* b. 6 Jan. 1950, Stellenboch; s. of Anton Rupert and Huberte Rupert; m. Gaynor Rupert; three c.; ed Paul Roos Gymnasium, Univ. of Stellenbosch; worked at Chase Manhattan Bank 1975–79; Business Apprentice, Lazard Freres, New York, USA 1976–79; Founder and CEO Rand Merchant Bank 1979–84; apptd Gen. Man. Rembrandt Group Ltd 1985, Vice-Chair. 1989–92, Chair. 1992–; Chair. (non-exec.) Gold Fields Ltd 1997–; f. VenFin Ltd 2000, Chair. (non-exec.) 2006–; Founder-Chair. (non-exec.) Remgro Ltd 2000–; CEO Compagnie Financiere Richemont SA (luxury goods) 2000–04, 2010–13, Chair. 2002–, mem. Group Man. Cttee 1988–; Chair. (non-exec.) Access Freight International (Pty) Ltd; Chair. Peace Parks Foundation, South African PGA Tour, Rembrandt Controlling Investments Ltd, South African Golf Devt Bd; Founder Small Business Devt Corpn 1979–, Laureus Sport for Good Foundation 1990–, Vendôme Luxury Group 1990–; owner Rupert & Rothschild and L'Ormarins wine estates; Developer, Leopard Creek Golf Club, Mpumalanga; Dir (non-exec.) Rothmans Int. Plc 1988–; Chancellor, Stellenbosch Univ. 2009–; f. Franschhoek Motor Museum; fmr Trustee, Southern African Nature Foundation; Hon. Vice-Pres., European Golf Tour 2010–; Officier, Ordre national de la Légion d'honneur; Dr hc (Stellenbosch Univ.) 2004, (Nelson Mandela Metropolitan Univ.) 2008, (Univ. of St Andrews, Scotland); Businessman of the Year, Sunday Times 1988, 1996, Business Leader of the Year, Die Burger newspaper, Cape Town Chamber of Commerce 1990, M.S. Louw Award, Afrikaanse Handelsinstituut 1993, Free Market Award, Free Market Foundation of South Africa 1999, Man. Excellence Award, Wits Business

School 2009, Int. Wine Entrepreneur of the Year 2009, Voted South Africa's Most Admired Business Leader 2010. *Address:* Compagnie Financiere Richemont SA, 50, Chemin De La Chênaie, Geneva, Switzerland (office); Office of the Chancellor, Stellenbosch University, Private Bag X1, Matieland 7602, South Africa (office). *Telephone:* 227153500 (Switzerland) (office); (21) 808 4896 (South Africa) (office). *E-mail:* mvdl@sun.ac.za (office). *Website:* www.richemont.com (office).

RUPNIK, Jacques, MA PhD; French political scientist and academic; *Director of Research, National Foundation for Political Science, Centre for International Studies and Research (CERI);* b. 21 Nov. 1950, Prague, Czech Republic; s. of Anton Rupnik and Micheline Bauvillain-Rupnik; m.; ed Harvard Univ., USA, Univ. of Paris (Sorbonne), Institut d'Etudes Politiques de Paris; Research Assoc., Russian Research Center, Harvard Univ. 1974–75; Eastern Europe specialist BBC World Service 1977–82; Prof., Institut d'Etudes Politiques de Paris 1982–96; adviser to Czech Pres. Vaclav Havel 1990–92; Exec. Dir Int. Comm. for Balkans, Carnegie Endowment for Int. Peace 1995–96; mem. Ind. Int. Comm. on Kosovo 1999–2000; Visiting Prof., Coll. of Europe 1999–, Harvard Univ. 2006; currently Research Dir Nat. Foundation for Political Science, Centre for Int. Studies and Research (CERI), Prof. 1982–; adviser to EC 2007–; mem. Scientific Council, Faculty of Social Sciences, Charles Univ. 1998–, Prague Inst. of Int. Relations, Inst. for Historical Justice and Reconciliation, Research Council of Int. Forum for Democracy Studies, Washington, DC 2013–; Sr Fellow, Davis Center 2008, Center for European Studies, Harvard Univ. 2011; Ordre Nat. du Mérite 1995, Order of T.G. Maseryk, Czech Repub. 2002. *Television includes:* writer and presenter, The Other Europe (6-part documentary series) (Channel 4 TV, UK) 1988. *Publications include:* The Other Europe 1988, Unfinished Peace 1996, Le Europe en face à l'élargissement 2004, Les Banlieues de l'Europe, les politiques de voisinage de l'UE 2007, The Western Balkans and the EU: The Hour of Europe 2011, Europe and the New International System 2013; numerous articles focused on central and Eastern Europe, and the Balkans. *Address:* Centre for International Studies and Research (CERI), 56 rue Jacob, 75006 Paris, France (office). *Telephone:* 1-58-71-70-51 (office); 1-49-57-08-54 (home). *Fax:* 1-58-71-70-90 (office). *E-mail:* rupnik@ceri -sciences-po.org (office); jacquesrupnik@hotmail.com (home). *Website:* www.ceri -sciencespo.com/cherlist/rupnik.htm (office).

RUPP, George, AB, BD, PhD; American professor of religion, university president and international organization official; b. 22 Sept. 1942, Summit, NJ; m. Nancy Katherine Farrar 1964; two d.; ed Univ. of Munich, Germany, Princeton Univ., Yale Divinity School, Univ. of Sri Lanka, Harvard Univ.; Faculty Fellow in Religion, Johnston Coll., Univ. of Redlands, Calif., 1971–73, Vice-Chancellor 1973–74; Asst Prof. of Theology, Divinity School, Harvard Univ. 1974–76, Assoc. Prof. of Theology and Chair. Dept of Theology 1976–77, Dean and John Lord O'Brian Prof. of Divinity 1979–85; Dean for Acad. Affairs and Prof. of Humanistic Studies, Univ. of Wisconsin-Green Bay 1977–79; Pres. and Prof. of Religious Studies, Rice Univ. 1985–93; Pres. and Prof. of Religion, Columbia Univ., New York 1993–2002; Pres. and CEO Int. Rescue Cttee 2002–13; Chair. Bd of Govs International Baccalaureate 2015–; mem. Bd Inst. of Int. Educ., Council on Foreign Relations, Interaction, Henry Luce Foundation, Josiah Macy Foundation and other orgs; Hon. DD (Austin Coll.) 1992, (Gen. Theological Seminary) 2011; Hon. DLit (Columbia) 1993; Hon. DHumLitt (Univ. of Redlands) 1994, (George-town Univ.) 2001; Hon. LLD (Hamilton Coll.) 1995; Danforth Grad. Fellowship, Yale and Harvard Univs 1964–71; Honors Scholarship, Yale Univ. 1964–65, Dwight Fellowship, Yale Univ. 1966–67, Center for the Study of World Religions travel grant, Harvard Univ. 1969–70, Ford Foundation summer research grant, Univ. of Redlands 1972, Asscn of Theological Schools research grant for leave in Tübingen, Germany, Harvard Univ. 1976, Alexander Hamilton Medal, Columbia Univ. 2002, Centennial Medal for Contrib. to Society, Harvard Univ. Grad. School of Arts and Sciences 2004, Gold Medal, Nat. Inst. of Social Sciences 2005, Woodrow Wilson Award, Princeton Univ. 2006. *Publications:* Christologies and Cultures: Toward a Typology of Religious Worldviews 1974, Culture-Protestantism: German Liberal Theology at the Turn of the Twentieth Century 1977, Beyond Existential-ism and Zen: Religion in a Pluralistic World 1979, Commitment and Community 1989, Globalization Challenged 2006; numerous book chapters and articles. *Address:* IB Global Centre, 7501 Wisconsin Avenue, Suite 200, West Bethesda, MD 20814, USA (office). *Website:* www.ibo.org (office).

RUPPRECHT, Rudolf, DipEng; German fmr business executive; b. 12 Jan. 1940, Berlin; ed Munich Tech. Univ.; began career as sales engineer, MAN Group 1966, various positions including Tech. Dir MAN subsidiary in Argentina, Exec. Dir Diesel Engines Div. 1981–84, apptd mem. Exec. Bd MAN B&W Diesel AG, Augsburg 1984, Chair. Exec. Bd 1989–93, Chair. Exec. Bd MAN Nutzfahrzeuge AG, Munich 1993–96, Chair. Exec. Bd MAN Aktiengesellschaft, Munich 1996–2004, mem. Supervisory Bd 2005–11; mem. Supervisory Bd Bayerische Staatsforsten AöR, KME AG, Salzgitter AG, SMS GmbH (also Chair.); retd.

RUPRECHT, William F.; American auctioneer and business executive; *Chairman, Invaluable;* b. St Louis, Mo.; ed Univ. of Colorado, Univ. of Vermont; began career as apprentice to furniture maker, Vermont; joined Sotheby's 1980, Dir of Marketing Sotheby's Inc., New York 1986–92, Dir of Marketing Sotheby's Worldwide 1992–94, Man. Dir Sotheby's N and S America 1994–2000, Pres., CEO and Dir Sotheby's Holdings, Inc. 2000–14; Chair. Invaluable 2016–. *Address:* Invaluable, 38 Everett Street, Allston, MA 02134, USA. *Telephone:* (617) 746-9800. *Website:* www.invaluable.com.

RUS, Ioan, PhD; Romanian engineer, academic and politician; b. 21 Feb. 1955, Urisor, Cluj Co.; m.; two c.; ed Faculty of Mechanical Eng, Technical Univ. of Cluj-Napoca; mil. service 1976–77, attained rank of Lt Col; engineer at TSMA, Cluj 1982–84; Research Engineer, Polytechnic Inst. of Cluj 1984–85; Asst Prof., Tech. Univ. of Cluj-Napoca 1985–90, Lecturer 1990–94, Assoc. Prof. 1995–2000, Prof. and Dept Co-ordinator of Computation and Construction Vehicles 2002, PhD supervisor 2003; Gen. Dir SC RMB Inter-Auto SRL (Representation of Mercedes-Benz Transilvania) 1993–2000, Man. 2004–12; mem. Party of Social Democracy of Romania (Partidul Democraţiei Sociale din România—PDSR) 1994–98; Prefect of Cluj Co. Aug.–Dec. 1996, Chair. Cluj Co. Council June–Dec. 2000; mem. Exec. Cabinet of Adrian Nastase 2000–03; Minister of the Interior 2000–03; Deputy Prime Minister 2003–04; Pres. Cluj Co. Org. of Social Democratic Party (Partidul Social Democrat—PSD) 2001–02, Vice-Pres. of the party 2002–04; campaigned for election as Mayor of Cluj; resigned as Pres. of PSD Cluj 2007; Minister of Admin

and the Interior May–Aug. 2012; mem. of several professional asscns in Romania and abroad, including Gen. Asscn of Engineers in Romania, Soc. of Automotive Engineers of Romania, Romania Asscn of Agricultural Mechanical Engineers, Soc. of Automotive Engineers (USA), Romanian Asscn for the Club of Rome, Societé des Ingenieurs de l'Automobile (France); Kt, Order of the Romanian Star 2002. *Publications include:* author or co-author of 14 books and numerous papers and scientific articles.

RUSBRIDGER, Alan, BA, MA; British journalist, editor and publishing executive; *Principal of Lady Margaret Hall, University of Oxford;* b. 29 Dec. 1953, Lusaka, Zambia; s. of G. H. Rusbridger and B. E. Rusbridger (née Wickham); m. Lindsay Mackie 1982; two d.; ed Cranleigh School, Magdalene Coll., Cambridge; reporter, Cambridge Evening News 1976–79; reporter, The Guardian 1979–82, diary ed. and feature writer 1982–86, special writer 1987–88, launch ed., Weekend Guardian 1988–89, Features Ed. 1989–93, Deputy Ed. 1993–95, Ed. 1995–2015, TV critic and feature writer, The Observer 1986, Exec. Ed. 1996–2015, apptd mem. Bd Guardian Newspapers Ltd 1994, Guardian Media Group 1999, Trustee, Scott Trust (owner of Guardian Media Group) 1997–2016 (resgnd); Washington Corresp., London Daily News 1987; fmr Visiting Fellow, Nuffield Coll., Oxford; Prin. of Lady Margaret Hall, Oxford 2015–; Chair. Inst. Steering Cttee, Reuters Inst. for the Study of Journalism, Univ. of Oxford 2016–; fmr Visiting Prof. of History, Queen Mary's London, Cardiff Univ., Asian Coll. of Journalism, Chennai, India; Chair. Nat. Youth Orchestra 2004–13; fmr Chair. Photographers' Gallery, London; Dr hc (Univ. of Lincoln) 2009, (Univ. of Kingston) 2010, (Univ. of Oslo) 2014; Ed. of the Year, What the Papers Say Awards (Granada TV) 1996, 2001, Nat. Newspaper Ed., Newspaper Industry Awards 1996, Editor's Ed., Press Gazette 1997, Judges' Award, What the Papers Say 2006, Goldsmith Career Award for Excellence in Journalism, Kennedy School of Govt, Harvard Univ. 2012, Right Livelihood Award 2014, Ortega y Gasset Award 2014, European Press Prize 2014, Tully Award for Free Speech, Newhouse School, Syracuse Univ. 2014, Columbia Journalism Award 2014, Marie Colvin Prize 2015, British Media Award 2016. *Television:* presenter, What the Papers Say (Granada TV) 1983–94, co-writer (with Ronan Bennett), Fields of Gold (BBC TV) 2001. *Publications include:* New World Order (ed.) 1991, Altered State (ed.) 1992, Guardian Year 1994, Play it Again 2013; children's books: The Coldest Day in the Zoo 2004, The Wildest Day at the Zoo 2005, The Smelliest Day at the Zoo 2007. *Leisure interests:* golf, music (playing clarinet), painting. *Address:* Office of the Principal, Lady Margaret Hall, University of Oxford, Oxford, OX2 6QA, England (office). *Telephone:* (1865) 274300 (office). *Website:* www.lmh.ox.ac.uk/Tutors/The-Principal (office); alanrusbridger .com.

RUSCHA, Edward (Ed) Joseph; American artist; b. 16 Dec. 1937, Omaha, Neb.; s. of Edward Joseph Ruscha and Dorothy Driscoll; m. Danna Knego 1967; one s.; ed Chouinard Art Inst., Los Angeles; first solo exhbn Los Angeles 1963; produced films Premium 1970, Miracle 1975; maj. exhbns include San Francisco Museum of Modern Art 1982, Musée St Pierre, Lyon, France 1985, Museum of Contemporary Art, Chicago 1988, Centre Georges Pompidou, Paris 1989, Serpentine Gallery, London 1990, Museum of Contemporary Art, Los Angeles 1990, Robert Miller Gallery, New York 1992, Thaddaeus Ropac, Salzburg, Austria 1992, Hayward Gallery, London 2009, Museum of Contemporary Art, Florida 2012; first public comm., for Miami Dade Cultural Center's Main Library, Miami, Fla 1985; other comms. include Great Hall, Denver Cen. Library 1994–95, Auditorium Getty Center, Los Angeles 1997; represented in numerous perm. collections; Guggenheim Foundation Fellowship 1971; mem. American Acad. of Arts and Letters 2001; Artistic Excellence Award, Americans for the Arts 2009. *Publications include:* 12 books, including Twenty-six Gasoline Stations 1963, The Sunset Strip 1966. *Website:* www.edruscha.com.

RUSH, Geoffrey Roy; Australian actor; b. 6 July 1951, Toowoomba, Queensland; s. of Roy Baden Rush and Merle Kiehne; m. Jane Menelaus 1988; one s. one d.; studied at Jacques Lecoq School of Mime, Paris, began professional career with Queensland Theatre Co.; Hans Christian Andersen Amb. 2005–; became the 19th actor to win the 'Triple Crown of Acting': Academy, Tony and Emmy Awards; Pres. Australian Acad. of Cinema and Television Arts 2011–17; Patron, Melbourne Int. Film Festival, Toowoomba's Empire Theatre Foundation, Spina Bifida Foundation Victoria; Australian Centenary Medal 2001; Hon. DLitt (Univ. of Queensland); Sidney Myer Performing Arts Awards 1994, Supporting Actor of the Year, Hollywood Film Festival 2003, Global Achievement Award, Australian Film Inst. 2003, Chauvel Award, Brisbane Int. Film Festival 2004, Longford Life Achievement Award, Australian Film Inst. 2009, Montecito Award, Santa Barbara Int. Film Festival 2011, Helpmann Award 2011, Australian of the Year 2012. *Theatre includes:* Hamlet 1994, The Alchemist 1996, The Marriage of Figaro 1998, The Small Poppies 1999, Exit the King (Tony Award for Best Actor 2009) 2009; also dir of numerous productions. *Films include:* The Wedding 1980, Starstruck 1981, Twelfth Night 1985, Midday Crisis 1994, Dad and Dave on our Selection 1995, Shine (Academy Award for Best Actor 1997, BAFTA Award, Australian Film Inst. Award, Golden Globe Award, numerous other awards) 1996, Children of the Revolution 1996, Les Miserables 1997, Elizabeth 1998, Shakespeare in Love (BAFTA Award for Best Supporting Actor) 1998, Mystery Men 1999, House on Haunted Hill 1999, Quills 1999, The Magic Pudding (voice) 2000, Tailor of Panama 2001, Lantana 2001, Frida 2002, The Banger Sisters 2002, Swimming Upstream 2003, Ned Kelly 2003, Finding Nemo (voice) 2003, Pirates of the Caribbean: The Curse of the Black Pearl 2003, Intolerable Cruelty 2003, Harvie Krumpet (voice) 2003, The Life and Death of Peter Sellers (Best Actor in a Miniseries or TV Movie, Golden Globe Awards 2005, Screen Actors Guild Awards 2005, Emmy Award for Best Actor in a Mini-Series or Movie 2005) 2004, Swimming Upstream 2005, Munich 2005, Candy 2006, Pirates of the Caribbean: Dead Man's Chest 2006, Pirates of the Caribbean: At World's End 2007, Elizabeth: The Golden Age 2007, $9.99 2008, Bran Nue Dae 2009, The King's Speech (British Independent Film Award for Best Supporting Actor, Central Ohio Film Critics Asscn Award for Best Supporting Actor, Nat. Soc. of Film Critics Award for Best Supporting Actor, BAFTA Award for Best Supporting Actor 2011) 2010, Legend of the Guardians: The Owls of Ga'Hoole 2010, The Warrior's Way 2010, The Eye of the Storm 2011, Pirates of the Caribbean: On Stranger Tides 2011, Green Lantern (voice) 2011, The Eye of the Storm 2011, Deception 2013, The Book Thief 2013, The Daughter 2015, Holding the Man 2015, Gods of Egypt 2016. *Television includes:* Menotti 1980–81, The Burning Piano 1992, Mercury 1996, Bonus Mileage 1996, Twisted (series)

1996, Frontier (mini-series) 1997, Kath & Kim (series) 2004, Lowdown (series) 2010–12. *Address:* c/o Shanahan Management, PO Box 478, King's Cross, NSW 2011, Australia.

RUSHAILO, Col-Gen. Vladimir Borisovich; Russian politician and international organization official; *Vice-President, Transneft;* b. 28 July 1953, Tambov; m.; three c.; ed Omsk Higher School of Militia, USSR Ministry of Internal Affairs; militiaman 1972–76; investigator Moscow Dept of Internal Affairs 1976–88, later Head Moscow Dept of Internal Affairs; Head Dept for Struggle against Organized Crime 1988–93, 1998–99, Head Regional Dept for Struggle against Organized Crime 1993–96; Counsellor Council of Fed. 1996–98; Deputy Minister of Internal Affairs 1998–99, Minister of Internal Affairs 1999–2001; Sec. Security Council of Russia 2001–04; Exec. Sec. and Chair. Exec. Cttee CIS 2004–07; Head, CIS mission to observe presidential election in Belarus 2006; Vice-Pres. Transneft 2013–; mem. Presidium of Russian Govt, Security Council 2001–04, Council of Fed., Fed. Ass. 2007–13; Order of Sign of Honour, Order for Personal Courage and numerous other decorations. *Address:* Transneft, 57 Bolshaya Polyanka, 119180 Moscow, 57 Bolshaya Polyanka, Russian Federation (office). *Telephone:* (495) 950-81-78 (office). *Fax:* (495) 950-89-00 (office). *E-mail:* transneft@ak.transneft.ru (office). *Website:* www.en.transneft.ru (office).

RUSHDIE, Sir (Ahmed) Salman, Kt, MA, FRSL; British writer and academic; *University Distinguished Professor, Emory University;* b. 19 June 1947, Bombay (now Mumbai), India; s. of Anis Ahmed Rushdie and Negin Rushdie (née Butt); m. 1st Clarissa Luard 1976 (divorced 1987, died 1999); one s.; m. 2nd Marianne Wiggins 1988 (divorced 1993); one step-d.; m. 3rd Elizabeth West 1997 (divorced); one s.; m. 4th Padma Lakshmi 2004 (divorced 2007); ed Cathedral and John Connon Boys' High School, Bombay, Rugby School, England, King's Coll., Cambridge; mem. Footlights revue, Univ. of Cambridge 1965–68; actor, fringe theatre, London 1968–69; advertising copywriter 1969–73; wrote first published novel Grimus 1973–74; part-time advertising copywriter while writing second novel 1976–80; mem. Int. PEN 1981–, Soc. of Authors 1983–, Exec. Cttee Nat. Book League 1983–, Council Inst. of Contemporary Arts 1985–, British Film Inst. Production Bd 1986–, PEN American Center (Pres. 2004–06); Distinguished Writer-in-Residence, then Univ. Distinguished Prof., Emory Univ., Atlanta 2007–; Exec. mem. Camden Cttee for Community Relations 1977–83; Distinguished Fellow in Literature, Univ. of East Anglia 1995; Distinguished Writer-in-Residence, Arthur L. Carter Journalism Inst., New York Univ. 2015; Foreign Hon. mem. American Acad. of Arts and Letters 2008–; Hon. Prof. MIT 1993; Hon. Spokesman Charter 88 1989; Commdr, Ordre des Arts et des Lettres 1999; Hon. DLitt (Bard Coll.) 1995; Arts Council Literature Bursary 1981, Kurt Tucholsky Prize Sweden 1992, Prix Colette Switzerland 1993, Austrian State Prize for European Literature 1994, British Book Awards Author of the Year 1996, London Int. Writers Award 2002, James Joyce Award 2008, Kitty Carlisle Hart Award for Outstanding Contrib. to the Arts, Americans for the Arts 2009, PEN Pinter Prize 2014, Hans Christian Andersen Literature Award 2014, Mailer Prize for Lifetime Achievement 2015. *Television film screenplays:* The Painter and the Pest 1985, The Riddle of Midnight 1988. *Film appearances:* Then She Found Me 2007, River of Fundament 2014. *Publications include:* Grimus 1975, Midnight's Children 1981 (Booker McConnell Prize for Fiction, English Speaking Union Literary Award 1981, James Tait Black Memorial Book Prize 1981, Booker of Bookers Prize 1993, 2008) 1981, Shame (Prix du Meilleur Livre Etranger 1984) 1983, The Jaguar Smile: A Nicaraguan Journey 1987, The Satanic Verses 1988, Is Nothing Sacred (lecture) 1990, Haroun and the Sea of Stories (novel) 1990, Imaginary Homelands: Essays and Criticism 1981–91 1991, The Wizard of Oz 1992, East, West (short stories) 1994, The Moor's Last Sigh (novel) (Whitbread Fiction Award 1996) 1995, The Vintage Book of Indian Writing 1947–97 (ed. with Elizabeth West) 1997, The Ground Beneath Her Feet 1999, Fury 2001, Step Across the Line: Collected Non-Fiction 1992–2002 2002, Telling Tales (contrib. to charity anthology) 2004, Shalimar the Clown 2005, The Enchantress of Florence 2008, Luka and the Fire of Life 2010, Joseph Anton (memoir) 2012, Two Years Eight Months and Twenty-Eight Nights 2015, The Golden House 2017; articles for New York Times, Washington Post, The Times and Sunday Times. *Leisure interests:* films, chess, table tennis, involvement in politics, especially race relations. *Address:* c/o Wylie Agency (UK) Ltd, 17 Bedford Square, London, WC1B 3JA, England (office). *Telephone:* (20) 7908-5900 (office). *Fax:* (20) 7908-5901 (office). *E-mail:* mail@wylieagency.co.uk (office). *Website:* www.wylieagency.co.uk (office); www.salmanrushdie.com.

RUŠKO, Pavol; Slovak politician; b. 20 Aug. 1963, Liptovský Hrádok; m. Viera; two c.; ed Comenius Univ.; Sports Ed. Slovak TV 1985, Head Dept of Program Research, Head of Transmitting Centre and Deputy of Gen. Dir 1989–94; with Lottop Co. 1994–96; Gen. Dir and Co-Owner TV Markiza 1995–2000, Chair. STS Markiza Bd of Owners 2000–; Dir-Gen. Slovenska Televizna Spolocnost; Chair. New Citizens' Alliance (NCA) (Aliancia nového občana—ANO) 2001–07; Vice-Chair. Nat. Council of Slovak Repub. 2002–03; Deputy Prime Minister and Minister of the Economy, and Admin and Privatization of Nat. Property 2003–05; European Crystal Globe award 2002.

RUSMAJLI, Ilir; Albanian lawyer and politician; b. 24 April 1965, Elbasan; ed Univ. of Tirana; fmrly Minister of Foreign Affairs; Deputy Prime Minister 2005–07; Minister of Justice 2007 (resgnd); Deputy, Kuvendi Popullor (People's Assembly); mem. Parl. Ass., Council of Europe 2009.

RUSNOK, Jiří, MEcon; Czech politician, economist and central banker; *Governor, Česká národní banka (Czech National Bank);* b. 16 Oct. 1960, Ostrava-Vítkovice; three c.; ed Univ. of Economics, Prague; various positions in state admin.; Econ. Adviser, Czech-Moravian Confed. of Trade Unions 1992–98; mem. Czech Social Democratic Party (CSDP) 1998–2010; Deputy Minister for Labour and Social Affairs 1998–2001; Minister of Finance 2001–02, of Industry and Trade 2002–03; Chief Economist and Exec. Adviser to the Man. Cttee and Dir of Pensions, ING Insurance Czech Repub./Slovak Repub. 2003–13; Pres. Czech Pension Funds Asscn 2005–12, Audit Public Oversight Council of Czech Repub. 2009–13; mem. Nat. Econ. Council of Govt; Prime Minister 2013–14; Gov. Czech Nat. Bank (Česká národní banka) 2016–. *Leisure interests:* gardening, nature, history, sport. *Address:* Česká národní banka (Czech National Bank), Na Příkopě 28, 115 03 Prague 1, Czech Republic (office). *Telephone:* 224411111 (office). *Fax:* 224412404 (office). *E-mail:* podatelna@cnb.cz (office). *Website:* www.cnb.cz (office).

RUSSELL, David Owen; American film director and screenwriter; b. 20 Aug. 1958, New York; s. of Bernard Russell and Maria Russell (née Muzio); m. Janet Grillo 1992–2007; ed Amherst Coll., Mass; mem. Bd of Dirs Ghetto Film School, South Bronx, New York; Career Tribute, Gotham Independent Film Awards 2012, Indie Impact Award, Variety 2012, Screenwriters Tribute Award, Nantucket Film Festival 2013. *Films directed include:* Bingo Inferno (also writer and producer) 1987, Hairway to the Stars 1990, Spanking the Monkey (also writer and exec. producer) (Independent Spirit Award for Best First Screenplay) 1994, Flirting with Disaster (also writer) 1996, Three Kings (Boston Soc. of Film Critics Award for Best Dir) 1999, I Heart Huckabees (also writer and producer) 2004, The Fighter 2010, Silver Linings Playbook (also writer) (BAFTA Award for Best Adapted Screenplay 2013) 2012, American Hustle (BAFTA Award for Best Original Screenplay 2014) 2013, Joy 2015. *Television:* Outer Space Astronauts (series) (executive producer) 2009. *Address:* c/o WME Entertainment, 9601 Wilshire Boulevard, Beverly Hills, CA 90210-5213, USA (office). *Website:* www.davidorussell.com (office).

RUSSELL, Sir George, Kt, CBE, BA, FRSA, CBIM, FID; British business executive; b. 25 Oct. 1935; s. of William H. Russell and Frances A. Russell; m. Dorothy Brown 1959; three d.; ed Gateshead Grammar School, Univ. of Durham; Vice-Pres. and Gen. Man. Welland Chemical Co. of Canada Ltd 1968, St Clair Chemical Co. Ltd 1968; Man. Dir Alcan UK Ltd 1976; Asst Man. Dir Alcan Aluminium (UK) Ltd 1977–81, Man. Dir 1981–82; Man. Dir and CEO British Alcan Aluminium 1982–86; Dir Alcan Aluminiumwerke GmbH, Frankfurt 1982–86, Alcan Aluminium Ltd 1987–2000; Group Chief Exec. Marley PLC 1986–89, Chair. and CEO 1989–93, Chair. (non-exec.) 1993–97; Deputy Chair. Channel Four TV 1987–88; Chair. Ind. TV News (ITN) 1988; Chair. Ind. Broadcasting Authority (IBA) 1989–90, Ind. Television Comm. (ITC) 1991–96; Chair. Camelot Group PLC 1995–2002; Chair. Luxfer Holdings Ltd 1976; mem. Bd of Dirs Northern Rock Building Soc. (now Northern Rock PLC) 1985–2006, 3i Group PLC 1992–2001 (Chair. non-exec. 1993–2001), Taylor Woodrow PLC 1992–2004 (Deputy Chair. 2000–03); Chair. Northern Devt Co. 1994–99; Deputy Chair. Granada PLC 2002–04, ITV PLC 2003–09; Chair. Comm. on Public Service Reform in the North East 2007–09; Dir Wildfowl & Wetlands Trust 2002–08, Vice-Pres. 2008–; Visiting Prof., Univ. of Newcastle-upon-Tyne 1978; mem. Northern Industrial Devt Bd 1977–80, Washington Devt Corpn 1978–80, IBA 1979–86, Megaw Cttee of Enquiry into Civil Service Pay 1981–82, Council CBI 1984–85, Widdicombe Cttee of Inquiry into Conduct of Local Authority Business 1985; mem. of Court, Univ. of Newcastle 2004–10, now Hon. Life Mem.; Fellow, Inst. of Industrial Mans; Trustee, Beamish Devt Trust 1985–90, Thomas Bewick Birthplace Trust; Hon. FRIBA 1993; Hon. FRTS 1994; Hon. FRAM 2001; Hon. DEng (Newcastle upon Tyne) 1985; Hon. DBA (Northumbria) 1992; Hon. LLD (Sunderland) 1995, (Durham) 1997. *Leisure interests:* tennis, badminton, bird watching. *Address:* 46 Downshire Hill, London, NW3 1NX, England.

RUSSELL, Ian, CBE, BCom; British chartered accountant and business executive; *Chairman, Johnston Press plc;* b. 16 Jan. 1953, Edinburgh, Scotland; s. of James Russell and Christine Clark; m. Fiona Russell 1975; one s. one d.; ed Univ. of Edinburgh; Finance Dir HSBC Asset Man., Hong Kong 1987–90; Dir Finance Control, Tomkins, London 1991–94; Finance Dir Scottish Power plc 1994, Deputy CEO 1998–2001, CEO 2001–06; apptd Industrialist in Residence, 3i Group (pvt. equity firm) 2007, apptd Chair. Advanced Power AG Advisory Bd (after 3i investment in Advanced Power) 2007, mem. Bd of Dirs –2014; mem. Bd of Dirs Johnston Press PLC 2007– (Chair. 2009–), JPMorgan Fleming Mercantile Investment Trust PLC 2007–, British Assets Trust PLC 2008–, Remploy Ltd (Chair. 2007–), British Polythene Industries PLC 2011–, HICL Infrastructure Co. Ltd 2013–; Adviser, Clyde Bergemann Power Group; Chair. Campaign Bd, Univ. of Edinburgh; Head Govt Comm. on Nat. Youth Volunteering Strategy 2004–05; mem. Edinburgh Int. Festival Council, Scottish Council of the Prince's Trust. *Leisure interests:* golf, rugby. *Address:* Johnston Press plc, Orchard Brae House, 30 Queensferry Road, Edinburgh, EH4 2HS, Scotland (office). *Telephone:* (131) 311-7500 (office). *Website:* www.johnstonpress.co.uk (office).

RUSSELL, Kurt (von Vogel); American actor; b. 17 March 1951, Springfield, Mass; s. of Bing Oliver Russell and Louise Julia Russell (née Crone); m. Season Hubley 1979 (divorced); one s.; pnr Goldie Hawn; one s.; lead role in TV series The Travels of Jamie McPheeters 1963–64; child actor in many Disney shows and films; professional minor league baseball player 1971–73; numerous TV guest appearances; mem. Professional Baseball Players' Asscn, Stuntman's Asscn; Co-founder Cosmic Entertainment (production co.) 2003; recipient five acting awards, ten baseball awards, one golf championship. *Films include:* Follow Me, Boys! 1966, Mosby's Marauders 1967, Guns in the Heather 1968, The One and Only, Genuine, Original Family Band 1968, The Horse in the Gray Flannel Suit 1968, The Computer Wore Tennis Shoes 1969, The Barefoot Executive 1971, Fools' Parade 1971, Now You See Him, Now You Don't 1972, Charley and the Angel 1973, Superdad 1973, The Strongest Man in the World 1975, The Captive: The Longest Drive 2 1976, Used Cars 1980, Escape from New York 1981, The Thing 1982, Silkwood 1983, Swing Shift 1984, Mean Season 1985, Best of Times 1986, Big Trouble in Little China 1986, Overboard 1987, Tequila Sunrise 1988, Winter People 1989, Tango & Cash 1989, Backdraft 1991, Unlawful Entry 1992, Captain Ron 1992, Tombstone 1993, Stargate 1994, Executive Decision 1996, Escape from LA 1996, Breakdown 1997, Soldier 1998, 3000 Miles to Graceland 2001, Vanilla Sky 2001, Interstate 60 2002, Dark Blue 2002, Miracle 2004, Jiminy Glick in La La Wood 2004, Dreamer 2005, Sky High 2005, Poseidon 2006, Grindhouse 2007, Death Proof 2007, Cutlass 2007, Touchback 2011, The Art of the Steal 2013, Fast & Furious 7 2015, Bone Tomahawk 2015, The Hateful Eight 2015. *Television series include:* Sugarfoot 1957, Travels with Jamie McPheeters 1963–64, The New Land 1974, The Quest 1976. *Television films include:* Search for the Gods 1975, The Deadly Tower 1975, Christmas Miracle in Caulfield USA 1977, Elvis 1979, Amber Waves 1988. *Telephone:* (310) 275-8080 (Cosmic Entertainment).

RUSSELL, Paul; British lawyer and music industry executive; b. 3 July 1944, London; m. Elizabeth Russell; three s. two d.; ed Coll. of Law; fmrly band mem. Red Diamond; fmrly with law firm Balin & Co.; joined CBS UK as Dir, Business Affairs 1973, moved to New York 1976, held several positions at CBS including Vice-Pres., Admin, CBS Records Int., Man. Dir, CBS Australia 1979–82, returned to England to become Man. Dir, CBS Records UK, apptd CEO 1985, Chair. 1989, Sony Corpn purchased CBS Records from CBS Inc. 1987 and co. was renamed Sony Music Entertainment, apptd Pres. Sony Music Europe 1993, Chair. Sony Music Europe 1997–2000, apptd Sr Vice-Pres. Sony Music Entertainment Inc. 2000, Chair. Sony ATV Music Publishing 2000, Chair. Sony ATV Music Publishing 2000; Founding Partner, R2M Music LPP & LLC 2005 (sold to Bertlesman 2012); mem. BPI Council 1985–92; Chair. BRIT Awards 1989–92; f. Platinum Europe Awards; mem. Bd of Dirs Honey Jam Barbados, Inc. 2013–. *Leisure interests:* music, films, theatre, golf, swimming, all sports. *Website:* www.honeyjambarbados.com.

RUSSELL, Stuart J., BA, PhD, FAAS; British computer scientist and academic; *Professor of Computer Science, University of California, Berkeley;* b. 1962, Portsmouth; ed St Paul's School, London, Wadham Coll., Oxford, Stanford Univ., USA; Programmer, IBM Systems Eng Centre, Warwick 1978–80; Programmer, graphics research project, IBM Scientific Center, Los Angeles 1981; Teaching Asst, Computer Science Dept, Stanford Univ. 1983, Research Asst 1985–86; Asst Prof., Computer Science Div., Univ. of California, Berkeley 1986–91, Assoc. Prof. 1991–96, Prof. 1996–, apptd Michael H. Smith and Lotfi A. Zadeh Chair in Eng 2001, Chair. Computer Science Div. 2006–14, Chair. Dept of Electrical Eng and Computer Sciences 2008–10, also Dir Center for Intelligent Systems; Adjunct Prof., Neurological Surgery, Univ. of California, San Francisco 2008–; Founder and Vice-Pres. Bayesian Logic Inc. 2011–; Prof. Invité, Université Pierre et Marie Curie, Paris 2012–14; Prof., Fondation de l'École Normale Supérieure, Paris 2012–14; Fellow, American Asscn for Artificial Intelligence 1997– (mem. Exec. Council 1997–2000), Asscn for Computing Machinery 2003–; mem. British Scientists Abroad (Chair. 1993–96); numerous awards including NSF Presidential Young Investigator Award 1990, IJCAI Computers and Thought Award (co-winner) 1995, Chaire Blaise Pascal 2012–14. *Publications:* over 150 papers on artificial intelligence; The Use of Knowledge in Analogy and Induction 1989, Do the Right Thing: Studies in Limited Rationality (with Eric Wefald) 1991, Artificial Intelligence: A Modern Approach (with Peter Norvig) 1995. *Address:* Computer Science Division, 387 Soda Hall, University of California, Berkeley, CA 94720-1776, USA (office). *Telephone:* (510) 642-4964 (office). *Fax:* (510) 642-5775 (office). *E-mail:* russell@cs.berkeley.edu (office). *Website:* www.cs.berkeley.edu/~russell (office); www.bayesianlogic.com.

RUSSELL, William (Willy) Martin; British writer, songwriter and playwright; b. 23 Aug. 1947; s. of William Russell and Margery Russell; m. Ann Seagroatt 1969; one s. two d.; ed St Katharine's Coll. of Educ., Liverpool; hairdresser 1963–69; teacher 1973–74; Fellow in Creative Writing, Manchester Polytechnic 1977–78; Founder-mem. and Dir Quintet Films; f. The Willy Russell Centre for Children and Adults Who Stammer 1990; TV and radio plays; Hon. Dir Liverpool, Playhouse; Hon. MA (Open Univ.) 1983, Hon. DLit (Liverpool Univ.) 1990. *Plays include:* Blind Scouse (three short plays) 1971, When the Reds (adaptation) 1972, John, Paul, George, Ringo and Bert (musical) 1974, Breezeblock Park 1975, One for the Road 1976, Stags and Hens 1978, Educating Rita (Laurence Olivier Award for Best New Comedy 1980) 1979, Blood Brothers (musical) (Laurence Olivier Award for Best New Musical 1983) 1983, Our Day Out (musical) 1983, Shirley Valentine (Laurence Olivier Award for Best New Comedy 1988) 1986, Our Day Out–The Musical 2009–10. *Screenplays include:* Educating Rita 1981, Shirley Valentine (Evening Standard British Film Award for Best Screenplay 1990) 1988, Dancing Through the Dark 1989. *Publications include:* Breezeblock Park 1978, One for the Road 1980, Educating Rita 1981, Our Day Out 1984, Stags and Hens 1985, Blood Brothers 1985, Shirley Valentine 1989, The Wrong Boy (novel) 2000, Hoovering the Moon 2003; songs and poetry. *Leisure interests:* playing the guitar, composing songs, gardening, cooking. *Website:* www.willyrussell.com.

RUSSELL BEALE, Simon, CBE, BA; British actor; b. 12 Jan. 1961, Penang, Malaya; s. of Lt-Gen. Sir Peter Beale and Lady Beale; ed Gonville and Caius Coll., Cambridge; Assoc. Artist of RSC 1986; Cameron Mackintosh Visiting Prof. of Contemporary Theatre, St Catherine's Coll., Oxford 2015; Pres. Anthony Powell Soc.; Patron, English Touring Theatre, South London Theatre, London Symphony Chorus, For Short. Theatre co., Diamond Fund for Choristers; Patron, English Touring Theatre, South London Theatre, London Symphony Chorus, For Short Theatre Company; Hon. Bencher, Middle Temple 2010; Freedom of the City of London 2011; Hon. DLitt (Univ. of Warwick) 2005, Dr hc (Open Univ.) 2010; Premio Shakespeare Award 2018. *Theatre includes:* (Traverse Theatre, Edin.): Die House, Sandra/Manon, Points of Departure, The Death of Elias Sawney; (Lyceum, Edin.): Hamlet (Royal Court, London): Women Beware Women, The Duchess of Malfi, Volpone, Rosencrantz and Guildenstern are Dead, Candide (Olivier Award for Best Actor in a Musical 2000), Money 1999, Sommerfolk, Hamlet (Royal Nat. Theatre) 2000, Uncle Vanya (Olivier Award for Best Actor 2003; Donmar Warehouse, London) 2002, Macbeth (Almeida, London) 2005, The Philanthropist (Evening Standard Award for Best Actor 2005) (Donmar Warehouse, London) 2005, Monty Python's Spamalot (Palace Theatre, London) 2005–06, London Assurance (Royal Nat. Theatre) 2010, Timon of Athens (Royal Nat. Theatre) 2012, Privates on Parade (part of Michael Grandage's new West End season at the Noël Coward Theatre) 2012–13, The Hothouse (Trafalgar Studios) 2013, King Lear (Royal Nat. Theatre) 2014, Temple 2015, Mr. Foote's Other Leg 2015, The Lehman Trilogy 2018. *RSC productions include:* The Winter's Tale, The Art of Success, Everyman in his Humour, The Fair Maid of the West, The Storm, Speculators, The Constant Couple, The Man of Mode, Restoration, Mary and Lizzie, Some Americans Abroad, Playing with Trains, Troilus and Cressida, Edward II (title role), Love's Labours Lost, The Seagull, Richard III (title role), The Tempest, King Lear, Ghosts, Othello. *Films include:* Orlando 1992, Persuasion 1995, Hamlet 1996, An Ideal Husband 1999, Blackadder Back & Forth (short) 1999, The Gathering 2003, Deep Water (voice) 2006, 1320 2011, The Deep Blue Sea 2011, My Week with Marilyn 2011, Into the Woods 2014, Cunk on Shakespeare 2016, The Legend of Tarzan 2016, My Cousin Rachel 2017, The Death of Stalin (British Ind. Film Award for Best Supporting Actor, Evening Standard British Film Award for Best Supporting Actor 2017) 2017, Museum 2018, Operation Finale 2018. *Radio includes:* played George Smiley in BBC Radio 4 adaptation of all the John Le Carré novels in which Smiley featured 2009–10, Discovering Music (presenter) 2011, Collaborators 2012, Copenhagen 2013. *Television includes:* Time and the Conways (film) 1985, A Very Peculiar Practice (series) 1988, Downtown Lagos (mini-series) 1992, The Mushroom Picker (mini-series) 1993, A Dance to the Music of Time (mini-series) (Royal TV Soc. Award for Best Actor 1997, BAFTA Award for Best Actor 1998) 1997, The Temptation of Franz Schubert (film) 1997, Alice in Wonderland (film) 1999, The Young Visiters (film) 2003, Dunkirk (documentary) 2004, The American Experience (series documentary) 2006, Sacred Music (series presenter) 2007, Sacred Music 2 (series presenter) 2009, Spooks 2010, Alice's Adventures in Wonderland (film) 2011, Symphony (series) 2011, God's Composer (presenter) 2011, The Hollow Crown (BAFTA Award for Supporting Actor for his performance as Falstaff in BBC series of TV films about Shakespeare's historical dramas Richard II; Henry IV, Part 1; Henry IV, Part 2 and Henry V 2013) 2012, Parkinson – Masterclass 2013, Penny Dreadful (series) 2014–16. *Leisure interests:* medieval history, music, history of religion. *Address:* c/o The Richard Stone Partnership, Suite 3, De Walden Court, 85 New Cavendish Street, London, W1W 6XD, England (office). *Telephone:* (20) 7497-0849 (office). *Fax:* (20) 7497-0869 (office). *E-mail:* mpoole@thersp.com (office). *Website:* www.therichardstonepartnership.co.uk/artist-details/simon_russell_beale (office).

RUSSO, Patricia F., BA; American communications industry executive; *Chairwoman, Hewlett Packard Enterprise;* b. (Patricia Fiorello), 12 June 1952, Trenton, NJ; m.; two step-c.; ed Lawrence High School, Georgetown Univ., Harvard Business School; Sales and Marketing Man. Exec., IBM 1973–81; joined AT&T, Murray Hill, NJ 1981, Pres. business unit, Business Communications Systems 1992–96, Exec. Vice-Pres. Strategy Business Devt and Corp. Operations 1997–99, Exec. Vice-Pres. and CEO Service Provider Networks Group 1999–2000, Pres. and CEO Lucent Technologies Inc. (spin-off of AT&T) 2002–03, Chair. and CEO 2003–06, CEO jt Alcatel-Lucent co. (following Alcatel acquisition of Lucent) 2006–08; Chair. Avaya, Inc. (fmr Business Communications Systems unit of Lucent Technologies) –2001; Pres. and COO Eastman Kodak 2001–02; Chair. Hewlett Packard Enterprise 2015–; mem. Bd of Dirs, Xerox Corpn, Schering-Plough Corpn (Chair. Governance Cttee), New Jersey Manufacturers Insurance Co., General Motors, Georgetown Univ.; Vice-Chair. Nat. Security Telecommunications Advisory Cttee 2003–06; mem. Network Reliability Interoperability Council; Trustee, Georgetown Univ.; Hon. DEng (Stevens Inst. of Tech.); Dr hc (Columbia Coll., SC). *Address:* Hewlett Packard Enterprise, 3000 Hanover Street, Palo Alto, CA 94304-1185, USA (office). *Telephone:* (650) 857-2246 (office). *Fax:* (650) 857-5518 (office). *E-mail:* investor.relations@hpe.com (office). *Website:* www.hpe.com (office).

RUSSO, Rene; American actress; b. 17 Feb. 1954, Burbank, Calif.; d. of Shirley Russo; one d.; fmr model, Eileen Ford Agency. *Film appearances include:* Meanwhile in Santa Monica 1988, Major League 1989, Mr Destiny 1990, One Good Cop 1991, Freejack 1992, Lethal Weapon 3 1992, In the Line of Fire 1993, Major League II 1994, Outbreak 1995, Get Shorty 1995, Tin Cup 1996, Ransom 1996, Buddy 1997, Lethal Weapon 4 1998, The Thomas Crown Affair 1999, The Adventures of Rocky and Bullwinkle 2000, Showtime 2002, Big Trouble 2002, 2 for the Money 2005, Yours, Mine & Ours 2005, Thor 2011, Nightcrawler 2014, The Intern 2015, Villa Capri 2017. *Television appearance:* Sable (series) 1987. *Address:* c/o Progressive Artists Agency, 400 South Beverly Drive, Suite 216, Beverly Hills, CA 90212, USA.

RUST, Edward (Ed) B., Jr, BA, MBA, JD; American insurance industry executive; b. 3 Aug. 1950, Ill.; m. Sally Rust; one s.; ed Illinois Wesleyan Univ., Southern Methodist Univ.; joined Tex. Regional Office, State Farm 1975, Pres. and CEO State Farm Insurance Cos 1985–87, Chair. and CEO 1987–2015, Chair. 2015–16, also Chair. and CEO State Farm Mutual Automobile Insurance Co., Pres. and CEO State Farm Fire and Casualty Co.; mem. Bd of Dirs Caterpillar Inc., Peoria, Helmerich and Payne Inc., McGraw-Hill Cos Inc.; Vice-Chair. US Chamber of Commerce; mem. Bd America's Promise Alliance, James B. Hunt, Jr Inst. for Educational Leadership, Achieve, Inc.; Co-Chair. The Business Roundtable for seven years (currently mem. Exec. Cttee); Chair. Emer. Illinois Business Roundtable, Business Higher Educ. Forum, The Business Roundtable's Educ. Initiative; fmr Chair. American Enterprise Inst., Financial Services Roundtable, Nat. Alliance for Business, Insurance Inst. for Highway Safety; Dir Achieve, Nat. Center for Educational Accountability; mem. Business Advisory Council, Illinois Coll. of Commerce and Business Admin; fmr mem. Advisory Council Stanford Univ. Grad. School of Business, Bd of Overseers Inst. for Civil Justice, Nat. (Glenn) Comm. on Math. and Science Teaching for the 21st Century, No Child Left Behind Comm.; Trustee, The Conference Bd, Cttee for Econ. Devt, Illinois Wesleyan Univ.; fmr Trustee, American Inst. for Property and Liability Underwriters; mem. Tex. and Ill. Bar Asscns; Owen B. Butler Education Excellence Award. *Address:* c/o State Farm Insurance Cos, 1 State Farm Plaza, Bloomingon, IL 61710-0001, USA. *E-mail:* info@statefarm.com.

RUSTAMOV, Elman Siraj oglu, CandEconSci, DEconSci; Azerbaijani economist and central banker; *Governor, Central Bank of Azerbaijan;* b. 29 June 1952, Jabrail dist; m.; three c.; ed Azerbaijan Nat. Economy Inst. (named after D. Bunyadzade); economist, Scientific Research Inst. of Economy, USSR State Planning Cttee July–Dec. 1973, Head Economist 1980–90, Doctorantura 1990–92; with Azerbaijan Nat. Economy Inst. 1973–78; mil. service, Smolensk, USSR 1974–75; Chief of Dept of Economy, Baku Fine Broadcloth Union of Azerbaijan SSR, Ministry of Light Industry 1978–80; Chief Adviser, Presidential Apparatus of Azerbaijan Repub. 1991–92; First Deputy Chair. Man. Bd Central Bank of Azerbaijan 1992–93, Deputy Chair. Man. Bd Agrarian – Industrial Union Jt Stock Bank 1993–94, First Deputy Chair. Man. Bd Cen. Bank of Azerbaijan 1994–95, Admin. for Azerbaijan at World Bank Group, MIGA and EBRD 1995, Chair. Man. Bd Cen. Bank of Azerbaijan 1995–, Gov. 2010–; Pres. Azerbaijan Chess Fed. 2007–; Order of Glory for services in development of banking in Azerbaijan. *Address:* Central Bank of Azerbaijan, 90 Rashid Behbudov street, 1014 Baku, Azerbaijan (office). *Telephone:* (12) 493-43-20 (office). *Fax:* (12) 493-55-41 (office). *E-mail:* mail@cbar.az (office). *Website:* en.cbar.az (office).

RUTAN, Elbert L. (Burt), BS; American aerospace engineer; *Chairman Emeritus, Scaled Composites, LLC;* b. 17 June 1943, Portland, Ore.; m. 4th Tonya Rutan; ed Calif. Polytechnic Univ.; first solo flight in Aeronca Champ aeroplane aged 16 1959; flight test project engineer, USAF, Edwards Air Force Base 1965–72; Dir Bede Test Center for Bede Aircraft, Newton, Kan. 1972–74; f. Rutan Aircraft Factory to develop light aircraft for homebuilt aircraft market 1974; f. Scaled Composites, LLC 1982, Pres. and CEO 1982–2008, Chair. Emer. 2008–; mem. Nat. Acad. of Engineering 1989–; Dr hc (Daniel Webster Coll.), (California Polytechnic Univ.), (Lewis Univ.), (Delft Univ. of Tech.); Presidential Citizen's Medal of Honor 1986, Collier Trophy 1987, Leroy Randle Grumman Medal for outstanding scientific achievement 1989, Structural Dynamics and Materials Award, AIAA 1992, Lloyd P. Nolan Achievement in Aviation Award 1993, Ansari X Prize for making two flights in SpaceShipOne within two weeks 29 Sept. and 4 Oct. 2004, NAS Award 2005. *Achievements include:* designed several aircraft including Voyager aircraft that his brother Dick and Jeana Yeager flew in first nonstop, unrefuelled flight around the world 1986, SpaceShipOne (first pvt. vehicle to achieve suborbital, 62.5 miles/100 km, spaceflight), Raytheon Beechcraft Starship, Proteus, VariEze, Long-EZ, Quickie, Quickie 2, Defiant, and Boomerang. *Address:* Scaled Composites, LLC, 1624 Flight Line, Mojave, CA 93501, USA (office). *Telephone:* (661) 824-4541 (office). *Fax:* (661) 824-4174 (office). *Website:* www.scaled.com (office).

RUTELLI, Francesco; Italian politician; *Leader, Alleanza per l'Italia;* b. 14 June 1954, Rome; m. Barbara Palombelli; four c.; mem. Camera dei Deputati (Parl.) (Radicals) 1983–93, then mem. Green Party, then Founder-mem. Democrats party; Minister for Environment (resgnd after one day) 1993; Mayor of Rome 1993–2001; mem. European Parl. 1999–2004; Pres. Democrazia è Libertà—La Margherita (Democracy is Liberty—The Daisy) 2001–07; Deputy Prime Minister and Minister of Cultural Assets and Activities 2006–08; Chair. Parl. Cttee for the Security of the Repub. (COPASIR) 2008–09; Leader Alleanza per l'Italia 2009–. *Address:* Alleanza per l'Italia, Largo Fontanella Borghese 84, 00186 Rome, Italy (office). *Telephone:* (06) 91712000 (office). *Fax:* (06) 68802560 (office). *E-mail:* info@alleanzaperlitalia.it (office). *Website:* www.alleanzaperlitalia.it (office).

RUTHVEN, Kenneth Knowles, PhD; British academic; b. 26 May 1936; ed Univ. of Manchester; Asst Lecturer, Lecturer, Sr Lecturer, Univ. of Canterbury, Christchurch, NZ 1961–72, Prof. of English 1972–79; Prof. of English, Univ. of Adelaide, Australia 1980–85, Univ. of Melbourne, Vic., Australia 1985–99, Prof. Emer. 2000–; Visiting Prof. of English, Univ. of Adelaide 2002–. *Publications:* A Guide to Ezra Pound's Personae 1969, The Conceit 1969, Myth 1976, Critical Assumptions 1979, Feminist Literary Studies: An Introduction 1984, Ezra Pound as Literary Critic 1990, Beyond the Disciplines: The New Humanities (ed.) 1992, Nuclear Criticism 1993, Faking Literature 2001, The Complete Poems of William Barnes, Vol. 1 (co-ed.) 2013; editor: Southern Review (Adelaide) 1981–85, Interpretations series (gen.) 1993–96 (19 vols). *Address:* 27 Fairleys Road, Rostrevor, SA 5073, Australia (home). *Telephone:* (8) 8336-6348 (home). *E-mail:* kenruthven@bigpond.com (home). *Website:* www.hss.adelaide.edu.au/english (office).

RUTSKOY, Maj.-Gen. Aleksandr Vladimirovich, CandEconSc; Russian politician and military officer; b. 16 Sept. 1947, Proskurov, Kamenets Podolsk Region (now Khmelnitsky, Ukraine); s. of Vladimir Alexandrovich Rutskoy and Zinaida Iosifovna Rutskaya; m. 3rd Irina Rutskaya; three s. one d.; ed Higher Air Force Coll., Barnaul, Y. Gagarin Higher Air Force Acad., Acad. of Gen. Staff; fmr mem. CPSU (expelled 1991); Regimental Commdr, Afghan War 1985–86; Deputy Commdr Army Air Force 1988; RSFSR People's Deputy, mem. Supreme Soviet, mem. Presidium of Supreme Soviet 1990–91; Leader Communists for Democracy (renamed People's Party of Free Russia 1991, renamed Russian Social Democratic Party 1994); Vice-Pres. RSFSR (now Russian Fed.) 1991–93; Head Centre for Operational Supervision of Progress of Reforms 1991–93; Leader Civic Union coalition 1992–93; declared Acting Pres. of Russia by Parl. Sept. 1993; arrested as one of organizers of failed coup d'état Oct. 1993; freed on amnesty Feb. 1994; Chair. Social-Patriotic Movt Derzhava 1994; Gov. of Kursk Region 1996–2000; mem. Council Europe Parl. 1996–2000; Pro-Rector Moscow State Sociological Univ. 2001; Hero of Soviet Union 1988, Order of Lenin, seven Russian and Afghan orders; 15 medals. *Publications include:* Agrarian Reform in Russia 1992, Unknown Rutskoy 1994, About Us and Myself 1995, Finding Faith 1995, Lefortovo Protocols 1995, March Records 1995, Bloody Autumn 1996, Liberal Reforms – Strong Power 1996. *Leisure interests:* painting, gardening, designing, fishing.

RUTTE, Mark, MA; Dutch business executive and politician; *Prime Minister;* b. 14 Feb. 1967, The Hague; ed Univ. of Leiden; joined Unilever 1992, various positions within group, including Human Resources Man., Personnel Man., Van den Bergh Nederland (Calvé) 1997–2000, Dir of Human Resources, IGLOMora Group BV 2002; mem. Tweede Kamer (House of Reps) Jan.–May 2003, 2006–10; mem. Volkspartij voor Vrijheid en Democratie (VVD—People's Party for Freedom and Democracy), Parl. Leader 2006–10; Sec. of State for Social Affairs and Employment 2002–04, for Educ., Culture and Science 2004–06; Prime Minister of the Netherlands 2010–12 (resgnd), re-elected 2012–; Minister of Gen. Affairs 2010–12, 2012– (following re-election); guest teacher (part-time), Johan de Witt group of schools, The Hague 2008–. *Address:* Office of the Prime Minister, Ministry of General Affairs, Binnenhof 20, PO Box 20001, 2500 EA The Hague, Netherlands (office). *Telephone:* (70) 3564100 (office). *Fax:* (70) 3564683 (office). *Website:* www.government.nl/ministeries/az (office); www.vvd.nl (office).

RUTTENSTORFER, Wolfgang, DEcon; Austrian business executive; *Chairman, Telekom Austria Group;* b. 1950, Vienna; m.; three c.; ed Univ. of Econs and Business Admin, Vienna; joined OMV AG 1976, with Planning and Control Dept 1985, Head of Strategic Devt 1989–90, Head of Marketing 1990, mem. Exec. Bd 1992–97, 2000– (as Deputy Chair.), CEO and Chair., Exec. Bd 2002–11; Deputy Minister of Finance 1997–2000; Chair. CA Immobilien Anlagen AG 2009–, TelekomAustria, Vienna 2015–; mem. Supervisory Bd Flughafen Wien AG 2011–, RHI AG 2012–; mem. Admin. Bd Naftna industrija Srbije, Novi Sad 2012–. *Address:* Telekom Austria Group, Lassallestrasse 9, 1020 Vienna, Austria (office). *E-mail:* konzernkommunikation@telekomaustria.com (office). *Website:* www.telekomaustria.com (office).

RUTTER, Deborah F., MBA; American arts administrator; *President, John F. Kennedy Center for the Performing Arts;* b. 1956, Pennsylvania; m. 2nd Peter Ellefson; one d.; ed Stanford Univ., Univ. of Southern California; studied piano and violin from an early age; began career as Orchestra Man., Los Angeles Philharmonic Orchestra; Exec. Dir, Los Angeles Chamber Orchestra 1986–92; Exec. Dir, Seattle Symphony Orchestra 1992–2003; Pres., Chicago Symphony Orchestra Asscn 2003–14; Pres., John F. Kennedy Center for the Performing Arts 2014–; fmr mem. Bd of Dirs Arts Alliance Illinois, Chicago Grant Park Conservancy, Solti Foundation, After School Matters, Cultural Advisory Council for the City of Chicago; mem. Bd of Overseers, Curtis Inst. of Music; mem. Bd of Dirs and Pres., Washington State Arts Alliance; fmr Chair., Policy Cttee, League of American Orchestras. *Address:* John F. Kennedy Center for the Performing Arts, 2700 F Street, NW, Washington, DC 20566, USA (office). *Telephone:* (202) 467-4600 (office). *Website:* www.kennedy-center.org (office).

RUTTER, Sir Michael Llewellyn, Kt, CBE, MD, FRS, FRCP, FRCPsych; British physician and academic; *Professor of Developmental Psychopathology, King's College London;* b. 15 Aug. 1933; s. of Llewellyn Charles Rutter and Winifred Olive Rutter; m. Marjorie Heys 1958; one s. two d.; ed Univ. of Birmingham Medical School; practised at Maudsley Hosp. 1958–61; Nuffield Medical Travelling Fellow, Albert Einstein Coll. of Medicine, New York 1961–62; scientist with MRC Social Psychology Research Unit 1962–65; Sr Lecturer, then Reader, Inst. of Psychiatry, King's Coll. London 1966–73, Prof. of Child Psychiatry 1973–98, Research Prof. 1998, now Prof. of Developmental Psychopathology, Dir MRC Research Centre for Social, Genetic and Developmental Psychiatry 1994–98, consultant psychiatrist, Maudsley Hosp. 1966, now Hon. Consultant; est. Medical Research Council Child Psychiatry Research Unit, Hon. Dir 1984–98, Social, Genetic and Developmental Psychiatry Research Centre, Hon. Dir 1994–98; Deputy Chair. Wellcome Trust 1999–2004; European Ed. Journal of Autism and Developmental Disorders 1974–94; Fellow, Center for Advanced Study in Behavioral Sciences, Stanford Univ. 1979–80; Pres. Soc. for Research in Child Devt 1999–2001 (Pres. 1997–99); Founding Fellow, Acad. of Medical Sciences, Clinical Vice-Pres. 2004–07; Research Adviser, Wave Trust; Patron, Autistica; Hon. Fellow, British Psychological Soc. 1978, American Acad. of Pediatrics 1981, Royal Soc. of Medicine 1996; Dr hc (Leiden) 1985, (Catholic Univ. of Leuven) 1990, (Birmingham) 1990, (Edinburgh) 1990, (Chicago) 1991, (Minnesota) 1993, (Jyväskylä) 1996, (Warwick) 1999, (East Anglia) 2000, (Sussex) 2014. *Publications include:* Children of Sick Parents 1966: A Neuropsychiatric Study in Childhood (jtly) 1970, Education, Health and Behaviour (ed. jtly) 1970, Infantile Autism (ed.) 1971, Maternal Deprivation Reassessed (ed.) 1981, The Child with Delayed Speech (jtly) 1972, Helping Troubled Children (jtly) 1975, Cycles of Disadvantage (jtly) 1976; Child Psychiatry (ed. jtly) 1976, (2nd edn as Child and Adolescent Psychiatry 1985), Autism (ed. jtly) 1978, Changing Youth in a Changing Society (jtly) 1979, Fifteen Thousand Hours: Secondary Schools and Their Effect on Children 1979, Scientific Foundations of Developmental Psychiatry (ed.) 1981, A Measure of Our Values: Goals and Dilemmas in the Upbringing of Children (jtly) 1983, Lead versus Health (jtly) 1983, Juvenile Delinquency 1983, Developmental Neuropsychiatry (ed.) 1983, Stress, Coping and Development (ed. jtly) 1983, Depression and Young People (ed. jtly) 1986, Studies of Psychosocial Risk: The Power of Longitudinal Data (ed.) 1988, Parenting Breakdown: The Making and Breaking of Intergenerational Links (jtly) 1988, Straight and Devious Pathways from Childhood to Adulthood (ed. jtly) 1990, Biological Risk Factors for Psychosocial Disorders (ed. jtly) 1991, Developing Minds (jtly) 1993, Development Through Life: A Handbook for Clinicians (ed. jtly) 1994, Stress, Risk and Resilience in Children and Adolescents (ed. jtly) 1994, Psychological Disorders in Young People 1995, Antisocial Behaviour by Young People (jtly) 1998, Genes and Behaviour: Nature-Nurture Interplay Explained 2006. *Leisure interests:* fell walking, tennis, wine tasting, theatre. *Address:* C1.37, SGDP Research Centre, Institute of Psychiatry, King's College London, De Crespigny Park, London SE5 8AF (office); 190 Court Lane, Dulwich, London, SE21 7ED, England (home). *Telephone:* (20) 7848-0882 (office). *Fax:* michael.rutter@kcl.ac.uk (office). *Website:* www.kcl.ac.uk/ioppn/index.aspx (office).

RÜÜTEL, Arnold, PhD, DrAgrSc; Estonian politician, agronomist and fmr head of state; *Honorary Chairman, Estonian People's Union;* b. 10 May 1928, Laimjala, Saaremaa Island; s. of Feodor Rüütel and Juulia Rüütel; m. Ingrid Rüütel (née Ruus) 1935; two d.; ed Jäneda Agric. Coll., Estonian Agricultural Acad.; Sr Agronomist, Saaremaa Dist, Estonian SSR 1949–50; mil. service 1950–55; teacher, Tartu School of Mechanization of Agric. 1955–57; Deputy Dir Estonian Inst. of Livestock-breeding and Veterinary Sciences 1957–63; mem. CPSU 1964–90; Dir Tartu Model State Farm 1963–69; Rector Estonian Agric. Acad. 1969–77; Agricultural Sec. of Cen. Cttee of Estonian CP 1977–79; First Deputy Chair. Council of Ministers of Estonia 1979–83; Chair. Presidium of Supreme Soviet of Estonian SSR 1983–90, of Supreme Council of Repub. of Estonia 1990–92; Deputy Pres. of USSR Presidium of Supreme Soviet 1984–91; mem. Constitutional Ass. 1991–92; Founder, Dir Inst. for Nat. Devt and Cooperation 1993–2001; Founder and Chair. Estonian Rural People's Party (Maarahva) 1994–99, Chair. Estonian People's Union 1999–2000, Hon. Chair. 2006–; mem. Riigikogu (Parl.) 1995–2001, Vice-Chair. 1995–97, Chair. ruling coalition's council 1995–99; Head Del. of Riigikogu to Baltic Ass. 1995–99, mem., alternately Chair. Presidium 1995–99; presidential cand. 1996; Pres. of Estonia 2001–06; Chair. Estonian Soc. for Nature Protection 1981–88, Keep Estonian Sea Clean, Forselius (educational org.); Pres. Estonian Green Cross 1993–2001; mem. Tallinn City Council 1993–2001; Chair. Estonian Soc. for Nature Conservation 1981–88 (Hon. mem. 1989–), B.G. Forselius Soc. 1989–2002, Hon. Chair. 2002–, Movt 'Protect the Estonian Sea' 1993–2002 (Hon. Chair. 2002–); apptd Pres. Estonian Nat. Org. of the Green Cross Int. 1993–2001, 2006; Foreign mem. Ukranian Acad. of Agrarian Sciences 2002; Associated Fellow, UNITAR, UN(O) 2007–; Hon. mem. Estonian Academic Agricultural Soc. 2002–, Int. Raoul Wallenberg Foundation 2002–; Collar of Order of Grand Cross of Terra Mariana (Estonia) 2001, Grand Cross Order of the White Rose with Collar (Finland) 2001, Grand Cross Order of the White Eagle (Poland) 2002, Grand Cross Royal Order of St Olaf (Norway) 2002, Grand Cross Order of Merit (Hungary) 2002, Grand Cross Order of Adolph de Nassau (Luxembourg) 2003, Grand Collar Order of Infant D. Henrique (Portugal) 2003, Grand Collar Nat. Order of Merit (Malta) 2003, Grand Collar Nat. Order of Merit (Romania) 2003, Grand Collar Order of Makarios III (Cyprus) 2004, Grand Cross with Collar, Order of Merit (Italy) 2004, Order of Falcon (Iceland) 2004, Order of 1st Class of Vytautas the Great (Lithuania) 2004, Order of 1st Class White Double Cross (Slovak Repub.) 2005; Dr hc (Bentley Coll.) 1991, (Estonian Agricultural Univ.) 1991, (Univ. of Helsinki) 2002, (Nat. Agricultural Univ. of Ukraine) 2002, (Univ. of Naples II) 2002, (Szent Istvan Univ., Hungary) 2004, (L.N. Gumilyov Eurasian Nat. Univ. of Kazakhstan) 2004, (Yerevan, Armenia) 2004; Rotary Foundation Distinguished Service Award 2002, Andres Bello Commemorative Medal 2002. *Publications:* Tuleviku taassünd (The Rebirth of the Future) (memoirs) 2003. *Leisure interests:* nature protection, sports. *Address:* Roheline Aas 1, 10150 Tallinn, Estonia (office). *E-mail:* ryytel.office@vpk.ee (office). *Telephone:* 6316291 (office).

RUVKUN, Gary Bruce, BS, PhD; American molecular biologist, geneticist and academic; *Professor, Department of Genetics, Harvard Medical School;* b. 26 March 1952, Berkeley, Calif.; ed Univ. of California, Berkeley, Harvard Univ., Massachusetts Inst. of Tech.; currently Prof., Dept of Genetics, Harvard Medical School; mem. NAS 2008, American Acad. of Arts and Sciences 2009, Inst. of Medicine 2009; Lewis S. Rosenstiel Award for Distinguished Work in Medical Research, Brandeis Univ. (co-recipient) 2005, Warren Triennial Prize, Massachusetts Gen. Hosp. (co-recipient) 2007, Albert Lasker Award for Basic Medical Research (co-recipient) 2008, Benjamin Franklin Medal in Life Science (co-recipient) 2008, Gairdner Foundation Int. Award (co-recipient) 2008, Louisa Gross Horwitz Prize, Columbia Univ. (co-recipient) 2009, Massry Prize, Keck School of Medicine, Univ. of Southern California (co-recipient) 2009, Dan David Prize 2011, 2012 Dr Paul Janssen Award for Biomedical Research (co-recipient) 2012, Gruber Genetics Prize (co-recipient) 2014, Wolf Prize in Medicine (co-recipient) 2014, Breakthrough Prize in Life Sciences (co-recipient) 2015. *Publications:* more than 150 papers in professional journals. *Address:* Department of Molecular Biology, Massachusetts General Hospital, Simches CPZN7806, 185 Cambridge Street, Boston, MA 02114, USA (office). *Telephone:* (617) 726-5959 (office). *Fax:* (617) 726-5949 (office); (617) 726-5973 (office). *E-mail:* ruvkun@molbio.mgh.harvard.edu (office). *Website:* www.hms.harvard.edu/dms/bbs (office); ccib.mgh.harvard.edu/ruvkun (office); molbio.mgh.harvard.edu/laboratories/ruvkun (office).

RUYS, Anthony; Dutch business executive; b. 20 July 1947, Antwerp, Belgium; m. Melanie E. van Haaften; two s.; ed Univ. of Utrecht, Harvard Business School; marketing trainee Van den Bergh & Jurgens 1974–80; Marketing Dir Cogra Lever S.A. 1980–84, Chair. 1984–87; Chair. Van den Bergh Italy; mem. Bd Italian Unilever Cos 1987–89; Chair. Van den Bergh Netherlands; mem. Bd Dutch Unilever Cos 1989–92; Sr Regional Man. Food Exec., North European Region, Unilever NV 1992–93; mem. Exec. Bd Heineken NV 1993–96, Vice-Chair. 1996–2002, Chair. 2002–05; Dir TRN, BAT Europe (Netherlands) BV, Rembrandt Foundation, Gtech Corpn, NH Hotels SA 1994–2003; Pres. Supervisory Bd Rijksmuseum, Amsterdam 2004–12, Stop Aids Now Foundation, ECR Europe 2004–06; Chair. Supervisory Bd Madurodam miniature city 2009–; mem. Supervisory Bd Gtech Holdings Corpn (now Lottomatica Italy), USA, ABN Ambro Bank, Sara Lee Int. B.V., Rijksmuseum, Amsterdam, Tourism Recreation Netherlands, Aiesec Netherlands 1996–2004, Veerstichting 1997–2007, Nat. Fund for the Preservation of Art Treasures, Stichting laluz; mem. Bd of Dirs Netherlands Asscn for Int. Affairs, Int. Chamber of Commerce Netherlands, Nationaal Fonds Kunstbehoud, British American Tobacco PLC 2006–14, Luchthaven Schipol NV, Rothmans Europe 1997–2001, Robeco Group NV 2001–04, Trilateral Comm. 2003–06, European Round Table of Industrialists 2004–05, SIFE Netherlands; mem. Bd Netherlands Soc. for Int. Affairs; mem. European Advisory Bd Harvard Business School 2003–07; mem. Int. Council INSEAD; Commdr, Order of Civil Merit (Spain), Officer,Order of Orange Nassau (Netherlands). *Website:* www.madurodam.nl.

RUZHO, Cui; Chinese painter; b. 1944, Beijing; ed Cen. Acad. of Fine Arts (with Li Kuchan); specializes in ink painting and finger painting; teacher Acad. of Arts and Design 1970s; moved to USA 1981; apptd Vice-Pres. Chinese Art Asscn, NY 1982; returned to China 1996; mentor National Acad. of Art; 'The Grand Snowing Mountainous Jiangnan Landscape' became the most expensive work of a living Chinese artist sold at auction (US $40 million) 2015; Pres. Int. Chinese Calligraphy Asscn, Painting Collectors' Asscn; Dr hc (Dewey Univ., Puerto Rico). *Publication:* The Artwork of Cui Ruzhuo. *Website:* www.cuiruzhuo.com (office).

RUZICKA, Karel Zdenek; Czech musician and composer; b. 2 June 1940, Prague; s. of Zdenek Ruzicka and Vlasta Ruzicka; m. Marie-José; one s.; ed Conservatory of Prague; pianist, Semafor Theatre, Prague 1960–66; mem. Prague Radio Big Band 1966–90; teacher Conservatory of Jaroslav Jezek, Prague 1969; imprisoned for political activities 1969; pianist, composer, arranger, conductor 1970–2000; f. Karel Ruzicka Jazz Quartet; has toured and performed in Canada, Poland, Cuba, France and Czech Repub.; has collaborated with Laco Deczi's Jazz Cellula septet, Czech–Polish Big Band, Veleband All-Stars and with numerous musicians including Rudolf Dasek (guitarist), Jarmo Sermila (trumpeter), Jiri Stivin (flutist), Wilson de Oliveira (saxophonist); Celebration Jazz Mass and Te Deum compositions performed during The Prague Spring Music Festival and also in Europe and USA; Monte Carlo Int. Jazz Festival composition awards (Interlude) 1977, (Echoes) 1978, (Triste) 1979; numerous awards from the Czech Composers Soc. and Musical Acad. of Monaco; Ministry of Culture Prize 1989. *Recordings:* 10 albums, 100 compositions, including Fata Morgana, Going Home, Flight, Celebration Jazz Mass, Te Deum. *Publications:* Jazz Echoes, Best of Arta, In the Garden of Time. *Leisure interest:* literature. *Address:* c/o Conservatory of Jaroslav Jezek, Roskotova 4/1692, 14000 Prague 4 (office); Devonska 1, 15200 Prague 5, Czech Republic (home). *E-mail:* karuz@barr.cz (home); karuzjazz@gmail.com (home).

RUZIMATOV, Farukh Sadilloyevich; Tajikistani ballet dancer and ballet director; *Artistic Director, Mikhailovsky Theater Ballet Company;* b. 26 June 1963, Tashkent; ed Vaganova Acad. of Russian Ballet; soloist State Academic Mariinsky Theatre 1981–86, Prin. Dancer 1986–2007; guest dancer Bolshoi Theatre, Moscow; Prin. Guest Dancer, American Ballet Theater 1990–91; Artistic Dir Mikhailovsky Theater Ballet Company, St Petersburg 2007–; Pres. Farukh Ruzimatov The Renaissance of the Dance Art Foundation 2006–; chevalier, Order For the Spiritual Renaissance of Russia; Silver Medallist, Sixth Varna Int. Competition 1983, awarded special diploma by Paris Acad. of Dance, Honoured Artist of Russia 1995, Golden Sofit Award 1995, Baltika Prize 1998, People's Artist of Russia 2000. *Principal roles include:* Albert in Giselle, Siegfried in Swan Lake, Basil in Don Quixote, The Prince in The Nutcracker, José in Carmen, Golden Slave in Sheherazade, Désiré Prince in Sleeping Beauty, James in La Sylphide, Solor in Bayadere, Ali in Corsair, Abderahman in Raymonda, Ferhad in Fokin's The Legend about love, Tariel in Vinogradov's The Knight in Tiger Skin. *Address:* Mikhailovsky Theatre, Arts Square, 1, St Petersburg, Russia (office). *Telephone:* (812) 595-43-05 (office). *E-mail:* pr@mikhailovsky.ru (office). *Website:* www.mikhailovsky.ru (office).

RUZOWITZKY, Stefan; Austrian film director and screenwriter; b. 25 Dec. 1961, Vienna; m.; two d.; ed Univ. of Vienna; began career by directing documentaries and commercials and also music videos for N'Sync, Scorpions and Die Prinzen.

Films: writer and dir: Tempo (Max Ophüls Preis) 1996, Die Siebtelbauern (The Inheritors; aka The One-Seventh Farmers) (Best Picture, Rotterdam Film Festival, Flanders Film Festival, prize at Int. Film Festival, Valladolid) 1998, Anatomie (Anatomy) 2000, All the Queen's Men (Die Männer Ihrer Majestät) 2001, Anatomie 2 2003, Die Fälscher (The Counterfeiters) (Academy Award for Best Foreign Language Film 2008) 2007, Hexe Lilli: Der Drache und das magische Buch (Lilly the Witch: The Dragon and the Magic Book) 2009; dir: All the Queen's Men 2001, Deadfall 2012, Die Hölle 2017, Patient Zero 2017. *Television:* Monte Video 1994.

RWANGOMBWA, John; Rwandan politician and government official; *Governor, National Bank of Rwanda;* fmr Chair. School of Finance and Banking, Kigali; fmr Vice-Chair. Rwanda Revenue Authority, Bralirwa SA; apptd Deputy Dir of Customs, Revenue Authority 1994; Chair. Devt Partners Consultative Group; joined as Dir of Nat. Treasury Dept, Ministry of Finance and Econ. Planning 2002, later Accountant Gen. 2005, Perm. Sec., and Sec. to Treasury 2006–09, Minister of Finance and Econ. Planning 2009–13; Gov. Nat. Bank of Rwanda 2013–; Dir East African Devt Bank. *Address:* National Bank of Rwanda, ave Paul VI, BP 531, Kigali, Rwanda (office). *Telephone:* 250575282 (office). *Fax:* 250572551 (office). *E-mail:* info@bnr.rw (office). *Website:* www.bnr.rw (office).

RYABOV, Nikolai Timofeyevich; Russian politician, lawyer and diplomatist; b. 9 Dec. 1946, Salsk, Rostov Region; ed Rostov Univ.; mem. CPSU 1968–91; worked as tractor driver, engineer Salsk Agricultural Machine Factory 1966–72; taught in higher educ. school of Rostov Region 1973–90; People's Deputy of Russia 1990–93; mem. Supreme Soviet 1990–92, Chair. Sub-Cttee for legis. 1990–91; Chair. Council of Repubs 1991–92, Deputy Chair. Supreme Soviet 1992–93; Deputy Chair. Constitutional Comm. 1991–93, Chair. Cen. Election Comm. of Russian Fed. 1993–96; Amb. to Czech Repub. 1996–2000, to Azerbaijan 2000–04, to Moldova 2004–06.

RYABOV, Vladimir Vladimirovich, PhD; Russian composer and pianist; *Composer-in-Residence, Moscow Symphony Orchestra;* b. 15 Sept. 1950, Chelyabinsk; m. 1st; one d.; m. 4th Ellen Levine; ed Moscow State Conservatory (expelled twice for non-conformist attitudes), Gnessin Pedagogical Inst. of Music (under Aram Khachaturyan), Leningrad State Conservatory; taught composition in Leningrad and Sverdlovsk conservatories 1977–81; Artistic and Repertoire Consultant, Moscow Symphony Orchestra 1993–; toured as pianist in Russia, Finland, USA, Germany, Austria, Hungary, Italy and Spain, performing standard repertoire and own compositions; mem. Int. Informatization Acad.; winner First S. Prokofiev Int. Composers' Competition 1991, Merited Artist of Russia 1995, Pushkin Gold Medal 1999. *Film:* The Life of Frederic Chopin (pianist) 1992. *Compositions include:* over 30, including 4 symphonies (Nine Northern Tunes 1977, Pushkin 1980, Listen! 1981, In Memoriam of J. Brahms 1983), 5 string quartets, works for full and chamber orchestras, sonatas and other compositions for piano, violin, viola, organ, choir, song cycles on Russian poetry and English, American, Spanish and German poetry in Russian trans., transcriptions of classical music and folk songs, 6 cycles of sacred music, European Cathedrals (7 cycles for different chamber ensembles), Norwegian Suite for symphony orchestra. *Leisure interests:* reading Russian poetry on stage, collecting illustrations of owls. *Address:* Novoyasenevsky pr. 14, kor. 2 Apt. 48, Moscow 117574, Russia (home); Orisaarentie 6E, 00840 Helsinki, Finland (home). *Telephone:* (495) 143-97-13 (Moscow) (home); (9) 6984059 (Helsinki) (home). *E-mail:* moscowsymphonyorchestra@mtu-net.ru (office). *Website:* www.moscowsymphony.ru (office).

RYACUDU, Gen. (retd) Ryamizard; Indonesian army officer and government official; *Minister of Defence;* b. 21 April 1950, Palembang; s. of Zuhariah Ryacudu; m. Nora Tristyana; three s.; ed Armed Forces Acad.; army service including as Chief of Staff, Army Strategic Reserve Command (Kostrad) Div. II 1997, Chief of Staff, Mil. Command (Kodam) II, Sriwijaya 1997–98, Commdr, Infantry Div. II April–July 1998, Kostrad Chief of Staff 1998–99, Commdr, Kodam V, Brawijaya Mil. Command Area Jan.–Nov. 1999, Commdr, Kodam Jaya, Jakarta 1999–2000, Commdr, Army Strategic Reserve Command 2000–02, Chief of Staff of Army 2002–05; involved in Operation Seroja (Indonesian mil. campaign in East Timor) and operations against Free Aceh Movt and Free Papua Org.; Minister of Defence 2014–; Bintang Kartika Eka Paksi, Bintang Mahaputera Pratama; numerous awards including GOM VIII/Dharma Pala, Dwija Sista, Garuda XII/Canti Dharma, UN Awards. *Publications:* Perang Modern 2004. *Address:* Ministry of Defence, Jalan Medan Merdeka Barat 13–14, Jakarta Pusat 10110, Indonesia (office). *Telephone:* (21) 3840889 (office). *Fax:* (21) 3828500 (office). *E-mail:* ppid@kemhan.go.id (office). *Website:* www.kemhan.go.id/menhan (office).

RYAN, Alan James, BA, MA, DLitt, FBA; British political scientist, academic and writer; *Professor Emeritus of Political Theory, Princeton University;* b. 9 May 1940, London, England; s. of James W. Ryan and Ivy Ryan; m. Kathleen Alyson Lane 1971; one d.; ed Christ's Hosp., Horsham, Balliol Coll. Oxford, Univ. Coll., London; Asst Lecturer, then Lecturer, Keele Univ. 1963–66; Lecturer, Univ. of Essex 1966–; Fellow and Tutor in Politics, New Coll., Oxford 1969, Univ. Lecturer in Politics 1969–78, Reader ad honinem 1978–88; Prof. of Politics, Princeton Univ., USA 1988–96, now Prof. Emer.; Mellon Fellow, Inst. for Advanced Study, Princeton, NJ 1991–92; Warden, New Coll., Oxford 1996–2009; Visiting Prof., CUNY 1967, Univ. of Texas 1972, Univ. of California, Santa Cruz 1977, Univ. of Witwatersrand, SA 1973, 1978, ANU 1974–75; Univ. of Cape Town, SA 1982–84; Visiting Fellow, ANU 1979; Fellow, Center for Advanced Studies in the Behavioral Sciences, Stanford Univ., USA 2002–03; Official mem. CNAA 1975–83; Del., Oxford Univ. Press 1982–87; Sr Consulting Ed., Bertrand Russell Project 1987; mem. Exec. Cttee Conf. for the Study of Political Thought 1988–; Chair. Conf. for the Study of Political Thought 1992–96; Almoner, Christ's Hosp. 1998–2004; Dr hc (Oxford) 1993; coll. prizes in philosophy and politics, Powell English Essay Prize, de Carle Lecturer, Univ. of Otago, NZ 1983, Convocation Lecturer, Lawrence Univ. 1993 Whidden Lecturer, McMaster Univ. 1993. *Publications:* The Philosophy of John Stuart Mill 1970, The Philosophy of the Social Sciences 1970, J. S. Mill 1974, Property and Political Theory 1984, Property 1987, Russell: A Political Life 1988, John Dewey and the High Tide of American Liberalism 1995, Liberal Anxieties and Liberal Education 1998. *Leisure interests:* dinghy sailing, long train journeys. *Address:* 21 Cunliffe Close, Oxford, OX2 7BJ, England (home). *Telephone:* (7908) 620784 (home). *E-mail:* alan.ryan@new.ox.ac.uk (office).

RYAN, Arthur (Art) Frederick; American insurance industry executive; b. 14 Sept. 1942, Brooklyn, New York; s. of Arthur Ryan and Gertrude Wingert; m. Patricia Kelly; two s. two d.; ed Providence Coll.; Area Man. Data Corpn Washington, DC 1965–72; Project Man. Chase Manhattan Corpn and Bank, New York 1972–73, Second Vice-Pres. 1973–74, Vice-Pres. 1974–75, Operations Exec. 1978, Exec. Vice-Pres. 1982, later Vice-Chair., Pres. 1990–94; CEO Prudential Insurance Co. of America (now Prudential Financial Inc.) 1994–2007, Chair. 1994–2008; mem. Bd of Dirs Citizens Financial Group, Inc. 2009–, Regeneron Pharmaceuticals 2003–, Royal Bank of Scotland Group PLC 2008–13; mem. Bd of Trustees, Providence Coll. 1995–11; mem. American Bankers Asscn; Dr hc (Providence Coll.) 1990, New Jersey Inst. of Tech.

RYAN, Frederick J. (Joseph), Jr, BA, JD; American lawyer, publishing executive and fmr government official; *Publisher, The Washington Post;* b. 12 April 1955, Tampa, Fla; s. of Frederick Joseph Ryan and Cordelia Ryan (née Hartman); m. Genevieve McSweeney 1985; three d.; ed Univ. of Southern California; mem. California Bar 1980, DC Bar 1986; Assoc., Hill, Farrer & Burrill (law firm) 1980–82; Staff mem., Ronald Reagan Presidential Campaign 1980; Deputy Dir, later Dir of Presidential Appointments & Scheduling, The White House 1982–87, Dir of Pvt. Sector Initiatives 1985–87, Asst to Pres. Ronald Reagan 1987–89, Chief of Staff to fmr Pres. Ronald Reagan 1989–95; Vice-Chair., Allbritton Communications Co. (TV, cable and internet co.) 1995–98, Pres. and COO 1998–2013, Pres. and CEO, Politico.com & Politico Newspaper 2007–13; Publr, The Washington Post 2014–; columnist, Legal Briefs 1980–82; Chair. Bd of Trustees Ronald Reagan Presidential Foundation 1995–; mem. Bd of Advisors, Ronald Reagan Inst. of Emergency Medicine, George Washington Univ. Medical Center; mem. Bd of Dirs Ford's Theater, Washington, DC, Town Hall of California, Nancy Reagan Foundation; mem. ABA, White House Historical Asscn; Commdr, Order of Merit (Italy), Chevalier, Ordre des Arts et Lettres 1986, Commdr, Ouissam Alaouite (Morocco); Presidential Commendation for Pvt. Sector Initiatives 1986, Golden Ambrosiana Medal (Italy) 1987, Lion of Venice Medal 1987, Ronald Reagan Distinguished Service Award 1999, Univ. of Southern California Alumni Merit Award. *Publications include:* Ronald Reagan: The Wisdom and Humor of the Great Communicator (Ed.) 1995, Ronald Reagan: The Great Communicator (Ed.) 2001. *Leisure interests:* skiing, tennis. *Address:* The Washington Post, 1301 K Street, NW, Washington, DC 20071, USA (office). *Telephone:* (202) 334-6000 (office). *Fax:* (202) 496-3954 (office). *Website:* www.washingtonpost.com (office).

RYAN, Meg; American actress; b. (Margaret Mary Emily Anne Hyra), 19 Nov. 1961, Fairfield, Conn.; m. Dennis Quaid 1991 (divorced); one s.; ed New York Univ.; fmrly appeared in TV commercials; TV appearances in As the World Turns, One of the Boys, Amy and the Angel, The Wild Side, Charles in Charge; f. Prufrock Pictures (production co., fmrly Fandango Films) 1994. *Films include:* Rich and Famous 1981, Amityville III-D, Top Gun, Armed and Dangerous, Innerspace, D.O.A., Promised Land, The Presidio, When Harry Met Sally, Joe Versus the Volcano, The Doors, Prelude to a Kiss, Sleepless in Seattle, Flesh and Bone, Significant Other, When a Man Loves a Woman, I.Q., Paris Match, Restoration, French Kiss 1995, Two for the Road 1996, Courage Under Fire 1996, Addicted to Love 1997, City of Angels 1998, You've Got Mail 1998, Hanging Up 1999, Lost Souls 1999, Proof of Life 2000, Kate & Leopold 2001, In the Cut 2003, Against the Ropes 2004, In the Land of Women 2007, The Deal 2008, My Mom's New Boyfriend 2008, The Women 2008, Serious Moonlight 2009, Fan Girl 2015, Ithaca 2016. *Television includes:* Web Therapy (series) 2013.

RYAN, Paul Davis, BA; American politician; b. 29 Jan. 1970, Janesville, Wis.; s. of Paul Murray Ryan and Elizabeth A Ryan (née Hutter); m. Janna Little; two s. one d.; ed Miami Univ., Ohio; began political career as aide to Senator Bob Kasten, US Senate 1992; econ. advisor and speechwriter, Empower America 1993–95; Legis. Dir to Rep. Sam Brownback, House of Reps 1995–97; marketing consultant, Ryan Inc. Central (site-work contractors) 1997–98; mem. US House of Reps from 1st Wis. Dist, Washington, DC 1999–2019, Chair. House Budget Cttee 2011–15, House Ways and Means Cttee Jan.–Oct. 2015, Speaker, House of Reps 2015–19; Republican party nominee for Vice-Pres. of US during presidential campaign 2012; Republican. *Publications include:* Young Guns: A New Generation of Conservative Leaders (with Eric Cantor and Kevin McCarthy) 2010, The Way Forward: Renewing the American Idea 2014.

RYAN, Thomas M. (Tom), BS; American pharmacist and retail executive; *Operating Partner, Advent International Corporation;* b. 15 Aug. 1952, NJ; m. Cathy Ryan; four c.; ed Univ. of Rhode Island; began career as pharmacist, CVS Pharmacy Inc. 1975, various man. and professional positions including Pres. and CEO CVS Pharmacy Inc. 1994–2007, Vice-Chair. and COO CVS Corpn 1996–98, Chair. 1999–2007, CEO CVS Caremark Corpn (following merger of Caremark Rx Inc. and CVS Corpn 2007) 1998–2011, Pres. CVS Caremark Corpn 1998–2010, Chair. 2007–11; Operating Partner, Advent Int. Corpn 2011–; mem. Bd of Dirs Reebok Int. Ltd 1998–2005, Yum! Brands Inc. 2002–, Bank of America Corpn 2004–10; Co-Chair. Blue Ribbon Steering Cttee, Univ. of RI, Chair. Leadership Gifts Cttee, URI Convocation Center; Hon. DHumLitt (Univ. of Rhode Island) 1999. *Address:* Advent International Corporation, 75 State Street, Boston, MA 02109, USA (office). *Telephone:* (617) 951-9400 (office). *Website:* www.adventinternational.com (office).

RYBAK, Volodymyr Vasylovych, DEconSci; Ukrainian politician; b. 3 Oct. 1946, Stalino (now Donetsk); ed Donetsk State Univ.; Chair. Donetsk City Council, Exec. Cttee and Mayor of Donetsk 1993–2002; first Leader, Party of Regional Revival of Ukraine (predecessor of Party of Regions); Co-organizer and first Chair. Party of Regions 1997–2001; mem. Verkhovna Rada (Parl.) 1998–2006, 2007–, Chair. (Speaker) 2012–14 (resgnd); First Deputy Prime Minister and Minister of Construction, Architecture and Housing and Utility 2006–07; Deputy Prime Minister March–Dec. 2007; Merited Builder of Ukraine 1995, Order of Prince Yaroslav the Wise 2011. *Address:* Verkhovna Rada, 01008 Kyiv, vul. M. Hrushevskoho 5, Ukraine. *E-mail:* umz@rada.gov.ua. *Website:* www.rada.gov.ua; partyofregions.ua.

RYBKIN, Ivan Petrovich, DrPolitSch, CandTechSc; Russian politician; b. 20 Oct. 1946, Semigorovka, Voronezh Region; m.; two d.; ed Volgograd Inst. of Agric. Acad. of Social Sciences at Cen. Cttee CPSU; Sr Engineer Kolkhoz Zavety Ilyicha Volgograd Region 1968–69; Lecturer, Prof., Head of Chair, Deputy Dean, Volgograd Inst. of Agric. 1970–87; Sec. Party Cttee 1983–87, First Sec. CPSU Dist Cttee in Volgograd, Second Sec. Volgograd Regional Cttee CPSU 1987–91; Head of Div. Cen. Cttee CP of RSFSR 1991; People's Deputy of Russia 1990–93; co-founder and Co-Chair. Communists of Russia faction 1990–91; mem. Agrarian Party, concurrently co-founder Socialist Party of Workers 1991–93; Deputy in State Duma (Parl.) 1993–96, Chair. 1994–95; mem. Council on Personnel Policy of Pres. Yeltsin 1994–95, mem. Security Council 1994–96, Sec. 1996–98; head of group negotiating with Chechen leaders 1996–98; Deputy Prime Minister 1998; Plenipotentiary Rep. of Russian Pres. to CIS states 1998; Chair. Political Union Regions of Russia, concurrently of Election Bloc 1995–96; Chair. Political Consultative Council of Pres. of Russia 1999–2000; cand. in 2004 presidential elections; Prize for Contribution to Peace with Chechnya (Ichkeria) 1996. *Publications:* State Duma, Fifth Attempt, We are Doomed to Consensus, Russia and the World: The Way to Security; numerous articles.

RYCHETSKÝ, Pavel, JuDr; Czech politician and judge; *Chairman, Constitutional Court;* b. 17 Aug. 1943, Prague; m.; three c.; ed Charles Univ.; Sr Lecturer and Asst Prof., Dept of Civil Law, Charles Univ. Law School, Prague 1966–70, compelled to leave for political reasons; worked as; co. lawyer for Fortuna commercial agency, Mladá fronta publrs and for housing devt co-operative; mem. CP 1966–69; Co-founder and signatory Charter 77; Co-founder Civic Forum, Rep. Civic Forum Liberal Club and later of Civic Movt; Public Prosecutor-Gen. of Czech Repub. 1990; Deputy Prime Minister and Chair. Legis. Council of the then Czech and Slovak Fed. Repub. 1990; f. solicitor's practice 1992; Lecturer in Political Sciences, Prague School of Econs Faculty of Int. Relations 1992; joined Czech Social Democrat Party 1995; elected Senator for Strakonice Constituency No. 12, later Chair. Constitutional Law Cttee of the Senate; Deputy Prime Minister of Czech Repub. and Chair. Govt Legis. Council 1998–2003; Chair. Govt Council for Research and Devt 1998–2002, Govt Council for Roma Community Affairs 1998–2002, Govt Council for Ethnic Minorities 1998–2002; Minister of Justice 2000–01, 2002–03; Chair. Constitutional Court, Brno 2003–; Chair. Czech Lawyers' Asscn 1990–92; Pres. Bd of Trustees Pro-Bohemia Foundation 1992–98; Founder Prácheňsko Region Citizens' Endowment Fund; Officier, Légion d'honneur 2005. *Address:* The Constitutional Court of the Czech Republic, Jostova 8, 660 83 Brno 2, Czech Republic (office). *Telephone:* (54) 2214360 (office). *Fax:* (54) 2218326 (office). *E-mail:* pavel.rychetsky@usoud.cz (office). *Website:* www.usoud.cz (office).

RYCROFT, Matthew John, CBE; British diplomatist; *Permanent Secretary, Department for International Development;* b. 16 June 1968, Southampton, Hants.; m. Alison Rycroft; three d.; ed Univ. of Oxford; joined FCO 1989; spent several months in Geneva, Switzerland and then on NATO desk in London; served at British Embassy, Paris 1991–95; Head of Political Section, Eastern Adriatic Dept, FCO 1995–96, mem. British del. to Dayton peace talks on Bosnia and Herzegovina; mem. Policy Planning Staff, FCO covering European and trans-Atlantic issues 1996–98; served at British Embassy, Washington, DC 1998–2002; Pvt. Sec. for Foreign Affairs, NI and Defence Issues to Prime Minister Tony Blair 2002–04; Amb. to Bosnia and Herzegovina 2005–08; EU Dir, FCO 2008–11, COO 2011–14, Perm. Rep. to UN, New York 2015–18, Perm. Sec. Dept for Int. Devt 2018–. *Leisure interests:* spending time with family, football, music (plays the double bass). *Address:* Department for International Development, 22 Whitehall, London, SW1 2EG, England (office). *Telephone:* (20) 70230000 (office). *Fax:* (20) 70230012 (office). *Website:* www.gov.uk/government/organisations/department-for-international-development (office).

RYDBERG-DUMONT, Josephine, MBA; Swedish business executive; b. 1955; ed Gothenburg School of Econs, Univ. of San Francisco, USA; served as Man. IKEA Catalogue Production to Gen. Man. IKEA of Sweden, responsible for purchasing and product devt of IKEA Group, Man. Dir IKEA of Sweden 2000–07, Head of IKEA Communication and Global Positioning –2008, mem. IKEA's Group Man. 2000–08; mem. Bd of Dirs Cederoth Intressenter AB, Skanska AB 2010–.

RYDER, Guy, CBE; British trade union official and international organization official; *Director-General, International Labour Organization;* b. 3 Jan. 1956, Liverpool; m. Carine Verstichel; ed Univ. of Cambridge; Asst, Int. Dept, TUC, London 1981–85; Sec., Industry Trade Section, Int. Fed. of Commercial, Clerical, Professional and Tech. Employees (FIET), Geneva, Switzerland 1985–88; Asst Dir, then Dir ICFTU, Geneva 1988–98, Gen. Sec. 2002–06, Gen. Sec. Int. Trade Union Confed. (formed after merger of ICFTU with World Confed. of Labour and eight nat. trade union orgs) 2006–10; Sec., Workers' Group, ILO 1993–96, 1996–98, Int. Labour Conf. 1994–98, Dir of Bureau for Workers' Activities 1998–99, Chief of Cabinet 1999–2001, Special Adviser to Dir-Gen. –2001, Exec. Dir Standards and Fundamental Principles and Rights at Work Sector 2010–12, Dir-Gen. ILO 2012–. *Address:* International Labour Organization, 4 route des Morillons, 1211 Genève 22, Switzerland (office). *Telephone:* 227996019 (office). *Fax:* 227998533 (office). *E-mail:* cabinet@ilo.org (office). *Website:* www.ilo.org (office).

RYDER, Winona; American actress; b. (Winona Horowitz), 29 Oct. 1971, Winona, Minn.; d. of Michael Horowitz and Cynthia Istas; ed Petaluma Jr High School, San Francisco and acting classes at American Conservatory Theatre, San Francisco. *Films include:* Lucas 1986, Square Dance 1987, Beetlejuice 1988, '1969' 1988, Heathers 1989, Great Balls of Fire! 1989, Welcome Home, Roxy Carmichael 1990, Edward Scissorhands 1990, Mermaids 1990, Night on Earth 1991, Bram Stoker's Dracula 1992, The Age of Innocence 1993, The House of the Spirits 1993, Reality Bites 1994, Little Women 1994, How to Make an American Quilt 1995, Boys 1996, The Crucible 1996, Looking for Richard 1996, Alien Resurrection 1997, Celebrity 1998, Girl, Interrupted 1999, Autumn in New York 2000, Lost Souls 2000, Mr Deeds 2002, S1m0ne 2002, The Day My God Died (voice) 2003, The Heart is Deceitful Above All Things 2004, The Darwin Awards 2006, A Scanner Darkly 2006, The Ten 2007, Sex and Death 101 2007, Welcome 2007, Water Pills 2008, The Last Word 2008, The Informers 2009, The Private Lives of Pippa Lee 2009, Star Trek 2009, Stay Cool 2009, Black Swan 2010, The Dilemma 2011, Frankenweenie 2012, Homefront 2013, Experimenter 2015, Destination Wedding 2018. *Television includes:* The Simpsons (episode: Lisa's Rival, voice) 1994, Dr Katz, Professional Therapist (episode: Monte Carlo, voice) 1996, From the Earth to the Moon (mini-series) 1998, Strangers with Candy (episode: The Last Temptation of Blank) 2000, Friends (episode: The One with Rachel's Big Kiss) 2001, When Love Is Not Enough:

The Lois Wilson Story 2010, Stranger Things 2016–. *Address:* c/o Thruline Entertainment, 9250 Wilshire Blvd, Beverly Hills, CA 90212, USA (office). *Telephone:* (310) 595-1500 (office). *E-mail:* info@thrulinela.com (office). *Website:* www.thruline.com (office).

RYDER OF WENSUM, Baron (Life Peer), cr. 1997, of Wensum in the County of Norfolk; **Richard Andrew Ryder**, OBE, PC, BA; British politician and company director; b. 4 Feb. 1949; s. of Richard Stephen Ryder, DL, JP and Margaret MacKenzie; m. Caroline Mary Stephens, CVO, MBE 1981; one s. (deceased) one d.; ed Radley Coll., Magdalene Coll., Cambridge; journalist 1972–75; Political Sec. to Margaret Thatcher, Leader of the Opposition and Prime Minister 1975–81; MP for Mid-Norfolk 1983–97; Parl. Pvt. Sec. to Financial Sec. to the Treasury 1984, Parl. Pvt. Sec. to Foreign Sec. 1984–86; Govt Whip 1986–88; Parl. Sec. Ministry of Agric. 1988–89; Econ. Sec. to Treasury 1989–90; Paymaster Gen. 1990; Parl. Sec. to Treasury and Govt Chief Whip 1990–95; Chair. Conservative Foreign and Commonwealth Council 1984–89; Chair. Eastern Counties Radio 1997–2001, Inst. of Cancer Research 2005–13, UNCANDOIT 2011–14, Child Bereavement UK 2013–; Vice-Chair. BBC Govs 2002–04, Chair. (Acting) 2004; Dir Great Bradley Farms and Estates, also dir of other family businesses. *Address:* House of Lords, Westminster, London, SW1A 0PW, England (office).

RYDIN, Bo, BSc; Swedish business executive; *Honorary Chairman, Svenska Cellulosa Aktiebolaget SCA;* b. 7 May 1932; s. of Gunnar Rydin and Signe Rydin (née Höög); m. 1st Monika Avréus 1955 (died 1992); m. 2nd Françoise Yon 1997; with Stockholms Enskilda Bank 1956–57; Marma-Långrör AB 1957–60; AB Gullhögens Bruk 1960, Pres. 1965–71; Pres. and CEO Svenska Cellulosa AB SCA 1972–88, Chair. and CEO 1988–90, Chair. 1990, Hon. Chair. 2002–; Chair. AB Industrivärden, Graningeverken, Skanska AB –2002; Vice-Chair. Svenska Handelsbanken, mem. Bd SAS Ass. of Reps; Vice-Chair. Volvo 1988–93; Chair. Fed. of Swedish Industries 1993–94; mem. Skandia 1983–93; mem. Royal Swedish Acad. of Eng Sciences, Royal Swedish Acad. of Agric. and Forestry; King's Medal 12th Dimension of Order of the Seraphim, Chevalier, Légion d'Honneur; Hon. DEcon; Hon. DTech. *Leisure interests:* golf, hunting, opera. *Address:* AB Industrivärden, Storgatan 10, Box 5403, 114 84 Stockholm (office); Karlavägen 3, 114 24 Stockholm, Sweden (home).

RYLANCE, Sir Mark, Kt; British actor, director and playwright; b. 18 Jan. 1960, Ashford, Kent, England; s. of David Waters and Anne Waters (née Skinner); ed Royal Acad. of Dramatic Art and Chrysalis Theatre School, Balham, London; family moved to USA 1962, first to Connecticut and then to Wis. 1969; took stage name of Mark Rylance; returned to England 1978; joined The Citizen's Theatre, Glasgow 1980; has since worked with RSC, Royal Nat. Theatre, Royal Opera House, Scottish Ballet, Shared Experience, Bush Theatre, Tricycle Theatre, London Theatre of Imagination, Contact Theatre, Oxford Playhouse, Project Theatre, Dublin, Mermaid Theatre, Royal Court, American Repertory Theatre, Boston, Theatre for a New Audience, New York, Pittsburgh Playhouse, Thelma Holte; now assoc. actor, RSC; Artistic Dir Shakespeare's Globe 1996–2005; Artistic Dir Phoebus Cart; Patron London Int. Festival of Theatre, Peace Direct, Stop the War Coalition; named in the TIME 100 list of the most influential people in the world 2016. *Theatre includes:* Much Ado About Nothing (Olivier Award for Best Actor 1994) 1993, title role in Phoebus Cart's production of Macbeth (also Dir) 1995, Proteus in The Two Gentlemen of Verona, Shakespeare's Globe's Prologue Season 1996, title role in Henry V in Shakespeare's Globe's opening season 1997, Bassanio in The Merchant of Venice and Hippolito in The Honest Whore, Shakespeare's Globe 1998, Cleopatra in Antony and Cleopatra, Shakespeare's Globe 1999, Life x3 2000, Twelfth Night, Shakespeare's Globe 2002, Vincentio in Measure for Measure, Shakespeare's Globe 2004, Peer Gynt (Minneapolis) 2008, Boeing Boeing (Tony Award for Best Performance by a Leading Actor in a Play) 2008, Jerusalem (Critics' Circle Theatre Award for Best Actor 2009) (Royal Court Theatre) 2009, 2010, La Bete (Comedy Theatre, London) 2010, (Broadway) 2010, Twelfth Night (Tony Award for Best Featured Actor in a Play) 2014, Farinelli and the King 2015, Nice Fish 2016–17. *Films include:* Prospero's Books 1991, Angels and Insects 1995, Institute Benjamenta 1995, Hearts of Fire 1987, Intimacy 2001, The Other Boleyn Girl 2008, Anonymous 2011, Days and Nights 2014, The Gunman 2015, Bridge of Spies (BAFTA Award for Best Supporting Actor 2016, Academy Award for Best Supporting Actor 2016) 2015, The BFG 2016, Dunkirk 2017, Ready Player One 2018. *Television appearances include:* The Grass Arena, Love Lies Bleeding 1993, In Lambeth, Incident in Judea, Leonardo 2003, Richard II 2003, The Government Inspector (British Academy TV Award for Best Actor) 2005, Bing (series) 2014–, Wolf Hall (mini-series) (BAFTA Award for Best Leading Actor 2016) 2015. *Address:* c/o Christian Hodell, Hamilton Hodell Talent Management, 20 Golden Square, London, W1F 9JL, England (office). *Telephone:* (20) 7636-1221 (office). *Fax:* (20) 7636-1226 (office). *E-mail:* christian@hamiltonhodell.co.uk (office). *Website:* www.hamiltonhodell.co.uk (office); www.markrylance.co.uk.

RYLKO, HE Cardinal Stanisław; Polish ecclesiastic; *Archpriest of the Basilica of Santa Maria Maggiore;* b. 4 July 1945, Andrychów; ordained priest of Kraków 1969; fmr Prof. of Pastoral Theology, Kraków Theological Acad.; apptd Head of Youth Section of Pontifical Council for the Laity 1988, responsible for planning celebrations for World Youth Day; later served as official of Vatican Secr. of State; apptd Titular Archbishop of Novica and Sec. Pontifical Council for the Laity 1995, Pres. Pontifical Council for the Laity 2003–05, 2005–13, 2013–16; cr. Cardinal (Cardinal-Deacon of Sacro Cuore di Cristo Re) 2007; participated in Papal Conclave 2013; Archpriest of the Basilica of Santa Maria Maggiore 2016–. *Address:* 00120 Città del Vaticano, Italy. *Website:* www.catholic-hierarchy.org.

RYMBAI, J. Dringwel, BA, BEd; Indian politician; *Chairman, Meghalaya Economic Development Council;* b. 26 Oct. 1934; m. Peggymon Pathaw; two s. three d.; high school teacher –1988; elected mem. Meghalaya Legis. Ass. representing Jirang constituency in Ri-Bhoi 1988, later Deputy Speaker, re-elected 1993, 2008, Speaker 1993, resgnd 2008; Minister of Food and Civil Supply 1993, held portfolios of Consumer Affairs, Taxation, Information Tech. and Tourism and Fisheries 2003–06, Minister for Parl. Affairs –2006; elected Leader, Congress Legislature Party 2006, resgnd 2008 and joined UDP; Chief Minister of Meghalaya with responsibility for Cabinet Affairs, Industries, Personnel, Planning, Political Programme Implementation and Taxation 2006–07; apptd Chair. Meghalaya Econ. Devt Council 2007. *Address:* Meghalaya Economic Development Council, Planning Department, Government of Meghalaya, Shillong 793 001, India (office). *Telephone:* (364) 2225470 (office); (364) 2224388 (home). *E-mail:* planning-shil-meg@nic.in. *Website:* megplanning.gov.in/medc.htm (office).

RYSALIYEV, Maj.-Gen. Zarylbek; Kyrgyzstani police official and politician; b. 19 Dec. 1960, Urmaral village, Talas Oblast, Kyrgyz SSR, USSR; ed Kyrgyz State Inst. of Physical Culture, Kyrgyz State Nat. Univ.; engineer, Admin of Corrective Labour Insts, Ministry of Internal Affairs 1985–95; Commdr 'Berkut' unit, Internal Affairs Unit, Alamadun Dist 1995–96; Sr Official, Criminal Investigation Dept, Ministry of Internal Affairs 1996–99, Sr Official for Serious Affairs 1999–2000, Dir Main Criminal Investigation Dept 2000–01, Sr Official for Serious Affairs, Main Inspectorate for the Combating Organized Crime 2001, Sr Official for Serious Affairs, Main Criminal Investigation Dept 2001–02, Dir Dept for Combating Organized Crime Groups 2002–04, Deputy Dir Ministry of Internal Affairs, Jalal-Abad Oblast 2004–05, Deputy Dir Main Criminal Investigation Dept, Ministry of Internal Affairs 2005–08, Dir Dept for Combating Narcotics 2008, Head of Section for Combating Organized Crime, Chief Criminal Investigation Dept 2008–09, Head of 9th Section, Ministry of Internal Affairs 2009, Head of Internal Affairs Section, Sverdlovsk Dist, Bishkek 2009–10, Head of Main Internal Affairs Section, Bishkek May–Sept. 2010, Minister of Internal Affairs Sept. 2010–12 (resgnd); apptd Chair. State Service for Punishment Execution 2012; Deputy, Jogorku Kenesh (Parl.) 2017–. *Address:* Jogorku Kenesh, 720053 Bishkek, Abdymomunov 207, Kyrgyzstan (office). *Telephone:* (312) 61-16-04 (office). *Fax:* (312) 62-50-12 (office). *E-mail:* zs@kenesh.gov.kg (office). *Website:* www.kenesh.kg (office).

RYZHKOV, Vladimir Aleksandrovich, DHist; Russian politician and academic; *Professor, National Research University Higher School of Economics;* b. 3 Sept. 1966, Altai Territory; m.; one d.; ed Altai State Univ.; Deputy Head, Altai Territory Soc. of Encouraging Perestroika 1988–90; Deputy Chair. Altai Territory Movt Democratic Russia 1990–91; Vice-Gov. Altai Territory; mem. State Duma (Parl.) 1993–2007, mem. Cttee on Fed. and Regional Policy 1994–95, First Deputy Chair. State Duma 1997–99, ind. mem. 2000–05; Deputy Chair. Russia Our Home faction 1996–97, Chair. 1999–2000; Founding mem. Democratic Alternative 2004, Co-Chair. Republican Party of Russia 2006, now associated with The Other Russia coalition; Prof., Nat. Research Univ. Higher School of Econs, Moscow 2008–; Co-Chair. Respublikanskaya Partiya Rossii—Partiya Narodnoi Svobody (Republican Party of Russia—Party of People's Freedom) 2006–; political columnist, Novaya Gazeta, Moscow Times; Chair. public movement Vibor Rossii. *Publications include:* Chetvertaya respublika (The Fourth Republic in Russia) 1999; more than 80 articles on contemporary policy. *Address:* National Research University Higher School of Economics, 101000 Moscow, Myasnitskaya ul., 20, Russia, (office). *Telephone:* (495) 772-95-90 (office). *E-mail:* ryzhkov-office@yandex.ru (office). *Website:* www.hse.ru (office); parnasparty.ru; www.ryzkov.ru (office).

S

SAAB, Elias Bou, BBA, MA; Lebanese business executive and politician; *Minister of National Defence;* b. 8 Sept. 1967, Dhour El Choueir, Mount Lebanon; s. of Nicolas Bou Saab and Janette Owayjan; m. Julia Boutros; two s.; ed American Coll., London, Boston Univ.; Founder and Exec. Vice Pres., American Univ. in Dubai 1995–; Owner, Sawt al-Mada radio station; Pres. (Mayor) of Dhour El Choueir village 2010–12; Minister of Educ. 2014–16; Adviser to Pres. Michel Aoun on Int. Cooperation 2017–; mem. Nat. Ass. (parl.) for Metn Dist 2018–; Minister of Nat. Defence 2019–; mem. Clinton Global Initiative 2005–; mem. Free Patriotic Movt (Tayar al-Watani al-Horr). *Address:* Ministry of National Defence, Yarze, Beirut, Lebanon (office). *Telephone:* (5) 420000 (office). *Fax:* (5) 951014 (office). *E-mail:* cmd@army.gov.lb (office). *Website:* www.lebarmy.gov.lb (office).

SAAB, Elie; Lebanese fashion designer; b. 4 July 1964, Beirut; m. Claudine Saab; three s.; began sewing as a child aged nine; moved to Paris to study fashion 1981, returned and launched Beirut-based fashion label 1982; first non-Italian designer to become mem. Italian Camera Nazionale della Moda 1997; showed first collection outside Lebanon in Rome 1997; started ready-to-wear in Milan 1998; showed first haute couture collection in Paris 2000; showed first ready-to-wear Spring-Summer collection in Paris 2006; launched first fragrance 'Le Parfum' 2011; Corresp. mem. Chambre Syndicale de la Haute Couture 2006; Chevalier, Ordre Nat. du Cèdre 2003. *Address:* Elie Saab Building, 2021-4516 Beirut Central District, Lebanon (office). *Telephone:* (1) 981982 (office). *Fax:* (1) 981983 (office). *E-mail:* hautecouture-lb@eliesaab.com (office). *Website:* www.eliesaab.com (office).

SAAB, Najib; Lebanese architect, publisher and international organization official; *Secretary-General, Arab Forum for Environment and Development;* b. 1953; ed American Univ. of Beirut; work experience ranges from designing for multinationals including General Motors and lecturing on corporate architecture at American Univ. of Beirut, to advising various govts and agencies on environment and writing on sustainable devt and tech.; Ed.-in-Chief Al-Bia Wal-Tanmia (Environment and Development); currently Sec.-Gen. Arab Forum for Environment and Devt; UNEP Global 500 Award for environmental achievement 2003, Zayed Int. Prize for Environment (co-recipient) 2011, Distinguished Alumni Award, American Univ. of Beirut 2014. *Publications include:* Environment: From One Catastrophe to Another (in Arabic) 1999, Arab Environmentalists, Unite! (in Arabic) 2001, Arab Environment: Climate Change Impact of Climate Change on Arab Countries (co-ed.), Nature Book (Book of the Year Award, Beirut Arab Book Fair) 2002, Environmental Agenda (in Arabic) 2006, Arab Environment: Future Challenges (co-ed.) 2008, Environment in Arab Media (in Arabic) 2008, Impact of Climate Change on Arab Countries (co-ed.) 2009, Arab Environment: Water Sustainable Management of a Scarce Resource (co-ed.) 2010, Green Economy: Sustainable Transition in a Changing Arab World (co-ed.) 2010, Water: Sustainable Management of a Scarce Resource 2010. *Address:* Arab Forum for Environment and Development, Eshmoun Building, Rue de Damas, PO Box 113-5474, Downtown Beirut, Lebanon (office). *Telephone:* (1) 321800 (office). *Fax:* (1) 321900 (office). *E-mail:* nsaab@mectat.com.lb; nsaab@afedonline.org (office). *Website:* www.afedonline.org (office); www.najibsaab.com.

SAAD, Stephen, BComm, CA; South African business executive; *Group CEO, Aspen Pharmacare Holdings Ltd;* b. 23 June 1964, Durban; m.; four d.; ed South Africa Inst. of Chartered Accountants, Univ. of Natal (now Univ. of KwaZulu-Natal); fmr Articled Clerk, Cooper and Lybrand, Durban; Co-owner of Quickmed 1990s; Co-founded Aspen Pharmacare Holdings Ltd 1997, then Jt Chief Exec., Group CEO 1999–, mem. Bd of Dirs 1999–; Owner, Covan Zurich; Chair. The Sharks rugby union team, Durban 2012–; Dr hc (Nelson Mandela Metropolitan Univ.) 2014; inducted into Ernst & Young Entrepreneur of the Year Hall of Fame 2005, Business Leader of the Year 2012. *Address:* Aspen Pharmacare Holdings Ltd, PO Box 25125, Gateway 4321, Umhlanga, South Africa (office). *Fax:* (31) 5808647 (office). *Website:* www.aspenpharma.com (office).

SAADAWI, Nawal el-, MA, MD; Egyptian physician and writer; b. 27 Oct. 1931, Kafr Tahla; m. 1st Ahmed Helmi (divorced); m. 2nd (divorced); m. 3rd Sherif Hetata 1964; one s. one d.; ed Cairo Univ., Columbia Univ., New York, USA; physician at University Hospital and Ministry of Health 1955–65; Dir-Gen. of Health Educ. Dept, Ministry of Health 1966–72; Researcher, Faculty of Medicine, Ain Shams Univ., Cairo 1973–78, also writer, High Inst. of Literature and Science; Head of Women's programme, UN Econ. Comm. for Africa, Addis Ababa 1978–79, UN Econ. Comm. for Africa, Beirut 1978–80; arrested and detained in Egypt for three months 1981; Founder, Arab Women's Solidarity Asscn 1982, Pres. 1982–91 (prohibited by Egyptian govt); fled to USA 1991, returned to Egypt 1996; Distinguished Visiting Prof., Duke Univ. 1993–96, taught at Univ. of Washington 1995, Univ. of Illinois, Chicago 1998, Florida Atlantic Univ. 1999, Montclair Univ. 2001–02, Univ. of Southern Maine 2003, Univ. of Autonoma, Barcelona 2004, Smith Coll., 2004 Claremont Univ. 2005, Spelman Coll. (Cosby Chair) 2007–09; formally charged with apostasy 2007, court dismissed all charges; fmr Ed.-in-Chief, Health magazine; fmr Asst Gen. Sec. Medical Asscn; First Degree Decoration of the Republic of Libya 1989; Hon. DUniv (York) 1994, (Univ. of Illinois, Chicago) 1996, (Univ. of St Andrews, Scotland) 1997, (Univ. of Tromso, Norway) 2003, Dr hc (Université libre de Bruxelles) 2007, (Flemish Univ.) 2007, (French Univ.) 2007, (Universidad Nacional Autónoma de México) 2010; High Council of Literature Award 1974, Short Story Award 1974, Franco-Arab Literary Award 1982, Literary Award of Gubran 1988, XV Premi Int. Catalunia Award 2003, North South Prize, Council of Europe 2004, Inana Int. Prize 2005, African Literature Asscn Award, Univ. of West Virginia 2007, Pan African Writers Asscn Literary Award 2009, Stig Dagerman Prize 2012. *Publications include:* Memoirs of a Woman Doctor 1958, Two Women in One 1968, Women and Sex 1971, She Has No Place in Paradise (short story) 1972, Woman at Point Zero 1975, God Dies by the Nile 1976, The Hidden Face of Eve: Women in the Arab World (non-fiction) 1977, The Circling Song 1977, The Veil (short story) 1978, Death of an Ex-Minister 1979, Memoirs from the Women's Prison 1983, My Travels Around the World 1986, The Fall of the Imam 1987, The Innocence of the Devil 1992, Nawal el-Saadawi in the Dock 1993, The Well of Life and The Thread: Two Short Novels 1993, The Nawal el-Saadawi Reader 1997, A Daughter of Isis: The Autobiography of Nawal el-Saadawi 1999, Love in the Kingdom of Oil 2001, Walking Through Fire: A Life of Nawal el-Saadawi 2002, The Novel 2005, God Resigns in the Summit Meeting 2007, Zeina 2009; contrib. to newspapers and magazines. *Leisure interests:* swimming, walking. *Address:* 19 Maahad Nasser Street, Bldg 1, Shoubra Gardens, 11241, Cairo, Egypt. *Telephone:* 2022279. *Fax:* 2035001. *E-mail:* shns@tedata.net.eg; nawalalsaadawi@yahoo.com.

SAAKASHVILI, Mikheil, LLM, SJD; lawyer, politician and fmr head of state; b. 21 Dec. 1967, Tbilisi, Georgian SSR, USSR; s. of Nikoloz Saakashvili and Giuli Alasania; m. Sandra Roelofs; two s.; ed Faculty of Int. Relations, Kyiv State Univ., Ukraine, Columbia Univ. Law School, New York, USA, George Washington Univ., Washington, DC, USA, Int. Inst. of Human Rights, Strasbourg, France, Norwegian Inst. of Human Rights; worked for Patterson, Belknap, Webb & Tyler (law firm), New York 1994; returned to Ukraine 1995; mem. Parl. (Union of Citizens of Georgia) 1995, Chair. Parl. Cttee responsible for creating new electoral system, ind. judiciary and non-political police force 1995–2000; Vice-Pres. Parl. Ass. of Council of Europe 2000; Minister for Justice 2000–01 (resgnd); resgnd from Sakartvelos Mokalaketa Kavshiri (Citizens' Union of Georgia) 2001; f. Natsionaluri Modzraoba (Nat. Movt) opposition party 2001, subsequently Chair. Ertiani Natsionaluri Modzraoba (ENM—United Nat. Movt); elected Head, City Council of Tbilisi 2002–03; Pres. of Georgia 2004–13; charges of abuse of office filed against him by Prosecutor-Gen. of Georgia July 2014, Tbilisi City Court ordered pre-trial detention in absentia Aug. 2014, wanted by on multiple criminal charges, denies as politically motivated; Lecturer and Sr Statesman, Fletcher School of Law and Diplomacy, Tufts Univ., USA 2014–15; Head of Ukraine's Int. Advisory Council on Reforms 2015–16; Gov. Odesa Oblast, Ukraine 2015–16 (resgnd); stripped of Georgian citizenship Dec. 2015; announced creation of new political party Rukh Novykh Sil (Movement of New Forces) Nov. 2016; stripped of Ukrainian citizenship July 2017; deported to Poland, later relocated to Netherlands 2018. *Address:* c/o Rukh Novykh Sil, 01033 Kyiv, provulok Muzeyny 4, Ukraine. *Telephone:* (44) 237-08-02 (office). *E-mail:* info@rns.org.ua. *Website:* rns.org.ua; saakashvilimikheil.com.

SAATCHI, Charles; British advertising executive and art collector; b. 9 June 1943, Baghdad, Iraq; s. of Nathan Saatchi and Daisy Saatchi (née Ezer); brother of Maurice Saatchi (q.v.); m. 1st Doris Lockhart Dibley 1973 (divorced 1990); m. 2nd Kay Hartenstein 1990 (divorced 2001); one d.; m. 3rd Nigella Lawson 2003 (divorced 2013); one step-s. one step-d.; ed Christ's Coll. Finchley, London Coll. of Communication; fmr jr copywriter, Benton & Bowles (US advertising agency), London; Assoc. Dir Collett Dickenson Pearce 1966–68; with Ross Cramer formed freelance consultancy, Cramer Saatchi, Dir 1968–70; Co-founder (with Maurice Saatchi), of Saatchi & Saatchi (advertising agency) 1970, (Saatchi & Saatchi PLC 1984), Dir 1970–93, Pres. 1993–95; Co-founder and Partner, M&C Saatchi Agency 1995–; f. Saatchi Gallery 2003, donated gallery and more than 200 works of art to the British public 2010; Co-founder with his brother, Saatchi Shul (ind. Orthodox Jewish synagogue), Maida Vale, London 1998. *Television:* School of Saatchi (BBC) 2009. *Publication:* My Name is Charles Saatchi and I Am an Artoholic 2009, Known Unknowns 2014, DEAD, A Celebration of Mortality 2015, Beyond Belief: Racist, Sexist, Rude, Crude and Dishonest: The Golden Age of Madison Avenue 2015. *Address:* Saatchi Gallery, Duke of York's Square HQ, King's Road, London, SW3 4RY, England (office). *Telephone:* (20) 7730-8135 (office). *Website:* www.saatchigallery.com (office); www.mcsaatchi.com (office).

SAATCHI, Baron (Life Peer), cr. 1996, of Staplefield in the County of West Sussex; **Maurice Nathan Saatchi,** BSc; British advertising executive and politician; *Partner, M&C Saatchi;* b. 21 June 1946, Baghdad, Iraq; s. of Nathan Saatchi and Daisy Saatchi; brother of Charles Saatchi (q.v.); m. 1st Gillian Osband 1972 (divorced 1984); m. 2nd Josephine Hart 1984 (deceased 2011); one s.; one step-s.; ed London School of Econs; started career with Haymarket Publications; Co-Founder Saatchi & Saatchi Co. 1970, Chair. Saatchi & Saatchi Co. PLC 1980–94, Dir –1994; Co-Founder and Partner, M&C Saatchi Agency 1995–; Chair. Megalomedia PLC 1995–; Dir (non-exec.) Loot 1998–; Shadow Treasury Minister in House of Lords 1999–2003, Cabinet Office Minister 2001–03; Co-Chair. Conservative Party 2003–05; Chair., Centre for Policy Studies 2009–13, Finsbury Foods PLC; Dir Centre for Policy Studies; mem. Council RCA 1997–2000; Gov. LSE 2003–13; Trustee, Victoria and Albert Museum 1988–96, Museum of Garden History; MacMillan Prize for Sociology 1967, St George's Soc. Medal of Honour. *Publication:* The War of Independence 1999, Happiness Can't Buy Money 1999, The Bad Samaritan 2000, Poor People! Stop Paying Tax! 2001, The Science of Politics 2001, If This is Conservatism, I Am a Conservative 2005, In Praise of Ideology 2006, The Sleeping Beauty of America 2007, Enemy of the People 2008, The Myth of Inflation Targeting 2009. *Address:* M&C Saatchi, 36 Golden Square, Soho, London, W1F 9EE, England (office). *Telephone:* (20) 7543-4500 (office). *Fax:* (20) 7543-4501 (office). *E-mail:* maurices@mcsaatchi.com (office). *Website:* www.mcsaatchi.com (office).

SAAVEDRA-ALESSANDRI, Pablo, LLM, JSD; Chilean lawyer and international organization executive; *Secretary, Inter-American Court of Human Rights (Corte Interamericana de Derechos Humanos);* ed Univ. Diego Portales, Univ. of Notre Dame Law School, USA; Lawyer, Nat. Corpn for Reparation and Reconciliation, Santiago 1992–94; Partner, Buzeta, Ilabaca, Saavedra (law firm), Santiago 1993–96; Rómulo Gallegos Fellow, Inter-American Human Rights Comm., Washington, DC 1996–97, Lawyer 1998–2001; Deputy Sec., Inter-American Court of Human Rights (Corte Interamericana de Derechos Humanos) 2001–03, Sec. 2003–. *Address:* Corte Interamericana de Derechos Humanos, Apdo Postal 6906-1000, San José, Costa Rica (office). *Telephone:* 2527-1600 (office). *Fax:* 2234-0584 (office). *E-mail:* pablosaavedra@corteidh.or.cr (office). *Website:* www.corteidh.or.cr (office).

SAAVEDRA SOTO, Rubén Aldo; Bolivian lawyer and politician; b. La Paz; ed Universidad Mayor de San Andrés; fmr Prof., Catholic Univ. of Bolivia; Dir of Civil Registry, Departmental Electoral Court of La Paz; Exec. Dir Financial Intelligence Unit and Departmental Man. of Legal Services, Contraloría General (nat. audit office), Santa Cruz –2010; Minister of Nat. Defence 2010–11, 2011–15; Man. Dir

Dirección Estratégica de Reivindicación Marítima April–Sept 2011. *Address:* c/o Ministry of National Defence, Calle 20 de Octubre 2502, esq. Pedro Salazar, La Paz, Bolivia.

SABAH, Sheikh Ahmad al-Fahad al-Ahmad al-, BSc; Kuwaiti politician; b. 12 Aug. 1963, Kuwait City; ed Univ. of Kuwait, Kuwait Mil. Acad.; officer in Kuwaiti Army 1985–90, reaching rank of Maj.; Pres. Kuwait Olympic Cttee 1990–2001, Olympic Council of Asia 1991–; Deputy Chair. Public Authority for Youth and Sports 1992–2000, Chair. (rank of cabinet minister) 2000; Chair. Afro-Asian Games Council 1998–2003; Sr Vice-Pres. Islamic Solidarity Sports Fed. 1999–; Minister of Information 2000, of Energy 2002; fmr Chair. Kuwait Petroleum Corpn; Sec.-Gen. OPEC 2003–05; Minister of Energy 2003–06; Minister of National Security 2006; Dir Nat. Security Apparatus 2006; Pres. Asian Handball Fed.; Vice-Pres. Int. Handball Fed.; mem. IOC 2001–, mem. of comms: Sport for All 1992–95, Olympic Movt (as NOCs Rep. 1995–2001), 'IOC 2000' (Exec. Cttee 1999), Olympic Solidarity 2000–11, Int. Relations 2002–14, Pres. Olympic Solidarity Comm. 2012–; fmr Chair. Nat. Council for Culture, Arts and Literature; Hon. Citizen of Hiroshima; Hon. Pres. of several Kuwait, Arab and Asian Clubs; Saudi Sports Order by HRH Prince Sultan; Hon. PhD (Dong-A Univ., South Korea, Taipei Univ., Taiwan, American Acad.); Kingdom of Saudi Arabia Sports Medal, Special Forces, Bravery Award, US Army, Sports Merit Award, Pres. of Turkey, Highest Civilian Award, Pres. of Kazakhstan, Gen. Dir of Saudi Youth and Sports. *Leisure interest:* sports, especially equestrian sports and shooting. *Address:* Olympic Council of Asia, PO Box 6706, Hawalli, 32042 Kuwait City, Kuwait. *Telephone:* 22274277. *Fax:* 22274280. *E-mail:* info@ocasia.org. *Website:* www.ocasia.org.

SABAH, Ahmad Homoud al-Jaber al-; Kuwaiti politician; Minister of the Interior 1991–92, of Defence 1994, First Deputy Prime Minister and Minister of the Interior 2011–13. *Address:* c/o Ministry of the Interior, POB 11, 13001 Safat, Kuwait.

SABAH, Lt-Gen. Ahmad Khaled al-Hamad al-; Kuwaiti army officer and government official; Chief of Staff of Kuwait Army –2012; Deputy Prime Minister and Minister of Defence 2012–13. *Address:* c/o Ministry of Defence, POB 1170, 13012 Safat, Kuwait City, Kuwait.

SABAH, Sheikh Jaber Mubarak al-Hamad al-; Kuwaiti politician; *Prime Minister;* b. 1948; Head of Admin. Affairs, Ministry of Amiri Diwan 1971–75; Gov. Hawally prov. 1979–85, Al-Ahmadi prov. 1985–86; Minister of Social Affairs 1986–88, of Information 1988–90; Deputy Prime Minister and Minister of Defence 2001–06; First Deputy Prime Minister and Minister of Defence 2006–11, Prime Minister 2011–12 (resgnd), Feb. 2012–; Medal of King Issa First Class 2007, Grand Cordon, Order of the Rising Sun, Japan 2009. *Address:* Diwan of the Prime Minister, POB 1397, 13014 Kuwait City, Kuwait (office). *Telephone:* 22000000 (office). *Fax:* 22223150 (office). *E-mail:* contact@pm.gov.kw (office). *Website:* www.pm.gov.kw (office).

SABAH, Lt-Gen. (retd) Khalid Al-Jarrah al-; Kuwaiti politician and fmr army officer; *Deputy Prime Minister and Minister of the Interior;* Army Chief of Staff 2012–13; Deputy Prime Minister and Minister of Defence 2013–16, Deputy Prime Minister and Minister of the Interior 2016–. *Address:* Ministry of Defence, POB 11, 13001 Safat, Kuwait City, Kuwait (office). *Telephone:* 22430500 (office). *Fax:* 22435487 (office). *E-mail:* contact@moi.gov.kw (office). *Website:* www.moi.gov.kw (office).

SABAH, Muhammad Khalid al-Hamad al-; Kuwaiti politician; b. 1955; s. of Sheikh Khalid al-Hamad al-Sabah and Mouza bint Ahmad al-Sabah; m. twice; one s. nine d.; several roles in Ministry of Interior including Asst, Gen. Register Dept, Secretarial Man., Dir of Public Registry Man., Dir, Dept of Naturalization, Dir, Dept of Citizenship and Travel Documents, Acting Asst Under-Sec. for Nationality Affairs and Travel Documents; Gov., Hawalli Prov. 1991–96; Minister of the Interior 1996–2003, 2013, also Deputy Prime Minister 2013; Adviser to the Royal Court (Diwan) 2003; Head of Nat. Security Apparatus 2009–13; Special envoy of the Amir 2009–13; Minister of Awqaf and Islamic Affairs May–Oct. 2014; Deputy Prime Minister and Minister of Defence 2016–17. *Address:* c/o Ministry of Defence, POB 1170, 13012 Safat, Kuwait City, Kuwait (office).

SABAH, Muhammad Sabah al-Salem al-, PhD; Kuwaiti politician and diplomatist; b. 1955; ed Univ. of California and Harvard Univ., USA; Lecturer in Econs, Faculty of Commerce, Economy and Political Sciences, Kuwait Univ. 1979–85, Kuwaiti Inst. of Scientific Research 1987–88; Amb. to USA 1993–2001; Minister of State for Foreign Affairs 2001–03; Minister of Foreign Affairs 2003–12; Deputy Prime Minister 2006–12; Order of Bahrain of the First Class 2004, Order of the Republic of Sudan of the First Class 2009; Hon. DIur (Claremont Mckenna Coll., USA) 2010, Dr. hc (Univ. for Foreigners of Perugia, Italy) 2011, Hon. DScS (Corvinus Univ., Budapest) 2013; The Salvatori Scholar Prize 1978, Robert and JoAnn Bendetson Global Leadership Award in Public Diplomacy, Tufts Univ. 2014. *Address:* c/o Ministry of Foreign Affairs, POB 3, Gulf Street, 13001 Safat, Kuwait City, Kuwait (office).

SABAH, Sheikh Nasser al-Muhammad al-Ahmad al-; Kuwaiti government official and diplomatist; b. 1940; m.; two s.; ed secondary education in Britain; Univ. of Geneva, Switzerland; began career at Ministry of Foreign Affairs 1964, Perm. Rep. to UN, Geneva 1965–68, Consul-Gen., Embassy in Switzerland 1967–68, Amb. to Iran 1968–79; Under-Sec., Ministry of Information 1979–85, Minister of Information 1985–88, of Social Affairs and Labour 1988–90, of State for Foreign Affairs 1990–98, of Amiri Diwan Affairs 1998–2006; Prime Minister of Kuwait 2006–11 (resgnd). *Website:* www.sheikhnasser.org.kw.

SABAH, Nasser Sabah al-Ahmad al-; Kuwaiti politician; *First Deputy Prime Minister and Minister of Defence,*b. 27 April 1948; s. of Sheikh Sabah al-Ahmad al-Sabah (Amir of Kuwait) and Sheikha Fatuwah bint Salman al-Sabah; m. Sheikha Hissa Sabah al-Salem al-Sabah; fmr Special Chancellor of his Highness the Crown Prince and His Highness the Prime Minister 1999; Minister of Amiri Diwan Affairs (head of the royal court) 2006–; First Deputy Prime Minister and Minister of Defence 2017–; f. Al Fotouh Holding Co., Kuwait Projects Holding Co.; f. Dar al-Athar al-Islamiyyah (cultural org. operating al-Sabah archaeological collection); Founder mem. Kuwaiti Public Funds Protection Cttee; mem. Bd of Dirs Metropolitan Museum, New York. *Address:* Ministry of Defence, POB 1170, 13012 Safat, Kuwait City, Kuwait (office). *Telephone:* 24848300 (office). *Fax:* 24846059 (office). *E-mail:* mod_info@mod.gov.kw (office). *Website:* www.mod.gov.kw (office).

SABAH, HH Sheikh Nawaf al-Ahmad al-Jaber al-; Kuwaiti government official; b. 25 June 1937, Kuwait City; s. of Amir Sheikh Ahmed al-Jaber al-Sabah and Yamama; m. Sharifa Sulaiman al-Jasem; four s. one d.; ed univ in UK; Gov. of Hawalli 1962–78; Minister of the Interior 1978–88, of Defence 1988–92; Deputy Prime Minister and Minister of the Interior from 2003, First Deputy Prime Minister 2003–06; proclaimed Crown Prince 20 Feb. 2006–; Kt Grand Cross, Order of Civil Merit (Spain) 2008. *Address:* Diwan of HH The Crown Prince, PO Box 4, 13001 Safat, Kuwait (office).

SABAH, HH Sheikh Sabah al-Ahmad al-Jaber al-, (Amir of Kuwait), GCB; b. 16 June 1929, Kuwait City; s. of Ahmad al-Jaber al-Sabah and Munira al-Ayyar; m. Fatuwah bint Salman al-Sabah (died 1990); three s. (one died 1969) one d. (died 2002); ed Mubarakiyyah Nat. School, Kuwait and privately; mem. Supreme Cttee 1955–62; Minister of Public Information and Guidance and of Social Affairs 1962–63, of Foreign Affairs 1963–91, acting Minister of Finance and Oil 1965, Minister of the Interior 1978; Deputy Prime Minister 1978–91; acting Minister of Information 1981–84; fmrly First Deputy Prime Minister and Minister of Foreign Affairs; Prime Minister 2003–06; Amir of Kuwait 2006–; Hon. Trustee, Metropolitan Museum of Art, New York; Hon. Citizen of Tirana, Albania 2008; Sovereign Grand Master, Order of Mubarak the Great, Sovereign Grand Master, Order of Kuwait, Sovereign Grand Master, Order of Nat. Defence, Sovereign Grand Master, Mil. Duty Order; Distinguished First Class, Order of Abdulaziz as-Sa'ud (Saudi Arabia) 2000, First Class, Order of Merit (Colombia) 2002, Collar of Abdulaziz as-Sa'ud (Saudi Arabia) 2006, Collar, Order of Khalifa (Bahrain) 2006, Collar of Independence (Qatar) 2006, Order of Zayed (UAE) 2006, Grand Croix, Légion d'honneur 2006, Grand Order of Mugunghwa (South Korea) 2007, Collar, Order of Civil Merit (Spain) 2008, Extraordinary Grade, Lebanese Order of Merit 2009, Heydar Aliyev Order (Azerbaijan) 2009, First Class, Order of Merit (Ukraine) 2009, First Class, Civil Order of Oman 2009, Kt Grand Cross, Order of Merit of the Italian Repub. 2010, Grand Cordon, Order of Civil Merit (Syria) 2010, Grand Cordon, Order of the Star of Jordan 2010, Order of Merit of the FRG 2010, Grand Cordon, Nat. Order of the Cedar (Lebanon) 2010, Order of the Liberator Gen. San Martín (Argentina) 2011, Order of the Chrysanthemum (Japan) 2012, Order of Lakandula (Philippines) 2012, Skanderbeg's Order (Albania) 2012; Hon. LLD (George Washington Univ., USA) 2005; UN Humanitarian Leadership 2014. *Address:* Bayan Palace, Amiry Diwan, Kuwait.

SABAH, Sabah al-Khalid al-Hamad al-, BA; Kuwaiti diplomatist and politician; *Deputy Prime Minister and Minister of Foreign Affairs;* b. 3 March 1953; m. Ayda Salim al-Ali al-Sabah; one s. one d.; ed Univ. of Kuwait; joined Ministry of Foreign Affairs as Diplomatic Attaché 1978, with Arab Affairs Desk, Political Dept 1978–83, posted to Perm. Mission to UN, New York 1983–89, Deputy Dir, Arab World Dept 1989–92, Dir, Under-Sec.'s Office 1992–95 Amb. to Saudi Arabia 1995–98, Chief of Nat. Security Apparatus 1998–2006; Minister of Labour and Social Affairs 2006–07, of Information 2007–09, also Minister of Justice and Awqaf and Islamic Affairs April–May 2009, Deputy Prime Minister and Minister of Foreign Affairs 2011–; Chair. Kuwait Fund for Arab Econ. Devt; mem. Nat. Security Council, Supreme Council of Petroleum, Supreme Council for Planning and Devt, Supreme Council of the Environment Public Authority. *Address:* Ministry of Foreign Affairs, POB 3, 13001 Safat, Gulf Street, Kuwait (office). *Telephone:* 22425141 (office). *Fax:* 22420429 (office). *E-mail:* mofa.site@mofa.gov.kw (office). *Website:* www.mofa.gov.kw (office).

SABAH, Sheikh Salem Abd al-Aziz Sa'ud al-, BA (Econs); Kuwaiti government official and fmr central banker; b. 1 Nov. 1951; ed American Univ. of Beirut, Lebanon; worked in Econ. Analyst Studies Section, Foreign Operations Dept, Cen. Bank of Kuwait 1977–78, Head of Dept 1978–80, Deputy Man. and Head of Investment and Studies Section 1980–84, Deputy Man. and Head of Inspection Section, Banking Supervision Dept March–Aug. 1984, Man. Banking Supervision Dept 1984–85, Exec. Dir for Banking Supervision and Monetary Policy 1985–86, Deputy Gov. Feb.–Sept. 1986, Gov. and Chair. Bd of Dirs 1986–2012; Deputy Prime Minister and Minister of Finance Aug.–Dec. 2013; Chair. Inst. of Banking Studies; Alternate Gov. of the State of Kuwait, IMF and Arab Monetary Fund; mem. Higher Planning Council, Higher Petroleum Council; mem. Bd of Dirs Kuwait Investment Authority, Higher Cttee for Econ. Devt and Reform; Gov. of the Year Award, Euromoney magazine 1988, Personality in Banking Management Award, Arab Research Center 1997. *Publications include:* Casting Light on the Monetary Policy and the Kuwaiti Economy 1988, Recent Issues of Central Bank Policy in Kuwait 1989, Prominent Landmarks in the Operation of the Central Bank of Kuwait 1995, Monetary Policy and the Role of the Central Bank of Kuwait: Current Concerns and Future Prospects 1997. *Address:* c/o Ministry of Finance, POB 9, 13001 Safat, al-Morkab Street, Ministries Complex, Kuwait City, Kuwait.

SABAN, Haim; American/Israeli media executive; *Chairman and CEO, Saban Capital Group, Inc.;* b. Alexandria, Egypt; m. Cheryl Saban; four c.; ed agricultural school, Israel; fled to Tel-Aviv with his parents aged 12 after Suez War 1956; served in Israeli Defense Force; est. leading tour business; relocated to France 1975, est. ind. record co. that sold over 18 million records in eight years; moved to Los Angeles, USA 1983, launched chain of recording studios that became leading suppliers of music for TV; f. Saban Entertainment 1988, merged with Fox Kids Network 1995, acquired Fox Family Channel (restructured as Fox Family Worldwide) 1997, sold to Walt Disney Co. 2001; Founder, Chair. and CEO Saban Capital Group, Inc. (SCG) 2002–; acquired ProSiebenSat.1 Media AG, Chair. Supervisory Bd –2007 (co. sold); with group of investors acquired Bezeq The Israel Telecommunication Corp., Ltd 2005, Univision Communications Inc. 2007; apptd to California Bd of Regents 2002–13; Founder Saban Inst. for the Study of the American Political System, Univ. of Tel-Aviv; f. Saban Family Foundation 1999; f. Saban Center for Middle East Policy, Brookings Inst. 2002, currently Chair. Int. Advisory Bd; mem. Bd of Trustees, Brookings Inst. *Address:* Saban Capital Group, Inc., 10100 Santa Monica Blvd, Los Angeles, CA 90067, USA (office). *Telephone:* (310) 557-5100 (office). *Website:* www.saban.com (office).

SABANCI, Güler; Turkish business executive; *Chairman and Managing Director, Hacı Ömer Sabancı Holding A.Ş.;* b. 1955, Istanbul; d. of İhsan Sabancı and Yüksel Sabancı; ed TED Ankara Coll. and Bosphorus Univ.; worked for

LASSA Tyre Manufacturing and Trading Co., Kocaeli Prov. 1978; Gen. Man. and mem. Bd KORDSA Tyre Cord Manufacturing and Trading Co. 1985–99, led teams that set up several jt ventures for Sabancı Group such as Brisa, Beksa and Dusa International LLC, Pres. Tire and Reinforcement Materials Group –2004, Chair. Hacı Ömer Sabancı Holding A.Ş. (also Head of Human Resources Cttee) 2004–; Founder and Chair. Bd of Trustees Sabancı Univ. 2002–; Chair.-Elect Sabancı Foundation, VAKSA; Order of Civil Merit, Encomienda de Numero (Spain) 2009; Woman of Distinction Award, Daughters of Atatürk 2006. *Leisure interest:* running vineyard producing wine under her own brand name. *Address:* Hacı Ömer Sabancı Holding A.Ş., Sabancı Center 4.Levent, 34330 Istanbul, Turkey (office). *Telephone:* (212) 2816600 (office); (212) 2816611 (office). *Fax:* (212) 2810272 (office). *E-mail:* info@sabanci.com (office). *Website:* www.sabanci.com (office).

SABBAGH, Nemeh Elias, MA, MBA; Jordanian banking executive; *CEO, Arab Bank Plc;* ed Institut d'Études Politiques, France, Austin Coll., Johns Hopkins Univ. and Univ. of Chicago, USA; worked for First National Bank, Chicago, USA 1974–76; joined Industrial Bank in Kuwait 1976; worked with National Bank of Kuwait 1979–98, Gen. Man. Int. Banking Group in charge of bank's int. activities, branches and subsidiaries world-wide; also worked with World Bank, Washington, DC; Man. Dir and CEO Arab National Bank, Riyadh, Saudi Arabia 1998–2006; Exec. Gen. Man. BankMed Sal 2006–09; mem. Bd of Dirs Arab Bank Plc 2010–, CEO 2012–; Dir (non-exec.) Europe Arab Bank plc 2010–, Oger Telecom Ltd; Dir, Arab National Bank –2005, BankMed Sal 2006–09, Jordan Mortgage Refinance Co. PLC 2011–, Jordan loan Guarantee Corp., Al-Hussein Fund for Excellence, Jordan Univ. of Science and Tech., American Univ. of Beirut. *Address:* Arab Bank Plc, PO Box 950545, Amman 11195, Jordan (office). *Telephone:* (6) 560-0000 (office). *Fax:* (6) 560-6793 (office). *E-mail:* info@arabbank.com (office). *Website:* www.arabbank.com (office).

SABBAGH, Rachid; Tunisian judge and politician; ed Ez-Zitouna Univ., Tunis; fmr judge (specialist in Islamic law); fmr Pres. Cour de Cassation (Supreme Court); Head of Cabinet of Ministers of Justice Mohamed Bellalouna 1971–73, Slaheddine Baly 1973–80; joined transitional govt of Beji Caid Essebsi as Pres. Higher Islamic Council 2011; Minister of Nat. Defence 2013–14.

SABBAH, Michel, PhD; ecclesiastic; *Latin Patriarch Emeritus of Jerusalem;* b. 19 March 1933, Nazareth; ed Patriarchate Seminary of Beit-Jala and in Beirut and Paris; ordained priest for Latin Patriarchate, Jerusalem 1955; fmr Dir Gen. of Schools, Patriarchate of Jerusalem –1967; taught Arabic and Islamic studies in Djibouti –1973; priest, Misdar, nr Amman; apptd Pres. Frères Univ. Bethlehem 1980; Latin (Roman Catholic) Patriarch of Jerusalem 1988–2008, Emer. Patriarch 2008–; fmr Pres. Bishops Conf. for Arab Countries, Pax Christi; Grand Prior, Equestrian Order of the Holy Sepulchre of Jerusalem. *Publication:* Lire et Vivre la Bible au Pays de la Bible 2003; eight pastoral letters. *Address:* Office of the Latin Patriarch, POB 14152, 91141 Jerusalem, Israel (office). *Telephone:* 2-6282323 (office). *Fax:* 2-6271652 (office). *E-mail:* chancellery@latinpat.org (office). *Website:* www.lpj.org (office).

SABBIONI, Enrico; Italian biochemist and academic; b. 28 May 1942, Milan; m.; one d.; ed Inst. for Periti Chimici Industriali 'E.Molinari', Univ. of Pavia; Researcher, then Scientific Officer, Inst. for Health and Consumer Protection, EC Jt Research Center, Ispra, Italy 1962–2007; Sr Researcher, Unit of Immunotoxicology and Allergic Diseases, Center for Science of Aging (CESI), Foundation Univ. 'G. d'Annunzio' Univ., Chieti 2007–; Consultant, Veneto Nanotech SCpA, Padua 2010–14; Chief Adviser, European Center for the Sustainable Impact of Nanotechnology 2010–; Task Leader, Inst. for Health and Consumer Protection; Pres., Società Italiana di Nanotossicologia 2010–; mem. European Centre for Validation of Alternative Methods; mem. Int. Soc. for Trace Element Research in Humans; Fellow, Int. Union of Pure and Applied Chem.; mem. Editorial Bd Science of the Total Environment, Alternatives to Laboratory Animals; mem. Bd of Dirs Università Carlo Cattaneo (LIUC); Commemorative Medal of Charles Univ. of Prague 1993, Hevesy Medal 2002. *Address:* Via Gramsci 25, Biandronno, 21024 Italy (home). *Telephone:* (338) 3754492 (mobile). *E-mail:* enrico.sabbioni@alice.it.

SABETI, Pardis Christine, BS, MS, DPhil, MD; Iranian/American biologist, geneticist and academic; *Associate Professor of Organismic and Evolutionary Biology, Center for Systems Biology, Harvard University;* b. 25 Dec. 1975, Tehran, Iran; d. of Parviz Sabeti and Nancy Sabeti; m. John Rinn; ed Massachusetts Inst. of Tech., Univ. of Oxford, UK, Harvard Medical School; Graduate Research Fellow, Univ. of Oxford 1997–2000; Post-doctoral Fellow in Genomics and Infectious Disease, Broad Inst., MIT and Harvard 2003, Asst Prof., Center for Systems Biology, Harvard Univ. 2008–12, Assoc. Prof. of Organismic and Evolutionary Biology 2012–, Sr Assoc. Mem. Broad Inst. 2008–, Assoc. Prof., Center for Communicable Disease Dynamics (CCDD), Harvard School of Public Health 2012–; Howard Hughes Medical Inst. Investigator 2015–; Corp. mem., Bd of Trustees, Massachusetts Inst. of Tech. Corpn 1999–2004; fmr mem. NAS Cttee on Women in Science, Medicine, and Engineering; mem. American Soc. of Composers; Smithsonian American Ingenuity Award for Natural Science, Vilcek Prize for Creative Promise, NIH Innovator Award, Packard Fellowship, Ellis Island Medal of Honor, L'Oréal USA For Women In Science Fellow 2004, named as Trailblazer by Science Spectrum Magazine 2006, Burroughs Wellcome Career Award in Biomedical Science 2006, named World Economic Forum Young Global Leader 2012. *Achievements include:* investigations into human genome to study disease, including analysis of Lassa virus, sequenced Ebola genome following 2014 outbreak in Africa. *Music:* lead singer and co-songwriter of rock band Thousand Days; five-song CD Headlight Waves (Billboard Songwriting Contest Hon. Mention 2006). *Address:* Northwest Lab, Room 469.30, 52 Oxford Street, Cambridge, MA 02138 (office); Broad Institute of Massachusetts Institute of Technology and Harvard, 415 Main Street, Cambridge, MA 02142, USA (office). *Telephone:* (617) 384-5335 (office). *E-mail:* pardis@broadinstitute.org (office). *Website:* www.sabetilab.org (office).

SABHARWAL, Sharat, BA, MA; Indian diplomatist (retd); b. 23 Sept. 1952; joined Foreign Service 1975, served in various positions including Perm. Mission to UN, Geneva and missions in Madagascar, France and Mauritius, Dir/Jt Sec., Ministry of External Affairs 1990–95, Deputy High Commr to Pakistan 1995–99, Deputy Perm. Rep. to UN, Geneva 1999–2002, Amb. to Uzbekistan 2002–05, Special Sec. in charge of Admin, Consular, Passport and Visa Affairs, Ministry of External Affairs 2005–09, High Commr to Pakistan 2009–13 (retd); Information Commr, Central Information Comm., New Delhi 2013–17.

SABIA, Michael J., BA, MA, MPh; Canadian telecommunications industry executive; *President and CEO, Caisse de dépôt et placement du Québec;* b. 1954, St Catharines, Ont.; m. Hilary M. Pearson; one d.; ed Trinity Coll., Univ. of Toronto, Yale Univ., USA; began career with Canadian Fed. Public Service, held various sr positions including Dir-Gen., Tax Policy, Dept of Finance, Deputy Sec. of the Cabinet (Plans), Privy Council Office –1993; Vice-Pres. Corp. Devt, Canadian Nat. Railway Authority (CN) 1993, Exec. Vice-Pres. and Chief Financial Officer 1995–99; Vice-Chair. and CEO Bell Canada Int. Inc. 1999–2000, Exec. Vice-Pres. Bell Canada Enterprises (BCE) Inc. and Vice-Chair. Bell Canada 2000, Pres. and COO BCE Inc. March–April 2002, COO Bell Canada March–May 2002, Pres. and CEO BCE Inc. 2003–08, also CEO Bell Canada; Pres. and CEO Caisse de dépôt et placement du Québec 2009–; mem. Canadian govt's Advisory Council on Economic Growth, Canada-Mexico Leadership Group, Asia Business Leaders Advisory Council; Trustee Foreign Policy Asscn of New York. *Address:* Caisse de dépôt et placement du Québec, Édifice Price, 65, rue Sainte-Anne, 14th Floor, Québec, PQ G1R 3X5, Canada (office). *Telephone:* (418) 684-2334 (office). *Fax:* (418) 684-2335 (office). *Website:* cdpq.com/en (office).

SABIT, Abdul Jabar; Afghan lawyer and government official; b. 1945, Nangarhar Prov.; legal adviser, Ministry of the Interior –2006; Attorney-Gen. 2006–08; fmr Asst Dir of Afghan Islamic Univ.; fmr Legal Adviser to Attorney Gen.; also worked as Reporter for Voice of America; mem. official del. that visited Afghan prisoners held by US Govt in Guantánamo Bay detainment camp, Cuba 2006.

SABOURIN, Louis, LLL, PhD, FRSC; Canadian academic; *Professor of International Economic Organizations and Director, Groupe d'Etude de Recherche et de Formation Internationales, Ecole Nationale d'Administration Publique, University of Québec;* b. 1 Dec. 1935, Québec City; s. of Rolland Sabourin and Valeda Caza; m. Agathe Lacerte 1959; one s. two d.; ed Univ. of Ottawa, Univ. of Paris, France, Institut d'Etudes Politiques de Paris, France, Columbia Univ., USA; Prof., Dir Dept of Political Science, Univ. of Ottawa, Dean of Faculty of Social Science; Founder and Dir Inst. of Int. Co-operation and Devt, Visiting Sr Research Fellow, Jesus Coll., Oxford and Queen Elizabeth House, England 1974–75; Pres. OECD Devt Centre, Paris 1977–82; Prof. of Int. Econ. Orgs, Ecole Nationale d'Admin Publique, Univ. of Québec 1983–, Dir Groupe d'Etude, de Recherche et de Formation Internationales 1983–; Visiting Prof., Univ. of Paris (Sorbonne) 1982, Univ. of Notre Dame and Stanford Univ. 1992, Hanoi, Viet Nam 2000; Founding mem. Asia-Pacific Foundation, Montreal Council of Foreign Relations; mem. Pontifical Comm. on Justice and Peace; Pres. Soc. de droit int. économique 1995 1988, Hon. Pres. 1995; Legal Counselor, Hudon, Gendron, Harris, Thomas 1989–; Ford Int. Fellow 1962, Canada Council Scholar 1963; Visiting Fellow, European Univ. Inst., Florence 1999; mem. Pontifical Acad. of Social Sciences, Rome 1994; Chevalier, Pléiade de la Francophonie 1988; Chevalier, Légion d'honneur; Dr hc (Univ. of Paris—Sorbonne) 1998; Prix d'excellence pour la contribution à l'Afrique 1995, V9); Titulaire de la Chaire UNESCO de l'Institut international Jacques-Maritain: Treviso-Rome 2000–08; Prix d'excellence de l'Institut canadien d'administration publique 2010. *Publications include:* Le système politique du Canada 1969, Dualité culturelle dans les activités internationales du Canada 1970, Canadian Federalism and International Organizations 1971, Le Canada et le développement international 1972, Allier la théorie à la pratique: le développement de la Chine nouvelle 1973, International Economic Development: Theories, Methods and Prospects 1973, The Challenge of the Less Developed Countries 1981, La crise économique: contraintes et effets de l'interdépendance pour le Canada 1984, Passion d'être, désir d'avoir, le dilemme Québec-Canada dans un univers en mutation 1992, Les organisations économiques internationales 1994, The Social Dimensions of Globalization 2000, Globalization and Inequalitites 2002, The Governance of Globalization 2004; numerous articles. *Leisure interests:* music, travel, wine-tasting (Grand officier du Tastevin), skiing, tennis, cycling. *Address:* GERFI-ENAP, 4750 avenue Henri-Julien, Montreal, PQ H2T 3E5, Canada (office). *Telephone:* (514) 849-3989 (office); (514) 735-2878 (home). *Fax:* (514) 849-3369 (office). *E-mail:* lsabourin@hotmail.com (office). *Website:* www.enap.ca (office).

SABRI, Naji, MA, PhD; Iraqi journalist, editor, diplomatist and government official; b. 1951; Foreign Ed. and Man. Ed. al-Thawra Daily 1968–75; Lecturer in English, Coll. of Arts, Univ. of Baghdad 1969–75; Councillor, Embassy in London 1975–80; Founder and Dir Iraqi Cultural Centre, London 1977–80; Founder and Ed.-in-Chief, UR (journal of modern Arab arts) 1977–80; Dir-Gen. Dar al-Mamun House (trans. and publishing) 1980–90; Ed.-in-Chief, Baghdad Observer 1980–98; Founder and Ed.-in-Chief Gilgamesh (journal of modern Iraqi arts) 1986–95; Vice-Pres. Iraqi Nat. Cttee of Educ., Science and Culture 1986–95; Dir-Gen. of Foreign Information, Ministry of Information and Culture 1990–91, Deputy Minister of Information and Culture 1991–95, Adviser to Minister of Information and Culture 1997–98; Lecturer, Coll. of Arts, Univ. of Mustansiriya 1995–99; Adviser, Presidential Office 1995–98; at Ministry of Foreign Affairs, Baghdad 1998, Amb. to Austria and Perm. Rep. to IAEA, UNIDO and UN Office, Vienna 1999–2001, Amb. to Slovakia (non-resident) 2000–01, Minister of State for Foreign Affairs April–Aug. 2001, Minister of Foreign Affairs 2001–03; currently teaches journalism in Qatar. *Publications include:* trans. into Arabic: The Genius of Show (Michael Holroyd), Aspects of Biography (André Maurois), Lectures on Literature (Vladimir Nabokov); several Iraqi political books into English; Iraq's Year Book (Ed.-in-Chief) 1988, 1990, 1995, 1998, 1999.

SABU, Mohamad; Malaysian politician; *Minister of Defence;* b. 14 Oct. 1954, Tasek Gelugor, Penang; m. Normah Alwi; three c.; ed Univ. Teknologi MARA; mem. Dewan Rakyat (Parl.) (PAS) for Nilam Puri, Kelantan 1990–95, (PAS) for Kubang Kerian, Kelantan 1995–99, (PAS) for Kuala Kedah, Kedah 1999–2004, (Amanah) for Kota Raja, Selangor 2018–; Minister of Defence 2018–; mem. Parti Islam Se-Malaysia (PAS, Islamic Party of Malaysia) 1981–2015, Deputy Pres. 2011–15; Founding Pres. Parti Amanah Negara (Amanah) 2015. *Address:* Ministry of Defence, Wisma Pertahanan, Jalan Padang Tembak, 50634 Kuala Lumpur, Malaysia (office). *Telephone:* (3) 26924007 (office). *Fax:* (3) 26914163 (office). *E-mail:* portal@mod.gov.my (office). *Website:* www.mod.gov.my (office); mohamadsabu.com.

SACA GONZÁLEZ, Elías Antonio (Tony); Salvadorean politician, business executive and fmr head of state; b. 9 March 1965, Usulután; m. Ana Ligia Mixco Sol de Saca; three c.; ed Instituto San Agustín de Usulatán, Colegio Cristóbal Colón; fmr sports commentator and journalist; launched TV channel and several radio programmes 1990s including Radio América (with Alfonso Rivas) 1987, Radio Astral 1993; Pres. Asociación Salvadoreña de Radiodifusores (ASDER) 1997–2001, Vice-Pres.; Pres. Asociación Nacional de Empresa Privada (ANEP; National Private Enterprise Asscn) 2001–04; fmr Pres. Círculo de Informadores Deportivos (CID); Pres. FEDEPRICAP (Fed. of Cen. American and Dominican Repub. Business Execs); Pres. of El Salvador 2004–09; cand. in presidential election Feb. 2014; mem. Alianza Republicana Nacionalista (ARENA) –2010, Gran Alianza por la Unidad Nacional (GANA) 2010–; pleaded guilty to charges of embezzlement and money laundering, and sentenced to 10 years in prison 2018; Micrófono de Oro 1991, Distinguished Broadcaster Award 2003.

SACCO, Desmond, BSc; South African geologist and business executive; *Chairman and Managing Director, Assore Ltd;* b. 22 Sept. 1942, Johannesburg; s. of Guido Sacco; m.; two c.; ed Univ. of the Witwatersrand; joined Assore Ltd 1968, mem. Bd of Dirs 1974, Chair. and Man. Dir 1992–; Dir African Mining and Trust Co. Ltd 1975, Chair. 1992–; Chair. Ore and Metal Co. Ltd 1992–; Deputy Chair. Assmang Ltd 1992–99, Chair. 1999–; Fellow, Geological Soc. of South Africa, Inst. of Dirs; Italian Business Man of the Year, Italian Chamber. *Publication:* The Desmond Sacco Collection. *Address:* Assore Ltd, Private Bag X03, Northlands 2116, South Africa (office). *Telephone:* (11) 7706800 (office). *Fax:* (11) 2686040 (office). *E-mail:* info@assore.com (office). *Website:* www.assore.com (office).

SACCOMANI, Fabrizio; Italian banking executive and government official; b. 22 Nov. 1942, Rome; m.; ed Bocconi Univ. (degree in econs), Princeton Univ., USA; joined Bank of Italy 1967, with Supervision Office 1967–70, with Int. Econ. Corpn Dept, then Econ. Research Dept 1975–84, Head of Foreign Dept 1984–97, Cen. Man. for Int. Affairs 1997–2003, Dir-Gen. 2006–13; Minister of Economy and Finance 2013–14; Rep. at Int. Relations Cttee, European Cen. Bank, Cttee on the Global Financial System, BIS, Econ. and Finance Cttee, EU; with Economist, Exchange and Trade Relations Dept, then Asst to Exec. Dir for Italy, IMF 1970–75; Chair. Foreign Exchange Policy Sub-Cttee, European Monetary Inst. 1991–97; Vice-Pres. EBRD 2003–06; mem. Bd of Dirs Einaudi Inst. for Econs and Finance, Istituto Italiano di Tecnologia; mem. Istituto Affari Internazionali, Società Italiana degli Economisti. *Address:* c/o Ministry of the Economy and Finance, Via XX Settembre 97, 00187 Rome, Italy.

SACHINIDIS, Philippos, MEconSc, PhD; Greek economist, academic and politician; b. 27 March 1963, Vancouver, BC, Canada; m. Ourania Karageorgou 1990; one s.; ed Univ. of Piraeus Grad. School of Industrial Studies, Queens Coll., City Univ. of New York, USA, Univ. of Manchester, UK; Lecturer in Econs, Manchester School of Man. 1991–94; fmr Researcher, Foundation of Econ. and Industrial Research (IOBE), Athens 1996; Sr Economist, Strategic Planning Div., Nat. Bank of Greece 1997–2000, 2004–07; fmr Special Adviser, Econ. Office of Prime Minister Konstantinos Simitis 2000–04; mem. (Panhellenic Socialist Movt—PASOK) of the Vouli (Parl.) for Larissa 2007–14, mem. Parl. Standing Cttee of Production and Trade 2007–09; Deputy, then Alt. Minister of Finance 2009–12, Minister of Finance March–May 2012; mem. Nat. Council and Sec. PASOK Devt Cttee 2007–09; resgnd from PASOK Jan. 2015, co-f. Movement of Democratic Socialists 2015–. *Publications:* several articles in academic journals and newspapers. *Address:* 1 Defkalionos str., 41222 Larisa, Greece (office). *Telephone:* (241) 0530848 (office). *Fax:* (241) 0252810 (office). *E-mail:* philippos@sachinidis.gr (office).

SACHS, Jeffrey David, BA, MA, PhD; American economist, writer and academic; *Quetelet Professor of Sustainable Development and Health Policy and Management and Director, The Earth Institute, Columbia University;* b. 5 Nov. 1954, Detroit, Mich.; s. of Theodore Sachs and Joan Sachs; m. Sonia Ehrlich; one s. two d.; ed Harvard Univ.; Research Assoc. Nat. Bureau of Econ. Research, Cambridge, Mass. 1980–85; Asst Prof. of Econs, Harvard Univ. 1980–82, Assoc. Prof. 1982–83, Galen L. Stone Prof. of International Trade 1984–2001, Dir Harvard Inst. for International Devt 1995–2002, Center for International Devt –2002; Quetelet Prof. of Sustainable Devt and Prof. of Health Policy and Man. and Dir The Earth Inst., Columbia Univ. 2002–; Adviser, Brookings Inst., Washington, DC 1982–; Special Adviser to UN Sec.-Gen. on Millennium Devt Goals 2002–, Dir Millennium Project 2002–06; Founder Millennium Villages Project; Founder and Co-Pres. Millennium Promise Alliance; Founder and Chair. Exec. Cttee Inst. of Econ. Analysis, Moscow 1993–; Chair. Comm. on Macroeconomics and Health, WHO 2000–01; Co-Chair. Advisory Bd The Global Competitiveness Report; mem. International Financial Insts Advisory Comm., US Congress 1999–2000; econ. adviser to various govts in Latin America, Eastern Europe, the fmr Soviet Union, Asia and Africa, Jubilee 2000 movt; fmr consultant to IMF, World Bank, OECD and UNDP; Adviser to Pres. of Bolivia 1986–90; Fellow, World Econometric Soc.; Research Assoc. Nat. Bureau of Econ. Research; syndicated newspaper column appears in more than 50 countries; mem. American Acad. of Arts and Sciences, Harvard Soc. of Fellows, Brookings Panel of Economists, Bd of Advisers, Inst. of Medicine, Fellows of the World Econometric Soc., Nat. Bureau of Econ. Research, Bd of Advisors Chinese Economists Soc., among other international orgs; Distinguished Visiting Lecturer, LSE, Univ. of Oxford, Tel-Aviv, Jakarta, Yale Univs; Hon. Prof., Universidad del Pacifico, Peru; Commdr's Cross, Order of Merit (Poland) 1999; Hon. PhD (St Gallen, Switzerland) 1990, (Universidad del Pacífico, Peru) 1997, (Lingnan Coll., Hong Kong) 1998, (Varna Econs Univ., Bulgaria) 2000, (Iona Coll., New York) 2000; hon. degrees from Pace Univ., State Univ. of New York, Kraków Univ. of Econs, Ursinus Coll., Whitman Coll., Mount Sinai School of Medicine, Ohio Wesleyan Univ., Coll. of the Atlantic, Southern Methodist Univ., Simon Fraser Univ., McGill Univ., Southern New Hampshire Univ., St John's Univ.; Frank E. Seidman Award in Political Econ. 1991, Berhard Harms Prize (Germany) 2000, Distinguished Public Service Award, Sec. of State's Open Forum 2002, Sargent Shriver Award for Equal Justice 2005, Padma Bhushan, Govt of India 2007, Cardozo Journal of Conflict Resolution International Advocate for Peace Award 2007, Centennial Medal, Harvard Grad. School of Arts and Sciences for his contribs to society 2007, BBC Reith Lecturer 2007, first holder of Royal Prof. Ungku Aziz Chair in Poverty Studies, Centre for Poverty and Devt Studies, Univ. of Malaya, Kuala Lumpur, Malaysia 2007–09, gave commencement address to

Lehigh Univ.'s Class of 2009, James Madison Award for Distinguished Public Service 2009, Blue Planet Prize 2015. *Publications include:* Economics of Worldwide Stagflation (with Michael Bruno) 1985, Developing Country Debt and the Economic Performance (ed.) 1989, Global Linkages: Macroeconomic Interdependence and Cooperation in the World Economy (with Warwick McKibbin) 1991, Peru's Path to Recovery (with Carlos Paredes) 1991, Macroeconomics in the Global Economy (with Felipe Larrain) 1993, Poland's Jump to the Market Economy 1993, The Transition in Eastern Europe (with Olivier Blanchard and Kenneth Froot) 1994, Russia and the Market Economy (in Russian) 1995, Economic Reform and the Process of Global Integration (with A. Warner) 1995, The Collapse of the Mexican Peso: What Have we Learned? (co-author) 1995, Natural Resource Abundance and Economic Growth (with A. Warner) 1996, The Rule of Law and Economic Reform in Russia (co-ed.) 1997, Economies in Transition (co-ed.) 1997, The End of Poverty 2005, Common Wealth: Economics for a Crowded Planet 2008, The Price of Civilization 2011, To Move the World: JFK's Quest for Peace 2013, The Age of Sustainable Development 2015; more than 200 scholarly articles. *Leisure interests:* skiing, biking, watching ballet. *Address:* The Earth Institute at Columbia University, 314 Low Library, 535 West 116th Street, MC 4335, New York, NY 10027, USA (office). *Telephone:* (212) 854-8704 (office). *Fax:* (212) 854-8702 (office). *Website:* www.earth.columbia.edu/about/director (office); jeffsachs.org.

SACKETT, Penny Diane, PhD; Australian (b. American) physicist, astronomer, strategic analyst and academic; *Adjunct Professor, College of Physical and Mathematical Sciences, Australian National University;* b. 28 Feb. 1956, Lincoln, Neb.; ed Univ. of Nebraska, Univ. of Pittsburgh; fmr reporter for Science News; fmr J. Seward Johnson Fellow, Inst. of Advanced Study, Princeton; fmr Program Dir Nat. Science Foundation; fmr Prof., Univ. of Groningen, Netherlands; fmr Researcher and Prof. of Astronomy, Kapteyn Astronomical Inst., Netherlands; Dir ANU Research School of Astronomy and Astrophysics 2002–07; also Dir Mount Stromlo and Siding Spring Observatories 2002–06, Adjunct Prof., Coll. of Physical and Math. Sciences 2011–; Chief Scientist of Australia 2008–11 (resgnd); mem. Bd of Dirs Asscn of Univs for Research in Astronomy, Giant Magellan Telescope –2008; mem. Australian Astronomical Soc., American Astronomical Soc., Int. Astronomical Union, Asscn for Women in Science; Int. Fellow, Royal Astronomical Soc. *Address:* College of Physical and Mathematical Sciences, Australian National University, Level 2, Peter Baume Building, 42 Linnaeus Way, Canberra, ACT 2601, Australia (office). *E-mail:* Penny.Sackett@anu.edu.au (office). *Website:* science.anu.edu.au (office).

SACKS, Lord Jonathan Henry Sacks, PhD; British rabbi; b. 8 March 1948, London; s. of Louis Sacks and Louisa (Libby) Sacks (née Frumkin); m. Elaine Taylor 1970; one s. two d.; ed Christ's Coll. Finchley, Gonville & Caius Coll., Cambridge, New Coll., Oxford, Univ. of London, Jews' Coll., London and Yeshivat Etz Hayyim, London; Lecturer in Moral Philosophy, Middlesex Polytechnic 1971–73; Lecturer in Jewish Philosophy, Jews' Coll., London 1973–76, in Talmud and Jewish Philosophy 1976–82, Chief Rabbi Lord Jakobovits Prof. (first incumbent) in Modern Jewish Thought 1982–, Dir Rabbinic Faculty 1983–90, Prin. 1984–90; Chief Rabbi, United Hebrew Congregations of British Commonwealth of Nations 1991–2013 (retd); Assoc. Pres. Conf. of European Rabbis 2000; Ingeborg and Ira Rennert Global Distinguished Prof. of Judaic Thought, New York Univ.; Kressel and Ephrat Family Univ. Prof. of Jewish Thought, Yeshiva Univ.; Prof. of Law, Ethics and the Bible, at King's Coll.; Visiting Prof., King's Coll. London 1998–, Birkbeck Coll. 2008–; Visiting Prof. of Philosophy, Univ. of Essex 1989–90; fmr Visiting Prof. of Philosophy, Hebrew Univ., Jerusalem; Rabbi, Golders Green Synagogue, London 1978–82, Marble Arch Synagogue, London 1983–90; Ed. Le'ela (journal) 1985–90; mem. CRAC; Presentation Fellow, King's Coll. London 1993; mem. (Crossbench) House of Lords 2009–; Trustee, Tuck Trust, Aria Trust; Hon. Fellow, Gonville and Caius Coll., Cambridge 1993; Hon. DD (Cantab.) 1993, (Archbishop of Canterbury) 2001, Dr hc (Middx Univ.) 1993, (Haifa Univ., Israel) 1996, (Yeshiva Univ., New York) 1997, (St Andrews Univ.) 1998, Hon. LLD (Univ. of Liverpool) 1997; Sherman Lecturer, Manchester Univ. 1989, Reith Lecturer 1990, Jerusalem Prize 1995, Cook Lecturer 1997, Grawemeyer Prize for Religion (USA) 2004, Norman Lamm Prize, Yeshiva Univ. (USA) 2010, Sanford St Martin's Trust Personal Award 2013. *Publications include:* Torah Studies 1986, Tradition and Transition (essays) 1986, Traditional Alternatives 1989, Tradition in an Untraditional Age 1990, The Persistence of Faith (Reith Lecture) 1991, Orthodoxy Confronts Modernity (Ed.) 1991, Crisis and Covenant 1992, One People?: Tradition, Modernity and Jewish Unity 1993, Will We Have Jewish Grandchildren? 1994, Faith in the Future 1995, Community of Faith 1995, The Politics of Hope 1997, Morals and Markets 1999, Celebrating Life 2000, Radical Then Radical Now 2001, The Dignity of Difference: How To Avoid the Clash of Civilizations 2002, The Chief Rabbi's Hagadah 2003, To Heal a Fractured World 2005, The Home We Build Together–Recreating Society 2007, Koren Sacks Siddur 2009, Covenant & Conversation: A Weekly Reading of the Jewish Bible (American Nat. Jewish Book Award 2009) 2009, Future Tense: Jews, Judaism, and Israel in the Twenty-first Century 2009, The Great Partnership: God, Science and the Search For Meaning 2011, The Koren Sacks Rosh HaShana Mahzor 2011, The Koren Sacks Pesah Mahzor (American Nat. Jewish Book Award 2014) 2013. *Leisure interests:* walking, music. *Address:* House of Lords, Westminster, London, SW1A 0PW, England. *Telephone:* (20) 7286-6391. *Fax:* (20) 7219-5979. *E-mail:* sacksj@parliament.uk.

SADA SOLANA, Carlos Manuel; Mexican industrial engineer and diplomatist; *Undersecretary for North America;* b. 15 Aug. 1952, Oaxaca, Oaxaca State; ed Ibero-American Univ., Newcastle Univ., UK, Univ. of Delft and Inst. of Public Admin, The Hague, The Netherlands; Adviser to Undersecretary of Educ. and Technological Research, Secr. of Public Educ. 1980–81; Exec. Mem.-at-Large, Public Investment Planning and Control Comm., Govt of State of Oaxaca 1982–83; Sec. of State Programs, Govt of State of Oaxaca 1983–86; Sec. of Econ. and Social Devt, Govt of State of Oaxaca 1986–89; Consul-Gen. in Toronto 1989–92; Municipal Pres. of Oaxaca de Juárez, Oaxaca 1993–95; Consul-Gen. in San Antonio, Tex. 1995–2000, Consul-Gen. in Chicago, Ill. 2000–07, Minister, Embassy in Washington, DC 2007–11, Consul-Gen. in New York 2011–13, Consul-Gen. in Los Angeles 2013–16, Amb. to USA 2016–17, UnderSec. for N America, Secr. of State for Foreign Affairs 2017–. *Address:* Secretariat of State for Foreign Affairs, Plaza Juárez 20, Col. Centro, Del. Cuauhtémoc, 06010 México DF, Mexico (office).

Telephone: (55) 3686-5100 (office). *Fax:* (55) 3686-5582 (office). *E-mail:* atencionciudadanasre@sre.gob.mx (office). *Website:* www.sre.gob.mx (office).

SADANG, Elbuchel, BS; Palauan politician; *Minister of Finance;* b. 6 March 1955; s. of Sadang Etibek and Dirrabang Delmau Sadang; m. Shangrang Wenty; four c.; ed Grand Valley State Univ., Mich., USA; legislator for Ngaraard State 1990–2001; Dir Bureau of Nat. Treasury, Ministry of Finance 1994–2001; Minister of Finance 2001–08, 2016–, also Gov. for Asian Devt Bank and IMF on behalf of Palau; mem. Asian Pacific Asscn for Fiduciary Studies, Island Govt Finance Officers Asscn; fmr mem. Bd of Trustees Civil Service Pension Plan, charged with pension fraud 2008 along with other bd mems; Chief of Staff to Pres. 2013. *Address:* Ministry of Finance, PO Box 6011, Koror, PW 96940, Palau (office). *Telephone:* 767-2501 (office). *Fax:* 767-2168 (office). *E-mail:* bpss@palaugov.net (office). *Website:* palaugov.pw/executive-branch/ministries/finance (office).

SADIK, Nafis, MD; Pakistani physician and UN official; b. 18 Aug. 1929, Jaunpur, India; d. of Mohammad Shoaib and Iffat Ara; m. Azhar Sadik 1954; one s. two d. and two adopted d.; ed Loretto Coll. Calcutta, Calcutta Medical Coll., Dow Medical Coll. Karachi and Johns Hopkins Univ.; Intern, Gynaecology and Obstetrics, City Hosp., Baltimore, Md 1952–54; civilian medical officer in charge of women's and children's wards in various Pakistani armed forces hosps. 1954–63; Resident, Physiology, Queen's Univ., Kingston, Ont. 1958; Head, Health Section, Planning Comm., on Health and Family Planning, Pakistan 1964; Dir of Planning and Training, Pakistan Cen. Family Planning Council 1966–68, Deputy Dir-Gen. 1968–70, Dir-Gen. 1970–71; Tech. Adviser, UN Population Fund (UNFPA) 1971–72, Chief, Programme Div. 1973–77, Asst Exec. Dir 1977–87, Exec. Dir UNFPA 1987–2000; fmrly UN Under-Sec.-Gen.; Sec.-Gen. Int. Conf. on Population and Devt 1994; UN Special Envoy for HIV/AIDS in Asia 2002–12; Pres. Soc. for Int. Devt 1994–97; Fellow ad eundem, Royal Coll. of Obstetricians and Gynaecologists; Order of Merit, First Class (Egypt) 1994, Hilal-I-Imtiaz (Pakistan); Hon. DHumLitt (Johns Hopkins) 1989, (Brown) 1993, (Duke) 1995; Hon. LLD (Wilfrid Laurier) 1995; Hon. DSc (Mich.) 1996, (Claremont) 1996, (Long Island) 1997, (Tulane) 1999, (Univ. of the West Indies) 2000; Hon. DLitt (Nepal Tribhuvan) 1998; Hon. DEcon (Nihon) 1999; Dr hc (Al-Ahfad) 2000; Bruno H. Schubert-Stiftung Prize 1995, Hugh Moore Award 1976, Women's Global Leadership Award 1994, Peace Award (UNA) 1994, Prince Mahidol Award 1995, Population Award, UN 2001, Defender of Democracy, Peoples Global Action 2006. *Publications:* Population: National Family Planning Programme in Pakistan 1968, Population: The UNFPA Experience (ed.) 1984, Population Policies and Programmes: Lessons Learned from Two Decades of Experience 1991, Making a Difference: Twenty-five Years of UNFPA Experience 1994; articles in professional journals. *Leisure interests:* bridge, reading, theatre, travel. *Address:* c/o Special Envoy of the UN Secretary-General for HIV/AIDS in Asia, 300 East 56th Street, 9J, New York, NY 10022, USA (office).

SADIQ, Mohammad, MA, MIA, MS; Pakistani diplomatist; m.; two d.; ed Peshawar Univ., Columbia Univ., New York; Nat. Defence Univ., Islamabad; Dir CIS Dept, Ministry of Foreign Affairs 1993–94; First Sec./Counsellor, Embassy in Brussels 1994–98; Counsellor, Embassy in Beijing 1998–2000; Dir Kashmir Affairs Dept 2001–02; Minister/Deputy Chief of Mission, Embassy in Washington, DC 2002–05; Dir-Gen. (Personnel) Jan.–July 2006, June–Dec. 2007; Spokesman, Ministry of Foreign Affairs 2007–09; Amb. to Afghanistan 2009–14; mem. UN Election Observer Team that oversaw elections in South Africa 1994.

SADIQ, Sardar Ayaz, BCom; Pakistani politician; b. 17 Oct. 1954, Lahore; s. of Sheikh Muhammad Sadiq; m. Reema Ayaz 1977; two s. one d.; ed Aitchison Coll., Hailey Coll. of Commerce, Punjab Univ.; began political career from Pakistan Tehreek-e-Insaf 1996, left the party after differences with its leader Imran Khan 1998, joined Pakistan Muslim League (N) (PML-N) 2001; mem. Nat. Ass. (Parl.) 2002–18, Speaker 2013–18; Pres., CPA 2015–16; fmr Pres. Asscn of SAARC Speakers and Parliamentarians; Chair. Sardar Trust Eye Hosp. 1994–. *Address:* c/o Office of the Speaker, National Assembly of Pakistan, Parliament House, Islamabad, Pakistan (office). *E-mail:* assembly@na.gov.pk (office). *Website:* www .na.gov.pk (office).

SADOUN, Arthur, MBA; French advertising executive; *Chairman and CEO, Publicis Groupe;* b. 23 May 1971; m. Anne-Sophie Lapix 2010; ed European Business School Paris, INSEAD; f. Z Group (advertising agency), Chile 1992; Head of Int. Strategic Planning and Head of Devt, TBWA, Paris 1997–2000, Man. Dir 2000–03, CEO 2003–06; CEO, Publicis Conseil 2006, Publicis France 2009, Man. Dir Publicis Worldwide 2011, CEO 2013, CEO, Publicis Communications 2015–17, Chair. and CEO Publicis Groupe 2017–; mem. Bd of Dirs numerous cos including Fnac Darty SA –2018, Sichuan Yongyang Advertising Co., Ltd 2016–, BBH Holdings Ltd, UK, Proximedia SA, Belgium, Publicis Brazil, G/B2 Inc., Canada, Cyber Media Group SA, Luxembourg, Kitchen Reklamebyra AS, Norway, LAP Agências de Comunicação, Portugal, Poke London Ltd, Publicis Ltd, UK, Publicis Canada Inc., MSL France SA (fmrly F2SCom); Chevalier, Nat. Order of Merit 2014; Ad Age's Agency Exec. of the Year 2016, Personality of Year, Grand Prix des Agences de l'Année 2016. *Address:* Publicis Groupe, 133 avenue des Champs Elysées, 75008 Paris, France (office). *Telephone:* 1-44-43-70-00 (office). *Website:* www.publicisgroupe.com (office).

SADOVNICHIY, Victor Antonovich, D.Phys-MathSc; Russian mathematician and university administrator; *Rector, Moscow State University 'M. V. Lomonsov';* b. 3 April 1939, Krasnopavlovka, Kharkov Region; m.; three c.; ed Moscow State Univ. 'M. V. Lomonsov'; Asst, Docent, Deputy Dean Chair of Mechanics and Math., Moscow State Univ. 'M. V. Lomonsov' 1972–78, Prof., Prorector 1982–84, First Pro-Rector 1982–92, Rector 1992–, also Chair. Dept of Math. Analysis; Pres. Russian Union of Rectors (mem. Perm. Cttee), Eurasia Univ. Asscn; Corresp. mem. Russian Acad. of Sciences 1994, mem. 1997, mem. Presidium, Vice-Pres. 2008; Dir Inst. of Math. Problems of Complex Systems 1995–; Prof., Int. Acad. of Marketing; mem. Russian Acad. of Tech. Sciences; Sec.-Gen. Asscn of USSR Univs. 1987–91; Vice-Pres. Int. Acad. of Higher School 1992–; mem. Yedinaya Rossia (United Russia) party; Hon. Citizen of Moscow City; Hon. mem. Russian Acad. of Educ.; Order of Merit for the Country, Class II, III, IV, two Orders of the Red Banner of Labour, Order St Prince Daniil Moskovsky II, Order of Venerable Sergius of Radonezh I, Commdr, Legion d'honneur, Order For Merit (Ukraine), Order Dostyk, Order of Francysk Skaryna (Belarus), Order Danaker (Kyrgyzstan), Order Dostyk

(Kazakhstan), Order of the Rising Sun (Japan), Order of Honour (South Ossetia); Lomonosov Prize 1973, USSR State Prize laureate 1989, Russian Fed. State Prize for Science and Tech. 2002, Medal for Distinguished Labour, Medal for the 850th Anniversary of Moscow, Kazakhstan State Prize 2004. *Address:* Moscow State University 'M. V. Lomonsov', Leninskie Gory, 119992 Moscow, Russia (office). *Telephone:* (495) 939-27-29 (office). *Fax:* (495) 939-01-26 (office). *E-mail:* rector@ rector.msu.ru (office). *Website:* www.msu.ru/en (office).

SADOVY, Andriy Ivanovych, BEng, MA; Ukrainian electronics engineer and politician; *Leader, Samopomich (Self-Help);* b. 19 Aug. 1968, Lviv, Ukrainian SSR, USSR; m. Kateryna Kit; four s.; ed Lviv Tech. School of Radioelectronics, Lviv Polytechnic State Univ., Acad. of State Governance; mil. service in Soviet Army 1987–89; began working as radio-electronics technician, Lvivprylad Mfrs 1989; Deputy Dir Lviv br. of Social Adaptation of Youth Fund under auspices of Cabinet of Ministers of Ukraine 1992–95; Chair. Pivdenzakhidelectromerezhbud Jt Stock Co. 1997–2005; Chair. Lviv Oblast Devt Fund 1997–2001; Dir Lviv Devt Inst. 2002–03; Chair. TRK Lux Jt Stock Co. 2002–; Head of Social Org., Samopomich (Self-Help) 2005–, Leader, Samopomich political party 2012–; Mayor of Lviv 2006–; mem. Nasha Ukraina (Our Ukraine) 2006–10; Ind. 2010–13; Chair. Man. Council, Metropolitan Andrey Sheptytsky Art and Culture Fund of Greek Church of Ukraine 2000–02; mem. Ukrainian-Polish Co-operation Capitul; elected a Deputy Head of 'Mosty na Skhid' (Bridges to the West) Inst. Council (Poland) 2003. *Address:* Samopomich, 79012 Lviv, vul. Sakharova 42, Ukraine (office). *Telephone:* (44) 206-56-65 (office). *E-mail:* a.sadovyy@city-adm.lviv.ua (office); samopomich@ samopomich.in.ua (office). *Website:* samopomich.ua (office); city-adm.lviv.ua/lmr/ profiles/andrii-sadovyi (office).

SADR, Moqtada as-; Iraqi religious leader; b. 12 Aug. 1973, Baghdad; s. of Grand Ayatollah Muhammad al-Sadr; f. al-Hawzah weekly newspaper; est. Mahdi Army (Shiite resistance group) and Sadr Bureau in Sadr City, suburb of Baghdad 2003; went on self-imposed exile 2007, returned from exile 2011.

ŠADŽIUS, Rimantas, LLM; Lithuanian physicist, lawyer and politician; b. 8 Oct. 1960, Vilnius; m. Dalia Šadžiuvienė; one s. one d.; ed Lomonosov Moscow State Univ., Russia and Vilnius Univ.; began career as scientific researcher specialising in quantum chem. and solid-state physics; Deputy Minister of Social Security and Labour 2003–04, of Health 2004–06, of Finance 2006–07; Minister of Finance 2007–08, 2012–16; Lecturer, Vilnius Pedagogical Univ. 2009–12; mem. European Court of Auditors 2016–; Officer's Cross, Vytautas Magnus Order. *Address:* European Court of Auditors, 12 rue Alcide De Gasperi, 1615 Luxembourg, Luxembourg (office). *Telephone:* 4398-45746 (office). *E-mail:* rimantas.sadzius@ eca.europa.eu (office). *Website:* www.eca.europa.eu (office).

SÆBØ, Magne, DTheol; Norwegian fmr professor of Old Testament theology; *Professor Emeritus of Old Testament Theology, Free Faculty of Theology;* b. 23 Jan. 1929, Fjelberg; s. of Samson Sæbø and Malla Ølfaernes; m. Mona Uni Bjørnstad 1953; three s.; ed Free Faculty of Theology, Oslo and Univ. of Oslo; studied Old Testament and Semitic languages in Jerusalem, Kiel and Heidelberg; teacher of Biblical Hebrew, Univ. of Oslo 1961–70; Lecturer in Old Testament, Free Faculty of Theology (now Norwegian School of Theology) 1969–70, Prof. 1970–99, Dean 1975–77, 1988–90, currently Prof. Emer.; Ed.-in-Chief int. project on Hebrew Bible/Old Testament: The History of Its Interpretation I–III; Ed.-in-Chief Tidsskrift for Teologi og Kirke (Univ. Press), Oslo 1977–94; mem. Bd Norwegian Bible Soc. 1965–91, Chair. O.T. Trans. Cttee 1968–78, Gen. Trans. Cttee 1978–91; Chair. Norwegian Israel Mission 1978–87; mem. WCC Consultation on the Church and the Jewish People 1976–81; Chair. Lutheran European Comm. on the Church and the Jewish People, Hanover 1979–82; Pres. Int. Org. for the Study of Old Testament 1995–98; mem. Royal Soc. of Science and Letters, Trondheim, Norwegian Acad. of Science and Letters, Oslo, Nathan Söderblom Soc., Uppsala; received on 65th birthday Festschrift Text and Theology 1994; Kt 1st Class of Royal Norwegian Order of St Olav 1994; Fridtjof Nansen Award for Eminent Research 1995. *Publications include:* Sacharja 9-14. Untersuchungen von Text und Form 1969, Gjennom alle tider 1978, Ordene og Ordet. Gammeltestamentlige studier 1979, Salomos ordspråk, Forkynneren, Høysangen, Klagesangene (Commentary) 1986, On the Way to Canon: Creative Tradition History in the Old Testament 1998, The Book of Esther, (Ed.), Megilloth, Edn Biblia Hebraica Quinta Editione 2004; articles in int. journals and theology books. *Leisure interests:* biographies, stamp collecting, mountain walking. *Address:* The Free Faculty of Theology, POB 5144, Majorstua, N-0302 Oslo (office); Lars Muhles vei 34, N-1338 Sandvika, Norway (home). *Telephone:* 22-59-05-00 (office); 67-54-38-06 (home). *Fax:* 22-69-18-90 (office); 67-54-38-06 (home). *E-mail:* msabo@mf.no (office); m -saebo@online.no (home).

SAEED, Abdullah, BA (Hons), LLM; Maldivian lawyer and judge; b. 25 Sept. 1964, Meedhoo, Seenu Atoll; s. of Mohamed Saeed and Maumoona Mohammed Didi; descendant of Dhiyamigili dynasty of the Maldives; comes from a family of scholars, jurists and educators, eight of whom have filled the office of Chief Justice of the Maldives since 16th century; m. Moomina Nafiz; one s. one d.; ed early educ. in India, English Preparatory and Secondary School, Malé, higher secondary educ. in Cairo, Egypt, Faculty of Sharia and Law, Al-Azhar Univ., Cairo, IMO Int. Maritime Law Inst., Malta, legal drafting course at Lok Sabha, India; admitted as advocate 1995; began legal career with Attorney Gen.'s Office, State Attorney 1995–2000, Dir 2001–05, Asst Dir Gen., Public Prosecutions June–Sept. 2005, represented the State in lower courts and High Court and advised govt depts on legal matters; Dir Inst. of Shari'ah and Law, Maldives Coll. of Higher Educ. 2000–01, First Dean, Faculty of Shari'ah and Law Feb.–April 2001, also taught law at Faculty of Shari'ah and Law, of Man. and Computing, Coll. of Islamic Studies; Chief Justice of the Maldives 2008–10, mem. Supreme Court 2010–14, Chief Justice 2014–18; mem. Council for the Protection of the Rights of Children 1996–98, 2002–05, Law Comm. of Repub. of Maldives 1997–2002. *Address:* c/o Supreme Court of the Maldives, Theemuge, Orchid Magu, Malé, Maldives (office). *Telephone:* 3009990 (office). *Fax:* 3008554 (office). *E-mail:* info@ supremecourt.gov.mv (office). *Website:* www.supremecourt.gov.mv (office).

SAEED, Fathimath Dhiyana, LLB, LLM; Maldivian lawyer, politician and international organization official; b. 22 Nov. 1974, S. Hulhudhoo (now Addu City), Southern Prov.; m. Abdullah Jabir; two s.; ed Univ. of Tasmania, Australia, Grad. School of Law and Politics, Osaka Univ., Japan; began legal career as State

Attorney in Attorney-Gen.'s Office, responsible for providing legal opinions to Govt and for reviewing draft laws and regulations, Exec. Dir 2005–08; Attorney-Gen. of first multi-party Govt 2008–11; apptd to People's Majlis (Parl.) and mem. People's Special Majlis (Constitutional Ass.) 2005–11; served as Maldivian Govt Envoy for South Asia 2010–11; Sec.-Gen. SAARC 2011–12; Founding mem. Dhivehi Rajyithunge Party, served as mem. Exec. Council; later joined Jumhooree Party, elected Leader of Women's Wing. *Leisure interests:* jogging, reading contemporary Asian writing.

SAEED, Hassan, PhD; Maldivian politician and lawyer; b. 14 Jan. 1970, Seenu Feydhoo; s. of Mohmed Saeed and Khadeeja Hussein; m. Fatin Yusof; ed Int. Islamic Univ. Malaysia, Univ. of Queensland, Australia; Chief Judge, Criminal and Juvenile Courts 2003; Attorney-Gen. of Maldives 2003–07 (resgnd); Pres. Maldives Alumni Asscn of Int. Islamic Univ. Malaysia; mem. and Deputy Leader Dhivehi Rayyithunge Party (DRP—Maldivian People's Party) -2007; mem. New Maldives Movt 2007–; Special Adviser to the Pres. 2009; apptd Pres. Dhivehi Qaumee Party (DQP—Maldivian Nat. Party) 2009 (party dissolved by Election Comm., status yet to be confirmed by Supreme Court); currently Partner, Raajje Chambers (law firm); unsuccessful cand. in presidential elections 2008. *Address:* Rajje Chambers, M. Maahi, 2nd Floor, Boduthakurufaanu Magu, Malé 20-188, The Maldives (office). *Telephone:* 3343842 (office). *Fax:* 334 3844 (office). *E-mail:* info@raajjechambers.com.mv (office). *Website:* raajjechambers.com.mv (office).

SAEED, Maeen Abdulmalik, PhD; Yemeni politician; *Prime Minister;* b. 1976, Taiz; worked in planning and construction in Cairo; Consultant, Yemeni Islands Promotion and Devt Authority 2004–05; fmr Asst Prof., Faculty of Eng, Dhamar Univ.; Minister of Public Works and Highways April–Oct. 2018; Prime Minister 2018–. *Address:* Office of the Prime Minister, San'a, Yemen (office).

SAEED ABU EL-NOUR, Mumtaz; Egyptian fmr central banker and government official; fmr Dir Central Bank of Egypt (as Ministry of Finance Rep.); long career with Ministry of Finance, returned from retirement July 2011 to serve as deputy to Finance Minister Hazem al-Beblawi; Minister of Finance 2011–13.

SÁENZ ABAD, Alfredo; Spanish banker; b. Nov. 1942, Getxo, Vizcaya; ed Univ. of Valladolid, Deusto Univ., Bilbao; mem. Bd of Dirs and Exec. Vice-Pres. Tubacex (Basque steel pipe producer) 1965–80; Dir of Planning, Banco de Vizcaya 1981; Man. Dir Banca Catalana 1983, Chair. –1993; Man. Dir Banco Bilbao Vizcaya 1988, First Vice-Pres. 1990–93; Chair. Banco Español de Crédito (Banesto) 1994–2002; Second Vice-Chair. and CEO Santander Central Hispano SA (subsequently Banco Santander SA) 2002–13 (resgnd); Vice-Chair. Compañía Española de Petróleos (CEPSA) 2002–; mem. Bd Dirs San Paolo IMI SpA, Auna Operadores de Telecomunicaciones SA; Dir (non-exec.) France Telecom España SA; chosen as second best CEO of the European banking sector, Institutional Investor magazine 2013. *Address:* c/o Ciudad Grupo Santander, Edificio Pereda, 1st Floor, Avenida de Cantabria s/n, 28660 Boadilla del Monte, Madrid, Spain. *E-mail:* info@gruposantander.com.

SÁENZ DE SANTAMARÍA ANTÓN, (María) Soraya, LLB; Spanish lawyer and politician; *Deputy Prime Minister;* b. 10 June 1971, Valladolid; m. Iván Rosa 2006; one s.; ed Univ. of Valladolid; Chief State Lawyer, León Prov. 1999–2000; State Lawyer before the High Court of Justice, Madrid 2004; Adviser to Cabinet of First Vice-Pres. of the Govt, Ministry of the Presidency and Ministry of Home Affairs 2000–03; Assoc. Prof. of Admin. Law, Carlos III Univ., Madrid 2002–03; mem. (Partido Popular) of Congreso de los Diputados (Parl.) for Madrid 2004–, Deputy Spokesperson of Constitutional Comm. 2004–08, Parl. Spokesperson of Partido Popular 2008–11; Exec. Sec. for Regional and Local Policy 2004–08; Deputy Prime Minister, Minister of the Presidency 2011–, also Govt Spokesperson 2011–16; Acting Minister of Justice 23–29 Sept. 2014. *Address:* Office of the President of the Government, Complejo de la Moncloa, Avenida de Puerta de Hierro s/n, 28071 Madrid, Spain (office). *Telephone:* (91) 3214000 (office). *Fax:* (91) 3900429 (office). *E-mail:* secretariapresidente@presidencia.gob.es (office). *Website:* www.la-moncloa.es (office).

SÆTRE, Eldar, MA; Norwegian oil industry executive; *President and CEO, Statoil ASA;* b. 8 Feb. 1956, Vartdal, Ørsta; m.; three c.; ed Norwegian School of Econs and Business Admin (NHH), Bergen; joined Statoil 1980, Exec. Vice-Pres. and Chief Financial Officer 2003–10, played key role during merger of Statoil with Hydro Oil & Gas 2007, Exec. Vice-Pres. of Marketing, Processing and Renewable Energy 2011–14, Interim Pres. and CEO Statoil ASA 2014–15, Pres. and CEO 2015–; mem. Bd of Dirs, Strømberg Gruppen AS, Trucknor AS. *Address:* Statoil ASA, Forusbeen 50, 4035 Stavanger, Norway (office). *Telephone:* 51-99-00-00 (office). *Fax:* 51-99-00-50 (office). *E-mail:* statoil@statoil.com (office). *Website:* www.statoil.com (office).

SAEZ, Emmanuel, BA, MD, PhD; French academic; *E. Morris Cox Professor of Economics and Director, Center for Equitable Growth, University of California, Berkeley;* b. 26 Nov. 1972; ed Ecole Normale Superieure, Massachusetts Inst. of Tech.; Asst Prof. of Econs, Harvard Univ. 1999–2002; Visiting Asst Prof., Univ. of California, Berkeley 2001–02, Asst Prof. of Econs 2002–03, Assoc. Prof. 2003–05, Prof. 2005–10, E. Morris Cox Prof. of Econs 2010–, Dir Center for Equitable Growth 2010–; Visiting Prof., Dept of Econs, MIT 2009; Nat. Fellow, Hoover Inst., Stanford Univ. 2004–05, Fellow, Center for Advanced Study in Behavioral Sciences 2007–08; Fellow, American Acad. of Arts and Sciences 2010, MacArthur Foundation 2010; Faculty Research Fellow, Public Econs Group, Nat. Bureau of Econ. Research 1999–2003, Research Assoc. Public Econs Program 2003–; Research Affiliate, Public Policy Group, Centre for Econ. Policy Research 2001–04, Research Fellow, Public Policy Program 2004–, Co-Dir 2009–; Research Affiliate, CESifo 2002–05, Research Fellow 2005–; Research Fellow, Inst. for Study of Labor 2009–; Alfred P. Sloan Doctoral Dissertation Fellowship 1998, Alfred P. Sloan Research Fellowship 2003; Dissertation Prize, Nat. Tax Asscn 1999, CESifo Prize in Public Econs 2002, Best Grad. Teacher Award, Econ. Grad. Students Asscn, Univ. of California, Berkeley 2002, Purvis Memorial Prize, Canadian Econ. Asscn 2006, John Bates Clark Medal, American Econ. Asscn 2009. *Publications include:* contrib. to several journals. *Address:* University of California, Department of Economics, 530 Evans Hall, #3880, Office 623, 6th floor, Berkeley, CA 94720, USA (office). *Telephone:* (510) 642-4631 (office). *Fax:* (510) 643-0413 (office). *E-mail:* saez@econ.berkeley.edu (office). *Website:* elsa.berkeley.edu/~saez (office).

SAFADI, Ayman Hussein Abdullah al-, BA, MA; Jordanian journalist and politician; *Minister of Foreign and Expatriates Affairs;* b. 1962, Az-Zarqā; ed Yarmouk Univ., Baylor Univ., USA; began professional career in journalism and communications mid 1980s; fmr CEO Abu Dhabi Media Co.; fmr Dir-Gen. Jordan Radio and Television Corpn; fmr Deputy Prime Minister, Minister of State and Spokesperson for the Govt; fmr Dir Royal Directorate of Communications and Information; Spokesperson UN Assistance Mission to Iraq 2004; Adviser to HM King Abdullah II 2008; Founder and CEO Path Arabia (political and communication strategy group), Abu Dhabi; mem. Senate 2016–17; Minister of Foreign and Expatriates Affairs 2017–; fmr Ed. several newspapers including the Jordan Times and Al-Ghad; regular commentator on Middle Eastern affairs for regional and int. media. *Address:* Ministry of Foreign and Expatriates Affairs, POB 35217, Amman 11180, Jordan (office). *Telephone:* (6) 5735150 (office). *Fax:* (6) 5735163 (office). *E-mail:* inquiry@mfa.gov.jo (office). *Website:* www.mfa.gov.jo (office).

SAFADI, Mohammad A., BBA; Lebanese business executive and politician; b. 28 March 1944, Tripoli; m. Mona Sidaoui; five c.; ed American Univ. of Beirut; Chair. Safadi Group Holding SAL; mem. Majlis al-Nuab (Nat. Ass.) 2000–; Minister of Public Works and Transport 2005–08, Acting Minister of Water and Energy 2007–08, Minister of Economy and Trade 2008–11, of Finance 2011–14; f. Safadi Foundation (non-profit NGO) 2001, currently Hon. Pres.; mem. Bd of Trustees Al Jinan Univ., Tripoli, Entrepreneurial Training Foundation, American Community School at Beirut; mem. Dean's Council, John F. Kennedy School of Govt, Harvard Univ.; Bundesverdienstkreuz (Germany). *Address:* c/o Ministry of Finance, MOF Bldg, place Riad el-Solh, Beirut, Lebanon (office). *Website:* www.mohammad-safadi.com.

SAFAR, Adel Ahmad, PhD; Syrian politician, biotechnologist and academic; b. 1953, Damascus; m.; four c.; ed Damascus Univ., Ecole Nationale Supérieur de l'Agric. et des Industries Alimentaires (ENSAIA), Nancy, France, Int. Centre for Agricultural Research in the Dry Areas; agricultural engineer, Arab Centre for the Studies of Arid Zones and Dry Lands (ACSAD) 1978–81; Deputy Lecturer, ENSAIA 1981–87; Deputy Dean for Admin. Affairs, Faculty of Agric., Damascus Univ. 1992–97, mem. Perm. Cttee for Agricultural Research 1996–2001, Dean of Faculty of Agric. 1997–2000; Deputy Rapporteur, Comm. for Scientific Agricultural Research and Veterinary Medicine, Supreme Council of Sciences 1997–2001; mem. Advisory Cttee Agricultural Productivity Admin, Productive Projects Admin 1999–2003; Sec., Damascus Univ. Br. of al-Baath Arab Socialist Party 2000–02; Head of Nat. Cttee for Man and the Biosphere Program in Syria 2000–04, Arab Network of Man and Biosphere Program in the Arab World 2001–04; Dir-Gen. ACSAD 2002–03; Minister of Agric. and Agrarian Reform 2003–11 (resgnd with rest of cabinet at Pres.'s request following popular protests); Prime Minister of Syria 3 2011–12; mem. Econ. Cttee, High Council for Investment; mem. Baath Party 1990–.

SAFAROV, Safar Ghaiurovich; Tajikistani diplomatist and politician; *First Deputy Chairman, Hizbi Halki-demokratii Tojikiston (People's Democratic Party of Tajikistan);* b. 22 May 1947, Danghara Dist; m.; five c.; ed Tech. Univ. of Tashkent; fmr Chief Engineer, cotton ginning plant, Kulob; fmr Chief-Engineer-Controller, Economy of Governmental Control, Exec. Cttee of Danghara Dist; fmr Second Sec. Komsomol Cttee, Danghara Dist; fmr Head of Propaganda and Agitation Dept and Educational Works, Komsomol Cttee of Qurghonteppa Region; fmr Instructor, Org. Dept, Party Cttee of Qurghonteppa Region; fmr Deputy Head of Org. Dept of Party Cttee, Qurghonteppa Region, Second Sec. Party Cttee and First Sec. of Soviet Dist Party Cttee; fmr Deputy Chair. Majlisi Oli's Cttee on Economy and Budget, later Chair.; Deputy of Supreme Soviet, Twelfth Convocation of Tajikistan 1990–95, People's Deputy, Majlisi Oli's First Convocation 1995–2000, Chair. Cttee on Economy, Budget, Finance and Tax, Head of Exec. Apparatus of Pres.; elected Deputy for N 26 constituency, Kurgan Tube; Amb. to Russian Fed. –2007; apptd Deputy Sec. Gen., Shanghai Cooperation Org., Beijing 2007; currently First Deputy Chair., Hizbi Halki-demokratii Tojikiston (People's Democratic Party of Tajikistan); Honoured Worker of Tajikistan; Glory Award (First Category). *Address:* Hizbi Halki-demokratii Tojikiston (People's Democratic Party of Tajikistan), 734000 Dushanbe, Xiyoboni Rudaki 107, Tajikistan (office). *Telephone:* (372) 21-05-45 (office). *Fax:* (372) 21-25-36 (office). *E-mail:* admin@hhdt.tj (office). *Website:* www.tribun.tj (office).

SAFAYEV, Sodyk Solihovich; Uzbekistani academic, politician and diplomatist; b. 3 Feb. 1954, Tashkent; m. (divorced 2001); ed Tashkent State Univ., Harvard Univ., USA; Lecturer, later Sr Lecturer, Tashkent State Univ. 1976–87; Head, Communist Party of Uzbekistan 1987–90; Sr Research Fellow, Inst. for Productive Forces, Acad. of Sciences of Uzbekistan 1990–91; Sr Consultant and Head, Dept of Int. Econ. Relations of Pres. of Uzbekistan 1991–92; First Deputy Minister of External Econ. Relations –1993; Minister of Foreign Affairs 1993–94, 2003–05, First Deputy Minister 2001–03; Amb. to Germany 1994–96, to USA 1996–2001; Rep. to Afghanistan 2001–03; Minister of Foreign Affairs 2003–05; Chair. Foreign Affairs Cttee, Senate of the Oliy Majlis 2005–09, 2010, First Deputy Chair. of Senate 2016–; Order of Mekhnat Shukhrati 2004; Memorial Order of Uzbekiston Mustakilligiga 15 yil 2006. *Address:* Senat, 100078 Tashkent, Mustaqillik maydoni 6, Uzbekistan (office). *Telephone:* (71) 238-26-38 (office). *Fax:* (71) 238-29-01 (office). *E-mail:* info@senat.uz (office); senat@tps.uz (office). *Website:* www.senat.uz (office).

SAFFA, Jacob Jusu; Sierra Leonean economist and politician; *Minister of Finance and Economic Development;* fmr Devt Economist/Evaluation Specialist, World Bank, Sierra Leone; mem. Sierra Leone People's Party (SLPP), Nat. Sec.-Gen. 2006–11, Chair. SLPP Nat. Voter Registration Cttee 2017, Chair. SLPP Election Man. Cttee 2018; Minister of Finance and Econ. Devt 2018–. *Address:* Ministry of Finance and Economic Development, George St, Freetown, Sierra Leone (office). *Telephone:* (22) 222211 (office). *E-mail:* info@mofed.gov.sl (office). *Website:* mofed.gov.sl (office).

SAFIN, Marat Mikhailovic; Russian professional tennis player (retd) and politician; b. 27 Jan. 1980, Moscow; s. of Mikhail Alexeivich Safin and Rausa Islanova; brother of professional tennis player Dinara Safina (retd 2014); started playing tennis aged six; moved to train in Valencia, Spain aged 14; turned professional 1997; winner ATP Tennis Masters Series, Toronto 2000, Paris 2000, 2002, 2004, Madrid 2004, Beijing 2004; winner US Open 2000, Australian Open

2005; retd 2009; Official, Russian Tennis Fed. 2009–; mem. Russian Olympic Cttee 2009–; mem. State Duma (Parl. (United Russia Party) for Nyzhny Novgorod region 2011–; ATP Newcomer of the Year 1998, ATP Most Improved Player 2000, Newcomer of the Year Laureus World Sports Awards, Monte Carlo 2000, inducted into Int. Tennis Hall of Fame 2016. *Address:* State Duma (Gosudarstvennaya Duma), 103265 Moscow, Okhotnyi ryad 1 (office); Tennis Federation of Russia, 101000 Moscow, st. Myasnitskaya 22/2/5, Russia. *Telephone:* (495) 692-80-00 (Duma) (office); (495) 232-13-81 (Tennis Fed.). *Fax:* (495) 203-42-58 (Duma) (office); (495) 624-64-27 (Tennis Fed.). *E-mail:* stateduma@duma.ru (office). *Website:* www.duma.gov.ru (office); www.tennis-russia.ru.

SAFONOVA, Yelena Vsevolodovna; Russian actress; b. 14 June 1956, Leningrad; d. of Vsevolod Safonov; m. 1st C. Labartona; m. 2nd Samuel Labarthe 1992 (divorced 1997); two c.; ed All-Union Inst. of Cinematography, Leningrad Inst. of Theatre, Music and Cinema; actress Mosfilm Studio 1986–; mem. of jury, Cannes Film Festival 1988. *Films include:* Looking For My Destiny 1974, Return of Butterfly 1982, Winter Cherries 1985, Dark Eyes (David di Donatello Prize 1988) 1987, Winter Cherries 2 1990, Winter Cherries 3 1995, Music for December 1995, The President and His Woman 1996, Princess on a Bean 1997, Sofia Kovalevskaya, Secret of the Earth, Strange Call, Confrontation, Sleuth, Continuation of the Clan, Taxi Blues, Butterflies, All Red, Alissa 1998, Woman's Own 1999, The Sky Will Fall 2000, Poklonnik 2001, Zayats nad bezdnoy 2006, La Traductrice 2006, Vy ne ostavite menya 2006, Kakraki 2009, Moscow Never Sleeps 2015. *Plays:* Pay forward (The Seagull-99 Award), Rumors, Dangerous Liaisons, Hen Party. *Television includes:* Schastlivyy (mini-series) 2005, V ritme tango (mini-series) 2006, Oduvanchik (film) 2011. *Address:* Taganskaya pl. 31/22, Apt. 167, 109004 Moscow, Russia. *Telephone:* (495) 278-07-36.

SAFRA, Joseph; Brazilian banker; *Chairman, Grupo Safra SA;* b. 1 Dec. 1939, Aleppo, Syria; s. of Jacob Safra and Esther Safra; m. Vicky Safra (neé Sarfatty); two s.; currently Chair. Grupo Safra SA, family business group that includes Banco Safra SA (f. 1967), Banco JS de Investimento (f. 1998), Bank Jacob Safra, Switzerland (f. 2000), Safra Nat. Bank of New York, Safra Asset Man. Corpn, Banque Safra-Luxembourg SA, Banque Safra-France SA, Banco Safra (Cayman Islands) Ltd, Safra Int. Bank and Trust Ltd, Aracruz Celulose SA; Pres. Safra Cultural Inst.; Perm. mem. Advisory Council, Albert Einstein Soc.; charged with tax corruption 2016. *Website:* www.safra.com.br (office).

SAGAWA, Masato, BA, MA, DrEng; Japanese electrical engineer and business executive; *President, Intermetallics Company Ltd;* b. 3 Aug. 1943; ed Kobe and Tohoku Univs; worked for Fujitsu Co. 1972–82; with Sumitomo Special Metals (SSM) 1982–88; Founder and Pres. Intermetallics Co. Ltd 1988–; Pres. NDFEB Corpn 2012–; consultant for several cos, including Ugimag SA (France), Showa Denko (Japan); Osaka Prize 1984, Agency Award, Minister of Science and Tech. 1985, Int. Prize for New Materials, American Physical Soc. 1986, Asahi Prize 1990, Japan Magnetics Soc. Award 1991, J. Herbert Hollomon Award, Acta Matellurgica 1999, Honda-kinen Prize 2003, Kato-kinen Prize 2006, Japan Prize (co-recipient) 2012. *Address:* Intermetallics Company Ltd, Kyodaikatsura #2211, 1-39 Goryo Ohara, Nishikyo-Ku, Kyoto, 615-8245, Japan (office). *Telephone:* (75) 392-8637 (office). *Fax:* (75) 392-8634 (office). *E-mail:* info@intermetallics.co.jp (office). *Website:* www.intermetallics.co.jp (office).

SAGDEEV, Roald Zinnurovich, DSc; Russian physicist and academic; *Distinguished University Professor and Director, East-West Space Science Center, University of Maryland;* b. 26 Dec. 1932, Moscow; m. Susan Eisenhower (grand-d. of US Pres. Dwight Eisenhower) 1990 (deceased 2008); ed Moscow State Univ.; Research Worker, Inst. of Atomic Energy, USSR Acad. of Sciences 1956–61; Head of Lab., Inst. of Nuclear Physics, Siberian Dept, Acad. of Sciences 1961–70, Inst. of High Temperature Physics of USSR Acad. of Sciences 1970–73; Prof., Novosibirsk State Univ. 1964–73; Dir Inst. of Space Research 1973–88, Sr Researcher 1988; Distinguished Univ. Prof., Univ. of Maryland, USA 1990–, Founder and Dir East-West Space Science Center 1992–; Corresp. mem. USSR (now Russian) Acad. of Sciences 1964, mem. 1968–; mem. Council of Dirs Int. Fund for Survival and Devt of Mankind 1988–; Head of Scientific-Methodical Centre for Analytical Research, Inst. of Space Research 1988; mem. NAS Swedish Royal Acad., Max Planck Soc.; USSR People's Deputy 1989–91; Order of October Revolution, Order of Red Banner and other decorations; Dr hc (Tech. Univ., Graz, Austria) 1984; Hero of Socialist Labour 1986; Lenin Prize 1984. *Address:* 2309A Computer and Space Sciences Building, University of Maryland, College Park, MD 20742, USA (office). *Telephone:* (301) 405-8051 (office). *E-mail:* rzs@umd.edu (office). *Website:* www.umdphysics.umd.edu (office).

SAĞINTAEV, Bakıtjan Äbdirulı; Kazakhstani politician; b. 13 Oct. 1963, Üşaral, Talas Dist, Jambıl Oblast, Kazakh SSR, USSR; m.; two d.; ed Kazakh S.M. Kirov State Univ. (now Kazakh Al-Farabi National Univ.); taught at Almatı Inst. of Nat. Economy 1985–88; Deputy Akim (Gov.) of Jambıl Oblast 1998–99 Deputy Chair. Republican Agency for Support of Small Businesses June–Oct. 1999; Chair. 'Fund for Devt of Small Enterprises' 1999–2001; Chair. Republican Agency for the Regulation of Natural Monopolies 2004–07; Head of the Chancellery of the Prime Minister 2007–08; Akim of Pavlodar Oblast 2008–12; Minister of Econ. Devt and Trade 2012–13; First Deputy Prime Minister 2013–16, Prime Minister 2016–19 (resgnd), also Minister of Regional Devt Jan.–Nov. 2013; First Deputy Chair. Nur Otan Xalıqtıq Demokratïyalıq Partïyası (Light of the Fatherland Nat. Democratic Party) 2012–; Kurmet Order and anniversary medals. *Publications:* several scientific works, publs on state regulation of the natural monopolies, small and medium-size business devt. *Address:* c/o Office of the Prime Minister, 010000 Nur-Sultan, Orynbor kosh. 6, Kazakhstan (office).

SAGLIO, Jean-François; French mining engineer; b. 29 July 1936, Toulon; s. of Georges Saglio; m. Odile Bertrand 1968; two s. one d.; ed Ecole Polytechnique and Ecole Supérieure des Mines, Paris; engineer, govt del., Algiers 1960–61; mining engineer, Mines de Metz 1961–66; Founder Dir Agence de Bassin Rhin-Meuse, Metz 1966–69; Adviser, Cabinet of Pres. of France 1969–73; Head, Perm. Secr. for Study of Water Problems of Paris 1971–73; Dir in charge of Pollution and Nuisance, Ministry of Environment 1973–78; Pres. Dir-Gen. Agence Foncière et Technique de la Région Parisienne 1979–81; Dir of Innovation and Valorization of Research, Elf Aquitaine, also Dir of New Projects 1981–84; Pres. Dir-Gen. INOVELF 1981–84; Asst Dir-Gen. Soc. Elf-France 1984; Asst Dir-Gen. Refineries and Distribution, Soc. Nat. Elf Aquitaine 1984; Dir-Gen. of Industry, Ministry of Industry, Posts & Telecommunications and Tourism 1987–88; Dir Soc. Roussel-Uclaf 1989–91; Vice-Pres. SCH Consultants; Pres. Admin. Council Rhin-Meuse 1992–97, ERSO 1993; Dir-Gen. CEA Industrie 1992–94; Pres. Dexter SA 1992–99, Inst. français de l'environnement 1995–98; Pres. BNFL SA 1996; Pres. AIRPARIF 2006–12; mem. Conseil Général des Mines 1991–99; mem. Bd of Dirs and Strategy Cttee, Gascogne SA; Officier, Légion d'honneur, Ordre nat. du Mérite, Croix de la Valeur militaire. *Address:* 143 rue de la Pompe, 75116 Paris, France (home). *Telephone:* 1-45-53-05-44 (home).

SAHAKYAN, Bako; Armenian government official; *President of the 'Republic of Nagornyi Karabakh';* b. 30 Aug. 1960, Stepanakert, Nagornyi Karabakh Autonomous Oblast, Azerbaijan SSR, USSR; m.; two c.; ed Stepanakert High School, Artsakh State Univ.; served in Soviet Army 1978–80; metalworker and mechanical engineer, Stepanakert Mechanical Works 1981–83; worked on restoration of historical monuments 1983–87; worked for Stepanakert council 1987–90; various roles within 'Repub. of Nagornyi Karabakh' Self Defence Forces including Deputy Commdr of External Relations and Commdr of HQ 1990–97; Asst to Minister for Home Affairs and Nat. Security 1997–99; Minister for Home Affairs 1999–2001; Head, State Dept for Nat. Security 2001–07; Pres. of 'Repub. of Nagornyi Karabakh' 2007–; Fighting Cross Order, Sparapet Vazgen Sargsyan, Order of Peter the Great (Russia). *Address:* Office of the President of the 'Republic of Nagornyi Karabakh', 75000 Stepanakert, Petrvari 20 poghots 3, Nagornyi Karabakh, Azerbaijan (office). *Telephone:* (47) 94-52-22 (office). *Fax:* (47) 94-52-22 (office). *E-mail:* ps@president.nkr.am (office). *Website:* www.president.nkr.am (office).

SAHAKYAN, Galust; Armenian philologist, teacher and politician; b. 8 April 1948, Yerevan, Armenian SSR, USSR; m.; two c.; ed Yerevan State Univ.; metalworker, Yerevan Silk Complex 1970–72; teacher, School No. 30, Deputy Headmaster, School No. 94, School No. 153, Headmaster, School No. 3 and School No. 185 1972–91; Deputy Chair., later First Deputy Chair. Exec. Cttee, Mashtots Dist Council, Yerevan 1991–96; Deputy (Hayastani Hanrapetakan Kusaktsutyun—HHK—Republican Party of Armenia), Nat. Ass. for Electoral Dist No. 32 1995–99, mem. Hanrapetutyun (Republic) faction, then of Yerkrapah (Homeland Defenders) deputy group and Miasnutyun (Unity) alliance 1999–2003, Vice-Chair. Standing Cttee on Science, Educ., Culture and Youth Affairs, mem. Miasnutyun faction, later Head of faction 2003–07, mem. Standing Cttee on State and Legal Affairs, Head of HHK faction, Deputy of Nat. Ass. (proportional electoral system) 2007–, mem. Standing Cttee on Defence, Nat. Security and Internal Affairs 2007–08, Head of HHK faction 2012–14, HHK Deputy Head, mem. HHK Exec. Body and Council, HHK Deputy Head, Pres. (Speaker), Nat. Ass. (Azgayin Zhoghov) 2014–17; YVU 'Sparapet Vazgen Sargsyan' Order 2015; 'Co-operation' Order of CIS Inter-Parl. Ass. 2015; Medal of Honour of the Nat. Ass. 2004, Vazgen Sargsyan Medal 2005, Prime Minister's Commemorative Medal 2006, Commemorative Medal 'Hon. Mem. of the Educational Centre' of P. Yavorov School No. 131 2007, Mesrop Mashtots Medal 2008, Eagle of Mountainous Armenia Golden Commemorative Medal 2008, Khachatur Abovyan Medal 2008, Fridtjof Nansen Commemorative Gold Medal 2010, Mkhitar Gosh Medal 2011, 90th Anniversary Armenian State Pedagogical Univ. Medal 2012, Garegin Nzhdeh' Medal, Ministry of Defence 2013, 'Armenian Eagle' Commemorative Gold Medal 2014, 'YVU 20 Years' Jubilee Medal 2014, Medal of Fed. Council 20th Anniversary of the FC Fed. Ass. of the Russian Fed. 2015, First Grade Medal 'For Services Contributed to Motherland' 2016. *Address:* Hayastani Hanrapetakan Kusaktsutyun (Republican Party of Armenia), 0010 Yerevan, M. Adamyan poghots 2, Armenia (office). *Telephone:* (10) 58-00-31 (office). *Fax:* (10) 50-12-59 (office). *E-mail:* hhk@hhk.am (office). *Website:* www.hhk.am (office).

SAHGAL, Nayantara, BA; Indian journalist and novelist; b. 10 May 1927, Allahabad; d. of Ranjit Sitaram Pandit and Vijaya Lakshmi Pandit; m. 1st Gautam Sahgal 1949 (divorced 1967); one s. two d.; m. 2nd E. N. Mangat Rai 1979 (died 2003); ed Wellesley Coll., USA; Adviser, English Language Bd, Sahitya Akademi (Nat. Acad. of Letters), New Delhi 1972–75; Scholar-in-Residence, holding creative writing seminar, Southern Methodist Univ., Tex. 1973, 1977; mem. Indian Del. to UN Gen. Ass. 1978; Vice-Pres. Nat. Exec., People's Union for Civil Liberties 1980–85; Fellow, Radcliffe Inst. (Harvard Univ.) 1976, Wilson Int. Center for Scholars, Washington, DC 1981–82, Nat. Humanities Center, NC 1983–84; mem. jury, Commonwealth Writers' Prize 1990, Chair. Eurasia Region 1991; mem. American Acad. of Arts and Sciences 1990; Foreign Hon. mem. American Acad. Arts and Sciences 1990; Hon. DLitt (Univ. of Leeds) 1997; Diploma of Honour, Int. Order of Volunteers for Peace, Salsomaggiore, Italy 1982, Sinclair Prize 1985, Doon Ratna Citizens' Council Prize 1992, Annie Besant Memorial Lecturer, Banaras Hindu Univ. 1992, Arthur Ravenscroft Memorial Lecturer, Univ. of Leeds 1993, Wellesley Coll. Alumni Achievement Award 2002, Pride of Doon Award 2002, Woodstock School Alumni Achievement Award 2004, Nanjanagudu Thirumalamba Award 2008, Zee TV Awadh Samman 2009. *Publications include:* Prison and Chocolate Cake 1954, A Time to Be Happy 1958, From Fear Set Free 1962, This Time of Morning 1965, Storm in Chandigarh 1969, History of the Freedom Movement 1970, The Day in Shadow 1972, A Situation in New Delhi 1977, A Voice for Freedom 1977, Indira Gandhi's Emergence and Style 1978, Indira Gandhi: Her Road to Power 1982, Rich Like Us (Sinclair Prize 1985, Sahitya Akad. Award 1987, returned in 2015) 1985, Plans for Departure 1985 (Commonwealth Writers' Prize 1987), Mistaken Identity 1988, Relationship: Extracts from a Correspondence 1994 (co-author), Point of View 1997, Before Freedom: Nehru's Letters to His Sister 1909–47 (ed.) 2000, Lesser Breeds 2003, Jawaharlal Nehru: Civilizing a Savage World 2010, Indira Gandhi: Tryst with Power 2012, The Story of India's Freedom Movement 2013, The Political Imagination 2014, Day of Reckoning 2015, Nehru's India: Essays on the Maker of a Nation 2015, When the Moon Shines by Day 2017; contribs to newspapers and magazines including India Today. *Leisure interests:* walking, reading, music. *Address:* 181B Rajpur Road, Dehra Dun, 248 009, India (home). *Telephone:* (135) 2734278 (home).

ŞAHIN, Mehmet Ali; Turkish politician; b. 16 Sept. 1950, Karabük; m.; four c.; ed Faculty of Law, Istanbul Univ.; early career as lawyer; fmr Mayor, Fatih Municipality, Istanbul; Founding mem. AK Party; mem. Büyük Millet Meclisi (Grand Nat. Ass. 1995–, Speaker 2009–11, Deputy Prime Minister and Minister of State responsible for Sport and Youth Affairs 2002–07, Minister of Justice

2007–09. *Address:* Büyük Millet Meclisi, TBMM 06543, Ankara, Turkey (office). *Telephone:* (312) 4205754 (office). *Fax:* (312) 4206943 (office). *E-mail:* mehmetali.sahin@tbmm.gov.tr (office). *Website:* www.tbmm.gov.tr (office).

SAHINGUVU, Yves, MD, MSc (Tech.); Burundian ophthalmologist and politician; b. 20 Dec. 1949, Bukeye, Muramvya Prov.; m.; two s., one d.; ed Univ. of Kinshasa, Catholic Univ. of Leuwen, Belgium; physician in pvt. practice in Kinshasa 1984–97; fmr Asst Prof., Faculty of Medicine, Univ. of Kinshasa; mem. Parl. (Union for Nat. Progress) for Muramvya 1998–2000, 2005–07, 2010–15, mem. Cttee on Good Governance; Senator 2000–05, First Vice-Pres. of Burundi 2007–10, also Chair. Cttee on the Strategic Framework for Peacebuilding for Burundi; currently Chair. SOCAR Insurance Co.; currently Pres. Asscn for Friendship Chine-Burundi; currently mem. Bd of Dirs Parl. Network on the World Bank, IMF; currently District Gov., Lions Club District 2007–08; Lions Club Int. Melvin Jones Fellow Award 2009. *Leisure interests:* tennis, swimming. *Address:* Assemblée Nationale, Bujumbura (office); 63 Avenue de la Révolution, Bujumbura, Burundi (home). *Telephone:* 76644645 (office); 79350350 (home). *E-mail:* yvesahi@yahoo.fr.

SAHL, Morton (Mort) Lyon, BS; American comedian; b. 11 May 1927, Montreal, Canada; s. of Harry Sahl; m. 1st Sue Babior 1955 (divorced 1957); m. 2nd China Lee; one c.; ed Compton Jr Coll., Univ. of Southern California; Ed. Poop from the Group; magazine writing; many night club engagements; radio and TV performances, including Comedy News TV show, Steve Allen Show, Jack Paar Show, Eddie Fisher Show, Nightline, Wide Wide World; monologues on long-playing records; in Broadway revue, The Next President 1958; one-man show Broadway 1987; Mort Sahl: The Loyal Opposition (TV) 1989; Visiting Lecturer, Claremont McKenna Coll. 2007. *Films include:* In Love and War 1958, All the Young Men 1960, Johnny Cool 1963, Doctor, You've Got to be Kidding 1967, (TV) Inside the Third Reich 1982, Nothing Lasts Forever 1984. *Publication:* Heartland 1976. *Address:* 142 Throckmorton Theatre, PO Box 1058, Mill Valley, CA 94942, USA. *Website:* www.mortsahl.com.

SAHLIN, Mona; Swedish politician; b. 9 March 1957, Sollefteå; d. of Hans Andersson; m. Bo Sahlin 1982; three c.; ed Correspondence School, Swedish Cooperative Movt 1978–80; Vice-Chair. Swedish Pupils' Asscn 1976–77; Sec. State Employees' Union 1980–82; Mem. Parl. (Riksdag) 1982–90; Minister of Employment 1990–91; Gen. Sec. Sveriges Socialdemokratiska Arbetareparti (SAP—Social Democratic Party of Sweden) 1992–94, Chair. 2007–11; Govt Rep. Bd of Swedish Sports Confed. 1983–90; Chair. Cttee on Working Hours 1982–90; mem. Bd Centre for Working Life 1982–90; Deputy Prime Minister and Minister with Special Responsibility for Equality Issues 1994–95; self-employed 1995–98; Minister, Ministry of Industry, Employment and Communications 1998–2002; Minister (Democracy and Integration Issues), Ministry of Justice 2002–04, Minister for Sustainable Devt 2004–06; nat. coordinator for 'struggle against violent extremists' 2014–.

SAID, Davlatali; Tajikistani fmr civil servant, diplomatist and politician; *First Deputy Prime Minister;* b. (Davlatali Saidov), 30 March 1970, Dushanbe, Tajik SSR, USSR; ed Tajik State Univ.; served in USSR Armed Forces 1988–89; worked in State Cttee for Investment and the Man. of State Property –2004, Chair. 2009–13; Head of Govt Cttee for Youth Affairs, Sport and Tourism 2005–07; Amb. to Japan 2007–09; First Deputy Prime Minister 2013–; Gov., Islamic Devt Bank, Asian Devt Bank; Sharaf Order. *Address:* Secretariat of the Prime Minister, 734023 Dushanbe, Xiyoboni Rudaki 80, Tajikistan (office). *Telephone:* (372) 21-18-71 (office). *Fax:* (372) 21-51-10 (office).

SAID, HH Sayyid Fahd bin Mahmoud al-; Omani government official; *Deputy Prime Minister for the Council of Ministers;* b. 1944; m. Sayyidah Berthe Fahad Al-Said; Deputy Prime Minister for Legal Affairs 1980–97, Deputy Prime Minister for the Council of Ministers 1998–. *Address:* Diwan of the Royal Court, POB 632, Muscat 113, Oman. *Telephone:* 24738711. *Fax:* 24739427.

SAÏD, Wafic Rida; Canadian (b. Syrian) business executive and philanthropist; *Chairman, Saïd Foundation;* b. 21 Dec. 1939, Damascus, Syria; s. of Dr Rida Said; m. Rosemary Thompson; one s. one d. (and one s. deceased); ed Collège de Notre Dame de Jamhour, Lebanon and at Inst. of Banking, London, UK; began banking career at UBS, Geneva 1962; f. TAG System Construction for design and construction projects in Saudi Arabia 1969; became Saudi Arabian citizen 1981; f. Said Holdings Ltd 1987 and Sagitta Asset Man. (Bermuda) Ltd 1995; mem. Bd Banque Libano-Française, Oxford Univ. Court of Benefactors; Trustee, Said Business School Foundation; apptd Amb. and Perm. Del. of Saint Vincent and the Grenadines to UNESCO 1996, Amb. to the Holy See 2012; f. Saïd Foundation 1982, now Chair.; Foundation Fellow, Somerville Coll. Oxford; Hon. Fellow, Trinity Coll. Oxford; Grand Commdr, Ordre de Mérite du Cèdre (Lebanon), Ordre Chérifien (Morocco); Sheldon Medal, Univ. of Oxford 2003. *Leisure interests:* music, architecture and art. *Address:* Saïd Foundation, 24 Queen Anne's Gate, London, SW1H 9AA, England. *Telephone:* (20) 7593-5420. *Fax:* (20) 7593-5429. *E-mail:* admin@saidfoundation.org. *Website:* www.saidfoundation.org; www.waficsaid.com.

SAÏD HASSANE, El-Anrif, PhD; Comoran diplomatist and politician; b. Fassi, Mitsamiouli; ed univ. in Jordan, Univ. Paris-IV (Sorbonne), France; Political Counsellor, Embassy in Paris 2007–13; Minister of External Relations and Co-operation, with responsibility for the Diaspora, and for Francophone and Arab Relations 2013–15; mem. Bd of Dirs Rassemblement des Mitsamiouliens, Paris. *Address:* c/o Ministry of External Relations and Co-operation, BP 428, Moroni, Comoros (office).

SAÏD PANGUINDJI, Dominique; Central African Republic magistrate and politician; *Government Spokesperson;* fmr magistrate; fmr Attorney-Gen., Bangui Court of Appeal; fmr Chef de cabinet, Ministry of Public Security; Central African Repub. Del. to VII Congress of Italian Ministry of Justice, Rome 2012; Minister of Public Security, Emigration and Immigration Jan.–Oct. 2015, also Govt Spokesperson 2015–, Minister of Justice Oct. 2015–16.

SAIDENOV, Anvar Galimullaevich, MS; Kazakhstani economist, banking executive and fmr central banker; b. 19 Sept. 1960; ed Moscow State Univ. M. G. Lomonsov, Russia, School of Oriental and African Studies, Univ. of London, UK; Researcher, Dzhambul Irrigation and Civil Engineering Inst. 1982–84, Prof. of Econ. Theory 1987–93; Consultant, EBRD, London 1993–96; Deputy Gov. Nat. Bank of Kazakhstan 1996–98; Exec. Dir State Cttee on Investments 1998–99; Chair. Nat. Agency on Investment Jan.–Aug. 1999; Vice-Minister of Finance 1999–2000; Chair. Man. Bd Halyk Savings Bank of Kazakhstan 2000–02, Acting Chair. then Chair. Bd of Dirs Jan.–June 2002; First Deputy Gov., Nat. Bank of Kazakhstan 2002–04, Gov. 2004–09; Chair. Man. Bd BTA Bank 2009–11, Chair. Bd of Dirs 2011–13; Chair. Supervisory Bd SB Capital LLC 2013–16, Chair. Sky Bridge Invest (subsidiary) 2013–16; Chair. Almaty International Airport 2014–16; mem. Bd of Dirs Bank RBK 2012–, Halyk Savings Bank of Kazakhstan 2014–; Order of the First Pres. of the Repub. of Kazakhstan Nursultan Nazarbayev 2006.

SAIF, HE Abdulla Hassan; Bahraini banker and government official; *Vice-Chairman, Islamic Bank of Asia;* b. 10 March 1945, Muharraq; ed Inst. of Cost and Man. Accountants, UK, IMF Inst.; joined Bahrain Petroleum Co. as apprentice, 1957, served in various depts –1971; Head of Finance and Admin., Civil Aviation Directorate 1971–74; Deputy Dir-Gen. Bahrain Monetary Agency 1974–77, Dir-Gen. 1977, fmr Gov.; Chair. Gulf Int. Bank BSC; Minister of Finance and Nat. Economy 1999–2005; Econ. Affairs Adviser to Prime Minister 2005–; Chair. then Vice-Chair. Islamic Bank of Asia 2005–; mem. Bd of Dirs Gulf Air Co., Org. for Social Insurance, Civil Service Pension Bd; Alt. Gov. IMF; Fellow, Chartered Inst. of Man. Accountants, UK; Dr hc (DePaul Univ., USA) 2002. *Address:* Islamic Bank of Asia, 45th Floor, West Tower, Bahrain Financial Harbour, PO Box 1317, Manama, Bahrain (office). *Telephone:* 1710 2050 (office). *Fax:* 1710 4990 (office). *Website:* www.islamicbankasia.com (office).

SAIF, Linda J., BA, MS, PhD; American veterinary microbiologist and academic; *Distinguished University Professor, College of Veterinary Medicine, Ohio State University;* ed Coll. of Wooster, Ohio State Univ.; Postdoctoral Fellow, Ohio Agricultural Research and Devt Center, Ohio State Univ., Wooster 1976–79, Asst Prof. 1979–85, Assoc. Prof. 1985–90, Prof. 1990–2002, Distinguished Univ. Prof. 2002–; mem. NAS 2003; Fellow, AAAS 1995; Hon. Diplomate, American Coll. of Veterinary Microbiologists 1990; Dr hc (Ghent Univ., Belgium) 2003; Honors Scholarship and Honors in Biology, Coll. of Wooster 1965–69, Grad. Research Fellowships, Dept of Molecular Biology, Case Western Reserve Univ. 1969–70, Dept of Microbiology, Ohio State Univ. 1972–76, Invited Distinguished Visiting Prof., Coll. of Veterinary Medicine, Univ. of Guelph 1987, Beecham Labs Award for Research Excellence, Coll. of Veterinary Medicine, Ohio State Univ. 1989, Distinguished Sr Scientist Research Award, OARDC, Ohio State Univ. 1992, Fulbright Scholar, Inst. of Virology, INTA, Buenos Aires, Argentina 1992, Univ. Distinguished Scholar Award, Ohio State Univ. 1995, Distinguished Veterinary Immunologist Award, American Asscn of Veterinary Immunologists 1995, Impact Awards Honoree, AARP Magazine 2005, Wolf Prize in Agric. 2015. *Publications include:* 42 book chapters and more than 220 papers in professional journals. *Address:* Food Animal Health Research Program, Ohio Agricultural Research and Development Center, Ohio State University, 1680 Madison Avenue, Wooster, OH 44691 (office); College of Veterinary Medicine, Ohio State University, 1900 Coffey Road, Columbus, OH 43210, USA (office). *Telephone:* (330) 263-3742 (office). *Fax:* (330) 263-3677 (office). *E-mail:* saif.2@osu.edu (office). *Website:* vet.osu.edu/saif-linda-j (office); oardc.osu.edu/lsaiflab (office); cmib.osu.edu (office).

SAIFULLAH KHAN, Javed, BA, MBA; Pakistani business executive; ed Carnegie Mellon Univ., Univ. of Pittsburgh, USA; joined Saif Group of Cos 1973, apptd Chair. Saif Holdings 1990, holding co. of Saif Group consisting of interests in telecommunications, information tech., cement and textiles, including Pakistan Mobile Communications Pvt. Ltd, Saif Telecom Ltd, Transworld Assocs Pvt. Ltd, Saif Textile Mills Ltd; Sr Adviser Galen Capital Group LLC, USA; mem. Bd of Dirs, Pakistan International Airlines Corpn 2003–, Pakistan Mobile Communications Ltd (Mobilink), Habib Bank Ltd; mem. Exec. Cttee Pakistan Petroleum Exploration and Production Cos; fmr mem. Bd of Investment, Govt of Pakistan; fmr Chair. Cen. Man. Cttee, All Pakistan Textile Mills Asscn; fmr mem. Task Force, Information Tech. and Telecommunication Advisory Bd, Ministry of Science and Tech.; Sitara I Imtiaz 2007. *Address:* c/o Saif Group, Kulsum Plaza, 42 West, Jinnah Aveneu, Blue Area3rd Floor, City Centre, Plot No-40, Main Bank Road, Saddar, Islamabad 44000, Pakistan.

SAIGOL, Mian Naseem; Pakistani business executive; *Chairman, Pak Electron Ltd;* s. of M. Yousuf Saigol; Chair. Saigol Group of Companies, conglomerate with interests in automobiles, eng, power, information tech., Chair. Kohinoor Energy Ltd, Pak Electron Ltd, Kohinoor Industries Ltd, Azam Textile Mills Ltd, Saritow Spinning Mills Ltd, Kohinoor Power Co.; est. Union Bank 1991; mem. Commonwealth Business Council, mem. Bd of Dirs 2006–08; fmr Pres. Faisalabad Chamber of Commerce and Industry, fmr Vice-Pres. Lahore Chamber of Commerce and Industry. *Address:* Pak Electron Ltd, 17 Aziz Avenue, Canal Bank, Gulberg V, Lahore (office); Kohinoor Energy Ltd, Near Tablighi Ijtima, Raiwind Bypass, Lahore, Pakistan. *Telephone:* (42) 5717364-5 (PEL) (office); (42) 35392317 (office). *Fax:* (42) 5715105 (PEL) (office); (42) 35393415 (office). *Website:* www.pel.com.pk (office); www.kel.com.pk (office).

SAIKHANBILEG, Chimediin, LLM; Mongolian politician; b. 1969, Dornod; ed Univ. of Humanities of Moscow, Russia, Nat. Univ. of Mongolia, George Washington Univ., USA; Officer, Mongolian Youth Fed. 1991, Sec. and Chair, Ulan Bator city br. 1991–97, Pres., Mongolian Youth Fed. 1997–2002; mem. Mongolian Great Khural (Parl.) 1996–2000, 2008–, Leader of Democratic Party caucus 2008–12; Minister for Enlightenment 1998–99; Dir, E & T Law Firm 2002–04; Chief, Information, Communication and Tech. Agency 2004–08; Press Spokesperson, Govt of Mongolia 2004; Chief of Cabinet Secr. 2012–14; Prime Minister 2014–16; Polar Star Order 2006, Order of Red Banner of Labour 2011. *Address:* c/o Prime Minister's Office, State Palace, Sükhbaataryn Talbai 6, Ulan Bator, Mongolia (office). *E-mail:* saikhanbileg@parliament.mn (office). *Website:* www.saikhanbileg.mn.

SAINSBURY, Keith J., BS, PhD; New Zealand marine research scientist; *Professor of Marine Systems Management, University of Tasmania;* b. 22 Feb. 1951, Christchurch; ed Univ. of Canterbury; research scientist, NZ Ministry of Agric. and Fisheries 1975–76; research scientist, CSIRO, Australia 1977–78, project leader and Man. Australian Tropical Fisheries Resources 1978–79, Man. Pelagic Fisheries Resources Program and Multi-Div. Program for Design and Evaluation of Marine Man. Strategies 1990–97, Man. Multiple Use Man. of

Exclusive Econ. Zone program 1997–2002, Sr Prin. Research Scientist and Program Leader, Div. of Marine Research 2002–06; Prof. of Marine Systems Management, Univ. of Tasmania 2006–; mem. Bd of Commrs Australian Fisheries Man. Authority 2004–, Bd Fisheries Research and Devt Corpn 2008–12; Pres. SainSolutions, Tasmania, Dir SainSolutions Pty Ltd 2006; Vice-Chair. Marine Stewardship Council, mem. Tech. Advisory Bd; Award for Outstanding Design and Production of an Australian Book, Australian Book Publrs' Asscn 1985, Japan Prize for contrib. to understanding of shelf ecosystems and their sustainable utilization 2004, Swedish Seafood Award in the Sustainable Fisheries for contrbiution to the Ecosystem Approach to Fishery Management 2011. *Publications:* Continental Shelf Fishes of Northern and Northwestern Australia (co-author) 1985; contrib. numerous chapters in books and articles in journals including Science and Journal of Marine Science. *Address:* Institute for Marine and Antarctic Studies, 15-21 Nubeena Crescent, Taroona, Tasmania 7053, Australia (office). *Telephone:* (3) 6229-1767 (office). *E-mail:* ksainsbury@netspace .net.au (home). *Website:* www.utas.edu.au/profiles/staff/imas/Keith-Sainsbury (office).

SAINSBURY, (Richard) Mark, DPhil, FBA; British academic; *Professor of Philosophy, University of Texas;* b. 2 July 1943, London, England; s. of Richard Eric Sainsbury and Freda Margaret Horne; m. 1st Gillian McNeill Rind 1969 (divorced); one s. one d.; m. 2nd Victoria Goodman 2000; ed Sherborne School, Corpus Christi Coll., Oxford; Radcliffe Lecturer in Philosophy, Magdalen Coll., Oxford 1968–70; Lecturer in Philosophy, St Hilda's Coll., Oxford 1970–73; Radcliffe Lecturer in Philosophy, Brasenose Coll., Oxford 1973–75; Lecturer in Philosophy, Univ. of Essex 1975–78, Bedford Coll., Univ. of London 1978–84, King's Coll., London 1984–87, Reader 1987–89, Stebbing Prof. of Philosophy 1991–2003; Prof. of Philosophy, Univ. of Texas at Austin 2002–; Ed. Mind 1990–2000; Radcliffe Fellow 1987–88; Fellow, King's Coll., London 1994, British Acad. 1998; Leverhulme Sr Research Fellow 2000–02; Hon. Fellow, Corpus Christi Coll., Oxford 2013. *Publications:* Russell 1979, Paradoxes 1988 (3rd edn 2009), Logical Forms 1991 (2nd edn 2001), Departing From Frege 2002, Reference Without Referents 2005, Fiction and Fictionalism 2009, Seven Puzzles of Thought (with Michael Tye) 2012, Thinking About Things 2018. *Leisure interest:* baking bread. *Address:* Department of Philosophy, WAG 403A, 1 University Station, University of Texas, Austin, TX 78712, USA (office). *Telephone:* (512) 417-5433 (office). *E-mail:* marksainsbury@austin.utexas.edu (office). *Website:* www .marksainsbury.net (home).

SAINSBURY OF PRESTON CANDOVER, Baron (Life Peer), cr. 1989, of Preston Candover in the County of Hampshire; **John Davan Sainsbury,** KG, MA; British business executive; b. 2 Nov. 1927, London; s. of A. J. (later Baron) Sainsbury and Drury Lane; m. Anya Linden 1963; two s. one d.; ed Stowe School and Worcester Coll., Oxford; Dir J Sainsbury Ltd 1958–92, Vice-Chair. 1967–69, Chair., CEO 1969–92, Pres. 1992–; f. Linbury Trust 1973; Chair. Anglo-Israel Asscn 2001–; Dir Royal Opera House, Covent Garden 1969–85 (Chair. 1987–91), The Economist 1972–80, Royal Opera House Trust 1974–84, 1987–97; Chair. Friends of Covent Garden 1969–81, Benesh Inst. of Choreology 1986–87; Vice-Pres. Contemporary Arts Soc. 1984–96, Vice-Patron 1998–2000; Chair. Rambert School Devt Cttee, Rambert School of Ballet and Contemporary Dance 2002–03, Rambert School Steering Cttee 2005–09, Rambert School Trust 2005–10; Dir Centre for Policy Studies 2009–12, Friends of Nelson Mandela Children's Fund 1996–2000; mem. Council, Retail Consortium 1975–79, Pres. 1993–97; mem. Nat. Cttee for Electoral Reform 1976–85; Fellow, Inst. of Grocery Distribution 1973; Gov. Royal Ballet School 1965–76, 1987–91, Royal Ballet 1987– (Chair. 1995–); Trustee Nat. Gallery 1976–83, Westminster Abbey Trust 1977–83, Tate Gallery 1982–83, Rhodes Trust 1984–98, Prince of Wales Inst. of Architecture 1992–96, Said Business School Foundation 2003–; mem. Bd of Trustees, Dulwich Picture Gallery 1994–2000, Patron 2004–; Jt Hon. Treas., European Movement 1972–75, Hon. Fellow, Worcester Coll., Oxford 1982, British School, Rome 2002, Hon. Bencher, Inner Temple 1985, Hon. Vice-Pres. Royal Opera House 2009–; Hon. DSc (London) 1985; Hon. DLitt (South Bank) 1992; Hon. LLD (Bristol) 1993; Albert Medal, RSA 1989, Hadrian Award, World Monuments Fund 2000, Sheldon Medal, Univ. of Oxford 2010, Presidential Award, Gjergj Kastrioti-Skenderbeg 2014. *Address:* c/o 33 Holborn, London, ECIN 2HT, England. *Telephone:* (20) 7695-6000. *Website:* www.john-sainsbury.com.

SAINSBURY OF TURVILLE, Baron (Life Peer), cr. 1997, in the County of Buckinghamshire; **David John Sainsbury,** BA, MBA, FRS; British business executive and fmr government official; *Chancellor, University of Cambridge;* b. 24 Oct. 1940; s. of Sir Robert Sainsbury and Lisa Ingeborg (née Van den Bergh); m. Susan Carroll Reid 1973; three d.; ed King's Coll., Cambridge and Columbia Univ., New York, USA; joined J Sainsbury 1963, Finance Dir 1973–90, Deputy Chair. J Sainsbury PLC 1988–92, Chair. and CEO 1992–98; Parl. Under-Sec. of State for Science and Innovation 1998–2006; mem. Cttee of Review of Post Office (Carter Cttee) 1975–77; Trustee, Social Democratic Party (SDP) 1982–90; mem. Gov. Body, London Business School 1985–98 (Chair. 1991–98); Visiting Fellow, Nuffield Coll., Oxford 1987–95; Chancellor Univ. of Cambridge 2011–; mem. IPPR Comm. 1995–97; Chair. Transition Bd, Univ. for Industry 1998–99; Chair., Inst. for Govt 2009–; f. Gatsby Charitable Foundation 1967 (one of Sainsbury Family Charitable Trusts); mem. (Labour), House of Lords 1997–, Leave of Absence 2013–; Hon. FREng 1994; Hon. LLD (Cambridge) 1997; Dr hc (Oxford), (Manchester), (Imperial Coll., London), (Rockefeller Univ.); Andrew Carnegie Medal of Philanthropy (on behalf of Sainsbury family), Carnegie Inst. 2003. *Publications:* Government and Industry: A New Partnership 1981, Wealth Creation and Jobs (with C. Smallwood) 1987, A Race to the Top: a Review of Government's Science and Innovation Policies 2007, Progressive Capitalism: How to Achieve Economic Growth, Liberty and Social Justice 2013. *Address:* House of Lords, London, SW1A 0PW, England. *Telephone:* (20) 7072-4405. *E-mail:* tracy.mattinson@gayfere.org.uk.

ST ARNAUD, Bill, BEng, MEng, PEng; Canadian computer engineer; b. 1951; ed Carleton Univ. School of Eng; Consultant and Chief Engineer, Switzer Engineer-ing 1975–79; Project Man., Motorola, Inc. 1979–81; Founder and Pres. TSA Proforma 1981–88; consultant for several high-tech start-ups 1988–92; Project Dir, Vision 2000 1992–93; Sr Dir of Network Projects, CANARIE Inc. 1993–2009, led devt, coordination and implementation of world's first nat. optical R&D Internet network, CA*net3, Chair. CA*net 3 Tech Applications Cttee 1994, then Chief Architect of CA*net4; currently consultant; mem. various cttees and bds, including Bd of Trustees for The Internet Society (ISOC), NomComm Cttee for Internet Corpn for Assigned Names and Numbers (ICANN), UKlight Steering Cttee, GLORIAD Policy Cttee, Neptune Canada Oversight Cttee, Global Lambda Integrated Facility Policy Cttee, Steering Cttee SPIE Tech. Group on Optical Networks 2000–, amongst others; NSF Reviewer; Ed. CAnet-3-NEWS@canarie.ca; mem. Editorial Bd Optical Networking Magazine; Globecomm Fellow, Center for Global Communications 2000; World Tech. Award in Communication Tech., The World Tech. Network 2005. *Publications:* numerous scientific papers in profes-sional journals. *E-mail:* bill.st.arnaud@gmail.com (home). *Website:* billstarnaud .blogspot.com.

SAINT-GEOURS, Frédéric; French civil servant and business executive; *Vice-President, Conseil national de l'industriel;* b. 20 April 1950, Clamart (Hauts-de-Seine); s. of Jean Saint-Geours, fmr Pres. Comm. des opérations de bourse; m. Eva Bettan; three c.; ed Institut d'Etudes Politiques and Ecole Nationale d'Admin, Paris; joined Ministry of Finance 1975, worked as forecaster for Finance Minister Jacques Delors, held series of govt posts in finance, including adviser to Pres. of Nat. Ass., finally Chief Tech. Adviser to Sec. of State for the Budget, Henri Emmanuelli 1984–86; Deputy Chief Financial Dir PSA Peugeot-Citroën 1986–88, Financial Dir 1988–90, Deputy Dir-Gen. Automobiles Peugeot 1990, oversaw Jean Todt's successful Peugeot 905 sports car campaigns 1991, 1992, 1993, Dir-Gen. Automobiles Peugeot 1998–2007; Chair. Union des Industries et Métiers de la Métallurgie 2007–14; Pres. Groupement des fédérations industrielles (Group of Industrial Federations) 2013–14; Chair. Supervisory Bd SNCF 2014–; Vice-Pres. Conseil national de l'industriel 2016–. *E-mail:* contact.cni@finances.gouv.fr (office). *Website:* www.entreprises.gouv.fr/conseil-national-industrie/cni (office).

SAINT-JACQUES, Guy; Canadian diplomatist; m. Sylvie Cameron; posting to Embassy in Washington, DC 1994, Dir-Gen. Personnel Man. Bureau, Dept of Foreign Affairs 2003, Deputy High Commr to UK 2003–06, Acting High Commr 2006–08, Deputy Head of Mission, Embassy in Washington, DC 2008–10, Chief Negotiator and Amb. for Climate Change 2010–12, Amb. to China 2012–16; Sr Fellow China Inst., Univ. of Alberta; Dir GS + J Groupe-conseil Inc. 2017–.

SAINT MALO DE ALVARADO, Isabel, MBA; Panamanian diplomatist and politician; *Vice-President and Minister of Foreign Affairs;* b. 27 June 1968, Panamá City; m. Omar Alvarado; two s. one d.; ed St Joseph's Univ., Nova Southeastern Univ., USA; intern, Embassy in Washington, DC 1988; worked for UNDP in Panama 1994–98, becoming Country Programme Man. and Asst Resident Rep. 2006; worked at Perm. Mission to UN, New York, becoming Alt. Amb.; ind. devt consultant, Stratego Consultores SA; Vice-Pres. and Minister of Foreign Affairs 2014–; mem. Nat. Council of Foreign Affairs of Panama, Advisory Council, Central American Inst. for Research on Fiscal Policy, Aspen Global Leadership Network; mem. bd of dirs, BBVA Bank, Fundación Democracia y Libertad, Women Corp. Dirs Asscn of Panama; Panamanian Business Execs. Asscn Woman of the Year Award 2012, Award for Promotion of Peace, Harry S. Truman Inst. 2015. *Address:* Ministry of Foreign Affairs, Edif. 26, Palacio Bolívar, Calle 3, San Felipe, Panamá 4, Panama (office). *Telephone:* 511-4100 (office). *Fax:* 511-4200 (office). *E-mail:* prensa@mire.gob.pa (office). *Website:* www.mire.gob.pa (office).

SAITO, Akihiko, PhD; Japanese engineer and business executive; m.; three s.; ed Nagoya Univ.; joined Toyota Motor Corpn 1968, responsible for several tech. assignments, including work in vibration testing, chassis design, product planning and production eng, mem. team that handled product planning work for Toyota's best-selling car, the Corolla 1980, served as Chief Engineer in devt of sixth and seventh generation Corollas, Gen. Man. Product Planning Div. 1987–91, apptd mem. Bd of Dirs 1991, Man. Dir 1996–98, Sr Man. Dir 1998–2001, Exec. Vice-Pres. 2001–05; Pres. Int. Fed. of Automotive Eng Socs 2006–08; Vice-Chair. DENSO Corpn 2005–07, Chair. 2007–09. *Leisure interests:* skiing, golf, music and art.

SAITO, Atsushi (Andy); Japanese business executive; *Chairman, KKR Japan;* ed Keio Univ.; joined Nomura Securities Co. Ltd 1963, apptd Dir 1986, Vice-Pres. 1995–98 (retd); Pres. Sumitomo Life Investment Co. Ltd 1998–2002, Chair. 2002–03; Pres. and CEO Industrial Revitalization Corpn of Japan 2003–07; apptd Pres. and CEO Tokyo Stock Exchange Group (TSE) 2007, merger between TSE and Osaka Securities Exchange, Ltd to form Japan Exchange Group, Inc. 2013, Group CEO and Rep. Exec. Officer, Japan Exchange Group, Inc. 2013–15 (retd); Chair. KKR Japan 2015–. *Address:* KKR, Yasuda Seimei Building, 2-1-1 Marunouchi, Chiyoda-ku, Tokyo 100-0005, Japan (office). *Telephone:* (3) 6268-6000 (office). *Website:* www.kkr.com (office).

SAITO, Gunzi, PhD; Japanese chemist and academic; *Professor Emeritus, Department of Chemistry, Graduate School of Science, Kyoto University;* b. 10 March 1945, Otaru, Hokkaido; s. of Nenosuke Saito and Toyo Saito; m. Atsuko Nishikawa 1971; three s.; ed Otaru Choryo High School, Hokkaido Univ.; Postdoctoral Fellow, Emory Univ., Atlanta, Georgia, USA 1973–74, Guelph Univ., Ont., Canada 1975–76; Welch Fellow Univ. of Tex., Dallas, USA 1977–78; Research Assoc., Inst. for Molecular Science, Okazaki 1979–84; Assoc. Prof., Inst. for Solid State Physics, Tokyo Univ. 1984–89; Prof., Dept of Chem., Graduate School of Science, Kyoto Univ. 1989–2008, now Prof. Emer.; mem. Science Council, Ministry of Educ., Sport and Culture 1996–2003; Inoue Award 1988, Nishina Award 1988, Japan Surface Science Award 1991, The Chemical Soc. of Japan Award 2003, Medal with Purple Ribbon Award 2009. *Publications include:* Organic Superconductors (co-author) 1998; more than 500 scientific articles on organic superconductors, organic metals and other organic functional materials. *Address:* 35-1-504 Kakinoki-cho, Nishigamo, Kita-ku, Kyoto 603-8821, Japan (home). *Telephone:* (75) 493-1046 (home). *Fax:* (75) 493-1046 (home).

SAITO, Jiro; Japanese business executive, government official and fmr diploma-tist; ed Univ. of Tokyo; joined Ministry of Finance 1959, worked in budget and tax bureaus, Vice-Minister of Finance 1993–95 (resgnd); also worked as diplomat in Germany; Pres. and CEO Tokyo Financial Exchange Inc. –2010; Pres. and CEO Japan Post Holdings Co. Ltd 2010–13, Outside Dir, Japan Post Network Co. Ltd. *Address:* c/o Japan Post Holdings Co. Ltd, 1-3-2 Kasumigaseki, Chiyoda-ku, Tokyo 100-8798, Japan.

SAITO, Katsutoshi; Japanese insurance industry executive; *Chairman and Representative Director, Dai-ichi Life Insurance Company Limited;* ed Hitotsubashi Univ., Harvard Business School Advanced Man. Program, USA; joined Dai-ichi Life Insurance Co. 1967, Gen. Man., Int. Planning Dept 1989–91, Gen. Man., Research Dept 1991–94, Dir and Gen. Man. 1994–95, Dir, Chief Gen. Man. (Corp. Planning, Public Relations) and Gen. Man., Research Dept 1995–97, Man. Dir 1997–2001, Sr Man. Dir 2001–03, Sr Man. Dir (Rep. Dir) 2003–04, Pres. 2004–10, Vice-Chair. 2010–11, Chair. 2011–; Chair. Life Insurance Asscn of Japan; mem. Bd of Dirs, Japan Cancer Soc. *Address:* Dai-ichi Life Insurance Co. Ltd, 13-1, Yurakucho 1-chome, Chiyoda-ku, Tokyo 100-8411, Japan (office). *Telephone:* (3) 3216-1211 (office). *E-mail:* info@dai-ichi-life.co.jp (office). *Website:* www.dai-ichi-life.co.jp (office).

SAITO, Tetsuo, BSc, MSc, DEng; Japanese engineer, academic and politician; b. 5 Feb. 1952, Ōchi Dist, Shimane Pref.; ed Tokyo Inst. of Tech.; joined Shimizu Corpn 1976; Visiting Fellow, Princeton Univ., USA 1986–89; mem. House of Reps for Chugoku Dist 1993–Chair. Cttee on Educ., Culture, Sports, Science and Tech.; Parl. Sec., Vice-Minister for Science and Tech. 1999–2004; Chair. Policy Research Council of New Komeito Party 2006–08; Minister of the Environment 2008–11. *Leisure interest:* swimming. *Address:* House of Representatives, 1-7-1 Nagatacho, Chiyoda-ku, Tokyo 100-0014, Japan (office). *Telephone:* (3) 3581-3111 (office). *E-mail:* webmaster@shugiin.go.jp (office). *Website:* www.shugiin.go.jp/internet/index.nsf/html/index_e.htm (office); www.saitotetsuo.com.

SAITO, Toshitsugu, BA, MBA; Japanese politician; b. 27 Dec. 1944; m.; two c.; ed Sophia Univ., Univ. of Washington; Pres. Japan Jr Chamber 1984; mem. House of Reps for Shizuoka Prefecture, 5th Electoral Dist 1986–Parl. Vice-Minister, Ministry of Posts and Telecommunications 1992, Chair. Standing Cttee on Commerce and Industry 1997, Standing Cttee on Local Admin 1999; fmr Minister of State and Dir-Gen. of Defence Agency; Dir Youth Div., Party Org. HQ, Liberal Democratic Party 1991, Dir Communications Div., Policy Research Council 1995, Dir-Gen. Information Research Bureau 1996, Deputy Chair. Diet Affairs Cttee 1996, Acting Chair. Public Relations HQ 1999, Dir-Gen. Int. Bureau 2001. *Address:* Liberal Democratic Party (Jiyu-Minshuto), 1-11-23, Nagata-cho, Chiyoda-ku, Tokyo 100-8910, Japan (office). *Telephone:* (3) 3581-6211 (office). *E-mail:* koho@ldp.jimin.or.jp (office). *Website:* www.jimin.jp (office).

SAITO, Yasuo; Japanese fmr diplomatist; b. 5 Jan. 1948, Okayama; m. Chieko Saito; two c.; ed Univ. of Tokyo; joined Ministry of Foreign Affairs 1971, positions included Dir-Gen. European Affairs Bureau; served as Amb. to UNESCO, Consul-Gen. in Atlanta, USA, Amb. to Saudi Arabia 2003, Amb. to Russia 2006–09, to France 2009–11; Outside Dir, Ajinomoto Co., Inc. 2012–; Grand Officier, Ordre nat. du Mérite 2012. *Address:* Ajinomoto Co., Inc., 15-1, Kyobashi 1-chome, Chuo-ku, Tokyo 104-8315, Japan (office). *Telephone:* (3) 5250-8111 (office). *Website:* www.ajinomoto.co.jp (office).

SAJI, Nobutada, MBA; Japanese business executive; *Chairman and CEO, Suntory Ltd;* b. 25 Nov. 1945; s. of Keizo Saji; m.; ed Keio Univ., Univ. of California, Los Angeles, USA; began career at Sony Trading Co.; joined Suntory Ltd (family business) 1974, CEO 2001–, Chair. 2009–, Pres. 2009–14, fmr Pres. Suntory Int. Corpn, USA; Chair. Advertising Council of Japan. *Leisure interest:* swimming. *Address:* Office of the Chairman, Suntory Holdings Limited, Dojimahama 2-1-40, Kita-ku, Osaka City, Osaka 530-8203, Japan (office). *Telephone:* (6) 6346-1131 (office). *Fax:* (6) 6345-1169 (office). *Website:* www.suntory.com (office).

SAJJADPOUR, Seyed Mohammad Kazem, PhD; Iranian diplomatist and academic; ed George Washington Univ., USA; Post-doctoral Fellow, Harvard Univ.; taught at Coll. of Int. Relations, Tehran Univ., Azad Univ., Nat. Defence Univ. of Iran; fmr Dir Inst. for Political and Int. Studies, Ministry of Foreign Affairs, currently Sr Faculty Member, School of International Relations (think-tank); fmr Amb. and Deputy Perm. Rep. to UN and other int. orgs, Geneva; mem. Bd of Advisers, Dialogues: Islamic World-US-The West program, New York Univ.; fmr Dir-Gen. Inst. for Political and Int. Studies (IPIS), Tehran, later Sr Fellow; currently Ed.-in-Chief Inst. for Strategic Research Journals; mem. Bd of Advisors Center for Dialogues, New York Univ. *Address:* Center for Dialogues, New York University, 194 Mercer Street, 4th Floor, New York, NY 10012, USA (office). *Telephone:* (212) 998-8693 (office). *Website:* islamuswest.org/about_Dialogues_Islam_US_West (office).

SAJJAN, Lt-Col Harjit Singh, PC; Canadian army officer (retd), police officer and politician; *Minister of National Defence;* b. Bombeli, Hoshiarpur Dist, Punjab, India; s. of Kundan Singh Sajjan and Vidya Kaur; m. Kuljit Kaur Sajjan; one s. one d.; ed Combat Training Centre, CFB Gagetown, New Brunswick; emigrated to Canada from India with family aged six; joined Army Reserve as Trooper 1989, commissioned in BC Regt (Duke of Connaught's Own) 1991, deployed with Canadian peacekeeping forces to Bosnia-Herzegovina during Operation Palladium 1997, Aide-de-Camp to Lt-Gov. of BC 2001, served as liaison officer to Afghan police with 1st Bn, Royal Canadian Regt Battle Group during Operation Medusa offensive, Kandahar 2006, apptd Officer Commanding Reconnaissance Squadron 2007, then Regimental Second-in-Command 2009, returned to Afghanistan as special adviser, Feb.–Nov. 2009, Nov. 2010–March 2011, apptd Commdr, BC Regt (Duke of Connaught's Own) 2012, attained rank of Capt. 1995, Maj. 2005, Lt-Col 2011; joined Vancouver Police Dept as detective 1999, becoming Detective-Constable with Gang Crime Unit, specializing in organized crime; mem. House of Commons for Vancouver South 2015–; Minister of Nat. Defence 2015–; mem. Liberal Party of Canada; numerous awards including Canada Forces Decoration, Meritorious Service Medal, Order of Mil. Merit. *Address:* Department of National Defence, National Defence HQ, Maj.-Gen. George R. Pearkes Bldg, 101 Colonel By Drive, Ottawa, ON K1A 0K2, Canada (office). *Telephone:* (613) 995-2534 (office). *Fax:* (613) 992-4739 (office). *E-mail:* information@forces.gc.ca (office). *Website:* www.forces.gc.ca (office); www.sajjan.ca.

SAKAGUCHI, Chikara, MD; Japanese politician; b. 1 April 1934, Mie Prefecture; ed Mie Univ.; elected mem. House of Reps (Komeito) for Tokai Dist 1976, fmr Dir Finance Cttee; Minister of Labour 1993–94, of Health, Labour and Welfare 2000–04; fmr Chair. Komeito Policy Bd, now Deputy Dir. *Address:* Komeito, 17, Minami-Motomachi, Shinjuku-ku, Tokyo 160-0012, Japan (office). *Telephone:* (3) 3353-0111 (office). *Website:* www.komei.or.jp (office).

SAKAKI, Hiroyuki, BS, MS, PhD; Japanese scientist and academic; *Professor, Institute of Industrial Science, University of Tokyo;* b. 6 Oct. 1944, Aichi; s. of Yoneichiro Sakaki and Fumiko Sakaki; m. Mutsuko Sakaki 1973; one s. four d.; ed Univ. of Tokyo; Assoc. Prof., Inst. of Industrial Science, Univ. of Tokyo 1973–87, Prof. 1987–, Prof., Research Center for Advanced Science and Tech. 1988–98; Visiting Scientist, IBM T. J. Watson Research Center (group of Dr Leo Esaki) 1976–77; Dir Quantum Wave Project (Japan's government project for Exploratory Research for Advanced Tech.) 1988–93; Dir Japan–US Jt Research Project on Quantum Transition 1994–98; Outstanding Achievement Award (jtly) 1974, Applied Physics Soc. Award 1983, Japan Applied Physics Soc. Prize 1983, 1990, Japan IBM Science Prize 1989, Hattori-Hokokai Prize 1990, Shimazu Science Prize, Outstanding Achievement Award, Inst. of Electronic Communications Engineers of Japan 1991, David Sarnoff Award, IEEE 1996, Fujiwara Prize 2000, Medal with Purple Ribbon (Japan) 2001, Esaki Award (jtly) 2004, Japan Acad. Prize (jtly) 2005. *Leisure interests:* listening to classical music, looking at paintings. *Address:* Sakaki Laboratory, Ee-403, Institute of Industrial Science, University of Tokyo, 4-6-1 Komaba, Meguro-ku, Tokyo 153-8505 (office); 1-41-5 Kagahara, Tsuzukiku, Yokohama 224, Japan (home). *Telephone:* (3) 5452-6235 (office); (45) 943-1539 (home). *E-mail:* sakaki@iis.u-tokyo.ac.jp (office). *Website:* quanta.iis.u-tokyo.ac.jp (office).

SAKAMOTO, Ryûichi, MA; Japanese composer, musician and actor; b. 17 Jan. 1952, Tokyo; m. Akiko Yano 1979; ed Shinjuku High School, Composition Dept, Tokyo Fine Arts Univ.; began composing aged 10; mem. group Yellow Magic Orchestra 1978–83; worked with David Sylvian 1982–83; solo recording artist, composer 1982–; conductor, arranger, music for Olympic Games opening ceremony, Barcelona, Spain 1992; Order of the Cavaleiro Admissão (Brazil), Ordre des Arts et des Lettres 2009; UN Environment Programme's Echo Award, Golden Pine Award for Lifetime Achievement, Int. Samobor Film Music Festival 2013. *Film appearances:* Merry Christmas Mr Lawrence 1982, The Last Emperor 1987, New Rose Hotel 1998. *Film soundtracks include:* Merry Christmas Mr Lawrence (BAFTA Award 1983) 1982, Daijôbu, mai furendo 1983, Koneko monogatari 1986, The Last Emperor (with David Byrne and Cong Su, Academy Award, Golden Globe Award, Grammy Award) 1987, Ôritsu uchûgun Oneamisu no tsubasa 1987, The Laser Man (title song) 1988, The Handmaid's Tale 1990, The Sheltering Sky (Golden Globe Award) 1990, Tacones lejanos 1991, Topâzu 1992, Wuthering Heights 1992, Wild Palms (TV series) 1993, Little Buddha 1993, Rabbit Ears: Peachboy 1993, Wild Side 1995, Snake Eyes 1998, Love is the Devil 1998, Gohatto 1999, Poppoya (theme) 1999, Femme Fatale 2002, Alexei to izumi 2003, Derrida 2003, Los Rubios 2003, Life Is Journey 2003, Appurushîdo 2004, Original Child Bomb 2004, Hoshi ni natta shonen 2005, Zarin 2005, Tony Takitani 2007, Silk 2007, The Revenant (with Carsten Nicolai) 2015. *Recordings include:* albums: Thousand Knives 1978, B-2 Unit 1980, Hidariudeno (A Dream Of The Left Arm) 1981, Coda 1983, Ongaku Zukan (A Picture Book Of Music) 1984, Illustrated Musical Encyclopedia 1984, Esperanto 1985, Miraiha Yarô (A Futurist Chap) 1986, Media Bahn Live 1986, Oneamisno Tsubasa (The Wings Of Oneamis) 1986, Neo Geo 1987, Playing The Orchestra 1988, Tokyo Joe 1988, Sakamoto Plays Sakamoto 1989, Grupo Musicale 1989, Beauty 1989, Heartbeat 1991, Neo Geo (with Iggy Pop) 1992, Sweet Revenge 1994, Soundbites 1994, Hard To Get 1995, 1996 1996, Music For Yohji Yamamoto 1997, Smoochy 1997, Discord 1998, Love Is The Devil 1998, Raw Life 1999, Intimate 1999, Space 1999, BTTB 1999, Gohatto 1999, Complete Index of Gut 1999, Cinemage 2000, Casa 2002; singles: Bamboo Houses (with David Sylvian) 1982, Forbidden Colours (with David Sylvian) 1983, Field Work (with Thomas Dolby) 1986, Risky 1988, We Love You 1991, Moving On 1994, Prayer/Salvation 1998, Anger 1998, O Grande Amor 2001, World Citizen 2003, Sala Santa Cecillia 2005, Revep 2006, Koko 2008, Nord 2009, Three 2013. *Website:* www.sitesakamoto.com.

SAKANE, Masahiro; Japanese business executive; *Counselor, Komatsu Ltd;* b. 7 Jan. 1941, Shimane Pref.; ed Osaka City Univ.; joined Komatsu Ltd 1963, COO Komatsu Dresser Co. 1990–94, Man. Dir 1994–97, Exec. Man. Dir 1997–99, Exec. Vice-Pres. 1999–2001, Pres. 2001–07, CEO 2003–07, Chair. and Rep. Dir 2007–10, Chair. 2010–13, Counselor 2013–; Vice-Chair. Japan Construction Equipment Mfrs Asscn 2001–04, apptd Chair. 2004; mem. Bd of Exec. Dirs Keidanren (Japan Business Fed.), Chair. Sub-Saharan Africa Cttee 2003, Deputy Chair. Japan-Russia (NIS) Business Cooperation Cttee 2003, apptd Vice-Chair. 2010; mem. Bd of Dirs Tokyo Electron Ltd 2008–16, Nomura Holdings, Inc. 2008–, Asahi Glass Co. Ltd 2011–, Takeda Pharmaceutical Co. Ltd 2014–, Kajima Corpn 2015–; Japan Inst. of Invention and Innovation Nat. Commendation for Invention 2003. *Address:* Komatsu Ltd, 2-3-6 Akasaka, Minato-ku, Tokyo 107-8414, Japan (office). *Telephone:* (3) 5561-2687 (office); (3) 5561-2616 (office). *Fax:* (3) 3505-9662 (office). *E-mail:* info@komatsu.com (office). *Website:* www.komatsu.com (office).

SAKINE, Ahmat Awad; Chadian politician and diplomatist; m. Mariam Sakine; Dir-Gen. of the Treasury –2004; Minister of the Economy and Finance 2004–05; Amb. to Belgium 2011–13. *Address:* Ministry of External Relations and African Integration, BP 746, N'Djamena, Chad (office). *Telephone:* 22-51-80-50 (office). *Fax:* 22-51-45-85 (office). *E-mail:* tchaddiplomatie@gmail.com (office). *Website:* www.tchad-diplomatie.org (office).

SAKMANN, Bert, BA, MD, PhD; German physician and academic; *Inaugural Scientific Director and Research Group Leader, Max Planck Florida Institute;* b. 12 June 1942, Stuttgart; s. of Berthold Sakmann and Annemarie Schaeffer Sakmann; m. Dr Christiane Wulfert 1970; two s. one d.; ed Univ. of Tübingen, Univ. of Munich, Univ. Hosp., Munich, Univ. of Göttingen; Research Asst, Max-Planck-Institut für Psychiatrie, Munich 1969–70; British Council Fellow, Dept of Biophysics, Univ. Coll., London 1971–73; Research Asst, Max-Planck-Institut für biophysikalische Chemie, Univ. of Göttingen 1974–79, Research Assoc., Membrane Biology Group 1979–82, Head, Membrane Physiology Unit 1983–85, Dir 1985–87, Prof. Dept of Cell Physiology 1987–89, Dir Dept of Cell Physiology, Max-Planck-Institut für medizinische Forschung, Heidelberg 1989–2008, apptd Research Group Leader 2008, apptd Inaugural Scientific Dir and Research Group Leader, Max Planck Florida Inst. for Neuroscience 2012; Prof. of Physiology, Univ. of Heidelberg 1990–; mem. Akademie der Naturforscher Leopoldina, Halle, Münchner Akademie der Wissenschaften, Göttinger Akademie der Wissenschaften, Heidelberger Akademie der Wissenschaften; Foreign mem. NAS 1993, Royal Soc. (UK) 1994; Orden Pour le Mérite; Dr hc (Univ. of Alicante), (Univ. of Liverpool), (Univ. of Bordeaux), (Univ. of Munich), (Univ. of Colorado), (Univ. College London), (Weizmann-Institute), (Univ. of Melbourne), (Mahidol Univ.,

Bangkok); Nernst Prize 1977, Feldberg Prize 1979, Magnes Award 1981, Spencer Prize 1983, Adolf Fick Prize 1984, Zottermann Prize 1984, Gross-Horwitz Prize 1986, Leibniz Prize 1986, Louis Jeantet Prize 1988, Gairdner Prize 1989, Ernst Hellmut Vits Prize 1990, Carus Medal 1991, Harvey Prize 1991, Gerard Prize 1991, Landesforschungspreis (Ministerium für Wissenschaft und Kunst, Baden-Württemberg) 1991, Nobel Prize for Medicine (jtly) 1991 (for discoveries about single-ion channels in cells), Int. Ellis Island Medal of Honor 2015. *Publications include:* The Visual System: Neurophysiology, Biophysics and Their Clinical Applications 1972 (contrib.), Advances in Pharmacology and Therapeutics 1978 (contrib.), Single Channel Recording 1983 (co-author), Membrane Control of Cellular Activity 1986 (contrib.), Calcium and Ion Channel Modulation 1988 (contrib.), Neuromuscular Junction 1989 (contrib.). *Leisure interests:* music, reading, tennis, skiing. *Address:* Max Planck Florida Institute, One Max Planck Way, Jupiter, FL 33458, USA (office). *Telephone:* (561) 972-9400 (office). *Fax:* (561) 972-9001 (office). *E-mail:* bert.sakmann@maxplanckflorida.org (office); bsakmann@neuro.mpg.de (office). *Website:* www.maxplanckflorida.org (office); www.neuro.mpg.de (office).

SAKO, Soumana, PhD, MPA; Malian politician, civil servant and international civil servant; b. 23 Dec. 1950, Nyamina; s. of Sayan Sako and Djeneba Traore; m. Cisse Toure; two s. two d.; ed Univ. of Pittsburgh, Pa, USA, Ecole Nationale d'Admin du Mali; Staff mem. Gen. Inspectorate, Office of the Pres. of Repub. of Mali 1974; Admin. and Finance Man., Operation Puits Project 1975–76; Staff mem. Ministry of Industrial Devt and Tourism 1981; Adviser Ministry of Foreign Affairs and Int. Co-operation 1981–82; Sr Adviser Ministry of Planning and Econ. Man. 1982–84; Dir of Sr Staff, Ministry of State-Owned Enterprises 1985–87; Minister of Finance and Commerce Feb.–Aug. 1987; Deputy Controller-Gen. Office of the Pres. 1988–89; UNDP official serving in Cen. African Repub. 1989–91, Sr Economist for Madagascar and Comoros Islands 1993–97; Prime Minister of Mali 1991–92; Prof. of Devt Econs and Public Finance, Univ. of Mali 1997–2000; int. consultant 1998–; Exec. Sec. African Capacity Bldg Foundation, Harare 2000–08; presidential cand. 2012; Commdr, Nat. Order of Mali 2000, Grand-Officer 2005; AFGRAD Distinguished Alumnus 1992, Sennen Andriamirado Prize of Excellence 2000. *Publication:* Determinants of Public Policy—A Comparative Analysis of Public Expenditure Patterns in African States Trade Related Capacity Building. *Leisure interests:* soccer, chess, gardening. *Address:* Villa f4 bis 48, Sema Gexco Bamako, Mali (home); BP 433, Bamako, Mali. *Telephone:* 236196 (home). *Fax:* 229748.

SAKOVÁ, Denisa, PhD; Slovak politician; *Minister of the Interior;* b. 17 April 1976, Nitra, Slovak Socialist Repub., Czechoslovak Socialist Repub.; divorced; one c.; ed Bratislava Univ. of Econs; Consultant, DELTA ES 1998–2001; Sr Consultant, Cap Gemini Ernst & Young, Bratislava and Berlin 2001–03; Dir of Application Div., E.ON IT Slovakia, sro 2003–07, Head, Service Coordination Dept 2011–12; Gen. Dir, Informatics, Telecommunications and Security Dept, Ministry of the Interior 2007–10, Sec.-Gen. 2012–16, Sec. of State 2016–18, Minister of the Interior 2018–; mem. Smer-Sociálna Demokracia (Direction-Social Democracy). *Address:* Ministry of the Interior, Pribinova 2, 812 72 Bratislava, Slovakia (office). *Telephone:* (2) 5094-1111 (office). *Fax:* (2) 5094-4397 (office). *Website:* www.minv.sk (office).

SAKSKOBURGGOTSKI, Simeon; Bulgarian politician and fmr King of Bulgaria; b. 16 June 1937, Sofia; s. of King Boris III and Queen Joanna; m. Margarita Gómez y Acebo 1962; four s. one d.; ed in England, Victoria Coll., Alexandria, Egypt, Lycée Français, Spain and Valley Forge Mil. Acad., USA; proclaimed King of Bulgaria 1943, deposed 1946; sought refuge in Egypt in 1947; has since lived mainly in Spain; Constitutional Court ruled in 1998 that confiscation of royal property by communist regime had been illegal; returned to Bulgaria 1996; Founder and Leader, Nat. Movt for King Simeon II (renamed Nat. Movt for Stability and Progress 2007) 2001–09 (resgnd); Prime Minister of Bulgaria 2001–05. *Address:* c/o National Movement for Stability and Progress (Natsionalno dvizhenie za stabilnost i vazhod), 1000 Sofia, ul. Vrabcha 23, Bulgaria.

SAKURADA, Kengo; Japanese business executive; *Representative Director, Group CEO, President and Executive Officer, Sompo Japan Nipponkoa Insurance, Inc.;* b. 11 Feb. 1956; joined Yasuda Fire & Marine Insurance Co. Ltd (Sompo Japan Insurance Inc.) 1978, Gen. Man. Consolidated Planning Dept 2000–01, Gen. Man. Consolidated Planning Dept and Dai-Ichi Life Office Integration Planning Dept 2001–02, Gen. Man. Business Strategy Planning Dept April–June 2002, Gen. Man. Corporate Planning Dept 2002, Exec. Officer and Gen. Man. Financial Insts Dept 2005–07, Man. Exec. Officer April–June 2007, Dir and Man. Exec. Officer 2007–10, Dir and Exec. Officer, NKSJ Holdings, Inc. (following establishment of jt holding co. by Sompo Japan Insurance Inc. and Nipponkoa Insurance Co. Ltd 2010) 2010–12, Rep. Dir, Pres. and Exec. Officer 2012–14, Rep. Dir, Chair. and Exec. Officer, Sompo Japan Nipponkoa Insurance Inc. 2014–15, Rep. Dir and Chair. April–July 2015, Group CEO, Rep. Dir, Exec. Officer and Pres. 2015–, Dir 2016–. *Address:* Sompo Holdings, Inc., 26-1, Nishi-Shinjuku 1-chome, Shinjuku-ku, Tokyo 160-8338, Japan (office). *Telephone:* (3) 3349-3000 (operator) (office); (3) 3349-3111 (office). *Fax:* (3) 3349-4697 (office). *Website:* www.sompo-hd.com (office).

SAKURAI, Masamitsu, CBE, BSc; Japanese business executive; b. 8 Jan. 1942, Tokyo; m. Yokohama Sakurai; ed Faculty of Science and Tech., Waseda Univ.; joined Ricoh Co. Ltd 1966, Gen. Man. of Eng Admin Office 1980–84, Pres. Ricoh UK Products Ltd 1984–92, apptd Dir 1992, Gen. Man. of Purchasing Div. 1992–93, Pres. Ricoh Europe BV 1993–94, Man.-Dir Ricoh Co. Ltd 1994–95, Gen. Man. Research and Devt Group 1995–96, Pres., COO and CEO 1996–2007, Rep. Dir and Chair. 2007–13; apptd Chair. Japan Business Machine and Information System Industries Asscn 2004; Chair. Japanese Soc. for Quality Control 2005–06; fmr Chair. Keizai Doyukai, Coca-Cola West Co. Ltd; fmr Corporate Auditor of San-Ai Oil Co. Ltd; Dir Tokio Marine Holdings Inc. 2002, Yamaha Motor Co. Ltd 2011–; World Environment Center Award 2003. *Leisure interests:* travel, golf, reading.

SAKYI, Maj.-Gen. Delali Johnson, BPA; Ghanaian military commander and UN official; b. 10 March 1954, Saviepe-Gborgame, Volta Region; ed Ghana Inst. of Man. and Public Admin, Sr Staff Coll., Ghana Armed Forces Staff Coll., Fort Bragg Mil. Acad., USA; commissioned as Infantry Officer, 2nd Infantry Bn, Ghana Army 1978, various command positions from platoon to brigade level in Ghana Armed Forces and operational-level HQ 1979–2011, including as Commdr of Ghana contingent in several peacekeeping missions: Second UN Emergency Force (UNEF II) 1979, UN Interim Force in Lebanon (UNIFIL) 1986, 1993, UN Protection Force 1995, Econ. Community of W African States Monitoring Group, Liberia and Sierra Leone 1998–99; served with UN Org. Mission in Democratic Repub. of Congo 2002–03; Abidjan Sector Commdr, UN Operation in Côte d'Ivoire 2008; Asst Commdt, Ghana Armed Forces Command and Staff Coll. (Jr Div.) Jan.–Dec. 2012; Force Commdr, UN Mission in S Sudan 2012–14; Chief Mil. Observer and Head, UN Mil. Observer Group in India and Pakistan 2014–16.

SALA, Marius, PhD; Romanian linguist and academic; *Director, Institutul de Lingvistică 'Iorgu Iordan – Al Rosetti', Bucharest;* b. 8 Sept. 1932, Vașcău, Bihor Co.; s. of Sabin Sala and Eleonora Tocoianu; m. Marina Sala 2003; one d.; ed Coll. of Philology, Bucharest Univ.; Researcher, Institutul de Lingvistică 'Iorgu Iordan – Al Rosetti', Bucharest 1955–90, Deputy Dir 1990–94, Dir 1994–; Prof., Faculty of Foreign Languages, Bucharest; Visiting Prof., Heidelberg 1971, Málaga 1968, 1970, 1973, 1979, Madrid 1978, 1981, 1987, Mexico City 1981, Cologne 1984, Frankfurt 1992, Oviedo 1994, Nancy 1999; apptd mem. Romanian Acad. 1993, Full mem. 2001, Vice-Pres. 2005–; Corresp. mem. Royal Acad. Spain 1978, Mexican Inst. of Culture 1981, Acad. Nacional de Letras, Montevideo 1994–, Academia Peruana de la Lengua, Lima 2004–, Int. Cttee of Onomastic Studies 1969; mem. Int. Cttee of the Mediterranean Linguistic Atlas 1960; mem. Man. Junta of the Int. Asscn of Hispanists 1974–80; mem. Cttee Soc. of Romance Linguistics 1974–80, 1989–1995, apptd Hon. mem. 2003; mem. Perm. Int. Cttee of Linguists 1987–92; Prize of Romanian Acad. 1970, Prize of Mexican Acad. Centennial 1976. *Publications include:* Contribuţii la fonetica istorică a limbii române (Contributions to the Historical Phonetics of the Romanian Language) 1970, Phonétique et Phonologie du Judéo-Espagnol de Bucarest 1971, Le judéo-espagnol 1976, Contributions à la phonétique historique du roumain 1976, El léxico indígena del español americano, Apreciaciones sobre su vitalidad (co-author) 1977, El español de América, (Vol. 1), Léxico (co-author) 1982, Limbile lumii. Mică enciclopedie (The Languages of the World: A Concise Encyclopaedia) (co-author), 1981, Les langues du monde (Petite Encyclopédie) (co-author) 1984, Etimologia și Limba Română (Etymology and the Romanian Language) (co-author) 1987, Vocabularul Reprezentativ Al Limbilor Romanice (The Representative Vocabulary of the Romance Languages) (co-author) 1988, Enciclopedia Limbilor Romanice (Encyclopaedia of the Romance languages) (co-author) 1989, Unité des langues romanes 1996, Limba română, limbă romanică (Romanian Language, Romance Language) 1997, Limbi în contact (Languages in Contact) 1997, Introducere în etimologia limbii române (Introduction to the Etymology of Romanian) 1999, May We Introduce the Romanian Language to You? (co-author) 1999, Du latin au roumain 2000, Limbile Europei (The Language of Europe) (jtly) 2001, Ratengo kara rumaniago he – rumania goshi 2001, Made in Spain 1 – Logos, Made in Spain 2 – Packaging 2002, Made in Spain 3 – Editorial 2002, Made in Spain 4 2003, Made in Spain 5 2003, From Latin to Romanian: The Historical Development of Romanian in a Comparative Romance Context 2005. *Leisure interests:* philately, cooking. *Address:* Institutul de Lingvistică, Calea 13 Septembrie 13, 79515 Bucharest, B.O. 42-37 (office); Aleea Bistra 1, E1, 39, Bucharest, Romania (home). *Telephone:* 3182452 (office); 3182416 (office); 7457564 (home). *Fax:* 3182417 (office). *E-mail:* inst@lingv.ro (office).

SALA-I-MARTÍN, Xavier, MA, PhD; Spanish economist and academic; *Jerome and Matthew Grossman Professor of Development Economics, Columbia University;* b. 17 June 1963, Barcelona; ed Univ. Autònoma, Barcelona, Harvard Univ., USA; Asst Prof., Yale Univ., USA 1990–93, Assoc. Prof. 1993–96; Prof. of Econs, Columbia Univ., USA 1996–2008, Jerome and Matthew Grossman Prof. of Devt Econs 2008–; Visiting Prof., Univ. Pompeu Fabra, Barcelona 1994–2006, Harvard Univ. 2003–04; Research Assoc., Nat. Bureau of Econ. Research, Cambridge, Mass 1991–; Founder and Pres. Umbele Foundation: A Future for Africa 2004–; Forum Fellow, World Econ. Forum 2001–, Sr Econ. Advisor 2002–06, Chief Econ. Advisor 2006–; consultant, IMF 1993–2007, World Bank 1996–98, 2001; Assoc. Ed. Journal of Economic Growth 1994–; Advisory Ed. Economics Letters, Harvard Univ. 1997–; mem. Bd of Dirs Barcelona Football Club 2006–10; Patron Fundació Catalunya Oberta 2000–; Hon. Prof., Central Univ. of Beijing, China 2005; NSF Award 1998, King Juan Carlos I Prize for Social Sciences 1998, Kenneth Arrow Prize 1999, King Juan Carlos I Prize for Econs 2004, Lenfest Award 2006, Carpenter Prize, Babson Coll. 2011. *Publications include:* Apuntes de Crecimiento Económico 1994, Economic Growth 1995, Economia Liberal para No Economistas y No Liberales, Converses amb Xavier Sala-i-Martin 2007; co-ed. Global Competitiveness Report annual series; numerous articles in learned journals. *Address:* Columbia University, Department of Economics, 420 West 118th Street, #1005, New York, NY 10027, USA (office). *Telephone:* (212) 854-7055 (office). *Fax:* (212) 854-8059 (office). *E-mail:* xs23@columbia.edu (office). *Website:* www.columbia.edu/~xs23 (office); salaimartin.com.

SALADÍN SELIN, Roberto B.; Dominican Republic diplomatist and politician; b. 23 July 1936, Santo Domingo; ed Universidad de Santo Domingo; public sector experience includes postings as Commercial Attaché, Embassy in Bonn (also Chargé d'affaires a.i.), Admin. Sec. of Perm. Del. to UNESCO, Paris, and rep. at various int. forums; has been involved in academic programmes in Germany, France, Japan and USA; Co-founder Dominican Export Promotion Center (CEDOPEX), Exec. Dir early 1980s; Sec. of State for Finance 1986–87; Gov. Cen. Bank and Pres. Monetary Bd 1987–89; presidential cand. with support of the Christian Popular Party 1990; journal columnist and frequent guest speaker on TV; fmr Producer daily programme Diario Económico 1991–96; CEO Banco de Reservas 1996–99; Amb. to USA 1999–2002, 2009–11; Alt. Exec. Dir representing the Dominican Repub. and Mexico on Bd of Dirs at IDB Bank 2004–09. *Publications include:* two books on Banco de Reservas. *Address:* c/o Secretariat of State for Foreign Affairs, Avenida Independencia 752, Estancia San Gerónimo, Santo Domingo, DN, Dominican Republic (office). *Telephone:* 987-7001 (office). *Fax:* 987-7002 (office). *E-mail:* relexteriores@serex.gob.do (office). *Website:* www .serex.gov.do (office).

SALADINO ARANDA, Irving Jahir; Panamanian athlete; b. 23 Jan. 1983, Colón; World and Olympic men's long jump Champion; Silver Medal, World Indoor Championships, Moscow 2006 (set South American indoor record of 8.29m); won five (Oslo, Rome, Zurich, Brussel, Berlin) out of six Golden League events in same season 2006; jumped 8.56m May 2006 (South American record); jumped 8.53m (–0.2m/s wind) to win Grande Prêmio Rio Caixa de Atletismo, Rio de Janeiro 13 May 2007; Gold Medal, World Championships, Osaka 2007 (jump of 8.57m); set new personal record of 8.73m (+1.2m/s wind) during FBK-Games, Hengelo May 2008; Gold Medal, Olympic Games, Beijing 2008 (jump of 8.34m); Panama's first Olympic gold medallist.

SALAH, Lt-Gen. Ahmed Gaid; Algerian army officer and government official; *Deputy Minister of National Defence and Chief of Staff of Algerian People's National Army;* b. 31 Jan. 1940, Batna; m.; seven c.; ed Vystrel Mil. Acad. of Artillery; Commdr 21st, 29th, 31st Bn, Nat. Liberation Army (NLA) 1957–; promoted to Maj.-Gen. 1993, apptd Commdr of Land Forces 1994, Chief of Staff of Algerian People's National Army (ANP) 2004, promoted to the rank of Lt-Gen. 2006, Gen. of Army Corps 2006, other mil. functions include Artillery Group Commdr, Brigade Commdr and Commdr, Operational Sector Centre, Commdr, Reserve Officers Training School, South Operational Sector of Tindouf, Deputy Commdr, 5th Mil. Region, Commdr, 2nd Mil. Region, 3rd Mil. Region; Deputy Minister of Nat. Defence and Chief of Staff of ANP 2013–; NLA medal, 2nd ANP medal, Medal of Mil. Merit, Medal of Honour. *Address:* Ministry of National Defence, Les Tagarins, el-Biar, Algiers, Algeria (office). *Telephone:* (21) 71-15-15 (office). *Fax:* (21) 72-51-73 (office). *Website:* www.mdn.dz.

SALAKHOV, Tair Teimur ogly; Azerbaijani/Russian painter; b. 29 Nov. 1928, Baku, Azerbaijan; s. of Teimur and Sona Salakhov; m. Varvara Salakhova; three d.; ed Azerbaijan Azim-zade Higher School of Fine Arts, Moscow State Inst. of Fine Arts; Docent, Prof. Azerbaijan State Inst. of Arts 1963–74, also teacher Baku Aliyev Art School; Chair. Exec. Bd Azerbaijan Union of Artists 1972–74; Head of Studio Moscow State Inst. of Fine Arts 1974–92; First Sec. Exec. Bd USSR Union of Artists 1973–91; mem. Exec. Bd USSR Acad. of Fine Arts, Sec. 1986–; author of numerous portraits, landscapes, theatre decorations; Sec. Academician for painting section Russian Acad. of Arts 1979–, apptd Vice-Pres. Russian Acad. of Arts 1996; mem. Acad. of Arts of Kyrghyz Repub., Azerbaijan Acad. of Arts; Corresp. mem. French Acad. of Fine Arts 1986–, San Fernando Royal Academy of Fine Arts (Spain), Real Academia San Fernando, Madrid –1998; Hon. Pres. Int. Asscn of Art, Paris, Int. Asscn of Art attached to UNESCO; Hon. mem. Austrian Soc. of Fine Arts 1975, Acad. of Fine Arts, Kazakhstan, Acad. of Fine Arts, Kyrgyzstan, Union of Artist, Germany, Montana Arts, USA; Hon. citizen Trenton, NJ, Santa Fe, NM and Billings, Mont.; Order of Istiglal of Azerbaijan 1998, Order of Za Zaslugi pered Otechestvom (3rd class) (Russia) 1998, Orders of Poland, Bulgaria, Mongolia, France; Prize of Cen. Komsomol Cttee 1959, Akhundov Prize of Azerbaijan SSR 1964, USSR State Prize 1968, State Prize of Azerbaijan 1970 (for picture New Sea), Grekov's Gold Medal 1977, Hero of Socialist Labour 1989, People's Painter of Russia 1996, Plastov Prize (Global Names category), Russia 2012. *Address:* 3 Mamedyarov lane, h.1 'Icheri Sheher', Baku, Azerbaijan (home); Kutizovskiy pr. 18, ap.29, 121151 Moscow, Russia (home). *Telephone:* (495) 637-39-71 (home). *Fax:* (495) 637-39-71 (home).

SALAKHOVA, Aidan; Azerbaijani artist; b. 1964, Moscow; ed Surikov Art Inst.; Curator and Co-dir First Gallery, Moscow 1989–92; f. Aidan Gallery, Moscow 1992; collections at Rudolf Budja Gallery, Vienna, Orel Art, Paris, XL Gallery, Moscow, D137 – The Gallery of Contemporary Art, St Petersburg. *Address:* Aidan Gallery, Winzavod, 4th Syromyatnicheskiy lane 1/6, Moscow 150120, Russian Federation (office). *Telephone:* (495) 228-1158 (office). *Fax:* (495) 228-1158 (office). *E-mail:* info@aidangallery.ru (office). *Website:* www.aidangallery.ru (office).

SALAM, Tamman Saeb, BEcons, BBA; Lebanese politician; *Prime Minister;* b. 13 May 1945, Beirut; s. of Saeb Salam (fmr Prime Minister of Lebanon) and Tamima Mardam Beik; m. Lama Badreddine; three c.; ed Broummana High School, Haigazian Univ., Beirut, American Univ. of Beirut, univ. in UK; f. reformist Ruwwad Al Islah movt 1974 (disbanded at outbreak of Civil War 1975); Dir Makassed Philanthropic Islamic Asscn of Beirut (non-profit educational, health-care and social org.) 1978–, Chair. 1982–2000, now Hon. Chair.; mem. Majlis al-Nuab (Nat. Assembly) (list of Rafik Hariri) 1996–2000, (list of Saad Hariri) for Beirut Third Dist 2009–, currently ind. mem.; Minister of Culture 2008–09; apptd Pres. Council of Ministers (Prime Minister) Desig. April 2013, Pres. Council of Ministers 2014–; Chair. Saeb Salam Foundation for Culture and Higher Educ.; Légion d'honneur 1998. *Address:* Office of the President of the Council of Ministers, Grand Sérail, place Riad el-Solh, Beirut, Lebanon (office). *Telephone:* (1) 746800 (office). *Fax:* (1) 983065 (office). *E-mail:* Conseilm@pcm.gov.lb (office). *Website:* www.pcm.gov.lb (office); www.tammamsalam.net.

SALAMA, Hussein Samir Abdul-Rahman, BSc, MSc, PhD, DSc; Egyptian entomologist and academic; *Research Professor Emeritus, National Research Centre;* b. 26 Jan. 1936, Gharbia; m.; two c.; ed Ain Shams Univ., Cairo Univ.; Research Asst, Entomology Research Unit, Nat. Research Centre (NRC) 1956–62, Researcher 1962–67, Assoc. Research Prof. 1967–73, Research Prof. of Entomology, NRC 1973, Vice-Pres. NRC, Pres. 1988–92, Research Prof. Emer. 1996–; fmr Vice-Pres. Research Council for Basic Sciences, Egyptian Acad. of Scientific Research and Tech., Nat. Cttee for Biological Sciences; Vice-Pres. Egyptian Inst. for Scientific Culture 1991; fmr Pres. Int. Union of Biological Sciences, now mem. Exec. Cttee; Vice-Pres. Entomological Soc. of Egypt; mem. Bd Egyptian Acad. of Sciences, African Acad. of Sciences; Post-Doctoral Fellow, Dept of Entomology, Univ. of Alberta 1963–65, Fellow, Alexander Von Humboldt Foundation, Univ. of Munich 1974–76, Islamic Acad. of Sciences 1987, African Acad. of Sciences 1990, TWAS 1994; State Prize for Biological Sciences 1973, Golden Medal of NRC 1981, Golden Medal of the Entomological Soc. of Egypt 1982, State Prize for Sciences Prize for Agricultural Sciences 1983, African Acad. of Sciences Prize for Agric. 1991, Recognition State Prize for Basic Sciences 1994 and numerous other awards. *Publications include:* 230 scientific publs and review articles. *Address:* 76 Mohyee Abonlezz str., Dokki, Cairo, Egypt (home). *Telephone:* (2) 3377399 (home). *E-mail:* hsarsalama@hotmail.com.

SALAMATIN, Dmytro; Ukrainian/Russian politician; b. 26 April 1965, Karaganda, Kazakh SSR, USSR; ed Karaganda Polytechnic Inst., Moscow Mining Inst.; worked in Russia 1991–99; moved to Ukraine 1999; Deputy (Party of Regions) to Verkhovna Rada (Parl.) 2006; Dir-Gen. Ukrspetsexport (state arms exporter) 2010–11; Dir-Gen. of newly created Ukroboronprom state concern 2011–12; Minister of Defence Feb.–Dec. 2012; apptd Adviser to Pres. 2012.

SALAMÉ, Ghassan, MPhil, PhD; Lebanese/French politician, academic and fmr UN official; *Special Representative and Head, United Nations Support Mission in Libya (UNSMIL);* b. 18 May 1951, Kfarzebian, Mount Lebanon; m.; two d.; ed Lyon Univ. in Beirut, Saint-Joseph Univ., Beirut, Paris III Univ., Paris I Univ.; taught Political Science at Saint-Joseph Univ., Beirut, American Univ. of Beirut and Paris I Univ.; Rockefeller Fellow in Int. Relations, Brookings Inst., Washington, DC 1981, Visiting Fellow 1985–86; mem. Social Science Research Council, New York 1985–90, Co-Dir 'State, Nation and Integration in the Arab World' study program 1986–91; Minister of Culture 2000–03; Prof. of Int. Relations, Institut d'Etudes Politiques (Sciences Po), Paris 1988–2015, Dean, Paris School for Int. Affairs 2010–15, Prof. Emer. 2015–; Visiting Prof., Columbia Univ., New York, USA; Co-founder and Chair. Euro-Mediterranean Studies, European Univ. Inst., Florence, Italy; Sr Adviser to UN Sec.-Gen. 2003–06; Co-Chair. Int. Crisis Group 2004–16, Humanitarian Dialogue Center 2011–15; Special Rep. and Head UN Support Mission in Libya (UNSMIL) 2017–; mem. Rakhin State Comm. 2016–17; Chevalier, Légion d'honneur 2003. *Publications:* author or ed. 12 books, including Al-mujtama' wa al-dawla fi al-mashriq al-arabi (State and Society in the Arab Levant) 1987, The Foundations of the Arab State 1987, The Politics of Arab Integration 1988, Democracy without Democrats: Politics of Liberalization in the Arab and Muslim World (ed.) 1994, Appels d'empire: ingérences et résistances à l'âge de la mondialisation (Phoenix Award, APELF Award) 1996, Quand L'Amerique refait le monde 2005, and others; articles published in several periodicals, including La Revue Française de Science Politique, Foreign Policy, The Middle East Journal, Security Dialogue. *Address:* Department of Political Affairs, United Nations, New York, NY 10017, USA (office). *Telephone:* (212) 963-1234 (office). *Fax:* (212) 963-4879 (office). *Website:* www.un.org/Depts/dpa (office); unsmil.unmissions.org (office).

SALAMEH, Riad T., BA (Econs); Lebanese central banker; *Governor, Banque du Liban;* b. 17 July 1950, Beirut; s. of Toufic Salameh and Renée Salameh; ed Jesuits' Coll. Notre Dame de Jamhour, American Univ. of Beirut; with Merrill Lynch, Beirut 1973–76, 1978–85, Paris 1976–78, Sr Vice-Pres. and Financial Counsellor, Paris 1985–93; Gov. Banque du Liban 1993–, mem. Bd of Govs IMF, Arab Monetary Fund (Chair. 2013); Co-Chair. Financial Stability Bd Regional Consultative Group for the Middle East and North Africa 2013–15; Kt, Légion d'honneur 1997, Officier, Légion d'honneur 2009; Dr hc (Lebanese American Univ. of Beirut) 2009, Hon. DHumLitt (Lebanese Univ.) 2010; Arab Creativity Award in Economics, Best Arab Banker Award, Euromoney 1996, Man of the Year, Best Cen. Bank Gov., Euromoney 2003, World's Best Cen. Bank Gov., Euromoney 2006, Hon. Sash and Shield Award (Hariri Canadian Univ.) 2011, Banker Magazine Best Central Bank Governor in the Middle East 2012. *Address:* Banque du Liban, Hamra, rue Masraf Loubnan, PO Box 11-5544, Beirut, Lebanon (office). *Telephone:* (1) 750000 (office). *Fax:* (1) 747600 (office). *E-mail:* bdlfx@bdl.gov.lb (office). *Website:* www.bdl.gov.lb (office).

SALAMI, Alawi Salih as-, BA; Yemeni politician and fmr central banker; b. 21 Dec. 1945, Radaa; ed Univ. of Baghdad, Iraq; Gen. Man. Financial and Admin. Affairs, Ministry of Educ. 1970–73; fmr Chair. Ministerial Cttee for Crude Oil Marketing; Gen. Man. Budget Gen. Office 1973–75; Deputy, Budget Div. 1975–86, with rank of Vice-Minister 1986; Minister of Finance 1986–94, 1997–2001; Gov. Yemen Cen. Bank 1994–97; Deputy Prime Minister and Minister of Finance 2001–06.

ŞALARU, Anatol; Moldovan politician; b. 7 Feb. 1962; m.; two c.; ed State Univ. of Medicine and Pharmacy, Moldovan Inst. of Scientific Research; Researcher, Moldovan Inst. of Scientific Research 1985–90; mem. Parlamentul (Parl.) 1990–94, 2009, 2014–15; Dir Ascom Grup SA, Chişinău 1996–97, Dir-Gen. and Rep. in Turkmenistan of Ascom Grup SA 1997–99, Project Man., Financial-Industrial Div., Ascom Grup SA 2002–03, Head of Representation of Ascom Grup SA in Iraq 2003–08; Minister of Transport and Roads Infrastructure 2009–13, Minister of Defence 2015–16; mem. Partidul Liberal (PL), Sr Vice-Pres. 2013–14. *Address:* c/o Ministry of Defence, 2021 Chişinău, şos. Hînceşti 84, Moldova (office).

SALAS COLLANTES, Javier; Spanish association executive; b. 1948, Lisbon, Portugal; ed Faculty of Econs, Univ. of Madrid; joined Instituto Nacional de Industria 1973, Pres. 1990–95; Chair. Iberia 1993–95; mem. Bd of Dirs Telvent, Red Eléctrica de España –2012, Abengoa; fmr Pres. Fundación Entorno; apptd Pres. Asociación Profesional de Empresas de Limpieza (ASPEL) 2005, European Fed. of Industrial Cleaning (FENI/EFCI) 2007–10; Founding Partner and Dir SAGA Servicios Financieros SA, Madrid; Counselor, GED Capital; mem. Advisory Bd Young & Rubicam. *Leisure interest:* hill-trekking. *Address:* SAGA Servicios Financieros C/Marqués de Riscal, 12 4ª Planta, 28010 Madrid, Spain (office). *Telephone:* (91) 7020986 (office). *Fax:* (91) 3105512 (office). *Website:* www.saga-sf.com (office).

SALAS FALGUERAS, Margarita, PhD; Spanish molecular biologist and academic; *Professor ad honorem, Severo Ochoa Centre for Molecular Biology, Universidad Autónoma de Madrid;* b. 30 Nov. 1938, Canero, Oviedo (Asturias); m. Dr Eladio Viñuela (died 1999); one d.; ed Univ. Complutense of Madrid; Post-doctoral work, Dept of Biochemistry, New York Univ. 1964–67; Prof. of Molecular Genetics, Complutense Univ. of Madrid 1968–92; Prof. in Research, Severo Ochoa Centre for Molecular Biology, Consejo Superior de Investigaciones Científicas-Universidad Autónoma de Madrid (CSIC-UAM), Madrid 1974–, Dir 1992–93; Pres. Spanish Inst. 1995–2003, Social Council of Oviedo Univ. 1999–2003, Fundación Severo Ochoa, Royal Bd of Nat. Library of Spain; mem. Bd, Cervantes Inst. 1996–; mem. External Advisory Bd of Oviedo Univ., Inst. of Predictive and Personalized Medicine of Cancer, Barcelona, Nat. Centre of Cardiovascular Research, Madrid; mem. Spanish Acad. of Sciences 1988, Spanish Acad. of Language 2003, Royal Spanish Acad., European Molecular Biology Org. (EMBO), Academia Europaea, Academia Scientiarum et Artium Europaea, American Acad. of Microbiology, American Acad. of Arts and Sciences; Foreign mem. NAS; Hon. Pres. Royal Acad. of Medicine of Asturias and Leon 1996; Hon. mem. Spanish Soc. of Biochemistry and Molecular Biology 1998; Great Cross of the Civil Order of Alfonso X el Sabio 2003; Prof. ad honorem, Spanish Nat. Research Council; Dr hc (Oviedo) 1996, (Tech. Univ. of Madrid) 2000, (Univ. of Extremadura) 2002, (Univ. of Murcia) 2003, (Univ. of Cádiz) 2004, (Universidad Rey Juan Carlos) 2008, (Univ. of Malaga) 2009, (Universidad Nacional de Educación a Distancia) 2011, (Universidad Internacional Menendez Pelayo) 2011, (Jaén) 2012; numerous prizes and distinctions, including Severo Ochoa Prize of Research, Carlos J. Finlay of UNESCO, Rey Jaime I of Research, Mexico Prize of Science and Tech., L'Oréal-UNESCO Prize 'Women in Science', Nat. Prize of Research, Santiago Ramón y Cajal, Gold Medal of Madrid Community, Honour Medal, UIMP and Complutense Univ., Madrid, Human Values Prize, Correo Group, Health Prize, Fund Inbev-Baillet Latour (Belgium), named Marquise of Canero, Echegaray Medal, Royal Acad. of Exact, Physical and Natural Sciences. *Publications:* more than 400 articles in scientific journals on DNA replication and control of gene expression using the bacterial virus ø29 as a model system. *Address:* Severo Ochoa Centre for Molecular Biology, Universidad Autónoma de Madrid, Nicolás Cabrera 1, Cantoblanco, 28049 Madrid, Spain (office). *Telephone:* (91) 1964675 (office); (91) 1964402 (office). *Fax:* (91) 1964420 (office). *E-mail:* msalas@cbm.csic.es (office). *Website:* www.cbm.csic.es (office).

SALAYEV, Eldar Unis ogly, D.Phys-Math.Sc; Azerbaijani physicist and politician; b. 31 Dec. 1933, Nakhichevan City; s. of Yunis Sala oglu Salayev and Telly Tahir kizi Salayeva; m. Dilara Ashraf Guseynova; two s.; ed Azerbaijan Univ.; mem. CPSU 1963–91; Jr Researcher then Deputy Dir Inst. of Physics, Azerbaijan Acad. of Sciences 1956–73, Dir 1973–83, currently Chief Scientific Worker; apptd Corresp. mem. Acad. of Sciences of Azerbaijan 1980, Full mem. 1983, Pres. 1983–97, fmr Chair. Repub. Council, Presidium of Acad. of Sciences of Azerbaijan; mem. Council on co-ordination of scientific activities of Acads of Sciences, Presidium of USSR Acad. of Sciences 1985–91; Ed.-in-Chief Doklady Akademii Nauk Azerbaijana; Deputy to USSR Supreme Soviet 1985–89; USSR People's Deputy 1989–91; accused of preparing the return of Rasul Quliyev to Azerbaijan and imprisoned 2005 but released; Merited Worker of Arts of Azerbaijan. *Publications include:* Dynamics and Statistics, Non-linear Effects on Layer Crystals, Type of Selenite Gallium 1993; more than 200 scientific publs in numerous journals. *Leisure interest:* sport. *Address:* Institute of Physics, 33, H.Javid Avenue, 1143 Baku, Azerbaijan (office). *Telephone:* (12) 4326143 (office); (12) 4959310 (home). *Fax:* (12) 4325229 (office). *E-mail:* azhep@physics.ab.az (office). *Website:* www.elm.az/en/physic (office).

SALAZAR, Ken Lee, BA, JD; American lawyer, politician and government official; *Partner, Wilmer Cutler Pickering Hale and Dorr LLP;* b. 2 March 1955, Alamosa, Colo; s. of Henry Salazar and Emma Salazar; m. Hope Salazar; two d.; ed Centauri High School, Conejos Co., St Francis Seminary, Colorado Coll., Univ. of Michigan Law School; worked as a farmer for more than 30 years, helped establish El Rancho Salazar partnership 1981; Assoc. Sherman & Howard (law firm), Denver Colo 1981–86; Chief Legal Counsel to Gov. of Colo 1986–90, apptd Exec. Dir Colo Dept of Natural Resources 1990–94; returned to pvt. law practice 1994–98; elected Colo Attorney Gen. 1999–2005; Dir Parcel, Mauro, Hultin & Spaanstra 1994–98; Senator from Colo 2005–08; US Sec. of the Interior, Washington, DC 2009–13; Partner, Wilmer Cutler Pickering Hale and Dorr LLP, Denver 2013–; mem. ABA, American Judicature Soc., Hispanic Bar Asscn, Denver Bar Asscn, Colorado Bar Asscn, American Farmland Trust, Pres.'s Council; mem. Bd of Trustees Colorado Coll.; Democrat; Hon. LLD (Colorado Coll.) 1993, (Univ. of Denver) 1999, (Univ. of Massachusetts – Lowell) 2012; Distinguished Alumni Award, Univ. of Michigan Law School 2002, Anti-Defamation League Civil Rights Award 2002, President's Award, League of United Latin American Citizens (LULAC) 2005, Nat. Farmers Union Golden Triangle Award 2006, Cuban American Nat. Council's Outstanding Hispanic Leader Award 2007, Smithsonian Latino Center Award for Leadership 2007, Annual Leadership Award, Golda Meir Center for Political Leadership 2011, Cesar Chavez Legacy Award 2012, Colorado Conservation Trust Lifetime Achievement Award 2013, Ansel Adams Award, Wilderness Society 2013. *Address:* Wilmer Cutler Pickering Hale and Dorr LLP, 1225 17th Street, Suite 1660, Denver, CO 80202, USA (office). *Telephone:* (720) 274-3131 (office). *E-mail:* ken.salazar@wilmerhale.com (office). *Website:* www.wilmerhale.com (office).

SALAZAR GÓMEZ, HE Cardinal Rubén, LicDogTheol, LicSacrTheol; Colombian ecclesiastic; *Archbishop of Bogotá;* b. 22 Sept. 1942, Bogotá; ed seminary of Ibague, Pontifical Gregorian Univ. and Pontifical Biblical Inst., Rome; ordained priest, Archdiocese of Ibagué 1967; held various positions, including pastor, seminary prof., Dir Dept of Social Pastoral of Colombian Episcopal Conf., Vicar for Pastoral Care; Bishop of Cúcuta 1992–99; Archbishop of Barranquilla 1999–2010; Archbishop of Bogotá 2010–; cr. Cardinal (Cardinal-Priest of San Gerardo Maiella) 2012; Pres., Latin American Bishops Conference 2015, Colombian Episcopal Conf.; mem. Pontifical Comm. for Latin America 2013–, Pontifical Council for Justice and Peace 2013–. *Address:* Arzobispado, Carrera 7a N. 10-20, Bogota DC, Colombia (office). *Telephone:* (1) 350-5511 (office). *Fax:* (1) 350-7290 (office). *E-mail:* sistemas@arquidiocesisbogota.org.co (office). *Website:* www.arquidiocesisbogota.org.co (office).

SALDIVAR, John Birchman, BSc, MSc; Belizean politician; *Minister of National Security;* ed Minnesota State Univ., Florida State Univ., USA; mem. House of Reps (Parl.) for Cayo South constituency 2003–08, for Belmopan constituency 2008–; Minister of the Public Service, Governance Improvement and Elections and Boundaries 2008–12, of Nat. Security 2012–16, 2018–; mem. United Democratic Party. *Address:* Ministry of National Security, Curl Thompson Building, Belmopan, Belize (office). *Telephone:* 822-2817 (office). *Fax:* 822-2195 (office). *E-mail:* minofnatsec@mns.gov.bz (office).

SALEEM, Ahmed; Maldivian diplomatist and international organization official; b. 26 May 1949, Malé; m. Ayesha Saleem; four c.; joined Foreign Service 1968, held several positions including Chief of Protocol and Head of Multilateral Div., served at High Comm. in Sri Lanka and Perm. Mission to UN, New York; with Ministry of Finance 1977, served as Alt. Gov. to World Bank, IDA, Asian Devt Bank; apptd Dir SAARC Secr. 1990, Sec.-Gen. SAARC 2012–14; mem. Human Rights Comm. of the Maldives 2003–10 (Pres. 2006–10); fmr mem. Maldivian Democratic Party. *Publications include:* numerous articles on human rights, int. affairs and regionalism. *Address:* c/o Ministry of Foreign Affairs, Henveiru, Block 77, Boduthakurufaanu Magu, Malé 20-077, Maldives.

SALEH, Ali Bin Saleh al-, BCom; Bahraini business executive and government official; *Chairman, Shura Consultative Council;* b. 28 Dec. 1942; s. of Saleh Al Saleh; m. Afaf Radhi Salman Almousawi 1970; one s. two d.; ed Ain Shams Univ., Egypt; mem. Founding Council 1973, Nat. Ass. 1973–75; Deputy Chair. Bahrain Chamber of Commerce and Industry 1975–93; Deputy Chair. Shura (Consultative Council) 1993–95, Chair. 2006–; Minister of Commerce 1995–2006; Chair. Bahrain Promotions and Marketing Bd 1995–2000, Bahrain Convention and Exhbn Bureau, Bahrain Stock Exchange; mem. Bd of Trustees Univ. of Bahrain 1985–95, Bahrain Centre for Studies and Research, Econ. Devt Bd. *Leisure interests:* reading, music, travel. *Address:* Office of the Chairman, Shura Council, PO Box 2991, Manama, Bahrain (office). *Telephone:* 17748888 (office). *E-mail:* info@shura.bh (office). *Website:* www.shura.bh (office).

SALEH, Amrullah; Afghan government official and politician; b. 1 Oct. 1972, Panjshir Prov.; ed high school educ., Afghanistan; served as trans. between CIA officers and Northern Alliance leader Ahmad Shah Massoud 2001; fmr Chief Liaison Officer with foreign mil. and diplomatic corps, Kabul; fmr political officer, spokesman and relief co-ordinator; fmr Deputy Chief of Afghanistan Intelligence, focused on foreign relations; Sr mem. Nat. Security Directorate, Head of Directorate 2004–10; Founder and Leader, Rawand-e Sabz-e Afghanistan (Afghanistan Green Trend) party 2010–; Acting Minister of Interior Affairs 2018–19 (resgnd); Hon. DSc (Cleary Univ., Mich.) 2005.

SALEH, Jaime Mercelino, LLM; Dutch government official, chief justice and university professor; b. 20 April 1941, Bonaire; m. Marguerite Marie Halabi; two s. two d.; ed State Univ. of Utrecht; Deputy Public Prosecutor, Netherlands 1967–68, Curaçao 1968–74; attorney-at-law, Curaçao 1971–74; Deputy mem. High Court of the Netherlands Antilles 1974–76; Justice 1976–79; Chief Justice High Court of Justice of the Netherlands Antilles and Aruba 1979–90, Vice-Pres. Dutch Navy Mil. Court for the Netherlands Antilles 1978–79, Pres. Dutch Navy Mil. Court for the Netherlands Antilles and Aruba 1979–90; Gov.-Gen. of Netherlands Antilles 1990–2002; apptd Minister of State 2004; Prof., Univ. of Utrecht 2005–11; Order of Merit of Corps Consulaire 1989; Order of Libertador en el grado de Gran Cordón, Venezuela 1996; Order of Knighthood of the Dutch Lion; Commdr, Order of Orange Nassau 2002; Royal Medal 1980, Almirate Luis Brion Naval Medal 1994, Dutch ICN Dales Award for Integrity 2004, Dutch Lawyers Asscn Award 2008. *Publications:* various works on law and politics, with particular reference to the Netherlands Antilles. *Address:* B7 Villapark Zuurzak, Willemstad, Curaçao (home). *Telephone:* (9) 7382800 (home). *Fax:* (9) 7382801 (home). *E-mail:* jaime.saleh@gmail.com (home).

SALEH ABBAS, Youssouf, LLM; Chadian politician; b. 1953, Abéché, Ouaddai Region; Head, Multilateral Co-operation Div. and Dir of Int. Co-operation, Ministry of Foreign Affairs 1979–81; Diplomatic Adviser to Pres. 1981; Dir Cabinet of Head of State 1981–82; Adviser to Dir-Gen., Ministry of Foreign Affairs 1992–96; Vice-Pres. Sovereign Nat. Conf. Jan.–April 1993; Dir-Gen. Ministry of Planning and Co-operation 1996–97; mem. Movt for Democracy and Justice in Chad 1998–2001; Pres.'s Special Rep. to UN Mission in the Central African Republic and Chad (MINURCAT) and EUFOR (EU peacekeepng force) 2007–08; Adviser to Pres. on Int. Relations and Co-operation 2006–08; Prime Minister 2008–10 (resgnd).

SALEHI, Ali Akbar, BSc, PhD; Iranian physicist, international organization official and government official; *Head, Atomic Energy Organization of Iran;* b. 24 March 1949, Karbala, Iraq; m. Zahra Rad; ed American Univ. of Beirut, Lebanon, Massachusetts Inst. of Tech., USA; fmr Full Prof., Sharif Univ. of Tech., Tehran, Chancellor 1982–85, 1989–93; Iranian Rep. to IAEA 1998–2003; Scientific Adviser to Ministry of Foreign Affairs 2004; Deputy Sec.-Gen. Org. of the Islamic Conf. 2007–09; Head, Atomic Energy Org. of Iran 2009–10, 2013–; Minister of Foreign Affairs 2011–13; mem. Acad. of Sciences of Iran, Int. Centre for Theoretical Physics, Italy. *Publications:* more than 20 scientific publs. *Address:* Atomic Energy Organization, Amir Abad, Tehran, Iran (office). *Telephone:* 88221203 (office). *Fax:* 88221209 (office). *E-mail:* head_office@aeoi.org.ir (office). *Website:* www.aeoi.org.ir (office).

SALEM, Elie Adib, PhD; Lebanese politician, academic and university administrator; *President, University of Balamand;* b. 5 March 1930, Bterram Kurah; s. of Adib Salem and Lamia Salem (née Malik); m. Phyllis Sell (died 2001); two s. two d.; ed American Univ. of Beirut, Univ. of Cincinnati, USA, Johns Hopkins Univ., USA; Instructor in Public Admin, American Univ. of Beirut 1954–56, Assoc. Prof. of Political Studies and Public Admin 1962–68, Asst Dean of Arts and Sciences 1966–68, Chair. Middle East Area Program and Prof. of Political Studies and Public Admin 1969–74, Chair. Dept of Political Studies and Public Admin 1972–74, Dean of Arts and Sciences 1974–82; Asst Prof. of Middle East Politics, School of Advanced Int. Studies, Johns Hopkins Univ. 1956–62; Visiting Prof., Dept of Govt and Research Scholar Int. Devt Research Centre, Ind. Univ. 1968–69; Deputy Prime Minister and Minister of Foreign Affairs 1982–84; Adviser to Pres. on Foreign Affairs 1984–88; Founder and fmr Pres. Lebanese Centre of Policy Studies; Pres. Univ. of Balamand 1993–. *Publications include:* The Arab Public Administrative Conference 1954, Political Theory and Institutions of the Khawarij 1956, Modernization without Revolution: Lebanon's Experience 1973, 'Rusum Dar al-Khilafah al Abbasiyah' manuscript by Hlal al Sab' (trans.) 1977, Violence and Diplomacy in Lebanon 1982–88 1994, My American Bride: A Tale of Love and War 2008; articles in professional journals. *Leisure interests:* tennis, swimming, table tennis. *Address:* Université de Balamand, PO Box 100, Tripoli, Lebanon (office). *Telephone:* (6) 930250, ext. 103 (office). *Fax:* (6) 930278 (office). *E-mail:* president@balamand.edu.lb (office). *Website:* www.balamand.edu.lb (office).

SALERNO, F. Robert; American car rental industry executive; b. Springfield, Mass; m.; one d.; ed Marquette Univ.; Vice-Pres., Eastern Region and Zone Devt, Avis Rent-a-Car 1982–87, Vice-Pres. Field Operations 1987–90, Sr Vice-Pres. and Gen. Man. 1990–95, Exec. Vice-Pres. of Operations 1995–96, Pres. and COO 1996–2002; Pres. and COO Cendant Car Rental 2002–03, CEO Cendant Vehicle Rental Services Div. 2003–05; Pres. and COO Avis Budget Group Inc. (cr. after Cendant separated into four units) 2005–10, Vice-Chair. 2010–11 (retd); mem. Bd of Dirs Avis Budget Group Inc. 2006–, Norwegian Cruise Line Holdings Ltd 2014–, NCL Corpn Ltd 2014–.

SALES, Wayne C.; American business executive; b. 28 Dec. 1949; served in several sr marketing, merchandising and store operations leadership positions with US div. of Kmart Corpn until 1991; joined Canadian Tire Corpn Ltd 1991, Pres. and CEO 2000–06, Vice-Chair. 2006–10; Dir (non-exec.) Supervalu Inc. 2006–12, Exec. Dir 2012–, Chair. (non-exec.) 2010–12, Exec. Chair., Pres. and CEO 2012–13; currently Limited Partner, IncWell, LLC; Dir and Chair. Compensation

Cttee Tim Hortons Inc.; Dir, Axiall Corpn (fmrly Georgia Gulf Corpn) 2007–12, Discovery Air Inc. 2008–12; Chair, Communications and Media, for the United Way of Greater Toronto's 2002 campaign; several awards, including Distinguished Retailer of the Year, Retail Council of Canada 2004, CEO of the Year, Canadian Business Magazine 2005, also inducted into Canadian Marketing Hall of Legends 2009. *Address:* IncWell, LLC, 1000 South Old Woodward Avenue, Suite #105, Birmingham, MI 48009, USA (office). *E-mail:* info@incwell.net (office). *Website:* theincwell.net (office).

SALGADO, Sebastião Ribeiro, Jr, PhD; Brazilian photographer; b. 8 Feb. 1944, Aimorés, Minas Gerais; m. Lélia Deluiz Wanick 1967; two s.; ed São Paulo Univ., Vanderbilt Univ., USA, Univ. of Paris, France; with Brazilian Ministry of Finance 1968–69; with Investment Dept, Int. Coffee Org., London 1971–73; photojournalist working in Europe, Africa and Latin America 1973–, with Sygma News Agency of Paris 1974, with Gamma Agency 1975–79, mem. Magnum Photos 1979–; UNICEF Goodwill Amb. 2001; collections at Musée de l'Elysée, Lausanne, Switzerland, Nat. Museum of Modern Art, Japan, Tokyo Metropolitan Museum of Photography, Japan, Ville du Port, Ile de la Réunion, France, Glasgow Arts Centre, Scotland, Fundação Cultural de Curitiba, Brazil, Bibliothèque Nationale de France, France, Maison Européenne de la Photographie, France, Museum für Moderne Kunst, Germany, Australian Nat. Gallery, Australia, San Francisco Museum of Modern Art, USA, New York Museum of Modern Art, USA, Chicago Art Inst., USA, Minneapolis Museum of Art, USA Museum of Photographic Arts, USA, Smithsonian Inst., Washington, DC, USA, Los Angeles County Museum of Art, USA, Deutsche Börse, Germany, Museu Historico Abilio Barreto, Belo Horizonte, Brazil, J. Paul Getty Museum, USA, Centre Pompidou, France; Hon. mem. American Acad. of Arts and Sciences, Hon. Fellow, Royal Photographic Soc. of Great Britain, England; Commdr, Order of Rio Branco 2004; Dr hc (Univ. of Evora, Portugal) 2001, Univ. of Nottingham) 2002, Hon. DFA (New School Univ., New York) 2001, (Lesley Univ., Boston) 2001; Eugene Smith Award 1982, Oskar Barnack Prize, World Press Photo Award 1985, Photojournalist of the Year Award, Int. Centre of Photography, New York 1986, 1988, Photographer of the Year Award, American Soc. of Magazine Photographers 1987, Olivier Rebbot Award, Overseas Press Club, New York 1987, King of Spain Award 1988, Erich Salomon Award, Germany 1988, Erna and Victor Hasselblad Award, Sweden 1989, Centenary MedalAward, Royal Photographic Soc. of Great Britain, England 1994, Award of Excellence, Soc. of Newspaper Design, USA, Silver Medal, Art Directors Club, USA 1995, Germany 1995, 1998, Prêmio Nacional de Fotografia, Brazil 1997, Principe de Asturias Award for Arts, Spain 1998, UNESCO Prize for Culture in Brazil 1999, Presidenza della Repubblica Italiana Medal, Int. Research Centre, Italy 2000, Int. Award, Photographic Soc. of Japan 2003, Gold Medal Award for Photography, Nat. Arts Club, New York 2005, Faz Diferença Prize, Rio de Janeiro, Brazil 2008, Excellence in Reporting of Social Issues Award, American Sociological Asscn, USA 2010, NANPA Lifetime Achievement Award, North American Nature Photography Asscn, USA, Save the Children Int. Prize, Spain 2010, Gold Medal of Honour 2010, Al-Thani Award for Photography, Qatar 2010. *Publications include:* several books of photographs and exhbn catalogues, including Autres Amériques (Prix de la Ville de Paris et Kodak) 1986, Sahel: L'Homme en Détresse (Prix du Livre) 1986, Les Cheminots 1988, Sahel: El Fin del Camino 1988, Workers: An Archaeology of the Industrial Age (World Hunger Year Harry Chapin Media Award) 1993, Terra: Luta dos Sem-Terra (Prêmio Jabuti) 1997, Exodus 2000, O Fím do Pálio 2003, Um Incerto Estado de Graça 2004, O Berço da Desigualdade 2005, Africa 2007. *Address:* c/o Amazonas Images, 93 Quai de Valmy, 75010 Paris, France (office). *Telephone:* 1-42-09-90-68 (office). *Fax:* 1-42-09-76-64 (office). *E-mail:* amazonas@amazonasimages.fr (office). *Website:* www.amazonasimages.com (office).

SALIH, Lt-Gen. Bakri Hassan; Sudanese military officer and government official; *First Vice-President;* b. 1949, Dongola; ed Sudanese Mil. Acad.; Commdr, Special Forces 1985–87, 1988–89; Mil. Officer, Revolutionary Command Council for Nat. Salvation (RCC–NS) 1989–; Dir, Nat. Security Service 1990–95; Minister of the Interior 1995–98, Minister of Nat. Defence 2000–05, Minister of Presidential Affairs 2005–13; First Vice-Pres. 2013–, also Prime Minister 2017–18; Deputy Sec.-Gen., Islamic Movement 2012–; mem. Nat. Congress. *Website:* www.presidency.gov.sd (office).

SALIH, Barham, BE; Iraqi politician and head of state; *President;* b. 12 Sept. 1960, Kurdistan; m. Sarbagh Salih; one s. one d.; ed Univ. of Cardiff, Univ. of Liverpool, UK; joined Patriotic Union Kurdistan (PUK) 1976, served as spokesman in London, UK; Rep. to US, Patriotic Union Kurdistan and Kurdistan Regional Govt 1991–2001; Regional Admin. Sulaimaniya; Deputy Prime Minister for Nat. Security Affairs 2004–05, 2006–09; Minister of Planning and Devt Co-operation 2005–06; Prime Minister, Kurdistan Regional Govt 2009–12; Pres. of Iraq 2018–; Founding mem. Coalition for Democracy and Justice 2017–. *Address:* Office of the President, Al Radwaniyah Presidential Complex, Baghdad, Iraq. *Website:* www.barhamsalih.net.

SALIH, Khaled, BA, MA, PhD; Iraqi academic and government official; *Senior Adviser to Prime Minister, Kurdistan Regional Government;* b. 16 Feb. 1957, Sulaimania, Kurdistan; ed Gothenburg Univ., Sweden; fmr Lecturer in Int. and Middle E Politics, Dept of Political Science, Gothenburg Univ. 1989–97; Sr Lecturer, Univ. of Linkøping, Sweden 1997–98; Assoc. Prof. in Middle E Politics, Centre for Contemporary Middle E Studies, Univ. of Southern Denmark, Odense 1998–; mem. Kurdistan Int. Constitutional Advisory Team 2003, also served as political adviser to Kurdistan Regional Govt and Kurdistan Nat. Ass.; apptd Official Spokesperson for Kurdistan Regional Govt 2006; currently Sr Adviser to Prime Minister and Minister of Natural Resources, Kurdistan Regional Govt; fmr Advisory Ed. Democratiya (journal). *Publications include:* State-Making, Nation-Building and the Military: Iraq, 1941–1958 1996, The Future of Kurdistan in Iraq (co-ed.) 2005. *Address:* Kurdistan Regional Government, Council of Ministers Building, Erbil, Iraq (office). *Website:* www.krg.org (office).

SALIH, Muhammad; Uzbekistani writer, poet and politician; *Chairman, O'zbekiston Erk Demokratik Partiyasi (Freedom Democratic Party of Uzbekistan);* b. 20 Dec. 1949, Xorazm, Uzbek SSR, USSR; m.; five c.; ed Tashkent State Univ., Moscow High Literary Inst., Russian SFSR; mil. service in army 1968–70; worked as screenwriter in 1980s; wrote letter to Politburo protesting at political situation in Uzbekistan 1984; work published in Soviet newspapers 1985–86; elected Chair. Union of Writers of Uzbekistan 1988; co-f. Birlik (Unity People's Movt) 1988; f. O'zbekiston Erk Demokratik Partiyasi (Freedom Democratic Party of Uzbekistan) 1990, currently Chair.; Deputy, Supreme Ass. (Oliy Majlis—Parl.) 1990–92 (resgnd); presidential cand. 1991; f. Democratic Forum 1992; refused offer of Deputy Prime Minister in return for dissolution of Democratic Forum 1992, arrested and jailed for three days, and subsequently put under house arrest, left Uzbekistan to continue political activity abroad 1992; received sentence in absentia of 15½ years 1999; flew to Prague from Amsterdam at invitation of Radio Free Europe Nov. 2001, arrested by Czech police and Interpol at Ruzyně Airport under int. arrest warrant issued by Uzbekistan Interpol bureau alleging his participation in terrorist activities; lived in exile in Norway with political asylum status; f. Nat. Salvation Cttee 2005; arrested and detained by the Swedish police at Stockholm-Arlanda Airport under same int. arrest warrant May 2006, released the next day after Norwegian Govt confirmed his asylum status; currently based in Turkey, plot to assassinate him reported to be discovered by the Turkish police Dec. 2015. *Publications:* The Golden Head of the Avenger (screenplay), more than 20 books, including: Oydinlik sari 1993, E'tikodning chorrahasi bolmaydi 1994, Ikror 1995, Devlet sirlari (in Turkish) 1997, Turkistan suuru (in Turkish) 1997, Agaclar sair olsa (in Turkish) 1997, Yolnoma (in Uzbek) 1999, Yo'lnoma (in Turkish) 2002, The Articles 2003, Valfajr, Ko'men nashriyoti, Konya 2005, Publisistika, Izdatelstvo Bilgeoguz 2005. *Address:* c/o O'zbekiston Erk Demokratik Partiyasi (Freedom Democratic Party of Uzbekistan), 100055 Tashkent, Ipakchi ko'ch. 38, Uzbekistan (office). *Telephone:* 216-4152887 (Turkey, mobile). *E-mail:* m.salih@uzbekistanerk.com (office); admin@uzbekistanerk.org (office). *Website:* www.uzbekistanerk.com (office); muhammadsalih.com.

SALIH MUHAMMAD, Osman, BSc; Eritrean politician; *Minister of Foreign Affairs;* b. 1948; ed Haile Selassie I Univ. (Addis Ababa Univ.), Ethiopia; Head, Eritrean People's Liberation Front refugee schools, Sudan 1983–87; Head, Educ. Dept 1987; Commr for Eritrean Refugees' Affairs 1987–92; mem. Nat. Ass. 1993–; Minister of Educ. 1993–2007, of Foreign Affairs 2007–; mem. People's Front for Democracy and Justice (PFDJ), mem. Exec. Bd 1993–, mem. Cen. Ass. 1993–. *Address:* Ministry of Foreign Affairs, PO Box 190, Asmara, Eritrea (office). *Telephone:* (1) 127838 (office). *Fax:* (1) 123788 (office). *E-mail:* tesfai@wg.eol (office).

SALIJ, Rev. Jacek, MA, PhD; Polish ecclesiastic and professor of theology; *Director, Chair of Dogmatic Theology, Cardinal Stefan Wyszyński University;* b. 19 Aug. 1942, Budy; ed Acad. of Catholic Theology, Warsaw; ordained priest 1966; Asst Acad. of Catholic Theology (now Cardinal Stefan Wyszyński Univ.), Warsaw 1970–71, Asst Prof. 1971–90, Extraordinary Prof. 1990–99, Ordinary Prof. 2000–, currently Dir of the Chair of Dogmatic Theology; Co-Founder Gaudium Vitae Movt 1979–; mem. Council of Educ. attached to the Pres. of Poland 1992–95, Main Council of Higher Educ. 1993–96; consultant to Educ. of Faith Comm. of Episcopate of Poland 1997–; mem. Polish Soc. of Philosophy 1982–, PEN Club 1989–, Cttee for Theological Studies, Polska Akademia Nauk; Order of Polonia Restituta 2007; FENIKS Award 2004. *Publications include:* Modlitwa za świętych w liturgii rzymskiej 1974, Królestwo Boże w was jest 1980, Legendy dominikańskie (composition and translation) 1982, Rozpacz pokonana 1983, Rozmowy ze św. Augustynem 1985, Pytania nieobojętne 1986, Dekalog 1989, Wiara na co dzień 1994, Nadzieja poddawana próbom 1995, Nasze czasy są OK. 1997, Praca nad wiarą 1999, Divinations, Astrology, Reincarnation (in Russian). *Leisure interest:* cycling. *Address:* Cardinal Stefan Wyszyński University, ul. Dewajtis 5, 01-815 Warsaw, Poland (office). *Telephone:* (22) 5618 00 (office). *Website:* www.uksw.edu.pl (office).

SALIKHOV, Shavkat Ismailovich; Uzbekistani biochemist; *President, Uzbek Academy of Sciences;* b. 12 Dec. 1944, Tashkent; ed Tashkent State Univ. (now Nat. Univ. of Uzbekistan); fmr Dir Sadykov Inst. of Bioorganic Chemistry; fmr CHAP/Uzbekistan Program Man.; apptd Academician, Uzbek Acad. of Sciences 1995, Pres. 2006–; apptd Senator 2006; Chair. Bd of Trustees, Center of High Technologies, Nat. Univ. of Uzbekistan 2011–; Order El-Yurt Khurmatu 2008; Honored Scientist of Repub. of Uzbekistan 1998. *Publications:* over 350 scientific publications, including 2 monographs, 56 inventions, and 40 patents. *Address:* Uzbek Academy of Sciences, ul. Acad. Yahya Gulyamov, 70, 100047 Tashkent, Uzbekistan (office). *Telephone:* (71) 233-68-47 (office). *Fax:* (71) 233-74-82 (office). *E-mail:* academy@academy.uz (office). *Website:* academy.uz/en (office).

SALIM, Anthoni; Indonesian business executive; *President and CEO, Salim Group;* m.; three c.; ed Ewell County Technical Coll., UK; currently Pres. and CEO Salim Group (family business conglomerate); Propr, Universal Integrated Corpn Consumer Products Pte Ltd; CEO PT Indofood Sukses Makmur Tbk PT 2004–; Dir First Pacific Co. Ltd 1981–, Chair. (non-exec.) 2004–; Pres. Commr and Commr Fastfood Indonesia PT; Dir (non-exec.) Futuris Corpn Ltd 2003–; Dir Elders Australia Ltd; fmr Pres. Commr and Commr PT Indomobil Sukses Internasional TBK; mem. Int. Advisory Bd and Jt Advisory Council Allianz AG; mem. Advisory Bd Rabobank (Netherlands); fmr mem. Int. Advisory Bd GE International; mem. Asia Business Council 2004–. *Address:* Office of the President, Salim Group, Sudirman Plaza, Indofood Tower, Jawa Barat, Jakarta 12910, Indonesia (office). *Telephone:* (21) 57958822 (office). *Fax:* (21) 57935960 (office).

SALIM, Salim Ahmed; Tanzanian journalist and diplomatist; b. 23 Jan. 1942, Pemba Island, Zanzibar; m. Amne Salim; two s. one d.; ed Lumumba Coll., Zanzibar, Univ. of Delhi, India, Columbia Univ., USA; Publicity Sec., UMMA Party and Chief Ed. of Sauti ya UMMA 1963; Exec. Sec., United Front of Opposition Parties and Chief Ed. of its newspaper; Sec.-Gen. All-Zanzibar Journalists Union 1963; Amb. to UAR 1964–65, High Commr to India 1965–68, Dir African and Middle East Affairs Div., Ministry of Foreign Affairs 1968–69, Amb. to China and Democratic People's Repub. of Korea June–Dec. 1969, Amb. and Perm. Rep. to UN, New York 1970–80 (Pres. of Gen. Ass. 1979, Chair. UN Security Council Cttee on Sanctions against Rhodesia Jan.–Dec. 1975, Chair. UN Special Cttee on Decolonization 1972–80), also High Commr to Jamaica, accred to Guyana, Trinidad and Tobago, Barbados and Amb. to Cuba 1971–80, Minister of Foreign Affairs 1980–84; Prime Minister of Tanzania 1984–85, Deputy Prime Minister, Minister of Defence and Nat. Service 1986–89; Sec.-Gen. OAU 1989–2001; African Union Special Envoy for Darfur Talks and Chief Mediator for the Inter-Sudanese Peace Talks on the Darfur Conflict 2004–08; African Water Amb. 2002–; Chair. Advisory Bd, Inst. Security Studies, Pretoria, South Africa,

Advisory Bd of Trustees, Inst. of Peace, Leadership and Governance, Africa Univ., Mutare, Zimbabwe; Chair. Bd of Trustees, Mwalimu Nyerere Foundation 2002–, International Bd of Trustees, Africa Humanitarian Action, Addis Ababa, Ethiopia; mem. Bd of Dirs South Centre (inter-governmental body) 2002–05; Chancellor Hubert Kairuki Memorial Univ.; Hon. LLD (Univ. of Philippines) 1980, Hon. DH (Univ. of Maiduguri, Nigeria) 1983, Hon. DCL (Univ. of Mauritius) 1991, Hon. Dr of Arts (Univ. of Khartoum, Sudan) 1995, Hon. PhD (Univ. of Bologna, Italy) 1996, Hon. DJur (Univ. of Cape Town) 1998; Order of the United Republic of Tanzania 1985, Order of Mille Collines, Rwanda 1993, Grande Croix de l'Ordre Congolais du Dévouement, Republic of Congo 1994, Grand Officier de l'Ordre du Mérite, Central African Republic 1994, Grand Officier de l'Ordre National du Lion, Senegal 2000, Order of the Two Niles, Sudan 2001, Ordre El-Athir, Algeria 2001, Ordre du Mono, Togo 2001, Commandant de l'Ordre Nat., Mali 2001; Star of Africa, Liberia 1980, Medal of Africa, Libya 1999. *Address:* Mwalimu Nyerere Foundation, 6 Sokoine Drive, POB 71000, Dar es Salaam, Tanzania (office). *Telephone:* (22) 2118354 (office). *Fax:* (22) 2119216 (office). *E-mail:* mnf-tanzania@raha.com (office). *Website:* www.nyererefoundation.org (office).

SALINAS DE GORTARI, Carlos, PhD; Mexican economist, academic, government official and fmr head of state; b. 1948, Mexico City; m.; six c.; ed Nat. Univ. of Mexico, Harvard Univ., USA; apptd Asst Prof. of Statistics, Nat. Univ. of Mexico 1970; Research Asst, Harvard Univ. 1974; taught Public Finance and Fiscal Policy in Mexico 1976, 1978; Asst Dir of Public Finance, Ministry of Finance 1971–74, Head of Econ. Studies 1974–76, Asst Dir of Financial Planning 1978, Dir-Gen. 1978–79; Dir-Gen. of Econ. and Social Policy, Ministry of Programming and Budget 1979–81; Dir-Gen. Inst. of Political, Social and Econ. Studies 1981–82; Minister of Planning and Fed. Budget 1982–87; named as pres. cand. by Partido Revolucionario Institucional 1987, Pres. of Mexico 1988–94. *Publications include:* Mexico: The Policy and the Politics of Modernization 2002; numerous articles and essays.

SALINAS PLIEGO, Ricardo B., BA, MBA; Mexican business executive; *Chairman and President, Grupo Elektra SA de CV;* b. 1955; m. María Laura Medina; three c.; ed Instituto Tecnológico y de Estudios Superiores de Monterrey, Tulane Univ., USA; fmrly with Arthur Andersen, Brinkman Co.; joined Grupo Elektra Sa de CV 1981, Pres. 1989–, Chair. 1993–, business interests in retail, broadcasting, telecommunications and financial services, including TV Azteca, Banco Azteca, Elektra, Iusacell, Unefon; Chair. Exec. Cttee Grupo Salinas 1999–; est. Empresario Azteca Program, Empresario Azteca Asscn; f. Fundación Azteca 1997; mem. Business Advisory Bd International Organization for Migration. *Address:* Grupo Elektra, SA de CV, Avenida Insurgentes Sur 3579, Colonia, Tlalpán La Joya, 14000 México DF, Mexico (office). *Telephone:* (55) 1720-7000 (office). *Fax:* (55) 1720-7822 (office). *Website:* www.grupoelektra.com.mx (office); www.ricardosalinas.com.

SALISBURY, David Murray, MA; British financial services industry executive; b. 18 Feb. 1952; s. of Norman Salisbury and Isobel Sutherland Murray; m. Lynneth Mary Jones 1977; two d.; ed Harrow School, Trinity Coll., Oxford; joined J. Henry Schroder Wagg & Co. Ltd 1974, Chief Exec. Schroder Capital Man. Int. Inc. 1986–2001, Jt Chief Exec. Schroder Investment Man. Ltd 1995–97, Chair. 1997–2001, CEO Schroders PLC 2000–01; mem. Bd of Dirs Dimensional Fund Advisors Inc. 1988–96, CEO Dimensional Fund Advisors Ltd 2002–09, apptd Chair. 2002; Gov. Harrow School 1996–99, 2001–06. *Leisure interests:* tennis, skiing. *Address:* Dimensional Fund Advisors Ltd, Dimensional Place, 6300 Bee Cave Road, Building One, Austin, TX 78746, USA (office). *Website:* us.dimensional .com (office).

SALISBURY, 7th Marquess of; **Most Hon. Robert Michael James Gascoyne-Cecil,** PC, DL; British politician and university chancellor; *Chancellor, University of Hertfordshire;* b. 30 Sept. 1946; s. of 6th Marquess of Salisbury; m. Hannah Ann Stirling 1970; two s. three d.; ed Eton Coll., Univ. of Oxford; MP for Dorset S 1979–87; mem. House of Lords (Conservative) 1992–, sits in House of Lords as Lord Gascoyne-Cecil 1999–, on leave of absence 2002–, retd 2017; Parl. Under-Sec. of State for Defence 1992–94; Lord Privy Seal 1994–97; Shadow Leader of House of Lords 1997–98; Chair. Council of Royal Veterinary Coll. 1999–2007, Combined Clinical Science Foundation 2004–, Court of Patrons, Thrombosis Research Inst. 2010–; Chancellor Univ. of Hertfordshire 2005–; Gov. The Charterhouse 2009–; fmr Pres. Royal Agricultural Soc. of England; DL Herts. 2007. *Address:* Hatfield House, Hatfield, Herts., AL9 5NF, England (home). *Telephone:* (20) 7351-7458 (office). *Fax:* (20) 7351-7450 (office).

SALJE, Ekhard Karl Hermann, MA, PhD, FRS, FGS, FInstP, FRSA; British/German scientist and academic; *Professor Emeritus of Mineralogy and Petrology, University of Cambridge;* b. 26 Oct. 1946, Hanover; s. of Gerhard Salje and Hildegard Salje (née Drechsler); m. Elisabeth Démaret; one s. four d.; ed Univ. of Hanover, Univ. of Cambridge, UK; Prof. of Crystallography, Univ. of Hanover 1983–86; Lecturer in Mineral Physics, Univ. of Cambridge 1986–92, Prof. 1992–94, apptd Prof. of Mineralogy and Petrology 1994, now Prof. Emer., apptd Head, Dept of Earth Sciences 1998; Pres. Clare Hall, Cambridge 2002–08; Visiting Prof. in Paris, Grenoble, Le Mans (France), Nagoya (Japan), Bilbao (Spain), Max Planck Institute for Mathematics, Leipzig 2008–09, Univ. of Paris VII 2009; Pres. Alexander von Humboldt Asscn (UK) 2004–, European Trust UK; Programme Dir Cambridge-MIT Inst. CMI 2001–03; mem. Bd Univ. of Hamburg, Germany 2004–; mem. Working Party on Nuclear Waster, Royal Soc., British Pugwash Group, Wissenschaftsrat Germany; Bd mem. EIT Poland 2008, Parl. Office for Science and Tech.; Fellow, Akad. Leopoldina (Germany); Hon. Fellow, Darwin Coll., Cambridge 2001, Clare Hall 2008; Bundesverdienstkreuz 2006, Chevalier des Palmes académiques; Abraham-Gottlieb-Werner Medal 1997, Schlumberger Medal 1997, Humboldt Research Prize 1999, Ernst Ising Prize 2000, Gold Medal, Univ. of Hamburg 2002, Agricola Medal for Mineralogy 2006, Leverhulme Emer. Fellowship 2016. *Publications:* over 400 scientific publs including book on phase transitions in ferroelastic and co-elastic crystals. *Leisure interests:* music, painting. *Address:* Department of Earth Sciences, University of Cambridge, Downing Street, Cambridge, CB2 3EQ, England (office). *Telephone:* (1223) 768321 (office). *E-mail:* es10002@esc.cam.ac.uk (office). *Website:* www.esc.cam.ac.uk (office).

SALKIND, Ilya; Mexican film producer; b. 27 July 1947, Mexico City; s. of Alexander Salkind; ed Univ. of London; Assoc. Producer, Cervantes, The Light at the Edge of the World, Spain, 1974; f. Illya Salkind Co., Los Angeles (film production co.), currently CEO and Pres. *Films produced include:* Bluebeard 1972, The Three Musketeers 1973, The Four Musketeers 1974, The Twist 1976, The Prince and the Pauper 1977, Superman 1978, Superman II 1980, Superman III 1983, Supergirl 1984, Santa Claus: The Movie 1985, Christopher Columbus: The Discovery 1992, Heads N TailZ 2005, Young Alexander the Great 2010. *Television includes:* Superboy (series) 1988–92. *Website:* www.ilyasalkindcompany.net.

SALL, Macky; Senegalese geologist, politician and head of state; *President;* b. 11 Dec. 1961, Fatick; m.; three c.; ed Université Cheikh Anta Diop, Institut Français du Pétrole, Paris; Head of Div., Société des Pétroles du Sénégal 1993–2002, Dir-Gen. 2000–01; fmr Special Adviser to the Pres. on Energy and Mining; Minister of Energy, Mining and Hydraulics 2001–03, concurrently Minister for Equipment and Transport Oct.–Nov. 2002; Minister of State, Minister of the Interior and Local Communities, Govt Spokesperson 2003–04; Prime Minister of Senegal 2004–07; Pres. Nat. Ass. 2007–08; Mayor of Fatick 2002–08, 2009–; Pres. of Senegal 2012–; fmr mem. Parti démocratique sénégalais; Grand Croix de l'Ordre nat. du Lion, Grand Officier, Ordre de la Pléade, Ordre de la Francophonie, Légion d'honneur. *Address:* Office of the President, ave Léopold Sédar Senghor, BP 168, Dakar, Senegal (office). *Telephone:* 33-880-8080 (office). *Website:* www.presidence.sn (office).

SALLAH, Halifa; Gambian politician, sociologist and editor; *Leader, People's Democratic Organization for Independence and Socialism;* currently Leader (jtly), People's Democratic Org. for Independence and Socialism and Coordinator (Nat. Alliance for Democracy and Devt), represents constituency of Serrekunda Central; expelled from Nat. Ass. for membership of two political parties 2005, re-elected later same year; unsuccessful cand. in presidential election 2006; mem. Pan-African Parl.; Co-Ed. Foroyaa (newspaper). *Publications include:* The Sene-Gambia Confederation 1985, Where We Differ in Principle 1986, Are We For or Against Unity Among Opposition Forces? (with Sam Sarr) 1987, Hope Never Dies Where the Just are Alive 2006; numerous other books and articles. *Address:* People's Democratic Organization for Independence and Socialism (PDOIS), POB 2306, 1 Sambou Street, Churchill, Serrekunda, The Gambia (office). *Telephone:* 4393177 (office). *Fax:* 4393177 (office). *E-mail:* foroyaa@qanet.gm (office). *Website:* www.foroyaa.gm.

SALLAH, Ousman Ahmadou, BA; Gambian diplomatist and business executive; *Managing Director, Dandimayo Enterprise;* b. 26 July 1938, Kudang; s. of Ahmadou Jabel Sallah and Haddy Sallah; m. Ramou Sallah 1966; two s. two d.; ed Trinity Coll., Hartford, Conn., School of Int. Affairs, Columbia Univ., New York, London School of Econs; Asst Sec., Prime Minister's Office 1967; Asst Sec. Ministry of External Affairs 1967–68, Deputy Perm. Sec. 1973–74; First Sec., Head of Chancery and Acting High Commr, London 1971; Amb. to Saudi Arabia (also accred to Egypt, Iran, Kuwait, Qatar and UAE) 1974–79, to USA 1979–83; Perm. Rep. to UN 1979–83; Perm. Sec., Ministry of External Affairs and Head of Gambian Diplomatic Service 1982–87, Amb. to USA and Perm. Rep. to UN, New York 1987–94; Consultant, World Bank 1996–99; Man. Dir Dandimayo Enterprise 1999–; Hon. LLD (Trinity Coll., Hartford); Diploma in Int. Relations and Diplomacy from UNITAR. *Leisure interest:* tennis. *Address:* PO Box 667, Banjul, The Gambia. *Telephone:* 820-39-12 (office); 820-39-13 (home); 653-82-64. *Fax:* 820-39-06 (office). *E-mail:* torodo@sentoo.sn (office); sallahlamtoro@yahoo.com.

SALLAL, Jamal Abdullah Al-, BS, MA; Yemeni diplomatist and government official; b. 1 Jan. 1960, Sana'a; m. Nadia Abdallah Ali Al-Dabbi; three c.; ed Ain Shams Univ., Egypt, Johns Hopkins Univ., USA; Deputy to Perm. Rep., League of Arab States, Cairo 1994–98, mem. Arabic Dept, Ministry of Foreign Affairs 1998–2000, Dir North American Dept and Canadian Affairs 2000–02, Vice-Chair. North and South American Dept 2002–04, Consul-Gen., Consulate in Mumbai 2004–05, in Dubai and Northern Emirates, UAE 2005–06, Amb. to Iran (also accred to Azerbaijan) 2006–11, Amb. and Perm. Rep. to UN, New York 2011–14; Minister of Foreign Affairs June–Nov. 2014. *Address:* c/o Ministry of Foreign Affairs, POB 1994, San'a, Yemen (office).

SALLE, David, BFA, MFA; American artist; b. 28 Oct. 1952, Norman, Okla; s. of Alvin S. Salle and Tillie D. Salle (née Brown); ed California Inst. of Arts; retrospective exhbn Museum of Contemporary Art, Chicago 1987; Guggenheim Fellow 1986; works in public collections at Dallas Museum of Art, Dallas, Guggenheim Museum, New York, Metropolitan Museum of Art, New York, Museum of Modern Art, New York, Nat. Gallery of Australia, Australia, Indianapolis Museum of Art, Indianapolis, Museo di Arte Moderna e Contemporanea, Italy, Museum of Contemporary Art, Chicago, Museum of Contemporary Art, Los Angeles, North Carolina Museum of Art, Raleigh, Tate Gallery, England, Tel Aviv Museum of Art, Israel, Virginia Museum of Fine Arts, Richmond. *Films:* Search and Destroy (directed) 1995. *Publication:* How to See (essays) 2016. *Address:* David Salle Studio, 81 Hanson Place, Brooklyn, NY 11217, USA. *Telephone:* (718) 254-0460. *Fax:* (718) 254-8770. *E-mail:* studio@davidsallestudio .net. *Website:* www.davidsallestudio.net.

SALLEH, Dato' Seri Mohd Nor, BSc, MSc, PhD; Malaysian scientist and academic; b. 20 Oct. 1940, Negeri Sembilan; s. of Mohammed Nor and Nyonya Nor; m. Habiba Alias 1966; two s. one d.; ed Univ. of Adelaide, Australia, Australian Forestry School, Canberra, ITC Delft, Netherlands, Michigan State Univ., USA; Deputy Conservator of Forests, Forest Dept Peninsular Malaysia 1965, Dir Forest Inventory 1971; Dir Forestry Research Inst., Kepong 1977–85; Dir-Gen. Forest Research Inst. of Malaysia 1985–95 (retd); Adjunct Prof., Univ. Putra Malaysia 1994–96, Univ. Malaysia Sabah 2001–; Vice-Pres. Int. Union of Forest Research Orgs 1986–90, Pres. 1991–95; apptd Pres. Malaysian Nature Soc. 1978; mem. Nat. Environment Quality Council 1995; fmr Vice-Pres. then Sec.-Gen. Malaysian Acad. of Sciences; mem. Advisory Cttee Nat. Science Center, Nat. Planetarium and Nat. Park; mem. Malaysian Human Rights Comm. 2000–02; mem. Bd of Dirs Forest Trends, CIFOR, Inter Acad. Council; mem. Panel of Eminent Experts on Ethics in Food and Agricultural of FAO 2000, Scientific and Tech. Advisory Panel of Global Environmental Facility, FAO High-Level Panel of External Experts on Forestry (Chair. 2003), Ind. Panel to Review the Tropical Forestry Action Plan; Chair. International Union for Conservation of Nature East Asia Group on Sustainable Use Initiative; fmr Chair. Asia Pacific Asscn of Forest Research Insts; Trustee, Int. Network on Bamboo and Rattan; Dr hc (Nat. Univ. of Malaysia) 1992,

(Aberdeen) 1993; KMN 1981, DSNS 1989, Award of Third World Network of Scientific Orgs for Public Understanding of Science 1991, Langkawi Environmental Award 1991, Nat. Science Award 1993. *Publications include:* The Tropical Garden City 1990, The Malaysian Marine Heritage 1991, over 100 articles and contribs. to seminars, books and journals. *Leisure interests:* squash, badminton, reading, nature-oriented activities.

SALLENAVE, Danièle; French novelist, journalist and academic; b. 28 Oct. 1940, Angers; worked for Le Monde, Le Messager européen (review), Temps modernes; taught literature and film history at Univ. of Paris-X Nanterre 1968–2001; weekly columnist, France Culture 2009–14; seventh woman since 1635 to become mem. of Acad. française (Seat 30 of Maurice Druon) April 2011; Chair. Haut Comité, Commémorations Nationales; mem. jury of several prizes including Prix Femina, Prix Simone de Beauvoir, Prix de la langue française de la ville de Brive, Prix du roman historique des Rendez-vous de l'histoire de Blois; Grand prix de littérature de l'Acad. française 2005. *Publications include:* novels: Paysages de ruines avec personnages 1975, Le voyage d'Amsterdam ou les règles de la conversation 1977, Les Portes de Gubbio (Prix Renaudot 1980) 1980, Un printemps froid 1983, La vie fantôme 1986, Rome 1986, Conversations conjugales 1987, Adieu 1988, Le don des morts 1991, Le théâtre des idées 1991, Passages de l'Est 1991, Villes et villes 1991, Le principe de ruine 1991, Lettres mortes 1995, Les trois minutes du diable 1994, Viol 1997, À quoi sert la littérature? 1997, L'Amazone du grand Dieu 1997, Carnets de route en Palestine occupée: Gaza-Cisjordanie 1997, Stock 1998, D'amour 2002, Nos amours de la France – République, identités, régions (with Perico Legasse) 2002, dieu.com 2003, La Fraga (Grand Prix Jean Giono 2005) 2004, Quand même (Prix Marguerite Duras 2006) 2006, Castor de guerre (Prix Jean Monnet de littérature européenne du département de Charente 2008) 2008, Nous, on n'aime pas lire 2009, La vie éclaircie: Réponses à Madeleine Gobeil 2010, Sibir: Moscou-Vladivostok 2012, Dictionnaire amoureux de la Loire 2014, Le fond de l'air est frais 2015, L'églantine et le muguet 2018; trans. of Italian, including The Divine Mimesis by Pier Paolo Pasolini. *Address:* c/o Editions Gallimard, 5 rue Gaston-Gallimard, 75328 Paris Cedex 07, France. *Telephone:* 1-49-54-42-00. *Fax:* 1-45-44-94-03. *Website:* www.gallimard.fr/Contributeurs/Daniele-Sallenave.

SALLES, Walter; Brazilian film director and screenwriter; b. 12 April 1956, Rio de Janeiro; s. of Walther Moreira Salles and Elisa Margarida Gonçalves; m.; one s.; mem. jury, Cannes Film Festival 1999, 2002. *Films include:* Socorro Nobre (Fipa d'Or 1996) 1995, Foreign Lane (Grand Prix du Public Rencontres de Cinéma de Paris 1995), Central do Brasil (co-directed) (Golden Bear Berlin Int. Film Festival, Best Screenplay Sundance Inst.-NHK, Best Foreign Film British Acad. Awards, Best Foreign Film Golden Globes) 1998, O Primeiro Dia (co-directed) (Best Latin-American Film Mexican Acad. Awards) 1998, Abril Despedaçado (Little Golden Lion Award Venice Film Festival) 2001, Diarios de Motocicleta (The Motorcycle Diaries) 2004, Dark Water 2005, Paris, Je T'aime 2006, Linha de Passe 2008, On the Road 2012, Venice 70: Future Reloaded (documentary) 2013, Jia Zhang-ke by Walter Salles (documentary) 2014. *Achievements include:* competed as a kart driver winning Rio de Janeiro's championship twice. *Address:* c/o William Morris Endeavor Entertainment, 9601 Wilshire Boulevard, Beverly Hills, CA 90210, USA.

SALLINEN, Aulis Heikki; Finnish composer and academic; b. 9 April 1935, Salmi; s. of Armas Rudolf Sallinen and Anna Malanen; m. 1st Pirkko Holvisola 1955 (died 1997); four s.; m. 2nd Maija Lokka 1999; ed Sibelius Acad.; primary school teacher 1958–60; Man. Finnish Radio Orchestra 1960–70; Prof. of Arts, Sibelius Acad. 1965–76; mem. Bd of Dirs TEOSTO (Finnish Composers' Copyright Soc.) 1970–84, Chair. 1988–90; mem. Swedish Royal Music Acad. 1979–; mem. Finnish Composers' Soc., Sec. 1958–73, Chair. 1971–73; fmr mem. Bd Finnish Nat. Opera; apptd Prof. of Arts for Life (by the Finnish Govt) 1981; Hon. DPhil (Turku) 1991, (Helsinki) 1994; Nordic Council Music Prize 1978, Wihuri Int. Sibelius Prize 1983. *Compositions include:* eight symphonies, violin concerto, cello concerto, flute concerto, horn concerto and other orchestral music, five string quartets and other chamber music; film score for The Iron Age 1983. *Operas include:* The Horseman 1975, The Red Line 1978, The King Goes Forth to France 1982, Kullervo 1988, The Palace 1993, King Lear 1999.

SALLING, Augusta; Greenlandic politician; b. 1954; m. Jens Salling; two c.; ed Greenland Coll. of Educ.; teacher, deputy head then man. head of school, Qeqertarsuaq 1980–86; Gen. Man. Disko Havfiskeri SpA 1986–93; mem. Qeqertarsuaq Local Council 1993–2001; Mayor of Qeqertarsuaq 1993–97; mem. Landtag (Atassut) 1999–, Chair. 2002–05; Minister of Economy 2001–02; Vice-Premier and Minister of Finance 2003; Vice-Chair., Landsting and Deputy, Nordic Council, Del. from Greenland 2005–, also Deputy Centre Group. *Address:* Nordic Council, Delegation from Greenland, Grønlands Landstings Bureau, POB 1060, 3900 Nuuk, Greenland (office). *Telephone:* 345000 (office). *Fax:* 324606 (office). *E-mail:* aus@gh.gl (office). *Website:* www.nanoq.gl (office).

SALLOUKH, Fawzi; Lebanese government official and diplomatist; b. 1931, Qammatieh; m. Hind Basma; three c.; ed American Univ. Beirut; Prof. 1955–57; Dir of Public Relations, Franklin Publishing 1957–60; Amb. to Sierra Leone 1964–71, Cen. Dept, Ministry of Foreign Affairs 1971–78, Amb. to Nigeria 1978–85, to Algeria 1985–87, Dir of Econ. Affairs 1987–90, Amb. to Austria 1990–94, to Belgium 1994–95; Sec.-Gen. Islamic Univ. 1998–; Minister of Foreign Affairs and Emigrants 2005–06 (resgnd, resignation not accepted), 2008–09. *Address:* c/o Ministry of Foreign Affairs and Emigrants, al-Sultana Building, al-Jnah, Sultan Ibrahim, Beirut, Lebanon. *E-mail:* director@emigrants.gov.lb.

SALMAN, Sheikh Ali; Bahraini politician; *President, Al-Wefaq (Islamic National Accord Association—INAA);* b. 30 Oct. 1965, Bilad Al Qadeem; ed in Qom; Shia cleric; exiled to Dubai 1995, then sought asylum in London, returned to Bahrain 2001; currently Pres. Al-Wefaq (Islamic Nat. Accord Asscn—INAA); mem. Parl. for Jid Hafas 2006–. *E-mail:* webmaster@alwefaq.org. *Website:* www.alwefaq.org.

SALMON, Peter Andrew, BA; British broadcasting executive; *Chief Creative Officer, Endemol Shine Group;* b. 15 May 1956, Burnley; m. Sarah Lancashire; four s.; ed Univ. of Warwick; fmr Dir of Programmes, Granada TV and Controller of Factual Programmes, Channel 4; fmr producer and series Ed. BBC TV, later Head of Features, BBC Bristol, Controller, BBC One 1997–2000, Dir BBC Sport 2000–05; CEO The Television Corpn 2005–06; Chief Creative Officer, BBC Vision

2006–08, Dir BBC North, Salford 2008–14, Dir BBC England 2014–16, also mem. Exec. Team and responsible for BBC Academy, Birmingham; Chief Creative Officer, Endemol Shine Group 2016–; mem. Bd Liverpool Culture Co. 2005–; mem. Creative Skillset, Manchester International Festival, Comic Relief, North Arts Council Boards. *Leisure interests:* cycling, football, tennis. *Address:* Endemol Shine Group, The Shepherds Building, Charecroft Way, London, W14 0EE, England (office). *Telephone:* (870) 333-1700 (office). *Website:* www.endemolshinegroup.com (office).

SALMOND, Alexander (Alex) Elliot Anderson, MA; British politician; b. 31 Dec. 1954, Linlithgow, Scotland; s. of Robert F. Salmond and Mary S. Milne; m. Moira McGlashan; ed Linlithgow Acad., St Andrews Univ.; Vice-Pres. Fed. of Student Nationalists 1974–77, St Andrews Univ. Students' Rep. Council 1977–78; founder-mem. Scottish Nat. Party (SNP) 79 Group 1979, mem. SNP Nat. Exec. Cttee 1981–82, 1983–18, SNP Exec. Vice-Convener for Publicity 1985–87, SNP Nat. Convener (Leader) 1990–2000, 2004–14, resigned from SNP 2018; Asst Economist, Dept of Agric. and Fisheries 1978–80; Economist, Bank of Scotland 1980–87; MP for Banff and Buchan 1987–2010, for Gordon 2015–17, SNP Parl. Spokesperson on Constitution and Fishing 1997–99; MSP for Banff and Buchan 1999–2001, for Gordon 2007–11, for Aberdeenshire East 2011–16; First Minister of Scotland 2007–14 (resgnd following No-vote in independence referendum); Visiting Prof. of Econs, Univ. of Strathclyde; Patron Aberdeen Univ. Shinty Club 2011. *Leisure interests:* golf, reading, horseracing.

SALOLAINEN, Pertti Edvard, CBE, MSc (Econ); Finnish diplomatist and politician; *Vice-Chairman, Foreign Affairs Committee, Eduskunta (Parliament of Finland);* b. 19 Oct. 1940, Helsinki; s. of Edvard Paavali Salolainen and Ella Elisabeth Salolainen; m. Anja Sonninen 1964 (died 2005); one s. one d.; ed Helsinki School of Econs; TV journalist, Finnish Broadcasting Co. 1962–65, producer 1965–66, corresp. in London 1966–69, mem. Working Cttee, Supervisory Bd 1970–87; journalist, BBC, London 1966; Head of Dept, Finnish Employers' Confed. 1969–89; mem. Parl. (Eduskunta) 1970–96, 2007–, Chair. Foreign Affairs Cttee 2007–11, Vice-Chair. 2011–; Minister for Foreign Trade 1987–95; Deputy Prime Minister 1991–95; Head, negotiating team for entry of Finland into EU 1993–95, negotiating team of GATT (Uruguay Round); Amb. to UK 1996–2004; Chair. Finance Cttee IPU 1982–87; Hon. Founder Worldwide Fund for Nature (WWF) Finland 1972, Chair. WWF Finland; mem. Supervisory Bd's Working Cttee Outokumpu Mining Co. 1979–91; mem. Supervisory Bd Suomi-Salama Insurance Co. 1980–91, Finnair 1995–2002; mem. Legal Cttee Nordic Council 1982–87, Finnish Defence Forces Evaluation Team 2011–; holds mil. rank of Maj.; Nat. Coalition Party (Leader 1991–94); several solo exhbns of nature photographs in Finland, Germany and UK; Freeman of the City of London 1998; Grand Cross of the Lion of Finland 1994, Grand Cross of the Nordstjerna Order (Sweden) 1996, Grand Cross of FRG, of Hungary, of Austria, of Estonia (Maaria Maa); Medal of Merit, Finnish Defence Force 1997; Int. Conservation Award, Worldwide Fund for Nature, Gold Medal of Merit, Finnish Asscn for Nature Conservation, Jaakko Honko Medal, School of Econs, Helsinki. *Leisure interests:* nature conservation, nature photography, sports, tennis, swimming, foreign and security policy. *Telephone:* (50) 5122270 (office). *E-mail:* pertti.salolainen@eduskunta.fi (office).

SALOMÃO, Tomaz Augusto, BA MA; Mozambican economist and fmr international organization official; b. 16 Oct. 1954, Inhambane Prov.; m.; ed Commercial and Industrial School Vasca da Gama-Inhambane, Commercial Inst. of Lurenco Marques, Eduardo Mondlane Univ., Johns Hopkins Univ., USA; expert for study unit of Montepio Savings Bank of Mozambique 1974–76; expert at Ministry of Industry and Trade 1976–78; head of production unit at CIFEL 1978–81; Sec. of State for Nat. Defence 1983–89; Lecturer, Eduardo Mondlane Univ. 1990–93; Deputy Minister of Planning and Finance 1990–94, Minister of Planning and Finance, Gov. for Mozambique at African Devt Bank, IMF, World Bank 1994–99; Chair. SADC Transport and Communications Ministers' Cttee 2000–02, Chair. SADC Ministers' Cttee on ICTs 2002–03; Chair. African Union Ministers' Cttee on ICTs 2003–04; Minister of Transport and Communications of Mozambique 2000–04; Exec. Sec. SADC 2005–13; Chair. Standard Bank Mozambique; Visiting Research Fellow, Univ. of the Witwatersrand 2013–. *Leisure interests:* music, swimming, soccer, jogging, tennis, reading, gardening. *Address:* Standard Bank Mozambique, Praça 25 de Junho 1, CP 2086, Maputo, Mozambique (office). *Website:* www.standardbank.co.mz (office).

SALOMON, Jude Alix Patrick; Haitian civil servant and politician; b. 28 Oct. 1958, Port-au-Prince; ed Institut Nat. d'Admin, de Gestion et des Hautes Études Internationales, École Nat. d'Admin Publique du Québec (ENAP); joined Civil Service 1982, with Directorate of Treasury 1982–86, becoming Asst Head of Section then Head of Section –1984, Deputy Dir, Directorate of Budgetary Control 1995, Dir, Directorate of Public Debt –1999, Dir Gen., Directorate Gen. of Budget 1999–2005, Special Adviser with rank of Deputy Dir-Gen., Programming Dept, Ministry of Finance, Dir Gen., Gen. Inspectorate of Finance 2008; Minister of the Economy and Finance 2017–18; Prof. of Math., Budgeting and Public Finance, Univ. of Haiti 1994–; taught Budget Management in Public Admin Master Program, École Nat. d'Admin Publique du Québec (ENAP), Haiti; mem. World Bank Consultative Group for Haiti (Coordination of Int. Assistance). *Address:* c/o Ministry of the Economy and Finance, Palais des Ministères, rue Mgr Guilloux, Port-au-Prince, Haiti (office).

SALONEN, Esa-Pekka, FRCM; Finnish conductor and composer; *Principal Conductor and Artistic Adviser, Philharmonia Orchestra;* b. 30 June 1958, Helsinki; ed Sibelius Acad., Helsinki, studied composition with Rautavaara and conducting with Panula, studied composition with Niccolò Castiglioni and Franco Donatoni in Italy; conducting debut with Finnish Radio Symphony Orchestra 1979; London conducting debut with the Philharmonia Orchestra 1983, Prin. Guest Conductor 1984–94, Prin. Conductor and Artistic Adviser 2008–(21); Prin. Guest Conductor, Oslo Philharmonic Orchestra 1985–; Music Dir and The Walt and Lilly Disney Chair, Los Angeles Philharmonic Orchestra 1992–2009; Prin. Conductor, Swedish Radio Symphony Orchestra 1985–95, Conductor Laureate 2018–; Music Dir, San Francisco Symphony (2020–); Artistic Adviser, New Stockholm Chamber Orchestra 1986; Artistic Dir, Helsinki Festival 1995–96; Co-founder and Artistic Dir Baltic Sea Festival 2003–18; Creative Chair, Tonhalle Zurich Orchestra 2014–15; Marie-Josée Kravis Composer-in-Residence, New York Philharmonic 2015–; Artist in Asscn, Finnish Nat. Opera and Ballet 2016–; Hon.

mem. American Acad. of Arts and Sciences 2010; Officier, Ordre des Arts et des Lettres 1998, Pro Finlandia Medal of the Order of the Lion of Finland; Dr hc (Sibelius Acad.) 2003, (Hong Kong Acad. of Performing Arts) 2009, (Univ. of Southern California) 2010, (Royal Coll. of Music, London) 2011; Siena Prize, Accad. Chigiana 1993, Royal Philharmonic Soc. Opera Award 1995, Litteris et Artibus Medal (Sweden) 1996, Royal Philharmonic Soc. Conductor Award 1997, Helsinki Medal 2005, Musical America Musician of the Year 2006, Artist of the Year, Int. Classical Music Awards 2011, 2014 Nemmers Composition Prize 2014. *Compositions include:* orchestral: Concerto for alto saxophone and orchestra 1980–81, Giro 1982–97; chamber music: YTA I for alto flute 1985, YTA II for piano 1985, YTA III for cello 1986, Floof for soprano and chamber ensemble (UNESCO Rostrum Prize) 1990, Mimo II 1992, LA Variations 1996, Gambit 1998, Five Images after Sappho 1999, Mania 2000, Foreign Bodies 2001, Insomnia for orchestra 2002, Wing on Wing for soprano and orchestra 2004, Helix for orchestra 2005, Piano Concerto 2007, Nyx Violin Concerto (Univ. of Louisville Grawemeyer Award for Musical Composition 2012) 2009, Nyx for orchestra 2011, Karawane for orchestra and choir 2014. *Recordings include:* numerous recordings, including Rite of Spring 2007, Orango 2009, Passion De Simone 2012, R Strauss Elektra (Gramophone Award for Best Opera Recording 2015) 2014, Zappa: 200 Motels—The Suites 2015, Pollux 2018. *Film appearance:* Sketches of Frank Gehry 2006. *Address:* c/o Fidelio Arts Ltd, 103 Whitecross Street, No 5, London, EC1Y 8JD, England (office); Philharmonia Orchestra, 6th Floor, The Tower Building, 11 York Road, London, SE1 7NX, England (office). *Telephone:* (07733) 011145 (office); (20) 7921-3900 (office). *E-mail:* jessica@fidelioarts.com (office); mark@fidelioarts.com (office); orchestra@philharmonia.co.uk (office). *Website:* www.fidelioarts.com (office); www .philharmonia.co.uk (office); www.esapekkasalonen.com. *Fax:* (20) 7921-3950 (office).

SALOVEY, Peter, AB, AM, MS, MPhil, PhD; American psychologist, academic and university administrator; *President, Yale University;* b. 21 Feb. 1958, Cambridge, MA; s. of Ronald Salovey and Elaine Salovey; m. Marta Elisa Moret 1986; ed Stanford Univ., Yale Univ.; mem. Faculty, Yale Univ. 1986–, Chair. Dept of Psychology 2000–03, Chris Argyris Prof. of Psychology 2001–, Dean Grad. School of Arts and Sciences 2003–04, Dean Yale Coll. 2004–08, holds secondary faculty appointments in Schools of Man. and Public Health, Inst. for Social and Policy Studies, and Sociology Dept, Provost of Yale Univ. 2008–13, Pres. 2013–; co-developed, with John D. Mayer, framework called Emotional Intelligence; Fellow, Nat. Acad. of Medicine 2013–, American Acad. of Arts and Sciences 2013–; Dr hc (Univ. of Pretoria, South Africa) 2009, (Shanghai Jiao Tong Univ., China) 2014, (Nat. Tsing Hua Univ., Taiwan) 2014, (Harvard Univ.) 2015; Rensselaer Medal 1976, William Clyde DeVane Medal for Distinguished Scholarship and Teaching, Yale Coll. 2000, Lex Hixon '63 Prize for Teaching Excellence in the Social Sciences 2002, Lifetime Achievement Award, Connecticut Psychological Asscn 2015. *Publications include:* has written or edited more than a dozen books; hundreds of journal articles and essays, focused primarily on human emotion and health behaviour. *Address:* President's Office, Yale University, PO Box 208229, New Haven, CT 06520-8229, USA (office). *Telephone:* (203) 432-2550 (office). *Fax:* (203) 432-7105 (office). *E-mail:* peter.salovey@yale.edu (office). *Website:* president.yale .edu (office).

SALTYKOV, Boris Georgievich; Russian politician and economist; *President, Polytechnical Museum;* b. 27 Dec. 1940, Moscow; s. of Georgy Saltykov and Evdokia M. Saltykova (née Pukaleva); m. Lubov N. Klochkova 1972; two d.; ed Moscow Inst. of Physics and Tech.; researcher, Head of lab., Head of Div. Cen. Inst. of Econ. and Math. USSR (now Russian) Acad. of Sciences 1967–86; Head of Div. Inst. of Econ. and Forecasting of Progress in Science and Tech. (now Forecasting of Econ.) USSR Acad. of Sciences 1986–91; Deputy Dir Analytical Centre USSR Acad. of Sciences 1991; Minister of Science, Higher School and Tech. Policy of Russian Fed. 1991–92; Deputy Prime Minister of Russian Fed. 1992–93; Minister of Science and Tech. Policy 1993–96; apptd Pres. Russian House of Int. Science and Tech. Cooperation 1996; currently Pres. Polytechnical Museum; Chair. Russian Comm. for UNESCO 1992–97; Dir-Gen. Fed. State Unitary Co. Russian Technologies 1998–2000; mem. State Duma (Parl.) 1993–95; mem. Supervisory Council, RUSNANO Fund for Infrastructure and Educational Programs; Hon. Foreign mem. American Acad. of Arts and Letters 1999–. *Leisure interest:* cars. *Address:* Polytechnical Museum, 129223 Moscow, 119 Mira Avenue, (VDNKh), bldg. 46, (office); Protochny per. 11, ap. 99, 121099 Moscow, Russia (home). *E-mail:* info@ polymus.ru (office). *Website:* polymus.ru (office).

SALTZ, Jerry; American art critic; *Senior Art Critic and Columnist, New York Magazine;* b. 19 Feb. 1951, Oak Park, Ill.; m. Roberta Smith; Sr Art Critic, The Village Voice 1998–2007; Sr Art Critic and Columnist, New York Magazine 2006–; fmr visiting critic, Columbia Univ., Yale Univ., Museum of Modern Art, New York, Solomon R. Guggenheim Museum, New York, San Francisco Museum of Modern Art, Cleveland Art Inst.; Advisor, Whitney Biennial, Whitney Museum of American Art 1995; f. NAME Gallery, Chicago 1973; contributing ed. Art in America; Dr hc (School of the Art Inst. of Chicago) 2008. *Publications include:* Seeing Out Loud: The Village Voice Art Columns 1998–2003 2003, Seeing Out Louder: Art Criticism 2003–2009 2009, Sketchbook with Voices (co–author) 2011. *Address:* New York Media, 75 Varick Street, New York, NY 10013, USA (office). *Telephone:* (212) 508-0700 (office). *E-mail:* jerry_saltz@newyorkmag.com (office). *Website:* nymag.com (office).

SALVADOR CRESPO, María Isabel; Ecuadorean politician; b. 1962; Minister of Tourism 2005–07, of External Relations, Trade and Integration 2007–08 (resgnd); Amb. and Perm. Rep. to OAS, Washington, DC 2010–12, also Chair Perm. Council; Pres. Governing Council of the Galapagos 2013–. *Address:* Ministry of Foreign Relations, Trade and Integration, Avenida 10 de Agosto y Carrión E1-76, Quito, Ecuador (office). *Telephone:* (2) 299-3200 (office). *Fax:* (2) 299-3273 (office). *E-mail:* gabminis@mmrree.gob.ec (office). *Website:* www.mmrree.gob.ec (office).

SALVATORI, Carlo; Italian business executive; *Chairman, Lazard S.r.l.;* b. 7 July 1941, Sora, Frosinone; m.; three c.; ed Univs of Bologna and Siena; began career with Banca Naz. del Lavoro (BNL); Deputy Gen. Man. Cassa di Risparmio di Parma 1980–87; Gen. Man. in charge of Business Devt Div., BNL 1987–90; Gen. Man., then Man.-Dir, Banco Ambrosiano Veneto 1990–96; Gen. Man. and Dir Cariplo 1996–98; Man.-Dir Banca Intesa 1998–2000; Chair. UniCredito Italiano SpA 2002–06; CEO Unipol Gruppo Finanziario 2006–10; Chair. SeaChange

International 2009–, Lazard Italy 2010–; Deputy Chair. Mediobanca SpA –2006, Inst. for Int. Political Studies; mem. Bd of Dirs Riunione Adriatica di Sicurtà, Abi, Ras; mem. Man. Bd and Gen. Council, Assonime; Grand Officer of the Order of Merit of the Italian Republic 1993. *Address:* Lazard S.r.l., Via Dell'Orso 2, 20121 Milan, Italy (office). *Website:* www.lazard.com (office).

SALVINI, Matteo; Italian journalist and politician; *Deputy Prime Minister and Minister of the Interior;* b. 9 March 1973, Milan; m. Fabrizia Ieluzzi 2001 (divorced), one s.; one d. with Giulia Martinelli; ed Univ. of Milan; mem. Milan City Council 1993–2012; worked as reporter for Padania (daily newspaper) 1997 and for Radio Padania Libera (radio station of Lega Nord) 1999–; mem. European Parl. for North-West Italy (non-aligned, later Europe of Nations and Freedom Group) 2004–18; mem. Chamber of Deputies (Camera dei Deputati, lower house of parl.) for Lombardy constituency 1 2008–09, 2013; mem. Senate (upper house of parl.) for Calabria 2018–; Deputy Prime Minister and Minister of the Interior 2018–; mem. Lega Nord (Northern League) 1990–, Fed. Sec. 2013–. *Address:* Palazzo Chigi, Piazza Colonna 370, 00187 Rome, Italy (office). *Telephone:* (06) 67791 (office). *Fax:* (02) 6454475 (office). *E-mail:* ufficio_stampa@governo.it (office). *Website:* www .governo.it (office).

SALWAI, Charlot; Ni-Vanuatu accountant and politician; *Prime Minister;* accountant, Union Electrique du Vanuatu Ltd (electricity and water co.) 1987–88; accountant, Development Bank of Vanuatu 1988–90; accountant, Melanesia Shell Products Ltd 1990–91; Private Sec. to Prime Minister Carlot Korman 1991–95; Second Sec., Ministry of Finance 1996, First Sec., Ministry of Educ. 1997–98, First Political Adviser, Ministry of Trade 1998–99, First Political Adviser, Ministry of Youth 2000–02; mem. Parl. for Pentecost constituency 2002–, Deputy Leader of Opposition 2004–05, Opposition Whip 2005–07; Minister of Lands Aug.–Dec. 2004, of Educ. 2007, of Justice and Community Services Jan.–Oct. 2012, of Finance and Econ. Man. 2012–13, of Internal Affairs 2014, Prime Minister 2016–; mem. Union of Moderate Parties 2002–12, fmr Vice-Pres. (expelled 2012); mem. Reunification Movement for Change 2012–. *Address:* Prime Minister's Office, PMB 9053, Port Vila, Vanuatu (office). *Telephone:* 22413 (office). *Fax:* 26301 (office). *Website:* www.governmentofvanuatu.gov.vu (office).

SALYANOVA, Aida Jenishbekovna, LLB; Kyrgyzstani lawyer and government official; b. 6 Aug. 1972, Naryn; m. Bakyt Abdykaparov; one s. one d.; ed Frunze Coll. of Soviet Trade, Bishkek, Kyrgyz State Nat. Univ.; Teacher, Bishkek Commercial Coll. 1992–96; Prof., Chui Univ., Bishkek 1996–97; Adviser, Jogorku Kenesh (Supreme Council, Parl.) 1997–2005, Head of Legal Dept (responsible for constitutional law, govt, rule of law and judicial reform) 2005–08; Sec. of State, Ministry of Justice 2008–10; Minister of Justice April–Dec. 2010; Plenipotentiary Rep. of Pres. in Jogorku Kenesh 2010–12; Acting Prosecutor-Gen. March–April 2011, Prosecutor-Gen. April 2011–15 (resgnd); State Counsellor of Justice, Third Class.

SALZ, Sir Anthony Michael Vaughan, Kt, LLB, FRSA; British lawyer; *Executive Vice-Chairman, N M Rothschild & Sons Ltd;* b. 30 June 1950, Tavistock, Devon, England; s. of Michael H. Salz and Veronica Edith Dorothea Elizabeth Salz (née Hall); m. Sally Ruth Hagger 1975; one s. two d.; ed Summerfields School, Oxford, Radley Coll. and Univ. of Exeter; articled clerk, Kenneth Brown Baker Baker 1972–74, Asst Solicitor 1974–75; Asst Solicitor, Freshfields 1975–77, seconded to Davis Polk & Wardwell, New York, USA 1977–78, solicitor, Freshfields 1978–80, Partner 1980–96, Sr Partner 1996–2000, Co-Sr Partner, Freshfields Bruckhaus Deringer 2000–06; Vice-Chair. Bd of Govs, BBC 2004–06, Acting Chair. 2006; Exec. Vice-Chair. N M Rothschild & Sons (investment bank) 2006–; Chair. Bloomsbury Publishing Plc 2013–, Freeformers Holdings Ltd 2016–; Chair. Teach First, Business leaders Council 2012–, Ind. Comm. on Youth Crime and Anti-Social Behaviour 2008–10; mem. Bd of Dirs, Habitat for Humanity GB 2004–10, Scott Trust 2009–, Guardian Foundation 2013–, Forward Inst. 2014; mem. Tate Gallery Corp. Advisory Group 1997– (Chair. 1997–2002); mem. Advisory Panel, Swiss Re Centre for Global Dialogue 2006–11; mem. Advisory Bd, Univ. of Exeter School of Business and Econs 2003–; Financial Services Knowledge Transfer Network 2010–14; Co-Chair. Educ. and Employers Taskforce 2009–10; mem. Business Action on Homelessness Exec. Forum –2006, Business in the Community Nat. Educ. Leadership Team 2007–10; apptd to lead review of business practices at Barclays following Libor rigging scandal 2012; Lead Ind. Bd mem. (non-exec.), Dept for Educ. 2010–12; Gov. Wellington Coll. Acad. Trust 2008; Trustee, Tate Foundation 2000–, Paul Hamlyn Foundation 2005–, Conran Foundation 2007, Media Standards Trust 2008–15, Royal Opera House Covent Garden Foundation 2008–16, Reprieve 2011–, The High Street Fund 2011–13, Foundation for Future London, 2015–, Eden Trust 2002–15 (Chair. 2009–15), SHINE, Supreme Court of UK Arts Trust 2016–: Support and Help in Educ. 2008–10. *Publications include:* contribs to various legal books and journals. *Leisure interests:* fishing, soccer, sports, theatre, arts. *Address:* N M Rothschild & Sons Ltd, New Court, St Swithin's Lane, London, EC4N 8AL, England (office). *Telephone:* (20) 7280-5186 (office). *Website:* www.rothschild.com (office).

SALZA, Enrico; Italian banking executive; *Chairman, Tecno Holding SpA;* b. 25 May 1937, Turin; Deputy Chair. and CEO Il Sole 24 Ore 1971–89; Deputy Chair. Sanpaolo 1984–95; CEO Cerved SpA 1995–2002; Dir and mem. Exec. Cttee Sanpaolo IMI SpA (now Intesa Sanpaolo SpA) 1998–2001, Deputy Chair. Man. Bd 2001–04, Chair. Sanpaolo IMI Group 2004–07, Chair. Man. Bd Intesa Sanpaolo SpA 2007–10; Chair. Tecno Holding SpA, Italconsult SpA, Techno Investments Ltd; Founder and first Chair. Confindustria Young Entrepreneurs; fmr Chair. Turin Chamber of Commerce, Unioncamere Piemontese, Chairman ASP (Asscn for Scientific and Technological Devt of Piedmont); Dir Centro Congressi Torino Incontra, Nomisma; fmr Dir Union Bank of Switzerland, Compagnia di San Paolo; mem. Exec. Council ICC; Hon. Chair. Associazione Sviluppo Scientifico e Tecnologico of Piedmont; Cavaliere del Lavoro, Cavaliere di Gran Croce dell'Ordine al Merito della Repubblica 2007; hon. degree in Man. Eng (Politecnico di Torino). *Address:* Tecno Holding SpA, Piazza Sallustio 9, 00187 Rome, Italy (office). *Telephone:* (06) 42011629 (office). *Fax:* (06) 42814495 (office). *E-mail:* info@ tecnoholding.it (office). *Website:* www.tecnoholding.it (office).

SAM-SUMANA, Samuel, BSc; Sierra Leonean business executive and politician; b. 17 April 1962, Koidu Town, Kono Dist; s. of Chief Sam-Sumana and Haja Sia Hawa Sam-Sumana; m.; three c.; ed Metropolitan State Univ., Minn., USA,

America Inst. of Diamond Cutting and Polishing, Deerfield Beach, Fla, USA, Knollwood Computer and Business School, St Louis Park, Minn.; fmr System Officer of network support for Prudential Financial Group, USA; fmr Vice-Pres. Network Support System, Allina Health Services and Seagate Technologies, USA; served as Regional Man. for C-12 International, Tex., USA (co. engaged in diamond buying in Sierra Leone, Guinea and Liberia); fmr Man. Dir United Diamond Mining Co., Kodu Town, Kono Dist; CEO Aries Rehabilitation Construction and Supplies (ARCS) SL Ltd –2007; mem. All People's Congress party, mem. 'Five-Man Committee'; Vice-Pres. of Sierra Leone 2007–15; Coalition for Change presidential cand. 2018; Vice-Chair. Kono-Union Chapter USA, Minn.

SAMA, Koffi, DMV; Togolese lawyer and politician; b. 1944, Amoutchou, Ogou Prefecture; m.; ed Lycée Bonnecarrère, Lomé and Ecole Nat. Vétérinaire de Toulouse, France; qualified as a veterinary surgeon 1972; Minister of Youth, Sport and Culture 1981–84; Dir-Gen. SOTOCO (Société Togolaise de Coton) 1990–96; Minister of Health 1996–99, of Nat. Educ. and Research 1999–2002, Prime Minister of Togo 2002–05; Special Adviser to Pres. 2005; Head of regional observation mission to presidential election in Burkina Faso 2010, to presidential and legislative elections in Niger 2011; apptd mem. Jt African Union–ECOWAS High-Level Mission to Senegal 2012, also Leader, ECOWAS Observation Mission to Senegal's 2012 presidential election; mem. Rassemblement du peuple togolais—RPT (fmr Sec.-Gen.); Officier, Ordre de Mono, Grand Officier, Ordre du Mérite agricole.

SAMAAN, Alice Thomas; Bahraini diplomatist and politician; b. 1 Jan. 1939, Manama; single; ed British Lebanese Training Coll., Beirut, Univ. of Southern California, USA; fmr teacher, American Mission School, Bahrain; fmr producer, presenter and dir of radio programmes for a religious radio station in Beirut, Lebanon; fmr Head of Overseas and Local Training, Ministry of Health; fmr Int. Program Officer for UNICEF in Bahrain and Oman; fmr Ed., Producer and Presenter of News, Bahrain Radio and TV Station; mem. Shura Council (Advisory Council) 2000–02, presided over as most sr mem. in absence of Chair. and two Deputy Chairs (first non-Muslim to act as Chair.) 2005, later Second Deputy Chair. Majlis ash-Shoura, mem. Services Cttee for initial term, Vice-Chair. for second and fourth sessions of first legis. term; mem. Ad-hoc Cttee for Women and Children for first term; Amb. to UK 2011–15; mem. Exec. Bd, American Mission Hosp., Bd of Dirs Al-Raja School for one term, Supreme Council for Vocational Training in Bahrain for one term, Bd of the Coll. of Health Sciences, Ministry of Health, Exec. Cttee, Nat. Program for Mother and Child Care, Oman.

SAMAKUVA, Isaías Henrique Gola; Angolan politician; *President, União Nacional para a Independência Total de Angola (UNITA);* b. 8 July 1946, Cunje; fmr Treas., União Nacional para a Independência Total de Angola (UNITA), Chief of Logistics mid-1980s, Rep. in Paris 1998–2002, fmr Interim Leader, Pres. 2003–. *Address:* União Nacional para a Independência Total de Angola (UNITA), Rua 28 de Maio, 1ª Travessa 2, Maianga, Luanda, Angola (office). *Telephone:* 222331215 (office). *E-mail:* info@unitaangola.org (office). *Website:* www.unitaangola.com (office); www.kwacha.net (office); www.samakuva.org.

SAMAR, Sima, OC, DMed; Afghan politician, physician and human rights activist; *Chairperson, Afghanistan Independent Human Rights Commission;* b. 3 Feb. 1957, Jaghori, Ghazni; m. Abdul Raoof; one s. one d.; ed Kabul Univ.; exiled in Pakistan following Soviet invasion; Founder and Dir Shuhada Org., f. Shuhada hosp. for Afghan women and children, Quetta, Pakistan 1989, founder of three medical clinics, four hosps and girls' schools in rural Afghanistan (also providing medical training, literacy programmes and food aid), f. school for refugee girls in Quetta, f. Shuhada Org.; mem. Women Living Under Muslim Law; political activist and opponent of women's subjugation under Taliban regime; Vice-Chair. and Minister of Women's Affairs, Afghan Interim Admin 2001–02; currently Chair. Afghanistan Ind. Human Rights Comm.; UN Special Rapporteur for Human Rights in Sudan 2005–09; mem. Truth and Justice Party 2011; Hon. LLD (Univ. of Alberta) 2004, (Univ. of Carleton) 2010; Hon. DHumLitt (Brown Univ.) 2005, (Salem State Univ., USA) 2013; numerous awards, including Community Leadership Award, Ramon Magsaysay Award Foundation 1994, Global Leader for Tomorrow, World Econ. Forum 1995, 100 Heroines Award 1998, Paul Gruniger Human Rights Award 2001, Voice of Courage Award, Women's Comm. for Refugee Women and Children 2001, Best Social Worker, Mailo Trust Foundation, Pakistan 2001, Int. Human Rights Award, Int. Human Rights Law Group 2002, Freedom Award, Women's Asscn for Freedom and Democracy, Spain 2002, Lawyers Cttee for Human Rights Award 2002, Silver Banner Award, Italy 2002, Women for Peace, Together for Peace Foundation, Rome 2002, Silver Rose Award, Brussels 2003, Perdita Huston Human Rights Award 2003, UN Asscn of the Nat. Capital Area 2003, Paul Schiller Stiftung Award 2004, Global Women's Rights Award 2007, Ypres Peace Prize 2008, Asia Democracy and Human Rights Award 2008, Don and Arvonne Fraser Human Rights Award, Advocates for Human Rights 2009, Politikens Freedom Prize (Denmark) 2009, Geuzen Medal (Netherlands) 2011, Tipperary Peace Prize (Ireland) 2011, Stephen J. Solarz Award for Commitment to Peace, Justice and Security, Int. Crisis Group, New York 2011, Right Livelihood Award 2012, Allard Prize for Int. Integrity (Canada) 2013. *Address:* Afghanistan Independent Human Rights Commission, Pul-i-Surkh, Karti 3, Kabul (office); Darulaman Road, Street No. 9, House No. 566, 6th District, Kabul, Afghanistan (home). *Telephone:* (20) 2500676 (office); 700-276283 (mobile). *Fax:* (20) 2500677 (office). *E-mail:* aihrc@aihrc.org.af (office); sima_samar@yahoo.com (home). *Website:* www.aihrc.org.af (office).

SAMARAS, Antonis C., BA, MBA; Greek economist and politician; b. 23 May 1951, Athens; s. of Prof. Constantine Samaras and Lena Samaras (née Zannas); m. Georgia Kretikos; one s. one d.; ed Athens Coll., Amherst Coll. and Harvard Business School, USA; mem. Nea Demokratia (ND—New Democracy) –1993, Sec. 1989–92, rejoined party 2004, Pres. ND 2009–15; mem. Parl. (Vouli) for Pref. of Messenia 1977–93, 2007–, Leader of the Opposition 2009–11 (then supported Govt of Lucas Papademos), 2015–, mem. Econ. Affairs and European Affairs Cttees 2007–; Minister of Finance July–Oct. 1989, of Foreign Affairs 1989–90, of Culture Jan.–Oct. 2009; Prime Minister of Greece following formation of coalition govt with Panellínio Socialistiko Kinima (PASOK—Panhellenic Socialist Movt) and Dimokratiki Aristera (DIMAR—Democratic Left) 2012–15; mem. Messinian Political Spring 1993–, Pres. –2004; mem. European Parl. 2004–09, mem. Budget Cttee, Cttee on Econ. and Monetary Policy, Comm. for the Lisbon Strategy, Cttee on Parl. Co-operation EU-Russia. *Address:* 18 Odos Rigillis, 106 74 Athens; Parliament (Vouli), Parliament Building, Leoforos Vassilissis Sofias 2, 100 21 Athens, Greece (office). *Telephone:* (210) 3707000 (office). *Fax:* (210) 3707814 (office). *E-mail:* asamaras@parliament.gr (office). *Website:* www.hellenicparliament.gr (office).

SAMARASEKERA, Indira V., OC, BSc, MS, PhD, DSc, FRSC, FCAE; Canadian (b. Sri Lankan) professor of metals and materials engineering and university administrator; *President Emeritus, University of Alberta;* b. 11 April 1952, Colombo, Sri Lanka; m.; two c.; ed Univ. of Ceylon, Univ. of California, USA, Univ. of British Columbia; fmr mechanical engineer, Refinery of Ceylon Petroleum Corpn; emigrated to Canada 1977; fmr Hays-Fulbright Scholar; fmr Dir of Student Affairs, Minerals, Metals and Materials Soc. of AIME; apptd Prof. Dept of Metals and Materials Eng and Centre for Metallurgical Process Eng, Univ. of British Columbia 1980, first Dofasco Chair in Advanced Steel Processing 1996, Vice-Pres. Research 2000–05; Pres. and Vice-Chancellor Univ. of Alberta 2005–15, Pres. Emer. 2015–; mem. Bd of Dirs Scotiabank 2008–, Discovery Parks Inc., Genome British Columbia, Canadian Microelectronics Corpn, Michael Smith Foundation for Health Research, The Stem Cell Network, Canadian Genetics Diseases Network, Provincial Health Services Authority; E.W.R. Steacie Fellow 1991; advisor to Canadian Minister of Environment at Copenhagen Summit 2009; moderator and speaker at World Econ. Forum in Davos 2010, 2011, 'Summer' Davos in China; mem. Science and Eng Advisory Cttee, Alberta Ingenuity Fund, Presidential Advisory Cttee, MIT, Carnegie Mellon Univ.; Vice-Chair. UNESCO Forum Scientific Cttee for Europe and N America; fmr Pres. Metallurgical Soc. of CIM; fmr mem. Nat. Research Council of Canada, Nat. Advisory Bd on Minerals and Metals, British Columbia Research Inst. for Children and Women's Health, Killam Selection Cttee for Canada Council for the Arts, Int. Review Cttee for Ontario Challenge Fund, Aquanet-NCE; fmr mem. Bd Children and Women's Health Centre of BC, TRIUMF; Fellow, Canadian Inst. of Mining, Metallurgy and Petroleum; Dr hc (Univ. of British Columbia, Univ. of Waterloo, Univ. of Montreal, Western Univ., Queen's Univ., Belfast, NI); Iron and Steel Soc. of AIME Robert W. Hunt and Charles H. Herty Best Paper Awards (jtly), UK Materials Soc. Williams Prize and Ablett Prize, TMS Extraction and Processing Technology Award, Univ. of British Columbia, Killam Prize and McDowell Medal for research excellence, British Columbia Science Council Award for New Frontiers in Research, Canadian Learning Partnership Award 2008, Peter Lougheed Leadership Award, Public Policy Forum (Canada) 2012, Leadership Award, CASE Dist VII (USA) 2012. *Address:* 3014 West 24th Avenue, Vancouver, BC, V6L 1R6, Canada.

SAMARASINGHE, Hudson; Sri Lankan journalist, broadcasting executive and fmr politician; b. Peradeniya; ed Arethusa Coll., Howard Univ., USA; has worked in various positions for Sri Lanka Broadcasting Corpn for 40 years, including broadcaster, Chair. (for fourth time) 2010–15; mem. Parl. (UNP) for Colombo East constituency 1992–94.

SAMARASINGHE, Maj.-Gen. M. C. Mendaka P., MSc, MPh; Sri Lankan army officer; b. 1 April 1958, Colombo; ed St Thomas' Coll., Mount Lavinia, Coll. of Mil. Eng, India, Royal Mil. Coll. of Science, UK, Fort Leonardswood, USA, Madras Univ., India; joined Sri Lanka Mil. Acad. as Officer Cadet 1978, passed out 1980, rank of 2nd Lt 1980, joined 1st Field Engineer Regt, becoming Commdr Combat Engineers, later Col-Gen. Staff, 55 Infantry Div., Gen. Officer Commanding, 22 Div., Trincomalee, Chief Instructor, Army Command and Staff Coll., Brig.-Gen. Staff Security Forces, Commdr Security Forces, Jaffna –2009, Army Chief of Staff 2009–10, transferred to Jt Operations Command 2010; mem. Advisory Group to Govt of Sri Lanka Del. during peace talks with Liberation Tigers of Tamil Eelam (LTTE), Geneva, Switzerland Feb. 2006; Rana Wickrama Padakkama, Rana Sura Padakkama for gallantry during operations, Utthama Seva Padakkama for meritorious service; Sri Lanka Mil. Acad. Sword of Honour for Best All Round Cadet 1980.

SAMARASINGHE, Adm. Thisara Sugeeshwara Gunasekara; Sri Lankan naval officer (retd) and diplomatist; b. 16 July 1954, Colombo; s. of Francis Samarasinghe and Umawathie Samarasinghe; m. Malathie Samarasinghe; one s. one d.; ed Royal Coll., Colombo (Sr Prefect and Regimental Sergeant Maj. of the Cadet Corps), Naval and Maritime Acad., Britannia Royal Naval Coll., UK, Navigation and Direction School, INS Venduruthy, India, Naval Staff Coll. (Class 38), Naval War Coll., Newport, RI, USA, Nat. Defence Coll., New Delhi; joined Sri Lanka Navy as an Officer Cadet 1974; served on board Short Patrol Craft, Long Patrol Craft and in command of one of first two Dvora-Mk I Fast Attack Crafts 1985; later served on board Fast Gun Boats of 3rd Fast Gun Boats Squadron and Surveillance Command Tender and Surveillance Command Ship (then the Flagship) of 7th Surveillance Command Squadron; shore commands included a naval base in northern naval area and of two training establishments; also served in several Staff and Deputy Dir/Dir appointments at Naval HQ; ADC to HRH The Prince of Wales during his state visit to Sri Lanka for 50th Anniversary Independence Day Celebrations 1998; as a Cdre, posted as Deputy Area Commdr of Northern Naval Area, Eastern Naval Area and Southern Naval Area, before being apptd Commdr of Southern Naval Area 2002–04; first Dir, Gen. Services, and concurrently Dir Naval Projects and Plans, Naval Asst to Commdr of the Navy and Prin. Staff Officer of Jt Operations HQ under the Chief of Defence Staff 2004–05; led Naval dels to India, Russia, Israel and USA on bilateral issues 1995–2006; rank of Rear Adm. 2005; Acting Commdr Northern Naval Area 2005–06; Dir-Gen. Naval Operations 2006–07; Commdr Eastern Naval Area during Eastern operations and in 2008, Commdr Northern Naval Area during Northern offensive 2007–09; apptd Chief of Staff of the Navy 2009, Commdr of the Navy 2009–11; rank of Rear Adm. 2005, Vice-Adm. 2009, Adm. 2011 (retd); High Commr to Australia 2011–15; mem. Prime Ministerial del. on state visit to Indonesia 2006, of Presidential del. on state visit to Libya 2009; Rana Sura Padakkama (RSP) for gallantry in combat, Vishista Seva Vibhushanaya (VSV) and Uttama Seva Padakkama (USP) service medals, Sri Lanka Armed Services Long Service Medal, Purna Bhumi Padakkama Medal, North and East Operations Medal, and others; won Sword of Honour of 4th intake at Naval and Maritime Acad., Best Int. Midshipman Award, Britannia Royal Naval Coll. 1976, five commendation letters from four Commdrs of the Navy 1977–2006.

SAMARAWEERA, Mangala, BA; Sri Lankan politician; *Minister of Finance and Mass Media;* b. 21 April 1956, Matara; s. of Mahanama Samaraweera and Khema Samaraweera; ed Central St Martin's School of Art, UK; returned to Sri Lanka after studies in UK 1982, worked as Visiting Lecturer, Inst. of Aesthetic Studies, Univ. of Kelaniya, also served as Design Consultant, Nat. Design Centre of Sri Lanka; Organizer for Matara, Sri Lanka Freedom Party (SLFP) 1983, apptd mem. SLFP Central Political Cttee 1993, Treas. SLFP 2002–04, then Asst Sec., Founder and Leader, SLFP—Mahajana Wing 2007; mem. Parl. (SLFP) for Matara Dist 1989–2010, for Matara Dist (United National Party—UNP) 2010–, Chief Opposition Whip 2001–04; Minister of Posts and Telecommunications 1994–2000, Minister of Media and Information and Govt Spokesman 1997–2000, Minister of Urban Devt, Construction and Public Utilities 2000–01, Minister of Ports and Aviation and Media and Deputy Minister of Educ. 2004–07, Minister of Information 2004, of Foreign Affairs 2005–07, 2015–17, of Finance and Mass Media 2017–; Head of UNP media and communications unit 2011–, mem. UNP Leadership Council 2012–; mem. Exec. Cttee of UNESCO representing Sri Lanka 2004–06. *Address:* Ministry of Finance and Mass Media, 163, Asi Disi Medura, Kirulapone Mawatha, Polhengoda, Colombo 5 (office); Francis Samaraweera Mawatha, Hakmana Road, Matara, Sri Lanka (home). *Telephone:* (11) 2513459 (office). *E-mail:* samaraweera_m@parliament.lk (office). *Website:* www.media.gov.lk (office).

SAMARDŽIC, Vice-Adm. Dragan; Montenegrin naval officer and government official; b. 14 May 1963, Kotor; m. Branka Samardžic; s. one d.; ed Naval Acad., Gen. Staff School, War Coll., Belgrade; commissioned as Ensign in Montenegrin Navy, served aboard 401-type missile gun boats as Weapons Officer, XO, CO and Commdr of Squadron 1985–95; various positions in 18th Flotilla HQ including Chief of Staff and Deputy Flotilla Commdr 1995–2001, Flotilla Commdr 2001–03; Deputy of Mil. Cabinet to Pres. of State Union of Serbia and Montenegro, Belgrade 2003; Chief of Staff Naval Corps and promoted to Flag Officer 2003–05; C-in-C Serbia and Montenegro Navy 2005–06; Deputy Chief of Gen. Staff, Army of Montenegro 2006–07, Chief of Gen. Staff 2008–17; Asst Minister for Material Resources, Ministry of Defence 2007–08; Cavaliere dell'Ordine 'Al Merito (Italy) 2006, numerous decorations from Montenegrin Govt.

SAMAWI, Khalid al-; Syrian banker and gallery owner; *Founder, Ayyam Gallery;* fmr banker based in London and Switzerland –2006; Founder Ayyam Gallery, Damascus 2006, also of sister galleries in Dubai, Beirut, Jeddah, London and Cairo; Entrepreneur of the Year, Arabian Business Achievement Awards 2009. *Address:* Ayyam Gallery, Mezzeh West Villas 30, Chile Street, Samawi Building, Damascus, Syria (office). *Telephone:* (11) 6131088 (office). *Fax:* (11) 6131087 (office). *E-mail:* info@ayyamgallery.com (office). *Website:* www.ayyamgallery.com (office).

SAMBA-PANZA, Catherine, DESS; Central African Republic lawyer and politician; b. 26 June 1954, Fort Lamy, French Equatorial Africa (now N'Djamena, Chad); m. Cyriaque Samba-Panza; three c. from previous m.; ed Panthéon-Assas Univ., France; early career as lawyer with Central African Repub. br. of Allianz Group; Mayor of Bangui 2013–14; Interim Pres. of Central African Repub. 23 Jan. 2014–Feb. 2016; mem. Asscn des femmes juristes de Centrafrique, Asscn des maires francophones. *Address:* c/o Office of the President, Palais de la Renaissance, Bangui, Central African Republic (office).

SAMBI, Ahmed Abdallah; Comoran politician, business executive and fmr head of state; b. 5 June 1958, Mutsamudu, Anjuouan; m. Hadjira Djoudi 1988; two s. five d.; ed in Saudi Arabia, Sudan and Hawzat Al Qaaim Coll., Iran; f. madras for girls 1986, imprisoned for 21 days following riot after closure of school by authorities in 1987; co-f. Ulézi Radio and TV Ulézi 1990; co-f. National Front for Justice Party 1990, soon left politics to concentrate on business activities; owner of factories producing mattresses, bottled water, and perfume; Pres. of Comoros 2006–11. *Leisure interests:* basketball, football, tennis.

SAMBIA, Brig-Gen. Pierre Chrysostome; Central African Republic politician; Dir-Gen. of Nat. Gendarmerie –2015; Minister of Public Security, Emigration and Immigration 2015–16. *Address:* c/o Ministry of Public Security, Emigration and Immigration, Bangui, Central African Republic (office).

SAMBLES, J(ohn) Roy, BSc, PhD, FRS; British physicist and academic; *Professor of Experimental Physics, University of Exeter;* b. 14 Oct. 1945, Callington, Cornwall; s. of Charles Henry Sambles and Georgina Sambles (née Deeble); m. Sandra Elizabeth Sambles; two s. one d.; ed Imperial Coll., London; Postdoctoral Research Assoc. in Surface Physics, Imperial Coll., London 1970–72; Lecturer in Physics, Univ. of Exeter 1972–91, Prof. of Experimental Physics 1991–, currently Academic Lead of Electromagnetic and Acoustic Materials Research Group; Council mem. Eng and Physical Sciences Research Council 2008–14, Chair. Resource Audit Cttee 2010–14; Pres., Inst. of Physics 2015–17; Distinguished Visitor, Nat. Physical Lab. 2017; consultant, Defence Scientific Advisory Council 2005–11, DSAC Independent (ISTA mem.) 2011–, Atlas Electronics 2012; Hon. Fellow, Inst. of Physics 2018; George William Gray Medal, British Liquid Crystal Soc. 1998, Thomas Young Medal and Prize, Inst. of Physics 2003, Faraday Medal and Prize, Inst. of Physics 2012. *Publications include:* The Optics of Thermotropic Liquid Crystals (co-ed.) 1998, Modern Plasmonics (co-ed.) 2014; more than 530 papers in professional journals, 20 patents. *Address:* Department of Physics and Astronomy, University of Exeter, Stocker Road, Exeter, EX4 4QL, England (office). *Telephone:* (1392) 724103 (office). *Fax:* (1392) 724111 (office). *E-mail:* j.r.sambles@exeter.ac.uk (office). *Website:* emps.exeter.ac.uk/physics-astronomy (office); newton.ex.ac.uk/staff/JRS (office).

SAMBO, Namadi, BSc, MArch; Nigerian architect and politician; b. 2 Aug. 1954, Kaduna; m. Amina Sambo; six c.; ed Govt Secondary School (now Alhuda-Huda Coll.), Zaria, Ahmadu Bello Univ., Zaria; with Ministry of Works and Housing Nat. Youth Service Corps, Oyo State 1978–79; Commr for Works, Transport and Housing, Kaduna State 1988–90; pvt practice as architect in 1990s with Coplan Assocs, Nalado Nigeria Ltd, Manyatta Engineering Services Ltd; mem. People's Democratic Party; Gov. Kaduna State 2007–10; Vice-Pres. of Nigeria 2010–15.

SAMBROOK, Richard, BA, MSc, FRSA, FRTS; British media executive and academic; *Professor of Journalism and Director, School of Journalism, Media and Cultural Studies, Cardiff University;* b. 24 April 1956, Canterbury; m.; two c.; ed Oakwood Grammar School, Maidstone, Reading Univ., Birkbeck Coll. London Univ.; trainee journalist Thomson Regional Newspapers 1977; spent three years with Celtic Press in Welsh Valleys and South Wales Echo; joined BBC as sub-ed. in

radio newsroom 1980, later producer and programme ed. on nat. TV news, sr producer and deputy ed. Nine O'Clock News, News Ed. BBC Newsgathering 1992–96, Head of Newsgathering 1996–99, Deputy Dir News Div. 1999–2001, Dir BBC News 2001–04, Dir World Service and Global News Div. 2004–10; Global Vice-Chair. and Chief Content Officer, Edelman (public relations co.) 2010–12; Prof. of Journalism and Dir Centre for Journalism, Cardiff Univ. 2012–, also, Deputy Head, School of Journalism, Media and Cultural Studies; Fellow, Reuters Inst. for the Study of Journalism. *Publication:* Global Voice: Britain's Future in International Broadcasting 2007. *Address:* Cardiff School of Journalism, Media and Cultural Studies, Room 0.32, Bute Building, King Edward VII Avenue, Cardiff, CF10 3NB, Wales (office). *Telephone:* (29) 2087-0982 (office). *E-mail:* sambrookrj@cardiff.ac.uk (office). *Website:* www.cardiff.ac.uk/jomec (office).

SAMBÚ, Soares; Guinea-Bissau politician; Pres. Cttee on Agric., Fisheries, Natural Resources, Environment and Tourism 1997–98; mem. Cen. Cttee Partido Africano da Independência da Guiné e Cabo Verde (PAIGC), Dir election campaign 2004; mem. Nat. Ass., Deputy Speaker –2003, PAIGC MP for Bafata e Cosse constituency 2009–; Minister of Foreign Affairs, Int. Co-operation and Communities 2004–05, of Natural Resources 2007–09, Minister of the Economy and Regional Integration 2013–16, of Foreign Affairs and Int. Co-operation 2016, Minister of State of the Presidency of the Council of Ministers 2017–18. *Address:* Partido Africano da Independência da Guiné e Cabo Verde, CP 106, Bissau, Guinea-Bissau (office). *Website:* www.paigc.org (office).

SAMIOS, Nicholas Peter, AB, PhD; American physicist and academic; *Senior Scientist Emeritus, Brookhaven National Laboratory;* b. 15 March 1932, New York, NY; s. of Peter Samios and Niki Samios; m. Mary Linakis 1958; two s. one d.; ed Columbia Coll., Columbia Univ., New York; Instructor, Dept of Physics, Columbia Univ. 1956–59, Adjunct Prof. 1970–95; Asst Physicist, Brookhaven Nat. Lab. Dept of Physics 1959–62, Assoc. Physicist 1962–64, Physicist 1964–68, Group Leader 1965–75, apptd Sr Physicist 1968, Chair. Div. of Particles and Fields 1975–76, Chair. PEP Experimental Program Cttee (of SLAC & LBL) 1976–78, Chair. Dept of Physics 1975–81, Deputy Dir 1981, Acting Dir 1982, Dir 1982–97, apptd Distinguished Sr Scientist 1997, Deputy Dir RIKEN BNL Research Center 1998–2003, Dir 2003–14, now Sr Scientist Emer.; Adjunct Prof., Stevens Inst. of Tech. 1969–75; mem. Bd of Dirs Stony Brook Foundation 1989–2004, Adelphi 1989–97, Long Island Asscn 1990–97; mem., fmr mem. or fmr chair. numerous specialist cttees and bds; Corresp. mem. Akademia Athenon 1994–, NAS 1982–; Fellow, American Physical Soc. 1964 (mem. Exec. Cttee 1976–77), American Acad. of Arts and Sciences, AAAS; E.O. Lawrence Memorial Award 1980, New York Acad. of Sciences Award in Physical and Math. Sciences 1980, AUI Distinguished Scientist 1992, W.K.H. Panofsky Prize 1993, Bruno Pontecorvo Prize, Jt Inst. for Nuclear Research, Moscow 2001, G.C. Wick Gold Medal 2009. *Address:* RIKEN BNL Research Center, Building 510A, Room 1-70, Physics Department, Brookhaven National Laboratory, Upton, NY 11973-5000, USA (office). *Telephone:* (631) 344-6281 (office). *Fax:* (631) 344-4906 (office). *E-mail:* samios@bnl.gov (office). *Website:* www.bnl.gov/riken (office).

SAMMONS, Mary F., BA; American retail executive; b. 1947, Portland, Ore.; ed Maryhurst Coll.; began career with Fred Meyer Inc. 1973, held several sr positions, including as Exec. Vice-Pres., in all areas of operations and merchandising 1985–97, Pres. and COO Fred Meyer Stores (food, drug and gen. merchandise retailer and subsidiary of The Kroger Co.) 1998–99, Pres. and CEO April–Dec. 1999; mem. Bd of Dirs, Pres. and COO Rite Aid Corpn 1999–2003, Pres. and CEO 2003–08, Chair. 2007–12, CEO 2008–10, Dir 2012–13, Pres. The Rite Aid Foundation; mem. Bd of Dirs StanCorp Financial Group, Inc. (currently Lead Ind. Dir) 2008–, Magellan Health, Inc. 2011–; fmr mem. Bd of Dirs First Horizon National Corpn; mem. Exec. Cttee Nat. Asscn of Chain Drug Stores (fmr Chair.). *Address:* Lead Director, Corporate Secretary, P12B, StanCorp Financial Group, Inc., PO Box 711, Portland, OR 97207, USA.

SAMMUT, Salv; Maltese trade union official (retd); b. (Saviour Lawrence), 4 March 1947, Lija; m. Doris Sammut; two s. one d.; ed diploma in Social Studies and Industrial Relations, Univ. of Malta; mem. Nat. Comm. for Health and Safety 1994, Bd Health and Safety Authority 2001–09; Vice-Pres. General Workers' Union (GWU) 1999–2001, Pres. 2001–09, represented GWU at int. congresses and confs relating to EU issues on matters of health and safety dealing with trade unions; fmr mem. EU Advisory Cttee on Health and Safety; Substitute mem. Bilbao Agency on Health and Safety; Sec. Maltese Poets Soc. *Plays:* 12 short plays. *Radio:* readings of three novels and several short stories and poems have been broadcast; 100 short stories broadcast in Australia. *Publications include:* nine long novels, three books of poetry (Second Place, Prize of the Year nat. award) 2000, book of verse 2008; essays and articles for journals. *Leisure interests:* reading, writing literature. *Address:* 'The Quest', Maisonette 2, Block R, Trejqet il-Gilju, Mtarfa, MTF 1430, Malta (home). *Telephone:* 21454903 (home); 79-864550 (mobile). *E-mail:* sammutsalv2@gmail.com.

SAMPAIO, Jorge Fernando Branco de; Portuguese politician, fmr head of state and fmr UN official; b. 18 Sept. 1939; m. Maria José Ritta; one s. one d.; ed Univ. of Lisbon; leader of students' union and led protests against govt as student in Lisbon 1960–61; following graduation as lawyer defended several political prisoners; fmr mem. Socialist Left Movt then joined Socialist Party (PS), elected Deputy to Nat. Parl. 1979, Pres. Parl. Bench 1986–87, Sec.-Gen. 1989–91; mem. European Comm. for Human Rights 1979–84; Mayor of Lisbon 1989–95; Pres. of Portugal 1996–2006; Special Envoy of the Sec.-Gen. to Stop Tuberculosis, UN 2006–13, High Rep. of the Sec.-Gen. for the Alliance of Civilizations, UN 2006–12; Order of the Three Stars (Latvia), Order of the White Eagle (Poland) 1997, Order of the White Double Cross, First Class (Slovakia) 2003, Grand Cordon of the Order of Leopold (Belgium) 2005, Grand Master, Order of the Tower and Sword (Portugal), Kt Grand Cross with Grand Cordon of the Order of Merit (Italy), Collar of the Order of the Cross of Terra Mariana (Estonia), Kt Grand Cross of the Order of St Olav (Norway), Kt Grand Cross of the Order of St Michael and St George (UK), Grand Cross of the Order of Vytautas the Great (Lithuania); Council of Europe North–South Prize 2008. *Leisure interests:* music, golf. *Address:* Socialist Party (PS), Largo do Rato 2, 1269-143 Lisbon (office); Tapada das Necessidades, 1350-213 Lisbon, Portugal. *Telephone:* (21) 3822000 (office); (21) 3931440. *Fax:* (21) 3822022 (office); (21) 3965079. *E-mail:* portal@ps.pt (office); tp.olagerodasac@lareg. *Website:* www.ps.pt (office); jorgesampaio.pt.

SAMPANTHAN, Rajavarothiam, LLB; Sri Lankan lawyer and politician; *Leader, Tamil National Alliance;* b. 5 Feb. 1933; s. of A. Rajavarothiam; m. Leeladevi Sampanthan; two s. one d.; ed St Patrick's Coll., St Sebastian's Coll., Ceylon Law Coll.; practised as an attorney; elected to Parl. (Tamil United Liberation Front, for Trincomalee) 1977, boycotted parl. along with other TULF MPs 1983, mem. of Parl. 2001–, Leader of Opposition 2015–; Leader, Tamil Nat. Alliance 2001–, Illankai Tamil Arasu Kachchi ITAK (main constituent of Tamil Nat. Alliance) 2004–. *Address:* Tamil National Alliance, 32 A, Retreat Road, Colombo 4, Sri Lanka (office). *Telephone:* (11) 2559352 (office); (21) 2223576 (office). *E-mail:* sampanthan_r@parliament.lk (office). *Website:* tnapolitics.org (office).

SAMPATH, Veeravalli Sundaram; Indian civil servant and government official; b. 16 Jan. 1950; joined the Admin. Service 1973, Dist Collector 1975–86; apptd Food and Public Distribution Dept, Industries Dept, Finance Dept 1989, apptd Sec., Agriculture Dept 1990; fmr Prin. Sec., Energy Dept, Finance Dept, served in Ministry of Rural Devt; Man. Dir Godavari Fertilizers and Chemicals Ltd –2004; apptd Dir-Gen. Nat. Inst. of Rural Devt 2005; fmr Sec. Chemicals and Petrochemicals, Ministry of Power; Election Commr 2009–12, Chief Election Commr 2012–15 (retd); fmr Man. Dir Apex Co-operative Bank, Handloom Marketing Soc., Oil Seeds Fed.

SAMPER PIZANO, Ernesto, BA; Colombian lawyer, politician, international organization official and fmr diplomatist; *Secretary-General, Union of South American Nations (UNASUR);* b. 3 Aug. 1950, Bogotá; s. of Andrés Samper Gnecco and Helena Pizano Pardo; m. 1st Silvia Arbeláez 1972 (divorced 1975), one s.; m. 2nd Jacquin Strouss Lucena 1979, two s.; ed Pontifical Xavierian Univ. of Bogotá, Columbia Univ., USA; mem. Regional Ass., Cundinamarca 1982–84; mem. Bogotá city council 1982–86; mem. Senate (upper house of Parl.) for Bogotá 1986–90; Minister of Econ. Devt 1990–91; Amb. to Spain 1991–93; Pres. of Colombia 1994–98; Sec.-Gen., Non-Aligned Movt 1995–98; Coordinator, Foro de Biarritz 2001–12; Sec.-Gen., Union of South American Nations (UNASUR) 2014–; mem. Partido Liberal Colombiano. *Publications include:* Colombia sale adelante! 1989, Apertura & modernización 1992, 100 días del salto social 1994, El tiempo de la gente 1994, Colombia en Alemania 1996, Escritos 1998, Aquí estoy y aquí me quedo 2000. *Address:* UNASUR, Av. Manuel Córdova Galarza, Mitad del Mundo, Quito, Ecuador (office). *Telephone:* (2) 399-0900 (office). *E-mail:* secretaria.general@unasursg.org (office). *Website:* www.unasursg.org (office).

SAMPERMANS, Françoise, MA, LèsL; French business executive; *President, France Générosités;* b. 10 July 1947, Paris; d. of Jacques Durand and Jeannine Behot; one s. one d.; joined CIT-TRANSAC 1974; est. public relations service, Chapelle Darblay 1978; Head of Public Relations, Entreprise et Crédit 1981; Dir of Communications, Transmission, Group Thomson 1982; subsequently Deputy Dir, Dir of Communications, Alcatel CIT; Dir of Communications, Alcatel NV 1987, Alcatel Alsthom 1987; Dir-Gen. Générale Occidentale 1991–95; Pres. Dir-Gen. Groupe Express 1992–95; Vice-Pres. Québecor-Europe 1996–2000; apptd Pres., Dir-Gen. Nouvel Economiste 1999; apptd Dir-Gen. Marianne and L'Evènement du Jeudi 1999; Vice-Pres. Nouvelles Messageries de la Presse Parisienne 2000–04; apptd Pres. Asscn for radiation of Chateau de Vincennes 2008; Pres. Baroque Music Centre of Versailles 1989–2009; Pres. France Générosités (asscn of foundations and philanthropic orgs) 2012–; mem. Bd UPM-Kymmene (Finland) 2004–09; Chevalier, Ordre des Arts et des Lettres. *Address:* France Générosités, 15/17, rue Albert, 75013 Paris (office); 18 rue Charles Silvestri, 94300 Vincennes, France. *Website:* www.francegenerosites.org (office).

SAMPHAN, Khieu (see KHIEU, Samphan).

SAMPOERNA, Putera; Indonesian business executive; *Chairman, Putera Sampoerna Foundation;* b. 13 Oct. 1947, The Netherlands; m. Katie Sampoerna; four c.; ed Univ. of Houston, USA; began career with family-owned palm oil and rubber plantations in Malaysia 1970–80; took over family tobacco business PT Hanjaya Mandala Sampoerna Tbk 1986 (sold to Philip Morris International 2005); currently Dir PT Sampoerna Strategic Group holding co.), business interests include Sampoerna Agro (palm plantation); Founder and Chair. Putera Sampoerna Foundation (educational charity) 2001–; Peace Through Commerce Medal Award, US Int. Trade Admin 2011. *Leisure interest:* football. *Address:* Putera Sampoerna Foundation, Sampoerna Strategic Square, North Tower, 27th Floor, Jl. Jendral Sudirman, Kav. 45, Jakarta 12930, Indonesia (office). *Telephone:* (21) 5772340 (office). *Fax:* (21) 5772341 (office). *Website:* www.sampoernafoundation.org (office).

SAMPRAS, Pete; American fmr professional tennis player; b. 12 Aug. 1971, Washington, DC; s. of Sam Sampras and Georgia Sampras; m. Brigette Wilson 2000; two s.; turned professional 1988; holds US men's record for most Grand Slam singles titles (14); US Open Champion 1990, 1993, 1995, 1996, 2002; Grand Slam Cup Winner 1990; IBM/ATP (Asscn of Tennis Professionals) Tour World Championship—Frankfurt Winner 1991; US Pro-Indoor Winner 1992; Wimbledon Singles Champion 1993, 1994, 1995, 1997, 1998, 1999, 2000; European Community Championships Winner 1993, 1994; ranked No. 1 1993–98 (record); Winner Australian Open 1994; RCA Championships 1996, ATP Tour World Championships, 1996, Australian Open 1997; Winner San José Open 1997, Philadelphia Open 1997, Cincinnatti Open 1997; Munich Open 1997, Paris Open 1997, Hanover Open 1997, Advanta Championship 1998; mem. US Davis Cup Team 1991, 1995; won 64 US Tour singles titles, two doubles titles and US $43,280,489; Chair. ATP Tour Charities Programme 1992; investor, partner and special consultant, Tennis Magazine 2003–; Co-founder Pure Sports Management, LLC 2007; f. Acres for Charity Fund; Jim Thorpe Tennis Player of the Year 1993, ATP Tour Player of the Year 1993–97, US Olympic Cttee Sportsman of the Year 1997, inducted into Int. Tennis Hall of Fame 2007. *Publication:* A Champion's Mind: Lessons from a Life in Tennis (autobiography) 2009. *Leisure interests:* golf, basketball, Formula 1 racing. *Address:* c/o Pure Sports Management, LLC, 904 Silver Spur Road, #350, Rolling Hills, CA 90274, USA (office). *Telephone:* (424) 241-3151 (office). *Fax:* (310) 807-9255 (office). *E-mail:* info@puresportsmgmt.com (office). *Website:* www.puresportsmanagement.com (office); www.petesampras.com.

SAMS, Jeremy Charles; British director, writer, composer and translator; b. 12 Jan. 1957, Croydon, Surrey, England; s. of Eric Charles Sydney Sams and Enid Sams (née Tidmarsh); one c.; ed Whitgift School, Magdalene Coll., Cambridge, Guildhall School of Music; Hon. FRAM; Hon. DUniv (Birmingham City Univ.). *Plays directed:* The Wind in the Willows (Tokyo) 1993, 1995, (Old Vic) 1995, Neville's Island (Nottingham Playhouse and West End), Forty Years On (West Yorks. Playhouse), Maria Friedman by Special Arrangement (Donmar Warehouse and West End), Enjoy (Nottingham Playhouse), Wild Oats (Royal Nat. Theatre) 1995, Passion (West End) 1996, Marat/Sade (Royal Nat. Theatre) 1997, 2 Pianos 4 Hands (Birmingham Repertory and West End) 1999, Spend Spend Spend (Plymouth and West End) 1999–2000, (tour) 2001, Noises Off (Royal Nat. Theatre) 2000, (West End, Broadway and tour) 2001, What The Butler Saw (Theatre Royal Bath and tour) 2001, Benefactors (West End) 2002, Water Babies (Chichester Festival Theatre) 2003, Little Britain Live (tour) 2005, Donkey's Years (West End) 2006, The Sound of Music (West End, Toronto and UK tours) 2006, 13 (Broadway) 2008, The King and I (Royal Albert Hall) 2009, Educating Rita (Menier Chocolate Factory) 2010, The Wizard of Oz (Palladium) 2011, (Toronto) 2012. *Plays translated:* Leonce and Lena, Saturday, Sunday … & Monday, The Rehearsal, Becket, The Miser, Time and the Room, The Park, Mary Stuart, The Orchestra, Les Parents Terribles, Le Visiteur, Don Juan on Trial, Enigma Variations, A Fool and His Money, Colombe, The Coffee House, Seven Doors, Scapino, Oscar, Partners In Crime, Jealousy, Zerlina's Tale. *Music composed for stage:* Ring Round The Moon, The Country Wife, Jumpers, Don Carlos, Edward II, As You Like It, Some Americans Abroad, Ghetto, The Wind in the Willows, The Scarlet Pimpernel, Talking Heads, Kean, The Rehearsal, Arcadia, Merry Wives of Windsor, The Break of Day, Honour, Absolutely! (perhaps), False Servant, Billy Liar; composed for BBC: Nativity Blues, Welcome Home Comrades, Uncle Vanya, Old Times, Down Town Lagos, Persuasion (BAFTA for Best Original Television Music), Have Your Cake. *Film music:* The Mother (2003), Enduring Love (Ivor Novello Award for Best Film Score) 2004, Hyde Park on Hudson 2012, Le Weekend 2013. *Television includes:* composed for BBC: Nativity Blues, Welcome Home Comrades, Uncle Vanya, Old Times, Down Town Lagos, Have Your Cake, Persuasion (BAFTA for Best Original TV Music). *Address:* c/o The Agency (London) Ltd, 24 Pottery Lane, Holland Park, London, W11 4LZ, England (office). *Telephone:* (20) 7727-1346 (office). *Fax:* (20) 7727-9037 (office). *E-mail:* info@theagency.co.uk (office). *Website:* www.theagency.co.uk (office).

SAMSONOWICZ, Henryk, PhD; Polish politician, historian and academic; *Professor, Instytut Historyczny, University of Warsaw;* b. 23 Jan. 1930, Warsaw; m. Agnieszka Lechowska; one s. one d.; ed Univ. of Warsaw; joined staff, Univ. of Warsaw 1950, Asst Lecturer then Sr Asst Lecturer 1950–60, Asst Prof. 1960–69, Prof., History Inst. 1969–, Vice-Dean 1967–69, Dean Dept of History 1969–74, Dir 1975–80, Rector 1980–82; mem. Civic Cttee attached to Lech Wałęsa (q.v.), Chair. Science and Educ. Comm., Solidarity Trade Union 1988–89; Head of Dept of Social Sciences, Polish Acad. of Sciences 2001–; participant, Round Table plenary debates, mem. group for political reforms and team for science, educ. and tech. progress Feb.–April 1989; Minister of Nat. Educ. 1989–90; Deputy Head of Scientific Research Cttee 1994–97; mem. Polish Historical Soc. (Chair. Gen. Bd 1977–82), Soc. for Advancement and Propagation of Sciences 1980–, Academia Europaea 1992–94, Acad. des Belles Lettres, Polish Acad. of Sciences 1994–; Hon. citizen Pultusk and Ostrowiec Świętokrzyski; Gold Cross (Hungary), Commdr's Cross, Order of Polonia Restituta, Gold Cross of Merit, Officier, Légion d'honneur 1984, Order of White Eagle 2010; Dr hc (Duquesne Univ., USA, High School of Educ., Kraków, Nicolaus Copernicus Univ., Toruń, Marie Curie-Skłodowska Univ., Lublin); Nat. Educ. Comm. Medal. *Publications include:* Bürgerkapital in Danzig des XV Jh 1970, Złota jesień polskiego Średniowiecza (Golden Autumn of the Polish Middle Ages) 1971, Dzieje miast i Polscę (History of the Towns of Poland) 1984, Republic of Nobles 1990, Dziedzictwo Średniowiecza (Heritages of the Middle Ages) 1994, Miejsce Polski w Europie (Poland's Place in Europe) 1996, Europe – North-South 1999, Studia z dziejów miast w średniowieczu 2014, Studia nad postrzeganiem przestrzeni przez ludzi średniowiecza 2016; numerous articles in professional journals. *Address:* Instytut Historyczny Uniwersytetu Warszawskiego, ul. Krakowskie Przedmieście 26/28, 00-927 Warsaw (office); ul. Wilcza 22 m. 5, 00-544 Warsaw, Poland (home). *Telephone:* (22) 8261988 (office); (22) 6214061 (home). *Fax:* (22) 8261988 (office). *E-mail:* wydzial1@pan.pl (office); h.samsonowicz@gmail.com (home). *Website:* www.ihuw.pl (office).

SAMUELI, Henry, BS, MS, PhD; American electrical engineer, computer scientist, academic and business executive; *Chief Technical Officer, Broadcom Inc.;* b. 20 Sept. 1954, Buffalo, NY; s. of Aron Samueli and Sala Samueli; m. Susan Samueli; three c.; ed Fairfax High School, Univ. of California, Los Angeles; Prof. of Electrical Eng, UCLA 1985–, also mem. Advisory Bd Henry Samueli School of Eng and Applied Science; Co-founder and Chief Tech. Officer, Broadcom Corpn 1991–2014, Chair. 1991–2008, 2011–14; Chief Tech. Officer, Broadcom Inc., also mem. Bd 2016–; mem. Nat. Acad. of Eng 2003; Distinguished Adjunct Prof., Dept of Electrical Eng and Computer Science, Univ. of California, Irvine 2003–; Co-owner (with his wife) Anaheim Ducks professional ice hockey team 2005–; mem. Exec. Cttee Nat. Hockey League Bd of Govs 2016–; f. Samueli Foundation; Hon. Fellow, Nat. Acad. of Inventors 2017; Hon. DSc (Technion-Israel Inst. of Tech.) 2005, Dr hc (Nat. Chiao Tung Univ.) 2017; IEEE Circuits and Systems Soc. Industrial Pioneer Award 2000, Presidential Medal, Univ. of California 2000, Univ. of California, Irvine Medal 2000, Alumnus of the Year Award, UCLA School of Eng and Applied Science 2000, UCLA Medal 2010, Dr Morris Chang Exemplary Leadership Award, Global Semiconductor Alliance 2011, Marconi Prize and Fellowship 2012. *Publications:* more than 100 technical papers in professional journals on digital signal processing and communications systems engineering; 70 US patents. *Address:* Broadcom Inc., 1320 Ridder Park Drive, San Jose, CA 95131, USA (office). *E-mail:* czegarel@broadcom.com (office). *Website:* www.broadcom.com (office).

SAMUELSEN, Anders; Danish politician; *Minister of Foreign Affairs;* b. 1 Aug. 1957; s. of Ole Samuelsen and Anna Holm; two s.; ed Aarhus Univ.; Temporary MP (Vejle Co. constituency) 1997–2001, MP (West Zealand Co. constituency) 2001–04, (Greater East Jutland constituency) 2007–11, (Greater North Zealand constituency) 2011–; mem. European Parl. 2004–07; Minister of Foreign Affairs 2016–; currently mem. Liberal Alliance, apptd Chair. 2009; fmr mem. Social Liberal Party, New Alliance; mem. Bd of Rep., Danish Arts Council 2009–11, Danish Arts Foundation 2009–11, CARE Denmark 2010–. *Publications:* Vejen til et bedre Europa: en bro mellem ja og nej (The Road to a Better Europe: a bridge between Yes and No) 2004, Europas stemmer (European Voices) 2005, Breve fra Europa: de første år i Bruxelles (Letters from Europe: the first years in Brussels) 2006, Det

Danmark jeg drømmer om: Danmark i et større perspektiv (The Denmark I dream of: Denmark in a broader perspective) 2015. *Address:* Ministry of Foreign Affairs, Asiatisk Pl. 2, 1448 Copenhagen K, Denmark (office). *Telephone:* 33-92-00-00 (office). *Fax:* 32-54-05-33 (office). *E-mail:* um@um.dk (office). *Website:* www.um.dk.

SAMUELSSON, Bengt Ingemar, DMS, MD; Swedish medical chemist and academic; *Professor Emeritus of Physiological Chemistry, Karolinska Institutet;* b. 21 May 1934, Halmstad; s. of Anders Samuelsson and Stina Nilsson; m. Inga Bergstein 1958; two c.; ed Karolinska Inst., Stockholm; Asst Prof., Karolinska Inst. 1961–66, apptd Prof. of Physiological Chemistry 1972, now Prof. Emer., Chair. Dept of Physiological Chem. 1973–83, Dean, Faculty of Medicine 1978–83, Rector 1983–95; Research Fellow, Harvard Univ., USA 1961–62; Prof. of Medical Chem., Royal Veterinary Coll., Stockholm 1967–72; mem. Nobel Cttee of Physiology or Medicine 1984–89, Chair. 1987–89; Chair. Nobel Foundation 1993–2005; mem. Bd of Dirs Svenska Handelsbanken AB, Pharmacia & Upjohn, The Liposome Co., NicOx; mem. Advisory Bd Odlander Fredrikson & Co. AB; mem. Research Advisory Bd Swedish Govt 1985–88, Nat. Comm. on Health Policy 1987–90, European Science and Tech. Ass. 1994; Special Advisor to Commr for Research and Educ., EC 1995; mem. Royal Swedish Acad. of Sciences 1981–; Foreign Assoc. NAS; Foreign mem. Royal Soc. (London), Mediterranean Acad. of Sciences, Acad. Europaea, French Acad. of Sciences, Spanish Soc. of Allergology and Clinical Immunology, Royal Nat. Acad. of Medicine (Spain), Int. Acad. of Sciences; Hon. Prof., Bethune Univ. of Medical Sciences, Changchun, China 1986, UMC Beijing, China 2016; Hon. mem. Asscn of American Physicians 1982, AAAS 1982, Swedish Medical Asscn 1982, American Soc. of Biological Chemists, Italian Pharmacology Soc., Acad. Nat. Medicina de Buenos Aires, Int. Soc. of Haematology; Hon. DSc (Chicago) 1978, (Illinois) 1983, (Louisiana State Univ.) 1993; Dr hc (Rio de Janeiro) 1986, (Complutense Univ., Madrid) 1991, (Milan) 1993; Hon. DUniv (Buenos Aires) 1986; Jubilee Award, Swedish Medical Asscn 1968, 1981, Anders Jahres Award, Oslo Univ. 1970, Louisa Gross Horwitz Award, Columbia Univ. 1975, Intrascience Medalist 1976, Albert Lasker Basic Medical Research Award 1977, Ciba Geigy Drew Award 1980, Lewis S. Rosenstiel Award 1981, Gairdner Foundation Award 1981, Heinrich Wieland Prize 1981, Bror Holmberg Medal, Swedish Chemical Soc. 1982, Medical Chemistry Award, ACS 1982, Waterford Bio-Medical Science Award 1982, Int. Asscn of Allergology and Clinical Immunology Award 1982, Nobel Prize in Physiology or Medicine (jtly) 1982, Abraham White Science Achievement Award 1991, City of Medicine Award 1992, Maria Theresa Medal 1996. *Publications include:* numerous articles in professional journals. *Address:* Karolinska Institutet, Department of Medical Biochemistry and Biophysics, C2, Departments, Physiological Chemistry II, Scheeles Väg 2, 171 77 Stockholm, Sweden (office). *Telephone:* (8) 524-87-60 (office). *Fax:* (8) 736-04-39 (office). *E-mail:* Bengt.Samuelsson@ki.se (office). *Website:* kikatalogen.ki.se (office).

SAMUKAI, Brownie J.; Liberian government official and fmr army officer; ed Univ. of Liberia, American Univ.; served with Armed Forces of Liberia 1980–91 (retd with rank of Col); Dir Liberian Nat. Police 1991–94; Deputy Minister for Operations, Ministry of Defence 1994–95; Deputy Minister of State for Admin, Ministry of State for Presidential Affairs 1995–97; Security Officer, UN Dept of Peacekeeping Operations, East Timor 1999–2000; Field Safety Advisor, UNHCR, Kibando, Tanzania 2000–03; Field Security Coordinator, UNDP, Dar es Salaam, Tanzania 2003–06; Minister of Defence 2006–18. *Address:* c/o Ministry of Defence, Benson Street, POB 10-9007, 1000 Monrovia, Liberia (office).

SAMURA, Sorious; Sierra Leonean journalist and documentary filmmaker; b. 1964; mem. Bd Insight News Television, London; mem. Bd of Dirs; Dr hc (Univ. of East Anglia) 2003; CNN African Journalist of the Year 1999, Rory Peck Award 1999, Mohamed Amin Award 1999, Amnesty International Media Award for TV Documentary 2000, George Foster Peabody Award 2000, ICRC Dignity in Conflict Award 2000, Columbia-DuPont Award 2001, BAFTA Award for News and Current Affairs Journalism 2001, TV Documentary Award, One World Media Awards 2000, 2001, two Emmy Awards, two further Amnesty International Media Awards, Prix Europa, Japan Prize, Harry Chapin Media Award, three Overseas Press Club of America Awards, Golden Nymph, Monte Carlo Television Festival, Bronze World Medal, New York Festivals. *Film documentaries include:* Cry Freetown 1999, Return to Freetown 2000, Exodus from Africa 2001, 21st Century War 2002, Living with Hunger 2003, Living with Illegals 2006, Africa's Last Taboo 2010. *E-mail:* info@sorioussamurafoundation.org. *Website:* sorioussamurafoundation.org.

SAMYN, Gilles; French/Belgian banking executive; *Chairman, Compagnie Nationale à Portefeuille (CNP);* b. 2 Jan. 1950, Cannes; m. Myriam Goethals; five c.; ed Solvay Business School, Université Libre de Bruxelles; Asst Solvay Business School 1969–75, Lecturer 1975; Adviser, Mouvement Co-operatif Belge 1972–74; with Groupe Bruxelles Lambert 1974–82; Ind. Adviser 1982–83; joined Groupe Frère-Bourgeois 1983, becoming Man. Dir Erbe SA 1986, Dir Cie Nationale à Portefeuille 1988, then apptd CEO and mem. Exec. Cttee, then Chair., CNP, also currently Man. Dir Groupe Frère; mem. Bd of Dirs Groupe Bruxelles Lambert, Pargesa Holding, Transcor, Astra Group, Groupe Flo, Entremont Alliance, Gruppo Banca Leonardo, M6, Affichage Holding, Imetal, CLT-UFA, Grand Hôpital de Charleroi, Acide Carbonique Pur. *Address:* Compagnie Nationale à Portefeuille, Rue de la Blanche Borne 12, 6280 Loverval, Gerpinnes, Belgium (office). *Telephone:* (71) 60-60-60 (office). *Fax:* (71) 60-60-70 (office). *E-mail:* cnp@cnp.be (office). *Website:* www.cnp.be (office); www.npm-cnp.be (office).

SAN GIACOMO, Laura; American actress; b. 14 Nov. 1962, West Orange, NJ; d. of John San Giacomo and MaryJo San Giacomo; m. 1st Cameron Dye 1990 (divorced 1998); one s.; m. 2nd Matt Adler 2000; ed Morris Knolls High School, NJ, Carnegie Mellon Univ.; started career in regional theatre productions; co-f. CHIME Charter Elementary School 2001. *Theatre includes:* North Shore Fish, Beirut, The Love Talker, Italian American Reconciliation. *Films include:* Sex, Lies and Videotape (New Generation Award, LA Film Critics' Asscn) 1989, Pretty Woman 1990, Vital Signs 1990, Quigley Down Under 1990, Once Around 1991, Under Suspicion 1991, Where the Day Takes You 1992, Nina Takes a Lover 1994, Stuart Saves His Family 1995, Eat Your Heart Out 1997, Suicide Kings 1997, Apocalypse 1997, With Friends Like These 1998, Mom's on the Roof, House on a Hill 2003, Havoc 2005, Checking Out 2005, Least Among Saints 2012. *Television includes:* The Stand (mini-series) 1994, Just Shoot Me (series) 1997–2003, Sister

Mary Explains It All 2001, Jenifer 2001, Saving Grace (series) 2007–10, NCIS 2016. *Leisure interests:* horse riding, playing piano, gymnastics, ballet.

SAN MIGUEL RODRÍGUEZ, Walker, BA; Bolivian lawyer, government official and international organization official; *Secretary-General, Andean Community;* b. 6 Aug. 1963, La Paz; m. Tatiana Núñez Ormachea; two c.; ed Universidad Mayor de San Andrés, Catholic Univ. of Valparaiso, Chile, Univ. of Salamanca, Spain; Prof. of Law, Universidad Mayor de San Andrés, Catholic Univ., Bolivian Andes Univ., Universidad Andina Simón Bolívar, La Paz 1998–2005; mem. Law Offices Moreno Baldivieso 1990–2002; Founder and Prin. San Miguel Walker SC Abogados Consultores Associates 2002–05; Minister of State for Defence 2006–10, also Acting Minister of Foreign Affairs and Minister of Justice; Gen. Consul (with rank of Amb.), Chile 2010–11; Founder and Prin. San Miguel Abogados Soc. Civil 2012–; Exec. Chair. Colegio de Abogados de La Paz (Bar Association La Paz) 2003–06; Sec.-Gen. The Andean Community 2016–; fmr Vice-Chair. Colegio Nacional de Abogados de Bolivia; mem. Nat. Acad. of Judicial Sciences of Bolivia, Inter-American Fed. of Lawyers. *Address:* Comunidad Andina, Av. Paseo de la República 3895, San Isidro, Lima 27, Peru. *Telephone:* (1) 7106400 (office). *Fax:* (1) 2213329 (office). *E-mail:* correspondencia@comunidadandina.org (office). *Website:* www.comunidadandina.org (office).

SANADER, Ivo, PhD; Croatian politician; b. 8 June 1953, Split; m. Mirjana Sanader 1978; two d.; ed Univ. of Innsbruck, Austria; Programme Ed., later Ed.-in-Chief, Logos publishing house, Split 1983–88; mem. Editorial Bd Mogućnosti (Possibilities) magazine 1987–90; man. own cos, Innsbruck 1988–91; Gen. Man. Croatian Nat. Theatre, Split 1991–92; mem. Parl. (House of Reps of Croatian Parl.) 1992–, Minister of Science and Tech. 1992–93; Deputy Minister of Foreign Affairs 1993–95; Chief of Staff to Pres. of Repub. of Croatia and Sec.-Gen. Defence and Nat. Security Council 1995–96; Deputy Minister of Foreign Affairs 1996–2000; Prime Minister of Croatia 2003–09 (resgnd); Pres. Croatian Democratic Union (HDZ) 2000–09; Deputy Chair. Foreign Affairs Cttee 2000; mem. Croatian Writers' Asscn, Croatian-PEN; attempted a political comeback inside HDZ but was ejected from party membership Jan. 2010; charged by Croatian authorities in two corruption indictments Dec. 2010, convicted and sentenced to nine years in prison. *Publications:* author of several books on literary history and contemporary politics. *Leisure interests:* golf, reading, music.

SANAKOYEV, Dimitri; Georgian government official; *Head of Administration of South Ossetia;* b. 10 May 1969, Tskhinvali, S Ossetian Autonomous Oblast, Georgian SSR, USSR; ed A. Tibilov South Ossetian State Univ.; fought on Ossetian side during Georgian–Ossetian conflict 1991–92; Minister of Defence in break-away region of S Ossetia 2000; Prime Minister 2001–03; apptd Pres. of the Provisional Admin of S Ossetia by Georgian Pres. Mikheil Saakashvili 2007–; mem. The Salvation Union of S Ossetia (political party). *Address:* 14/16 Gagarin str., Tbilisi, Georgia (home). *Telephone:* 95-958119 (mobile) (office); (32) 2998990 (office). *E-mail:* so_frede@yahoo.com (office). *Website:* www.soa.gov.ge (office).

SANBAR, Samir H., BBA; Lebanese international civil servant and consultant; b. 9 March 1934, Haifa; s. of Habib Sanbar and Georgette Khoury; ed American Univ. of Beirut; Deputy Ed. Al Howadeth, Al-Sayyad (Arab weeklies) and journalist with various Lebanese, Arab and int. media; Political Ed. Al-Usbu Al Araby (pan-Arab weekly), Beirut 1954–65; Information Officer of Special Rep. of Sec.-Gen. for UNYOM 1964, Special Asst to Personal Rep. of Sec.-Gen. of UNITAR 1965–70, Special Asst to Exec. Dir UNITAR 1970–73, accompanied UN Sec.-Gen. on all visits to Middle East 1973–87, Dir UN Information Centre, Beirut, Chief, Information Services of ECWA and Co-ordinator of UN public information activities in Gulf countries 1975–82, special assignment to assist Office of Sec.-Gen. in liaison and media functions during establishment of UNIFIL 1978–82, Chief, UN Centres Services 1982–87, mem. and Chair. UN Appointment and Promotions Bd 1986–96, Dir UN Information Centres, Dept of Public Information 1987–93, Special Rep. of UN Sec.-Gen. to head UN mission to verify Referendum in Eritrea 1993, Asst Sec.-Gen., UN Dept of Public Information 1994–98, mem. Bd of Dirs UN International School 1994–96, Chair. Joint UN Information Committee 1996–98, UN Staff Recreation Council 1996–98; mem. Bd of Dirs Dag Hammarsk-jold Tower, International Council of the Nat. Acad. of TV Arts and Sciences; currently Exec. Ed. UNforum. *Publications include:* Hold on to Your Dreams, Inside the United Nations: In a Leaderless World 2016; (short stories in Arabic): Characters From Ras Beirut, Aleikum Salam (Greetings). *Website:* www.unforum.com.

SANCAR, Aziz, MD, PhD; Turkish biochemist, physician and academic; *Sarah Graham Kenan Professor of Biochemistry, University of North Carolina;* b. 1946, Savur; m. Gwen Boles Sancar; ed Istanbul Medical School, Univ. of Texas, Dallas, USA; Assoc. Prof. of Biochemistry, Univ. of North Carolina, Chapel Hill 1982–, Sarah Graham Kenan Prof. 2001–; co-f. (with his wife) Carolina Turk Evi (perm. Turkish centre close to univ. campus); Distinguished Visiting Prof., Academia Sinica 2014; mem. NAS 2005; Fellow, American Acad. of Arts and Sciences 2004, Turkish Acad. of Sciences 2006, Third World Acad. of Science; NSF Presidential Young Investigator Award 1984–89, American Soc. for Photobiology Award 1990, Basic Science Award, Turkish Scientific Research Council 1995, NIH Merit Award 1966, Turkish Koç Award 2007, Distinguished Alumni Award, Univ. of Texas at Dallas 2009, Nobel Prize in Chem. (co-recipient with Tomas Lindahl and Paul Modrich) 2015. *Publications:* numerous papers in professional journals. *Address:* Department of Biochemistry and Biophysics, University of North Carolina School of Medicine, 120 Mason Farm Road, CB# 7260, 3073 Genetic Medicine, Chapel Hill, NC 27599-7260, USA (office). *Telephone:* (919) 962-0115 (office). *E-mail:* aziz_sancar@med.unc.edu (office). *Website:* www.med.unc.edu/biochem (office); www.med.unc.edu/biochem/asancar-lab (office).

SÁNCHEZ CERÉN, Salvador; Salvadorean politician and head of state; *President;* b. 18 June 1944, Quezaltepeque; s. of Antonio Alfonso Sánchez and Dolores Rodas; m. Margarita Villalta; ed Univ. Salvadoreña Alberto Masferrer; began career as teacher; mem. Frente Farabundo Martí para la Liberación Nacional (FMLN), guerrilla leader in civil war 1980–92, Commanding Gen. of FMLN 1984; mem. Legis. Ass. (FMLN) 2000, re-elected 2003 and 2006; Vice-Pres. of El Salvador 2009–14, Pres. 2014–(19). *Address:* Ministry for the Presidency, Alameda Dr Manuel Enrique Araujo 5500, San Salvador, El Salvador (office).

Telephone: 2248-9000 (office). *Fax:* 2248-9370 (office). *Website:* www.presidencia.gob.sv (office); sanchezceren.com.

SANCHEZ, Felix; Dominican Republic athlete (retd); b. 30 Aug. 1977, New York, NY USA; ed Univ. City High School, San Diego, Calif., Mesa Community Coll. and Univ. of Southern California, USA; sprinter and 400m hurdler; represents Dominican Republic (birthplace of his parents); 400m hurdles personal best 47.25 seconds (Paris, France Aug. 2003), 400m 44.90 seconds (Gateshead, UK Aug. 2001), 200m 20.87 seconds (Irvine, California May 2001); gold medal, 400m hurdles (1st Dominican Republic World Championship medal), World Championships 2001, 2003, 400m hurdles, Pan-American Games 2003; gold medal, 400m hurdles, Olympic Games, Athens 2004; silver medal, 400m hurdles, World Championships 2007, 4x400m relay, Pan American Games 2011; bronze medal, 4x400m relay, Pan American Games 2003, 4x400m relay, Pan American Games 2007; gold medal, 400m hurdles, Olympic Games, London 2012; retd 2016; won 43 consecutive 400m hurdles races 2001–04; hurdles coach, Harvard-Westlake School, Calif. 2001–16, sprint/relay coach 2012–16; commentator, ESPN 2016–; Central American and Caribbean Confed.'s Male Athlete of the Year 2002, 2003, Latin American Sportsman of the Year 2003, Laureus World Comeback of the Year 2013.

SÁNCHEZ ARVELAIZ, Maximilian, MSc; Venezuelan communications consultant and diplomatist; ed Inst. for Study of the Americas, Univ. of London, UK; fmr Adviser to Pres. Hugo Chávez; fmr Minister Counsellor, Perm. Mission of Venezuela to UN, New York; Dir-Gen., Int. Presidential Relations –2010; Amb. to Brazil 2010–13; Presidential Commr for Int. Affairs 2013–14. *Address:* Ministry of Foreign Affairs, Torre MRE, al lado del Correo de Carmelitas, Avda Urdaneta, Caracas 1010, Venezuela (office). *Telephone:* (212) 806-4400 (office). *Fax:* (212) 861-2505 (office). *Website:* www.mre.gov.ve (office).

SÁNCHEZ DE LOZADA, Gonzalo; Bolivian politician; b. 1 July 1930; m. Ximena Iturralde Monje; one s. one d.; ed Univ. of Chicago, USA; Founder and Man. Telecine Ltda (documentary and commercial film production co.) 1953–57; Founder and Gen. Man. Andean Geo-Services Ltd 1957–62; Founder and Pres. Compañía Minera del Sur (COMSUR) 1962–79, Pres. 1980–82; mem. Parl. 1979–80, 1982–85; Senator for Cochabamba and Pres. Senate 1985–86; Minister for Planning and Coordination 1986–88; Presidential cand. 1989; Leader, Movimiento Nacionalista Revolucionario (Histórico) (MNR) 1988–2006 (resgnd); Pres. of Bolivia 1993–97, 2002–03; currently in exile in USA; mem. Club de Madrid.

SÁNCHEZ GALÁN, (José) Ignacio; Spanish industrial engineer and business executive; *Chairman and CEO, Iberdrola SA;* b. Sept. 1950, Salamanca; m.; four c.; ed Eng Tech. School (ICAI), Universidad Pontificia de Comillas, Madrid; Commercial Dir SE Acumulador Tudor SA, Operations Man., Man. Dir Industrial Batteries Div., Pres. and CEO several cos in Grupo Tudor 1972–91; Gen. Man. and CEO ITP 1991–95; CEO Airtel Movil 1995–2001; Vice-Chair. and CEO Iberdrola SA 2001, Chair. and CEO 2001–, Chair. Iberdrola Renovables SA –2011, Iberdrola Immobiliaria SA, El Desafio Español 2007 SA (co. that manages participation of Spanish boat in America's Cup), Chair. Scottish Power Ltd (part of Iberdrola Group) 2007–; Dir Page Ibérica, Bodegas Matarromera; mem. Bd Nutreco Holding BV, Page Iberica, GALP, Red Electrica de España, Bodegas Matarromera, Corporación IBV, Puleva Biotech and other cos; mem. Advisory Bd Accenture Energy; mem. Advisory Cttee Prince of Asturias Endowed Chair in Information Tech., Univ. of New Mexico; mem. Círculo de Empresarios Vascos, Círculo de Empresarios (Madrid), Círculo de Economía, Asociación para el Progreso de la Dirección, American Man. Asscn; Trustee, Fundación Universitaria Pontificia de Salamanca, Fundación Atapuerca, Fundación Consejo España-Estados Unidos, Fundación de Estudios Financieros, Fundación Premysa, Fundación Iberdrola; fmr Prof., School of Industrial Engineers, ICAI; Best CEO in European Utilities sector, Institutional Investor magazine 2007, Top Exec. of the Year, Platts Global Energy Awards 2006, three Best CEO awards, Investor Relations magazine, Business Leader of the Year, Spain-US Chamber of Commerce 2008, Premio Internacional de Economía, Fundación Cristóbal Gabarrón 2008. *Leisure interests:* hunting, horse riding. *Address:* Iberdrola SA, Plaza Euskadi 5, 48009 Bilbao, Spain (office). *Telephone:* (94) 4151411 (office). *Fax:* (94) 4663194 (office). *E-mail:* informacion@iberdrola.com (office). *Website:* www.iberdrola.com (office); www.iberdrola.es (office).

SÁNCHEZ VARGAS DE RIOS, Ana María Liliana; Peruvian diplomatist and politician; b. 28 Jan. 1959, Lima; ed Pontificia Universidad Católica del Perú, Diplomatic Acad. of Peru; joined Diplomatic Service as Third Sec. of Chancellery, Sub-Secr. for Econ. Affairs and Integration 1983–84, becoming Third Sec. of Chancellery, Sub-Secr. of Foreign Policy 1984, Third Sec. of Chancellery, Río de la Plata Basin Dept 1984–91, Third Sec., Embassy in Hungary 1985–86, Third Sec. and Vice-Consul, Consulate-Gen. in Sao Paulo, Brazil 1986, Second Sec., America I Dept 1991, Second Sec., Directorate-Gen. for Admin 1992–97, First Sec., Consul of Peru in Mexico City 1993, First Sec. and Head, Central America and Caribbean Dept 1997–99, Counsellor and Head of Andean Community Dept 1999–2001, Counsellor, Dept of Political Cooperation and Integration 2001–03, Minister-Counsellor, Perm. Mission to OAS 2003, Minister-Counsellor, Coordinating Cabinet of Vice-Minister and Sec.-Gen. 2003–09, Minister, Under-Secr. for Econ. Affairs 2009, Minister, Perm. Mission to OAS 2009, Dir, Andean Community Dept, Directorate-Gen. of South American Community and Under-Secr. for Econ. Affairs 2009–10, Dir of Devt and Border Integration, Nat. Border Devt Directorate (part of Under-Secr. for American Affairs) 2010–11, Minister and Dir of Integration, Directorate-Gen. for Econ. Affairs 2011–12, Head of Cabinet of Minister of Foreign Affairs 2012–14, Minister of Foreign Affairs 2015–16; Commdr, Mil. Order of Ayacucho 2008. *Address:* c/o Ministry of Foreign Affairs, Jirón Lampa 535, Lima 1, Peru (office).

SÁNCHEZ-VICARIO, Arantxa; Spanish fmr professional tennis player; b. 18 Dec. 1971, Barcelona; d. of Emilio Sánchez and Marisa Vicario; m. 1st Juan Vehils (divorced 2001); m. 2nd Jose Santacana 2008; one d. one s.; turned professional in 1984 and won first professional title at Brussels 1988; winner of French Open 1989, 1994, 1998, Wimbledon 1995 (doubles), US Open 1993 (doubles), 1994 (singles and doubles), Australian Open 1992, 1995, 1996 (all doubles); Olympics: silver medal (doubles) 1992, bronze medal (singles) 1992, silver medal (singles) 1996, bronze medal (doubles) 1996; winner Int. Championships of Spain 1989, 1990, Virginia Slims Tournaments Newport 1991, Washington 1991, Canadian Open 1992; named Int. Tennis Fed. World Champion 1994;, Spanish Fed. Cup team 1986–98, 2000–01; winner of 14 Grand Slam titles, 96 WTA Tour titles and over US $16 million in prize money at retirement Nov. 2002; Capt. Spanish Fed Cup Team 2012; Professional coach 2015–, trained Caroline Wozniacki; mem. Spanish Olympic Cttee 2001, Sánchez Vicario Foundation, Fundación Alex; mem. Bd of Trustees, Fundación Laureus; Infiniti Commitment to Excellence Award 1992, Tennis Magazine Comeback Player of the Year 1998, Principe de Asturiasi Award (Spain) 1998, Int. Tennis Fed. Award of Excellence 2001, Philippe Chatrier Award 2012. *Publication:* The Young Tennis Player: A Young Enthusiast's Guide to Tennis 1996. *Leisure interests:* soccer, water skiing, reading, horse riding, languages.

SANCHO-ROF, Juan, DChemEng; Spanish business executive; *Vice-President, Técnicas Reunidas Internacional SA;* b. 9 Feb. 1940, Madrid; m. Paloma Suils; two s. three d.; ed Universidad Complutense de Madrid and Instituto de Estudios Superiores de la Empresa, Barcelona; Technical–Commercial post Petronor SA (Petróleos del Norte) 1970–76, Deputy Gen. Man. 1976–85; Chair. and CEO Repsol Petróleo SA 1985, Pres. 1995, then Pres. Petronor and Exec. Vice-Pres. of Downstream, Repsol YPF 1992–2003; mem. Bd of Dirs Gas Natural SDG 2003; currently Vice-Pres. Técnicas Reunidas Internacional, SA; Pres. Gen. Council of the Colls of Chemists of Spain. *Publications include:* several technical works. *Address:* Técnicas Reunidas Internacional SA, Arapiles 13, Madrid, Spain, (office). *Telephone:* (91) 5920300 (office). *Fax:* (91) 5920397 (office). *Website:* www.tecnicasreunidas.es (office).

SANDAGIRI, Adm. (retd) Daya, MSc; Sri Lankan naval officer (retd) and university administrator; *Chancellor, General Sir John Kotelawala Defence University;* b. 1 Sept. 1947, Veyangoda; ed St Mary's Coll. Veyangoda, Kegalu Maha Vidyalaya; joined Royal Ceylon Navy (now Sri Lanka Navy) 1966, Sub-Lt 1973, Commdr of the Navy 2001–05, promoted to rank of Adm. 2005; Chief of Defence Staff 2004–06; apptd Deputy Sec., Ministry of Defence 2006, suspended June 2006 accused of engaging in malpractice in arms purchases; Chair. Lanka Phosphate Ltd 2011–13; Chancellor, General Sir John Kotelawala Defence Univ. 2015–; served as Pres. Sri Lanka Navy Buddhist Asscn, National Basketball Fed. and Sr Vice-Pres. National Volleyball Fed.; Vishista Seva Vibhushanaya, Utthama Seva Padakkama, Republic of Sri Lanka Armed Services Medal, Sri Lanka Armed Services Long Service Medal and Clasp, President's Inauguration Medal, Sri Lanka Navy 50th Anniversary Medal and Clasp, 50th Independence Anniversary Commemoration Medal, North & East Operations Medal and Clasp, Purna Bhumi Padakkama, Vadamarachchi Operation Medal, Riviresa Campaign Service Medal. *Address:* Office of the Chancellor, General Sir John Kotelawala Defence University, Kandawala Road, Rathmalana, Sri Lanka (office). *Telephone:* (11) 2635268 (office). *E-mail:* kdudefence@kdu.ac.lk (office). *Website:* www.kdu.ac.lk/chancellor (office).

SANDBERG, Per; Norwegian politician; b. 1960, Levanger, Nord-Trøndelag; s. of Rolf Sandberg and Rannveig Ertsås; m. Line Miriam Haugan; three c.; waiter/bartender, Ustaoset Høyfjellshotell 1977–80; Tyre production worker, Viking Askim AS 1980–81; joined Norske Skog AS (pulp and paper co.) as Process Operator 1982, becoming Man. 1995–96; served with UN Interim Force in Lebanon (UNIFIL) 1986; mem. Nord-Trøndelag County Council 1995–97; mem. Storting (Parl.) for Nord-Trøndelag 1997–2005, for Sør-Trøndelag 2005–, Chair., Standing Cttee on Transport and Communications 2005–09, Standing Cttee on Justice 2009–13, mem., Standing Cttee on Foreign Affairs and Defence 2013–; Minister of Fisheries 2015–18; mem. Fremskrittspartiet (Progress Party), mem. Cen. Exec. Cttee 2000–05, Sec. Group Steering Cttee 2001–05, First Vice-Chair., Group Steering Cttee 2005–09, First Deputy Leader, Fremskrittspartiet 2006–18. *Address:* c/o Ministry of Trade, Industry and Fisheries, Kongens gate 8, 0153 Oslo, Norway (office).

SANDBERG, Sheryl Kara, AB, MBA; American business executive; *Chief Operating Officer, Facebook Inc.;* b. 28 Aug. 1969, Washington, DC; d. of Joel Sandberg and Adele Sandberg; m. 1st Brian Kraff (divorced 2004); m. 2nd David Goldberg 2004 (died 2015); two c.; ed Harvard Coll., Harvard Business School; grew up in North Miami Beach, Fla; taught aerobics while at high school 1980s; economist, World Bank 1991–93; Man. Consultant, McKinsey & Co. 1995–96; Chief of Staff to Sec., US Dept of Treasury, Washington, DC 1996–2001; Vice-Pres. Global Online Sales and Operations, Google Inc. 2001–08; COO Facebook Inc. 2008–, mem. Bd of Dirs 2012–; f. Lean In Foundation 2013– (renamed Sheryl Sandberg & Dave Goldberg Family Foundation 2016); mem. Bd of Dirs eHealth Inc. 2006–08, Starbucks 2009–12, Walt Disney Co. 2010–; mem. Bd Brookings Inst., Women for Women International, V-Day, Ad Council; John H. Williams Prize for top graduating student in econs, Harvard Coll. 1991. *Publications:* Lean In: Women, Work, and the Will to Lead 2013, Option B: Facing Adversity, Building Resilience and Finding Joy (with Adam Grant) 2017. *Address:* Facebook Inc., 156 University Avenue, Suite 300, Palo Alto, CA 94301, USA (office). *Telephone:* (650) 543-4800 (office). *Fax:* (650) 543-4801 (office). *Website:* www.facebook.com (office).

SANDER, Jean-Marie; French business executive and politician; b. 23 Dec. 1949, Ohlungen, Alsace; engaged in industrial action with Jeunes Agriculteurs, Canton of Haguenau 1971; Pres. Jeunes Agriculteurs du Bas-Rhin 1972; elected City Councillor and Deputy Mayor of Ohlungen 1983, Mayor 1995; mem. Bd of Dirs, Crédit Agricole SA 1999–2015, Vice-Chair. 2003–10, Chair. 2010–15, Chair. Strategic Cttee and mem. Appointments and Governance Cttee; Chair. CRCAM d'Alsace-Vosges from 1993, CICA, Grameen Crédit Agricole Foundation, Caisse d'Assurance Accidents du Bas Rhin; Deputy Chair. SAS Sacam Développement; mem. Bd, Fédération nationale du Crédit agricole, Chair. 2003–10, Deputy Chair. 2010–15; Dir, SAS Rue La Boétie, SAS SACAM Participations, SCICAM, 'Pays de France' Crédit Agricole Foundation, 'Un Avenir Ensemble' Foundation, Société Electricité de Strasbourg; mem. Man. Cttee Gecam (GIE); Pres. Chambre d'agric. d'Alsace 1989–. *Address:* c/o Crédit Agricole SA, 91–93 boulevard Pasteur, 75015 Paris, France. *E-mail:* info@credit-agricole-sa.fr.

SANDER, Heidemarie Jiline (Jil); German fashion designer; b. 27 Nov. 1943, Wesselburen; stylist on fashion magazine; designs clothes for working women; owns own co. Jil Sander, fmr Chair.; opened flagship store Hamburg 1968, Paris

1993, Tokyo 1999, New York 2008; launched first women's collection 1973; launched first fragrances Woman Pure and Man. Pure 1979; f. Jil Sander Italia SpA, Milan 1994, Jil Sander America, Inc. 1995; launched first men's collection 1997; introduced menswear range Jan. 1997; left Jil Sander AG 2000 after co. sold to Prada, returned as Chief Designer 2003, left again 2004, signed with Japanese firm Fast Retailing Co. to design +J for Uniqlo line, returned to Jil Sander 2012. *Leisure interests:* modern art, gardening. *Address:* Jil Sander, Via Beltrami 5, 20121 Milan, Italy (office). *Telephone:* (80) 69131 (office). *E-mail:* info@JilSander .de (office). *Website:* www.jilsander.com (office).

SANDERS, Bernard (Bernie), BS; American politician; *Senator from Vermont;* b. 8 Sept. 1941, Brooklyn, NY; m. Dr Jane O'Meara Sanders; two s. two d.; ed James Madison High School, Brooklyn, Brooklyn Coll., Univ. of Chicago; moved to Vt 1964; worked as carpenter and journalist; political career began when he joined anti-Viet Nam War Liberty Union Party 1971, resgnd 1977; unsuccessful ind. cand. for election to Senate 1972, 1974, and for Gov. of Vt 1972, 1976, 1986; worked as writer and Dir American People's Historical Soc.; Mayor of Burlington 1981–86; cand. in elections for US House of Reps 1988, mem. House of Reps for Vermont-At Large Dist 1991–2006 (first ind. mem. of House since 1950, longest-serving ind. mem. of the House), mem. Cttee on Financial Services, Cttee on Govt Reform; Co-founder House Progressive Caucus, chaired group for its first eight years; Senator from Vermont 2007–; mem. Faculty, Harvard Univ. 1989, Hamilton Coll. 1991; Ind. (caucuses with Democrats and is counted as Democrat for purposes of cttee assignments); cand. for Democratic party nomination for US Pres. 2015–16. *Radio:* regular guest appearances on Thom Hartmann radio programme for Friday segment Brunch with Bernie. *Publication:* Outsider in the House (autobiography) 1997. *Address:* 332 Dirksen Senate Office Building, Washington, DC 20510, USA (office). *Telephone:* (202) 224-5141 (office). *Fax:* (202) 228-0776 (office). *E-mail:* bernie@bernie.org. *Website:* sanders.senate.gov (office); berniesanders.com (office).

SANDERS, Donald Neil, AO, CB, BEcons; Australian banker; b. 21 June 1927, Sydney; s. of L. G. Sanders and R. M. Sanders; m. Betty Elaine Constance 1952; four s. one d.; ed Wollongong High School, Univ. of Sydney; with Commonwealth Bank of Australia 1943–60; with Australian Treasury 1956; with Bank of England 1960–61; with Reserve Bank of Australia 1961–87, Supt, Credit Policy Div. of Banking Dept 1964–66, Deputy Man. of Banking Dept 1966–67, of Research Dept 1967–70, Chief Man. of Securities Markets Dept 1970–72, of Banking and Finance Dept 1972–74, Adviser and Chief Man. 1974–75, Deputy Gov. and Deputy Chair. of Bd 1975–87; with Australian Embassy, Washington, DC 1968; Man. Dir Commonwealth Banking Corpn 1987–91; Man. Dir CEO Commonwealth Bank of Australia 1991–92; Chair. H-G Ventures Ltd 1995–2000; Dir Lend Lease Corpn Ltd, MLC Ltd 1992–99, Queensland Investment Corpn 1992–98, Australian Chamber Orchestra Pty Ltd 1992–99. *Publications:* Collected Speeches 1969–92. *Leisure interests:* golf, music. *Address:* 106 Blaxland Road, Wentworth Falls, NSW 2782, Australia (home). *Telephone:* (2) 4757-3900 (home).

SANDERS, Jeremy Keith Morris, CBE, BSc, PhD, ScD, FRS; British chemist, academic, university administrator and editor; *Editor-in-Chief, Royal Society Open Science;* b. 3 May 1948, London, England; s. of Sidney Sanders and Sylvia Sanders (née Rutman); m. Louise Elliott 1972; one s. one d.; ed Wandsworth School, Imperial Coll. London, Univ. of Cambridge; Research Assoc. in Pharmacology, Stanford Univ., USA 1972–73; Demonstrator in Chem., Univ. of Cambridge 1973–78, Lecturer 1978–92, Reader 1992–96, Prof. of Chem. 1996–2015, Head of Dept of Chem. 2000–06, Deputy Vice-Chancellor, Univ. of Cambridge 2006–10, Head of School of Physical Sciences 2009–11, Pro-Vice-Chancellor (Institutional Affairs) 2011–15, Chair. Chem. Sub-panel, 2008 Research Assessment Exercise 2004–08, Fellow, Selwyn Coll., Cambridge 1976–; Ed.-in-Chief, Royal Soc. Open Science (open access journal) 2016–; Visiting Fellow, Japan Soc. for the Promotion of Science 2002; Visiting Prof., Pole Balard Chimie, Montpellier, France 2013; mem. Editorial Bd Magnetic Resonance in Chemistry 1984–92, Journal of the Chemical Society Perkin Transactions 1988–93; mem. Editorial Advisory Bd Chemical Society Reviews 1996–2002, Chair. 2000–02; Assoc. Ed. New Journal of Chemistry 1998–2000; mem. Int. Supervisory Bd Nat. Research Consortium on Catalysis (Netherlands) 1999–2009; mem. Scientific Bd Inst. of Chemical Research of Catalonia 2002–12; mem. Scientific Advisory Bd Cresset BioMolecular Discovery Ltd 2002–07; mem. Editorial Advisory Bd Journal of American Chemical Society 2009–12; mem. Int. Advisory Bd Israel Journal of Chemistry 2010–12, Chemistry sub-panel, 2014 Research Excellence Framework 2011–14; Meldola Medal, Royal Inst. of Chem. 1975, RSC Hickinbottom Award 1981, Pfizer Award 1984, 1988, RSC Josef Loschmidt Prize 1994, RSC Pedler Lecturer 1996, Izaat Christensen Award, USA 2003, AstraZeneca Lecturer, Univ. of Alberta, Canada 2003, Merck-Frosst Lecturer, Simon Fraser Univ. 2003, IAP Lecturer, Columbia Univ. 2003, J. Clarence Karcher Lecturer, Univ. of Oklahoma 2005, Barré Lecturer, Univ. of Montreal 2007, Davy Medal, Royal Soc. 2009, Diamond Jubilee Anniversary Day Lecturer, Nat. Chemical Lab., India 2010, Pres. 'Burgenstock' Stereochemistry Conf., Switzerland 2011, Novartis Lecturer, Scripps Inst. 2011, Bender Distinguished Lecturer, Northwestern Univ., USA 2013. *Publications:* Modern NMR Spectroscopy (with B. K. Hunter, second edn) 1993; numerous papers in scientific journals. *Address:* Royal Society Open Science, The Royal Society, 6–9 Carlton House Terrace, London, SW1Y 5AG, England (office). *Telephone:* (20) 7451-2654 (office). *Website:* rsos.royalsocietypublishing.org (office).

SANDERS, Sir Ronald Michael, Kt, KCMG, KCN, MA; Antigua and Barbuda diplomatist, international relations consultant, business executive and writer; *Senior Research Fellow, Institute of Commonwealth Studies, School of Advanced Study, University of London;* b. 26 Jan. 1948, Guyana; m. Susan Ramphal 1975; ed Sacred Heart RC School, Guyana, Boston Univ., USA, Univ. of Sussex, UK; Man. Dir Guyana Broadcasting Service, Public Affairs Adviser to Prime Minister of Guyana 1973–76; Lecturer in Communications, Univ. of Guyana 1975–76; Consultant to Pres. of Caribbean Devt Bank, Barbados 1977–78; Special Adviser to the Minister of Foreign Affairs of Antigua and Barbuda 1978–82; Deputy Perm. Rep. of Antigua and Barbuda to the UN, New York 1982–83; Antigua and Barbuda Amb. Extraordinary and Plenipotentiary accred to UNESCO 1983–87; Antigua and Barbuda High Commr in UK 1984–87, 1995–2004 (also accred to FRG 1986–87, 1996–2004, to France 1996–2004), Chief Foreign Affairs Rep. with Ministerial Rank 1999–2004; Deputy Chair. Caribbean Financial Action Task Force 2002–; Pres. Caribbean Broadcasting Union 1975–76; Chair. Caribbean Sub-

Group at UNESCO 1983–85; mem. Bd Dirs of Caribbean News Agency 1976–77; mem. Inter-Governmental Council of the Int. Programme for the Devt of Communications at UNESCO 1983–87; mem. Exec. Bd UNESCO 1985–87; Visiting Fellow, Univ. of Oxford 1987–89; Sr Research Fellow, Inst. of Commonwealth Studies, Univ. of London, UK 2012–16; freelance broadcaster with BBC World Service 1987–89; Consultant (Int. Relations) Atlantic Tele-Network, US Virgin Islands 1989–97; mem. Bd of Dirs Swiss American Nat. Bank of Antigua 1990–97, Guyana Telephone and Telegraph Co. 1991–97, Innovative Communication Corpn, US Virgin Islands 1998 (Exec. Dir for Int. Relations 2004); mem. Advisory Council Commonwealth Broadcasting Asscn 2005–; mem. Eminent Persons Group 2010–; currently columnist, Antigua Sun newspaper. *Publications include:* Broadcasting in Guyana 1978, Antigua and Barbuda: Transition, Trial, Triumph 1984, Inseparable Humanity: Anthology of Reflections of the Commonwealth Secretary-General (ed.) 1988, Antigua Vision: Caribbean Reality, Perspectives of Prime Minister Lester Bird (ed.) 2002, Crumbled Small: The Commonwealth Caribbean in World Politics 2005; numerous articles on media ownership and control, communication and development and Antarctica. *Leisure interests:* reading, West Indian history, cinema. *Address:* Institute of Commonwealth Studies, School of Advanced Study, University of London, Second Floor, South Block, Senate House, Malet Street, London, WC1E 7HU, England. *Telephone:* (20) 7862-8853. *Fax:* (20) 7862-8813. *E-mail:* ronaldsanders29@ hotmail.com. *Website:* commonwealth.sas.ac.uk; www.sirronaldsanders.com.

SANDERSON, Bryan Kaye, CBE, BSc; British business executive; b. 14 Oct. 1940, Co. Durham; s. of Eric Sanderson and Anne Sanderson; m. Sirkka Kärki 1966; one s. one d.; ed Dame Allan's School, London School of Econs, UK, International Man. Inst. Lausanne, Switzerland; VSO 1962–64; joined British Petroleum (BP) 1964, Sr Rep. for SE Asia and China 1984–87, CEO BP Nutrition 1987–90, CEO BP Chemicals, then BP Amoco Chemicals 1990–97, mem. Bd BP 1992–2000; Dir (non-exec.) Corus (fmrly British Steel) 1994–2000, Six Continents hotel group 2001–03, Argus Media Ltd 2012–; Chair. (non-exec.) BUPA 2001–06; Dir (non-exec.) Standard Chartered PLC 2002–03, Exec. Chair. 2003–06; mem. Advisory Group to the Labour Party on Industrial Competition Policy 1997–98, Dept for Trade and Industry (DTI) Advisory Group on Competitiveness 1998, King's Fund Man. Cttee 1999, DTI Co. Law Steering Group 1998, DTI Industrial Devt Advisory Bd 2000–04; Pres. European Chemical Industry Council 1998–2000; Chair. Learning and Skills Council 2000–04, Sunderland Urban Regeneration Co. 2001–08, QGS Synergy (now Business Impact UK Ltd) 2007–08, Northern Rock PLC 2007–08, Cella Energy –2014; mem. Bd of Dirs Glodyne Technoserve Ltd 2011–, Sunderland Football Club PLC 1998– (Chair. 1998–2004), Durham Co. Cricket Club 2005–, Argus Media 2012–; mem. Court of Govs LSE 1997– (Vice-Chair. 1998–2004); mem. Commonwealth Business Council; Trustee, Economist 2006–, Florence Nightingale Foundation 2008–; Hon. FIChemE 2002; Hon. DBA (Sunderland) 1998, (York) 1999. *Leisure interests:* reading, golf, walking, gardening.

SANDERSON, Hon. Kerry Gaye, AC, BSc, BEcons; Australian public servant, business executive and state government official; b. 21 Dec. 1950, Subiaco, Western Australia; m. Lancelot (Lance) John Sanderson (died 2007); two s.; ed Churchlands Senior High School, Univ. of Western Australia; served in sr positions in Dept of the Treasury, Govt of Western Australia for 17 years and as Deputy Dir Dept of Transport for four years, CEO Fremantle Ports 1991–2008, Agent-Gen. for Western Australia 2008–11; entered pvt. sector 2011–14, Dir (non-exec.), Downer EDI, St John of God Health Care, Atlas Iron; also holds positions with several charities and non-profit orgs; Adjunct Prof., Curtin Univ.'s Business School 2013–; Gov. of Western Australia (first woman) 2014–18; Centenary Medal 2001; Hon. LLD (Univ. of Western Australia) 2005; Telstra Business Woman of the Year (Western Australia) 1996.

SANDIFORD, Rt Hon. Sir Lloyd Erskine, PC, JP, MA (Econs); Barbadian politician and diplomatist; b. 24 March 1937; s. of Cyril G. Sandiford and Eunice Sandiford; m. Angelita P. Ricketts 1963; one s. two d.; ed Coleridge-Parry Secondary School, Harrison Coll., Barbados, Univ. Coll. of the West Indies, Jamaica and Univ. of Manchester, UK; Asst Master, Modern High School, Barbados 1956–57, Kingston Coll., Jamaica 1960–61; part-time Tutor and Lecturer, Univ. of the West Indies, Barbados 1963–65; Sr Grad. Master, Harrison Coll. 1964–66; Asst Tutor, Barbados Community Coll. 1976–86; mem. Barbados Senate 1967–71, MP for St Michael S 1971–99; Personal Asst to Prime Minister 1966–67; Minister of Educ. 1967–71, of Educ., Youth Affairs, Community Devt and Sport 1971–75, of Health and Welfare 1975–76; Deputy Prime Minister and Minister of Educ. and Culture 1986–87; Prime Minister of Barbados and Minister of Finance 1987–93, Prime Minister and Minister of Econ. Affairs and the Civil Service 1987–94, also of Defence; Amb. to People's Repub. of China 2010–14; Pres. Sandiford Centre for Public Affairs; Visiting Scholar, Pennsylvania State Univ., Harrisburg, Pa, USA; Founder, Acad. of Politics; mem. Democratic Labour Party, also Asst Sec., Gen. Sec., Pres. 1974–75; mem. Council of Freely Elected Presidents and Prime Ministers, Carter Center, Atlanta; mem. Global Peace Council, Universal Peace Fed.; Life mem. Barbados Cricket Asscn; tutor, Barbados Community Coll.; Order of the Liberator (Venezuela), Kt of St Andrew 2000; Hon. LLD (Univ. of the West Indies) 2009; Barbados Scholar 1956, Distinguished Fellow, Sir Arthur Lewis Inst. of Social and Econ. Studies, Univ. of the West Indies 1999, Pres.'s Medal of Excellence, Bowie State Univ., Maryland. *Poetry:* Ode to the Environment, When She Leaves You. *Publications include:* The Essence of Economics 1997, Caribbean Politics and Society 2000, Speeches (six vols). *Leisure interests:* choral singing, reading, gardening, swimming, cricket. *Address:* c/o Ministry of Foreign Affairs, 1 Culloden Road, St Michael, Barbados; Hillvista, Porters, St James, Barbados (home). *Telephone:* 422-3458 (home). *Fax:* 422-0281 (home). *E-mail:* lesandiford@carbsurf.com.

SANDILA, Adm. (retd) Mohammad Asif, BSc, MSc; Pakistani naval officer (retd); *Chief Executive, Moawin Foundation;* b. 15 Nov. 1954, Shaikhupura; ed Cadet Coll., Pakistan Naval Acad., Britannia Royal Naval Coll., UK, Nat. Defence Univ., Naval Command and Staff Coll., Indonesia; joined Navy as Cadet 1972, Sub-Lt Naval Operations Branch 1975, Div. Officer, Pakistan Naval Acad., Fleet Operations Officer to Commdr Fleet, Flag Lt to Chief of Staff, Dir Project (Plans), Asst Chief of Naval Staff (Plans), Prin. Sec. to Chief of Naval Staff, Commdr, 25th Destroyer Squadron, DG Maritime Security Agency, Commdr of Naval Logistics,

Commdr, Pakistan Fleet 2008, Deputy Chief of Naval Staff Operations, Chief of Staff 2010–11, Chief of Naval Staff 2011–14 (retd); currently Chief Exec. Moawin Foundation, Islamabad; Chevalier, II Ordre national du Mérite 2004; Nishan-e-Imtiaz. *Leisure interests:* golf, reading. *Address:* Moawin Foundation, House No. B-9, Navy Housing Scheme, F-11/1, Islamabad, Pakistan (office). *Telephone:* (51) 9260931 (office). *E-mail:* mas@moawinfoundation.org.pk (office). *Website:* moawinfoundation.org.pk (office).

SANDLE, Michael Leonard, FRBS, DFA, ARA; British artist and fmr professor of art; b. 18 May 1936, Weymouth, Dorset; s. of Charles E. Sandle and Dorothy G. Sandle (née Vernon); m. 1st Cynthia D. Koppel 1971 (divorced 1974); m. 2nd Demelza Spargo 1988 (divorced 2004); one s. one d.; ed Douglas High School, Isle of Man, Douglas School of Art and Tech. and Slade School of Fine Art; studied lithography, Atelier Patris, Paris 1960; began sculpture 1962; held various teaching posts in UK 1961–70; Lecturer Coventry Coll of Art 1964–68; resident in Canada 1970–73; Visiting Prof., Univ. of Calgary 1970–71; Visiting Assoc. Prof., Univ. of Victoria, British Columbia 1972–73; Lecturer in Sculpture, Fachhochschule für Gestaltung, Pforzheim, FRG 1973–77, Prof. 1977–80; Prof., Akad. Für Bildenden Künste, Germany 1980–99 (retd); mem. RA 1990–97 (resgnd), re-elected 2004; Fellow, Kenneth Armitage Foundation 2004–06; designed architecture and executed sculpture for the Malta Siege Memorial, Grand Harbour, Valletta 1989–92; designed Int. Memorial for Seafarers at International Maritime Org's HQ, London 2001; works in many public collections in UK, Germany, Australia, USA; Nobutaka Shikanai Prize, 1st Rodin Grand Prize Exhbn, Japan 1986, Henry Hering Memorial Medal, Nat. Sculpture Soc. of America 1995.

SANDLER, Adam, BFA; American actor and screenwriter; b. 9 Sept. 1966, Brooklyn, New York; s. of Stanley Sandler and Judy Sandler; m. Jacqueline Samantha Titone; two d.; ed New York Univ.; f. Happy Madison Productions; People's Choice Award 2000. *Albums:* They're All Gonna Laugh at You! 1993, What the Hell Happened to Me? 1996, What's Your Name? 1997, Stan and Judy's Kid 2000, Shhh.. Don't Tell 2004. *Films include:* Going Overboard 1989, Shakes the Clown 1992, Coneheads 1993, Airheads 1994, Mixed Nuts 1994, Billy Madison 1995, Happy Gilmore 1996, Bulletproof 1996, The Wedding Singer 1998, The Water Boy 1998, Big Daddy 1999, Little Nicky 2000, Punch-Drunk Love 2002, Mr Deeds 2002, Anger Management 2003, 50 First Dates 2004, Spanglish 2004, The Longest Yard 2005, Click 2006, Reign Over Me 2007, I Now Pronounce You Chuck and Larry 2007, You Don't Mess with the Zohan 2008, Funny People 2009, Grown Ups 2010, Just Go with It 2011, That's My Boy 2012, Hotel Transylvania (voice) 2012, Grown Ups 2 2013, Blended 2014, Men, Women & Children 2014, The Cobbler 2014. *Television appearances include:* actor, writer, Saturday Night Live 1990–95. *Screenplays:* (co-writer) Billy Madison, Happy Gilmore, The Water Boy, You Don't Mess with the Zohan. *Publications:* Little Nicky 2000. *Address:* Happy Madison Productions, 10202 West Washington Blvd., Judy Garland Bldg, Culver City, CA 90232; William Morris Endeavor Entertainment, 9601 Wilshire Blvd., 10th Floor, Beverly Hills, CA 90210, USA. *Website:* www.adamsandler.com.

SANDLER, Joanne; American international organization official; ran consulting business that provided organizational devt support to women's orgs, New York; joined UNIFEM 1997, fmr Chief of Organisational Learning and Resource Devt and Deputy Dir for Programmes, Deputy Exec. Dir 2011–11, Ad-Interim Exec. Dir –2008; part of transition team for UN Women 2010–11; mem. bd of dirs of several orgs including Asscn for Women's Rights in Devt, Gender at Work, Women Make Movies, Breakthrough, Women Win.

SANDLER, Ron, CBE, MA, MBA; South African business executive; *Executive Chairman, Towry Holdings Ltd;* b. 5 March 1952, Durban; s. of Bernard M. Sandler and Carla Sandler; m. Susan Lee 1977; two s.; ed Queens' Coll. Cambridge, Stanford Univ., USA; worked at Boston Consulting, Los Angeles, USA, then Booz Allen, London, England; f. own man. consultancy firm 1988; apptd. Chair. Quadrex Holdings 1990; joined Lloyd's of London 1994, Chief Exec. 1995–99; COO Nat. Westminster Bank PLC 1999–2000; apptd Chair. Kyte Group 2000; Chair. Computacenter 2001–08; Chair. (non-exec.) Northern Rock PLC 2008–10, Exec. Chair. Feb.–Oct. 2008, 2010–11; Exec. Chair. Towry Holdings Ltd 2014–; Chair. Paternoster Ltd, Phoenix Group Holdings, Ironshore Inc.; Adviser, Palamon Capital Partners, LP; Deputy Chair. KiFin Ltd; Trustee, Royal Opera House 1999–; Head, Inquiry into Long-term Savings 2001; led Govt-sponsored review of UK Long Term Savings Industry 2002; fmr Pres. Chartered Inst. of Bankers; Hon. CBE; Dr hc City University London 2012. *Leisure interests:* poker, opera, golf, skiing. *Address:* Towry House, Western Road, Bracknell, RG12 1TL (office); 5 Southside, Wimbledon, London, SW19 4TG, England (home). *Telephone:* (20) 8946-1179 (home). *E-mail:* info@towry.com (office). *Website:* www.towry.com (office).

SANDMO, Agnar, DrOecon; Norwegian economist and academic; *Professor of Economics Emeritus, Norwegian School of Economics and Business Administration;* b. 9 Jan. 1938, Tønsberg; m. Tone Sverdrup 1959; two s. one d.; ed Tønsberg Gymnasium, Norwegian School of Econs and Business Admin. (NHH); Grad. Fellow, NHH 1963–66, Asst Prof. of Econs 1966–71, Prof. of Econs 1971–2007, Prof. Emer. 2007–, Vice-Rector 1985–87; Visiting Fellow, Catholic Univ. of Louvain 1969–70; Visiting Prof., Univ. of Essex 1975–76; mem. Petroleum Price Bd 1976–80, several govt bds and cttees on social science and gen. research policy; Pres. European Econ. Asscn 1990; mem. Norwegian and Swedish Acads of Science; Fellow, Econometric Soc.; Order of St Olav 1997; Dr hc (Oslo) 1997, (Uppsala) 2008; Research Council of Norway Prize for Outstanding Research 2002. *Publications:* articles and books on econs and econ. policy. *Address:* Norwegian School of Economics and Business Administration, Helleveien 30, 5045 Bergen (office); Måseskjærveien 8, 5035 Bergen, Norway (home). *Telephone:* 55-95-92-76 (office); 55-25-65-86 (home). *E-mail:* agnar.sandmo@nhh.no (office). *Website:* www.nhh.no (office).

SANDOVAL, Arturo; American (b. Cuban) musician (trumpet); b. 6 Nov. 1949, Artemisa, Cuba; m. Marianela Sandoval; one s.; ed Nat. School of Art; began playing trumpet aged 12 and made first public appearances in Cuba aged 13; played in group with Chucho Váldez until 1981; formed own group, Irakere, in 1981; granted political asylum in USA 1990; apptd Prof. of Music, Florida Int. Univ., now Prof. Emer.; opened Arturo Sandoval Jazz Club, Miami Beach 2006; festival appearances at Tokyo, Newport, Montreux, Antibes, Chicago, The Hague and the Hollywood Bowl; Dr hc (Univ. of Notre Dame) 2016; 10 Grammy Awards, six Billboard Awards, Emmy Award, Presidential Medal of Freedom 2013, Hispanic Heritage Award 2015. *Recordings include:* albums: Havana (with David Amram) 1976, New York (with David Amram) 1977, Irakere 1979, To a Finland Station (with Dizzy Gillespie) 1982, Breaking the Sound Barrier 1983, No Problem 1986, Tumbaito 1987, Straight Ahead 1988, Classics 1989, Arturo Sandoval 1989, Flight to Freedom 1991, I Remember Clifford 1992, Danzón 1993, Dream Come True 1993, Passion 1993, Cubano 1994, Arturo Sandoval y el Tren Latino 1995, Double Talk (with Ed Calle) 1996, Swingin' 1996, Just Music 1997, Hot House 1998, Americana 1999, Sunset Harbour (with Ed Calle) 1999, Los Elefantes (with Wynton Marsalis) 1999, For Love or Country 2000, Piedras y Flores (with Amaury Gutiérrez) 2001, L.A. Meetings 2001, My Passion for the Piano 2002, From Havana With Love 2003, Trumpet Evolution 2003, Rumba Palace (Latin Grammy Award for Best Latin Jazz Album 2007) 2007, Arturo Sandoval & the Latin Jazz Orchestra 2007, A Time for Love (Latin Grammy Award for Best Instrumental Album) 2010, Dear Diz (Grammy Award for Best Large Jazz Ensemble Album 2013) 2012, Live at Yoshi's 2016. *Website:* www.arturosandoval.com.

SANDOVAL, Brian Edward, BA, JD; American lawyer and politician; b. 5 Aug. 1963, Redding, Calif.; s. of Ronald L. Sandoval and Gloria Sandoval; m. Kathleen Teipner; one s. two d.; ed Bishop Manogue High School, Reno, Nev., Univ. of Nevada, Ohio State Univ. Moritz Coll. of Law; entered pvt. practice with several Reno law firms: McDonald, Carano, Wilson, McCune Bergin, Frankovich & Hicks 1989–91, Robinson, Belaustegui, Robb & Sharp 1991–95, Gamboa, Sandoval & Stovall 1995–99; est. Sandoval Law Office, Reno 1999–2003; mem. Nevada State Ass. representing 25th Legis. Dist 1995–97, served on Judiciary, Taxation and Natural Resources Cttees, also served on Nev. Legis. Comm., Advisory Comm. on Sentencing, Juvenile Justice Comm., Advisory Council on Community Notification of Sex Offenders, Tahoe Regional Planning Agency Oversight Cttee; mem. Nevada Gaming Comm. 1998–2001, Chair. 1999–2001 (youngest ever chair.); Attorney Gen. of Nev. 2003–05; Judge, US Dist Court for Dist of Nevada 2005–09; Gov. of Nevada 2011–19; mem. Bd of Trustees, Children's Cabinet, Reno, St Jude's Ranch for Children, Washoe Co. Law Library; Republican; several awards and certificates, including Hispanics in Politics Broche de Oro Award 1996, Torch of Liberty Award, Anti-Defamation League 2003, Access to Justice Public Lawyer Award, Nevada State Bar 2004, Most Influential Hispanic in the US Award, The Latino Coalition 2004, Alumnus of the Year Award, Univ. of Nevada 2004, Excellence in Leadership Award, Latino Coalition 2010. *Leisure interests:* running, travelling, spending time with his family. *Address:* c/o Office of the Governor, State Capitol, 101 N Carson Street, Carson City, NV 89701, USA (office). *Website:* www.briansandoval.com.

SANDOVAL CÓRDOVA, Wellington, MD, PhD; Ecuadorean physician, government official and diplomatist; ed Universidad Central del Ecuador, Univ. of Michigan, USA, Univ. of Toronto, Canada; dir of mobile hosp. during Paquisha war 1981; cardiovascular and thoracic surgeon, Armed Forces Hosp., Quito 1977–91; Dir Hospital Metropolitano, Quito 1992–2005, currently cardiothoracic surgeon; apptd Prof. and Head of Surgery, Faculty of Medical Sciences, Universidad Internacional del Ecuador 2004; Minister of Public Health April–Dec. 2005; Pres. Inst. for Social Security 2006–07; Minister of Nat. Defence 2007–08 (resgnd); Amb. to Argentina 2008–13. *Address:* Hospital Metropolitano, Av. Mariana de Jesús s/ny Nicolás Arteta, C1 CONS # 48, Ext. 348, Quito EC170129, Ecuador (office). *E-mail:* wsancor39@hotmail.com. *Website:* www.hospitalmetropolitano.org (office).

SANDOVAL GONZÁLEZ, Luis Crescencio, DEM; Mexican army officer and politician; *Secretary of National Defence;* b. 7 Feb. 1960, Ensenada, BC; ed Heroic Mil. Coll.; has served as Chief Commdr of several mil. units; joined Secr. of Foreign Affairs as Mil. Attaché, Embassy in Washington, DC, USA; fmr Deputy Chief of Cabinet; held numerous positions at the Secr. of Nat. Defence, including Asst to a senior official, Deputy Chief of the Nat. Defence Staff, later Sec. of Nat. Defence 2018–; Chevalier de l'Ordre national du Mérite (France), Condecoración de Perseverancia, Condecoración Miguel Hidalgo; Meritorious Service Medal (USA). *Address:* Secretariat of National Defence, Blvd Manuel Ávila Camacho, esq. Avenida Industria Militar, Col. Lomas de Sotelo, 11200 México, Mexico (office). *Telephone:* (55) 2122-8800 (office). *E-mail:* atn.ciudadana@sedena.gob.mx (office). *Website:* www.gob.mx/sedena (office).

SANDOVAL ÍÑIGUEZ, HE Cardinal Juan; Mexican ecclesiastic; *Archbishop Emeritus of Guadalajara;* b. 28 March 1933, Yahualica, Jalisco; s. of Esteban Sandoval and María Guadalupe Iñiguez; ed Seminario Diocesano de Guadalajara, Pontifica Universidad Gregoriana; ordained as a Catholic priest 1957; teacher Seminario de Guadalajara 1961, Prof. of Philosophy, Vice-Rector 1971, Rector 1980; Bishop's Coadjutor, Juárez 1988, Bishop of Juárez 1992; Archbishop of Guadalajara 1994–2011, Archbishop Emer. 2011–; cr. Cardinal (Cardinal-Priest of Nostra Signora di Guadalupe e San Filippo Martire in Via Aurelia) 1994; participated in Papal Conclave 2005, 2013; mem. IV Latin American Archbishop's Conf., Santo Domingo 1992, Congregation for Insts of Consecrated life and Societies of Apostolic Life, Congregation for Catholic Educ., Pontifical Council for Culture, Pontifical Comm. for Latin America, Prefecture for Econ. Affairs of the Holy See, Cardinal Comm. for the Supervision, Inst. for Works of Religion, Special Council for America, Gen. Secr. of the Synod of Bishops. *Address:* Arzobispado, Calle Liceo 17, Apdo. 1-331, 44100 Guadalajara, Mexico (office). *Telephone:* (3) 614-5504 (office). *Fax:* (3) 658-2300 (office). *Website:* www.arquidiocesisgdl.org.mx (office).

SANDRE, Didier (Didier de Maffre); French actor; b. 17 Aug. 1946, Paris; s. of Pierre Maffre and Geneviève Gevril; m. 2nd Nada Strancar 1990; one d.; ed Lycée Gustave Monod, Enghien-les-Bains, Collège Estienne, Paris; internship roles include: Don Juan, The Tempest, The Winter's Tale, Phaedra, L'Ecole des Femmes, The Misanthrope, Tartuffe, The Screens, Fake Next, Foreign Land, Martyrdom of Saint Sebastian, Madame de Sade, The Marriage Figaro, Le Soulier de Satin, Ivanov, The Way Solitaire, Sharing Midi, An Ideal Husband, Dinner with Friends, Thomas Becket, Berenice, Histoire du Soldat, My Life with Mozart, Dance of Death, The Cherry Orchard, RER, Collaboration, Tartuffe, Romeo et Juliette, Fourberies de Scapin, Les Damnés, Poussiere, Créanciers; mem. Comédie Française Co.; Chevalier des Arts et des Lettres, Ordre nat. du Mérite, Chevalier, Légion d'honneur; Prix Syndicat de la Critique, Molière Prize for Best Actor 1996,

Prix du Brigadier 2013, Notes d'automne Prize 2013. *Plays by:* Molière, Racine, Shakespeare, J. Ford, H. Ibsen, T. Mann, M. Yourcenar, J. Lenz, W. Witkiewicz, Marivaux, Beaumarchais, Y. Mishima, J. Genet, J. Anouilh, A. Gatti, D. Margulies, G. Feydeau, A. Strindberg, A. Schnitzler, P. Claudel, E. Bond, O. Wilde, A. Moravia, R. Schimmelpfennig, E.A. Schmitt, J.M. Besset, Chekhov, R. Harwood. *Films include:* La java des ombres 1983 Train d'enfer 1985, Code Name: Emerald 1985, Woman of My Life 1986, Vent de galerne 1989, Les mannequins d'osier 1989, Boulevard des hirondelles 1992, The Lie 1993, 3000 Scenarios Against a Virus 1994, Mazeppa (voice) 1993, I Can't Sleep (voice) 1994, Petits arrangements avec les morts 1994, An Autumn Tale 1998, The Mystery Paul 2000, La légende de Parva (voice) 2003, Hell 2006, Montparnasse 2009, Memory Lane 2009, 38 témoins 2012, A.L.F. 2012, Foto 2012, Au bout du conte 2013, Pas son genre 2014. *Television includes:* Médecins de nuit (series) 1978, Le misanthrope (film) 1980, Peer Gynt (film) 1981, Saint Louis ou La royauté bienfaisante (film) 1982, Conrad Killian, le fou du désert (series) 1982, Deux amies d'enfance (mini-series) 1983, Capitaine X (mini-series) 1983, Two Childhood Friends 1983, Richelieu ou La journée des dupes (film) 1983, La fausse suivante (film) 1985, L'année terrible (film) 1985, Manon Roland (film) 1989, Eurocops (series) 1989, Liberté, Libertés (film) 1989, Jeanne d'Arc, le pouvoir de l'innocence (film) 1989, Les grandes familles (mini-series) 1989, Le chemin solitaire (film) 1990, Ivanov (film) 1990, Turbulences (film) 1992, Flash – Der Fotoreporter (series) 1993, L'amour assassin (film) 1993, Turbulence 1992, 3000 scénarios contre un virus (series) 1994, Une famille formidable (series) 1992–96, Sandra princesse rebelle (mini-series) 1995, L'allée du roi (mini-series) 1996, L'uomo che ho ucciso (film) 1996, La femme d'un seul homme (film) 1998, Passion interdite (film) 1998, Intime conviction (film) 1998, Deux frères (film) 2000, L'enfant éternel (film) 2002, Saint-Germain ou La négociation (film) 2003, Les amants du Flore (film) 2006, Le sang noir (film) 2007, Moi, Louis, enfant de la mine (film) 2007, Sous un autre jour (film) 2009, À la recherche du temps perdu (film) 2011, Nicolas Le Floch (series) 2012, Les années perdues (film) 2015. *Leisure interests:* music, gardening, reading. *Address:* c/o Laurence Bagoe, 10 rue Louvois, 75002 Paris, France (office). *Telephone:* 6-70-70-18-37 (mobile) (office). *E-mail:* laurencebagoe@gmail.com (office). *Website:* www.didiersandre.info.

SANDRI, HE Cardinal Leonardo, BCL; Argentine ecclesiastic; *Prefect of the Congregation for the Oriental Churches;* b. 18 Nov. 1943, Buenos Aires; born to parents of Italian descent; ordained priest in Buenos Aires 1967; entered Vatican diplomatic corps 1974, served at Vatican Embassy in Madagascar, worked at Secr. of State 1977–89, assigned to Nunciature in USA 1989–91, returned to the Vatican 1991–97; apptd Titular Archbishop of Aemona 1997; Apostolic Nuncio to Venezuela 1997–2000, to Mexico 2000; Substitute (Sostituto) Sec. for Gen. Affairs, Secr. of State 2000–07; Prefect of the Congregation for the Oriental Churches 2007–; cr. Cardinal (Cardinal-Deacon of Santi Biagio e Carlo ai Catinari) 2007; participated in Papal Conclave 2013; mem. Congregation for the Doctrine of the Faith, Congregation for the Evangelization of Peoples, Pontifical Council for Promoting Christian Unity, Pontifical Council for Interreligious Dialogue, Pontifical Council for Legis. Texts, Pontifical Comm. for Latin America, Pontifical Comm. for Vatican City State, Congregation for Bishops 2010–, Apostolic Signatura 2011–, Congregation for Catholic Educ. 2012–; named by Pope Benedict XVI as Co-Pres. of special Synod of Bishops for the Middle East, The Vatican Oct. 2010. *Address:* Congregation for the Oriental Churches, Via della Conciliazione 34, Palazzo del Bramante, 00193 Rome, Italy (office). *Telephone:* (06) 6988-4281 (office). *Fax:* (06) 6988-4300 (office). *E-mail:* cco@orientchurch.va (office). *Website:* www.vatican.va/roman_curia/congregations/orientchurch (office).

SANDS, Peter A., MPA; British business executive; *Senior Fellow, Mossavar-Rahmani Center for Business and Government, Kennedy School of Government, Harvard University;* b. 8 Jan. 1962; m.; four c.; ed Univ. of Oxford, Harvard Univ., USA (Harkness Fellow); grew up in Asia; worked for FCO –1988; joined McKinsey & Co. 1988, worked extensively in banking and tech. sectors, Pnr 1996–2002, mem. Bd of Dirs 2000–02; Group Finance Dir and Group Exec. Dir Standard Chartered PLC 2002–06, Group Chief Exec. 2006–15; Sr Fellow, Mossavar-Rahmani Center for Business and Govt, Kennedy School of Govt, Harvard Univ. 2015–; Chair. Comm. on Global Health Risk Framework, NAS 2015–; Co-Chair. UK-India CEO Forum 2010–15; apptd Lead Non-Exec. Dir, UK Dept of Health 2011; mem. Bd of Dirs Int. Inst. of Finance 2007–15, Int. Monetary Conference 2010–15, World Economic Forum 2012–15; mem. Int. Advisory Bd, Monetary Authority of Singapore 2010–15. *Address:* John F. Kennedy School of Government, Mailbox NR, 79 JFK Street, Cambridge, MA 02138, USA (office). *Telephone:* (776) 877-3975 (office). *E-mail:* peter_sands@hks.harvard.edu (office). *Website:* www.hks.harvard.edu (office).

SANDS, Philippe, BA, LLM, QC; French/British lawyer, commentator, writer and academic; *Professor of Law and Director, Centre on International Courts and Tribunals, University College of London;* b. 17 Oct. 1960, London; m.; three c.; Research Fellow, St Catharine's Coll., Univ. of Cambridge 1984–88; taught at King's Coll. London 1988–93, School of Oriental and African Studies, Univ. of London 1993–2001; Global Prof. of Law, New York Univ. 1995–2003; Co-founder, Foundation for Int. Environmental Law and Devt; Founder mem. Matrix Chambers, currently Lawyer; Prof. of Law and Dir Centre on Int. Courts and Tribunals, Univ. Coll. London 2002–; commentator, BBC, Sky News, Al Jazeera, CNN; contrib. to Financial Times, The Guardian, London Review of Books, Vanity Fair; Visiting Prof., Univ. of Toronto 2005, Univ. of Melbourne 2005, Université de Paris I, Sorbonne 2006, 2007; apptd Judge, Guardian First Book Prize Award 2007; currently Vice-Pres. Hay Festival of Arts and Literature; mem. of Bd Tricycle Theatre 2008–, English PEN 2013–; mem. Advisory Bd, European Journal of Int. Law, Review of European Community and Int. Environmental Law; Hon. DJur (Univ. of Lincoln) 2015; Henri Rolin Medal 1999, Elizabeth Haub Prize 2005. *Publications:* Principles of International Environmental Law 1995, The Manual of International Courts and Tribunals (with Shany and Mackenzie) 1999, Lawless World: America and the Making and Breaking of Global Rules 2005, Torture Team: Rumsfeld's Memo and the Betrayal of American Values 2008, East West Street: On the Origins of Genocide and Crimes against Humanity (Baillie Gifford Prize for Non-Fiction 2016, Jewish Quarterly Wingate Prize 2017) 2016, City of Lions 2016. *Leisure interest:* football. *Address:* University College of London, Laws, Bidborough House, 38–50 Bidborough Street, London, WC1H 9BT, England (office). *Telephone:* (20) 3108-8375 (office). *E-mail:* p.sands@ucl.ac.uk (office). *Website:* www.laws.ucl.ac.uk (office).

SANDS, Sarah; British editor and writer; b. (Sarah Harvey), 3 May 1961, Cambridge; m. 1st Julian Sands; one s.; m. 2nd Kim Fletcher; two c.; ed Goldsmiths Coll., London; worked at Kent and Sussex Courier 1983–86; worked at Evening Standard, London, as diary reporter, Ed. of the Londoner's Diary, later Features Ed., then Assoc. Ed. 1986–95; Deputy Ed. The Daily Telegraph 1996–2005, responsible for The Daily Telegraph Saturday edn, Ed. The Sunday Telegraph 2005–06; Consulting Ed. The Daily Mail 2006–08; Ed.-in-Chief Reader's Digest UK 2008–09; Deputy Ed., London Evening Standard 2009–12, Ed. 2012–17; Ed. Today programme (BBC Radio 4) 2017–. *Publications include:* novels: Playing the Game 2003, Hothouse 2005, Chiswick Wives 2006. *Address:* Today Programme, W1 NBH 03C, BBC Broadcasting House, Portland Place, London, W1A 1AA, England (office). *E-mail:* today@bbc.co.uk (office). *Website:* www.bbc.co.uk/programmes/b006qj9z (office).

SANDSTRÖM, Sven, BA, MBA, PhD; Swedish banker and international finance official; ed Univ. of Stockholm, Stockholm School of Econs, Royal Inst. of Tech.; consultancy work 1966–68; Research Assoc., MIT and Harvard Business School, USA 1969–72; joined IBRD (World Bank) 1972, Project Analyst, Urban Projects Dept 1973, Deputy Div. Chief 1977, Div. Chief 1979, Div. Chief Urban Devt and Water Supply, S Asia Projects 1986, Dir Southern Africa Dept 1987–90, Dir Office of Pres. 1990–91, Man. Dir 1991–2001, Chair. Operation Cttee, Chair. Information and Knowledge Man. Council; Secr. Dir International Task Force on Global Public Goods, Stockholm 2003–06; Vice-Chair. Voluntary Replenishment Mechanism, Global Fund to Fight AIDS, Tuberculosis and Malaria; Treas., World Conservation Union 2004–08, also mem. Governing Council; Coordinator and Chair. for the replenishment of African Devt Fund, African Devt Bank; fmr Special Adviser to EU, also fmr Adviser to World Bank; mem. Bd of Dirs AES Corpn 2002–15, Hifabgruppen AB; Adviser to Hand in Hand, India, then CEO Hand in Hand International 2011–14.

SANDU, Maia; Moldovan economist and politician; *Leader, Partidul Acţiune şi Solidaritate;* b. 24 May 1972, Risipeni, Făleşti Dist, Moldovan SSR, USSR; ed Acad. of Econ. Studies of Moldova, Acad. of Public Admin, Chişinău, John F. Kennedy School of Govt at Harvard Univ., USA; worked as Adviser to Exec. Dir of World Bank, Washington, DC 2010–12; Minister of Educ. 2012–15; mem. Partidul Liberal Democrat din Moldova (PLDM—Liberal Democratic Party of Moldova) 2012–15; Leader Partidul Acţiune şi Solidaritate (Action and Solidarity Party) 2016–; second-placed cand. in presidential election 2016; Global Partnership for Social Accountability Award. *Address:* Partidul Acţiune şi Solidaritate (Action and Solidarity Party), Chişinău, str. A. Mateevici 31, Moldova (office). *Telephone:* 78-999800 (mobile) (office). *E-mail:* unpaspentrumoldova@gmail.com (office). *Website:* unpaspentru.md (office).

SANDY, Brig. (retd) John C. E., BSc, MSc; Trinidad and Tobago diplomatist and fmr army officer; m. Jacqueline Sandy 1971; one s. three d.; ed Univ. of the West Indies, Springfield Coll., USA; joined Trinidad and Tobago Defence Force 1966, served 36 years in various positions including Contingent Commdr, CARICOM peacekeeping forces in Haiti 1994–95, Defence and Mil. Attaché, Embassy in Washington, DC 1997–2000, Chief of Defence Staff 2000–02, Exec. Chair. Exercise Tradewinds 2002; fmr Security Consultant, CL Financial Group, Colonial Life Insurance Co. (Trinidad) Ltd; Man. Dir and CEO Premium Security Services Ltd; Chief Security Liaison Officer with Trinidad and Tobago Nat. Football Team at FIFA World Cup Finals 2006; Minister of Nat. Security 2010–12; apptd Perm. Rep. to UN Offices at Geneva and to WTO 2012; mem. People's Partnership coalition; US Meritorious Service Medal. *Leisure interests:* cricket, basketball.

SANÉ, Pierre Gabriel Michel, MSc, MBA; Senegalese administrator and UN official; *President, Imagine Africa Institute;* b. 7 May 1948, Dakar; s. of Nicolas Sané and Thérèse Carvalho; m. Ndeye Coumba Sow 1981; two s. one d.; ed Lycée Van Vollenhoven, Dakar, Ecole Supérieure de Commerce de Bordeaux, France, Ecole Nouvelle d'Organisation Economique et Sociale, Paris, London School of Econs, UK, Carleton Univ., Ottawa, Canada; Vice-Pres. Fédération des Etudiants d'Afrique Noire en France 1971–72; auditor with audit firms in France 1973–77; Deputy Gen. Man. Société Sénégalaise Pharmaceutique (Senepharma) 1977–78; joined Int. Devt Research Centre (IDRC) 1977, various positions Ottawa, Nairobi and Dakar, to Regional Dir W and Cen. Africa, Dakar 1988–92; mem. Amnesty International 1988–, Sec.-Gen. 1992–2001; Asst Dir-Gen. UNESCO, Paris 2001–10; Founder and Exec. Pres. Imagine Africa Inst., Paris 2010–; winner, Concours Nat. de Commercialisation, France 1972. *Publications:* books on poverty and regional integration; papers and reports on African devt, science and tech. and human rights research man. for IDRC. *Leisure interests:* reading, travelling, music, museums, arts. *Address:* Imagine Africa Institute, 1 de l'Indépendance, Dakar, Senegal (office). *Telephone:* 33-842-2681 (office). *E-mail:* contact@imagineafricainstitute.com (office). *Website:* www.imagineafricainstitute.com (office).

SANEJOUAND, Jean-Michel, DenL; French painter; b. 18 July 1934, Lyon; s. of Henri Felix Sanejouand and Angèle Fardel; m. Michelle Bourgeois 1957; two s.; ed Institut d'études politiques, Faculté de Droit, Lyon; self-taught in art; worked as artist, Lyon 1955–59, Paris 1959–93, Vaulandry 1993–; 'charges-objets' (assemblage works) 1963–67, 'organisations d'espaces' (environmental works) 1967–75, 'calligraphies d'humeurs' (calligraphic works on canvas) 1968–77, 'espaces-peintures' (painted and drawn works) 1978–86, black and white paintings 1987–93, sculptures 1988–, colour paintings 1993–96; 'sculptures-peintures' (paintings of sculptures) 1997–2002; retrospective exhbn Centre Georges Pompidou, Paris 1995; Espaces critiques (imaginary landscapes organised with earlier works) 2002–. *Address:* Belle-Ville, 49150 Vaulandry, France. *Telephone:* (2) 41-82-88-71. *E-mail:* web-site@sanejouand.com (office). *Website:* www.sanejouand.com (office).

SANFORD, Marshall Clement (Mark), Jr, BBA, MBA; American business executive and politician; b. 28 May 1960, Fort Lauderdale, Fla; s. of Marshall Clement Sanford, Sr and Peggy Sanford (née Pitts); m. Jennifer Sullivan 1989 (divorced 2010); four s.; ed Furman Univ., Greenville, SC, Univ. of Virginia Darden Grad. School of Business Admin; attained rank of Eagle Scout in Boy Scouts of America; assoc. for Coldwell Banker 1983; worked as project supervisor for

Beachside Real Estate, Isle of Palms 1984–86; training positions with Goldman Sachs 1987–88; Financial Analyst, Chemical Realty Corpn 1988–90; Prin. Southeastern Partners 1989–93; real estate broker Brumley Co., Charleston, SC 1990–91; Propr Norton & Sanford Real Estate Investment 1992, Prin. 1993–95, 2001–02; mem. from 1st S Carolina Dist, US House of Reps, Washington, DC 1995–2001, 2013–; Gov. of SC 2003–11; Chair. Republican Govs Asscn 2008–09 (resgnd); medical admin officer, USAF Reserve; mem. Preservation Soc., Charleston; Republican; Taxpayers' Best Friend Award, Nat. Taxpayers Union, Deficit Hawk Award, Concord Coalition Citizens Council, Taxpayer Hall of Fame, Taxpayers for Common Sense, Golden Bulldog Award, Watchdogs of the Treasury Inc., Spirit of Enterprise Award, US Chamber of Commerce, Congressional Youth Leadership Council Award. *Publication:* The Trust Committed to Me 2000. *Leisure interests:* windsurfing, running. *Address:* 2201 Rayburn House Office Building, Washington, DC 20515-4001, USA (office). *Telephone:* (202) 225-3176 (office). *Website:* sanford.house.gov (office).

SANGAJAVYN, Bayartsogt, MSc; Mongolian economist and politician; b. 28 March 1967, Selenge; m.; two c.; ed Lomonosov Moscow State Univ., Baden-Wuerttemberg Acad. for Foreign Trade, Nat. Univ. of Mongolia, Columbia Univ.; Sec. Youth Comm., Nat. Central Hospital 1980–82; Vice-Chair. Mongolian Youth Comm. Cttee 1990–91; mem. State Baga Hural (Parl.) 1990–92; Pres. Mongolian Youth Union 1991–97; mem. Great Hural (Parl.) 1996–2000, 2004–06, 2008–; Cabinet mem. and Minister of Nature and Environment 1998; adviser to Tovhon Khan Ltd 2002–04; Chief, Cabinet Secr. of Govt 2004–06; Minister of Finance 2008–12. *Address:* c/o Ministry of Finance, Government Building 2, United Nations Street - 5/1, Chingeltei District, Ulan Bator, Mongolia.

SANGAKKARA, Kumar Chokshanada; Sri Lankan professional cricketer; b. 27 Oct. 1977, Matale; s. of Kshema Sangakkara and Kumari Sangakkara; m. Yehali Sangakkara 2003; one s. one d. (twins); ed Trinity Coll., Kandy, law student at Sri Lanka Law Coll.; wicketkeeper; left-handed batsman; right-arm off-break bowler; ambidextrous; plays for Nondescripts Cricket Club 1997–, Sri Lanka 2000–15 (Vice-Capt. 2006, Capt. 2009–11), World XI One-Day Team 2005, Warwicks. 2007, Kings XI Punjab 2008–10, Deccan Chargers 2011–12, Sunrisers Hyderabad 2013, Durham 2014, Surrey 2015–, Hobart Hurricanes 2015–; First-class debut: 1997/98; Test debut: Sri Lanka v S Africa, Galle 20–23 July 2000; One-Day Int. (ODI) debut: Sri Lanka v Pakistan, Galle 5 July 2000; T20I debut: England v Sri Lanka, Southampton 15 June 2006; has played in 134 Tests and scored 12,400 runs (38 centuries, 52 half-centuries), highest score 319, average 57.40; ODIs: 404 matches, scored 14,234 runs, highest score 169, average 41.98; T20Is: 56 matches, scored 1,382 runs, highest score 78, average 31.40; captained Sri Lanka to reach final of ICC Cricket World Cup, losing to India, Mumbai 2 April 2011, stepped down as Capt. of Sri Lanka in one-day formats 5 April 2011; completed 12,000 runs in ODIs while playing Asia Cup match against Pakistan Feb. 2014; retd from T20 ints after playing ICC World T20 2014; retd from ODIs during ICC Cricket World Cup 18 March 2015; retd from int. cricket 23 Aug. 2015; Trinity Lion Award, Trinity Coll., Kandy 1996, Ryde Medallist, Trinity Coll. 1996, Test Batsman of the Year, Sri Lanka Cricket Awards 2006, ICC Test World XI 2006, 2007, 2008, 2010, 2011, 2012, Test Batting Prize, Cricinfo Awards 2007, Outstanding Young Persons of Sri Lanka Award (Personal Improvement and Accomplishment category) 2008, ICC ODI Player of the Year 2011, LG People's Choice Award, ICC Awards 2011, Wisden Leading Cricketer in the World 2011, 2014, ICC ODI World XI 2011, 2012, 2013, 2014, 2015, honoured as one of the top-five Wisden Cricketers of the Year 2012, ICC Outstanding One-Day Player in the World 2013, Outstanding Achievement in Sport, The Asian Awards 2015, CEAT Int. Cricketer of the Year 2015. *Achievements include:* shared record-breaking partnership of 624 with Mahela Jayawardene (world record in both Test and First-class cricket, first case of partnership of 600 or more in First-class or Test match innings) July 2006; became sixth man in history to score back-to-back double centuries with consecutive unbeaten innings of 200 and 222 in second and third Tests against Bangladesh; named as new No. 1 batsman in LG ICC Test player rankings with a rating of 938 Dec. 2007; first batsman ever to score in excess of 150 in four consecutive tests Dec. 2007; ranked first on Test batting rankings Sept. 2009; only fourth batsman in history to score seven consecutive 50s in Tests June 2014. *Address:* c/o Sri Lanka Cricket, Sinhalese Sports Club, Colombo, Sri Lanka. *E-mail:* info@srilankacricket.lk. *Website:* www.srilankacricket.lk; www.kumarsangakkara.lk.

SANGALA, Aaron; Malawi politician; b. 1958; worked for Lever Brothers 1974–81; mem. Parl. for Blantyre Ndirande Malabada 2004–; Deputy Minister of Health 2006–07; Deputy Minister of Women and Child Devt 2007–08; Minister of Nat. Defence 2008–09 (reappointed 2011); of Home Affairs and Internal Security 2009–11; mem. Democratic Progressive Party, currently Director of Foreign Affairs; Trustee Jacaranda Foundation. *Address:* Democratic Progressive Party, Lilongwe 3, Malawi. *Website:* dppmw.org.

SANGARE, Oumou; Malian singer and songwriter; b. 25 Feb. 1968, Bamako; m. Ousmane Haidara; one c.; began singing aged five; first performance at Stade des Omnisports aged six; mem. Nat. Ensemble of Mali; mem. Djioliba percussion 1986–89; solo artiste with own backing group 1989–; regular concert tours in W Africa and Europe; first US concert 1994; campaigner for women's rights; apptd Amb. to FAO 2003; Performance of the Year 1993, IMO-UNESCO Int. Music Prize 2001, Grammy Award for Best Pop Collaboration with Vocals (with Herbie Hancock) 2011; Songlines Awards for Africa and Middle East 2018, for Best Artist 2018; numerous African Music Awards. *Recordings include:* Moussolou (Women) (Best Selling Album of the Year 1990) 1990, Ko Sira (Marriage Today) (European World Music Album of the Year 1993) 1993, Worotan 1996, Moussolou 1999, Ko Sira 2000, Oumou (compilation) 2003, Seya 2009, Kounadia 2012, Mogoya 2017; appears on African Blues 1998, Beloved 1998; also recordings with Ali Farka Touré, Trilok Gurtu, Herbie Hancock.

SANGARE, Tiémoko, PhD; Malian politician; b. 1957, Sanankourouni; m.; three c.; ed Moscow Inst. of Geodesy Eng, Aerial Photography and Cartography; began career as Lecturer, École nat. d'ingénieurs de Bamako (ENI), becoming Deputy Dir-Gen., ENI 1991–92; mem. Nat. Ass. (parl.) 1992–97; Technical Adviser, Ministry of State Property and Land Affairs 2003; Minister of Agric. 2007–09, of the Environment and Sanitation 2009–12, of Mines and Petroleum 2016–18, Minister of Defence and War Veterans 2018–19; fmr mem. Mouvement pour l'Indépendance, la Renaissance et l'Intégration Africaine (MIRIA) 1994, First

Admin. Sec. 1994–2001; mem. Alliance pour la Démocratie au Mali—Parti Pan-Africain pour la Liberté, la Solidarité et la Justice (ADEMA-PASJ), Deputy Sec.-Gen. 2004. *Address:* c/o Ministry of Defence and War Veterans, route de Koulouba, BP 2083, Bamako, Mali (office).

SANGAY, Lobsang, LLB, BA (Hons), LLM, SJD; Tibetan legal scholar and politician; *Prime Minister, Central Tibetan Administration (Tibetan Government-in-Exile);* b. 1968, village in Darjeeling, India; s. of Kelsang Choden; m. Kesang Yangdon Shakchang 1998; one d.; ed Tibetan Refugee High School, Darjeeling, Univ. of Delhi, India, Harvard Univ., USA; expert on Tibet and int. human rights law; fmr mem. of radical Tibetan Youth Congress, took part in protests against Chinese rule in Tibet; organized five confs between Chinese and Tibetan scholars, including a meeting between the Dalai Lama and 35 Chinese scholars at Harvard Univ. 2003; became the first Tibetan (among six million) to earn a doctorate degree from Harvard Law School; Visiting Research Fellow, East Asian Legal Studies Program, Harvard Law School; elected as the next Kalon Tripa, or Prime Minister, of the Cen. Tibetan Admin (Tibetan Govt-in-Exile) 26 April 2011, succeeding the 5th Samdhong Rinpoche, took oath of office 8 Aug. 2011–; Tibetan Fulbright Fellowship for study at Harvard Law School 2004; Yong K. Kim' 95 Prize of Excellence for his dissertation, Democracy in Distress: Is Exile Polity a Remedy? A Case Study of Tibet's Government-in-Exile 2004, selected as one of the 24 Young Leaders of Asia by the Asia Soc. 2006. *Publications:* We Sing a Song of Sadness – Tibetan Political Prisoners Speak Out (co-ed.) 2006; several articles in scholarly journals. *Address:* Office of the Kalon Tripa, Kashag Secretariat, Central Tibetan Administration, Dharamshala 176215, Himachal Pradesh, India (office). *Telephone:* (1892) 222218 (office); (1892) 222713 (office); (1892) 223546 (office). *Fax:* (1892) 224914 (office). *E-mail:* katri-pa@gov.tibet.net (office); katri-pa@tibet.net (office); kadrung@gov.tibet.net (office). *Website:* www.tibet.net (office).

SANGHELI, Andrei; Moldovan business executive and fmr politician; *Director-General, Limagrain Moldova SRL;* b. 20 July 1944, Grinautsy; m.; one s.; ed Kishinev Agric. Inst., Kishinev Higher CP School; mem. CPSU 1967–91; agronomist, Deputy Dir, then Dir of collective farms, Moldova 1971–75, Sec., Kamenka Regional CP Cttee 1975–79, Vice-Chair. Council of Collective Farms of Moldova 1979–80; Chair. Dondushansk Regional Exec. Cttee; First Sec., Regional CP Cttee 1980–86; First Deputy-Chair. Council of Ministers, Chair. State Agric.-Industrial Cttee 1986–89, First Deputy Prime Minister of Moldova; Minister of Agric. and Food 1990–92; Prime Minister of Moldova 1992–96; currently Dir-Gen. Limagrain Moldova SRL (agricultural co.); Chair. Union of Agrarians 1997–. *Address:* Limagrain Moldova SRL, 2004 Chisinau, blvd Stefan cel Mare, 162, Moldova (office). *Telephone:* (22) 21-00-49 (office). *Fax:* (22) 21-00-67 (office). *E-mail:* limagrain@moldovacc.md (office).

SANGMA, Conrad Kongkal, MBA; Indian politician and businessman; *Chief Minister of Meghalaya;* b. 28 Jan. 1978, Tura, West Garo Hills, Meghalaya; s. of Purno Agitok Sangma and Soradini Kongkal Sangma; m. Mehtab Agitok Sangma 2009; two c.; ed Univ. of Pennsylvania, Imperial Coll., Univ. of London; mem. Legislative Ass., Meghalaya 2008–13, Leader of Opposition 2009–13; Cabinet Minister of Finance, Power and Tourism, Govt of Meghalaya 2008–09; mem. Lok Sabha (Parl.) (Tura Constituency) 2016–18, mem. Standing Cttee on Energy 2016–; Chief Minister of Meghalaya 2018–; Pres. Nat. People's Party 2016–; Pres., Meghalaya Cricket Asscn and Sports Acad., P.A. Sangma Foundation. *Leisure interest:* reading, music, travelling. *Address:* Office of Chief Minister of Meghalaya, Main Secretariat Building, Shillong 793001 Meghalaya (office); Walbakgre, PO Tura, West Garo Hills, 794001 Meghalaya, India (home). *Telephone:* (364) 2222454 (office); (91) 9856001009. *E-mail:* conradsangma@gmail.com. *Website:* www .meghalaya.gov.in (office).

SANGMA, Mukul M., MB BS; Indian physician and politician; b. 20 April 1965, Chengkompara, Ampati, West Garo Hills Dist; s. of Binoy Bhushan M. Marak and Roshanara M. Sangma; ed Govt High School, Ampati, West Garo Hills, St Anthony's Coll., Shillong, Regional Inst. of Medical Sciences (RIMS), Imphal, North Eastern Regional Medical Coll., Imphal; mem. Youth Congress as a student; held different positions in Governing Body of Students Council of RIMS; practised as pvt. medical practitioner at pvt. clinic at Tura 1990–91; joined and served as Medical and Health Officer, Zikzak PHC, West Garo Hills under Govt of Meghalaya 1991; left Govt Service to enter into politics 1993, elected as Ind. MLA from 58-Ampatigre L.A. Constituency 1993, re-elected as a Rep. of Indian Nat. Congress 1998, 2008, 2010, 2013, currently Leader of Opposition; Chair. Meghalaya Transport Corpn Feb.–Sept. 1993; posts held have included Parl. Sec., Govt of Meghalaya 1996–98, Cabinet Minister in charge of depts including Co-operation, Fisheries, Taxation and others, Govt of Meghalaya 1998–99, Cabinet Minister in charge of portfolios including Taxation, IPR and others, Govt of Meghalaya 2001–03, Cabinet Minister, Govt of Meghalaya and looked after Taxation, PWD, Home (P), Educ. (both Higher and Tech. Educ. and Elementary and Mass Educ.), Forest and Environment, Information Tech., Election, IPR and other Depts 2003–05; Deputy Chief Minister, Govt of Meghalaya April–Oct. 2005; Deputy Chief Minister in charge of Planning, IPR, Election, PID, Power, including Non-Conventional Energy, Reorganization Depts 2007–08; Deputy Chief Minister in charge of Finance, Power and Non-Conventional Energy, Health and & Family Welfare, IPR, Labour, Horticulture, Home (Passport) Admin. Reforms 2009–10; Chief Minister of Meghalaya 2010–18; held various posts as Party functionary of Indian Nat. Congress in State of Meghalaya; Sec., Dist Congress Cttee, West Garo Hills 1998–99; apptd Chair. North Eastern Regional Power Committee Cttee 2010; Pres. Dist Congress Cttee, West Garo Hills 1998–2000; Gen. Sec. Meghalaya Pradesh Congress Cttee, in charge of Frontal Wings 2000–, involved in mobilization of Frontal Wings of Indian Nat. Congress in State of Meghalaya; Chief Patron Ampati Youth Welfare Club; Founder-mem. Mirachel Foundation; contested parl. elections 2004, Gen. Election, by-election for Tura Lok Sabha seat 2006. *Telephone:* (0364) 2500634 (office); 98-6080845 (mobile). *Website:* megassembly.gov.in.

SANGUINETTI CAIROLO, Julio María; Uruguayan lawyer, politician, international organization official and fmr head of state; *President, Circulo de Montevideo;* b. 1936; m. Marta Canessa; one s. one d.; began career in journalism 1953, worked as ed., reporter and columnist for various newspapers including El día, Acción, Semanarios Canelones, Correo de los Viernes, El País; mem. Gen. Ass. 1962–73; Minister of Industry and Labour 1969–72, of Educ. and Culture 1972–73;

Pres. Comisión Nacional de Artes Plásticas 1967–73; Pres. UNESCO Comm. for promotion of books in Latin America 1975–84; Pres. of Uruguay 1985–89, 1995–2000; Senator 2005–10; Leader (Foro Batllista) Colorado Party 1989–94; apptd Pres. of the Council, Universidad para la Paz de Naciones Unidas 2007; Founding mem. and Pres. Circulo de Montevideo; Founding mem. Club de Madrid; mem. InterAcción Council; Hon. Pres. Centro Latinoamericano de journalism (CELAP) 1997, Club Atlético Peñarol; numerous hon. degrees; Lifetime Achievement Award, Cristóbal Gabarrón Foundation 2007, Pluma de Honor, Academia Argentina de Periodismo 2008, Premio Security 2011, Premio Giovanni Battista Cuneo de la Región Liguore (Italy) 2012. *Publications include:* La Agonía de una Democracia (Premio Bartolomé Hidalgo de la Cámara del Libro de Uruguay) 2009. *Address:* Circulo de Montevideo, José Luis Zorrilla de San Martín 248, Montevideo, Uruguay. *E-mail:* secretaria@circulodemontevideo.com. *Website:* www.circulodemontevideo.com.

SANKARANARAYANAN, Kateekal; Indian politician; b. 15 Oct. 1932, Kerala; s. of A. Sankaran Nair and K. Lekshmi Amma; m. Radha Sankaranarayanan; one d.; active mem. students' org. from 1946; elected to 5th Kerala Legis. Ass. (KLA) from Thrithala, 6th KLA from Sreekrishnapuram, 8th KLA from Ottappalam, 11th KLA from Palghat Constituency, as Indian Nat. Congress mem.; Convenor United Democratic Front 1985–2001; Minister for Agric., Animal Husbandry and Dairy Devt and Community Devt 11–25 April 1977, 27 April–Oct. 1978; Chair. Cttee on Govt Assurances 1980–82, Cttee on Public Accounts 1989–91; Minister for Finance and Excise 2001–04, continued as MLA –2006; served as minister in state govt of Kerala; Gov. of Nagaland 2007–09, of Arunachal Pradesh (Additional Charge) during absence on leave of S. K. Singh 2007–08, of Assam June–July 2009, Gov. of Jharkand 2009–10, of Maharashtra 2010–14, of Goa 2011–14.

SANKEY, John Anthony, CMG, PhD; British fmr diplomatist; b. 8 June 1930, London, England; m. Gwendoline Putman 1958; two s. two d.; ed Cardinal Vaughan School, Kensington, Peterhouse, Cambridge, NATO Defence Coll., Rome, Univ. of Leeds; served in Colonial Office 1953, UK Mission to UN, New York, USA 1961, FCO 1964, Guyana 1968, Singapore 1971, Malta 1973, The Hague 1975, Special Counsellor for African Affairs, FCO 1980–82; High Commr in Tanzania 1982–85; Perm. Rep. to the UN in Geneva 1985–90; Sec.-Gen. Soc. of London Art Dealers 1991–96; Dir Int. Art and Antiques Loss Register 1993–96; Chair. Tanzania Devt Trust 1999–2004; mem. Exec. Cttee, St Francis Leprosy Guild –2014. *Publication:* Thomas Brock, Forgotten Sculptor of the Victoria Memorial (ed.). *Leisure interest:* Victorian sculpture. *Address:* 108 Lancaster Gate, London, W2 3NW, England (home). *Telephone:* (20) 7723-2256 (home).

SANNEH, Amadou; Gambian accountant and politician; m. Haddijatou Sanneh; f. A. A. Co. (private auditing business); Auditor-Gen., Nat. Agricultural Research Inst. 2010; fmr Accountant-Gen. of The Gambia; sentenced to five years' imprisonment on two counts relating to sedition for his role in supporting an asylum application Dec. 2013, released by presidential pardon Jan. 2017; Minister of Finance and Econ. Affairs 2017–18; mem. United Democratic Party 1995–, fmr party Treas. *Address:* c/o Ministry of Finance and Economic Affairs, The Quadrangle, POB 9686, Banjul, Gambia (office).

SANNIKAU, Andrey Alegavich; Belarusian politician; b. 8 March 1954, Minsk, Belarusian SSR, USSR; m. Iryna Khalip; two s.; ed Minsk State Linguistic Univ., Diplomatic Acad. of Ministry of Foreign Affairs of Russian Fed., Moscow; worked for a Soviet oil co. in Pakistan and worked on construction of an aluminium plant in Egypt; worked at Union of Soviet Socs for Friendship and Cultural Relations with Foreign Countries; served at UN Secr., New York, USA 1982–87; worked in Ministry of Foreign Affairs of Belorussian SSR; headed del. on Nuclear and Conventional Weapons Armament Negotiations 1992, retained authority of signature on behalf of Belarus until 1995; also served as adviser to Belarusian diplomatic mission in Switzerland; Deputy Minister of Foreign Affairs with rank of Amb. 1995–96 (resgnd); Co-founder of civil initiative Khartiya-97 (Charter '97), becoming its int. co-ordinator, opposition group to Lukashenko party in Belarus; cr., with Hienadz Karpienka, The Coordinating Council (Rada) of the Congress of Democratic Forces of Belarus 1999; initiated, with other politicians, civil campaign European Belarus advocating joining country with EU 2008; unsuccessful presidential cand. 2010; imprisoned in a Minsk KGB facility for protesting at a demonstration after the elections, named a prisoner of conscience by Amnesty International, sentenced to five years' imprisonment on charges of organizing mass disturbances May 2011, pardoned and released by Pres. Lukashenka 14 April 2012; Bruno Kreisky Prize 2005. *E-mail:* charter97@gmail.com. *Website:* www.charter97.org.

SANO, Seiichiro; Japanese business executive; b. 20 Nov. 1952, Osaka; ed Kwansei Gakuin Univ.; joined SANYO Electric Co. Ltd 1977, Human Resources Div., Audio Business 1977–89, Labour Admin Div., Human Resources HQ 1989–92, Man. Labour Admin Div. 1992–97, Man. Human Resouces Dept 1997–2000, Gen. Man., Gen. Affairs/Human Resources 2000–07, Gen. Man. Human Resources Group 2001–03, Gen. Man. Corp. Admin Dept 2003–05, Vice-Pres. 2005–07, Exec. Dir and Pres. 2007–12 (Sanyo acquired by Panasonic Corpn 2009), Sr Corp. Auditor, Panasonic Corpn 2012–. *Address:* Panasonic Corporation, 1006, Oaza Kadoma, Kadoma-shi, Osaka 571-8501, Japan (office). *Website:* www.panasonic.com (office).

SANOGO, Capt. Amadou Haya; Malian army officer; b. 1972, Ségou; ed mil. training in USA including Lackland Air Force Base, Tex., Fort Huachuca, Ariz., Fort Benning, Ga, Quantico Marine Corps Base, Va; fmr English teacher; instructor, Koulikoro Mil. Coll. –2012; led coup d'état which displaced Pres. Amadou Toumani Touré 22 March 2012; Chair. Nat. Cttee for the Restoration of Democracy and State (head of state) March–April 2012 (stood down 6 April under agreement brokered by ECOWAS); imprisoned on charge of complicity in murder (during uprising of Sept. 2013) Feb. 2014.

SANON, Jean Gustave; Burkinabè economist and politician; several years with Ministry of the Economy and Finance, including as Dir of Studies and of Financial Legislation, also Dir of Monetary and Financial Affairs, Minister of the Economy and Finance 2014–16; Dir of Public Finance, Comm. of W African Econ. and Monetary Union (UEMOA) 2001, Tech. Adviser to Auditor of Political Economy and Tax Authorities for UEMOA region 2013–14; worked for IMF including as Resident Consultant for Man. of Public Finance, IMF Regional Centre for Tech. Assistance, first for Central Africa based in Libreville, Gabon, subsequently for W Africa based in Abidjan, Côte d'Ivoire. *Address:* c/o Ministry of the Economy and Finance, 395 avenue Ho Chi Minh, 01 BP 7008, Ouagadougou 01, Burkina Faso (office).

SANT, Alfred, MSc, MBA, DBA; Maltese politician, consultant and author; b. 28 Feb. 1948; one d.; ed Univ. of Malta, Inst. Int. d'Admin Publique, France, Boston Univ. and Harvard Business School, USA; Founding mem. experimental drama group Xsenuru 1967–68; Second Sec., First Sec., Malta Mission to European Communities, Brussels 1970–75; Adviser on gen. and financial man., Ministry of Parastatal and People's Industries, Valletta 1977–78; Man. Dir Medina Consulting Group 1978–80; Exec. Deputy Chair. Malta Devt Corpn 1980–82; consultant to pvt. and public sectors 1982–; Chair. Metal Fond Ltd, Bottex Clothing 1982–84, First Clothing Cooperative 1983–87; Lecturer, Man. Faculty, Univ. of Malta 1984–87; Adviser to Prime Minister on econ. and diplomatic affairs 1985–87; Chair. Dept of Information, Malta Labour Party 1982–92; Pres. Malta Labour Party 1984–88, Leader 1992–2008; MP 1987–2013; Prime Minister of Malta 1996–98, Leader of the Opposition 1998–2008; mem. European Parl. 2014–. *Plays:* Fid-Dell Tal-Katidral 1994, Qabel Tiftah L-Inkjesta 1999. *Publications include:* Min Hu Evelyn Costa? (plays) 1979, L-Ewwel Weraq tal-Bajtar (novel), Silg fuq Kemmuna (novel) 1985, Malta's European Challenge (essay) 1995, Bejgh u Xiri (novel) 1999, La Bidu, La Tmiem (novel) 2001, Confessions of a Maltese European 2003, L-Ghalqa tal-Iskarjota (novel) 2009 (English trans., The Iscariot Field 2011), Pupu bil-Bahar (short stories) 2009, Bhal f'Dizzjunarju 2011, Malta and the Euro 2012, George Bush f'Malta 2013, Cpar 2013; contrib. articles in the press and professional publs. *Leisure interests:* travel, reading, writing, listening to music. *Address:* European Parliament, 60, rue Wiertz, Altiero Spinelli 14G146, 1047 Brussels, Belgium (office); 18A, Victory Street, B'Kara, Malta (home). *Telephone:* (2149) 5742 (office). *E-mail:* info@alfredsant.eu (office). *Website:* www.alfredsant.eu.

SANTANA, Carlos; Mexican musician; b. 20 July 1947, Autlán de Navarro; s. of José Santana; m. Cindy Blackman 2010; played Tijuana night clubs; debut with the Santana Blues Band 1966, played at Woodstock Festival Aug. 1969; guitarist, Santana Man. 1987–; Prin. Guts and Grace Records 1993; performed with Mike Bloomfield, Al Kooper, Buddy Miles, McCoy Turner, Jose Feliciano, Herbie Hancock, Wayne Shorter, Alice Coltrane, Aretha Franklin, Mahavishnu, John McLaughlin; Co-founder Milagro Foundation supporting young people in the arts, health and education 1998; Santana Band first to earn CBS Records' Crystal Globe Award, multiple Best Pop-Rock Guitarist in Playboy Magazine's Readers' Poll, Grammy for Best Rock Instrumental Performance 1988, Nosotros Golden Eagle Legend Award 1992, Recording Acad. (NARAS) tribute concert and induction into Hollywood Rock Walk, Billboard Magazine Century Award 1996, ten Bay Area Music Awards, BAMMY Hall of Fame, Chicano Music Awards Latino Music Legend of the Year 1997, inducted into Rock 'n' Roll Hall of Fame 1998, also won nine Grammys Feb. 2000, Latin Recording Acad. Person of the Year 2004; numerous civic and humanitarian commendations. *Films:* Viva Santana 1988, Sacred Fire 1993, A History of Santana: The River Of Color And Sound 1997, A Supernatural Evening With Santana 2000. *Recordings include:* albums: Santana 1969, Abraxas 1970, Santana III 1971, Greatest Hits 1974, Moonflower 1977, Inner Secrets 1978, Zebop! 1981, Shango 1982, Freedom 1987, Freedom 1987, Viva Santana 1988, Milagro 1992, Sacred Fire 1993, Dance Of The Rainbow Serpent 1995, Live At The Fillmore 1997, Best of Santana 1998, Supernatural 1999, All That I Am 2005, Guitar Heaven: The Greatest Guitar Classics of All Time 2010, Shape Shifter 2012, Corazón 2014. *Publication:* The Universal Tone: Bringing My Story to Light 2014, Santana IV 2016. *Address:* Creative Artists Agency, 2000 Avenue of the Stars, Los Angeles, CA 90067, USA (office); Santana Management, PO Box 10348, San Rafael, CA 94912, USA (office). *E-mail:* info@jensencom.com. *Website:* www.santana.com (office); www.milagrofoundation.org.

SANTANA LOPES, Pedro; Portuguese lawyer and politician; b. 29 June 1956, Lisbon; five c.; ed Univ. of Lisbon; joined Social Democratic Party 1976; elected mem. Parl. 1976, Deputy Prime Minister, IV Constitutional Govt 1978, 1979; Legal Adviser to the Prime Minister 1980–81; Chair. Inst. of Political Studies 1983–87; mem. European Parl. 1987–89; Sec. of State for Culture 1990–94; Mayor of Figueira da Foz 1998–2002; Chair. Congress, General Council of the Nat. Asscn of Portuguese Municipalities, Central Region 1998–2001; Mayor of Lisbon 2002–July 2004, Feb.–Oct. 2005; Vice-Chair. Cttee of the Regions 2002–04; Prime Minister of Portugal July 2004–Feb. 2005 (resgnd); Pres. Sporting Club de Portugal 1995–96; elected Vice-Pres., Social Democratic Party 1996, then Pres. 2004–05; Alderman, City of Lisbon 2009–13; Attorney, Global Lawyers 2010–; Provedor, Santa Casa da Misericórdia de Lisboa 2011–17.

SANTER, Jacques, DenD; Luxembourg politician and banker; b. 18 May 1937, Wasserbillig; s. of Josef Santer and Marguerite Santer; m. Danièle Binot; two s.; ed Athénée de Luxembourg, Univs of Paris and Strasbourg and Inst. d'Etudes Politiques, Paris; advocate, Luxembourg Court of Appeal 1961–65; attaché, Office of Minister of Labour and Social Security 1963–65; Govt attaché 1965–66; Parl. Sec. Parti Chrétien-Social 1966–72, Sec.-Gen. 1972–74, Pres. 1974–82; Sec. of State for Cultural and Social Affairs 1972–74; mem. Chamber of Deputies 1974–79; Municipal Magistrate, City of Luxembourg 1976–79; Minister of Finance, of Labour and of Social Security 1979–84; Prime Minister, Minister of State and Minister of Finance 1984–89, Prime Minister, Minister of State, of Cultural Affairs and of the Treasury and Financial Affairs 1989–94, now Hon. Minister of State; MEP 1975–79, 1999–2004, Vice-Pres. 1975–77; Pres. European Comm. 1994–99; Pres. Robert Schuman Foundation 1998–; currently Pres. Fondation Mérite Européen; Chair. Bd CLT-UFA 2004–; apptd Chair. Bd Unicredit International Bank 2005, mem. Bd RTL Group 2005–, mem. Bd Unicredit Luxembourg 2009–15, mem. Bd European Sovereign Bond Protection Facility; Hon. LLD (Wales) 1998, (Miami Univ.), (Sacred Heart Univ., Ohio), (Univ. of Urbino, Italy), (Kyoto Univ., Japan) and others; Prince of Asturias Prize (Spain) 1998, Robert Schumann Prize, Jean Monnet Medal (Lausanne, Switzerland) and others. *Leisure interests:* walking, swimming. *Address:* 33 blvd F.D. Roosevelt, 2450 Luxembourg (office); 69 rue J.-P. Huberty, 1742 Luxembourg (home). *Telephone:* 24-78-81-55 (office); 42-00-40 (home). *Fax:* 26-27-08-37 (office); 26-43-09-99 (home). *E-mail:* jacques.santer@me.etat.lu (office).

SANTER, Rt Rev. Mark, MA, DD; British ecclesiastic (retd); b. 29 Dec. 1936, Bristol; s. of Rev. Canon E. A. R. Santer and Phyllis C. Barlow; m. 1st Henriette Cornelia Weststrate 1964 (died 1994); m. 2nd Sabine Böhmig Bird 1997; one s. two d.; ed Marlborough Coll., Queens' Coll. and Westcott House, Cambridge; curate, All Saints Cuddesdon 1963–67; tutor, Cuddesdon Coll. Oxford 1963–67; Dean and Fellow, Clare Coll. Cambridge 1967–72; Asst Lecturer in Divinity, Univ. of Cambridge 1968–72; Prin. Westcott House 1973–81; Area Bishop of Kensington, London 1981–87; Bishop of Birmingham 1987–2002; Hon. Asst Bishop Diocese of Worcester 2002–; Co-Chair. Anglican/RC Int. Comm. 1983–99; Hon. Fellow, Clare Coll. Cambridge 1987, Queens' Coll. Cambridge 1991; Hon. DD (Birmingham) 1998, (Lambeth) 1999, Hon. DUniv (Univ. of Cen. England) 2003. *Publications include:* Documents in Early Christian Thought (with M. F. Wiles) 1975, Their Lord and Ours (ed.) 1982. *Address:* 81 Clarence Road, Birmingham, B13 9UH, England (home). *Telephone:* (121) 441-2194 (home). *E-mail:* msanter@btinternet.com (home).

SANTO DE CARVALHO, Evaristo do Espírito (see Carvalho, Evaristo do Espírito Santo de).

SANTORUM, Richard (Rick) John, BA, MBA, JD; American lawyer and politician; b. 10 May 1958, Winchester, Va; s. of Aldo Santorum and Catherine Santorum (née Dughi); m. Karen Garver 1990; seven c. and one s. (deceased); ed Carmel High School, Mundelein, Ill., Pennsylvania State Univ., Univ. of Pittsburgh and Dickinson Law School; called to the Bar of Pa 1986; Admin. Asst to Pa State Senator Doyle Corman, Harrisburg, Pa 1981–86, Exec. Dir Local Govt Cttee, Pa State Senate 1981–84, Transport Cttee 1984–86; Assoc. Attorney, Kirkpatrick and Lockhart, Pittsburgh 1986–90; mem. US House of Reps from 18th Pa Dist, Washington, DC 1991–95; Senator from Pennsylvania 1995–2007, Chair. Senate Republican Conf. 2001–07; joined Eckert Seamans Cherin & Mellott, LLC law firm 2007; Sr Fellow, Ethics and Public Policy Center, Washington, DC 2007–11, est. and directed America's Enemies programme; unsuccessful cand. for Republican US presidential nomination 2012, 2016; contrib. to Fox News 2007–11; Co-f. Patriot Voices (nonprofit org.); columnist, Word Net Daily website 2012–13; CEO EchoLight Studios (film production co.) 2013–; Republican. *Publications include:* It Takes a Family: Conservatism and the Common Good 2005, Rick Santorum 2005, Darwin's Nemesis: Phillip Johnson and the Intelligent Design Movement (foreword) 2006, American Patriots 2012, Blue Collar Conservatives: Recommitting to an America That Works 2014, Bella's Gift: How One Little Girl Transformed Our Family and Inspired a Nation 2015. *Leisure interests:* golf, cross-country skiing, racquet sports. *Address:* Patriot Voices, PO Box 247, Verona, PA 15147, USA (office). *E-mail:* info@patriotvoices.com (office). *Website:* www.patriotvoices.com (office); www.ricksantorum.com (office); www.echolight.com (office).

SANTOS CALDERÓN, Francisco; Colombian journalist, politician and diplomatist; *Ambassador to USA;* b. 14 Oct. 1961, Bogotá; m. María Victoria García; four c.; ed Univ. of Kansas, Univ. of Texas, USA; reporter, El Tiempo (daily newspaper) 1984–86, Int. Ed. 1986–87, Night Ed. 1987–88, Asst Ed. 1988–91, Man. Ed. 1991–2000; taught journalism and US–Latin American relations at several Colombian univs including Universidad Central, Universidad Javeriana, Universidad Jorge Tadeo Lozano 1987–89; kidnapped with other journalists by Pablo Escobar, leader of Medellín drug cartel 1990, held for eight months; Nieman Fellow, Harvard Univ. 1992; co-f. Fundación Pais Libre (Free Country Foundation) to assist victims of kidnapping and their families; moved to Madrid, Spain and worked as journalist for daily newspaper El País and BBC 2000–02; Vice-Pres. of Colombia 2002–10; Dir RCN RADIO Morning News on RCN Radio 2010–12; unsuccessful cand. in election for Pres. of Colombia 2014; Amb. to USA 2018–; Paul Harris Medal, Rotary Int. *Address:* Embassy of Colombia, 1724 Massachusetts Ave, NW, Washington, DC 20036, USA (office). *Telephone:* (202) 387-8338 (ext. 300) (office). *Fax:* (202) 232-8643 (office). *E-mail:* emwas@colombiaemb.org (office). *Website:* www.colombiaemb.org (office).

SANTOS CALDERÓN, Juan Manuel; Colombian politician and fmr head of state; b. 10 Aug. 1951, Bogotá; m. María Clemencia Rodríguez; two s. one d.; ed Cartagena Naval Acad. of Colombia, Univ. of Kansas, USA, London School of Econs, UK, Harvard Univ., USA; fmr leader Colombian Del. to Int. Coffee Org. negotiations, London; fmr journalist, Deputy Dir and Pres. Editorial Bd El Tiempo (daily); apptd Minister of Foreign Trade 1991; Vice-Pres. 1993; apptd Minister of Finance and Public Credit 2000; managed Pres. Alvaro Uribe's re-election campaign 2006; Minister of Nat. Defence 2006–09 (resgnd); Pres. of Colombia 2010–18; Pres. UNCTAD 1992–96, UN ECLA 1997–99; fmr Vice-Pres. Press Freedom Comm. of Inter-American Press Soc.; Founder and Chair. Fundación Buengobierno; Bernardo O'Higgins en el Grado de Comendador 1996, Gran Oficial de la Orden Nacional Francesca del Mérito 2001; Fulbright and Neiman Fellowships, King of Spain Prize for journalism, Nobel Peace Prize for negotiating a peace treaty with FARC guerillas despite losing a popular referendum on the deal 2016. *Publications include:* several books including The Third Way, An Alternative for Colombia. *Address:* c/o Office of the President, Palacio de Nariño, Carrera 8, No 7-26, Bogotá, DC, Colombia (office).

SANTOS LÓPEZ, Samuel; Nicaraguan politician; b. 13 Dec. 1938, Managua; s. of Samuel Santos Fernández and Lucila López Bermúdez; m. Annelly Molina de Santos; early business career with several managerial roles including roles at Publicidad Noble y Asociados, Honduras, Hotel Best Western Las Mercedes, Inversiones Inmobiliarias Acuario S.A., Inmobiliarios Penta S.A., Inmobiliarios Alpha S.A., Inmobiliarios Beta S.A; Founder and fmr Dir Stock Market of Nicaragua; mem. Nat. Govt for Reconstruction 1979–85; Vice-Pres. Nat. Devt Bank 1979–80; Minister in charge of Reconstruction of Managua 1980–85; Mayor of Managua 1984–85; Chair. ADYSA and Editorial El Amanecer 1986–92; Finance Sec. Frente Sandinista de Liberación Nacional 1992, Exec. Sec. –2001, Int. Relations Spokesperson 2001–06; Minister of Foreign Affairs 2007–17; Founding mem. Nicaragua Wall Street; mem. Chamber of Commerce, Chamber of Tourism, Union of Latin American Capital Cities, Exec. Cttee of the Bolivian Congress for Town Devt, Works Comm. for the Inter-Oceanic Canal of Nicaragua; Order of Friendship (South Ossetia) 2010.

SANTOS ORDÓÑEZ, Elvin Ernesto, BSc; Honduran engineer, business executive and politician; b. 18 Jan. 1963, Tegucigalpa; s. of Elvin Santos Lozano and Sonia Ordóñez de Santos; m. Becky Manzanares de Santos; four c.; ed Lamar Univ., USA; CEO Santos y Compañia Construction Co.; fmr Consul in Austin, Tex.; fmr Chair. Honduras Chamber of Industry and Construction, Dir Honduras Pvt. Enterprise Council, Nat. Asscn of Industrialists; mem. Partido Liberal de Honduras; Vice-Pres. of Honduras 2006–08 (resgnd); Partido Liberal candidate in 2009 presidential election; mem. Colegio de Ingenieros Civiles de Honduras, American Soc. of Civil Engineers.

SANTOS PAIS, Marta, BA, MA; Portuguese diplomatist and UN official; *Special Representative of the Secretary-General on Violence against Children, United Nations;* b. 1952; m.; two c.; ed Univ. of Lisbon; more than 25 years' experience on human rights issues and engagement in intergovernmental processes; Rapporteur, UN Cttee on the Rights of the Child 1991–97, served as Vice-Chair. Co-ordinating Cttee on Childhood Policies, Council of Europe; Dir of Evaluation, Policy and Planning, UNICEF 1997–2001, served as Co-Chair. UN Devt Group Working Group on Human Rights, Dir UNICEF Innocenti Research Centre, Florence, Italy 2001–09; Special Rep. on Violence against Children at level of Asst Sec.-Gen. 2009–; held several advisory positions on human rights and legal issues in Portugal; served as Special Adviser to Machel Study on children affected by armed conflict and to UN Study on Violence against Children. *Publications:* numerous studies and publs. *Address:* 633 Third Avenue, Room 6053, New York, NY 10017, USA (office). *Telephone:* (212) 824-6322 (office). *Website:* srsg.violenceagainstchildren.org (office).

SANTOS PEREIRA, Álvaro, BA, MSc, PhD; Portuguese/Canadian economist, academic and politician; *Director, Country Studies Branch, Economics Department, Organisation for Economic Co-operation and Development;* b. 1972, Viseu; ed Univ. de Coimbra, Exeter Univ., Simon Fraser Univ., Vancouver, Canada; Lecturer, Simon Fraser Univ., Vancouver 2000–04, concurrently Visiting Prof., Dept of Econs, Univ. of British Columbia 2000–04; Prof. of Econs and European Econ. Devt, Dept of Econs, Univ. of York, UK 2004–07; Minister of the Economy and Employment 2011–13; Dir, Country Studies Br., OECD Econs Dept 2014–; columnist for several newspapers including O Diário de Notícias, Jornal Público, Diário Económico, Expresso, Exame, Jornal de Notícias; author of Desmitos blog; Ind. *Publications include:* Portugal na Hora da Verdade, Os Mitos da Economia Portuguesa 2007, Diário de um Deus Criacionista, O Medo do Insucesso Naciona 2009, Portugal's Moment of Truth: New Economic Policy for Portugal 2011. *Address:* OECD 2, rue André Pascal, 75775 Paris cedex 16, France (office). *Telephone:* (1) 45-24-82-00 (office). *Fax:* (1) 45-24-85-00 (home). *Website:* www.oecd.org/eco/alvaro-pereira.htm (office).

SANTOS SILVA, Augusto Ernesto, PhD; Portuguese academic and politician; *Minister of Foreign Affairs;* b. 1956, Porto; m.; three c.; ed Inst. for Labour and Business Sciences, Univ. of Porto; Lecturer in Econs, Univ. of Porto 1981, Sr Prof., also Head, Academic Council, Faculty of Econs 1998–99, Deputy Vice-Rector 1998–99; mem. Partido Socialista (PS) 1990–, mem. Nat. Cttee 1998–, Nat. Political Cttee 2002–05, 2006, Nat. Secr. 2006, Dir Acção Socialista (official PS journal) 2002–05; elected mem. Assembléia da República (Parl.) for Porto constituency 2002, Co-ordinator, PS Parl. Group for Culture, Science and Higher Educ. 2002–05; Sec. of State for Educ. Admin 1999–2000, Minister of Educ. 2000–01, of Culture 2003–06, Minister for Parl. Affairs 2005–06, Minister of Nat. Defence 2009–11, of Foreign Affairs 2015–; columnist, Jornal de Notícias 1978–86, Público (newspaper) 1992–99, 2002–05, TSF-Rádio Jornal 1997–98; mem. Nat. Educ. Council 1996–99; mem. Bd Fundação José Fontana 2002–05, Fundação Res Publica 2008; Grand Cross, Ordine al Merito della Repubblica Italiana 2002, Order of Charles III (Spain) 2016, Order of Honour (Greece) 2017, Orden de Isabel la Católica (Spain) 2018. *Publications include:* Entre a Razão e o Sentido: Durkheim, Weber e a Teoria das Ciências Sociais 1988, Educação de Adultos, Educação para o Desenvolvimento 1990, Tempos Cruzados: um Estudo Interpretativo da Cultura Popular 1994, De que Vale Ter Poder? Crónicas no Público 1995–97 1997, Cultura e Desenvolvimento: Estudos sobre a Relação entre Ser e Agir 2000, A Sociologia e o Debate Público: Estudos sobre a Relação entre Conhecer e Agir 2006, Os valores da esquerda democrática: Vinte teses oferecidas ao escrutínio crítico 2010, Os porquês da esperança: Ideias a favor do futuro em Portugal 2015. *Address:* Ministry of Foreign Affairs, Palácio das Necessidades, Largo do Rilvas, 1399-030 Lisbon, Portugal (office). *Telephone:* (21) 3946000 (office). *Fax:* (21) 3946070 (office). *E-mail:* gabinete.ministro@mne.gov.pt (office). *Website:* www.portugal.gov.pt (office).

SANTOS SIMÃO, Leonardo, LicMed, MSc; Mozambican politician and medical practitioner; *Executive Director, Joaquim Chissano Foundation;* b. 6 June 1953, Mandlakaze; s. of Antonio Santos Simão Sitoi and Amélia Muchanga; m. Josephine P. Simão; two d.; ed Liceu Salazar, Maputo, Eduardo Mondlane Univ., Univ. of London, UK, Boston Univ., USA; Dir Centre of Dist Formation of Chicumbane, Gaza 1981–82; Prov. Health Dir Zambezia Prov. 1982–84; Dir Prov. Hosp. of Quelimane, Zambezia Prov. 1984–88; Minister of Health 1988; apptd Prof. of Medicine, Eduardo Mondlane Univ. 1988; Minister of Foreign Affairs and Co-operation 1994–95; currently Exec. Dir Joaquim Chissano Foundation; Chair. Nat. Mine Clearance Comm., Muyake SA; mem. Cen. Cttee Frelimo Party; mem. Medical Asscn of Mozambique, Mozambique Asscn of Public Health; Great Cross, Order of Rio Branco (Brazil) 1996, Order of Good Hope, II Grade (South Africa) 1997, Great Cross, Order of Merit (Portugal) 1998, Order of Eduardo Mondlane (Mozambique) 2005, Diploma of Honour (Mozambique) 2005. *Leisure interests:* music, reading, swimming. *Address:* The Joaquim Chissano Foundation, 954, Av. Zimbabwe, Maputo, Mozambique (office). *Telephone:* (21) 484000 (office). *Fax:* (21) 484001 (office). *E-mail:* l.simao@fjchissano.org.mz (office). *Website:* www.fjchissano.org.mz (office).

SANUSI II, HRH The Emir of Kano; **Muhammad,** BSc, MSc, CON; Nigerian ruler and fmr central banker; *Emir of Kano;* b. (Sanusi Lamido Sanusi), 31 July 1961, Kano; s. of Muhammad Lamido Sanusi; great nephew of the later emir, Dr Ado Abdullahi Bayero; m. Sadiya, Maryam, Rakiya; c.; ed King's Coll., Lagos, Ahmadu Bello Univ., Zaria, Int. Univ. of Africa, Khartoum; Lecturer in Econs, Ahmadu Bello Univ. 1983–85; began banking career with Icon Ltd (merchant banker) 1985; joined Credit and Risk Man. Div., United Bank for Africa PLC 1997, becoming Gen. Man.; Exec. Dir in charge of Risk and Man. Control, First Bank of Nigeria PLC 2005–09, Group Man. Dir (CEO) 2009; Gov. Cen. Bank of Nigeria 2009–14 (suspended by Pres. Jonathan on govt charges of financial recklessness and misconduct); crowned Emir of Kano 8 June 2014–; fmr Chief Risk Officer with UBA PLC; fmr Chair. Kakawa Discount House; fmr Dir FBN Bank (UK) Ltd; Fellow, Chartered Inst. of Bankers of Nigeria; Cen. Bank Gov. of the Year and Cen. Bank Gov. of the Year for Africa, Banker magazine 2010. *Publications include:* numerous papers in academic journals, books and newspapers. *Address:* Gidan Rumfa (Palace of the Emir), Kano, Kano State, Northern Nigeria.

SAPARBAEV, Berdibek, DEcon; Kazakhstani economist and politician; b. 9 Feb. 1953, Talap (now Besaryk), Qizilorda Oblast, Kazakh SSR, USSR; ed Alma-Ata (now Almatı) Inst. of Nat. Economy; began career as economist in state admin of nat. savings banks; continued in Ministry of Finance 1977–88, later Head of Planning and Econs Dept; Deputy Minister of Public Educ. 1988–93; Head of Finance, Dept of Labour and Social Protection of Population, Presidential Service and in Cabinet 1993–94; Head of Cabinet Service March–Sept. 1995; Gov. Qizilorda Oblast Sept. 1995–99, of Southern Kazakhstan Oblast 1999–2002; Chair. Customs Control Agency and Vice-Minister of Finance 2002–06; Minister of Labour and Social Protection of Population 2005–07; Deputy Head of Prime-Minister's Office and Govt Rep. in Majlis (Ass.) 2006–07; Vice-Minister of Economy and Budget Planning Feb.–Aug. 2007; Akim (Gov.) of Eastern Kazakhstan Oblast 2009–14; Deputy Prime Minister 2014–15. *Address:* c/o Office of the Prime Minister, 010000 Nur-Sultan, Beibitshilik kosh. 11, Kazakhstan.

SAPIN, Michel, BA, MPhil; French politician; b. 9 April 1952, Boulogne-Billancourt (Hauts-de-Seine); m. Yolande Millan 1982; three c.; ed Lycée Henri IV, Paris-Sorbonne Univ., École Normale Supérieure, Institut d'études politiques de Paris, École nationale d'admin, Strasbourg; joined Parti Socialiste 1975; elected Deputy Nat. Ass. for Indre 1981–86, 2007–12, for Hauts-de-Seine 1986–91, Sec. 1983–84, Vice-Pres. 1984, Chair. of the Cttee for Law 1988–91, currently mem. Finance Cttee; town councillor, Nanterre 1989–94; Minister Del. for Justice 1991–92; Minister of Economy and Finance 1992–93, of Civil Service, of Admin. Reform 2000–02; Regional Councillor, Île de France 1992–94; mem. Council for Monetary Policy of Banque de France 1994–95; Mayor of Argenton-sur-Creuse 1995–2004, Deputy Mayor 2004–08; Gen. Councillor of Indre 1998–; Pres. Centre Regional Council 1998–2000, 2004–07, Vice-Pres. 2000–01; First Vice-Pres. Asscn of the Regions of France 1998–2000; Nat. Sec. on Economy, Parti Socialiste 2007–; Minister of Labour, Employment, Professional Training and Social Dialogue 2012–14, of Finance and Nat. Accounts 2014–16, of Economy and Finance 2016–17. *Publications:* L'Etat en mouvement 2002, La France peut s'en sortir! 2012, L'Ecume et l'océan: chronique d'un ministre du travail par gros temp 2014. *Address:* Parti Socialiste, 10 rue de Solférino, 75333 Paris Cedex 07, France (office). *Telephone:* 1-45-56-77-00 (office). *Fax:* 1-47-05-15-78 (office). *E-mail:* interps@parti-socialiste.fr (office). *Website:* www.parti-socialiste.fr (office).

ŠAPOKA, Vilius, BEcons, MEcons; Lithuanian economist and government official; *Minister of Finance;* b. 14 Dec. 1978, Šiauliai; m.; two s.; ed Vilnius Univ.; Client Man., Financial Analyst, Customer Service Man., AB Lithuania Savings Bank 1999–2001; Sr Specialist, later Chief Specialist and Deputy Head, Financial Markets Dept, Ministry of Finance 2002–06; Deputy Chair., Securities Comm. (VPK) 2006–12; Dir, Financial Services and Markets Dept, Lietuvos Bankas (central bank) 2012–16; Minister of Finance 2016–. *Address:* Ministry of Finance, Lukiškių g. 2, Vilnius 01512, Lithuania (office). *Telephone:* (5) 239-0000 (office). *Fax:* (5) 279-1481 (office). *E-mail:* finmin@finmin.lt (office). *Website:* finmin .lrv.lt (office).

SAPUTO, Emanuele (Lino), CM; Canadian business executive; *Chairman, Saputo Inc.;* b. 10 June 1937, Sicily, Italy; s. of Giuseppe Saputo and Maria Saputo; m. Mirella Saputo; two s. one d.; family emigrated to Canada 1952; with parents f. dairy processor Saputo Inc. 1954, Chair. 1969–, Pres. 1969–2004, CEO 1998–2004; mem. Bd of Dirs Arbec Forest Products Inc. 1996–, Tembec Inc. 2006–07; mem. Bd of Trustees TransForce Income Fund 2008–; f. Jolina Capital (investment co.). *Address:* Saputo Inc., 6869 Metropolitain Boulevard East, Montreal, PQ H1P 1X8, Canada (office). *Telephone:* (514) 328-6662 (office). *Fax:* (514) 328-3364 (office). *Website:* www.saputo.com (office).

SAR, Kheng; Cambodian politician; *Deputy Prime Minister and Minister of the Interior;* b. 15 Jan. 1951, Prey Veng; m. Nhem Sakhan; mem. Cen. Cttee Cambodian People's Party 1984–, Pres. Org. Comm. 1990–; Deputy Prime Minister 1992–, Co-minister of the Interior 1998–2006, Minister of the Interior 2006–; fmr Acting Prime Minister; fmr Chair. Nat. Census Cttee; fmr Co-Chair. Nat. Cttee to Support Commune/Sangkat; Membership Award, Natural Sciences Acad. of the Russian Fed. 2002. *Address:* Ministry of the Interior, 275 Blvd Norodom, Khan Chamkarmon, Phnom-Penh, Cambodia (office). *Telephone:* (23) 721190 (office). *Fax:* (23) 726052 (office). *E-mail:* info@interior.gov.kh (office). *Website:* www .interior.gov.kh (office).

SARABI, Habiba; Afghan politician, haematologist, pharmacist and women's rights activist; b. 5 Dec. 1957, Mazar-e Sharif; m.; two s. one d.; ed Aisha Durani High School, Kabul Univ.; licensed pharmacist; with Nat. Inst. of Medicine, Kabul 1983–87; teacher, Intermediate Medical Inst., Kabul 1988–96; exile in Pakistan 1996–2001; Prof. and Gen. Man. Afghanistan Inst. of Learning 1997–2001; medical aid to women and children in refugee camps on Afghanistan-Pakistan border 2001; Dir of Humanitarian Assistance for the Women and Children of Afghanistan, Peshawar 2002; Minister of Women's Affairs 2002–04; Gov. of Bamiyan Prov. (first female gov. in Afghanistan) 2005–13 (resgnd); unsuccessful cand. for Second Vice-Pres. of Afghanistan on ticket with Zalmai Rassoul 2014; Advisor on Women's Affairs and Youth to Ministry of Women's Affairs to CEO (Prime Minister) of Afghanistan 2015–; est. Band-e Amir Nat. Park; WHO Fellowship Training Programme, All India Inst. of Medical Science 1998; Commdr, Ordre national du Mérite 2007; Jason Award, Children's Square, USA 2005, Malalai Maiwand Medal from Pres. Karzai 2007, named by Time magazine a Hero of the Environment 2008, Ramon Magsaysay Award 2013. *Website:* ceo.gov.af/en.

SARACENO, Chiara, PhD; Italian sociologist and academic; *Honorary Fellow, Collegio Carlo Alberto;* b. 20 Oct. 1941, Milan; m.; two d.; ed Catholic Univ. of Milan; Assoc. Prof. then Full Prof., Faculty of Sociology, Univ. of Trento 1971–90, Vice-Rector Univ. of Trento 1989–90; Prof. of Sociology of the Family, Faculty of Political Sciences, Univ. of Turin 1990–2008, Chair. Dept of Social Sciences 1991–97, Chair. Univ. Gender and Women Studies Centre (CIRSDe) 1997–2006, Chair. PhD Programme in Comparative Social Research 1996–2005; Chair. Italian

Poverty Comm. 1999–2001; mem. High-Level Expert Group on the Measurement of Econ. Progress and Social Performance; Research Prof., Wissenschaftszentrum Berlin fuer Sozialforschung 2006–11, Prof. Emer. 2011–; Corresp. Fellow, British Acad. 2011; Hon. Fellow, Collegio Carlo Alberto, Turin 2011; Grand'ufficiale della Repubblica Italiana. *Publications:* Genere. La costruzione sociale del femminile e del maschile (co-ed) 1996, Separarsi in Italia (with Marzio Barbagli) 1998, Sociologia della famiglia (co-author) 2001, Età e corso della vita 2001, Commissione d'indagine sull'esclusione sociale, Rapporto sulle politiche contro la povertà e l'esclusione sociale. 1997–2001 2002, Social Assistance Dynamics in European Welfare States (ed.) 2002, Diversi da chi? Gay, lesbiche, transessuali in un'area metropolitana (ed.) 2003, Mutamenti della famiglia e politiche sociali in Italia 2003, Dinamiche assistenziali in Europa (ed.) 2004, Quality of Life in the Enlarged European Union (co-ed.) 2007, Povertà e benessere (co-ed.) 2007, Childhood – Changing Contexts (co-ed.) 2008, Families, Aging and Social Policy (ed.) 2008, Dimensioni della disuguaglianza in Italia: povertà, salute, abitazione (co-ed.) 2009, Coppie e famiglie. Non è questione di natura 2011 (second edn 2016), Il lavoro non basta. La povertà in Europa negli anni della crisi 2015, Mamme e papà. Gli esami non finiscono mai 2016, L'equivoco della famiglia 2017; numerous scientific papers in academic journals on comparative family changes, gender patterns, family and social policies, poverty and anti-poverty policies in comparative perspective; writes regularly for major Italian newspapers. *Leisure interests:* reading, theatre and movie going, walking and swimming, spending time with my grandchildren, knitting. *Address:* Collegio Carlo Alberto, Piazza Arbarello 8, 10122 Torino, Italy (office). *E-mail:* chiara.saraceno@unito.it (office). *Website:* www.carloalberto.org/ people/faculty/honorary/chiara-saraceno (office).

SARAGA, Peter, CBE, OBE, FIEE, FREng; British engineer and academic; m. Anne Coffey MP (Stockport); one s. one d.; ed Univ. of Cambridge, Imperial Coll. London; early career as research scientist specializing in robotics and image processing; Man. Dir Philips Research Laboratories UK 1992–2002; currently consultant; Visiting Prof. and mem. Strategic Advisory Group, Dept of Electric and Electronic Eng, Imperial Coll. London, Adviser to Inst. of Biomedical Eng; Chair. School of Electronics and Physical Sciences Advisory Bd, Univ. of Surrey; mem. Council and Dir of Sussex Intellectual Property Ltd, Univ. of Sussex 2003–, Vice-Chair. Council 2007–09; mem. of Court, Brunel Univ.; Vice-Pres. and Hon. Sec. for Int. Activities, Royal Acad. of Eng; Pres.-elect Inst. of Physics 2005–06, Pres. 2006–08, Past Pres. 2008–09; mem. Bd Higher Educ. Funding Council for England 2002–, Chair. Business and the Community Cttee; has also served on UK Govt cttees relating to tech. issues and acted as adviser to UK research councils. *Publications:* numerous papers in professional journals. *Address:* Room 1108, Control and Power Group, Electrical and Electronic Engineering, Imperial College, South Kensington Campus, London, SW7 2AZ (office). *Telephone:* (20) 7594-6272 (office). *Fax:* (20) 7594-6282 (office). *E-mail:* peter.saraga@imperial.ac .uk (office). *Website:* www.imperial.ac.uk/controlandpower (office).

SARAH, HE Cardinal Robert; Guinean ecclesiastic; *Prefect of the Congregation for Divine Worship and the Discipline of the Sacraments;* b. 15 June 1945, Ourous; ed Seminary of Bingerville, Ivory Coast, Seminary of Dixinn, Seminary Jean XXIII, Grand Seminary of Nancy, France, Sébikotane, Senegal, Pontifical Gregorian Univ., Rome, Studium Biblicum Franciscanum of Jerusalem, Israel; returned to Guinea 1974; ordained priest, Diocese of Conakry 1969; Archbishop of Conakry 1979–2001; Sec. Congregation for the Evangelization of Peoples 2001–10; Pres. Pontifical Council 'Cor Unum' 2010–13, 2013–14; Prefect of the Congregation for Divine Worship and the Discipline of the Sacraments 2014–; cr. Cardinal (Cardinal-Deacon of San Giovanni Bosco in via Tuscolana) 2010; participated in Papal Conclave 2013. *Address:* Palazzo delle Congregazioni, Piazza Pio XII 10, 00193 Rome, Italy (office). *Telephone:* (06) 69884005 (office); (06) 69884416. *Fax:* (06) 69883499 (office). *Website:* www.vatican.va/roman_curia/congregations/ccdds/ index.htm (office).

SARAIVA MARTINS, HE Cardinal José; Portuguese ecclesiastic; *Cardinal-Bishop of Palestrina;* b. 6 Feb. 1932, Gagos de Jarmelo, Guarda; ed Pontifical Gregorian Univ., Pontifical Univ. of St Thomas Aquinas, Rome; ordained priest 1957, Bishop 1988; fmr teacher Claretianum, Rome; fmr teacher Pontifical Urbanian Univ., Rector 1977–80, 1980–83, 1986–88; Titular Archbishop of Thuburnica 1988; Prefect of the Congregation for the Causes of Saints 1998–2008, Prefect Emer. 2008–; cr. Cardinal 2001, apptd Cardinal-Deacon of Nostra Signora del Sacro Cuore 2001; Cardinal-Bishop of Palestrina 2009–. *Address:* c/o Congregation for the Causes of Saints, Palazzo delle Congregazioni, Piazza Pio XII 10, 00193 Rome, Italy.

SARAN, Pankaj, BA (Hons), MA; Indian diplomatist; *Ambassador to Russia;* m. Preeti Saran; two s.; ed Univ. of Delhi; joined Foreign Service 1982, Third Sec. (language trainee)/Second Sec. (Political), Embassy in Moscow 1984–86, Under-Sec., East Europe Div., Ministry of External Affairs 1986–89, Second, then First Sec., High Comm. in Dhaka 1989–92, First Sec. (Political), Embassy in Washington, DC 1992–94, Deputy Sec. in Foreign Sec.'s Office, New Delhi 1994–95, Deputy Sec./Dir, Prime Minister's Office 1995–99, Counsellor (Political and Commercial), Embassy in Cairo 1999–2002, Counsellor (Political), Head of Chancery and Minister (Political), Perm. Mission to UN, Geneva 2002–05, Jt Sec., Northern Div. dealing with Nepal and Bhutan, Ministry of External Affairs 2005–07, Jt Sec., Prime Minister's Office 2007–12, High Commr to Bangladesh 2012–15, Amb. to Russian Fed. 2016–. *Leisure interests:* tennis, golf, bridge, reading. *Address:* Embassy of India, 101000 Moscow, ul. Vorontsovo Pole 6–8, Russia (office). *Telephone:* (495) 783-75-31 (office). *Fax:* (495) 916-34-47 (office). *E-mail:* amb.moscow@mea.gov.in (office); amboffice.moscow@mea.gov.in (office). *Website:* www.indianembassy.ru (office).

SARANDJI, Simplice Mathieu; Central African Republic politician and fmr academic; b. 4 April 1955, Baoro; ed Univ. of Bangui, Univ. Michel de Montaigne Bordeaux III, France; Head, Dept of History and Geography, Univ. of Bangui, becoming Dean, Faculty of Letters and Social Science and Sec. Gen., Univ. of Bangui; Nat. Campaign Dir, then five years as Cabinet Dir to Prime Minister Faustin Archange Touadéra 2008–13; Prime Minister 2016–19 (resgnd). *Address:* c/o Office of the Prime Minister, BP 932, Bangui, Central African Republic (office).

SARANDON, Susan Abigail; American actress; b. 4 Oct. 1946, New York; d. of Philip Tomalin and Lenora Criscione; m. Chris Sarandon 1967 (divorced 1979); one

d. with Franco Amurri; fmr pnr Tim Robbins (q.v.); two s.; ed Catholic Univ. of America; numerous TV appearances; UNICEF Goodwill Amb. 1999–; FAO Goodwill Amb. 2010–. *Films include:* Joe 1970, Lady Liberty 1971, The Rocky Horror Picture Show 1974, Lovin' Molly 1974, The Great Waldo Pepper 1975, The Front Page 1976, Dragon Fly 1976, Walk Away Madden, The Other Side of Midnight 1977, The Last of the Cowboys 1977, Pretty Baby 1978, King of the Gypsies 1978, Loving Couples 1980, Atlantic City 1981, Tempest 1982, The Hunger 1983, Buddy System 1984, Compromising Positions 1985, The Witches of Eastwick 1987, Bull Durham 1988, Sweet Hearts Dance 1988, Married to the Mob, A Dry White Season 1989, The January Man 1989, White Palace, Thelma and Louise 1991, Light Sleeper 1991, Lorenzo's Oil, The Client, Little Women 1995, Safe Passage 1995, Dead Man Walking (Acad. Award for Best Actress 1996) 1996, James and the Giant Peach 1996, Illuminata 1998, Twilight 1998, Stepmom 1999, Anywhere But Here 1999, The Cradle Will Rock 1999, Rugrats in Paris 2000, Joe Gould's Secret 2000, Cats and Dogs 2001, Igby Goes Down 2002, The Banger Sisters 2003, The Nazi Officer's Wife 2003, Last Party 2000 2003, Noel 2004, Shall We Dance? 2004, Alfie 2004, Elizabethstown 2005, Romance & Cigarettes 2005, Irresistible 2006, In the Valley of Elah 2007, Mr. Woodcock 2007, Emotional Arithmetic 2007, Bernard and Doris 2007, Enchanted 2007, Speed Racer 2008, The Lovely Bones 2009, Wall Street: Money Never Sleeps 2010, Jeff, Who Lives At Home 2011, That's My Boy 2012, Cloud Atlas 2012, Tammy 2014, The Meddler 2015, 3 Generations 2015, Mothers and Daughters 2016, Ace the Case 2016, A Bad Moms Christmas 2017, Viper Club 2018, The Death and Life of John F. Donovan 2018. *Television includes:* A.D. (mini-series) 1985, Mussolini and I (series) 1985, Women of Valor (film) 1986, Earthly Possessions (film) 1999, Children of Dune (mini-series) 2003, The Exonerated (film) 2005, Rescue Me (series) 2006–07, You Don't Know Jack (film) 2010, The Big C (series) 2012, Cassius and Caly (film) (voice) 2016, Feud (series) 2017, Skylanders Academy (series) 2016–17, Neo Yokio (series) 2017–19. *Stage appearances include:* A Coupla White Chicks Sittin' Around Talkin', An Evening with Richard Nixon, A Stroll in the Air, Albert's Bridge, Private Ear, Public Eye, Extremities, Exit the King. *Address:* c/o Shani Rosenzweig, United Talented Agency, 888 Seventh Avenue, Seventh Floor, New York, NY 10106, USA (office). *Telephone:* (212) 659-2600 (office). *Website:* www.unitedtalent.com (office).

SARANDOS, Theodore (Ted) Anthony; American business executive and producer; *Chief Content Officer, Netflix, Inc.;* b. 30 July 1964, Phoenix, Ariz.; m. Nicole Alexandra Avant; one s. one d.; Vice-Pres., Product & Merchandising, Video City 1983–88; Western Regional Dir, Sales & Operations and Gen. Man., ETD (video distributor) 1988–2000; Vice-Pres., Content and Chief Content Officer, Netflix, Inc. 2000–; mem. Exec. Cttee, Acad. of Television Arts & Sciences 2015; mem. Bd of Dirs Spotify Investors 2016–17, MediaRights.org; mem. Film Advisory Bd Tribeca and Los Angeles Film Festivals; mem. Retail Advisory Bd Digital Entertainment Group; Henry Crown Fellow, Aspen Inst.; mem. Bd of Trustee Exploring The Arts; Trustee Int. Documentary Asscn; Hon. mem. Harvard Lampoon; Humanitarian Award, Simon Wiesenthal Center 2014, Brandon Tartikoff Legacy Award, NAPTE 2015, Pioneer Award, Int. Documentary Asscn 2015, Showman of the Year, Variety magazine 2017. *Films:* The Do-Over 2016, The Ridiculous 6 2016, Crouching Tiger, Hidden Dragon: Sword of Destiny 2016, First They Killed My Father 2017, Sandy Wexler 2017, Okja 2017, War Machine 2017, Death Note 2017, Bright 2017, Mute 2018. *Address:* Netflix, Inc, 100 Winchester Circle, Los Gatos, CA 95032, USA (office). *Telephone:* (408) 540-3700 (office). *E-mail:* tsarandos@netflix.com (office). *Website:* www.netflix.com (office).

SARASSORO, Fidèle, BEcons, MEcons, PhD; Côte d'Ivoirian UN official; b. 1960; m.; three d.; ed Université de Côte d'Ivoire, Univ. of Illinois, Urbana-Champaign, USA; served as UN Capital Devt Fund Program Specialist, USAID Regional Office, Abidjan 1988–91, Sr Portfolio Man., UN Office for Project Services (UNOPS) Regional Office, Abidjan 1997–2001, Acting Chief 2001–02, UN Resident Coordinator and UNDP Resident Rep., Togo 2002–06, UN Resident and Humanitarian Coordinator and UNDP Resident Rep., Ethiopia 2006–09, Deputy Special Rep. of Sec.-Gen. for Democratic Repub. of the Congo and Head, UN Org. Stabilization Mission in the Democratic Repub. of the Congo (MONUSCO) 2010–12; currently working in the Security Sector and disarmament, demobilization and reintegration (DDR) in Office of the Pres. 2012–. *Address:* Office of the President, 01 BP 1354, Abidjan 01, Côte d'Ivoire (office). *Telephone:* 20-22-02-22 (office). *Fax:* 20-21-14-25 (office). *Website:* www.cotedivoirepr.ci (office).

SARASTE, Jukka-Pekka; Finnish conductor; *Chief Conductor, WDR Symphony Orchestra;* b. 22 April 1956, Heinola; m. Marja-Lisa Ollila; three s. one d.; ed Sibelius Acad., Helsinki; debut with Helsinki Philharmonic 1980; Prin. Conductor, Scottish Chamber Orchestra 1987–91; Prin. Conductor and Music Dir Finnish Radio Symphony Orchestra 1987–2001, now Conductor Laureate; Music Dir Toronto Symphony Orchestra 1994–2001; Prin. Guest Conductor, BBC Symphony Orchestra 2002–05; Chief Conductor and Music Dir Oslo Philharmonic Orchestra 2006–13, Conductor Laureate 2013–; Artistic Adviser, Lahti Symphony Orchestra 2008–11, Artistic Dir Lahti Sibelius Festival 2008–11; Chief Conductor, WDR Symphony Orchestra, Cologne 2010–; Founder and Artistic Dir Finnish Chamber Orchestra, also f. the orchestrás annual Tammisaari Festival; has been guest conductor with Boston Symphony Orchestra, Cleveland Orchestra, San Francisco Orchestra, Frankfurt Radio Orchestra, NY Philharmonic Orchestra, London Philharmonic Orchestra, Orchestre Philharmonique de Radio France, BBC Symphony Orchestra, Munich Philharmonic Orchestra; has toured Japan, Hong Kong, Taiwan, Germany, USA, Canary Islands Festival; Dr hc (Univ. of York), (Sibelius Acad.); Pro Finlandia Prize, Sibelius Medal, Finnish State Prize for Music. *Recordings include:* numerous recordings, including complete Sibelius symphonies 1995 (with Finnish Radio Symphony Orchestra), Mussorgsky (with Toronto Symphony Orchestra), Nielsen Symphonies 4&5 (with Finnish Radio Symphony Orchestra), Romeo and Juliet Suite (Prokofiev), Bruckner's Symphony No. 8 2016. *Address:* c/o Lothar Schacke, KünstlerSekretariat am Gasteig, Montgelasstrasse 2, 81679 Munich, Germany (office). *Telephone:* (89) 4448879-0 (office). *E-mail:* lothar.schacke@ks-gasteig.de (office). *Website:* jukkapekkasaraste.com.

SARAYA, Osama, BA; Egyptian journalist and editor; b. 24 March 1952; ed Cairo Univ.; has held various positions at Al-Ahram (state-owned daily newspaper) since 1975, including Econs Ed., Supervisor of the Econ. Page (weekly edn), Dir of Arab Econs Dept, Man. of Al-Ahram Regional Press Inst., Dir of Al-Ahram office in Saudi Arabia, Ed.-in-Chief 2005–11, supervised training programmes for Egyptian, Arab and African journalists of Al-Ahram Regional Press Inst., represented Al-Ahram in Arab and int. conventions, est. The Devt and Environment Media Unit in Al-Ahram Regional Press Inst.; mem. Egyptian Journalists Syndicate, fmr Sec.-Gen. and Treas.; helped establish Nat. Democratic Party—NDP (ruling party), mem. sub-cttee of NDP's policy secr.; Gen. Union for Egyptians Abroad Unity Prize 2005.

SARBANES, Paul Spyros, BA, LLB; American lawyer and fmr politician; b. 3 Feb. 1933, Salisbury, Md; s. of Spyros P. Sarbanes and Matina (née Tsigounis) Sarbanes; m. Christine Dunbar 1960 (deceased 2009); two s. one d.; ed Princeton Univ., Balliol Coll., Oxford, UK, Harvard Law School; Rhodes Scholar, Balliol Coll., Oxford 1954–57; admitted to Maryland Bar 1960; law clerk to circuit judge 1960–61; Assoc., Piper and Marbury, Baltimore 1961–62; Admin. Asst to Chair. Council of Econ. Advisers 1962–63; Exec. Dir Charter Revision Comm., Baltimore 1963–64; Assoc., Venable, Baetjer & Howard, Baltimore 1965–70; mem. Maryland House of Dels 1967–71, House of Reps 1971–76; Senator from Maryland 1977–2007 (retd), co-author Sarbanes-Oxley Act; mem. American Acad. of Arts and Sciences 2004–; Democrat; John V. Kabler Memorial Award 2002, Paul H. Douglas Ethics in Govt Award, Univ. of Illinois 2003, Cox, Richardson, Coleman Award 2004, Woodrow Wilson Award, Princeton Univ. 2007, Reginald V. Truitt Environmental Award 2007. *Address:* Tower 1, Suite 1710, 100 South Charles Street, Baltimore, MD 21201, USA.

SARCINELLI, Mario; Italian banker, economist, academic and business executive; b. 9 March 1934, Foggia; m. Giovanna Longardi; two s.; ed Univ. of Pavia, Univ. of Cambridge; joined Bank of Italy 1957, Econ. Adviser to Italian Del. to UN 1960, fmr Head Data Processing and Information Systems Dept, Cen. Man. for Banking Supervision 1976, apptd Deputy Dir-Gen. 1976, alt. mem. EEC Cttee of Govs of Cen. Banks 1978–81, Bd of Dirs BIS 1978–81, Dir-Gen. Treasury 1982–91; Minister of Foreign Trade April–July 1987; Vice-Pres. EBRD 1991–94; Chair. Monetary Cttee 1989–90, Banca Nazionale del Lavoro SpA 1994–98; Chair. Diners Club Sim p.a. 1999–2001; Prof. of Int. Monetary Econs, Università degli Studi di Roma 'la Sapienza' 1998–2002; Lecturer in Global Banking, LUISS Guido Carli 2001–04, Pres. Centro di Ricerca per il Diritto d'Impresa (CERADI) 1999–2004; Chair. Dexia Crediop, Rome 2007–14; Pres. Gesac SpA 2010–15; Officier Légion d'honneur, Cavaliere del Lavoro 1996; Dr hc (Univ. of Bari). *Address:* Dexia Crediop, Via Venti Settembre 30, 00187 Rome, Italy (office). *Telephone:* (06) 47711 (office). *Fax:* (06) 47715961 (office). *E-mail:* mario.sarcinelli@dexia-crediop.it (office). *Website:* www.dexia-crediop.it (office); www.aeroportodinapoli.it/en (office).

SARDESAI, Rajdeep, BA, MA, BCL; Indian journalist and television presenter; *Consulting Editor, India Today Group;* b. 24 May 1965, Gujarat; s. of Dilip Sardesai and Nandini Sardesai; m. Sagarika Ghose; two c.; ed St Xavier's Coll., Mumbai, Univ. of Oxford; Asst Ed. then City Ed. and Chief of News Service, Times of India, Mumbai 1988–94; Special Corresp. and Political Ed., New Delhi TV (NDTV) 1994–2002, Man. Ed. NDTV 24x7 and NDTV India 2002–05; Co-Founder IBN18 Network 2005, Ed.-in-Chief CNN-IBN 2005–14; Consulting Ed., India Today Group 2014–, Host, Headlines Today; apptd Pres. Eds Guild of India 2008; mem. Population Council; Padma Shri 2008, Int. Broadcasters Award, Ramnath Goenka Excellence in Journalism Award 2007, Asian TV Award, News Anchor of the Year, Indian TV Acad. Academy (six years). *Address:* India Today Group, Mediaplex FC-8, Sector 16A, Film City, Noida 201 301, India (office). *E-mail:* rajdeepsardesai52@gmail.com. *Website:* indiatoday.intoday.in (office); www.indiatodaygroup.com (office); www.rajdeepsardesai.net.

SARDI, HE Cardinal Paolo, STL; Italian ecclesiastic; b. 1 Sept. 1934, Ricaldone, Prov. of Alessandria; ed Università Cattolica del Sacro Cuore, Milan; ordained priest 1958; taught moral theology in Turin –1976; called to the Vatican to work in Secr. of State 1976; Vice-Councillor for Gen. Affairs 1992–96; Apostolic Nuncio with special responsibilities 1996–2004; Titular Archbishop of Sutrium 1996–; Vice-Chamberlain of the Apostolic Chamber 2004–11; Patron of the Sovereign Mil. Order of Malta 2010–14; cr. Cardinal (Cardinal-Deacon of Santa Maria Auxiliatrice in via Tuscolana) 2010; participated in Papal Conclave 2013. *Address:* c/o Apostolic Chamber, Palazzo Apostolico, 00120 Città del Vaticano, Rome, Italy (office). *Telephone:* (06) 69883554 (office). *Website:* www.vatican.va (office).

SARDJOE, Ramdien; Suriname politician; *Honorary Chairman, Vooruitstrevende Hervormings Partij;* b. 10 Oct. 1935, Dist Suriname; s. of Sewsanker Sardjoe and Mangri Bissumbhar; m. 1st Sawitrie Bindraban 1958; one s.; m. 2nd Darmatie Ilse Biharie; three s. one d.; worked as teacher 1953–72; Lecturer, Instituut voor de Opleiding van Leraren (Inst. for the training of teachers) 1972–96; fmr Deputy Sec., Ministry of Educ. (also Acting Perm. Sec.); mem. Parl. 1964–80, 1987–2005, Speaker 2001–05; Chair. Vooruitstrevende Hervormings Partij 2001–11, then Hon. Chair.; Vice-Pres. of Suriname 2005–10; Co-Pres. ACP-EU Jt Parl. Ass. 2003–04; Patron, Machu Picchu; Large Ribbon, Hon. Order of the Yellow Star, Officer, Hon. Order of the Yellow Star, Grand Officer, Hon. Order of the Yellow Star, Officer, Hon. Order of Oranje Nassau, Award as Guest of Honour, Parwasie Bharatya Divas. *Address:* Commissaris Roblesweg 3, Paramaribo, Suriname (home). *Telephone:* 550540 (home). *Fax:* 455201 (home). *E-mail:* ramsardjoe@gmail.com (home). *Website:* ramdiensardjoe.com (office).

ŠAREC, Marjan; Slovenian politician and fmr broadcaster; *Prime Minister;* b. 2 Dec. 1977, Ljubljana, fmr Yugoslavia; m. Barbara Iskra Šarec 2005; two c.; ed Acad. of Theatre, Radio, Film and Television, Ljubljana; fmr journalist, political commentator and editor; worked as comedian and political satirist on Radiotelevizija Slovenija (RTV Slo, nat. broadcaster), with appearances on radio show Radio Ga-Ga and TV show Hri-bar; Mayor of Kamnik 2010–18; fmr mem. Pozitivna Slovenija (PS, Positive Slovenia), Chair. PS Kamnik Municipal Cttee; Founder and Pres. Lista Marjana Šarca (List of Marjan Šarec) 2014–; cand. in presidential election 2017; Prime Minister 2018–. *Address:* Office of the Prime Minister, 1000 Ljubljana, Gregorčičeva 20–25, Slovenia (office). *Telephone:* (1) 4781000 (office). *Fax:* (1) 4781721 (office). *E-mail:* gp.kpv@gov.si (office). *Website:* www.kpv.gov.si (office); www.sarec.si (office).

SAREVA, Jarmo, MA, MSc; Finnish UN official and fmr diplomatist; b. 1959; m.; two d.; ed Univ. of Turku, Johns Hopkins Univ. School of Advanced Int. Studies,

USA; served several years with Ministry of Foreign Affairs including as Dir of Disarmament, Arms Control and Non-proliferation, later First Sec., Embassy in Washington, DC, Counselor, Mission to CSCE, Deputy Chief of Mission, Embassy in Moscow 1996–98, Minister Counsellor, Perm. Mission to UN, New York 1998–2000; Chef de Cabinet, Office of the Pres., 55th session of UN Gen. Ass. 2000–01; Special Asst to Exec. Chair., UN Monitoring, Verification and Inspection Comm. 2001–02; Amb. and Deputy Perm. Rep. to UN, New York –2006; Chief of Disarmament and Peace Affairs Br., Dept for Gen. Ass. and Conf. Management 2006–09, also Sec., First Cttee (Disarmament and Int. Security) of UN Gen. Ass. 2006–09, Deputy Sec.-Gen., Conf. on Disarmament, UN Office for Disarmament Affairs 2009–14, Dir, UN Inst. for Disarmament Research 2015–18.

SARFATI, Alain; French architect and town planner; b. 23 March 1937, Meknès, Morocco; s. of Maurice Sarfati and Sarah Levy de Valencia; two d.; ed Lycée Poeymirau, Meknès, Lycée Laknal, Sceaux, Ecole des Beaux Arts, Paris and Inst. d'Urbanisme, Univ. de Paris; town planner, Inst. d'Urbanisme, Paris region 1966; Founder of review A.M.C. and Atelier de Recherche et d'Etudes d'Amènagement (AREA) (now Sarea Alain Sarfati Architecture) 1967, currently Head; Prof. of Architecture, Nancy 1969; Prof. and Head of Dept, Ecole des Beaux Arts, Paris-Conflans 1979; architectural adviser, Ministry of Public Works, Urban Devt, Housing and Transport 1985–; Vice-Pres. of Construction Planning, Ministry of Public Works, Housing, Transport and the Sea 1988–; mem. Consultative Cttee, Centre Scientifique et Technique du Bâtiment 1990–; Vice-Pres. Ordre Nat. des Architectes 1992–96; work includes housing, schools, hosps, leisure centres and Centre des Archives du Monde du Travail, Roubaix 1993; also designed French Embassy in China 2011; Chevalier, Ordre du Mérite, Légion d'Honneur, Officier, Ordre des Arts et Lettres; winner, Palmarès nat. de l'habitat, Institut de France. *Leisure interests:* opera, cinema, art, golf, skiing. *Address:* Atelier de Recherche et d'Etudes d'Amènagement, 43 rue Maurice Ripoche, 75014 Paris (office); 79 rue du Cherche-Midi, 75006 Paris, France (home). *Telephone:* 1-58-14-24-00 (office). *Fax:* 1-58-14-24-13 (office). *E-mail:* sarea@sarea.fr (office). *Website:* www.sarea.fr (office).

SARGENT, Ronald (Ron) L., BA, MBA; American retail executive; *Chairman and CEO, Staples Inc.;* b. 1956; ed Harvard Univ., Harvard Business School; began retail career with The Kroger Co., man. positions in operations, human resources, strategy, sales and marketing –1989; Regional Vice-Pres. of Operations, Staples Inc. 1989–91, Head of Staples Direct 1991, Vice-Pres. Staples 1991–94, Pres. Staples Contract & Commercial 1997, Pres. N American Div. 1997–98, Pres. and COO Staples Inc. 1998–2002, Pres. and CEO 2002–05, Chair. and CEO 2005–16; fmr mem. Bd of Dirs Literacy Volunteers of America; mem. Bd of Dirs The Kroger Co., Mattel, Inc., Yankee Candle Co., Wells Fargo 2017–, Bd of Advisers Boston Coll. Carroll School of Man.

SARGENT, Thomas (Tom) John, BA, PhD; American economist and academic; *William R. Berkley Professor of Economics, New York University;* b. 19 July 1943, Pasadena, Calif.; ed Univ. of California, Berkeley, Harvard Univ.; Research Assoc., Carnegie Inst. of Tech. 1967–68; First Lt and Capt., US Army 1968–69, served as Staff mem. and Acting Dir, Econs Div., Office of Asst Sec. of Defense (Systems Analysis) 1968–69; Assoc. Prof. of Econs, Univ. of Pennsylvania 1970–71; Assoc. Prof. of Econs, Univ. of Minnesota 1971–75, Prof. of Econs 1975–87; Research Assoc., Nat. Bureau of Econ. Research 1970–73, 1979–; mem. Brookings Panel on Econ. Activity 1973; Ford Foundation Visiting Research Prof. of Econs, Univ. of Chicago 1976–77, David Rockefeller Prof. of Econs 1991–98; Advisor, Fed. Reserve Bank of Minneapolis 1971–87; Visiting Prof. of Econs, Harvard Univ. and Research Assoc., Nat. Bureau of Econ. Research 1981–82; Visiting Scholar, Hoover Inst., Stanford Univ., Calif. 1985–87, Sr Fellow, Hoover Inst. 1987–, Donald Lucas Prof. of Econs, Stanford Univ. 1998–2002, Prof. Emer. 2002–; first William R. Berkley Prof. of Econs and Business, New York Univ. 2002–; mem. American Econ. Asscn (mem. Exec. Cttee 1986–88, Vice-Pres. 2000–01, Pres.-elect 2006, Pres. 2007), Econometric Soc. (mem. Council 1987–92, 1995–99, Second Vice-Pres. 2003, First Vice-Pres. 2004, Pres. 2005); Pres. Soc. for Econ. Dynamics and Control 1989–92; Fellow, Econometric Soc. 1976, NAS 1983, American Acad. of Arts and Sciences 1983; Corresp. Fellow, British Acad. 2011; Dr hc (Stockholm School of Econs) 2003; Hon. DEcon (European Univ. Inst.) 2008; Univ. Medallist as Most Distinguished Scholar in Class of 1964, Univ. of California, Berkeley, Mary Elizabeth Morgan Prize for Excellence in Econs, Univ. of Chicago 1979, Erwin Plein Nemmers Prize in Econs, Northwestern Univ. 1996–97, NAS Award for Scientific Reviewing 2011, CME Group-MSRI Prize in Innovative Quantitative Applications 2011, Nobel Prize in Econs 2011. *Publications:* Macroeconomic Theory 1979 (second edn 1987), Rational Expectations and Econometric Practice (co-ed. with Robert E. Lucas, Jr) 1981, Energy, Foresight and Strategy (ed.) 1985, Dynamic Macroeconomic Theory 1987, Exercises in Dynamic Macroeconomic Theory (with Rodolfo Manuelli) 1987, Rational Expectations Econometrics (with Lars Hansen) 1991, Rational Expectations and Inflation (reprinted articles, second edn) 1992, Bounded Rationality in Macroeconomics 1993, The Conquest of American Inflation 1999, The Big Problem of Small Change (with François Velde) 2002, Recursive Macroeconomic Theory (second edn, with Lars Ljungqvist) 2004, Robustness (with Lars Peter Hansen) 2008; numerous papers in professional journals. *Address:* Department of Economics, New York University, 19 West Fourth Street, Sixth Floor, New York, NY 10012-1119 (office); Leonard N. Stern School of Business, Kaufman Management Center, 44 West Fourth Street 7-75, New York, NY 10012 (office); 434 Galvez Mall, Stanford University, Stanford, CA 94305-6010, USA (office). *Telephone:* (212) 998-8900 (New York) (office); (650) 723-0965 (Stanford) (office). *Fax:* (212) 998-4186 (New York) (office). *E-mail:* thomas .sargent@nyu.edu (office); tsargent@stern.nyu.edu (office). *Website:* econ.as.nyu .edu (office); files.nyu.edu/ts43/public (office); www.hoover.org (office); www.stern .nyu.edu (office).

SARGSYAN, Aram; Armenian politician; b. 2 Jan. 1961, Ararat; m.; three c.; ed Yerevan School of Arts, Yerevan Polytechnical Inst.; army service 1981–83; various positions with Araratstroytrust 1989–93; Asst Dir-Gen., then Deputy Dir-Gen. Araratcement 1993–98, Exec. Dir 1998–99; mem. Republican Party of Armenia, Yerkrapah Union of Volunteers; Prime Minister of Armenia 1999–2000; in pvt. business; mem. Hanrapetutyun Kusaktsutyun (Republic Party), fmr Chair. *Address:* Hanrapetutyun Kusaktsutyun (Republic Party), 0002 Yerevan, Mashtotsi Avenue 37/30, Armenia (office). *Telephone:* (10) 53-86-34 (office). *E-mail:* republic@arminco.com (office).

SARGSYAN, Armen, CandPhys-MathSc; Armenian physicist, academic, diplomatist and head of state; *President;* b. 23 June 1953, Yerevan, Armenian SSR, USSR; m.; two s.; ed Yerevan State Univ.; Prof. of Physics, Yerevan State Univ., Founder Dept of Computer Modelling of Complex Systems at Univ.'s Dept of Theoretical Physics 1976–84; Visiting Research Fellow, Univ. of Cambridge, UK 1984–85; Lecturer, Yerevan State Univ. 1985–90; Prof., Inst. of Math., Univ. of London 1989–91; apptd. Chargé d'affaires a.i., then Amb. to UK 1991–95, 1998–99, 2013–18; Amb. and Perm. Rep. to EU (also accred to Belgium, the Netherlands, Luxembourg and Holy See (Vatican City)) 1991–99, Head of Mission to the EU 1995–96; Prime Minister of Armenia 1996–97; Special Advisor to Pres. of EBRD and Gov. of EBRD 1993–2000; Founding Pres. Eurasia House International 2000; Founder and Dir Eurasia Centre, Univ. of Cambridge's Judge Business School 2001–11; Pres. of Armenia 2018–; Initiator of Eurasian Media Forum (Astana) 2002; Founder High Power Annual Conf., Univ. of Cambridge 2003; Sr Advisor, British Petroleum, Alcatel, Telefonica, Bank of America Merrill Lynch and other multinational corpns 2001–13; Chair. Global Council on Energy Security (WEFForum); Vice-Chair. East West Inst. (EWI); Comm. mem. Euro-Atlantic Security Initiative (Chair. of Energy Security); Founding Pres. British-Armenian All Party Parl. Group; mem. Bd Global Leadership Foundation; mem. Dean's Advisory Council, Kennedy School of Govt, Harvard Univ., Dean's Advisory Council, Harris School of Public Policy Studies, Univ. of Chicago; mem. John Smith Trust, London, Int. Econ. Alliance, Global Leadership Foundation; Hon. mem. Royal Soc. of Int. Relations and Cen. of Strategic Studies, Univ. of Oxford; Hon. Sr Research Fellow, School of Math. Sciences, Queen Mary and Westfield Coll., London; Dr hc (Nat. Acad. of Sciences of Armenia); Order of Merit for the Fatherland (1st degree) 2017; St Gregory the Great Award from His Holiness Pope John Paul II 1997, St Gregory the Illuminator Medal from His Holiness Karekin II, Catholicos Patriarch of All Armenians 2008. *Publications include:* numerous articles on politology, theoretical physics, astronomy and math. modelling. *Address:* Office of the President, 0077 Yerevan, Marshal Baghramyan poghota 26, Armenia (office). *Telephone:* (10) 58-87-12 (Chief of Staff) (office); (10) 52-53-94 (office). *Fax:* (10) 58-87-12 (Chief of Staff) (office); (10) 52-53-94 (office). *E-mail:* press@president.am (office). *Website:* www.president.am (office).

SARGSYAN, Serzh; Armenian philologist, politician and fmr head of state; b. 30 June 1954, Stepanakert, Nagornyi Karabakh Autonomous Oblast, Azerbaijan SSR, USSR; m. Rita Sargsyan 1983; two d.; ed Yerevan State Univ., Armenian SSR; served in USSR army 1972–74; metal turner, Electrical Devices Factory, Yerevan 1975–79; Komsomol Sec., Head of Propaganda section City Cttee, Stepanakert 1979–88; Head of Self-Defence Cttee, 'Repub. of Nagornyi Karabakh' 1989–93; Deputy Supreme Council (Parl.) 1990–93, Minister of Defence 1993–95, 2000–07, of Nat. Security 1995–96, 1999, of Internal Affairs and Nat. Security 1996–99; Chief of Staff to Pres. 1999–2000; Sec. Council of Nat. Security 1999–2007; mem. Hayastani Hanrapetakan Kusaktsutyun (HHK—Republican Party of Armenia) 2006–, Chair. Party Council 2006–07, Chair. HHK 2007–; Prime Minister 2007–08, 17–23 April 2018; Pres. of Armenia 2008–18; Chair. Bd of Trustees, Yerevan State Univ.; Chair. Chess Fed. of Armenia; Order of Martakan Khach (First Degree); Kt of Voske Artsiv (Golden Eagle) Order; Hero of Artsakh; Armenian Battle Cross 'Tigran Mets'; First Class of the Order of Prince Yaroslav the Wise (Ukraine) 2011; Order of the Repub. of Serbia 2013; Chevalier, Ordre nat. du Mérite 2014. *Address:* Hayastani Hanrapetakan Kusaktsutyun, 0010 Yerevan, M. Adamyan poghots 2, Armenia (office). *Telephone:* (10) 58-00-31 (office). *Fax:* (10) 50-12-59 (office). *E-mail:* hhk@hhk.am (office). *Website:* www.hhk.am (office); www .serzhsargsyan.am.

SARGSYAN, Tigran, PhD; Armenian politician, diplomatist and fmr central banker; *Chairman, Eurasian Economic Commission;* b. 29 Jan. 1960, Kirovakan (now Vanadzor), Armenian SSR; m.; two s. one d.; ed Tech. Coll. No. 14, Yerevan, Inst. of Nat. Economy, Planning and Economy Dept, Yerevan, Voznesenskii Financial and Econ. Inst., Leningrad (now St Petersburg), Russian SFSR, Int. Inst. of Law, Washington, DC, USA; Chief of Dept for Foreign Econ. Relations, Scientific Research Inst. of Econ. Planning 1987–90; Chair. Republican Council of Young Specialists and Scientists 1988–93; mem. Supreme Council of the Repub. of Armenia and Chair. of Standing Comm. for Financial, Credit and Budget Affairs 1990–95; Reader in Banking Man., Yerevan State Univ. 1993–94; Dir of Scientific Research, Inst. of Social Reforms 1995–98; Chair. Armenian Banks Asscn 1995–98; Chair. Cen. Bank of Armenia 1998–2008, Interstate Bank Council 2005–07; Dir Transition Soc. Inst. 1995–2008; Prime Minister of Armenia 2008–14 (resgnd); Amb. to USA 2014–16; Chair. Eurasian Econ. Comm., Eurasian Econ. Union 2016–; holds mil. rank of Reserve Officer; Anania Shirakatsi Medal, First Degree Medal 'For Services to Motherland' 2012; Dr hc (State Econs Univ.). *Publications include:* more than 20 scientific articles. *Address:* Eurasian Economic Commission, 3/5 Smolensky Blvd, building 1, Moscow, 119121, Russia (office). *Telephone:* (495) 669-24-00 (office). *Fax:* (495) 669-24-15 (office). *E-mail:* info@ eecommission.org (office). *Website:* www.usa.mfa.am (office); www .eurasiancommission.org.

SARGSYAN, Vigen Alexander; Armenian politician; b. 10 May 1975; m.; two d.; ed St Petersburg State Univ. of Man., USSR, Yerevan State Univ., Tufts Univ. Fletcher School of Law and Diplomacy, USA; Asst and Adviser to Chair. of Nat. Ass. (Parl.) 1995–98; Asst to Minister of Defence 2000–03; Lecturer, American Univ. of Armenia 2001–11; Asst to Pres. of Armenia 2003–09, Deputy Chief of Staff to the Pres. 2009–11, Chief of Staff 2011–16; Minister of Defence 2016–18 (resgnd); mem. Hayastani Hanrapetakan Kusaktsutyun (HHK—Republican Party of Armenia); Founding mem. Cambridge–Yerevan Twin City Asscn Council; Chevalier, Ordre Nat. du Mérite; Movses Khorenatsi Medal, Andranik Ozanyan Medal.

SARIEV, Qaxraman; Uzbekistani statistician and government official; *Chairman of the Council of Ministers of the Sovereign Republic of Qoraqalpog'iston;* b. 1 Jan. 1980, To'rtkul Dist, Kara-Kalpak ASSR (now Sovereign Repub. of Qoraqalpog'iston), Uzbek SSR, USSR; ed Tashkent State Inst. of Oriental Studies, Acad. of State and Social Construction at the Office of the Presidency; worked in Dept of Statistics of Foreign Econ. Relations, Tashkent City Statistical Dept 2004–06, Deputy Head, then Head of Dept 2007–09; Economist in Dept of Foreign Econ.

Relations and Interstate Relations, State Statistics Cttee 2006–07, Acting Head of Dept, then Head of Dept, of Information Preparation of Domestic Trade Statistics 2009–10, Deputy Head, then Head, Statistical Dept of Foreign Econ. Activity 2010–11, Head of Dept of Summary Statistical Works 2012–13, Head of Dept of Collective Reference Work 2013–14; Minister of Economy of Sovereign Repub. of Qoraqalpog'iston 2014–16; currently Chair. Council of Ministers of Sovereign Repub. of Qoraqalpog'iston. *Address:* Office of the Chairman, Council of Ministers of the Sovereign Republic of Qoraqalpog'iston, 230100 Qoraqalpog'iston, Nukus, G'arezsizlik ko'ch. 50, Uzbekistan (office). *Telephone:* (361) 222-15-68 (office); (361) 222-00-14 (office). *Fax:* (361) 222-26-46 (office). *E-mail:* info@sovminrk.gov.uz (office). *Website:* sovminrk.gov.uz (office).

SARIN, Arun, BTech, MS, MBA; American/Indian telecommunications industry executive; b. 21 Oct. 1954, Pachmarhi, MP; s. of Krishan Sarin and Ramilla Sarin; m. Rummi Anand; two c.; ed Indian Inst. of Tech., Kharagpur, Univ. of California, Berkeley; several corp. positions, including Chief Strategy Officer, Pacific Telesis Group 1984–93; Sr Vice-Pres. of Corp. Strategy and Devt, AirTouch Communications (upon demerger from Pacific Telesis), Pres. and CEO AirTouch Int., Pres. AirTouch Communications, CEO USA and Asia Pacific region 1993–2000 (upon acquisition of AirTouch by Vodafone Group Plc); CEO InfoSpace, Inc. 2000; CEO Accel-KKR Telecom 2001–03; Group CEO Vodafone Group plc 2003–08; mem. Bd of Dirs The Gap, Inc. 1999–2003, Charles Schwab Corpn –2009, Court of the Bank of England 2005–09, Cisco Systems 2009–, Safeway Inc. 2009–15, Aricent Inc. 2010–, Accenture 2015–, Blackhawk Networks 2009–, Ola 2015–, Pine Labs 2016–; fmr Sr Advisor, Kohlberg Kravis Roberts & Co.; Hon. KBE 2010; B.C. Roy Gold Medal 1975, Haas School Business Leader of Year 2000, Univ. of California Trust (UK) Award 2003. *Leisure interests:* golf, travel.

SARIYEV, Temir, BA; Kyrgyzstani business executive and politician; b. 17 June 1963, Tosh Bulak, Sokuluk Dist, Frunze (now Chui) Oblast, Kyrgyz SSR, USSR; m.; two c.; ed Kyrgyz State Nat. Univ.; began career with freight forwarder Alamedin fur factory 1983, becoming Sr Economist 1987; Instructor with Komsomol (Soviet youth org.), later Head, Youth Work Dept 1987–89; Party work, becoming Deputy Chair., Alamedin Exec. Cttee 1989–91; Founder and Pres. Kyrgyzstan Commodity and Raw Materials Exchange 1991–95; CEO Totoni financial and industrial firms 1995; mem. Jogorku Kenesh (Supreme Council, Parl.) 2000–07, mem. Budget and Finance Cttee; mem. Constitutional Council 2005; acting Deputy Chair. Provisional Govt 2010 (resgnd); Minister of Finance 2010 (resgnd), of Econs and Anti-monopoly Policy 2011–15; Prime Minister of Kyrgyzstan 2015–16; Co-Chair. For Reforms! Movement 2007; Co-Chair. Ak Shumkar Union of Democratic Forces Party 2007; Chair. White Falcon Political Party (Ak Shumkar) 2008–; Ind.; Order of Manas (Third Degree). *Address:* c/o Office of the Government, 7200003 Bishkek, Dom Pravitelstva, Kyrgyzstan. *E-mail:* ps@mail.gov.kg.

SARKAR, Manik, BCom; Indian politician; b. 22 Jan. 1949, Radhakishorepur; m. Panchali Bhattacharya; ed Maharaja Bir Bakram Coll., Calcutta Univ.; mem. Communist Party of India—Marxist 1968–, mem. State Cttee 1972, State Secr. 1978, mem. Central Cttee 1985, State Sec. 1993, State Left Front Convenor, mem. Politburo 1998; mem. Tripura Legis. Ass. 1980–, also Leader of Opposition; Chief Minister of Tripura 1998–2018. *Website:* www.tripuraassembly.nic.in.

ŠARKINAS, Reinoldijus; Lithuanian economist and fmr central banker; b. 16 July 1946, Toliūnų Village, Ukmergės Dist; m.; two d.; ed Vilnius Univ.; Chief Engineer, Spindulys factory and Head, Div. of Labour and Earnings, Lithuanian Chemicals Co. 1968–72; Deputy Head, Dept of Planning and Finance, Head, Financial Accounting Dept, Ministry of Educ. 1972–80; Finance Adviser, Ministry of Educ., Repub. of Cuba 1980–82; Deputy Head, Head of Culture and Health Care Financing Dept, Dir Budget Dept, Ministry of Finance 1983–90; Deputy Minister and Sec., Ministry of Finance 1991–95, Minister of Finance 1995–96; mem. Bd Bank of Lithuania 1992–95, Chair. Bd of Govs 1996–2011; Commdr's Cross, Order of Lithuanian Grand Duke Gediminas 2003.

SARKISOV, Ashot Arakelovich; Russian nuclear energy specialist; *Adviser, Nuclear Safety Institute, Russian Academy of Sciences;* b. 30 Jan. 1924, Tashkent, USSR; s. of Arakel A. Sarkisov and Evgeniya B. Grigoryan; m. Nelli G. Sarkisov 1951; two s.; ed F. Dzerzhinsky Higher Marine Eng School, Leningrad Univ.; worked as engineer Baltic fleet; Chair. Higher Marine School, Sevastopol; Deputy Dir Naval Acad.; Chair. Scientific-Tech. Council of the Navy; Head of Dept, Inst. for Nuclear Safety; currently Chair. Expert Council on Naval and Shipbuilding Problems of Higher Certification Comm., Int. Russian-American Scientific-Technical Program of International Science and Technology Center; Chair. Panel of Experts, Int. Scientific and Engineering Program on Radioactive Waste; apptd Academician, Russian Acad. of Sciences (RAS) 1994, mem. and Adviser, Nuclear Safety Inst. 1990–, currently also Deputy Chair Scientific Council on Atomic Energy; research in theory of dynamic processes and automatic protection of nuclear plants, problems of safety and security in nuclear energy; currently Chief-Ed. Arctic: Economics & Ecology (professional magazine); ten Orders of the USSR and of Russia; more than 30 state medals, including Aleksandrov Gold Medal, Russian Acad. of Sciences 2007, Global Energy Prize (jtly) 2014. *Publications include:* Dynamics of Nuclear Power Plants of Submarines 1964, Nuclear Propulsion Power Plants 1968, Dynamic Regimes in the Operation of Nuclear Propulsion Power Plants 1971, Physics of Transitional Processes in Nuclear Reactors 1983, Nuclear Propulsion Power Plants and Steam Generators 1985, Thermo-Electric Generators with Nuclear Sources of Heat 1987, Physical Principles of Nuclear Steam-Productive Plants 1989, Nuclear Submarine Decommissioning and Related Problems 1996, Analysis of Risks Associated with Nuclear Submarine Decommissioning, Dismantling and Disposal 1999, Remaining Issues in the Decommissioning of Nuclear Powered Vessels 2003, Overcoming Impediments to US–Russian Cooperation on Nuclear Nonproliferation 2004, Status, Problems and Priorities of NS Complex Decommissioning in the North-West Russia (Basic Provisions of Strategic Master Plan Initial Phase) 2004, Strategic Approaches in Solving Decommissioning Problems of Retired Russian Nuclear Fleet in the Northwest Region: Executive Summary of Strategic Master Plan, Phase 1 2004, Strengthening US–Russian Cooperation on Nuclear Nonproliferation Recommendations for Action 2005, Scientific and Technical Issues in the Management of Spent Nuclear Fuel of Decommissioned Nuclear Submarines 2006, Atomic Legacy of the Cold War at the Artic Seabed. Radioecological Consequences

and Technical and Economic Problems of Radiation Remediation at the Arctic Seas 2006, Strategic Master Plan for Decommissioning of the Retired Russian Nuclear Fleet and Environmental Rehabilitation of Its Supporting Infrastructure in Northwest Russia. Priority Project Programme 2006, Strategic Master Plan for Decommissioning of the Retired Russian Nuclear Fleet and Environmental Rehabilitation of Its Supporting Infrastructure in Northwest Russia. Executive Summary 2007, The Nuclear Legacy of the "Cold War" at the Bottom of the Arctic 2008, Expected Radiation and Radioecological Consequences from Floating NPPs' Use 2008, The Salient Need to Develop New Approaches to Address Nuclear Weapons Proliferation Issues, Future of the Nuclear Security Environment in 2015 2009, Nuclear and Radiation Safety Challenges at the Disposal Sites of the Nuclear Fleet in the Far East of Russia 2010,. International Cooperation in Cold War Legacy Elimination in the Arctic Region of Russia 2011, Low-power NPPs - a New Development Trend of Nuclear Energy 2011, Risk Assessment and Safeguard of Industry and Energy Facilities. Integrative approach 2011. *Leisure interests:* tennis, history of the navy. *Address:* Nuclear Safety Institute, Russian Academy of Sciences, 115191 Moscow, B. Tulskaya str. 52, Russia (office). *Telephone:* (495) 952-24-21 (office), (495) 955-22-80 (office). *Fax:* (495) 958-00-40 (office). *E-mail:* sarkisov@ibrae.ac.ru (office). *Website:* www.ibrae.ac.ru (office).

SARKÖZY DE NAGY BOCSA, Nicolas Paul Stéphane, LLM; French politician, barrister, civil servant and fmr head of state; *President, Union pour un Mouvement Populaire (UMP);* b. 28 Jan. 1955, Paris; s. of Paul Sarközy de Nagy Bocsa and Andrée Mallah; m. 1st Marie-Dominique Culioli 1982 (divorced 1996); two s.; m. 2nd Cecilia Ciganer-Albeniz 1996 (divorced 2007); one s.; m. 3rd Carla Bruni 2008; one d.; ed Inst. of Political Studies, Paris, Paris Univ.; barrister, Paris 1981–87; Assoc., Leibovici Claude Sarközy 1987; mem. Neuilly-sur-Seine Municipal Couincil 1977–83, Mayor of Neuilly-sur-Seine 1983–2002; Vice-Chair. Hauts-de-Seine Gen. Council, responsible for Educ. and Culture 1986–88, Chair. 2004; RPR Deputy to Nat. Ass. from Hauts-de-Seine 1988–2002; Govt Spokesman 1993–95; Minister of the Budget 1993–95, of Communications 1994–95, of the Interior, Internal Security and Local Freedoms 2002–04, of the Economy, Finance and Industry 2004, of the Interior and Town and Country Planning 2005–07 (resgnd); Pres. of France 2007–12, Co-Prince of Andorra 2007–12; Nat. Sec. RPR responsible for Youth and Training 1988, for Activities, Youth and Training 1989, Deputy Gen. Sec. responsible for local brs 1992–93, mem. Political Bureau 1993, Gen. Sec. RPR 1998, Interim Pres. April–Oct. 1999, Pres. RPR Regional Cttee of Hauts-de-Seine 2000; Leader RPR-DL List, European Elections 1999; Pres. Union pour un Mouvement Populaire—UMD (Les Républicains from 2015) 2004–07, 2014–16; charged with corruption and accepting illegal campaign finance from Libyan govt March 2018–; Chevalier, Légion d'honneur 2004, Grand'Croix, Légion d'honneur 2007, Grand'Croix, Ordre nat. du Mérite 2007, Stara Planina (Bulgaria) 2007, Commdr, Ordre de Léopold (Belgium), Hon. GCB (UK) 2008, Commdr, Order of Prince Yaroslav the Wise (Ukraine) 2010, Kt, Order of Golden Fleece (Spain) 2011. *Publications include:* Georges Mandel, moine de la politique 1994, Au bout de la passion, l'équilibre (co-author) 1995, Libre 2001, La République, les Religions, l'Espérance 2004, Témoignage 2006. *Leisure interests:* tennis, cycling.

SARMADI, Morteza, BSc, MA; Iranian politician and diplomatist; b. July 1954, Tehran; m. Fatima Hosseini 1982; four d.; ed Sharif Univ., Tehran; joined Ministry of Foreign Affairs 1981, Dir-Gen. of Press and Information 1982–89, Deputy Foreign Minister for Communication 1989–97, Deputy Foreign Minister for Europe and America 1997, Amb. to UK 2000–05, Deputy Foreign Minister for Euro-American Affairs 2005; Sr Del. Iran-Iraq peace talks; Exec. Dir, Indian Ocean Rim Asscn for Regional Co-operation (IOR-ARC) –2012; Trustee, Islamic Thought Foundation, Islamic Repub. News Agency, Islamic High Council of Propagation Policy, Inst. for Political and Int. Studies. *Publications:* numerous political articles. *Leisure interests:* reading, writing, watching TV, spending time with family. *Address:* Ministry of Foreign Affairs, Imam Khomeini Square, Tehran, Iran (office). *Telephone:* (21) 61151 (office). *Fax:* (21) 66743149 (office). *E-mail:* matbuat@mfa.gov.ir (office). *Website:* www.mfa.gov.ir (office).

SARMI, Massimo, BEng; Italian postal service executive; *CEO, Milano Serravalle — Milano Tangenziali;* b. 4 Aug. 1948, Malcesine; ed Univ. of Rome; began career in Italian Air Force; then joined SIP as Head Buyer and Head of Operations –1995; Gen. Man. TIM 1995–98, Telecom India 1998–2001; CEO Siemens, Italy 2001–02; CEO and Man. Dir Poste Italiane SpA 2002–14; CEO Milano Serravalle — Milano Tangenziali 2014–; Prof., Univ. 'La Sapienza' and Univ. 'Luiss', Rome; mem. Admin. Bd Univ. Bocconi, Milan 2006–; Bd mem. of several Italian and int. cos including Int. Post Corpn; fmr Vice-Pres. Federcomin; fmr mem. Exec. of Confindustria; Cavaliere del Lavoro 2009; American Chamber of Commerce Business and Culture Award 2006, Business and Culture Award 2006, GEI Award 2007. *Address:* Milano Serravalle Milano Tangenziali SpA, via del Bosco Rinnovato 4/a Palazzo U9, Assago 20090, Italy (office). *Telephone:* (02) 575941 (office). *Fax:* (02) 57594334 (office). *E-mail:* info@serravalle.it (office). *Website:* www.serravalle.it (office).

SARNA, Navtej, BCom, LLB; Indian journalist, writer and diplomatist; *Ambassador to USA;* b. 2 Dec. 1957; m. Dr Avina Sarna; one s. one d.; ed Univ. of Delhi; joined Foreign Service 1980, IFS Probationer, Ministry of External Affairs 1980–82, Third Sec., Embassy in Moscow 1982–83, Officer on Special Duty (PR), Ministry of External Affairs 1983–85, Second, then First Sec., Embassy in Warsaw 1985–89, First Sec., Embassy in Thimphu, Bhutan 1989–92, Deputy Chief of Protocol, Ministry of External Affairs 1992–93, Deputy Sec. (UN) 1993–94, Counsellor, Perm. Mission to UN, Geneva 1994–97, Counsellor, Embassy in Tehran 1997–98, Minister/Counsellor, Embassy in Washington, DC 1998–2002, Official Spokesperson, Ministry of External Affairs 2002–08, Amb. to Israel 2008–12, Additional Sec. (Int. Orgs and Political), Ministry of External Affairs 2012–13, Special Sec. (Int. Orgs and Political) 2013–14, Sec. (West) 2014–16, High Commr to UK Jan.–Oct. 2016, Amb. to USA 2016–. *Publications include:* Folk Tales of Poland 1991, The Book of Nanak 2003, We Weren't Lovers Like That (novel) 2003, The Exile (novel) 2008, Zafarnama (trans.) 2011, Winter Evenings – Short Stories 2012, Savage Harvest – Short Stories (trans.) 2013, Indians at Herod's Gate: A Jerusalem Tale 2014, Second Thoughts: On Books, Authors and the Writerly Life 2015; regular contrib. to Times Literary Supplement (UK) and several Indian journals. *Address:* Embassy of India, 2107 Massachusetts Avenue, NW, Washington, DC 20008, USA (office). *Telephone:* (202) 939-7000 (office). *Fax:*

(202) 265-4351 (office). *E-mail:* indembwash@indiagov.org (office). *Website:* www.indianembassy.org (office).

SARNAK, Peter Clive, BSc, BSc, PhD, FRS; South African/American mathematician and academic; *Eugene Higgins Professor of Mathematics, Princeton University;* b. 18 Dec. 1953, Johannesburg, South Africa; ed Univ. of the Witwatersrand, South Africa, Stanford Univ., USA; Asst Prof., Courant Inst., New York Univ. 1980–83, Assoc. Prof. 1983, Prof. 2001–05; Assoc. Prof., Stanford Univ. 1984–87, Prof. 1987–91; Prof., Princeton Univ. 1991–, H. Fine Prof. 1995–96, Chair. Dept of Math. 1996–99, Eugene Higgins Prof. of Math. 2002–; mem. School of Math., Inst. for Advanced Study, Princeton, NJ 1999–2002, 2005–07, Prof. 2007–; mem. Bd of Adjudicators and Selection Cttee for the Math. Award, under auspices of the Shaw Prize; Ed. Annals of Mathematics (mem. Editorial Bd 1996–2012); mem. Editorial Bd, Communications in Mathematical Physics –2008, Forum Mathematics –2011, Cambridge University Press, Duke Mathematics Journal, GAFA (Geometric & Functional Analysis), Compositio Mathematics, Journal of Experimental Mathematics, IMRN, Colloquium Series, American Math. Soc.; mem. American Acad. of Arts and Sciences 1991, NAS 2002, American Philosophical Soc. 2008; Foreign mem. Academia Europea 2013; Trustee, Math. Sciences Research Inst.; Dr hc (Hebrew Univ. of Jerusalem) 2010, (Shandong Univ., China) 2014; Hebert LeMay Prize, Univ. of the Witwatersrand 1974, William Cullen Medal, Univ. of the Witwatersrand 1974, Unisco Chemical Co. Gold Medal, Univ. of the Witwatersrand 1975, Sloan Fellow 1983–85, Presidential Young Investigator 1985–90, George Pólya Prize, Soc. of Industrial and Applied Math. (co-recipient) 1998, Ostrowski Prize (co-recipient) 2001, Levi L. Conant Prize, American Math. Soc. (co-recipient) 2003, Aisenstadt Chair, CRM, Canada 2004, Rothchild Chair, Isaac Newton Inst., Cambridge, UK 2004, Frank Nelson Cole Prize, American Math. Soc. 2005, Lester Ford Prize MAA 2012, Wolf Prize in Math. 2014. *Publications include:* Some Applications of Modular Forms 1990; (co-ed.): Extremal Riemann Surfaces 1997, Random Matrices, Frobenius Eigenvalues and Monodromy 1998, Selected Works of Ilya Piatetski-Shapiro (Collected Works) 2000, Elementary Number Theory, Group Theory and Ramanujan Graphs 2003, Selected Papers Vol. I-Peter Lax 2005, Automorphic Forms and Applications 2007; numerous papers in professional journals. *Address:* Department of Mathematics, 1101 Fine Hall, Princeton University, Washington Road, Princeton, NJ 08544-1000 (office); Simonyi Hall 113, School of Mathematics, Institute for Advanced Study, Einstein Drive, Princeton, NJ 08540, USA (office). *Telephone:* (609) 258-4229 (Univ.) (office); (609) 734-8117 (IAS) (office). *Fax:* (609) 258-1367 (Univ.) (office); (609) 951-4459 (IAS) (office). *E-mail:* sarnak@math.princeton.edu (office); sarnak@math.ias.edu (office). *Website:* www.math.princeton.edu/directory/peter-sarnak (office); www.math.ias.edu/people/faculty/sarnak (office).

SARNEY, José; Brazilian politician and author; b. 24 April 1930, Pinheiro, Maranhão; s. of Sarney de Araújo Costa and Kyola Ferreira de Araújo Costa; m. Marli Macieira Sarney; two s. one d.; Asst to Maranhão State Gov. 1950; Maranhão State Rep. 1956, re-elected 1958, 1962; elected Gov. of Maranhão 1965; State Senator (Arena Party, now Partido Democrático Social—PDS) 1970; Nat. Pres. Arena 1970; fmr Chair. PDS; mem. Partido Frente Liberal 1984, PMDD; Acting Pres. of Brazil March–April 1985, Pres. 1985–90; Senator 1971–85, 1991–2015, Pres. of Fed. Senate 2003–05, 2009–13; fmr Pres. Nat. Congress; mem. Academia Brasileira de Letras (Brazilian Acad. of Letters); Brazilian Union of Writers Aluízio de Azevedo Award 2003. *Publications include:* A canção inicial 1952, Norte das Águas (Tales of Rain and Sunlight) 1970, Os maribondos de fogo 1978, O Dono do Mar (The Master of the Sea) 1995, Saraminda 2003, Saudades Mortas 2004, Tempo de Pacotilha 2004. *Leisure interests:* literature, painting. *Website:* www.josesarney.org.

SAROIAN, Konstantin R., PhD; Armenian economist and business executive; *Secretary-General, Federation of Euro-Asian Stock Exchanges;* b. 14 June 1978; m. Viktorya Avetisyan; ed Yerevan State Univ.; started career 1999, heading marketing and strategic planning depts in several Armenian banks, as well as in clearing and settlement dept of Central Depository of Armenia; exec. positions with Armswissbank 2004–11, including Head of Internal Audit –2006, mem. Bd of Man. 2006–11, man. several depts including marketing, PR, human resources, strategic planning and business devt 2006–11; CEO NASDAQ OMX Armenia (stock exchange) 2011–17; Sec.-Gen. Fed. of Euro-Asian Stock Exchanges (FEAS) 2017–; Lecturer, French Univ. of Armenia, Yerevan. *Address:* Federation of Euro-Asian Stock Exchanges, 0010 Yerevan, 5b Mher Mkrtchyan, Armenia (office). *Telephone:* (44) 737-727 (office). *E-mail:* secretariat@feas.org (office). *Website:* www.feas.org (office).

SAROTA, Angelina, DrIur; Polish civil servant and business executive; ed Faculty of Law and Admin of Jagiellonian Univ., Nat. School of Public Admin, Leon Koźmiński Admin; employed in Court Representation Dept and Restructuring and Public Help Dept, Ministry of State Treasury 2001–03; adviser to Minister of Science and Information Tech. 2003, Deputy Dir Dept of Strategy and Science Devt 2003–05, acted as Law Dir 2005; Dir of Law Dept, Chancellery of Prime Minister 2005–08; Sec. Supervisory Bd, PKN Orlen 2008–13, Chair. 2013–18; mem. Man. Bd Coll. of Europe, Warsaw 2013–; fmr Vice-Chair. Supervisory Bd, Warsaw Tech. Park; fmr mem. Supervisory Bd, Cerg Ltd, Gliwice, Chemar Ltd, Kielce.

ŠAROVIĆ, Mirko, LLB; Bosnia and Herzegovina politician; *Deputy Chairman of the Government and Minister of Foreign Trade and Economic Relations;* b. 16 Sept. 1956, Rogatica, People's Repub. of Bosnia and Herzegovina, Fed. People's Repub. of Yugoslavia; m. Stojanka Sarović; two s.; ed Faculty of Law, Sarajevo Univ.; mem. Srpska Demokratska Stranka (Serb Democratic Party); mem. Nat. Ass., Republika Srpska, Bosnia and Herzegovina 1996–98; Vice-Pres. of Republika Srpska, Bosnia and Herzegovina 1998–2000, de facto Pres. 2000–02; Mem. of the Presidency of Bosnia and Herzegovina 2002–03 (resgnd facing accusations of organizing illegal mil. trade with Iraq), barred from holding any political office 2004; Minister of Foreign Trade and Econ. Relations 2012–; Deputy Chair. of the Govt 2015–; several decorations including Serbian Order of the Repub. 2012; numerous honours, awards and prizes. *Leisure interest:* collecting old books. *Address:* Ministry of Foreign Trade and Economic Relations, 71000 Sarajevo, Musala 9 (office); 71123 Istočno Sarajevo, Lukavica b.b., Bosnia and Herzegovina (home). *Telephone:* (33) 220093 (office). *Fax:* (33) 220091 (office); (51) 312805 (home). *E-mail:* nfo@mvteo.gov.ba (office). *Website:* www.mvteo.gov.ba (office).

SARR, HE Cardinal Théodore-Adrien; Senegalese ecclesiastic; *Archbishop Emeritus of Dakar;* b. 28 Nov. 1936, Fadiouth; ordained priest of Dakar 1964; Bishop of Kaolack 1974–2000; Archbishop of Dakar 2000–14, Archbishop Emer. 2014–; cr. Cardinal (Cardinal-Priest of Santa Lucia a Piazza d'Armi) 2007; participated in Papal Conclave 2013; first Vice-Pres. Symposium of Episcopal Confs of Africa and Madagascar; also served as Pres. Bishops' Conf. of Senegal, Mauritania, Cabo Verde and Guinea-Bissau. *Address:* Archeveche, BP 1908, Avenue Jean XXIII, Dakar, Senegal (office). *Telephone:* 8890600 (office). *Fax:* 8234875 (office).

SARRAF, Yaacoub Riyad, BEng, BArch; Lebanese/French politician; b. 1961, Meniara, Akkar; s. of Riyad Sarraf; m. Hala Merhej; two c.; ed American Univ. of Beirut; fmr Asst Dir with several Greek, French, and Moroccan companies and institutions; Gov. of Beirut 1999, of Mount Lebanon 2003; Minister of the Environment 2005–08; Acting Minister of Nat. Defence (following attempt on Minister Elias Murr's life) 2005, Minister of Nat. Defence 2016–19; mem. Lebanese Order of Engineers; mem. Free Patriotic Movement, mem. FPM Political Council. *Address:* c/o Ministry of National Defence, Yarze, Beirut, Lebanon (office).

SARRAJ, Fayez al-; Libyan engineer, business executive and politician; *Prime Minister, Government of National Accord;* b. 20 Feb. 1960, Tripoli; s. of Mustafa al-Sarraj; ed Al-Fateh Univ., Tripoli; worked as engineer in project man.; mem. Gen. Nat. Congress (GNC) 2012–14; Deputy, Chamber of Reps (new legislature which replaced GNC) for Tripoli 2014–; fmr mem. Nat. Alliance Party; apptd Prime Minister-desig., Govt of Nat. Accord (recognized by UN as legitimate governing authority for Libya) 2016, took office April 2016, also Chair. Presidential Council of Libya March 2016–; Founder mem. Office of Tripoli Consulting Engineers.

SARRIS, Michalis, BSc (Econs), DEcon; Cypriot banker and government minister; b. 14 April 1946, Nicosia; ed London School of Econs, UK, Wayne State Univ., USA; joined research dept of Central Bank of Cyprus 1972; moved to Bank of Cyprus 1974; Dir World Bank 1975–2004; Minister of Finance 2005–08, Feb.–April 2013, of Defence (acting) 2007–08; apptd Dir (non-exec.) FxPro Financial Services Ltd 2010; mem. Bd of Dirs Marfin CLR Public Co. Ltd –2005, Logicom Public Ltd, Laiki Group; fmr mem. Bd of Govs European Investment Bank.

SARTORIUS, Norman H., MD, PhD; German/Croatian psychiatrist and psychologist; *President, International Association for the Improvement of Mental Health Programmes;* b. 28 Jan. 1935, Münster, Germany; s. of Prof. F. Sartorius and Prof. Dr F. Fischer-Sartorius; m. Vera Pecikozić 1963; one d.; ed Univ. of Zagreb, Univ. of London; Consultant, Dept of Psychiatry, Univ. of Zagreb 1959–64; Research Fellow, Inst. of Psychiatry, Univ. of London, UK 1964–65; WHO medical officer in psychiatric epidemiology 1967–68; Medical Officer in charge of Epidemiological and Social Psychiatry and Standardization of Psychiatric Diagnosis, Classification and Statistics, WHO 1969–73, Chief, Office of Mental Health 1974–76, Dir Div. of Mental Health 1976–93; Pres. World Psychiatric Asscn (WPA) 1993–99, Scientific Dir WPA Global Programme Against Stigma and Discrimination because of Schizophrenia 1999–2006; currently Pres. Int. Asscn for Improvement of Mental Health Programmes; Pres. AEP 1999–2001; Visiting Prof., Univ. of Zagreb, Univ. of London, St Louis Univ., Univ. of Beijing, Univ. of London; mem. Council of WPA; Corresp. mem. Royal Spanish Acad. of Medicine, Croatian Acad. of Arts and Science; Hon. Fellow, Royal Coll. of Psychiatrists (UK), Royal Australian and NZ Coll. of Psychiatrists, Amercan Coll. of Psychiatry; Distinguished Fellow, American Psychiatric Asscn; Hon. mem. Peruvian Acad. of Medicine, Croatian Medical Acad. and of numerous professional and scientific orgs; Hon. DrMed (Umeå), (Prague); Hon. DSc (Bath), (Copenhagen), (Timisoara, Romania); Rema Lapouse Medal, Prince Mahidol Prize for Medicine 2005, Harvard Prize in Psychiatric Epidemiology, Burgholzli Prize. *Publications include:* more than 400 articles, numerous books (author or ed.) on schizophrenia, transcultural psychiatry, mental health policy, scientific methodology, ethics, human rights and stigma. *Leisure interests:* chess, reading, history. *Address:* Association for the Improvement of Mental Health Programmes (AMH), 14 Chemin Colladon, 1209 Geneva, Switzerland (office). *Telephone:* (22) 7882331 (office). *Fax:* (22) 7882334 (office). *E-mail:* sartorius@normansartorius.com (office). *Website:* www.aim-mental-health.org (office).

SARTZETAKIS, Christos A., LLD; Greek lawyer and fmr head of state; b. 6 April 1929, Salonika; m. Efi Argyriou; one d.; ed Salonika Univ., Univ. of Paris (Sorbonne) Law Faculty; joined Faculty of Law, Univ. of Thessaloniki 1946; called to Bar 1954; apptd JP 1955, Judge of 1st Instance 1956; Investigating Magistrate in Lambrakis affair (which inspired Vasilis Vasilikos' novel Z, later made into film) 1963–64; postgraduate studies Paris 1965–67; mem. Société de Législation Comparée, Paris 1966–; fmr mem. Admin. Council Hellenic Humanistic Soc.; arrested and detained on unspecified charges 1969; reinstated as Appeal Judge 1974; Sr Appeal Judge, Nauplion 1981, Justice of Supreme Court 1982–85; Pres. of Greece 1985–90; mem. Société de Législation Comparée, Paris 1966–; fmr mem. Admin. Council Hellenic Humanistic Soc.; Hon. mem. High Court of Portugal, Literary Soc. of Thessalonica, Hon. Prof., Dimokrition Univ. of Thrace. *Address:* Aghias Sophias street 6, 152 36 Nea Penteli, Greece (home). *Website:* www.sartzetakis.gr.

SARUNGI, Philemon, MD, MCh; Tanzanian surgeon and politician; ed Bugema Coll., Medical Univ. of Szeged, Hungary, Univ. of Vienna, Austria, Univ. of Shanghai, China; Medical Officer, Muhimbili Hosp. 1971–72; Lecturer in Surgery, Univ. of Dar es Salaam 1972–76; Prof. and Head of Dept of Orthopaedics/Trauma, Muhimbili Medical Centre 1977–84, Dir-Gen. 1984–90; Minister for Health 1990–95; Regional Commr, Coast Region 1996–97, Kilimanjaro Region 1998–2000; mem. Parl. for Tarime Constituency 2000–, Minister for Defence and Nat. Service 2000–06; Founding Pres. Dr Mwl. J.K. Nyerere Golden Award on Science & Technology Achievements.

SARWAN, Ramnaresh Ronnie; Guyanese professional cricketer (retd); b. 23 June 1980, Wakenaam Island, Essequibo; right-handed batsman; right-arm leg-break bowler; played for West Indies (Capt. 2007–08, Vice-Capt. 2008), Glos. 2005, Guyana (domestic) 1996–2014, Kings XI Punjab 2008, Leicestershire 2012–14, Stanford Superstars, Georgetown Cricket Club; First-class debut: 1995/96; Test debut: West Indies v Pakistan, Bridgetown 18–22 May 2000; One-Day Int. (ODI) debut: England v West Indies, Nottingham 20 July 2000; T20I debut: S Africa v West Indies, Johannesburg 11 Sept. 2007. *Achievements include:* youngest West

Indian to score 5,000 runs 2008; equalled record for most centuries (13) in fourth innings 2009.

SARWAR, Mohammad; Pakistani (b. British) politician; *Governor of Punjab;* b. 18 Aug. 1952, Roda, Faisalabad; m. Perveen Sarwar; three s. one d.; ed Govt Coll., Faisalabad; moved to Scotland 1976; elected Labour councillor for Pollokshields East 1987, 1992; Co-founder Man. Dir, United Wholesale Grocers Ltd (now United Wholesale (Scotland) Ltd after division of business 2002) 1982–97; MP (Labour) for Glasgow Govan 1997–2005, for Glasgow Central 2005–10; mem. Scottish Affairs Select Cttee 2004–13 (apptd Chair. 2005); Gov. of Punjab (renounced British citizenship upon taking up post) 2013–15 (resgnd), 2018–; mem. Senate for Punjab March–Sept. 2018; mem. Pakistan Tehreek-e-Insaf (PTI) (Pakistan Movement for Justice) 2015–; Dr hc (Univ. of the West of Scotland) 2014. *Address:* Governor House, Mall Road, Lahore 54000 (office). *E-mail:* governor.sectt@punjab.gov.pk (office). *Website:* punjab.gov.in (office); www.sarwar.pk.

SASAE, Kenichiro, LLB; Japanese diplomatist (retd); b. 25 Sept. 1951; ed Hiroshima Univ., Tokyo Univ.; joined Ministry of Foreign Affairs 1974, postings overseas include Embassies in Washington, DC and London, Perm. Mission to Int. Orgs, Geneva, Deputy Dir-Gen. Asian Affairs Bureau 1999, Exec. Asst to Prime Minister for Foreign Affairs 2000, Deputy Dir-Gen. Foreign Policy Bureau 2001, Dir-Gen., Econ. Affairs Bureau 2002–05, Dir-Gen., Asian and Oceania Affairs Bureau 2005–08, Deputy Minister for Foreign Affairs 2008–10, Vice-Minister for Foreign Affairs 2010–12, Amb. to USA 2012–18. *Address:* c/o Embassy of Japan, 2520 Massachusetts Ave, NW, Washington, DC 20008-2869, USA (office).

SASAKAWA, Yohei; Japanese foundation executive; *Chairman, The Nippon Foundation;* b. 1939, Tokyo; s. of Ryoichi Sasakawa; ed Meiji Univ.; Trustee, Nippon Foundation 1981–88, Acting Pres. 1988–89, Pres. 1989–2005, Chair. 2005–; Founder and Trustee, Sasakawa Memorial Health Foundation 1974, US-Japan Foundation 1980, Scandinavia-Japan Sasakawa Foundation 1984, GB Sasakawa Foundation 1985, Sasakawa Peace Foundation 1986, Sasakawa Africa Asscn 1986, Sasakawa Young Leaders Fellowship Fund 1987, Sasakawa Pacific Island Nations Fund 1989, Sasakawa Cen. Europe Fund 1990, Foundation Franco-Japonaise Sasakawa 1990, Sasakawa Pan Asia Fund 1992; Vice-Chair. Sasakawa Japan-China Friendship Fund 1990; adviser, Tokyo Foundation, AsiaResearch Fund; WHO Global Alliance for Elimination of Leprosy (GAEL) 2001, WHO Goodwill Amb. for Leprosy Elimination 2004; Goodwill Amb. for the Human Rights of People Affected by Leprosy, Ministry of Foreign Affairs 2007; Goodwill Amb. for the Welfare of the Nat. Races in Myanmar 2012; Special Envoy of Govt of Japan for Nat. Reconciliation in Myanmar 2013; Hon. Prof., Yanbian Univ. 2000, China Medical Univ. 2003, Harbin Medical Univ. 2004, Heilongjiang Univ. 2004, Shanghai Maritime Univ. 2004; Grand Officier, Ordre du Mono (Togo) 1989, La Grande Etoile de Djibouti 1995, Order of Merit for Distinguished Service, Third Grade (Peru) 1996, Order of Friendship (Russian Fed.) 1996, Al Hussein Bin Ali Decoration for Accomplishment, First Degree (Jordan) 1998, Order of Merit in the Rank of Grand Officer (Romania) 2000, Officier, Ordre Nat. (Madagascar) 2003, Commdr, Ordre Royal du Monisaraphon (Cambodia) 2003, Commdr, Ordre Nat. du Mali 2006, Coast Guard Legion of Honour (Degree of Maginoo) 2007, Polestar Order (Mongolia) 2007, Commdr, Order of the White Rose of Finland 2010, The Patriarch's Chart of the Patriarch of Moscow and All Russia Kirill 2010, Dr Norman E. Borlaug Medallion of the World Food Prize 2010, Kt, Order of the Dannebrog (Denmark) 2010, Grand Cross, Order of the Falcon with Star (Iceland) 2010, Ordem de Timor-Leste 2010, Commdr, Order of the Defender of the Realm (Panglima Mangku Negara) Tan Sri (Malaysia) 2010, Commdr, First Class, Royal Order of the Polar Star (Sweden) 2010, Ethiopian Millenium Gold Medal 2010, Commdr, Royal Norwegian Order of Merit 2010, Commdr, Medal of Gratitude Cen. Africa 2010, Royal Order of Sahametrei Class Maha Sirivudha (Grand Cross) (Cambodia) 2011, Friendship Medal, State of Viet Nam 2013, Gold Medal of Merit (Serbia) 2013; Dr hc (Univ. of Bucharest) 2000, (Univ. of Cape Coast) 2000, (Acad. of Man., Mongolia) 2003, (World Maritime Univ.) 2004; Diploma of an Academician, Russian Acad. of Natural Sciences 2010; Hon. DH (Univ. of Malaya, Malaysia Univ.) 2012; Hon. DUniv (York, UK) 2013; Medal for Merits, Third Degree (Ukraine) 1996, Frantsiska Scarina Medal (Belarus) 1996, China Health Medal 1997, WHO Health-for-All Gold Medal 1998, Decerne la Medaille d'Honneur de Menerbes (France) 2000, Int. Leprosy Union Millennium Gandhi Award 2001, Vaclav Havel Memorial Medal 2001, Nat. Construction Medal (Cambodia) 2003, Yomiuri Int. Cooperation Prize (Japan) 2004, Int. Gandhi Award (India) 2006, Science for Society Award, Hungarian Acad. of Sciences 2009, The Rule of Law Award, Int. Bar Asscn 2014, Int. Maritime Prize 2014, Int. Gandhi Peace Prize 2018. *Publications (in English):* Those with Wisdom Fail for Wisdom 1996, Real Faces of the World Unknown to the Ministry of Foreign Affairs 1998, This Country and That Country 2004, The Day Leprosy is Eradicated from the World 2004. *Address:* The Nippon Foundation, 1-2-2 Akasaka, Minato-ku, Tokyo 107-8404, Japan (office). *Telephone:* (3) 6229-5121 (office). *Fax:* (3) 6229-5120 (office). *Website:* www.nippon-foundation.or.jp (office).

SASAKI, Hajime, MSc; Japanese computer industry executive; *Executive Adviser, NEC Corporation;* b. 6 April 1936; ed Univ. of Tokyo; joined NEC Corpn 1961, designed integrated circuits for communications applications 1961–82, Gen. Man. VLSI Devt Div. 1982–84, Gen. Man. Microcomputer Products Div. 1984–86, Vice-Pres. 1986–88, Assoc. Sr Vice-Pres. 1988–91, Exec. Vice-Pres. 1994–96, Sr Exec. Vice-Pres. 1996–99, Chair. and Rep. Dir 1999–2008, Chair. 2008–10, currently Exec. Adviser; Exec. Dir Semiconductor Industry Research Inst. Japan 1994–96; Pres. Semiconductor Leading Edge Technologies Inc. 1996–98; Chair. Communications Industry Asscn of Japan (CIAJ) 1999–2000, Japan Electronics and Information Technology Industries Asscn 2003–04, Cttee on Global Environment and Energy Policy, Japan Asscn of Corporate Execs 2003–06; apptd Chair. Nanotechnology Business Creation Initiative 2005; fmr Pres. NEC C&C Foundation, now Counselor; mem. Bd of Dirs Komatsu Ltd, Asunaro Aoki Construction Co. Ltd, Bull SA; Sheffield Fellowship, Yale Univ. 2006; IEEE Fellow 1996, IEEE Life Fellow 2001; Foreign Assoc. Nat. Acad. of Eng 2000; Fellow, Inst. of Electronics Information and Communications Engineers (IEICE) 2000; Chevalier, Légion d'honneur 2006; Science and Tech. Agency Award, Govt of Japan 1997, IEEE Third Millennium Medal 2000, IEICE Achievement Award 2001, IEEE Robert N. Noyce Medal 2001, Deming Prize for Individuals 2005. *Address:* NEC Corporation, 7-1 Shiba 5-chome, Minato-ku, Tokyo 108-8001, Japan (office). *Telephone:* (3) 3457-7711 (office). *Fax:* (3) 3798-7818 (office). *E-mail:* a-shikimori@ay.jp.nec.com (office); Lwojtecji@necusa.com (office). *Website:* www.nec.com (office).

SASAKI, Mikio, DEng; Japanese business executive; *Senior Corporate Adviser, Mitsubishi Corporation;* b. 8 Oct. 1937, Tokyo; m.; c.; ed Waseda Univ.; joined Mitsubishi Corpn 1960, various man. positions including assignments in Chile 1973, Iran 1979–83, USA 1980s, Germany and UK 1990s, apptd Dir Mitsubishi Corpn and Mitsubishi Heavy Industries Ltd 1992, Man. Dir 1994–98, Pres. and CEO 1998–2004, Chair. 2004–10, Sr Corp. Adviser 2010–, mem. Bd of Dirs Mitsubishi Electric Corpn –2016, Mitsubishi Motors Corpn –2016; Vice-Chair. Tokyo Chamber of Commerce and Industry 2000–07, Nippon Keidanren 2007–11; Chair. Japan-Philippines Economic Cooperation Committee 2000–12, International Chamber of Commerce Japan 2002–, Japan Foreign Trade Council Inc. 2004–08; mem. Advisory Council of Japan Finance Corpn (aka Japan Bank for Int. Co-operation); mem. Bd of Dirs Mitsubishi Research Inst. Inc. 2010–, Tokio Marine Holdings Inc. 2011–, Nissin Foods Holdings Co. Ltd (Nissin Food Products Co. Ltd; Medal of Merit, Philippines–Japan Soc. 2015. *Address:* Mitsubishi Corporation, Mitsubishi Shoji Building, 3-1, Marunouchi 2-chome, Chiyoda-ku, Tokyo 100-8086, Japan (office). *Telephone:* (3) 3210-2121 (office). *Fax:* (3) 3210-8583 (office). *E-mail:* info@mitsubishicorp.com (office). *Website:* www.mitsubishicorp.com (office).

SASAKI, Norio; Japanese business executive; b. 1 June 1949; ed Waseda Univ.; joined Toshiba Corpn 1972, Tech. Exec., Nuclear Energy Systems, Power Systems and Services Co. 2001–03, Vice-Pres., Nuclear Energy Systems and Services Div., Industrial and Power Systems and Services Co. 2003–05, Corp. Vice-Pres., Exec. Vice-Pres., Industrial and Power Systems and Services Co. 2005–06, Corp. Vice-Pres., Pres. and CEO Power Systems Co. 2006–07, Corp. Exec. Vice-Pres. and CEO Infrastructure Systems Group 2007–08, Rep. Exec. Officer, Corp. Sr Exec. Vice-Pres. and Dir 2008–09, Rep. Exec. Officer, Pres., CEO and Dir 2009–13, Vice-Chair. 2013–15 (resgnd). *Address:* c/o Toshiba Corpn, 1-1, Shibaura 1-chome, Minato-ku, Tokyo 105-8001, Japan.

SASSE, Benjamin (Ben) Eric, AB, MA, PhD; American academic, government official and politician; *Senator from Nebraska;* b. 22 Feb. 1972, Plainview, Neb.; s. of Gary Sasse and Linda K. Sasse (née Dunklau); m. Melissa McLeod; three c.; ed Harvard Univ., St John's Coll., Yale Univ., Univ. of Oxford, UK; Assoc. Consultant, Boston Consulting Group 1994–95; Chief of Staff, Office of Legal Policy, US Dept of Justice, Washington, DC 2003–05; Chief of Staff to Rep. Jeff Fortenberry, US House of Reps 2005; Counsellor to Sec., US Dept of Health and Human Services 2006–07, Asst Sec. for Planning and Evaluation 2007–09; Asst Prof. of Public Affairs, Lyndon B. Johnson School of Public Affairs, Univ. of Texas 2009–10; Pres. and Prof. of History, Midland Univ. 2010–14; Senator from Nebraska 2015–; Republican; Theron Rockwell Field Prize, George Washington Egleston Prize. *Address:* B40E Dirksen Senate Office Building, Washington, DC 20510, USA (office). *Telephone:* (202) 224-4224 (office). *Website:* www.sasse.senate.gov (office).

SASSEN, Saskia, MA, PhD; American (b. Dutch) sociologist and academic; *Robert S. Lynd Professor of Sociology and Co-Chair, Committee on Global Thought, Columbia University;* b. (Saskia Sassen Van Elsloo), 5 Jan. 1947, The Hague, Netherlands; d. of Willem Sassen Van Elsoo and Mara Van de Voort; m. Richard Sennett; one s.; ed Univ. of Notre Dame, Université de Poitiers, France, Harvard Univ.; Prof. of Sociology, Queens Coll., CUNY, New York 1976–85; Prof. of Urban Planning, Columbia Univ., New York 1985–98, Robert S. Lynd Prof. of Sociology 2007–, mem. Cttee on Global Thought 2007– (Co-Chair. 2010–); Ralph Lewis Prof. of Sociology, Univ. of Chicago 1998–2007; Visiting Centennial Prof., LSE, UK 1998–2006; Helen McCahn Fellow, Girton Coll., Cambridge; Chair. Information Tech. and Int. Cooperation Cttee of the Social Science Research Council; Dir Transnationalism Project, Univ. of Chicago; mem. Global Chicago Project, Bd Urban Age of LSE, Panel on Urban Population Dynamics, Cttee on Population, NAS; participant, expert for MasterCard Worldwide Centers of Commerce Index; mem. Council on Foreign Relations, Sociological Research Asscn, European Acad. of Sciences; Hon. Geographer 2012; Hon. Global Devt Scholar, ISA 2012; Dr hc (Delft Univ., Netherlands), (De Paul Univ., Chicago), (Université de Poitiers, France), (Royal Swedish Tech. Inst.), (Univ. of Ghent, Belgium), (Univ. of Warwick, UK), (Univ. of Murcia, Spain); First Most Distinguished Alumnus (Arts and Sciences), Univ. of Notre Dame; Best Book awards in several categories, recipient of awards from the Ford Foundation, Mellon Foundation, Tinker Foundation, Revson Foundation, Chicago Inst. for Architecture and Urbanism, Twentieth Century Fund, Nat. Prize of the American Inst. of Certified Planners, Distinguished Lecturer, Inst. for Advanced Studies, Vienna, Henry Luce Lecturer, Clark Univ., Georg Simmel Lectures, Humboldt Univ., Eilert Sundt Lecture, Univ. of Oslo, Sheril Lecturer and Storrs Lecturer, Yale Univ. Law School, Luhman Lecturer, Bielefeld Univ., Germany, Zygmund Baumann Inst. Fellow, named by Foreign Policy Magazine as one of the Top 100 Global Thinkers of 2011, Prince of Asturias Award for Social Sciences 2013, numerous other awards and honours. *Publications include:* author: The Mobility of Labor and Capital 1988, The Global City 1991, Cities in a World Economy 1994 (fourth revised edn 2011), Losing Control? Sovereignty in an Age of Globalization 1996, Migranten, Siedler, Flüchtlinge 1996, Globalization and its Discontents – Selected Essays 1984–98 1998, Guests and Aliens 1999, Territory, Authority, and Rights: From Medieval to Global Assemblages (Distinguished Book Award, American Sociological Asscn 2007, Robert Jervis and Paul Schroeder Best Book Award, American Political Science Asscn 2007) 2006, A Sociology of Globalization 2007, Expulsions, Brutality and Complexity in the Global Economy 2014; editor: Global Networks/Linked Cities 2002, Deciphering the Global: Its Spaces, Scales and Subjects 2007; co-editor: Digital Formations 2005; books translated into 21 languages. *Address:* Department of Sociology, Columbia University, 713 Knox Hall, 606 West 122nd Street, New York, NY 10027, USA (office). *Telephone:* (212) 854-0790 (office). *Fax:* (212) 854-2963 (office). *E-mail:* sjs2@columbia.edu (office). *Website:* www.sociology.columbia.edu (office); www.columbia.edu/~sjs2 (office); www.saskiasassen.com; cgt.columbia.edu (office).

SASSER, Hon. James (Jim) Ralph, JD; American lawyer, fmr diplomatist, academic and fmr politician; *Professor of the Practice, Department of Public Policy, University of North Carolina;* b. 30 Sept. 1936, Memphis, Tenn.; s. of Joseph Ralph Sasser and Mary Nell Sasser (née Gray); m. Mary Ballantine Gorman 1962; one s.

one d.; ed Vanderbilt Univ.; served in US Marine Corps Reserve 1958–65; Partner, Goodpasture, Carpenter, Woods & Sasser, Nashville, Tenn. 1961–76; Chair. Tennessee Democratic State Cttee 1973–76; Senator from Tennessee 1977–95; Amb. to People's Repub. of China 1995–2001; Foreign Policy Adviser to Vice-Pres. Al Gore 2000; J.B. and Maurice C. Shapiro Prof., Elliott School of Int. Affairs, George Washington Univ. 2000–02; currently Sr Advisor to FedEx Corpn and Sr Counselor to APCO Worldwide, Washington, DC; mem. Bd of Dirs GreenHunter Energy, Inc. 2008–; Vice-Chair. Cttee on US-China Relations, US-China Foundation; mem. Council on Foreign Relations, ABA, UN Asscn, Int. Advisory Bd of the Culture and Civilization of China, Yale Univ.; Trustee, Nat. Geographic Soc.; Fellow, John F. Kennedy School of Government, Harvard Univ. 1995; currently Prof. of the Practice, Dept of Public Policy and Sr Fellow, Global Research Inst., Univ. of North Carolina. *Address:* Department of Public Policy, University of North Carolina, Campus Box 3435, Chapel Hill, NC 27599, USA (office). *Telephone:* (919) 962-1600 (office). *E-mail:* jmsasser@live.unc.edu (office). *Website:* publicpolicy.unc.edu (office).

SASSOON, David; British fashion designer; b. 5 Oct. 1932, London; s. of George Sassoon and Victoria Gurgi; ed Chelsea Coll. of Art and Royal Coll. of Art; designer, Belinda Bellville 1958; first ready-to-wear collection 1963; Dir Belinda Bellville 1964; Licensee Vogue Butterick USA 1966 (became Bellville Sassoon 1970), Dir Bellville Sassoon 1983; Trustee, Fashion and Textile Museum; UK Fashion Export Award in Women's Fashion 2005, Lifetime Achievement Award, Asscn of Design Professionals, Chicago 2008. *Publication:* The Glamour of Bellville Sassoon 2009. *Leisure interests:* theatre, ballet.

SASSOU-NGUESSO, Gen. Denis; Republic of the Congo army officer and head of state; *President;* b. 1943, Edou; joined Congolese Armed Forces 1960, mil. training in Cen. Africa, Algeria and France 1961–68; mem. Parti Congolais du Travail (PCT) 1970–, First Vice-Pres., Mil. Cttee, co-ordinator of PCT activities 1977–79, Pres. 1979–, Leader, Forces Démocratiques Unies (alliance of six parties including PCT) 1994–95; apptd Minister of Defence 1975; Pres. of the Republic of the Congo 1979–92, 1997–; Chair. African Union 2006–07. *Address:* Palais du Peuple, Brazzaville, Republic of the Congo (office). *Telephone:* 22-281-17-11 (office). *Website:* www.presidence.cg (office).

SASTRY, S(osale) Shankar, B.Tech, MS, MA, PhD; Indian electrical engineer, computer scientist and academic; *Dean and Roy W. Carlson Professor of Engineering and Director, Richard C. Blum Center for Developing Economies, University of California, Berkeley;* ed Indian Inst. of Tech., Bombay, Univ. of California, Berkeley, USA; Asst Prof., MIT 1980–82; Asst Prof., Univ. of California, Berkeley 1983–84, Assoc. Prof., 1984–88, Prof. 1988–, Dir, Electronics Research Lab., Univ. of Calif., Berkeley 1996–99, Prof. of Bioengineering 1999–, Chair., Dept of Electrical Eng 2001–04, Nippon Electronics Corporation (NEC) Distinguished Professorship in Coll. of Eng and Walter A. Haas School of Business 2002–, Dean, Coll. of Eng 2007–, apptd Roy W. Carlson Prof. of Eng, Professor of Mechanical Eng 2007–, Dir Richard C. Blum Center for Developing Economies 2007–, Dir Center for Information Tech. in the Interest of Soc. 2005–07, Dir Emer. 2007–, Dir NSF Science and Technology Center 'TRUST: Team for Research in Ubiquitous Security Technologies' 2005–; Gordon McKay Prof., Harvard Univ. 1994; fmr Visiting Prof., ANU, Univ. of Rome, Univ. of Pisa, Inst. Nat. Polytechnique de Grenoble, Center for Intelligent Control Systems, MIT; Chair., Int. Computer Science Inst. 2004–; fmr Assoc. Ed., IEEE Transactions on Automatic Control, IMA Journal of Control and Information, Journal of Biomimetic Systems and Materials, International Journal of Adaptive Control and Signal Processing; Fellow, IEEE 1994–; mem. Bd of Dirs Fed. of American Scientists 2002–08, CrossBow, Inc. 2007–11, C3 LLC 2009–, HCL Technologies, Inc. 2012–; mem. Scientific Advisory Bd Finmeccanica, SPROUT 2007–11, Scientific Systems Inc. 2006–07, Singapore National Research Foundation 2009–12, Interwest Partners 2011–, Eriksholm Technologies, Denmark 2014–, Scientific Advisory Bd of UN Sec.-Gen. 2014–; mem. Science and Technology Advisory Bd for Thai Prime Minister 2009–12; mem. Nat. Acad. of Eng 2001–, American Acad. of Arts and Sciences 2004–; Hon. MA (Harvard) 1994; Hon. PhD (Royal Inst. of Tech., Stockholm) 2007; numerous awards including Pres. of India Gold Medal 1977, Eckman Award, American Automatic Control Council 1990, Ragazzini Award 2005, Chang Lin Tien Educational Leadership Award 2010. *Publications include:* has co-authored more than 550 technical papers; books include Essays in Mathematical Robotics (jt author), Adaptive Control: Stability, Convergence and Robustness (jt author) 1989, A Mathematical Introduction to Robotic Manipulation (jt author) 1994, Nonlinear Systems: Analysis, Stability and Control 1999, An Invitation to 3D Vision: From Images to Models (jt author) 2003. *Address:* Dean's Office, College of Engineering, 320 McLaughlin Hall 1700, University of California, Berkeley, CA 94720-1770, USA (office). *Telephone:* (510) 642-5771 (office). *E-mail:* sastry@coe .berkeley.edu (office); sastry@eecs.berkeley.edu (office). *Website:* www.eecs .berkeley.edu/Faculty/Homepages/sastry (office); robotics.eecs.berkeley.edu/ ~sastry (office).

SATCHIDANANDAN, Koyamparambath, BA, MA, PhD; Indian poet and writer; b. 28 May 1946, Pullut, Thrissur Dist, Kerala; s. K C Sankara Menon and K. Kunjikutty Amma; m. Tulasi Devi T. P.; two d.; ed Univ. of Kerala, Univ. of Calicut; writer in Malayalam and English; Lecturer, then Prof. of English, Christ Coll., Kerala 1977–92; Ed. Indian Literature journal 1992–96; Pres. Sahitya Akademi 1996–2006; fmr consultant, India Dept of Higher Educ., Nat. Trans. Mission; Dir School of Translation Studies and Training, IGNOU, Delhi 2011–12; Nat. Fellow, Inst. of Advanced Study, Shimla; Cavaliere, Ordine al Merito della Repubblica Italiana; Kerala Sahitya Akademi Award 1984, 1989, 1999, 2001, Oman Cultural Centre Award, UAE 1993, Mahakavi Ulloor Award 1996, Mahakavi P. Kunhiraman Nair Award 1997, Bharatiya Bhasha Parishad Samvatsar Award 1998, Kumaran Asan Award 2000, Odakkuzhal Award 2001, Baharain Kerala Samaj Award, UAE 2002, Gangadhar Meher Nat. Award, Sambalpur Univ., Orissa 2002, Pandalam Kerala Verma Award 2005, Bappureddy Nat. Award 2005, Vayalar Award 2005, India-Poland Friendship Medal, Govt of Poland 2005, K.Kuttikrishnan Memorial Award 2007, Subrahmanya Shenoi Memorial Award 2008, NTR Nat. Literary Award 2009, Kusumagraj Award 2011, National Sahitya Akademi Award 2013, Kuvempu Award 2013, Kerala Sahitya Parishat Award 2013, State Bank of India Golden Award 2014, Muttatthu Varky Award 2014, Int. Poetry for Peace Award 2015, V. Aravindakshan Award 2016,

Nehru Memorial Coll. Golden Jubilee Award 2016. *Plays:* Saktan Thampuran 1983, Gandhi 1995. *Publications include:* poetry: Anchu Sooryan 1971, Atmagita 1974, Kavita 1977, Indian Sketchukal 1978, Ezhuthachan Ezhutumbol 1979, Peedana Kalam 1981, Venal Mazha 1982, Randu Deergha Kavyangal 1983, Satchidandante Kavithakal 1962–82 1983, Socrateesum Kozhiyum 1984, Ivanek-koodi 1987, Veedumattam 1988, Kayattam 1990, Kavibuddhan 1992, Ente Satchidanandan Kavitakal 1993, Desatanam 1994, Malayalam 1996, Apoornam 1998, Theranjedutha 1999, Sambhashanathinu Oru Sramam 2000, Vikku 2002, Sakshyangal 2004, Satchidanandante Kavitakal 1965–2005 2006, Onaam Padham 2006, Anantam 2007, Ente Kavita 2008, Marannu Vecha vastukkal 2009, Bahuroopi 2011, Tathagatam 2013, Nilkkunna Mnushyan 2015, Satchidanandante Kavitakal, 1965–2015 2016; non-fiction: Kurukshetram 1970, Janatayum Kavitayum 1982, Marxian Soundarya Sadtram 1983, Thiranjedutha Lekhanangal 1985, Samvadangal 1986, Sameepanangal 1986, Samskarathinte Rashtreeyam 1989, Sambhashanangal 1989, Brechtinte Kala 1989, Padavukal 1990, Kazhcha-kal, Kazhachappadukal 1991, Anveshanangal 1991, Veenduvicharangal 1992, Soundaryavum Adhikaravum 1993, Muhurtangal 1996, Pala Lokam, Pala Kalam 1998, Kalayum Nishedhavum 1999, Moonnu Yatra 2004, Kizhakkum Padinjarum 2005, Adithattukal 2006, Mukjamukham 2006; prose: Kurukshetram 1970, Janatayum Kavitayum 1982, Marxian Soundarya Sastram 1983, Thiranjedutha Lekhanangal 1985, Pablo Neruda 1985, Samvadangal 1986, Sameepanangal 1986, Samskarathinte Rashtreeyam 1989, Sambhashanangal 1989, Brechtinte Kala 1989, Padavukal 1990, Kazhchakal, Kazhachappadukal 1991, Anveshanangal 1991, Veenduvicharangal 1992, Soundaryavum Adhikaravum 1993, Muhurtangal 1996, Pala Lokam, Pala Kalam 1998, Kalayum Nishedhavum 1999, Indian Literature: Positions and Propositions 1999, Bharateeya Kavitayile Pratirodha Paramparyam 2002, Moonnu Yatra 2004, Kizhakkum Padinjarum 2005, Adithat-tukal 2006, Mukhamukham 2006, Indian Literature: Paradigms and Praxis 2008, Indian Literature and Beyond 2009, Darshanangalude Ritubhedangal 2011, Vithum Vrikshavum 2013, Orma, Anubhavam, Yatra 2014. *E-mail:* satchida@ gmail.com. *Website:* satchidanandan.blogspot.com.

SATHASIVAM, Palanisamy, BA; Indian lawyer and fmr judge; *Governor of Kerala;* b. 27 April 1949, Kadappanallur, Erode Dist, Tamil Nadu; s. of Palanisamy Sathasivam and Natchiamma Sathasivam; m. Saraswathi Sathasivam; ed Govt Law Coll., Chennai; enrolled as an advocate at Madras 1973, apptd as Additional Govt Pleader and further as Special Govt Pleader in Madras High Court, also worked as legal adviser for several state-owned transport corpns, municipalities, nationalized banks etc., apptd as a perm. Judge of the Madras High Court 1996, transferred to the Punjab and Haryana High Court 2007, Judge of Supreme Court 2007–14, Chief Justice of India 2013–14 (retd); Gov. of Kerala 2014–. *Address:* Office of the Governor, Thiruvananthapuram, Kerala, India (office). *Telephone:* (471) 2721100 (office). *Fax:* (471) 2720226 (office). *Website:* www.rajbhavan.kerala .gov.in (office).

SATHIRATHAI, Surakiart, LLM, MALD, SJD; Thai lawyer, economist, politician and academic; *Chairman, Siam Premier International Law Office Ltd;* b. 7 June 1958, Bangkok; m. Thanpuying Dr Suthawan Sathirathai; one s.; ed Chulalongkorn Univ., Tufts Univ., Harvard Univ., USA; policy adviser to Prime Minister 1988–92, to Nat. Ass. 1989–91, to Prime Minister on econ. affairs 1991–92; Co-founder Siam Premier Int. Law Office Ltd 1990, Chair. Exec. Bd 1990–2001, currently Chair.; Dean and Assoc. Prof., Chulalongkorn Univ. 1992–95, currently Distinguished Scholar, Faculty of Law; Chair. Crown Property Bureau, Securities Exchange Comm., House Select Cttee on Budget Review 1995–96, PTTEP Co. Ltd 1998–2000, Laem Thong Bank Co. Ltd 1998–99, Petroleum Authority of Thailand, Thai Oil Co. Ltd 1999–2000; Minister of Finance 1995–96; Vice-Chair. of Prime Minister's Advisory Council on Econ. and Foreign Affairs 1996–97; Councillor of State 1997–2001; Pres. Inst. of Social and Econ. Policy (ISEP) 1997–2001, Chair. ISEP Foundation 1999–2001; chosen mem. Parl. (Party List) 2001; Minister of Foreign Affairs 2001–05; Deputy Prime Minister 2005–06; Visiting Scholar, Harvard Law School, 2007–09, Sr Fellow, Belfer Center for Science and International Affairs, John F. Kennedy School of Govt, Harvard Univ. March–Dec. 2007; mem. Advisory Council, Global Law and Policy Inst., Harvard Law School; Kt Grand Cordon (Special Class) of the Most Noble Order of the Crown of Thailand, Kt Grand Cross (First Class) of the Most Exalted Order of the White Elephant, Genesis Decoration; Red Cross Medal, Psalm Scout Medal, Tertiary Military Academy Magic. *Publications include:* Third World Attitudes Toward International Law: An Introduction (with Frederick Snyder) 1987, Thailand and International Trade Law, The Role of International Trade Law 2010. *Address:* Siam Premier International Law Office Ltd, 26th Floor, The Offices at Central World, 999/9 Rama 1 Road, Pathumwan, Bangkok 10330, Thailand (office). *Website:* siampremier.com (office).

SATO, Hiroshi; Japanese engineer and business executive; *Senior Advisor, Kobe Steel Ltd (KOBELCO);* ed Kyusyu Univ.; joined Kobe Steel Ltd in 1970, acted as Head of Tech. Devt Div. and Material Research Centre, served as Exec. Vice-Pres., Tech. Devt Group, Pres., CEO and Rep. Dir, Kobe Steel Ltd (KOBELCO) 2009–13, Chair. and CEO 2013–16, Sr Advisor 2016–. *Address:* Kobe Steel Ltd, Shinko Building, 10-26 Wakinohamacho 2-chome, Kobe 651-8585, Japan (office). *Telephone:* (78) 261-5111 (office). *Fax:* (78) 261-4123 (office). *E-mail:* info@kobelco.co.jp (office). *Website:* www.kobelco.co.jp (office).

SATO, Humitaka, PhD; Japanese astrophysicist and academic; b. 23 March 1938, Yamagata; s. of Mokichi Sato and Kane Sato; m. Keiko Okazaki 1965; one s. one d.; ed Kyoto Univ.; Prof. of Astrophysics and Relativity, Kyoto Univ. 1974–2006, Dean Faculty of Sciences 1993, Prof. Emer. 2001–, Dir Yukawa Inst. for Theoretical Physics 1976–80; Pres. Physical Soc. of Japan 1998–2000, Yukawa Memorial Foundation; Prof. of Physics, Konan Univ. 2001–14; fmr Visiting Physicist, Univ. of California, Berkeley; fmr Ed. Progress of Theoretical Physics and other journals; fmr Chair. Physics Cttee, Science Council of Japan, C19 of IUPAP; Order of the Sacred Treasure 2013; Nishina Prize 1973, Matsunaga Prize 1975, Asahi Scientific Subsidy 1983, First Award for Essay on Gravitation 1985, Purple Medal of Honour 1999. *Publications include:* Black Holes 1976, Discovery of Big Bang 1983, Invitation to Cosmology 1988, Dark Matter in the Universe 1990; 140 papers on astrophysics, Theory of General Relativity, Theory of Expanding Universe. *Address:* Yukawa Memorial Foundation, Yukawa Institute of Theoretical Physics, Kyoto University, Kitasirakawa, Sakyo-ku, Kyoto 606-

8502, Japan (office). *E-mail:* sato@tap.scphys.kyoto-u.ac.jp (office). *Website:* www.kyoto-u.ac.jp (office).

SATO, Mikio, BSc, PhD; Japanese mathematician and academic; *Professor Emeritus, Research Institute for Mathematical Sciences, Kyoto University;* b. 1928; ed Univ. of Tokyo; Lecturer, Univ. of Tokyo 1960–63, Prof. 1968–70; Prof., Osaka Univ. 1963–68; Prof., Research Inst. for Math. Sciences (RIMS), Kyoto Univ. 1970–92, Prof. Emer. 1992–, Dir RIMS 1987–91; mem. NAS 1993–; Asahi Prize of Science 1969, Japan Acad. Prize 1976, Fujiwara Prize 1987, Rolf Schock Prize in Math., Royal Swedish Acad. of Sciences 1997, Wolf Prize 2003. *Publications:* numerous articles in math. journals on algebraic analysis and theory of hyperfunctions. *Address:* Research Institute for Mathematical Sciences, Kyoto University, Kyoto 606-8502, Japan (office). *Fax:* (75) 7537276 (office). *E-mail:* sato@kurims.kyoto-u.ac.jp (office). *Website:* www.kurims.kyoto-u.ac.jp (office).

SATO, Ryuzo, PhD, DEcon; Japanese economist and academic; b. 5 July 1931, Akita-ken; m. Kishie Hayashi 1959; one s. one d.; ed Hitotsubashi Univ., Tokyo, Johns Hopkins University, USA; Fulbright Scholar, Johns Hopkins Univ. 1957–62; Prof., Univ. of Hawaii, Manoa 1962–67; Prof. of Econs, Brown Univ. 1967–85; C. V. Starr Prof. of Econs, New York Univ. 1985–2006 (retd), Dir Center for Japan–US Business and Econ. Studies, Stern School of Business –2006; Adjunct Prof. of Public Policy, John F. Kennedy School of Govt, Harvard Univ. 1983; apptd Visiting Prof. of Econs, Univ. of Tokyo 2003; Guggenheim Fellow; Ford Foundation Fellow; Rondan Prize, Yomiuri (newspaper), Economics Award (Nikkei Prize), Nihon-Keizai (newspaper). *Publications include:* Theory of Technical Change and Economic Invariance 1981, Research and Productivity (with G. Suzawa) 1983, The Chrysanthemum and the Eagle (Rondansho Prize) 1991, Growth Theory and Technical Change 1996, Global Competition and Integration (with R. V. Ramachandran and Kazuo Mino) 1998, Symmetry and Economic Invariance (with R. V. Ramachandran) 1998, Production, Stability and Dynamic Symmetry 1999, Biased Technical Change and Economic Conservation Laws 2010. *Leisure interests:* skiing, music, gardening. *E-mail:* rsato@stern.nyu.edu.

SATO, Tsutomu, BEng; Japanese politician; b. 20 June 1952, Tochigi; ed Univ. of Nihon; Deputy, Tochigi Prefectural Ass. 1987–99; mem. House of Reps 1996–, Chair. House of Reps Gen. Affairs Cttee 2006; mem. LDP, Vice-Chair. LDP Diet Policy Cttee 2002–05, Chair. LDP Gen. Affairs Div. 2005; Vice-Minister of Health, Labour and Welfare 2001, Vice-Minister of Internal Affairs and Communications 2007, Minister of State, Chair. Nat. Public Safety Comm. 2008–09, Minister of State in charge of Okinawa and N Territories and Disaster Man. 2008–09, Minister of Internal Affairs and Communications 2009, also Minister of State for Decentralization Reform. *Address:* House of Representatives, 1-7-1 Nagatacho, Chiyoda-ku, Tokyo 100-0014, Japan (office). *Telephone:* (3) 3581-3111 (office). *E-mail:* g02103@shugiin.go.jp; webmaster@shugiin.go.jp (office). *Website:* www.shugiin.go.jp/internet/index.nsf/html/index_e.htm (office); www.satoben.jp.

SATO, Yasuhiro; Japanese business executive; *Representative Director, President and CEO, Mizuho Financial Group, Inc.;* b. 15 April 1952; ed Univ. of Tokyo; joined Mizuho Financial Group 1976, worked in New York late 1980s, Exec. Officer/Sr Corp. Officer, Int. Banking Unit, Mizuho Corp. Bank Ltd 2003–04, Man. Exec. Officer 2004–06, Man. Dir/Head of Corp. Banking Unit 2006–07, Deputy Pres./Chief Auditor 2007–09, Pres. and CEO 2009–13, Dir of Mizuho Financial Group, Inc. 2009–, Deputy Pres. and Chief Auditor Mizuho Bank Ltd 2007–09, Pres. and CEO 2009–14, Dir 2011–, Rep. Dir, Pres. and CEO Mizuho Financial Group, Inc. (Group CEO) 2011–, Dir Mizuho Trust & Banking Co. 2014, Mizuho Securities Co.; Dir The Fuji Fire and Marine Insurance Co., Ltd. *Address:* Mizuho Financial Group, Inc., Marunouchi 2-chome Building, 2-5-1, Marunouchi, Chiyoda-ku, Tokyo 100-8333, Japan (office). *Telephone:* (3) 5224-1111 (office). *Fax:* (3) 3215-4616 (office). *E-mail:* info@mizuho-fg.co.jp (office). *Website:* www.mizuho-fg.co.jp (office).

SATO, Yoshio; Japanese insurance industry executive; *President, CEO and Representative Director, Sumitomo Life Insurance Company;* Man. Dir Sumitomo Life Insurance Co. –2007, apptd Pres., CEO and Rep. Dir 2007, Chair. and Rep. Exec. Officer 2014–; mem. Bd of Dirs Life Insurance Asscn of Japan; Trustee Japan Inst. of Life Insurance; mem. Audit & Supervisory Bd Panasonic Corpn 2014. *Address:* Sumitomo Life Insurance Co., 1-4-35 Shiromi, Chuo-ku, Osaka 540-8512, Japan (office). *Telephone:* (6) 6937-1435 (office). *E-mail:* info@sumitomolife.co.jp (office). *Website:* www.sumitomolife.co.jp (office).

SATOH, Yukio, BA; Japanese diplomatist; *Vice-Chairman, Japan Institute of International Affairs;* b. 6 Oct. 1939; m.; two c.; ed Tokyo Univ., Univ. of Edinburgh, UK; entered Foreign Service 1961, with Ministry of Foreign Affairs, Tokyo, then Embassy, Washington, DC –1976, Dir Div. of Security Affairs, American Affairs Bureau, Ministry of Foreign Affairs 1976–77, Pvt. Sec. to the Foreign Minister 1977–79, Counsellor, London 1981–84, also Consul-Gen., Dir Policy Coordination Div. 1985–87, Asst Vice-Minister for Parl. Affairs, Ministry of Foreign Affairs 1987–88; Chief of Prefectural Police, Miyazaki 1984–85; Consul-Gen., Hong Kong 1988–90; Dir-Gen. North American Affairs Bureau and Dir-Gen. Information Analysis, Research and Planning Bureau, Ministry of Foreign Affairs 1990–94, Amb. to the Netherlands 1994–96, to Australia 1996–98; Perm. Rep. to the UN 1998–2002; Pres. The Japan Inst. of Int. Affairs 2002–09, Vice-Chair. 2009–. *Publications:* numerous articles on Japanese foreign and security policy. *Address:* The Japan Institute of International Affairs, Kasumigaseki Building 11 Floor, 3-2-5 Kasumigaseki, Chiyoda-ku, Tokyo, 100-6011, Japan (office). *Telephone:* (3) 3503-7295 (office). *Fax:* (3) 3503-7411 (office). *E-mail:* satoh@jiia.or.jp (office). *Website:* www.jiia.or.jp (office).

SATOMI, Susumu, MD; Japanese surgeon, academic and university administrator; *President, Tohoku University;* b. June 1948, Kagoshima Pref.; ed School of Medicine, Tohoku Univ.; Lecturer, Second Dept of Surgery, Tohoku Univ., then Prof. 1995–, Prof., Div. of Advanced Surgical Science and Tech., Grad. School of Medicine, Dir Tohoku Univ. Hosp. 2004–05, Vice-Pres. Tohoku Univ. 2005–08, Dir Innovation of New Biomedical Eng Centre 2008–12, Pres. Tohoku Univ. 2012–; Pres. Japan Surgical Soc. 2008–12, Japan Asscn of Nat. Univs. *Address:* Office of the President, Tohoku University, 1-1 Katahira, 2-chome, Aoba-ku, Sendai 980-8577, Japan (office). *Telephone:* (22) 217-4807 (office). *E-mail:* ssatomi@bureau.tohoku.ac.jp (office). *Website:* www.tohoku.ac.jp (office).

SATRAPI, Marjane, MA; Iranian writer, illustrator and film director; b. (Marjan Ebrahimi-Ripa), 22 Sept. 1969, Rasht; ed Visual Communication School of Fine Arts, Tehran, École des Arts Decoratifs de Strasbourg, France; Dr hc (Katholieke Universiteit Leuven, Université catholique de Louvain) 2009; Gat Perich Award. *Films include:* Persepolis (dir and writer with Vincent Paronnaud) (Sutherland Trophy, British Film Inst. Awards 2007, Jury Prize, Cannes Film Festival 2007, Special Jury Prize, Cinemanila Int. Film Festival 2007, César Award for Best First Work 2007, Audience Award, Rotterdam Int. Film Festival 2008, Audience Award, São Paulo Int. Film Festival 2007, Most Popular Film, Vancouver Int. Film Festival 2007) 2007, Poulet aux prunes 2011, La bande des Jotas 2012, The Voices 2014. *Publications include:* Persepolis: The Story of a Childhood (four vols) (Angoulême Coup de Coeur Award 2001, Angoulême Prize 2002) 1999–2002, Persepolis 2: The Story of a Return (adapted as screenplay 2007) 2005, Embroideries 2005, Chicken with Plums (Angoulême Best Comic Book Award) 2006, The Sigh 2011; several children's books; contrib. illustrations to French magazines and periodicals. *Address:* 13 rue de Thorigny, 75003 Paris, France (home). *Telephone:* 6-64-99-04-52 (home). *Fax:* 1-42-72-65-15 (home). *E-mail:* marjanesatrapi@yahoo.fr (home).

SATTAR, Abdul, MA; Pakistani diplomatist (retd); b. 10 July 1931, Narowal; m. Yasmine Sattar 1955; one s. two d.; ed Forman Christian Coll., Lahore, Punjab Univ., Fletcher School of Law and Diplomacy, Tufts Univ., USA; served in Pakistan Missions in Saudi Arabia, Sudan and the USA; Rep. of Pakistan to IAEA and Amb. to Austria 1975–78; Amb. to India 1978–82, 1990–92, to USSR 1988–90; Dir, then Dir-Gen. and Additional Sec. at Foreign Office, for Asia 1982–86; Foreign Sec., Islamabad 1986–88; Sr Del. to Geneva Talks on Afghanistan 1988; Minister of Foreign Affairs 1999–2002; mem. Nat. Security Council. *Publications include:* Pakistan's Foreign Policy: A Concise History 1947–2007 2007; articles in learned journals on nuclear non-proliferation and regional studies; columns in Pakistani newspapers. *Address:* House 7, College Road, F-7/3, Islamabad, Pakistan (home). *Telephone:* (51) 2611144 (home). *E-mail:* sattara@comsats.net.pk.

SATTERFIELD, David M., BA; American diplomatist and international organization official; *Acting Assistant Secretary of State for Near Eastern Affairs;* b. Baltimore, Md; ed Univ. of Maryland, Georgetown Univ.; joined US State Dept 1980, served in Saudi Arabia, Tunisia, Lebanon and Syria and staff mem. Bureau of Near Eastern Affairs, Bureau of East Asian and Pacific Affairs and Intelligence and Research, Dir for Exec. Secretarial Staff and for Near East and South Asian Affairs, Nat. Security Council 1993–96, Dir Office of Israel and Arab-Israeli Affairs 1996–98, Amb. to Lebanon 1998–2001, Deputy Asst Sec. for Near Eastern Affairs 2001–04, Prin. Deputy Asst Sec. of State for Near Eastern Affairs 2004–05, Deputy Chief of Mission, Embassy in Baghdad 2005–06, Sr Advisor to Sec. of State and Coordinator for Iraq 2006–09 (retd); Dir-Gen., Multinational Force and Observers (MFO), Rome, Italy 2009–17; Acting Asst Sec. of State for Near Eastern Affairs 2017–; Presidential Meritorious Exec. Rank Award, Dept of State Distinguished Honor Award, Dept Sr Performance Award, six Dept of State Superior Honor Awards. *Address:* US Department of State, Harry S Truman Bldg, 2201 C Street, Northwest, Washington, DC 20520, USA (office). *Website:* www.state.gov (office).

SATYANAND, Rt Hon Sir Anand, GNZM, QSO, KStJ, LLB; New Zealand lawyer, judge and ombudsman; b. 22 July 1944, Auckland; m. Susan Satyanand 1970; three c.; ed Univ. of Auckland Law School; admitted to the Bar 1970; practised law with Crown Solicitors' Office and Partner, pvt. law practice; Dist Court Judge, Palmerston N and Auckland, with specialist warrant for criminal jury trials 1982–94; Parl. Ombudsman 1995–2005; Gov.-Gen. of New Zealand 2006–11; Chair. Confidential Forum for Fmr In-Patients of Psychiatric Hosps –2006; Registrar of Pecuniary Interests of Mems of Parl. –2006; Chair. Commonwealth Foundation 2013–16; fmr mem. Bd of Dirs New Zealand Inst. of International Affairs, now mem. Standing Cttee; mem. Advisory Council, Transparency International; fmr exec. New Zealand Rugby League; Hon. mem. Royal Order of the Crown by the King of Tonga 2011, Hon. Advisor, Asia New Zealand Foundation; Distinguished Companion, New Zealand Order of Merit 2005, Principal Companion, New Zealand Order of Merit (redesignated Grand Commdr, New Zealand Order of Merit 2009) 2006; Hon. LLD (Auckland Univ.) 2006; New Zealand Commemoration Medal 1990, Pravasi Bharatiya Samman Award 2011. *Leisure interests:* sport, reading, int. affairs. *Address:* c/o PO Box 9062, Marion Square, Wellington 6141, New Zealand (office).

SATYARTHI, Kailash; Indian children's rights activist; b. 11 Jan. 1954, Vidisha, MP; m.; one s. one d.; active in Indian movt against child labour since 1980s; has been involved with Global March Against Child Labour and its int. advocacy body, Int. Centre on Child Labour and Educ., and also Global Campaign for Educ.; Founder and mem. Exec. Cttee, Bachpan Bachao Andolan; est. Rugmark (now known as Goodweave) as first voluntary labelling, monitoring and certification system of rugs manufactured without use of child labour in South Asia; fmr mem. Bd Fast Track Initiative (now the Global Partnership for Educ.); Aachener Int. Peace Award (Germany) 1984, Trumpeter Award (USA) 1985, Robert F. Kennedy Human Rights Award (USA) 1995, Friedrich Ebert Stiftung Award (Germany) 1999, Wallenberg Medal, University of Michigan 2002, Freedom Award (USA) 2006, recognized by US State Dept in list of Heroes Acting to End Modern Day Slavery 2007, Medal of the Italian Senate 2007, Alfonso Comin Int. Award (Spain) 2008, Defenders of Democracy Award (USA) 2009, Nobel Peace Prize (shared with Malala Yousafzai) 2014. *Address:* Bachpan Bachao Andolan, L- 6, Kalkaji, New Delhi 110 019, India (office). *Telephone:* (11) 49211111 (office). *Fax:* (11) 49211138 (office). *E-mail:* info@bba.org.in (office); info@kailashsatyarthi.net. *Website:* www.bba.org.in (office); www.kailashsatyarthi.net.

SATYBALDIYEV, Jantoro Joldoshevich; Kyrgyzstani politician; b. 6 Jan. 1956, Mirza-Aki village, Uzgen dist, Osh Oblast; m.; four c.; fmr First Deputy Minister of Transport, later Minister of Transport; headed town admin of Osh; Pres.'s Special Rep. on Electroenergy Security for southern Kyrgyzstan 2003–05; removed as Gov. of Osh dist due to deficiencies in his work and legal case launched against him accusing him of misusing an official position 2007; later apptd Regional Dir of TRACECA (project to develop Europe-Caucasus-Asia transport corridor); fmr Head of Directorate to rebuild and develop Osh and Jalal-Abad; Head of Pres.'s Office 2011–12; Prime Minister of Kyrgyzstan 2012–14; Medal in honour of 300th anniversary of the foundation of St Petersburg (Russia) 2004.

Address: c/o Office of the Government, 720003 Bishkek, Dom Pravitelstva, Kyrgyzstan.

SA'UD, Abdullah bin Faisal al-; Saudi Arabian engineer, business executive and diplomatist; b. 1951, Taif; s. of Faisal bin Turki bin Abdullah bin Saud as-Sa'ud and Luluwah bint Abdulaziz as-Sa'ud; m.; four c.; ed eng studies in UK; began professional career as an engineer with newly est. Royal Comm. for Jubail and Yanbu where he held tech. and managerial positions, Acting Sec.-Gen. Royal Comm. 1985–87, Sec.-Gen. 1987–91, Chair. and CEO 1991–2000; Gov. Saudi Arabian Gen. Investment Authority 2000–04; Chair. Saudi Italian Devt Co. –2015; Amb. to USA 2015–17.

SA'UD, HRH Prince Bandar bin Sultan bin Abd al-Aziz al-, MA; Saudi Arabian diplomatist and army officer; b. 2 March 1949, Taif; s. of HRH Crown Prince Sultan bin Abd al-Aziz al-Sa'ud; m. HRH Princess Haifa bint Faisal bin Abd al-Aziz al-Sa'ud; four s. four d.; ed RAF Coll., Cranwell, USAF Advanced Program and Johns Hopkins Univ.; fighter pilot, Royal Saudi Air Force 1969–82; in charge of special Saudi Arabian liaison mission to USA for purchase of AWACS and other defence equipment 1981; Defence and Mil. Attaché, Saudi Arabian Mil. Mission to USA 1982–83; Amb. to USA 1983–2005; promoted to rank of Minister 1995; Sec.-Gen. Nat. Security Council 2005–15; Dir-Gen. Saudi Intelligence Agency 2012–14; numerous medals and decorations, including Hawk Flying Medal of Aviation, King Faisal Medal, King Abdul Aziz Sash, as well as honours from other nations. *Leisure interests:* flying, racquetball, reading.

SA'UD, HRH Prince; Khalid bin Salman bin Abd al-Aziz; Saudi Arabian diplomatist and politician; *Deputy Minister of Defence;* b. 1988, Riyadh; s. of HM King Salman bin Abd al-Aziz al-Sa'ud and Fahda bint Falah bin Sultan al-Hithalayn; m. HRH Hayfa bint Abdullah al-Sa'ud; two c.; ed King Faisal Air Acad., Harvard Univ.; served in the Royal Saudi Air Force; Senior Civilian Adviser, Ministry of Defence; Adviser, Royal Embassy of Saudi Arabia, Washington DC 2016–17; Amb. to USA 2017–19; Deputy Minister of Defence 2019–. *Address:* Ministry of Defence, POB 26731, Airport Rd, Riyadh, 11165, Saudi Arabia (office). *Telephone:* (11) 478-9000 (office). *Fax:* (11) 401-336 (office). *Website:* www.mod.gov .sa (office).

SA'UD, HRH Prince Muhammad bin Nawaf bin Abd al-Aziz al-; Saudi Arabian diplomatist; *Ambassador to UK;* b. 22 May 1953, Riyadh; m. HH Princess Fadwa bint Khaled bin Abdallah bin Abdulrahman; five c.; ed The Capital Inst. High School, Riyadh, School of Foreign Service, Georgetown Univ. and John F Kennedy School of Govt, Harvard Univ., USA; worked for Royal Comm. for Jubail and Yanbu for two years; transferred to Ministry of Foreign Affairs where he held several positions, including the Minister's Cabinet before being promoted to Insp. Gen.; Amb. to Italy and Malta 1995–2005, to UK 2005–; Pres. Council of Admin for the Islamic Cultural Centre of Italy 1998; fmr Dean of Arab Ambs' Corps. *Address:* Embassy of Saudi Arabia, 30 Charles Street, Mayfair, London, W1J 5DZ, England (office). *Telephone:* (20) 7917-3000 (office). *Fax:* (20) 7917-3113 (office). *E-mail:* ukemb@mofa.gov.sa (office). *Website:* www.saudiembassy.org.uk (office).

SA'UD, HRH Crown Prince Muhammad bin Salman bin Abd al-Aziz al-, LLB; Saudi Arabian royal and government official; *Crown Prince, Deputy Prime Minister, Minister of Defense and Secretary-General of the Royal Court;* b. 31 Aug. 1985, Riyadh; s. of HM King Salman bin Abd al-Aziz al-Sa'ud and Fahda bint Falah bin Sultan al-Hithalayn; m. Sara bint Mashoor bin Abdulaziz al-Sa'ud 2008; four c.; ed King Sa'ud Univ.; acted as special adviser to his father Prince Salman while he was Gov. of Riyadh Prov. 2009–11 and Crown Prince 2012–15; Pres. Crown Prince's Court and special adviser with rank of Minister 2013–15; State Minister and mem. Council of Ministers 2014; Minister of Defense and Sec.-Gen. of Royal Court 2015–, also Deputy Prime Minister 2017–; Deputy Crown Prince April 2015–17, apptd Crown Prince 21 June 2017; Chair. Council for Econ. and Devt Affairs 2015–; Founding Chair. Prince Mohammed bin Salman Foundation; Chair. Prince Salman Youth Centre; Sec.-Gen. Riyadh Competitiveness Centre; Nishan-e-Pakistan 2019. *Address:* Crown Prince Court, POB 11111, Riyadh, Saudi Arabia (office). *Telephone:* (1) 488-2222 (office). *Fax:* (1) 480-3572 (office). *E-mail:* admin@ cpc.gov.sa (office).

SA'UD, Prince Muhammad bin Nayef bin Abd al-Aziz al-, BA; Saudi Arabian government official; b. 30 Aug. 1959, Jeddah; s. of Nayef bin Abd al-Aziz al-Sa'ud (Crown Prince of Saudi Arabia) and Al Jawhara bint Abdulaziz bin Musaed al-Jiluwi; brother of Prince Sa'ud bin Nayef; nephew of Salman bin Abd al-Aziz al Sa'ud (King of Saudi Arabia); m. Reema bint Sultan al-Sa'ud; two d.; ed Al-Asemah Inst., Riyadh; worked in the private sector –1999; Asst Minister of Interior for Security Affairs 1999–2004, Minister 2004–12, Deputy Minister of the Interior July–Nov. 2012, Minister 2012–17; Deputy Crown Prince Jan.–April 2015, Crown Prince 29 April 2015–21 June 2017; Second Deputy Prime Minister Jan.–April 2015, First Deputy Prime Minister 2015–17; Chair. Council for Political and Security Affairs 2015–17; mem. Supreme Information Council 1999–, Supreme Economic Council 2009–; mem. Nat. Anti-Narcotics Cttee, High Comm. of Prince Nayef bin Abd al-Aziz Al-Sa'ud Award for Prophet's Sunnah and Contemporary Islamic Studies; King Abd al-Aziz Sash, First Class 2008. *Leisure interests:* shooting, equestrianism, swimming. *Address:* Royal Diwan, Riyadh 11165, Saudi Arabia (office).

SA'UD, HRH Prince Muqrin bin Abd al-Aziz al-; Saudi Arabian politician and fmr air force pilot; b. 15 Sept. 1945, Riyadh; s. of King Abd al-Aziz al-Sa'ud and Baraka Al Yamaniyah; half-brother of King Salman bin Abd al-Aziz al-Sa'ud; m. Abta bint Hamoud al-Rashid; six s. eight d.; ed Riyadh Model Inst., Royal Air Force Coll., UK, Gen. Staff Course, USA; joined Royal Saudi Air Force (RSAF), rank of Flight Lt 1968, named Commdr RSAF 2nd Air Squadron 1970, served in several positions 1973–77, apptd Adjutant to Dir of Air Operations 1977, then Pres. RSAF Operations and Planning –1980; Gov. of Hail Prov. 1980–99, of Madinah Prov. 1999–2005; Dir-Gen. Al Mukhabarat Al A'amah (Saudi Intelligence Agency) 2005–12; apptd King Abdullah's Adviser and Special Envoy with rank of Minister 2012–; Second Deputy Prime Minister 2013–15; Deputy Crown Prince 2014–15, Crown Prince and First Deputy Prime Minister Jan.–April 2015. *Leisure interests:* astronomy, literature, Arabic poetry, collecting books. *Address:* Royal Diwan, Riyadh 11165, Saudi Arabia.

S'AUD, HRH Princess; Reema Bint Bandar Al-, BA; Saudi Arabian royal, entrepreneur and diplomatist; *Ambassador to USA;* b. 1975, Riyadh; d. of HRH Prince Bandar bin Sultan bin Abd al-Aziz al-S'aud and HRH Princess Haifa bint Faisal bin Abd al-Aziz al-S'aud; one s. one d.; ed Mount Vernon Coll., George Washington Univ.; CEO Alf Int. 2008–15; Founder and CEO Alf Khair 2013–; Vice-Pres. Devt and Planning, Gen. Sports Authority 2016–, also Vice-Pres. of Women's Affair; Amb. to USA 2019–; apptd Pres. Mass Participation Fed. 2017; Founder and Creative Dir, Baraboux (luxury handbag brand); founding mem., Zahra (Saudi Breast Cancer Asscn); launched 10KSA (event for breast cancer); mem. Saudi Nat. Int. Olympic Cttee's Women in Sports Comm., Saudi Arabian Olympic Comm., Advisory Bd Creative Initiative; Patron, Arab Women's Awards; Young Global Leader, World Economic Forum 2015, Sheikh Mohammed bin Rashid Al Maktoum Creative Sport Award 2017. *Address:* 601 New Hampshire Avenue, NW, Washington, DC 20037, USA (office). *Telephone:* (202) 342-3800. *Fax:* (202) 295-3625. *E-mail:* citizen@saudiembassy.net. *Website:* www.saudiembassy.net.

SA'UD, HM The King of Saudi Arabia Salman bin Abd al-Aziz al-; Saudi Arabian politician and head of state; *Head of State and Prime Minister;* b. 13 Dec. 1935; s. of King Abd al-Aziz al-Sa'ud and Hussah bint Ahmad al-Sudairi; half-brother of King Abdullah ibn Abd al-Aziz as-Sa'ud; m. 1st Princess Sultana bint Turki al-Sudairi (deceased); m. 2nd Sarah bint Faisal al-Subai'ai; m. 3rd Fahda bint Falah bin Sultan al-Hithalayn; 13 c.; Gov. of Riyadh 1955–60, 1963–2011; Minister of Defence and Civil Aviation 2011–15, also First Deputy Prime Minister 2012–15; Prime Minister 2015–; named Crown Prince (following death of brother Nayef ibn Abd al-Aziz as-Sa'ud) 18 June 2012; succeeded to throne following death of half-brother Abdullah bin Abd al-Aziz al-Sa'ud 23 Jan. 2015; Chair. Bd Riyadh Water and Sanitary Drainage Authority and numerous other orgs; est. Prince Salman Centre for Disability Research, Prince Fahd bin Salman Charitable Soc. for Care of Kidney Patients; also active in Abdul Aziz Foundation. *Leisure interest:* reading. *Address:* Royal Diwan, Riyadh 11165, Saudi Arabia (office).

SA'UD, HRH Prince Sa'ud bin Abdullah bin Thunayan al-, BSc; Saudi Arabian business executive; *Chairman, Saudi Basic Industries Corporation (SABIC);* ed King Sa'ud Univ.; early career as engineer, Riyadh Municipality, becoming Dir-Gen. for Survey and Drawings and Dir-Gen. for Operations and Maintenance; Under-Sec. for Planning and Programmes, Ministry of Municipality and Rural Affairs 1989; Chair. Admin. Bd Saudi Basic Industries Corpn (SABIC) 2003–; Chair. Royal Comm. for Jubail and Yanbu, Utility and Water Co. of Jubail and Yanbu; Deputy Chair. Prince Salman Social Centre; mem Bd Royal Family Bd; mem several cttees formed by Royal Decree to regulate needs of Al-Jouf, Jizan, northern border and Hail areas in Saudi Arabia, in addition to villages and areas in western coast and needs of people of Yanbu Governorates; mem jt cttee that supervises co-ordination and follows work between Ministry of Municipality and Rural Affairs, Ministry of Transportation, Ministry of Agric. and Higher Cttee for Childhood. *Address:* Saudi Basic Industries Corporation, PO Box 5101, Riyadh 11422, Saudi Arabia (office). *Telephone:* (1) 225-8000 (office). *Fax:* (1) 225-9000 (office). *E-mail:* ztalsaud@thunayan-al-saud.com (office). *Website:* www.sabic.com (office); www.thunayan-al-saud.com.

SA'UD, HRH Prince Turki al-Faisal bin Abd al-Aziz al-, LLB, MA; Saudi Arabian diplomatist; *Chairman, King Faisal Center for Research and Islamic Studies;* b. 15 Feb. 1945; s. of King Faisal bin Abd al-Aziz al-Sa'ud; m. HRH Princess Nouf bint Fahad; three s. three d.; ed Lawrenceville School, NJ, Princeton and Georgetown Univs, USA, Univs of Cambridge and London, UK; adviser to Royal Court 1973–77; Dir-Gen. Saudi Arabian Intelligence Dept 1977–2001; Del. to Afghanistan 1997–98; Amb. to UK 2003–05, to USA 2005–06; Co-founder King Faisal Foundation; Chair. Bd of Dirs King Faisal Center for Research and Islamic Studies; Trustee Effat Coll., Jeddah. *Address:* King Faisal Center for Research and Islamic Studies, PO Box 51049, Riyadh 115434, Saudi Arabia (office). *Telephone:* (1) 465-2255 (office). *Fax:* (1) 465-9993 (office). *E-mail:* sjameel@kff.com (office). *Website:* www.kfcris.com (office); www.kff.com (office).

SAUDARGAS, Algirdas; Lithuanian politician, biophysicist and diplomatist; b. 17 April 1948, Kaunas; m. Laima Saudargenė; one s. one d.; ed Kaunas Inst. of Medicine; Research Asst Inst. of Math. and Information Tech., Lithuanian Acad. of Sciences 1972–77; Sr Lecturer, Lithuanian Acad. of Agriculture 1977–82; Researcher Kaunas Inst. of Medicine (now Acad.) 1982–90; Founder-mem. Sąjūdis Movt, Chair. Sąjūdis Seimas (Parl.) Political Cttee 1988–90; elected to Supreme Soviet Repub. of Lithuania 1990; Minister of Foreign Affairs 1990–92, 1996–99; mem. official del. to negotiations with Soviet Union; mem. Seimas, Cttee on Foreign Affairs, mem. Seimas del. to European Parl. 1992–2004, elected again 2014, Chair. Sub-cttee on European Affairs 1995–2004; Chair. Lithuanian Christian Democratic Party 1995– (mem. 1989–); mem. Seimas Del. to OSCE 2003–04; Amb. to the Holy See, Vatican City 2004–08; mem. European Parl. 2009–. *Leisure interest:* reading. *Address:* Street Theatre, 8-17A, 03107 Vilnius, Lithuania (office). *Telephone:* (85) 261-0480 (office). *E-mail:* algirdas.saudargas@europarl .europa.eu (office); info@asaudargas.lt. *Website:* www.algirdassaudargas.lt.

SAUDEK, Jan; Czech photographer; b. 13 May 1935, Prague; s. of Gustav Saudek and Pavla Saudková; m. 1st Marie Geislerová 1958 (divorced 1973); m. 2nd Marie Šrámková 1974 (died 1993); two s. three d.; studied reproduction photography at graphic school; factory worker 1953–83; over 500 solo exhbns world-wide, over 500 jt exhbns; works include Hey Joe! 1956, Life (Man Holding New Born Child) 1966, Destiny 1969, Artist's Father on the Jewish Cemetery 1972, Marie nr. 1 1974, Hungry for Your Touch 1975, 120 km/hr. 1975, Mothers and Daughters 1979, Walkman 1984, Desire 1985, Playcards 1986, The Death of an Soldier 1987, F. Sisters 1987, Hommage to Great Vincent 1989, The Wedding 1990, Black Sheep & White Crow 1993, The Deep Devotion 1994, Pretty Girl I Loved 1995, Joan of Arc 1998, Pimp & Hooker 2000; Chevalier, Ordre des Arts et des Lettres 1990; Award for album cover 'Soul Asylum' 1999, Int. Award of Photography 2012 (Photo Festival, Spillimbergo, Italy). *Television:* Jan Saudek (Czech TV project GEN) 1993, Brothers Saudek (Czech TV) 2001. *Films include:* Jerôme du Missolz, France 1991, Jan Saudek – Czech Photographer (documentary); Telewizia Wroslaw, Poland 1997, V pekle svých vášní 2008. *Publications include:* Il Teatro de la Vita 1980, The World of Jan Saudek 1983, Jan Saudek – 200 Photographs 1953–1986 1987, Life, Love, Death and Such Other Trifles 1992, Theatre of the Life 1992, The Letter 1995, Jubilations and Obsessions 1995, Album 1997, Jan Saudek... 1998, Love is a 4 Letter Word 1999, Single, Married, Divorced, Widower 1999, Realities

2002, Saudek 2005, Best of Jan Saudek 2005, Chains of Love 2007, Le allegorie dell Umanita (co-author) 2012. *Leisure interests:* women, running long distances, painting, drinking. *Address:* Ke hrbitovu 11, 152 00 Prague 5, Czech Republic (home). *Telephone:* 737960682 (office). *E-mail:* jan@saudek.com; sarah@saudek.com. *Website:* www.saudek.com.

SAUER, Fernand Edmond; French international official, pharmacist and lawyer; *Honorary Director for Public Health, European Commission;* b. 14 Dec. 1947, St Avold, Moselle; m. Pamela Sheppard; one s. two d.; ed Univs of Strasbourg and Paris II; fmr hosp. pharmacist and pharmaceutical insp. French Ministry of Health; joined European Comm., Brussels, Head of Pharmaceuticals 1986; Exec. Dir European Agency for Evaluation of Medicinal Products (EMEA), London 1994–2000; Dir for Public Health, EC, Luxembourg 2001–06, Hon. Dir 2006–; mem. Coll., Haut-Conseil de santé publique (High Council for Public Health), Paris 2007–11; mem. Académie Nationale de Pharmacie 2000–; Hon. Fellow, School of Pharmacy, Univ. of London, Hon. mem. Royal Pharmaceutical Soc.; Chevalier, Légion d'honneur, Ordre national du Mérite. *Address:* 12, avenue de la Marne, 13260 Cassis, France (home). *Telephone:* 4-91-52-77-98 (home). *E-mail:* fernandsauer@hotmail.com.

SAUER, Louis, FAIA; American/Canadian fmr architect, urban planner and professor of architecture; *Visiting Professor, School of Architecture and Design, Royal Melbourne Institute of Technology;* b. 15 June 1928, Forest Park, Ill.; s. of Frank J. Sauer and Jeanne LaFazia; m. 1st Elizabeth Mason 1956; two c.; m. 2nd Perla Serfaty 1990; ed Univ. of Pennsylvania, Int. School of City Planning, Venice, Italy, Illinois Inst. of Tech.; Prin. Louis Sauer Assoc. Architects, Phila, Pennsylvania 1961–79; Prof. of Architecture, Univ. of Pennsylvania 1974–79, Carnegie-Mellon Univ., Pittsburgh, Pennsylvania 1979–85, Univ. of Colorado 1985–89; Commr, Ville de Montreal Jacques Viger Comm. 1991–; Pnr, Archiris Inc., Pittsburgh 1981–84; Prin. Louis Sauer Architect, Boulder,Colorado 1985–89; Dir of Urban Design, Daniel Arbour and Assocs, Montreal, Canada 1989–2000; currently Visiting Prof., School of Architecture and Design, Royal Melbourne Inst. of Technology, Australia; currently also Chair Design Advisory Panel, Mornington Peninsula Shire; fmr consultant to USAID to advise govts of Lebanon, Egypt and Portugal on low-income housing devt; works include: Water Plaza and high-rise housing, Cincinnati, renewal plan for Fells Point waterfront, public open-space landscape, pvt. housing and housing for the elderly, Baltimore, new town devt for Golf Course Island, Reston, Virginia, Oaklands Mills Village Centre, Columbia, Maryland, housing at Society Hill, Philadelphia; work in Canada includes master-plans for Verdun Nuns Island 1991, Bois-Franc St-Laurent New Town 1992, Ville de Laval 1993, Angus C. P. Rail Rosemont Community 1993, Gatineu City Town Centre 1993, Ile Bizard Town Centre 1993; Nat. Endowment for the Arts Design Fellowship 1978, over 50 design and public service awards. *Leisure interests:* gardening, fishing. *Address:* School of Architecture and Design, Royal Melbourne Institute of Technology, PO Box 2476V, Melbourne, Vic. 3001, Australia (office). *Telephone:* (3) 9925-3555 (office). *Fax:* (3) 9925-3507 (office). *E-mail:* archdes@rmit.edu.au (office). *Website:* www.rmit.edu.au (office).

SAUL, John Ralston, CC, PhD; Canadian essayist, writer and philosopher; b. 19 June 1947, Ottawa; m. Adrienne Clarkson 1999; ed McGill Univ., King's Coll., London, UK; Corresp., Arts Review magazine 1972–75; Special Asst to the Chair., Petro-Canada 1976–78, Policy Advisor 1978–79; Pres. Canadian PEN 1990–92, co-creator, Canadian PEN Writers In Exile Network 2004, Pres. Int. PEN 2009–15; Sr Fellow, Massey Coll., Univ. of Toronto 1999–2005, Chair. LaFontaine-Baldwin Symposium; Co-Chair Inst. for Canadian Citizenship; Founder and Hon. Chair. Le français pour l'avenir/French for the Future, LaFontaine-Baldwin symposium; Patron, PLAN; mem. Royal Soc. of Canada 2014–; mem. Council of Writers and Experts, Int. Cities of Refuge Network (ICORN), Norway; Chevalier, Ordre des Arts et des Lettres 1996; numerous hon. degrees including McGill Univ. 1997, Herzen State Pedagogical Univ., St Petersburg (Russia) 2003, Univ. of Ottawa 2004, Université de Moncton 2011, Univ. of Winnipeg 2014; Pablo Neruda Medal, Chile, Manhae Gutenberg Galaxy Award for Literature 2002, Grand Prize for Literature, South Korea 2010. *Publications include:* non-fiction: Voltaire's Bastards: The Dictatorship of Reason in the West 1992, The Doubter's Companion: A Dictionary of Aggressive Common Sense 1994, The Unconscious Civilization (Gov. Gen.'s Literary Award for Non-Fiction 1996, Gordon Montador Award for Best Canadian Book on Social Issues 1996) 1995, Le citoyen dans un cul-de-sac?: Anatomie d'une société en crise 1995, Reflections of a Siamese Twin 1997, On Equilibrium: Six Qualities of the New Humanism 2001, The Collapse of Globalism and the Reinvention of the World 2005, Joseph Howe and the Battle for the Freedom of Speech 2006, A Fair Country: Telling Truths about Canada 2008, Louis-Hippolyte LaFontaine and Robert Baldwin 2010, The Comeback 2014; fiction: The Paradise Eater (Premio Lettarario Internazionale, Italy 1990), The Birds of Prey 1977, Baraka or The Lives, Fortunes and Sacred Honor of Anthony Smith 1983, The Next Best Thing 1986, The Paradise Eater 1988, De Si Bons Americains 1994, Dark Diversions 2012, other: Gen. Ed., Penguin Extraordinary Canadians Series; contrib. articles and essays to magazines and anthologies. *Address:* c/o Andrea Damiani, Westwood Creative Artists, 94 Harbord Street, Toronto, ON M5B 1G6, Canada (office); 12 Admiral Road, Toronto, ON M5R 2L5, Canada. *Telephone:* (416) 964-3302 (office). *Fax:* (416) 975-9209 (office). *E-mail:* wca_office@wcaltd.com (office); jrs.ahouse12@rogers.com. *Website:* www.wcaltd.com (office); www.johnralstonsaul.com.

SAUMAREZ SMITH, Sir Charles Robert, Kt, CBE, PhD, FSA; British gallery administrator; *Secretary and CEO, Royal Academy of Arts;* b. 28 May 1954, Redlynch, Wilts.; s. of William Hanbury Saumarez Smith and Alice Elizabeth Harness Saumarez Smith (née Raven); m. Romilly Le Quesne Savage 1979; two s.; ed King's Coll., Cambridge, Harvard Univ., USA, Univ. of London, Warburg Inst.; Christie's Research Fellow in Applied Arts, Christ's Coll. Cambridge 1979–82; apptd Asst Keeper Victoria & Albert (V&A) Museum 1982, with special responsibility for V&A/RCA MA course in History of Design, Head of Research 1990–94; Dir Nat. Portrait Gallery 1994–2002, Nat. Gallery 2002–07; Sec. and CEO Royal Academy of Arts 2007–; Slade Prof., Univ. of Oxford 2002; Chair. English Art Museum Dir's Conf. 1999–2003; Pres. Museum Asscn 2004–06; mem. Advisory Council, Warburg Inst. 1997–2003, Inst. of Historical Research 1999–2004, Expert Panel for Museums, Libraries and Archives of the Heritage Lottery Fund 1998–2002; Gov. Univ. of the Arts 2005–13; Prof. of Cultural History, Queen Mary, Univ. of London 2007–; Chair. Advisory Bd, Fondazione Palazzo Strozzi 2008–13; Hon. Fellow, RCA 1991; Hon. FRIBA 2000; Hon. DLitt (Univ. of E Anglia) 2001, (Westminster) 2002, (London) 2003, (Sussex) 2003, (Essex) 2005. *Publications include:* The Building of Castle Howard (Alice Davis Hitchcock Medallion) 1990, Eighteenth Century Decoration 1993, The National Portrait Gallery 1997, The National Gallery 2009, The Company of Artists: The Origins of the Royal Academy of Arts 2012. *Address:* Royal Academy of Arts, Burlington House, Piccadilly, London, W1J 0BD, England (office). *Telephone:* (20) 7300-8020 (office). *E-mail:* chiefexecutive@royalacademy.org.uk (office). *Website:* www.royalacademy.org.uk (office).

SAUNDERS, Jennifer; British actress and writer; b. 6 July 1958, Sleaford, Lincs., England; m. Adrian Edmondson; three d.; ed Cen. School of Speech and Drama, London; Hon. Rose, Montreux 2002, Acad. Fellowship, BAFTA 2009. *Theatre:* An Evening with French and Saunders (nat. tour) 1989, Me and Mamie O'Rourke 1993, French and Saunders Live in 2000 (nat. tour) 2000. *Films include:* The Supergrass 1985, Dangerous Brothers Present: World of Danger (video) 1986, Eat the Rich 1987, Prince Cinders (voice) 1993, In the Bleak Midwinter 1995, Muppet Treasure Island 1996, Spice World: the Movie 1997, Fanny and Elvis 1999, Maybe Baby 2000, Shrek 2 (voice) 2004, L'Entente cordiale 2006, Coraline (voice) 2009, Minions (Voice) 2015, Absolutely Fabulous: The Movie 2016. *Television includes:* The Comic Strip (short) 1981, The Young Ones (series) 1982–84, The Comic Strip Presents. . . 1982–2011, The Lenny Henry Show (series) 1984, Happy Families (series) 1985, Girls on Top 1985–86, Saturday Live (series) 1986, French and Saunders 1987–2005, The Storyteller (series) 1988, The Jim Henson Hour (series) 1989, Rita Rudner (series) 1990, The Tale of Little Pig Robinson (film) 1990, Absolutely Fabulous (Emmy Award 1993, BAFTA Award for Best Comedy 1993, Writers' Guild of Great Britain Award TV for Situation Comedy 1993, BAFTA Award for Best Female Performance in a Comedy Programme 2012) 1992–2012, French and Saunders Live (video) 1993, Queen of the East (film) 1995, Roseanne (series) 1996, Absolutely Fabulous: Absolutely Not! (video) 1998, Friends (series) 1998, Let Them Eat Cake (series) 1999, The Magician's House (series short) 1999, The Nearly Complete and Utter History of Everything (film) 1999, French & Saunders Live (video) 2000, Mirrorball (short) 2000, Pongwiffy (series) 2002, Comic Relief 2003: The Big Hair Do (film) 2003, Comic Relief: Red Nose Night Live 05 (film) 2005, Jam and Jerusalem 2006–09, The Life and Times of Vivienne Vyle (series) 2007, A Bucket o' French and Saunders (series) 2007, The Vivienne Vyle Show (film) 2007, French & Saunders Still Alive (video) 2008, Comic Relief 2009 (film) 2009, Comic Relief: Uptown Downstairs Abbey (film) 2011, This is Jinsy (series) 2011, Blandings (series) 2012. *Publications:* A Feast of French and Saunders (with Dawn French) 1992, Absolutely Fabulous: The Scripts 1993, Absolutely Fabulous 'Continuity' 2001, Bonkers: My Life in Laughs (autobiography) 2013. *Address:* c/o Maureen Vincent, United Agents, 12–26 Lexington Street, London, W1F 0LE, England (office). *Telephone:* (20) 3214-0800 (office). *Fax:* (20) 3214-0801 (office). *E-mail:* info@unitedagents.co.uk (office). *Website:* unitedagents.co.uk (office).

SAUNDERS, Stuart John, MD, FRCP; South African physician, professor of medicine and university administrator; b. 28 Aug. 1931, Cape Town; s. of Albert Frederick Saunders and Lilian Emily; m. 1st Noreen Merle Harrison 1956 (died 1983); one s. one d.; m. 2nd Anita Louw 1984; ed Christian Brothers Coll. and Univ. of Cape Town; Registrar in Pathology and Medicine, Groote Schuur Hosp. and Univ. of Cape Town 1955–58, Lecturer and Sr Lecturer 1961–70, Prof. and Head of Medicine Dept 1971–80, Deputy Principal for Planning, Univ. of Cape Town 1978–80, Vice-Chancellor and Prin. Univ. of Cape Town 1981–96, Vice-Chancellor Emer. 1996–, Co-founder Liver Clinic and Liver Research Unit; Research Asst Royal Postgraduate Medical School, London 1959–60; Fellow in Medicine, Harvard Medical School and Massachusetts Gen. Hosp. 1963–64; fmr Sr Advisor for South Africa program, Andrew W. Mellon Foundation; Past Pres. South Africa Inst. of Race Relations; Fellow, Royal Soc. of South Africa 1995, Coll. of Medicine of South Africa 1996; Life Fellow, Univ. of Cape Town; mem. Faculty of Consulting Physicians of South Africa; Grand Counsellor, Order of the Baobab; Hon. LLD (Aberdeen), (Sheffield), (Princeton), (Rhodes), Hon. DSc (Toronto), (Cape Town). *Publications include:* Access to and Quality in Higher Education: A Comparative Study 1992, Vice-Chancellor on a Tightrope 2000; numerous scientific publications particularly in the field of liver diseases. *Leisure interests:* reading, fishing. *Address:* 45 Belvedere Avenue, Oranjezicht, 8001 Cape Town, South Africa (home). *Telephone:* 453035 (home). *Fax:* 4620047 (home).

SAUPER, Hubert, BA; Austrian film director, producer and writer; b. Kitzbühel, Tyrol; ed Univ. of Performing Arts, Vienna, Univ. of Paris VIII. *Films as writer/director include:* On the Road with Emil (documentary) (Int. Festival, Würzburg Best Short Film 1994, Prix Max Ophülz for Best Documentary Nexon, France 1995) 1993, So I Sleepwalk in Broad Daylight (also producer) (Premio da casa da Figueira da Foz, Portugal 1995, Best First Film, Best Film School Production) 1994, Lomographer's Moscow 1995, Kisangani Diary (documentary, also producer) (seven int. awards) 1998, Alone With Our Stories (documentary) 2000, Darwin's Nightmare (documentary, also producer) (six int. awards, including European Film Awards Best Documentary and Vienna Film Prize) 2004, We Come as Friends (documentary) 2014. *Films as director include:* Wer fürchtet sich vorm schwarzen Mann 1988, Era Max 1989, Piraten in Österreich 1990, Blasi, Der 1990, Ich habe die angenehme Aufgabe 1993. *Films as actor:* In the Circle of the Iris, Blue Distance. *E-mail:* hubert.sauper@free.fr.

SAURA, Carlos; Spanish film director; b. 4 Jan. 1932, Huesca; s. Antonio Saura Pacheco and Fermina Torrente; m. 1st Adela Medrano 1957; two s.; m. 2nd Mercedes Pérez 1982; three s.; ed Inst. of Cinema Research and Studies; professional photographer 1949–; teacher, Instituto de Investigaciones y Experiencias Cinematograficos, Madrid 1957–64, dismissed for political reasons; Lifetime Achievement Award, European Film Awards 2004. *Films include:* Cuenca 1958, Los golfos 1959, Llanto por un bandido 1964, La Caza (Silver Bear, Berlin Film Festival) 1966, Peppermint Frappé (Silver Bear, Berlin Film Festival 1968) 1967, Stress-es tres-tres 1968, La madriguera 1969, El jardín de las delicias 1970, Ana y los lobos 1972, La Prima Angelica (Jury Prize, Cannes Film Festival 1974) 1973, Cría cuervos (Grand Prix of the Jury, Cannes Film Festival 1976) 1975, Elisa, vida mía 1977, Los ojos vendados 1978, Mamá cumple cien años 1979, Deprisa, Deprisa (Silver Bear, Berlin Film Festival 1981) 1980, Bodas de Sangre

1981, Sweet Hours 1982, Carmen (Technical Grand Prize and Award for Best Artistic Contribution, Cannes Film Festival, BAFTA Award) 1983, El Dorado 1987, The Dark Night 1989, Ay Carmela! 1990, Sevillanas 1992, Dispara! 1993, Flamenco 1995, Taxi 1996, Pajarico 1997, Tango 1998, Esa Luz! 1998, Goya en Burdeos 1999, Buñuel y la mesa del rey Salomón 2001, Salome 2002, El Séptimo día 2004, Iberia 2005, Fados 2007, Sinfonía de Aragón (documentary) 2008, Io, Don Giovanni 2009, Flamenco, Flamenco (documentary) 2010, Argentina (documentary) 2015, Jota de Saura (documentary) 2016. *Website:* www.carlos-saura.com.

SAUVAGE, Jean-Pierre, BEng, PhD; French chemist and academic; *Professor Emeritus, Institut de Science et d'Ingénierie Supramoléculaires, University of Strasbourg;* b. 21 Oct. 1944, Paris; s. of Camille Sauvage and Lydie Angèle Arcelin; m. Simone Carmen Boni; one s.; ed Ecole Nationale Supérieure de Chimie, Strasbourg, Université Louis Pasteur; Post-doctoral Researcher, Univ. of Oxford, UK 1973–74; Research Asst, CNRS, Strasbourg 1971–75, Research Assoc. 1975–79, Master of Research 1979, Sr Researcher 1979–81, Univ. Prof. 1981–85, CNRS Dir of Research 1988–2009, now Prof. Emer., Univ. of Strasbourg and CNRS Dir of Research Emer.; Visiting Prof., Univ. of Zurich 2009–10; Distinguished Visiting Scholar, Northwestern Univ., Evanston, USA 2010–12; Chair. 21st Solvay Conf. in Chem., From Non-covalent Assemblies to Molecular Machines, Brussels 2007; mem. Acad. des sciences 1997, Japanese Soc. for the Promotion of Science 1994; Fellow, European Acad. of Sciences 2012; Chevalier, Légion d'honneur 2000; Dr hc (Zurich) 2010; Bronze Medal, CNRS 1978, Award in Coordination Chemistry, Soc. Française de Chimie 1979, Jean-Baptiste Dumas Award, Acad. des sciences 1980, Award in Organic Chem., Soc. Française de Chimie 1987, Silver Medal, CNRS 1988, Izatt-Christensen Award in Macrocyclic Chem. 1991, Prelog Gold Medal, ETH-Zurich (Switzerland) 1994, World Nessim Habif Award, Univ. of Geneva 1995, Centenary Lecturer and Medal, RSC (UK) 2000, Pierre Süe Prize, Soc. Française de Chimie 2005, Catalan Sabatier Prize, Royal Spanish Soc. of Chem. 2005, R.B. Woodward Award in Porphyrin Chem. 2008, Japan Coordination Chem. Award 2009, 'Luigi Tartufari' Int. Prize, Accad. Nazionale dei Lincei (Italy) 2012, Blaise Pascal Medal in Chem., European Acad. of Sciences 2012, Grand Prix de la Fondation de la Maison de la Chimie 2014; ISI HighlyCited chemist 2015; named lectures: Albright and Wilson Lecturer, Univ. of Warwick, UK 1988, Donders Lectureship, Univ. of Utrecht, Netherlands 1992, Univ. of Pavia, Italy 1992, Univ. of Bern, Switzerland 1992, Univ. of Bologna, Italy 1993, The Pfizer Lecturer, Univ. of Sheffield, UK 1993, Univ. of Louvain la Neuve, Belgium 1994, Andrews Lecturer, Univ. of Sydney, Australia 1994, Earl Muetterties Memorial Lecturer, Univ. of Berkeley, USA 1995, H.H. King Lecturer, Kansas State Univ., USA 1995, Reilly Lecturer, Notre Dame Univ., USA 1996, Frontiers in Chemical Research Lecturer, Texas A&M Univ., USA 1996, Morris S. Kharasch Lecturer, Univ. of Chicago, USA 1998, Taft Lecturer, Univ. of California, Irvine, USA 1999, Barré Lecturer, Univ. of Montréal 1999, Centenary Lecturer, RSC (UK) 2000, Descartes Lecturer, Royal Netherlands Acad. of Arts and Sciences 2000, Univ. of La Laguna, Spain 2001, Univ. of Santiago de Compostela, Spain 2001, Musher Lecturer, The Hebrew Univ. of Jerusalem, Israel 2001, Les Power Lecturer, James Cook Univ., Townsville, Australia 2004, Steinhofer Lecturer 2006, Tech. Univ. of Kaiserslautern, Germany 2007, Univ. of Hokkaido, Sapporo, Japan 2010, Inst. for Molecular Science, Okazaki, Japan 2010, The Heinlen Hall Lectures, Bowling Green State Univ., USA 2012, Univ. of Geneva, Switzerland 2012, The R.J.P. Williams Lecture, Univ. of Oxford 2013, Nobel Prize in Chem. (co-recipient with Sir James Fraser Stoddart and Bernard Feringa) 2016. *Publications include:* more than 500 publs 1969–2014; more than 600 lectures and seminars at nat. and int. meetings, in univs and in industrial or governmental research centres on supramolecular chemistry. *Address:* Institut de Science et Ingénierie Supramoléculaires, 8 Allée Gaspard Monge, Université de Strasbourg, 67000 Strasbourg, France (office). *Telephone:* (3) 68-85-51-43 (office). *E-mail:* jpsauvage@unistra.fr (office). *Website:* chimie.unistra.fr (office).

SAVAGE, Francis (Frank) Joseph, CMG, LVO, OBE; British administrator, diplomatist and consultant; *Adviser, Foreign and Commonwealth Office;* b. 8 Feb. 1943, Preston, Lancs., England; s. of Francis Fitzgerald Savage and Mona May Savage (née Parsons); m. Veronica Mary McAleenan 1966; two s.; ed St Stephen's RC School, Welling, N Kent Coll., Dartford; joined Foreign Office 1961, Embassy, Cairo 1967–70, Washington, DC 1971–73, Vice-Consul, Aden 1973–74, Foreign Office 1974–78, Consul, Düsseldorf 1978–82, Consul, Peking (now Beijing) 1982–86, First Sec., Lagos and Consul, Benin 1987–90; First Sec./Counsellor, Foreign Office 1990–93; Gov. of Montserrat 1993–97, of the British Virgin Islands 1998–2002; Chair. Friends of British Virgin Islands 2005–; adviser to FCO 2003–; freelance consultant 2003–; mem. Bd Visar Trust 2002–; adviser on overseas territories to FCO; Pres. Soc. of London Ragamuffins 2008–09; Trustee, Montserrat Foundation 2008–; Kt Commdr, Pontifical Order of St Gregory the Great 2002; Montserrat Badge of Honour 2000. *Leisure interests:* cricket, travel, volcano watching. *Address:* Foreign and Commonwealth Office, King Charles Street, London, SW1A 2AH (office); 19 Cleeve Park Gardens, Sidcup, Kent, DA14 4JL, England (home). *Telephone:* (20) 8309-5061 (home). *E-mail:* frank.savage@fco.gov.uk (office); fjsavage@savagef.fsnet.co.uk (home).

SAVAGE-RUMBAUGH, (Emily) Sue, MS, PhD; American primatologist, academic and writer; *Associate Program Director, Great Ape Trust;* b. 1946; m. Duane Rumbaugh; ed Southern Methodist Univ., Univ. of Oklahoma; fmr Asst Research Prof., Yerkes Regional Primate Research Center, Emory Univ., Assoc. Research Prof. 1984–92; associated with Language Research Center, Georgia State Univ. 1981–2005, also Adjunct Assoc. Prof. of Biology 1983–92, Prof. of Biology and Psychology 1992–2005; Dir Bonobo Research, Great Ape Trust 2005–08, Assoc. Program Dir and Scientist with Special Standing 2008–; Dr hc (Chicago) 1997, (Missouri State) 2008; Leighton A. Wilkie Award in Anthropology, Indiana Univ. 2000. *Publications include:* Ape Language: From Conditioned Response to Symbol 1986, Kanzi: The Ape at the Brink of the Human Mind (co-author) 1995, Apes, Language and the Human Mind (co-author) 1996; numerous articles in professional journals. *Address:* Great Ape Trust, 1515 Linden Street, Suite 220, Des Moines, IA 50320, USA (office). *Telephone:* (515) 243-9367 (office). *Fax:* (515) 243-9367 (office). *E-mail:* info@greatapetrust.org (office). *Website:* www.greatapetrust.org (office).

SAVARIN, Charles Angelo; Dominican politician and diplomatist; *President;* b. 2 Oct. 1943, Portsmouth; m. Clara Etienne; one s. two d.; ed Dominica Grammar School, Roseau, Ruskin Coll., Oxford, UK; Asst Master, Dominica Grammar School 1963–70; Gen. Sec., Dominica Civil Services Assen 1966–83; Senator, House of Ass. 1979–85, 2005–13; Minister without Portfolio, Prime Minister's Office 1983–85; Minister Counsellor, Dominica High Comm., London 1985–86; Perm. Rep. of Dominica to EU, Brussels 1986–93, concurrently Amb. to Belgium and Perm. Rep. to UN, Geneva 1986–93; Gen. Man. Nat. Devt Corpn 1993–95; mem. Parl. for Roseau Cen. Constituency 1995–2005; Leader, Freedom Party 1996–2006; Minister of Tourism 2000–05, of Foreign Affairs, Trade and Labour 2005–07, Minister for the Public Service 2005–, Minister of Public Utilities, Energy and Ports 2007–09, of Nat. Security, Immigration and Labour 2009–13; Pres. 2013–; Sisserou Award of Honour 2006, Dominica Award of Honour 2013. *Address:* Office of the President, Morne Bruce, Roseau, Dominica (office). *Telephone:* 4482054 (office). *Fax:* 4498366 (office). *E-mail:* presidentsoffice@dominica.gov.dm (office). *Website:* presidentoffice.gov.dm (office).

SAVART, Michel; French business executive; *Chairman and CEO, Foncière Euris SA;* ed Ecole Polytechnique, Ecole Nationale Supérieure des Mines de Paris; began career at Havas 1986; successively in charge of missions at Bank Louis Dreyfus 1987; managed projects then adviser to Man. Bd/Exec. Bd Banque Arjil (Lagardère Group) 1988–94; Man. Dir Mergers & Acquisitions, Dresdner Kleinwort Benson (DKB) 1995–99; joined Euris-Rally as a Dir-Adviser to the Pres. 1999, within Euris Group, served as Adviser to Chair. of Rallye SA, Perm. Rep. of Rallye on Board of Groupe Go Sport (listed co.), Rep. of Foncière Euris: Chair. Marigny Belfort SAS, Marigny Elysées SAS, Marigny Foncière SAS, Matignon Abbeville SAS, Matignon Bail SAS, Matignon Corbeil Centre SAS, Man. of SCI Sofaret and SCI Les Herbiers, Rep. of Marigny Foncière, Chair. Mat-Bel 2 SAS, Co-Man. SNC Centre Commercial Porte de Châtillon, SCI Les Deux Lions, SCI Palais des Marchands, SCI Ruban Bleu Saint-Nazaire and Man. SCI Pont de Grenelle, Rep. of Matignon Abbeville and Man. of Centrum K Sarl, Centrum J Sarl, and Centrum Z Sarl, Rep. of Centrum NS Luxembourg Sarl and Man. of Manufaktura Luxembourg Sarl, Co-Man. of Alexa Holding GmbH, Alexa Shopping Centre GmbH, Alexanderplatz Voltairestrasse GmbH, Einkaufszentrum am Alex GmbH, Guttenbergstrasse BAB5 GmbH, HBF Königswall GmbH, Loop 5 Shopping Centre GmbH, Man. (category A) of Centrum NS Luxembourg Sarl, Rep. of Foncière Euris, Chair. Marigny Expansion, and Man. of SNC Alta Marigny Carré de Soie, Rep. of Matignon Abbeville and Chair. of Mat-Bel 2 SAS, Rep. of Marigny Elysées and Co-Man. of SCCV des Jardins de Seine 1, SCCV des Jardins de Seine 2, SNC Centre Commercial du Grand Argenteuil, Chair. and CEO Foncière Euris SA 2010–; outside Euris Group, served as mem. Bd Groupe Go Sport; Perm. Rep. of Parande SAS on Bd of Matussière et Forest SA; Co-Man. SNC Centre Commercial Porte de Chatillon, SCI Les Deux Lions, SCI Palais des Marchand, amongst others; Man. EURL Montmorency, EURL Aubriot Investissements; mem. Bd of Dirs Casino Guichard Perrachon & Cie SA 2005–, C Discount SA 2005–, Mercialys SA 2010–. *Address:* Foncière Euris SA, 83 rue du Faubourg Saint-Honoré, 75008 Paris, France (office). *Telephone:* 1-44-71-14-00 (office). *Fax:* 1-44-71-14-50 (office). *E-mail:* info@fonciere-euris.fr (office). *Website:* www.fonciere-euris.fr (office); www.rallye.fr.

SAVÉANT, Jean-Michel, DèsSc; French chemist and academic; *Emeritus Research Director, Centre National de la Recherche Scientifique, Université Paris 7 - Denis Diderot;* b. 19 Sept. 1933, Rennes; ed Ecole Normale Supérieure, Paris, Instituto di Chimica Fisica dell'Universita de Padova, Italy; Asst Dir, Chem. Lab., Ecole Normale Supérieure, Paris 1968–70; Prof., Univ. Paris 7 – Denis Diderot 1971–85, CNRS Research Dir 1985–2000, Research Dir Emer. 2000–, currently also Sr Scientist; Prof., California Inst. of Technology, USA 1988–89; mem. Editorial Bd Journal of the American Chemical Society, Inorganic Chem., Journal of Physical Organic Chem., ChemPhysChem, Journal of Electroanalytical Chem.; mem. Acad. des Sciences 2000–; Foreign Assoc. mem. NAS 2001–; French Chemical Soc. Prix Louis Ancel 1966, CNRS Silver Medal 1976, Royal Soc. of Chem. Faraday Medal 1983, Medaglia Luigi Riccoboni 1983, Prix Emile Jungfleisch, Acad. des sciences 1989, Electrochemical Soc. Palladium Medal 1993, Oscar K. Rice Distinguished Lecturer, Univ. of North Carolina, Chapel Hill 1995, Societa Chimica Italiana Luigi Galvani Medal 1997, Nelson Leonard Distinguished Lecturer, Univ. of Illinois, Urbana-Champaing 1999, Manuel Baizer Award, Electrochemical Soc. 2002, Baker Lecturer, Cornell Univ. 2002, Bruno Breyer Medal, Royal Australian Chemical Inst. 2005. *Publication:* Elements of Molecular and Biomolecular Electrochemistry 2006. *Address:* Laboratoire d'Electrochimie Moléculaire UMR CNRS - P7 7591, Université Paris Diderot - Paris 7, 15 rue Jean-Antoine de Baïf, 7e Etage - case 7107, 75205 Paris, Cedex 13, France (office). *Telephone:* 1-57-27-87-95 (office). *Fax:* 1-57-27-87-88 (office). *E-mail:* saveant@univ-paris-diderot.fr (office). *Website:* www.lemp7.cnrs.fr (office).

SAVELYEV, Oleg Genrikhovich; Russian politician; *Minister of Crimean Affairs;* b. 27 Oct. 1965, Leningrad (now St Petersburg); ed Leningrad Polytechnic Inst.; First Deputy Minister of Econ. Devt 2008–14, Co-Chair. fifth meeting of Working Group on co-operation of special economy zone between China and Russia 2013; Minister of Crimean Affairs, responsible for integration of annexed Crimea into Russian Fed. 2014–; mem. Bd of Dirs Gazprom 2014–; mem. Bd of Regents, Northern (Arctic) Fed. Univ.; travel bans and assets freeze imposed on him by EU April 2014, placed on Sanctions List Against the Russian Fed. by US Govt Aug. 2014. *Address:* Ministry of Crimean Affairs, Office of the Government, 103274 Moscow, Krasnopresnenskaya nab. 2, Russia (office). *Website:* government.ru/department/296 (office); government.ru/en/gov/persons/382/events (office).

SAVELYEVA, Lyudmila Mikhailovna; Russian actress; b. 24 Jan. 1942, Leningrad (now St Petersburg); m. Aleksandr Zbruyev 1965 (divorced); one c.; ed Vaganova Ballet School, Leningrad; soloist, Kirorskiy (Mariinskiy) Theatre 1961–65; People's Artist of the RSFSR 1985. *Films include:* Sleeping Beauty 1964, War and Peace 1967, The Sunflowers (de Sica) 1971, Flight 1971, The Headless Horseman 1973, The Seagull 1973, Yulia Vrevskaya 1978, The Hat 1982, The Fourth Year of War 1983, Success 1985, Another's Belaya and Ryaboy 1986, White Rose–Emblem of Grief, Red Rose–Emblem of Love 1989, The Mystery of Nardo 1999, The Tender Age 2000. *Television:* Anna Karenina (mini-series) 2009. *Theatre productions include:* The Price (Miller), M. Rozovsky theatre. *Address:* Tverskaya Str. 19, Apt. 76, 103050 Moscow, Russia. *Telephone:* (495) 299-99-34.

SAVI, Toomas, PhD; Estonian fmr physician and politician; b. 30 Dec. 1942, Tartu; s. of Kaarel Savi and Salme Savi Moistus; m. Kirsti Savi; two d.; ed Tartu

State Univ.; Chief Physician, USSR light athletics team, concurrently Sr Researcher Tartu State Univ. 1970–80; nat. team physician, Olympic Games, Munich 1972, Montreal 1976, Moscow 1980, Lillehammer 1994; Chief Physician, Tartu Medical Centre of Physical Educ. 1979–93; Asst Medical Officer, Kuopio Univ. Hosp. and Kajaani Hosp., Finland 1991–92; mem. Tartu Town Council 1989–93, 1996–97, 1999–2000; Deputy Mayor of Tartu 1993–95; mem. Eesti Reformierakond (Estonian Reform Party) 1994–; Speaker of Riigikogu (State Ass.) 1995–2003, Deputy Speaker 2003–04; Observer, European Parl. 2003–04; mem. European Parl. (Group of the Alliance of Liberals and Democrats for Europe) 2004–09, Del. for Relations with Canada, mem. Cttee on Devt, Substitute mem. Cttee on Regional Devt, Del. to the ACP-EU Jt Parl. Ass.; Founder-mem. Estonian Olympic Cttee 1989–, Vice-Pres. 2008–12; Pres. Estonian Skiing Asscn 1999–2011; mem., Tartu Rotary Club 1993–, Bd Eluterve Eesti exercise asscn 1994–, Bd Estonian Asscn 2001–, Supervisory Bd of Tartu St Mary's Church Foundation 2003–; Grand Cross, Royal Norwegian Order of Merit 1998, Nat. Order of Merit (Malta) 2001, Grand Cross, Ordre nat. du Mérite (France) 2001, Commdr Grand Cross, Order of the Lion (Finland) 2002, Badge of the Order of the Nat. Coat of Arms (Second Class) (Estonia) 2003, Grand Officer, Order of Infante Dom Henrique (Portugal) 2003. *Leisure interests:* sport. *Address:* Näituse 22-8, 50 407 Tartu, Estonia. *E-mail:* toomas.savi@mail.ee (home).

SAVILL, Dame Rosalind Joy, DBE, CBE, FBA, FSA; British museum director; *Curator Emeritus, The Wallace Collection;* b. 12 May 1951, Hants.; d. of Guy Savill and Lorna Williams; one d.; ed Wycombe Abbey School, Chatelard School, Montreux and Univ. of Leeds; Museum Asst, Ceramics Dept, Victoria & Albert Museum 1973–74; Museum Asst and Sr Asst, The Wallace Collection 1974–78, Asst to Dir 1978–92, Dir 1992–2011, Curator Emer. 2011–; Pres. French Porcelain Soc. 1999–; mem. Arts Panel, Nat. Trust 1995–2015, Art Advisory Cttee, Nat. Museums & Galleries of Wales 1998–2003, Museums and Collections Advisory Cttee English Heritage 1998–2002, Royal Mint Advisory Cttee 1999–2007; Visiting Prof., Univ. of Arts in London 2008–; Gov. Camden School for Girls 1996–2008; Syndic, Fitzwilliam Museum, Cambridge 2015–; mem. Bd of Dirs and mem. of Council, Alpha Plus Schools 2012–; Trustee, Somerset House 1997–2004, Campaign for Museums 1999–2009, Holburne Museum of Art, Bath 2004–08, Samuel Courtauld Trust 2008–16, Buccleuch Living Buccleuch Trust 2009–, Wallace Collection Foundation 2012–, Royal Collection Trust 2012–; Professional Research Fellow, Univ. of Buckingham 2011; Officier, Ordre des Arts et des Lettres 2013; Dr hc (Buckinghamshire and Chiltern Univ. Coll.); Hon. DLit (Univ. of Buckingham) 2013; Leverhulme Scholar 1975, Getty Scholar 1985, Nat. Art Collections Fund Prize 1990, European Women of Achievement Award 2005, Iris Foundation Award for Outstanding Contribution to the Decorative Arts, Bard Graduate Center, New York 2014. *Publications include:* The Wallace Collection Catalogue of Sèvres Porcelain (three vols) 1988; articles, reviews, contrib. to exhbn catalogues etc. *Leisure interests:* music, birds, wildlife, gardening. *Address:* The Wallace Collection, Manchester Square, London, W1U 3BN, England (office). *Website:* rosalindsavill@hotmail.com (office).

SAVISAAR, Edgar; Estonian politician; b. 31 May 1950, Harjumaa, Harju Co., Estonian SSR, USSR; m. 1st Kaire Savisaar; one s.; m. 2nd Liis Savisaar; one s. one d.; m. 3rd Vilja Savisaar (divorced 2009); one d.; ed Tartu Secondary School, Tartu State Univ.; worked in governmental insts dealing with planning of economy 1980–88; Academic Dir Mainor consultancy co. 1988–89; mem. CP –1990; Leader Estonian Popular Front; Vice-Chair. Council of Ministers of Estonian SSR and Head of State Plan Cttee 1989 (resgnd), Chair. Council of Ministers 1990–91, then Prime Minister of Repub. of Estonia following independence 1991–92; Minister of Economy 1990; Deputy Speaker of Riigikogu 1992–95; Chair. Eesti Keskerakond (Estonian Centre Party) –1995 (resgnd), re-appointed Chair. following split in party 1996–2016; Deputy Prime Minister and Minister of the Interior April–Nov. 1995, dismissed from posts following scandal over taped conversations; Chair. Tallinn City Council 1996–99; Mayor of Tallinn 2001–04, 2007–15 (suspended); briefly Prime Minister of Estonia following legis. election 2003; Minister of Econ. Affairs and Communications 2005–07; Order of State Coat of Arms 2001. *Publications include:* four books. *Address:* Eesti Keskerakond (Estonian Centre Party), Toom-Rüütli 3/5, Tallinn 10130, Estonia (office). *Telephone:* 627-3460 (office). *Fax:* 627-3461 (office). *E-mail:* keskerakond@keskerakond.ee (office); tallinnalinnapea@hotmail.com (office). *Website:* www.keskerakond.ee (office); linnapea.tallinn.ee (office).

SAVOLA, Kai Kari Akseli; Finnish theatre director, actor and translator; b. 30 Sept. 1931, Helsinki; s. of Tauno Savola and Hilppa Korpinen; m. Terttu Byckling 1958; two s. one d.; ed Helsinki Univ.; worked as critic 1957–60; Admin. Dir Helsinki Student Theatre 1959–62; Man. Dir Finnish Drama Agency 1962–65; Literary Man. Helsinki City Theatre 1965–68; Dir-Gen. Tampere Workers' Theatre 1968–73; Dir Finnish Nat. Theatre 1973, Dir-Gen. 1974–92; stage direction of Finnish, English, Romanian, Russian and Japanese drama; designed the two experimental stages of the Finnish Nat. Theatre (with Prof. Heikki Siren) 1976, 1987; mem. Bd of Dirs Foundation of Finnish Nat. Theatre; Hon. Prof. 1983; Commdr, Order of White Rose of Finland 1991, Golden Medal of Honour of Tampere 1973, Golden Medal, Helsinki 1992, Ida Aalberg Medal. *Plays:* as director: A Taste of Honey, Friends (Kobo Abe); as actor: L'Invasion (Adamov). *Publications include:* translations of English and German plays into Finnish. *Leisure interest:* farming. *Address:* Laivurinkatu 39 A 12, 00150 Helsinki, Finland (home). *Telephone:* (9) 636939 (home); (40) 5846454 (home). *E-mail:* t.savola@kolumbus.fi (home).

SAVOSTYANOV, Maj.-Gen. Yevgeny Vadimovich; Russian politician; b. 28 Feb. 1952, Moscow; m. Julia Savostyanova; two s.; ed Moscow Mining Inst.; Jr Researcher, Inst. of Physics of the Earth, USSR Acad. of Sciences 1975–77; Researcher, Inst. for Problems of Complex Use of Mineral Wealth 1975–90; Founder and Co-Chair. Club of Voters of Acad. of Sciences for election of Andrey Sakharov and other scientists as people's deputies from Acad. of Sciences; Asst to Chair., Moscow City Soviet, then Dir-Gen. Dept Moscow Mayor's Office 1990–91; mem. Co-ordination Council Movt Democratic Russia; mem. Org. Cttee of Democratic Reforms 1991; Deputy Dir Russian Fed. Service of Counterespionage, Head of Dept Moscow and Moscow Region 1991–94; Adviser to Chair. Russian Fed. of Independent Trade Unions 1995–96; Deputy Head, Admin. of Russian Presidency 1996–98; Vice-Pres. Moscow Oil and Gas Co. 1999–2005; Pres. Metro-Navtika; Deputy Chief Exec., Centre for Assisting Rapprochement Between Russia and USA; Chair. Supervisory Bd Kemerovo Mining Co. 2000; mem. Bd of Dirs Sibir Energy PLC 2004; unsuccessful cand. for Pres. of Russian Fed. 2000; Head, Coordination Council on Intellectual Property Protection –2015; mem. Public Council, Ministry of Culture –2015 (resgnd).

SAVOY, Guy; French chef and restaurateur; *Proprietor, Restaurant Guy Savoy;* b. 24 July 1953, Nevers; m. Marie Danielle Amann 1975; one s. one d.; for three years Chef at La Barrière de Clichy, Paris; Propr Restaurant Guy Savoy, Paris 1980–, Restaurant Le Bistrot de l'Etoile Troyon 1989–, Restaurant Le Bistrot de l'Etoile-Niel 1989–, Restaurant Le Bistrot l'Etoile-Lauriston 1991, Restaurant La Butte Chaillot 1992, Les Bookinistes 1994, Le Cap Vernet, Paris 1995; Légion d'honneur. *Publications include:* Les Légumes gourmands 1985, La Gourmandise apprivoisée 1987, Vegetable Magic 1989, La Cuisine de mes bistrots 1998, 120 recettes comme à la maison 2000, Guy Savoy: Simple French Recipes for the Home Cook 2004. *Leisure interest:* modern painting. *Address:* Restaurant Guy Savoy, 11, quai de Conti, 75006 Paris, France (office). *Telephone:* 1-43-80-40-61 (office). *Fax:* 1-46-22-43-09 (office). *Website:* www.guysavoy.com (office).

SAWA, Metropolitan Michał Hrycuniak, MA, ThD; Polish ecclesiastic; *Metropolitan of Warsaw and All Poland; Primate of the Polish Autocephalous Orthodox Church;* b. 15 April 1938, Śniatycze; ed Christian Acad. of Theology, Warsaw, Univ. of Belgrade; teacher Orthodox Seminary, Warsaw 1962–, Rector Int. Section 1964–65; Rector Orthodox Theological Seminary, Jabłeczna 1970–79; Assoc. Prof. and Prof. Christian Acad. of Theology, Warsaw 1966–, Prof. of Theological Sciences 1990–; ordained deacon 1964; ordained priest 1966; Dir Chancellery of Metropolitan of Warsaw and All Poland 1966–70; Superior Monastery of St Onufrey at Jabłeczna 1970–79; ordained Bishop 1979, Bishop of Łódź and Poznań 1979–81, of Białystok and Gdańsk 1981–99; Archbishop 1987; Metropolitan of Warsaw and All Poland, Primate of the Polish Autocephalous Orthodox Church 1998–; Orthodox Ordinary of the Polish Armed Forces 1994–98, rank of Brig.-Gen. 1996; f. quarterly publs of Diocese of Białystok and Gdańsk and of Orthodox Ordinate of Polish Armed Forces; Dean and Prof. of Chair of Orthodox Theology, Univ. in Białystok 1999–; Ed.-in-Chief Kalendarz Polskiego Autokefalicznego Kościoła Prawosławnego, Elpis, Rocznik Teologiczny (annual), Cerkiewny Wiestnik (quarterly), Wiadomości Polskiego Autokefalicznego Kościoła Prawosławnego (monthly); Hon. Prof. of Theological Sciences; Dr hc (St Vladimir's Orthodox Seminary, New York) 2000, (Univ. in Bialystok, Poland) 2001, (Univ. of Thessaloniki, Greece) 2002, (Theological Acad., Minsk, Belarus) 2003. *Publications include:* Prawosławne pojmowanie małżeństwa (The Orthodox Understanding of Marriage) 1994, Chrystus najwierniejszy przyjaciel człowieka (Christ the Only Beloved Friend) 2003, Slova (Speeches) 2004. *Address:* Al. Solidarności 52, 03-402 Warsaw, Poland (office). *Telephone:* (22) 6190886 (office). *Fax:* (22) 6190886 (office). *Website:* www.orthodox.pl (office).

SAWANT, Pramod; Indian physician and politician; *Chief Minister of Goa;* b. 24 April 1973, Goa; s. of Pandurang Sawant and Padmini Sawant; m. Sulakshana Sawant; ed Ganga Ayurvedic Medical Coll., Kolhapur, Tilak Maharashtra Univ.; practised as doctor of alternative medicine, Goa; fmr Chair. Goa State Infrastructure Development Corpn; mem. Goa Legis. Ass. for Sanquelim constituency (BJP) 2012–, Speaker, Goa Legis. Ass. 2017–19; Chief Minister of Goa 2019–; mem. Bharatiya Janata Party, fmr BJP youth leader. *Address:* Office of the Chief Minister, Secretariat, Panaji 403 001, Goa, India (office). *Telephone:* (832) 2223970 (office). *Fax:* (832) 2223648 (office). *E-mail:* cmgoa@goa.nic.in (office). *Website:* www.goa.gov.in (office).

SAWERS, Sir (Robert) John, Kt, GCMG, BSc; British diplomatist, business executive and fmr crown servant; *Partner and Chairman, Macro Advisory Partners LLP;* b. 26 July 1955, Warwick, England; m. Shelley Sawyers; three c.; ed City of Bath Boys' School (later Beechen Cliff School), Univ. of Nottingham, spent periods at Univs of St Andrews, the Witwatersrand, South Africa and Harvard, USA; joined FCO 1977, served in Yemen and Syria on behalf of MI6, Political Officer in Damascus 1982–84, Desk Officer, EU Dept, FCO 1984–86, Pvt. Sec. to the Minister of State 1986–88, served in Pretoria, then Cape Town 1988–91, Head of EU Presidency Planning Unit, FCO 1991–93, Prin. Pvt. Sec. to the Foreign Sec. 1993–95; Int. Fellow, Harvard Univ. 1995; served at Embassy in Washington, DC 1996–98, Foreign Affairs Adviser to the Prime Minister 1999–2001, Amb. to Egypt 2001–03, Political Dir, FCO 2003–07, Amb. and Perm. Rep. to UN, New York 2007–09; Chief, Secret Intelligence Service (MI6) 2009–14; Partner and Chair. Macro Advisory Partners LLP 2015–; Visiting Prof., Dept of War Studies, King's Coll. London 2014; Gov., Ditchley Foundation. *Leisure interests:* theatre, hiking, sport (especially tennis and cycling). *E-mail:* info@macroadvisorypartners.com (office). *Website:* www.macroadvisorypartners.com (office).

SAWIRIS, Naguib Onsi; Egyptian business executive and politician; *Executive Chairman and CEO, Orascom Telecom Media and Technology Holding S.A.E.;* b. 15 June 1954; s. of Onsi Sawiris; m.; four c.; ed German Evangelical School, Cairo, Swiss Inst. of Tech. (ETH), Zurich, Switzerland; joined Orascom 1979, Chair. and CEO Orascom Telecom Holding S.A.E. (after Orascom split into separate operating cos) 1997–2011, Exec. Chair. and CEO Orascom Telecom Media and Technology Holding S.A.E. 2011–, also Chair. Orascom TMT Investments S.à r.l., La Mancha Inc., Accelero Capital; f. Weather Investments (now Wind Telecom SpA) 2005; Founder Free Egyptians Party 2011; Jt Chair. Italian-Egyptian Business Council 2006–07; Chair. Egyptian Co. for Mobile Services (MobiNil); Pres. German-Arab Chamber of Industry and Commerce 2008–09; mem. Bd of Dirs Arab Thought Foundation, Egyptian Council for Foreign Affairs, Consumer Rights Protection Asscn, Cancer Soc. of Egypt; apptd mem. Int. Advisory Cttee New York Stock Exchange 2005; mem. Int. Advisory Bd, Nat. Bank of Kuwait; Trustee and Head of Financial Cttee, French Univ. in Cairo; Légion d'honneur, Commdr, Order of Stella della Solidarietà Italiana 2011; Sitara-e-Quaid-e-Azam Award 2006, CIC Globalist of the Year 2011. *Address:* Orascom Telecom Media and Technology Holding S.A.E, 2005A Nile City Towers, South Tower, Cornish El Nile Ramlet Beaulac, Cairo 11221, Egypt (office). *E-mail:* info@otmt.com (office). *Website:* otmt.com/en-us/home.aspx (office).

SAWIRIS, Nassef, BA; Egyptian business executive; *CEO, Orascom Construction Industries (OCI N.V);* b. 1961; s. of Onsi Sawiris; m.; four c.; ed Univ. of Chicago, USA; CEO Orascom Construction Industries (OCI S.A.E.) 1998–2013, Chair.

2010–13, CEO OCI N.V 2013–; mem. Bd of Dirs 1998–; Chair. Building Materials and Refractory Council, Fed. of Egyptian Industries; mem. Bd of Dirs Cairo Stock Exchange 2004–07, Alexandria Stock Exchanges 2004–07, Lafarge SA, Dubai International Financial Exchange, NNS Holding, Luxembourg, Besix, Belgium, NASDAQ Dubai 2008–10, LafargeHolcim Ltd 2015–, Nile City Investments, The Egyptian Fertilizer Co., NNS Holding; mem. American Chamber of Commerce, German-Arab Chamber of Industry and Commerce, Business Secr. of Egyptian Nat. Democratic Party. *Address:* Orascom Construction Industries N.V, Honthorststraat 19, 1071 DC Amsterdam, Netherlands (office). *Telephone:* (20) 7234500 (office). *Website:* www.oci.nl (office).

SAWIRIS, Onsi, BSc; Egyptian business executive; *Chairman Emeritus, Orascom Construction Industries;* b. 1930; m. Youssreya Loza Sawiris; three s.; ed Cairo Univ.; est. Orascom Construction Industries (fmrly Orascom Onsi Sawiris & Co.) 1976, currently Chair. Emer. and Dir (non-exec.); currently also Hon. Chair. and mem. Bd of Dirs MobiNil; fmr Chair. for AIG Insurance Co., Egypt, YMCA, Cairo, Egyptian-Scandinavian Business Asscn in Egypt; Advisor to Bd, Sawiris Foundation for Social Development; Commdr in the Order of the Crown (Belgium), L'Order de Leopold 1998, Royal Order of the Polar Star (Sweden) 2008. *Address:* Orascom Construction Industries, Nile City Towers, 2005A, Corniche El Nil, Cairo 11221, Egypt (office). *Telephone:* (2) 24611111 (office). *Website:* www.orascom.com (office).

SAWIRIS, Samih; Egyptian/Montenegrin business executive; *Chairman, Orascom Development Holding;* b. 28 Jan. 1957, Cairo; s. of Onsi Sawiris; m.; one s. three d.; ed German School, Cairo, Technical Univ. of Berlin, Germany; f. Nat. Marine Boat Factory, Orascom Projects for Touristic Devt 1996, Orascom Hotel Holdings 1997, El Gouna Beverages Co. (sold in 2001) 1997; CEO Orascom Devt Holding –2011, now Chair.; mem. Bd of Dirs Beltone Financial, Guggenheim Museum, Jordan Projects for Tourism Devt Co.; Founder-mem. Sawiris Foundation for Social Devt 2001–. *Address:* Orascom Development Holding, Gotthardstrasse 12, 6460 Altdorf, Switzerland (office). *Telephone:* (41) 8741717 (office). *Fax:* (41) 8741707 (office). *Website:* www.orascomdh.com (office).

SAWYER, Amos, BA, MA, PhD; Liberian academic and political activist; *Chairman, Governance Commission Liberia;* b. 1945; s. of Abel Sawyer and Sarah Sawyer; ed Univ. of Liberia, Northwestern Univ., USA; Chair. Constitution Drafting Comm. 1980s; installed as Leader of Interim Govt of Nat. Unity (by nat. conf. of Liberian leaders that included leaders of political parties, civil soc. orgs and of combined guerrilla forces which overthrew regime of fmr Pres. Samuel Doe 1990) Aug. 1990, inaugurated Nov. 1990; fmr Leader Liberian People's Party; fmr Dir Inst. of Research and Dean Coll. of Social Science and Humanities, Univ. of Liberia; Co-Dir and Research Scholar, Workshop in Political Theory and Policy Analysis, Indiana Univ. 2000–09; currently Chair. Governance Comm. of Liberia; mem. Panel of Eminent Persons, African Peer Review Mechanism 2010–14 (Chair. 2012–13); Distinguished Service Order and Grand Cordon of the Knighthood of Most Venerable Order of Pioneers; Dr hc (Indiana Univ.) 2018; Gusi Peace Prize 2011. *Publications include:* The Emergence of Autocracy in Liberia: Tragedy and Challenge 1992, Beyond Plunder: Toward Democratic Governance in Liberia 2005. *Address:* Governance Commission, S.D. Cooper Road, Paynesville, Liberia (office). *E-mail:* acsawyer45@aol.com (office). *Website:* governancecommissionlr.org (office).

SAWYER, Diane, BA; American broadcast journalist; b. 22 Dec. 1945, Glasgow, Ky; d. of Erbon Powers 'Tom' Sawyer and Jean W. Sawyer (née Dunagan); m. Mike Nichols 1988 (died 2014); ed Seneca High School, Louisville, Ky, Wellesley Coll.; toured country as America's Junior Miss to promote Coca-Cola Pavilion at 1964–65 New York World's Fair 1962–65; reporter, WLKY-TV, Louisville, Ky 1967–70; Admin. White House Press Office 1970–74; mem. Nixon-Ford transition team 1974–75; Asst to Richard Nixon (fmr US Pres.) 1974, 1975; Gen. Reporter, later State Dept Corresp., CBS News 1978–81, apptd Co-Anchor Morning News 1981, Co-Anchor Early Morning News 1982–84, Corresp. and Co-Ed. 60 Minutes 1984–89; Co-Anchor PrimeTime Live (now Primetime Thursday), ABC News 1989–99, Good Morning America 1999–2009, Anchor, ABC World News with Diane Sawyer 2009–14, now works on news specials and selected interviews; won America's Junior Miss scholarship pageant as rep. from State of Kentucky, nine Emmy awards, Nat. Headliner Awards, George Foster Peabody Award for Public Service, Robert F. Kennedy Journalism Award, Special Dupont Award, Ohio State Award, IRTS Lifetime Achievement Award, inducted TV Acad. of Fame 1997, Peabody Award for work on A Hidden America: Children of the Mountains 2009. *Address:* ABC News, 47 West 66th Street, New York, NY 10023, USA (office). *Website:* abcnews.go.com/wn (office).

SAWYERS, Charles Lazelle, BA, MD, PhD; American physician, oncologist and academic; *Marie-Josée and Henry R. Kravis Chair in Human Oncology and Pathogenesis, Memorial Sloan-Kettering Cancer Center;* b. 26 Jan. 1959, Nashville, Tenn.; m.; two c.; ed Princeton Univ., Johns Hopkins Medical School; Residency, Univ. of California, San Francisco; worked at Jonsson Cancer Center, UCLA for nearly 18 years; currently Marie-Josée and Henry R. Kravis Chair in Human Oncology and Pathogenesis, Memorial Sloan-Kettering Cancer Center, New York; a Howard Hughes Medical Inst. Investigator; Past Pres. American Soc. of Clinical Investigation; mem. Bd of Dirs Novartis AG 2013–; mem. Bd of Scientific Councilors, Nat. Cancer Inst.; mem. Inst. of Medicine, NAS; Fellow, UCLA; numerous honours and awards, including the Doris Duke Distinguished Clinical Scientist Award 2001, Richard & Hinda Rosenthal Foundation Award, American Asscn of Cancer Research 2005, David A. Karnofsky Award, American Soc. of Clinical Oncology 2005, Dorothy P. Landon-AACR Prize for Translational Cancer Research 2009, Lasker-DeBakey Award for Clinical Medical Research (co-recipient) 2009, Breakthrough Prize in Life Sciences (co-recipient) 2013, BBVA Foundation Frontiers of Knowledge Award in Biomedicine (co-recipient) 2014. *Achievements include:* developed, with Brian J. Druker and Nicholas B. Lydon, imatinib (or Gleevac) and dasatinib – targeted treatments for chronic myeloid leukemia. *Publications:* numerous papers in professional journals. *Address:* Memorial Sloan-Kettering Cancer Center, 1275 York Avenue, New York, NY 10065, USA (office). *Telephone:* (646) 888-2138 (office); (646) 888-3462 (office). *Fax:* (646) 888-3407 (office). *E-mail:* sawyersc@mskcc.org (office). *Website:* www.mskcc.org/research/lab/charles-sawyers (office).

SAXENA, Ashutosh, BTech, MS, PhD; American (b. Indian) computer scientist, academic and entrepreneur; *Alfred P. Sloan Fellow and Microsoft Faculty Fellow, Stanford University;* b. 11 Feb. 1984; ed Indian Inst. of Tech. (IIT), Kanpur, Stanford Univ.; Research Intern, Bose Corpn April–July 2003; Researcher, CSIRO, Sydney, Australia May–Sept. 2004; Research Intern, Microsoft May–July 2005; Co-founder and Chief Tech. Officer, ZunaVision 2008–10; Advisor and Consultant, Sony Ericsson Mobile Communications 2010–12; Chief Scientist, Holopad, New York 2010–13; Asst Prof., Cornell Univ. 2009–14; Alfred P. Sloan Fellow, Stanford Univ. 2011–, Microsoft Faculty Fellow 2012–; Co-founder Cognical Zibby 2012–14; Dir, RoboBrain Project, Stanford Univ. and Cornell Univ. 2014–16; Founder and CEO Brain of Things 2015–; Google Faculty Research Award 2012, CUAir at AUVSI'12: First Prize, Mission Performance, Best Cognitive Robotics Paper, IROS'14, Best Student Paper, RSS'13, NSF Career Award 2013, RSS Early Career Award 2014, The 50 years of Shakey at AAAI-RSS Blue Sky Ideas Award 2015, Eight Innovators to Watch in 2015, Smithsonian Inst. 2015, World Tech. Award (IT Software) 2015. *Address:* Gates Building 138, Stanford Computer Science, Stanford University, 353 Serra Mall, Stanford, CA 94305, USA (office). *E-mail:* asaxena@cs.stanford.edu (office); info@brainoft.com (office). *Website:* www.cs.stanford.edu (office); brainofthings.com (office).

SAYALATH, Maj.-Gen. Sengnouane; Laotian army officer and government official; Deputy Minister of Nat. Defence –2014, Minister of Nat. Defence (acting) May–July 2014, Minister of Nat. Defence 2014–16. *Address:* c/o Ministry of National Defence, avenue Kaysone Phomvihane, Ban Phone Kheng, Vientiane, Laos (office).

SAYARI, Sheikh Hamad Sa'ud al-, MA; Saudi Arabian economist and fmr central banker; b. 1941; ed Univ. of Maryland, USA; taught econs at Inst. of Public Administration, Riyadh; Dir-Gen. Saudi Industrial Devt Fund 1979–80; Controller Gen., Saudi Arabian Monetary Agency (SAMA) 1979–80, Vice-Gov. 1980–83, Acting Gov. 1983–85, Gov. 1985–2009, also Chair. Bd of Dirs; mem. Supreme Econ. Council; mem. Bd of Dirs Public Investment Fund (Sec.-Gen. 1973–74), Gulf Investment Corpn; mem. Regional Advisory Group (Middle East), IMF.

SAYAVONG, Khammy; Laotian government official; b. 9 April 1944, Khai Village; m. Boun Ngiem; ed Inst. of Party, Moscow, Russia; Head of Propaganda and Training Div., Vientiane Prov. 1992–95; Vice-Chair. Propaganda and Training Cen. Cttee 1996–98; Vice-Chair. Cen. Control Cttee 1999–2000; Pres. People's Supreme Court 2001–11. *Address:* Sisavat Village, Chanthabouly District, Vientiane Municipality, Laos (home). *Telephone:* (21) 212355 (home).

SAYED, Ahmad Mohamed al-, LLB, MBA; Qatari lawyer and business executive; *Minister of State and Adviser to the Emir;* b. 1976; ed Boston Univ., New York Univ., USA; legal counsel, Qatar Holding LLC –2009, Man. Dir and CEO 2009–13; Vice-Chair. Qatar Exchange 2009–; CEO Qatar Investment Authority (sovereign wealth fund) 2013–14; Minister of State 2013–; Adviser to the Emir 2014–; mem. Int. Advisory Bd Russian Direct Investment Fund; Dir (nonexec.) Canary Wharf Group PLC 2009–; fmr Dir Qatar Oman Investment Co. *Address:* c/o Qatar Holding LLC, Q-Tel Tower, Diplomatic Area Street, West Bay, POB 23224, Doha, Qatar (office).

SAYED, Karimat El-, PhD; Egyptian physicist and academic; *Professor Emeritus of Solid State Physics, Ain-Shams University;* m.; two s. one d.; ed Ain-Shams Univ., Univ. Coll. London, UK; joined Faculty, Ain-Shams Univ., Cairo 1965, now Prof. Emer. of Solid State Physics; UNESCO-L'Oréal Award for Women in Science 2003. *Address:* Physics Department, Faculty of Science, Ain-Shams University, Elkhalifa Elmaamoon Street, Abbassia, Cairo, Egypt (office). *Telephone:* (2) 282-2189 (office). *Fax:* (2) 284-2123 (office). *E-mail:* karima@frcu.eun.eg (office). *Website:* sci.shams.edu.eg (office).

SAYED, Mostafa Amr el-, BSc, PhD, FAAS; American (b. Egyptian) chemical physicist and academic; *Julius Brown Chair and Regents Professor and Director, Laser Dynamics Laboratory, School of Chemistry and Biochemistry, Georgia Institute of Technology;* b. 8 May 1933, Zifta, Egypt; s. of Amr el-Sayed and Zakia Ahmed; m. Janice Jones 1957; two s. two d.; ed Ain Shams Univ., Cairo, Egypt, Florida State, Yale and Harvard Univs, Calif. Inst. of Tech.; Prof., UCLA 1961–94; Julius Brown Prof. and Dir Laser Dynamics Lab., Georgia Inst. of Tech. 1994–, Regents Prof. 2000–; Visiting Prof., American Univ. of Beirut 1968, Univ. of Paris 1976, 1991; Mem.-at-Large, US Nat. Research Council Cttee for IUPAC 1987–91 (Chair. 1990–92); Alexander von Humboldt Sr Fellow, Tech. Univ. of Munich 1982; mem. Bd of Trustees Assoc. Univs Inc. 1988–91; mem. Advisory Bd, NSF Chem. Div. 1990–93; mem. Dept of Energy Basic Energy Sciences Advisory Cttee; apptd by Pres. Obama as mem. Pres.'s Nat. Medal of Science Cttee 2014; Ed.-in-Chief, Journal of Physical Chemistry 1980–2004; Ed. International Reviews in Physical Chemistry 1988–94, Proceedings of the National Academy of Sciences 2006; mem. NAS 1980, Third World Acad. of Sciences 1984, NSF 2000; Fellow, American Acad. of Arts and Sciences 1986, American Physical Soc. 2000, AAAS 2000; Hon. Fellow, Chinese Chem. Soc. 2009, Indian Chem. Soc. 2009; Inaugural Fellow, ACS 2009; Medal of the Egyptian Repub. (First Class) 2009; Dr hc (Hebrew Univ. 1993, Alexandria Univ. Medical School, Ain Shams Univ., Mansoura Univ., Beni-Suef Univ. 2008); Hon. DHumLitt (American Univ. of Beirut) 2011; Fresenius Nat. Award in Pure and Applied Chem. 1967, Guggenheim Foundation Fellow 1967–68, Alexander von Humboldt Sr US Scientist Award, 1982, King Faisal Int. Prize in Sciences (Chem.) 1990, Harris Award, Univ. of Nebraska 1995, Nat. Medal of Science 2007, Ahmed Zewail Prize in Molecular Sciences 2009, Glenn T. Seaborg Medal 2009, Thomson Reuters Highly Cited Researcher 2015, ACS Priestley Medal 2016, and many other honours and awards. *Publications:* over 630 articles in scientific and medical journals. *Leisure interest:* travelling. *Address:* Department of Chemistry and Biochemistry, Office 104-B (LDL), Georgia Institute of Technology, 901 Atlantic Drive, Atlanta, GA 30332 (office); 579 Westover Drive, Atlanta, GA 30305, USA (home). *Telephone:* (404) 894-0292 (office); (404) 352-0453 (home). *Fax:* (404) 894-7452 (office). *E-mail:* melsayed@gatech.edu (office); mostafa.el-sayed@chemistry.gatech.edu (office); mostafa.elsayed@chemistry.gatech.edu (office). *Website:* www.chemistry.gatech.edu/faculty/El-Sayed (office); ldl.gatech.edu (office).

SAYED-KHAIYUM, Aiyaz, LLB, LLM, BSc; Fijian lawyer and politician; *Attorney-General and Minister for Economy, Public Enterprises, Civil Service and Communications;* s. of Sayed Abdul Khaiyum; m. Ela Gavoka; two s.; ed Univ.

of Hong Kong, Univ. of New South Wales, Univ. of Wollongong, Australian Nat. Univ., Australia; worked with Minter Ellison (law firm), Sydney; fmr Sr Legal Officer, Office of Dir of Public Prosecutions, Suva; Gen. Man., Group Legal and Compliance Div. and Co. Sec., Colonial Group of Companies, Suva 2002–07; Attorney-Gen. 2007–14 and fmr Minister for Justice, Anti-Corruption, Public Enterprises, Communications, Civil Aviation, Tourism, Industry and Trade; Attorney-Gen. and Minister for Economy, Public Enterprises, Civil Service and Communications 2014–; mem. Parl. 2014–; Pres. Fiji Young Lawyers Asscn; mem. Bd Transparency Int. Fiji; mem. FijiFirst Party, currently Gen. Sec. *Address:* Office of the Attorney-General, Government Bldgs, Victoria Parade, POB 2213, Suva (office); Ministry of Economy, Government Bldgs, Victoria Parade, POB 370, Suva, Fiji. *Telephone:* 3309866 (office); 382001 (Ministry of Economy) (office). *Fax:* 3305421 (office); 3300834 (Ministry of Economy) (office). *E-mail:* psfinance@govnet.gov.fj (office). *Website:* www.ag.gov.fj (office); aiyazsayedkhaiyum.org.

SAYEED, Hafiz Mohammad; Pakistani military leader; b. 5 June 1950, Sargodha, Punjab; s. of Kamal-ud-Deen Sayeed; ed Univ. of Panjab, King Saud Univ.; apptd to Council on Islamic Ideology by Gen. Mohammad Zia-ul-Haq; joined as Lecturer of Islamic Studies, Univ. of Tech. and Eng, Lahore, promoted to Prof., later Chair. Dept of Islamic Studies; fmr Guest Speaker, Nat. Inst. of Public Administration (NIPA), Lahore; served as Visiting Faculty at several Colls. and Univs. including Punjab Univ., Lahore, Karachi Univ., Karachi, Agricultural Univ., Faisalabad; Co-Founder and Leader, Lashkar-e-Taiba (banned militant group), Founder and Leader Jamaat-ud-Dawa; detained, then placed under house arrest 2002, released Nov. 2002.

SAYEF, Abdul Rasul; Afghan politician and academic; *Leader, Tanzim-i Dawat-i Islami (Organization for Invitation to Islam);* ed Kabul Univ., Al-Azhar Univ., Cairo, Egypt; fmr Prof. of Islamic Law, Shariat in Kabul –1973, tenure ended when he plotted with Burhanuddin Rabbani, Ahmed Shah Massoud and Gulbuddin Hekmatyar to overthrow Pres. Daoud Khan from Panjshir Valley; fmr mem. Akhwan-ul-Muslimeen (Muslim Brotherhood); fought against Soviet occupying forces Afghanistan during 1980s, chair. first rebel alliance 1980, one of the most important resistance leaders during Soviet invasion that ended in 1992; Leader Islamic Union for the Liberation of Afghanistan (Ittihad-i Islami Bara-yi Azadi—only anti-Taliban Pashtun leader to be part of Northern Alliance), now called Tanzim-i Dawat-i Islami (Org. for Invitation to Islam) 2005–; mem. constitutional Loya Jirga 2003–04; elected to Wolasi Jirga (House of People, Nat. Ass.); cand. in presidential election 2014.

SAYEGH, Bishop Selim Wahban, PhD; Jordanian ecclesiastic; *Titular Bishop of Aquae in Proconsulari;* b. 15 Jan. 1935, Jordan; s. of Wahban Sayigh; ed Lateran Univ., Rome; Pres. of the Latin Patriarchal Court, Jerusalem 1967–79; Rector of the Latin Patriarchal Seminary 1976–81; apptd Auxiliary Bishop of Jerusalem 1981, Auxiliary Bishop Emer. 2012–; Titular Bishop of Aquae in Proconsulari and Vicar Gen. for Transjordan 1982–; Commdr of the Equestrian Order of the Holy Sepulchre of Jerusalem. *Publications:* Le Statu Quo des Lieux-Saints 1971, The Christian Family's Guidebook. *Leisure interests:* chess, table tennis, volleyball, history, ecclesiastical law. *Address:* Latin Vicariate, PO Box 851379, Amman 11185, Jordan. *Telephone:* (6) 5929546. *Fax:* (6) 5920548.

SAYEH, Antoinette Monsio, PhD; Liberian economist, government official and international organization official; b. 12 July 1958, Monrovia; one s.; ed Swarthmore Coll., Fletcher School, Tufts Univ., USA; fmrly with Ministry of Planning, Ministry of Finance; worked for 17 years at World Bank, positions included Country Dir for Benin, Niger and Togo 2000–03 and working on public finance man. and civil service reform in Pakistan; Minister of Finance 2006–08; Dir African Dept, IMF 2008–16; currently Distinguished Visiting Fellow, Centre for Global Devt; Lucretia Mott Award, Swarthmore Coll., Service to Country Award, Govt of Niger. *Address:* Centre for Global Devt, 2055 L Street, NW, Fifth Floor, Washington, DC 20036, USA (office). *Telephone:* (202) 416-4000 (office). *Fax:* 416-4050 (office). *Website:* www.cgdev.org (office).

SAYLES, John Thomas, BS; American writer, film director, actor and scriptwriter; b. 28 Sept. 1950, Schenectady, NY; s. of Donald John Sayles and Mary Sayles (née Rausch); pnr, Maggie Renzi; ed Williams Coll.; John D. MacArthur Award, Eugene V. Debs Award, John Steinbeck Award, John Cassavettes Award, Ian McLellan Hunter Award, LEAF Award for Lifetime Environmental Achievement in the Fine Arts 2012, Crystal Apricot Lifetime Achievement Award 2012, Lifetime Achievement PROGIE Award (co-recepient) 2013, Phylis Franklin Award for Public Advocacy of the Humanities, Modern Language Asscn 2014. *Films include:* Return of the Secaucus Seven (dir, screenwriter, actor, ed.) (Los Angeles Film Critics Award) 1980, Baby It's You (dir, screenwriter) 1983, Lianna (dir, screenwriter, actor, ed.) 1983, The Brother from Another Planet (dir, screenwriter, actor, ed.) 1984, Matewan (dir, screenwriter, actor) 1987, Eight Men Out (dir, screenwriter, actor) 1989, Bruce Springsteen: Video Anthology 1978–1988 (dir videos Born in the USA, Glory Days, I'm on Fire), City of Hope (dir, screenwriter, actor, ed.) 1991, Passion Fish (dir, screenwriter, actor, ed.), The Secret of Roan Inish (dir, screenwriter, ed.) 1994, Lone Star (dir, screenwriter, ed.) 1996, Men With Guns (dir, screenwriter, ed.) 1997, Limbo (dir, screenwriter, ed.) 1999, Santitos (producer) 1999, Sunshine State (dir, screenwriter, ed.) 2002, Casa de los babys (dir, screenwriter, ed.) 2003, Silver City (dir, screenwriter, ed.) 2004, Honeydripper (dir, screenwriter, actor, ed.) (Jury Prize for Best Screenplay, San Sebastian Film Festival 2007, NAACP Image Award for Outstanding Ind. or Foreign Film 2008) 2007, My Mexican Shivah (producer) 2007; writer: Piranha 1978, The Lady in Red 1979, Battle Beyond the Stars 1980, The Howling 1981, Alligator 1981, The Challenge 1982, Enormous Changes at the Last Minute 1983, The Clan of the Cave Bear 1986, Something Wild 1986, Wild Thing 1987, Breaking In 1989, Men of War 1994, The Spiderwick Chronicles 2008, Amigo (screenwriter, dir, ed.) 2010, Go for Sisters (screenwriter, dir, ed.) 2013; actor: Malcolm X 1992, Straight Talk 1992, Matinee 1993, My Life's in Turnaround 1993, Gridlock'd 1997, Girlfight (also producer) 2000, The Toe Tactic 2008, In the Electric Mist 2009, The Normals 2012. *Television includes:* writer: A Perfect Match 1980, Unnatural Causes 1986, Shannon's Deal (also dir) 1989, Piranha 1995; as actor: Scene by Scene 2003. *Publications:* Pride of the Bimbos 1975, Union Dues 1979, Thinking in Pictures 1987, I-80 Nebraska, M.490-M.205 (O. Henry Award) 1975, Breed, Golden State (O. Henry Award) 1977, Hoop, The Anarchists' Convention 1979, New Hope for the Dead (play) 1981, Turnbuckle (play), Los Gusanos 1991, Dillinger in Hollywood 2004. *Address:* c/o Lucy Stille, Paradigm, 360 N Crescent Drive, North Building, Los Angeles, CA 90210, USA (office). *Website:* johnsaylesblog.com.

SCACCHI, Greta; Italian/Australian actress; b. 18 Feb. 1960, Milan, Italy; d. of Luca Scacchi Gracco and Pamela Carsaniga; m. 1st Vincent D'Onofrio 1991 (divorced 1993); one d.; one s. by Carlo Mantegazza; ed Bristol Old Victoria Drama School; Kt, Order of Merit of the Italian Republic 2013. *Films:* Das Zweite Gesicht, Heat and Dust, Defence of the Realm, The Coca-Cola Kid, A Man in Love, Good Morning Babylon, White Mischief, Paura e Amore (Three Sisters), La Donna della Luna, Presumed Innocent, Shattered, Fires Within, Turtle Beach, The Player, Salt on Our Skin, The Browning Version, Jefferson in Paris 1994, Country Life 1995, Emma 1996, The Serpent's Kiss 1997, The Red Violin 1998, Ladies Room 1999, The Manor 1999, Tom's Midnight Garden 2000, Looking for Alibrandi 2000, One of the Hollywood Ten 2000, Cotton Mary 2000, Festival in Cannes 2002, Baltic Storm 2003, Sotto falso nome 2004, Beyond the Sea 2004, Flightplan 2005, The Book of Revelation 2006, The Handyman 2006, Icicle Melt 2006, L'Amour caché 2007, Hidden Love 2007, Brideshead Revisited 2008, Shoot on Sight 2008, Miss Austen Regrets 2008, Ways to Live Forever 2010, Un altro mondo 2010, The Falling 2014, La Tenèrezza 2017, La ragazza nella nebia 2017, Operation Finale 2018, Amanda 2018. *Television:* The Ebony Tower, Dr Fischer of Geneva, Waterfront (Australia), Rasputin (Emmy Award 1996), The Odyssey (series) 1996, Macbeth 1998, The Farm (Australia) 2000, Daniel Deronda, Jeffrey Archer – The Truth 2002, Maigret: Lombra cinese 2004, Marple: By the Pricking of My Thumbs 2006, Broken Trail 2006, Nightmares and Dreamscapes: From the Stories of Stephen King (miniseries) 2006, The Trojan Horse (miniseries) 2008, Hindenburg (film) 2011, Agatha Christie: Poirot (series) 2013, War & Peace (series) 2016, The Terror (series) 2018. *Theatre:* Cider with Rosie, In Times Like These, Airbase, Uncle Vanya 1988, A Doll's House, Miss Julie, Simpatico, A Midsummer Night's Dream, Easy Virtue, The Guardsman 2000, Old Times 2000, The True-Life Fiction of Mata Hari 2002, The Deep Blue Sea 2008, A Little Night Music 2010, Bette and Joan 2011, King Lear 2013, The Seagull 2014, The Glass Menagerie 2015, The entertainer 2016. *Address:* c/o Nicola van Gelder, Conway van Gelder, Third Floor, 8/12 Broadwick Street, London, W1F 8HW, England (office). *Telephone:* (20) 7287-0077 (office). *E-mail:* nicki@conwayvg.co.uk (office). *Website:* www.conwayvangeldergrant.com (office).

SCACE, Arthur Richard Andrew, CM, QC, LLB, LLD; Canadian lawyer, banking executive and company director; b. 22 July 1938, Toronto, Ont.; m. Susan Margaret Kernohan; one s. one d.; ed Univ. of Toronto, Univ. of Oxford, UK, Harvard Univ., USA, Osgoode Hall; called to the Bar, Ont. 1967; began career at McCarthy Tétrault (law firm) 1967, became Partner 1972, Man. Partner, Toronto 1989–96, Nat. Chair. 1997–99, currently Counsel; mem. Bd of Dirs Scotiabank (Nat. Bank of Nova Scotia) 1997–2009, Chair. 2004–09; Dir The Canada Life Assurance Co., Canada Life Financial Corpn 2000–04; fmr Chair. Canadian Opera Co., now Pres. Bd of Dirs Canadian Opera House Corpn; fmr Chair. Henry White Kinnear Foundation; fmr Treas. Law Soc. of Upper Canada; mem. Bd of Dirs Garbell Holdings Ltd, Gardiner Group Capital Ltd, Gerdau Ameristeel Corpn, Lallemand Inc., N.M. Davis Corpn Ltd, Sceptre Investment Counsel Ltd, WestJet Airlines Inc.; fmr mem. Bd of Dirs The Canada Life Assurance Co., Canada Life Financial Corpn, Brompton Equity Split Corpn, Brompton Split Banc Corpn, Univ. of Toronto Schools; Sec., Rhodes Scholarships in Canada; Hon. DIur (Law Soc. of Upper Canada, York Univ.); Robinette Medal, Osgoode Hall Law School 2003. *Publication:* The Income Tax Law of Canada (co-author) 1972. *Address:* Canadian Opera House Corporation, 145 Queen Street West, Toronto, ON M5H 4G1, Canada. *Telephone:* (416) 368-4227. *Website:* www.coc.ca.

SCAGLIA, Silvio; Italian telecommunications industry executive; *Founder and Chairman, Pacific Global Management Group (PGM Group);* b. 1958, Lucerne, Switzerland; m.; three c.; ed Polytechnic Univ. of Turin; began career at Aeritalia Spazio, then worked for Arthur Andersen Management Consulting; later Consultant with McKinsey & Co. and Bain & Co.; apptd Gen. Man. Motovespa 1991, then Sr Vice-Pres.; fmr CEO Omnitel (now Vodafone Italy); f. Fastweb (fibre-to-the-home broadband co.) 1999, CEO 1999–2003, Chair. 2003–07; Founder and Chair. Babelgum (on-demand TV over the internet service) 2007–12; Founder and Chair. Pacific Global Management Group (PGM Group) (holding co.), also Exec. Chair. La Perla (subsidiary). *Address:* La Perla, Via Mattei 10, Bologna 40136, Italy (office). *Website:* www.laperla.com (office).

SCAIFE, Brendan Kevin Patrick, PhD, DSc (Eng), MRIA, CEng, FIET, CPhys, FInstP; Irish electrical engineer and academic; b. 19 May 1928, London, England; s. of James Scaife and Mary Kavanagh; m. Mary Manahan 1961; three s. one d.; ed Cardinal Vaughan Memorial School, London, Chelsea Polytechnic and Queen Mary Coll. London; with GEC Research Labs, Wembley 1953–54; Scholar, School of Theoretical Physics, Dublin Inst. for Advanced Studies 1954–55; Inst. for Industrial Research and Standards, Dublin 1955–56; Electricity Supply Bd Dublin 1956; Coll. of Tech., Dublin 1956–61; Lecturer in Electronic Eng, Trinity Coll. Dublin 1961–66, Fellow 1964, Reader 1966, Assoc. Prof. 1967–72, Prof. of Eng Science 1972–86, Prof. of Electromagnetics 1986–88, Sr Fellow 1987–88, Fellow Emer. 1988–; Visiting Prof., Univ. of Salford 1969–82; Fellow, Inst. of Engineers of Ireland, Inst. of Eng and Tech.; Boyle Medal, Royal Dublin Soc. 1992. *Publications include:* Complex Permittivity (compiler) 1971, Studies in Numerical Analysis (ed.) 1974, Principles of Dielectrics (revised edn) 1998, The Mathematical Papers of Sir William Rowan Hamilton Vol. IV (ed.) 2000. *Address:* Department of Electronic and Electrical Engineering, Trinity College, Dublin 2 (office); 6 Trimleston Avenue, Booterstown, Blackrock, Co. Dublin, Ireland (home). *Telephone:* (1) 8961580 (office); (1) 2693867 (home). *Fax:* (1) 6772442 (office). *E-mail:* bscaife@eircom.net (home).

SCALES, Prunella Margaret Rumney, CBE; British actress; b. (P. M. R. Illingworth), 22 June 1932, Sutton Abinger, Surrey; d. of John Richardson Illingworth and Catherine Scales; m. Timothy West (q.v.) 1963; two s.; ed Moira House, Eastbourne, Old Vic Theatre School, London, Herbert Berghof Studio, New York; in repertory, Huddersfield, Salisbury, Oxford, Bristol Old Vic etc.; seasons at Stratford and Chichester 1967–68; numerous radio broadcasts, readings, poetry recitals, fringe productions; has directed plays at numerous theatres including Bristol Old Vic, Arts Theatre, Cambridge, Nottingham Playhouse, W Yorkshire Playhouse (Getting On); Pres. Council for the Protection of Rural England 1997–2002; Amb. Howard League for Penal Reform 2007–; Freeman of the City of

London 1990; Hon. DLitt (Bradford) 1995, (East Anglia) 1996. *Plays include:* The Promise 1967, Hay Fever 1968, The Wolf 1975, Make and Break 1980, An Evening with Queen Victoria 1980, The Merchant of Venice 1981, Quartermaine's Terms 1981, When We Are Married 1986, Single Spies (double bill) 1988, School for Scandal, Long Day's Journey into Night (Nat. Theatre), Happy Days 1993, Staying On 1996, Some Singing Blood (Royal Court), The Mother Tongue, The Editing Process 1994, The Birthday Party 1999, The Cherry Orchard 2000, The External 2001, Too Far to Walk (King's Head) 2002, A Woman of No Importance 2004, Gertrude's Secret, New End Theatre 2007. *Films include:* Laxdale Hall 1953, Waltz of the Toreadors 1962, What Every Woman Wants 1954, Hobson's Choice 1954, The Crowded Day 1954, The Hound of the Baskervilles 1978, The Boys from Brazil 1978, The Wicked Lady 1983, The Lonely Passion of Judith Hearne 1987, Consuming Passions 1988, A Chorus of Disapproval 1988, Howards End 1992, Freddie as F.R.O.7 (voice) 1992, Sherwood's Travels 1994, Second Best 1994, Wolf 1994, An Awfully Big Adventure 1994, Phoenix 1997, An Ideal Husband 1998, Stiff Upper Lips 1998, Mad Cows 1999, The Ghost of Greville Lodge 2000, Brand Spanking (short) 2004, Helix (short) 2006, Think. What Does it Take to Change a Habit? (short) 2007, Horrid Henry: The Movie 2011. *Radio includes:* After Henry 1985–89, Smelling of Roses 2000, Ladies of Letters 2001, 2004, 2010, Rumpole 2007. *Television includes:* Pride and Prejudice (mini-series) 1952, What Every Woman Wants 1954, The Crowded Day 1954, French for Love 1955, Room at the Top (uncredited) 1959, The New Man 1960, The Secret Garden (series) 1960, The Seven Faces of Jim – The Face of Genius 1961, Coronation Street 1961, Marriage Lines (series) 1961–66, On the Margin (series) 1966, Blues in the Morning 1971, Seven of One – One Man's Meat 1973, Comedy Playhouse – The Big Job 1974, Decisions, Decisions 1975, The Apple Cart 1975, Fawlty Towers (series) 1975, 1979, Escape from the Dark 1976, Mr Big (series) 1977, Pickersgill People (series) 1978, Target 1978, Doris and Doreen 1978, Bergerac 1981, Grand Duo 1982, S.W.A.L.K. (series) 1982, Never the Twain 1982, Outside Edge 1982, The Merry Wives of Windsor 1982, Wagner (mini-series) 1983, Mapp and Lucia (series) 1985–86, Absurd Person Singular 1985, Unnatural Causes 1986, What the Butler Saw 1987, When We Are Married 1987, After Henry (series) 1988–92, Beyond the Pale 1989, A Question of Attribution 1991, My Friend Walter 1992, The Rector's Wife (series) 1994, Fair Game 1994, Look at the State We're In! (mini-series) 1995, Signs and Wonders 1995, Searching (series) 1995, Lord of Misrule 1996, Emma 1996, Dalziel & Pascoe 1996, Breaking the Code 1996, The Tale of Mrs Tiggy-Winkle and Mr Jeremy Fish (voice) 1998, Midsomer Murders – Beyond the Grave 2000, Silent Witness – Faith 2001, Station Jim 2001, Dickens (series) 2002, Looking for Victoria (film) 2003, Essential Poems for Christmas 2004, Casualty (series) 2004, Where the Heart Is (series) 2005, Mr. Loveday's Little Outing (film) 2006, The Shell Seekers 2006, Marple: A Pocket Full of Rye (film) 2008, The Royal (series) 2008, Great Canal Journeys (series) 2014. *Publication:* So You Want To Be An Actor?. *Leisure interests:* gardening, crosswords, canal boat. *Address:* Conway van Gelder Grant Ltd, 3rd Floor, 8–12 Broadwick Street, London, W1F 8HW, England (office). *Telephone:* (20) 7287-0077 (office). *Fax:* (20) 7287-1940 (office). *E-mail:* vena@conwayvg.co.uk (office). *Website:* www.conwayvangeldergrant.com (office).

SCALFARI, Eugenio, DIur; Italian editor and journalist; b. 6 April 1924, Civitavecchia; m. 1st Simonetta de Benedetti 1959 (died 2006); two d.; m. 2nd Giuliana Rossetti 2008; Dir L'Europeo (news magazine) 1945–54, Ed.-in-Chief –1963; Co-founder Partito Radicale 1958; Ed.-in-Chief L'Espresso 1963–68, Man. Dir 1970–75; Co-founder, La Repubblica newspaper 1976, Ed.-in-Chief 1976–96; Deputy to Parl. 1968–72; fmr columnist, La Repubblica and L'Espresso; Siena Award 1985, Journalist of the Year Award 1986, Premio Ischia alla Carriera 1996, Premio St Vincent alla Carriera. *Publications include:* Rapporto sul Neocapitalismo in Italia 1961, Il Potere Economico in URSS 1962, L'Autunno della Repubblica 1969, Razza Padrona (co-author) 1974, Interviste ai Potenti 1979, L'Anno di Craxi 1984, Incontro con Io 1994, Alla ricerca della morale perduta 1995, Il Labirinto 1998, La ruga sulla fronte 2001, La Ruga Sulla Fronte 2001, Le Prince inconstant (co-author) 2003, L'uomo che non credeva in Dio 2008, La Sera Andavamo in Via Veneto 2009, Per l'alto mare aperto 2010, Scuote l'anima mia Eros 2011, Racconto autobiografico 2014, L'allegria, il pianto, la vita 2015. *Address:* c/o La Repubblica, Via Cristoforo Colombo 90, 00147 Rome, Italy. *Telephone:* (06) 49821. *Website:* www.repubblica.it/protagonisti/Eugenio_Scalfari.

SCAPARROTTI, Gen. Curtis Michael; American army officer and international organization official; *Supreme Allied Commander Europe (SACEUR), NATO;* b. 5 March 1956, Logan, Ohio; s. of Michael Scaparrotti and Betty Brown Scaparrotti; m. Cindy Bateman; one s. one d.; ed US Mil. Acad., West Point, Univ. of South Carolina; commissioned as Second Lt in US Army infantry 1978, tactical officer and aide-de-camp to Superintendent, US Mil. Acad., West Point 1985–88, Operations Officer, 1st Bn, 325th Airborne Combat Team, Southern European Task Force, Vicenza, Italy 1989, Operations Officer, 1st Bn, 87th Infantry Regt 1989–92, with Office of Army Chief of Staff, Washington, DC 1992–94, Commdr, 3rd Bn, 325th Airborne Combat Team, Southern European Task Force, Vicenza, Italy 1994–96, Operations Officer, 10th Mountain Div. 1996, Chief of Army Initiatives Group, Office of Deputy Chief of Staff for Plans and Operations, Washington, DC 1998, Commdr, 2nd Brigade, 82nd Airborne Div., Fort Bragg 1999–2001, Asst Deputy Dir for Jt Operations on Jt Staff, Washington, DC 2001–03, Asst Div. Commdr (Maneuver), 1st Armored Div. during Operation Iraqi Freedom 2003–04, Commandant of Cadets, US Mil. Acad., West Point 2004–06, Dir of Operations for US Command 2006, Commdr, 82nd Airborne Div. 2008 (served as Commanding Gen. Combined Jt Task Force 82 and Regional Command East, Afghanistan), Commdr, I Corps and Jt Base Lewis–McChord, Fort Lewis, Washington 2010, Commdr, Int. Security Assistance Force Jt Command and Deputy Commdr, US Forces, Afghanistan 2011–12, Dir of Jt Staff 2012–13, Commdr, United Command, Combined Forces Command and United Forces Korea 2013–16, Supreme Allied Commdr Europe (SACEUR), NATO 2016–; numerous mil. awards including Jt Meritorious Unit Award with three oak leaf clusters, Nat. Defense Service Medal with two bronze service stars, Armed Forces Expeditionary Medal, Korea Defense Service Medal, NATO Medal for fmr Yugoslavia with two bronze service stars, Order of Nat. Security Merit, Tong-il Medal (Repub. of Korea). *Address:* NATO Supreme Headquarters Allied Powers Europe, Casteau, Belgium (office). *Telephone:* 65-44-3872 (office). *Website:* www.shape.nato.int (office).

SCARAMUZZI, Franco; Italian agricultural scientist; *Professor Emeritus, University of Florence;* b. 26 Dec. 1926, Ferrara; s. of Donato Scaramuzzi and Alberta Rovida; m. Maria Bianca Cancellieri 1955; one s. one d.; Prof. of Pomology, Univ. of Pisa 1959, Univ. of Florence 1969, now Prof. Emer.; Rector Magnificus, Univ. of Florence 1979–91, later Prof. Emer.; Pres. Int. Soc. of Horticultural Science 1986–90, Accad. dei Georgofili 1986–2014 (then Hon. Pres.), Società di San Giovanni Battista 2001–05; mem. Soviet (now Russian) Acad. of Agricultural Sciences 1982–; Hon. Pres. Italian Horticultural Soc. 1976–, Italian Acad. of Vine and Wine; Hon. mem. Rotary International; Cavaliere di Gran Croce 1998; Dr hc (Bucharest); Gold Medal of the Minister of Educ. 1983, Gold Medal, Univ. of Florence. *Publication:* Fruit Pomology. *Address:* University of Florence, Piazza S.Marco, 4, 50121 Florence, Italy (office). *Fax:* urp@unifi.it (office). *Website:* www.unifi.it/changelang-eng.html (office).

SCARDINO, Dame Marjorie Morris, DBE, BA, JD, FRSA; American/British journalist, lawyer and business executive; b. 25 Jan. 1947, Flagstaff, Ariz., USA; d. of Robert Weldon Morris and Beth Lamb Morris; m. Albert James Scardino 1974; two s. one d.; ed Baylor Univ., Univ. of San Francisco; started career as reporter, Associated Press; Partner, Brannen, Wessels & Searcy law firm, Savannah, Ga 1975–85; Co-founder (with husband) and Publr The Georgia Gazette Co. (won Pulitzer Prize) 1978–85; Pres. The Economist Newspaper Group Inc., New York 1985–93, Chief Exec. The Economist Group, London 1993–97, mem. Bd of Dirs and CEO Pearson PLC 1997–2012; Dir (non-exec.) Nokia Corpn 2001–12, Vice-Chair. 2007–12, Chair. Corp. Governance and Nomination Cttee, mem. Personnel Cttee; mem. Bd of Dirs International Consolidated Airlines Group 2013–, Twitter Inc. 2013–; mem. Bd of Trustees The MacArthur Foundation, Carter Center, Victoria & Albert Museum; Hon. Fellow, London Business School, City and Guilds of London Inst., RSA; Hon. LLD (Univ. of Exeter, St Andrews Univ.); Hon. DHumLitt (New School Univ.); Dr hc (Heriot-Watt Univ., Brunel Univ.); Veuve Clicquot Businesswoman of the Year Award 1998, Benjamin Franklin Medal, RSA 2001. *Leisure interests:* horse riding, playing golf, watching Manchester United football team.

SCARFE, Gerald A., CBE; British cartoonist; b. 1 June 1936, London; m. Jane Asher; two s. one d.; joined Daily Mail as political cartoonist 1966; political cartoonist, London Sunday Times 1967–; contributed cartoons to Punch 1960–, Private Eye 1961–, Time 1967–, has also worked for The New Yorker magazine; animation and film directing BBC 1969–; designer and dir of animation for Pink Floyd The Wall concerts and film 1975–78; consultant designer and character design for film Hercules 1997; Hon. Fellow, London Inst. 2001; Hon. LLD (Liverpool) 2001, (Dundee) 2007; Zagreb Prize for BBC film Long Drawn Out Trip 1973, BAFTA Award for Scarfe on Scarfe 1987, Olivier Award for Absolute Turkey 1993, Cartoonist of the Year, British Press Awards 2006. *Television includes:* dir and presenter Scarfe on Art 1991, Scarfe on Sex 1991, Scarfe on Class 1992, Scarfe in Paradise 1992; subject of Scarfe and His Work with Disney (South Bank Special). *Theatre design:* Ubu Roi (Traverse Theatre) 1957, What the Butler Saw (Oxford Playhouse) 1980, No End of Blame (Royal Court, London) 1981, Orpheus in the Underworld (English ENO, Coliseum) 1985, Who's a Lucky Boy (Royal Exchange, Manchester) 1985, Born Again 1990, The Magic Flute (Los Angeles Opera) 1992, An Absolute Turkey 1993, Mind Millie for Me (Haymarket, London) 1996, Fantastic Mr. Fox (Los Angeles Opera) 1998, Peter and the Wolf (Holiday on Ice, Paris and world tour) 2000, The Nutcracker 2002. *Publications include:* Gerald Scarfe's People 1966, Indecent Exposure 1973, Expletive Deleted: The Life and Times of Richard Nixon 1974, Gerald Scarfe 1982, Father Kissmass and Mother Claus 1985, Scarfe by Scarfe (autobiog.) 1986, Gerald Scarfe's Seven Deadly Sins 1987, Line of Attack 1988, Scarfeland 1989, Scarfe on Stage 1992, Scarfe Face 1993, Hades: The Truth at Last 1997, Heroes & Villains 2003, Drawing Blood: Forty-five Years of Scarfe Uncensored 2005, Monsters: How George Bush Saved The World & Other Tall Stories 2008, The Making of Pink Floyd's The Wall 2010. *Leisure interests:* drawing, painting, sculpting. *Address:* c/o Simpson Fox Associates, 6 Beauchamp Place, London, SW3 1NG, England (office). *Website:* www.geraldscarfe.com (office).

SCARGILL, Arthur; British trade union official and fmr coal miner; *General Secretary, Socialist Labour Party;* b. 11 Jan. 1938, Worsborough, Yorks.; s. of Harold Scargill and Alice Scargill; m. Anne Harper 1961; one d.; ed White Cross Secondary School; worked first in a factory, then Woolley Colliery 1955; mem. Barnsley Young Communist League 1955–62; mem. Nat. Union of Mineworkers (NUM) 1955–, NUM Br. Cttee 1960, Br. del. to NUM Yorks. Area Council 1964, mem. NUM Nat. Exec. 1972–, Pres. Yorks. NUM 1973–82, Pres. NUM 1981–2002, Hon. Pres. and Consultant 2002–, involved in litigation over membership of NUM 2010–; Chair. NUM Int. Cttee; Pres. Int. Miners Org. 1985–; mem. Labour Party 1966–95; mem. TUC Gen. Council 1986–88; f. Socialist Labour Party 1996, Gen. Sec. 1996–; contested Newport East 1997, Hartlepool 2001. *Address:* Socialist Labour Party, PO Box 706, Barnsley, S70 9LE, England (office). *Telephone:* (1226) 212951 (office). *E-mail:* slpscot@btinternet.com (office); info@socialist-labour-party.org.uk (office). *Website:* www.socialist-labour-party.org.uk (office).

SCARLETT, Sir John McLeod, Kt, KCMG, OBE, MA; British crown servant; b. 18 Aug. 1948, London; s. of James Henri Stuart Scarlett and of Clara Dunlop Scarlett (née Morton); m. Gwenda Mary Rachel Stilliard 1970; one s. three d. (and one s. deceased); ed Epsom Coll., Magdalen Coll., Oxford; with Secret Intelligence Service 1971–2001, FCO London 1971–73, 1977–84, 1988–91, 1994–2001 (Dir of Security and Public Affairs 1999–2001), Third Sec., Nairobi 1973–74; language student 1974–75; Second, later First Sec., Moscow 1976–77; First Sec., Paris 1984–88, Political Counsellor, Moscow 1991–94; Chair. Jt Intelligence Cttee and Intelligence and Security Dir, Cabinet Office 2001–04; Chief, Secret Intelligence Service (MI6) 2004–09; Strategic Adviser, Statoil ASA 2011; Chair. Bletchley Park Trust; mem. Bd of Dirs Times Newspapers Ltd 2011–; Officier, Légion d'Honneur 2011. *Leisure interests:* history, family. *Address:* Bletchley Park Ltd, The Mansion, Bletchley Park, Milton Keynes, MK3 6EB, England (office). *E-mail:* info@bletchleypark.org.uk (office). *Website:* www.bletchleypark.org (office).

SCARONI, Paolo, MBA; Italian business executive; *Deputy Chairman, N.M. Rothschild & Sons Limited;* b. 28 Nov. 1946, Vicenza; m.; three c.; ed Univ. of Bocconi, Milan, Columbia Univ., New York, USA; staff mem. Chevron 1969–71; consultant, McKinsey & Co. 1972–73; joined Saint Gobain Group 1973, various exec. positions including Financial Man. St German Italia, Gen. Man. Balzaretti & Modigliani SpA, Chair. Borma SpA and Air Industrie SpA –1978; Gen. Del. St

Gobain Venezuela, Colombia, Ecuador and Peru, Caracas 1978–81; Gen. Del. St Gobain Italia 1981–84; Chair. St Gobain Flat Glass Div., Paris 1984; Chair. and Man. Dir St Gobain Vitrage SA; CEO St Gobain Group –2002; Chair. Fabbrica Pisana SpA, Vegla GmbH, Cristaleria Espanola SA, Saint Roch SA; Vice-Chair. and Man. Dir Techint 1985; Vice-Chair. Falck SpA 1986–88; Man. Dir SIV SpA 1993–95; Group CEO Pilkington PLC 1996–2002; CEO and COO Enel SpA 2002–05; CEO Eni SpA 2005–14; Deputy Chair. N.M. Rothschild & Sons Ltd 2014–; Chair. Alliance Unichem (UK) 2005–06; Vice-Chair. Sadi SpA; Dir (non-exec.) Assicurazioni Generali, Veolia Environnement; Deputy Chair. (non-exec.) London Stock Exchange Group; mem. Bd of Overseers of Columbia Business School and Fondazione Teatro alla Scala; mem. Bd AC Milan (Exec. Chair. 2018–); Cavaliere del Lavoro della Repubblica Italiana 2004; Officier, Légion d'honneur 2007, Commdr 2013. *Publication:* Professione manager 1985. *Leisure interests:* reading, skiing, golf, football. *Address:* N.M. Rothschild & Sons Ltd, New Court, St Swithin's Lane, London, EC4P 4DU, England (office). *Telephone:* (20) 7280-5000 (office). *Fax:* (20) 7929-1643 (office). *E-mail:* info@rothschild.com (office). *Website:* www.rothschild.com (office).

SCAZZIERI, Roberto, MLitt, DPhil; Italian economist and academic; *Professor of Economics, University of Bologna;* b. 1 May 1950, Bologna; s. of Guerrino Scazzieri and Fosca Lambertini; m. Maria Cristina Bacchi 1983; one s.; ed Liceo Minghetti, Bologna, Univ. of Bologna, Univ. of Oxford, UK; Asst Lecturer, Univ. of Bologna 1974–79, Lecturer in Theory and Policy of Econ. Growth 1980–83, in Econ. Principles 1983–86, in Advanced Econ. Analysis 1985–87, Assoc. Prof. of Econs, Faculty of Political Sciences 1986–87, Full Prof. of Econs, Faculty of Econs and Commerce and Dept of Econs 1990–, mem. Teaching Bd, PhD Programme in Science, Tech. and Humanities 2007–10, PhD Programme in Science, Cognition and Tech. 2011–; Prof. of Econs, Faculty of Statistics, Univ. of Padua 1987–90; Sr Research Assoc., Centre for Financial History, Newnham Coll., Cambridge 2012–; Visiting Scholar, Dept of Applied Econs, Univ. of Cambridge 1987, 1989, Research Assoc. 1992–93; Visiting Fellow, Clare Hall 1992, Life mem. 1992–; Visiting Fellow, Gonville and Caius Coll. 1999, Sr mem. 1999–, Centre for Research in the Arts, Social Sciences and Humanities, Univ. of Cambridge 2004; Visiting Prof., Interdisciplinary Research Centre 'Beniamino Segre', Accad. Nazionale dei Lincei 2012–15; Resident Fellow, Bologna Inst. of Advanced Study 1997, Founding Scientific Dir 2000–03, Deputy Scientific Dir 2003–06; Visiting Prof., Univ. of Lugano, Switzerland 1997; Visiting Research Fellow, Centre for History and Econs, King's Coll., Cambridge 2005, Visiting Scholar, Gonville and Caius College and Clare Hall 2007–08; Faculty Advisor, Market Square-The Polity, Economy and Society, Cambridge Research Group, Centre for Research in the Arts, Social Sciences and Humanities, Univ. of Cambridge 2011–; Man. Ed. Structural Change and Economic Dynamics 1990–; Assoc. Ed. Journal of Economic Methodology 2003–05, Economia Politica, Journal of Analytical and Institutional Economics 2006–14; mem. Steering Cttee Bologna-Cambridge-Harvard Sr Seminars Network, Bologna Inst. for Advanced Study, European Consortium of Humanities Centres and Insts, Cambridge Seminar in the History of Econ. Analysis (CAMHIST), Clare Hall 2008–, Cambridge Research Seminar in Political Economy, Emmanuel Coll. 2013–; mem. Man. Bd European Summer School in Structural Change and Econ. Dynamics, Selwyn Coll., Cambridge 1995–97; mem. Scientific Cttee Int. Centre for the History of Univs and Science 1994–, Scientific Cttee Research Centre in Econ. Analysis and Int. Econ. Devt (CRANEC), Catholic Univ. of Milan, Scientific Cttee Centre for Research on Complex Automated Systems (CASY), Univ. of Bologna 2002–; mem. Man. Bd 'Federigo Enriques' Centre for Epistemology and History of Sciences, Univ. of Bologna, Int. Microfinance Observatory, Univ. of Bologna; Foundation Fellow, Kyoto Univ.; Rector's Del., Bologna-Clare Hall Fellowship 1993–; mem. Bologna Acad. of Sciences 1994–, Istituto Lombardo Accad. di Scienze e Lettere 2010–, Accad. Nazionale dei Lincei 2013–; Bonaldo Stringher Prize Scholarship (Bank of Italy) 1974, St Vincent Prize for Econs 1985, Linceo Prize for Econs, Nat. Lincei Acad. 2004. *Publications:* Efficienza produttiva e livelli di attività 1981, Protagonisti del pensiero economico (co-author) 1977–82, Sui momenti costitutivi dell'economia politica 1983 (co-author), Foundations of Economics: Structures of Inquiry and Economic Theory 1986, The Economic Theory of Structure and Change 1990, A Theory of Production: Tasks, Processes and Technical Practices 1993, Production and Economic Dynamics 1996, Incommensurability and Translation. Kuhnian Perspectives on Scientific Communication and Theory Change 1999, Knowledge, Social Institutions and the Division of Labour 2001, Economics of Structural Change (co-author) 2003, Reasoning, Rationality, and Probability (co-author) 2008, Markets, Money and Capital – Hicksian Economics for the Twenty First Century (co-author) 2008, Migration of Ideas (co-author) 2008, Capital, Time and Transitional Dynamics (co-author) 2009, Fundamental Uncertainty – Rationality and Plausible Reasoning (co-author) 2011, L'illuminismo delle riforme civili: il contributo degli economisti lombardi (co-author) 2014, The Political Economy of the Eurozone (co-author) 2017, The Palgrave Handbook of Political Economy (co-author) 2018; numerous articles. *Leisure interests:* reading and conversation, art and classical music, walking and travelling. *Address:* Università degli Studi di Bologna, Piazza Scaravilli 2, 40126 Bologna (office); Via Garibaldi 5, 40124 Bologna, Italy (home). *Telephone:* (051) 2098146 (office). *Fax:* (051) 2098040 (office). *Website:* www.dse.unibo.it (office); www.lincei.it (office); www.clarehall.cam.ac.uk (office); www.crassh.cam.ac.uk (office); www.accademiascienzebologna.it (office).

SCHAAKE, Marietje, MSc; Dutch politician; b. 28 Oct. 1978, Leiden; ed Wittenberg Univ., Ohio, Univ. of Amsterdam; began career as ind. adviser to govts, diplomats, businesses and NGOs; mem. European Parl. (Democraten 66/Group of the Alliance of Liberals and Democrats for Europe) 2009–, mem. Cttee on Int. Trade; Founder European Parl. Intergroup on the Digital Agenda for Europe, Intergroup on New Media and Tech.; mem. Global Comm. on the Stability of Cyberspace; mem. World Econ. Forum Global Future Council on Future of Digital Economy; named World Econ. Forum Young Global Leader 2014. *Address:* European Parliament, Rue Wiertz 60, 1047 Brussels, Belgium (office). *Telephone:* (2) 284-56-17 (office). *E-mail:* marietje.schaake@europarl.europa.eu (office). *Website:* www.marietjeschaake.eu (office).

SCHAAL, Barbara A., BS, MPh, PhD; American/German plant biologist and academic; *Mary-Dell Chilton Distinguished Professor, Department of Biology and Dean, Faculty of Arts and Sciences, Washington University in St Louis;* b. 1947, Berlin, Germany; ed Univ. of Illinois, Chicago, Yale Univ.; became US citizen in 1956; grew up in Chicago; mem. Faculty, Univ. of Houston, Ohio State Univ. –1980; Assoc. Prof., Dept of Biology, Washington Univ. in St Louis 1980–86, apptd Prof. 1986, Spencer T. Olin Prof. in Arts and Sciences 2001–09, Mary-Dell Chilton Distinguished Prof. 2009–, Dir Tyson Research Center 2011–, Dean of the Faculty of Arts and Sciences 2013–, Chair. Dept of Biology 1993–97; Assoc. Ed. Molecular Biology and Evolution, The American Journal of Botany, Molecular Ecology, Conservation Genetics; Pres. Botanical Soc. of America 1995–96; fmr Pres. Soc. for Study of Evolution; mem. Bd of Trustees St Louis Acad. of Sciences, Missouri Chapter of Nature Conservancy; mem. Advisory Bd, Science and Entertainment Exchange; Fellow, AAAS; mem. NAS 1999–, Vice-Pres. NAS 2005–; mem. President's Council of Advisors on Science and Technology 2009–; Distinguished Scientist Award, American Inst. of Biological Sciences 2011–12. *Achievements include:* recognized for work on genetics of plant species, particularly for studies using DNA sequences to understand evolutionary processes such as gene flow, geographical differentiation, and domestication of crop species. *Publications:* numerous scientific papers in professional journals. *Address:* South Brookings 205, Department of Biology, Washington University in St Louis, Campus Box 1137, One Brookings Drive, St Louis, MO 63130-4899, USA (office). *Telephone:* (314) 935-6822 (office). *E-mail:* schaal@biology.wustl.edu (office). *Website:* www.biology.wustl.edu/faculty/schaal (office).

SCHABRAM, Hans, DPhil; German professor of English; *Professor Emeritus, Abteilung für Englische Sprache und Literatur des Mittelalters, University of Göttingen;* b. 27 Sept. 1928, Berlin; s. of Paul Schabram and Lucia Schabram; m. Candida Larisch 1956; two s. one d.; ed Univs of Berlin and Cologne; Asst, English Dept, Univ. of Heidelberg 1957–63; Prof. of Medieval English Language and Literature, Univ. of Giessen 1964–67; apptd Prof., Abteilung für Englische Sprache und Literatur des Mittelalters, Univ. of Göttingen 1968, currently Prof. Emer.; mem. Akad. der Wissenschaften, Göttingen. *Publications:* 55 publs on English Philology since 1956. *Address:* Seminar für Englische Philologie, Abteilung für Englische Sprache und Literatur des Mittelalters, Georg-August-Universität, Käte-Hamburger Weg 3, 37073 Göttingen (office); Heinz-Hilpert-Str. 6, 37085 Göttingen, Germany (home). *Telephone:* (551) 55444 (home). *Website:* www.uni-goettingen.de (office).

SCHACHT, Henry Brewer, MBA; American business executive; *Managing Director and Senior Advisor, Warburg Pincus LLC;* b. 16 Oct. 1934, Erie, Pa; s. of Henry Schacht and Virginia Schacht; m. Nancy Godfrey 1960; one s. three d.; ed Yale and Harvard Univs; Investment Man. Irwin Man. Co. 1962–64; Vice-Pres. Finance, Subsidiaries and Int. Areas, Cummins Engine Co., Inc. 1964–69; Pres. Cummins Engine Co., Inc. 1969–77, Chair. 1977–95, CEO 1977–94; Man. Dir Warburg Pincus LLC, New York 1995, Man. Dir and Sr Advisor 2004–; Chair. and CEO Lucent Techs, Murray Hill, NJ 1995–98, 2000–03; fmr mem. Bd of Dirs CBS, AT&T, Chase Manhattan Corpn, Chase Manhattan Bank NA, Johnson & Johnson, New York Times Co., Avaya, Aluminum Company of America (Alcoa); fmr mem. Business Council; Trustee, Metropolitan Museum of Art; fmr Chair. Bd of Trustees Ford Foundation; fmr Trustee Yale Univ., Brookings Inst., Business Enterprise Trust, Calver Educ. Foundation; fmr Sr mem. The Conference Board. *Address:* Warburg Pincus LLC, 450 Lexington Avenue, New York, NY 10017, USA (office). *Telephone:* (212) 878-0600 (office). *Fax:* (212) 878-9351 (office). *Website:* www.warburgpincus.com (office).

SCHACK, Bo, BL, MBA; Danish lawyer and UN official; *Director, UNRWA Operations in Gaza;* b. 1955; m.; three c.; ed Univ. of Copenhagen, European Coll., Bruges, Belgium, Open Univ., UK; Assoc. Attorney, Ministry of Industry –1985; worked for UNHCR in Senegal 1985–88, in Hong Kong 1988–91, at Asia Bureau HQ 1991–94, Special Operation in fmr Yugoslavia 1994–97, in Sri Lanka 1997–2000, Deputy Rep. in Tehran, Iran 2000–03, Head of Policy Unit, Europe Bureau, UNHCR HQ, Geneva 2003–07, Rep. in Burundi 2007–09; Deputy Special Rep. of the Sec. Gen. in Central African Repub. and UN Resident Co-ordinator, Humanitarian Co-ordinator and Resident Rep., UN Integrated Peacebuilding Office in Cen. African Repub. (BINUCA) 2010–11, Special Adviser to Deputy Special Rep. of Sec.-Gen. in UN Mission in Côte d'Ivoire (ONUCI) April–July 2012, Rep. and Country Dir in Afghanistan, UNHCR 2013–15; Dir UNRWA Operations in Gaza 2015–. *Address:* UNRWA, PO Box 61, Gaza City, Palestinian Territories (office). *Telephone:* (8) 2887457 (office). *Fax:* (8) 2887219 (office). *E-mail:* gazapio@unrwa.org (office). *Website:* www.unrwa.org (office).

SCHAEFER, George A., Jr, BS, MBA; American business executive; *Independent Lead Director, Anthem Inc.;* ed US Mil. Acad. at West Point, Xavier Univ.; mem. Bd of Dirs Fifth Third BanCorp 1988, now Dir Emer., Pres. Fifth Third BanCorp 1990–2006, CEO 1990–2007, Chair. Fifth Third BanCorp 2006–08, Pres. and CEO Fifth Third Bank, Cincinnati, Ohio (subsidiary of Fifth Third BanCorp) from 1990, Pres. Fifth Third Leasing Co., Pres. and CEO Fifth Third Bank of Northeastern Ohio; mem. Bd of Dirs, WellPoint, Inc. 2001–, formed from merger of WellPoint Health Networks, Inc. and Anthem, Inc. 2004, WellPoint, Inc. renamed Anthem, Inc. 2014–, Chair. 2013–15, Ind. Lead Dir 2015–; Chair. Bd of Univ. of Cincinnati; mem. Bd of Dirs, Anthem Insurance (subsidiary of WellPoint, Inc.) 1995–2003, Ashland Inc. 2003–, Kenton Co. Airport; mem. Advisory Bd, Federal Reserve Bank of Cleveland; mem. Bd of Trustees, Univ. of Cincinnati, Children's Hosp., Cincinnati. *Address:* Anthem, Inc., 120 Monument Circle, Indianapolis, IN 46204, USA (office). *Telephone:* (317) 532-6000 (office). *Fax:* (317) 488-6028 (office). *E-mail:* boardofdirectors@antheminc.com (office). *Website:* www.antheminc.com (office).

SCHAEFER, Henry Frederick, III, BS, PhD; American chemist, researcher and academic; *Graham-Perdue Professor of Chemistry and Director, Center for Computational Chemistry, University of Georgia;* b. 8 June 1944, Grand Rapids, Mich.; s. of Henry Frederick Schaefer, Jr and Janice Christine Trost Schaefer; m. Karen Regine Rasmussen; three s. two d.; ed Massachusetts Inst. of Tech., Stanford Univ.; Prof. of Chem., Univ. of Calif., Berkeley 1969–87; Wilfred T. Doherty Prof. and Dir Inst. for Theoretical Chem., Univ. of Tex. 1979–80; Graham-Perdue Prof. of Chem. and Dir Center for Computational Chem., Univ. of Ga 1987–; Ed. Molecular Physics 1991–2005, Encyclopedia of Computational Chem. 1995–2004; Pres. World Asscn of Theoretical and Computational Chemists 1996–2005; Alfred P. Sloan Research Fellow 1972–74; John Simon Guggenheim Fellow 1976–77; Fellow, American Physical Soc. 1977–, AAAS, American Acad. of

Arts and Sciences 2004–, Royal Soc. of Chemistry 2005–, American Chemical Soc. 2009, Int. Union of Pure and Applied Chemistry 2013; mem. Int. Acad. of Quantum Molecular Sciences; numerous lectureships including Guelph-Waterloo Distinguished Lecturer, Univ. of Guelph and Univ. of Waterloo, Ont., Canada 1991, John M. Templeton Lecturer, Case Western Reserve Univ. 1992, Herbert H. King Lecturer, Kansas State Univ. 1993, Francis A. Schaeffer Lectures, Washington Univ., St Louis 1994, Mary E. Kapp Lecture, Va Commonwealth Univ. 1996, Abbott Lectures, Univ. of ND 1997, C.S. Lewis Lecture, Univ. of Tenn. 1997, Joseph Frank McGregory Lecture, Colgate Univ. 1997, Kenneth S. Pitzer Lecture, Univ. of Calif. at Berkeley 1998, Donald F. Othmer Lectures in Chem., Tokyo 2000, Israel Pollak Lectures, Technion-Israel Inst. of Tech., Haifa 2001, Coochbehar Lectures, Indian Asscn for the Cultivation of Science, Kolkata 2001, Lise Meitner Lecture, Hebrew Univ., Jerusalem 2001, Oakley Vail Lecture, Wake Forest Univ. 2002, Lawrence J. Schaad Lecture, Vanderbilt Univ. 2002, Annual Lecture of the Croatian Chemical Soc., Zagreb 2002, The Pres.'s Lecture, Univ. of Texas at Arlington 2002, Distinguished Theory Lecturer, Max Planck Inst., Mülheim, Germany 2003, John Marks Templeton Lecture, Princeton Univ. 2004, The New Coll. Lectures, Univ. of New South Wales 2004, Nanqiang Lecture, Xiamen Univ. 2005, C. V. Raman Memorial Lecture, Calcutta 2007, Per-Olov Löwdin, Univ. of Uppsala 2007, Herman Hotz Trust Lecture, Univ. of Arkansas 2008, Steven Adelman Lectures, Purdue Univ. 2009, Russel Pitzer Lecture, Ohio State Univ. 2009, Coll. of Sciences Distinguished Lecturer, Univ. of Cen. Florida, Orlando 2011, Distinguished Lecturer, Texas A&M Univ. 2011, William E. Palke Lecture, Univ. of Calif., Santa Barbara 2013, Science at the Edge Lecture Series, Michigan State Univ., East Lansing 2013, Jan Almlöf – Odd Gropen Lectures, Univ. of Tromsø and Univ. of Oslo 2013, Australian Asscn of Theoretical and Computational Chemists Lecture, Australian Nat. Univ. and Univ. of Sydney 2014, James William McBain Lecture, Nat. Chemical Lab., Pune, India 2014, Inst. Lecture, Indian Inst. of Tech. Bombay, Mumbai 2014; 27 hon. degrees; ACS Award in Pure Chem. 1979, Leo Hendrik Baekeland Award (ACS) 1983; Schroedinger Medal, World Asscn of Theoretical Organic Chemists 1990, Centenary Medal, RSC, London 1992, ACS Award in Theoretical Chem. 2003, ACS Ira Remson Award 2003, Joseph O. Hirschfelder Prize 2006, Chemical Pioneer Award 2013, ACS Peter Debye Award in Physical Chemistry 2014. *Publications:* The Electronic Structure of Atoms and Molecules 1972, Modern Theoretical Chemistry 1977, Quantum Chemistry 1984, A New Dimension to Quantum Chemistry 1994, Science and Christianity: Conflict or Coherence? 2013; more than 1,450 publs in scientific journals. *Leisure interests:* Bible study, hiking. *Address:* Center for Computational Chemistry, University of Georgia, 1004 Cedar Street, Athens, GA 30602-2525, USA (office). *Telephone:* (706) 542-0364 (office); (706) 542-2067 (office). *Fax:* (706) 542-0406 (office). *E-mail:* qc@uga.edu (office). *Website:* ccqc.uga.edu (office).

SCHAEFER, Michael, PhD; German diplomatist and foundation executive; *Chairman, BMW Foundation Herbert Quandt;* b. 6 March 1949, Paderborn; m.; three c.; ed Ludwig-Maximilian Univ., Munich, Max Planck Inst., Heidelberg, Univ. of Mannheim; Second State Exam Law, Heidelberg 1978; joined Foreign Service 1978, postings include UN Missions in New York and Geneva, Singapore, Head of Western Balkans Task Force, Fed. Foreign Office, Berlin 1999–2001, Special Envoy for S Eastern Europe and Deputy Political Dir 2001–02, Head, Legal Dept 2002, Political Dir 2002–07, rank of Amb. 2002–, Amb. to People's Repub. of China 2007–13 (retd); Chair. BMW Foundation Herbert Quandt 2013–; mem. Bd of Dirs United Nations Asscn of Germany (DGVN); mem. Advisory Bd, Mercator Inst. for China Studies; mem. German Group of Trilateral Comm., Comm. on Global Security, Justice and Governance; Hon. Prof., China Univ. of Political Science and Law; Officier, Légion d'honneur 2007. *Publications:* Der Sicherheitsmechanismus der Vereinten Nationen 1980, Berufsbild Diplomat: Auswahl und Ausbildung im Auswärtigen Dienst 1995; contrib. to Südosteuropa Mitteilungen, Zeitschrift Vereinte Nationen. *Address:* BMW Stiftung Herbert Quandt, Reinhardtstrasse 58, 10117 Berlin, Germany (office). *Telephone:* (30) 3396-3500 (office). *E-mail:* info@bmw-foundation.de (office). *Website:* bmw-foundation.org (office).

SCHAEFFER, Bogusław, DPhil; Polish/Austrian composer, music critic, playwright and pianist; b. 6 June 1929, Lwów (now Lviv, Ukraine); s. of Władysław Schaeffer and Julia Schaeffer; m. Mieczysława Hanuszewska 1953; one s.; ed State Higher School of Music (student of A. Malawski), Jagiellonian Univ., Kraków (student of Zdzisław Jachimecki); wrote first dodecaphonic music for orchestra in Eastern Europe, Music for Strings: Nocturne 1953; Assoc. Prof., State Higher School of Music, Kraków 1963–98, Ordinary Prof. of Composition, Higher School of Music, Mozarteum, Salzburg 1986–89, Prof. 1989–; Chief Ed. Forum Musicum 1967–; leads int. summer courses for new composition in Salzburg and Schwaz, Austria 1976–; Hon. mem. Int. Soc. for Contemporary Music 1998, Pro Sinfonica 2003; Gold Cross of Merit 1969; Kt's Cross of Polonia Restituta Order 1972; numerous prizes include G. Fitelberg Prize 1959, 1960, 1964, A. Malawski Prize 1962, Minister of Culture and Arts Prize 1971, 1980, Union of Polish Composers Prize 1977, Alfred Jurzykowski Award 1999. *Main compositions:* Extrema, Tertium datur, Scultura, S'alto for alto saxophone, Collage and Form, Electronic Music, Visual Music, Heraclitiana, Missa Electronica, Jangwa, Missa Sinfonica, eight Piano Concertos, Maah, Sinfonia, Hommage à Guillaume for two cellos and piano 1995, Sinfonietta for 16 instruments 1996, Symphony in One Movement 1997, Enigma for Orchestra 1997, Four Psalms for choir and orchestra 1999, Musica Omogènea for 32 violins 1999, Si Quaeris Miracula for soprano and orchestra 2000, Model XXI (Wendepunkt) for piano 2000, De Profundis for soprano and chamber orchestra 2000, Monophonie VIII for 24 violins 2000, Ave Maria for soprano and orchestra 2000, opera Liebesblicke 2000, five violin concertos, three cello concertos, Concerto for vibraphone and orchestra 2001, Concerto for harp, Celtic harp and orchestra 2002, Concerto for saxophone, piano and orchestra 2002, 9th Symphony 2003, Concert for piano and choir 2004, For violin and electronics 2004, Blues VII for piano and orchestra 2004, Quartet for four cellos 2005, Panorama for orchestra 2005, Fragment III for two actors, clarinet, cello, piano and electronic media 2005, Second Symphony in One Movement 2005, OCSENOT for soprano and ensemble of seven instruments, Impresiónes Liricas for piano and electro-acoustic medias 2005, Model XXXIII for piano 2005, Contemporaneamente o Alternatamente for violin and piano 2005, Model XXXIV for piano 2006, Concerto for viola and 12 various instruments 2007, Quartet for four violins and chamber orchestra 2009, 10th Symphony 2010, SaVi for saxophone and violin 2011, Mini opera, also film and theatre music, Miserere, Organ Concerto, 17 string quartets, Orchestral and Electronic Changes, Concerto for Violin, Piano and Orchestra, Symphony/Concerto for 15 solo instrumentalists and orchestra, Heideggeriana, Winter Musik for horn and piano, Concerto for percussion, electronic media and orchestra. *Plays:* 46 stage plays including: Three Actors 1970, Darknesses 1980, Screenplay for Sins of Old Age 1985, The Actor 1990, Rehearsals 1990, Séance 1990, Tutam 1991, Rondo 1991, Together 1992, Toast 1991, Harvest 1993, Promotion 1993, Gloss 1993, Daybreak 1994, Multi 1994, Largo 1996, Blockheads 1997, Stage Demon 1998, Alles 1998, Advertisement 1998, Walks Through Parc 1998, InOut 1998, Farniente 1998, Chance 1999, Dwa Te (Two Te) 2000, Skala 2000, Scale 2008, Something Multimedial 2009, Case; plays trans. into 17 languages. *Publications:* Nowa Muzyka. Problemy współczesnej techniki kompozytorskiej (New music. Problems of Contemporary Technique in Composing) 1958, Klasycy dodekafonii (Classics of Dodecaphonic Music) 1964, Leksykon kompozytorów XX wieku (Lexicon of 20th Century Composers) 1965, W kręgu nowej muzyki (In the Sphere of New Music) 1967, Mały informator muzyki XX wieku 1975, Introduction to Composition (in English) 1975, Historia muzyki (Story of Music) 1980, Kompozytorzy XX wieku (20th Century Composers) 1990, Trzy rozmowy (kompozytor, dramaturg, filozof) (Three Conversations: Composer, Playwright and Philosopher) 1992. *Leisure interests:* literature, theatre. *Address:* Osiedle Kolorowe 4, m.6, 31-938 Kraków, Poland; St. Julienstrasse 7A, Apartment 27, 5020 Salzburg, Austria. *Telephone:* (12) 6441960 (Poland) (home). *E-mail:* bsch@ceti.pl (office).

SCHAEFFER, Leonard D., BA; American business executive and academic; *Judge Robert Maclay Widney Chair, Sol Price School for Public Policy, University of Southern California;* b. 28 July 1945, Chicago, Ill.; m. Pamela Schaeffer (née Sidford); two c.; ed Princeton Univ.; Man. Consultant, Arthur Andersen & Co. 1969–73; Deputy Dir of Man. Illinois Mental Health and Developmental Disabilities, Springfield, Ill. 1973–75; Dir Ill. State Bureau of Budget 1975–76; Vice-Pres. Citibank NA, New York 1976–78; Asst Sec., Man and Budget, US Dept of Health and Human Services, Washington, DC 1978, Admin. Health Care Financing Admin 1978–80; Exec. Vice-Pres. and COO Student Loan Marketing Asscn 1980–82; Pres. and CEO Group Health Inc., Minneapolis, Minn. 1983–86; Chair. and CEO Blue Cross of Calif. 1986–96, managed transition to WellPoint, Chair. and CEO WellPoint Health Networks Inc. (now WellPoint Inc.) 1993–2004, Chair. 2004–05; Dir Allergan, Inc. 1993–; est. Calif. Endowment and Calif. HealthCare Foundation 1996; currently Sr Advisor TPG Capital (Pvt. investment firm); also currently Judge Robert Maclay Widney Chair and Prof., Sol Price School of Public Policy, Univ. of Southern California; mem. Bd of Dirs Quintiles Transnational Corpn, scPharmaceuticals, Inc., Amgen Inc. 2004–13; fmr Chair. Nat. Inst. for Health Care Man., Health Insurance Asscn of America, Nat. Health Foundation; Founding Chair. Coalition for Affordable and Quality Healthcare; mem. Inst. of Medicine, Nat. Acad. of Science; Chair. Bd of Trustees, Brewster Foundation: mem. Bd of Trustees, The Brookings Inst., RAND Corpn, Univ. of Southern California; mem. Bd of Fellows and Co-Chair., Advisory Council, Dept of Healthcare Policy, Harvard Medical School; mem. Advisory Council Dept of Economics, Princeton Univ.; Citation for Outstanding Service, American Acad. of Paediatrics, Distinguished Public Service Award, US Dept of Health, Educ. and Welfare, Exec. Leadership Award, UCLA Anderson School of Man. 2003. *Address:* USC Sol Price School of Public Policy, University of Southern California, Lewis Hall 312, Los Angeles, CA 90089-0626, USA (office). *Website:* priceschool.usc.edu (office).

SCHAFER, Edward (Ed) Thomas, BA, MBA; American business executive, government official and fmr politician; b. 8 Aug. 1946, Bismarck, ND; s. of Harold Schafer and Marian Schafer; m. Nancy Jones 1992; four c.; ed Univ. of North Dakota and Univ. of Denver; quality control insp., Gold Seal 1971–73, Vice-Pres. 1974, Chair. Man. Cttee 1975–78, Pres. 1978–85; Owner/Dir H & S Distribution 1976; Pres. Dakota Classics 1986, TRIESCO Properties 1986, Fish 'N Dakota 1990–94; Gov. of N Dakota 1993–2000; Civilian Aide to US Sec. of the Army 2002; Co-founder and CEO Extend America (wireless communications co.) 2000–08; advisor, Americans for Prosperity 2006–08; Trustee Investors Real Estate Trust (IRET) 2006–07, 2009–11; US Sec. of Agric., Washington, DC 2008–09; consultant to Bion 2009–10; Chair. Theodore Roosevelt Medora Foundation; Co-Chair. China–US Agriculture Uplift Program; mem. Bd of Dirs Continental Resources Inc. 2011–, North Dakota Tax Payers Asscn; mem. Advisory Cttee, Impact Red River Valley; Advisor, Yangling Agriculture High Tech Demonstration Zone; Republican.

SCHÄFERKORDT, Anke; German television executive; *CEO, RTL Mediengruppe Deutschland GmbH;* b. 1962; began career at Bertelsmann AG in 1988; Exec. Asst for Sales Controlling and Strategic Planning, RTL Television GmbH, Cologne 1991–92, Head, Controlling Dept 1992–93, Dir in charge of Corp. Planning and Controlling Div. 1993–95, Head of Business Affairs, VOX Television 1995–97, Program Dir 1997–99, CEO VOX Television 1999–, COO and Deputy CEO of RTL Television Feb.–Sept. 2005, CEO Sept. 2005–, Co-CEO RTL Group 2012–, currently CEO Mediengruppe RTL Deutschland GmbH; mem. Supervisory Bd BASF SE 2010–, Software AG 2010–. *Address:* RTL Television GmbH, Picassoplatz 1, 50679 Cologne, Germany (office). *Telephone:* (221) 456-0 (office). *Fax:* (221) 456-1690 (office). *Website:* www.rtl-television.de (office).

SCHÄFERS, Reinhard; German diplomatist; b. 27 May 1950; m.; two c.; ed Ecole Nationale d'Admin, Paris; joined Fed. Ministry of Foreign Affairs 1977, Second Sec. 1979, Consul, Embassy in Prague 1979–82, Deputy Head of Mission, Embassy in Mogadishu, First Sec. and Counsellor, Ministry of Foreign Affairs 1985–88, Counsellor, Embassy in Moscow 1988–91, Counsellor, USSR Div., Ministry of Foreign Affairs 1991–92, Head of Cen., E and SE Europe Div. 1992–98, Minister, Embassy in Paris 1998–2000, Perm. Rep. to WEU 2000, to EU Political and Security Cttee 2001, Amb. to Ukraine 2006–08, to France 2008–12, to Italy 2012–15. *Address:* Federal Ministry of Foreign Affairs, 11013 Berlin, Germany (office). *Telephone:* (30) 18170-0 (office). *Fax:* (30) 18173402 (office). *E-mail:* poststelle@auswaertiges-amt.de (office). *Website:* www.auswaertiges-amt.de (office).

SCHALLER, George Beals, PhD; American zoologist, academic and author; *Vice-President, Panthera Inc.;* b. 26 May 1933, Berlin, Germany; s. of George Ludwig Schaller and Bettina Iwersen (née Byrd); m. Kay Suzanne Morgan 1957;

two s.; ed Univ. of Alaska, Univ. of Wisconsin-Madison; moved to USA in his teens; Fellow, Dept of Behavioral Sciences, Stanford Univ. 1962–63; Research Assoc., Johns Hopkins Univ., Baltimore 1963–66; Adjunct Assoc. Prof., Rockefeller Univ., New York 1966–72; Research Zoologist, Wildlife Conservation Soc. 1966–, Dir Int. Conservation Program, New York Zoological Soc. 1979–88, then Vice-Pres. Science and Exploration Program and Ella Millbank Foshay Chair in Wildlife Conservation, now Sr Conservationist; Vice-Pres. Panthera Inc.; Adjunct Prof., Peking Univ.; Research Assoc., American Museum of Natural History; Fellow, Guggenheim Foundation 1971; Hon. Dir Explorers' Club 1991; Order of Golden Ark (Netherlands) 1978; Int. Cosmos Prize (Japan) 1996, Tyler Prize for Environmental Achievement 1997, Gold Medal, World Wildlife Fund 1980, Beebe Fellowship, Wildlife Conservation Soc. 2006, Lifetime Achievement Award, Nat. Geographic Soc. 2007, Indianapolis Prize 2008. *Achievements include:* recognized as one of the world's leading field biologists, studying wildlife throughout Africa, Asia and S America. *Publications include:* The Mountain Gorilla 1963, The Year of the Gorilla 1964, The Deer and the Tiger 1967, The Serengeti Lion (Nat. Book Award 1973) 1972, Mountain Monarchs 1977, Stones of Silence 1980, The Giant Pandas of Wolong (co-author) 1985, The Last Panda 1993, Tibet's Hidden Wilderness 1997, Wildlife of the Tibetan Steppe 1998, Antelopes, Deer and Relatives (co-ed.) 2000, Giant Pandas in the Wild: Saving an Endangered Species (jtly) 2005, A Naturalist and Other Beasts: Tales from a Life in the Field 2007, Tibet Wild: A Naturalist's Journey on the Roof of the World 2012. *Leisure interests:* photography, reading. *Address:* Panthera, Inc., 8 West 40th Street, 18th Floor, New York, NY 10018 (office); Wildlife Conservation Society, 2300 Southern Boulevard, Bronx, New York, NY 10460, USA (office). *Telephone:* (646) 786-0400 (Panthera) (office). *E-mail:* info@panthera.org; asiaprogram@wcs.org (office). *Website:* www.panthera.org (office); www.wcs.org (office).

SCHALLY, Andrew Victor, PhD; American medical researcher and academic; *Distinguished Medical Research Scientist, Department of Veterans' Affairs;* b. 30 Nov. 1926, Wilno, Poland (now Vilnius, Lithuania); s. of Casimir Peter Schally and Maria Schally (née Lacka); m. 1st Margaret Rachel White; one s. one d.; m. 2nd Ana Maria de Medeiros-Comaru 1976 (died 2004); m. 3rd Maria Rasmussen 2011; ed Bridge of Allan, Scotland and Univ. of London, UK, McGill Univ., Montreal, Canada; Asst Prof. of Physiology and Asst Prof. of Biochemistry, Baylor Univ. Coll. of Medicine, Houston, Tex. 1957–62; Chief, Endocrine and Polypeptide Labs, Veterans Admin. Hosp., New Orleans, La 1962–2005; Sr Medical Investigator, Veterans Admin. 1973–99, Distinguished Medical Research Scientist, Dept of Veterans Affairs 1999–; Assoc. Prof. of Medicine, Tulane Univ. School of Medicine, New Orleans, La 1962–67, Prof. of Medicine 1967–2005; Distinguished Leonard Miller Prof. of Pathology, Prof., Div. of Hematology/Oncology and Div. of Endocrinology, Dept of Medicine, Miller School of Medicine, Univ. of Miami; mem. NAS, AAAS and numerous other socs and nat. acads; Chevalier, Légion d'honneur 2004; decorations from USA, Spain, France, Ecuador and Venezuela; more than 30 hon. degrees, including Hon. MD and Hon. DSc; Charles Mickle Award 1974, Gairdner Foundation Award 1974, Edward T. Tyler Award 1975, Borden Award in the Medical Sciences (Asscn of American Medical Colls) 1975, Lasker Award 1975, shared Nobel Prize for Physiology or Medicine with Roger Guillemin (q.v.) for discoveries concerning peptide hormones 1977, US Govt Distinguished Service Award 1978. *Publications:* more than 2,500 scientific papers, particularly concerning hormones and cancer. *Leisure interests:* swimming, soccer. *Address:* Veterans Administration Hospital Research Service, 1201 NW 16th Street, Room 2A123, Miami, FL 33125 (office); 3801 Collins Avenue, Apt 1506, Miami Beach, FL 33140, USA (home). *Telephone:* (305) 575-3477 (office); (305) 575-7000 (office). *Fax:* (305) 575-3126 (office). *E-mail:* andrew.schally@va.gov (office); barbara.bueno@va.gov (office).

SCHAMA, Sir Simon Michael, Kt, CBE, MA, FBA, FRSL; British historian, academic, writer and art critic; *University Professor of Art History and History, Columbia University;* b. 13 Feb. 1945, London; s. of Arthur Schama and Gertrude Steinberg; m. Virginia Papaioannou 1983; one s. one d.; ed Christ's Coll., Cambridge; Fellow and Dir of Studies in History, Christ's Coll., Cambridge 1966–76; Fellow and Tutor in Modern History, Brasenose Coll., Oxford 1976–80; Prof. of History (Mellon Prof. of the Social Sciences), Harvard Univ. 1980; Univ. Prof. of Art History and History, Columbia Univ. 1997–; art critic, New Yorker 1995–; Contributing Ed., Financial Times 2009–; Vice-Pres. Poetry Soc.; American Historical Asscn 1978, Nat. Cash Register Book Prize for Non-Fiction (for Citizens) 1990. *Television:* documentaries: Rembrandt: The Public Eye and the Private Gaze (BBC) 1995, A History of Britain (series) (BBC) 2000–01, Murder at Harvard (PBS) 2003, The Power of Art (series) 2006, The American Future: A History (series) (BBC) 2008, Obama's America (BBC) 2009, Shakespeare (BBC) 2012, Story of the Jews (BBC) 2013, Civilisations (BBC) 2018. *Publications include:* Patriots and Liberators: Revolution in the Netherlands 1780–1813 (Wolfson History Prize, Leo Gershoy Prize) 1977, Two Rothschilds and the Land of Israel 1979, The Embarrassment of Riches: An Interpretation of Dutch Culture in the Golden Age 1987, Citizens: A Chronicle of the French Revolution 1989, Dead Certainties (Unwarranted Speculations) 1991, Landscape and Memory 1995, Rembrandt's Eyes 1999, A History of Britain Vol. 1: At the Edge of the World? 3000 BC–AD 1603 2000, Vol. 2: The British Wars 1603–1776 2001, Vol. 3: The Fate of Empire 1776–2001 2002, Hang-Ups: Essays on Painting 2004, Rough Crossings: Britain, the Slaves and the American Revolution 2005, Power of Art 2006, The American Future: A History 2008, Scribble, Scribble, Scribble 2010, The Story of the Jews Vol. 1 2013, The Story of the Jews Vol. 2 2017. *Leisure interests:* wine, Dutch bulbs, children's fiction. *Address:* Department of History, 522 Fayerweather Hall, Columbia University, New York, NY 10027, USA (office). *Telephone:* (212) 854-4593 (office). *E-mail:* sms53@columbia.edu (office). *Website:* www.columbia.edu/cu/arthistory/faculty/Schama.html (office).

SCHAPIRO, Morton, BEcons, PhD; American economist, academic and university administrator; *President, Northwestern University;* m. Mimi Schapiro; one s. two d.; ed Hofstra Univ., Univ. of Pennsylvania; Prof. of Econs and Asst Provost, Williams Coll. 1980–91, Pres. Williams Coll. 2000–09; Chair. Dept of Econs, Univ. of Southern California 1991–94, Dean Coll. of Letters, Arts and Sciences 1994–2000, Vice-Pres. for Planning 1998–2000; Prof. of Econs, Judd A. and Marjorie Weinberg Coll. of Arts and Sciences, Northwestern Univ. 2009–, also holds appointments in Kellogg School of Man. and School of Educ. and Social Policy, Pres. Northwestern Univ. 2009–; Fellow, American Acad. of Arts and Sciences 2010. *Publications include:* Keeping College Affordable: Government and Educational Opportunity 1991, Paying the Piper: Productivity, Incentives and Financing in Higher Education (co-author) 1993, The Student Aid Game: Meeting Need and Rewarding Talent in American Higher Education 1998; College Success: What It Means and How to Make It Happen (ed.) 2008, College Access: Opportunity or Privilege? (ed.) 2006; more than 100 articles. *Address:* Office of the President, Northwestern University, 2-130 Rebecca Crown Center, 633 Clark Street, Evanston, IL 60208, USA (office). *Telephone:* (847) 491-7456 (office). *Fax:* (847) 467-3104 (office). *E-mail:* nu-president@northwestern.edu (office). *Website:* www.northwestern.edu/president (office).

SCHARIOTH, Klaus, MA, MALD, PhD; German diplomatist; *Dean, Mercator College for International Affairs;* b. 8 Oct. 1946, Essen, North Rhine-Westphalia; m.; three c.; ed studies in Caldwell, Ida, USA, in Bonn and Freiburg, Germany, and in Geneva, Switzerland, Fletcher School of Law and Diplomacy, Harvard Law School, John F. Kennedy School of Govt; mil. service 1966–67; entered Foreign Service 1976, Asia Div., Press Div. and State Sec.'s Office, Fed. Foreign Office 1977–79, Embassy in Quito, Ecuador 1979–82, Policy Planning Staff, Fed. Foreign Office 1982–86, Perm. Mission to UN, New York, Vice-Chair. UN Legal and Charter Cttees 1986–90, Int. Law Div., Fed. Foreign Office 1990–93, Chef de Cabinet (Dir pvt. office) to NATO Sec.-Gen., Brussels 1993–96, Head of Defence and Security Policy Div., Fed. Foreign Office 1996–97, Office of the Foreign Minister 1997–98, Head of Office April 1998, Head of Int. Security and N America Directorate 1998–99, Political Dir and Head of Political Directorate-Gen. 1999–2002, State Sec. of the Foreign Office 2002–06, Amb. to USA 2006–11; Dean, Mercator Coll. for Int. Affairs 2011–; Prof. of Practice, The Fletcher School, Tufts Univ. *Address:* Mercator College for International Affairs, College Ring 6-7, 28759 Bremen, Germany (office). *Telephone:* (421) 2005302 (office). *Website:* www.stiftung-mercator.de (office).

SCHARP, Anders, MSc; Swedish business executive; b. 8 June 1934; s. of John Henry Scharp and Esther Scharp; m. Maud Hermansson 1957; ed Royal Inst. of Tech., Stockholm; joined AB Electrohelios 1960 (merged with AB Electrolux 1963), Exec. Vice-Pres. (Production and Research & Devt) 1974; apptd Pres. AB Electrolux 1981, CEO 1986; Chair. Saab-Scania 1990–95; Chair. Saab AB 1995–2006, AB Nederman; Chair. and CEO AB SKF 1992–2008; Chair. Incentive AB 1992–98; Chair. White Consolidated Industries 1993–98, fmrly CEO; mem. Bd of Dirs Investor AB 1988–, Vice Chair. 2005–; fmr Chair. AB Nederman & Co.; fmr mem. Bd of Dirs Swedish Asscn of Metalworking Industries, Swedish Metal Trades Employers' Asscn, Swedish Employers' Confed.; Bd mem. Fed. of Swedish Industries, Asscn of Swedish Engineering Industries; mem. Royal Swedish Acad. of Engineering Sciences; Great Gold Medal, Royal Swedish Acad. of Engineering Sciences 2017.

SCHARPING, Rudolf; German politician; *CEO, Rudolf Scharping Strategie Beratung Kommunikation GmbH;* b. 2 Dec. 1947, Niederelbert, Westerwald; m. 1st Jutta Scharping (divorced 2000); three c.; m. 2nd Countess Kristina Pilati Borggreve 2000; ed Univ. of Bonn; joined Social Democratic Party (SPD) 1966; State Chair. and Nat. Deputy Chair. Jusos (Young Socialists) 1966; mem. State Parl. of Rhineland-Palatinate 1975–94; Party Leader of SPD in Rhineland-Palatinate 1985; Leader of Opposition in Rhineland-Palatinate 1987; Minister-Pres. of Rhineland-Palatinate 1991–94; mem. Bundestag (German Parl.) 1994–2005; Leader, SPD 1993–95, Deputy Chair. 1995–2003, Chair. SPD Parl. Group, Leader of the Opposition 1994; Chair. Social Democratic Party of Europe –2003; Minister of Defence 1998–2002; Deputy Chair. Party of European Socialists 1995–2001; currently CEO Rudolf Scharping Strategie Beratung Kommunikation GmbH; Research Asst to mems of Bundestag and European Parl. Deutsch 1969–75; Visiting Prof., Fletcher School for Law and Diplomacy, Tufts Univ. 2004–06; Pres. Bundes Deutscher Radfahrer (Fed. of German Cyclists) 2005–. *Publications include:* Was Jetzt Butun Ist 1994, Wir Dürfer Nicht Wegsehen – Der Kosovo-Krieg und Europa 1999; numerous articles on German and European politics. *Address:* Rudolf Scharping Strategie Beratung Kommunikation GmbH, Freiherr-vom-Stein-Str. 11, 60323 Frankfurt, Germany (office). *Telephone:* (69) 6612770 (office). *Fax:* (69) 66127712 (office). *E-mail:* info@rsbk.de (office). *Website:* www.rsbk.de (office).

SCHATZ, Brian Emanuel, BA; American politician and organization executive; *Senator from Hawaii;* b. 20 Oct. 1972, Ann Arbor, Mich.; s. of Irwin Schatz; m. Linda Kwok Kai Yun; one s. one d.; ed Punahou School, Pomona Coll., Claremont, Calif., spent a term studying in Kenya as part of the Int. Training Program; family moved to Hawaii 1974; taught at Punahou before taking other positions in the non-profit sector; active in Youth for Environmental Services 1980s; CEO Helping Hands Hawaii 2002–10; fmr Dir Makiki Community Library and of the Center for a Sustainable Future; mem. Hawaii House of Reps from the 24th Dist 1998–2002, from the 25th Dist 2002–06; Chair. Democratic Party of Hawaii 2008–10; Lt-Gov. of Hawaii 2010–12; Senator from Hawaii (to fill the vacancy caused by the death of Daniel Inouye) 2012–, mem. Cttee on Commerce, Science and Transportation, Cttee on Energy and Natural Resources, Cttee on Indian Affairs; Democrat. *Address:* G11 Dirksen Senate Office Building, Washington, DC 20510, USA (office). *Telephone:* (202) 224-3934 (office). *Website:* schatz.senate.gov (office); brianschatz.com.

SCHATZBERG, Alan Frederic, BS, MD; American psychiatrist, neuroscientist and academic; *Kenneth T. Norris, Jr Professor of Psychiatry and Behavioral Sciences, School of Medicine, Stanford University;* b. 17 Oct. 1944, New York; Nancy R. Silverman 1972; two c.; ed New York Univ.; Internship, Lenox Hill Hosp., NY 1968–69; Resident in Psychiatry, Massachusetts Mental Health Center, Boston 1969–72, Clinical Dir 1988–91; Clinical Fellow in Psychiatry, Harvard Medical School 1969–72, Asst Prof. in Psychiatry 1977–82, Assoc. Prof. 1982–88, Prof. 1988–91; Service Chief, McLean Hospital, Belmont, Mass 1982–84, 1986–88, Dir Depression Research Facility 1985–91, Interim Psychiatrist-in-Chief 1984–86; Kenneth T. Norris, Jr Prof. of Psychiatry and Behavioral Sciences, School of Medicine, Stanford Univ. 1991–, Chair. Dept of Psychiatry and Behavioral Neuroscience 1991–2009, Dir Stanford Mood Disorder Center; Pres. American Psychiatric Asscn 2009–10; Founder Corcept Therapeutics; mem. Inst. of Medicine of NAS 2003; Hon. DrMed (Medical Univ. of Vienna) 2011; Gerald L. Klerman, MD Lifetime Research Award, Nat. Depressive and Manic Depressive Asscn 1998, Klerman Award, Cornell Medical Coll. 2001, Edward A. Strecker, MD Award,

Univ. of Pennsylvania School of Medicine 2001, Mood Disorders Research Award, American Coll. of Psychiatrists 2002, Research Award, American Psychiatric Asscn 2002, Distinguished Service in Psychiatry Award, American Coll. of Psychiatrists 2005, Falcone Award, Nat. Alliance for Research in Schizophrenia and Affective Disorders 2005, Anna Monika Prize, Anna Monika Foundation 2013, Golden Kraepelin Medal, Max-Planck-Gesellschaft (co-recipient) 2014. *Publications:* numerous papers in professional journals. *Address:* Stanford University School of Medicine, 291 Campus Drive, Li Ka Shing Building, Stanford, CA 94305-5101 (office); Psychiatry Department, 401 Quarry Road, MC 5723, Stanford, CA 94305, USA (office). *Telephone:* (650) 723-6811 (School of Medicine) (office); (650) 723-8335 (Psychiatry Dept) (office). *Fax:* (650) 498-5294 (Psychiatry Dept) (office). *E-mail:* afschatz@stanford.edu (office). *Website:* med.stanford.edu/profiles/alan -schatzberg (office).

SCHAUB, Alexander, DJ; German lawyer and civil servant; *Of Counsel, Freshfields Bruckhaus Deringer;* b. 14 June 1941, Duisburg; s. of Franz Schaub and Gertrud Stockert; m. Nicole Van der Meulen 1974; one s. two d.; ed Univs of Freiburg, Lausanne, Cologne and Bonn and Coll. of Europe, Bruges; with Fed. Ministry of Econ. Affairs 1971; mem. Secr. of Ralf Dahrendorf 1973; mem. Secr. and Deputy Chef de Cabinet of Guido Brunner 1974–78; Deputy Chef de Cabinet Messrs Davignon and Burke 1980, of Pres. Gaston Thorn 1981; Chef de Cabinet of Willy de Clercq 1985–89; Dir DG External Relations and Trade Policy, EC 1989–90, Deputy Dir-Gen. DG Internal Market and Industrial Affairs 1990–93, Deputy Dir-Gen. DG Industry 1993–95, Dir-Gen. for Competition 1995–2002; Dir-Gen. DG Internal Market and Services 2002–06 (retd); Of Counsel, Freshfields Bruckhaus Deringer, Brussels 2007–; mem. Schindler Group 2007–10; Grosses Silbernes Ehrenzeichen mit Stern (Austria), Verdiensthrent 1 klasse des Verdinstordens der Bundesrepublik Deutschland. *Publications include:* Die Anhörung des Europäischen Parlaments in Rechtsetzungsverfahren der EWG 1971, Food Quality in the Internal Market 1993, Gentechnik im Lebensmittelber-eich – Die Politik der EG-Kommission 1994 and numerous contribs to legal and professional journals, articles in newspapers etc. *Leisure interests:* tennis, skiing. *Address:* Freshfields Bruckhaus Deringer, Bastion Tower, Place du Champ de Mars/Marsveldplein 5, 1050 Brussels, Belgium (office). *Telephone:* (2) 504-76-57 (office). *Fax:* (2) 404-76-57 (office). *E-mail:* alexander.schaub@freshfields.com (office). *Website:* www.freshfields.com (office).

SCHÄUBLE, Wolfgang, DrIur; German politician and lawyer; *President of the Bundestag;* b. 18 Sept. 1942, Freiburg; s. of Karl Schäuble and Gertrud Schäuble (née Göhring); m. Ingeborg Hensle 1969; one s. three d.; ed Univs of Freiburg and Hamburg; Regional Pres., Junge Union, S Baden 1969–72; worked in admin. of taxes, Baden-Württemberg 1971–72; mem. Bundestag 1972–, Exec. Sec. CDU/CSU Parl. Group 1981–84, Vice-Chair. in charge of Foreign Security and European Policies 2002–05; mem. parl., European Council 1975–84; Chair. CDU Cttee on Sport 1976–84; Regional Vice-Pres. S Baden CDU 1982–95, mem. Federal Exec. Cttee CDU, mem. Presidium CDU 2000–; Federal Minister with special responsibility and Head of Chancellery 1984–89, of Interior 1989–91, 2005–09, of Finance 2009–17; Pres. Bundestag 2017–; Deputy Chair. Bd of Supervisory Dirs KfW Bankengruppe 2011; CDU Parl. Leader 1991–2000, Leader 1998–2000; legal practice in Offenburg 1978–84; Chair. Arbeitsgemeinschaft Europäischer Grenz-regionen (AGEG) 1979–82; Ordine al Merito della Repubblica Italiana 1986, Grosses Bundesverdienstkreuz 1991, Commandeur de la Légion d'honneur 1998, Ordre de la couronne de chêne (Luxembourg) 2011, Kissinger Prize 2017. *Publications:* Der Vertrag 1991, Und der Zukunft zugewandt 1994, Und sie bewegt sich doch 1998, Mitten im Leben 2000, Scheitert der Westen? 2003, Zukunft mit Maß 2009, Anders gemeinsam (with M. Sapin) 2016. *Leisure interests:* chess, music. *Address:* Bundestag, Platz der Republik 1, 11011 Berlin, Germamy (office). *Telephone:* (30) 2270 (office). *Fax:* (30) 22736979 (office). *E-mail:* mail@bundestag.de (office). *Website:* www.bundestag.de (office).

SCHAVAN, Annette; German politician, theologian and diplomatist; *Ambassador to the Holy See (Vatican City);* b. 10 June 1955, Jüchen; ed Univ. of Düsseldorf; Scientific Adviser, Religious Studies Dept, Cusanuswerk Inst., Bonn 1980–84, Dir 1988–95; Lecturer, Univ. of Düsseldorf 1980–95; Dept Leader for Further Educ., Parish of Aachen 1984–87; Leader, CDU Women's Union 1987–88, Vice-Chair. CDU 1998–; Baden-Württemberg Regional Minister for Culture, Youth and Sport 1995–2005; elected mem. Bundestag 2005; Fed. Minister of Educ. and Research 2005–13 (resgnd following revocation of her doctorate); Amb. to the Holy See (Vatican City) 2014–; Officier, Légion d'honneur 2002; Else Mayer Award 2006. *Leisure interests:* rambling. *Address:* Embassy of Germany, Via di Villa Sacchetti 4–6, 00197 Rome, Italy (office). *Telephone:* (06) 809511 (office). *Fax:* (06) 80951227 (office). *Website:* www.vatikan.diplo.de (office); www.annette-schavan .de.

SCHECK, Adolf; German business executive; joined Edeka AG Sparkasse Offenburg 1965, completed training as retail trade buyer 1969, various posts as dept man. within regional co., took over parent's Edeka business 1979, Man. Dir Scheck-, In-Einkaufscenter GmbH, Edeka Handelsgesellschaft Südwest mbH (Chair.), Bau & Grün AG (Chair.), Edeka AG Sparkasse Offenburg/Ortenau –2010, mem. Supervisory Bd Edeka AG 2002–16, Chair. Supervisory Bd Edeka AG and Edeka Zentrale AG & Co. KG 2010–16; mem. Supervisory Bd Ava Allgemeine Handelsgesellschaft Der Verbraucher AG (fmrly Ava AG) 2004–; Bundesver-dienstkreuz (with ribbon) 2017.

SCHECKTER, Jody David; South African business executive and fmr racing driver; b. 29 Jan. 1950, East London, nr Durban; m. Pam Bailey; two s.; raced karts from age of 11, graduated to motorcycles and racing cars; won SA Formula Ford Sunshine Series in 1970, competed in Britain from 1971; Formula One World Champion 1979, runner-up 1977, third place 1974 and 1976; Grand Prix wins: 1974 Swedish (Tyrrell-Ford), 1974 British (Tyrrell-Ford), 1975 South African (Tyrrell-Ford), 1976 Swedish (Tyrrell-Ford), 1977 Argentine (Wolf-Ford), 1977 Monaco (Wolf-Ford), 1977 Canadian (Wolf-Ford), 1979 Belgian (Ferrari), 1979 Monaco (Ferrari), 1979 Italian (Ferrari); retd from motor racing 1980; est. business in Atlanta, Ga, designing and building simulation equipment for firearms training, later retd; currently Owner, Laverstoke Park Farm (organic farm), UK; International Jewish Sports Hall of Fame 1983. *Leisure interest:* keeping fit. *Address:* Laverstoke Park Offices, Overton, Hants., RG25 3DR, England (home). *Telephone:*

(1256) 772800 (home). *Fax:* (1256) 772809 (home). *E-mail:* info@laverstokepark.co .uk (home). *Website:* www.laverstokepark.co.uk (home).

SCHEEPBOUWER, Adrianus (Ad) Johannes; Dutch telecommunications industry executive; b. 22 July 1944, Dordrecht; Pres. Air Freight Div. Pakhoed Holding NV (later Pandair Group) 1976–88; Man. Dir PTT Post 1988–98; mem. Bd of Man. Royal KPN NV (fmr holding co. of PTT Post and PTT Telecom) 1992–98, Chair. and CEO TPG 1998–2001, Chair. Bd of Man. and CEO Royal KPN 2001–11, CEO Getronics 2010; currently Prin., AJS Holdings B.V.; Chair. Supervisory Bd Havenbedrijf Rotterdam NV, Supervisory Council of Maasstad Hosp.; mem. Supervisory Bd RFS Holland Holding BV (Wehkamp), Bank Oyens & van Eeghen; mem. Advisory Bd ECP. NL; Chair. Audit Cttee 'Sleutelgebieden' of the Innovationplatform; mem. Supervisory Council of Foundation for Nat. Art Collection; Amb. 'Randstad Urgent' (Project International City The Hague). *Address:* AJS Holdings B.V., Gustav Mahlerlaan 310, 1082 ME Amsterdam, Netherlands (office).

SCHEER, Andrew James, PC, BA; Canadian politician; *Leader, Conservative Party of Canada;* b. 20 May 1979; s. of James Scheer and Mary Scheer (née Enright); m. Jill Ryan; five c.; ed Univ. of Ottawa, Univ. of Regina; began career as insurance broker, Shenher Insurance, Regina; worked as Constituency Sec. for Alliance MP Larry Spencer; MP (Conservative) for Regina-Qu'Appelle 2004–, Speaker, House of Commons (youngest ever) 2011–15, Official House Leader of the Opposition 2015; mem. Conservative Party of Canada, Leader 2017–. *Address:* Conservative Party of Canada, 130 Albert Street, Suite 1720, Ottawa, ON K1P 5G4, Canada (office). *Telephone:* (613) 755-2000 (office). *Fax:* (613) 755-2001 (office). *Website:* www.conservative.ca (office).

SCHEER, François, DèsSc; French diplomatist (retd); b. 13 March 1934, Strasbourg; s. of Alfred Scheer and Edmée Lechten; m. 2nd Nicole Roubaud 1985; one s. one d.; one s. three d. from 1st m.; ed Faculty of Law, Univ. of Paris, Inst. d'Etudes Politiques de Paris, Ecole Nat. d'Admin; Second Sec., Embassy in Algiers 1962–64, Direction des Affaires Economiques et Financières, Admin Cen. 1964–67, Cultural Attaché, Embassy in Tokyo 1967–71, Deputy Dir for Budget 1971, also for Financial Affairs 1972–76, Amb. to Mozambique and Swaziland 1976–77, Deputy Perm. Rep. to European Community 1977–79, Dir of Cabinet to Pres. of European Parl. 1979–81, Dir of Cabinet of Minister of Foreign Affairs 1981–84, Amb. to Algeria 1984–86, Amb. and Perm. Rep. to EC (now EU) 1986–88, 1992–93, Sec.-Gen., Ministry of Foreign Affairs 1988–92, Amb. to FRG 1993–99; mem. Cttee for Atomic Energy 1988–92; Admin. Cie générale des matières nucléaires (Cogema) 1989–93; mem. Conseil d'Admin. Ecole Nat. d'Admin. 1991–95; Adviser, Pres. of Cogema 1999–2001; Pres. Exec. Bd Areva 2001–11; Commdr, Légion d'honneur, Ordre nat. du Mérite. *Address:* 10 square Adanson, 75005 Paris, France (home). *Telephone:* 1-45-81-35-84 (home). *E-mail:* francoischeer@orange.fr.

SCHEEREN, Ole; German architect; *Principal and Chief Designer, Büro Ole Scheeren;* b. 6 Jan. 1971, Karlsruhe; s. of Dieter Scheeren; ed Karlsruher Institut für Technologie, École Polytechnique Fédérale, Lausanne, School of Architecture, Architectural Asscn, London; joined Office of Metropolitan Architecture 1995, Pnr and Dir 2002–10; f. Büro Ole Scheeren 2010, currently Principal and Chief Designer; Visiting Prof., Univ. of Hong Kong 2010–. *Major works include:* Barclay Village, Canada, Empire City, Viet Nam, 1500 West Georgia, Canada, Riverpark Tower, Germany, Guardian Art Centre, China, The Interlace, Singapore (Best Architecture, Asia Pacific Property Awards 2010, Urban Habitat Award, Council on Tall Buildings and Urban Habitat 2014), China Central Television Station, China (Best New Global Design, Int. Architecture Awards 2008, Best Tall Building Worldwide, Council on Tall Buildings and Urban Habitat 2013), DUO, Singapore, Angkasa Raya, Malaysia, Maha Nakhon, Thailand (Best Mixed-Use Development, Asia Pacific Property Awards 2015), Archipelago Cinema, Italy, Collaborative Cloud, Germany, Dean and DeLuca Stage, USA, Olympicopolis, UK, Studio ZX, China, Television Cultural Centre, China, Prada Epicentre, USA, The Scotts Tower, Singapore, Taipei Performing Arts Centre, Taiwan, Mirage City Cinema, United Arab Emirates, Marfa Drive-in, Tex., Shenzhen Crystal Island, China, Crystal CG Media Centre, China, Beijing Books Building, China, Penang Tropical City, Malaysia, Los Angeles County Museum of Art, Calif. *Address:* Büro Ole Scheeren, Unit 1006, Tower A Jianwai SOHO 39 Dongsanhuan ZhongLu Chaoyang Dist, Beijing 100022, People's Republic of China (office). *Telephone:* (10) 59001989 (office). *E-mail:* beijing@buro-os.com (office). *Website:* buro-os.com.

SCHEFFER, Ingrid, MB BS, PhD, FRACP; Australian paediatrician, medical scientist and academic; *Chair of Paediatric Neurology Research, University of Melbourne;* Chair of Paediatric Neurology Research, Univ. of Melbourne, Prof., Depts of Medicine and Paediatrics, Sr Prin. Research Fellow, Florey Neuroscience Insts; Dir of Paediatrics, Austin Health, Heidelberg, Vic., Dir Children's Epilepsy Program; Paediatric Neurologist and Epileptologist, Neurosciences, Monash Medical Centre, Clayton, Vic., Dept of Neurology, Royal Children's Hosp., Parkville, Vic.; Hon. Fellow of Genetic Health Services, Vic.; Hon. Research Fellow, Murdoch Children's Research Inst.; Nat. Health and Medical Research Council (NHMRC) Medical Postgraduate Scholar 1992–94, Jr Investigator Award, American Epilepsy Soc. 1993, Commendation for Premier of Vic.'s Award for Medical Research 1998, Harbison-Higinbotham Research Scholarship, Univ. of Melbourne 1998, Chancellor's Prize, Univ. of Melbourne 1999, Nat. Asscn of Research Fellows of NHMRC Post-Doctoral Investigator Award 2003, Henry Dunn Lecturer, Vancouver Gen. Hosp., Canada 2008, MacKeith Lecturer, British Paediatric Neurology Asscn 2009, Prof. R. Gulati Oration, Postgraduate Inst. of Medical Educ. and Research, Chandigarh, India 2009, Tibbles Lecturer, Annual 46th Congress of the Canadian Neurological Sciences Fed. 2011, Jacobsen Lecturer, Royal Victoria Infirmary, Newcastle, UK 2011, NHMRC Program Grant Chief Investigator 2002–15, NHMRC Practitioner Fellowship 2001–05, 2011–15, Research Recognition Award for Clinical Research, American Epilepsy Society 2007, Eric Susman Prize, Royal Australasian Coll. of Physicians 2009, L'Oréal-UNESCO For Women in Science Award (Asia-Pacific) (for identifying genes involved in some forms of epilepsy) 2012. *Publications:* numerous papers in professional journals. *Address:* Epilepsy Research Centre, Level 2, Melbourne Brain Centre, 245 Burgundy Street, Austin Health, Heidelberg, Vic. 3084, Australia (office). *Telephone:* (3) 9035-7344 (office). *Fax:* (3) 9496-2291 (office).

E-mail: scheffer@unimelb.edu.au (office). *Website:* www.brain.org.au/epilepsyresearch/staff/profiles/i_scheffer.htm (office); www.ingridscheffer.com.

SCHEFFLER, Matthias Robert, Dr rer. nat; German physicist and academic; *Director, Theory Department, Fritz Haber Institute;* b. 1951, Berlin; ed Technische Universität Berlin; Scientific Staff mem., Physikalisch-Technische Bundesanstalt, Braunschweig 1978–88; Researcher, IBM T.J. Watson Research Center, Yorktown Heights, NY, USA 1979–80; Researcher, Max-Planck-Inst., Stuttgart 1982; Dir, Theory Dept, Fritz Haber Inst., Berlin 1988–; Visiting Scientist, Instituto de Fisica, Universidade de Sao Paulo, Brazil 1995; Visiting Scientist, Kavli Inst. for Theoretical Physics, Univ. of Calif., Santa Barbara, USA 2002; Hon. Prof., Technische Universität Berlin 1989–, Freie Universitat Berlin 2001–, Visiting Prof., Dalian Inst. of Chem. Physics, Chinese Acad. of Sciences 2004–, Distinguished Visiting Prof., Univ. of California, Santa Barbara 2004–; Dr hc; Max-Planck Research Award for Int. Co-operation 2001, Medard W. Welch Medal and Prize, American Vacuum Soc. 2003, Max Born Medal and Prize 2004, Ernst Mach Hon. Medal, Acad. of Sciences of the Czech Repub. 2008, Rudolf Jaeckel Prize, German Vacuum Soc. 2010. *Publications:* Walter Kohn: Personal Stories and Anecdotes Told by Friends and Collaborators (co-ed.) 2003; 409 articles in scientific journals. *Address:* Fritz-Haber-Institut der Max-Planck-Gesellschaft, Faradayweg 4–6, 14195 Berlin-Dahlem, Germany (office). *Telephone:* (30) 8413-4711 (office). *Fax:* (30) 8413-4701 (office). *E-mail:* scheffler@fhi-berlin.mpg.de (office). *Website:* th.fhi-berlin.mpg.de/site (office).

SCHEIBER, Harry N., AB, MA, PhD; American academic, writer and editor; *Stefan A. Riesenfeld Professor Emeritus of Law and History and Director, Institute for Legal Research, University of California, Berkeley;* b. 1935, New York, NY; ed Columbia Univ., Cornell Univ.; Instructor to Assoc. Prof., Dartmouth Coll. 1960–68, Prof. of History 1968–71; Fellow, Centre for Advanced Study in the Behavioural Sciences, Stanford 1967, 1971; Prof. of American History, Univ. of California, San Diego, 1971–80, Prof. of Law, Univ. of California, Berkeley 1980–, Assoc. Dean 1990–93, 1996–99, Stefan A. Riesenfeld Prof. of Law and History 1991, now Prof. Emer. and Chancellor's Emer. Prof., Dir Center for the Study of Law and Society 2000–01, Earl Warren Legal Inst. 2002–05, Inst. for Legal Research 2005–, Sho Sato Program in Japanese and US Law, Law of the Sea Inst. 2004–16; Fulbright Distinguished Sr Lecturer, Australia 1983; Visiting Research Prof., Univ. of Uppsala, Sweden 1995; Ed. Yearbook of the California Supreme Court Historical Society 1994–2008; mem. American Historical Asscn, California Supreme Court Historical Soc., Economic History Asscn, Law and Society Asscn, Org. of American Historians, American Acad. of Arts and Sciences 2003–, American Soc. for Legal History (Pres. 2003–05); mem. Bd of Advisors, National Sea Grant Legal Center 2004–14; mem. Scientific Advisory Bd, Joint Ocean Commission Initiative 2007–15; Fellow, Japan Soc. for the Promotion of Science 2001; Hon. MA (Dartmouth Coll.) 1965; Hon. DJur (Uppsala) 1998; Guggenheim Fellowships 1971, 1988, Rockefeller Foundation Fellowship 1979, Nat. Endowment for the Humanities Fellowship 1985–86, Riesenfeld Award in Int. Law 2012, Univ. of California, Berkeley Citation 2012, Faculty Service Award, Univ. of California, Berkeley 2015. *Publications include:* The Wilson Administration and Civil Liberties 1960, United States Economic History 1964, America: Purpose and Power (co-author) 1965, The Condition of American Federalism 1966, The Frontier in American Development (co-ed.) 1969, The Old Northwest 1969, The Ohio Canal Era 1820–1861 1969 (revised edns 1987, 2012), Black Labor in American History 1972, Agriculture in the Development of the Far West 1975, American Economic History (co-author) 1976, American Law and the Constitutional Order 1978, Perspectives on Federalism (ed.) 1987, Power Divided (co-ed.) 1989, Federalism and the Judicial Mind (ed.) 1993, Legal Culture and the Legal Profession (co-author) 1995, The State and Freedom of Contract 1998, Law of the Sea: The Common Heritage and Emerging Challenges 2000, Inter-Allied Conflicts and Ocean Law, 1945–1952 2001, Bringing New Law To Ocean Waters (co-ed.) 2004, Earl Warren and the Warren Court (ed.) 2007, Japanese Family Law (co-ed.) 2009, Oceans in the Nuclear Age (co-ed.) 2010, Japanese Legal System (co-ed.) 2012, Regions, Institutions and Law of the Sea 2013, Science, Technology and Law of the Sea 2016, Bayonets in Paradise: Martial Law in Hawaii during World War II (with Jane Scheiber) 2016, Constitutionalism and Judicial Power: History of the California Supreme Court 2016, Law of the Sea: Fifty Years of Debates 2018; 220 contribs to professional journals in law, history and social science. *Address:* School of Law, 306 Boalt Hall, Univ. of California, Berkeley, CA 94720, USA (office). *Telephone:* (510) 643-9788 (office). *Fax:* (510) 643-2698 (office). *E-mail:* scheiber@berkeley.edu (office). *Website:* www.law.berkeley.edu (office).

SCHEID, HE Cardinal Eusébio Oscar, SCI, DTheol; Brazilian ecclesiastic; *Archbishop Emeritus of Saõ Sebastião do Rio de Janeiro;* b. 8 Dec. 1932, Bom Retiro, Joaçaba; s. of Alberto Reinaldo Scheid and Rosalia Joana Scheid; ed Congregation of Priests of Sacred Heart of Jesus (Dehonian Fathers') Seminary, Seminary of Priests of Heart of Jesus, Corupa, Pontifical Gregorian Univ., Rome, Italy; ordained priest 1960; Prof. of Theology, Christ the King Seminary and Northeast Regional Seminary, Recife 1964–65 Prof. of Dogma and Liturgy, Theological Inst. of Taubate 1965–81; Prof. of Religious Culture, Pontifical Catholic Univ. of Saõ Paulo 1966–68; Coordinator of Catechesis, Taubate 1970–74; Dir Faculty of Theology, Taubate; Bishop of São José dos Campos 1981–91; Archbishop of Florianópolis 1991–2001; attended Fourth Gen. Conf. of Latin American Episcopate, Santo Domingo, Dominican Repub. 1992, Ninth Ordinary Ass. of World Synod of Bishops, Vatican City 1994, Tenth Ordinary Ass. 2001; Archbishop of Saõ Sebastião do Rio de Janeiro and Bishop of Brazil, Faithful of the Oriental Rites 2001–09, Archbishop Emer. 2009–; cr. Cardinal (Cardinal Priest of SS Bonifacio ed Alessio) 2003; Pres. South Region IV of Brazilian Bishops' Conf., currently Counsellor, Pontifical Comm. for Latin America; mem. Pontifical Council for Social communications, Pontifical Comm. for Latin America, Council of Cardinals. *Address:* Archdiocese of São Sebastião do Rio de Janeiro, Rua Benjamin Constant 23/502, Gloria, C.P. 1362, 20241-150 Rio de Janeiro, RJ, Brazil (office). *Telephone:* (21) 292-3132 (office). *Fax:* (21) 242-9295 (office). *Website:* www.arquidiocese.org.br (office).

SCHEIFELE, Bernd, LLM; German business executive; *Chairman of the Managing Board, HeidelbergCement;* b. 5 May 1958, Freiburg; m.; four c.; ed Univ. of Freiburg, Univ. of Dijon, France; worked with Gleiss Lutz Hootz Hirsch law firm, Stuttgart 1988–94; as attorney, prepared incorporation of Phoenix

Pharmahandel AG & Co. KG, Mannheim, Chair. Phoenix 1994–2005, currently Chair. Advisory Bd; Chair. Man. Bd HeidelbergCement 2005–; Chair. Supervisory Bd Tamro Group, Vantaa (Finland); Deputy Chair. Supervisory Bd Georg von Holtzbrinck publishing group; mem. Bd of Dirs Helaba (Landesbank Hessen-Thüringen); Fulbright Scholarship 1984. *Address:* HeidelbergCement, Berliner Strasse 6, 69120 Heidelberg, Baden-Württemberg, Germany (office). *Telephone:* (6221) 481-0 (office). *Fax:* (6221) 481-554 (office). *E-mail:* info@heidelbergcement.com (office). *Website:* www.heidelbergcement.com (office).

SCHEIFF, Dieter Christian, BA, MBA; German business executive; *Managing Partner, Ufenau Capital Partners AG;* b. 8 June 1952, Koblenz; m.; three c.; ed Univ. of Applied Sciences (Fachhochschule) Aachen; held various sales and marketing roles at 3M 1987–98; joined Johnson and Johnson Cordis 1998, becoming Vice-Pres. for Europe 2001; Head of Sales and Marketing, DIS Deutscher Industrie Service AG 2001–02, CEO 2002–06, CEO Adecco Management & Consulting SA (following acquisition of DIS by Adecco) 2006–09; joined Ufenau Capital Partners AG 2010, Man. Partner 2013–. *Address:* Ufenau Capital Partners AG, Huobstrasse 3, Pfäffikon, Schwyz 8808, Switzerland (office). *Telephone:* (78) 635-96-96 (office); (44) 482-66-66 (office). *Fax:* (44) 482-66-63 (office). *E-mail:* d.scheiff@ucp.ch (office). *Website:* ucp.ch (office).

SCHEKMAN, Randy Wayne, PhD; American biologist and academic; *Professor of Cell and Developmental Biology, University of California, Berkeley;* b. 30 Dec. 1948, St Paul, Minn.; m. Nancy Walls; one s. one d.; ed Univ. of California, Los Angeles and Stanford Univ. School of Medicine; Cystic Fibrosis Postdoctoral Fellow, Biology Dept, Univ. of California, San Diego, La Jolla 1974–76; Asst Prof., then Assoc. Prof., then Prof., Dept of Biochemistry, Univ. of California, Berkeley 1976–89, Prof. of Cell and Developmental Biology, Dept of Molecular and Cell Biology 1989–, Head, Div. of Biochemistry and Molecular Biology 1990–94, Investigator, Howard Hughes Medical Inst. 1990–, Co-Chair. Dept of Molecular and Cell Biology 1997–2000; Chair. FASEB Conf. on Protein Folding in the Cell 1992, Gordon Conf. on Molecular Membrane Biology 1997; mem. Bd of Scientific Advisors, Jane Coffin Childs Memorial Fund for Medical Research 1992–2000, Scientific Dir 2002–; mem. Eli Lilly Award Cttee 1988–90, Chair. 1990; mem. Advisory Cttee, Pew Scholars Program 1996–2002; Ed.-in-Chief Ann. Rev. Cell & Developmental Biology 1999–, eLife 2012–; Assoc. Ed. Molecular Cell Biology 1988–91, Molecular Biology of the Cell 1992–99 (later Ed. 1999), Annual Reviews of Cell and Developmental Biology 1993–98, Journal of Cell Biology (later Ed.) 1993); mem. Editorial Bd Journal of Cell Biology 1985–92, Journal of Membrane Biology 1986, Biochemistry 1986–93, Cell 2001–; mem. NAS 1992 (apptd Chair. Biochemistry Section 2002, Ed.-in-Chief Proceedings of the National Academy of Sciences 2007–11), NIH Cell Biology (Study Section), American Soc. for Microbiology, American Acad. for Microbiology, American Soc. for Biochemistry and Molecular Biology, American Soc. for Cell Biology (Council mem. 1991–94); Foreign Assoc., European Molecular Biology Org. 2001, Royal Soc. of London 2013; Foreign mem. Accademia Nazionale dei Lincei, Italy 2010; Hon. mem. Japanese Biochemical Soc. 1993; Dr hc (Geneva) 1997, (Univ. of Regensburg, Germany) 2005; Undergraduate Research Award, UCLA Zoology Dept 1970, Woodrow Wilson Fellow 1970, Guggenheim Fellowship 1982–83, Lewis S. Rosenstiel Award in Basic Biomedical Science 1994, Gairdner Foundation International Award 1996, Amgen Award Lecturer Protein Society 1999, Berkeley Faculty Research 1999, Albert Lasker Award for Basic Medical Research 2002, Louisa Gross Horwitz Prize, Columbia Univ. 2002, Keith Porter Lecture, American Soc. for Cell Biology 2005, Dickson Prize in Medicine, Univ. of Pittsburgh 2008, Massry Prize 2010, Nobel Prize in Medicine (with James E. Rothman and Thomas C. Sudhof) 2013. *Publications include:* more than 200 articles in scientific journals on mechanism and control of intracellular protein transport. *Address:* Schekman Lab, Department of Molecular and Cell Biology, University of California, Berkeley, 475D Li Ka Shing Center #3370, Berkeley, CA 94720-3370, USA (office). *Telephone:* (510) 642-5686 (office). *Fax:* (510) 642-7846 (office). *E-mail:* schekman@berkeley.edu (office). *Website:* mcb.berkeley.edu/labs/schekman (office).

SCHELL, Orville Hickok, BA, MA, PhD; American journalist, writer and academic; *Arthur Ross Director, Center on US-China Relations, Asia Society;* b. 20 May 1940, New York, NY; m.; three s.; ed Stanford Univ., National Taiwan Univ., Harvard Univ., Univ. of California, Berkeley; Overseas Development Training Associate Fellowship, Ford Foundation, Jakarta, Indonesia 1964–66; Foreign Area Training Fellowship, Center for Chinese Studies, Univ. of California 1967–68; Co-Dir Bay Area Inst. 1968–71; Founder and Ed.-in-Chief, Pacific News Service 1970–71; China Correspondent, New Yorker magazine 1975; Research Assoc. Univ. of California, Berkeley 1986, Regents' Lecturer 1990, Dean, Graduate School of Journalism 1996–2007; Sr Fellow, Center on Communication Leadership, Annenberg School for Communication, Univ. of Southern California 2007–; Arthur Ross Dir, Center on US-China Relations, Asia Soc. 2007–; Visiting Distinguished Prof., Chico State Univ. 1987; Moderator, Issues and Perspectives on China, Voice of America 1995–97; Ed., Project Syndicate China column 2000–; Sr Fellow, Freedom Forum Media Studies Center, Columbia Univ. 1995; mem. Bd of Dirs World Affairs Council of San Francisco 1999–, Current Media 2005–, Homelands Productions; mem. Media Council, World Economic Forum 1998–; mem. Authors Guild, Council on Foreign Relations 1992–, Global Business Network, Human Rights Watch Board, Pacific Council, PEN, National Committee on US-China Relations 1984–; Dr hc (Dominican Univ.) 2001; Alicia Patterson Foundation Journalism Fellowship 1981, MacDowell Colony Fellowship 1983, 1986, Guggenheim Fellowship 1989–90, Emmy Award (for 60 Minutes report Made In China) 1992, Overseas Press Club of American Award 1993, George Foster Peabody Award (as producer of WGBH-Frontline documentary The Gate of Heavenly Peace) 1997, Shorenstein Journalism Award for Covering Asia, Shorenstein Center on the Press, Politics and Public Policy and Stanford Univ. Asia-Pacific Research Center 2003, Fred Cody Lifetime Achievement Award, Northern California Book Awards 2005. *Publications include:* The China Reader (with Frederick Crews) 1970, Modern China: The Story of a Revolution 1972, The Town That Fought to Save Itself 1976, In the People's Republic 1976, Brown 1978, Watch Out for the Foreign Guests: China Encounters the West 1981, Modern Meat: Antibiotics, Hormones and the Pharmaceutical Farm 1983, To Get Rich is Glorious: China in the 1980s 1984, Discos and Democracy: China in the Throes of Reform 1988, Mandate of Heaven: A New Generation of Entrepreneurs, Dissidents, Technocrats, and Bohemians Grasp for Power in China 1994, The China

Reader: The Reform Years (ed. with David Shambaugh) 1999, Virtual Tibet: The West's Fascination with the Roof of the World 1999, Wealth and Power: China's Long March to the Twenty-first Century (co-author) 2013; contributions: numerous books, reviews, and journals. *Address:* Center on US-China Relations, Asia Society, 725 Park Avenue, New York, NY 10021, USA (office). *E-mail:* info@ asiasociety.org (office). *Website:* www.asiasociety.org/center-us-china-relations (office); orvilleschell.com.

SCHELLER, Richard H., BS, PhD; American medical scientist, academic and business executive; *Chief Scientific Officer and Head of Therapeutics, 23andMe, Inc.;* b. 30 Oct. 1953, Milwaukee, Wis.; m. Prof. Susan McConnell; ed Univ. of Wisconsin, California Inst. of Tech.; Postdoctoral Fellow in Molecular Neurobiology, Coll. of Physicians and Surgeons, Columbia Univ. 1981–82; Asst Prof., Dept of Biological Sciences, Stanford Univ. 1982–87, Assoc. Prof. 1987–90, Assoc. Prof., Dept of Molecular and Cellular Physiology 1990–93, Prof. 1993–2002, Assoc. Investigator, Howard Hughes Medical Inst., Stanford Univ. Medical Center 1990–94, Investigator 1994–2001; Adjunct Prof., Dept of Biochemistry and Biophysics, Univ. of California, San Francisco 2004–10; Postdoctoral Fellow in Biology, Calif. Inst. of Technology (also mem. Bd of Trustees); Sr Vice-Pres., Genentech, Inc. 2001–03, Exec. Vice-Pres. of Research 2003–09, Chief Scientific Officer and Exec. Vice-Pres. of Research 2008–09, Exec. Vice-Pres., Genentech Research and Early Development and mem. Enlarged Roche Corp. Exec. Cttee 2009–15; Chief Scientific Officer and Head of Therapeutics, 23andMe, Inc. 2015–; mem. NAS 2000; Foreign mem. Norwegian Acad. of Science and Letters 2010; Fellow, American Acad. of Arts and Sciences 1998; Hon. Fellow, Norwegian Acad. of Science and Letters; Alan T. Waterman Award 1989, W. Alden Spencer Award 1993, NAS Award in Molecular Biology 1997, Kavli Prize in Neuroscience (co-recipient) 2010, Life Sciences Distinguished Alumni Award, Univ. of Wisconsin 2013, Albert Lasker Award for Basic Medical Research (co-recipient) 2013, Distinguished Alumni Award, Calif. Inst. of Tech. 2014, Nat. Academies of Science 2015. *Publications:* more than 280 papers in professional journals. *Address:* 23andMe, Inc., 899 West Evelyn Avenue, Mountain View, CA 94041, USA (office). *Telephone:* (800) 239-5230 (office). *Website:* www.23andme.com (office).

SCHELLING, Hans Jörg; Austrian academic, business executive and politician; b. 27 Dec. 1953, Hohenems, Vorarlberg; m.; two d.; ed Johannes Kepler Univ.; Asst Prof., Inst. for Retail, Sales and Marketing, Johannes Kepler Univ., Linz 1978–81; joined Kika-Leiner Unternehmensgruppe (furniture retailer) 1981, becoming Man. Dir 1988–90; self-employed business consultant, Schelling GmbH 1990–2014; Man. Dir XXXLutz GmbH (furniture retailer), Wels 1992–2005; Man. Partner Big Deal Marken und MarketingberatungsgesmbH 1999–2014; Vice-Pres. Wirtschaftskammer Österreich (Austrian Fed. Econ. Chamber) 2004–14; Man. Dir XLA GmbH, Wels 2005–08, mem. Bd of Dirs 2005–11; mem. Nationalrat (Parl.) 2007–08; Chair. Asscn of Austrian Social Security Insts 2009–14; Chair. Volksbank AG 2012–14; Chair. Social Security Pension AG 2013–14; Fed. Minister of Finance 2014–17; mem. Österreichische Volkspartei (ÖVP—Austrian People's Party). *Address:* c/o Federal Ministry of Finance, Johannesgasse 5, 1010 Vienna, Austria (office).

SCHELLNHUBER, Hans Joachim, PhD (Habil.); German physicist and academic; *Director, Potsdam Institute for Climate Impact Research;* b. 7 June 1950, Ortenburg, Passau; m. Margret Boysen; one c.; ed Vilshofen Secondary School, Univs of Regensburg and Oldenburg; Student Asst, Physics Dept, Univ. of Regensburg 1971–76, Scientific Asst 1976–81; Postdoctoral Fellow, Inst. for Theoretical Physics, Univ. of California, Santa Barbara, USA 1981–82; Asst Prof., Physics Dept, Univ. of Oldenburg 1982–87, Prof. of Theoretical Physics 1988–93, Man. Dir Interdisciplinary Inst. for Coastal Environment Studies 1992; Founder and Dir Potsdam Inst. for Climate Impact Research, in conjunction with a Chair of Theoretical Physics at Univ. of Potsdam 1992–; Research Dir, Tyndall Centre for Climate Change Research (Distinguished Science Adviser 2005–09) and Prof., Environmental Sciences School, Univ. of East Anglia, Norwich, UK 2001–09; External Prof., Santa Fe Inst., USA 2010–; Visiting Prof., Inst. of Nonlinear Sciences, Univ. of California, Santa Cruz, USA 1987–88; Visiting Prof. in Physics and Visiting Fellow of Christ Church Coll., Oxford 2005–09; Co-Chair. German Advisory Council on Global Change (WBGU); mem. Intergovernmental Panel on Climate Change; Amb. of Int. Geosphere-Biosphere Programme 2003; Amb. of Science, State of Brandenburg 2009; mem. Max Planck Soc., German Nat. Acad. (Leopoldina), NAS, Leibniz Science Asscn, Geological Soc. of London, Int. Research Soc. Sigma Xi, Academia Europaea; Fellow, Heisenberg Programme of the German Science Foundation 1987–89; Hon. CBE 2004, Order of Merit (Roter-Adler-Orden), State of Brandenburg 2008, Order of Merit of FRG 2011; Dr hc (Copenhagen) 2011, (Technische Universität Berlin) 2012; Bavarian Scholarship for Exceptionally Gifted 1970, Heisenberg Fellow, German Science Foundation 1987, Wolfson Research Merit Award and Research Fellow, Royal Soc. 2002, German Environment Prize 2007, Environment Prize of Bundesdeutscher Arbeitskreis für Umweltbewusstes Management e.V. 2008, Times Higher Education Award: Research Project of the Year, Univ. of East Anglia 2008, Volvo Environment Prize 2011, Pioneer of German Energy Transformation (Wirtschaftswoche) 2011, Wilhelm Foerster Prize, URANIA Potsdam 2013, Blue Planet Prize 2017. *Publications:* numerous papers in professional journals. *Address:* Potsdam Institute for Climate Impact Research, PO Box 601203, 14412 Potsdam, Germany (office). *Telephone:* (331) 2882502 (office). *Fax:* (331) 2882600 (office). *E-mail:* director@pik-potsdam.de (office). *Website:* www.pik-potsdam.de/members/john (office).

SCHENKER, Joseph G., MD; Israeli physician; b. 20 Nov. 1933, Kraków, Poland; s. of Itzhak Schenker; m. Ekaterina Idels 1959; two s.; ed Herzlia High School, Tel-Aviv and Hebrew Univ. of Jerusalem; Exec. Chief of Teaching Obstetrics and Gynaecology, Hebrew Univ. Medical School 1977–84; Chair. Dept of Obstetrics and Gynaecology, Hadassah Univ. Hosp., Jerusalem 1978; Prof. of Obstetrics and Gynaecology, Hebrew Univ. Jerusalem 1979–; Pres. Israel Soc. of Obstetrics and Gynaecology 1984–92, Deputy Pres. and Sec. 1993–; Pres. Israel Medical Asscn, Jerusalem br. 1984–; Chair. of Directory, Bd Examination in Obstetrics and Gynaecology, State of Israel 1979–83, of Advisory Cttee 1979–86; Acting Chair. of Hadassah Org. of Heads of Depts 1983–; Chair. Residency Programme, Medical Council 1987, of Cttee Licensing Physicians, Ministry of Health 1987; Pres. of Int. Soc. for Study of Pathophysiology 1983; Chair. European

Residency Exchange Programme, Extended European Bd of Gynaecology and Obstetrics 1993– (Pres. of Bd 1994–), Cttee for European Examination for Excellence in Gynaecology and Obstetrics 1993–, FIGO (Int. Fed. of Gynaecology and Obstetrics) Cttee for Study of Ethical Aspects of Human Reproduction 1994–2004 (mem. Exec. Bd FIGO 1991–); Pres. Int. Acad. of Human Reproduction 1996–; Deputy Pres. and Sec. Israel Medical Council 1985–, European Asscn of Gynaecology and Obstetrics 1996–2000; Founder mem. European Soc. of Human Reproduction, Int. Soc. of Gynaecological Endocrinology, Int. Soc. of Study of Pathophysiology of Pregnancy and other orgs; mem. exec. bds and cttees, hon. mem. or mem. numerous int. professional orgs; mem. Editorial Bd Human Reproduction (Oxford), Int. Journal of Gynaecology and Obstetrics (USA), Int. Journal of Foeto-Maternal Medicine (Germany), European Journal of Obstetrics, Gynaecology and Reproductive Biology and several other journals; Hon. Fellow, American Coll. of Obstetricians and Gynaecologists, Royal Coll. of Obstetricians and Gynaecologists and other int. orgs, Hon. Citizen of City of Jerusalem; Award for Outstanding Contrib. to the Field of Human Reproduction 1999. *Publications include:* Recent Advances in Pathophysiological Conditions in Pregnancy (ed.) 1984, The Intrauterine Life-Management and Therapy 1986, Female and Male Infertility 1997, Pregnancy and Delivery 1998, Textbook of Gynecology 2000; more than 550 articles in medical journals on obstetrics and gynaecology, new tech. in reproduction, ethical and legal aspects of IVF etc. *Leisure interests:* history, chess. *Address:* Department of Orbital Gynaecology, Hadassah Medical Centre, PO Box 12000, Jerusalem 91120 (office); 5 Mendele Street, Jerusalem 91147, Israel (home). *Telephone:* 2-6777779 (office); 2-637775 (home). *Fax:* 2-6432445 (home). *E-mail:* joseph.schenker@mail.huji.ac.il (office).

SCHEPISI, Frederic Alan, AO; Australian film writer, director and producer; b. 26 Dec. 1939, Melbourne; s. of Frederic Thomas Schepisi and Loretto Ellen Schepisi (née Hare); m. 1st Joan Mary Ford 1960; two s. two d.; m. 2nd Rhonda Elizabeth Finlayson 1973 (divorced 1983); two d.; m. 3rd Mary Rubin 1984; one s.; ed Assumption Coll., Kilmore, Victoria, Marist Brothers' Juniorate, Macedon, Victoria, Marcellin Coll., Melbourne; Carden Advertising, Melbourne, Press TV Production; Patron Advisory Service, Melbourne 1961–64; Victorian Man. Cinesound Productions, Melbourne 1964–66; Man. Dir, The Film House, Melbourne 1966–79, Chair. 1979–92; Dr hc (Griffith Univ., Australia) 1995; Raymond Longford Award 1991, Chauvel Award 1994, Outstanding Achievement Award 2003. *Television:* Empire Falls (Golden Globe Award 2005, Emmy Award 2005) 2003. *Films include:* A Devil's Playground (Australian Film Inst. Award for Best Direction) 1975, The Chant of Jimmie Blacksmith (Writers Guild Award) 1978, Barbarosa 1981, Iceman 1983, Plenty 1985, Roxanne (Writers Guild Award 1988) 1986, Evil Angels (Australian Film Inst. Award for Best Film 1989) (also known as A Cry in the Dark (Longford Award 1991) 1990, The Russia House 1990, Mr. Baseball 1991, Six Degrees of Separation 1993, IQ 1994, Fierce Creatures 1997, That Eye the Sky (exec. producer), Last Orders 2001, It Runs in the Family 2002, The Eye of the Storm 2011, Words and Pictures 2013. *Television includes:* Empire Falls 2005. *Leisure interests:* tennis, swimming. *Website:* fredschepisi.com.

SCHERAGA, Harold A., PhD; American scientist and academic; *George W. and Grace L. Todd Professor Emeritus, Department of Chemistry and Chemical Biology, Cornell University;* b. (Abraham Harold Scheraga), 18 Oct. 1921, Brooklyn, NY; s. of Samuel Scheraga and Etta Scheraga; m. Miriam Kurnow 1943; one s. two d.; ed City Coll. of New York and Duke Univ.; ACS Postdoctoral Fellow, Harvard Medical School 1946–47; Instructor of Chem., Cornell Univ. 1947–50, Asst Prof. 1950–53, Assoc. Prof. 1953–58, Prof. 1958–92, George W. and Grace L. Todd Prof. 1965–92, Prof. Emer. 1992–; Chair. Chem. Dept 1960–67; Guggenheim Fellow and Fulbright Research Scholar, Carlsberg Lab., Copenhagen 1956–57, Weizmann Inst., Rehovoth, Israel 1963; NIH Special Fellow, Weizman Inst., Rehovoth, Israel 1970; Visiting Lecturer, Wool Research Labs, CSIRO, Australia 1959; Visiting Prof., Weizmann Inst., Rehovoth, Israel 1972–78, Japan Soc. for the Promotion of Science 1977; Regional Dir Nat. Foundation for Cancer Research 1982–; mem. NAS, American Acad. of Arts and Sciences; Vice-Chair. Cornell Section ACS 1954–55, Chair. 1955–56, Councillor 1959–62; mem. Advisory Panel in Molecular Biology NSF 1960–62; mem. editorial bd of numerous scientific journals; mem. Biochemical Training Cttee, NIH 1963–65, Fogarty Scholar 1984, 1986, 1988, 1989, 1990, 1991; mem. Comm. on Molecular Biophysics Int. Union for Pure and Applied Biophysics 1967–69; mem. Comm. on Macromolecular Biophysics, Int. Union for Pure and Applied Biophysics 1969–75, Pres. 1972–75; mem. Comm. on Subcellular and Macromolecular Biophysics, Int. Union for Pure and Applied Biophysics 1975–81; mem. Exec. Comm. Div. of Biological Chem. ACS 1966–69; Vice-Chair. Div. of Biological Chem. ACS 1970, Chair. 1971; mem. Council Biophysical Soc. 1967–70; mem. Research Career Award Cttee NIH 1967–71; mem. Bd Govs Weizmann Inst., Rehovoth, Israel 1970–97; Fellow, Biophysical Soc. 1999; Hon. Life Mem. New York Acad. of Sciences 1985, Hon. Mem. Hungarian Biophysical Soc. 1989; Hon. ScD (Duke Univ.) 1961, (Univ. of Rochester) 1988, (Univ. of San Luis) 1992, (Technion) 1993, (Univ. of Gdansk) 2006; ACS Eli Lilly Award in Bio chem. 1957, Welch Foundation Lecturer 1962, Harvey Lecturer 1968, Gallagher Lecturer 1968–69, Townsend Harris Medal, CCNY 1970, Lemieux Lecturer 1973, Nichols Medal, NY Section, ACS 1974, Hill Lecturer 1976, City Coll. Chem. Alumni Scientific Achievement Award Medal 1977, ACS Kendall Award in Colloid Chem. 1978, Venable Lecturer 1981, Linderstrøm-Lang Medal 1983, Kowalski Medal 1983, Pauling Medal, ACS 1985, Mobil Award, ACS 1990, Repligen Award, ACS 1990, Stein and Moore Award, Protein Soc. 1995, ACS Award for Computers in Chemical and Pharmaceutical Research 1997, Hirschmann Award in Peptide Chem., ACS 1999, Ramachandran Lecturer 2002. *Publications include:* Protein Structure 1961, Theory of Helix-Coil Transitions in Biopolymers 1970; more than 1,200 articles in profession journals on the physical chem. of proteins and other macromolecules, structure of water, and the chem. of blood clotting and growth factors. *Leisure interest:* golf. *Address:* 223 Forest Home Drive, Ithaca, NY 14850 (home); Department of Chemistry and Chemical Biology, 136A Baker Laboratory, Ithaca, NY 14853-1301, USA (office). *Telephone:* (607) 272-5155 (home); (607) 255-4034 (office). *Fax:* (607) 254-4700 (office). *E-mail:* has5@cornell.edu (office). *Website:* www.chem.cornell.edu (office).

SCHERBAK, Yuri, MD, PhD, DSc; Ukrainian diplomatist, politician, environmentalist and academic; b. 12 Oct. 1934, Kiev; m. Maria Scherbak; two c.; ed Kiev Medical Inst.; worked as social and political publicist in Ukrainian and Soviet media 1988–91; began active political career 1989, won seat in USSR Supreme Soviet, Chair. Sub-cttee on Energy and Nuclear Safety; f. Ukrainian Green Movt, Leader, Zeleny Svit (Green World) 1988, Leader, Green Party of Ukraine 1990; Minister of Environmental Protection 1991–92; Amb. to Israel 1992–94, to USA 1994–98 (also accred to Mexico 1997), to Canada 2000–03; Foreign Policy Adviser to Pres. of Ukraine 1998–2000; Int. Affairs Adviser to Volodymyr Lytvyn, Speaker of Verkhovna Rada (Parl.) –2006; fmr Prof., Vernadsky Inst. for Sustainable Devt, Moscow; mem. Nat. Security and Defence Council 1991; mem. Acad. of Ecological Sciences of Ukraine, Writers' Union of Ukraine (mem. Bd 1987–89), Cinematographers' Union of Ukraine; Hon. mem. Scientific Studies Inst., Harvard Univ., USA; Yuri Yanovski Literary Prize 1984, Olexander Dovzhenko Prize in Cinematography 1985. *Publications include:* Chornobyl (eye-witness account) 1986, The Strategic Role of Ukraine 1998, Ukraine: Challenge and Choice 2004; 20 books of poetry, prose, plays and essays; over 200 publs on epidemiology, theoretical issues in medicine and ecology.

SCHERER, Frederic M. (Mike), AB, MBA, PhD; American economist and academic; *Aetna Professor Emeritus of Public Policy and Corporate Management, John F. Kennedy School of Government, Harvard University;* b. (Frederic Walter Scherer), 1 Aug. 1932, Ottawa, Ill.; s. of Walter K. Scherer and Margaret Lucey Scherer; m. Barbara Silbermann 1957; one s. two d.; ed Univ. of Michigan, Harvard Univ.; served in US Army Counter-Intelligence Corps 1954–56; research asst then assoc. Harvard Business School 1958–63; professorial appointments, Princeton Univ. 1963–66, Univ. of Michigan 1966–72, Int. Inst. of Man. 1972–74, Northwestern Univ. 1976–82, Swarthmore Coll. 1982–89; Chief Economist, US Fed. Trade Comm. 1974–76; Aetna Prof. of Public Policy and Corp. Man., John F. Kennedy School of Govt, Harvard Univ. 1989–2000, Prof. Emer. 2000–; Ludwig Erhard Visiting Prof., Univ. of Bayreuth 2000; Lecturer, Woodrow Wilson School of Public and International Affairs, Princeton Univ. 2000–05; Visiting Prof., Haverford Coll. 2004–06; Co-founder European Asscn for Research in Industrial Econs; Dr hc (Hohenheim Univ.); Lanchester Prize, Operations Research Soc. of America 1964, O'Melveny & Myers Centennial Research Prize 1989, Distinguished Fellow, Industrial Org. Soc. 1999, Lifetime Achievement Award, American Antitrust Inst. 2002, Baker Scholar, Copeland Award, Harvard Business School. *Achievements include:* pioneering work on theory of research and devt strategy and timing. *Publications include:* The Weapons Acquisition Process: Economic Incentives 1964, Industrial Market Structure and Economic Performance 1970, The Economics of Multi-Plant Operation 1975, Mergers, Sell-offs, and Economic Efficiency 1987, Innovation and Growth: Schumpeterian Perspectives 1984, Industry Structure, Strategy and Public Policy 1996, Quarter Notes and Bank Notes: The Economics of Music Composition in the 18th and 19th Centuries 2004. *Leisure interest:* 17th–19th century music. *Address:* 53 Standish Street, Unit 2, Cambridge, MA 02138, USA (home). *Telephone:* (617) 497-4345 (home). *E-mail:* mike_scherer@hks.harvard.edu (office). *Website:* www.hks.harvard.edu/fs/fmscherer (office).

SCHERER, HE Cardinal Odilo Pedro, PhD; Brazilian ecclesiastic; *Archbishop of São Paulo;* b. 21 Sept. 1949, São Francisco; s. of Edwin Scherer and Francisca Wilma Scherer; ed Pontifical Brazilian Coll., Pontifical Gregorian Univ.; ordained priest in Toledo, Paraná 1976; served as pastor in Diocese of Toledo, taught at and served as rector of several seminaries and religious insts in southern Brazil; worked as official of Vatican's Congregation for Bishops 1994–2001; Auxiliary Bishop of São Paulo and Titular Bishop of Novi 2001–02; Sec.-Gen. Brazilian Bishops' Conf. 2003–; Archbishop of São Paulo 2007–; cr. Cardinal (Cardinal-Priest of San Andrea al Quirinale) 2008; participated in Papal Conclave 2013; named one of two Secs, Fifth Gen. Conf. of Bishops of Latin America and the Caribbean, Brazil 2007; Grand Chancellor Pontifical Catholic University of São Paulo (PUC-SP). *Address:* Archdiocese of São Paulo, Avenida Higienopolis 890, 01238-908 São Paulo (office); CP 1670, 01064-970 São Paulo, Brazil. *Telephone:* (11) 3826-0133 (office). *Fax:* (11) 3825-4414 (office). *E-mail:* imprensa@arquidiocesedesaopaulo.org.br (office). *Website:* www.arquidiocesedesaopaulo.org.br (office).

SCHERPENHUIJSEN ROM, Willem; Dutch business executive; b. 1933, Utrecht; ed Univ. of Amsterdam; Chair. NMB Postbank 1976–92; Chair. Int. Nederlande (formed by merger of NMB Postbank and Internationale Nederlande Groep in 1991) 1992; mem. and Treas. (for Europe) Trilateral Comm.; Founding mem. and Deputy Chair. Institut für Sozialforschung MAITRI e.V; mem. Anthroposophical Soc. 1992–; mem. Advisory Bd Arleen Auger Memorial Fund.

SCHERRER, Anton, BSc, Dr Sci.Techn.; Swiss business executive; b. 1942; ed Swiss Inst. of Tech. (ETH-Zurich); headed biological research lab. and experimental brewery at Swiss brewing industry trial facility 1970–73; Plant Man. and Deputy Man. Eglisau (mineral spring) and Deputy Head Tech. Dept Unifontes Group 1973–76; held several man. positions at Brauerei Hürlimann 1977–91, including Deputy Man. and Master Brewer 1977–82, apptd Chief Tech. Officer 1983, Chair. Exec. Bd 1984–89; apptd Chair. Retail Trade Cttee Migros Cooperative Asscn 2001, Chair. Admin. Del. 2001–03; Chair. Exec. Bd Migrosbank 2003–05; Vice-Chair. Swisscom AG 2005–06, Chair. 2006–11; mem. Bd of Dirs Hürlimann Holding AG 1984–91, Orior AG 2007–13; mem. Exec. Bd economiesuisse 2006–11; mem. Advisory Bd Capvis Equity Partners AG, Theo Müller Gmbh & Co., Germany –2008; mem. Bd of Trustees, Agrovision Foundation Muri, Swiss Inst. of Technology Zurich Foundation –2011; mem. Managerial Cttee Inst. for Marketing and Trade, Univ. of St Gallen –2011; mem. Nat. Comm. for Tech. and Innovation 2012. *Telephone:* (44) 7150660 (home). *E-mail:* anton@scherrer.com (home).

SCHETYNA, Grzegorz Juliusz; Polish politician; *President, Platforma Obywatelska (Civic Platform);* b. 18 Feb. 1963, Opole; ed Wrocław Univ.; fmr mem. Solidarność Walcząca (Fighting Solidarity); Chair. Niezależne Zrzeszenie Studentów (NZS—Ind. Students' Union), Wrocław Univ. 1986–89, later mem. Presidium NZS Nat. Co-ordinating Cttee; Dir Voivodship Office, Wrocław 1990, Deputy Voivod 1991–92; Chair. Kongres Liberalno-Demokratyczny (Liberal and Democratic Congress), Wrocław 1991, later becoming Sec.-Gen.; mem. Unia Wolności (Freedom Union) 1994–2001; Co-founder Platforma Obywatelska (Civic Platform) 2001, Pres. 2016–; mem. Sejm (Parl.) for Legnica 1997–, Marshall of the Sejm 2010–11, Chair. Foreign Affairs Cttee 2011–14; Deputy Prime Minister and Minister of the Interior and Admin 2007–09; Acting Pres. of Poland 8 July–6 Aug. 2010; Minister of Foreign Affairs 2014–15; launched Radio Eska, Wrocław 1993. *Leisure interests:* basketball, football, travelling, American literature. *Address:* Platforma Obywatelska, 00-490 Warsaw, ul. Wiejska 12A (office); Wiejska 4/6/8, 00-902 Warsaw, Poland. *Telephone:* (22) 4596400 (office). *Fax:* (22) 4596431 (office). *E-mail:* biuro@schetyna.pl (office); biuro@platforma.org (office). *Website:* www.platforma.org (office).

SCHIEFFER, Robert (Bob), BA; American broadcast journalist; b. 25 Feb. 1937, Austin, Tex.; m. Patricia Penrose; two d.; ed Texas Christian Univ.; reporter, Fort Worth Star-Telegram; news anchor, WBAP-TV, Dallas; began work at CBS News 1969, Pentagon Corresp. 1970–74, White House Corresp. 1974–79, Chief Washington Corresp. 1982–2015, anchor, CBS Sunday Nightly News 1973–74, Sunday ed. CBS Evening News, then Sun. Ed. 1976, anchor, Saturday ed. CBS Evening News 1976–96, co-anchor, CBS Morning News 1985, anchor and moderator, Face the Nation, CBS News 1991–2015 (retd), interim anchor, CBS Evening News 2005–06, now political analyst; six Emmy Awards and two Sigma Delta Chi Awards, Broadcaster of the Year, Nat. Press Foundation 2002, Paul White Award from Radio-TV News Dirs Asscn 2003, Int. Radio and TV Soc. Foundation Award 2004, American News Women's Club Helen Thomas Award for Excellence in Journalism 2004, and numerous other awards. *Publications include:* The Acting President (with Gary P. Gates) 1989, This Just In: What I Couldn't Tell You On TV 2003, Face the Nation: My Favorite Stories from the First 50 Years of the Award-Winning News Broadcast, Bob Schieffer's America. *Address:* CBS News, 2020 M Street, NW, Washington, DC 20036, USA (office). *Website:* www.cbsnews.com/team/bob-schieffer (office).

SCHIEFFER, J(ohn) Thomas (Tom), BA, MA; American lawyer, politician, diplomatist and business executive; *Founder and Principal, Envoy International LLC;* b. 4 Oct. 1947, Fort Worth, Tex.; m. Susanne Silber 1979; one s.; ed Arlington Heights High School and Univ. of Texas; worked in offices of Tex. State Senator Don Kennard and Tex. Gov. John Connally; elected to Tex. House of Reps 1972, served three terms; admitted to Tex. Bar 1979; Pnr with George W. Bush and Edward W. (Rusty) Rose in ownership of Texas Rangers (Major League Baseball club) 1989–99, Pnr-in-Charge of Ballpark Devt 1990, Pres. 1991–99; Pres. J. Thomas Schieffer Man. Co., Pablo Operating Co. –2001; Amb. to Australia 2001–05, to Japan 2005–09; apptd Sr Counsel, Akin Gump Strauss Hauer & Feld LLP, Dallas 2010; Founder and Prin., Envoy International LLC (consultancy); apptd by Major League Baseball Commr Bud Selig to oversee Los Angeles Dodgers' business and financial operations 2011; mem. Bd Dirs Maureen and Mike Mansfield Foundation; mem. Bd Councilors US-Japan Council; mem. Advisory Bd US Studies Centre, Univ. of Sydney, Japan-America Soc. of Dallas/Fort Worth; fmr mem. Bd Dirs Maureen and Mike Mansfield Foundation, Drew Industries; fmr mem. Advisory Bd JP Morgan Chase Bank, Fort Worth; fmr Tarrant Co. Coordinator for Gov. Mark White; has served on numerous charitable and civic bds, including The Penrose Foundation, Dallas Co. Community Coll. Foundation, Dallas 2012 Olympic Cttee, Tarrant Co. Coll. Foundation, Winston School; fmr mem. Exec. Cttee Dallas Chamber of Commerce; Trustee, Tarrant Co. Jr Coll. 1987; Hon. Order of Australia; Grand Cordon, Order of the Rising Sun (Japan) 2013; honoured by FBI for efforts to combat int. scourge of child pornography, Nat. Intelligence Reform Medal, Dir of Nat. Intelligence, CIA Donovan Award, Defense Intelligence Agency Director's Award Medal, Nat. Security Agency Director's Distinguished Service Medal, Nat. Geospatial-Intelligence Agency Medallion for Excellence, Dept of Defense Medal for Distinguished Public Service 2009. *Address:* Envoy International LLC, 306 West Seventh Street, Suite 850, Fort Worth Club Building, Fort Worth, TX 76102, USA.

SCHIFANI, Renato Giuseppe, LLB; Italian lawyer and politician; b. 11 May 1950, Palermo; m. Franca Schifani; two s.; lawyer, Court of Appeal; f. Siculabrokers 1979, becoming Dir; f. GMS (credit agency) 1992; fmr mem. Partito della Democrazia Cristiana; mem. Forza Italia 1995–, Pres. 2001–06; mem. Popolo della Libertà (People of Freedom) 2007–; mem. Senato (Upper House) for Sicily constituency 1996–, Pres. 2008–13, Head of Area Popolare coalition 2015–16; Pres. Nuovo Centrodestra (New Centre-Right) party 2013, now mem. Forza Italia. *Address:* Senato della Repubblica, Piazza Madama, 00186 Rome, Italy (office). *Telephone:* (6) 67061 (office). *E-mail:* schifani_r@posta.senato.it (office). *Website:* www.senato.it (office).

SCHIFF, Sir András, Kt; British (b. Hungarian) pianist; b. 21 Dec. 1953, Budapest; s. of Odon Schiff and Klara Schiff (née Csengeri); ed Franz Liszt Acad. of Music, Budapest with Pal Kadosa, Gyorgy Kurtag and Ferenc Rados, pvt lessons with George Malcolm, England; recitals in London, New York, Paris, Vienna, Munich, Florence; concerts with New York Philharmonic, Chicago Symphony, Vienna Philharmonic, Concertgebouw, Orchestre de Paris, London Philharmonic, London Symphony, Philharmonia, Royal Philharmonic, Israel Philharmonic, Berlin Philharmonic, Cleveland, Philadelphia, Washington Nat. Symphony; played at Salzburg, Edinburgh, Aldeburgh, Feldkirch Schubertiade, Lucerne and Tanglewood Festivals; f. Musiktage Mondsee Festival 1989 (Artistic Dir 1989–98); f. orchestra Cappella Andrea Barca 1999; Special Supernumerary Fellow, Balliol Coll., Oxford, UK 2011–; Hon. Prof., Music Schools in Budapest, Detmold and Munich 2011–; Mem. of Honour, Vienna Konzerthaus 2012; Ordre pour le Mérite for Sciences and Arts 2012; Prizewinner at Tchaikovsky Competition, Moscow 1974 and Leeds Piano Competition 1975, Liszt Prize 1977, Premio dell'Accad. Chigiana, Siena 1987, RPS/Charles Heidsieck Award for best concert series of 1988–89, Wiener Flötenuhr 1989, Bartók Prize 1991, Instrumentalist of the Year, Royal Philharmonic Soc. 1994, Claudio Arrau Memorial Medal 1994, Kossuth Prize 1996, Sonning Prize, Copenhagen 1997, Palladio d'Oro della Città di Vicenza 2003, Musikfest Prize, Bremen 2003, Abbiati Prize 2007, RAM Bach Prize 2007, Wigmore Medal 2008, Klavier-Festival Ruhr Prize for outstanding achievements and to honour a lifetime's work as a pianist 2009, Schumann Prize, City of Zwickau 2011, Gold Medal, Royal Philharmonic Soc. 2013. *Recordings include:* Bach Goldberg Variations, Bach Partitas, Bach Piano Concertos, Mendelssohn Concertos 1 and 2, all the Schubert Sonatas, Schubert Trout Quintet, Schumann and Chopin 2, all the Mozart Concertos, Bach Two- and Three-part Inventions, Bach Well-Tempered Klavier, Beethoven Violin and Piano Sonatas with Sandor Vegh, Beethoven Piano Concertos, Bartók Piano Concertos, Tchaikovsky Piano Concerto, Bach English Suites (Grammy Award 1990), Bach French Suites, Lieder with Peter Schreier, Robert Holl and Cecilia Bartoli, etc., Beethoven Piano Sonatas Op. 2 Nos 1–3 and Op. 7 No. 4 2005, Beethoven Piano Sonatas Op. Nos 6–8 2008,

Schumann Geistervariationen (Int. Classical Music Award for Recording of the Year and Best Solo Instrument Recording 2012) 2011, Franz Schubert: Sonatas, Impromptus & Moments Musicaux (Int. Classical Music Award for Solo Instrument 2016) 2015. *Television:* The Wanderer – A Film About Schubert with András Schiff (BBC Omnibus, narrator), Chopin with András Schiff (BBC Omnibus, narrator). *Leisure interests:* literature, languages, soccer, theatre, cinema, art. *E-mail:* info@askonasholt.co.uk (office). *Website:* www.askonasholt.co.uk (office).

SCHIFFER, Claudia; German actress and fmr fashion model; b. 25 Aug. 1970, Düsseldorf; m. Matthew Vaughn 2002; one s. two d.; fashion model for Karl Lagerfeld 1990, model for Revlon 1992–96, Chanel –1997; has appeared on numerous covers for magazines and journals; designs calendars; appears on TV specials; has share in Fashion Café, New York 1995–; announced retirement from modelling 1998; mem. US Cttee UNICEF 1995–98, UK Goodwill Amb. 2006–. *Films include:* Richie Rich 1994, Pret-a-Porter 1994, The Blackout 1997, And She Was 1999, Friends and Lovers 1999, Black and White 2000, Chain of Fools 2000, Reckless + Wild 2001, Life Without Dick 2001, Love Actually 2003. *Publication:* Memories 1995. *Address:* c/o Heidi Gross GmbH & Co., KG Hartungstrasse 5, 20146 Hamburg, Germany (office). *Telephone:* (49) 40440555 (office). *Fax:* (49) 404500885 (office). *E-mail:* info@model-management.de (office). *Website:* claudiaschiffer.com (office).

SCHIFRES, Michel Maurice René; French journalist; b. 1 May 1946, Orléans; s. of Jacques Schifres and Paulette Mauduit; m. Josiane Gasnier (divorced); two c.; ed Lycée du Mans, Lycée de Caen, Faculté des Lettres de Caen, Centre de Formation des Journalistes; journalist with Combat 1970–72, with Monde 1972–74; Head of Political Affairs Quotidien de Paris 1974–76; Asst Head of Political Affairs France-Soir 1976; Head of Political Affairs Journal du Dimanche 1977, Deputy Ed. 1979–82, Ed. 1982–86, Deputy Editorial Dir 1985–89; mem. Comm. on quality of radio and TV broadcasts 1977–79; Editorial Dir France-Soir 1989–92, Asst Dir-Gen. 1992; Asst Editorial Dir Le Figaro (newspaper) 1992–98, Man. Dir 1998–2000, Man. Ed. Le Figaro magazine 2005–07, Vice-Pres. Editorial Cttee 2000–; mem. Editorial Cttee La Revue de l'Intelligent 2003–; columnist, L'Opinion; Chevalier, Ordre nat. du Mérite. *Television:* L'Elysée 1988, Ville de Chiens 1989, Un Siecle d'Ecrivain: Jules Romains 1998. *Publications include:* La CFDT des militants 1972, D'une France à l'autre 1974, L'enaklatura 1987, L'Elysée de Mitterrand 1987, La désertion des énarques 1999. *Leisure interest:* antiques. *Address:* 150 avenue Emile Zola, 75015 Paris, France (home). *Telephone:* 1-40-58-16-64 (home); 6-07-59-40-91 (mobile). *E-mail:* mschifres@noos.fr (home).

SCHIFTER, Richard, BA, LLB; American lawyer, diplomatist and politician; *Chairman, American Jewish International Relations Institute;* b. 31 July 1923, Vienna, Austria; m.; five c.; ed Coll. of the City of New York, Yale Law School; served in US Army 1943–46; practising attorney, Washington, DC 1951–84; Rep. to UN Human Rights Comm. 1983–86, Deputy Rep. to UN Security Council (with rank of Amb.) 1984–85; Asst Sec. of State for Human Rights and Humanitarian Affairs 1985–92, Counsellor, Nat. Security Council (organized SE Europe Cooperative Initiative 1996), Dept of State Rep. to CSCE, Special Advisor to Sec. of State 1993–2001; Chair. Centre for Democracy and Reconciliation in SE Europe 2001–08; currently Chair. American Jewish International Relations Inst.; Grand Decoration of Honour in Gold (Austria) 1998, Order Stara Planina (Bulgaria), Commdr, Order of the Star of Romania; Distinguished Service Award of the Sec. of State. *Publication:* Human Rights, Perestroika and The End of the Cold War (co-author) 2009. *Address:* American Jewish International Relations Institute, PO Box 42732, Washington, DC 20015, USA (office). *Telephone:* (301) 229-0357 (home). *E-mail:* rschifter@aol.com (office). *Website:* www.ajiri.us (office).

SCHILLER, Vivian, MA; American media executive; b. 13 Sept. 1961; m. Phil Frank; two c.; ed Cornell Univ., Middlebury Coll.; Russian interpreter and tour guide, Moscow 1984–88; Production Co-ordinator, Turner Broadcasting System Inc., Moscow 1988, Supervising Producer, Sr Producer, then Vice-Pres. and Gen. Man., Turner Original Productions, Turner Entertainment Networks 1994–2002, fmr Exec. Vice-Pres. CNN Productions, Turner Broadcasting System Inc.; Sr Vice-Pres. and Gen. Man. Discovery Times Channel, The New York Times Co. 2002–05, Sr Vice-Pres. TV and Video 2005–06, Exec. Vice-Pres. and Gen. Man. Discovery Times Channel 2005–06; Sr Vice-Pres. and Gen. Man. NYTimes.com 2006–08; Pres. and CEO, National Public Radio, Washington, DC 2009–11 (resgnd); Sr Vice-Pres. and Chief Digital Officer, NBC News 2011–14; Head of News, Twitter Inc. Jan.–Oct. 2014; currently ind. media and tech. consultant; mem. Bd of Trustees Investigative News Network 2011–, Soc. for Science and the Public 2011–, Int. Center for Journalists 2012–; mem. Advisory Bd CUNY Grad. School of Journalism 2012–, Reuters Inst. for the Study of Journalism 2014–; mem. Council on Foreign Relations; five Emmy Awards, two Peabody Awards, two Alfred I. DuPont-Columbia Univ. Awards, CableACE Award, Int. Documentary Asscn Award. *Television includes:* as supervising producer: A Century of Women 1994, Moon Shot 1994; as sr producer: Hank Aaron: Chasing the Dream 1995, Hollywood's Amazing Animal Actors 1996, Biker Women 1996, Survivors of the Holocaust 1996, Animal ER 1996, Pirate Tales 1997, Twin Stories 1997, Warner Bros. 75th Anniversary: No Guts, No Glory 1998, Dying to Tell the Story 1998; as exec. producer: Word Wars 2004, Off to War 2005.

SCHILLEROVÁ, Alena, JUDr, PhD; Czech lawyer, public servant and politician; *Minister of Finance;* b. 18 March 1964, Brno, Czechoslovak Socialist Repub. (now Czech Repub.); ed Masaryk Univ., Brno; External employee, Dept of Financial Law and Nat. Econs, Faculty of Law, Masaryk Univ., Brno 1994–, Lecturer, Faculty of Law 2006–, Expert Asst 2011–14; Lawyer, Brno Financial Office 1991–94, Head of Legal and Enforcement Dept June–Dec. 1994, Deputy Man., Brno Financial Office 1995–2006, Man. 2006–12; Deputy Man. and Head of Methodology and Tax Enforcement Dept, South Moravia Regional Financial Office 2013–14, Man., Legal and Tax Process Dept, Gen. Directorate of Finance 2014–15; Deputy Minister of Finance for Tax and Customs 2016–17, Minister of Finance 2017–. *Address:* Ministry of Finance, Letenská 15, 118 10 Prague1, Czech Republic (office). *Telephone:* 257041111 (office). *E-mail:* 257042788 (office). *Website:* podatelna@mfcr.cz (office); www.mfcr.cz (office).

SCHILTZ, Jean-Louis; Luxembourg lawyer and politician; *Partner, Schiltz & Schiltz;* b. 14 Aug. 1964, Luxembourg; m.; three c.; ed Université Paris I Panthéon Sorbonne; worked for Schiltz & Schiltz (law firm), Luxembourg 1989–2004, Partner 2009–; Academic Asst, Law Faculty Université Paris I Panthéon Sorbonne 1989–90; mem. Cttee Young Bar Asscn 1990, Chair. 1997–98, then mem. Bar Council; elected mem. Parl. 2004; Minister for Devt Cooperation and Humanitarian Action, Minister for Communications and Minister of Defence 2004–09; apptd Gov. Asian Development Bank for Luxembourg 2004; Sec.-Gen. Parti Chrétien Social (Chrëschtlech Sozial Vollekspartei) (PCS/CSV) (Christian Social Party), Pres. 2009–11; First Asst, then Chargé de Cours, Centre universitaire de Luxembourg 1991–2004; currently Visiting Prof., Univ. of Luxembourg; Co-ed. Assurances et Responsabilité 1994–2004; mem. Editorial Bd European Lawyer, Int. Bar Asscn; fmr mem. Legal Comm., Nat. Olympic Cttee. *Sport achievements:* Luxembourg team fencing champion 1983. *Leisure interests:* running, biking. *Address:* Schiltz & Schiltz, 2, rue du Fort Rheinsheim, 2419, Luxembourg. *E-mail:* schiltz@schiltz.lu (office). *Website:* schiltz.lu (office).

SCHILY, Otto; German lawyer and politician; b. 20 July 1932, Bochum; s. of Franz Schily; m. (divorced); two d.; ed Univs of Munich, Hamburg and Berlin; mem. Bundestag 1983–86, 1987–89, 1990–2009; Co-founder Green Party 1980; mem. SPD 1990–, Deputy Chair. 1994–; Minister of the Interior 1998–2005; f. Otto Schily Rechtsanwaltsgesellschaft mbH 2006; mem. Presidium Neue Gesellschaft für bildende Kunst; Adviser, Humanist Union; Bavarian Order of Merit 2001; Leo Baeck Medal 2005.

SCHIMMEL, Paul Gordon; American museum curator; *Partner and Vice-President, Hauser & Wirth;* b. 1954, New York; m. Yvonne Schimmel; ed Syracuse Univ., New York Univ.; internship, Contemporary Arts Museum, Houston, Tex. 1975–78, then mem. curatorial staff; Curator, Newport Harbor Art Museum 1981–89; Chief Curator, Museum of Contemporary Art, Los Angeles 1990–2012; Partner and Vice-Pres. Hauser & Wirth 2013–, also Prin. Hauser Wirth & Schimmel (gallery), Los Angeles; fmr Co-Dir and Chair. Mike Kelley Foundation for the Arts; has lectured at Kanazawa Museum of Modern Art, Japan, RCA, London, Centre Georges Pompidou, Paris, Whitney Museum of American Art, J. Paul Getty Museum, Los Angeles Co. Museum of Art, and others; panelist, Nat. Endowment for the Arts; Bard Coll. Center for Curatorial Studies Award for Curatorial Excellence. *Publications include:* Ecstasy: In and About Altered States (co-ed with Lisa Gabrielle Mark); contrib.: articles in journals and magazines including The Art Book. *Address:* Hauser Wirth & Schimmel, 2121 E 7th Place, Unit 115, Los Angeles, CA 90021, USA (office). *Telephone:* (213) 537-0858 (office). *Fax:* (213) 221-7119 (office). *E-mail:* losangeles@hauserwirthschimmel.com (office). *Website:* hauserwirthschimmel.com (office).

SCHINDLER, David W., OC, BSc, DPhil, FRS, FRSC; Canadian biologist, ecologist and academic; *Killam Memorial Professor Emeritus of Ecology, University of Alberta;* b. 3 Aug. 1940, Fargo, ND, USA; ed North Dakota State Univ., Univ. of Oxford, UK; Asst Prof. of Biology, Trent Univ., Canada 1966–68; Founder and Dir Experimental Lakes Project, Canadian Dept of Fisheries and Oceans 1968–89; Killam Memorial Prof. of Ecology, Univ. of Alberta 1989–2013, Prof. Emer. 2013–, Chair. Limnology Lab. 1993–2012; Chair. Alberta Br., Safe Drinking Water Foundation; mem. Bd of Dirs Canadian Arctic Resources Cttee (Chair. Cumulative Effects Sub-Cttee); mem. Scientific Advisory Cttee and Aquatic Sciences Cttee, Yukon to Yellowstone; mem. NAS 2002–; Foreign mem. Royal Swedish Acad. of Eng Science 2003–; Assoc. Ed. Canadian Journal of Fisheries and Aquatic Sciences; mem. Editorial Bd Aquatic Sciences, Proceedings of the National Academy of Sciences; mem. Advisory Bd Ecosytems (journal); Queen's Golden Jubilee Medal 2002, Alberta Order of Excellence 2008; Hon. DSc (N Dakota State Univ., Acadia Univ., Brock Univ., Queen's Univ. and Univs of Victoria, Athabasca, Winnipeg and Lethbridge); Hon. DLaws (Univ. of Windsor, Trent Univ.); Outstanding Achievement Award, American Inst. of Fisheries Research Biologists 1984, Frank Rigler Award, Canadian Soc. of Limnologists 1984, Hutchinson Medal, American Soc. of Limnology and Oceanography 1985, Naumann-Thieneman Medal, Int. Limnology Soc. 1989, First Stockholm Water Prize, Stockholm Water Foundation 1991, Manning Distinguished Achievement Award 1993, First Romanowski Medal, RSC 1994, Walter Bean–Canada Trust Award for Environmental Science 1996, Volvo Environment Prize 1998, J. Gordin Kaplan Award for Excellence in Research, Univ. of Alberta 1999, Distinguished mem., Int. Water Acad., Norway 1999, Alberta Science and Tech. Award for Outstanding Leadership in Alberta Science 1999, Natural Sciences and Eng Research Council (NESRC) Award of Excellence 2000, 2001, Douglas H. Pimlott Award for Conservation, Canadian Nature Fed. 2001, NESRC Gerhard Herzberg Canada Gold Medal for Science and Eng 2001, Environment Canada, EcoLogo/Natural Marine Environmental Award 2002, Award of Distinction, City of Edmonton 2002, Killam Prize 2003, Tyler Prize for Environmental Achievement (co-recipient) 2006, David Schindler Endowed Professorship in Aquatic Sciences est. at Trent Univ. 2008, Sandford Fleming Medal, Royal Canadian Inst. 2009. *Publications:* more than 280 articles and reports, more than 20 of them in Science and Nature magazine. *Address:* University of Alberta, Room Z 811, Biological Sciences Building, Edmonton, AB T6G 2R3, Canada (office). *Telephone:* (780) 492-1291 (office). *Fax:* (780) 492-9234 (office). *E-mail:* d.schindler@ualberta.ca (office). *Website:* www.biology.ualberta.ca (office).

SCHINZLER, Hans-Jürgen, DJur; German insurance industry executive; *Honorary Chairman of the Supervisory Board, Münchener Rückversicherungsgesellschaft AG (Munich Re);* b. 12 Oct. 1940, Madrid, Spain; m. Monika Somya; three c.; ed Univs of Munich and Würzburg; training at Bayerische Vereinsbank 1968–69; joined Münchener Rückversicherungsgesellschaft AG (Munich Re) 1968, mem. Bd of Man. 1981–93, Chair. Bd of Man. 1993–2003, Chair. Supervisory Bd 2004–12, Hon. Chair. 2013–, Chair. Munich Reinsurance America, Inc. 1997–2003, Chair. Bd of Trustees Munich Re Foundation; Chair. Wittelsbacher Ausgleichsfonds; Deputy Chair. Allgemeine Kreditversicherung AG, Mainz, Allianzversicherung AG, Munich; Chair. Supervisory Bd ERGO Versicherungsgruppe AG –2003, MR Beteiligungen AG, Grafelfing, Bonn Metro AG, MRE Beteiligungen AG, Munich; Deputy Chair. Supervisory Bd Stuttgart, Metro AG, Dusseldorf Aventis SA, Schiltigheim, France –2004, Bayerische Hypo- und Vereinsbank 2004–05; Deputy Chair. and mem. Supervisory Bd HVB Group (holding co. of Bayerische Hypo-und Vereinsbank AG); mem. Supervisory Bd Man AG –2003, Sanofi-Aventis AG 1999–2004, METRO AG 2002–, Bayerische Hypo- und Vereinsbank AG 2003–05, Deutsche Telekom AG from 2003; mem. Bd of Man. Freundeskreis des Bayerischen Nationalmuseums e.V.; fmr Deputy Chair.

Supervisory Bd Man AG; Vice-Chair. Statutory Supervisory Bd Allianz Lebensversicherungs AG –2002, Dresdner Bank AG –2002; Ind. Dir, UniCredit SpA 2005–; Dir, Munich Reinsurance America, Inc. (fmrly American Re Corpn) 1996–; mem. Bd Deutscher Verein für Versicherungswissenschaft e.V.; mem. Bd of Dirs Munich-American Holding Corpn, Del.; mem. Bd of Trustees Gemeinnützige Hertie-Stiftung, Hypo-Kulturstiftung, State of Bavaria of Stifterverband für die Deutsche Wissenschaft, Stiftung Demoskopie Allensbach, Stiftung Pinakothek der Moderne; mem. Comparable German and Foreign Corp. Bd of Business Enterprises of Aventis SA; mem. Insurance Advisory Council Bundesanstalt fur Finanzdienstleistungsaufsicht; Treas. and mem. Senate of Max-Planck-Gesellschaft zur Förderung der Wissenschaften e.V. *Address:* Munich Re Group, Königinstrasse 107, 80802 Munich, Germany (office). *Telephone:* (89) 38913534 (office). *Fax:* (89) 399056 (office). *Website:* www.munichre.com (office).

SCHIZER, David M., BA, MA, JD; American professor of law; *Dean Emeritus and the Harvey R. Miller Professor of Law and Economics, Columbia University;* ed Yale Univ.; Exec. Ed. Yale Law Journal; clerk for Judge Alex Kozinski of US Court of Appeals for the Ninth Circuit 1993–94, for US Supreme Court Assoc. Justice Ruth Bader Ginsburg 1994–95; worked at Davis Polk & Wardwell –1998; Wilbur H. Friedman Prof. of Tax Law, Columbia Law School –2004, Lucy G. Moses Prof. of Law and Dean of Columbia Law School 2004, now Dean Emer. and Harvey R. Miller Prof. of Law and Econs, also Co-Dir Richard P. Richman Center for Business, Law, and Public Policy, Charles Evans Gerber Transactional Studies Center, Center for Israeli Legal Studies; also currently Martin D. Ginsburg Visiting Prof., Georgetown Law Center; mem. Bd of Dirs Seacor Holdings Inc.; mem. Exec. Cttee and Co-Chair. Cttee on Financial Insts, NY State Bar Asscn Tax Section; Willis L.M. Reese Prize for Excellence in Teaching, Columbia Law School. *Publications:* more than 25 books and numerous articles on taxation, financial instruments and regulation. *Address:* Jerome L. Greene Hall, Room 903, Columbia University Law School, 435 West 116th Street, New York, NY 10027, USA (office). *Telephone:* (212) 854-2599 (office). *Fax:* (212) 854-9746 (office). *E-mail:* david .schizer@law.columbia.edu (office). *Website:* www.law.columbia.edu (office).

SCHJELDAHL, Peter; American art critic and poet; *Senior Art Critic, The New Yorker;* b. 1942, Fargo, ND; m. Brooke Alderson; ed Carleton Coll., The New School, Manhattan; fmr Lecturer, Dept of Visual and Environmental Studies, Harvard Univ.; columnist, The Village Voice 1990–98; Contributing Ed. Art in America; Sr Art Critic, The New Yorker magazine 1998–; regular art critic for The New York Sunday Times, Vanity Fair, Seven Days; Guggenheim Fellowship for poetry, Cooper Union Frank Jewett Mather Award for art criticism, Clark Prize for Excellence in Arts Writing 2008, Harold D. Vursell Memorial Award 2010. *Publications include:* White Country 1968, An Adventure of the Thought Police 1971, Dreams 1973, Since 1964: New and Selected Poems 1978, Art of Our Time Volume 1 1984, The Seven Days Art Columns 1991, Hydrogen Jukebox: Selected Writings of Peter Schjeldahl 1978–1990 1991, De Kooning and Dubuffet: The Late Works 1993, Columns & Catalogues 1994, Let's See: Writings on Art from The New Yorker 2008. *Address:* The New Yorker, 4 Times Square, New York, NY 10036-7448, USA (office). *Telephone:* (212) 286-5400 (office). *Website:* www.newyorker .com/contributors/peter-schjeldahl (office).

SCHLAGMAN, Richard Edward, FRSA; British publisher; b. 11 Nov. 1953, London, England; s. of Jack Schlagman and Shirley Schlagman (née Goldston); m. Mia Hagg; two s.; ed Univ. Coll. School, Hampstead, Brunel Univ.; Co-Founder, Jt Chair., Man. Dir Interstate Electronics Ltd 1973–86; purchased Bush from Rank Org., renamed IEL Bush Radio Ltd 1981, floated on London Stock Exchange 1984, sold as Bush Radio PLC 1986; acquired Phaidon Press Ltd 1990, Chair. and Publr 1990–2012; mem. Exec. Cttee Patrons of New Art, Tate Gallery 1994–97, Glyndebourne Festival Soc.; Patron Bayreuther Festspiele, Salzburger Festspiele, Salzburger Osterfestspiele, Schubertiades, Lucerne Festival, Bayerische Staatsoper; Pres. Judd Foundation, MARFA, Tex. 1999–2001, mem. Bd 2001–09; Acquired Cahiers du Cinema 2009. *Leisure interests:* music, art, architecture. *Address:* Piazza Grande 26, 6600 Locarno, Switzerland (office). *Telephone:* 917596000 (office). *Fax:* 917596006 (office). *E-mail:* rs.office@quoig.com (office).

SCHLANGER, Marvin O.; American business executive; *Chairman, Ceva Logistics BV;* joined Lyondell Chemical Worldwide Inc. (fmrly ARCO Chemical Co.) as an Officer 1987, Vice-Pres., Worldwide Business Man. 1988–89, Sr Vice-Pres. and Chief Financial Officer 1989–92, Sr Vice-Pres. and Pres. ARCO Chemical Americas Co. 1992–94, Exec. Vice-Pres. and COO Lyondell Chemical Worldwide Inc. 1994–98, Pres. and CEO May–Oct. 1998, Chair. Supervisory Bd LyondellBasell Industries 2010–13; Prin., Cherry Hill Chemical Investments, LLC 1998–; CEO Resolution Performance Products Inc. (holding co. of Resolution Performance Products LLC) 2000–05, Pres. RPP LLC and RPP Capital Corpn –2001, CEO 2001; Interim Pres. OneChem Ltd 1999–2000; Chair. CEVA Group Plc 2009–, CEO Ceva Logistics BV 2012–14; Chair. Berry Plastics Corpn (fmrly Covalence Specialty Materials Corpn) 2006–07, Resolution Specialty Materials Co. 2004–05, Resolution Performance Products LLC and its subsidiary RPP Capital Corpn 2000; Vice-Chair. Hexion Specialty Chemicals Inc. (now Momentive Specialty Chemicals Inc.) 2005–10; mem. Bd of Dirs UGI Utilities Inc 1998–, UGI Corpn 1998–, Wellman Inc. 1999, OneChem Ltd 2002–, Momentive Specialty Chemicals Inc. 2005–10, Momentive Performance Materials Holdings Inc. 2006–10, AmeriGas Propane Inc. (Gen. Partner of AmeriGas Partners, LP) 2009–, Taminco Global Chemical Corporation 2012–, RPP Capital. *Address:* Ceva Logistics BV, Siriusdreef 20, PO Box 483, 2132 WT Hoofddorp, Netherlands (office). *Telephone:* (23) 568-3300 (office). *Fax:* (23) 568-3301 (office). *E-mail:* info@cevalogistics.com (office). *Website:* www.cevalogistics.com (office).

SCHLECKER, Anton; German retail executive; *CEO, Fa. Anton Schlecker;* b. 1944; m.; two c.; began career as apprentice butcher in father's co. 1965, built first self-service dept store in Ehingen 1967, opened first drugstore in Kirchheim 1975, began expanding into other European countries 1987, currently CEO Fa. Anton Schlecker. *Address:* Fa. Anton Schlecker, Talstrasse 12, 89579 Ehingen, Germany (office). *Telephone:* (73) 91 584-0 (office). *Fax:* (73) 91 584-300 (office). *Website:* www .schlecker.com (office).

SCHLESSINGER, Joseph, BS, MSc, PhD; American molecular biologist, biochemist and academic; *William H. Prusoff Professor and Chairman, Department of Pharmacology, School of Medicine, Yale University;* b. 26 March 1945, Topusko, Croatia; s. of Ehud Schlessinger and Avner Schlessinger; m. Dr Irit Lax; ed The Hebrew Univ., Jerusalem and The Weizmann Inst. of Science, Rehovot, Israel; Postdoctoral Assoc., Dept of Chem., School of Applied and Eng Physics, Cornell Univ., Ithaca, NY 1974–76; Visiting Scientist, Immunology Br., Nat. Cancer Inst., NIH, Bethesda, Md 1977–78; Sr Scientist, Dept of Chemical Immunology, The Weizmann Inst. of Science 1978–80, Assoc. Prof. 1980–85, Prof. 1985–91, The Ruth and Leonard Simon Prof. of Cancer Research, The Weizmann Inst. of Science 1985–91; Research Dir Rorer Biotechology, Inc., Rockville, Md and King of Prussia, Pa 1985–90; The Milton and Helen Kimmelman Prof. and Chair. Dept of Pharmacology, New York Univ. Medical Center 1990–2001; William H. Prusoff Prof. and Chair. Dept of Pharmacology, Yale Univ. School of Medicine, New Haven, Conn. 2001–; Founder SUGEN, Inc. 1991, Plexxikon 2000; Dir Cancer Biology Inst.; mem. Editorial Bd European Molecular Biology Organization (EMBO) Journal, Cell, Molecular Cell, Genes and Development, Molecular Biology of the Cell, Journal of Biological Chemistry, Cancer Research, Journal of Cell Biology, Growth Factors, Protein Engineering, Cell Growth and Differentiation, Structure; mem. EMBO 1982, NAS 2000, American Acad. of Arts and Sciences 2001, European Acad. of Sciences 2004, Inst. of Medicine, NAS 2005, Russian Acad. of Sciences 2006, Croatian Acad. of Sciences 2008; Hon. mem. Japanese Biochemical Soc. 1999; Michael Landau Prize for PhD Thesis 1973, Sara Leedy Prize 1980, Hestrin Prize 1983, Levinson Prize 1984, Keynote Presidential Lecturer, The Endocrine Soc. 1986, Lamport Lecturer, Univ. of Seattle 1993, E. Fisher Lecturer, Univ. of Geneva 1993, E.J. Cohn Lecturer, Harvard Univ. Medical School 1993, Randall Lecturer, Univ. of Pennsylvania 1994, Feigen Lecturer, Stanford Univ. Medical School 1994, Opening Keynote Lecturer, American Soc. for Biochemistry and Molecular Biology 1994, Deans Lecturer, Mount Sinai Medical School 1994, Harvey Lecturer, Rockefeller Univ. 1994, Antoine Lacassagne Prize 1995, Drew-Ciba Prize 1995, Opening Keynote Lecturer, Whitehead Inst. Symposium 1995, Howard Hughes Medical Inst. Symposium on Signal Transduction 1995, Sigma-Tau Lecturer 1995, Lindner Lecturer, The Weizmann Inst. of Science 1996, Burroughs Wellcome Lecturer, Indiana Univ. 1997, Juan March Lecturer 1998, 6th Ray A. and Robert L. Kroc Lecturer, Univ. of Massachusetts Medical School 1999, Bayer Lecturer, Univ. of California, Berkeley 1999, Distinguished Service Award, Miami Nature Biotechnology 1999, 16th Annual Kenneth F. Naidorf Memorial Lecturer, Columbia Univ. 2000, Distinguished Speakers Program, Univ. of Texas Health Science Center 2000, NIH Director's Lecturer 2000, The Taylor Prize 2000, Dan David Prize 2006, Inaugural Pfizer Lecturer, Univ. of Michigan 2006, Keith Porter Lecturer, ASCB San Diego 2006, NIH-WALS Lecturer 2008, Helen Coley-Nauts Lecturer, Moscow 2008, Medal of Danica Hrvatska Order (Croatia) 2009, AACR International Award for Cancer 2010, BBVA Foundation Frontiers of Knowledge Award 2014. *Publications:* more than 450 articles in scientific journals. *Address:* Department of Pharmacology, Yale University School of Medicine, Sterling Hall of Medicine, PO Box 208066, 333 Cedar Street, B-204, New Haven, CT 06520-8066, USA (office). *Telephone:* (203) 785-7395 (office). *Fax:* (203) 785-3879 (office). *E-mail:* joseph.schlessinger@yale.edu (office); Laura.copela@yale.edu (office). *Website:* info .med.yale.edu/pharm (office).

SCHLETTWEIN, Carl-Hermann Gustav (Calle), BSc, MSc; Namibian politician; *Minister of Finance;* b. 13 June 1954, Otjiwarongo, Otjozondjupa Region; ed Univ. of Stellenbosch; Researcher 1981–90; served as Perm. Sec. at various ministries including Ministry of Agric., Fisheries, Water and Rural Devt 1990–91, Ministry of Fisheries and Marine Resources 1991–93, Ministry of Youth and Sport 1993–96, Ministry of Labour 1996–2003, Ministry of Finance 2003–10; Deputy Minister of Finance 2010–12, Minister of Trade and Industry 2012–15, Minister of Finance 2015–; bd mem. Millennium Challenge Account 2010–; bd mem. numerous orgs including Namibian Black Empowerment Cttee, Fisheries Advisory Council, Namibia Regional Trust Fund, Nat. Council for Higher Educ., Luderitz Waterfront Devt Co., Namibia Sports Comm., Namibian Tender Bd, Diamond Bd of Namibia, Namibia Devt Corpn, Bank of Namibia; mem. Council and Senate, Univ. of Namibia; Most Excellent Order of the Eagle (2nd class) 2014. *Leisure interests:* photography, sport, outdoor activities, environment. *Address:* Ministry of Finance, Fiscus Bldg, John Meinert Street, PMB 13295, Windhoek, Namibia (office). *Telephone:* (61) 2099111 (office). *Fax:* (61) 227702 (office). *Website:* www .mof.gov.na (office).

SCHLIFSKE, John E., BA, MA; American business executive; *Chairman, President and CEO, Northwestern Mutual;* b. 27 March 1959, Milwaukee, Wis.; m.; six c.; ed Carleton Coll., Kellogg Grad. School of Man., Northwestern Univ.; joined Northwestern Mutual as an investment specialist 1987, held positions of increasing authority in Securities and Real Estate Depts, later Exec. Vice-Pres. Northwestern Mutual and mem. Man. Cttee, Exec. Vice-Pres.– Investment Products and Services 2004–08, Interim Pres. and CEO Russell Investment Co. (subsidiary) 2008–09, Interim Pres. Feb.–March 2009, Pres. Northwestern Mutual 2009–10, Chair., Pres. and CEO 2010–, mem. Bd of Trustees; Co-Chair. Milwaukee Succeeds 2011–; Dir Russell Investment Co.; mem. Bd, Froedtert and Community Health 2010–, Metropolitan Milwaukee Asscn of Commerce 2010–, Children's Hosp. of Wisconsin 2011–, Greater Milwaukee Cttee 2011–, Kohl's Department Stores 2011–. *Address:* Northwestern Mutual, 720 East Wisconsin Avenue, Milwaukee, WI 53202-4797, USA (office). *Telephone:* (414) 271-1444 (office). *E-mail:* info@northwesternmutual.com (office). *Website:* www .northwesternmutual.com (office).

SCHLINK, Bernhard; German judge, academic and writer; *Professor Emeritus of Public Law and Legal Philosophy, Humboldt University of Berlin;* b. 6 July 1944, Grossdornberg, North Rhine-Westphalia; s. of Prof. Dr Edmund Schlink; ed Heidelberg, Berlin, Darmstadt, Bielefeld and Freiburg Univs; Prof., Univ. of Bonn 1981–91; Judge, Constitutional Law Court of North Rhine-Westphalia, Münster 1987–2005; Prof., Univ. of Frankfurt 1991–92; Prof., Humboldt Univ. of Berlin 1992–; Visiting Prof. of Law, Benjamin Cardozo School of Law, Yeshiva Univ., New York 1994–; qualified as masseur in Calif.; began writing fiction in 1980s; Verdienstorden der Bundesrepublik Deutschland 2004; Die Literarische Welt Literary Prize 1999, Park Kyong-ni Prize (South Korea) 2014. *Publications include:* fiction: Selbs Justiz (with Walter Popp, trans. as Self's Punishment) 1987, Die Gordische Schleife 1988, Selbs Betrug (trans. as Self's Betrayal) 1992, Der Vorleser (trans. as The Reader) (Grinzane Cavour Prize 1997, Prix Laure Bataillon 1997, Hans Fallada Prize 1998, Evangelischer Buchpreis, German Asscn of

Protestant Libraries 2000) 1995, Liebesfluchten (short stories; trans. as Flights of Love) 2001, Selbs Mord (trans. as Self's Murder) 2005, Die Heimkehr (trans. as Homecoming) 2006, Das Wochenende (trans. as The Weekend) 2008, Guilt About the Past 2009, Summer Lies 2012, Die Frau auf der Treppe 2014; non-fiction: Weimar: A Jurisprudence of Crisis (with Arthur Jacobson), several books on constitutional law, fundamental separation of powers and admin. law. *E-mail:* schlink@rewi.hu-berlin.de (office). *Website:* schlink.rewi.hu-berlin.de (office).

SCHLISSEL, Mark S., BA, MD, PhD; American medical scientist, academic and university administrator; *President, University of Michigan;* b. 24 Nov. 1957, Brooklyn, NY; m. Monica Schwebs; four c.; ed Princeton Univ., Johns Hopkins Univ. School of Medicine; residency training in internal medicine at Hopkins Hosp.; postdoctoral research as Bristol-Myers Cancer Research Fellow, Whitehead Inst., MIT; began ind. research career at Johns Hopkins Univ. School of Medicine 1991, earned several awards and fellowships; Assoc. Prof., Dept of Molecular and Cell Biology, Univ. of California, Berkeley 1999–2002, Prof. 2002–11, Chair. Grad. Admission Cttee 2001, Vice-Chair. Dept of Molecular and Cell Biology 2002–07, Dean of Biological Sciences 2008–11; Provost, Brown Univ. 2011–14, Chair. Academic Priorities Cttee, Univ. Resource Council; Pres. Univ. of Michigan 2014–; mem. Immunobiology Study Section, NIH 2002–04, Chair. 2004–06; mem. Scientific Review Bd, Howard Hughes Medical Inst.; mem. American Asscn of Immunologists 1992, American Soc. of Clinical Investigators 1998. *Publications:* about 100 papers in professional journals on developmental biology of B lymphocytes. *Address:* Office of the President, University of Michigan, 2074 Fleming Administration Building, 503 Thompson Street, Ann Arbor, MI 41809-1340, USA (office). *Telephone:* (734) 764-6270 (office). *Fax:* (734) 936-3529 (office). *E-mail:* presoff@umich.edu (office). *Website:* president.umich.edu (office).

SCHLÖGL, Herwig, PhD; German government official and international organization official; b. 17 Aug. 1942; ed Univ. of Marburg; mem. German Perm. Representation to European Econ. Union, Brussels 1969–72; mem. staff, Industrial Policy Div., Ministry of Econs 1972–76, Head of Foreign Econ. Affairs Div. of Industry Dept 1980–84, Head Div. for Foreign Econ. Policy, Export Promotion 1984–96; Head, Econs Dept, German-American Chamber of Commerce, New York 1976–80; Deputy Dir-Gen. for Trade Policy, Bonn 1996–98; Deputy Sec.-Gen. OECD, Paris 1998–2006. *Publications include:* books and articles on competition policy and trade issues.

SCHLÖGL, Robert, PhD; German chemist; *Director, Fritz Haber Institute and Institute for Chemical Energy Conversion Max-Planck-Gesellschaft;* b. 23 Feb. 1954, Munich; ed Ludwig Maximilian Univ. of Munich; Full Prof. of Inorganic Chemistry, J.W. Goethe-Universität 1989–94; Dir Fritz-Haber-Institut der Max-Planck-Gesellschaf 1994–, Vice-Chair. Chemisch-Physikalisch-Technische Sektion des Wissenschaftlichen Rates der Max-Planck-Gesellschaft 2002–03, Chair. 2004–06; Founding Dir Max Planck Inst. for Chemical Energy Conversion 2011–; mem. Berlin-Brandenburgischen Akademie der Wissenschaften 1995–, AAAS, ACS, American Carbon Soc., Gesellschaft für chemischeTechnik und Biotechnologie m.b.H., Deutsche Bunsengesellschaft, Deutsche Gesellschaft für Elektronenmikroskopie, Deutsche Gesellschaft für Erdöl, Erdgas und Kohle, Deutsche Physikalische Gesellschaft, Freunde der Hebräischen Universität Jerusalem, Gesellschaft deutscher Chemiker, The Electrochemical Soc., ICHEME Working Party on Chemical Reaction Eng; Tetelman Fellow, Yale Univ. 2004, Fellow, Royal Soc. of Chemistry, UK 2005; Hon. Prof. Technische Universität Berlin 1994–, Hon. Prof. Humboldt-Universität zu Berlin 1998–, Hon. Prof. Universität Duisburg-Essen 2012–, Hon. Prof. Ruhr-Universität Bochum 2015–; Schunck Award for Innovative Materials 1989, Otto Bayer Prize 1994, Dechema Medal 2010, Max Planck Communitas Award 2013, Alwin Mittasch Award 2015, Innovation Prize State North-Rhine Westphalia 2016. *Achievements include:* registered inventor for more than 20 families of patents and/or patent applications. *Publications include:* Chemical Energy Storage 2012; more than 1,000 publications. *Address:* Fritz Haber Institute of the Max Planck Society, Department of Inorganic Chemistry, Faradayweg 4-6, D-14195 Berlin (office); Max Planck Institute for Chemical Energy Conversion, Stiftstr. 34-36, 45470 Mülheim an der Ruhr, Germany (office). *Telephone:* (30) 84134400 (Berlin) (office); (20) 83063595 (office). *Fax:* (30) 84134401 (Berlin) (office). *E-mail:* acsek@fhi-berlin.mpg.de (office); robert .schloegl@cec.mpg.de (office). *Website:* www.fhi-berlin.mpg.de (office); www.mpg .de/5869732/chemische_energiekonversion_wissM3 (office).

SCHLÖNDORFF, Volker; German film director; b. 1939, Wiesbaden; m. Margarethe von Trotta 1971 (divorced 1991); m. 2nd Angelika Schlöndorff; one d.; ed Institut des Hautes Etudes Cinematographique (IDHEC), Paris, France; has directed numerous cinema and TV films; mem. German PEN Centre; Officier, Ordre Nat. de la Légion d'Honneur 2002; Prize of the Int. Film Critics, Cannes 1966, Konrad-Wolf-Prize 1997, Blue Angel Award for Best European Film 2000. *Films include:* Der junge Törless, Mord und Totschlag, Michael Kohlhaas, Der plötzliche Reichtum der armen Leute von Kombach, Baal, Die Moral der Ruth Halbfass, Strohfeuer, Die Ehegattin, Übernachtung in Tirol, Die verlorene Ehre der Katharina Blum, Die Blechtrommel (The Tin Drum) (Golden Palm of Cannes, Acad. Award for Best Foreign Film) 1979, Die Fälschung 1981, Circle of Deceit 1982, Eine Liebe von Swann (Swann in Love) 1984, Death of a Salesman 1985, The Handmaid's Tale 1989, Voyager 1991, The Ogre 1996, Palmetto 1997, Die Stille nach dem Schuss 2000, Ten Minutes Older: The Cello (segment) 2002, Der Neunte Tag (The Ninth Day) 2004, Strike 2006, Ulzhan 2007, Calm at Sea 2011, Diplomacy 2014. *Television includes:* Death of a Salesman 1985, Enigma: Eine uneingestandene Liebe 2005, Billy Wilder Speaks 2006.

SCHLÜTER, Poul Holmskov, LLB; Danish lawyer and fmr politician; b. 3 April 1929, Tønder; s. of Johannes Schlüter; m. 1st Lisbeth Schlüter 1979 (died 1988); two s. one d.; m. 2nd Anne Marie Vessel Schlüter 1989; ed Univs of Århus and Copenhagen; barrister and Supreme Court Attorney; Leader of Conservative Youth Movt (KU) 1944, Nat. Leader 1951; Del. to Int. Congress of World Asscn of Youth 1951, 1954; Chair. Young Conservatives, mem. Exec. Cttee Conservative Party 1952–55, 1971, Nat. Chair. Jr Chamber 1961, Vice-Pres. Jr Chamber Int. 1962; mem. Folketing (Parl.) 1964–94, Prime Minister of Denmark 1982–93; Chair. Jt Danish Consultative Council on UN 1966–68; MP Foreign Affairs Cttee 1968, Chair. 1982; mem. Council of Europe 1971–74; fmr Chair. Conservative People's Party 1974–77, 1981–93; Chair. Danish Del. to Nordic Council and mem.

Presiding Cttee 1978–79; Dir Nat. Cleaning Group 1993, Int. Service System (ISS); Co-founder Danish Centre for Political Studies 2004.

SCHMID, Samuel; Swiss lawyer and politician; b. 8 Jan. 1947; m.; three s.; ed Univ. of Bern; with Swiss Fed. Finance Admin 1973; joined legal practice, Bern 1973; independent advocate and notary, Lyss 1978–; solicitor with Kellerhals & Pnrs LLC, Bern 1998–; adviser to econ. and trade asscns; local councillor 1972–74, Pres. Municipality of Rueti 1974–82; mem. Berni Greater Council 1982–93, Chair. Cttee for new Berni State Canton Constitution, mem. Finance Cttee; mem. Nat. Council 1994–98; Pres. Swiss People's Party (Schweizerische Volkspartei) Parl. Group of the Presidential Election Council 1998–99, currently mem. Conservative Democratic Party (Bürgerlich-Demokratische Partei); mem. Comm. for Foreign Policy 1999– (also Vice-Pres.), Comm. for Econs and Deliveries, Comm. for Social Security and Health, Nat. Political Comm.; elected mem. Upper House of Parl. 2001; mem. Fed. Council 2001–08 (resgnd), Head of Fed. Dept of Defence, Civil Protection and Sport 2001–08; Vice-Pres. Swiss Confed. 2004, Pres. 2005; Pres. Berni Trade Asscn 1990; mem. Exec. Cttee Swiss Trade Asscn 1991; Col, Commdt of infantry regiment 1993–96, Commdt Stv F Div. 3 1998–99.

SCHMID, Walter Jürgen, DrIur; German lawyer and diplomatist; b. 1946; ed Univ. of Tübingen, studied law at Munich and Aix-en-Provence; served in mil. 1966–67; jr court lawyer 1973–75; Attaché, Minister of Foreign Affairs 1976–78, Adviser to Minister of State 1978–79; served in embassies in Montevideo 1979–82, Ankara 1982–85; Senate Dir, Senatskanzlei Freie and Hamburg 1986–91; Amb. to Guinea 1992–94; served at Royal Coll. of Defence Studies, London, UK 1995; Disarmament Dept, Ministry of Foreign Affairs 1996–2000, Deputy Rep. for Disarmament and Arms Control 2000–03, Commr for Disarmament and Arms Control 2003–05; Amb. to Russia 2005–10, to the Holy See (Vatican City) 2010–11. *Address:* Federal Ministry of Foreign Affairs, 11013 Berlin, Germany (office). *Telephone:* (30) 5000-0 (office). *Fax:* (30) 18173402 (office). *E-mail:* poststelle@ auswaertiges-amt.de (office). *Website:* www.auswaertiges-amt.de (office).

SCHMIDBAUR, Hubert, Dr rer. nat; German chemist, academic and consultant; *Professor Emeritus, Technische Universität München;* b. 31 Dec. 1934, Landsberg; s. of Johann B. Schmidbaur and Katharina S. Ehelechner; m. Rose-Marie Fukas; one s. one d.; ed Univ. of Munich; Asst Prof., Univ. of Munich 1960–64; Assoc. Prof., Univ. of Marburg 1964–69; Prof., Univ. of Würzburg 1969–73; Prof. of Chem. and Head of Dept, Tech. Univ. of Munich 1973–2002, Dean, Faculty of Science 1983–86, Prof. Emer. 2002–; Assoc. Prof., Univ. of Stellenbosch, SA 2002–06, Nat. Univ. of Singapore 2008, King Abdulaziz Univ., Jeddah, Saudi Arabia 2012–; mem. Göttingen, Leopoldina, Bavarian and Finnish Acads, Acatech, Senate, German Science Foundation; Bundesverdienstkreuz 1st Class 1991, Maximiliansorden für Wissenschaft & Kunst 2010; Dr hc (Westfälische Wilhelms-Universität Münster) 2005; F. S. Kipping Award, ACS 1974, A. Stock Prize, German Chemical Soc. 1982, G. W. Leibniz-Preis, Deutsche Forschungsgemeinschaft 1986, Dwyer Memorial Medal, Univ. of New South Wales 1986, J. C. Bailar Medal, Univ. of Illinois 1987, Centenary Medal, RSC 1991, Ludwig Mond Medal, RSC 1994, Wacker Silikon Preis 1996, Bonner Chemie-preis 1998, Birch Medal, ANU 1999, Blaise Pascal Medal in Chem., European Acad. of Sciences 2014. *Publications include:* about 850, including books, monographs and scientific papers on inorganic, metalorganic and analytical chem. *Address:* Technische Universität München, Department Chemie, Lichtenbergstrasse 4, 85747 Garching (office); Königsbergerstr. 36, 85748 Garching, Germany (home). *Telephone:* (89) 28913130 (office). *Fax:* (89) 28913125 (office). *E-mail:* h.schmidbaur@lrz.tum.de (office). *Website:* aac.anorg.chemie.tu -muenchen.de (office).

SCHMIDT, Andreas; German singer (baritone) and academic; *Kammersänger Professor, Hochschule für Musik und Theater, Munich;* b. 30 June 1960, Düsseldorf; m. Jeanne Pascale 2003; two s. four d.; ed studied piano, organ, conducting in Düsseldorf, singing in Düsseldorf and Berlin; youngest mem. Deutsche Oper Berlin 1983; debut Hamburg State Opera 1985, Munich State Opera 1985, Covent Garden London 1986, Vienna State Opera 1988, Geneva Opera 1989, Salzburg Festival 1989, Aix-en-Provence Festival 1991, Metropolitan New York 1991, Edin. Festival 1991, Paris Bastille 1992, Paris Garnier 1993, Glyndebourne Festival 1994, State Opera Berlin 1995, Amsterdam Opera 1995, Bayreuth Festival 1996; has sung with major orchestras, including Berlin, Geneva, Vienna, Munich, Hamburg, London, Paris, Rome, Amsterdam, Copenhagen, Stockholm, Helsinki, New York, Israel Philharmonic orchestras, Cincinnati, Cleveland, Chicago, San Franciso and Philadelphia Symphony orchestras, La Scala, Milan, and with conductors including Bernstein, Solti, Levine, Barenboim, Sinopoli, Thielemann, Conlon, Eschenbach, Masur, Nagano and others; fmr Prof., Hochschule für Musik 'Carl Maria von Weber', Dresden; Prof., Hochschule für Musik und Theater, Munich 2010–; Hon. mem. Richard-Wagner-Verband; awarded title Kammersänger, Hansestadt Hamburg 1997; First Prize, Deutscher Musikwettbewerb, several German and int. awards and prizes. *Recordings include:* more than 130 CDs. *Leisure interests:* fly-fishing, golf, literature, art. *Address:* c/o Hartmut Haase, Artists Management, Aalgrund 8, 31275 Lehrte, Germany (office). *Telephone:* (5175) 953232 (office). *Fax:* (5175) 953233 (office). *E-mail:* artists@t-online.de (office). *Website:* www.artists-haase.de (office).

SCHMIDT, Benno C., Jr; American academic and university administrator; *Chairman, Avenues: The World School;* b. 20 March 1942, New York; s. of Benno Charles Schmidt, Sr and Martha Chastain; m. 2nd Helen Cutting Whitney 1980; one d. (one s. one d. by previous marriage); ed Yale Coll. and Yale Law School; clerk to US Supreme Court Chief Justice Earl Warren 1966–67; with US Dept of Justice 1967–69; mem. Faculty, Columbia Univ. Law School 1969–86, Harlan Fiske Stone Prof. of Constitutional Law 1982, Dean 1984–86; Pres. and Prof. of Law, Yale Univ. 1986–92; Pres. and CEO The Edison Project (now Edison Schools) 1992–98, also Chair.; Chair. Avenues: The World School, New York 2011–; Chair. Nations Acad. 2007–, Council on Aid to Educ.; Chair. Bd of Trustees, CUNY; Dir Nat. Humanities Center, Chapel Hill, NC 1985–; mem. Council on Foreign Relations, The American Acad. of Arts and Sciences; Trustee, Ewing Marion Kauffman Foundation 2007– (interim Pres. and CEO 2012); Hon. Master of Bench, Gray's Inn 1988, Hon. AO 1991. *Publications include:* Freedom of the Press versus Public Access 1976, The Judiciary and Responsible Government 1910–1921 (with A. M. Bickel) 1984; papers on constitutional law, freedom of the press and first amendment issues. *Address:* Avenues: The World School, 11 East 26th Street, 17th Floor, New York,

NY 10010-1420, USA (office). *Telephone:* (212) 935-5000 (office). *Fax:* (646) 625-7600 (office). *Website:* www.avenues.org (office).

SCHMIDT, Brian Paul, AC, BS, AM, PhD, FRS, FAA; American/Australian astronomer and academic; *Australian Research Council Laureate Fellow, Distinguished Professor and Vice-Chancellor, Australian National University;* b. 24 Feb. 1967, Missoula, Mont.; s. of Dana Charles Schmidt and Donna Pentz Schmidt; m. Jennifer Margaret Gordon; two s.; ed Univ. of Arizona, Harvard Univ.; Post-doctoral Fellow, ANU 1993–94, Post-doctoral Fellow, ANU Mount Stromlo and Siding Spring Observatories 1995–96, Research Fellow 1997–99, Fellow, Research School of Astronomy and Astrophysics 1999–2002, Australian Research Council Professorial Fellow 2003–05, Australian Research Council Fed. Fellow 2005–09, Australian Research Council Laureate Fellow and Distinguished Prof. 2009–, Vice-Chancellor of ANU 2016–, Scientific Leader, SkyMapper Telescope and Southern Sky Survey; Chair. LOC and SOC of Astronomical Soc. of Australia's AGM 2002, Australian Time Allocation Cttee (Gemini/AAT/UK-Schmidt) 2002–03, Australia Telesope Nat. Facility Time Allocation Cttee 2002–04, Australian Nat. Acad. LOFAR Working Group 2003, Australian Decade Plan Working Group on Int. Facilities 2004; mem. Major Nat. Research Facility Selection Panel 2001, Council of Astronomical Soc. of Australia 2001–03, Australian Square Kilometre Array Steering Cttee 2001–, Anglo Australian Telescope Bd 2004–; Dir (non-exec.), Astronomy Australia Ltd 2007–; mem. Australian Decadal Working Group on Int. Facilities, Mid Term Review of the Australian Astronomy Decadal Plan, Bd of Australian Wine Research Inst. 2013–; Fellow, Japanese Soc. for the Promotion of Science 1999, NAS 2008; Glenn C. Purviance Scholarship, Univ. of Arizona 1988, Vesto Slipher Scholarship, Univ. of Arizona 1988–89, Most Outstanding Student in Physics, Univ. of Arizona 1989, Danforth Award for Excellence in Teaching, Harvard Univ. 1991, NASA Grad. Student Researchers Program Fellowship Recipient 1992–93, Science Magazine's 'Breakthrough of the Year' 1998, Bok Prize for Outstanding Astronomical Thesis, Harvard Univ. 2000, Inaugural Malcolm McIntosh Prize, Australian Govt 2000, Pawsey Medal, Australian Acad. of Sciences 2001, Harley Wood Lecturer, Astronomical Soc. of Australia 2001, Burbidge Lecturer, Auckland Astronomical Soc. 2001, Inaugural Oliphant Lecturer, Australian Acad. of Science 2001, Vainu Bappu Medal, Astronomical Soc. of India 2002, Dean's Lecturer, Univ. of Western Australia 2004, Australian Academy of Science 50th Anniversary Lecture 2004, Bulletin Magazine's Scientist of the Year 2004, Marc Aaronson Memorial Lecturer 2005, Shaw Prize in Astronomy (co-recipient) 2006, Gurevitch Lecture, Portland State Univ. 2007, Niels Bohr Lecturer, Copenhagen 2007, Gruber Prize for Cosmology (co-recipient) 2007, Sackler Lecturer, Princeton Univ. 2008, ISI Most Cited Australian in Space Sciences 1997–2007 2008, Oxford Univ. Halley Lecturer 2010, Nobel Prize in Physics (co-recipient) 2011, Diract Medal 2012, Breakthrough Prize in Fundamental Physics (co-recipient) 2015. *Publications include:* more than 110 scientific papers in professional journals on observational cosmology, studies of supernovae, gamma ray bursts, large surveys, photometry and calibration. *Leisure interest:* winemaker and vigneron. *Address:* Research School of Astronomy and Astrophysics, ANU Mount Stromlo Observatory, via Cotter Road, Weston Creek, ACT 2611, Australia (office). *Telephone:* (2) 6125-8042 (office). *Fax:* (2) 6125-0260 (office). *E-mail:* denise.sturgess@anu.edu.au (Sec.); brian.schmidt@mso.anu.edu.au (office). *Website:* www.mso.anu.edu.au/~brian (office).

SCHMIDT, Chauncey Everett, BS, MBA; American banker and business executive; b. 7 June 1931, Oxford, Ia; s. of Walter F. Schmidt and Vilda Saxton; m. Anne Garrett McWilliams 1954 (deceased); one s. two d.; ed US Naval Acad., Harvard Graduate School of Business Admin.; with First Nat. Bank of Chicago 1959–75, Vice-Pres. 1965, Gen. Man., London 1966, Gen. Man. for Europe, Middle East and Africa 1968, Sr Vice-Pres. 1969–72, Exec. Vice-Pres. 1972, Vice-Chair. 1973, Pres. 1974–75; Chair. and CEO Bank of Calif. 1976–84; Chair., Pres. and CEO BanCal Tri-State Corpn 1976–84; apptd Chair. Cybernet Software Systems 2004; Founder and Chair. C. E.Schmidt and Assocs Inc.; mem. Bd of Dirs Docuton, Barry Financial, UBS Asset Man., Amfac Ltd, Calif. Bankers Clearing House Asscn, Calif. Roundtable, Bay Area Council; mem. Exec. Bd San Francisco Bay Area Council of Boy Scouts of America; mem. Bd of Govs San Francisco Symphony; mem. Fed. Advisory Council of Fed. Reserve System, Advisory Council of Japan-US Econ. Relations, SRI International, Council, Int. Monetary Conf., Asscn of Reserve City Bankers, American Bankers Asscn; mem. Advisory Bd Pacific Rim Bankers Program. *Address:* 40 Why Worry Farm, Woodside, CA 94062, USA (home).

SCHMIDT, Christian, PhD, DSc (Econ), PhD; French economist and academic; *President, European Neuroeconomics Association;* b. 20 July 1938, Neuilly-sur-Seine; s. of Paul Schmidt and Jeanne Loriot; m. Marie-Pierre de Cossè Brissac 1988; ed Facultés de lettres, droit, sciences, Institut d'etudes politiques, Paris, Institut des hautes études de défense nationale, École des hautes études en sciences sociales, Acad. of Int. Law, The Hague; Research Asst Inst. of Applied Econ. Sciences Laboratoire Coll. de France 1964–67; Asst La Sorbonne 1967–70; Chargé de Mission Forecasting Admin. Ministry of Finances 1970–72; f. Dir Econ. Perspectives 1969–86; Asst Dir French Inst. of War Studies 1980–82; Pres. Charles Gide Asscn for the Study of Econ. Thought 1981–90; Consultant on Econ. Aspects of Disarmament UN 1980; Prof. of Econs, Univ. of Paris IX (Paris Dauphine) 1983–2012, Prof. Emer. 2012–, Dir Lab. of Econs and Sociology of Defence Orgs (LESOD) 1984–2005; Founder and Pres. Asscn française des économistes de défense 1981–2001, Int. Defence Econ. Asscn 1985–; Co-Dir (Research Group) CNRS 1990–; Chair. Scientific Council of European Soc. of Econ. Thought; Pres. European Neuroeconomics Asscn 2011–; mem. Council French Econs Asscn 2000–04, Soc. d'Economie Politique 2000–; mem. various editorial bds; Officier, Légion d'honneur; Prix de L'institut (Acad. des Sciences Morales et Politiques) 1986, 1993, Prix Risques 2010. *Publications include:* Conséquences Economiques et Sociales de la Course aux Armaments 1983, Essai sur l'Economie Ricardienne 1984, La Semantique Economique en Question 1985, Peace, Defence and Economic Analysis 1987, The Economics of Military Expenditures 1989, Penser la Guerre, Penser l'Economie 1991, Game Theory and International Relations 1994, Uncertainty and Economic Thought 1996, Game Theory and International Relations (co-ed.) 1996, The Rational Foundations of Economic Behaviour (co-ed.) 1996, La Theorie des Jeux: Essai d'Interpretation 2001, Game Theory and Economic Analysis 2002, Neuroeconomie: Comment les neurosciences transforment l'analyse economique 2010, Comprendre nos interactions: une perspective neuroéconomique 2014; numerous articles in learned journals. *Leisure interests:* theatre, opera. *Address:* Université Paris Dauphine, Place du Maréchal de Lattre de Tassigny, 75775 Paris Cedex 16 (office); 109 rue de Grenelle, 75007 Paris, France (home). *Telephone:* 1-45-51-01-78 (home); 6-07-62-89-51 (mobile). *Fax:* 1-45-51-22-70 (home). *E-mail:* christian.schmidt@dauphine.fr (office); schmidtchristian.fr@gmail.com (home).

SCHMIDT, Eric E., BS, MS, PhD; American computer industry executive; *Executive Chairman, Alphabet Inc.;* b. 27 April 1955, Washington, DC; m. Wendy Schmidt; two c.; ed Princeton Univ., Univ. of California, Berkeley; began career with Bell Labs and Zilog; mem. Research Staff Computer Science Lab., Xerox Palo Alto Research Center (PARC) 1979–83; Software Man. Sun Microsystems 1983–84, Software Dir 1984–85, Vice-Pres. Software Products 1985–88, Vice-Pres. Gen. Systems Group 1988–91, Chief Tech. Officer 1994–97, Pres. Sun Tech. Enterprises 1991–94; Chair. and CEO Novell Inc. 1997–2001; CEO Google Inc. 2001–11, Exec. Chair. 2001–04, 2007–15, Exec. Chair. Alphabet Inc. (newly formed holding co. containing Google and new ventures) 2015–; co-Chair. World Econ. Forum Annual Meeting, Davos 2015; mem. Bd of Dirs Siebel Systems Inc., Integrated Archive Systems, Tilion, Apple Computer Inc. 2006–09 (resgnd), Khan Acad. 2012–, The Economist 2013–; Chair. New America Foundation 2008–; mem. Pres. Obama's Council of Advisors on Science and Tech., Prime Minister's Advisory Council (UK); Trustee, Inst. for Advanced Study, Princeton, NJ 2008–; mem. IEEE, Asscn of Computing Machinery, Nat. Acad. of Eng 2006; Fellow, American Acad. of Arts and Sciences 2007. *Publications:* The New Digital Age: Transforming Nations, Businesses and Our Lives (co-author) 2013, How Google Works (co-author) 2014. *Address:* Alphabet Inc., 1600 Amphitheatre Parkway, Mountain View, CA 94043, USA (office). *Telephone:* (650) 330-0100 (office). *Fax:* (650) 618-1499 (office). *Website:* www.google.com (office); plus.google.com/+EricSchmidt/posts.

SCHMIDT, Klaus, PhD; German economist and academic; *Professor, Faculty of Economics, Ludwig-Maximilians-Universität München;* b. 16 June 1961, Koblenz; m. Monika Schnitzer; three d.; ed Univs of Marburg, Hamburg and Bonn and London School of Econs, UK; Teaching Asst, Univ. of Bonn 1987–88, 1989–91; Visiting Asst Prof., MIT, USA 1992; Asst Prof., Univ. of Bonn 1993–95; Full Prof. of Econs, Ludwig-Maximilians-Universität München 1995–, Dean, Faculty of Econs 2002–04, Dean of Research 2009–; Visiting Prof., Stanford Univ. 2000, Yale Univ. 2004–05, Univ. of California, Berkeley 2009, Harvard Univ. 2013; Ed. European Economic Review 1999–2002; Dir Review of Economic Studies Ltd 2001–03; Assoc. Ed. RAND Journal of Economics 1995–2009, Journal of the European Economic Association 2004–11, Management Science 2011–15; Sr Ed. Economic Policy 2015–; mem. Editorial Bd Review of Economic Studies 1993–2003; Fellow, European Economic Asscn 2008–, Econometric Soc. 2010–; mem. Advisory Bd German Federal Minister for Economics and Technology 2012–; mem. Berlin-Brandenburg Acad. of Sciences 2005–; mem. Scientific Council of Social Science Research Center Berlin (WZB) 2010–; Gossen Prize, German Econ. Asscn 2001, Prize of the Berlin-Brandenburg Acad. of Sciences 2001. *Address:* Department of Economics, Ludwig-Maximilians-Universität München, Room 08, Ludwigstr. 28, 80539 Munich, Germany (office). *Telephone:* (89) 21802250 (office). *Fax:* (89) 21803510 (office). *E-mail:* klaus.schmidt@lmu.de (office). *Website:* www.vwl.uni-muenchen.de (office).

SCHMIDT, Maarten, PhD, ScD; Dutch astronomer and academic; *Francis L. Moseley Professor Emeritus of Astronomy, California Institute of Technology;* b. 28 Dec. 1929, Groningen; s. of W. Schmidt and A. W. Haringhuizen; m. Cornelia J. Tom 1955; three d.; ed Univs of Groningen and Leiden, Yale Univ., USA; Scientific Officer, Univ. of Leiden Observatory 1949–59; Carnegie Fellow, Mount Wilson Observatory, Pasadena 1956–58; Assoc. Prof., Calif. Inst. of Tech. 1959–64, Prof. of Astronomy 1964–81, Inst. Prof. 1981–87, Francis L. Moseley Prof. 1987–96, Francis L. Moseley Prof. Emer. 1996–, Exec. Officer for Astronomy 1972–75, Chair. Div. of Physics, Math. and Astronomy 1976–78, Dir Hale Observatories 1978–80; Pres. American Astronomical Soc. 1984–86; mem. Norwegian Acad. of Science and Letters; Helen B. Warner Prize 1964, Rumford Award, American Acad. of Arts and Sciences 1968, Karl Schwarzschild Medal 1968, Jansky Prize, Nat. Radio Astronomy Observatory 1979, Royal Astronomy Soc. Gold Medal 1980, James Craig Watson Medal, NAS 1991, Bruce Medal 1992, Kavli Prize 2008. *Achievements include:* discovered large red shifts in spectra of quasi-stellar radio sources (quasars). *Leisure interest:* classical music. *Address:* California Institute of Technology, 288 Cahill Center for Astronomy and Astrophysics, 1216 East California Boulevard, Pasadena, CA 91125, USA (office). *Telephone:* (626) 395-4671 (office). *E-mail:* mxs@astro.caltech.edu (office). *Website:* www.astro.caltech.edu (office).

SCHMIDT, Renate; German fmr politician; b. 12 Dec. 1943, Hanau/Main; m. 2nd Hasso von Henninges 1998; three c.; worked as programmer, systems analyst and mem. of works cttee of mail-order co.; mem. SPD 1972–, Chair. SPD Bavaria 1991–2000, Deputy Chair. SPD 1997; mem. Bundestag (Parl.) 1980–94, 2005–09; Deputy Chair. SPD Parl. Party in Bundestag (Chair. of Equal Rights for Woman and Man working group) 1987–90, Vice-Pres. Bundestag 1990–94; directly elected mem. of Parl. for Nuremberg North in Bavarian Landtag; Chair. SPD Parl. Party in Bavarian Landtag 1994–2002; Federal Minister for Family Affairs, Senior Citizens, Women and Youth 2002–05; currently Ombudsman for Data Protection and Anti-Corruption, Vodafone D2; Pres. Bavarian Red Cross 1993–2002, Deutscher Familienverband May–Oct. 2002, Zentralstelle für Recht und Schutz der Kriegsdienstverweigerer aus Gewissensgründen e.V. 2002; mem. HBV, AWO, Socialist Youth Germany 'Die Falken', Bund Naturschutz, AIDS-Hilfe, Bd of Trustees of the Deutscher Kinderschutzbund; Chair. Nestle Future Forum on Nutrition; Consultant for Roche on Rheumatoid Arthritis. *Address:* Rohrmattenstr. 18, 90480 Nuremburg, Germany. *Fax:* (911) 407641. *E-mail:* renate.schmidt@vodafone.com. *Website:* www.renateschmidt.de.

SCHMIDT-HOLTZ, Rolf; German lawyer and music company executive; *Co-founder and Chairman, Just Software AG;* b. 31 Aug. 1948, Martinsreuth; ed Univs of Erlangen and Kiel, Germany; journalist, television correspondent, Ed.-in-Chief and Publisher, magazines, newspapers; television exec.; Ed.-in-Chief WDR (German public broadcaster) 1986–88; Publr Gruner + Jahr's Stern news magazine 1988, Ed.-in-Chief 1990, mem. Exec. Bd Gruner + Jahr 1989–94; CEO UFA (Bertelsmann TV c.) 1994, CEO CLT-UFA (after merger with CLT) 1997, then merger with Pearson Television to form RTL Group 2000; Chair. and CEO BMG 2001–04, Non-Exec. Chair. Sony BMG (following merger with Sony Music Entertainment) 2004–06, Chair. Man. Bd and CEO 2006–11; Co-founder and Chair. Just Software AG; mem. Exec. Bd Bertelsmann SE & Co. 2000–06, Bertelsmann Stiftung Bd of Trustees 2005–; Co-Chair. Advisory Bd Art Dirs Club Inst., Berlin 2004–; mem. Supervisory Bd L. Possehl & Co. MbH 2008–, Gruner & Jahr AG, Druck-und Verlagshaus; mem. Bd of Dirs RTL Group SA 2002–.

SCHMIDT-JORTZIG, Edzard, DrIur; German academic, politician and lawyer; *Of Counsel, Schmidt-Jortzig Petersen Penzlin;* b. 8 Oct. 1941, Berlin; s. of Rear-Adm. Friedrich-Traugott Schmidt and Carla Freiin von Frydag; m. Marion von Arnim 1968; two d. two s.; ed Univs of Bonn, Lausanne and Kiel; early career as municipal lawyer; Asst Lecturer, then Prof., Univ. of Göttingen 1977; Prof. of Public Law, Univs of Münster and Kiel 1977–2007, Head of Law Dept, Univ. of Kiel 1992; judge, Higher Admin. Courts of Lüneburg and Schleswig and at Constitutional Court of Saxony 1989–94; mem. Bundestag (FDP) 1994–2002; Fed. Minister of Justice 1996–98; Chair. German Ethical Council (Deutscher Ethikrat) 2008–12; currently Of Counsel, Schmidt-Jortzig Petersen Penzlin, Hamburg; Bundesverdienstkreuz 2002. *Publications include:* Zur Verfassungsmässigkeit von Kreisumlagesätzen 1977, Kommunale Organisationshoheit 1979, Die Einrichtungsgarantien der Verfassung 1979, Kommunalrecht 1982, Gemeindliches Eigentum an Meereshäfen 1985, Reformüberlegungen für die Landessatzung Schleswig-Holstein 1988, Handbuch des Kommunalen Finanz und Haushaltsrechts (with J. Makswit) 1991, Staatsangehörigkeit im Wandel 1997, Wann ist der Mensch tot? 1999, Rechtsfragen der Biomedizin 2003. *Address:* Schmidt-Jortzig Petersen Penzlin, Rechtsanwälte Partnerschaftsgesellschaft, Alstertor 9, 20095 Hamburg, Germany (office). *Telephone:* (40) 3095496 (office). *Fax:* (40) 309549650 (office). *E-mail:* info@sjpp.de (office). *Website:* www.sjpp.de (office); www.uni-kiel.de/oeffrecht/schmidt-jortzig (office).

SCHMITT, Allison Rodgers; American swimmer; b. 7 June 1990, Pittsburgh, Pa; d. of Ralph Schmitt and Gail Schmitt; started swimming at the age of nine, four-time champion in 200 and 500-yard freestyle swimming events, Nat. Collegiate Athletic Asscn (NCAA); trained at North Baltimore Aquatic Club with Michael Phelps; bronze medal, 4x200m freestyle relay, qualified to semifinals in 200m freestyle, Beijing Olympics 2008; silver medal, 200m freestyle, 4x200m freestyle relay, World Aquatics Championships 2009; gold medal, 200m and 400m freestyle, Duel in the Pool, Manchester 2009; gold medal, 200m freestyle, 4x200m freestyle relay, finished fourth in 400m freestyle, Pan Pacific Championships 2010; gold medal, 200m freestyle, USA Nat. Championships 2010; gold medal, 4x200m freestyle relay, World Aquatics Championships 2011; gold medal, 200m and 400m freestyle, Santa Clara Int. Grand Prix 2011; gold medal, 200m freestyle (Olympic Record), 4x100m medley relay, 4x200m freestyle relay, silver medal, 400m freestyle, bronze medal, 4x100m freestyle relay, London Olympics 2012; attends Univ. of Georgia; mem. Club Wolverine. *Address:* c/o Club Wolverine, PO Box 130229, Ann Arbor, MI 48113, USA. *Website:* swimallison.com.

SCHMITT, Harrison H., BS, PhD; American geologist, business executive, fmr politician and fmr astronaut; b. 3 July 1935, Santa Rita, NM; s. of Harrison A. Schmitt and Ethel Hagan Schmitt; m. Teresa Fitzgibbons 1985; ed California Inst. of Tech., Univ. of Oslo, Norway and Harvard Univ.; Fulbright Fellowship 1957–58, Kennecott Fellowship in Geology 1958–59, Harvard Fellowship 1959–60, Harvard Travelling Fellowship 1960, Parker Travelling Fellowship 1961–62, NSF Postdoctoral Fellowship, Dept of Geological Sciences, Harvard 1963–64; has done geological work for Norwegian Geological Survey, Oslo, for US Geological Survey, New Mexico and Montana and in Alaska 1955–56; with US Geological Survey Astrogeology Dept –1965; Project Chief on photo and telescopic mapping of moon and planets; selected as scientist-astronaut by NASA 1965; completed flight training 1966; Lunar Module pilot Apollo XVII 1972; Chief, Astronaut Office, Science and Applications, Johnson Space Center 1974; Asst Admin., Energy Programs, NASA, Washington, DC 1974–76; Senator from New Mexico 1977–83; mem. Pres.'s Foreign Intelligence Advisory Bd 1984–85, Army Sciences Bd 1985–89, Army Research Lab. Tech. Review Bd 1993–; co-leader group to monitor Romanian elections 1990; Chair., Pres. Annapolis Center for Science-Based Public Policy 1994–98, now Chair. Emer.; Chair. NASA Advisory Council 2005–08; Adjunct Prof., Univ. of Wisconsin 1995–; Fellow, American Geophysical Union, AAAS, AIAA, American Asscn of Petroleum Geologists; Republican; Hon. Fellow, Geological Soc. of America 1984, Hon. mem. American Inst. of Mining, Metallurgical and Petroleum Engineers, New Mexico Geological Soc.; numerous awards, including Arthur S. Fleming Award 1973, First Extraterrestrial Field Geologist Award, Geological Soc. of America 1973, Manned Spacecraft Center Superior Achievement Award 1973, NASA Distinguished Service Award 1973, Engineer of the Year Award, Nat. Soc. of Professional Engineers 1981, Nat. Security Award 1981, Public Service Award, American Asscn of Petroleum Geologists 1982, Lovelace Award, NASA 1989, Gilbert Award, GSA 1989, Award for Excellence, Presbyterian Healthcare Foundation 1990, Aviation Week Legend Award 2002, Eugene M. Shoemaker Memorial Award, Arizona State Univ. 2007, Pick and Gavel Award, American Asscn of State Geologists 2008, Columbia Medal, Aerospace Division of American Soc. of Civil Engineers 2010, Leif Erikson Award 2015, inducted into Astronaut Hall of Fame, International Space Hall of Fame. *Publications include:* Return to the Moon: Exploration, Enterprise, and Energy in the Human Settlement of Space 2006. *Leisure interests:* writing, skiing, fishing, carpentry, hiking, handball, squash, running. *Website:* americasuncommonsense.com.

SCHMITT, Pál, PhD; Hungarian diplomatist, international organization official, sportsman, politician and fmr head of state; b. 13 May 1942, Budapest; m. Katalin Makray; ed Univ. of Econs; hotel manager 1965–80; mem. Hungarian Nat. Fencing Team 1965–77; won Team Épée Gold Medal at Olympic Games, Mexico City 1968, Munich 1972; Deputy Under-Sec. of State for Sport 1981–90; mem. IOC 1983–, First Sec., Hungarian Olympic Cttee 1983–89, Chair. 1989–2010, Vice-Chair. Athletes Comm. of IOC 1984–88, mem. IOC Exec. Bd 1991–99, Chair. Sport and Environment Comm. of IOC 1995–, Vice-Pres. IOC 1995–99; Pres. World Olympians Asscn 1999–2007; Amb. to Spain 1993–97, to Switzerland 1998–2002; mem. Fidesz—Hungarian Civic Union, Vice-Chair. 2003–07; mem. European Parl. (Group of the European People's Party) 2004–10, Vice-Chair. Cttee on Culture and Educ. 2004–09, Chair. Del. to EU-Croatia Jt Parl. Cttee 2004–09, Vice-Pres.

European Parl. 2009–10; Speaker of the Nat. Ass. (Országgyülés) May–Aug. 2010; Pres. of Hungary 2010–12 (resgnd). *Address:* c/o Office of the President, 1014 Budapest, Szent György tér 1–2, Hungary.

SCHMITTER, Philippe, BA, PhD; American academic; *Professor Emeritus, European University Institute;* b. 19 Nov. 1936, Washington, DC; m. (divorced); one s. one d.; ed Dartmouth Coll., Univ. Nacional Autónoma de México, Mexico, Univ. of Geneva, Switzerland, Univ. of California, Berkeley; Research Asst, Univ. of California, Berkeley 1961–62, Fellowship Coordinator, Inst. of Int. Studies 1964, Research Political Scientist 1966–67; Lecturer, Sacramento State Coll. 1967; Asst Prof., Dept of Political Sciences, Univ. of Chicago 1967–71, Chair. Cttee on Latin American Studies 1970–73, 1974–76, Assoc. Prof. 1971–75, Founding Chair. Cttee on Western Europe 1974–77, Prof. 1975–84; Dir European Univ. Inst. (EUI) Summer School, Florence, Italy 1983, Prof. Dept of Social and Political Sciences 1982–86, Prof. of Political Science –2004, Prof. Emer. 2004–; Prof., Stanford Program-in-Paris 1993; Prof., Dept of Political Science, Stanford Univ. 1985–98, Prof. Emer. 1999–; Visiting Prof., Univ. of Brazil 1965–66, INTAL, Buenos Aires 1969, Harvard Univ. 1970, Univs of Geneva 1973–74, Paris I 1976, Mannheim 1977–78, Zurich 1978, Barcelona 1984, Univ. Autónoma de Madrid 1990, Univ. Menendez Pelayo, Valencia 1993, Inst. of Political Studies, Paris 1994, Bilkent Univ., Ankara 1995, Univ. of Siena 1999–2002; Recurring Visiting Prof., Central European Univ. 2005–; mem. Editorial Bd Comparative Political Studies 1974–77, Armed Forces and Society 1976–82, Historical Social Research 1976–83, Papers: Revista de Sociologia 1979–85, Politics and Soc. 1982–86, Stato e mercato 1983–86, 1997–, Journal of Democracy 1992–, The Encyclopedia of Democracy 1992–, Review Internationale de Politique Comparée 1993–, Swiss Political Science Review 1995–, Politique et Sociétés 1995–; mem. numerous academic advisory bds; mem. Société Tocqueville 1977–, Asscn Française de Science Politique 1981–, Schweizerische Vereinigung für Politische Wissenschaft 1981–, Società italiana di scienza politica 1982–, Deutsche Vereinigung für Politische Wissenschaft 1982–; mem. Research Cttee on European Unification, Int. Political Science Asscn 1993–; Int. Fellow, Council on Foreign Relations, New York 1972–73, Fellow, Alexander von Humboldt Stiftung 1977, J.S. Guggenheim Foundation 1978, Center for Advanced Studies in the Behavioural Sciences 1991–92, Collegium Budapest 2005–06, and others; Hon. Prof., Konstanz Univ. 1999–2002; numerous grants, Dissertation Prize, Univ. of California, Berkeley 1968, ECPR Lifetime Acheivement Prize 2008, EUSA Contrib. to European Integration Prize 2009, IPSA Mattei Doggan Award 2009, Johan Skytte Prize, Univ. of Uppsala 2009. *Publications include:* Corporatism and Public Policy in Authoritarian Portugal 1975, Trends Toward Corporatist Intermediation (co-author) 1984, Patterns of Corporatist Policy-Making (co-author) 1982, La politica degli interessi nei paesi industrializzati (co-author) 1984, Private Interest Government and Public Policy (co-ed.) 1985, Transitions from Authoritarian Rule: Tentative Conclusions about Uncertain Democracies (co-author) 1986, Transitions from Authoritarian Rule: Prospects for Democracy, Vols I-IV (co-author) 1986, Neocorporativismo (co-author) 1992, Sustainable Democracy (co-author) 1995, Governance in the European Union (co-author) 1996, El fin del siglo del corporativismo (co-author) 1998, Portugal: do autoritarismo à democracia 1999, Come democratizzare l'Unione Europea...e perché 2000; numerous articles in professional journals and chapters in books. *Address:* Department of Social and Political Sciences, European University Institute, Badia Fiesolana, Via dei Roccettini, 9, 50016 San Domenico di Fiesole (FI), (office); Via di Monteloro 31/A, 50069 Le Sieci (FI), Italy (home). *Telephone:* 055 4685274 (office); 055 8300613 (home). *Fax:* 055 4685201 (office). *E-mail:* philippe.schmitter@iue.it (office). *Website:* www.iue.it (office).

SCHMÖGNEROVÁ, Brigita, PhD; Slovak international organization official and politician; b. 17 Nov. 1947, Bratislava; m.; one s.; ed School of Econs, Bratislava; teacher, Univ. of Athens, Greece, Georgetown Univ., USA; Researcher, Inst. of Econs, Slovak Acad. of Sciences; Lecturer, Univ. of Econs, Bratislava; Econ. Adviser to Pres. of Slovak Repub. 1993; Deputy Prime Minister 1994; mem. Parl. 1995–98; Minister of Finance 1998–2002; Exec. Sec., UN Econ. ECE 2002–05; adviser to IMF, IBRD and EBRD; apptd Vice-Pres. EBRD 2005; World Finance Minister of the Year Award, Euromoney Inst. Investor 2000. *Publication:* Kniha o vládnutí 2016. *Address:* European Bank for Reconstruction and Development, One Exchange Square, London, EC2A 2JN, England (office). *Telephone:* (20) 7338-6000 (office). *Fax:* (20) 7338-6910 (office). *Website:* www.ebrd.com (office).

SCHNABEL, Julian, BFA; American painter and film director; b. 26 Oct. 1951, Brooklyn, New York; ed Univ. of Houston, Whitney Museum Ind. Study Program, New York. *Films:* Basquiat (writer, dir) 1996, Before Night Falls (producer, writer, dir) 2000, Sketches of Frank Gehry 2006, Le Scaphandre et le Papillon (Best Dir, Cannes Film Festival 2007, Best European Film, San Sebastian Film Festival 2007, Best Foreign Film, Nat. Bd of Review 2007, Golden Globe for Best Foreign Language Film, Golden Globe for Best Dir 2008) 2007, Berlin 2007, Miral 2010. *Publication:* Nicknames of Maître D's and Other Excerpts From Life 1988. *Address:* c/o PaceWildenstein Gallery New York, 32 East 57th Street, New York, NY 10022, USA.

SCHNACKENBERG, Gjertrud, BA; American poet and writer; b. 27 Aug. 1953, Tacoma, Wash.; d. of Walter Charles Schnackenberg and Doris Ione Schnackenberg (née Strom); m. Robert Nozick 1987 (died 2002); ed Mount Holyoke Coll.; Fellow in Poetry, The Radcliffe Inst. 1979–80; Christensen Fellow, Saint Catherine's Coll., Oxford 1997; Visiting Scholar, Getty Research Inst., J. Paul Getty Museum 2000; Fellow, American Acad. of Arts and Sciences 1996, Civitella Ranieri 2012, William B. Hart Poet in Residence, The American Acad. in Rome 2014; Dr hc (Mount Holyoke Coll.) 1985; Glascock Award for Poetry 1973, 1974, Acad. of American Poets Lavan Younger Poets Award 1983, American Acad. and Inst. of Arts and Letters Rome Prize 1983–84, Amy Lowell Traveling Prize 1984–85, Nat. Endowment for the Arts grant 1986–87, Guggenheim Fellowship 1987–88, American Acad. of Arts and Letters Award in Literature 1998, Daimler Chrysler Berlin Prize Fellow, American Acad., Berlin 2004. *Publications:* Portraits and Elegies 1982, The Lamplit Answer 1985, A Gilded Lapse of Time 1992, The Throne of Labdacus (Los Angeles Times Book Prize in Poetry 2001) 2000, Supernatural Love: Poems 1976–1992 2000, Heavenly Questions (Griffin Int. Poetry Prize 2011) 2010; contrib. to books and journals. *Address:* c/o Farrar, Straus & Giroux Inc., 18 West 18th Street, New York, NY 10011, USA (office). *Telephone:* (212) 741-6900 (office). *Website:* us.macmillan.com/FSG.aspx (office).

SCHNAPPER, Dominique, PhD; French sociologist, academic and writer; *Professor, École des Hautes Études en Sciences Sociales;* b. 9 Nov. 1934, Paris; d. of Raymond Aron and Suzanne Gauchon; m. Antoine Schnapper 1958; three c.; ed Institut d'Études Politiques de Paris, Sorbonne, Université Paris V; Prof. and Dir of Studies, École des Hautes Études en Sciences Sociales, Paris 1980–; currently Pres. Musée d'art et d'histoire du Judaïsme; mem. Comm. Marceau Long on reform of nation 1987, Comm. 2000 1989, Comm. on Drugs Henrion 1994, Comm. on Educ. Fauroux 1995–96; mem. Steering Cttee of French Soc. of Sociology 1991–95, Pres. 1995–99; mem. Conseil Constitutionnel (Supreme Court) 2001–10; Hon. mem. Conseil Constitutionnel; Officier, Légion d'honneur, des Arts et des Lettres, Ordre nat. du Mérite; Prix de l'Assemblée Nat. 1994, Balzan Prize for Sociology 2002. *Publications include:* La Communauté des citoyens 1994, La Rélation a l'autre 1998, Qu'est ce que la citoyenneté? 2000, La Démocratie providentielle 2002, Diasporas et nations 2006, Qu'est ce que l'intégration? 2007, La condition juive en France 2009, Une sociologue au Conseil constitutionnel 2010, Travailler et aimer 2013, L'esprit démocratique des lois 2014, La citoyenneté l'épreuve, les juifs et la démocratie 2018. *Address:* Maison des Sciences de l'Homme, 105 boulevard Raspail, 75007 Paris, France (office). *Telephone:* 1-53-63-51-51 (office). *E-mail:* schnappe@ehess.fr (office).

SCHNEIDER-AMMANN, Johann Niklaus, BEng, MBA; Swiss business executive and politician; b. 18 Feb. 1952, Sumiswald; m. Katharina Schneider-Ammann; one s. one d.; ed Swiss Federal Inst. of Tech., Zurich, European Inst. of Business Admin (INSEAD), France; Project Leader, Oerlikon Bührle 1978–81; Asst, Ammann-Unternehmungen 1981–84, Dir U. Ammann Maschinenfabrik AG 1984–89, Pres. and Del., Ammann Group Holding AG (mechanical eng co.), Langenthal 1990–; mem. Nationalrat (Nat. Council) 1999–2010; mem. Federal Council 2010–18, Head, Federal Dept of Econ. Affairs, Educ. and Research 2010–18, Vice-Pres. 2015, Pres. 2016–17; mem. Free Democratic Party. *Address:* c/o Federal Department of Economic Affairs, Education and Research, Schwanengasse 2, 3003 Bern, Switzerland (office).

SCHNEIDER, Cynthia Perrin, BA, PhD; American professor of art history and fmr diplomatist; *Distinguished Professor in Practice of Diplomacy, School of Foreign Service, Georgetown University;* b. 16 Aug. 1953, Pennsylvania; m. Thomas J. Schneider; two c.; ed Harvard Univ., Oxford Univ.; Asst Curator of European Paintings, Museum of Fine Arts, Boston 1980–84; Asst Prof. of Art History, Georgetown Univ. 1984–90, apptd Assoc. Prof. 1990, Distinguished Prof. in Practice of Diplomacy, School of Foreign Service 2004–, Pfizer Medical Humanities Scholar in Residence, Public Policy Inst. and Dir Life Sciences and Society Initiative 2004–06; Vice-Chair. Pres.'s Cttee on the Arts and Humanities 1994–98; Amb. to Netherlands 1998–2001; mem. Bd of Advisors, Inst. for Cultural Diplomacy, Sustainable Preservation Initiative, Center on Policy for Emerging Technologies, Singapore Technologies Telemedia (ST Telelemedia) Eircom; mem. Supervisory Bd, Royal Ahold, Zaandam, Netherlands 2001–05; Non-resident Sr Fellow, Saban Center for Middle East Policy, Brookings Inst. 2006–08, Coordinator, Arts and Culture Initiative 2006–08, Co-Convener of Action Group, US-Islamic World Forum 2014, Co-Dir Timbuktu Renaissance Initiative 2014–15; Co-f. and Co-Dir Muslims on Screen and Television (MOST) resource center; presented TED talk titled The surprising spread of Idol TV 2009; fmr mem. Bd of Dirs Nat. Museum of Women in the Arts, Australian-American Leadership Dialogue, Peace Research Endowment; Honor Award, Dept of Treasury, US Secret Service 2001, Flevo Award 2001, Exceptional Public Service Award, Office of the Sec. of Defense 2001, Rockefeller Foundation Grant 2003. *Publications:* Rembrandt's Landscapes 1990, Rembrandt's Landscapes: Drawing and Prints 1990. *Address:* Georgetown University, 3700 O Street, NW, Washington, DC 20057 (office); 17201 Norwood Road, Sandy Spring, MD 20860, USA (home). *Telephone:* (301) 706-9260 (office). *E-mail:* schneidc@georgetown.edu (office). *Website:* www.georgetown.edu (office); cynthiapschneider.org.

SCHNEIDER, Etienne; Luxembourg economist and politician; *Deputy Prime Minister and Minister of the Economy and of Health;* b. 29 Jan. 1971, Dudelange; ed Inst. catholique des hautes études commerciales, Brussels, Belgium, Greenwich Univ., London, UK; Research Asst, European Parl., Brussels 1995–96; Municipal Councillor, Kayl 1995–2005, First Alderman 2005–10; economist for LSAP parl. group 1996–97, Sec.-Gen. 1997–2004; Project Leader with NATO, Brussels 1997; Govt Adviser to Ministry of the Economy and Foreign Trade, responsible for Directorates of Energy, E-Commerce and Internet Security 2004, Sr Govt Adviser responsible for Directorates of Econ. Devt, Infrastructures and Energy 2009, for Directorate-Gen. of Econ. Devt, Industry and Businesses 2011; Minister of Economy and Foreign Trade 2012–13, Deputy Prime Minister and Minister of the Economy 2013–, of Internal Security and of Defence 2013–18, of Health 2018–; Chair. and Man. Dir Société électrique de l'Our 2005; Chair. Exec. Bd Cegedel SA 2004; Chair. Enovos International SA, Enovos Deutschland AG 2010–12; Chair. and Man. Dir Creos (grid co.) 2010–12; Vice-Chair. Société nationale de crédit et d'investissement (SNCI) 2010–12; mem. Lëtzebuerger Sozialistesch Arbechterpartei (LSAP). *Address:* Ministry of the Economy, 19–21 blvd Royal, 2449 Luxembourg, Luxembourg (office). *Telephone:* 247-82478 (office). *Fax:* 46-04-48 (office). *E-mail:* info@eco.public.lu (office). *Website:* www.eco.public.lu (office).

SCHNEIDER, Manfred, Dr rer. pol; German business executive; b. 21 Dec. 1938, Bremerhaven; m.; one d.; ed Univs of Freiburg, Hamburg and Cologne; fmr Asst to Prof. of Business Man., Aachen Tech. Univ.; joined Bayer AG, Leverkusen 1966, Head Finance and Accounting Dept of subsidiary co. Duisburger Kupferhütte, later Chair. of Bd, returned to Bayer AG 1981, apptd Head of Regional Coordination, Corp. Auditing and Control 1984, mem. Bd of Man. 1987–2002, Chair. 1992–2002, Chair. Supervisory Bd 2002–12; Chair. Supervisory Bd, RWE AG 2009–16, Linde AG 2001–16; mem. Supervisory Bd, Daimler AG, Stuttgart (mem. Chair.'s Council 2001–), TUI AG Hanover; mem. Jt Advisory Council, Allianz SE 2007–15; Pres. German Chemical Industry Asscn (VCI) 1999–2001. *Address:* c/o RWE International SE, Opernplatz 1, 45128 Essen, Germany. *E-mail:* info@rwe.com.

SCHNEIDER, Peter; German politician and business executive; *President, Sparkassenverband Baden-Württemberg;* b. 27 July 1958, Riedlingen; m. Rose Marie Schneider 1978; two s.; mem. CDU 1976–; with Co. Dept Sigmaringen 1986–88; Pvt. Sec. to Ministry of Interior Dietmar Schlee 1988–92; worked for Biberach Dist 1992–2006; mem. State Parl. of Baden-Württemberg 2001–; Pres. Sparkassenverband Baden-Württemberg (Savings Bank Asscn of Baden-Württemberg), Stuttgart 2006–; mem. Supervisory Bd Landesbank Baden-Württemberg, Chair. –2010; Dist Chair. German Red Cross Biberach. *Address:* Sparkassenverband Baden-Württemberg, Am Hauptbahnhof 2, 70173 Stuttgart (office); Landesbank Baden-Württemberg, Am Hauptbahnhof 2, 70173 Stuttgart, Germany (office). *Telephone:* (711) 127-0 (office). *Fax:* (711) 12743544 (office). *E-mail:* Peter.Schneider@sv-bw.de (office); Peter.Schneider@CDU.landtag-bw.de (office). *Website:* www.sv-bw.de (office); www.peter-schneider-bc.de.

SCHNEIDER, Ulf Mark, Lic. oec., PhD, MBA; German business executive; *CEO, Nestlé SA;* ed Univ. of St Gallen, Switzerland, Harvard Univ., USA; held several exec. positions with Franz Haniel & Cie. GmbH from 1989; Group Finance Dir Gehe UK plc (pharmaceutical wholesale and retail distributor), Coventry, UK; joined Fresenius 2001, Chief Financial Officer Fresenius Medical Care 2001–03, Chair. Man. Bd Fresenius SE 2003–16; CEO Nestlé SA 2016–. *Address:* Nestlé Suisse SA, Rue d'Entre-deux-Villes 12, 1814 La Tour-de-Peilz, Switzerland (office). *Telephone:* (21) 924-51-11 (office). *Website:* www.nestle.com (office).

SCHNEIDERHAN, Gen. Wolfgang; German army officer; b. 26 July 1946, Riedlingen, Baden-Württemberg; m. Elke Schneiderhan (née Speckhardt); three s. two d.; ed Bundeswehr Command and Staff Coll., Hamburg; began career with Bundeswehr (German Armed Forces) 1966; Youth Information Officer, 10th Armoured Div., Sigmaringen 1972–74; Co. Commdr Armoured Bn 293, Stetten am Kalten Markt 1974–77; Asst Br. Chief, Mil. Intelligence, Armed Forces Staff 1979–81; Asst Chief of Staff, G-3 Operations, Home Defence Brigade 55, Böblingen 1981–83; Sr Officer, G-3, Operations, NATO Cen. Europe HQ, Brunssum, The Netherlands 1983–86; CO Armoured Bn 553, Stetten am Kalten Markt 1986–88; Chief of Staff, 4th Mechanized Div., Regensburg 1988–90; Sr Officer, Arms Control, NATO HQ, Brussels 1990–92; Dir Faculty of Army Doctrine, Bundeswehr Command and Staff Coll. 1992–94; CO Armoured 39 Brigade Thüringen, Erfurt 1994–97; Asst Chief of Staff, Planning, Fed. Ministry of Defence 1997–99; Chief of Policy and Advisory Staff 2000–02; Chief of Staff of the Bundeswehr 2002–09; Insp. Gen. of the Bundeswehr 2002–09; rank of Brig. Gen. 1996, Maj. Gen. 1999, Lt-Gen. 2000, Gen. 2002; Order of Merit, First Class; Gold Cross of Honour of the Bundeswehr; Chevalier, Légion d'honneur; Legion of Merit (USA); Grand Officer, Order of the Crown (Belgium); Eagle's Cross, First Class (Estonia); Medal of Merit, First Class, Ministry of Defence (Czech Repub.); Grand Gross of Mil. Merit (Jordan). *Leisure interests:* contemporary history, music. *Address:* Federal Ministry of Defence, Stauffenbergstr. 18, 10785 Berlin, Germany (office). *Telephone:* (30) 1824000 (office). *Fax:* (30) 18245357 (office). *E-mail:* poststelle@bmvg.bund.de (office). *Website:* www.bmvg.de (office).

SCHNIEDERS, Richard J., BA; American food distribution industry executive; *Co-founder and CEO, MoGro;* b. 6 March 1948, Remsen, Ia; s. of Bob Schnieders and Helen Schnieders; m. Beth Schnieders; two d.; ed Univ. of Iowa; began career at Randall's Super Valu Stores, Iowa City; with John Morrell & Co., Des Moines, Bettesdorf and Memphis; joined Exec. Devt Program, Hardin's-Sysco, Memphis 1982, Pres. and CEO 1989–90, Chair., Pres. and CEO 1990–92, apptd Sr Vice-Pres. Merchandising Sysco Corpn, Houston, Tex. 1992, mem. Bd of Dirs and Sr Vice-Pres., Merchandising and Multi-unit Sales 1997–2009, Exec. Vice-Pres., Foodservice Operations 1999–2000, COO Jan.–July 2000, Pres. and COO July 2000–03, Chair. and CEO 2003–March 2009, Pres. 2005–07, Chair. March–June 2009 (retd); Co-founder (with wife) and CEO MoGro (non-profit mobile grocery truck firm) 2010–; mem. Bd of Dirs Revolution Foods, Save The Children Federation, Stone Barns Center for Food and Agriculture. *Address:* MoGro, 901 Menaul Blvd NE, Albuquerque, NM 87107, USA (office). *Telephone:* (505) 216-8611 (office). *E-mail:* info@MoGro.net (office). *Website:* www.mogro.net (office).

SCHOCKEMÖHLE, Alwin; German show jumper (retd) and horse breeder; b. 29 May 1937, Osterbrock, Kreis Meppen; s. of Aloys Schockemöhle and Josefa Schockemöhle (née Borgerding); m. 2nd Rita Wiltfang; two s. one d.; two d. from previous m.; began riding 1946, in public events 1948; trained in mil. riding 1954–55; reserve for Mil. and Showjumping, Melbourne Olympics 1956; specialized in showjumping 1956–77; first Derby win, riding 'Bachus', Hamburg 1957; continually in int. showjumping events 1960–77; currently Owner, Gestüt und Rennstall Alwin Schockemöhle (stud and racing stables); Showjumping Champion FRG four times; second in European Championship three times; European Champion riding Warwick 1975, 1976; gold medal (Team Award) Rome Olympics 1960; gold medal (Individual Award) and silver medal (Team Award) riding Warwick, Montreal Olympics 1976. *Publication:* Sportkamerad Pferd (A Horse for Sports Companions). *Address:* Münsterlandstraße 53, 49453 Mühlen, Germany (office). *Telephone:* (54) 923823 (office). *Fax:* (54) 923794 (office). *E-mail:* info@alwin-schockemoehle.de (office). *Website:* www.alwinschockemoehle.de (office).

SCHOEN, Serge, MSc, MBA; French business executive; *Executive Chairman, Louis Dreyfus Commodities Holdings Group;* ed Ecole Nationale Superieure des Telecommunications de Paris, Sloan School of Man. at Massachusetts Inst. of Tech., USA; with Boston Consulting Group, Paris 1992–99; CEO Louis Dreyfus Commodities 2006–13, Adviser, Louis Dreyfus Holding BV June 2013–, mem. Supervisory Bd Louis Dreyfus Commodities Holdings BV, Chair. Sept. 2013–; Dir, Neuf Cegetel SA. *Address:* Louis Dreyfus Commodities BV, Westblaak 92, 3012 Rotterdam, The Netherlands (office). *E-mail:* DRH-Paris@louisdreyfus.fr (office). *Website:* www.ldcom.com (office); www.louisdreyfus.com (office).

SCHOLAR, Sir Michael Charles, Kt, KCB, BA, MA, PhD, ARCO; British civil servant, academic and college principal; b. 3 Jan. 1942, Merthyr Tydfil, Wales; s. of Richard Scholar and Blodwen Scholar (née Jones); m. Angela Sweet 1964; three s. one d. (deceased); ed St Olave's and St Saviour's Grammar School, St John's Coll., Cambridge, Univ. of California, Berkeley, Harvard Univ., USA; worked at HM Treasury 1969–93; Sr Int. Man. Barclay's Bank 1979–81; Pvt. Sec. to Prime Minister 1981–83; Perm. Sec., Welsh Office 1993–96; Perm. Sec. Dept of Trade and Industry 1996–2001; Pres. St John's Coll., Oxford 2001–12; Dir (non-exec.) Council of Man., Nat. Inst. of Econ. and Social Research 2001–05, Legal and General Investment Man. 2002–07; Chair. Benton Fletcher Advisory Cttee 2004–; Chair. UK Statistics Authority 2007–12; Hon. Fellow, Univ. of Wales (Aberystwyth) 1996, St John's Coll., Cambridge, Cardiff Univ.; Dr hc (Univ. of Glamorgan). *Leisure interests:* playing the organ and piano, opera, long-distance walks.

SCHOLES, Myron S., BA, MBA, PhD; American/Canadian professor of finance and business executive; b. 1 July 1941, Timmons, Ont., Canada; two d.; ed McMaster Univ., Canada, Univ. of Chicago, USA; instructor at Business School, Univ. of Chicago 1967–68; Asst Prof., MIT Man. School 1968–72, Assoc. Prof. 1972–73; Assoc. Prof. Univ. of Chicago 1973–75, Prof. 1975–79, Edward Eagle Brown Prof. of Finance 1979–82, Dir Center for Research in Security Prices 1975–81; Prof., Business School and the Law School, Stanford Univ. 1983–96, Frank E. Buck Prof. Emer. of Finance 1996–; Man. Dir Salomon Bros 1991–93; Sr Research Fellow, Hoover Inst., Stanford Univ. 1988–; Co-founder and Prin. Long-Term Capital Man. (hedge fund) 1994–99; f. Platinum Grove Asset Man. 1999, Chair. –2009 (retd); Dir Capital Preservation Fund, Capital Preservation Fund II; Research Assoc. NBER; fmr Dir The Chicago Mercantile Exchange; mem. American Econ. Asscn American Finance Asscn; Dr hc (Univ. of Paris-Dauphine) 1989, (McMaster Univ.) 1990, (Katholieke Universiteit Leuven) 1998; shared Nobel Prize for Econs 1997 for devising Black-Scholes Model for determining value of derivatives. *Leisure interests:* skiing, golf. *Address:* Stanford Graduate School of Business, Knight Management Center, Stanford University, 655 Knight Way, Stanford, CA 94305-7298, USA (office). *Telephone:* (650) 723-2146 (office). *E-mail:* mscholes@pgamlp.com (office). *Website:* www.gsb.stanford.edu (office).

SCHOLEY, Sir David (Gerald), Kt, CBE, FRSA; British banker; *Senior Adviser, UBS Investment Bank;* b. 28 June 1935, Chipstead, Surrey; s. of Dudley Scholey and Lois Scholey; m. Alexandra Beatrix Drew 1960; one s. one d.; ed Wellington Coll., Berks. and Christ Church, Oxford; served in RAC, 9th Queen's Royal Lancers (Nat. Service) 1953–55, TA Yorks Dragoons 1955–57, 3/4 CLY (Sharp-shooters) 1957–61, Metropolitan Special Constabulary (Thames Div.) 1961–65; with Thompson Graham & Co. (Lloyd's Brokers) 1956–58; Dale & Co. (Insurance Brokers), Canada 1958–59; Guinness Mahon & Co. Ltd 1959–64; joined S.G. Warburg & Co. Ltd 1965, Dir 1967–95, Deputy Chair. 1977–80, Jt Chair. 1980–84, Chair. 1985–95; Chair. S.G. Warburg Group plc (now UBS Investment Bank) 1985–95, SBC Warburg July–Nov. 1995, Sr Adviser 1995–; mem. Bd of Dirs Mercury Securities plc 1969–86, Chair. 1984–86; mem. Bd of Dirs Orion Insurance Co. Ltd 1963–87, Stewart Wrightson Holdings Ltd 1972–81, Union Discount Co. of London Ltd 1976–81, Bank of England 1981–98, British Telecom plc 1986–94, Chubb Corpn, USA 1991–2008, Gen. Electric Co. 1992–95, J Sainsbury plc 1996–2000, Vodafone Group plc 1998–2005, Anglo American plc 1999–2005; Sr Adviser, International Finance Corpn 1996–2005, Financial Services Authority 2010–; mem. Export Guarantees Advisory Council 1970–75, Deputy Chair. 1974–75; Chair. Construction Exports Advisory Bd 1975–78; mem. Institut International d'Etudes Bancaires 1976–94 (Pres. 1988), Cttee on Finance for Industry, Nat. Econ. Devt Office 1980–87, IISS Studies Council 1984–93 (Hon. Treas. 1984–90), Business in the Community, Pres.'s Cttee 1988–91, General Motors European Advisory Council 1988–97, Save the Children Fund, Industry and Commerce Group 1989–95 (Lord Mayor's Appeal Cttee 2002–03), London First 1993–96, London Symphony Orchestra Advisory Council 1998–2004, Fitch Int. Services Advisory Cttee 2001–, Mitsubishi Int. Advisory Cttee 2001–07, Sultanate of Oman Financial Advisory Group 2002–06; Gov. Wellington Coll. 1978–88, 1996–2004 (Vice-Pres. 1998–2004); Dir, BBC 1994–2000, Nat. Inst. for Econ. and Social Research 1984; Trustee, Glyndebourne Arts Trust 1989–2002, Nat. Portrait Gallery (Chair.) 1992–2005; Hon. DLitt (Guildhall) 1993; Hon. DSc (UMIST) 1999. *Address:* UBS Investment Bank, 1 Finsbury Avenue, London, EC2M 2PP (office); Heath End House, Spaniards Road, London, NW3 7JE, England (home). *Telephone:* (20) 7568-2400 (office). *Fax:* (20) 7568-4225 (office). *E-mail:* david.scholey@ubs.com (office). *Website:* www.ubs.com (office).

SCHOLL, Hermann, DrIng; German business executive; *Honorary Chairman, Bosch Group;* b. 21 June 1935, Stuttgart; m.; one d.; ed Univ. of Stuttgart; joined Robert Bosch GmbH, Advanced Eng Dept, Automotive Tech. 1962, Chief Engineer, Electronic Fuel Injection 1968–71, Dir of Eng, Electrical and Electronic Engine Equipment 1971–73, Assoc. mem. Bd of Man. 1973–75, Deputy mem. 1975–78, mem. 1978–2003, Chair. 1993–2003, Man. Partner, Robert Bosch Industrietreu-hand KG (holding co.) 1995–2003, Chair. Supervisory Council, Robert Bosch GmbH 2003–12, Hon. Chair. Bosch Group 2012–; mem. Supervisory Bd, BASF AG; conferred with title of Prof. by Gov. of Baden-Württemberg 2005; Hon. DrIng (Kettering Univ., Mich., USA) 1988, (Tech. Univ. of Munich) 1993. *Address:* Robert Bosch GmbH, Postfach 106050, 70049 Stuttgart, Germany (office). *E-mail:* info@bosch.com (office). *Website:* www.bosch.com (office).

SCHOLZ, Olaf; German politician and lawyer; *Vice-Chancellor and Federal Minister of Finance;* b. 14 June 1958, Osnabrück; m. Britta Ernst; ed Univ. of Hamburg; joined SPD youth wing 1975; Deputy Chair. Socialist Youth Org. 1982–88; Vice-Pres. Int. Union of Socialist Youth 1987–89; Partner, Zimmermann, Scholz & Partners (law firm), Hamburg 1985–; mem. Bundestag (parl.) for Hamburg Altona 1998–2001, 2002–11, Vice-Chair. SPD Parl. Group 2009–11; Minister of the Interior, City of Hamburg May–Oct. 2001; Mayor of Hamburg 2011–18; Gen. Sec. SPD 2002–04, Vice-Chair. 2009–, also Acting Chair. Feb.–April 2018; Fed. Minister of Labour and Social Affairs 2007–09, of Finance 2018–; Vice-Chancellor 2018–; Legal adviser to Cen. Asscn of German Consumer Cooperatives 1990–98. *Publication:* Hoffnungsland – Eine neue deutsche Wirklichkeit 2017. *Address:* Federal Ministry of Finance, Wilhelmstr. 97, 10117 Berlin, Germany (office). *Telephone:* (30) 186820 (office). *Fax:* (30) 186823260 (office). *E-mail:* poststelle@bmf.bund.de (office). *Website:* www.bundesfinanzministerium.de (office); www.olafscholz.de.

SCHOLZ, Rupert, DJur; German lawyer, professor of public law and politician; *Of Counsel, Gleiss Lutz;* b. 23 May 1937, Berlin; m.; ed Free Univ. of Berlin, Univ. of Heidelberg; Prof. of Public Law, Free Univ. of Berlin 1972–78; Chair of Public Law, Univ. of Munich 1978–2005, Prof. Emer. 2005–; Senator for Justice, W Berlin 1981–88, for Fed. Affairs 1983–88; Minister of Defence 1988–90; mem. Bundestag 1990–2002, Chair. legal affairs cttee 1998–2002; Of Counsel, Gleiss Lutz (law firm), Berlin 2005–; mem. CDU 1983–. *Address:* Gleiss Lutz, Friedrichstrasse 71, 10117 Berlin, Germany (office). *Telephone:* (30) 800979171 (office). *Fax:* (30) 800979979 (office). *E-mail:* rupert.scholz@gleisslutz.com (office). *Website:* www.gleisslutz.com (office).

SCHOLZE, Peter, BA, MA, Dr rer. nat; German mathematician and academic; *Professor, University of Bonn;* b. 11 Dec. 1987, Dresden; ed Heinrich-Hertz-Gymnasium, Berlin-Friedrichshain, Univ. of Bonn; made a Full Prof. at Rheinische Friedrich Wilhelms Univ. of Bonn shortly after completing his doctoral thesis (youngest full prof. in Germany); Hausdorff Chair 2012–13; Fellow, Clay Math. Inst. (USA) 2011–16; Dir Max Planck Inst. for Math. 2018–; mem. German Acad. of Sciences Leopoldina 2017, Berlin-Brandenburg Acad. of Sciences 2017, North Rhine-Westphalia Acad. of Sciences and Arts 2018; participated in Int. Math. Olympiad, winning three gold medals and one silver medal, SASTRA Ramanujan Prize 2013, Clay Research Award, Clay Math. Inst. 2014, Fermat Prize 2015, Frank Nelson Cole Prize in Algebra 2015, Ostrowski Prize 2015, Leibniz Prize 2016, Fields Medal 2018. *Publications:* numerous papers in professional journals on Shimura varieties, p-adic Hodge theory and Langlands program. *Address:* Room 4.029, Mathematisches Institut, Universität Bonn, Endenicher Allee 60, 53115 Bonn, Germany (office). *Telephone:* (228) 7362237 (office). *E-mail:* scholze@math.uni-bonn.de (office). *Website:* www.math.uni-bonn.de/people/scholze (office).

SCHÖNBERG, Claude-Michel; French composer; b. 6 July 1944; s. of Adolphe Schönberg and Julie Nadás; one s. two d.; m. Charlotte Talbot 2003; started as producer for EMI France and as pop song writer 1967–72; recording his own songs in France 1974–77; recipient of Tony, Grammy, Evening Standard and Laurence Olivier Awards, French 'Molière' and 'Victoires de la musique' for musicals; Grammy Award for Outstanding Contrib. to the Creative Community. *Ballet:* Wuthering Heights with the Northern Ballet Theatre 2002, cr. Cleopatra 2011. *Films:* Les Misérables (screenplay) 2012. *Compositions:* musicals: La Révolution Française 1973, Les Misérables 1980–85, Miss Saigon 1989, Martin Guerre 1996–, Pirate Queen 2006–, Marguerite 2008; for cinema: Les Misérables 2012. *Address:* c/o Cameron Mackintosh Limited, 1 Bedford Square, London, WC1B 3RA, England (office). *Telephone:* (20) 7637-8866 (office).

SCHÖNBORN, HE Cardinal Christoph, OP; Austrian ecclesiastic; *Archbishop of Vienna;* b. 22 Jan. 1945, Skalsko (now in Czech Repub.); ordained priest 1970; student pastor, Univ. of Graz 1973–75; Assoc. Prof. of Dogma, Univ. of Fribourg 1975–76, Prof. of Theology 1976–81, Prof. of Dogmatic Theology 1981–91; apptd Auxiliary Bishop of Vienna 1991, Coadjutor 1995, Archbishop of Vienna 1995–; cr. Cardinal (Cardinal-Priest of Gesù Divin Lavoratore) 1998; Pres. Austrian Bishop's Conf. 1998–; participated in Papal Conclave 2005, 2013; curial mem. Congrega-tions for the Doctrine of the Faith, Oriental Churches, and Catholic Educ.; mem. Pontifical Council on Culture, Comm. on the Cultural Heritage of the Church, Special Council for European of the Gen. Secr. of the Synod of Bishops; mem. Pontifical Council for Promoting the New Evangelization 2011–; Ordinary for the faithful of Byzantine Rite in Austria. *Address:* Archdiocese of Vienna, Wollzeile 2, 1010 Vienna, Austria (office). *Telephone:* (1) 515-52-0 (office). *Fax:* (1) 515-52-3760 (office). *Website:* stephanscom.at; www.cardinalschonborn.com.

SCHÖNE, Albrecht, DPhil; German philologist and professor of German philology; *Professor Emeritus, University of Göttingen;* b. 17 July 1925, Barby; s. of Friedrich Schöne and Agnes Moeller Schöne; m. Dagmar Haver 1952; one s. one d.; ed Univs of Freiburg, Basle, Göttingen and Münster; Extraordinary Prof. of German Literature, Univ. of Münster 1958–60; Prof. of German Philology, Univ. of Göttingen 1960–90, Prof. Emer. 1990–; Pres. Int. Asscn for Germanic Studies 1980–85; mem. Akad. der Wissenschaften, Göttingen, Deutsche Akad. für Sprache und Dichtung, Bayerische, Nordrhein-Westfäl. Akad. der Wissenschaften, Austrian and Netherlands Acads; Hon. mem. Modern Language Asscn of America, Foreign Hon. mem. American Acad. of Arts and Sciences; Officier, Ordre nat. du Mérite, Grand Cross with Star of Merit (Germany), Order Pour le mérite for Sciences and Arts; Hon. DPhil, Hon. DTheol; several prizes. *Publications:* numerous books and articles on German literature and philology. *Leisure interests:* riding, hunting, painting. *Address:* Grotefendstrasse 26, 37075 Göttingen, Germany (home). *Telephone:* (551) 56449 (home).

SCHÖNHOLZER, Annette, MA; Swiss/American arts administrator and con-sultant; b. 1964; ed Univ. of Zürich, Int. Centre for Culture and Man., Austria; mem. Program Cttee and Curator, VIPER Int. Film, Video and Multimedia Festival, Basel 1994–98; worked for various public and private orgs promoting the arts; Co-Head of Cultural Competence Center, Aargau Canton 1997–2001; Project Man. BIOPOLIS show, Expo 02 (Swiss nat. exhbn) 2000–02; Show Man. Art Basel Miami Beach Int. Art Show, USA 2002, then Co-Dir Miami and Basel editions, also Dir Operations and Finance, Art Basel, Dir of New Initiatives 2012–14; Founder connect the dots (consultancy), Basel 2014–. *Address:* connect the dots, Leonhardsstr. 34, 4051 Basel, Switzerland (office).

SCHOTTE, Gerrit Fransisco; Curaçao business executive and politician; *Leader, Movementu Futuro Kòrsou (Movement for the Future of Curaçao);* b. 9 Sept. 1974, Willemstad; s. of Hendrik Schotte and Maria Ruiz; ed Peter Stuyvesant Coll.; f. The Shoppers (purchasing office) 1995–2000; Founding Dir Bad Boyz Toyz NV; mem. Nat. Professional Paintball League 1997–99; Founding Dir Food4U Delivery Service 2000–02; Gen. Man. Lido Hotel Resort & Casino NV 2001–05; fmr mem. Frente Obrero; co-f. Movementu Patriotiko Kòrsou (MPK), fmr Pres.; mem. Curaçao Parl. 2007–10, 2010–; fmr Commr in charge of Tourism, Econ. Affairs, Agric., Husbandry and Fishery, Curaçao Exec. Council; mem. Netherlands Antilles Parl. Jan.–Aug. 2010 (parl. dissolved); f. Movementu Futuro Kòrsou (MFK—Movt for the Future of Curaçao) 2010; Prime Minister of Curaçao Oct. 2010–12 (first Prime Minister following dissolution of Netherlands Antilles); f. Fundashon Gerrit Schotte. *Address:* Movementu Futuro Korsou, Salinja Lind-bergweg z/n, Willemstad, Curaçao (office). *Telephone:* (9) 461-7766 (office). *E-mail:* info@mfk.an (office). *Website:* www.gerritschotte.com.

SCHRADER, Hans Otto; German business executive; *Chairman of the Executive Board and CEO, Otto Group;* b. 8 Dec. 1956, Bevensen; m.; two c.; joined Otto Group 1977, becoming Deputy Head, Hong Kong Office, Vice-Pres. for Import, Vice-Pres. for Merchandising 1993–99, mem. Exec. Bd Otto GmbH & Co. KG 1999–, Otto Group 2005–, Chair. Exec. Bd and CEO 2007–. *Address:* Otto Group, Wandsbeker Strasse 3–7, 22172 Hamburg, Germany (office). *Telephone:* (40) 6461401 (office). *Fax:* (40) 64618571 (office). *E-mail:* info@ottogroup.com (office). *Website:* www.ottogroup.com (office).

SCHRADER, Paul Joseph, MA; American screenwriter and director; b. 22 July 1946, Grand Rapids, Mich.; s. of Charles A. Schrader and Joan Schrader (née Fisher); m. 1st Jeannine Oppewall 1969 (divorced 1976); m. 2nd Mary Beth Hurt

1983; ed Calvin Coll. and Univ. of California, Los Angeles; film critic for Los Angeles Free Press magazine 1970–72; Ed. Cinema magazine 1970; fmr Prof., Columbia Univ. *Films include:* screenplays: The Yazuka 1974, Taxi Driver 1976, Obsession 1976, Rolling Thunder 1977, Old Boyfriends (also producer) 1979, Raging Bull 1981, The Mosquito Coast 1986, Light of Day 1987, The Last Temptation of Christ 1988, City Hall 1996, Affliction 1997, Bringing Out the Dead 1999, The Walker (also dir) 2007, Dying of the Light 2014, First Reformed (also dir) (Gotham Independent Film Award for Best Screenplay 2018, New York Film Critics Circle Award for Best Screenplay 2018) 2017, The Jesuit (also producer) 2018; directed: Bluecollar (also co-writer) 1978, Hardcore 1978, American Gigolo (also co-writer) 1979, Cat People 1982, Mishima (also co-writer) 1985, Patty Hearst 1989, The Comfort of Strangers 1990, Light Sleeper (also writer) 1991, Witch-hunt 1994, Touch 1997, Forever Mine (also writer) 1999, Auto Focus 2002, Paul Schrader's Exorcist: The Beginning 2005, Adam Resurrected 2008, The Canyons (Melbourne Underground Film Festival for Best Foreign Dir 2013) 2013, Venice 70: Future Reloaded 2013, Dog Eat Dog (also actor) 2016. *Publications include:* Transcendental Style in Film: Ozu, Bresson, Dreyer 1972, Schrader on Schrader (with Kevin Jackson) 1990, Collected Screenplays 2002, A Hundred Years of Japanese Film (with Donald Richie) 2005. *Address:* c/o Johnnie Planco, Parseghian Planco 322, 8th Avenue, Suite 601, New York, NY 10001, USA. *Telephone:* (212) 777-7786. *Fax:* (212) 777-8642. *E-mail:* schraderproductions@gmail.com. *Website:* paulschrader.org.

SCHRAMECK, Olivier Claude Martin; French politician, diplomatist and civil servant; *President, Report and Studies Section, Conseil d'État;* b. 27 Feb. 1951, Paris; s. of Jean Schrameck and Stéphanie Schrameck (née Epstein); m. Hélene Rioust de Largentaye 1980; one s. one d.; ed Lycées Carnot, Paris and Pasteur, Neuilly-sur-Seine, Univ. of Paris II (Université Panthéon Assas), Ecole Nat. d'Admin., Inst. d'Etudes Politiques, Paris; several roles within Conseil d'État including Auditor 1977–83, Governing Commr, Litigation and Judgements Section 1981–82, 1987–88, Master of Petitions 1983–95, mem. Ass. and Perm. Comm. 1995, 2005–, currently Pres., Report and Studies Section; Tech. Adviser to Minister of State, Minister of the Interior and Decentralization 1982–84; Chief of Staff, Sec. of State of Ministry of Nat. Educ., with responsibility for Univs 1984–85, Dir of Higher Educ. 1985–86; Chief of Staff, Minister of State, Ministry of Nat. Educ., Youth and Sports 1988–91; Assoc. Prof., Univ. of Paris I (Panthéon-Sorbonne) 1991–97, 2005–; Assoc. Prof., Sciences-Po Paris; Gen. Reporter to High Council for Integration 1991–93; Sec.-Gen. Constitutional Council 1993–97; Chief of Staff to Prime Minister 1997–2001; Amb. to Spain 2002–05; Vice-Pres. World Bank Appeals Cttee 2010–12; Pres. Superior Council of Audio-Visual 2013–19; mem. Supreme Council of the Judiciary 2019–; mem. Admin. Council, Nat. Caisse of Historic Monuments 1992–97, Cttee for Institutional Reform 2007–; Officier, Légion d'honneur 2016, Chevalier, Ordre nat. du Mérite. *Publications include:* Les Cabinets ministériels 1995, La Fonction publique territoriale 1995, Matignon, Rive Gauche 1997–2001, Mémoire d'Alternance: L'Espagne de Zapatero 2005, Dans l'Ombre de la République: Les Cabinets Ministériels 2007; numerous articles on decentralization, law, immigration and constitutional law. *Address:* Conseil d'État, 1 place du Palais Royal, 75001 Paris, France (office). *Telephone:* 1-40-20-83-90 (office). *E-mail:* olivier.schrameck@conseil-etat.fr (office). *Website:* www.conseil-etat.fr (office).

SCHREIBER, Stuart L., BA, PhD; American chemist and academic; *Scientific Co-Director, Harvard Center for Genomics Research;* b. 6 Feb. 1956; ed Univ. of Virginia, Harvard Univ.; Asst Prof., Yale Univ. 1981–84, Assoc. Prof. 1984–86, Prof. 1986–88; Morris Loeb Prof., Harvard Univ. 1988–, Co-Dir, Harvard Inst. of Chem. and Cell Biology 1997–, Scientific Co-Dir, Harvard Center for Genomics Research 1998–, Assoc. mem. Harvard Univ. Medical School, Molecular and Cell Biology Div. 1988–; Investigator, Howard Hughes Medical Inst., Chevy Chase, Md 1994–, Assoc. mem., Dept of Molecular and Cellular Biology 1994–; Founder and Co-Chair. Scientific Advisory Bd Infinity Pharmaceuticals 2002–06; Founder and Chair. Bd of Scientific and Medical Advisors ARIAD Pharmaceuticals 1991–, Founder ARIAD Gene Therapeutics 1994–; Founder and mem. Scientific Advisory Bd Vertex Pharmaceuticals 1988–90; Advisor, Theravance 2000–04; consultant to Pfizer 1983–91; Founder and Co-Ed. Chemistry and Biology 1993–2004, Founding Ed. 2005–; mem. Bd of Consulting Eds Tetrahedron Publications 1983–; mem. Editorial Bd or Advisory Ed. The Scientist 2005–, Proceedings of NAS 1995–98, Current Biology, Topics in Stereochemistry, Comprehensive Organic Synthesis, Current Opinion in Chemical Biology, Nature Chemical Biology, ACS Chemical Biology, ChemBioChem, Synthesis Letters, Journal of Organic Chemistry, Journal of Medicinal Chemistry, Bioorganic and Medicinal Chemistry Letters, Bioorganic and Medicinal Chemistry; mem. NAS 1995–, American Acad. of Arts and Sciences 1995–; Trustee Rockefeller Univ. 1999–2004; Founding mem. Broad Inst., Dir Chemical Biology Program; numerous awards, including ICI Pharmaceuticals Award for Excellence in Chem. 1986, Arthur C. Cope Scholar Award, ACS 1986, Award in Pure Chem., ACS 1989, Arun Guthikonda Memorial Award, Columbia Univ. 1990, Ciba-Geigy Drew Award for Biomedical Research 1992, Thieme-IUPAC Award in Synthetic Organic Chem. 1992, NIH Merit Award 1992, Rhone-Poulenc Silver Medal, Royal Soc. of Chem. 1992, Eli Lilly Award in Biological Chem., ACS 1993, Leo Hendrik Baekeland Award, ACS 1993, Nat. Cancer Inst. Derek Barton Medal 1999, William H. Nichols Medal 2001, Chiron Corpn Biotechnology Research Award, American Acad. of Microbiology 2001 Soc. for Biomolecular Screening Achievement Award 2004, Asscn of American Cancer Insts Distinguished Scientist Award 2004, Academic Scientist of the Year, Finalist for the 2005 Pharmaceutical Achievement Awards 2005, Thomson Laureate Award in Chem. (with Gerald R. Crabtree) 2006, ACS Authur C. Cope Award 2014, Wolf Prize in Chem. (co-recipient) 2016. *Address:* Schreiber Research Laboratory, 7 Cambridge Center, Cambridge, MA 02142 (office); Department of Chemistry and Chemical Biology, Harvard University, 12 Oxford Street, Cambridge, MA 02138-2902, USA (office). *Telephone:* (617) 324-4380 (Lab.) (office); (617) 495-5318 (office). *Fax:* (617) 324-9601 (Lab.) (office); (617) 495-0751 (office). *E-mail:* stuart_schreiber@harvard.edu (office). *Website:* www.fas.harvard.edu/~biophys/Stuart_L_Schreiber.htm (office); www.broad.harvard.edu/chembio/lab_schreiber/home.php (office).

SCHREIER, Ethan J., BSc, PhD, FAAS; American astronomer; b. New York, NY; ed Bronx High School of Science, City Coll. of New York, Massachusetts Inst. of Tech.; Researcher, American Science and Eng Inc. 1970–73; Sr Scientist, Harvard-Smithsonian Center for Astrophysics 1973; Co-founder, Space Telescope Science Inst., Baltimore, Md 1981, becoming Chief Data and Operations Scientist, Assoc. Dir for Next Generation Space Telescope, and Head of Strategic Planning and Devt; currently Adjunct Prof., Dept of Physics and Astronomy, Johns Hopkins Univ.; Exec. Vice-Pres., Associated Universities Inc. 2001–04, Pres. 2004–17, then Sr Advisor; mem. Bd of Dirs Atacama Large Millimeter/submillimeter Array, Cerro Chajnantor Atacama Telescope, Virtual Astronomical Observatory (VAO); mem. numerous NASA advisory cttees, including VAO Exec. Cttee, Int. Virtual Observatory Alliance Exec.; Distinguished Scientist of the Year, North American-Chilean Chamber of Commerce 2014. *Address:* Associated Universities Inc., 1400 16th Street, NW, Washington, DC 20036-2252, USA (office). *Telephone:* (202) 462-1676 (office). *Fax:* (202) 232-7161 (office). *E-mail:* ejs@aui.edu (office). *Website:* www.aui.edu (office).

SCHREYER, Rt Hon. Edward Richard, CC, PC, CMM, CD, MA, LLD; Canadian politician and diplomatist; b. 21 Dec. 1935, Beausejour, Manitoba; s. of John J. Schreyer and Elizabeth Gottfried; m. Lily Schulz 1960; two s. two d.; ed Beausejour Collegiate, United Coll., St John's Coll. and Univ. of Manitoba; elected mem. Manitoba Legislature for Brokenhead 1958, re-elected 1959, 1962; Prof. of Political Science and Int. Relations, Univ. of Manitoba 1962–65; mem. Manitoba Prov. Legis. Ass. for Springfield constituency 1965–68, for Selkirk 1968; Leader, Manitoba New Democratic Party 1969–78; Premier of Manitoba, Minister of Dominion-Provincial Relations 1969–77, Prov. Minister of Hydro 1971–77, of Finance 1972–74; Leader of the Opposition 1977–78; Gov.-Gen. of Canada 1979–84; High Commr to Australia, also accred to Papua New Guinea and Solomon Islands 1984–88; Amb. to Vanuatu 1984–88; Distinguished Visiting Prof., Univ. of Winnipeg 1989–90, Simon Fraser Univ. 1991; Distinguished Fellow, Inst. of Integrated Energy Systems, Univ. of Victoria 1992–94, Dept of Geography, Univ. of BC 1995–96; apptd Chair. Canadian Shield Foundation 1984; apptd Dir Perfect Pacific Investments 1989, China Int. Trust and Investment Corpn (Canada) Ltd 1991, Swan-E-Set Bay Resort and Country Club 1991, Habitat for Humanity Canada 1992–, Sask. Energy Conservation and Devt Authority 1993–96, Alt. Fuel Systems Inc. (Calgary) 1994, Cephalon Oil and Gas Resource Corp. (Calgary) 1994–95; mem. Int. Asscn of Energy Econs, Churchill Econ. Advisory Cttee, Pacific Inst. of Deep Sea Tech.; Counsellor, Canada West Foundation 1989; Sr Adviser, Summit Council for World Peace (World Peace Fed.), Washington DC 1991; Chancellor, Brandon Univ. 2002–08; Hon. Dir Sierra Legal Defence Fund 1991–, Hon. Patron, John Diefenbaker Soc. 1991–, Hon. Adviser, Canadian Foundation for the Preservation of Chinese Cultural and Historical Treasures 1994–; Hon. LLD (Manitoba) 1979, (Mount Allison) 1983, (McGill) 1984, (Simon Fraser) 1984, (Lakehead) 1985; Gov.-Gen. Vanier Award 1975. *Leisure interests:* reading, golf, sculpting, woodworking. *Address:* 250 Wellington Center, Unit 401, Winnipeg, Man. R3M 0B3, Canada.

SCHRIEFFER, John Robert, BS, MS, PhD; American physicist and academic; b. 31 May 1931, Oak Park, Ill.; s. of John Henry Schrieffer and Louise Anderson; m. Anne Grete Thomson 1960; one s. two d.; ed Massachusetts Inst. of Tech., Univ. of Illinois; NSF Fellow, Univ. of Birmingham, UK and Univ. Inst. for Theoretical Physics, Copenhagen 1957–58; Asst Prof., Univ. of Chicago 1957–60, Univ. of Illinois 1959–60; Assoc. Prof., Univ. of Illinois 1960–62; Prof., Univ. of Pennsylvania 1962, Mary Amanda Wood Prof. of Physics 1962–79, Mary Amada Wood Prof. of Physics 1964–79; Andrew D. White Prof.-at-Large, Cornell Univ. 1969–75; Prof. of Physics, Univ. of California, Santa Barbara 1980–91, Essan Khashoggi Prof. of Physics 1985, Dir Inst. for Theoretical Physics 1984–89, Chancellor's Prof. 1984–91; Prof., Florida State Univ., Tallahassee 1992–2006, Chief Scientist Nat. High Magnetic Field Lab. 1992–2006, Univ. Eminent Scholar, Florida State Univ. System 1996–2006 (retd); Vice-Pres. American Physical Soc. 1994–96, apptd Pres. 1996; fmr Chair. Scientific Council of the Int. Centre for Theoretical Physics; mem. Int. Advisory Editorial Bd Current Applied Physics journal (Elsevier); mem. NAS, American Acad. Arts and Sciences, American Philosophical Soc. 1974, Royal Danish Acad. of Science and Letters, Nat. Medal of Science Cttee 1996–; Guggenheim Fellow 1967–68; Fellow, American Physical Soc. (Pres. 1997); sentenced to two years in prison after a vehicular manslaughter incident 2005; Dr hc (Technische Hochschule, Munich, Univs of Geneva, Pennsylvania, Illinois, Cincinatti, Tel-Aviv, Alabama); Oliver E. Buckley Solid State Physics Prize 1968, Comstock Prize, NAS 1968, Nobel Prize for Physics (with J. Bardeen and L.N. Cooper) 1972, John Ericsson Medal, American Soc. of Swedish Engineers 1976, Alumni Achievement Award, Univ. of Ill. 1979, Nat. Medal of Science 1985, Superconductivity Award of Excellence, World Congress of Super-conductivity 1996, Robert A. Holton Medal for Distinguished Research Service, Florida State Univ. 2004. *Publication:* Theory of Superconductivity 1964.

SCHROCK, Richard R., AB, PhD; American chemist and academic; *Frederick G. Keyes Professor of Chemistry, Massachusetts Institute of Technology;* b. 4 Jan. 1945, Berne, Ind.; m. Nancy F. Carlson 1971; two s.; ed Univ. of California, Riverside, Harvard Univ., Univ. of Cambridge, UK; Research Chemist, Cen. Research and Devt Dept, E.I. du Pont de Nemours & Co. 1972–75; Asst Prof. of Chem., MIT 1975–78, Assoc. Prof. 1978–80, Prof. 1980–89, Frederick G. Keyes Prof. of Chem. 1989–; Sherman T. Fairchild Scholar, Calif. Inst. of Tech. 1986, Science and Eng Research Council Visiting Fellow, Univ. of Cambridge 1991; ACS Award in Organometallic Chem. 1985 and Harrison Howe Award 1990, Inorganic Chem. Award 1996, Bailar Medal, Univ. of Ill. 1998, ACS Cope Scholar Award 2001, RSC Sir Geoffrey Wilkinson Medal 2002, Nobel Prize in Chem. (co-recipient) 2005. *Publications:* numerous papers in scientific journals. *Address:* Department of Chemistry, 6-331, Massachusetts Institute of Technology, 77 Massachusetts Avenue, Cambridge, MA 02139, USA (office). *Telephone:* (617) 253-1596 (office). *Fax:* (617) 253-7670 (office). *E-mail:* rrs@mit.edu (office). *Website:* web.mit.edu/rrs/www/home.html (office); web.mit.edu/chemistry/www/faculty/schrock.html (office).

SCHRÖDER, Gerhard, LL.B.; German business executive and fmr politician; *Chairman, Nord Stream AG* and *Chairman, Rosneft;* b. 7 April 1944, Mossenburg, Lippe; s. of Fritz Schröder and Erika Schröder; m. 1st Eva Schubach; m. 2nd Anna Taschenmacher; m. 3rd Hiltrud Hensen 1984; m. 4th Doris Köpf 1997; one adopted d. one adopted s.; ed Univ. of Göttingen; apprentice as shop asst 1961; joined SPD 1963, Chair. 1999–2004; lawyer, Hanover 1976; Nat. Chair. of Young Socialists 1978–80; mem. Bundestag 1980–86; Leader of Opposition in State Parl. of Lower

Saxony 1986; Minister-Pres. of Lower Saxony 1990–98; Chancellor of Germany 1998–2005; consultant to Ringier Group (publr) 2005; Adviser, Rothschild Group 2006–; apptd Chair. Nord Stream AG (consortium owned by OAO Gazprom, BASF AG, E.On AG for construction and operation of planned Nord Stream submarine pipeline) 2006, now Exec. Dir; Chair. Rosneft 2017–; mem. Bd of Dirs TNK BP Ltd 2009–14; mem. InterActionCouncil, 21st Century Council, Council for the Future of Europe; Patron Aladdin Project, Gesicht Zeigen! Für ein weltoffenes Deutschland, Hilfe für ALS-kranke Menschen; Hon. Chair. Nah- und Mittelostvereins (NuMOV); Mittelstandspreis 1997, Quadriga Award 2007. *Address:* Nord Stream AG, 114435 Moscow, ul. Malaya Pirogovskaya 3; Rosneft, 117997 Moscow, Sofiiskaya nab. 26/1, Russian Federation. *Telephone:* (495) 777-06-76 (Nord Stream) (office); (499) 517-88-99 (Rosneft) (office). *Fax:* (499) 921-34-58 (Nord Stream) (office); (499) 517-72-35 (Rosneft) (office). *E-mail:* info@nord-stream.com (office); postman@rosneft.ru (office). *Website:* www.nord-stream.com (office); www.rosneft.com (office).

SCHRØDER, Søren Wølck, BA (Econ); American business executive; b. Aarhus, Denmark; ed Connecticut Coll.; worked for more than 15 years at Continental Grain and Cargill; joined Bunge 2000, served in a variety of agribusiness leadership roles in USA and Europe, CEO Bunge North America 2010–13, mem. Bd of Dirs and CEO Bunge Ltd 2013–19.

SCHROEDER, Barbet; French film producer, director and actor; b. 26 Aug. 1941, Tehran, Iran; s. of Jean-William Schroeder and Ursula Schroeder; m. Bulle Ogier; ed Univ. of Paris (Sorbonne); worked as jazz tour operator Europe, photo journalist India, critic for Cahiers du Cinéma and L'Air de Paris 1958–63; Asst to Jean-Luc Godard on Les Carabiniers 1963; f. own production co. Les Films du Losange 1964; worked as actor and producer. *Films produced:* Méditerranée 1963, La Carrière de Suzanne 1963, La Boulangère de Monceau 1963, Nadja à Paris 1964, Paris vu par… 1965, Fermière à Montfaucon 1967, La Collectionneuse 1967, More 1969, Ma nuit chez Maud 1969, Le Genou de Claire 1970, Sing-Sing 1971, Maquillages 1971, Le Cochon aux patates douces 1971, L'Amour l'après-midi 1972, Céline et Julie vont en bateau 1974, Marquise von O…, Die 1976, Chinesisches Roulette 1976, Perceval le Gallois 1978, Le Pont du Nord 1981, Flügel und Fesseln 1985, Barfly 1987, Single White Female 1992, Kiss of Death 1995, Never Talk to Strangers 1995, Before and After 1996, Desperate Measures 1998, Shattered Image 1998, La Virgen de los sicarios 2000, Murder by Numbers 2002. *Films directed:* More 1969, Sing-Song (documentary) 1971, Le Cochon aux patates douces 1971, La Vallée 1972, General Idi Amin Dada (documentary) 1974, Maîtresse 1976, Koko, the Talking Gorilla (documentary) 1978, Tricheurs 1984, Charles Bukowski (50 four-minute videos) 1985, Barfly 1987, Reversal of Fortune 1990, Single White Female 1992, Kiss of Death 1995, Before and After (also producer) 1996, Desperate Measures 1998, La Virgen de los Sicarios 2000, Murder by Numbers 2002, L'Avocat de la terreur (French César, Best Documentary) 2007, Inju: The Beast in the Shadow 2008, Amnesia 2015. *Films as actor:* La Boulangère de Monceau 1963, Les Carabiniers 1963, Paris vu par... 1965, Out 1, noli me tangere 1971, Out 1: Spectre 1972, Céline et Julie vont en bateau 1974, Roberte 1979, L'Amour par terre 1984, The Golden Boat 1990, La Reine Margot 1994, Beverly Hills Cop III 1994, Mars Attacks! 1996, La Virgen de los sicarios 2000, Ne fais pas ça 2004, Une aventure 2005, Paris, je t'aime (segment) 2006, Ne touchez pas la hache 2007, The Darjeeling Limited 2007, The Counsel 2010, Par exemple, Electre 2013, Portrait of the Artist 2014.

SCHROEDER, Patricia Nell Scott, JD; American organization executive and fmr politician; b. 30 July 1940, Portland, Ore.; m. James W. Schroeder; one s. one d.; ed Univ. of Minn., Harvard Law School; mem. US House of Reps 1972–96, served on House Armed Services and Judiciary Cttees and several other cttees, Chair. House Select Cttee on Children, Youth and Families 1991–93; Prof., Woodrow Wilson School of Public and Int. Affairs, Princeton Univ. Jan.–June 1997; Pres. and CEO Asscn of American Publrs 1997–2009; mem. Bd Marguerite Casey Foundation (currently Vice-Chair.), ABA Center for Human Rights; Chair. Peace PAC, Council for a Livable World; elected to Nat. Women's Hall of Fame, Seneca Falls, New York 1995. *Publications:* Champion of the Great American Family 1989, 24 Years of House Work and the Place is Still a Mess 1998. *Address:* 621 Nadina Place, Orlando, FL 34747, USA (home).

SCHROEDER, Steven Alfred, MD; American physician and academic; *Distinguished Professor of Health and Health Care, Department of Medicine, University of California, San Francisco;* b. 26 July 1939, New York, NY; s. of Arthur E. Schroeder; m. Sally Ross Schroeder 1967; two s.; ed El Cerrito High School, Stanford Univ., Harvard Univ.; Fellow, Harvard Community Health and Medical Care and Instructor Harvard Medical School 1970–71; Asst Prof. of Medicine and Health Care Sciences, later Assoc. Prof., The George Washington Univ. Medical Center 1971–76, Medical Dir The George Washington Univ. Health Plan 1971–76; Assoc. Prof. of Medicine, Univ. of Calif., San Francisco 1976–80, Prof. 1980–90, Chief, Div. of Gen. Internal Medicine 1980–90, Distinguished Prof. of Health and Health Care, Dept of Medicine 2003–, Dir Smoking Cessation Leadership Center 2003–; Clinical Prof., Univ. of Medicine and Dentistry of NJ, Robert Wood Johnson Medical School 1991–2002; Pres. Robert Wood Johnson Foundation 1990–99, Pres. and CEO 1999–2003; Founding Chair. Int. Advisory Cttee of The Health Services, Ben-Gurion Univ. of the Negev, Israel 1996–2009; mem. Bd of Dirs American Legacy Foundation 2000–05 (Vice-Chair. 2001–03, Chair. 2003–05), James Irvine Foundation 2004–, Charles R. Drew Univ. of Medicine and Science 2005–09, Marin Gen. Hosp. 2009–, Mathematica Policy Research 2011–, Marin Community Foundation 2013–; mem. Bd of Overseers, Harvard Coll. 2000–06; mem. Editorial Bd New England Journal of Medicine 1994–2013; Visiting Prof., Dept of Community Medicine, St Thomas's Hosp. Medical School, London 1982–83; Pres. Harvard Medical Alumni Asscn 2005–06; numerous hon. degrees; numerous awards. *Publications include:* more than 300 articles. *Leisure interests:* climbing, hiking, tennis, gardening, literature, history. *Address:* Smoking Cessation Leadership Center, University of California, 3333 California Street, Suite 430, San Francisco, CA 94143 (office); Box 1211, University of California, San Francisco, San Francisco, CA 94143-1211 (office); 10 Paseo Mirasol, Belvedere Tiburon, CA 94920, USA (home). *Telephone:* (415) 502-1881 (office); (415) 435-3872 (home). *Fax:* (415) 502-5739 (office). *E-mail:* schroeder@medicine.ucsf.edu (office). *Website:* smokingcessationleadership.ucsf.edu (office).

SCHROTT, Erwin; Uruguayan singer (bass-baritone); b. 21 Dec. 1972, Montevideo; one s. with Anna Netrebko; ed studied singing with Franca Mattiucci; operatic debut as Roucher in Andrea Chénier, Montevideo aged 22; with Teatro Municipal, Santiago, Chile –1996, sang Timur in Turandot, Colline in La Bohème, Sparafucile in Rigoletto and Ramfis in Aida; Italian stage debut at Teatro Regio di Torino in Boris Godunov 1996; debut at Vienna State Opera as Banquo in Verdi's Macbeth 1999; debut at New York Metropolitan Opera as Colline in La Bohème 2000; debut at Royal Opera House as Leporello in Don Giovanni 2003; debut at Salzburg Festival as Leporello 2008; has sung his interpretation of title role in Mozart's Don Giovanni at Royal Opera, Covent Garden, Teatro alla Scala, Maggio Musicale Fiorentino, Washington Opera, Los Angeles Opera, as well as in Seville and Turin and with Metropolitan Opera on tour to Japan; has sung in numerous operatic theatres including Teatro alla Scala, Metropolitan Opera, Opera Nat. de Paris, Washington Opera, Vienna State Opera, Teatro Colon of Buenos Aires, Royal Opera, Covent Garden, Maggio Musicale Fiorentino, Hamburg State Opera, Theatre Royale de la Monnaie, Teatro Comunale, Firenze, Teatro Carlo Felice, Genoa, Los Angeles Opera, numerous others; numerous concert appearances including jt concert with Anna Netrebko conducted by Plácido Domingo in Centro de Bellas Artes, San Juan, Puerto Rico 2007, gala concert for 5th Abu Dhabi Music and Arts Festival, with Anna Netrebko and Elīna Garanča 2008, solo concert at Münchner Residenz 2008, jt concerts with Anna Netrebko and Jonas Kaufmann at Waldbühne, Berlin, Stadthalle, Wien and Königsplatz, Munich 2011, with Anna Netrebko and Ramon Vargas, Albert Hall, London 2012, solo concerts at Salzburger Festspiele 2014 and Los Angeles Opera 2015; 2016 roles included title role in Don Giovanni, Opera di Genova, Teatro Colón, Münchner Opernfestspiele, Theater an der Wien, Hungarian State Opera; Escamillo in Carmen, Teatro San Carlo, Naples 2017; scholarship for studies in Italy 1996; first prize in Plácido Domingo Operalia Singing Competition 1998; named Distinguished Citizen of Montevideo 2015. *Opera repertoire includes:* major Mozart roles of Don Giovanni, Leporello and Figaro, Pagano in Verdi's I Lombardi, title role in Verdi's Attila, Banquo in Macbeth, Escamillo in Carmen, Méphistophélès in Gounod's Faust and title role in Boito's Mefistofele. *Recordings include:* Rojotango (Echo Klassik Award 2012) 2011, Arias 2012, Don Giovanni (Festpielhaus Baden Baden recording) 2014, Les Vêpres Siciliennes (Royal Opera House recording) 2015. *Address:* c/o Alan Green, Zemsky Green Artists Management, 104 West 73rd Street, New York, NY 10023, USA (office). *Telephone:* (212) 579-6700 (office). *E-mail:* agreen@zemskygreen.com (office). *Website:* www.zemskygreen.com (office); www.erwinschrott.com (office).

SCHUBARTH, Martin, DrIur; Swiss lawyer, judge and academic; *Avocat-Conseil, Rusconi & Associés;* b. 9 June 1942, Basel; m. Musa Retschmedin 1944; one d.; ed Univ. of Basel; began practising as lawyer, Basel 1969–83; mem. Bar of Basel 1969–83; Guest Lecturer, Univ. of St.Gallen 1974; Lecturer, Univ. of Basel 1975–78; Prof. Univ. of Bonn 1976–80, Univ. of Hanover 1980–83; Fed. Judge 1983–2004, Pres. Fed. Supreme Court 1999–2000, Pres. Criminal Court 1999–2002; Judge, Court of Cassation 1987–2004; Avocat-Conseil, Rusconi & Associés, Lausanne 2004–; working visits to Supreme Court of Yugoslavia 1984, Lausanne of the European Court of Human Rights, Lausanne 1992, 1996, 2000, Austrian Supreme Court 1995, Fed. Constitutional Court 1997, Constitutional Court 2001, Fed. Constitutional Court, Karlsruhe 2001, Constitutional Court, Vienna 2002, Liechtenstein Tribunal 2002; Chair. Swiss Inst. for Alcohol and Other Drug Issues 1985–2003; mem. Bd of Dirs Swiss working group for Criminology 1989–2003. *Publication:* Kommentar zum Schweizerischen Strafrecht 1982 ff. *Address:* Rusconi & Associés, 4 rue de la Paix, CP 7268, 1002 Lausanne (office); Ch. du Levant 44, 1005 Lausanne, Switzerland (home). *Telephone:* (21) 321-50-80 (office); (21) 728-83-82 (home). *Fax:* (21) 320-29-60 (office). *E-mail:* info@rusconi-avocats.ch (office); m.schubarth@bluewin.ch (home). *Website:* www.rusconi-avocats.ch; www.martinschubarth.ch.

SCHUBERT, John Michael, AO, PhD; Australian business executive; *Chairman, Great Barrier Reef Foundation;* b. 11 Dec. 1942, Adelaide, South Australia; m. Prudence Schubert; two c.; began career at ESSO in Australia 1969, held numerous positions at ESSO in Australia and internationally, fmr Chair. and Man. Dir Esso Australia Ltd; fmr Man. Dir and CEO Pioneer International Ltd, led business to merger at Hanson Plc 2000; mem. Bd of Dirs Commonwealth Bank of Australia 1991–2010, Deputy Chair. 2000–04, Chair. 2004–10; Chair. G2 Therapies Pty Ltd 2000–13; joined Worley Parsons Ltd (fmrly Worley Group Ltd) as Chair. Advisory Bd 2000, Chair. (non-exec.) 2002–05; Dir BHP Ltd 2000–, Ind. Dir, BHP Billiton plc 2001–, Dir (non-exec.) BHP Billiton Ltd 2001–, Dir BHP Billiton Group; Ind. Dir (non-exec.) Qantas Airways Ltd 2000–12; mem. Bd of Dirs Hanson Ltd 2000–03; Chair. Great Barrier Reef Research Foundation; Chair. Garvan Inst. of Medical Research 2013–; fmr Pres. Business Council of Australia; Dir Australian Grad. School of Man., Salvation Army Advisory Bd; Fellow, Acad. of Technological Science and Eng, Inst. of Engineers; Hon. mem. Business Council of Australia. *Address:* Great Barrier Reef Foundation, PO Box 1362, Brisbane, Queensland 4001, Australia (office). *Telephone:* (7) 3252-7555 (office). *E-mail:* johnmschubert@bigpond.com; frances.grant2@bigpond.com. *Website:* www.barrierreef.org (office).

SCHULMAN, Amy Weinfeld, BA, JD; American lawyer and business executive; *CEO, Lyndra, Inc.;* b. 16 Oct. 1960, New York; d. of Alvin Harold Schulman and Ann Schulman; m. David Eli Nachman; three s.; ed Wesleyan Univ., Yale Law School; law clerk to Judge Harold Ackerman 1989; Assoc., Cleary Gottlieb 1990–97; Of Counsel, Piper & Marbury 1997, Pnr, Piper Rudnick 1998–2004, Pnr, DLA Piper Rudnick Gray Cary (litigation practice) 2005–08; Gen. Counsel Pfizer Inc. 2008–13, Exec. Vice-Pres. 2010–13; CEO Arsia Therapeutics Inc. 2014–16, mem. Bd; Venture Pnr Polaris Partners 2014–18, Entrepreneur Pnr 2018–; Co-founder and CEO Lyndra, Inc. 2015–; mem. Bd of Dirs Brooklyn Acad. of Music 2002–, Wesleyan Univ.; Visiting Prof., Harvard Law School; mem. Fed. Bar Council, ABA, Int. Asscn of Defense Counsel, Defense Research Inst.; Margaret Brent Women Lawyers of Achievement Award, ABA 2012. *Address:* 65 Grove Street, Suite 301, Watertown, MA 02472, USA (office). *Telephone:* (857) 304-4512 (office). *E-mail:* media@lyndra.com. *Website:* www.lyndra.com (office).

SCHULMAN, Joshua G.; American business executive; *President and CEO, Coach brand;* b. Beverly Hills, Calif.; Sr Account Exec., Perry Ellis Int. 1991–93; Vice-Pres. and Dir Sales and Marketing, Richard Tyler 1993–97; Worldwide Dir

Women's Ready to Wear for Gucci brand, Gucci Group 1997–2000, Exec. Vice-Pres. Worldwide Merchandising and Wholesale for Yves Saint Laurent brand, Gucci Group 2000–05; Man. Dir of Int. Strategic Alliances and Sr Vice-Pres. Int. Product Devt and Merchandising Gap Inc. 2005–06; Pres. Kenneth Cole Productions, Inc. New York brand 2006–07; CEO Jimmy Choo (shoe label) 2007–12; Pres. Bergdorf Goodman, Neiman Marcus Group 2012–14, Pres. NMG International, including responsibility for Bergdorf Goodman and int. subsidiaries 2014–17; Pres. and CEO Coach brand 2017–. *Address:* Coach Inc., 10 Hudson Yards, New York, NY 10001, USA. *Website:* www.coach.com/company-information.html (office).

SCHULTE-NOELLE, Henning, MBA, DrJur; German insurance executive; b. 26 Aug. 1942, Essen; m.; one s. one d.; ed Univs of Tübingen, Bonn, Cologne, Edinburgh, UK and Pennsylvania, USA; attorney, Eckholt, Westrick & Partners, Frankfurt 1974; joined Allianz Group 1975, Head of Chair.'s Office, Munich 1979–83, Head of Regional Office for North Rhine-Westphalia, Cologne 1984–87, mem. Man. Bd Allianz Versicherung 1988–90, Allianz Leben 1988–90 (Chair. 1991), Chair. Allianz AG (renamed Allianz SE 2006) 1991–2003, Chair. Supervisory Bd 2003–12; mem. Supervisory Bd E.ON AG; fmr mem. Supervisory Bd Thyssen Krupp AG, Siemens AG, BASF AG, Linde AG, Vodafone AG and others; Bavarian Order of Merit 2001; Manager of the Year, Manager Magazine 1996. *Address:* c/o Allianz SE, Königinstrasse 28, 80802 Munich, Germany. *E-mail:* info@allianz.com.

SCHULTZ, Howard, BS; American business executive; b. 19 July 1953, Brooklyn, New York; m. Sheri Kersch Schultz; one s. one d.; ed Canarsie High School and Northern Michigan Univ.; began career as sales trainee for Xerox; Vice-Pres. of US Sales, Hammerplast (subsidiary of Swedish-based Perstorp); joined Starbucks Coffee Co. (now Starbucks Corpn) in Sales and Marketing Dept 1982, Chair. 1987–2018 (after buying out original owners), CEO 1987–2000, 2008–17, also Chief Global Strategist; Co-founder Maveron (venture capital firm) 1998, mem. Bd of Dirs Pinkberry Inc.; Co-Founder Schultz Family Foundation; fmr Owner, Seattle SuperSonics professional basketball team (Nat. Basketball Asscn) and Seattle Storm professional basketball team (Women's Nat. Basketball Asscn); Israel 50th Anniversary Tribute Award 1998, National Leadership Award 1999, International Distinguished Entrepreneur Award 2004, FIRST Responsible Capitalism Award 2007, Rev. Theodore M. Hesburgh, C.S.C., Award for Ethics in Business 2007, named 'Businessperson of the Year' by Fortune Magazine 2011, Nat. Equal Justice Award 2017. *Publications include:* Pour Your Heart Into It: How Starbucks Built a Company One Cup at a Time (with Dori Jones Yang) 1997, Onward: How Starbucks Fought for Its Life Without Losing Its Soul (with Joanne Gordon) 2011, For Love of Country: What Our Veterans Can Teach Us About Citizenship, Heroism, and Sacrifice 2014.

SCHULTZ, Peter G., BS, PhD; American chemist and academic; *CEO and Professor of Chemistry, The Scripps Research Institute;* b. 23 June 1956, Cincinnati, Ohio; ed California Inst. of Tech., Massachusetts Inst. of Tech.; Asst Prof., Dept of Chem., Calif. Inst. of Tech. 1985–87, Assoc. Prof. 1987–89, Prof. 1989–99; Prin. Investigator, Lawrence Berkeley Lab. 1985–; Founding Scientist and Chair., Scientific Advisory Bd, Affymax Research Inst., Palo Alto, Calif. 1988–; Investigator, Howard Hughes Medical Inst. 1994–98; Founder and Dir Symyx Technologies, Palo Alto 1995–; Scripps Prof. of Chem., Scripps Research Inst., La Jolla, Calif. 1999–, CEO 2015–; Inst. Dir Genomics Inst., Novartis Research Foundation, La Jolla 1999–2010; mem. Bd of Dirs Nanosphere 2005–; Founder and Dir Syrrx Inc. 2000–, Kalypsys 2001–, Phenomix 2002–, Ambrx 2003–, Ilypsa 2004–; Dir Calif. Inst. for Biomedical Research (Calibr) 2012–; mem. American Acad. of Arts and Sciences 1990–, NAS 1993–, Caltech Chem. Advisory Cttee 1998–, Searle Advisory Cttee 1995–, Welch Foundation Scientific Advisory Bd 2002–, Daman Runyon Advisory Bd 1999–2004, Princeton Chem. Advisory Cttee 1994–96; Dr hc (Uppsala Univ., Sweden) 1994; numerous awards including NSF Presidential Young Investigator Award 1985, Alan T. Waterman Award 1988, ACS Award in Pure Chem. 1990, Eli Lilly Award in Biological Chem. 1991, Humboldt Research Award 1992, Wolf Prize in Chem. 1994, Calif. Scientist of the Year 1995, Alfred Bader Award in Bioorganic and Bioinorganic Chem. 2000, Ludwig Darmstaedter Prize 2002, Paul Ehrlich Prize 2003, Arthur C. Cope Award, ACS 2006, G. K. Gilbert Award 2012, Solvay Prize 2013. *Publications include:* co-authored nearly 600 scientific publications. *Address:* The Scripps Research Institute, 10550 North Torrey Pines Road, La Jolla, CA 92037, USA (office). *Telephone:* (858) 784-1000 (office). *Website:* schultz.scripps.edu (office).

SCHULTZ, Wolfram, FRS, PhD; German neurobiologist; *Wellcome Principal Research Fellow, Professor of Neuroscience, Cambridge University;* b. 27 Aug. 1944, Meissen; s. of Robert Schultz and Herta Schultz (née Beegen); m. Gerda Baumann 1972; two s. one d.; ed Univs of Hamburg and Heidelberg, Germany, Univ. of Fribourg, Switzerland; Medical Internship 1972–73; Postdoctoral Collaborator, Neurobiology Section, Max Planck Inst. for Biophysical Chemistry, Göttingen 1973–75; Postdoctoral Collaborator (Research Asst Prof.), Neurobiology Lab., Dept of Physiology, State Univ. of New York at Buffalo, USA 1975–76; Postdoctoral Collaborator, Swedish Medical Research Council, Dept of Histology, Karolinska Inst., Stockholm, Sweden 1976–77; Chef de Travaux, Inst. of Physiology, Univ. of Fribourg 1977–81, Privat-docent 1981, Asst, later Assoc. Prof. 1986–96, Prof. and Chair of Neurophysiology 1996–2001; Wellcome Prin. Research Fellow, Dept of Physiology, Devt and Neuroscience, Univ. of Cambridge 2001–, Prof. of Neuroscience 2002–; Fellow, Churchill Coll. Cambridge 2004–; Visiting Research Assoc., California Inst. of Tech., Pasadena; Visiting Prof., Tamagawa Univ., Tokyo; Swiss Societies for Neurology, Neurosurgery and Neuropathology Ellermann Prize 1984, Swiss Acad. of Medical Sciences Theodore-Ott-Prize (jt winner) 1997, Minerva Foundation Golden Brain Award 2002, Ipsen Prize for Neuronal Plasticity (jt winner) 2005, European Journal of Neuroscience Award of the Fed. of European Neuroscience Societies (EJN FENS Award) 2010, Gertrud Reemtsma Foundation Zülch Prize (jt winner) 2013, Lundbeck Foundation Brain Prize (jt winner) 2017. *Address:* Department of Physiology, Development and Neuroscience, University of Cambridge, Downing Street, Cambridge, CB2 3DY, England (office). *Telephone:* (1223) 333779 (office). *Fax:* (1223) 333840 (office). *E-mail:* ws234@cam.ac.uk (office). *Website:* research.pdn.cam.ac.uk/staff/schultz/index.shtml (office).

SCHULZ, Ekkehard D., Dr-Ing; German business executive; b. 24 July 1941, Bromberg, Westpreussen; m.; two c.; ed Clausthal Mining Acad., Clausthal Univ.; mem. scientific staff and Chief Engineer, Inst. for Gen. Metallurgy and Casting, Clausthal Univ. 1967–72; joined Thyssen Group 1972, Deputy Mem. (Production) Exec. Bd, Thyssen Stahl AG 1985, mem. (Production) 1986, (Tech.) 1988, Chair. 1991; mem. Exec. Bd, Thyssen AG 1991, Chair. 1998, Chair. Exec. Bd, ThyssenKrupp Stahl AG 1997, ThyssenKrupp AG 1999–2011, Thyssen Krupp Steel AG 1999–2001, apptd mem. Supervisory Bd ThyssenKrupp AG 2011; mem. Supervisory Bd RWE Plus AG, MAN AG, Bayer AG; mem. int. advisory Bd, Salomon Smith Barney, New York; mem. Exec. Cttee and Bd, Wirtschaftsvereinigung Stahl und VDEh; mem. Advisory Council of BDI (Vice-Pres.); Hon. Prof. (Clausthal Univ.) 1999; Hon. Dr rer. pol (Berlin) 2004; Hon. Dr-Ing. (Aachen) 2005.

SCHULZ, Martin; German politician and fmr bookseller; b. 20 Dec. 1955, Hehlrath; m. Inge Schulz; two c.; began career as apprentice in publishing trade 1975–77, worked in various bookshops 1977–82, bookshop propr, Würselen 1982–94; mem. SPD 1974–, Chair. Aachen Dist SPD 1996–2010, mem. SPD Fed. Exec. 1999–, Chair. SPD 2017–18; mem. Würselen town council 1984–99, Mayor of Würselen 1987–98; mem. European Parl. 1999–2017, Leader, SPD Group in European Parl. 2000–04, Leader, Progressive Alliance of Socialists and Democrats 2004–12, Pres. European Parl. 2012–17; mem. Bundestag 2017–; Dr hc (Staatlichen Technischen Univ. Kaliningrad) 2009, (İstanbul Bilgi Univ.) 2012, (Hebrew Univ.) 2013, (Pädagogischen Hochschule Karlsruhe) 2014; Bundesverdienstkreuz (1st Class) 2006, Grosses Goldenes Ehrenzeichen am Bande für Verdienste um die Republik Österreich 2015, Grosses Verdienstkreuz mit Stern und Schulterband 2016. *Leisure interests:* reading, football. *Address:* Sozialdemokratische Partei Deutschlands, Willy-Brandt-Haus, Wilhelmstr. 141, 10963 Berlin, Germany (office). *Telephone:* (30) 25991500 (office). *Fax:* (30) 25991507 (office). *E-mail:* parteivorstand@spd.de (office). *Website:* www.spd.de (office); www.martin-schulz.info (office).

SCHULZE, Ingo; German writer; *Director, Literary Section, Akademie der Künste, Berlin;* b. 15 Dec. 1962, Dresden; s. of Christa Schulze; m. Jutta Müller-Tamm; two d.; ed Univ. of Jena; Dramatic Producer, Theatre of Altenburg 1988–90; Founder of weekly newspaper in Altenburg 1990–92, weekly newspaper in St Petersburg 1993; writer in Berlin 1993–; mem. Akad. der Künste, Berlin, Akad. für Deutsche Sprache und Dichtung, Darmstadt, Sächsische Akad., Dresden; Alfred-Döblin Prize 1995, Aspekte Literature Prize 1995, Berlin Literature Prize 1998, Johannes Bobrowski Medal 1998, Joseph Breitbach Prize 2001, Peter Weiss Prize 2006, Thuringia Literature Prize 2007, Leipzig Book Fair Prize 2007, Premio Grinzane Cavour 2008, Stadtschreiber Mainz 2011, Bertolt-Brecht Prize 2013, Int. Manhae Prize for Culture (S Korea) 2013, Rheingau Literatur Preis 2017. *Television:* Rettung aus dem Regenwald? – Die Wiederentdeckung der Terra Preta (documentary, with Christine Traber) (ZDF/3SAT) 2011. *Publications:* 33 Augenblicke des Glücks (Aspekte-Literatur Prize for best debut) 1995, Simple Storys: Ein Roman aus der ostdeutschen Provinz 1998, Von Nasen, Faxen und Ariadnefäden, Fax-Briefe (with Zeichnungen von Helmar Penndorf) 2000, Telling Tales (contrib. to charity anthology) 2004, Neue Leben (novel) 2005, Handy – 13 Geschichten in alter Manier (stories) 2007, Adam und Evelyn (novel) 2008, Der Herr Augustin (with Julia Penndorf), Tausend Geschichten sind nicht genug (essays), Was Wollen Wir? (essays) 2009, Orangen und Engel (with photos by Matthias Hoch) (stories) 2010, Unsere schönen neuen Kleider (essay) 2012, Henkerslos. Ein Märchenbrevier (stories/fairy tales written together with Christine Traber) 2013; contrib. to Granta 100 (anthology) 2010, Einübung ins Paradies 2016, Peter Holz-sein glückliches Leben erzählt von ihm selbst (novel) 2017. *Address:* c/o S. Fischer Verlag, Hedderichstraße 114, 60596 Frankfurt am Main, Germany (office). *Telephone:* 69 6062-0 (office). *E-mail:* thomas.rohde@hanser.de (office). *Website:* www.hanser-literaturverlage.de (office); www.ingoschulze.com (office).

SCHULZE, Richard (Dick) M.; American retail executive; b. St Paul, Minn.; m.; one d.; ed St Paul Cen. High School; tech. electronics training with USAF and Minn. Air Nat. Guard; began career as ind. mfrs rep. for consumer electronics brands 1960s; f. Sound of Music (stereo component retail stores chain) 1966, Chair. and Dir 1966–83; f. Best Buy Co. Inc. (consumer electronics retailer) 1983, mem. Bd Dirs, Chair. and CEO 1983–2002, Chair. 2002–12 (resgnd); mem. Minn. Business Partnership; mem. Bd Dirs Pentair Inc., The Nat. Entrepreneur of the Year Inst., Bd Overseers Carlson School of Man., Advisory Bd Science and Tech. Center; Trustee, Univ. of St Thomas, Chair. Exec. and Institutional Advancement Cttee; Chair. Bd of Govs Univ. of St Thomas Business School, Best Buy Children's Foundation 1994–; Hon. PhD (Univ. of St Thomas) 1998; Dealer's Pride Award, Dealerscope Merchandising 1997, Corp. Leader of the Year, Juvenile Diabetes Foundation 1999, America's Promise Red Wagon Award for Community Service 1999, Lifetime Achievement Award, Ernst & Young 1999, Outstanding Marketing Exec. of the Year, Minn. DECA 2000.

SCHULZE, Svenja; German politician; *Federal Minister of the Environment, Nature Conservation and Nuclear Safety;* b. 29 Sept. 1968, Düsseldorf; ed Ruhr-Univ. Bochum; Freelance advertising and PR work 1993–97; North Rhine-Westphalia (NRW) State Chair. JUSOS (Working Group of Young Socialists in the SPD) 1993–97; mem. NRW Regional Ass. 1997–2000, 2004–18; business consultant with focus on public sector 2000–04; NRW State Minister of Innovation, Science and Research 2010–17; Fed. Minister of the Environment, Nature Conservation and Nuclear Safety 2018–; mem. Social Democratic Party (SPD) 1988–, NRW Regional SPD Sec.-Gen. 2017–18, mem. SPD Exec. Bd 2017–. *Address:* Federal Ministry of the Environment, Nature Conservation, Building and Nuclear Safety Stresemannstr. 128–130, 10117 Berlin, Germany (office). *Telephone:* (30) 183050 (office). *Fax:* (30) 183052044 (office). *E-mail:* service@bmub.bund.de (office). *Website:* www.bmub.bund.de (office); svenja-schulze.de.

SCHUMACHER, Joel, BA; American film director and producer; b. 29 Aug. 1939, New York City; s. of Francis Schumacher and Marian Kantor; ed Parsons School of Design, New York; began to work in fashion industry aged 15; later opened own boutique Paraphenalia; costume designer for Revlon in 1970s; also set and production designer; wrote screenplays Sparkle, Car Wash, The Wiz; also wrote and directed for TV. *Films include:* The Incredible Shrinking Woman 1981, DC Cab (also screenplay) 1983 St Elmo's Fire (also screenplay) 1985, The Lost Boys 1987, Cousins 1989, Flatliners 1990, Dying Young 1991, Falling Down 1993, The Client 1994, Batman Forever 1995, The Babysitter 1995 (producer), A Time to Kill 1996, Batman and Robin 1997, Eight Millimeter 1999, Flawless (also screenplay and producer) 1999, Gossip (producer) 2000, Tigerland 2000 Phone Booth 2002, Bad Company 2002, Veronica Guerin 2003, The Phantom of the Opera 2004, The Number 23 2007, Blood Creek 2009, Twelve 2010, Man in the Mirror 2011, Trespass 2011; as writer: Amateur Night at the Dixie Bar and Grill 1979, Sparkle 2012. *Address:* Joel Schumacher Productions, 400 Warner Blvd, Burbank, CA 91522, USA (office).

SCHUMACHER, Michael; German motor racing driver; b. 3 Jan. 1969, Hürth-Hermülheim; s. of Rolf Schumacher and Elisabeth Schumacher; m. Corinna Betsch 1995; one d. one s.; began professional career 1983; 2nd place, Int. German Formula 3 Championship 1989; driver for Mercedes 1990; Int. German Champion, Formula 3 Championship 1990; European Formula 3 Champion 1990; World Champion, Formula 3, Macau and Fiji 1990; Formula 1 racing driver for the Jordan team 1991, Benetton team 1992–95, Ferrari team 1996–2006 (retd); ended retirement to sign for Mercedes GP team 2010–12 (retd); Grand Prix wins: Argentina 1998, Australia 2000, 2001, 2002, 2004, Austria 2002, 2003, Bahrain 2004, Belgium 1992, 1995, 1996, 1997, 2001, 2002, 2004, Brazil 1994, 1995, 2000, 2002, Britain 1998, 2002, 2004, Canada 1994, 1997, 1998, 2000, 2002, 2003, 2004, China 2006, Europe 1994, 1995, 2000, 2001, 2004, 2006, France 1994, 1995, 1997, 1998, 2001, 2002, 2004, 2006, Germany 1995, 2002, 2004, 2006, Hungary 1994, 1998, 2001, 2004, Italy 1996, 1998, 2000, 2003, 2006, Japan 1995, 1997, 2000, 2001, 2002, 2004, Malaysia 2000, 2001, 2004, Monaco 1994, 1995, 1997, 1999, 2001, Pacific 1994, 1995, Portugal 1993, San Marino 1994, 1999, 2000, 2002, 2003, 2004, 2006, Spain 1995, 1996, 2001, 2002, 2003, 2004, USA 2000, 2003, 2004, 2005, 2006; Formula One World Champion 1994, 1995, 2000, 2001, 2002, 2003, 2004 (record seven times); placed in a medically induced coma after suffering a severe head injury in skiing accident in French Alps 29 Dec. 2013, left hosp. 16 June 2014. *Publications:* Schumacher: Driving Force 2003, Schumacher 2006, 7 91 2009. *Leisure interests:* football, skiing, motorbiking, climbing. *Address:* c/o Sabine Kehm, The MS Office, Avenue du Mont-Blanc 14B, 1196 Gland, Switzerland (office). *Telephone:* (22) 999-68-00 (office). *Fax:* (22) 999-68-09 (office). *Website:* www.michael-schumacher.de.

SCHUMANN, William H., III, BS, MS; American business executive; *Chairman, Avnet, Inc.;* ed Univ. of California, Los Angeles, Marshall School of Business, Univ. of Southern California; with Sunkist Growers, Inc. and Hughes Helicopter –1981; Dir of Pension Investments, FMC Corpn 1981, served in various man. positions throughout 1980s, including as Treas. 1987, Dir of North American Operations, Agricultural Products Group and Exec. Dir of Corp. Devt 1991–93, Vice-Pres. and Gen. Man. Agricultural Products Group 1995–98, Vice-Pres. of Corp. Devt 1998–99, Sr Vice-Pres. and Chief Financial Officer (CFO) 1999–2001 (until creation and spin-off of FMC Technologies), Exec. Vice-Pres. and CFO, FMC Technologies, Inc. 2001–11; mem. Bd of Dirs, Avnet, Inc. 2010–, Chair. 2012–; mem. Bd of Dirs Great Lakes Advisors, Inc. 1992–2011, AMCOL International 2012–14, McDermott International 2012–, URS Corpn March–Oct. 2014, Tesoro Corpn (now Andeavor) 2016–; voted one of the top CFOs in oilfield service and equipment by sell side analysts 2010. *Address:* Avnet, Inc., 2211 South 47th Street, Phoenix, AZ 85034, USA (office). *Telephone:* (480) 643-2000 (office). *E-mail:* info@avnet.com (office). *Website:* www.avnet.com (office).

SCHUMER, Charles (Chuck) Ellis, BA, JD; American politician; *Senate Minority Leader;* b. 23 Nov. 1950, Brooklyn, New York; s. of Abraham Schumer and Selma Schumer (née Rosen); m. Iris Weinshall 1980; two d.; ed Madison High School, Harvard Coll. and Harvard Law School; called to the NY Bar 1975; mem. staff, US Senator Claiborne Pell 1973; Assoc., Paul, Weiss, Rifking, Wharton & Garrison (law firm) 1974; mem. New York State Ass. 1975–80, Chair. Sub-cttee on City Man. and Governance 1977, Cttee on Oversight and Investigation 1979; elected to US Senate 1998, Sr Senator from New York 2000–, Chair. Democratic Senatorial Campaign Cttee 2005–09, Cttee on Rules and Admin 2009–, mem. Banking, Housing, and Urban Affairs Cttee, Judiciary Cttee (Chair. Subcommittee on Immigration, Refugees, and Border Security), Finance Cttee, Jt Cttee on the Library; Senate Minority Leader 2017–; Chair. Democratic Policy and Communications Center 2010–; Vice-Chair. Democratic Conf. 2006–; Democrat. *Publication:* Positively American: Winning Back the Middle-Class Majority One Family at a Time (with Daniel Squadron) 2007, Positively American: How the Democrats Can Win in 2008 2008. *Address:* 322 Hart Senate Office Building, Washington, DC 20510, USA (office). *Telephone:* (202) 224-6542 (office). *Fax:* (202) 228-3027 (office). *Website:* www.schumer.senate.gov (office); www.chuckschumer.com.

SCHÜSSEL, Wolfgang, DJur; Austrian politician; *President, Österreichische Gesellschaft für Außenpolitik und die Vereinten Nationen (ÖGAVN);* b. 7 June 1945, Vienna; m.; two c.; ed Univ. of Vienna; Sec. Parl. Group, Austrian People's Party (ÖVP) 1968–75, Sec.-Gen. Austrian Business Fed. 1975–91, Chair. ÖVP 1995–2007, Chair. Parl. Group 2006–08, Group Leader in Parl. 2007–11; mem. Parl. 1979–2011 (retd); Minister of Econ. Affairs 1989–95; Vice-Chancellor of Austria and Minister of Foreign Affairs 1995–2000; Pres. EU Council of Gen. and Foreign Affairs July–Dec. 1998; Chancellor of Austria 2000–07; Pres. EU July–Dec. 2006; Minister of the Interior Jan. 2007; Pres. Österreichische Gesellschaft für Außenpolitik und die Vereinten Nationen (ÖGAVN) (Austrian Soc. for Foreign Policy and the United Nations) 2008–; mem. Supervisory Bd RWE AG 2010–; mem. Bd of Dirs United Europe; mem. Scientific Cttee, European House – Ambrosetti; mem. Bd of Trustees, Bartelsmann Foundation 2007–, Allensbach Inst.; Hon. Citizen, Tirana, Albania; Grand Cross of the Royal Order of Merit (Norway) 1996, Grand Cross with Diamonds of the Order of Merit (Liechtenstein) 2001, Grand Cross of the Order of the Star (Romania) 2004, Grand Cross of Order of Merit (Poland) 2006, Grand Cross of Merit (Hungary) 2006, Bavarian Order of Merit 2007; Medal of Baden-Württemberg 2007. *Publications:* several books on issues relating to democracy and economics. *Address:* Österreichische Gesellschaft für Außenpolitik und die Vereinten Nationen (ÖGAVN), Hofburg/Stallburg Reitschulgasse 2/2. OG, 1010 Vienna, Austria (office). *E-mail:* office@oegavn.org (office). *Website:* www.oegavn.org (office).

SCHUSTER, Rudolf, PhD; Slovak politician, diplomatist, writer and engineer; b. 4 Jan. 1934, Košice; s. of Alojz Schuster and Mária Benediková; m. Irene Trojáková (died 2008); one s. one d.; ed Slovak Tech. Univ., Bratislava, Tech. Univ. Košice; designer, Regional Agric. Inst., Bratislava 1960; Asst Hydrology and Hydraulic Inst., Slovak Acad. of Sciences 1960–62; Dir Energy Investment Dept and Tech. Dir E Slovak Steelworks 1963–74; Vice-Mayor of Košice 1975–83, Mayor 1983–86,

1994–99, Chair. E Slovak Region Nat. Cttee 1986–89; Chair. Nat. Council 1989–90; Amb. of Czech Repub. and Slovakia to Canada 1990–92; with Ministry of Foreign Affairs 1993–94; Mayor of Košice 1994–99; Pres. of Slovakia 1999–2004; Hon. Citizen, Miskolc 1999; Order of Labour 1988 and many other decorations; Dr hc (Tech. Univ. Košice) 1998, (Wuppertal) 1999, (Moscow) 2001, (Kraków) 2002, (Bratislava) 2002, (St Petersburg) 2002, (Sofia) 2002, (Kiev) 2002, (Ottawa) 2003, (Ostrava) 2003, (Liptovský Mikuláš) 2003, (Nitra) 2006, (Prešov) 2014; Merit Award for Peace and Democratic Achievement 2000 and numerous other decorations. *Achievements:* open-air performance of Bocatius, eight broadcast performances and 21 literary sessions. *Publications:* Ultimatum (memoirs, translated into eight languages) 1997, more than 40 books (travel, crime fiction and detective novels, memoirs); numerous screenplays. *Leisure interests:* documentaries, literature, collecting historical photocameras, film-cameras and cine-projectors.

SCHUWIRTH, Gen. (retd) Rainer; German army officer (retd); *Chairman, Deutsche Gesellschaft für Wehrtechnik;* b. 12 July 1945, Regensburg, Bavaria; m. Barbara Hackbarth; one s., one d.; enlisted into Fed. Armed Forces 1964; trained as Artillery Officer 1964–66; assignments as Artillery Officer and Honest John Battery Commdr 1966–76; Fed. Armed Forces Command and Staff Coll., Hamburg 1976–78; G2 Staff Officer (Intelligence Estimates), HQ Centag, Heidelberg 1978–81; G3 Staff Officer (Operations) at III Corps, Koblenz 1981–83; Commdr Missile Artillery Bn 150 (Lance), Wesel 1983–85; Asst Br. Chief, Mil. Leadership and Civic Educ., Armed Forces Staff, Fed. Ministry of Defence, Bonn 1985–88, Br. Chief of Mil. Policy 1990–91; Mil. Asst to Fed. Minister of Defence 1988–90; Commdr Armoured Brigade 8, Luneberg 1991–93; Head of Mil. Policy Div., Perm. Mission to NATO 1994–96; Asst Chief of Staff, Armed Forces Staff Politico-Mil. Affairs and Operations, Ministry of Defence 1996–99; Commdg Gen. IV Corps, Potsdam 1999–2001; Dir-Gen., EU Mil. Staff 2001–04; Chief of Staff, SHAPE 2004–07 (retd); contracted by European Defence Agency to produce draft concept for EU to exploit Network Enabled Capabilities (NEC) in support of crisis-man. operations 2007; work with Stiftung Wissenschaft und Politik, Berlin 2008–; currently Chair. Deutsche Gesellschaft für Wehrtechnik eV; Silver Cross of Honour, Fed. Armed Forces, Gold Cross of Honour, Fed. Armed Forces, Cross of Order of Merit, Cross of Order of Merit (First Class), Commdr de l'Ordre nat. de Mérite, Gold Medal, Polish Armed Forces DWT Studienpreis 2016. *Publications include:* The Importance of Civil–Military Integration 2008. *Address:* Deutsche Gesellschaft für Wehrtechnik, Bertha-von-Suttner-Platz 1-7, 53111 Bonn, Germany (office). *Website:* www.dwt-sgw.de (office).

SCHWAB, Charles Robert, BA (Econs), MBA; American business executive; *Chairman, Charles Schwab Corporation;* b. 29 July 1937, Sacramento, Calif.; m. Helen O'Neill; five c.; ed Stanford Univ., Stanford Grad. School of Business; f. Charles Schwab Corpn, San Francisco 1971, Chair. 1986–, CEO 1986–97, 2004–08, Co-CEO 1998–2003, also Chair. Charles Schwab & Co., Inc. and Charles Schwab Bank, Trustee Charles Schwab Family of Funds, Schwab Investments, Schwab Capital Trust, Schwab Annuity Portfolios; Chair. San Francisco Museum of Modern Art; apptd Chair. President's Advisory Council on Financial Literacy (now President's Advisory Council on Financial Capability) 2008; mem. Bd of Dirs Yahoo! Inc. 2014–; fmr mem. Bd of Dirs The Gap Inc., Transamerica Corpn, AirTouch Communications, Siebel Systems, Inc.; mem. World Business Forum, CEO Org., San Francisco CEO Cttee on Jobs; mem. Bd and Treas. Nat. Park Foundation; mem. Bd of Trustees, Stanford Univ.; Co-founder and Chair. Charles and Helen Schwab Foundation 1987–; mem. San Francisco Golf Club. *Publications:* How To Be Your Own Stockbroker 1984, Charles Schwab's Guide to Financial Independence 1998, It Pays To Talk (co-author), You're Fifty — Now What?. *Leisure interests:* golf. *Address:* Charles Schwab Corporation, 211 Main Street, San Francisco, CA 94105 (office); Charles and Helen Schwab Foundation, 530 Lytton Avenue, Suite 200, Palo Alto, CA 94301, USA (office). *Telephone:* (415) 667-7000 (office). *Website:* www.schwab.com (office).

SCHWAB, Klaus, DEcon, DrIng, MPA; German foundation director and academic; *Executive Chairman, World Economic Forum;* b. 30 March 1938, Ravensburg; m. Hilde Schwab; one s. one d.; ed Swiss Federal Inst. of Tech., Univ. of Fribourg, Harvard Univ.; Founder and Exec. Chair. World Econ. Forum 1971–; Prof. of Business Policy, Univ. of Geneva 1972–2002; fmr mem. UN High-Level Advisory Bd on Sustainable Devt; fmr Vice-Chair. UN Cttee for Devt Planning; fmr mem. Earth Council; co-f. The Schwab Foundation for Social Entrepreneurship 1998; f. The Forum of Young Global Leaders 2004; Trustee, Peres Center for Peace, Israel; Hon. Prof., Ben Gurion Univ., Israel; Hon. KCMG, Grosses Goldenes Ehrenzeichen für Verdienste um die Republik Österreich 1997, Grosses Verdienstkreuz mit Stern 2012, Mexican Order del Aguila Azteca 2012, Grand Cordon Order of the Rising Sun (Japan) 2013, Colombian Order of San Carlos 2014; 13 hon. doctorates, including from Bishops Univ., Quebec, Canada, Univ. Autonoma de Guadalajara, Mexico, LSE, UK, Nankai Univ., Tianjin, People's Repub. of China, Vietnam Nat. Univ.; The Candlelight Award Foundation for Prevention and Early Resolution of Conflict 2001. *Publications:* several books and The Global Competitiveness Report (annually 1979–). *Leisure interests:* cross-country ski marathons, mountain climbing. *Address:* World Economic Forum, 91–93 route de la Capite, 1223 Cologny/Geneva, Switzerland (office). *Telephone:* (22) 869-1212 (office). *Fax:* (22) 786-2744 (office). *E-mail:* chairman@weforum.org (office). *Website:* www.weforum.org (office).

SCHWAB, Susan Carroll, PhD; American academic administrator and fmr government official; *Strategic Advisor, Mayer Brown LLP;* b. 23 March 1955, Washington, DC; m. Curtis Carroll (died 2006); ed Int. School Bangkok, Williams Coll., Stanford Univ., George Washington Univ.; agricultural trade negotiator, Office of US Trade Rep. 1977–79; Trade Policy Officer, US Foreign Service, Embassy in Tokyo 1979–81; Chief Econ. and Legis. Asst, Office of US Senator John C. Danforth 1981–86, Legis. Dir 1986–89; Asst US Sec. of Commerce and Dir Gen., US and Foreign Commercial Service, US Dept of Commerce, Washington, DC 1989–93; Dir of Corp. Business Devt, Motorola Inc. 1993–95; Dean, School of Public Affairs, Univ. of Md 1995–2003, Pres. and CEO Univ. of Md Foundation 2004–05, Prof., School of Public Policy 2009–; Deputy US Trade Rep., Washington, DC 2005–06, US Trade Rep. 2006–09; Strategic Advisor, Mayer Brown LLP (global law firm) 2010–; mem. Bd of Dirs Calpine Corp. 1997–2005, Caterpillar Inc. 2009–, FedEx Corpn 2009–, Boeing 2010–, Marriott International Inc. 2015–, Signature

Theatre; mem. Bd of Advisors, Perella Weinberg Partners LP 2016–, Miller Buckfire; mem. Council on Foreign Relations, Aspen Strategy Group; Fellow, Nat. Acad. of Public Admin; Trustee, The Conference Board. *Publications:* Trade-Offs: Negotiating the Omnibus Trade Act 1994; numerous articles in magazines and journals. *Address:* Mayer Brown LLP, 1999 K Street, NW, Washington, DC 20006-1101 (office); School of Public Policy, University of Maryland, 4105 Van Munching Hall, College Park, MD 20742, USA. *Telephone:* (202) 2630-3331 (Mayer Brown) (office); (301) 405-6347. *Fax:* (202) 263-3300 (Mayer Brown) (office); (301) 403-4675. *E-mail:* sschwab@mayerbrown.com (office); sschwab@umd.edu. *Website:* www.mayerbrown.com (office); www.publicpolicy.umd.edu.

SCHWAN, Gesine Marianne, Dr rer. pol; German political scientist, professor of political science and university administrator; *President, Humboldt-Viadrina School of Governance;* b. 22 May 1943, Berlin; d. of Hildegard Schneider (née Olejak) and Hans R. Schneider; m. 1st Alexander Schwan 1969 (died 1989); m. 2nd Peter Eigen 2004; one s. one d.; ed Lycée Français de Berlin, Free Univ. of Berlin; Asst Prof., Dept of Political Sciences, Free Univ. of Berlin 1971–77, Prof. 1977–; Fellow, Woodrow Wilson Int. Center for Scholars 1980–81; apptd By-Fellow, Robinson Coll., Cambridge, UK 1984; Chair. German Asscn for Political Science 1985–87, Bd mem. 1994–2000; Dean, Otto-Suhr Inst. 1992–95; Pres. Europa-Univ. Viadrina 1999–2008; unsuccessful candidate for Pres. of Germany 2004, 2008; Chair. Scientific Advisory Bd, Centre Marc Bloch in Berlin 2001–; Co-Chair. German-Polish Forum 2002–09; Co-ordinator for civil social cooperation near to Repub. of Poland 2005–09; Co-founder and Pres. Humboldt-Viadrina School of Governance 2010–; mem. of Senate, Max Planck Soc. 2005–; mem. Scientific Advisory Bd, Centre d'études et de recherche Interdisciplinary sur l'Allemagne 2006–; mem. Académie de Berlin 2006–; mem. Bd of Trustees, German Inst. of Poland, Theodor-Heuss-Stiftung 1994–, Haniel Foundation 2006–, Stone Award, Alfred Töpfer Foundation 2007–, Science Center Berlin 2008–; Fed. Cross of Merits 1993, Verdienstkreuz (1st class) 2002; Dr hc (European Univ. Inst., Florence) 2006, Golden Badge of Honour, Bridge Foundation Award 2010; Urania Medal 1999, Marion Dönhoff Award 2004, Asscn of Berlin Foreign Press Award 2004, Pauline Staegemann Award 2004, Women in Europe Award, Network European Movt Germany 2005, Tolerance Award, Tolerance Ecumenical Foundation 2005. *Publications include:* Leszek Kolakowski, Eine Philosophie der Freiheit nach Marx 1971, Die Gesellschaftskritik von Karl Marx 1974, Sozialdemokratie u. Marxismus (with Alexander Schwan) 1974, Sozialismus in der Demokratie; Eine Theorie Konsequent sozialdemokratischen Politik 1982, Der normative Horizont moderner Politik I und II (with Alexander Schwan) 1985, Politik und Schuld: Die zerstörerische Macht des Schweigens 1997; Jahrbuch für Politik (co-ed.) 1991–. *Leisure interests:* music, theatre, travelling. *Address:* Humboldt-Viadrina School of Governance, Wilhelmstraße 67, 10117 Berlin (office); Teutonenstrasse 6, 14129 Berlin, Germany (home). *Telephone:* (30) 200597123 (office); (30) 8038366 (home). *Fax:* (30) 200597111 (office). *Website:* www.humboldt-viadrina.org (office).

SCHWAN, Severin, Mag.rer.soc.oec., MagIur, DrIur; Austrian pharmaceuticals industry executive; *CEO, Roche Group;* b. 1967; m.; three c.; ed Univ. of Innsbruck, Univs of York and Oxford, UK, Univ. of Louvain, Belgium; trainee, Corp. Finance, Roche, Basel 1993–95, Head of Finance and Admin, Roche, Brussels 1995–98, Head of Finance and Informatics, Roche, Grenzach, Germany and mem. Exec. Bd, Roche Deutschland Holding GmbH 1998–2000, Head of Global Finance and Services, Roche Diagnostics, Basel 2000–04, Head of Asia Pacific Region, Roche Diagnostics, Singapore 2004–06, CEO Roche Diagnostics Div. 2006–08, CEO Roche Group 2008–, mem. Bd of Dirs, Roche Holding Ltd 2013–; Chair. Genentech, Inc. 2014–; mem. Bd of Dirs, Credit Suisse Group AG 2014–; mem. Int. Business Leaders Advisory Council for the Mayor of Shanghai 2009–, European Round Table of Industrialists 2013–. *Address:* Roche Holding Ltd, Grenzacherstrasse 124, 4070 Basel, Switzerland (office). *Telephone:* (61) 688-11-11 (office). *Fax:* (61) 691-93-91 (office). *E-mail:* info@roche.com (office). *Website:* www.roche.com (office).

SCHWARTZ, Gerald W. (Gerry), OC, BCom, LLB, MBA; Canadian financial services industry executive; *Chairman, President and CEO, Onex Corporation;* b. 24 Nov. 1941, Toronto, Ont.; m. Heather Reisman 1982; four c.; ed Univ. of Manitoba, Harvard Univ. Grad. School of Business Admin; fmr specialist in mergers and acquisitions, investment banking firm, New York; Co-founder and Pres. CanWest Capital (renamed CanWest Global Communications) –1983; f. Onex Corpn 1983, Chair., Pres. and CEO 1983–, mem. Bd of Dirs 1987; Vice-Chair. and mem. Exec. Cttee, Mount Sinai Hosp.; Gov. Jr Achievementof Metro Toronto; Trustee, The Simon Wiesenthal Center; mem. Bd of Dirs, Celestica Inc. 1998–2016, Bank of Nova Scotia 1999–2007, Indigo Books and Music Inc. 2001–, Canadian Council of Christians and Jews; mem. Cttee of Univ. Resources, Harvard Univ. Bd of Overseers, Business School, Canadian Council of Christians and Jews; Hon. Dir Bank of Nova Scotia 2008–; Hon. LLD (Univ. of Manitoba) 2016, (St Francis Xavier Univ.), Hon. DPhil (Tel-Aviv Univ.); inducted into Canadian Business Hall of Fame. *Address:* Onex Corpn, 161 Bay Street, PO Box 700, Toronto, ON M5J 2S1, Canada (office). *Telephone:* (416) 362-7711 (office). *E-mail:* info@onex.com (office). *Website:* www.onex.com (office).

SCHWARTZ, Jonathan Ian, BA; American business executive; *CEO, CareZone Inc.;* b. 20 Oct. 1965; ed Wesleyan Univ., Carnegie Mellon Univ.; Assoc., McKinsey & Co., New York 1986–89; Co-founder and CEO Lighthouse Design –1996, joined Sun Microsystems Inc. 1996 after Sun's acquisition of Lighthouse, held several sr positions including Vice-Pres., Venture Fund, Vice-Pres., Developer Products, Vice-Pres., Enterprise Software, Dir of Product Marketing, Javasoft, Sr Vice-Pres. of Corp. Strategy and Planning –2002, Exec. Vice-Pres. for Software 2002–04, Pres. and COO 2004–06, Pres. and CEO 2006–10; Co-Founder and CEO CareZone Inc. 2010–; mem. Bd of Dirs Taleo Corpn 2010–12, Silver Spring Networks 2011–, Inst. on Aging 2013–, Jut, Inc. 2014–, VeriFone 2014–. *Leisure interests:* golf, ice hockey. *Address:* CareZone Inc., 1463 East Republican Street, Suite 198, Seattle, WA 98112, USA (office). *E-mail:* jonathan@carezone.com (office). *Website:* carezone.com (office).

SCHWARTZ, Maxime; French scientist (retd) and writer; b. 1 June 1940, Blois; ed Ecole Polytechnique; joined Inst. Pasteur 1963, Head of Lab. 1973–84, mem. Scientific Council 1973–85, Head of Dept of Molecular Biology 1984–85, Deputy Dir 1985–87, Dir-Gen. 1988–99; Dir Dept Lab. Programming, l'Agence Française de Sécurité Sanitaire des aliments (AFSSA) –2007. *Publications include:* How the Cows Turned Mad 2001, Microbes or Man, Who Will Win? (in French) 2008. *Address:* L'Institut Pasteur, 25–28 rue du Dr. Roux, 75015 Paris, France (office). *Telephone:* 1-44-38-93-38 (office). *E-mail:* maxime.schwartz@pasteur.fr (office). *Website:* research.pasteur.fr/en/member/maxime-schwartz (office).

SCHWARTZENBERG, Roger-Gérard, DenD; French politician and professor of law; b. 17 April 1943, Pau, Pyrénées-Atlantiques; s. of André Schwartzenberg and Simone Gutelman; ed Inst. d'Etudes Politiques, Paris; Prof., Univ. de Droit, d'Économie et de Sciences Sociales de Paris II 1969–, Inst. d'Etudes Politiques 1972–83; Pres., Mouvement des Radicaux de Gauche 1981–83, Hon. Pres. 1983–; mem. European Parl. 1979–83; Sec. of State, Ministry of Educ. 1983–84; Sec. of State responsible for univs, Ministry of Educ. 1984–86; Deputy to Nat. Ass. for Val de Marne 1986–2000, 2002–07; Sec. to Nat. Ass. 1988–92, 1993–97, Vice-Pres. Foreign Affairs Comm. 1992–2000; Mayor of Villeneuve-Saint-Georges 1989–95, 2001–08; Deputy Judge, High Court of Justice and Court of Justice of the Repub. 1993–97; Pres., Groupe parlementaire radical, citoyen et vert 1999–2000; Minister of Research 2000–02; Chevalier, Légion d'honneur 2009, Grand Officer, Order of Merit (Germany), Grand Decoration of Honour (Austria). *Publications:* books on political and legal topics including La Campagne présidentielle de 1965 1967, L'Autorité de la chose décidée ou la Force juridique des décisions administratives 1969, La Guerre de succession ou les élections présidentielles de 1969 1969, Traité de sociologie politique 1971, L'Etat spectacle, Essai sur et contre le star-system en politique 1977, La Droite absolue 1981, La Politique mensonge 1998, 1788: Essai sur la maldémocratie 2006, L'Etat spectacle 2 2009. *Leisure interest:* tennis. *Address:* Université de Droit de Paris, 12 Place du Panthéon, 75005 Paris, France (office).

SCHWARZ-SCHILLING, Christian, DPhil; German politician, consultant and fmr UN official; *Senior Advisor, Dr Schwarz-Schilling and Partner GmbH;* b. 19 Nov. 1930, Innsbruck, Austria; s. of Rheinhard Schwarz-Schilling and Duzsa Schwarz-Schilling; m. Marie Luise Jonen 1957; two d.; ed Univs of Berlin and Munich; mem. Landtag, Hesse, FRG 1966–76; Sec.-Gen. Hesse CDU 1966–80, Deputy Chair. 1967–96; Chair. Coordinating Cttee for Media Policy CDU/CSU 1975–83; mem. Bundestag 1976–2002; Minister of Posts and Telecommunications 1982–92; Deputy Chair. CDU/CSU Fed. Medium and Small Business Asscn 1977–97; Pres. Exec. Cttee European Medium and Small Business Union 1979–82; Chair. Inquiries Cttee Bundestag New Information and Communication Technologies 1981–82; Chair. Bundestag Subcttee on Human Rights and Humanitarian Aid 1995–98, Deputy Chair. 1998; Int. Mediator-Arbitrator for Fed. of Bosnia and Herzegovina 1996–98, also for Repub. Srpska 1997; Founder and Pres. Dr Schwarz-Schilling and Pnr GmbH 1993, now Sr Advisor; Chair. Bd Prima Com AG, Mainz, 1999–, Mox Telecom AG Ratingen 1999–; High Rep. UN Mission in Bosnia and Herzegovina 2006–07; Prof. of Politics, Univ. of Sarajevo 2009–; Hon. Citizen of Büdingen 2004; Grosses Bundesverdienstkreuz mit Stern; Hon. DUniv (Bryant Coll., USA) 1997; Achievement Cross with Star of the Order of Achievement (Germany) 1992, Manfred Wörner Medal 2005, Hessian Peace Prize 2007. *Publication:* Unsere Geschichte Schicksal oder Zufall, Lansfristig Sichere Rente. *Leisure interests:* swimming, skiing, piano. *Address:* Dr Schwarz-Schilling and Partner GmbH, Joseph-Schumpeter-Allee 25, 53227 Bonn (office); Am Dohlberg 10, 63654 Büdingen, Germany (home). *Telephone:* (228) 76367990. *E-mail:* css@schwarz-schilling.de (office). *Website:* www.schwarz-schilling.de (office).

SCHWARZENBERG, Prince of Schwarzenberg, Count of Sulz, Princely Landgrave in Klettgau and Duke of Krumlov; **Karel;** Czech/Swiss politician; b. (Karl Johannes Nepomuk Josef Norbert Friedrich Antonius Wratislaw Menas von Schwarzenberg), 10 Dec. 1937, Prague, Czechoslovakia; s. of Prince Karl VI of Schwarzenberg of the minor line and Princess Antonie von Fürstenberg; m. Therese von Hardegg 1967 (divorced 1988, re-married 2008); two s. one d.; ed Univs of Vienna and Graz, Austria, Univ. of Munich, Germany; family exiled to Austria after Communist takeover of Czechoslovakia 1948; Pres. Int. Helsinki Cttee for Human Rights (concerned with human rights issues in fmr USSR, Bulgaria, fmr Yugoslavia (Kosovo) and Czechoslovakia) 1984–91; est. Czechoslovak Documentation Centre (archive of prohibited literature) with Dr Vilém Prečan in Bavaria, Germany 1985; returned to Czechoslovakia 1990; Chancellor, Office of the Pres. 1990–92; Head of first OSCE del. to Nagorno Karabakh 1992; mem. Senate (Civic Democratic Alliance, ODA) 2004–08; mem. Poslanecká sněmovna (TOP 09) 2010; Chair. Foreign Affairs, Defence and Security Cttee 2005–07, Alt. mem. Perm. Del. of Parl. to Parl. Ass. of Council of Europe 2005; mem. Perm. Czech del. to Parl. Ass., NATO 2006; mem. Caucus of Open Democracy 2006–07; Minister of Foreign Affairs 2007–09, 2010–13; Deputy Prime Minister 2010–13; Chair. Tradice, Odpovědnost, Prosperita 09 (TOP 09—Tradition, Responsibility, Prosperity 09) party 2009–15, Hon. Chair. 2015–, mem. Poslanecká sněmovna (TOP 09) 2013, Chair. Foreign Affairs Cttee 2013–15; unsuccessful cand. in presidential election 2013; mem. Bd of Dirs Forum 2000 2005–07; Kt, Order of the Golden Fleece (Austrian br.) 1991, Order of Tomáš Garrigue Masaryk (Third Class) 2002, Decoration for Services to the Repub. of Austria in Silver with Sash 2005, Grand Cross of the Fed. Cross of Merit (Germany) 2008, Sächsischer Verdienstorden 2012; Prize for Human Rights, Council of Europe (with Lech Wałęsa) 1989, Marietta and Friedrich Torberg Medal 2015. *Address:* Tradice, Odpovědnost, Prosperita 09 (TOP 09—Tradition, Responsibility, Prosperity 09), Michnův palác, budova č. 2, Újezd 450/40, Malá Strana, 118 00 Prague 1, Czech Republic (office). *Telephone:* (2) 55790999 (office). *Fax:* (2) 55790899 (office). *E-mail:* info@top09.cz (office). *Website:* www.top09.cz (office); www.karelschwarzenberg.cz.

SCHWARZENEGGER, Arnold Alois, BA; American (b. Austrian) actor, business executive, fmr politician and fmr bodybuilder; b. 30 July 1947, Thal, nr Graz, Austria; s. of Gustav Schwarzenegger and Aurelia Schwarzenegger (née Jadrny); m. Maria Owings Shriver 1985 (divorced 2011); two s. two d. and one s. with Mildred Baena; ed Santa Monica Coll., Univ. of Wisconsin-Superior; went to USA 1968, naturalized 1983; Nat. Weight Training Coach Special Olympics, later Global Amb.; Bodybuilding Champion 1965–80; volunteer, prison rehabilitation programmes; Chair. Pres.'s Council on Physical Fitness and Sport 1990; Nat. Chair. Nat. Inner-City Games Foundation; Gov. of Calif. (after recall of Gov. Gray Davis) 2003–11; Governor Downey Prof. of State and Global Policy, Schwarzenegger Inst. for State and Global Policy, Univ. of Southern California 2012–; Republican; First Prize, Styrian Jr Weightlifting Championships 1964, First Prize, German Austrian Weightlifting Championships 1965, Jr Mr Europe 1965, Best Built Man of Europe 1966, Mr Europe 1966, First Prize, Int. Powerlifting

Championships 1966, Mr International 1968, Mr Universe (amateur) 1967, Mr Universe (professional) 1968, 1969, 1970, First Prize, German Powerlifting Championships 1968, Mr Olympia 1970–75, 1980, Nat. Theater Owners' Int. Star of the Decade, 1993, Simon Wiesenthal Center Nat. Leadership Award, ShoWest Humanitarian of the Year Award 1997, Boys and Girls Town Father Flanagan Service to Youth Award 2000, American Film Marketing Association (AFMA) World Wide Box Office Champ 2002, Muhammad Ali Humanitarian Award 2002, and numerous other prizes. *Film appearances include:* Stay Hungry 1976 (Golden Globe Award), Pumping Iron 1977, The Jayne Mansfield Story 1980, Conan the Barbarian 1982, Conan The Destroyer 1984, The Terminator 1984, Commando 1985, Raw Deal 1986, Predator 1987, Running Man 1987, Red Heat 1988, Twins 1989, Total Recall 1990, Kindergarten Cop 1990, Terminator II: Judgment Day 1991, Last Action Hero 1993, Dave (cameo) 1993, True Lies 1994, Junior 1994, Eraser 1996, Jingle All the Way 1996, Batman and Robin 1997, End of Days 1999, The Sixth Day 2000, Collateral Damage 2002, Terminator 3: Rise of the Machines 2003, Around the World in 80 Days 2004, The Expendables (uncredited) 2010, The Expendables 2 2012, The Last Stand 2013, Escape Plan 2013, Sabotage 2014, The Expendables 3 2014, Maggie 2015, Terminator Genisys 2015. *Publications:* Arnold: The Education of a Bodybuilder 1977, Arnold's Bodyshaping for Women 1979, Arnold's Bodybuilding for Men 1981, Arnold's Encyclopedia of Modern Bodybuilding 1985, Arnold's Fitness for Kids (co-author) 1993, Total Recall: My Unbelievably True Life Story (autobiography) 2012. *Website:* www .schwarzenegger.com.

SCHWARZMAN, Stephen A., BA, MBA; American investment banker; *Chairman and CEO, The Blackstone Group;* b. 14 Feb. 1947, Philadelphia; m. Christine Hearst; three c. from previous marriages; ed Yale Univ., Harvard Business School; began career in Mergers and Acquisitions (M&A) at Lehman Brothers 1977–84, at age 31, elected Man. Dir 1978–84, Chair. M&A Cttee 1981–84; Co-founder, Chair. CEO The Blackstone Group 1985–; Chair. Bd John F. Kennedy Center for the Performing Arts, Washington, DC 2004–10; Chair. Pres.'s Strategic and Policy Forum Jan.–Aug. 2017; mem. Council on Foreign Relations; mem. Bd New York City Ballet, New York Public Library, Film Soc. of Lincoln Center, Harvard Business School Visiting Cttee, JPMorgan Chase Nat. Advisory Bd, New York City Partnership Bd of Dirs; Trustee Frick Collection. *Address:* The Blackstone Group, 345 Park Avenue, New York, NY 10154, USA (office). *Telephone:* (212) 583-5000 (office). *Fax:* (212) 583-5712 (office). *Website:* www.blackstone.com (office).

SCHWEBEL, Stephen Myron, BA, LLB; American judge, lawyer, arbitrator and mediator; b. 10 March 1929, New York, NY; s. of Victor Schwebel and Pauline Pfeffer Schwebel; m. Louise I. N. Killander 1972; two d.; ed Harvard Coll., Univ. of Cambridge, UK, Yale Law School; attorney 1954–59; Asst Prof. of Law, Harvard Univ. 1959–61; Asst Legal Adviser, then Special Asst to Asst Sec. of State for Int. Org. Affairs 1961–67; Exec. Vice-Pres. and Exec. Dir American Soc. of Int. Law 1967–73; Consultant, then Counsellor on Int. Law, Dept of State 1967–74, Deputy Legal Adviser 1974–81; Prof. of Int. Law, then Edward B. Burling Prof. of Int. Law and Org., Johns Hopkins Univ., Washington, DC 1967–81; Legal Adviser to US Del. and Alt. Rep. in 6th Cttee, UN Gen. Ass. 1961–65; Visiting Lecturer or Prof., Univ. of Cambridge 1957, 1983, ANU 1969, Hague Acad. of Int. Law 1972, Inst. Univ. de hautes études int., Geneva 1980 and various American univs 1987–; rep. in various cttees UN 1962–74; Assoc. Rep., Rep., Counsel or Deputy Agent in cases before Int. Court of Justice 1962–80; Judge, Int. Court of Justice 1981–2000, Vice-Pres. 1994–97, Pres. 1997–2000; mem. Int. Law Comm. 1977–81, Perm. Court of Arbitration, The Hague 2006–; arbitrator or chair. in int. commercial arbitrations 1982–; mem. Tribunal in Eritrea-Yemen Arbitration 1997–99, Ethiopia-Eritrea Boundary Comm. 2000–; Pres. Barbados-Trinidad and Tobago Arbitration Tribunal 2004; Pres. Admin. Tribunal, IMF 1994–2010, World Bank 2011–17; Pres. Southern Blue Fin Tuna Arbitration 2000, Pakistan-India Indus Waters Arbitration 2011–; mem. Panels of Arbitrators and of Conciliators of the Int. Centre for the Settlement of Investment Disputes of the World Bank 2000–; mem. Bd of Eds, American Journal of Int. Law 1967–81, 1994–; mem. Council on Foreign Relations, Inst. of Int. Law; mem. Bars of State of New York, Dist of Columbia, Supreme Court of the USA; Hon. Bencher, Gray's Inn 1998–, Hon. Fellow, Lauterpacht Centre for Int. Law, Univ. of Cambridge; Hon. Fellow, Trinity Coll. Cambridge 2005; Hon. LL (Bhopal Univ.) 1983, (Hofstra Univ.) 1997, (Univ. of Miami) 2002; Gherini Prize, Yale Law School 1954, Medal of Merit, Yale Law School 1997, Manley O. Hudson Medal, American Soc. of Int. Law 2000. *Publications:* The Secretary-General of the United Nations 1952, The Effectiveness of International Decisions (ed.) 1971, International Arbitration: Three Salient Problems 1987, Justice in International Law 1994; author of some 175 articles in legal periodicals and the press on problems of international law and relations. *Leisure interests:* music, cycling. *Address:* 1917 23rd Street NW, Washington, DC 20008, USA (home). *Telephone:* (202) 232-3114 (home). *Fax:* (202) 797-9286 (home). *E-mail:* judgeschwebel@aol.com (office).

SCHWEIGER, Til; German actor, producer and director; b. 19 Dec. 1963, Freiburg; m. Dana Schweiger; four c.; ed acting acad., Cologne; Best Actor Award, Moscow Film Festival 1997. *Films include:* Manta Manta 1991, Ebbie's Bluff (Max Ophuls Prize for Best Actor) 1992, Der Bewegte Mann 1994, Maennerpension, Das Superweib, Brute 1996, Knocking on Heaven's Door 1996 (also producer and co-writer), Replacement Killers, Judas Kiss 1997, Der Eisbär (also producer), Der grosse Bagarozy 1998, Magicians 1999, Investigating Sex, Driven 2000, Was tun wenn's brennt 2000, Jetzt oder Nie (producer) 2000, Auf Herz und Nieren (producer) 2000, Joe and Max 2001, Tomb Raider 2 2002, King Arthur 2003, A Surprise Period 2003, The Daltons vs. Lucky Luke 2004, Barfuss 2005, Deuce Bigalow: European Gigolo 2005, Bye Bye Harry! 2006, Wo ist Fred? 2006, Video Kings 2007, Body Armour 2007, Keinohrhasen 2007, Already Dead 2007, Der Rote Baron 2008, Far Cry 2008, 1 1/2 Ritter 2008, Inglourious Basterds 2009, This Means War 2012, The Necessary Death of Charlie Countryman 2013, Kokowääh 2 2013, Tschiller: Off Duty 2016, Unsere Zeit ist jetzt 2016. *Television:* Tatort (series) 2013–16. *Address:* c/o Players Agentur Management GmbH, Sophienstr. 21, 10178 Berlin, Germany (office). *Telephone:* (30) 2851680 (office). *Fax:* (30) 2851686 (office). *E-mail:* mai@players.de (office). *Website:* www.players.de (office).

SCHWEIKER, Mark, BSc, MA; American business executive and fmr politician; *Senior Vice-President and Chief Relationship Officer, Renmatix Inc.;* b. 31 Jan. 1953, Bucks Co., Pa; s. of John Schweiker and Mary Schweiker; m. Katherine Schweiker; two s. one d.; ed Bloomsberg Univ., Rider Univ.; began career with Merrill Lynch, then McGraw-Hill; first elected to public office as Middletown Township Supervisor 1979; Bucks Co. Commr 1987–94; Lt-Gov. of Pennsylvania 1994–2001, Gov. 2001–03; Pres. and CEO Greater Philadelphia Chamber of Commerce 2003–09 (resgnd), Pres. PRWT Business Process Solutions 2009–12, now mem. Bd of Dirs; Sr Vice-Pres. and Chief Relationship Officer, Renmatix Inc. 2012–; Sr Advisor, Stradley Ronon (law firm) 2013–; mem. Bd of Dirs minSEC Holdings Inc., Network of Victim Assistance; mem. Bd of Visitors Smeal Coll. of Business, Pennsylvania State Univ.; Dr hc (Rider Univ.); Bloomsburg Univ. Alumnus of the Year 1990, Pennsylvania Nature Conservancy Award for Outstanding Service to Conservation 1993, Tech. Council of Pennsylvania Advocate of the Year 1996, Pennsylvania Econ. League Commitment to Excellence in Local Govt Award 1998, Pennsylvania League of Cities Outstanding Public Service Award 1999, Life Sciences Public Official of the Year, Speaker of the Year for Communications Excellence, Tech. Advocate of the Year. *Address:* Renmatix Inc., 660 Allendale Road, King of Prussia, PA 19406, USA (office). *Telephone:* (484) 751-4000 (office). *Fax:* (484) 751-4001 (office). *E-mail:* mschweiker@stradley.com (office). *Website:* www.stradley.com (office).

SCHWEIKERT, Emile Alfred, PhD; American (b. Swiss) chemist and academic; *Director, Center for Chemical Characterization, Department of Chemistry, Texas A&M University;* b. 10 Sept. 1939, Flawil, Switzerland; s. of Emil Martin Schweikert and Olga Elisa Schweikert-Niederer; m. Marta Teresa Guzman de Schweikert; one s. two d.; ed Univ. of Paris; fmr Head, Dept of Chem. Texas A&M Univ., currently Prof., also Dir Center for Chemical Characterization; mem. Program Advisory Cttee, Nat. Inst. of Standards and Tech. (NIST) Center for Neutron Research, Gaithersburg, Md 1997–98; George Hevesy Medal 1986. *Address:* Department of Chemistry, Texas A&M University, College Station, TX 77843-3255, USA (office). *Telephone:* (979) 845-2341 (office). *Fax:* (979) 845-1655 (office). *E-mail:* schweikert@mail.chem.tamu.edu (office). *Website:* www.chem .tamu.edu/faculty/schweikert (office); www.chem.tamu.edu/rgroup/schweikert (office).

SCHWEISGUT, Hans Dietmar, MA, DrIur; Austrian lawyer and diplomatist; *European Union Ambassador to People's Republic of China;* b. 16 March 1951, Zams; m. Kaoru Schweisgut; one c.; ed Univ. of Innsbruck, Southern Methodist Univ., Dallas, Texas, USA, Diplomatic Acad., Vienna; Ministry of Foreign Affairs 1977–79, Second Sec., Perm. Mission of Austria to UN, New York 1979–83; Head of Office of State Sec. for Econ. Co-ordination, Fed. Chancellery 1983–84; Sec., later Head of Office of Fed. Minister for Public Economy and Transport 1984–86; Econ. Advisor Fed. Federal Minister of Finance 1986–87; Minister, Embassy in Tokyo 1987–91; Dir-Gen. for Econ. Integration and Customs, Fed. Ministry of Finance 1991–99; Amb. to Japan 1999–2003, to People's Repub. of China 2003–07, Perm. Rep. of Austria to EU, Brussels 2007–10, EU Amb. to Japan 2011–14, EU Amb. to People's Repub. of China 2014–. *Address:* Delegation of the European Union to People's Republic of China, 15 Dongzhimenwai Dajie, Sanlitun, 100600 Beijing, People's Republic of China (office). *Telephone:* (10) 84548000 (office). *Fax:* (10) 65321720 (office). *E-mail:* delegation-china@eeas.europa.eu (office). *Website:* eeas .europa.eu/delegations/china/index_en.htm (office).

SCHWEITZER, Brian David, BS, MS; American rancher and fmr politician; b. 4 Sept. 1955, Havre, Mont.; s. of Adam Schweitzer and Kathleen (Kay) Schweiter (née McKernan); m. Nancy Hupp 1981; two s. one d.; ed The Abbey School, Holy Cross Abbey, Canon City, Colo, Colorado State Univ., Montana State Univ.; began career in irrigation devt working in Africa, Asia, Europe and S America 1981–86; returned to Montana to raise family and build ranching and irrigation business 1986; apptd by Sec. of Agric. to serve on Montana State Dept of Agric. Farm Service Agency Cttee 1993–99; apptd to Montana Rural Devt Partnership Bd 1996, Nat. Drought Task Force 1999; cand. in US Senate elections 2000; Gov. of Montana 2005–13; fmr Chair. Western Govs Asscn, Democratic Govs Asscn; fmr Pres. Council of State Govts; Democrat; Sec. of Agric. Award for outreach efforts to Native Americans 1995.

SCHWEITZER, Louis, LenD; French business executive; *Chairman, High Authority against Discrimination and for Equality (HALDE);* b. 8 July 1942, Geneva, Switzerland; s. of Pierre-Paul Schweitzer and Catherine Hatt; m. Agnes Schmitz 1972; two d.; ed Inst. d'Etudes Politiques, Paris, Faculté de Droit, Paris and Ecole Nat. d'Admin; Insp. of Finance 1970–; special assignment, later Deputy Dir, Ministry of the Budget 1974–81; Dir du Cabinet to Minister of Budget 1981–83, of Industry and Research 1983, to Prime Minister 1984–86; Prof. Inst. d'Etudes Politiques de Paris 1982–86; Vice-Pres. for Finance and Planning Régie Renault SA 1986–90, Chief Finance Officer 1988–90, Exec. Vice-Pres. 1989–90, Pres. and COO 1990, Chair. and CEO 1992–2005, Chair. 2005–08; mem. Bd of Dirs Volvo Group 2001–12, Chair. 2010–12; mem. Bd of Dirs AstraZeneca PLC 2004–12, Chair. (non-exec.) 2005–12; Chair. Haute autorité de lutte contre les discriminations et pour l'égalité (HALDE—High Authority against Discrimination and for Equality) 2005–; Admin., Société Générale 1989–93, UAP 1988–94, Inst. Pasteur 1988–94, Péchiney 1989–92, IFRI 1989–, Réunion des Musées Nat. 1990–96, Renault Véhicules Industriels 1992–2001, BNP Paribas SA 1993–, Roussel UCLAF 1994–97, Crédit Nat. (now Natexis) 1995–99, Philips 1997–, Électricité de France SA 1999–2008, Véolia Environnement SA 2003–, L'Oréal SA 2005–; Chair. Ecole des mines de Nancy 1999–; Chair. Supervisory Bd Groupe Le Monde 2008–10; Pres. Festival d'Avignon 2005–; Commr Gen. for Investment 2014–; Officier, Légion d'honneur, Commdr 2005, Grand Officier 2013; Officier, Ordre nat. du Mérite, Grand Officier 2007. *Publications:* Mes Années Renault. Entre Billancourt et le marché mondial 2006, Les Discriminations en France 2009; magazine articles. *Address:* 1 rue Dauphine, 75006 Paris (home); La Halde, 11 rue Saint Georges, 75009 Paris, France (office). *Website:* defenseurdesdroits.fr (office).

SCHWERY, HE Cardinal Henri; Swiss ecclesiastic; *Bishop Emeritus of Sion;* b. 14 June 1932, St Léonard, Valais; s. of Camille Schwery and Marguerite Terroux; ed Lycée-Coll. de Sion, Valais, Faculty of Sciences, Univ. de Fribourg, Grand Séminaire de Sion and Pontificia Università Gregoriana, Rome; ordained priest 1957; teacher of science, math. and religious studies, Lycée-Coll. de Sion 1961–; Rector 1972–77; Dir Pensionnat de la Sitterie (Petit Séminaire) de Sion 1968–72; Diocesan Chaplain, Action Catholique de Jeunesse Etudiante 1958–66; Mil. Chaplain 1958–77; Bishop of Sion 1977–95, Bishop Emer. 1995–; cr. Cardinal 1991; Cardinal-Priest of Ss. Protomartiri a Via Aurelia Antica 1991–; Kt of the

Grand Cross, Order of the Holy Sepulchre of Jerusalem. *Publications:* Un Synode extraordinaire 1986, Chemin de Croix, chemin de lumière, L'Année Mariale dans le diocèse de Sion 1987, Sentiers Pastoraux 1988, Sentiers épiscopaux – Regards sur nos familles (two vols) 1992, Magnificat (in collaboration) 1992, Chrétien au quotidien 1996. *Leisure interest:* spirituality. *Address:* Diocèse de Sion, 12 rue de la Tour, PO Box 2124, 1950 Sion 2, Switzerland (office). *Telephone:* (27) 3291818 (office). *Fax:* (27) 3291836 (office). *E-mail:* diocese.sion@cath-vs.ch (office). *Website:* www.cath-vs.ch (office).

SCHWIMMER, David, BS; American actor, writer and director; b. 12 Nov. 1966, New York; s. of Arthur Schwimmer and Arlene Schwimmer; m. Zoe Buckman 2010; one d.; ed Beverly Hills High School and Northwestern Univ.; Co-founder Lookingglass Theater Co., Chicago 1988; mem. Bd of Dirs Rape Foundation for Rape Treatment Center of Santa Monica. *Theatre includes:* West, The Odyssey, Of One Blood, In the Eye of the Beholder all with Lookingglass Theater Co.), The Master and Margarita (all with Lookingglass Theater Co.), Some Girl(s) (Gielgud Theatre, London) 2005, The Caine Mutiny Court-Martial (Broadway) 2006. *Theatre directed includes:* The Jungle (six Joseph Jefferson Awards), The Serpent, Alice in Wonderland (Edin. Festival, Scotland). *Films include:* Flight of the Intruder 1990, Crossing the Bridge 1992, Twenty Bucks 1993, The Waiter 1993, Wolf 1994, The Pallbearer 1996, Shooting the Moon (exec. producer) 1996, Apt Pupil 1998, Kissing a Fool (exec. producer) 1998, Six Days Seven Nights 1998, The Thin Pink Line 1998, All the Rage 1999, Picking Up the Pieces 2000, Hotel 2001, Dogwater (also Dir), Duane Hopwood 2005, Madagascar (voice) 2005, Big Nothing 2006, Run, Fat Boy, Run (dir) 2007, Nothing But the Truth 2008, Madagascar Escape 2 Africa (voice) 2008, Trust (dir) 2011, Madagascar 3: Europe's Most Wanted (voice) 2012, The Iceman 2012, John Carter 2012, Irreversible 2015. *Television includes:* The Wonder Years 1988, Monty 1993, NYPD Blue 1993, Friends 1994–2004, L.A. Law, The Single Guy (NBC), Happy Birthday Elizabeth: A Celebration of Life 1997, Breast Men 1997, Since You've Been Gone (dir) 1998, Band of Brothers (mini-series) 2001, Uprising 2001, Curb Your Enthusiasm (series) 2004, Web Therapy (series) 2012, Irreversible (film) 2014, American Crime Story (series) 2016. *Leisure interests:* writing, playing softball and basketball. *Address:* c/o The Gersh Agency, PO Box 5617, Beverly Hills, CA 90210 (office); Lookingglass Theatre Company, 821 North Michigan Avenue, Chicago, IL 60611, USA. *Telephone:* (312) 337–0665. *E-mail:* box@lookingglasstheatre.org. *Website:* www.lookingglasstheatre.org.

SCHWIMMER, Walter, LLD; Austrian lawyer, politician and international organization official; *Co-Chairman, Dialogue of Civilizations Research Institute, Berlin;* b. 16 June 1942, Vienna; s. of Walter Schwimmer and Johanna Schwimmer; m. Martina Pucher-Schwimmer; two s.; ed Univ. of Vienna; mem. Nationalrat (Austrian Parl.) 1971–99, Chair. Parl. Cttee on Health 1989–94, on Justice 1995–96; Vice-Chair. Parl. Group, Austrian People's Party (ÖVP) 1986–94; mem. Council of Europe Parl. Ass. 1991–, Vice-Pres. Council of Europe 1996, Jan.–Sept. 1999, Sec.-Gen. 1999–2004; Chair. European People's Party Group–Christian Democrats 1996–99; Dir and Exec. Vice-Pres. Vienna Health Insurance Fund 1979–99; Chair. World Public Forum – Dialogue of Civilizations (DOC) 2005–13, Co-Chair. DOC Research Inst., Berlin 2016–; Pres. European Democracy Forum, Strasbourg 2006–, Megatrend Univ., Belgrade 2010–12; mem. Bd Crans Montana Forum 2004–09; consultant on int. relations and European affairs 2004–; Hon. Sec.-Gen., Maison de la Méditerranée 2004–; Leopold-Kunschak Award 1975, Peter the Great Int. Prize of the Russian Fed., European Pro Humanitate European Foundation for Culture Prize, Germany, Medal of the European Inst. of Moscow, Person of the Year Award (Ukraine) 2002. *Publications include:* Christian Trade Unions in Austria 1975, Social Consequences of Inflation 1988, A Union Goes Down in History 1993, Der Traum Europa 2003, The European Dream 2004, Sognare l'Europa 2004, San Evropa 2004. *Leisure interests:* books, history, stamps, art. *Address:* Dialogue of Civilizations Research Institute, Neustiftgasse 67-69, Top 24, 1070 Vienna (office); Consultancy Office, Dietschen 2, 3400 Klosterneuburg, Austria (office). *Telephone:* (1) 513-01-38-2 (Vienna) (office); (2243) 87694 (Klosterneuburg) (office). *Fax:* (1) 513-01-38-4 (Vienna) (office); (2243) 87649 (Klosterneuburg) (office). *E-mail:* w.schwimmer@wpfdc.at (office); schwimmer.consult@aon.at (office). *Website:* www.wpfdc.org (office); www.socialstudies.at (office).

SCHYGULLA, Hanna; German actress; b. 25 Dec. 1943, Chorzów, Poland; d. of Joseph Schygulla and Antonie (née Mzyk); Bundesverdienstkreuz Erster Klasse; Hon. Award, Antalya Golden Orange Film Festival 2007, Berlin Film Festival Hon. Golden Bear 2010. *Stage appearances include:* Mother Courage 1979. *Films include:* Die Ehe der Maria Braun (Silberner Bär Berlinale 1979) 1979, Die Dritte Generation 1979, Lili Marleen 1980, Die Fälschung 1981, La Nuit de Varennes 1982, Eine Liebe in Deutschland 1983, The Story di Piera (Cannes Film Festival Award for Best Actress 1983) 1983, Miss Arizona 1987, The Summer of Mr. Forbes, Dead Again 1991, Beware of a Holy Whore 1993, The Merchant of Four Seasons 1998, Werckmeister Harmonies 2001, Die Blauwe Grenze 2005, Vendredi ou un autre jour 2005, Winterreise 2006, The Edge of Heaven 2007, Faust 2011, Avanti 2012, Pandemia 2012, Lullaby to My Father 2012, Lucky 2017, Fortunata 2017, The Prayer 2018. *Television appearances include:* 8 Stunden sind kein Tag (series) 1972, Absolitude 2001, Das unreine Mal 2006, Clara, une passion française 2009. *Leisure interests:* travel, painting. *Address:* c/o Agence Anne Alvares Correa, 34 rue Jouffroy d'Abbans, 75017 Paris, France. *Telephone:* 1-42-67-80-85. *Fax:* 1-44-09-00-27. *E-mail:* arac2@wanadoo.fr. *Website:* www.agence-annealvarescorrea.com.

SCICLUNA, Edward, BA, MEconSc, DEcon; Maltese economist and politician; *Minister of Finance;* b. 12 Oct. 1946, Naxxar; m. Astrid Bartoli; one s. one d.; ed Univ. of Malta, Univ. of Oxford, UK, Univ. of Toronto, Canada; Prof. and Head, Dept of Econs, Univ. of Malta 1981–90; Electoral Commr 1987–93; Dir Central Bank of Malta 1996–2003; Chair. Malta Financial Services Authority 1997–99; mem. Council of Europe's Devt Bank Auditing Cttee 1997–2000; Chair. Malta Council of Econ. and Social Devt 1999–2003; mem. Nat. Euro Change-over Cttee 2005–08; mem. European Parl. 2009–13, also Vice-Chair. Econ. and Monetary Affairs Cttee and Reps, European Statistical Advisory Bd; mem. House of Reps (Parl.) for 5th and 8th Dists 2013–; Minister of Finance 2013–; fmr Chair. CWG PLC, HSBC's Malta Funds Sicav PLC, Structured Funds Sicav PLC; fmr Dir San Antonio Hotel and Spa; mem. Partit Laburista (PL, Labour Party) 2009–. *Address:* Ministry of Finance, 30 Maison Demandols, South Street, Valletta VLT 1102, Malta (office). *Telephone:* 25998259 (office). *Fax:* 25998429 (office). *E-mail:* info.mfin@gov.mt (office). *Website:* mfin.gov.mt (office); www.edwardscicluna.com.

SCICLUNA, Martin, BCom; British accountant and business executive; *Chairman, RSA Insurance Group;* b. 1952, Malta; s. of William Scicluna and Miriam Scicluna; two s. one d.; ed Berkhamsted School, Univ. of Leeds; joined Deloitte (fmrly Touche Ross) 1973, Articled Clerk 1973–76, Audit Partner Deloitte & Touche LLP (formerly Touche Ross & Co.) 1982–2008, Group Partner 1985–90, Head of London Audit Div. 1990–95, Partner, Chair. Deloitte UK 1995–2007; Dir (non-exec.), Worldpay 2013–; Chair. Great Portland Estates 2009–; Chair. Royal and Sun Alliance (RSA) Insurance Group PLC 2013–; mem. Bd of Dirs Deloitte Touche Tohmatsu 1998–2007, Lloyds Banking Group PLC 2008–13; Gov. Berkhamsted School 2008–; mem. Financial Services Trade and Investment Bd 2013–15; Freeman of the City of London; Hon. LLD (Leeds) 2008. *Leisure interests:* Arsenal Football Club, wine, gardening. *Address:* RSA Insurance Group plc, 20 Fenchurch Street, London EC3M 3AU, England (office). *Website:* www.rsagroup.com (office).

SCINDIA, Jyotiraditya Madhavrao, MBA; Indian politician; *General Secretary for Uttar Pradesh West, Indian National Congress;* b. 1 Jan. 1971, Mumbai; s. of Madhavrao Scindia and Madhavi Raje Scindia; m. Priyadarshini Raje Scindia 1994; one s. one d.; ed Campion School, Mumbai, The Doon School, Dehradun, Harvard Univ., USA, Stanford Graduate School of Business; fmr Financial Analyst, Morgan Stanley Asia Ltd, Hong Kong and Mumbai; fmr Summer Intern with UN, New York and Merrill Lynch, Los Angeles; elected to 13th Lok Sabha (lower house of Parl.) for Guna Dist constituency 2002, re-elected to 14th Lok Sabha 2004, 15th Lok Sabha 2009, 16th Lok Sabha 2014–, mem. Cttee on Finance 2002–04, Cttee on External Affairs 2002–04, Cttee on Defence 2004; Union Cabinet Minister of State for Communications and Information Tech. 2008, for Commerce and Industry 2009–12, for Power 2012–14; Pres. Madhya Pradesh Cricket Asscn; Gov. Madhav Inst. of Tech. & Science, Gwalior; mem. Indian Nat. Congress (Congress), Gen. Sec. for Uttar Pradesh West 2018–; mem. Cttee on Privileges, Standing Cttee on Finance, Consultive Cttee, Ministry of Home Affairs. *Leisure interests:* cricket, swimming, reading, wild life conservation. *Address:* Uttar Pradesh Congress Committee, Nehru Bhawan, 10, Mall Avenue, Lucknow, Uttar pradesh (office); Jai Vilas Palace, Lashkar, Gwalior 470 004, Madhya Pradesh (home); 27, Safdarjung Road, New Delhi 110 001, India (home). *Telephone:* (522) 2238858 (Uttar Pradesh) (office); (522) 2238859 (Uttar Pradesh) (office); (11) 23792174 (Delhi) (home); (751) 2322390 (Madhya Pradesh) (home). *Fax:* (522) 2239825 (Uttar Pradesh) (office); (751) 230411 (Madhya Pradesh) (home); (11) 23013148 (Delhi) (home). *E-mail:* upcclko@hotmail.com (office); scindia1@gmail.com (office); officeofscindia@gmail.com (office). *Website:* uttarpradeshcongress.com; jyotiradityamscindia.com (office).

SCIOLI, Daniel Osvaldo; Argentine business executive and politician; b. 13 Jan. 1957, Villa Crespo, Buenos Aires; m. Karina Rabolini; one d. from previous relationship; ed Escuela Superior de Comercio Carlos Pellegrini, Universidad Argentina de la Empresa; Dir Electrolux Argentina 1994–97; mem. Chamber of Deputies (Justicialist Party) for Buenos Aires 1997–2002, Pres. Sports Cttee; Sec. of Sports and Tourism 2001–03; Vice-Pres. of Argentina and Pres. of the Senate 2003–07; Gov., Buenos Aires Prov. 2007–15; Frente para la Victoria candidate in presidential election 2015; Founding mem. Partido Justicialista, Pres. 2010–14. *Achievements include:* fmr speedboat racing world champion (won numerous int. offshore powerboat racing championships in various categories). *Leisure interest:* football.

SCLATER, John G., BS, PhD, FRS; British geophysicist and professor of geophysics; *Professor of Geophysics, Scripps Institution of Oceanography, University of California, San Diego;* b. 17 June 1940, Edinburgh, Scotland; s. of John G. Sclater and Margaret Bennett Glen; m. 1st Fredrica R. Sclater 1968 (divorced 1985); two s.; m. 2nd Paula Ann Edwards 1985 (divorced 1991); m. 3rd Naila G. Burchett 1992; ed Stonyhurst Coll., Univs of Edinburgh and Cambridge; Postdoctoral Research Geophysicist, Scripps Inst. of Oceanography, Univ. of California, San Diego 1965–67, Asst Research Geophysicist 1967–72, Prof. of Geophysics 1991–; Assoc. Prof., MIT 1972–77, Prof. 1977–83, MIT Dir, Jt Program in Oceanography with the Woods Hole Oceanographic Inst. 1981–83; Assoc. Dir Inst. for Geophysics, Univ. of Texas at Austin, Prof., Dept of Geological Sciences and Shell Distinguished Chair. in Geophysics 1983–91; mem. NAS 1989; Fellow, Geological Soc. of America 1975, American Geophysical Union 1977; Swiney Lecturer, Edin. Univ. 1976; Guggenheim Fellow 1998–99; Rosenstiel Award 1978, Walter H. Bucher Medal, American Geophysical Union 1985. *Leisure interests:* running, swimming, golf. *Address:* Scripps Institution of Oceanography, Geosciences Research Division, University of California, San Diego, 9500 Gilman Drive, La Jolla, CA 92093, USA (office). *Telephone:* (619) 534-3051. *E-mail:* jsclater@ucsd.edu (office). *Website:* grd.ucsd.edu (office).

SCLATER, John Richard, CVO, MA, MBA; British company chairman and farmer; *Managing Partner, Sutton Hall Farms;* b. 14 July 1940, Camborne, Cornwall, England; s. of Arthur William Sclater and Alice Sclater (née Collett); m. 1st Nicola Mary Gloria Cropper 1967 (divorced); one s. one d. (deceased); m. 2nd Grizel Elizabeth Catherine Dawson MBE 1985; ed Charterhouse, Gonville and Caius Coll., Cambridge and Yale and Harvard Univs, USA; Commonwealth Fellow 1962–64; Glyn, Mills & Co. 1964–70; Dir Williams, Glyn & Co. 1970–76; Man. Dir Nordic Bank 1976–85, Chair. 1985–87; Dir and Deputy Chair. Guinness Peat Group PLC 1985–87, Jt Deputy Chair. 1987; Dir and Deputy Chair. Guinness Mahon & Co. Ltd 1987, Chair. 1987; Dir Foreign & Colonial Investment Trust PLC 1981–2002, Chair. 1983–2002; Chair. Foreign & Colonial (now Graphite) Enterprise Trust PLC 1986–2009, Foreign & Colonial Ventures Ltd 1990–98, Berisford PLC 1990–2000 (Dir 1986–2000), Hill Samuel Bank Ltd 1992–96, (Dir 1990–96, Vice-Chair. 1990–92), Foreign & Colonial (now Graphite) Pvt. Equity Trust PLC 1994–2002, Finsbury Life Sciences Investment Trust PLC (renamed Finsbury Emerging Biotechnology Trust PLC 2005, then The Biotech Growth Trust PLC 2007) 1997–2012, Argent Group Europe Ltd 1998–2012; Man. Partner, Sutton Hall Farms 2012–; Pres. Equitable Life Assurance Soc. 1994–2001 (Dir 1985–2001); Deputy Chair. Yamaichi Int. (Europe) Ltd 1985–97, Union (fmrly Union Discount Co. of London) PLC 1986–96 (Dir 1981–96, Chair. 1996), Grosvenor Group Ltd (fmrly Grosvenor Group Holdings Ltd) 2000–05 (Dir 1999),

Grosvenor Estate Holdings 1989–2002; Dir, Berner Nicol & Co. Ltd 1968 (Chair. 2002–04, 2005–, co. renamed Sclater Estates Ltd 2015), James Cropper PLC 1972–2008, Holker Estates Co. Ltd 1974–2013, Angerstein Underwriting Trust PLC 1985–96, Foreign & Colonial Group (Holdings) Ltd 1989–2001, Fuel Tech (Europe) 1990–98, Millennium & Copthorne Hotels PLC 1996–2007, Wates Group Ltd 1999–2004; Chair. Asscn of Consortium Banks 1980–82; Consultant RP&C Int. 1997–2003; First Church Estates Commr 1999–2001 (mem. Archbishops' Council and Gen. Synod, Church of England 1999–2001); Dir and Gov. Brambletye School 1976–2006; mem. City Taxation Cttee 1973–76, London Bd of Halifax Building Soc. 1983–90, Council of Duchy of Lancaster 1987–2000, CBI City Advisory Group 1988–99; Gov. Int. Students House 1976–99; Trustee, The Grosvenor Estate 1973–2005, The Coll. of Arms 1994–; Chair. Infinity Christmas Trees Ltd 2017–; Freeman of the City of London 1993–; Liveryman Goldsmiths' Co. 1993–. *Leisure interest:* country pursuits. *Address:* Sutton Hall, Barcombe, nr Lewes, East Sussex, BN8 5EB, England (home). *Telephone:* (1273) 400450 (home). *Fax:* (1273) 401086 (home). *E-mail:* john.sclater@newickandsuttonhall.com (home).

SCOFIDIO, Ricardo, BArch; American artist, architect and academic; *Professor Emeritus of Architecture, Cooper Union for the Advancement of Science and Art;* b. 1935, New York; m. 1st (divorced); m. 2nd Elizabeth Diller; ed Columbia Univ., Cooper Union; co-f. (with Elizabeth Diller q.v.), Diller & Scofidio (now Diller Scofidio + Renfro), New York 1979, cr. installations and electronic media projects; apptd Prof. of Architecture, The Cooper Union 1965, now Prof. Emer.; Fellow, American Acad. of Arts and Sciences 2009–, RIBA; Tiffany Foundation Award for Emerging Artists 1990, Progressive Architecture Award (for Slow House) 1991, Chrysler Award for Achievement and Design 1997, MacArthur Foundation Award 1999, Centennial Medal of Honor, American Acad. in Rome, National Design Award, Smithsonian, Brunner Prize, American Acad. of Arts and Letters 2003, Royal Acad. Architecture Prize 2019, AIA President's Award, AIA Medal of Honor, Obie Award. *Publications:* with Elizabeth Diller: Flesh 1995, Back to the Front: Tourisms of War 1996, Flesh: Architectural Probes 1998, Blur: The Making of Nothing 2002. *Address:* Diller Scofidio + Renfro, 601 West 26th Street, Suite 1815, New York, NY 10001, USA (office). *Telephone:* (212) 260-7971 (office). *E-mail:* disco@dsrny.com (office). *Website:* www.dsrny.com (office).

SCOGNAMIGLIO PASINI, Carlo Luigi, DEcon; Italian politician, economist and academic; *Professor of Economics, Libera Università Internazionale degli Studi Sociali Guido Carli;* b. 27 Nov. 1944, Varese; s. of Luigi Scognamiglio and Esther Scognamiglio (née Pasini); m. Cecilia Pirelli; one s. one d.; ed L. Bocconi Univ., Milan, London School of Econs; Asst Lecturer, L. Bocconi Univ., Asst Prof. of Industrial Econs 1968–73, Prof. 1973; Asst Prof. of Finance, Univ. of Padua 1973–79; Prof. of Econs and Industrial Policy, Libera Università Internazionale degli Studi Sociali Guido Carli, Rome 1979–, Dean and Rector 1984–92; Liberal Party cand. in Milan constituency, elected to Senate 1992, Chair. European Affairs Cttee, mem. Budget Cttee, re-elected to Senate 1994; Pres. of Senate 1994–96; Acting Pres. of Italy 1994–96; Pres. Rizzoli-Corriere della Sera 1983–84, later Vice-Pres.; Minister of Defence 1998–99; Co-Founder, Bocconi School of Business Admin 1979; Pres. Italian Liberal Party 2009–; fmr Pres. Aspen Inst. Italia, currently Hon. Chair. and life-time Trustee; Acad. of France Award for Econs 1988. *Publications include:* The Stock Exchange 1973, Industrial Crises 1976, The White Book on PPSS 1981, The White Book on the Italian Financial Market 1982, Theory and Policy of Finance 1987, Industrial Economics 1987, Report to Minister of Treasury of Commission for Privatization of Industry 1990, The Liberal Project 1996. *Leisure interests:* economics, history. *Address:* Department of Economics, Libera Università Internazionale degli Studi Sociali Guido Carli, Viale Romania 32, 00197 Rome, Italy (office). *Website:* economiaefinanza.luiss.it/en (office).

SCOLA, HE Cardinal Angelo, PhD, DTheol; Italian ecclesiastic; b. 7 Nov. 1941, Malgrate; s. of Carlo Scola and Regina Colombo; ed Catholic Univ. of Sacred Heart, Milan, Seminary of Saronno, Milan, Seminary of Venegono, Milan, Univ. of Fribourg, Switzerland; ordained priest 1970; successively, until 1991, active collaborator of Comunione e Liberazione, Dir Inst. of Studies for Transition, Milan, collaborator in establishment and mem. Exec. Cttee Italian edn of Rivista Internazionale Communio, pastoral work in Italy and abroad; Research Asst to Chair of Political Philosophy 1979, later Asst to Chair of Fundamental Moral Theology, Univ. of Fribourg; Prof. of Theological Anthropology, Pontifical John Paul II Inst. for Studies on Marriage and Family, Pontifical Lateran Univ., Rome 1982, later Prof. of Contemporary Christology, Faculty of Theology, Rector Magnifico Pontifical Lateran Univ. and Pres. Pontifical John Paul II Inst. for Studies on Marriage and the Family 1995; attended Seventh Ordinary Ass. of World Synod of Bishops as an asst to Special Sec., Vatican City 1987; Bishop of Grosseto 1991–95 (resgnd); Patriarch of Venice 2002–11; Archbishop of Milan 2011–17; cr. Cardinal (Cardinal Priest of Santi XII Apostoli) 2003; participated in Papal Conclave 2005, 2013; Relator Gen. 11th Gen. Ordinary Ass. of World Synod of Bishops 2005.

SCOLARI, Luiz Felipe; Brazilian/Italian professional football manager and fmr professional footballer; b. 9 Nov. 1948, Passo Fundo, Rio Grande do Sul; defender; pyouth player, Aymoré de São Leopoldo-RS 1966–73; sr player for Caxias 1973–79, Juventude 1980, Novo Hamburgo 1980–81, Centro Sportivo Alagoano (CSA) 1981; Man. CSA 1982 (won Campeonato Alagoano 1982), Juventude 1982–83, Brasil de Pelotas 1983, Al-Shabab 1984–85, Brasil de Pelotas 1986, Juventude 1986–87, Grêmio 1987, 1993–96 (won Campeonato Gaúcho 1987, 1995, 1996, Copa do Brasil 1994, Copa Libertadores 1995, Campeonato Brasileiro Série A 1996, Recopa Sudamericana 1996), Goiás 1988, Al Qadisiya 1988–90 (won Kuwait Emir Cup 1989), Kuwait 1990 (won Gulf Cup of Nations 1990), Criciúma 1991 (won Copa do Brasil 1991), Al-Ahli 1991, Al Qadisiya 1992, Júbilo Iwata 1996–97, Palmeiras 1997–2000 (won Copa do Brasil 1998, Copa Mercosur 1998, Copa Libertadores 1999, Torneio Rio-São Paulo 2000), Cruzeiro 2000–01 (won Copa Sul-Minas 2001); Man. Brazilian nat. team 2001–02 (led Brazil to record fifth FIFA World Cup June 2002, resgnd July 2002), 2012–14 (resgnd following record 7–1 defeat by Germany in World Cup semifinal at home and a further 3–0 in Third Place Playoff match by the Netherlands July 2014); Man. Portuguese nat. team 2003–08; Man. Chelsea FC, London 2008–09, FC Bunyodkor, Tashkent, Uzbekistan 2009–10, Palmeiras (won the Copa do Brasil 2012) 2010–12; Medal of Merit, Order of the Immaculate Conception of Vila Viçosa (House of Braganza); South American Coach of the Year 1999, 2002. *Address:* c/o Confederação Brasileira de Futebol, Avenida Luis Carlos Prestes 130, Barra da Tijuca, Rio de Janeiro 22775-055, Brazil. *E-mail:* info@cbf.com.br. *Website:* www.cbf.com.br.

SCOLES, Giacinto, MSc, FRS; Italian physicist and academic; *Donner Professor Emeritus of Science, Princeton University;* b. 2 April 1935, Turin; ed Univ. of Genoa, Univ. of Leiden, Netherlands; began career in Physics Dept, Univ. of Genoa –1961; mem. staff, Univ. of Leiden 1961–64; Prof. of Chem. and Physics, Univ. of Waterloo, Canada –1986, Acting Dir Guelph-Waterloo Centre for Grad. Work in Chem. 1974–75, Dir Centre for Molecular Beams and Laser Chem. 1982–85; Prof. of Solid State Physics, Univ. of Trento 1975–82; Donner Prof. of Science, Princeton Univ. Chem. Dept and Princeton Materials Inst. 1987–2008, Donner Prof. Emer. of Science 2008–; Prof., Depts of Biophysics and Condensed Matter Physics, Int. School for Advanced Studies, Trieste 2003–; Elettra Synchrotron Lab., Trieste 2003–09; Distinguished Visiting Prof., Univ. of Florida, Gainesville 2003; Moscowitz Lecturer, Univ. of Minnesota 2004; Distinguished Adjunct Prof. of Biology, Temple Univ., Phila 2008–; apptd Sr Consultant to International Center for Science and High Technology, UNIDO 2009; Foreign mem. Royal Acad. of Arts and Sciences, Netherlands 2000, American Chemical Soc.; Fellow, Optical Soc. of America, American Physical Soc., Chemical Inst. of Canada; Dr hc (Univ. of Genova) 1996, (Univ. of Waterloo, Canada) 2000; Lippincott Award, Optical Soc. of America, Coblentz Soc., Soc. for Applied Spectroscopy 1995, Peter Debye Award, American Chemical Soc. 2002, E.K. Plyler Prize 2003, Creativity Award 2005, Benjamin Franklin Medal in Physics (co-recipient) 2006. *Publications:* numerous scientific papers in professional journals on the devt of helium droplet spectroscopy. *Address:* Department of Chemistry, Princeton University, Washington Road, Princeton, NJ 08544-1009, USA (office). *Telephone:* (609) 258-5570 (office). *E-mail:* gscoles@princeton.edu (office). *Website:* www.princeton.edu/~gscoles (office); prism.princeton.edu (office).

SCORSESE, Martin Charles, BA, MA; American film director, producer, actor and screenwriter; b. 17 Nov. 1942, Queens, NY; s. of Charles Scorsese and Catherine Scorsese (née Cappa); m. 1st Laraine Marie Brennan 1965 (divorced 1971); one d.; m. 2nd Julia Cameron 1976 (divorced 1977); one d.; m. 3rd Isabella Rossellini (q.v.) 1979 (divorced 1982); m. 4th Barbara DeFina 1985 (divorced 1991); m. 5th Helen Morris 1999; ed Cardinal Hayes High School, New York Univ.; Faculty Asst and Instructor, Film Dept, New York Univ. 1963–66, instructor 1968–70; dir and writer of films: What's a Nice Girl Like You Doing in a Place Like This? 1963, It's Not Just You, Murray 1964, Who's That Knocking At My Door? 1968, The Big Shave 1968; dir play The Act 1977–78; dir and writer of documentaries; Supervising Ed. and Asst Dir Woodstock 1970; Assoc. Producer and Post-Production Supervisor Medicine Ball Caravan 1971; Order of Merit (Italy) 2001, Légion d'honneur 2005; Dr hc (Nat. Film School, Łódź) 2011; Edward J. Kingsley Foundation Award 1963, 1964, First Prize, Rosenthal Foundation Awards of Soc. of Cinematologists 1964, named Best Dir, Cannes Film Festival 1986, First Prize, Screen Producer's Guild 1965, Brown Univ. Film Festival 1965, shared Rosellini Prize 1990, Award American Museum of Moving Image 1996, American Film Inst. Lifetime Achievement Award 1997, Int. Fed. of Film Award for Preservation 2001, Kennedy Center Honor 2007, honoured by Nat. Italian American Foundation 2007, Cecil B. DeMille Award for Lifetime Achievement 2010, BAFTA Fellowship 2012, Princess of Astorias Award for Arts, Spain 2018. *Films include:* Street Scenes 1970, Boxcar Bertha 1972, Mean Streets 1973, Italianamerican 1974, Alice Doesn't Live Here Any More 1974, Taxi Driver 1976, New York, New York 1977, The Last Waltz 1978, Raging Bull 1980, King of Comedy 1981, After Hours 1985, The Color of Money 1986, The Last Temptation of Christ (Courage in Filmmaking Award, LA Film Teachers Asscn 1989) 1988, Good Fellas 1989, Made in Milan 1990, Cape Fear 1991, The Age of Innocence 1993, Casino 1995, Kundun 1997, Bringing Out the Dead 1999, Gangs of New York (Golden Globe for Best Dir 2003) 2002, The Aviator 2004, The Departed (Nat. Bd of Review Award for Best Dir 2006, Golden Globe for Best Dir 2007, Dirs' Guild of America Award 2007, Acad. Award for Best Picture, Best Dir 2007) 2006, Shine a Light 2007, Shutter Island 2010, Public Speaking (documentary) 2010, George Harrison: Living in the Material World (documentary) 2011, Hugo (Golden Globe Award for Best Dir 2012) 2011, The Wolf of Wall Street 2013, The 50-Year Argument 2014, Silence 2016, Rolling Thunder Revue: A Bob Dylan Story 2019, The Irishman 2019; exec. producer: The Crew 1989, Naked in New York 1994, Grace of My Heart 1996, Kicked in the Head 1996, You Can Count on Me 2000, Deuces Wild 2002, Soul of a Man 2003, Something to Believe In 2004, Brides 2004, The Aviator 2004, Life Itself (documentary) 2014, Revenge of the Green Dragons 2014, The Third Side of the River 2014, The Wannabe 2014; producer: The Grifters 1989, Naked in New York 1994, Casino 1996, Kundun 1998, Bringing Out the Dead 1999, Gangs of New York 2002; co-producer Mad Dog and Glory 1993; acted in Cannonball 1976, Triple Play 1981, Dreams 1990, The Muse 1999. *Television includes:* Lady by the Sea: The Statue of Liberty 2004, No Direction Home: Bob Dylan 2005, American Masters (series documentary) 2005, 2010, A Letter to Elia 2010; exec. producer The Blues (mini-series) 2003, Boardwalk Empire (Emmy Award for Outstanding Directing for a Drama Series 2011) 2010–13. *Publications include:* Scorsese on Scorsese 1989, The Age of Innocence: The Shooting Script (with Jay Cocks) 1996, Casino (with Nicholas Pileggi) 1996. *Address:* c/o Artists Management Group, 9465 Wilshire Boulevard, Suite 519, Los Angeles, CA 90212 (office); Jeff Doolly Starr & Co., 350 Park Avenue, 9th Floor, New York, NY 10022, USA (office).

SCOTLAND, Barton Umax Adolphus; Guyanese lawyer and fmr diplomatist; *Speaker, National Assembly;* ed Univ. of London, UK; numerous years of pvt. legal practice, specializing in the areas of natural resources, investment law and int. law; mem. Bars of Guyana, Barbados, St Kitts and Nevis, England and Wales; fmrly worked in Ministry of Foreign Affairs as Sr Diplomatist and Adviser; fmr Head, Dept of Int. Econ. Co-operation; fmr Commr, CARICOM Competition Comm., later becoming Chair.; Speaker, Nat. Ass. 2015–; Cacique Crown of Honour. *Address:* National Assembly, Parliament Building, Georgetown, Guyana (office). *Telephone:* 226-8458 (office). *Fax:* 226-8458 (office). *E-mail:* info@parliament.gov.gy (office). *Website:* parliament.gov.gy (office).

SCOTLAND OF ASTHAL, Baroness (Life Peer), cr. 1997, of Asthal in the County of Oxfordshire; **Patricia Janet Scotland,** PC, QC, LLB; British barrister and politician; *Secretary-General, The Commonwealth;* b. 19 Aug. 1955, Dominica; d. of

Arthur Leonard Scotland and Dellie Marie Genevieve; m. Richard Mawhinney 1985; two s.; ed Mid Essex Tech. Coll., Chelmsford (pursued external Univ. of London law degree); called to the Bar, Middle Temple 1977, QC 1991 (first black woman), Bencher 1997; mem. the Bar, Antigua, Recorder 2000; mem. Privy Council 2001; Parl. Under-Sec. of State, Foreign and Commonwealth Office 1999–2001; Parl. Sec., Lord Chancellor's Dept 2001–03; Alt. UK Govt Rep. of the European Convention 2002–03; Minister of State, Home Office 2003–07; Attorney-Gen. for England and Wales (first woman) 2007–10, Attorney-Gen. for NI 2007–10, Advocate Gen. for NI 2010; Shadow Attorney-Gen. 2010–11; Sec.-Gen. The Commonwealth and CEO of the Commonwealth Secr. 2016–; fmr mem. Comm. for Racial Equality, Gen. Council Bar Race Relations Cttee, Professional Conduct Cttee, Judicial Studies Bd Ethnic Minority Advisory Cttee, House of Commons Working Party on Child Abduction, Legal Advisory Panel on the Nat. Consumer Council, Ind. Cttee for the Supervision of Standards of Telephone Information Services, Nat. Advisory Cttee on Mentally Disordered Offenders; Commr Millennium Comm. 1994–; Chair. HMG Caribbean Advisory Group; Dominican Rep. of Council of The British Commonwealth Ex-Service League; Chancellor, Univ. of Greenwich 2014–; Founder-mem. and fmr Head of Chambers, 1 Gray's Inn Square; fmr Chair. Inner London Educ. Authority Disciplinary Tribunal; fmr mem. BBC World Service Consultative Group; Hon. Pres. Trinity Hall Law Soc.; Hon. Fellow, Cardiff Univ., Soc. for Advanced Legal Studies, Wolfson Coll. Cambridge; Dame, Sacred Mil. Constantinian Order of St George; Dr hc (Westminster, Buckingham, Leicester, East London 2005, Newman Univ. Coll., Birmingham); Black Woman of the Year (Law) 1992, Peer of the Year, House Magazine Awards 2004, Peer of the Year, C4 Political Awards 2004, Parliamentarian of the Year, Political Studies Association Awards 2004, The Spectator Parliamentarian of the Year Awards 2005. *Leisure interests:* church, sport, dancing, theatre. *Address:* Commonwealth Secretariat, Marlborough House, Pall Mall, London, SW1Y 5HX (office); House of Lords, Westminster, London, SW1A 0AP, England. *Telephone:* (20) 7747-6500 (office). *Fax:* (20) 7930-0827 (office). *E-mail:* info@commonwealth.int (office). *Website:* www.thecommonwealth.org (office).

SCOTT, Adam Derek; Australian professional golfer; b. 16 July 1980, Adelaide, SA; m. Marie Kojzar; ed Univ. of Nevada, Las Vegas, USA; turned professional 2000; plays mainly on PGA Tour; winner Alfred Dunhill Championship 2001, Qatar Masters 2002, Gleneagles Scottish PGA Championship 2002, Scandic Carlsberg Scandinavian Masters 2003, Deutsche Bank Championship 2003, The Players Championship 2004, Booz Allen Classic 2004, Nissan Open 2005, Johnnie Walker Classic 2005, Singapore Open 2005, 2006, The Tour Championship 2006, Shell Houston Open 2007, Commercialbank Qatar Masters 2008, EDS Byron Nelson Championship 2008, Australian Open 2009, Valero Texas Open 2010, Barclays Singapore Open 2010, WGC-Bridgestone Invitational 2011, Talisker Masters 2012, 2013, Masters Tournament 2013, Australian PGA Championship 2013, The Barclays 2013, PGA Grand Slam of Golf (US unofficial money event) 2013, ISPS Handa World Cup of Golf (team with Jason Day) 2013, Crowne Plaza Invitational at Colonial 2014, Honda Classic 2016; WGC-Cadillac Championship 2016; represented Australia in World Cup 2001, 2002, 2013 (winners); represented Int. team in Presidents Cup 2003 (tie), 2005, 2007, 2009, 2011, 2013, 2015, 2017; PGA Tour of Australasia Order of Merit winner 2005, 2013. *Address:* c/o The Adam Scott Company Pty Ltd, PO Box 671, Sanctuary Cove, Qld 4212, Australia. *Telephone:* (7) 5514-8148 (home). *E-mail:* jmillington@adamscott.com (home). *Website:* www.adamscott.com.au.

SCOTT, Charles Thomas, CA; British business executive; b. 22 Feb. 1949; with Binder Hamlyn 1967–72; Chief Accountant, ITEL Int. Corpn 1972–77; Controller, IMS Int. Inc. 1978–84, Chief Financial Officer 1985–89; Chief Financial Officer, Saatchi & Saatchi Co. (later Cordiant PLC, now Cordiant Communications Group PLC) 1990–91, COO 1991–92, CEO 1993–95, Chair. 1995–2003; Chair. Bates Worldwide 1997; Sr Exec. Dir William Hill PLC 2002–04, Chair. (non-exec.) 2004–07, Chair. 2007–10; mem. Bd of Dirs InTechnology PLC 2001–, TBI Ltd (fmrly TBI PLC) 1998–2005, Emcore Corpn 1998–, Flybe Group PLC, Kircal Ltd; fmr Chair. Robert Walters PLC. *Leisure interests:* golf, tennis.

SCOTT, Guy Lindsay, BA (Econs), PhD; Zambian politician; b. 1 June 1944, Livingstone; s. of Alexander Scott; m. 1st (divorced), three c.; m. 2nd Charlotte Scott, one d.; ed Trinity Hall, Cambridge, Univ. of Sussex; joined Ministry of Finance as planner 1965; f. Walkover Estates (agribusiness venture) 1970; co-f. Mpongwe Devt Co. 1978; mem. Movement for Multi-Party Democracy 1990–96; co-f. Lima Party 1996; elected mem. Nat. Ass. for Mpika constituency 1991, for Lusaka Central constituency 2006–; Minister of Agric., Food and Fisheries in 1990s; Vice-Pres. of Zambia 2011–14, Acting Pres. (following death of Pres. Michael Sata) 28 Oct. 2014–25 Jan. 2015; mem. Patriotic Front 2001–.

SCOTT, James, MSc, FRS, FRCP, FMedSci, FIBiol; British physician and professor of cardiovascular medicine; *Professor of Cardiovascular Medicine, National Heart and Lung Institute, Imperial College, London;* b. 13 Sept. 1946, Ashby-de-la-Zouch; s. of Robert B. Scott and Iris O. Scott (née Hill); m. Diane M. Lowe 1976; two s. one d.; ed Univ. of London, London Hosp. Medical Coll.; house surgeon London Hosp. 1971–72; House Physician Hereford Co. Hosp. July–Dec. 1972; Sr House Officer Queen Elizabeth Hosp., Midland Centre for Neurosurgery and Neurology, Birmingham Jan.–Dec. 1973; Registrar Gen. Hosp., Birmingham Jan.–Dec. 1974, Royal Free Hosp., Academic Dept of Medicine 1975–76; Hon. Sr Registrar, MRC Research Fellow Hammersmith Hosp., Dept of Medicine 1976–80; Postdoctoral Fellow Univ. of California, Dept of Biochemistry and Biophysics 1980–83; Clinical Scientist, Head Div. of Molecular Medicine, MRC Research Centre 1983–91; Hon. Consultant Physician Northwick Park Hosp., Harrow 1983–91, Hammersmith Hosp. 1992–97; Prof., Chair. of Medicine Royal Postgraduate Medical School 1992–97; Hon. Dir MRC Molecular Medicine Group 1992–; Dir of Medicine Hammersmith Hosps NHS Trust, Dir Div. of Medical Cardiology 1994–97; Prof. of Medicine, Imperial Coll. School of Medicine 1997–, Deputy Vice-Prin. for Research 1997–, Founder-Dir Genetics and Genomics Research Inst., Imperial Coll. 2000, currently Prof. of Cardiovascular Medicine, Nat. Heart and Lung Inst.; Consultant LondonMedical; Founder-mem. Acad. of Medical Sciences, European Molecular Biology Org.; Fellow, Inst. of Biology 1998, Queen Mary and Westfield Coll. 1998; European Ed. Arteriosclerosis, Thrombosis and Vascular Biology (Journal of American Heart Asscn); Hon. Fellow, Asscn of Physicians of Great Britain and Ireland 1998; several prizes and awards include Graham Bull Prize (Royal Coll. of Physicians) 1989, Squibb Bristol Myers Award for Cardiovascular Research 1993, A–plus Distinction Award 1996, etc. *Publications:* numerous articles on molecular medicine, molecular genetics, atherosclerosis, RNA modification, RNA editing and gene expression. *Leisure interests:* family and friends, the twentieth-century novel, British impressionist and modern painting, long distance running, swimming. *Address:* Genetics and Genomics Research Institute, The Flowers Building, Imperial College, London, SW7 2AZ, England (office). *Telephone:* (20) 7594-1345 (office). *Fax:* (20) 7594-3653 (office). *E-mail:* j.scott@imperial.ac.uk (office). *Website:* www3.imperial.ac.uk (office).

SCOTT, Keith; British diplomatist; *High Commissioner to Papua New Guinea;* m. Carly Scott; two c.; Desk Officer, Political Union/Institutional Reform, European Community Dept (Internal), FCO 1991–93, Desk Officer, Transcaucasus/Central Asia Section, Eastern Dept 1993–94, Second Sec. (Political), High Comm. in Nigeria 1994–95, Desk Officer, Bosnia and Herzegovina Eastern Adriatic Dept 1995–98, Head of Section for Yugoslavia, Croatia, Albania and Macedonia 1998; served in Exec. Office of UN Sec. Gen., New York 1998–99; Regional Man for West and Central Africa, Dept of Trade and Industry 1999–02, First Sec., Embassy in Iraq 2004–05, Embassy in Afghanistan 2005–07, Head of North Africa and Maghreb Team 2002–04, Head of Political and Communications Section, Embassy in Zimbabwe 2007–12, Head of Network Devt, Finance Directorate 2012–15, Deputy Migration Envoy, Mediterranean Migration Unit, Econ. Diplomacy Directorate 2016–18, High Commr to Papua New Guinea 2018–. *Address:* British High Commission, Sec 411 Lot 1,2, Kiroki Street, Waigani National Capital District 131, Port Moresby, Papua New Guinea (office). *Telephone:* 3037600 (office). *Fax:* 3253547 (office). *E-mail:* uk.inpng@fco.gov.uk (office). *Website:* www.gov.uk/world/organisations/british-high-commission-port-moresby (office).

SCOTT, (Harold) Lee, Jr, BBA; American retail executive; *Operating Partner, Solamere Capital LLC;* b. 14 March 1949, Joplin, Mo.; s. of Harold Lee Scott and Avis Viola Scott (née Parsons); m. Linda Gale Aldridge 1969; two s.; ed Pittsburg State Univ., Pittsburg, Kan.; Br. Man. Yellow Freight System, Springdale 1972–78; Man. Queen City Warehouse, Springfield 1978–79; joined Wal-Mart Stores, Inc., Bentonville 1979, Dir of Transportation 1979–83, Vice-Pres. of Distribution, Sr Vice-Pres. of Logistics, Exec. Vice-Pres. of Logistics, Pres. and CEO Wal-Mart Stores Div. 1996, COO and Vice-Chair. 1999–2000, Pres. and CEO 2000–09, Chair. Exec. Cttee 2009–11 (retd); Operating pnr Solamere Capital LLC 2009–, also mem. Investment Cttee; mem. Bd of Dirs Pvt. Truck Council, Washington, DC 1985–86, Goldman Sachs Group 2010–11, Cooper Industries Inc., United Negro Coll. Fund, Yahoo! Inc. 2014–; Bd mem. Tsinghua Univ., China 1999–, currently also mem. Advisory Bd, School of Economics and Man.; mem. Republican party. *Leisure interests:* reading, quail hunting. *Address:* Solamere Group LLC, 137 Newbury Street, Seventh Floor, Boston, MA 02116 (office); 611 Prairie Creek Road, Rogers, AR 72756-3019, USA (home). *Telephone:* (857) 362-9205 (office). *Website:* investorrelations@solameregroup.com (office); www.solameregroup.com (office).

SCOTT, Mark, AO, BA, MA, MPA; Australian/American public servant, academic and fmr media executive; *Secretary, New South Wales Department of Education;* b. 9 Oct. 1962, Los Angeles, CA; s. of Brian Scott; grand-s. of Sir Walter Scott (govt adviser); m. Briony Scott; ed Univ. of Sydney, Harvard Univ.; Editorial Dir John Fairfax Publs –2006, Ed.-in-Chief Metropolitan Newspapers 2003–05, Regional and Community Newspapers 2005; also worked for Sydney Morning Herald, Sun Herald, Age and Sunday Age; Man. Dir Australian Broadcasting Corpn (ABC) 2006–16 (retd); Sec., NSW Dept of Educ. 2016–. *Address:* NSW Department of Education, 105 Phillip Street, Parramatta, NSW 2150, Australia (office). *Telephone:* (2) 7814-1530 (office). *E-mail:* DECinfo@det.nsw.edu.au (office). *Website:* education.nsw.gov.au (office).

SCOTT, Peter Denys John, CBE, MA, QC; British lawyer and arbitrator; b. 19 April 1935; s. of John Ernest Dudley Scott and Joan G. Steinberg; ed Monroe High School, Rochester, New York, USA, Balliol Coll., Oxford; called to Bar 1960, QC 1978; Chair. of Bar 1987 (Vice-Chair. 1985–86); Standing Counsel to Dir-Gen. of Fair Trading 1974–78, to Dept of Employment 1973–78; mem. Interception of Communications Tribunal 1986–2000, Lord Chancellor's Advisory Cttee on Legal Educ. and Conduct 1991–94; Chair. Inst. of Actuaries Appeal Bd 1995–2000; Judicial Chair. City Disputes Panel 1997–; Chair. Panel on Takeovers and Mergers 2000–10; Harmsworth Scholar of Middle Temple; Bencher of Middle Temple; Chair. Kensington Housing Trust 1999–2002; Chair. Bd of Trustees, Nat. Gallery 2000–08, Scott Review (NI) 2007–; mem. Investigatory Powers Tribunal 2000–10. *Leisure interests:* art, gardening, theatre. *Address:* 4 Eldon Road, London, W8 5PU, England (home). *Telephone:* (20) 7937-3301 (home). *Fax:* (20) 7376-1169 (home).

SCOTT, Phil, BS; American business executive and politician; *Governor of Vermont;* b. 4 Aug. 1958, Barre, Vt; s. of Howard Scott and Marian Scott; m. Diana McTeague Scott; two d.; ed Univ. of Vermont; Co-owner, Debois Construction 1986–; Co-owner, Shoneys Restaurant; mem. Vermont State Senate for Washington Dist 2001–11; elected Lt-Gov. of Vermont 2011, Gov.-elect of Vermont 2016–17, Gov. 2017–; mem. Asscn of Gen. Contractors (Pres. 1997–98); Republican. *Leisure interests:* stock car racing, cycling. *Address:* Office of the Governor, Pavilion Office Building, 109 State Street, Montpelier, VT 05609, USA (office). *Telephone:* (802) 828-3333 (office). *Fax:* (802) 828-3339 (office). *Website:* governor.vermont.gov (office); www.philscott.org.

SCOTT, Richard Lynn (Rick), BBA, LLB; American lawyer, business executive, politician and fmr state governor; *Senator from Florida;* b. 1 Dec. 1952, Bloomington, Ill.; m. Ann Scott (née Frances Annette Holland) 1972; two d.; ed Univ. of Missouri-Kansas City, Southern Methodist Univ.; raised in Kansas City, Mo.; served in USN on USS Glover as radar technician 1971–74; while a student, bought two Kansas City doughnut shops; practised law in Dallas, Tex.; Pnr, Johnson & Swanson (law firm), Dallas; Partner, HM Capital Partners, Dallas; helped found Columbia Hospital Corpn 1987 (merged with Hospital Corpn of America to form Columbia/HCA 1989, later became largest pvt. for-profit health care co. in USA), forced to resign as Chair. and CEO of Columbia/HCA amid questions over co.'s business and Medicare billing practices 1997; Partner of George W. Bush in ownership of Texas Rangers professional baseball team 1990s; Founder and CEO Richard L. Scott Investments, LLC, Naples, Fla (originally in

Stamford, Conn.) 1997–; Co-founder and Chair. Solantic Corpn, Jacksonville 2001–; mem. Bd of Dirs Associated Industries of Florida, CyberGuard 2001–03, Secure Computing Corpn 2006–08, Envestnet Asset Management, Continental Structural Plastics, Inc.; f. Conservatives for Patients Rights 2009; Gov. of Florida 2011–19; Senator from Florida 2019–; mem. Nat. Bd of The United Way 1997–2003, Business Council, Business Roundtable, Healthcare Leadership Council; Republican; Second Century Award for Excellence in Health Care, Columbia Univ. School of Nursing 1995, Silver Award for the CEO of the Year, Financial World magazine 1995, Entrepreneurship Award, George Washington Univ. 2007. *Address:* 716 Hart Senate Building, Washington, DC 20510 (office); Richard L. Scott Investments, LLC, 1400 Gulfshore Blvd North, Suite 148, Naples, FL 34102, USA. *Telephone:* (202) 224-5274 (senate) (office); (239) 263-9030 (office). *Fax:* (202) 228-2183 (senate) (office); (239) 263-9031 (office). *Website:* www.rlsi.net (office); rickscott.senate.gov (office).

SCOTT, Sir Ridley, Kt; British film director and film producer; b. 30 Nov. 1937, South Shields, Tyne and Wear; ed Royal Coll. of Art; Dir of numerous award-winning TV commercials since 1970; Co-founder (with Tony Scott) RSA Films (production co.) 1968; Hon. DLitt (Sunderland) 1998; Dr hc (Royal Coll. of Art, London) 2015; BAFTA Award for Outstanding British Contribution To Cinema 1995, inducted into Science Fiction Hall of Fame 2007. *Films include:* Boy and Bicycle (dir, producer) 1965, The Duellists (dir) (Cannes Best Debut Film Award 1977) 1977, Alien (dir) (Best Director, Saturn Awards, Best Science Fiction film 1979) 1979, Blade Runner (dir, co-producer) 1982, Legend (dir) 1985, Someone to Watch Over Me (dir, exec. producer) 1987, Black Rain (dir) 1989, Thelma and Louise (dir, producer) 1991, 1492: Conquest of Paradise (dir, producer) 1992, Monkey Trouble (exec. producer) 1994, The Browning Version (producer) 1994, White Squall (dir, exec. producer) 1996, G.I. Jane (dir, producer) 1997, Clay Pigeons (producer) 1998, Where the Money Is (producer) 2000, Gladiator (dir, exec. producer) (Acad. Award for Best Picture) 2000, Hannibal (dir, producer) 2001, Black Hawk Down (dir, producer) 2001, Six Bullets from Now (producer) 2002, The Hire: Hostage (exec. producer) 2002, The Hire: Beat the Devil (exec. producer) 2002, The Hire: Ticker (exec. producer) 2002, Matchstick Men (dir, producer) 2003, Kingdom of Heaven (dir, producer) 2005, In Her Shoes (producer) 2005, Domino (producer) 2005, Tristan & Isolde (exec. producer) 2006, A Good Year (dir, producer) 2006, American Gangster (dir, producer) 2007, Body of Lies (dir, producer) 2008, Tell-Tale 2009, Robin Hood 2010, Prometheus 2012, The Counsellor (dir, producer) 2013, Exodus: Gods and Kings (dir, producer) 2014, The Martian (dir, producer) (Golden Globe Award for Best Motion Picture–Musical or Comedy 2015) 2015, Alien: Covenant 2017, All the Money in the World 2017. *Television includes:* Z Cars (dir, series) 1962, The Troubleshooters (dir, series) 1965, Adam Adamant Lives! (dir, series) 1966, The Informer (dir, series) 1966, Robert (dir, film) 1967, The Hunger (exec. prod., series) 1997, RKO 281 (exec. prod., series) 1999, The Last Debate (exec. prod., film) 2000, AFP: American Fighter Pilot (exec. prod., series) 2002, The Gathering Storm (exec. prod., film) (Emmy Award for Best Made-for-TV Film) 2002, Numb3rs (exec. prod., series) 2005, The Good Wife (exec. producer, series) 2009–15, The Vatican (dir, exec. producer) 2013, Galyntine (exec. producer) 2014, Killing Jesus (exec. producer) 2015, Taboo (series, exec. producer) 2016. *Address:* RSA Films, 634 North La Peer Drive, Los Angeles, CA 90069, USA. *Website:* www.rsafilms.com.

SCOTT, Robert G., BA, MBA; American business executive; *Chairman, Genpact Ltd;* b. 1946, Montclair, NJ; m. Karen Scott; ed Williams Coll., Stanford Graduate School of Business; investment banker, Morgan Stanley 1970–79, Man. Dir 1979–97, Dir Capital Market Services 1985–92, Corp. Finance 1992–94, Investment Banking 1994–96, Chief Financial Officer and Exec. Vice-Pres. Morgan Stanley Dean Witter (now Morgan Stanley) 1997–2001, Pres. and COO 2001–03, currently Advisory Dir; Chair. (non-exec.) Genpact Ltd 2011–; mem. Bd of Dirs 2006–; Exec. Vice-Pres. Greater New York Council of Boy Scouts of America 1992–2004; mem. Bd of Dirs NYSE Euronext, Intercontinental Exchange Inc.; mem. Advisory Council, Stanford Graduate School of Business; Trustee, The Seeing Eye Inc. 1984–2004, New York-Presbyterian Hospital, Williams Coll., Naples Children and Education Foundation; fmr Trustee, Japan Soc. of New York; fmr Chair. American Museum of Fly Fishing; Excellence in Leadership Award, Stanford Business School 2004. *Leisure interests:* flu fishing, golf, downhill skiing. *Address:* Genpact Ltd, 105 Madison Avenue, 2nd Floor, New York, NY 10016-7418, USA (office). *Website:* www.genpact.com (office).

SCOTT, Timothy (Tim), AADipl; British sculptor; b. 18 April 1937, Richmond, Surrey, England; s. of A. C. Scott and Dorothea Scott; m. Yvonne Jeanne Malkanthi Wirekoon 1958; two s. three d.; ed Lycée Jaccard, Lausanne, Architectural Asscn and St Martin's School of Art, London; worked at Atelier Le Corbusier-Wogenscky and others, Paris 1959–61; Sr Lecturer Canterbury Coll. of Art 1975–76; Head of Fine Art Dept, Birmingham Polytechnic 1976–78; Head Dept of Sculpture, St Martin's School of Art 1980–86; Prof. of Sculpture, Akad. der Bildenden Künste Nürnberg 1993–2002; numerous visiting lectureships in USA, Canada, Australia, Germany, UK, Chile. *Leisure interests:* music, architecture, travel, Sri Lanka, Indian culture, food. *Address:* 'High House', 71 Gangawata Para Anniewatte, Kandy, Sri Lanka (office); Keeper's Cottage, Troutsdale, N Yorks., YO13 9PS (home); 50 Clare Court, Judd Street, London, WC1H 9QW, England (home). *Telephone:* (81) 2226913 (Sri Lanka) (office); (1723) 859087 (UK) (home). *E-mail:* timscottsculptor@yahoo.com (office).

SCOTT, Timothy (Tim), BS; American politician and business executive; *Senator from South Carolina;* b. 19 Sept. 1965, Charleston, South Carolina; s. of Ben Scott, Sr and Frances Scott; ed Presbyterian Coll., Charleston Southern Univ.; owns an insurance agency and works as a financial adviser; Partner, Pathway Real Estate Group, LLC; mem. Charleston Co. Council from the 3rd Dist 1995–2009; mem. S Carolina House of Reps from the 117th Dist 2009–11; mem. US House of Reps for the 1st Congressional Dist of S Carolina 2011–13, mem. Cttee on Transportation, Cttee on Small Business, Cttee on Rules; Senator from S Carolina 2013–; Republican. *Address:* 113 Hart Senate Office Building, Washington, DC 20510, USA (office). *Telephone:* (202) 224-6121 (office). *Website:* scott.senate.gov (office).

SCOTT, Hon. W(illiam) Alexander, CBE, JP, BFA; Bermudian politician; b. 1940; s. of Willard Scott and Edith Lucille Scott; m. Olga Scott 1969; one s. one d.; ed Temple Univ., USA; Owner public relations agency; Founder-mem. and fmr Chair. Big Brothers; mem. Pitt Comm. investigating causes of riots 1977; apptd to Senate 1985, Opposition Leader in the Senate 1989; elected to Parl. 1993, Deputy Leader of the Opposition Progressive Labour Party 1996, currently MP for Warwick South East Constituency, Minister of Works and Eng 1998–2003, Premier of Bermuda and Govt Leader 2003–06. *Leisure interest:* photography. *Address:* Progressive Labour Party, Alaska Hall, 16 Court Street, Hamilton, HM 17, Bermuda (office). *Telephone:* 236-8633 (office). *E-mail:* ascott@plp.bm (office). *Website:* www.plp.bm (office).

SCOTT, Walter, Jr, BS; American business executive; *Chairman Emeritus, Peter Kiewit Sons Inc.;* b. 21 May 1931; m. Suzanne Scott (deceased); three s. three d.; ed Colorado State Univ.; began career with Peter Kiewit Sons Inc., Omaha 1953, Man. Cleveland Dist 1962–64, Vice-Pres. 1964–65, Exec. Vice-Pres. 1965–79, Pres. 1979–97, Chair. Emer. 1998–, mem. Bd of Dirs 1964–2014, Chair. Level 3 Communications (cr. after spinoff from Peter Kiewit Sons) 1979–2014; Chair. MidAmerican Energy Holdings (renamed Berkshire Hathaway Energy 2014) 1992–93, currently mem. Bd of Dirs; Pres. Joslyn Art Museum, Omaha 1987–97, currently Dir; mem. Bd of Dirs George Industries Inc. 1981–, Valmont Industries 1981–, Burlington Resources 1988–, Commonwealth Telephone Enterprises Inc. 1993–, WorldCom 1996–97, RCN Corpn 1997–, ConAgra Inc.; currently Chair. Bd of Trustees, Open World Leadership Center; Chair. Bd of Policy Advisors, Peter Kiewit Inst. for Information Science, Tech. and Eng, Heritage Services, Omaha Zoological Soc.; Dir Neb. Game and Parks Foundation, Horatio Alger Asscn, Nat. Forest Asscn; f. Suzanne and Walter Scott Foundation; Hon. mem. Chi Epsilon Soc. 1986; Hon. DLitt (Univ. of Nebraska) 1983, Hon. DHumLitt (Coll. of Saint Mary) 1988, Hon. DComm (Bellevue Univ.) 1996; Nebraska Builder Award, Univ. of Nebraska 1983, Outstanding Achievement in Construction Award 1986, Brotherhood Award, Nat. Conf. of Christians and Jews 1986, Philanthropist of the Year, Nat. Soc. of Fund-Raising Executives 1987, Man of the Year, Mid-America Council Boy Scouts of America 1988, Spirit of Youth Award 1988, Perry W. Branch Distinguished Service Award, Univ. of Nebraska Foundation 1989, Golden Plate Award, American Acad. of Achievement 1991, Golden Apple Award, Metropolitan Community Coll. Foundation 1993, Headliner Award, Greater Omaha Chamber of Commerce 1996, Horatio Alger Award 1997, Distinguished Eagle Scout Award 1991, Nebraskalander Award, Nebraskaland Foundation 1998, Manresa Award, Creighton Univ. 1998, Community Builder Award, Greater Omaha Chamber of Commerce 1999, Midlander of the Year, Omaha World-Herald 2000.

SCOTT, W(illiam) Richard, PhD; American sociologist and academic; *Professor Emeritus and Senior Scholar, Global Projects Center and John Garner Center, Stanford University;* b. 18 Dec. 1932, Parsons, Kan.; s. of Charles H. Scott and Hildegarde Hewit; m. Joy Lee Whitney 1955; three c.; ed Parsons Jr Coll., Kan., Univ. of Kansas, Univ. of Chicago; Asst Prof., Dept of Sociology, Stanford Univ. 1960–65, Assoc. Prof. 1965–69, Prof. 1969–99, Prof. Emer. 1999–, Chair. Dept of Sociology 1972–75, Dir Orgs. Research Training Program 1972–89; Dir Stanford Center for Orgs. Research 1988–96; Prof. by courtesy, Dept of Health Research and Policy, School of Medicine 1972– and of Educ., School of Educ. and of Organizational Behaviour, Graduate School of Business, Stanford Univ. 1977–, Sr Scholar, John W. Gardner Center for Youth and Their Communities 2002–08, 2013–16, Collaboratory for Global Research; Sr Researcher, Nat. Center for Health Services Research, Dept of Health, Educ. and Welfare, Washington, DC 1975–76; Visiting Prof., Kellogg Grad. School of Man., Northwestern Univ. 1997, Hong Kong Univ. of Science and Tech. 2000; Visiting Distinguished Scholar, Singapore Management Univ. 2006; Visiting Prof., Said Business School and Green Coll., Univ. of Oxford 2008; Ed. Annual Review of Sociology 1986–91; mem. Gov. Bd, Comm. on Social and Behavioral Sciences and Educ., NAS 1990–96; Woodrow Wilson Fellow 1954–55; Social Science Research Council Fellow 1958–59, Fellow, Center for Advanced Study in the Behavioral Sciences 1989–90; Resident Fellow, Bellagio Center 2002; mem. Inst. of Medicine 1975; Dr hc (Copenhagen Business School) 2000; Hon. DEcon (Helsinki School of Econs) 2001; Dr Scientiarum Socialium (Århus Univ., Denmark) 2010; Distinguished Scholar Award, OMT Div. of Acad. of Man. 1988, Richard D. Irwin Award for Distinguished Scholarly Career, Acad. of Man. 1996, Distinguished Educator Award, OMT Div. of Acad. of Man. 2013, Eminent Scholar of the Year, Acad. of Int. Business 2016. *Publications:* Metropolis and Region (co-author) 1960, Formal Organizations (co-author) 1962, Social Processes and Social Structures 1970, Evaluation and the Exercise of Authority (co-author) 1975, Organizations: Rational, Natural and Open Systems 1981 (fifth edn 2003), Organizational Environments (co-author) 1983, Hospital Structure and Performance (co-author) 1987, Institutional Environments and Organizations: Structural Complexity and Individualism (co-author) 1994, Institutions and Organizations 1995 (third edn 2008), Institutional Change and Healthcare Organizations: From Professional Dominance to Managed Care (co-author) 2000, Organizations and Organizing (co-author) 2007, Organizations and Organizing: Rational, Natural and Open System Perspectives 2007, Between Movement and Establishment (co-author) 2009, Global Projects: Institutional and Political Challenges (co-author) 2011, Higher Education and Silicon Valley: Connected but Conflicted (co-author) 2017. *Leisure interests:* reading, gardening, hiking. *Address:* Department of Sociology, Stanford University, Building 120, Stanford, CA 94305 (office); 940 Lathrop Place, Stanford, CA 94305, USA (home). *Telephone:* (650) 723-3416 (office); (650) 857-1834 (home). *Fax:* (650) 725-6471 (office). *E-mail:* scottwr@stanford.edu (office). *Website:* www.stanford.edu/dept/soc (office).

SCOTT BROWN, Denise, MArch, MCP, RIBA, Int. FRIBA; American architect, planner, urban designer, writer and academic; *Principal, VSBA, LLC;* b. (Denise Valda Lakofski), 3 Oct. 1931, Nkana, Zambia; d. of Simon Lakofski and Phyllis Hepker; m. 1st Robert Scott Brown 1955 (died 1959); m. 2nd Robert Venturi 1967 (died 2018); one s.; ed Univ. of Witwatersrand, South Africa, Architectural Asscn, UK, Univ. of Pennsylvania; Arts Instructor, Univ. of Pennsylvania School of Fine Arts 1960, Asst Prof. 1961–65; Assoc. Prof., UCLA 1965–68, Regents Lecturer 1972; Visiting Critic, Rice Univ. 1969; mem. Venturi, Scott Brown & Assocs, Inc. (now VSBA, LLC), Philadelphia 1967–, Pnr 1969–89, Prin. 1989–; Chair. Evaluation Cttee for Industrial Design Program, Philadelphia Coll. of Art 1972; Visiting Prof., Univ. of California, Berkeley 1965, Yale Univ. 1967–71, Univ. of Pennsylvania 1982–83; mem. MIT School of Architecture and Urban Planning Visiting Cttee 1973–83; Eliot Noyes Visiting Critic, Harvard Univ. 1990; Distinguished Prof., Asscn of Collegiate Schools of Architecture 1991; Kassler Lecturer and Whitney J. Oates Fellow, Humanities Council, School of Architecture 2006; Jury mem., Prince of Wales Prize in Urban Design 1993; mem. Advisory Bd, Carnegie Mellon Univ. Dept of Architecture 1992–, Bd of Overseers for Univ. Libraries, Univ. of Pennsylvania 1995–2004; Consulting Adviser, Architecture, Landscape and Horticulture Initiative 1998; Adviser to Bd of Visitors, Tyler School of Art and Architecture, Temple Univ. 2008–; mem. Bd of Trustees Chestnut Hill Acad. 1985–89; Fellow, Morse Coll. 1970, Butler Coll., Princeton Univ. 1983–; numerous other academic and professional appointments; Honoree, French–American Chamber of Commerce, Philadelphia 2000; Chevalier de l'Ordre des Arts et Lettres 2000; Hon. DEng (Tech. Univ. of Nova Scotia) 1991, Hon. DHumLitt (New Jersey Inst. of Tech.)1984, (Pratt Inst.) 1992, (Lehigh Univ.) 2002, (Drexel Univ.) 2012; Hon. DFA (Oberlin Coll.) 1977, (Parsons School of Design) 1985, (Philadelphia Coll. of Art) 1985, (Univ. of Pennsylvania) 1994; Hon. DLit (Univ. of Nev.) 1998; Dr hc (Univ. of the Witwatersrand) 2011; Hazlett Memorial Award for Excellence in the Arts, Commonwealth of Pennsylvania 1983, President's Medal, Architectural League of NY 1986, Chicago Architecture Award 1987, Commendatore of the Order of Merit, Repub. of Italy 1987, Nat. Medal of Arts 1992, Trustees of the Philadelphia Award 1993, John Harbeson Distinguished Service Award, Philadelphia Chapter of the American Inst. of Architects 1993, Benjamin Franklin Medal Award (RSA) 1993, Topaz Medallion, ACSA–AIA Jt Award for Excellence in Architecture Educ. 1996, Giants of Design Award, House Beautiful Magazine 2000, Joseph Pennell Medal, Philadelphia Sketch Club 2000, Edith Wharton Women of Achievement Award for Urban Planning 2002, Vincent J. Scully Prize, National Building Museum (with R. Venturi) 2002, Visionary Woman Award, Moore Coll. of Art and Design 2003, Inaugural Design Philadelphia Luminary Award, (with R. Venturi) 2005, Harvard Radcliffe Inst. Medal 2005, Master Builder Award, Carpenters' Co. (with R. Venturi) 2005, The Founder's Award, Historical Soc. of Pennsylvania (with R. Venturi) 2006, Philadelphia Artistic Legacy Award, Woodmere Art Museum (with R. Venturi) 2006, Vileck Prize 2007, Athena Award 2007, Nat. Design Mind Award, Cooper Hewitt Nat. Design Museum (with R. Venturi) 2007, Anne d'Harnoncourt Award for Artistic Excellence, Arts & Business Council of Greater Philadelphia (with R. Venturi) 2010, Int. Award, Soc. of American Registered Architects, Philadelphia 2010, Edmund N. Bacon Prize, Ed Bacon Foundation 2010, The Mario Pani Award, Mexico 2013, National Planning Award for a Planning Pioneer, American Planning Asscn (with R. Venturi) 2014, Medal of Honor, The American Inst. of Architects (with R. Venturi) 2014, Gold Medal, American Inst. of Architects (with R. Venturi) 2016, Medal of Distinction, Philadelphia Chapter of the American Inst. of Architects 2016, ECC Architecture Award, European Cultural Centre 2016, Jane Drew Prize for Women in Architecture 2017, Soane Medal, Sir John Soane's Museum, London 2018, and numerous other awards. *Publications include:* Learning from Las Vegas (with R. Venturi and S. Izenour) 1977, A View from the Campidoglio: Selected Essays, 1953–84 (with R. Venturi) 1984, Urban Concepts 1990, Architecture and Decorative Arts: Two Naifs in Japan (with R. Venturi) 1991, Architecture as Signs and Systems for a Mannerist Time (with R. Venturi) 2004, Supercrit 2 2007, AA Words 4: Having Words 2009; articles in professional journals. *Leisure interests:* travelling, writing, teaching, lecturing. *Address:* VSBA Architects & Planners, 116 Shurs Lane, Philadelphia, PA 19127, USA (office). *Telephone:* (215) 487-0400 (office). *E-mail:* info@vsba.com (office). *Website:* www.vsba.com (office); venturiscottbrown.org (office).

SCOTT OF FOSCOTE, Baron (Life Peer), cr. 2000, of Foscote in the County of Buckinghamshire; **Richard Rashleigh Folliott Scott,** BA, LLB; British lawyer; b. 2 Oct. 1934, Dehra Dun, India; s. of Lt-Col C. W. F. Scott and Katharine Scott (née Rashleigh); m. Rima E. Ripoll 1959; two s. two d.; ed Michaelhouse Coll. Natal, Univ. of Cape Town, Trinity Coll., Cambridge, Univ. of Chicago; called to Bar, Inner Temple 1959; practising barrister, Chancery Bar 1960–83; QC 1975; Attorney-Gen. to Duchy of Lancaster 1980–83; Bencher, Inner Temple 1981; Chair. of the Bar 1982–83 (Vice-Chair. 1981–82); High Court Judge, Chancery Div. 1983–91; Vice-Chancellor, County Palatine of Lancaster 1987–91; a Lord Justice of Appeal 1991–94; Vice-Chancellor of the Supreme Court of Justice 1994–2000; Head of Civil Justice 1995–2000; mem. (Crossbench), House of Lords 2000–16 (retd); Lord of Appeal in Ordinary 2000–09; non-Perm. Judge, Hong Kong Court of Final Appeal 2004–12; Judge, Civil and Commercial Court of Qatar 2010–15; conducted inquiry into the sale of arms to Iraq 1992–96; Ed.-in-Chief Supreme Court Practice 1996–2001; Hon. mem. American Bar Asscn, Canadian Bar Asscn; Hon. LLD (Birmingham) 1996, (Buckingham) 1999. *Publications:* Report of the Inquiry into the Export of Defence Equipment and Dual-Use Goods to Iraq and the Related Prosecutions; articles in legal journals. *Leisure interests:* equestrian activities, tennis, bridge. *Address:* The Old Rectory, Foscote, Buckingham, MK18 6AE, England. *Telephone:* (1280) 813142. *E-mail:* rima.scott@gmail.com (home). *Website:* www.parliament.uk/biographies/lords/lord-scott-of-foscote/2557.

SCOTT OF NEEDHAM MARKET, Baroness (Life Peer), cr. 2000, of Needham Market in the County of Suffolk; **Rosalind Carol (Ros) Scott,** BA; British politician; b. (Rosalind Carol Leadbeater), 10 Aug. 1957, Bath, Somerset, England; d. of Kenneth Vincent Leadbeater and Carol Leadbeater; m. 1st (divorced); one s. one d.; m. 2nd Mark Valladares 2008; ed Whitby Grammar School, Kent School, Univ. of East Anglia; Councillor, Mid-Suffolk Dist Council 1991–94, Suffolk Co. Council 1993–2005 (Vice-Chair. 1996–97); Chair. Local Govt Asscn Transport Exec. 2002–05; mem. (Liberal Democrat) House of Lords 2000–, mem. Appointments Comm. 2010–; Liberal Democrat Whip 2001–02, Deputy Chief Whip 2002, Spokesperson for Transport, Local Govt and the Regions 2001–02, for Transport 2002–04, for Office of the Deputy Prime Minister/Communities and Local Govt 2004–09, currently Chair. House of Lords EU Scrutiny Cttee D; Pres. Liberal Democrat Party 2009–10; mem. North Sea Comm. 1997–2005, Council of European Municipalities and Regions 1997–2003, Congress of Local and Regional Authorities in Europe 1997–2003, EU Cttee of the Regions 1998–2002, Inter-Parl. Union 2000–, Commonwealth Parl. Asscn 2000–; Bd mem. Audit Comm. 2004–06; Dir (non-exec.) Lloyd's Register, ITV Anglia, Entrust, the Landfill Tax regulator; mem. Comm. for Integrated Transport (think-tank); Lecturer for Dod's 'Westminster Explained'; mem. Bd Harwich Haven Authority 2013–; Hon. Pres. East Coast Sailing Trust. *Address:* House of Lords, Westminster, London, SW1A 0PW, England (office). *Telephone:* (20) 7219-8660 (office). *Fax:* (20) 7219-5979 (office). *E-mail:* scottrc@parliament.uk (office).

SCOTT THOMAS, Dame Kristin Ann, DBE; British/French actress; b. 24 May 1960, Redruth, Cornwall, England; d. of Lt Commdr Simon Scott Thomas and Deborah Scott Thomas (née Hurlbatt); m. François Olivennes 1987 (divorced 2005); two s. one d.; ed Cheltenham Ladies' Coll., St Antony's Leweston, Sherborne, Dorset, Cen. School of Speech and Drama, London, École nationale supérieure des arts et techniques du théâtre, Paris; stage debut in Schnitzler's La Lune Déclinante Sur 4 ou 5 Personnes Qui Danse while student in Paris; has lived in France since age of 19; Chevalier, Légion d'honneur 2005. *Theatre includes:* La Lune déclinante sur 4 ou 5 personnes qui dansent (Festival de Semur en Auxois) 1983, Terre étrangère (Théâtre Nanterre-Amandiers) 1984, Naïves Hirondelles (Festival d'Avignon) 1984, Yes, peut-être (in a field in Burgundy) 1985, Bérénice (Festival de Perpignan and Festival d'Avignon plus nat. tour) 2001, Three Sisters (Playhouse Theatre, London) 2003, As You Desire Me (Playhouse Theatre, London) 2005–06, The Seagull (Royal Court Theatre, London; Olivier Award for Best Actress 2008) 2007, Betrayal (Comedy Theatre, London) 2011, Old Times (Harold Pinter Theatre London) 2013, Electra (The Old Vic, London) 2014, The Audience (Apollo Theatre, London) 2015. *Films include:* Charly 1985, Under the Cherry Moon 1986, Djamel et Juliette 1987, L'Agent Troublé 1987, La Méridienne, A Handful of Dust (Evening Standard British Film Award for Most Promising Newcomer) 1988, Force Majeure 1989, Bille en Tête 1989, The Bachelor 1990, Bitter Moon 1992, Four Weddings and a Funeral (BAFTA Award for Best Actress in a Supporting Role, Evening Standard British Film Award for Best Actress) 1994, Angels and Insects (Evening Standard Film Award for Best Actress) 1995, Richard III 1995, The English Patient 1996, Amour et Confusions 1997, The Horse Whisperer 1998, Random Hearts 1999, Up at the Villa 2000, Gosford Park 2001, Life as a House 2001, Petites Coupures 2003, Résistantes 2004, The Three Ages of the Crime 2004, Arsène Lupin 2004, Man to Man 2005, Keeping Mum 2005, La Doublure 2006, Ne le dis à personne 2006, The Walker 2007, The Golden Compass (voice) 2007, I've Loved You So Long 2008, The Other Boleyn Girl 2008, Seuls two 2008, Easy Virtue 2008, Largo Winch 2008, Confessions of a Shopaholic 2009, Partir (Leaving) 2009, Nowhere Boy 2010, Contre Toi 2010, Salmon Fishing in the Yemen 2011, The Woman in the Fifth 2011, Bel Ami 2012, In the House 2012, Looking for Hortense 2012, Only God Forgives 2013, The Invisible Woman 2013, Before the Winter Chill 2013, Suite française 2014, My Old Lady 2014, The Kitchen Boy 2015, Darkest Hour 2017. *Television includes:* Mistral's Daughter (mini-series) 1984, Sentimental Journey (film) 1987, La tricheuse (film) 1987, The Tenth Man (film) 1988, The Endless Game (series) 1989, Spymaker: The Secret Life of Ian Fleming (film) 1990, Framed (film) 1990, Titmuss Regained (mini-series) 1991, Look at It This Way (mini-series) 1992, Weep No More, My Lady (film) 1992, Body & Soul (mini-series) 1993, Belle Époque (mini-series) 1995, Gulliver's Travels (film) 1996, Absolutely Fabulous (series) 2003. *Address:* c/o TESS Management, 4th Floor, 9–10 Market Place, London, W1W 8AQ, England (office). *Telephone:* (20) 7557-7100 (office). *Fax:* (20) 7557-7101 (office). *E-mail:* info@tessmanagement.com (office). *Website:* www.tessmanagement.com (office).

SCOTTO, Renata; Italian singer (soprano); b. 24 Feb. 1935, Savona; m. Lorenzo Anselmi; one s. one d.; ed Giuseppe Verdi Conservatory with Emilio Ghiriardini; debut as Violetta, Teatro Nuovo, Milan 1953; joined La Scala opera co. from 1954; London debut at the Stoll Theatre 1957; US debut in Chicago 1960; Covent Garden debut 1962, as Madama Butterfly; roles at the Metropolitan Opera from 1965, directed Butterfly at the Metropolitan 1986 and sang there for the last time in 1987; numerous festival appearances; sang roles in Adriana Lecouvreur, Andrea Chénier, Anna Bolena, Cavalleria Rusticana, Der Rosenkavalier (Marschallin), Elektra (Klytämnestra), Edgar, Falstaff, Gilda, I Capuleti e i Montecchi, I Lombardi, I Puritani, I Vespri Siciliani (Helena), L'Elisir d'amore, La Bohème, La Sonnambula (Amina), La Straniera, La Traviata, La Voix Humaine, Lucia di Lammermoor, Madama Butterfly, Manon Lescaut, Otello, Pagliacci, Pirata, Robert le Diable, The Medium, Tosca, Trittico, Turandot; as stage dir: Il Pirata, Bellini Festival, Catania, Madama Butterfly, Arena di Verona, Genoa, Thessaloniki, Ancona, Dallas Opera, Lucia di Lammermoor, Thessaloniki, Tosca, Traviata, Sonnambula, Florida Grand Opera, Sonnambula, Detroit; est. Renata Scotto Opera Program, Opera Naples, Fla 2016; Commendatore della Reppublica; Dr hc (Saint John's Univ.); Metropolitan Opera Guild Opera News Award 2007. *Publication:* More Than a Diva (autobiog.) 1984. *Address:* Piper Anselmi Artists Management, 777 Westchester Avenue, Suite 101, White Plains, NY 10604 (office); c/o Robert Lombardo Associates, 61 West 62nd Street, Suite 6F, New York, NY 10023, USA (office). *Telephone:* (212) 586-4453 (office). *Fax:* (212) 581-5771 (office). *E-mail:* lewis@rlombardo.com (office). *Website:* piperanselmi.com/portfolio/renata-scotto (office); www.lombardoassociates.org/renata-scotto (office).

SCOTTY, Ludwig Derangadage; Nauruan politician and fmr head of state; b. 20 June 1948, Anabar; ed Univ. of South Pacific, Fiji; mem. Parl. for Anabar Dist 1983–, Speaker –2000, 2010–13; Pres. and Minister of Foreign Affairs May–Aug. 2003 (removed in a no-confidence vote), mem. of Opposition 2003–04, re-elected Pres. 2004–07 (removed in a no-confidence vote), also fmr Minister of Civil Aviation, of Customs and Immigration and of Public Service. *Address:* Parliament of Nauru, Parliament House, Yaren, Nauru (office). *Telephone:* 557-3133 (office). *E-mail:* parliament.info@naurugov.nr (office). *Website:* www.naurugov.nr/parliament/index.html (office).

SCOWCROFT, Lt-Gen. Brent, PhD; American consultant, fmr government official and air force officer (retd); *President, Scowcroft Group;* b. 19 March 1925, Odgen, Utah; s. of James Scowcroft and Lucile Balantyne Scowcroft; m. Marian Horner 1951 (died 1995); one d.; ed US Mil. Acad., West Point and Columbia Univ.; Operational and Admin. positions in USAF 1948–53; taught Russian history as Asst Prof., Dept of Social Sciences, US Mil. Acad., W Point 1953–57; Asst Air Attaché, US Embassy, Belgrade 1959–61; Assoc. Prof., Political Science Dept, USAF Acad., Colorado 1962–63, Prof., Head of Dept 1963–64; Plans and Operations Section, Air Force HQ, Washington 1964–66; various Nat. Security posts with Dept of Defense 1968–72; Mil. Asst to Pres., The White House 1972, Deputy Asst to Pres. for Nat. Security Affairs 1973–75, Asst to Pres. for Nat. Security Affairs 1975–77, 1989–93, mem. Pres.'s Gen. Advisory Cttee on Arms Control 1977–81; Vice-Chair. Kissinger Associates, Inc. 1982–89; Pres. Forum for Int. Policy 1993–; Pres. The Scowcroft Group 1994–; Dir Atlantic Council, US Bd of Visitors USAF Acad. 1977–79, Council on Foreign Relations, Rand Corpn, Mitre Corpn; Vice-Chair. UNA/USA; Chair. Presidential Comm. on Strategic Forces 1983–89; mem. Cttee to Advise Dir of CIA 1995–; Chair. Pres.'s Foreign

Intelligence Advisory Bd 2001–04, Eisenhower Inst. 2004–; mem. Cttee of Enquiry into Nat. Security Council 1986–87; Defense DSM, Air Force DSM (with two oak leaf clusters), Legion of Merit (with oak leaf cluster), Air Force Commendation Medal, Nat. Security Medal; Hon. KBE 1993, Grand Cross of the Order of Merit (Germany) 2009; Hon. DIur (Columbia Univ.) 2005, Hon. DH (Weber State Univ.) 2010; Presidential Medal of Freedom 1991, Ewald von Kleist Award 2013. *Publications:* A World Transformed (with George Bush) 1998, America and the World: Conversations on the Future of American Foreign Policy (with Zbigniew Brzezinski) 2008. *Address:* The Scowcroft Group, Suite 900, 900 17th Street, NW, Washington, DC 20006, USA (office). *Telephone:* (202) 296-9312 (office). *Fax:* (202) 296-9395 (office). *Website:* www.scowcroft.com (office).

SCRIVENER, Christiane; French public official and mediator; b. 1 Sept. 1925, Mulhouse; d. of Pierre Fries and Louise Fries; m. Pierre Scrivener 1944; one s. (deceased); ed Harvard Business School, USA, Univ. of Paris; involved since 1958 in org. of French tech. co-operation with more than 100 countries, devt of int. tech. and industrial exchanges and promotion of French tech. abroad; State Sec. for Consumer Affairs 1976–78; MEP 1979–89; mem. Union pour la Démocratie (UDF); EEC Commr for Taxation and Customs Union and Consumers' Interests 1989–95; Pres. Ombudsman Société Générale 1996, Plan Int. France 1997; mem. Bd Alliance Française 1995–97; Grand Officier, Légion d'honneur; Grand-croix Ordre de Leopold (Belgium); Grand-croix de Mérite (Luxembourg); Officier de Polonia Restituta (Poland). *Publications:* Le rôle et la responsabilité à l'égard du public 1978, L'Europe, une bataille pour l'avenir 1984, Histoires du petit Troll 1986. *Leisure interests:* skiing, music. *Address:* 21 avenue Robert-Schuman, 92100 Boulogne-Billancourt, France. *Telephone:* 1-48-25-44-11 (home). *E-mail:* ch .scrivener@wanadoo.fr (home).

SCRIVER, Charles Robert, OC, CC, MD, CM, FRS, FRSC, FAAS; Canadian paediatrician and geneticist; *Alva Professor Emeritus of Human Genetics, McGill University;* b. 7 Nov. 1930, Montreal; s. of Walter DeMoulpied and Jessie Marion Boyd; m. Esther Peirce 1956; two s. two d.; intern Royal Victoria Hosp. Montreal 1955–56, Resident 1956–57, Resident Montreal Children's Hosp. 1956–57, Chief Resident (Pediatrics) 1960–61, physician 1961–; Children's Medical Center, Boston, USA 1957–58; McLaughlin Travelling Fellow, Univ. Coll., London, UK 1958–60; Asst Prof. of Pediatrics, McGill Univ. 1961, Markle Scholar 1961–66, f. deBelle Lab. for Biochemical Genetics 1961, Assoc. Prof. 1965–69, Prof. of Pediatrics, Genetics and Biology 1969–, Co-Dir MRC Genetics Group 1972–95, Alva Prof. of Human Genetics 1994, Alva Prof. Emer. of Human Genetics 2002–; Assoc. Dir Canadian Genetic Diseases Network 1989–98; Pres. Canadian Soc. for Clinical Investigation 1974–75, Soc. for Pediatric Research 1975–76, American Soc. Human Genetics 1986, American Pediatric Soc. 1994–95; mem. Medical Advisory Bd/Scientific Advisory Bd Howard Hughes Medical Inst. 1981–88; Hon. DSc (Manitoba) 1992, (Glasgow, Montreal) 1993, (Utrecht) 1999, (British Columbia) 2002, (Montreal); Allen Award, American Soc. of Human Genetics 1978, Gairdner Foundation Int. Award 1979, McLaughlin Medal, Royal Soc. of Canada 1981, Canadian Rutherford Lectureship, Royal Soc., London 1983, Ross Award, Canadian Pediatric Soc. 1990, Award of Excellence, Genetic Soc. of Canada 1992, Prix du Québec 1995, Friesen Award 2001, Querci Prize (Italy) 2001, ASHG Award for Excellence in Human Genetics Educ. 2001, John Howland Award, American Pediatric Soc. 2010, Pollin Prize for Pediatric Research 2010, Victor A. McKusick Leadership Award 2015, American Soc. of Human Genetics. *Publications:* Amino Acid Metabolism and its Disorders (co-author) 1973, Garrod's Inborn Factors in Disease (co-author) 1989, Metabolic Basis of Inherited Disease (6th, 7th, 8th edns, online, Sr Ed.) (co-author) 1989–; author or co-author of more than 500 scientific articles. *Leisure interests:* literature, music, photography. *Address:* Department of Human Genetics, McGill University, Room W-315, Strathcona Anatomy & Dentistry Building, 3640 rue University, Montreal, PQ H3A 0C7 (office); 232 Strathearn Avenue, Montreal, PQ H4X 1Y2, Canada (home). *Telephone:* (514) 412-4417 (office). *E-mail:* charles.scriver@mcgill.ca (office); thomas.leslie@mcgill.ca (office). *Website:* www.mcgill.ca (office).

SCRUTON, Sir Roger Vernon, Kt, BA, PhD, FRSL, FBA; British philosopher and writer; b. 27 Feb. 1944, Buslingthorpe, Lincs.; s. of John Scruton and Beryl C. Haines; m. 1st Danielle Laffitte 1975 (divorced 1983); m. 2nd Sophie Jeffreys 1996; ed High Wycombe Royal Grammar School, Jesus Coll. Cambridge and Inner Temple, London; Fellow, Peterhouse, Cambridge 1969–71; Lecturer in Philosophy, Birkbeck Coll. London 1971–79, Reader 1979–86, Prof. of Aesthetics 1986–92; Prof. of Philosophy, Boston Univ. 1992–95; Founder and Dir The Claridge Press 1987–2004; Ed. The Salisbury Review 1982–2000, now on Editorial Bd; currently Visiting Prof. of Philosophy, Univ. of Oxford; Sr Fellow, Ethics & Public Policy Center, Washington DC; mem. Editorial Bd, British Journal of Aesthetics, Arka (Kraków); Dr hc (Adelphi Univ.) 1995, (Masaryk Univ., Brno, Czech Repub.) 1998, (Hillsdale Coll., Michigan, USA) 2012; Medal of Merit, First Class (Czech Repub.) 1998. *Compositions:* The Minister (opera in one act) 1994, Violet (opera in two acts) 2006. *Television:* Why Beauty Matters (BBC) 2009. *Publications:* Art and Imagination 1974, The Aesthetics of Architecture 1979, The Meaning of Conservatism 1980, The Politics of Culture and Other Essays 1981, Fortnight's Anger (novel) 1981, A Short History of Modern Philosophy 1982, A Dictionary of Political Thought 1982, The Aesthetic Understanding 1983, Kant 1983, Untimely Tracts 1985, Thinkers of the New Left 1986, Sexual Desire 1986, Spinoza 1987, A Land Held Hostage: Lebanon and the West 1987, The Philosopher on Dover Beach (essays) 1989, Francesca (novel) 1991, A Dove Descending and Other Stories (short stories) 1991, Conservative Texts: An Anthology 1991, Xanthippic Dialogues (fiction) 1993, Modern Philosophy 1993, The Classical Vernacular 1994, Modern Philosophy 1996, Animal Rights and Wrongs 1996, An Intelligent Person's Guide to Philosophy 1997, The Aesthetics of Music 1997, On Hunting 1998, Town and Country (co-ed.) 1998, An Intelligent Person's Guide To Modern Culture 1998, Perictione in Colophon (fiction) 2000, England: An Elegy 2000, The West and the Rest: Globalization and the Terrorist Threat 2002, Death-Devoted Heart: Sex and the Sacred in Wagner's Tristan and Isolde 2004, News from Somewhere: On Settling 2004, Gentle Regrets (autobiog.) 2005, A Political Philosophy 2006, Culture Counts: Faith and Feeling in a World Besieged 2007, Beauty 2009, Understanding Music: Philosophy and Interpretation 2009, I Drink Therefore I Am 2009, The Uses of Pessimism and the Danger of False Hope 2010, Green Philosophy 2012, The Face of God 2012, How to Think Seriously About the Planet: The Case for an Environmental Conservatism 2012, Our Church 2012, The Soul of

the World 2014, How to Be a Conservative 2014, Notes from Underground (fiction) 2014, Fools, Frauds and Firebrands: Thinkers of the New Left 2015, The Disappeared (fiction) 2015, Confessions of a Heretic: Selected Essays 2016, Conversations with Roger Scruton (with Mark Dooley) 2016, The Ring of Truth: The Wisdom of Wagner's Ring of the Nibelung 2016, On Human Nature 2017, Where we are: The State of Britain Now 2017. *Leisure interests:* music, literature, hunting. *Address:* Sunday Hill Farm, Brinkworth, Wilts., SN15 5AS, England. *Website:* www.roger-scruton.com.

SCULLY, Marlan Orvil, BS, MS, PhD; American physicist and academic; *Burgess Distinguished Professor, Physics and Astronomy, Texas A&M University;* b. 3 Aug. 1939, Casper, Wyoming; ed Casper Coll., Univ. of Wyoming, Rensselaer Polytechnic Inst., Yale Univ.; Instructor, Yale Univ. 1961–62; Asst Prof., Massachusetts Inst. of Tech. 1967–69, Assoc. Prof. 1969–71; Prof., Univ. of Arizona 1969–80; Distinguished Prof., Univ. of New Mexico 1980–92; External Scientist, Max Planck Inst. for Quantum Optics 1980–; Univ. Prof., Texas A&M Univ. 1992–96, Burgess Distinguished Prof. 1996–; Visiting Burgess Prof. (Chem.), Princeton Univ. 2003–05, Lecturer with rank of Prof. 2005–; mem. NAS, Academia Europaea, Max Planck Soc.; Fellow, American Acad. of Arts and Sciences, AAAS, American Physical Soc., Optical Soc. of America; Dr hc (Ulm); numerous awards, including Schawlow Prize, American Physical Soc., Townes Award, Optical Soc. of America, IEEE Quantum Electronics Award, Elliott Cresson Medal, Franklin Inst., Lomb Medal, Optical Soc. of America, Humboldt Sr Faculty Prize, named Harvard Loeb Lecturer, Hebert Walther Award, Optical Soc. of America/Deutsche Physikalische Gesellschaft, Guggenheim Fellowship, Alexander von Humboldt Distinguished Faculty Prize. *Publications:* Laser Physics (co-author), Quantum Optics (co-author); more than 700 papers in professional journals. *Address:* Department of Physics and Astronomy, Texas A&M University, 4242 TAMU, College Station, TX 77843-4242 (office); Department of Mechanical and Aerospace Engineering, Princeton University, Room D416, Engineering Quadrangle, Princeton, NJ 08544, USA. *Telephone:* (979) 862-2333 (College Station) (office); (609) 258-3962 (Princeton) (office). *Fax:* (979) 845-2590 (Princeton) (office). *E-mail:* scully@tamu.edu (office); mscully@princeton.edu (office). *Website:* physics.tamu.edu (office); iqse.tamu.edu (office); www.princeton.edu/ mae/people/faculty/scully (office).

SCULLY, Sean Paul, BA; Irish/American artist; b. 30 June 1945, Dublin, Ireland; s. of John Anthony Scully and Holly Scully; m. Catherine Lee; ed Croydon Coll. of Art, Newcastle Univ., UK, Harvard Univ., USA; mem. staff, Fine Art Dept, Newcastle Univ. 1967–71; Lecturer, Harvard Univ. 1972–73; Lecturer, Chelsea School of Art and Goldsmiths' School of Art, London 1973–75; Lecturer, Princeton Univ. 1978–83; Lecturer in Painting, Parsons School of Design, New York 1983–; works in public collections in UK, USA, Australia, Germany, Ireland; Hon. mem., London Inst. 1994; Hon. DFA (Massachusetts Coll. of Art) 2003, (Nat. Univ. of Ireland) 2003; Stuyvesant Foundation Prize 1970, 1972 Prize John Moores Liverpool Exhbn 8, 1974 Prize John Moores Liverpool Exhbn 9, Guggenheim Fellowship 1983, Artist's Fellowship, Nat. Endowment for the Arts. *Address:* c/o Kerlin Gallery, Anne's Lane, South Anne Street, Dublin 2, A028, Ireland. *Website:* www.kerlingallery.com/artists/sean-scully.

SEABRA, Antônio Luíz; Brazilian business executive; *Chairman, Natura Cosméticos;* b. 1943, São Paulo; began career as trainee in Human Resources Dept, Remington Brazil, Man. 1964–66; f. Natura Cosméticos 1969, mem. Bd of Dirs 1998–, co-Chair. 2001–; Most Valuable Exec. Award, Valor Econômico 2003. *Address:* Natura Cosméticos S.A, Rodavia Régis Bittencourt, km 293, Building 1, Potuverá, 06882-700 Itapecerica da Serra, São Paulo, Brazil (office). *Telephone:* (11) 5694-7655 (office). *Website:* www.natura.net (office).

SEACREST, Ryan John; American radio personality, television host and producer; b. 24 Dec. 1974, Atlanta, Ga; s. of Gary Lee Seacrest and Constance Marie Seacrest (née Zullinger); ed Univ. of Georgia; hosted first season of ESPN's Radical Outdoor Challenge 1993; host of talent competition American Idol since 2002; host and Exec. Producer of On Air with Ryan Seacrest 2004, Los Angeles morning drive-time radio show for Clear Channel's 102.7 KIIS-FM, also of American Top 40 radio show; hosted the 59th Primetime Emmy Awards 2007; f. The Ryan Seacrest Foundation 2010; launched clothing and lifestyle brand Ryan Seacrest Distinction (in retail partnership with Macy's) 2014; launched men's skincare line Polished (with Dr Harold Lancer) 2017; Man. Ed. E! News; mem. Bd of Trustees Los Angeles County Museum of Art 2014–; Hon. Chair Grammy Foundation Bd 2014; Hon. DHumLitt (Univ. of Georgia) 2016; Daytime Emmy Award for co-hosting the Walt Disney World Christmas Day Parade with Regis Philbin and Kelly Ripa 2005, Emmy Award for producing ABC TV show Jamie Oliver's Food Revolution. *Television includes:* host: Click 1997, Ultimate Revenge 2002, American Juniors 2003, American Idol Rewind 2007–08, The Million Second Quiz (also exec. producer) 2013, Knock Knock Live 2015; exec. producer: Paradise City 2007, Crash My School (TV movie) 2007, Keeping Up with the Kardashians (also creator) 2007–17, Bank of Hollywood 2009–10, Kourtney and Kim Take New York 2011, Married to Jonas 2012, The Wanted Life 2013, Ryan Seacrest with Selena Gomez (TV movie documentary) 2013, Mixology 2014, Shades of Blue 2016–18, Life of Kylie 2017, Live with Kelly and Ryan (also co-host) 2017–. *Address:* Ryan Seacrest Productions, 5750 Wilshire Boulevard, 4th Floor, Los Angeles, CA 90036, USA (office). *Telephone:* (323) 954-2400 (office). *Website:* ryanseacrest.com (office); www.onairwithryan.iheart.com.

SEAGA, The Most Hon. Edward Philip George, BA, ON, PC; Jamaican academic and fmr politician; *Chancellor, University of Technology;* b. 28 May 1930, Boston, Mass, USA; s. of Philip Seaga and Erna Seaga (née Maxwell); m. 1st Marie Elizabeth Constantine 1965 (divorced 1995); two s. one d.; m. 2nd Carla Frances Vendryes 1996; one d.; ed Wolmers Boys' School, Kingston, Harvard Univ., USA; Field Researcher with Inst. of Social and Econ. Research (Univ. of West Indies) on devt of child and revival spirit cults; nominated to Upper House, Legis. Council 1959; Asst Sec. to Jamaican Labour Party 1960, Sec. 1962; MP for Western Kingston 1962–2005; Minister of Devt and Social Welfare 1962–67, of Finance and Planning 1967–72; Leader of Jamaican Labour Party 1974–2005; Leader of Opposition 1974–80, 1989–2005; Prime Minister 1980–89; Minister of Finance and Planning, Information and Culture 1980–89, of Defence 1987–89; Chair. Premium Group 1989; Distinguished Fellow, Univ. of the West Indies at Mona 2005–, Man. Dir Edward Seaga Research Inst.; Chancellor Univ. of Technology 2010–; Chair.

Premier League Players Asscn; Grand Cross, Order of Merit (FRG) 1982, Order of the Nation 2002 (Jamaica), Grand Collar de Libertador (Venezuela), Grand Gwangwa Medal, Order of Diplomatic Service (South Korea), Order of the Aztec Eagle (Mexico); Hon. LLD (Univ. of Miami), (Tampa Univ.), Univ. of South Carolina), (Boston Univ.), (Univ. of Hartford); Hon. DLitt (Univ. of Technology); Gold Mercury Int. Award (Venezuela) 1981, Dr Martin Luther King Humanitarian Award 1984, Enviromental Leadership Award, UNEP 1987, American Friendship Medal, Freedom Foundation, and other awards. *Publications include:* Development of the Child, Revival Spirit Cults, Faith Healing in Jamaica, My Life and Leadership- Volume 1: Clash of Ideologies 1930–1960 2010. *Leisure interests:* classical music, reading, hunting, sports, futurology. *Address:* Office of the Chancellor, University of Technology, 237 Old Hope Road, Kingston 6 (office); 24–26 Grenada Crescent, New Kingston, Kingston 5, Jamaica (home). *Telephone:* (876) 927-1680 (office). *Fax:* (876) 977-4388 (office). *E-mail:* websupport@utech.edu.jm (office); edward.seaga@uwimona.edu.jm (office). *Website:* www.utech.edu.jm (office).

SEAGAL, Steven; American/Russian/Serbian actor, producer and martial arts expert; b. 10 April 1951, Lansing, Mich.; s. of Samuel Steven Seagal and Patricia Seagal; m. 1st Miyako Fujitoni 1974 (divorced 1987); one s. one d.; m. 2nd Kelly Le Brock 1987 (divorced 1996); one s. two d.; m. 3rd Erdenetuya Batsukh 2009; ed Fullerton Coll., Orange Coast Coll.; moved to Japan aged 17 remaining there for 15 years; established martial arts acads (dojo) in Japan and Los Angeles; CEO Steamroller Productions; granted Russian citizenship 2016; Special Rep. for Russian Foreign Ministry in charge of Russian–US humanitarian ties 2018–; PETA Humanitarian Award 1999. *Television:* Steven Seagal: Lawman 2009–14 (producer), True Justice (producer) 2010–12. *Films include:* Above the Law 1988, Hard to Kill 1990, Marked for Death 1990, Out for Justice 1991, Under Siege 1992, On Deadly Ground (dir) 1994, Under Siege 2 1995, The Glimmer Man 1996, Executive Decision 1996, Fire Down Below 1997, The Patriot 1998, Get Bruce 1999, Ticker 2001, Exit Wounds 2001, Ticker 2001, Half Past Dead 2002, The Foreigner 2003, Out for a Kill 2003, Belly of the Beast 2003, Clementine 2004, Out of Reach 2004, Into the Sun 2005, Mercenary for Justice 2006, Attack Force 2006, Flight of Fury 2007, Urban Justice 2007, Pistol Whipped 2008, Kill Switch 2008, Against the Dark 2009, The Keeper 2009, A Dangerous Man 2010, Born to Raise Hell 2010, Skin Trade 2011, Maximum Conviction (also producer) 2012, Force of Execution (also producer) 2013, A Good Man (also co–producer) 2014, Gutshot 2014, Mercenary: Absolution (also producer) 2015, Killing Salazar (also producer) 2016, Sniper: Special Ops (also exec. producer) 2016, Code of Honor (also exec. producer) 2016, The Asian Connection (also exec. producer) 2016, The Perfect Weapon 2016, End of a Gun (also producer) 2016. *Recording:* Songs from The Crystal Cave 2004, Mojo Priest (album) 2007. *Website:* www.stevenseagal.com.

SEAL, Basil (see BARNES, Julian Patrick).

SEAMAN, Christopher, MA, ARCM; British conductor; b. 7 March 1942, Faversham, Kent; s. of Albert Edward Seaman and Ethel Margery Seaman (née Chambers); ed Canterbury Cathedral Choir School, The King's School, Canterbury, King's Coll., Cambridge; Prin. Timpanist, London Philharmonic Orchestra 1964–68; Asst Conductor BBC Scottish Symphony Orchestra 1968–70, Chief Conductor 1971–77; Chief Conductor Northern Sinfonia Orchestra 1973–79; Prin. Conductor BBC Robert Mayer Concerts 1978–87; Conductor-in-Residence, Baltimore Symphony Orchestra 1987–98; Chief Guest Conductor Utrecht Symphony Orchestra 1979–83; Music Dir Naples Philharmonic Orchestra, Fla 1993–, Rochester Philharmonic Orchestra, NY 1998–2011; Artistic Advisor, San Antonio Symphony; Dir Symphony Australia Conductor Programme; appears as guest conductor world-wide and has appeared in USA, Germany, France, the Netherlands, Belgium, Italy, Portugal, Spain, Australia and throughout UK; Hon. FGSM 1972. *Publication:* Inside Conducting 2013. *Leisure interests:* people, reading, shopping, theology. *Address:* c/o Harrison Parrott, The Ark, 201 Talgarth Road, London, W6 8BJ, England (office). *Telephone:* (20) 7229 9166 (office). *E-mail:* info@harrisonparrott.co.uk (office). *Website:* www.harrisonparrott.com/artist/profile/christopher-seaman (office).

SEARLE, John R., BA, MA, DPhil; American academic; *Willis S. and Marion Slusser Professor Emeritus of Philosophy of the Mind and Language, University of California, Berkeley;* b. 31 July 1932, Denver, Colo; s. of George W. Searle and Hester Beck Searle; m. Dagmar Carboch 1958; two s.; ed Univ. of Wisconsin, Univ. of Oxford, UK; Asst Prof. of Philosophy, Univ. of California, Berkeley 1959–64, Assoc. Prof. 1964–67, Prof. 1967–, later Slusser Prof. of Philosophy, then Prof. Emer., Chair. Dept of Philosophy 1973–75, Special Asst to Chancellor for Student Affairs 1965–67; mem. Scholar Council, Library of Congress 2000–; mem. Editorial Bd Journal of Psycholinguistic Research, Linguistics and Philosophy, Philosophy and Artificial Intelligence, Journal of Consciousness Studies, Cognitive Science Series, Harvard Univ.Press; mem. American Acad. of Arts and Sciences 1976–, Cognitive Science Group, Univ. of California, Berkeley 1981–, European Acad. of Science and Art 1993–, Scientific Bd, Vilem Mathesius Centre, Charles Univ., Prague 1994–, Nat. Council of Nat. Endowment of Humanities 1992–96; mem. Bd of Dirs American Council of Learned Socs 1979–87; mem. Bd of Trustees Nat. Humanities Center 1976–90; Fellow and Lecturer, World Econ. Forum, Davos 1991, 1995, 1998, 2001; Educ. TV series in Calif. 1960–74; Advisor to Pres.'s Comm. on Student Unrest (Scranton Comm.) 1970; Hon. Prof., Tsinghua Univ., Beijing 2007, East China Normal Univ., Shanghai 2007; Dr hc (Adelphi) 1993, (Wisconsin) 1994, (Bucharest) 2000, (Torino) 2000, (Lucano) 2003; Rhodes Scholar 1952, Reith Lecturer 1984, Tasan Award, South Korean 2000, Jean Nicod Prize 2000, Jovellanos Prize 2000, Nat. Humanities Medal 2005, Mind and Brain Prize, Torino, Italy 2006, Puffendorf Medal, Sweden 2006. *Publications include:* Speech Acts 1969, The Campus War 1972, Expression and Meaning 1979, Intentionality 1983, Minds, Brains and Science 1984, The Foundations of Illocutionary Logic (with D. Vanderveken) 1985, The Rediscovery of the Mind 1992, (On) Searle on Conversation 1992, The Construction of Social Reality 1995, Mystery of Consciousness 1997, Mind, Language and Society 1998, Conversations with John Searle 2001, La Universidad Desafiada 2002, Consciousness and Language 2002, Liberté et Neurobiologie (trans. as Freedom and Neurology) 2004, Mind, A Brief Introduction 2004, Making the Social World 2010, Thinking About the Real World 2011, Seeing Things as They Are: A Theory of Perception 2015. *Leisure interests:* literature, opera, skiing, travel. *Address:* Department of Philosophy, 314 Moses Hall 2390, University of California, Berkeley, CA 94720-2390, USA (office). *Telephone:* (510) 642-2722 (office). *Fax:* (510) 642-4164 (office). *E-mail:* searle@berkeley.edu. *Website:* philosophy.berkeley.edu (office).

SEARS, Hon. Alfred M., BA, JD; Bahamian politician and lawyer; b. 13 Jan. 1953, Fort Charlotte; s. of Winifred Sears; m. Marion Bethel 1987; three c.; ed Boys' Industrial School, St Augustine Coll., Columbia Univ. and New York Law School, USA, Univ. of the West Indies, Jamaica; f. Interdenominational Christian Youth Asscn (ICYA); Lecturer in Caribbean Politics, Hunter Coll., City Univ. of New York 1977–87; fmr Attorney, Civil Court of Manhattan, USA, Berthan Macaulay, Jamaica, Gibson & Co., The Bahamas; Founder and Pnr, Sears & Co. (law firm) 1992–; Attorney-Gen. and Minister of Educ. 2002–07; Head of Caribbean Financial Action Task Force (CFTAF) 2002. *Address:* Sears & Co., POB N-3645, Nassau, The Bahamas (office). *Telephone:* 326-3481 (office). *Fax:* 326-3483 (office). *E-mail:* info@searschambers.com (office). *Website:* www.searschambers.com (office); alfredsears.org.

SEARS, Malcolm, MB, ChB, FRACP, FRCPC, FAAAAI; New Zealand professor of medicine, physician and academic; b. 8 Feb. 1942, New Plymouth, New Zealand; ed Univ. of Otago, Dunedin; mem. Faculty, Univ. of Otago 1973–90; Dir Firestone Regional Chest and Allergy Unit (forerunner of Firestone Inst. of Respiratory Health), Dir of Respiratory Medicine, St Joseph's Healthcare and Prof., Dept of Medicine, McMaster Univ. 1990–2002, stepped down as Clinical Dir and became Research Dir, Firestone Inst. 2002–09, holds an endowed Astra Zeneca Chair in Respiratory Epidemiology; Founding Dir CIHR/AllerGen-funded Canadian Healthy Infant Longitudinal Devt (CHILD) Study following more than 3,000 infants from pregnancy through childhood; Fellow, Royal Australasian Coll. Physicians, Royal Coll. of Physicians of Canada, American Acad. of Allergy, Asthma and Immunology; Wunderly Orator, Thoracic Soc. of Australia and NZ 1997, Christie Memorial Lecturer, Canadian Thoracic Soc. 2011, Award for Leadership in Health Research, Asthma Soc. of Canada 2015, J. Allyn Taylor Int. Prize in Medicine (co-recipient) 2016. *Publications:* more than 300 peer-reviewed papers and book chapters in professional journals. *Address:* c/o Room T3219, St Joseph's Healthcare, McMaster University, 50 Charlton Avenue East, Hamilton, ON L8N 4A6, Canada (office). *Telephone:* (905) 525-9140 (ext. 33286) (office). *Fax:* (905) 521-6132 (office). *E-mail:* searsm@mcmaster.ca (office). *Website:* fhs.mcmaster.ca/medicine/respirology (office).

SEATON, David T.; American business executive; *Chairman and CEO, Fluor Corporation;* b. 1962; ed Univ. of South Carolina, Advanced Man. Program, Wharton School of Business, Int. Man. Program, Thunderbird Univ.; joined Fluor Corpn (eng, procurement, construction and maintenance services co.) 1984, held numerous exec. positions in both operations and sales globally, including Sr Group Pres., Energy and Chemicals, Govt and Power Groups, was responsible for Fluor's activities in China and the Middle East, led co.'s global business activities, including ICA Fluor (jt venture in Mexico) also served as Sr Vice-Pres. and Group Exec. for global corp. sales, COO Fluor Corpn 2009–11, mem. Bd of Dirs and CEO 2011–, Chair. 2012–, Chair. Stork Holding B.V. (subsidiary) 2016–; Vice Chair. Nat. Asscn of Manufacturers 2017–, mem. Nat. Petroleum Council 2011–; mem. Bd of Dirs Mosaic Co.; mem., Business Roundtable, Bd American Petroleum Inst., US-Saudi Arabian Business Council, World Econ. Forum's Partnering Against Corruption Initiative (Co-Chair. Forum's Global Agenda Council on Corruption); South Carolina State Guard Lifetime Achievement Award 2016. *Address:* Fluor Corporation, 6700 Las Colinas Blvd, Irving, TX 75039, USA (office). *Telephone:* (469) 398-7000 (office). *Fax:* (469) 398-7255 (office). *E-mail:* info@fluor.com (office). *Website:* www.fluor.com (office).

SEBAN, Alain Pierre; French arts organization executive; b. 15 July 1964, Toulouse; ed École Polytechnique, ENSAE ParisTech (École nationale de la statistique et de l'admin économique), Inst. d'Études Politiques de Paris; auditor, Conseil d'État 1991, Maître de requêtes 1994, Govt Commr 1997; adviser to the Minister of Culture 1995–97, Media Devt Dir 2002–05; Chargé de mission, Ministry of Foreign Affairs 2002–05; adviser on culture and education to Pres. Jacques Chirac 2005–07; Pres. Centre Georges Pompidou, Paris 2007–15; Conseiller juridique, Musée du quai Branly 1997–2002; Vice-Pres. Exec. Cttee, Opéra de Paris pension fund 1997; Lecturer, École nationale d'admin 1996–99; Commdr des Arts et des Lettres 2002; Chevalier, Légion d'honneur 2011.

SEBASTIANI, HE Cardinal Sergio; Italian ecclesiastic; *President Emeritus, Prefecture for Economic Affairs of The Holy See;* b. 11 April 1931, Montemonaco (Ascoli-Piceno); s. of Angelo Sebastiani and Lucia Valeri; ed Pontifical Gregorian Univ., Pontifical Lateran Univ., Pontifical Ecclesiastical Acad.; ordained priest 1956; Sec. of Apostolic Nunciature, Peru 1960; Sec. of Apostolic Nunciature, Brazil 1962; Uditore, Apostolic Nunciature, Chile 1966, Office Chief, Vatican Secr. of State, Counsellor Apostolic Nunciature in Paris, with special assignment to Council of Europe 1974; ordained Titular Archbishop of Cesarea in Mauritania; Apostolic Pro-Nuncio to Madagascar and Apostolic Del. to Réunion and Comoros 1976, Apostolic Nuncio to Turkey 1985; Sec.-Gen. Cen. Cttee of Great Jubilee Year 2000 1994; Pres. Pref. for Econ. Affairs of The Holy See 1997–2008 (resgnd), Pres. Emer. 2008–; apptd Cardinal-Deacon of St Eustachio 2001, Cardinal-Priest of St Eustachio 2011–; Commendadore Order of Merit, Italy, Nat. Order of Madagascar, Grand Cross Order O'Higgins, Chile. *Publications:* La Chiesa all'uomo del XX secolo, La Sapienza nell'Antico Testamento. *Address:* Prefecture for the Economic Affairs of the Holy See, Palazzo delle Congregazioni, Largo del Colonnato 3, 00193 Rome (office); Via Rusticucci 13, 00193 Rome, Italy (home). *Telephone:* (06) 69884263 (office). *Fax:* (06) 69885011 (office).

SEBELIUS, Kathleen, MPA; American fmr government official and fmr politician; *Co-Chairman, Aspen Health Strategy Group;* b. 15 May 1948, Ohio; d. of fmr Ohio Gov. John Gilligan; m. Gary Sebelius; two s.; ed Trinity Coll., Conn., Univ. of Kansas, Trinity Washington Univ.; first woman employee in Kan. Dept of Corrections 1975–87; mem. Kan. State House of Reps 1987–94, mem. Ethics Comm.; Insurance Commr, Kan. 1994–2002; Gov. of Kan. 2003–09; Sec. of Health and Human Services, Washington, DC 2009–14; Co-Chair. Aspen Health Strategy Group (health policy forum) 2015–; Democrat. *Leisure interest:* jazz music. *Address:* Aspen Health Strategy Group, Aspen Institute, One Dupont Circle, NW, Suite 700, Washington, DC 20036-1133, USA.

ŠEBRLE, Roman; Czech fmr decathlete; b. 26 Nov. 1974, Lanškroun, Czechoslovakia; m. Eva Kasalová 2000; one s. one d.; ed Gymnázium Františka Martina Pelcla, Rychnov nad Kněžnou, Gymnázium Pardubice, extension course of Information Science and Computer Tech.; competed in first decathlon competition in Týniště nad Orlicí, reaching 5,187 points 1991; met coach Jiří Čechák; compulsory military service in Czech Armed Forces 1995–97; joined army sports club TJ Dukla Praha of which he is still a mem.; achieved a score of more than 8,000 points for the first time, reaching 8,210 points at a meeting in Prague 1996; won World Univ. Games in Sicily 1997; came ninth at World Championships, Athens 1997; mem. Czech Olympic athletics team, Sydney 2000 (silver medal for decathlon); set world record for decathlon (9,026 points, lasted until 2012), World Championships, Götziz, Austria May 2001; gold medals in decathlon, Universiade, Catania 1997, heptathlon, World Indoor Championships, Lisbon 2001, heptathlon, European Indoor Championships, Vienna 2002, Madrid 2005, Birmingham 2007, decathlon, European Championships Munich 2002, Gothenburg 2006, heptathlon, World Indoor Championships, Budapest 2004, decathlon, Olympic Games, Athens 2004 (set Olympic record with 8,893 points), World Championships, Osaka 2007; silver medal in heptathlon, European Indoor Championships, Ghent 2000, decathlon, World Championships, Paris 2003, Helsinki 2005; bronze medal, heptathlon, World Indoor Championships, Maebashi 1999, Birmingham 2003, Moscow 2006, heptathlon, European Indoor Championships, Turin 2009, Paris 2011; Men's Decathlon European record holder 2001–; Men's Heptathlon European record holder 2004–; retd June 2013; Czech Athlete of the Year 2002, 2003, 2004, 2005, 2006, World's Greatest Athlete 2004, No. 8 on TIME's list of 100 Olympic Athletes To Watch 2008. *Leisure interests:* computers, the Internet, football, sci-fi, music, spaghetti. *Address:* c/o Czech Olympic Committee, Benesovská 6, 10100 Prague 10; Česká sportovní a.s., Na Příkopě 9/11, 110 00, Prague 1, Czech Republic. *Telephone:* (2) 71734734 (Czech Olympic Committee); (2) 24233725 (Česká sportovní). *E-mail:* info@olympic.cz; sekretariat@ceskasportovni.cz. *Website:* www.ceskasportovni.cz; www.iaaf.org/athletes/czech-republic/roman-sebrle-130083.

SECHIN, Igor Ivanovich, PhD; Russian politician and business executive; *Chairman of the Management Board, CEO and Deputy Chairman of the Board of Directors, Rosneft;* b. 7 Sept. 1960, Leningrad (now St Petersburg), Russian SFSR, USSR; m.; one d.; ed Leningrad State Univ.; army service 1984–86; leading instructor, Exec. Cttee, Dept of Foreign Econ. Relations, Leningrad City Soviet 1988–91; Chief Expert, Asst to Head of Admin to First Vice-Mayor, Chair. Cttee on Foreign Relations, Office of Mayor of Leningrad 1991–96; Expert, Deputy Head of Div., Public Relations Dept, Dept of Foreign Affairs 1996–97; Head, Gen. Admin Dept, Adviser to Deputy Head then Head Chief Control Dept, Admin of the Russian Pres. 1998–99; Head, Secr. of First Deputy Chair., later Chair., Govt of Russian Fed. 1999–2000; Deputy Chief of Staff, Presidential Exec. Office 2002–08, Aide to the Pres. 2004–08; Deputy Chair. of the Govt (Deputy Prime Minister), in charge of industry devt, nuclear power and environment 2008–12; Dir (non-exec.), Rosneft Oil Co. 2004–11, Chair. 2004–11, Chair. Man. Bd and CEO 2012–, Deputy Chair. Bd of Dirs 2013–; Chair. OJSC Rosneftegaz, Nat. Oil Consortium, United R&D Centre (RN-CIR); Chair. Supervisory Bd CSKA PHC; Pres. RN Management; mem. Bd of Dirs TNK-BP Ltd; sanctioned by US Govt in response to Russia's involvement in Ukraine March 2014. *Address:* Rosneft, 117997 Moscow, Sofiiskaya nab. 26/1, Russian Federation (office). *Telephone:* (499) 517-88-99 (office). *Fax:* (499) 517-72-35 (office). *E-mail:* postman@rosneft.ru (office). *Website:* www.rosneft.com (office).

SECK, Fodé, MA; Senegalese diplomatist; *Permanent Representative to United Nations;* b. 1 Sept. 1950, Koungheul; m.; six c.; ed Univ. Cheikh Anta Diop, Dakar; First Counsellor Senegalese Embassy, USSR 1978–81, in Nigeria 1981–86; held several posts in Ministry of State and Foreign Affairs 1986–2002, Chief Tech. Adviser 2002–06; Chargé d'affaires, Saudi Arabia Dec. 2006–Sept. 2007, Amb. to Brazil 2007–10; Perm. Rep. to UN Office and other int orgs in Geneva Feb.–Sept. 2014, Perm. Rep. to UN, New York 2014–. *Address:* Permanent Mission of Senegal, 229 E 44th Street, New York, NY 10017, USA (office). *Telephone:* (212) 517-9030 (office). *Fax:* (212) 517-3032 (office). *E-mail:* senegal.mission@yahoo.fr (office). *Website:* www.un.int/senegal (office).

SECK, Idrissa; Senegalese politician; *Mayor of Thies;* b. 9 Aug. 1959, Thies; m.; three c.; ed Institut d'Etude Politique, Paris, Princeton Univ., USA; consultant with Price Waterhouse 1986–92; mem. Parti démocratique sénégalais—PDS (Democratic Party), fmr Deputy Sec.-Gen.; fmr Minister Without Portfolio; Sec. of State and Dir Office of the Pres. 2000–02; Prime Minister of Senegal 2002–04; elected Mayor of Thies 2002, 2009; unsuccessful cand. for Pres. 2007.

SEDAKA, Neil; American singer, pianist, songwriter and record producer; b. 13 March 1939, Brooklyn, NY; s. of Mac Sedaka and Eleanor Appel; m. Leba M. Strassberg 1962; one s. one d.; ed Juilliard School of Music, New York; recipient of numerous gold records and recording industry awards, Ivor Novello Special Int. Award 2010. *Compositions include:* popular songs: Breaking Up Is Hard To Do, Stupid Cupid, Calendar Girl, Oh! Carol, Stairway to Heaven, Happy Birthday Sweet Sixteen, Laughter in the Rain, Bad Blood, Love Will Keep Us Together, Lonely Night (Angel Face). *Recordings include:* Rock with Sedaka 1959, Circulate 1961, Neil Sedaka Sings His Greatest Hits 1963, Smile 1965, Sounds of Sedaka 1969, Workin' on a Groovy Thing 1969, Emergence 1971, Solitaire 1972, The Tra-La Days Are Over (UK) 1973, Sedaka's Back 1974, The Hungry Years 1975, Steppin' Out 1976, A Song 1977, All You Need Is The Music 1978, In the Pocket 1980, Neil Sedaka Canta en Espanol 1983, Come See About Me 1984, All Time Greatest Hits 1988, Oh! Carol and Other Hits 1990, Timeless – The Very Best of Neil Sedaka 1991, Tales of Love (and Other Passions) 1998, The Show Goes On 2003, Neil Sedaka in Italiano 1999, The Singer and His Songs 2000, RCA 100th Anniversary Series: The Very Best of Neil Sedaka 2001, Brighton Beach Memories – Neil Sedaka Sings Yiddish 2003, Oh! Carol: The Complete Recordings, 1955–66 2003, Stairway to Heaven: The Best of Neil Sedaka 2004, Love Songs 2005, The Very Best of Neil Sedaka: The Show Goes On 2006, Neil Sedaka: Live at the Royal Albert Hall – The Show Goes On (2 DVD set filmed in London) 2006, The Definitive Collection 2007, Oh! Carol (LT Series album, compilation of 1970s hits recorded live in concert) 2007, The Miracle of Christmas 2008, Waking Up Is Hard to Do 2009, Flashback (compilation of Italian recordings) 2009, The Music of My Life (UK) 2009, The Miracle of Christmas: The Deluxe Edition 2009, The Music of My Life 2010, Neil Sedaka Sings Little Devil and His Other Hits/The Many Sides of Neil Sedaka 2010, The Real Neil 2012, I Do It For Applause 2014. *Address:* c/o Leba Sedaka, Robert Cotto, Neil Sedaka Music, 641 Lexington Avenue, 14th Floor, New York, NY 10022, USA (office). *Fax:* (212) 593-0526 (office). *E-mail:* leba@neilsedaka.com (office); rob@neilsedaka.com (office). *Website:* www.neilsedaka.com (office).

SEDGWICK, (Ian) Peter; British business executive (retd); b. 13 Oct. 1935; m. Verna Mary Sedgwick 1956; one s. one d.; with Nat. Provincial Bank 1952–59, Ottoman Bank Africa and Middle East 1959–69, J. Henry Schroder Wagg & Co. Ltd 1969–90; Dir Schroders Nominees Ltd 1981–95, CEO Schroder Investment Man. Ltd 1985–94, Dir Schroder Unit Trusts Ltd 1987–95, Group Man. Dir Investment Man. Schroders PLC 1987–95, Deputy Chair. (Chair. Desig.) 1995–2000, Chair. 2000–03, CEO (interim) 2001, Dir (non-exec.) Schroder & Co. Inc. 1991–99, Chair. 1996–2002, Pres. and CEO Schroders Inc., New York 1996–2000, Chair. Schroder All-Asia Fund 1991–99, Schroder UK Growth Fund 1994, Pres. CEO Schroder US Holdings Inc. 1996; Dir (non-exec.) Equitable Life Assurance Soc. 1991–2001, INVESCO City & Commercial Investment Trust PLC (fmrly New City & Commercial Trust PLC) 1992–2001; Co-founder and Advisor, Frank Investments 2005; Chair. Queen Elizabeth Foundation 2007–10 (Trustee 2002–10); mem. European Advisory Bd JER Pnrs. *Leisure interests:* golf, grandchildren, theatre.

SEDIQ, Khalilullah, BA; Afghan central banker; *Governor, Da Afghanistan Bank (Central Bank of Afghanistan);* b. 1949, Logar Prov.; m.; three d.; ed Kabul Univ.; joined Da Afghanistan Bank (Central Bank of Afghanistan) 1971, has held several sr man. positions, including Dir-Gen. Foreign Trade Dept 1980–81, Dir-Gen. Research Dept 1981–82, First Deputy Gov. 1982–86, Adviser to Gov. 1986–89, Gov. Da Afghanistan Bank 1990–91, 2015–; with Sun Trust Bank, Silver Spring, Md, USA 2003–06; returned to Afghanistan 2006, CEO Afghanistan International Bank 2006–15; Chair. Afghanistan Banks Asscn; mem. Bd of Dirs Harakat (Afghanistan Investment Climate Facility) 2009–15, Private Banks Asscn 2012, American Chamber of Commerce in Afghanistan 2013–14, Afghanistan Inst. of Banking and Finance 2011–14. *Address:* Da Afghanistan Bank (Central Bank of Afghanistan), Ibne Sina Wat, Kabul, Afghanistan (office). *Telephone:* (20) 2104146 (office). *Fax:* (20) 2100305 (office). *E-mail:* info@centralbank.gov.af (office). *Website:* dab.gov.af (office).

ŠEDIVÝ, Jaroslav, CSc, DPhil; Czech politician and diplomatist (retd); b. 12 Nov. 1929, Prague; s. of Jaroslav Šedivý and Marie Šedivý; m. Marie Poslušná 1962; one s. one d.; ed Charles Univ., Prague; with Czech Acad. of Sciences 1954–57; scientist, Inst. of Int. Policy and Econ. 1957–70; imprisoned on charges of subversion of the state 1970–71; worker, driver, window cleaner 1972–88; researcher, Prognostic Inst., Prague 1989; adviser to Minister for Foreign Affairs 1989–90; Amb. to France 1990–95, to Belgium, Luxembourg and NATO 1995–97; Perm. Rep. to UNESCO 1993–95; Minister for Foreign Affairs 1997, Jan.–July 1998; Amb. to Switzerland 1998–2002; Adviser, Analysis Section, Ministry of Foreign Affairs 2002–03; Grand Officier, Ordre nat. du Mérite 1994, Chevalier de la Légion d'honneur 2005, Ordre of Merit (Czech Repub.) 2005; Dr hc (J.F. Kennedy Univ., Buenos Aires) 1998. *Publications include:* Policy and Relations 1969, Humiliated Revolution (published under pseudonym Y. Heřtová) 1978, Palace Černín in the Year Zero 1997, Metternich contra Napoleon 1998, Secrets and Sins of the Knights Templar 1999, Decembrists: Anatomy of an Unsuccessful Coup 2000, Ambassador to the Eiffel Tower, 1990–1994: Prague-Paris in Foreign Policy 2008, Diplomacy is the Art of Compromise: The Path to NATO, the EU and Other Stories: 1995–2002 2009, Jaroslav Šedivý: My Wandering Bewildered Century 2012, Fatal Alliance 2015. *Telephone:* (2) 41431707 (home). *E-mail:* sedivay@seznam.cz (home).

SEDLEY, Rt Hon. Sir Stephen John, Kt, PC, BA; British judge and writer; b. 9 Oct. 1939; s. of William Sedley and Rachel Sedley; m. 1st Ann Tate 1968 (divorced 1995); one s. two d.; m. 2nd Teresa Chaddock 1996; ed Mill Hill School, Queens' Coll., Cambridge; writer, musician, trans. 1961–64; called to Bar, Inner Temple 1964, Bencher 1989, QC 1983, Lord Justice of Appeal 1999–2011; mem. Int. Comm. on Mercenaries, Angola 1976; Visiting Professorial Fellow, Univ. of Warwick 1981; Pres. Nat. Reference Tribunals for the Coalmining Industry 1983–88; Visiting Fellow, Osgoode Hall Law School, Canada 1987, Visiting Prof. 1997; Dir Public Law Project 1989–93; Chair. Sex Discrimination Cttee, Bar Council 1992–95; Judge of the High Court of Justice, Queen's Bench Div. 1992–99; Distinguished Visitor, Hong Kong Univ. 1992; Visiting Fellow, Victoria Univ. of Wellington, NZ 1998; Judicial Visitor, Univ. Coll. London 1999–; Pres. British Inst. of Human Rights 2000–, British Tinnitus Asscn 2006–; Chair. British Council Advisory Cttee on Governance 2002–05; mem. Admin. Law Bar Asscn (Hon. Vice-Pres. 1992–), Haldane Soc. (Sec. 1964–69); Hon. Prof., Univ. of Wales, Cardiff 1993–, Univ. of Warwick 1994–; Hon. Fellow, Inst. for Advanced Legal Studies 1997; Dr hc (North London) 1996; Hon. LLD (Nottingham Trent) 1997, (Bristol) 1999, (Warwick) 1999, (Durham) 2001, (Hull) 2002, (Southampton) 2003, (Exeter) 2004, (Essex) 2007. *Publications include:* Whose Child? 1987, The Making and Remaking of the British Constitution (with Lord Nolan) 1997, Freedom, Law and Justice 1999, Human Rights: A New World or Business as Usual 2000; editor: Seeds of Love (anthology) 1967, A Spark in the Ashes 1992; translator: From Burgos Jail, by Marcos Ana and Vidal de Nicolas 1964; contrib. essays to numerous books, including Freedom of Expression and Freedom of Information 2000, Judicial Review in International Perspective 2000, Discriminating Lawyers 2000; contrib. to periodicals and journals, including Civil Justice Quarterly, Industrial Law Journal, Journal of Law and Society, Journal of Legal Ethics, Law Quarterly Review, London Review of Books, Modern Law Review, Public Law. *Address:* Cloisters, Temple, London, EC4Y 7AA, England (office).

SEDNEY, Jules; Suriname academic and politician; b. 28 Sept. 1922, Paramaribo; s. of Eugene Edwin Leonard Sedney and Marie Julia Linger; m. Ina Francis Waaldyk 1951 (divorced 1985); two s. two d.; one d. by A. Calor; ed Graaf van Zinzendorfschool, Mulo and Univ. of Amsterdam; fmr teacher; held sr post with Cen. Bank of Suriname 1956–58, Pres. 1980; Minister of Finance 1958–63; Dir Industrial Devt Corpn of Suriname and Nat. Devt Bank 1963; left Nationale Partij Suriname (NPS) and joined Progressieve Nationale Partij (PNP) 1967; Prime Minister and Minister of Gen. Affairs 1970–73; Prof. of Econs, Univ. of Suriname 1976–80; Chair. Nat. Planning Council 1980; fmr Dir Suriname Trade and Industry Asscn 1990–92; Chair. Monitoring Group Suriname Structural Adjustment Programme 1992–96, Tripartite Advisory Bd to Govt of Suriname 1994–98, Seniority Bd of Econ. Advisers to Pres. of the Repub. 1998–2000, Center for the Promotion and Protection of Democracy and Civil Soc. 1999; Gran Cordón Simón Bolívar (Venezuela), Groot-Officier Oranje Nassau (Netherlands), Kt, Nederlandse Leeuw (Netherlands). *Publications:* Growth Without Development 1978, To Choose and To Divide 1980, The Future of Our Past 1998. *Leisure interests:* bridge, golf. *Address:* Maystreet 34, Paramaribo, Suriname. *Telephone:* (597) 439114. *Fax:* (597) 421029.

SEDWILL, Sir Mark Philip, KCMG, BSc (Hons), MPhil, FRGS, FIoD; British public servant and fmr diplomatist; *Cabinet Secretary and Head of the Civil Service;* b. 21 Oct. 1964, Ealing, London; m.; one d.; ed Bourne Grammar School, St Andrews Univ., St Edmund Hall, Oxford; joined FCO 1989, with Security Coordination Dept and Gulf War Emergency Unit 1989–91, Second Sec., Egypt 1991–94, Resource Man. Group, FCO 1994–96, First Sec. and UN Weapons Inspector, Iraq 1996–97, First Sec., Political-Mil. and Counter-Terrorism, Cyprus 1997–99, Europe and Middle East Press Officer, FCO 1999–2000, Pvt. Sec. to Foreign Sec. Robin Cook and Foreign Sec. Jack Straw 2000–02, British Govt Spokesman on Middle East 2002, Deputy High Commr in Pakistan 2003–04, Deputy Dir Middle East and North Africa, FCO 2005, Int. Dir, UK Border Agency 2006–08, Amb. to Afghanistan 2009–10, NATO Sr Civilian Rep. in Afghanistan 2010–11, Prime Minister's Special Rep. for Afghanistan and Pakistan, FCO 2011–, Dir-Gen. (Political) 2012–13; Perm. Sec., Home Office 2013–17; Nat. Security Adviser 2017–; Cabinet Sec. 2018–; Head of the Civil Service 2018–; NATO Meritorious Service Medal, US Distinguished Service Medal, NATO Afghanistan Medal, UK Afghanistan Civilian Service Medal. *Address:* Cabinet Office, 70 Whitehall, London, SW1A 2AS, England (office). *Telephone:* (20) 7276-1234 (office). *E-mail:* publiccorrespondence@cabinetoffice.gov.uk (office). *Website:* www.gov.uk/government/organisations/cabinet-office (office).

SEEBACH, Dieter, BS, PhD, FRSC; German chemist and academic (retd); *Professor Emeritus, Eidgenössische Technische Hochschule Zürich;* b. 31 Oct. 1937, Karlsruhe; m. Ingeborg Reichling (deceased); three c.; ed Univ. of Karlsruhe; Post-doctoral Fellow and Lecturer in Chem., Harvard Univ., USA 1965–66; Prof., Justus Liebig Universität, Giessen 1971–77; Prof., ETH, Zürich 1977–2003, Prof. Emer. 2003–; Visiting Prof. at numerous int. univs including Harvard Univ. 2007; mem. Advisory Bd Synthesis 1984–, Angewandte Chemie 1985–94, Chimia 1985–, Helvetica Chimica Acta 1986–91; mem. Schweizerischer Chemiker Verband 1981–92, Chemische Gesellschaft, European Chemical Soc., ACS, Gesellschaft Deutscher Chemiker, Chemical Soc. of Japan, ACS, Deutsche Akad. der Naturforscher Leopoldina 1984, Neue Schweizerische Chemische Gesellschaft 1992–95 (Hon. mem. 2004), Einzelmitglied der Schweizerischen Akad. der Technischen Wissenschaften 1998; Corresp. mem. Akad. der Wissenschaften und Literatur, Mainz 1990, Academia Mexicana de Ciencias 2001; Fellow, Japan Soc. for the Promotion of Science 1985–; Foreign Assoc. NAS (USA) 2007–; Dr hc (Montpellier) 1989; hon. lecturer at numerous int. univs; numerous awards, including Univ. of Karlsruhe Wolf Prize 1964, Stichting Havinga Fonds Havinga Medal 1985, Gesellschaft Deutscher Chemiker Karl Ziegler Prize 1987, Harvard Univ. Tischler Prize 1990, King Faisal Int. Prize in Science (Saudi Arabia) 1999, Marcel Benoist Prize (Switzerland) 2000, Yamada Prize (Japan) 2000, Nagoya Medal (Japan) 2002, A.W. von Hofmann Medal 2003, Tetrahedron Prize 2003, American Peptide Soc. Vincent du Vigneaud Award 2004, Ryoji Noyori Prize 2004, Max Bergmann Medal 2005, EuCheMS Award 2006. *Publications:* more than 800 research papers and more than 1,000 lectures world-wide. *Address:* Laboratorium für Organische Chemie, Eidgenössische Technische Hochschule, Hönggerberg HCI H 331, Vladimir-Prelog-Weg 3, 8093 Zürich, Switzerland (office). *Telephone:* (44) 632-2990 (office). *Fax:* 44) 632-1144 (office). *E-mail:* seebach@org.chem.ethz.ch (office). *Website:* infosee.ethz.ch/seebach/seebach.html (office).

SEEDER, Helir-Valdor; Estonian economist and politician; *First Vice-President, Riigikogu;* b. 7 Sept. 1964, Viljandi, Estonian SSR, USSR; m.; four s.; ed Estonian Acad. of Agric.; began career as teacher, Vana-Võidu Tehnikum 1990–91; Econ. Advisor to Viljandi City Govt 1991–92, Deputy Mayor of Viljandi 1992, Mayor 1992–93, Gov., Viljandi Co. 1993–2003; mem. Baltic Ass. 2003–07; mem. Riigikogu (parl.) for Järva and Viljandimaa 2003–, First Vice-Pres. 2019–; Minister of Agric. 2007–14; mem. Exec. Cttee, Estonian Olympic Cttee 2012–; mem. Isamaaliit (Pro Patria Union) 1991–2006, mem. Isamaa ja Res Publica Liit (IRL—Union of Pro Patria and Res Publica) (following merger) 2006–18, renamed Isamaa (Pro Patria) 2018, Chair. of IRL 2017–18, of Isamaa 2018–; Order of the White Star (III Class) 2001; Baltic Ass. Medal 2007. *Address:* State Assembly (Riigikogu), Lossi plats 1a, Tallinn 15165, Estonia (office); Isamaa, Paldiski mnt. 13, Tallinn 10137, Estonia (office). *Telephone:* 631-6311 (office); 624-0403 (office). *Fax:* 631-6334 (office). *E-mail:* helir-valdor.seeder@riigikogu.ee (office); info@isamaa.ee (office). *Website:* www.riigikogu.ee (office); isamaa.ee (office).

SEEHOFER, Horst Lorenz; German politician; *Federal Minister of the Interior;* b. 4 July 1949, Ingolstadt; m. Karin Seehofer 1985; one s. three d.; ed Verwaltungs- und Wirtschaftsakademie, Munich; began career in local govt, Ingolstadt and Eichstätt; joined Christlich-Soziale Union (CSU) 1971; mem. Parl. for Ingolstadt 1980–2008, CSU Speaker on Social Affairs 1983–89; Parl. Sec. of State, Ministry of Employment 1989–92; Minister of Health 1992–98; Vice-Chair. CSU 1994–2008, Chair. 2008–; Vice-Chair. CDU/CSU Parl. Group 1998–2004, Regional Chair., Christlich Soziale Arbeitnehmerschaft 2000–08; Minister of Food, Agric. and Consumer Protection 2005–08; Minister-Pres. of Bavaria 2008–18; Fed. Minister of the Interior 2018–; Pres. Bundesrat 2011–12; Acting Pres. of Germany following resignation of Pres. Christian Wulff 17 Feb.–18 March 2012. *Address:* Federal Ministry of the Interior, Alt-Moabit 101, 10559 Berlin, Germany (office). *Telephone:* (30) 186811002 (office). *Fax:* 30) 186811018 (office). *E-mail:* mb@bmi.bund.de (office). *Website:* www.bmi.bund.de (office); www.csu.de/seehofer/aktuell (office).

SEELE, Rainer, PhD; German chemist and business executive; *Chairman of the Executive Board and CEO, OMV Group;* b. 1960; ed Univ. of Göttingen; Research Scientist, BASF AG, Ludwigshafen 1987–91, Head of Group Chemical Research 1991–94, Head of Planning and Controlling 1994–96, mem. Exec. Bd 2000; Head of Strategic Planning Dept, Wintershall AG, Kassel 1996–2000, Man. Dir and Head of Sales Dept, WINGAS GmbH, Kassel 2000–02, Chair. Exec. Bd and Head of Gas Man. Div. 2002–09, Chair. and CEO Wintershall AG 2009–15, also Head of Natural Gas Trading, mem. Bd of Exec. Dirs, Wintershall Holding GmbH; Chair. Exec. Bd and CEO OMV AG 2015–; Dir, OJSC Severneftegazprom, South Stream Transport BV; mem. Shareholder Cttee, Nord Stream AG; mem. Supervisory Bd, VNG-Verbundnetz Gas AG 2002–14, Chair. 2009–14. *Address:* OMV AG, Trabrennstrasse 6–8, 1020 Vienna, Austria (office). *Telephone:* (1) 40440-21950 (office). *Fax:* (1) 40440-27900 (office). *E-mail:* info@omv.com (office). *Website:* www.omv.com (office).

SEELERT, Robert (Bob) Louis; American business executive; *Chairman, Saatchi & Saatchi Worldwide;* b. 1 Sept. 1942, Manchester, Conn.; m. Sarah Seelert; ed Harvard Univ.; Gen. Man. Gen. Foods 1966–86, Pres. Coffee and Int. Foods Div. 1986–89; Pres. and CEO Kayser-Roth (hosiery group) 1991–94; Pres. and CEO Topco American (grocery co.) 1989–91; Chief Exec. Cordiant Communications Group PLC (fmrly Saatchi & Saatchi, later Cordiant PLC) 1995–97; CEO Saatchi & Saatchi Worldwide 1997–, currently Chair. (non-exec.). *Publication:* Start With the Answer 2009. *Address:* Saatchi & Saatchi Worldwide, 375 Hudson Street, New York, NY 10014-3620, USA (office). *Telephone:* (212) 463-2000 (office). *Fax:* (212) 462-2267 (office). *Website:* www.saatchi.com (office).

SEEMAN, Nadrian (Ned) Charles, BS, PhD, FRSC; American chemist, crystallographer and academic; *Margaret and Herman Sokol Professor of Chemistry, New York University;* b. 16 Dec. 1945, Chicago, Ill.; s. of Herman Seeman and Emma Seeman; ed Univs of Chicago and Pittsburgh; Postdoctoral researcher, Columbia Univ., New York 1970–72, MIT, Cambridge, Mass 1972–77; Asst Prof., Dept of Biology, State Univ. of NY, Albany 1977–83, Assoc. Prof. 1983–88; Prof., Dept of Chem., New York Univ. 1988–, Margaret and Herman Sokol Chair in Chem. 2001–; Founding Pres. Int. Soc. for Nanoscale Science, Computation and Eng; Einstein Prof., Chinese Acad. of Science 2012; Fellow, AAAS 1998; Hon. Prof., Universidad Peruana Cayetano Heredia 1998; NATO Advanced Study Fellow 1970, Damon Runyon Fellow 1972–73, NIH Postdoctoral Fellow 1973–76, Sidhu Award 1974, Basil O'Connor Fellow 1978–81, NIH Research Career Devt Award 1982–87, Popular Science Magazine Science and Tech. Award 1993, Feynman Prize in Nanotechnology 1995, Discover Magazine Emerging Tech. Award 1997, Margaret and Herman Sokol Faculty Award in the Sciences 1999, Rozenberg Tulip Award in DNA-Based Computation 2004, MERIT Award, Nat. Inst. of Gen. Medical Sciences 2005, Nano50 Award, Nanotech Briefs 2005, World Tech. Award in Biotechnology, The World Tech. Network 2005, Nichols Medal, New York Section of ACS 2008, Frontiers of Science Award 2009, Alexander Rich Medal 2010, Kavli Prize 2010, Guggenheim Fellow 2010–11, ISNSCE Award 2011, Distinguished Alumnus, Univ. of Pittsburgh 2012, Benjamin Franklin Medal in Chem. 2016. *Publications include:* numerous scientific papers in professional journals on DNA nanotechnology, macromolecular design and topology, biophysical chem. of recombinational intermediates, DNA-based computation, and crystallography. *Address:* Room 1066, Department of Chemistry, New York University, New York, NY 10003-6688, USA (office). *Telephone:* (212) 998-8395 (office). *Fax:* (212) 995-4475 (office). *E-mail:* ned.seeman@nyu.edu (office). *Website:* seemanlab4.chem.nyu.edu (office).

SEEPERSAD-BACHAN, Carolyn, BSc, MSc; Trinidad and Tobago engineer and politician; *Leader, Congress of the People;* b. San Fernando; m. Suresh Bachan; one s. one d.; ed Univ. of the West Indies; began career as Lecturer in Eng, Univ. of the West Indies, also mem. Bd of Eng Inst.; Opposition Senator 2002–06; mem. House of Reps for San Fernando West 2010–15; Minister of Energy and Energy Affairs 2010–11, of Public Admin 2011–15; fmr Chair. Nat. Petroleum Co. Ltd; fmr dir of several private cos; mem. Congress of the People, Leader 2017–. *Address:* Congress of the People, Res Integra Building, 151 A Southern Main Road, Edinburgh Village, Chaguanas, Trinidad and Tobago (office). *Telephone:* 349-1395 (office). *E-mail:* secretariat@coptnt.com (office). *Website:* www.congresstt.com (office).

SEFAJ, Flamur, MSc; Kosovo politician; b. 8 Oct. 1972; ed Univ. della Svizzera italiana; began career in Marketing Dept, IBSA Inst. Biochimique SA, Pambio Noranco 2003; Librarian, Lugano Univ. Library 2003–04; Inter-cultural Mediator, Swiss Fed. Office for Refugees 1998–2004; Head of Corp. Staff of Group Pres., Mabetex Project Engineering, Lugano 2005–17; Project Man., General Studio SA (software co.), Lugano 2008–10; Minister of Internal Affairs 2017–18 (dismissed); mem. Nisma për Kosovën (NISMA—Initiative for Kosovo). *Address:* c/o Ministry of Internal Affairs, 10000 Prishtina, Rruga Luan Haradinaj, Kosovo (office). *Telephone:* (38) 213007 (office). *Fax:* (38) 20019640 (office). *E-mail:* zip-mpb@rks-gov.net (office). *Website:* mpb.rks-gov.net (office).

ŠEFČOVIČ, Maroš, JUDr, PhD; Slovak lawyer, diplomatist, politician and EU official; *Commissioner for Energy Union and Vice-President, European Commission;* b. 24 July 1966, Bratislava, Czechoslovak Socialist Repub. (now Slovakia); m. Helena Šefčovič; three c.; ed Univ. of Econs, Bratislava, Moscow State Inst. of Int. Relations, USSR, Comenius Univ., Bratislava, Université d'eté de Perpignan, France, Hoover Inst., Stanford Univ., USA, Alliance française, Harare, Zimbabwe, Salzburg Global Seminar, Austria, Ulpan Akiva, Netanya and Dale Carnegie Assocs, Tel-Aviv, Israel; Adviser to First Deputy Foreign Minister, Ministry of Foreign Affairs, Prague, Czechoslovakia 1990; Desk Officer, Dept of EU and NATO countries, Ministry of Foreign Affairs, Slovak Repub., Bratislava 1995, Deputy Dir 1996, Deputy Dir, Office of the Foreign Minister 1997, Dir 1998, Dir-Gen., Bilateral Cooperation Section 2002, Dir-Gen., European Affairs Section 2003–04; overseas postings include Third Sec. and Consul, Embassy of the Czech and Slovak Fed. Repub., Zimbabwe 1991–92; Deputy Chief of Mission and Second Sec., Embassy of the Slovak Repub., Ottawa, Canada 1992, Deputy Head of Mission, Mission to the EC, Brussels 1998; Amb. to Israel 1999; Amb. and Perm. Rep. to EU, Brussels 2004–09; Commr for Educ., Training, Culture and Youth 2009–10, Vice-Pres. EC responsible for Inter-Institutional Relations and Admin 2010–14, Interim Vice-Pres. EC responsible for Inter-Institutional Relations and Admin and Health and Consumer Policy Oct.–Nov. 2012, Commr for Energy Union and Vice-Pres. EC 2014–(19); Chatam Sofer Medal for promotion of Slovak-Israeli relations. *Publications:* various articles on issues related to European integration. *Leisure interests:* sport (tennis, jogging, skiing), biographies. *Address:* European Commission, Rue de la Loi/Wetstraat 200, 1049 Brussels, Belgium (office). *Telephone:* (2) 299-11-11 (switchboard) (office). *E-mail:* cab-sefcovic-web@ec.europa.eu (office). *Website:* ec.europa.eu/commission/2014-2019/sefcovic_en (office).

SEFRIOUI, Anas; Moroccan business executive; *President and Director-General, Douja Promotion Groupe Addoha SA;* b. 16 May 1957, Fes; s. of Haj Abdeslam Sefrioui; m.; three c.; left school to work with father in Gassoul (Moroccan clay) business; est Douja Promotion Groupe Addoha SA 1988, currently Pres. and Dir-Gen., also Chair. Ciments de l'Atlas; Vice-Chair. Supervisory Bd, Banque Populaire de Casablanca; Chair. and CEO Immolog; mem. Bd of Dirs Lasry Maroc; mem. Supervisory Bd, Maroc Assistance; mem. Gen. Confed. of Moroccan Enterprises Foundation. *Address:* Douja Promotion Groupe Addoha SA, Km 7 Route De Rabat, Casablanca, Morocco (office). *Telephone:* (52) 2679900 (office). *Website:* www.groupeaddoha.com (office).

SEGAL, Anthony (Tony) Walter, MD, PhD, DSc, FRS, FRCP, FMedSci; British medical scientist and consultant physician; *Charles Dent Professor of Medicine and Director, Centre for Molecular Medicine, Department of Medicine, University College London;* b. 24 Feb. 1944, Johannesburg, S Africa; s. of Cyril Segal and Doreen Segal (née Hayden); m. Barbara Miller 1966; three d.; ed Univ. of Cape Town, S Africa and Univ. of London; House Physician and Surgeon, Groote Schuur Hosp., Cape Town 1968–69; Registrar in Cardiology, Wentworth Hosp., Durban Feb.–July 1969; Casualty Officer, Hammersmith Hosp., London Aug. 1970–Feb 1971, Sr House Officer of Rheumatology Feb.–Aug. 1971, Sr Registrar, Dept of Medicine 1975–76; Clinical Research Registrar, Gen. Medicine & Gastroenterology, Northwick Park Hosp., Harrow 1971–74; Scientific Officer, Medical Research Council, Harrow June–Sept. 1974; Clinical Scientist, Clinical Research Centre 1976–79; Sr Clinical Fellow, Wellcome Trust 1979–86; Charles Dent Prof. of Medicine, Univ. Coll., London 1986–, also Head of Centre for Molecular Medicine and Hon. Consultant Physician, Univ. Coll. Hosp.; UCL Prize Lecture in Clinical Science 2014. *Publications include:* more than 240 articles in professional journals. *Leisure interests:* golf, sculpture, theatre, art. *Address:* Department of Medicine, University College London, 2nd Floor, The Rayne Building, 5 University Street, London, WC1E 6JJ (office); 48B Regents Park Road, London, NW1 7SX, England (home). *Telephone:* (20) 7679-6175 (office); (20) 7586-8745 (home). *Fax:* (20) 7679-0967 (office). *E-mail:* t.segal@ucl.ac.uk (office). *Website:* www.ucl.ac.uk/CMM (office).

SEGAL, George, BA; American actor and producer; b. 13 Feb. 1934, New York, NY; s. of George Segal and Fanny Segal (née Bodkin); m. 1st Marion Sobol 1956 (divorced 1983); two d.; m. 2nd Linda Rogoff 1983 (deceased); m. 3rd Sonia Schulz; ed Haverford Coll., Columbia Coll. *Films include:* The Young Doctors 1961, Act One 1962, The Longest Day 1962, Invitation to a Gunfighter 1964, The New Interns (Golden Globe Award for New Star of the Year 1965) 1964, Ship of Fools 1965, King Rat 1965, Who's Afraid of Virginia Woolf? 1966, The Quiller Memorandum 1966, Bye Bye Braverman 1968, No Way to Treat a Lady 1968, The Bridge at Remagen 1969, She Couldn't Say No 1969, The Southern Star 1969, Loving 1970, Where's Poppa? 1970, The Owl and the Pussy Cat 1970, Born to Win 1972, The Hot Rock 1972, Blume in Love 1972, A Touch of Class (Golden Globe Award for Best Performance by an Actor in a Motion Picture-Comedy or Musical 1974) 1973, The Terminal Man 1973, California Split 1973, Blackbird 1974, Russian Roulette 1975, The Duchess and the Dirtwater Fox 1976, Fun with Dick and Jane 1976, Rollercoaster 1977, Who is Killing the Great Chefs of Europe? 1978, Lost and Found 1979, The Last Married Couple in America 1980, Stick 1983, The Endless Game (TV) 1989, Look Who's Talking 1990, The Clearing, For The Boys 1991, The Mirror has Two Faces 1996, Flirting with Disaster 1996, The Cable Guy 1996, The November Conspiracy 1997, Heights 2004, 2012 2009, Love & Other Drugs 2010, The Tale of the Princess Kaguya (voice) 2013, Elsa & Fred 2014. *Play:* Art, New York 1999, West End, London 2001. *Television includes:* Just Shoot Me (series) 1996–2003, Houdini 1998, The Linda McCartney Story 2000, The Goldbergs 2013–. *Leisure interest:* banjo playing.

SEGAL, Graeme Bryce, BSc, MA, DPhil, FRS; British mathematician and academic; *Emeritus Fellow, All Souls College, Oxford;* b. 21 Dec. 1941; ed Univ. of Sydney, Australia, Balliol Coll., Oxford, St John's Coll., Cambridge; Jr Research Fellow, Worcester Coll., Oxford 1964–66, Jr Lecturer in Math., Univ. of Oxford 1965–66, CUF Lecturer 1966–70, Science Research Council Research Assoc. 1971–75, Univ. Lecturer 1975–78, Reader 1978–89, Prof. of Math. (ad hominem) 1989–90, Fellow, St Catherine's Coll., Oxford 1966–90, Sr Research Fellow, All Souls Coll., Oxford 1999–2009, Emer. Fellow 2009–; Lowndean Prof. of Astronomy and Geometry and Fellow of St John's Coll., Cambridge 1990–99; Pres. London Math. Soc. 2011–13; mem. Inst. for Advanced Study 1969–70; Ed. Topology 1970–90; Pólya Prize, London Math. Soc. 1990, Sylvester Medal, Royal Soc. 2010. *Publications:* Loop Groups (co-author) 1986; numerous papers in professional journals. *Address:* Room N3.07, Mathematical Institute, University of Oxford, Andrew Wiles Building, Radcliffe Observatory Quarter, Woodstock Road, Oxford, OX2 6GG (office); All Souls College, Oxford, OX1 4AL, England. *Telephone:* (1865) 615193 (office). *E-mail:* graeme.segal@all-souls.ox.ac.uk (office). *Website:* www.maths.ox.ac.uk (office); www.all-souls.ox.ac.uk (office).

SEGAL, Julian, BSc (ChemEng), MBA; Australian business executive; *Managing Director and CEO, Caltex Australia Ltd;* ed Israel Inst. of Tech., Macquarie Grad. School of Man.; held several sr man. positions at Orica, including Man. of Strategic Market Planning, Gen. Man.– Australia/Asia Mining Services, and Sr Vice-Pres.– Marketing for Orica Mining Services 1999–2005; Man. Dir and CEO Incitec Pivot Ltd (global chemicals co.) 2005–09; Man. Dir and CEO Caltex Australia Ltd 2009–; Dir Australian Inst. of Petroleum Ltd 2009–. *Address:* Caltex Australia Ltd, Level 24, Market Street, Sydney, NSW 2000, Australia (office). *Telephone:* (2) 9250-5000 (office). *Fax:* (2) 9250-5742 (office). *E-mail:* info@caltex.com.au (office). *Website:* www.caltex.com.au (office).

SEGAL, Uriel (Uri); Israeli orchestral conductor and academic; *Adjunct Senior Lecturer in Music (Orchestral Conducting), Jacobs School of Music, Indiana University;* b. 7 March 1944, Jerusalem; s. of Alexander Segal and Nehama Segal; m. Ilana Finkelstein 1966; one s. three d.; ed Rubin Acad., Jerusalem and Guildhall School of Music, UK; debut with Tivoli Orchestra, Copenhagen 1969; Prin. Conductor Bournemouth Symphony Orchestra 1980–82, Philharmonia Hungarica 1981–85; Music Dir Israeli Chamber Orchestra, Chautauqua Festival, NY 1990–2007, Louisville Orchestra, Ky 1998–2004; Founder/Chief Conductor, Century Orchestra, Osaka, Japan 1990–98, Laureate Conductor 1998–; Adjunct Sr Lecturer in Music (Orchestral Conducting), Jacobs School of Music, Ind. Univ. 2004–; fmr Prin. Guest Conductor, Stuttgart Radio Symphony; orchestras conducted include Berlin Philharmonic, Stockholm Philharmonic, Concertgebouw, Orchestre de Paris, Vienna Symphony, Israel Philharmonic, London Symphony, London Philharmonic, Philharmonia, Orchestre de la Suisse Romande, Warsaw Philharmonic, Spanish Nat. Orchestra, Pittsburgh Symphony, Chicago Symphony, Detroit Symphony, Dallas Symphony, Houston Symphony, Montréal Symphony and Rochester Symphony; tours have included Austria, Switzerland, Spain, Italy, France, UK, Scandinavia and the Far East; operatic debut conducting The Flying Dutchman at Sante Fe Opera 1973, has since conducted opera in Italy, France, Germany, Japan, Israel and USA; First Prize, Int. Mitropoulos Conducting Competition, New York 1969. *Recordings include:* Mahler Symphony No. 4 (with NZ Symphony Orchestra), music by Britten (Bournemouth Symphony), Stravinsky's Firebird Suite and Symphony in C with the Suisse Romande Orchestra), Mozart Piano Concertos with Radu Lupu and the English Chamber Orchestra, Schumann's Piano Concerto with Ashkenazy and the London Symphony, Beethoven Piano Concertos with Rudolf Firkusny and the Philharmonia, Mozart Piano Concertos with Alicia de Larocha and Wiener Symphoniker. *Leisure interests:* reading, photography, cooking. *Address:* Michal Schmidt Artists Management, 59 East 54th Street, Suite 83, New York, NY 10022, USA (office). *Telephone:* (212) 421-8500 (office); (54) 801-9086 (Israel) (home). *E-mail:* mws@schmidtart.com (office); uriel@urielsegal.com; usegal@indiana.edu. *Fax:* (77) 332-5508 (office). *Website:* www.urisegal.com; music.indiana.edu.

SEGLIŅŠ, Mareks; Latvian lawyer and politician; b. 4 July 1970, Aizpute; m. Kristin Šegliņu (divorced); two c.; ed Aizputes Secondary School, Univ. of Latvia; worked in prosecutor's office and court of Liepāja City; worked in law office Pomerancis un Kreicis 1994–98; mem. Saeima (Parl.) 1998–2011, mem. Parl. (People's Party Parl. Group), Chair. Legal Affairs Cttee, Sub-cttee on Drafting Criminal Procedure Law of the Legal Affairs Cttee, Deputy Chair. Nat. Security Cttee, mem. Baltic Affairs Sub-cttee of Foreign Affairs Cttee, Sports Sub-cttee of Educ., Culture and Science Cttee, Latvian del. to Baltic Ass., Latvia Interparliamentary Co-operation Groups with Australia and NZ, Azerbaijan, Canada, Chile, China, Ecuador, Germany, Italy, Kuwait, Taiwan, Turkey, UK and USA; Minister of Interior 1999–2002, 2007–09, Minister of Justice 2009–10; elected Chair. Tautas partija (People's Party) 2008 (dissolved 2011); fmr mem. Bd of Dirs Rigas nami.

SEGUELA, Jacques Louis, PhD; French advertising executive; *Chief Creative Officer, Havas Advertising;* b. 23 Feb. 1934, Paris; s. of Louis Seguela and Simone Le Forestier; m. Sophie Vinson 1978; one s. four d.; ed Lycée de Perpignan, Faculté de Pharmacie de Montpellier; reporter, Paris Match 1960; with France Soir group's leisure magazines 1962; produced several TV programmes; joined Delpire 1964, then Axe; f. Roux Seguela Agency; co-f. Roux Seguela Cayzac & Goudard (RSGC) 1978; Vice-Pres. (Euro-RSCG) 1991–96; Chief Creative Officer, Havas Advertising 1996–, also Vice-Pres.; est. Bleu comme bleu (restaurant), Paris 1995; Co-founder Havas Tunisia 2010; Chevalier, Légion d'honneur 2008, Chevalier des Arts et des Lettres; César winner. *Publications:* Terre en rond 1961 (Prix littérature sportive), Ne dites pas à ma mère que je suis dans la publicité, elle me croit pianiste dans un bordel 1979, Hollywood lave plus blanc 1982, Fils de pub 1984, Cache Cache Pub, Demain il sera tros star 1989, C'est gai la pub 1990, Vote au-dessus d'un nid de cocos 1992, Pub Story 1994, La parole de Dieu 1995, le Futur a de l'avenir 1996, 80 ans de publicité Citroën et toujours 20 ans 1999, Le Vertige des urnes 2000, Job Guide des métiers de demain 2001, Tous ego: Havas, moi et les autres 2005, Soeur Courage 2006, La prise de l'Elysée: Les campagnes présidentielles de la Ve République 2007, Autobiographie non autorisée 2009, Génération QE 2009, Le pouvoir dans la peau 2011. *Address:* Havas, 29-30, Quai de Dion Bouton, 92817 Puteaux Cedex, France (office). *Telephone:* 1-58-47-90-20 (office). *Fax:* 1-58-47-90-25 (office). *E-mail:* js@jacques-seguela.com. *Website:* www.jacques-seguela.com; www.havas.com (office).

SEHGAL, Tino; British/German artist; b. 1976, London, England; ed studied political economy and dance in Berlin and Essen with Xavier Le Roy and Jerome Bel; grew up mostly in Düsseldorf and Paris; began to work as an artist in 2000; works ('constructed situations') involve one or more people carrying out instructions conceived by the artist; has exhibited at several venues, including Inst. of Contemporary Arts (ICA), London, Tate Gallery, Manifesta 4 and Venice Biennale 2005; first major exhbn in Italy presented by Nicola Trussardi Foundation at Galleria d'Arte Moderna, Villa Reale, Milan 2008; Bâloise Prize, Art Basel, Switzerland 2004, Golden Lion for the Best Artist in the Int. Exhibition Il Palazzo Enciclopedico, Venice Biennale 2013.

SEHWAG, Virender; Indian professional cricketer (retd); b. 20 Oct. 1978, Delhi; s. of Krishan Sehwag and Krishna Sehwag; m. Aarti Ahlawat 2004; two s.; ed Arora Vidya School; right-handed opening batsman; occasional right-arm off-break bowler; played for Delhi beginning 1997, India 1999–2013 (Vice-Capt. 2005–06, 2008–09), Leics. 2003, Int. Cricket Council (ICC) World XI 2005, Asian Cricket Council XI 2005, Delhi Daredevils 2008, India Blue, Rajasthan Cricket Asscn Pres.'s XI; First-class debut: 1997/98; Test debut: South Africa v India, Bloemfontein 3–6 Nov. 2001; One-Day Int. (ODI) debut: India v Pakistan, Mohali 1 April 1999; T20I debut: S Africa v India, Johannesburg 1 Dec. 2006; mem. winning Indian cricket team in ICC Cricket World Cup against Sri Lanka 2011; highest score made by an Indian in Test cricket (319), which was also fastest triple century in history of int. cricket (reached 300 off only 278 balls); holds record for highest individual score in ODI matches (219 off 149 balls, v West Indies at Indore) 2011; one of three batsmen in the world to have surpassed 300 runs twice in Test cricket, only cricketer to score two triple centuries and take a five-wicket innings haul; scored fastest century ever by an Indian in ODI cricket, from 60 balls; opened vegetarian restaurant, Sehwag Favourites, Delhi 2005; retd from int. cricket in 2015; mem., Cricket Affairs Cttee, Delhi & Dist Cricket Asscn (DDCA) –2018; Padma Shri 2010; Arjuna Award 2002, Wisden Leading Cricketer of the World 2008, 2009, ICC Test Player of the Year 2010.

SEIDELMAN, Susan, MFA; American film director; b. 11 Dec. 1952, nr Philadelphia, Pa; d. of Florence Seidelman; m. Jonathan Brett; one s.; ed Drexel Univ. and New York Univ. Film School; directing debut with And You Act Like One Too (Student Acad. Award, Acad. of Motion Picture Arts and Sciences); then Dir Deficit (short film funded by American Film Inst.) and Yours Truly, Andrea G. Stern, The Dutch Master; Adjunct Prof. New York Univ.; mem. Jury Berlin Int. Film Festival 1994; Hon. PhD (Drexel); Mary Pickford Award for Best Female Dir 2002. *Films:* Smithereens (dir, producer, co-scriptwriter) 1982, Desperately

Seeking Susan 1985, Making Mr Right 1987, Cookie 1989, She-Devil 1989, Confessions of a Suburban Girl 1992, Dutch Master 1994, Tales of Erotica 1996, Gaudi Afternoon 2001, The Boynton Beach Club 2005, Musical Chairs 2011, The Hot Flashes 2013, Cut in Half (short) 2017. *Television:* The Barefoot Executive 1995, Sex and The City (pilot episode) 1998, A Cooler Climate 1999, Now and Again (series) 1999, Power and Beauty 2002, The Ranch 2004, The Electric Company 2009. *Leisure interest:* travel. *Address:* c/o Michael Shedler, 350 Fifth Avenue, New York, NY 10118; c/o Gary Pearl Pictures, 10956 Weyburn Avenue, Suite 200, Los Angeles, CA 90024, USA. *E-mail:* stonehedge185@aol.com.

SEIDENBERG, Ivan G., BA, MBA; American telecommunications industry executive; *Advisory Partner, Perella Weinberg Partners LP;* b. 1946; m. Phyllis Seidenberg; two c.; ed Lehman Coll., City Univ. of New York, Pace Univ.; began career in communications as cable splicer's asst 1965; sr exec. positions at AT&T; fmr govt affairs dir Bell Atlantic; mem. Bd of Dirs NYNEX Inc. 1991–97, CEO (oversaw merger between NYNEX and Bell Atlantic 1997) –1997; CEO Bell Atlantic (oversaw merger between Bell Atlantic and GTE 1999) 1997–99; co-f. Verizon Wireless (cr. from merger of wireless assets of Bell Atlantic, GTE and Vodafone Airtouch) 1999, Co-CEO 1999–2002, Pres. and CEO Verizon Communications Inc. 2002–03, Chair. and CEO 2004–11, Chair. Aug.–Dec. 2011; Advisory Partner, Perella Weinberg Partners LP (investment banking firm) 2012–; mem. or fmr mem. Bd of Dirs Honeywell, Museum of TV and Radio, Viacom Inc., Verizon Foundation, Wyeth (pharmaceuticals co.), BlackRock Inc.; named by Pres. George W. Bush to Nat. Security Telecommunications Advisory Cttee 2007; Chair. Business Roundtable 2009–11; apptd by Pres. Obama to Pres.'s Export Council 2010; fmr Chair. US Telecom Asscn; mem. New York Acad. of Sciences' Pres.'s Council; Trustee, New York Presbyterian Hosp., The New York Hall of Science, Pace Univ., Paley Center for Media; Steven J. Ross Award 2002, Nat. Bridge Award 2004, Lifetime Achievement Award, Nat. Acad. of TV Arts and Sciences 2009, Distinguished Alumnus Award, American Asscn of State Colleges and Universities 2013. *Address:* Perella Weinberg Partners LP, 767 Fifth Avenue, New York, NY 10153, USA (office). *Telephone:* (212) 287-3200 (office). *Fax:* (212) 287-3201 (office). *E-mail:* kfindlay@pwpartners.com (office). *Website:* www.pwpartners.com (office).

SEIERSTAD, Åsne; Norwegian journalist and writer; b. 10 Feb. 1970, Oslo; ed Univ. of Oslo; mem. staff, ITAR-TASS news agency, Moscow; covered wars in Chechnya, Kosovo, Afghanistan, Iraq for several Scandinavian newspapers 1994–2004; correspondent, Norwegian television news 1998–2000; award for television reporting from Kosovo, Chechnya and Afghanistan, Gullruten Award 1999, Fritt Ord Honorary Award 2001, Årets Frilanser Award 2002, Journalist of the Year, Norway 2003, EMMA Award, London 2004, Bookseller's Prize, France 2004. *Publications include:* non-fiction: With Their Backs to the World 2000, The Bookseller of Kabul 2002, A Hundred and One Days: A Baghdad Journal 2004, Angel of Grozny: Inside Chechnya 2008, En Av Oss (One of Us: The Story of Anders Breivik and the Massacre in Norway) 2013, Two Sisters: Into the Syrian Jihad 2018. *Leisure interests:* skiing, nature. *Address:* Tidemands gt. 20, 0260 Oslo, Norway (home). *E-mail:* aaseie@frisurf.no.

SEIF, Valiollah, BSc, MSc, PhD; Iranian economist and central banker; *Assistant Professor, Department of Accounting, Allameh Tabatabaei University;* b. 1 Jan. 1952, Nahavnd; m.; ed Petroleum Univ. of Tech., Allameh Tabatabaei Univ.; Acting Under-Sec., Ministry of Commerce 1982–83; CEO and Chair., Bank Mellat 1984–86, Saderat Bank 1989–96, Sepah Bank 1996–2000, Bank Melli Iran 2000–05, Future Bank of Bahrain 2006–10, Karafarin Bank 2010–13; Gov. Bank Markazi Jomhouri Islami Iran 2013–18; Vice-Pres. Mostazafan Foundation 1986–89, Industrial Devt and Renovation of Iran (IDRO) 2005–06; mem. Finance Dir and Man. Bd, IDRO 1981–82; mem. Accounting and Man., Faculty of Allameh Tabatabaei Univ. 1991–, currently Asst Prof., Dept of Accounting; Gold Medal for Public Relations 2011. *Leisure and interests:* professional reading and sports activities. *Website:* simap.atu.ac.ir (office).

SEIKE, Tomio; Japanese artist and photographer; b. 13 July 1943, Tokyo; m. Junko Seike; ed Sapporo Jr Coll., Japan Photographic Acad.; asst photographer, Japan 1970–74; moved to England 1974; freelance photographer, Tokyo 1975–; public collections at Bibliothèque Nationale Paris, Maison Européenne de la Photographie, Jane Voorhees Zimmerli Art Museum, Rutgers Univ., Museum of Fine Arts, Houston. *Publications include:* Portrait of Zoe, Paris, Waterscape 2003. *Address:* Hamiltons Gallery, 13 Carlos Place, London, W1 2EU, England. *Telephone:* (20) 7499-9494. *Fax:* (20) 7629-9919. *E-mail:* art@hamiltonsgallery.com. *Website:* www.hamiltonsgallery.com/artists/42-tomio-seike/overview.

SEILLIÈRE de LABORDE, Ernest-Antoine; French business executive and fmr civil servant; b. 20 Dec. 1937, Neuilly-sur-Seine; s. of Jean Seillière de Laborde and Renée de Wendel; m. Antoinette Barbey 1971; two s. three d.; ed Ladycross Coll., Lycée Janson-de-Sailly, Faculty of Law, Paris, Nat. School of Admin.; attaché, High Comm. of Algeria 1962; with Ministry of Information 1963, Sec. for Foreign Affairs 1966, mem. French del. at negotiations for EEC, Brussels and Gen. Agreement on Tariffs and Trade, Geneva 1966–69; Adviser on Foreign Affairs 1969, Adviser to the Prime Minister 1969–72, Tech. Adviser to Minister for Foreign Affairs 1972–73; Minister of Armed Forces 1973–74; Lecturer, Centre for Int. Affairs, Harvard Univ. 1975; Jt Dir-Gen. of Industrial Politics, Marine-Wendel 1976, Pres. 1992–2002, Pres. Wendel Investissement 2002–13 (following merger of CGIP and Marine Wendel, now Wendel Group); Gen. Dir, Admin. CGIP 1978–87, Pres., Dir-Gen. 1987–2002; Vice-Pres. Carnaud SA (later CMB Packaging) 1984–91; Vice-Chair. Cap Gemini 2000–; Vice-Pres. Fed. of Mechanical Industries 1985; Vice-Pres. Nat. Council of French Employers (CNPF) 1988–97, Pres. 1997, Pres. MEDEF (newly named CNPF) 1997–2005; Pres. Business Europe (European business lobby group fmrly known as UNICE) 2005–09; currently Chair. Legrand Holding, Supervisory Bd Oranje-Nassau Groep BV; mem. Supervisory Bd Editis Holding, Peugeot SA, Hermès Int; Commdr, Légion d'honneur, Officier, Ordre nat. du Mérite. *Address:* Wendel Group, 89 rue Taitbout, 75009 Paris, France. *Telephone:* 1-42-85-30-00 (office). *Fax:* 1-42-80-68-67 (office). *Website:* www.wendelgroup.com (office).

SEIN, Lt-Gen. Win; Myanma air force officer and government official; *Minister of Defence;* ed Burma Officer Training School; headed newly created Air Defence Office under Ministry of Defence 2002, served in several command roles, becoming Chief of Staff of Air Defence 2010–15, Minister of Defence 2015–. *Address:* Ministry of Defence, Bldg 20, Nay Pyi Taw, Myanmar (office). *Website:* www.mod.gov.mm (office).

SEINFELD, Jerome (Jerry) Allen; American comedian; b. 29 April 1954, Brooklyn, New York; s. of Kalmen Seinfeld and Betty Seinfeld; m. Jessica Sklar 1999; three c.; ed Queens Coll., New York; fmrly salesman; stand-up comedian 1976–; joke-writer Benson (TV series) 1980; cr. (with Larry David) The Seinfeld Chronicles (later Seinfeld) 1989, actor Seinfeld (TV series) 1990–98, also co-writer, producer; Emmy Award Outstanding Comedy Series (for Seinfeld) 1993, American Comedy Award 1988, 1992. *Films include:* Pros & Cons 1999, A Uniform Used to Mean Something 2004, Hindsight Is 20/20 (short, writer) 2004, The Thing About My Folks 2005, Bee Movie (voice, writer and producer) 2007, New Family (video short) 2008. *Television includes:* Benson (series) 1980–81, The Ratings Game (film) 1984, The Seinfeld Chronicles 1989, One Night Stand (series) 1990, Seinfeld (series) 1990–98, Carol Leifer: Gaudy, Bawdy & Blue (film) 1992, The Larry Sanders Show (series) 1993, I'm Telling You for the Last Time 1998, Larry David: Curb Your Enthusiasm (film) 1999, Dilbert (series) 2000, Curb Your Enthusiasm (series) 2004–09, Sincerely, Ted L. Nancy (film, creator) 2008, The Marriage Ref (series writer and exec. producer) 2010–11, Colin Quinn Long Story Short (film) (exec. producer) 2011. *Publications:* Seinlanguage 1993, Halloween (juvenile) 2002. *Leisure interests:* Zen, yoga. *Address:* c/o Creative Artists Agency, 2000 Avenue of the Stars, Los Angeles, CA 90067, USA. *Website:* www.caa.com; www.jerryseinfeld.com.

SEINO, Satoshi; Japanese transport industry executive; *Chairman, East Japan Railway Company;* b. 1947; ed Tohoku Univ.; joined Japanese Nat. Railways (predecessor of East Japan Railway Co.) 1970, served as Head of Human Resources Div. and as Man. Dir East Japan Railway Co., Exec. Vice-Pres., Corp. Planning HQ and IT Business Devt HQ, East Japan Railway Co. 2002–06, Pres. and CEO 2006–12; Chair. 2012–; fmr Chair. Int. Union of Railways; Outside Dir Japan Post Holdings Co. 2014–. *Address:* East Japan Railway Co., 2-2-2 Yoyogi, Shibuya-ku, Tokyo 151-8578, Japan (office). *Telephone:* (3) 5334-1150 (office); (3) 5334-1310 (office). *Fax:* (3) 5334-1110 (office); (3) 5334-1297 (office). *E-mail:* ir@jreast.co.jp (office); bond@jreast.co.jp (office); info@jreast.co.jp (office). *Website:* www.jreast.co.jp (office).

SEIP, Anne-Lise, DPhil; Norwegian historian and academic; *Professor Emerita of Modern History, University of Oslo;* b. 6 Nov. 1933, Bergen; d. of Edvin Thomassen and Birgit Thomassen; m. Jens Arup Seip 1960 (died 1992); one s. one d.; ed Univ. of Oslo; Rep., Bærum Council 1964–71; Sr Lecturer Inst. of Criminology and Penal Law, Univ. of Oslo 1974–75, Dept of History 1975–85, Prof. of Modern History 1985, now Prof. Emer.; mem. Broadcasting Council 1974–81; mem. Norwegian Acad. of Science, Det kongelige danske videnskabernes selskab. *Publications include:* Videnskap og virkelighet T.H. Asehehoug 1974, Eilert Sundt. 1983, Sosialhjelpstaten blir til 1984, Veier til velferdsstaten 1994, Norges historie, Vol. 8 1830–70 1997, Demringstid. Johan Sebastian Welhaven og nasjonen 2007; numerous articles. *Leisure interests:* books, music, gardening. *Address:* Gamle Drammensvei 144, 1363 Høvik, Norway (home). *Telephone:* 67-53-40-39 (home).

SEITERS, Rudolf; German politician; *President, German Red Cross;* b. 13 Oct. 1937, Osnabrück; s. of Adolf Seiters and Josefine Gördel; m. Brigitte Kolata; three c.; ed Univ. of Münster; qualified as lawyer; joined Junge Union and CDU 1958, Regional Chair. Junge Union, Osnabrück-Emsland 1963–65, Chair. CDU Land Asscn Hanover 1965–68, mem. Junge Union Fed. Exec. Cttee 1967–71, Sr Chair. CDU Land Asscn Lower Saxony 1968–70; Head Econ. and Housing Dept, Office of Regierungspräsident (Regional Gov.), Osnabrück 1967–69; mem. Deutscher Bundestag 1969–; mem. CDU Fed. Exec. Cttee 1971–73; Parl. Party Man. CDU/Christian Social Union (CSU) Parl. Party in Bundestag 1971–76, Sr Parl. Man. 1984–89; Parl. Party Man. 1982–84; Fed. Minister for Special Tasks and Head of Fed. Chancellery 1989–91, of the Interior 1991–93; Deputy Chair. CDU/CSU in Bundestag 1994–; Vice-Pres. Bundestag 1998–2002; Pres. German Red Cross 2003–17; Hon. Dr rer. pol; Grosses Bundesverdienstkreuz mit Stern 1995, Grosses Silbernes Ehrenzeichen (Austria) 1995, Officier, Légion d'honneur 1996, Grosses Verdienstkreuz mit Stern 2018, Schulterband des Verdienstordens der Bundesrepublik Deutschland 2018; Dr Rainer-Hildebrandt-Medaille 2008. *Publications include:* Aussenpolitik im 21. Jahrhundert 1996, In der Spur Bleiben 2005, Vertrauensverhältnisse 2016. *Address:* Deutschen Roten Kreuzes Generalsekretariat, Carstenstr. 58, 12205 Berlin, Germany (office). *Telephone:* (30) 85404275 (office). *E-mail:* praesidium@drk.de (office). *Website:* www.drk.de (office).

SEITZ, John N., BSc, MSc; American geologist and petroleum industry executive; *Chairman and CEO, GulfSlope Energy, Inc.;* ed Univ. of Pittsburgh, Rensselaer Polytechnic Inst., Univ. of Pennsylvania Wharton School of Business; Sr Exploration Geologist, Anadarko Petroleum Corpn 1977–82, Chief Geologist 1982–83, Gen. Man. 1983–89, Vice-Pres. of Exploration and Production 1989–95, Sr Vice-Pres. of Exploration 1995–97, Exec. Vice-Pres. of Exploration and Production 1997–99, mem. Bd of Dirs 1997–2003, Pres. and COO 1999–, then CEO –2003; f. North Sea Oil Ventures 2003; Co-founder Endeavour Int. (cr. after merger of North Sea Oil Ventures and Continental Southern Resources), Houston, Tex 2003, Co-CEO 2003–06, then Vice-Chair.; Chair. and CEO GulfSlope Energy, Inc. 2013–, Chief Financial Officer 2013–14; mem. Bd of Dirs ION Geophysical Corpn 2003–, Constellation Energy Partners LLC 2004–, Gulf United Energy 2011–, Input/Output Inc., Elk Resources Inc., Casa Exploration. LLC; mem. Advisory Bd Spindletop; mem. American Asscn of Petroleum Geologists, Geological Soc. of America, American Inst. of Professional Geologists, Houston Geological Soc., Soc. of Petroleum Engineers; Trustee, American Geosciences Inst. Foundation. *Address:* GulfSlope Energy, Inc., 2500 CityWest Blvd, Suite 800, Houston, TX 77042, USA (office). *Telephone:* (281) 918-4100 (office). *Website:* www.gulfslope.com (office).

SEITZ, Konrad, MA, DrPhil; German diplomatist (retd) and writer; b. 18 Jan. 1934, Munich; m. Eva Kautz 1965; ed Univ. of Marburg, The Fletcher School of Law and Diplomacy, Tufts Univ., USA; Prof. of Classics, Univs of Marburg and Munich 1956–64; entered Foreign Office 1965; served in New Delhi 1968–72, UN Mission, New York 1972–75; main speech writer for Minister of Foreign Affairs 1975; Head, Policy Planning Staff, Foreign Office 1980–87; Amb. to India 1987–90; Co-Chair. Comm. Economy 2000, Baden-Württemberg 1992–93; Amb. to Italy

1992–95, to China 1995–99; Grosses Bundesverdienstkreuz 1996, Baden-Württemberg Medal of Honour 1998. *Publications include:* The Japanese-American Challenge: Germany's Hi-tech Industries Fight for Survival 1990, The Aimless Elites: Are the Germans Losing the Future? (with others), Europa: Una Colonia Tecnológica? 1995, Race into the 21st Century: The Future of Europe Between America and Africa 1998, China: A World Power Comes Back 2000, Mughal and Deccani Painting (co-author) 2010; contribs to foreign and econ. journals and newspapers. *Leisure interests:* history of ideas, literature, art, collecting Indian miniature paintings. *Address:* Dahlienweg 4, 53343 Wachtberg-Pech, Germany. *Telephone:* (228) 327811. *Fax:* (228) 9325154. *E-mail:* k.seitz@freenet.de.

SEITZ, Hon. Raymond George Hardenbergh; American fmr diplomatist and business executive; b. 8 Dec. 1940, Honolulu, Hawaii; m. Caroline Gordon Richardson; two s. one d.; ed Yale Univ.; joined Foreign Service 1966, served as Political Officer in Montreal, Political Officer, Embassy in Nairobi, also Vice-Consul, Seychelles 1968–70; Prin. Officer, Bukavu, Zaire 1970–72; served on Secretariat Staff, Washington, DC 1972 then Dir of Staff; Special Asst to Dir-Gen. Foreign Service 1974; Political Officer, London 1975–79; Deputy Exec. Sec., Dept of State 1979–81, Sr Deputy Asst Sec. for Public Affairs 1981–82, Exec. Asst to Sec. Shultz 1982–84; Minister, Embassy in London 1984–89; Asst Sec. of State for European and Canadian Affairs 1989–91; Amb. to UK 1991–94 (retd); Vice-Chair. Lehman Bros. Int. (Europe) (now Lehman Bros. Europe Ltd) 1995–2003; Chair. (non-exec.) Sun-Times Media Group Inc., Chicago 2003–08; mem. Bd of Dirs Chubb Corpn 1994–2007, British Airways PLC 1995–2002, Cable and Wireless 1995–, Rio Tinto 1996–2003, Authoriszor Inc. 1999–, PCCW Ltd 2005–, Marconi PLC, Hollinger Int.; Contributing Ed. Conde Nast Traveller magazine (UK) 2004–; Trustee, Nat. Gallery 1996–2001; fmr Trustee, Royal Acad. of Arts and the World Monuments Fund; Gov. Ditchley Foundation; Hon. DUniv (Herriot-Watt) 1994, Dr hc (Open Univ.) 1997, received several hon. degrees from Univs of Durham, Newcastle upon Tyne, Bath, Buckingham, Royal Holloway, Leeds, Reading Univ., Leicester Univ.; Presidential Award 1986, 1988, Benjamin Franklin Medal 1995, Churchill Medal of Honour 1999, Freedom of the City of London 1999. *Publication:* Over Here 2001.

SEJDIU, Fatmir, PhD; Kosovo politician, academic and fmr head of state; b. 23 Oct. 1951, Pakashticë/Pakaštica, nr Podujevë/Podujevo; m. Nezafete Sejdiu; three c.; ed Univ. of Prishtina; Prof. of Law, Univ. of Prishtina; mem. Ass. of Kosovo –2006, fmr mem. Cttee for Rules and Procedures of Ass., Cttee for Int. Cooperation and EU Integration; Pres. of Kosovo 2006–10 (resgnd); mem. Democratic League of Kosovo, Chair. –2010; Skanderbeg's Order (Albania); Dr hc (Tirana). *Publications:* The History of State and Law (co-author) 2000, 2005, Agrarian Politics as an Instrument of National Repression (monograph) 2000, Constitutional Framework of Kosovo (co-author) 2001, Glossary of Parliamentary and Legal Terms (co-author) 2005. *Address:* Lidhja Demokratike e Kosovës, 10000 Prishtina, Kompleksi Qafa, Kosovo (office). *Telephone:* (38) 242242 (office). *Fax:* (38) 245305 (office). *E-mail:* info@ldk-ks.eu (office). *Website:* www.ldk-ks.eu (office).

SEJIMA, Kazuyo, MArch; Japanese architect; *Principal, SANAA/Kazuyo Sejima & Ryue Nishizawa Associates;* b. 29 Oct. 1956, Ibaraki Pref.; ed Japan Women's Univ.; worked for Toyo Ito Architect & Assocs 1981–87; f. Kazuyo Sejima & Assocs 1987; Founder and Prin. (with Ryue Nishizawa), SANAA Ltd/Kazuyo Sejima & Ryue Nishizawa Assocs 1995–; apptd Dir of Architecture Sector Venice Biennale 2010; teacher, Dept of Architecture, Univ. of Illinois, USA; Officier de l'Ordre des Arts et des Lettres 2009; Winner, Competition for MCH House 1990, Second Prize, Nasunogahara Harmony Hall Design Competition 1991, Second Prize, GID Competition 1992, Second Prize, Commercial Space Design Award 1992, Young Architect of the Year, Japan Inst. of Architects 1992, Grand Prize, Commercial Space Design 1994, Architect of the Year 1994, Vincenzo Scamozzi Architecture Award 2003, Rolf Schock Prize in Visual Arts (with Ryue Nishizawa) 2005, Minister of Education's Art Encouragement Prize 2006, StellaRe Prize 2009, Pritzker Prize (with Ryue Nishizawa) 2010. *Works include:* MCH House (Kajima Prize, SD Review) 1990, Platform One Katsuura, Platform Two Yamanashi, Platform Three Tokyo, Castelbajac Sports Store, Saishunkan Seiyaku Women's Dormitory (Kenneth F. Brown Asia Pacific Culture and Architecture Award, Univ. of Hawaii 1995), Pachinko Parlors I, II & III (Grand Prize, Commercial Space Design Award 1994), Y-House Katsuura, Chino Villa in the Forest, Police Box at Chofu Station, N-House Kumamoto, Yokohama Int. Port Terminal, Apartment Bldg in Gifu, Expo Tokyo 96, Oogaki Multi Media Studio, U Office Building, Small House, Kozankaku Student Residence, hhstyle.com Store, Asahi Shimbun Yamagata Office Bldg, House in a Plum Grove (Japan Architecture Award 2006), Onishi Civic Center, Theater and Artscentre, Almere, The Netherlands, New Museum, New York City, Shibaura House, Louvre-Lens, Lens, France, Sumida Hokusai Museum. *Exhibitions include:* Nat. Panasonic Gallery, Tokyo 1989, Artpolis, Kumamoto 1992, Sezon Museum 1993, MA Gallery, Tokyo 1993, Nat. Museum of Modern Art, Seoul, Korea 1994. *Address:* SANAA Ltd/Kazuyo Sejima, Ryue Nishizawa & Associates, 7-A Shinagawa-Soko, 2-2-35 Higashi-Shinagawa, Shinagawa-ku, 140 Tokyo, Japan. *Telephone:* (3) 34501757. *E-mail:* sanaa@sanaa.co.jp.

SEJKO, Gent; Albanian economist and central banker; *Governor, Bank of Albania (Banka e Shqipërisë);* ed Univ. of Tirana, Univ. of Glasgow, Scotland; Head of Credit Div., Nat. Commercial Bank 1992; Insp., Supervision Dept, Bank of Albania (Banka e Shqipërisë) 1993–95, Supt 1997–98, Head of Div. for On-Site Examinations 2002–04; Audit Man., Deloitte & Touche 1998–2000; Head of Internal Audit and Compliance Div., American Bank of Albania 2001–02; Head of Internal Audit Div., Raiffeisen Bank Albania 2004–06, Dir-Gen., Raiffesen Leasing Albania 2006–08, Head of Corp. Banking 2008–10; Deputy Gen. Man. and Head of Retail Dept and Branches Network, Societe Generale 2010–15; Gov. Bank of Albania (Banka e Shqipërisë) 2015–, also Chair. Supervisory Council, mem. Bd of Govs IMF. *Address:* Bank of Albania (Banka e Shqipërisë), Sheshi Skënderbej 1, 1001 Tirana, Albania (office). *Telephone:* (4) 2419301 (office). *Fax:* (4) 2419408 (office). *E-mail:* public@bankofalbania.org (office). *Website:* www .bankofalbania.org (office).

SEKERAMAYI, Sydney Tigere, MB, ChB, DTM; Zimbabwean politician; b. 30 March 1944; m.; fmr govt positions include Minister for Lands and Resettlement, Minister of State Security, Energy Minister, Intelligence Dir; Minister of Defence 2001–09, 2013–17; mem. Parl. (Zanu-PF) for Marondera E 2005–08; Senator from Marondera-Hwedza 2008–09; Minister of State for Nat. Security 2009–13. *Address:* c/o Ministry of Defence, Defence House, cnr Kwame Nkuruma and 3rd Streets, Harare, Zimbabwe (office).

ŠEKERINSKA JANKOVSKA, Radmilla, BSc, MA; Macedonian politician; *Deputy Prime Minister and Minister of Defence;* b. 10 June 1972, Skopje, Socialist Repub. of Macedonia, Socialist Fed. Repub. of Yugoslavia; d. of Aleksandar Šekerinski and Jelena Šekerinska; m. Bozidar Jankovski; ed Skopje Univ., Fletcher School of Law and Diplomacy, Tufts Univ., USA; fmr Public Relations Asst, Open Soc. Inst.; Asst, Faculty of Electrical Eng, Skopje Univ.; started political career with Social Democratic Youth of Macedonia 1992, Pres. 1995; mem. Skopje City Council 1996–98; mem. Parl. 1998–2002, 2006–, Ass. Del. to Inter-Parl. Union, Ass. Group for Cooperation with the European Parl. 1998–2002; Deputy Prime Minister, with responsibility for European Integration 2002–06, 2017–, Acting Prime Minister Nov.–Dec. 2004; Deputy Coordinator, Spokesperson and mem. Socijaldemokratski Sojuz na Makedonija (Social Democratic Alliance of Macedonia), Vice-Chair., Chair. 2006–08, now Vice-Pres.; Pres. Nat. Council for European Integration 2007–14; Minister of Defence 2017–; mem. Advisory Council Acad. for Cultural Diplomacy; Young Global Leader, World Econ. Forum 2004. *Publications include:* scientific articles. *Address:* Ministry of Defence, 1000 Skopje, North Macedonia (office). *Telephone:* (2) 3282042 (office). *Fax:* (2) 3283991 (office). *E-mail:* info@morm.gov.mk (office). *Website:* www.morm.gov.mk (office).

SEKHAMANE, Tlohang, BA.Ed, MPhil; Lesotho government official; b. 30 May 1955, Mokhotlong; m.; two c.; ed Nat. Univ. of Lesotho, Univ. of Cambridge, UK; began career as Clerk, Vaal Reefs Mines, Orkney, S Africa 1976; Group Supervisor for data collection, Thaba-Tseka Rural Devt Project 1979; Headmaster, Mapholaneng High School, Mokhotlong 1982–85; Sr Curriculum Officer, Nat. Curriculum Devt Centre 1986; Asst Private Sec. to King Moshoeshoe II 1986–90; Lecturer, Nat. Univ. of Lesotho 1991, Head, Dept of Devt Studies, also mem. Senate and mem. Council 1994–95; Dir Nat. Teacher Training Coll. 1991–93; Educ. Officer, UNICEF 1995–97; Sr Consultant and Acting Dir, Inst. of Devt Studies 1997, Country Dir 1998–2000; Prin. Sec., Ministry of Educ. 2000–01; Govt Sec. and Head of the Public Service 2001–15; mem. Nat. Ass. for Mokhotlong 2012–; Minister of Foreign Affairs and Int. Relations 2015–17; mem. Democratic Congress, mem. Nat. Exec. Cttee. *Address:* c/o Ministry of Foreign Affairs and International Relations, Qhobosheaneng Government Complex, Griffith Hill Road, POB 1387, Maseru 100, Lesotho (office).

SEKIGUCHI, Ken-ichi; Japanese insurance industry executive; *Senior Advisor, Meiji Yasuda Life Insurance Company;* Gen. Man. Aomori Br. Meiji Yasuda Life Insurance Co. 1994–96, Gen. Man. Int. Investment Dept, Meiji Yasuda Life Insurance Co. 1996–97, Gen. Man. Global Investment Dept 1997–2000, Gen. Man. Financial Planning Dept 2000–03, later Man. Dir, mem. Bd of Dirs 1999–, Chair. and Rep. Exec. Officer 2005–13, Sr Advisor 2013–, mem. Nominating Cttee, Compensation Cttee, Chief Exec. New Market Devt; mem. Bd Dirs UBS Wealth Man., USA (fmrly Paine Webber Group Inc.) 1999–. *Address:* Meiji Yasuda Life Insurance Co., 1-1, Marunouchi 2-chome, Chiyoda-ku, Tokyo 100-0005, Japan (office). *Telephone:* (3) 3283-8293 (office). *Fax:* (3) 3215-8123 (office). *E-mail:* info@meijiyasuda.co.jp (office). *Website:* www.meijiyasuda.co.jp (office).

SEKIMIZU, Koji, BS, MS; Japanese engineer and fmr international organization official; b. 3 Dec. 1952, Yokohama; m.; one s. one d.; ed Osaka Univ.; joined Ministry of Transport 1977, Ship Inspector 1977–79, Tech. Official 1979–80, Special Tech. Researcher, Shipbuilding Research Asscn 1981–82, Deputy Dir Environment Div. 1982–84; Deputy Dir, Second Int. Orgs Div., Econ. Affairs Bureau, Ministry of Foreign Affairs 1984–86; Deputy Dir Safety Standards Div., Maritime Tech. and Safety Bureau, Ministry of Transport 1986–89; Tech. Official, Maritime Safety Div., IMO 1989–97, Sr Deputy Dir Marine Environment Div. 1997–2000, Dir Marine Environment Div. 2000–04, Dir Maritime Safety Div. 2004–12, Sec.-Gen. IMO 2012–15; mem. Japan Soc. of Naval Architects and Ocean Engineers; Fellow, Royal Inst. of Naval Architects; Hon. mem. Int. Fed. of Shipmasters' Asscns 2012, Master Mariners Asscn, Gdynia (Poland) 2014; Order of Maritime Merit (France) 2014; Dr hc (Batumi State Maritime Acad., Georgia) 2012, (Nikola Vaptsarov Naval Acad., Varna, Bulgaria) 2014; Golden Anchor Award for Lifetime Achievement (Turkey) 2012, Halert C. Shepherd Award American Chamber of Shipping 2013. *Publications:* The Marine Electronic Highway in the Straits of Malacca and Singapore – An Innovative Project for the Management of Highly Congested and Confined Waters 2001, GESAMP and GMA – Constructing a New System for Evaluation of the Marine Environment 2003, Marine Electronic Highway Project as a New Management System for Sea Areas 2004. *Leisure interests:* golf, playing guitar, composing songs. *Address:* c/o International Maritime Organization, 4 Albert Embankment, London, SE1 7SR, England (office).

SEKIZAWA, Tadashi, BEng; Japanese business executive; *Senior Executive Adviser, Fujitsu Ltd;* b. 6 Nov. 1931, Tokyo; m. Misako Sekizawa; two s.; ed Tokyo Univ.; joined Fujitsu Ltd 1954, Gen. Man. Switching Systems Group 1982–84, Bd Dir 1984, Man. Dir 1986–88, Exec. Dir 1988–90, apptd Pres. and Rep. Dir 1990, later Chair., currently Sr Exec. Adviser; Vice-Chair. Communication Industry Asscn of Japan 1990–98, apptd Chair. 1998, Japan Electronic Industry Devt Asscn 1990. *Leisure interests:* literature, travel, motoring. *Address:* Fujitsu Ltd, Shiodome City Center, 1-5-2, Higashi-Shimbashi, Minato-ku, Tokyo 105-7123, Japan (office). *Telephone:* (3) 6252-2220 (office). *Fax:* (3) 6252-2783 (office). *Website:* www.fujitsu.com (office).

ŠEKS, Vladimir, LLB; Croatian lawyer and politician; b. 1 Jan. 1943, Osijek; m. Anica Resler-Šeks; one s. one d.; ed Univ. of Zagreb; trainee, Municipal Public Prosecutors Office, Vinkovci 1967–69; Deputy Municipal Public Prosecutor, Vinkovci 1970; Municipal Court Judge, Osijek 1970–71; Deputy Regional Public Prosecutor, Osijek 1971; barrister in prt. law firm 1972–81; sentenced to seven-month prison term for conspiracy against the state 1981; mem. Croatian Democratic Union (Hrvatska demokratska zajednica—HDZ), Vice-Chair. 1989–91, 1995–99, Chair. Rep. Group 1995, Acting Chair. Jan.–April 2000, Chair. Parl. Group 2000, Deputy Chair. Cen. Cttee 2002–03; elected mem. Sabor (Parl.) 1990, Deputy Pres. 1992–2000, Pres. 2003–08; Public Prosecutor of Croatia 1992; Chair. State Amnesty Comm. 1996–2000; Chair. Cttee on Constitutional Affairs

1990–92, Deputy Chair. 1995–99; mem. Defence and Nat. Security Council 1995–99, Council for Strategic Decisions of the Pres. 1995–99; Founder and Co-Chair. Yugoslav Helsinki Cttee 1987; mem. Amnesty International; Grand Order of King Dmitar Zvonimir, Order of Ante Starčević, Order of Stjepan Radić, Order of the Croatian Trefoil, Vukovar Medal, Veleredom kralja Petra Krešimira IV. s lentom i Danicom 2008. *Publications include:* Expression of Opinion Treated as Offence, Contemplations on the Freedom of Conscience, Dangerous Times, Reminiscences from Prison; over 20 professional papers on law and politics. *Address:* Hrvatska demokratska zajednica (Croatia Democratic Union), trg Žrtava fašizma 4, 10000 Zagreb, Croatia (office). *Telephone:* (1) 4553000 (office). *Fax:* (1) 4552600 (office). *E-mail:* hdz@hdz.hr (office). *Website:* www.hdz.hr (office).

SELA, Michael, PhD; Israeli immunologist, chemist and academic; *W. Garfield Weston Chair of Immunology, Weizmann Institute of Science;* b. (Mieczysław Salomonowicz), 6 March 1924, Tomaszow, Poland; s. of Jakob Salomonowicz and Roza Salomonowicz; m. 1st Margalit Liebman 1948 (died 1975); two d.; m. 2nd Sara Kika 1976; one d.; ed Hebrew Univ., Jerusalem and Univ. of Geneva, Switzerland; joined Weizmann Inst. of Science 1950, Head Dept of Chemical Immunology 1963–75, Vice-Pres. 1970–71, Dean Faculty of Biology 1970–73, mem. Bd of Govs 1970–, Pres. 1975–85, Deputy Chair. 1985–, W. Garfield Weston Prof. of Immunology 1966–, currently also W. Garfield Weston Chair of Immunology; Visiting Scientist, NIH, Bethesda 1956–57, 1960–61; Visiting Prof. of Molecular Biology, Univ. of Calif., Berkeley 1967–68; Visiting Prof., Dept of Medicine, Tufts Univ. School of Medicine, Boston 1986–87; Inst. Prof. 1985; Fogarty Scholar-in-Residence, Fogarty Int. Center, Bethesda, Maryland 1973–74; mem. WHO Expert Advisory Panel of Immunology 1962–; Chair. Council, European Molecular Biology Org. 1975–79; Pres. Int. Union Immunological Socs 1977–80; Chair. Scientific Advisory Cttee European Molecular Biology Lab., Heidelberg 1978–81; WHO Advisory Cttee on Medical Research 1979–82, WHO Special Programme for Research and Training in Tropical Diseases 1979–81; mem. Council Paul Ehrlich Foundation (Frankfurt) 1980–97; mem. Advisory Bd UCLAF, France 1980–92; Founding mem. Bd of Dir Int. Foundation for Survival and Devt of Humanity, Moscow and Washington, DC 1988–92; Nat. mem. Gen. Cttee Int. Council of Scientific Unions 1984–93; mem. Scientific Advisory Group of Experts, Programme for Vaccine Devt, WHO 1987–92; mem. Int. Guidance Panel, Israel Arts and Science Acad. 1987–; Vice-Pres. Asscn Franco-Israélienne pour Recherche Scientifique et Technologique 1992–98; mem. Exec. Bd Int. Council of Human Duties, Trieste 1995–; mem. other int. bodies; serves on many editorial bds, including Exec. Advisory Bd of Dictionary for Science and Tech. 1989–, Ed. Acad. of the Int. Journal of Molecular Medicine 1997, Int. Advisory Bd of Russian Journal of Immunology 2000, Int. Ed. Bd Reviews in Auto-immunity 2001, Cambridge Encyclopedia of the Life Sciences, Handbook of Biochemistry and Molecular Biology, Experimental and Clinical Immunogenetics, Receptor Biology Reviews, Encyclopedia of Human Biology, Encyclopedia of the Life Sciences; mem. Israel Acad. of Sciences and Humanities 1971, Pontifical Acad. of Sciences 1975, Deutsche Akad. der Naturforscher Leopoldina 1989; Foreign mem. Max-Planck Soc., Freiburg 1967, French Acad. of Sciences 1995, French Acad. of Medicine 2008; Active mem. European Acad. of Sciences and Arts 2004; Foreign Assoc. NAS 1976, Russian Acad. of Sciences 1994, Italian Acad. of Sciences 1995, American Philosophical Soc. 1995; Fellow, Polish Acad. of Arts and Sciences 1998; Hon. mem. American Soc. Biological Chemists 1968, American Asscn of Immunologists 1973, Scandinavian Soc. for Immunology 1971, Harvey Soc. 1972, French Soc. for Immunology 1979, Chilean Soc. for Immunology 1981, Romanian Acad. 1991, Romanian Acad. of Medical Sciences 1991, Romanian Soc. for Immunology; Foreign Hon. mem. American Acad. Arts and Sciences 1971; Hon. Fellow, The Open Univ. of Israel 2004; Commdr's Cross of Order of Merit Award (FRG) 1986, Officier, Légion d'honneur 1987, Commdr 2011, Caballero, Order of San Carlos (Colombia) 1997, Gran Ufficiale of Italian Solidarity Star 2007; Dr hc (Bordeaux II) 1985, (Nat. Autonomous Univ. of Mexico) 1985, (Tufts Univ.) 1989, Colby Coll. 1989, (Univ. Louis Pasteur) 1990, (Hebrew Univ. of Jerusalem) 1995, (Tel-Aviv) 1999, (Ben Gurion Univ. of the Negev) 2001; awarded NIH Lectureship 1973; Israel Prize Natural Sciences 1959, Rothschild Prize for Chem. 1968, Otto Warburg Medal, German Soc. of Biological Chem. 1968, Emil von Behring Prize, Phillipps Univ. 1972, Gairdner Int. Award, Toronto 1980, Prize, Inst. de la Vie Fondation Electricité de France, Lille 1984, Prix Jaubert, Faculty of Science, Univ. of Geneva 1986, Interbrew-Baillet Latour Health Prize 1997, Karl Landsteiner Medal, Toronto 1986, Albert Einstein Gold Medal 1995, Harnak Medal, Max-Planck-Soc. 1996, Wolf Prize in Medicine 1998. *Publications include:* more than 800 in immunology, biochemistry and molecular biology; Ed. The Antigens (seven vols published). *Address:* Weizmann Institute of Science, Wolfson Building for Biological Research, Room no 708, Rehovot, 76100, Israel (office). *Telephone:* (8) 9344021 (office); (8) 9344022 (office); (8) 9471132 (home). *Fax:* (8) 9469713 (office). *E-mail:* michael.sela@weizmann.ac.il (office). *Website:* www.weizmann.ac.il/immunology/SelaPub.html (office).

SELANGOR, HRH The Sultan of; Tuanku Sharafuddin Idris Shah Salahuddin Abdul Aziz Shah, DK; Malaysian; b. 24 Dec. 1945, Klang; s. of Sultan Salahuddin Abdul Aziz Shah and Raja Shaidatul Ihsan binti Tengku Badar Shah; m. 1st Raja Zarina binti Raja Zainul 1968 (divorced 1986); m. 2nd Lisa Davis (Puan Nur Lisa Abdullah) 1988 (divorced 1997); two d. one s.; m. 3rd Norashikin Abdul Rahman Tengku Permaisuri Norashikin; ed Hale School, Perth, Australia and Langhurst Coll., Surrey, England; fmr Regent of Selangor, proclaimed ninth Sultan of Selangor on the death of his father Nov. 2001; held various admin. posts in state and fed. govt services, including Selangor State Secr., Dist Office and Royal Malaysian Police Dept, Kuala Lumpur 1968–; mem. The Conf. of Rulers, Malaysia; Pro-Chancellor Universiti Teknologi MARA 2000–05; Captain-in Chief, Captain, Royal Malaysian Navy 2001, Captain-in Chief, Rear Admiral 2002; Chancellor Universiti Putra Malaysia 2002–; Chair. Semi-Professional Football Asscn; Chair. Bd of Trustees Yayasan Seni Selangor (Selangor Art Foundation), Galeri Shah Alam; Patron Malaysian branch of the Royal Asiatic Soc., Royal Selangor Club; circumnavigated the world on his yacht, S. Y. Jugra 1995–96; participated in Peking to Paris Challenge vintage car race 1997; Hon. Life Pres. Selangor Football Asscn, Hon. Major, Rejimen Askar Wataniah 1974, Hon. Commdr, Royal Malaysian Navy Volunteer Reserve 1998; recipient of multiple decorations Kt Grand Commdr of the Order of the Crown of Johor, Johor 1975, Grand Master of the Order of Sultan Salahuddin Abdul Aziz Shah, Selangor 2001, Royal Family Order of Perak, Perak 2002, Order of the Crown of the Realm, Malaysia 2003, Perlis Family Order of the Gallant Prince Syed Putra Jamalullail, Perlis 2005, Commdr Order of the Legion of Honour, France 2012; Dr hc (Universiti Teknologi MARA) 2001. *Website:* www.selangor.gov.my.

SELBORNE, 4th Earl, cr. 1882; **John Roundell Palmer,** GBE, BA, MA, FRS, FIBiol, FLS; British peer and business executive; b. 24 March 1940, Henstridge, England; s. of Capt. William Palmer, Viscount Wolmer and Priscilla Egerton-Warburton; m. Joanna van Antwerp James 1969; three s. one d.; ed Eton Coll., Christ Church, Oxford; Man. Dir Blackmoor Estate Ltd 1962–2005; Treas. King Edward's School, Witley 1972–83; Chair. Hops Marketing Bd 1978–82, Agricultural and Food Research Council 1983–89; Pres. Royal Agricultural Soc. of England 1987–88; Chair. Jt Nature Conservation Cttee 1991–97; Chair. House of Lords Select Cttee on Science and Tech. 1993–97, 2014–; mem. Govt Panel on Sustainable Devt 1994–97; Chair. AMC 1994–2002, UK Chemical Stakeholder Forum 2000–09; Dir Lloyds TSB Group 1995–2006; Chancellor Univ. of Southampton 1996–2006; Pres. Royal Agricultural Soc. of England 1987–88, Royal Inst. of Public Health and Hygiene 1991–97, Royal Geographical Soc. (with Inst. of British Geographers) 1997–2000; Vice-Pres. Royal Soc. for the Protection of Birds 1996–2007; elected Hereditary mem. House of Lords 1999–, Chair. Sub-cttee D (Agric. and Environment), House of Lords EU Select Cttee 1999–2003; Chair. Bd of Trustees, Royal Botanic Gardens, Kew 2003–09; Chair. Council of the Foundation for Science and Tech. 2006–18, Rank Prize Funds 1992–2014; mem. World Comm. on the Ethics of Science and Tech., UNESCO 1999–2003; Patron Inst. of Ecology and Environmental Man.; Fellow, Inst. of Biology; Conservative; Master of the Worshipful Co. of Mercers 1989; Hon. LLD (Bristol) 1988; Hon. DSc (Cranfield) 1991, (East Anglia) 1996, (Southampton) 1996, (Birmingham) 2000; Massey-Ferguson Nat. Award for Services to UK Agric. 1990. *Address:* House of Lords, Westminster, London, SW1A 0PW (office); Temple Manor, Selborne, Alton, Hants., GU34 3LR, England (home). *Telephone:* (20) 7219-6171 (office); (1420) 473646 (home). *E-mail:* selbornejr@gmail.com (home); selbornejr@parliament.uk (office).

SELEŠ, Monica; American/Hungarian (born Yugoslav) fmr professional tennis player; b. 2 Dec. 1973, Novi Sad, Yugoslavia (now Serbia and Montenegro); d. of Karolj Seleš and Ester Seleš; moved to USA 1986; became US citizen 1994; semi-finalist, French Open 1989; won French Open 1990, 1991, 1992; Virginia Slims Championships 1990, 1991, 1992; US Open 1991, 1992; Australian Open 1991, 1992, 1993, 1996; Canadian Open 1995, 1996; winner LA Open 1997, Canadian Open 1997, Tokyo Open 1997; bronze medal Olympic Games, Sydney 2000; quarter-finalist, Wimbledon Championships 1990; off court for over two years after being stabbed by spectator during Hamburg quarter-final 1993; 59 WTA Tour titles, nine Grand Slam titles and US $14,891,762 in prize money; mem. winning US Fed. Cup team 1996, 1999, 2000; retd 2008; partner, the All-Star Café; Goodwill Amb. of Laureus Sports Foundation, Intergovernmental Inst. for the use of Microalgae Spirulina Against Malnutrition; Ted Tinling Diamond Award 1990, Associated Press Athlete of the Year 1990–91, Tennis Magazine Comeback Player of the Year 1995, Flo Hyman Award 2000, Sanex Hero of the Year award 2002, elected to Int. Tennis Hall of Fame 2009. *Publication:* Monica: From Fear to Victory 1996, Getting A Grip: On My Body, My Mind, My Self 2009. *Leisure interests:* ice skating, horse riding, basketball, guitar, swimming, reading autobiographies. *Address:* c/o International Management Group, 1360 E, 9th Street, Suite 100, Cleveland, OH 44114, USA.

SELF, Colin Ernest, DFA; British artist; b. 17 July 1941, Rackheath; s. of Ernest Walter Self and Kathleen Augustine Self (née Bellamy); m. 1st Margaret Ann Murrell 1963; m. 2nd Jessica Prendergast 1978; one s. two d.; ed Norwich Art School, Slade School of Fine Art, London Univ.; Drawing Prize, Biennale de Paris 1967, Giles Bequest Prize, Bradford Biennale 1969, Tolly Cobbold Prize 1979. *Leisure interests:* nature study, music. *Address:* c/o James Hyman Gallery, 16 Savile Row, London, W1S 3PL; 31 St Andrew's Avenue, Thorpe, Norwich, NR7 0RG, England. *Website:* www.jameshymangallery.com/artists/4650/biography/colin-self.

SELF, William (Will) Woodward, MA; British writer, cartoonist and academic; b. 26 Sept. 1961, London; s. of Peter John Otter Self and Elaine Rosenbloom; m. 1st Katharine Sylvia Anthony Chancellor 1989 (divorced 1996); one s. one d.; m. 2nd Deborah Jane Orr 1997; two s.; ed Christ's Coll., Exeter Coll., Oxford; cartoon illustrations appeared in New Statesman and City Limits 1982–88; Publishing Dir Cathedral Publishing 1988–90; Contributing Ed. London Evening Standard magazine 1993–95; columnist, The Observer 1995–97, The Times 1997–99, Ind. on Sunday 2000–, Evening Standard 2002–, The Independent 2003–; Prof. of Contemporary Thought, Brunel Univ. 2012–; Geoffrey Faber Memorial Prize 1992. *Publications:* short stories: Quantity Theory of Insanity 1991, Grey Area 1994, A Story for Europe 1996, Tough Tough Toys for Tough Tough Boys 1998, Dr Mukti and Other Tales of Woe 2003, Liver 2008; novellas: Cock and Bull 1992, The Sweet Smell of Psychosis 1996; novels: My Idea of Fun 1993, Great Apes 1997, How the Dead Live 2000, Perfidious Man 2000, Feeding Frenzy 2001, Dorian 2002, Dr Mukti 2004, The Book of Dave 2006, Umbrella 2012, Shark 2014, Phone 2017; non-fiction: Junk Mail (selected journalism) 1995, Sore Sites (collected journalism) 2000, Psychogeography (collected journalism) 2007, The Butt 2008, Psycho Too (with Ralph Steadman) 2009, Walking to Hollywood 2010; collected cartoons 1985. *Leisure interest:* walking. *Address:* c/o The Wylie Agency, 17 Bedford Square, London, WC1B 3BA, England (office); Gaskell Building, 134 Brunel University, Uxbridge, UB8 3PH, England. *E-mail:* will.self@brunel.ac.uk; info@will-self.com. *Website:* will-self.com.

SÉLI, Mbogo Ngabo, MSc; Chadian banking executive and government official; b. 12 Aug. 1975, N'Djamena; m.; four c.; ed Univ. of Ouagadougou; Asst to Dir-Gen., Loterie Nationale Burkinabé (LONAB), Ouagoudougou 1999–2000, Dir LONAB 2000–02; Dir and Chair., Audit Cttee, Commercial Bank Tchad 2001–13; Head of Documentation, Publications and Website Admin, Banque des Etats de l'Afrique centrale (BEAC), Yaoundé 2002–06, with Office of the Gov., BEAC 2006–09; with Marketing Dept, Banque Int. d'Industrie et l'Agriculture du Burkina Faso 2008–09; Chef de Cabinet to Minister of Finance and the Budget 2010–13, to Minister of Urban Affairs, Housing and Land Devt 2013–14; Deputy Dir-Gen., Société Générale du Tchad 2014–15; Minister of Land Use and Urban Affairs 2015–16, of Finance and the Budget 2016–17; Dir for Chad, Fonds Africain de garantie et de coopération Economique 2012–13; Dir (representing Minister of Finance and the Budget), Musée National N'Djamena 2012–13.

SELIGMAN, Joel, AB, JD; American lawyer, academic and university administrator; b. 11 Jan. 1950, New York, NY; m. 2nd Delores Conway 2012; one s. two d.; ed Univ. of California, Los Angeles, Harvard Law School; attorney, Accountability Research Group, Washington, DC 1974–77; Prof., Northeastern Univ. School of Law 1977–83; Prof., George Washington Univ. Law School 1983–86; Prof., Univ. of Michigan Law School 1987–95; Dean and Samuel M. Fegtly Prof. of Law, Univ. of Arizona Coll. of Law 1995–99; Dean and Ethan A.H. Shepley Univ. Prof., School of Law, Washington Univ., St Louis 1999–2005; Pres. Univ. of Rochester 2005–18; mem. Bd of Govs Financial Industry Regulatory Authority 2007–15; reporter, Nat. Conf. of Commrs on Uniform State Laws, Revision of Uniform Securities Act 1998–2002; Chair. SEC Advisory Cttee on Market Information 2000–01; consultant to US Fed. Trade Comm., Washington, DC 1979–82, US Dept of Transportation 1983, Office of Tech. Assessment 1988–89; Dir Nat. Asscn of Securities Dealers 2004–07; mem. American Law Inst., State Bar of Calif., American Inst. of Certified Public Accountants (mem. Professional Ethics Exec. Cttee 2000–02). *Publications include:* author or co-author of 20 books, including (co-author with the late Louis Loss) Securities Regulation (11 vols) and The Transformation of Wall Street: A History of the Securities and Exchange Commission and Modern Corporation Finance; over 50 articles.

SELIGMAN, Nicole Kay, BA, JD; American lawyer and electronics industry executive; b. 1956; m. Joel I. Klein 2000; ed Radcliffe Coll., Harvard Law School; edited the Harvard Law Review; Assoc. Editorial Page Ed. Asian Wall Street Journal, Hong Kong 1978–80; law clerk for Judge Harry T. Edwards, US Court of Appeals, DC Circuit, Washington, DC 1983–84; law clerk to Justice Thurgood Marshall, US Supreme Court, Washington, DC 1984–85; Pnr, Williams & Connolly LLP (law firm), Washington, DC –2001; Exec. Vice-Pres. and Gen. Counsel, Sony Corpn of America, New York 2001–12, Pres. 2012–16, Corp. Exec. Officer, Sony Corpn 2003–14, Group Deputy Gen. Counsel 2003–05, Exec. Vice-Pres. and Gen. Counsel, Sony Corpn 2005–14, Sr Legal Counsel, Sony Group and Pres. Sony Entertainment, Inc. 2014–16; Sears Prize.

SELINGER, Benjamin (Ben) Klaas, AO, AM, Dr rer. nat, DSc; Australian chemist, environmental consultant and academic; *Professor Emeritus of Chemistry, Australian National University;* b. 23 Jan. 1939, Sydney, NSW; s. of Herbert Selinger and Hilde Wittner; m. Veronica Hollander 1967; two s.; ed Sydney Boys High School, Univ. of Sydney, Tech. Univ. Stuttgart, Germany, Australian Nat. Univ.; Lecturer in Physical Chem., ANU 1966–71, Sr Lecturer 1971–78, Head, Dept of Chem. 1988–91, Prof. of Chem. 1992–98, Prof. Emer. 1999–; Chair. Bd of Nat. Registration Authority for Agric. and Veterinary Chemicals 1993–97; mem. numerous Govt bodies, advisory cttees, etc.; Deputy Chair. ANZAAS 1994–96; Chair. Australian Science Festival Ltd 2001–; Fellow, Royal Australian Chem. Inst., Royal Inst. of GB, Australian Acad. of Tech. Sciences and Eng, Australian Acad. of Forensic Sciences; mem. CHOICE (Council Australian Consumers Asscn) 2000–, Life mem. 2007; consultant, Versel Scientific Consulting; columnist, Canberra Times 1972–2005, Burke's Backyard magazine 2000–05; Alexander von Humboldt Fellow; numerous awards and distinctions, including Archibald Olle Prize 1979, Special Eureka Prize for Science Communication (ABC/Australian Museum) 1991, ANZAAS Medallist 1993. *Film:* appeared as a forensic expert in An Act of Necessity, Film Australia 1991. *Radio:* Dial-a-Scientist, ABC, talk back radio. *Television:* has appeared in ABC World Series Debates on Science Is a Health Hazard, Home and Away (BBC) 1991, many interviews on environmental questions. *Publications include:* Chemistry in the Market Place 1975–2017 (now in sixth edn), Thinking with Fourier 1992, Expert Evidence 1992, Why the Watermelon Won't Ripen in Your Armpit 2000. *Leisure interests:* bushwalking, science museums, communication, forensic science, consumer science. *Address:* 2005/71–73 Spring Street, Bondi Junction, NSW 2022, Australia (office). *E-mail:* benselinger39@gmail.com (office). *Telephone:* (2) 9389-8595 (home); 407-460339 (mobile) (home).

SELINGER, Greg, BA, MPA, PhD; Canadian politician; m. Claudette Toupin; two s.; ed Univ. of Manitoba, Queen's Univ., Kingston, Ont., London School of Econs, UK; fmr Assoc. Prof., Faculty of Social Work, Univ. of Manitoba; elected to Winnipeg City Council 1989, becoming mem. Exec. Policy Cttee and Chair. Finance Cttee; unsuccessful cand. for Mayor of Winnipeg 1992; mem. Manitoba Legis. Ass. as MP for St Boniface 1999–; Manitoba Prov. Minister of Finance 1999–2001, also Minister responsible for French Language Services and for Crown Corpns Public Review and Accountability Act 1999–2001, Minister of Civil Service Comm. 2001–06, Minister responsible for Manitoba Hydro 2006–09, also responsible for Liquor Control Comm. and Manitoba Lotteries Corpn 2007–09, Premier of Manitoba 2009–16, also Pres., Exec. Council and Minister of Fed.-Prov. Relations; mem. New Democratic Party of Manitoba, Leader 2009–. *Address:* c/o Office of the Premier, 204 Legislative Building, 450 Broadway, Winnipeg, MB R3C 0V8, Canada (office).

SELIVON, Mykola Jedosovych, PhD; Ukrainian lawyer, judge and diplomatist; b. 30 Oct. 1946, Shestovytsya, Chernigiv Region; one s. one d.; ed Faculty of Law, Kyiv Taras Shevchenko State Univ.; Research Fellow, Inst. of State and Law, Acad. of Sciences of Ukraine 1973; apptd Sr Asst Govt Legal Group 1979, later Chief of Legal Dept; fmr Deputy Minister of Cabinet of Ministers, later First Deputy Minister –1996; Judge, Constitutional Court of Ukraine 1996–99, Deputy Chair. 1999–2002, Chair. 2002–06; Amb. to Kazakhstan 2006–10; Academician, Ukrainian Acad. of Law Sciences; mem. Perm. Court of Arbitration, The Hague; Order for Service, Third Class; Distinguished Lawyer of Ukraine. *Leisure interests:* classical music, theatre, sport.

SELKOE, Dennis J., BA, MD; American neurologist and professor of neurology; *Vincent and Stella Coates Professor of Neurologic Diseases, Harvard Medical School;* b. 25 Sept. 1943, New York; ed Columbia Univ., Univ. of Virginia School of Medicine; US Public Health Service Summer Research Fellow in Pediatrics, Michael Reese Medical Research Inst., Chicago 1966, US Public Health Service Summer Research Fellow in Neurochemistry, McLean Hosp., Belmont, Mass 1968; Intern in Medicine, Hosp. of the Univ. of Pennsylvania, Phidelphia 1969–70; Research Assoc., Nat. Inst. of Neurological Disorders and Stroke, NIH, Bethesda, Maryland 1970–72; Resident in Neurology, Peter Bent Brigham, Children's and

Beth Israel Hosps Boston, Mass 1972–75, Chief Resident in Neurology, Peter Bent Brigham and Children's Hosps 1974–75, United Cerebral Palsy Fellow, Children's Hosp. 1974–75; NIH Postdoctoral Fellow in Neuroscience, Children's Hosp., Harvard Medical School, Boston 1975–78, Research Assoc. in Neuroscience, Children's Hosp. Medical Center 1975–78, Instructor in Neurology, Harvard Medical School 1975–78, Asst Neurologist Children's Hosp. and Brigham and Women's Hosp. 1975–82, Asst Prof. of Neurology, Harvard Medical School 1978–82 (Faculty mem. Div. on Aging 1979–, Program in Neuroscience 1985–), Assoc. Physician (Neurology), Children's Hosp. and Brigham and Women's Hosp. 1982–85, Assoc. Prof. of Neurology 1982–85, Assoc. Prof. of Neurology (Neuroscience) 1985–90, Physician (Neurology), Brigham and Women's Hosp. 1985–92, Co-Dir Center for Neurologic Diseases, Brigham and Women's Hosp. 1985–, Prof. of Neurology (Neuroscience), Harvard Medical School 1990–, Sr Physician (Neurology), Brigham and Women's Hosp. 1992–99, Clinical Assoc. in Neurology, Massachusetts Gen. Hosp. 1997–, Sr Neurologist, Brigham and Women's Hosp. 1999–, Vincent and Stella Coates Prof. of Neurologic Diseases, Harvard Medical School 2001–, currently also Co-Dir Center for Neurologic Diseases; Assoc. Neuropathologist, McLean Hosp., Belmont 1978–85; Investigator, Huntington's Disease Research Center Without Walls, Boston 1980–83; Andrew Floud Memorial Lecturer, Neurological Inst. 1984; Arling Lecturer, Univ. of Cincinnati Medical Center 1991; Distinguished Alumnus/Keynote Speaker, Univ. of Virginia Medical Alumni Symposium 1994; Wellcome Visiting Professorship in the Basic Medical Sciences, Louisiana State Univ. Medical School 1995; Royston C. Clowes Annual Memorial Lecturer, Univ. of Texas, Dallas 1996; Lowell O. Randall Lecturer in Pharmacology, Univ. of Pennsylvania School of Medicine 1996; Frank A. Elliott Lecturer, Penn Neurological Inst., Univ. of Pennsylvania Health System 1999; Rotary Chair for Alzheimer's Disease, Univ. of Leiden (Netherlands) 2000; Co-Chair. Governance Cttee and Chair. Harvard Center for Translational Neurology Research, Harvard Center for Neurodegeneration and Repair, Harvard Medical School 2000–; mem. Medical and Scientific Advisory Bd Alzheimer's Asscn (USA) 1983–90; mem. Exec. Cttee Massachusetts Alzheimer's Disease Research Center 1984–; Founding mem. Dana Alliance for Brain Initiatives 1992–; mem. Scientific Review Bd (Neuroscience) Howard Hughes Medical Inst. 1995–; mem. NIH Nat. Advisory Council on Aging 1998–; Consulting Ed. Journal of Clinical Investigation 1998–; mem. Editorial Bd Neurobiology of Aging 1983–93, Alzheimer's Disease 1986–, Neurodegeneration 1990–93, Neuron 1993–99, Neurobiology of Disease 1993–, Amyloid 1994–, American Journal of Alzheimer's Disease 1997–; mem. Editorial Advisory Bd Synapse 1994–; mem. Editorial Cttee Annual Review of Neuroscience 1996–2001; Editorial Advisor, Neurology, BioMed Central 2000–; mem. American Soc. for Neurology 1973, Soc. for Neuroscience 1980, Massachusetts Neurologic Asscn 1980, AAAS 1982, American Soc. for Neurochemistry 1983, American Asscn for Neuropathologists 1983, American Neurological Asscn 1983, World Fed. of Neurology 1985, American Soc. for Investigative Pathology 1992, American Soc. for Cell Biology 1998; Fellow, American Acad. of Neurology 1996 (Chair. Potamkin Prize Cttee 1998–); Matthew and Marcia Simons Lecturer, Alzheimer's Asscn; Hon. MA (Harvard) 1991; Neuropathology Award, Univ. of Virginia School of Medicine 1966, Medical Student Research Award in Experimental Neurology (First Prize), American Acad. of Neurology 1968, Nat. Foundation Merit Award 1968, Univ. Research and Devt Prize, Univ. of Virginia 1969, Teacher Investigator Devt Award, NIH (NINDS) 1978–83, Wood Kalb Foundation Prize for Research on Alzheimer's Disease 1984, Metropolitan Life Foundation Award for Medical Research 1986, McKnight Foundation Award for Neuroscience Research 1988–91, Leadership and Excellence in Alzheimer's Disease (LEAD) Award, NIH Nat. Inst. on Aging 1988–95, Potamkin Prize, American Acad. of Neurology 1989, NIH MERIT Award, Nat. Inst. on Aging 1991, Commonwealth of Massachusetts 1992, Lifetime Science Award, Inst. for Advanced Studies in Immunology and Aging, Washington, DC 1992, Rita Hayworth Award, Alzheimer's Asscn 1995, Arthur Cherkin Memorial Award, UCLA 1996, Leonard Berg Hon. Symposium on Alzheimer's Disease, Washington Univ. School of Medicine 1997, Mathilde Solowey Award in the Neurosciences, NIH Foundation for Advanced Education in the Sciences 1998, Boerhaave Medal, Univ. of Leiden 1998, Robert J. Huebner Memorial Symposium, Kimmel Cancer Center, Jefferson Univ. 1999, Pioneer Award, Alzheimer's Asscn 1999. *Publications:* more than 630 articles in medical journals. *Address:* Harvard Institutes of Medicine, Ann Romney Center for Neurologic Diseases, Room 730, 4 Blackfan Street, Boston, MA 02115, USA (office). *Telephone:* (office); (617) 525-5200 (office). *Fax:* (617) 525-5252 (office). *E-mail:* dselkoe@partners.org (office). *Website:* www.hms.harvard.edu/dms/neuroscience/fac/selkoe.html (office); selkoelab.bwh.harvard.edu (office).

SELLA, Phillippe; French rugby union player (retd) and business executive; *Co-Director, Sella Communications;* b. 14 Feb. 1962, Tonneins; centre/wing; 111 appearances with French nat. team 1982–95, fmr world record number of caps, scored 30 tries including one in every game of the 1986 Five Nations Championship; appeared in three World Cups, retd from nat. team 1995; with English club Saracens 1995–97; fmrly co-coach of Barbarians; Consultant, CANAL+ 1998–2012; Man. France Under-20 team 2007–11; Rugby Dir Sporting Union Agen Lot-et-Garonne 2012–; co-Dir Sella Communications 1993–; Ordre du national du mérite 1994. *Address:* Sella Communications, 1 rue du Parc des Princes, 47300 Villeneuve-sur-Lot, France (office). *Telephone:* 5-53-40-15-22 (office). *Fax:* 5-53-36-70-10 (office). *E-mail:* contact@sellacommunication.com (office). *Website:* www.sellacommunication.com (office).

SELLAL, Abdelmalek; Algerian politician and fmr diplomatist; b. 1 Aug. 1948, Constantine; ed Ecole Nat. d'Admin, Algiers; Admin. and Chief of Staff, Guelma Wilaya (Dist) 1975; Tech. Adviser, Ministry of Nat. Educ. 1976; Chief, Daïra Tamanrasset and Arzew Dists 1977–84, Boumerdes, Adrar, Sidi Bel, Abbes, Oran and Laghouat Dists 1984–89; Adviser to Minister of the Interior 1989–94; Chief of Staff to Minister of Foreign Affairs 1994–95, Dir-Gen. of Resources, Ministry of Foreign Affairs 1995–96, Amb. to Hungary 1996–97; Minister of the Interior, Local Govt and Environment 1998–99, of Youth and Sports 1999–2001, of Public Works 2001–02, of Transport 2002–04, of Water Resources 2004–12; Prime Minister 2012–14, 2014–17.

SELLAL, Pierre, LenD; French diplomatist; b. 13 Feb. 1952, Mulhouse; ed Lycée Albert Schweitzer, Mulhouse, Faculté de Droit et de Sciences Economiques de Strasbourg, Ecole Nationale d'Admin; Sec. of Foreign Affairs, Ministry of Foreign Affairs 1977–80; Tech. Counsellor, Office of Minister of External Trade 1980–81;

Counsellor, Perm. Mission of France to EC, Brussels 1981–84; Head of Services, Ministry of Industrial Redeployment and Foreign Trade (Directorate of Hydrocarbons) 1984–85; Asst Sec.-Gen. SGCI (Secrétariat général du comité interministériel—Interministerial Cttee for Questions of European Econ. Co-operation) 1985–90; Minister-Counsellor, Embassy in Rome 1990–92, Asst Perm. Rep. 1992–97, Dir European Co-operation 1997, Cabinet Dir 1997–2002, Amb. and Perm. Rep. to EU, Brussels 2002–09, 2014–17, Sec.-Gen. Ministry of Foreign and European Affairs 2009–14; Commdr, Ordre nat. du Mérite 1993, Chevalier, Légion d'honneur 2002, Officier 2011.

SELLARS, Peter, BA; American theatre and opera director and professor of theatre and arts; *Professor, Department of World Arts and Cultures, University of California, Los Angeles;* b. 27 Sept. 1957, Pittsburgh, Pa; ed Harvard Univ.; Dir, Boston Shakespeare Co. 1983–84; Dir and Man., American Nat. Theater at J.F. Kennedy Center, Washington, DC 1984–86; Artistic Advisor, Boston Opera Theatre 1990; currently Prof., Dept of World Arts and Culture, UCLA; Fellow, MacArthur Foundation, Chicago 1983; fmr Visiting Prof., Center for Theatre Arts, Univ. of California, Berkeley; Artistic Dir, New Crowned Hope Festival 2006–; Erasmus Prize 1998, The Dorothy and Lillian Gish Prize 2005, Opera News Award for invaluable contrib. to opera 2011, Polar Music Prize 2014, Musical America Award 2014. *Libretto:* Doctor Atomic (Adams). *Productions include:* Ajax, Armida, Così fan tutte, The Death of Klinghoffer, Die Zauberflöte, Don Giovanni, The Electrification of the Soviet Union, Le Grand Macabre, Idomeneo, The Lighthouse, The Marriage of Figaro, Mathis der Maler, Merchant of Venice, The Mikado, El Niño, Nixon in China, Orlando, The Rake's Progress, Saul and Orlando, St François d'Assise, Tannhäuser, Theodora, Zangezi, Mozart's Zaide (Mostly Mozart Festival at Lincoln Center, New York 2006), Saariaho's La Passion de Simone 2006, Adams' A Flowering Tree 2006, Othello (New York City's Public Theater) 2009, Adams' Nixon in China (Metropolitan Opera) 2011, Vivaldi's Griselda (Santa Fe Opera) 2011, Tristan and Isolde (Helsinki Festival) 2012, (Toronto) 2013, (Real Opera Madrid) 2014, (Paris Opera) 2014, Johannes-Passion (Baden-Baden) 2014. *Address:* Department of World Arts and Cultures, UCLA, Glorya Kaufman Hall 114, 120 Westwood Plaza, Suite 150, PO Box 951608, Los Angeles, CA 90095-1608, USA (office). *Telephone:* (310) 825-3951 (office). *E-mail:* djmalecki@aol.com. *Website:* www.wac.ucla.edu (office).

SELLECK, Tom; American actor and producer; b. 29 Jan. 1945, Detroit, Mich.; s. of Robert D. Selleck and Martha Selleck; m. 1st Jackie Ray 1970 (divorced 1982); one step-s.; m. 2nd Jillie Mack 1987; one d.; ed Univ. of Southern California; mem. Bd Michael Josephson Inst. of Ethics, Nat. Rifle Asscn 2005–18, Advisory Bd Character Counts Coalition (fmr Nat. Spokesperson), Student/Sponsor Partnership Program, New York, Cttee of John F. Kennedy Center for the Performing Arts; fmr Hon. Chair. Skin Cancer Foundation; Spokesman for Nat. Fatherhood Initiative; fmr spokesperson for Los Angeles Mission to Help the Homeless; Hon. LLD (Pepperdine Univ.) 2004; Distinguished American Award, Horatio Alger Asscn 2004. *Films include:* Myra Breckenridge, Midway, Coma 1978, Seven Minutes, High Road to China 1983, Runaway 1984, Lassiter 1984, Three Men and a Baby 1987, Her Alibi 1988, Quigley Down Under 1990, An Innocent Man 1989, Three Men and a Little Lady 1991, Folks 1991, Mr Baseball 1991, Christopher Columbus: The Discovery 1992, In & Out 1997, The Love Letter 1999, Running Mates 2000, Meet the Robinsons (voice) 2007, Killers 2010. *Television includes:* The Rockford Files 1978–79, The Sacketts 1979, Magnum PI 1980–88 (Emmy Award for Outstanding Lead Actor In A Drama Series 1984, Golden Globe Award for Best Performance by an Actor in TV Series 1985), Friends (series), 1996, 2000, Ruby, Jean and Joe, Broken Trust 1995, The Closer series) 1998–99, Washington Slept Here 2000, Louis L'Amour's Crossfire Trail 2000, Monte Walsh 2003, 12 Mile Road 2003, Reversible Errors 2004, Ike, Countdown to D Day 2004, Stone Cold 2005, Jesse Stone: Night Passage 2006, Jesse Stone: Death in Paradise 2006, Jesse Stone: Sea Change 2007, Las Vegas (series) 2007–08, Jesse Stone: Thin Ice 2009, Killers 2010, Jesse Stone: No Remorse 2010, Jesse Stone: Innocents Lost 2011, Jesse Stone: Benefit of the Doubt 2012, Jesse Stone: Lost in Paradise 2015, Blue Bloods (series) 2010–16. *Leisure interests:* volleyball (Hon. Capt. US Men's Volleyball Team for 1984 Olympic Games), outrigger canoe specialist, baseball, horseback riding. *Address:* c/o Esme Chandlee, 2967 Hollyridge Drive, Los Angeles, CA 90068, USA. *Telephone:* (323) 962-5704 (office). *Fax:* (323) 962-5705 (office).

SELLERT, Wolfgang, DJur; German legal scholar and professor of history; *Professor Emeritus, University of Göttingen;* b. 3 Nov. 1935, Berlin; s. of Horst-Günther Sellert and Else Kaiser; m. Dr Urte Wenger 1962; two d.; Asst in Dept for History of German Law, Univ. of Frankfurt 1965–72, Prof. 1972–77; apptd Prof. of History of German Law and Civil Law, Georg-August Univ., Göttingen 1977, Dean of the Law Faculty 1984–85, Chair. Comm. of Göttingen Acad. of Sciences 'Die Funktion des Gesetzes in Vergangenheit und Gegenwart' (The function of the law in past and present) 1990–2002, Man. Dir Univ. of Göttingen 1991–2000, Chair. Univ. of Göttingen Universitätsbundes e. V. 2000–06, Prof. Emer. 2002–; Dir German-Chinese Inst. of Econ. Law, Univ. of Nanjing 1995–2000; Chair. Göttinger Vereinigung zur Pflege der Rechtsgeschichte eV 2006–; mem. Exec. Bd Göttinger Zentrum für Mittelalter- und Frühneuzeitforschung 1999–2002; mem. Göttinger Rechtswissenschaftliche Gesellschaft 1978–, Akad. der Wissenschaften, Göttingen 1984–. *Publications include:* Über die Zuständigkeitsabgrenzung von Reichshofrat und Reichskammergericht 1965, Prozessgrundsätze über Stilus Curiae am Reichshofrat 1973, Die Ordnungen des Reichshofrats 1980, Studien- u. Quellenbuch zur Geschichte der dt. Strafrechtspflege 1989, Recht u. Gerechtigkeit in der Kunst 1991. *Leisure interests:* collecting old manuscripts and baroque literature. *Address:* Konrad-Adenauer-Strasse 25, 37075 Göttingen; Juridicum, Räume 131-133, Platz der Göttinger, Sieben 6, 37073 Göttingen, Germany (office). *Telephone:* (551) 3919795. *E-mail:* wseller@gwdg.de.

SELMAYR, Martin, PhD; German lawyer and EU official; *Secretary-General, European Commission;* b. 5 Dec. 1970, Bonn; s. of Gerhard Selmayr and Silke Selmayr; m.; ed Univ. of Geneva, Univ. of Passau; Legal Adviser, European Central Bank, Frankfurt am Main 1998–2000; Visiting Official, Legal Dept, IMF Jan.–April 2000; Dir, Govt Relations and Legal Adviser, Bertelsmann AG, Brussels 2001–03, Vice-Pres., Govt Relations and Legal Adviser 2003–04; Lecturer in Econ. Law, Univ. of Saarland 2001–10, Prof. 2010–; Co-Dir, Centre for European Law, Univ. of Passau 2001–; joined European Comm. (EC) as civil servant 2004, EC Spokesman 2004–10, Chef de Cabinet to EU Commr for Justice 2010–14, Head of Transition Team of EC Pres.-elect Jean Claude Juncker July–Oct. 2014, Chief of Staff to EC Pres. 2014–18, Sec.-Gen., EC 2018–; mem. Christen-Democratisch en Vlaams (CD&V) (Christian Democratic and Flemish) (Belgian political party) 2014–. *Address:* European Commission, 200 rue de la Loi, 1049 Brussels, Belgium (office). *Telephone:* (2) 299-11-11 (office). *Fax:* (2) 295-01-38 (office). *E-mail:* martin.selmayr@ec.europa.eu (office). *Website:* ec.europa.eu (office).

SEMAGO, Vladimir Vladimirovich; Russian politician; *Leading Expert, Accounts Chamber of the Russian Federation;* b. 10 Jan. 1947; m. Olga Valentinovna Myasnikova; one s. one d.; ed Moscow Inst. of Construction Eng, All-Union Acad. of Foreign Trade; with Mosoblstroi 1973–77; joined Goskominturist 1977; Deputy CEO Solnechny 1979–81; accountant, tourist co., commerce Dept, State Cttee of Tourism 1981–83; Deputy Chair., Domodedovo Dist Consumers' Union 1983–86; Chief Engineer, State Cttee of Science and Tech. of USSR Council of Ministers 1986–87; Founder Jt Venture Moscow Commercial Club 1990; co-f. Ecology and Energy Resources 1992; mem. State Duma 1993–99, 2003–07, mem. State Duma Cttee on Int. Affairs 1999; mem. CP of Russian Fed. 1993–2004; apptd Chair. Rosebusinesbank 1995; Founder and leader New Left (political movt) 1999; mem. Presidium, Co-ordination Council Round Table of Russian Business; elected mem. United Russia (UR) (Yedinaya Rossiya) 2006; Leading Expert, Accounts Chamber of the Russian Fed. 2007–. *Films include:* as actor: Vstretimsya na Taiti 1991, The Rifleman of the Voroshilov Regiment 1999, V avguste 44-go 2001, Tycoon 2002; as producer: V avguste 44-go 2001. *Leisure interests:* travelling, collecting modern paintings. *Address:* Accounts Chamber of the Russian Federation, 119991 Moscow, Zubovskaya street 2, Russia (office). *Telephone:* (495) 986-05-09 (office). *Fax:* (495) 986-09-52 (office). *E-mail:* info@ach.gov.ru (office). *Website:* www.ach.gov.ru (office).

SEMAKULA KIWANUKA, Matia Mulumba, PhD; Ugandan government official and diplomatist; m.; several c.; ed Makerere Univ. and Univ. of London, UK; fmr univ. lecturer, researcher and admin.; Sr Presidential Adviser 1979–81; worked with UNEP 1985–87; Counterpart Chief Tech. Adviser and Dir of Planning and Project Co-ordination for a UNDP project on capacity-building and institutional strengthening 1988–90; Dean, Makerere Univ. School of Post grad. Studies and Research 1991–94; Exec. Dir Man. Training and Advisory Centre, Uganda 1994–96; Amb. and Perm. Rep. to UN, New York 1996–2003, Chair. Gen. Ass.'s Fourth Cttee (Special Political and Decolonization) 2000; Minister of State in Charge of Luwero 2003–05, of Investment 2005; fmr Minister of Culture, Royal Kingdom of Buganda; mem. Royal Council.

SEMASHKA, Uladzimir I.; Belarusian politician; b. 20 Nov. 1949, Kalinkovichi, Gomel Oblast; m.; two d.; ed Belarusian Polytechnic Inst.; mil. service 1972–74; Design Engineer, then Head of Design Bureau No. 44, then Chief Engineer of Special Mechanical Eng Design Bureau, then Chief Engineer of Mechanical Eng Dept, Dzerzhinsky Plant, Research and Production Asscn Integral 1974–96; Gen. Man. Minsk Production Asscn Horizont, Dir, Minsk Plant Horizont 1996–2001; Minister of Energy 2001–03; Acting Deputy Prime Minister July–Dec. 2003; First Deputy Prime Minister Dec. 2003–14; Chair. Supervisory Bd Beltransgaz 2007–10; Order of Honour 2008. *Address:* c/o Office of the Council of Ministers, 220010 Minsk, vul. Savetskaya 11, Belarus. *E-mail:* contact@government.by.

SEMEDO, Rui Mendes; Cabo Verde politician; b. 7 Oct. 1956, Praia, Santiago; fmr Prof. of Elementary and Secondary Educ.; fmr Dir Office of the Parl. Group of Partido Africano da Independência de Cabo Verde (PAICV—African Party of Independence of Cape Verde), fmr Sec.-Gen. and Vice-Pres. PAICV; mem. Nat. Council, mem. Standing Cttee; Minister of Parl. Affairs 2006–16, also Minister of Nat. Defence 2014–16. *Address:* c/o Ministry of National Defence, Palácio do Governo, Várzea da Companhia, Praia, Santiago, Cabo Verde (office).

SEMEL, Terry, BS; American media executive; *Chairman and CEO, Windsor Media;* b. 24 Feb. 1943, New York; s. of Ben Semel and Mildred Semel (née Wenig); m. 1st Maryann Semel (divorced); m. 2nd Jane Bovingdon 1977; one s. two d.; ed Long Island Univ., City Coll. of New York; Domestic Sales Man. CBS Cinema Center Films, Studio City, Calif. 1970–72; Vice-Pres., Gen. Man. Walt Disney's Buena Vista, Burbank, Calif. 1972–75; Pres. W.B. Distribution Corpn, Burbank 1975–78; Exec. Vice-Pres., COO Warner Bros. Inc., Burbank 1979–80, Pres., COO 1980–96, Chair., CEO 1994–99; Chair., Co-CEO Warner Music Group Inc. 1995–99; Chair., CEO and Dir Yahoo! Inc. 2001–07, Chair. (non-exec.) 2007–08; Founder, Chair., CEO Windsor Media 2008–; Co-Chair. Los Angeles County Museum of Art; Vice-Chair. San Diego Host Cttee for Republican Nat. Convention 1996; mem. Bd of Dirs Polo Ralph Lauren Corpn, Guggenheim Museum, Emerson Coll.; Trustee The Paley Center for Media; mem. Chancellor's Cttee, UCLA, Think Long Cttee for California of Berggruen Inst. on Governance; Vanguard Award from Producers Guild of America 2005, UCLA Medal 2005, Legend in Leadership Award, Yale School of Man. 2005.

SEMENOV, Victor Aleksandrovich; Russian politician and business executive; *Chairman of the Supervisory Board, Belaya Dacha Group;* b. 14 Jan. 1958, Novokuryanovo, Moscow Region; m.; one s. one d.; ed Moscow K. Timiryazev Acad. of Agric.; on state farm, later Agric. Co. Belaya Dacha 1980–85; instructor Agric. Dept, Lyubertsy Town CP Cttee 1987–88; f. Belaya Dacha Group, Pres. and Dir-Gen. Belaya Dacha 1989–98, currently Chair. Supervisory Bd; Minister of Agric. and Food of Russian Fed. 1998–99; mem. State Duma (Otechestvo faction) 1999–; Chair. Union of Agricultural Scientific Complex Asscns of the Russian Fed. (ASSAGROS); Pres. Russian Interregional Asscn for Assistance of Field Experiments (AAFEI); Chair. Agricultural Cttee, Chamber of Commerce; founder-mem. Agricultural Asscn; mem. Russian Acad. of Agricultural Sciences. *Leisure interests:* travelling, fishing, horse-riding. *Address:* Belaya Dacha Group, 2, Yanichkin Proezd, Kotelniki, Lubertsy District, Moscow 140053, Russia (office). *Telephone:* (495) 995-90-00 (office). *Fax:* (495) 554-10-90 (office). *E-mail:* info@belaya-dacha.ru (office). *Website:* www.belaya-dacha.ru (office); www.viktor-semenov.ru.

SEMENOV, Yuri Pavlovich; Russian mechanical engineer (retd); b. 20 April 1935, Toropets, Kalinin region; m.; two d.; ed Dnepropetrovsk State Univ.; worked in rocket and space industry as engineer, head of group, Leading Designer 1967–72, Chief Designer 1972–78, Deputy Gen. Designer, Chief Designer 1978–81; First Deputy Gen. Designer, Chief Designer of BURAN Orbiter, Manned

Spacecrafts and Stations 1981–89, Gen. Designer of ENERGIA Scientific and Production Asscn (NPO ENERGIA) 1989–91, Dir Gen., Gen. Designer 1991–94; Gen. Designer and Pres. S. P. Korolev RSC ENERGIA 1994–2005 (retd); mem. Int. Acad. of Astronautics 1986; Corresp. mem. USSR (now Russian) Acad. of Sciences 1987, mem. 2000–; Hero of Socialist Labour 1976, Lenin Prize 1978, USSR State Prize 1985, USSR Acad. of Sciences K. Tsyolkovsky Gold Medal 1987, Alan De Emil IAF State Prize 1991, State Prize of Russian Fed. 1999, François-Xavier Bagnoud Aeropace Prize 1999, RAS S.P. Korolev Gold Medal 2001 and others. *Achievements include:* responsible for devt and operation of Buran reusable vehicle, devt, manufacture and operation of Soyuz, Progress-type vehicles, Salyut and Mir in-orbit complexes, rocket segment of the Sea Launch rocket and space complex-RSC, satellite systems based on YAMAL spacecraft of new generation communication satellites and devt of Russian segment of Int. Space Station and its main modules, devt and construction of the AURORA/ONEGA RSC). *Publications:* more than 360 publs including S.P. Korolev Rocket and Space Corporation Energia 1946–96 1996, S.P. Korolev Rocket and Space Corporation ENERGIA at the Turn of Two Centuries 1996–2001 2001. *Leisure interests:* sports.

SEMENYAKA, Lyudmila Ivanovna; Russian ballerina; b. 16 Jan. 1952, Leningrad (now St Petersburg); m. (divorced); one s.; ed Vaganova Ballet Acad., Leningrad (now St Petersburg); danced with Kirov Ballet 1970–72; Prima Ballerina, Bolshoi Theatre Co., Moscow 1972–96, debuted as choreographer 1999; has worked with English Nat. Ballet 1990–91 and Scottish Nat. Ballet; ballet teacher 1994–, with Moscow State Acad. of Choreography 1999–, coach at Bolshoi Theatre 2000–, works with Svetlana Zakharova, Elena Andrienko, Anastasia Meskova, Anastasia Goryacheva, Anna Nikulina, Eugenia Obraztsova, Viktorya Osipova, Darya Hochlova and others; trained as actress, Studio Theatre of Modern Dramaturgy 2001–03; mem. jury, several int. ballet competitions; performed in Europe, USA and Argentina; winner, Moscow Int. Ballet competition 1969, 1972, Varna 1972, Tokyo (First Prize and Gold Medal) 1976, Anna Pavlova Prize, Paris 1976, USSR State Prize 1977, USSR People's Artist 1986, Evening Standard Prize 1986. *Films include:* Ludmila Semenyaka Danse, The Bolshoi Ballerina, Spartacus, The Stone Flower, Raymonda, The Nutcracker, Fantasy on the Theme of Casanova and others. *Plays:* An Excellent Medicine for Anguish, The Seagull. *Roles include:* all of classical repertoire, debut in Odette/Odile, Swan Lake, Moscow; all of Y. Grigorovitch ballets: Phrygia (Spartak), Anastasia (Ivan the Terrible), Katerina (Stony Flower) etc; roles in ballets by Balanchin, Petit, Lavrovsky, Vassilyev, Boccadoro, Ben Stivenson, May Murdmaa; has partnered Mikhail Baryshnikov, Vladimir Vassilyev, Irek Mukhamedov, Farukh Ruzimatov etc; as balletmaster has staged performances of Fountain of Bakhchisarai, Astrakhan 2008, Giselle, Ekaterinburg 2009, Swan Lake, Ekaterinburg 2010. *Address:* Bolshoi Theatre, Moscow 125009, Teatralnaya ploshchad 1, Russia. *Telephone:* (499) 151-26-75 (home). *Fax:* (499) 151-26-75 (home). *Website:* www .bolshoi.ru (office).

SEMENZA, Gregg L., AB, MD, PhD; American professor of paediatrics, physician and academic; *Michael Armstrong Professor of Pediatrics and Director, Vascular Biology Program, Institute for Cell Engineering, Johns Hopkins University;* b. July 1956, New York; m. Laura Kasch-Semenza; ed Harvard Univ., Univ. of Pennsylvania; residency in Pediatrics, Duke Univ. Medical Center; performed postdoctoral research in Medical Genetics at Johns Hopkins Univ. School of Medicine, mem. Faculty 1990–, currently C. Michael Armstrong Prof. of Pediatrics, Prof. of Biological Chem., Prof. of Medicine, Prof. of Radiation Oncology and Molecular Radiation Sciences, Dir Vascular Biology Program, Inst. for Cell Eng; Visiting Prof., Dept of Physiology, Medical Coll., Wisconsin 1998; Ed.-in-Chief, Journal of Molecular Medicine; mem. Editorial Bd Cancer Research 2003, Molecular and Cellular Biology 2008; mem. Soc. for Pediatric Research 1991, American Soc. for Clinical Investigation 1995, NAS 2008, Asscn of American Physicians 2008, Inst. of Medicine 2012; Founding Fellow, American Coll. of Medical Genetics; Research Prof., American Cancer Soc. 2012–16; Lucille P. Markey Scholar Award in Biomedical Science, Markey Trust 1989, Established Investigator Award, American Heart Asscn 1994, Jean and Nicholas Leone Award, Children's Brain Tumor Foundation 1999, E. Mead Johnson Award for Research in Pediatrics, Soc. for Pediatric Research 2000, Canada Gairdner Award 2010, Stanley J. Korsmeyer Award, American Soc. for Clinical Investigation 2012, Lefoulon-Delalande Grand Prize, Institut de France 2012, Albert Lasker Basic Medical Research Award, Lasker Foundation (co-recipient) 2016. *Publications:* Transcription Factors and Human Disease 1998; several book chapters and more than 250 research articles in professional journals. *Address:* Vascular Biology Program, Institute for Cell Engineering, Johns Hopkins University School of Medicine, Edward D. Miller Research Building, 733 North Broadway, Baltimore, MD 21205-1832, USA (office). *E-mail:* hopkinsice@jhmi.edu (office). *Website:* www .hopkinsmedicine.org (office); www.hopkinsmedicine.org/research/labs/gregg -semenza-lab (office).

ŠEMETA, Algirdas Gediminas; Lithuanian economist, fmr government official and fmr EU official; *Business Ombudsman for Ukraine's Anti-Corruption Initiative;* b. 23 April 1962; m.; three c.; ed Univ. of Vilnius; Economist (Younger Fellowship), Lithuanian Economy Inst. 1985–90; Head of Subdivision of the Economy Devt Strategy Div., Ministry of the Economy 1990–91, Adviser on Privatization 1991–92; Chair. Securities Comm., Ministry of Finance 1992–96, Chair. Securities Comm. of Lithuania 1996–97; Minister of Finance 1997–99, 2008–09; Vice-Pres. AB Nalšia June–Nov. 1999; Govt Sec. Office of the Govt 1999–2001; Dir-Gen. Dept of Statistics 2001–08; Commr for Financial Programming and Budget, EC, Brussels 2009–10, for Taxation and Customs Union, Audit and Anti-Fraud 2010–14; Business Ombudsman for Ukraine's Anti-Corruption Initiative 2014–; mem. Knowledge Economy Forum. *Address:* European Union Anti-Corruption Initiative, 01001 Kyiv, 4V Volodymyrskyi descent, Ukraine (office). *E-mail:* info@ukraine-aci.com (office). *Website:* euaci.eu (office).

SEMIGIN, Gennady Yuryevich, Dr rer. pol; Russian business executive and politician; *Leader, Patriots of Russia (Patrioty Rossii);* b. 23 March 1964; m.; three c.; ed Riga Higher Mil. Political School, Moscow Juridical Inst., Acad. of Finance; army service 1985–90; f. Centre of Econs and Russian AKROS 1990; f. Russian Group of Finance and Industry 1991; mem. Council on Business, Russian Presidency 1992–; mem. Exec. Bd Russian Union of Businessmen, Pres. Russian Group of Finance and Industry 1991–; f. Nat. Public Scientific Fund 1996; Founder

and Head, Inst. of Comparative Politology, Russian Acad. of Sciences; Pres. Congress of Russian Business Circles; mem. CP 1998; mem. State Duma (Agrarian faction, then CP faction) 1999–, Deputy Chair. 2000–03; Founder and Leader Patriots of Russia (Patrioty Rossii) 2002–, Head Rodina faction 2007–; mem. Comm. on Regulation of Labour and Social Relations, Russian Acad. of Social Sciences, Acad. of Political Sciences; corresp. mem. Acad. of Natural Sciences. *Publications:* Social Partnership in the Contemporary World, Political Stability of Society, ed. New Philosophical Encyclopedia (4 Vols). *Leisure interests:* swimming, tennis, running, classical music, boxing, history, philosophy, art, economics. *Address:* Patriots of Russia (Patrioty Rossii), 119121 Moscow, Smolensky Blvd 11/2 (office); State Duma, Okhotny Ryad 1, 103205 Moscow, Russia (office). *Telephone:* (495) 692-15-50 (Patrioty Rossii) (office); (495) 292-76-75 (office). *Fax:* (495) 692-15-50 (Patrioty Rossii) (office). *E-mail:* partia-korn@rambler.ru (office). *Website:* www .patriot-rus.ru (office); www.duma.ru (office).

SEMIZOROVA, Nina Lvovna; Russian ballerina; b. 15 Oct. 1956, Krivoi Rog, Ukraine; d. of Lev Alexandrovich Semizorov and Larisa Dmitrievna Semizorova; m. 1st Maris Liepa 1980; m. 2nd Mark Peretokin 1988; one d.; ed Kiev Choreographic School; danced with Shevchenko Theatre of Opera and Ballet, Kiev 1975–78, with Bolshoi Ballet, Moscow 1978–2000, Teacher-Repetiteur 2009–; Repetiteur, Kremlevsky Ballet Theater 2000–03; Asst to Dir Choreographer, Krasnoyarsk State Opera 2003–09; teacher, then Prof., Russian Acad. of Theatrical Arts 1996–; First Prize, Int. Ballet Competition, Moscow 1977, Artist of Merit of Ukrainian SSR 1977, Honoured Artist of Russia 1987, Laureate of Moscow Komsomol 1987, Soul of Dance Prize, Ballet magazine 2007. *Roles include:* Odette/Odile (Swan Lake), Giselle, Aurora (Sleeping Beauty), Kitri (Don Quixote), Raymonda, Mistress of the Copper Mountain (The Stone Flower), Lady Macbeth (Macbeth), Aegina and Phrygia (Spartacus), Luska (The Golden Age). *Leisure interest:* reading. *Address:* Bolshoi Theatre, Moscow 125009, Teatralnaya Square 1 (office); 2 Zhukovskaya Street, Apt. 8, Moscow, Russia (home). *Telephone:* (495) 923-40-84 (home). *Fax:* (495) 923-40-84 (home). *Website:* www.bolshoi.ru/en (office).

SEMJÉN, Zsolt, DTheol; Hungarian theologian, sociologist and politician; *Deputy Prime Minister for Hungarian Communities Abroad, Church Affairs and Nationalities;* b. 8 Aug. 1962, Budapest; s. of Dr Miklós Semjén and Erzsébet Niklász; m.; two s. one d.; ed High School Szilágyi Erzsébet, Budapest, Pázmány Péter Catholic Theological Acad., Sociology Faculty, Eötvös Loránd Univ.; worked for Termeltető Craft Co., Budapest 1981–84; Co-founder Kereszténydemokrata Néppárt (KDNP—Christian Democratic People's Party) 1989, Pres. 1990, mem. Exec. Cttee 1990–91, Chair. Disciplinary and Ethics Cttee 1993–94, Vice-Pres. KDNP 1997, left party to join Magyar Demokrata Fórum (MDF—Hungarian Democratic Forum) 1997, rejoined 2002, Pres. KDNP 2003–, Leader Parl. Group 2006, 2010; Dist Municipal Councillor, Budapest II 1990–94; mem. Parl. 1994–98, 2002–; State Sec. for Church Affairs and Vice-Chair. Cttee on Human Rights, Ministry of Nat. Cultural Heritage 1998–2002; Deputy Prime Minister and Minister without Portfolio 2010–, responsible for Hungarian Communities Abroad, for Nat. Policy 2010–18, for Communities Abroad, Church Affairs and Nationalities 2018–; mem. Pontifical Acad. of Tiberina 1999; Hon. Assoc. Prof. 1996; Winner, Pro Caritate and Pro Ecclesia Hungariae. *Address:* Cabinet Office of the Prime Minister, 1357 Budapest, Pf. 1, Hungary (office). *Telephone:* (1) 896-1747 (office). *Fax:* (1) 795-0893 (office). *E-mail:* mk@mk.gov.hu (office). *Website:* www.kormany.hu (office); semjenzsolt.hu.

SEMPÉ, Jean-Jacques; French cartoonist; b. 17 Aug. 1932, Bordeaux; s. of Ulysse Sempé and Juliette Marson; one s. one d.; ed Ecole Communale à Bordeaux; started career as toothpaste salesman; then apprentice in wine trade; published first drawings 1950; work has appeared in various publications including: L'Express magazine, Paris-Match, Punch (now defunct), New Yorker, New York Times; has produced an album annually for 30 years for Editions Denoël; Officier des Arts et des Lettres. *Publications include:* Le Petit Nicolas series from 1960, Rien n'est simple 1962, Tout se complique 1963, Sauve qui peut 1964, Monsieur Lambert 1965, La grande panique 1966, St Tropez 1968, Information-Consommation 1968, Des Hauts et des Bas 1970, Face à Face 1972, Bonjour Bonsoir 1974, L'Ascension Sociale de Mr Lambert 1975, Simple question d'equilibre 1977, Un léger décalage 1977, Les Musiciens 1979, Comme par hasard 1981, De bon matin 1983, Vaguement compétitif 1985, Luxe, calme et volupté 1987, Par Avion 1989, L'Histoire de Monsieur Sommer (with Patrick Süsskind) 1991, Ames Soeurs 1991, Insondables Mystères 1993, Raoul Taburin 1995, Les Musiciens 1996, Grands rêves 1997, Beau Temps 1999, Multiples intentions 2003, Sentiments distingués 2007.

SEMPLE, Sir John Laughlin, KCB, BSc (Econ), MA (Cantab.); British fmr civil servant; b. 10 Aug. 1940, Belfast, Northern Ireland; s. of J. E. Semple and of Violet E. G. Semple; m. Maureen Anne Kerr 1970; two s. one d.; ed Campbell Coll., Belfast and Corpus Christi Coll., Cambridge; joined Home Civil Service, Ministry of Aviation 1961, transferred to Northern Ireland Civil Service 1962, succession of posts relating to industrial training, financial planning, community relations, physical planning, Belfast Devt and housing policy, Perm. Sec., Northern Ireland Dept of Finance and Personnel 1988–97, Head, Northern Ireland Civil Service 1997–2000, (also Second Perm. Sec., Northern Ireland Office 1998–99), Sec. to Northern Ireland Exec. Cttee 1999–2000; mem. Consumer Council for Postal Services 2000, Regional Chair. for Northern Ireland 2000–01; Dir of Northern Ireland Affairs, Royal Mail Group plc 2001–06; Chair. Bd of Trustees, Northern Ireland Police Fund 2001–05; Head, Independent Affordability Review, Dept for Social Devt 2006–07. *Leisure interests:* golf, tennis, skiing, history. *Address:* 24 Ailsa Road, Cultra, Holywood, Co. Down, BT18 0AS, Northern Ireland. *Telephone:* (28) 9042-1078. *E-mail:* johnsemple1@btinternet.com.

SEN, Amartya Kumar, BA, MA, PhD, FBA; Indian economist and academic; *Thomas W. Lamont University Professor and Professor of Economics and Philosophy, Harvard University;* b. 3 Nov. 1933, Santiniketan, Bengal; s. of Ashutosh Sen and Amita Sen; m. 1st Nabaneeta Dev 1960 (divorced 1975); two d.; m. 2nd Eva Colorni 1978 (died 1985); one s. one d.; m. 3rd Emma Rothschild 1991; ed Presidency Coll., Calcutta and Trinity Coll., Cambridge; Prof. of Econs, Jadavpur Univ., Calcutta 1956–58; Fellow, Trinity Coll., Cambridge 1957–63; Prof. of Econs, Univ. of Delhi 1963–71, Chair. Dept of Econs 1966–68; Hon. Dir Agricultural Econs Research Centre, Delhi 1966–68, 1969–71; Prof. of Econs, LSE

1971–77, Univ. of Oxford 1977–80, Drummond Prof. of Political Economy 1980–88; Thomas W. Lamont Univ. Prof., Harvard Univ. 1987–98, 2004–, Prof. Emer. 1998–2004, Prof. of Econs and Philosophy 2004–; Master Trinity Coll., Cambridge 1998–2003; Visiting Prof., Univ. of Calif., Berkeley 1964–65, Harvard Univ. 1968–69; Andrew D. White Prof.-at-Large, Cornell Univ. 1978–84; Pres. Int. Econ. Asscn 1986–89; Fellow, Econometric Soc., Pres. 1984; Hon. Prof., Delhi Univ., Foreign Hon. mem. American Acad. of Arts and Sciences, Hon. Fellow, Inst. of Social Studies, The Hague, Hon. Fellow LSE, Inst. of Devt Studies; Hon. CH 2000, Grand Cross, Order of Scientific Merit (Brazil) 2000, Commdr, Légion d'honneur 2013; Hon. DLitt (Univ. of Saskatchewan, Canada) 1979, (Visva-Bharati Univ., India) 1983, (Oxford) 1996; Hon. DUniv (Essex) 1984, (Caen) 1987; Hon. DSc (Bath) 1984, (Bologna) 1988; Dr hc (Univ. Catholique de Louvain) 1989, (Padua) 1998, numerous others; Senator Giovanni Agnelli Inst. Prize for Ethics 1989, Nobel Memorial Prize in Econ. Sciences 1998, Bharat Ratna 1999, UN Econ. and Social Comm. for Asia and the Pacific (UNESCAP) Lifetime Achievement Award 2007, Nat. Humanities Medal 2012, inaugural Charleston-EFG John Maynard Keynes Prize 2015, Univ. of Oxford Bodley Medal 2019. *Publications include:* Choice of Techniques: An Aspect of Planned Economic Development 1960, Growth Economics 1970, Collective Choice and Social Welfare 1970, On Economic Inequality 1973, Employment, Technology and Development 1975, Poverty and Famines 1981, Utilitarianism and Beyond (jtly with Bernard Williams) 1982, Choice, Welfare and Measurement 1982, Resources, Values and Development 1984, Commodities and Capabilities 1985, On Ethics and Economics 1987, The Standard of Living 1988, Hunger and Public Action (with Jean Drèze) 1989, Social Security in Developing Countries (jtly) 1991, Inequality Re-examined 1992, The Quality of Life (jtly) 1993, Development as Freedom 1999, The Argumentative Indian: Writings on Indian History, Culture and Identity 2005, Identity and Violence: The Illusion of Destiny 2006, The Idea of Justice 2009, Peace and Democratic Society 2011, An Uncertain Glory: India and its Contradictions (with Jean Drèze) 2013, Bhartiya Arthatantra Itihas Aur Sanskriti 2013, The Country of First Boys: And Other Essays (with Gopalkrishna Gandhi) 2015; articles in various journals in econs, philosophy and political science. *Address:* Department of Economics, 1805 Cambridge Street, Littauer Center 205, Harvard University, Cambridge, MA 02138, USA (office). *Telephone:* (617) 495-1871 (office). *Fax:* (617) 496-5942 (office). *E-mail:* asen@fas.harvard.edu (office). *Website:* www.economics .harvard.edu (office).

SEN, Laura J.; American retail executive; *Chairman (non-Exec.), BJ's Wholesale Club, Inc.;* ed Boston Coll.; several positions in mass retailing, including service with Zayre Corpn and Jordan Marsh Co.; Vice-Pres. of Logistics, BJ's Wholesale Club, Inc. 1989–93, Sr Vice-Pres. of Gen. Merchandise 1993–97, Exec. Vice-Pres. of Merchandising and Logistics 1997–2003, 2007–08, COO BJ's Wholesale Club, Inc. 2008–09, mem. Bd of Dirs and Pres. 2008–, CEO 2009–16, Chair. (non-Exec.) 2016–; Prin. of Sen Retail Consulting 2003–06; mem. Bd Saint Coletta and Cardinal Cushing Schools of Massachusetts, Inc.; mem. Bd of Dirs Abington Bancorp Inc. (and its subsidiary Abington Savings Bank) 2001, Massachusetts Mutual Life Insurance Co. 2017, Massachusetts Port Authority 2017–; provides support to non-profit orgs, including the Women's Inn at Pine Street, the Neely House and the Cardinal Cushing Centers Springtime Event. *Address:* BJ's Wholesale Club, Inc., One Mercer Road, Natick, MA 01760, USA (office). *Telephone:* (508) 651-7400 (office). *Fax:* (508) 651-6114 (office). *E-mail:* info@bjs .com (office). *Website:* www.bjs.com (office).

SENANAYAKE, Lt-Gen. Mahesh, BSc, RWP, RSP, USP; Sri Lankan army officer; *Commander of Army;* m.; one s. two d.; ed Colombo Ananda Coll. US Army Command and General Staff Coll., Jawaharlal Nehru Univ., India; joined Sri Lanka Army as Officer Cadet 1981, posted to 1 Plant Engineer Regiment 1983, Squadron Commdr 1st Special Forces Regiment 1989, later 3rd Special Forces Regiment, later Regimental Center Commdt and Commdr, Officer Instructor Sri Lanka Military Acad. Commdr 211 Infantry Brigade-Vavuniya, Col-Gen. Staff 52 Division, Brig.-Gen. Staff, Security Force Headquarters, Jaffna (SFHQ-J), Commdr SHGQ-J, Commdr of Army 2017–; Sr Man. Project Man. of Afghan Operations and Strategic Planning, Civil Reserved Air Fleet, US Army. *Address:* Sri Lanka Army, Directorate of Media, 4th Floor, Premier Pacific Building No. 28, R.A. De Mel Mawatha, Colombo 4, Sri Lanka (office). *Telephone:* (11) 2432682 (office). *E-mail:* slarmymedia@gmail.com (office). *Website:* dmedia@army.lk (office); www.army.lk (office).

SENARD, Jean-Dominique, MA; French business executive; *Chairman, Renault SA;* b. 7 March 1953; m.; three c.; ed HEC (Hautes Études Commerciales) business school, Paris; early career serving in various financial and operational positions with Total 1979–87, then with Saint Gobain 1987–96, mem. Bd of Dirs 2012–, Lead Independent Dir 2017–, also Chair. Strategy and Corporate Social Responsibility Cttee; mem. Group Exec. Council and Chief Financial Officer Pechiney 1996–2001, also head of Pechiney's Primary Metal section –2004, mem. Exec. Cttee Alcan, in charge of integrating Pechiney and served as Chair. Pechiney SA; joined Michelin as Chief Financial Officer and mem. Michelin Group Exec. Council 2005, Man. Partner, Michelin Group 2007–11, Man. Gen. Partner alongside Michel Rollier 2011–12, Man. Gen. and CEO 2012–19; Chair. Renault SA 2019–; mem. Bd of Dirs SEB SA 2009–13. *Address:* Renault SA, 13–15 quai Le Gallo, 92513 Boulogne-Billancourt Cedex, France. *Telephone:* 1-76-84-50-50 (Paris) (office). *Fax:* 1-41-04-51-49 (Paris) (office). *Website:* www.renault.com (office).

SENDANYOYE RUGWABIZA, Valentine, BSc, MSc; Rwandan diplomatist, business executive, international organization executive and government official; *Permanent Representative, United Nations;* b. 25 July 1963; m. John Paulin Sendanyoye; ed Nat. Univ. of Zaïre (now Democratic Repub. of the Congo); sr man. with major Swiss multinational co., first as head of its commercial devt and marketing operations for Cen. Africa, based in Yaoundé, Cameroon, and then as its regional man. for Cen. and West Africa, based in Abidjan, Côte d'Ivoire 1989–97; managed her own co. 1997–2000; joined govt 2000, served simultaneously as Perm. Rep. to UN in Geneva, Head of Del. to WTO and Amb. to Switzerland 2002–05; Deputy Head of Del. for Rwanda's first Trade Policy Review 2004; adviser, Council of Econ. and Social Affairs, Office of Pres. of Rwanda, Kigali –2005; Deputy Dir-Gen. WTO 2005–13, Coordinator of African Group in WTO; CEO Rwanda Development Bd 2013–14; Minister for the Ministry of East African Community 2014–16, mem. Cabinet of Rwanda 2016–; Perm. Rep. to UN, New York 2016–; mem. East African Legis. Ass. 2012–17; founding mem. Rwandese Pvt. Sector Fed., Rwanda Women Entrepreneurs' Org., Rwandese Women Leaders' Caucus; one of two Ambs representing Least Developed Countries in Integrated Framework Working Group. *Address:* Permanent Mission of Rwanda to United Nations, 124 East 39th Street, New York, NY 10016, USA (office). *Telephone:* (212) 679-9010 (office). *Fax:* (212) 679-9133 (office). *E-mail:* ambanewyork@minaffet.gov.rw (office).

SENDOV, Blagovest Hristov, PhD, DSc; Bulgarian mathematician, academic, politician and diplomatist; *Researcher, Bulgarian Academy of Sciences;* b. 8 Feb. 1932, Assenovgrad; s. of Christo Sendov and Marushka Sendov; m. 1st Lilia Georgieva 1958 (divorced 1982); two d.; m. 2nd Anna Marinova 1982; one s.; ed gymnasium in Assenovgrad, Sofia Univ., Moscow State Univ. and Imperial Coll., London, UK; cleaner in Sofia 1949–52; teacher in Boboshevo and Elin Pelin 1956–58; Asst, Dept of Algebra, Univ. of Sofia 1958–60, Asst in Numerical Analysis and Computer Science 1960–63, Asst Prof. of Computer Sciences 1963–67, Prof. of Computer Science 1967, Dean, Faculty of Math. 1970–73, Rector 1973–79; mem. Parl. 1976–90, 1994–, Pres. of Parl. 1995–97, Vice-Pres. 1997–2003; Amb. to Japan 2003–09; Vice-Pres. Bulgarian Acad. of Sciences 1980–82, Vice-Pres. and Scientific Sec.-Gen. 1982–88, Dir Centre for Informatics and Computer Tech. 1985–90, Pres. 1988–91; Pres. Comm. of Science 1986–88; Vice-Pres. Int. Fed. for Information Processing 1985–88, Pres. 1989–91; Vice-Pres. World Peace Council 1983–86, IIP—UNESCO 1986–90; Extraordinary Vice-Pres. ICSU 1990–93; mem. Exec. Cttee and Bd of Dirs Int. Foundation for Survival and Devt of Humanity 1988–2003; Hon. Pres. Int. Asscn of Univs 1985–; two Orders of People's Repub. of Bulgaria and many others; Dr hc 1969, 1977, 2005, 2010, 2012; Dimitrov Prize for Science, Honoured Scientist 1984. *Publications:* Numerical Analysis, Old and New 1973, Hausdorff Approximation 1979, Averaged Moduli of Smoothness (monograph); textbooks and more than 200 articles in learned journals. *Leisure interests:* tennis, gardening, travelling. *Address:* 5 Plachkoviza Str., 1126 Sofia, Bulgaria (home). *Telephone:* (2) 862-6083 (home). *Fax:* (2) 870-8494 (office). *E-mail:* sendov2003@yahoo.com (home); acad@sendov.com (office). *Website:* www.sendov .com.

SENEQUIER, Dominique, DEA; French investment manager and business executive; *Chairman and CEO, Ardian;* b. 1953, Toulon; m.; one s. one d.; ed Ecole Polytechnique, Univ. of Paris (Sorbonne); worked for French Insurance Comm. 1975–80; Group Acquisitions Man., Groupe GAN (insurance co.) 1980–87, Founder and Dir GAN Participations 1987–95; joined AXA Investment Managers 1996, Founder of subsidiary AXA Private Equity (now Ardian), Chair. and CEO 1997–; mem. Bd of Dirs Hewlett-Packard 2011–12, Cytheris, Alitheia Capital; non-voting mem. Bd Bourbon 2009–; mem. Institut des Actuaries Français, Int. Actuarial Asscn; acquired Chateau Kirwan and Chateau Clinet wineries in Bordeaux; Chevalier, Légion d'honneur 2012; named by European Dow Jones (Awards for Excellence in Private Equity) "the most influential woman of capital investment" 2010. *Leisure interests:* playing the piano, opera. *Address:* Ardian, 20 place Vendôme, 75001 Paris, France (office). *Telephone:* 1-41-71-92-00 (office). *Fax:* 1-41-71-92-99 (office). *E-mail:* press@ardian.com (office). *Website:* www.ardian.com (office).

ŞENER, Abdüllatif, DEcon; Turkish politician and academic; b. 1954, Yıldızeli, Sivas; ed Ankara Univ., Gazi Univ.; served in several academic posts at Gazi Univ. and Hacettepe Univ.; also worked in Ministry of Interior Affairs, Turkish Employment Agency, and as a tax inspector, Ministry of Finance; mem. Parl. (Refah Partisi) 1991–2007; Minister of Finance 1996–97, Deputy Prime Minister and Minister of State 2002–07; mem. Refah Partisi 1991–98, Fazilet Partisi 1998–2001, Founding mem. Justice and Progress Party (AKP) 2001–07 (fmr Deputy Chair.), Founder and Leader, Türkiye Partisi 2009–12; apptd Assoc. Prof., TOBB Univ. of Econs and Tech. 2007, Pres. TOBB Union of Chambers and Commodity Exchanges; also mem. Faculty, Dept of Public Finance, Hacettepe Univ.; Pres. Exec. Cttee, e-Transformation Turkey. *Address:* Union of Chambers and Commodity Exchanges, TOBB, Dumlupınar Bulvarı No:252 (Eskişehir Yolu 9. Km.), 06530 Ankara, Turkey (office). *Website:* www.tobb.org.tr/Sayfalar/Eng/TicaretBorsalari.php (office).

SENEVIRATNE, Hon. Athauda; Sri Lankan teacher and politician; b. 19 Sept. 1931, Kegalle; m.; mem. Parl. (United Peoples Freedom Alliance) for Kegalle; Minister of Labour Relations and Foreign Employment –2010, of Justice and Law Reforms 2010, Sr Minister of Rural Affairs 2010–15; Pres. Jana Sahana Foundation. *Address:* C 78, Gregories Avenue, Colombo 07, Sri Lanka (home). *E-mail:* seneviratne_a@parliament.lk (office).

SENEVIRATNE, (Welathanthirige Don) John; Sri Lankan lawyer and politician; b. 15 Jan. 1941, Kahawatta, Ratnapura; s. of Welathanthirige Podi Appuhami and Soma Wijesundara; ed Sri Lanka Law Coll., Palmadulla Gangkanda Vidyalaya, Horana Thakshilawa, Aquinas Coll.; entered politics 1977; MP (Sri Lanka Freedom Party) for Ratnapura 1990–, Chair. Parl. Cttee on Public Expenditure (COPE) 2008, currently Chief Opposition Whip; Deputy Minister of Educ. 1995–97, Minister of Labour 1997–2000, of Health 2000–04, of Justice and Judicial Reforms 2004–05, of Power and Energy 2005–10, of Public Admin and Home Affairs 2010–15. *Address:* Parliament of Sri Lanka, Parliamentary Complex, Sri Jayawardenapura, Sri Lanka (office). *Telephone:* (11) 2777100 (office). *Fax:* (11) 2777564 (office). *E-mail:* senewiratne_w@parliament.lk (office). *Website:* www.parliament.lk (office).

SENGHAAS, Dieter, DPhil; German professor of social science; *Professor of Peace, Conflict and Development Research, University of Bremen;* b. 27 Aug. 1940, Geislingen; m. Eva Knobloch 1968; one d.; ed Univs of Tübingen, Ann Arbor and Frankfurt and Amherst Coll.; Research Fellow, Center for Int. Affairs, Harvard Univ. 1968–70; Research Dir, Peace Research Inst., Frankfurt 1971–78; Prof. of Int. Relations, Univ. of Frankfurt 1972–78; Prof. of Peace, Conflict and Devt Research, Univ. of Bremen 1978–; mem. several nat. and int. scientific orgs; Dr hc (Tübingen) 2000; Lentz Int. Peace Research Award 1987, Göttingen Peace Award 1999, Villa Ichon Culture and Peace Prize 2006, Leopold Kohr Prize 2010. *Publications include:* Aggressivität und kollektive Gewalt 1972, Aufrüstung durch Rüstungskontrolle 1972, Gewalt-Konflikt-Frieden 1974, Abschreckung und Frieden (3rd edn) 1981, Rüstung und Militarismus (2nd edn) 1982, Von Europa lernen 1982, The European Experience 1985, Die Zukunft Europas 1986, Europas Entwicklung und die Dritte Welt 1986, Weltwirtschaftsordnung und Entwicklungspolitik (5th edn) 1987, Konfliktformationen im internationalen System 1988, Europa 2000: Ein Friedensplan 1990, Friedensprojekt Europa 1992, Wohin driftet die Welt 1994, Zivilisierung wider Willen 1998, Klaenge des Friedens 2001, The Clash Within Civilizations 2001, Zum irdischen Frieden 2004, On Perpetual Peace 2007, Weltordnung in einer zerklüfteten Welt 2012, Dieter Senghaas Pioneer of Peace and Development Research 2013, Frieden hoeren 2013; ed. or co-ed. of 33 books related to political science, int. affairs, music, etc. *Leisure interest:* music. *Address:* University of Bremen, Fachbereich 8/ InIIS, Postfach 330440, 28334 Bremen (office); Freiligrathstrasse 6, 28211 Bremen, Germany (home). *Telephone:* (421) 21867489 (office); (421) 230436 (home). *Fax:* (421) 21867491 (office); (421) 249169 (home). *E-mail:* tmenge@iniis.uni-bremen.de (office); senghaas@uni-bremen.de (home). *Website:* www.iniis.uni-bremen.de/homepages/senghaas (office).

SENGHORE, Aboubacar Abdullah, PhD; Gambian academic and politician; b. 1968, Fass Njaga Choi, North Bank Region; fmr Lecturer in Comparative Law, Dept of Islamic Law, Faculty of Islamic Revealed Knowledge and Human Sciences, Int. Islamic Univ., Malaysia; Legal and Research Officer and Head of Legal and Research Dept, African Centre for Democracy and Human Rights Studies, Banjul 1999–2002; fmr Assoc. Lecturer, Management Devt Inst., Banjul; Sr Lecturer in Law, Governance and Int. Politics and Dean, Faculty of Law, Univ. of the Gambia –2013, also fmr Dean, Faculty of Social Sciences; Minister of Foreign Affairs, Int. Co-operation and Gambians Abroad 2013–April 2014, May–Sept. 2014; Contrib. African Human Rights Law Journal; Gusi Peace Prize (Philippines) 2013. *Address:* c/o Ministry of Foreign Affairs, International Co-operation and Gambians Abroad, 4 Marina Parade, Banjul, Gambia (office).

SENGOKU, Yoshito; Japanese lawyer and politician; b. 15 Jan. 1946, Tokushima; ed Tokyo Univ.; pvt. practice as lawyer 1971–; mem. House of Reps (Democratic Party of Japan) for Tokushima Pref. 1990–93, 1996–2012, fmr Chair. Parl. Cttee on Audit and Oversight of Admin; fmr mem. Social Democratic Party of Japan; fmr Next (Shadow) Minister of State for Econ. and Fiscal Policy, fmr Shadow Chair. Econ. Strategy Meeting; Minister of State for Admin. Innovation and for Civil Service Reform 2009–10; Chief Cabinet Sec. 2010–11, also Minister of State for the Abduction Issue; Minister of Justice 2010–11.

SENTAMU, Most Rev. Rt Hon John Tucker Mugabi, LLB, MA, PhD, FRSA, PC; Ugandan/British ecclesiastic; *Archbishop of York;* b. 1949; m. Margaret Sentamu; two c.; ed Makerere Univ., Univ. of Cambridge, UK; trained barrister and Advocate of the High Court of Uganda; Asst Chaplain Selwyn Coll. Cambridge; ordained 1979; Chaplain, Latchmere Remand Centre 1979–82; curate, St Andrew's Ham in Southwark 1979–82; curate, St Paul's, Herne Hill 1982–83; Priest-in-Charge, Holy Trinity, Tulse Hill 1983–84; Parish Priest St Matthias, Upper Tulse Hill 1983–84; Vicar Holy Trinity and St Matthias, Tulse Hill 1985–96; mem. Gen. Synod 1985–96, 2005–, mem. Standing, Policy and Appointments Cttees; mem. Archbishop's Comm. for Urban Priority Areas 1988–92; mem. Revision Cttee for the Ordination of Women to the Priesthood; Priest-in-Charge, St Saviour, Brixton Hill 1987–89; mem. Family Welfare Asscn 1989–; mem. Decade of Evangelism Steering Group; mem. Exec. Springboard; Prolocutor Convocation of Canterbury 1990–96; Chair. Cttee for Minority Ethnic Anglican Concerns 1990–99; Area Bishop of Stepney 1996–2002; Bishop of Birmingham 2002–05, Archbishop of York 2005–; Adviser to the Stephen Lawrence Judicial Inquiry 1997–99; Gov. Univ. of North London 1998–2002; Pres. and Chair. London Marriage Guidance Council 2000–04; Chair. Review into the murder investigation of Damilola Taylor 2001–02; Chancellor, York St John Univ. 2006–, Univ. of Cumbria 2007–; Pres. Youth for Christ, YMCA England; Chair. NHS Haemoglobinopathy Screening Programme, EC1 New Deal Devt Programme; Sponsor of the Fairness Commission in York, then Chair. ind. Comm. on future of the Living Wage 2013; mem. Health Advisory Cttee HM Prisons, CTE Forum, Birmingham Hosp. NHS Trust, Yorkshire Soc. 2009–; Custodian Trustee, Birmingham Diocesan Fund; Trustee, Tower Hamlets Summer Univ.; Deputy Chair. Comm. on Urban Life and Faith 2003; Tourism Amb. Visit York 2010; Fellow, Univ. Coll., Christ Church, Canterbury, Queen Mary, Univ. of London; Hon. Fellow Selwyn Coll. Cambridge, Hon. Canon Southwark Cathedral 1993–96; Hon. Master Bencher, Grays Inn 2007; Freeman of the City of London 2000, Freeman of the City of Montego Bay 2007; Dr hc (Open Univ.), (Birmingham City Univ.), (York) 2010; Hon. DPhil (Gloucestershire); Hon. DD (Birmingham), (Hull), (Cambridge), (Nottingham), (Wycliffe Coll., Toronto), (Univ. of the South, Sewanee, TN) 2010, (London) 2010; Hon. LLD (Leicester), (Teeside), (Leeds) 2010; Hon. DL (Sheffield), (Univ. of the West Indies); Hon. DCL (Northumbria); Hon. DTheol (Univ. of Chester) 2009; Midlander of the Year 2003, Yorkshire Man of the Year 2007, Speaker of the Year 2007. *Leisure interests:* music, cooking, reading, athletics, rugby, football. *Address:* Bishopthorpe Palace, Bishopthorpe, York, YO23 2GE, England (office). *Telephone:* (1904) 707021 (office). *Fax:* (1904) 709204 (office). *E-mail:* office@archbishopofyork.org (office). *Website:* www.archbishopofyork.org (office).

ŞENTOP, Mustafa, PhD; Turkish politician and academic; *Chairman of the Grand National Assembly;* b. 6 Aug. 1968, Tekirdağ; m.; four c.; ed Istanbul Univ., Marmara Univ.; prof. 2011; Vice-Dean, Marmara Univ., also mem. Exec. Bd; Pres. Ekonomik Ve Sosyal Araştırmalar Merkezi; mem. Grand Nat. Ass. 2011–, Deputy Chair. 2018–19, Chair. 2019–; Deputy Chair., Justice and Devt Party 2012–15. *Address:* Grand National Assembly, TBMM 06543, Main Building E Block, Bakanlıklar, Ankara, Turkey (office). *Telephone:* (312) 4205151 (office). *Fax:* (312) 4205146 (office). *E-mail:* mustafa.sentop@tbmm.gov.tr (office). *Website:* www.tbmm.gov.tr (office); baskanlik.tbmm.gov.tr/ozgecmis.aspx.

SEPE, HE Cardinal Crescenzio; Italian ecclesiastic; *Archbishop of Naples;* b. 2 June 1943, Carinaro, Aversa; ed Pontifical Lateran Univ., Univ. of Rome La Sapienza.; taught theology at Lateran and Urbanian Pontifical Univs; ordained priest 1967; apptd Assessor for Gen. Affairs, Secr. of State 1987; consecrated Bishop 1992; apptd Titular Archbishop of Grado 1992; apptd Sec. Congregation for the Clergy 1992; Chair. Peregrinatio ad Petri Sedem 1997–2001; cr. Cardinal (Cardinal-Priest of Dio Padre misericordioso) 2001; Prefect of Congregation for the Evangelization of Peoples, Roman Curia 2001–05, 2005–06; Archbishop of Naples 2006–; participated in Papal Conclave 2005, 2013; currently also Grand Chancellor, Pontifical Urban Univ.; Int. Witness of Holiness Award, Tu es Petrus Asscn, Battipaglia 2010. *Address:* Curia of Naples, Largo Donnaregina 22, 80138 Naples (office); Villa Betania, Via Urbans VIII 16, 00165 Rome, Italy (home). *Telephone:* (081) 5574111 (office). *E-mail:* internet@chiesadinapoli.it (office). *Website:* www.chiesadinapoli.it (office).

SEPÚLVEDA-AMOR, Bernardo, LLB; Mexican lawyer, judge and politician; b. 14 Dec. 1941, Mexico City; s. of Bernardo Sepúlveda and Margarita Sepúlveda; m. Ana Yturbe 1970; three s.; ed Nat. Univ. of Mexico and Queen's Coll., Cambridge; fmrly taught int. law, El Colegio de México and Faculty of Political Science, Univ. of Mexico; Asst Dir of Juridical Affairs, Ministry of Presidency 1968–70; Dir-Gen. of Int. Financial Affairs, Ministry of Finance 1976–81; Int. Adviser, Minister of Programming and Budget 1981; Amb. to USA March–Dec. 1982; Sec. of Foreign Affairs 1982–88; Amb. to UK 1989–93; Foreign Affairs Adviser to Pres. of Mexico 1993–; mem. UN Int. Law Comm. 1996–2005; fmr Judge ad hoc, Int. Court of Justice, Judge 2006–15, Vice-Pres. 2012–15; Sec. Int. Affairs Institutional Revolutionary Party (PRI) 1981–82; Pres. to UN Sixth Comm. on Transnational Corpns 1977–80; Hon. Fellow, Queens' Coll., Cambridge 1991; Dr hc (Univ. of San Diego), (Univ. of Leningrad); Premio Príncipe de Asturias, Premio Simón Bolivar. *Publications:* Foreign Investment in Mexico 1973, Transnational Corporations in Mexico 1974, A View of Contemporary Mexico 1979, Planning for Development 1981. *Address:* Rocas 185, México, DF 01900, Mexico. *Telephone:* (5) 652-0641. *Fax:* (5) 652-9739.

SEQUEIRA, José Agostinho, (Somotxo); Timor-Leste politician and fmr resistance fighter; b. 25 Oct. 1960, Loré, Lautém; Mil. Sec./Chief of Staff to Commdr in Chief, Falintil (mil. wing of Fretilin) during war of independence mid 1990s; worked to compile archive of Timor-Leste resistance with Mário Soares Foundation (FMS), Lisbon 2002; Inaugural Dir, Archive & Museum of East Timorese Resistance 2005; returned to Timor-Leste May 2006; Vice Minister of Interior 2006–07; Pres. Falintil Veterans Foundation; mem. State Council 2012–17; mem. Nat. Parl. 2017–; Minister of Defence and Security 2017–18; mem. Frente Revolucionária do Timor Leste Independente (FRETILIN) (Revolutionary Front for an Independent East Timor political party). *Address:* FRETILIN, Rua dos Mártires da Pátria, Dili, Timor-Leste (office). *Telephone:* 7287080 (office). *E-mail:* fretilin.media@gmail.com (office). *Website:* fretilinmedia.blogspot.com (office).

SEQUEIRA, Luis, BA, MA, PhD; American plant biologist and academic; *Professor Emeritus, Department of Plant Pathology, University of Wisconsin, Madison;* b. 1 Sept. 1927, San José, Costa Rica; s. of Raul Sequeira and Dora Jenkins; m. Elisabeth Steinvorth 1954; one s. three d.; ed Harvard Univ.; Teaching Fellow, Harvard Univ. 1949–52; Parker Fellow, Harvard and Instituto Biológico, São Paulo, Brazil 1952–53; Plant Pathologist, Asst Dir, then Dir Coto Research Station, United Fruit Co., Costa Rica 1953–60; Research Assoc., North Carolina State Univ., Raleigh, North Carolina 1960–61; Assoc. Prof., then Prof., Dept of Plant Pathology, Univ. of Wis., Madison 1961–78, Prof., Depts of Bacteriology and Plant Pathology 1978–82, apptd J.C. Walker Prof. 1982, currently Prof. Emer.; Consultant Agracetus, Madison 1982–93; Chief Scientist, Competitive Grants Office, USDA, Washington, DC 1987–88; Fellow, American Phytopathological Soc. (Pres. 1985–86), American Acad. of Microbiology; mem. NAS, Linnean Soc. of London, Nat. Science Bd 1991–; Hon. Prof., Univ. of Queensland 1997; Award of Distinction, American Phytopathological Soc. 1994, E.M. Stakman Award. *Publications:* approximately 260 publs in journals and covering plant pathology, bacteriology, biochemistry and genetics. *Leisure interests:* classical music, cross-country skiing. *Address:* 10 Appomattox Court, Madison, WI 53705, USA (home). *Telephone:* (608) 833-3440 (home); (608) 262-1393 (office). *Fax:* (608) 263-2626 (office). *E-mail:* lzs@plantpath.wisc.edu (office).

SEQUEIRA, Gen. Salviano de Jesus, (Kianda); Angolan army officer and politician; *Minister of National Defence;* b. 31 Dec. 1945; m.; participated in MPLA guerrilla campaign 2nd Political-Military Region, Cabinda Prov. 1968–74, Commdr troops stationed in city of Cabinda 1974–75, Commdr Artillery Group of 9th Brigade, Chief of Artillery Brigade, Chief of Staff 1975–77, promoted to Maj. 1976, Chief of Staff 1st Military Region (provinces of Bengo, Kwanza Norte, Uíge, Malange, Zaire) 1976–77, promoted to Col 1979, Chief of Staff 5th Military Region (provinces of Namibe, Huíla, Cunene) 1979–81, Commdr Troops of 5th Military Region 1981–85, promoted to Maj.-Gen. 1988, Deputy Commdr North Front (1st, 2nd, 3rd, 7th, 9th, 10th Military Regions) 1988–90, Head Tanks and Transportation, Directorate of Gen. Staff 1990–92, promoted to Gen. (two stars) 1992, Commdr South Military Region 1992–93, apptd for special missions abroad namely exploration of sources of weapons supplies, combat techniques, other military equipment, inspection, and shipment to Angola 1993–96, promoted to Gen. (three stars) 1996, Commdr Angolan Armed Forces (FAA) Logistics and Infrastructure 1996–2003, Deputy Chief of Staff Operations, FAA 2003–09; Deputy Minister of Nat. for Defence Material Resources and Infrastructure 2010–12, Sec. of State for Material Resources and Infrastructures 2012–17, Minister of Nat. Defence 2017–. *Address:* Ministry of National Defence, Rua 17 de Setembro, Luanda, Angola (office). *Telephone:* 222330354 (office). *Fax:* 222334276 (office). *E-mail:* geral@minden.gov.ao (office). *Website:* www.minden.gov.ao (office).

SEQUI, Ettore Francesco, BA; Italian diplomatist; *Ambassador to China;* b. 13 Feb. 1956, Ghilarza, Oristano, Sardinia; ed Univ. of Cagliari; joined Italian Foreign Service 1985, with Dept for Econ. Affairs, Ministry of Foreign Affairs 1985–88, with Cabinet of Dir-Gen. of Econ. Affairs 1988–89, Consul in Tehran 1989–94, Counsellor, Perm. Representation to UN, New York 1994–98, Counsellor, Cabinet of Minister of Foreign Affairs, Rome 1998–2000, First Counsellor, Deputy Head of Mission, Embassy in Tirana 2000–04, Amb. to Afghanistan 2004–09, EU Special Rep. for Afghanistan 2008–09, for Afghanistan and Pakistan 2009–10, Head of EU Del. to Albania 2011–14, Chief of Cabinet, Ministry of Foreign Affairs 2014–15, Amb. to China 2015–; Officer, Order of Merit of the Italian Repub., Encomienda de Numero, Order of Isabel the Catholic (Spain), Medal of Ghazi Mir Bacha Khan (Afghanistan). *Publication:* Italy in the UN 1993–1999 (with others). *Leisure interests:* tennis, sailing, literature, history. *Address:* Embassy of Italy, 2 Dong Er Jie, San Li Tun, Beijing 100600, People's Republic of China (office). *Telephone:* (10) 85327600 (office). *Fax:* (10) 65324676 (office). *E-mail:* ambasciata.pechino@esteri.it (office). *Website:* www.ambpechino.esteri.it (office).

SERAGELDIN, Ismail, BSc, MRP, PhD; Egyptian international organization official; *Director, Bibliotheca Alexandrina;* b. 9 May 1944, Guiza; m.; one s.; ed Cairo Univ., Harvard Univ.; fmr lecturer Cairo and Harvard Univs; fmr consultant in city and regional planning; joined World Bank 1972, held numerous positions including Economist in Educ. and Human Resources 1972–76, Div. Chief for Tech. Assistance and Special Studies 1977–80, for Urban Projects in Europe, the Middle E and N Africa 1980–83, Dir for Programs in W Africa 1984–87, Co-Dir for Cen. and Occidental Africa 1987–89, Tech. Dir for Sub-Saharan Africa 1990–92, Vice-Pres. for Environmentally and Socially Sustainable Devt 1992–98, Co-Chair. Non Governmental Org.-Bank Cttee 1997–99, Vice-Pres. for Special Programs 1998–2000; Chair. Global Water Partnership 1996–2000, World Comm. for Water in the 21st Century 1998–2000; currently Dir Bibliotheca Alexandrina (Library of Alexandria); Amb. Alliance of Civilizations; also Chair. Exec. Council, World Digital Library; Prof., Int. Chair Savoirs contre pauvreté (Knowledge Against Poverty), Collège de France; Chair. and mem. of numerous advisory cttees including Egyptian Acad. of Science, Acad. of Sciences for the Developing World, Indian Nat. Acad. of Agricultural Sciences, European Acad. of Sciences and Arts; Foreign Fellow, Bangladesh Acad. of Sciences; fmr Distinguished Univ. Prof. Univ. of Wageningen, Netherlands; Officier, Ordre des Arts et des Lettres 2003, Order of the Rising Sun (Gold and Silver Star), Japan 2008, Ordre national de la Légion d'honneur 2008, Commandeur, Ordre des Arts et des Lettres 2011; Grameen Foundation Award, USA 1999, Pablo Neruda Medal of Honor, Chile 2004, Jamnalal Bajaj Award 2006, Champion of Youth Award, World Youth Congress, Quebec 2008, M. S. Swaminathan Award for Environmental Protection 2010, Millennium Excellence Award, Excellence Awards Foundation, Ghana 2010, Public Welfare Medal, NAS 2011, Calouste Gulbenkian Prize 2013; Hon. DSc (Indian Agricultural Research Inst.) 1997, (Punjab Agricultural Univ.) 1998, (Tamil Nadu Veterinary and Animal Sciences Univ.) 1998, (Tamil Nadu Agricultural Univ.) 1999, (Egerton Univ., Kenya) 1999, (SNHU, Manchester, NH) 2002, (McGill Univ., Montreal) 2003, (Azerbaijan State Economic Univ., Baku) 2007, numerous other hon. degrees. *Publications:* Nurturing Development 1995, Sustainability and the Wealth of Nations 1996, Architecture of Empowerment 1997, Rural Well-Being: From Vision to Action (jtly) 1997, The Modernity of Shakespeare 1998, Biotechnology and Biosafety (jtly) 1999, Very Special Places 1999, Promethean Science (jtly) 2000 and numerous other books and articles. *Address:* Bibliotheca Alexandrina, POB 138, El Shatby, Alexandria, 21526, Egypt (office). *Telephone:* (203) 4839999 (office). *Website:* www.bibalex.org (office); www .serageldin.com.

ŞERBAN, Andrei; Romanian theatre and opera director; *Professor and Director, Oscar Hammerstein II Center for Theatre Studies, Columbia University;* b. 21 June 1943, Bucharest; s. of Gheorghe Şerban and Elpis Şerban; m.; two c.; ed Bucharest Theatrical and Cinematographic Art Inst.; int. scholarships Ford 1970, Guggenheim 1976, Rockefeller 1980; associated with Robert Brustein's American Repertory Theatre Company for more than 20 years 1970–; worked also with LaMama Theatre, Public Theater, Lincoln Center, Circle in the Square, Yale Repertory Theatre, Guthrie Theatre, ACT, New York City, Seattle and Los Angeles Operas; in Europe: at Paris, Geneva, Vienna, and Bologna Opera Houses, Welsh Nat. Opera, Covent Garden, Théâtre de la Ville, Helsinki Lilla Teatern, Comédie Française, among others; worked with Shiki Co. of Tokyo, Japan; has delivered numerous lectures; Gen. Man. Nat. Theatre of Romania 1990–93; Prof. and Dir, Oscar Hammerstein II Center for Theatre Studies, Columbia Univ., New York 1992–; Order of the Star of Romania (Steaua Romȃniei); Prize for the Best Performance, World Students' Theatre Festival, Zagreb 1965, Obie Awards, Tony Award, George Abbott Award, Soc. of Stage Dirs and Choreographers, prizes at Avignon, Belgrade and Shiraz Festivals. *Productions include:* (in Romania) Ubu Roi 1966, Julius Caesar 1968, Jonah 1969, An Ancient Trilogy (Medea, The Trojan Women, Elektra) 1990; (in USA) Medea (Euripides) 1972, Fragments of a Trilogy (Medea, Elektra, The Trojan Women) 1974, As You Like It 1976, The Cherry Orchard 1977, Uncle Vanya 1979, The Umbrellas of Cherbourg 1980, The Seagull 1981, Three Sisters 1983, The King Stag 1985, The Miser 1988, Twelfth Night 1989, Sweet Table at the Richelieu 1989, Hamlet 1999 (in France, at the Comédie Française), L'Avare 2000, Le Marchand de Venise 2001, Lysystrata 2002 Pericles 2003, Cleansed 2006, Uncle Vanya 2005, King Lear 2006, Cries and Whispers (in Romania, three UNITER Awards including Best Dir 2011) 2011, Hedda Gabler 2012, Angels in America (in Hungary, Best Dir, Hungarian Theatre Critics Asscn 2013) 2013, Chung Young 2014. *Opera productions include:* Eugene Onegin 1980, Turandot 1984, Norma 1985, Fidelio (Covent Garden) 1986; Paris Opera: L'Ange de feu 1991, Lucia Di Lammermoor 1995, The Puritans 1997, L'Italienne à Alger 1998, Les Indes Galantes 1999, La Khovantchina 2001, Les Vêpres Siciliennes 2003, Otello 2004; Wiener Staatsoper: Les Contes d'Hoffman 1993, Die Lustige Witwe 1999, Werther 2005, Manon 2007, etc. *Address:* Oscar Hammerstein II Center for Theatre Studies, Columbia University, 601C Dodge Hall, Mail Code 1807, 2960 Broadway, New York, NY 10027, USA (office). *Telephone:* (212) 854-3408 (office). *Fax:* (212) 854-3344 (office). *E-mail:* as160@columbia.edu (office). *Website:* arts.columbia.edu/theatre-arts (office).

SERDENGEÇTİ, Süreyya, BS, MA; Turkish economist, academic and fmr central banker; *Director, Stability Institute, Economic Policy Research Foundation of Turkey (TEPAV);* b. 1952, Istanbul; m. Çiğdem Son Deniz; ed Middle East Tech. Univ., Ankara, Vanderbilt Univ., USA; with Central Bank of Turkey 1980–2006, positions included Foreign Exchange, Markets, External Relations, Communication Depts, Vice-Gov. 1998–2001, Gov. 2001–06; Sr Lecturer, Dept of Econs, TOBB Univ. of Econs and Tech., Ankara 2006–; Dir Stability Inst., Econ. Policy Research Foundation of Turkey 2006–. *Address:* TEPAV Söğütözü Cd 43, 43 Tobb-Etü Yerleşkesi 2. Kısım, Ankara 06560, Turkey (office). *Telephone:* (312) 2925500 (office). *Fax:* (312) 292 5555 (office). *E-mail:* serdengecti@tepav.org.tr (office); serdengecti@etu.edu.tr (office). *Website:* www.tepav.org.tr/en (office).

SERDYUKOV, Anatolii Eduardovich, DEcon; Russian business executive and politician; *Chairman of Board of Directors, Technodinamika JSC;* b. 8 Jan. 1962, Kholmskii village, Abin Dist, Krasnodar Krai; m. Yuliya Zubkova; two c.; ed Leningrad (now St Petersburg) Inst. of Soviet Trade and St Petersburg State Univ.; mil. service 1984–85; worked in furniture shop 1985–95, then Marketing Dir and Dir-Gen. St Petersburg furniture market 1995–2000; Deputy Head, Dist Inspectorate of Taxes, Ministry of Taxes and Dues 2000–01; Deputy Head then Head, St Petersburg Tax Authority 2001–04; Deputy Minister of Taxes and Dues Feb.–July 2004, Head of Fed. Tax Service 2004–07; Minister of Defence 2007–12; Chair. JSC Chimprom Volgograd 2007–10; Aviation Cluster Industrial Dir Rostec State Corpn 2015–, Chair. Bd of Dirs Technodinamika JSC (subsidiary) 2016–; mem. Bd of Dirs UNC (United Engine Corpn) JSC, KRET JSC, Russian Helicopters JSC. *Address:* Technodinamika JSC, 115184 Moscow, 35/5 Bolshaya Tatarskaya Street, Russia (office). *Telephone:* (495) 627-10-99 (office). *E-mail:* info@technodinamika.ru (office). *Website:* technodinamika.ru (office).

SEREBRIAN, Oleg, PhD; Moldovan politician, diplomatist and writer; *Ambassador to Germany;* b. 1969; ed Universitatea Pedagogică de Stat Ion Creangă, European Inst. of High Int. Studies, France; Spokesperson, Ministry of Foreign Affairs 1998–99; Deputy Rector, Free Univ. of Moldova 1999–2002; Chair. Social Liberal Party 2001, then First Deputy Chair. Democratic Party; mem. Parl. 2005–10; Amb. to France 2010–15, to Germany 2015–. *Publications include:* Geopolitics of the Black Sea Region 1998, Politosphere 2001, Politics and Geopolitics 2004, Dictionary of Geopolitics 2006, About Geopolitics 2009, Song of the Sea (novel) 2011, Russia at the Crossroads 2014. *Address:* Embassy of Moldova, Gotlandstr. 16, 10439 Berlin, Germany (office). *Telephone:* (30) 44652970 (office). *Fax:* (30) 44652972 (office). *E-mail:* office@botschaft-moldau.de (office). *Website:* www.germania.mfa.md (office).

SEREBRIER, José, MA; American conductor and composer; b. 3 Dec. 1938, Montevideo, Uruguay; s. of David Serebrier and Frida Serebrier (née Wasser); m. Carole Farley 1969; one d.; ed Univ. of Minnesota, Curtis Inst. of Music, studied composition with Aaron Copland and Vittorio Giannini and conducting with Antal Dorati and Pierre Monteux; started conducting at age of 12; moved to USA 1956; guest conductor in USA, S America, Australia and Europe; Assoc. Conductor, American Symphony Orchestra, with Leopold Stokowski 1962–68; conducted alongside Leopold Stokowski world première of Charles Ives' Fourth Symphony, Carnegie Hall, New York 1964; conducted first performance in Poland of Charles Ives' Fourth Symphony 1971 and premieres of over 500 works; Rockefeller Foundation Composer-in-Residence with Cleveland Orchestra 1968–70; Music Dir Cleveland Philharmonic Orchestra 1968–71; Artistic Dir Int. Festival of the Americas, Miami 1984–, Miami Festival 1985– (also Founder), Festival Miami; toured frequently with Russian Nat. Orchestra in S America and China; two Guggenheim Fellowships, Ford Foundation Conducting Award, Nat. Endowment for the Arts Comm. Award 1969, Ditson Award for Promotion of New Music, Columbia Univ. 1980, Deutsche Schallplatten Critics' Award 1991, UK Music Retailers' Asscn Award for Best Symphony Recording (for Mendelssohn symphonies) 1991, Diapason d'Or Recording Award, France, Best Audiophile Recording (for Scheherazade), Soundstage 2000, BMI Award, Koussevitzky Foundation Award, Latin Grammy for Best Classical Album of 2004 (for Carmen Symphony with Barcelona Symphony Orchestra). *Compositions include:* Solo Violin Sonata 1954, Quartet for Saxophones 1955, Pequeña música (wind quintet) 1955, Symphony No. 1 1956, Momento psicológico (string orchestra) 1957, Solo Piano Sonata 1957, Suite canina (wind trio) 1957, Symphony for Percussion 1960, The Star Wagon (chamber orchestra) 1967, Nueve (double bass and orchestra) 1970, Colores mágicos (variations for harp and chamber orchestra) 1971, At Dusk, in Shadows (solo flute), Andante Cantabile (strings), Night Cry (brass), Dorothy and Carmine (flute and strings), George and Muriel (contrabass), Winter (violin concerto) 1995, Winterreise (for orchestra) 1999; composed music for several films; all compositions published and recorded; over 350 recordings to date. *Television includes:* int. TV broadcast of Grammys Ceremony, LA 2002, conducting suite from Bernstein's West Side Story. *Recordings include:* more than 300 recordings with major orchestras. *Publications include:* orchestration of 14 songs by Edvard Grieg 2000, orchestration of Gershwin's works 2002, Suite from Janacek's Makropoulos Case 2004; more than 100 works published. *Leisure interests:* reading, swimming, football. *Address:* 20 Queensgate Gardens, London, SW7 5LZ, England (office). *Fax:* (212) 662-8073 (New York) (office). *E-mail:* caspi123@aol.com (office). *Website:* www.joseserebrier.com.

SERETSE, Brig. Dikgakgamatso Ramadeluka; Botswana lawyer, politician and fmr army officer; m. Sandra Seretse; served as Brig. in Botswana Defence Force, mem. Parl. for Serowe North East (Botswana Democratic Party) 2004–14; Minister for Lands and Housing –2008, for Defence, Justice and Security 2008–10 (resgnd), 2011–14. *Address:* c/o Ministry for the Administration of Justice, Gaborone, Botswana.

SERETSE, Vincent, BA; Botswana business executive and politician; *Minister of International Affairs and Cooperation;* m. Michelle Seretse; three d.; ed Univ. of Botswana and Swaziland, Boston Univ., New York Univ.; started his career as Govt Town Planner 1982, becoming Sr Urban Planner; fmr Property Man. with Knight Frank & Rutley Botswana (property consultancy); fmr CEO Botswana Housing Corpn; CEO, Botswana Telecommunications Corpn 2004–08; Group Man. Dir RPC DataBotswana (ICT co.) 2008; Exec. Chair. Kwena Property Services (Pty) Ltd –2009, now non-Exec. Chair.; joined Nat. Ass. (Parl.) as Specially Elected MP 2009, mem. various Parl. Cttees including Commonwealth Parl. Cttee, Public Accounts Cttee, elected as MP for Lentsweletau/Mmopane constituency 2014–; Asst Minister of Finance and Devt Planning 2011–14, Acting Minister of Youth, Sport and Culture April–Nov. 2014, Minister of Investment, Trade and Industry 2014–18, Minister of Int. Affairs and Cooperation 2018–; fmr Chair. Standard Chartered Bank of Botswana; Dir Dikgang (PTY) Ltd 1993–2003, also fmr Chair.; fmr mem. Comm. on Review of Public Service Pay Structures; mem. Real Estate Inst. of Botswana, South African Inst. of Valuers. *Address:* Ministry of International Affairs and Co-operation, Government Enclave, PMB 00365, Gaborone, Botswana (office). *Telephone:* 3600700 (office). *Fax:* 3913366 (office). *E-mail:* mofaic-admin@lists.gov.bw (office). *Website:* www.mofaic.gov.bw (office).

SERGEANT, Carol, CBE, BA, MBA; British banking executive and financial officer; b. 7 Aug. 1952, Berlin, Germany; d. of Frank Hawksworth and Norah MaCauley; m. Philip Sergeant; one s. one d.; ed Newnham Coll. Cambridge, City Univ. Business School; joined Bank of England 1970s, various positions in research, negotiations with IMF, EEC issues, foreign exchange –1998; joined Financial Services Authority 1998, held various positions including Dir Strategic Change, Man. Dir responsible for Regulatory Processes and Risk Directorate, Deputy Chair. Building Societies Comm., Dir Banks and Building Societies, mem. Bd 2001–03 (resgnd); Chief Risk Dir and mem. Group Exec. Cttee, Lloyds TSB 2004–11; consultant to various banks 2011–13; Chair. Standards Policy and

Strategy Cttee, British Standards Inst. 2013–; Chair. Ind. Project Bd, Asscn of British Insurers 2014; Chair. Bd of Trustees, Public Concern at Work (charity); led HM Treasury–sponsored project on Simple Financial Products 2012–13; mem. Bd of Dirs Martin Currie Holdings, Secure Trust Bank 2011–, Danske Bank A/S 2013–, Tullett Prebon plc 2015–; mem. Advisory Bd and Strategy Cttee, Cass Business School; mem. Trustee and Audit Cttee, Court of Int. Guild of Bankers; Trustee Lloyd's Register Foundation. *Leisure interest:* fencing. *Address:* Standards Policy and Strategy Committee, British Standards Institution, 389 Chiswick High Road, London, W4 4AL, England (office). *E-mail:* cservices@bsigroup.com (office). *Website:* www.bsigroup.com (office).

SERGEYEV, Victor Mikhailovich, DHist; Russian mathematician, political scientist and professor of political studies; *Professor of Comparative Politics and Director, Centre for International Research, Moscow State Institute of International Relations;* b. 22 April 1944, Moscow; m. Marina Alekseyevna Sergeyeva; one s.; ed Moscow Inst. of Energy, Moscow State Univ.; Sr Researcher All-Union Research Inst. of Meteorological Service, USSR State Cttee of Standards 1975–78, Problem Lab. of System Analysis, Moscow State Inst. of Int. Relations 1978–86, Prof. of Comparative Politics and Dir Centre for Int. Research 1998–; Head of Lab. Inst. of USA and Canada, USSR (now Russian) Acad. of Sciences 1986–90; Deputy Dir Analytical Centre on Scientific and Industrial Policy, Ministry of Science and Tech. 1998–; Visiting Prof. and Fellow, Leiden Univ., Santa Fe Inst., Netherlands Inst. for Advanced Studies, Svedish Collegium for Advanced Studies in Social Science, Uppsala Univ., Leeds Univ.; mem. Russian Acad. of Nat. Sciences, Asscn of Political Studies, Kant Soc., Russian Asscn of Artificial Intellect, Exec. Bd Centre of Philosophy, Psychology and Sociology of Religion; Hon. mem. Leeds Univ., UK. *Publications include:* numerous scientific works published in Russia and abroad on political and religious culture, cognitive studies, including The Wild East 1998, Limits of Rationality 1998. *Leisure interest:* foreign languages. *Address:* Centre for International Research, Moscow State Institute of International Relations, prospekt Vernadskogo 76, 119454 Moscow, Russia (office). *Telephone:* (495) 434-20-44 (office). *Fax:* (495) 434-20-44 (office). *E-mail:* tsmi@mgimo.ru (office); av205@comtv.ru.

SERGIENKO, Valentin Ivanovich, MS, PhD, DSc; Russian chemist; *Chairman, Far East Branch, Russian Academy of Sciences;* b. 18 Aug. 1944, Novosysoyevka, Primorsky territory; m.; two c.; ed Far East State Univ., Vladivostok; has held numerous positions at Inst. of Chemistry, Far East Br., Russian Acad. of Sciences 1970–92, including Jr Researcher, Sr Researcher, Head of Group, Head of Lab., Head of Div., Deputy Dir, Acting Dir, Deputy Chair. Far East Br. of Russian Acad. of Sciences 1992–2001, Chair. 2001–, concurrently Head of Div., Inst. of Chem., Far East Br. of Russian Acad. of Sciences 2002–, Dir Natural School 2011–14; Scientific Head, Inst. of Engineering and Social Ecology, Far East State Technical Univ.; Dir Far East Br. of Agency for Man. of Property, Russian Acad. of Sciences; mem. Russian Acad. of Sciences, Corresp. mem. 1997–2000, Academician 2002–, Vice-Pres. 2013–; Bd mem. Russian Foundation for Basic Research; mem.-at-large, Asscn of Acads and Socs of Sciences in Asia; Order of Labour Red Banner, Order of Honor 2012; Prize of Russian Fed. Govt in the field of science and technology. *Publications include:* over 160 scientific papers, monographs on theoretical chemistry, spectrochemistry, structure of fluorides, technology of purification and utilization of waste; owner of six patents. *Address:* Presidium of Far Eastern Branch, Russian Academy of Sciences, Svetlanskaya street 50, Vladivostok 690950, Russia (office). *Telephone:* 4232-22 86 30 (office). *E-mail:* sergienko@hg.febras.ru (office). *Website:* www.febras.ru (office).

SERJEANT, Graham Roger, CMG, OJ, MD, FRCP; British medical research scientist and academic; *Chairman, Sickle Cell Trust (Jamaica);* b. 26 Oct. 1938, Bristol; s. of Ewart E. Serjeant and Violet E. Serjeant; m. Beryl E. King 1965; ed Sibford School, Banbury, Bootham School, York, Clare Coll., Cambridge, London Hosp. Medical School and Makerere Coll. Kampala; House Physician, London Hosp. 1963–64, Royal United Hosp. Bath 1965–66, Hammersmith Hosp., London 1966; Registrar, Univ. Hosp. of the West Indies 1966–67; Wellcome Research Fellow, Dept of Medicine, Univ. Hosp. of the West Indies 1967–71; Visiting Prof., Dept of Biochemistry, Univ. of Tennessee, USA 1971; mem. scientific staff, MRC Abnormal Haemoglobin Unit, Cambridge 1971–72, Epidemiology Research Unit, Jamaica 1972–74; Dir MRC Labs, Jamaica 1974–99; Prof. of Epidemiology, Faculty of Medicine, Univ. of the West Indies 1981–99, Prof. Emer. 1999–; Visiting Prof., London School of Hygiene and Tropical Medicine 1999, Guy's, King's and St Thomas' Combined Medical School, London 1999; Chair. Sickle Cell Trust (Jamaica); Hon. FRCPE 1998; Hon. Prof., Dept of Public Health, Guy's Hosp., London 1999; Hon. CD (Jamaica), Ordre du Mérite Congolais; Vice-Chancellor's Award for Excellence 1999, Pan American Health Org. Jamaican Hero of Health 2002. *Publications include:* The Clinical Features of Sickle Cell Disease 1974, Sickle Cell Disease (3rd edn) 2001; more than 400 papers on sickle cell disease in medical journals. *Leisure interests:* squash, music. *Address:* 14 Milverton Crescent, Kingston 6, Jamaica (home). *Telephone:* 970-0077 (office); 927-2300 (home). *Fax:* 970-0074 (office). *E-mail:* grserjeant@cwjamaica.com (home). *Website:* www.sicklecelltrustjamaica.com (office).

SEROTA, Sir Nicholas Andrew, Kt, CH, MA; British art gallery director; *Chairman, Arts Council England;* b. 27 April 1946, Hampstead, London, England; s. of Stanley Serota and Baroness Serota; m. 1st Angela M. Beveridge 1973 (divorced 1995); two d.; m. 2nd Teresa Gleadowe 1997; ed Haberdashers' Aske's School, Hampstead and Elstree, Christ's Coll., Cambridge and Courtauld Inst. of Art; Regional Art Officer and Exhbn Organizer, Arts Council of GB 1970–73; Dir Museum of Modern Art, Oxford 1973–76; Dir Whitechapel Art Gallery 1976–88; Dir The Tate Gallery, London 1988–2016; Chair. Arts Council England 2016–; Chair. British Council Visual Arts Advisory Cttee 1992–98 (mem. 1976–98); Sr Fellow, Royal Coll. of Art 1996; Trustee Public Art Devt Trust 1983–87, Architecture Foundation 1991–99, The Little Sparta Trust 1995–2007; Commr Comm. for Architecture and the Built Environment 1999–2006; mem. Olympic Delivery Authority 2006–12; Hon. Fellow, Queen Mary and Westfield Coll., Univ. of London 1988, RIBA 1992, Goldsmiths Coll., Univ. of London 1994; Hon. DArts (City of London Polytechnic) 1990; Hon. DLitt (Plymouth) 1993, (Keele) 1994, (South Bank) 1996, (Exeter) 2000; Hon. DUniv (Surrey) 1997. *Publication:* Experience or Interpretation: The Dilemma of Museums of Modern Art 1997. *Address:* Arts Council England, 21 Bloomsbury Street, London, WC1B 3HF, England (office). *Website:* www.artscouncil.org.uk (office).

SERPA SOARES, Miguel de; Portuguese lawyer and UN official; *Under-Secretary-General for Legal Affairs and Legal Counsel, United Nations;* b. 1967, Angola; ed Univ. of Lisbon, Collège d'Europe, Belgium; Asst Lecturer of Law, Univ. of Lisbon 1989–93; practised as assoc. at Portuguese law firm 1992–96; Chief of Staff of Deputy Minister for Infrastructure, Planning and Territorial Admin 1996–99; Legal Adviser to Perm. Representation to EU, Brussels 1999–2008, mem. Perm. Bilateral and Assessment Cttees, Ministry of Foreign Affairs, later Dir-Gen. Dept of Legal Affairs 2008–13; Under-Sec.-Gen. for Legal Affairs and UN Legal Counsel 2013–; mem. Perm. Court of Arbitration, The Hague 2010–; Judge, Portuguese Univ. Moot Court of International Law 2011–; Chair. Supervisory Bd of Lisbon Port Authority 1997–98; represented Portugal at various int. forums, including Sixth Cttee of UN Gen. Ass., Cttee of Public Law Legal Advisers of Council of Europe, Int. Criminal Court Ass. of State Parties; Ed. Portuguese Yearbook of International Law; mem. Portuguese Bar. *Address:* Office of Legal Affairs, United Nations Headquarters, New York, NY 10017, USA (office). *Telephone:* (212) 963-1234 (office). *Fax:* (212) 963-6430 (office). *Website:* legal.un.org/ola (office).

SERRA, José; Brazilian politician, economist and academic; b. 19 March 1942, São Paulo; m. Monica Serra; two c.; ed Univ. of São Paulo, CEPAL-ILPES, Santiago, Chile, Univ. of Chile, Cornell Univ., USA; Leader of Nat. Students' Union 1963–64; forced to flee to Chile for opposing Brazil's mil. regime in early 1970s, in exile for 14 years; Prof. of Econs, Univ. of Chile 1968–73; mem. Inst. for Advanced Study, Princeton Univ., USA 1976–78; Prof., Univ. of Campinas; Sec. for Economy and Planning, São Paulo 1983–86; Co-founder and mem. Brazilian Social Democratic Party (PSDB) 1988–; elected mem. Nat. Congress of Brazil (Chamber of Deputies) 1986–94; elected Senator 1994–; Minister of Planning 1995–96. Minister of Health 1998–2002, Minister of Foreign Affairs 2016–17; unsuccessful presidential cand. 2002, 2010; Mayor of São Paulo 2004–06; Gov. State of São Paulo 2007–10. *Address:* Partido da Social Democracia Brasileira (PSDB), SGAS, Quadra 607, Edif. Metrópolis, Asa Sul, 70200–670 Brasília, DF Brazil (office). *Telephone:* (61) 3424-0500 (office). *Fax:* (61) 3424-0515 (office). *E-mail:* tucano@psdb.org.br (office). *Website:* www.psdb.org.br (office).

SERRA, Maj. Gen. Paolo, BSc, MSc; Italian army officer and UN official; *Military Adviser, Permanent Mission of Italy to the UN;* b. 7 April 1956, Turin; s. of Carlo Serra and Maria Serra; m. Antonella Filippi; one d.; ed Italian Mil. Acad., Modena, Univ. of Turin, Army War Coll., Carlisle, Pa, USA, patrol and paratrooper courses in Pisa, Long Range Patrol Course in Weingarten, Germany, skiing and climbing courses for instructors in Aosta, 114th Jr and Sr Staff Courses in Civitavecchia, Rome; Cadet, Italian Mil. Acad., Modena 1975–77, Cadet, Italian Army Jr Officers Advanced School, Turin 1977–79, commissioned as 'Alpini' Lt 1979; Platoon Leader, Alpini Bn 'Saluzzo', Cuneo 1979–80; Anti-Tank Co. Commdr, Alpini Brigade 'Taurinense', Turin 1980–90; rank of Capt. 1990; Staff Officer, Alpini Brigade 'Orobica', Merano 1990–91; apptd Anti-Tank Co. Commdr in Italian Contingent of ACE Mobile Force – AMF(L); Staff Officer, Alpini Brigade 'Tridentina', Bressanone 1991–93; Jr Asst to Chief of Cabinet, Gen. Staff, Rome 1993–94; rank of Lt Col 1994; Commdr of 'Susa' Alpini Bn 1994; Bn Commdr, Alpini Bn 'Susa', Pinerolo 1994–96; Asst to Defence Chief of Staff, Defence Gen. Staff, Rome 1996–99; rank of Col 1999; commanded 9th Alpini Regt, deployed in Kosovo 1999; Regt Commdr 9th Alpini Regt, L'Aquila 1999–2000; Int. Fellow, US Army War Coll. 2000–01; with NATO Rapid Deployment Corps 2001–03; Exec. to Army Chief of Staff, Rome 2003–04; rank of Brig. Gen. 2005; Army Attaché, Embassy in Washington, DC 2004–07; Brigade Commdr 'Julia' Alpini Brigade and Multinational Land Force, Udine 2007–08; Regional Command West Commdr within ISAF mission, Herat, Afghanistan 2008–09; rank of Maj. Gen. 2009; Chief of Staff of NATO Rapid Deployable Corps – Italy, Solbiate Olona (Varese) 2009–10; Chief of 4th Logistic Div. and Chief of Land Transformation Dept, Army Gen. Staff, Rome 2010–12; Commdr UN Interim Force in Lebanon (UNIFIL) and Force Commdr in South Lebanon 2012–14; Mil. Adviser, Perm. Mission of Italy to UN, New York 2014–; participated in second Italian expedition to Antarctica 1987–88; numerous awards and decorations including Silver Cross for Meritorious Service (Army) 2002, Kt, Mil. Order 2011, 'Mauriziana' Medal for Meritorious Service, Meritorious Medal for the Mission in Afghanistan, Meritorious Cross for Peace Operations in Kosovo, Meritorious Cross for Peace Operations in Lebanon, UN Medal for the Mission in Lebanon (UNIFIL), NATO Medal for the Mission in Afghanistan, NATO Medal for the Mission in Kosovo, Antarctica Scientific Expedition Medal, Légion d'Honneur, Commendatore, Ordine al merito della Repubblica italiana 2014. *Address:* Permanent Mission of Italy to the United Nations, 885 Second Avenue (One Dag Hammarskjold Plaza), 49th Floor, New York, NY 10017, USA (office). *Telephone:* (212) 486-9191 (office). *Fax:* (212) 486-1036 (office). *Website:* www.italyun.esteri.it/rappresentanza_onu (office).

SERRA, Richard, BA, BFA, MFA; American sculptor; b. 2 Nov. 1939, San Francisco, Calif.; m. Clara Weyergraf-Serra; ed Univ. of California, Berkeley, Univ. of California, Santa Barbara, Yale Univ.; works in numerous perm. collections including Whitney Museum of Modern Art, Guggenheim Museum, Museum of Modern Art, New York, Art Gallery of Ontario, Stedelijk Museum, Amsterdam, Dia Center for the Arts, New York, Colby Coll.; John Simon Guggenheim Memorial Foundation Fellowship 1970; Chevalier, Légion d'honneur 2015; Hon. DFA (Calif. Coll. of Arts and Crafts, Oakland) 1994, (Williams Coll.) 2008, Harvard Univ.) 2010; Skohegan School Medal 1975, Japan Art Asscn Praemium Imperiale 1994. *Publications:* Weight and Measure 1992, Writings/Interviews 1994. *Address:* c/o Gagosian Gallery, 980 Madison Avenue, New York, NY 10075, USA. *Website:* www.gagosian.com/artists/richard-serra.

SERRA RAMONEDA, Antoni, PhD; Spanish economist, academic and fmr university rector; *Professor Emeritus, Department d'Economia de l'Empresa, Universitat Autònoma of Barcelona;* b. 20 July 1933, Barcelona; s. of Antoni Serra Riera and Enriqueta Ramoneda Ruis; m. Margarita de la Figuera Buñuel 1958; one s. two d.; ed Lycée Français, Barcelona and Univ. Complutense de Madrid; Sec., Faculty of Econ. Sciences, Univ. of Barcelona 1960–64; Founding mem. Universitat Autònoma de Barcelona and Dept d'Economia de l'Empresa, Univ. Autónoma de Barcelona, Sec.-Gen. 1960–72, Dir Inst. of Educ. Sciences 1977–78, Rector 1980–85, Full Prof. of Managerial Econs and mem. Business Efficiency and

Competitiveness Group –2003, Prof. Emer. 2003–; currently Pres. Generalitat de Catalunya's Managing Council for University-System Quality; Treas. Institut d'Estudis Catalans (IEC) 1992–98, Vice-Pres. 1998–2001; Pres. Caixa Catalunya 1984–2005; Pres. Comisión de Control Caja de Pensiones para la Vejez y de Ahorros 1979–82, Sec.-Gen. 1982–84; Pres. Caja de Ahorros de Cataluña 1984; Officier and Chevalier de l'Ordre du Mérite, Premi Creu de Sant Jordi 2005; Medalla al Mèrit Científic, Medalla Narcís Monturiol al Mèrit Científic i Tecnològic. *Publications include:* Libro Blanco sobre los efectos para Cataluña del ingreso de España en la CEE, La industria textil algodonera y el Mercado Común Europeo, Sistema Económico y Empresa. *Address:* Pl. Bonanova 5, Barcelona 08022, Spain (home). *Telephone:* (93) 2478101 (home).

SERRA REXACH, Eduardo, LLB; Spanish business executive and fmr politician; *President, Eduardo Serra y Asociados SL;* b. 19 Dec. 1946, Madrid; m. 1st; one s.; m. 2nd Luz del Carmen Municio; ed Complutense Univ., Madrid; began career as state lawyer; mem. staff Ministry of Energy and Industry 1977–79; Under-Sec. of Defence 1979–84, Sec. of State for Defence 1984–87, Minister of Defence 1996–2000; Chair. Telettra 1986; Chair. Cubiertas y MZOV 1989–91, Chair. 1991; Chair. Peugeot Spain 1992, Airtel 1994–96; Chair. UBS Warburg Spain 2000–06; currently Founder and Pres. Eduardo Serra y Asociados (ESYA) SL; Pres. Everis, Pres. Transforma España Foundation; mem. Bd of Dirs PharmaMar, Aula de Dirigentes (Instituto de Empresa); Chair. Bd of Trustees, Prado Museum, Madrid 2000–; Chair. Elcano Royal Inst., Madrid 2001–05; Patron, Real Instituto Elcano for Int. and Strategic Studies. *Address:* Eduardo Serra y Asociados SL, Ayala, 7, 2º izq, 28001 Madrid, Spain (office). *Telephone:* (91) 7817700 (office). *Fax:* (91) 5766057 (office). *E-mail:* ndemiguel@esya.es (office); secretaria@esya.es (office).

SERRA SERRA, Narcís, DEcon; Spanish politician, business executive and academic; *President, Institut Barcelona d'Estudis Internacionals;* b. 30 May 1943, Barcelona; m. Conxa Villalba i Ibáñez; ed Univ. of Barcelona, London School of Econs, UK, Universidad Autónoma de Barcelona; Prof. of Econ. Theory, Autonomous Univ. of Barcelona 1976–77; Regional Minister of Public Works in Catalan Autonomous Govt 1977–79; Mayor of Barcelona 1979–82; mem. Parl. for Barcelona 1986–2004; Minister of Defence 1982–91, Deputy Prime Minister 1991–95; Gen. Sec. Catalan Socialist Party 1996–2000; Pres. CatalunyaCaixa Capital, SA 2005–10; apptd Vice-Pres. Telefónica Chile 2005; currently Councillor, Telecomunicaciones de São Paulo SA; Pres. Institut Barcelona d'Estudis Internacionals (IBEI) 2004–; Chair. Bd of Trustees, Museu Nacional d'Art de Catalunya 2004-11; mem. Bd of Dirs Center for Int. Relations and Devt Studies (Pres. 2000–12); Hon. Fellow, LSE 1991. *Publications include:* Guerra y paz en el siglo XXI – una perspectiva Europea 2003, Europa en construcción – integración, identidades y seguridad 2004, Visiones sobre el Desarrollo en América Latina 2007, Hacia un nuevo pacto social. Políticas económicas para un desarrollo integral en América Latina 2008, The Washington Consensus Reconsidered: Towards a New Global Governance (with Joseph Stiglitz) 2008, La transición militar. Reflexiones en torno a la reforma democrática de las fuerzas armadas 2008, The Military Transition – Democratic Reform of the Armed Forces 2010. *Address:* Institut Barcelona d'Estudis Internacionals, Elisabets 10, 08001 Barcelona, Spain (office). *Telephone:* (93) 3180807 (office). *Fax:* (93) 3427550 (office). *E-mail:* lmoya@cidob.org (office). *Website:* www.ibei.org (office).

SERRANO ELIAS, Jorge, PhD; Guatemalan business executive and fmr head of state; b. 26 April 1945, Guatemala City; s. of Jorge Adán Serrano and Rosa Elías; m. Magda Bianchi de Serrano; three s. two d.; ed Univ. of San Carlos, Stanford Univ., USA; Pres. Advisory Council of State 1982–83; Pres. of Guatemala 1991–93, left office after failed self-coup d'etat attempt, has been living in Panama 1993–, Panama refused extradition request 1994.

SERRE, Jean-Pierre, BSc, PhD, DèsSc; French mathematician and academic; *Honorary Professor, Collège de France;* b. 15 Sept. 1926, Bages; s. of Jean Serre and Adèle Serre (née Diet); m. Josiane Heulot 1948; one d.; ed Lycée de Nîmes, Ecole Normale Supérieure, Université de Paris; worked at Centre National de la Recherche Scientifique, Paris 1948–54, Université de Nancy 1954–56; Prof. of Algebra and Geometry, Coll. de France 1956–94 (retd), Hon. Prof. 1994–; mem. Acad. des Sciences 1977, acads in the Netherlands 1978, USA 1979, Sweden 1987, Russia 2003, Norway 2009, Taiwan 2010, Turin 2010; Foreign mem. Royal Soc., London 1974; Fellow, American Math. Soc. 2012; Hon. mem. London Math. Soc. 1973; Grand Croix, Légion d'honneur, Ordre nat. du Mérite; Dr hc (Cambridge) 1978, (Stockholm) 1980, (Glasgow) 1983, (Athens) 1996, (Harvard) 1998, (Durham) 2000, (London) 2001, (Oslo) 2002, (Oxford) 2003, (Bucharest, Barcelona) 2004, (Madrid) 2006; Fields Medal 1954, Prix Gaston Julia 1970, Médaille Émile Picard, Académie des Sciences 1971, Balzan Prize 1985, Médaille d'or du CNRS 1987, American Math. Soc. Steele Prize 1995, Wolf Prize 2000, Abel Prize 2003. *Publications include:* Homologie singulière des espaces fibrés 1951, Faisceaux algébriques cohérents 1955, Groupes algébriques et corps de classes 1959, Corps Locaux 1962, Cohomologie galoisienne 1964, Abelian *l* -adic representations 1968, Cours d'arithmétique 1970, Représentations linéaires des groupes finis 1971, Arbres, amalgames, SL2 1977, Lectures on the Mordell-Weil Theorem 1989, Topics in Galois Theory 1992, Collected Papers (four vols) 1949–1998, Local Algebra 2000, Correspondence Grothendieck-Serre 2004, Lectures on NX 2012, Finite Groups: An Introduction 2016. *Address:* Collège de France, 11, place Marcelin Berthelot, 75231 Paris Cedex 05 (office); 6 avenue de Montespan, 75116 Paris, France (home). *Telephone:* 1-44-27-17-90 (office). *Fax:* 1-44-27-17-04 (office). *E-mail:* serre@noos.fr (office). *Website:* www.college-de-france.fr (office).

SERREAU, Coline; French film director, film writer and actress; b. 29 Oct. 1947, Paris; d. of Jean-Marie Serreau and Geneviève Serreau; m. Benno Besson (deceased 2006); one c.; has acted in several stage plays including Lapin, lapin in Paris; wrote and acted in Bertuccelli's On s'est trompé d'histoire d'amour 1973; directed Oedipus the King for Italian TV; f. trapeze school in Canada. *Television:* Pont dormant 1972, La folie des bêtes 1974. *Films include:* A Little, a Lot, Passionately 1971, The Lion's Share 1971, We Were Mistaken About a Love Story 1974, Mais qu'est-ce qu'elles veulent? (documentary) 1975, Sept morts sur ordonnance 1975, Pourquoi pas! 1976, Le fou de mai 1980, Qu'est-ce qu'on attend pour être heureux! 1982, Trois hommes et un couffin (Three Men and a Cradle – also screenwriter) 1985, Romuald et Juliette 1989, Mama, There's a Man in Your Bed 1990, La crise 1992, La belle Verte 1996, Chaos (also screenwriter) 2003, 18 ans après (also screenwriter) 2003, Saint-Jacques... La Mecque (also screenwriter) 2005, Solutions locales pour un désordre global (documentary) 2010, Tout est permis (documentary) 2014.

SERRY, Robert H.; Dutch diplomatist and UN official; b. 1950, Calcutta, India; m.; three c.; ed Univ. of Amsterdam; led Middle Eastern Affairs Div., Ministry of Foreign Affairs, The Hague, participated in events leading to Middle East Peace Conf., Madrid during Netherlands EC presidency 1991, diplomatic postings in Bangkok, Moscow, New York (UN) and Kyiv, also held position of Deputy Asst Sec.-Gen. for Crisis Man. and Operations, NATO, fmr Amb. to Ireland; UN Special Coordinator for Middle East Peace Process, Sec.-Gen.'s Personal Rep. to Palestine Liberation Org. and Palestinian Authority, and Sec.-Gen.'s Envoy to Quartet 2007–15. *Publications:* Standplaats Kiev 1997; several articles on political and peacekeeping topics, ranging from the Middle East to Eastern Europe. *Address:* c/o Office of the Secretary-General, UN Headquarters, First Avenue at 46th Street, New York, NY 10017, USA.

SERSALE DI CERISANO, R(enato) Carlos, MIA, PhD; Argentine diplomatist and fmr UN official; *Ambassador to UK;* ed Univ. of Buenos Aires, Columbia Univ., USA, Univ. of Salvador, Buenos Aires; teaching experience at univ. level in Buenos Aires, at Nat. Univ. of Buenos Aires and Nat. Univ. of La Plata; pvt. consultant for econ. and financial man. of contracts of large public investment projects; joined Foreign Service as Third Sec. 1979, rep. to UN food and agricultural orgs (FAO, IFAD, WFP and World Food Council) in Rome, Vice-Pres. Exec. Bd, UNDP/UNFPA (UN Population Fund) 1994–95, mem. Argentine Del. to UN Security Council 1994–95, Pres. Council 1995, Special Adviser on UN and Inter-Governmental Affairs to Admin. of UNDP 1996–97, Special Rep. of Dir-Gen. and Asst Dir-Gen. for UN Affairs, UNIDO, New York 1998–99, with Under-Secr. of Int. Econ. Affairs of Prov. of Buenos Aires 2000, Dir-Gen. of Human Rights, Ministry of Foreign Affairs 2001–03, Dir of Int. Security, Nuclear and Space Affairs 2003–06, Amb. to South Africa 2006–16, to UK 2016–; Pres. Missile Tech. Control Regime 2003–04. *Publications:* several articles and papers on co-operation for devt and int. affairs issues. *Address:* Embassy of Argentina, 65 Brook Street, London, W1K 4AH, England (office). *Telephone:* (20) 7318-1321 (office). *Fax:* (20) 7318-1301 (office). *E-mail:* ambassadorsoffice@argentine-embassy-uk.org (office). *Website:* www.argentine-embassy-uk.org (office).

SERTIĆ, Željko; Serbian business executive and government official; b. 1967, Sečanj; ed in Novi Sad and Union Univ., Belgrade; expert on small and medium-sized enterprises; Owner Komrad co.; mem. Bd of Dirs, Evrokomore; Pres. Serbian Chamber of Commerce 2013–; Minister of the Economy 2014–16; voted one of Best Mans of SE and Cen. Europe. *Address:* c/o Ministry of the Economy, 11000 Belgrade, Kneza Miloša 20, Serbia. *E-mail:* kabinet@privreda.gov.rs.

SERULLE RAMIA, José A.; Dominican Republic academic and diplomatist; *Ambassador to Trinidad and Tobago;* b. 11 June 1950, San Francisco de Macoris; m. Jacqueline Boin; fmr Vice-Rector, teacher of Int. Economy, Univ. of Santo Domingo; Amb. to Haiti 2005–08, to Trinidad and Tobago 2009–; Founder Fundación Ciencia y Arte Inc., fmr Pres. *Publications include:* 14 books, including as co-author (with wife): El proceso del capitalism en la República Dominicana 1979, Inversion de capitales imperialistas en la República Dominicana: elementos de crítica a la "teoría de la dependencia" 1981, Fondo Monetario Internacional: deuda externa y crisis mundial 1984. *Address:* Embassy of Dominican Republic, Suite 101, 10B Queen's Park West, Port of Spain, Trinidad and Tobago (office). *Telephone:* 624-7930 (office). *Fax:* 623-7779 (office). *E-mail:* embadom@hotmail.com (office).

SERVATIUS, Bernhard, DJur; German lawyer; *Partner, Servatius Rechtsanwälte;* b. 14 April 1932, Magdeburg; s. of Rudolf Servatius and Maria Servatius; m. Ingeborg Servatius 1985; ed Univs of Fribourg, Hamburg and other univs; Sr Partner, Dr Servatius & Partner (legal firm), then Partner, Servatius Jenckel Noelle; currently Partner, Servatius Rechtsanwälte, Hamburg; Man. Pnr Treubesitz GmbH, Hamburg (trust co.); legal adviser to Axel Springer and Springer Publishing Group 1970; Chair. Axel Springer Verlag AG, Berlin 1985–2002; Chair. Supervisory Bd Rheinische Merkur GmbH; Chief Rep. of Axel Springer and Acting Chair. of Man. Admin. Verlagshaus Axel Springer 1984; Prof. Hochschule für Musik und Theater, Hamburg; Deputy Chair. Supervisory Bd AWD Holding AG –2008; Chair. German Foundation for Monument Protection 2002–10; mem. Supervisory Bd equitrust Aktiengesellschaft; mem. Advisory Bd EnBW Energie Baden-Württemberg AG, Hapag-Lloyd AG; Hon. Prof., Univ. of Music and Theatre, Hamburg 1984; Federal Cross of Merit, Bavarian Order of Merit; Hon. DPhil (Weizmann Inst. of Science, Israel) 2000; Austrian Medal for Science and Art. *Address:* Servatius Rechtsanwälte Partnerschaftsgesellschaft, Gänsemarkt 50, 20354 Hamburg, Germany (office). *Telephone:* (40) 35016145 (office). *Fax:* (40) 35016100 (office). *E-mail:* bernhard.servatius@servatius-law.de (office). *Website:* www.servatius-rechtsanwaelte.de (office).

SESAY, Sheku Sambadeen, BA, MA (Econs); Sierra Leonean economist and central banker; b. 20 Aug. 1949, Kambia; ed Howard Univ., USA; Econ. Devt and Planning Officer, Ministry of Planning and Econ. Devt Aug.–Dec. 1978; Part-time Lecturer, History of Econ. Thought and Money and Banking, Fourah Bay Coll., Univ. of Sierra Leone 1978–84; Sr Project Officer, Nat. Devt Bank 1979–84; joined ADB as Loans Officer 1984, becoming Sr Country Economist, Prin. Country Economist, Chief Country Economist, North Region 1984–2000, Div. Man., Country Operations Div. 2000–01, Div. Man. 2001–04, Resident Rep., ADB Tanzania Country Office 2004–07; Financial Sec., Ministry of Finance 2007–09; Gov., Bank of Sierra Leone (central bank) 2009–14. *Publications:* several. *Leisure interests:* reading, sports. *Address:* c/o Office of the Governor, Bank of Sierra Leone, Siaka Stevens Street, POB 30, Freetown, Sierra Leone (office).

ŠEŠELJ, Vojislav, DJur; Serbian lawyer, writer and politician; *President, Srpska Radikalna Stranka (Serbian Radical Party);* b. 11 Oct. 1954, Sarajevo, People's Repub. of Bosnia and Herzegovina, People's Fed. Repub. of Yugoslavia; s. of Nikola Šešelj and Danica Šešelj (née Misita); m. 1st Vesna Mudreša; m. 2nd Jadranka Pavlović 1992; four s.; ed Univs of Sarajevo and Belgrade; Docent, Sarajevo Univ. 1981–84; Prof., Prishtina Univ. 1991–, was persecuted by authorities for nationalistic activities, arrested and sentenced to eight years' imprisonment 1984, released after 22 months; later arrested twice 1990, 1994–95; Head of Četnik (royalist) Movt 1989; Founder and Pres. Srpska Radikalna Stranka

(Serbian Radical Party) 1990–; supported war against Croatia 1991; mem. Narodna skupština (People's Ass.—Parl.) 1993–98, 2000–03, 2016–, Leader of the Opposition 2016–; cand. for presidency of Serbia 1997; Deputy Prime Minister 1998–2000; worked and lectured in European countries, USA, Canada; indicted by Int. Criminal Tribunal for the fmr Yugoslavia (ICTY) for crimes against humanity and war crimes Feb. 2003, trial began Nov. 2007, trial suspended because of alleged witness intimidation 2009, trial resumed Jan. 2009, sentenced to a further 15 months in custody for not respecting the court 24 July 2009, trial resumed Jan.–March 2010, permitted to return to Serbia for medical treatment Nov. 2014, acquitted of all charges March 2016 and released, pending appeal, acquittal partially overturned Apr. 2011, but released owing to sentence being already served. *Publications:* more than 100 books including Political Essence of Militarism and Fascism 1979, Dusk of Illusions 1986, Democracy and Dogma 1987, Debrozovisation of Public Mentality 1990, Destruction of Serbian National Being 1992, Actual Political Challenges 1993, Are We Threatened with Slobotomia 1994, Selected Works 1994. *Address:* Srpska Radikalna Stranka, 11080 Belgrade, Zemun, Magistratski trg 3, Serbia (office). *Telephone:* (11) 3164621 (office). *E-mail:* info@srpskaradikalnastranka.rs (office); info@vseselj.com. *Website:* www.srpskaradikalnastranka.org.rs (office); www.vseselj.com.

SESHADRI, Conjeevaram Srirangachari, BA, PhD, FRS; Indian mathematician and academic; *Director Emeritus, Chennai Mathematical Institute;* b. 29 Feb. 1932; m. Sundari Seshdri 1962; two s.; ed Loyola Coll., Madras Univ., Tata Inst. of Fundamental Research, Bombay Univ.; Research Scholar, Tata Inst. of Fundamental Research, Bombay 1953, Prof., 1965–75, Sr Prof., 1975–84; Sr Prof., Inst. of Math. Sciences, Madras 1984–89; Prof. and Founding Dir Chennai Math. Inst. 1989, now Dir Emer.; Visiting Prof., Univ. of Paris 1957–60, Harvard Univ. 1974–75, Inst. for Advanced Study, Princeton 1975–76, UCLA, Brandeis Univ., Univ. of Bonn, Kyoto Univ.; Fellow, Indian Nat. Science Acad.; Hon. DSc (Banaras Hindu Univ.); Shanti Swarup Bhatnagar Award 1972, Srinivasa Ramanujan Medal, Indian Acad. of Sciences, Third World Acad. of Sciences Science Award, Trieste Science Prize in Math. (co-recipient) 2006, Padma Bhushan 2009. *Publications:* numerous papers in professional journals on algebraic geometry. *Leisure interest:* Carnatic music. *Address:* Chennai Mathematical Institute, Plot H1, SIPCOT IT Park, Siruseri, Kelambakkam, 603 103, India (office). *E-mail:* css@cmi.ac.in (office). *Website:* www.cmi.ac.in (office).

SESSIONS, Jefferson Beauregard, III, BA, JD; American lawyer and politician; b. 24 Dec. 1946, Selma, Ala; s. of Jefferson Beauregard Sessions and Abbie Sessions (née Powe); m. Mary Montgomery Blackshear 1969; one s. two d.; ed Huntingdon Coll., Montgomery and Univ. of Alabama; admitted to the Ala Bar 1973; Assoc., Guin, Bouldin & Porch, Russellville, Ala 1973–75; Asst US Attorney, US Dept of Justice, Mobile, Ala 1975–77, US Attorney 1981–93; Assoc. Pnr, Stockman & Bedsole Attorneys, Mobile 1977–81; mem. US Attorney-Gen.'s Advisory Cttee 1987–89, Vice-Chair. 1989; Pnr, Stockman, Bedsole & Sessions 1993–94; Attorney-Gen. for Ala 1996; Senator from Alabama 1997–2017, mem. Environment and Public Works Cttee, Judiciary Cttee; US Attorney-Gen. 2017–18; mem. Bd of Trustees, Exec. Cttee Mobile Bay Area Partnership for Youth 1981–; Chair. Advisory Bd, Ashland Place United Methodist Church, Mobile 1982; First Vice-Pres. Mobile Lions Club 1993–94; Capt. US Army Reserves 1975–85; mem. ABA, Ala Bar Asscn, Mobile Bar Asscn; US Attorney-Gen.'s Award 1992. *Address:* c/o Office of the Attorney-General, Department of Justice, 950 Pennsylvania Ave, NW, Washington, DC 20530-0001 USA (office).

SESSIONS, William S., JD; American lawyer, government official and judge; *Partner, Holland & Knight LLP;* b. 27 May 1930, Fort Smith, Ark.; s. of William A. Sessions and Edith A. Steele; m. Alice June Lewis 1952; three s. one d.; ed Baylor Univ.; called to Texas Bar 1959; Pnr, McGregor & Sessions, Waco, Tex. 1959–61; Assoc. Tirey, McLaughlin, Gorin & Tirey, Waco 1961–63; Pnr, Haley, Fulbright, Winniford, Sessions & Bice, Waco 1963–69; Chief, Govt Operations Section, Criminal Div. Dept of Justice 1969–71; US Attorney, US Dist Court (Western Dist) Texas, San Antonio 1971–74, US Dist Judge 1974–80, Chief US Dist Judge 1980–87; Dir Fed. Bureau of Investigation (FBI) 1987–93; Pnr, Sessions & Sessions 1995–2000, Holland & Knight LLP 2000–; apptd Vice-Chair. Gov.'s Task Force on Homeland Security for the State of Texas 2002; mem. Gov.'s Anti- Crime Comm. 2002, Judiciary Relations Cttee for the State Bar of Texas; fmr Pres. Waco-McLennan Co. Bar Asscn, Fed. Bar Asscn of San Antonio, Dist Judges' Asscn of the Fifth Circuit; fmr mem. Bd of Dirs Fed. Judicial Center, Washington, DC; mem. Steering Cttee of Coastal Texas 2020, Innocence Project of Nat. Capital Region, Innocence Comm. for Virginia, Texas Comm. on Judicial Efficiency 1995–97, Texas Comm. on a Rep. Student Body 1997–98; serves as arbitrator and mediator for American Arbitration Asscn, Int. Center for Dispute Resolution, CPR Inst. of Dispute Resolution (Dist Panelist), Nat. Panel of Distinguished Neutrals, Arbitration Appeal Panel; mem. DC Bar, State Bar of Texas, San Antonio Bar Asscn, Fed. Bar Asscn, ABA (Initial Chair. Cttee on Independence of the Judiciary 1997, Hon. Co-Chair. Comm. on the 21st Century Judiciary 2002, mem. Advisory Comm. to Standing Cttee on the Law Library of Congress), American Bar Foundation, Judicature Soc., William S. Sessions American Inn of Court, Nat. Asscn of Fmr United States Attorneys; mem. Bd of Trustees, Nat. Environmental Educ. and Training Foundation Inc. 2001–; Hon. Dir Martin Luther King Jr Fed. Holiday Comm. 1991–93, 1994–; several hon. degrees; Baylor Univ. Law School Lawyer of the Year 1988, Price Daniel Distinguished Public Service Award 2002, listed in The Best Lawyers In America for Alternative Dispute Resolution 2005–06, Chesterfield Smith Award, Holland & Knight 2008, Constitution Project's Inaugural Constitutional Champion Award 2008. *Publications:* articles in professional journals. *Leisure interests:* climbing, hiking, canoeing. *Address:* Holland & Knight LLP, 2099 Pennsylvania Avenue, NW, Suite 100, Washington, DC 20006, USA (office). *Telephone:* (202) 419-2410 (office). *Fax:* (202) 955-5564 (office). *E-mail:* william.sessions@hklaw.com (office). *Website:* www.hklaw.com (office).

SESTER, Sven; Estonian business executive and politician; *Chairman, Economic Affairs Committe, Riigikogu;* b. 14 July 1969, Tallinn; ed Tallinn Secondary School No. 24 (Kopli Art School), Tallinn Univ. of Tech.; data processing specialist and coordinator of data processing, Mainor Centre for Public Opinion Research (later EMOR) 1990–91; Sales Man. and Man. Selected Daily Mail Joint Enterprise 1991–92; Man. ERI Real Estate Ltd 1993–99, Dir, Vice-Chair., later Chair. Supervisory Bd, Baltic Real Investments (fmr ERI Real Estate Ltd) 1999–2015; Chair. Supervisory Bd, Eesti Loto 2003–05, Roosikrantsi Hotell Ltd 2007–15; mem. Isamaa ja Res Publica Liit (IRL—Union of Pro Patria and Res Publica) 1999–, mem. Bd IRL; Deputy Chair. Finance Cttee, Tallinn City Council 2002–03; mem. Riigikogu (Parl.) for Tallinn constituency of Kesklinn, Lasnamäe and Pirita 2003–15, Deputy Chair. Econ. Affairs Cttee 2003–07, Chair. 2017–, mem. Econ. Affairs Cttee 2009, Chair. Finance Cttee 2009; Minister of Finance 2015–17; Pres. Estonian Tournament Bridge League; mem. Bd, Lions Club Tallinn VIA; Vice-Pres. Asscn of Estonian Small and Medium Businesses. *Address:* Riigikogu, Lossi plats 1A, 15165 Tallinn, Estonia. *Telephone:* 631-6432 (office); 504-9222 (mobile). *E-mail:* sven.sester@riigikogu.ee (office). *Website:* www.riigikogu.ee; www.svensester.ee.

SETCH, Terry, RA, RWA, DFA; British artist; b. 11 March 1936, Lewisham, London, England; s. of Frank Setch and Florence Skeggs; m. Dianne Shaw 1967; one d.; ed Sutton and Cheam School of Art, Slade School of Fine Art, Univ. Coll., London; Sr Lecturer in Painting, School of Art, Univ. of Wales Inst. 1964–2001; Visiting Lecturer, Emily Carr Coll. of Art, Vancouver, Canada 1981; Artist in Residence, Victorian Coll. of Art, Melbourne, Australia 1983; elected to the Faculty of Painting, British School at Rome 1984; Examiner BA, Slade School of Art, Univ. Coll. London 1985–87; Examiner in Painting MA, Chelsea School of Art, London 1986–89; elected to Faculty of Fine Arts, British School at Rome 1987; External Examiner BA, Faculty of Art, Univ. of Reading 1989–92; mem. Derek Williams Cttee, Nat. Museum and Galleries of Wales 1996–2005; elected to Royal West of England Acad. 2002, Royal Acad. of Art, London 2009; Welsh Arts Council comm. for large-scale hoarding poster print 1968, Royal Nat. Eisteddfod Main Prizewinner 1968, Welsh Arts Council Painting Award 1971, John Moores 8 Prizewinner 1972, Welsh Arts Council Comm. Award for Coleg Harlech 1972, Welsh Arts Council Major Artist Award 1978, Print Comm., Royal Nat. Eisteddfod 1978, Third Prize, John Moores Exhbn 1985, shortlist prizewinner, Athena Awards 1988, comm. for a painting for restaurant in Nat. Museum of Wales, Cardiff 1993, Bryan Robertson Trust Award 2009. *Radio:* Art Work: Terry Setch (BBC Radio 3) 2000, Terry Setch – How I Spend My Sundays (Radio Wales) 2001, Inspired – Sisley and his Work in Penarth (BBC Radio Wales) 2007, Pitch (Cardiff Radio) 2011. *Television:* Statements (BBC 2 Wales) 1990, A Word in Your Eye (HTV Wales) 1997, Catalyst (BBC 1 Wales) 1997, Painting the Dragon (BBC Wales) 2000, Jamie Owen Welsh Journeys (BBC 1) 2006, Picturing the Century (BBC Wales), Inspired, Sisley and his Work in Penarth, Framing Wales (presented by Kim Howells, BBC 2 Wales) 2011. *Publications include:* New Work by Terry Setch 1992, Terry Setch: A Retrospective 2001, Terry Setch 2009. *E-mail:* setch@terrysetch.co.uk. *Website:* www.terrysetch.co.uk.

SETCHELL, David Lloyd, MA, FCA; British chartered accountant; b. 16 April 1937, Anston, Yorks., England; s. of Raymond Setchell and Phyllis Jane Lloyd; m. Muriel Mary Davies 1962 (deceased); one s. one d.; ed Woodhouse Grammar School and Jesus Coll., Cambridge; Peat Marwick 1960–64; Shawinigan Ltd 1964–71; Vice-Pres. Gulf Oil Chemicals (Europe) 1971–82; Man. Dir Gulf Oil (GB) Ltd 1982–98; Pres. Inst. of Petroleum 1996–98, Oil Industries Club 1993–95; Council mem. Univ. of Gloucestershire 1994–2007, Chair. 2002–07; Gov. Cheltenham Coll. 1998–2004; Dir Cheltenham Arts Festivals 1994–2005, RAF Personnel and Training Command Bd 2000–06; Fellow Energy Inst.; Dr hc (Univ. of Gloucestershire). *Leisure interests:* golf, music, theatre. *Address:* South Hayes, Sandy Lane Road, Cheltenham, Glos., GL53 9DE, England. *Telephone:* (1242) 571390.

SETH, Nikhil; Indian diplomatist; *Executive Director, United Nations Institute for Training and Research;* m.; two c.; ed Delhi Univ.; Lecturer in Econs, St Stephen's Coll., Delhi Univ. 1977–79; joined diplomatic service 1980, assignments included posts at embassies in Geneva, Democratic Repub. of Congo, Central African Repub., Gabon and Equatorial Guinea, Del. at Perm. Mission to UN, New York 1990–93; joined UN 1993, Special Asst and Chief of Office to Under-Sec.-Gen. for Econ. and Social Affairs 1993–2001, Chief of Policy Coordination Br., ECOSOC Support and Coordination Div. 2001–03, Sec., ECOSOC and UN Gen. Ass. Second Cttee 2004–06, Dir, Office for ECOSOC Support and Coordination 2006–11, Dir, Div. for Sustainable Devt, Dept of Econ. and Social Affairs 2011–15, Exec. Dir UN Inst. for Training and Research 2015–. *Achievements include:* as Head, Rio+20 Secr., spearheaded preparations for UN Conf. on Sustainable Devt in Rio 2012. *Address:* United Nations Institute for Training and Research, International Environment House, Chemin des Anémones 11–13, Châtelaine, 1219 Geneva, Switzerland (office). *Telephone:* (22) 917-8400 (office). *Fax:* (22) 917-8047 (office). *Website:* www.unitar.org (office).

SETH, Vikram, CBE, MA, PhD; Indian author and poet; b. 20 June 1952, Calcutta (now Kolkata); s. of Premnath Seth and Leila Seth; ed Doon School, India, Tonbridge School, UK, Corpus Christi Coll., Oxford, UK, Stanford Univ., USA, Nanjing Univ., People's Repub. of China; Hon. Fellow, Corpus Christi Coll., Oxford 1994; Chevalier des Arts et des Lettres 2001; Pravasi Bharatiya Samman 2005, Padma Shri 2007. *Publications include:* Mappings 1980, From Heaven Lake: Travels Through Sinkiang and Tibet (non-fiction) (Thomas Cook Travel Book Award) 1983, The Humble Administrator's Garden (Commonwealth Poetry Prize) 1985, All You Who Sleep Tonight (trans.) 1985, The Golden Gate: A Novel in Verse 1986, Three Chinese Poets (trans.) 1992, A Suitable Boy (novel) (W. H. Smith Literary Prize 1994, Commonwealth Writers Prize 1994) 1993, Arion and the Dolphin (libretto) 1994, Beastly Tales (animal fables) 1994, An Equal Music (novel) (EMMA BT Ethnic and Multicultural Media Award 2001) 1999, Two Lives (biog.) 2005, The Rivered Earth (non-fiction) 2011, A Suitable Girl (fiction) 2018; several vols of poetry. *Leisure interests:* Chinese calligraphy, music, swimming. *Address:* c/o Jonny Geller, Curtis Brown, Haymarket House, 28–29 Haymarket, London, SW1Y 4SP, England (office). *Telephone:* (20) 7393-4400 (office). *Fax:* (20) 7393-4401 (office). *E-mail:* cb@curtisbrown.co.uk (office).

SETHI, Geet, BA, MBA; Indian billiards player (retd); b. 17 April 1961, Delhi; m. Kiran Sethi; two c.; ed St Xavier's Coll., Ahmedabad, B.K School of Business Man.; Nat. Billiards Champion 1982, 1985, 1986, 1987, 1988, 1997, 2007; Nat. Snooker Champion 1985‘ 1986‘ 1987, 1988; Int. Pontins Snooker Champion 1984, World Amateur Billiards Champion 1985, 1987, 2001, Asian Billiards Champion 1986, World Professional Billiards Champion 1992, 1993, 1995, 1998, 2006, Asian Games (gold medal), Bangkok 1998, Asian Billiards Champion 1987, World Team Snooker Masters Champion 2006, Asian Indoor Games (silver medal), Macau 2007; Co-

Founder and mem. Bd of Dirs Olympic Gold Quest programme, Mumbai, Foundation for Promotion of Sports and Games; Padma Shri 1986, Arjuna Award 1986, Rajiv Gandhi Khel Ratna 1992–93, K.K. Birla Award 1993, Billiards Player of the Year, World Professional Billiards and Snooker Asscn 1999. *Publication:* Success vs Joy 2005. *Address:* Olympic Gold Quest, Dalamal Chambers, Vitthaldas Thackersey Marg, New Marine Lines, Marine Lines, Mumbai, Maharashtra 400 020, India (office). *E-mail:* geetsethi@olympicgoldquest.com (office). *Website:* www.olympicgoldquest.in (office).

SETHNESS, Charles Olin, AB, MBA; American government official, financial executive, university administrator and investment banker; b. 24 Feb. 1941, Evanston, Ill.; s. of C. Olin Sethness and Alison Louise Burge; four c. and step-c.; ed New Trier High School, Princeton Univ. and Harvard Business School; Sr Credit Analyst, American Nat. Bank and Trust Co. of Chicago 1963–64; Research Asst, Harvard Business School 1966–67; with Morgan Stanley & Co. 1967–73, 1975–81, Vice-Pres. 1972–73, Man. Morgan & Cie Int. SA, Paris 1971–73, Man. Dir 1975–81; Exec. Dir World Bank Group and Special Asst to Sec. of Treasury 1973–75; Assoc. Dean for External Relations, Harvard Business School, Boston 1981–85; Asst Sec. of the Treasury for Domestic Finance 1985–88; Dir Capital Markets Dept, Int. Finance Corpn 1988–89; Chief Financial Officer IDB 1990–2004; apptd Vice-Pres., Monitoring and Evaluation, interim CEO, Vice-Pres., Accountability, Sr Investment Counsellor and Resident Country Dir, Millennium Challenge Corpn 2005; Alexander Hamilton Medal, US Treasury Dept 1988. *Leisure interests:* Washington Inst. of Foreign Affairs, Washington Recorder Soc., Nat. Cathedral Choral Soc. *Address:* 14525 SW Millikan, #80479, Beaverton, OR 97005-2343, USA (home). *Telephone:* (678) 7756740 (home). *E-mail:* charlessethness@aol.com (home).

SETIAWAN, Boenjamin, MD, PhD; Indonesian pharmacologist and business executive (retd); b. 1943; m.; two c.; ed Univ. of Indonesia, Univ. of California, San Francisco, USA; co-f. Kalbe Farma Tbk (now Kalbe Group) with five siblings 1966, becoming Pres. Commr –2008; Adviser, Faculty of Pharmacology, Univ. of Indonesia, Stem Cell Inst. of Indonesia; mem. Bd of Dirs KOMNAS Lansi; mem. Advisory Bd GP Farmasi, KOMNAS Perempuan; Co-founder and Treas., Yayasan Pengembangan Kreativitas Indonesia; mem. Supervisory Bd Kehati (Indonesian Biodiversity Foundation); Lifetime Achievement Entrepreneur of the Year 2005. *Address:* Kalbe Farma Tbk, Gedung Kalbe, Jl. Let. Jend Suprapto Kav 4, Cemp. Putih Tim., Cemp. Putih, Kota Jakarta Pusat, Daerah Khusus Ibukota, Jakarta 10510, Indonesia (office). *Telephone:* (21) 89907333 (office). *Fax:* (21) 89907360 (office). *Website:* www.kalbe.co.id (office).

SETUBAL, Roberto Egydio, BEng, MEng; Brazilian banking executive; *Vice-Chairman and CEO, Itaú Unibanco Holding SA;* ed Coll., Univ. Escola Politécnica of Universidade de São Paulo, Stanford University; Gen. Man. Itaú Unibanco SA 1990–94, CEO 1994–, Dir-Gen. 1994–2014, mem. Bd of Dirs 1995–2003, Dir-Gen. for Retail 2014–; Chair. Banco Itaú BBA SA 2003–; Exec. Vice-Pres., Itaúsa – Investimentos Itaú SA 1994–, Chair. Accounting Policies Cttee 2008–11; Vice-Chair. and CEO Itaú Unibanco Holding SA 2003–; CEO Unibanco – União de Bancos Brasileiros SA 2008–; Chair. Itauseg Participação SA 2005–; Pres. Brazilian Fed. of Banks (Fenaban) 1997–2001, Brazilian Fed. of Bank Asscns (Febraban) 1997–2001; co-Chair. World Econ. Forum Annual Meeting, Davos 2015; Vice-Pres. Int. Inst. of Finance; mem. Bd Int. Monetary Conf., Int. Advisory Cttee of Fed. Reserve Bank of New York, Int. Advisory Cttee of the New York Stock Exchange (NYSE) 2005–. *Address:* Itaú Unibanco Holding SA, Praça Alfredo Egydio de Souza Aranha 100, Torre Olavo Setubal, Parque Jabaquara, São Paulo 04344-902, Brazil (office). *Telephone:* (11) 5019-1677 (office). *Fax:* (11) 5019-1114 (office). *E-mail:* info@itau.com.br (office). *Website:* www.itau.com.br (office).

ŞEULEANU, Dragoş, BA, MBA; Romanian radio journalist, public relations consultant and organization executive; b. 29 Jan. 1962; ed Acad. of Econ. Studies, Bucharest, Romanian-American Business School, Univ. of Washington at Seattle; apptd Pres. Trade-Tourism Dept, Romanian Chamber of Commerce and Industry 2001, Vice-Pres. Romanian Chamber of Commerce and Industry May–Dec. 2007, Interim Pres. 2007; fmr Pres. Gen. Man. Romania's Radio Broadcasting Corpn (ROR) where he served as Deputy Dir for Programming, later Human Resources Dir, later Sec.-Gen., later CEO during a 15-year career, active radio journalist at ROR, covered Democratic and Republican conventions 2000, 2004–05; est. Effective Management Solutions (public relations co.); apptd Pres. Foundation for Democracy, Culture and Liberty 2005; apptd Gen. Man. S.C. Economix News SA 2006; currently partner ELI-NP (Magurele High Tech Cluster project); Adjunct Fellow (non-resident), New European Democracies Project, Center for Strategic and Int. Studies, Washington, DC; mem. Int. Press Inst., Vienna; Founding mem. Romanian Chapter of Transparency International, Romanian Asscn of Public Relations Professionals; mem. Bd European Broadcasting Union; fmr Vice-Chair. Forum of the Information Society (Romanian Acad.); expert on ethnic politics, governance, business, information tech. and communications, and regional security; Hon. Adviser, Ministry of the Interior 2000; Hon. mem. Romanian Acad. of Scientists, Foundation of the Romanian Gendarmerie Magazine; Young European for 1994 Prize, Del. of EC in Romania 1994, Medal for 'Faithful Service' in the rank of Cavalier, Pres. of Romania. *Address:* c/o ELI-NP, PO Box MG-6, Bucharest, Magurele, Romania. *Telephone:* (21) 4042301. *Fax:* (21) 4574440. *E-mail:* dragos.seuleanu@eli-np.ro. *Website:* www.eli-np.ro.

SEVAN, Benon Vahe, MA; Cypriot fmr UN official; b. 18 Dec. 1937; m.; one d.; ed Melkonian Educational Inst., Columbia Coll. and School of Int. and Public Affairs, Columbia Univ., USA; joined UN 1965, with Dept of Public Information 1965–66, with Secr. of Special Cttee on Decolonization 1966–68, served in W Irian (Irian Jaya), Indonesia 1968–72, with Secr. of UN Econ. and Social Council 1973–88, Dir and Sr Political Adviser to Rep. of Sec.-Gen. on Settlement of Situation relating to Afghanistan 1988–89, Personal Rep. of Sec.-Gen. in Afghanistan and Pakistan 1989–92, Rep. of Sec.-Gen. on Implementation of Geneva Accords on Afghanistan 1990–92, Dir Office for Co-ordination of UN Humanitarian and Econ. Assistance Programmes in Afghanistan 1991–92, Asst Sec.-Gen., Dept of Political Affairs 1992–94, Asst Sec.-Gen. for Conf. and Support Services 1994–97, Asst Sec.-Gen. Office of Security Co-ordination 1994–2002, Exec. Dir Office of Iraq Programme 1997–2004, Head, Oil-for-Food Programme 1996–2003, resgnd from UN 2005, charged in 2007 of bribery and conspiracy to commit wire fraud, in connection with the UN Oil-for-Food Program, returned to Cyprus 2005; Founding mem. Asscn of Former International Civil Servants (AFICS) – Cyprus, currently Auditor. *Address:* Association of Former International Civil Servants (AFICS) – Cyprus, c/o UNFICYP Registry, PO Box 21642, 1590 Nicosia, Cyprus.

SEVELE, Lord Sevele of Vailahi; Feleti (Fred), BSc, BA, MA, PhD; Tongan economist, politician, business executive and academic; b. 7 July 1944, Ma'ufanga, Nuku'alofa; s. of Viliami Vaka'uta Sevele and Mele Yarnton; m. Ainise Manu; three c.; ed Univ. of Canterbury, New Zealand, Univ. of Cambridge, UK; Bd Sec., Tonga Commodities Bd 1973–74, CEO 1974–78; Chief Economist, South Pacific Comm. 1978–84; Dir of Catholic Educ., Catholic Diocese of Tonga 1984–90; consultant to Cen. Planning Dept of Govt of Tonga 1990–92; advisor to ANZ Bank 1993–94; mem. Legis. Ass. 1999–2010, Minister of Labour, Commerce, Industries 2005–08; Interim Prime Minister Feb.–March 2006, Prime Minister (first non-noble) 2006–10, Minister of Finance and Defence 2009–10; est. numerous business ventures, including commercial farming, agricultural exports, retail and wholesale, financial and consultancy services, real estate; Sec.-Gen. Tonga Amateur Sports Asscn and Nat. Olympic Cttee 1990–96; apptd Life Peer by HM King George Tupou V 2010.

SEVERIANO TEIXEIRA, Nuno, PhD; Portuguese academic and politician; *Vice-Rector and Full Professor of International Relations, New University of Lisbon;* b. 5 Nov. 1957, Bissau; ed Univ. of Lisbon, European Univ. Inst., Florence, Italy, New Univ. of Lisbon; Researcher, European Univ. Inst., Florence 1989–92; Visiting Prof., Dept of Govt, Georgetown Univ., USA 2000; Visiting Fellow, Center for European Studies, Univ. of Calif., Berkeley, USA 2003; Prof., Dept of Political Sciences and Int. Relations, Faculty of Social and Human Sciences, New Univ. of Lisbon, currently Vice-Rector and Full Prof. of Int. Relations, Dir Portuguese Inst. of Int. Relations; Dir Inst. of Nat. Defence 1996–2000; Minister of Internal Admin 2000–02, of Nat. Defence 2006–09; Ordem do Infante D. Henrique Comendados 2000, Grande Oficial 2006. *Publications include:* O Ultimatum Inglês. Política Externa e Política Interna no Portugal de 1890 1990, O Poder e a Guerra. Objectvos nacionais e estratégias políticas na entrada de Portugal na Grande Guerra 1914–1918 1996, The International Politics of Democratization (ed.) 2011, The Europeanization of Portuguese Democracy (co-ed.) 2012, Heróis do Mar, História dos Símbolos Nacionais; numerous articles in professional journals. *Address:* Universidade Nova de Lisboa, Avenida de Berna, 26-C, 1069-061, Lisbon, Portugal (office). *Telephone:* 213845133. *Fax:* 213845134. *E-mail:* nst@unl.pt (office). *Website:* www.unl.pt (office).

SEVERIN, (Giles) Tim, MA, BLitt; British traveller and writer; b. 25 Sept. 1940, Jorhat, Assam, India; s. of Maurice Watkins and Inge Severin; m. Dorothy Virginia Sherman 1966 (divorced 1979); one d.; ed Tonbridge School, Keble Coll., Oxford; Commonwealth Fellow, USA 1964–66; expeditions: led motorcycle team along Marco Polo's route 1961, canoe and launch down River Mississippi 1965, Brendan Voyage from W Ireland to N America 1977, Sindbad Voyage from Oman to China 1980–81, Jason Voyage from Greece to Soviet Georgia 1984, Ulysses Voyage, Troy to Ithaca 1985, Crusade: on horseback from Belgium to Jerusalem 1987–88, Travels on horseback in Mongolia 1990, China Voyage: bamboo sailing raft Hong Kong-Japan-Pacific 1993, Spice Islands Voyage in Moluccas, E Indonesia 1996, Pacific travels in search of Moby Dick 1998, Latin America travels seeking Robinson Crusoe sources 2000; historical novelist 2005–; Hon. DLitt (Trinity Coll., Dublin) 1996, (Nat. Univ. of Ireland) 2003; Royal Geographical Soc. Gold Medal, Royal Scottish Geographical Soc. Livingstone Medal. *Publications include:* Tracking Marco Polo 1964, Explorers of the Mississippi 1967, The Golden Antilles 1970, The African Adventure 1973, Vanishing Primitive Man 1973, The Oriental Adventure 1976, The Brendan Voyage 1978, The Sindbad Voyage 1982, The Jason Voyage 1984, The Ulysses Voyage 1987, Crusader 1989, In Search of Genghis Khan 1991, The China Voyage 1994, The Spice Islands Voyage 1997, In Search of Moby Dick 1999, Seeking Robinson Crusoe 2002, Viking: Odinn's Child (novel) 2004, Viking: Sworn Brother 2005, Viking: King's Man 2005, Pirate: Corsair 2007, Privateer 2014, Buccaneer 2008, Sea Robber 2009, The Book of Dreams 2013, The Emperor's Elephant 2014, The Pope's Assassin 2015. *Address:* Inchy Bridge, Timoleague, Co. Cork, Ireland (home). *Telephone:* (23) 8846127 (home). *E-mail:* severin.tim@gmail.com (home). *Website:* www.timseverin.net (home).

SEVERINO DI BENEDETTO, Paola; Italian lawyer, academic and politician; *Vice-President and Professor of Criminal Law, LUISS Guido Carli University;* b. 22 Oct. 1948, Naples; ed La Sapienza Univ., Rome; fmr Assoc. Prof. of Criminal Law, Faculty of Economy and Trade, Univ. of Perugia, later Chair. of Criminal and Commercial Law 1987, Full Prof., Faculty of Econs 1995–; Lecturer and Chair. of Criminal Law, LUISS Guido Carli Univ., Rome 1987–90, Asst Prof. 1990–95, Prof. 1998–, Dean, Faculty of Law 2003–06, apptd Deputy Vice-Chancellor 2006, Rector 2016–18, Vice-Pres. 2018–, Pres. Scientific Council mem. Strategic Group of the LUISS School of European Political Economy, Dir Master in Criminal Law of Business, in Compliance and Prevention of Corruption in Public and Private Sectors, in Cybersecurity: Public policies, regulations and Man.; apptd Special Rep. Italian OSCE Presidency for the Fight against Corruption 2018; Vice-Pres. Military Council of the Magistracy 1997–2001; Minister of Justice (in Mario Monti's 'govt of technocrats') 2011–13; fmr Lecturer in Criminal Law, Scuola Ufficiali Carabinieri, Rome; Chair. Technical-Scientific cttee mem. Editorial Bd Enciclopedia giuridica Treccani; legal adviser to numerous cos, banks and trade asscns; mem. Avvocati di Roma (bar asscn) 1975–, Reflection and Strategic Address cttee, Ministry of Foreign Affairs and Int. Cooperation 2015–, Italian-French cttee, Ethics cttee, Veronesi Foundation, Scientific cttee Vodafone Foundation, Ernst & Young, Confindustria, Silvia Sandano asscn, Arel; mem. Scientific cttee Archivio penale, Guardia di Finanza, Rivista del diritto della navigazione, The Future of Science and Ethics; fmr mem. several ministerial cttees on reform of criminal law and criminal procedure; Dr hc Univ. of Glasgow 2018; Minerva Prize 2003, Marisa Bellisario Award 2009, Dell'Andro Award 2012, Scanno Prize-Law Section 2015, Guido Prize Carli 2018, Il Perugino Prize 2018. *Address:* Department of Law, LUISS Guido Carli University, Viale Porec, 11, 00198 Rome, Italy (office). *Telephone:* (06) 85225294 (office). *Fax:* (06) 85225852 (office). *E-mail:* pseverino@luiss.it (office). *Website:* didattica.giurisprudenza.luiss.it (office).

SEVIGNY, Chloë Stevens; American actress; b. 18 Nov. 1974, Darien, Conn.; d. of H. David Sevigny and Janine Sevigny (née Malinowski); early career as fashion model, New York; film debut in Kids 1995; has also designed several vintage-style clothing collections 2006–. *Films include:* Kids 1995, The Last Days of Disco 1998, Boys Don't Cry (Satellite Award for Best Supporting Actress in a Drama, Sierra

Award for Best Supporting Actress, Independent Spirit Award for Best Supporting Actress) 1999, A Map of the World 1999, American Psycho 2000, Demonlover 2002, Dogville 2003, The Brown Bunny 2003, Shattered Glass 2003, Melinda and Melinda 2004, Broken Flowers 2005, Sisters 2006, The Killing Room 2009, Barry Munday 2010, Mr Nice 2010, The Wait 2011, Lovelace 2013, Love & Friendship 2016, Antibirth 2016. *Television:* Will & Grace 2004, Big Love (Golden Globe Award for Best Supporting Actress 2010) 2006–11, Louie 2012, Hit and Miss 2012, American Horror Story: Asylum 2012–13, Portlandia 2013, The Mindy Project 2013. *Address:* Endeavor, 9601 Wilshire Blvd, Beverly Hills, CA 90210, USA (office). *Telephone:* (310) 248-2000 (office).

SEVÓN, Leif, LLM; Finnish judge (retd) and foundation executive; *Chairman, Sigrid Jusélius Stiftelse;* b. 31 Oct. 1941, Helsinki; s. of Enzio Sevón and Ulla Sevón; m. (divorced); one s. one d.; ed Univ. of Helsinki; Asst, Univ. of Helsinki 1966–71, Asst Prof. 1971–74; Counsellor of Legislation, Ministry of Justice 1973–78; Sr Judge, Chamber Pres., City Court of Helsinki 1979–80; Dir of Legislation, Ministry of Justice 1980–86, Dir-Gen. Dept of Legislation 1986–91; Judge, Supreme Court of Justice 1991; Counsellor, Dept of Trade, Ministry of Foreign Affairs 1991–92; Pres. EFTA Court 1994; Judge, Court of Justice of European Communities 1995–2002; Pres. Supreme Court of Finland 2002–05 (retd); mem. Bd of Dirs Sigrid Jusélius Stiftelse 2002–, Chair. 2008–; Commdr, Grand Cross Order of White Rose of Finland 2003, Nordstjärncorden (Sweden) 2003; Hon. LLD (Stockholm) 1999, (Helsinki) 2000. *Publications:* books, articles and translations. *Address:* Sigrid Jusélius Stiftelse, Alexandersgatan 48 B, 00100 Helsinki, Finland (office). *Website:* www.sigridjuselius.fi (office).

SEWELL, Rufus Frederick; British actor; b. 29 Oct. 1967, Twickenham; s. of Bill Sewell; ed Central School of Speech and Drama, London; London Critics' Circle Best Newcomer 1992, Broadway Theatre World Award 1995, London Evening Standard Award for Best Actor 2006. *Stage appearances include:* Royal Hunt of the Sun, Comedians, The Lost Domain, Peter and the Captain, Pride and Prejudice, The Government Inspector, The Seagull, As You Like It, Making it Better, Arcadia, Translations, Rat in the Skull, Macbeth, Luther, Rock 'N' Roll (London Critics' Circle Best Actor 2006, Best Actor, Laurence Olivier Awards 2007). *Television appearances include:* The Last Romantics, Gone to Seed, Middlemarch, Dirty Something, Citizen Locke, Cold Comfort Farm, Henry IV, Charles II: The Power and the Passion 2003, Taming of the Shrew 2005, Eleventh Hour (series) 2008–09, The Pillars of the Earth (series) 2010, Zen (series) 2011, Masterpiece Mystery (series) 2011, Parade's End (series) 2012, Restless 2012, Dangerous Liaisons 2014, Killing Jesus 2014, The Man in the High Castle (series) 2015, Victoria (series) 2016. *Film appearances include:* Twenty-One 1991, Dirty Weekend 1993, A Man of No Importance 1994, Victory 1995, Carrington 1995, Hamlet 1996, The Woodlanders 1997, Dangerous Beauty 1998, Dark City 1998, Martha, Meet Frank, Daniel and Laurence 1998, Illuminata 1998, At Sachem Farm 1998, In a Savage Land 1999, Bless the Child 2000, A Knight's Tale 2001, Extreme Ops 2002, Victoria Station 2003, The Legend of Zorro 2005, Tristan + Isolde 2006, The Illusionist 2006, Paris, je t'aime 2006, Amazing Grace 2006, The Holiday 2006, Vinyan 2008, Downloading Nancy 2008, The Tourist 2010, Abraham Lincoln: Vampire Hunter 2012, Hotel Noir 2012, The Brunchers 2013, All Things to All Men 2013, The Sea 2013, I'll Follow You Down 2013, Hercules 2014, The Devil's Hand 2014, Blinky Bill the Movie 2015. *Address:* c/o Julian Belfrage Associates, 3rd Floor, 9 Argyll Street, London, W1F 7TG, England (office). *Telephone:* (20) 7287-8544 (office). *Fax:* (20) 7287-8832 (office). *E-mail:* renata@rufussewell.net (office). *Website:* www.rufussewell.net (office).

SEWERYN, Andrzej; Polish actor and theatre director; b. 25 April 1946, Heilbronn, Germany; s. of Zdzisław Seweryn and Zofia Seweryn; m. 1st Krystyna Janda (divorced 1979); m. 2nd Laurence Seweryn (divorced); m. Mireille Maalouf 1988; two s. one d.; ed State Higher School of Drama, Warsaw; actor, Athenaeum Theatre, Warsaw 1968–82, Peter Brook's Group 1984–88, perm. mem. Comédie Française, Paris 1993–; mem. SPATiF (Asscn of Polish Theatre and Film Actors) 1969–82; Prof., School of Theatre National de Chaillot, Nat. School of Arts and Technical Theatre, Lyon; Prof. of Drama, Nat. Conservatory of Dramatic Art, Paris 2001–; Chevalier des Arts et des Lettres 1995, Kt's Cross, Order of Polonia Restituta 1997, Ordre Nat. du Mérite 1999; Prize Berlin Int. Film Festival for Conductor 1979, Best Actor, French Film Awards for Unpleasant Man 1996, Prize of Le Syndicat professionnel de la Critique dramatique et musicale de France 1996, Polish TV Award, Polish Film Festival, Gdańsk 2000. *Films include:* Zenon in The Border 1977, Rościszewski in Without Anaesthetic 1978, Ksiądz in The Brute 1979, Kung-fu 1979, Conductor 1979, Mahabharata 1988, French Revolution 1989, Schindler's List 1994, Journey to the East 1994, Total Eclipse 1995, Unpleasant Man 1996, With Fire and Sword 1998, Billboard 1998, Pan Tadeusz (The Last Foray in Lithuania) 1999, The Primate 2000, The Revenge 2002, Par amour (TV) 2003, A ton image 2004, Who Never Lived (dir) 2006, Nightwatching 2007, Possibility of an Island 2008, Little Rose 2010, Entanglement 2011, You Ain't Seen Nothin' Yet 2012, The Vulture 2013, Close-ups 2014, Anatomia zla 2015, Ostatnia rodzina 2016. *Theatre:* (actor) leading roles in Don Carlos, Peer Gynt, Don Juan; (dir) Le Mariage forcé by Molière, Comédie Française 1999, Le Mal court by Jacques Audiberti, Comédie Française 2000, Tartuffe 2002. *Television series:* Kliefhorn in Polish Roads 1977, Marek in On the Silver Globe 1976–79, Bukacki in Połaniecki's Family 1977, Roman in Roman and Magda 1979, Ekipa 2007, 39 i pól 2009, Little Rose 2010, Uwiklanie 2011, Vous n'avez encore rien vu 2012; numerous other roles on TV. *Address:* Comédie Française, Place Colette, 75001 Paris, France (office). *E-mail:* informations@comedie-francaise.org (office); www.comedie-francaise.fr (office).

SEWING, Christian; German banking executive; *CEO, Deutsche Bank AG;* b. 22 April 1970; m.; four c.; ed Bankakademie Bielefeld and Hamburg; joined Deutsche Bank 1989, worked in Singapore, later Jr Corp. Account Man. in Toronto, Head of Lending Operations in Tokyo, six years in London, Chief Credit Officer, Deutsche Bank AG 2010–12, Deputy Chief Risk Officer 2012–13, Head of Group Audit 2013–14, mem. Man. Bd 2015–, assumed responsibility for Deutsche Bank Private & Commercial Bank (including Postbank) 2015–18, CEO, Deutsche Bank AG 2018–; mem. Man. Bd Deutsche Genossenschafts-Hypothekenbank 2005–07. *Address:* Deutsche Bank AG, Theodor-Heuss-Allee 70, 60486 Frankfurt, Germany (office). *Telephone:* (69) 9100 (office). *Fax:* (69) 91034225 (office). *E-mail:* deutsche.bank@db.com (office). *Website:* www.deutsche-bank.de (office).

SEXTON, John Edward, BA, MA, PhD, JD; American lawyer, professor of law and university administrator; b. 1944, Brooklyn, NY; m. Lisa E. Goldberg (died 2007); one s. one d.; ed Fordham Coll., Fordham Univ., Harvard Law School; Prof. of Religion, St Francis Coll., Brooklyn 1966–73, Dept Chair. 1970–75; Law Clerk, Judges David Bazelon and Harold Leventhal Court of Appeals 1979–80, to Chief Justice Warren Burger, Supreme Court 1980–81; joined Law Faculty, New York Univ. (NYU) 1981, apptd Dean 1988, currently Dean Emer. of Law School, Benjamin Butler Prof. of Law and Pres. NYU 2002–15; served as Special Master Supervising Pretrial Proceedings in Love Canal Litigation 1983–93; Founding Chair. NASD Dispute Resolution 2000–02; Chair. New York Acad. of Sciences, Comm. of Ind. Colls and Univs of New York, Fed. Reserve Bank of New York 2003–06, Fed. Reserve Systems Council of Chairs 2006; mem. Bd of Dirs Nat. Asscn of Securities Dealers 1996–98, New York State Comm. on Higher Educ., American Council on Educ., Inst. of Int. Educ., Asscn for a Better New York; fmr Pres. American Asscn of Law Schools; mem. Asscn of American Univ. Presidents, Council on Foreign Relations; Fellow, American Acad. of Arts and Sciences, Foreign Policy Asscn, New York; mem. Advisory Bd Genesis Prize Foundation; Chevalier, Légion d'honneur 2008; Dr hc (Fordham Univ., St Francis Coll., St John's Univ., Syracuse Univ., Katholieke Universiteit Leuven, St Joseph's Coll., Univ. of Rochester, Univ. of Surrey, Univ. of Warwick); Vol. 60 of NYU's Annual Survey of American Law dedicated in his honour, named by Emory University as "Outstanding High School Debate Coach of the Last 50 Years" for work he did from 1960–75, honoured at Harvard Law Review Annual Banquet, named Alumnus of the Year, Fordham Univ. and Brooklyn Prep, NASPA President's Award 2012. *Publications:* Redefining the Supreme Court's Role: A Theory of Managing the Federal Court System, Civil Procedure: Cases and Materials (co-author), Baseball as a Road to God: Seeing Beyond the Game 2013; numerous book chapters and articles. *Address:* c/o Office of the President, New York University, 70 Washington Square South, New York, NY 10012, USA.

SEXWALE, (Gabriel) Tokyo; South African business executive and politician; b. 5 March 1953, Orlando West, Soweto; s. of Frank Sexwale; m. Judy Moon; one s. one d.; ed Univs of Botswana, Lesotho, Swaziland; joined African Nat. Congress (ANC) in 1970s; went into exile and underwent officers' mil. training in Soviet Union 1975; returned to South Africa as underground fighter in ANC's Spear of the Nation armed wing 1976, imprisoned for 13 years on Robben Island for guerrilla activities; returned to Johannesburg, served as Head Public Liaison Dept of ANC HQ, then apptd Head Special Projects under Mil. HQ 1989; elected mem. Exec. Cttee ANC, Pretoria-Witwatersrand-Vereeniging (now Gauteng) Prov. 1990, Chair. 1994–97, Premier 1994–97; Minister of Human Settlements 2009–13; mem. ANC Nat. Exec. Cttee 1991–97; left politics for business sector and co-f. Mvelaphanda Mining, expanded into Mvelaphanda Holdings Pty Ltd (now Mvelaphanda Group Ltd), Chair. 2002–07, Chair. (non-exec.) 2007, currently Exec. Chair., also Chair. of related cos Trans Hex Group Ltd, Mvelaphanda Resources Ltd, Northam Platinum Ltd; Owner, Jonga Entabeni; CEO Batho Bonke; mem. Bd of Dirs GFI-SA, Gold Fields Ltd, ASBA Group, Allied Electronics Corpn Ltd, Desta Power Matla, Voltex, De Montfort Univ., UK; Pres. South African/Russian Business, Technological and Cultural Asscn; Vice-Pres. South African/Japanese Business Forum; Chancellor Vaal Univ. of Technology; Trustee, Nelson Mandela Foundation, Business Trust, Robben Island Ex-Prisoners Trust, Global Philanthropists Circle, Synergos Inst.; Patron Johannesburg Child and Family Welfare Soc., Streetwise South Africa, Save the Family Fund, The Sky is No Limit; Hon. Consul General of Finland in South Africa; Légion d'honneur, Cross-of-Valour (Ruby Class) (South Africa), Order of the Freedom of Havana (Cuba); Dr hc (Univ. of Nottingham, UK, De Montfort Univ.); Reach and Teach Leadership Award, USA. *Address:* Mvelaphanda Group Ltd., POB 1639, Rivonia 2128, South Africa (office). *Telephone:* (11) 2904200 (office). *Website:* www.mvelagroup.co.za (office).

SEYDOUX FORNIER DE CLAUSONNE, Jérôme; French business executive; *Co-President, Pathé;* b. 21 Sept. 1934, Paris; s. of René Seydoux Fornier de Clausonne and Geneviève Schlumberger; m. 1st (divorced); three s. one d.; m. 2nd Sophie Desserteaux-Bessis 1988; one s.; ed Lycées Montaigne, Louis-le-Grand and Buffon; financial analyst Istel, Lepercq and Co. Inc. NY 1962–63; sleeping pnr Bank of Neuflize, Schlumberger, Mallet 1964, Pnr 1966, mem. Bd of Dirs 1969–70; Admin. Schlumberger Ltd 1969, Exec. Vice-Pres. 1970, Dir-Gen. 1975–76; Admin. Compagnie Deutsch 1964–; mem. Bd of Dirs Danone (fmrly BSN) 1970–2005, fmr Admin.; Pres. Pricel 1976; Pres. Chargeurs 1980–96, later Vice-Pres., Dir-Gen., currently Vice-Chair., CEO and Dir; Pres. Admin. Council of France 5 1986; Pres., Dir-Gen. Pathé Palace (fmrly Pathé Cinema) 1991–2000, Chair. Supervisory Cttee 2000–02, Co-Pres. 2002–; Vice-Pres. Advisory Bd, Mont-Blanc Co. 2000–; Chair. BSkyB 1998–99; owner Libération newspaper; Officier, Légion d'honneur. *Leisure interests:* skiing, golf. *Address:* Pathé, 2 rue Lamennais, 75008 Paris, France (office). *Website:* www.pathe.com (office).

SEYDOUX FORNIER DE CLAUSONNE, Michel; French business executive and film producer; *Chairman and President, Lille OSC Football Club;* b. 11 Sept. 1947, Paris; grand-s. of Marcel Schlumberger; brother of Jerome and Nicolas Seydoux Fornier de Clausonne; ed École Alsacienne; began career as Asst to Pres. of Org. centrale des camps et activités de jeunesse 1968–71; Founder and Pres. Caméra One (production co.); Pres. Air Littoral 1992–98; Admin., Gaumont; mem. Bd of Trustees, Pathé; co-owns, with Pierre Gagnaire, Le Gaya rive gauche (seafood restaurant), Paris; Chair. and Pres. Lille OSC football club 2002–; mem. Council of Admin, Ligue de football professionelle (LFP) 2005–, Bureau of LFP 2007–, Pres. Marketing Comm. 2008–; Chevalier des Arts et des Lettres. *Films produced:* Lily aime-moi 1974, F… comme Fairbanks 1976, Don Giovanni 1979, Hôtel de France 1987, Cyrano de Bergerac 1990, Urga 1991, Prospero's Books 1991, Anna 1992, Toxic Affair 1993, Smoking/No Smoking 1993, Soleil trompeur 1994, On connaît la chanson 1997, Le Barbier de Sibérie 1999, René 2002, Le Filmeur 2005, Les Ambitieux 2006. *Address:* LOSC Lille Métropole, Domaine de Luchin, Grand Rue BP 79, 59780 Camphin-en-Pévèle, France (office). *Telephone:* (8) 92-68-56-72 (office). *Fax:* (3) 20-17-71-78 (office). *E-mail:* info@losc.fr (office). *Website:* www.losc.fr (office).

SEYDOUX FORNIER DE CLAUSONNE, Nicolas Pierre, LenD; French business executive; *President-Director-General, Gaumont;* b. 16 July 1939, Paris; s. of René Seydoux Fornier de Clausonne and Geneviève Schlumberger; m. Anne-

Marie Cahen-Salvador 1964; two c.; ed Lycée Buffon, Faculté de Droit, Paris, New York Business School and Inst. d'Etudes Politiques, Paris; Head of Legal Service, Cie Int. pour l'Informatique, Paris 1967–70; financial analyst, Morgan, Stanley & Co. Inc., New York 1970–71, Morgan & Cie Int. SA, Paris 1971–74; Vice-Pres.-Dir-Gen. Gaumont 1974, Pres.-Dir-Gen. 1975–; Pres. Fédération Nat. des Distributeurs de Films 1988–2001, Bureau de liaison des industries cinématographiques (BLIC) 2000, Asscn de Lutte contre la Piraterie Audiovisuelle (ALPA), Asscn des Producteurs Indépendants (API); Chair. Forum d'Avignon—Culture, Economy, Media 2008–; Vice-Chair. Supervisory Bd Arte France; mem. Bd of Dirs Schlumberger 1982–; Officier Légion d'honneur. *Leisure interests:* vintage cars, skiing. *Address:* Gaumont, 30 Avenue Charles de Gaulle, 92200 Neuilly-sur-Seine (office); 5 place du Palais-Bourbon, 75007 Paris, France (home). *Telephone:* 1-46-43-24-24 (office). *Fax:* 1-46-43-21-25 (office). *Website:* www.gaumont.com (office).

SEYMOUR, Lynn, CBE; Canadian fmr ballet dancer and choreographer (retd); b. 8 March 1939, Wainwright, Alberta; d. of E.V. Springett; m. 1st Colin Jones 1963 (divorced 1974); three s.; m. 2nd Philip Pace 1974; m. 3rd Vanya Hackel 1983 (divorced 1988); ed Sadler's Wells School and Royal Ballet School, UK; graduated into Royal Ballet 1957; promoted to Soloist rank 1958, to Prin. 1958; prima ballerina Berlin Opera Ballet 1966–69; Principal Guest Ballerina Artist, Royal Ballet 1971–78; Artistic Dir Munich State Opera Ballet 1978–80, Ballet Bayerische Staatsoper 1979–80, Greek Nat. Opera Ballet 2006–07 (resgnd); Guest Artist with other cos including Alvin Ailey; Evening Standard Drama Award 1977. *Ballets:* The Burrow 1958, Swan Lake 1958, Giselle 1958, The Invitation 1960, The Two Pigeons 1961, Symphony 1963, Romeo and Juliet 1965, Anastasia 1967, Dances at a Gathering, The Concert, The Seven Deadly Sins, Flowers 1972, Shukumei, The Four Seasons 1975, Side Show, Rituals 1975, Manon Lescaut 1976, A Month in the Country 1976, Mayerling 1978, Manon 1978, Choreography for Rashomon 1976, The Court of Love 1977, Intimate Letters 1978, Mae and Polly, Boreas, Tattooed Lady, Wolfy, the Ballet Rambert 1987. *Films:* as actress: Dancers 1987, Wittgenstein 1993, Relative Values 2000. *Television:* Tempo 1965, The Little Vampire 1986–87, Dance for the Camera 1998. *Publication:* Lynn: Leaps and Boundaries (autobiography with Paul Gardner) 1984.

SEZER, Ahmet Necdet, BA, LLM, PhD; Turkish judge and fmr head of state; b. 13 Sept. 1941, Afyon; m.; three c.; ed Univ. of Ankara; served in mil. service at Land Forces Acad.; Judge in Ankara, then Dicle and Yerköy; fmr Supervisory Judge, High Court of Appeal, Ankara; apptd mem. High Court of Appeal 1983; mem. Constitutional Court 1988–2000, Chief Justice 1998–2000; Pres. of Turkey 2000–07.

SEZGIN, Aydin Adnan, BA; Turkish diplomatist; b. 1956, Aydin; m.; one c.; ed Ankara Tevfik Fikret High School, Ankara Hacettepe Univ., Univ. of Law and Econs, Paris; joined Ministry of Foreign Affairs (MFA) and worked in Dept of Int. Econ. Orgs 1982–84, Third, then Second Sec., Perm. Mission to EEC, Brussels 1984–87, Second, then First Sec., Embassy in Baghdad 1987–89, First Sec., Gulf and Islamic Countries Dept, MFA 1989–91, First Sec., Perm. Mission to UN Office in Geneva 1991–94, First Sec. and Special Adviser, Presidential Admin 1995–96, Acting Head of Dept, European Council and Human Rights Dept, MFA 1996–97, Dir Gen. of Press and Information, Office of the Prime Minister 1997–2003, Consul Gen. in Paris 2003–06, Envoy/Deputy Dir Gen. for Research, MFA 2007–09, Dir-Gen. for Research and Intelligence 2009–10, Amb. to Russia 2010–14, to Italy 2014–16; mem. İyi Parti: (Good Party), Vice-Chair. (Int. Affairs) 2018–. *Address:* İyi Parti: (Good Party), Mustafa Kemal Dist 2120, Cadde, No.9, Çankaya 06520, Ankara, Turkey (office). *Telephone:* (312) 408-08-08 (office). *Website:* iyiparti.org.tr (office).

SEZIBERA, Richard, MA, MBChB; Rwandan physician and politician; *Minister of Foreign Affairs and International Co-operation;* b. 5 June 1964, Kigali; m. Eustochie Sezibera; five c.; ed Makerere Univ., Georgetown Univ.; began career as doctor at Mbuya Hosp., Kampala, Uganda; worked in Dept of Obstetrics and Gynaecology, Mbale Regional Referral Hosp., Eastern Uganda; Field Medical Officer, Rwanda Patriotic Front/Rwanda Patriotic Army (RPF/RPA) 1990, rank of Maj. 1993; apptd Physician and Mil. Aide to Pres. of the Repub. 1994; mem. Parl. 1995–99, Pres. Parl. Comm. on Social Affairs, mem. Comm. on Defence and Nat. Security; Amb. to USA 1999–2003; Presidential Special Envoy to African Great Lakes Region 2003–08; Minister of Health 2008–11; Sec. Gen., East African Community 2011–16; Senator for Southern Region 2016–18; Minister of Foreign Affairs and Int. Co-operation 2018–; mem. Rwanda Medical Asscn, GAVI (Global Alliance for Vaccine) (fmr Chair. GAVU Programme and Policy Cttee); fmr Fellow Inst. for Advanced Studies in the Humanities, Edinburgh. *Publications:* published widely in medical journals, political science journals and int. media outlets. *Address:* Ministry of Foreign Affairs and International Co-operation, Kimihurura, 5th and 6th Floors, ave du lac Muhazi, POB 179, Kigali, Rwanda (office). *Telephone:* 252599128 (office). *Fax:* 252599129 (office). *E-mail:* info@minaffet.gov.rw (office). *Website:* www.minaffet.gov.rw (office).

SGOUROS, Dimitris; Greek pianist; b. 30 Aug. 1969, Athens; s. of Sotirios Sgouros and Marianthi Sgouros; ed Univ. of Athens, Athens Conservatory of Music, Univ. of Maryland, USA, St Peter's Coll., Oxford and Royal Acad. of Music, London, UK; debut in Piraeus aged seven; numerous concerts in Europe from 1980; solo piano recital aged 11, to audience of 4,000 at Herodes Atticus Theatre of Athens 1981; first US appearance aged 12, with Nat. Symphony Orchestra of Washington, Carnegie Hall, New York 1982; appeared at Prague Spring Festival with Sir Charles Mackeras and the Czech Philharmonic Orchestra playing Beethoven's Piano Concerto No. 4 1986; played 12 different piano concertos over six nights with Singapore Symphony Orchestra, Sgouros Festival, Singapore 1990; has played in all the major cities and concert houses and on all the major radio and TV stations world-wide; repertoire of 45 piano concertos and large number of solo piano and chamber music works; took part in cultural events at Los Angeles Olympics 1984, Athens Olympics 2004, Beijing Olympics 2008; opening recital, Newport Music Festival, RI 2011; European tours with Budapest Festival Orchestra 2013, 2015–16; numerous awards, including Rotary Club of Athens Award 1981, Acad. of Athens Award 1982, Los Angeles 1984, Athens Conservatory Gold Medal 1984, Tom Brandley Award, Los Angeles 1984, Leonardo da Vinci Int. Prize, The Lions: Melvin Jones Fellow 2000, Chopin Diploma (Poland) 2010, UNESCO Prize for Arts, Sciences and Literature (Greece) 2014. *Television:* Chopin's Piano Concerto No. 1 with Simon Bolivar Youth Orchestra, Conservatory of Music, Caracas (televised nationally on American A&E Network) 1982. *Recordings include:* works by Schumann, Brahms, Rachmaninov, Tchaikovsky, Liszt, Mozart and Chopin with the Berlin Philharmonic, London Philharmonic and Sofia Philharmonic Orchestras and the Radio Orchestra of Slovenia, Capriccio's Elysium Recordings (USA), Grieg Piano Concerto with Borusan Istanbul Philharmonic Orchestra 2000, Rachmaninov Piano Concertos Nos 2 and 3 with Cyprus State Orchestra (for Steinway Club 150th anniversary, recorded live). *Leisure interests:* mathematics, conducting opera, languages. *Address:* Tompazi 28, 18537 Piraeus (home); Sahturi 25, 18535 Piraeus, Greece (office). *Telephone:* 693-2265110 (mobile) (home); (210) 8959778 (office). *Fax:* (210) 8956477 (home). *E-mail:* info@sgouros-pianist.com (office). *Website:* www.sgouros-pianist.com (office).

SGRECCIA, HE Cardinal Elio; Italian ecclesiastic; *President Emeritus of the Roman Curia;* b. 6 June 1928, Arcevia, Prov. of Ancona, Marche region; ordained priest 1952; Titular Bishop of Zama Minor 1992–; Sec. Pontifical Council for the Family 1992–96; Pres. Pontifical Acad. for Life 2005–08, Pres. Emer. of the Roman Curia 2008–; apptd Cardinal-Deacon of S. Angelo in Pescheria, cr. Cardinal (non-voting) 20 Nov. 2010. *Address:* c/o Pontifical Academy for Life, Via della Conciliazione 1, 00193 Rome, Italy. *Telephone:* (06) 69882423. *E-mail:* pav@acdlife.va. *Website:* www.vatican.va/roman_curia/pontifical_academies/acdlife; www.academiavita.org.

SHA, Ming; Chinese business executive; Gen. Man. Xinxing Cathay International Group Co. Ltd (fmrly Xinxing Ductile Iron Pipes Co. Ltd). *Address:* Xinxing Cathay International Group, 27F Office Tower, Beijing Fortune Plaza, 7 Dongsanhuan Zhong Road, Beijing 100020, People's Republic of China (office). *Telephone:* (10) 59290000 (office). *Fax:* (10) 59290029 (office). *E-mail:* service@xxpgroup.com (office). *Website:* english.xxcig.com (office).

SHA, Zukang; Chinese diplomatist and UN official; b. 24 Sept. 1947, Jiangsu prov.; m.; one s.; ed Nanjing Univ.; staff mem., Embassy in London 1971–74, in Sri Lanka 1974–80, Attaché and Third Sec., Embassy in Delhi 1980–85, Deputy Div. Dir and First Sec. Dept of Int. Orgs and Confs 1985–88, Adviser and Deputy Dir-Gen. 1992–95, First Sec. and Adviser, Perm. Mission to UN, New York 1988–92, Amb. for Disarmament Affairs and Deputy Perm. Rep. to UN Office and Other Int. Orgs, Geneva, Switzerland 1995–97, Dir-Gen. Dept of Arms Control 1997–2001, Perm. Rep. to UN, Geneva 2001–07; Under-Sec.-Gen. for Econ. and Social Affairs, UN, New York 2007–12, Sec.-Gen. Rio+20 (UN Conf. on Sustainable Devt 2012) 2010–12. *Address:* c/o Office of the Under-Secretary-General for Economic and Social Affairs, United Nations, Room DC2-2320, New York, NY 10017, USA.

SHAABAN, Mohammad Shaaban, PhD; Egyptian diplomatist and UN official; b. 13 June 1942, Port Said; m.; three c.; ed Free Univ. of Brussels; joined foreign service, rep. to ECOSOC, UNDP and various other cttees 1984–88, Amb. to Belgium and Luxembourg 1993–97, to Denmark and Lithuania 1998–2000, Head of Perm. Mission to EU, Brussels 1993–97, Deputy Minister of Foreign Affairs responsible for Africa 1997–98, Deputy Minister for Information, Research and Assessment 2000–01, Deputy Minister for Foreign Affairs responsible for Europe 2001–04, Co-ordinator of First Session of Euro-Mediterranean Parl. Ass. 2005, Adviser to Minister of Foreign Affairs 2004–07, Nat. Co-ordinator for Reform Initiatives in Middle East 2004–07, Diplomatic Adviser to Speaker of the House, Egyptian Parl. 2004–07; Under-Sec.-Gen., Dept for Gen. Ass. and Conf. Man., UN, New York 2007–12; Visiting Lecturer, Diplomatic Acad. of London, Univ. of Westminster 2002–; Order of Merit (Egypt) 1977, Chevalier, Ordre nat. du Mérite 1978, Grand Croix de l'Ordre de la Couronne (Belgium) 1997. *Publications include:* The United Nations Secretary-General: The Man and the Post 1971, The Analysis of International Relations (in Arabic) 1984. *Leisure interests:* tennis, swimming, reading.

SHAATH, Nabeel A., BA, MBA, PhD, DJur; Palestinian politician, diplomatist, consultant and academic; *Senior Adviser on Foreign Affairs to President of Palestinian National Authority;* b. Aug. 1938, Safad; m.; two s. two d.; ed Univ. of Alexandria, Egypt, Univ. of Pennsylvania, Wharton School of Business, USA; fmr Business School Prof., taught Finance and Econs, Univ. of Pennsylvania, USA 1961–65, academic positions at Univs of Cairo and Alexandria 1965–69; Dean, School of Business Admin, American Univ. in Beirut 1969–75; consultant to several govts, in Org. of Shuaiab industrial zone, Kuwait, power sector in Saudi Arabia, public transportation in Gulf Area; est. Engineering and Management Inst. and Arab Centre for Admin. Devt in Beirut, Cairo and 14 brs in other Arab countries; mem. Fatah Cen. Cttee 1990–2016, del. to Middle E Peace Conf., Madrid 1991; First Head of PLO Del. to UN, Adviser to Yasser Arafat, wrote his speech to UN Gen. Ass. 1974; mem. PLO–Israel peace negotiations, Oslo, Norway and Washington, DC 1993–95; Palestinian Authority Minister of Planning and Int. Co-operation 1994–2003, Minister of Foreign Affairs 2003–05; Deputy Prime Minister 2005–06; Pres. Constitution Drafting Comm., PLO 2002–11; elected to Palestinian Legis. Council, Rep. of Khan Younis, Gaza Strip 1996; Rep. of Palestine to world media confs, including World Econ. Forum; Acting Prime Minister of Palestinian Authority 2005, currently Sr Adviser to Pres. of Palestinian Nat. Authority; Commr Gen., Fateh Foreign Relations Comm. 2009–17. *Address:* c/o Fatah, Ramallah, Palestinian Autonomous Areas.

SHACKLETON OF BELGRAVIA, Baroness (Life Peer), cr. 2010, of Belgravia in the City of Westminster; **Fiona Shackleton,** LVO, LLD; British solicitor; *Partner, Payne Hicks Beach;* b. (Fiona S. Charkham), 26 May 1956, London; d. of Jonathan Charkham and Moira Elizabeth Frances Charkham (née Salmon); Salmon family co-owners of J. Lyons & Co. cornerhouse empire, cousin to Nigella and Dominic Lawson and George Monbiot; m. Ian Shackleton (relative of Antarctic explorer Sir Ernest Shackleton); two d.; ed Benenden School, Kent, Univ. of Exeter; qualified as a solicitor 1980; Partner, Brecher & Co. 1981–84; Partner, Farrer & Co. 1986–2001; Partner, Payne Hicks Beach 2001–, Solicitor for Prince William and Prince Harry; Gov., Benenden School 1986–2007; Hon. Bencher, Inner Temple 2011; Hon. LLD (Exeter) 2010. *Publications:* The Divorce Handbook 1992. *Leisure interests:* travel, opera, fashion. *Address:* Payne Hicks Beach, 10 New Square, Lincoln's Inn, London, WC2A 3QG (office); House of Lords, Westminster, London, SW1A 0PW, England. *Telephone:* (20) 7465-4300 (office); (20) 7219-5353 (House of Lords). *Fax:* (20) 7465-4329 (office); (20) 7219-5979 (House of Lords). *E-mail:* fshackleton@phb.co.uk (office). *Website:* www.paynehicksbeach.co.uk (office).

SHADIYEV, Askarbek; Kyrgyzstani economist and politician; b. 31 Jan. 1969, Leilek Dist, Batken Region; m.; five c.; ed Frunze Polytechnic Coll., Kyrgyz State Univ.; Deputy Chief Accountant, Sfaera (industrial and commercial co.) 1993–94; Commercial Dir LLC Aznur Ltd 1995; Vice-Pres. LLC Datka Corpn 1995–2000; mem. Jogorku Kenesh (Supreme Council, parl.) 2000–02, 2005–10, 2015–; Deputy Minister of Finance 2002–03, also Chair., Ministry of Finance Revenue Cttee 2002–03; Gov. Batken Oblast 2003–05; Minister of Energy 2010–11, of Energy and Industry 2011–12; First Deputy Prime Minister 2017–18; Honoured Economist of the Kyrgyz Repub. *Address:* c/o Office of the Government, 720003 Bishkek, Dom Pravitelstva, Kyrgyzstan (office).

SHAFAI, Lotfollah, PhD, FRSC; Canadian electronics engineer and academic; *Distinguished Professor and Canada Research Chair in Applied Electromagnetics, University of Manitoba;* ed Univ. of Tehran, Univ. of Toronto; moved to Canada from Iran 1964; Lecturer, Dept of Electrical and Computer Eng, Univ. of Manitoba 1969, currently Distinguished Prof. and Canada Research Chair in Applied Electromagnetics; Fellow, IEEE, Canadian Acad. of Engineers, Eng Inst. of Canada; IEE Maxwell Premium Award 1990, IEEE R.W.P. King Award 1996, Killam Prize in Eng, Canada Council for the Arts 2011, IEEE Antennas and Propagation Soc. John Kraus Antenna Award 2013. *Achievements include:* early work led to development of first generation picoterminals for the Canadian Hermes satellite – ultra-small fully portable satellite ground stations with antennas now in use around the globe, making direct satellite broadcasting accessible to the public; recent work has focused on electromagnetic mapping of Arctic sea ice to provide data for understanding effects of climate-warming trends. *Publications:* numerous papers in professional journals. *Address:* Room E3-404C, Engineering and Information Technology Complex, University of Manitoba, 75 Chancellor's Circle, Winnipeg, MB R3T 5V6, Canada (office). *Telephone:* (204) 474-9615 (office). *E-mail:* shafai@umanitoba.ca (office); shafai@cc.umanitoba.ca (office). *Website:* umanitoba.ca/ece (office).

SHAFEEU, Ismail; Maldivian politician; fmr Minister of Planning, Human Resources and Environment; Minister of Educ. 2002–03, of Home Affairs and Environment 2003–04, of Defence and Nat. Security 2004–08; fmr Chair. Dhiraagu Ltd.

SHAFIK, Dame Nemat Talaat, (Minouche), DBE, BA, MSc, DPhil; British (b. Egyptian) economist and international official; *Director, London School of Economics;* b. 1962, Alexandria, Egypt; m. Raffael; twin c.; ed Univ. of Massachusetts, Amherst, USA, London School of Econs, Univ. of Oxford, UK; Economist, Int. Econs Dept, World Bank 1990, Economist, World Devt Report 1992, Country Economist, Cen. European Dept 1992–94, Sr Economist, Office of the Chief Economist 1994–95, Middle East and N Africa (MENA) Region 1996–97, Dir Pvt. Sector and Finance, MENA 1997–99, Vice-Pres. Pvt Sector Devt and Infrastructure 1999–2003, Vice-Pres. Infrastructure 2003–04; Dir-Gen. Country Programmes, Dept for Int. Devt, UK 2004–08, Perm. Sec. 2008–11; Deputy Man. Dir IMF 2011–14; Deputy Gov., responsible for Markets and Banking, Bank of England 2014–17; Dir LSE 2017–; Adjunct Prof., Econs Dept, Georgetown Univ. 1989–94; Chair. Consultative Group to Assist the Poorest 1999–2004, InfoDev 1999–2004, Global Water and Sanitation Program 1999–2004, Pvt. Participation in Infrastructure Advisory Facility 1999–2004, Energy Sector Man. and Advisory Program 1999–2004; Visiting Assoc. Prof., Wharton School, Univ. of Pennsylvania 1996; mem. Bd of Advisory Eds, The Middle East Journal 1996–2002; mem. Bd, Operating Council, Global Alliance for Workers and Communities, Int. Youth Fed. 1999–2003, Calderon Comm. on New Climate Economy 2014; Trustee, British Museum 2016; Hon. DJur (Warwick) 2012, (Reading) 2016, (Glasgow) 2017; Woman of the Year in Global Leadership and Global Diversity 2009. *Publications:* several books; numerous articles in academic journals on int. econs, development, the Middle East and environment; various blogs and newspaper columns. *Address:* London School of Economics, Houghton Street, London, WC2A 2AE, England (office). *Telephone:* (20) 7955-7100 (office). *E-mail:* director@lse.ac.uk (office). *Website:* www.lse.ac.uk (office).

SHAH, Amitbhai (Amit) Anilchandra, BSc; Indian politician; *President, Bharatiya Janata Party;* b. 22 Oct. 1964, Mumbai, Maharashtra; s. of Anilchandra Gokaldas Shah; m. Sonal Shah; one s.; ed CU Shah Science Coll., Gujarat Univ.; briefly ran his father's PVC pipe business and worked as stockbroker and with co-operative banks in Ahmedabad; joined Rashtriya Swayamsevak Sangh (RSS) aged 14, apptd Sec., Akhil Bharatiya Vidyarthi Parishad (student wing of RSS) 1983; joined Bharatiya Janata Party (BJP) 1986, later Sec., BJP Ahmedabad unit, then held several party positions in Gujarat unit, Nat. Treas., Bharatiya Janata Yuva Morcha (BJP youth wing) 1997 and later Vice-Pres. BJP Gujarat State unit, apptd Gen. Sec. BJP Gujarat State unit 2010, head of BJP Lok Sabha election efforts in UP during 2014 election, Pres. BJP 2014–; MLA for Sarkhej constituency 1995–2012, for Naranpura constituency 2012–; apptd Chair. Gujarat State Financial Corpn 1995, apptd Minister of State in Gujarat 2002, assigned numerous portfolios including Transport, Police, Housing, Border Security, Civil Defense, Gram Rakshak Dal, Home Guards, Prison, Prohibition, Excise, Law and Justice, Parl. Affairs and Home Ministry (resgnd 2010 after arrested on charges of having ordered a series of 'encounter' killings by State Police, subsequently cleared of all charges); apptd Chair. Ahmedabad District Co-Operative Bank 2000; Vice-Pres. Gujarat Cricket Asscn 2009–14, Pres. 2014–; fmr Pres. Gujarat State Chess Asscn. *Address:* Bharatiya Janata Party, 11 Ashoka Road, New Delhi 110 001 (office); 10, Shivkunj Society, Near Sanghavi High School, Vijaynagar Road, Naranpura, Ahmedabad 380 013, India (home). *Telephone:* (11) 48005700 (office); (79) 27499070 (home). *Fax:* (11) 48005787 (office). *E-mail:* amitshah.bjp@gmail.com. *Website:* www.bjp.org (office).

SHAH, HRH Haji Ahmad Shah al-Musta'in Billah ibni al-Marhum Sultan Abu Bakar Ri'ayatuddin al-Mu'adzam Shah, DKP; Malaysian; b. 24 Oct. 1930, Istana Mangga Tunggal, Pekan; m. Tengku Hajjah Afzan binti Tengku Muhammad 1954 (died 1988); m. 2nd Kalsom binti Abdullah 1991; ed Malay Coll., Kuala Kangsar, Worcester Coll., Oxford and Univ. Coll., Exeter, UK; named Tengku Mahkota (Crown Prince) 1944; Capt. 4th Bn, Royal Malay Regt 1954; Commdr 12th Infantry Battalion of Territorial Army 1963–65, Lt-Col; mem. State Council 1955; Regent 1956, 1959, 1965; succeeded as Sultan 1974; abdicated 14 Jan. 2019; Timbalan Yang di Pertuan Agong (Deputy Supreme Head of State of Malaysia) 1975–79, Yang di Pertuan Agong (Supreme Head of State) 1979–84,

1985; Constitutional Head of Int. Islamic Univ. 1988; Pres. Malaysian Football Asscn 1984–2014; numerous int. decorations; Hon. DLitt (Malaya) 1988; Hon. LLD (Northrop, USA) 1993. *Address:* Istana Abu Bakar, Pekan, Pahang, Malaysia.

SHAH, Pir Karam Ali; Pakistani politician; first elected unopposed as mem. Northern Areas Advisory Council 1970, three decades as mem. Northern Areas Legis. Council (now Gilgit-Baltistan Legis. Ass.), fmr Deputy Chief Exec.; Gov. Gilgit-Baltistan 2011–15; mem. Pakistan People's Party.

SHAH, Prakash, BA, LLB, MCom; Indian diplomatist; *Chairman, PRS International Consultants;* b. 4 July 1939, Bombay; s. of H. Shah; m. Radhika; two d.; joined Indian Foreign Service 1961; Third Sec. EEC 1962–64; Second Sec. Washington, DC 1964–67; Ministry of External Affairs 1967–69; Ministry of Finance 1969–71; First Sec., Petroleum Counsellor, Embassies, Iran and Gulf States 1971–75; Dir Ministry of Petroleum 1975–77; Dir Indian Petrochemicals Ltd, Petrofils Co-operatives Ltd 1976–77; Dir/Jt Sec. Ministry of External Affairs 1977–78; Jt Sec. to Prime Minister 1978–80; High Commr in Malaysia and Brunei 1980–83; Amb. to Venezuela and Consul-Gen. to Netherlands Antilles 1983–85; Jt Sec. Ministry of External Affairs 1985–88, Additional Sec. 1989–90; Dir Kudremakh Iron Ore Ltd 1986; Amb. and Perm. Rep. to UN, Geneva 1991–92; Amb. to Japan 1992–95; Perm. Rep. to UN, New York 1995–97; Special Rep. of UN Sec.-Gen. to Iraq 1998; Dir Pathfinder Int.; Adviser Dodsal Group, UPS, Washington, USA, Sloan Global Consultants, Washington, DC; mem. Bd Khandwala Securities Bombay, Global Educ. Man., Indo-American Arts Council, Hinduja Group, Falcon Corp. Advisors, Symbiosis Int. Educ. Soc.; mem. Indo-Japan Eminent Persons Group; Chair. PRS Int. Consultants; del. to numerous int. confs. *Publications:* articles in professional journals. *Leisure interests:* cricket, tennis, golf, bridge. *Address:* G-20, Athashree, Magarpatta Road, Hadapsar, Pune 411 028, India (home). *Telephone:* (22) 23676714 (office); (22) 23676717 (home). *Fax:* (22) 24974208 (office). *E-mail:* prakashun@yahoo.com (office); prakash4739@gmail.com (office).

SHAH, Syed Mehdi; Pakistani politician; b. Skardu; mem. Pakistan Peoples Party (PPP), Acting Pres. PPP Gilgit-Baltistan; Chief Minister of Gilgit-Baltistan (first chief minister of Gilgit-Baltistan following its new constitutional position) 2009–14; unsuccessful cand. for Gilgit-Baltistan Legis. Ass. seat for Skardu-1 2015.

SHAH, Syed Murad Ali, BEng, MSc; Pakistani engineer and politician; *Chief Minister of Sindh;* b. 11 Aug. 1962, Karachi; s. of Syed Abdullah Shah (fmr Chief Minister of Sindh); m.; two c.; ed NED Univ. of Eng and Tech., Karachi, Stanford Univ., USA; Jr Engineer, Water and Power Devt Authority (WAPDA) 1986–89; Engineer, Hyderabad Devt Authority 1986; Exec. Engineer, Port Qasim Authority, Karachi 1990; fmr Project Dir Karachi Fisheries Harbour Authority; worked for Citibank in Pakistan and London; fmr Vice-Pres. Gulf Investment Corpn, Kuwait; mem. Sindh Provincial Ass. (Pakistan Peoples Party) from PS-77 Jamshoro-cum-Dadu constituency 2002–07; fmr Sindh Minister for Irrigation, Sindh Minister of Finance 2008; Chief Minister of Sindh 2016–May 18, July 2018–. *Address:* Office of the Chief Minister, Secretariat House, Karachi, Pakistan (office). *Website:* www.cmsindh.gov.pk (office).

SHAH, Syed Qaim Ali, BA, LLB; Pakistani lawyer and politician; b. 1935, Khairpur dist; s. of Syed Ramzan Ali Shah; m. 1st (deceased); m. 2nd (deceased); m. 3rd; four s. seven d. from three marriages; ed Univ. of Karachi, SM Law Coll., Karachi; elected Chair. Dist Council, Khairpur in Ayub Khan's era; pioneer mem. Pakistan People's Party (PPP) 1967; elected mem. Nat. Ass. 1970; Fed. Minister for Industries and Kashmir Affairs during Zulfikar Ali Bhutto's premiership; Pres. PPP Sindh 1973–77, 1987–97, 2004–16; elected mem. Prov. Ass. 1990, later Leader of Sindh Ass., re-elected five times; elected Senator 1997; Chief Minister of Sindh 1988–90, 2008–13, 2013–16 (resgnd). *Address:* c/o Jilani House, Khairpur, Pakistan (office).

SHAHEED, Ahmed, PhD; Maldivian diplomatist, politician, government official and UN official; *Special Rapporteur on Freedom of Religion or Belief, United Nations;* b. 1964; m.; one s. two d.; ed Univ. of Wales, Aberystwyth, UK, Univ. of Queensland, Australia; joined Ministry of Foreign Affairs 1982, Attaché, Perm. Mission to UN, New York 1982–84, est. Research and Analysis section, Ministry of Foreign Affairs 1989–91, Officer, Bilateral Relations Dept 1995–96, Head of SAARC Div. 1996–98, Head of Multilateral Affairs Dept 1998–99, Perm. Sec. 1999–2004; speech writer for Pres. 1996; Chief Govt Spokesman 2004–05; Minister of Foreign Affairs 2005–07 (resgnd), 2008–10, 2010–11; UN Special Rapporteur on the Situation of Human Rights in the Islamic Repub. of Iran 2011–16, on Freedom of Religion or Belief 2016–, Human Rights Centre, Univ. of Essex, UK 2012–; Visiting Prof. CUNY; mem. Dhivehi Rayyithunge Party (DRP—Maldivian People's Party), Co-founder and Leader New Maldives faction; Co-founder and Patron Open Soc. Asscn 2006–; Chair. Universal Rights Group, Geneva 2014–; Muslim Democrat of the Year Award, Centre for the Study of Islam and Democracy, Washington, DC 2009. *Address:* OHCHR – Palais Wilson, United Nations Office at Geneva, 1211, Geneva 10, Switzerland (office). *Fax:* (22) 9179006 (office). *E-mail:* freedomofreligion@ohchr.org (office). *Website:* www.ohchr.org (office).

SHAHEEM, Gen. Qadam Shah; Afghan military officer; b. 1963, Tashkan dist, Badakhshan Prov.; m.; six c.; ed Jamiat-i-Islami Military Univ., Pakistan; fought with Jamiat-e Islami against Soviets in early 1980s, then fought against Taliban; apptd Commdr 82nd Regt in Qargha 1993, apptd Brig. 1996 (appointments by mujahidin Islamic State administration of Burhanuddin Rabbani), apptd Commdr 37th Brig. of commandos 2001, Commdr 111st Div., Kabul 2011–15, Chief of Gen. Staff, Afghan Nat. Army 2015–17.

SHAHEEN, C. Jeanne, BA, MSc; American politician and fmr state governor; *Senator from New Hampshire;* b. 28 Jan. 1947, St Charles, Mo.; d. of Ivan Bowers and Belle Bowers; m. William H. Shaheen; three d.; ed Shippensburg Univ., Univ. of Mississippi; taught high school in Miss. and NH; fmr small business owner; directed several New Hampshire statewide political campaigns; mem. NH Senate 1990–96; Gov. of NH (first woman) 1997–2003; mem. Democratic Nat. Cttee Comm. on Presidential Nomination Timing and Scheduling 2004; Nat. Chair. Kerry-Edwards Campaign for Pres. 2004; Sr Fellow, Inst. of Politics, Kennedy School of Govt, Harvard Univ., Dir 2005–07; Senator from New Hampshire 2009–, mem. Cttee on Foreign Relations, Cttee on Energy and Natural Resources, Cttee on Armed Services, Cttee on Small Business and Entrepreneurship; mem. Bd of Dirs Nellie Mae Educ. Foundation; fmr Sr Fellow, Coll. of Citizenship and Public Service, Tufts Univ.; Democrat. *Address:* 506 Hart Senate Office Building, Washington, DC 20510, USA (office). *Telephone:* (202) 224-2841 (office). *Fax:* (202) 228-3194 (office). *Website:* shaheen.senate.gov (office); www.jeanneshaheen.org.

SHAHI, Manarup, BA; Nepalese business executive; *Executive Director, Shahi Global Careers Pvt. Ltd;* b. 31 July 1966, Raskot Municipality-1, Kalikot dist; s. of Birkha Bahadur Shahi and Kalika Shahi; m. Usha Shah; two s.; apptd Treas., Social Welfare Council 2007; Exec. Chair. Nepal Airlines Corpn 2011–12; Dir, Civil Aviation Authority of Nepal 2011–12; currently Exec. Dir Shahi Global Careers Pvt. Ltd; Council mem. Nepal Devt Council, Nat. Planning Comm.) 2006–. *Publications:* four books of poetry and six other training and development related books. *Telephone:* (1) 5151067 (office); (1) 5250750. *Fax:* (1) 5151025 (office). *E-mail:* ed@shahicareers.com (office). *Website:* www.shahicareers.com (office). *Address:* Satdobato Chowk-15, Ringroad, Lalitpur, Nepal (office).

SHAHID, Abdulla, BA, MA; Maldivian civil servant and politician; *Minister of Foreign Affairs;* b. 26 May 1962, Malé; m.; three c.; ed Canberra Coll. of Advanced Educ., Australia, Fletcher School of Law and Diplomacy, Tufts Univ., USA; began civil service career in Foreign Ministry 1983; mem. Constitutional Ass. 1994; mem. People's Majlis (Parl.) 1995–, Speaker 2009–14; Exec. Sec. to the Pres. 1995–2005; Minister of State for Foreign Affairs 2005–07, Minister of Foreign Affairs 2007–08, 2018–; mem. Dhivehi Rayyithunge Party –2013, joined Maldivian Democratic Party 2014. *Leisure interests:* soccer, badminton, writing Dhivehi poetry. *Address:* Ministry of Foreign Affairs, Henveiru, Blk 77, Boduthakurufaanu Magu, Malé 20-077 (office); Maldivian Democratic Party, H. Sharasha, 2nd Floor, Sosun Magu, Malé 20-059, The Maldives (office). *Telephone:* 3323400 (office); 3340044 (office). *Fax:* 3323841 (office); 3322960 (office). *E-mail:* admin@foreign.gov.mv (office); secretariat@mdp.org.mv (office). *Website:* foreign.gov.mv; www.mdp.org.mv (office).

SHAHRANI, Nematullah, PhD; Afghan politician and scholar; b. 1941, Jorm Dist, Badakhshan; ed Abu Hanifa School, Kabul Univ., Al-Azhar Univ., Egypt, George Washington Univ., USA; fmr Prof. of Sharia, Kabul Univ.; fmr Ed.-in-Chief, Sharayat magazine; Vice-Pres. Transitional Authority 2002–04; Dir Constitutional Drafting Cttee 2002; Minister of Hajj and Religious Affairs 2004–08. *Publications include:* more than 30 books, including Quran Shenaasy (Knowing the Holy Quran), Feqeh Islami Wa Qanoon e Gharb (Islamic Fiqh and Western Law); several hundred articles on Sharia law.

SHAIBANI, Mohammed al-, BA; United Arab Emirates government official and business executive; *Director-General, Ruler's Court, Dubai;* started professional career with Dubai Ports Authority and Jebel Ali Free Zone; four years as Man. Dir, Al Khaleej Investments, Singapore; Pres. Dubai Office (pvt. man. office for Dubai royal family) 1998–; currently Dir-Gen., Ruler's Court, Dubai; Vice-Chair. Supreme Fiscal Cttee of Dubai; Chair. Dubai Islamic Bank; CEO and Exec. Dir Investment Corpn of Dubai (govt investment holding co.); Dir Dubai World 2010–, Dubai Aerospace Enterprise Ltd, The Knowledge Fund, International Humanitarian City. *Address:* HH Ruler's Court, POB 90300, Dubai, United Arab Emirates (office). *Website:* www.dubai.ae (office).

SHAIKH, Abdul Hafeez, PhD; Pakistani economist and politician; *Adviser to the Prime Minister on Finance;* b. 26 Dec. 1954, Jacobabad, Sindh; s. of Abdul Nabi Shaikh and Afroz Nabi Shaikh; m. Nadene Nichols Shaikh; ed Boston Univ., USA; worked at Harvard Univ., USA; served as country head of World Bank's operations in Saudi Arabia 1990s, led assignments and advised more than 18 countries of Europe, Latin America, Asia and Africa as a Sr World Bank official, also led teams for successful privatization in many countries in fields of telecommunication, electricity, transport, aviation, banking and manufacturing; Pnr, New Silk Route (pvt. equity firm); Minister for Finance, Planning and Devt, Sindh govt 2000–02; Fed. Minister for Privatization and Investment 2003–06, of Finance, Planning and Devt, Econ. Affairs, Revenue and Statistics 2010–13; elected mem. Senate 2012, fmr Chair. Senate Cttee on World Trade Org.; Adviser to the Prime Minister on Finance, Revenue, Econ. Affairs, Statistics and Planning and Devt March–June 2010, 2019–; mem. Advisory Bd BMG Financial Group. *Publications include:* numerous publs, including book Argentina's Privatisation. *Website:* hafeezshaikh.com (office).

SHAIMIYEV, Mintimer Sharipovich; Russian engineer and politician; b. 20 Jan. 1937, Anyakovo, Aktanyshski Dist, Tatar ASSR; s. of Sharip Shaimiev and Naghima Safioullina; m. Sakina Shaimiyeva; two s.; ed Kazan Inst. of Agric.; Engineer, Chief Engineer Service and Repair Station, Mouslyumovski Dist, Tatar ASSR 1959–62; Man. Selkhoztekhnika Regional Asscn, Tatar ASSR 1962–67; Instructor, Deputy Chief of Agricultural Dept, Tatar Regional Cttee of CPSU, Tatar ASSR 1967–69; Minister of Land Improvement and Water Man., Tatar ASSR 1969–83; First Deputy Chair. Council of Ministers, Tatar ASSR 1983, Chair. 1985–89; Sec. Tatar Regional Cttee of CPSU 1983–85, First Sec. 1989–90; Chair. Supreme Soviet, Tatar ASSR 1990–91; Pres. of Tatarstan 1991–2010; Tatarstan State Counsellor; Chair. Bd of Trustees, The Republican Foundation for the Revival of Historical and Cultural Monuments of the Repub. of Tatarstan 2010–; f. All Russia political movt 1999, now part of United Russia (Yedinaya Rossiya); mem. Acad. of Tech. Sciences; Co-Chair., Higher Council, United Russia Party; Hon. mem. Presidium, Int. Parl. of World Confed. of Kts (under auspices of UN), Int. Acad. of Informatization; Hon. Prof., Moscow State Inst. of Int. Relations; Order of Lenin 1966, Order of Red Banner of Labour 1971, Order of Oct. Revolution 1976, Order of Friendship of Peoples 1987, Order for Services to the Fatherland, Grade II 1997, Kazakhstan Order of Friendship, First Class 2010; Silver Avitsenna Medal, UNESCO 2001. *Leisure interests:* chess, gardening, skiing. *Address:* c/o Office of the President, 420014 Tatarstan, Kazan, Kreml, Russia.

SHAKAR, Karim Ebrahim ash-, BA; Bahraini diplomatist; *Under-Secretary for International Affairs;* b. 23 Dec. 1945, Manama; m. Fatima Al-Mansouri 1979; three d.; ed Univ. of New Delhi; joined Ministry of Foreign Affairs 1970; mem. Perm. Mission to the UN, rising to rank of Second Sec. 1972–76; Chief of Int. Relations and Orgs Section, Bahrain 1977–82; apptd First Sec., Ministry of Foreign Affairs 1978, Counsellor 1981; Perm. Rep. to the UN Office, Geneva and Consul-Gen., Switzerland 1982–87; Perm. Rep. to the UN Office, Vienna 1984–87; Perm. Rep. to the UN Office 1987–90; Amb. to UK (also accred to Ireland, Netherlands, Denmark) 1990–95; Dir Int. Directorate, Ministry of Foreign Affairs, Bahrain 1995–2001; Amb. to People's Repub. of China (also accred to Malaysia, Philippines, Thailand) 2001–07; Amb.-at-Large, Ministry of Foreign Affairs 2007–09; Under-Sec. for Int. Affairs, Ministry of Foreign Affairs 2009–; Shaikh Isa Bin Salman Al-Khalifa Medal of Merit 2001. *Leisure interests:* reading, travelling. *Address:* Ministry of Foreign Affairs, PO Box 547, Government House, Government Road, Manama, Kingdom of Bahrain. *Telephone:* 17227555 (office). *Fax:* 17212603 (office). *E-mail:* kalshakar@mofa.gov.bh (office). *Website:* www.mofa.gov.bh (office).

SHAKED, Ayelet, BSc; Israeli computer engineer and politician; *Minister of Justice;* b. (Ayelet Ben Shaul), 7 May 1976; m.; two c.; ed Tel-Aviv Univ.; began career as software engineer in Tel-Aviv high-tech industry; fmr Marketing Man., Texas Instruments; Office Dir, Office of Leader of Opposition Benjamin Netanyahu 2006–08; co-f. My Israel (extra-parl. movt) 2011, Leader 2010–12; mem. Knesset (Parl.) 2013–, mem. Knesset House Cttee, Econ. Affairs Cttee, Cttee on Foreign Workers; Minister of Justice 2015–; mem. Jewish Home Party (HaBayit HaYehudi) 2012–; Abramowitz Israeli Prize for Media Criticism 2012. *Address:* Ministry of Justice, POB 49029, 29 Salahadin Street, Jerusalem 91010, Israel (office). *Telephone:* 2-6466527 (office). *Fax:* 2-6285438 (office). *E-mail:* pniot@justice.gov.il (office). *Website:* www.justice.gov.il (office).

SHAKED, Shaul, PhD; Israeli professor of Iranian studies and comparative religion; *Schwarzmann University Professor Emeritus, Hebrew University of Jerusalem;* b. (Shaul Scharf), 5 March 1933, Debrecen, Hungary; s. of Joshua Scharf and Irma Scharf; m. Miriam Schächter 1960; one s. two d.; ed Hebrew Univ. Jerusalem and School of Oriental and African Studies, Univ. of London; Asst Lecturer, SOAS 1964–65, Lecturer 1964–65; Lecturer, Assoc. Prof., Prof., Hebrew Univ., Jerusalem 1965–2001, Chair. Dept of Indian, Iranian and Armenian Studies 1971–72, 1974–75, Chair. Dept of Comparative Religion 1972–74, 1977–79, Chair. Ben Zvi Inst. for Study of Jewish Communities in the East 1975–79, Inst. of Asian and African Studies 1981–85, Chair. Academic Bd, Centre for the Study of Christianity 1999–2001, currently Schwarzmann Univ. Prof. Emer.; Visiting Prof., Univ. of California, Berkeley 1969–70, Columbia and New York Univs 1980–81, Univ. of Heidelberg 1987–88; Visiting Fellow, Wolfson Coll., Cambridge, Netherlands Inst. for Advanced Study; Vice-Pres. Societas Iranologica Europaea 1995–99, Int. Academic Union 1998–2001, Pres. 2001–04, Hon. Pres. 2004–; mem. Israel Acad. of Sciences and Humanities 1986 (Chair. Section of Humanities and Social Sciences 1995–2001), Magyar Tudományos Akadémia 2013; Hon. Fellow, Univ. Coll. London 1995–; Yoram Ben-Porat Prize for Distinguished Research 1993, Israel Prize in Linguistics 2000, Scheiber Medal, Hungary 2012. *Publications include:* A tentative bibliography of Geniza documents 1964, Amulets and Magic Bowls (with J. Naveh) 1985, Dualism in Transformation 1994, From Zoroastrian Iran to Islam 1995, Magische Texte aus der Kairoer Geniza (with P. Schäfer) (three vols) 1994–99, Aramaic Documents from Ancient Bactria (with J. Naveh) 2012, Aramaic Bowl Spells 1 (with J. N. Ford and S. Bhayro) 2013; articles and book chapters. *Address:* Dept of Islamic and ME Studies, The Hebrew University, Mount Scopus, Jerusalem 91905, Israel (office). *Telephone:* (2) 6416005 (home); 549456417 (home). *Fax:* (2) 6416005 (home). *E-mail:* shaul.shaked@huji.ac.il (office). *Website:* religions.huji.ac.il (office).

SHAKESPEARE, Frank; American fmr diplomatist and fmr radio and television executive; b. 9 April 1925, New York; s. of Frank J. Shakespeare, Sr and Frances Hughes Shakespeare; m. Deborah Ann Spaeth Shakespeare 1954; one s. two d.; ed Holy Cross Coll.; with Liberty Mutual Insurance Co., Washington, DC 1947–49; with Procter and Gamble Co. 1949–50; worked for Radio Station WOR, New York 1950, CBS 1950; Gen. Man. WXIX-TV, Milwaukee, Wis. 1957–59; Vice-Pres. and Gen. Man. WCBS-TV, New York 1959–63; Vice-Pres. and Asst to Pres. CBS-TV Network 1963–65; Exec. Vice-Pres. CBS-TV Stations 1965–67; Pres. CBS Television Service Div. 1967–69; Dir US Information Agency 1969–73; Exec. Vice-Pres. Westinghouse Electric Co. 1973–75; Pres. RKO Gen. 1975–83, Vice-Chair. 1983–85; Chair. Radio Free Europe/Radio Liberty Inc. 1982–85; Amb. to Portugal 1985–86, to the Holy See 1986–89; Trustee, Heritage Foundation 1979, now Hon. Trustee, Chair. 1981–85; Trustee, Lynde and Harry Bradley Foundation, Milwaukee, Wis.; Kt Grand Cross with Palm, Order of the Holy Sepulchre and other honours; nine hon. degrees. *Address:* c/o The Heritage Foundation, 214 Massachusetts Avenue, NE, Washington, DC 20002-4999, USA.

SHAKHANBEH, Abed Ali, LLM, PhD; Jordanian lawyer, judge and politician; b. 1950, Jdaideh-Madba; ed Damascus Univ., Syria, Jordan Univ., Cairo Univ., Egypt; civil servant, lawyer, then judge 1973–93; Sec.-Gen. Court of Control and Admin. Audit 1993–95, Pres. of Court 1995–2001; Pres. Court of Audit 2003; Minister of State for Judiciary Affairs 2001–03, 2003–05; Minister of Justice 2005–07; Head, Anti-Corruption Comm., Amman –2015. *Address:* c/o Anti-Corruption Commission, PO Box 5000, 11953 Amman, Jordan (office).

SHAKHNAZAROV, Karen Georgyevich; Russian film director; *Chairman and Director-General, Mosfilm Cinema Concern;* b. 8 July 1952, Krasnodar; s. of Georgy Shakhnazarov and Anna Shakhnazarova; m. (divorced); two s. one d.; ed All-Union Inst. of Cinematography; Asst Film Dir Mosfilm Studio 1973–75; on staff Mosfilm 1976–; Artistic Dir VI Creative Union 1987; Chair. Bd of Dirs Courier Studio at Mosfilm 1991–, Dir-Gen. Mosfilm Cinema Concern 1998–, currently also Chair.; Boris Polevoy Prize 1982, Special Prize of the Jury (Grenoble) 1984, Silver Medal of Int. Film Festival, Lodz 1984, Prize of Int. Film Festival in Moscow for Courier 1986, Comsomol Prize 1986, Brothers Vassilyev State Prize 1988, Special Prize of Karlovy Vary Film Festival for Day of Full Moon 1998, Merited Worker of Arts of Russia, People's Artist of the Russian Fed. 2002. *Film scripts:* debut as scriptwriter Ladies Invite Partners 1981. *Films include:* God Souls 1980, Jazzmen (Diplomas of Int. Film Festivals in London, Chicago, Belgrade 1984) 1983, Winter Night in Gagra 1985, Courier 1986, Town Zero 1989, Assassin of the Tsar (Grand Prix of Int. Film Festival in Belgrade 1991) 1991, Dreams 1993, American Daughter 1995, Day of Full Moon 1998, Poisons or the World History of Poisoning 2001, Rider Named Death 2004, The Vanished Empire 2008, Ward Number 6 (Crystal Simorgh Awards, Int. Film Festival, Tehran) 2009, White Tiger 2012, Anna Karenina: Vronsky's Story 2017. *Leisure interests:* swimming, driving. *Address:* 119991 Moscow, Mosfilmovskaya str. 1, Russian Federation (office).

Telephone: (499) 143-95-93 (office). *Fax:* (495) 705-93-03 (office). *E-mail:* referent@ mosfilm.ru (office). *Website:* www.mosfilm.ru (office).

SHAKHRAY, Sergey Mikhailovich, LLD; Russian politician and university administrator; *Deputy President, Lomonosov Moscow State University;* b. 30 April 1956, Simferopol, Crimea, USSR; s. of Mikhail A. Shakray and Zoya A. Shakray; m. Tatyana Shakhray 1985; two s. one d.; ed Rostov State Univ.; fmr Head of Law, Moscow State Univ.; People's Deputy of Russia 1990–92; Chair. of the Legis. Cttee of Russian Supreme Soviet 1990; State Councillor on legal issues of Russian Fed. 1991–92; Vice-Prime Minister of Russia 1991–92, 1993, 1994–95; Chair. State Cttee for nat. problems; Founder and Chair. Party of Russian Unity and Consent (PRES) 1993–; Head interim admin in zone of emergency situation in N Ossetia and Ingushetia 1992–93; mem. State Duma (Parl.) 1993; Minister for Nationalities and Nat. Problems 1994–95; Deputy Head of Pres. Yeltsin's Admin, Pres.'s Rep. at Constitutional Court 1996–98; Deputy Chair. Political Consultative Council of Pres. Yeltsin; adviser to Prime Minister 1998–; Prof., Moscow State Inst. of Int. Relations 1999–; Deputy Head, Parl. Accounts Chamber Admin 2001–04, Head 2004–13; currently Deputy Pres. Lomonosov Moscow State Univ., mem. Academic Council, Academic Adviser, School of State Audit; Honoured Jurist of the Russian Fed. *Publications:* Constitution of the Russian Federation. Encylopaedic Dictionary (co-author) 1995, Constitutional Justice in the System of Russian Federalism 2002, Constitutional Law of the Russian Federation 2003, Globalization in the Contemporary World – Political-Legal Aspects 2003, Globalization State Law 2003. *Leisure interests:* fishing, bicycling, badminton, Russian baths. *Address:* School of State Audit, Lomonosov Moscow State University, Moscow, GSP-1, Leninskiye Gory, 119991 Moscow, Russian Federation (office). *Telephone:* (495) 986-19-83 (office). *E-mail:* office@audit.msu.ru (office). *Website:* audit.msu.ru (office).

SHAKIRA; Colombian singer, songwriter, dancer, record producer and choreographer and model; b. (Shakira Isabel Mebarak Ripoll), 2 Feb. 1977, Barranquilla; d. of William Mebarak Chadid and Nidia Ripoll; wrote first song aged eight, signed recording contract with Sony Music Colombia aged 13; f. Fundación Pies Descalzos (Barefoot Foundation) 1997; Founding mem. Fundación América Latina en Acción Solidaria; apptd UNICEF Goodwill Amb. 2003; helped organize Live Aid Latino series of concerts 2008–; Hon. Chair. for Educ. Action Week, Global Campaign for Educ. April 2008; mem. White House Initiative on Educational Excellence for Hispanics 2011; Latin Grammy Awards for Best Female Vocal Performance 2000, for Best Music Video (for Suerte) 2002, five MTV Video Awards 2002, MTV Europe Music Award for Best Female 2005, American Music Award for Favorite Latin Music Artist 2005, 2006, Billboard Music Awards for Latin Song of the Year (for La Tortura), for Latin Pop Album Artist of the Year 2005, MTV Video Award for Best Choreography 2006, MTV Latin America Music Award for Song of the Year (for Hips Don't Lie) 2006, Latin Grammy Awards for Best Song (for La Totura), for Record of the Year (for La Totura) 2006, for Record of the Year and Song of the Year (both for La Bicicleta, with Carlos Vives) 2016, MTV Video Music Award for Best Collaboration (for Beautiful Liar with Beyoncé) 2007, Latin Recording Academy Person of the Year 2011, Premios Lo Nuestro Award for Artist of the Year 2012, Premios Lo Nuestro Award for Female Artist of the Year 2012, Premios Lo Nuestro Award for Song of the Year (for Rabiosa) 2012, American Music Award for Favourite Artist-Latin 2017. *Recordings include:* albums: Magia 1991, Peligro 1993, Pies Descalzos 1996, ¿Dónde Están Los Ladrones? 1998, Laundry Service 2002, Washed And Dried: Laundry Service Limited Edition 2002, Fijación Oral Vol. 1 (Billboard Music Award for Latin Pop Album of the Year 2005, Grammy Award for Best Latin Rock/Alternative Album 2006, Latin Grammy Awards for Best Album and Best Female Pop Vocal Album 2006) 2005, Fijación Oral (Vol. 2) 2005, She Wolf 2009, Sale el Sol (Premios Lo Nuestro Award for Album of the Year 2012) 2010, Shakira 2014, El Dorado (Grammy Award for Best Latin Pop Album 2018) 2017. *Television includes:* El oasis (Colombian TV drama series) 1996, Taina (series) 2002, coach and judge on The Voice (NBC) 2013, 2014. *Address:* c/o ROC Nation, 1411 Broadway, New York, NY 10018, USA (office). *Telephone:* (212) 292-8500 (office). *Website:* www.rocnation.com (office); www.shakira.com.

SHAKOOR, Aishath Azima; Maldivian lawyer, politician and government official; mem. Parl. apptd by Pres. Maumoon Abdul Gayoom; Deputy Minister of Home Affairs 2005–07; Attorney-Gen. 2007–08, 2012–13; Special Adviser to the Pres. Dr Mohamed Waheed 2013; currently with Avant-Garde Lawyers, Malé; Pres. Women's Wing, Dhivehi Rayyithunge Party (Maldivian People's Party). *Address:* Avant-Garde Lawyers, Sosun Magu, Malé, Maldives.

SHAKOORU, Uza Aishath Azima; Maldivian lawyer and government official; served as Attorney-Gen. under Pres. Maumoon Abdul Gayoom, then Attorney-Gen. 2012–13. *Address:* c/o Attorney-General's Office, Velaanaage, 6th Floor, Ameer Ahmed Magu, Malé 20-096, Maldives.

SHAKUROV, Sergey Kayumovich; Russian actor; b. 1 Jan. 1942, Moscow; ed Theatre School of Cen. Children's Theatre; with K. Stanislavsky Drama Theatre 1978–88; USSR State Prize 1980, prizes of All-Union Film Festivals for Best Actor 1988, 1991, People's Actor of Russia 1991. *Stage roles include:* Ivanov (Chekhov), Hamlet and others. *Films include:* Svoy sredi chuzhikh, chuzhoy sredi svoikh (At Home among Strangers) 1974, Sto dney posle detstva (100 Days after Childhood) 1975, The Taste of Bread 1979, Portret zheny khudozhnika (Portrait of the Artist's Wife) 1982, Retsept yeyo molodosti (Recipe of Her Youthfulness) 1984, Dogs' Feast 1991, Szwadron (Squadron) 1992, Hagy-Trager 1993, Declaration of Love 1995, Cranberries in Sugar 1995, Armaviz 1998, Pan Tadeusz 1999, Rozhdestvenskaya mysterya 2000, Dikarka 2001, Antikiller 2002, Dnevnik kamikadze (Diary of a Kamikaze) 2003, Antikiller 2: Antiterror 2003, Sdvig 2006, Junk 2006, Konservy 2007, Paragraph 78 2007, O, Luckyman! 2009, Zvorykin-Muromets 2010, Vysotskiy. Spasibo, chto zhivoy 2011, Sokrovishcha O.K. 2013, Ded 005 2013, Käshbasshy zholy 2013, Flight Crew 2016. *Television includes:* Vizit k Minotavru (Visit to Minotaurus) (mini-series) 1987, Chyornaya komnata 2000, Brezhnev 2005, Master i Margarita (mini-series) 2005, Na puti k serdtsu 2007, Petr Perviy. Zaveshanie 2011, Lyubov za lyubov (mini-series) 2013, Velikaya (series) 2015. *Address:* Bibliotechnaya str. 27, Apt. 94, 109544 Moscow, Russia (home). *Telephone:* (495) 270-15-32 (home).

SHALALA, Donna Edna, PhD; American academic, fmr government official, fmr university president and foundation executive; *President and CEO, Bill, Hillary*

and Chelsea Clinton Foundation; b. 14 Feb. 1941, Cleveland, Ohio; d. of James A. Shalala and Edna Smith; ed Western Coll. and Syracuse Univ.; volunteer, Peace Corps, Iran 1962–64; Asst to Dir Metropolitan Studies Program, Syracuse Univ. 1965–69; Instructor and Asst to Dean, Maxwell Grad. School, Syracuse Univ. 1969–70; Asst Prof. of Political Science, Bernard Baruch Coll., CUNY 1970–72, Prof. of Political Science and Pres. Hunter Coll. 1980–88; Assoc. Prof. of Politics and Educ., Teachers' Coll., Columbia Univ. 1972–79; Asst Sec. for Policy Devt and Research, US Dept of Housing and Urban Devt Washington, DC 1977–80; Chancellor and Prof. of Political Science, Univ. of Wis., Madison 1988–92; US Sec. of Health and Human Services 1993–2001; Pres. Univ. of Miami 2001–15; Pres. and CEO, Bill, Hillary and Chelsea Clinton Foundation 2015–; Dir Inst. of Int. Econs 1981–93, Ditchley Foundation 1981–93; mem. Bd of Dirs Gannett Co. 2001–11, Lennar Corpn, Mednax Inc.; mem. American Acad. of Arts and Sciences, American Soc. for Public Admin., Council on Foreign Relations, NAS; 24 hon. degrees; Nelson Mandela Award for Health and Human Rights, Harry S. Truman Legacy of Leadership Award, inducted into Nat. Women's Hall of Fame, Presidential Medal of Freedom 2008. *Publications:* Neighborhood Governance 1971, The City and the Constitution 1972, The Property Tax and the Voters 1973, The Decentralization Approach 1974. *Leisure interests:* tennis, mountain-climbing, reading, spectator sports. *Address:* Bill, Hillary and Chelsea Clinton Foundation, 1271 Avenue of the Americas, 42nd Floor, New York, NY 10020, USA (office). *Telephone:* (212) 348-8882 (office). *Website:* www.clintonfoundation .org (office).

SHALAMANOV, Velizar, PhD; Bulgarian politician; b. 24 Dec. 1961, Karlovo; m. Bonka Shalamanov; one d.; ed Benkovsky Bulgarian Air Force Acad., Rakovsky Defence Staff Coll., Kiev Higher School, USSR, George C. Marshall European Center for Security Studies, Germany; 14 years in Bulgarian Armed Forces (including two years in Intelligence and Electronic Warfare Div. of Main Land Forces HQ) 1984–98; Deputy Minister of Defence for Policy, Planning and Integration 1998–2001; various positions in Bulgarian Acad. of Sciences as Adviser on Nat. Security and Defence to Chair. of the Acad., also Dir, C4 Programme, Centre for Nat. Security and Defence Research, Asst Dir, Space Research Inst., Head of C4 Dept and Jt Training Simulation and Analysis Centre, Inst. of Parallel Processing 2001–09; Dir in charge of cooperation with NATO Consultation, Command and Control Agency, Brussels 2009–12, Dir, Demand Management for NATO Communications and Information Agency 2013–14; Minister of Defence (in caretaker govt) Aug.–Nov. 2014; mem. Int. Advisory Bd, Geneva Center for Democratic Control of Armed Forces 2002–12; fmr part-time lecturer at Sofia Univ., Univ. of Nat. and World Economy and New Bulgarian Univ.; Co-founder George Marshall Asscn–Bulgaria; Chair. TEREM Stock Holding Co. 1998–2001; mem. Bd of Dirs Armed Forces Communications and Electronics Asscn 2013–; mem. European Security Research and Innovation Forum 2008–10. *Address:* c/o Ministry of Defence, 1092 Sofia, ulitsa Dyakon Ignatiy 3, Bulgaria (office).

SHALGAM, Abd ar-Rahman Muhammad, BA; Libyan government official, diplomatist and fmr newspaper editor; b. 22 Nov. 1949, Al-Ghrefa; s. of Mohamed Shalgam and Rahma Shalgam; m. Mabrouk el-Araby; three s.; ed Cairo Univ., Egypt; Ed. Al-Fajr Al-Jadid newspaper 1973–75, Ed.-in-Chief 1975–77; Ed.-in-Chief Al-Usbu Al-Thaqafi (cultural weekly) and Al-Usbu Al-Siaysi (political weekly) newspapers 1977–79; Dir Gen. Jamahiriya News Agency (JANA) 1979–89; Sec. (Minister) of Information 1981–83; Sec. (Amb.), Libyan People's Bureau, Rome (Libyan Embassy) 1984–95; Sec. of Foreign Affairs, Secr. of the Gen. People's Congress 1998–2000, Sec. of the Gen. People's Cttee for Foreign Liaison and Int. Co-operation 2000–09; Amb. and Perm. Rep. to UN, New York 2009–13, Pres. of the Security Council March 2009; Chair. Jt Libyan Italian Co.; mem. Cultural Innovation Cttee, Libyan Arabic Language Acad.; El-Fatah Medal. *Publications include:* Al-Huruf (Words) – Articles in Literature and Politics, The Future Africa – Studies in African Literature, Art, and History, Asrar (Secrets) (poetry anthology), Revelations from the Conscience to the Destiny, Articles and Quotations 2009, I Decided to be Happy, Poems 2009; several articles published in Libyan papers and magazines on political and cultural issues. *Leisure interests:* music, playing the lute and piano. *Address:* Ministry of Foreign Affairs, Tripoli, Libya (office). *Telephone:* (21) 3402121 (office). *E-mail:* info@foreign.gov.ly (office). *Website:* www.foreign.gov.ly (office).

SHALHOUB, Anthony (Tony) Marcus, MA; American actor; b. 9 Oct. 1953, Green Bay, Wis.; s. of Joe Shalhoub and Helen Shalhoub; m. Brooke Adams 1992; two d.; ed Univ. of Southern Maine, Yale School of Drama; spent four seasons with American Repertory Theatre, Cambridge, Mass 1980–84. *Films include:* Longtime Companion 1990, Big Night (Best Supporting Actor Nat. Soc. of Film Critics) 1996, Men in Black 1997, Primary Colors 1998, A Civil Action 1998, The Siege 1998, Galaxy Quest 1999, Impostor 2001, Spy Kids 2001, Spy Kids 2 2002, Men in Black II 2002, Spy Kids 3-D 2003, Against the Ropes 2004, The Great New Wonderful 2005, Careless 2007, American East 2007, Feed the Fish 2009, How Do You Know 2010, Pain & Gain 2013, Guns for Hire 2015, Custody 2016, Breakable You 2017, Cars 3 2017, Rosy 2018. *Television includes:* Wings (series) 1991–97, Stark Raving Mad (series) 1999, Monk (also exec. producer) (Best Actor in a Comedy Acad. of TV Arts and Sciences 2003, 2005, Golden Globe 2003, SAG Award 2004, 2005) 2002–10, Too Big to Fail (TV film) 2011, Friday Night Dinner (TV film) 2012, We Are Men (series) 2013, Nurse Jackie (series) 2015, BrainDead (series) 2016, The Marvelous Mrs. Maisel (series) (SAG Award for Outstanding Performance by a Male Actor in a Comedy Series 2019) 2017–. *Stage:* As You Like It 1980, The Marriage of Figaro 1981, Three Sisters 1982, The Odd Couple 1986, The Heidi Chronicles 1989, The Old Neighborhood 1997, The Scene 2007, Golden Boy 2012, Happy Days 2015, The Band's Visit (Tony Award for Best Performance by a Leading Actor in a Musical 2018) 2016, The Price 2017.

SHALOM, Silvan, BA, MA, LLB, CPA; Israeli politician and journalist; b. 1958, Tunisia; m. Judy Shalom Nir-Mozes; five c.; ed Tel-Aviv Univ., Ben Gurion Univ.; attained rank of Sergeant during mil. service; mem. Knesset 1992–; Deputy Minister of Defence 1997, Minister of Science and Tech. 1998, Deputy Prime Minister and Minister of Finance 2001–03, Deputy Prime Minister and Minister of Foreign Affairs 2003–06 (resgnd), Vice-Prime Minister 2009–13, Minister for Regional Co-operation and the Devt of the Negev and Galilee 2009–15, Minister of Energy and Water Resources 2013–15, Minister of the Interior May–Dec. 2015 (resgnd); Chair. Israel Electric Co., Dir-Gen. Ministry of Energy and Infrastructure; Deputy Chair. Public Council for Youth Exchange; mem. Exec. of the Broadcasting Authority; Adviser to Ministers of Finance, Econ., Planning and Justice; Israel Airport Authority, Dir Sun d'Or International Airlines; mem. Likud. *Publications:* numerous articles on the Israeli press. *Address:* Knesset, HaKiryah, Jerusalem 91950, Israel (office). *Website:* www.knesset.gov.il (office).

SHAMANOV, Lt-Gen. (retd) Vladimir Anatolyevich; Russian army officer (retd) and politician; *Chairman of the Defence Committee, State Duma;* b. 15 Feb. 1957, Barnaul, Altai territory; m.; one s. one d.; ed Ryazan Higher Military School of Paratroopers, M. Frunze Military Acad. of General Army, Military Acad. of General Staff; Commdr of artillery platoon, Pskov region 1978–85, Bn Commdr 1985–87; Deputy Regt Commdr Kishinev, Moldova 1990–91; Regt Commdr Kirovabad, Azerbaijan 1991–93, Regt moved to Ulyanovsk 1994; Head of Staff Novorossiysk div. 1994–95, transferred to Chechnya as Commdr operation group; Deputy Commdr army group, Ministry of Defence 1995–96; Head of Staff 20th Gen. Troops Army, Voronezh 1998–99; Commdr 58th Army N Caucasus Mil. Command 1999, W Direction of United Group of Fed. Forces 1999; participated in devt and realization of Operation Hunting for Wolves, Grozny, Chechnya 2000; Commdr 58th Army 2000; Gov. Ulyanovsk Region 2001–04; fmr Counselor to Minister of Defence Sergei Ivanov; Co-Chair. US-Russia Jt Comm. on POW/MIAs –2007; apptd Head, Armed Forces Combat Training Directorate 2007, Commdr Russian Airborne Troops 2009–16 (retd); mem. State Duma 2016–, Chair. Defence Cttee 2016–; Hon. Citizen of Makhachkala, Dagestan; Hero of Russia 1999, Order of Courage, Order of Saint George 2008, Order for Service to the Homeland in the Armed Forces of the USSR. *Address:* State Duma (Gosudarstvennaya Duma), 103265 Moscow, Okhotnyi ryad 1, Russia (office). *Telephone:* (495) 692-62-66 (office). *Fax:* (495) 697-42-58 (office). *E-mail:* stateduma@duma.gov.ru (office). *Website:* www.duma.gov.ru (office).

SHAMASK, Ronaldus; Dutch fashion designer; b. 24 Nov. 1945, Amsterdam; self-educated in design; window-dresser for dept store in Melbourne, Australia 1959; fashion illustrator, The Times and The Observer newspapers, London 1967–68; set and costume designer, Company of Man (multi-media artists' org.) Buffalo, New York 1968–71; subsequently undertook design and clothing commissions for pvt. clients in New York; Founder-Partner with Murray Moss, Moss Shamask Fashion Co., New York 1978–89; opened Moss boutique, Madison Avenue, New York, presented first collection 1979; costume designer, Lucinda Childs Dance Co. premiere of Available Light, Next Wave Fall Festival, Brooklyn Acad. of Music 1983; launched own co. Shamask 1996; work in perm. collection of Smithsonian Inst.; American Fashion Critics Coty Award 1981, Conf. Internationale du Lin Fil d'Or Award 1985, 1987, 1989, Council of Fashion Designers of America Award 1987, Woolmark Award 1989. *Address:* Shamask LLC, PO Box 287464, New York, NY 10128, USA (office). *E-mail:* info@shamask.com (office). *Website:* www.shamask.com (office).

SHAMBA, Sergei Mironovich, PhD; Georgian (Abkhaz) politician; *Chairman, Ertiani Apkhazetis (United Abkhazia);* b. 15 March 1951, Gudauta, Abkhazian ASSR, Georgian SSR, USSR; ed Yerevan Inst. of Archeology; Head of Aidgylara –1992; First Deputy Minister of Defence during war in Abkhazia 1992–93; Minister of Foreign Affairs of Abkhazia 1997–June 2004 (resgnd), Dec. 2004–10; attained rank of Amb. 2001; unsuccessful presidential cand. 2004, 2011; co-f. Social-Democratic Party of Abkhazia 2004; Prime Minister of the 'Republic of Abkhazia' Feb. 2010–Sept. 2011; mem. Nat. Ass. of 'Republic of Abkhazia' (Parl.) 2014–; Chair. United Abkhazia 2016–. *Address:* National Assembly of the 'Republic of Abkhazia,' 384900 Sukhumi, ul. Zvanba 1, Abkhazia, Georgia (office). *Telephone:* (840) 226-56-16 (office). *E-mail:* mail@parlamentra.org (office). *Website:* www.parlamentra.org (office).

SHAMGAR, Meir; Israeli lawyer, fmr government official and fmr judge; b. 13 Aug. 1925, Danzig (now Gdańsk, Poland); s. of Eliezer Sterenberg and Dina Sterenberg; m. Geula Shamgar 1955 (deceased); two s. one d.; ed Balfour Coll. Tel-Aviv, Hebrew Univ. and Govt Law School, Jerusalem and Univ. of London; served in Israeli army attaining rank of Brig.-Gen. 1948–68; Mil. Advocate-Gen. 1961–68; Legal Adviser, Ministry of Defence April–Aug. 1968; Attorney-Gen. of Israel 1968–75; Justice, Supreme Court 1975, Deputy Chief Justice 1982, Pres. of Supreme Court (Chief Justice of Israel) 1983–95, Pres. Emer. 1995–; Chair. Comm. of Inquiry into Judiciary in Mil. Justice 1977, into Hebron Massacre 1994, into Murder of Prime Minister Yitzhak Rabin 1995, into Appointment and Powers and Duties of Attorney-Gen. of Israel 1999, into Pollution on Kishon River 2001; Head, govt cttee drafting code for ministers' ethics 2007; mem. Perm. Court of Arbitration, The Hague; mem. Council Open Univ. of Israel, World Jurist Asscn (Peace Through Law); Hon. Fellow, Open Univ. of Israel; Hon. Chair. Council for Ethiopian Jewry; Dr hc (Weizman Inst.) 1987, (Hebrew Univ. Jerusalem) 1990, (Ben Gurion Univ., Beer-Sheva) 1996, (Tel-Aviv Univ.) 1997, (Bar Ilan Univ.) 1998; Israel Prize for Special Service to Society and State 1996, Ben Gurion Prize 1998, Democracy Award, Israel Democracy Inst. 2008. *Publications:* The Military Government of the Territories Administered by Israel 1967–80: The Legal Aspects 1982; numerous articles and essays in legal publs. *Address:* Kiriat Ben Gurion, Rehov Shaare Mishpat 1, Jerusalem 91909, Israel (office).

SHAMI, Ali Hussein al-, PhD; Lebanese academic (retd) and politician; b. 21 April 1945, Jarjouh; ed Lebanese Univ., Univ. of Grenoble, Switzerland; fmr Prof. of Law and Political Science, Lebanese Univ.; mem. Amal (Hope—Afwaj al-Muqawamah al-Lubnaniyyah—Lebanese Resistance Detachments); Minister of Foreign Affairs and Emigrants 2009–11 (resgnd). *E-mail:* info@amal-movement .com. *Website:* www.amal-movement.com.

SHAMI, Misbah-Ud-Din, BSc, MSc, PhD; Pakistani chemist, academic and university administrator; b. 1 Oct. 1930, Jalandhar, India; m.; four c.; ed Punjab Univ., Washington State Univ., USA; Postdoctoral Fellowship, Royal Soc. 1969; apptd Prof., Punjab Univ. 1970, Dean, Faculty of Natural Sciences, Eng and Pharmacy 1973, Pro-Vice-Chancellor 1974–76; mem. Univs Grants Comm. 1976–80; Chair. Pakistan Science Foundation 1980–90; Ed. Pakistan Journal of Science 1972–79; Adviser to Chancellor, Hamdard Univ., Karachi 1998; mem. and fmr Pres. Pakistan Asscn for the Advancement of Science, Pakistan Asscn of Scientists and Scientific Professions, Scientific Soc. of Pakistan; Founding Fellow, Islamic Acad. of Sciences, mem. Council 1994–99; Fellow, Pakistan Acad. of Sciences, Treas. 2005; Fellow and Past-Pres. Pakistan Inst. of Chemical Engin-

eers; Allama Iqbal Centenary Commemorative Medal, 1979, Nat. Award of the Pakistan Talent Forum 1987, UNESCO Kalinga Prize 1990, Sitara-Imtiaz 1990, UNESCO Niels Bohr Medal 1990, Pakistan Acad. of Sciences Golden Jubilee Medal 2002.

SHAMIR, Shimon, PhD; Israeli historian, academic and fmr diplomatist; *Professor Emeritus, Department of Middle Eastern and African History, Tel-Aviv University;* b. 15 Dec. 1933, Romania; m. Daniela (née Levin) Shamir 1958; one s. two d.; ed Hebrew Univ. of Jerusalem and Princeton Univ.; Instructor, Lecturer in Modern History of the Middle East, Hebrew Univ. of Jerusalem 1960–66, Fellow, Inst. for Advanced Studies 1978–79; Sr Lecturer, Modern History of the Middle East, Tel-Aviv Univ. 1966, Head of Dept of Middle Eastern and African History 1966–71, Head of Shiloah Center for Middle Eastern and African Studies 1966–73, Assoc. Prof. of Modern History of the Middle East 1970, Head of Grad. School of History 1973–76, mem. Bd of Govs 1974–77, Head of Dept of Middle Eastern and African History 1978–79, apptd Full Prof. 1979, Kaplan Chair in the History of Egypt and Israel 1980, now Prof. Emer., Head of Tami Steinmetz Center for Peace Research 1992–95; Dir Israeli Academic Center, Cairo 1982–84, mem. Bd of Dirs 1985–93; Amb. to Egypt 1988–90, to Jordan 1995–97; Fellow, Center for Middle Eastern Studies, Harvard Univ. 1968–69; Visiting Assoc. Prof. of Oriental Studies and Political Science, Univ. of Pennsylvania 1976–77, Dept of Near Eastern Studies, Cornell Univ. 1982; Distinguished Fellow, US Inst. of Peace 1991–92; mem. Council for Higher Educ. 1971–76. *Publications:* A Modern History of the Arabs in the Middle East, 1798–1918 1965, Egypt Under Sadat: The Search for a New Orientation 1978, Self-Views in Historial Perspective in Egypt and Israel 1981, The Jews of Egypt: A Mediterranean Society in Modern Times 1987, Egypt from Monarchy to Republic (ed.) 1995. *Address:* Gilman Building, Room 405, Department of Middle Eastern and African History, Tel-Aviv University, Ramat-Aviv, 69978 Tel-Aviv, Israel (office). *Telephone:* (3) 6409313 (office). *Fax:* (3) 6415802 (office). *E-mail:* shimons@post.tau.ac.il (office). *Website:* en-mideast -africa.tau.ac.il (office).

SHAMKHANI, Rear-Adm. Ali, BSc, MSc, MA; Iranian military officer; *Secretary, Supreme National Security Council;* b. 29 Sept. 1955, Ahvaz, Khuzestan; ed Univ. of Ahvaz, Univ. of State Man. Org.; held various military posts in Iran-Iraq War including Commdr Islamic Revolution's Guards Corps (IRGC) of Khuzestan province 1981–82, Deputy Commdr of IRGC 1982–89, Chief Commdr of ground force 1984–89, Deputy chiefs of staff of the armed forces in charge of intelligence and operations 1987–89, IRGC Minister 1988–89, Head of implementation cttee of UN Resolution 598 on ending Iran-Iraq War 1988–89; Commdr of IRGC Naval Forces 1989–97; Minister of Defence and Armed Forces Logistics 1997–2005, then Head of Centre for Strategic Defense Research, Tehran; Sec., Supreme Nat. Security Council 2013–, Sr Coordinator for Political, Mil. and Security Affairs with Syria and Russia 2016–. *Address:* Ministry of Defence, Shadid Yousuf Kaboli Street, Sayed Khandan Area, Tehran, Iran.

SHAMLAN, Ali Abdullah ash-, BSc, MSc, PhD; Kuwaiti geologist, academic and administrator; b. 8 March 1945; m.; ed Univ. of Puget Sound and Univ. of Texas at El Paso, USA, Kuwait Univ.; apptd Demonstrator, Kuwait Univ. 1967, Asst Prof. of Geology 1973, Assoc. Prof. 1978, apptd Prof. 1985, Chair. Geology Dept 1975–78, Asst Dean Faculty of Science 1978–82, Dean 1982–84; apptd Dir-Gen. Kuwait Foundation for the Advancement of Sciences 1985; Chair. Science Coll. Council of Kuwait; Minister of Higher Educ. 1988–92; mem. Higher Cttee for the Evaluation of the Educational System; mem. Arabian Gulf Univ., Bahrain, Gulf Univ. for Science and Tech., Kuwait, Oxford Center for Islamic Studies, Oxford Univ., UK, Prince Charles School of Traditional Arts, American Soc. of Petroleum Geologists, Soc. of Econ. Palaeontologists and Mineralogists; Founding Fellow, Islamic Acad. of Sciences 1986–; Trustee, American Univ. of Sharjah; Dr hc (Univ. of Massachusetts, USA).

SHAMOLIN, Mikhail; Russian business executive; *President and Chairman, Segezha Group;* b. 1970; ed Russian Acad. of Public Admin, Wharton Business School, Univ. of Pennsylvania, USA; worked at McKinsey & Co. 1998–2004; Man. Ferroalloys Div., Interpipe Corpn (Ukraine) 2004–05; joined MTS as Vice-Pres. for Sales and Customer Service 2005–06, Vice-Pres. and Head of MTS Russia business unit 2006–08, Pres. and CEO MTS Group 2008–11; Pres. and CEO, Exec. Bd, Dir and Chair. Man. Bd AFK Sistema 2011–18; Pres. and Chair. Man. Bd Segezha Group 2018–. *Address:* Segezha Group, 115432 Moscow, building 9, 18, Andropova Avenue, Russia (office). *Telephone:* (499) 962-82-00 (office). *Website:* www.segezha -group.com (office).

SHAMS, Mohammad Jalil, PhD; Afghan economist, academic and politician; ed Sultan Ghias-ud-din Ghoori High School, Herat, Cairo Univ., Egypt, Bochum Univ., Germany; Asst Prof., School of Econs, Kabul Univ. 1964–66; Vice-Pres. Banke Milli-e-Afghan, Hamburg, Germany 1969–71; Man. Dir Afghan Nat. Bank, London, UK 1971–74; Lecturer in Econs, Essen Polytechnic Germany 1973–74; Deputy Minister of Foreign Affairs 1992–94 (resgnd in protest against internal conflict in Afghanistan); Deputy Minister of Energy and Water 2005–06; Minister of Economy 2006–09, then CEO Da Afghanistan Brishna Shirkat (Afghanistan Electricity Co.).

SHANAHAN, Patrick, BS, MS, MBA; American government official and former business executive; *Acting Secretary of Defense;* b. 27 June 1962, Seattle, Washington; s. of Michael Shanahan and Jo-Anne Shanahan; divorced; three c.; ed Univ. of Washington, Massachusetts Inst. of Tech., MIT Sloan School of Man.; joined The Boeing Co. as engineer 1986, various roles including with Computer Services Div. and Boeing 777 program, fmr Vice Pres. and Gen. Man., Boeing Commercial Airplanes 757 program, also Dir 767 Manufacturing Business Unit and Dir Tooling Business Unit, Fabrication Div., Vice Pres. and Gen. Man. RotorcraftSystems, Philadelphia, Vice Pres. and Gen. Man. Boeing Missile Defense Systems 2004–06, Vice Pres. and Gen. Man. 787 Dreamliner program 2007–08, Sr Vice Pres. and Gen. Man. Airplane programs for Boeing Commercial Airplanes 2008, becoming Sr Vice Pres., Supply Chain & Operations 2016–17; Deputy Sec. of Defense 2017–19, Acting Sec. of Defense 2019–; Fellow Soc. of Manufacturing Engineers 2004, Royal Aeronautical Soc. 2005; Assoc. Fellow American Inst. of Aeronautics and Astronautics. *Address:* Department of Defense, 1400 Defense Pentagon, Washington, DC 20301-1400, USA (office). *Telephone:* (703) 571-3343 (office). *Website:* www.defense.gov (office).

SHANG, Bing, BSc, MBA, DBA; Chinese economist and business executive; *Executive Director and Chairman, China Mobile Communications Corporation;* b. Dec. 1955, Liaoning Prov.; ed Shenyang Chemical Industry Inst., State Univ. of New York, USA, Hong Kong Polytechnic Univ.; fmr Dir Industrial Tech. Devt Centre, Liaoning Prov.; fmr Gen. Man. Econ. and Technological Devt Co., Liaoning Prov.; fmr Gen. Man. China United Telecommunications Corpn, Liaoning Br., then Dir, Vice-Pres. and Pres. China United Telecommunications Corpn, then Exec. Dir and Pres. China United Telecommunications Corpn Ltd and China Unicom Ltd, then Vice-Pres., then Exec. Dir, Pres. and COO China Telecom Corpn Ltd –2015, mem. Bd of Dirs, Exec. Dir and Chair. China Mobile Communications Corpn and China Mobile Communication Co. Ltd 2015–; fmr Vice-Minister of Industry and Information Tech. *Address:* China Mobile Communications Corporation, 29 Financial Street, Xicheng District, Beijing 100032, People's Republic of China (office). *Telephone:* (10) 3121-8888 (office). *Fax:* (10) 2511-9092 (office). *E-mail:* info@chinamobileltd.com (office). *Website:* www.chinamobileltd.com (office); www.chinamobile.com (office).

SHANG, Fulin, PhD; Chinese banker; b. 13 Nov. 1951, Jinan, Shandong Province; ed Beijing Finance and Trade Coll., Southwestern Univ. of Finance and Economics, Chengdu; soldier, PLA 1969–73; worker, Municipal Br., Agricultural Bank of China, Beijing, Yingtaoyuan 1973–78, Deputy Div. Dir Financial Planning Dept, Agricultural Bank of China 1982, then Div. Dir, then Deputy Dept Dir, then Dept Dir; Asst Gov. People's Bank of China 1994–96, Deputy Gov. 1996–2001, Head of Monetary Policy Cttee 1997, Del. to Bank for Int. Settlements (BIS) 1998; Gov. Agricultural Bank of China 2001–03; Chair. China Securities Regulatory Comm. 2002–11; Vice-Chair. Exec. Cttee, Int. Securities Regulatory Comm. 2008–11; Chair. China Banking Regulatory Comm. 2011–17; Alt. mem. 16th CCP Cen. Cttee 2002–07; mem. 17th CCP Cen. Cttee 2007–12, 18th CCP Cen. Cttee 2012–17. *Publications:* China's Monetary Policy and Credit System of China 1995, The Operation, Efficiency and Development of Central Banks 1996, China's Success in Controlling Inflation and Its Future Policy Orientation 1997, Encyclopedia of Financial Guarantees 1999, A Study on the Transmission Mechanism of Monetary Policy 2000, The Situational Analysis on State-Owned Commercial Banks 2002. *Address:* c/o China Banking Regulatory Commission, No. 15 Financial Street, Xicheng District, Beijing 100033, People's Republic of China.

SHANGHVI, Dilip S., BCom; Indian pharmaceutical industry executive; *Managing Director, Sun Pharmaceutical Industries Ltd.;* b. Amreli, Gujarat; m.; two c.; ed Univ. of Calcutta; Founder and Man. Dir Sun Pharmaceutical Industries Ltd 1983–, Chair. 1999–2012; Chair. Bd of Dirs Caraco Pharmaceutical Labs Ltd 1997–; Dir Sun Speciality Chemicals Pvt. Ltd, Sun Resins & Polymers Pvt. Ltd, Sun Fastfin Services Pvt. Ltd, Sun Petrochemicals Pvt. Ltd, SPARC Bio-Research Pvt. Ltd, Sun Pharma Global Inc., British Virgin Island, Sun Pharma De Mexico SA DE CV, SPIL De Mexico SA DE CV, Shantilal Shanghvi Foundation; mem. Advisory Cttee Global Bio Pharma Conf. Group; Ernst & Young Entrepreneur of the Year in Health Care and Life Sciences 2005, Entrepreneur of the Year Award, The Economic Times 2008, CEO of the Year, The Business Standard, First Generation Entrepreneur of the Year, CNBC-TV 18 India Business Leader Awards 2007, Lifetime Honour, Indian Merchants Chamber 2008. *Leisure interests* reading, travelling, listening to music. *Address:* Acme Plaza, Andheri–Kurla Road, Andheri East, Mumbai 400 059, India (office). *Telephone:* (22) 56455645 (office). *Fax:* (22) 56455685 (office). *E-mail:* piedadedsouya@sunpharma.com (office). *Website:* www.sunpharma.com (office).

SHANKAR, Ramamurti, BTech, PhD; American (b. Indian) physicist and academic; *John Randolph Huffman Professor of Physics, Yale University;* b. 28 April 1947, New Delhi; ed Indian Inst. of Tech. (ITT), Madras, Univ. of California, Berkeley, USA; Jr Fellow, Harvard Soc. of Fellows 1974–77; J.W. Gibbs Instructor of Physics, Yale Univ. 1977–79, Asst Prof. 1979–83, Assoc. Prof. 1983–88, Prof. 1988, Chair., Dept of Physics 2001, John Randolph Huffman Prof. of Physics 2004–; Visiting Assoc. Prof., Ecole Normale Supérieure, Paris, France 1982; A.P. Sloan Fellow 1982–86; Visiting Prof., Inst. for Theoretical Physics, Santa Barbara, Calif. 1989; Distinguished Visiting Prof., IIT Madras 2015–; mem. Editorial Bd Journal of Statistical Physics 1988–90; mem. Aspen Center for Physics 1998–2003, Trustee 2004–10; mem. Advisory Bd, Center for Correlated Electrons and Magnetism, Augsburg, Germany 2007–, Kavli Inst. of Physics 2010–13; mem. American Acad. of Arts and Sciences 2014–; Cttee of Visitors, NSF 1999, Dannie Heineman Prize Cttee 1997–98; Fellow, American Physical Soc. 2001–; Byrnes and Sewel Teaching Prize, Yale Univ. 2005, Julius Edgar Lilienfeld Prize, American Physical Soc. 2009, Distinguished Alumnus Award, IIT Madras 2013. *Publications* include: Principles of Quantum Mechanics 1980, Basic Training in Mathematics 1995; numerous journal articles. *Address:* 55 Sloane Physics Laboratory, Department of Physics, Yale University, POB 208120, New Haven, CT 06520, USA (office). *Telephone:* (203) 432-6917 (office). *Fax:* (203) 432-6175 (office). *E-mail:* r.shankar@yale.edu (office). *Website:* campuspress.yale.edu/rshankar (office).

SHANKAR, Uday, MPhil; Indian journalist and media executive; *Chairman and CEO, Star India;* b. 16 Sept. 1962; m.; ed Jawaharlal Nehru Univ., New Delhi, Times School of Journalism; worked at The Times of India, Sunday Mail, India Today and Sahara (launched news div. of Sahara TV); fmr Ed. and News Dir Aaj Tak, launched Aaj Tak Headlines Today; joined Star News as CEO Media Content and Communications Services, Star Group 2004–07, COO Star India May–Oct. 2007, CEO Oct. 2007–, Chair. 2016–; Pres. Indian Broadcasting Foundation 2014–16; Pres. 21st Century Fox, Asia 2017–; Vice-Pres. Fed. of Indian Chambers of Commerce and Industry 2018–; mem. Bd of Dirs Tata Sky Ltd, Media Content and Communication Services (India) Pvt. Ltd, Asianet Communications Ltd, Indian Broadcasting Foundation, STAR CJ Network India Pvt. Ltd, Vijay Television Pvt. Ltd, Star CJ Home Shopping Company Ltd, ESPN Star Sports; Industry Leadership Award, 8th Annual Indian Film Festival Los Angeles 2010. *Address:* Star India, 1st Floor, Central Wing, Thapar House, 124 Janpath, New Delhi 110 001, India (office). *Telephone:* (11) 42494900 (office). *Fax:* (11) 41049490 (office). *E-mail:* info@star.co.in (office). *Website:* www.star.co.in (office); www .indya.com (office).

SHANKS, Ian Alexander, OBE, PhD, FRS, FIEE, FRSA, FRSE; British scientist; *Honorary Professor, University of Glasgow;* b. 22 June 1948, Glasgow; s. of Alexander Shanks and Isabella A. Beaton; m. Janice Coulter 1971; one d.; ed Dumbarton Acad., Univ. of Glasgow and Portsmouth Polytechnic; Projects Man.

Scottish Colorfoto Labs Ltd, Alexandria 1970–72; Jr Research Fellow, Royal Signals and Radar Establishment, Malvern, later Sr Scientific Officer, Prin. Scientific Officer 1973–82; Sr Scientist, later Prin. Scientist/Sr Man. Unilever Research Lab., Sharnbrook, Beds. 1982–86, Divisional Science Adviser 1994–2000, Vice-Pres. Physical and Eng Sciences 2001–03, Vice-Pres. Physical and Eng Sciences 2001–; Chief Scientist, Thorn EMI PLC 1986–94; Visiting Prof. of Electrical and Electronic Eng, Univ. of Glasgow 1985–, now Hon. Prof.; Founder Optoelectronics Coll.; Vice-Pres. The Royal Soc. 1989–91; Chair. Inter-Agency Cttee for Marine Science and Tech. 1991–93; Pres. Asscn for Science Educ., Scotland 2007–08; mem. Optoelectronics Cttee, Rank Prize Fund 1985–, Steering Group for Science and Eng Policy Studies Unit 1988–90, Science Consultative Group, BBC 1989–91; mem. Advisory Bd for Research Councils 1990–93, Science Advisory Group for Nat. Physical Lab. (currently Chair.), Royal Acad. of Eng Science 1998–2007, Advisory Bd for Inst. of Nanotechnology 2001–06; Fellow, Royal Acad. of Eng; Hon. Fellow, Inst. of Nanotechnology 2005; Hon. DEng (Univ. of Glasgow) 2002; Clifford Paterson Medal and Prize, Inst. of Physics 1984. *Achievements include:* over 75 patents mainly on liquid crystals, displays and biosensors. *Leisure interests:* music, collecting antique pocket watches, scientific instruments and art deco figures. *Address:* Kings Close, 11 Main Road, Biddenham, Bedford, MK40 4BB, England (home). *Telephone:* (1234) 328773 (home).

SHANMUGAM, K(asiviswanathan), LLD; Singaporean lawyer and politician; *Minister for Home Affairs and Minister for Law;* b. 1959, Singapore; ed Raffles Inst., Nat. Univ. of Singapore; admitted to Singapore Bar as advocate and solicitor 1985; several years' private legal practice, becoming Sr Partner and Head of Litigation and Dispute Resolution, Allen & Gledhill LLP (law firm); apptd Sr Counsel, Supreme Court of Singapore 1998; MP for Nee Soon Group Representation Constituency 1988–; Minister for Law 2008–, Second Minister for Home Affairs 2008–11, also Minister for Foreign Affairs 2011–15, of Home Affairs 2015–; mem. Singapore Indian Devt Asscn (Pres. 2002–09); mem. People's Action Party; mem. Advisory Bd Faculty of Law, Raffles Inst.; mem. Bd of Govs., Media Devt Authority, Sembawang Corporation Industries Ltd. *Address:* Ministry of Home Affairs, New Phoenix Park, 28 Irrawaddy Road, Singapore 329560, Singapore (office). *Telephone:* 64787010 (office).. *Fax:* 62546250 (office). *E-mail:* mha_feedback@mha.gov.sg (office). *Website:* www.mha.gov.sg (office).

SHANMUGANATHAN, V., MPhil; Indian civil servant; b. 21 Nov. 1949, Thanjavur, Tamil Nadu; ed Raja Serfoji Government Coll., Nat. Coll., Tiruchi, Univ. of Madras; joined Rashtriya Swayamsevak Sangh (voluntary Hindu charitable non-govt org.) 1962, fmr State Sec. in Chennai; also participated in various activity-oriented forums including Movt for Nat. Unity and Integrity, Tamil Valarchi Mandram (promoting Tamil literature), Bhakthar Peravai (charitable trust); Gov. of Meghalaya May 2015–17, of Manipur 2015–16, also of Arunachal Pradesh 2016–17; mem. Bharatiya Janata Party (BJP), fmr Additional Sec. and Prabhari (official) for BJP Overseas Affairs. *Publications include:* over 600 articles in leading newspapers and magazines; five books including Karyakarta Nirman, The Remarkable Political Movement.

SHANMUGARATNAM, Tharman, MPhil, MPA; Singaporean politician and economist; *Deputy Prime Minister and Co-ordinating Minister for Economic & Social Policies;* b. 1957, London, England; m. Jane Yumiko Ittogi; three s. one d.; ed London School of Econs, Univ. of Cambridge, UK, Harvard Univ., USA; early professional career as Man. Dir Monetary Authority of Singapore (MAS), Chair. 2011–; mem. Parl. for Jurong GRC (Taman Jurong) 2001–; Sr Minister of State, Ministry of Trade and Industry and Ministry of Educ. 2001–03, Minister for Educ. 2003–08, Second Minister of Finance 2006–07, Minister of Finance 2007–15, Minister for Manpower 2011–12, Deputy Prime Minister 2011–, also Co-ordinating Minister for Econ. & Social Policies 2015–; first Asian apptd Chair. of Int. Monetary and Financial Cttee (policy steering cttee of IMF) 2011–; Chair. Ong Teng Cheong Labour Leadership Inst.; Chair. Bd of Trustees, Singapore Indian Devt Asscn (SINDA), Tripartite Skills Future Council, Nat. Productivity Council, Int. Academic Advisory Panel; Lucius N. Littauer Fellow Award, Harvard Univ., Singapore Public Admin Gold Medal 1999. *Address:* Ministry of Finance, The Treasury 100 High Street, #10-01, Singapore 179434 (office). *Telephone:* 63322717 (office). *Fax:* 63367001 (office). *E-mail:* tharman_s@mof.gov.sg (office). *Website:* www.mof.gov.sg (office).

SHANNON, M. Frances, BSc, PhD; Irish biochemist and academic; *Emeritus Professor, Australian National University;* ed Univ. Coll. Dublin; Postdoctoral Fellow, Univ. of Adelaide, then Founding mem. Hanson Centre for Cancer Research, Inst. of Medical and Veterinary Science, Adelaide; joined faculty as Prof., ANU, Deputy Dir John Curtin School of Medical Research (JCSMR) 2007–08, Interim Dir 2008–09, also served as head of Div. of Molecular Bioscience and Group Leader, Gene Expression and Epigenomics Lab., now Prof. (hon.); Deputy Vice-Chancellor, Research, Univ. of Canberra 2010–18; Pres. Lorne Genome Conference Inc. 2007–09, Australian Soc. for Biochemistry and Molecular Biology 2011–12; Emer. Prof. Australian Nat. Univ. 2018–; mem. Editorial Bd FEBS Letts (journal of Fed. of European Biochemical Socs); Australian Soc. for Biochemistry and Molecular Biology Boehringer Medal, Lorne Genome Meeting Julian Wells Medal. *Address:* Australian National University, Canberra, ACT 2600, Australia (office). *E-mail:* frances.shannon@anu.edu.au (office). *Website:* www.anu.edu.au (office).

SHANNON, Michael Corbett; American actor; b. 7 Aug. 1974, Lexington, Ky; s. of Donald Sutherlin Shannon and Geraldine Hine; partner Kate Arrington 2002; two d.; started professional stage career in Chicago at Illinois Theatre Center; worked with Steppenwolf, The Next Lab, the Red Orchid Theatre. *Plays include:* Fun/Nobody (Joseph Jefferson Award for Actor in a Principal Role 1992) 1992, Simpatico (Joseph Jefferson Award for Actor in a Principal Role 2013) 2013, 99 Homes 2015, Long Day's Journey Into Night (Drama Desk Award for Outstanding Featured Actor in a Play 2016, Outer Critics Circle Award for Outstanding Featured Actor in a Play 2016) 2016. *Films include:* Groundhog Day 1993, Chain Reaction 1996, Chicago Cab 1997, The Ride 1997, Jesus' Son 1999, The Photographer 2000, Cecil B. DeMented 2000, Tigerland 2000, Pearl Harbor 2001, New Port South 2001, Vanilla Sky 2001, High Crimes 2002, 8 Mile 2002, Kangaroo Jack 2003, Bad Boys II 2003, Grand Theft Parsons 2003, The Woodsman 2004, Criminal 2004, Dead Birds 2004, Water 2004, Marvelous 2006, Bug 2006,

World Trade Center 2006, Let's Go to Prison 2006, Shotgun Stories 2007, Blackbird 2007, Lucky You 2007, Before the Devil Knows You're Dead (Satellite Award for Best Supporting Actor 2008) 2007, Revolutionary Road (Santa Barbara Int. Film Festival Virtuoso Award, Satellite Award for Best Supporting Actor in a Motion Picture) 2008, The Missing Person 2009, The Greatest 2009, Bad Lieutenant 2009, My Son, My Son, What Have Ye Done 2009, The Runaways 2010, 13 2010, Jonah Hex 2010, Return 2011, Take Shelter (Saturn Award for Best Actor 2011, Austin Film Critics Asscn Best Actor, Chicago Film Critics Asscn Best Actor, New York Film Critics Online Best Actor, San Diego Film Critics Soc. Best Actor, Toronto Film Critics Asscn Best Actor) 2011, The Broken Tower 2011, Machine Gun Preacher 2011, Mud 2012, Premium Rush 2012, The Iceman 2012, Man of Steel 2013, Can't Come Out to Play 2013, Bad Land: Road to Fury 2014, They Came Together 2014, She's Funny That Way 2014, 99 Homes (Los Angeles Film Critics Asscn Award for Best Supporting Actor 2015, San Francisco Film Critics Circle Award for Best Supporting Actor 2015) 2014, Freeheld 2015, The Night Before 2015, Complete Unknown 2016, Frank & Lola 2016, Midnight Special 2016, Batman v Superman: Dawn of Justice 2016, Wolves 2016, Poor Boy 2016, Elvis & Nixon (also producer) 2016, Loving 2016, Salt and Fire 2016, Nocturnal Animals 2016. *Television includes:* Overexposed (film) 1992, Angel Street (film) 1992, Early Edition (series) 1998–99, Boardwalk Empire (series) (Screen Actors Guild Award for Outstanding Performance by an Ensemble in a Drama Series 2011, 2012) 2010–14. *Address:* Byron Wetzel Management, 200 Park Avenue South, 8th Floor, New York, NY 10003, USA (office). *Telephone:* (646) 783-9443 (office).

SHANTSEV, Valery Pavlinovich; Russian politician; b. 1947, Susanino Kostroma Region; m.; one s. one d.; ed Moscow Aviation School, Moscow Inst. of Radiotech., Electronics and Automation, Acad. of Nat. Econs; asst to master factory Salut 1968–75; instructor Perov Dist CP Cttee, Deputy Head Machine Construction Dept Moscow City CP Cttee 1975–85; Chair. Exec. Cttee Perov Dist Soviet, First Sec. Perov Dist CP Cttee, Chair. Perov Dist Soviet of People's Deputies 1985–90; Sec. Moscow City CP Cttee 1990–91; Deputy of Perovo District Council of People's Deputies 1983–93; Deputy of Moscow Soviet 1987–93; Commercial Dir Hockey Club Dynamo 1991–94; Prefect of S Admin. Dist of Moscow 1994–96; Vice-Mayor of Moscow, First Deputy Prime Minister, Moscow Govt and Head of Social Complex 1996–99; Vice-Mayor of Moscow, First Deputy Prime Minister, Moscow Govt and Head of Econ. Policy and Devt Complex 1999–2001; Vice-Mayor of Moscow and Head of Econ. Policy and Devt Complex 2001–05; Gov. Nizhny Novgorod Region 2005–17. *Address:* c/o Office of the Governor, Kremlin, Corpus 1 and 2, Nizhny Novgorod 603082, Russia.

SHAO, Lt-Gen. Huaze; Chinese journalist, army officer and government official; *Honorary Chairman, All-China Journalists Association;* b. June 1933, Chun'an Co., Zhejiang Prov.; ed PLA Political Cadres' School No. 2, Chinese People's Univ.; joined PLA 1950, CCP 1957; Ed. Jiefangjun Ribao (PLA Daily) 1964; Vice-Dir Jiefangjun Ribao 1981; Dir Propaganda Dept PLA Gen. Political Dept 1985; rank of Maj.-Gen. 1988, Lt-Gen. 1992; Ed.-in-Chief Renmin Ribao (People's Daily) 1989–92, Dir 1992–2000; Chair. All-China Journalists' Asscn 1996–2006, now Hon. Chair.; Dean, School of Journalism and Mass Communication, Peking Univ. 2002–13; Vice-Chair. China Great Wall Soc.; mem. 14th CCP Cen. Cttee 1992–97, 15th CCP Cen. Cttee 1997–2002; mem. Standing Cttee 9th CPPCC Nat. Cttee 1998–2003; fmr Hon. Pres. Chinese Soc. of News Photography, Chinese Newspapers Asscn. *E-mail:* sjc18@pku.edu.cn (office). *Website:* www.xinhuanet.com/zgjx/ldr.htm.

SHAPIRO, Bernard, OC, BA, PhD; Canadian (b. American) academic administrator and fmr government official; *Principal Emeritus, McGill University;* b. 8 June 1935, Montreal; s. of Maxwell Shapiro and Mary Tafler; twin brother of Harold T. Shapiro (q.v.); m. Phyllis Schwartz 1957 (died 2005); one s. one d.; ed McGill Univ., Harvard Univ., USA; started career as Assoc. Dean, School of Educ., Boston Univ.; Dean, Faculty of Educ., Univ. of Western Ontario 1976, Vice-Pres. (Academic) and Provost 1978; Dir Ontario Inst. for Studies in Educ. 1980–86; Deputy Minister of Educ., Ont. Prov. 1986–89, of Skills Devt 1988–89; Deputy Sec. of Prov. Cabinet, Ont. 1989–90, Deputy Minister and Sec., Man. Bd 1990–91, of Colls and Univs 1991–93; Prof. of Educ. and Public Policy, Univ. of Toronto 1992–94; Prin. and Vice-Chancellor McGill Univ. 1994–2003, now Prin. Emer.; Ethics Commr of Canada 2004–07 (resgnd); apptd mem. Concordia Univ. external governance review cttee 2011; Officer, Order of Canada 1999, Grand Officier, Nat. Order of Quebec 2004; Hon. LLD (McGill) 1988, (Toronto) 1994, (Ottawa) 1995, (Yeshiva) 1996, (Montreal) 1998, (Edin.) 2000, (Glasgow) 2001, (Bishop's) 2001, Dr hc (McMaster), (Nipissing), (Melbourne).

SHAPIRO, Ehud (Udi), BA, BSc, PhD; Israeli computer scientist and academic; *Harry Weinrebe Professorial Chair of Computer Science and Biology, Weizmann Institute of Science;* b. 28 Feb. 1955, Jerusalem; ed Tel-Aviv Univ., Yale Univ., USA; Postdoctoral Fellow, Dept of Computer Science and Applied Math., Weizmann Inst. 1982–93, co-operated closely with Japanese Fifth Generation Computer Systems project to invent high-level programming language for parallel and distributed computer systems, named Concurrent Prolog, on leave of absence 1993–98, Assoc. Prof., Depts of Computer Science and Applied Math., and Biological Chem., holds Harry Weinrebe Professorial Chair of Computer Science and Biology 1998–; Founder and CEO Ubique Ltd (Israeli internet software co., sold to AOL 1995, sold again to IBM in 1988 following man. buy-out in 1997); World Tech. Award in Biotechnology, The World Tech. Network 2004, Research Leader in Nanotechnology, Scientific American 50 2004. *Achievements include:* studied molecular biology in attempt to build biomolecular computer to operate inside the living body ('Doctor in a Cell'); has also developed method for tracing 'genealogy' of cells in the human body. *Publications:* Algorithmic Program Debugging 1983, Inductive Inference of Theories from Facts 1986, The Art of Prolog: Advanced Programming Techniques (with L. Sterling) 1986 (translated into Japanese, Dutch, French, German and Russian, second edn 1994), Concurrent Prolog: Collected Papers, Vols 1 and 2 (ed.) 1987, Hebrew Prolog for Beginners (with Z. Scherz and O. Maler; in Hebrew) 1988; several scientific papers in professional journals; five US patents. *Address:* Department of Computer Science and Applied Mathematics, Weizmann Institute of Science, Rehovot 76100, Israel (office). *Telephone:* (8) 934-4506 (office). *Fax:* (8) 947-1746 (office). *E-mail:* ehud.shapiro@weizmann.ac.il (office). *Website:* www.wisdom.weizmann.ac.il/~udi (office).

SHAPIRO, Harold Tafler, MA, PhD; American university president and professor of economics; *Professor of Economics and Public Affairs, Department of Economics and Woodrow Wilson School of Public and International Affairs, Princeton University;* b. 8 June 1935, Montreal, Canada; s. of Maxwell Shapiro and Mary Tafler; twin brother of Bernard Shapiro (q.v.); m. Vivian Shapiro; four d.; ed McGill Univ., Canada, Princeton Univ. Grad. School; Harold Helm Fellow, McGill Univ. 1961–64, Harold Dodds Sr Fellow 1963–64; apptd Asst Prof. of Econs, Univ. of Mich. 1964, Assoc. Prof. 1967, Prof. 1970, Vice-Pres. for Academic Affairs 1977, Pres. Univ. of Mich. 1980–88; Pres. Princeton Univ. 1988–2001, Pres. Emer. 2001–, Prof. of Econs and Public Affairs, Dept of Econs and Woodrow Wilson School of Public and Int. Affairs 1988–; currently Chair. Cttee on Organizational Structure of NIH; mem. Conf. Bd Inc., Bretton Woods Cttee; mem. Pres.'s Council of Advisors on Science and Tech. 1990–92; Chair. Nat. Bioethics Advisory Comm. 1996–2001; Dir Dow Chemical Co., Nat. Bureau of Econ. Research; mem. Bd of Dirs, DeVry, Inc. 2001– (Chair. 2008–), Inst. for Advanced Study 2009–, Hastings Center; Chair. InterAcademy Council Cttee on the Review of International Panel on Climate Change 2010–; mem. Inst. of Medicine of NAS, American Philosophical Soc., Nat. Insts of Health Council 2007–10; mem. Bd of Overseers, Robert Wood Johnson Medical Center, Bd of Trustees Educational Testing Service 1994–2000, Univ. Corpn for Advanced Internet Devt 2000–; Fellow, American Acad. of Arts and Sciences 1990, Coll. of Physicians of Philadelphia 2000, American Asscn for the Advancement of Science 2006; Trustee, Alfred P. Sloan Foundation, Univ. of Pennsylvania Medical Center, Univs Research Asscn, Educational Testing Service; Hon. DSc (Michigan Technological Univ., Michigan) 1980, Hon. LLD (Wayne State Univ., Michigan) 1980, (Grand Valley State Colleges, Michigan) 1983, (Albion College, Michigan) 1985, (Michigan State Univ., Michigan) 1987, (Univ. of Michigan, Michigan) 1987, (Rutgers Univ., New Jersey) 1988, (Yale Univ., Connecticut 1988), (McGill Univ., Quebec, Canada) 1988, (Centenary Coll., New Jersey 1992, (Univ. of Toronto, Ontario, Canada) 1994, Hon. DHL (Yeshiva Univ., New York) 1996, Dr hc (Univ. of Edinburgh) 2000, Carnegie Mellon Univ., Pennsylvania 2009, Thomas Edison State Coll., New Jersey 2009; Lieutenant Gov.'s Medal in Commerce 1956, William D. Carey Lectureship Award 2006, Clark Kerr Award, Univ. of California 2009, Public Welfare Medal, NAS 2012. *Address:* Department of Economics and The Woodrow Wilson School of Public and International Affairs, 359 Wallace Hall, Princeton University, Princeton, NJ 08544-0015 (office); 10 Campbelton Circle, Princeton, NJ 08540, USA (home). *Telephone:* (609) 258-6184 (home). *Fax:* (609) 258-7120 (office). *E-mail:* hts@princeton.edu (office). *Website:* www.princeton.edu/~hts (office).

SHAPIRO, Irwin I., PhD, FAAS; American physicist and academic; *Timken University Professor, Department of Astronomy, Harvard University;* b. 29 Oct. 1929, New York; s. of Esther Feinberg and Samuel Shapiro; m. Marian Helen Kaplun 1959; one s. one d.; ed Cornell and Harvard Univs; mem. staff, MIT Lincoln Lab. 1954–70, Prof. of Geophysics and Physics 1967–80; Redman Lecturer, McMaster Univ. 1969; Sherman Fairchild Distinguished Scholar, Calif. Inst. of Tech. 1974; Schlumberger Prof., MIT 1980–85, Prof. Emer. 1985–; Sr Scientist, Smithsonian Astrophysical Observatory 1982–; Paine Prof. of Practical Astronomy and Prof. of Physics, Harvard Univ. 1982–97, Timken Univ. Prof., Dept of Astronomy 1997–, Dir Harvard-Smithsonian Center for Astrophysics 1983–2004 (Chair. Bd 1980–81); mem. Editorial Bd Celestial Mechanics 1969–75, Annals of Physics 1977–82; Assoc. Ed. Icarus 1969–75; Fellow, American Geophysical Union, American Physical Soc.; mem. Int. Astronomical Union, NAS 1974, American Acad. of Arts and Sciences 1969, American Astronomical Soc., American Philosophical Soc. 1998, AAAS; mem. Radio Science Teams, Mariner Venus–Mercury, Viking and Pioneer–Venus Missions 1970–79, Space Science Bd (NAS) 1977–80, NSF Astronomy Advisory Cttee 1983–86, Task Group on Astronomy and Astrophysics of Nat. Research Council Space Science Bd Study 'Major Directions for Space Science: 1995–2015' 1984–86, Tech. Oversight Cttee of Nat. Earth Orientation Service 1986–, NASA Advisory Council 1987–90; Chair. NASA Astrophysics Sub-cttee 1988–92, mem. 1992–96; Albert A. Michelson Medal of Franklin Inst. 1975, Benjamin Apthorp Gould Prize of NAS 1979, John Simon Guggenheim Fellowship 1982, New York Acad. of Sciences Award in Physical and Math. Sciences 1982, Dannie Heineman Award of American Astronomical Soc. 1983, John C. Lindsay Lecturer, NASA Goddard Space Flight Center 1986, Whitten Medal (American Geophysical Union) 1991, Bowie Medal (American Geophysical Union) 1993, Einstein Medal 1994, Gerard Kuiper Award 1997, Sec.'s Gold Medal for Exceptional Service, Smithsonian Inst. 1999, Einstein Prize, American Physical Soc. 2013. *Publications:* over 350 including Prediction of Ballistic Missile Trajectories from Radar Observations 1958; Ed. of trans. of Mathematical Foundations of Quantum Statistics (Khinchin) 1960; numerous scientific articles, tech. reports and text books for students. *Address:* Perkin Lab, P-217 Harvard-Smithsonian Center for Astrophysics, 60 Garden Street, MS-51, Cambridge, MA 02138 (office); 17 Lantern Lane, Lexington, MA 02421, USA (home). *Telephone:* (617) 495-7300 (office). *E-mail:* shapiro@cfa.harvard.edu (office). *Website:* www.cfa.harvard.edu (office); astronomy.fas.harvard.edu (office).

SHAPIRO, Joel, BA, MA; American sculptor; b. 27 Sept. 1941, New York, NY; s. of Dr Joseph Shapiro and Dr Anna Shapiro; m. Ellen Phelan; one d.; ed New York Univ., Peace Corps in India; teacher, Princeton Univ. 1974–75, 1975–76, School of Visual Arts 1977–82; group exhbns in UK, USA, Australia, France, Germany, Spain, the Netherlands, Switzerland, China, Singapore 1969–2012; Nat. Endowment for the Arts 1975; mem. Swedish Royal Acad. of Art 1994, American Acad. of Arts and Letters 1998; Chevalier des Arts et des Lettres 2005; Visual Arts Fellowship, Visual Arts Program, Nat. Endowment for the Arts 1975, Brandeis Univ. Creative Arts Award 1984, Skowhegan Medal for Sculpture 1986, Award of Merit Medal for Sculpture, American Acad. and Inst. of Arts and Letters, New York 1990, Resident in the Visual Arts, American Acad. in Rome 1998–99, Smithsonian Archives of American Art Award 2008, Distinguished Alumni, New York Univ. 2010, Gabarron Int. Award for Visual Art 2012, Nat. Art Award, Americans for the Arts 2013. *Film:* 20 Elements 2005, Michael Blackwood. *Radio:* Giornale radio (interview with Peter Boswell, Radio RAI, Italy) 1999, New York and Company (interview with Leonard Lopate, WNYC-AM, New York) 2001, Leonard Lopate Remote, Whitney Museum of American Art (WNYC-AM) 2002, Art Talk (interview with Edward Goldman, KCRW-FM, Los Angeles) 2004. *Television:* Julião Sarmento/Joel Shapiro 1997, L'Exposition Impossible, Musée d'Orsay, Paris 2005, Joel Shapiro: Twenty Elements (Michael Blackwood Productions, Inc., New

York) (DVD) 2006, Getty Museum Audio Tour Interview on Matisse, Nasher Museum 2006. *Publications:* numerous exhbn catalogues with text by others. *Address:* c/o The Pace Gallery, 32 East 57th Street, New York, NY 10022, USA. *Telephone:* (212) 421-3292 (office). *E-mail:* studio@jeshapiro.com (office). *Website:* www.thepacegallery.com (office).

SHAPIRO, Larry J., AB, MD; American geneticist, paediatrician and academic; b. 6 July 1946, Chicago, Ill.; m. Carol-Ann Uetake; one s. two d.; ed Washington Univ. in St Louis; intern, St Louis Children's Hosp. 1971–72, resident 1971–73; Research Assoc., Nat. Inst. of Arthritis, Metabolism and Digestive Diseases, Bethesda, Md 1973–75; Asst Prof. of Pediatrics, UCLA 1975–79, Assoc. Prof. 1979–83, Prof. of Pediatrics and Biological Chemistry 1983–91; Investigator, Howard Hughes Medical Inst. 1987–91, also W.H. and Marie Wattis Distinguished Prof.; Prof. and Chair. Dept of Pediatrics, Univ. of California, San Francisco School of Medicine 1991–2003, also Chief of Pediatric Services, Univ. of California, San Francisco Children's Hosp.; Spencer T. and Ann W. Olin Distinguished Prof., Exec. Vice Chancellor for Medical Affairs and Dean, School of Medicine, Washington Univ. in St Louis 2003–15; Fellow, AAAS, American Acad. of Pediatrics; mem. NAS Inst. of Medicine (currently Vice-Chair.), American Acad. of Arts and Sciences, American Pediatric Soc. (Pres. 2003–04), American Soc. for Clinical Investigation, American Soc. for Human Genetics (Pres. 1997), Asscn of American Physicians, Soc. for Inherited Metabolic Disease (Pres. 1986–87), Western Soc. for Pediatric Research (Pres. 1989–90), Soc. for Pediatric Research (Pres. 1991–92); numerous awards including Ross Award, Western Soc. for Pediatric Research 1981. *Address:* c/o Office of the Dean, School of Medicine, Washington University in St Louis, 660 South Euclid Avenue, St Louis, MO 63110, USA.

SHAPIRO, Robert Leslie, BS, JD; American lawyer; *Senior Partner, Glaser Weil Fink Howard Avchen & Shapiro LLP;* b. 2 Sept. 1942, Plainfield, New Jersey; m. Linell Shapiro; two s. (one deceased); ed Univ. of California, Los Angeles, Loyola Univ. Law School; called to the Bar, Calif. 1969, US Court of Appeals 1972, US Dist Court, Calif. 1982; Deputy Dist Attorney, Los Angeles 1969–72; sole practice 1972–87; Counsel, Bushkin, Gaims, Gaines, Jonas 1987–88; with Christensen, White, Miller, Fink & Jacobs 1988–95, currently Sr Partner, Glaser Weil Fink Jacobs Howard Avchen & Shapiro LLP and Head, White-Collar Criminal Defense Section; f. Trial Lawyers for Public Justice 1982; mem. Nat. Asscn of Criminal Defence Lawyers, Calif. Attorneys for Criminal Justice, Bar Asscn; Founder and Chair. Brent Shapiro Foundation for Drug Awareness; Co-founder LegalZoom.-com, ShoeDazzle.com; American Jurisprudence Award, Bancroft Whitney 1969; Best Criminal Defence Lawyer, Bar Asscn 1993, Lawyer of the Year 1995, Bruce K. Gould Award, Touro Law Center 1997, Author of One of the Ten Best Legal Articles of the Decade, Calif. State Bar Journal, Pro-Bono Lawyer of the Year, Nevada, 100 Most Influential Lawyers in America, Nat. Law Journal 2013. *Publications include:* Search for Justice 1996, Misconception (novel) 2001. *Address:* Glaser Weil Fink Jacobs Howard Avchen and Shapiro LLP, 10250 Constellation Blvd, 19th Floor, Los Angeles, CA 90067, USA (office). *Telephone:* (310) 556-7886 (office). *Fax:* (310) 556-2920 (office). *E-mail:* rs@glaserweil.com (office). *Website:* www.robertshapiro.com (office); www.brentshapiro.org.

SHAPOSHNIKOV, Air Marshal (retd) Yevgeny Ivanovich; Russian air force officer (retd) and government official; b. 3 Feb. 1942, Bolshoy Log, Rostov region; s. of Ivan Sevastinovich Shaposhnikov and Klavdia Stepanova Shaposhnikova; m. Zemfira Nikolayevna Shaposhnikova 1980; one s. two d.; ed Kharkov Higher Aviation School, Y. Gagarin Aviation Acad., Gen. Staff Acad.; joined Soviet Army 1959, Head, Soviet Air Force in Germany 1987–88, apptd First Deputy Commdr, All-Union Soviet Air Force 1988, Commdr 1990–91; Minister of Defence and Head Soviet Armed Forces Aug.–Dec. 1991, C-in-C of the Armed Forces of the CIS 1991–93, Sec. of Security Council, resgnd 1993; apptd Rep. of Pres. Yeltsin in Rosvooruzhenie (state-owned armaments exports co.); Gen. Dir Aeroflot 1995–97; Asst to Russian Fed. Pres. 1997–2004; mem. Bd Democratic Reforms Movt 1993–98. *Leisure interests:* literature, theatre, tennis.

SHAPOVALYANTS, Andrei Georgiyevich; Russian economist; b. 23 Feb. 1952, Moscow; m.; two d.; ed Moscow Plekhanov Inst. of Nat. Econs; Researcher, Inst. Elektronika, Main Computation Centre, USSR State Planning Cttee, Head of Div., USSR State Planning Cttee 1969–90; Head, Div. of Financial-Credit Policy, USSR Ministry of Econs and Prognosis 1991; Deputy, First Deputy Minister of Econs and Finance of Russian Fed. 1991–93; Acting Minister of Econs and Finance, First Deputy Minister 1993–98, Minister of Econs 1998–99; mem. Presidium, Russian Govt 1998; Man. Black Sea Bank of Trade and Devt 1999; apptd Pres. Bd of Dirs KAMAZ co. 1999; Dir-Gen. Centre of Reconstruction and Devt of Enterprises 2001; mem. Bd of Dirs Murmansk Commercial Seaport.

SHAPPS, Rt Hon. Grant, PC; British politician and business executive; b. 14 Sept. 1968, Watford, Herts., England; m. Belinda Goldstone 1997; three c.; ed Watford Grammar School for Boys, Cassio Coll., Manchester Polytechnic (now Manchester Metropolitan Univ.); f. PrintHouse Corpn, London 1990; contested North Southwark and Bermondsey constituency in Gen. Election 1997, Welwyn Hatfield 2001; MP for Welwyn Hatfield 2005–, mem. Public Admin Select Cttee 2005–07; Shadow Minister for Housing (attending Shadow Cabinet) 2007–10; Minister of State for Housing and Local Govt, Dept for Communities and Local Govt 2010–12; mem. Speaker's Cttee on Electoral Comm. 2010–; Minister without Portfolio, Cabinet Office 2012–15; Minister of State for Int. Devt May–Nov. 2015 (resgnd); Br. Chair. Barnhill, Brent North 1995–99; mem. Conservative Friends of Israel 1995, Selsdon Group 1996, Conservative Foreign Affairs Forum 1996; Vice-Pres. North Southwark and Bermondsey Asscn 1997; Vice-Chair. (Campaigning) Conservative Party 2005–09, Co-Chair. Conservative Party 2012–15; has used the name Michael Green in his Internet marketing businesses. *Address:* House of Commons, Westminster, London, SW1A 0AA (office); Constituency Office, Welwyn Hatfield Conservative Association, Maynard House, The Common, Hatfield, AL10 0NF, England. *Telephone:* (20) 7219-8497 (Westminster) (office); (1707) 262632 (Hatfield). *Fax:* (20) 7219-0659 (Westminster); (1707) 263892 (Hatfield). *E-mail:* shappsg@parliament.uk (office); sandra@welhatconservatives.com. *Website:* www.parliament.uk/biographies/commons/grant-shapps/1582 (office); www.shapps.com.

SHARA', Farouk al-, BA; Syrian politician and diplomatist; *Vice-President, responsible for Foreign Affairs and Information;* b. 10 Dec. 1938; m.; one s. one d.; ed Damascus Univ., Univ. of London, UK; fmr Head, state-owned Syrian Arab Airlines, London 1963–76; Amb. to Italy 1976–80; Minister of State for External Affairs 1980–84, Acting Minister of Information 1983, Minister of Foreign Affairs 1984–2006, Deputy Prime Minister 2001–03; Vice-Pres., responsible for Foreign Affairs and Information 2006–; mem. Regional Leadership of Al-Baath Socialist Party 2000–13. *Publication:* The Missing Account 2015. *Address:* Office of the Vice-President, Abu Rummaneh, Almadfaa Square, Damascus, Syria (office).

SHARAF, Essam, MSc, PhD; Egyptian engineer, professor of civil engineering and politician; b. 1952, Giza; ed Cairo Univ., Purdue Univ., USA; Visiting Asst Prof., School of Civil Eng, Purdue Univ. 1984–85; Asst Prof. of Highway and Traffic Eng, Cairo Univ. 1985–90; Asst Prof. of Civil Eng, King Saud Univ., Saudi Arabia 1990–96; Minister of Transport 2004–05; Prime Minister of Egypt March–Nov. 2011 (resgnd); fmr Adviser to Roads and Transport Authority of Dubai; co-f. Egypt Scientific Soc.; Fellow, Chartered Inst. of Logistics and Transport (UK) 2007; Acad. of Scientific Research and Tech. State Prize in Eng Sciences 1987, 1997, First Class State Medal of Excellence 1995, Purdue Univ. Excellence Award in Eng 2005.

SHARANSKY, Natan; Israeli (b. Soviet) politician and human rights activist; *Chairman of the Executive, Jewish Agency for Israel;* b. 20 Jan. 1948, Donetsk, USSR (now Ukraine); s. of Ida Milgrom; m. Natalya (now Avital) Stiglitz 1974; two d.; ed Physical Tech. Inst., Moscow; leading spokesman for Jewish emigration movt in USSR; arrested by Soviet authorities for dissident activities 1977; received 13-year prison sentence on charges of treason 1978, released him in exchange for spies held in West, took up residence in Israel Feb. 1986; apptd Pres. Zionist Forum 1988; Assoc. Ed. The Jerusalem Report 1990–96; co-f. Peace Watch 1994; mem. Knesset 1996–2006 (resgnd); Minister of Trade and Industry 1996–99, of the Interior 1999–2000, of Housing and Construction and Deputy Prime Minister 2001–03; Minister without Portfolio responsible for Jerusalem, Social and Diaspora Affairs 2003–05; Inst. Chair. and Distinguished Fellow, Adelson Inst. for Strategic Studies, Shalem Center 2006–; Chair. of the Exec., Jewish Agency for Israel 2009–; Chair. One Jerusalem, Beit Hatefutsot (Jewish diaspora museum), Tel-Aviv; fmr Visiting Prof., Brandeis Univ., Waltham, Mass.; Founder and fmr Leader, Yisrael B'Aliya Party 1996 (merged with Likud 2003); US Congressional Medal of Honor, US Presidential Medal of Freedom, Israel Prize. *Publications include:* Fear No Evil 1988, The Case for Democracy: The Power of Freedom to Overcome Tyranny and Terror (with Ron Dermer) 2005, Defending Identity: It's Indispensable Role in Protecting Democracy 2008. *Address:* Jewish Agency for Israel, POB 92, 3 Haaskan Street, Jerusalem 9426218, Israel (office). *Telephone:* (2) 444-3210 (office). *E-mail:* larissa.ruthman@gmail.com (office). *Website:* www.jewishagency.org (office).

SHARAPOVA, Maria Yuryevna; Russian professional tennis player; b. 19 April 1987, Nyagan, Siberia, USSR; d. of Youri Sharapov and Yelena Sharapova; turned professional 2001; Women's Tennis Asscn (WTA) singles titles include Tokyo 2003, 2004, 2005, Quebec City 2003, Birmingham 2004, 2005, Seoul 2004, WTA Championships, Los Angeles 2004, Doha 2005, Italian Open 2011, 2012, BNP Paribas Open, Indian Wells 2013, Porsche Tennis Grand Prix, Stuttgart 2013, 2014, Mutua Madrid Open 2014, China Open, Beijing 2014; WTA Championships, Istanbul 2012; Grand Slam results: winner, Wimbledon 2004 (second-youngest Wimbledon Champion in Open era, fourth-youngest winner of any Grand Slam title), US Open 2006, Australian Open 2008, French Open 2012, 2014, finalist, Australian Open 2007, 2012, 2015, Wimbledon 2011, semi-finalist, French Open 2007, 2011; silver medal, Olympic Games, London 2012; WTA doubles titles, Luxembourg 2003 (with Tamarine Tanasugarn), Japan Open 2003 (with Tanasugarn), Birmingham 2004 (with Maria Kirilenko); highest ranking: World No. 1 22 Aug. 2005; coached by father and by Robert Lansdorp; signed with IMG Models 2003; has won five Grand Slam titles; apptd UNDP Goodwill Amb. 2007; provisionally suspended from tennis March 2016 after failing drugs test after 2016 Australian Open; WTA Newcomer of the Year 2003, WTA Player of the Year 2004, WTA Most Improved Player of the Year 2004, ESPY Best Female Tennis Player 2005, 2007, 2008, named the country's best female player for the year by Russia's tennis fed. 2005, 2006, Master of Sports of Russia 2005, Prix de Citron Roland Garros 2005, Whirlpool 6th Sense Player of the Year 2006, ESPY Best Int. Female Athlete 2007, named the January 2008 female Athlete of the Month by the US Sports Acad. for her performance at the Australian Open 2008. *Leisure interests:* fashion, singing, dancing, movies. *Address:* IMG, 200 5th Avenue, 7th Floor, New York, NY 10010, USA. *Website:* www.mariasharapova.com.

SHARAR, Muhammad Dhaifallah, LLB; Kuwaiti lawyer and government official; *Advisor at Al-Diwan Al-Amiri;* b. 1948; ed Kuwait Univ.; pvt. law practice 1985–90; elected to Nat. Ass. 1996, Minister of Justice, Awqaf and Islamic Affairs –1998, State Minister for Nat. Ass. Affairs 1998, State Minister for Cabinet and Nat. Ass. Affairs 2001–06; currently Advisor at Al-Diwan Al-Amiri (advisor to Amir Sheikh Sabah al-Ahmad al-Jaber al-Sabah, Amir of Kuwait). *Address:* Al Diwan Al Amiri, Sief Palace, Building 100, Safat, 13001, Kuwait (office). *Website:* www.da.gov.kw/eng (office).

SHAREEF, Mohammed Hussain; Maldivian government official; *Ambassador to Sri Lanka;* fmr Chair. State Trading Org. plc; fmr Dir-Gen. Post and Telecommunications Section, Ministry of Communication, Science and Tech.; fmr Chief Govt Spokesman; apptd Minister of Human Resources, Youth and Sports 2012; Amb. to Japan April–Aug. 2017, to Sri Lanka 2017–. *Address:* Embassy of the Maldives, Iikura IT Bldg, 8/F, 1-9-10, Azabudai, Minato-ku, Tokyo 106-0041, Japan (office). *Telephone:* (3) 6234-4315 (office). *Fax:* (3) 6234-4316 (office). *E-mail:* info@maldivesembassy.jp (office). *Website:* www.maldivesembassy.jp (office).

SHAREEF UMAR, Adam, MA; Maldivian politician and fmr teacher; ed Univ. of East Anglia, UK; started career as primary teacher 1981; Lecturer, Faculty of Educ., Maldives Nat. Univ. 1992–2000; Dir-Gen., Centre for Continuing Educ. 2010–12; Dir-Gen., Nat. Inst. of Educ. 2012–; State Minister for Educ. 2014–15; Minister of Defence and Nat. Security 2015–18; mem. Progressive Party of Maldives. *Address:* c/o Ministry of Defence and National Security, Ameer Ahmed Magu, Malé 20-126, Maldives (office).

SHARER, Kevin W., BS, MS, MBA; American business executive and academic; b. 2 March 1948; s. of Keith Sharer and Heather Sharer; m. Carol Sharer; five c.; ed US Naval Acad., Univ. of Pittsburgh; fmr Consultant, McKinsey & Co.; fmr Exec.,

Gen. Electric Corpn; Exec. Vice-Pres. and Pres. of Business Markets Div., MCI Communications Corpn –1992; COO and mem. Bd of Dirs Amgen 1992–2000, Pres. 1992–2010, CEO 2000–12, Chair. 2001–12; Exec. Partner, Foundation Medical Partners (venture capital firm) 2013–; Sr Lecturer of Business Administration, Harvard Business School 2013–; mem. Bd of Dirs Chevron, Northrop Grumman Corpn, US Naval Acad. Foundation; Chair. Bd of Trustees, LA Co. Museum of Natural History; mem. The Business Council. *Address:* Foundation Medical Partners, 105 Rowayton Avenue, Rowayton, CT 06853 (office); Division of Faculty and Research, Harvard Business School, Soldiers Field, Boston, MA 02163, USA (office). *Telephone:* (617) 495-6353 (Harvard) (office). *E-mail:* ksharer @ foundmed .com (office). *Website:* www.foundmed.com (office); www.hbs.edu (office).

SHARIATMADARI, Hossein; Iranian journalist and newspaper industry executive; *Managing Director and Editor-in-Chief, Kayhan;* imprisoned in Tehran before Islamic Revolution of 1979; served as Revolutionary Guards Commdr during war with Iraq; currently Man. Dir and Ed.-in-Chief Kayhan (daily newspaper); Pres. Kayhan Inst.; apptd Rep. of the Supreme Leader of the Islamic Revolution 1993. *Address:* Kayhan, POB 11365/9631, Martyr Shah Cheraghi Street, Tehran 11444, Iran (office). *Telephone:* (21) 33110251 (office). *Fax:* (21) 33111120 (office). *Website:* kayhan.ir/en (office).

SHARIF, Maimunah Mohd, BSc, MSc; Malaysian local government administrator and UN official; *Executive Director, United Nations Human Settlements Programme (UN-Habitat);* b. 26 Aug. 1961, Kuala Pilah, Negeri Sembilan; m. Adli Lai Abdullah; two d.; ed Univ. of Wales Inst. of Science and Tech., Univ. of Science, Malaysia; Town Planning Officer, Municipal Council of Penang Island 1985–2003, Dir Dept of Planning and Devt 2003–09, Mayor City Council of Penang Island July 2017–Jan. 2018; Founder and Gen. Manager George Town World Heritage Inc. 2009–11, also mem. Bd of Dirs; Pres. Municipal Council of Seberang Perai 2011–17; Exec. Dir UN Human Settlements Programme (UN-Habitat) 2018–; Planner of The Year, Malaysian Inst. of Planners 2014, Global Human Settlements Outstanding Contribution Award 2016. *Address:* United Nations Human Settlements Programme (UN-Habitat), PO Box 30030, Nairobi, Kenya (office). *Telephone:* (20) 621234 (office). *Fax:* (20) 624266 (office). *E-mail:* infohabitat@ unhabitat.org (office). *Website:* www.unhabitat.org (office).

SHARIF, Mian Mohammed Nawaz; Pakistani politician and industrialist; b. 25 Dec. 1949, Lahore; s. of Mian Muhammad Sharif; brother of Mian Mohammed Shebaz Sharif; m. Kulsoom Nawaz (deceased) 1971; two s. two d.; ed Govt Coll. and Punjab Univ. Law Coll., Lahore; started work in Ittefaq faction industrial group 1969; joined Panjab Advisory Council 1981; Finance Minister, Govt of the Punjab 1981–85, Chief Minister of Punjab 1985–90; Prime Minister 1990–93 (dismissal ruled unconstitutional), resgnd July 1993, Prime Minister 1997–99, concurrently Minister of Defence and Finance (removed in coup by Gen. Pervez Musharraf), Prime Minister 2013–17, Minister of Defence June–Nov. 2013; sentenced to life imprisonment for terrorism and hijacking April 2000; released from imprisonment, went into exile in Jeddah, Saudi Arabia Dec. 2000, allowed to return to Pakistan Aug. 2007; Pres. Pakistan Muslim League, Punjab 1985, Islami Jamhoori Ittehad 1988; Leader, Pakistan Muslim League—Nawaz (PML—N) 1993–99, 2011–18; ordered Pakistan's nuclear tests in response to those of India May 1998; barred by Supreme Court from contesting elections or holding public office early 2009, defied house arrest to lead anti-govt protests March 2009. *Leisure interests:* social work, photography, hunting, playing cricket. *Address:* c/o Pakistan Muslim League—Nawaz, House 20-H, Street 10, Sector F-8/3, Islamabad (office); 180–181-H, Ittefaq Colony, Model Town, Lahore, Pakistan (home). *Telephone:* (51) 2852662 (office). *Fax:* (51) 2852662 (office). *E-mail:* info@pmln.org (office). *Website:* pmln.org (office).

SHARIF, Mian Muhammad Shehbaz; Pakistani politician; *President, Pakistan Muslim League—Nawaz;* b. 23 Sept. 1951, Lahore, Punjab Prov.; brother of Mian Mohammed Nawaz Sharif, fmr Prime Minister of Pakistan; m. 1st Nusrat Shahbaz 1973 (died 1993); two s. three d.; m. 2nd Nargis Khosa 1993 (deceased); m. 3rd Aaliya Honey 1993 (divorced); m. 4th Tehmina Durrani 2003; m. 5th Kalsoom Hayi 2012; elected to Provincial Ass. (Constituency PP-122) 1988, (Constituency PP-124) 1990, (Constituency PP-125) 1993, (Constituency PP-125) 1997; elected to Nat. Ass. of Pakistan (Constituency NA-96) 1990, (Constituency NA-96) 1993, 1997, Chair. Public Accounts Cttee 2018–; Chief Minister of Punjab 1997–99 (ousted in mil. coup of Gen. Pervez Musharraf 1999), 2008–March 2013, June 2013–18; Pres. Pakistan Muslim League—Nawaz 2002–11, Pres. 2018–; lived in exile in Saudi Arabia and London before being allowed to return to Pakistan 2007. *Address:* Pakistan Muslim League—Nawaz, House 20-H, Street 10, Sector F-8/3, Islamabad, Pakistan (office). *Telephone:* (51) 2852662 (office). *Fax:* (51) 2852662 (office). *E-mail:* cmshehbaz@pmln.org (office). *Website:* pmln.org (office).

SHARIF, Osama Al, BA; Jordanian/Canadian publisher, journalist, columnist and media consultant; *Chairman, Media-Arabia;* b. 14 June 1960, Jerusalem, Jordan; s. of Mahmoud Al Sharif and Aida Al Sharif; m. Ghada Yasser Amr 1984; one s. one d.; ed Univ. of Missouri, USA; Chief Ed. The Jerusalem Star 1985–88; Pres. Info-Media, Jordan 1989–; Publr, Chief Ed. and weekly columnist, The Star, Jordan 1990–; Publr Arabian Communications & Publishing (ACP) 1994–97, BYTE Middle East 1994–97, Al Tiqaniyyah Wal 'Amal 1995–97; Chief Ed. and Dir General Arabia.com 1999–2002; Chief Ed. Addustour Newspaper 2003–06; Ed. Al-Ittihad daily newspaper, Abu Dhabi, UAE Jan.–June 2009; Chair. Media-Arabia 2006–; mem. Royal Cttee for the Nat. Agenda, Amman, Jordan 2005. *Leisure interests:* novel and short-story writing, travel, photography, horse riding. *Address:* PO Box 9313, Amman 11191, Jordan (office). *Telephone:* (6) 5922161 (office). *Fax:* (6) 5922161 (office). *E-mail:* osama@mediaarabia.com (office). *Website:* www.mediaarabia.com (office).

SHARIF, Gen. Raheel; Pakistani army officer (retd); *Commander-in-Chief, Islamic Military Alliance;* b. 16 June 1956, Quetta; s. of Maj. Muhammad Sharif; m.; two s. one d.; ed Govt Coll., Lahore, Pakistan Mil. Acad., Bundeswehr Univ., Germany, Nat. Defense Univ., Canadian Army Command and Staff Coll., Canada, Royal Coll. of Defense Studies, UK; commissioned into 6th Bn, Frontier Force Regt 1976, joined infantry brigade in Gilgit, Adjutant, Pakistan Mil. Acad., Gen. Officer Commanding, 11th Infantry Div., Lahore, commanded several infantry units, including 6 Frontier Force Regt, Kashmir, 26 Frontier Force Regt, Commdt, Pakistan Mil. Acad., Chief of Staff, 30 Corps, 12 Corps; Commdr, Gujranwala 30

Corps, Prin. Staff Officer to Ashfaque Parvez Kayani and Insp. Gen. for Training and Evaluation, Pakistan Army –2013, Chief of Army Staff 2013–16 (retd), mem. Faculty, Command and Staff Coll., Quetta; C-in-C, (39-Nation) Islamic Military Alliance 2017–; Hilal-e-Imtiaz, Nishan-e-Imtiaz 2013, Order of Abdulaziz Al Saud. (Saudi Arabia), Order of Merit (Brazil) 2015, and several others. *Leisure interests:* reading, swimming, hunting. *Address:* c/o Ministry of Defence, Pakistan Secretariat, No. II, Rawalpindi 46000, Pakistan.

ŞÄRIFOV, Samir Rauf oğlu, MA; Azerbaijani economist and government official; *Minister of Finance;* b. 7 Sept. 1961; m.; two c.; ed Kiev State Univ.; foreign econ. relations specialist in USSR 1983–91; Deputy Chief, Dept of Int. Econ. Relations, Ministry of Foreign Affairs 1991–95; Chief of Dept, then Exec. Dir Nat. Bank of Azerbaijan 1995–2001; Exec. Dir State Oil Fund of Repub. of Azerbaijan (SOFAZ) 2001–06, also Azerbaijan Rep. and Dir Black Sea Trade and Devt Bank 2001–06; Chair. Govt Comm. on Extractive Industries Transparency Initiative 2003–06; Minister of Finance 2006–. *Address:* Ministry of Finance, 1022 Baku, Samed Vurghun küç. 83, Azerbaijan (office). *Telephone:* (12) 493-30-12 (office). *Fax:* (12) 493-05-62 (office). *E-mail:* office@maliyye.gov.az (office). *Website:* maliyye .gov.az (office).

SHARKEY, Baron (Life Peer), cr. 2010, of Niton Undercliff in the County of Isle of Wight; **John Sharkey;** British/Irish management consultant and advertising executive; *Chairman, Sharkey Associates Ltd;* b. 24 Sept. 1947; Co-founder and fmr Chair. Bainsfair Sharkey Trott advertising agency; fmr Jt Man. Dir Saatchi & Saatchi UK; fmr Deputy Chair. Saatchi International; fmr Chair. BDDP Holdings Ltd, Highland Partners Europe; fmr COO Blue Arrow Plc; Adviser to Nick Clegg, Leader of Liberal Democratic Party, on Strategic Communications 2008–10, Chair. Liberal Democrat Gen. Election campaign 2010; Chair. Sharkey Assocs Ltd (man. consultancy) 1998–; mem. Council of Hansard Soc. 2004–, Hon. Treas. 2007–10; mem. (Liberal Democrat) House of Lords 2010–. *Address:* Sharkey Associates Ltd, Carmelite, 50 Victoria Embankment, Blackfriars, London, EC4Y 0LS (office); House of Lords, Westminster, London, SW1A 0PW, England. *Telephone:* (20) 7219-5353 (Westminster). *Fax:* (20) 7219-5979 (Westminster). *E-mail:* sharkeyjk@ parliament.uk.

SHARMA, Damodar Prasad, MCom, LLM; Nepalese judge; b. 10 Oct. 1949, Kathmandu; joined Judicial Service as Section Officer, Supreme Court 1974; Dist Judge 1975–85; Personal Sec. of Chief Justice 1984–86; Zonal Court Judge 1986–91; Judge, Appellate Court 1991–2004, apptd Chief Judge 2004; apptd Justice, Supreme Court 2005, Acting Chief Justice 2013–14, Chief Justice April–Oct. 2014; Pres. Revenue Tribunal 1999–2002; mem. Special Court 2002–03.

SHARMA, Janardan, (Prabhakar); Nepalese army officer (retd) and politician; ed Tribhuvan Univ.; fmrly one of the four Deputy Supreme-Commdrs of the People's Liberation Army of Nepal; mem. Communist Party of Nepal (Maoist Centre) (CPN—MC); elected to the Rukum-2 constituency 2008; Minister of Energy 2016–17, Minister of Home Affairs 2017–18; currently Chair. Central Natural Disaster Relief Cttee. *Address:* c/o Ministry of Home Affairs, Singha Durbar, Kathmandu, Nepal (office). *Telephone:* (1) 4211214 (office). *Fax:* (1) 4211286 (office). *E-mail:* gunaso@moha.gov.np (office). *Website:* www.moha.gov.np (office); www.janardansharma.com.

SHARMA, Kamalesh; Indian diplomatist and international organization official; b. 30 Sept. 1941; m. Babli Sharma; one s. one d.; ed St Stephen's Coll., Delhi Univ., King's Coll. Cambridge, UK; joined Indian Foreign Service 1965, Head of Divs of Econ. Relations, Int. Orgs and Policy Planning, Head of Div. Ministry of Finance, postings in Bonn, Hong Kong, Saudi Arabia and Turkey, Amb. to fmr GDR, Kazakhstan, Kyrgyzstan, Amb. to UN, Geneva, also Amb. for Disarmament and Spokesman for developing countries in UNCTAD, Perm. Rep. to UN, New York 1997–2002; Special Rep. of UN Sec.-Gen. for East Timor (now Timor-Leste) and Head of UN Mission of Support in East Timor (UNMISET) 2002–04; Dir Int. Peace Acad., New York; High Commr to UK 2004–08; Sec.-Gen. The Commonwealth 2008–16; Chancellor, Queen's Univ. Belfast 2009–15; Fellow, Weatherhead Center for Int. Affairs, Harvard Univ.; mem. US Foreign Policy Asscn; fmr mem. Bd of Dirs Peace Acad., New York, Education Consultants India Ltd; Gov. Ditchley Foundation; Hon. LLD (De Montfort Univ., UK); Medal of US Foreign Policy Asscn. *Publications include:* Mille Fleurs: Poetry from Around the World (compilation of poems by diplomats and officials) (ed.), Imagining Tomorrow: Rethinking the Global Challenge. *Leisure interests:* literature, cosmology, cricket, Indian and western classical music and jazz. *Address:* c/o Commonwealth Secretariat, Marlborough House, Pall Mall, London, SW1Y 5HX, England.

SHARMA, Konkona Sen, BA; Indian actress; b. 3 Dec. 1979, New Delhi; d. of Mukul Sharma and Aparna Sen Sharma; m. Ranvir Shorey 2010; ed St Stephen's Coll., Univ. of Delhi; hosted TV show My Brilliant Brain 2007. *Films include:* Indira 1983, Picnic 1989, The Girl Ria 2000, Mr and Mrs Iyer (Nat. Film Award 2003) 2002, Chai Pani Etc. 2004, Amu Kaju 2005, Page 3 (Kalakar Award 2005) 2005, Karkat Rashi 2005, 15 Park Avenue 2005, Dosar (Mahindra Indo-American Arts Council Film Festival Award 2007) 2005, Mixed Doubles 2005, The Companion 2006, Yun Hota Toh Kya Hota 2006, Omkara (Nat. Film Award 2007) 2006, Deadline: Sirf 24 Ghante 2006, Meridian Lines 2007, Life in a Metro (Filmfare Award 2008, Popular Award 2008) 2007, Traffic Signal 2007, Aaja Nachle 2007, Laaga Chunari Mein Daag (Filmfare Best Supporting Actress Award 2007) 2007, Zeinab 2008, Dil Kabaddi 2008, The President Is Coming 2009, Wake Up Sid 2009, Atithi Tum Kab Jaoge 2010, Right Ya Wrong 2010, Mirch 2010, Goynar Baksho (Filmfare Best Actor Female Award 2013) 2013, A Death In The Gunj (Director, Int. Indian Film Acad. Award for Best Debut Director 2018) 2017. *Play:* The Blue Mug 2009.

SHARMA, Lt-Gen. (retd) Nirbhay, MSc, MPhil; Indian state official and fmr army officer; b. 1946; m. Jyotsna Sharma; one s. one d.; ed Nat. Defence Acad., Univ. of Madras; commissioned into Indian Army 1966, service included combat in Indo-Pakistani War 1971 as part of Airborne Assault Group, later roles include Dir Gen. (Perspective Planning) at Army HQ, Master Gen. of Ordnance, Corps Commdr and Security Adviser to Govt of Jammu and Kashmir, retd from army 2008; mem. Union Public Service Comm. of India 2008–13; Gov. of Arunachal Pradesh 2013–15, of Mizoram 2015–18; Distinguished Fellow, Observer Research Foundation, New Delhi; mem. Indian Nat. Congress; numerous mil. awards including Param Vishisht Seva Medal, Uttam Yudh Seva Medal, Ati Vishisht Seva

Medal, Vishisht Seva Medal. *Address:* c/o Office of the Governor, Raj Bhavan, Aizawl 796 001, India (office). *Website:* mizoram.nic.in/gov/governor.htm.

SHARMA, R. S.; Indian energy industry executive; *Managing Director, Bajaj Power Ventures Private Ltd;* ed Govt Eng Coll., Rewa, MP; apptd Dir (Finance) Oil and Natural Gas Corpn (ONGC) Ltd 2002, Acting Chair. and Man. Dir May–Aug. 2006, Chair. and Man. Dir 2006–11; joined Nat. Thermal Power Corpn (NTPC) 1980, Gen. Man. of Singrauli (Northern Region), Exec. Dir Corporate Planning –2008, Chair. and Man. Dir Ltd 2008–10; Man. Dir Jindal Power Ltd 2010–15; Man. Dir Bajaj Power Ventures Private Ltd (holding co. including Bajaj Energy Private Ltd and Lalitpur Power Generation Co. Ltd) 2015–; mem. Bd of Dirs ONGC Videsh Ltd 2002–, PTC India Ltd 2004–08, Mangalore Refinery and Petrochemicals Ltd –2011, ONGC Mittal Energy Services Ltd, NTPC Vidyut Vyapar Nigam Ltd, Indian Oil Corpn Ltd –2007; Fellow and mem. Inst. of Cost and Works Accountants of India; Assoc. mem. Indian Inst. of Bankers; Hon. Fellow, All India Man. Asscn 2010; India Chief Financial Officer Award 2005 – Excellence in Finance in a PSU, CNBC-TV18 CFO Award 2006 for Excellence in Finance in Oil and Allied Services, Amity Leadership Award for Corp. Excellence in Oil & Gas Industry, Amity Business School 2009. *Address:* Bajaj Power Ventures Private Ltd, Bajaj Bhavan, 2nd Floor, Jamnalal Bajaj Marg, 226 Nariman Point, Mumbai 400 021, India (office). *Website:* www.bajajenergy.com (office).

SHARMA, Sheel Kant, MS, PhD; Indian diplomatist and international organization executive; b. 10 Jan. 1950; m. Meenu Sharma; ed Indian Inst. of Tech., Mumbai; joined Indian Foreign Service 1973, served as Third Sec., Embassy in Kuwait and Second Sec., Embassy in Riyadh 1976–77, Under-Sec., Middle East Desk, Ministry of External Affairs 1978–81, Fellow, Inst. of Defence Studies and Analysis, New Delhi 1981–82, Deputy Sec. (North), Ministry of External Affairs 1982–83, First Sec. (Disarmament), Perm. Mission to UN, Geneva and Alt. Rep. to UN Conf. on Disarmament 1983–86, Counsellor and Deputy Chief of Mission, Embassy in Algiers 1986–89, Dir (UN Div.) and Disarmament Head, Ministry of External Affairs, New Delhi 1989–91, Jt Sec. (South and Disarmament) in charge of India's relations with ASEAN, Indo-China and South Pacific 1991–94, seconded to IAEA, Vienna, served as sr professional in External Relations and Policy Coordination Div. 1994–2000, Jt Sec. (Disarmament and Int. Security Affairs) 2000–03, Additional Sec. (Int. Orgs), Ministry of External Affairs 2003–04, Amb. to Austria and Perm. Rep. to all Int. Orgs, Vienna 2004–08, Chair. G-77 Vienna Chapter 2005, Sec.-Gen. SAARC 2008–11; columnist, The Indian Express, Inst. of Peace and Conflicts Studies; mem. India Int. Centre, India Habitat Centre; Distinguished Aluminus Award, Indian Inst. of Tech. Mumbai 2007. *Publications include:* UN Report on Verification (co-author) 1991, UN Report on Defensive Security Concepts (co-author) 1992, UNIDIR Monograph on Verification of Fissile Materials Cut-Off and Non-use of Nuclear Weapons 1992, article in IAEA Bulletin 1995, paper presented at Pugwash Conf. on Energy in Malta 1995, UN panel's report on missile in all their aspects (co-author) 2002; articles in scientific journals and in newspapers and periodicals. *Leisure interests:* literature, readings on science and tech., basketball, tennis, swimming, yoga, chess.

SHARMA, Shikha; Indian banking executive; b. 19 Nov. 1958; m. Sanjaya Sharma; ed Lady Shriram Coll., Indian Inst. of Man., Ahmedabad; began career with Industrial Credit and Investment Corpn India Ltd in 1980, was instrumental in setting up group's investment banking business, Head of ICICI Prudential Life Insurance Co. Ltd –2009; Man. Dir and CEO Axis Bank Ltd (India's third-largest pvt. bank) 2009–18; numerous business awards, including Entrepreneur of the Year, E&Y Entrepreneur Awards 2007, Businesswoman of the Year, Economic Times Awards 2008, Transformational Business Leader of the Year, AIMA Managing India Awards 2012, Woman Leader of the Year, UTV Financial Leadership Awards 2012, Businessworld's Banker of the Year Award 2012.

SHARMAN, Baron (Life Peer), cr. 1999, of Redlynch in the County of Wiltshire; **Colin Morven Sharman,** OBE, FCA, CIMgt; British chartered accountant and business executive; b. 19 Feb. 1943; s. of Col Terence John Sharman and Audrey Emmiline Newman; m. Angela M. Timmins 1966; one s. one d.; ed Bishops Wordsworth School, Salisbury; qualified as accountant with Woolgar Hennel & Co. 1965; joined Peat Marwick Mitchell 1966 (later KPMG Peat Marwick, now KPMG), Man. Frankfurt Office 1970–72, The Hague Office 1972–81 (Partner 1973, Partner-in-Charge 1975), London Office 1981–, Sr Partner, Nat. Marketing and Industry Groups 1987–90, Sr Man. Consultancy Partner 1989–91, Sr Regional Partner, London and SE 1990–93, Sr Partner 1994–98, Chair. KPMG Int. 1997–99; Deputy Chair. Aegis Group plc 1999, Chair. 1999–2008; Deputy Chair. (non-exec.) Group 4 Securicor (now G4S) plc 2003, 2004–05, Chair. (non-exec.) Nov. 2003–04; mem. Bd of Dirs Aviva plc 2005–12, Chair. (non-exec.) 2006–12; Pres. GamCare 2011–; Dir (non-exec.) AEA Technology plc 1996–2002, Young & Co.'s Brewery plc 1999–2002, BG Group PLC 2000–11, Reed Elsevier plc 2002–11; mem. Supervisory Bd ABN AMRO Holding NV 2003–07; mem. Industrial Soc.; completed a study of Cen. Govt Audit and Accountability commissioned by Chief Sec. to The Treasury 2002; Hon. mem. Securities Inst.; Dr hc (Cranfield Univ.) 1998. *Publication:* Living Culture 2001. *Leisure interests:* food and wine, sailing, opera. *Address:* House of Lords, Westminster, London, SW1A 2PW, England (office). *Telephone:* (20) 7219-8622 (office).

SHARMAN, Helen Patricia, CMG, OBE, BSc, MA, CChem, FRAeS, FRGS, FBIS, MSCI, FIST; British fmr manager, astronaut and industrial scientist; *UK Outreach Ambassador, Imperial College, London;* b. 30 May 1963, Sheffield; d. of John David Sharman and Lyndis Mary Sharman; ed Univ. of Sheffield and Univ. Coll., London; Engineer and Section Head, Marconi Osram Valve 1984–87; Research Technologist, Mars Confectionery Ltd 1987–89; selected to be first Briton in space as part of Juno Space Mission 1989, travelled to Mir space station 1991; science communicator and broadcaster 1991–99; Group Leader, Surface and Nanoanalysis Group, Nat. Physical Lab. 2010–13; Faculty Tech. Man., Kingston Univ. 2013–15; Departmental Operations Man., Dept of Chem., Imperial Coll., London 2015–18, UK Outreach Amb. 2019–; apptd Pres. Inst. of Science and Tech. 2017; Hon. FRSC; Freedom of the City of Sheffield 1991. *Publications:* Seize the Moment 1993, The Space Place 1997. *Address:* Imperial College London, Exhibition Road, London, SW7 2AZ, England (office); c/o DBA Speakers, Landmark House, Station Road, Hook, Hampshire, RG27 9HA, England (office). *E-mail:* h.sharman@imperial.ac.uk (office); info@dbaspeakers.com (office). *Website:* www.helensharman.com; www.dbaspeakers.com (office). *Telephone:* (19) 3222-8544 (office).

SHARMARKE, Omar Abdirashid Ali, BA, MA; Somali/Canadian diplomatist and politician; b. 18 June 1960, Mogadishu; s. of Abdirashid Ali Shermarke (fmr Pres. of Somalia assassinated in 1969) and Ruqia Dahir Ali Boss; m.; ed Carleton Univ., Canada; consultant to Coca Cola, Somali Bottling Co., Mogadishu 1984–90; Project Consultant, Somali Devt Bank 1988–90; with Centre for Peace and Democratic Initiatives, Ottawa, Canada 1993–2000; worked for UN in various capacities including Political/Civil Affairs Officer, Civil Affairs Division, UNAMSIL (Sierra Leone) 2000–05, UNMIS (Sudan) 2006, Political Adviser, Darfur-Darfur Dialogue and Consultations 2006–07; Foreign Policy Adviser, Transitional Fed. Govt of Somalia 2007–09; Amb.-designate to USA 2009; Prime Minister 2009–10 (resgnd), 2014–17; Amb. to USA July–Dec. 2014; cand. in presidential election 2017.

SHARP, Hon. John Randall; Australian politician (retd) and company director; b. 15 Dec. 1954, Sydney; s. of J.K. Sharp; m. Victoria Sharp 1986; two s. one d.; ed The King's School, NSW, Orange Agricultural Coll.; fmr farmer; mem. House of Reps for Gilmore, NSW 1984–93; MP (Nat. Party of Australia) for Hume, NSW 1993–98, Shadow Minister for Tourism and Sport 1988, for Tourism, Sport and Youth Affairs 1988–89, for Land Transport and Shipping 1989–90, for Shipping and Waterfront Reform 1990–93, for Transport 1993–96; Minister for Transport and Regional Devt 1996–97, Deputy Man. of Opposition Business in the House 1990–94; Exec. Dir Linfox (now ADI–Fox) 1999–2001, Corp. adviser 1999–2001; Founder and Chair. Thenford Consulting (transport consulting co.) 1998; Chair. Aviation Safety Foundation of Australasia (later named Flight Safety International) 2003–10, Power and Data Corpn 2004–15; Deputy Chair. Regional Express Airlines 2005–; Chair. Pel Air 2006–; mem. Bd of Dirs EADS Australia Pacific (renamed Airbus Group Australia Pacific) 2001–15, Sky Traders 2005–13; fmr mem. Bd of Dirs French-Australian Chamber of Commerce and Industry; mem. Advisory Council, Parsons Brinckerhoff 2007–10; mem. Univ. of Wollongong Vice-Chancellor's Advisory Bd; mem. Nat. Party of Australia, Hon. Fed. Treas. 2000–05; Chair. Winifred West Foundation 2001; Co-Chair. Cancer Council of NSW, Southern Highlands Br.; Fellow, Chartered Inst. of Transport; apptd mem. Climate Change Authority 2015; Trustee John McKeown House; Hon. Sec. Nat. Party of Australia. *Leisure interests:* rugby union, scuba diving, skiing, tennis, aviation. *Address:* Thenford Consulting, 413A Nowra Road, Moss Vale, NSW 2577; Climate Change Authority, GPO Box 1944, Melbourne, VIC 3001, Australia. *E-mail:* enquiries@climatechangeauthority.gov.au. *Website:* www.climatechangeauthority.gov.au.

SHARP, Phillip Allen, PhD; American biologist, academic and academic administrator; *Institute Professor, Massachusetts Institute of Technology;* b. 6 June 1944, Falmouth, Ky; s. of Joseph W. Sharp and Katherin A. Sharp; m. Ann H. Holcombe 1964; three d.; ed Union Coll., Ky, Univ. of Illinois, California Inst. of Tech. and Cold Spring Harbor, New York; Research Asst, Dept of Chem., Univ. of Ill. 1966–69; Postdoctoral Fellow, Lab. of Prof. Norman Davidson, Calif. Inst. of Tech. 1969–71, Cold Spring Harbor Lab. 1971–72, Sr Research Investigator 1972–74; Assoc. Prof., Center for Cancer Research and Dept of Biology, MIT 1974–79, Prof. 1979–99, Inst. Prof. 1999–; Assoc. Dir Center for Cancer Research 1982–85, Dir 1985–91, Head of Dept of Biology 1991–99; Founding Dir The McGovern Inst. for Brain Research 2000–04; Co-founder and Chair. Scientific Bd Biogen Idec, Inc. –2002, mem. Bd of Dirs –2009; mem. Bd of Dirs Alnylam Pharmaceuticals, Whitehead Inst., MIT 2005–, Syros Pharmaceuticals, Vir Biotechnology; mem. Scientific Advisory Bd, Fidelity Biosciences Group 2004–; Chair. Gen. Motors Cancer Research Foundation Awards Ass. 1994–2006, Scientific Advisory Cttee Dana-Farber Cancer Inst. 1996, Scientific Review Council Cancer Prevention and Research Inst. of Texas 2009–12, Scientific Advisory Cttee, SU2C Project, AACR 2008–; Co-Chair. NRC Cttee on A New Biology for the 21st Century: Ensuring the United States Leads the Coming Biology Revolution, NAS 2008–10, MIT's Production in an Innovation Economy (PIE) Comm. 2010–; mem. Cttee on Science, Eng and Public Policy 1992–95, Pres.'s Advisory Council on Science and Tech. 1991–97, Nat. Cancer Advisory Bd, NIH (Presidential appointment) 1996, Scientific Bd of Advisors, Van Andel Inst. 1996–, Scientific Cttee Ludwig Inst. for Cancer Research 1998–2008, Bd of Scientific Govs, Scripps Research Inst. 1999–, Bd FDA's Reagan-Udall Foundation 2008–, Howard Hughes Medical Inst. Medical Advisory Bd and Review Cttee 2011–; mem. and Trustee Alfred P. Sloan Foundation 1995–2004; mem. Bd Trustees Massachusetts Gen. Hosp. 2002–10, Cttee Research and Educ., Partners HealthCare Systems Inc. 2003–, Bd Advisors Polaris Ventures; mem. NAS, NAS Inst. of Medicine, American Acad. of Arts and Sciences, American Philosophical Soc.; Pres. AAAS 2014; Foreign Fellow, Royal Soc. (UK); Hon. mem. Nat. Acad. of Sciences, Repub. of Korea; Hon. Academician, Academia Sinica, Repub. of China (Taiwan); Hon. DSc (Univ. of Kentucky), (Univ. of Tel-Aviv), (Thomas More Coll., Ky), (Univ. of Glasgow), (Albright Coll., Pa), (Rippon Coll., Wis.), (Univ. of Minnesota); Hon. MD (Uppsala Univ.); Dr hc (Union Coll., Ky), (Univ. of Buenos Aires), (McGill Univ.), (Scripps Research Inst.); Howard Ricketts Award, Eli Lilly Award, NAS US Steel Foundation Award, Gen. Motors Research Foundation Alfred P. Sloan, Jr Prize for Cancer Research, Gairdner Foundation Int. Award, New York Acad. of Sciences Award in Biological and Medical Sciences, Louisa Gross Horwitz Prize, Albert Lasker Basic Medical Research Award, Dickson Prize (Univ. of Pittsburgh), Nobel Prize in Physiology or Medicine (with Richard J. Roberts) 1993, Benjamin Franklin Medal, American Philosophical Soc. 1999, Walter Prize, Museum of Science, Boston, Nat. Medal of Science 2004, Inaugural Double Helix Medal for Scientific Research, Cold Spring Harbor Lab., AACR Irving Weinstein Distinguished Lectureship Award 2006, Karl Friedrich Bonhoeffer Lecture, Max Planck Inst., Göttigen, Germany, Winthrop-Sears Award, Chemists' Club of New York 2007, Othmer Gold Medal 2015, Raymond and Beverly Sackler Award for Sustained Nat. Leadership 2017. *Publications:* numerous papers in scientific journals. *Leisure interests:* family, reading, sports. *Address:* Room 76-461, Koch Institute for Integrative Cancer Research, Massachusetts Institute of Technology, 500 Main Street, Cambridge, MA 02139, USA (office). *Telephone:* (617) 253-6425 (office). *Fax:* (617) 253-3867 (office). *E-mail:* sharppa@mit.edu (office). *Website:* web.mit.edu/sharplab (office).

SHARPE, William Forsyth, PhD; American economist and academic; *STANCO 25 Professor Emeritus of Finance, Graduate School of Business, Stanford University;* b. 16 June 1934, Cambridge, Mass; s. of Russell Thornley Sharpe and Evelyn Forsyth Maloy Sharpe (née Jillson); m. 1st Roberta Ruth Branton 1954 (divorced 1986); one s. one d.; m. 2nd Kathryn Dorothy Peck 1986; one step-s. one step-d.; ed Univ. of California, Los Angeles; Economist, RAND Corpn 1957–61; Asst Prof. of Econs, Univ. of Washington 1961–63, Assoc. Prof. 1963–67, Prof. 1967–68; Prof., Univ. of Calif., Irvine 1968–70; Timken Prof. of Finance, Stanford Univ. 1970–89, Prof. Emer. 1989–92, Prof. of Finance 1993–95, STANCO 25 Prof. of Finance 1995–99, Prof. Emer. 1999–; Pres. William F. Sharpe Assocs 1986–92; Founder and Chair. Financial Engines Inc. 1996–2003; Hon. DHumLitt (De Paul Univ.) 1997, Dr hc (Alicante Univ.) 2003, (Univ. of Vienna) 2004, Hon. DSc (Econs) (London Business School) 2008; Graham and Dodd Award 1972, 1973, 1986, 1988, Nicholas Molodovsky Award 1989, Nobel Prize for Econ. Sciences 1990, UCLA Medal 1998. *Publications include:* Economics of Computers 1969, Portfolio Theory and Capital Markets 1970, Asset Allocation Tools 1987, Investments 1999, Fundamentals of Investments (second edn) 2000, Investors and Markets 2007. *Leisure interests:* sailing, all kinds of music. *Address:* Graduate School of Business, Stanford University, Stanford, CA 94305, USA (office). *E-mail:* wfsharpe@stanford.edu (office). *Website:* www.stanford.edu/~wfsharpe (office).

SHARPLESS, K(arl) Barry, BA, PhD; American chemist and academic; *W.M. Keck Professor of Chemistry, Scripps Research Institute;* b. 28 April 1941, Philadelphia, Pa; s. of Dr E. Dallett Sharpless and Evelyn Anderson Sharpless; m. Jan Sharpless; two s. one d.; ed Dartmouth Coll., New Hampshire, Stanford Univ., Harvard Univ.; mem. Chem. Faculty, MIT 1970–77, 1980–90, Arthur C. Cope Prof. 1987–90; mem. Chem. Faculty, Stanford Univ. 1977–80; W.M. Keck Prof. of Chem., The Scripps Research Inst. (TSRI), La Jolla, Calif. 1990–, Skaggs Inst. for Chemical Biology, TSRI 1996–; mem. AAAS 1984, American Acad. of Arts and Sciences 1984, NAS 1985; Hon. mem. RSC 1998; numerous hon. degrees, including Dr hc (Dartmouth Coll.) 1995, (Royal Inst. of Tech., Stockholm) 1995, (Tech. Univ., Munich) 1995, (Catholic Univ. of Louvain) 1996, (Wesleyan Univ.) 1999; numerous fellowships, including A.P. Sloan Foundation Fellow 1973, Camille and Henry Dreyfus Foundation Fellow 1973, Simon Guggenheim Foundation Fellow 1987, ten prizes from the ACS including Arthur C. Cope Scholar 1986, and Award 1992, San Diego Scientist of the Year 1992, Roger Adams Award in Organic Chem. 1997; Janssen Prize 1986, Prelog Medal, ETH, Zürich 1988, Sammet Award, Goethe Univ., Frankfurt 1988, Chemical Pioneer Award (American Inst. of Chemists) 1988, Scheele Medal (Swedish Acad. of Pharma Sciences) 1991, Tetrahedron Prize 1993, King Faisal Prize for Science (Saudi Arabia) 1995, Microbial Chem. Award, Kitasato Inst., Tokyo 1997, Harvey Science and Tech. Prize, Israel Inst. of Tech. 1998, Organic Reactions Catalysis Soc. Richard Rylander Award 2000, NAS Chemical Sciences Award 2000, Chirality Medal, Italian Chemical Soc. 2000, Nobel Prize in Chem. 2001 (jt recipient), Benjamin Franklin Medal Medal, Philadelphia 2001, Wolf Prize in Science (jtly) 2001, Rhône-Poulenc Medal (UK) 2001, John Scott Prize and Medal, Philadelphia 2001. *Publications:* more than 300 publs in learned journals and 20 patents. *Address:* Scripps Research Institute, 10550 North Torrey Pines Road, BCC-315, La Jolla, CA 92037, USA (office). *Telephone:* (858) 784-7505 (office). *Fax:* (858) 784-7562 (office). *E-mail:* sharples@scripps.edu (office). *Website:* www.scripps.edu/chem/sharpless (office).

SHARPLESS, Norman (Ned) E., MD; American academic; *Director, National Cancer Institute;* b. 20 Sept. 1966, Greensboro, North Carolina; m. Julie L. Sharpless; two c.; ed Univ. of North Carolina, Chapel Hill; Research Scholar, Howard Hughes Medical Inst. 1990–91, also Post-Doctoral Research Fellow 1998–2001; Resident in Medicine, Mass Gen. Hosp., Boston 1993–96; Instructor in Medicine, Harvard Medical School 2000–02; Physician, Brigham and Women's Hosp. 2000–02, Dana Farber Cancer Inst. 2000–02; John Motley Morehead Scholar, Univ. of North Carolina, Chapel Hill 1984–88, Asst Prof. of Medicine and Genetics 2002–08, then Assoc. Prof. 2008–11, Prof. 2011–12, co-founder and co-dir, Mouse Phase 1 Unit 2006–, co-dir Experimental Therapeutics Program, Lineberger Comprehensive Cancer Center 2007, now Dir 2014–, Assoc. Dir for Basic Science in Aging, Center for Aging and Health 2007–, Wellcome Prof. of Cancer Research 2012–; Dir Nat. Cancer Inst. 2017–; Paul Beeson Physician Faculty Scholar, Aging and Research 2003–2006; Deputy Ed. Journal of Clinical Investigation 2012–; elected Councilor, Nat. Insts of Aging, Md 2016; mem. Bd of Oncology, American Bd of Internal Medicine 1999–; mem. Scientific Advisory Bd, Adenoid Cystic Carcinoma Research Foundation 2005–; mem. Editorial Bd, Aging Cell 2008–, Impact Aging; mem. American Soc. of Clinical Investigation 2008–, council mem. 2011–14; mem. Bd of Dirs, Asscn of American Cancer Inst. 2016–; Cancer Research Scholar Award, Sidney Kimmel Foundation 2003, New Scholar Award, Ellison Medical Foundation 2005, Jefferson-Pilot Fellowship in Academic Medicine 2007, Clinical Scientist in Translational Research Award, Burroughs-Wellcome Fund 2007, Phillip and Ruth Hettleman Prize for Artistic and Scholarly Achievement, Univ. of North Carolina, Chapel Hill 2009, Glenn Award for Research in Biological Mechanisms of Aging, Glenn Foundation for Medical Research 2010, Health Care Innovator of the Year, Triangle Business Journal 2012. *Publications include:* more than 170 reports, reviews and book chapters. *Address:* Office of the Director, National Cancer Institute, 31 Center Drive, Bethesda, MD 20814, USA (office). *Telephone:* (240) 781-3300 (office). *E-mail:* norman.sharpless@nih.gov (office). *Website:* www.cancer.gov (office).

SHARQI, HH Sheikh Hamad bin Muhammad ash-, (Ruler of Fujairah); United Arab Emirates; b. 25 Sept. 1948; s. of Sheikh Mohammed bin Hamad ash-Sharqi and Sheikha Fatima bint Rashid an-Nuaimi; m. Fatima bint Thani al-Maktoum; three s. three d.; ed Eastbourne School of English, UK, Mons Mil. Acad., Hendon Police Coll.; Minister of Agric. and Fisheries, UAE Fed. Cabinet 1971–74; Ruler of Fujairah 1974–; mem. Supreme Council 1974–. *Address:* Emiri Court, PO Box 1, Fujairah, United Arab Emirates.

SHASHKIN, Dimitri; Georgian politician; b. 8 Aug. 1975, Tbilisi; m.; two c.; ed Tbilisi State Univ.; Insp., Weapons Office, Ministry of Internal Affairs 1992–93; Lt, Akhaltsikhe Mil. Base, Georgian Armed Forces –1996; Program Asst, ABA, Tbilisi 1997–98; Asst Program Officer, Int. Republican Inst., Tbilisi 1998–2001, Resident Program Officer 2001–07, Resident Country Dir 2007–09; Minister of Corrections and Legal Assistance Feb.–Dec. 2009, of Educ. and Science 2009–12, of Defence July–Oct. 2012. *Address:* c/o Ministry of Defence, 0112 Tbilisi, Gen. Kvinitadze 20, Georgia. *E-mail:* pr@mod.gov.ge.

SHATNER, William, BA; American (b. Canadian) actor and film director; b. 22 March 1931, Montreal; s. of Joseph Shatner and Anne Shatner; m. 1st Gloria Rand 1956 (divorced 1969); m. 2nd Marcy Lafferty 1973 (divorced 1996); m. 3rd Nerine Kidd 1997 (died 1999); three d.; m. 4th Elizabeth Martin 2001; ed McGill Univ.; appeared at Montreal Playhouse 1952, 1953; juvenile roles, Canadian Repertory Theatre, Ottawa 1952–53, 1953–54; appeared at Shakespeare Festival, Stratford, Ont. 1954–56; Broadway appearances include: Tamburlaine the Great 1956, The World of Suzie Wong 1958, A Shot in the Dark 1961, Shatner's World: We Just Live In It (one-man show) 2012; Founder and Presenter Hollywood Charity Horse Show, Los Angeles 1991–; CEO C.O.R.E. Digital Pictures, Inc., Toronto 1994–; Hon. DLit (McGill Univ.) 2011; Tyrone Guthrie Award 1956, Theatre World Award 1958, Prism Award 2009, Streamy Award 2009, Governor General's Performing Arts Award 2011, NASA Distinguished Public Service Medal 2014. *Films include:* The Brothers Karamazov 1957, The Explosive Generation 1961, Judgment at Nuremberg 1961, The Intruder 1962, The Outrage 1964, Dead of Night 1974, The Devil's Rain 1975, Star Trek 1979, The Kidnapping of the President 1979, Star Trek: The Wrath of Khan 1982, Star Trek III: The Search for Spock 1984, Star Trek IV: The Voyage Home 1986, Star Trek V: The Final Frontier (also dir) 1989, Star Trek VI: The Undiscovered Country 1991, National Lampoon's Loaded Weapon 1993, Star Trek: Generations 1994, Ashes of Eden 1995, Star Trek: Avenger 1997, Tek Net 1997, Free Enterprise 1999, Miss Congeniality 2000, Groom Lake (also dir and co-writer) 2002, Dodgeball 2004, Miss Congeniality 2: Armed & Fabulous 2005, Stalking Santa (voice) 2006, The Wild (voice) 2006, Over the Hedge (voice) 2006, Fanboys 2009. *Albums:* The Transformed Man 1968, Has Been 2004. *TV appearances include:* Star Trek (series) 1966–69, TekWar (also exec. producer and dir of two episodes), T.J. Hooker (series) 1982–86, 3rd Rock from the Sun (series) 1999–2000, Boston Legal (series) (Best Supporting Actor in a Series, Mini-series or TV Movie, Golden Globe Awards 2005, Emmy Award for Best Supporting Actor in a Drama 2005) 2004–08, The Practice (Emmy Award for Outstanding Guest Actor in a Drama Series 2004) 2004, Everest (mini-series) 2007, $#*! My Dad Says (series) 2010–11. *Publications include:* TekWar 1989, Star Trek Memories (jtly) 1993, Star Trek Movie Memories 1994, Ashes of Eden (jtly) 1995, Man O' War 1996, Tek Kill 1996, The Return 1996, Avenger 1997, Delta Search: Quest For Tomorrow 1997, Delta Search: In Alien Hands 1998, Step into Chaos 1999, Dark Victory 1999, Step Into Chaos 1999, Get a Life (jtly) 1999, The Preserver 2000, Spectre 2000, Up Till Now: The Autobiography (with David Fisher) 2008, Shatner Rules (with Chris Regan) 2011. *Leisure interests:* tennis, yoga, skiing, riding, horse breeding, scuba diving, parasailing. *Website:* www.williamshatner.com.

SHATTER, Alan Joseph, LLB; Irish lawyer and politician; b. 14 Feb. 1951, Dublin; m. Carol Shatter; two c.; ed Trinity Coll., Dublin, Europa Instituut, Univ. of Amsterdam; mem. Dáil Éireann (Fine Gael, FG) for Dublin South 1981–2002, 2007–, FG Front Bench Spokesperson on Law Reform 1982, 1987–88, on the Environment 1989–91, on Labour 1991, Justice 1992–93, Equality and Law Reform 1993–94, Health and Children 1997–2000, Justice, Law Reform and Defence 2000–02, on Children 2007–10; mem. Dublin County Council 1991–99; Minister for Justice, Equality and Defence 2011–14; Partner, Gallagher Shatter (legal practice) 1977–; fmr Consultant on Family Law to Law Soc. of Ireland; Fellow, Int. Acad. of Matrimonial Lawyers. *Publications include:* Family Law in the Republic of Ireland 1977, Family Planning Irish Style 1979, Laura (novel) 1989. *Address:* c/o Gallagher Shatter, 4 Upper Ely Place, Dublin 2, Ireland.

SHATTUCK, Mayo A., III, BA, MBA; American energy industry executive; *Chairman, Exelon Corporation;* b. 7 Oct. 1954, Boston, Mass; s. of Mayo Adams Shattuck, Jr and Jane Bergwall; m. 1st Jennifer W. Budge (divorced); two c.; m. 2nd Molly George Shattuck (divorced 2014); three c.; ed Williams Coll., Stanford Univ. (Arjay Miller Scholar); analyst, Morgan Guaranty Trust Co. 1976–78; Man. Bain & Co. 1980–83; Pres., COO and Dir Alex Brown Inc. 1991–97; Vice-Chair. Bankers Trust Corpn 1997–99; Co-Chair. and Co-CEO Deutsche Banc Alex Brown Inc. 1999–2001; Pres. and CEO Constellation Energy Group Inc. 2001–12, Chair. 2002–12 (acquired by Exelon Corpn 2012), Chair. Exelon Corpn 2012–, mem. Exec. Cttee 2007–; Chair. Baltimore Gas and Electric Co. 2002–; mem. Bd of Dirs Constellation Holdings Inc. 1994–98, Gap Inc. (Chair. Audit and Finance Cttee) 2002–, Capital One Financial Corpn (Chair. Compensation Cttee) 2003–, Edison Electric Inst. (Chair. Finance Cttee), Nuclear Energy Inst., Inst. of Nuclear Power Operations, Walters Art Museum; Chair. Bd of Visitors Univ. of Maryland, Baltimore Co. 2004–16; Co-Chair. Center for Strategic & Int. Studies Comm. on Nuclear Policy; Chair. United Way of Central Maryland campaign; mem. Bd, Advisory Council, Grad. School of Business, Stanford Univ., Gilman School, U.S. Ski Team Foundation; mem. Bd of Trustees, Seagram Co. Ltd 1997, Johns Hopkins Medicine; Vice-Chair. and Dir Bankers Trust Corpn 1997–99; mem. Exec. Cttee Council on Competitiveness; mem. Bd of Dirs, Alarm.com; mem. Nat. Bd, The First Tee; Dr hc (Univ. of Maryland, Baltimore Co.); Business Leader of the Year, Loyola Univ., Master Entrepreneur of the Year, Ernst & Young, Distinguished Graduate Award, Noble & Greenough, Boy Scouts Distinguished Citizen Award, Philanthropist of the Year, United Way of Central Maryland. *Leisure interests:* tennis, golf. *Address:* Exelon Corporation, 10 S. Dearborn Street, 48th Floor, PO Box 805398, Chicago, IL 60680-5398, USA (office). *Telephone:* (800) 483-3220 (office). *E-mail:* info@exeloncorp.com (office). *Website:* www.exeloncorp.com (office).

SHAVA, Frederick Musiiwa Makamure, MSc, MPhil, PhD; Zimbabwean politician and diplomatist; *Permanent Representative to United Nations;* ed Univ. of Zimbabwe, Royal Holloway Coll., Imperial Coll.; Minister of Labour, Manpower Planning and Devt 1981–86, Minister of State for Political Affairs 1987; Consultant, Zimbabwe's Parliamentary Reform 2003–04; Amb. to China 2007–14; Perm. Rep. to UN 2014–. *Address:* Permanent Representative to United Nations, 128 E 56th Street, New York, NY 10022, USA (office). *Telephone:* (212) 980-9511 (office). *Fax:* (212) 308-6705 (office). *E-mail:* zimnewyork@gmail.com (office).

SHAW, Audley, BA, MA; Jamaican politician; *Minister of Industry, Commerce, Agriculture and Fisheries;* b. 13 June 1952, Christiana, Manchester; m. Susan Duhaney; four d.; ed Northern Illinois Univ., USA; began career as Lab. Technician, Jamaica Milk Products; worked for Jamaica Promotions Ltd; fmr Area Literacy Officer, JAMAL Movt; MP for Manchester N E 1993–, served as

Shadow Minister of Information and Culture, of Public Utilities and Transport, of Industry and Commerce, fmr Chair. Public Accounts Cttee, Shadow Minister of Finance and Public Service 1997–2007, Minister of Finance and Public Service 2007–12, of Finance, Planning and Public Service 2016–18, of Industry, Commerce, Agriculture and Fisheries 2018–; Deputy Leader, Labour Party 1999– (fmr Gen. Sec.). *Address:* Ministry of Industry, Commerce, Agriculture and Fisheries, 4 St Lucia Ave, Kingston 5 (office); The Jamaica Labour Party, 20 Belmont Road, Kingston 5, Jamaica (office). *Telephone:* 968-7116 (Ministry) (office); 964-3300 (office). *Fax:* 960-7422 (Ministry) (office). *E-mail:* communications@miic.gov.jm (office); fitzalbert_2@yahoo.com (office); nemanchester@hotmail.com (office). *Website:* www.miic.gov.jm (office); www.audleyshawjamaica.com (office).

SHAW, Bernard Leslie, PhD, FRS; British scientist and academic; *Professor Emeritus and Honorary Research Professor, School of Chemistry, University of Leeds;* b. 28 March 1930, Springhead, Yorks., England; s. of Tom Shaw and Vera Shaw; m. Mary Elizabeth Neild 1951 (died 2003); two s.; ed Hulme Grammar School, Oldham and Manchester Univ.; Sr DSIR Fellow, Torry Research Station, Aberdeen 1953–55; Research Scientist, Ministry of Defence 1955–56; Research Scientist, ICI Ltd 1956–61; Lecturer, School of Chem., Univ. of Leeds 1962–65, Reader 1965–71, Prof. 1971–94, Research Prof. 1995, now Prof. Emer. and Hon. Research Prof.; Visiting Prof., Univ. of Western Ont., Carnegie Mellon Univ. 1969, ANU 1983, Univ. of Auckland 1986, Univ. of Strasbourg 1993; mem. Science and Eng Research Council Chem. Cttee 1975–78, 1981–84; research consultant, Union Carbide Corpn, USA for 31 years; Chemical Soc. Award in Transition Metal Chem. 1975, Tilden Lecturer, Chemical Soc. 1975, Liversidge Lecturer, Royal Soc. of Chem. (RSC) 1987–88, RSC Ludwig Mond Lecturer and Prizewinner 1992–93, Sir Edward Frankland Lecturer and Prizewinner 1995, Calabria Prize for Science 2001. *Publications:* Inorganic Hydrides, Organo-Transition Metal Compounds and Related Aspects of Homogeneous Catalysis and over 400 research papers; several patents. *Leisure interests:* walking, pottery, gardening, tennis, classical music, opera. *Address:* School of Chemistry, University of Leeds, Leeds, LS2 9JT (office); 14 Monkbridge Road, Leeds, West Yorks., LS6 4DX, England (home). *Telephone:* (113) 343-6454 (office); (113) 275-5895 (home). *Fax:* (113) 343-6565 (office). *E-mail:* B.L.Shaw@Leeds.ac.uk (office). *Website:* www.chem.leeds.ac.uk (office).

SHAW, Caroline Adelaide, BMus, MMus; American violinist, singer, composer and academic; b. 1982, Greenville, North Carolina; ed Rice Univ., Yale Univ.; musician since early childhood; fmr Thomas J. Watson Fellow; Doctoral Fellow in Composition, Princeton Univ. 2010–; mem. Roomful of Teeth (vocal quartet); also performs as violinist with American Contemporary Music Ensemble; has worked with Trinity Wall Street Choir, Alarm Will Sound, Wordless Music, Signal, The Yehudim, Victoire, Mark Morris Dance Group Ensemble, Opera Cabal, Yale Baroque Ensemble, Kanye West; work has been performed by So Percussion, Brentano String Quartet, Edward T. Cone Performers-in-Residence (Princeton); regular collaboration with artist Jane Philbrick as part of permanent landscape installation 'The Expanded Field' at Massachusetts Museum of Contemporary Art; Musician-in-Residence, Dumbarton Oaks 2014–15; residency with Vancouver's Music on Main 2014–16; Pulitzer Prize for Music (for composition Partita for 8 Voices) 2013. *Recordings include:* Roomful of Teeth 2012. *E-mail:* hello@carolineshaw.com. *Website:* carolineshaw.com; www.roomfulofteeth.org.

SHAW, Fiona, BA, FRSA; Irish actress; b. 10 July 1958, Cork; d. of Dr Denis Joseph Wilson and Mary Teresa Flynn; ed Univ. Coll. Cork, Royal Acad. of Dramatic Art (RADA); joined RSC 1985; Hon. Prof. of Drama, Trinity Coll. Dublin; Officier des Arts et des Lettres 2001; Hon. CBE 2002; Hon. DUniv (Open Univ.) 1999; Hon. LLD (Nat. Univ. of Ireland) 2000; Hon. DLitt (Trinity Coll. Dublin) 2002, (Ulster) 2004; RADA Tree Prize 1982, RADA Ronson Award 1982, Olivier Award, Evening Standard Award for Machinal 1995, Evening Standard Award for Best Actress 2001, RADA Bancroft Gold Medal, OBIE Award, New York 2002, William Shakepeare Award, Washington, DC 2003. *Plays include:* debut in Love's Labours Lost, Julia in The Rivals, Nat. Theatre, Mary Shelley in Howard Brenton's Bloody Poetry (Hampstead), appeared with RSC as Celia in As You Like It, Tatyana in Gorky's Philistines, Madame des Volonges in Les Liaisons Dangereuses, Beatrice in Much Ado About Nothing, Portia in The Merchant of Venice, Kate in The Taming of the Shrew, Mistress Carol in James Shirley's Hyde Park and as Sophocles's Electra; appeared as Rosalind in As You Like It, Old Vic 1990, as Shen Te/Shui Ta in Brecht's The Good Person of Sichuan (Nat. Theatre) 1990 (Olivier Award for Best Actress 1990, London Critics' Award for Best Actress 1990), in Hedda Gabler (Abbey Theatre, Dublin and West End) 1991 (London Critics' Award 1992), in Beckett's Footfalls 1994, as Richard II in Richard II and in The Waste Land 1996, The Prime of Miss Jean Brodie, Royal Nat. Theatre 1998, Widower's Houses 1999, Medea (Abbey Theatre, Dublin) 2000, (West End) 2001, The Power Book (Nat. Theatre) 2002, The Seagull (Edinburgh Festival) 2003, Julius Caesar (Barbican) 2005, My Life is a Fairy Tale (Lincoln Centre) 2005, Readings (Nat. Theatre of Challot, Paris) 2005, Woman and Scarecrow (Royal Court Theatre) 2006, Happy Days (Royal Nat. Theatre) 2007, Mother Courage and Her Children 2009, London Assurance 2010, John Gabriel Borkman (Abbey Theatre, Dublin) 2010. *Films include:* The Man Who Shot Christmas 1984, Sacred Hearts 1985, My Left Foot 1989, Mountains of the Moon 1990, 3 Men and a Little Lady 1990, London Kills Me 1991, Super Mario Brothers 1992, Undercover Blues 1993, The Waste Land 1995, Persuasion 1995, Jane Eyre 1996, The Avengers 1997, The Butcher's Boy 1997, Anna Karenina 1997, The Last September 1999, The Triumph of Love 2000, Harry Potter and The Philosopher's Stone 2001, Doctor Sleep 2001, The Triumph of Love 2001, Harry Potter and The Chamber of Secrets 2002, Harry Potter and the Prisoner of Azkaban 2004, El sueño de una noche de San Juan (A Midsummer Night's Dream) (voice; English version) 2005, The Black Dahlia 2006, Catch and Release 2006, Fracture 2007, Harry Potter and the Order of the Phoenix 2007, Dorian Gray 2009, Harry Potter and the Deathly Hallows: Part 1 2010, The Tree of Life 2011, The English Teacher (narrator) 2013, The Hippopotamus 2017, Colette 2018, Lizzie 2018. *Radio includes:* Transfiguration 2000, Aiding and Abetting 2000. *Television includes:* The Adventures of Sherlock Holmes: The Crooked Man 1984, Love Song 1985, Iphigenia at Aulis 1990, For the Greater Good 1991, Maria's Child 1992, Shakespeare: The Animated Tales—Twelfth Night 1992, Hedda Gabler 1993, Seascape 1994, Richard II 1997, RKO 281 1999, Gormenghast (BBC) (mini-series) 1999, Mind Games 2001, The Sweetest Thing 2002, Empire (mini-series) 2005, The British Face 2006, Trial and Retribution XIV: Mirror Image 2007, True Blood (series) 2011, Maigret (series) 2016, Emerald City (series) 2017, Inside No. 9 (series) 2017, Mrs Wilson (series) 2018, Killing Eve (series) 2018–, Fleabag (series) 2019. *Leisure interests:* opera, running, snorkling. *Address:* Eglantine, Montenotte, Cork, Ireland (home). *E-mail:* shawassist@aol.com (home).

SHAW, Yu-Ming, PhD; Taiwanese historian, academic and media executive; *Chairman, Public Television Service;* b. 3 Nov. 1938, Harbin; m. Shirley Shiow-jyu Lu; one s. one d.; ed Nat. Chengchi Univ., Tufts Univ. and Univ. of Chicago, USA; Asst Prof. of History, Newberry Coll., SC 1967–68, 1972–73; Assoc. Prof. of History, Univ. of Notre Dame 1973–82; held various research posts in Asian studies in USA; Dir Asia and World Inst., Taiwan 1983–84; Dean, Grad. School of Int. Law and Diplomacy, Nat. Chengchi Univ. 1984, Dir Inst. of Int. Relations 1984–87, 1994, Prof. of History 1991; Dir-Gen. Govt Information Office and Govt spokesman 1987–91; currently Prof., Chinese Culture Univ., Pres. Cultural Foundation of the United Daily News Group 1992; apptd Chair. Coordination Council for North American Affairs 2009; apptd Chair. Taiwan's Public Television Service 2013; awards from American Council of Learned Socs, Asia Foundation, Inst. of Chinese Culture, USA and others. *Publications include:* China and Christianity 1979, Problems in Twentieth Century Chinese Christianity 1980, Twentieth Century Sino-American Relations 1980, History and Politics in Modern China 1982, International Politics and China's Future 1987, Beyond the Economic Miracle 1988, An American Missionary in China: John Leighton Stuart and Chinese-American Relations 1993. *Website:* eng.pts.org.tw (office).

SHAWAIS, Rozh Nuri, DEng; Iraqi engineer and politician; b. 1947; Head, Kurdish Student Union, Germany; returned to Iraq to join Kurdish rebellion 1979; Deputy Prime Minister, Jt Kurdistan Regional Govt 1996; Prime Minister, Kurdistan Regional Govt Arbil 1996–99; Pres. Iraqi Kurdistan Nat. Ass. 1999–2004; Interim Vice-Pres. 2004–05; Deputy Prime Minister 2005–06, 2009–15; mem. Political Bureau, Kurdistan Democratic Party.

SHAWCROSS, William; British journalist, writer and broadcaster; b. 28 May 1946, Sussex; s. of Baron Shawcross; m. 1st Marina Warner 1972 (divorced 1980); one s.; m. 2nd Michal Levin 1981 (divorced); one d.; m. 3rd Olga Forte 1993; ed Eton, Univ. Coll., Oxford; freelance journalist in Czechoslovakia 1968–69; corresp. for The Sunday Times, London 1969–72; Chair. Article 19, Int. Centre on Censorship 1986–96, Charity Comm. 2012–; mem. Bd Int. Crisis Group 1995–, mem. Exec. Cttee 2000–; mem. Council of Disasters Emergency Cttee 1997–2002; mem. Informal Advisory Bd UNHCR 1995–2000. *Publications include:* Dubček 1970, Crime and Compromise: Janos Kadar and the Politics of Hungary Since Revolution 1974, Sideshow: Kissinger, Nixon and the Destruction of Cambodia 1979, Quality of Mercy: Cambodia, the Holocaust and Modern Conscience 1984, The Shah's Last Ride 1989, Kowtow: A Plea on Behalf of Hong Kong 1989, Murdoch 1992, Cambodia's New Deal 1994, Deliver Us from Evil: Warlords & Peacekeepers in a World of Endless Conflict 2000, Queen and Country 2002, Allies: The United States, Britain, Europe and the War in Iraq (aka Allies: The US, Britain and Europe in the Aftermath of the Iraq War) 2003, Queen Elizabeth The Queen Mother 2009, Justice for the Enemy 2011; contrib. to newspapers and journals. *Leisure interests:* sailing, walking. *Address:* c/o Janklow and Nesbit Ltd, 13a Hillgate Street, London, W8 7SP, England (office). *Telephone:* (20) 7243-2975 (office). *Fax:* (20) 7243-4339 (office). *E-mail:* queries@janklow.co.uk (office). *Website:* www.gov.uk/government/organisations/charity-commission.

SHAWN, Wallace, BA; American actor and playwright; b. 12 Nov. 1943, New York; s. of William Shawn and Cecille Lyon; brother-in-law of Jamaica Kincaid (q.v.); pnr Deborah Eisenberg; ed Harvard Univ., Magdalen Coll., Oxford, UK; mem. Advisory Bd Jewish Voice for Peace; Gold Medal, American Acad. of Arts and Letters 2016. *Films include:* Manhattan 1979, My Dinner with André (also writer) 1981, The Princess Bride 1987, The Moderns 1988, Scenes from the Class Struggle in Beverly Hills 1989, We're No Angels 1989, Shadows and Fog 1992, Mom and Dad Save the World 1992, Nickel and Dime 1992, The Cemetery Club 1993, Vanya on 42nd Street 1994, Mrs Parker and the Vicious Circle 1994, Clueless 1995, Canadian Bacon 1995, Toy Story (voice) 1995, The Wife 1995, House Arrest 1996, All Dogs Go To Heaven II (voice), Critical Care 1997, My Favorite Martian 1999, Toy Story 2 (voice) 1999, The Prime Gig 2000, Blonde 2001, The Curse of the Jade Scorpion 2002, Love Thy Neighbor 2002, Personal Velocity: Three Portraits 2002, Duplex 2003, The Haunted Mansion 2003, Teacher's Pet (voice) 2004, Melinda and Melinda 2004, The Incredibles (voice) 2004, Chicken Little (voice) 2005, Southland Tales 2006, Tom and Jerry: Shiver Me Whiskers (voice) 2006, Happily N'Ever After (voice) 2007, New York City Serenade 2007, Kit Kittredge: An American Girl 2008, Mia and the Migoo (voice) 2008, Jack and the Beanstalk 2010, Furry Vengeance 2010, Toy Story 3 (voice) 2010, Cats & Dogs: The Revenge of Kitty Galore (voice) 2010, The Speed of Thought 2011, Vamps 2012, A Late Quartet 2012, Admission 2013, The Double 2013, A Master Builder 2013, Don Peyote 2014, Maggie's Plan 2015, Drawing Home 2016, Animal Crackers 2017. *Television includes:* Clueless (series) 1996–97, Blonde 2001, Crossing Jordan 2001–06, Mr. St. Nick 2002, Monte Walsh 2003, Karroll's Christmas 2004, Crossing Jordan (series) 2001–06, Gossip Girl 2008, The L Word 2008–09, Gossip Girl (series) 2008–12, Kung Fu Panda: Legends of Awesomeness (series) 2011–14, The Stinky & Dirty Show 2016–18. *Plays:* as writer: The Hotel Play 1970, A Thought in Three Parts 1976, Marie and Bruce 1979, Aunt Dan and Lemon 1985, The Fever 1990, The Designated Mourner 1996, Our Late Night 1999, Grasses of a Thousand Colours 2009, Evening at the Talk House 2015. *Stage appearances include:* A Thought in Three Parts, Marie and Bruce 1979, Aunt Dan and Lemon 1985, The Fever 1991. *Publications:* Essays 2009, Night Thoughts 2017. *Address:* c/o William Morris Endeavor Entertainment, 1325 Avenue of the Americas, New York, NY 10019, USA (office).

SHAYE, Robert Kenneth, MBA, JD; American lawyer, actor, film producer and film director; *Co-Chairman and Co-CEO, New Line Cinema Corporation;* b. 3 March 1939, Detroit, Mich.; s. of Max Shaye and Dorothy Shaye; m. Eva G. Lindsten 1970; two c.; ed Univ. of Michigan, Columbia Univ. Law School; won First Prize in Soc. of Cinematologists' Rosenthal Competition for Best Film Directed by American Under 25; wrote, produced, directed and edited short films and TV commercials, including award-winning shorts, Image and On Fighting Witches; f. New Line Cinema Corpn 1967, Co-Chair. and Co-CEO; mem. Bd of Trustees, Neuroscience Inst., Motion Picture Pioneers, American Film Inst., Legal Aid Soc.; mem. New York State Bar; Trustee, Columbia Coll. *Films include:* as producer:

Stunts (also writer) 1977, Polyester 1981, Alone in the Dark (also writer) 1982, XTRO 1983, The First Time 1983, Critters 1986, Quiet Cool 1986, My Demon Lover 1987, A Nightmare on Elm Street (parts 1–6) 1984–2010, The Hidden 1987, Stranded 1987, Critters 2 1988, Hairspray 1988, Heart Condition 1990, Blink 1994, Frequency 2000, Lord of the Rings trilogy 2001–03, Freddy Vs. Jason (also actor) 2003, The Last Mimzy (also dir) 2007, The Golden Compass 2007, The Mortal Instruments 2012, Shiver 2012, The Mortal Instruments: City of Bones 2013; as dir: Image 1963, On Fighting Witches 1965, Book of Love 1990; as actor: Quiet Cool 1986, A Nightmare on Elm Street 4: The Dream Master 1988, Freddy's Dead: The Final Nightmare 1991, Man's Best Friend 1993, Festival in Cannes 2001, Cellular 2004. *Television:* Freddy's Nightmare: The Series (exec. producer) 1988–90, Shadowhunters: The Mortal Instruments 2016 (series exec. producer) 2016. *Leisure interest:* cooking. *Address:* New Line Cinema Corporation, 110 Leroy Street, New York, NY 10014-3911, USA (office). *Telephone:* (212) 924-4044 (office). *Website:* www.newline.com (office).

SHCHEGOLEV, Igor Olegovich; Russian government official and fmr journalist; *Plenipotentiary Representative of President of Russian Federation in Central Federal District;* ed Moscow State Inst. of Foreign Languages, Germanic Studies Faculty, Univ. of Leipzig, Germany; ITAR-TASS Corresp., Paris, France 1993–97, Ed. of European News, ITAR-TASS, Moscow 1997–98, later Deputy Head of ITAR-TASS; Deputy Head of Dept of State Information, Russian Govt 1998; Press Sec. to the Prime Minister, later Head of Dept of State Information 1998–2002; Head of Presidential Press Service 2000–02; Head of Protocol Office of Pres. of Russian Fed. 2002–08; Minister of Communications and the Mass Media 2008–12, apptd mem. Bd of Dirs Rostelecom 2011; Plenipotentiary Rep. of Pres. of Russian Fed. in Cen. Fed. Dist 2018–; Aide to the President (external adviser). *Address:* Office of the President, 103132 Moscow, Staraya pl. 4, Russia. *Website:* www.cfo.gov.ru (office).

SHCHERBAKOV, Vladimir Ivanovich, DEconSc; Russian business executive; *Head, Avtotor Investment Group;* b. 5 Dec. 1949, Novo-Sysoyevka, Primorsky territory; s. of Ivan Shcherbakov and Elena Shcherbakova; m. Natalia Shcherbakova; one s.; ed Togliatti Polytech. Inst., Higher Comsomol School; engineer-mechanic; mem. CPSU 1970–91; party work in Togliatti 1971–74; engineer, controller, Chief Planning and Econ. Dept, Volga Motor Car Plant 1970–82; Deputy Dir-Gen., Dir Econ. and Planning Dept, Kama Big Lorries Plant 1982–85; Chief Machine Bldg and Metal Trade Plant Dept, USSR State Cttee for Labour and Social Affairs 1985–88; First Deputy Chief Nat. Economy Man. Dept, USSR Council of Ministers 1988–89; Minister of Labour and Social Affairs 1989–91; Deputy Prime Minister, later First Deputy Prime Minister, Minister of Economy and Planning of the USSR March–Aug. 1991; Pres. Interprivatization Fund 1991–; Head, Avtotor Investment Group 1995–; Chair. Russian United Industrial Party 1995–97; Vice-Pres. Russian Union of Mfrs and Entrepreneurs 1996–2011; Vice-Pres. Free Econ. Soc. of Russia 1997–; mem. Russian Acad. of Natural Sciences; Hon. Consul of Greece in Kaliningrad. *Publications include:* about 50 monographs and articles, concerning Big Economic Complexes: Mechanism of Management, Industrial Labour and its Remuneration, New Mechanisms of Labour Remuneration etc. *Leisure interests:* hunting, sports. *Address:* Avtotor Holding, 109028 Moscow, 3/3 Solyanka Street, Russia (office). *Telephone:* (495) 624-60-61 (office). *E-mail:* scherbakov@avtotor.ru (office). *Website:* www.avtotor.ru (office).

SHE, Lulin, BSc (Pharm), MBA; Chinese business executive; *Non-Executive Chairman, China National Pharmaceutical Group Corporation (Sinopharm);* ed Nanjing Pharmaceutical Inst. (now China Pharmaceutical Univ.), Tsinghua Univ.; served successively as Deputy Head of Gen. Man.'s Office, Asst to Gen. Man., Deputy Gen. Man. and Gen. Man. China Nat. Pharmaceutical Group Guangzhou Corpn 1982–96, Vice-Chair. and Gen. Man. China Nat. Pharmaceutical Group Corpn (Sinopharm) 1998–2004, Dir, Gen. Man. and Sec. of Party Cttee 2004–09, Vice-Chair., Gen. Man. and Sec. of Party Cttee 2009–, Pres. and Legal Rep. of Sinopharm Industrial Investment Co. Ltd 2008–, Chair. Sinopharm Group Holdings Co. Ltd 1998–2001, Dir (non-exec.) 2003–, Chair. (non-exec.), Sinopharm Group Co. Ltd 2007–. *Address:* Sinopharm, 20 Zhichun Road, Beijing 100088, People's Republic of China (office). *Telephone:* (10) 82287727 (office). *Fax:* (10) 62033332 (office). *E-mail:* webmaster@sinopharm.com (office). *Website:* www .sinopharm.com (office).

SHEA, Jamie Patrick, BA, DPhil; British international organization official and university professor; *Deputy Assistant Secretary General for Emerging Security Challenges, NATO;* b. 11 Sept. 1953, London, England; m.; two c.; ed Univ. of Sussex, Lincoln Coll., Oxford; joined NATO 1980, Administrator in Council Operations Section, Exec. Secr. 1980–82, Head of Youth Programmes 1982–85, Head of External Relations Confs and Seminars 1985–88, Asst to Sec.-Gen. for Special Projects (speechwriting, press releases, official communiqués), also adviser to Sec.-Gen. on political and mil. issues 1988–91, Deputy Head and Sr Planning Officer, Policy Planning Unit and Multilateral Affairs Section, Political Directorate, also Speechwriter to Sec.-Gen. 1991–93, Spokesman and Deputy Dir of Information and Press 1993–2001, Dir 2000–03, Temporary Spokesman 2003–04, Deputy Asst Sec.-Gen. for External Relations 2003–05, Dir Policy Planning, Pvt. Office of the Sec.-Gen. 2005–10, Deputy Asst Sec.-Gen. for Emerging Security Challenges 2010–; currently Visiting Prof., European Political and Administrative Studies Dept, Coll. of Europe; Visiting Lecturer, Sussex Univ.; Prof. of Int. Relations, Assoc. Prof. of Int. Relations, American Univ., Washington, DC; Lecturer, Brussels School of Int. Studies, Univ. of Kent; Adjunct Assoc. Prof. of Int. Relations, James Madison Coll., Michigan State Univ. also Dir MSU Summer School in Brussels; Chair of Transatlantic Programme, Royal Holloway Coll., Univ. of London; Bd mem., Geneva Centre for Security Policy; mem. Advisory Council Int. Relations Studies and Programme, Université Libre de Bruxelles and Jean Monnet Visiting Prof.; Visiting Prof., LSE; Sr Transatlantic Fellow, German Marshall Fund of USA; mem. Academic Advisory Council, Vesalius Coll., Brussels; mem. Advisory Council European Policy Centre, Brussels; Founder and mem. Security and Defence Agenda, Brussels; mem. Centre for European Policy Studies, European-Atlantic Movt, Int. Studies Asscn; mem. Advisory Bd, Centre for Defence Studies, Estonia; Assoc. mem. Institut Royal des Relations Internationales, Brussels; 30th Anniversary Fellow, Univ. of Sussex; Hon. Fellow, Security and Strategy Inst., Univ. of Exeter; Golden Eagle (Albania), Gold Londen Medal (Czech Repub.), NATO Medal for Meritorious Service; Hon. PhD (Nat. School of

Political and Admin. Studies, Bucharest) 2012; European Communicator of the Year 1999. *Address:* NATO, Boulevard Leopold III, 1110 Brussels, Belgium (office). *Telephone:* (2) 707-44-13 (office). *E-mail:* shea.jamie@hq.nato.int (office). *Website:* www.nato.int (office).

SHEARER, Alan, CBE, OBE, DL; British fmr professional footballer and fmr professional football manager; b. 13 Aug. 1970, Gosforth, Newcastle upon Tyne, England; s. of Alan Shearer and Anne Shearer; m. Lainya Shearer 1991; one s. two d.; striker; coached as a child at Wallsend Boys' Club –1986; yout player for Southampton 1986–88; sr player for Southampton 1988–92, Blackburn Rovers 1992–96 (won Premier League 1994–95), becoming the only player in English football ever to score 30 or more goals in three consecutive seasons; signed by Newcastle United for then world record transfer fee of £15 million 1996, Capt. 1999–2006, player-Coach 2005–06 (retd); played for England U-21 team 1990–92, England B team 1992, England nat. team 1992–2000 (63 caps, 30 goals), Capt. 1996–2000, won Tournoi de France 1997; first player to score 200 Premiership goals and first to score 100 League goals for two different clubs; Premiership all-time leading scorer with 260 goals in 441 games; record for most Premier League goals (34) in a 42-game season 1992–95; Sporting Amb. for Newcastle United 2006–07; football commentator, Match of the Day and other BBC broadcasts 2006–; Man. Newcastle United Football Club April–May 2009 (retd); Patron, Sir Bobby Robson Foundation 2009–; Freeman of Newcastle upon Tyne 2000; Hon. DCL (Northumbria Univ.) 2006, (Newcastle Univ.) 2009; Southampton FC Player of the Season 1990–91, Euro 96 Golden Boot Winner (five goals) 1996, UEFA Cup top scorer 2003/04, 2004/05, Professional Footballers Asscn Players' Player of the Year 1995, 1997, Football Writers' Asscn Footballer of the Year 1994, (Football Asscn) Hall of Fame 1998, inducted into English Football Hall of Fame 2004, Newcastle United FC Player of The Year 2005, named by Pelé as one of the 125 greatest living footballers, Premier League 10 Seasons Awards (1992/93–2001/02): Domestic and Overall Player of the Decade, Domestic and Overall Team of the Decade, Outstanding Contribution to the FA Premier League, Top Goalscorer (204), *Leisure interest:* golf. *Address:* Match of the Day, BBC Sport, Quay House, BBC MediaCity UK, Salford, M50 2QH (office); The Alan Shearer Foundation, St Cuthberts House, West Road, Newcastle upon Tyne, NE15 7PY, England. *Website:* www.alanshearerfoundation.org.uk.

SHEARER, David James, MBE, BSc, MSc; New Zealand UN official and fmr politician; *Secretary-General's Special Representative for South Sudan and Head, United Nations Mission in South Sudan (UNMISS);* b. 28 July 1957, Papatoetoe, Auckland; m. Anuschka Meyer; two c.; ed Univ. of Auckland, Univ. of Canterbury; teacher, Massey High School 1983–84, Onehunga High School 1987; consultant, Tainui Trust Bd 1987–89; several sr positions with UN, including Co-ordinator for Humanitarian Operations in Africa and the Balkans 1989, also Head, Save the Children Fund in Rwanda, Somalia, Northern Iraq and Sri Lanka 1989, Sr Humanitarian Adviser to UN Assistance Mission in Afghanistan (UNAMA) 2002, Head of UN Humanitarian Office, Jerusalem 2003–07, Humanitarian Coordinator in Lebanon 2006, Sec.-Gen.'s Deputy Special Rep., Resident Coordinator and Humanitarian Coordinator, UN Assistance Mission for Iraq (UNAMI) 2007–09, Special Rep. for South Sudan and Head, UN Mission in South Sudan (UNMISS) 2016–; Research Assoc., Int. Inst. of Strategic Studies, London 1996–99; Adviser to Minister for Foreign Affairs and Trade 2000–02; MP for Mount Albert 2009–16; mem. Labour Party, Leader 2011–13; Save the Children Int. Award for Gallantry 1994. *Publications:* numerous publs in the areas of conflict resolution, effective interventions for peace and humanitarian affairs. *Address:* United Nations Mission in South Sudan, POB 29, Juba 081111, South Sudan (office). *Telephone:* 91206-2000 (office). *Fax:* 91206-6200 (office). *E-mail:* unmiss-spokesperson@un .org (office). *Website:* www.un.org/en/peacekeeping/missions/unmiss (office).

SHEBBEARE, Sir Thomas (Tom) Andrew, Kt, KCVO, BA; British charity administrator; *Director, Virgin Money Giving Ltd;* b. 25 Jan. 1952; s. of Robert Austin Shebbeare and Frances Dare Graham; m. Cynthia Jane Cottrell 1976; one s. one d.; ed Malvern Coll., Univ. of Exeter; with World Univ. Service 1973–75; Gen. Sec. British Youth Council 1975–80; Admin. Council of Europe 1980–85; Exec. Dir European Youth Foundation 1985–88; Exec. Dir Prince's Trust 1988–99, CEO 1999–2003; apptd Dir Royal Jubilee Trusts 1988; Dir The Prince's Charities 2004–11; Chair. Virgin Money Giving Ltd (not-for-profit subsidiary within Virgin Group) 2004–, Virgin StartUp 2004–; Chair. Spring Films Ltd 2011–; Trustee, InKind Direct, School Food Trust, Turquoise Mountain Foundation, UK Skills; mem. Bd of Dirs CIM Investments, Delphis Eco Ltd; Barclay Fellow, Green Templeton Coll., Oxford; Trustee, The Prince's Charities Foundation (China), Turquoise Mountain (Afghanistan), Royal Parks Foundation (currently Chair.); mem. Council Queen's Coll. 1999–; Amb., Studio Schools Trust; Hon. LLD (Univ. of Exeter) 2005. *Leisure interests:* family, cooking, food and drink. *Address:* Virgin Money Giving, 28 Saint Andrews Square, Edinburgh, EH1 2AF, Scotland (office). *Telephone:* (34) 5609-1046 (office). *Website:* uk.virginmoneygiving.com (office); www.virginstartup.org (office); www.springfilms.tv.

SHECHTMAN, Dan, BSc, MSc, PhD; Israeli/American materials scientist and academic; *Distinguished Professor Emeritus of Materials Science and Engineering, Technion Israel Institute of Technology;* b. 24 Jan. 1941, Tel-Aviv; m. Zipora Shechtman; four c.; ed Technion Israel Inst. of Tech., Haifa; Nat. Research Council Fellow, Wright Patterson Air Force Base, OH, USA 1973–75; Dept of Materials Eng, Technion Israel Inst. of Tech., Haifa 1975–, becoming Philip Tobias Prof. of Materials Science, currently Distinguished Prof. Emer.; Distinguished Prof., Dept of Materials Science and Eng, Iowa State Univ., USA 2004–; Head, Int. Scientific Council, Tomsk Polytechnic Univ. 2014–; Research Fellow, Johns Hopkins Univ., Baltimore 1981–83; Researcher, Nat. Inst. of Standards and Tech. (NIST), Gaithersburg, Md 1992–94; mem. Israel Acad. of Sciences 1996, Nat. Acad. of Eng (USA) 2000, European Acad. of Sciences 2004, AAAS; Foreign mem. Russian Acad. of Sciences; Hon. mem. Materials Research Soc. of India 1997, ISIS-Symmetry (Int. Soc. for Interdisciplinary Sciences 1998, Israel Soc. for Microscopy 1998, Israel Crystallographic Asscn 1999, French Physical Soc. 2000, Japan Inst. of Metals 2005; Friedenberg Fund for the Advancement of Science and Educ. Physics Award 1986, American Physical Soc. Int. Award for New Materials 1987, Technion England Academic Award for Academic Excellence 1987/88, Rothchild Prize in Eng 1990, Weizmann Prize in Science 1993, Israel Prize in Physics 1998, Wolf Prize for Physics 1999, Swedish Royal Acad. of Sciences Gregori Aminoff

Prize 2000, EMET Prize in Chem. 2002, Nobel Prize in Chem. 2011. *Address:* Technion Israel Institute of Technology, Room 617, Technion City, Haifa 32000, Israel (office). *Telephone:* (4) 8294299 (office). *Fax:* (4) 8295677 (office). *E-mail:* dannys@tx.technion.ac.il (office). *Website:* materials.technion.ac.il/dan-shechtman-quasi-crystals-nobel (office).

SHECTMAN, Stephen A., BS, PhD; American astronomer; *Staff Member, Carnegie Observatories;* b. 25 Sept. 1949, New York; s. of Arthur Shectman and Dorothy Shectman; divorced; one s. one d.; ed Yale Univ., California Inst. of Tech. (Caltech); Post-Doctoral Scholar in Astronomy and Lecturer in Physics, Univ. of Michigan 1973–75; Alfred P. Sloan Research Fellow 1984–88; staff mem. Carnegie Observatories, Pasadena, California 1975–, Project Scientist, Magellan Telescope Project 1986–2004; mem. American Acad. of Arts and Sciences 1997, NAS 2014; Weber Award for Astronomical Instrumentation, American Astronomical Soc. 2005, Jackson-Gwilt Medal, Royal Astronomical Soc. 2008, Muhlmann Award, Astronomical Soc. of the Pacific 2015. *Publications include:* numerous articles in astronomical journals. *Leisure interests:* opera, cycling. *Address:* Carnegie Observatories, 813 Santa Barbara Street, Pasadena, CA 91101, USA (office). *Telephone:* (626) 577-1122 (office). *Fax:* (626) 795-8136 (office). *E-mail:* shec@obs.carnegiescience.edu (office). *Website:* obs.carnegiescience.edu/users/shec (office).

SHEEHAN, (Cornelius Mahoney) Neil, AB; American journalist and author; b. (Cornelius Mahoney Sheehan), 27 Oct. 1936, Holyoke, Mass; s. of Cornelius Sheehan and Mary O'Shea; m. Susan Margulies 1965; two d.; ed Harvard Univ.; Viet Nam Bureau Chief, UPI, Saigon 1962–64; reporter, New York Times, New York, Jakarta, Saigon, Washington, DC 1964–72, obtained classified Pentagon Papers from Daniel Ellsberg 1971, subsequently published in New York Times winning newspaper Pulitzer Prize; Guggenheim Fellow 1973–74; Adlai Stevenson Fellow 1973–75; Fellow, Lehrman Inst. 1975–76; Rockefeller Foundation Fellow 1976–77; Fellow, Woodrow Wilson Center for Int. Scholars 1979–80; mem. Soc. of American Historians, Acad. of Achievement; Hon. LittD (Columbia Coll., Chicago) 1972; Hon. LHD (American Int. Coll.) 1990, (Lowell Univ.) 1991; recipient of numerous awards for journalism. *Publications include:* The Arnheiter Affair 1972, A Bright Shining Lie: John Paul Vann and America in Viet Nam (Nat. Book Award 1988, Pulitzer Prize for Non-fiction 1989, J.F. Kennedy Award 1988, 1989, After the War Was Over: Hanoi and Saigon 1992, A Fiery Peace in a Cold War: Bernard Schriever and the Ultimate Weapon 2009; contrib. to The Pentagon Papers 1971; articles and book reviews for popular magazines. *Address:* 4505 Klingle Street, NW, Washington, DC 20016, USA (home).

SHEEHY, Sir Patrick, Kt; British business executive (retd); b. 2 Sept. 1930; s. of Sir John Francis Sheehy and Jean Sheehy (née Newton); m. Jill Patricia Tindall 1964; one s. one d.; ed Ampleforth Coll., Yorks.; served in Irish Guards 1948–50; joined British-American Tobacco Co. 1950, first appointment, Nigeria, Ghana 1951, Regional Sales Man. Nigeria 1953, Ethiopian Tobacco Monopoly 1954, Marketing Dir Jamaica 1957, Gen. Man. Barbados 1961, Netherlands 1967; Dir British-American Tobacco 1970–82, mem. Chair.'s Policy Cttee and Chair. Tobacco Div. Bd 1975; Deputy Chair. BAT Industries 1976–81, Vice-Chair. 1981–82, Chair. 1982–95; Chair. BAT Financial Services 1985–90, Barder Marsh (now Marlborough) 1995–96, Perpetual Income Investment Trust Ltd 1996–2007; Dir Eagle Star Holdings 1984–87, British Petroleum 1984–98, The Spectator Ltd 1988, Cluff Resources 1992–96, Celtic Football Club 1996; Dir (non-exec.) British Petroleum Co. Plc 1984–98, Asda Property Holdings Plc 1994, Abdela Holdings UK Ltd 1996, Sherritt Int. Corpn 1996, EFG Private Bank Ltd 1996, Cluff Mining 1997, Pvt. Bank and Trust Co. 1996; Chair. Council of Int. Advisors Swiss Bank Corpn 1985–97; Chair. UK Home Office Inquiry into Police Responsibilities and Rewards 1992–93; CEO Rainbow 1993; fmr mem. Pres.'s Cttee, CBI, European Roundtable of Industrialists, Action Cttee for Europe; mem. Trade Policy Research Centre 1984–89, Task Force on Urban Regeneration; Chevalier, Légion d'honneur 1995. *Leisure interests:* golf, reading, skiing. *Address:* 11 Eldon Road, London, W8 5PU, England. *Telephone:* (20) 7937-6250.

SHEEN, Charlie; American actor; b. (Carlos Irwin Estevez), 3 Sept. 1965, New York, NY; s. of Martin Sheen (q.v.) and Janet Sheen (née Templeton); brother of Emilio Estevez; m. 1st Donna Peele 1995 (divorced 1996); m. 2nd Denise Richards 2002 (divorced 2006); two d.; m. 3rd Brooke Mueller 2008 (divorced 2011); two s.; one c. with Paula Profit; ed Santa Monica High School; first film appearance aged nine in father's film The Execution of Private Slovik 1974; launched Sheen Kidz children's clothing line 2006; nationwide tour, My Violent Torpedo of Truth/Defeat is Not An Option 2011; partner in business venture of electronic cigarettes, NicoSheen 2011. *Films include:* Red Dawn 1984, The Boys Next Door 1986, Lucas 1986, Ferris Bueller's Day Off 1986, Platoon 1986, The Wraith 1986, Wisdom 1986, A Life in the Day 1986, No Man's Land 1987, Three for the Road 1987, Grizzly II: The Predator 1987, Young Guns 1988, Wall Street 1987, Eight Men Out 1988, Major League 1989, Comicitis 1989, Catchfire 1989, Cadence 1990, Men at Work 1990, Courage Mountain 1990, Navy SEALS 1990, The Rookie 1990, Stockade (dir), Secret Society, Hot Shots! 1991, Beyond the Law 1992, Hot Shots! Part Deux 1993, Deadfall 1993, The Three Musketeers 1993, The Chase 1994, Major League II 1994, Terminal Velocity 1994, All Dogs Go To Heaven II (voice) 1996, The Arrival (aka Shockwave) 1996, Shadow Conspiracy 1997, Loose Women 1997, Money Talks 1997, The Fireman 1997, Bad Day on the Block 1997, Postmortem 1998, No Code of Conduct 1998, Free Money 1998, A Letter From Death Row 1998, Five Aces 1999, Being John Malkovich 1999, Rated X 2000, Good Advice 2001, Scary Movie 3 2003, Deeper Than Deep 2003, Scary Movie 3 2003, The Big Bounce 2004, Scary Movie 4 (uncredited) 2006, Foodfight! (voice) 2009, Wall Street: Money Never Sleeps (uncredited) 2010, Due Date 2010, Winning Recipes (short) 2011, She Wants Me 2012, A Glimpse Inside the Mind of Charles Swan III 2012, Scary Movie 5 2013. *Television includes:* The Execution of Private Slovik (film) 1974, Silence of the Heart (film), The Boys Next Door (film), Sugar Hill 1999, Spin City (Golden Globe for Best Actor 2002) 2000–02, Two and a Half Men (series) 2003–11, Anger Management (series) 2012–14. *Leisure interests:* baseball, music, film-making. *Address:* c/o Jeffrey Ballard Public Relations, 4814 Lemara Avenue, Sherman Oaks, CA 91403, USA (office). *Website:* www.charliesheen.com.

SHEEN, Ching-Jing; Taiwanese business executive; *Chairman, Core Pacific Group;* b. 1947, Nanjing, China; moved with family to Taiwan 1947; mil. service 1969–71; worked on cargo ships 1971–73; govt clerk 1974; est. Wei Yung Enterprise co. to buy and sell textile quotas 1974, f. Core Pacific property co. 1985, Core Pacific Securities 1988, acquired Yamaichi Company (securities co.) 1988, obtained franchise of BES Engineering Inc. and China Petrochemical Development Corpn 1994, co. changed name to Core Pacific–Yamaichi International (H.K.) Ltd (CPY), negotiated merger between Core Pacific Securities and Yuanta 2000, CPY restructured to become wholly-owned subsidiary of Core Pacific Group 2006, currently Chair. Core Pacific Group; Chair. Sheen Chuen-Chi Cultural and Educational Foundation 1988–. *Address:* Core Pacific Group, 5F, No.12, Dongxing Road., Songshan District, Taipei City 105, Taiwan (office). *Website:* www.corepacific.com.tw (office).

SHEEN, Martin; American actor; b. (Ramon Estevez), 3 Aug. 1940, Dayton, Ohio; s. of Francisco Estevez and Mary Ann Phelan; m. Janet Templeton 1961; three s. one d.; Hon. Mayor of Malibu 1989–, Hon. Life mem. Law Soc., Univ. Coll. Dublin 2011–; Hon. DLitt (Marquette Univ.) 2003, Hon. DHumLitt (Univ. of Dayton) 2015; Laetare Medal, Univ. of Notre Dame 2008. *Stage appearances:* The Connection (début, New York and European tour), Never Live Over A Pretzel Factory, The Subject Was Roses, The Crucible. *Films include:* The Incident, Catch-22, Rage, Badlands, Apocalypse Now, Enigma, Gandhi, The King of Prussia, That Championship Season, Man, Woman and Child, The Dead Zone, Final Countdown, Loophole, Wall Street, Nightbreaker, Da 1988, Personal Choice 1989, Cadence (also Dir) 1990, Judgement in Berlin 1990, Limited Time, The Maid 1990, Cadence (also Dir), Hear No Evil, Hot Shots Part Deux (cameo), Gettysburg 1993, Trigger Fast, Hits!, Fortunes of War, Sacred Cargo, The Break, Dillinger & Capone, Captain Nuke and the Bomber Boys, Ghost Brigade, The Cradle Will Rock, Dead Presidents, Dorothy Day, Gospa, The American President, The War At Home, Spawn, Storm 1999, Monument Avenue, Free Money, Lost & Found 1999, Apocalypse New Redux 2001, Catch Me If You Can 2003, Milost mora 2003, The Commission 2003, Jerusalemski sindrom 2004, The Departed 2006, Bobby 2006, Bordertown 2007, Flatland: The Movie 2007, Talk to Me 2007, Love Happens 2009, The Way 2010, The Amazing Spider-Man 2012, Bhopal: Prayer for Rain 2014, Selma 2014, Ask Me Anything 2014, The 33 2015, Trash 2015, The Vessel 2015. *Television appearances include:* The Defenders, East Side/West Side, My Three Sons, Mod Squad, Cannon, That Certain Summer, The Execution of Private Slovik, Missiles of October, The Last Survivors, Blind Ambition, Shattered Spirits, Nightbreaker, The Last P.O.W.?, Roswell, The West Wing (Golden Satellite Award 2000, Golden Globe Award 2000, Screen Actors Guild Award 2001) 1999–2006, Anger Management (series) 2012–14, The Whale 2014, Grace and Frankie 2015. *Publication:* Along the Way (memoir with son Emilio Estevez) 2012.

SHEEN, Michael; British actor; b. 5 Feb. 1969, Newport, Gwent, Wales; s. of Meyrick Sheen and Irene Sheen; one c.; ed Royal Acad. of Dramatic Art; Hon. Fellow, (Swansea Metropolitan Univ.) 2009, (Univ. of Wales, Newport) 2009, (Swansea Univ.) 2012, (Aberystwyth Univ.) 2012; Evening Standard Award for Best Actor 2003, Variety Award, British Independent Film Awards 2008, Actor of the Year, GQ Magazine 2009, BAFTA Britannia Award for British Artist of the Year 2010, Theatre Award UK for Best Dir (co-recipient for The Passion) 2011, James Joyce Award, Literary and Historical Soc., Univ. Coll. Dublin 2011. *Films include:* Othello 1995, Mary Reilly 1996, Wilde 1997, Heartlands 2002, The Four Feathers 2002, Bright Young Things 2003, Underworld 2003, Timeline 2003, Laws of Attraction 2004, The Banker 2004, Dead Long Enough 2005, Kingdom of Heaven 2005, The League of Gentlemen's Apocalypse 2005, Underworld: Evolution 2006, The Queen (Los Angeles Film Critics Asscn Award for Best Supporting Actor 2006, Kansas City Film Critics Circle Award for Best Supporting Actor 2006) 2006, Blood Diamond 2006, Music Within 2007, Airlock, or How to Say Goodbye in Space 2007, Frost/Nixon 2008, Underworld: Rise of the Lycans 2009, The Damned United 2009, My Last Five Girlfriends 2009, New Moon 2009, Unthinkable 2010, Alice in Wonderland (voice) 2010, Beautiful Boy 2010, The Special Relationship 2010, Tron Legacy 2010, Resistance 2010, Midnight in Paris 2010, Few Options, All Bad 2012, Jesus Henry Christ 2012, The Twilight Saga: Breaking Dawn Part 2 2012, The Curse of the Midas Box 2012, The Gospel of Us 2012, Admission 2013, Kill the Messenger 2014, Far from the Madding Crowd 2015, Alice Through the Looking Glass (voice) 2016, Nocturnal Animals 2016, Norman 2016, Passengers 2016, Home Again 2017, Brad's Status 2017, Apostle 2018, Slaughterhouse Rulez 2018. *Theatre includes:* Neon Gravy 1991, When She Danced 1991, Romeo and Juliet 1992, Ion 1993, Look Back In Anger 1993, Moonlight 1993, Don't Fool With Love 1993, Charley's Aunt 1994, Livre de Spencer 1994, Peer Gynt 1994, Look Back In Anger 1994–95, Ends of the Earth 1995, The Dresser 1995, The Seagull 1995, The Homecoming 1996–97, Henry V 1997, Amadeus 1998, Caligula 2003, The Un Inspector 2005, Frost/Nixon 2006,Hamlet 2011, The Passion 2011. *Television includes:* Gallowglass 1993, The Grand 1997, Lost in France 1998, The Deal 2003, Maigret 2003, Dirty Filthy Love 2004, Kenneth Williams: Fantabulosa! (Royal TV Soc. Award for Best Actor 2006) 2006, Ancient Rome: The Rise and Fall of an Empire 2006, HG Wells: War with the World 2006, The Battle for Rome 2006, A Child's Christmases in Wales (voice) 2009, 30 Rock (two episodes) 2010, Masters of Sex (series) 2013–16, The Spoils of Babylon (series) 2014, Under Milkwood 2015, 7 Days in Hell (film) 2015, The Spoils Before Dying (mini-series) 2015, Aberfan: The Green Hollow (film) 2016, Michael Bolton's Big, Sexy Valentine's Day Special (variety musical) 2017, The Simpsons (series) 2017, To Provide All People (film) 2018, Animals (series) 2018. *Address:* c/o Roxanne Vacca Management, 61 Judd Street, London, WC1H 9QT, England (office). *Telephone:* (20) 7383-5971 (office). *E-mail:* info@roxanevacca.co.uk (office). *Website:* www.roxanevacca.co.uk (office).

SHEERAN, Josette, BA; American newspaper editor, diplomatist and international organization official; *President and CEO, Asia Society;* b. Orange, NJ; m. Whitney Shiner (divorced); three c.; ed Univ. of Colorado, Boulder; Deputy Man. Ed., Washington Times newspaper 1985–92, Man. Ed. 1992–97; Man. Dir Starpoint Solutions, NY; fmr Pres. and CEO Empower America; Deputy US Trade Rep., Office of US Trade Rep. –2005; Under-Sec. of State for Econ., Business and Agricultural Affairs, US State Dept 2005–07; apptd to UN High-Level Panel on System-wide Coherence in Devt, Humanitarian Assistance and the Environment, Exec. Dir UN WFP 2007–12, Chair. UN High-Level Cttee on Man., mem. UN Devt Group, UN High-Level Task Force on the Global Food Crisis; mem. World Econ. Forum, fmr Chair. Global Agenda Council on Food Security, Vice-Chair. World Econ. Forum 2012–13, UN Sec.-Gen.'s Special Envoy of Haiti 2017–; Pres. and CEO Asia Soc. 2013–; mem. Council on Foreign Relations; mem. Bd of Dirs Overseas Pvt. Investment Corpn; mem. Council on Foreign Relations, served on its

Washington Advisory Bd; fmr mem. Washington Bd, Urban League, United Negro Coll. Fund; Grand Official, Order of Rio Branco (Brazil); Commdr, Ordre du Mérite agricole; Press Award for Journalistic Achievement, Nat. Order of Women Legislators, nat. award for developing and promoting African-American journalists, Niigata International Food Award (Japan), Game Changer Award, Huffington Post 2011. *Address:* Asia Society, 725 Park Avenue (at 70th Street), New York, NY 10021, USA (office). *Telephone:* (212) 288-6400 (office). *Fax:* (212) 517-8315 (office). *E-mail:* info@asiasociety.org (office). *Website:* www.asiasociety.org (office).

SHEETZ, Michael Patrick, BS, PhD; American cell biologist and academic; *William R. Kenan, Jr Professor of Cell Biology and Chair of Biological Sciences, Columbia University;* b. 11 Dec. 1946, Pennsylvania, USA; m. Linda Jean Kenney; ed Albion Coll., California Inst. of Tech.; Postdoctoral Fellow, Univ. of California, San Diego; began career at Univ. of Connecticut Health Center; Washington Univ. in St Louis Medical School 1985–90; Chair of Cell Biology, Duke Medical Center 1990–2000; William R. Kenan, Jr Professor of Cell Biology and Chair of Biological Sciences, Columbia Univ. 2000–, Prin. Investigator for Nanomedicine Center for Mechanical Biology; Distinguished Prof. and Founding Exec. Dir Mechanobiology Inst., Nat. Univ. of Singapore; Ed.-in-Chief MBInfo; L.L.M. van Deenen Prize in Membrane Biology 2004, Wiley Prize in Biomedical Sciences 2012, Albert Lasker Award for Basic Medical Research 2012, Massry Prize 2013, Keith R. Porter Lecture to American Society for Cell Biology 2014. *Publications:* numerous papers in professional journals. *Address:* Department of Biological Sciences, Columbia University, 713 Fairchild Center, MC 2408, 1212 Amsterdam Avenue, New York, NY 10027, USA (office); Mechanobiology Institute, Singapore National University of Singapore, T-Lab, Level 10, 5A Engineering Drive 1, Singapore 117411 (office). *Telephone:* (212) 854-4857 (New York) (office); (65) 9827 2429 (Singapore) (office). *Fax:* (212) 865-8246 (New York) (office). *E-mail:* ms2001@columbia.edu (office). *Website:* www.columbia.edu/cu/biology (office); www.mbi.nus.edu.sg/michael-sheetz/ (office); www.mechanobio.info/Home/mbinfoteam/michael-sheetz (office).

SHEHATA, Hassan; Egyptian fmr footballer and football coach; b. 19 June 1949, Kafr El-Dawwar; footballer (forward), Zamalek SC 1967–68, 1971–83; mem. Egyptian Nat. Football Team 1972–80; man. of several teams including Zamalek SC 1983–85, Al Wasl 1986–88, Shourta 1990–92, 1993–94, Menia 1996–97, Egypt U20 2001–03, Egyptian Nat. Team 2004–11, Zamalek 2011–12, Al-Arabi, Qatar 2012, Difaâ El Jadidi 2014, El Mokawloon 2014–15; Hon. Pres. SATUC Cup (charity) 2015–; several awards including Best Footballer in African Cup 1974, Best Footballer in Egypt 1976, Egyptian Merit of Sport 1980. *Website:* www.satucfootballcup.org.

SHEIKH AHMED MOHAMED, Abdiweli, MA, PhD; Somali/Canadian economist and politician; b. 1959, Bardera; m.; c.; ed Somali Nat. Univ., Univ. of Ottawa, Canada; Dir-Gen., Livestock Marketing and Health Agency, Mogadishu 1984–90; CEO, MISK Enterprises (livestock exporting firm) 1991–98; Programme Man., African Union Red Sea Livestock Trade Comm., Nairobi 2003–06; Sr Livestock and Pastoralism Adviser, COMESA (Common Market for Eastern and Southern Africa), Lusaka 2007–09; Sr Agric. and Rural Devt Officer, Islamic Devt Bank 2010–13; Prime Minister 2013–14; over 20 years' experience with regional and int. devt orgs including Islamic Devt Bank, World Bank, USAID, African Union/IBAR, COMESA, European Union; mem. Canadian Econs Soc., Int. Livestock and Pastoralism Devt Network, Arab-African Int. Devt Professionals.

SHEIKH MOHAMUD, Hassan; Somali politician and fmr head of state; b. 29 Nov. 1955, Jalalaqsi, Central Hiran Region; m. Qamar Ali Omar; three c.; ed Somali Nat. Univ., Bhopal Univ. (now Barkatullah Univ.), India; began career as teacher, Lafole Technical Secondary School; Prof., Somali Nat. Univ. 1981; consultant with various NGOs, UN agencies and devt projects during civil war; Educ. Officer, UNICEF, Cen. and S Somalia 1993–95; co-f. Somali Inst. of Man. and Admin (SIMAD), Mogadishu 1999, Dean –2010; Consultant, Ministry of Planning and Int. Cooperation, Transitional Fed. Govt 2009–10; Founder and Chair. Peace and Devt Party 2011; mem. newly-formed Fed. Parl. 2012–; Pres. of Somalia 2012–17.

SHEIN, Ali Mohammed, MSc, PhD; Tanzanian physician and politician; *President of Zanzibar and Chairman of Revolutionary Council;* b. 13 March 1948, Chokocho, Pemba Island; m. Mwanamwema Shein; ed Odessa State Univ., USSR, Univ. of Newcastle Medical School, UK; Clerk, Ministry of Educ. and Asst to Deputy Prin. Sec. May–Sept 1969; Head, Dept of Diagnosis and Dept of Pathology, Ministry of Health 1976–84, Specialist in Diagnosis and Head, Dept of Pathology 1989–91, Programme Man., AIDS Prevention Project 1991–95; mem. Zanzibar House of Reps 1995; Deputy Minister of Health 1995–2000, Minister of State, Pres.'s Office, Constitution and Good Governance, Zanzibar 2000–01; Vice-Pres. of Tanzania 2001–10; Pres. of Zanzibar and Chair. of Revolutionary Council 2010–; mem. Chama Cha Mapinduzi (CCM). *Address:* Office of the President, State House, PO Box 2422, Zanzibar, Tanzania (office). *Telephone:* (24) 2230814 (office). *E-mail:* info@ikuluzanzibar.go.tz (office). *Website:* www.ikuluzanzibar.go.tz (office).

SHEINWALD, Sir Nigel Elton, Kt, MA, CMG, GCMG, KCMG; British diplomatist and academic; *Visiting Professor, Department of War Studies, Kings College London;* b. 26 June 1953, London, England; s. of Leonard Sheinwald and Joyce Sheinwald; m. Dr Julia Dunne; three s.; ed Harrow Co. Grammar School, Balliol Coll., Univ. of Oxford; joined Diplomatic Service 1976, Japanese Desk, FCO 1976–77, Embassy in Moscow 1978–79, mem. Lancaster House Conf. team on Zimbabwe 1979–80, Head of Anglo-Soviet Section, FCO 1981–83, Embassy in Washington, DC 1983–87, Deputy Head of Policy Planning Staff, FCO 1987–89, Deputy Head of EC Dept 1989–92, Perm. Rep. to EU, Brussels 1993–95, Head of News Dept, FCO 1995–98, Dir EU Div. 1998–2000, Amb. and Perm. Rep. to EU, Brussels 2000–03; Foreign Policy and Defence Adviser to the Prime Minister and Head, Cabinet Office Defence and Overseas Secr. 2003–07; Amb. to USA 2007–12; Visiting Prof., Dept of War Studies, King's Coll. London 2012–, also mem. Governing Council; apptd Prime Minister's Special Envoy on Intelligence and Law Enforcement Data Sharing 2014; Gov., Ditchley Foundation; mem. Advisory Bd Centre for European Reform; mem. Bd of Dirs (non-exec.) Royal Dutch Shell 2012–, Invesco Ltd 2015–; Hon. Fellow, Balliol Coll., Univ. of Oxford. *Address:* Department of War Studies, 6th Floor, King's College London, Strand, London, WC2R 2LS, England (office). *E-mail:* nigel.sheinwald@kcl.ac.uk (office). *Website:* www.kcl.ac.uk/sspp/departments/warstudies (office).

SHELAH, Saharon, PhD; Israeli mathematician and academic; *Professor Emeritus, Hebrew University of Jerusalem;* b. 3 July 1945, Jerusalem; s. of Yonatan Ratosh; m. Yael Shelah; three c.; ed Tel-Aviv Univ. and Hebrew Univ. of Jerusalem; mil. service, Israel Defence Forces Army 1964–67; Teaching Asst, Inst. of Math., Hebrew Univ. of Jerusalem 1967–69, Instructor 1969, Asst Prof. 1971–72, Assoc. Prof. 1972–74, apptd Prof. 1974, apptd A. Robinson Chair for Math. Logic 1978, now Prof. Emer.; Head, Model Theory Group, Inst. for Advanced Studies, Princeton NJ 1980–81; Lecturer, Dept of Math., Princeton Univ., 1969–70; Asst Prof., UCLA 1970–71; Visiting Prof., Univ. of Wis. 1977–78, Univ. of California, Berkeley 1978, 1982, Dept of Electrical Eng and Computer Science, Univ. of Mich 1984–85, Simon Fraser Univ., Burnaby, BC, Canada 1985, Rutgers Univ., New Brunswick, NJ 1985–86; Distinguished Visiting Prof., Rutgers Univ. 1986–; Chair. European Research Confs: Infinite Combinatorics and its Impact to Algebra, Hattingen, Germany 1999; Vice-Chair. European Science Foundation Meeting, Barcelona, Spain 1997; Head, Israeli Del., US-Israel Conf. in Classification Theory, Chicago, Ill. 1984; Ed. Proceedings American Math. Soc. Summer Conf. on Set Theory, Boulder, Colo 1983, Fundamenta Mathematicae 1994–, Journal of Applied Analysis 1996–, Asian Journal of Mathematics 1998–; mem. Gen. Editorial Bd Journal D'Analyse Mathématique 1992–, Israel Journal of Mathematics 1992; mem. Asscn of Symbolic Logic, Israel Math. Soc., American Math. Soc., Israeli Acad. of Science and Humanities 1988–; Foreign hon. mem. American Acad. of Arts and Sciences 1991; hon. mem. Hungarian Acad. of Sciences 2013–; Hon. Ed. Mathematica Japonica 1994–; Erdös Prize 1977, Rothschild Prize in Math. 1982, C. Karp Prize, Asscn for Symbolic Logic 1983, Conf. in Honour of S. Shelah, Tulane Univ., New Orleans 1987, George Polya Prize in Applications of Combinatorial Math., Soc. for Industrial and Applied Math. 1991, Plenary Lecturer, Canadian Math. Soc. Annual Meeting 1992, Plenary Lecturer, European Logic Colloquium, Haifa, Israel 1995, Gödel Lecturer, Asscn for Symbolic Logic Annual Meeting, Madison, WI 1996, Israel Prize in Math. 1998, Japanese Asscn of Math. Sciences Prize 1999, Janos Bolyai Prize, Hungarian Acad. of Sciences 2000, Wolf Foundation Prize in Math. 2001, Emet Prize for Art, Science and Culture (Math. jtly) 2011, Leroy P. Steele Prize for Seminal Contribution to Research 2013. *Publications:* Classification Theory and the Number of Nonisomorphic Models 1978; more than 840 articles in math. journals. *Address:* Einstein Institute of Mathematics, Hebrew University of Jerusalem, Edmond Safra Campus, Givat Ram, Kaplun 205, 91904 Jerusalem, Israel (office). *Telephone:* (2) 658-41-22 (office). *Fax:* (2) 563-07-02 (office). *E-mail:* shelah@math.huji.ac.il (office); shelah@math.rutgers.edu (office). *Website:* shelah.logic.at (office).

SHELBY, Richard Craig, BA, LLB; American lawyer and politician; *Senator from Alabama;* b. 6 May 1934, Birmingham, Ala; s. of Ozie Houston Shelby and Alice L. Shelby (née Skinner); m. Annette Nevin 1960; two s.; ed Univ. of Alabama; law clerk, Supreme Court of Ala 1961–62; law practice, Tuscaloosa, Ala 1963–78; Tuscaloosa City Prosecutor 1963–71; US Magistrate, Northern Dist of Ala 1966–70; Special Asst Attorney-Gen., State of Ala 1969–71; Pres. Tuscaloosa Co. Mental Health Asscn 1969–70; mem. Ala State Senate 1970–78; mem. US House of Reps from 7th Ala Dist 1979–87; Senator from Alabama 1987–, Chair. Senate Banking Cttee 2003–07; fmr mem. Exec. Cttee Ala State Democratic Party; joined Republican Party 1994; mem. ABA; Republican. *Address:* 304 Russell Senate Office Building, Washington, DC 20510 (office); 1414 High Forest Drive, North Tuscaloosa, AL 35406, USA (home). *Telephone:* (202) 224-5744 (office). *Fax:* (202) 224-3416 (office). *Website:* shelby.senate.gov (office).

SHELDRICK, George Michael, MA, PhD, FRS; British scientist and academic; *Professor Emeritus of Structural Chemistry, University of Göttingen;* b. 17 Nov. 1942, Huddersfield, England; s. of George Sheldrick and Elizabeth Sheldrick; m. Katherine Elizabeth (née Herford) 1968; two s. two d.; ed Huddersfield New Coll. and Jesus Coll., Cambridge; Fellow, Jesus Coll. Cambridge and Univ. Demonstrator/Lecturer, Univ. of Cambridge 1966–78; Prof. of Structural Chem., Univ. of Göttingen 1978–2011, now Prof. Emer.; mem. Akad. der Wissenschaften zu Göttingen 1989; Fellow, American Crystallographic Asscn 2011; RSC Meldola Medal 1970, RSC Corday-Morgan Medal 1978, RSC Award for Structural Chem. 1981, Leibniz Prize, Deutsche Forschungsgemeinschaft 1987, Patterson Prize, American Crystallographic Asscn 1993, mineral Sheldrickite named after him 1996, Carl-Hermann Medal, Deutsche Gesellschaft für Kristallographie 1999, Dorothy Hodgkin Prize, British Crystallographic Asscn 2004, Max Perutz Prize, European Crystallographic Asscn 2004, Gregori Aminoff Prize, Royal Swedish Acad. of Science 2009, Ewald Prize, Int. Union of Crystallography 2011. *Achievements include:* author of widely used computer programme for crystal structure determination (SHELX); author of most-cited scientific paper in all subjects of period 2006–10 (http://info.scopus.com/topcited). *Publications:* 830 scientific papers. *Leisure interests:* chess, tennis. *Address:* Department of Inorganic Chemistry, University of Göttingen, Tammannstr. 4, 37077 Göttingen, Germany. *Telephone:* (551) 393021 (office). *Fax:* (551) 3922582 (office). *E-mail:* gsheldr@shelx.uni-ac.gwdg.de (office). *Website:* shelx.uni-ac.gwdg.de (office).

SHELLEY, Howard Gordon, OBE; British concert pianist and conductor; b. 9 March 1950, London; s. of Frederick Gordon Shelley and Anne Taylor; m. Hilary MacNamara 1975; one s. one step-s.; professional debut at Wigmore Hall, London 1971; soloist with all London and prov. British orchestras; regular tours to USA and Canada, Australia, Hong Kong and Europe; three piano concertos written for him (Cowie, Chapple, Dickinson); conducting debut with London Symphony Orchestra 1985; Assoc. Conductor, London Mozart Players 1990–92, Prin. Guest Conductor 1992–98, Conductor Laureate 2013–; Music Dir and Prin. Conductor, Uppsala Chamber Orchestra, Sweden 2001–03; opera conducting debut 2002; current engagements as conductor or soloist or combined role of conductor/soloist; Hon. FRCM 1993; Dannreuther Concerto Prize 1971. *Repertoire:* from Mozart through Liszt to Gershwin; first pianist to perform in concert complete solo piano works of Rachmaninov 1983. *Recordings include:* more than 150 recordings, including complete solo piano music of Rachmaninov (nine vols) and complete Rachmaninov song-cycle (three vols), vols of solo piano music by Chopin and Schumann, Hummel solo piano works, the complete Clementi sonatas (six double CDs) and a survey of Mendelssohn's music for piano solo, piano concertos of many British composers including Alwyn, Lennox Berkeley, Carwithen, Dickinson,

Ferguson, Leighton, Rubbra, Tippett, Vaughan Williams and Britten, the symphonies of Alice Mary Smith, Gershwin's piano concerto and rhapsodies, piano concertos of Balakirev, Korngold (Left Hand), Liapounov, Hindemith's Four Temperaments, Szymanowski's Symphony No. 4 and Messiaen's Turangalila; conducting from the keyboard, has recorded Mendelssohn's piano concertos and Mozart piano concertos (six vols); Hummel piano concertos (eight vols), Cramer piano concertos with London Mozart Players; with Tasmanian Symphony Orchestra, piano concertos by Moscheles, Herz, Hiller, Kalkbrenner, Pixis, Döhler & Dreyschock, Rosenhain & Taubert, Godard; with Ulster Orchestra, first two vols of classical piano series: Dussek, Steibelt; with Orchestra of Opera North: Schumann, Grieg and Saint-Saëns piano concertos and the complete works for piano and orchestra of Beethoven (two-CD set); conducting the Royal Philharmonic Orchestra has recorded Mozart symphonies 35 and 38 and Schubert symphonies 3 and 5; with Tasmanian Symphony Orchestra: Reinecke symphonies 2 and 3; with Orchestra Svizzera Italiana in Lugano: Haydn's London symphonies and symphonies of Spohr. *Television includes:* documentary on Ravel with Tasmanian Symphony Orchestra (Australian Broadcasting Co.) featured as presenter, conductor and pianist (Gold Medal for Best Arts Biog., 40th New York Festival Awards); documentary on Rachmaninov by Hessische Rundfunk (Channel 4). *Address:* Caroline Baird Artists, Stable Cottage, High Street, Culham, Oxon. OX14 4NA, England (office); 38 Cholmeley Park, London, N6 5ER, England (home). *Telephone:* (1235) 521771 (office). *E-mail:* caroline@carolinebairdartists.co.uk (office). *Website:* www.carolinebairdartists.co.uk (office).

SHELOV-KOVEDYAYEV, Fedor Vadimovich, PhD; Russian politician and academic; *Head, Russian Public Policy Centre;* b. 15 June 1956, Moscow; m.; two c.; ed Moscow State Univ.; Researcher, Inst. of History of USSR (now Russian) Acad. of Sciences; mem. Club of Moscow Intellectuals Moskovskaya Tribuna 1989–91; RSFSR People's Deputy; mem. Cttee on Human Rights, Supreme Soviet 1990–93; First Deputy Minister of Foreign Affairs 1991–92; mem. State Duma 1993–95; mem. Political Council, Democratic Choice of Russia Party 1993–96; Dir Inst. of Contemporary Policy and Economics 1995–98; Prof., Moscow School of Econs, M.V. Lomonosov Moscow State Univ. 2005–07; Co-Chair., Int. Russian Club; Vice-Pres. Expert Fund of Social Research (ELF); currently Head, Russian Public Policy Centre; mem. Constitutional Comm. on Regional Policy and Co-operation; mem. Parl. Block Coalition of Reforms. *Publications:* History of the Bosphorus from 6th to 14th Century BC and over 90 scientific works.

SHELTON, Gen. H(enry) Hugh, MSc; American fmr army officer; *Chairman, Red Hat Corporation;* b. 2 Jan. 1942, Tarboro, NC; s. of Hugh Shelton and Sarah Shelton (née Laughlin); m. Carolyn L. Johnson; three s.; ed North Carolina State Univ., Auburn Univ., Harvard Univ., Air Command and Staff Coll., Nat. War Coll.; commissioned into Infantry 1963; served in mainland USA, Hawaii, 2 tours of Vietnam; fmrly Commdr 3rd Bn 60th Infantry Div., Fort Lewis, Wash., Asst Chief of Staff for Operations 9th Infantry Div., Commdr 1st Brigade 82nd Airborne Div., Fort Bragg, NC, Chief of Staff 10th Mountain Div., Fort Drum, NY; rank of Brig.-Gen. 1987; Deputy Dir for Operations, Nat. Mil. Command CTR, Jt Staff Operations Directorate 1987–89; Asst Div. Commdr for Operations 101st Airborne Div. (Air Assault) (including during Operations Desert Shield and Desert Storm 1990–91) 1989–91; rank of Maj.-Gen. 1991; Commdr 82nd Airborne Div., Fort Bragg, NC 1991–93; rank of Lt-Gen. 1993; Commdr XVIIIth and Fort Bragg Airborne Corps 1993, Commdr Jt Task Force for Operation Restore Democracy, Haiti 1994; attained rank of Gen. 1996; C-in-C US Special Operations Command 1996–97; Chair. Jt Chiefs of Staff 1997–2001 (retd); Pres. International Operations, M.I.C. Corpn 2001–05; Founder and Exec. Dir Shelton Leadership Center, North Carolina State Univ. 2002–; Chair. Red Hat Corpn 2010– (mem. Bd of Dirs 2003–); mem. Bd of Dirs Anheuser-Busch Cos 2001–08, CACI Int. Inc., Ceramic Protection Corpn, Anteon Int. 2001–07, Professional Products of America 2005–09, L-3 Communications 2011–, Hugh and Carolyn Shelton Military Neurotrauma Foundation; recipient Defense DSM (with 2 oak leaf clusters) 1989, 1994, 1997, DSM 1994, Legion of Merit (with oak leaf cluster) 1985, 1991, Bronze Star Medal (with V device, 3 oak leaf clusters) 1968, 1969, 1991, Purple Heart 1967, Congressional Gold Medal and numerous other decorations Charlotte (NC) World Affairs Council World Citizen Award 2002, Eisenhower Award, Golden Plate Award, Intrepid Freedom Award, Doughboy Award, Army Infantry 2008, Man of the Year Award, Army Special Operations Professionals 2009. *Publications:* Secrets of Success: North Carolina Values-Based Leadership 2009, Without Hesitation: The Odyssey of an American Warrior (autobiography) 2010. *Leisure interests:* jogging, woodworking, reading, playing guitar. *Address:* Shelton Leadership Center, North Carolina State University, Campus Box 7401/210 McKimmon Center, Raleigh, NC 27695-7401 (office); Red Hat Corporation, 100 E Drive, Raleigh, NC 27601, USA (office). *Telephone:* (919) 513-0148 (Shelton Leadership Center) (office); (919) 754-4950 (Red Hat Corporation) (office). *Fax:* (919) 513-4813 (Shelton Leadership Center) (office); (919) 800-3804 (Red Hat Corporation) (office). *Website:* www.redhat.com (office); sheltonleadership.ncsu.edu (office); www.hughshelton.com.

SHELTON, Robert Neal, BS, MS, PhD; American physicist, academic and university administrator; *President, Research Corporation for Science Advancement;* b. 5 Oct. 1948, Phoenix, Ariz.; m. Adrian Shelton (née Millar) 1969; two s. one d.; ed Stanford Univ., Univ. of California, San Diego; Asst Research Physicist, Univ. of California, San Diego 1975–78; Asst Prof. of Physics, Iowa State Univ. 1978–81, Assoc. Prof. 1981–84, Prof. 1984–87; Prof. of Physics, Univ. California, Davis 1987–2001, Chair. Dept of Physics 1987–90, Vice Chancellor for Research 1990–96, Vice Provost for Research, 1996–2001; Prof. of Physics, Univ. of North Carolina, Chapel Hill 2001–06, Exec. Vice Chancellor and Provost 2001–06; Pres. Univ. of Arizona 2006–11, also Prof. of Physics; Exec. Dir Arizona Sports Foundation 2011–14; Pres. Research Corpn for Science Advancement 2014–; Fellow, American Physical Soc., AAAS; fmr Ed. Journal of Physics and Chemistry of Solids; fmr Co-Chair. NASA Presidential Working Group for American Asscn of Universities; mem. Bd of Dirs Asscn of Universities for Research in Astronomy; fmr mem. Bd of Dirs Triangle Research Libraries Network, Triangle Universities Center for Advanced Studies, Los Alamos Foundation, California Inst. on Energy Efficiency, Bay Area Science Infrastructure Consortium, California Asscn for Research in Astronomy (governing bd for Keck Telescope Facility, Chair. 1997–2000); fmr mem. Space Telescope Inst. Council, Space Telescope Science Inst. (Hubble Space Telescope); Student Advocate Award, Univ. of North Carolina, Chapel Hill 2004. *Publications:* over 240 publs. *Address:* Research Corporation for Science Advancement, 4703 East Camp Lowell Drive, Suite 201, Tucson, AZ 85721, USA (office). *Telephone:* (520) 571-1111 (office). *Fax:* (520) 571-1119 (office). *E-mail:* awards@rescorp.org (office). *Website:* rescorp.org (office).

SHELTON-COLBY, Sally, BA, MA; American international organization official and fmr diplomatist; *Treasurer, Pan American Health and Education Foundation;* b. 29 Aug. 1944, San Antonio, Tex.; m. William Colby 1984 (died 1996); ed Univ. of Missouri, Johns Hopkins School of Advanced Int. Studies, Institut des Sciences Politiques, France; fmr Deputy Asst Sec. of State for Inter-American Affairs; fmr mem. Perm. Mission to UN, New York; Amb. to Grenada, Barbados and other Caribbean nations 1979–81; Sr Fellow and Adjunct Prof., Center for Latin American Studies, Georgetown Univ.; Asst Admin. for Global Problems, US Agency for Int. Devt 1994–99; Deputy Sec.-Gen. OECD 1999–2002; fmr Vice-Pres. Bankers Trust Co., New York; fmr Dir Valero Energy Corpn, Baring Brother & Co. Ltd's Puma Fund; Pres. Helen Keller International/Europe 2002, then Chair.; Bd mem. Pan American Health and Education Foundation 2008–, currently Treasurer; Fulbright scholar, Institut d'Études Politiques de Paris; Founder and fmr Chair. Joint UN Programme on HIV/AIDS (UNAIDS); mem. American Acad. of Diplomacy 2002–; adviser to several multi-nat. corpns on int. trade and investment strategies; fmr Co-Ed. Global Assessment (econ. journal); Dr hc (Univ. of Missouri), (St Mary's Coll.). *Address:* Pan American Health and Education Foundation, PO Box 27733, Washington, DC 20038-7733, USA (office). *E-mail:* education@pahef.org (office). *Website:* www.pahef.org (office).

SHEMYAKIN, Mikhail Mikhailovich; Russian sculptor and painter; b. (Kardanov), 4 May 1943, Moscow; ed Il'ya Repin Inst. of Painting, Sculpture and Architecture, Leningrad (now St Petersburg); started career at Hermitage Museum; solo exhbn, Leningrad 1962; arrested for dissident activities, interned in lunatic asylums; emigrated in 1971; lived in Paris 1971–81; living in USA 1981–; f. Foundation for Helping Soviet Veterans of the War in Afghanistan 1989; visited Russia frequently after citizenship was restored 1990; Chief Designer on Gofmaniada film project, Soyuzmultfilm 2006–; mem. European Acad. of Arts, Paris, New York Acad. of Sciences and Arts; private collections at Metropolitan Museum, New York, State Russian Museum, St Petersburg, Tretyakov Gallery, Moscow; public works include: double-faced Sphinxes on Robespierre Embankment, St Petersburg, Architects-Founders of Petersburg (at the graveyard of Sampsonievsky Monastery), St Petersburg, Peter the First, Peter and Paul Cathedral, St Petersburg, Children as the Victims of Vices of Adults, Bolotnaya square, Moscow, Cybele: the Goddess of Fertility, New York, The Carnival of St Petersburg, Paris, In memory of the 200th anniversary of the death of Casanova, Venice; Ordre des Arts et des Lettres, Order of Friendship (Russia); Dr hc (San Francisco); State Prize 1993, Pres. of Russia Prize 1995. *Publication:* Two Destinies.

SHEN, Dali; Chinese historian and translator; b. 4 Sept. 1938, Yan'an, Shanbei region, Shaanxi Prov.; s. of Shen Xu and Song Ying; m. Dong Chun 1993; one s. one d.; ed Beijing Foreign Languages Univ.; Prof. titulaire and Dir Doctoral Theses, French Dept, Beijing Foreign Languages Univ. 1960–2010; trans. at UNESCO, Paris 1979–81, réviseur 1985; Chinese del. WIPO 1984; visiting scholar in France 1990–91; Prof., Univ. of Montreal, Canada 1994, 2005; Prof., INALCO, Paris 1995, Univ. of Aix and Marseille 2003, 2007; Président du Jury 'Grands Reportages', FIPA 1996; del. to Cultural Comm. CIO, Lausanne, Switzerland 1997; mem. Chinese Writers' Asscn 1982–, Editorial Cttee Revue des Deux Mondes (France) 1999–2009; Chevalier, Ordre des Arts et des Lettres 1991, Croix de vermeil du Mérite et Dévouement français 1996; awarded title 'Membre d'honneur' by L'Asscn des Amis de la Commune de Paris 1981. *Translations include:* Le temps des cerises, Montserrat, Selected Poems of Eugene Pottier (additional trans): Les fleurs jumelles (play) 1982, L'epreuve (novel) 1985, Les trésors de la cité interdite 1986, Poésies choisies de la Commune de Paris 1986, l'Internationale, la Marseillaise, Le Chant du départ, N'a qu'un oeil, La paix du ménage, Le Vésuve, Les couteaux, Les yeux de demain, La vraie Dame aux camélias, Byron et les femmes 2002, Bruges la morte 2002, Biographie de Victor Hugo 2003. *Publications:* The Humble Violet (novel) 1980, The Meteor (novel) 1981, The Children of Yenan (novel, also in French and Italian) 1985, Les fleurs du rêve (poetry) 1986, Les lys rouges (novel) 1987, La flûte des Titans (play) 1987, Le rêve dans le pavillon d'azur, Le temps des cigales, Le tableau de Paris (prose) 1989, L'etoile filante (novel) 1993, (augmented edn) 1995, Voyage en Europe et en Amérique du Nord 1996, La rose de Jéricho (film) 1999; painting and poetry (in Italian, French and English): Matisse/Frasnedi 2001, Chagall/Vangeli 2001, Renoir/Zejtlin 2005, Rublev/Ambrosino 2006, Michelangelo/Günter Roth 2006, Les lettres et arts en France (essay) 2003, Les Amoureux du lac (novel) 2004, Biographie de Berlioz 2005, Lega/Vacca 2008, Roberto Panichi 2009, Su Manshu et Paul Verlaine (comparative study), Biographie de Frida Kahlo 2010, Le Jardin latin (essay) 2010. *Leisure interest:* music. *Address:* Building No. 49-1-4, Dongdaqiaolu, Beijing 100020, People's Republic of China (home). *Telephone:* (10) 65007458 (home). *Fax:* (10) 65007458 (home). *E-mail:* chun.shen@free.fr (home).

SHEN, Guofang; Chinese forestry engineer and university professor; b. 15 Nov. 1933, Jiashan, Zhejiang Prov.; ed Leningrad Forestry Inst.; currently Prof., Beijing Forestry Univ. (Pres. 1986–93); Pres. Chinese Soc. of Forestry 1993–97; Fellow, Chinese Acad. of Eng, Beijing Forestry Univ. 1995–, Vice-Pres. 1998–2006; Ed.-in-Chief Scientia Silvae Sinicae; Nat. Award of Science and Tech. Progress 1986, Ministry of Forestry Award of Science and Tech. Progress 1981, 1987, 1989, Nat. May 1 Medal 1996. *Publication:* Silviculture (Chief Ed.) 1961, Silviculture of Main Tree Species of China (Co-Ed.) 1978, The Influence of Site Factor on the Growth of Pinus Tabulaeformis, IUFRO proceedings 1981, Techniques for Rehabilitation of Sylvo-pastoral Ecosystem in Arid Zones, 10th World Forestry Congress Proceedings, Volume. 3 1991, Silvicultural Techniques of China 1993. *Address:* Beijing Forestry University, Qinghuadong Road Beijing 100083, People's Republic of China (office). *Telephone:* (10) 62338940 (office). *E-mail:* shengf@beilin.bjfu.edu.cn (office).

SHEN, Hao; Chinese engineer and business executive; *Chairman, Shaanxi Yanchang Petroleum (Group) Company Limited;* has been leader of several govt depts and state-owned enterprises that engage in oil and natural gas exploration and exploitation and coal and chemical production and operation; fmr Pres.

Tongchuan Mining Bureau of Shaanxi, Vice-Gen. Man. Shaanxi Coal Transportation of Marketing (Group) Ltd, Chair. Shaanxi Binchang Mining Development and Construction Co., Chair. Shaanxi Coal Industrial Group, Chair. Shaanxi Coal Chemical and Industrial Group Ltd; Dir-Gen. and Sec. Yanchang Oil Mine Admin. Bureau; Exec. Dir Shaanxi Yanchang Petroleum (Group) Co. Ltd 2010–, Chair. and Sec. of Party Cttee 2011–; Exec. Vice-Pres. China Petroleum Enterprise Asscn 2009; Rep. of 17th Nat. Congress of CCP, of 11th Prov. Party Congress and Alt. mem. Comm. of CP of Shaanxi Prov.; Rep. of 9th and 11th People's Congress of Shaanxi Prov.; mem. Cttee, 9th CPPCC. *Address:* Shaanxi Yanchang Petroleum (Group) Co. Ltd, 75 Keji Road, Xi'an 710075, Shaanxi, People's Republic of China (office). *Telephone:* (29) 88899666 (office). *Fax:* (29) 88899669 (office). *E-mail:* webmaster@sxycpc.com (office). *Website:* www.sxycpc.com (office).

SHEN, Heting; Chinese engineer and business executive; b. Aug. 1954; ed Tianjin Commercial Coll., Postgraduate School of Party School of CCP; fmr Asst Man., Deputy Man. and Man. Furnace Construction Co. of 22nd China Metallurgical Construction Corpn, Gen. Man. 1997–2004, fmr Dir, Deputy Sec. of Party Cttee and Legal Rep., China Metallurgical Group Corpn, Pres. 2008–13, Exec. Dir 2008–14; mem. Bd of Dirs Resourcehouse Ltd 2010–; Nat. Labour Day Prize 2004. *Address:* c/o China Metallurgical Group Corpn, 28 Shuguangxili, Chaoyang, Beijing, People's Republic of China (office).

SHEN, Jerry, MEng; Taiwanese computer industry executive; ed Nat. Taiwan Univ.; spent 10 years holding several sr R&D positions at computer cos and IT research insts; Pres. AOOP (ASUS Open Optimal Platform) Group for Motherboard (MB), Graphics Card (VGA), Desktop, Chassis, Digital Home, EMS and Server businesses 1994–2007, CEO ASUSTeK Computer 2008–18.

SHEN, Jianhua, PhD; Chinese automotive industry executive; *Deputy Chairman, SAIC Motor Corporation Limited;* b. March 1953; ed Tongji Univ.; served as Office Dean of Shanghai Motorcycle Plant, Section Head and Deputy Dean of Gen. Man. Office, Shanghai Automotive and Tractor Industry Jt Business Co., Gen. Man. Shenzhen Zhongrui Automotive Machinery Industry Co. Ltd, Dean of Pres.'s Office, Vice-Chief Economist, Pres.'s Asst, Vice-Pres. Shanghai Automotive Industry Corpn (Group), Vice-Pres. SAIC Motor Corpn Ltd, Chair. auto parts business –2007, mem. Bd of Dirs, Pres. and Deputy Sec. Party Cttee 2007–14, Deputy Chair. Deputy Sec. Party Cttee, also Vice-Chair. HUAYU Automotive Systems Co. Ltd. *Address:* SAIC Motor Corporation Ltd, 5/F Building A, 563 Songtao Road, Zhangjiang, High Technology Park, Pu Dong, Shanghai 201203 (office); SAIC Motor Corporation Ltd, 489 Weihai Road, Shanghai 200041, People's Republic of China (office). *Telephone:* (21) 50803757 (office); (21) 22011688 (office). *Fax:* (21) 50803780 (office); (21) 22011188 (office). *E-mail:* info@saicgroup.com (office). *Website:* www.saicgroup.com (office); www.saicmotor.com (office).

SHEN, Lyushun, LLB, MA, PhD; Taiwanese diplomatist and academic; ed Nat. Chung-Hsing Univ., Univ. of Pennsylvania, USA; Research Assoc., School of Law, Univ. of Maryland, USA 1981–82; Staff Consultant, Congressional Liaison Coordination Council for North American Affairs (CCNAA), USA 1982–88; Sr Specialist and Chief of First Section, Dept of N American Affairs, Ministry of Foreign Affairs (MFA), Taipei 1988–91; Dir-Gen., CCNAA Office in Kansas City 1991–93, Dir Political Affairs Div., CCNAA 1993–94, Dir Public Affairs (Congressional Liaison) Div., Taipei Econ. and Cultural Rep. Office in USA (TECRO, fmrly CCNAA) 1994–96; Dir-Gen., Dept of N American Affairs, MFA 1996–99; Deputy Rep., TECRO 1999–2003; Dir-Gen. (rank of Amb.), Taiwan Cultural and Econ. Del., Geneva 2003–08; Rep., Taipei Rep. Office in EU and Belgium, Brussels 2008–09; Deputy Minister of Foreign Affairs 2009–11; Rep., Taipei Rep. Office in UK 2011–14, Taipei Economic and Cultural Rep. Office in the USA 2014–16; Visiting Adjunct Prof. of Int. Studies, Univ. of Kansas, USA 1992–93; Hon. PhD (Park Univ., Missouri) 1993.

SHEN, Rong; Chinese writer; b. (Shen Derong), Oct. 1936, Hankou, Hubei Prov.; worked as a translator, music ed. and school teacher, later became a professional writer; Perm. mem. Chinese Writers' Asscn 1985–, China PEN 1986–; mem. Chinese Int. Exchange Asscn 1990–. *Publications:* Forever Green (novel) 1975, A Middle-aged Woman 1980, Wrong, Wrong, Wrong! 1984, No Way Out, Light and Dark, True and False, The Secret of Taizi Village,. *Address:* Chinese Writers' Association, 25 East Tucheng Road, Chaoyang District, Beijing 100013, People's Republic of China (office).

SHEN, Wenrong; Chinese engineer, economist and business executive; *Chairman and President, Jiangsu Shagang Group Inc.;* b. 1946, Zhangjiagang, Jiangsu province; fmr steelworker; built Jiangsu Shagang into one of China's largest steelmakers, currently Chair., Pres. and Party Chief, Jiangsu Shagang Group Inc., took 45% stake in Australian iron ore prospector Grange Resources, merged it with its Australian iron ore unit, Australian Bulk Minerals; Exec. Vice-Chair. Promotion Asscn for Pvt. Enterprises in Jiangsu Prov.; Chair. Metallurgical Industry Asscn of All-China Fed. of Industry and Commerce; Vice-Chair. China Iron and Steel Asscn; mem. 17th CCP Cen. Cttee 2007–12; Nat. Model Worker of China. *Address:* Jiangsu Shagang Group Inc., Jin feng, Zhang, Jiagang City 215625, Jiangsu Province, People's Republic of China (office). *Telephone:* (512) 58568800 (office). *E-mail:* shagang@mx.js.cei.gov.cn (office). *Website:* www.sha-steel.com (office).

SHENG, Datuk Seri Panglima Andrew Len Tao, LLD, FCA; Malaysian/Chinese economist and financial regulator; *President, Fung Global Institute;* b. 26 Aug. 1946; m. Lim Suan Poh; ed Sabah Coll., Kota Kinabalu, Sabah, Univ. of Bristol, UK; began career as trainee accountant with Arthur Andersen, London; Chief Economist and Asst Gov., Bank and Insurance Regulations, Bank Negara Malaysia 1976–89; Sr Man., Dept of Financial Sector Devt, World Bank, Washington, DC 1989–93; Deputy Chief Exec., Dept of Reserves Man. and External Affairs, Hong Kong Monetary Authority 1993–98; Chair. Hong Kong Securities and Futures Comm. 1998–2005; Chief Adviser, China Bank Regulatory Comm.; Pres. Fung Global Inst., Hong Kong 2011–; Pro-Chancellor, Universiti Tun Abdul Razak 2009–; Hon. Fellow, Hong Kong Securities and Investment Inst. 2013; Silver Bauhinia Star, Yang di-Pertua Negeri Sabah 2005. *Publication:* From Asian to Global Financial Crisis: An Asian Regulator's View of Unfettered Finance in the 1990s and 2000s 2009. *Address:* Fung Global Institute, Cyberport 1, Level 12, 100 Cyberport Road, Hong Kong Special Administrative Region, People's Republic of China (office). *Telephone:* 23002728 (office). *Fax:* 23002729 (office). *E-mail:* as@andrewsheng.net (office). *Website:* www.fungglobalinstitute.org (office).

SHENG, Huaren; Chinese politician; b. 1935, Xieyang Co., Jiangsu Prov.; joined CCP 1954; Office Sec. CCP Party Cttee, Nanjing Chemical Industry Corpn, Jiangsu Prov.; mem. Exec. Council China Council for the Promotion of Peaceful Reunification; Deputy Office Dir CCP Party Cttee, Chemical Fertilizer Industry Corpn, Ministry of Chemical Industry 1965; Deputy Head, Long-Term Planning Group, Ministry of Fuel and Chemical Industries 1970; Deputy Dir, later Dir Planning Dept, Ministry of Chemical Industry; Deputy Gen. Man., later Exec. Deputy Gen. Man. Sinopec Corpn 1983 (Deputy Sec. CCP Leading Party Group), Gen. Man. 1990–98; Vice-Pres. China-ROK Non-Governmental Econ. Asscn; Minister of State Econ. and Trade Comm. 1998–2001; Del., 14th CCP Nat. Congress 1992–97, 15th CCP Nat. Congress 1997–2002; Vice-Chair. and Sec.-Gen. 10th Standing Cttee of NPC 2003–08; mem. State Leading Group for Science and Tech. 1998; mem. 9th Standing Cttee of NPC 1998–2003.

SHENGELAIA, Eldar; Georgian film director and fmr politician; *Chairman, State Council of Heraldry at the Parliament of Georgia;* b. 26 Jan. 1933, Georgia; s. of Nikolai Shengelaia and Nato Vachnadze; brother of Georgiy Nikolayevich Shengelaia (q.v.); m. 1st Ariadna Shengelaia (Shprink) 1957 (divorced 1980); two d.; m. 2nd Nelly Davlianidze 1981; one d.; ed Moscow Inst. of Cinematography; Dir at Mosfilm 1958–59, at Kartuli Pilmi film studio, Georgia 1960–; mem. CPSU 1966–90; apptd Chair. Georgian Filmmakers Union 1976; fmr sec. USSR Filmmakers' Union; teacher, Tbilisi Theatre Inst., Tbilisi State Univ., Head of Film and TV Dept; Deputy, Supreme Soviet of Georgian SSR 1980–85, 1986–90, mem. Presidium 1989–90; elected to Supreme Soviet of Georgian Repub. (representing Democratic Centre) 1990–91; People's Deputy of USSR, USSR Supreme Soviet 1989–91; fmr mem. State Council; mem. Georgian Parl. 1990–2004, fmr Deputy Chair.; Chair. Cultural Comm.; Chair. State Council of Heraldry at Parl. of Georgia 2008–; People's Artist of Georgia 1979, People's Artist of USSR 1987, Saint George's Order of Victory 2009; USSR Prize 1985, numerous other prizes. *Films include:* The Legend of the Ice Heart 1957, The Snow Fairy Tale 1958, White Caravan 1963, Mikela 1965, An Extraordinary Exhibition 1968, The Screwballs 1974, Stepmother of Samanishvili 1978, Blue Mountains or an Improbable Event 1984, Tbilisi 9 April Chronicles 1989, Express Information 1994, Dog Rose 1996. *Address:* State Council of Heraldry at the Parliament of Georgia, 4, Sanapiro str, 0114 Tbilisi (office); Ioseliani Street 37, Flat 58, 380091 Tbilisi, Georgia (home). *Telephone:* (32) 293-20-99 (office). *E-mail:* heraldika@parliament.ge (office). *Website:* heraldika.ge (office).

SHENGELAIA, Georgiy Nikolayevich; Georgian film director and actor; b. 11 May 1937, Tbilisi; s. of Nicolai Shengelaia and Nato Vachnadze; brother of Eldar Shengelaia (q.v.); m. 1st Sofiko Chiaureli 1957 (divorced); m. 2nd Ketevan Ninya 1985; three s.; ed Moscow Inst. of Cinematography; freelance artist; mem. Parl., Deputy Chair. 2000; Georgian State Prize 1980. *Films include:* as dir: Alaverdoba 1960, Matsi Khvitia 1966, Pirosmani 1969, Veris Ubnis Melodiebi 1973, Kvishani Darchebian 1976, Sikvaruli Kvelas Unda 1980, Akhalgazrda Kompozitoris Mogzauroba (also writer) 1986, Khareba Da Gogia (also writer) 1987, Orpeosis Sikvdili (also writer) 1996, Kahdzhi Murat (also writer) 1996, Midioda Matarebeli (also writer) 2005; as actor: In Our Courtyard 1956, Otaraant Qvrivi 1958, Rats Ginakhavs, Vegar Nakhav 1965, Ambavi Erti Kalishvilisa 1960, Kvishani Darchebian 1976; as producer: Tsre 1992, Aslani da Elza 1992, Gilotsavt Akhal Tsels 1995.

SHEPHARD OF NORTHWOLD, Baroness (Life Peer), cr. 2005, of Northwold in the County of Norfolk; **Gillian Patricia Shephard,** PC, JP, MA, DL; British politician; b. 22 Jan. 1940; d. of Reginald Watts and Bertha Watts; m. Thomas Shephard 1975; two step-s.; ed North Walsham High School for Girls, St Hilda's Coll., Oxford; Educ. Officer and Schools Inspector 1963–75; Lecturer, Univ. of Cambridge Extra-Mural Bd 1965–87; Councillor Norfolk Co. Council 1977–89 (Chair. Social Services Cttee 1978–83, Educ. Cttee 1983–85); Chair. W Norfolk and Wisbech Health Authority 1981–85, Norwich Health Authority 1985–87; MP for SW Norfolk 1987–97, for Norfolk SW 1997–2005; Co-Chair. Women's Nat. Comm. 1990–91; Parl. Pvt. Sec. to Econ. Sec. to the Treasury 1988–89; Parl. Under-Sec. of State Dept of Social Security 1989–90; Minister of State (Treasury) 1990–92; Sec. of State for Employment 1992–93, for Agric., Fisheries and Food 1993–94, for Educ. 1994–95, for Educ. and Employment 1995–97; Shadow Leader of House of Commons and Shadow Chancellor of Duchy of Lancaster 1997–99; Opposition Spokesman on Environment, Transport and the Regions 1998–99; Deputy Chair. Conservative Party 1991–92, 2002–03; Vice-Pres. Hansard Soc. 1997–2003; mem. Council Univ. of Oxford 2000–06, Bd mem. Dept for Continuing Educ., Univ. of Oxford; Hon. Fellow, St Hilda's Coll. 1991, Queen Mary, Univ. of London; Chevalier, Légion d'honneur 2009. *Publications:* The Future of Local Government 1991, Shephard's Watch 2000, Knapton Remembered (ed.) 2007. *Leisure interests:* music, gardening, France. *Address:* House of Lords, Westminster, London, SW1A 0PW, England (office). *Telephone:* (20) 7219-4457 (office). *E-mail:* westm@parliament.uk (office).

SHEPHERD, Cybill; American actress; b. 18 Feb. 1950, Memphis, Tenn.; d. of William Jennings Shepherd and Patty Shobe Micci; m. 1st David Ford 1978 (divorced); one d.; m. 2nd Bruce Oppenheim 1987 (divorced 1990); one s. one d.; fmr magazine cover girl; eight years of commercials for L'Oréal Préférence. *Films include:* The Last Picture Show 1971, The Heartbreak Kid 1973, Daisy Miller 1974, At Long Last Love 1975, Taxi Driver 1976, Special Delivery 1976, Silver Bears 1977, The Lady Vanishes 1978, Earthright 1980, The Return 1986, Chances Are 1988, Texasville 1990, Alice 1990, Once Upon A Crime 1992, Married to It 1993, The Last Word 1995, Open Window 2005, Another Harvest Moon 2009, Expecting Mary 2010, Family Jewels 2010, Listen to Your Heart 2010, Another Harvest Moon 2010, Annie and the Gypsy 2012, She's Funny That Way 2014, Do You Believe? 2015, Being Rose 2017. *Plays include:* A Shot in the Dark 1977, Vanities 1981, The Muse 1999, Marine Life 2000. *Television includes:* The Yellow Rose 1983–84, Moonlighting (Emmy Award 1985) 1985–89, Cybill 1994–98, Due East 2002, Martha Inc.: The Story of Martha Stewart (film) 2003, The Detective 2004, Martha Behind Bars (film) 2005, Psych (series) 2008–13, Eastwick (series) 2009–10, The Client List (film) 2010, My Freakin' Family (film) 2011, The Client List (series) 2012–13. *Albums include:* Cybill Getz Better 1978, Vanilla 1979, Moonlighting 1984, Somewhere Down the Road 1990, Songs from the Cybill Show

2003, At Home with Cybill 2004. *Publication:* Cybill Disobedience 2000. *E-mail:* info@tomcroxonmanagement.co.uk (office). *Website:* www.tomcroxonmanagement.co.uk (office); www.cybill.com.

SHER, Sir Antony, Kt, KBE; British actor, artist and author; b. 14 June 1949, Cape Town, South Africa; civil partnership with Gregory Doran 2005, m. 2015; ed Webber Douglas Acad. of Dramatic Art; numerous appearances at Nat. Theatre, RSC (RSC Assoc. Artist 1982–) and in West End; directorial debut with Fraser Grace's play Breakfast with Mugabe at The Other Place, Stratford-upon-Avon; Hon. DLitt (Liverpool) 1998 (Exeter) 2003, (Warwick) 2007, (Cape Town) 2010; Best Actor Awards from The Evening Standard Awards, for performance as Richard III (RSC) 1985, Olivier Award for Best Actor, Soc. of West End Theatres, for performances as Richard III, as Arnold in Torch Song Trilogy 1985, for Stanley 1997, Best Actor Award, Martini TMA Awards, for performance as Titus Andronicus 1996, Peter Sellers Evening Standard Film Award for performance as Disraeli in Mrs. Brown 1998. *Plays include:* John, Paul, Ringo and Bert (Lyric Theatre), Teeth 'n' Smiles, Cloud Nine, A Prayer for My Daughter (Royal Court Theatre), Goosepimples (Hampstead and Garrick Theatres), King Lear, Tartuffe, Richard III, Merchant of Venice, The Revenger's Tragedy, Hello and Goodbye, Singer, Tamburlaine the Great, Travesties, Cyrano de Bergerac, The Winter's Tale, Macbeth, The Roman Actor, The Malcontent, Othello, The Tempest (RSC), Torch Song Trilogy (Albery Theatre), True West, Arturo Ui, Uncle Vanya, Titus Andronicus, Travelling Light, The Captain of Köpenick (Nat. Theatre), Stanley (Nat. Theatre, Circle in the Square Theater, New York), Mahler's Conversion (Aldwych Theatre), ID (Almeida Theatre) 2003, Primo (Nat. Theatre, London) 2005, (Music Box Theater, New York), (New York Drama Desk and Outer Critics' Circle Awards for Best Solo Performance 2005–06, S. Africa Fleur du Cap Award for Best Solo Performance 2005) 2005, Kean (Apollo Theatre) 2007, The Tempest (on tour) 2008, An Enemy of the People (Sheffield Crucible) 2010, Broken Glass (Kilburn Tricycle) 2010. *Films include:* Mark Gertler: Fragments of a Biography 1981, Shadey 1985, The Young Poisoner's Handbook 1995, Alive and Kicking (aka Indian Summer) 1996, Mrs. Brown 1997, Shakespeare in Love 1998, Churchill: The Hollywood Years 2004, Three and Out 2008, The Wolfman 2010. *Television includes:* ITV Playhouse – Cold Harbour, Pickersgill People – The Sheik of Pickersgill 1978, Collision Course 1979, The History Man 1981, Tartuffe 1983, Changing Step 1990, The Land of Dreams 1990, The Comic Strip Presents. . . – The Crying Game 1992, Genghis Cohn 1993, Moonstone 1996, Hornblower: The Frogs and the Lobsters 1999, Macbeth 2001, The Jury (mini-series) 2002, Home 2003, Murphy's Law – Jack's Back 2004, Primo 2007, God on Trial 2008, The Shadow Line 2011. *Publications:* Year of the King (theatre journal) 1986, Middlepost (novel) 1988, Characters (paintings and drawings) 1989, Changing Step (screenplay) 1989, The Indoor Boy (novel) 1991, Cheap Lives (novel) 1995, Woza Shakespeare! (theatre journal, co-written with Gregory Doran) 1996, The Feast (novel) 1998, Beside Myself (auto-biog.) 2001, I.D. (play) 2003, Primo (play) 2005, Primo Time (theatre journal) 2005, The Giant (play) 2007. *Address:* c/o Mic Cheetham Literary Agency, 50 Albemarle Street, London, W1S 4BD, England (office). *Telephone:* (20) 7495-2002 (office). *E-mail:* simon@miccheetham.com (office). *Website:* www.miccheetham.com (office).

SHERCHAN, Amik; Nepalese politician; b. 1949; three s. one d.; Chair. People's Front Nepal (Janamorcha Nepal) –2008 (deposed); Deputy Prime Minister and Minister of Health and Population 2006–07; joined Unified Communist Party of Nepal (Maoist) 2009, mem. Standing Cttee; mem. Constituent Ass. from Chitwan-5 2008–.

SHERIMKULOV, Medetkan; Kyrgyzstani politician, diplomatist and academic; b. 17 Nov. 1939, Tchapaevo (Kyrgyzia); m.; three d.; ed Kyrgyz Univ., Moscow Univ.; mem. CPSU 1962–91; Instructor, Div. of Science, Cen. Cttee CP of Kyrgyzia 1971–73; Sec., Party Cttee, Kyrgyz Nat. Univ. 1973–76; Sec., Issyk-Kul Regional CP Cttee 1976–80; Head, Div. of Propaganda, Cen. Cttee CP, Kyrgyz SSR 1986–90; Chair. Supreme Soviet (now Uluk Kenesh) of Repub. of Kyrgyzstan 1990–94; apptd Lecturer, Kyrgyz Nat. Univ. 1995, Prof., Centre of Strategic Studies and Political Sciences, Kyrgyz Nat. Univ. 1998; cand. for presidency of Kyrgyzstan 1995; Amb. to Turkey 1996–2002, to Iran 2007–11.

SHERMAN, Bernard (Barry) Charles, BSc, MS, PhD; Canadian pharmaceuticals industry executive; *Chairman and CEO, Apotex Inc.;* b. 1942; m. Honey Sherman; four c.; ed Univ. of Toronto, Massachusetts Inst. of Tech., USA; fmr Pres. and major shareholder of Barr Laboratories, New York; f. Apotex Inc. 1974, currently Chair. and CEO; Chair. Cangene Corpn 1995–2006; mem. Bd of Govs Mount Sinai Hospital, Baycrest Centre for Geriatric Care, Toronto; Hon. PhD (Technion Univ., Israel) 2004. *Address:* Apotex Inc., 150 Signet Drive, Toronto, ON M9L 1T9, Canada (office). *Telephone:* (800) 268-4623 (office). *Fax:* (800) 609-9444 (office). *Website:* www.apotex.com (office).

SHERMAN, Cindy, BA; American artist and photographer; b. 19 Jan. 1954, Glen Ridge, NJ; d. of Charles Sherman and Dorothy Sherman; m. Michel Auder 1984 (divorced 1999); ed State Univ. Coll., Buffalo; perm. collections at Museum of Contemporary Art, Los Angeles, Museum of Modern Art, New York, Philadelphia Museum of Art, Philadelphia, San Francisco Museum of Modern Art, San Francisco, Solomon R. Guggenheim Museum, New York, Whitney Museum of American Art, New York, Albright-Knox Art Gallery, Buffalo, Corcoran Gallery of Art, Washington, DC, Metropolitan Museum of Art, New York, Museum Ludwig, Cologne, Germany, Tate Gallery, London, UK, Victoria and Albert Museum, London, UK, Art Gallery of Ontario, Toronto, Canada, Centre Georges Pompidou, Paris, France, Centro de Arte Reina Sofia, Madrid, Spain, Louisiana Museum, Humlebaek, Denmark, Musée d'art Contemporain, Montréal, Canada, Museum Boymans-van Beuningen, Rotterdam, The Netherlands; MacArthur Fellowship 1995; Hon. mem. Royal Academy of Arts 2010; Dr hc (RCA, London) 2013; Nat. Arts Award 2001, American Acad. of Arts and Sciences Award 2003, Lifetime Achievement Award for Visual Arts, Guild Hall Acad. of the Arts 2005, Jewish Museum's Man Ray Award 2009, Roswitha Haftmann Prize 2012, Centennial Medal, American Acad. in Rome 2014, Praemium Imperiale 2016, Max-Beckmann-Prize 2019. *Film:* Office Killer (as Dir) 1997. *Address:* c/o Metro Pictures, 519 West 24th Street, New York, NY 10011, USA. *Telephone:* (212) 206-7100. *E-mail:* gallery@metropictures.com. *Website:* www.metropictures.com/artists/cindy-sherman/.

SHERMAN, Wendy R., BA, MA; American diplomatist and government official; *Senior Counselor, Albright Stonebridge Group;* ed Smith Coll., Boston Univ., Univ. of Maryland; Asst Sec. for Legis. Affairs, Dept of State 1993–96, Counselor and Special Advisor to Pres. Clinton and Policy Coordinator on N Korea 1997–2001; Vice-Chair. Albright Stonebridge Group (global strategy firm) 2001–11, mem. Investment Cttee of Albright Capital Management (affiliated investment advisory firm), Sr Counselor 2016–; served on US Dept of Defense's Defense Policy Bd; apptd by Congressional Leadership to serve on Comm. on Prevention of Weapons of Mass Destruction, Proliferation and Terrorism 2008; Under-Sec. of State for Political Affairs, Dept of State 2011–15, Acting Deputy Sec. of State Nov. 2014–Jan. 2015; Sr Fellow, Belfer Center for Science and Int. Affairs, Kennedy School of Govt, Harvard Univ. 2015–; mem. President's Intelligence Advisory Bd 2016–; fmr Pres. and CEO Fannie Mae Foundation; fmr Chair. Oxfam America; National Security Medal. *Address:* Albright Stonebridge Group, 601 Thirteenth Street, NW, 10th Floor, Washington, DC 20005, USA (office). *Telephone:* (202) 759-5100 (office). *Fax:* (202) 759-5101 (office). *Website:* www.albrightstonebridge.com (office).

SHERPAO, Aftab Ahmad Khan; Pakistani politician; *Leader, Qaumi Watan Party;* b. 20 Aug. 1944; f. Pakistan People's Party—PPP (Sherpao Group), breakaway faction, faction rejoined PPP 2002; fmr Chief Minister of North-West Frontier Prov.; fmr Minister of Water and Power, of Inter-Prov. Co-ordination and of Kashmir Affairs, Northern Areas and State and Frontier Regions; Minister of the Interior 2004–07; Leader, Qaumi Watan Party 2012–. *Address:* Qaumi Watan Party, 5-F, Rehman Baba Road, University Town, Peshawar, Pakistan (office). *Telephone:* (91) 5846091 (office). *Fax:* (91) 5846093 (office). *E-mail:* qaumisecretariat@hotmail.com (office). *Website:* qwp.org.pk (office).

SHERRINGTON, David, BSc, Dip.Adv.Stud.Sci, PhD; British physicist and academic; *Wykeham Professor Emeritus of Physics, University of Oxford;* b. 29 Oct. 1941, Blackpool, Lancs.; s. of James A. Sherrington and Elfreda Cameron; m. Margaret Gee-Clough 1966; one s. one d.; ed St Mary's Coll. Middlesbrough and Univ. of Manchester; Asst Lecturer in Theoretical Physics, Univ. of Manchester 1964–67, Lecturer (on leave) 1967–69; Asst Research Physicist, Univ. of Calif., San Diego 1967–69; Lecturer in Solid State Physics, Imperial Coll. London 1969–74, Reader 1974–83, Prof. of Physics 1983–89; Cadre Supérieur, Inst. Laue Langevin, Grenoble 1977–79; Wykeham Prof. of Physics, Univ. of Oxford 1989–2008, Prof. Emer. 2008–; Ulam Scholar, Los Alamos Nat. Lab., USA 1995–96; Fellow, New Coll. Oxford 1989–; Visiting Prof., Hong Kong Univ. of Science and Tech. 1994, Ecole Normale Supérieure, Paris 2003; External Prof., Santa Fe Inst. 2004–; Visiting Scientist, IBM 1975, Schlumberger-Doll Research 1984, Inst. for Advanced Study, Princeton 2003, Univ. of California, Santa Barbara 2003, Univ. of California, San Diego 2008, Los Alamos Nat. Lab.; Ed. Communications in Physics 1975–76, Advances in Physics 1984–, Journal of Physics A 1989–93; mem. Editorial Bd, Journal of Physics C 1981–85, Oxford Monographs in Physics 1995–, Quantitative Finance; Del., Oxford University Press; Fellow, American Physical Soc., European Acad. of Sciences, Academia Europeae; Bakerian Lecture, Royal Soc. 2001, Dirac Medal and Prize, Inst. of Physics 2007, Scott Lectureship, Cambridge 2009, Blaise Pascal Medal, European Acad. of Sciences 2010. *Publications:* numerous articles in scientific journals, co-ed. of several books. *Leisure interests:* travel, wine, theatre, walking, science, history, art. *Address:* Rudolf Peierls Centre for Theoretical Physics, 1 Keble Road, Oxford, OX1 3NP, England (office). *Website:* www2.physics.ox.ac.uk/contacts/people/sherr (office).

SHERSTYUK, Col-Gen. Vladislav Petrovich; Russian security official and academic; *Director, Institute of Information Security Issues, Lomonosov Moscow State University;* b. 16 Oct. 1940, Novoplastunovskaya, Krasnodar Region; m.; one s.; ed Moscow State Univ., Higher KGB School; with KGB 1966–; Head Dept of Radioelectronic Espionage Telecommunications, Fed. Agency of Govt Telecommunications and Information 1995–98, Deputy Dir-Gen. 1998, Dir-Gen. 1998–99; First Deputy Sec., Security Council 1999; Dir Fed. Agency of Govt Communications and Information (FAPSI) 2001–02; currently Dir Inst. of Information Security Issues, Lomonosov Moscow State Univ.; Order of Labour Red Banner 1975, Order for Service to Motherland 1996 and numerous other decorations USSR State Prize 1978, State Prize of Russian Fed. 1996, Red Star 1988. *Address:* Institute of Information Security Issues, Lomonosov Moscow State University, 119192 Moscow, Michurinsky pr. 1, Russia (office). *Telephone:* (495) 932-89-58 (office). *Fax:* (495) 939-20-96 (office). *E-mail:* iisi@iisi.msu.ru (office). *Website:* www.iisi.msu.ru (office).

SHERWIN, Susan, BA, PhD, FRSC, FCAHS; Canadian academic; *Research Professor Emerita, Department of Philosophy and Department of Gender and Women's Studies, Dalhousie University;* b. 6 June 1947, Toronto; ed York Univ., Stanford and Case Western Reserve Univs, USA; Asst Prof., Dept of Philosophy, Dalhousie Univ. 1974–80, Assoc. Prof. 1980–90, Chair. Dept of Philosophy 1982–87, Prof. 1990, Univ. Research Professor 2002–08, now Prof. Emer., Co-ordinator Women's Studies 1987–88, 1996–2000, also taught in Gender and Women's Studies Program, Faculty of Health Professions; mem. Canadian Comm. for UNESCO (Ethics Cttee 2001–03, Sectoral Comm. on Natural and Social Sciences 2001–03), Canadian Soc. for Women in Philosophy (Co-ordinator 1985–86, 1994–95), Canadian Philosophical Asscn (Exec. Cttee 1983–85), Canadian Research Inst. for Advancement of Women, Nova Scotia Women's Health Educ. Network, Canadian Soc. of Bioethics, Int. Asscn of Bioethics (Bd mem. 1995–2000), Int. Feminist Approaches to Bioethics (Jt Coordinator 2001–03); mem. Ethics and Equity Cttee, Royal Coll. of Physicians and Surgeons of Canada, Research Council, Canadian Inst. of Advanced Research 2002–05, CIHR Standing Cttee on Ethics 2000–06; CAUT Sarah Shorten Award 2000, American Soc. for Women and Philosophy Distinguished Woman Philosopher 2004, Killam Prize in Humanities 2006, Canadian Bioethics Soc. Lifetime Achievement Award 2007. *Publications:* Moral Problems in Medicine (co-ed.) 1983, No Longer Patient: Feminist Ethics and Health Care 1992, Health Care Ethics in Canada (co-ed.) 1995, The Politics of Women's Health: Exploring Agency and Autonomy (ed.), Women 1992, Medicine, Ethics, and the Law (co-ed.) 2002; Engaged Philosophy (co-ed.) 2007, Agency and Embodiment (co-ed.) 2009; contribs: numerous articles in journals including Journal of Medicine and Philosophy, Humane Medicine, Bioethics, Politeia. *Address:* Department of Philosophy, Dalhousie University, Halifax, NS B3H 4P9, Canada (office). *Telephone:* (902)

494-3393 (office). *Fax:* (902) 494-3518 (office). *E-mail:* susan.sherwin@dal.ca (office). *Website:* philosophy.dal.ca (office).

SHERWOOD, James Blair, BEcons; American business executive; b. 8 Aug. 1933; s. of William Earl Sherwood and Florence Balph Sherwood; m. Shirley Angela Masser Cross 1977; two step s.; ed Yale Univ.; Lt USN 1955–58; Man. French Ports, later Asst Gen. Freight Traffic Man., US Lines Co. 1959–62; Gen. Man. Container Transport Int. Inc. 1963–64; Founder and Pres. Sea Containers Ltd 1965–2006 (resgnd); Founder and Chair. Orient-Express Hotels Ltd 1987–2007, Dir 2007–11, Chair. Emer. 2011–; with Mark Birley est. Harry's Bar Club, London 1979; Dir James Sherwood Ltd 1991–; Dir Hotel Cipriani SpA; Propr Capannelle Wine Estate Gaiole, Chianti, Italy 1997–; Trustee, Solomon R. Guggenheim Foundation 1989, Oxford Philomusica Trust; mem. Council to Save Venice, Inc., President's Council on Int. Activities; Hon. Citizen of Venice, Italy 1990; Order of the Southern Cross (Brazil) 2004. *Achievements include:* restored and brought into service Venice Simplon-Orient-Express 1982. *Publication:* James Sherwood's Discriminating Guide to London 1975, Orient-Express: A Personal Journey (co-author) 2012. *Leisure interests:* skiing, tennis, sailing, golf. *Address:* Hinton Manor, Hinton Waldrist, Oxon., SN7 8SA, England (home). *Telephone:* (1865) 820260 (home).

SHERZAI, Gul Agha; Afghan politician; b. (Mohammad Shafiq), 1954; s. of Haji Abdul Latif; Gov. of Kandahar prior to Taliban takeover, in exile in Quetta, Pakistan 1994–2001, reinstated as Gov. of Kandahar 2002–04, Gov. of Nangarhar 2004–13; Minister of Urban Affairs 2003; fmr Minister of Urban Devt and Housing; Minister of Public Works –2004; fmr ministerial adviser to Pres. Hamid Karzai; cand. in presidential election 2014.

SHESHINSKI, Eytan, BA, MA, PhD; Israeli economist and academic; *Sir Isaac Wolfson Professor Emeritus of Public Finance and Lecturer Emeritus, Department of Economics, Hebrew University of Jerusalem;* b. 29 June 1937, Haifa; s. of Alice Sheshinski and Baruch Sheshinski; m. Ruth H. Sheshinski 1960; four d.; ed Hebrew Univ. Jerusalem, Mass Inst. of Tech., USA; Asst Prof., Harvard Univ. 1966–67; Lecturer, then Assoc. Prof. 1971–74, apptd Prof. of Econs 1974, then Sir Isaac Wolfson Prof. Emer. of Public Finance, Hebrew Univ. of Jerusalem, now Sir Isaac Wolfson Prof. of Public Finance and Lecturer Emer.; Visiting Prof. at numerous univs, including Harvard Univ., Stanford Univ., MIT, Columbia Univ., Brown Univ.; fmr Chair. Koor Industries Ltd, Khevrat Ha'Ovdim 1989–92; Chair. cttee appointed by Govt on fiscal policy regarding offshore gas and oil drills; Pres. Israel Econ. Asscn 2004–06; Econs Policy Program Fellow, Taub Center for Social Policy Studies in Israel; Fellow, Econometric Soc.; Foreign mem. Royal Swedish Acad. of Sciences, American Acad. of Arts and Sciences; Dr hc (Stockholm School of Econs) 1984; American Acad. of Arts and Sciences Award. *Publications:* The Optimal Linear Income Tax (Review of Economic Studies 1972), Inflation and Costs of Price Adjustment (Review of Economic Studies 1977), Optimum Pricing, Inflation and the Costs of Price Adjustments (ed.) 1993. *Leisure interests:* hiking, sailing. *Address:* Hebrew University of Jerusalem, Mount Scopus, 91905 Jerusalem, Israel (office). *Telephone:* (2) 5883144 (office); (2) 6242442 (home). *Fax:* (2) 5883357 (office); (2) 6255571 (home). *E-mail:* mseytan@mscc.huji.ac.il (office). *Website:* economics.huji.ac.il/sheshinski (office).

SHESTAKOV, Sergey Vasilyevich; Russian biologist; *Chief Scientific Officer, Moscow State University;* b. 23 Nov. 1934, Leningrad; s. of Vasily Ivanovich Shestakov and Ludmila Shestakova; m. Galina A. Grigorieva 1964; one s.; ed Moscow State Univ.; on staff, Moscow State Univ. 1957–, Chair. Dept of Genetics 1980–2009, now Chief Scientific Officer; Dir Int. Biotechnology Centre 1991–2003; Dir N. Vavilov Inst. of Genetics, USSR (now Russian) Acad. of Sciences 1988–91; Corresp. mem. USSR (now Russian) Acad. of Sciences 1987, mem. 2000; Chair. Scientific Council on Genetics 1988–2004, Scientific Council on Life Sciences, Moscow State Univ. 1998–; mem. Int. Acad. of Science; Visiting Prof., Michigan State Univ., USA 1992; Visiting Researcher, Chicago Univ., USA 1994, Univ. of Wales, UK 1998; Ed.-in-Chief Russian Journal of Genetics 2011–16; Hon. Distinguished Scientist of Russian Fed. 1995; Hon. Prof. (Univ. of Wales) 2000; Hon. Distinguished Worker of Higher School of Russian Fed. 2011; Fulbright-Hays Fellowship 1975 UNESCO Fellowship Award 1985, USSR State Prize 1988, Lomonosov Prize 1995, N. Vavilov Gold Medal 1997, P. Ehrlich Medal (Germany) 2006. *Publications include:* papers and articles on microbial and plant molecular genetics of DNA repair and recombination, photosynthesis, nitrogen-fixation, resistance to stresses, functional genomics, photobiotechnology. *Leisure interest:* sports. *Address:* Department of Genetics, Moscow State University, 119899 Moscow, Russia (office). *Telephone:* (495) 939-09-75 (office). *Fax:* (495) 939-43-09 (office). *E-mail:* shestakovgen@mail.ru (office).

SHESTAKOVA, Tatyana Borisovna; Russian actress; b. 23 Oct. 1948, Leningrad; d. of Boris Shestakov and Aleksandra Shestakova; m. Lev Dodin 1972; ed Leningrad Theatre Inst.; Leningrad Theatre for Children 1972–75; Leningrad Comedy Theatre 1975–80; Bolshoi Drama Theatre 1980–83; Maly Drama Theatre 1984–; also played for Moscow Arts Theatre; toured abroad 1983, 1987–2001; apptd Dir Stars In the Morning Sky 2005; USSR State Prize 1986, RSFSR Merited Artist 1987, Nat. 'Triumph' Prize 1992. *Films include:* Tsarevich Prosha 1974, Solyonyy Pyos 1975, Chelovek, Kotoromu Vezlo 1978, Idi i Smotri 1985, Podsudimyy 1986. *Theatre roles include:* Liza (The House) 1980, Sonya (Uncle Vanya) 1982, She (The Meek One) 1985, Anfisa (Brothers and Sisters) 1986, Anna (Stars of the Morning Sky) 1987, Lebyadkina (The Possessed), Lubov Andreevna (The Cherry Orchard) 1994, Dame Elegant (Roberto Zucco) 1994, Katya and Ivanova (Claustrophobia) 1994, Anna Petrovna (Play Without a Name) 1997, Sonya (Chevengur) 2000, Arcadina (The Seagull) 2001. *Television:* Na vsyu ostavshuyusya zhizn... (mini-series). *Leisure interests:* travelling, books, music. *Address:* Maly Drama Theatre, ul. Rubinshteyna, 18, St Petersburg (office); Michurinskaya St 1-140, St Petersburg 191002, Russia (home). *Telephone:* (812) 713-20-78 (office). *E-mail:* teatr@mdt-dodin.ru (office). *Website:* www.mdt-dodin.ru/eng (office).

SHETREET, Shimon, LLB, LLM, LLD; Israeli politician, legal scholar and academic; *Professor of Law, Hebrew University of Jerusalem;* b. 1 March 1946, Erfoud, Morocco; m. Miri Shetreet; four c.; ed Hebrew Univ., Univ. of Chicago, USA; Sec., Council for Public Justice; Chair. Cttee on Broadcasting Authority Law; Chair. Int. Conf. on Legal Matters; Prof. of Law, Hebrew Univ. 1973–, Chair., Asscn of Lecturers 1974–77, currently also Greenblatt Chair of Public and International Law, fmr Pres. Sacher Inst. of Legislative Research and Comparative Law; Chair. Mishan, Old Age Home Enterprise 1986–88, Int. Inst. for Devt, Cooperation and Labour Studies, Afro-Asian Inst. 1988–92; mem. Bd of Dirs Bank Leumi 1987–89; Visiting Prof. of Law, Univ. of Manitoba 1977–78, Wuerzburg Univ., Germany 1980, Univ. of San Diego School of Law 1983, New York Univ. Law School 1983–84, School of Law, Case Western Reserve Univ. 1999; Minister of Economy and Planning 1992–95, Science and Tech. 1992–93, in charge of Second Television and Radio Authority 1993–95, of Religious Affairs 1995–96; Sr Deputy Mayor of Jerusalem 1998–2003; Visiting Sr Fellow, Inst. of Advanced Legal Studies, Univ. of London 1999; mem. Knesset 1988–96; served on numerous cttees 1988–92, including Landau Comm. on Israeli Court System, Council for Admin. Courts, plenum of Israel Broadcasting Authority 1984–87; Dir Leumi Bank; mem. Labour Party; Ethics Prize 1994, Int. Jurists Award 2010. *Publications include:* The Good Land Between Power and Religion, Judges on Trial 1976, Justice in Israel 1994, Women in Law 1998; and articles on legal matters. *Leisure interest:* Bible study. *Address:* Hebrew University of Jerusalem, Mount Scopus, Jerusalem 91905 (office); 6 Hahavtacha Street, Jerusalem, Israel (home). *Telephone:* 2-5882534 (office); 2-5866444 (home). *Fax:* 2-5883042 (office); 2-5864503 (home). *E-mail:* mshetree@mscc.huji.ac.il (office); shetreet@gmail.com (home). *Website:* law.huji.ac.il/eng (office).

SHETTAR, Jagadish, BCom, LLB; Indian lawyer and politician; b. 17 Dec. 1955, Badami Taluk, Bagalkot District; s. of Shivappa Shivamurthappa Shettar; m. Shilpa Shettar 1984; two s.; ed Jagadguru Gangadhar Coll. of Commerce, Hubli, Karnatak Univ., Dharwad; practised for 20 years as lawyer, Hubli Bar; mem. Karnataka Legis. Ass. from Hubli rural segment 1994–, Leader of the Opposition 1999, Speaker 2008–09; Revenue Minister, Karnataka State Govt 2006, Minister of Rural Devt and Panchayat Raj 2009; Chief Minister of Karnataka 2012–13; mem. Bharatiya Janata Party (BJP), Pres. Hubli Rural Constituency BJP 1990–94, Head of Dharwad BJP District Unit 1994–96, BJP State Sec. 1996–99, BJP State Pres. 2005. *Address:* Bharatiya Janata Party (BJP), 11 Ashok Road, New Delhi 110 001, India (office). *Telephone:* (11)-23005700 (office). *Fax:* (11)-23005787 (office). *E-mail:* webmaster@bjp.org (office). *Website:* www.bjp.org (office); jagadishshettar.com.

SHETTY, Devi Prasad, MB BS, MS, FRCS; Indian cardiologist, philanthropist and entrepreneur; *Chairman, Narayana Hrudayalaya Hospitals;* b. 8 May 1953, Mangalore; m.; four c.; ed Kasturba Medical Coll., Manipal, Univ. of Mysore; sr house officer in cardiothoracic surgery, Killing Beck Hosp., Leeds, UK 1983–84, Brompton Hosp., London, July–Sept. 1984; Registrar in Cardiothoracic Surgery, West Midlands Cardiothoracic Rotation programme between Walsgrave Hosp., Coventry and East Birmingham Hosp. 1984–86; Registrar in Cardiothoracic Surgery, Guy's Hosp., London 1986–89; Chief Cardiac Surgeon and Clinical Dir, B.M. Birla Heart Research Centre, Kolkata 1989–97; Chief Cardiac Surgeon and Vice-Chair. Manipal Heart Foundation, Bangalore 1997–2001; Founder, Chair. and Sr Consultant Cardiac Surgeon, Narayana Hrudayalaya Group of Hosps 2001–; hon. degree (Univ. of Minnesota) 2011, (Indian Inst. of Tech. Madras) 2014; Padma Shri 2003, Padma Bhusan 2012; Rajyotsava Award 2002, Sir M. Visvesvaraya Memorial Award 2003, Ernst & Young Entrepreneur of the Year 2003, Dr B.C. Roy Award 2004, Citizen Extraordinaire, Rotary International 2004, Social Entrepreneurship Award, World Econ. Forum 2005, Commendation for driving affordable and quality healthcare for all, Healthcare Awards Program presented by ICICI Lombard & CNBC TV18 2010, Indian of the Year 2010 from NDTV 2011, Business Process Award Winner, The Economist's Innovation Awards 2011, Economic Times Entrepreneur of the Year Award 2012, FICCI Healthcare Excellence Lifetime Achievement Award 2012, Indian of the Year (Public Service category), CNN-IBN 2012. *Address:* Narayana Hrudayalaya, No. 258/A, Bommasandra Industrial Area, Anekal Taluk, Bangalore 560 099, India (office). *Telephone:* (80) 27835000 (office); (80) 27835018 (office). *Fax:* (80) 27832648 (office). *E-mail:* devishetty@nhhospitals.org (office). *Website:* www.nhhospitals.in (office).

SHETTY, Salil, BCom, MBA, MSc; Indian international organization official; *Secretary-General, Amnesty International;* b. 3 Feb. 1961, Mumbai; s. of V. T. Rajashekhar and Hemlatha Shetty; m. Bina Rani Shetty; one s. one d.; ed Bangalore Univ., Indian Inst. of Man., Ahmedabad, London School of Econs, UK; joined ActionAid 1985, postings to Africa and India, CEO 1998–2003; Dir UN Millennium Campaign 2003–10; Sec.-Gen. Amnesty Int. 2010–; mem. Bd The Overseas Devt Inst., London, Agence France-Presse Foundation, Paris, Inst. of Devt Studies, Sussex; mem. Advisory Council, American India Foundation, New York, Strategic Planning Group of Amnesty Int., Global Leadership Council of the Tech. Museum of Innovation, San Jose, Calif. *Address:* Amnesty International, 1 Easton Street, London, WC1X 0DW, England (office). *Telephone:* (20) 7413-5500 (office). *Fax:* (20) 7956-1157 (office). *E-mail:* sct@amnesty.org.uk (office); contactus@amnesty.org (office). *Website:* www.amnesty.org (office).

SHEVCHENKO, Andrei Mikolayovich; Ukrainian football manager and professional footballer (retd); b. 29 Sept. 1976, Dvrkivshchyna, Yahotynskyi Raion, Kiev Oblast, USSR; m. Kristen Pazik; two s.; striker; family forced to abandon home and relocate to coast to escape Chernobyl disaster 1986; competitive boxer in LLWI Ukrainian jr league for a time; youth player, Dynamo Kiev 1986–94; sr player for Dynamo Kiev 1994–99, 2009– (128 league appearances, 64 goals, won Ukrainian Premier League 1994/95, 1995/96, 1996/97, 1997/98, 1998/99, Ukrainian Cup 1996, 1998, 1999, CIS Cup 1996, 1997, 1998), AC Milan, Italy 1999–2006, 2008–09 (208 appearances, 127 goals, won Serie A 2003/04, Coppa Italia 2002/03, Supercoppa Italiana 2004, UEFA Champions League 2003, UEFA Super Cup 2003, Dubai Challenge Cup 2009), Chelsea 2006–09 (won League Cup 2007, FA Cup 2007, World Football Challenge 2009, FA Community Shield 2009); played for Ukraine U-18 1994–95, Ukraine U-21 1994–95, Ukraine 1995– (92 caps, 43 goals); Asst Ukraine men's nat. football team 2012–16, Head Coach 2016–; Ukrainian Footballer of the Year 1997, 1999–2001, 2004–05, CIS Cup Top Scorer 1997, Ukrainian Premier League Top Scorer 1998–99, UEFA Champions League Top Scorer 1998–99, 2000–01, 2005–06, UEFA Champions League Best Forward 1998–99, Serie A Top Scorer 1999–2000, 2003–04, Serie A Foreign Footballer of the Year 2000, Ballon d'Or (European Footballer of the Year) 2004, named in FIFA 100 2004, FIFPro World XI 2004–05, Ukraine nat. team all-time top scorer, AC Milan second all-time scorer. *Leisure interests:* pool, tennis, cars. *Website:* www.ffu.org.ua/eng; www.sheva7.com.

SHEVCHENKO, Col-Gen. Yuri Leonidovich, DMed; Russian politician and physician; b. 7 April 1947, Yakutsk; m.; two c.; ed Leningrad Acad. of Mil. Medicine; teacher, then Prof., then Head of Chair., Leningrad Mil. Acad. of Medicine 1980–92, Head of Acad. 1992–99; Chief Cardiosurgeon St Petersburg and Leningrad Region, Head, Regional Centre of Cardiac Surgery 1992–99; Minister of Public Health 1999–2004; Rep. of Russian Fed. to WHO Exec. Cttee –2004; apptd Pres. Nat. Medical-Surgical Centre 2004; Vice-Pres. Russian Acad. of Natural Sciences; Vice-Pres. Peter's Acad. of Sciences and Arts; mem. Bd F. Lang Scientific Soc. of Cardiologists; Corresp. mem. Russian Acad. of Medical Sciences. *Publications:* over 300 articles.

SHEVCHUK, Yevgenii Vasilyevich; Moldovan (ethnic Ukrainian) lawyer and politician; b. 19 June 1968, Rybnitsa (Rîbniţa), Moldavian SSR, USSR; Deputy to Supreme Soviet of 'Transnistrian Moldovan Repub.' 2000–11; Speaker of Transnistria Supreme Soviet 2005–09 (resgnd); Leader of opposition party Obnovleniye (Renewal) –2010, led a reform drive by his party to introduce changes to Transnistria's electoral code prior to 2005; has worked both in government and in pvt. business; banned by European Parl. from entering EU countries; Pres. of the 'Transnistrian Moldovan Republic' 2011–16. *Address:* c/o Office of the President of the 'Transnistrian Moldovan Republic', 3300 Tiraspol, ul. Karla Marksa 187, Moldova. *E-mail:* psp@president.gospmr.org.

SHEYNIS, Viktor Leonidovich, DrSc; Russian historian, politician and economist; *Chief Research Fellow, Institute of World Economy and International Relations;* b. 16 Feb. 1931, Kiev; s. of Leonid M. Sheynis and Liah O. Kimelfeld; m. Alla K. Nazimova 1953; ed Leningrad Univ.; history teacher in secondary school 1953–56; manual worker, Kirov factory, Leningrad 1958–64; teacher, Leningrad Univ. 1966–75; on staff as researcher at Inst. of World Economy and Int. Relations (IMEMO) 1975–92, Chief Research Fellow 2000–; co-author of Russian Constitution and electoral laws 1993–99; People's Deputy 1990–93, mem. State Duma (Parl.) 1993–99; mem. Supreme Soviet of Russia 1991–93; Co-Founder Consent in Name of Progress faction 1992–93; mem. Council of Reps of 'Democratic Russia' Movt 1990–93, Yabloko Movt 1993–95, Yabloko Party 1995–, Political Bureau and Fed. Council; mem. Cttee on Legislation and Reform of the Judicial System; Imre Nagy Medal (Hungary) 1993. *Publications include:* Developing Nations at the Turn of the Millennium 1987, Capitalism, Socialism and Economic Mechanism of Present-day Production 1989, Die Präsidentenwahlen in Russland: Ergebnisse und Perspektiven, Osteuropa 1996, O caminho histórico da Revolução de Outubro visto sob a prisma de 1997 1997, Il tormentato cammino della Constituzione russa 1998, Wie Russland gewaklt hat: Osteuropa 2000, The Constitution: In Between Dictatorship and Democracy 2004, The Rise and Fall of Parliament: Watershed Years in Russian Politics 1985–93 (two vols) 2005. *Leisure interests:* tourism, cinematography, reading. *Address:* Institute of World Economy and International Relations, 117859 Moscow, Profsoyuznaya str. 23 (office); 117335 Moscow, Vavilova str. 91, corp. 1, Apartment 41, Russia (home). *Telephone:* (495) 120-52-36 (office); (495) 132-73-15 (home). *Fax:* (495) 120-65-75 (office). *E-mail:* imemoran@imemo.ru (office); nazimova@mtu-net.ru (home). *Website:* www.imemo.ru (office).

SHHAIDEH, Sevil; Romanian civil servant and politician; b. (Sevil Cambek), 4 Dec. 1964, Constanţa; family belongs to Turkish and Tatar minorities of Romania; m. Akram Shhaideh 2011; ed Acad. of Econ. Sciences, Ovidius Univ. of Constanţa, Faculty of Econ. Planning and Cybernetics, obtained specialization as expert in public admin and int. org. from USAID; programmer analyst, Trust for Agricultural Mechanization, Constanţa 1987–91; Man., Information Systems, Dept of Labour and Social Protection, Constanţa Co. 1991–93; Dir, Sevil Shhaileh Information Systems, Constanţa Co. Council 1993–2007, led Gen. Directorate of Projects 2007–12; fmr Co-ordinator, Nat. Union of County Councils of Romania (UNCJR); State Sec., Minister of Regional Devt and Public Admin 2012–15; Deputy Prime Minister and Minister of Regional Devt and Public Admin May–Nov. 2015; nominated as Prime Minister Dec. 2016 but nomination rejected by Pres. Klaus Johannis; Deputy Prime Minister June–Oct. 2017, Minister of Regional Devt, Public Admin and EU Funds Jan.–Oct. 2017; Pres. Nat. Asscn of Public Admin 2000. *Address:* c/o Ministry of Regional Development, Public Administration and European Union Funds, 050706 Bucharest 5, Str. Libertăţii 16, North Wing, Romania (office).

SHI, Dahua; Chinese railway industry executive; ed Southwest Jiaotong Univ., Cen. Communist Party School; joined China Railway Group Ltd 1997, Deputy Sec. to CCP Cttee, China Railway Construction Corpn 1995–97, Deputy Sec. to CCP Cttee, China Railway Eng Corpn (CRECG) 1997–98, Sec. 1998–2007, Deputy Gen. Man. CRECG 2002–06, Chair. 2006–10, Chair. and Exec. Dir China Railway Group Ltd 2007–10; Alt. mem. 16th CCP Cen. Cttee 2002–07, 17th CCP Cen. Cttee 2007–12; Dir of Transportation Professionals Co-operation Cttee of Consultant Council for the Promotion of Econ. and Tech. Cooperation of China-Spain Forum; Deputy Dir Steering Cttee of Nat. Construction Enterprise Career Man. Certification and Construction Enterprises Qualifications Admin and Research; recognized as a sr economist by Ministry of Personnel 2007.

SHI, Guangsheng; Chinese politician; b. Sept. 1939, Changli, Hebei Prov.; ed Beijing Inst. of Foreign Trade; joined CCP 1965; clerk, Deputy Section Dir, later Deputy Gen. Man. China Metals and Minerals Import and Export Corpn 1974–86; Special Commr Ministry of Foreign Econ. Relations and Trade, Shanghai 1986–88; Dir Import and Export Dept, Ministry of Foreign Trade 1988–91, Asst Minister of Foreign Econ. Relations and Trade 1991–93; Vice-Minister of Foreign Trade and Econ. Co-operation 1993–98, Minister 1998–2003; fmr Pres. China Asscn of Enterprises with Foreign Investment; fmr Exec. Vice-Chair. World Econ. Devt Declaration Conf.

SHI, Jiliang; Chinese economist and banker; b. Feb. 1945; ed Cen. Inst. of Banking and Finance; Vice-Pres. Heilongjiang br., Agricultural Bank of China 1983–88, Vice-Pres. Tianjing br. 1988–91, Pres. Tianjing br. 1991–94, Pres. Agricultural Bank of China 1994–97; Vice-Pres. People's Bank of China 1997–2003; Vice-Chair. China Banking Regulatory Comm. 2003–05; Chair. Bd of Supervisors China Merchants Bank Co. Ltd –2010; mem. 10th Nat. Cttee CPPCC.

SHI, Jiuyong, MA; Chinese lawyer, professor of international law and judge (retd); b. 9 Oct. 1926, Ningbo, Zhejiang Prov.; m. Zhang Guoying 1956; one s.; ed St John's Univ., Shanghai and Columbia Univ., New York, USA; Asst Research Fellow, Inst. of Int. Relations, Beijing 1956–58; Sr Lecturer, Assoc. Prof. of Int. Law, Foreign Affairs Coll. Beijing 1958–64; Research Fellow in Int. Law, Inst. of Int. Law, Beijing 1964–73, Inst. of Int. Studies, Beijing 1973–80; Prof. of Int. Law, Foreign Affairs Coll. Beijing 1984–93, Foreign Econ. Law Training Centre of Ministry of Justice; Legal Adviser, Ministry of Foreign Affairs 1980–93, Chinese Centre of Legal Consultancy, Office of Chinese Sr Rep. Sino-British Jt Liaison Group (on question of Hong Kong) 1985–93; Adviser to Chinese Soc. of Int. Law –2003, Fellow; mem. American Soc. of Int. Law; mem. Standing Cttee Beijing Cttee of CPPCC 1988–93, mem. 8th Nat. Cttee 1993–98; mem. Int. Law Comm. 1987–93, Chair. 1990; Judge, Int. Court of Justice, The Hague 1994–2010, Vice-Pres. 2000–03, Pres. 2003–06; mem. Advisory Bd, The Global Community Yearbook of Int. Law and Jurisprudence; Pres. Curatorium Xiamen Acad. of Int. Law 2005–; Hon. Prof., Eastern China Univ. of Political Science and Law 2001–; Hon. Pres. Chinese Soc. of Int. Law 2004–. *Publications:* numerous publs on int. law. *Leisure interest:* classical music. *Address:* c/o International Court of Justice, Peace Palace, Carnegieplein 2, 2517 KJ The Hague, Netherlands. *E-mail:* info@icj-cij.org.

SHI, Mingde; Chinese diplomatist; *Ambassador to Germany;* b. Dec. 1954, Shanghai; m.; one c.; ed studies in GDR; posted to Embassy in Berlin, GDR 1976–81, employed in service office for diplomats in Beijing 1981–86, Second Sec., Embassy in Berlin, GDR 1986–90, Deputy Head of West Europe Dept, Ministry of Foreign Affairs (MFA) 1990–93, Counsellor, Embassy in Bonn, FRG 1993–97, Counsellor, Policy Planning Staff and Deputy Dept Man. for Western Europe, MFA 1997–2002, Amb. to Germany 2002–06, Dir Gen. Cen. Office for Foreign Affairs, CCP Cen. Cttee 2006–10, Amb. to Austria 2010–12, to Germany 2012–. *Address:* Embassy of the People's Republic of China, Märkisches Ufer 54, 10179 Berlin, Germany (office). *Telephone:* (30) 27588-0 (office). *Fax:* (30) 27588-221 (office). *Website:* www.china-botschaft.de (office).

SHI, Xiushi; Chinese politician; b. July 1942, Shangqiu, Henan Prov.; ed Beijing Civil Eng Inst.; joined CCP 1978; technician and engineer, later Deputy Dir Building Materials Research Inst. 1964–80; Engineer and Deputy Chief, Building Materials Industry Div., Heavy Industry Bureau, State Econ. Comm. 1980–86; Deputy Div. Chief, later Div. Chief, Office of Tourist Industry Coordination 1986–88; Deputy Dir, later Dir Bureau of the State Council 1988–96; Deputy Sec.-Gen. State Council 1996–2000; Vice-Gov. of Guizhou 2001, Gov. 2001–06; Deputy Sec. Guizhou Prov. Cttee 2000–06; mem. 16th CCP Cen. Cttee 2002–07; Deputy Dir 10th Financial and Econ. Cttee of NPC 2006–08; Chair. 11th Financial and Econ. Cttee of NPC 2008–13.

SHI, Adm. Yunsheng; Chinese fmr naval officer; b. Jan. 1940, Fushun City, Liaoning Prov.; ed PLA Air Force Aviation School and PLA Navy Acad.; joined PLA 1956, CCP 1960; pilot, Squadron Leader, Deputy Group Commdr and Deputy Regt Commdr Naval Aviation 1962–70; Deputy Commdr Naval Fleet Aviation 1976–81; Div. Commdr Naval Aviation 1981–83; Commdr Naval Fleet Aviation 1983–90; Deputy Commdr PLA Naval Aviation Dept 1990–92; Deputy Commdr PLA Navy 1992–96, Commdr 1996–2003; rank of Adm. 2000; Del. 13th CCP Nat. Congress 1987–92; mem. 15th CCP Cen. Cttee 1997–2002, 16th CCP Cen. Cttee 2002–07.

SHI, Zhengrong, BSc, MSc, PhD; Chinese/Australian electrical engineer, research scientist and business executive; *Executive Chairman and Chief Strategy Officer, Suntech Power Holdings Company Ltd;* b. 1963, Yangzhong, Jiangsu Prov.; m.; two c.; ed Changchun Univ. of Science and Tech., Shanghai Inst. of Optics and Fine Mechanics, Chinese Acad. of Sciences, Univ. of New South Wales, Australia; Sr Research Scientist and Leader, Thin Film Solar Cells Research Group, Centre of Excellence for Photovoltaic Eng, Univ. of NSW, Australia 1992–95; Research Dir and Exec. Pacific Solar Pty, Australia 1995–2001, acquired Australian citizenship 2001; Founder, Chair. and CEO Suntech Power Holdings Co., Ltd (manufacturer of photovoltaic cells for use in solar panels), Wuxi, China 2001–13, Exec. Chair. and Chief Strategy Officer 2013–; Wuxi Prize for Excellence in Innovation and Pioneering, Nat. Prize for Excellent Achievements by Homecoming Chinese. *Publications:* numerous scientific papers. *Address:* Suntech Power Holdings Company Ltd, 9 Xinhua Road, New District, Wuxi 214028, Jiangsu Province, People's Republic of China (office). *Telephone:* (86510) 85318888 (office). *Fax:* (86510) 85343321 (office). *E-mail:* ir@suntech-power.com (office). *Website:* www.suntech-power.com (office).

SHI, Zhong-ci; Chinese computer scientist and professor of mathematics; *Chairman, Academic Committee, Institute of Computational Mathematics and Scientific/Engineering Computing, Chinese Academy of Sciences;* b. 5 Dec. 1933, Ningpo Co., Zhejiang Prov.; ed Fudan Univ., Steklov Inst. of Math., Moscow; Asst Research Fellow, Inst. of Computing Tech., Chinese Acad. of Sciences 1961–64; Lecturer, Univ. of Science and Tech. 1965–77, Assoc. Prof. 1978–79, Prof. 1980–86, Chair. Dept of Math. and Dir of Computer Center 1984–88, Dir Inst. of Computational Math. and Scientific/Engineering Computing (fmrly Computer Center), Chinese Acad. of Sciences 1987–91, Sr Research Fellow 1987–94; currently Vice-Dean Coll. of Sciences, Zhejiang Univ., also Researcher Center of Mathematical Sciences; currently Chair. Academic Cttee, Lab. of Scientific and Eng Computing (LSEC), Chair. Academic Cttee, Inst. of Computational Mathematics and Scientific/Engineering Computing (ICMSEC); Vice-Pres. Chinese Math. Soc. 1988–95; Vice-Pres. Chinese Soc. of Computational Math. 1985–89, Pres. 1994–; Chief Scientist Nat. Key Project for Fundamental Research; mem. Chinese Sciences Acad. 1992–; also served as Visiting Prof. to numerous univs; 2nd Prize Award, Chinese Acad. of Sciences 1980, 1st Prize Award, Chinese Acad. of Sciences 1986, Nat. Natural Science Award 1987. *Leisure interests:* travel, classical music. *Address:* Institute of Computational Mathematics and Scientific/Engineering Computing, Chinese Academy of Sciences, No.55, ZhongGuanCun DongLu, POB 2719, Beijing 100090, People's Republic of China (office). *Telephone:* 62587583 (office). *Fax:* 62542285 (office). *E-mail:* shi@lsec.cc.ac.cn (office). *Website:* www.cc.ac.cn (office); lsec.cc.ac.cn/~shi/homepage.html.

SHI, Zongyuan; Chinese politician; b. July 1946, Baoding, Hebei Prov.; ed Northwest Ethnic Inst.; worker, People's Govt, Hezheng Co., Gansu Prov. 1968–80, CCP Co. Cttee 1978–80; joined CCP 1978; fmrly clerk in various govt offices in Hezheng Co., Gansu Prov.; Deputy Magistrate Hezheng Co. (Dist)

People's Court 1981–82, Magistrate 1981–84; Deputy Chief Magistrate Linxia Hui Autonomous Pref., Gansu Prov., Deputy Sec. and then Sec. CCP Linxia Hui Autonomous Pref. Cttee 1984–93; Dir Propaganda Dept of CCP Gansu Prov. Cttee 1993–98; Dir Propaganda Dept of CCP Jilin Prov. Cttee, also Vice-Sec. CCP 1998–2000; Dir Press and Publications Admin and Dir State Bureau of Copyrights 2000–05; Sec. Guizhou Provincial CCP Cttee 2005–10; apptd Chair. Provincial People's Congress Standing Cttee, Guizhou Prov. 2006; Vice-Chair. 11th Internal and Judicial Affairs Cttee NPC 2010; Alt. mem. 14th CCP Cen. Cttee 1992–97, 15th CCP Cen. Cttee 1997–2002, mem. 16th CCP Cen. Cttee 2002–07; mem. 17th CCP Cen. Cttee 2007–12.

SHIARLY, Vassos; Cypriot banker and government official; b. 1948, London, UK; ed LSE, Wayne State Univ.; worked for 19 years in various accounting firms in London, becoming Sr Man., Coopers & Lybrand –1985; joined Bank of Cyprus Group 1985, becoming Sr Man., Customer Man. Services Unit, Group Gen. Man., Branch Banking 1998–2003, Group Gen. Man., Domestic Banking 2003–09, Sr Group Gen. Man. 2009–10, Group Chief Gen. Man. 2010–11, also Head, Domestic Corporate Banking and Int. Corporate Lending; Minister of Finance 2012–13; Chair. Asscn of Cyprus Banks 2009–10; fmr Group Adviser and Chair. Cypriot Health Insurance Org.; mem. Bd of Dirs Nicosia Junior School 1986–92.

SHIBATA, Ai; Japanese swimmer (retd); b. 14 May 1982, Fukuoka Pref.; ed Nat. Inst. of Fitness and Sports, School of Physical Educ. Univ.; gold medal, 800m freestyle, Athens Olympics 2004; silver medal, 400m freestyle, bronze medal, 800m freestyle, World Championships, Montreal 2005; bronze medal, 400m freestyle, bronze medal, 1500m freestyle, World Championships, Melbourne 2007; gold medal, 400m freestyle, silver medal, 800m freestyle, bronze medal, 1500m freestyle, Pan Pacific Championships, Victoria 2006; swims for Team Arena Club; retd in 2008. *Address:* Japan Amateur Swimming Federation, Kishi Memorial Hall, 1-1-1 Jinnan, 1-chome, Shibuyo-Ku, Tokyo 150-8050, Japan. *Telephone:* (3) 3481-2306. *Fax:* (3) 3481-0942. *Website:* www.descente.co.jp/arena-jp/fan/ai.html.

SHIBIBI, Sinan Muhammad Rida ash-, MA, PhD; Iraqi economist; ed Univs of Manchester and Bristol, UK; consultant on trade, debt and finance; Head, importation and marketing section, Ministry of Oil 1975–77; served in Iraqi Ministry of Planning 1977–80; taught at Baghdad Univ. and Mustansiryah Univ., Iraq; Sr Economist, UNCTAD –2001, consultant 2001–03; Gov. Cen. Bank of Iraq 2003–12; spoke at Senate hearings on Iraq Aug. 2002, on disappearance of Iraqi middle class under sanctions, and reconstruction of Iraq, and at AEI Conf. on post-Saddam Iraq Oct. 2002 (mem. follow-up cttee Dec. 2002); sentenced in 2014 to seven years in prison for corruption during tenure as Gov. Cen. Bank of Iraq. *Publications:* OPEC Aid: Issues and Performance 1987, The Arab Share in OPEC Aid: Some Related Facts 1988, Prospects for the Iraqi Economy: Facing the New Reality 1997, Globalisation of Finance: Implications for Macroeconomic Policies and Debt Management 2001.

SHIELDS, Brooke Christa Camille, BA; American actress and model; b. 31 May 1965, New York; d. of Francis Shields and Teri Schmon; m. Andre Agassi 1997 (divorced 1999); m. Chris Henchy 2001; two d.; ed Princeton Univ.; began modelling in Ivory Soap commercials 1966, later for Calvin Klein jeans and Colgate toothpaste. *Theatre includes:* Grease (Broadway) 1994–95, Wonderful Town (Broadway) 2004, Chicago (Adelphi Theatre, London) 2005. *Films:* Communion (aka Alice, Sweet Alice) 1976, Pretty Baby 1977, King of the Gypsies 1978, Wanda Nevada 1978, Just You and Me, Kid 1978, Tilt 1979, The Blue Lagoon 1979, Endless Love 1980, Sahara 1983, The Muppets Take Manhattan 1984, Brenda Starr 1986, Speed Zone! 1988, Backstreet Dreams (aka Backstreet Strays) 1989, Running Wild 1992, Freaked 1993, The Seventh Floor 1993, Freeway 1996, The Misadventures of Margaret 1998, The Weekend 1999, Black and White 1999, The Bachelor 1999, After Sex 2000, Mariti in affitto 2004, The Easter Egg Adventure 2005, Bob the Butler 2005, The Midnight Meat Train 2008, Furry Vengeance 2010, Chalet Girl 2011, The Greening of Whitney Brown 2011, The Hot Flashes 2013, Daisy Winters 2017. *Television:* After the Fall (film) 1974, The Prince of Central Park (film) 1977, Wet Gold (film) 1984, The Diamond Trap (film) 1988, I Can Make You Love Me (film) 1993, Un Amore americano (film) 1994, Nothing Lasts Forever (mini series) 1995, Suddenly Susan (series) 1996, The Almost Perfect Bank Robbery (film) 1998, What Makes a Family (film) 2001, Widows (mini series) 2002, Miss Spider's Sunny Patch Kids (film, voice) 2003, Gone But Not Forgotten (mini series) 2004, Hannah Montana (series) 2007–09, Lipstick Jungle (series) 2008–09, The Middle 2010–18, Army Wives (series) 2013, A Monsterous Holiday (film, voice) 2013, Mr. Pickles (series, voice) 2013–18, Creative Galaxy (series, voice) 2014–18, Flower Shop Mystery: Mum's The Word (film) 2016, Flower Shop Mystery: Snipped in the Bud (film) 2016, Flower Shop Mystery: Dearly Depotted (film) 2016, Law & Order: Special Victims Unit (series) 2017–18. *Publication:* The Brooke Book 1978, On Your Own 1985, Down Came the Rain: A Mother's Story of Depression and Recovery 2005, It's the Best Day Ever, Dad! 2009, There Was a Little Girl: The Real Story of My Mother and Me 2014. *Leisure interests:* pottery.

SHIGA, Shigenori; Japanese business executive; b. 13 Dec. 1953; joined Toshiba Corpn 1979, Vice-Pres., Power Systems Co. 2008–11, Exec. Officer, Corp. Sr Vice-Pres. 2011–14, Exec. Officer, Corp. Exec. Vice-Pres. 2014–15, Rep. Exec. Officer, Corp. Sr Exec. Vice-Pres. 2015–16, Dir, Rep. Exec. Officer and Chair. 2016–17. *Address:* c/o Toshiba Corporation, 1-1, Shibaura 1-chome, Minato-ku, Tokyo 105-8001, Japan (office).

SHIGA, Toshiyuki; Japanese automotive industry executive; *Vice-Chairman, Nissan Motor Co. Ltd;* Head of China operations, Nissan Motor Co. Ltd –2007, Rep. Dir 2005–, COO and Sr Vice-Pres., Nissan Motor Co. Ltd 2005–13, Vice-Chair., External and Govt Affairs, Intellectual Asset Man., Corp. Governance 2013–; Chair. Japan Automobile Mfrs Asscn Inc. –2012. *Address:* Nissan Motor Co. Ltd, 1-1, Takashima 1-chome, Nishi-ku, Yokohama-shi, Kanagawa 220-8686, Japan (office). *Telephone:* (45) 523-5523 (office). *Website:* www.nissan-global.com (office).

SHIGEHARA, Kumiharu, BL; Japanese economist; *President, International Economic Policy Studies Association;* b. 5 Feb. 1939, Maebashi; s. of Seizaburo Shigehara and Rutsu Tanabe; m. Akiko Yoshizawa 1965; one s. one d.; ed Maebashi High School, Univ. of Tokyo, Univ. of Poitiers, France; Economist, Bank of Japan 1962–70; Economist, OECD 1970–71, Sr Economist 1971–72, Head, Monetary Div. 1972–74; Councillor for Policy Planning, Bank of Japan 1974–76; Man. Int. Affairs 1976–80; Deputy Dir-Gen., Econs Branch, OECD 1980–82; Gen.

Man. Bank of Japan 1983–87; Dir-Gen., Econs Branch, OECD 1987–89; Dir-Gen. Inst. for Monetary and Econ. Studies and Chief Economist, Bank of Japan 1989–92; Head, Econs Dept and Chief Economist, OECD 1992–97, Deputy Sec.-Gen. OECD 1997–99; Special Adviser, Int. Friendship Exchange Council 2000–; Head, Int. Econ. Policy Studies Group 2002–08; Pres. Int. Econ. Policy Studies Asscn 2008–; Dr hc (Liège) 1998; Hozumi Special Award, Univ. of Tokyo 1960. *Publications include:* The Role of Monetary Policy in Demand Management (co-author) 1975, Europe After 1992 1991, The Problems of Inflation in the 1990s (ed.) 1992, Evolving International Trade and Monetary Regimes 1992, Causes of Declining Growth in Industrialised Countries 1992, Price Stabilization in the 1990s 1993, Long-term Tendencies in Budget Deficits and Debt 1995, The Options regarding the Concept of a Monetary Policy Strategy 1996, Monetary and Economic Policy: Then and Now 1998, Causes and Implications of East Asian Financial Crises 1998, International Aspects of Competition Policy 1999, Monetary Policy and Economic Performance 2001, Looking for Models in Pursuit of Economic Prosperity 2002, Managing the International Economic Crisis 2008, Surveillance by International Institutions: Lessons from the Global Financial and Economic Crisis (with Paul Atkinson) 2011, The Limits of Surveillance and Financial Market Failure: Lessons from the Euro-area Crisis 2014. *Leisure interests:* golf, tennis, hiking. *E-mail:* office.shigehara@online.fr (office). *Website:* office.shigehara.online.fr (office).

SHIGEMOTO, Hiroshi (Hiro), BA, BSc; Dutch politician; b. 22 June 1970, Sint Maarten, Netherlands Antilles; s. of Jesiman Veronica Lake; m. Zetsia Robin Shigemoto-Duncan; one s.; ed Christelijke Hogeschool, Netherlands, Univ. of Tampa, USA; Head of Finance, Island Govt of Sint Maarten 2003–06, Dir of Resources 2006–10; Minister of Finance (first holder after dissolution of Netherlands Antilles) 2010–12 (resgnd); on trial for fraud Oct. 2014; mem. United People's Party; numerous awards for participation in lectures and seminars. *Leisure interests:* gardening, music appreciation.

SHIH, Chi-Yang, LLM, DJur; Taiwanese politician; b. 5 May 1935, Taichung City; m. Jeanne Tchong-Koei Li 1968; ed Nat. Taiwan Univ., Univ. of Heidelberg, Germany; Asst, Dept of Law, Nat. Taiwan Univ. 1959–62, Assoc. Prof. 1967–71, Prof. (part-time) 1971–84; Research Asst, Inst. of Int. Relations, Nat. Chengchi Univ. 1967–69, Research Fellow 1969–71; Deputy Dir 5th Section, Cen. Cttee, Kuomintang 1969–72, Deputy Dir Dept of Youth Activities 1972–76; Admin. Vice-Minister, Ministry of Educ. 1976–79; Political Vice-Minister, Ministry of Educ. 1979–80, Ministry of Justice 1980–84; Minister of Justice 1984–88; Vice-Premier 1988–93; Sec.-Gen. Nat. Security Council 1993–94; Pres. Judicial Yuan 1994–99.

SHIH, Choon Fong, MSc, PhD; Singaporean scientist, fmr university administrator and professor of mechanical engineering; b. 23 Oct. 1945; ed Singapore Polytechnic, Harvard Univ., USA; Research Fellow, Harvard Univ. 1973–74; Leader, Fracture Research Group, Corp. Research Lab., General Electric, NY 1974–81; Visiting Assoc. Prof., Brown Univ. 1981–83, Assoc. Prof. 1983–86, Prof. 1986–97; Visiting Prof., Japan Soc. for Promotion of Science, Tokyo Univ. 1989; Fellow, Applied Mechanics Div., ASME 1999; Founding Dir Inst. of Materials Research and Eng, Singapore 1996–99; Founding Pres. Materials Research Soc. of Singapore; Deputy Vice-Chancellor Nat. Univ. of Singapore 1997–2000, Vice-Chancellor and Pres. 2000–08; Founding Pres. King Abdullah Univ. of Science and Tech. (KAUST) 2008–13; Chair. Emer. Asscn of Pacific Rim Univs (APRU), fmr Chair. Governing Bd, APRU World Inst.; Dir Agency for Science, Tech. and Research, Biomedical Research Council, Science and Eng Research Council, Inst. of Policy Studies, Singapore Int. Fed.; Foreign Assoc., Nat. Acad. of Eng (USA) 2004; fmr Founding Pres. Materials Research Soc. of Singapore; fmr consultant to NASA, Oak Ridge Nat. Lab., Nuclear Regulatory Comm.; fmr mem. Singapore Int. Foundation; Foreign Hon. mem. American Acad. of Arts and Sciences 2006, Hon. mem. Medical Alumni Asscn, Singapore 2007; Chevalier, Légion d'honneur 2005; Dr hc (Loughborough Univ.) 2005, (Waseda Univ.) 2007, (Brown Univ.) 2008; George Rankin Irwin Medal, American Soc. for Testing and Materials 1986, Swedlow Award, American Soc. for Testing and Materials 1998, Chief Exec. Leadership Award, Council for Advancement and Support for Educ. 2007, Ted Belytschko Applied Mechanics Award, American Soc. for Mechanical Engineers 2008, Harvard Centennial Medal 2018. *Publications:* more than 200 papers in academic journals. *Address:* c/o King Abdullah University of Science & Technology, Thuwal 23955-6900, Saudi Arabia.

SHIH, Jonney, BSc, MBA; Taiwanese business executive; *Chairman, ASUSTeK Computer Inc.;* b. 1951; ed Nat. Taiwan Univ., Nat. Chao-Tung Univ.; fmr research and devt engineer at Acer Inc.; Chair. and CEO ASUSTeK Computer Inc. 1993–2008, Chair. 2008–; Outstanding Tech. Man. Award, Chinese Soc. for Man. of Tech. 2006, Outstanding Entrepreneur Award, Chinatimes and Taiwan DHL 2006, Pan Wen Yuan Prize 2012. *Address:* ASUSTeK Computer Inc., 15 Li-Te Road, Peitou, Taipei 112, Taiwan (office). *Telephone:* (2) 2894-3447 (office). *Fax:* (2) 2892-6140 (office). *E-mail:* info@asus.com (office). *Website:* www.asus.com (office).

SHIH, Ming-Teh; Taiwanese politician; b. 15 Jan. 1941, Kaohsiung; s. of Shih Kuo-tsui; m. 1st Chen Li-chu (divorced); m. 2nd Linda Gail Arrigo; ed Kaohsiung Jr High-School, Kaohsiung's Chung-Cheng Sr High School; fmr political prisoner in Taiwan, spent 25 years in prison, 13 years in solitary confinement and over four years on hunger strike; reporter, Liberty Times; Chair. Democratic Progressive Party 1994–96; mem. Taiwan Legis. Council; initiated Million Voices Against Corruption-Chen Must Go campaign 2006. *Address:* Room 601, 10 Tsingtao East Road, Taipei, Taiwan.

SHIH, Dato Stan, PhD; Taiwanese computer industry executive; *Honorary Chairman, Acer Inc.;* b. 18 Dec. 1944, Chang-Hwa; m. Carolyn Yeh; two s. one d.; ed Nat. Chiao Tung Univ.; with Unitron Industrial Corpn 1971–72, Qualitron Industrial Corpn 1972–76; f. Acer Inc. (electronics co. previously known as Multitech) 1976, Chair. and CEO 1976–2004 (retd), Chair. and Pres. 2013–14, now Hon. Chair.; Founder-Chair. iD SoftCapital 2004–; Chair. Nat. Culture and Arts Foundation; Founder and Chair. Stans Foundation; mem. Bd of Dirs BenQ, Wistron, Taiwan Semiconductor Manufacturing Co., Nan Shan Life Insurance Co., National Chiang Kai-Shek Cultural Center, Taiwan Public Television Service Foundation; mem. Asia Business Council (fmr Chair.); mem. Int. Advisory Panel, Malaysia's Multimedia Super Corridor; Gov. Asian Inst. of Man.; apptd Special Rep. of Pres. to APEC Meeting, Australia 2007; Hon. Fellow, Univ. of Wales; Hon.

Chair. Brand Int. Promotion Asscn; Order of the Brilliant Star with Grand Cordon 2011; Dr hc (National Chiao Tung Univ.) 1992, (Hong Kong Polytechnic Univ.) 1997, (American Grad. School of Int. Man., Thunderbird School of Global Man.) 2000; Int. Business Exec. of the Year, Acad. of Int. Business 1999, Outstanding Contribution to Brand Building Award 2003, Asian Star of the Year, Businessweek magazine 2004, named as one of Asian Heroes, Time magazine 2006, Lifetime Achievement Reward of the 4th Pan Wen Yuan Prize 2011, Industrial Technology Research Inst. Laureate 2012. *Publications include:* more than 100 articles on man., marketing etc. *Address:* Acer Inc., 8f, 88, Sec. 1, Hsin Tai Wu Road, Hsichih, Taipei 221, Taiwan (office). *Telephone:* (2) 26961234 (office). *Fax:* (2) 26963535 (office). *Website:* www.acer.com (office).

SHIH, Yen-Shiang, PhD; Taiwanese politician and business executive; b. 1950; m. Ei-Wang Chang; ed Nat. Taiwan Univ., Massachusetts Inst. of Tech., USA; Assoc. Prof. and Prof. of Chemical Eng and Tech., Nat. Taiwan Inst. of Tech. (now Nat. Taiwan Univ. of Science and Tech.) 1979–89, Head of Dept of Chemical Eng and Tech. 1981–86; Prof., Grad. Inst. of Tech. and Innovation Man., Nat. Cheng-Chih Univ. 1996–2002; Deputy Dir Office of Science and Tech. Advisors (now Dept of Industrial Tech.), Ministry of Econ. Affairs 1986–87, later Dir, Dir-Gen. Small and Medium Enterprises Admin 1992–95, Dir-Gen. Industrial Devt, Bureau 2001–02; Dir-Gen. Taiwan Tobacco and Wine Bureau (now Taiwan Tobacco and Liquor Co.) 1995–2000; Chair. CPC Corpn March–Sept. 2009; Deputy Minister of Econ. Affairs 2002–09, Minister of Econ. Affairs 2009–13. *Address:* c/o Ministry of Economic Affairs, 15 Foo Chou Street, Taipei 10015, Taiwan. *E-mail:* minister@moea.gov.tw.

SHIHAB, Hussain, MSc; Maldivian politician, diplomatist and business executive; b. 1949; m.; six c.; ed Wesley Coll., Colombo, Kuban State Agric. Univ., USSR, Int. Training Inst., Sydney, Australia; Under-Sec., Ministry of Home Affairs and Social Services 1975, Ministry of Agric. 1976–78; Man. TV Maldives 1978–81, Deputy Dir, then Dir 1985; Dir of Environmental Affairs, Ministry of Home Affairs and Social Services 1986–88, Dir of Environmental Affairs, Ministry of Planning and the Environment 1988–93, Deputy Minister 1993–95, July–Sept. 1998; Dir South Asia Co-operative Environment Programme 1995–98; Amb. and Perm. Rep. to UN, New York 1998–2002; del. to numerous UN meetings on the environment, including Conf. on Environment and Devt 1992 and Global Conf. on the Sustainable Devt of Small Island Developing States 1994; fmr Deputy Minister of Foreign Affairs; Minister of State for the Arts 2005–07; Amb. to Saudi Arabia and OIC 2007–10, High Commr to Sri Lanka 2010–14 (also accred to Australia and as Amb. to the Philippines); Owner and CEO, Gulfaam Films 2000–; consultant for media, public relations and foreign affairs 2014–; formulated Maldives' first nat. environmental action plan; Silver Pen Award 1987. *Films:* Fidhaa 1985, Hadmiya 1993, Rihun 2002, Vissaradmuni 2005. *Publications:* Ochid Eyanarse Maa (short stories) 1983; papers on the environment and sustainable devt presented at int. confs. *Leisure interests:* film, reading, writing. *Address:* Ministry of Foreign Affairs, Boduthakurufaanu Magu, Malé 20-077, Maldives (office). *Telephone:* 3323400 (office). *Fax:* 3323841 (office). *E-mail:* admin@foreign.gov.mv (office). *Website:* www.foreign.gov.mv (office).

SHIHAB, Mohamed, BEcons; Maldivian economist and politician; b. 2 Oct. 1957, Malé; s. of Ibrahim Shihab and Jameela Ibrahim; ed James Cook Univ. of N Queensland, Australia; Project Officer, Nat. Planning Agency, Malé 1980–81, Asst Dir 1981–82; Under-Sec., Ministry of Planning and Devt 1982–85, Sr Under-Sec. 1985–89, Dir of External Resources 1989–94; Dir Maldives Transport and Contracting Co. Ltd 1994–99; fmr sr mem. Maldivian Democratic Party; MP (Jumhooree Party) for Dhaal Atoll 1985–2005, for Malé 2005–, Speaker of People's Majlis 2008–09; Minister of Home Affairs 2009–10 (resgnd), of Finance Jan.–Mar. 2012; Man. Dir Maldives Post Ltd 2006; mem. Bd of Dirs Maldives Transport and Contracting Co. Ltd 1991–99, Bank of Maldives 1994–96, Maldives Tourism Devt Corpn PLC 2007–08. *Address:* c/o Ministry of Finance and Treasury, Ameenee Magu, Malé 20-379, Maldives.

SHIHAB-ELDIN, Adnan, BSc, MSc, PhD; Kuwaiti engineer and international organization official; *Director General, Kuwait Foundation for Advancement of Sciences;* b. 1943; ed Univ. of California, Berkeley, USA; trained as nuclear engineer; Asst Prof. of Physics, then Vice-Rector of Academic Affairs, Kuwait Univ. 1970–80; Dir-Gen. Kuwait Inst. for Scientific Research 1976–86; Dir of UNESCO Regional Office for Science and Tech. and UNESCO Rep. in Egypt, Sudan and Yemen 1991–99; Dir Africa, E Asia and Pacific Div., Dept of Tech. Cooperation, Int. Atomic Energy Agency (IAEA) 1999–2001; Dir Research Div., OPEC 2001–06, Acting Sec.-Gen. 2005; currently Dir Gen. Kuwait Foundation for Advancement of Sciences; also currently Sr Research Advisor, Oxford Inst. for Energy Studies, UK, Energy Advisor, Energy Inst., Schlumberger Business Consulting, France; Advisor to and mem. Kuwait Nat. Nuclear Energy Cttee; mem. Bd of Dirs Al-Dorra Oil Services Co.; mem. Bd of Trustees American Univ. of Kuwait, Gulf Research Center Foundation, Geneva; mem. UN Advisory Cttee on Science and Tech. for Devt, Arab Thought Forum, Jordan, Int. Scientific Council for Science and Tech. Policy Devt, UNESCO. *Address:* Office of the Director General, Kuwait Foundation for Advancement of Sciences, Ahmad Al Jaber Street, Sharq, Kuwait (office). *E-mail:* info@kfas.org.kw (office). *Website:* www.kfas.org (office).

SHIIMI, Ipumbu Wendelinus, BCom, MSc; Namibian economist and central banker; *Governor, Bank of Namibia;* ed Univ. of Western Cape, Univ. of Stellenbosch, Wits Business School, South Africa, Univ. of London, UK, Maastricht School of Man., Netherlands; several years with Bank of Namibia (central bank), including as Head of Research and Sr Man., Banking Supervisor, Dir, Financial Intelligence Centre, becoming Asst Gov., responsible for overseeing Reserve Man., Banking Supervision, Financial Stability and Financial Intelligence 2006–10, Gov. 2010–. *Address:* Office of the Governor, Bank of Namibia, 71 Robert Mugabe Avenue, POB 2882, Windhoek, Namibia (office). *Telephone:* (61) 2835111 (office). *Fax:* (61) 2835067 (office). *E-mail:* jerome.mutumba@bon.com.na (office). *Website:* www.bon.com.na (office).

SHIKAPWASHA, Rev. Lt-Gen. Ronnie; Zambian politician and fmr air force officer; b. 25 Dec. 1947; m.; MP for Keembe constituency 2003–, mem. Reforms and Modernisation Cttee 2015–, Nat. Security and Foreign Affairs Cttee 2015–; Minister of Home Affairs 2003–05, 2006–08, of Foreign Affairs 2005–06, of Information and Broadcasting Services 2008–11, Acting Health Minister 2006; resigned from Movement for Multi-party Democracy (MMD) and joined Patriotic Front (PF) party 2016. *Address:* National Assembly of Zambia, Parliament Buildings, PO Box 31299, Lusaka (office); Jesus is Life Church, PO Box 36259, Lusaka, Zambia. *E-mail:* rshikapwasha@parliament.gov.zm (office); ltgenronnie@yahoo.com. *Website:* www.parliament.gov.zm (office).

SHIKHMURADOV, Boris Orazovich; Turkmenistani diplomatist and politician; b. 25 May 1949, Aşgabat, Turkmen SSR, USSR; m. Tatyana Shikhmuradova; two s.; ed Moscow State Univ., Diplomatic Acad.; journalist, Press Agency Novosti and USSR Ministry of Foreign Affairs 1971–72; various positions in missions abroad, then on staff, USSR Ministry of Foreign Affairs 1983–86; worked in embassies in Pakistan, India, missions to Turkey, Afghanistan, USA, China, Singapore; Deputy, then First Deputy Minister of Foreign Affairs of Turkmenistan May 1992; Deputy Chair. Cabinet of Ministers of Turkmenistan 1992; Minister of Foreign Affairs 1995–2000; Amb. to People's Repub. of China March–Nov. 2001; emigrated to Moscow 2001; est. opposition people's movt of Turkmenistan 2002; returned to Aşgabat Dec. 2002, arrested and sentenced to life imprisonment on charges of conspiracy to organize assassination of Pres. Niyazov; nothing has been heard of him since 2007, thought to be still imprisoned or may have died in prison.

SHILLER, Robert James, BA, SM, PhD; American economist and academic; *Sterling Professor of Economics, Yale University;* b. 29 March 1946, Detroit, MI; ed Univ. of Michigan, Massachusetts Inst. of Tech.; Asst Prof. of Econs, Univ. of Minnesota 1972–74; Assoc. Prof. of Econs, Univ. of Pennsylvania 1974–80; Research Fellow, Nat. Bureau of Econs Research, Cambridge, Mass 1980–81; Visiting Prof., MIT 1981–82; apptd Stanley B. Resor Prof. of Econs, Yale Univ. 1982, currently Sterling Prof. of Econs, also Prof., School of Man.; Co-founder Case Shiller Weiss Inc., Cambridge, Mass 1991, Macro Securities Research LLC 1999; research in behavioural finance and behavioural macroecons at Nat. Bureau of Econ. Research; Guggenheim Fellowship 1991, Paul Samuelson Award 1996, Commonfund Prize 2000, Nobel Prize in Econs (with Eugene Fama and Lars Peter Hansen) 2013. *Publications:* Market Volatility 1989, Macro Markets: Creating Institutions for Managing Society's Largest Economic Risks 1993, Irrational Exuberance 2000, The New Financial Order 2003, Animal Spirits: How Human Psychology Drives the Economy, and Why It Matters for Global Capitalism 2009, Finance and the Good Society 2012, Phishing for Phools: The Economics of Manipulation and Deception 2015. *Address:* Yale University, POB 208281, New Haven, CT 06520-8281 (office). *Telephone:* (203) 432-3708 (office). *Fax:* (203) 432-6167 (office). *E-mail:* robert.shiller@yale.edu (office). *Website:* som.yale.edu (office).

SHILOV, Aleksandr Maksovich; Russian artist; b. 6 Oct. 1943, Moscow; s. of Ludmila Sergeevna Pazhenova; ed V.I. Surikov Inst. of Fine Arts, Moscow; f. Moscow State A. Shilov Picture Gallery 1997, currently Art Dir; mem. Acad. of Social Sciences 1997–, Council for Culture and Art 1999–; Corresp. mem. Russian Acad. of Arts 1997–2001, mem. 2001–; Order for Services to the Motherland (Fourth Degree) 1997, (Third Degree) 2004, Order of Francisk Skorina (Belarus) 2003; numerous awards including Lenin Komsomol Prize 1977, People's Artist of RSFSR 1981, People's Artist of USSR 1985. *Achievements include:* asteroid named after him 1992. *Address:* Romanov per. 3, Apartment 71, 103009 Moscow, Russia. *Telephone:* (495) 203-42-08. *Fax:* (495) 203-69-75 (office). *E-mail:* shilov_gallery@mail.ru (office). *Website:* amshilov.ru (office).

SHILTON, Peter Leslie, MBE, OBE; British fmr professional footballer; b. 18 Sept. 1949, Leicester, England; s. of Les Shilton and May Shilton; m. Sue Shilton 1970; two s.; ed King Richard III School, Leicester; goalkeeper; youth player, Leicester CIty 1963–66; sr player, Leicester City 1966–74 (won Football League Second Div. 1970/71, FA Charity Shield 1971), Stoke City 1974–77, Nottingham Forest 1977–82 (won First Div. League Championship 1977/78, FA Charity Shield 1978, League Cup 1979, European Cup 1979, 1980, European Super Cup 1979), Southampton 1982–87 (won Trofeo Ciudad de Vigo 1983), Derby County 1987–92, Plymouth Argyle 1992–95, Wimbledon 1995, Bolton Wanderers 1995, Coventry City 1995–96, West Ham United 1996, Leyton Orient 1996–97 (retd); Man. Plymouth Argyle FC 1992–95; mem. England U-23 team 1968–72, England 1970–90 (125 caps—record), won Rous Cup 1986, 1988, 1989; first England goalkeeper to win more than 100 caps at European Championships 1988; record English league appearances (1,005); conceded only 80 int. goals; holds all-time record for most competitive appearances in world football; Southampton FC Player of the Season 1984/85, 1985/86, Professional Footballers' Asscn (PFA) Players' Player of the Year 1978, PFA Order of Merit 1990, Football Writers' Tribute Award 1991, Inaugural Inductee into English Football Hall of Fame 2002, Contribution to League Football Award 2013. *Address:* c/o Champions (UK) PLC, Barrington House, Leake Road, Costock, Loughborough, Leics., LE12 6XA, England (office). *Telephone:* (845) 3313031 (office). *E-mail:* Info@championsukplc.com (office). *Website:* championsukplc.com (office); www.petershilton.com.

SHIMALI, Mustafa Jassem al-; Kuwaiti civil servant and politician; served in several sr govt posts, including Under-Sec. for Econ. Affairs 1986–2006 and Under-Sec. for Finance 2006–07; Minister of Health 2011–12, of Finance 2012–13, Deputy Prime Minister and Minister of Oil 2013–14; fmr Chair. Kuwait Investment Authority. *Address:* c//o Ministry of Oil, PO Box 5077, 13051 Safat, Kuwait City, Kuwait (office).

SHIMAMURA, Yoshinobu; Japanese politician; b. 27 March 1934, Edogawa; ed Gakushuin Univ.; with Nippon Oil Corpn 1956–71; fmr Parl. Vice-Minister of Agric., Forestry and Fisheries; mem. House of Reps (LDP) for Tokyo 16th Dist 1976–2005, fmr Chair. Cttee on Transport; Minister of Educ. 1995–96, of Agric., Forestry and Fisheries 1997–98, 2004–05; fmr Chair. LDP Diet Affairs Cttee.

SHIMIZU, Shinobu; Japanese transport industry executive; *Executive Corporate Adviser, Tokyu Corporation;* m.; ed Dept of Econs, Hitotsubashi Univ.; joined Tokyu Corpn 1953, Pres. Tokyo Express Electric Railway 2001, Chair. and Rep. Dir –2005, currently Exec. Corp. Adviser; Sr Vice-Pres. Japan Airline System Corpn 2002; Chair. Asscn of Japanese Pvt. Railways 2001–; mem. Man. Council, Devt Bank of Japan 2004–, Registers of Council. *Address:* Tokyu Corporation, 5-6 Nanpeidai-cho, Shibuya-ku, Tokyo 150-8511, Japan (office). *Telephone:* (3) 3477-6111 (office). *Fax:* (3) 3462-1690 (office). *Website:* www.tokyu.co.jp (office).

SHIMIZU, Yasuyuki; Japanese mining executive; Exec. Vice-Pres. Nippon Mining and Metals Co. 1999; Exec. Vice-Pres. Toho Titanium Co. 1999–2000, Pres. 2000–01; Sr Man. Dir and Chief Div. Officer, Corp. Support Div., Nippon Mining Holdings, Inc. (fmrly Japan Energy Co.) 1998–2001, Chair. and Rep. Dir 2001–03, CEO 2003, Pres. and Rep. Dir 2003–06, Chair. and Rep. Dir 2006–10 (following merger with Nippon Oil Corpn to form JX Holdings 2010); Chair. Japan Titanium Soc. *Address:* c/o JX Holdings, Inc., 2-6-3, Ote-machi, Chiyoda-ku, Tokyo 100-0004, Japan. *E-mail:* info@hd.jx-group.co.jp.

SHIMOKOBE, Kazuhiko, LLB; Japanese lawyer and business executive; *Head of the Steering Committee, Nuclear Damage Liability Facilitation Fund;* ed Kyoto Univ.; worked for Japan Post Holdings Co. Ltd and Chori Co. Ltd; fmr bankruptcy lawyer serving as Head of Steering Cttee of Nuclear Damage Liability Facilitation Fund state bailout facility; Ind. Chair. Tokyo Electric Power Co. (TEPCO), Inc. 2012–14, Chair. Audit Cttee, mem. Nominating Cttee, Compensation Cttee. *Address:* c/o Tokyo Electric Power Co., Inc., 1-1-3 Uchisaiwai-cho, Chiyoda-ku, Tokyo 100-8560, Japan. *E-mail:* info@tepco.co.jp.

SHIMOMURA, Hakubun; Japanese politician; *Minister of Education;* b. 23 May 1954, Takasaki, Gunma Pref.; ed Waseda Univ.; mem. Tokyo Metropolitan Ass. 1989–97; mem. House of Reps (lower house of Parl.) for Tokyo No. 11 constituency (LDP) 1996–, mem. Council Foreign Affairs Cttee, Exec. Cttee on Legal Affairs, Cttee on Rules and Admin; Deputy Chief Cabinet Sec. 2006; Minister of Educ., Culture, Sports, Science and Tech. and for Rebuilding Educ. 2012–; mem. Japanese Nat. Comm. for UNESCO; Vice-Chair. Ashinaga (non-profit org.); mem. Liberal Democratic Party (LDP), Deputy Chair. LDP Policy Research Council. *Address:* Ministry of Education, Culture, Sports, Science and Technology, 3-2-2, Kasumigaseki, Chiyoda-ku, Tokyo 100-8959, Japan (office). *Telephone:* (3) 5253-4111 (office). *Fax:* (3) 3595-2017 (office). *Website:* www.mext.go.jp (office).

SHIMOMURA, Setsuhiro; Japanese business executive; *Chairman, Mitsubishi Electric Corporation;* b. 1945, Tottori Pref.; joined Mitsubishi Electric Corpn in 1969, first served as an engineer in Himeji Works, named to Mitsubishi Electric's Bd of Dirs 2001–, Exec. Vice-Pres. and Group Pres. of Building Systems 2004–06, Rep. Exec. Officer, Pres. and CEO Mitsubishi Electric Corpn 2006–10, Chair. 2010–14, Exec. Corp. Adviser 2014–; Head Vice-Chair. Japan Electronics and Information Tech. Industries Asscn 2009–; Outside Dir Toda Corpn. *Address:* Mitsubishi Electric Corpn, Tokyo Bldg, 2-7-3, Marunouchi, Chiyoda-ku, Tokyo 100-8310, Japan (office). *Telephone:* (3) 3218-2111 (office). *E-mail:* info@mitsubishi.com (office). *Website:* www.mitsubishi.com (office).

SHIN, Chang-jae, MD, PhD; South Korean physician and business executive; *Chairman and CEO, Kyobo Life Insurance Co. Ltd;* b. 1953, Seoul; s. of Shin Yong-ho; m.; two c.; ed Seoul Nat. Univ.; began career as obstetrician; fmr Prof. of Medicine, Seoul Nat. Univ.; Chair. Daesan Foundation 1993–, Vice-Pres. Kyobo Life Insurance Co. Ltd 1996–98, Pres. 1998–99, Chair. 1999–2000, CEO and Chair. 2000–; Vice-Chair. Korea Mecenat Asscn; several awards including Best CEO Award, Korea Man. Asscn 2001, Presidential Citation for Service Quality Innovation 2006, Korean Montblanc de la Culture Arts Patronage Award 2010. *Address:* Kyobo Life Insurance Co. Ltd, Jongno-1ga, Jongno-gu, Seoul 110-714, Republic of Korea (office). *Telephone:* (2) 721-2121 (office). *Fax:* (2) 737-9970 (office). *Website:* www.kyobo.co.kr (office).

SHIN, Dong-bin, BEcons, MBA; South Korean retail executive; *Chairman, Lotte Shopping Company Limited;* b. 1955, Japan; s. of Shin Kyuk-ho and Shigemitsu Hatsuko; m.; three c.; ed Aoyama Gakuin Univ., Japan, Columbia Univ., USA; Asst Man. Dir Honam Petrochemical Corpn –2006; Vice-Chair. Lotte Group, CEO, Lotte Shopping Co. Ltd 2006–18, Dir 2006–, Chair. 2015–; sentenced to 2½ years' imprisonment for bribery and embezzlement Feb. 2018, sentence suspended Oct. 2018; Chair. Visit Korea Year Cttee; Co-Chair. Asia Soc. Korea Center. *Address:* Lotte Shopping Co. Ltd (Chul Woo Lee), Sogongdong 1, Jung-gu, Seoul, Republic of Korea (office). *Telephone:* (2) 2118-2021 (office). *Fax:* (2) 2118-2028 (office). *Website:* www.lotte.co.kr (office).

SHIN, Heon-cheol, BA, MBA; South Korean business executive; ed Busan Nat. Univ., Yonsei Univ.; joined SK Corpn as Head Man. of Business Team, Pres.'s Office 1985–89, Sr Man. in charge of developing man. skills 1989–91, Dir 1991, Head, Metropolitan Marketing Br. SK Telecom Co. Ltd 1995–98, Sr Man. Dir 1998, Sr Vice-Pres. and Man. Dir SK Telink Co. Ltd 1998–2002, Man. Dir SK Gas Co. Ltd 2002–05, Pres. and CEO SK Corpn 2004–, apptd Vice-Chair. and Co-CEO 2006, mem. Bd of Dirs 2004–, mem. Bd of Dirs SK Energy Co. Ltd 2007, currently CEO and Pres.; Vice-Chair. Korea Listed Companies Asscn; mem. Bd of Dirs Korea YMCA. *Address:* SK Corporation, 99 Seorin-dong, Jongno-gu, Seoul 110-110, Republic of Korea (office). *Telephone:* (2) 2121-5114 (office). *Fax:* (2) 2121-7001 (office). *Website:* www.skcorp.com (office).

SHIN, In-ryung, PhD, LLM; South Korean professor of law and fmr university president; *Professor Emeritus, Ewha Women's University;* ed Coll. of Law, Ewha Women's Univ.; Exec. Sec. in charge of Educ., Korea Dialogue Acad. 1971–80, Dir 2003–; part-time Lecturer in Labor Law, Coll. of Law, Lecturer in Women's Studies, Dept of Women's Studies, Ewha Women's Univ. 1974–84, Asst Prof. Coll. of Law 1985–87, Assoc. Prof. 1987–92, apptd Prof. 1992, Dean 2000–02, Dir Law Div. 1992–94, Pres. Ewha Women's Univ. 2002–06, now Prof. Emer.; Visiting Research Prof., Hitotsubasi Univ., Japan 1994–95; Visiting Scholar, Univ. of Wash. School of Law, USA 1998–99; Exec. Dir Korean Soc. of Labor Law 1990–97, Deputy Pres. 1998–2001, Pres. 2001–02; Deputy Pres. Korean Industrial Relations Research Asscn 1995–96; Co-Pres. Korean Fed. for Environmental Movement 2003; Chair. Cttee of Women's Affairs, Advisory Council on Democratic and Peaceful Unification 2003–; mem. Comm. for the Prevention of Corruption, Bd of Audit and Inspection of Korea 1999, Lawyers Disciplinary Cttee, Ministry of Justice 2000–02, Comm. for the Evaluation of Unification Policy, Ministry of Unification 2001–02; non-exec. mem. Nat. Labor Relations Comm. 1997–98, 1999–2002; Adviser Constitutional Court of Korea 2003–, Presidential Advisory Council on Korea Unification 2003–05; mem. Bd of Dirs Samsung Dream Scholarship Foundation, Korea Dialogue Acad., Korea Advanced Inst. of Science and Tech., Sungkok Acad. and Cultural Foundation, Korea Inst. of Science and Tech., I-Sang Yoon Peace Foundation, Korea Research Foundation; mem. Commrs Bd Korea Independent Comm. against Corruption 2004; mem. Presidential Cttee on Judicial Reform 2005, Prosecutor's Office Policy Advisory Bd 2005. *Publications include:* Women Labor Law 1985, A Research on Fundamental Rights of Labor 1985, Labor Law and Labor Campaigns 1987, The Overcoming of the Division of the Korean Peninsula, and Korean Women Emancipation Campaigns 1989, Law and Women Studies 1989, Law and Modern Society 1992, Law and Social Justice 1992, A Research on Labor Law Cases – Cases on Labor Union Campaigns 1995, Human Rights of Labor and the Law of Labor 1996, An Introduction to Korean Law 1998, The Historical Development of Korean Labor Legislations 1999, The Globalization and Women's Rights of Labor 2002.

SHIN, Jong-kyun, BS; South Korean electronics engineer and business executive; *President and CEO, Samsung Electronics;* b. 16 Jan. 1956; ed Kwangwoon Univ.; Head, R&D Team, Mobile Communications Business, Samsung Electronics 2006–08, Head, Mobile Communications Business 2009–11, Head, IT and Mobile Communications Div. 2011–12, Pres. and Head, IT and Mobile Communications 2012–, Pres., CEO and Rep. Dir, Samsung Electronics 2013–. *Address:* Samsung Electronics Building, 1320-10 Seocho-2-dong, Seocho-gu, Seoul 137-857, Republic of Korea (office). *Telephone:* (2) 2255-0114 (office). *Fax:* (2) 2255-2133 (office). *Website:* www.samsung.com (office).

SHIN, Kyuk-ho; South Korean business executive; b. 4 Oct. 1922, Ulsan, S Kyungsang Prov.; m.; three c.; ed Waseda Univ.; went to Japan to study 1941; est. factory to manufacture cutting oil 1944, factory destroyed in World War II; f. Lotte Group (maker of bubble gum), Japan 1948, Chair. –2010, Pres. –2011, mem. Bd of Dirs; f. Lotte Confectionery Co. Ltd 1967, now a leading food and leisure group spanning hotels, confectionary and an amusement park, Standing Dir Lotte Shopping Co. Ltd 2009–17, also Chair. Lotte Chilsung Beverage Co. Ltd, Canon Korea Business Solutions Inc. *Address:* c/o Lotte Confectionery Co. Ltd, 23, 4-ga, Yangpyeong-dong, Yeongdeungpo-gu, Seoul, Republic of Korea (office). *Telephone:* (2) 670-6114 (office). *Fax:* (2) 6672-6600 (office). *Website:* www.lotte.com (office); www.lottetown.com (office).

SHIN, Kyung-sook; South Korean writer; b. 12 Jan. 1963, Jeong-eup, Jeolla Prov.; m. Nam Jin-wo; ed Seoul Inst. of the Arts; Today's Young Artist Award from Ministry of Culture and Sports, Dong-in Literary Award (for When Will He Come) 1997, 21st Century Literary Prize (for The Place Where He Doesn't Know) 2000, Yi Sang Literature Prize (for Buseok Temple) 2001, Oh Young-soo Literary Prize (for Linden Tree in Front of the Castle Gate) 2006. *Publications include:* novels: Deep Sorrow 1994, A Lone Room (Manhae Literature Prize 1996, Prix de l'Inapercu 2009) 1995, The Train Departs at 7 1999, Violet 2001, Yi Jin 2007, Please Look After Mom (Man Asian Literary Prize 2012) 2009, Somewhere A Phone Is Ringing For Me 2010, I'll Be Right There 2014, The Girl Who Wrote Loneliness 2015; novella: Winter Fables (Munye Joongang New Author Prize) 1985; short story collections: Until It Turns into River 1990, Where the Harmonium Once Stood 1992, Potato Eaters 1997, Strawberry Fields 2000, The Sound of Bells 2003; non-fiction: Beautiful Shade 1995, Sleep, Sorrow 2003. *Address:* Barbara J. Zitwer Agency, 525 West End Avenue, Suite 11H, New York, NY 10024, USA (office). *E-mail:* zitwer@gmail.com (office). *Website:* www.barbarajzitweragency.com (office).

SHIN, Yoshiaki; Japanese business executive; *Chairman, Mitsui Sumitomo Insurance Group Holdings, Inc.;* Sr Man. Dir and Sr Exec. Officer, Mitsui Sumitomo Insurance Group Holdings, Inc. –2006, Rep. Dir, Pres. and Co-CEO 2006–08, Chair. 2008–. *Address:* Mitsui Sumitomo Insurance Group Holdings, Inc., 27-2 Shinkawa 2-chome, Chuo-ku, Tokyo 104-8252, Japan (office). *Telephone:* (3) 3297-1111 (office). *Fax:* (3) 3297-6888 (office). *E-mail:* info@msig.com (office). *Website:* www.msig.com (office); www.ms-ins.com (office).

SHIN, Young-soo, MD; South Korean health official and international organization official; *Regional Director for the Western Pacific, World Health Organization;* b. 15 Oct. 1943, Seoul; m.; one s. two d.; ed Coll. of Medicine, Seoul Nat. Univ., School of Public Health, Yale Univ., USA; began career as Research Asst in Preventive Medicine, Coll. of Medicine, Seoul Nat. Univ., becoming Prof. of Health Policy and Man. 1978–; three years as medical officer in Korean Navy; several positions with Ministry of Health and Welfare in 1990s, including Pres., Korea Inst. of Health Services Man. 1992–99, Dir Nat. Health Insurance Review and Assessment Service 2002–03; mem. WHO Exec. Bd as rep. from Repub. of Korea 1995–98, Dir Regional Office for W Pacific, WHO 2009–; Pres. Korean Soc. of Preventive Medicine 2005–06, Korean Soc. of Quality Assurance in Health Care 2006–08; Nat. Order of Merit, Moran Medal 2003. *Address:* World Health Organization Regional Office for the Western Pacific, PO Box 2932, Manila 1000, Philippines (office). *Telephone:* (2) 528-8001 (office). *Fax:* (2) 521-1036 (office); (2) 526-0279 (office). *E-mail:* pio@wpro.who.int (office). *Website:* www.wpro.who.int (office).

SHINDE, Sushilkumar Sambhaji Rao, BA, LLB; Indian politician and lawyer; b. 4 Sept. 1941, Solapur, Maharashtra; s. of Sambhaji Rao Shinde and Sakhubai Shinde; m. Ujwala Shinde; three d.; ed Law Coll., Pune, Sangameshwar and Dayanand Coll., Solapur, Shivaji Univ., Kolhapur, New Law Coll., Univ. of Mumbai; Boy Peon, then Court Peon and then Court Clerk, Sessions Court Solapur 1956–65; officer Mumbai Police Crime Investigation Dept 1965–71; mem. Rajya Sabha 1992–98, 2006; elected to Lok Sabha 1998–2014; fmr Minister of Finance and Planning, of Industry, of Urban Devt and of Youth and Social Welfare, Maharashtra; Chief Minister of Maharashtra 2003–04; Gov. of Andhra Pradesh 2004–06 (resgnd); Minister of Power 2006–12, of Home Affairs 2012–14; mem. Congress Party; Nat. Citizens Award 1993, 1994. *Leisure interests:* reading, travelling. *Address:* 19, Ashok Nagar, Jai-Jui, Vijapur Road, Solapur, 413 001, India (home).

SHINDO, Kosei; Japanese business executive; *Representative Director and President, Nippon Steel & Sumitomo Metal Corporation;* fmr Gen. Man. Corp. Planning Div., Nippon Steel Corpn, Exec. Vice-Pres., Nippon Steel & Sumitomo Metal Corpn 2012–14, Rep. Dir and Pres. Nippon Steel & Sumitomo Metal Corpn 2014–; Chair. Nippon Steel Arts Foundation; Dir, Nippon Steel Corpn, Nippon Steel & Sumitomo Metal Corpn; fmr Statutory Auditor, Nippon Coke and Engineering Co. Ltd (Mitsui Mining Co. Ltd). *Address:* Nippon Steel & Sumitomo Metal Corporation, Marunouchi Park Building, 6-1, Marunouchi 2-chome, Chiyoda-ku, Tokyo 100-8071, Japan (office). *Telephone:* (3) 6867-4111 (office). *Fax:* (3) 6867-5607 (office). *E-mail:* info@nssmc.com (office). *Website:* www.nssmc.com (office).

SHINDO, Yoshitaka, BA; Japanese politician; b. 20 Jan. 1958, Kawaguchi, Saitama Pref.; ed Meiji Univ.; worked in city planning, Kawaguchi Municipal Office 1980–90; mem. Kawaguchi Municipal Ass. 1991–95; mem. House of Reps (lower house of Parl.) for 2nd Dist, Saitama Pref. (LDP 1996–2003, 2005–), Chair. Cttee on Audit and Oversight of Admin 2011; Vice-Minister for Internal Affairs and Communications 2001–02, for Foreign Affairs 2002, Minister of Economy, Trade and Industry 2007, Minister for Internal Affairs and Communications 2012–14, for Regional Revitalization and for Regional Govt (Doshu-Sei), and Minister of State for Decentralization Reform 2012–14; Dir LDP Nat. Defence Div. 2005, Chair. Cttee on Orgs Involved with Land Devt and Construction 2006. *Address:* House of Representatives, 1-7-1 Nagatacho, Chiyoda-ku, Tokyo 100-0014, Japan (office). *Website:* www.shugiin.go.jp (office).

SHINEFIELD, Henry Robert, BA, MD; American pediatrician and vaccine researcher; *Clinical Professor of Pediatrics and of Dermatology, University of California, San Francisco;* b. 11 Oct. 1925, Paterson, NJ; s. of Louis Shinefield and Sarah Shinefield (née Kaplan); m. Jacqueline Walker 1983; one s. three d.; ed Columbia Univ.; Asst Resident Pediatrician, New York Hosp. (Cornell) 1950–51, Pediatrician Outpatients 1953–59, Instructor in Pediatrics 1959–60, Asst Prof. 1960–64, Assoc. Prof. 1964–65; Chief of Pediatrics, Kaiser-Permanente Medical Center, San Francisco 1965–89, Chief Emer. 1989–; Co-Dir Kaiser Permanente Pediatric Vaccine Study Center, Calif.; currently Adjunct Investigator, Div. of Research, Kaiser Permanente N Calif.; Assoc. Clinical Prof. of Pediatrics, Univ. of Calif., San Francisco 1966–68, Clinical Prof. of Pediatrics 1968–, Clinical Prof. of Dermatology 1970–; mem. Inst. of Medicine, NAS 1980, American Bd of Pediatrics; Fellow, American Acad. of Pediatrics. *Leisure interests:* skiing, tennis, travel. *Address:* Kaiser Permanente, 4131 Geary Boulevard, San Francisco, CA 94118 (office); 2705 Larkin Street, San Francisco, CA 94109, USA (home). *Telephone:* (415) 202-3597 (office); (415) 771-5372 (home). *E-mail:* henry.shinefield@kp.org (office). *Website:* www.dermatology.ucsf.edu (office).

SHINKAI, Seiji, BS, PhD; Japanese chemist and academic; *Professor, Sojo University;* b. 5 July 1944, Fukuoka; ed Kyushu Univ.; Lecturer, Kyushu Univ., Fukuoka City 1972, Asst Prof. 1975–87, Prof. 1988–2008, Prof. Emer. 2008–, Leader, Kyushu Univ. Centre of Excellence (COE) Project 'Design and Control of Advanced Molecular Assembly Systems' 1998–2002, 21st Century COE Project 'Functional Innovation of Molecular Informatics' 2002–06; Asst Prof., Nagasaki Univ. 1976; currently Prof., Sojo Univ.; Project Leader, Research Devt Corpn of Japan/Exploratory Research for Advanced Tech. Project (ERATO) 'Shinkai Chemirecognics Project', Kawaguchi City 1990–95; Research Dir Japan Science and Tech. Corpn/Int. Collaboration Project (ICORP) 'Chemotransfiguration' 1997–2001, Japan Science and Tech. Corpn/Solution Oriented Research for Science and Tech. (SORST) 'Gene Manipulators Based on the Polysaccharide-Polynucleotide Interactions' 2002–04; Pres. Inst. of Systems, Information Technologies and Nanotechnologies; mem. Editorial Bd Bioorganic Chemistry 1986–, Journal of the Chemical Society, Perkin Transactions 1992–2001, Supramolecular Chemistry 1992–, Nanotechnology 1993–, Current Opinion in Chemical Biology 1997–, Angewandte Chemie 1999–, European Journal of Organic Chemistry 2000–; Postdoctoral Fellow, Dept of Chem., Univ. of California, Santa Barbara, USA 1972–74; Chemical Soc. of Japan Award for Advanced Research 1978, Soc. of Polymer Science Award 1985, Izatt-Christensen Int. Award, ISMC Cttee 1998, Backer Lecture Award, Univ. of Groningen 1999, Vielberth Lectureship Award, Univ. of Regensburg 2002. *Publications include:* more than 750 articles in scientific journals and more than 131 book chapters and reviews on host/guest chem., molecular recognition, liquid crystals/organic gelators, sugar sensing/sugar-based combinatorial chem., polysaccharide-polynucleotide interactions, sol-gel transcription and inorganic combinatorial chem. *Address:* Sojo University, 4-22-1 Ikeda, Kumamoto 860, Japan (office). *Telephone:* (96) 326 3111 (office). *Fax:* (96) 326 3000 (office). *Website:* www.sojo-u.ac.jp (office).

SHINMACHI, Toshiyuki; Japanese airline industry executive; *Resident Adviser, Japan Airlines (JAL) International Co. Ltd;* b. 20 Jan. 1943; ed Gakushuin Univ.; joined Japan Airlines Corpn 1965, Deputy Dir Cargo Export, Tokyo Regional Cargo Sales Office 1987–88, Dir 1988–89, Regional Man. Cargo Sales, New York Regional Cargo Sales Office 1989–91, Gen. Man., Admin, JAL Cargo 1991–93, Vice-Pres. JAL Cargo, Tokyo Regional Cargo Sales Office 1993–95, Vice-Pres. JAL Cargo Sales, Japan Region 1995–97, apptd mem. Bd of Dirs 1997, Sr Vice-Pres. Japan Airlines 1997–2000, Man. Dir 2000–01, Sr Man. Dir 2001–03, Sr Man. Dir Japan Airlines System Corpn 2002–03, Exec. Vice-Pres. Japan Airlines and Japan Airlines System Corpn 2003–04, Pres. Japan Airlines and Japan Airlines Corpn 2004–05, CEO JAL Group 2005–06, Chair. JAL Group 2006–08 (retd), Resident Adviser, JAL International Co. Ltd 2008–. *Address:* Japan Airlines International Co. Ltd, 4-11, Higashi-shinagawa 2-chome, Shinagawa-ku, Tokyo 140-8637, Japan (office). *Telephone:* (3) 5460-6600 (office). *E-mail:* info@jal.com (office). *Website:* www.jal.com/en/outline/corporate (office).

SHINODA, Masahiro; Japanese film director and screenwriter; b. 9 March 1931, Gifu Pref.; m. Shima Iwashita 1967; ed Waseda Univ., Tokyo; started career as Asst Dir, Ofuna Studio, Shochiku 1953; worked as asst to Ozu 1957; directing career 1960–2003 (retd); Izumi Kyōka Prize 2010. *Films include:* as dir: Koi no katamichi kippu (One-Way Ticket for Love) 1960, Kawaita mizummi (Dry Lake) 1960, Yuhi ni akai ore no kao (My Face Red in the Sunset) 1961, Waga koi no tabiji (Epitaph to My Love) 1961, Watakushi-tachi no kekkon (Our Marriage) 1961, Shamisen to otobai (Love Old and New or Shamisen and Motorcycle) 1961, Namida o shishi no tategami ni (Tears on the Lion's Mane) 1962, Yama no sanka: moyuru wakamono tachi (Glory on the Summit: Burning Youth) 1962, Kawaita hana (Pale Flower) 1964, Ansatsu (The Assassin) 1964, Utsukushisa to kanashimi to (With Beauty and Sorrow, UK) 1965, Ibun sarutobi sasuke (Samurai Spy) 1965, Shokei no shima (Punishment Island) 1966, Akane-gumo (Clouds at Sunset, USA) 1967, Shinjû: Ten no amijima (Double Suicide) 1969, Buraikan (The Scandalous Adventures of Buraikan) 1970, Chinmoku (Silence) 1971, Sapporo Orinpikku (Sapporo Winter Olympics) 1972, Kaseki no mori (The Petrified Forest) 1973, Himiko 1974, Sakura no mori no mankai no shita (Under the Cherry Blossoms) 1975, Hanre Goze Orin (Ballad of Orin, USA, Melody in Gray) 1977, Yashagaike (Demon Pond) 1979, Akuryo-To (Akuryo Island) 1981, Setouchi shonen yakyu dan (MacArthur's Children) 1984, Yari no gonza (Gonza the Spearman) (Silver Bear Award, Berlin) 1986, Maihime (The Dancer) 1989, Shonen jidai (Childhood Days) (several prizes at Japanese Acad. Awards) 1990, Sharaku 1995, Setouchi munraito serenade (Setouchi Moonlight Serenade) 1997, Fukuro no shiro (Owls' Castle, USA) 1999, Spy Sorge 2003; screenplays: Waga koi no tabiji (Epitaph to My Love) 1961, Watakushi-tachi no kekkon (Our Marriage) 1961, Namida o shishi no tategami ni (Tears on the Lion's Mane) 1962, Kawaita hana (Pale Flower) 1964, Shinjû: Ten no amijima (Double Suicide) 1969, Himiko 1974, Hanre Goze Orin (Ballad of Orin, USA or Melody in Gray) 1977, Maihime (The Dancer) 1989, Sharaku 1995, Spy Sorge 2003; Music for the Movies: Tom Takemitsu (as himself) 1994.

SHINOHARA, Yoshiko; Japanese business executive; *President, Tempstaff Co. Ltd;* b. Kanagawa Pref.; ed Takagi High School of Commerce, studied languages and secretarial skills in Switzerland and UK; with Mitsubishi Heavy Industries Ltd 1953–57; spent time in Japan before moving to Australia in 1971; joined P.R.S.A. Inc. (marketing co.) as asst to Pres. 1971–73; Founder, Rep. Dir and Pres. Tempstaff Co. Ltd 1973–; mem. Exec. Council Japan Staffing Business Assen 1986–; Dir Health Insurance Soc. for Temporary Workers; Flower Award, 14th Econ. Awards 1989, Veuve Clicquot Business Woman of the Year 1992, Venture of The Year in Female Entrepreneurs 1993, Harvard Business School's Business Stateswoman of the Year 2001. *Address:* Tempstaff Co. Ltd, Shinjuku Maynds Tower, 2-1-1, Yoyogi, Shibuya-ku, Tokyo 151-0053, Japan (office). *Telephone:* (3) 5350-1212 (office). *Fax:* (3) 5350-1219 (office). *Website:* www.tempstaff.co.jp (office).

SHINSEKI, Gen. (retd) Eric Ken, BS, MA; American army officer (retd) and fmr government official; b. 28 Nov. 1942, Lihue, Kauai, Hawaii; m. Patricia Shinseki; two c.; ed US Mil. Acad., Duke Univ., Nat. War Coll., Fort Lesley J. McNair, Washington, DC; commissioned 2nd Lt in US Army 1965, Forward Observer B battery 2nd Battalion, 9th Artillery, 3rd Brigade, 25th Infantry Div., Viet Nam 1965–66; Asst S1 Base Defense Command, XXIV Corps, Viet Nam 1969–70, Commdr A Troop, 3rd Squadron, 5th Cavalry, 9th Infantry Div., Viet Nam 1970 Personnel Staff Officer US Army Pacific, Fort Shafter, Hawaii 1971–74, Instructor, Dept of English, US Mil. Acad., West Point 1976–78, Commdr 3rd Squadron, 7th Cavalry, 3rd Infantry Div. then Asst Chief of Staff, G-3, US Army Europe and 7th Army, Germany 1982–85, Commdr 2nd Brigade, 3rd Infantry Div. then Asst Chief of Staff G3 VII Corps, US Army Europe and 7th Army 1987–90, Deputy Chief of Staff, Admin/Logistics, Allied Land Forces, Southern Europe, Germany 1990–92, Asst Div. Commdr, 3rd Infantry Div., US Army and 7th Army Europe, Germany 1992–93, Commanding Gen. 1st Cavalry Div., Fort Hood, Tex. 1994–95, Asst Deputy Chief of Staff for operations and plans then Deputy Chief of Staff, US Army, Washington, DC 1995–97, Commdr in Chief and Commdr Stabilization Force, US Army Europe and 7th Army in Bosnia-Herzegovina 1997–98, Vice-Chief of Staff, Washington, DC 1998–99, Chief of Staff 1999–2003 (retd); Sec. of Veterans Affairs, Washington, DC 2009–14 (resgnd); mem. Bd of Dirs First Hawaiian Bank 2006–08, 2015–; Defense Distinguished Service Medal, Distinguished Service Medal, Legion of Merit with oak leaf cluster, Bronze Star with V device with three oak leaf clusters, Purple Heart with oak leaf cluster, Meritorious Service Medal with two oak leaf clusters, Air Medal, Army Commendation Medal with oak leaf cluster, Army Achievement Medal.

SHINYO, Takahiro, PhD; Japanese political scientist, academic and diplomatist; *Vice-President, Kwansei Gakuin University;* b. 11 Jan. 1950, Kagawa; ed Faculty of Law, Osaka Univ., Univ. of Göttingen, Germany; joined Ministry of Foreign Affairs 1972, int. law studies 1973–75, served at Embassies in Berne, Beijing and Bonn 1975–89, Head of Div. for Disarmament and later for UN Policy, Ministry of Foreign Affairs 1989–93, Minister, Embassy in Berlin 1996–99, Deputy Dir-Gen., European and Oceanian Affairs Bureau, Ministry of Foreign Affairs 1999–2001, Deputy Dir-Gen., European Affairs Bureau 2001–02, Consul-Gen. in Düsseldorf, Germany Jan. 2002, Amb. and Dir-Gen., Global Issues Dept, Ministry of Foreign Affairs Jan. 2005, Amb. and Deputy Perm. Rep. to UN 2006–09, Amb. to Germany 2009–12; Vice-Pres. Kwansei Gakuin Univ. 2012–; Visiting Prof., Ritsumeikan Univ., Kyoto 1992–95, Grad. School, Tokyo Univ. 2000–01; Prof., Osaka School of Int. Public Policy, Osaka Univ. 1993–96. *Publications:* Atarashii Kokusai Chitsujo wo Motomete (Looking for a New World Order) (co-author) 1994, Shin Kokuren Ron (New UN Theory) 1995, Kokusai Heiwa Kyoryoku Nyumon (Introduction to International Peace Co-operation) (ed.) 1995, Yobou Gaikou (Preventive Diplomacy) (co-author) 1996, Kokusai Kiki to Nihongaikou (International Crisis and Japanese Diplomacy) 2005. *Address:* Kwansei Gakuin University, Public Relations Office, 1-155 Uegahara-1bancho, Nishinomiya, Hyogo 662-8501, Japan (office). *Telephone:* (798) 546017 (office). *Fax:* (798) 510912 (office). *E-mail:* ciec@kwansei.ac.jp (office). *Website:* global.kwansei.ac.jp (office).

SHIOZAKI, Yasuhisa, MPA; Japanese politician; b. 7 Nov. 1950; m.; two s.; ed Univ. of Tokyo, John F. Kennedy School of Govt, Harvard Univ.; with Bank of Japan 1975–86; Political Asst to Minister of State for Econ. Planning Agency 1982–83, to Minister of State for Man. and Coordination Agency 1990; mem. House of Reps (Ehime 1st Dist) 1993–95, 2000–, apptd Dir Standing Cttee on Judicial Affairs 2001, Chair. Standing Cttee on Judicial Affairs 2004–05, apptd Dir Cttee on Budget 2010; mem. House of Councillors (Ehime Dist) 1995–2000, apptd Dir Standing Cttee on the Budget 1996, Standing Cttee on Audit 1996–97, Chief Dir Standing Cttee on Justice 1999–2000; Parl. Vice-Minister of Finance 1997–98; Sr Vice-Minister for Foreign Affairs 2005–06; Chief Cabinet Sec. and Minister of State for the Abduction Issue 2006–07; Chair. Liberal Democratic Party (LDP) Judicial Affairs Div., Policy Research Council (PRC) 1999–2000, Foreign Affairs Div. 2000–01, Treasury and Finance Div. 2002–03, apptd Deputy Chair. LDP PRC 2003, Chief Sec. Party Reform and Task Force HQ, Man. Admin. Reform HQ, Vice-Chair. Research Cttee on the Financial Issues, Chair. Sub-cttee on Int. NGOs, Sub-cttee on Corp. Accounting, Sub-cttee on Commercial Law, Man. Research Cttee on the Tax System, PRC, Chair. Press Bureau 2011; Minister of Health, Labour and Welfare 2014–17; Sec.-Gen. Japan-Thailand Parliamentarians' Friendship League, Japan-Singapore Parliamentarians' Friendship League, Japan-US Parliamentarians' Friendship League; Pres. KSG Club of Japan. *E-mail:* shiozaki@y-shiozaki.or.jp. *Website:* www.y-shiozaki.or.jp.

SHIPLEY, Rt Hon. Dame Jennifer Mary (Jenny), DNZM, FNZIM; New Zealand politician, company director, consultant and fmr prime minister; *Managing Director, Jenny Shipley NZ Ltd;* b. (Jennifer Mary Robson), 4 Feb. 1952, Gore; d. of Leonard Cameron Robson and Adele Doreen Goodall; m. Burton Shipley

1973; one s. one d.; fmr primary school teacher; farming partnership 1973–88; joined Nat. Party 1975; fmr Malvern Co. Councillor; MP for Ashburton (now Rakaia) 1987–; Minister of Social Welfare 1990–93 and of Women's Affairs 1990–98, of Health 1993–96, of State Services 1996–97, also of State Owned Enterprises, of Transport, of Accident Rehabilitation and Compensation Insurance, Minister Responsible for Radio New Zealand; Minister in Charge of NZ Security Intelligence Service 1997–99; Prime Minister of NZ 1997–99; Leader of the Opposition 1999–2001; Man. Dir Jenny Shipley NZ Ltd; Chair. Genesis Energy, SMI; mem. Bd of Dirs China Construction Bank, ISI, Momentum, Mainzeal Group Ltd –2013; Vice-Pres. Club of Madrid; mem. World Women's Leaders' Council; Fellow, NZ Inst. of Man.; Dame Companion, NZ Order of Merit. *Leisure interests:* family, int. affairs, gardening, sailing. *Address:* PO Box 6636, Auckland, New Zealand (home). *Telephone:* (9) 358-5360 (office). *E-mail:* jenny@jsnz.com (office). *Website:* www.national.org.nz (office).

SHIRAKAWA, Hideki, BS, PhD; Japanese chemist and academic; *Professor Emeritus, Institute of Materials Science, University of Tsukuba;* b. 20 Aug. 1936, Tokyo; s. of Hatsutarou Shirakawa and Fuyuno Shirakawa; m. Chiyoko Shibuya 1966; two s.; ed Tokyo Inst. of Tech.; Asst Chemical Resources Laboratory, Tokyo Inst. of Tech. 1966; pioneered work on conductive polymers; Assoc. Prof., Inst. of Materials Science, Univ. of Tsukuba 1979–82, Prof. 1982–2000, Prof. Emer. 2000–, Chair Master's School in Sciences and Eng, Grad. School 1991–93; Provost 3rd Cluster of Colls 1994–97; elected mem. Council for Science and Tech. Policy, Japanese Cabinet Office 2001; Soc. of Polymer Science Award, Japan 1983, Award for Distinguished Service in Advancement of Polymer Science, Soc. of Polymer Science 2000, Nobel Prize for Chem. (jt recipient) 2000, Person of Cultural Merit 2000, Special Award, Chemical Soc. of Japan 2001. *Address:* Institute of Materials Science, University of Tsukuba, 1-1-1 Ten-nodai, Tsukuba, Ibaraki 305-8573, Japan (office). *Telephone:* (298) 53-2111 (office). *Fax:* (298) 53-6012 (office). *E-mail:* hideki@ims.tsukuba.ac.jp (office). *Website:* www.ims.tsukuba.ac.jp (office).

SHIRAKAWA, Masaaki, BA, MA; Japanese economist, academic and fmr central banker; *Professor, Aoyama Gakuin University;* b. 27 Sept. 1949, Kitakyushu; ed Univ. of Tokyo, Univ. of Chicago, USA; joined Nippon Ginko (Bank of Japan) 1972, held various positions including Dir and Head of Financial System 1990–93, Head of Planning Div., Policy Planning Dept 1993–94, Gen. Man. Oita Br. 1994–95, Gen. Man. for Americas, New York 1995–96, Deputy Dir-Gen. Inst. for Monetary and Econ. Studies 1996–97, Deputy Dir-Gen. Int. Dept 1997, Adviser to Gov. Credit and Market Man. Dept 1997, Adviser to Gov. Financial Markets Dept 1998, Adviser to Gov. Policy Planning Dept 2000–02, Exec. Dir 2002–06, Deputy Gov. 2008, Gov. 2008–13 (resgnd); Prof., Kyoto Univ. School of Govt 2006–08, Aoyama Gakuin Univ. 2013–; Chevalier, Legion d'honneur 2012. *Publications include:* numerous papers on Japanese monetary policy. *Address:* Aoyama Gakuin University, Aoyama Campus, 4-4-25 Shibuya, Shibuya-ku, Tokyo 103-8660, Japan (office). *Website:* www.aoyama.ac.jp/en (office).

SHIRDON, Abdi Farah, BEcons; Somali politician, economist and business executive; b. 1958, Dhusamareb, central Galguduud region; m. Asha Haji Elmi; four c.; ed Somali Nat. Univ.; briefly worked as economist at Ministry of Finance and Ministry of Agric. during Siad Barre admin 1983–85; left govt to pursue business career; est. Shirdon International and served as CEO; moved to Nairobi, Kenya following outbreak of civil war in Somalia 1991 and est. import-export business; Co-founder Rajo Forum (Somali civil society inst.), apptd Chair. 2012; Prime Minister of Somalia 2012–13; Ind.

SHIRE, Bare Adan; Somali politician; commdr Marehan Somali National Front during civil war; fmr Minister of Reconstruction and Resettlement and fmr Minister of Defence in Transitional Fed. Govt 2004; Chair. Juba Valley Alliance (JVA) 1998–2006.

SHIRINOV, Abdujabbor; Tajikistani mathematician, banker and diplomatist; b. 20 June 1953, Khatlon region; m.; five c.; ed Tajik State Nat. Univ.; computer programmer, later Head of Dept for Designing Automatic Control Systems, Data-Processing Centre, Tajik State Univ. 1974–92; Chief Engineer, later Dir Settlement Dept, Nat. Bank of Tajikistan 1992–98; Deputy Chair., later First Deputy Chair. Exec. Bd Jt Stock Commerce Agro-Industrial Investment Bank 1998–2000; Deputy Chair., later First Deputy Chair. Nat. Bank of Tajikistan 2000–06, Chair. 2012–15; Chair. State Financial Control Cttee 2006–07; First Deputy Dir Agency for State Finance Control and Struggle Against Corruption 2007; Amb. to USA 2007–12; Honoured Worker of Tajikistan.

SHIRLEY, Donna Lee, BA, BS, MS; American aeronautical engineer, academic and consultant; *President, Managing Creativity;* b. 1941, Wynnewood, Okla; m. (divorced); one d.; ed Univ. of Oklahoma, Univ. of Southern California; specifications writer, McDonnell Aircraft, St Louis, Mo. 1963; joined NASA Jet Propulsion Lab. 1966, mission analyst for Mariner 10 mission to Venus and Mercury 1970–74, Energy and Environmental System Man. 1974–79, Task Man. 1979–81, Man. Mission Design Section 1981–82, Man. Space Station Program Office 1982–85, Man. Automation and Robotics Office 1985–87, Man. Rover Concept Team 1987–90, Leader, Surface Transportation Vehicle Systems Eng 1989–91, Man. Exploration Initiative Studies 1990–91, project engineer, Cassini Mission 1991–92; Man. Mars Pathfinder Microrover Flight Experiment 1992–94, Man. Mars Exploration Program 1994–98; Asst Dean of Eng for Advanced Program Devt, Coll. of Eng, Univ. of Oklahoma 1999–2002, now mem. Bd of Visitors; Pres. Managing Creativity (consulting firm) 1997–; Sr Fellow, School of Public Policy, UCLA 1997; Dr hc (Susquehanna Univ.) 2004; NASA Group Achievement Awards, including for Telerobotics Tech. Team 1991 and Pathfinder Mars Rover Devt Team 1997, NASA Outstanding Leadership Medal 1997, Pres.'s Award, Soc. for Tech. Technical Communication 1997, inducted into Women in Tech. Int. Hall of Fame 1997, Holley Medal for Lifetime Achievement, ASME 1998, Judith Resnick Award, Soc. of Women Engineers 1998, Washington Award for Eng Achievement, Western Engineer Soc. 2000, Leadership in Tech. Man. Award 2001, Wernher Von Braun Memorial Award, Nat. Space Soc. 2001, Oklahoma Byliners Award 2002, inducted into Oklahoma Women's Hall of Fame 2003, Kathryn Wright Award 2009. *Publication:* Managing Martians – The Extraordinary Story of a Woman's Lifelong Quest to Get to Mars and of the Team Behind the Space Robot That Has Captured the Imagination of the World (memoir) 1998, The Land That Lost Its Green 2012. *Leisure interests:* acting, painting, playing the guitar, sailing. *Address:* Managing

Creativity, 1591 Swan Drive, Tulsa, OK 74120, USA (office). *Telephone:* (918) 910-0466 (office). *E-mail:* dshirley1941@gmail.com (office). *Website:* www.managingcreativity.com (office).

SHIRLEY, George Irving, BEd; American singer (tenor) and academic; *Joseph Edgar Maddy Distinguished University Professor Emeritus of Music (Voice), School of Music, Theatre and Dance, University of Michigan;* b. 18 April 1934, Indianapolis, Ind.; s. of Irving E. Shirley and Daisy Shirley (née Bell); m. Gladys Lee Ishop 1956; one s. one d.; ed Wayne State Univ.; New York premiere with Amato Opera in Verdi's Aroldo 1961; debuts with Metropolitan Opera, New York Opera, Festival of Two Worlds (Spoleto, Italy), Santa Fé Opera 1961, Teatro Colón, Buenos Aires 1965, La Scala, Milan 1965, Glyndebourne Festival 1966, Royal Opera, Covent Garden, Scottish Opera 1967, Vienna Festival 1972, San Francisco Opera 1977, Chicago Lyric Opera 1977, Théâtre Municipal d'Angers 1979, Edin. Festival 1979, Nat. Opera Ebony, Philadelphia 1980, Spoleto Festival, Charleston, SC 1980, Tulsa Opera, Okla 1980, Ottawa Festival 1981, Deutsche Oper 1983, Guelph Spring Festival 1983, Bregenz Festival, Austria 1998; Glimmerglass Opera, Cooperstown, NY 1999, Eugene Opera, Ore. 2009; Prof. of Voice, Univ. of Maryland 1980–87; Prof. of Music, Univ. of Michigan School of Music, Theatre & Dance 1987–2007, Joseph Edgar Maddy Distinguished Univ. Prof. of Music (Voice) 1992–2007, Prof. Emer. 2007–, also Dir Emer., Vocal Arts Div.; mem. Bd Santa Fe Opera, Sullivan Foundation, Voice Foundation; mem. Univ. of Michigan Soc. of Fellows 1989, American Acad. of Teachers of Singing 1990; Hon. HDH (Wilberforce Univ.) 1967, Hon. LLD (Montclair State Coll.) 1984, Hon. DFA (Lake Forest Coll.) 1988, Hon. DHumLitt (Northern Iowa) 1997, (Wayne State Univ.) 2012, Hon. DM (Univ. of Michigan) 2015; numerous awards including Nat. Arts Club Award 1960, Concorso di Musica e Danza (Vercelli, Italy) 1960, Grammy Award (for recording of Mozart's Così fan tutte) 1968, Distinguished Scholar-Teacher Award, Univ. of Md 1985–86, Univ. of Mich. School of Music Alumni Asscn Distinguished Achievement Award 2005, Opera Noire Grazioso Award, New York 2005, Dr Charles H. Wright Legacy Award for Excellence in Fine Arts, Detroit 2006, Nat. Asscn for Study and Performance of African American Music Trail Blazer Award 2007, Lifetime Achievement Award, Nat. Asscn of Teachers of Singing 2014, Nat. Medal of Arts 2015, Nat. Opera Asscn Lifetime Achievement Award 2016. *Leisure interests:* golf, sketching and cartoons, photography, writing. *Address:* c/o Robert Mirshak, Mirshak Artists Management, 1173 Second Avenue, #313, New York, NY 10065, USA (office); 3027 Earl V. Moore Building, University of Michigan School of Music, 1100 Baits Drive, Ann Arbor, MI 48109, USA (office). *Telephone:* (917) 282-0687 (office). *Fax:* (646) 395-1368 (office). *E-mail:* Robert@MirshakArtists.com (office); gis@umich.edu (office). *Website:* www.mirshakartists.com/ (office); www.music.umich.edu (office).

SHIRO, Hiruta; Japanese business executive; b. 1942; joined Asahi Kasei Corpn 1964, held several sr positions including Man. Dir, Sr Man. Dir, Exec. Vice-Pres. 2002–03, Pres. 2003–10, also Presidential Exec. Officer of Research and Devt and mem. Group Advisory Cttee, Adviser 2010–, apptd Dir Asahi Chemical Industry Co. Ltd 1998; Special Adviser at Iwato Partners Co., Ltd; mem. Bd of Dirs Olympus Corpn 2012–; fmr Pres. Petrochemical Industry Asscn. *Address:* Asahi Kasei Corporation, Jinbocho-Mitsui Building, 1-105 Kanda Jinbocho, Chiyoda-Ku, Tokyo 101-8101, Japan (office).

SHIRVINDT, Alexander Anatolyevich; Russian actor and screenwriter; *Artistic Director, Moscow Academic Theatre of Satire;* b. 19 July 1934, Moscow; m. Natalya Belousova; one s.; ed Shchukin School of Theatre Art; actor, Moscow Theatre of Lenin's Comsomol 1957–70, actor Moscow Academic Theatre of Satire 1957–, Artistic Dir 2000–; teacher, Shchukin School of Theatre Art; mem. Union of Cinematographers; People's Artist of Russia 1989, Order of Merit for the Fatherland, Order of Friendship of Peoples. *Films include:* Once Again for Love 1968, Inkognito iz Peterburga 1977, A Railway Station for Two 1983, Shantazhist 1988, Candide 1994, Privet, duralei! 1996, Andersen. Zhizn bez lyubvi 2006, Ironiya sudby. Prodolzhenie 2007, Pestrye sumerki 2010. *Stage appearances include:* Trigorin (The Seagull), Dobchinsky (The Government Inspector), King Louis (Bondage of Hypocrites), Akhmed Ryza (Crank), Count Almaviva (The Marriage of Figaro), Press Secretary (Burden of Decisions), Molchalin (Misfortune from Intellect), Nehrish (Red Horse with Small Bells), President of the Reportage (Bug). *Plays produced include:* Small Comedies of a Big House, Melancholy, Shut Up, Wake Up and Sing; two-man variety shows with M. Derzhavin. *Leisure interest:* fishing. *Address:* Moscow Academic Theatre of Satire, Triumfalnaya pl. 2, 103050 Moscow (office); Kotelnicheskaya nab. 1/15, korp. A, Apartment 50, 109240 Moscow, Russia (home). *Telephone:* (495) 699-63-05 (office); (495) 916-49-82 (home). *Fax:* (495) 699-36-42 (office). *Website:* www.satire.ru (office).

SHISHKIN, Mikhail Pavlovich; Russian author; b. 18 Jan. 1961, Moscow; ed Moscow State Pedagogical Inst.; journalist for Rovesni 1982–85; teacher of English and German 1985–95; debut as writer with short story Calligraphy Lesson 1993; contrib., Znamya magazine. *Publications include:* novels: One Night Befalls Us All 1993, The Taking of Izmail (Russian Booker Prize 2000) 1999, Maidenhair (Big Book Award 2006, Nat. Best-Seller Prize 2006, Int. Literature Award 2011) 2005, Pismovnik (Big Book Award 2011, Haus der Kulturen der Welt International Literature Award 2011) 2010; novella: Blind Musician 1994; short stories: Saved Language 2001; non-fiction: Russian Switzerland 2000, Montreux-Missolunghi-Astapovo, in the Steps of Byron and Tolstoy (Prix du Meilleur Livre Étranger 2005) 2002. *Address:* Banke, Goumen & Smirnova Literary Agency, St Petersburg 195220, Nauki pr. 19/2, fl. 293, Russia (office). *E-mail:* goumen@bgs-agency.com (office). *Website:* bgs-agency.com/authors/shishkin-mikhail (office).

SHISLER, Arden L.; American insurance industry executive; b. 1941, Massillon, Ohio; ed Dalton High School, Ohio State Univ.; served in US Army; COO K&B Transport Inc. 1986–92, Pres. and CEO 1992–2003, Consultant 2003–04; mem. Bd of Dirs Nationwide Mutual Insurance Co. 1984–2008, Chair. 1992–2008, mem. Bd of Dirs Nationwide Financial Services Inc., Chair. 2003–09, later also Chair. Nationwide Mutual Fire Insurance Co., Nationwide Life Insurance Co.; fmr Pres. Ohio Agricultural Marketing Asscn; mem. Bd of Dirs Ohio 4-H Foundation; mem. Advisory Cttee, Ohio State Univ. Agric. Tech. Inst.; mem. Wayne Co. Farm Bureau, Cornerstone Community Church; Trustee, Aberdeen Select Equity Fund 2000–, Nationwide Variable Insurance Trust 2000–, Nationwide Mutual Funds 2000–, Gartmore Variable Insurance Trust 2000–, Dreyfus Gvit International

Value Fund 2000–; fmr Trustee, Aberdeen Funds, Natiowide NVIT Mid Cap Growth Fund, Aberdeen Health Sciences Fund, Gartmore Convertible Fund.

SHIYAM, Maj.-Gen. Ahmed; Maldivian army officer; *Chief of National Defence Force;* m.; one s. three d.; ed Royal Mil. Acad., UK, Nat. Defence Coll., India, Command and Staff Coll., Pakistan; started career as Instructor, Girifushi Training Center, CO of the Unit, Commdt; CO, Defence Inst. for Training and Educ.; joined Nat. Defence Force 1986, CO, Northern Regional HQ, CO, Southern Regional HQ, CO, Regional HQ, Exec. Officer for Chief of Defence Force and Minister of Defence, CO, Electrical and Mechanical Engineers, CO, Support Battalion II, Commdr Rapid Reaction Forces, First Commdt Marine Corps, Nat. Defence Force 2009, Commdr Cen. Area, Second Commdt, Coast Guard 2011–12, Chief of Nat. Defence Force 2012–; Distinguished Service Medal, Presidential Medal, Defence Force Service Medal, Dedicated Service Medal, Good Conduct Medal, Nov. 3rd Medal, Centenary Medal. *Address:* Maldives National Defence Force Headquarters, Bandaarakoshi, Ameer Ahmed Magu, Malé, Maldives (office). *Telephone:* 3322607 (office). *Fax:* 3322496 (office). *E-mail:* media@mndf.gov.mv (office). *Website:* www.mndf.gov.mv (office).

SHKOLNIK, Vladimir Sergeyevich; Kazakhstani mining engineer and politician; b. 17 Feb. 1949, Serpukhov, Moscow Oblast, Russian SFSR, USSR; m.; two c.; ed Moscow Inst. of Physics and Math.; various posts from engineer to Deputy Dir, Mañğistaw Energy Complex 1973–92; Dir-Gen. Agency of Atomic Energy Repub. of Kazakhstan 1992–94; Minister of Science and New Tech. 1994–96, of Science 1996–99, of Energy and Mineral Resources 1999–2001, 2005, of Industry and Trade –2007; Vice-Chair. Pres.'s Admin 2007; Pres. JSC Kazatomprom NAC 2009–14; Minister of Energy 2014–16; mem. Kazakhstan Acad. of Sciences, Pres. 1996–. *Address:* c/o Ministry of Energy, 010000 Nur-Sultan, Kabanbai batyr kosh. 19, Kazakhstan. *E-mail:* bogdanova@mgm.gov.kz.

SHLAPAK, Oleksandr Vitalyovych; Ukrainian economist and politician; b. 1 Jan. 1960, Irkutsk; m. Oksana Markovna; two d.; ed Lviv Polytechnic Inst., Ukrainian State Univ. of Finance and Int. Trade; began career as software engineer at Lviv Polytechnic Inst. 1982–84, Sec., Lviv Polytechnic Inst. Komsomol Cttee 1984–90; Chair., Lviv Regional Council of Democratic Youth Union 1990–93; Dir Lviv Br. and Deputy Chair., PrivatBank 1993–98; Chief Econ. Adviser to Deputy Prime Minister 1998–2000; Deputy Minister of Economy 2000–01, Minister of Economy 2001–02; Deputy Chair., Nat. Bank of Ukraine 2003–05; Chair. State Treasury 2005–06; Head of Socio-Econ. Devt Service in Presidential Secr. 2006–07, First Deputy Head of Presidential Secr. 2007–10; Vice-Pres. IMG International Holding Co. 2010–14; Minister of Finance March–Dec. 2014; Honoured Economist of Ukraine 2008, Order of Prince Yaroslav the Wise 2010, Friendship Order of the Socialist Repub. of Vietnam 2011. *Address:* c/o Ministry of Finance, 01008 Kyiv, vulitsa M. Hrushevskoho 12/2, Ukraine.

SHMAKOV, Mikhail Viktorovich; Russian trade union official; *Chairman, Federation of Independent Trade Unions of Russia;* b. 12 Aug. 1949, Moscow; m.; one s.; ed Bauman Moscow State Tech. Univ.; engineer in defence industry factories 1972–75, 1977–86; army service 1975–77; Chair. Moscow City Trade Union of Workers in Defence Industry 1986–90; Chair. Moscow City Council of Trade Unions (later transformed into Moscow Fed. of Trade Unions) 1990–93; Chair. Fed. of Ind. Trade Unions of Russia 1993–; Pres. Gen. Confed. of Trade Unions 2004–; mem. Exec. Bureau and Gen. Council, International Trade Union Confed. 2006–, Pres. Pan-European Regional Council 2007–; Titular mem. Governing Body, ILO 2010–; mem. Organizational Cttee Otechestvo Movt; Order of Honour 1985, Order of Merit for the Fatherland, IV degree 1999, Order of Merit for the Fatherland, III degree 2006; Person of the Year 2009. *Leisure interest:* sports. *Address:* Federation of Independent Trade Unions of Russia, Leninsky Prospekt 42, 119119 Moscow, Russia (office). *Telephone:* (495) 938-73-12 (office). *Fax:* (495) 137-06-94 (office). *E-mail:* shmakov@fnpr.ru (office). *Website:* www.fnpr.ru (office).

SHMATKO, Sergei Ivanovich; Russian government official; b. 26 Sept. 1966, Stavropol; ed Faculty of Political Economy, Ural State Univ., Mil. Acad., Jt Staff VS of Russia; worked as auditor in BDO Binder 1992–94; Dir RFI GmbH (official rep. of Russian Fed. Property Fund in EU) 1994–95; scientific employee, Inst. of Problems of Investment 1995–97, supervised man. of external relations of All-Russia devt bank of regions; Head of Analytical Centre of Econ. Strategy, Rosenergoatom 1997–99; adviser on econ. strategy to Gen. Dir All-Russian Scientific Research Inst. for Nuclear Power Plant Operation (VNIIAES) 1999–2001; Chair. State fund of conversion 2002–05; adviser to Chair. Gazprombank Feb.–June 2005; adviser to Vice-Pres. Atomstroyexport (jt stock co.) Feb.–June 2005, Pres. Atomstroyexport 2005–08; Minister of Energy 2008–12.

SHNAIDER, Alexander, BA; Canadian (b. Russian) business executive; b. 1969, Leningrad (now St Petersburg), USSR; m.; three c.; ed York Univ.; est. steel-trading business in Belgium, expanded business by trading with steel mills in Soviet Union; Co-f. (with Eduard Shifrin) Midland Resources (later Midland Group) 1994, bought large stakes in Zaporizhstal steel mill, Ukraine, nat. electricity grid, Armenia and now has interests in steel, shipping, construction, real estate in Russia, Ukraine and worldwide; Chair. Talon International Development Corpn, Royal Laser Corpn 2006–; bought Jordan Grand Prix racing team 2005, renamed Midland Racing, sold team 2006; fmr mem. Bd of Dirs Magellan Energy Ltd. *Address:* Midland Resources Holding Ltd, Havelet House, South Esplanade, St Peter Port GY1 3AN Guernsey, Channel Islands.

SHOCHAT, Avraham, BSc; Israeli construction engineer, company director and fmr politician; b. 14 June 1936, Tel-Aviv; ed Haifa Technion; fmr paratrooper in Israel Defence Forces; Br. Dir Solel Boneh (Histadrut construction co.); Co-f. City of Arad, Mayor of Arad 1967–89, Chair. Citizens' Cttee Arad, Devt Towns Council, Econ. Cttee, Finance Cttee, Deputy Chair. Union of Local Authorities; mem. Knesset (Parl.) 1988–2003; Minister of Finance 1992–96, 1999–2001, of Nat. Infrastructure 2000–01; Chair. Investment Cttee, Israel Infrastructure Fund, IDI Technologies Ltd; mem. Bd of Dirs Alon USA Energy Inc. 2005–, Israel Chemicals Ltd 2006–, Kali Capital Markets Insurance Agency Ltd, Mizrahi Tefahot Bank Ltd 2006–, Direct Insurance Financial Investments Ltd, ICL Fertilizers Ltd, ICL Industrial Products; fmr mem. Bd of Dirs Israel Aircraft Industries, Desalination Engineering; headed Govt Cttee on higher educ. reforms 2007; mem. Labour Party. *Address:* Israel Infrastructure Fund, Adgar Tower 360, 26th floor, 2 Hashlosha Street, Tel-Aviv 6109301, Israel.

SHOEMAKER, Sydney S., BA, PhD, FBA; American academic; *Susan Linn Sage Professor Emeritus of Philosophy, Cornell University;* b. 29 Sept. 1931, Boise, Idaho; s. of Roy Hopkins Shoemaker and Sarah Anderson Shoemaker; m. Molly McDonald 1960; one s.; ed Reed Coll., Edinburgh Univ., Cornell Univ.; instructor, Ohio State Univ. 1957–60; Santayana Fellow, Harvard Univ. 1960–61; Asst then Assoc. Prof., Cornell Univ. 1961–67, apptd Prof. 1970, Susan Linn Sage Prof. 1978, currently Prof. Emer.; Assoc. Prof., Rockefeller Univ. 1967–70; ed. The Philosophical Review, many terms 1964–; Gen. Ed. Cambridge Studies in Philosophy 1982–90; Vice-Pres. Eastern Div. American Philosophical Asscn 1992–93, Pres. 1993–94; John Locke Lecturer, Univ. of Oxford 1972; Josiah Royce Lecturer, Brown Univ. 1993; Fulbright Scholar 1953–54, mem. American Philosophical Asscn; Fellow, Center for Advanced Study in Behavioral Sciences 1973–74, Nat. Endowment for the Humanities Fellowship 1980–81, Nat. Humanities Center 1987–88, American Acad. of Arts and Sciences. *Publications include:* Self-Knowledge and Self-Identity 1963, Identity, Cause and Mind 1984, Personal Identity (with Richard Swinburne) 1984, The First Person Perspective 1996, Physical Realization 2007. *Leisure interests:* music, reading, gardening. *Address:* Sage School of Philosophy, 218 Goldwin Smith Hall, Cornell University, Ithaca, NY 14853-3201 (office); 104 Northway Road, Ithaca, NY 14850, USA (home). *Telephone:* (607) 255-3687 (office); (607) 257-7382 (home). *Fax:* (609) 255-8177 (office). *E-mail:* ss56@cornell.edu (office); philosophy@cornell.edu (office). *Website:* philosophy.cornell.edu/people/philosophy-faculty.cfm (office).

SHOEMATE, Charles Richard (Dick), MBA; American business executive; b. 10 Dec. 1939, LaHarpe, Ill.; s. of Richard Osborne Shoemate and Mary Jane Shoemate (née Gillette); m. Nancy Lee Gordon 1962; three s.; ed Western Illinois Univ., Univ. of Chicago; Comptroller, Corn Products Unit, CPC Int. 1972–74, Plant Man. 1974–76, Vice-Pres. of Operations 1976–81, Corpn Vice-Pres. 1983–88, Pres. 1988–98, Chair. and CEO 1990–98, Chair., Pres., CEO Bestfoods (fmrly CPC Int.) 1998–2000; Pres. Canada Starch Co. 1981–83, mem. Bd of Dirs 1981–88; mem. Bd of Dirs Corn Refiners Asscn 1985–88, CIGNA Corpn 1991–2005, Chevron-Texaco, Inc. (now Chevron Corpn) 1998–2012; Ind. Dir Int. Paper Co. 1994–2005; Advisory Dir Unilever 2001–03; fmr Chair. Conference Board; mem. Business Roundtable, Cttee for Econ. Devt; mem. Advisory Council Indian River Medical Center Foundation.

SHOICHET, Molly S., BSc, MSc, PhD, FRSC; Canadian chemical engineer and academic; *University Professor and Canada Research Chair in Tissue Engineering, University of Toronto;* b. Toronto; ed Toronto French School, Massachusetts Inst. of Tech. and Univ. of Massachusetts, USA; began career at CytoTherapeutics Inc, Providence, RI 1992–95; Adjunct Faculty mem., Dept of Molecular Pharmacology and Biotechnology, Brown Univ. 1992–95; joined faculties of Dept of Chemical Engineering and Applied Chemistry and Dept of Chemistry, Univ. of Toronto 1995, currently Univ. Prof., Prin. Investigator, Shoichet Lab.; Vice-Pres., Founding Scientist and Dir, BoneTec Corpn 1998–2003; f. matREGEN Corpn, Toronto 2002; Consultant, Chemical Engineering Research Consultants Ltd, Toronto; mem. Heart and Stroke Foundation Center for Stroke Recovery, AIChE, ACS, Soc. for Biomaterials, Canadian Biomaterials Soc., Chemical Inst. of Canada, Soc. for Neuroscience, Tissue Eng and Regenerative Medicine Int. Soc., Materials Research Soc. 1990–91, 2000; Fellow, American Inst. for Medical and Biological Eng 2006, Biomaterials Science and Eng 2008, AAAS 2011, Canadian Acad. of Eng 2012, Canadian Acad. of Health Sciences 2012; Order of Ont. 2011; Univ. Faculty Award, Natural Sciences and Eng Research Council 1995–2000, Canada's Top 40 under 40 2001 (awarded 2002), Young Explorer's Award, Canadian Inst. for Advanced Research 2002, Career Award, Canada Foundation for Innovation 2003, Syncrude Canada Innovation Award, Canadian Soc. for Chemical Eng 2003, Canada Research Chair in Tissue Eng, Tier II 2001–06, McLean Award, Univ. of Toronto 2004, RSC UK-Canada WISET Lectureship 2005, Canada Research Chair in Tissue Eng, Tier I 2006–13, 2013–(19), RSC Rutherford Memorial Medal in Chem. 2006, Steacie Fellowship, Natural Sciences and Eng Research Council 2003–05, Clara Benson Award, Canadian Soc. for Chem. 2009, Woman of Action, Israel Cancer Research Fund (co-recipient) 2010, Killam Research Fellowship, Canada Council for the Arts 2008–10, Clemson Award for Contribs to Literature, Soc. for Biomaterials (USA) 2012, Innovation of the Year Award, Univ. of Toronto 2012, Award of Int. Fellows of Tissue Eng and Regenerative Medicine 2013, Queen Elizabeth II Diamond Jubilee Award 2013, Laureate, L'Oréal-UNESCO Awards for Women in Science (North America) 2015. *Publications:* numerous papers in professional journals. *Address:* Room 514, Chemical Engineering and Applied Chemistry, Faculty of Applied Science and Engineering, University of Toronto, 160 College Street, Toronto, ON M5S 3E5, Canada (office). *Telephone:* (416) 978-1460 (office). *Fax:* (416) 978-8287 (office). *E-mail:* molly.shoichet@utoronto.ca (office). *Website:* www.chem-eng.utoronto.ca (office); www.ecf.utoronto.ca/~molly/home.html (office).

SHOIGU, Col Gen. Sergei Kuzhugetovich, Cand. Sc. (Econ); Russian engineer and politician; *Minister of Defence;* b. 21 May 1955, Chadan, Tuva ASSR (now Repub. of Tyva), Russian SFSR, USSR; s. of Kuzhuget Sereevich Shoigu and Alexandra Yakovlevna Shoigu; m. Irina Shoigu; two d.; ed Krasnoyarsk Polytech. Inst.; engineer, Sr master construction trust in Krasnoyarsk 1977–78; man. construction trusts Achinskalyuminstroi, Sayanalyuminstroi, Abakanvagonstroi 1979–88; Second Sec. Abakan City (Khakass Autononous Okrug, then in Krasnoyarsk Krai, now Repub. of Khakasiya) CP Cttee, insp. CP Cttee Krasnoyarsk Krai 1989–90; Deputy Chair. State Cttee on Architecture and Construction RSFSR 1990–91; Chair. State Cttee of Russian Fed. on Civil Defence, Emergencies and Natural Disasters 1991–94; Minister of Civil Defence, Emergencies and Clean-up Operations 1994–2012; Deputy Prime Minister Jan.–May 2000; Gov. Moscow Oblast May–Nov. 2012; Minister of Defence Nov. 2012–; Pres. Russian Geographical Soc. 2009–; mem. Security Council of Russia; Co-founder and leader pre-election bloc (then party) Yedinstvo (Unity) 1999–2001; Co-Chair. of Yedinstvo i Otechestvo-Yedinaya Rossiya (Unity and Fatherland-United Russia, later Yedinaya Rossiya—United Russia) 2001–05; mem. Gosudarstvennaya Duma (State Duma) 1999; Hon. Citizen of Kemerovo Oblast 2005; Order for Personal Courage (Russia) 1994, Danaker Order (Kyrgyzstan) 2002, Order of St Sava (1st class) (Serbia) 2003, Order of Merit for the Fatherland (3rd class)

(Russia) 2005, Order of Honour (Russia) 2009, Order of Merit for the Fatherland (2nd class) (Russia) 2010; Medal 'Dank' (Kyrgyzstan) 1997, Hero of Russian Fed. 1999, Nat. Public Prize of Peter the Great 1999, Moscow Medal, Merited Rescuer of the Russian Fed. 2005. *Leisure interests:* singing, playing guitar, football (supports Spartak Moscow), collecting swords, daggers and Japanese samurai swords, watercolour painting and graphics, manufacturing handicrafts made of wood. *Address:* Ministry of Defence, 119019 Moscow, ul. Znamenka 19, Russia (office). *Telephone:* (495) 696-71-71 (office); (495) 696-84-36 (office). *Website:* eng.mil.ru/en/management/minister.htm (office); government.ru/en/gov/persons/25/events (office).

SHOISMATOV, Ergash Rahmatullayevich; Uzbekistani politician; apptd Minister of Power Eng and Electrification 2000; Chair. Uzbekenergo (state energy co.) –2006; apptd Deputy Prime Minister various changing energy responsibilities 2006, including responsibility for Geology, the Fuel-Energy Complex, and the Chemical and Petroleum Industries and Metallurgy.

SHOKHIN, Aleksandr Nikolayevich; Russian politician; *President, Russian Union of Industrialists and Entrepreneurs;* b. 25 Nov. 1951, Savinskoye, Arkhangelsk Region; m. Tatyana Valentinovna Shokhina; one s. one d.; ed Moscow Univ.; mem. staff, Inst. of Econ., State Planning Cttee, Inst. of Labour, State Cttee of Labour 1974–82; Researcher, Cen. Econ.-Math. Inst. and Inst. for Industrial Prognostics, USSR Acad. of Sciences 1982–87; adviser, Head of Dept of Int. Econ. Relations, Ministry of Foreign Affairs 1987–91; Dir Inst. of Employment Problems May–Aug. 1991; Russian Minister of Labour Aug.–Nov. 1991; Deputy Chair. of Russian Govt 1991–94; Minister of Labour and Employment 1991–92, of Foreign Econ. Relations 1992–93, of Econs 1994; Man. for Russia, IMF and IBRD 1992–94; mem. Bd State Specialized Export-Import Bank 1995; Pres. Higher School of Econs 1995; mem. Bd Russian Party of Unity and Consent 1993–95; Co-ordinator pre-election Union 'Our Home Russia' 1995, Chair. 1997–98; mem. State Duma (Parl.) 1993–97, First Deputy Chair. 1996–97; Deputy Prime Minister Sept. 1998 (resgnd); Chair. Interdepartmental Comm. of Security Council for Econ. Security 1998–99; apptd Pres. Bureau of Russian Union of Industrialists and Entrepreneurs 2003, Pres. RSPP International Council for Cooperation and Investment 2008, Russia-US Council on Business Cooperation 2009; Chair. Coordinating Council of Employers' Unions of Russia 2008–; Ind. Dir LUKoil, TNK-BP Management, TMK and Russian Railways; Chair. Supervisory Bd, Renaissance Capital (investment group) 2002–06, Expert Council, Fed. Comm. on Securities Market 2003; Ind. mem. Cttee of Credit Org. and Financial Markets 1999, then currently Chair.; mem. Nat. Council of Corp. Governance 2003–; apptd Perm. mem. Russian part of Russian-French Council on Economic, Financial, Industrial and Trade Matters 2007; Order of Distinguished Service (4th degree) (Russia), Medal of Honor. *Publications:* several books including Social Problems of Perestroika 1989, Consumer's Market 1989, Interactive of Powers in the Legislative Process 1997; over 200 scientific articles. *Address:* Russian Union of Industrialists and Entrepreneurs, 17 Kotel'nicheskaya naberezhnaya, 109240 Moscow, Russia (office). *Telephone:* (495) 663-04-04 (office). *Fax:* (495) 663-04-32 (office). *E-mail:* rspp@rspp.ru (office). *Website:* www.rspp.ru (office).

SHOKIN, Yurii Ivanovich; Russian mathematician and academic; *Director, Institute of Computational Technologies, Russian Academy of Sciences;* b. 9 July 1943, Kansk; m. 1968; two d.; ed Novosibirsk State Univ.; Sr Researcher, Head of Lab. Computers, Cen. Siberian br., USSR Acad. of Sciences 1969–76, Head of Lab., Inst. Theoretical and Applied Mechanics (Siberian br.) 1976–83, Dir Computers, Cen. Siberian br. in Krasnoyarsk 1983–90; Dir Inst. of Computational Technologies (Siberian br.), Russian Acad. of Sciences 1990–, Gen. Scientific Sec. (Siberian br.) 1992–97, Gen. Dir United Inst. of Informatics 1997–2003, Chair. Scientific Council on Nano- and Information Technologies 2008–; Dir Technopark, Novosibirsk 1998–; Corresp. mem. USSR (now Russian) Acad. of Sciences 1984, mem. 1994; research in computational math., numerical methods of mechanics, applied math., informatics, telecommunication, math. simulation; Order of Merit 1982, Order of Friendship 1999, Badge of Repub. of Kazakhstan for services in Devt of Science 2002, Order of Honour 2004, Medal For Belief and Good 2006. *Publications:* Interval Analysis 1981, Numerical Modelling of Tsunami Waves 1983, Method of Differential Approximation: Application in Gas Dynamics 1985, Methods of Interval Analysis 1986, Fortran 90 for the Fortran Programmer 1995, Numerical Simulation of Environmental Problems 1997, Modelling of Jet Flows in Steel Converters 2000, Numerical Modelling of Fluid Flows with Surface Waves 2001, Methods of Riemann's Geometry in Construction Problems of Computational Meshes 2005, Modeling and Optimization of Systems with Distributed Parameters 2006, Construction of Differential Meshes by Means of Beltrami Equations Diffusion 2007, Differential Meshes and Coordinate Transformations for Computational Solution of Singular Perturbed Problems 2008; numerous scientific articles. *Address:* Lavrentyev av. 6, 630090 Novosibirsk 90 (office); Voevodskogo 10, 630090 Novosibirsk 90, Russia (home). *Telephone:* (383) 235-33-45 (office). *Fax:* (383) 235-12-42 (office). *E-mail:* shokin@adm.ict.nsc.ru (office); i.shokin@g.nsu.ru (office). *Website:* www-sbras.nsc.ru (office).

SHOMAN, Abdel Hamid Abdul Majeed, BSc; Palestinian banking executive; b. 1 Jan. 1947; s. of Abdul Majeed Shoman; m.; three c.; ed American Univ. of Beirut; first joined Arab Bank 1970, Asst Gen. Man. Arab Bank plc, later Deputy Chair. and CEO 2001–05, Chair. and CEO 2005–10, Exec. Chair. 2010–12 (resgnd), also Chair. Islamic International Arab Bank (Amman), Arab Bank (Switzerland) Zurich 2002–12, Europe Arab Bank 2005–12, Al Arabi Investment Group Co. 2004, AB Capital 2005, Arab National Leasing Co. LLC 2004, Commercial Buildings Co., Lebanon 2005, Abdul Hamid Shoman Foundation 2007; mem. Senate (Upper House of Parl.) of Jordan 2005–11; mem. Bd of Trustees, King Hussein Cancer & Biotechnology Inst.; Arabian Business Magazine Banker of the Year Award 2008.

SHONEKAN, Chief Ernest Adegunle Oladeinde, LLB, CBE; Nigerian lawyer, business executive, politician and fmr head of state; *Co-Founder and Non-Executive Partner, African Capital Alliance;* b. 9 May 1936, Lagos; m. Beatrice Oyelayo Oyebola 1965; two s. three d.; ed Church Missionary Soc. (CMS) Boys' School, Lagos, CMS Grammar School, Lagos and Univ. of London, UK; legal asst, UAC of Nigeria Ltd 1964–67, Asst Legal Adviser 1967–73, Deputy Legal Adviser 1974–75, Legal Adviser 1975–78, Dir 1976, Chair. 1980; Gen. Man. Bordpak Premier Packaging Co. 1978–79; Chair. Transitional Council of Nigeria Jan.–Aug. 1993; Pres. of Nigeria and Head of Interim Govt Aug.–Nov. 1993; Co-Founder and Non-Exec. Partner, African Capital Alliance (investment firm), Lagos 1997–; Bd mem. Nigerian-German Chemicals plc, MAERSK Line Nigeria Ltd; Grand Officier, Ordre national de la Légion d'honneur. *Address:* African Capital Alliance, 8th Floor, C & C Towers, Plot 1684, Sanusi Fafunwa Street, Victoria Island, Lagos (office); 12 Alexander Avenue, Ikoyi, Lagos, Nigeria (home). *Telephone:* (1) 2706909 (office); 681437 (home). *Fax:* (1) 2706908 (office). *E-mail:* info@aca-web.com (office). *Website:* www.aca-web.com (office).

SHOR, Peter Williston, BS, PhD; American mathematician and academic; *Morss Professor of Applied Mathematics, Department of Mathematics, Massachusetts Institute of Technology;* b. 14 Aug. 1959, New York; m. Jennifer S. Collins Shor; two d.; ed California Inst. of Tech., Massachusetts Inst. of Tech.; Post-doctoral Fellow, Math. Sciences Research Inst., Berkeley, Calif. 1985; mathematician, AT&T Bell Labs 1986, with Information Sciences Research Lab., AT&T Fellow 1998; Morss Prof. of Applied Mathematics, Dept of Math., MIT 2003–; specialises in algorithms, quantum computing and quantum information theory; mem. NAS; Fellow, American Acad. of Arts and Sciences 2011–; Nevanlinna Award 1998, Int. Quantum Communications Award 1998, Goedel Prize (shared) 1999, Dickson Prize in Science 1999, MacArthur Fellowship 1999, King Faisal Int. Prize in Science (shared) 2002, Distinguished Alumni Award, Caltech 2007. *Publications:* frequent contribs to professional journals. *Address:* Room 2-375, Massachusetts Institute of Technology, 77 Massachusetts Avenue, Cambridge, MA 02139, USA (office). *Telephone:* (617) 253-4362 (office). *Fax:* (617) 253-4358 (office). *E-mail:* shor@math.mit.edu (office). *Website:* math.mit.edu/~shor (office).

SHORATS, Andrey Viktorovich; Belarusian engineer and government official; *Chairman, Minsk City Executive Committee;* b. 12 April 1973, Vitebsk (Viciebsk), Belarusian SSR, USSR; ed Vitebsk State Technological Univ., Acad. of Public Admin under aegis of Pref. of Repub.; engineer, Vitebsk Instruments Plant 1995–97; First Sec., Kastrychnitski dist Cttee, Belarusian Patriotic Youth Union, Vitebsk 1997–98; official with Vitebsk Oblast Consumer Socs Asscn 1999–2002; Head of Power Generation, Transport and Communications Dept, Vitebsk Oblast Exec. Cttee 2002–05, Head of Housing and Utilities Dept 2005–10; Deputy Minister of Housing and Utilities 2010–11, Minister of Housing and Utilities 2011–14; Chair. Minsk City Exec. Cttee 2014–. *Address:* Minsk City Executive Committee, pr. Nezalezhnasti 8, 220030 Minsk, Belarus (office). *Telephone:* (17) 2180001 (office). *E-mail:* mgik@minsk.gov.by (office). *Website:* minsk.gov.by (office).

SHORE, Howard, OC; Canadian film score composer; b. 18 Oct. 1946, Toronto, Ont.; ed Berklee Coll. of Music, Boston; f. rock band Lighthouse; Musical Dir Saturday Night Live TV comedy show 1970s; began composing film music 1978; has collaborated on films by David Cronenberg, Peter Jackson; mem. ASCAP; Officier, Ordre des Arts et des Lettres; Dr hc (Berklee Coll. of Music), Hon. DLitt (York Univ., Toronto) 2007; Career Achievement for Music Composition Award, Nat. Bd of Review of Motion Pictures, ASCAP Lifetime Achievement Award 2004, Max Steiner Film Music Achievement Award, City of Vienna 2010. *Film scores include:* I Miss You, Hugs and Kisses 1978, The Brood 1979, Scanners 1980, Videodrome 1983, Nothing Lasts Forever 1984, After Hours 1985, Fire with Fire 1986, The Fly 1986, Heaven 1987, Nadine 1987, Dead Ringers 1988, Big 1988, Signs of Life 1989, She-Devil 1989, The Local Stigmatic 1989, An Innocent Man 1989, Made in Milan 1990, The Lemon Sisters 1990, Naked Lunch 1991, The Silence of the Lambs 1991, A Kiss Before Dying 1991, Prelude to a Kiss 1992, Single White Female 1992, Philadelphia 1993, Mrs Doubtfire 1993, Guilty As Sin 1993, Sliver 1993, M. Butterfly 1993, Nobody's Fool 1994, The Client 1994, Ed Wood (Los Angeles Film Critics' Asscn Award) 1994, Se7en 1995, Moonlight and Valentino 1995, White Man's Burden 1995, Before and After 1996, The Truth About Cats and Dogs 1996, Striptease 1996, Looking For Richard 1996, Crash 1996, That Thing You Do! 1996, The Game 1997, Cop Land 1997, Gloria 1999, Existenz 1999, Dogma 1999, Analyze This 1999, The Yards 2000, High Fidelity 2000, Esther Kahn 2000, The Cell 2000, Camera 2000, The Score 2001, The Lord of the Rings: The Fellowship of the Ring (Acad. Award for Best Original Score 2002, Grammy Award for Best Soundtrack) 2001, Spider 2002, Panic Room 2002, The Lord of the Rings: The Two Towers 2002, Gangs of New York 2002, The Lord of the Rings: The Return of the King (Golden Globe Award for Best Original Score 2004, Acad. Award for Best Song, for 'Into the West' 2004) 2003, The Aviator (Golden Globe Award for Best Original Score 2005) 2004, The Departed 2006, The Last Mimzy 2007, Eastern Promises 2007, Doubt 2008, The Betrayal 2008, The Twilight Saga: Eclipse 2010, Edge of Darkness 2010, A Dangerous Method 2011, Hugo (Frederick Loewe Award) 2011, The Spider 2011, The Rise of Theodore Roosevelt 2011, The Hobbit: An Unexpected Journey 2012, Cosmopolis 2012, Rosewater 2014, Denial 2016. *Opera:* The Fly. *Address:* Gorfaine/Schwartz Agency Inc, 4111 West Alameda Avenue, Suite 509, Burbank, CA 91505-4161, USA (office). *Telephone:* (818) 260-8500 (office). *Website:* www.gsamusic.com (office); www.howardshore.com.

SHORT, Rt Hon. Clare, PC, BA; British politician and international organization official; *Chair, Cities Alliance and Welfare Association;* b. 15 Feb. 1946, Birmingham; d. of Frank Short and Joan Short; m. 1st 1964 (divorced 1974); one s.; m. 2nd Alex Lyon 1981 (died 1993); ed Univs of Keele and Leeds; with Home Office 1970–75; Dir All Faith for One Race 1976–78, Youthaid and Unemployment Unit 1979–83; MP for Birmingham Ladywood 1983–2010, mem. Select Cttee on Home Affairs 1983–85; Shadow Employment Spokesperson 1985–89, Social Security Spokesperson 1989–91, Environment Protection Spokesperson 1992–93, Spokesperson for Women 1993–95; Shadow Sec. of State for Transport 1995–96, for Overseas Devt 1996–97; Sec. of State for Int. Devt 1997–2003; resgnd from the Govt 2003, resgnd Labour whip 2006; Vice-Chair All-Party Parl. Group on Trafficking of Women and Children; Chair All Party Group on Race Relations 1985–86, Int. Advisory Bd of Cranfield Masters in Security Sector Man. Programme; mem. Nat. Exec. Cttee Labour Party 1988–98, Chair Women's Cttee 1993–97; Vice-Pres. Socialist International Women 1992–97; mem. Advocacy Panel of Cities Alliance 2006–16; Chair. Extractive Industries Transparency Initiative 2011–16; Chair Cities Alliance 2016–(19); mem. UNISON; Trustee, Africa Humanitarian Action, Hope (serving destitute asylum seekers), Welfare Asscn (Chair); Dr hc (Bradford Peace Studies, Cardinal Wiseman Coll., Coventry Univ., Univ. of Wolverhampton); Order of Volta Companion 2008; Spectator Campaigning MP of the Year 1992, Channel 4 Politician's Politician Award 2002,

Wilberforce Medal 2004. *Publication:* An Honourable Deception? New Labour, Iraq and the Misuse of Power (Channel 4 Political Book of the Year 2005) 2004. *Leisure interests:* books, family, swimming. *Address:* 23 Larkhall Rise, London, SW4 6JB, England (home). *Telephone:* (20) 7720-1525 (office). *E-mail:* shortclare@gmail.com (office). *Website:* www.clareshort.org (office).

SHORT, Nigel David; British chess player, writer, coach and commentator; b. 1 June 1965, Leigh, Lancs.; s. of David Short and Jean Gaskell; m. Rea Karageorgiou 1987; one s. one d.; ed Bolton School, Leigh Coll.; at age of 12 beat Jonathan Penrose in British championship; Int. Master 1980, Grandmaster 1984; British Champion 1984, 1987, 1998, English Champion 1991; Pres. Grandmasters' Asscn 1992; defeated Anatoly Karpov 1992; defeated by Kasparov 1993; chess columnist, The Daily Telegraph 1991, The Sunday Telegraph 1996–2006; stripped of int. ratings by World Chess Fed. June 1993, reinstated 1994; resgnd from Fédération Internationale des Echecs (FIDE) and est. Professional Chess Asscn (PCA) with Garry Kasparov 1993, left PCA 1995; Commonwealth Champion 2004, 2006, 2008; EU Champion 2006; Pres. Commonwealth Chess Asscn 2006–08; Hon. Fellow, Univ. of Bolton 1993–; Hon. MBE 1999. *Publication:* Learn Chess with Nigel Short 1993. *Leisure interests:* guitar playing, cricket, history, olive farming, swimming. *E-mail:* nigelshort@gmail.com (office).

SHORT, Roger Valentine, AM, ScD, FAA, FRS, FRCPE, FRANZCOG, FRSE, FRCVS, FRCOG, FAAS; Australian/British professor of reproductive biology and academic; *Honorary Professorial Fellow, Faculty of Medicine, University of Melbourne;* b. 31 July 1930, Weybridge, Surrey, England; s. of F. A. Short and M. C. Short; m. 1st Dr Mary Bowen Wilson 1958 (divorced 1981); one s. three d.; m. 2nd Prof. Marilyn Bernice Renfree 1982; two d.; ed Sherborne School, Univs of Bristol and Cambridge, Univ. of Wisconsin, USA; mem. ARC Unit of Reproductive Physiology and Biochemistry, Cambridge 1956–72; Lecturer, then Reader, Dept of Veterinary Clinical Studies, Univ. of Cambridge 1961–72, Fellow, Magdalene Coll. 1961–72; Dir MRC Unit of Reproductive Biology, Edinburgh, Scotland 1972–82; Prof. of Reproductive Biology, Monash Univ., Australia 1982–95; currently Hon. Professorial Fellow, Faculty of Medicine, Univ. of Melbourne; J. D. White Visiting Prof., Cornell Univ., USA 2002, Regent's Prof., Univ. of California 2001; Chair. Family Health Int., NC 1985–95 (Bd mem. 1983–97); Fellow, American Acad. of Arts and Sciences, Royal Coll. of Veterinary Surgeons, Royal Australian and NZ Coll. of Obstetricians and Gynaecologists; Hon. Prof., Univ. of Edin. 1976–82; Hon. DSc (Guelph, Bristol, Edin.). *Achievements include:* holder of patents for use of melatonin to control jet lag 1983, 1986, 1987, and of topical oestriol administration to the foreskin to prevent HIV infection 2009. *Publications include:* Reproduction in Mammals, Vols 1–8 (with C. R. Austin) 1972–86, Contraceptives of the Future 1976, Ever Since Adam and Eve: The Evolution of Human Sexuality (with M. Potts) 1999; contrib. to numerous scientific journals. *Leisure interests:* gardening, wildlife, history of biology. *Address:* Level 4, 766 Elizabeth Street, University of Melbourne, Melbourne, Vic. 3010 (office); 18 Gwingana Crescent, Glen Waverley, Vic. 3150, Australia (home). *Telephone:* (3) 8344-3370 (office); (3) 9561-8873 (home). *Fax:* (3) 9347-8939 (office). *E-mail:* r.short@unimelb.edu.au (office). *Website:* www.unimelb.edu.au (office).

SHORTEN, Bill, BA, LLB, MBA; Australian lawyer and politician; *Leader of the Opposition;* b. 12 May 1967, Melbourne; s. of William Robert Shorten and Ann Shorten (née McGrath); m. Chloe Shorten; three c.; ed Monash Univ., Melbourne Business School; mil. service, Australian Army Reserve 1985–86; 18 months as lawyer with Maurice Blackburn Cashman; Organiser, Australian Workers' Union 1994, State Sec. (Vic.) 1998, Nat. Sec. 2001–07; Dir, Australian Super (formerly Superannuation Trust Australia) 1998–2007; Dir Victorian Funds Man. Corpn 2005–07; mem. House of Reps (Parl.) for Maribyrnong 2007, 2010, 2013, 2016–; Parl. Sec. for Disabilities and Children's Services 2007–10, for Victorian Bushfire Reconstruction 2009–10, Asst Treas. 2010–11, Minister for Financial Services and Superannuation 2010–13, for Employment and Workplace Relations 2011–13, for Educ. and for Workplace Relations July–Sept. 2013; Leader of the Opposition 2013–; mem. Australian Labor Party (ALP), ALP State Pres. (Vic.) 2005–08, mem. ALP Nat. Exec. 2004–, Leader, Federal Parl. Labor Party 2013–; Centenary Medal 2003. *Leisure interests:* running, reading, spending time with family. *Address:* Australian Labor Party, Suite 1A, 12 Hall Street, Moonee Ponds, Vic. 3039, Australia (office). *Telephone:* (3) 9326-1300 (office). *E-mail:* Bill.Shorten.MP@aph.gov.au (office). *Website:* www.alp.org.au (office); www.billshorten.com.au.

SHORTER, Wayne, BA; American jazz musician (saxophone); b. 25 Aug. 1933, Newark, New Jersey; ed New York Univ.; served in US Army 1956–58; played saxophone with Art Blakey 1959–63, Miles Davis 1964–70, Weather Report 1970–86, Miles Davis Tribute Band 1992; solo artist 1962–, and with Wayne Shorter Quartet; Hon. DMus (Berklee Coll. of Music) 1999, (New York Univ.) 2010; winner of numerous Down Beat Magazine Awards, Best Soprano Sax 1984, 1985, Grammy Awards for Best Jazz Instrumental Performance (for A Tribute to Miles) 1994, for Best Jazz Instrumental Solo (for In Walked Wayne) 1999, for Best Instrumental Composition (for Sacajawea) 2003, for Best Improvised Jazz Solo (for Orbits) 2014, Jazz Journalists' Asscn Awards for Lifetime Achievement in Jazz 2013, for Musician of the Year 2014, for Soprano Saxophonist of the Year 2013, for Small Ensemble 2013, for Midsize Ensemble 2014, 2015, NEA Jazz Master Award 1998, Kennedy Center Honor for Lifetime Contribution to American culture through the performing arts 2018. *Recordings include:* albums: solo: Blues á la Carte 1959, Introducing Wayne Shorter 1959, Second Genesis 1960, Free Form 1961, Wayning Moments 1962, Search for a New Land 1964, Night Dreamer 1964, Some Other Stuff 1964, JuJu 1964, Speak No Evil 1964, The Soothsayer 1965, Et Cetera 1965, The Collector 1965, The All Seeing Eye 1965, Adam's Apple 1966, Schizophrenia 1967, Super Nova 1969, Moto Grosso Felo 1970, Odyssey of Iska 1970, Shorter Moments 1972, Wayne Shorter 1974, Native Dancer 1974, Atlantis 1985, Phantom Navigator 1986, Joy Ryder 1988, High Life (Grammy Award for Best Contemporary Jazz Album 1996) 1994, Portrait 2000, All or Nothing at All 2002, Footprints Live! 2002, Alegría (Grammy Award for Best Jazz Instrumental Album by an Individual or Group) 2003, Footprints 2005, Beyond the Sound Barrier (Grammy Award for Best Jazz Instrumental Album by an Individual or Group 2006) 2005, Without a Net (Jazz Journalists' Asscn Award for Record of the Year 2014) 2013, Emanon 2018; with Weather Report: Weather Report 1971, I Sing the Body Electric 1972, Sweetnighter 1973, Mysterious Traveler 1974, Tail Spinnin' 1975, Black Market 1976, Black Market/Heavy Weather 1978, Mr Gone 1978, 8.30 (Grammy Awards for Best Jazz Fusion Performance) 1979, Night Passage 1980, Procession 1983, Domino Theory 1984, Sportin' Life 1985, This is This! 1986. *E-mail:* info@imnworld.com (office). *Website:* www.imnworld.com (office); www.wayneshorter.com.

SHOSTAKOVICH, Maksim Dmitriyevich; American (b. Russian) conductor and pianist; b. 10 May 1938, Leningrad (now St Petersburg); s. of Dmitriy Shostakovich and Nina Varzar; m. 1st; one s.; m. 2nd Marina Tisie 1989; one s. one d.; ed Cen. Music School, Moscow Conservatory, studied conducting under Rabinovich, Gauk, Rozhdestvensky; Asst Conductor, Moscow Symphony Orchestra; Conductor, State Academic Symphony Orchestra; piano debut age 19 in father's Second Piano Concerto; Prin. Conductor and Artistic Dir USSR Radio and TV Symphony Orchestra; requested and granted political asylum in USA while on tour with USSR Radio and TV Symphony Orchestra, Nuremberg 1981; conducted Nat. Symphony Orchestra, on Capitol steps, Washington, DC, USA 1981; apptd Prin. Guest Conductor, Hong Kong Philharmonic 1982; Music Dir New Orleans Symphony Orchestra 1986–91; toured Western Europe with USSR Radio and TV Symphony Orchestra, Japan, USA 1971–81; has conducted all major N American orchestras and many in Europe, Asia, S America; conducted premiere of father's 15th Symphony and recorded virtually all father's symphonies in USSR; has performed with leading soloists, including Emil Gilels, Oistrakh, Rostropovich; Hon. Music Dir Louisiana Philharmonic Orchestra 1993–94. *Address:* Judie Janowski, Columbia Artists Management LLC, 5 Columbus Circle at 1790 Broadway, New York, NY 10019-1412, USA (office). *E-mail:* info@cami.com (office).

SHOTWELL, Gwynne, BS, MS; American business executive; *President and Chief Operating Officer, SpaceX (Space Explorations Technologies Corporation);* ed Northwestern Univ.; originally enrolled in Chrysler Corpn's man. training programme; began work at El Segundo, Calif. research centre of Aerospace Corpn 1988, did tech. work on mil. space research and devt contracts 1988–98; Dir Space Systems Div., Microcosm Inc. 1998–2002; joined SpaceX 2002, now Pres. and COO; World Technology Prize (Space) 2011, Women in Technology Int. Hall of Fame 2012. *Address:* Space Exploration Technologies Corporation (SpaceX), 1 Rocket Road, Hawthorne, CA 90250, USA (office). *Telephone:* (310) 363-6000 (office). *E-mail:* media@spacex.com (office). *Website:* www.spacex.com (office).

SHOUKRY, Sameh; Egyptian diplomatist and politician; *Minister of Foreign Affairs;* b. 20 Oct. 1952; m.; two s.; ed Ain Shams Univ.; joined diplomatic corps 1976, served in Embassies in London and Buenos Aires as well as at Perm. Mission to UN, New York, Head of Dept of the US and Canada, Ministry of Foreign Affairs 1994–95, Sec. for Information and Follow-up for Pres. Hosni Mubarak 1995–99, Amb. to Austria and Perm. Rep. to Int. Orgs, Vienna 1999–2003, Dir of Cabinet for Minister of Foreign Affairs 2004–05, Perm. Rep. to UN, Geneva 2005–08, Amb. to USA 2008–12 (retd); Minister of Foreign Affairs 2014–. *Address:* Ministry of Foreign Affairs, Corniche en-Nil, Cairo (Maspiro), Egypt (office). *Telephone:* (2) 25796334 (office); (2) 25749820 (office). *Fax:* (2) 25767967 (office). *E-mail:* contactus@mfa.gov.eg (office). *Website:* www.mfa.gov.eg (office).

SHOWALTER, Elaine, MA, PhD, FRSL; American academic, literary critic and writer; *Professor Emerita of English, Princeton University;* b. 14 Jan. 1941, Cambridge, Mass.; d. of Paul Cottler and Violet Cottler (née Rottenberg); m. English Showalter 1963; one s. one d.; ed Bryn Mawr Coll., Brandeis Univ.; Teaching Asst, Dept of English, Univ. of Calif. 1964–66, Assoc. Prof. 1967–78; Prof. of English, Rutgers Univ. 1978–84; Avalon Foundation Prof. of Humanities, Princeton Univ. 1984–2003, Prof. Emer. 2003–; columnist and writer, The Guardian newspaper, UK 2003–; R. Stanton Avery Distinguished Fellow, Huntington Library 2004–05; Visiting Prof. of English and Women's Studies, Univ. of Del. 1976–77; Visiting Prof., School of Criticism and Theory, Dartmouth Coll. 1986; Guggenheim Fellow 1977–78; Rockefeller Humanities Fellow 1981–83; Chair. Man Booker Int. Prize jury 2007 mem. Modern Language Asscn; Dr hc (Univ. of St Andrews) 2012; Howard Behrman Humanities Award, Princeton Univ. 1989. *Publications include:* A Literature of Their Own 1977, The Female Malady 1985, Sexual Anarchy 1990, Sister's Choice 1991, Hysteria Beyond Freud (jt author) 1993, Hystories 1997, Faculty Towers: The Academic Novel and Its Discontents 2005, A Jury of Her Peers (Truman Capote Award for Literary Criticism) 2009; also ed. of several feminist publs and writer of numerous articles and reviews.

SHOYAMA, Etsuhiko, BS; Japanese electronics industry executive; *CEO, Hitachi China Ltd;* b. 9 March 1936, Niigata Pref.; ed Tokyo Inst. of Tech.; began career as power plant engineer, Hitachi Works 1959–82, Deputy Gen. Man. Hitachi Works 1982–85, Gen. Man. Kokubu Works 1985–87, Gen. Man. Tochigi Works 1987–90, Gen. Man. Household Appliances Div. 1990–1991, elected to Bd of Dirs Hitachi Ltd 1991, Gen. Man. Consumer Electronics Div. 1991–93, Exec. Man. Dir 1993–95, Sr Exec. Man. Dir 1995–97, Exec. Vice-Pres. and Rep. Dir 1997–99, Pres. and Rep. Dir 1999–2003, Pres. and CEO 2003–06, Chair. and Dir 2006–07, Chair. and Advisor 2007–09, mem. Bd of Dirs and CEO Hitachi China Ltd 2006–, Chair. Hitachi Europe Ltd, Chair. Hitachi America Ltd 2006–07; Chair. Babcock-Hitachi K.K.; mem. Bd of Dirs Nippon Mining Holdings, Inc. (JX Nippon Oil & Energy Corpn since 2010); Outside Dir, JX Holdings, Inc. 2010–13; fmr Vice-Chair. Nippon Keidanren; Chair. Information and Communications Council, Ministry of Internal Affairs and Communications 2005–; fmr Chair. Exec. Bd Japan Electronics and Information Tech. Industries Asscn; mem. Council for Science and Tech., Policy Cabinet Office 2006–; Officier, Légion d'honneur 2007. *Address:* Hitachi China Ltd, 4/F, North Tower, World Finance Centre, Harbour City, Tsimshatsui, Kowloon, Hong Kong Special Administrative Region, People's Republic of China (office). *Telephone:* 2735-9218 (office). *Fax:* 2375-3192 (office). *E-mail:* service@cm.hbi.co.jp (office). *Website:* www.hitachi.com.cn (office).

SHPAK, Col-Gen. (retd) Georgy Ivanovich; Russian army officer and politician; b. 6 Sept. 1943, Osipovichi, Mogilev Region, Ukraine; m.; one s. (deceased) one d.; ed M. Frunze Mil. Acad., Mil. Acad. of Gen. Staff; commdr paratrooper regt, head of staff, deputy commdr paratrooper div., commdr of div. 1978–88; Deputy Commdr of Army Odessa Mil. Command 1988–89; Army Commdr, First Deputy Commdr Turkestan Mil. Command 1989–92; First Deputy Commdr Volga Mil. Command; Commdr Airborne Troops 1996–2003; elected mem. State Duma 2004;

Gov. Ryazan Oblast 2004–08 (retd); three orders, ten medals. *Leisure interests:* countryside, fishing.

SHPEK, Roman Vasilyevich; Ukrainian economist, diplomatist and banking executive; *Chairman, Independent Association of Banks of Ukraine (NABU);* b. 10 Nov. 1954, Broshniv, Ivano-Frankivsk Region; m. Maria Romanivna Shpek; one s. one d.; ed Forestry Eng Inst., Lviv, Int. Inst. of Wood Man., Kiev, Dalover Univ.; processing engineer and head of woodworking manufacturing plant, Ivano-Frankivsk Region 1976–78, Chief Engineer, wood and woodworking plant 1978–81, Dir 1981–89; Deputy Minister of Forestry, Woodworking and Furniture Industry, Ukrainian SSR 1989–92; Minister of Privatization, Ukraine April–Oct. 1992; First Deputy Minister of the Economy of Ukraine 1992–93, Minister 1993–95, Deputy Prime Minister on Econ. Policy 1995–96; Head Nat. Agency for Devt and European Integration 1996–2000; Co-Chair. Ukrainian-German Council on Econ. Co-operation, Ukrainian-Italian Council on Econ. Co-operation, Comm Kuchma-Gor on Econ. Devt Cttee; Acting Gov., then Gov. for Ukraine, World Bank Group; Chair. Currency and Finance Council to Cabinet of Ministers of Ukraine; Nat. Co-ordinator of Tech. Assistance Programme for Ukraine 1993–2000; Ukrainian Rep. to UNDP 1996; Amb. and Head of Mission of Ukraine to EU 2000–07; Vice-Pres. Alfa Bank (Ukraine) 2008–10, then Sr Advisor; Advisor to Pres. of Ukraine 2010–; mem. Supervisory Bd, National Bank of Ukraine; Chair. Independent Asscn of Banks of Ukraine (NABU) 2014–; Order for Merits, 3rd Degree (Ukraine). *Leisure:* oil painting, classical music, travelling, sport (football, boxing). *Address:* Independent Association of Banks of Ukraine (NABU), 72 Velyka Vasylkivska Street, Entrance 3, floor 3, office 6, Kyiv 03150, Ukraine (office). *E-mail:* info@ukrbanki.com.ua (office); roman.shpek@gmail.com. *Website:* nabu.ua/en (office).

SHRESTHA, Ambica, BA; Nepalese business executive; *Managing Director, Kathmandu Travels and Tours Limited;* b. 12 Feb. 1933, Kathmandu; two d.; ed in India; Man. Dir Kathmandu Travels and Tours Ltd, Nepal Trek and Natural History Expeditions; Dir Davs Enterprises Pvt. Ltd; Pres. Dwarika's Hotel; mem. Transparency Int. Nepal anti-corruption organisation (Pres. Exec. Cttee 1996–); Pres. Int. Fed. of Business and Professional Women; Hon. Consul of Spain; Order of the Gorkha Dakshina Bahu, Prakhyat Trisakti Patta, Birendra-Aishwarya Sewa Padak, Cross of Order of Civil Merit (Spain), Cross, Orden de Isabel La Catolica (Spain); Pata Heritage Award, Business and Professional Women's Club 1980, Rotary Int. Service Above Self Award 2012–13, Golden Mike Award, Radio and TV Asscn of Spain, Badge of Honour, BPW Int., Public Admin Asscn of Nepal Bahadur Malla Award. *Address:* Kathmandu Travels and Tours Ltd, PO Box 459, Battisputali, Kathmandu, Nepal (office). *Telephone:* (1) 471577 (office). *Fax:* (1) 471379 (office). *E-mail:* info@dwarikas.com (office); ktt@mail.com.np (office). *Website:* dwarikas.com (office).

SHRESTHA, Gopal Man; Nepalese politician; *Deputy Prime Minister, Minister of Education and Minister of Law, Justice and Parliamentary Affairs;* b. Putalibazar, Syanja Dist; elected twice to the House of Reps (Pratinidhi Sabha— Lower House of Parl.); served as acting Pres. of Nepali Congress Party— Democratic (now Nepali Congress Party—NCP), sr mem. in the Central Cttee; Deputy Prime Minister, Minister of Education and Minister of Law, Justice and Parliamentary Affairs 2017–. *Address:* Ministry of Education, Singha Durbar, Kathmandu, Nepal (office). *Telephone:* (1) 4200340 (office). *Fax:* (1) 4200375 (office). *E-mail:* info@moe.gov.np (office). *Website:* www.moe.gov.np (office).

SHRESTHA, Indra Bahadur; Nepalese business executive; fmr Pres. CCI Makawanpur; Chair. Hetauda Cement Industries Ltd –2014; fmr Pres. Lalitpur Chamber of Commerce and Industry; mem. Nat. Exec. Cttee, Amnesty Int. Nepal 2004. *Address:* c/o Hetauda Cement Industries Ltd, POB 24, Hetauda, Makawanpur, Nepal.

SHRESTHA, Kalyan, DL, MA; Nepalese judge (retd); b. 14 April 1951, Baglung; m. Urmila Shrestha; one s. one d.; ed , Inst. of Social Sciences, Netherlands; Section Officer, Supreme Court of Nepal 1972–74; Dist Judge (various dists) 1979–83; UnderSec., Ministry of Law and Justice 1983–85; Judge, Zonal Courts 1985–90; Judge, Appellate Courts 1990–2005; Chief Judge, Appellate Court Jumla 2005; Justice, Supreme Court of Nepal 2005–16, Chief Justice 2015–16; Exec. Dir Nat. Judicial Acad. 2004; Chair. Constituent Ass. Court; Pres. South Asian Asscn for Regional Co-operation in Law, Judges Soc. Nepal; mem. Judicial Council, Judicial Service Comm.; Prasiddha Prabal Janasewashree-Second Class 2014; Lok Raj Gyawanli Gold Medal, Tribhuvan Univ., Mahendra Vidya Bhusan, Tribhuvan Univ., Subikhyat Trishakti Patta, Suprabal Gorkha Dakshin Bahu. *Publications:* Constitution of Nepal and its Analysis (co-author) 1996, Constitutional Law of Nepal (co-author) 1997.

SHRESTHA, Narayan Kaji; Nepalese politician; b. Jaubari village, Gorkha; s. of Megh Narayan Shrestha and Jyoti Maya Shrestha; Lecturer in math., Siddhartha Vanasthali Inst. in 1980s; imprisoned as political leader in 1980, 1986; mem. Constituent Ass. (Janamorcha Nepal) 2008–; Deputy Prime Minister and Minister of Home Affairs 1 Aug.–29 Aug. 2011; Deputy Prime Minister and Minister of Foreign Affairs 2011–13; currently Sr Leader, Unified Maoists Party. *Address:* c/o Ministry of Foreign Affairs, Narayanhiti, Kathmandu, Nepal.

SHRESTHA, Rt Hon Ram Prasad, LLB, MA; Nepalese judge; b. 5 May 1956, Palpa; ed Tribhuvan Univ.; joined judicial service, Asar 1971; Judge, Dist Courts of Sangjya, Parsa, Kaski 1975–84; Judge, Zonal Courts of Mahakali, Koshi and Veri 1984–91; Judge, Appellate Courts of Patan, Nepalgunj 1991–96; Chief Judge, Appellate Courts of Nepalgunj, Pokhara 1996–2003; Justice Supreme Court 2003–10, Chief Justice 2010–11 (retd).

SHRESTHA, Raman Kumar, BL, BEd; Nepalese lawyer and government official; *Attorney-General;* b. 28 May 1960, Baglung; s. of Raj Kumar Shrestha and Buddhi Kumari; ed Tribhuwan Univ.; mem. Supreme Court Bar Asscn 1991–92; mem. Central Cttee, Nepal Bar Asscn 1993–96, Gen. Sec. 2007–10, mem. Central Advisory Cttee 2010–; Attorney-Gen. 2016–. *Address:* Office of the Attorney-General, Ramshah Path, Kathmandu, Nepal (office). *Telephone:* (1) 4240210 (office). *Fax:* (1) 4262582 (office). *E-mail:* info@attorneygeneral.gov.np (office). *Website:* www.attorneygeneral.gov.np (office).

SHREVE, Susan Richards, MA; American writer and academic; *Professor of Creative Writing, George Mason University;* b. 2 May 1939, Toledo, Ohio; d. of Robert Richards and Helen Richards; m. 1st Porter Shreve (divorced 1987); m. 2nd Timothy Seldes 1987; two s. two d.; ed Univs of Pennsylvania and Virginia; Prof. of Creative Writing, George Mason Univ., Fairfax, Va 1976–; Visiting Prof., Columbia Univ., New York 1982–; Princeton Univ. 1991, 1992, 1993; fmr Pres. PEN/Faulkner Foundation, currently Co-Chair.; producer, The American Voice for TV 1986–; Essayist, MacNeil/Lehrer Newshour; George Washington Univ. Jenny Moore Award 1978, Guggenheim Fellowship 1980, Nat. Endowment for the Arts Fellowship 1982. *Publications include:* A Fortunate Madness 1974, A Woman Like That 1977, Children of Power 1979, Miracle Play 1981, Dreaming of Heroes 1984, Queen of Hearts 1986, A Country of Strangers 1989, Daughters of the New World 1992, The Train Home 1993, Skin Deep: Women and Race 1995, The Visiting Physician 1995, The Goalie 1996, Narratives on Justice (co-ed.) 1996, Outside the Law 1997, How We Want to Live (co-ed.) 1998, Plum and Jaggers 2000, A Student of Living Things 2006, Warm Springs: Traces of a Childhood at FDR's Polio Haven 2007, Kiss Me Tomorrow 2007, Trout and Me 2009, Under the Watsons' Porch 2009, The Lovely Shoes 2011, You Are the Love of My Life 2012; juvenile: The Flunking of Joshua T. Bates 1993, Jonah, The Whale 1997, Ghost Cats 1999, The End of Amanda, The Good 2000. *Address:* Graduate Creative Writing Program, Department of English, George Mason University, 4400 University Drive, Fairfax, VA 22030 (office); 3319 Newark Street, NW, Washington, DC 20008, USA (home). *Telephone:* (703) 993-1180 (office). *Fax:* (703) 993-1161 (office). *E-mail:* writing@gmu.edu (office); srshreve@aol.com. *Website:* creativewriting.gmu.edu (office); www.susanshreve.com.

SHRIVER, Maria Owings, BA; American broadcaster and journalist; b. 6 Nov. 1955, Chicago, Ill.; d. of Robert Sargent Shriver and Eunice Mary Shriver (née Kennedy); m. Arnold Schwarzenegger 1986 (divorced 2014); two s. two d.; ed Stone Ridge School of the Sacred Heart, Bethesda, Md, Georgetown Univ.; began career as writer and producer on TV news at KYW-TV, Philadelphia 1977; journalist on Evening Magazine, WJZ-TV, Baltimore 1978–80; Nat. Corresp. on PM Magazine 1981–83; W Coast Reporter for CBS Morning News, then Co-Presenter, New York 1985–86; joined NBC News 1986, Co-Presenter Sunday Today 1987–90, Main Street 1987, Yesterday, Today and Tomorrow 1989, Presenter NBC Nightly News Weekend Edition 1989–90, Cutting Edge with Maria Shriver 1990, First Person with Maria Shriver 1991–2003; writer and presenter of many news programmes, documentaries and TV specials including The Baby Business, Men, Women, Sex and AIDS, Wall Street: Money, Greed and Power, and Fatal Addictions (Christopher Award 1990); exclusive interviews with King Hussein of Jordan, Fidel Castro, US Vice-Pres. J. Danforth Quayle and Pres. Corazón Aquino of the Philippines (Exceptional Merit Media Award, Nat. Women's Political Caucus); First Lady of Calif. 2003–11. *Publications include:* Ten Things I Wish I'd Known Before I Went Out into the Real World 2000, What's Wrong With Timmy? 2001, What's Happening to Grandpa? (juvenile) 2004, And One More Thing Before You Go… 2005, What's Heaven? 2007, Just Who Will You Be?: Big Question, Little Book, Answer Within 2008. *E-mail:* info@mariashriver.com. *Website:* www.mariashriver.com.

SHTAUBER, Zvi Meir, PhD; Israeli diplomatist, academic and fmr military officer; *Chairman, Israel Intelligence Heritage and Commemoration Center (IICC);* b. 15 July 1947; s. of Yisrael Shtauber and Jaffa Shtauber; m. Nitza Rousso; two s. one d.; ed Harvard Business School, Fletcher School of Law and Diplomacy, Tufts Univ., USA; with Israel Defence Forces 1970–95, Head of Strategic Planning Div. 1995, retd with rank of Brig.-Gen. 1995; Vice-Pres. Ben-Gurion Univ. of the Negev 1996–99; Foreign Policy Adviser to Prime Minister Ehud Barak 1999–2000; Amb. to UK 2001–04; apptd Head, Jaffee Center for Strategic Studies, Tel-Aviv Univ. 2005, Dir Inst. for Nat. Security Studies (incorporated Jaffee Center) –2008; Chair. Israel Intelligence Heritage and Commemoration Center (IICC) 2012–. *Address:* Israel Intelligence Heritage and Commemoration Center (IICC), PO Box 3555, Ramat Hasharon 47134, Israel (office). *E-mail:* Contact@intelligence.org.il (office). *Website:* www.iicc.org.il (office).

SHTAYYEH, Mohammed, BA, MA, PhD; Palestinian economist and politician; *Prime Minister and Minister of the Interior;* b. 17 Jan. 1958, Nablus; ed Birzeit Univ., Univ. of Sussex; Prof. of Econ. Devt, Birzeit Univ. 1989–91, Dean of Student Affairs 1991–93; Founder and mem. Bd of Dirs Palestinian Housing Council 1991–2000; Sec.-Gen. Palestinian Nat. Authority Central Elections Comm. 1995–98; Gov. for Palestine, Islamic Devt Bank 2005–; Minister of Public Works and Housing 2005–06, 2008–10; Minister, Palestinian Econ. Council for Devt and Reconstruction (PECDAR) 2009–; mem. Palestinian Cen. Council 2014; Prime Minister and Minister of the Interior 2019–; mem. World Innovation Foundation; Chair. Bd of Trustees American Arab Univ.; mem. Cen. Cttee Fatah; Chevalier, Ordre Nat. du Mérite (France) 1999; Samaritan Medal 2009. *Publications:* several books on economics, politics and history. *Address:* Office of the Prime Minister, Ramallah, Palestinian Territories (office).

SHU, Frank H., BS, PhD; American (b. Chinese) astrophysicist, astronomer and academic; *Professor Emeritus of Astronomy, University of California, San Diego;* b. (Shu Hsia-San), 2 June 1943, China; s. of Shien-Siu Shu; ed Massachusetts Inst. of Tech., Harvard Univ.; has held faculty appointments at State Univ. of NY, Stony Brook and Univ. of California, Berkeley; Emer., Chair. Astronomy Dept, Univ. of California, Berkeley 1984–88; Pres. Nat. Tsing Hua Univ. 2002–06; apptd Distinguished Prof. of Physics, Univ. of California, San Diego 2006, now Prof. Emer. and Distinguished Prof.; Pres. American Astronomical Soc. 1994–96; mem. NAS 1987, Academia Sinica 1990, American Acad. of Arts and Sciences 1992, American Philosophical Soc. 2003, TWAS, Acad. of Sciences for Developing World 2006; Foreign Assoc., Royal Astronomical Soc. 2005; Hon. DrSc (Stony Brook Univ.) 2017; Warner Prize, American Astronomical Soc. 1977, Oort Prof., Leiden Univ. 1996, Brouwer Award, Div. of Dynamical Astronomy 1997, Bruno Rossi Lecturer, Arcetri Observatory, Italy 1999, Heineman Prize, American Inst. of Physics and American Astronomical Soc. 2000, Faculty Research Lecturer, Univ. of California, Berkeley 2001, Outstanding Scholar Award, Taiwan 2002–06, Ta-You Wu Lecturer, Univ. of Michigan 2007, Caroline Herschel Lecturer, Space Telescope Science Inst. 2007, Centennial Medal, Harvard Univ. 2008, Shaw Prize in Astronomy (co-recipient) 2009, Catherine Wolfe Bruce Gold Medal, Astronomical Soc. of the Pacific 2009, main-belt asteroid 18238 Frankshu named in his honour. *Publications:* numerous papers in professional journals on the origin of meteorites, the birth and early evolution of stars and the structure of spiral galaxies. *Address:* Department of Physics, University of California, San Diego, SERF 427, 9500 Gilman Drive, La Jolla, CA 92093, USA (office). *Telephone:* (858) 822-1214 (office). *E-mail:* fhshu@ucsd.edu (office). *Website:* www-physics.ucsd.edu (office).

SHU, Qi; Taiwanese actress and fmr model; b. (Lin Li-Hui), 16 April 1976, Xindian, Taipei Co. (now New Taipei City); moved to Hong Kong aged 17; appeared on cover of Penthouse Hong Kong and Chinese edn of Playboy magazine; came under management of Hong Kong producer Manfred Wong; selected by Kenzo for advertising campaign for fragrance Flower by Kenzo 2006–09; also worked as a spokesperson for Shiatzy Chen; represents Frederique Constant in Asia as brand amb. 2008–; jury mem. Berlinale (Berlin Int. Film Festival) 2008, Cannes Film Festival 2009. *Films include:* Sex & Zen II 1996, Viva Erotica (Best New Performer and Best Supporting Actress, Hong Kong Film Awards, Best Supporting Actress, Golden Bauhinia Awards 1996) 1996, Growing Up 1996, Street Angels 1996, Till Death Do Us Laugh 1996, A Queer Story 1996, The Fruit is Swelling (cameo) 1997, Love: Amoeba Style 1997, Those Were the Days 1997, Love Is Not a Game, But a Joke 1997, My Dad Is a Jerk 1997, L-O-V-E... Love 1997, The Lucky Guy 1998, Young and Dangerous 5 1998, The Storm Riders 1998, Love Generation Hong Kong 1998, Bishonen 1998, City of Glass 1998, Young & Dangerous: The Prequel 1998, Portland Street Blues (Best Supporting Actress, Hong Kong Film Awards 1998) 1998, Another Meltdown 1998, Extreme Crisis 1998, Your Place or Mine (Best Supporting Actress, Golden Horse Awards 1998) 1998, Gorgeous 1999, True Woman 1999, A Man Called Hero 1999, Iron Sister 1999, The Island Tales 1999, When I Look Upon the Stars 1999, Metade Fumaca 1999, My Loving Trouble 7 1999, Unexpected Challenges 2000, Hidden Whisper 2000, Born to Be King 2000, Flyin' Dance 2000, Skyline Cruisers 2000, Dragon Heat 2000, My Name is Nobody 2000, For Bad Boys Only 2000, Martial Angels 2001, Millennium Mambo 2001, Visible Secret 2001, Love Me, Love My Money 2001, Beijing Rocks 2001, The Wesley's Mysterious File 2002, Women From Mars 2002, So Close 2002, Just One Look (cameo) 2002, The Transporter 2002, Haunted Office 2002, Looking for Mr. Perfect 2003, The Foliage 2003, The Eye 2 2004, Seoul Raiders 2005, Three Times (Best Actress, Golden Horse Awards 2005) 2005, Home Sweet Home 2005, Hong Fu Nu 2006, Confession of Pain 2006, My Wife is a Gangster 3 2006, Forest of Death 2007, Blood Brothers 2007, If You Are the One 2008, Look for a Star 2009, New York, I Love You 2009, City Under Siege 2010, Legend of the Fist: The Return of Chen Zhen 2010, If You Are the One 2 2010, A Beautiful Life 2011, Chinese Zodiac 2012, Journey to the West 2013, The Assassin 2015. *Other:* Hong Kong (audio walking tour by Louis Vuitton and Soundwalk) 2008.

SHU, Shengyou; Chinese politician; b. Dec. 1936, Yushan Co., Jiangxi Prov.; joined CCP 1959; Mayor of Jingdezhen City; Vice-Gov. Jiangxi Prov. 1991, Gov. 1996–2001; Vice-Sec. CCP Jiangxi Prov. Cttee 1995–2001; mem. 15th CCP Cen. Cttee 1997–2002; mem. Standing Cttee 9th CPPCC Nat. Cttee 1998–2003.

SHU, Yinbiao, BSc, MSc, PhD; Chinese business executive; *Chairman, State Grid Corporation of China;* b. May 1958, Zhuozhou City, Hebei Prov.; ed North China Electric Power Univ., Wuhan Univ., Hubei Prov.; Deputy Dir, Finance Div., Nat. Electric Power Dispatching and Communication Centre, State Electric Power Corpn 1989–91, Dir 1991–94, Gen. Engineer, Nat. Electric Power Dispatching and Communication Centre 1994–2001, Deputy Dir 1998–2001; Deputy Dir, Eng Construction Dept, State Grid Corpn of China 2001–02, Dir 2002–04, Asst Gen. Man., State Grid Corpn of China 2004–05, Deputy Gen. Man. 2005–13, mem. Leading Party Group, State Grid Corpn of China CCP 2005–, mem. Bd of Dirs, State Grid Corpn of China 2013–, Gen. Man. State Grid Corpn of China 2013–16, Chair. 2016–. *Address:* State Grid Corporation of China, 86 West Chang'an Street, Xicheng District, Beijing 100031, People's Republic of China (office). *Telephone:* (10) 66598583 (office). *Fax:* (10) 66598794 (office). *E-mail:* sgcc-info@sgcc.com.cn (office). *Website:* www.sgcc.com.cn (office).

SHUE, Elisabeth; American actress; b. 6 Oct. 1963, Wilmington, Del.; d. of James Shue and Anne Wells; m. Davis Guggenheim 1994; one s. two d.; ed Wellesley Coll., Harvard Univ.; studied with Sylvie Leigh, Showcase Theater; appeared in Broadway plays including Some Americans Abroad, Birth and After Birth. *Films include:* The Karate Kid 1984, Link 1986, Adventures in Babysitting 1987, Cocktail 1988, Body Wars 1989, Back to the Future Part II 1989, Part III 1990, Soapdish 1991, The Marrying Man 1991, Twenty Bucks 1993, Heart and Souls 1993, Radio Inside 1994, Blind Justice 1994, The Underneath 1995, Leaving Las Vegas (Chicago Film Critics Asscn Award for Best Actress, Dallas-Fort Worth Film Critics Asscn Award for Best Actress, Independent Spirit Award for Best Lead Female, Los Angeles Film Critics Asscn Award for Best Actress, Nat. Soc. of Film Critics Award for Best Actress) 1995, The Trigger Effect 1996, The Saint 1996, Palmetto 1997, Deconstructing Harry 1997, Cousin Bette 1997, Molly 1998, Hollow Man 2000, Amy and Isabelle 2001, Leo 2004, Mysterious Skin 2004, Hide and Seek 2005, Gracie 2007, Don McKay 2009, Waking Madison 2010, House at the End of the Street 2012, Chasing Mavericks 2012, Behaving Badly 2014, Battle of the Sexes 2017, Death Wish 2018. *Television includes:* The Royal Romance of Charles and Diana 1982, Call to Glory (series) 1984–85, Double Switch 1987, Hale the Hero 1992, Blind Justice 1994, Dreamer 2005, CSI: Crime Scene Investigation (series) 2012–15, The Boys (series) 2019. *Address:* c/o Creative Arts Agency, 9830 Wilshire Boulevard, Beverly Hills, CA 90212, USA.

SHUGAIRI, Ahmad al-, MBA; Saudi Arabian TV presenter; b. 17 July 1973, Jeddah; m. 1st 1995 (divorced); m. 2nd Rola Dashisha; two s.; ed California State Univ., Northridge, USA; began studying with cleric Adnan al-Zahrani; TV debut 2002, presenter, TV program Khawatir 2005–15, currently presenter, Qomrah; opened Andalucia Café, Jeddah; Mohammed Bin Rashid Al Maktoum Knowledge Award 2015. *Publications include:* Khawater, My Trip with Ghandi. *Address:* c/o Middle East Broadcasting Center (MBC), POB 76267, Dubai, United Arab Emirates (office).

SHULEVA, Lidiya Santova, BE, MA; Bulgarian economist, business executive and fmr politician; *Managing Partner, Business Intellect Ltd;* b. 23 Dec. 1956, Velingrad; m. (widowed); two c.; ed Tech. Univ., Sofia, Univ. of Nat. and World Economy, Man. Acad., Germany; worked in man. and finance, Japan; fmr man. consultant, EEC, Greece; Founder and Man. Business Intellect Ltd 1992–96, now Man. Partner; Exec. Man. Albena Invest Holding AD 1995–2001; Chair. Asscn of Industrial Capital 2000; Minister of Labour and Social Policy 2001; Deputy Prime Minister and Minister of the Economy 2001–05; mem. Governing Bd Assistance to Charity Foundation 2000; elected mem. Nat. Ass. 2005, Observer in European Parl. 2005–06, mem. European Parl. Jan.–May 2007; adviser for Ukrainian govt and consultant on investment projects 2011–12; mem. Council of Women in Business. *Address:* Business Intellect Ltd, 9A Pozitano Street, Floor 4, Office 12, 1000 Sofia, Bulgaria (office). *Telephone:* (2) 444-66-51 (office). *E-mail:* office@business-intellect.com (office). *Website:* www.business-intellect.com (office).

SHULKIN, David Jonathon, BA, MD, FACP; American physician, health administrator and government official; b. 22 June 1959, Bala Cynwyd, Pa; m. Merle Bari; ed Medical Coll. of Pennsylvania, Yale Univ. School of Medicine, Univ. of Pittsburgh School of Medicine; Clinical Scholar, Robert Wood Johnson Foundation, Univ. of Pennsylvania 1990–91, Chief Medical Officer, Hosp. of the Univ. of Pennsylvania 1990–99, Chief Medical Officer, Univ. of Pennsylvania Health System 1991–99, Chief Medical Officer, Medical Coll. of Pennsylvania 2002–04; CEO doctorquality 1999–2003; Vice-Dean, Chair of Medicine and Chief Quality Officer, Drexel Univ. School of Medicine 2003–04; Chief Medical Officer, Temple Univ. Hosp. 2004–05; Pres. and CEO Beth Israel Medical Center 2005–09; Pres. Morristown Medical Center 2010–15; Under-Sec. of Health, US Dept of Veterans Affairs 2015–17, Sec. of Veterans Affairs 2017–18; Sr Fellow, Leonard Davis Inst. in Health Econs, Univ. of Pennsylvania; Nat. Health Policy Fellow, US Senate Cttee on Aging. *Publications:* Questions Patients Need to Ask 2008; 25 peer-reviewed journal articles and numerous professional publications. *Address:* c/o Department of Veterans Affairs, 810 Vermont Avenue, NW, Washington, DC 20420, USA (office).

SHULMAN, Alexandra, CBE, OBE, BA; British journalist and editor; b. 13 Nov. 1957, London; d. of Milton Shulman and Drusilla Beyfus; m. Paul Spike 1994; one s.; ed St Paul's Girls' School and Univ. of Sussex; Sec., Over-21 magazine; joined Condé Nast 1982, Writer and Commissioning Ed., later Features Ed. Tatler 1982–87; Ed. Women's Page, Sunday Telegraph 1987, later Deputy Ed. 7 Days current affairs photo/reportage; Features Ed. Vogue 1988; Ed. GQ 1990; Ed.-in-Chief British Vogue 1992–2017; Trustee, Nat. Portrait Gallery, London 1999–2008, Arts Foundation 2001–10, Royal Marsden Hospital cancer campaign 2009–; Hon. MA (Univ. for the Creative Arts) 2010; Editors' Editor of the Year, British Society of Magazine Editors 2004, 2017. *Publication:* Can We Still Be Friends 2012. *Address:* c/o Condé Nast Publications, Vogue House, Hanover Square, London, W1S 1JU, England.

SHULMAN, Robert Gerson, MA, PhD; American biophysicist; *Sterling Professor Emeritus of Molecular Biophysics and Biochemistry, Yale University;* b. 3 March 1924, New York; s. of Joshua S. Shulman and Freda Shulman (née Lipshay); m. 1st Saralee Deutsch 1952 (died 1983); three s.; m. 2nd Stephanie S. Spangler 1986; ed Columbia Univ.; Research Assoc., Columbia Univ. Radiation Lab., New York 1949; AEC Fellow in Chem., Calif. Inst. of Tech. 1949–50; Head, Semiconductor Research Section, Hughes Aircraft Co. Culver City, Calif. 1950–53; mem. tech. staff, Bell Labs, Murray Hill, NJ 1953–66, Head, Biophysics Research Dept 1966–79; Prof. of Molecular Biophysics and Biochemistry, Yale Univ. 1979–94, Dir Div. of Biological Sciences 1979–94, apptd Sterling Prof. of Biophysics and Biochemistry 1994, currently Sterling Prof. Emer. and Sr Research Scientist, Diagnostic Radiology, fmr Emissary for Clinical Research; mem. NAS, Inst. of Medicine; Guggenheim Fellow, Cambridge 1961–62. *Address:* Department of Molecular Biophysics and Biochemistry, Yale University, 300 Cedar Street, PO Box 208024, New Haven, CT 06520-8024, USA (office); (203) 432-1333 (home). *Telephone:* (203) 785-6201 (office). *Fax:* (203) 785-7979 (office). *E-mail:* robert.shulman@yale.edu (office). *Website:* www.mbb.yale.edu (office).

SHULTZ, George Pratt, BA, PhD; American economist, academic and fmr government official; *Thomas W. and Susan B. Ford Distinguished Fellow, Hoover Institution, Stanford University;* b. 13 Dec. 1920, New York, NY; s. of Birl E. Shultz and Margaret Lennox Pratt Shultz; m. 1st Helena M. O'Brien 1946; two s. three d.; m. 2nd Charlotte Mailliard Swig 1997; ed Princeton Univ. and Massachusetts Inst. of Tech.; Assoc. Prof. of Industrial Relations, MIT 1955–57; Sr Staff Economist, Pres.'s Council of Econ. Advisors 1955–56; Prof. of Industrial Relations, Grad. School of Business, Univ. of Chicago 1957–68, Dean, Grad. School of Business 1962–68; Pres. Industrial Research Asscn 1968; US Sec. of Labor 1969–70; Dir Office of Man. and Budget, Exec. Office of the Pres. 1970–72; US Sec. of Treasury, Washington, DC 1972–74; Chair. Council on Econ. Policy 1973–74; Sec. of State 1982–89; Exec. Vice-Pres. Bechtel Corpn 1974–75, Pres. 1975–77, Vice-Chair. 1977–81, Pres. Bechtel Group Inc. 1981–82; Prof. of Man. and Public Policy, Grad. School of Business, Stanford Univ. 1974–82, of Int. Economy 1989–91, Prof. Emer. 1991–; Chair. JP Morgan Chase Int. Council, Accenture Energy Advisory Bd 2003–07, Advisory Council Inst. of Int. Studies, Stanford, Govs' Econ. Policy Advisory Bd, Calif., Gov.'s Council of Econ. Advisors 2004–11; mem. Bd Bechtel Group Inc. 1989–2007; Chair. Pres. Reagan's Econ. Policy Advisory Bd 1981–82; Chair. Advisory Bd Precourt Inst. for Energy Efficiency; Chair. External Advisory Bd MIT Energy Initiative; mem. Bd of Trustees, Center for Advanced Study in the Behavioral Sciences, Stanford, Calif.; Distinguished Fellow, Hoover Inst., Stanford Univ. 1989–, Thomas W. and Susan B. Ford Distinguished Fellow, Hoover Inst. 2001–, Distinguished Fellow, American Econ. Asscn 2005; Grand Cordon, Order of the Rising Sun 1989; Jefferson Award 1989, Presidential Medal of Freedom 1989, Seoul Peace Prize 1992, Eisenhower Medal 2001, Reagan Distinguished American Award 2002, Ralph J. Bunche Award for Diplomatic Excellence 2002, Nat. World War II Museum American Spirit Award 2006, George Marshall Award 2007, Truman Medal for Econ. Policy 2007, American Acad. of Arts and Sciences Rumford Prize 2008, Commdt's Leadership Award, Marine Corps-Law Enforcement Foundation 2009, Congressional Medal of Honor Soc.'s Distinguished Citizen Award 2011, Nat. Endowment for Democracy Service Medal 2012, Dwight D. Eisenhower Award, American Nuclear Soc. 2015. *Publications include:* Pressures on Wage Decisions, Labor Problems, The Dynamics of a Labor Market, Management Organization and the Computer, Strategies for the Displaced Worker, Guidelines, Informal Controls and the Market Place, Workers and Wages in the Urban Labor Market, Leaders and Followers in an Age of Ambiguity, Economic Policy beyond the Headlines, Turmoil and Triumph: My Years as Secretary of State 1993, Putting Our House in Order: A Guide to Social Security and Health Care Reform (with John Shoven) 2008, Ideas & Action, Featuring 10 Commandments of Negotiations 2010, Issues on My Mind: Strategies for the Future 2013,

Game Changers: Energy on the Move (co-ed with Robert C. Armstrong) 2014. *Leisure interest:* golf. *Address:* Hoover Institution, Stanford, CA 94305-6010, USA (office). *Telephone:* (650) 725-3492 (office). *Fax:* (650) 723-5441 (office). *Website:* www-hoover.stanford.edu (office).

SHUMEIKO, Vladimir Filippovich, DEcon; Russian economist and politician; b. 10 Feb. 1945, Rostov Don; m.; two d.; ed Krasnodar Polytech. Inst.; worked in factories as foreman, engineer, chief engineer, Dir-Gen. Concern Krasnodar Factory of Measuring Instruments −1991; People's Deputy of Russia 1990–92; Vice-Chair. Supreme Soviet of Russia 1991–92, First Deputy Prime Minister of Russia 1992–93; Pres. Confed. of Entrepreneurs' Unions of Russia 1992–93; mem. Council of Fed. (Upper House of Parl.) 1993–96, Chair. 1994–96; Founder and Chair. Reforms-New Course Movt 1996; Lecturer, Acad. of Border Service; apptd Chair. Interregional Auction and Stock Corpn 1998, Moskva Bank 2002. *Publication:* Russian Reforms and Federalism 1995, Pelmeny po Protocoly 2001. *Leisure interests:* fishing, woodworking, collecting small bells.

SHUMLIN, Peter Elliott; American business executive and politician; b. 24 March 1956, Brattleboro, Vt; s. of George J. Shumlin and Kitty Shumlin (née Weber); m. 1st Deborah Holway 1989 (divorced 2013); two d.; m. 2nd Kate Hunt 2015; ed Buxton School, Wesleyan Univ.; mem. Windham Co. Democratic Cttee 1980—90; mem. Comm., Windham Regional Community 1983–85; Chair. Putney Bd Selectmen 1983–89; helped found Landmark Coll., Putney, Vt; apptd to fill vacancy in Vt House of Reps from Putney Dist 1990–92; mem. Vt Senate for Windham Dist 1992–2002, 2007–11, Senate Minority Leader 1992–94, Pres. Pro Tempore 1994–2002, 2006–11; unsuccessful cand. for Lt Gov. 2002; returned to family business, Putney Student Travel 2003–06; Gov. of Vermont 2011–17; Chair. Nat. Democratic Govs Asscn 2013; mem. River Valley Arts Center, River Valley Playhouse (Founder); Democrat. *Address:* c/o Office of the Governor, Pavilion Office Building, 109 State Street, Montpelier, VT 05609, USA (office).

SHUNEVICH, Col Ihar Anatolievich; Belarusian police officer and government official; *Minister of Internal Affairs;* b. 27 March 1967, Luhansk Oblast, Ukrainian SSR, USSR; ed Acad. of Ministry of Internal Affairs; has held several different positions in law enforcement services of Belarus; began career as an ordinary investigator, rose to position of Deputy Chief of Dept of Internal Affairs, Minsk Oblast Exec. Cttee; worked in State Security Committee 2007–12, headed Investigative Dept, later headed Bureau of Counterintelligence Security of Law Enforcement and Supervisory Authorities, Anti-Corruption Drive and Combating Organized Crime; First Deputy Minister of Internal Affairs − Chief of Criminal Police Office Jan.–May 2012, Minister of Internal Affairs May 2012–. *Address:* Ministry of Internal Affairs, 220030 Minsk, vul. Gorodskoy Val 4, Belarus (office). *Telephone:* (17) 218-79-89 (office); (17) 218-78-08 (office). *Fax:* (17) 218-70-35 (office). *E-mail:* uiosmvd@yandex.ru (office); miapress@mia.by (office). *Website:* www.mvd.gov.by (office).

SHUSHKEVICH, Stanislaw, DSc; Belarusian physicist, politician and fmr university rector; *Chairman, Belorusian Social Democratic Party (Hramada);* b. 15 Dec. 1934, Minsk, Byelorussian SSR, USSR; s. of Stanislaw Shushkevich and Helena Romaouskaya; m. Irina Kuzminichna Shushkevich; one s. one d.; ed Belarus State Univ.; CPSU 1967–91; researcher, Inst. of Physics, Belarus Acad. of Sciences 1959–60; engineer Minsk Radio Plant 1960–61; Chief Engineer, Head of Section Belarus Univ. 1961–67; Prof. and Pro-Rector Minsk Radiotechnical Inst. 1966–69; Head of Chair., Belarus Univ. 1969–86, Pro-Rector 1986–90; began involvement in politics 1989 as critic of Govt negligence in aftermath of Chernobyl accident; mem. Supreme Soviet 1990–91; Chair. Supreme Soviet 1991–94, mem. −1996; Dir Centre of Political and Econ. Studies, European Humanitarian Inst. 1994–; mem. Civil Action faction; cand. in presidential elections 1994; Chair. Belarusian Social Democratic Party (Hramada) 1997–; Corresp. mem. Belarus Acad. of Sciences 1991–; Highest Order of Lithuanian Repub. for contrib. to democratic transformation of Lithuania 1989–94, Order of Korea of ISCP for contrib. to peace 2019, Order of Lithuania for promoting the democratization of Lithuania and Vilnius 2019; hon. doctorates from four univs; State Prize of Byelorussian SSR 1986, Govt of USSR Prize 1988, Ukrainian Int. Pylyp Orlyk Award, Jan Nowak-Jezioranski Award, Medal of Truman-Reagan Freedom Award 2012. *Publications include:* Belarus − Self-Identification and Statehood, Belorussian Newcommunism, My Life, Collapse and Revival USSR, My Life, Collapse and Revival USSR, 25 Years After; more than 100 articles and papers on problems of nuclear electronics and political problems. *Leisure interest:* building with his own hands. *Address:* c/o Belaruskaya Satsyal-demakratychnaya Partya (Hramada), 220013 Minsk, vul. Kulman 4 (home); Masherova avenue 78-14, 220035 Minsk, Belarus (home). *Telephone:* (17) 319-70-71 (home); (29) 339-66-86 (office). *E-mail:* stastashu@mail.ru (home).

SHUVALOV, Igor Ivanovich; Russian politician and lawyer; *Chairman, Vnesheconombank;* b. 4 Jan. 1967, Bilibino, Chukot Nat. (now Autonomous) Okrug (then part of Magadan Oblast), Russian SFSR, USSR; m. Olga Viktorovna Shuvalova; two s. two d.; ed Moscow State Univ.; lab. worker, EKOS Research Inst., Moscow 1984–85; army service 1985–87; attaché, Ministry of Foreign Affairs, Russian Fed. 1993; Sr Legal Adviser, Stock Co. (ALM) Consulting Moscow 1993–95; Dir Advocates' Bureau (ALM) 1995–97; Head, Dept of State Cttee on Man. of State Property 1997–98; Deputy Minister of State Property 1998; Chair., Russian Foundation of Fed. Property 1998–2000; Head of Govt Admin and Minister Without Portfolio 2000–02, Deputy Head of Presidential Admin 2003–08; First Deputy Chair. of the Govt, in charge of external econ. relations and foreign trade, WTO negotiations and small business 2008–18; Head of Organizing Cttee for the 27th World Summer Universiade 2009–13; Head of Russia's bid cttee to host the 2018 FIFA World Cup 2009–10, co-ordinated the organization, preparation and holding of the World Cup in 2018; Chair. Vnesheconombank (State Corporation Bank for Devt and Foreign Econ. Affairs) 2018–; Hon. Citizen of the City of Kazan 2013; Hon. Diploma, Govt of the Russian Fed. 2003; Order for Service to the Repub. of Tatarstan 2013, Order of Aleksandr Nevskii 2013. *Address:* Vnesheconombank, 107996 Moscow, pr. Akademika Sakharova 9, Russia (office). *Telephone:* (495) 721-18-63 (office). *Fax:* (495) 721-92-91 (office). *Website:* www.veb.ru (office).

SHUVALOV, Vladimir A.; Russian biologist; *Director, Institute of Basic Biological Problems, Russian Academy of Sciences;* b. 13 Oct. 1943, Omsk; m.;

two c.; ed Lomonosov Moscow State Univ.; Sr Lab Worker, then Jr Researcher, Bach Inst. of Biochemistry 1968–72; Sr Researcher, Inst. of Soil Science and Photosynthesis, USSR (now Russian Acad. of Sciences) 1972–79, Head of Lab. 1979, Dir Inst. of Basic Biological Problems 1996–; Co-Pres. Russian Soc. for Photobiology 1996–2011; Head of A.N. Belozersky Scientific Research Inst. of Physical-Chemical Biology, Lomonosov Moscow State Univ. 1997–2003; mem. Ed. Bd Biochimica et Biophysica Acta −2008; Order of Friendship 1999, Order of Honour 2004; State Prize 1991. *Publications include:* author of more than 150 scientific papers on primary light energy transformation at photosynthesis, including The Primary Photoreactions in the Complex P-890-bacteriophophylin 760 1976, Burning of a Narrow Spectral Note at 1.7 K in the Absorption Band of the Primary Electron of Rhodosendomous Vividis Reaction Centres with Blocked Electron Transfer 1988. *Address:* Institute of Basic Biological Problems, Russian Academy of Sciences, Pushchino, Russia (office). *E-mail:* shuvalov@issp.serpukhov.su (office). *Website:* www.ibpn.ru (office).

SHVYDKOI, Mikhail Yefimovich, PhD, DFA; Russian theatre scholar and government official; *Special Envoy of the President for International Cultural Cooperation;* b. 5 Sept. 1948, Kyrgyzia; m. Marina Shvydkaya; two s.; ed Moscow Lunacharsky Inst. of Theatre Art; reviewer, Radio Co., Deputy Ed.-in-Chief Theatr magazine 1973–90; Ed.-in-Chief Publrs Co. Kultura, Russian Fed. Ministry of Culture 1990–93; Deputy Minister of Culture 1993–97; Prof. of Foreign Theatre, Acad. of Humanitarian Sciences; commentator on cultural problems on Russian TV; Deputy Chair. Russian TV and Radio Co., Ed.-in-Chief Cultura TV Channel 1997–98; Chair. All-Russian State Radio and TV Holding 1998–2000; Minister of Culture 2000–04; Head, Fed. Agency of Culture and Cinematography 2004–08; Special Envoy for International Cultural Cooperation 2008–; elected Pres. Russian Acad. of Television 2008; Chair. Nat. Comm. World Decade of Culture at UNESCO, mem. Bd of Dirs Pervyi Kanal 2004–; mem. Russian International Affairs Council; Order "For Merit to the Fatherland", IV Class 2008; Govt Award of the Russian Fed. for Literature and Art 1999; numerous awards, prizes and decorations from France, Poland, Ukraine, Kazakhstan and Russian Fed. *Television:* broadcaster on Cultural Revolution (Cultura TV channel) 2002–, Life is Wonderful (STS TV channel) 2004–. *Publications include:* Dramatic Composition: Theatre and Life, Secrets of Lonely Comedians, Sketches on Foreign Theatre of the Late 20th Century; numerous articles on history and contemporary state of theatre in Russian and foreign periodicals. *Address:* c/o 7/6 Maliy Gnezdnikovskiy per., Moscow 125009, Russia (office). *Telephone:* (495) 629-23-11 (office). *Fax:* (495) 629-22-48 (office).

SHWAYRI, Ramzi; Lebanese chef; *General Director, Al-Kafaàt Catering School;* b. 1971, Beirut; m. Tanya Jamous; ed Univ. of Lyon, France, Univ. of London, UK; studied econs and law in France; received training in France with Int. French Chef, Jean Masson; Lebanon's first TV chef, live programmes three times weekly on Future Television; joined Al-Kafaàt Foundation (f. by his father) 1992, mem. Bd of Trustees, Gen. Dir Hotel Management Inst. (now Al-Kafaàt Catering School) 1995–; est. 'Chef Ramzi' (co. for production of Chef Ramzi ready-to-eat meal dishes for int. export and distribution) 2001; est. 'Chef Ramzi' magazine 2003; Hon. mem. French Syndicate of Baking and Dessert Making Arts. *Television:* Alam Al Sabbah (Future Television Network) 1994. *Publication:* Chef Ramzi 1998, Chef Ramzi from the Lebanese Heritage 2001. *Address:* Al-Kafaàt Catering School, Mansourieh, Moutazah Street, Beit Mery (office); Al-Kafaàt Foundation, PO Box 47, Hadath, Lebanon (office). *Telephone:* (961) 1879301 (office). *Fax:* (961) 1879307 (office). *E-mail:* cheframzi@gmail.com; cheframzi@cheframzi.com.lb. *Website:* www.al-kafaat.org (office); www.cheframzi.com.lb.

SHYAMALAN, M. Night, BA; Indian film director, screenwriter, actor and producer; b. (Manoj Nelliyattu Shyamalan), 6 Aug. 1970, Pondicherry, Tamil Nadu Prov.; s. of Nelliyattu C. Shyamalan and Jayalakshmi Shyamalan; m. Bhavna Vaswani 1993; two d.; ed New York Univ.; Co-founder M. Night Shyamalan Foundation; Distinguished Alumni Award, Episcopal Academy 2001, Padma Shri Award 2008. *Films:* Praying with Anger (writer, dir, actor, producer) 1992, Wide Awake (writer, dir) 1998, The Sixth Sense (writer, dir, actor) 1999, Stuart Little (screenplay writer) 1999, Unbreakable (writer, dir, actor, producer) 2000, Signs (writer, dir, producer) 2002, The Village (writer, dir, producer) 2004, Lady in the Water (writer, dir, producer) 2006, The Happening 2008, The Last Airbender 2010, After Earth (writer, dir, producer) 2013, The Visit 2015, Split 2017. *Television includes:* Wayward Pines (series, exec. producer) 2015. *Publications:* juvenile: Stuart Finds His Way Home (with Kitty Richards) 1999, Stuart and the Stouts (with Greg Brooker) 2001, Stuart and Snowbell (with Greg Brooker) 2001. *Leisure interest:* comic books. *Address:* Creative Artists Agency, 2000 Avenue of the Stars, Los Angeles, CA 90057, USA (office). *Telephone:* (424) 288-2000 (office). *Fax:* (424) 288-2900 (office). *Website:* www.caa.com (office); www.mnightshyamalan.com.

SIAL, Amjad Hussain B., MSc; Pakistani diplomatist and international organization official; *Secretary-General, South Asian Association for Regional Cooperation;* b. 20 June 1956, Karachi; s. of Barkat Ali D. Sial; m. Shama Amjad; ed Nat. Defence Univ., Islamabad; joined Foreign Service of Pakistan 1983, Section Officer, Foreign Service HQ 1984–87, 1991–93, served at Embassy in Vienna 1987–90, Dir, Foreign Service HQ 1993–94, 2000–02, served at Embassy in Harare 1994–96, posted to Mission in New York 1996–2000, Dir-Gen., Foreign Service HQ 2006–09, 2011, Amb./Alt. Perm. Rep., Perm. Mission to UN, New York 2009–11, Amb. to Tajikistan 2011–14, Additional Foreign Sec. 2014, Special Foreign Sec. 2015–16; Dir for Pakistan, South Asian Asscn for Regional Cooperation (SAARC) Secr. 2003–06, Sec.-Gen., SAARC 2017–. *Leisure interests:* badminton, photography, sightseeing. *Address:* SAARC Secretariat, POB 4222, Tridevi Sadak, Kathmandu, Nepal (office). *Telephone:* (1) 4221785 (office). *Fax:* (1) 4227033 (office). *E-mail:* sg@saarc-sec.org (office). *Website:* www.saarc-sec.org (office).

SIALE BILEKA, Silvestre; Equatorial Guinean lawyer and politician; fmr Minister of Justice and Religion; Prime Minister and Head of Govt of Equatorial Guinea 1991–93, 1993–95; Minister of Foreign Affairs and Francophone Affairs 1991–92; Pres. Supreme Tribunal 2000–04; later Presidential Councillor on Human Rights; mem. Partido Democrático de Guinea Ecuatorial.

SIBAL, Kanwal, MA, LLB; Indian fmr diplomatist; b. 18 Nov. 1943, Baddomalhi, British India; m. Elisabeth Sibal; one s. one d.; joined Foreign Service 1966, Third Sec., then Second Sec., Embassy in Paris 1968–73, Under-Sec. Ministry of

External Affairs 1973–75, Jt Sec. 1986–89, Deputy High Commr, High Comm. in Dar-es-Salaam 1976–79, Counsellor, Embassy in Lisbon 1980–82, Deputy Chief of Mission, Embassy in Kathmandu 1982–85, Amb. to Turkey 1989–92, Deputy Chief of Mission, Embassy in Washington, DC 1992–95, Amb. to Egypt 1995–98, to France 1998–2002, Foreign Sec. 2002–04, Amb. to Russia 2004–07; mem. Nat. Security Advisory Bd 2008–10; Pres. Asscn of Indian Diplomats; apptd Chair. EADS India; Dean, Centre for International Relations and Diplomacy and mem. Advisory Bd, Vivekananda Int. Foundation; mem. Bd of Dirs East-West Inst., New York, Green Ventures; Dir JSC Sitronics 2010–12; Grand Officier, Ordre nat. du Mérite. *Address:* 171 Jor Bagh, New Delhi 110 003, India. *Telephone:* (11) 24644755. *E-mail:* kanwalsibal@gmail.com.

SIBAL, Kapil, LLB, MA, LLM; Indian lawyer and politician; b. 8 Aug. 1948, Jalandhar, Punjab; s. of H.L. Sibal; m. 1st Nina Sibal 1973 (died 2000); two s.; m. 2nd Promila Sibal 2005; ed St John's High School, Chandigarh, Univ. of Delhi, Harvard Law School, USA; joined Bar Asscn 1970, set up own law practice, designated Sr Lawyer 1983; Additional Solicitor Gen. of India 1989–90; mem. Rajya Sabha (upper house of Parl.) for Bihar 1998–2004; mem. Lok Sabha (lower house of Parl.) (Congress Party) for Chandni Chowk constituency 2004–14; Union Minister for Science, Tech. and Earth Sciences 2004–10, Minister of Human Resource Devt 2009–12, Minister of Communications and Information Tech. 2010–14, of Law and Justice May 2014; Pres. Supreme Court Bar Asscn 1995–96, 1997–98, 2001–02; mem. Bd of Man., Indira Gandhi Nat. Open Univ. 1993; mem. Exec. Council, Inst. of Constitutional and Parl. Studies 2001; mem. Business Advisory Cttee 2001, Cttee on Home Affairs 2002, Bd of International AIDS Vaccine Initiative 2002, Programme Bd of Bill and Melinda Gates Foundation of Indian AIDS Initiative 2003, Human Rights Comm. Working Group on Arbitrary Detention, Geneva; Living Legend of the Law, International Bar Asscn 1994, Padma Bhushan Award 2006. *Publications include:* poems: I Witness: Partial Observation 2008; numerous articles on issues including security, terrorism and nuclear proliferation. *Address:* c/o Ministry of Communications and Information Technology, Electronic Niketan, CGO Complex, Lodhi Road, New Delhi 110 003, India. *Website:* kapilsibalmp.com.

SIBBETT, Wilson, CBE, BSc, PhD, FRS, FRSE; British physicist and academic; *Emeritus Professor, University of St Andrews;* b. 15 March 1948, Portglenone, Co. Antrim, Northern Ireland; s. of John Sibbett and Margaret Sibbett (née McLeister); m. Barbara Anne Brown 1979; three d.; ed Ballymena Tech. Coll., Queen's Univ. Belfast, Imperial Coll.; Post-doctoral Research Fellow, Imperial Coll., London, later Lecturer and Reader in Physics; Prof. of Natural Philosophy, Univ. of St Andrews 1985–2013, Emer. Prof. 2013–; Chair. Scottish Science Advisory Cttee 2002–06; Fellow, Optical Soc. of America 1998, European Optical Soc. 2007; Hon. DSc (Dundee), (Glasgow), (London City), Hon. ScD (Trinity Coll. Dublin), Hon. DUniv (Strathclyde); Schardin Gold Medal 1978, Inst. of Physics Boys Medal and Prize 1993, Rank Prize for Optoelectronics 1997, Royal Soc. Rumford Medal 2000, European Physical Soc. Quantum Electronics Prize 2002, Royal Medal, Royal Soc. of Edinburgh 2009, Charles Hard Townes Award 2011. *Publications:* 390 papers published in scientific journals. *Leisure interests:* golf, DIY, gardening. *Address:* School of Physics and Astronomy, University of St Andrews, North Haugh, St Andrews, KY16 9SS (office); 1 Lawhead Road East, St Andrews, KY16 9ND, Scotland (home). *Telephone:* (1334) 463100 (office); (1334) 472778 (home). *Fax:* (1334) 463104 (office). *E-mail:* ws@st-andrews.ac.uk (office). *Website:* www.st-andrews.ac.uk/physics (office).

SIBER, Sibel; Turkish-Cypriot politician and fmr physician; b. 13 Dec. 1960, Nicosia; m.; two c.; ed Istanbul Univ., Univ. of Virginia, Rush Univ. Medical Center, USA; early career as physician; resident in internal medicine, Şişli Etfal Hosp., Istanbul 1987; est. private medical practice; mem. Legis. Ass. (Parl.) 2009–, Pres. (Speaker) 2013–18; Prime Minister (first female) June–Aug. 2013; cand. in presidential election April 2015; mem. Cumhuriyetçi Türk Partisi (Republican Turkish Party). *Address:* Assembly of the TNRC, Badr Demirel Avenue, Lefkoşa, Mersin 10, Turkey (office). *E-mail:* info@cm.gov.nc.tr (office). *Website:* www.cm.gov .nc.tr (office).

SIBLEY, Dame Antoinette, CBE, DBE; British ballerina; b. 27 Feb. 1939, Bromley, Kent; d. of Edward G. Sibley and Winifred Smith; m. 1st Michael Somes 1964 (divorced 1973, died 1994); m. 2nd Panton Corbett 1974; one s. one d.; joined the Royal Ballet 1956, Soloist 1959, Prin. Ballerina 1960–; Vice-Pres. Royal Acad. of Dance 1989–91, Pres. 1991–2012 (retd). *Ballets:* leading roles in: Swan Lake, Sleeping Beauty, Coppelia, The Nutcracker, La Fille Mal Gardée, Romeo and Juliet, Jabez and the Devil (cr. role of Mary), The Dream (cr. Titania), Jazz Calendar (cr. Friday's Child), Enigma Variations (cr. Dorabella), Thais (cr. Thais), Triad (cr. the Girl), Manon (cr. Manon), Soupirs (cr. pas de deux), Symphonic Variations, Daphnis and Chloë, Varii Capricci (cr. La Capricciosa), The Good-Humoured Ladies, A Month in the Country, L'Invitation au Voyage (cr. a lead role), Anastasia (cr. Kschessinska pas-de-deux), Pavane (cr. pas-de-deux). *Television:* Cinderella (TV movie), The Rosalina Neri Show 1959, The London Palladium Show 1967. *Films:* The Turning Point 1978, Mime Matters (video). *Publications:* Sibley and Dowell 1976, Antoinette Sibley 1981, Reflections of a Ballerina 1985. *Leisure interests:* doing nothing, opera, cinema, reading.

SIDDARAMAIAH, K., BSc, LLB; Indian lawyer, politician and government official; b. 12 Aug. 1948, Siddaramanahundi, Varuna Hobli, Mysore Dist; s. of Siddarame Gowda and Boramma; m. Parvathi Siddaramaiah; two s.; ed Univ. of Mysore; a leader of the Kuruba Gowda community in Karnataka; was a junior under a lawyer in Mysore and later taught law; began political career when elected to Mysore Taluka 1978; contested on a Bharatiya Lok Dal ticket from Chamundeshwari constituency and entered 7th Karnataka Legis. Ass. 1983; joined ruling Janata Party and became first Pres. Kannada Watchdog Cttee (Kannada Kavalu Samiti) set up to supervise the implementation of Kannada as an official language; re-elected from same constituency 1985; Minister for Animal Husbandry and Veterinary Services from 1985, handled portfolios including Sericulture, Animal Husbandry and Transport at different times, defeated in Ass. elections 1989; apptd Sec.-Gen. of Janata Dal 1992; elected again in state elections 1994; Minister for Finance in Janata Dal Govt 1994–96; Deputy Chief Minister of Karnataka 1996–99, 2004–06; joined Janata Dal (Secular) faction of Deve Gowda following split in the Janata Dal and became Pres. of its state unit, defeated in state elections 1999; expelled from JD (S) 2006; joined the Nat. Congress; elected

mem. Karnataka Legis. Ass. (Chamundeshwari constituency) 2006; re-elected for Varuna constituency 2008, 2013; elected Leader of the Congress Legis. party in Karnataka Ass. 2013; Chief Minister of Karnataka 2013–18.

SIDDIQUI, Nazim Hussain, BA, LLM; Pakistani fmr judge; b. 30 June 1940; s. of Mukarram Hussain Siddiqui; ed Univs of Hyderabad and Karachi; lawyer, Hyderabad 1961–67; fmr Civil Judge, Sr Civil Judge, Customs Judge, Special Judge; apptd Judge, High Court of Sindh 1992, Chief Justice 1999–2000; Judge, Supreme Court 2000–05, Chief Justice 2004–05 (retd); Chair. Cen. Zakat Council of Pakistan; mem. Selection Bd, Quaid-i-Azam Univ.

SIDDIQUI, Brig. Rashid; Pakistani army officer (retd) and business executive; ed Command and Staff Coll., Nat. Defence Coll., Islamabad; army service 1971–2002, becoming Dir of Military Intelligence and Faculty mem., Nat. Defence Coll., Islamabad; Exec. Dir (Admin) Pakistan Nat. Shipping Corpn 2002–, Chair. 2009–11; Sitara-i-Imtiaz (Mil.). *Leisure interests:* golf, jogging. *Address:* Pakistan National Shipping Corporation, PNSC Building, M.T. Khan Road, PO Box No. 5350, Karachi 74000 (office); House No 35-B, North Circular Avenue, Phase I, DHA, Karachi, Pakistan (home). *Telephone:* (21) 9204029 (office); (300) 8221869 (mobile); (21) 5380379 (home). *Fax:* (21) 99203974 (office). *E-mail:* communication@pnsc.com.pk (office); siddiqi06@hotmail.com. *Website:* pnsc.com .pk (office).

SIDEROV, Volen Nikolov; Bulgarian journalist and politician; *Leader, Partiya Ataka (Ataka—Attack Party);* b. 19 April 1956, Yambol; m. Kapka Siderova (separated); one s.; partner Denitsa Gadzheva; ed degree in Applied Photography in Sofia; worked as photographer at Nat. Literature Museum –1989; mem. Movt for Human Rights 1990; Ed.-in-Chief Democracy (official newspaper of Democratic Party) 1990–92; journalist, 168 Hours (weekly newspaper); press attaché for Sasho Donchev (Srpska Radikalna Stranka—Serbian Radical Party), Topenergy and Overgas mid-1990s; journalist, Monitor (newspaper) –2003; hosted talk show on cable TV channel SKAT 2003–05; Founder and Leader, Ataka (Attack) Nat. Union (later Ataka) 2005–; mem. Parl. 2005–; unsuccessful presidential cand. 2006; mem. and Spokesperson for United Patriots (alliance of VMRO—Balgarsko natsionalno dvizhenie (VMRO—BND) (IMRO—Bulgarian Nat. Movt), Natsionalen Front za Spasenie na Bulgaria (NFSB—Nat. Front for the Salvation of Bulgaria and Attack Party) 2016–; known for hardline attitude towards minorities in Bulgaria; Union of Bulgarian Journalists Award 2000. *Leisure interests:* collecting books and maps related to Bulgaria. *Address:* Partiya Ataka (Ataka—Attack Party), 1000 Sofia, ul. Vrabcha 1, Bulgaria (office). *Telephone:* (2) 980-55-70 (office). *Fax:* (2) 980-55-70 (office). *E-mail:* volenataka@abv.bg (office); atakacentrala@abv.bg (office). *Website:* www.ataka.bg (office).

SIDHWA, Bapsi; American/Pakistani writer and academic; b. 11 Aug. 1939, Karachi; d. of Peshotan Bhandara and of Tehmina Bhandara; m. 1st (divorced); m. 2nd Nosher Rustam Sidhwa; two d. one s.; ed Kinnaird Coll. for Women, Lahore; self-published first novel The Crow Eaters 1978; Asst Prof., Creative Writing Program, Univ. of Houston 1985; Bunting Fellowship, Radcliffe Coll., Harvard Univ. 1986–87; Asst Prof., Writing Div., Columbia Univ. 1989; Visiting Scholar, Rockefeller Foundation Centre, Bellagio, Italy 1991; Prof. of English and Writer-in-Residence, Mount Holyoake Coll., South Hadley, Mass 1997; Fannie Hurst Writer-in-Residence, Brandeis Univ., Mass 1998–99; Postcolonial Teaching Fellowship, Univ. of Southampton, UK 2001; Chair. Commonwealth Writers' Prize 1993; mem. Advisory Cttee to Prime Minister Benazir Bhutto on Women's Devt –1996, Punjab Rep., Asian Women's Conf., Alma Ata; Sec. Destitute Women's and Children's Home, Lahore; Sitara-I-Imtiaz 1991, Nat. Award for English Literature, Pakistan Acad. of Letters 1991, Patras Bokhari Award for Literature 1992, Lila Wallace Reader's Digest Award 1993, Excellence in Literature Award, Zoroastrian Congress 2002, South Asian Excellence Awards for Literature 2008, HCC Asian-American Legacy Award 2008. *Play:* Sock 'em With Honey 1993. *Film:* Earth (film of Ice-Candy-Man aka Cracking India) 1999. *Publications include:* The Crow Eaters (David Higham Award) 1978 (commercially published 1980), The Bride 1982, Ice-Candy-Man (aka Cracking India) (Notable Book of the Year, New York Times) 1991, An American Brat 1993, Bapsi Sidhwa Omnibus 2001, Water: A Novel (Premio Mondello for Foreign Authors 2007) 2006, City of Sin and Splendour: Writings on Lahore 2006, The Pakistani Bride 2008, Their Language of Love: Collection of Short Stories 2013; numerous short stories and reviews. *Leisure interests:* reading, theatre, cinema, cooking, bridge. *Address:* Milkweed Editions, 1011 Washington Avenue, South Suite 300, Open Book, Minneapolis, MN 55415 (office); 5442 Cheena Drive, Houston, TX 77096, USA (home). *Telephone:* (612) 332-3192 (office); (713) 283-0811 (home). *Website:* hometown.aol .com/bsidhwa; bapsisidhwa.com.

SIDIBÉ, Cissé Mariam Kaïdama; Malian civil servant and politician; b. 4 Jan. 1948, Timbuktu, French Sudan; m.; four c.; ed École nat. d'admin, Bamako, École int. de Bordeaux, France, École nat. d'admin publique, Québec, Canada; civil servant in Ministère de Tutelle des Socs et Entreprises d'Etat (Ministry of Oversight for State Cos and Socs) 1974–89, becoming Asst to Minister 1987–89; Special Adviser to Pres. 1991, 2001; Minister of Planning and Int. Co-operation 1991–92, also Minister of Agric. May–June 1992; Exec. Sec., Interstate Cttee on the Fight Against Desertification in the Sahel (Cilss), Ouagadougou 1993–2000; Minister of Rural Devt March–June 2002; Pres. Admin Council, Soc. nat. des tabacs et allumettes du Mali (govt-owned tobacco corpn) 2003–11; Prime Minister of Mali (first woman) 2011–12 (deposed in coup d'état and reported to be detained by junta forces 22 March); mem. Réseau des femmes ministres et parlementaires du Mali, Alliance contre la faim, Asscn pour la sauvegarde de Tombouctou.

SIDIBÉ, Michel, MA; Malian UN official; *Executive Director, UNAIDS;* b. 1952; m.; four c.; ed Blaise Pascal Univ. Clerment-Ferrand, France; joined UNICEF, Zaire (now Democratic Repub. of the Congo) 1987, served as UNICEF country rep. in several African countries, including Burundi, Swaziland and Uganda; apptd Dir Country and Regional Support Dept, UNAIDS 2001, Deputy Exec. Dir of Programmes, UNAIDS and UN Asst Sec.-Gen. 2007–09, Exec. Dir UNAIDS and UN Under-Sec.-Gen. 2009–; mem. Bd of Dirs Grassroot Soccer 2011; Hon. Prof., Stellenbosch Univ. of South Africa 2007; Order of St Charles (Monaco) 2009, Chevalier, Légion d'honneur 2010; Emerging Leader Award 2010. *Address:* UNAIDS, 20, Avenue Appia, 1211 Geneva 27, Switzerland (office). *Telephone:* 227913666 (office). *Fax:* 227914187 (office). *Website:* www.unaids.org (office).

SIDIBÉ, Modibo, LLM; Malian politician; *Leader, Forces Alternatives pour le Renouveau et l'Emergence;* b. 4 Nov. 1952, Bamako; brother of Mandé Sidibé; m.; five c.; ed Univ. of Reims, Univ. of Aix-en-Provence, France; Inspector Gen. of Police –2001 (retd); Chef de Cabinet for Minister Del. of Nat. Defence 1989–91; Cabinet Dir for Minister Del. of Internal Security 1991; Cabinet Dir for Pres. of Transitional Cttee for Health 1991–92; Minister of Health, Solidarity and the Elderly 1992–97, of Foreign Affairs and Malians Abroad 1997–2002; Sec.-Gen., Office of the Pres. 2002–07; Prime Minister 2007–11 (resgnd); Pres. Foreign Affairs Council, Econ. Community of West African States (ECOWAS) 1999–2001, Pres. Mediation and Peace Council 1999–2001; currently Leader, Forces Alternatives pour le Renouveau et l'Emergence; unsuccessful cand. for Pres. of Mali 2014; Commandeur, Ordre National du Mali, Commandeur, Légion d'Honneur. *Website:* www.president-modibosidibe.com (office).

SIDIBÉ, Saidou; Niger economist and politician; *President, Audit Court;* Minister of Finance in transitional Conseil de Réconciliation Nationale (CRN) govt 1999–2000; fmr Minister-Del. to Minister of Finance in charge of Budget; fmr Pres., Dispositif Nat. de Prévention et de Gestion des Crises Alimentaire (nat. body for prevention of food crises); Chief of Staff to Pres. of Repub. 2013, to Prime Minister 2014; Minister of Finance 2015–16; Pres. Audit Court 2016–; fmr Gov. or Vice-Gov. of multilateral insts, including IMF, ADB, Islamic Devt Bank. *Publications include:* author or co-author of several publications on economic reforms including: Reform of the Parastatal Sector in Niger 1994, Public Development Aid: A Tool 2004, Economic and Financial Reform in Niger: The Other Face 2012. *Address:* Cour des Comptes, rue 239, pl. Nelson Mandela, BP 14034, Niamey, Niger (office). *Telephone:* 20-72-68-00 (office). *Fax:* 20-72-68-03 (office). *E-mail:* courdescomptes@courdescomptes.ne (office). *Website:* www.courdescomptes.ne (office).

SIDIKOU, Maman Sambo, PhD; Niger journalist, government official, UN official and diplomatist; m. Fatima Djibo-Sidikou; two c.; ed Universidad de Madrid, Spain, Université de Dakar, Senegal, Univ. of Texas, Austin and Florida State Univ., Tallahassee, USA; worked as journalist at Ministry of Information's Office de Radiodiffusion et Télévision du Niger (ORTN) 1976–79, Dir of nat. television for ORTN 1979–81; Dir in Cabinet of the Prime Minister 1983; Research Assoc. with Center for Int. Studies, Learning Systems Inst., Florida State Univ. early 1990s; Human Devt Man. with USAID, Niamey 1994–95; Minister Advisor, Office of the Presidency 1996–97; Minister managing Niger's external relations, including negotiations with int. and bilateral partners, Ministry of Foreign Affairs and African Integration 1997–99; Minister and Dir Cabinet of the Presidency 1999; Chief of Educ., Water and Sanitation with UNICEF, Abuja, Nigeria 2000–01, Team Leader for UNICEF Back-To-School Campaign, Kabul, Afghanistan 2001–02; Sr Educ. Specialist with World Bank, Washington, DC 2002–05; UN Cluster Co-ordinator for Educ. and Culture with UNICEF Programme Irak, Amman, Jordan 2005–07; Chief of Educ. for UNICEF in Nigeria 2007–10; Country Dir for Rwanda 2010, Democratic Repub. of the Congo 2010–11, working with USAID, UN, World Bank and Save the Children to coordinate programming and dialogue with devt partners; Amb. to USA 2011–14; Special Rep. of the Chair. of the African Union Comm. for Somalia (SRCC) and Head of AMISOM 2014–15; Special Rep. for the Democratic Repub. of the Congo and Head of the UN Stabilization Mission in the Democratic Repub. of the Congo (MONUSCO) 2015–18.

SIDIMÉ, Lamine; Guinean lawyer, politician and judge; b. 1944; ed studied law in Paris; lecturer, Univ. of Dakar 1980, Senegal, Univ. of Conakry 1984, Prof. of Law 1985–; mem. Constitutional Council 1990; Pres. Supreme Court 1992–99, 2004; Prime Minister of Guinea, Co-ordinator of Govt Affairs 1999–2004; mem Parti de l'Unité et du Progrès (PUP). *Address:* c/o Supreme Court, Corniche-Sud, Camayenne, Conakry, Guinea (office). *Telephone:* 30-41-29-28 (office).

SIDLIN, Murry, MM; American conductor and academic; b. 6 May 1940, Baltimore, Md; ed Academia Chigiana, Siena, Cornell Univ., Peabody Conservatory of Music, Johns Hopkins Univ.; Asst Conductor, Baltimore Symphony Orchestra 1971–73; Dir Maryland Ballet Co. 1971–73; Prin. Conductor, Baltimore Chamber Players 1971–73; Resident Conductor, Nat. Symphony Orchestra under Dorati 1973–77, Wolf Trap American Univ. Music Acad. 1974; Host and Conductor, Children's TV series Music is... 1977; Music Dir Tulsa Philharmonic Orchestra 1978–80; Music Dir New Haven Symphony 1977–88, Long Beach Symphony 1980–88, Resident Conductor, Aspen Music Festival 1978–93; Resident Conductor, Oregon Symphony Orchestra 1994–2002; Dean, Benjamin T. Rome School of Music, Catholic Univ., Washington, DC 2002–10, currently Prof. of Conducting; currently Founder-Pres. Defiant Requiem Foundation; Co-founder, Assoc. Dir and Program Coordinator, American Acad. of Conducting, Aspen; Artistic Dir Cascade Festival of Music; guest conductor with St Louis Symphony, orchestras of San Francisco, Pittsburgh, Minnesota, Atlanta, Colorado, Utah, Florida, Jerusalem, orchestras of Madrid, I Solisti Veneti, Honolulu, Seattle, Monte Carlo, Vancouver, Victoria, and Edmonton and Quebec, George Enescu Philharmonic of Bucharest, Czech Nat. Symphony, MVD Orchestra of Budapest, Iceland Symphony, Boston Pops, San Antonio Symphony and Opera, Houston Symphony; regular performances with Lindberg Orchestra of Holland; mem. Int. Bd of Govs Jerusalem Acad. of Music and Dance 2013–; winner, Baltimore Symphony Orchestra Young Conductor's Competition 1962, Educator of the Year, Nat. Assn of Ind. Schools of Music in America 1997, Distinguished Alumnus Award, Peabody Conservatory of Music, Johns Hopkins Univ. 2011, Excellence in Arts Award, City Choir of Washington 2011, Medal of Valor, Simon Wiesenthal Center 2013. *Television:* Music Is... *Telephone:* (212) 977-6779 (office); (202) 244-0220 (office). *E-mail:* hughkaylor@msn.com (office); msidlin@defiantrequiem.org. *Address:* Defiant Requiem Foundation, PO Box 6242, Washington, DC 20015, USA (office). *Website:* www.defiantrequiem.org; www.murrysidlin.com.

SIDORSKY, Syarhey Syarheyovich, DEngSci; Belarusian politician; b. 13 March 1954, Gomel; m.; two d.; ed Belarus Inst. of Railway Transport Engineers; worked as electrical fitter and electrician; foreman of assembly shop, head of lab., head of dept, Deputy Dir Gomel Radio Equipment Plant 1976–91, Dir 1991–92; Gen. Man. Gomel Scientific Production Assn RATON 1992–98; Deputy Chair. and First Deputy Chair. Gomel Oblast Admin 1998–2001; Deputy Prime Minister 2001–02, First Deputy Prime Minister 2002–03, Acting Prime Minister July–Dec. 2003, Prime Minister 2003–10; Academician, Int. Eng Acad.; Honoured Workman of Industry (Belarus). *Publications include:* more than 40 scientific publs and monographs.

SIEBERT, Bernd, Dr rer. nat (Habil.); German mathematician and academic; *Professor of Mathematics, University of Texas at Austin;* b. 5 March 1964, Berlin-Wilmersdorf; ed Univs of Erlangen, Bonn and Göttingen; worked at Courant Inst. of Math. Sciences, New York Univ., USA; mem. Faculty, Univ. of Bochum 1993–94; Visiting Scholar, MIT 1997–98; DFG-Heisenberg Fellow, Univ. of Paris VI/Univ. of Paris VII 2000–02; Prof., Albert Ludwigs Univ. of Freiburg 2002–08; Prof. of Math., Univ. of Hamburg 2008–18, Head of Graduiertenkolleg Math. Inspired by String Theory and QFT; Prof. of Math., Univ. of Texas at Austin 2018–; Clay Research Award, Clay Math. Inst. (co-recipient) 2016. *Publications:* numerous papers in professional journals. *Address:* Department of Mathematics, Robert Lee More Hall 9.160, University of Texas at Austin, 2515 Speedway Stop C1200, Austin, TX 20146, USA (office). *Telephone:* (512) 471-7711 (office). *E-mail:* siebert@math.utexas.edu (office). *Website:* www.ma.utexas.edu (office).

SIEGEL, François; French editor, newspaper executive and publisher; *Co-founder, We Demain;* s. of Maurice Siegel; Ed. VSD (Vendredi Samedi Dimanche) group 1981–96; Ed. Le Monde2 –2004; Co-founder with Jean-Dominique Siegel of GS Presse, We Demain 2012–. *Address:* Rédaction We Demain – GS Editions, 92 avenue Victor Cresson, 92442 Issy-les-Moulineaux, France (office). *Telephone:* 1-40-95-57-16 (office). *E-mail:* francois.siegel@wedemain.fr (office). *Website:* www.wedemain.fr (office).

SIEGERT, Theo, MBA, PhD; German business executive; *Managing Partner, de Haen Carstanjen & Söhne;* b. 8 April 1947, Düsseldorf; m.; two c.; ed Univ. of Munich; joined Franz Haniel & Cie. GmbH 1975, held several sr positions including in Controlling Dept, then Head of Strategic Planning Dept, Dir of Finance and Mergers & Acquisitions, Deputy Mem. Managing Bd 1994–96, mem. 1996–2005, Chair. 2005; Chair. Supervisory Bd Metro AG 2004–06; Man. Partner, de Haen Carstanjen & Söhne, Dusseldorf 2006–; mem. Supervisory Bd Commercial Pharmaceutique S.A., Saint-Ouen/France –2002, Merck KGaA 2006–, Deutsche Bank AG 2006–12, Henkel AG & Co. 2009–, E.ON AG 2009–, Ergo Versicherungsgruppe AG –2010; mem. Bd of Dirs DKSH, ERGO Insurance Group AG 2009–10; mem. Bd of Partners, E. Merck KG 2014–; Chair. Foundation Council, Stiftung Marktwirtschaft; Hon. Prof. of Financial Analysis and Co. Man., Ludwig-Maximilians Univ. of Munich. *Address:* de Haen-Carstanjen & Söhne, Königsallee 24, 40212 Düsseldorf, Germany (office). *E-mail:* siegert@dhcs.de (office). *Website:* www.dhcs.de (office).

SIELICKI, Tomasz, BEcons; Polish business executive; ed Warsaw Univ. of Tech.; joined ComputerLand 1991, Pres., Man. Bd 1992–2005, Pres. Computer-Land Group (now Sygnity Group after merger with Emax 2007) 2005–07, Vice-Chair. Supervisory Bd 2007–17, Bd; Pres. Polish Chess Fed. 2009–13; mem. Man. Bd Polish Confed. of Pvt. Employers LEWIATAN; mem. Supervisory Bd Agora SA; Vice-Pres. European Chess Union; mem. Bd World Chess Fed., Polish Olympic Cttee 2013–, Foundation Bd of bridge24.pl.; mem. Polish Confed. of Private Employers, Council of Inst. of Public Affairs, Council of Information Soc. Development Foundation, Council of European Forum for New Ideas, Program Council of Acad. of Capital Market Leaders operating at Lesław Paga Foundation, Council of United Way; Kt's Cross, Orderu Odrodzenia Polski 2013; INFO-STAR prize, Global Leader for Tomorrow Prize 1999. *Leisure interests:* chess. *Address:* c/o Sygnity Group, Royal Wilanow Business Centre, ul. F. Klimczak 1, 02-797 Warsaw, Poland (office). *Telephone:* (22) 2908800 (office). *Website:* www.sygnity.pl (office).

SIEMIĄTKOWSKI, Zbigniew, DH; Polish politician; b. 8 Oct. 1957, Ciechanów; m.; one d.; ed Univ. of Warsaw; Sr Asst, Univ. Warsaw 1981; Deputy to Sejm (Parl.) 1991–2005, mem. Comm. for Nat. and Ethnic Minorities, Comm. of Justice; mem. Polish United Workers' Party (PZPR) 1978–90; mem. Social Democracy of Polish Repub. (SDRP) 1990–99; Minister of Internal Affairs 1996; mem. Council of Ministers 1997; mem. Democratic Left Alliance (SLD) 1999–; Sec. of State in Chancellery of Prime Minister 2001; Acting Head, Office of State Protection (Urzad Ochrony Panstwa—UOP) 2001–02, Head, Foreign Intelligence Agency (Agencji Wywiadu—AW) (following absorption of UOP into AW and Interior Security Agency (Agencja Bezpieczenstwa Wewnetrznego—AWB)) 2002–04 (resgnd); Ordre National du Mérite, France 1996, Commdr, Legion of Merit (USA) 2004. *Publications:* Intelligence and Power: The Role of the Civil Intelligence in the PRZ Government Political System. *Leisure interest:* family, tourism.

SIEMONIAK, Tomasz; Polish communications industry executive and politician; b. 2 July 1967; m.; one s., one d.; ed Warsaw School of Econs; fmrly with Ind. Student Assn; Chair. in Main School of Planning and Statistics; fmr Sec., Nat. Coordination Cttee; Dir Office for Field Branches, Telewizja Polska SA (Polish public television) and Gen. Dir Channel 1 1994–96; Coordinator, Media and Democracy Programme, Inst. of Public Affairs 1997; Dir Press and Information Office, Ministry of Nat. Defence 1998–2000; Deputy Chair. Supervisory Bd of Polish News Agency 1998–2002; mem. Warsaw-City Centre District Council 1998–2000; Deputy Chair. of Culture Cttee 1998–2000; Deputy Mayor of Warsaw 2000–02; mem. Man. Bd Polskie Radio SA (Polish public radio) 2002–06; Deputy Marshal, Marshal's Office of Mazowieckie Voivodeship 2006–07; Sec. of State, Ministry of Interior and Admin 2007–11; Minister of Nat. Defence 2011–15, Deputy Prime Minister 2014–15. *Address:* c/o Ministry of National Defence, 00-909 Warsaw, ul. Klonowa 1, Poland.

SIENKIEWICZ, Bartłomiej Henryk; Polish politician; b. 29 July 1961, great-grandson of novelist and journalist Henryk Sienkiewicz; m.; three s. one d.; ed Faculty of Philosophy and History, Jagiellonian Univ.; participated in Kraków opposition movt early 1980s; co-f. Office for State Protection 1990; co-f. Centre for Eastern studies (think-tank) 1990, Vice-Pres. for Programme Affairs 1991–93, 1996–2001, currently Chair. Centre for Eastern Studies; worked in pvt. sector in early 2000s; f. Sienkiewicz i Wspólnicy (now ASBS Othago); adviser to Speaker of the Sejm (Parl.) 2003–05; fmr Lecturer, Nat. Defence Univ.; mem. Programme Bd, Polish Inst. of Int. Affairs; mem. Bd Internal Security Agency Central Training Centre; Minister of the Interior 2013–14. *Address:* c/o Ministry of the Interior, 02-591 Warsaw, ul. Stefana Batorego 5, Poland. *E-mail:* kancelaria.glowna@mswia.gov.pl.

SIEVERT, Frederick J., BA, MA; American fmr insurance industry executive; m.; five c.; ed Amherst Coll., Wayne State Univ.; fmr secondary school teacher; Sr Vice-Pres. Royal Maccabees Life Insurance Co.; joined New York Life Insurance Co. as Sr Vice-Pres. and Chief Financial Officer with responsibility for Financial Man. Dept of Individual Operations 1992–95, also responsible for Individual Life, Individual Annuity and Disability Income Depts 1994, Exec. Vice-Pres. 1995–97, Vice-Chair. 1997–2004, Pres. 2002–07 (retd); mem. Bd of Dirs Reinsurance Group of America Inc. 2010–, CNO Financial Group Inc. 2011–; fmr Chair. Bd of Trustees, The American Coll., currently Trustee; mem. American Acad. of Actuaries; Fellow, Soc. of Actuaries.

SIEVERTS, Thomas C. W., DiplIng; German architect and town planner; b. 8 June 1934, Hamburg; s. of Rudolf Sieverts and Elisabeth Sieverts (née Ronnefeldt); m. Heide Pawelzick 1966; one s. two d.; ed in Stuttgart, Liverpool and Berlin; with Kossak and Zimmermann f. Freie Plannungsgruppe Berlin 1965; Prof. of Town Planning Dept of Architecture, Hochschule der Künste, Berlin 1967–70; Guest Prof., Grad. School of Design, Harvard Univ., USA 1970–71; Prof. of Town Planning, Dept of Architecture, Tech. Hochschule, Darmstadt 1971–99, now Prof. Emer.; Special Prof. of Urban Design, Inst. of Planning Studies, Univ. of Nottingham, UK 1978–83; in practice as architect and town planner, skt umbaukultur, Bonn 1978–; Fellow, Inst. for Advanced Study, Berlin 1995–96; Regent's Prof., Univ. of California, Berkeley 2005; mem. Scientific Advisory Council World Exhbn, 'Expo 2000', Hanover 1989–99, Sächsische Akad. der Künste; Deubau Prize (Essen) 1969, Verdienstzeichen in Gold (Vienna) 1988, Bauherren Prize 1992, Deutsche Städtebau Prize 1993. *Buildings:* town planning consultant to the City of Vienna, planning Danubia area 1973–78, the Gürtel area 1984–88; Dir of Int. Bldg Exhbn Emscher Park (Ruhr) 1989–94. *Publications:* Zwischenstadt (3rd edn) 1999 (English edn: Cities Without Cities – An Interpretation of the Zwischenstadt 2004), Fünfzig Jahre Städtebau – Reflektion und Praxis 2001; many contribs to periodicals and books. *Leisure interest:* drawing. *Address:* skt umbaukultur, Thomas-Mann-Strasse 41, 53111 Bonn, Germany. *Telephone:* (228) 22723620 (office). *Fax:* (228) 22723629 (office). *E-mail:* info@umbaukultur.eu (office). *Website:* www.skt-umbaukultur.eu (office).

SIEW, Vincent C., LLM; Taiwanese diplomatist, fmr government official and research institute administrator; b. (Siew Wan-chang), 3 Jan. 1939, Chiayi City, Taiwan; m. Susan Chu; three d.; ed Nat. Chengchi Univ., Georgetown Univ.; Vice-Consul, Kuala Lumpur, Malaysia 1966–69, Consul 1969–72; Section Chief, Asia Pacific Affairs Dept, Ministry of Foreign Affairs 1972; Deputy Dir 4th Dept Bd of Foreign Trade, Ministry of Econ. Affairs 1972–74, Dir 1974–77, Deputy Dir-Gen. Bd of Foreign Trade 1977–82, Dir-Gen. 1982–88; Vice-Chair. Council for Econ. Planning and Devt, Exec. Yuan 1988–89; Dir-Gen. Dept of Organizational Affairs, Kuomintang Cen. Cttee 1989–90, Vice-Chair. Kuomintang 2000–05; Minister of Econ. Affairs 1990–93; Minister of State, Chair. Council for Econ. Planning and Devt, Exec. Yuan 1993–94; Minister of State, Chair. Mainland Affairs Council, Exec. Yuan 1994–95; legislator 1996–97; Premier of Taiwan 1997–2000; Vice-Pres. of Taiwan 2008–12; Eisenhower Fellow, USA 1985; Chair. Chung-Hua Inst. for Econ. Research, Convenor Presidential Econ. Advisory Panel 2003–04; fmr Chair. Cross-Straits Common Market Foundation; Prof. Nat. Chengchi Univ.; Hon. Chair. Cross-Straits Common Market Foundation; Hon. DMan (Nat. Chia-Yi Univ.); Hon. DEcon (Sung Kyun Kwan Univ., Seoul); Hon. PhD (Rangsit Univ., Thailand); Hon. Dr Public Service (Ohio State Univ., USA). *Publications:* One Plus One is Greater than Two: The Road to the Cross-Straits Common Market, To Govern the Nation with Expertise.

SIFAKIS, Joseph, PhD; Greek/French computer scientist, institute director and consultant; *Director, Centre de la Recherche Intégrative;* b. 26 Dec. 1946, Heraklion, Crete; ed Nat. Technical Univ. of Athens, Univ. of Grenoble, France; Research Dir, CNRS, Founder Verimag Lab., Grenoble, Dir 1993–2006, now Sr Researcher Emer.; Prof., Ecole Polytechnique Fédérale de Lausane, Switzerland 2011–; Dir Centre de la Recherche Intégrative (CRI), Grenoble 2009–; Scientific Coordinator ArtistDesign Network of Excellence on Embedded Systems Design; Chair. Chamber B (Public Research Orgs) of ARTEMISIA (industrial asscn within the ARTEMIS European Tech. Platform on Embedded Systems); mem. Bd of Dirs CARNOT Inst. 'Intelligent Software and Systems', Grenoble; Co-founder Int. Conf. on Computer Aided Verification (CAV); Pres. Greek Nat. Council for Research and Technology 2014–; mem. Steering Cttee EMSOFT (Embedded Software) Conf.; mem. editorial bds of several journals; mem. Academia Europea, French Nat. Acad. of Engineering, French Acad. of Sciences; Foreign Hon. Mem., American Academy of Arts and Sciences 2015–; Hon. Prof., Univ. of Patras; Grand Officier, Ordre national du Mérite, Commdr, Ordre national de la Légion d'honneur, Commdr, Order of the Phoenix (Greece); Dr hc (Ecole Polytechnique Fédérale de Lausanne) 2009, (Univ. of Athens), (Int. Hellenic Univ.); CNRS Silver Medal 2001, Turing Award (co-recipient) 2007, Leonardo da Vinci Medal 2012. *Achievements include:* developed theory and tech. for the SCADE tool used for design and validation of critical real-time systems, de facto standard for aeronautics; recognized for pioneering work on both theoretical and practical aspects of Concurrent Systems Specification and Verification. *Publications:* numerous scientific papers in professional journals on component-based design, modelling, and analysis of real-time systems with focus on correct-by-construction techniques. *Address:* Centre de la Recherche Intégrative, Bâtiment CTL, 7 allée de Palestine, 38610 Gières, France (office). *Telephone:* (4) 56-52-04-47 (office). *Fax:* (4) 56-52-04-46 (office). *E-mail:* joseph.sifakis@imag.fr (office). *Website:* www-verimag .imag.fr/~sifakis (office); cri-grenoble.com (office).

SIGALOVA, Alla Mikhailovna; Russian choreographer, ballet dancer and academic; *Professor, Chekhov Moscow Art Theatre (MKhAT);* b. 28 Feb. 1958, Volgograd; d. of Stalov Mikhail Petrovich and Viogina Tamara Aleksandrovna; m. Kozak Roman Yefimovich; one s. one d.; ed Leningrad Vaganova School of Choreography, Russian Acad. of Theatre Arts; teacher, Russian Acad. of Theatre Arts 1982–2004; choreographer, Theatre Satirikon 1987–89; Artistic Dir Theatre Ind. Troupe of Alla Sigalova 1989–97, Choreography Theatre of Alla Sigalova 2001–; Prof. and Head, Faculty of Eurhythmics, Studio School of Chekhov Moscow Art Theatre (MKhAT) 2004–; choreographer of New Year TV shows for ORT and NTV channels 1996–99; Honoured Artist of Russia, Golden Mask Nat. Theatre Award 2008. *Dance:* Othello 1990, Queen of Spades 1991, Salomea 1991. *Productions choreographed include:* Moscow Mayakovsky Theatre: Diary of an Ordinary Girl 1984, Bed-Bug 1986; Moscow Satirikon Theatre: Serving Girls 1988; Moscow Mossoviet Theatre: Banana 1994; Theatre of Lower Saxony: Yvonne, the Princess of Burgundy; Nuremberg Theatre: Money-bank; Ekaterinburg City Ballet: Nutcracker; Latvian Nat. Opera: Duets, Yellow Tango, Bolero; Samara Theatre of Opera and Ballet: Visions of Ivan the Terrible; New Opera Theatre: Traviata; Lithuanian Opera and Ballet Theatre: Seven Deadly Sins; Theatre of Popular Genre: Dreams of Love; Pushkin Theatre: Romeo and Juliet, Djan; Pushkin Theatre: Nights of Cabiria, Madame Bovary; Moscow Chekhov Theatre: Carmen. Etudes. *Address:* Chekhov Moscow Art Theatre (MKhAT), 3 Kamergerskiy Pereulok, Moscow 103 (office); Prechistenka str. 25/13, Apartment 10, Moscow, Russia (home). *Telephone:* (495) 629-87-60 (office); (495) 201-44-36 (home). *Fax:* (495) 201-44-36 (home). *E-mail:* mhat@theatre.ru (office); asigalova@mail.ru (home). *Website:* art.theatre.ru (office); www.en.allasigalova.ru.

SIGFÚSSON, Steingrímur J., BSc; Icelandic politician; *Speaker of Althingi;* b. 4 Aug. 1955, Thistilfjordur; m. Bergný Marvinsdóttir; four c.; ed Univ. of Iceland; mem. Althingi (Parl.) 1983–, Chair. People's Alliance Parl. Group 1987–88, mem. Cttee on Fisheries 1991–98 (Chair. 1995–98), on Economy and Trade 1991–99, on Social Affairs 1999–2003, on Foreign Affairs 1999–2009, Special Cttee on Constitutional Affairs 2004–05, mem. Del. to W Nordic Council 1991–95, to Nordic Council 1996–2005, 2006–07, to Parl. Ass. of the Council of Europe 2007–13, Chair. PACE Cttee on Equal Opportunities 2008–13, Deputy Speaker 2013–16, 2017, Speaker 2016–17, 2017–; Founding Chair. Left-Green Movement 1999–2013; Minister of Agric. and Communications 1988–91, of Fisheries and Agric. Feb.–May 2009, of Finance 2009–11, of Econ. Affairs Jan.–Sept. 2012, of Fisheries and Agric. Jan.–Sept. 2012, of Industries and Innovation Sept. 2012–13. *Publications:* Róvið á ny mið: Sóknarfæri iíslensks sjavarutvegs 1996, Við öll: Íslenskt velferðarsamfélag á tímamótum 2006, Steingrímur J.: Frá hruni og heim 2013; numerous newspaper and magazine articles. *Address:* Skrifstofa Alþingis, Kt. 420169-3889, 101 Reykjavík (office); c/o Vinstrihreyfingin–grænt framboð (Left-Green Movement),-Túngötu 14, 101 Reykjavík, Iceland. *Telephone:* 5630500 (office). *Fax:* 5630550 (office). *E-mail:* sjs@althingi.is (office). *Website:* www.althingi.is (office).

SIGUA, Tengiz Ippolitovich, DTechS; Georgian engineer and politician; b. 9 Nov. 1934, Lentekhi; s. of Ipolite Sigua and Lidia Schavdia; m. Nina Iwania 1975; one d.; ed Georgian Polytechnical Inst.; engineer and Dir Metallurgy Inst. Georgian Acad. of Sciences 1962–90, mem. Georgian Acad. of Sciences; fmr leading mem. Round Table—Free Georgia Alliance, Chair. All-Georgia Rustaveli Soc.; apptd Head of Govt by Zviad Gamsakhurdia, Nov. 1990, resigned Aug. 1991 and joined the opposition; mem. State Council March–Oct. 1992; mem. Supreme Soviet 1992–95; apptd Prime Minister by Mil. Council 1992–93 (resgnd), joined Parl. Opposition; Vice-Pres. Georgian Rustaveli Soc. 1989, Pres. 1992–93; arrested with Tengiz Kitovani after an attempted march of armed Georgian refugees on Abkhazia to retake breakaway region 1995, later released. *Leisure interests:* sport, art.

SIGURÐARDÓTTIR, Jóhanna; Icelandic politician; b. 4 Oct. 1942, Reykjavík; m. 1st Þorvaldur Steinar Jóhannesson 1970 (divorced); two s.; civil partner Jónína Leósdóttir 2002, m. 2010; ed Commercial Coll. of Iceland; fmr flight attendant, Loftleiðir; fmr office worker; elected Social Democratic Party mem. of Althing (Parl.) (Social Democratic Party) 1978, Deputy Speaker 1979, 1983–84, 2003–07; Vice-Chair. Social Democratic Party 1984–93; Minister of Social Affairs and Social Security 1987–94, 2007–09; f. Þjóðvaki party 1994–2000; mem. Social Democratic Alliance 2000–13; Prime Minister 2009–13; Bd mem. Commercial Workers' Union 1976–83. *Address:* c/o Social Democratic Alliance, Hallveigarstíg 1, 101 Reykjavík, Iceland.

SIGURDSSON, Jón, MSc(Econ); Icelandic politician and economist; b. 17 April 1941, Ísafjörður; s. of Sigurdur Gudmundsson and Kristin Gudjona; m. Laufey Thorbjarnardóttir; four c.; ed Akureyri Coll., Univ. of Stockholm, Sweden and London School of Econs, UK; Econ. Inst. of Iceland 1964–71 (Dir Econ. Research 1970–71); Chief Econ. Research Div. Econ. Devt Inst. 1972–74; Man. Dir Nat. Econ. Inst. and Econ. Adviser to Govt 1974–80, 1983–86; Exec. Dir for Nordic Countries IMF 1980–83, Alt. Gov. IMF for Iceland 1974–87; Assoc. Jt IBRD/IMF Devt Cttee 1974–80; IBRD Gov. for Iceland 1987–; EBRD Gov. for Iceland 1991–; mem. Althing (SDP) 1987–; Minister of Justice and Ecclesiastical Affairs 1987–88, of Commerce 1987–93, of Industry 1988–93, of Nordic Co-operation 1988–89; Chair. OECD Council of Ministers 1989, Nordic Council of Ministers 1989; mem. Salaries Arbitration Court 1970–80; Rep. for Iceland Econ. and Devt Review Cttee OECD 1970–80, 1983–86; Gov. and Chair. Bd of Dirs, Cen. Bank of Iceland 1993–94; Pres. and CEO Nordic Investment Bank 1994–2005, mem. Bd of Dirs 1976–87, Chair. 1984–86; currently financial and econ. consultant.

SIILASMAA, Risto, MSc (Eng); Finnish business executive; *Chairman, Nokia Corporation;* b. 1966; ed Helsinki Univ. of Tech.; Founder, Pres. and CEO F-Secure Corpn 1988–2006, Chair. 2006–; mem. Bd of Dirs Nokia Corpn 2008–, Chair. 2012–, interim CEO 2013–14; mem. Bd of Dirs Blyk Ltd, Mendor Ltd, Elisa Corpn 2007–12 (Chair. 2008–12), Efecte Oy 2008–12 (Chair. 2007–08), Ekahau Oy 2008–11 (Chair. 2007–08), Ekahau, Inc. 2008–11 (Chair. 2006–08), Nexit Ventures Oy 1999–2009, Fed. of Finnish Tech. Industries; fmr Chair. Fruugo Inc.; several awards, including The Leader of the Decade 2003, Most Influential IT Leader 2007, Nordic Chairman of the Year 2009. *Address:* Nokia Corporation, Keilalahdentie 4, 00045 Espoo (office); F-Secure Corporation, Tammasaarenkatu 7, PL 24, 00181 Helsinki, Finland. *Telephone:* (7180) 08000 (Espoo) (office); (9) 2520-0700 (Helsinki) (office). *Fax:* (7180) 38226 (Espoo) (office); (9) 2520-5001 (Helsinki) (office). *E-mail:* info@nokia.com (office); info@f-secure.com (office). *Website:* www .nokia.com (office); www.f-secure.com (office).

SIIMANN, Mart; Estonian fmr politician; b. 21 Sept. 1946, Kilingi-Nõmme; m.; two c.; ed Tartu State Univ.; psychologist, Deputy Head Lab. of Scientific Org. of Work and Man. 1971–75; Sr research Asst Tartu State Univ. 1975–82; broadcaster, Deputy Dir-Gen., Ed.-in-Chief Estonian TV 1982–87, Dir-Gen. 1989–92; Dir-Gen. Estonian Radio 1987–89; Man. Dir commercial TV station ReklamTV 1992–95; mem. Riigikugu (Parl.) 1995–97, 1999–2003; Chair. Coalition Party 1997–99; Prime Minister of Estonia 1997–99; fmr Counsellor to Pres. of Estonia on Domestic Policy; Pres. Estonian Olympic Cttee 2001–12. *Leisure interests:* sport, literature, fishing, philosophy.

SIKHARULIDZE, Vasil; Georgian physician, psychiatrist and diplomatist; *Chairman, Atlantic Council of Georgia;* b. 30 May 1968, Tbilisi; m. Anna Tsagareli; one d.; ed Tbilisi State Medical Univ.; physician and psychiatrist, Inst. of Psychiatry 1993–95; Exec. Dir Atlantic Council of Georgia 1995–96; worked in Georgian Parl. as specialist on Cttee of Defence and Security 1996–2000; Head of NATO Div., Ministry of Foreign Affairs and Deputy Head of Georgian Mission to NATO, Brussels 2000–02; NATO Fellow 2001–03; Under-Sec. Nat. Security Council of Georgia March–July 2004; Deputy Minister of Defence 2004–05, First Deputy Minister of Defence, responsible for Policy and Planning, Int. Relations and Legal Affairs 2005–06; Amb. to USA 2006–08; Minister of Defence 2008–09; Foreign Policy Adviser to Pres. 2009–; currently Chair. Atlantic Council of Georgia. *Address:* Atlantic Council of Georgia, 0186 Tbilisi, 8, Jurkha Nadiradze str, Georgia (office). *Telephone:* (70) 10-52-51 (office). *E-mail:* office@atlanticcouncil.ge (office). *Website:* www.acge.ge (office).

SIKORSKI, Radosław (Radek) Tomasz, BA, MA; Polish journalist and politician; b. 23 Feb. 1963, Bydgoszcz; m. Anne Applebaum; two s.; ed Pembroke Coll., Oxford, UK; involved in Solidarity social movt early 1980s; Chair. student strike cttee Bydgoszcz 1981; political refugee in UK 1981–89; journalist reporting on wars in Afghanistan and Angola 1986–89; Deputy Minister of Nat. Defence 1992; Under-Sec. of State in Ministry of Foreign Affairs 1998–2002; Fellow, American Enterprise Inst. and Exec. Dir New Atlantic Initiative, Washington, DC 2002–05; elected to Senate for Bydgoszcz (Law and Justice Party), Minister of Nat. Defence 2005–07, of Foreign Affairs 2007–14; Deputy in the Sejm (Parl.) for Bydgoszcz 2007–, Marshal of the Sejm 2014–15; Vice-Chair. Civic Platform party 2010–; 'Millennium Star' Medal (Lithuania) 2008, Nat. Order of Merit, Grade of Companion (Malta) 2009, Order of Merit, First Class (No. 407) (Ukraine) 2009, Royal Order of the Polar Star (Sweden) 2011, Order of Prince Jaroslaw the Wise, Third Class (Ukraine) 2011, Commdr's Grand Cross, Royal Order of the Polar Star (Sweden) 2011, Grand Officier, Légion d'honneur 2012; World Press Photo Prize 1987, The Spectator and The Sunday Telegraph Young Writers' Awards 1988, Odznaka Zasłużony Działacz Kultury (Polish award for the promotion of culture), Wiktor Award for "most popular politician" 2006, Lithuanian Millennium Star Medal 2008, Gold Badge, Asscn of Poles in Lithuania 2010, named by the Foreign Policy magazine as one of the Top 100 Global Thinkers 2012. *Television:* cr. TV programme Wywiad Miesiąca (interview of the month). *Publications:* Prochy Świętych – podróż do Heratu w czas wojny (Dust of the Saints – A Journey to Herat in Time of War) 1989, The Polish House: An Intimate History of Poland 1998, Strefa Zdekomunizowana 2007; ed. of series of analytical publs entitled European Outlook. *Address:* Sejm, 00-902 Warsaw, ul. Wiejska 4/6/8, Poland (office). *Telephone:* (22) 6942500 (office). *Fax:* (22) 6941446 (office). *E-mail:* zjablon@sejm .gov.pl (office). *Website:* www.sejm.pl (office); www.radeksikorski.pl.

SIKUA, David Derek, DipEd, BEd, MEPA, PhD; Solomon Islands educator and politician; b. 10 Sept. 1959; ed Univ. of the South Pacific, Fiji, Univ. of Southern Queensland, Australia, Monash Univ., Univ. of Waikato, New Zealand; teacher and Deputy Headmaster Pawa Secondary School 1982–84; teacher and Deputy Prin., Waimapuru, Nat. Secondary School 1984–86; Prin. Educ. Officer, Implementation and Planning Unit, Ministry of Educ. and Human Resources Devt 1986–87, Dir Implementation and Planning Unit 1988–90, Dir Secondary School Div. Jan.–Feb. 1993, UnderSec. Minister of Educ. and Human Resources Devt 1993–94, Perm. Sec. 1994–97; Perm. Sec. Ministry of Forests, Environment and Conservation 1997–98; Perm. Sec. (Special Duties), Ministry of Educ. and Human Resources Devt May–Sept. 2003, Perm. Sec. 2003–05; mem. Parl. for North East Guadalcanal 2006–, Leader of the Opposition 2011–14; Minister for Educ. and Human Resources Devt 2006–07, re apptd 2014; Prime Minister 2007–10; Chair. Solomon Islands Nat. Comm. for UNESCO 2006; Chair. Nat. Educ. Planning Cttee 1989–90, Nat. Library Bd 1993–94; Deputy Chair. Solomon Islands Coll. of Higher Educ. Council 1994–97; mem. USP Council Exec. Cttee 2007–. *Leisure interests:* reading, writing, soccer, cricket, rugby, bushwalking, bird watching. *Address:* National Parliament, POB G19, Honiara, Solomon Islands (office). *Telephone:* 28520 (office). *Fax:* 24272 (office). *Website:* www.parliament.gov.sb (office).

SILAJDŽIĆ, Haris, PhD; Bosnia and Herzegovina academic and politician; b. 1 Oct. 1945, Sarajevo; m.; one s.; ed Garyounis Univ., Libya; has held several academic positions including Arabic Language Prof., Univ. of Prishtina, Prof., Faculty of Philosophy and Dept of History, Univ. of Sarajevo, Andrew D. White Prof. at Large, Cornell Univ., New York, Guest Lecturer, Harvard Univ. and Univ. of Maryland, Chatham House (Royal Inst. for Int. Affairs), London, Carnegie Foundation, Woodrow Wilson Center, and other univs; Minister of Foreign Affairs, Repub. of Bosnia and Herzegovina 1990–93, Prime Minister 1993–96, Co-Chair. Council of Ministers of Bosnia and Herzegovina 1997–2000; Bosniak mem. Tripartite State Presidency 2006–10, Chair. (Pres. of Bosnia and Herzegovina) March–Nov. 2008, March–Nov. 2010; fmr mem. and Vice-Pres. Party of Democratic Action; Founder Party for Bosnia and Herzegovina (Stranka za Bosnu i Hercegovinu), Pres. 1996–2012; Sitara-e-Pakistan 2018; Dr hc (Geneva School of Diplomacy and Int. Relations) 2005; Rabbi Marc H. Tanenbaum Memoral Lecturer 1997, Lifetime Achievement Award, Advisory Council for Bosnia and Herzegovina (ACBH) 2018. *Publications:* several books and papers on int. relations, including relations between USA and Albania. *Address:* Party for Bosnia and Herzegovina, 71000 Sarajevo, Fra Grge Martića 2/II, Bosnia and Herzegovina (office). *Telephone:* (33) 573470 (office). *Fax:* (33) 475597 (office). *E-mail:* zabih@zabih.ba (office). *Website:* www.zabih.ba (office).

SILANYO, Ahmed Mohamed, BEcons, MEcons; Somali politician; b. 1936, Burao; ed Univ. of Manchester, UK; Jr Official, Ministry of Planning and Co-ordination, Mogadishu 1965–69, Minister of Planning and Co-ordination 1969–73, of Commerce 1973–78, 1980–82; Chair. Nat. Econ. Bd 1978–80; in exile in UK 1982 until Somaliland's declaration of independence from Somalia 1991; Chair. Somali Nat. Movt 1982–90; mem. House of Reps, Somaliland 1993–97, Somaliland Minister of Finance 1997–99, of Planning and Coordination 1999–2001; currently Chair. Peace, Unity and Devt Party (Kulmiye); unsuccessful cand. in presidential election 2003; Pres. of self-proclaimed ' Repub. of Somaliland' (NW Somalia) 2010–17. *Address:* c/o Office of the President, Hargeisa, Somaliland (office).

SILAYEV, Ivan Stepanovich; Russian politician; b. 21 Oct. 1930; m.; two c.; ed Kazan Aviation Inst.; mem. CPSU 1959–91; foreman, shop supt, deputy chief engineer, chief engineer, plant dir in Gorky 1954–74; Deputy Minister of Aircraft Industry of USSR 1974–77, First Deputy Minister 1977–80, Minister 1981–85; Minister of Machine Tool and Instrument-Making Industry of USSR 1980–81; Deputy to USSR Supreme Soviet 1981–89; Deputy Pres. Council of Ministers of USSR 1985–89; Pres. Council of Ministers of RSFSR 1989–91; Pres. Inter-Republican Econ. Cttee of USSR 1991; Russian Perm. Rep. to EC (now EU) 1991–94; Pres. Bd of Dirs Ecology of Russia Consortium 1995; Chair. Moscow Interregional Commercial Bank 1996, Int. Union of Mechanical Engineers 1997; Pres. Russian Union of Machine-Builders 2002–; mem. Bd of Dirs Yukos Corp. 2005–, Int. Business Club; mem. CPSU Cen. Cttee 1981–91; Order of Lenin 1971, 1975, Hero of Socialist Labour 1975, Order of the October Revolution 1981; Lenin Prize 1972, Nat. Prize of Peter the Great 2002.

SILBERBERG, Reinhard; German diplomatist; b. 1953; m.; four c.; ed social sciences, philosophy, Romance languages and literature studies; joined Foreign Service 1978, Desk Officer for Cultural and Media Affairs, Embassy in Dhaka, Bangladesh 1980–84, Political Directorate-Gen., Fed. Foreign Office, Bonn 1984–87, Deputy Head of Mission, Embassy in Guatemala 1987–90, Desk Officer for Political Affairs, Perm. Representation to European Communities 1990–92, Deputy Head of Basic European Policy Issues Div., Fed. Foreign Office 1992–95, Deputy Head of Fed. Foreign Office Task Force for EU Intergovernmental Conf. (Treaty of Amsterdam) 1995–96, Head of Fed. Foreign Office Task Force for EU Intergovernmental Conf. 1996–97, Head of Fed. Foreign Office Task Force for EU Enlargement 1997–98, Dir Gen. for European Affairs, Fed. Chancellery 1998–2005, State Sec., Fed. Foreign Office 2006–09, Amb. to Spain 2009–14, Amb. and Perm. Rep. to EU, Brussels 2014–18.

SILBERMAN, Laurence Hirsch, LLB; American judge, banker, diplomatist and academic; *Senior Judge, United States Court of Appeals for the DC Circuit;* b. 12 Oct. 1935, York, Pa; s. of William Silberman and Anna Hirsch; m. Rosalie Gaull 1957; one s. two d.; ed Dartmouth Coll., Harvard Law School; with Moore, Torkildson & Rice, Quinn & Moore (law firm) 1961–64; Pnr, Moore, Silberman & Schulze 1964–67; lawyer, Nat. Labor Relations Bd 1967–69; solicitor, Labor Dept 1969–70, Under-Sec. for Labor Affairs 1970–73; Pnr, Steptoe & Johnson 1973–74; Deputy Attorney-Gen., Dept of Justice 1974–75; Amb. to Yugoslavia 1975–77 (withdrawn); Man. Pnr, Morrison and Foerster, Washington, DC 1978–79, 1983–85; Exec. Vice-Pres. Legal and Govt Affairs Div., Crocker Nat. Bank 1979–83; Sr Fellow, American Enterprise Inst. for Public Policy Research, Washington, DC 1977–78, Visiting Fellow 1978–85; Vice-Chair. Advisory Council on Gen. Govt, Republican Nat. Comm. 1977–80; mem. US Gen. Advisory Cttee on Arms Control and Disarmament 1981–85; Assoc. Prof. of Admin. Law, Georgetown Univ., Washington, DC 1987–94, 1999–2001, currently Adjunct Prof. and Distinguished Visitor from the Judiciary; Assoc. Prof., New York Univ. 1995–96, Harvard Univ. 1998; Judge, US Court of Appeals, DC Circuit 1985–2000, Sr Judge 2000–; Co-Chair. Pres.'s Comm. on Intelligence Capabilities of the US Regarding Weapons of Mass Destruction 2004–05; Presidential Medal of Freedom 2008. *Address:* US Court of Appeals, DC Circuit, 333 Constitution Avenue, NW, Washington, DC 20001, USA. *Website:* www.cadc.uscourts.gov (office).

SILES DEL VALLE, Juan Ignacio; Bolivian politician, diplomatist, academic and poet; b. 1961; ed Univ. of Chile, Univ. of Georgia, USA; fmr Univ. Prof. of Literature, Greater Univ. of San Andrés; Head of Educative Reform initiative 1994–95; Alternating Perm. Rep. to UN, Vienna and Rome; Vice-Pres. UN Comm. for Drug Control, representing Latin American and Caribbean Countries, Vienna 2001; Dir Summit Coordination in charge of Cooperation of Latin American Summits 2002; Nat. Coordinator of XIIIth Latin American Summit of Heads of State and Govt 2003; fmr Dir Diplomatic Acad.; fmr Dir Cultural Subjects, Minister of Foreign Affairs and Culture 2003–05; currently working at Ibero-American General Secretariat, Madrid. *Publications include:* Con las manos vacías de mariposas muertas 1987, Medulamor 1993, Canción de cuna para la muerte de mi madre 1995, Los últimos días del Che. Que el sueño era tan grande (essays) 2007. *Address:* Ibero-American General Secretariat Headquarters, Paseo de Recoletos, 8, 28001 Madrid, Spain. (office). *Telephone:* (91) 5901980 (office). *E-mail:* info@segib.org (office). *Website:* segib.org/en (office).

SILEVITCH, Michael B., BSEE, MSEE, PhD; American engineer and academic; *Robert D. Black Professor, College of Engineering Distinguished Professor, Electrical and Computer Engineering, Northeastern University;* ed Northeastern Univ., Brandeis Univ.; joined Faculty, Northeastern Univ. 1972, Prof. then Distinguished Prof., Robert D. Black Endowed Chair in Eng 2003–, Coll. of Eng Distinguished Prof. with dual appointments in Electrical and Computer Prof. as well as Civil and Environmental Prof.; Co-Dir Awareness and Localization of Explosives-Related Threats (ALERT), Dept of Homeland Security Center of Excellence; Dir Bernard M. Gordon Center for Subsurface Sensing and Imaging Systems (Gordon-CenSSIS), NSF Eng Research Center; Research Trans. Leader, Puerto Rico Testsite to Explore Contamination Threats (PROTECT) programme; Dir Center for Enhancement of Science and Math. Educ. (CESAME) 1987–96; fmr Dir Center for Electromagnetics Research, Gordon Eng Leadership Program; a Co-PI of Mass Statewide Systemic Initiative Project, PALMS (Partnerships Advancing the Learning of Math. and Science) 1990–2000; Life Fellow, IEEE 2003; Gordon Prize, Nat. Acad. of Eng (co-recipient) 2015. *Publications:* approx. 65 papers in professional journals. *Address:* Gordon Center, 360 Huntington Avenue, 302 Stearns Center, Boston, MA 02115, USA (office). *Telephone:* (617) 373-3033 (office). *E-mail:* m.silevitch@neu.edu (office). *Website:* www.ece.neu.edu (office); www.censsis.neu.edu (office).

SILIÉ VALDEZ, Rubén Arturo; Dominican Republic sociologist, diplomatist and international organization official; fmr prof. at several univs and ists; fmr Vice-Rector Nat. Univ. of Santo Domingo; Dir Latin American Faculty for Social Sciences (FLACSO) 1996–; Adviser to the Vice-Pres. and Sec. of State for Educ. 2001–; apptd Amb., Ministry of Foreign Affairs 2001; Sec.-Gen. Asscn of Caribbean States 2004–08; Amb. to Haiti 2009–17; mem. Bd Batey Relief Alliance.

SILJA, Anja; German singer (soprano) and producer; b. 17 April 1940, Berlin; m. Christoph von Dohnányi (divorced); one s. two d.; ed studied with Egon van Rijn; began concert career aged ten at Berlin Titania Palace; stage debut Brunswick 1956, as Rosina; mem. Stuttgart and Frankfurt operas 1958–59; sang the Queen of Night at Aix 1959; sang at Bayreuth Festival 1960–67, as Senta, Elsa, Eva, Elisabeth and Venus; London debut at Sadler's Wells Theatre as Leonore/Fidelio

1963; Covent Garden debut as Leonore 1969, returned as Cassandre in Les Troyens, Senta, Marie in Wozzeck, Kostelnicka in Jenůfa; Metropolitan Opera debut 1972, returned as Salome, Marie and Kostelnicka; with Vienna Staatsoper 1959–, in roles including Queen of Night, Salome, Elektra, Lulu; Paris Opéra 1964–, as Salome and Brünnhilde; Glyndebourne Opera debut as Kostelnicka 1989; sang the Nurse in Die Frau ohne Schatten at San Francisco 1989; debut as opera producer at Brussels with Lohengrin 1990; sang Emilia Marty at Glyndebourne 1995; season 1997 in The Makropulos Case at Glyndebourne and as Herodias at Covent Garden; Geschwitz in Lulu at Düsseldorf 2000; Clytemnestra at Madrid, Geschwitz and Herodias at Amsterdam, The Makropulos Case at Aix and The Bassarids in Amsterdam, Pierrot Lunaire by Schoenberg at Aix 2003; season 2004 as Madame de Croissy in Milan and Mère Marie in Hamburg and Paris (both in Dialogues des Carmélites), Emilia Marty in Berlin, Clytemnestra (Elektra) in Oviedo, Gräfin Geschwitz (Lulu) in Munich; season 2005 as Kostelnicka in Lyon and Barcelona, Emilia Marty in Lyon and Berlin, Janáček's Osud in Vienna, and Gräfin Geschwitz in Munich; Kammersängerin; Bundesverdienstkreuz 1988; Janacek Medal, Opera News Award for invaluable contrib. to opera 2012. *Recordings include:* Der fliegende Holländer, Tannhäuser, Lohengrin and Parsifal from Bayreuth, Lulu, Wozzeck, Jenůfa (Grammy Award) 2001, Pierrot Lunaire, Salome, Erwartung, The Makropoulos Case. *Publication:* Die Sehnsucht nach dem Unerreichbaren (autobiog.) 1999. *Address:* Artists Management Zürich, Rütistrasse 52, 8044 Zürich-Gockhausen, Switzerland (office). *Telephone:* (1) 8218957 (office). *Fax:* (1) 8210127 (office). *E-mail:* schuetz@artistsman.com (office). *Website:* www.artistsman.com (office).

SILK, John M.; Marshall Islands lawyer and politician; *Minister of Foreign Affairs;* b. 15 Sept. 1956, Kwajalein; m. Mary Silk; five c.; ed Regis Univ., Denver, Colo, USA; Ed. Marshall Islands Journal 1979–81; Legal Adviser, Micronesian Legal Services Corpn 1981–90; with Stege and Assocs (law firm) 1990–93; Minister of Resources and Devt 2000–07, of Foreign Affairs 2009–12, 2016–; Senator, Ebon Atol 2000–; Del. to Marshall Islands Constitutional Convention 1991; mem. Marshall Islands Bar Asscn, Marshall Islands Law Soc. *Leisure interests:* tennis, baseball, fishing. *Address:* Ministry of Foreign Affairs, PO Box 1349, Majuro, MH 96960, Marshall Islands (office). *Telephone:* (625) 3181 (office). *Fax:* (625) 4979 (office). *E-mail:* mofasec@ntamar.net (office).

SILLARD, Yves; French aerospace engineer; b. 5 Jan. 1936, Coutances, Manche; s. of Roger Sillard and Madeleine Sillard (née Guerrand); m. 1st Annick Legrand 1966 (divorced); m. 2nd Hélène Benech-Badiou 1982 (divorced); m. 3rd Martine Gautry 1999; ed Ecole Massillon, Ecole Polytechnique, Ecole nat. Supérieure de l'Aéronautique; Test Eng and then Head of Colomb-Béchard unit of Centre d'Essais en Vol 1960–62, Tech. Dir of Cazeaux annex 1963–64; Head of Concorde Programme at Secrétariat général à l'Aviation civile 1965; Head of Div. setting up French Guiana Space Centre, Kourou 1966–68; Tech. Dir and then Dir Space Centre, Kourou 1968–72; Dir of Launchers, Centre Nat. des Etudes Spatiales 1973–76, Man. Dir 1976–82; Chair. and Man. Dir Centre nat. pour l'exploitation des océans 1982–85; Chair. Conseil d'administration de l'institut français de recherche pour l'exploitation de la mer 1985–89; French Nat. Co-ordinator for EUREKA Programme 1986–89; Gen. Del., Armaments 1989–93; mem. Atomic Energy Cttee 1989–93; Chair., Man. Dir Défence conseil international 1993–97; Asst Sec.-Gen. for Scientific Affairs and Environment, NATO 1998–2001; Head of Steering Cttee, Groupe d'études et d'information sur les phénomènes aérospatiaux non identifiés (GEIPAN) 2005–09; mem. Nat. Acad. for Aeronautics and Space; Commdr, Légion d'honneur, Chevalier, Ordre nat. du Mérite, Commdr Merit (FRG); Médaille de l'Aéronautique. *Publications include:* Phénomènes aérospatiaux non identifiés, un défi à la Science 2007. *Address:* 8 rue de la Forge, 17800 Brives sur Charente, France (home). *Telephone:* (5) 46-95-01-56 (home). *E-mail:* ysillard@club-internet.fr (home).

SILNOV, Andrey Alexandrovich; Russian athlete and politician; b. 9 Sept. 1984, Shakhty, Rostov Oblast; men's high jumper; Gold Medal, European Championships, Gothenburg 2006 (jump of 2.36m); jumped 2.37m in Monaco a week later (world leading jump in 2006); Silver Medal, World Athletics Final, Stuttgart 2006, World Cup, Athens 2006; jumped new personal best of 2.38m in London Grand Prix July 2008; Gold Medal, Olympic Games, Beijing 2008 (jump of 2.36m); coached by Sergey Starykh and Yevgeniy Zagorulko; mem. Rostov Region Legis. Ass. 2014–. *Address:* Legislative Assembly, 344050, Rostov-on-Don, Street Socialist, 112, Russia. *E-mail:* zsrnd@zsro.ru. *Website:* www.zsro.ru/en.

SILUANOV, Anton Germanovich; Russian economist and politician; *First Deputy Chairman and Minister of Finance;* b. 12 April 1963, Moscow, Russian SFSR, USSR; m.; one s.; ed Moscow Finance Inst.; Economist, later Sr Economist, Ministry of Finance 1985–87, Leading Economist and Subdivision Deputy Dir 1989–92, Deputy Dir Budget Dept 1992–97, Dir Macroeconomic Policy and Banking Dept 1997–2003, mem. Finance Ministry Bd 2001–, Deputy Minister of Finance 2003–04, 2005–11, Dir Inter-budget Relations Dept 2004–05, Acting Minister of Finance Sept.–Dec. 2011, Minister of Finance Dec. 2011–; First Deputy Chair. 2018–; Decree of the Pres. of the Russian Fed. 2002, Minister of Finance's Decree 2002, Order 'For Merit to the Fatherland' (IVth Degree) 2011; Hon. Diploma, Ministry of Finance 2001. *Address:* Ministry of Finance, 109097 Moscow, ul. Ilinka 9, Russia (office). *Telephone:* (495) 987-91-01 (office). *Fax:* (495) 625-08-89 (office). *Website:* minfin.ru (office); government.ru/en/gov/persons/166/events (office).

SILUNGWE, Hon. Mr Justice Annel Musenga, LLM; Zambian judge and barrister; b. 10 Jan. 1936, Mbala; s. of Solo Musenga Silungwe and Janet Nakafunda Silungwe; m. Abigail Nanyangwe Silungwe 1960; one s. four d.; ed Univs of Zambia and London, Inner Temple, London; Resident Magistrate 1967, Sr Resident Magistrate (Class II) 1968, (Class I) 1970; Judge of the High Court 1971; nominated MP and apptd Minister of Legal Affairs and Attorney-Gen. 1973; State Counsel 1974; Chief Justice 1975–92; Judge, Court of Appeal, Seychelles 1992–2003; Judge of High Court and Acting Judge of Supreme Court, Namibia 1999; Dir Justice Training Centre, Namibia 1994–99; Chair. Judicial Services Comm. 1975–92, Council of Legal Educ. 1975–92, Council of Law Reporting 1975–92, apptd Tech. Cttee on Drafting the Zambian Constitution 2011; Regional Chair. Southern African Region of Nat. Cheshire Int. Homes and Foundations 1998; Dist Gov. Rotary Int. 1982–83; mem. Council World Jurist Asscn of World Peace Through Law Center 1985; mem. Bd Dirs The Commonwealth Judicial Educ. Inst., Halifax, Canada 1997–; Rotary Int. Award for Community Service 1989. *Leisure interests:* music, golf, photography. *Address:* c/o Technical Committee on Drafting the Zambian Constitution, Government Complex Conference Centre, PO Box 50106, Lusaka 10101, Zambia.

SILVA, Artur António da; Guinea-Bissau engineer and politician; b. 1956; ed Rural Fed. Univ. of Pernambuco, Brazil, Univ. of Hull, UK, School of Maritime Affairs, Bordeaux, France; early career as maritime engineer; Minister of Fisheries 1994–99; Sec. of State for Int. Co-operation 2008–09; Minister of Defence –Oct. 2009, of Culture, Educ., Science, Youth and Sports 2009–12, of Foreign Affairs and International Co-operation 2015–16; Prime Minister Jan.–April 2018; mem. Partido Africano da Independência da Guiné e Cabo Verde (PAIGC). *Website:* www.gov.gw (office).

SILVA, Hon. Sarath Nanda, LLM; Sri Lankan judge; ed Univ. of Brussels, Belgium; Advocate of the Supreme Court of Sri Lanka 1967; Crown Counsel, Attorney Gen.'s Dept 1968, Sr State Counsel 1975, Deputy Solicitor Gen. 1979; Lecturer, Sri Lanka Law Coll. 1981–87; Judge, Court of Appeal 1987–94, Pres. 1994; Judge of the Supreme Court 1995–99, Chief Justice of Sri Lanka 1999–2009; Lecturer in Civil Law, Sri Lanka Law Coll. 1981–87; apptd Attorney Gen. 1996; Pres.'s Counsel 1996.

SILVA, Tilvin; Sri Lankan politician; b. 26 Feb. 1956; Gen. Sec. Janatha Vimukthi Peramuna (People's Liberation Front) 1995–, currently also Sec. on Education. *Address:* Janatha Vimukthi Peramuna, 464/20 Panchikawattha Road, Pelawatta, Battaramulla, Colombo 10, Sri Lanka (office). *Telephone:* (11) 2785612 (office). *Fax:* (11) 2786050 (office). *E-mail:* media@jvpsrilanka.com (office). *Website:* www.jvpsrilanka.com (office).

SILVA BARBEIRO, Marciano; Guinea-Bissau politician; *Ministry of Public Works, Housing and Town Planning;* Minister of Educ. 2004–05, of Nat. Defence 2007–09, of Public Works, Housing and Town Planning 2016–; Chief, Casa Civil da Presidência (Civil House of the Presidency) 2014–16; mem. Partido Africano da Independência da Guiné e Cabo Verde (PAIGC). *Address:* Ministry of Public Works, Housing and Town Planning, Av. dos Combatentes da Liberdade da Pátria, CP 14, Bissau, Guinea-Bissau (office). *Telephone:* 443206575 (office).

SILVA E LUNA, Gen. Joaquim; Brazilian army officer and government official; b. 10 Dec. 1949; ed Academia Militar das Agulhas Negras, Escola Agrotécnica Federal de Barreiros-PE, Escola de Aperfeiçoamento de Oficiais, Escola de Comando e Estado-Maior do Exército, Centro de Instrução de Guerra na Selva; began as Officer of Eng Weapons 1972, promoted to rank of 2nd Lt 1973, 1st Lt 1975, worked as Army Construction Engineer, promoted to rank of Maj. 1985, Lt-Col 1990, mem. Brazilian Mil. Instruction Mission in Paraguay (also Eng Adviser) 1992–94, promoted to the rank of Col 1995, commanded 6th Bn of Construction Eng 1996–98, Attaché of Defense, Naval, Army and Aeronautical in Israel 1999–2001, promoted to Brig.-Gen. 2002, Commdr, 16th Jungle Infantry Brigade, Tefé-AM 2002–2004, Heritage Dir 2004–06, promoted to Div.-Gen. 2006, Chief of Staff of Army Commdr 2007–11, promoted to Army-Gen. Chief of Staff of Army 2011–14; worked as Sec. of Personnel Education, Health and Sports, Sec.-Gen. 2015–18; Minister of Defence 2018–19. *Address:* c/o Ministry of Defence, Esplanada dos Ministérios, Bloco Q, 70049-900 Brasília, DF, Brazil (office).

SILVA LUJÁN, Gabriel; Colombian politician and diplomatist; b. 5 Oct. 1957; m. Mariana Espinosa de Silva; four c.; ed Univ. of the Andes, Bogotá, Paul H. Nitze School of Advanced Int. Studies, Johns Hopkins Univ., USA; Adviser on Political Affairs to fmr Pres. Virgilio Barco 1986–90; Adviser on Int. Politics to fmr Pres. Cesar Gaviria 1990–93; Amb. to USA 1993–94, 2010–12; pursued several entrepreneurial projects, including co-founding Newbridge Andean Partners investment fund; Founding Partner and mem. Bd of Dirs PetroColombia SA; Founding Pres. Global Tuition and Education Insurance Corpn and Global Life Insurance SA 1995–2002; Gen. Man. Federación Nacional de Cafeteros de Colombia (FEDERACAFÉ—nat. coffee growers fed.) 2002–09; Minister of Defence 2009–10; fmr columnist, El Tiempo newspaper; mem. bd several non-governmental orgs dedicated to environmental conservation and protection, including Fundacion Natura and ProSierrra Foundation; Hon. Fellow, Ford Foundation. *Publications:* has authored several books on Colombia.

SILVA ROSA, Sérgio Ricardo; Brazilian banker and mining industry executive; b. 1959; ed Universidade de São Paulo; joined Caixa de Previdência dos Funcionários do Banco do Brasil (PREVI) (investment fund) as Exec. Dir 2000, Pres. and CEO 2003–10; mem. Bd of Dirs Companhia Vale do Rio Doce (CVRD, now called Vale) 2003–11, Chair. 2003–11; Exec. Officer, Litel Participações SA (Litel); Legislator at Municipality of São Paulo 1995–96; Dir, Brasil Telecom 2000–03, Sauípe SA 2001–, Valepar SA, Associação Brasileira das Entidades de Previdência Privada (ABRAPP); Pres. Confederação Nacional dos Bancários (CNB/CUT) 1994–97, 1997–2000; Vice Chair. Brasil Foods SA 2013–15; mem. Exec. Cttee UN's 'Principles for Responsible Investment' programme.

SILVA VAZ DE LIMA, (Maria Osmarina) Marina, BA; Brazilian politician and environmentalist; b. 8 Feb. 1958, Seringal Bagaço, Acre; d. of Pedro Augusto da Silva and Maria Augusta da Silva; m. 1st Raimundo Souza (divorced); one s. one d.; m. 2nd Fábio Vaz de Lima; two d.; ed Fed. Univ. of Acre; Co-founder rubber tapping trade union with Chico Mendes 1984; mem. Partido dos Trabalhadores (PT) 1985–2009, Nat. Sec. for Environment and Devt 1995–97; secondary school history teacher, Rio Branco 1985–87; Visiting Lecturer, Fed. Univ. of Acre 1986; Councillor, Rio Branco Municipal Govt 1988–90; State Deputy, Acre 1990–94; Senator for Acre 1995–2002, re-elected 2003; Minister of the Environment 2003–08; joined Partido Verde (Green Party) 2009, unsuccessful cand. for Pres. of Brazil 2010; f. Rede Sustentabilidade (Sustainability Network) party 2013; cand. for Vice-Pres. of Brazil for Partido Socialista Brasileiro (Brazilian Socialist Party) 2014, then cand. for Pres. after death of presidential cand. Eduardo Campos; mem. Editorial Bd Esquerda 21 magazine; Hon. Citizen of São Paulo 1995, Hon. Assoc., Chico Mendes Foundation 2001; Order of Merit, Belo Horizonte Council 1995; Goldman Environmental Prize 1996, named as one of UNEP's 25 Women Environmental Leaders 1997, Woman of the Year, Nat. Women's Council of Brazil 1998, Almirante Tamandaré Medal, Brazilian Navy 1999, Jorge Marskell Award 1999, FASE Prize 2001, named by UNEP a Champion of the Earth 2007; numerous other environmental awards. *Address:* Partido Socialista Brasileiro, SCLN 304,

Bloco A, Sobreloja 1, Entrada 63, 70736-510 Brasília, DF, Brazil (office). *Telephone:* (61) 3327-6405 (office). *E-mail:* psb@psbnacional.org.br (office). *Website:* www.psbnacional.org.br (office).

SILVEIRA GODINHO, José António da; Portuguese fmr politician, economist and business executive; b. 16 Oct. 1943, Lisbon; s. of Raul Catarino Godinho and Angela da Silveira Godinho; m. Isabel Maria Canhoto Segura de Faria 1972; three s.; ed Lisbon Tech. Univ.; Asst Prof. Lisbon School of Econs 1967–77; Sr Vice-Pres. Banco de Portugal 1975–79, mem. Bd of Dirs 2004–; mem. Man. Bd Banco Pinto & Sotto Mayor 1979–82; Sec. of State for Finance 1980–81; mem. Exec. Bd Banco Espírito Santo 1982–93; Sec. of State for Nat. Defence 1986–87; Minister of Internal Affairs 1987–90; Amb. to OECD 1993–96; mem. Bd of Dirs Espírito Santo, Ca. de Seguros SA 1996–, AdvanceCare, SA 1999–; mem. Gen. Council Asscn of Portuguese Economists 1999–. *Leisure interests:* reading, travelling, music, sport. *Address:* c/o Board of Directors, Banco de Portugal, R. do Ouro, 148, 1100-150 Lisbon, Portugal (office).

SILVER, Joan Micklin, BA; American film and theatre director and screenwriter; b. 24 May 1935, Omaha, Neb.; d. of Maurice Micklin and Doris Shoshone; m. Raphael Silver 1956; three d.; ed Sarah Lawrence Coll.; began career as writer for educational films; original screenplay for Limbo purchased by Universal Pictures; commissioned by Learning Corpn of America to write and direct short narrative film The Immigrant Experience 1972 and wrote and dir two children's films for same co.; Dir plays: Album and Maybe I'm Doing it Wrong; also Dir for TV. *Films include:* Hester Street (dir and screenplay), Between the Lines (dir), On the Yard (producer), Head Over Heels (dir and screenplay, retitled Chilly Scenes of Winter), Crossing Delancey (dir), Loverboy (dir), Big Girls Don't Cry, They Get Even (dir), Fish in the Bathtub 1997. *Television includes:* Bernice Bobs Her Hair (dir and screenplay), A Private Matter (dir) 1992, In the Presence of Mine Enemies (dir) 1996, Invisible Child (dir) 1998, Charms for the Easy Life (dir) 2002, Hunger Point (dir) 2003. *Radio:* Great Jewish Short Stories from Eastern Europe and Beyond (dir) 1995. *Address:* Silverfilm Productions Inc., 510 Park Avenue, Suite 9B, New York, NY 10022-1105, USA (home). *E-mail:* jmicksil@aol.com (office).

SILVER, Joel; American film producer; b. 14 July 1952, South Orange, NJ; m. Karyn Fields; one s.; ed Tisch School of Arts, New York Univ.; fmrly Asst to Lawrence Gordon, Pres. Lawrence Gordon Productions; producer, Vice-Pres. Universal Pictures; currently runs Silver Pictures 1985– and (with Robert Zemeckis) Dark Castle Entertainment 1999–. *Films:* The Warrior 1979, Xanadu 1980, 48 Hours 1982, Jekyll & Hyde... Together Again 1982, Streets of Fire 1984, Brewster's Millions 1985, Weird Science 1985, Commando 1985, Jumpin' Jack Flash 1986, Lethal Weapon 1986, Predator 1987, Action Jackson 1988, Die Hard 1988, Lethal Weapon 2 1989, Roadhouse 1989, Ford Fairlane 1990, Die Hard 2 1990, Predator 2 1990, Hudson Hawk 1991, Ricochet 1991, The Last Boy Scout 1991, Lethal Weapon 3 1992, Demolition Man 1993, The Hudsucker Proxy, Richie Rich 1994, Demon Knight 1994, Assassins 1995, Fair Game 1995, Executive Decision 1996, Conspiracy Theory, Father's Day, Lethal Weapon 4 1998, Romeo Must Die 1999, Made Men 1999, The Matrix 1999, The House on Haunted Hill 1999, Romeo Must Die 2000, Dungeons & Dragons 2000, Ritual 2001, Exit Wounds 2001, Proximity 2001, Swordfish 2001, Thir13en Ghosts 2001, Ghost Ship 2002, Cradle 2 the Grave 2003, The Animatrix: Final Flight of the Osiris 2003, The Matrix Reloaded 2003, The Matrix Revolutions 2003, Gothika 2003, Kiss, Kiss, Bang, Bang 2005, V for Vendetta 2005, The Reaping 2007, The Invasion 2007, The Brave One 2007, Fred Claus 2007, Speed Racer 2008, RocknRolla 2008, Orphan 2009, Whiteout 2009, Ninja Assassin 2009, Sherlock Holmes 2009, The Book of Eli 2010, The Losers 2010, Unknown 2011, Sherlock Holmes: A Game of Shadows 2011, The Apparition 2012, Dragon Eyes 2012, Stash House 2012, The Factory 2012, Enemies Closer 2013, Non-Stop 2014, The Nice Guys 2016, Collide 2016, Superfly 2018. *Television:* Tales from the Crypt, Two Fisted Tales, Parker Can, W.E.I.R.D. World, Freedom, Next Action Star, Veronica Mars 2004–07, Moonlight 2007–08. *Address:* Silver Pictures, c/o Warner Bros Pictures, 4000 Warner Boulevard, Building 90, Burbank, CA 91522-0001, USA.

SILVER, (Sidney Alexander) Sandy, BEduc; Canadian politician and fmr teacher; *Premier of Yukon;* b. 15 Oct. 1969, Antigonish, Nova Scotia; ed St Francis Xavier Univ., Univ. of Maine, USA; fmr Head, Math. Dept, Robert Service School, Dawson City; mem. Yukon Legis. Ass. for Klondike 2011–, mem. Standing Cttee on Public Accounts, Standing Cttee on Appointments to Major Govt Bd and Cttees, Mem.s' Services Bd; Premier of Yukon 2016–; mem. Yukon Liberal Party, Leader 2012–; fmr Pres. Dawson City Music Festival. *Address:* Office of the Premier, Administration Bldg, 2071 Second Avenue, POB 2703, Whitehorse, YT Y1A 2C6, Canada (office). *Telephone:* (867) 667-8660 (office). *Fax:* (867) 393-6252 (office). *E-mail:* premier@gov.yk.ca (office). *Website:* www.yukonpremier.ca (office).

SILVERMAN, Benjamin (Ben) Noah, BA; American television executive; *Founder and Chairman, Electus;* b. 15 Aug. 1970, Pittsfield, Mass; s. of Stanley Silverman and Mary Silverman; ed Tufts Univ.; began career as Asst, CBS and Warner Bros; Devt Exec. New World/Marvel Entertainment 1993–95; Head of Packaging Div., William Morris Agency 1995–2002; Founder and CEO Reveille Productions (ind. production and distribution co.) 2002–07; Co-Chair. NBC Entertainment and NBC Universal TV Studio (later Universal Media Studios) 2007–09; Founder and Chair. Electus (multimedia entertainment studio) 2009–; mem. Bd of Govs Cedars-Sinai Hospital; mem. Bd of Dirs Best Buddies; Excellence in Digital Innovation Award, 2014. *Television includes:* Exec. Producer: The Office 2005–13, The Biggest Loser 2005–, Ugly Betty 2006–10, The Tudors 2007–10, Mob Wives 2012–13, Fashion Star 2012–13, Massholes 2012–13, Dog and Beth: On the Hunt 2013, Roll Models 2013, The Hero 2013, Marco Polo 2014, Candid Camera 2014, Southern Justice 2014, Jane the Virgin 2014–15, Fameless 2015, Food Fighters 2015, Casanova 2015. *Website:* www.electus.com (office).

SILVERMAN, Sir Bernard Walter, Kt, BA, BTh, MA, PhD, DPhil, DSc, FRS; British professor of statistics and college president; *Chief Scientific Adviser, Home Office;* b. 22 Feb. 1952, London; s. of Elias Silverman and Helen Silverman; m. Rowena Fowler 1985; one s.; ed City of London School, Jesus Coll., Cambridge; Research Fellow, Jesus Coll., Cambridge 1975–77; Calculator Devt Man., Sinclair Radionics 1976–77; Weir Fellow, Univ. Coll., Oxford 1977–78, also Jr Lecturer, Univ. of Oxford; Lecturer, then Reader, then Prof. of Statistics, Univ. of Bath 1978–93, Head of School of Math. Sciences 1988–91; Prof. of Statistics, Univ. of Bristol 1993–99, Head of Statistics Group 1993–97, 1998–99, Henry Overton Wills Prof. of Math. 1999–2003, Provost Inst. for Advanced Studies 2000–03; Master, St Peter's Coll. Oxford and Prof. of Statistics, Univ. of Oxford 2003–09; Chief Scientific Adviser to the Home Office 2010–; visiting appointments include Dept of Statistics, Princeton Univ., USA 1978, 1979, Univ. of Paris VI 1979, Sonderforschungsbereich 123, Univ. of Heidelberg 1980, Math. Research Center, Univ. of Wisconsin-Madison 1981, Dept of Statistics, Johns Hopkins Univ. 1981, Depts of Statistics and Biostatistics, Univ. of Washington 1984, Univ. of Frankfurt 1984, Univ. of California, San Diego 1985, CSIRO Div. of Math. and Statistics, Canberra, Sydney, Melbourne and Perth, Australia 1985, Math. Sciences Research Inst., Berkeley, Calif. 1991, Dept of Linguistics and English Language, Univ. of Lancaster; Fellow, Center for Advanced Study in the Behavioral Sciences, Stanford, Calif. 1997–98; Chartered Statistician, Royal Statistical Soc., mem. Research Section Cttee 1979–82, mem. Council 1982–90, Hon. Sec. 1984–90, mem. Working Party on Official Statistics, Chair. Research Section 1991–93, Pres. 2010; Fellow, Inst. of Math. Statistics 1987, mem. Council 1991–94, 1997–2000, Pres. 2000–01, Acad. of Social Sciences 2014; Fellow, Int. Statistical Inst./Bernoulli Soc. 1986, mem. Bernoulli Soc. European Regional Cttee 1986–92 Chair. 1988–90, mem. Bernoulli Soc. Council 1999–2003; Assoc. Fellow, Green Templeton Coll., Oxford; Fellow, Royal Soc. 1997, mem. Council 2009–10, mem. several cttees, including Research Grants Cttee A 1997–2000 (Chair. 1999–2000), Sectional Cttee 1 1998–2001 (Chair. 2001), Conf. Grants Cttee 1998–2001, Dorothy Hodgkin Fellowships Cttee A 1999–2004 (Chair. 2003), Wolfson Merit Awards Cttee 2006–09; Ed. Oxford University Press Statistical Science Series 1983–87, International Statistical Review 1991–96, Chapman & Hall Monographs on Statistics and Applied Probability 1985–97, Interdisciplinary Statistics Series 1993–97, Wiley Statistics Series 1997–2001, IMS Bulletin 2002–06, Cambridge University Press Statistics Series 2003–10, Annals of Statistics 2007–09; Assoc. Ed. Annals of Statistics 1982–85, Journal of the Royal Statistical Society, Series B 1980–84; Sr Ed. Statistics and Computing 1990–2005; mem. Editorial Bd Inverse Problems 1998–2000; mem. Founding Editorial Cttee Annual Review of Statistics and Its Application 2012–; mem. Science and Eng Research Council Statistics Panel 1990–94; frequent reviewer for US NSF, Natural Sciences and Eng Research Council of Canada, Australian Research Council, etc. Eng and Physical Sciences Research Council Math. Coll. 1994–97, 2000–03; mem. Scientific Cttee, EURANDOM, Netherlands 1997–2003, Statistics Research Assessment Panel for Higher Educ. Funding Council for England (HEFCE) Research Assessment Exercise 2001, Scientific Steering Cttee, Isaac Newton Inst. 2003–06, Steering Group, Int. Review of UK Math. 2003–04 (Chair. Subpanel 22 (Statistics) and mem. Panel F (Math.)), HEFCE Research Assessment Exercise 2008; Patron Royal Inst. Wessex Math. Master Classes; Chair. Jt Math. Council of the UK 2003–06, UK Math. Trust 2004–08; consultant to UK Govt Inquiry (the 'Lessons Learned' Inquiry) into the Foot and Mouth Epidemic 2002, Statistics Commission 2003; consultancies with Nuclear Electric, Nat. Audit Office, Ministry of Defence, Agilent Technologies, Mass Spec Analytical Ltd; mem. Advisory Bd Statistics Dept, Carnegie-Mellon Univ. 2002, Academic Chair. 2006; mem. GM Science Review Panel 2002–03, Owner's Advisory Bd (non-exec. dir) Defence Analytical Services Agency 1998–2009; Chair. Peer Review Panel on the Project for the Sustainable Devt of Heathrow 2005–06; mem. Academia Europaea 2001; ordained deacon (Church of England) 1999–, priest 2000–; Hon. Fellow, Jesus Coll., Cambridge 2003, St Chad's Coll., Durham 2014; Dr hc (Univ. of St Andrews) 2014; First Prize, Int. Math. Olympiad 1970, Mayhew Prize for Math. Tripos Part III, Univ. of Cambridge 1974, Smith's Prize, Univ. of Cambridge 1976, Guy Medal in Bronze, Royal Statistical Soc. 1984, Guy Medal in Silver 1995, Special Invited Paper, Inst. of Math. Statistics 1985, Technometrics Special Discussion Paper, American Statistical Asscn 1988, Pres.' Award, American Statistical Asscn, Inst. of Math. Statistics, Biometric Soc. (ENAR and WNAR) and Statistical Soc. of Canada for "the outstanding statistician under forty" (COPSS Award) 1991, Fulkerson Lecturer, Cornell Univ. 1993, Special Invited Paper, Inst. of Math. Statistics 1999, Henri Willem Methorst Medal, Int. Statistical Inst. 1999, Corcoran Lecturer, Univ. of Oxford 2000, Original Mem. Highly Cited Researchers database, Information Sciences Inst. 2002. *Publications include:* Density Estimation for Statistics and Data Analysis 1986, Industrial Quality and Productivity with Statistical Methods: A Joint Symposium of the Royal Society and the Royal Statistical Society (co-ed.) 1989, Nonparametric Regression and Generalized Linear Models: A Roughness Penalty Approach (with P. J. Green) 1994, Functional Data Analysis (with J. O. Ramsay) 1997, (revised and expanded second edn 2005), Wavelets: The Key to Intermittent Information? (co-ed.) 2000, Applied Functional Data Analysis (with J. O. Ramsay) 2002; more than 80 papers in peer-reviewed journals and numerous research contribs and govt reports. *Website:* www.gov.uk/government/people/bernard-silverman (office); www.bernardsilverman.com.

SILVERMAN, Fred, MA; American producer and broadcasting executive; *President, Fred Silverman Company;* b. 13 Sept. 1937, New York; m. Cathy Kihn; one s. one d.; ed Syracuse Univ., Ohio State Univ.; with WGN-TV Chicago; exec. position WP1X-TV New York; Dir Daytime Programmes CBS-TV New York, Vice-Pres. Programmes 1970–75; Pres. ABC Entertainment 1975–78; Pres. and CEO NBC 1978–81; ind. film producer 1981–; Pres. The Fred Silverman Co. 1986–. *Address:* Fred Silverman Company, 1648 Mandeville Canyon Road, Los Angeles, CA 90025, USA (office). *Telephone:* (310) 471-4676 (office). *Fax:* (310) 471-3295 (office).

SILVERMAN, Henry Richard, BA, JD; American lawyer and business executive; *Founder and CEO, 54 Madison Partners, LLC;* b. 2 Aug. 1940, New York; s. of Herbert Silverman and Roslyn Silverman (née Moskowitz); m. 1st Susan H. Herson 1965 (divorced 1977); two d.; m. 2nd Nancy Ann Kraner 1978 (divorced); one d.; m. 3rd Karen Hader 2012; one s.; ed Hackley School, Tarrytown, NY, Williams Coll., Univ. of Pennsylvania Law School; with USNR 1965–73; called to Bar NY 1965; with US Tax Court 1965; with US Court of Appeals 1965; law practice 1965–66; with White, Weld & Co. 1966; Gen. Pnr, Oppenheimer & Co. 1966–70; Pres., CEO ITI Corpn 1970–72; f., Pres. Trans-York Securities Corpn 1972; CEO Vavasseur America Ltd 1974–75; Gen. Pnr,Brisbane Pnrs 1976–77; prin. in various investment groups 1977–, Silverman Energy Co. 1977, NBC Channel 20 1977–83, ABC Channel 9 1977–81, Delta Queen Steamboat 1977–86, also Dir; apptd Pres., CEO Reliance Capital Corpn (subsidiary Reliance Group Holdings Inc.) 1982, Sr Vice-Pres. Business Devt Reliance Group Holdings Inc.

1982–90; Gen. Pnr, Blackstone Group 1990–91; Founder, Chair., CEO HFS Inc. 1990–97; CEO Cendant Corpn 1997–2005, Pres. 1997–2004, Chair. 1998–2005 (co. split into four separate cos including Realogy), Chair. and CEO Realogy Corpn 2004–07, Chair. 2007; Vice-Chair. and COO, Apollo Global Man. 2007–11; Sr Advisor and Vice-Chair. Investment Man. Business, Guggenheim Partners 2012, Global Head, Real Estate and Infrastructure 2013–15; Founder and CEO 54 Madison Partners, LLC 2014–; Chair. Business Roundtable's Fiscal Policy Task Force; Dir NY Univ. Hosp. 1987–, New York Univ. Child Study Center; Commr and Vice-Chair. Port Authority of New York and New Jersey 2002–12; Trustee, New York Univ. (NYU) Langone Medical Center; mem. JP Morgan's Nat. Advisory Bd, G-100; American Heritage Award, Anti-Defamation League 1998, Jackie Robinson Foundation award 2001, US Hispanic Chamber of Commerce award 2003. *Leisure interest:* tennis. *Address:* 54 Madison Partners, LLC, 520 Madison Avenue, New York, NY 07054, USA (office). *Telephone:* (212) 468-5000 (office). *Fax:* (212) 468-5099 (office). *E-mail:* info@54madison.com (office). *Website:* www.54madison.com (office).

SILVERMAN, Marcia, MEconSc; American business executive; one s.; ed Univ. of Pennsylvania; fmr employee Nat. Labour Relations Bd; worked in Public Relations Div., J. Walter Thompson 1978–81; joined Washington office, Ogilvy & Mather Public Affairs 1981, Head of Washington Office 1990–2000; Pres. of the Americas, Ogilvy Public Relations Worldwide 2000–02, CEO 2002–10, apptd CEO Ogilvy PR 2010; mem. Faculty, Georgetown Univ. School of Continuing Studies; Public Relations Star Award, Inside PR.

SILVERSTONE, Alicia; American actress; b. 4 Oct. 1976, San Francisco, Calif.; d. of Monty Silverstone and Didi Silverstone; m. Christopher Jarecki 2005, one s.; stage debut in play Carol's Eve at Met Theatre, LA; starred in three Aerosmith videos including Cryin'; starred in various TV commercials; Broadway debut with The Graduate 2002; f. First Kiss Productions (production co.); Heart of Green Award 2009, Voice of Compassion Award 2010. *Films:* The Crush (MTV Award for Best Villain, for Breakthrough Performance 1994) 1993, The Babysitter 1995, True Crime 1995, Le Nouveau Monde 1995, Hideaway 1995, Clueless (National Board of Review Award for Best Breakthrough Performance 1995) 1995, Batman and Robin 1997, Excess Baggage (also producer) 1997, Free Money 1998, Love's Labour's Lost 1999, Blast from the Past 1999, Rock My World 2002, Scorched 2003, Scooby Doo 2: Monsters Unleashed 2004, Beauty Shop 2005, Silence Becomes You 2005, Alex Rider: Stormbreaker 2006, The Art of Getting By 2011, Butter 2011, Vamps 2012, Ass Backwards 2013, Angels in Stardust 2014, King Cobra 2016, Catfight 2016, Diary of A Wimpy Kid: The Long Haul 2017, The Killing of A Sacred Deer 2017, Book Club 2018, The Lodge 2019. *Plays:* Carol's Eve 1993, Scorched 2003, Boston Marriage 2007, Time Stands Still 2009–10, The Performers 2012, Of Good Stock 2015. *Television includes:* Torch Song 1993, Shattered Dreams 1993, The Cool and the Crazy 1994, The Wonder Years 1997, Bareface (series) (also exec. producer) 2001–03, Miss Match (series) 2003, Pink Collar 2006, The Singles Table (series) 2007, Bad Mother's Handbook 2008, Suburgatory (series) 2012, HR 2014, American Woman (series) 2018. *Publications:* The Kind Diet (with Victoria Pearson) 2009, The Kind Mama 2014. *Website:* thekindlife.com.

SILVESTRINI, HE Cardinal Achille; Italian ecclesiastic; *Prefect Emeritus, Congregation for Oriental Churches, Roman Curia;* b. 25 Oct. 1923, Brisighella; ordained priest 1946, consecrated Bishop 1979, elected Archbishop of Novaliciana, Mauritania 1979; Sec. Council for Public Affairs of the Church 1979; cr. Cardinal-Deacon of S. Benedetto fuori Porta S. Paolo 1988–99, Cardinal-Priest of S. Benedetto fuori Porta S. Paolo 1999–; Prefect of the Supreme Tribunal of the Apostolic Signatura 1988–91; Prefect of the Congregation for Oriental Churches, 1991–2000, Prefect Emer. and Grand Chancellor of the Pontifical Eastern Inst. 2000–; mem. Congregation for the Doctrine of the Faith, for the Oriental Churches, for the Causes of the Saints, for the Bishops, for the Evangelization of Peoples, for Catholic Educ.; mem. Pontificial Council for the Interpretation of Legislative Texts, for Inter-Religious Dialogue. *Address:* Palazzina della Zecca, 00120 Vatican City, Italy (home). *Telephone:* (06) 69884838 (home). *Fax:* (06) 69881311. *E-mail:* asilvestrini@org.va (office).

SILVESTROV, Valentin Vasilyevich; Ukrainian composer; b. 30 Sept. 1937, Kiev; ed Kiev State Conservatory, studied with Boris Lyatoshinsky and Lev Revutsky; took courses at an evening music school while training to become a civil engineer 1955–58; compositions performed in USSR and numerous countries in Europe and in USA; Visiting Composer, Almeida Music Festival, London 1989, Gidon Kremer's Lockenhaus Festival, Austria 1990, and at other festivals in Denmark, Finland, and the Netherlands; Visiting Fellow, German Academic Exchange Service, Berlin 1998–99; S. Koussevitsky Prize (USA) 1967, Prize of Gaudeamus Soc. (Netherlands) 1970. *Compositions include:* five symphonies for large symphony orchestra 1963–82, Symphony for baritone with orchestra Echo Momentum on verses of A. Pushkin 1987, Sixth Symphony 2002, Symphony No. 7 2002–03, Symphony No. 8 2016, string quartets 1978, 1988, Dedication – symphony for violin and orchestra 1991, Mertamusica for piano and orchestra 1992, numerous chamber ensembles, piano pieces, vocal cycles, choruses, Metamusic 1993, Dedication for violin and orchestra 1993. *Address:* Entuziastov str. 35/1, Apt. 49, 252147 Kiev, Ukraine (home). *Telephone:* (44) 517-04-47 (home).

SILVIA, HM The Queen of Sweden; b. (Silvia Renate Sommerlath), 23 Dec. 1943, Heidelberg, Germany; d. of Walther Sommerlath and Alice Toledo; m. King Carl XVI Gustaf 1976; two d., Crown Princess Victoria Ingrid Alice Désirée b. 14 July 1977, Princess Madeleine Thérèse Amelie Josephine b. 10 June 1982; one s., Prince Carl Philip Edmund Bertil b. 13 May 1979; ed Munich School of Interpreting; lived in São Paulo, Brazil 1947–57, returned to FRG 1957; fmr mem. staff Argentine Consulate, Munich; mem. Organizing Cttee, Munich Olympics 1971–73, Deputy Head of Protocol, Organizing Cttee, Winter Olympics, Innsbruck, Austria 1973; Chair. Royal Wedding Fund, Jubilee Fund; est. Silvia Home, Drottningholm; Patron First World Congress Against Commercial Sexual Exploitation of Children, Stockholm 1996; f. World Childhood Foundation; Hon. mem. Menton Foundation, Swedish Amateur Athletic Asscn, Children's Cancer Foundation of Sweden, Swedish Save the Children Fed.; Royal Order of the Seraphim 1976; Royal Family Order of King Carl XVI Gustaf of Sweden 1976; HM King Carl XVI Gustaf 50th Anniversary Medal 1996; Commemorative Ruby Jubilee Medal of HM The King 2013; Grand Cross, Order of the Southern Cross (Brazil); Grand Cross with Collar, Order of the White Rose of Finland; Grand Croix, Légion d'honneur; Grand Cross, Order of Merit of FRG; Grand Cordon, Order of the Precious Crown (Japan); Kt, Order of the Crown of the Realm (Malaysia); Kt Grand Cross, Order of the Netherlands Lion; Grand Cross, Royal Norwegian Order of St Olav; Grand Cross, Order of the White Eagle (Poland); Dame, Order of the Smile (Poland); Cordon, Order of Stara Planina (Bulgaria); Dame Grand Cross (First Class), Order of Chula Chom Klao (Thailand); Grand Cordon, Order of Leopold (Belgium) 1977; Grand Star, Decoration of Honour for Services to the Repub. of Austria 1979; Dame Grand Cross, Order of Isabella the Catholic (Spain) 1979; Kt Grand Cross, Order of the Falcon (Iceland) 1981; Kt, Order of the Elephant (Denmark) 1985; Grand Cross, Order of Christ (Portugal) 1987; Grand Cordon, Supreme Order of the Renaissance (Jordan) 1989; Kt Grand Cross, Order of Merit of the Italian Repub. 1991; Order of the Cross of Terra Mariana, First Class (Estonia) 1995; Commdr, Grand Cross, Order of Three Stars (Latvia) 1995; Grand Cross, Order of Vytautas the Great (Lithuania) 1995; Grand Cross, Order of Honour (Greece) 2008; Kt, Order of the Gold Lion of the House of Nassau (Luxembourg) 2008; Grand Cross, Order of Prince Henry (Portugal) 2008; Grand Cross, Order of the Star of Romania (Romania) 2008; Order of the White Star, First Class (Estonia) 2011; Dr hc (Åbo Univ.) 1990, (Karolinska Institutet) 1993, (Univ. of Linköping) 1994, (Göteborg Univ.) 1999; Deutsche Kulturpreis 1990, Chancellor's Medal, Univ. of Mass, Shaikha Fatima Bint Mubarak Motherhood and Childhood Award (UAE) 2016. *Leisure interests:* theatre, opera, concerts, skiing. *Address:* Royal Court of Sweden, Kungl. Slottet, 107 70 Stockholm, Sweden. *Telephone:* (8) 4026000. *Fax:* (8) 4026062. *E-mail:* info@royalcourt.se. *Website:* www.kungahuset.se.

SIM, Wong Hoo; Singaporean business executive; *Chairman and CEO, Creative Technology Ltd;* ed Ngee Ann Polytechnic; f. Creative Technology Ltd, Singapore 1981, currently Chair. and CEO; f. Creative Labs, USA; launched Sound Blaster PC card 1989, Sound Blaster Pro 1991; Chair. Technopreneurship 21 Pvt. Sector Cttee. *Publication:* Chaotic Thoughts from the Old Millennium. *Address:* Creative Technology Ltd, 31 International Business Park, Creative Resource, 609921, Singapore (office). *Telephone:* 6895-4000 (office). *Fax:* 6895-4999 (office). *Website:* www.creative.com (office).

SIMAI, Mihály; Hungarian economist; *Professor of International Economics, Corvinus University;* b. 4 April 1930, Budapest; s. of Mátyás Simai and Jolán Rosenberg; m. Vera Bence 1953; one d.; ed Univ. of Econs, Budapest; postgraduate studies in Geneva and Paris; Fellow, UN Econ. Comm. for Europe 1959–60, Staff mem. UN Center for Devt Econs, Projections and Policies, New York 1964–68; Prof. of Int. Econs and Nat. Business, Univ. of Econs, Budapest 1971–, Dir of Grad. Studies in Int. Business and Strategy 1987–, in Int. Relations 1991–; Prof. of Int. Econs, Corvinus Univ.; mem. Hungarian Acad. of Sciences, Budapest 1979–, Deputy Dir of Research, Inst. for Econs 1973–87, Dir 1987–91, now Research Prof. Emer.; Pres. Hungarian UN Ass.; Chair. Council UN Univ. 1990–92; Vice-Pres. Int. Studies Asscn 1988–90; fmr Pres. Ed. Cttee Acta Oeconomica; Dir UN Univ. World Inst. for Devt Econs Research 1993–96; mem. Governing Council, Nat. Studies Asscn 1984–90, Advisory Bd for UN TNCs 1990–, Editorial Bd Environmental Econs 1991–; Randolpf Jenkins Fellow, US Inst. for Peace 1991–92; Hon. Pres. World Fed. of UN Asscns 1982–; Labour Order of Merit (Golden Degree), Order of the Star of Hungary (Golden Degree), Order of the Flag of the Hungarian Repub. 1990; UN Meritorious Service Award, Szechenyi Award. *Publications include:* Capital Export in the Contemporary Capitalist System 1962, The World Economic System of Capitalism, 1965, View from the 26th Floor 1969, The United States before the 200th Anniversary 1974, The United Nations and the Global Problems 1977, Interdependence and Conflicts in the World Economy 1981, Economic Decolonization and the Developing Countries 1981, The United Nations Today and Tomorrow 1985, Power, Technology and the World Economy of the 1990s 1990, Foreign Direct Investments in Hungary 1991, The Future of Global Governance: Managing Risk and Change in the International System 1994, International Business Policy 1996, The Democratic Process and the Market (ed.) 1999, The Reintegration of the Former Socialist Countries in Europe, China and Vietnam into the Global Economy 2000, The Ages of Global Transformations 2001, United States in the Global Economy 2005, The World Economy in the Age of Turbulence 2008, Russia between Two Worlds 2011; more than 250 articles on int. econ. and political issues. *Leisure interests:* hiking, skiing. *Address:* Institute for World Economics, Hungarian Academy of Sciences, Budapest 1112, Budaörsi ut 45 (office); Department of World Economy, Corvinus University, 1093 Budapest, Fővám tér 8, Hungary (office). *Telephone:* 30-8487069 (mobile) (office); 20-9179768 (mobile) (office). *Fax:* (1) 309-2624 (office). *E-mail:* mihalysimai@gmail.com (office). *Website:* www.vki.hu (office).

SIMELUM, Maki Stanley, BA, MBOS; Ni-Vanuatu accountant and politician; b. 3 March 1972, Ambrym; ed Malapoa Coll., Univ. of the South Pacific, Univ. of Tech., Australia; Accounts Supervisor, Moore Stephens (accountancy firm), Port Vila 1990–92; Finance Man., Devt Bank of Vanuatu (DBV) 1992–99; Finance and Planning Man., Nat. Bank of Vanuatu 1999–2001; CEO Asset Management Unit (govt agency) 2001–12; mem. Parl. for Ambrym 2012–; Minister of Justice and Social Welfare March–May 2013, of Finance 2013–15; mem. Vanua'aku Pati (VP); fmr Governor Asian Devt Bank. *Address:* Parliament of Vanuatu, PMB 9052, Port Vila, Vanuatu (office). *Telephone:* 33060 (office); 822229 (office).

SIMÉON, Jean-Pierre; French poet, playwright, novelist and artistic director; *Artistic Director, Printemps des poètes;* b. 6 May 1950, Paris (13th arrondissement); taught at Institut universitaire de formation des maîtres, Clermont-Ferrand; contrib. to numerous literary journals (Commune, Jungle, Faites entrer l'infini, Les Cahiers de l'Archipel, etc.); co-directs, with Jean-Marie Barnaud, the collection Grands Fonds at Cheyne éditeur; literary critic and dramatic for l'Humanité; Assoc. Poet, Nat. Drama Centre, Reims for six years; currently at Théâtre Nat. Populaire, Villeurbanne; Artistic Dir Printemps des poètes; Prix Theophile Briant 1978, Prix Maurice-Scève 1981, Grand Prix du Mont-Saint-Michel 1999, Prix Goncourt de la Poésie (Printemps des poètes) 2016. *Publications include:* Traquer la louve 1978, Hypnose du silence 1981, Fuite de l'immobile (Prix Artaud 1984) 1984, Un Essaim amoureux 1986, Passage du Désir 1988, Les Douze louanges 1990, Eva R 1992, Le sentiment du monde (Prix Apollinaire 1994) 1993, Traité de la juste merveille (illustrated by Martine Mellinette) 1996, L'homme clos 1996, Les petits jardins 1996, Poèmes du corps traversé 1998, Matière nuit 1998, Ouvrant le pas 1998, Le sourire du chien 1999, D'entre les morts 2000, Stabat

Mater Furiosa (suivi de) Soliloques 2000, La Lune des pauvres, 2001, Quoique. Chroniques citoyennes 2002, Fresque peinte sur un mur obscur 2002, Charles Juliet, la conquête dans l'obscur 2003, Sermons joyeux (De la lente corruption des âmes dans la nuit tombante) 2004, Lettre à la femme aimée au sujet de la mort (Prix Max-Jacob 2006) 2005, Le bois de hêtres, précédé de Le sentiment du monde, suivi de La question et la preuve 2005, Algues, sable, coquillages et crevettes: Lettre d'un poète a des comédiens et a quelques autres passeurs 2006, Le Petit Ordinaire (Cabaret macabre) 2006, Odyssée, dernier chant 2006, Témoins à charge: Ou La comparution d'Eros et Thanatos devant les hommes 2007, Quel théâtre pour aujourd'hui? 2007, Usages du poème 2008, Philoctète 2009, Le Testament de Vanda 2009, Traité des sentiments contraires 2011, Théâtre 1999–2004 2013, La poésie sauvera le monde 2015; for children: À l'aube du buisson 1985, La nuit respire 1987, L'étrange, curieuse, bizzare, étonnante, stupéfiante, inquiétante, fabuleuse et véridique histoire de Népomucène, d'Iphigénie et du poivron flottant (with Anne Siméon, Stéphane Queyriaux and Frédéric Siméon) 1995, Contes et légendes d'Auvergne 1996, La Mouche qui lit (illustrated by Isabelle Simon) 1998, Un homme sans manteau 2000, Sans frontières fixes 2001, Aïe! Un poète (illustrated by Nicole Claveloux, Henri Galeron and Tina Mercié) 2003, Ceci est un poème qui guérit les poissons (illustrated by Olivier Tallec) 2005, Ici 2009. *Address:* c/o Jean-François Manier and Martine Mellinette, Cheyne éditeur, 43400 Le Chambon-sur-Lignon, France. *Telephone:* (4) 71-59-76-46. *Fax:* (4) 71-65-89-00. *E-mail:* cheyne-editeur@wanadoo.fr. *Website:* www .cheyne-editeur.com.

SIMEONOV, Valeri; Bulgarian engineer and politician; *Deputy Prime Minister for Economic and Demographic Policy;* b. 14 March 1955, Dolni Chiflik; widower; two c.; ed Sofia Tech. Univ.; began career as Asst Tech. Man., Transstroy (civil eng and construction co.); three years as electromechanic on board Atlantic Ocean fishing trawlers; f. SKAT cable network, Burgas 1992, also SKAT TV (cable TV co.) 1994; Chair. Burgas municipal council 2007–09; mem. Nat. Ass. (Parl.) for 2–Burgas 2014–17; Deputy Prime Minister for Econ. and Demographic Policy 2017–; apptd Head, Bulgarian Council on Ethnic Minority Integration 2017; mem. Ataka (Attack) Party 2005–09; co-f. Natsionalen Front za Spasenie na Bulgaria (Nat. Front for the Salvation of Bulgaria) 2011–, currently Pres.; Medal of Honour of the Repub. of Armenia. *Address:* Office of the Council of Ministers, 1594 Sofia 1, bul. Dondukov 1, Bulgaria (office). *Telephone:* (2) 940-29-99 (office). *Fax:* (2) 980-21-01 (office). *E-mail:* gis@government.bg (office). *Website:* www.government.bg (office).

SIMHON, Shalom, BA; Israeli politician, social worker and business executive; *Chairman, Demeter-AWE Holdings, Ltd;* b. 1956, Kfar Saba; m.; two c.; ed Univ. of Haifa; Sergeant Maj. in Israel Defence Forces; Exec. Dir Youth Section, Moshav Movt 1985–91, Chair. Social Dept 1991–93, Pension Fund 1993–2001, Sec.-Gen. 1993–2001; mem. Knesset (Labour Party) 1996–2011, (Ha'atzmaut) 2011–13; Chair. Agric. Cttee 1996; mem. Econ. Cttee and Finance Cttee 1996–2002 (Chair. 2003–04); Chair. Finance Cttee 1999; Minister of Agric. and Rural Devt 2001–03, 2006–11, of the Environment 2005–06, of Industry, Trade and Labour 2011–13, also Minister of Minority Affairs 2011–13; Sec.-Gen. Agricultural Centre 1997–2001; fmr Chair. Bd of Tnuva (food conglomerate); Co-founder and Chair. Demeter-AWE Holdings, Ltd (consulting and investment firm) 2013–. *Address:* Demeter-AWE Holdings, Ltd, 3 Rothschild Bld, Tel-Aviv 66881, Israel (office). *E-mail:* info@demeter-awe.com (office). *Website:* www.demeter-awe.com (office).

SIMIĆ, Charles, BA; American poet, writer and academic; *Professor Emeritus of English, University of New Hampshire;* b. 9 May 1938, Belgrade, Yugoslavia (now Serbia); s. of George Simic and Helen Matijevich; m. Helen Dubin 1965; one s. one d.; ed Oak Park High School, Chicago, Univ. of Chicago, New York Univ.; arrived in USA 1954; army service 1961–64; worked for Chicago Sun-Times as proofreader; later business Man. Aperture Magazine 1966–69; Lecturer, Calif. State Univ., Hayward 1970–73; Assoc. Prof., later Prof. of English, Univ. of New Hampshire 1973, now Prof. Emer.; elected a Chancellor of Acad. of American Poets 2000; Poet Laureate of USA 2007–08; PEN Int. Award for Translation 1970, 1980, Guggenheim Fellowship 1972, Nat. Endowment for the Arts Fellowships 1974, 1979, Edgar Allan Poe Award 1975, American Acad. of Arts and Letters Award 1976, Harriet Monroe Poetry Award 1980, Fulbright Fellowship 1982, Ingram Merrill Foundation Fellowship 1983, John D. and Catherine T. MacArthur Foundation Fellowship 1984, Acad. of American Poets Fellowship 1998, Wallace Stevens Award 2007, Frost Medal 2011, Vilcek Prize in Literature 2011, The Zbigniew Herbert Int. Literary Award 2014, Golden Wreath of the Struga Poetry Evenings 2017. *Publications include:* poetry: What the Grass Says 1967, Somewhere Among Us A Stone Is Taking Notes 1969, Dismantling the Silence 1971, White 1972, Return to a Place Lit by a Glass of Milk 1974, Biography and a Lament 1976, Charon's Cosmology 1977, Brooms: Selected Poems 1978, School for Dark Thoughts 1978, Classic Ballroom Dances 1980, Shaving at Night 1982, Austerities 1982, Weather Forecast for Utopia and Vicinity: Poems 1967–82 1983, The Chicken Without a Head 1983, Selected Poems 1985, Unending Blues 1986, The World Doesn't End (prose poems) (Pulitzer Prize for Poetry 1990) 1989, In the Room We Share 1990, The Book of Gods and Devils 1990, Selected Poems: 1963–83 1990, Hotel Insomnia 1992, A Wedding in Hell 1994, Walking the Black Cat 1996, Jackstraws 1999, Night Picnic 2001, The Voice at 3:00AM 2003, Selected Poems 1963–2003 (Griffin Int. Poetry Prize) 2005, That Little Something 2008, Sixty Poems 2008, Monster Loves His Labyrinth 2008, The Renegade: Writings on Poetry and a Few Other Things 2009, Master of Disguises 2010, The Horse Has Six Legs: An Anthology of Serbian Poetry 2010, Confessions of a Poet Laureate 2010, New and Selected Poems 1962–2012 2013, The Lunatic 2015, Scribbled in the Dark 2017; prose: The Uncertain Certainty 1985, Wonderful Words, Silent Truth 1990, Dimestore Alchemy 1992, The Unemployed Fortune Teller 1994, Orphan Factory (essays) 1997, A Fly in the Soup 2000, The Renegade: Writings on Poetry and a Few Other Things 2009, Dime-Store Alchemy: The Art of Joseph Cornell 2011, The Life of Images: Selected Prose 2015; ed.: Another Republic: 17 European and South American Writers (with Mark Strand) 1976, The Essential Campion 1988, The Best American Poetry 1992; many trans of French, Serbian, Croatian, Macedonian and Slovenian poetry. *Address:* Department of English, University of New Hampshire, 229 Hamilton Smith Hall, 95 Main Street, Durham, NH 03824, USA (office). *Telephone:* (603) 862-3991 (office). *Fax:* (603) 862-3563 (office). *E-mail:* charles.simic@unh.edu (office). *Website:* cola.unh.edu/english (office).

SIMIĆ, Slavko; Kosovo politician; *Vice-President, Kosovo Assembly;* b. 29 June 1984; m.; ed Faculty of Sports and Physical Educ.; fmr Leader of SL deputies in Kosovo Ass., currently mem. Cttee on Rights, Interests of Communities and Returns, Vice-Pres. Kosovo Ass. 2017–; Leader of Srpska Lista (SL—Serb List) (coalition of reps of local brs of Serb groups, including Srpski Pokret Obnove (SPO—Serbian Renewal Movt) and Socijaldemokratska Partija Srbije (SPS—Social Democratic Party of Serbia, fmrly Srpska Lista za Kosovo i Metohiju (Serb List for Kosovo and Metohija)) 2015–17. *Address:* Srpska Lista (Serb List), Mitrovica, Kosovo (office). *Telephone:* (49) 568832 (office). *E-mail:* medjusobnopostovanje@gmail.com (office). *Website:* www.kuvendikosoves.org/?cid=2,102,861 (office).

SIMICSKÓ, István, LLD, PhD; Hungarian lawyer and politician; b. 29 Nov. 1961, Tiszalök; m.; three c.; ed Coll. of Commerce, Catering and Tourism, Eötvös Loránd Univ., Zrínyi Miklós Nat. Defence Univ.; mem. Nat. Ass. for Újbuda (Budapest constituency XVI) 1998–, Deputy Chair. Nat. Defence Cttee, mem. Foreign Affairs Cttee 1998–2000, Chair. Nat. Security Cttee 2006–10; Sec. of State for Civil Service/Nat. Security 2000–02, Sec. of State for Defence 2010–12, Sec. of State for Sports in Ministry of Human Resources 2012–15, Minister of Defence 2015–18; Lecturer, Nat. Univ. of Public Service 2010–; mem. Fidesz—Magyar Polgári Szöevetség (Fed. of Young Democrats—Hungarian Civic Alliance) 1998–2006; mem. Kereszténydemokrata Néppárt (KDNP, Christian Democratic People's Party) 2006–; mem. Hungarian Asscn of Mil. Science 1993–. *Leisure interest:* Chinese martial arts. *Address:* c/o Ministry of Defence, 1055 Budapest, Balaton u. 7–11, Hungary (office).

SIMION, Eugen Ioan, PhD; Romanian literary critic; *President, Department of Literature and Philology, Romanian Academy;* b. 25 May 1933, Chiojdeanca, Prahova Co.; s. of Dragomir Simion and Sultana Simion; m. Adriana Manea 1957; one d.; ed I. L.Caragiale High School, Ploiesti, Faculty of Philology, Bucharest Univ.; Researcher, Romanian Acad. 1957–62, Corresp. mem. 1991, mem. 1992, Vice-Pres. 1994–98, Pres. 1998–2006, Pres. Dept of Literature and Philology 2006–; Ed. Gazeta literară 1962–68; Asst Lecturer, Bucharest Univ. 1964, Assoc. Prof. 1971, Prof. of Romanian Literature 1990–; Visiting Prof., Sorbonne, Paris 1970–73; Dir Caiete critice (cultural review) 1991–; mem. Bd Romanian Writers' Union; Vice-Pres. Intergovernmental Cttee for the World Decade for Cultural Devt—UNESCO 1992, then Pres.; Pres. Nat. Council for the Certification of Diplomas and Univ. Certificates; mem. Academia Europaea 1992–, Acad. of Sciences of Moldavia 1999, Int. Union of Literary Critics; Dr hc (Jassy, Galati, Târgoviste, Arad); prizes of Romanian Writers' Union (five times), Prize of Romanian Acad. 1977. *Publications include:* Eminescu's Fiction 1964, Trends in Today's Literature 1965, E Lovinescu the Sceptic Saved 1971, The Romanian Writers Today Vol. I 1974, Vol. II 1976, Vol. III 1983, Vol. IV 1989; A Time to Live, a Time to Confess (Paris Diary), The Morning of Poets 1980, Defying Rhetoric 1985, Mercutio's Death 1993, Talking to Petru Dumitriu 1994, Mircea Eliade, A Spirit Amplitude 1995, The Return of the Author 1996, Critical Fragments I–IV 1998–2000; more than 3000 articles. *Address:* Romanian Academy, Calea Victoriei 125, Sector 1, 010071 Bucharest (office); Dr Lister 8, Bucharest, Romania (home). *Telephone:* (1) 2128640 (office); (1) 4109748 (home). *Fax:* (1) 2116608 (office); (1) 3365855 (home). *E-mail:* eugen.simion@fnsa.ro (office); mdc@rnc.ro (home).

SIMITIS, Constantine (Costas), DJur; Greek lawyer and politician; b. 23 June 1936, Athens; s. of George Simitis and Fani Cristopoulou; m. Daphne Arkadiou; two c.; ed Univ. of Marburg and London School of Econs; lawyer at Supreme Court 1961–; taught in W German univs 1971–75; Prof. of Commercial Law, Univ. of Athens 1977; mem. Nat. Council of Panhellenic Liberation Movt (PAK) during colonels' dictatorship, mem. Pasok 1974–, mem. Cen. Cttee of Pasok, Pres. 1996–2004; mem. Parl. 1985–2004; Minister of Agric. 1981–85, of Nat. Economy 1985–87, of Educ. and Religious Affairs 1989–90, of Industry, Energy, Tech. and Trade 1993–95; Prime Minister of Greece 1996–2004. *Publications include:* Politics is a Creative Greece 1996–2004 2005, Objectives, Strategies and Prospects 2007, Democracy in Crisis? 2007, The Crisis 2008, The Derailment 2012; numerous articles on legal and econ. topics. *Address:* Akademias 35, Athens 10672, Greece. *Telephone:* (210) 3708213. *Fax:* (210) 3708220. *E-mail:* contact@costas-simitis.gr. *Website:* www.costas-simitis.gr.

ŠIMKO, Ivan, IngEcon, DIur; Slovak politician; b. 1 Jan. 1955, Bratislava; m.; four c.; ed Univ. of Econs, Bratislava, Comenius Univ., Bratislava; mem. staff, Inst. for Planning, Bratislava 1978–79, Dept of Chief Architect, Bratislava 1979–89; Adviser to Deputy Prime Minister 1990; mem. Parl. 1990–; Founding mem. Christian Democratic Movt (KDH) 1990–2000, left to co-found Slovak Democratic and Christian Union 2000–04, returned to KDH 2010–; Vice-Chair. Legis. Council 1992; Minister of Justice 1992; Deputy Prime Minister 1994; mem. Nat. Council for the Slovak Repub. 1994–2001, 2003–06; Minister of the Interior 2001–02, of Defence 2002–03; Founder Slobodné fórum (SF—Free Forum Party) 2004, left to form Mission 21 – New Christian Democracy 2004–10; mem. Nat. Council Cttee for Constitutional Law. *Leisure interests:* sport, literature. *Address:* KDH, Bajkalská 25, 821 01 Bratislava, Slovakia (office). *Telephone:* (2) 58233431 (office). *Fax:* (2) 58233434 (office). *E-mail:* sekretariat@kdh.sk (office). *Website:* kdh.sk (office).

SIMMA, Bruno, DJur; German lawyer, academic and judge; *Professor of Law, University of Michigan;* b. 29 March 1941, Quierschied, Saar; ed Univ. of Innsbruck; called to the Bar, Innsbruck 1967; Asst, Faculty of Law, Univ. of Innsbruck 1967–72; Expert, Directorate of Legal Affairs, Council of Europe 1972; Prof. of Int. Law and EC Law, Univ. of Munich 1973–2003, Dir Inst. of Int. Law 1973–2003, Dean Faculty of Law 1995–97; Dir of Studies, Hague Acad. of Int. Law 1976, 1982, Lecturer 1995, 2009; Lecturer in Int. Law, Training Centre for Jr Diplomats, Ministry of Foreign Affairs 1981–89; Visiting Prof., Univ. of Siena, Italy 1984–85; Visiting Prof., Univ. of Michigan Law School, USA 1986, 1995, Prof. of Law 1987–92, mem. Affiliate Overseas Faculty 1997, Prof. of Law (part-time) 2012–; Judge, Int. Court of Justice, The Hague 2003–12; mem. UN Cttee on Econ., Social and Cultural Rights 1987–96, UN Int. Law Comm. 1996–2003; Distinguished Global Law School Fellow; New York Univ. Law School 2005; Co-founder and Ed. European Journal of Int. Law; Founding Pres. European Soc. of Int. Law; Assoc. Institut de Droit international; Counsel for Germany in various legal cases 1994–2003; int. arbitrator, consultant, mem. numerous legal advisory bds and professional asscns; Certificate of Merit, American Soc. of Int. Law 1996; Dr hc (Univ. of Macerata, Italy) 2006, (Univ. of Glasgow); Manley O. Hudson Medal,

American Soc. for Int. Law 2013. *Publications:* numerous books and articles in professional journals. *Address:* 437 Hutchins Hall, University of Michigan, South State Street, Ann Arbor, MI 48109, USA (office). *Telephone:* (734) 763-3806 (office). *E-mail:* simmab@umich.edu (office). *Website:* www.law.umich.edu (office).

SIMMEL, Peter; German business executive; b. 7 June 1959; heads regional Edeka store chain with 32 stores in Saxony, Thuringia and Bavaria, Chair. Supervisory Bd Edeka Zentrale AG & Co. KG, Hamburg 2005–10, mem. Supervisory Bd 2010–. *Address:* Edeka Zentrale AG & Co. KG, New-York-Ring 6, 22297 Hamburg, Germany (office). *Telephone:* (40) 63-77-0 (office). *Fax:* (40) 63-77-22-31 (office). *E-mail:* info@edeka.de (office). *Website:* www.edeka.de (office).

SIMMEN, Jeannot, Dr habil.; Swiss/German art critic and curator; *Director, Club Bel Etage Berlin;* b. 14 Sept. 1956, Zürich; s. of Georges Simmen and Clara Brüngger; m. Dr Brigit Blass 1988; two d.; ed Univ. of Zürich, Free Univ. of Berlin; Prof., Univs of Wuppertal, Kassel, Essen 1990–2000; exhbn projects include: Licht: Objekt/Medium, Telematic, Net-Modern-Navigation; Curator Schwerelos (exhbn), Grosse Orangerie, Charlottenburg Palace, Berlin 1991–92, Die Macht des Alters – Strategien der Meisterschaft (exhbn), Kronprinzen-Palais, Berlin 1998; Dir media future project Ars Digitalis, Acad. of Fine Arts, Berlin 1996, Club Bel Etage Berlin 2005–; Design-Preis Schweiz 01 für 'Interaction Design', Design Center Langenthal, Switzerland. *Publications:* Kunst – Ideal oder Augenschein 1980, Der Fahrstuhl 1983, Vertigo 1990, Schwerelos 1991, Vertikal 1994, Kasimir Malewitsch 1998, 1999, Kidai Shôran (CD) 2000, Telematik 2002, TotalSchaden 2006, Berlin-2010.eu/Von WestBerlin zur Kultur-Metropole Eurplas 2010. *Leisure interests:* art and the media. *Address:* Club Bel Etage Berlin GmbH, Pariser-Strasse 44, 10707 Berlin, Germany (office). *Telephone:* (30) 88550136 (office). *E-mail:* simmen@club-bel-etage.de (office); simmen@snafu.de. *Website:* www.jeannot-simmen.eu; www.club-bel-etage.de/Jeannot_Simmen (office).

SIMMONDS, Rt Hon. Kennedy Alphonse, PC; Saint Kitts and Nevis physician and politician; b. 12 April 1936; s. of Arthur Simmonds and Bronte Clarke; m. Mary Camella Matthew 1976; three s. two d.; ed Basse-Terre Boys' School, St Kitts-Nevis Grammar School and Univ. of the West Indies; Intern, Kingston Public Hosp., Jamaica 1963; Registrar in Internal Medicine, Princess Margaret Hosp., Bahamas 1966–68; Resident in Anaesthesiology, Pittsburgh 1968–69; medical practice in St Kitts and Anguilla 1964–66, in St Kitts 1969–80; Founder mem. People's Action Movt 1965, Pres. 1976, unsuccessfully contested elections 1966, 1971, 1975; elected to Parl. 1979; Premier 1980–83; Minister of Home and External Affairs, Trade, Devt and Industry 1980–84, of Finance, Home and Foreign Affairs 1984–95; Prime Minister 1983–95; currently Dir of Medical Services, Anguilla; Fellow, American Coll. of Anaesthesiologists. *Leisure interests:* cricket, tennis, football. *Address:* Ministry of Social Development, 3rd Floor, D3 Building, Caribbean Commercial Complex, PO Box 60, The Valley, Anguilla.

SIMMONS, David, BA, MEd; Australian organization executive and fmr politician; *Chairman, Western NSW Medicare Local Ltd;* b. 7 Nov. 1947, Broken Hill, NSW; m. Kaye Simmons; one s. one d.; ed Univ. of New England, NSW; Head of Social Science Dept, Bathurst High School, NSW; Alderman, Bathurst City Council 1978–83; MP for Calare, NSW 1983–96, mem. House of Reps Cttee on Finance and Public Admin. 1985–89; Minister for Defence, Science and Personnel 1989–90, for Arts, Tourism and Territories 1990–91, for Local Govt and Family Support 1991–93; Chair. House of Reps. Cttee on Banking, Finance and Public Admin. 1994; Exec. Dir Hunter Regional Tourism Org. 1996–97; Gen. Man. Newcastle Regional Chamber of Commerce 1997–98; CEO Newcastle & Hunter Business Chamber 1998–2001; Chair. Western NSW Medicare Local Ltd 2012–; Dir Daskay Pty Ltd 2001–, GP Training Valley to Coast Pty Ltd 2010–, Pacific Link Housing Ltd 2010–; Pres. Heart Foundation (NSW), also Dir Nat. Bd. *Leisure interests:* golf, stamp collecting, arts, travel. *Address:* Western NSW Medicare Local Ltd, Level 2/258–260 Macquarie Street, Dubbo, NSW 2830, Australia (office). *Telephone:* (2) 6884-0197 (office). *Fax:* (2) 6884-0198 (office). *E-mail:* admin@wml.org.au (office). *Website:* www.wml.org.au (office).

SIMMONS, Hardwick (Wick), AB, MBA; American business executive; b. 1940; m. Sloan T. Miller; five c.; ed Harvard Univ., Harvard Business School; with US Marine Corps Reserve 1960–66; Financial Adviser, Hayden Stone 1966–69, Vice-Pres. Data Processing and Communications Div. 1969–70, Man. Boston office 1970–73, Exec. Vice-Pres. for Shearson Hayden Stone Retail Sales and Admin. 1973–77, Sr Exec. Vice-Pres. for Marketing and Sales, Shearson/American Express 1977, Pres. Pvt. Client Group, Shearson Lehman Brothers, Inc. –1991; Pres. and CEO Prudential Securities, Inc. 1991–2001; CEO, Chair. Nasdaq Stock Market Inc. 2001–03; Dir New York City Partnership and Chamber of Commerce, Inc.; mem. Bd Nat. Acad. Foundation; mem. Bd of Dirs Raymond James Financial Inc. 2003– (Lead Dir 2006), Geneva Acquisition Corpn 2006–, Lions Gate Entertainment Corpn 2005–; Co-founder Longwing, mem. Bd of Advisors 2003–06; fmr Dir Chicago Bd Options Exchange; mem. and fmr Chair. Securities Industry Asscn; mem. and fmr Pres. Bond Club of New York, Inc.; mem. NY City Public/Pvt. Initiatives (PPI) Bd; mem. Harvard Univ. John King Fairbank Center for E Asian Research; Trustee South Street Seaport Museum; Pres. Bd of Trustees Groton School; Trustee Woods Hole Oceanographic Inst., Rippowan Cisqua School.

SIMMONS, J(onathan) K(imble); American actor; b. 9 Jan. 1955; m. Michelle Schumacher; three c.; ed Univ. of Montana; early career in musical theatre, including as Broadway actor and singer; fmr mem. Seattle Repertory Theatre. *Theatre includes:* Birds of Paradise 1987, Guys and Dolls 1992, Das Barbecu 1994, Carousel. *Films include:* Popeye Doyle 1986, The Ref 1994, The First Wives Club 1996, Extreme Measures 1996, Crossing Fields 1997, The Jackal 1997, Anastasia 1997, The Cider House Rules 1999, For Love of the Game 1999, Autumn in New York 2000, The Gift 2000, The Mexican 2001, Spider-Man 2002, Disposal 2003, Hidalgo 2004, The Ladykillers 2004, Spider-Man 2 2004, Thank You for Smoking 2005, The Closer 2005, Spider-Man 3 2007, Juno 2007, Rendition 2007, Burn After Reading 2008, Red Sands 2009, Aliens in the Attic 2009, Up in the Air 2009, Jennifer's Body 2009, Crazy on the Outside 2010, An Invisible Sign 2010, A Beginner's Guide to Endings 2010, True Grit 2010, Cats & Dogs: The Revenge of Kitty Galore 2010, The Music Never Stopped 2011, The Good Doctor 2011, The Words 2012, Contraband 2012, Jobs 2013, Labor Day 2013, Dark Skies 2013, The Heeler 2013, The Magic Bracelet 2013, Whiplash (Nat. Soc. of Film Critics Award for Best Supporting Actor 2014, New York Film Critics Circle Award for Best Supporting Actor 2014, Toronto Film Critics Asscn Award for Best Supporting Actor 2014, Golden Globe Award for Best Supporting Actor – Motion Picture 2015, Critics' Choice Movie Award for Best Supporting Actor 2015, London Film Critics' Circle Award for Supporting Actor of the Year 2015, Screen Actors Guild Award for Outstanding Performance by a Male Actor in a Supporting Role 2015, Acad. Award for Best Supporting Actor 2015) 2014, Barefoot 2014, Break Point 2014, The Boxcar Children 2014, The Rewrite 2014, Men, Women & Children 2014, The Meddler 2015, Worlds Apart 2015, Zootopia (voice) 2016. *Television includes:* Law & Order 1994–2010, New York Undercover 1996–98, Third Watch 2000, Law & Order: Special Victims Unit 2000–01, Law & Order: Criminal Intent 2002, Path to War 2002, Oz 1997–2003, ER 2004, The D.A. 2004, Nip/Tuck 2004, Justice League 2004–06, The Closer 2005–12, The West Wing 2006, Men at Work 2012–14, Growing Up Fisher 2014, Counterpart 2017–18. *Address:* The Gersh Agency, 9465 Wilshire Boulevard, Beverly Hills, CA 90212, USA (office). *Telephone:* (310) 274-6611 (office). *E-mail:* info@gershla.com (office). *Website:* www.gershagency.com (office).

SIMMONS, Robert Malcolm, PhD, FRS; British biophysicist and academic; *Professor Emeritus, Randall Division of Cell and Molecular Biophysics, King's College, London;* b. 23 Jan. 1938, London; s. of Stanley Laurence Simmons and Marjorie Simmons (née Amys); m. Mary Ann (Anna) Ross 1967; one s. one d.; ed King's Coll., London, Royal Inst., Univ. Coll., London; Lecturer, Univ. Coll. London 1967–81; MRC Staff Scientist, King's Coll. London 1981–83, Prof. of Biophysics 1983–2002, Dir Randall Inst. 1995–99, Randall Div. of Cell and Molecular Biophysics 1999–2001, Prof. Emer. 2002–. *Publication:* Muscular Contraction 1992. *Leisure interests:* music, fishing. *Address:* 1 Woodborough Road, Pewsey, Wilts., SN9 5NH, England (home). *Telephone:* (1672) 562281 (home). *E-mail:* simmons.bob@btinternet.com (home).

SIMMONS, Ruth J., PhD; American academic and university administrator; *President, Prairie View A&M University;* b. 3 July 1945, Grapeland, Tex.; m. Norbert Alonzo Simmons (divorced); one s. one d.; ed Dillard Univ., Harvard Univ.; fmr Asst Prof. of French, Univ. of New Orleans, Asst Dean Coll. of Liberal Arts –1977; Visiting Assoc. Prof. of Pan-African Studies, Calif. State Univ., Northridge 1977–79, also Acting Dir Int. Programmes; Asst, then Assoc. Dean of Grad. Studies, Univ. of Southern Calif. 1979–83; Dir Afro-American Studies, Princeton Univ. 1985–87, Assoc. Dean 1986–90, Vice-Provost 1992–95; Provost, Spelman Coll., Atlanta 1990–91; Pres. Smith Coll. 1995–2001; Pres. Brown Univ. 2001–12, Pres. Emerita and Prof. of Comparative Literature and Africana Studies 2012–14; Pres. Prairie View A&M Univ. 2017–; Chevalier, Légion dHonneur 2013; 25 hon. doctorates; numerous awards including President's Award, United Negro College Fund 2001, Fulbright Lifetime Achievement Medal 2002, Eleanor Roosevelt Val-Kill Medal 2004, Ellis Island Medal of Honor 2010, Foreign Policy Asscn Award 2010. *Address:* Office of the President, Prairie View A&M University, PO Box 519, Prairie View, TX 77446, USA (office). *Telephone:* (936) 261-2111 (office). *E-mail:* dmesters@pvamu.edu (office). *Website:* www.pvamu.edu/president (office).

SIMMS, Sir Neville Ian, Kt, BSc, MEng, FREng, FRSA, FICE; British business executive and chartered civil engineer; *Deputy Chairman, GDF Suez Energy International;* b. 11 Sept. 1944, Glasgow, Scotland; s. of Arthur Neville Simms and Anne Davidson Simms (née McCulloch); ed Queen Elizabeth Grammar School, Crediton, Newcastle Univ and Univ of Glasgow; Structural Engineer, Ove Arup and Partners 1966–69; joined Tarmac PLC 1970, Chief Exec. Tarmac Construction Ltd 1988–92, Group Chief Exec. Tarmac PLC 1992–99, (Deputy Chair. 1994–99); Group Chair. Carillion PLC 1999–2004; mem. Bd of Dirs International Power PLC 1998–2011, Chair. 2000–11 (co. acquired by GDF Suez 2012), Deputy Chair. GDF Suez Energy International 2011–; Dir Bank of England 1995–2002; Chair. BITC West Midlands 1998–2001, Chair BITC Solent Region 2005–07; Dir (non-exec.) Courtaulds 1994–98, Pvt. Finance Panel Ltd 1994–99, Nat. Power 1998–2000, Sustainable Procurement Task Force 2006; Chair BRE Trust 2006–; mem. New Deal Task Force 1999–2001; Gov. Stafford Grammar School 1997–2004, Ashridge Man. Coll. 2000–11; Hon. DTech (Wolverhampton) 1997; Dr hc (Edin.) 2000; Hon. DEng (Glasgow) 2001; Pres.'s Medal, Chartered Inst. of Bldg 1995; Prince of Wales Amb. Award 2001. *Publications:* Building Towards 2001; numerous speeches and articles on industry-related topics. *Address:* GDF Suez Energy International, Senator House, 85 Queen Victoria Street, London, EC4V 4DP, England (office). *Telephone:* (20) 7320-8600 (office). *Fax:* (20) 7320-8700 (office). *E-mail:* neville.simms@gdfsuez.com (office). *Website:* www.gdfsuez.com (office).

SIMON, Carly; American singer, songwriter and musician (piano, guitar); b. 25 June 1945, New York; d. of Richard Simon; m. 1st James Taylor 1972 (divorced 1983); one d. one s.; m. 2nd James Hart 1987 (divorced 2007); ed Sarah Lawrence Coll.; Grammy Award for Best New Artist 1971, Acad. Award (for Let The River Run) 1989, Golden Globe Award for Best Original Song (for Let the River Run) 1990. *Film appearance:* No Nukes 1980. *Compositions include:* Romulus Hunt (opera) 1993; film scores for Heartburn 1986, Working Girl 1988, Postcards From the Edge 1990, This Is My Life 1992; theme tunes for Torchlight 1985, Phenom (TV) 1993; contrib. songs to other films. *Recordings include:* albums: Carly Simon 1971, Anticipation 1972, No Secrets 1973, Hotcakes 1974, Playing Possum 1975, Another Passenger 1976, Boys In The Trees 1978, Spy 1979, Come Upstairs 1980, Torch 1981, Hello Big Man 1983, Spoiled Girl 1985, Coming Around Again 1987, My Romance 1990, Have You Seen Me Lately? 1991, This Is My Life 1992, Letters Never Sent 1994, Clouds In My Coffee 1965–95 1996, Film Noir 1997, The Bedroom Tapes 2000, This Kind of Love 2008, Never Been Gone 2009, Songs from the Trees: A Musical Memoir Collection 2015. *Publications include:* Boys in the Trees: A Memoir 2015; juvenile: Amy the Dancing Bear 1989, The Boy of the Bells 1990, The Fisherman's Song 1990, The Nighttime Chauffeur 1993, Midnight Farm 1997, Basket Full of Rhymes 2000, Take Me Out to the Ball Game 2011, Boys in the Trees (memoir) 2015; several songbooks. *Address:* Ciancia Management, 5419 Evergreen Heights Drive, Evergreen, CO 80439, USA (office). *Telephone:* (213) 925-7117 (office). *Fax:* (310) 388-5353 (office). *E-mail:* larry@cianciamanagement.com (office). *Website:* www.cianciamanagement.com (office); www.carlysimon.com.

SIMON, David, BA; American screenwriter, TV producer and fmr journalist; b. 1960, Washington, DC; m. Laura Lippman; ed Bethesda-Chevy Chase High School, Univ. of Maryland; police reporter at Baltimore Sun newspaper 1982–95; f. Blown Deadline Productions; Fellow, John D. and Catherine T. MacArthur

Foundation 2010. *Television includes:* Homicide: Life on the Street (producer, writer) (Writers Guild of America Award) 1993–99, NYPD Blue (writer) 1996, The Corner (producer, writer) (three Emmy Awards) 2000, The Wire (producer, writer) 2002–08, Generation Kill (producer, writer) 2008, Treme 2010–13, Show Me a Hero 2015, The Deuce 2017. *Publications include:* Homicide: A Year on the Killing Streets (Edgar Award 1992) 1991, The Corner: A Year in the Life of an Inner-City Neighborhood (co-author) (Notable Book of the Year, New York Times) 1997. *Website:* www.davidsimon.com.

SIMON, Lou Anna Kimsey, PhD; American university president; ed Indiana State Univ., Michigan State Univ.; joined faculty of Mich. State Univ. (MSU) 1974, Asst Dir Office of Institutional Research, then Asst Provost for Gen. Academic Admin, Assoc. Provost, Provost (also for MSU Coll. of Law), Vice-Pres. for Academic Affairs 1993, Interim Pres. MSU May–Sept. 2003, Pres. 2005–18, has taught seminars at Coll. of Educ.; mem. Exec. Cttee, Cttee on Institutional Cooperation 1999– (Chair. 2000–05); Chair. Exec. Cttee Nat. Collegiate Athletic Asscn 2012–14. *Publications include:* Serving Children and Families through Community-University Partnerships, Universities and Communities: Remaking Professional and Interprofessional Education for the Next Century, Learning to Serve: Promoting Civil Society through Service Learning (co-ed.) 2002. *Address:* c/o Office of the President, Michigan State University, 426 Auditorium Road, Hannah Administration Building, East Lansing, MI 48824-1046, USA (office).

SIMON, Paul F., BA; American singer and composer; b. 13 Oct. 1941, Newark, NJ; s. of Louis Simon and Belle Simon; m. 1st Peggy Harper (divorced); one s.; m. 2nd Carrie Fisher 1983 (divorced 1984, died 2016); m. 3rd Edie Brickell 1992; two s. one d.; ed Queens Coll., Brooklyn Law School; mem. singing duo Simon & Garfunkel (with Art Garfunkel) 1964–71; solo artist 1972–; Co-founder (with Dr Irwin Redlener) Children's Health Fund 1986; Hon. DMus (Berklee Coll.) 1986, (Yale) 1996, (Queens Coll.) 1997; Emmy Award (for Paul Simon Special, NBC) 1977, inducted into Songwriters Hall of Fame 1982, Simon & Garfunkel inducted into Rock and Roll Hall of Fame 1990, inducted as solo artist 2001, Kennedy Center Honor 2002, Grammy Lifetime Achievement Award 2003, Gershwin Prize for Popular Song, US Library of Congress 2007, Polar Music Prize (Sweden) 2012. *Compositions:* The Capeman (musical) (Antoinette Perry Award for Best Original Score Written for the Theatre 1998) 1997. *Film appearances:* Annie Hall 1977, The Rutles (TV) 1978, All You Need Is Cash 1978, One-Trick Pony 1980. *Recordings include:* albums: as Simon & Garfunkel: Wednesday Morning 3AM 1964, Sounds Of Silence 1966, Parsley, Sage, Rosemary And Thyme 1966, The Graduate (film soundtrack) (two Grammy Awards) 1968, Bookends 1968, Bridge Over Troubled Water (six Grammy Awards 1971) 1970, Concert In Central Park (live) 1982, Early Simon & Garfunkel 1993, Old Friends 1997; solo: The Paul Simon Songbook 1965, Paul Simon 1972, There Goes Rhymin' Simon 1973, Live Rhymin': Paul Simon In Concert 1974, Still Crazy After All These Years (two Grammy Awards) 1975, One-Trick Pony 1980, Hearts And Bones 1983, Graceland (Grammy Award 1987) 1986, Negotiations And Love Songs 1988, Rhythm Of The Saints 1990, Paul Simon's Concert In The Park 1991, Songs From The Capeman 1997, You're The One 2000, Surprise 2006, So Beautiful or So What 2011, Live in New York City 2012, Stranger to Stranger 2016, In the Blue Light 2018. *Publications:* The Songs of Paul Simon 1972, New Songs 1975, One-Trick Pony (screenplay) 1980, At The Zoo (juvenile) 1991. *Address:* c/o C. Vaughn Hazell, Paul Simon Music, Suite 500, 1619 Broadway, New York, NY 10019, USA. *Website:* www.paulsimon.com.

SIMON MUNARO, Yehude; Peruvian politician and fmr teacher; b. 18 July 1947, Lima; ed Univ. Nacional Pedro Ruiz Gallo; teacher, Colegio San Vicente de Paul 1966–72; Pres. Fed. of Teachers, Univ. Nacional Pedro Ruiz Gallo 1981–85; Sec.–Gen. United Left, Lambayeque 1984; mem. Parl. for Lambayeque 1985–90; Gov. of Lambayeque 2003–06; Prime Minister of Peru 2008–09; mem. Congress (Parl.) 2011–, Second Vice-Pres. 2011–12; Pres. Lambayeque Defence Front 1984–90; Pres. Movimiento Humanista Peruano 2000. *Address:* Congress, Plaza Bolívar, Av. Abancay s/n, Lima, Perú. *E-mail:* ysimon@congreso.gob.pe (office); yehudesimon@hotmail.com (office). *Website:* www4.congreso.gob.pe/pvp/2011/ysimon.asp (office).

SIMON OF HIGHBURY, Baron (Life Peer), cr. 1997, of Canonbury in the London Borough of Islington; **David Alec Gwyn Simon,** Kt, CBE, MA, MBA; British business executive; b. 24 July 1939, London, England; s. of Roger Simon and Barbara Hudd; m. 1st Hanne Mohn 1964; two s.; m. 2nd Sarah Smith 1992; ed Gonville and Caius Coll., Cambridge; joined BP 1961, Marketing Dir, Holland 1972–75, Marketing Co-ordinator, European Region 1975–80, Marketing Dir, Oil UK 1980–82, Man. Dir, Oil Int. Ltd 1982–85, Man. Dir BP Co. PLC 1986–95, Deputy Chair. 1990–95, Group Chief Exec. 1992–95, Chair. 1995–97; Dir Bank of England 1995–97; Minister of State Responsible for Trade and Competitiveness in Europe (attached to Dept of Trade and Industry and Treasury) 1997–99; Dir (non-exec.) and Deputy Chair. Unilever 2000–04, 2005–09; Dir Centre for European Policy Studies 2002–; Sr Adviser, GDF SUEZ 2001– (also Non-exec. Dir); Lay mem. and Deputy Chair., Univ. Council, Univ. of Cambridge 2005–10; mem. Int. Advisory Bd Dana Gas Corpn 2006–, Advisory Bd Montrose Assocs 2008–; Trustee, Hertie Foundation, Germany, Cicely Saunders International 2001–10; mem. Inst. of Dirs, Centre for European Policy Studies, Brussels, Inst. for Strategic Dialogue; Grand Commdr, Order of Leopold II (Belgium); Hon. DEcon (Hull) 1993, (Birmingham) 2003; Dr hc (Univ. of N London) 1995; Hon. LLD (Bath) 1998. *Leisure interests:* golf, books, music. *Address:* 1 St James's Square, London, SW1Y 4PD, England (office). *Telephone:* (20) 7496-5821 (office). *Fax:* (20) 7496-4436 (office). *E-mail:* sjs1@bp.com (office).

SIMONETI, Marko, BA, MA, PhD; Slovenian economist, financial executive and academic; *Professor of Money and Finance, Law School, University of Ljubljana;* b. 8 July 1958; m.; ed Univ. of Ljubljana, Cornell Univ., USA; Sr Research Fellow, Inst. for Econ. Research 1982–90; Under-Sec. of State in Fed. Govt 1989; Man. Dir Agency for Privatization, Ljubljana 1990–93; Co-founder CEEPN (Cen. and Eastern European Privatization Network) 1993, Chair. Steering Cttee 1991–92, Exec. Dir 1993–2004; served as Vice-Chair. Board of the Securities and Exchange Comm., mem. Supervisory Bd of Ljubljana Stock Exchange and Chair. Govt Comm. for privatization of largest bank in Slovenia; served as pvt. sector devt adviser to various int. orgs (IBRD, EBRD, OECD, UNDP, UN-ECE); Pres. and CEO Ljubljanska Borza d.d. (Ljubljana Stock Exchange) 2005–09; Chair. Supervisory Bd Nova Ljubljanska banka 2009–12; Prof. of Money and Finance, Law

School, Univ. of Ljubljana 1997–; mem. Econ. Asscn of Slovenia, European Asscn for Comparative Econ. Studies. *Publications include:* Investment Funds as Intermediaries of Privatization (CEEPN Workshop Series, Vol. 5) (co-ed.) 1994, Bank Rehabilitation and Enterprise Restructuring (CEEPN Workshop series, Vol. 6) (co-ed.) 1995, The Governance of Privatization Funds: Experiences of the Czech Republic, Poland and Slovenia (co-ed.) 1999; numerous book chapters, reports and articles in professional journals. *Address:* Law School, University of Ljubljana, Poljanski nasip 2, 1000 Ljubljana, Slovenia (office). *E-mail:* marko.simoneti@pf.uni-lj.si (office). *Website:* www.pf.uni-lj.si (office).

SIMONIA, Nodari Aleksandrovich, CandEconSc, DHist; Russian political economist; *Professor, Moscow State Institute of International Relations (MGIMO);* b. 30 Jan. 1932, Tbilisi, Georgia; m.; one d.; ed Moscow Inst. of Int. Relations; Corresp. mem. Russian Acad. of Sciences 1990, mem. 1997–; Acad. Sec., Dept of Int. Relations, Jr Researcher, Sr Researcher, Prof. and Head of Sector, Head of Div., Deputy Dir, Inst. of Oriental Studies 1955–86; Deputy Dir Inst. of World Econ. and Int. Relations (IMEMO), Russian Acad. of Sciences 1986–2000, Dir 2000, currently Adviser; Prof., Moscow State Inst. of Int. Relations (MGIMO); Prof., Centre of Slavic Studies, Hokkaido Univ., Japan; main research in comparative studies: Russia and developing countries; mem. Presidium, Russian Acad. of Sciences, Scientific Council Ministry of Foreign Affairs, European Acad. of Sciences, Arts and Literature; Special Rep. of Pres. of Russian Fed. for Relations with African States' Leaders in the G-8 Framework 2002–06. *Publications:* over 260 scientific works, including 16 books, articles and papers on the devt of capitalism including within modern Russia. *Address:* IMEMO, Profsoyuznaya str. 23, 117997 Moscow, GSP-7, Russia (office). *Telephone:* (499) 120-84-50 (office); (495) 434-15-68 (home). *Fax:* (499) 120-65-75 (office). *E-mail:* imemoran@imemo.ru (office). *Website:* www.imemo.ru/eng (office).

SIMONIS, HE Cardinal Adrianus Johannes; Dutch ecclesiastic; *Archbishop Emeritus of Utrecht;* b. 26 Nov. 1931, Lisse; ed Hageveld (high school) and Warmond seminaries, Haarlem, Biblicum (Papal Inst. for the Bible), Rome and Jerusalem; ordained priest, Rotterdam 1957; consecrated Bishop of Rotterdam 1971; apptd Coadjutor Archbishop of Utrecht 1983, Archbishop of Utrecht 1983–2007, now Archbishop Emer.; cr. Cardinal (Cardinal-Priest of S. Clemente) 1985; mem. Congregation for the Catholic Educ., Congregation for the Insts of the Consecrated Life and the Societies of Apostolic Life, Pontifical Council for the Promotion of the Unity Among Christians, Conf. of European Bishops; Orde van de Nederlandse Leeuw 1976, Grootkruis Oranje-Nassau. *Publications:* Op de adem van het leven 1997, Een hart om te denken 2007. *Telephone:* 2334244 (office); (73) 5115976 (office); (30) 2338030. *Fax:* 2332103 (office); (30) 2311962. *Website:* www.rkkerk.nl (office).

SIMONIS, Heide, MA; German politician; b. 4 July 1943, Bonn; d. of Dr Horst Steinhardt and Sophia Brück; m. Prof. Udo E. Simonis 1967; tutor in German, Univ. of Zambia 1967–69, Goethe Inst. and Nat. TV and Radio Service, Tokyo 1970–72; mem. Bundestag 1976–88; Minister of Finance, Schleswig-Holstein 1988–93, Minister-Pres. 1993–2005; Head of UNICEF Deutschland 2005–08; mem. Social Democratic Party (SPD); Orden wider den tierischen Ernst, Aachen 1998, Order of the Cross of Terra Mariana (Estonia) 2006, Order of the Rising Sun (Japan) 2010; Bambi Award 1993, Schlitzorh Prize 1997. *Publications include:* Kein Blatt vorm Mund 1998, Unter Männern (autobiog.) 2003, Ausgeteilt, eingesteckt 2007, Drei Rheintöchter (co-author) 2008, Verzockt! Warum die Karten von Markt und Staat neu gemischt werden müssen 2010. *Leisure interests:* music, literature. *Address:* Büro Heide Simonis, Kleiner Kuhberg 28-30, 24103 Kiel; Düsternbrooker Weg 70, 24105 Kiel, Germany. *Telephone:* (431) 9882000. *Fax:* (431) 9881960. *E-mail:* heide.simonis@stk.landsh.de (office); tokio70@web.de (home). *Website:* www.heide-simonis.de.

SIMONITI, Vasko, PhD; Slovenian historian, academic and politician; b. 23 March 1951, Ljubljana; ed Univ. of Ljubljana; Lecturer in History, Univ. of Ljubljana 1989–2000, now Prof.; mem. Slovenian Democratic Party 2000–; Minister of Culture 2004–08. *Publications include:* Vojaška organizacija 1991, Slovenska zgodovina do razsvetljenstva 1995, Turki so v deželi že, Turški vpadi na slovensko ozemlje 1996, Fanfare nasilja 2003, Slovenska povjest do prosvetiteljstva 2004 (co-author), Slowenische Geschichte: Gesellschaft, Politik, Kultur (co-author) 2008. *Address:* Department of History, University of Ljubljana, Kongresni trg 12, 1000 Ljubljana, Slovenia (office). *Website:* www.zgodovina-ff-uni-lj.net (office).

SIMONOV, Aleksey Kirillovich; Russian film director, interpreter and human rights activist; *President, Glasnost Defence Foundation;* b. 8 Aug. 1939, Moscow; s. of Konstantin Simonov (writer and poet); m.; two s.; ed Inst. of Oriental Languages at Moscow State Univ., courses for film dirs; worked in lab. at Inst. of Permafrost Studies 1956–58; translator, USSR State Cttee for Int. Econ. Relations in Indonesia 1963–64; Ed., Khudozhestennaya Literatura 1964–67; film Dir EKRAN TV Studio 1970–91; Lecturer, All-Russian Inst. of Cinematography 1991–93; Sec., USSR Union of Cinematographists 1991; f. Konf 1991; Co.-Chair. Licence Cttee of Russian Fed. 1992–93; mem. Movt of Democratic Reforms 1991–93; mem. Public Chamber of Russian Presidency; Co-founder Movt for Mil. Reform 1995; Pres. Glasnost Defence Foundation 1991–; Vice-Pres. Russian PEN Centre 2009–; Chair. jury for Sakharov prize for Journalism, Stalker Film Festival; mem. Editorial Bd, Sovyetsky Ekran (magazine) 1988–92, Rossia (weekly) 1992–96; mem. Moscow Helsinki Group 1998–; Founder Dossier on Censorship (quarterly) 1997–, Law and Practice (monthly) 1995–2003; Moscow Int. Press Club 1997, Femida Prize (for Glasnost Defence Foundation) 1999, Nat. Endowment for Democracy 2005. *Films:* directed over 25 feature films and documentaries including Detachment 1985. *Publications:* Private Collection 1999 (prose), End of the Holyday of Disobedience 2004, Guy from Sivtsev-Vrajek (prose) 2009; edited numerous book; numerous articles in newspapers and magazines Yunost, Ogonyok, Moskva; currently columnist, Russkaya Misl, Paris, Izvestia, Moscow; translator of English plays, Indonesian and African poetry. *Leisure interest:* collecting turtles. *Address:* 119121 Moscow, Zubovski blvd. 4, apt. 438 (office); Moscow, Leningradski prosp. 60-A, apt. 2, Russia (home). *Telephone:* (495) 637-44-20 (office); (499) 155-38-39 (home). *Fax:* (495) 637-49-47 (office). *E-mail:* fond@gdf.ru (office); simonov@gdf.ru (home). *Website:* www.gdf.ru (office).

ŠIMONOVIĆ, Ivan, DJur; Croatian diplomatist, civil servant, academic, politician and UN official; *Special Adviser on the Responsibility to Protect, United Nations;* b. 2 May 1959, Zagreb; m.; two c.; ed Univ. of Zagreb; staff mem. Social Research Inst., Zagreb; mem. Faculty of Law, Univ. of Zagreb 1986–93, Asst Prof., then Assoc. Prof. in Dept for Theory of Law and State 2004–05, Prof. and Vice-Dean of Law Faculty 2005–08, Head of Dept of Gen. Theory of Law and State 2006–08, Vice-Rector Univ. of Zagreb 2006–08; Guest Lecturer at univs in Graz, Austria, Kraków, Poland and Yale Univ., Pittsburg, Montana and N Dakota, USA; Fulbright Scholar, Yale Univ. Law School 1993–94; with Ministry of Foreign Affairs, serving as Asst Minister of Foreign Affairs in charge of Consular and Int. Legal Affairs 1992–93, Multilateral Affairs 1994–95, First Asst Minister and Deputy Minister of Foreign Affairs 1995–96, mem. Croatian Del. at Dayton Peace Talks 1995, Deputy Minister of Foreign Affairs 2003–04; Minister of Justice 2008–10; UN Asst Sec.-Gen. for Human Rights 2010–16; Special Adviser on the Responsibility to Protect 2016–; mem. numerous Govt comms including Jt Comm. on Search for Missing Persons and Mortal Remains under auspices of ICRC, Comm. for Detained and Missing Persons, State Comm. for UN Protection Force (UNPROFOR); Perm. Rep. to UN, New York 1997–2003; Co-Chair. Hungarian-Croatian Jt Cttee 2003–; apptd Agent of Govt of Croatia to Int. Court of Justice in its case against Fed. Repub. of Yugoslavia for alleged genocide 2000; Sr Vice-Pres. ECOSOC 2001–02, Pres. 2002–03; Vice-Pres. Bureau of Preparatory Cttee of Int. Conf. on Financing for Devt 2002; currently Visiting Sr Research Scholar, Faculty of Int. and Public Affairs, School of Int. and Public Affairs; Officier, Légion d'honneur 2004. *Publications include:* author and ed. of more than 50 publs including books, book chapters and articles in scholarly journals, in Croatian and English. *Address:* New York Office of the UN High Commissioner for Human Rights, United Nations, New York, NY 10017, USA (office). *Telephone:* (212) 963-5931 (office). *E-mail:* InfoDesk@ohchr.org (office). *Website:* www.ohchr.org (office).

SIMONS, Benjamin David, PhD; British theoretical physicist and academic; *Herchel Smith Chair in Physics, Cavendish Laboratory, University of Cambridge;* ed Univ. of Cambridge; began career researching high temperature superconductivity, undertook post-doctoral research in quantum mesoscopic physics at MIT and NEC Research Inc., Princeton, NJ, USA; Royal Soc. Research Fellowship 1994; Lecturer, Imperial Coll., London 1994–95; moved to Cavendish Lab., Univ. of Cambridge 1995, Chair in Theoretical Condensed Matter Physics 2002, Herchel Smith Chair in Physics 2011–, also currently Head of Theory of Condensed Matter (TCM) physics group, affiliated to Wellcome Trust/Cancer Research UK Gurdon Inst. and Wellcome Trust –MRC Cambridge Stem Cell Inst., Fellow, St John's Coll., Cambridge; Sr Investigator Award, Wellcome Trust, Gabor Medal, Royal Soc. 2015. *Publications:* numerous papers in professional journals. *Address:* Cavendish Laboratory, TCM, University of Cambridge, 19 J.J. Thomson Avenue, Cambridge, CB3 0HE, England (office). *Telephone:* (1223) 337253 (office); (1223) 337254 (office). *Fax:* (1223) 337356 (office). *E-mail:* bds10@cam.ac.uk (office). *Website:* www.tcm.phy.cam.ac.uk (office); www.stemcells.cam.ac.uk (office).

SIMONS, John Philip, PhD, ScD, FRS; British chemist and academic; *Dr Lee's Professor Emeritus of Chemistry, University of Oxford;* b. 20 April 1934, London; s. of Mark Simons and Rose Simons; m. 1st Althea Screaton (died 1989); m. 2nd Elizabeth Corps; three s.; ed Sidney Sussex Coll., Cambridge; fmr Prof. of Photochemistry, Univ. of Birmingham; fmr Prof. of Physical Chem., Univ. of Nottingham; fmr Prof. of Chem., Univ. of Oxford, now Dr Lee's Prof. Emer., Emer. Professorial Fellow, Exeter Coll., Oxford; Miller Visiting Prof., Univ. of California, Berkeley; Erskine Fellow, Univ. of Canterbury, New Zealand; Hon. Citizen, Toulouse, France; Hon. DSc (Birmingham); Davy Medal, Royal Soc., Humphry Davy Lecturer, Royal Soc., RSC Liversidge, Tilden, Polanyi and Spiers Medals, Chemical Dynamics Award, Pimentel Lecturer, Univ. of California, Berkeley. *Publications include:* numerous scientific papers in professional journals on photochemistry, molecular reaction dynamics, spectroscopy, interactions and structures of biologically important molecules in the gas phase. *Leisure interests:* reading, writing. *Address:* Physical and Theoretical Chemistry Laboratory, University of Oxford, South Parks Road, Oxford, OX1 3QZ, England (office). *Telephone:* (1865) 275400 (office). *Fax:* (1865) 275410 (office). *E-mail:* john.simons@chem.ox.ac.uk (office).

SIMONYI, András, PhD; Hungarian economist, consultant and fmr diplomatist; *Managing Director, Center for Transatlantic Relations, Paul H. Nitze School of Advanced International Studies, Johns Hopkins University;* b. 16 May 1952, Budapest; s. of Denes Simonyi and Maria Balazs; m. Nada Pejak; one s. one d.; ed Karl Marx Univ. of Econs (now Budapest Univ.); worked in 1980s with different orgs in field of youth exchange, particularly promoting East–West contacts, including programmes with American Council of Young Political Leaders; mem. staff Foreign Relations Dept, Socialist Workers Party 1984–89; Head of Nordic Dept, Ministry of Foreign Affairs 1989–91; Deputy Chief of Mission Embassy of Hungary, The Hague 1991–92, Hungarian Mission to EC and NATO, Brussels 1992–95; Head, Hungarian NATO Liaison Office, Brussels 1995–99; Perm. Rep. to NATO Council (first Hungarian Perm. Rep.) 1999–2001, rep. on North Atlantic Council during Kosovo campaign; Amb. to USA 2002–07; ran own consulting co. Danison Ltd 2001–02; Man. Dir Center for Transatlantic Relations, The Paul H. Nitze School of Advanced Int. Studies, The Johns Hopkins Univ. 2012–; Imre Nagy Award, Hungary–Ohio Partnership for Educ. *Publications include:* numerous articles on the accession process to NATO, trans-Atlantic relations and European security and the war on terror. *Leisure interest:* blues music (plays electric guitar). *Address:* SAIS Center for Transatlantic Relations, 1717 Massachusetts Avenue NW, Suite 525, Washington, DC 20036, USA (office). *Telephone:* (202) 663-5880 (office). *Fax:* (202) 663-5879 (office). *E-mail:* asimonyi@jhu.edu (office). *Website:* transatlantic.sais-jhu.edu/about/bios/Andras%20Simonyi (office).

ŠIMONYTĖ, Ingrida, BBA, MA; Lithuanian economist and politician; *Deputy Chair, Bank of Lithuania;* b. 15 Nov. 1974, Vilnius; m.; ed Vilnius Secondary School No. 7, Vilnius Univ.; Chief Economist of Tax Div., Fiscal Policy Dept, Ministry of Finance 1997–98, Head of Indirect Taxes Div. 1998–2001, Dir Tax Dept 2002–04, Under-Sec., Ministry of Finance 2004–09, Minister of Finance 2009–12; Deputy Chair. Bank of Lithuania 2013–. *Address:* Lietuvos bankas, Gedimino pr. 6, Vilnius 01103, Lithuania (office). *Telephone:* (5) 268-0029 (office). *E-mail:* info@lb.lt (office). *Website:* www.lb.lt (office).

SIMOR, András; Hungarian financial consultant and fmr central banker; *Senior Vice-President, Chief Financial Officer and Chief Operating Officer, European Bank for Reconstruction and Development;* b. 17 May 1954, Budapest; s. of János Simor and Zsuzsanna Beretvás; divorced; three c.; ed Budapest Univ. of Econs; Exec. Foreign Exchange Man. Dept, Hungarian Nat. Bank (Magyar Nemzeti Bank—MNB) 1976–79, with Hungarian Int. Bank Ltd, London (subsidiary) 1979–85, Gov. MNB 2007–13; CEO Creditanstalt Értékpapír Rt, Budapest 1989–97; Exec. Chair. CA IB Investmentbank AG, Vienna 1997–98; Chair. Budapest Stock Exchange 1998–2002; Chair. Deloitte Hungary 1999–2007, Chair. and Office Man. Partner Deloitte & Touche Rt, Budapest 2000–07, also mem. Bd of Dirs Deloitte & Touche Cen. Europe 2002–06; Vice-Pres. Policy, EBRD 2013–16, Chief Financial Officer 2014–, Sr Vice-Pres. and COO 2016–; named by Euromoney as Banker of the Year in the emerging Europe region 2010. *Address:* EBRD, One Exchange Square, London EC2A 2JN, England (office). *Telephone:* (20) 73386000 (office). *Website:* www.ebrd.com (office).

SIMPSON, Alan Kooi, BS, JD; American lawyer and fmr politician; *Partner, Simpson, Kepler & Ewards;* b. 2 Sept. 1931, Cody, Wyo.; s. of Milward Lee Simpson and Lorna Simpson (née Kooi); m. Ann Schroll 1954; two s. one d.; ed Univ. of Wyoming; called to Wyo. Bar 1958, US Supreme Court 1964; Asst Attorney Gen. Wyo. State 1959; Attorney for Cody 1959–69; mem. Wyo. House of Reps 1964–77; Senator from Wyoming 1978–97, Asst Majority Leader 1985–87, Asst Minority Leader 1987–97; currently Partner, Simpson, Kepler & Ewards (div. of Burg Simpson Eldredge Hersh and Jardine), Cody, Wyo.; consultant, Tongour, Simpson, Holsclaw Group, Washington, DC; Visiting Lecturer, Lambard Chair., Shorenstein Center, Harvard Univ. 1997–2000; Visiting Lecturer, Univ. of Wyo. 2000–; mem. Iraq Study Group, US Inst. of Peace 2006; Co-Chair. Nat. Comm. on Fiscal Responsibility and Reform 2010–; Trustee, Buffalo Bill Historical Center (now Chair.), Cody, Gottsche Foundation Rehabilitation Center; mem. Wyo. Bar Asscn, ABA, Asscn of Trial Lawyers of America, American Asscn for Justice, Park County Bar Asscn; Hon. LLD (Calif. Western School of Law) 1983, (Colo Coll.) 1986, (Notre Dame Univ.) 1987; Hon. JD (Rocky Mountain Coll.) 1996, (Univ. of Wyo.) 1999, (American Univ.; Centennial Alum Award (Wyo. Univ.) 1987, Thomas Jefferson Award in Law, Univ. of Va 1998. *Publication:* Right in the Old Gazoo: A Lifetime of Scrapping with the Press 1997. *Address:* Burg, Simpson, Eldredge, Hersh & Jardine, 1135 14th Street, PO Box 490, Cody, WY 82414, USA (office). *Telephone:* (307) 527-7891 (office). *E-mail:* asimpson@burgsimpson.com (office). *Website:* www.burgsimpson.com (office).

SIMPSON, John, CBE, MA, FRGS; British broadcaster and writer; *World Affairs Editor, BBC;* b. (John Cody Fidler-Simpson), 9 Aug. 1944, Cleveleys; s. of Roy Fidler-Simpson and Joyce Leila Vivien Cody; m. 1st Diane Petteys 1965 (divorced 1996); two d.; m. 2nd Adèle Krüger 1996; one s.; ed St Paul's School, London, Magdalene Coll. Cambridge; joined BBC 1966, Foreign Corresp. in Dublin, Brussels, Johannesburg 1972–78, Diplomatic Corresp., BBC TV 1978–80, Political Ed. 1980–81, Diplomatic Ed. 1982–88, Foreign Affairs Ed. (now World Affairs Ed.) 1988–; Contributing Ed. The Spectator 1991–95; columnist, Sunday Telegraph 1995–; Chancellor, Roehampton Univ. 2005–; Hon. Fellow, Magdalene Coll., Cambridge 2000; Hon. DLitt (De Montfort) 1995, (Univ. of E Anglia) 1998; Dr hc (Nottingham) 2000; Golden Nymph Award Cannes 1979, BAFTA Reporter of the Year 1991, 2001, Royal TV Soc. Dimbleby Award 1991, Peabody Award 1998, Emmy Award (for coverage of the fall of Kabul) 2002, Bayeux War Correspondents' Prize 2002, Int. Emmy Award, New York 2002. *Publications:* The Best of Granta 1966, The Disappeared 1985, Behind Iranian Lines 1988, Despatches from the Barricades 1990, From the House of War 1991, The Darkness Crumbles 1992, In the Forests of the Night 1993, Lifting the Veil: Life in Revolutionary Iran 1995, The Oxford Book of Exile 1995, Strange Places, Questionable People (autobiography) 1998, A Mad World, My Masters 2000, News from No Man's Land: Reporting the World 2002, Days from a Different World: A Memoir of Childhood (autobiography) 2005, Twenty Tales from the War Zone 2007, Not Quite World's End 2007, Unreliable Sources: How the 20th Century was Reported 2010, We Chose to Speak of Love and Strife 2016. *Leisure interests:* travel, scuba diving, book collecting. *Address:* BBC World Affairs Unit, Broadcasting House, Portland Place, London, W1A 1AA, England.

SIMPSON, Patricia Ann, BSc (Hons), PhD, FRS; British research scientist; *Professor Emeritus, Department of Zoology, University of Cambridge;* b. 9 Dec. 1945, Poona, India; d. of James Simpson and Peggy Simpson; ed Univ. of Southampton, Univ. Pierre et Marie Curie, Paris; ind. researcher, CGM, Gif sur Yvette 1975–80; Research Dir CNRS Strasbourg 1981–2000; Wellcome Trust Prin. Fellow, Dept of Zoology, Univ. of Cambridge 2000–11, Prof. of Comparative Embryology 2002–11, Prof. Emer. 2012–; mem. European Molecular Biology Org. (EMBO) 1990; Fellow, AAAS 2012; Honorary Fellow, Newnham Coll., Cambridge 2016; Silver Medal, CNRS, France 1993, Waddington Medal, British Soc. for Developmental Biology 2008. *Publication:* The Notch Receptors 1994. *Leisure interests:* woodwork, boating, hiking, travel, gardening. *Address:* Department of Zoology, University of Cambridge, Downing Street, Cambridge, CB2 3EJ (office); 25 Temple End, Great Wilbraham, Cambs., CB21 5JF, England (home). *Telephone:* (1223) 336600 (office); (1223) 880664 (home). *Fax:* (1223) 336676 (office). *E-mail:* reception@zoo.cam.ac.uk (office). *Website:* www.zoo.cam.ac.uk (office).

SIMPSON-MILLER, Most Hon. Portia Lucretia, BPA; Jamaican politician; b. 12 Dec. 1945, Wood Hall, St Catherine; m. Errald Miller; ed St Martin's High School, Union Inst., Miami, Fla; Councillor in Kingston, People's Nat. Party (PNP) 1974, 1976; Vice-Pres. PNP 1978–2006, Pres. 2006–, mem. Exec. Council and Nat. Exec. Council PNP; PNP Spokesperson on Women's Affairs, Pensions, Social Security, Consumer Affairs 1983–89; MP for SW St Andrew 1989–2017; fmr Parl. Sec., Ministry of Local Govt, later in Office of the Prime Minister; Minister of Labour, Welfare and Sports 1989–93, of Labour and Welfare 1993–95, of Labour, Social Security and Sports 1995–2000, of Tourism and Sports 2000–02, of Local Govt and Sport 2002–06; Prime Minister (first woman) of Jamaica 2006–07, Prime Minister and Minister of Defence, Devt, Information and Sports 2012–16; Leader of the Opposition 2007–12, 2016–17; Vice-Pres. Socialist International 2013–; mem. Council of Women World Leaders; Jamaican Order of the Nation 2006; Dr hc (Union Inst.); World Women and Sport Trophy, IOC 2007, named Person of the Year by The Gleaner and Observer in the Gleaner Awards 2011. *Address:* People's National Party, 89 Old Hope Rd, Kingston, 6, Jamaica (office). *Telephone:* 978-1337 (office). *Fax:* 978-5851 (office). *E-mail:* secretariat@peoplesnationalparty.org (office). *Website:* www.pnp.org.jm (office).

SIMPSON OF DUNKELD, Baron (Life Peer), cr. 1997, of Dunkeld in Perth and Kinross; **Rt Hon. George Simpson,** FCIS, FCCA, FRSA; British business executive and company director; b. 2 July 1942, Scotland; s. of William Simpson and Eliza Jane Simpson (née Wilkie); m. Eva Chalmers 1963; one s. one d.; ed Morgan Acad., Dundee, Dundee Inst. of Technology; Sr Accountant Scottish Gas 1964–68; Cen. Audit Man. British Leyland 1969–73, Financial Controller, Leyland Truck and Bus Div. 1973–76, Dir of Accounting, Leyland Cars 1976–78, Finance and Systems Dir, Leyland Trucks 1978–80; Man. Dir Coventry Climax Ltd 1980–83, Freight Rover Ltd 1983–86; CEO Leyland DAF 1986–88; Man. Dir Rover Group 1989–91, Chair. 1991–94, CEO 1991–92; Dir BAe 1990–94, Deputy CEO 1992–94; Chair. Ballast Nedam Construction Ltd 1992–94, Arlington Securities 1993–94; CEO Lucas Industries PLC 1994–96; Man. Dir Marconi PLC (fmrly GEC PLC) 1996–99, CEO 1999–2001; mem. Supervisory Bd and Dir (non-exec.) Pilkington PLC 1992–99, Northern Venture Capital 1992–2000, Pro Share 1992–4, ICI PLC 1995–2001, Nestlé SA 1999–2003; mem. Bd of Dirs Triumph Group Inc. 2003–; Dir (non-exec.) Alstom SA 1997–2004, Bank of Scotland 2000–02; mem. Exec. Cttee SMMT 1986– (Vice-Pres. 1986–95, Pres. 1995–96); Industrial Prof., Univ. of Warwick 1991–; Gov. Nat. Inst. of Econ. and Social Research 1997–; Fellow, Univ. of Abertay; mem. European Round Table of Businessmen 1997–2001, Mayor of Shanghai's Business Advisory Council 1998–2000; Hon. Fellow, London Business School; hon. degrees from Univs of Warwick and Aston. *Leisure interest:* golf. *Address:* House of Lords, London, SW1A 0PW, England (office). *E-mail:* lordsimps@aol.com (home).

SIMS, Christopher A., BA, PhD; American economist and academic; *John J. F. Sherrerd '52 University Professor of Economics, Princeton University;* b. 21 Oct. 1942; ed Harvard Coll., Univ. of California, Berkeley, Harvard Univ.; Instructor in Econs, Harvard Univ. 1967–68, Asst Prof. of Econs 1968–70; Assoc. Prof. of Econs, Univ. of Minnesota 1970–74, Prof. of Econs 1974–90, mem. Grad. Faculty in Statistics 1973–90; Henry Ford II Prof. of Econs, Yale Univ. 1990–99, Dir of Grad. Studies, Dept of Econs 1992–94; Prof. of Econs, Princeton Univ. 1999–, Harold H. Helm '20 Prof. of Econs and Banking 2004–12, John J. F. Sherrerd '52 Univ. Prof. of Econs 2012–, Dir of Grad. Studies, Dept of Econs 2003–08, 2013–14, Assoc., Princeton Dept of Operations Research and Financial Eng 2012–, Co-Dir Griswold Center for Econ. Policy Studies 2014–; Research Fellow, Nat. Bureau of Econ. Research 1970–71; Visiting Prof., Yale Univ. 1974, MIT 1979–80; part-time consultant, Control Data Business Advisors 1981–83; consultant, Fed. Reserve Bank of Minneapolis 1983, 1986–87, Fed. Nat. Mortgage Asscn 1999–2002; Dir Inst. for Empirical Macroeconomics, Minneapolis 1987–91; Visiting Scholar, Fed. Reserve Bank of Atlanta most years since 1995, Fed. Reserve Bank of New York 1994–97, 2004–, Fed. Reserve Bank of Philadelphia 2000–03, IMF 2003; Resident Scholar, Fed. Reserve Bank of New York 2012–13; Chair. Section 54, Econ. Sciences, NAS 2006–09; Co-Chair. Program Cttee, World Congress of Econometric Soc. 1990; mem. NSF Econs Advisory Panel 1973–75, American Econ. Asscn 1974–75 (Pres. 2012), American Statistical Asscn Advisory Cttee to Census 1976–81, Fellows Nominating Cttee of Econometric Soc. 1980, 1985, Program Cttee for World Congress of Econometric Soc. 1980, Brookings Panel of Econ. Activity 1975–76, 2001–02 (Sr Advisor 1977–), Cttee on Nat. Statistics of Nat. Research Council, NAS 1982–85, Panel on Natural Gas Statistics of Cttee on Nat. Statistics 1982–85, Program Cttee, Summer Meetings of the Econometric Soc. 1971, 1984, 1998, NSF Program Advisory Cttee for Advanced Scientific Computing 1984–86, SIAM FCCSET Workshop on Research in Large Scale Computational Science and Eng 1987, Search Cttee for Dir of Minnesota Supercomputer Inst. 1987–88, Comm. for Behavioral and Social Sciences and Educ., Nat. Research Council 1992–98, Nat. Acad. of Sciences Report Review Cttee 2000–03; mem. Bd Barcelona Grad. School of Econs 2007–; American Econometrics Ed. Review of Economic Studies 1973–75; Co-Ed. Econometrica 1977–81; Assoc. Ed. Journal of Applied Econometrics 1986–89, Journal of Business and Economic Statistics 1986–93; mem. Editorial Bd Annals of Economic and Social Measurement 1975, Journal of Economics and Philosophy 1985–94, International Journal of Supercomputer Applications 1987–89, Proceedings of the National Academy of Sciences 1996–2000; mem. Council of the Econometric Soc. 1979–80, 1990–92, Exec. Cttee of Econometric Soc. 1992, Second Vice-Pres. Econometric Soc. 1993, First Vice-Pres. 1994, Pres. 1995; mem. American Acad. of Arts and Sciences 1988, NAS 1989; Fellow, Econometric Soc. 1975, Minnesota Supercomputer Inst. 1987–91; Fisher-Schultz Lecturer, European Meetings of the Econometric Soc. 1977, Nobel Prize in Econs (with Thomas Sargent) 2011. *Publications:* numerous papers in professional journals on econometric theory for dynamic models and macroeconomic theory and policy. *Address:* Department of Economics, 104 Fisher Hall, Princeton University, Princeton, NJ 08544-1021 (office); 276 Dodds Lane, Princeton, NJ 08540, USA (home). *Telephone:* (609) 258-4033 (office); (609) 688-1001 (home). *Fax:* (609) 258-6419 (office). *E-mail:* sims@princeton.edu (office). *Website:* www.princeton.edu/~sims (office).

ŞIMŞEK, Mehmet, BS, MPhil; Turkish economist and politician; b. 1 Jan. 1967, Batman prov.; ed Ankara Univ., Univ. of Exeter, UK; fmr Research Asst, Int. Econs and Econ. Devt Dept, Ankara Univ.; Sr Economist, US Embassy, Ankara 1993–97; worked for UBS Bank, New York 1997; Sr Economist and Bank Analyst, Deutsche Securities 1998–2000; joined Merrill Lynch, London, UK 2000, Chief Economist and Strategist for emerging Europe, Middle East and Africa region 2005–07; mem. Grand Nat. Ass. 2007–, Deputy Prime Minister 2015–18; Minister of State and Head of Treasury 2007–09, Minister of Finance 2009–15; mem. Parl. (AKP—Adalet ve Kalkinma Partisi/Justice and Devt Party) 2007–. *Address:* Adalet ve Kalkınma Partisi (AKP) (Justice and Development Party), Söğütözü Cad. 6, Çankaya, Ankara, Turkey (office). *Telephone:* (312) 2045000 (office). *Fax:* (312) 2045044 (office). *E-mail:* rte@akparti.org.tr (office). *Website:* www.akparti.org.tr (office).

SIMUKANGA, Stephen, BMinSc, MMinSc, PhD, CEng, FIMMM, FSAIMM, FEIZ; Zambian metallurgist, academic and university administrator; *Director-General, Higher Education Authority of Zambia;* b. 20 May 1957, Mufulira; ed Univ. of Zambia, Univ. of Strathclyde, UK; began career in Luanshya mine of Zambia Consolidated Copper Mines Ltd 1982; Visiting Prof., Univ. of Cape Town for ten years; Prof. of Metallurgy and Mineral Processing, Univ. of Zambia, Vice-Chancellor 2007–15, Coordinator of Mineral Resources Unit of UNU-INRA, School of Mines; Dir-Gen. Higher Educ. Authority of Zambia 2016–; Operating Unit Coordinator, United Nations Univ.; consultant and researcher in areas of mine and quarry evaluation, mineral processing and the environment; Chair. Nat. Inst. for Scientific and Industrial Research, Examinations Council of Zambia; Fellow, Inst. of Materials, Minerals and Mining, Southern African Inst. of Mining and Metallurgy, Eng Inst. of Zambia; mem. Royal Acad. of Eng. *Address:* Higher Education Authority of Zambia, PO Box 50795, Ridgeway Dedan Kimathi Road, Lusaka, Zambia (office). *Telephone:* (21) 227084 (office). *E-mail:* info@hea.org.zm (office). *Website:* www.hea.org.zm.

SIMUUSA, Wylbur C., MSc, MBA; Zambian mining engineer and politician; *Ambassador to Republic of Korea;* b. 9 Sept. 1962; m. Beatrice Simuusa; mem. Nat. Ass. (Parl.) for Nchanga constituency 2007–; Minister of Mines 2011, of Lands, Natural Resources and Environmental Protection –2013, of Foreign Affairs 2013–14, of Agric. and Livestock 2014–15; Chair. Regional Center for Mapping of Resources for Devt Conf. of Ministers 2013; Amb. to Republic of Korea 2017–; mem. Patriotic Front. *Address:* Embassy of Zambia, 44–gil, 2 Hoenamu-ro, Yongsan-gu, Seoul, Republic of Korea (office). *Telephone:* (2) 793-1961 (office). *E-mail:* zamembseoul@gmail.com (office).

SINAI, Yakov G., PhD; Russian mathematician and academic; *Professor of Mathematics, Princeton University;* b. 21 Sept. 1935, Moscow; s. of Gregory Sinai and Nadezda Kagan; m. Elena Vul; one s.; ed Moscow State Univ.; Scientific Researcher, Lab. of Probabilistic and Statistical Methods, Moscow State Univ. 1960–71, Prof. of Math. 1971–93; Prof. of Math., Princeton Univ., NJ, USA 1993–, Thomas Jones Prof. 1997–98; Sr Researcher, Landau Inst. of Theoretical Physics, Russian Acad. of Sciences 1971–; Chair. Fields Medal Cttee, Int. Math. Union 2001; Foreign mem. Hungarian Acad. of Sciences 1993, Brazilian Acad. of Sciences 2000, Polish Acad. of Sciences 2009; Foreign Assoc. NAS 1999; mem. Academia Europaea 2008, Royal Soc. of London 2009; Foreign Hon. mem. American Acad. of Arts and Sciences 1983; Hon. mem. London Math. Soc. 1992; Dr hc (Warsaw) 1993, (Budapest Univ. of Tech. and Econs) 2002, (Hebrew Univ. of Jerusalem) 2005, (Warwick) 2010; Loeb Lecturer, Harvard Univ. 1978, Plenary Speaker, Int. Congress on Math. Physics, Berlin 1981, Marseilles 1986, Boltzman Gold Medal 1986, Distinguished Lecturer, Israel 1989, Heineman Prize 1989, Markov Prize 1990, S. Lefshetz Lecturer, Mexico 1990, Plenary Speaker, Int. Congress of Mathematicians, Kyoto 1990, Dirac Medal, Int. Centre for Theoretical Physics, Trieste 1992, Landau Lecturer, Hebrew Univ. of Jerusalem 1993, Wolf Foundation Prize in Math. 1997, Plenary Speaker, First Latin American Congress in Math. 2000, Brazilian Award of Merits in Sciences 2000, Andreewski Lecturer, Berlin 2001, Jürgen Moser Lecture Prize, Soc. for Industrial and Applied Math. 2001, Bowen Lecturer, Univ. of California, Berkeley 2001, Alaoglu Lecturer, California Inst. of Tech. 2002, Frederic Esser Nemmers Prize in Math. 2002, Lagrange Prize 2008, Henri Poincaré Prize, Int. Asscn of Math. Physics 2009, Dobrushin Int. Prize, Inst. of Information Transmission, Russian Acad. of Sciences 2009, AMS Steele Prize for Lifetime Achievement 2012, Abel Prize, Norwegian Acad. of Science and Letters 2014. *Publications:* Probability Theory: An Introductory Course 1992, Classical Nonintegrability, Quantum Chaos (jtly) 1997, Selected Works of Eberhard Hopf with Commentaries (co-ed.) 2003; more than 140 articles in math. journals on dynamical systems (Kolmogorov-Sinai entropy). *Address:* Department of Mathematics, Princeton University, 708 Fine Hall, Washington Road, Princeton, NJ 08544-1000, USA (office). *Telephone:* (609) 258-4200 (office); (609) 258-4199 (office). *Fax:* (609) 258-1367 (office). *E-mail:* sinai@math.princeton.edu (office). *Website:* www.math.princeton.edu (office).

SINAISKY, Vassily Serafimovich; Russian conductor; b. 20 April 1947, Abez, Komi Autonomous Repub., Russia; m. Tamara Grigoryevna Sinayskaya; one s.; ed Leningrad State Conservatory; Artistic Dir and Chief Conductor Novosibirsk State Symphony 1971–73; Latvian State Symphony 1975–89; Moscow State Philharmonic Orchestra 1991–96; State Symphony Orchestra of Russia 2000–02; Prin. Guest Conductor BBC Philharmonic 1996–2011, Conductor Emer. 2012–; worked with Orchestre Nat. de France, Berlin Philharmonic Orchestra, Orchestre Philharmonic du Luxembourg, Royal Scottish Nat. Orchestra and Finnish Radio Symphony; apptd Principal Conductor, Malmö Symphony Orchestra 2007, now Hon. Conductor; Conductor-in-Residence, Bolshoi Theatre 2009–10, Music Dir 2010–13; Prof. of Conducting, St Petersburg Conservatoire; Gold Medal and First Prize, Karajan Competition, Berlin 1973, People's Artist of Latvia 1981. *Address:* c/o Jessica Ford, Intermusica Artists' Management Ltd, 36 Graham Street, Crystal Wharf, London, N1 8GJ, England (office). *E-mail:* jford@intermusica.co.uk (office). *Website:* vassilysinaisky.com.

SINAMENYE, Mathias; Burundian economist, politician and fmr central banker; Second Vice-Pres. of Burundi for Econ. and Social Affairs 1998–2002; apptd Exec. Dir World Bank Group, in charge of the African region; Head of Del. to UN Gen. Ass. Special Session on HIV/AIDS, New York June 2001; fmr Gov. Banque de la République du Burundi; mem. Bd of Dirs African Trade Insurance Agency.

SINATAMBOU, Marie Joseph Noël-Etienne Ghislain, BA, DEA; Mauritian lawyer and politician; *Minister of Social Security, National Solidarity and the Environment and Sustainable Development;* b. 1964; s. of Georges Sinatambou and Claire Chantal; m. 1st Manisha Bissoon (divorced), one s.; m. 2nd Sandyana Sinatambou, one d.; ed Collège Royal de Curepipe, Balliol Coll., Oxford; fmr Assoc. Research Fellow, Inst. of Advanced Legal Studies, Univ. of London; Owner, Sinatambou Chambers (law firm), Port Louis; mem. Nat. Ass. for Constituency no 16 (Vacoas-Floréal) 2005–, Deputy Speaker 2008; Minister of Information Tech. 2005–08, of Foreign Affairs, Regional Integration and Int. Trade 2014–16, of Technology, Communication and Innovation 2016, of Environment, Sustainable Devt and Disaster and Beach Man. 2016–17, of Social Security, Nat. Solidarity and the Environment and Sustainable Devt 2017–; fmr mem. Parti Travailliste; mem. Alliance Lepep (Alliance MSM/PMSD/ML) 2014–. *Address:* Ministry of Social Security, National Solidarity and the Environment and Sustainable Development, Renganaden Seeneevassen Building, 13th Floor, cnr Jules Koenig and Maillard Sts, Port Louis, Mauritius (office). *Telephone:* 207-0625 (office). *Fax:* 212-8190 (office). *E-mail:* mss@mail.govmu.org (office). *Website:* socialsecurity.govmu.org (office).

SINCKLER, Christopher Peter, BA, MA; Barbadian civil servant, politician and academic; m. Arlyn Mayers; two s. one d.; ed Univ. of the West Indies; worked on econ. policy issues with IBRD (World Bank), IMF, IDB, WTO, CARICOM, African, Caribbean and Pacific Group of States, EU, among others; Lecturer in Govt and Political Science, Univ. of the West Indies 1990–94, 2006; Exec. Dir Caribbean Policy Devt Centre (coalition of Caribbean non-governmental orgs) 1999–2008, also Prin. Liaison for global NGOs to Exec. Bd of World Bank 1999–2003; mem. Democratic Labour Party, currently Gen. Sec.; MP for St St Michael NW; Minister of Foreign Affairs, Foreign Trade and Int. Business 2008, of Social Care, Constituency Empowerment and Urban Devt 2008–10, of Finance and Econ. Affairs 2010–18. *Leisure interests:* reading, cycling and tennis. *Address:* c/o Ministry of Finance and Economic Affairs, East Wing, Warrens Office Complex, St Michael, Bardados (office). *E-mail:* csinckler@sunbeach.net.

SINCLAIR, Charles James Francis, CBE, BA, FCA; British business executive; *Chairman, Associated British Foods plc;* b. 4 April 1948; s. of Sir George Sinclair and Lady Sinclair; m. Nicola Bayliss 1974; two s.; ed Winchester Coll. and Magdalen Coll., Oxford; Voluntary Service Overseas, Zambia 1966–67; with Deardon Farrow, chartered accountants 1970–75; with Associated Newspapers Holdings Ltd 1975, Man. Dir 1988, Group Chief Exec. Daily Mail and Gen. Trust plc (after merger with Associated Newspapers) 1988–2008; Chair. Associated British Foods plc 2009–; mem. Bd of Dirs (non-exec.) Euromoney Institutional Investor PLC 1985–2008, SVG Capital 2009–13, Schroders PLC 1990–2005, Reuters Group PLC 1994–2005; fmr mem. Voluntary Service Overseas UK, Reuters Inst. for the Study of Journalism (Bd mem.); Chair. Bd of Trustees Minack Theatre Trust, Porthcuno, Cornwall; Gov., Courtauld Inst. of Art 2011–; Fellow, Winchester Coll. 2010, Warden 2014–. *Leisure interests:* opera, fishing, skiing. *Address:* Associated British Foods plc, Weston Centre, 10 Grosvenor Street, London, W1K 4QY, England. *Website:* www.abf.co.uk.

SINCLAIR, Sir Clive Marles, Kt; British inventor; b. 30 July 1940, London; s. of George William Carter Sinclair and Thora Edith Ella Sinclair (née Marles); m. 1st Ann Trevor-Briscoe 1962 (divorced 1985, died 2004); two s. one d.; m. 2nd Angie Bowness 2010 (divorced 2017); ed St George's Coll., Weybridge; Ed. Bernards Publrs Ltd 1958–61; Chair. Sinclair Radionics Ltd 1962–79, Sinclair Research Ltd 1979, Sinclair Browne Ltd 1981–85, Cambridge Computer 1986–90, Retro Computers Ltd 2014–; Chair. British Mensa 1980–98, Hon. Pres. 2001–; Visiting Fellow, Robinson Coll., Cambridge 1982–85; Visiting Prof., Imperial Coll., London 1984–92; Dir Shaye Communications Ltd 1986–91, Anamartic Ltd; Hon. Fellow, Imperial Coll., London 1984; Hon. DSc (Bath) 1983, (Warwick, Heriot Watt) 1983, (UMIST) 1984; Royal Soc. Mullard Award 1984. *Publications:* Practical Transistor Receivers 1959, British Semiconductor Survey 1963. *Leisure interests:* music, poetry, mathematics, science, poker. *Address:* Retro Computers Ltd, The Hat Factory, 65-67 Bute Street, Luton, Bedfordshire, LU1 2EY, England (office). *Website:* retro-computers.co.uk (office).

SINCLAIR, Rt Hon. Ian McCahon, AC, PC, BA, LLB; Australian consultant, lawyer, farmer, company director and fmr politician; *Chairman, Foundation for Rural and Regional Renewal;* b. 10 June 1929, Sydney, NSW; s. of George Sinclair and Hazel Sinclair; m. 1st Margaret Tarrant 1956 (died 1967); one s. two d.; m. 2nd Rosemary Edna Fenton 1970; one s.; ed Knox Grammar School, Wahroonga and Sydney Univ.; barrister 1952–; mem. Legis. Council in NSW Parl. 1961–63, House of Reps 1963–98; Minister for Social Services 1965–68; Minister Assisting Minister for Trade and Industry 1966–71; Minister for Shipping and Transport 1968–71, for Primary Industry 1971–72; Deputy Leader Country Party (now Nat. Party) 1971–84, Fed. Parl. Leader 1984–89, Party Spokesman on Defence, Foreign Affairs, Law and Agric. 1973–75, Opposition Spokesman on Agric., Leader of Opposition in House of Reps 1974–75; Minister for Agric. and Northern Australia Nov.–Dec. 1975, for Primary Industry 1975–79, for Communications 1980–82, for Defence 1982–83; Leader of Govt in House of Reps 1975–82; Leader of Opposition in House of Reps 1983–87, Opposition Spokesman for Defence 1983–87, for Trade and Resources 1987–89; Shadow Special Minister of State 1994; mem. Jt Cttee of Foreign Affairs, Defence and Trade 1991–98, Chair. 1996–98; Chair. Australian Constitutional Convention 1998; Speaker, House of Reps, Fed. Parl. 1998; Adjunct Prof. of Political Science, Univ. of New England 2000–; Man. Dir Sinclair Pastoral Co. 1953–, Grazier 1953–; Dir Farmers' and Graziers' Co-operative Co. Ltd 1962–65; Chair. Australian Rural Summit 1999, Australia Taiwan Business Council 2000–10, Foundation for Rural and Regional Renewal 2000–, CRC for Sheep 2001–08, Good Beginnings Australia 2001–10; Pres. Austcare 2000–09; Pres. Scouts Australia (NSW) 2001–, Murray-Darling Basin Comm. 2003–08; Chair. NSW Native Vegetation Reform Implementation Group 2003–06; Co-Chair. NSW Health Care Advisory Council 2005–11; Dir Regional Australia Inst. 2011–18; Patron Sir Roden Cutler Charities 2004–11; Hon. DUniv (Univ. of New England); Hon. DLitt (Southern Cross Univ.). *Leisure interests:* surfing, walking, farming. *Address:* PO Box 27, Cundletown, NSW 2430 (home); 'Mulberry Farm', Dumaresq Island, NSW 2430 (home); PO Box 41, Bendigo, Vic. 3552, Australia (office). *Telephone:* (2) 6553-8276 (home); (3) 5430-2303 (office). *E-mail:* iansinclair@ozemail.com.au (home). *Website:* www.frrr.org.au (office).

SINDAYIGAYA, Gaspard; Burundian politician and banker; *Director-General, Banque Commerciale du Burundi SM (BANCOBU);* fmr mem. Nat. Assembly for Rutana constituency (Front pour la Démocratie au Burundi); various posts with Burundi banking insts including CEO Banque Nationale pour le Developpement Economique SARL; Gov. Banque de la République du Burundi (central bank) 2007–12; Dir-Gen. Banque Commerciale du Burundi 2012–. *Address:* Banque Commerciale du Burundi SM, 84 chaussée Prince Louis Rwagasore, BP 990, Bujumbura, Burundi (office). *Telephone:* 22265200 (office). *Fax:* 22221018 (office). *E-mail:* info@bancobu.com (office). *Website:* www.bancobu.com (office).

SINDI, Hayat, PhD; Saudi Arabian biotechnologist and academic; b. 1967, Makkah; ed King's Coll., London and Univ. of Cambridge, UK, Massachusetts Inst. of Tech. and Harvard Univ., USA; left Saudi Arabia in her teens to become first Saudi and Muslim woman from Gulf region to earn PhD in biotechnology; Visiting Scholar, Harvard Univ. 2006–11; Co-founder and mem. Bd of Dirs Diagnostics For All 2007–; f. i2nstitue for Imagination and Ingenuity (helps local scientists create business plans and find investors for their ideas) 2011; mem. Saudi Arabia Shura Council 2013–; fmr PopTech Fellow in both Science and Social Innovation; apptd UNESCO Goodwill Amb. for Sciences 2012–; mem. UN Sec.-Gen.'s Scientific

Advisory Bd; announced by National Geographic as National Geographic Emerging Explorer, Mekkah Al Mukaramah Prize for scientific innovation 2010, ranked by Arabian Business amongst the Power 500: The World's Most Influential Arabs (19th) 2012, Arabian Business Award for Medicine 2013, Leadership in Civil Society Prize, Clinton Global Initiative 2014. *Address:* Diagnostics For All, 840 Memorial Drive, Cambridge, MA 02139, USA (office). *Telephone:* (617) 494-0700 (office). *E-mail:* info@dfa.org (office). *Website:* www.dfa.org (office); www .i2institute.org (office); hayatsindi.blogspot.co.uk.

SINEGAL, James (Jim) D.; American retail executive; b. 1 Jan. 1936; m. Janet Sinegal; two s. one d.; ed Helix High School, La Mesa, Calif., San Diego City Coll., San Diego State Univ.; joined FedMart 1954, held several exec. positions including Exec. Vice-Pres. Merchandising and Operations; fmr Exec. Vice-Pres. The Price Club; Pres. Sinegal, Chamberlain & Assocs –1983; Co-founder (with Jeff Brotman), Pres. and COO Costco 1983–93, CEO 1988–93, merged with The Price Club 1993, mem. Bd Dirs 1993–, Pres. and CEO Costco Wholesale Corpn 1993–2011 (retd), non-officer employee 2012–13; mem. Educ. Cttee, Washhington Business Roundtable; Trustee, Seattle Univ.; LCB Visionary Award – Trendsetter of the Year, Lundquist School of Business, Univ. of Oregon 2000, Business Achievement Award, Seattle Univ. 2002. *Address:* Costco Wholesale Corporation, 999 Lake Drive, Issaquah, WA 98027, USA (office). *Telephone:* (425) 313-8100 (office). *Fax:* (425) 313-8103 (office). *E-mail:* info@costco.com (office). *Website:* www.costco.com (office).

SINEMA, Kyrsten, BA, JD, MSW, PhD; American social worker, lawyer and politician; *Senator from Arizona;* b. 12 July 1976, Tucson, Ariz.; d. of Dan Sinema and Marilyn Sinema; m. Blake Dain (divorced); ed Brigham Young Univ., Ariz. State Univ.; social worker, Washington Elementary School Dist, Phoenix 1995–2002, Sunnyslope Community; Adjunct Prof., School of Social Work, Ariz. State Univ. 2002–; Attorney, Private Practice 2005–; Faculty mem., Center for Progressive Leadership 2006–, also Bd mem.; Dir Family Resource Center, Shaw Butte Elementary School; mem. State House of Reps, Ariz. 2004–10, Senator 2010–12; mem. US House of Reps for 9th Congressional Dist of Ariz. 2012–19, Senator from Arizona 2019–; Chair. Arizona Together 2005–; Pres. of Bd, Community Outreach and Advocacy for Refugees 2005–; mem. Bd Ariz. Death Penalty Forum 2003–, Girls for a Change 2005–, Progressive Democrats of America 2005–, Comm. to Prevent Violence Against Women 2006–; mem. Precinct Cttee, Ariz. Democratic Party 2005–; mem. Ariz. Educ. Asscn, Human Rights Fund, Civil Liberties Union, Nat. Org. of Women, Planned Parenthood, League of Women Voters; mem. of numerous congressional caucuses including Social Work, Travel & Tourism, Arts, Career and Tech. Educ. (CTE), LGBT Equality, Fire Services and Military Families; Planned Parenthood Legis. Choice Award, Legislator of the Year, AZ Public Health Asscn, Civil Rights Award, Nat. Asscn for the Advancement of Colored People. *Publication:* Unite and Conquer: How to Build Coalitions that Win and Last 2009. *Leisure interests:* ultra-marathon, iron man finisher, politics, reading, running, hiking. *Address:* United States Senate, 317 Hart Senate Office Building, 120 Constitution Avenue NE, Washington, DC 20002, USA (office). *Telephone:* (202) 224-4521 (office). *Website:* www.sinema .senate.gov (office); www.kyrstensinema.com.

SINGAY, Lyonpo Jigme, MBBS, MPH; Bhutanese politician; b. 5 May 1954, Themnangbi, Mongar Dist; ed Delhi Univ., India, San Diego State Univ., USA; Deputy Dir Public Health Div., Dept of Health Services 1987–89, Jt Dir, Dept of Health Services 1989–1993, Dir Div. of Health Services 1994–98; Sec. Royal Civil Service Comm. 1998–2003; Minister of Health 2003–07 (resgnd); mem. People's Democratic Party; Red Scarf (Dasho) 1997, Orange Scarf (Lyonpo) 2003.

SINGER, Isadore Manuel, PhD; American mathematician and academic; *Institute Professor, Department of Mathematics, Massachusetts Institute of Technology;* b. 3 May 1924, Detroit, Mich.; s. of Simon Singer and Freda Rose; m. Sheila Ruff 1961; five c.; ed Univs of Michigan and Chicago; C.L.E. Moore Instructor at MIT 1950–52; Asst Prof., UCLA 1952–54; Visiting Asst Prof., Columbia Univ. 1954–55; Visiting mem. Inst. for Advanced Study, Princeton 1955–56; Asst Prof., MIT 1956, Assoc. Prof. 1958, Prof. of Math. 1959, Norbert Wiener Prof. of Math. 1970–79, John D. MacArthur Prof. of Math. 1983–, Inst. Prof. 1987–; Visiting Prof. of Math., Univ. of Calif., Berkeley 1977–79, Prof. 1979–83, Miller Prof. 1982–83; mem. NAS, American Math. Soc., Math. Asscn of America, American Acad. of Arts and Sciences, American Philosophical Soc., American Physical Soc.; Sloan Fellow 1959–62, Guggenheim Fellow 1968–69, 1975–76; Bôcher Memorial Prize 1969, 1975–76, Nat. Medal of Science 1985, Wigner Prize, Int. Congress of Mathematicians 1989, Abel Prize (jtly with Sir Michael Atiyah) 2004. *Publications:* Lecture Notes on Elementary Topology and Geometry; author of research articles in functional analysis, differential geometry and topology. *Leisure interests:* literature, hiking, tennis. *Address:* Department of Mathematics, Massachusetts Institute of Technology, Room 2-387, 77 Massachusetts Avenue, Cambridge, MA 02139, USA (office). *Telephone:* (617) 253-5601 (office). *Fax:* (617) 253-8000 (office). *E-mail:* ims@math.mit.edu (office). *Website:* www-math.mit.edu (office).

SINGER, Maxine, PhD; American biochemist; *President Emerita, Carnegie Institution of Washington;* b. 15 Feb. 1931, New York; d. of Hyman Frank and Henrietta Perlowitz Frank; m. Daniel M. Singer 1952; one s. three d.; ed Swarthmore Coll., Yale Univ.; Research Chemist, Enzymes and Cellular Biochemistry Section, Nat. Inst. of Arthritis and Metabolic Diseases, NIH, Bethesda, Md 1958–74, Chief, Nucleic Acid Enzymology Section, Lab. of Biochemistry, Div. of Cancer Biology and Diagnosis, Nat. Cancer Inst. 1974–79, Chief, Lab. of Biochemistry 1979–87, Research Chemist 1987–88, Scientist Emer. 1988–; Pres. Carnegie Inst. of Washington 1988–2002, now Pres. Emer., Sr Scientific Advisor and mem. Bd of Trustees; Visiting Scientist, Dept of Genetics, Weizmann Inst. of Science, Rehovot, Israel 1971–72; Dir Foundation for Advanced Educ. in Sciences 1972–78, 1985–86; mem. Yale Corpn 1975–90; Chair. Smithsonian Council 1992–94 (mem. 1990–94); Chair. Comm. on the Future of the Smithsonian 1994–96; mem. Editorial Bd Journal of Biological Chemistry 1968–74, Science 1972–82; Chair. Editorial Bd Proceedings of NAS 1985–88; Scientific Council Int. Inst. of Genetics and Biophysics, Naples 1982–86, mem. Bd of Govs Weizmann Inst., Human Genome Org. 1989–, Cttee on Science, Eng and Public Policy, NAS 1989–91, Int. Advisory Bd, Chulabhorn Research Inst. 1990–; mem. Bd of Dirs Johnson & Johnson; mem. NAS, American Soc. of Biological Chemists, American

Soc. of Microbiologists, ACS, American Acad. of Arts and Sciences, Inst. of Medicine of NAS, American Philosophical Soc., New York Acad. of Sciences; Trustee, Wesleyan Univ. 1972–75, Whitehead Inst. 1985–94; Hon. DSc (Wesleyan Univ.) 1977, (Swarthmore Coll.) 1978, (Univ. of Md) 1985, (Brandeis Univ.) 1988, (Radcliffe Coll.) 1990, (Williams Coll.) 1990, (Franklin and Marshall Coll.) 1991, (George Washington Univ.) 1992, (New York Univ.) 1992, (Lehigh Univ.) 1992, (Dartmouth) 1993, (Yale) 1994, (Harvard) 1994; Dir's Award, NIH 1977, Nat. Medal of Science 1992, NAS Public Welfare Medal 2007. *Publications include:* molecular biology textbooks (with Paul Berg), Why Aren't Black Holes Black? (with Robert Hazen), George Beadle: An Uncommon Farmer (with Paul Berg) 2005, and numerous articles in major scientific journals. *Leisure interests:* scuba diving, cooking, literature. *Address:* 5410 39th Street, NW, Washington, DC 20015, USA (home). *Telephone:* (202) 939-1119.

SINGER, Miroslav, PhD; Czech economist and fmr central banker; b. 14 May 1968, Prague; m.; two c.; ed Univ. of Econs, Prague, Univ. of Pittsburgh, USA; Researcher and Lecturer, later Deputy Dir for Research, Econs Inst. of Czech Acad. of Sciences and Centre for Econ. Research and Graduate Educ., Charles Univ. 1993–95; Chief Economist, Expandia Finance 1995, Man. Dir Expandia Investment Co. 1998–99, Man. Dir Expandia Holding 2000–01; Dir of Business Services Group, PricewaterhouseCoopers Czech Repub. 2001; apptd mem. Bd Czech Nat. Bank (central bank) 2005, Vice-Gov. 2005–10, Gov. 2010–16; Lecturer, Centre for Econ. Research and Graduate Educ., Charles Univ., Univ. of Econs, Prague; mem. Supervisory Bd/Bd of Dirs Česká pojišťovna, Expandia Finance, Expandia Banka, Expandia Holding, Chemofond, Jitona, Vigona, Vlnap; mem. Editorial Bd Finance a úvěr (Journal of Economics and Finance), Business Central Europe; Central Banker of the Year Award for Central and Eastern Europe 2013, Central Banker of the Year Award for Europe 2014.

SINGER, Peter Albert David, AC, BPhil, MA; Australian philosopher, writer and academic; *DeCamp Professor of Bioethics, Princeton University;* b. 6 July 1946, Melbourne, Vic.; s. of Ernest Singer and Cora Oppenheim; m. Renata Diamond 1968; three d.; ed Scotch Coll., Univ. of Melbourne, Univ. Coll., Oxford, UK; Radcliffe Lecturer, Univ. Coll., Oxford 1971–73; Visiting Asst Prof., Dept of Philosophy, New York Univ. 1973–74; Sr Lecturer, Dept of Philosophy, La Trobe Univ., Bundoora, Vic., Australia 1974–76; Prof., Dept of Philosophy, Monash Univ., Clayton, Vic. 1977–99, Dir Centre for Human Bioethics 1981–91, Deputy Dir 1992–99; DeCamp Prof. of Bioethics, Princeton Univ., NJ, USA 1999–; Laureate Prof., Centre for Applied Philosophy and Public Ethics, Univ. of Melbourne 2005–; Prof., New Coll. of the Humanities, London 2011–; various visiting positions in USA, Canada, Italy and NZ. *Publications:* Democracy and Disobedience 1973, Animal Rights and Human Obligations (ed. with Thomas Regan) 1975, Animal Liberation: A New Ethics for Our Treatment of Animals 1975, Practical Ethics 1979, Marx 1980, The Expanding Circle: Ethics and Sociobiology 1981, Test-Tube Babies (co-ed.) 1982, Hegel 1983, The Reproduction Revolution: New Ways of Making Babies (with Deane Wells, aka Making Babies: The New Science and Ethics of Conception) 1984, In Defence of Animals (ed.) 1985, Should the Baby Live?: The Problem of Handicapped Infants (with Helga Kuhse) 1985, Applied Ethics (ed.) 1986, Animal Liberation: A Graphic Guide (with Lori Gruen) 1987, Animal Factories (with Jim Mason) 1990, Embryo Experimentation (ed.) 1990, Companion to Ethics (ed.) 1991, How Are We to Live? 1993, The Great Ape Project: Equality Beyond Humanity (ed. with Paola Cavalieri) 1993, Rethinking Life and Death 1994, Ethics (ed.) 1994, The Greens 1996, Ethics into Action 1998, A Companion to Bioethics (with Helga Kuhse) 1998, A Darwinian Left 1999, Writings on an Ethical Life 2000, One World 2002, Pushing Time Away: My Grandfather and the Tragedy of Jewish Vienna 2003, The President of Good and Evil: Taking George W. Bush Seriously 2004, The Moral of the Story (co-ed.) 2005, Eating: What We Eat and Why it Matters (with Jim Mason) 2006, The Life You Can Save 2009, The Point of View of the Universe: Sidgwick and Contemporary Ethics (co-author) 2014, One World Now 2016, Ethics in the Real World 2016, Utilitarianism: A Very Short Introduction (co-author) 2017. *Leisure interests:* bushwalking, reading, surfing. *Address:* University Center for Human Values, 5 Ivy Lane, Princeton, NJ, 08544-1013, USA (office). *Telephone:* (609) 258-2202 (office). *Fax:* (609) 258-1285 (office). *E-mail:* psinger@princeton.edu (home). *Website:* www.petersinger.info (office); www.thelifeyoucansave.org.

SINGH SINGHA, Maj.-Gen. Iqbal; Indian army officer and UN official; b. 1956; m.; two s.; ed Nat. Defence Acad., Army War Coll., Madras Univ.; Chief Logistics Officer, UN Mission in Eritrea and Ethiopia (UNMEE) 2003–05; Col-Gen. Staff Sub-Conventional Operations, Army Training Command 2005–06, Pres. Army Standing Establishment Cttee 2007–09, Brig.-Gen. Staff Operations 2009–10, Gen. Officer, Commanding Infantry Div. 2010–12; Head of Mission and Force Commdr UN Disengagement Observer Force (UNDOF) 2012–15. *Address:* c/o United Nations Disengagement Observer Force (UNDOF), Department of Peacekeeping Operations, United Nations, New York, NY 10017, USA (office).

SINGH, Lt-Gen. (retd) Ajai, MSc; Indian army officer (retd) and government official; b. 20 Nov. 1935, Rajasthan; s. of Raj Dalpat Singh; ed Mayo Coll., Ajmer, Madras Univ.; joined Indian Army, Tank Commdrs Course, Czechoslovakia 1966, Defence Services Staff Course, Wellington 1972, Higher Command Course, Coll. of Combat, Mhow 1979–80, Royal Coll. of Defence Studies, London, UK 1983, Discussions at RAND Co-operation, USA 1983, 1989, saw action in Indo-Pak wars 1965, 1971; Commdr Ind. Armed Brigade, Ambala 1980–82, BGS I-Corps, Mathura 1982–84, Dir-Gen. WE, Army HQ, New Delhi 1985–87, GOC 31 Armoured Div., Jhansi 1987–89, Dir-Gen. Mechanised Forces, Army HQ, New Delhi 1989–90, GOC 4 Corps, Tezpur, Assam 1990–92, Dir-Gen. Combat Vehicles, Army HQ, New Delhi 1992–93, CCR&D, Defence Research & Devt Org., Ministry of Defence 1993–95; Gov. of Assam 2003–08; fmr Chair. North Eastern Council; Indian Mil. Acad. Sword of Honour and Silver Medal, (Best All Round Gentleman Cadet of June 1956 Batch), Mentioned in Despatches for Gallantry, Indo-Pak War 1965; Ati Vishist Seva Medal for Gallantry 1986, Param Vishist Seva Medal for Gallantry 1992. *Leisure interests:* tennis, squash, hockey, football, cricket, polo, golf, oil and crayon painting, landscaping, music, wildlife and Environment, time and personnel management techniques and resource optimization.

SINGH, Lt-Gen. (retd) Ajay Kumar, MSc, M.Phil; Indian government official and fmr army officer; s. of Chowdhry Jai Narain Singh and Shrimati Tripti Devi; m. Suneeti Singh; two s.; ed Sainik School, Staff Coll., Camberley, UK, Malinovski Tank Acad., Russia, Royal Coll. of Military Science, UK, Nat. Defence Acad.; commissioned into 7th Light Cavalry 1973, commanded 7th Cavalry, T-90 Tank Brigade, Armoured Div., Strike 1 (Corps), Gen. Officer Commanding-in-Chief, Southern Command (covering 10 States and four Union Territories) 2011–13 (retd); Lt Gov., Andaman and Nicobar Islands 2013–16, Lt Gov., Puducherry 2014–16; Param Vishisht Seva Medal, Ati Vishisht Seva Medal, Vishisht Seva Medal, Sena Medal. *Leisure interests:* cycle polo, horse riding.

SINGH, Capt. Amarinder; Indian politician and fmr army officer; *Chief Minister of Punjab;* b. 11 March 1942, Patiala, Punjab; s. of HH Maharaja Yadavindra Singh of Patiala and HH Rajmata Mohinder Kaur; m. Maharani Preneet Kaur; one s. one d.; ed Doon School, Dehradun, Nat. Defence Acad., Kharakvasla, Indian Mil. Acad., Dehradun; officer in Indian army 1963–66; mem. Lok Sabha (Parl.) 1980–84, 2014–16; elected mem. Legis. Ass. for Talwandi Sabo 1985–92, for Samana 1992–97, for Patiala Town 2002–14, for Patiala Urban 2017–; Chief Minister of Punjab 2002–07, 2017–; Pres. Punjab Pradesh Congress Cttee 1998–2002, 2010–13, 2015–; Founder and Pres. Shiromani Akali Dal (Panthik) 1991–98; mem. Marylebone Cricket Club, UK, Naval and Mil. Club, London, Golf Club, Delhi, Gymkhana Club, Patiala, Officers Inst., Patiala. *Publications include:* A Ridge Too Far: War In The Kargil Heights 1999, Lest We Forget 1999, The Last Sunset: Rise and Fall of the Lahore Durbar 2010. *Leisure interests:* gardening, shooting, sports. *Address:* Office of the Chief Minister, Govt of Punjab, 45, Sector 2, Chandigarh, India (office). *Telephone:* (172) 2740325 (office). *Fax:* (172) 2740769 (office). *E-mail:* cm@punjabmail.gov.in (office).

SINGH, Arun K., MA; Indian diplomatist; m. Dr Maina Chawla Singh; one d.; ed Univ. of Delhi; taught at Univ. of Delhi for two years; joined Foreign Service 1979, posted to Embassy in Moscow 1981–82, Second Sec., Embassy in Addis Ababa 1982–85, First Sec., Embassy in Tokyo 1985–88, Deputy Sec./Dir in charge of East Asia and Pakistan Divs, Ministry of External Affairs 1988–91, Head of Offices of Foreign Sec. and Minister of External Affairs 1991–93, Counsellor in charge of Multilateral Social and Econ. Negotiations, Perm. Mission to UN, New York 1993–97, Counsellor/Minister, Embassy in Moscow 1997–2000, Jt Sec. in charge of UN Policy, then Pakistan, Afghanistan and Iran Divs, Ministry of External Affairs 2000–05, Amb. to Israel 2005–08, Deputy Chief of Mission, Embassy in Washington, DC 2008–13, Amb. to France 2013–15, to USA 2015–16; Distinguished Non-Residential Sr Fellow, Asia Program German Marshall fund of the United States 2016–; Diplomat-in-Residence, School of Int. Service, American Univ. 2017, also, fmr Visiting Faculty; Distinguished Visiting Fellow, Emory Univ., Centre for Advanced Study of India, Univ. of Pennsylvania.

SINGH, Ashni Kumar, PhD; Guyanese government official; ed Queens Coll., Lancaster Univ., UK; fmr Deputy Auditor Gen., Office of the Auditor Gen.; fmr Commr Gen. Guyana Revenue Authority; Dir of the Budget, Ministry of Finance –2006; Minister of Finance 2006–15; fmr mem. Governing Council, Univ. of Guyana. *Address:* c/o Ministry of Finance, 49 Main and Urquhart Streets, Kingston, Georgetown, Guyana.

SINGH, Lt-Gen. (retd) Bhopinder; Indian government official and fmr army officer; b. 20 March 1946, Allahabad, UP; s. of Brig. Rajmohan Singh; m. Bhawanee Singh; ed Nat. Defence Acad.; commissioned into Rajput Regt 1965, held several command, staff and instructional appointments, commanded troops in Indo-Pak wars 1965, 1971, led counter-insurgency operations in Jammu and Kashmir, Mizoram and Assam, has been an Instructor at Indian Mil. Acad., held Gen. Staff tenures at Kargil and Kashmir Valley, commanded 17 Rajput Bn, commanded Rajput Regimental Centre, Fategarh, UP; fmr Mil., Naval and Air Attaché in Addis Ababa; as Maj.-Gen. was Additional Dir-Gen. of Org. (AG's Br.), Army HQ; Mil. Sec. to Pres. of India and Col of Pres.'s Bodyguard 1997–; Col, Rajput Regt 2002; Lt-Gov. of Andaman and Nicobar Islands 2006–13, of Puducherry 2008; Param Vishisht Seva Medal (PVSM), Ati Vishisht Seva Medal (AVSM); Army Commdr's Commendation, Ethiopian Govt Commendation Certificate. *Leisure interests:* sports, outdoor adventure activities. *Address:* House No 593, Sector 16-D, Chandigarh 160 015, India (home). *E-mail:* lgandaman@hotmail.com; lgandaman@yahoo.com.

SINGH, Gen. (retd) Bikram, M.Phil; Indian fmr army officer; m. Surjeet Kaur; two c.; ed Nat. Defence Acad., Indian Mil. Acad., Defence Services Staff Coll., Indore Univ., Army War Coll., USA; commissioned into Sikh Light Infantry regiment 1972, served as GOC Eastern Command, 15 Corps, Rashtriya Rifles, UN Peacekeeping Mission in Congo, UN Observer in Nicaragua and El Salvador, Deputy Dir-Gen. Perspective Planning (Strategy), Additional Dir-Gen. Army's Think Tank, Dir-Gen. Staff Duties, Directorate Gen. of Mil. Operations, Chief of Army Staff 2012–14 (retd); Hon. ADC to Pres.; Jammu and Kashmir Rifles Gold Medal, Param Vishisht Seva Medal, Uttam Yudh Seva Medal, Ati Vishsht Seva Medal, Sena Medal, Vishisht Seva Medal; Shrinagesh Trophy, Commando Dagger, Gold Medal for 'Tactics and Leadership'. *Leisure interests:* cricket, athletics, hockey.

SINGH, Buta, BA, MA, PhD; Indian politician; b. 21 March 1934, Jalandhar Punjab; s. of Sardar Bir Singh and Sardarni Beant Singh; m. Manjit Kaur 1964; two s. one d.; ed Lyallpur Khalsa Coll., Jalandhar, Guru Nanak Khalsa Coll., Bombay and Bundelkhand Univ., Jhansi; elected to Lok Sabha 1962, 1967, 1971, 1980, 1984, 1999; Union Deputy Minister for Railways 1974–76, for Commerce 1976–77; Minister of State in Ministry of Shipping and Transport 1980–81; Minister of Supply and Rehabilitation 1981–82, of Sport 1982–83, Cabinet Minister in charge of several ministries 1983–84, Minister of Agric. 1984–86, of Home Affairs 1986–89, of Civil Supplies, Consumer Affairs and Public Distribution 1995–96, of Communications 1998; Gov. of Bihar 2004–06; mem. Nat. Small Savings Cttee 1973–74, Senate, Punjab Univ. 1974–80, Planning Comm. 1985; Gen. Sec. Indian Nat. Congress 1978–80; Pres. All India Confed. of Farmers Asscns 1969–70, Amateur Athletic Fed. of India 1976–84, Bharat Ekta Andolan 1991; fmr Pres. Dr B. R. Ambedkar All India Inst. of Social Sciences; Chair. Nat. Comm. for Scheduled Castes 2007–10; Vice-Pres. Asian Amateur Athletics Asscn 1979. *Publications include:* Punjabi Speaking State: A Critical Analysis. *Leisure interests:* reading, writing, swimming, shooting, hiking. *Address:* Jallowal, Jalandhar, 144 001, India (home). *Telephone:* (11) 24625378 (office). *Fax:* (11) 24634743 (office).

SINGH, Digvijay, BEng; Indian politician; b. 28 Feb. 1947, Indore; s. of Balbhadra Singh; m. Amrita Rai; one s. four d.; ed Shri Govindram Seksaria Inst. of Technology and Science; mem. Madhya Pradesh Legis. Ass. 1977–84, 1994–2008; Minister, Irrigation, Agric., Fisheries and Animal Husbandry, Madhya Pradesh 1984–89; mem. Lok Sabha 1984–89, 1991–93; Chief Minister of Madhya Pradesh 1993–2003; mem. Rajya Sabha 2014–; Gen. Sec. Madhya Pradesh Youth Congress 1978–79; Pres. Madhya Pradesh Congress Cttee 1980, Council 1984, 1992. *Address:* Rajya Sabha, Parliament House Annexe, New Delhi 110 001 (office); Fort Raghogarh, Guna District, Madhya Pradesh, India (home). *Telephone:* (11) 23034695 (office). *Fax:* (11) 23792940 (office). *E-mail:* secygen.rs@sansad.nic.in (office). *Website:* rajyasabha.nic.in (office).

SINGH, Gurjit, BA; Indian diplomatist and author; m.; two c.; ed Mayo Coll., Ajmer, St Xavier's Coll., Kolkata, School of Int. Studies, Jawaharlal Nehru Univ., New Delhi, programmes at Indian Inst. of Foreign Trade, Indian Inst. of Mass Communications and Indian School of Business; joined Foreign Service 1980, served in missions in Tokyo (twice), Colombo, Nairobi (Deputy Perm. Rep. to UNEP and UN-HABITAT), Rome and was Amb. to Ethiopia, Djibouti, Rep. of India to African Union, ECA and IGAD, Amb. to Indonesia (also accred to Timor-Leste and to ASEAN) –2016, to Germany 2016–17. *Publications include:* The Abalone Factor: An Overview of India–Japan Business Relations (Bimal Sanyal Award for Research by a Foreign Service officer) 1997, The Injera and the Parantha: Enhancing the Ethio-India Relationship 2009, Masala Bambu 2015, comic book on the legacy of the India–Indonesia relationship; contrib. on econ., developmental and trade issues to various books and journals. *Leisure interest:* cricket (qualified umpire with Kenya Cricket Asscn).

SINGH, Harpal, BA, BS, MPA; Indian business executive; *Chairman, Save the Children India;* ed The Doon School, St Stephen's Coll., New Delhi, Univ. of California, Hayward, USA; has held sr positions in Tata Admin. Service, Hindustan Motors, Telco, and Bd-level responsibility at Shaw Wallace; Sr Advisor (Corp. Projects), Mahindra and Mahindra; fmr Chair. Fortis Healthcare Ltd, Fortis Financial Services Ltd, Fortis Securities Ltd, now Chair. Emer.; Chair. (non-exec.) Ranbaxy Labs Ltd 2007–08; mem. Bd of Dirs Religare Technologies 2010–15; mem. Senate, Baba Farid Univ. of Health Sciences; mem. Punjab Chief Minister's Advisory Cttee on Industrial Growth and Development of Relevant Infrastructure; mem. Confederation of Indian Industry (CII) Nat. Cttee on Healthcare and CII Nat. Cttee on Primary and Secondary Educ., Chair. CII Punjab State Council; Chair. Save the Children; Founder Chair. Trustee, Nanhi Chhaan Foundation, Chronic Care Foundation; mem. Bd of Dirs Public Health Foundation of India; Co-Chair. India-US Strategic Working Group on Healthcare; mem. Bd of Advisors NIIT Univ.; mem. India-UK Round Table. *Address:* Save the Children, Bal Raksha Bharat, 1st & 2nd Floor, Plot No. 91, Sector - 44, Gurgaon, Haryana, 122 003, India (office). *Website:* www.savethechildren.in (office).

SINGH, Harsha Vardhana, MA, MPhil, PhD; Indian economist, academic and international organization executive; *Senior Associate for Strategic Research and Policy Analysis, International Centre for Trade and Sustainable Development;* b. 30 Aug. 1956, Delhi; m. Veena Jha; two c.; ed Delhi Univ., Univ. of Oxford, UK (Rhodes Scholar); worked as consultant with Bureau of Industrial Costs and Prices, New Delhi and with ILO and UNCTAD, Geneva; worked in GATT/WTO Secr. in various capacities, including Econ. Research and Analysis Unit 1985–89, Trade Policy Review Div. 1989–91, Rules Div. 1991–95, Trade and Environment and Tech. Barriers to Trade Div. 1995–96, Office of WTO Dir-Gen. 1996–97, served as Chair. of dispute settlement panels, Deputy Dir-Gen. WTO 2005–13; Econ. Advisor, Telecom Regulatory Authority of India (TRAI) 1997–2001, Sec. cum Prin. Advisor and Head of TRAI Secr. 2001–05; Sr Fellow, Int. Inst. for Sustainable Devt 2013; currently Sr Assoc. for Strategic Research and Policy Analysis, Int. Centre for Trade and Sustainable Devt, Geneva; Adjunct Prof. of Int. and Public Affairs, School of Int. and Public Affairs, Columbia Univ. 2013–14; fmr mem. Visiting Faculty, TERI School of Advanced Studies for their Masters programme in Regulatory Studies; Hon. Prof., Indian Council for Research on Int. Econ. Relations. *Publications:* several papers on trade policy and regulatory issues. *Address:* International Centre for Trade and Sustainable Development, International Environment House 2, Chemin de Balexert 7, 1219 Châtelaine, Geneva, Switzerland (office). *E-mail:* ictsd@ictsd.ch (office). *Website:* www.ictsd.org (office).

SINGH, Iqbal, BA; Indian business executive and politician; s. of Shri Lal Singh and Santokh Kaur; m. Gurinder Bir Kaur; two s.; ed Punjab Univ.; represented Indian Nat. Youth Congress at Int. Youth Festival, Cuba 1978; fmr Gen. Sec. Punjab Youth Congress; has held several positions in Indian Nat. Congress, including Sec. All India Congress Cttee for 12 years, Perm. mem. Congress Working Cttee; mem. Parl. (Rajya Sabha) 1992–98, mem. Tourism, Steel, Scout and Raj Bhasha Cttees, Chair. Cttee constituted by Ministry of Shipping, Chair.-cum-Sec. Transport Cttee; Lt Gov. of Puducherry 2009–13; delivered address at World Hindi Conf., UN, New York; has delivered lectures in India and world-wide to promote Hindi as 'Raj Basha' (official language); attended and delivered lectures at Int. Punjabi Soc. confs in UK, USA and Canada; adviser for several trusts and educational insts; Trustee, Bhai Vir Singh Sadhan, K.L. Sehgal Memorial, B.D. Arya Educational Inst.; fmr Chief Patron Harballabh Sangeeth Maha Sabha; Founder All India Surjit Hockey Tournament; Chair. Punjab Sports Welfare Soc.; Hon. DLitt (Andhra Univ.) 2009. *Publications include:* Bhartiye Sanskriti Aur Kurukshetra (in Hindi; several awards), a book and several articles on the 10th Guru, Shri Guru Gobind Singh; several articles in leading dailies and magazines on social reforms and empowerment. *Leisure interests:* reading, writing, listening to music (especially that by Shri Sehgal, collector of his compositions), sports.

SINGH, Jagmeet, BSc, LLB; Canadian lawyer and politician; *Leader, New Democratic Party of Canada;* b. 2 Jan. 1979, Scarborough, Ont.; s. of Jagtaran Singh and Harmeet Kaur; ed Univ. of Western Ontario, Osgoode Hall Law School; Barrister and Solicitor, Pinkofskys Criminal Trial and Appeal Lawyers 2006–07; Barrister and Solicitor, Dhaliwal Law 2007–11; mem. Ont. Legis. Ass. for riding of Bramalea-Gore-Malton 2011–17, becoming Deputy House Leader; mem. New Democratic Party of Canada (NDP), Deputy Leader, Ont. NDP 2015–17, Leader NDP 2017–. *Address:* New Democratic Party of Canada, 279 Laurier Ave W, Suite 300, Ottawa, ON K1P 5J9, Canada (office). *Telephone:* (613) 236-3613 (office). *Fax:* (613) 230-9950 (office). *Website:* www.ndp.ca (office).

SINGH, Jaswant, BA, BSc; Indian politician, fmr army officer and writer; b. 3 Jan. 1938, Jasol, Rajasthan; s. of Thakur Sardar Singhji and Kunwar Baisa; m. Sheetal Kumari 1963; two s.; ed Mayo Coll., Ajmer, Jt Services Wing, Clement Town, Dehradun, Indian Mil. Acad., Dehradun; commissioned Cen. India Horse 1957; resgnd his comm. and elected to Rajya Sabha 1980; Minister of Finance and Company Affairs 1996, 2002–04; Deputy Chair., Planning Comm. 1998–99; Minister of External Affairs 1999, 2001–02, of Electronics Feb.–Oct. 1999, of Surface Transport Aug.–Oct. 1999, of Defence 2000–01; Chair. Consultative Cttee for the Ministry of External Affairs 2000–01; Leader of the House, Rajya Sabha 1999–2004, Leader of the Opposition 2004; mem. Lok Sabha from Darjeeling 2009; Outstanding Parliamentarian Award 2001. *Publications:* 23 books, including National Security: An Outline of Our Concerns 1996, Shauryo Tejo 1997, Defending India 1999, District Diary 2001, Khankhananama (Hindi) 2001, A Call to Honour: In Service of Emergent India 2006, Travels in Transoxiana 2006, Till Memory Serves 2007, Conflict & Diplomacy 2008, Our Republic – Post 6 December 1992 2008, Jinnah: India, Partition, Independence 2009, Audacity of Opinion 2012, India at Risk: Mistakes, Misconceptions and Misadventures 2013; contrib. of numerous articles on int. affairs, security and devt issues to Indian and foreign magazines, newspapers and journals. *Leisure interests:* horses, equestrian sports, reading, music, golf, chess.

SINGH, Gen. (retd) Joginder Jaswant, MSc, PVSM, AVSM, VSM; Indian army officer and government official; b. 17 Sept. 1945, Bahawalpur (now in Pakistan); s. of Jaswant Singh Marwah; m. Anupama Singh; one s. one d.; ed Nat. Defence Acad., Khadakwasla, Pune, Defence Services Staff Coll., Wellington, Nat. Defence Coll., New Delhi; joined Ninth Maratha Light Infantry (LI) 1964, served in Jammu and Kashmir, Nagaland, Arunachal Pradesh, Uttaranchal Pradesh, Col, Fifth Maratha LI, Defence Attaché to Algeria 1987–90, Commdr 79th (Ind.) Mountain Brigade, Baramula Sector, Jammu and Kashmir 1991–92, Deputy Dir-Gen. Operational Logistics, Army HQ 1993, Commdr Ninth Infantry Div. 1996–98, Additional Dir-Gen. Mil. Operations, Mil. Operations Directorate, Army HQ 1998, Commdr One 'Strike' Corps, Mathura, GOC-in-C, Army Training Command 2003, Western Command 2004, Chief of Army Staff 2005–07, fmr Chair. Jt Chiefs of Staff Cttee; Gov. of Arunachal Pradesh 2008–13; Hon. Col, Maratha Light Infantry; Hon. DLit (Shri Jagdishprasad Jhabarmal Tibrewala Univ.); Vishisht Seva Medal, War Wound Medal, Chief of Army Staff's Commendation, Param Vishisht Seva Medal 2004, Sikh of the Year Award, Sikh Forum UK 2007, Lifetime Achievement Award, Mother Teresa's Int. and Millennium Awards Cttee 2008, Punjabi Ratan Award, World Punjabi Org. 2009, GPS Achievers Lifetime Achievement Award, Global Punjabi Soc. 2010. *Publication:* A Soldier's General (autobiog.) 2012. *Leisure interests:* basketball, squash, golf, mountaineering. *E-mail:* genjjsingh@gmail.com (office).

SINGH, Kalyan, BCom; Indian politician and state official; *Governor of Rajasthan and of Himachal Pradesh;* b. 5 Jan. 1932, Madholi, Uttar Pradesh; s. of Tejpal Singh Lodhi and Sita Lodhi; m. Ramwati Singh 1952; one s. one d.; ed D.S Degree Coll., Aligarh; mem. Uttar Pradesh Legis. Ass. 1967–80, 1985–2004, mem. Cttee on Public Undertaking 1993–95, Leader of Opposition 1997; Minister, Dept of Health, UP 1977–79; Chief Minister of Uttar Pradesh 1991–92, 1997–99; mem. Bharatiya Janata Party (BJP) 1960s-2009, 2012– (following merger of Jan Kranti Party, which he formed after leaving BJP), State Gen. Sec. BJP, UP 1980, State Pres. 1987, 1994, Nat. Vice-Pres., BJP; mem. (BJP) Lok Sabha (Parl.) 2004–09, mem. (Ind.) for Etah 2009–14, Chair. Cttee on Rural Devt and Panchayati Raj, mem. Gen. Purposes Cttee, Consultative Cttee, Ministry of Health and Family Welfare, Cttee on Defence 2009; Gov. of Rajasthan 2014–, also of Himachal Pradesh 2015–. *Leisure interests:* reading, Kabbadi, tennis. *Address:* Raj Bhawan, Civil Lines, Jaipur 302 006 (office); 2 Mall Avenue, Lucknow, India (home). *Telephone:* (141) 2228716 (office); (522) 2237218 (home); 97-61837999 (mobile). *Fax:* (141) 2228737 (office). *E-mail:* dpr-comp-rj@nic.in (office). *Website:* www.rajasthan.gov.in/Government/Governor/Pages/Governor.aspx (office).

SINGH, Vice-Adm. Karambir; Indian naval officer; *Deputy Chief of Naval Staff;* b. 3 Nov. 1959, Jalandhar, Punjab; ed Defence Services Staff Coll., Tamil Nadu, Coll. of Naval Warfare; commissioned in Indian Navy 1980, served as helicopter pilot and Commdr of several warships including ICGS Chand Bibi, INS Vijaydurg, INS Rana and INA Delhi, also served on the Exec. Bd, Fleet Operations Officer of Western Fleet, then C-in-C 2017, staff positions included Joint Dir, Naval Air Staff, then Air Capt. and Officer-in Charge, Naval Air Station, Mumbai, Chief of Staff, Eastern Naval Command, then Chief of Staff, Tri-Services Unified Command, Andaman & Nicobar Islands, also Flag Officer Commanding Maharashtra and Gujarat Naval Area (FOMAG), currently Deputy Chief of Naval Staff, rank of Vice-Adm., Chief of Naval Staff-elect (June 2019–); Dir-Gen. Project Seabird; mem. Aircrew Instrument Rating and Categorization Bd (AIRCATS); Param Vishisht Seva Medal, Ati Vishist Seva Medal, Operation Vijay Medal, Operation Parakram Medal. *Address:* Integrated Headquarters of the Ministry of Defence, New Delhi 110 011, India (office). *Telephone:* (11) 23019665 (office). *E-mail:* pronavy.dprmod@nic.in (office). *Website:* www.indiannavy.nic.in (office).

SINGH, Karan, MA, PhD; Indian politician; b. 9 March 1931, Cannes, France; s. of Lt-Gen. HH Maharaja Sir Hari Singh, GCSI, GCIE, GCVO and Maharani Tara Devi, CI; m. Princess Yasho Rajya Lakshmi of Nepal 1950; two s. one d.; ed Doon School, Univ. of Jammu and Kashmir and Delhi Univ.; appointed Regent of Jammu and Kashmir 1949; elected Sadar-i-Riyasat (Head of State) by Jammu and Kashmir Legis. Ass. Nov. 1952, recognized by Pres. of India and assumed office 17 Nov. 1952, re-elected 1957 and 1962, Gov. 1965–67; Union Minister for Tourism and Civil Aviation 1967–73, for Health and Family Planning 1973–75, 1976–77, for Educ. 1979–80; re-elected mem. of Parl. 1977, 1980; Amb. to USA 1989–91; mem. Rajya Sabha (Upper House of Parl.) 2005–, Deputy Leader Congress Parl. Party, Chair. Ethics Cttee; currently Pres. Indian Council for Cultural Relations; also Chair. Auroville Foundation; led Indian Del. to World Population Conf., Bucharest; Vice-Pres. World Health Ass. 1975–76; fmr Chancellor, Jammu and Kashmir Univ., Banaras Hindu Univ., Jawaharlal Nehru Univ.; Vice-Chair. Jawaharlal Nehru Memorial Fund; fmr Chair. Delhi Music Soc., Indian Bd for Wild Life, Life Trustee of the India Int. Centre; Hon. Maj.-Gen. Indian Army, Hon. Col Jammu and Kashmir Regt 1962; Dr hc (Aligarh Muslim Univ.) 1963, (Banaras Hindu Univ., Soka Univ., Tokyo); Padma Vibhushan 2005, Outstanding Parliamentarian Award 2011. *Publications include:* Varied Rhythms (essays and poems)

1960, Shadow and Sunlight (folk songs) 1962, Prophet of Indian Nationalism: The Political Thought of Sri Aurobindo Ghosh 1893–1910 1963, Welcome the Moonrise (poems) 1965, Population, Poverty and the Future of India 1975, In Defence of Religion 1978, Religions of India 1983, One Man's World 1986, Bridge to Immortality 1987, Humanity at the Crossroads 1988, Autobiography 1989, Essays on Hinduism 1990, Brief Sojourn 1991, Hymn to Shiva and Other Poems 1991, The Mountain of Shiva (novel) 1994, India and the World 1995, Hinduism: the Eternal Religion 1999, A Treasury of Indian Wisdom 2010; and several books on political science, philosophical essays, travelogues, trans. of Dogra-Pahari folksongs and poems in English. *Leisure interests:* reading, writing, music. *Address:* Mansarovar, 3 Nyaya Marg, Chanakyapuri, New Delhi 110 003, India (home). *Telephone:* (11) 26111744 (home). *Fax:* (11) 2687 3171 (home). *E-mail:* karansingh@karansingh.com; karansi@sansad.nic.in (office). *Website:* www.karansingh.com.

SINGH, Kunwar Natwar, BA; Indian diplomatist, politician and writer; b. 6 May 1931, Bharatpur, Rajasthan; s. of Shri Govind Singhji and Shrimati Prayag Kaur; m. Shrimati Heminder Kumari 1967; one s. one d.; ed Univ. of Delhi, Univ. of Cambridge, UK, Peking Univ., People's Repub. of China; joined Foreign Service 1953; served in Peking 1956–58; Perm. Mission to UN 1961–66; mem. Bd UNICEF 1962–66, rapporteur 1963–65; mem. Prime Minister's Secr. 1966–71; Amb. to Poland 1971–73; Deputy High Commr to UK 1973–77; High Commr to Zambia 1977–80; Amb. to Pakistan 1980–82; mem. Lok Sabha 1984–89; Union Minister of State Dept of Steel, Dept of Fertilizers 1985–86; with Ministry of External Affairs 1986–89; mem. Cttee on External Affairs, on Public Accounts 1998–99; elected to Rajya Sabha 2002; mem. Cttee on External Affairs 2002–04; Minister of External Affairs 2004–05, Minister without Portfolio 2005 (resgnd); mem. Bd Dirs Air India 1982–84; Pres. UN Conf. on Disarmament and Devt, New York 1987; Padma Bhushan 1984, E. M. Forster's Literary Award 1989. *Publications include:* E. M. Forster: A Tribute 1964, The Legacy of Nehru 1965, Tales from Modern India 1966, Stories from India 1971, Maharaja Suraj Mal: 1707–63 1981, Curtain Raisers 1984, Profiles and Letters 1997, The Magnificent Maharaja Bhupinder Singh of Patiala: 1891–1938 1997, Heart to Heart 2003, My China Diary 1956–88 2009, Yours Sincerely 2009, Walking with Lions: Tales from a Diplomatic Past 2013, One Life is Not Enough: An Autobiography 2014; contribs to numerous newspapers and journals. *Address:* 'Govind Niwas', Bharatpur 321 001, India (home). *Telephone:* (11) 23013855 (home). *Fax:* (11) 23793704 (home).

SINGH, Manmohan, BA, MA, DPhil; Indian politician and economist; b. 26 Sept. 1932, Gah, Punjab (now Pakistan); s. of Gurumukh Singh and Amrit Kaur; m. Smt. Gursharan Kaur 1958; three d.; ed Panjab Univ., Chandigarh, Univs of Cambridge and Oxford, UK; Sr Lecturer in Econs, Panjab Univ. 1957–59, Reader in Econs 1959–63, Prof. of Econs 1963–65; Econ. Affairs Officer, UNCTAD, UN Secr., New York, USA 1966, Chief, Financing for Trade Section 1966–69; Prof. of Int. Trade, Delhi School of Econs, Delhi Univ. 1969–71; Econ. Adviser, Ministry of Foreign Trade 1971–72; Chief Econ. Adviser, Ministry of Finance 1972–76; Dir Reserve Bank of India 1976–80, Gov. 1982–85; mem. Econ. Advisory Council to the Prime Minister 1983–84; Mem.-Sec. Planning Comm. 1980–82, Deputy Chair. 1985–87, Chair. 2004–14; Sec.-Gen., Commr South Comm. 1987–90; econ. adviser to Prime Minister 1990–91; Chair. Univ. Grants Comm. March–June 1991; Minister of Finance 1991–96, Gov. of India on Bd of Govs of IMF and IBRD (World Bank) 1991–95; mem. Rajya Sabha (Parl.) for Assam 1991–, Chair. Parl. Standing Cttee on Commerce 1996–97, Leader of Opposition 1998–2004; Prime Minister of India and Minister-in-charge of Personnel, Public Grievances and Pensions, of Planning, of Atomic Energy, of Space 2004–14, also Minister of External Affairs 2005–06, Minister of Coal and of the Environment and Forests 2007–09, Minister of Finance 2008–09, June–July 2012, Minister of Culture 2009–11; Chair. India Cttee of Indo-Japan Jt Study Cttee 1980–83; Pres. Indian Econ. Asscn 1985; apptd by UN Sec.-Gen. mem. Group of Eminent Persons to advise him on Financing for Devt 2000; Leader of Indian del. to Aid India Consortium Meetings 1977–79, to Indo-Soviet Monitoring Group Meeting 1982, to Indo-Soviet Jt Planning Group Meeting 1980–82, to Commonwealth Heads of Govt Meeting, Cyprus 1993, to Human Rights World Conf., Vienna 1993, and mem. numerous other dels; Distinguished Fellow, LSE Centre for Asia Economy, Politics and Society 1994; Fellow, Nat. Acad. of Agricultural Sciences, New Delhi 1999; Hon. Prof., Jawaharlal Nehru Univ., New Delhi 1976, Delhi School of Econs, Univ. of Delhi 1996; Hon. Fellow, Indian Inst. of Bankers 1982, St John's Coll., Cambridge 1982, All India Man. Asscn 1994, Nuffield Coll., Oxford 1994; Grand Cordon of Order of Paulownia Flowers (Japan) 2014; Hon. DLitt (Panjab Univ., Chandigarh, Guru Nanak Univ., Amritsar, Delhi Univ., Sri Venkateswara Univ., Tirupathi, Univ. of Bologna, Italy, Univ. of Mysore, Chaudhary charan Singh Haryana, Kurukshetra Univ., Nagarjuna Univ., Nagarjunanagar, Osmania Univ., Hyderabad, Dr Bhimrao Ambedkar Univ. (fmrly Agra Univ.), Pt Ravishankar Shukla Univ., Raipur); Hon. DScS (Univ. of Roorkee); Hon. LLD (Univ. of Alberta, Edmonton); Hon. DSc (Agricultural Univ., Hisar), Thapar Inst. of Eng and Tech., Patiala, Indian School of Mines, Dhanbad (Deemed Univ.); Dr hc (Univ. of Cambridge) 2006, (King Saud Univ.) 2010, (Moscow State Inst. of Int. Relations) 2013; Univ. Medal, Panjab Univ. 1952, Uttar Chand Kapur Medal, Panjab Univ. 1954, Wright's Prize for distinguished performance, St John's Coll., Cambridge 1955, Adam Smith Prize, Univ. of Cambridge 1956, Wrenbury Scholar, Univ. of Cambridge 1957, Nat. Fellow, Nat. Inst. of Educ. (NCERT) 1986, Padma Vibhushan Award 1987, Finance Minister of the Year, Asiamoney Awards 1993, 1994, Finance Minister of the Year, Euromoney Awards 1993, Jawaharlal Nehru Birth Centenary Award, Indian Science Congress Asscn for 1994–95 1995, Nikkei Asia Prize for Regional Growth, Nihon Keizai Shimbun Inc. (NIKKEI) 1997, Justice K. S. Hegde Foundation Award for the Year 1996 1997, Lokmanya Tilak Award, Tilak Smarak Trust, Pune 1997, H.H. Kanchi Sri Paramacharya Award for Excellence from Shri R. Venkataraman (fmr Pres. of India) 1999, Annasaheb Chirmule Award, W.L.G. alias Annasaheb Chirmule Trust 2000, World Statesman Award, Appeal of Conscience Foundation 2010, Indira Gandhi Peace Prize 2018. *Publication:* India's Export Trends and Prospects for Self-Sustained Growth 1964; numerous articles in econ. journals. *E-mail:* manmohan@sansad.nic.in.

SINGH, Prakash Man, MA; Nepalese politician; *Co-General Secretary, Nepali Congress Party;* b. 3 April 1956, Chhetrapati, Kathmandu; s. of Ganesh Man Singh and Mangala Devi Singh; began political career 1977; Minister for Population and Environment 1996, later Minister for Supplies; Vice-Pres. Nepali Congress (Democratic) (after split with Nepali Congress Party—NCP) 2002, rejoined NCP 2007, currently Co-Gen. Sec.; mem. Constituent Ass. 2008–; fmr Minister for Physical Planning and Construction, Deputy Prime Minister and Minister of Federal Affairs and Local Devt 2014–15. *Address:* Nepali Congress Party, B. P. Smriti Bhavan, B. P. Nagar, Sanepa, Lalitpur, Nepal (office). *Telephone:* (1) 5555263 (office). *Fax:* (1) 5555188 (office). *E-mail:* ncparty@wlink.com.np (office). *Website:* www.nepalicongress.org (office).

SINGH, Radha Mohan, BA; Indian agriculturist and politician; *Minister of Agriculture;* b. 1 Sept. 1949, Narha Panapur Dist, East Champaran, Bihar; s. of Baidya Nath Singh and Jai Sundari Devi; m. Shanti Devi; one s. one d.; ed Bihar Univ.; mem. Bharatiya Janata Party (BJP), Gen. Sec., BJP, East Champaran, Bihar 1977–80, Gen. Sec., BJP, Bihar 1990–93, State Pres., BJP, Bihar 2006–09; mem. Lok Sabha (lower house of Parl.) for Motihari 1996–2004, for Paschim Champaran 2009–, mem. numerous cttees including Cttee on Estimates, Standing Cttee on Energy, Standing Cttee on Communications, Jt Cttee on Salaries and Allowances of MPs; Minister of Agric. 2014–; Dist Pres., Asscn of Bihar Cricket. *Address:* Ministry of Agriculture, Krishi Bhavan, Dr Rajendra Prasad Road, New Delhi 110 001, India (office). *Telephone:* (11) 23383370 (office). *Fax:* (11) 23384129 (office). *E-mail:* secy-agri@nic.in (office). *Website:* agricoop.nic.in (office).

SINGH, Raj Kishore, BTech (MechEng); Indian mechanical engineer and oil industry executive; ed Banaras Hindu Univ., Indian Inst. of Man., Ahmedabad, Admin. Staff Coll. of India, Hyderabad, Univ. of Tennessee, USA; joined Bharat Petroleum Corpn Ltd (BPCL) 1978, held various assignments at BPCL, both in Refinery and Marketing divs, Exec. Dir of LPG –2006, also headed a group constituted for transfer of technology of LPG equipment from Denmark/Italy, Dir of Refineries, BPCL 2006–10, Chair. and Man. Dir Bharat Petroleum Corpn Ltd 2010–13; Dir of Bharat Oman Refineries Ltd 2006–, Petronet LNG Ltd 2011–13, Bharat PetroResources Ltd, Premier Oil Cachar BV, Bharat Petro Resources Ltd, Numaligarh Refinery Ltd 2006–; Additional Dir, Oil and Natural Gas Corpn Ltd 2014–. *Address:* c/o Bharat Petroleum Corpn Ltd, Bharat Bhavan 1, Mumbai 400 001, India. *E-mail:* info@bharatpetroleum.com.

SINGH, Rajnath, MSc; Indian politician and farmer; *Minister of Home Affairs;* b. 10 July 1951, Bhabhora village, Tehsil Chakia of Varanasi dist, Uttar Pradesh; s. of Ram Badan Singh and Gujarati Devi; m. Savitri Singh; two s. one d.; ed Gorakhpur Univ.; Lecturer in Physics, K. B. Postgraduate Coll., Mirzapur, UP; served in various capacities with Rashtriya Swayamsevak Sangh (Nat. Volunteers' Union—Hindu nationalist org.) since 1964; Org. Sec. Akhil Bharthiya Vidyarthi Parishad (Gorakhpur Div.) 1969–71; apptd Sec. Bharatiya Jana Sangh's Mirzapur Unit 1974; joined JP Movt and was apptd its Dist Convenor; apptd Dist Pres. Jana Sangh 1975; jailed during Emergency 1975, remained in jail until elections 1977; elected as mem. Legis. Ass. from Mirzapur constituency 1977; held several positions in Bharatiya Janata Yuva Morcha (BJYM), UP State Unit as well as in Nat. Exec., BJP Sec. in UP 1983–84, State Pres. BJYM 1984–86, Nat. Gen. Sec. BJYM 1986–88, Nat. Pres. BJYM 1988, Vice-Pres. BJP, UP 1990, Pres. 1997–99, mem. Nat. Exec. BJP, Gen. Sec. Cen. BJP org. 2002–05, Pres. BJP 2005–09, 2013–14; mem. UP Legis. Council 1988–94; Minister of Educ. 1991–94; elected to Rajya Sabha 1994–99, 2003–08; Union Minister for Surface Transport 1999–2000; Chief Minister of UP 2000–02; Union Minister of Agric. 2002; elected to Lok Sabha 2009–; Minister of Home Affairs 2014–; mem. BJP, Advisory Cttee on Industry 1994–96, Consultative Cttee for Ministry of Agric., Business Advisory Cttee, House Cttee, Cttee on Human Resource Devt, Cttee on Ethics. *Publication:* book on the causes of and solutions to unemployment problems. *Leisure interests:* reading books on history, culture and science and tech. *Address:* Ministry of Home Affairs, North Block, Central Secretariat, New Delhi 110 001 (office); 04, Kalidas Marg, Lucknow 226 001, India (home). *Telephone:* (11) 23092011 (office); (522) 2236338 (home). *Fax:* (11) 23093750 (office). *E-mail:* websitemhaweb@nic.in (office). *Website:* mha.nic.in (office).

SINGH, Raman, BSc, BAMS; Indian medical practitioner and politician; b. 15 Oct. 1952, Thathapur, Kawardha Dist; s. of Vighnaharan Singh; m. Smt. Beena Singh; one s. one d.; ed Univ. of Ravishankar, Raipur; Ayurvedic medical practitioner; MLA 1990–92, 1993–98; mem. Bharatiya Janata Party (BJP) (Pradesh Mantri) 1996–; Pres. BJP Legislature Party 2003–; mem. Lok Lekha Samitti Public Accounts Samitti, Legis. Cttee; mem. Lok Sabha for Rajnandgaon 1990–, Chhattisgarh Legis. Ass. 2004–, later BJP Chief Whip; Union Minister of State for Commerce and Industry 1999–2003; Chief Minister of Chhattisgarh 2003–18 (resgnd). *Leisure interests:* sports, tourism, public welfare. *Address:* c/o Government of Chhattisgarh, New Mantralaya, Raipur 492 002, India (office).

SINGH, Sujatha, MA; Indian diplomatist; b. July 1954; d. of T. V. Rajeswar; m. Sanjay Singh; two d.; ed Lady Shri Ram Coll., Delhi School of Econs; joined Foreign Service 1976, served as Second Sec., Embassy in Bonn 1978–82, Under-Sec., Nepal, Ministry of External Affairs 1982–85, First Sec., High Comm. in Ghana 1985–89, Counsellor, Embassy in Paris 1989–92, Dir Econ. Co-ordination Unit, Ministry of External Affairs 1992–95, Jt Sec., Foreign Service Inst., New Delhi 1996–97, Consul-Gen. in Milan 2000–04, Jt Sec. (West Europe), Ministry of External Affairs –2007, High Commr to Australia 2007–12, Amb. to Germany 2012–13, Foreign Sec. 2013–15. *Address:* c/o Ministry of External Affairs, South Block, 110 011 New Delhi, India.

SINGH, Sukhmander, MS, PhD; American (b. Indian) civil engineer and academic; *Nicholson Family Professor of Civil Engineering, Santa Clara University;* b. 15 Sept. 1939, Lambi, Punjab, India; s. of Mahla Singh and Jangir Kaur; m. Charanjit Kaur 1967; one s. one d.; ed Punjabi Univ., Patiala, Punjab, Indian Inst. of Tech. (IIT), Delhi, Univ. of Ottawa and Carleton Univ., Ottawa, Canada, Rice Univ., Houston, Tex. and Univ. of Calif., Berkeley, USA; Assoc. Lecturer, IIT, Delhi 1966–67; Teaching Asst, Univ. of Ottawa 1967–68; Visiting Lecturer, Univ. of Alaska, Anchorage 1975, San Jose State Univ. 1978; Assoc. Prof. of Civil Eng, Calif. State Univ., LA 1983–86; Assoc. Prof. of Civil Eng, Santa Clara Univ., Calif. 1986–90, Chair. Dept of Civil Eng and Chair. Eng Mechanics 1990–, Nicholson Family Prof. of Civil Eng 1994–; professional work as engineer with John V. Lowney & Assocs, Palo Alto, Calif. 1969, Dames & Moore, San Francisco, London, Houston, Anchorage and Seattle offices 1969–83, as Consultant 1983–; Consultant with Purcell, Rhoades and Assocs, Hayward, Calif. 1987–, with Calpine/Kaiser 1989–; mem. numerous cttees on soil dynamics and geotechnical eng; Outstanding Immigrant Award, Researcher of the Year Award, Pres.'s Special Recognition

Award for scholarship, teaching and service. *Publications:* numerous scientific papers. *Leisure interests:* reading, hiking, volleyball playing. *Address:* Department of Civil Engineering, EC 238, Santa Clara University, Santa Clara, CA 95053, USA (office). *Telephone:* (408) 554-6869 (office). *Fax:* (408) 554-5474 (office). *E-mail:* ssingh@scu.edu (office). *Website:* www.ce.scu.edu (office).

SINGH, Urmila, BA, LLB; Indian government official; b. 6 Aug. 1946, Fingeshwar, Raipur Chhattisgarh; m. Virendra Bahadur Singh (deceased); two s. one d.; mem. MP state Legis. Ass. from Ghansaur (Seoni) constituency 1985–90, 1990–98, 1998–2003; Minister of State for Finance and Dairy Devt 1993–95, for Social Welfare and Tribal Welfare Depts 1998–2003; Chair. Nat. Comm. for Scheduled Tribes 2007–10; Gov. of Himachal Pradesh 2010–15; mem. Indian Nat. Congress party; Pres. MP Congress Cttee 1996–98; mem. Cen. Social Welfare Bd 1978–90 (Chair. 1988–89); mem. MP Scheduled Castes Welfare Advisory Cttee 1978–80, Nat. Food and Nutrition Bd 1986–88; Founder Pres. Ujjain Citizen Forum 1988–; Pres. MP Org. for Tribal Women 1993–; Chancellor, Himachal Pradesh Univ., Dr Y. S. Parmar Univ. of Horticulture & Forestry, Jaypee Univ. of Information Tech.; Pres. Indian Red Cross Soc., Himachal Pradesh State Branch, Himachal Pradesh State Council for Child Welfare, Rajya Sainik Welfare Bd, Himachal Pradesh. *Address:* Ghurwada, Tehsil-Lakhnadaun, Seoni 480 661, India (home).

SINGH, Vijay; Fijian professional golfer; b. 22 Feb. 1963, Lautoka; m. Ardena Seth; one c.; ed Univ. of N Carolina; turned professional 1982, joined PGA Tour 1983; PGA Tour victories: Buick Classic 1993, 1995, 2004, Phoenix Open 1993, Memorial Tournament 1997, Buick Open 1997, 2004, PGA Championship 1998, 2004, Sprint Int. 1998, 2004, Honda Classic 1999, Masters Tournament 2000, Shell Houston Open 2002, Phoenix Open 2003, Byron Nelson Championship 2003, John Deere Classic 2003, 2004, FUNAI Classic 2003, Pebble Beach Nat. Pro-Am 2004, New Orleans Classic 2004, Deutsche Bank Championship 2004, Canadian Open 2004, 84 Lumber Classic 2004, Chrysler Championship 2004, Sony Open 2005; int. victories: Malaysian PGA Championship 1984, Nigerian Open 1988, Swedish PGA 1988, Volvo Open di Firenze 1989, Ivory Coast Open 1989, Nigerian Open 1989, Zimbabwe Open 1989, El Bosque Open 1990, King Hassan Trophy, Morocco 1991, Turespaña Masters Open de Andalucía 1992, Malaysian Open 1992, Volvo German Open 1992, Bells Cup 1993, Scandinavian Masters 1994, Trophée Lancôme 1994, Passport Open 1995, South African Open 1997, Toyota World Match Play Championship 1997, Johnnie Walker Taiwan Open 2000, Singapore Masters 2001, Malaysian Open 2001; first player to win US$10 million in one year 2004; PGA Arnold Palmer Award 2003, PGA Tour Player of the Year 2004. *Leisure interests:* snooker, cricket, rugby, soccer, James Bond movies. *Address:* c/o International Management Group (IMG), 420 West 45th Street, New York, NY 10036, USA (office). *Telephone:* (212) 541-5640 (office). *Fax:* (212) 265-5483 (office). *Website:* www.imgworld.com (office).

SINGH, Gen. (retd) Vijay Kumar, PVSM, AVSM, YSM, ADC, MSc, MA, PhD; Indian politician and fmr army officer; *Minister of State of External Affairs;* b. 10 May 1951, Pune, Maharashtra; s. of Col Jagat Singh and Krishna Kumari; m. Bharti Singh; two d.; ed Birla Public School, Pilani, Madras Univ., Nat. Defence Acad., Defence Services Staff Coll., Wellington, US Army Rangers Course, USA, US Army War Coll., USA; third generation officer of Rajput Regt; commissioned in 2 Rajput (Kali Chindi) 1970; commanded same bn with distinction 1991–94; saw action in Liberation War of Bangladesh 1971 and Operation Pawan, Sri Lanka 1987; experience of various high profile command, staff and instructional appointments; GOC Counter Insurgency Force in Jammu and Kashmir; served in Mil. Operations Directorate, Army HQ, Col GS of Infantry Div. and was Brig. Gen. Staff of a Corps during Operation Parakram when Indian troops were mobilized on the border in the wake of attack on Parl. 2001; fmr Instructor at Infantry School, Mhow and Chief Instructor at JLW (Commando Wing), Belgaum; served as Instructor at Indian Mil. Training Team (IMTRAT) HQ, Bhutan; commanded Strike Corps Ambala-based 2 Corps in Punjab plains in Western Sector before taking over command of Eastern Army March 2008, Chief of the Army Staff 2010–12; Minister of State of External Affairs 2014–, of Overseas Indian Affairs 2014–, Minister of State (independent charge) for North East Region 2014–; social and civil society activist, formed Jantantra Morcha to Reclaim India; Yudh Seva Medal 1989, Ati Vishisht Seva Medal 2006, Param Vishisht Seva Medal 2009. *Leisure interests:* trekking, photography, sports. *Address:* Ministry of External Affairs, South Block, New Delhi 110 011 (office); Maitri Bhawan, Silokra Road, Gurgaon 122 001, India (home). *Telephone:* (11) 23011141 (office). *Fax:* (11) 23011425 (office). *E-mail:* singhvijay3940@gmail.com. *Website:* www.mea.gov.in.

SINGH, Virbhadra, BA, MA; Indian agriculturist, horticulturist and politician; b. 23 June 1934, Sarahan, Shimla Dist; s. of Padam Singh and Shanti Devi; m. Pratibha Singh; ed St Stephen's Coll., Delhi; mem. Indian del. to Gen. Ass. of UN, New York 1976; mem. Indian Nat. Congress 1962; elected to Lok Sabha 1962, 1967, 1972, 1980, 2009; Deputy Minister of Tourism and Civil Aviation 1976–77; Minister of State for Industries 1982–83; mem. Himachal Pradesh Legis. Ass. 1983–, Leader of Opposition 1998–2003, Chief Minister of Himachal Pradesh 1983–1990, 1993–98, 2003–07, 2012–17; Minister of Steel 2009–11, of Micro, Small and Medium Enterprises 2011–12; Pres. State Congress Cttee 1992–94; Pres. Sanskrit Sahitya Sammelan, Friends of Soviet Union Soc. (Himachal State Br.); Hon. Capt., Indian Army. *Leisure interests:* reading, meeting people. *Telephone:* 9418927775 (mobile). *E-mail:* virbhadra@nic.in. *Website:* www.hpvidhansabha.nic.in.

SINGH BENIWAL, Vijender, BA; Indian boxer; b. 29 Oct. 1985, Kalwas, Bhiwani Dist, Haryana; s. of Mahipal Singh Beniwal and Krishna Singh Beniwal; ed Vaish Coll., Bhiwani; middleweight boxer; all-India youth boxing champion 2003; wins include Afro-Asian Games, Hyderabad 2003 (silver medal), Summer Olympic Games, Athens 2004, Beijing 2008 (bronze medal), Commonwealth Games, Melbourne 2006 (silver medal), Asian Games, Doha 2006 (bronze medal), World Amateur Boxing Championships, Milan 2009 (bronze medal), Commonwealth Boxing Championship, India 2010 (gold medal); ranked by Int. Boxing Asscn as top-ranked boxer in middleweight category 2009; Rajiv Gandhi Khel Ratna 2009, Padma Shri 2010.

SINGH CASSIDY, Sukhinder; American internet industry executive; *Chairman, Joyus;* ed Richard Ivey School of Business, Univ. of Western Ontario, Canada; began internet career in strategy and business devt, working for Amazon.com and interactive TV provider OpenTV; Co-founder and Sr Vice-Pres. of Business Devt, Yodlee.com Inc. 1999–2003; joined Google as first Gen. Man. for Google Local & Maps 2003, later responsible for Google Books, Scholar, and Video, Pres. Asia-Pacific and Latin American Operations –2009; CEO-in-Residence Accel Partners (global venture and growth equity firm) 2009–11; CEO and Chair. Polyvore, Inc. 2010–11; Founder and Chair. Joyus (internet shopping site) 2011–; mem. Bd of Dirs TripAdvisor, Formspring, Inc.; Advisor, Twitter; mem. Advisory Council, Dept of Computer Science, Princeton Univ. *Address:* Joyus, 375 Alabama Street, Suite 325, San Francisco, CA 94110, USA (office). *Telephone:* (866) 856-9878 (office). *E-mail:* support@joyus.com (office). *Website:* www.joyus.com (office).

SINGH RAWAT, Trivendra, MA; Indian politician; *Chief Minister of Uttarakhand;* b. 20 Dec. 1960, Khairasain village, Pauri Garhwal Dist, Uttarakhand; s. of Pratap Singh; m. Sunita Rawat; two d.; ed Hemwati Nandan Bahuguna Garhwal Univ.; mem. Rashtriya Swayamsevak Sangh (nationalist org.) 1979–2002, Pracharak (apostle) for Dehradun region 1985, Organizing Sec. for Uttarakhand region (later state of Uttarakhand) 2000; mem. Uttarakhand Legis. Ass. for Doiwala 2002, 2017–; Uttarakhand Minister of Agric. 2007; Chief Minister of Uttarakhand 2017–; mem. Bharatiya Janata Party. *Address:* Chief Minister Secretariat, 4 Subash Road, Uttarakhand Secretariat, Fourth Floor New Building, Dehradun 248001, Uttarakhand, India (office). *Telephone:* (135) 2650433 (office). *Fax:* (135) 2712827 (office). *E-mail:* cm-ua@nic.in (office). *Website:* www.cm.uk.gov.in/ (office).

SINGH SUHAG, Lt-Gen. Dalbir; Indian fmr army officer; b. 28 Dec. 1954, Bishan, Haryana; s. of Ramphal Singh and Smt. Ishari Devi; m. Namita Suhag 1984; ed Nat. Defence Acad., Coll. of Defence Man., Nat. Defence Coll., Osmania Univ.; commissioned into 4th Bn of 5 Gorkha Rifles 1974; Company Commdr during Operation Pawan in Sri Lanka 1987, commanded 53 Infantry Brigade, Kashmir Valley 2003–05, 8 Mountain Div., Kargil 2007–08, Insp. Gen., Special Frontier Force 2009–11, apptd Col 5 Gorkha Rifles Regt 2011, Gen. Officer C-in-C Eastern Command 2012–13, Vice-Chief of Army Staff 2013–14, apptd Pres. Gorkha Brigade 2014, Chief of Army Staff 2014–16; also served as Instructor, Army School of Mechanical Transport, Bangalore, Indian Mil. Acad., Dehradun; Hon. Col, Brigade of Guards, Rashtriya Rifles, 61st Cavallry Regiment; Param Vishisht Seva Medal, Uttam Yudh Seva Medal, Ati Vishisht Seva Medal, Vishisht Seva Medal. *Leisure interests:* running, horse riding, golf.

SINHA, A. M. K.; Indian mechanical engineer and business executive; *Chairman, IndianOil Corporation Limited;* joined IndianOil 1977, Head of Corp. Planning and Econ. Studies –2014, Chair. IndianOil Corpn Ltd 2014–, also Dir (Planning and Business Devt); Chair. IndianOil Adani Gas Pvt. Ltd; Chair. (non-exec.) Green Gas Ltd; mem. Bd of Dirs Petronet LNG Ltd, IndOil Montney Ltd (inc. in Canada), IndOil Global BV (subsidiary in the Netherlands); fmr mem. Bd Lanka IOC Ltd, Indian Oil Tanking Infrastructure and Energy Services Ltd (IOTIESL). *Address:* IndianOil Corporation Ltd, Corporate Office, 3079/3, J.B. Tito Marg, Sadiq Nagar, New Delhi 110 049, India (office). *Telephone:* (11) 26260000 (office). *E-mail:* info@iocl.com (office). *Website:* www.iocl.com (office).

SINHA, Ashok, BTech, MBA; Indian petroleum industry executive; ed Indian Inst. of Tech., Kanpur, Indian Inst. of Man., Bangalore; with International Computers Pvt. Ltd 1973–75; joined Bharat Petroleum Corpn Ltd 1977, Finance Dir 1995–2005, Chair. and Man. Dir 2005–10; Chair. Indraprastha Gas Ltd 2005–07; mem. Bd of Dirs Bharat Oman Refineries Ltd from 1995 (Chair.), Kochi Refineries Ltd (part-time Chair. (non-exec.) 2005–10, acquired by Bharat Petroleum 2006), Numaligarh Refinery from 2001 (Chair.), Bharat Shell Ltd; Dir (non-exec.) Petronet LNG Ltd –2010, Ind. Dir (non-exec.) 2011–; Dir (non-exec.), Cipla Ltd 2013–; Econ. Intelligence Unit India/American Express India Chief Financial Officer Award for Information and Knowledge Management 2001, Alumnus of the Year Award, Indian Inst. of Man., Bangalore, Award for Customer Man., Technology Media Group. *Address:* Cipla Ltd, Mumbai Central, Mumbai 400 008, India (office). *Telephone:* (22) 2308-2891 (office). *Fax:* (22) 2307-0013 (office). *E-mail:* info@cipla.com (office). *Website:* www.cipla.com (office).

SINHA, Shantha, MA, PhD; Indian social activist and government official; *Chairperson, National Commission for Protection of Child Rights;* b. (Mamidipudi Shantha), 7 Jan. 1950, Nellore Dist, Andhra Pradesh; d. of Mamidipudi Anandam and Sita Anandam; ed St Anns High School, Osmania Univ., Jawaharlal Nehru Univ.; fmr faculty mem., Dept of Political Science, Hyderabad Cen. Univ., currently Prof.; Chair. Nat. Comm. for Protection of Child Rights 2007–; Founder, Sec., Trustee, Mamidipudi Venkatarangaiya Foundation (M.V. Foundation) 1981–; fmr Dir Shramik Vidya Peeth; mem. Nat. Cttee, Ministry of Labour, Ministry of Human Resource Devt, Planning Comm. on Issues relating to Child Labour, Universalisation of Elementary Educ. and Rural Devt; Padma Shri 1999, Albert Shanker Int. Award, Educ. Int. 1999, Ramon Magsaysay Award 2003. *Address:* M.V. Foundation, 201 Narayan Apartments, West Marredpally, Secunderabad 500 026, India (office). *Telephone:* (40) 27801320 (office); (40) 27700290 (office). *Fax:* (40) 27808808 (office); (40) 27701656 (office). *E-mail:* mvfindia@gmail.com (office). *Website:* www.mvfindia.in (office).

SINHA, Surendra Kumar, LLB; Bangladeshi judge; b. 1 Feb. 1951, Tilakpur, P.S-Kamalganj, Mulvibazar Dist; s. of Lalit Mohan Sinha and Dhanabati Sinha; ed Chittagong Univ.; Advocate, Dist Court, Sylhet 1974–77; Advocate, High Court Div. 1978–90, Appellate Div., Supreme Court 1990–99; Judge, High Court Div. 1999–2009; apptd Judge, Appellate Div. of Supreme Court 2009, Chief Justice, Supreme Court 2015–17; Chair. Bangladesh Judicial Service Comm. 2011.

SINHA, Yashwant, MA; Indian politician, teacher and civil servant; b. 6 Nov. 1937, Patna, Bihar; s. of Bipin Bihari Saran and Dhana Devi; m. Nilima Sinha 1961; two s. one d.; ed Patna Univ.; Lecturer in Political Science, Patna Univ. 1958–60; joined Admin. Service 1960; Deputy Comm. Santhal Paraganas; Chair. Drafting Cttee of UNCTAD Conf. on Shipping, Geneva; First Sec., Germany 1971–73, Consul-Gen. 1973–74; Prin. Sec. to Chief Minister, Bihar; Jt Sec. to Govt of India, Ministry of Shipping and Transport 1980–84; retd from Admin. Service and joined Janata Party 1984, Gen. Sec. 1986–88; mem. Rajya Sabha (Parl.) 1988, mem. Cttee on Petitions 1989; joined Janata Dal (Samajwadi) after split in Janata Dal 1990; mem. Bharatiya Janata Party from mid-1990s–2018 (Vice-Pres. –2009); mem. Lok Sabha (Parl.) 1998– (mem. Parl. Pay Cttee 1998–99, Chair. Standing

Cttee on External Affairs 2009, Cttee on Public Accounts 2009); Minister of Finance 1998–99, 2001–02, of External Affairs 2002–04; launched Rashtra Manch (non-party political action group) 2018; Pres. All India Tennis Asscn; mem. Press Council of India 2006–, Delhi Gymkhana Club; Officier de la Légion d'Honneur 2015; Golden Peacock Award. *Publications include:* Confessions of a Swadeshi Reformer: My Years as Finance Minister. *Leisure interests:* reading, travelling, listening to music, watching films. *Address:* Jasol House, Paotabarea, Jodhpur (home); Rishabh Vatika via College More, Village Rajgoda, Morangi, Thana - Mufassil, Demotand, Dist Hazaribagh, Jharkhand, India. *Telephone:* (6546) 233418. *E-mail:* ysinha2005@hotmail.com.

SINIORA, Fouad, MBA; Lebanese banking executive, government official and politician; b. 22 Nov. 1943, Sidon; m.; three c.; ed Nat. Evangelical Inst., American Univ. of Beirut; various positions at First Nat. City Bank, including clerk 1967, Head Credit Dept 1970–71, Credit Account Officer, Marketing Officer, mem. Credit Cttee 1970–72; Lecturer, Lebanese Univ., American Univ. Beirut 1971–77; concurrently several positions at Finance Bank including Man. Industry and Tourism loans, mem. Credit Cttee, Sec. Bd of Dirs 1972–75; Financial Adviser, Intra Investment 1975–77; Asst Gen. Man. Middle East Cement Co. 1975–77; Banking Control Commr, Central Bank 1977–82; Dir Arab Universal Insurance 1982–92; exec. positions at several cos including Al Mal, IRAD, Méditerranée Investors Group, Méditerranée Group Sevices, Banque de la Méditerranée, Saudi Lebanese Bank 1982–92; Minister of State for Financial Affairs, Acting Minister of Finance 1992–98; Minister of Finance –2004; Prime Minister 2005–09; mem. Majlis al-Nuab (Parl.) from Saida, Leader, Future Movt parl. group. *Address:* c/o Majlis al-Nuab, Place de l'Etoile, Beirut, Lebanon (office). *Website:* www.lp.gov.lb; www.fuadsiniora.com.

SINIRLIOĞLU, Feridun Hadi, PhD; Turkish politician and diplomatist; *Permanent Representative to United Nations;* b. 30 Jan. 1960, Görele, Giresun Province; m. Ayşe Sinirlioğlu; two c.; ed Ankara Univ., Boğaziçi Univ.; Third Sec. Directorate of Personnel, Multilateral Cultural Relations Dept, Ministry of Foreign Affairs (MFA) May–Oct. 1982, Third Sec./Second Sec. 1983–85; Second Sec./First Sec. Turkish Embassy, The Hague 1985–88, First Sec., Beirut 1988–90; First Sec. Special Adviser to Deputy Undersecretary for Bilateral Political Affairs, MFA 1990–92, Special Adviser to Prime Minister 1991–92; Political Counsellor, Perm. Mission to UN 1992–96; Chief Foreign Policy Adviser to Pres. 1996–2000; Minister & Deputy Dir-Gen. for Middle East and North Africa, MFA 2000–02; Amb. to Israel 2002–07; Deputy Undersecretary for Bilateral Political Affairs 2007–09, Undersecretary MFA 2009–15; Minister of Foreign Affairs 2015–16; Perm. Rep. to UN 2016–; Turkish military service Nov. 1982–Feb. 1983. *Address:* Permanent Mission of Turkey, One Dag Hammarskjöld Plaza, 885 Second Avenue, 45th Floor, New York, NY 10017, USA (office). *Telephone:* (212) 949-0150 (office). *Fax:* (212) 949-0086 (office). *E-mail:* tr-delegation.newyork@mfa.gov.tr (office). *Website:* www.turkuno.dt.mfa.gov.tr (office).

SINISCALCO, Domenico Giovanni, LLB, PhD; Italian economist, business executive, writer and fmr government official; *Vice-Chairman, Country Head (Italy) and Head of Government Coverage, Europe, Middle East and Africa, Morgan Stanley (Italy);* b. 15 July 1954, Turin; m.; two c.; ed Univ. of Turin, Univ. of Cambridge, UK; Prof. of Econs, Univ. of Turin 1990–2006 (on leave of absence); Dir-Gen. Treasury, Rome Oct. 2001–04, Minister of Economy and Finance 2004–05; Man. Dir and Vice-Chair. Morgan Stanley International, London 2006–07, Country Head and Chief Exec. Morgan Stanley (Italy) 2007–11, Vice-Chair., Country Head (Italy) and Head of Govt Coverage, Europe, Middle East and Africa (EMEA) 2011–; fmr teaching posts at LUISS, Rome, Univ. of Cagliari, Johns Hopkins Univ., USA, Univ. of Cambridge, UK, Univ. Catholique de Louvain, Belgium; Chair. Collegio Carlo Alberto, Turin 2006–; mem. Steering Cttee journals Equilibri, Mercato, Concorrenza and Regole; mem. Royal Swedish Acad. of Sciences, Beijer Inst. *Publications include:* New Directions in Economic Theory of the Environment (co-ed.), The Challenges of Privatization: An International Analysis 2004; more than 90 publs on privatization, environmental and industrial econs. *Address:* Morgan Stanley Investment Banking Division, Palazzo Serbelloni, Corso Venezia 16, 20121 Milan, Italy (office). *Telephone:* (02) 7633-5672 (office). *Fax:* (02) 7633-6174 (office). *E-mail:* domenico.siniscalco@morganstanley.com (office). *Website:* www.morganstanley.com (office).

SINN, Hans-Werner, Dr rer. pol; German economist and academic; b. 7 March 1948, Brake, Lower Saxony; m. Gerlinde Sinn (née Zoubek) 1971; two s. one d.; ed Helmholtz-Gymnasium, Bielefeld, Univ. of Münster, Univ. of Mannheim; Lecturer, Univ. of Münster 1972–74, Univ. of Mannheim 1974–78, Sr Lecturer 1979–83, Assoc. Prof. 1983–84; Visiting Asst Prof., Univ. of Western Ont. 1978–79; Prof. of Econs and Insurance, Univ. of Munich 1984–94, Dir Centre for Econ. Studies 1991–2016, Prof. of Econs and Public Finance 1994–2016; mem. Council of Econ. Advisers, Fed. Ministry of Econs 1989–; Chair. Verein für Socialpolitik (German Econ. Asscn) 1997–2000; Pres. Ifo Inst. for Econ. Research 1999–2016; Pres. Int. Inst. of Public Finance 2006–09; Order of Merit 1999, 2005; Venia Legendi 1983; Hon. Dr rer. pol (Univ. of Magdeburg) 1999; Dr hc (Helsinki) 2011, (Leipzig); Yrjö Jahnsson Lecturer, Univ. of Helsinki 1999, Stevenson Lecturer on Citizenship, Univ. of Glasgow 2000, Prize of Advisory Council of the Union 2003, Econ. Book Prize, Financial Times Deutschland 2003, Int. Book Prize CORINE 2004, The World Economy Annual Lecturer, Univ. of Nottingham 2005, Jelle Zijlstra Lecturer, Univ. of Amsterdam 2006, Europe Award, Univ. of Maastricht 2008, D.B. Doran Lecturer on Population, Resources and Development, Hebrew Univ. of Jerusalem 2010, 10th European Economy Lecturer, College of Europe, Bruges 2011. *Publications include:* Economic Decisions under Uncertainty 1980, Capital Income Taxation and Resource Allocation 1985, Jumpstart: The Economic Unification of Germany 1991, The German State Banks – Global Players in the International Financial Markets 1999, The New Systems Competition 2002, Ist Deutschland noch zu retten? 2003–05 (English version: Can Germany be Saved? 2007), Kasino-Kapitalismus 2009 (English version: Casino Capitalism 2010), Das grüne Paradoxon 2008 (English version: The Green Paradox 2012), Die Target-Falle 2012; numerous articles on public finance and other subjects; editor of several journals, including Economic Policy. *Address:* Ifo Institute-Leibniz Institute for Economic Research, Poschingerstr. 5, 81679 Munich, Germany (office). *Telephone:* (89) 92241279 (office). *E-mail:* sinn@ifo.de (office). *Website:* www .hanswernersinn.de (office).

SINNOTT, Kevin, MA; British artist; b. 4 Dec. 1947, Bridgend, Wales; s. of Myles Vincent Sinnott and Honora Burke; m. Susan Forward 1969; three s. one d.; ed St Robert's School, Royal Coll. of Art; teacher Canterbury Coll. of Art 1981–88, St Martin's School of Art, London 1981–93; solo exhbns at Bernard Jacobson Gallery 1986, 1988, 1990, Bernard Jacobson, New York 1987, 1989, Flowers East 1992, 1994, 1996, 1998, Flowers West, Los Angeles 1999, Caldwell/Snyder, New York 2000; work in numerous public collections (including Arts Council of GB, British Museum, British Council, Nat. Museum of Wales, Metropolitan Museum of Art, New York). *Publications:* Behind the Canvas (autobiog.) 2008. *Leisure interests:* cinema, books, walks, opera. *Address:* Tyr Santes Fair, Pont-y-Rhyl, Bridgend, CF32 8LJ, Wales (home). *Telephone:* (1656) 871854 (home). *Fax:* (1656) 871854 (home). *E-mail:* mail@kevinsinnott.co.uk (home). *Website:* www.kevinsinnott.co .uk (home).

SINYAVSKAYA, Tamara Ilyinichna; Russian singer (mezzo-soprano); b. 6 July 1943, Moscow; m. Muslim Magovaev 1974; ed Moscow Music Coll. and State Theatre Art Inst.; soloist with Bolshoi Theatre 1964–; studied at La Scala, Milan 1973–74; currently Head, Dept of Vocal Training, Russian Acad. of Theatre Arts (GITIS); Order of Merit 2001, Order of Lomonosov First Degree 2004; First Prize, Int. Singing Competition, Sofia 1968, Grand Prix Int. Singing Competition, Belgium 1969, First Prize, Int. Tchaikovsky Competition, Moscow 1970, People's Artist of RSFSR 1976, People's Artist of USSR 1982, Irina Arkhipova Prize 2004. *Opera roles include:* Olga in Tchaikovsky's Eugene Onegin, Carmen, Blanche and Frosya in Prokofiev's Gambler and Semyon Kotko, Vanya in Glinka's A Life for the Tsar, Ratmir in Glinka's Ruslan and Lyudmila, Lyubasha in Rimsky-Korsakov's The Tsar's Bride, Varvara in Not Love Alone. *Address:* Department of Vocal Training, Russian Academy of Theatre Arts (GITIS), Moscow, 125009, Malyy Kislovskiy pereulok, 6, Russia. *Website:* gitis.net.

SIPILÄ, Juha Petri, MEng; Finnish business executive and politician; *Prime Minister;* b. 25 April 1961, Veteli; m. Minna-Maaria Sipilä; five c. (one deceased); ed Univ. of Oulu; began career as Product Devt Man., Lauri Kuokkanen Ltd (electronics co.); Man. Dir, Solitra Oy (telecommunications components co.) 1992, Propr 1994–96; f. Fortel Invest Oy 1998; CEO Elektrobit Oyj 2002–05; mem. Eduskunta (Parl.) for Oulu 2011–; Prime Minister 2015–; mem. Municipal Council, Kempele 2013–15; mem. Suomen Keskusta (Finnish Centre Party), Chair. 2012–. *Address:* Prime Minister's Office, Snellmaninkatu 1a, POB 23, 00023 Helsinki, Finland (office). *Telephone:* (9) 16001 (office). *Fax:* (9) 16022165 (office). *E-mail:* info@vnk.fi (office). *Website:* www.vnk.fi (office); www.juhasipila.fi.

SIRAT, René-Samuel, Dr de Recherches; French/Israeli rabbi; *Vice-President, Conference of European Rabbis;* b. 13 Nov. 1930, Bône (now Annaba), Algeria; s. of Ichoua Sirat and Oureida Atlan; m. 1st Colette Salamon 1952; one s. two d.; m. 2nd Nicole Holzman 1978; ed Lycée St Augustin, Bône, Univs of Strasbourg and Paris (Sorbonne), Hebrew Univ. of Jerusalem, Ecole Nat. des Langues Orientales (ENLOV); Rabbi, Toulouse 1952–55; Chaplain, Jeunesse juive 1955–63; Prof. Emer., Institut Nat. des Langues et Civilisations Orientales (INALCO, fmrly ENLOV), Dir of Hebrew Studies 1965–96; Prof., Ecole Rabbinique de France 1965–70, 1977–80; Insp.-Gen. of Hebrew, Ministry of Educ. 1972–80; Pres. Hebrew Examining Bd, Certificate of Professional Aptitude and Higher Studies 1973–78; Dir Centre de Documentation et Recherches des Etudes Juives modernes et contemporaines 1974–; Pres. Hebrew Examining Bd, Agrégation 1978–80; Dir Ecole Hautes Etudes de Judaïsme 1985–; Pres. Centre Universitaire Rachi, Troyes 1989; Grand Rabbin of France 1981–87; Chief Rabbi, Consistoire Central 1988; Vice-Pres. Conférence des Rabbins européens 1989–; Pres. Acad. Hillel 1989–, Inst. des connaissances des religions du livre 1996–; Officier, Légion d'honneur 1998, Grand Officier, Ordre nat. du Mérite 2010, Commdr des Palmes Académiques, Commdr des Arts et des Lettres; Dr hc (Yeshiva Univ., USA) 1985, (Université Laval, Canada) 1992, (Université Cluj-Nepoca); Prix de Jérusalem. *Publications:* Omer Hasikha (co-ed.) 1973, Mélanges A. Neher (co-ed.) 1974, Mélanges Vajda 1974–80 (co-ed.), La joie austère 1990, La tendresse de Dieu 1996, Héritages de Rachi (proceedings of the int. scientific colloquium organized in Troyes in June 2005 on the occasion of the 900th anniversary of the disappearance of Rabbi Shelomo Itshaqie (Rachi) 2006, Chrétiens, Juifs, Musulmans: Lectures qui rassemblent lectures qui séparent (co-author) 2007. *Address:* 51 rue de Rochechouart, 75009 Paris, France (home).

SIRCAR, Muhammad Jamiruddin, LLB, MA; Bangladeshi barrister and politician; b. 1 Dec. 1931, Nayabari, Bhajanpur, PS: Tetulia, Dist: Panchagarh; m. Nur Akhter Sircar; two s. one d.; ed Univ. of Dhaka; Vice-Pres. Iqbal Hall (now Sergeant Johirul Hoque Hall), Univ. of Dhaka 1958–59; called to the Bar by East Pakistan High Court of Judicature 1960, Bar of England and Wales (including Commonwealth countries) 1967; Pres. Inns of Court Pakistan Soc., London 1963; Co-founder East Pakistan Soc. House, London; barrister, Supreme Court of Bangladesh in constitutional, civil and criminal law; contested Panchogarh constituency as ind. cand. in prov. parl. election 1970, as ind. cand. in Bangladesh Nat. Ass. Election 1973; Founding mem. Bangladesh Jatiyatabadi Dal (Bangladesh Nationalist Party) and mem. Standing Cttee; MP for Panchagarh-1, Seat-1 1979– (re-elected 1991, 1996, 2001, 2009), Speaker of Jatiyo Shongshod (Parl.) 2001–09; served as Minister of State of Public Works and Urban Devt (Habitat), as Minister of State for Foreign Affairs, as Minister of State for Land Admin and Law Reforms, as Minister for Science and Tech., as Minister for Educ., as Minister for Law, Justice and Parl.; Acting Pres. of Bangladesh 21 June–6 Sept. 2002; mem. Bangladesh del. to UN Gen. Ass. Session 1977, responsible for Legal Cttee 1977–80. *Publications include:* Glimpses of International Law 1997, Stronger United Nations for Peaceful Welfare World 2003, The Law of the Sea 2003, London-e Chatro andolon 2005, London-e Bondhu bandhob 2006, Oshtom shongshoder Speaker 2006, Pal Raj theke Plolashi ebong British Raj theke Bongo bhobon 2006, Law of the International Rivers and Other Water Courses 2007, Pakistan-er Gonotontrer Biporjoy ebong Shadhin Bangladesh-er Obbhuddoy 2008. *Address:* 21 Baily Rd, Ramna, Dhaka 1000, Bangladesh (home). *Telephone:* (2) 933480 (home). *Website:* public.jamiruddin.com.

SIREGAR, Mahendra, MA; Indonesian politician and diplomatist; *Ambassador to the USA;* b. 17 Oct. 1962, Jakarta; m. Ita Br Siregar; three c.; ed Univ. of Indonesia, Monash Univ.; joined Ministry of Foreign Affairs 1986, Third Sec., Embassy of Indonesia, London 1992–95, Information Counsellor, Washington DC 1998–2001, Amb. to the USA 2019–; Special Asst to Minister 2001, Deputy

Coordinating Minister, Int. Econ. and Financial Relations 2005–09, Vice-Minister of Trade 2009–11, of Finance 2011–13; Exec. Dir Council for Palm Oil Producing Countries; Chair. Eximbank, Indonesia Sep.–Dec. 2009, Indonesia Investment Coordinating Bd 2013–14, Bank Mandiri (Europe) Ltd; Asia Rep. UN Framework Convention on Climate Change Adaptation Fund Bd 2007–09; Chair. Bd of Supervisors Semen Indonesia 2012–17, Rajawali Nusantara Indonesia 2012–, mem. Bd of Supervisors Aneka Tambang 2008–09, AKR Corporindo 2015–, Sarana Multi Infrastruktur 2017–. *Address:* Embassy of the Republic of Indonesia, 2020 Massachusetts Avenue NW, Washington DC 20036 USA (office). *Telephone:* (202) 775-5200 (office). *Website:* www.embassyofindonesia.org (office).

SIRISENA, (Pallewatte Gamaralalage) Maithripala (Yapa); Sri Lankan politician and head of state; *President and Minister of Defence, of Mahaweli Development and Environment, of National Integration and Reconciliation, and of Law and Order;* b. 3 Sept. 1951; m. Jayanthi Pushpa Kumari; one s. two d.; ed Royal Coll., Polonnaruwa, Sri Lanka School of Agriculture, Kundasale, Maxim Gorky Acad., Russia; joined Sri Lanka Freedom Party (SLFP) 1967, apptd Dist Sec. 1979, Sec., All Island SLFP Youth Org. 1981–83, Chair. All Island SLFP (Youth Org.) 1983, Chief Organiser (Polonnaruwa seat), SLFP 1983, also Dist Leader (Polonnaruwa seat), Deputy Sec. 1997–2000, Vice-Chair. 2001, Gen. Sec. 2001–14, now Pres.; MP 1989–2015, Leader of the House 2004–05; Deputy Minister of Irrigation 1995, Cabinet Minister for Mahaweli Devt 1997, for Mahaweli Devt and Rajarata Devt 2004, for Agriculture, Irrigation, Mahaweli and Environment 2006, for Agricultural Devt and Agrarian Services 2007, for Health 2010–14; Pres. of Sri Lanka and Minister of Defence, of Mahaweli Devt and Environment, of Nat. Integration and Reconciliation 2015–, and of Law and Order 2018–; Harvard Ministerial Leadership in Health Award, Harvard School of Public Health and Kennedy School of Govt 2013. *Address:* President's Secretariat, Republic Square, Colombo 1, Sri Lanka (office). *Telephone:* (11) 2324801 (office). *Fax:* (11) 2430590 (office). *E-mail:* priu@presidentsoffice.lk (office). *Website:* www.president.gov.lk (office).

SIRIVADHANABHAKDI, Charoen; Thai business executive; *Chairman, Thai Beverage Public Co. Ltd;* m.; five c.; Owner, Thai Beverage Public Co. Ltd (ThaiBev), Chair 2003–; Chair. TCC Holding Co. Ltd 1987–, Beer Thai Public Co. Ltd 1991–, South East Group Co. Ltd 1997–, Berli Jucker Public Co. Ltd 2001–, TCC Land Co. Ltd 2002–, Red Bull Distillery Group of Cos 2004–, Fraser & Neave Ltd 2013–; other cos owned include Sang Som Group, Thai Charoen Corpn Group, Charoen Life (insurance co.), Sirivana Co. Ltd; Dr hc (Maejo Inst. of Agricultural Tech., Chandrakasem Rajabhat Univ., Huachiew Chalermprakiet Univ., Eastern Asia Univ., Mae Fah Luang Univ.); Kt Grand Cordon (Special Class), Most Exalted Order of the White Elephant, Kt Grand Cordon (Special Class), Most Noble Order of the Crown of Thailand, Kt Grand Cross (First Class), Most Admirable Order of the Diredgunabhorn, Kt Grand Commdr (Second Class, Higher Grade), Most Illustrious Order of Chula Chom Klao. *Address:* Thai Beverage Public Co. Ltd, 14 SangSom Building, Vibhavadee Rangsit Road, Chomphon, Chatuchak, Bangkok 10900, Thailand (office). *Telephone:* (2) 127-5555 (office). *Fax:* (2) 272-2328 (office). *Website:* www.thaibev.com (office).

SIRIWIT, Cherdpong, MA; Thai business executive and fmr government official; *Chairman of the Executive Board, The Thai Cane and Sugar Corporation;* b. 1 Sept. 1946; ed Thammasat Univ., Nat. Defence Coll., Georgetown Univ., USA; held positions in govt successively as Sec.-Gen. Office of the Cane and Sugar Bd, Deputy Dir-Gen., then Dir-Gen. Office of Industrial Econs, Dir-Gen. Dept of Mineral Resources, Sec.-Gen. Thai Industrial Standards Inst., Deputy Perm. Sec., Ministry of Industry, then Perm. Sec., Ministry of Energy; Chair. Thai Oil Public Co. Ltd 2005–08; currently Chair. Exec. Bd The Thai Cane and Sugar Corpn; Chair. Vithai Biopower Ltd 2011–, Electricity Generating Authority of Thailand 2003–04, Ratchaburi Electricity Generating Holding Public Co. Ltd 2003–07, PTT Chemical Public Co. Ltd 2004–08, Solartron Public Co. Ltd 2010–15; mem. Bd of Dirs Thoresen Thai Agency Public Co. Ltd, Evergreen Plus Co. Ltd, Thaioil Power Co. Ltd, Advance Finance Public Co. Ltd, IRPC Public Co. Ltd; Chair. Thai-Lao For Friendship Asscn 2004–; mem. Council of Trustees, Petroleum Inst. of Thailand (PTIT). *Address:* The Thai Cane and Sugar Corporation, 128/345-6, Payatai Plaza Building 32nd Floor, Phyathai Road, Rajthavee, Bangkok 10400, Thailand (office). *Telephone:* (2) 216-5155 (office). *Fax:* (2) 216-5161 (office). *E-mail:* tcsc@mweb.co.th (office).

SIRRINGHAUS, Henning, PhD; Swiss physicist, business executive and academic; *Hitachi Professor of Electron Device Physics, Optoelectronics Group, Cavendish Laboratory, University of Cambridge;* ed Inst. of Solid State Physics, ETH Zurich; Postdoctoral Research Fellow, Dept of Electrical Eng, Princeton Univ., USA 1995–97; postdoctoral research at Cavendish Lab., Univ. of Cambridge, UK 1998, Royal Soc. Univ. Research Fellowship 1998, Lecturer, Cavendish Lab. 2000–02, Reader 2002–04, Hitachi Prof. of Electron Device Physics, Optoelectronics Group and Head of Microelectronics Research Centre 2004–, Fellow of Churchill Coll.; Co-founder and Chief Scientist, Plastic Logic Ltd (tech. start-up co. commercializing printed organic transistor tech.) 2000–; Balzers Prize, Swiss Physical Soc. 1995, Silver Medal, ETH, Zurich 1996, Descartes Prize, EC 2000, Mullard Award, Royal Soc. 2003, Hughes Medal, Royal Soc. 2013, Faraday Medal, Inst. of Physics (UK) 2015. *Publications:* more than 70 publs and 20 patents/patent applications. *Address:* Optoelectronics Group, Cavendish Laborabory, University of Cambridge, JJ Thomson Avenue, Cambridge, CB3 0HE (office); Plastic Logic Limited, 34 Cambridge Science Park, Milton Road, Cambridge, CB4 0FX, England (office). *Telephone:* (1223) 337557 (office); (1223) 706000 (Plastic Logic) (office). *Fax:* (1223) 337706 (office); (1223) 706006 (Plastic Logic) (office). *E-mail:* hs220@cam.ac.uk (office); info@plasticlogic.com (office). *Website:* www.phy.cam.ac.uk/directory/sirringhaush (office); www-oe.phy.cam.ac.uk (office); www.plasticlogic.com (office).

SISI, Abd al-Fatah al-; Egyptian fmr army officer, politician and head of state; *President;* b. 19 Nov. 1954, Cairo; s. of Saeed Hussein Khalil al-Sisi; m. Entissar Amer 1977; three s. one d.; ed Egyptian Mil. Acad., Egyptian Command and Staff Coll., British Jt Command and Staff Coll., Higher War Coll. of Nasser Mil. Sciences Acad., US Army War Coll., Carlisle, Pa, USA; long career in Egyptian Armed Forces, beginning as infantry officer 1977, later becoming Defence Attaché, Embassy in Riyadh 1999–2000, Commdr, Northern Mil. Region 2008–10, Dir, Mil. Intelligence and Reconnaissance Dept and mem. Supreme Council of the Armed Forces 2010–12, Minister of Defence 2012–13, Commdr-in-Chief, Egyptian Armed Forces 2012–14, First Deputy Prime Minister and Minister of Defence and Mil. Production 2013–14, Pres. of Egypt 2014–; attained rank of Gen. 2012, Field Marshal 2014; Chair. African Union 2019–; numerous mil. awards, including 25 April Decoration (Liberation of Sinai), Distinguished Service Decoration, Mil. Duty Decoration (First and Second Class), Longevity and Exemplary Medal, Kuwait Liberation Medals (Kuwait and Egypt), Silver Jubilee of October War Medal, Golden Jubilee of 23 July Revolution, Silver Jubilee of Liberation of Sinai Medal, 25 January Revolution Medal, Mil. Courage Decoration, Republic's Mil. Decoration, Training Decoration, Army Day Decoration. *Address:* Ittehadiya Presidential Palace, Al Nadi, El-Montaza, Heliopolis, Cairo, Egypt (office).

SISILO, Robert, BA, MA; Solomon Islands politician and diplomatist; *Permanent Representative to United Nations;* b. 1956, Sikaiana; m. Priscilla Sisilo; two c.; ed Univ. of South Pacific in Suva, Fiji, Fletcher School of Law and Diplomacy, Tufts Univ., Univ. of Wollongong, Australia; joined Solomon Islands Ministry of Foreign Affairs 1983, served as Desk Officer, Chief Desk Officer, Sr Desk Officer 1983–85; Chargé d'affaires, Perm. Mission to UN 1986–91; Deputy Sec. of Foreign Affairs 1996; Amb. to EU, Belgium, France, Germany, Netherlands, UK 1996–2004, Perm. Rep. to WTO, Geneva 1996–2004; Perm. Rep. of Pacific Islands Forum to WTO, Geneva 2005–08; Acting Sec. for Foreign Affairs and Trade, Nauru 2009–10; Perm. Sec. Ministry of Foreign Affairs and External Trade July 2011–Feb. 2012; Ministry of Police, Nat. Security and Correctional Services March–May 2012, Trade Negotiations Envoy Ministry of Foreign Affairs and External Trade 2012–14; Perm. Rep. to UN 2017–. *Address:* Permanent Mission of Solomon Islands, 685 Third Avenue, Suite 1105, New York, NY 10017, USA (office). *Telephone:* (212) 599-6193 (office). *Fax:* (212) 661-8925 (office). *E-mail:* simun@solomons.com (office).

SISOLAK, Stephen (Steve) F., BA, MBA; American politician; *Governor of Nevada;* b. 26 Dec. 1953, Milwaukee, Wis.; s. of Edward F. Sisolak and Mary Sisolak; m. 1st Lori 'Dallas' Garland (divorced); two c.; m. 2nd Kathy Ong 2018; ed Univ. of Wis., Milwaukee, Univ. of Nev., Las Vegas; Chair. and Partner, American Distributing Co., Associated Industries; mem. Nev. Bd of Regents 1998; elected mem. Clark Co. Comm. 2009, Chair. 2013–18; Gov. of Nev. 2019–; mem. Bd of Dirs, Chamber of Commerce, Henderson, American Heart Asscn; mem. Nev. Tourism Infrastructure Cttee, Regional Planning Coalition; mem. Founders' Bd, Boys & Girls Clubs of America. *Address:* Office of the Governor, Grant Sawyer State Office Building, 555 E Washington Avenue, Suite 5100, Las Vegas, NV 89101, USA (office). *Telephone:* (702) 486-2500 (office). *Fax:* (702) 486-2505 (office). *Website:* www.gov.nv.gov (office).

SISOWATH, Prince Sirirath, BSc; Cambodian politician and diplomatist; b. 21 June 1946, Kampong Siem; s. of Sisowath Sirik-Matak and Norodom Kethneary; ed Univ. of Phnom Penh; fmr officer, Airborne Div., Cambodian Army; fmr Jt Minister of Defence; fmr Amb. and Perm. Rep. to UN, New York; mem. FUNCINPEC Party (United National Front for an Independent, Neutral, Peaceful and Co-operative Cambodia Party), apptd Second Vice-Pres. 2006; mem. Privy Council; Grand Cross, Kingdom of Cambodia, Commdr, Order of Sena Cheyisith, Commdr, Order of Queen Kossamak. *Leisure interests:* reading, swimming, jogging. *Address:* 37 Vithei Preah Suramarit, Sangkat Chaktomuk, Phnom-Penh, Cambodia (home). *Telephone:* (12) 845126 (home). *Fax:* (23) 211936 (home).

SISSOKO, Bouaré Fily; Malian economist and politician; b. 22 Aug. 1955, Dakar, Senegal; d. of Samba Sissoko; m.; two c.; ed Lycée technique de Bamako; Minister of State Property and Land Affairs 2000–02, of Communication 2002; several sr positions within Ministry of Finance, including State Comptroller-Gen., Deputy Dir-Gen. of Customs; economist with World Bank, Bamako –2013; Minister of the Economy and Finance 2013–15. *Address:* c/o Ministry of the Economy, Finance and the Budget, Bamako, Mali.

SISSOKO, Cheick Oumar, BA; Malian politician and filmmaker; *Leader, Parti de la solidarité africaine pour la démocratie et l'indépendance;* b. 1945, San Dist, Bamako; ed Ecole nat. de cinématographie Louis Lumière, Ecole des hautes études en sciences sociales; began career in Mali Civil Service; Minister of Culture 2002–07, of Minister of Nat. Educ. 2007; Asst Dir-Gen., later Dir-Gen. Centre nat. de la production cinématographique; f. Kora Films (producers asscn); Pres. Kayira (ind. radio station); Leader, Parti de la solidarité africaine pour la démocratie et l'indépendance. *Films include:* Nyamanton ou la leçon des ordures 1987, Finzan 1991, Guimba le tyran, une époque (Grand Prize, Fespaco Festival, Ouagadougou 1995) 1993, La Genèse 1999, Battu 2000. *Documentaries include:* Africa is Moving 1992, Etre jeune à Bamako (Youth in Mali) 1992, Building a Nation – Eritrea 1996, Malnutrition in the Sahel Region 1997. *Radio includes:* L'Afrique en question (producer, weekly programme for Kayira). *Address:* Parti de la solidarité africaine pour la démocratie et l'indépendance, Djélibougou, rue 246, porte 559, BP 3140, Bamako, Mali. *Telephone:* 224-10-04 (office).

SISSONS, Peter George, MA; British journalist, broadcaster and television news presenter (retd); b. 17 July 1942, Liverpool, England; s. of George Sissons and Elsie Evans; m. Sylvia Bennett 1965; two s. one d.; ed Liverpool Inst. High School for Boys and Univ. Coll., Oxford; grad. trainee, Independent TV News 1964, gen. reporter 1967, industrial corresp. 1970, industrial ed. 1972–78; presenter, News at One 1978–82, Channel Four News 1982–89; presenter, BBC TV news 1989–2009 (6 O'Clock News 1989–94, 9 O'Clock News 1994–2000, 10 O'Clock News 2000–03, BBC News 24 2003–09), Chair. BBC TV Question Time 1989–93; Hon. Fellow, Liverpool John Moores Univ. 1997; Hon. LLD (Liverpool); Queen's Silver Jubilee Medal 1977, Broadcasting Press Guild Award 1984, Royal Television Soc. Judges' Award 1988, Television and Radio Industries Club Newscaster of the Year 2000. *Publication:* When One Door Closes (autobiog.) 2011. *Leisure interests:* gardening. *Address:* c/o Knight Ayton Management, 29 Gloucester Place, London, W1U 8HX, England. *Telephone:* (20) 3795-1806. *Fax:* (20) 7831-4455. *E-mail:* info@knightayton.co.uk. *Website:* www.knightayton.co.uk.

SISTANI, Grand Ayatollah Al-Sayyid Ali Al-Husaini Al-; Iraqi (b. Iranian) religious leader; b. 4 Aug. 1930, Mashhad, Iran; s. of Sayyid Mohammad Baqir; joined Islamic seminary, Qom 1949; fmr Lecturer in Jurisprudence, Najaf Ashraf; after religious training in Iran moved to Iraq to become most senior Shia cleric; apptd head of network of schools, Najaf 1992. *Publications:* numerous religious works and treatises. *Address:* Office of the Grand Ayatollah Sistani, Muallim

Street, PO Box 371853514, Qom, Iran. *Telephone:* (253) 7741415. *Fax:* (253) 7741420. *E-mail:* english@sistani.org. *Website:* www.sistani.org.

SISULU, Beryl Rose; South African diplomatist; *High Commissioner to Australia;* adopted d. of Walter Sisulu and Nontsikelelo Albertina (Ma) Sisulu; Deputy CEO Oblivion Design 2002–15; Amb. to Norway 2009–12; served with Nat. Prosecution Service 2012–15; Amb. to Japan 2015–16, High Commr to Australia 2017–. *Address:* South Africa High Commission, cnr State Circle and Rhodes Pl., Yarralumla, ACT 2600, Australia (office). *Telephone:* (2) 6272-7300 (office). *Fax:* (2) 6273-1033 (office). *E-mail:* info.canberra@dirco.gov.za (office). *Website:* www.sahc .org.au (office).

SISULU, Lindiwe Nonceba, BA, MA, MPhil; South African politician; *Minister of International Relations and Co-operation;* b. 10 May 1954, Johannesburg; m.; ed St Michael's School, Swaziland, Waterford Kamhlaba, Swaziland, Univ. of Swaziland, Centre for Southern African Studies, Univ. of York, UK; African Nat. Congress (ANC) activist since 1970s, detained for political activities 1975–76, joined Umkhonto we Sizwe (MK) and worked for underground structures of ANC in exile 1977–78, obtained mil. training specializing in Intelligence 1977–79; teacher, Manzini Cen. High School 1981; Lecturer, Dept of History, Univ. of Swaziland 1982; sub-ed., The Times of Swaziland, Mbabane 1983; Lecturer, Manzini Teachers' Training Coll. 1985–87; Chief Examiner, History for Jr Certificate Examinations for Botswana, Lesotho and Swaziland 1985–87; returned to SA 1990; Personal Asst to Jacob Zuma, ANC Head of Intelligence 1990, Chief Admin. for ANC at Convention for Democratic South Africa (CODESA) 1991, Admin. of Intelligence, ANC Dept of Intelligence and Security 1992, mem. ANC Nat. Exec. Cttee, ANC Nat. Working Cttee; Dir Govan Mbeki Research Fellowship, Univ. of Fort Hare 1993; mem. Man. of Sub-Council on Intelligence, Transitional Exec. Council 1994; MP 1994–, Chair. Parl. Jt Standing Cttee on Intelligence 1995–96; consultant, Nat. Children's Rights Cttee, UNESCO 1992; mem. Man. Cttee, Policing Org. and Man. course, PDM, Univ. of the Witwatersrand 1993; Deputy Minister of Home Affairs 1996–2001; Minister of Intelligence 2001–04; Head of Command Centre for Emergency Reconstruction 2000–02; Minister of Housing 2004–09, of Defence and Mil. Veterans 2009–12, of Public Service and Admin 2012–14, of Human Settlements 2014–18, of Int. Relations and Co-operation 2018–; inaugural Chair. African Ministerial Conf. on Housing and Urban Devt 2005; mem. Bd of Dirs Nelson Mandela Foundation; Trustee, South African Democracy Educ. Trust, Albertina and Walter Sisulu Trust; Human Rights Centre Fellowship in Geneva 1992, The Presidential Award, Inst. for Housing of South Africa 2004, Science Award, Int. Asscn for Housing 2005. *Publications include:* South African Women in Agricultural Sector (pamphlet) 1990; book chapter and several articles. *Address:* Department of Foreign Affairs, Private Bag X152, Pretoria 0001 (office); Department of Foreign Affairs, East Wing, Union Building, 1 Government Avenue, Arcadia, Pretoria 0002, South Africa (office). *Telephone:* (12) 3511000 (office). *Fax:* (12) 3510165 (office). *E-mail:* minister@foreign.gov.za (office). *Website:* www.dfa.gov.za (office).

SISULU, Sheila Violet Makate, BA; South African diplomatist and UN official; b. 4 Dec. 1948, d.-in-law of Walter Max Ulyate Sisulu and Albertina Nontsikelelo Sisulu; m. Mlungisi Sisulu (died 2015); one s. two d.; ed Univ. of the Witwatersrand; various sr positions, South African Comm. for Higher Educ. 1978–88; Educ. Co-ordinator, African Bursary Fund, South African Council of Churches 1988–91; Dir Jt Enrichment Project 1991–94; Special Adviser, Ministry of Educ. 1994–97; Consul-Gen., South African Consulate-Gen., New York 1997–99; Amb. to USA 1999–2002; Deputy Exec. Dir UN World Food Programme 2003–08, Deputy Exec. Dir for Hunger Solutions 2008; Chancellor Amb. Walter Sisulu Univ. 2015–; mem. ANC Nat. Educ. Cttee, USA-South Africa Leadership Training Program, Community Bank Foundation; Dir, Worldwide Investment Holdings; mem. Council, Univ. of the Witwatersrand; Trustee, Equal Opportunity Foundation, Women's Devt Foundation, Women's Devt Bank, South African Broadcasting Corpn; Dr hc (Univ. of Maryland, CUNY). *Address:* Walter Sisulu University, Private Bag X1, Unitra 5117, South Africa. *Website:* www.wsu.ac.za (office).

SITAULA, Krishna Prasad; Nepalese politician; Spokesperson for Nepali Congress, arrested several times and ordered to be released by Supreme Court Feb. 2006; Minister of Home Affairs 2006–07, Interim Minister of Home Affairs 2007; chief govt negotiator at peace talks with Maoist rebels 2006.

SITHANEN, Ramakrishna, BSc, MSc, PhD; Mauritian politician, economist and business executive; *Chairman and Director, International Financial Services (IFS) Ltd;* b. 21 April 1954, Port Louis; m. three c.; ed London School of Econs, Brunel Univ., UK; fmr Research Officer, Centre for Labour Econs, LSE; fmr Research Officer, OECD, Paris; Educ. Officer 1979–80; Econ. Consultant, De Chazal Du Mee & Co. 1980–82; Transport Economist, Air Mauritius 1982–87, Dir of Planning 1987–90; Gen. Man., Planning and Devt, Rogers & Co. Ltd 1990–91; MP for Belle Rose/Quatre Bornes Constituency 1991–; Minister of Finance 1991–95, Vice Prime Minister and Minister of Finance and Econ. Empowerment 2005–10; currently Chair. and Director International Financial Services (IFS) Ltd, Ebene; Grand Commdr of the Star and Key; Academic Achievement Prize, LSE. *Leisure interests:* reading, football. *Address:* International Financial Services (IFS) Ltd., IFS Court 28, Ebene Cybercity, Mauritius (office). *Telephone:* 467-5278 (office). *Fax:* 467-3000 (office). *E-mail:* rama.sithanen@sannegroup.com (office). *Website:* www.sannegroup.com (office).

SITHARAMAN, Nirmala, MA, MPhil; Indian economist, social worker and politician; *Minister of Defence;* b. 18 Aug. 1959, Madurai, Tamil Nadu; d. of Narayanan Sitharaman and Shrimati Savitri; m. Parakala Prabhakar; one d.; ed Seethalakshmi Ramaswamy Coll., Tiruchirapalli, Tamil Nadu, Jawaharlal Nehru Univ.; fmr Sr Man. (Research & Analysis), Price Waterhouse, London; Deputy Dir, Centre for Public Policy Studies, Hyderabad 1992; mem. Nat. Comm. for Women 2003–05; Minister of State, Ministry of Finance May–Nov. 2014; Minister of State, Ministry of Corp. Affairs 2014; Minister of State (Ind. Charge), Ministry of Commerce and Industry 2014–17; Minister of Defence 2017–; mem. Rajya Sabha (upper house of parl.) for Andhra Pradesh 2014–16, for Karnataka 2016–; mem. Bharatiya Janata Party (BJP) 2008–, mem. BJP Nat. Exec. 2008–, Nat. BJP Spokesperson 2010–14. *Address:* Ministry of Defence, South Blk, New Delhi 110 011 (office); 15, Safdarjung Road, New Delhi 110 011, India (home). *Telephone:* (11)

23019030 (office); (11) 23793791 (home). *Fax:* (11) 23015403 (office). *E-mail:* ak .antony@sansad.nic.in (office). *Website:* www.mod.nic.in (office).

SITHOLE, Majozi Vincent; Swazi politician and central banker; *Governor, Central Bank of Eswatini;* ed Univ. of Botswana; Minister, Econ. Planning and Devt 1999–2001, Minister of Finance 2001–13; Gov. Central Bank of Swaziland (renamed Central Bank of Eswatini 2018) 2013–; mem. House of Ass. 1998. *Address:* Central Bank of Eswatini, Mahlokohla Street, POB 546, Mbabane, Eswatini (office). *Telephone:* 24082000 (office). *Fax:* 24040063 (office). *E-mail:* info@centralbank.org.sz (office). *Website:* www.centralbank.org.sz.

SITKOVETSKY, Dmitry; American/British violinist, conductor, arranger and television presenter; *Music Director, Greensboro Symphony Orchestra;* b. 27 Sept. 1954, Baku, USSR (now Azerbaijan); s. of Julian Sitkovetsky and Bella Davidovich; m. Susan Roberts; one d.; ed Moscow Conservatory, Juilliard School of Music, New York (Artistic Diploma); debut with Berlin Philharmonic 1980; appearances with Vienna Symphony Orchestra, Orchestre de Paris and the Amsterdam, Rotterdam, Munich and Royal Philharmonic Orchestras in Europe and the Chicago, Cincinnati, Detroit, Montréal and Toronto Symphony Orchestras in N America; Carnegie Hall debut 1986; Artistic Dir Korsholm Festival, Finland 1983–93, Seattle Int. Music Festival 1992–97; Music Dir and Prin. Conductor Ulster Orchestra, NI 1996–2001; Music Dir Tuscan Sun Festival, Cortona, Italy 2003–06; Artist-in-Residence, Orchestra de Castilla & Leon, Valladolid, Spain 2006–09; currently Music Dir Greensboro Symphony Orchestra, Greensboro, N Carolina; First Prize, Fritz Kreisler Competition, Vienna 1979, Avery Fisher Career grant 1983. *Television includes:* role of Arkady Greenberg in film Heavy Sand (Russian Moscow TV) 2008, presenter of series Visiting with Dmitry Sitkovetsky for the Kultura channel (Russia) 2014, 10-part series It Ain't Necessarily So... (Medici TV) 2016. *Recordings include:* Stravinsky: A Soldier's Tale 2012, Chopin: 12 Preludes 2013, Stravinsky Divertimento 2015; more than 50 transcriptions. *Publications include:* transcriptions: Bach – Goldberg Variations for String Trio 1985, 2012, Dohnányi – Serenade for string orchestra 1990, Shostakovich – String Symphony Op. 73 1991, Bach Sinfonias for string trio 2015. *Leisure interests:* movies, football. *Telephone:* (646) 709-6910 (office). *E-mail:* ab@ artsprimavera.com (office). *Website:* www.artsprimavera.com/primavera (office); www.dmitrysitkovetsky.com.

SITORUS, Martua, BEcons; Indonesian business executive; *Executive Deputy Chairman, Wilmar International;* b. 1960; m.; four c.; ed HKBP Nommensen Univ., Medan; began trading shrimp and other marine products 1978; bought first palm oil plantation 1994; co-f. Wilmar International (agribusiness) 1991, Exec. Deputy Chair. 2006–. *Address:* Wilmar International Ltd, 56 Neil Road, Singapore 088830, Singapore (office). *Telephone:* 62160244 (office). *Fax:* 68361709 (office). *E-mail:* info@wilmar.com.sg (office). *Website:* www.wilmar-international.com (office).

SITPHAXAY, Sonexay; Laotian central banker; *Governor, Bank of the Lao PDR;* several years as Man. Dir, Banque pour le Commerce Extérieur Lao (BCEL); Deputy Gov., Bank of the Lao PDR Sept.–Dec. 2018, Gov. Dec. 2018–; substitute mem. 10th Cen. Cttee, Lao People's Revolutionary Party. *Address:* Bank of the Lao PDR, rue Yonnet, BP 19, Vientiane, Laos (office). *Telephone:* (21) 213109 (office). *E-mail:* bol@bol.gov.la (office). *Website:* www.bol.gov.la (office).

SITTHIPHONG, Norkun, BEng (Mech), MS (MechEng), PhD; Thai business executive; *Chairman, Thai Oil Public Company Limited;* m. Bularat Sitthiphong; two d.; ed Chulalongkorn Univ., Oregon State Univ., USA, Nat. Defense Coll., Capital Market Acad., Thai Inst. of Dirs; Dean, Faculty of Eng, Chiang Mai Univ. 1985–97, Vice-Pres. for Research and Property Affairs 1989–2001, for Academic Affairs 2001–03, Sec. Chiang Mai Univ. Council; Advisor to the Bd of Dirs and Sec., The Eng Inst. of Thailand (Northern) 1986–95; Deputy Perm. Sec., Ministry of Energy 2003–10, Perm. Sec. 2010–; Chair. Electricity Generating Public Co. Ltd June–Oct. 2006; Chair. PTT Public Co. Ltd 2008–10, –2013, Chair. PTT Aromatics and Refining Public Co. Ltd 2010–11, IRPC Public Co. Ltd, PTT Exploration and Production Public Co. Ltd 2011–; Chair. Thai Oil Public Co. Ltd 2013–; fmr Dir, Electricity Generating Authority of Thailand; elected to Acad. of Distinguished Engineers, Oregon State Univ. 2005. *Address:* Thai Oil Public Co. Ltd, 555/1 Energy Complex Building A, 11th Floor, Vibhavadi Rangsit Road, Chatuchak, Bangkok 10900, Thailand (office). *Telephone:* (2) 797-2999 (office). *Fax:* (2) 797-2970 (office). *E-mail:* info@thaioilgroup.com (office). *Website:* www.thaioilgroup .com (office).

SIU, Hera K., BS, MBA; Chinese business executive; *Managing Director, Pearson China;* m.; two c.; ed Univ. of Hong Kong, Penn State Univ. and Univ. of Nevada, Reno, USA; appointments have included Marketing Man., RealNetworks, Marketing Specialist, Honeywell, Vice-Pres. and Regional Man., Computer Associates China, Sr Vice-Pres., Application Service Provider, Pacific Century Cyberworks (PCCW), Hong Kong; Corp. Vice-Pres. and Gen. Man. Nokia Telecommunications Ltd (mfg jt venture based in mainland China) –2010, also managed corp. affairs, govt relations, environmental sustainability and corp. social responsibility; Pres. SAP China (business software co.) 2010–14; Man. Dir for Greater China Region, Pearson China 2014–; mem. Bd of Dirs SITA. *Address:* Pearson China, Suite 1208, Tower D, Beijing Global Trade Center 36 North Third Ring Road East, Dongcheng District, Beijing 100013, People's Republic of China (office). *Telephone:* (10) 5735 5000 (office). *Fax:* (10) 5825 7950 (office). *Website:* www.edexcelchina.com (office).

SIWIEC, Marek Maciej; Polish politician and journalist; b. 13 March 1955, Piekary Śląskie; m.; one s. one d.; ed Akademia Górniczo-Hutnicza Univ. of Science and Tech., Kraków, postgraduate journalist studies at Acad. of Social Sciences – Centre for Educ., Foreign Service, Warsaw; Asst, Electronics Inst. of Akademia Górniczo-Hutnicza 1980–82; trainee, Gas & Fuel Corpn of Victoria, Australia 1981–82; Ed.-in-Chief 'Student' bi-monthly 1985–87, weekly ITD (weekly) 1987–90, Trybuna (daily) 1990–91; mem. Democratic Left Alliance in Poland (SLD) –2012, Vice-Chair. 2011–12; Deputy to Sejm (Parl.) 1991–97, Spokesman for SLD Parl. Party 1993; mem. Nat. Council for Radio and Television 1993–96; mem. Parl. Ass. of the Council of Europe 1993–96; Sec. of State, Chancellery of the Pres. of Poland 1996–2004; Chief of Nat. Security Office 1997–2004; Sec. of Nat. Security Council 2000–04; Vice-Chair. Consultative Cttee of the Presidents of Poland and Ukraine 1997–2004; mem. European Parl. 2004–, Head of nat. del. to the PSE in European Parl. 2004–06, Vice-Pres. European Parl. 2007–09, mem. Parl. Cttee for Foreign Affairs, Substitute mem. Cttee on Internal Market and Consumer

Protection, Coordinator of the S&D (Group of the Progressive Alliance of Socialists & Democrats) in Del. to Euronest Parl. Ass., mem. del. to EU-Ukraine Parl. Cooperation Cttee, Substitute mem. Del. to EU-Kazakhstan, EU-Kyrgyzstan and EU-Uzbekistan Parl. Cooperation Cttees, and for relations with Tajikistan, Turkmenistan and Mongolia; Pres. European Friends of Israel; Chair. Supervisory Bd Foundation to Counter Terrorism and Biological Threats; mem. Bd Yalta European Strategy Foundation (YES), Global Leadership Council Colorado; Head of Polish Asscn of Friends of the Peres Centre for Peace. *Leisure interests:* jogging, cycling, snow-boarding, skiing, triathlon, travelling. *Address:* ASP 15G142, 60 rue Wiertz, 1097 Brussels, Belgium (office). *Telephone:* (2) 284-76-53 (office). *Fax:* (2) 284-36-53 (office). *E-mail:* marek.siwiec-office@europarl.europa.eu (office). *Website:* www.mareksiwiec.pl (office).

SIZA VIEIRA, Álvaro (Joaquim Melo); Portuguese architect; b. 25 June 1933, Matosinhos; s. of Júlio Siza Vieira and Cassilda Ermelinda C. Carneiro de Melo Siza Vieira; m. Maria Antonia Marinho Leite 1940 (died 1973); two c.; ed Univ. of Porto; in pvt. practice 1954–; Lecturer, Univ. of Porto 1966–69, Prof. of Construction 1976–; Gold Medal, Alvar Aalto Foundation 1988, Gold Medal, Colegios de Arquitectos (Spain) 1988, Pritzker Architecture Prize 1992, Berlage Prize 1994, Gubbio Prize 1994, Nara World Architecture Exhbn Gold Medal 1995, Imperial Prize, Japan Arts Asscn 1998, Wolf Foundation Prize in Arts 2001, Royal Gold Medal, RIBA 2008, Int. Union of Architects Gold Medal 2011, Venice Architecture Biennale Golden Lion for lifetime achievement 2012. *Address:* Rua do Aleixo 53 2º, 4150-043 Porto, Portugal (office). *Telephone:* (22) 616-72-70 (office). *Fax:* (22) 616-72-79 (office). *E-mail:* geral@sizavieira.pt (office). *Website:* www.sizavieira.pt (office).

SJAASTAD, Anders Christian, PhD; Norwegian politician; *Research Fellow, Norwegian Institute of International Affairs;* b. 21 Feb. 1942, Oslo; s. of Andreas Sjaastad and Ingrid Sjaastad; m. Torill Oftedal Sjaastad 1969 (died 2000); one d.; ed Univ. of Oslo; Pres. Norwegian Students' Asscn, Univ. of Oslo 1967; Research Asst, Inst. of Political Science, Univ. of Oslo 1968–70; Research Assoc., Norwegian Inst. of Int. Affairs (NUPI) 1970–81, Dir of Information 1973–81, Research Fellow 1998–, Dir European Studies 1998–2004, Sr Adviser 2004–12; mem. Høyre (Conservative Party), Vice-Chair. Oslo Høyre 1977–88, Chair. 1996–2000; mem. Storting (Parl.) 1981–2001; Minister of Defence 1981–86; Pres. European Movt in Norway 1989–92; Chair. Defence and Security Cttee (North Atlantic Ass.) 1994–97; Vice-Chair. Standing Cttee on Justice (Stortinget) 1993–97; mem. Norwegian Nat. Defence Comm. 1974–78, Norwegian Cttee on Arms Control and Disarmament 1976–81, 2002–06, N Atlantic Ass. 1989–97; proxy mem. Nobel Peace Prize Cttee 2004–06. *Publications include:* Departmental Decision Making (co-author) 1972, Politikk og Sikkerhet i Norskehavsområdet (with J. K. Skogan) 1975, Norsk Utenrikspolitisk Arbok (ed.) 1975, Deterrence and Defence in the North (co-ed. and contrib.) 1985, Arms Control in a Multipolar World (contrib.) 1996, Maritime Security in Southeast Asia (contrib.) 2007. *Address:* Norwegian Institute of International Affairs (NUPI), C.J. Hambros plass 2D, PO Box 8159, Dep 0033 Oslo, Norway (office). *Telephone:* 22-99-40-32 (office); 95-92-48-94 (mobile) (home). *Fax:* 22-36-21-82 (office). *E-mail:* andersc.sjaastad@nupi.no (office). *Website:* www.nupi.no (office).

SKALICKÝ, Jiří; Czech politician; b. 26 April 1956, Kolín; m.; three s. one d.; ed Coll. of Advanced Chemical Tech., Prague; research worker with Astrid (state enterprise), Prague 1981–90; mem. Civic Democratic Alliance (ÇDA) 1990–98, Deputy Chair. 1990–92; Deputy to House of Nations, Fed. Ass. of ČSFR 1990–92; mem. Plan and Budget Cttee, House of Nations, Fed. Ass. 1990–92; Minister for Nat. Property Admin. and Privatization 1992–96, for the Environment 1996–98; Chair. Presidium of Nat. Property Fund 1992–96; Deputy Chair. Civic Democratic Alliance 1995–97, Chair. 1997–98; Deputy Prime Minister 1997; Senator 1998–2004. *Address:* Zahradnickova 1220, 150 00 Prague 5, Czech Republic (home). *E-mail:* jiriskalicky@volny.cz (home).

SKÁRMETA, Antonio, BA, MA; Chilean writer and diplomatist; b. 7 Nov. 1940, Antofagasta; m. Cecilia Boisier; two s.; ed Universidad de Chile, Columbia Univ., New York; Prof. of Philosophy, Instituto Nacional 1966–68, Universidad de Chile 1968–75; escaped military dictatorship in Chile, lived in Argentina, Portugal, West Germany, Nicaragua; Distinguished Prof. of Literature and Romance Languages, Washington Univ. of St Louis, USA 1988; Amb. to Germany 2000–03; Chevalier, Order des Arts et des Lettres 1986, Commendatore dell'Ordine (Italy) 1996, Grand Cross of Merit (Germany) 2003; Fulbright Scholarship, Guggenheim Fellowship, Premio Excelencia, Universidad de Artes y Ciencias de la Comunicación 1998, Goethe Medal (Germany) 2002, Premio Neruda 2004, Nat. Prize for Literature (Chile) 2014. *Radio:* Voy y Vuelo 2000. *Publications include:* El entusiasmo 1967, Desnudo en el Tejado (Premio Casa de Las Americas) 1969, Tiro Libre 1973, Soné que la nieve ardía 1975, No Pasó Nada (Boccaccio Europa Prize 1986) 1980, La Insurreción 1982, Ardiente paciencia (made into film Il Postino) 1985, Match Ball 1989, La Composición (Jane Adams Prize 2001, Premio Las Américas 2001, Gustav-Heinemann Peace Prize 2004) 1998, La Boda del Poeta (Premio Altazor 2000, Grinzane Cavour Prize 2000, Prix Médicis 2001) 1999, La Chica del Trombón (Premio Elsa Morante 2002, Premio de Narrativa José María Arguedas 2003) 2001, El Baile de la Victoria (Premio Planeta 2003, Premio Municipal de Literatura de la ciudad de Santiago 2004) 2003, Los días del arco iris (Premio Iberoamericano Planeta-Casa de América de Narrativa 2011) 2010; trans.: An American Dream, Norman Mailer 1968, The Pyramid, William Golding 1968, Typee, Herman Melville 1968, Visions of Gerard, Jack Kerouac 1969, Love, Roger, Charles Webb 1969, The Last Tycoon, F. Scott Fitzgerald 1969. *E-mail:* cordillero@gmail.com (office). *Website:* www.antonio-skarmeta.com.

SKARPHÉÐINSSON, Össur, BS, PhD; Icelandic journalist and politician; b. 19 June 1953, Reykjavik; ed Univ. of Iceland, Univ. of East Anglia, UK; ed., Þjóðviljinn newspaper 1984–87, Alþýðublaðið newspaper 1996–97, DV newspaper 1997–98; Asst Prof., Univ. of Iceland 1987–88; Deputy Dir Reykjavík Reinsurance 1989–91; mem. Althingi (Parl.) 1991–, Chair. Social Democratic Party Parl. Group 1991–93, Vice-Chair. 1995–96, Chair. Social Democratic Alliance Parl. Group 2006–07, mem. Cttee on Fisheries 1991–93, on Gen. Affairs 1991–93, on Industry 1991–93, on Agric. 1992–93, on Health and Social Security 1995–99 (Chair.) 1995–99, on Foreign Affairs 1995–99 (Vice-Chair. 1998–99), 2005–07, on the Environment 1999–2000, on the Budget 1999–2001, on Credentials 1999–2003, on Economy and Trade 2001–05, Chair. Del. to NATO Parl. Ass. 2005–07, Vice-Chair. Del. to WEU Ass. 1995–99, mem. Del. to EFTA and EEA Parl. Cttees 1991–93, 1999–2004, Parl. Ass. of the Council of Europe 2003–05; Minister for the Environment 1993–95, for Nordic Co-operation 2007–08, of Industry 2007–09, for Foreign Affairs and External Trade 2009–13; mem. Icelandic Delegation to NATO Parliamentary Ass. 2013– (Deputy Chair. 2013–). *Address:* c/o Samfylkingin (Social Democratic Alliance), Hallveigarstíg 1, 101 Reykjavík, Iceland. *E-mail:* ossur@althingi.is.

SKARSGÅRD, J. Stellan; Swedish actor; b. 13 June 1951, Göteborg; s. of J. Skarsgård and Gudrun Skarsgård; m. My Günther 1976; five s. one d.; with Royal Dramatic Theatre, Stockholm 1972–87; Best Actor, Berlin Film Festival 1982; twice Best Film Actor in Sweden; Best Actor, Rouen Film Festival 1988, 1992, Best Actor, Chicago Film Festival 1991, Jury's Special Prize, San Sebastián Film Festival 1995, European Film Award. *Films include:* Simple Minded Murderer 1982, Serpent's Way 1986, Hip Hip Hurrah 1987, The Unbearable Lightness of Being 1988, Good Evening Mr Wallenberg 1990, The Ox 1992, Wind 1992, The Slingshot 1993, Zero Kelvin 1994, Breaking the Waves 1995, Insomnia 1997, Amistad 1997, Good Will Hunting 1997, Ronin 1998, Deep Blue Sea 1998, Passion of Mind 1999, Kiss Kiss (Bang Bang) 2000, Signs & Wonders 2000, Timecode 2000, Dancer in the Dark 2000, Aberdeen (also assoc. producer) 2000, The Hire: Powder Keg 2001, Taking Sides 2001, The House on Turk Street 2002, City of Ghosts 2002, Dogville 2003, King Arthur 2004, Eiffeltornet 2004, Exorcist: The Beginning 2004, Pirates of the Caribbean: Dead Man's Chest 2006, Goya's Ghosts 2006, Pirates of the Caribbean: At World's End 2007, W Delta Z 2007, Arn-Tempelriddaren 2007, Mamma Mia! 2008, Arn-Riket vid vägens slut 2008, Angels and Demons 2009, Boogie Woogie 2009, Thor 2011, Melancholia 2011, The Girl with the Dragon Tattoo 2011, Avengers Assemble 2012, The Railway Man 2013, Thor: The Dark World 2013, The Physician 2013, Nymphomaniac: Vol. II 2013, Nymphomaniac: Vol. I 2013, In Order of Disappearance 2014, Hector and the Search for Happiness 2014, Cinderella 2015, Avengers: Age of Ultron 2015. *Television includes:* Hamlet 1984, Harlan County War 2000, Helen of Troy 2003, God on Trial 2008, Rouge Brésil (series) 2012, River (mini-series) 2015. *Address:* Hogbergsgatan 40, 118 26 Stockholm, Sweden.

SKARŻYŃSKI, Henryk, DMedHab, PhD, DSc; Polish medical scientist; *Director, Institute of Physiology and Pathology of Hearing;* b. 3 Jan. 1954, Rosochate Koscielne; s. of Józef Skarzynski and Janina Skarzynska; m. Bozena Bruska; two s.; ed Warsaw Medical Univ.; Researcher, Oto-rhino-laryngology Clinic, Warsaw Medical Univ. 1979–2000, Head Ward 1986–96, Asst Prof. 1991–93, Assoc. Prof. 1993–95, Full Prof. 1995–2000; Dir Diagnostic Treatment Rehabilitation Centre for the Deaf and Hearing-Impaired 1993–96; Dir Inst. of Physiology and Pathology of Hearing, Ministry of Health 1996–, Head, Otology Clinic 1999–2003, Head, Int. Centre of Hearing and Speech 2003–12, Head, Oto-Rhino-Laryngology Surgery Clinic 2003–, Head, World Hearing Center 2012–; Chair of Audiology and Phoniatrics Dept, F. Chopin Acad. of Music, Warsaw 2002–; mem. American Acad. of Audiology 1994–, Collegium of Oto-Rhino-Laryngologicum Amicitiae Sacrum 1994–, New York Acad. of Sciences 1995–, American Tinnitus Asscn 1995–, Int. Evoked Response Audiometry Study Group 1997–, European Acad. of Otology and Neuro-Otology 1998–; Corresp. mem. American Otological Soc. 2012–; Hon. mem. Slovak Asscn of Otolaryngology and Head and Neck Surgery 1998–; Hon. Prof. Audiology and Speech Therapy Dept, Brigham Young Univ., USA 1998–99; Officer's Cross, Order of Polonia Restituta 2004, Officer's Cross of Merite de l'Invention (Belgium) 2005, Knight's Cross, Order of Polonia Restituta 2006, Officier, Ordre du Mérite Européen de l'Innovation (Belgium) 2010, Order of Merit (Ukraine) 2010; Dr hc (Maria Grzegorzewska Acad. of Special Educ.) 2011, (Warsaw) 2012; Prize of the Prime Minister 2000, Prize of the Minister of Health and Social Welfare 2000, 2001, Prof. Jan Miodonski Award 1983, Stockholm Challenge Award 2000, Gold Medal of the Acad. of Polish Success 2001, Gold Medal, Brussels Eureka 2002, Award of Chair. of State Cttee for Scientific Research 2003, Golden Medal awarded during Lepine Competition, Paris 2003, Special Prize on behalf of Warsaw City Council 2003, Irlandia Award, High-Level Conf. on eHealth, Cork (Ireland) 2004, Gloria Medicinae Medal 2004, Golden Scalpel, Pulse of the Medicine journal 2010, 2014, Medal of Honour (Georgia) 2010, Hipocrates Statue, Polish Asscn of Family Medicine 2012, Copernicus Medal, Polish Acad. of Sciences 2012, Medal of the Warsaw University of Technology 2014, Man of Freedom Award 2014, Wiktor Television Academy Award 2015. *Achievements include:* pioneer work in developing first Polish Programme for the Treatment of Hearing Disorders, Cochlear and Brainstem Implants Programme. *Publications include:* co-author: Urazy kosci skroniowej (Damages of the Temporal Bone) 1999, Anatomia topograficzna kosci skroniowej dla potrzeb otochirurgii (Topographical Anatomy of the Temporal Bone for Otosurgery) 2000, Technika komputerowa w audiologii, foniatrii i logopedii (Informatic Techniques in Audiology Phoniatrics and Speech and Language Therapy) 2002, Objawy laryngologiczne w rzadkich zespolach chorobowych (Laryngological Symptoms in Rare Diseases) 2002; monographs: Kryteria kwalifikacji do zabiegów wszczepiania implantów slimakowych i program rehabilitacji calkowitej utraty sluchu u dzieci 1994, Implant nadziei. Nowe szanse dla osób nieslyszacych. Pytania i odpowiedzi (Implant of Hope. New Chances for the Hearing Impaired. Questions and Answers) 1994. *Leisure interests:* football, breeding doves. *Address:* Institute of Physiology and Pathology of Hearing, ul. Pstrowskiego 1, 01-943 Warsaw, Poland (office). *Telephone:* (22) 8356670 (office). *Fax:* (22) 8355214 (office). *E-mail:* sekretariat@ifps.org.pl (office). *Website:* www.ifps.org.pl (office); www.ifps.org.pl (office); henrykskarzynski.pl/en.

SKATOV, Nikolai Nikolayevich, DLit; Russian linguist; b. 2 May 1931; m.; one d.; ed Kostroma State Pedagogical Inst.; Sr Teacher, Acting Head, Chair of Literature, Kostroma State Pedagogical Inst. 1956–62; Sr Teacher, Leningrad State Pedagogical Inst. 1962, then Sr Researcher, Docent, Prof., Head of Dept of Literature; apptd Dir Inst. of Russian Literature (Pushkin House) 1987; Chair., Comm. on Literature and Educ., Russian Acad. of Sciences, Deputy Chair., Comm. on Russian Literature, Presidium Russian Acad. of Sciences, Corresp. mem. Russian Acad. of Sciences 1997–; Ed.-in-Chief Russkaya Literature (magazine). *Publications:* 12 books and over 200 scientific works.

SKEGG, Sir David C. G., KNZM, OBE, DCNZM, BMedSc, MB, ChB, DPhil, FRSNZ; New Zealand medical researcher, academic and university administrator; b. 16 Dec. 1947, Auckland; m. Dr Keren Skegg; two d.; ed King's Coll., Auckland,

Univ. of Otago, Balliol Coll., Univ. of Oxford, UK; Lecturer in Epidemiology, Univ. of Oxford 1976–79; Chair of Preventive and Social Medicine, Univ. of Otago 1980–2004, Vice-Chancellor, Univ. of Otago 2004–11; Pres. Royal Soc. of New Zealand 2012–15; Adviser to WHO's Special Programme of Research, Devt and Research Training in Human Reproduction; fmr Chair. NZ Public Health Comm. 1992–95, Health Research Council of NZ; NZ Commemoration Medal 1990, Sir Charles Hercus Medal, Royal Soc. of NZ 1999, Distinguished Research Medal, Univ. of Otago 2003. *Publications:* over 150 papers in academic journals. *Leisure interests:* books, art history, walking.

SKEHEL, Sir John James, Kt, PhD, FRS, FMedSci; British research scientist; *Emeritus Scientist, The Francis Crick Institute;* b. 27 Feb. 1941, Blackburn, Lancs.; s. of Joseph Skehel and Annie Skehel; m. Anita Varley 1962; two s.; ed St Mary's Coll., Blackburn, Univ. Coll. of Wales, Aberystwyth and UMIST; Postdoctoral Fellow, Marischal Coll. Aberdeen 1965–68; Fellow, Helen Hay Whitney Foundation 1968–71; mem. Scientific Staff and Head, Infection and Immunity, MRC Nat. Inst. for Medical Research 1971–84, 1984–2006, Dir 1987–2006, currently Visiting Worker; Emer. Scientist, The Francis Crick Inst.; Dir World Influenza Centre 1975–94; mem. Academia Europea 1992; Vice-Pres. and Biological Sec., Royal Society 2013–; Fellow, Acad. of Medical Science 1998, Vice-Pres. 2002–07; Fellow, Univ. of Aberystwyth 2007; Hon. Prof. of Virology, Univ. of Glasgow 1997–, Hon. Prof., University Coll., London 2002–, Liverpool John Moore's Univ. 2007–; Hon. DSc (University Coll., London) 2004, (Liverpool John Moore's Univ.) 2007, Laurea hc in Medicina e Chirurgia (Univ. of Padua) 2010; Feldberg Prize 1986, Robert Koch Prize 1987, Prix Louis Jeantet de Médecine 1988, ICN Int. Prize in Virology 1993, Royal Soc.'s Royal Medal 2003, Imperial Coll. Ernst Chain Prize 2004, Int. Union of Microbiological Socs Stuart Mudd Award for Basic Microbiology 2005, Int. Louis D, Institut de France Grand Prize (co-recipient) 2007. *Publications:* numerous articles in scientific journals. *Address:* National Institute for Medical Research, The Ridgeway, Mill Hill, London, NW7 1AA, England (office); 49 Homewood Road, St Albans, Herts., AL1 4BG, England (home). *Telephone:* (20) 8816-2256 (office); (1727) 860603 (home). *E-mail:* skeheljj@nimr.mrc.ac.uk (office). *Website:* www.crick.ac.uk/.

ŠĶĒLE, Andris; Latvian politician and business executive; b. 16 Jan. 1958, Aluksne District; m. Dzintra Šķēle; two c.; ed Latvian Acad. of Agric.; Head of Sector, Sr research Asst, Deputy Dir Research Assoc. Inst. of Latvian Agricultural Mechanization and Electrification 1981–90; First Deputy Minister of Agric. 1990–93; Prime Minister of Latvia 1995–97, 1999–2000; Founder and Chair. Tautas Partija (People's Party) 1998–2002, 2009–10; mem. Saeima (Parl.) 1998–2000, 2002–03.

SKELEMANI, Phandu; Botswana lawyer and politician; b. 1945; ed Univ. of Botswana, Lesotho and Swaziland; joined civil service as State Counsel 1973, becoming Sr State Counsel 1975, Prin. State Counsel 1978, Deputy Attorney-Gen. 1980–82, Attorney-Gen. 1992–2003; mem. Parl. for Francistown East, mem. Botswana Democratic Party (BDP) (Domkrag); Minister of Presidential Affairs and Public Admin. 2004–07, of Justice, Defence and Security 2007–08, of Foreign Affairs and Int. Co-operation 2008–14. *Address:* c/o Ministry of Foreign Affairs and International Co-operation, Private Bag 00368, Gaborone, Botswana.

SKERRIT, Roosevelt, BA, BSc; Dominican politician; *Prime Minister and Minister of Finance, Investments, Housing and Lands;* b. 8 June 1972, Vieille Case; m. Melissa Poponne; one s.; ed New Mexico State Univ., Univ. of Mississippi, USA; mem. of Young Freedom Movt (youth arm of Dominica Freedom Party) while a student; fmr high school teacher; Lecturer, Clifton-Dupigny Community Coll. –1999; mem. House of Ass. for Vieille Case constituency 2000–; Minister of Educ., Sports and Youth Affairs 2000–04; Prime Minister of Dominica 2004–, also Minister of Finance 2004–10, of Nat. Security and Econ. Planning 2004–07, 2008–10, of Social Security and Foreign Affairs 2007–08, of Finance, Foreign Affairs and Information Tech. 2010–14, of Nat. Security, Labour and Immigration 2010–14, of Finance, Investments, Housing and Lands 2014–; mem. Dominica Labour Party (DLP), Leader 2004–; Hon. DLitt (Lovely Professional Univ., India) 2016, (Duquesne Univ., USA) 2018. *Address:* Office of the Prime Minister, 6th Floor, Financial Centre, Kennedy Avenue, Roseau, Dominica (office). *Telephone:* 2663300 (office). *Fax:* 4488960 (office). *E-mail:* opm@dominica.gov.dm (office). *Website:* www.opm.gov.dm (office).

SKIDELSKY, Baron (Life Peer), cr. 1991, of Tilton in the County of East Sussex; **Robert Jacob Alexander Skidelsky,** MA, DPhil, FBA, FRHistS, FRSL; British professor of political economy; *Professor Emeritus of Political Economy, University of Warwick;* b. 25 April 1939, Harbin, China; s. of Boris Skidelsky and Galia Sapelkin; m. Augusta Hope 1970; two s. one d.; ed Brighton Coll. and Jesus Coll., Oxford; Research Fellow, Nuffield Coll. Oxford 1965; Assoc. Prof., Johns Hopkins Univ., USA 1970; Prof. of Political Economy, Univ. of Warwick 1990–, currently Emer. Prof.; Chair. Social Market Foundation 1991–2001; Chair. Hands Off Reading Campaign 1994–97; Conservative Front Bench Spokesman on Culture, Media and Sport 1997–98, on Treasury Affairs 1998–99; mem. Lord Chancellor's Advisory Council on Public Records 1988–93; mem. Schools Examination and Assessment Council 1992–93; mem. Bd Manhattan Inst. 1994–, Moscow School of Political Studies 1999–, Janus Capital Group Inc. 2001–11; mem. (Crossbench), House of Lords 1991–, mem. Select Cttee on Econ. Affairs 2006–08, 2012–15; Gov. Brighton Coll. 1998–2016; Chair., Wilton Park Academic Council 2004–, Centre for Global Studies 2002–; mem. EU Financial Affairs Sub-Cttee 2015–, Rusnano Capital 2009–15, Russneft 2016–; Hon. DLitt (Buckingham) 1997. *Publications include:* Politicians and the Slump 1967, English Progressive Schools 1970, Oswald Mosley 1975, John Maynard Keynes, Vol. 1 Hopes Betrayed 1883–1920 1983, Vol. 2 The Economist as Saviour, 1920–1937 (Wolfson Prize for History) 1992, Vol. 3 Fighting for Britain, 1937–1946 (Duff Cooper Prize, James Tait Black Memorial Prize for Biography, Lionel Gelber Prize for Int. Relations, Arthur Ross Council on Foreign Relations Prize for Int. Relations) 2000, (single-vol. abridgement) 2003, Interests and Obsessions 1993, The World After Communism 1995, Beyond the Welfare State 1997, The Politics of Economic Reform 1998, Keynes: the return of the master 2009, A World by Itself: A History of the British Isles 2010, How Much is Enough?: Money and the Good Book (with Edward Skidelsky) 2012, Britain Since 1900: A Success Story? 2014, The Essential Keynes (ed) 2015. *Leisure interests:* music, tennis. *Address:* House of Lords, Westminster, London, SW1A 0PW (office); Room 207, Fielden House, 13 Little College Street, London, SW1P 3SH, England. *Telephone:* (20) 7219-8721 (office). *E-mail:* skidelskyr@parliament.uk (office). *Website:* www.skidelskyr.com.

SKILBECK, Malcolm, AO, MA, PhD, FASSA; Australian educational researcher, consultant and author; *Professor Emeritus, Deakin University;* b. 22 Sept. 1932, Northam, WA; s. of Charles Harrison Skilbeck and Elsie Muriel Nash Skilbeck; m. 1st Elizabeth Robbins; one s. three d.; m. 2nd Dr Helen Connell 1984; one d.; ed Sydney Univ., Univ. of Illinois, USA, Univ. of London, UK; Prof. and Dean of Educ., Univ. of Ulster, NI 1971–75; Foundation Dir, Australian Curriculum Devt Centre 1975–81; Dir of Studies, Schools Council for Curriculum and Examinations for England and Wales 1981–83; Prof. of Curriculum Studies, Inst. of Educ., Univ. of London 1981–85; Vice-Chancellor and Prin. Deakin Univ. 1986–91, Prof. Emer. 1991–; Deputy Dir for Educ., Directorate of Educ., Employment, Labour and Social Affairs, OECD 1991–97; Dir Connell Skilbeck Int. Educ. Consultants 1997–2006; Consultant to OECD, UNESCO, nat. govts, British Council, Australian Int. Devt Assistance Bureau; Hon. DLitt. *Publications:* Culture and the Classroom 1976, A Core Curriculum for the Common School 1982, School Based Curriculum Development 1984, Evaluating the Curriculum for the Eighties 1984, Curriculum Reform 1990, The Vocational Quest 1994, Redefining Tertiary Education 1998, Access and Equity in Higher Education 2000, The University Challenged 2002. *Leisure interests:* gardens, books, art. *Address:* PO Box 278, Drysdale, Vic. 3222, Australia. *Telephone:* (3) 5253-3340. *E-mail:* skilbeck.connell@deakin.edu.au.

SKINNER, James (Jim) Alan; American food industry executive; *Executive Chairman, Walgreens Boots Alliance, Inc.;* b. 1944; served in USN for ten years; began career with McDonald's as trainee restaurant man. 1971, then numerous man. positions including dir of field operations, market man., regional Vice-Pres., US Sr Vice-Pres.; joined McDonald's int. man. team as Sr Vice-Pres. and Relationship Partner for Cen. Europe, the Middle East, Africa and India 1992, Exec. Vice-Pres. and Relationship Partner 1995–97, Pres. McDonald's Europe 1997–2001, fmr Pres. and COO for Europe/Asia/Pacific and the Middle East, fmr Pres. and COO McDonald's Restaurant Group, Vice-Chair. and CEO McDonald's Corpn 2004–12; mem. Bd of Dirs, Walgreen Co. 2005–, Chair. (non-exec.) 2012–14, Exec. Chair. Walgreens Boots Alliance, Inc. 2015–; mem. Bd Ronald McDonald House Charities, Illinois Tool Works, Hewlett Packard; mem. The Chicago Club, The Commercial Club of Chicago, The Economic Club of Chicago, The Executives' Club of Chicago, The Chicago Council on Global Affairs; mem. Bd of Trustees, Museum of Science and Industry; named by Dow Jones/Marketwatch as CEO of the Year 2007, named by Restaurants & Institutions magazine Executive of the Year 2007. *Address:* Walgreens Boots Alliance, Inc., 108 Wilmot Road, Deerfield, IL 60015, USA (office). *Telephone:* (847) 315-3700 (office). *E-mail:* investor.relations@wba.com (office). *Website:* www.walgreensbootsalliance.com (office).

SKINNER, Paul David, CBE, BA (Law), DpBA; British natural resources industry executive; b. 1944; m.; two s.; ed Univ. of Cambridge, Manchester Business School; joined The Royal Dutch/Shell Group of Cos 1966, sr appointments in UK, Greece, Nigeria, New Zealand and Norway, CEO Global Oil Products Business 1999–2003, Man. Dir Shell Transport and Trading Co. PLC 2000–03, also Group Man. Dir; Dir Rio Tinto plc and Rio Tinto Ltd 2001–09, Group Chair. 2003–09; Dir (non-exec.) Standard Chartered PLC 2003–15, Tetra Laval Group 2005–15, L'Air Liquide SA 2006–15; Chair. Governing Body ICC (UK) 2004–08, Commonwealth Business Council 2007–09; Chair. (non-exec.), Infrastructure UK 2009–13; mem. (non-exec.), Defence Bd, Ministry of Defence 2006–09, 2014–, Public Interest Body, PwC 2010–; Pres. UK Chamber of Shipping 1997–98; mem. Bd INSEAD Business School 1999–2011; mem. Advisory Bd Norton Rose Fulbright LLP 2014–. *Leisure interests:* skiing, other outdoor sports, opera, modern history. *Address:* Defence Equipment and Support, Ministry of Defence, Abbey Wood South, NH2 Maple 2c, #2219, Bristol, BS34 8JH, England (office). *Telephone:* (11) 7913-0545 (office). *E-mail:* des-chairman@mod.uk (office). *Website:* www.hm-treasury.gov.uk/infrastructure_about.htm (office).

SKINNER, Quentin Robert Duthie, MA, FBA; British historian and academic; *Barber Beaumont Professor of the Humanities, Queen Mary, University of London;* b. 26 Nov. 1940, Oldham, Lancs., England; s. of Alexander Skinner and Winifred Skinner (née Duthie); m. 2nd Susan James 1979; one s. one d.; ed Bedford School, Gonville and Caius Coll., Cambridge; Fellow, Christ's Coll., Cambridge 1962–2008, Vice-Master 1997–99, Hon. Fellow 2008–; Lecturer in History, Univ. of Cambridge 1967–78, Prof. of Political Science 1978–96, Regius Prof. of History 1996–2008, Pro-Vice-Chancellor 1999; Barber Beaumont Prof. of the Humanities, Queen Mary, Univ. of London 2008–; mem. Inst. of Advanced Study, Princeton, New Jersey 1974–75, 1976–79; mem. Academia Europaea 1989; Foreign mem. American Acad. of Arts and Sciences 1986, American Philosophical Soc. 1997, Royal Irish Acad. 1999, Accad. Nazionale dei Lincei 2007, Österreichische Akad. der Wissenschaften 2009, Royal Danish Acad. of Sciences and Letters 2015; Hon. DLitt (Chicago) 1992, (E Anglia) 1992, (Helsinki) 1997, (Oxford) 2000, (Leuven) 2004, (St Andrews) 2005, (Harvard) 2005, (Athens) 2007, (Aberdeen) 2007, (Santiago) 2009, (Oslo) 2011, (Copenhagen) 2014, (Kent) 2017, (Uppsala) 2018; Wolfson Literary Award 1979, Balzan Prize 2006, Sir Isaiah Berlin Prize 2006. *Publications include:* The Foundations of Modern Political Thought, Vol. I The Renaissance 1978, Vol. II The Age of Reformation 1978, Machiavelli 1981, Philosophy in History (co-ed. and contrib.) 1984, The Return of Grand Theory in the Human Sciences (ed. and contrib.) 1985, The Cambridge History of Renaissance Philosophy (co-ed. and contrib.) 1988, Machiavelli: The Prince (ed. and introduction) 1988, Meaning and Context: Quentin Skinner and His Critics (ed. James Tully) 1988, Machiavelli and Republicanism (co-ed. and contrib.) 1990, Political Discourse in Early-modern Britain (co-ed. and contrib.) 1993, Milton and Republicanism (co-ed.) 1995, Reason and Rhetoric in the Philosophy of Hobbes 1996, Liberty before Liberalism 1998, Visions of Politics, Vol. I Regarding Method 2002, Vol. II Renaissance Virtues 2002, Vol. III Hobbes and Civil Science 2002, Republicanism: A Shared European Heritage (co-ed. and contrib.) Vol. I Republicanism and Constitutionalism in Early Modern Europe 2002, Vol. II The Values of Republicanism in Early Modern Europe 2002, States and Citizens (co-ed. and contrib.) 2003, Thomas Hobbes: Writings on Common Law and Hereditary Right (co-ed.) 2005, Hobbes and Republican Liberty 2008, Sovereignty in Fragments (co-ed. and contrib.) 2010, Families and States in Western Europe (ed.) 2011, Freedom and the Construction of Europe, Volume I: Religious Freedom and Civil Liberty (co-ed.) 2011, Freedom and the Construction of Europe, Volume II: Free Persons and Free States (co-ed.) 2011, Forensic Shakespeare 2014, Popular Sovereignty in Historical Perspective (co-ed.) 2016, From Humanism to Hobbes 2018. *Address:* School of History, Queen Mary, University of London, Mile End Road, London, E1 4NS, England (office). *Telephone:* (20) 7882-8325 (office). *Fax:* (20) 8980-8400 (office). *E-mail:* q.skinner@qmul.ac.uk (office). *Website:* www.history.qmul.ac.uk (office).

SKODON, Emil, BA, MBA; American diplomatist (retd); b. 25 Nov. 1953, Chicago, Ill.; m.; two d.; ed Univ. of Chicago, Foreign Service Inst.; career mem. Sr Foreign Service with rank of Minister-Counselor, served in Embassy in Bridgetown, Barbados 1977–78, State Dept Office of Southern African Affairs 1982–84, assigned to econ. sections of embassies in East Berlin 1979–81, Vienna 1984–88, Counselor for Econ. Affairs, Embassy in Kuwait 1989–91, Acting Deputy Chief of Mission, Embassy in Baghdad 1990, US Consul-Gen., Perth 1991–95, Deputy Chief of Mission, Embassy in Singapore 1995–98, Dir State Dept Office of Australian, New Zealand, and Pacific Island Affairs 1998–2000, Foreign Policy Advisor to USAF Chief of Staff 2000–02, Deputy Chief of Mission, Embassy in Rome 2002–05, Amb. to Brunei 2005–08; Special Advisor, Anari Inc./WorldView 2010–; Project Leader, Compass Pro Bono Consulting 2010–12, Head of Project Leaders Advisory Group 2011–13, Project Evaluator 2013–; mem. Nat. Trust for Historic Preservation; several State Dept Superior Honor and Meritorious Honor awards, US Army Outstanding Civilian Service Medal, USAF Decoration for Exceptional Civilian Service. *Address:* Compass, 1720 N Street, NW, Washington, DC 20036, USA (office). *Telephone:* (202) 629-2354 (office). *Website:* compassprobono.org (office).

SKOL, Michael, BA; American diplomatist and business executive; *Principal, Skol & Serna;* b. 15 Oct. 1942, Chicago, Ill.; s. of Ted Skol and Rebecca Skol; m. Claudia Serwer 1973; ed Yale Univ.; joined US Foreign Service 1965, served in Buenos Aires, Saigon, Santo Domingo, Naples, Rome, San José and Bogotá (Deputy Chief of Mission) and as Desk Officer for Costa Rica, Paraguay and Uruguay, Deputy Dir for Policy Planning and Dir Andean Affairs, State Dept Bureau of Inter-American Affairs, Deputy Asst Sec. of State for S America, 1988–90, Amb. to Venezuela 1990–93; Prin. Deputy Asst Sec. Latin American/ Caribbean Dept of State 1993–95; Founding Chair. US-Colombia Business Partnership 1996–99; Sr Vice-Pres. Diplomatic Resolutions Inc., Washington, DC 1996–97; Founder and Pres. Skol and Assocs, Inc., Washington, DC 1998–; Sr Man. Dir for Latin America, DSFX, Washington, DC 1998–2005; Founder and Pres. Skol, Ospina & Serna LLC, Bogotá, Colombia 2000–03, Prin., Skol and Serna, Washington, DC and Bogotá 2003–; Sr Assoc., Manchester Trade Ltd; mem. Council on Foreign Relations; Order of the Liberator (Venezuela) 1993, Order of Nat. Merit (Paraguay) 1995. *Television includes:* co-creator and first co-host 'Choque de Opiniones', CNN Spanish TV network 1997. *Leisure interests:* collecting Latin American folk art, first editions of British children's books. *Address:* Manchester Trade Ltd, 1776 Eye Street, NW, 9th Floor, Washington, DC 20006 (office); 650 Park Avenue, Apartment 9, New York, NY 10065, USA (home). *Telephone:* (917) 843-9753 (office). *Fax:* (917) 477-6453 (office). *E-mail:* skolassoc@gmail.com (office). *Website:* ssadvisors.net (office).

ŠKOLČ, Jožef; Slovenian fmr politician; *General Secretary, Zveza za tehnično kulturo Slovenije;* b. 19 Aug. 1960, Breginje; ed Ljubljana Univ.; active in Socialist Youth League of Slovenia (ZSMS) 1979–84; mem. of Pres. Republican Conf. of Socialist Youth League (RKZSMS) 1984, Pres. 1988–92; Chair. Cttee for Constitution 1990; elected Deputy, Nat. Ass. for Ljubljana Moste-Polje (6) 1992, Pres. Nat. Ass. 1994–96; Leader of ZSMS Deputies' Club (later Liberal Democratic Party) 1990–94; Co-ordinator of Liberal Democracy of Slovenia; Minister of Culture 1997–2000; Chair. Comm. for Mandates and Elections 2000; Leader, Deputy Club of Liberal Democracy 2007–; State Sec. responsible for non-governmental orgs 2008–11, State Sec. at Ministry of Culture 2011; Gen. Sec. Zveza za tehnično kulturo Slovenije 2012–. *Address:* Zveza za tehnično kulturo Slovenije (Association for Technical Culture of Slovenia), Zaloška cesta 65, 1000 Ljubljana, Slovenia (office). *E-mail:* jozef.skolc@zotks.si (office). *Website:* www.zotks.si/ (office).

SKOLIMOWSKI, Jerzy; Polish film director, artist and actor; b. 5 May 1938, Warsaw; m. Joanna Szczerbic; ed Warsaw Univ. and State Superior Film School, Łódź; wrote scripts for Wajda's Innocent Sorcerers, Polanski's Knife in the Water and Łomnicki's Poślizg; Special Prize, Venice Film Festival 1985. *Films include:* Rysopis (Identification Marks: None) (also designer, author, editor, actor) 1964, Walkover (also screenwriter and actor) 1965, Bariera (Barrier) (also screenwriter) (Grand Prix, Int. Film Festival, Bergamo 1966) 1966, Le Départ 1967, Dialogue 20-40-60 1968, The Adventures of Gerard 1969, The Deep End 1971, King, Queen, Knave 1972, Lady Frankenstein (or Terminus) 1976, The Shout (Silver Palm, Cannes Film Festival 1978) 1978, Rece do góry (Hands Up!) (also screenwriter and actor) 1981, Moonlighting (British Film Award 1982) 1982, Success is the Best Revenge 1984, The Lightship 1985, Mesmerized (screenwriter) 1986, Torrents of Spring (screenwriter) 1989, Before and After Death 1990, 30 Door Key 1991, The Hollow Men, America 2008, A Short Film About Killing, Essential Killing 2011; as actor: Niewinni czarodzieje 1960, Boks 1961, Rysopis 1964, Walkower 1965, Sposób bycia 1966, Deep End 1971, Poslizg 1972, Rece do góry 1981, Die Fälschung 1981, White Nights 1985, Big Shots 1987, Torrents of Spring 1989, Mars Attacks! 1996, L.A. Without a Map 1998, Before Night Falls 2000, Eastern Promises 2007, Cztery noce z Anna (Four Nights with Anna) 2008, Essential Killing (also screenplay) 2010, 11 Minutes (also writer) 2015. *Publications:* poetry: Gdzieś blisko siebie (Somewhere Close to Oneself); play: Ktoś się utopił (Somebody Got Drowned).

SKOLL, Jeffrey (Jeff) S., OC, BS, MBA; American/Canadian business executive, foundation executive and film producer; *Chairman, Skoll Foundation;* b. 16 Jan. 1965, Montréal; ed Univ. of Toronto, Stanford Univ. Grad. School of Business; f. Skoll Eng (consulting firm), Toronto 1987, Micros on the Move Ltd (computer hire firm) 1990; Man. Knight-Ridder Information (online news information) internet distribution channels 1995; Co-founder and Pres. eBay Inc. 1996–98, then Vice-Pres., Strategic Planning and Analysis 1998; mem. Bd of Dirs eBay Foundation 1998–; Founder and Chair. Skoll Foundation 1999–; Founder and CEO Participant Productions (film production co.), Los Angeles 2004–; f. Gandhi Project 2005, Skoll Global Threats Fund, Capricorn Investment Group; mem. Bd of Dirs Community Foundation Silicon Valley; mem. Advisory Bd Stanford Grad. School of Business; Hon. LLD (Univ. of Toronto) 2003, Hon. Dr of Public Service (Santa Clara Univ.); Leafy Award (Canada) 1999, Software Devt Forum Visionary Award 2001, Asscn of Fundraising Professionals Silicon Valley Chapter Outstanding Philanthropist Award 2002, Int. Asscn of Fundraising Professionals Outstanding Philanthropist Award 2003, Nat. Leadership Award for Commonwealth Club Silicon Valley 2004, Wired Magazine's Rave Award 2006, Producers Guild of America Visionary Award 2009, Entertainment Industry Environmental Leadership Award, Global Green USA 2009, James G. Morgan Humanitarian Award 2011, John W. Gardner Leadership Award 2012, S. Roger Horchow Award for Greatest Public Service by a Private Citizen 2015. *Films produced include:* House of D 2004, Good Night, and Good Luck 2005, North Country 2005, American Gun 2005, Syriana 2005, An Inconvenient Truth 2006, Fast Food Nation 2006, The World According to Sesame Street 2006, Chicago 10 2007. *Publications include:* numerous articles in popular and professional journals. *Address:* Skoll Foundation, 250 University Avenue, Suite 200, Palo Alto, CA 94301, USA (office). *Telephone:* (650) 331-1031 (office). *Fax:* (650) 331-1033 (office). *Website:* skoll.org (office); www.jeffskollgroup.com (office); www.skollglobalthreats.org (office); www.participantmedia.com (office).

SKOMOROKHA, Viktor Yehorovych, Cand. of Law; Ukrainian judge; b. 1941, Matrosove Village, Solonyansk Dist, Dnipropetrovsk Region; m. Liudmyla Vasylivna; one s. one d.; ed Kharkiv Law Inst. (now Yaroslav Mudry Nat. Law Acad. of Ukraine); Judge, Krasny Luch Municipal Court, Luhansk Region 1967–70; mem. Luhansk Municipal Court 1970–76; Judge, Supreme Court of Ukraine 1976–96; apptd Judge, Constitutional Court of Ukraine 1996, Chair. 1999–2002; Order for Merits, Second Class 2000, First Class 2002; Cross of Honour for the Renaissance of Ukraine 2002; Veteran of Work Medal 1983, Distinguished Lawyer of Ukraine 1995. *Publications:* publs on Ukrainian constitutional issues, human rights and admin. reform. *Leisure interests:* history books, poetry, gardening.

SKORTON, David J., BA, MD; American cardiologist, computer scientist and university administrator; *Secretary, Smithsonian Institution;* b. 22 Nov. 1949, Milwaukee, Wis.; ed Northwestern Univ.; medical residency and cardiology fellowship, UCLA; Instructor, Univ. of Iowa 1980, Asst Prof. of Internal Medicine 1981, Asst Prof. of Electrical and Computer Eng 1982–84, Assoc. Prof. 1984–88, Prof. 1988–2003, Co-founder and Co-dir Adolescent and Adult Congenital Heart Disease Clinic, Univ. of Iowa Hosps and Clinics, Vice-Pres. for Research 1992, Interim Vice-Pres. for External Relations 2000–02, Vice-Pres. for Research and External Relations 2002–03, Pres. Univ. of Iowa 2003–06; Pres. Cornell Univ. 2006–15, held faculty appointments in Medicine and Medicine in Pediatrics at Weill-Cornell Medical Coll., New York City and in Biomedical Eng at Coll. of Eng on Ithaca campus; Sec., Smithsonian Inst., Washington, DC 2015–; Charter Past-Pres. Asscn for Accreditation of Human Research Protection Programs, Inc.; has served on bds and cttees of many other nat. orgs, including American Coll. of Cardiology, American Heart Asscn, American Inst. of Ultrasound in Medicine, American Soc. of Echocardiography, Asscn of American Univs, Council on Competitiveness, Korea America Friendship Soc.; Vice-Chair. Business-Higher Educ. Forum 2006–08, Chair. 2008–10; Life mem. Council on Foreign Relations, Advisory Council Nat. Inst. of Biomed Imaging and Bioengineering, NIH 2009–; Chair. Gov.'s Task Force on Diversifying the NY State Economy Through Industry-Higher Educ. Partnerships 2009, Advisory Council 10,000 Small Businesses 2009–, Council of Presidents, Univs Research Asscn 2010, NY Gov.-elect Andrew Cuomo's Transition Comm. on Econ. Devt and Labor 2010–11; Master, American Coll. of Cardiology. *Radio:* studied and played saxophone and flute in Iowa City and hosted a weekly jazz program, As Night Falls, on KSUI (Univ. of Iowa's public FM radio station). *Publications:* numerous articles, reviews, book chapters, and two major texts on cardiac imaging and image processing. *Address:* Office of the Secretary, Smithsonian Institution, Washington, DC 20013-7012, USA (office). *Website:* www.si.edu (office).

SKOTHEIM, Robert Allen, BA, MA, PhD; American historian and academic administrator; b. 31 Jan. 1933, Seattle, Wash.; s. of Sivert O. Skotheim and Marjorie F. Skotheim (née Allen); m. Nadine Vail 1953; one s. two d.; ed Univ. of Washington; Prof. of History, Univ. of Wash., Wayne State Univ., UCLA, Univ. of Colorado 1962–72; Provost and Faculty Dean, Hobart and William Smith Colls 1972–75; Pres. Whitman Coll. 1975–88; Dir Huntington Library, Art Collections, Botanical Gardens 1988–90, Pres. 1990–2001, now Pres. Emer.; Pres. Occidental Coll. 2008–09; mem. Advisory Bd Thomas C. Wales Foundation; Guggenheim Memorial Fellowship 1967–68; numerous hon. degrees. *Publications include:* American Intellectual Histories and Historians 1966, co-ed. Historical Scholarship in the United States and Other Essays 1967; ed. The Historian and the Climate of Opinion 1969, Totalitarianism and American Social Thought 1971, co-ed. American Social Thought: Sources and Interpretations (two vols) 1972. *Address:* 2126 Place Road, Port Angeles, WA 98363-9664, USA (home).

SKOTNIKOV, Leonid Alekseyevich; Russian diplomatist and judge; b. 26 March 1951, Kalinin; m.; one s.; ed Moscow State Inst. of Int. Relations; mem. staff, Consular Dept Ministry of Foreign Affairs 1974–77; attaché, Perm. Mission to the UN 1977–81; mem. staff, Legal Dept, Ministry of Foreign Affairs 1981–91, Dir 1991–92, 1998–2001; Amb. to the Netherlands 1992–98; Amb. and Perm. Rep. to UN Office and other Int. Orgs in Geneva, the Disarmament Conf. 2001–05; Judge, Int. Court of Justice 2006–15; mem. Panel of Ind. Experts to Assess Admin of Justice System of UN 2015–; Order of Friendship 2002.

SKOU, Søren, BBA, MBA (Hons); Danish shipping company executive; *CEO of Maersk Line and Group CEO, Maersk Group;* b. 20 Aug. 1964; m. Lene Skou; three c.; ed Copenhagen Business School, Int. Inst. for Man. Devt, Lausanne, Switzerland; joined Maersk 1983, held various positions in Maersk Line, with roles in Copenhagen, New York and Beijing, joined Maersk Tankers 1998, where he was CEO 2001–11, mem. Exec. Bd, A.P. Moller-Maersk Group 2007–, CEO Maersk Liner Business, encompassing Maersk Line, Safmarine, MCC and Seago Line 2012–, Group CEO Maersk Group 2016–; named as jt-second most influential person (with Nils Andersen) in int. shipping industry according to Lloyds List 2014. *Leisure interest:* cycling. *Address:* The Mærsk Group, Esplanaden 50, 1098 Copenhagen K, Denmark (office). *Telephone:* 33-63-33-63 (office). *Fax:* 33-63-30-03 (office). *E-mail:* info@maersk.com (office). *Website:* www.maersk.com (office).

SKOURAS, Thanos, PhD, FBIM; Greek economist and academic; *Professor Emeritus, Athens University of Economics and Business;* b. 21 Dec. 1943, Athens; s. of Spyros D. Skouras and Ismini Xanthopoulos; m. 1st Gella Varnava 1966 (divorced 1987); two s.; m. 2nd Savina Ioannides 1998; ed Athens Coll., King's Coll., Durham Univ. and London School of Econs, UK; Asst Lecturer, Lecturer, Sr Lecturer, Middlesex Polytechnic at Enfield, UK 1967–73; Prin. Lecturer and Head Econs Div., Thames Polytechnic 1974–77; Head Dept of Applied Econ. Studies, NE London Polytechnic (now Univ. of East London) 1978–86; Prof., Athens Univ. of Econs and Business 1986–2010, Prof. Emer. 2011–, Deputy Chair. Econs Dept 1987–89, Chair. Marketing and Communication Dept 2004–08, Vice-Rector 1989–92, Pres. Research Centre 1989–92; fmr Visiting Lecturer, Architectural Asscn School, London, Cambridge Univ., CEMI Beijing, Fudan Univ. Shanghai, Katholieke Univ. Leuven, Univ. of Athens; Adviser to Deputy Minister of Nat. Economy, Athens; mem. Council of Econ. Advisers 1986–88; Ed. Thames Papers in Political Economy 1974–86, British Review of Econ. Issues 1976–85; Assoc. Ed. Greek Econ. Review 1985–90; mem. Editorial Bd Int. Review of Applied Econs 1993–; Councillor Royal Econ. Soc., London 1982–86; mem. Governing Council Greek Centre of Planning and Econ. Research 1987–88; Chair. Cttee for Financing of Major Infrastructure Projects 1988; Council mem. Euro-China Research Asscn for Man. 1989–92; mem. Supreme Disciplinary Council, Econ. Chamber of Greece 1990–92; Consultant intra muros European Comm. DG XVI 1992–94; Chair. Abax Stockbroking 1991–94, Global New Europe Fund Portfolio Investments 2002–03, Credit M 2013–; mem. Bd Ergose 1996–97, Commercial Bank 1997, Greek Econ. Soc. 1998–99, Hellenic Centre for European Studies 2001–, Global New Europe Fund 2003–08, Acad. of Labour 2005–08, Greek State Scholarships Foundation 2008–09, Budget Cttee of European Univ., Florence 2008–09; Treas. Citizens' Movt for an Open Society 2007–10, Soc. for the Study of Greek History 2007–11; Hon. Research Fellow, Polytechnic of East London 1986–91. *Publications:* Land and its Taxation in Recent Economic Theory 1977, Post-Keynesian Economic Theory (co-ed.) 1985, The Greek Economy: Economic Policy for the 1990s (ed.) 1991, Production or Importation of Advanced Technology Manufactures? – The Case of Telecommunications Equipment (co-author) 1993, Economic Priorities on the Threshold of the 21st Century (co-ed.) 2000, The Economic Dimension of Mass Communication Media 2003; about 60 articles in professional journals. *Address:* Athens University of Economics and Business, 76 Patission Street, 104 34 Athens (office); 8 Chlois Street, 145 62 Athens, Greece. *Telephone:* (210) 8203432 (office). *Fax:* (210) 8082543 (office). *E-mail:* chlois@aueb.gr (office). *Website:* www.aueb.gr/gb (office).

SKOURIS, Vassilios; Greek judge and academic; *Professor, School of Law, Aristotle University of Thessaloniki;* b. 1948; ed Free Univ., Berlin, Hamburg Univ., Germany; Asst Prof., Univ. of Hamburg, Germany 1972–77; Prof. of Public Law, Univ. of Bielefeld, Germany 1978, Univ. of Thessaloniki 1982; Minister of Internal Affairs 1989, 1996; Judge, Court of Justice of the European Communities (now EU) 1999–2015, Pres. 2003–15; apptd Dir Centre for Int. and European Econ. Law, Thessaloniki 1997; mem. Acad. Council, Acad. of European Law, Trier 1995; Prof., School of Law, Aristoteleio Panepistimio Thessalonikis (Aristotle Univ. of Thessaloniki), Bucerius Law School, Hamburg, Germany 2012–; mem. Greek Nat. Research Cttee 1993–95, Scientific Cttee, Ministry of Foreign Affairs 1997–99; mem. Admin. Bd, Univ. of Crete 1983–87, Higher Selection Bd for Greek Civil Servants 1994–96, Admin. Bd, Greek Nat. Judges' Coll. 1995–96; Pres. Greek Asscn for European Law 1992–94, Greek Econ. and Social Council 1998; numerous hon. degrees. *Address:* School of Law, Aristotle University of Thessaloniki Campus, 541 24, Thessaloniki, Greece (office). *Website:* www.law.auth.gr/en (office).

SKOURLETIS, Panagiotis (Panos); Greek politician and business executive; *Secretary, SYRIZA;* b. 1 Jan. 1962, Exarcheia, Athens; m.; two s.; ed Univ. of Piraeus; became active in Rigas Feraios youth wing of Kommunistiko Komma Elladas—Esoterikou (Communist Party of Greece—Interior), mem. Cen. Council office; work experience in pvt. sector since 1986; mem. Synaspismos tis Aristeras ton Kinimátôo kai tis Oikologías (Synaspismos—Coalition of the Left, of Movements and Ecology) since 1990 and subsequently of Synaspismos Rizospastikis Aristeras (SYRIZA—Coalition of the Radical Left), Spokesman for SYRIZA 2009–15, Sec., SYRIZA 2018–; mem. Parl. for Athens B 2015–; Minister of Labour, Social Security and Social Solidarity 27 Jan.–18 July 2015, of Reconstruction of Production, Environment and Energy 18 July–28 Aug. 2015, of Environment and Energy Sept. 2015–Nov. 2016, of the Interior 2016–18. *Address:* SYRIZA, Pl. Eleftherias 1, 105 53 Athens, Greece (office). *Telephone:* (210) 3378400 (office). *Fax:* (210) 3217003 (office). *E-mail:* info@syriza.gr (office). *Website:* www.syriza.gr (office).

SKOVHUS, Bo; Danish singer (baritone); b. 22 May 1962, Ikast; s. of Freddy Jorgensen and Birthe Skovhus; one d.; ed Music Acad., Århus, Royal Music Acad. and Opera School, Copenhagen, and in New York; debut in Don Giovanni, Vienna Volksoper 1988, debut as Silvio, Pagliacci Vienna Staatsoper 1991; regular guest singer with all major orchestras and opera cos including Metropolitan, New York, San Francisco, Houston, Munich State Opera, Hamburg State Opera, Berlin, Cologne, Covent Garden, Dresden, etc.; many recitals in Europe, USA and Japan; numerous lieder recitals with Helmut Deutsch, Stefan Vladar, Yefim Bronfman, Lief Ove Andsnes, Christoph Eschenbach and Daniel Barenboim; repertoire includes Don Giovanni, Almaviva in Le Nozze di Figaro, Guglielmo in Così fan tutte, Wolfram in Tannhauser, Olivier in Capriccio, Barber in Schweigsame Frau, Wozzeck, Hamlet, Billy Budd, Eugene Onegin, Yeletsky in Pique Dame, Danilo in Lustige Witwe, Eisenstein in Die Fledermaus, Mandryka in Arabella, Beckmesser in Die Meistersinger von Nürnberg, Kurwenal in Tristan und Isolde, Storch in Intermezzo; Kammersänger (Austria) 1997; Kt's Cross, Order of the Dannebrog. *Recordings include:* Don Giovanni (twice), Le Nozze di Figaro (three times), The Merry Widow, Britten's War Requiem, Carmina Burana, Fidelio, Das Lied von der Erde, Wozzeck, Mirror of Perfection (Blackford), I Pagliacci, Der Waffenschmied (Lortzing), Maskarade (Nielsen), Venus (Schoek), Die Schöne Müllerin, Schwanengesang (Schubert), Dichterliebe (Schumann), Liederkreis Op. 24 (Schumann), Eichendorff Lieder (Wolf), Italienisches Liederbuch (Wolf), Faust (Spohr), Oberon (Weber), Die Orchesterlieder (Strauss), Lyrische Sinfonie (Zemlinsky) (twice), Lieder (Zemlinski), arias by Britten, Gounod, Korngold, Verdi, Wagner, Thomas, Massenet and Tchaikovsky, Don Carlos, Tote Stadt, Brahms Requiem and Triumphlied, Mahler Knaben Wunderhorn/Klenau, Rilke, Scandinavian Orchestra Songs, Orchestra Songs by Schubert, Frühe lieder, Rückert lieder, Abschied, aus Lied von der Erde (Mahler). *Address:* c/o Rudolf Balmer, Balmer & Dixon Management AG, Kreuzstrasse 82, 8032 Zurich, Switzerland (office). *Telephone:* (43) 2448644 (office). *Fax:* (43) 2448649 (office). *E-mail:* balmer@badix.ch (office). *Website:* www.badix.ch (office).

SKRINSKY, Aleksandr Nikolayevich, DSc; Russian physicist; *Scientific Leader, Budker Institute of Nuclear Physics;* b. 15 Jan. 1936, Orenburg; s. of Nikolay Alexandrovich Skrinsky and Galina Stepanovna Skrinskaya; m. Lydia Borisovna Golovanova; one s. one d.; ed Moscow State Univ.; Research Worker, Inst. of Nuclear Physics, Siberian Dept, USSR (now Russian) Acad. of Sciences, Head of Lab. 1959–, Deputy Dir 1971–77, apptd Dir Budker Inst. of Nuclear Physics 1977, now Scientific Leader, Chair. Joint Council for Scientists of Physics and Technical Sciences; Prof., Novosibirsk Univ. 1967–85; Corresp. mem. USSR (now Russian) Acad. of Sciences 1968–70, mem. 1970, Academician-Sec. Nuclear Physics Dept 1988–2002; mem. Int. Cttee for Future Accelerators (ICFA) 1983–90 (Chair. 1990–93), CERN Scientific Policy Cttee 1985–91; mem. Royal Swedish Acad. of Science 2002; Fellow, American Physical Soc. 1999–; Lenin Prize 1967, USSR State Prize 1989, Robert R. Wilson Prize 2002, Karpinsky Prize 2002. *Publications:* more than 200 scientific works in the field of accelerator physics and technology, elementary particle physics. *Leisure interests:* ski-running, swimming, music. *Address:* Office 327, Institute of Nuclear Physics, Novosibirsk 630090, 11, akademika Lavrentieva prospect, Russia (office). *E-mail:* A.N.Skrinsky@inp.nsk.su (office). *Website:* www.inp.nsk.su (office).

SKULACHEV, Vladimir Petrovich; Russian biologist and academic; *Director, A. Belozersky Institute of Physico-Chemical Biology, Moscow State University;* b. 21 Feb. 1935, Moscow; s. of Petr Stepanovich Skulachev and Nadezhda Aronovna Skulacheva; m. Severina Inna Isaakovna; four s. one d.; ed Moscow State Univ.; jr researcher, Head of Div., Head of Lab. Moscow State Univ., Dir A. Belozersky Inst. of Physico-Chemical Biology, Dean Faculty of Bioengineering Bioinformatics; Corresp. mem. USSR (now Russian) Acad. of Sciences 1974, mem. 1990–; research in biochemistry, bioenergetics, investigation of molecular mechanisms of energy transformation in membranes of bacteria, mitochondria and chloroplasts; USSR State Prize. *Publications:* Energy Accumulation in Cells 1969, Energy Transformation in Biomembranes 1972, Membranes Bioenergies 1988; numerous other books and articles. *Leisure interests:* badminton, skiing. *Address:* A. N. Belozersky Institute of Physico-Chemical Biology, Moscow State University, 119992 Moscow, Russia (office). *Telephone:* (495) 939-55-30 (office); (495) 939-01-47 (office). *Fax:* (495) 939-03-38 (office). *E-mail:* skulach@belozersky.msu.ru (office). *Website:* www.genebee.msu.su (office).

SKVERNELIS, Saulius; Lithuanian police officer and government official; *Prime Minister;* b. 23 Dec. 1970, Kaunas, Lithuanian SSR, USSR; m.; one d.; ed Vilnius Gediminas Tech. Univ., Mykolas Romeris Univ.; Asst, Police Law and Professional Tactics Dept, Lithuanian Police Acad. 1994–98; Commr Insp., Road Police, Trakai Dist Police HQ 1998–99, Road Police Service, Organizational Unit of Public Police, Police Dept under Ministry of the Interior 1999–2001; Commr, Road Patrols Team, Traffic Supervision Service, Lithuanian Public Police Bureau 2001–03, Lithuanian Police Escorting Team 2003–05; Chief of Lithuanian Police Traffic Supervision Service 2005–08; Deputy Police Commr Gen. 2008–11, Police Commr Gen. 2011–14; Minister of Interior 2014–16, also in charge of Civil Service Dept and Dept of Physical Educ. and Sports, Prime Minister of Lithuania 2016–; mem. Lithuania Section Bd, Int. Police Asscn. *Leisure interest:* sports. *Address:* Office of the Prime Minister, Gedimino pr. 11, Vilnius 01103 (office); Žircnūnus 38A -31, Vilnius, Lithuania (home). *Telephone:* (8) 706-63711 (office); (6) 984-2492 (home). *Fax:* (8) 706-63895 (office). *E-mail:* mptarnyba@lrv.lt (office). *Website:* www.lrv.lt (office).

SKYRMS, Brian, BA, MA, PhD; American academic; *UCI Distinguished Professor of Social Science, University of California, Irvine;* b. 11 March 1938, Pittsburgh, Pa; s. of Frederick John Skyrms and Marie Margaret Skyrms (née Schlipf); m. Pauline Jenkins 1972; two s.; ed Lehigh Univ., Univ. of Pittsburgh; Asst Prof., Calif. State Univ., Northridge 1964–65, Univ. of Del. 1965–66; Visiting Asst Prof., Univ. of Mich. 1966–67; Asst Prof. then Assoc. Prof., Univ. of Ill., Chicago 1967–70, Prof. 1970–80; Prof. of Philosophy, Univ. of Calif., Irvine 1980–97, Distinguished Prof. of Philosophy and Prof. of Econs 1997–, Dir Program in History and Philosophy of Science, UCI Distinguished Prof. of Social Sciences 1998–, Prof. of Philosophy, Stanford Univ. 2007–; mem. Governing Bd American Philosophical Asscn 1987–90, Philosophy of Science Asscn 1990–91, Pres. 2005–06; mem. several editorial bds including American Philosophical Quarterly and Philosophy of Science; Ed. Cambridge Studies in Probability, Induction and Decision Theory; Fellow Center for Advanced Study in the Behavioral Sciences 1993–94, American Acad. of Arts and Sciences 1994, NAS 1999; Guggenheim Fellow 1987–88; Fellow, Game Theory Soc. 2017; numerous science fellowships; Univ. of Calif. Pres.'s Research in the Humanities 1993–94; Pres. Pacific Div. American Philosophical Asscn 2000–01; FAAS 2004–; Lakatos Prize 1999, Paul Silverman Award 2006, Synthese Distinguished paper award 2010, Hempel Award 2016. *Publications include:* Choice and Chance: An Introduction to Inductive Logic 1966, Causal Necessity 1980, Pragmatics and Empiricism 1984, The Dynamics of Rational Deliberation 1990, Evolution of the Social Contract 1996, The Stag Hunt and the Evolution of the Social Structure 2004, Signals: Evolution, Learning and Information 2010, From Zeno to Arbitrage 2012, Social Dynamics 2014, Evolution of the Social Contract 2014, Ten Great Ideas about Chance (with Persi Diaconis) 2017; ed. or co-ed. seven books; numerous articles in learned journals. *Address:* School of Social Sciences, Office 767 SST, 3151 Social Science Plaza, University of California, Irvine, Irvine, CA 92697-5100, USA (office). *Telephone:* (949) 824-6495 (office). *Fax:* (949) 824-2379 (office). *E-mail:* bskyrms@uci.edu (office). *Website:* faculty.sites.uci.edu/skyrms (office).

SLACK, Paul Alexander, DPhil, DLitt, FBA; British historian and academic; *Professor Emeritus of Early Modern Social History, University of Oxford;* b. 23 Jan. 1943, Bradford, Yorks., England; s. of Isaac Slack and Helen Slack (née Firth); m. Diana Gillian Manby 1965 (deceased); two d.; ed Bradford Grammar School, St John's Coll., Oxford; Jr Research Fellow, Balliol Coll., Oxford 1966–69; Lecturer in History, York Univ. 1969–72; Fellow and Tutor in Modern History, Exeter Coll., Oxford 1973–96, Reader in Modern History, Univ. of Oxford 1990–96, Chair. Gen. Bd of Faculties 1995–96, Prin., Linacre Coll. Oxford 1996–2010, Prof. of Early

Modern Social History, Univ. of Oxford 1999–2010, Prof. Emer. 2010–, Pro-Vice-Chancellor 1997–2000, Pro-Vice-Chancellor (Academic Services) 2000–05. *Publications include:* The Impact of Plague in Tudor and Stuart England 1985, Poverty and Policy in Tudor and Stuart England 1988, The English Poor Law 1531–1782 1990, From Reformation to Improvement: Public Welfare in Early Modern England 1999, The Invention of Improvement: Information and Material Progress in Seventeenth-Century England 2015. *Leisure interests:* opera, fell-walking. *Address:* Linacre College, Oxford, OX1 3JA, England (office). *Telephone:* (1865) 271650 (office). *Fax:* (1865) 271668 (office).

SLADE, Rt Hon. Sir Christopher John, Kt; British judge (retd); b. 2 June 1927, London; s. of George Penkivil Slade, KC and Mary A. A. Slade; m. Jane G. A. Buckley 1958; one s. three d.; ed Eton Coll. (Scholar) and New Coll., Oxford (Scholar); called to Bar 1951, QC 1965; in practice at Chancery Bar 1951–75; Judge, High Court of Justice, Chancery Div. 1975–82; Judge of Restrictive Practices Court 1980–82, Pres. 1981–82; Lord Justice of Appeal 1982–91; mem. Gen. Council of Bar 1958–62, 1965–69; mem. Senate of Four Inns of Court 1966–69; Bencher, Lincoln's Inn 1973; mem. Lord Chancellor's Legal Educ. Cttee 1969–71; Treas. Lincoln's Inn 1994. *Leisure interests:* multifarious. *Address:* 40 Rivermead Court, Ranelagh Gardens, London, SW6 3RX, England (home). *Telephone:* (20) 7731-0938 (home). *E-mail:* slade151@talktalk.net (home).

SLADE, Tuiloma Neroni, LLB; Samoan lawyer, diplomatist and judge; b. 8 April 1941; m.; two d.; ed Victoria Univ. of Wellington, New Zealand, Hague Acad. of Int. Law; qualified as solicitor and barrister, worked in law practice in Wellington, NZ 1967–68; legal counsel, Office of Attorney-Gen., Wellington 1969–73; Parl. Counsel 1973–75; Head of Del. UN Conf. on the Law of the Sea 1973–76; Attorney-Gen. of Western Samoa 1976–82, also Chief Justice for periods between 1980–82; Asst Dir Legal Div. Commonwealth Secr., London 1983–93; Amb. to USA 1993–2003, also Perm. Rep. to the UN, New York and High Commr to Canada; Judge, Int. Criminal Court 2003–06; practiced as int. legal consultant 2007–08; Sec.-Gen. Pacific Islands Forum 2008–14; Chair. Alliance of Small Island States 1997–2003; Leader, Samoan del. to Preparatory Comm. for Int. Criminal Court, New York 1999–2002; Distinguished Diplomat in Residence, Temple Univ., Philadelphia 2003; Chair. first S Pacific Law Conf. 1986; legal consultant S Pacific Forum Fisheries Agency 1989; UNITAR Fellowship, Hague Acad. of Int. Law and UN Legal Office; Order of Samoa (Poloaiga Sili a Samoa) 2005; Laureate, Elizabeth Haub Award for Environmental Diplomacy 2001, Global Oceans Leadership Award 2003, Elisabeth Mann Borgese Medal for services to small island developing States and the oceans 2003. *Address:* c/o Office of the Secretary General, Pacific Islands Forum Secretariat, Private Mail Bag, Suva, Fiji.

SLAKTERIS, Atis; Latvian agricultural engineer and fmr politician; b. 21 Nov. 1956, Code Pagasts, Bauska Dist; m.; two c.; ed Latvian Acad. of Agric., Univ. of Minnesota, USA; began career as mechanic, later Chief Engineer Code Co. 1980–89; First Deputy Man. Bauskas Lauktehnika (state-owned co.) 1989–90; Chief Engineer, Bauska Agric. Dept 1990–94, Head, Agric. Consultation Bureau 1994–96; Minister of State for Cooperation, Ministry of Agric. 1996–97; mem. 7th Saeima 1998–2002, serving as Chair. Cttee on Economy, Agricultural Environment and Regional Policies 1998–99, Chair. Cttee on Privatisation 1999–2000; Parl. Sec., Ministry of Agric. 2000, Minister for Agric. 2000–02, Minister of Defence 2004, 2006–07, of Finance 2007–09; Chair. People's Party 2002–08; Pres. Latvijas ūdens motosporta federācijas (Latvian Water Motorsports Fed.). *Address:* Latvijas ūdens motosporta federācijas (Latvian Water Motorsports Federation), Dārzu iela 29, Jūrmala 2008, Latvia (office). *Website:* www.lumsf.lv/lv/jaunumi (office).

SLATER, Christian; American actor; b. (Christian Michael Leonard Hawkins), 18 Aug. 1969, New York; s. of Michael Gainsborough and Mary Jo Slater; m. 1st Ryan Haddon 2000 (divorced 2006); one s. one d.; m. 2nd Brittany Lopez 2013; ed LaGuardia High School of Music, Art and Performing Arts, New York; appeared at age of seven in TV series One Life to Live; professional stage debut at age of nine in touring production of The Music Man. *Stage appearances include:* Macbeth, David Copperfield, Merlin, Landscape of the Body, Side Man, One Flew Over the Cuckoo's Nest (Edinburgh Festival then Gielgud Theatre, London, Garrick Theatre, London 2006) (Theatregoers' Choice Award for Best Actor 2005) 2004–05, The Glass Menagerie (Ethel Barrymore Theatre, Broadway) 2005, Swimming with Sharks (Vaudeville Theatre, London) 2007. *Television appearances include:* Sherlock Holmes (film) 1981, Living Proof: The Hank Williams Jr. Story (film) 1983, The Haunted Mansion Mystery (film) 1983, Ryan's Hope (series) 1975, Secrets (film) 1986, Desperate for Love (film) 1989, Merry Christmas, George Bailey 1997, Prehistoric Planet (series) 2002, The West Wing (series) 2003, 2004, A Light Knight's Odyssey (film) 2004, My Name is Earl 2006, My Own Worst Enemy 2008, The Forgotten 2009, Breaking In 2011–12, Mind Games 2014, Mr. Robot (Golden Globe Award for Best Actor in a Supporting Role 2016) 2015–. *Films include:* The Legend of Billie Jean 1985, The Name of the Rose 1986, Twisted 1986, Tucker: The Man and his Dream 1988, Gleaming the Cube 1989, Heathers 1989, Beyond the Stars 1989, The Wizard 1989, Tales from the Darkside: The Movie 1990, Young Guns II: Blaze of Glory 1990, Pump up the Volume 1990, Robin Hood: Prince of Thieves 1991, Mobsters 1991, Star Trek VI: The Undiscovered Country 1991, Kuffs 1992, Ferngully: The Last Rainforest 1992, Where the Day Takes You 1992, Untamed Heart 1993, True Romance 1993, Jimmy Hollywood 1994, Interview with a Vampire 1994, Murder in the First 1995, Bed of Roses 1996, Broken Arrow 1996, Austin Powers: International Man of Mystery 1997, Julian Po 1997, Hard Rain (also producer) 1998, Basil (also co-producer) 1998, Very Bad Things (also producer) (Golden Slate Award) 1998, Love Stinks 1999, The Contender 2000, 3000 Miles to Graceland 2001, Who is Cletis Tout? 2001, Run for the Money 2002, Windtalkers 2002, Masked and Anonymous 2003, The Good Shepherd 2004, Mindhunters 2004, Churchill: The Hollywood Years 2004, Pursued 2004, Alone in the Dark 2005, The Deal (also producer) 2005, Hollow Man II 2006, Bobby 2006, Slipstream 2007, He Was a Quiet Man 2007, The Ten Commandments 2007, Igor (voice) 2008, Playback 2012, Soldiers of Fortune 2012, El Gringo 2012, Dawn Rider 2012, Rites of Passage 2012, Bullet to the Head 2012, The Power of Few 2013, Stranded 2013, Nymphomaniac 2013, Ask Me Anything 2014, Way of the Wicked 2014, Hot Tub Time Machine 2 2015, The Adderall Diaries 2015. *Website:* www.christianslater.com.

SLATER, Douglas, BSc, MD; Saint Vincent and the Grenadines physician and politician; b. 19 Aug. 1955, Clare Valley; m. Sherian Slater; two c.; ed Univ. of the West Indies, Univ. of Havana, Cuba; worked in medicine in Guyana, Jamaica and St Vincent and the Grenadines; Medical Officer of Health (Dir of Primary Health Care Service) 1994–98; Minister of Health and Environment –2010, of Foreign Affairs, Foreign Trade and Consumer Affairs 2010–13. *Address:* c/o Ministry of Foreign Affairs, Administrative Bldg, 3rd Floor, Bay St, Kingstown, St Vincent and the Grenadines.

SLATER, Adm. Sir Jock (John Cunningham Kirkwood), Kt, GCB, LVO, DL; British naval officer; b. 27 March 1938, Edinburgh, Scotland; s. of James K. Slater, OBE, MD, FRCPE and M. C. B. Slater (née Bramwell); m. Ann Frances Scott 1972; two s.; ed Edinburgh Acad., Sedbergh School, Royal Naval Coll. Dartmouth; Lt, HMS Soberton 1965, Lt Commdr, Equerry to HM The Queen 1968–71, Commdr, HMS Jupiter 1972–73, Capt., HMS Kent 1976–77, with Royal Coll. of Defence Studies 1978, Capt. HMS Illustrious 1981–83, Capt., School of Maritime Operations, HMS Dryad 1983–85, Rear Adm., Asst Chief of Defence Staff 1985–87, Flag Officer, Scotland, NI, Naval Base Commdr Rosyth 1987–89, Vice-Adm., Chief of Fleet Support 1989–91, Adm., C-in-C of Fleet, Allied C-in-C Channel and Eastern Atlantic 1991–92, Vice-Chief of Defence Staff 1993–95, Chief of Naval Staff and First Sea Lord 1995–98; Dir Vosper Thornycroft Holdings 1999–2004; Dir and Sr Mil. Adviser to Lockheed Martin (UK) Ltd 1999–2008; consultant, Bristow Helicopters Ltd 2001–04; Chair. Imperial War Museum 2001–06, RN Club 1765–1785 2001–04, White Ensign Asscn 2002–05, Royal Nat. Lifeboat Inst. 2004–08; Pres. American Air Museum in Britain 2001–06, RN&RM Charity 2008–11, RM Asscn Concert Band 2007, Droxford and Dist Br. RBL 1999–15; Gov. Sedbergh School 1997–2002; DL Hants. 1999; Freeman of the City of London 1989, Elder Brother, Trinity House 1995; Prime Warden, Worshipful Co. of Shipwrights 2011–12; Commdr, US Legion of Merit 1997; Hon. DSc (Cranfield) 1998, (Univ. of Southampton) 2008; Sword of Honour and The Queen's Telescope, BRNC Dartmouth 1958, Cheetham Hill Memorial Prize, HMS Dryad 1966. *Achievements include:* mem. Nat. Youth Orchestra 1955. *Publications include:* articles in professional publs. *Leisure interest:* outdoor. *Address:* c/o Naval Secretary, Leach Building, Whale Island, Portsmouth, Hants., PO2 8BY, England (home). *E-mail:* jock.slater@talk21.com (home).

SLATER, Kelly; American professional surfer; b. (Robert Kelly Slater), 11 Feb. 1972, Cocoa Beach, Fla; s. of Steve Slater and Judy Slater; one d.; joined professional surfing ranks in 1990; 11 times ASP World Champion 1992 (age 21, youngest ever), 1994, 1995, 1996, 1997, 1998, 2005, 2006, 2008, 2010, 2011; Winner, Mountain Dew Pipe Master, Hawaii 1999, Gotcha Tahiti Pro, Tahiti 2000, The Quiksilver, Hawaii 2002, Billabong Pro, Tahiti 2003, 2005, 2011, Billabong Pro, South Africa 2003, 2005, Billabong Pro, Mundaka, Spain 2003, Nova Schin Festival, Brazil 2003, Snickers Australian Open 2004, Energy Australia Open 2004, The Globe WCT, Fiji 2005, Boost Mobile Pro, Calif. 2005, 2007, 2008, Quiksilver Pro, Australia 2006, 2008, 2011, Rip Curl Pro, Australia 2006, 2008, 2010, Glove Pro, Fiji 2008, Billabong Pro J-Bay, South Africa 2008, Billabong Pipeline Masters, Hawaii 2008, Hang Loose Pro, Brazil 2009, Hurley Pro, Calif. 2010, 2011, Rip Curl Pro, Portugal 2010, Rip Curl Search, Puerto Rico 2010, Nike US Open, Calif. 2011; first surfer ever to be awarded two perfect scores for a total 20 out of 20 points under the ASP two-wave scoring system 2005; most successful champion in the history of the sport; starred in TV series Baywatch early 1990s and in numerous surf movies; inspiration for Kelly Slater Pro Surfer video game; Laureus World Action Sportsperson of the Year 2012. *Leisure interests:* golf, fishing, music, playing the guitar. *Address:* c/o Shelby Meade, Fresh and Clean Media, 12701 Venice Boulevard, Los Angeles, CA 90066, USA (office). *Telephone:* (310) 313-7200 (office). *Fax:* (310) 313-0277 (office). *E-mail:* shelby@freshcleanmedia.com (office). *Website:* www.freshcleanmedia.com (office); www.kellyslater.com.

SLATER, Rodney E., BS, JD; American lawyer and fmr government official; *Partner, Squire Patton BoggsLLP;* b. 23 Feb. 1955, Tutwyler, Miss.; m. Cassandra Wilkins; one c.; ed Eastern Michigan Univ., Univ. of Arkansas; Asst Attorney-Gen., Ark. 1980–82; Special Asst to Gov. of Ark. for community and minority affairs 1983–85, Exec. Asst for econ. and community programs 1985–87, Dir Intergovernmental Relations Ark. State Univ. 1987–93; Admin. Fed. Highway Admin. US Dept of Transportation, Washington, DC 1993–97; US Sec. of Transportation 1997–2001; Ark. Liaison Martin Luther King Jr Fed. Holiday Comm. 1983–87; Partner, Patton Boggs LLP (law firm, now Squire Patton Boggs LLP) 2001–; Chair. Audit Cttee, United Way of America 2003–; Pres. W. Harold Flowers Law Soc. 1985–92; Sec., Treasurer Ark. Bar Asscn 1989–93; Deputy Campaign Man. and Sr Travelling Advisor, Clinton for Pres. Campaign 1992, Deputy then Chair. Clinton/Gore Transition Team 1992–93; Special Counsel, Takata Corpn 2014; mem. Bd of Dirs Africare 2001–, Jt Center for Political and Econ. Studies 2001–, Verizon 2010–, WS Atkins 2011–; mem. Ark. Sesquicentennial Comm. 1986, Ark. State Highway and Transportation Comm. 1987–93, Chair. 1992–93. *Address:* Squire Patton Boggs, 2550 M Street, NW, Washington, DC 20037, USA (office). *Telephone:* (202) 457-5265 (office). *Fax:* (202) 457-6315 (office). *E-mail:* rodney.slater@squirepb.com (office). *Website:* www.squirepattonboggs.com (office).

SLATKIN, Leonard Edward; American conductor and pianist; *Music Director Emeritus, Detroit Symphony Orchestra;* b. 1 Sept. 1944, Los Angeles, Calif.; s. of Felix Slatkin and Eleanor Aller; m. 4th Cindy McTee 2011; one s. from previous marriage; ed Indiana Univ., Los Angeles City Coll., Juilliard School; studied violin, piano, viola, composition, conducting; debut Carnegie Hall 1966; Founder, Music Dir and Conductor St Louis Symphony Youth Orchestra 1979–80, 1980–81; Asst Conductor Youth Symphony of New York, Carnegie Hall 1966, Juilliard Opera, Theater and Dance Dept 1967, St Louis Symphony Orchestra 1968–71, Assoc. Conductor 1971–74, Music Dir and Conductor 1979–96; Prin. Guest Conductor Minn. Orchestra 1974–, Summer Artistic Dir 1979–80; Music Dir New Orleans Philharmonic Symphony Orchestra 1977–78; Music Dir Nat. Symphony Orchestra, Washington, DC 1996–2008; Prin. Conductor BBC Symphony Orchestra 2000–04; Prin. Guest Conductor Royal Philharmonic Orchestra 2005–, Pittsburgh Symphony Orchestra 2008–; Music Dir Detroit Symphony Orchestra 2008–18, Emer. 2018–; Music Dir Orchestre National de Lyon 2011–17; guest conductor with orchestras worldwide, including most major US orchestras, Montréal, Toronto, Vienna, Vienna State Opera, London Symphony, London Philharmonia, English Chamber, Concertgebouw, Royal Danish, Stockholm, Scottish Nat., NHK

Tokyo, Israel, Berlin, Stuttgart Opera; festivals include Tanglewood, Blossom, Mann Music Center, Mostly Mozart and Saratoga; Founder and Dir Nat. Conducting Inst.; currently teaches at Indiana University Jacobs School of Music, Manhattan School of Music, Juilliard School; Chevalier, Légion d'honneur, Declaration of Honour in Silver (Austria); Dr hc (Julliard School, Indiana Univ., Michigan State Univ., Washington Univ. in St Louis); seven Grammy Awards, Nat. Medal of Arts, Gold Baton Award, American Symphony Orchestra League. *Publication:* Conducting Business (ASCAP Deems Taylor Special Recognition Award 2013) 2012. *Address:* R. Douglas Sheldon, Columbia Artists Management Inc., 1790 Broadway, New York, NY 10019-1412, USA (office); Office of Leonard Slatkin, Detroit Symphony Orchestra, 3711 Woodward Avenue, Detroit, MI 48201, USA (office). *E-mail:* rdsheldon@cami.com (office). *Telephone:* (313) 576-5111 (office). *Fax:* (313) 576-5109 (office). *Website:* www.detroitsymphony.com (office); www.auditorium-lyon.com/L-Orchestre/Orchestre-national-de-Lyon; www .leonardslatkin.com.

SLAVESKI, Trajko, PhD; Macedonian economist, academic and politician; *Professor, Faculty of Economics, Ss. Cyril and Methodius University;* b. 1960, Ohrid; m.; two c.; ed Ss. Cyril and Methodius Univ., Skopje, State Univ. of Calif. and Harvard Univ., USA; currently Prof., Faculty of Econs, SS Cyril and Methodius Univ., Skopje; Visiting Prof., Arizona State Univ., USA 1997, Nat. and Capodistrian Univ., Athens, Greece 1999–; Minister of Devt 1999–2000; Adviser to Minister of Finance and Nat. Co-ordinator for Poverty Reduction Strategy 2000–02; mem. Parl. 2006–; Minister of Finance 2006–09; mem. Exec. Cttee Internal Macedonian Revolutionary Org.-Democratic Party for Macedonian Nat. Unity (VMRO-DPMNE) 2003–, Vice-Pres. 2005–. *Address:* Faculty of Economics, Ss. Cyril and Methodius University, Blvd. Goce Delchev 9V, 1000 Skopje, North Macedonia (office). *Telephone:* (2) 3286800 (office). *E-mail:* slaveski@eccf.ukim.edu.mk (office). *Website:* www.eccf.ukim.edu.mk (office).

SLAVITT, David Rytman, (David Benjamin, Henry Lazarus, Lynn Meyer, Henry Sutton), MA; American writer, poet, translator and academic; b. 23 March 1935, White Plains, NY; s. of Samuel Slavitt and Adele Slavitt; m. 1st Lynn Meyer 1956 (divorced 1977); two s. one d.; m. 2nd Janet Lee Abrahm 1978; ed Yale and Columbia Univs; Instructor in English, Georgia Inst. of Tech., Atlanta 1957–58; writer, Assoc. Ed., Newsweek 1958–65; Visiting Lecturer, Univ. of Maryland 1977; Visiting Assoc. Prof., Temple Univ. 1978–80; Lecturer in English and Comparative Literature, Columbia Univ. 1985–86; teacher of creative writing, Rutgers Univ. 1987; Lecturer in English and Classics, Univ. of Pennsylvania 1991–97; Visiting Lecturer in Creative Writing, Princeton Univ. 1996; Lecturer in English, Bennington Coll. 2000; Assoc. Fellow, Trumbull Coll., Yale Univ.; has lectured widely at US univs and other academic insts; Pennsylvania Council on the Arts Award 1985, Nat. Endowment for Arts Fellowship in Translation 1988, Nat. Acad. and Inst. of Arts and Letters Award 1989, Rockefeller Foundation Artist's Residence, Bellagio 1989, Umhoefer Award in the Humanities 2007, Kevin Kline Theater Award 2010, L. E. Phillabaum Poetry Award 2013. *Publications include:* fiction: Rochelle, or Virtue Rewarded 1967, King Saul (play) 1967, Feel Free 1968, The Cardinal Sins (play) 1969, Anagrams 1970, ABCD 1972, The Outer Mongolian 1973, The Killing of the King 1974, King of Hearts 1976, Jo Stern 1978, Cold Comfort 1980, Ringer 1982, Alice at 80 1984, The Agent 1986, The Hussar 1987, Salazar Blinks 1988, Lives of the Saints 1990, Short Stories Are Not Real Life 1991, Turkish Delights 1993, The Cliff 1994, Get Thee to a Nunnery: Two Divertimentos from Shakespeare 1999, Aspects of the Novel: A Novel 2003, The Duke's Man 2011, Overture 2012, L'Heure bleue 2013, Shiksa 2014, Walloomsac 2014, Fabrications 2015; as Henry Sutton: The Exhibitionist 1967, The Voyeur 1968, Vector 1970, The Liberated 1973, The Proposal 1980; as Lynn Meyer: Paperback Thriller 1975; as Henry Lazarus: That Golden Woman 1976; as David Benjamin: The Idol 1979; poetry: Suits for the Dead 1961, The Carnivore 1965, Day Sailing 1968, Child's Play 1972, Vital Signs: New and Selected Poems 1975, Rounding the Horn 1978, Dozens 1981, Big Nose 1983, Adrien Stoutenburg: Land of Superior Mirages: New and Selected Poems (ed.) 1986, The Walls of Thebes 1986, Equinox 1989, Eight Longer Poems 1990, Crossroads 1994, A Gift 1996, Epic and Epigram 1997, A New Pléiade: Seven American Poets 1998, PS3569.L3 1998, Falling from Silence: Poems 2001, Change of Address: Poems, New and Selected 2005, William Henry Harrison and Other Poems 2006, Seven Deadly Sins 2009, Civil Wars 2013, Choruses from the Lost Plays of Sophocles 2013; non-fiction: Understanding Social Life: An Introduction to Social Psychology (with Paul F. Secord and Carl W. Backman) 1976, Physicians Observed 1987, Virgil 1991, Re Verse: Essays on Poets and Poetry 2005, Blue State Blues 2006, George Sanders, Zsa Zsa and Me 2009; translator: The Eclogues of Virgil 1971, The Eclogues and the Georgics of Virgil 1972, The Tristia of Ovid 1985, Ovid's Poetry of Exile 1990, Seneca: The Tragedies 1992, The Fables of Avianus 1993, The Metamorphoses of Ovid 1994, Three Amusements of Ausonius 1998, The Persians of Aeschylus 1998, The Twelve Minor Prophets 1999, The Voyage of the Argo of Valerius Flaccus 1999, Sonnets of Love and Death of Jean de Sponde 2001, The Book of Lamentations 2001, The Elegies of Propertius 2001, The Poetry of Manuel Bandeira 2002, The Regrets of Joachim du Bellay 2004, The Phoenix and Other Translations 2004, Sophocles' Theban Plays 2007, De Rerum Natura of Lucretius 2008, Boethius' Consolation of Philosophy 2008, Ludovico Ariosto's Orlando Furioso 2009, Dante's Vita Nuova 2010, The Latin Eclogues of Giovanni Boccaccio 2010, Poems from the Greek Anthology 2010, The Gnat and other minor poems of Virgin 2011, The Latin Poems of John Milton 2011, The Love Letters, Poems, and Remedies of Ovid 2011, The Sonnets and Short Poems of Petrarch 2012, The Crooning Wind: Three Greenlandic Poets 2012, The Poetry of Guido Cavalcanti 2012, The Dhamapada of The Buddha 2012, Procne: A Poem in Voices by Gregorio Correr 2012, The Other Four Plays of Sophocles 2013, The Lays of Marie de France 2013, The Odes of Horace 2014, The Mahabharata 2015, From the Fragrant East by Pietro Bembo 2015; The Rig Veda: The First Mandala 2015, The Jungle Poems of Leconte de Lisle 2017; contrib. of book reviews, articles in journals and magazines. *Address:* 35 West Street, #5, Cambridge, MA 02139, USA (home). *Telephone:* (617) 497-1219 (home). *E-mail:* drslavitt@comcast.net.

ŠLECHTOVÁ, Karla; Czech economist, public servant and politician; b. 22 May 1977, Karlovy Vary; ed Univ. of West Bohemia; Project Portfolio Coordinator, Communications Dept, Deloitte Bulgaria 2001–04, Sr Consultant, Deloitte Bulgaria 2005–08, Sr Consultant, Deloitte Advisory sro 2005–10; Project Man., European Centre for Public Admin sro 2004–05; Project Man., Czech Social Security Admin 2010–11; Dir of Programming Preparations, Planning Dept, Ministry for Regional Devt 2011–14; Dir, EU Funds Dept, Office of the Czech Govt June–Sept. 2014; mem. Poslanecká Sněmovna (Chamber of Deputies) for Plzen constituency 2017–; Minister for Regional Devt 2014–17; Minister of Defence 2017–18. *Address:* c/o Ministry of Defence, Tychonova 221/1, 160 00 Prague 6, Czech Republic (office).

SLEEP, Wayne, OBE; British dancer, actor and choreographer; b. 17 July 1948, Plymouth; ed Royal Ballet School (Leverhulme Scholar); joined Royal Ballet 1966, Soloist 1970, Prin. 1973; roles in: Giselle, Dancers at a Gathering, The Nutcracker, Romeo and Juliet, The Grand Tour, Elite Syncopations, Swan Lake, The Four Seasons, Les Patineurs, Petroushka (title role), Cinderella, The Dream, Pineapple Poll, Mam'zelle Angot, 4th Symphony, La Fille Mal Gardée, A Month in the Country, A Good Night's Sleep, Coppelia; also roles in operas: A Midsummer Night's Dream, Aida; choreography and lead role, The Point: co-starred in Song and Dance 1982, 1990, Cabaret 1986; f. DASH co. 1980, The Wayne Sleep Foundation; dancer and jt choreographer, Bits and Pieces 1989; numerous TV appearances including series The Hot Shoe Show 1983, 1984; Show Business Personality of the Year 1983. *Films include:* The Virgin Soldiers, The First Great Train Robbery, Twelfth Night, Elizabeth, The Tales of Beatrix Potter. *Theatre includes:* Ariel in the Tempest, title role in Pinocchio, Genie in Aladdin, Soldier in The Soldier's Tale, Truffaldino in the Servant of Two Masters, Mr Mistoffelees in Cats. *Ballets include:* Sleeping Beauty, Tarantella, Swan Lake, Romeo and Juliet, Elite Syncopations, Swan Lake, Cinderella, The Dream, The Dream, Petrushka, Widow Simone,. *Publications:* Variations on Wayne Sleep 1983, Precious Little Sleep (autobiog.) 1996. *Leisure interest:* entertaining. *Address:* 22 Queensberry Mews West, London, SW7 2DY, England. *Telephone:* (1723) 500038. *E-mail:* info@waynesleep.org. *Website:* www.waynesleep.org.

SLEIMAN, Gen. Michel, BA; Lebanese politician, fmr army commander and head of state; b. 21 Nov. 1948, Amchit; m. Wafaa Sleiman; three c.; ed Lebanese Univ.; Chief Intelligence Br., Mount Lebanon 1990–91; Army Staff Sec.-Gen. 1991–93; Commdr 11th Infantry Brigade 1993–96, Sixth Infantry Brigade 1996–98; Commdr Lebanese Armed Forces 1998–2008; Pres. of Lebanon 2008–14; Kt and Grand Cordon, Nat. Order of the Cedar; Lebanese Order of Merit (First, Second, Third and Extraordinary Grades); Grade of Excellence, Syrian Order of Merit; Collar of King Abdul Aziz; Grand Cross, Italian Order of Merit; Collar of Moubarak the Great; Khalifite Collar, Zayed Order; Oman Mil. Order; Grand Croix, Légion d'honneur; Collar, Nat. Order of the Star of Romania; Collar, Order of Isabella the Catholic; Collar, Order 'Pro Merito Melitensi'; Collar, Order of Makarios III; Grand Collar, Nat. Order of the Southern Cross; Grand Cordon, Nat. Order of Umayya; Qatari Necklace of Independence; Kt Grand Cross, Order of St Charles; Grand Cross, Order of Rio Branco, Armenian Order of Honour; Grand Star, Decoration of Honour; Grand Cross, Order of the Redeemer; Grand Cross, Nat. Order of the Lion, Grand Cross, Nat. Order of Ivory Coast; Medal of War, Medal of Nat. Unity, Medal of Mil. Pride (Silver), Medal of Mil. Valour (Silver), Medal of Honour of the Arab Fed. for Mil. Sports, Medal of the Pres. of Repub. of Ukraine, Medal of the Defence Ministry of Fed. Repub. of Russia, Mil. Medal, Medal of Internal Security, Medal of General Security, Medal of State Security, Medal of the Dawn of South, Commemorative Medal of Confs 2002, Prize of HH Patriarch Alexey II 2012.

ŠLESERS, Ainārs; Latvian business executive and fmr politician; *Chairman, Riga Commercial Port LLC;* b. 22 Jan. 1970, Riga; m. Inese Šlesere; five c.; ed Rīga Secondary School No. 25, Rīga Industrial Polytechnics, Christian Folk Coll., Norway, Latvian Christian Acad.; Pres. Latvian-Norwegian jt venture Latvian Information and Commerce Centre, Norway 1992–96; Pres. Skandi Ltd 1993–96; Dir Gen. Varner Baltija Ltd 1994–98; Chair. Bd and Pres. JSC Supermarket Centres 1995–96, 1996–98; Dir Gen. Rimi Baltija Ltd 1996–97, Varner Hakon Invest Ltd 1996–98; mem. Saeima (Parl.) Oct.–Nov. 1998, 1999–2002, 2002–; Minister for Econs 1998–99; Deputy Prime Minister Nov. 2002–Jan. 2004, March–Dec. 2004; Minister of Transport 2004–09; Vice-Mayor of Rīga 2009–10; mem. Latvian First Party (LPP) 2002–11; resigned from politics 2010; currently Chair. Riga Commercial Port LLC and Head of Riga Port City Devt project; mem. Bd Baltic Stability Fund 1996–; mem. Bd 'For Spiritual Renaissance in Latvia' 2001–. *Address:* Riga Commercial Port, Andrejostas iela 10, Ziemeļu rajons, Rīga 1045, Latvia (office). *Telephone:* 6723-3633 (office). *Website:* www.rto.lv (office).

ŠLEŽEVIČIUS, Adolfas; Lithuanian politician and consultant; b. 2 Feb. 1948, Mirčiškės, Šiauliai Co.; ed Acad. of Nat. Econ., USSR Council of Ministers; Sr Engineer-Constructor, Chief Mechanic, Chief Engineer, Kaunas dairy factory 1971–77; Vice-Minister of Dairy and Meat Industry of Lithuania 1977–81; Chair. dairy production enterprise Pienocentras 1989–90; Vice-Minister of Agric. 1990–91; Pres. Lithuanian-Norwegian Jt Venture C. Olsen-Baltic 1991–93; Pres. Lithuanian Dairy Producers Asscn 1992–; mem. Democratic Labour Party; Prime Minister of Lithuania 1993–96, resgnd following corruption scandals; consultant to pvt. cos, including ATB-West. *Address:* c/o ATB-West, Rudaminos str. 1A, Vilnius 13275, Lithuania. *Telephone:* (5) 235-11-74. *Fax:* (5) 235-11-79. *E-mail:* info@atb-west.lt. *Website:* www.atb-west.lt.

SLIM DOMIT, Carlos, BBA; Mexican business executive; *Co-Chairman, América Móvil SAB de CV;* b. 1967; eldest s. of Carlos Slim Helú; m. María Elena Torruco 2010; ed Universidad Anáhuac; mem. Bd of Dirs Grupo Carso 1991–, currently Chair.; mem. Bd of Dirs, Teléfonos de Mexico (Telmex) (Chair.), Grupo Sanborns (Chair.), America Móvil SAB de CV (Co-Chair. 2013–), Group7, América Telecom, Carso Global Telecom, US Commercial Corpn and some subsidiaries of Grupo Carso. *Address:* América Móvil SAB de CV, Lago Zurich 245, Edificio Telcel, Col. Granada Ampliación, CP 11529 Mexico City, DF, Mexico (office). *Telephone:* (55) 2581-4449 (office). *Fax:* (55) 2581-4422 (office). *E-mail:* info@americamovil.com (office). *Website:* www.americamovil.com (office); www.carso.com.mx (office).

SLIM DOMIT, Patrick; Mexican telecommunications executive; *Co-Chairman, América Móvil SAB de CV;* b. 1969; s. of Carlos Slim Helú and Soumaya Domit; ed Univ. Anáhuac; Chair. América Móvil SAB de CV 2004–12, Co-Chair. (with Carlos Slim Domit) 2012–; Vice-Pres. Grupo Carso SAB de CV (fmr CEO); Vice-Chair. America Telecom –2004; fmr CEO Industrias Nacobre SAB de CV; Chair. Ferrosur SAB de CV; mem. Bd of Dirs Carso Global Telecom SAB de CV, Teléfonos de México SAB de CV (Telmex), Hoteles Calinda SAB de CV, Grupo Condumex SAB de CV, Empresas Frisco SAB de CV, Sears Roebuck de México SAB de CV, Cigarros La Tabacalera de México SAB de CV, Promotora Inbursa SAB de CV, Industrias Nacobre SAB de CV. *Address:* América Móvil SAB de CV, Lago Zurich 245, Edificio Telcel, Col. Granada Ampliación, CP 11529 Mexico City, DF, Mexico (office). *Telephone:* (55) 2581-4449 (office). *Fax:* (55) 2581-4422 (office). *E-mail:* info@americamovil.com (office). *Website:* www.americamovil.com (office).

SLIM HELÚ, Carlos; Mexican telecommunications industry executive and philanthropist; *Chairman, Teléfonos de México SA de C.V. (Telmex);* b. 28 Jan. 1940, Mexico City; s. of Julián Slim Haddad and Linda Helú; m. Soumaya Domit Gemayel 1967 (died 1999); six c.; ed Universidad Autónoma de México (UNAM); taught algebra and linear programming at UNAM while studying 1961; f. Grupo Carso 1961, expanded co. through series of acquisitions including Jarritos de Sur (bottling co.) 1970, Galas de México (cigarette manufacturer) 1976, Cigarrera La Moderna 1981, and many other cos, Chair. Teléfonos de México SA de C.V. (Telmex) 2002–, Grupo Financiero Inbursa, Hon. Lifetime Chair. Grupo Carso; Chair. Emer. América Móvil; fmr mem. Bd of Dirs, Altria, SBC Communications –2004, Alcatel SA 2000–06; f. Fundación del Centro Histórico de la Ciudad de México A.C. 2000, Chair. Exec. Cttee for the Restoration of the Historic Centre 2001–; f. Instituto Carso para la Salud 2007; heads the Latin America Devt Fund project; mem. Exec. Bd RAND Corpn (Research and Devt) 2008–; formed own oil co. Carso Oil & Gas 2015; Leopold II Commdr Medal (Belgium), Grand Officer, Nat. Order of the Cedar (Lebanon) 2008; Hon. Dr in Public Service (George Washington Univ.) 2012; Entrepreneurial Merit Medal of Honour, Mexican Chamber of Commerce 1985, CEO of the Year, Latin Trade magazine 2003, CEO of the Decade, Latin Trade magazine 2004, World Educ. and Devt Fund Award 2004, Alliance Award, Free Trade Alliance 2004, Hadrian Award, World Monuments Fund 2004, Real Estate Developers' Asscn Award 2004, Fashion Group Int. Prize for work in rescue of Historical Centre of Mexico City 2004, Galardon del Salon del Empresario, Impulsa and Grupo Editorial Expansión 2006, Life Achievement Award, World-wide Asscn of Mexicans Abroad (AMME) 2006, Golden Plate Award, American Acad. of Achievement 2007, Nat. Award to the Excellence Jaime Torres Bodet, Univ. Center Sun Group 2007, Industrialist of Year, Mexican Foundation for Health (Funsalud) 2007, recognized by Mexican Asscn of Professionals in Power of Attorney of Bottoms Chapter, Mexico City 2007, Man of the Year 2008, World Boxing Council 2009, ESADE award in recognition of his philanthropic and entrepreneurial management, ESADE Alumni, Barcelona 2009, George Washington Univ. Pres.'s Medal 2009. *Address:* Teléfonos de México SA de C.V., Parque Vía 190, Col Cuahtémoc, 06599 México DF, Mexico (office). *Telephone:* (1) 5222-1212 (office). *Fax:* (1) 5545-5550 (office). *E-mail:* info@telmex.com.mx (office). *Website:* www.telmex.com.mx (office); www.carlosslim.com.

SLIMANE, Hedi; French fashion designer, photographer and curator; *Artistic, Creative and Image Director, Céline;* b. 5 July 1968, Paris; ed 'Hypokhagne' Prépa Sciences-Po, École du Louvre; discovered photography aged 11; began making own clothes aged 16; studied art history and completed a tailor apprenticeship at a men's design house; assisted fashion consultant Jean-Jacques Picart 1992–95; apptd ready-to-wear director of men's collections at Yves Saint Laurent 1996, later Artistic Dir; took up a residency at Kunst-Werke Inst. for Contemporary Art, Berlin 2000–02; Creative Dir for Dior Homme (menswear line of Christian Dior) 2000–07, in charge of launch of Dior Homme's first fragrance named Higher 2001; cr. stagewear for groups including The Libertines, Daft Punk, Franz Ferdinand and The Kills and artists including Mick Jagger, Beck, Jack White; returned to fashion and portrait photography 2007; Creative Dir for Saint Laurent Paris (fmrly Yves Saint Laurent) 2011–16; Artistic, Creative and Image Dir, Céline 2018–; CFDA Award for Int. Designer (first menswear designer) 2002. *Publications:* Intermission 1 2002, Berlin 2003, Stage 2004, London Birth of a Cult 2005, Interzone: The Hedi Slimane Book 2005, Portrait of a Performer: Courtney Love 2006, Costa Da Caparica 1989 (exhbn catalogue) 2007, Rock Diary 2008, American Youth (DVD box set) 2009, Anthology of a Decade 2011. *Address:* c/o Almine Rech Gallery, 64 Rue de Turenne, 75003 Paris, France (office). *Telephone:* 1-45-83-71-90 (office). *E-mail:* press@hedislimane.com (office). *Website:* www.hedislimane.com.

SLISKA, Lyubov Konstantinovna; Russian lawyer and politician; b. 15 Oct. 1953, Saratov; m. Sergei Germanovich; ed Saratov Inst. of Law; lawyer, Soyuzpechat Saratov 1977–89; on staff, regional trade cttee of heavy machine construction industry workers 1992–96; Perm. Rep. of Govt in Regional Duma, Deputy Chair. Regional Govt 1996–2000; mem. State Duma (Yedinstvo Movt List) 1999; First Deputy Chair. (Speaker) of State Duma 2000–12; mem. United Russia 2001–12, fmr mem. Exec. Council; Order of Merit to Fatherland (III degree) 1997, Order for Service to Motherland; Hon. PhD. *Leisure interests:* countryside, fishing, theatre, chamber music, ballet.

SLIVA, Anatoly Yakovlevich, Cand.Jur.; Russian politician and judge; b. 10 Feb. 1940, Slavgorod, Belarus; m.; ed Moscow State Univ.; teacher and Dean, All-Union Juridical Inst. by correspondence; Sr Scientific Consultant, Deputy Head of Div. of local soviets, USSR Supreme Soviet 1988–92; Deputy Head of State Law Dept at Russian Presidency, concurrently Head of Div. on Interaction with Organs of Rep. and Exec. Power 1992–94; Official Rep. of Russian Pres. on legal problems to Supreme Soviet Russian Fed. 1992; mem. State Duma, Chair. Cttee on problems of local man. 1993–95; Rep. of Russian Pres. to Fed. Council 1996–98; apptd Justice, Constitutional Court of Russian Fed. 1998.

SLOAN, Timothy (Tim) J., BA, MBA; American banking executive; b. 30 May 1960, Cleveland; m.; three c.; ed Univ. of Michigan, Ann Arbor; began career with Continental Illinois Bank, Chicago 1984–87; joined Wells Fargo & Co. in Loan Adjustment Group 1987, various leadership roles in wholesale banking 1991–2006, Chief Admin. Officer 2010–11, Chief Financial Officer 2011–14, Head, Wholesale Banking 2014–15, Pres., Wells Fargo & Co. 2015–19, COO 2015–16, mem. Bd of Dirs and CEO 2016–19; mem. Bd of Overseers, Huntington Library; Trustee, City of Hope, California Inst. of Tech.; mem. Advisory Bd Univ. of Michigan Ross School of Business. *Address:* c/o Wells Fargo & Co., 420 Montgomery Street, San Francisco, CA 94104, USA.

SLONIMSKY, Sergey Michailovich, PhD; Russian composer, teacher and pianist; *Professor, St Petersburg Conservatoire;* b. 12 Aug. 1932, Leningrad (now St Petersburg); s. of Michail Slonimsky and Ida Slonimskaya (née Kaplan); m. Raisa Slonimskaya (née Zankisova) 1973; one s. one d.; ed Leningrad Conservatoire; mem. Teaching Faculty, Music Theory and Composition, Leningrad (now St Petersburg) Conservatoire 1958–, Prof. 1976–; mem. Bd CIS Composers' Union (also mem. St Petersburg Br.); Cavalier of Commdr's Cross of Poland; RSFSR Glinka State Prize 1983, RSFSR People's Artist 1987, State Prize of Russia 2002. *Works include:* 13 symphonies 1958–2004, orchestral and vocal works, chamber works, opera, ballet, songs and choral pieces, including Carnival Overture 1957, Concerto Buffa, chamber orchestra 1966, Antiphones (string quartet) 1969, Virinea opera 1969, Icarus (ballet in three acts) 1973, Master and Margarita (chamber opera in three acts) 1970–85, Merry Songs for piccolo, flute and tuba 1971, Sonata for violoncello and piano 1986, Mary Stuart (opera performed at 1986 Edinburgh Festival, USSR and abroad), Hamlet (opera) 1990–94, Cerch: dell'Inferno secondo Dante 1992, 24 Preludes and Fugues for piano 1994, Ivan the Terrible 1994 (opera premiered at Samara 1998), 24 Preludes and Fugues for piano 1995, King Lear (opera after Shakespeare) 2001, The Magic Nut (ballet) 2005. *Recordings include:* Requiem 2003, Magic Nut (ballet, libretto by Mihail Shemiakin) 2005. *Publications:* musicological study of Prokofiev's symphonies 1964, Burlesques, Elegies, Dithyrambs 2000, Free Dissonance 2005. *Leisure interest:* poetry, literature, painting. *Address:* St Petersburg Conservatoire of Music, 190000 St Petersburg, 3, Teatralnaya Square (office); 191186 St Petersburg, Canal Griboedova 9-97, Russia (home). *Telephone:* (812) 571-85-85 (home). *Fax:* (812) 571-58-11 (office). *E-mail:* sloh@rambler.ru (home). *Website:* eng.conservatory.ru (office).

SLOSAR, John Robert, BEcons; American airline industry executive; *Chairman, Cathay Pacific;* b. 1950, Ohio; ed Columbia Univ., Trinity Coll., Cambridge, UK; joined Swire Group (diversified group with interests in property, aviation, marine services, beverages, trade and industry) 1980, posted first to Thailand, then apptd Vice-Pres. for USA and Latin America, based in San Francisco, later Man. Dir, Hong Kong Aircraft Engineering Co. Ltd 1996–98, also Chair., Taikoo (Xiamen) Aircraft Engineering Co. (TAECO) 1996–98, Man. Dir, Swire Beverages Ltd 1998–2007, Chief Operating Officer, Cathay Pacific Airways Ltd 2007–11, also Chair., Swire Beverages, Hong Kong Dragon Airlines Ltd (Dragonair), CEO Cathay Pacific 2011–14, Chair. 2014–, Chair. John Swire & Sons (HK) Ltd 2014–18, Swire Pacific Ltd, Swire Properties Ltd, Hong Kong Aircraft Engineering Co. Ltd; mem. Bd of Dirs Swire Beverages 2006–, John Swire & Sons (HK) Ltd 2000–, Cathay Pacific Airways Ltd 2007–, Swire Pacific Ltd 2006–; Dir (non-exec.) Purecircle Ltd 2006–. *Address:* Cathay Pacific, One Pacific Place, 88 Queensway, Hong Kong Special Administrative Region, People's Republic of China (office). *Website:* www.swire.com (office).

SLOTA, Ján; Slovak engineer and politician; b. 14 Sept. 1953, Lietavská Lúčka; m.; three s. one d.; ed Faculty of Mining, Tech. Univ., Košice; Co-founder Slovak Nat. Party (SNS) 1990, Pres. 1994–99, 2003–12; Mayor of Žilina 1990–2006; mem. Fed. Ass. of Czechoslovakia 1990–92; mem. Parl. 1992–2002, 2006–12, mem. Cttee for Review of Decisions of Nat. Security Authority, Cttee on Human Rights, Minorities and Status of Women, Special Control Cttee of Activities of Slovak Intelligence Service; State Order of Andrej Hlinka (First Class), Cross of the Pres. (First Degree).

SLOTOVER, Matthew, OBE; British publisher, entrepreneur and arts executive; *Director, Frieze Art Fairs;* b. 1968; s. of Robert Slotover and Jill Slotover; grandson of Richard Kravitz; m.; three c.; ed St Paul's School, London, Univ. of Oxford; first became interested in contemporary art after visiting Young British Artists art exhbn 'Modern Medicine' 1990; Co-Publr, with Amanda Sharp, Frieze magazine 1991–; Co-owner, with Amanda Sharp, Frieze Art Fair (int. contemporary art fair taking place annually in Oct.), Regent's Park, London 2002–, Randall's Island, New York 2012–, also Frieze Masters (London), a fair with a contemporary approach to pre-21st century art 2012–; Co-founder Counter Editions 1999; Chair. Bd of Trustees, South London Gallery; mem. Jury, Turner Prize 2000; hon. degree (Univ. of the Arts London) 2009. *Address:* Frieze, 1 Montclare Street, London, E2 7EU, England (office). *Telephone:* (20) 3372-6111 (office). *E-mail:* info@frieze.com (office). *Website:* friezelondon.com (office).

SLYNGSTAD, Yngve; Norwegian banking executive; *CEO, Norges Bank Investment Management;* b. 3 Nov. 1962; ed Univ. of Oslo, Norwegian School of Econs, Univ. of Paris, France, Univ. of California, Santa Barbara, USA; started career as Researcher, Norges Bank 1993; fmr Chief Investment Officer, Asian Equities, Storebrand Asset Management; Head of Equities, Norges Bank Investment Man. (NBIM) 1998–2007, CEO NBIM 2008–. *Address:* Norges Bank Investment Management, Bankplassen 2, PO Box 1179 Sentrum, 0107 Oslo, Norway (office). *Telephone:* 24-07-30-00 (office). *E-mail:* contact@nbim.no (office). *Website:* www.nbim.no (office).

SMAGHI, Lorenzo Bini, BEcons, MA, PhD; Italian economist and business executive; *Chairman, Société Générale;* b. 29 Nov. 1956, Florence; m.; two c.; ed Lycée Français de Bruxelles, Catholic Univ. of Louvain, Belgium, Univ. of Southern California and Univ. of Chicago, USA; grew up in Brussels, Belgium; began career as economist, Research Dept, Banca d'Italia 1983; Head of Policy Div., European Monetary Inst. 1994–98; Dir Gen. for Int. Affairs, Italian Treasury 1998–2005; Chair. SACE SpA 2001–05; mem. Exec. Bd, European Cen. Bank 2005–11; Chair. (non-exec.), SNAM (Italy) 2013–16; Vice-Chair. Société Générale 2014–15, Chair. 2015–; Chair. Fondazione Palazzo Strozzi, Florence, Italian Chapter of Alumni of Univ. of Chicago, ChiantiBanca (Italy); Visiting Scholar, Weatherhead Center for Int. Affairs, Istituto Affari Internazionali; fmr mem. Bd, Finmeccanica, MTS, EIB, Morgan Stanley International; currently mem. A-List of Commentators for Financial Times. *Publications include:* Chi ci salva dalla prossima crisi finanziaria? 2000, Open Issues in European Central Banking (with Daniel Gros) 2000, L'Euro 1998 (third edn 2001), Il paradosso dell'euro. Luci e ombre dieci anni dopo 2008, Morire di Austerità, Democrazie europee con le spalle al muro 2013, Austerity, European Democracies Against the Wall 2013. *Address:* Société Générale, 29 boulevard Haussmann, 75009 Paris, France (office). *Telephone:* 1-42-14-20-00 (office). *E-mail:* info@socgen.com (office). *Website:* www.societegenerale.com (office); www.lorenzobinismaghi.com.

SMALE, Stephen, PhD; American mathematician and academic; *Distinguished University Professor, Department of Mathematics, City University of Hong Kong;* b. 15 July 1930, Flint, Mich.; ed Univ. of Michigan; Instructor, Univ. of Chicago 1956–58; NSF Postdoctoral Fellowship, Inst. for Advanced Study, Princeton, NJ and Instituto de Mathematica Pura e Aplicada Rio de Janeiro, Brazil 1958–60; Alfred P. Sloan Research Fellow 1960–62; Assoc. Prof. of Math., Univ. of California, Berkeley 1960–61, Prof. 1964–94, Prof. without Stipend, Dept of Econs 1976–, Faculty Research Lectureship 1983, Prof. of Math. and Econs Emer. 1994–; Distinguished Univ. Prof., City Univ. of Hong Kong 1995–2001, 2009–; Prof., Toyota Technological Inst., Chicago 2002–09; Professorship, Columbia Univ., New York 1961–64; Research Prof., Miller Inst. for Basic Research in Science, Berkeley 1967–68, 1979–80, 1990; visiting mem. Institut des Hautes Etudes Scientifiques, Paris 1969–70, 1972–73, 1976; Visiting Prof., Univ. of Paris 1972–73, Yale Univ. 1974, Instituto de Matematica Pura e Aplicada, Rio de Janeiro 1976, 1988, 1994, Columbia Univ. 1987; Visiting Scientist, IBM Corpn, Yorktown Heights 1987; Visiting Corpn, Collège de France, Paris 1962; Foreign mem. Brazilian Acad. of Science 1964; mem. American Acad. of Arts and Sciences 1967, NAS 1970; Fellow, The Econometric Soc. 1983, Japan Soc. for the Promotion of Science 1993; hon. mem. Instituto de Matematica Pura e Aplicada, Rio de Janeiro 1990, Trinity Math. Soc., Dublin 1991–92, Moscow Math. Soc. 1997, London Math. Soc. 1998; Hon. Prof., Univ. of Yunnan, Kunming 1997; Class of the Grand Cross of the Brazilian Nat. Order of Scientific Merit 1994; Hon. DSc (Univ. of Warwick, UK) 1974, (Queen's Univ., Kingston, Ont.) 1987, (Univ. of Mich.) 1996, (City Univ. of Hong Kong) 1997, (Rostov State Univ.) 1999, Dr hc (Université Pierre et Marie Curie, Paris) 1997, (Univ. of Genoa) 2004; Veblen Prize for Geometry, American Math. Soc. 1965, Fields Medal, Int. Congress of Mathematicians, Moscow 1966, Univ. of Mich. Sesquicentennial Award 1967, American Math. Soc. Colloquium Lecturer 1972, Chauvenet Prize, Math. Asscn of America 1988, Von Neumann Award, Soc. for Industrial and Applied Math. 1989, Bishop Berkeley Lecturer, Trinity Coll., Dublin 1991, Distinguished Lecturer, Fields Inst., Waterloo, Canada 1992, Nat. Medal of Science 1996, Jurgen Moser Prize, SIAM Activity Group on Dynamical Systems 2005, Wolf Foundation Prize in Math. 2007. *Publications:* more than 100 articles in math. journals. *Address:* Department of Mathematics, City University of Hong Kong, B6513 Academic 1, 83 Tat Chee Avenue, Kowloon, Hong Kong Special Administrative Region, People's Republic of China (office). *Telephone:* (852) 3442-5280 (office). *Fax:* (852) 3442-0250 (office). *E-mail:* smale@cityu.edu.hk (office). *Website:* www.cityu.edu.hk (office).

SMART, George M., BS, MBA; American energy industry executive; *Chairman, FirstEnergy Corporation;* b. 1946; ed Defiance Coll., Wharton School, Univ. of Pennsylvania; Staff Asst, Central States Can (division of Van Dorn Co.) 1969, Sales Rep. 1970–76, Dir of Marketing 1976–79, Pres. and CEO 1979–92; Chair. and Pres. Phoenix Packaging Corpn 1993–2001; Pres. Sonoco-Phoenix Inc. 2001–04; Chair. (non-exec.) FirstEnergy Corpn 2004–14, 2015–; fmr Chair. Can Manufacturers Inst.; mem. Bd of Dirs Ball Corpn, Ohio Edison Co. 1988–97; fmr mem. Bd of Dirs Unizan Financial Corpn, Belden & Blake Corpn, Commercial Intertech Corpn; Trustee, Defiance Coll. *Address:* FirstEnergy Corporation, 76 Main Street, Akron, OH 44308, USA (office). *Telephone:* (800) 646-0400 (office). *Fax:* (330) 384-3866 (office). *Website:* www.firstenergycorp.com (office).

SMEAL, Eleanor, MA; American feminist leader, political analyst and author; *President, Feminist Majority Foundation;* b. (Eleanor Marie Cutri), 30 July 1939, Ashtabula, OH; d. of Peter Anthony Cutri and Josephine E. Agresti; one s. one d.; ed Strong Vincent High School, Duke Univ., Univ. of Florida; joined Nat. Org. for Women 1970, Pres. 1977–82, 1985–87, currently mem. Bd; Founder and Pres. Feminist Majority Foundation 1986–; Publr Ms. magazine (owned and published by Feminist Majority Foundation) 2001–; launched Feminist Majority Foundation Online (www.feminist.org) 1995; mem. Bd Nat. Council for Research on Women; mem. Leadership Circle, Convention on the Elimination of all Forms of Discrimination Against Women; Hon. LLD (Duke Univ.); named by TIME Magazine as one of the "50 Faces for America's Future" 1979, chosen by The World Almanac as the fourth most influential woman in the USA 1983, featured as one of the six most influential Washington lobbyists in U.S. News and World Report, inducted into Nat. Women's Hall of Fame 2015. *Achievements include:* involved in several legislative initiatives, including Free Access to Clinic Entrances legislation (influenced by Madsen v. Women's Health Center) 1994, defeat of Proposition 209 in Calif., Pregnancy Discrimination Act, Equal Credit Act, Civil Rights Restoration Act, Violence Against Women Act, Freedom of Access to Clinic Entrances Act, Civil Rights Act 1991, and fight to amend Equal Rights Amendment. *Publications include:* How and Why Women Will Elect the Next President 1984. *Address:* Feminist Majority Foundation, 1600 Wilson Boulevard, Suite 801, Arlington, VA 22209, USA (office). *Telephone:* (703) 522-2214 (office). *Fax:* (703) 522-2219 (office). *E-mail:* info@feminist.org (office). *Website:* www.feminist.org (office).

SMETS, Jan; Belgian economist and central banker; *Governor, Banque Nationale de Belgique;* b. 2 Jan. 1951, Ghent; m. Martine Roegiers; two d.; ed Rijksuniversiteit Gent; joined Banque Nationale de Belgique as trainee 1973, apptd Attaché 1974, Asst Advisor (Head of Office) 1976, Economist (Head of Dept), Econs and Research Dept 1982, Advisor 1984, Head 1992–94, seconded to Cabinet of Vice-Prime Minister Jean-Luc Dehaene 1988–91, seconded to Cabinet of Prime Minister Wilfried Martens April–Dec. 1991, Insp.-Gen. Banque Nationale de Belgique 1991, First Advisor 1991, seconded to Cabinet of Prime Minister Jean-Luc Dehaene 1992–94, Asst Dir Banque Nationale de Belgique 1998, Dir 1999–2011, Gov. 2015–, also Gov. IMF 2015–, Alternate Gov. IBRD 2015–, mem. Governing Council and Gen. Council, European Cen. Bank 2015–; Chair. Indexcommissie 1986–92, Irving Fisher Cttee on Central Bank Statistics, BIS 2005–08; mem. Econ. Policy Cttee, OECD 1999–2015; mem. Gen. Bd, European Systemic Risk Bd 2015–; mem. Bd of Dirs Nat. Accounts Inst. 2015–. *Address:* Banque Nationale de Belgique, 14 Blvd de Berlaimont, 1000 Brussels, Belgium (office). *Telephone:* (2) 221-20-01 (office); (2) 221-20-96. *E-mail:* jan.smets@nbb.be (office); gisele.vanobberghen@nbb.be (office). *Website:* www.nbb.be (office).

SMILEY, Jane Graves, MFA, PhD; American writer and academic; b. 26 Sept. 1949, Los Angeles, Calif.; d. of James La Verne Smiley and Frances Nuelle Smiley (née Graves); m. 1st John Whiston 1970 (divorced); m. 2nd William Silag 1978 (divorced); two d.; m. 3rd Stephen Mark Mortensen 1987 (divorced 1997); one s.; ed Vassar Coll. and Univ. of Iowa; Asst Prof., Iowa State Univ. 1981–84, Assoc. Prof. 1984–89, Prof. 1989–90, Distinguished Prof. 1992–96; Visiting Prof., Univ. of Iowa 1981, 1987; mem. American Acad. of Arts and Letters 2001–; Fulbright Grant 1976, Nat. Endowment for the Arts grants 1978, 1987; Friends of American

Writers Prize 1981, O. Henry Awards 1982, 1985, 1988, Distinguished Alumni Award, Univ. of Iowa 2003. *Publications include:* Barn Blind 1980, At Paradise Gate 1981, Duplicate Keys 1984, The Age of Grief 1987, Catskill Crafts: Artisans of the Catskill Mountains (non-fiction) 1987, The Greenlanders 1988, Ordinary Love and Goodwill 1989, A Thousand Acres (Pulitzer Prize in Fiction 1992, Nat. Book Critics Circle Award 1992, Midland Authors Award 1992, Heartland Prize 1992) 1991, Moo: A Novel 1995, The All-True Travels and Adventures of Lidie Newton 1998, Horse Heaven 2000, Dickens (biog.) 2002, Good Faith 2003, A Year at the Races 2004, Thirteen Ways of Looking at the Novel (non-fiction) 2006, Ten Days in the Hills 2007, The Georges and the Jewels (children's fiction) 2009, Private Life 2010, The Man Who Invented the Computer: The Biography of John Atanasoff, Digital Pioneer 2010, Some Luck: A Novel 2014, Early Warning 2015, Golden Age 2015. *Leisure interests:* cooking, swimming, playing piano, quilting. *E-mail:* jane .smiley@sbcglobal.net. *Website:* www.therealjanesmiley.com.

SMIRNOV, Andrei Sergeyevich; Russian actor, film director and scriptwriter; b. 12 March 1941, Moscow; ed All Union State Inst. of Cinematography; numerous prizes at int. film festivals. *Films include:* dir: Hey, Anybody! (with B. Yashin) 1962, An Inch of Land (with B. Yashin) 1964, A Little Joke (TV film with B. Yashin) 1966, Somebody Else's Pain (TV film) 1966, Jacqueline Francois Sings (TV film) 1966, Angel 1987, Belorussian Railway Station 1970, Fall 1974, By Trust and Truth 1979, Unwillful Striptease 1983, Zhila-byla odna baba 2011; actor: Following, Chernov, Dreams of an Idiot, Mania of Giselle, Dnevnik ego zheny (Diary of His Wife) 2000, Persona non grata 2005, Elena 2011, Two Days 2011; scriptwriter: Autumn, Sentimental Journey, My Dear Relatives. *Television includes:* actor: Idiot (mini-series) 2003, Moskovskaya saga 2004, Master i Margarita (mini-series) 2005, The First Circle (mini-series) 2006, Apostol (mini-series) 2008, Ottepel (series) 2013. *Plays directed:* Late Supper (Moscow Art Theatre) 1994, Turgenev's Month in a Village (Comedy Francaise) 1997. *Publications include:* plays: Autumn, Sentimental Journey, My Dear Relative. *Address:* 121019 Moscow, Suvirivski boulevard 8, Apt, Russia (office). *Telephone:* (495) 299-34-93 (office).

SMIRNOV, Igor Nikolayevich, DEconSc; Russian politician; b. 23 Oct. 1941, Petropavlovsk-Kamchatskii, Kamchatka Oblast (now Kamchatka Krai), Russian SFSR, USSR; s. of Nikolai Stepanovich Smirnov and Zinaida Grigor'evna Smirnova; m. Zhannetta Nikolayevna Lotnik; two s.; ed Zaporizhzhya Machine Construction Inst., Ukrainian SSR; mem. CPSU 1963–90; early career as engineer, chief engineer, chief of shop; Deputy Dir Novo-Kakhova Electromash plant, Ukrainian SSR; Dir Tiraspol Electromash plant 1987–90, Moldovan SSR; Dir Tiraspol Jt Trade Union 1989–91, Chair. City Soviet and Tiraspol City Exec. Cttee 1990–91; Pres. Self-Declared 'Transnistrian Moldovan Repub.' (expelled from CPSU for separatism 1990) 1991–2011; People's Deputy of Moldova 1990–92; Academician, Ukrainian Economical-Cybernetics Acad.; mem. Int. Informatization Acad., Russian Acad. of Natural Sciences; Order of Repub. 1995, Medal, Order of Prince Daniyl of Moscow 1998, Order of Sergei Radonezhski 1999, Order for Benefit of Motherland, Russian Acad. of Sciences, Order of World Distributing Univ., Cross for Faith and Motherland (3rd Degree), Cross for Defence of 'Transnistrian Moldovan Repub.', Cross for Service to the Cossacks, Order of Lenin, Star of Hero, Order of Glory of Russia 2000, Order for Personal Courage 2001; Medal for Labour Prowess, Medal on 10th anniversary of 'Transnistrian Moldovan Repub.'. *Publications:* Human Beings, Science and Technical Progress in a Century of Information 2000, In Favour of the Republic 2000, To Live on Our Land (Sholohov Prize) 2004. *Leisure interest:* hunting. *Address:* c/o Office of the President of the 'Transnistrian Moldovan Republic', 3300 Tiraspol, ul. Gorkogo 53, Moldova. *E-mail:* psp.pmr@mail.ru.

SMIRNOV, Igor Pavlovich, DPhilSc; Russian literary scholar and academic; *Professor Emeritus, University of Konstanz;* b. 19 May 1941, Leningrad (now St Petersburg); s. of Pavel Smirnov and Valentina Lomakina; m. 2nd Nadezda Grigoryeva 2011; ed Leningrad Univ.; Research Assoc., Leningrad Inst. of Russian Literature; left USSR 1981; Prof., Univ. of Konstanz, Germany 1981–2006, Prof. Emer. 2006–; Vjazemski Prize 1998, Andrey Bely Prize 2000. *Publications include:* Meaning in Art and the Evolution of Poetic Systems 1977, Diachronic Transformations of Literary Genres and Motifs 1981, Essays on the History of the Typology of Culture (with Johanna Smirnov) 1982, The Emergence of the Inter-text 1985, Towards a Theory of Literature 1987, Being and Creating 1990, On Old Russian Culture, Russian National Specificity and the Logic of History 1991, Psychohistory of Russian Literature from Romanticism to the Present Day 1995, A Novel of Secrets – Dr. Zhivago 1996, Homo homini philosophus 1999, Megahistory 2000, Philosophy for Everyday 2003, Philosophical Sociology of Revolution 2004, Genesis 2006, A (Hypo)Theory of Genres 2008, Semantic History of Cinema 2009, How Literature Refers to Philosophy 2010, Praxeology 2012, Transformations of Sense 2015, On Limits of Mind 2017, A Contrario 2018. *Address:* Department of Russian, University of Konstanz, 78457 Konstanz (office); Kornblumenweg 14, 78465 Konstanz, Germany (home). *Telephone:* (7531) 882682 (office); (7531) 43583 (home). *Fax:* (7531) 4852 (office). *E-mail:* igor.smirnov@uni-konstanz.de (office).

SMIRNOV, Stanislav Konstantinovich, PhD; Russian mathematician and academic; *Professor, University of Geneva;* b. 3 Sept. 1970, Leningrad; ed St Petersburg Lyceum 239, St Petersburg State Univ., California Inst. of Tech., USA; has held research positions at Yale Univ., USA, Max Planck Inst. for Math., Germany, Inst. for Advanced Study, USA; at Royal Inst. of Tech., Stockholm, Sweden 1998–2003; Prof., Analysis, Math. Physics and Probability Group, Univ. of Geneva, Switzerland 2003–; also part-time at Chebyshev Lab., St Petersburg State Univ.; Fellow, American Math. Soc. 2012; jtly ranked first at Int. Math. Olympiad with perfect scores and gold medals on both occasions 1986, 1987, St Petersburg Math. Soc. Prize 1997, Clay Research Award 2001, Salem Prize (co-recipient) 2001, Göran Gustafsson Research Prize 2001, Rollo Davidson Prize 2002, Prize of European Math. Soc. 2004, Fields Medal (co-recipient) 2010. *Publications:* numerous papers in professional journals on complex analysis, dynamical systems and probability theory. *Address:* Section de mathématiques, University of Geneva, 2–4 rue du Lièvre, CP 64, 1211 Geneva 4, Switzerland (office). *Telephone:* (22) 3791149 (office). *Fax:* (22) 3791176 (office). *E-mail:* stanislav.smirnov@unige.ch (office). *Website:* www.unige.ch/~smirnov (office).

SMIRNOV, Vitaly Georgiyevich; Russian sport administrator; b. 14 Feb. 1935, Khabarovsk; m. Irina Aleksandrovna Smirnova; three s.; ed Cen. State Inst. of

Physical Culture; instructor, Head Div. of Sports Moscow Comsomol Cttee 1958–60; First Sec. Kuntzevo Regional Comsomol Cttee; Moscow Region 1960; Chair. Moscow Regional Council, Union of Sports Socs and Orgs 1960–62; Second Sec., then First Sec., Moscow Regional Comsomol Cttee 1962–68; First Sec., City Cttee of CPSU 1968–70; Deputy Chair., First Deputy Chair. USSR Cttee of Sports and Physical Culture 1970–75, Chair. Water Polo Fed. 1962–72; First Deputy Chair. Org. Cttee of Olympic Games 1980 in Moscow 1975–81; Chair. State Cttee on Sports and Physical Culture of Russian Fed. 1981–90; mem. IOC 1971–2015, Hon. Mem. 2016–, mem. Exec. Bd 1974–78, 1986–90, Vice-Pres. IOC 1978–82, 1990–94, 2001–05, Chair. Eligibility Comm. 1992–98, mem. Int. Relations Comm. 2002–15, Remuneration Working Group 2004–, 2009 Congress 2006–09, Public Affairs and Social Development through Sport 2015–, Chair. USSR Olympic Cttee 1990–92, Pres. Olympic Cttee of Russia 1992–2001, Hon. Pres. USSR Olympic Cttee 2001–; mem. Acad. of Creativity 1994–, Int. Acad. of Informatization, Peter's Acad. of Sciences and Arts; Order Sign of Honour 1966, 1970, 1976, Order Friendship of Nations 1980, Order Labour Red Banner 1985, Order of Honour 1994, Order For Services to Motherland 3rd degree 1966, Order for Services to Motherland 2nd degree 2001; orders and awards of international sports federations. *Publications:* numerous articles and papers on the devt of sports in Russia and the Olympic movt. *Leisure interests:* hunting, fishing, tennis. *Address:* Russian Olympic Committee, 119992 Moscow, Luzhnetskaya emb. 8, Russia. *Telephone:* (495) 725-45-01 (office). *Fax:* (495) 637-02-55 (office). *E-mail:* smirnov@roc.ru (office). *Website:* www.roc.ru (office).

SMIRNOV, Vladimir Nikolaevich; Russian biochemist; b. 17 May 1937, Cheliabinsk; m. 1st Valeriana Kreier 1956 (divorced 1973); m. 2nd Galina Chernonsova 1976; one s.; ed Leningrad Univ.; mem. CPSU 1976–91; postgraduate 1959–64; Jr, Sr Research Fellow at USSR Acad. of Med. Science Inst. of Medical Radiology 1964–68; Head of Biochemical Section, Ministry of Health 1968–72; Corresp. mem. of USSR (now Russian) Acad. of Sciences 1981; Prof. of Biological Science 1977; Head of Lab. at All-Union Scientific Centre for Cardiology (br. of USSR (now Russian) Acad. of Medical Science) 1973–76, Dir 1976–82; Dir of Inst. of Experimental Cardiography of Acad. of Medical Sciences 1982–; Corresp. mem., then mem. Acad. of Medical Sciences 1984–; USSR State Prize 1978. *Publications:* works on molecular biology, biochem. of the heart, cellular and molecular athero- and trombogenesis. *Leisure interests:* hunting, fishing. *Address:* Institute of Experimental Cardiology, Cardiology Research Centre, 112552 Moscow, 3rd Cherepkovskaya 15A, Russia. *Telephone:* (495) 415-00-35 (office); (495) 203-84-83 (home). *Fax:* (495) 415-29-62.

SMISEK, Jeffery (Jeff) A., AB, JD; American airline industry executive; b. 17 Aug. 1954, Washington, DC; m.; two c.; ed Princeton Univ., Harvard Law School; Pnr and Exec. Vice-Pres. Vinson & Elkins LLP, Houston 1983–95; Sr Vice-Pres. and Gen. Counsel, Continental Airlines Inc. 1995–96, Exec. Vice-Pres., Gen. Counsel and Sec. 1996–2001, Exec. Vice-Pres., Corp. 2001–03, Exec. Vice-Pres. 2003–04, Pres. 2004–10, COO 2008–09, Chair. and CEO Jan.–Oct. 2010, Pres. and CEO United Continental Holdings, Inc. (holding co. of United Airlines and Continental Airlines) Oct. 2010–15 (resgnd), Chair. 2013–15, Chair., Pres. and CEO United Airlines –2015; mem. Bd of Dirs National Oilwell Varco Inc., Varco International Inc., Orbitz Inc.; named Aviation Week's Person of the Year 2010.

SMIT, John William; South African fmr professional rugby union player; *Chief Executive Officer, The Sharks;* b. 3 April 1978, Pietersburg (now Polokwane), Limpopo Prov.; ed Pretoria Boys High School (Head Prefect); plays as hooker and prop; played in First XV, Pretoria Boys High School 1994–96, Univ. of Natal 1997, Natal Sharks 1998, Sharks (Super 14) 1998–2007, 2008–11, Clermont 2007–08, Saracens 2011, South African Nat. Rugby Union Team (Springboks) 2000–11; CEO, The Sharks team, South African rugby union 2013–; played his first Springbok game 2000, played in a record 46 consecutive Test matches for South Africa 2003–07, Capt. 2004–11; won Tri Nations 2004; captained South Africa to win Rugby World Cup, Paris 2007, series victory against British and Irish Lions 2009, Tri Nations 2009; currently most-capped capt. in int. rugby history; played his 100th Test (only the 15th player ever, and second South African) 2010. *Address:* Sharks Private Ltd., Kings Park, PO Box 307, Durban 4000, South Africa (office). *Telephone:* (31) 3088400 (office). *Fax:* (31) 3129197 (office). *E-mail:* yourview@sarugby.co.za. *Website:* www.sharksrugby.co.za (office); www.sarugby.co.za.

SMIT, Sir Timothy (Tim) Bartel, KBE; British (b. Dutch) business executive; *Co-Founder and Executive Vice-Chair, Eden Project;* b. 25 Sept. 1954, Scheveningen, The Netherlands; s. of Jan Smit; ed Durham Univ.; fmr rock and opera music composer; Co-Founder and Exec. Vice-Chair., Eden Project 1995, also Exec. Chair. Eden Project Int.; discovered "lost" gardens at Heligan, near St Austell, Cornwall 1990; hon. degrees from numerous univs.; Albert Medal, RSA 2003. *Publications:* The Lost Gardens Of Heligan 1997, Eden 2001. *Leisure interests:* reading, film, music, art. *Address:* Eden Project, Bodelva, Cornwall, PL24 2SG, England (office). *Telephone:* (1726) 811911. *Website:* www.edenproject.com.

SMITH, Ali, CBE, FRSL; British writer; b. 1962, Inverness, Scotland; partner Sarah Wood; ed Univ. of Aberdeen and Newnham Coll., Cambridge; fmr Lecturer, Univ. of Strathclyde; gave lecture on Angela Carter, Nat. Portrait Gallery, London 2004; Patron Visual Verse online anthology; Hon. DLitt (Aberdeen) 2007, (Anglia Ruskin, Cambridge) 2008; Scottish Arts Council Award 1995, inaugural Harriet Martineau Lecturer, in celebration of Norwich, UNESCO City of Literature 2013. *Plays:* The Seer 2001, Just 2005. *Publications:* Free Love and Other Stories (Saltire First Book Award) 1995, Like (novel) 1997, Other Stories and Other Stories 1999, Hotel World (novel) (Encore Prize, Scottish Arts Council Book Award, Scottish Arts Council Book of the Year 2002) 2001, The Whole Story and Other Stories 2003, The Accidental (novel) (Whitbread Novel of the Year 2005) 2004, The Reader 2006, Girl Meets Boy (SAC Sundial Novel of the Year 2008) 2007, The First Person and Other Stories 2008, There But For The 2011, Artful (non-fiction) 2012, Shire (non-fiction) 2013, How to Be Both (Goldsmiths Prize 2014, Novel Award, Costa Book Awards 2014, Baileys Women's Prize for Fiction 2015) 2014, Autumn 2016, Winter 2017; contrib. to TLS, The Scotsman, The Guardian. *Address:* c/o The Wylie Agency, 17 Bedford Square, London, WC1B 3JA, England (office). *Telephone:* (20) 7908-5900 (office). *Fax:* (20) 7908-5901 (office). *E-mail:* mail@wylieagency.co.uk (office). *Website:* www.wylieagency.co.uk (office).

SMITH, Andrew David; British politician; b. 1 Feb. 1951; m. Valerie Miles (died 2015); one step-s.; ed Reading Grammar School, St John's Coll., Oxford; joined Labour Party 1973; mem. Oxford City Council 1976–87; MP for Oxford East 1987–2017; Opposition Spokesman on Higher Educ. 1988–92, on Treasury and Econ. Affairs 1992–94; Shadow Chief Sec. to HM Treasury 1994–96; Shadow Transport Sec. 1996–97; Minister of State, Dept for Educ. and Employment 1997–99; Chief Sec. to HM Treasury 1999–2002; Sec. of State for Work and Pensions 2002–04 (resgnd); Chair. Bd Oxford Brookes Univ. (fmrly Oxford Polytechnic) 1987–93. *Address:* 4 Flaxfield Road, Blackbird Leys, Oxford, OX4 5QD, England (home). *Fax:* (1865) 305089 (office).

SMITH, Anthony David, CBE, MA; British author and broadcaster (retd) and administrator (retd); *Chairman, The Hill Foundation;* b. 14 March 1938; s. of Henry Smith and Esther Smith; ed Brasenose Coll., Oxford; Current Affairs Producer, BBC 1960–71; Fellow, St Antony's Coll., Oxford 1971–76; Dir British Film Inst. 1979–88, Fellow; Pres. Magdalen Coll., Oxford 1988–2005; Gov. British Inst. of Florence 2005–14; mem. Bd of Dirs, Channel Four TV 1980–84; mem. Acton Soc. Trust 1978–90; Chair. Writers and Scholars Educational Trust (Index on Censorship) 1989–99, Hill Foundation 1999–, Oxford–Russia Fund 2004–; mem. Arts Council 1990–94; Trustee, Prince of Wales Inst. of Traditional Arts 2005–09; Bd mem. The Sixteen Choir 2006–; mem. Council Royal Acad. of Dramatic Art 2007–16; Hon. Fellow, Brasenose Coll., Oxford 1994, Magdalen Coll., Oxford 2005–; Chevalier des Arts et des Lettres; Dr hc (Oxford Brookes Univ., Univ. of Lincoln). *Publications include:* The Shadow in the Cave: The Broadcaster, The Audience and the State 1973, British Broadcasting 1974, The British Press since the War 1976, Subsidies and the Press in Europe 1977, The Politics of Information 1978, Television and Political Life 1979, The Newspaper: An International History 1979, Newspapers and Democracy 1980, Goodbye Gutenberg – The Newspaper Revolution of the 1980s, The Geopolitics of Information 1980, The Age of the Behemoths 1991, From Books to Bytes 1993, The Oxford Illustrated History of Television 1995, Software for the Self: Culture and Technology 1996. *Address:* I:1, Albany, Piccadilly, London, W1J 0AX, England (home). *Telephone:* (20) 7734-5494 (home). *E-mail:* anthony@anthonysmith.net (office). *Website:* www.hillfoundationscholarships.org (office).

SMITH, Sir (Eric) Brian, Kt, MA, PhD, DSc, FRSC; British scientist and university vice-chancellor (retd); b. 10 Oct. 1933, Mold, North Wales; s. of Eric Smith and Dilys Olwen Hughes; m. 1st Margaret Barr 1957 (divorced 1978); two s. one d.; m. 2nd Regina Arvidson Ball 1983; two step-d.; ed Alun Grammar School, Mold, Wirral Grammar School, Univ. of Liverpool; Fellow, St Catherine's Coll. Oxford and Lecturer in Physical Chem., Univ. of Oxford 1960–88, now Hon. Fellow, Master St Catherine's Coll. 1988–93; Vice-Chancellor Cardiff Univ. 1993–2001; Dir ISIS Innovation Network 1988–97; mem. Bd Welsh Devt Agency 1998–2001, Wales European Centre 2001–03, Higher Educ. Funding Council for Wales 2002–; Gov. Univ. of Glamorgan 2002–06. *Publications:* Virial Coefficients of Pure Gases and Mixtures 1969, Basic Chemical Themodynamics 1973, Intermolecular Forces 1981, Forces Between Molecules 1986; papers in scientific journals. *Leisure interest:* mountaineering.

SMITH, Bruce Alfred, BS, MBA; American energy industry executive; b. 12 Oct. 1943, Coffeyville, Kan.; s. of George Alfred Smith and Isabel Smith (neé Andrews); m. 1st Cynthia Denton Smith (neé Doughat) 1969, divorced 1987; five s.; m. 2nd Gail Smith (neé Hutchison) 1990; ed Westminster Coll., Univ. of Kansas; served in US Army; worked as Financial Analyst, Ford Motor Co., Dearborn, Mich. 1967–69; Banking Officer, Metropolitan Div. Continental Ill. Nat. Bank and Trust Co., Chicago 1971–73, 2nd Vice-Pres. Multinational Div. 1973–75, Vice-Pres. Mining Div. 1975–77, Vice-Pres. and Section Man., Chicago and London 1977–80, Vice-Pres. and Man. Int. Energy Div., Chicago 1980–82, Vice-Pres. and Man. Southwest Group and Commercial Banking Houston 1983–86; Vice-Pres. and Treas. Valero Energy Corpn 1986–92; Chief Financial Officer Tesoro Corpn 1992–95, Exec. Vice-Pres. 1993–95, Pres. and CEO 1995–96, mem. Bd of Dirs 1995–2010, Chair., Pres. and CEO 1996–2010 (retd); mem. Bd of Dirs Noble Energy Inc., Nat. Petrochemical and Refiners Asscn.

SMITH, Carsten, DJur; Norwegian judge (retd); b. 13 July 1932, Oslo; s. of Oscar Smith and Julie Høyer; m. Lucy Dahl 1958; three d.; ed Univ. of Oslo; practised as attorney 1956–60; Deputy Judge 1960; Asst Prof., Univ. of Oslo 1957, Assoc. Prof. 1960, Prof. of Law 1964–91, Dir Inst. of Pvt. Law 1972–73, Dean, Faculty of Law 1977–79; Temporary Supreme Court Justice 1987, 1989–90, Chief Justice, Supreme Court of Norway 1991–2002; Chair. Saami Rights Comm. 1980–85, Comm. on Human Rights in Norwegian Legislation 1989–91, Comm. for reviewing Norwegian Court system 1996–99, Comm. on Nordic Saami Rights Convention 2003–05, Comm. on fishing rights in the ocean north of Norway for Saami People and other citizens 2006–08; mem. Perm. Court of Arbitration 1996–2004; Ed. Journal of Law 1963–73; mem. Norwegian Acad. of Science and Letters, Pres. 1991; apptd mem. UN Perm. Forum on Indigenous Issues 2008; Grand Cross of Royal Norwegian Order of St Olav 2003; hon. degrees from several univs; Nordic Lawyer Award 1996. *Television:* chief judge in TV show Double or Nothing 1963, 1966, 1985. *Publications include:* Law of Torts and Social Security (co-author) 1953, Law of Guarantees (Vols I–III) 1963–81, State Practice and Legal Theory 1978, Banking Law and State Regulations 1980, Contemporary Legal Reasoning 1992, The Law and the Life 1996, Surety Law 1997; other books and articles in fields of int. law, constitutional law, admin. law and pvt. law. *Address:* Høyesterett, PO Box 8016 Dep, 0030 Oslo, Norway. *Telephone:* 22-03-59-05. *Fax:* 22-33-23-55.

SMITH, Cindy, MSc, PhD; American academic and UN official; ed Univ. of California, Irvine, Nat. Univ., Irvine, American Univ.; Assoc. Prof. and Dir Masters Criminal Justice Program, Univ. of Baltimore 2000–05, Assoc. Prof. in Criminology 2008–10; Fulbright Sr Researcher, Turkey 2005–06; Chief of Int. Centre, Nat. Inst. of Justice, Washington, DC 2005–08; Lead Foreign Affairs Officer, US Dept of State 2011–12, Sr Coordinator for Int. Programs, Office to Monitor and Combat Trafficking in Persons 2012–15; Dir-Gen., UN Interregional Crime and Justice Research Inst. (UNICRI) 2015–17; Herbert Bloch Award, American Soc. of Criminology 2006. *Publications include:* Routledge Handbook of International Criminology (co-author) 2011. *Address:* c/o United Nations Interregional Crime and Justice Research Institute (UNICRI), Viale Maestri del Lavoro 10, 10127 Turin, Italy (office).

SMITH, Dan F., BSc; American petrochemical industry executive; *Chairman, Kraton Polymers LLC;* m. Sandy Smith; two c.; ed Lamar Univ.; Engineer ARCO (Atlantic Richfield Co.) 1968–82, Planning Man. 1982–84, Vice-Pres., Planning and Control, ARCO Metals Co. 1984–85, Exec. Vice-Pres. and COO 1991–93; Vice-Pres., Control and Admin Lyondell Chemical Co. 1985, Vice-Pres. then Pres. of Mfg Operations 1985–88, Exec. Vice-Pres. and Chief Financial Officer 1988–91, 1993–94, Pres. 1994–2007, CEO 1996–2007, Chair. 2007, CEO Partnership Governance Cttee, Equistar Chemicals LP 1997–2007, Millennium Chemicals Inc. 2004–07 (subsidiaries of Lyondell Chemical Co.); Chair. Kraton Polymers LLC 2008–; mem. Bd of Dirs Cooper Industries, Northern Tier Energy 2012–; Chair. Nexeo Solutions, LLC, Valerus Compression Services; mem. Lamar Univ. Coll. of Eng Advisory Council. *Address:* Kraton Polymers LLC, 700 Milam Street, 13th Floor, North Tower, Houston, TX 77002, USA (office). *Website:* www.kraton.com (office).

SMITH, Hon. (Daniel) Orlando, OBE, FRCS; British Virgin Islands physician and politician; b. 28 Aug. 1944, Tortola; s. of Joshua Smith and Eldra Smith (née Davies); m. Lorna Smith; ed British Virgin Islands High School, Univ. of the West Indies, Royal Coll. of Surgeons, Edinburgh, Royal School of Public Health, London and London School of Hygiene and Tropical Medicine, UK; trained as obstetrician; began medical career at Univ. Hosp. of the West Indies; intern, Princess Margaret Hosp., Nassau, Bahamas 1967–70; Chief Medical Officer of British Virgin Islands (BVI) 1979–96, also Surgeon, Peebles Hosp.; mem. Legis. Council (renamed House of Ass. 2007) 1999–; Leader of the Opposition 1999–2003; Chief Minister of British Virgin Islands 2003–07; Premier and Minister of Finance 2011–19; Founding mem. and Chair. Nat. Democratic Party 1998–2018; fmr Chair. British Virgin Islands Medical and Dental Asscn, Nat. Drug Advisory Council. *Leisure interests:* reading, squash, tennis. *Address:* c/o Office of the Premier, 33 Admin Drive, Wickham's Cay 1, Road Town, Tortola VG1110, British Virgin Islands (office).

SMITH, Delia Ann, CH, CBE, OBE, FRTS; British cookery writer and broadcaster; b. 18 June 1941, Woking, Surrey; m. Michael Wynn Jones; creator and presenter of several TV series since 1969; cookery writer, Evening Standard newspaper 1972–85; columnist, Radio Times; Consultant Food Ed., Sainsbury's Magazine; Dir Norwich City Football Club; UK's best-selling cookery author, with more than 21 million copies sold; signed, with Heston Blumenthal, by Waitrose supermarket chain to appear in a series of 40 commercials on UK television 2010; announced retirement from TV cookery programmes to concentrate on offering recipes online Feb. 2013; Hon. Fellow, St Mary's Coll., Univ. of Surrey 1996, John Moores Univ., Liverpool 2000; Dr hc (Nottingham) 1996, (East Anglia) 1999; Special Award, Andre Simon Memorial Fund 1994, BAFTA Special Award 2013. *Television:* Family Fare, Series 1 1973, Series 2 1974, Series 3 1975, Delia Smith's Cookery Course 1 1978–79, Delia Smith's Cookery Course 2 1980, Delia Smith's Cookery Course 3 1981, Delia Smith's One is Fun 1985, Delia Smith's Christmas 1990, Delia Smith's Summer Collection 1993, Delia Smith's Winter Collection 1995–96, Delia's Red Nose Collection 1997, Delia's How to Cook 1 1998, Delia's How to Cook 2 2000, Delia's How to Cook 3 2002, Delia's Chocolate C'Hunks 2001, Delia 2008, Delia's Classic Christmas 2009, Delia through the Decades 2010. *Publications:* How to Cheat at Cooking 1971, Country Fare 1973, Recipes from Country Inns and Restaurants 1973, Family Fare: Book 1 1973, Book 2 1974, Evening Standard Cookbook 1974, Country Recipes from Look East (regional TV programme) 1975, More Country Recipes from Look East 1976, Frugal Food 1976, Book of Cakes 1977, Recipes from Look East 1977, Food for Our Times 1978, Cookery Course: Part 1 1978, Part 2 1979, Part 3 1981, The Complete Cookery Course 1982, A Feast for Lent 1983, A Feast for Advent 1983, One is Fun 1985, Food Aid Cookery Book (ed.) 1986, A Journey into Prayer 1986, A Journey into God 1988, Delia Smith's Christmas 1990, Delia Smith's Summer Collection 1993, Delia Smith's Winter Collection 1995, Delia's Red Nose Collection 1997, How to Cook: Book 1 1998, How to Cook: Book 2 1999, How to Cook Book 3 2001, Delia's Chocolate Collection (for Comic Relief) 2001, Delia's Vegetarian Collection 2002, The Delia Collection: Soup, Fish, Chicken, Chocolate 2003, The Delia Collection: Pork, Italian 2004, The Delia Collection: Baking 2005, The Delia Collection: Puddings 2006, Delia's Kitchen Garden 2007, Delia's How to Cheat at Cooking (completely rewritten) 2008, Delia's Frugal Food 2008, Delia's Happy Christmas 2009, Delia's Cakes 2013. *Address:* c/o Deborah Owen, 78 Narrow Street, Limehouse, London, E14 8BP, England. *Telephone:* (20) 7987-5119. *Fax:* (20) 7538-4004. *E-mail:* do@deborahowen.co.uk (office). *Website:* www.deliaonline.com.

SMITH, Donnie; American business executive; *CEO, Tyson Foods Inc.;* joined Tyson Foods 1980, Sr Vice-Pres., Supply Chain Man. 2001–05, Sr Vice-Pres. and Chief Information Officer 2005–06, Sr Vice-Pres., Information Systems, Purchasing and Distribution 2006–07, Group Vice-Pres., Logistics and Operations Services 2007–08, Group Vice-Pres., Consumer Products 2008–09, Sr Group Vice-Pres., Poultry and Prepared Foods Jan.–Nov. 2009, Pres. and CEO Tyson Foods Inc. 2009–15, Dir 2014–, CEO 2016–. *Address:* Tyson Foods Inc., 2200 Don Tyson Parkway, Springdale, AR 72762, USA (office). *Telephone:* (479) 290-4000 (office). *Fax:* (479) 290-4061 (office). *E-mail:* info@tysonfoodsinc.com (office). *Website:* www.tysonfoodsinc.com (office).

SMITH, Elizabeth (Liz) A., BA, MBA; American business executive; *Chairman and CEO, Bloomin' Brands, Inc.;* ed Univ. of Virginia, Stanford Grad. School of Business; began career as a financial analyst at Paine Webber Inc. 1986; Asst Brand Man. Jell-O Ready-to-Eat-Snacks, Kraft Foods Inc. 1990–2000, also worked as Category Business Dir and Gen. Man. for Callard & Bowser-Suchard, Exec. Vice-Pres. and Gen. Man. Beverage Div. 2000–02, Pres. Beverages, Desserts and Cereals Group (div. of Kraft Foods Inc.) 2002–04, Group Vice-Pres. Kraft Foods North America and Pres. US Beverages and Grocery Sectors, Kraft Foods Inc. Jan.–Nov. 2004; joined American CareSource as Dir of Operations 2004, later Vice-Pres. of Operations, American Caresource Holdings, Inc.; Vice-Pres. of Field Operations, Furr's Restaurant Group Inc. from 2002; Exec. Vice-Pres. and Pres. N America and Global Marketing, Avon Products Inc. 2005–07, Pres. Avon Products Inc. 2007–09; mem. Bd of Dirs and CEO OSI Restaurant Partners LLC (now Bloomin' Brands, Inc.) 2009–, Chair. 2012–; fmr Business Services Man. for Visiting Nurse Asscn of Texas; Quality Man. for Tenet Healthcare Corpn –2004; mem. Bd of Dirs The William Carter Co. 2004–, Carter's Inc. 2004–08, Staples Inc. 2008–, Cosmetic, Toiletry & Fragrance Asscn, Personal Care Products Council; Dir of Big Brothers and Big Sisters of America; recognized by Advertising Age magazine as one of the top marketers in 1996. *Address:* Bloomin' Brands, Inc., 2202 North West Shore Boulevard, 5th Floor, Tampa, FL 33607, USA (office). *Telephone:* (813) 282-1225 (office). *Fax:* (813) 282-1209 (office). *Website:* www.bloominbrands.com (office).

SMITH, Sir Francis Graham (See GRAHAM-SMITH, Sir Francis).

SMITH, Frank Thomas, DPhil, FRS; British mathematician and academic; *Goldsmid Professor of Applied Mathematics, University College London;* b. 24 Feb. 1948, Bournemouth, Dorset, England; s. of Leslie Maxwell Smith and Catherine Matilda Smith; m. Valerie Sheila Hearn 1972; three d.; ed Bournemouth School, Jesus Coll. Oxford, Univ. Coll. London; Research Fellow, Southampton Univ. 1972–73; Lecturer in Math., Reader then Prof., Imperial Coll. London 1973–84; Goldsmid Prof. of Applied Math., Univ. Coll. London 1984–; Visiting Prof., Univ. of Western Ontario, Canada 1978–79, Ohio State Univ. 1990. *Publications:* Boundary-Layer Separation (co-ed.); numerous scientific papers, mostly on theoretical and computational fluid dynamics, industrial and biomedical applications and math. modelling. *Address:* Mathematics Department, University College, Gower Street, London, WC1E 6BT (office); 9 Woodham Park Road, Woodham, Addlestone, Surrey, KT15 3ST, England (home). *Telephone:* (20) 7679-2837 (office); (1932) 352394 (home). *Fax:* (20) 7383-5519 (office). *E-mail:* frankmath@ucl.ac.uk (office). *Website:* www.ucl.ac.uk/Mathematics (office).

SMITH, Geoff, BSc, PhD; Australian physicist and academic; *Professor Emeritus in Applied Physics and Senior Lecturer, School of Mathematical and Physical Sciences, University of Technology Sydney;* ed Monash Univ.; mem. staff, Univ. of Sussex, UK 1971–73; joined Univ. of Tech. Sydney 1973, now Prof. Emer. in Applied Physics and Sr Lecturer, School of Math. and Physical Sciences; has worked on renewable energy projects at Chalmers Univ. of Tech., Univ. of Uppsala, Sweden, Univ. of Houston, Texas, Lawrence Berkeley Lab., Calif., USA; carried out daylighting design and polymer roofing studies for Australia stadium at Sydney Summer Olympics 2000; contributed to Australia's Energy Efficient Building Codes and chairs its skylight and Roof Glazing Standards Cttee; mem. ABCB Tech. Cttee on glazing within energy efficiency building codes; Chair. Australian Standards Cttee for Skylights and Roof Glazing; Assoc. Ed., Journal of Nanophotonics; mem. Australian Optical Soc., SPIE (Int. Soc. for Optics and Photonics), Australian and NZ Solar Energy Soc., Optical Soc. of America; Affiliated to Skylight Industry Asscn; Fellow, Australian Inst. of Physics, Australian Inst. of Energy; Hon. PhD (Univ. of Uppsala); World Tech. Award (Environment) (co-recipient) 2015. *Publications:* more than 200 peer-reviewed papers in professional journals on science and technology in energy, coatings and nanotechnology; 15 patents. *Address:* University of Technology Sydney, City Campus, 15 Broadway, Ultimo, NSW 2007, Australia (office). *Telephone:* (2) 9514-2224 (office). *Fax:* (2) 9514-2219 (office). *E-mail:* geoff.smith@uts.edu.au (office). *Website:* www.uts.edu.au (office).

SMITH, George David William, MA, DPhil, FRS, FIMMM, FInstP, FRSC, CEng, CPhys; British metallurgist, materials scientist and academic; *Professor Emeritus of Materials Science, University of Oxford;* b. 28 March 1943, Aldershot, Hants.; s. of George Alfred William Smith and Grace Violet Hannah Dayton Smith; m. Josephine Ann Halford 1968 (died 2014); two s.; ed Corpus Christi Coll., Oxford; SRC Research Fellow, Dept of Materials, Univ. of Oxford 1968–70, Research Fellow 1970–75, Sr Research Fellow 1975–77, Lecturer 1977–92, George Kelley Reader in Metallurgy 1992–96, Prof. of Materials Science 1996–2010, Prof. Emer. 2010–, Head of Dept 2000–05, Fellow, St Cross Coll., Oxford 1977–91 (Fellow Emer. 1991–), Trinity Coll., Oxford 1991–2010 (Fellow Emer. 2010–); Man. Dir Kindbrisk Ltd (renamed Oxford NanoScience Ltd 2000) 1987–2002, Chair. 2002–04; Chair. Polaron plc 2004–06, Int. Review Panel for RCUK Nanoscience Programme 2009, Healthwatch Oxfordshire 2017–; consultant, Tokamak Energy 2012–; mem. Council Inst. of Materials 1998–2002 (Vice-Pres. 2002), UK Materials Foresight Panel 1998–2001, Council Inst. of Materials, Minerals and Mining 2003–05, Council Royal Soc. 2002–04, Scientific Advisory Panel, UK Environment Agency 2004, British Library Advisory Council 2004–11; Trustee, Sino-British Fellowship Trust 2016–; Liveryman of the Armourers' and Brasiers' Co.; Freeman of the City of London 1999; Hon. Fellow, Corpus Christi Coll. Oxford 2009; Beilby Medal and Prize 1985, Rosenhain Medal and Prize 1991, Nat. Award for Innovative Measurement 2004, Acta Materialia Gold Medal 2005, Inst. of Materials Platinum Medal 2006, Distinguished Physical Scientist Award, Microscopy Soc. of America 2016, William Hume Rothery Award, The Minerals, Metals and Materials Soc. (USA) 2017. *Publications:* Atom Probe Microanalysis (with M. K. Miller) 1989, Atom Probe Field Ion Microscopy (co-author) 1996; over 400 contribs to scientific journals. *Leisure interests:* walking, fishing, bird watching, grandchildren. *Address:* Department of Materials, University of Oxford, Parks Road, Oxford, OX1 3PH, England (office). *Telephone:* (1865) 273762 (office). *Fax:* (1865) 273738 (office). *E-mail:* george.smith@materials.ox.ac.uk (office). *Website:* www.materials.ox.ac.uk/peoplepages/smith.html (office).

SMITH, George E., BS, MS, PhD, FIEEE; American physicist and fmr inventor; b. 10 May 1930, White Plains, New York; m. E. Janet Carson 1955 (deceased); three c.; ed Univs of Pennsylvania and Chicago; served in Navy 1948–52; began career at Bell Labs in 1959, Head of Device Concepts Dept 1964, Head of VLSI Device Dept 1970–86 (retd); Founding Ed., IEEE Electron Device Letters; mem. Nat. Acad. of Eng; Fellow, American Physical Soc., Inst. for Electrical and Electronic Engineers (IEEE); Hon. Fellow, Royal Photographic Soc. 2015 IEEE Electron Devices Soc. Distinguished Service Award 1997, Stuart Ballentine Medal, Franklin Inst. (co-recipient) 1973, IEEE Morris N. Liebmann Memorial Award 1974, Progress Medal, Photographic Soc. of America 1986, IEEE Device Research Conf. Breakthrough Award 1999, Edwin H. Land Medal, Soc. for Imaging Science and Tech. 2001, C&C Prize (Computer and Communications), NEC Foundation, Tokyo 1999, Draper Prize (co-recipient) 2006, Nobel Prize in Physics (with Charles Kao and Willard S. Boyle) 2009, Progress Medal, Royal Photographic Soc. 2015. *Achievements include:* co-inventor (with Willard S. Boyle) charge-coupled device (CCD) 1970; completed a 17-year cruise aboard his sailing vessel, Apogee 2006. *Publications include:* holds 31 US patents; more than 40 papers in professional journals on electronic and thermoelectric properties of semi metals, optical devices, the silicon-diode-array camera tube and charge-coupled devices. *Address:* 221 Teaneck Road, PO Box 787, Barnegat, NJ 08005, USA (office). *E-mail:* apogee2@comcast.net.

SMITH, George Pearson, AB, PhD; American biologist; *Curators' Distinguished Professor Emeritus of Biological Sciences, University of Missouri;* b. 10 March 1941, Norwalk, Conn.; m. Marjorie Sable; two s.; ed Haverford Coll., Harvard Univ.; one year as teacher at high school, N Philadelphia 1963; worked as lab. technician; joined Faculty, Univ. of Missouri 1975, becoming Curators' Distinguished Prof. of Biological Sciences 2000–15, Prof. Emer. 2015–; Visiting Prof., Duke Univ.; Fellow AAAS 2001; Promega Biotechnology Research Award 2007, Nobel Prize in Chemistry (jtly with Greg Winter and Frances Arnold) 2018. *Publications:* author or co-author of more than 50 articles in scientific journals. *Address:* Division of Biological Sciences, 105 Tucker Hall, Columbia, MO 65211-7400, USA (office). *Telephone:* (573) 882-6659 (office). *Fax:* (573) 882-0123 (office). *E-mail:* smithgp@missouri.edu (office). *Website:* biology.missouri.edu/ (office).

SMITH, Hon. Godfrey, BL; Belizean lawyer and politician; *Partner and Senior Counsel, Marine Parade Chambers;* m. Valerie Woods; two c.; ed Univ. of the West Indies; Assoc. Attorney, Barrow & Williams, Belize City 1994–97; Chief of Staff Office of the Prime Minister 1998–99; Attorney-Gen. 1999–2006, concurrently Minister of Information; mem. House of Reps for Pickstock 2003–08; Minister of Foreign Affairs and Co-operation 2003–06; Minister of Tourism, and Nat. Emergency Man. 2006–08, of Information 2006–07; Sec-Gen. People's United Party, Belize City 1997–98, apptd Deputy Leader 2005; currently Partner and Sr Counsel, Marine Parade Chambers, Belize City; Founding Ed. Belize Law Reports, Belize Law Review, Belize Foreign Policy Yearbook; currently Lecturer, Univ. Coll. Belize; columnist, Belize Times 2006–. *Publications include:* Belize Law Report (ed.), Practical Guide to Gross Receipt Tax. *Address:* Marine Parade Chambers, Volta Building, Belize City, Belize (office). *Telephone:* 223-2428 (office). *Fax:* 223-3476 (office). *Website:* www.pupbelize.bz (office); marineparadechambers .weebly.com (office).

SMITH, Gordon Harold, BA, JD; American fmr politician; *President and CEO, National Association of Broadcasters;* b. 25 May 1952, Pendleton, Ore.; s. of Milan Dale Smith and Jessica Smith (née Udall); m. Sharon Lankford; two s. one d.; ed Brigham Young Univ. and Southwestern Univ.; law clerk to Justice H. Vern Payne, New Mexico Supreme Court; pvt. practice in Ariz.; Owner, Smith Frozen Foods; mem. Ore. State Senate 1992–95, Pres. 1995–96; Senator from Ore. 1997–2009, Pres. and CEO Nat. Assen of Broadcasters 2009–. *Address:* National Association of Broadcasters, 1771 N Street, NW, Washington, DC 20036, USA (office). *Telephone:* (202) 429-5300 (office). *E-mail:* nab@nab.org (office). *Website:* www.nab.org (office).

SMITH, Gordon Scott, PhD; Canadian diplomatist, academic and consultant; *Adjunct Professor, School of Public Administration, University of Victoria;* b. 19 July 1941, Montreal; s. of G. Meredith Smith and Helen Scott; m. Lise G. Lacroix; three s. one d.; ed Lower Canada Coll., Montreal, McGill Univ., Univ. of Chicago, Massachusetts Inst. of Tech.; joined Defence Research Bd 1966, transferred to Dept of External Affairs 1967; mem. Canadian Del. to NATO 1968–70; Special Adviser to Minister of Nat. Defence 1970–72; joined Privy Council Office 1972; Deputy Sec. to Cabinet (Plans) 1978–79; Deputy Under-Sec. Dept of External Affairs 1979; Assoc. Sec. to Cabinet, Privy Council Office 1980–81; Sec. Ministry of State for Social Devt 1981–84; Assoc. Sec. to Cabinet and Deputy Clerk of Privy Council 1984; Deputy Minister for Political Affairs, Dept of External Affairs 1985; Amb. and Perm. Rep. to NATO, Brussels 1985–90; Sec. to the Cabinet for Fed.-Prov. Relations, Govt of Canada 1990–91; Amb. to the EC 1991–94; Deputy Minister of Foreign Affairs 1994–97; Chair. Int. Devt Research Centre 1997–2007; Adjunct Prof., School of Public Admin, Univ. of Victoria 1997–, Exec. Dir Centre for Global Studies 1997–2012; Distinguished Fellow, Centre for Int. Governance Innovation 2010–; Visiting Prof., Diplomatic Acad., Univ. of Westminster, London, UK; mem. Int. Advisory Bd, Centre for Int. Governance Innovation, Waterloo, Ont.; Trudeau Mentor, Pierre Elliott Trudeau Foundation, Montreal; Pres. Gordon Smith International; Vanier Medal 2009, Inaugural Gordon Smith Lecture Series 2014. *Publication:* Altered States. *Leisure interests:* squash, tennis, sailing, skiing, antiques. *Address:* School of Public Administration, University of Victoria, Human & Social Development Building A302, 3800 Finnerty Road (Ring Road), Victoria, BC V8P 5C2 (office); 2027 Runnymede Avenue, Victoria, BC V8S 2V5, Canada. *Telephone:* (250) 472-4726 (office). *Fax:* (250) 472-4830 (office). *E-mail:* gssmith@ uvic.ca (office). *Website:* publicadmin.uvic.ca (office).

SMITH, Graeme Craig; South African professional cricketer; b. 1 Feb. 1981, Johannesburg, Transvaal; s. of Graham Smith and Janet Smith; ed King Edward VII School; opening batsman; left-handed batsman; right-arm off-break bowler; plays for Gauteng 1990–2000, Western Prov. 2000–04, Hampshire 2000, S Africa 2002–14 (Capt. Test side 2003–14, ODI side 2003–11, T20I side 2005–10), Cape Cobras 2004–, Somerset 2005 (Capt. for part of season), Rajasthan Royals 2008–10, Pune Warriors India 2011, Surrey (Capt.) 2013–, ICC (Int. Cricket Council) World XI, Africa XI, United Cricket Bd of S Africa Invitation XI and Western Prov. Boland; First-class debut: 1999/2000; Test debut: South Africa v Australia, Cape Town 8–12 March 2002; One-Day Int. (ODI) debut: S Africa v Australia, Bloemfontein 30 March 2002; T20I debut: S Africa v NZ, Johannesburg 21 Oct. 2005; has played in 117 Tests, taken 8 wickets and scored 9,265 runs (27 centuries, 38 half-centuries), highest score 277, average 48.25, best bowling (innings) 2/145, (match) 2/145; ODIs: 197 matches, took 18 wickets and scored 6,989 runs, highest score 141, average 37.98, best bowling (innings) 3/30, (match) 3/30; T20Is: 33 matches, scored 982 runs, highest score 89 (not out), average 31.67; announced retirement from int. cricket March 2014; South African Cricketer of the Year 2001/02. *Achievements include:* made double centuries in consecutive Test matches: 277 at Edgbaston (highest individual innings ever made for S Africa) and 259 at Lord's (highest score ever made at Lord's by an overseas player) 2008; added 415 for first wicket with Neil McKenzie against Bangladesh (world record opening partnership) 2008. *Address:* c/o Surrey County Cricket Club, The Kia Oval, Kennington, London, SE11 5SS, England. *E-mail:* enquiries@surreycricket.com. *Website:* www .kiaoval.com.

SMITH, Hamilton O., MD; American medical scientist and academic; *Founder and Co-Chief Scientific Officer, Synthetic Genomics, Inc.;* b. 23 Aug. 1931, New York; s. of Tommie Harkey and Bunnie Othanel Smith; m. Elizabeth Anne Bolton 1957; four s. one d.; ed Univ. of Illinois, Univ. of California at Berkeley, Johns Hopkins Univ. School of Medicine, Baltimore, Md; Internship, Barnes Hosp., St Louis, Mo. 1956–57; Lt in USNR, Sr Medical Officer 1957–59; Resident, Henry Ford Hosp., Detroit, Mich. 1960–62; Postdoctoral Fellow, Dept of Human Genetics, Univ. of Mich. 1962–64, Research Assoc. 1964–67; Asst Prof. of Microbiology, Johns Hopkins Univ. School of Medicine 1967–69, Assoc. Prof. 1969–73, Prof. of Microbiology 1973–81, Prof. of Molecular Biology and Genetics 1981, now Prof. Emer.; conducted work at Inst. for Genomic Research –1998; joined Celera Genomics 1998–2002; Scientific Dir Synthetic Biology and Biological Energy Groups, Venter Inst. 2002–; Founder and Co-Chief Scientific Officer Synthetic Genomics, Inc. 2005–; sabbatical year with Inst. für Molekular-Biologie, Univ. of Zurich, Switzerland 1975–76; Guggenheim Fellow 1975–76; mem. NAS 1980, AAAS; Nobel Prize for Physiology and Medicine (jtly) 1978. *Leisure interests:* piano, classical music. *Address:* Synthetic Genomics, Inc., 11149 North Torrey Pines Road, La Jolla, CA 92037 (office); 8222 Carrbridge Circle, Baltimore, MD 21204, USA (home). *Telephone:* (858) 754-2900 (office); (301) 821-5409 (home). *Fax:* (240) 238-0888 (office). *E-mail:* media@syntheticgenomics.com (office). *Website:* www.syntheticgenomics.com (office).

SMITH, Henry (Harry) Sidney, MA, FBA, DLit; British academic; *Professor Emeritus of Egyptology, University College London;* b. 14 June 1928, London; s. of Sidney Smith and Mary W. Smith (née Parker); m. Hazel Flory Leeper 1961 (died 1991); ed Merchant Taylors School, Sandy Lodge, Middx and Christ's Coll., Cambridge; Asst Lecturer in Egyptology, Faculty of Oriental Studies, Cambridge 1954–59, Lecturer 1959–63; Wallis Budge Fellow in Egyptology, Christ's Coll., Cambridge 1955–63; Field Dir Egypt Exploration Soc. Archaeological Survey of Nubia, Epigraphist at Nubian sites 1959–65; Reader in Egyptian Archaeology, Univ. Coll. London 1963–70, Edwards Prof. of Egyptology 1970–86, Prof. Emer. 1986–; Prin. Epigraphist and Site Supervisor, Egypt Exploration Soc., Saqqara, Egypt 1964–70, Field Dir, Sacred Animal Necropolis 1971–76, Anubieion 1976–81, Dir Memphis Project in Egypt 1981–88; Corresp. mem. Deutsches Archäologisches Institut; Medallist, Collège de France, Paris 1984. *Publications:* Preliminary Reports of the EES Archaeological Survey of Egyptian Nubia 1961, A Visit to Ancient Egypt: Memphis and Saqqara, c. 600–30 BC 1974, The Fortress of Buhen, II: The Inscriptions 1976, I: The Archaeological Report (with W. B. Emery and A. Millard) 1979, Saqqara Demotic Papyri I (with W. J. Tait) 1983, The Anubieion at Saqqara, Vols I and II (with D. G. Jeffreys and Lisa L. Giddy) 1988, 1992, The Sculpture from the Sacred Animal Necropolis at North Saqqara 1964–76 (with Elizabeth Anne Hastings) 1997, The Sacred Animal Necropolis at North Saqqara I: The Falcon Complex and Catacomb: The Archaeological Report II: The Main Temple Complex: The Archaeological Report (with Sue Davies) 2005, 2006, The Sacred Animal Necropolis at North Saqqara: The Mother of Apis Inscriptions (with C.A.R. Andrews and Sue Davies) (two vols) 2011; excavation reports, text publications and historical articles in int. journals. *Leisure interests:* varied. *Address:* Ailwyn House, High Street, Upwood, Huntingdon, Cambridgeshire, PE26 2QE, England (home). *Telephone:* (1487) 812196 (home).

SMITH, Hon. James Herbert, CBE, MA; Bahamian politician and business executive; *Deputy Chairman Bahamas Petroleum Company Plc;* b. 26 Oct. 1947, Nassau; s. of Bertram A. Smith and Rosalie B. Smith; m. Portia M. Campbell 1973 (deceased); two s. one d.; ed Ryerson Polytechnical Coll. and Univs of Windsor and Alberta, Canada; Deputy Perm. Sec., Ministry of Econ. Affairs 1977–79; Under-Sec., Cabinet Office 1980–84; Sec. for Revenue, Ministry of Finance 1984–85, Perm. Sec. 1985–86; fmr Chair. Bahamas Devt Bank; Gov. Cen. Bank of the Bahamas 1987–97; Amb. for Trade, Chief Negotiator, Free Trade Area of the Americas discussions 1997–2002; Minister of State for Finance 2002–07; Deputy Chair. Bahamas Petroleum Company PLC 2014–; fmr Chair. Bahamas Maritime Authority, Paradise Island Bridge Co., Bahamas Maritime Museum. *Address:* Bahamas Petroleum Company Plc, Building 3 Western Road, Mount Pleasant Village, PO Box SP-64135, Nassau, Bahamas (office); Bahamas Petroleum Company Plc, IOMA House, Hope Street, Douglas, IM1 1AP, Isle of Man (office). *E-mail:* info.nassau@bpcplc.com (office). *Website:* www.bpcplc.com (office).

SMITH, Jean Kennedy, BA; American foundation executive and diplomatist; b. 20 Feb. 1928, Boston, Mass; d. of Joseph P. Kennedy and Rose Kennedy (née Fitzgerald); m. Stephen E. Smith 1956 (died 1990); two s. two d.; ed Manhattanville Coll.; mem. Bd of Trustees, Joseph P. Kennedy Jr Foundation 1964–, currently also Sec., John F. Kennedy Center for the Performing Arts 1964– (Chair. Educ. Cttee 1964–74 and Founder of Center's children's programs); fmr mem. Bd IRC; f. Very Special Arts (int. program for people with disabilities) 1974; Amb. to Ireland 1993–98; Hon. Irish Citizen; several hon. degrees; Jefferson Award for Outstanding Public Service, American Inst. for Public Service, Margaret Mead Humanitarian Award, Council of Cerebral Palsy Auxiliaries, Irish American of the Year Award, Irish America Magazine 1995, Rotary One Int. Award, Rotary Club of Chicago 1997, Terence Cardinal Cooke Humanitarian Award 1997, Hadassch Volunteer of the Year Award 2003, Presidential Medal of Freedom 2011. *Publication:* Chronicles of Courage: Very Special Artists 1993. *Leisure interests:* the arts, tennis, golf, sailing, reading. *Address:* 4 Sutton Place, New York, NY 10022, USA. *Telephone:* (212) 758-3610. *Fax:* (212) 813-1871.

SMITH, Dame Jennifer Meredith, DBE, JP; Bermudian politician; b. 14 Oct. 1947; d. of Eugene O. Smith and Lillian E. Smith; began career as journalist; reporter, Bermuda Recorder 1970–74, Ed. 1974; on staff of Fame magazine, later Ed.; joined ZBM Radio and TV; art teacher at Sr Training School (attached to Bermuda Prison Service) for eight years; represented Bermuda as an artist at CARIFESTA in Jamaica; last exhbn in 1996; contested St George's N seat for Progressive Labour Party (PLP) in House of Ass. elections 1972, 1976, 1980; mem. Senate 1980–89; fmr Shadow Minister for Educ.; mem. House of Ass. (PLP) 1989, 1993, 1998–, Deputy Speaker 2003–; Leader of PLP 1996–2003; Prime Minister of Bermuda 1998–2003; Minister of Educ. 2010–12; fmr Exec. mem. Commonwealth Parl. Asscn; Fellow, Harvard Univ., Cambridge, USA 2015; Hon. DHumLitt (Mount St Vincent, Morris Brown Coll., Art Inst. of Pittsburgh); Outstanding Woman in Journalism Award 1972 and several other awards. *Publication:* Voice of Change 2003. *Leisure interests:* painting, dancing, reading, working with young people, writing, collecting match-book covers and first day stamp covers. *Address:* PO Box HM 2191, Hamilton HMHX, Bermuda (home). *Website:* voiceofchange.bm.

SMITH, Lt Gen. (retd) Joseph Henry; Ghanaian army officer (retd), government official and diplomatist; b. 9 Jan. 1945, Takoradi; m.; five c.; ed Ghana Mil. Acad.; Commdt Mil. Acad. and Training School 1992–93; Commdr 2nd Infantry Brigade Group 1993–96; Special Task Force Commdr to restore law and order in

Northern Ghana 1994; Co. Commdr UNEF 1996; Commdr Ghana Army 1996–2001; Chair. Nat. Insurance Comm. –2009; Minister of Defence 2009–13; Amb. to USA 2014–17; mem. Nat. Security Bd 1996–2001, Ghana Armed Forces Command and Staff Coll. Control Bd 1996–2001; Companion, Order of the Volta 2001, Legion of Merit (USA); Ghana/UN Peace Keeping Award 1976, West African Defense Minister of the Year, African Leadership magazine 2012, Golden Star Award for Distinguished Leadership, Security Watch Africa 2012, Legion of Merit (USA).

JOHNSON SMITH, Kamina, LLM; Jamaican lawyer and politician; *Minister of Foreign Affairs and Foreign Trade;* b. St Andrews; m. Jason Smith; ed LSE, Univ. of the West Indies; Govt Senator 2009–12, Opposition Senator 2012–16, fmr Leader of Govt Business and Chair. of Various Cttees; Minister of Foreign Affairs and Foreign Trade 2016–; Chair. Caribbean Forum of the African, Caribbean and Pacific Group of States 2016–17; Pres. Council of Ministers, African, Caribbean, and Pacific Group of States Feb.–July 2018; worked at Jamaican Bar; served as Co.-Sec. and Head of Corporate Affairs and Project, Cable & Wireless Jamaica Ltd; served on Corporate Governance Cttee, Private Sector Org. of Jamaica; Dir Factories Corpn of Jamaica, Early Childhood Comm.; mem. Jamaica Labour Party; fmr Opposition Whip, Spokesperson on Education and Youth. *Leisure interest:* sports, yoga, reading, dance. *Address:* Ministry of Foreign Affairs and Foreign Trade, 21 Dominica Drive., POB 624, Kingston 5, Jamaica (office). *Telephone:* 926-4220 (office). *Fax:* 929-6733 (office). *E-mail:* info@mfaft.gov.jm (office). *Website:* www.mfaft.gov.jm.

SMITH, Kevin Patrick; American director, film producer, screenwriter, author and actor; b. 2 Aug. 1970, Highlands, New Jersey; s. of Donald E. Smith and Grace Smith; m. Jennifer Schwalbach Smith 1994; one d.; ed Henry Hudson Regional High School, The New School, Vancouver Film School, Canada; Co-founder (with Scott Mosier) of View Askew Productions; Owner of Jay and Silent Bob's Secret Stash comic and novelty store in Red Bank, New Jersey; hosts a weekly podcast with Scott Mosier known as SModcast. *Films include:* Mae Day: The Crumbling of a Documentary 1992, Clerks 1994, Mallrats 1995, Drawing Flies (producer) 1996, A Better Place (producer) 1996, Good Will Hunting (producer) 1996, Overnight Delivery (writer) 1997, Chasing Amy 1997, Superman Lives (writer) 1998, Tail Lights Fade 1999, Big Helium Dog 1999, Dogma 1999, The Six Million Dollar Man (writer) 2000, Coyote Ugly (writer) 2000 Vulgar 2000, Scream 3 (actor) 2000, Jay and Silent Bob Strike Back 2001, The Concert for New York City 2001, The Flying Car 2001, Now You Know (actor) 2002, Daredevil (actor) 2003, Jersey Girl 2004, Reel Paradise (producer) 2005, Clerks II 2006, Small Town Gay Bar (producer) 2006, Doogal (actor) 2006, Bottoms Up (actor) 2006, Southland Tales (actor) 2006, Catch and Release (actor) 2007, Superman: Doomsday (actor) 2007, TMNT (actor) 2007, Degrassi Goes Hollywood (actor) 2007, Live Free or Die Hard (actor and writer) 2007, Zack and Miri Make a Porno 2008, Fanboys (actor) 2009, Cop Out 2010, Bear Nation (producer) 2010, 4.3.2.1 (actor) 2010, Red State 2011, Tusk (dir) 2014, Holidays (dir) 2015. *Television includes:* Hiatus (writer) 1996, Law & Order (actor) 2000, Clerks: The Animated Series (actor and producer) 2000, Duck Dodgers (actor) 2003, Yes, Dear (actor) 2004, Veronica Mars (actor) 2005, Joey (actor) 2005, Degrassi: The Next Generation (actor) 2005, Sucks Less with Kevin Smith (producer) 2006, Reaper (also producer) 2007, Phineas and Ferb (actor) 2010. *Music videos:* Can't Even Tell (Soul Asylum) as Silent Bob (also directed), Build Me Up Buttercup (The Goops) as Silent Bob, Because I Got High (Afroman) as Silent Bob, Kick Some Ass (Stroke 9) as Silent Bob. *Publications include:* books: Silent Bob Speaks 2005, My Boring Ass Life: The Uncomfortably Candid Diary of Kevin Smith 2007, Shootin' the Sh*t with Kevin Smith 2009, Tough Shit: Life Advice from a Fat, Lazy Slob Who Did Good 2012, Jay and Silent Bob's Blueprints For Destroying Everything 2014; comics: Spider-Man/Black Cat: The Evil that Men Do (with Terry Dodson) 2002, 2005–06, Green Arrow: Quiver (with Phil Hester) 2001–02, Green Arrow: The Sound of Violence (with Phil Hester) 2002, Batman: Cacophony (with Walt Flanagan) 2008–09, Batman: The Widening Gyre (with Walt Flanagan) 2009–10, Green Hornet (with Jonathan Lau) 2010, The Bionic Man (with Jonathan Lau and Phil Hester) 2011–12, Batman '66 Meets the Green Hornet (with Ty Templeton) 2014, Batman: Bellicosity (with Walt Flanagan) 2015. *E-mail:* viewaskew@viewaskew.com (office). *Website:* www.viewaskew.com (office); www.smodcast.com.

SMITH, Gen. (retd) Lance L., BA, MA; American army officer (retd); ed Virginia Polytechnic Inst., Cen. Michigan Univ., Air Command and Staff Coll., Ala, Army War Coll., Pa, Advanced Exec. Program, J.L. Kellogg Grad. School of Man., Northwestern Univ., Evanston, Ill.; entered USAF in 1970, commanded two fighter wings and led two air expeditionary force deployments to SW Asia: AEF III and the 4th Air Expeditionary Wing, served as Commdr of 7th Air Force, Pacific Air Forces, Air Component Commdr Repub. of Korea and US Combined Forces Command, Korea, Deputy Commdr US Forces, Korea, served two tours at the Pentagon and was Commdt of the NATO School at Supreme HQ Allied Powers Europe, Commdt of Air War Coll. and Commdr Air Force Doctrine Center, Deputy Commdr US Cen. Command, MacDill Air Force Base, Fla, Commdr US Jt Forces Command (USJFCOM) and NATO Supreme Allied Commdr for Transformation (ACT), Norfolk, Va 2005–07, retd 2008; flew more than 165 combat missions in SE and SW Asia in the A-1 Skyraider and the F-15E Strike Eagle, command pilot with more than 3,000 hours in the T-33, T-37, T-38, A-1, A-7, A-10, F-111F, F-15E and F-16 aircraft; rank of Second Lt 1970, First Lt, Capt. 1973, Maj. 1978, Lt-Col 1982, Col 1989, Brig.-Gen. 1995, Maj.-Gen. 1998, Lt-Gen. 2002, Gen. 2005; mem. Bd of Dirs North Carolina Military Foundation; Special Advisor, Rylex Consulting; Defense DSM, DSM, Silver Star with two oak leaf clusters, Defense Superior Service Medal, Legion of Merit with oak leaf cluster, DFC with two oak leaf clusters, Purple Heart, Meritorious Service Medal with three oak leaf clusters, Air Medal with one silver and four bronze oak leaf clusters, Aerial Achievement Medal with oak leaf cluster, Air Force Commendation Medal, Army Commendation Medal, Humanitarian Service Medal, Honor Cross of the Bundeswehr Medal (FRG), Order of Nat. Security Merit Gukseon Medal (Repub. of Korea), Order of Nat. Security Merit Cheonsu Medal (Repub. of Korea), Repub. of Viet Nam Gallantry Cross with Palm; Distinguished Achievement Award, Virginia Tech Univ. 2010. *Address:* c/o Rylex Consulting LLC, Landfall Executive Suites, 1213 Culbreth Drive, Wilmington, NC 28405, USA.

SMITH, Lanty Lloyd, BS, LLB; American lawyer and banking executive; *Chairman, Precision Fabrics Group, Inc.;* b. 11 Dec. 1942, Sherrodsville, Ohio; m. Margaret Smith; three d.; ed Wittenberg Univ., Duke Univ.; Assoc. Jones, Day, Cockley & Reavis (law firm), Cleveland 1967–73, Partner, Jones Day, Reavis & Pogue 1974–77; Exec. Vice-Pres. and Sr Gen. Counsel Burlington Industries, Greensboro, N Carolina 1977–86, Pres. 1986–88; Chair. Precision Fabrics Group Inc. (est. to purchase existing businesses of Precision Fabrics Div. of Burlington Industries) 1988–; apptd mem. Bd of Dirs Wachovia Corpn, Charlotte, N Carolina 1987, Lead Ind. Dir 2000–08, Chair. and interim CEO June–July 2008 Chair. July 2008; Co-founder and Chair. Exec. Cttee of Bd of Dirs The Greenwood Group, Inc. 1992; Chair. and CEO Tippet Capital (merchant banking firm), Raleigh, NC 2007–; Founder and Chair. Scion Neurostim (medical device devt co) 2007–; Pres. and CEO MediWave Star Tech Inc. 1999–; mem. Bd of Dirs Piedmont Pharmaceuticals 2007–, N Carolina Inst. of Medicine; f. Piedmont Angel Network; mem. Advisory Cttee Triad Health Project, Cen. N Carolina Chapter of Multiple Sclerosis Soc., Reading Connections; Trustee Emer., Duke Univ.; Americanism Award from Anti-Defamation League, Greensboro Outstanding Community Service Award, Class of 1914 Award, Wittenberg Univ. 2007. *Address:* Precision Fabrics Group, Inc., 301 North Elm Street, Greensboro, NC 27401, USA (office). *Telephone:* (800) 284-0000 (office). *Website:* www.precisionfabrics.com (office).

SMITH, Rt Hon. Sir Lockwood, Kt, KNZM, PhD; New Zealand diplomatist and fmr politician; m. Alexandra Smith; ed Auckland Grammar School, Massey Univ., Adelaide Univ. (Commonwealth Scholar); trained opera singer; ran a beef farming operation with his wife; fmr univ. lecturer; hosted educational children's TV shows in Australia and NZ; Marketing Man. for Cen. and SE Asia, New Zealand Dairy Board –1984; MP 1984–2013 (retd), Speaker, House of Reps 2008–13; served as Sr Minister in various portfolios, including Educ., Agric. and Trade; also served as Deputy Minister of Finance, Minister of Forestry, Minister of Tourism, Minister Responsible for Contact Energy Ltd, Minister Responsible for the Educ. Review Office and Minister Responsible for Nat. Library; High Commr to UK (also accred to Nigeria and Ghana and as Amb. to Ireland) 2013–17. *Leisure interest:* sports and fitness.

SMITH, Dame Maggie Natalie, CH, DBE; British actress; b. 28 Dec. 1934, Ilford, Essex; d. of Nathaniel Smith and Margaret Little; m. 1st Robert Stephens 1967 (divorced 1975, died 1995); two s.; m. 2nd Beverley Cross 1975 (died 1998); ed Oxford High School for Girls; first appeared with Oxford Univ. Dramatic Soc. (OUDS) in Twelfth Night 1952; appeared in revue New Faces New York 1956, Share My Lettuce 1957, The Stepmother 1958; with Old Vic Co. 1959–60 playing in The Double Dealer, As You Like It, Richard II, The Merry Wives of Windsor, What Every Woman Knows; other appearances include Rhinoceros 1960, Strip the Willow 1960, The Rehearsal 1961, The Private Ear and The Public Eye 1962, Mary, Mary 1963; with Nat. Theatre played in The Recruiting Officer 1963, Othello (Desdemona) 1964, The Master Builder 1964, Hay Fever 1964, Much Ado About Nothing 1965, Miss Julie 1965, A Bond Honoured 1966, The Beaux' Stratagem 1970, Hedda Gabler 1970, Three Sisters, Design for Living (Los Angeles) 1971, Private Lives, London 1972, USA 1974–75, Peter Pan 1973, Snap 1974; played 1976, 1977, 1978 and 1980 seasons, Stratford, Ont., Canada, Night and Day 1979, Virginia, London 1981, The Way of the World, Chichester Festival and London 1984–85, Interpreters, London 1985, The Infernal Machine 1986, Coming in to Land 1987, Lettice and Lovage, London 1987, New York 1990, The Importance of Being Earnest 1993, Three Tall Women 1994–95, Talking Heads 1996, A Delicate Balance 1997, The Lady in the Van 1999, The Breath of Life 2002, Talking Heads (Australian tour) 2004, The Lady from Dubuque 2007; Dir United British Artists 1992–; Hon. DLit (St Andrew's, Leicester) 1982, (Cambridge) 1993; Hon. DLitt (Bath) 1986; Evening Standard Best Actress Award 1962, 1970, 1982, 1985, 1994; Variety Club Actress of the Year 1963; LA Critics Award Best Actress 1970; Variety Club Award Best Stage Actress 1972 (plays); Acad. Award for Best Actress 1969, for Best Supporting Actress 1979; Best Actress Award from Soc. of Film and TV Arts (UK) 1969; Best Actress Award from Film Critics' Guild (USA) 1969 (films), BAFTA Award for Best Actress 1984, 1987, 1989, BAFTA Award for Lifetime Achievement 1992, BAFTA Award for Best Supporting Actress (for Tea with Mussolini); Tony Award 1990; Shakespeare Prize, FVS Foundation, Hamburg 1991. *Films include:* Child in the House (uncredited) 1956, Nowhere to Go 1958, Go to Blazes 1962, The V.I.P.s 1963, The Pumpkin Eater 1964, Young Cassidy 1965, Othello 1965, The Honey Pot 1967, Hot Millions 1968, The Prime of Miss Jean Brodie 1969, Oh! What a Lovely War 1969, Travels with My Aunt 1972, Love and Pain and the Whole Damn Thing 1973, Murder by Death 1975, Death on the Nile 1978, California Suite 1978, Quartet 1981, Clash of the Titans 1981, Better Late Than Never 1982, Evil Under the Sun 1982, Ménage à Trois 1982, The Missionary 1982, Lily in Live 1984, A Private Function 1984, A Room with a View 1985, The Lonely Passion of Judith Hearn 1987, Paris by Night 1988, Romeo-Juliet (voice) 1990, Hook 1991, Sister Act 1992, The Secret Garden 1993, Sister Act 2: Back in the Habit 1993, Richard III 1995, The First Wives Club 1996, Washington Square 1998, Tea with Mussolini 1999, Curtain Call 1999, The Last September 1999, Harry Potter and The Philosopher's Stone 2001, Gosford Park 2002, Divine Secrets of the Ya-Ya Sisterhood 2002, Harry Potter and the Chamber of Secrets 2002, Ladies in Lavender 2004, Harry Potter and the Prisoner of Azkaban 2004, Harry Potter and the Goblet of Fire 2005, Keeping Mum 2005, Becoming Jane 2007, Harry Potter and the Order of the Phoenix 2007, Harry Potter and the Half-Blood Prince 2009, From Time to Time 2009, Nanny McPhee and the Big Bang 2010, Gnomeo and Juliet 2011, Harry Potter and the Deathly Hallows: Part 2 2011, The Best Exotic Marigold Hotel 2011, Quartet 2012, My Old Lady 2014, The Best Exotic Marigold Hotel 2 2015, The Lady in the Van 2015. *Television includes:* Kraft TV Theatre (Night of the Plague) 1957, Hay Fever 1960, Much Ado About Nothing 1967, Play of the Month (Man and Superman 1968, The Seagull 1968, The Merchant of Venice 1972, The Millionairess 1972, Mrs. Silly 1983, Talking Heads (mini-series) 1987, Memento Mori 1992, Suddenly, Last Summer 1993, All the King's Men 1999, David Copperfield 1999, My House in Umbria (Emmy Award for Best Actress) 2003, Capturing Mary 2007, Downton Abbey (series) (Emmy Award for Outstanding Supporting Actress in a Mini-series or Movie 2011, 2012, 2016, Golden Globe Award for Best Performance by an Actress in a Supporting Role in a Series, Mini-Series or Motion Picture Made for TV 2013, Screen Actors Guild Award for Outstanding Performance by a Female Actor in a Drama Series 2014) 2010–15. *Leisure interest:* reading. *Address:* c/o Independent, Oxford House, 76

Oxford Street, London, W1D 1BS, England (office). *Telephone:* (20) 7636-6565 (office). *Fax:* (20) 7323-0101 (office). *E-mail:* info@independenttalent.com (office). *Website:* www.independenttalent.com (office).

SMITH, Martin (William) Cruz, BA; American writer; b. 3 Nov. 1942, Reading, Pa; s. of John Smith and Louise Lopez; m. Emily Arnold 1968; two d. one s.; ed Univ. of Pennsylvania; fmr newspaper reporter and ed.; CWA Golden Dagger Award 1981, Left Coast Crime Lifetime Achievement Award 2011. *Publications include:* The Indians Won 1970, Gypsy in Amber 1971, Analog Bullet 1972, Canto for a Gypsy 1972, Gorky Park (Gold Dagger Award, Crime Writers Asscn 1981) 1981, Nightwing 1977, Stallion Gate 1986, Polar Star 1989, Red Square 1992, Rose (Hammett Prize, Int. Asscn of Crime Writers 1996) 1996, Havana Bay (Hammett Prize, Int. Asscn of Crime Writers 1999) 1999, December 6 (aka Tokyo Station) 2002, Wolves Eat Dogs 2004, Stalin's Ghost 2007, Three Stations 2010, Tatiana 2013, The Girl from Venice 2016. *Address:* c/o Publicity Department, Simon & Schuster, Inc., 1230 Avenue of the Americas, New York, NY 10020, USA (office). *Website:* www.martincruzsmith.com.

SMITH, Michael, TD; Irish politician and fmr farmer; b. Nov. 1940, Roscrea, Co. Tipperary; m. Mary T. Ryan; one s. six d.; ed Univ. Coll. Cork; mem. Irish Farmers' Asscn 1969–; mem. Tipperary North Riding Co. Council 1967–88, Chair. 1986–87; mem. Dáil 1969–73, 1977–82, 1987–2007; Minister of State, Dept of Agric. 1980–81; Senator 1982–87, Agric. Panel 1982–83, Culture and Educ. Panel 1983–87; Minister of State, Dept of Energy 1987–88; Minister for Energy 1988–89; Minister of State, Dept of Industry and Commerce 1989–91; Minister for the Environment 1992–94, for Defence 1997–2004; mem. Fianna Fáil. *Address:* Lismackin, Roscrea, Co. Tipperary, Ireland (home). *Telephone:* (505) 43157 (home).

SMITH, Michael Roger Pearson, OBE, BSc; British banker; b. 10 Sept. 1956; m.; three c.; ed City Univ., London; joined HSBC Group 1978, Man. Planning, Hongkong and Shanghai Banking Corpn Ltd, Hong Kong 1984–85, Man. Wholesale Banking, Australia 1985–87, State Man., New South Wales 1987–90, with Planning Dept, Midland Bank (now HSBC Bank), UK 1990–93, Man. Dir Int., Midland Bank 1993–95, Exec. Dir and Deputy CEO Hongkong Bank Malaysia Berhad (now HSBC Bank Malaysia Berhad) 1995–97, CEO HSBC Argentina Holdings SA 1997–2000, Chair. 2000–03, HSBC Group Gen. Man. 2000–07, Pres. and CEO Hongkong and Shanghai Banking Corpn Ltd 2004–07, Chair. HSBC Bank Malaysia Berhad 2004–07, Chair. Hang Seng Bank Ltd 2005–07; Exec. Dir and CEO Australia and New Zealand Banking Group Ltd (ANZ) 2007–15, Adviser to Bd 2015–17; fmr mem. Bd Dirs Visa International Asia Pacific 2005–07; mem. Chongqing Mayor's Int. Econ. Advisory Council 2006–; Fellow, The Hong Kong Man. Asscn 2005–; Chevalier, Ordre du Mérite agricole 2007. *Leisure interests:* viniculture, golf, tennis, classic cars, art, antiques.

SMITH, Patti; American singer, songwriter, musician (guitar), poet and artist; b. 30 Dec. 1946, Chicago, Ill.; d. of Grant Smith and Beverly Smith; m. Fred 'Sonic' Smith 1980 (died 1994); two s.; ed Glassboro State Teachers Coll., NJ; avant-garde poet, singer and artist; fmr rock critic for Creem, Rock, Crawdaddy and Rolling Stone magazines 1970s; solo artist 1972–, forming Patti Smith Group 1974; Artistic Dir Meltdown Festival, South Bank Centre, London 2005; Commdr, Ordre des Arts et des Lettres 2005; Dr hc (Wesleyan Univ.) 2016; inducted into Rock and Roll Hall of Fame 2007, ASCAP Founders Award 2010, Polar Music Prize, Royal Swedish Acad. of Music 2011, Katharine Hepburn Medal, Bryn Mawr Coll. 2013. *Recordings include:* albums: Horses 1975, Radio Ethiopia 1976, Easter 1978, Wave 1979, Dream Of Life 1988, Gone Again 1996, Peace And Noise 1997, Gung Ho 2000, Land 1975–2002 2002, Twelve 2007, The Coral Sea (with Kevin Shields) 2008, Banga 2012. *Publications:* Seventh Heaven (poems) 1971, Kodak (poems) 1972, Cowboy Mouth (play, with Sam Shepard) 1972, Witt (poems) 1973, Babel 1978, Early Work 1970–1979 (poems) 1980, Woolgathering (short stories) 1993, The Coral Sea (prose poems in memory of Robert Mapplethorpe) 1996, Auguries of Innocence (poems) 2006, Just Kids (Nat. Book Award for Non-Fiction 2010) 2010, M Train 2015. *Website:* www.pattismith.net (home).

SMITH, Sir Paul Brierley, Kt, CBE; British fashion designer and retailer; b. 5 July 1946, Nottingham; s. of Harold B. Smith and Marjorie Smith; ed Beeston Fields School, Nottingham; first Paul Smith Shop opened, Nottingham 1970, others in London 1979, 1982, 1983, 1987, 1998, 2001, New York 1987, first Paul Smith franchise shop in Hong Kong 1990, flagship store Tokyo, Japan 1991 (now over 220 shops in Japan), first Milan shop 2001, first stand-alone accessories shop, London 2001, shop at London Heathrow Terminal 3 2002; first Paul Smith Collection Show, Paris 1976; launched Paul Smith for Women 1994; designed limited edn Mini 1998; launched fragrances range for men and women 2000, two fragrances 'Paul Smith Extreme' 2002, collection of furniture with Cappellini 2002; designed collection of rugs for The Rug Company 2002–03; launched collection of Swiss-made watches 2003, collection of writing instruments 2003; Royal Designer for Industry RCA 1991; Dr hc (Nottingham Polytechnic) 1991; Queen's Award for Industry 1995. *Address:* Paul Smith Ltd, 20 Kean Street, London, WC2B 4AS, England (office). *Telephone:* (20) 7836-7828 (office). *Fax:* (20) 7379-0241 (office). *Website:* www.paulsmith.co.uk (office).

SMITH, Robert Clinton, BA; American organization official and fmr politician; b. 30 March 1941, Trenton, New Jersey; s. of Donald Smith and Margaret Eldridge; m. Mary Jo Hutchinson 1966; two s. one d.; ed Lafayette Coll. and Long Beach State Univ.; Reservist, USN 1962–65, active duty including one year in Viet Nam 1965–67; served in Naval Reserve 1967–69; Owner and Man., Yankee Pedlar Realtors, Wolfeboro, New Hampshire 1975–85; mem. US House of Reps from 1st Dist of NH 1985–91; Senator from New Hampshire 1990–2002, fmr Chair. Cttee on Environment and Public Works, Cttee on Armed Services, Cttee on the Judiciary, Select Cttee on Ethics; unsuccessful campaign for Republican nomination for Senator from Fla 2004; Pres. Everglades Foundation 2004–07; Republican; Co-Chair. Cruz for President military coalition Vets for Ted 2015; Nat. Security Leadership Award, Airline Security Award, Allied Pilots Asscn, Golden Gavel Award, Honoree, Humane Soc. of the United States, Disabled Army Veterans, American Legion.

SMITH, Roberta, BA; American art critic; *Senior Art Critic, The New York Times;* b. New York City; d. of Thomas R. Smith and Eleanor Smith; m. Jerry Saltz 1992; ed Lawrence High School, Grinnell Coll.; participated in Whitney Museum's Ind. Study Program; became a studio asst to sculptor Donald Judd; also worked

with Paula Cooper during early years of SoHo gallery devoted to contemporary art; began working as a professional art critic 1970s, writing for journals such as Arts, Artforum and Art in America 1976–80; Art Critic for the Village Voice 1981–85, for New York Times 1986–, now Sr Art Critic; served as guest curator and catalogue essayist for exhbn Four Artists and the Map at Kansas Univ.'s Spencer Museum of Art 1981; Frank Jewett Mather Award for Art Criticism, Coll. Art Asscn 2003, Franklin D. Murphy Lecturer, Spencer Museum of Art and Kress Foundation Dept of Art History at Univ. of Kansas together with Nelson-Atkins Museum of Art, Kansas City 2004, Lifetime Achievement Award, Dorothea and Leo Rabkin Foundation 2019. *Address:* The New York Times, 620 Eighth Avenue, New York, NY 10018, USA (office). *Telephone:* (212) 556-1234 (office). *E-mail:* thearts@nytimes.com (office). *Website:* www.nytimes.com (office); www.nytimes.com/by/roberta-smith (office).

SMITH, Roland Hedley, CMG, MA; British fmr diplomatist; *Clerk, Wakefield & Tetley Trust;* b. 11 April 1943, Sheffield, Yorks.; s. of Alan Hedley Smith and Elizabeth Louise Smith; m. Katherine Jane Lawrence 1971; two d.; ed King Edward VII School, Sheffield, Keble Coll. Oxford; joined Diplomatic Service 1967; Second Sec. Moscow 1969–71; Second, later First Sec., UK Del. to NATO, Brussels 1971–74; at FCO, London 1974–78; First Sec. and Cultural Attaché, Moscow 1978–80; at FCO 1980–83; mem. staff Int. Inst. for Strategic Studies 1983–84; Political Adviser, British Mil. Govt, Berlin 1984–88; at FCO 1988–92; Minister, UK Del. to NATO, Brussels 1992–95; Dir Int. Security, FCO 1995–98; Amb. to Ukraine 1999–2002; Dir St Ethelburga's Centre for Reconciliation and Peace, London 2002–04; Clerk, Wakefield (now Wakefield & Tetley) Trust 2004–. *Leisure interests:* music, especially choral singing, football (Sheffield United), trams. *Address:* Wakefield & Tetley Trust, Oxford House, Derbyshire Street, London, E2 6HG, England (office). *Telephone:* (20) 7749-1118 (office). *E-mail:* roland.smith@wakefieldtrust.org.uk (office). *Website:* www.wakefieldtrust.org.uk (office).

SMITH, Rosamond (see OATES, Joyce Carol).

SMITH, Gen. Sir Rupert Anthony, Kt, KCB, DSO, OBE, QGM; British army officer (retd); b. 13 Dec. 1943; ed Imperial Service Coll., Royal Military Acad., Sandhurst; with Parachute Regt 1964; Deputy Commdt, Staff Col, Camberley 1989–90; Commdr 1st Armoured Div. BAOR, Gulf 1990–92; Asst Chief of Defence Staff (Operations) 1992–94; Commdr UN Protection Force, Bosnia-Herzegovina 1995; GOC and Dir of Mil. Operations, NI 1996–98; Deputy Supreme Allied Commdr in Europe 1998–2002; ADC Gen. to the Queen 2000–02; currrently consultant and adviser on security and defence matters; Visiting Prof., Dept of Politics and Int. Relations, Univ. of Reading; Order of Abdulaziz Al Saud 3rd Class (Saudi Arabia); Queen's Gallantry Medal 1978. *Publication:* The Utility of Force: The Art of War in the Modern World 2005. *Address:* Department of Politics and International Relations, University of Reading, Whiteknights, PO Box 218, Reading, Berks., RG6 6AA, England (office). *E-mail:* politics@reading.ac.uk (office). *Website:* www.reading.ac.uk/spirs (office).

SMITH, Stephen Francis, LLM; Australian politician; *Winthrop Professor of International Law, University of Western Australia;* b. 12 Dec. 1955, Narrogin, WA; ed Univ. of Western Australia, London Univ., UK; solicitor, lecturer and tutor 1978–83; Prin. Pvt. Sec. to State Attorney-Gen., WA 1983–87; mem. Australian Labor Party Nat. Exec. 1987–90, Jr Vice-Pres. 1989–90; Adviser to Treas. P. J. Keating 1991, to Minister for Science and Tech. R. V. Free 1991, to Prime Minister P. J. Keating 1991–92; MP for Perth 1993–2013, Shadow Minister for Trade 1996–97, for Resources and Energy 1997–98, for Communications 1998–2001, for Health and Ageing 2001–04, for Industry, Infrastructure and Industrial Relations 2004–06, for Educ. and Training 2006–07, Minister for Foreign Affairs 2007–10, for Defence 2010–13; Winthrop Prof. of Int. Law, Univ. of Western Australia 2014–. *Address:* Fauclty of Law, The University of Western Australia, 35 Stirling Highway, Crawley, Perth, WA 6009, Australia (office). *Telephone:* (8) 6488-2945 (office). *Fax:* (8) 6488-1045 (office). *Website:* www.law.uwa.edu.au/ (office).

SMITH, Steve; Australian cricketer; b. (Steven Peter Devereux Smith), 2 June 1989, Sydney, NSW; s. Peter Smith and Gillian Smith; m. Dani Willis 2018; right-handed batsman; right-arm leg spinner; played for NSW Blues 2007–, Royal Challengers Bangalore 2010, Worcestershire 2011, Kochi Tuskers Kerala 2011, Sydney Sixers 2011–, Pune Warriors India 2012–13, Antigua Hawksbills 2013, Rajasthan Royals 2014–15, Rising Pune Supergiants 2016–17; ODI debut: Australia vs West Indies, Melbourne 19 Feb. 2010; Test debut: Australia vs Pakistan, Lord's 13–16 July 2010; T20 debut: Australia vs Pakistan, Melbourne 5 Feb. 2010; Capt. Australian Test side 2015–18, One Day Int. (ODI) 2015–18, T20 Int. 2015–18; fastest Australian batsman to reach 10,000 int. runs; youngest Australian batsman to reach 6,000 runs in Test cricket; banned for 12 months from int. and domestic cricket for ball-tempering incident 2018; McGilvray Medal 2014, 2015, 2016, 2017, Sir Garfield Sobers Trophy 2015, ICC Test Player of the Year 2015, 2017, Allan Border Medal 2015, 2018, Australian Test Player of the Year 2015, 2018, Australian One-Day Int. Player of the Year 2015, Compton-Miller Medal 2017–18. *Address:* c/o Warren Craig, Turning Point Management, PO Box 624, Castle Hill, Sydney, NSW 1765, Australia (office). *Telephone:* (2) 9899-1339 (office); 412-311-074 (mobile) (office). *E-mail:* warren@tpmgt.com.au (office). *Website:* www.tpmgt.com.au (office).

SMITH, Tina Flint, BA, MBA; American politician; *Senator from Minnesota;* b. 4 March 1958, Albuquerque, New Mexico; m. Archie Smith; two c.; ed Stanford Univ., Dartmouth Coll.; began career with Marketing Dept, General Mills, Inc. 1980s; Partner, MacWilliams Cosgrove Smith Robinson (public relations co.) 1992–98; Vice Pres. of External Affairs, Planned Parenthood Minnesota, North Dakota, South Dakota 2003–06; Chief of Staff for Mayor of Minneapolis R. T. Rybak 2006–10; Campaign Man. for Rybak during gubernatorial campaign 2010; Chief of Staff for Gov. of Minn. Mark Dayton 2011–15; Lt-Gov. of Minn. 2015–18; Senator from Minn. 2018–; Democrat. *Address:* 309 Hart Senate Office Building, Washington, DC 20510, USA (office). *Telephone:* (202) 224-5641 (office). *Website:* www.smith.senate.gov (office).

SMITH, (Tony) Anthony David Hawthorn, BA BComm; Australian politician; *Speaker of House of Representatives;* b. 13 March 1967, Melbourne; s. of Alan Smith and Noel Smith; m. Pam Smith; two s.; ed Univ. of Melbourne; Research Asst, Inst. of Public Affairs 1989–90; Media Adviser to Peter Costello, MP 1990–98, Sr Political Adviser to the Treasurer 1998–2001; mem. House of Representatives

(Casey, Vic., Liberal) 2001–; Parl. Sec. to the Prime Minister 2007; Shadow Minister for Educ., Apprenticeships and Training from 2007–08, for Broadband, Communications and the Digital Economy 2009–10, Shadow Asst Treas. 2008–09, Shadow Parl. Sec. for Tax Reform 2010–13; Deputy Chair., Coalition Policy Devt Cttee 2010–13; Chair. Jt Standing Cttee on Electoral Matters 2013–15, Chair. Coalition Backbench Economics and Finance Policy Cttee 2013–15; Speaker of the House of Representatives 2015–. *Leisure interests:* rowing, history, football, restoring classic cars. *Address:* PO Box 6022, House of Representatives, Parliament House, Canberra, ACT 2600 (office); PO Box 40, Suite 1, 1 East Ridge Drive, Chirnside Park, VIC 3116, Australia (office). *Telephone:* (3) 9727-0799 (office); (2) 6277-4000 (office). *Fax:* (3) 9727-0833 (office); (2) 6277-2050 (office). *E-mail:* Tony.Smith.MP@aph.gov.au (home). *Website:* www.tonysmithmp.com (home); www.liberal.org.au (office); www.aph.gov.au (office).

SMITH, Vernon L., BSEE, MA, PhD, FAAS; American economist and academic; *George L. Argyros Endowed Chair in Finance and Economics and Professor of Economics and Law, Chapman University;* b. 1 Jan. 1927, Wichita; m. Candace Smith; ed Calif. Inst. of Tech., Univ. of Kansas and Harvard Univ.; Instructor in Econs Univ. of Kansas 1951–52; Economist, Harvard Econs Research Project 1954–55; mem. Man. Sciences Research Group, Purdue Univ. 1955–56, Asst Prof. 1956–58, Assoc. Prof. 1958–61, Prof. 1961–67, Krannert Outstanding Professorship 1964–67; Research Consultant Rand Corpn 1957–59; Contrib. Ed. Business Scope 1957–62; Visiting Prof. Stanford Univ. 1961–62; Prof. of Econs Brown Univ. 1967–68; Prof. of Econs Univ. of Mass. 1968–75; Visiting Prof. Univ. of Southern Calif. and Calif. Inst. of Tech. 1974–75; Prof. of Econs Univ. of Ariz. 1975–2001, Regents Prof. of Econs 1988–2001, McClelland Prof. of Econs 1998–2001; Research Dir Econ. Science Lab. 1986–2001; Prof. of Econs and Law George Mason Univ. (GMU), Arlington, Va 2001–08, now Prof. Emer., Dir and Research Scholar, Interdisciplinary Center for Econ. Science 2001, Research Fellow, Mercatus Center 2001; George L. Argyros Endowed Chair. in Finance and Economics and Prof. of Economics and Law, Chapman Univ. 2008–; Fellow, Econometric Soc. 1988, AAAS 1990, American Acad. of Arts and Sciences 1991; Distinguished Fellow, American Econ. Asscn 1992; mem. Editorial Bd American Econ. Review 1969–72, The Cato Journal, Journal of Economic Behavior and Organization (Assoc. Ed. 1985), Journal of Risk and Uncertainty, Science 1988–91, Economic Theory, Economic Design 1994, Games and Economic Behavior, Journal of Economic Methodology 1995; mem. NAS 1995–; mem. Acad. Advisory Council, Inst. of Econ. Affairs, UK 1993; Founding Pres. Econ. Science Asscn 1986–87; Pres. Public Choice Soc. 1988–90, Western Econ. Asscn 1990–91, Asscn for Pvt. Enterprise Educ. 1997, Int. Foundation for Research in Experimental Econs 1997; fmr Ford Foundation Faculty Research Fellow; Fellow, Center for Advanced Study in the Behavioral Sciences 1972–73; Sherman Fairchild Distinguished Scholar, Calif. Inst. of Tech. 1973–74; mem. Blue Ribbon Panel, Nat. Electricity Rehabilitation Council 1997; consultant on privatization of electric power in Australia and NZ and participated in numerous pvt. and public discussions on energy deregulation in the USA; Hon. DrMan (Purdue) 1989, Dr hc (Universidad Francisco Marroquín) 2004, Hon. DS (Univ. of Kansas) 2014; Andersen Consulting Prof. of the Year 1993, Asscn for Pvt. Enterprise Educ. Adam Smith Award 1995, Distinguished Alumni Award, Calif. Inst. of Tech. 1996, Nobel Prize for Econs 2002, Friedrich-August-von-Hayek-Gesellschaft e.V. Award 2008, Alumni Distinguished Achievement Award, Univ. of Kansas 2011, Thinker Award, Texas Tech Univ. 2014. *Publications include:* Economics: An Analytical Approach (jtly with K. Davidson and J. Wiley) 1958, Investment and Production 1961, Economics of Natural and Environmental Resources 1977, Papers in Experimental Economics (collected works) 1991, Experiments in Decision, Organization and Exchange 1993, Bargaining and Market Behavior: Essays in Experimental Economics (collected works) 2000, Research in Experimental Economics, Vols 1–3 (ed.) 1979, 1982, 1985, Schools of Economic Thought: Experimental Economics (ed.) 1990; over 200 articles on capital theory, finance, natural resource econs and experimental econs. *Address:* Economic Science Institute, Chapman University, Wilkinson Hall 103, One University Drive, Orange, CA 92866, USA (office). *Telephone:* (714) 628-2682 (office). *E-mail:* vsmith@chapman.edu (office). *Website:* www.chapman.edu/our-faculty/vernon-smith (office).

SMITH, Wilbur Addison, BComm; British novelist; b. 9 Jan. 1933, Zambia; m. 1st Danielle Antoinette Smith 1971 (died 1999); two s. one d.; m. 2nd Mokhiniso Rakhimova 2000; ed Michaelhouse, Natal and Rhodes Univ.; business exec. 1954–58; factory owner 1958–64; professional author 1961–. *Publications include:* When the Lion Feeds 1964, The Dark of the Sun 1965, The Sound of Thunder 1966, Shout at the Devil 1968, Gold Mine 1970, The Diamond Hunters 1971, The Sunbird 1972, Eagle in the Sky 1974, The Eye of the Tiger 1975, Cry Wolf 1976, A Sparrow Falls 1977, Hungry as the Sea 1978, Wild Justice 1979, A Falcon Flies 1980, Men of Men 1981, The Angels Weep 1982, The Leopard Hunts in Darkness 1984, The Burning Shore 1985, Power of the Sword 1986, Rage 1987, The Courtneys 1987, The Courtneys in Africa 1988, A Time to Die 1989, Golden Fox 1990, Elephant Song 1991, River God 1993, The Seventh Scroll 1995, Birds of Prey 1997, Monsoon 1999, Warlock 2001, Blue Horizon 2003, The Triumph of the Sun 2005, The Quest 2007, Assegai 2009, Those in Peril 2011, Desert God 2014, Golden Lion 2015, Predator 2016, Pharaoh 2016; contrib. to numerous journals and magazines. *Leisure interests:* fishing, wildlife, skiing, wing shooting. *Address:* Tibor Jones and Associates, Unit 12b, Piano House, 9 Brighton Terrace, London, SW9 8DJ, England (office). *E-mail:* enquiries@tiborjones.com (office). *Website:* www.wilbursmithbooks.com.

SMITH, Will; American actor and singer; b. (Willard Christopher Smith II), 25 Sept. 1968, Philadelphia, Pa; s. of Willard Smith, Sr and Caroline Smith; m. 1st Sheree Zampino 1992 (divorced); one s.; m. 2nd Jada Pinkett 1997; one s. one d.; ed Overbrook High School, Winfield, Pa; formed duo DJ Jazzy Jeff and the Fresh Prince; f. Overbrook Entertainment (production co.); developer and owner The Boom Boom Room (recording studio); with DJ Jazzy Jeff: Grammy Awards Best Rap Performance 1988, 1991; as solo artist: Grammy Awards Best Rap Solo Performance 1998, MTV Music Video Awards Best Male Video, Best Rap Video 1998, American Music Awards Favorite Pop/Rock Male Artist, Favorite Album, Favorite Male Soul/R&B Artist 1998, Favorite Pop/Rock Male Artist 2000; César d'honneur 2005, American Music Award for Favorite Male Pop/Rock Artist 2005, Kora All African Music Award for Best African American Diaspora Artist (for song, Switch) 2005. *Films include:* Where the Day Takes You 1992, Made in America 1993, Six Degrees of Separation 1993, Bad Boys 1995, Independence Day 1996, Men in Black 1997, Enemy of the State 1998, Wild Wild West 1999, Legend of Bagger Vance 2000, Ali 2002, Men in Black II: Alien Attack 2002, Bad Boys II 2003, Shark Tale (voice) 2004, I, Robot 2004, Hitch 2005, The Pursuit of Happyness 2006, I Am Legend 2007, Hancock 2008, Seven Pounds 2009, The Karate Kid (producer) 2010, Men in Black 3 2012, After Earth 2013, Winter's Tale 2014, Focus 2015, Concussion 2015, Suicide Squad 2016, Collateral Beauty 2016, Bright 2017, Aladdin 2019. *Television includes:* The Fresh Prince of Bel Air (series) 1990–96, Happily Ever After: Fairy Tales for Every Child (episode 'Pinocchio'; voice) 1997, All of Us Johnny (three episodes) 2003–04, Nur die Liebe zählt (episode) 2008. *Recordings include:* albums: as The Fresh Prince with DJ Jazzy Jeff: He's the DJ, I'm the Rapper 1988, And in This Corner… 1989, Homebase 1991, Rock the House 1991, Code Red 1993; solo: Big Willie Style 1997, Willennium 1999, Born to Reign 2002, Lost and Found 2005. *Publication:* Just the Two of Us (juvenile) 2005. *Address:* c/o Overbrook Entertainment, 450 North Roxbury Drive, 4th Floor, Beverly Hills, CA 90210 (office); c/o Ken Stovicz, Creative Artists Agency, 9830 Wilshire Boulevard, Beverly Hills, CA 90212, USA (office). *Telephone:* (310) 432-2400 (Overbrook) (office). *Fax:* (310) 432-2410 (Overbrook) (office). *Website:* www.overbrookent.com (office).

SMITH BASTERRA, Jaime, BA, MA; Spanish business executive; *Executive Director, Moldava Consulting SL;* b. 6 Sept. 1965; ed Univ. Comercial Deusto, Univ. of Exeter, UK; Dir of Equity Research, Benito & Monjardin SVB SA, Madrid 1989–98; Dir of Global Equities, Banesto (Banco Santander Group) 1989–99; Dir of Financial Planning, Telefónica Internacional 1999, Chief Financial Officer 1999–2000, Controller, Telefónica Group 2000–02, Chief Financial Officer, Telefónica de Espana 2002–05, Chair., Pres. and CEO O2 Czech Republic 2005–07, CEO Telefónica O2 Germany GmbH & Co., Munich 2007–09, Director of Industrial Alliances, Telefónica 2009–10, Telefonica Mexico, Central America and Venezuela 2010–12; Exec. Dir Moldava Consulting SL, Madrid 2013–; mem. Bd of Dirs I+D, Telyco, TTP, Telfisa; mem. Presiding Cttee BITKOM. *Address:* Moldava Consulting SL, Calle Comunidad de Canarias, 61, 28231 Las Rozas, Madrid, Spain (office). *Website:* moldava-consulting.pymes.com (office).

SMITH OF CLIFTON, Baron (Life Peer), cr. 1997, of Mountsandel in the County of Londonderry; **Trevor Arthur Smith,** Kt, BSc (Econ.), FRHistS, FAcSS; British university vice-chancellor (retd) and business executive; b. 14 June 1937, London; s. of Arthur J. Smith and Vera G. Cross; m. 1st Brenda Eustace 1960 (divorced 1973); two s.; m. 2nd Julia Bullock 1979; one d.; ed London School of Econs; schoolteacher, London 1958–59; Asst Lecturer in Politics, Univ. of Exeter 1959–60; Research Officer, Acton Soc. Trust 1960–62; Lecturer in Politics, Univ. of Hull 1962–67; Lecturer, Queen Mary Coll. London 1967, Sr Lecturer, Head Dept 1972–85, Dean of Social Studies 1979–82, Prof. of Politics 1983–91, Pro-Prin. 1985–87, Sr Pro-Prin. 1987–89, Sr Vice-Prin., Queen Mary & Westfield Coll. 1989–91; Vice-Chancellor, Univ. of Ulster 1991–99 and Hon. Prof.; Visiting Prof., Univ. of York 1999–2003, Univ. of Portsmouth 2000–01; Dir Joseph Rowntree Reform Trust Ltd 1975–2006 (Chair. 1987–99); Chair. Political Studies Asscn UK 1988–89, Vice-Pres. 1989–91, Pres. 1991–93; Dir Job Ownership Ltd 1978–85, New Society Ltd 1986–88, Statesman and Nation Publishing Co. Ltd 1988–90, Bell Educ. Trust Ltd 1988–93, Gerald Duckworth Ltd 1990–95; Deputy Pres. Inst. for Citizenship 1991–2001; Dir Irish Peace Inst. 1992–99; Pres. Belfast Civic Trust 1995–99; mem. Admin. Bd Int. Asscn of Univs 1995–96, Editorial Bd Government and Opposition journal 1995–2013, Bd A Taste of Ulster 1996–99; mem. N Yorks Health Authority 2000–02; mem. (Liberal Democrat), House of Lords 1997–2019, Liberal Democrat Spokesman on NI 2000–11, British Irish Parl. Ass. 2000–11, Chair. Lords Select Cttee on Animals in Scientific Procedures 2001–02; Trustee Stroke Asscn 2002–07; Academician Coll. of Learned Socs in the Social Sciences 2000; Hon. mem. of Senate (Fachhochschule Augsburg) 1994; Hon. Fellow, Queen Mary London 2003; Hon. LLD (Dublin) 1992, (Hull) 1993, (Belfast) 1995, (Nat. Univ. of Ireland) 1996; Hon. DHL (Alabama) 1998; Hon. DLitt (Ulster) 2002. *Publications:* Training Managers (with M. Argyle) 1962, Town Councillors (with A. M. Rees) 1964, Town and County Hall 1966, Anti-Politics 1972, The Politics of the Corporate Economy 1979, The Fixers (with Alison Young) 1996; contributed to numerous other publs. *Leisure interest:* water-colour painting. *Address:* c/o House of Lords, Westminster, London, SW1A 0PW, England (office). *Telephone:* (20) 7219-5353 (office). *Fax:* (20) 7219-5979 (office). *E-mail:* smitht@parliament.uk (office).

SMITH OF FINSBURY, Baron (Life Peer), cr. 2005, of Finsbury in the London Borough of Islington; **Rt Hon. Chris(topher) Robert Smith,** PC, PhD; British politician; *Master, Pembroke College Cambridge;* b. 24 July 1951, Barnet, London, England; s. of Colin Smith and Gladys Smith (née Luscombe); ed George Watson's Coll., Edinburgh, Pembroke Coll., Cambridge, Harvard Univ. (Kennedy Scholar 1975–76), USA; Devt Sec., Shaftesbury Soc. Housing Asscn 1977–80; Devt Co-ordinator Soc. for Co-operative Dwellings 1980–83; Councillor, London Borough of Islington 1978–83, Chief Whip 1978–79, Chair. Housing Cttee 1981–83; Labour MP for Islington S and Finsbury 1983–2005, mem. Cttee on Standards in Public Life 2001–05; Opposition Spokesman on Treasury and Econ. Affairs 1987–92; Prin. Opposition Spokesman on Environmental Protection 1992–94, on Nat. Heritage 1994–95, on Social Security 1995–96, on Health 1996–97; Sec. of State for Culture, Media and Sport 1997–2001; Chair. Labour Campaign for Criminal Justice 1985–88, Tribune Group of MPs 1988–89; mem. (Non-affiliated), House of Lords 2005–, Vice-Chair. British Museum Group 2005–; mem. Exec. Fabian Soc. 1990–96, Chair. 1996–97; Pres. SERA (Labour Environment Campaign) 1992–2007, Ramblers' Asscn 2004–08; Chair. Wordsworth Trust 2001–, Classic FM Consumer Panel 2001–07, Donmar Warehouse Theatre 2003–15, Judges, Man Booker Prize for Fiction 2004, London Cultural Consortium 2004–08, Advertising Standards Authority 2007–, Environment Agency 2008–14, Review of Film Policy for HM's Govt 2010–11, 2013, The Art Fund 2014–; Dir Clore Cultural Leadership Programme 2003–08; Master, Pembroke Coll. Cambridge 2015–; Dir (non-exec.), PPL (Phonographic Performance Ltd) 2006–, Spencer Ogden 2015–; Sr Assoc. Judge, Inst. in Man. Studies, Univ. of Cambridge 2001–07; Visiting Prof., Univ. of the Arts London 2002–14; Visiting Fellow, Ashridge Business Coll. 2007–09; Sr Fellow, RCA 2007; Vice-Pres. Christian Socialist Movt; Companion, Chartered Man. Inst. 2005–10; Trustee, The Sixteen 2013–; Patron The Food Chain, London; Hon. Life mem. BAFTA 2001; Hon. FRIBA 2001; Hon. RIAS 2013; Hon. Fellow, Pembroke Coll., Cambridge 2004, King's Coll., London 2008, Univ. of Cumbria

2010; Freedom of the Borough of Islington 2010; Dr hc (City) 2003, (Lancaster) 2011, (Westminster) 2015, (London Metropolitan) 2016. *Publications:* Creative Britain 1998, Suicide of the West (co-author) 2006. *Leisure interests:* mountaineering (first MP to climb all the 3,000 ft 'Munros' in Scotland), literature, theatre, music, art. *Address:* Master, Pembroke College, Cambridge, CB2 1RF (office); House of Lords, Westminster, London, SW1A 0PW, England (office). *Telephone:* (1223) 338129 (office); (20) 7219-5119 (office). *E-mail:* smithcr@parliament.uk (office); master@pem.cam.ac.uk (office). *Website:* www.pem.cam.ac.uk (office); www.parliament.uk/biographies/lords/lord-smith-of-finsbury/186 (office).

SMITH OF KELVIN, Baron (Life Peer), cr. 2008, of Kelvin in the City of Glasgow; **Rt Hon. Robert Haldane Smith,** Kt, KT, CH, CA; British business executive; b. 8 Aug. 1944; m. Alison Marjorie Bell 1969; two d.; ed Allan Glen's School, Glasgow; accountant, Robb Ferguson & Co., Glasgow 1963–68; with ICFC (later 3i Group PLC) 1968–82; with Royal Bank of Scotland 1983–85; Man. Dir Charterhouse Development Capital Ltd 1985–89; BBC Nat. Gov. for Scotland and Chair. Broadcasting Council for Scotland 1999–2004; Chair. and CEO Morgan Grenfell Private Equity 2001, also CEO Morgan Grenfell Asset Man. (renamed Deutsche Asset Man. 1999), Chair. Deutsche Asset Man. 2000–02; Exec. Dir Scottish and Southern Energy plc (now SSE plc) 2003–15, Deputy Chair. 2003–05, Chair. 2005–15; Chair. The Weir Group PLC 2002–13; Chancellor Paisley Univ. 2003– (named changed to Univ. of the West of Scotland following merger with Bell Coll., Hamilton 2007); Chair. Glasgow 2014 Ltd; Chair. Bd of Trustees, Nat. Museums of Scotland 1993–2002; Dir (non-exec.), 3i Group PLC, Standard Bank Group Ltd, Aegon UK PLC; fmr mem. Bd of Dirs, MFI Furniture Group PLC, Stakis PLC (also Chair. 1998–99), Bank of Scotland, Tip Europe PLC, Network Rail; Pres. British Asscn of Friends of Museums 1995–; fmr Pres. Inst. of Chartered Accountants of Scotland; mem. Financial Services Authority 1997–2000, Financial Reporting Council, Judicial Appointments Bd for Scotland, Council of Econ. Advisers to the First Minister of Scotland, Bd of Trustees, The British Council; mem. Museums and Galleries Comm. 1988–98 (Vice-Chair. 1996–98); Patron Scottish Community Foundation; Dr hc (Glasgow, Edinburgh and Paisley). *Address:* House of Lords, Westminster, London, SW1A 0PW, England (office). *Telephone:* (20) 7219-5353 (office). *Fax:* (20) 7219-5979 (office). *E-mail:* contactholmember@parliament.uk (office). *Website:* www.parliament.uk/biographies/lords/lord-smith-of-kelvin/3856 (office).

SMITH PERERA, Roberto, PhD; Venezuelan politician and business executive; b. 1958, Barquisimeto; s. of Roberto Smith Camacho; m. Marina Pocaterra; three d.; ed Universidad Simón Bolívar and Harvard Univ., USA; Man. Consultant, McKinsey & Co. Energy Group, Washington, DC 1987–89; Coordinator of Govt's 8th Plan for the Nation 1989–90; Minister of Transport and Communications 1990–92; Amb. to EU, Belgium and Luxembourg 1992–95; Pres. Impsat Venezuela 1995–96; Pres. Digitel Venezuela (telecoms co.) 1997–2002, f. Digicel in El Salvador and Guatemala (subsidiaries of Digitel) 1996–2003; Pres. Santa Fe Group 2000–; f. Microjuris.com (internet service); unsuccessful cand. in Vargas state gubernatorial elections 2004; Founder and Pres. Venezuela de Primera Party (Venezuela First) 2005–10, unsuccessful cand. in presidential elections 2006, currently mem. Voluntad Popular; f. Grupo HI 2006. *Publication:* Venezuela: Vision or Chaos 1995.

SMITS, Robert-Jan; Dutch EC official; *Director-General, Directorate-General for Research and Innovation, European Commission;* b. 1958; ed Utrecht Univ., Institut Universitaire d'Hautes Etudes Internationales, Switzerland, Fletcher School of Law and Diplomacy, USA; fmr Dir for European Research Area: Research Programmes and Capacity at EC's Directorate-Gen. for Research and Innovation (RTD), responsible for coordination of nat. research programmes, co-operation with intergovernmental research orgs (EIROforum, EUREKA, COST), Research Infrastructures, relations with European Investment Bank and the Structural Funds; Deputy Dir-Gen. Directorate-Gen. of Jt Research Centre, EC, responsible for Programmes and Stakeholder Relations, Resource Man., and Inst. for Energy, Inst. for Environment and Sustainability and Inst. for Prospective Technological Studies Feb.–June 2010; Dir-Gen. Directorate-Gen. for Research for Research and Innovation 2010–; Chair. several high-level cttees, including European Research Area Cttee (ERAC), Steering Cttee of the ERC (ERCEA). *Address:* Directorate-General for Research and Innovation, European Commission, Square frère Orban 8, 1000 Brussels, Belgium (office). *Telephone:* (2) 296-32-96 (office). *E-mail:* robert-jan.smits@ec.europa.eu (office).

SMOL, John P., OC, BS, MSc, PhD, FRSC; Canadian biologist and academic; *Professor of Biology and Canada Research Chair in Environmental Change, Queen's University;* b. Montréal; ed McGill Univ., Brock Univ., Queen's Univ.; post-doctoral work with Geological Survey of Canada, High Arctic; joined faculty of Dept of Biology and School of Environmental Studies, Queen's Univ., Kingston 1984, Prof. of Biology 1991–, Canada Research Chair in Environmental Change 2000–; Founding Dir Paleoecological Environmental Assessment and Research Lab., Queen's Univ.; Founding Ed. Journal of Paleolimnology 1987–2007; Ed. Environmental Reviews, Developments in Paleoenvironmental Research; Distinguished Fellow, Geological Asscn of Canada; Hon. LLD (St Francis Xavier Univ.) 2003; Dr hc (Helsinki) 2007; numerous awards including Botanical Soc. of America Darbaker Prize 1992, Nat. Research Council Steacie Prize 1993, Miroslaw Romanowski Medal 2001, NSERC Herzberg Gold Medal 2004, W. A. Johnston Medal 2005, G. Evelyn Hutchinson Award 2007, Flavelle Medal 2008, Canada Council for the Arts Killam Prize 2009, Premier of Ont. Discovery Award 2009, Nature Award for Mentoring in Science 2010, Ramon Margalef Award for Excellence in Education 2012. *Publications include:* over 350 journal articles and book chapters; 16 books, including Pollution of Lakes and Rivers: A Paleoenvironmental Perspective. *Address:* Department of Biology, Queen's University, Kingston, ON K7L 3N6, Canada (office). *Telephone:* (613) 533-6147 (office). *E-mail:* smolj@queensu.ca (office). *Website:* www.queensu.ca/research/environment/smol (office).

SMOOT, George Fitzgerald, III, BS (Phys), BS (Math.), PhD; American astrophysicist and cosmologist; *Professor of Physics and Director, Paris and Berkeley Centers for Cosmological Physics, University of California, Berkeley* and *Sorbonne Paris-Cité;* b. 20 Feb. 1945, Yukon, Fla; s. of George F. Smoot, Jr; ed Stetson Univ., Georgetown Univ., Massachusetts Inst. of Tech.; Post-doctoral researcher, MIT 1970; Research Physicist, Univ. of California, Berkeley Space Sciences Lab. 1971–74, jt appointment, Research Physicist, Lawrence Berkeley Nat. Lab. 1974–2016, Prof., Physics Dept, Univ. of California, Berkeley 1994–, Dir Berkeley Center for Cosmological Physics 2007–; Dir Inst. for the Early Universe and Distinguished Prof., Ewha Univ. and Acad. of Advanced Studies, Seoul, S Korea 2008–14; Chaire Blaise Pascal, Université de Paris, Diderot; Dir Paris Center for Cosmological Physics 2011–; Prof., Sorbonne Paris-Cité 2011–13; Helmut and Anna Pao Sohmen Prof. at Large, IAS Hong Kong Univ. of Science and Tech. 2017–; Dir Extreme Universe Lab., Moscow State Univ.; mem. American Physical Soc. Cttee on Safety of Commercial Nuclear Reactors 1974–75, Man. and Operations Working Group for Shuttle Astronomy 1976–80, Steering Group on Cosmic Background Explorer Satellite (Prin. Investigator on isotropy experiment—NASA) 1975–96, White Mountain Research Station Advisory Cttee 1982, Superconducting Magnet Facility for the Space Station Study Team 1985, Center for Particle Astrophysics at Univ. of California, Berkeley 1988, Radio Astronomy Lab. Advisory Cttee 1990; mem. American Physical Soc., American Astronomical Soc., AAAS, Int. Astronomical Union, NAS; Dr hc (Univ. of Marseille), (Reiko Univ.), (Miguel Hernandez Univ.), (Moscow State Univ.), (Bruno Giodano Global Shift Univ.), (Gustavus Adolphus Coll., Minn.); NASA Medal for Exceptional Scientific Achievement 1991, Popular Science Award 1992, Aerospace Laureate, Aviation Week & Space Technology 1993, Distinguished Scientist, ARCS Foundation, Inc. 1993, Kilby Award 1993, Gravity Research Foundation Essay First Award 1993, Productivity Group Award, Goddard Space Flight Center, NASA 1993, Golden Plate Award 1994, Lawrence Award 1995, Nobel Prize in Physics (with John C. Mather) 2006, Oersted Medal 2009. *Music:* Rhythms of the Universe with Mickey Hart and others. *Television:* The Big Bang Theory. *Publications:* Wrinkles in Time (co-author) 1993; more than 500 scientific papers in professional journals on astrophysics and cosmology. *Address:* Physics Department, University of California, Berkeley, 437 Old LeConte Hall, Berkeley, CA 94720-7300 (office); Ernest Orlando Lawrence Berkeley National Laboratory, 1 Cyclotron Road, Mail Stop 50R5005, Berkeley, CA 94720, USA (office). *Telephone:* (510) 486-5505 (office); (510) 486-5237 (office); (510) 642-9389 (office). *Fax:* (510) 486-7149 (office). *E-mail:* gfsmoot@lbl.gov (office). *Website:* www.physics.berkeley.edu/research/faculty/Smoot.html (office); aether.lbl.gov (office); pariscosmo.fr; ieu.ewha.ac.kr; bccp.lbl.gov (office).

SMOUT, Thomas Christopher, CBE, MA, PhD, FRSE, FBA, FSA (Scot.); British historian and academic; *Professor Emeritus of Scottish History, University of St Andrews;* b. 19 Dec. 1933, Birmingham; s. of Sir Arthur J. G. Smout and Lady Smout (Hilda Smout, née Follows); m. Anne-Marie Schøning 1959; one s. one d.; ed Leys School, Cambridge, Clare Coll., Cambridge; joined staff Edinburgh Univ. 1959, Prof. of Econ. History 1970–79; Prof. of Scottish History, Univ. of St Andrews 1980–91, Prof. Emer. 1991–; Dir St John's House Inst. for Advanced Historical Studies, Univ. of St Andrews 1992–97; Founder and Dir Inst. for Environmental History, Univ. of St Andrews 1992–2000; Visiting Prof., Univ. of Strathclyde 1991–95, Univ. of Dundee 1993–, Univ. of Stirling 1997–, Univ. of York 1998–99; Deputy Chair. Scottish Nat. Heritage 1992–97, mem. Bd 1992–98; Historiographer Royal in Scotland 1993–; mem. Bd Royal Comm. Ancient and Historical Monuments of Scotland 1986–2000, Nature Conservancy Council (Scotland) 1991–92, Royal Comm. on Historical Manuscripts 1999–2003, Advisory Council on Nat. Records and Archives 2003–04; Trustee Nat. Museums of Scotland 1991–94, Woodland Trust 1998–2004; Chair. Scottish Coastal Archaeology and the Problem of Erosion 2001–; Patron Scottish Native Woods 2004–; Hon. Fellow, Trinity Coll. Dublin 1994–; Dr hc (Queen's Univ., Belfast) 1995, (Edin.) 1996, (St Andrews) 1999, (Glasgow) 2001, (Stirling) 2002. *Publications:* Scottish Trade on the Eve of the Union 1963, History of the Scottish People, 1560–1830 1969, State of the Scottish Working Class in 1843 (with Ian Levitt) 1979, Scottish Population History from the 17th Century to the 1930s (with M. W. Flinn) 1976, Century of the Scottish People, 1830–1950 1986, Scottish Voices (with S. Wood) 1990, Prices, Food and Wages in Scotland (with A. Gibson) 1995, Nature Contested 2000, People and Woods in Scotland (ed.) 2002, History of the Native Woods of Scotland (with A. R. MacDonald and F. Watson) 2005. *Leisure interests:* birdwatching and other natural history, conservation, architecture. *Address:* Chesterhill, Shore Road, Anstruther, Fife, KY10 3DZ, Scotland. *Telephone:* (1334) 463300. *Fax:* (1333) 311193. *E-mail:* tcs1@st-andrews.ac.uk.

SMURFIT, Anthony P. J., BSc; Irish business executive; *Group CEO, Smurfit Kappa Group;* b. 19 Dec. 1963, Wigan; s. of Michael Smurfit; ed Univ. of Scranton, USA; mem. Bd Jefferson Smurfit Group (now Smurfit Kappa Group), apptd Chief Exec. Smurfit France 1996, later Deputy CEO Smurfit Europe, then CEO Smurfit Europe 1999–2002, COO Smurfit Kappa Group 2002–05, Pres. and Group COO Smurfit Kappa Group 2005–15, Group CEO 2015–; Dir C&C Group plc, Irish Nat. Stud Co.; Hon. Consul of Mexico to Ireland 2003, Chevalier, Légion d'honneur 2004. *Leisure interests:* golf, horse breeding. *Address:* Smurfit Kappa Group, Beech Hill, Clonskeagh, Dublin 4, Ireland (office). *Telephone:* (1) 202-7157 (office). *Fax:* (1) 202-7183 (office). *E-mail:* info@smurfitkappa.com (office). *Website:* www.smurfitkappa.com (office).

SMURFIT, Michael, Jr, MBA; Irish business executive; s. of Michael Smurfit; ed Univ. Coll. Dublin; fmr Vice-Pres. World Purchasing, Jefferson Smurfit Group, Pres. and Chief Exec., Smurfit Packaging Corpn (now Smurfit-Stone Container Corpn) 1996; currently CEO SF Investments (pvt. investment co.), Dublin; mem. Bd of Dirs CNG Travel Group plc, GameAccount Global Limited, Escher plc, The K Club Limited, Irish Youth Foundation; mem. Irish Advisory Bd Michael Smurfit Grad. Business School, Univ. Coll. Dublin.

SMURFIT, Sir Michael William Joseph, Kt, KBE; Irish business executive (retd); b. 7 Aug. 1936, St Helens, England; m. 1st Norma Treisman (divorced); two s. two d.; m. 2nd Birgitta Beimark; two s.; joined Jefferson Smurfit & Sons Ltd 1955, f. Jefferson Smurfit Packaging Ltd (Lancs.) 1961, rejoined Jefferson Smurfit Group, Dir 1964, Jt Man. Dir 1967, Deputy Chair. 1979, Chair. and CEO Jefferson Smurfit Group PLC, Dublin 1977–2002, Chair. 2002–07, also Chair. Jefferson Smurfit Corpn & Container Corpn of America; mem. Irish Advisory Bd Michael Smurfit Grad. Business School, Univ. Coll. Dublin; fmr Chair. Telecom Eireann; Hon. LLD (Trinity Coll., Dublin), (Univ. of Scranton, Pennsylvania, USA). *Address:* Le Sardanapale, 2 Avenue Princesse Grace, Monte Carlo 98000, Monaco (office). *Telephone:* (93) 157045 (office). *E-mail:* mwjsoffice@monaco.mc (office).

SNAPKOU, Mikalay Henodzyevich; Belarusian economist and politician; b. 1969, Mogilev (Mahiloŭ); ed Belarusian Agricultural Acad., Presidential Man. Acad.; worked as an economist, sr economist and accountant at agricultural establishments in Mogilev and Grodno Oblasts 1990–94; Economist, Sr Economist, Deputy Man., Drybyn br. (Mogilev Oblast) of Belagroprombank 1994–96; Deputy Chair. responsible for Econ. Affairs, Market Relations and Privatization, Horets Raion (dist) Exec. Cttee, Mogilev Oblast 1996–2000; Chief of Financial Dept, Mogilev Oblast 2000–07, Deputy Head, Mogilev Oblast Exec. Cttee 2007–09; Deputy Chair. of Presidential Admin Jan.–Dec. 2009; Minister of the Economy Dec. 2009–14. *Address:* c/o Ministry of the Economy, 220050 Minsk, vul. Bersona 14, Belarus. *E-mail:* minec@economy.gov.by.

SNEGUR, Mircea, DrAgriSc; Moldovan politician; b. 17 Jan. 1940, V. Trifăneşti, Soroca Dist; s. of Ion Snegur and Ana Snegur; m. Georgeta Snegur 1960; one s. one d.; ed Kishinau Inst. of Agric.; mem. CPSU 1964–90; work as agronomist, man. state and collective farms 1961–68, Chair. of Experimental Station 1968–73, Chief of Section Ministry of Agric. 1973–78; Dir-Gen. Research Production Asscn 'Selektsia', Balts 1978–81; Sec., CP Cttee, Yedinetsky Dist 1981–85; Sec., Cen. Cttee of CP of Moldavia 1985–89, Chair. Presidium of Supreme Soviet of Moldavia 1989–90; Pres. of Moldova 1990–96; Chair. Party of Resurrection and Accord (later Democratic Convention) 1995–2001; elected mem. of Parl. 1998, Constant Bureau of Parl. 1998–2001; Hon. Chair. Liberal Party 2002–; Insigna de Onoare 1966, Ordinul Republicii 2000; Diploma Academiei Europene de Arte 1995; Dr hc (Agrarian Univ., Chisinau) 1996, (Univ. of Ankara) 1996, (Free International Univ. of Moldova) 2001; Medalia Pentru Vitejie în Muncă 1976. *Publications include:* more than 100 articles on phytotechnical matters and the application of scientific procedures to production, Memories in Two Parts (monograph). *Leisure interests:* billiards, history and detective fiction, sports programmes, sport fishing.

SNEH, Brig.-Gen. Ephraim, MD; Israeli politician, physician and army officer (retd); *Chairman, S. Daniel Abraham Center for Strategic Dialogue, Netanya Academic College;* b. 19 Sept. 1944, Tel-Aviv; s. of Dr Moshe Sneh; m.; two c.; ed Tel-Aviv Univ. Medical School; Research Fellow, Walter Reed Army Medical Center; rank of Brig.-Gen., army service includes Medical Officer of Paratroops Brigade 1972–74; Chief Medical Officer of the Paratroops and Infantry Corps 1974–78; Commdr of the Medical Teams during the Entebbe Rescue Operation 1976; Commdr Israel Defense Forces (IDF) elite unit 1978–80; Chief Medical Officer, IDF Northern Command 1980–81; Commdr of Security Zone in S Lebanon 1981–82; Head of the Civil Admin. of the West Bank 1985–87; mem. (Labor Party) of Knesset (Parl.) 1992–2008; Minister of Health 1994–96, of Transportation 2001–02; Deputy Minister of Defence 1999–2001, 2006–07; est. Strong Israel Party 2008; Chair. S. Daniel Abraham Center for Strategic Dialogue, Netanya Academic Coll. 2008–; Pres. Silver Bullet Ltd. *Publication:* Navigating Perilous Waters 2005. *Address:* 6 Hachoshlim Street, PO Box 12006, Herzliya Pituach 46722 (office); 12 Hapalmach Street, Herzelia 46793, Israel (home). *Telephone:* (77) 6935612 (office). *Fax:* (77) 6935601 (office). *E-mail:* esneh@netvision.net.il (home). *Website:* sdc .netanya.ac.il (office); www.sneh.org.il.

SNEIDER, Tamás; Hungarian politician; *President, Movement for a Better Hungary;* b. 11 June 1972, Eger; m.; two s. one d.; ed Eszterházy Károly Coll.; mem. Magyar Igazság és Élet Pártja (Party of Hungarian Justice and Life) 2000–07; mem. Eger City Council 2002–06; Founding mem. Magyar Önvédelmi Mozgalom (Hungarian Self-Defence Movt) 2005; mem. Jobbik Magyarországért Mozgalom (Movt for a Better Hungary) 2007–, Vice-Pres. 2009–18, Pres. 2018–; mem. Nat. Ass. (Parl.) 2010–, Chair. Youth, Social and Family Policy Cttee 2010–14, Deputy Speaker 2014–. *Address:* Jobbik Magyarországért Mozgalom, 1113 Budapest, Villányi ú. 20a, Hungary (office). *Telephone:* (1) 365-1488 (office). *E-mail:* jobbik@ jobbik.hu (office). *Website:* www.jobbik.hu (office).

SNIDER, Stacey, BA, JD; American film industry executive; *Co-Chairman, Film Studio, 20th Century Fox;* b. 29 April 1961, Philadelphia, Pa; m. Gary Jones; two c.; ed Univ. of Pennsylvania, Univ. of California, Los Angeles; began career in post room, Triad Agency, later Asst; Asst, Simpson-Bruckheimer Productions; joined Guber-Peters Entertainment Co. as Dir of Devt 1986–90, Exec. Vice-Pres. 1990–92; Production Pres. TriStar Pictures 1992–96; Co-Pres. of Production, Universal Pictures 1996–98, Head of Production April–Nov. 1998, Pres. of Production and Co-Chair. 1998, Chair. and CEO Universal Pictures 1999–2006; Co-Chair. and CEO DreamWorks SKG 2006–14, also Prin. Partner; Co-Chair. of film studio, 20th Century Fox 2014–; mem. Bd of Dirs City Year, Special Olympics of Southern California, American Film Inst.; Dorothy and Sherrill C. Corwain Human Relations Award, American Jewish Cttee 2004. *Address:* 20th Century Fox Studios, 10201 West Pico Blvd, Los Angeles, CA 90064, USA (office). *Website:* www .foxstudios.com (office).

SNIPES, Wesley; American actor and producer; b. 31 July 1962, Orlando, Fla; one s.; ed High School for the Performing Arts, New York and State Univ. of New York, Purchase; fmr telephone repair man, New York; appeared in Martin Scorsese's video Bad 1987; Co-Founder Struttin Street Stuff puppet theatre mid-1980s; indicted on eight counts of US tax fraud Oct. 2006, convicted and sentenced to three years in prison 2008, released 2013; ACE Award for Best Actor for Vietnam War Stories (TV) 1989, Best Actor for One Night Stand, Venice Film Festival. *Films include:* Wildcats, Streets of Gold, Major League, Mo Better Blues 1990, Jungle Fever 1991, New Jack City, White Men Can't Jump, Demolition Man, Boiling Point, Sugar Hill, Drop Zone, To Wong Foo, Thanks for Everything, Julie Newmar 1995, The Money Train, Waiting to Exhale, The Fan 1996, One Night Stand, Murder at 1600, Blade (also producer) 1997, U.S. Marshals 1998, Down in the Delta (also producer) 1998, The Art of War 2000, Blade 2 2002, Undisputed 2002, Unstoppable 2004, Blade: Trinity 2004, Brooklyn's Finest 2009, Game of Death 2010, Gallowwalkers 2012, The Expendables 3 2014. *Broadway stage appearances:* Boys of Winter, Execution of Justice, Death and King's Horsemen.

SNODGRASS, Anthony McElrea, DPhil, FBA, FSA, FRSA; British archaeologist and academic; *Laurence Professor Emeritus of Classical Archaeology, Faculty of Classics, University of Cambridge;* b. 7 July 1934, London, England; s. of Maj. W. M. Snodgrass and Kathleen M. Snodgrass; m. 1st Ann Vaughan 1959 (divorced 1978); three d.; m. 2nd Annemarie Künzl 1983; one s.; ed Marlborough Coll. and Worcester Coll., Oxford; Nat. Service, RAF 1953–55; Lecturer in Classical Archaeology, Univ. of Edin. 1961–68, Reader 1968–75, Prof. 1975–76; Laurence Prof. of Classical Archaeology, Univ. of Cambridge 1976–2001, now Prof. Emer.; Sather Prof. in Classics, Univ. of Calif. at Berkeley 1984–85; Geddes-Harrower Prof. Univ. of Aberdeen 1995–96; Fellow, Clare Coll. Cambridge 1977–; Vice-Pres. British Acad. 1990–92; mem. Humanities Research Bd 1994–95; Chair. British Cttee for the Reunification of the Parthenon Marbles 2002–10; Foreign mem. Russian Acad. of Sciences 2002; Hon. Fellow, Worcester Coll., Oxford 2000; Hon. Fellow, Archaeological Inst. of America 2010; Hon. DLitt (Edinburgh) 2008; Hon. DHumLitt (Chicago) 2009. *Publications:* Early Greek Armour and Weapons 1964, Arms and Armour of the Greeks 1967, The Dark Age of Greece 1971, Archaeology and the Rise of the Greek State 1977, Archaic Greece: the Age of Experiment 1980, An Archaeology of Greece 1987, Homer and the Artists 1998, Archaeology and the Emergence of Greece 2006. *Leisure interests:* mountaineering, skiing. *Address:* Clare College, Trinity Lane, Cambridge, CB2 1TL, England (office). *Telephone:* (1223) 313599 (home). *Fax:* (1223) 313599 (home). *E-mail:* ams1002@cam.ac.uk (office). *Website:* www.classics.cam.ac.uk/directory/anthony-snodgrass (office).

SNOOK, Hans; German business executive; b. 1948; m. Etta Lai Yee Lau; worked in hotel industry and in real estate sales in Canada; joined Young Generation paging group, Hong Kong 1984; co. bought by Hutchinson Whampoa 1986; Founder and CEO Orange 1994–2001; Chair. (non-exec.) Carphone Warehouse PLC 2002–05, Monstermob Group PLC 2005–07; Dir (non-exec.) DDD Group PLC 2006–.

SNOOP DOGG, (Snoop Lion, Snoop Doggy Dogg); American rap artist and actor; b. (Calvin Cordozar Broadus, Jr), 20 Oct. 1971, Long Beach, Calif.; mem. 213 (with Warren G. and Nate Dogg) early 1990s, re-formed 2005; collaborations with Dr Dre, Rage Against the Machine, K-Ci, JoJo; Exec. Producer, satellite radio network, XM 2005; MTV Europe Music Award for Best Hip-hop 2005. *Songs for film:* In Prison My Whole Life 2008. *Film appearances:* Half Baked 1998, Caught Up 1998, Ride 1998, Da Game of Life 1998, Urban Menace 1999, The Wrecking Crew 1999, Hot Boyz 1999, 3 the Hard Way 1999, Tha Eastsidaz 2000, Baby Boy 2001, Training Day 2001, Bones 2001, The Wash 2001, Crime Partners 2000 2001, Snoop Dogg's Hustlaz: Diary of a Pimp 2002, Malibu's Most Wanted (voice) 2003, Starsky & Hutch 2004, Soul Plane 2004, Racing Stripes (voice) 2005, Boss'n Up 2005, The Tenants 2005, Arthur and the Invisibles (voice) 2007, Falling Up 2009, Arthur and the Revenge of Maltazard 2009, The Big Bang 2011, We the Party 2012, Mac and Devin Go to High School 2012, Turbo (voice) 2013, Scary Movie 5 2013, Pitch Perfect 2 2015, Meet the Blacks 2016. *Television includes:* The Boondocks (series) 2007–08, GGN: Snoop Dogg's Double G News Network (series) 2011–16. *Recordings include:* albums: solo: Doggystyle 1993, Tha Doggfather 1996, Da Game Is To Be Sold, Not To Be Told 1998, Top Dogg 1999, The Last Meal 2000, Death Row's Greatest Hits 2001, Paid Tha Cost To Be Da Boss 2002, Rhythm & Gangsta: The Masterpiece 2004, The Blue Carpet Treatment 2006, Ego Trippin' 2008, Malice n' Wonderland 2009, Doggumentary 2011, Reincarnated (as Snoop Lion) 2013, Bush 2015, Coolaid 2016; with 213: The Hard Way 2005. *Address:* c/o William Morris Endeavor Entertainment, 1325 Avenue of the Americas, New York, NY 10019, USA (office). *Telephone:* (212) 586-5100 (office). *Fax:* (212) 246-3583 (office). *Website:* www.wmeentertainment.com (office); snoopdogg.com.

SNOUSSI, Ahmed, PhD; Moroccan fmr diplomatist; b. 22 April 1929, Meknès; m. Farida Snoussi; three c.; ed Faculté de Droit, Univ. de Paris and Inst. des Hautes Etudes Politiques; Dir of Public Information, Govt of Morocco and ed. various publs on foreign affairs 1958–60; Sec.-Gen. Ministry of Tourism, Information and Fine Arts 1963; Minister of Information 1967–71 (Moroccan Commr-Gen. Expo '67, Montréal); Amb. to Nigeria 1965, to Cameroon 1966, to Tunisia 1971, to Algeria 1973, to Mauritania and Envoy of the King to Heads of State 1978–79; Head of Moroccan del. UN Security Council 1992–94; Amb. and Perm. Rep. to UN, New York 1997–2001; fmr Chair. Exec. Bd Somathon Tuna Fishing and Packing Corpn, Lafarge Maroc Group; fmr Pres. Cinouca Corpn, Asscn of Deep Sea Fishing Fleets, Nat. Producers Asscn; Chevalier, Order of Ouissam Alaouite, Commdr, Légion d'honneur. *Leisure interests:* poetry, painting, 'elucubrations de ma jeunesse'. *Address:* 3 Avenue de la Victoire, Rabat, Morocco (office). *Telephone:* (3) 7774141 (home). *Fax:* (3) 7777929 (home). *E-mail:* asnoussi51@yahoo.fr (home).

SNOW, David B., Jr, BSc, MS; American health care industry executive; *Chairman and CEO, Medco Health Solutions Inc.;* b. 1955; ed Bates Coll., Duke Univ.; began career working for Creighton Univ. Medical School, Memorial Hosp. of Burlington Co. then US Healthcare Inc.; Sr Vice-Pres. American Int. Healthcare 1988–89; Co-Founder, Pres. and CEO Managed Health Care Systems (later renamed AmeriChoice) 1989–93; Exec. Vice-Pres. Oxford Health Plans 1993–98; Pres. and COO WellChoice Inc. (fmrly Empire BlueCross BlueShield) 1999–2003; Pres. and CEO Medco Health Solutions Inc. March–June 2003, Chair. and CEO June 2003–; named by Institutional Investor Best CEO in Health Care Tech. and Distribution in its All-America Exec. Team rankings 2011. *Address:* Medco Health Solutions Inc., Express Scripts Holding Company, 1 Express Way, St. Louis, MO 63121, USA (office). *Telephone:* (800) 282-2881 (office). *Fax:* (201) 269-1109 (office). *E-mail:* info@medcohealth.com (office). *Website:* www.medcohealth.com (office).

SNOW, John W., LLB, PhD; American business executive and fmr government official; *Chairman, Cerberus Capital Management LP;* b. 2 Aug. 1939, Toledo, Ohio; ed Kenyon Coll., Univ. of Toledo, Univ. of Virginia, George Washington Univ.; Asst Prof. of Econs, Univ. of Maryland 1965–67; with Wheeler & Wheeler (law firm), Washington, DC 1967–72; Asst Gen. Counsel, US Dept of Transportation 1972–73; Adjunct Prof. of Law, George Washington Univ. Law School 1972–75; Deputy Asst Sec. for Policy, Plans and Int. Affairs 1973–74; Asst Sec. for Govt Affairs, US Dept of Transportation 1974–75, Deputy Under-sec. 1975–76; Admin., Nat. Highway Traffic Safety Admin. 1976–77; Visiting Prof. of Econs, Univ. of Virginia, 1977; Vice-Pres. of Govt Affairs, Chessie System Inc. (later part of CSX Corpn) 1977–80, Sr Vice-Pres. Corp. Services, CSX Corpn Richmond 1980–84, Exec. Vice-Pres. 1984–85, COO 1988–89, Pres. 1988–2001, CEO 1989–2003, Chair. 1991–2003; US Sec. of the Treasury 2003–06; Chair. Cerberus Capital Man. LP 2006–; Co-Chair. Nat. Comm. on Financial Inst. Reform, Recovery and Enforcement 1992–93; mem. Business Roundtable, Chair. 1995–96; mem. Bd of Dirs Sapient Corpn, Verizon, Johnson & Johnson, US Steel, Asscn of American Railroads, Carmax; mem. Bd of Trustees Johns Hopkins Univ., The Business Council, Va Business Council, Nat. Coal Council; Co-Chair. Conf. Bd Blue-Ribbon Comm. on Public Trust and Pvt. Enterprise; Chair. Kennedy Center Corp. Fund Bd; Hon. LLD (Kenyon Coll.) 1993; Marco Polo Award, US–China

Foundation for Int. Exchanges 2001. *Address:* Cerberus Capital Management LP, 299 Park Avenue, New York, NY 10171, USA (office). *Telephone:* (212) 891-2100 (office). *E-mail:* media@cerberuscapital.com (office). *Website:* www.cerberuscapital.com (office).

SNOW, Jonathan (Jon) George; British television journalist; b. 28 Sept. 1947; s. of Rt Rev. George Snow and Joan Snow; fmr pnr Madeleine Colvin; two d.; m. Precious Lunga 2010; ed St Edward's School, Oxford, Univ. of Liverpool; Voluntary Service Overseas, Uganda 1967–68; Co-ordinator New Horizon Youth Centre, London 1970–73 (Chair. 1986–); journalist, Independent Radio News, LBC 1973–76; reporter, ITN 1977–83, Washington Corresp. 1983–86, Diplomatic Ed. 1986–89; presenter, Channel Four News 1989–; Visiting Prof. of Broadcast Journalism, Nottingham Trent Univ. 1992–2001, Univ. of Stirling 2002–; Chair. Prison Reform Trust 1992–97; Trustee, Tate Modern Council 1999–2008, Nat. Gallery 1999–2008; Chancellor, Oxford Brookes Univ. 2001–08; Hon. FRIBA; Hon. DLitt (Nottingham Trent) 1994, Hon. DLitt (Open Univ.); Monte Carlo Golden Nymph Award, for Eritrea air attack reporting 1979, TV Reporter of the Year, for Afghanistan, Iran and Iraq reporting, Royal Television Soc. (RTS) 1980, Valiant for Truth Award, for El Salvador reporting 1982, Int. Award, for El Salvador reporting, RTS 1982, Home News Award, for Kegworth air crash reporting, RTS 1989, RTS Presenter of the Year 1994, 2002, BAFTA Richard Dimbleby Award 2005, RTS Journalist of the Year 2006, BAFTA Fellowship Award 2015. *Publications:* Atlas of Today 1987, Sons and Mothers 1996, Shooting History: A Personal Journey 2004; articles in The Guardian, Financial Times, Independent, Telegraph, New Statesman. *Leisure interests:* water colours, cycling. *Address:* Knight Ayton Management, 35 Great James Street, London, WC1N 3HB, England (office); Channel Four News, ITN, 200 Gray's Inn Road, London, WC1X 8HB, England (office). *E-mail:* info@knightayton.co.uk (office); jon.snow@itn.co.uk (office). *Telephone:* (20) 7430-4237 (office); (20) 7833-3000 (office). *Fax:* (20) 7430-4607 (office). *Website:* www.channel4.com/news/jon-snow (office); blogs.channel4.com/snowblog.

SNOW, Peter John, CBE; British television presenter, reporter and author; b. 20 April 1938, Dublin, Ireland; s. of Brig. John F. Snow, CBE and Peggy Pringle; m. 1st Alison Carter 1964 (divorced 1975); one s. one d.; m. 2nd Ann MacMillan 1976; one s. two d.; ed Wellington Coll. and Balliol Coll. Oxford; Second Lt, Somerset Light Infantry 1956–58; newscaster and reporter, ITN 1962–79, Diplomatic and Defence Corresp. 1966–79; Presenter BBC Newsnight 1979–97, Tomorrow's World 1997–2001, BBC Election Programmes 1983–2005, BBC Radio 4 Mastermind 1998–2000, Radio 4 Random Edition 1998–2009, Radio 4 Masterteam 2001–05, Battlefield Britain (BBC 2, jtly with s. Dan Snow) 2004, 20th Century Battlefields (jtly with s. Dan Snow) 2007; Judges' Award, Royal TV Soc. 1998. *Publications:* Leila's Hijack War (co-author) 1970, Hussein: A Biography 1972, Battlefield Britain 2004, The World's Greatest 20th Century Battlefields (with Dan Snow) 2007, To War with Wellington 2010, When Britain Burned the White House: The 1814 Invasion of Washington 2013. *Leisure interests:* sailing, skiing, model railways, photography. *Address:* c/o Lucas Alexander Whitley Ltd, 14 Vernon Street, London, W14 0RJ, England (office). *Telephone:* (20) 7471-7900 (office). *Fax:* (20) 7471-7910 (office). *E-mail:* p.snow@btconnect.com (office).

SNOWE, Olympia Jean, BA; American politician; b. 21 Feb. 1947, Augusta, Me; d. of George Bouchles and Georgia Goranites Bouchles; m. John Rettie McKernan 1969; ed Edward Little High School, Auburn, Univ. of Maine; mem. Maine House of Reps 1973–76, Maine Senate 1976–78; mem. 96th–103rd Congresses from 2nd Maine Dist 1979–95; Deputy Republican Whip; Senator from Maine 1995–2013 (retd), mem. Cttee on Small Business & Entrepreneurship, Select Cttee on Intelligence, Cttee on Commerce, Science, & Transportation, Cttee on Finance; Counsel to Asst Majority Leader 1997; Republican; Hon. LLD (Husson Coll.) 1981, (Maine) 1982, (Bowdoin Coll.) 1985, (Suffolk) 1994, (Colby Coll.) 1996, (Bates Coll.) 1998; numerous other awards and distinctions.

SNOWMAN, (Michael) Nicholas, OBE, MA; British music administrator and business executive; *Chairman, Wartski;* b. 18 March 1944, London; s. of Kenneth Snowman and Sallie Snowman (née Moghilevkine); m. Margo Michelle Rouard 1983; one s.; ed Hall School and Highgate School, London, Magdalene Coll., Cambridge; Asst to Head of Music Staff, Glyndebourne Festival 1967–69; Co-founder and Gen. Man. London Sinfonietta 1968–72; Admin. Music Theatre Ensemble 1968–71; Artistic Dir Institut de Recherche et de Coordination Acoustique/Musique (IRCAM), Centre d'Art et de la Culture Georges Pompidou 1972–86; Co-founder and Artistic Adviser, Ensemble Intercontemporain 1975–92, mem. Bd 1992–, Vice-Chair. 1998–; mem. Music Cttee, Venice Biennale 1979–86; Artistic Dir Projects in 1980, 1981, 1983, Festival d'Automne de Paris; Programme Consultant, Cité de la Musique, La Villette, Paris 1991–92; Gen. Dir (Arts), South Bank Centre, London 1986–92, Chief Exec. 1992–98; Gen. Dir Glyndebourne Opera 1998–2000, Opera Nat. du Rhin, Strasbourg 2002–09; Chair. Wartski (jewellers) 2002– (co. made wedding rings for Prince Charles and Camilla Parker-Bowles 2005 and for Prince William and Kate Middleton 2011); mem. British Section, Franco-British Council 1995–; Trustee, New Berlioz Edn 1996–; Gov. RAM, London 1998–; Chevalier, Ordre des Art et des Lettres (France) 1985, Officier 1990; Order of Cultural Merit (Poland) 1990; Chevalier, Ordre nat. du Mérite (France) 1995. *Radio:* Desert Island Discs (BBC Radio 4) 1990. *Publications:* The Best of Granta (co-ed.) 1967, The Contemporary Composers (series ed.) 1982–; papers and articles on music, cultural policy and France. *Leisure interests:* films, eating, spy novels. *Address:* Wartski, 14 Grafton Street, London, W1S 4DE, England (office); 9 rue de Bain Finkwiller, 67000 Strasbourg, France (home). *Telephone:* (20) 7493-1141 (office); (6) 64-77-81-30 (home). *Fax:* (20) 7409-7448 (office). *E-mail:* wartski@wartski.com (office). *Website:* www.wartski.com (office); www.ensembleinter.com.

SNOY ET D'OPPUERS, Baron; Bernard Baudouin Idesbalde Fernand Marie Ghislain, BA, DIur, PhD; Belgian economist, academic and international organization official; *Professor, Institute of European Studies, Catholic University of Louvain;* b. 11 March 1945, Ophain-Bois-Seigneur-Isaac; m. Christine de Weck 1971; three c.; ed Catholic Univ. of Louvain, Harvard Univ., USA; worked for World Bank 1974–86, Exec. Dir representing Austria, Belgium, Luxembourg, Turkey and countries in transition (Belarus, Czech Repub., Hungary, Kazakhstan, Slovakia and Slovenia) 1991–94; Econ. Adviser, EC 1986–88; Chief of the Cabinet, Belgian Minister of Finance, Philippe Maystadt 1988–91; mem. Bd of Dirs, EBRD,

London, representing Belgium, Luxembourg and Slovenia 1994–2002; Dir Working Table II (Econ. Reconstruction, Devt and Co-operation), Stability Pact for South Eastern Europe 2002–05; Co-ordinator OSCE Econ. and Environmental Activities 2005–08, Prof., Inst. of European Studies, Catholic Univ. of Louvain 2008–; Pres., Asscn of the Nobility of the Kingdom of Belgium 2008–, Snoy Family Asscn; Pres. Int., European Chair. Centre de Culture Européenne, Brussels, Europe Direct du Brabant Wallon, Waterloo Cttee of Belgium (Pres. 2008–), Robert Triffin Int. Foundation (Pres. 2013–), Festival Musical du Brabant Wallon 2002–05, Monetary Panel of the European League for Econ. Co-operation 1996–2002 (Chair. Neighbourhood Comm. 2009–10, Pres. Int. 2010–); mem. Ind. Comm. for the Reform of the Insts and Procedures of the EU (Andriessen Comm.) 1998–99; mem. Bd of Dirs, Soc. Royale d'Économie Politique de Belgique 1999–2007, Cofinimmo SA (and of Audit Cttee) 2002–05; mem. Advisory Bd, Fondation Scientifique Jean Bastin; Commdr, Grand Order of the Crown of Oak (Luxembourg) 2001; Commdr, Order of Léopold 2009; Golden Medal for services to the Repub. of Austria 2006. *Publications include:* Taxes on Direct Investment Income in the E.E.C.: A Legal and Economic Analysis 1975, Fragility of the Int. Financial System: How Can We Prevent New Crises in Emerging Markets? (Int. Financial Relations) (co-author) 2002. *Address:* Institute of European Studies, Catholic University of Louvain, 1 Place des Doyens, 1348 Louvain-la-Neuve (office); Château de Bois-Seigneur-Isaac, 1421 Braine-l'Alleud, Belgium (home). *Telephone:* (10) 47-85-45 (office); (67) 21-38-80 (home). *Fax:* (10) 47-85-49 (office). *E-mail:* bernard.snoy@uclouvain.be (office); snoy.bernard@skynet.be (home). *Website:* www.uclouvain.be/262383.html (office); www.bois-seigneur-isaac.be (home).

SNYDER, Allan Whitenack, BS, MS, DSc, PhD, FRS; American/Australian optical scientist and academic; *Foundation Director, Centre for the Mind, Australian National University and University of Sydney;* b. 23 Nov. 1940, Philadelphia, Pa; s. of E. H. Snyder and Zelda Cotton; ed Cen. High School, Pennsylvania State Univ., Massachusetts Inst. of Tech., Harvard Univ. and Univ. Coll., London, UK; Greenland Ice Cap Communications Project 1961; Consultant, Gen. Telecommunications and Electricity Research Lab. 1963–67, British Post Office and Standard Telecommunications Lab. 1968–70; Sr Research Fellow, later Prof. Fellow, ANU 1971–79, Chair. Optical Physics and Visual Sciences Inst. for Advanced Studies 1978–, Head Applied Math. 1979–82, Founder and Head Optical Sciences Centre 1983–, apptd Foundation Dir Centre for the Mind 1997, Peter Karmel Professorial Chair of Science and the Mind 1998–; Aniv Prof. of Science and the Mind, Univ. of Sydney 2000–; NSF Fellowship, Dept of Applied Physics, Yale Univ. Medical School, USA 1970–71; Guggenheim Fellow 1977, Foundation Fellow, Nat. Vision Research Inst. of Australia 1983, Royal Soc. Quest Research Fellow, Univ. of Cambridge, UK 1987; 150th Anniversary Chair of Science and the Mind, Univ. of Sydney; Assoc. Ed. Journal of Optical Soc. of America 1981–83; Research Medal, Royal Soc. of Vic. 1974, Thomas Rankin Lyle Medal, Australian Acad. of Science 1985, Edgeworth David Medal, Royal Soc. of NSW, Sutherland Memorial Medal, Australian Acad. of Technological Sciences 1991, CSIRO Research Medal 1995, Harrie Massey Medal and Prize, British Inst. of Physics 1996, Arthur E. Mills Oration and Medal, RACP 1966, Int. Australia Prize 1997, Clifford Patterson Lecturer, Royal Soc., London 2001, Marconi Int. Fellowship and Prize 2001, Centenary Medal 2003. *Publications include:* Photoreceptors Optics (co-author) 1975, Optical Waveguide Sciences (co-author) 1983, Optical Waveguide Theory (co-author) 1983, What Makes a Champion! (ed.). *Leisure interests:* art, thought and mind. *Address:* Centre for Mind, Main Quadrangle (A14), University of Sydney, Sydney, NSW 2006, Australia (office). *Telephone:* (2) 9351-8531 (office). *E-mail:* allan@centreforthemind.com (office). *Website:* www.centreforthemind.com (office).

SNYDER, Barbara, BA, JD; American lawyer, academic and university administrator; *President, Case Western Reserve University;* b. 23 July 1955, Columbus, Ohio; m. Michael Snyder; two s. one d.; ed Ohio State Univ., Univ. of Chicago Law School; called to the Ill. Bar 1980; Legal Clerk, US Court of Appeals for Seventh Circuit, Chicago 1980–82; with Sidley & Austin (law firm), Chicago –1983; Asst Prof., Case Western Reserve School of Law, Cleveland 1983–86, Assoc. Prof. 1986–88, Pres. Case Western Reserve Univ. 2007–; Assoc. Prof., Moritz Coll. of Law, Ohio State Univ. 1988–90, Prof. 1990–2000, Joanne W. Murphy Prof. 2000–07, Interim Exec. Vice-Pres. and Provost, Ohio State Univ. 2003–04, Exec. Vice-Pres. and Provost 2004–07; mem. American Law Inst. 2007–; Moritz Coll. of Law Outstanding Professor Award 1997. *Publications:* co-author: Ohio Evidence 1996, The Ohio Rules of Evidence Handbook (annual 1996–2005). *Address:* Office of the President, Case Western Reserve University, 10900 Euclid Avenue, Cleveland, OH 44106-7001, USA (office). *Telephone:* (216) 368-4344 (office). *Fax:* (216) 368-4325 (office). *E-mail:* barbara.snyder@case.edu (office). *Website:* www.case.edu/president (office).

SNYDER, Richard Dale (Rick), BGS, MBA, JD; American business executive, politician and fmr state governor; b. 19 Aug. 1958, Battle Creek, Mich.; s. of Dale F. Snyder and Helen Louella 'Pody' Snyder; m. Sue Snyder 1987; one s. two d.; ed Stephen M. Ross School of Business, Univ. of Michigan, Univ. of Michigan Law School; with Coopers & Lybrand 1982–91, began in tax dept in Detroit office 1982, Partner 1988–89, Partner-in-Charge of mergers and acquisitions practice in Chicago office 1989–91; Exec. Vice-Pres. Gateway 1991–96, Pres. and COO 1996–97, Chair. 2005–07, interim CEO 2006 (co. sold to Acer Inc. of Taiwan 2007); Co-founder, Pres. and CEO Avalon Investments Inc. (venture capital co.), Ann Arbor, Mich. 1997–2000; Co-founder Ardesta LLC (venture capital firm), Ann Arbor 2000, Chair. and CEO –2010; mem. Bd of Dirs Henry Ford Museum, Michigan chapter of the Nature Conservancy and several bds tied to Univ. of Michigan; fmr Adjunct Asst Prof. of Accounting, Univ. of Michigan; Gov. of Michigan 2011–18; Chair. Ann Arbor SPARK; mem. Bd Univ. of Michigan Coll. of Eng Nat. Advisory Cttee, mem. Tech. Transfer Nat. Advisory Cttee, Univ. of Michigan; mem. Gov. e-Michigan Advisory Council; mem. Advisory Bd Samuel Zell & Robert H. Lurie Inst. for Entrepreneurial Studies, NanoBusiness Alliance, Visiting Cttee Purdue Univ. School of Eng; mem. Michigan Bar Asscn, The Nature Conservancy, Michigan Chapter; Trustee, The Henry Ford Foundation; Republican. *Address:* c/o Office of the Governor, State Capitol Building, PO Box 30013, Lansing, MI 48909, USA (office).

SO, Hon. John, AO, JP; Australian business executive and politician; b. 2 Oct. 1946, Hong Kong; ed Univ. of Melbourne; taught physics at Fitzroy High School then opened Dragon Boat restaurant in Flinders Lane, Melbourne 1976, went on to establish businesses in Australia, Hong Kong and China; Councillor, City of Melbourne 1991–96, 1999–2001, served as Commr, Ethnic Affairs Comm. 1991–93; Lord Mayor of Melbourne 2001–08; Chair. World Chinese Economic Forum Global Business Council, Melbourne 2012–; Special Advisor, All-China Federation of Returned Overseas Chinese 2013–; mem. Cttee for Melbourne Bd, Cancer Council Bd, Shrine of Remembrance Bd, Victorian Community Council on Crime and Violence; fmr Vice-Pres. Melbourne Chinatown Traders Asscn; Patron Melbourne Jr Chamber of Commerce; Dr hc (Victoria Univ.) 2007; You Bring Charm to the World Award (among most influential Chinese in 2006) 2007, World Chinese Economic Forum Lifetime Achievement Award 2011, Sir Edward 'Weary' Dunlop Asia Medal 2013. *Website:* www.johnso.com.au.

SOAMES, Rt Hon. Sir (Arthur) Nicholas Winston, Kt, PC; British politician; b. (Arthur Nicholas Winston Soames), 12 Feb. 1948; s. of Baron and Lady Soames; grandson of Sir Winston Churchill; m. 1st Catherine Weatherall 1981 (divorced 1988); m. 2nd Serena Smith 1993; two s. one d.; ed St Aubyns, Sussex and Eton Coll.; commissioned into 11th Hussars, served in Germany and UK, subsequently Equerry to HRH The Prince of Wales; worked as stockbroker 1972–74; Personal Asst to Sir James Goldsmith 1974–76; legislative asst on staff of US Senator Mark Hatfield, Washington DC 1976–78; Asst Dir Sedgwick Group 1979–81; joined firm of Lloyds Brokers as a Dir; MP (Conservative) for Crawley 1983–97, for Mid-Sussex 1997–; Parl. Sec. and Minister of Food, Ministry of Agric., Fisheries and Food 1992–94; Minister of State for the Armed Forces 1994–97; served on Countryside and Rights of Way Bill Cttee, Hunting Bill Cttee; fmr mem. Exec. of 1922 Committee; fmr Chair. Conservative Middle East Council; Shadow Sec. of State for Defence 2003–05; Pres. East Grinstead Target Shooting Club, Haywards Heath Dist Scout Council, Haywards Heath Rugby Football Club, Staplefield Cricket Club, South of England Hound Show; Vice-Pres. St Catherine's Hospice; fmr mem. Commonwealth War Graves Comm., Court of Univ. of Sussex, Council of the South of England Agricultural Soc., Burgess Hill Business Parks Asscn; Trustee, Amber Foundation; Patron No. 24 Burgess Hill Detachment, Sussex Army Cadet Force; Hon. Pres. 172 Haywards Heath Squadron (air cadets). *Leisure interests:* reading, music, horse racing, country pursuits. *Address:* House of Commons, Westminster, London, SW1A 0AA, England (office). *Telephone:* (20) 7219-4143 (office). *Fax:* (20) 7219-2998 (office). *E-mail:* nicholas.soames.mp@parliament.uk (office). *Website:* www.parliament.uk/biographies/commons/sir-nicholas-soames/116 (office); www.nicholassoames.org.uk.

SOARES, Eugénio Lourenço; São Tomé and Príncipe politician and central banker; fmr MP from Mé-Zochi; Gov. São Tomé e Príncipe, ADB; Minister of Planning and Finance 2003–04; apptd Vice-Gov. and mem. Council of Admin, Banco Central de São Tomé e Príncipe 2006, Admin. 2019–.

SOARES, Commdt Lúcio; Guinea-Bissau politician; b. 13 Dec. 1951, Bolama; m. Ana Maria Soares; five d.; Minister of Defence 2001, of the Interior 2009–11.

SOARES ALVES, Francisco José, MA; Portuguese archaeologist; b. 18 April 1942, Lisbon; s. of José Augusto Ferreira Alves and Margaret Hellen Libbie Mason Soares; m. (divorced); one s.; ed D. João de Castro High School, Lisbon, Univ. of Paris, DEA—Institut d'Art et d'Archéologie, Paris; Dir archaeological campus, Braga (Bracara Augusta) 1976–80; Dir Portuguese Dept of Archaeology 1980–82; Dir Nat. Museum of Archaeology 1980–96; Dir Portuguese Centre for Underwater and Nautical Archaeology 1997–2007; Prof. of Nautical and Underwater Archaeology, Universidade Nova de Lisboa, Faculdade de Ciências Sociais e Humanas 2000–12, currently Associated Researcher, Instituto de Arqueologia e Paleociências; Chief Div. of Nautical and Underwater Archaeology, IGESPAR (Portuguese Heritage), Ministry of Culture 2007–11; Dir of underwater archaeology on sites of L'Océan (French flagship sunk in 1759) 1984, 15th Century shipwreck Ria de Aveiro A 1996–99, Senhora dos Mártires shipwreck (Indiaman lost in Tagus bar 1606) 1997–98, Lima river dugouts (3rd century BC) 2003, Colab of the rescue and research of the 16th century Portuguese Oranjemund, Namibia shipwreck 2008–09; mem. Advisory Bd of State Parties of the Convention on the Protection of Underwater Cultural Heritage, UNESCO, Paris 2001; Franco Papo Award, 8th Rassegna di Archeologia, Italy. *Leisure interest:* diving. *Address:* Instituto de Arqueologia e Paleociências (IAP), Avenida de Berna 26C, 1069 Lisbon, Portugal. *E-mail:* franciscojsalves@gmail.com (home); iap@fcsh.unl.pt (office).

SOBAI, Muhammad Khalifa Turki al-; Qatari business executive; *Managing Director and CEO, Qatar Intermediate Industries Holding Company Ltd;* Gen. Man. Qatar Jet Fuel Co. 1992; Vice-Chair. and Man. Dir Qatar Fuel (Woqod) 2002–14; currently Man. Dir and CEO, Qatar Intermediate Industries Holding Co. Ltd. *Address:* Qatar Intermediate Industries Holding Co Ltd, POB 28882, 37 Muhammad bin Thani Street, bin Omran Area, al-Maha Bldg, Doha, Qatar (office). *Telephone:* 44976454 (office). *Fax:* 44293440 (office). *E-mail:* qh@qh.com.qa (office). *Website:* www.qh.com.qa (office).

SOBEL, Dava; American science writer; b. 15 June 1947, New York, NY; d. of Samuel H. Sobel MD and Betty Sobel (née Gruber); divorced; one s. one d.; ed State Univ. of NY at Binghamton; fmr science reporter, New York Times; reported for several journals including Audubon, Discover, Life, The New Yorker; fmr Contributing Ed. Harvard Magazine; has lectured at The Smithsonian Inst., The Explorers Club, NASA Goddard Space Flight Center, Folger Shakespeare Library, Los Angeles Public Library, NY Public Library, Royal Geographical Soc. (London); numerous radio and TV appearances; mem. American Asscn of Univ. Women, Planetary Soc.; Fellow, American Geographical Soc.; Hon. DLit (Middlebury Coll., Vt) 2002, (Bath, UK) 2002; Nat. Media Award American Psychological Foundation 1980, Lowell Thomas Award Soc. of American Travel Writers 1992, Gold Medal Council for the Advancement and Support of Educ. 1994, Christopher Award 1999, Los Angeles Times Book Prize 2000, Nat. Science Bd Public Service Award 2001, Bradford Washburn Award Boston Museum of Science 2001, Nathaniel Bowditch Maritime Scholar 2003, Harrison Medal, Worshipful Co. of Clockmakers (UK) 2004, Klumpke-Roberts Award, Astronomical Soc. of the Pacific 2008. *Publications:* Is Anyone Out There? The Scientific Search for Extraterrestrial Intelligence (with Frank D. Drake) 1992, Longitude (several awards including Harold D. Vursell Memorial Award American Acad. of Arts and Letters 1996, UK Book of the Year 1996, Prix Faubert du Coton, Premio del Mare Circeo) 1995, Galileo's Daughter: A Historical Memoir of Science, Faith, and Love 1999, Letters to Father 2001, The Planets 2005, A More Perfect Heaven: How Copernicus Revolutionized the Cosmos 2011, The Glass Universe: How the Ladies of the Harvard Observatory Took the Measure of the Stars 2016. *Address:* c/o Michael Carlisle, InkWell Management, 521 Fifth Avenue, 26th Floor, New York, NY 10175, USA (office). *E-mail:* dava@davasobel.com. *Website:* www.davasobel.com.

SOBERANES FERNÁNDEZ, José Luis, LicenDer, LLD; Mexican lawyer and academic; b. 10 Jan. 1950, Santiago de Querétaro, Querétaro; ed law degree from Universidad Nacional Autónoma de México (UNAM), Universidad de Valencia, Spain; Sec.-Gen. Latin American univs' asscn 1985–90; Dir Instituto de Investigaciones Jurídicas, UNAM 1990–98, full-time researcher at UNAM; Prof., Nat. Univ. of San Marcos (Peru); Visiting Prof. of the Social Sciences, Univ. of Toulouse, France; apptd by Congress Pres. Comisión Nacional de los Derechos Humanos (Nat. Comm. for Human Rights) 1999–2009; Academician and fmr Fellow, Royal Acad. of Jurisprudence, Spain; Great Cross of San Raimundo de Peñafort (Spain). *Publications include:* more than 20 books, including Los tribunales de la Nueva España 1980, Sobre el origen de la Suprema Corte de Justicia de la Nación 1987, Historia del sistema jurídico mexicano 1990, Los bienes eclesiásticos en la historia constitucional de México 1999; numerous papers in academic journals.

SOBERÓN VALDÉS, Francisco, PhD; Cuban politician and fmr central banker; b. 18 April 1945; fmr Prof. of Social Sciences and Econ. Planning; Founder and Leader, Unión de jóvenes Party (UJC) 1962–64; apptd mem. Cen. Cttee CP Party of Cuba 1970; fmr Deputy in Nat. Ass. of People's Power; Pres. Nat. Bank of Cuba (renamed Cen. Bank of Cuba 1997) 1995–2009 (resgnd).

SOBERS, Sir Garfield (Gary) St Aubrun, Kt, AO; Barbadian/Australian fmr cricketer; b. 28 July 1936, St Michael; s. of Thelma Sobers and Shamont Sobers; m. Prudence Kirby 1969 (divorced 1990); two s. one adopted d.; ed Bay St School, Barbados; left-hand batsman, left-arm bowler, using all kinds of bowling; outstanding all-rounder; teams: Barbados 1952–74 (Capt. 1965–71), S Australia 1961–64, Notts. 1968–74 (Capt. 1968–71, 1973); Test debut: West Indies v England, Kingston 30 March–3 April 1954; only One-Day Int.: England v West Indies, Leeds 5 Sept. 1973; played in 93 Tests for W Indies 1953–74, 39 as Capt., scoring 8,032 runs (average 57.78) with 26 hundreds, including record 365 not out (record 1958–94), taking 235 wickets (average 34.03) and holding 109 catches, best bowling (innings) 6/73, (match) 8/80; scored First-class 28,314 runs (average 54.87) including 86 hundreds, took 1,043 wickets and held 407 catches, best bowling 9/49; hit six sixes in an over, Notts. vs Glamorgan at Swansea 1968; toured England 1957, 1963, 1966, 1969, 1973; Special Consultant Barbados Tourism Authority 1980; apptd tech. consultant to West Indies cricket coach 2004; became a dual Barbadian/Australian citizen through marriage in 1980; Hon. Life mem. MCC 1981; Order of the Caribbean Community 1998; West Indian Cricket Cricketer of the Year 1958–59, Wisden Cricketer of the Year 1964, The Cricket Soc. Wetherall Award for the Leading All-Rounder in English First-Class Cricket 1970, Walter Lawrence Trophy 1974, Barbados Nat. Hero 1998, selected as one of five Wisden Cricketers of the Century 2000, Sir Garfield Sobers Trophy inaugurated by Int. Cricket Council (ICC) 2004, selected retrospectively by Wisden as the Leading Cricketer in the World for the years 1958, 1960, 1962, 1964–66, 1968, 1970 2007. *Publications include:* Cricket Advance 1965, Cricket Crusader 1966, King Cricket 1967 (with J. S. Barker), Cricket in the Sun (with J. S. Barker) 1967, Bonaventure and the Flashing Blade 1967, Sobers: Twenty Years at the Top 1988, Sobers: The Changing Face of Cricket (with Ivo Tennant) 1995. *Leisure interest:* golf. *Address:* 23 Highgate Gardens, St Michael, Barbados (home).

SOBHI SAYED AHMED, Col-Gen. Sedki; Egyptian army officer and government official; b. 12 Dec. 1955; ed Egyptian Mil. Acad., US Army War Coll., USA; joined Egyptian Army 1976, several command roles with Third Field Army, including Commdr, Mechanized Infantry Bn, Chief of Staff, Mechanized Infantry Brigade, Chief, Operations Br., Commdr, Third Field Army 2009; Chief of Staff, Egyptian Armed Forces 2012–14; Deputy Chair. Supreme Council of Armed Forces of Egypt 2012–14; Minister of Defence and Supreme Commdr of Armed Forces 2014–18; attained rank of Maj.-Gen., Lt-Gen. 2012, Col-Gen. 2014; Fellow, Higher War Coll., Nasser Higher Mil. Acad. 2000; numerous mil. decorations including 25 April Decoration (Liberation of Sinai), Mil. Duty Decoration, First and Second Class, Liberation of Kuwait Medal, Golden Jubilee of 23 July Revolution, 25 Jan. Revolution Medal. *Address:* c/o Ministry of Defence, Sharia 23 July, Kobri el-Kobba, Cairo, Egypt (office).

SOBIROV, Ilgizar Matiakubovich, CandIur; Uzbekistani politician; b. 20 Feb. 1959, Urtaiap Kushkupir dist, Xorazm Viloyat; ed Law Faculty, Tashkent State Univ.; began career as mem. law collective, Kurshkupir dist; completed mil. service 1980; carried out pedagogical work in criminal law 1986–94; apptd Pro-Rector, Tashkent Legal Inst. 1994; fmr legal worker, Philosophy and Law Inst., Uzbek Acad. of Sciences; worked in Supreme Court, becoming Plenum Sec. and mem. Supreme Econ. Court; directed prov. admin of justice in Khorezm Prov.; Deputy, Oliy Majlis (Supreme Ass.) 2000–03, Deputy Chair. Cttee on Questions of Defence and Security 1999–2004, later Chair. Cttee on Legislation and Legal Questions; Hokim (Gov.), Kushkupir dist, Xorazm Viloyat 2003–05; elected Senator 2005–, Chair. Cttee on Questions of Defence and Security 2005–06, Chair. Senate 2006–15. *Address:* c/o Office of the Chairman of the Senate, 100029 Tashkent, Mustaqillik maydoni 6, Uzbekistan.

SOBOLEV, Col-Gen. Valentin; Russian government official; b. 11 March 1947, Kyzyl-Atrek Dist (Turkmen SSR); ed V. Kuibyshev Inst. of Engineering and Construction, Moscow and Fed. Security Services Acad.; began career as construction worker, Asgabat 1962; served in KGB; Deputy Dir Fed. Counter-intelligence Service 1994–97; First Deputy Dir Fed. Security Service 1997–99; Deputy Sec., Security Council of the Russian Fed. 1999–2012, Acting Sec. 2007–08.

SOBOTKA, Bohuslav, BLL; Czech lawyer and politician; b. 23 Oct. 1971, Telnice; m. Olga Sobotková 2003; two s.; ed Masaryk Univ., Brno; mem. Česká strana sociálně demokratická (ČSSD—Czech Social Democratic Party) 1989–, Chair. Deputies Club 2001–02, Acting Chair. ČSSD 2010–11, Chair. 2011–17; mem. Parl. for Jihomoravský (ČSSD) 1996–2002, 2002–06, 2006–; mem. Mandate (Proxy) and

Immunity Cttee 1996–98; Chair. Sub-cttee for Financial and Capital Markets, Budget Cttee 1998–2001; mem. Municipal Council of Slavkov, nr Brno 1998–2010; Chair. Interim Comm. for Pension Reform 2001; Minister of Finance 2002–06; First Deputy Prime Minister 2005–06; Prime Minister 2014–17. *Leisure interests:* history, literature, science fiction, theatre, cinema (especially Czech films), travel. *Address:* c/o Office of the Government, náb. Edvarda Beneše 4, 118 01 Prague 1 (office); 9. května 21, 682 01 Vyškov, Czech Republic. *E-mail:* bsobotka@socdem.cz; info@bohuslavsobotka.cz. *Website:* www.bohuslavsobotka.cz.

SOBOTKA, Přemysl, MUDr; Czech physician and politician; b. 18 May 1944, Mladá Boleslav; s. of Zdeněk Sobotka and Eliška Sobotka; ed Charles Univ., Prague; physician 1968–; councillor, Liberec 1990–96; Chief Physician, Hosp. Liberec 1990–98; mem. Civic Democratic Party (Občanská demokratická strana—ODS); Senator, Vice-Chair. of Senát (Senate) 1996–2002, Chair. 2004–10, mem. Cttee on Agenda and Procedure, Sub-cttee on Bestowing Decorations, Civic Democratic Party Caucus. *Publications:* papers in medical journals. *Leisure interests:* tennis, volleyball, travel. *Address:* Senát PČR, Valdštejnské nám. 4, 11801 Prague 1 (office); Nezvaolova 658, 460 16 Liberec, Czech Republic (home). *Telephone:* (2) 57072331 (office); (6) 02348371 (home). *Fax:* (2) 57534509 (office). *E-mail:* sobotkap@senat.cz (office). *Website:* www.mfcr.cz (office); www.premyslsobotka.cz.

SOBTI, Atul, BEcons (Hons); Indian business executive; *Chairman and Managing Director, Bharat Heavy Electricals Limited;* ed St Stephen's Coll., Univ. of Delhi, Indian Inst. of Man., Ahmedabad; has 30 years' experience in industries including durables, information tech. services, automobiles and pharmaceuticals; has worked for Xerox and Honda; Exec. Dir (Sales, Marketing, Finance and Human Resources) Hero Honda 1998–2005; Pres. (India, Middle East, Asia Pacific and the Global Consumer Healthcare Business) Ranbaxy Laboratories Ltd 2005–07, COO 2007–09, CEO and Man. Dir 2009–10 (resgnd); Dir Bharat Heavy Electricals Ltd 2013–, Dir, Power –2015, Finance 2015–16, Chair. and Man. Dir 2016–. *Address:* Bharat Heavy Electricals Ltd, Siri Fort, New Delhi 110049, India (office). *Telephone:* (11) 66337000 (office). *Fax:* (11) 26493021 (office). *Website:* www.bhel.com (office).

SOBYANIN, Sergei Semenovich, PhD; Russian politician; *Mayor of Moscow;* b. 21 June 1958, Nyaksumvol, Berezovo Dist, Khanty-Mansii Nat. (now Autonomous) Okrug, Tyumen Oblast, Russian SFSR, USSR; m. Irina Sobyanina (divorced 2014); two d.; ed Kostroma State Inst. of Tech.; metalworker and then foreman at Chelyabinsk Pipe Plant 1980–82; Head of Admin. Dept Lenin Dist Komsomol, Chelyabinsk 1982–84; party and admin. work in Khanty-Mansii Autonomous Okrug, Tyumen Oblast 1984–90; Head of State Tax Inspection Office, Kogalym, Khanty-Mansii Autonomous Okrug 1990–91; Mayor of Kogalym 1991–93; First Deputy Head Khanty-Mansii Autonomous Okrug 1993–94; Chair. Khanty-Mansii Autonomous Okrug Duma, mem. Fed. Council and Chair. Fed. Council Cttee on Constitutional Legislation and Judicial-Legal Matters 1994–2000; First Deputy to Presidential Plenipotentiary Envoy in Urals Fed. Okrug 2000–01; Gov. of Tyumen Oblast 2001–05; Chief of Staff, Presidential Exec. Office 2005–08; Deputy Chair. of the Govt, in charge of co-ordinating Fed. Agencies, also Head of Govt Staff 2008–10; Mayor of Moscow 2010–; Chair. TVEL (state nuclear power co.) 2006–; Order of Merit, Medal For Services to the Fatherland (Second Degree), Church Second Stage Order of St Prince Danil Moskovskii, Medal of Honour in Educ., Ordre du Mérite Agricole (France) 2003; Russia's Man of the Year: Politician Prize 2003. *Address:* Office of the Mayor and Prime Minister of the Government of Moscow City, 125032 Moscow, ul. Tverskaya 13, Russia (office). *E-mail:* ud@mos.ru (office). *Website:* www.mos.ru (office).

SÓCRATES CARVALHO PINTO DE SOUSA, José; Portuguese politician; b. 6 Sept. 1957, Vilar de Maçada; divorced; two c.; Chair. Castelo Branco Fed., Partido Socialista (Socialist Party) 1983–96, mem. Partido Socialista Secr. 1991–, Spokesperson on Environmental Affairs 1991–95, Sec.-Gen. 2004–11; mem. Parl. 1987–2011; mem. Covilha Municipal Ass. 1989–96; Deputy Minister to the Prime Minister 1995–99; Minister of Environmental Affairs 1999–April 2002, of Public Works Jan.–April 2002; Prime Minister of Portugal 2005–11 (resgnd); Chair. Advisory Council for Latin America, Octapharma AG (pharmaceutical co.) 2013–; Pres. World Conf. of Ministers Responsible for Youth 1998.

SODANO, HE Cardinal Angelo, STD, JCD; Italian ecclesiastic; *Dean, College of Cardinals, Roman Curia;* b. 23 Nov. 1927, Isola d'Asti; s. of Hon. Giovanni Sodano and Delfina Brignolo; ed Pontifical Gregorian Univ., Rome, Pontifical Lateran Univ., Rome and Pontifical Ecclesiastical Acad., Rome; ordained priest, Asti 1950; Sec. Apostolic Nunciatures in Ecuador, Uruguay and Chile 1961–68; official, Council for Public Affairs of Church, Vatican City State 1968–77; apptd Titular Archbishop of Nova Caesaris 1977; Apostolic Nuncio to Chile 1978–88; Sec. Council for Public Affairs of the Church 1988–89; Sec. for Relations with States of Secr. of State 1989–90; Pro-Sec. of State to His Holiness Pope John Paul II 1990–91; cr. Cardinal-Priest of S. Maria Nuova 1991; Sec. of State 1991–2005 (resgnd), re-apptd 2005–06 (resgnd); apptd Cardinal-Bishop of Albano 1994–, Cardinal-Bishop of Ostia 2005–; mem. Congregations for the Doctrine of the Faith, for the Bishops, Pontifical Comm. for Vatican City State; Vice-Dean Coll. of Cardinals 2002–05, Dean 2005–; numerous honours and awards. *Address:* 00120 Vatican City, Rome, Italy (office).

SØDERBERG, Jess, MBA; Danish business executive; *Deputy Chairman of the Supervisory Board, Carlsberg Breweries A/S;* b. 1944; ed Copenhagen Business School; joined A.P. Møller 1970, various positions finance in USA and Denmark, Pnr 1986–93, Pnr and Group CEO A.P. Møller-Mærsk A/S 1993–2007; Vice-Chair. Mærsk Olie og Gas A/S 2004; Deputy Chair. Carlsberg Breweries A/S 2009–; Adviser to Permira; fmr Chair. Dansk Supermarked A/S, F. Salling A/S, Ejendomsaktieselskabet; mem. Advisory Council, Danske Bank; Kt, Order of Dannebrog, Order of Bernardo O'Higgins (Chile). *Address:* Carlsberg Breweries A/S, 100 Ny Carlsberg Vej, 1799 Copenhagen V, Denmark (office). *Website:* www.carlsberggroup.com (office).

SODERBERG, Nancy E., BA, MS; American political scientist, academic, international organization official, fmr diplomatist and fmr government official; *Distinguished Visiting Scholar, Department of Political Science and Public Administration and Faculty Administrator, University of North Florida;* b. 13 March 1958, San Turce, Puerto Rico; d. of Lars Olof Soderberg and Nancy Soderberg (née MacGilvrey); ed Vanderbilt Univ., Georgetown Univ. School of Foreign Service; budget and reports analyst, Bank of New England, Boston 1980–82; Research Asst Brookings Inst., Washington, DC 1982–83; Research Asst, US Agency for Int. Devt, Washington, DC 1983; Del. Selection Asst, Mondale-Ferraro Cttee, Washington, DC 1983, Foreign Policy Adviser 1984 (unsuccessful US presidential campaign); Deputy Issues Dir, Foreign Policy, Dukakis for Pres. Cttee, Boston 1988; Foreign Policy Adviser to Senator Edward Kennedy, Washington, DC 1985–88, 1989–92; Foreign Policy Dir Clinton/Gore Transition, Little Rock 1992–93; Special Asst to Pres. for Nat. Security Affairs, Staff Dir Nat. Security Council, Washington, DC 1993–95, Deputy Asst to Pres. for Nat. Security Affairs 1995–2001; Alt. Rep. to UN with rank of Amb. 1997–2001; Vice-Pres. (Multilateral Affairs), Int. Crisis Group, New York 2001–05; Distinguished Visiting Scholar, Univ. of North Florida, Jacksonville 2006–, Faculty Admin., Political Science and Public Admin, Coll. of Arts and Sciences; Adjunct Prof., Columbia Univ. School of Int. and Public Affairs 2004; foreign policy analyst for MSNBC; mem. Council for Foreign Relations; mem. Bd of Dirs, Concern Worldwide, Member, Jacksonville Port Authority 2013–; mem. Advisory Bd, Nat. Cttee on American Foreign Policy, Tannenbaum Center; Pres. Sister Cities Program of the City of New York 2002–06, The Connect U.S. Fund, Washington, DC; Precinct Committeewoman, Duval Co. Democratic Exec. Cttee, Jacksonville, Fla 2008–; Chair. Public Interest Declassification Bd 2011–; cand. for the Florida Senate Dist #4 2012; mem. Bd of Dirs, Florida Democratic Party and Chair. Northeast Florida Democratic Leadership Council 2013–. *Publications:* The Superpower Myth: The Use and Misuse of American Might 2005, The Prosperity Agenda: What the World Wants from America—and What We Need in Return (co-author) 2008; numerous articles in professional journals. *Address:* University of North Florida, Department of Political Science and Public Administration, Building 51, Room 2114, Jacksonville, FL 32224-2645; 121 Lantern Wick Place, Ponte Vedra Beach, FL 32082, USA. *Telephone:* (904) 620-3926 (office); (904) 620-3926. *E-mail:* n.soderberg@unf.edu (office); nsoderberg@aol.com. *Website:* www.unf.edu/bio/N00445553 (office).

SODERBERGH, Steven; American film director, producer and screenwriter; b. 14 Jan. 1963, Atlanta; s. of Peter Andrew Soderbergh and Mary Ann Bernard; m. Elizabeth Jeanne Brantley 1989 (divorced 1994); m. 2nd Jules Asner 2003; ed high school and animation course at Louisiana State Univ.; aged 15 made short film Janitor; briefly ed. Games People Play (TV show); made short film Rapid Eye Movement while working as coin-changer in video arcade; produced video for Showtime for their album 90125; Co–founder Section Eight Productions 2001-07; signed six-film deal with 2929 Entertainment, releasing films simultaneously in cinemas, on DVD and on cable TV 2005–; Robert B. Aldrich Service Award, Dirs Guild of America 2014. *Films:* Winston (dir, screenplay) 1987, Sex, Lies and Videotape (dir, screenplay) (Cannes Palme d'Or) 1989, Kafka (dir) 1991, King of the Hill (dir, screenplay) 1993, Suture (exec. producer) 1993, Underneath (dir, screenplay) 1995, Gray's Anatomy (dir) 1996, Schizopolis (dir, screenplay) 1996, The Daytrippers (producer) 1996, Nightwatch (screenplay) 1997, Pleasantville (prod.) 1998, Out of Sight (dir) 1998, The Limey (dir) 1999, Erin Brockovich (dir) 2000, Traffic (dir) (Acad. Award for Best Dir) 2000, Ocean's Eleven (dir) 2001, Who is Bernard Tapie? (exec. producer) 2001, Tribute (exec. producer) 2001, Welcome to Collinwood (producer) 2002, Far from Heaven (exec. producer) 2002, Naqoyqatsi (exec. producer) 2002, Confessions of a Dangerous Mind (exec. producer) 2002, Insomnia (exec. producer) 2002, Full Frontal (dir) 2002, Solaris (dir, screenplay) 2002, Criminal (screenplay) 2004, Eros (dir, screenplay) 2004, Ocean's Twelve (dir) 2004, Able Edwards (exec. producer) 2004, Criminal (producer) 2004, Keane (producer) 2004, Bubble (dir, producer) 2005, The Big Empty (exec. producer) 2005, The Jacket (producer) 2005, Good Night and Good Luck (exec. producer) 2005, Rumor Has It (exec. producer) 2005, Syriana (producer) 2005, A Scanner Darkly (exec. producer) 2006, The Half Life of Timofey Berezin (producer) 2006, The Good German (dir, producer) 2006, Wind Chill (exec. producer) 2007, Ocean's Thirteen (exec. producer) 2007, Che 2008, The Informant! (dir) 2009, And Everything is Going Fine 2010, Haywire 2011, Magic Mike (dir) 2012. *Television as Director:* Fallen Angels (episode, The Quiet Room) 1993, K Street (series, also exec. producer) 2003, Unscripted (series pilot episode, also exec. producer) 2005, Behind the Candelabra (Outstanding Directorial Achievement in Movies for TV and Mini-Series, Dirs Guild of America 2014) 2013. *Address:* c/o Dollard Management & Productions, 21361 Pacific Coast Highway, #3, Malibu, CA 90265, USA.

SOEKNANDAN, Manorma P., LLB, PhD; Suriname lawyer and diplomatist; *Deputy Secretary-General, Caribbean Community (CARICOM);* b. Paramaribo; ed Anton de Kom Univ.; worked for 27 years as lawyer with Govt of Suriname, including in Dept of Legislation and Legal Advice, Ministry of Justice and Police, becoming Head, Judicial Dept 1995; Amb. to Guyana 2001–13, also accred to Jamaica and to Caribbean Community (CARICOM) 2002 (represented Suriname, including as head of del., at several meetings of CARICOM's organs and bodies including CARICOM Legal Affairs Cttee); Deputy Sec.-Gen., CARICOM Secr. 2016–; fmr teacher, Advanced Teacher Training Inst., Paramaribo; Visiting Prof. in Int. Law, Univ. of Suriname; Suriname Rep. on Working Group on Legal Educ. in the Caribbean 1999–. *Address:* Caribbean Community and Common Market (CARICOM), PO Box 10827, Georgetown, Guyana (office). *Telephone:* (2) 222-0001 (office). *Fax:* (2) 222-0171 (office). *E-mail:* registry@caricom.org (office). *Website:* www.caricom.org (office).

SOEMARNO, Rini Mariani, BEcons; Indonesian business executive and politician; *Minister of State-owned Enterprises;* b. 9 June 1958, Bethesda, Md, USA; m. Didik Soewandi (divorced); three c.; ed Wellesley Coll., USA; with Departemen Keuangan AS 1981; trainee, US Treasury Dept, Washington, DC, USA 1981–82; economist, Citibank 1982–89; Gen. Man. Finance Div., PT Astra International (Indonesia's main car maker) 1989, Dir of Finance 1990–98, Exec. Dir 1998–2000; Vice-Chair. Nat. Banking Penyehatan 1998; Vice-Pres. Commr PT United Tractors 1993; Commr Jakarta Stock Exchange 1995–2001; Commr PT Astra Agro Lestari 1995, Pres. Commr 1999; Pres. Commr PT Citra Motorindo 2000; Commr PT Agrakom 2000; Econ. Adviser to Minister of Finance 1997–98; Deputy Chair. Indonesian Bank Restructuring Agency April 1998; Minister of Industry and Trade 2001–04; Commr Aora TV 2008–; Minister of State-owned Enterprises 2014–. *Address:* Minister of State-owned Enterprises, Jalan Medan

Merdeka Selatan 13, Jakarta 10110, Indonesia (office). *Telephone:* (21) 29935678 (office). *Fax:* (21) 29935740 (office). *Website:* www.bumn.go.id (office).

SÕERD, Aivar; Estonian business executive and politician; b. 22 Nov. 1964, Haapsalu; pnr; three s.; ed Univ. of Tartu, Univ. of Oulu; Dir of Tartu Agency, AS Eesti Kindlustus 1990–93; Acting Head of Tax Policy Dept, Ministry of Finance 1993–96; Acting, then Perm. Gen. Dir Estonian Tax Bd 1996–2004; Chair. AS Vaba Maa 2004–05; Minister of Finance 2005–07, also Gov. of EIB for Estonia; Man. Dir Tallink Hotels 2007–11; mem. Riigikogu (Parl.) 2011–; mem. Estonian People's Union 2005–10, Estonian Reform Party 2010–; Order of The White Star (Fourth Class) 2003; Global Finance Minister of the Year (Financial Times Group magazine The Banker Award) 2007. *Leisure interests:* recreational sports, music. *Address:* State Assembly (Riigikogu), Lossi plats 1a, 15165 Tallinn, Estonia (office). *E-mail:* Aivar.Soerd@riigikogu.ee (office). *Website:* www.riigikogu.ee (office); www.aivarsoerd.ee.

SOERYADJAYA, Edwin, BBA; Indonesian business executive; *President Commissioner, PT Saratoga Investama Sedaya Tbk;* s. of William Soeryadjaya; m.; three c.; ed Univ. of Southern California, USA; Vice-Pres. and Dir PT Astra International Tbk (conglomerate) 1981–93; f. PT Saratoga Investama Sedaya 1991, Pres. Commr 1997–; Commr PT Aria West International 1995–2003; Chair. and Founding Pnr, Saratoga Capital 1998–; Chair. L & M Group Investments Ltd, Singapore 2009–; Chair. PT Adaro Energy Tbk (coal mine), PT Sapta Indra Sejati (mining contractor), PT Indonesia Bulk Terminal (coal terminal), PT Pulau Seroja Jaya (dry bulk barging), PT Mitra Global Telekomunikasi Indonesia (telecom operator), PT Makmur Sejahtera Wisesa (power plant); Co-Propr Recapital Asia; Chair. Christian Univ. of Indonesia Foundation (Yayasan Universitas Kristen Indonesia). *Address:* PT Saratoga Investama Sedaya Tbk., Menara Karya, 15th Floor Jl. H.R. Rasuna Said Block X-5 Kav. 1-2, Jakarta 12950, Indonesia (office). *Website:* saratoga-investama.com.

SOESATYO, Bambang, BPA, MBA; Indonesian politician and business executive; *Speaker, House of Representatives;* b. 10 Sept. 1962, Jakarta; m. Lenny Sri Mulyani; eight c.; ed Indonesia Open Univ., Sekolah Tinggi Ilmu Ekonomi Indonesia; fmr accountant, lecturer, publr; Man. Ed. Batu Karang Emas Sejati 1985; Journalist Vista Magazine 1989–92, Editorial Sec. 1989–92, Promotion Man. 1989–92; Dir Kodeco Timber 2007–13; mem. House of Reps. (Parl.) (Golkar) for Central Java 2009–, Speaker 2018–; fmr mem., Special Cttee, Corruption Eradication Comm.; mem. Partai Golkar 2014–, Chair. 2017–. *Address:* House of Representatives, Senayan, Jakarta 10270, Indonesia (office). *Telephone:* (21) 5715924 (office). *E-mail:* bag_humas@dpr.go.id (office). *Website:* www.dpr.go.id (office).

SOETJIPTO, Dwi, BChemEng, MA, PhD; Indonesian business executive; *President Director and CEO, PT Pertamina (Persero);* b. 10 Nov. 1955, Surabaya, East Java; m. Handini Soetjipto; four c.; ed Institut Teknologi Sepuluh Nopember, Surabaya, Univ. of Andalas, Univ. of Indonesia; began career in PT Semen Padang 1981, R&D Dir, PT Semen Padang 1995–2003, Pres. Dir 2003–05, Pres. Dir PT Semen Gresik (Persero) Tbk 2005–13, Pres. Dir PT Semen Indonesia (Persero) Tbk 2013–14; Pres. Dir and CEO PT Pertamina (Persero) 2014–; Commr, PT Bursa Efek Indonesia. *Address:* Pertamina Pusat, Jl. Medan Merdeka Timur 1A, Jakarta 10110, Indonesia (office). *Telephone:* (21) 3815111 (office); (21) 79173000 (office). *Fax:* (21) 3633585 (office); (21) 7972177 (office). *E-mail:* pcc@pertamina.com (office). *Website:* www.pertamina.com (office).

SOEUF, Mohamed El Amine; Comoran diplomatist and politician; *Minister of External Relations and International Co-operation, with responsibility for Comorans Abroad;* b. 28 July 1962, Moroni; Amb. to Egypt and Perm. Rep. to Arab League 1995–98; Minister of State, Minister of Foreign Affairs, Co-operation, Francophone Affairs, with Responsibility for Comorans Abroad 1999–2005; Deputy Union Ass. 2004; Perm. Rep. to UN, New York 2006; lived in exile in Paris from 2006; Minister of External Relations and Int. Co-operation, with responsibility for Comorans Abroad 2017–. *Publications:* Les Comores en mouvement 2008, Les grands défis de la politique étrangère des Comores 2009, Le Transport aérien aux Comores entre Souveraineté et Sécurité 2009, Discours et Images des Comores, Réflexions sur géopolitique de l'Océan indien. *Address:* Ministry of External Relations and Co-operation, BP 428, Moroni, Comoros (office). *Telephone:* 7732306 (office). *Fax:* 7732108 (office). *E-mail:* mirex@snpt.km (office). *Website:* www.diplomatie.gouv.km (office).

SOFAER, Abraham David, AB, LLD; American lawyer, fmr judge, academic and fmr government official; *George P. Shultz Senior Fellow in Foreign Policy and National Security Affairs, Hoover Institution, Stanford University;* b. 6 May 1938, Bombay, India; m. Marian Bea Scheuer 1977; five s. one d.; ed Yeshiva Coll. and New York Univ. School of Law; called to New York Bar 1965; law clerk, US Court of Appeals 1965–66, to Hon. J. Skelly and Hon. William J. Brennan, Jr, US Supreme Court 1966–67; Asst US Attorney, South Dist, New York 1967–69; Prof. of Law, Columbia Univ. 1969–79; Judge, US Dist Court for South Dist, New York 1979–85; Legal Adviser, State Dept, Washington, DC 1985–90; Partner, Hughes Hubbard & Reed 1991–94; George P. Shultz Distinguished Scholar, Sr Fellow in Foreign Policy and Nat. Security Affairs, Hoover Inst., Stanford Univ. 1994–, Prof. of Law (by Courtesy), Stanford Univ. 1996–; Distinguished Service Award, US State Dept 1988. *Recording:* CD on Jazz Standards. *Publications:* War, Foreign Affairs and Constitutional Power: The Origins 1976; articles in legal journals. *Leisure interests:* charitable activities, ancient coins, opera (amateur tenor with choruses, including Desoff and Stanford). *Address:* Hoover Institution, Stanford University, Stanford, CA 94305-6010 (office); 1200 Bryant Street, Palo Alto, CA 94301, USA (home). *Telephone:* (650) 725-3763 (office). *Fax:* (650) 723-8583 (office). *E-mail:* asofaer@stanford.edu (office). *Website:* www.abesofaer.com.

SOFIA, Michael (Mike) J., BA, PhD; American chemist, business executive and academic; *Chief Scientific Officer, Arbutus Biopharma, Inc.;* b. 1958; m.; ed Baltimore Polytechnic Inst., Cornell Univ., Univ. of Illinois, Urbana-Champaign; NIH Fellow, Columbia Univ.; Sr Research Scientist, Eli Lilly 1989–93; Vice-Pres. of Discovery Research, Transcell Technologies/Intercardia, Inc. 1993–99; Group Dir, New Leads Chem., Bristol-Myers Squibb 1999–2005; Sr Vice-Pres., Chem., Pharmasset, Inc. 2005–12; Sr Vice-Pres., Chem., Site Head and Sr Advisor, Gilead Sciences, Inc. 2012–13; Pres., Chief Scientific Officer and Co-founder OnCore Biopharma, Inc. 2012–15, Chief Scientific Officer, Arbutus Biopharma, Inc. (following merger of OnCore Biopharma and Tekmira) 2015–; Adjunct Prof., Drexel Univ. School of Medicine 2013–; Prof., Baruch S. Blumberg Inst. 2013–; Scientific Achievement Award, Pennsylvania BIO 2014, Global Thinkers Award, Foreign Policy Magazine 2014, Recognition Award for Scientific Achievement, Pennsylvania Senate and House of Reps 2014, ACS Heroes of Chem. Award 2015, IUPAC-Richter Prize 2016, Lasker~DeBakey Clinical Medical Research Award, Lasker Foundation (co-recipient) 2016. *Publications:* nine book chapters and more than 100 papers in professional journals; more than 30 patents. *Address:* Arbutus Biopharma, Inc., 100-8900 Glenlyon Parkway, Burnaby, BC V5J 5J8, Canada (office). *Telephone:* (604) 419-3200 (office). *Fax:* (604) 419-3201 (office). *E-mail:* info@arbutusbio.com (office). *Website:* arbutusbio.com (office).

SOFTIĆ, Senad, PhD; Bosnia and Herzegovina academic and central banker; *Governor, Central Bank of Bosnia and Herzegovina;* b. 10 Aug. 1963; Researcher–Expert Assoc., Inst. for Org. and Econs, Sarajevo 1987–95; joined Sarajevo Inst. of Econs as Researcher–Academic Assoc., then Head, Centre for Microeconomic Analyses 1995–2007; Asst Prof., School of Econs and Business, Univ. of Sarajevo, later Sr Asst Prof., then part-time Assoc. Prof. –2015, served as Chair. Governing Bd, Faculty of Econs; also served as Head of Master Studies, Sarajevo School of Econs and Business and Zagreb Faculty of Econs and Business; fmr Deputy Chair. Supervisory Bd, Investment Bank, FBiH Devt Bank; Gov. Cen. Bank of Bosnia and Herzegovina 2015–, also Chair. Governing Bd; mem. of Soc. of Economists, Sarajevo. *Publications include:* 13 books and monographs as author or co-author; 30 scientific papers in collections, journals, seminars and symposia. *Address:* Central Bank of Bosnia and Herzegovina, 71000 Sarajevo, Maršala Tita 25, Bosnia and Herzegovina (office). *Telephone:* (33) 278100 (office). *Fax:* (33) 278299 (office). *E-mail:* pr@cbbh.ba (office). *Website:* www.cbbh.ba (office).

SOGAVARE, Manasseh Damukana, BA; Solomon Islands politician; *Prime Minister;* b. 17 Jan. 1955; m. Emmy Sogavare; fmr Chair. Solomon Islands Nat. Provident Fund; Perm. Sec., Ministry of Finance 1994–96; mem. Nat. Parl. for East Choiseul 1997–2001; Minister of Finance and Treasury 1997–98, 2017–19; Prime Minister of the Solomon Islands 2000–01, 2006–07, 2014–17, 2019–; Deputy Prime Minister 2017–19; Pres. Ownership, Unity and Responsibility (OUR) Party. *Address:* Office of the Prime Minister, POB G1, Honiara, Solomon Islands (office). *Telephone:* 21863 (office). *Fax:* 28649 (office). *E-mail:* www.pmc.gov.sb (office).

SOGLO, Dieudonné Nicéphore, BA; Benin politician; b. 29 Nov. 1934, Lomé, Togo; two c.; ed Univ. of Paris (Sorbonne) and Ecole nat. d'admin, Paris, France; fmr Inspector-Gen. of Finances, Tech. Adviser, Finance Ministry; Head Finance Dept 1963; fmr Chair. Nat. Monetary Comm., other financial insts; Gov. IMF 1964; Prime Minister of Benin 1990–91, Pres. of Benin 1991–96; Leader Parti de la Renaissance de Benin (renamed La Renaissance du Bénin), now Hon. Pres.; Mayor of Cotonou 2003–15; Commander, Nat. Order of the Lion, Senegal 1986, Grand Croix, Légion d'Honneur 1995; Hon. DLitt (Clark Atlanta Univ.) 1995. *Address:* Zone Résidentielle, Lot G20, Les Cocotiers, Cotonou, Benin (home). *E-mail:* ndsoglo@yahoo.fr (home); ndsoglo@hotmail.com (home); nicephore.soglo@wanadoo.fr (home).

SOHI, Amarjeet, PC; Canadian community organizer and politician; *Minister of Natural Resources;* b. 8 March 1964, Banbhaura, Sangrur Dist, Punjab, India; m. Sarbjeet Sohi; one d.; emigrated to Canada with family 1981; returned to India to study 1988, joined activist group, imprisoned following political protest, Bihar 1988–90, case dismissed following int. campaign 1990, released and returned to Canada; worked as bus driver for Edmonton Transit System 1998–2007; Edmonton City Councillor 2007–10, 2010–15; fmr Vice-Pres., Alberta Urban Municipalities Assen and mem. Edmonton Police Comm.; fmr Adviser to REACH Edmonton Council for Safe Communities; mem. House of Commons (Parl.) for Edmonton Mill Woods 2015–; Minister of Infrastructure and Communities 2015–18, of Natural Resources 2018–; mem. Liberal Party of Canada; several awards in recognition of his community leadership. *Address:* Natural Resources Canada, 580 Booth Street, Suite 1100, Ottawa, ON K1A 0E4, Canada (office). *Telephone:* (613) 995-0947 (office). *E-mail:* questions@nrcan.gc.ca (office). *Website:* www.nrcan.gc.ca (office); amarjeetsohi.com.

SOHLMAN, Staffan A. R., BA; Swedish diplomatist and consultant; b. 21 Jan. 1937, Rome, Italy; s. of Rolf R. Sohlman and Zinaida Jarotskaja; m. Åsa Maria Carnerud 1961; one s. one d.; ed Sigtuna Humanistiska Laroverk, Washington and Lee Univ., USA, Stockholm and Lund Univs; Nat. Inst. for Econ. Research 1962–65; Ministry of Finance 1965–68; mem. Swedish Del. to OECD 1968–70; Ministry for Foreign Affairs, Dept for Devt Co-operation 1970–75, Head Multilateral Dept 1972, Project Leader Secr. for Futures Studies 1975–77, Head Transport Div. 1977–78; Deputy Dir-Gen. Nat. Bd of Trade 1978–84; Head Multilateral Dept of Ministry for Foreign Affairs Trade Dept 1984–88; Co-ordinator for Econ. Co-operation with Cen. and Eastern Europe, Ministry for Foreign Affairs 1989–90; Dir Cen. Bank 1989; Amb. and Perm. Rep., Swedish Del. to OECD 1991–95, Acting Sec.-Gen. OECD Oct.–Nov. 1994; Chair OECD Steel Cttee 1986–88, OECD Liaison Cttee with Council of Europe 1992, OECD Council Working Party on Shipbuilding 1993–95, Wassenaar Arrangement on Export Control for Conventional Arms and Dual-Use Goods and Technologies 1996–99; Amb. and Insp. Gen. of Mil. Equipment, Ministry for Foreign Affairs 1995, Amb. and Insp. Gen., Head Nat. Inspectorate of Strategic Products 1996; Amb. and Defence Co-ordinator, Ministry of Defence 2000–03; currently manages Sohlman Senior Consultants; Chair. Senior Power (think tank) 2009–12. *Publications:* Swedish Exports and Imports 1965–70, Resources, Society and the Future 1980, Swedish Defence Materials Administration 1996–2003, A Russian Family in Letters and Memoirs 1886–1961, Zina Sohlman and Her Russian Family, Ragnar Sohlman – Baku, Chicago, San Remo 2016. *Leisure interests:* music, art, architecture, literature. *Address:* Hornsgatan 51, 118 49 Stockholm, Sweden (home). *Telephone:* (8) 668-53-81 (home); 70-7516813 (mobile). *E-mail:* sasohlman@privat.utfors.se (office); srs1919@hotmail.com (office).

SOILIH, Soilih Mohamed; Comoran government official and diplomatist; *Permanent Representative to UN;* b. 1 Jan. 1964, Moroni; m.; three c.; ed Institut d'Etudes Politiques, Univ. of Aix-Marseilles; correspondent, Radio France Int. 1990–96; Dir-Gen. Radio Comores 1992–93; Press Attaché at Office of Pres. of Comoros 1991–92; in-charge of evaluation-orientation, Skills Assessment Centre, Mayotte 2002–04; Sec.-Gen. of Govt, Island of Ngazidja 2004–06, Special Del.,

Moroni City Hall 2006–07; Chief-of-Staff to Minister of Finance 2007–09, Political Counsellor of Minister of Foreign Affairs 2009–10; Dir-Gen., Office of Radio and TV of Comoros 2010–14; Perm. Rep. to UN, New York (also Amb. to USA) 2014–. *Address:* Permanent Mission of the United of Comoros, 866 United Nations Plaza, Suite 418, New York, NY 10017, USA (office). *Telephone:* (212) 750-1637 (office). *Fax:* (212) 750-1657 (office). *E-mail:* comoros@un.int (office). *Website:* www.un.int/comoros (office).

SOILIHI, Mohamed Ali; Comoran politician; Gov. World Bank 1997; Minister of Finance, Economy, Budget and Home Trade 1997, of Interior Jan.–March 2002, of Finance, Economy, Planning and Employment 2002–06, of Finance, Budget and Planning 2007, Vice-Pres., with responsibility for Finance, the Economy, the Budget and Investments and External Trading (Privatization) 2011–16; cand. in presidential election Feb. 2016. *Address:* c/o Ministry of Finance, the Budget and Investments, BP 324, Moroni, The Comoros (office).

SOINI, Timo, MPolSci; Finnish politician; *Minister of Foreign Affairs;* b. 30 May 1962, Rauma; m. Tiina Soini; two c.; ed Univ. of Helsinki; Sec.-Gen. and Chair. Kehittyvän Suomen Nuorten Liitto (youth league of developing Finland) 1983–92; mem. Suomen Maaseudun Puolue (Finnish Rural Party) 1979–95, Vice-Chair. 1989–92, Sec.-Gen. 1992–95 (party dissolved 1995); Co-founder Perussuomalaiset (Finns Party) 1995, Leader 1997–2017; mem. Espoo City Council 2000–; mem. Espoo City Bd 2007–08; mem. Eduskunta (Parl.) for Uusimaa 2003–09, 2011–, Chair. Foreign Affairs Cttee 2011–15, Cttee of Ministers, Council of Europe 2018–, Deputy mem. Grand Cttee 2011–15; Deputy Prime Minister 2015–17; Minister for Foreign Affairs 2015–; mem. European Parl. 2009–11; cand. in presidential election 2006, 2012. *Publications:* Maisterisjätkä 2008, Peruspomo 2014. *Address:* Ministry of Foreign Affairs, Merikasarmi, Laivastokatu 22, POB 176, 00023 Helsinki, Finland (office). *Telephone:* (9) 5350000 (office). *Fax:* (9) 629840 (office). *E-mail:* kirjaamo.um@formin.fi (office); timo.soini@eduskunta.fi. *Website:* www.um.fi (office); www.timosoini.fi.

SOIRON, Rolf, PhD; Swiss business executive; *Chairman, Lonza Group Ltd;* b. 31 Jan. 1945; ed Univ. of Basel, Harvard Business School, USA; served in several positions in human resources, finance and man. at Sandoz Group 1972–83, Group Vice-Pres. Agribusiness USA 1988–92, COO 1992–93; CEO and Pres. Protek Group 1983–88; CEO Jungbunzlauer Group, Basel 1993–2001, Man. Dir 2002–03; apptd mem. Bd of Dirs Holcim Ltd 1994, Chair. 2003–14; Chair. Lonza Group Ltd 2005–; Chair. Bd of Dirs Council of the European Union, Geneva 2014–; mem. Bd of Dirs Synthes-Stratec 1995–; Chair. Nobel Biocare 2003–10; Pres. (part-time) Univ. of Basel 1996–2005, Avenir Suisse (think-tank) 2009–14; mem. International Committee of the Red Cross 2009–, International Council of the Red Cross 2010–. *Address:* Lonza Group Ltd, Münchensteinerstrasse 38, 4052 Basel, Switzerland (office). *Telephone:* (61) 316-81-11 (office). *Website:* www.lonza.com (office).

SOISSON, Jean-Pierre Henri Robert, LenD; French politician; *Regional Counsellor for Burgundy;* b. 9 Nov. 1934, Auxerre (Yonne); s. of Jacques Soisson and Denise Soisson (née Silve); m. Catherine Lacaisse 1961; two s.; ed Lycée Jacques-Amyot, Auxerre, Faculté de Droit, Paris, Ecole nationale d'admin; auditor, Audit Office 1961; with del. to Algeria 1961–62; Lecturer, Institut d'Études Politiques de Paris 1962–68; tech. adviser to Sec.-Gen. of Merchant Navy 1964–65, to Sec. of State for Information, later for Foreign Affairs 1966–67, to Minister of Agric. 1967–68; Conseiller référendaire, Audit Office 1968–; Deputy to Nat. Assembly for Yonne 1968–74, 1978, 1981–88, 1993–; Deputy Sec.-Gen. Fédération nationale des républicains indépendants 1969–75, Vice-Pres. 1975–78; fmr Sec.-Gen. Parti Republicain; Co. Councillor, Auxerre sud-ouest 1970–76, Mayor 1971–98; Pres. Caisse d'Aide à l'équipement des collectivités locales 1973–74; fmr Pres. parl. group for rural Devt; Sec. of State for Univs 1974–76, for Professional Training 1976, to Minister of the Quality of Life (Youth and Sport) 1976–78; Minister for Youth, Sport and Leisure 1978–81, of Labour, Employment and Professional Training 1988–91, of State for the Civil Service and Admin. Reform 1991–92, of Agric. and Forests 1992–93; Vice-Pres., Conseil Général de l'Yonne 1982–88; Vice-Pres. Regional Council for Burgundy 1986–92, Pres. 1992–93, 1998–2004, Regional Counsellor 2004–; Pres. Comm. de surveillance de La Caisse des dépots et consignations; Sec.-Gen. United France 1991, Mouvement des Réformateurs 1992–2002; mem. Union pour un Mouvement Populaire 2002–; Croix de la valeur militaire; Commdr du Mérite agricole, des Palmes académiques, des Arts et Lettres; Grand Cross, German Order of Merit; Officer of various foreign orders. *Publications:* Le Piège (with Bernard Stasi and Olivier Stirn) 1973, La victoire sur l'hiver 1978, L'enjeu de la formation professionnelle 1987, Mémoires d'ouverture 1990, Politique en jachère 1992, #3, Voyage en Norvège 1995, Charles le Téméraire 1997, Charles Quint 2000, Marguerite, Princesse de Bourgogne 2002, Philibert de Chalon, Prince d'Orange 2005, Paul Bert, l'idéal républicain 2008. *Leisure interests:* tennis, skiing. *Address:* Conseil Régional de Bourgogne, 17 Boulevard de la Trémouille, BP 1602, 21035, Dijon Cedex (office); Assemblée Nationale, 75355 Paris; 2 place Robillard, 89000 Auxerre, France (home). *Telephone:* (3) 86-52-00-98 (office). *E-mail:* jpsoisson@cr-bourgogne.fr (office); jpsoisson@assemblee-nationale.fr (home); jp.soisson@wanadoo.fr (home). *Website:* www.cr-bourgogne.fr (office); www.assemblee-nationale.fr (office).

SOJO GARZA-ALDAPE, Eduardo, PhD; Mexican economist, academic and government official; b. 9 Jan. 1956, León, Guanajuato; ed Monterrey Inst. of Tech. and Advanced Studies, Univ. of Pennsylvania; fmr Researcher and Prof., Monterrey Inst. of Tech. and Advanced Studies, León; has held numerous positions in Fed. Public Admin including Tech. Dir and Short-Term Statistics Dir, Istituto Nacional de Estadística y Geografía (INEGI, Nat. Geography and Statistics Inst.) and Analyst Gen. Econ. and Social Policy Bureau 1979–82, Pres. 2008–15; Coordinator Guanajuato State Govt Econ. Cabinet during Vicente Fox Quesada admin 1995–2000; Advisers Coordinator during Fox's presidential electoral campaign, then Pres. Elect's Transition Team Econ. Coordinator –2000, Chief Econ. Adviser and Chief, Presidential Office for Public Policy 2000–06; Sec. of Economy 2006–08; Non-Resident Sr Assoc., Americas Program, Center for Strategic and Int. Studies 2017–; fmr Research Analyst, Univ. of Pa Link Project. *Publications include:* Guanajuato, Century XXI Study (co-author), De la alternancia al desarrollo, Políticas Públicas en Democracia; numerous articles in professional journals and research on combined time series and econometric modelling. *Address:* Center for Strategic and Int. Studies, 1616 Rhode Island Avenue, Washington, DC 20036, USA. *Telephone:* (202) 877-0200 (office). *Fax:* (202) 755-3199 (office). *E-mail:* webmaster@csis.org (office). *Website:* www.csis.org (office).

SOKAMBI, Aristide Dominique; Central African Republic lawyer and politician; ed Inst. de formation à la Médiation et à la Négociation, France; mem. Barreau de la République Centrafricaine (bar asscn); Assoc. mem. Brussels Bar; fmr Minister of Justice and Keeper of the Seals, Minister of Territorial Admin, Decentralization and Regionalization –2014, Minister of State, in charge of Nat. Defence, Restructuring of the Armed Forces, Former Combatants and War Victims 2014–15; Officier and Commdr, Ordre du Mérite Centrafricain. *Address:* c/o Ministry of National Defence and the Restructuring of the Armed Forces, Bangui, Central African Republic.

SOKOLOV, Aleksandr Sergeyevich, DFA; Russian musicologist and government official; *Rector, Moscow State Tchaikovsky Conservatory;* b. 8 Aug. 1949, Leningrad (now St Petersburg); m. Larisa Sokolova; one d.; ed Moscow State Tchaikovsky Conservatory; Lecturer, Moscow State Tchaikovsky Conservatory 1977, Prof. of Musical Theory 1992, Prorector 1992–2001, Rector 2001–04, 2009–; Minister of Culture and Mass Communications 2004–08; Pres. Moscow Conservatory Dissertation Bd 2006–; mem. Composers' Union of Russia; Order of the Hungarian Repub. with Star 2006, Order of St Sergiy Radonejsky 2006, For the Rebirth of Russia, 21st Century 2007, St Innocentius (2nd grade) 2007, Order of Stella d'Italia 2013, Order of the Rising Sun 2016; Honored Master of Art of the Russia 1999, State Prize for literature and art 2005, Honored Master of Culture of Buryatiya Repub. 2007. *Publications include:* Music Around Us 1996, Musical Composition of the XX Century: Dialectic of Creation 2002 (Spanish trans. 2005), Introduction to the Musical Composition of the XX Century 2004. *Leisure interests:* music, hunting, tourism. *Address:* Office of the Rector, Moscow State Tchaikovsky Conservatory, Bolshaya Nikitskaya ul., 13, Moscow 125009, Russia (office). *Telephone:* (495) 253-8491 (office). *Website:* www.mosconsv.ru (office).

SOKOLOV, Grigory Lipmanovich; Russian pianist; b. 18 April 1950, Leningrad (now St Petersburg); m. Inna Sokolova; ed Leningrad Conservatory (pupil of Moisey Halfin); numerous guest appearances in London, Paris, Vienna, Berlin, Madrid, Salzburg, Munich, Rome and New York; has worked with leading conductors including Myung-Whun Chung, Neeme Järvi, Herbert Blomstedt, Valery Gergiev, Sakari Oramo, Trevor Pinnock, Andrew Litton, Vassilly Sinajskij, Jukka-Pekka Saraste, Alexander Lazarev, John Storgards, Moshe Atzmon, Walter Weller and Evgeny Svetlanov; has performed with orchestras including New York Philharmonic, Montreal Symphony, Münchner Philharmoniker, Leipzig Gewandhaus, Philharmonia, Amsterdam Concertgebouw and Detroit Symphony; Prof., Leningrad (now St Petersburg) Conservatory 1975–; First Prize, Int. Tchaikovsky Piano Competition 1966, People's Artist of Russia 1988, ECHO Klassik Instrumentalist Award 2016. *Recordings include:* several live recordings including works by Bach, Beethoven, Brahms, Chopin, Rachmaninov, Prokofiev, Schubert, Schumann, Scriabin and Tchaikovsky; DVD of 2002 Paris recital directed by Bruno Monsaingeon, recital recorded live at 2008 Salzburg Festival 2015, Schubert/Beethoven 2016. *Address:* Artists Management Co., Piazza R. Simoni 1, 37122 Verona, Italy (office). *Telephone:* (80) 14041 (office). *E-mail:* panozzo@amcmusic.com (office); office@amcmusic.com (office). *Website:* www.amcmusic.com/artists/grigory-sokolov (office); www.grigory-sokolov.com (office).

SOKOLOV, Maksim Yur'yevich; Russian journalist; b. 10 Sept. 1959, Moscow; m.; ed Moscow State Univ.; worked as programmer in All-Union Centre of Transport, USSR State Cttee on Science and Tech. 1981–83; All-Union Research Inst. of Patent Information 1983–84; All-Union Research Inst. for Man. of Coal Industry 1985–87; Research Inst. of Gen. Plan of Moscow 1988–89; journalist since late 1980s; contrib. Commersant (weekly) 1989–97; political observer, Izvestiya 1998–2010 (resgnd), 2011–; publs in newspapers Nezavisimaya Gazeta, Atmoda, Segodnya, magazines Vek XX i Mir, Oktyabr, Soviet Analyst (UK); broadcaster, Russian Public TV Co. ORT; Gong 94 Journalism prize; Medal for the Defence of Free Russia 1991. *Leisure interests:* travelling, cooking, reading fiction, mushroom hunting. *Address:* Izvestiya, 127994 Moscow, Tverskaya str. 18/1, Russia. *E-mail:* m.sokolov@izvestia.ru (office). *Website:* izvestia.ru (office).

SOKOMANU, George, MBE; Ni-Vanuatu politician; *Chairman, Vanuatu Red Cross Society;* b. (George Kalkoa), 13 Jan. 1937, Vanuatu; m. Leitak Matautava 1960; four s. one d.; ed Lelean Memorial School; fmr Deputy Chief Minister and Minister of the Interior of New Hebrides; Pres. of Vanuatu 1980–88; arrested Dec. 1988; sentenced to six years' imprisonment March 1989, released April 1989; Sec.-Gen. South Pacific Comm. 1992–95; Deputy Prime Minister, Minister of Home Affairs, Local Govt, Police and Defence 1994–95; currently Chair. Vanuatu Red Cross Soc.; Patron, Pacific Peacebuilding Initiatives; Order of Merit, Vanuatu. *Address:* Vanuatu Red Cross Society, Rue d'Auvergne, PO Box 618, Port Vila, Vanuatu (office). *E-mail:* redcross@vanuatu.com.vu (office). *Website:* www.redcross.org.vu (office).

SOKUROV, Alexander Nikolayevich; Russian film director; b. 14 June 1951, Irkutsk; ed Gorky (now Nizhny Novgorod) Univ., All-Union Inst. of Cinematography; worked in Gorky (now Nizhny Novgorod) TV, Lenfilm Studio, directed feature and documentary films; Founder and Dir Experimental School of Young Cinema Vanguard; various prizes at int. film festivals. *Films include:* A Solitary Voice of a Man (Bronze Leopard, Locarno Int. Festival 1978), Mournful Callousness, Days of Eclipse (FIPRESSI Prize—Montreal Int. Festival), A Sonata for Hitler, Second Round, Elegy (about F. Shalyapin), Moscow Elegy (dedicated to A. Tarkovsky) Soviet Elegy, Russian Elegy, The Quiet Pages, The Spiritual Voices (Sony Prize, Locarno Int. Festival 1995), Oriental Elegy (Grand Prix Oberhausen Festival 1996), Mother and Son (prizes at Int. Festivals of Berlin, Moscow 1997), The Knot: Solzhenitsyn 1998, Moloch 1999, Sonata for Hitler 2000, Calf 2001, Russian Ark 2003, The Sun (Best Director Eurasia Int. Film Festival) 2005, Alexandra 2007, Faust (Venice Film Festival Golden Lion) 2011, We Need Happiness (documentary) 2011, Francofonia (documentary) 2015. *Address:* 199048 St Petersburg, Smolenskaya nab. 4, Apt. 222, Russia.

SOLAGH, Baqir, (Bayan Jabr); Iraqi politician; ed Baghdad Univ.; Sr Official, Supreme Council for the Islamic Revolution in Iraq (now Islamic Supreme Council), currently head of Citizen's bloc, fmr Head of Damascus office; Minister of

Construction and Housing 2003–04, of the Interior 2005–06, of Finance 2006–10. *E-mail:* info@almejlis.org. *Website:* www.almejlis.org.

SOLANA MADARIAGA, (Francisco) Javier, PhD; Spanish fmr physicist, politician and international organization official; *President, Madariaga – College of Europe Foundation;* b. 14 July 1942, Madrid; brother of Luis Solana Madariaga; m. Concepción Giménez; one s. one d.; ed Colegio del Pilar, Universidad Complutense de Madrid; joined Spanish Socialist Party 1964; won Fulbright scholarship to study physical sciences in USA until 1968; Asst to Prof. Nicolas Cabrera, Univ. of Va 1968–71, then at Universidad Autónoma de Madrid (where contract was cancelled allegedly for political reasons); mem. Exec., Federación Socialista Madrileña and Federación de Trabajadores de la Enseñanza, Unión General de Trabajadores; Prof. of Solid State Physics, Universidad Complutense de Madrid 1977; mem. Congress of Deputies for Madrid; mem. Fed. Exec. Comm., Partido Socialista Obrero Español, fmr Press Sec. and Sec. for Research and Programmes; Minister of Culture 1982–88; Govt Spokesman 1985–88; Minister of Educ. and Science 1988–92, of Foreign Affairs 1992–95; Sec.-Gen. NATO 1995–99, responsible for NATO Defence and Foreign Policy 1999; Sec.-Gen. and High Rep. for Common Foreign and Security Policy, Council of the EU 1999–2009; Sec.-Gen. WEU 1999–2009; Pres. European Defence Agency 2004–09; Pres. Madariaga –Coll. of Europe Foundation 1998–, Centre for Global Economy and Geopolitics, ESADE Business School, Barcelona 2009–; mem. Spanish Chapter of Club of Rome; Hon. KCMG 1999, Grand Cross of Isabel the Catholic, Kt of the Order of the Golden Fleece 2010; Dr hc (London School of Econs); Manfred Wörner Medal, Ministry of Defence (Germany), Vision for Europe Award 2003, Statesman of the Year Award, EastWest Inst. 2003, Premio Carlomagno 2006, Carnegie-Wateler Peace Prize 2006, Charlemagne Prize 2007, Charles V European Award, European Acad. of Yuste Foundation 2010, Ewald von Kleist Award 2010, Gold Medal, Jean Monnet Foundation for Europe 2011. *Publications:* more than 30 publs in field of solid-state physics. *Address:* Madariaga – College of Europe Foundation, Dijver 11, BE-8000 Bruges, Belgium (office). *Telephone:* (2) 496-58-35-80 (office). *E-mail:* info@madariaga.org (office); public.relations@consilium.eu.int. *Website:* www .madariaga.org (office).

SOLANKI, Kaptan Singh, MA, BEd; Indian academic and politician; *Governor of Tripura;* b. 1 July 1939, Garhpara, Bhind Dist, Madhya Pradesh; s. of Jimipal Singh and Parvati Bai; m. Rani Solanki; three s. two d.; ed Vikram Univ., Post-Graduate Basic Training Coll., Ujjain, Jiwaji Univ.; teacher, Morena Dist 1958–65; Prof., PGV Coll., Gwalior 1966–2000; mem. Rajya Sabha (Bharatiya Janata Party—BJP) for Madhya Pradesh State 2009–14; Gov. of Haryana 2014–18, also of Punjab 2015–16, also ex-officio Admin. of Chandigarh, Gov. of Tripura 2018–. *Address:* Office of the Governor, Raj Bhavan, Pushpavant Palace, Agartala 799 001, Tripura, India (office). *Telephone:* (381) 2224091 (office). *Fax:* (381) 2224350 (office). *E-mail:* rajbhavanagt@gmail.com (office). *Website:* tripura.gov.in/ government (office).

SOLANKI, Sushil Kumar; Indian wrestler; b. 26 May 1983, Najafgarh, Delhi; s. of Diwan Singh Solanki and Kamla Devi Solanki; World Cadet Games (gold medal) 1998, Asian Jr Wrestling Championship (gold medal) 2000, Asian Wrestling Championships (bronze medal) 2003, Commonwealth Wrestling Championships (gold medal), Commonwealth Wrestling Championships (gold medal) 2003, 2005, 2007, Asian Wrestling Championships (bronze medal) 2008, Beijing Olympics 2008 (bronze medal), Asian Wrestling Championships (gold medal) 2010, FILA World Wrestling Championships (gold medal) 2010, Commonwealth Games (gold medal), Delhi 2010; currently Asst Commercial Man., Indian Railways; Arjuna Award 2006, Rajiv Gandhi Khel Ratna 2009. *Address:* Railway Complex, Shivaji Bridge, Behind Shankar Market, New Delhi 110 001, India (office). *Telephone:* (11) 23411173 (office); (11) 23413627 (office).

SOLBERG, Erna; Norwegian politician; *Prime Minister;* b. 24 Feb. 1961, Bergen; d. of Asbjørn Solberg and Inger Wenche Torgersen; m. Sindre Finnes; two c.; ed Univ. of Bergen; Deputy mem. Bergen city council 1979–83, 1987–89; mem. Storting (Parl.) for Hordaland 1989–; Minister of Local Govt and Regional Devt 2001–05; Prime Minister 2013–; mem. Høyre (Conservative party), Deputy Leader 2002–04, Leader 2004–; apptd Co-Chair. Sustainable Development Goals Advocates 2016; Commdr, Order of St Olav 2005; Global World Leader Prize 2018. *Address:* Office of the Prime Minister, Glacisgt. 1, POB 8001 Dep., 0030 Oslo, Norway (office). *Telephone:* 22-24-90-90 (office). *Fax:* 22-24-95-00 (office). *E-mail:* postmottak@smk.dep.no (office). *Website:* www.regjeringen.no/smk (office).

SOLBERG, Monte, PC; Canadian fmr politician; *Principal, New West Public Affairs;* b. 17 Sept. 1958, Calgary; m. Debra LeClaire; two s.; fmr broadcaster and businessman; mem. Parl. for Medicine Hat, Alberta (Reform Party 1993–2001, Canadian Alliance 2001, then Conservative Party of Canada) 1993–2008, parl. positions held include Critic for Foreign Affairs, Nat. Revenue, Human Resources Devt, Vice-Chair. standing cttees on Finance, Human Resources Devt, Status of Persons with Disabilities, Foreign Affairs, Int. Trade; Minister of Citizenship and Immigration 2006–07, of Human Resources and Social Devt 2007–08; fmr Sr Adviser, Fleishman-Hillard Inc. (public relations agency); currently Prin., New West Public Affairs (consultancy), Calgary; Special Advisor, RCI Capital; columnist and contributor SUN News Network; fmr mem. Exec. Cttee Canada–USA Parl. Asscn; mem. Bd of Dirs Alberta Asscn of Broadcasters. *Address:* New West Public Affairs, Suite 316, 908-17th Avenue SW, Calgary, AB T2T 0A3, Canada (office). *Telephone:* (403) 457-1619 (office). *E-mail:* monte.solberg@ newwestpublicaffairs.ca (office). *Website:* newwestpublicaffairs.ca (office).

SOLBES MIRA, Pedro, DPolSci; Spanish economist and politician; b. 31 Aug. 1942, Pinoso, Alicante; m.; three c.; ed Univ. of Madrid, Inst. of European Studies of Free Univ., Brussels; civil servant, Ministry of Trade 1968–73, Commercial Counsellor to Spain's Perm. Mission to the EC 1973–78, Special Adviser to Minister for Relations with the EC 1978–79; Dir Gen. Commercial Policy, Ministry of Econs and Trade 1979–82; Gen. Sec. Ministry of Econs and Finance and mem. of task force for Spanish Accession negotiations to EC 1982–85; Sec. of State for Relations with the EC 1985; Pres. Internal Market Council during first Spanish presidency of EC 1989; Minister of Agric., Food and Fisheries 1991–93, of Economics and Finance 1993–96; Pres. Ecofin Council during Spanish presidency of EU 1995; mem. Spanish Parl. 1996; Pres. Jt Cttee of Spanish Parl. on EU 1996; European Commr for Econ. and Monetary Affairs 1999–2004; Second Deputy

Prime Minister and Minister of the Economy and Finance 2004–09; Pres. FRIDE (Fundación para las Relaciones Internacionales y el Diálogo Exterior) (think-tank), Madrid –2015.

SOLBRIG, Otto Thomas, PhD; American biologist and academic; *Bussey Professor Emeritus of Biology, Harvard University;* b. 21 Dec. 1930, Buenos Aires, Argentina; s. of Hans Solbrig and Rose Muggleworth; m. Dorothy Crosswhite 1969; one s. one d.; ed Colegio Nacional de Mar de La Plata, Univ. Nacional de La Plata and Univ. of Calif., Berkeley; Research Asst, Univ. of La Plata 1951–54; Teaching Fellow, Univ. of Calif., Berkeley 1956–58; Asst then Assoc. Curator, Gray Herbarium, Harvard Univ. 1960–66, Dir 1963–78; Assoc. Prof., then Prof., Univ. of Mich. 1966–69; Bussey Prof. of Biology, Harvard Univ. 1969–, now Prof. Emer., Faculty Assoc., Harvard Univ. Center for the Environment; Fellow, American Acad. of Arts and Sciences, AAAS; Guggenheim Fellow 1975–76; Hon. MA (Harvard) 1969, Extraordinary Prof. hc (Univ. of La Plata) 1991, Distinguished Prof. hc (Univ. of Buenos Aires) 1994, Hon. Drof Agronomy (Nat. University of Lomas de Zamora) 1997; Cooley Prize 1961, Congressional Antarctic Medal 1967, Willdenow Medal, Berlin Botanical Gardens 1979. *Publications include:* author or co-author of 21 books and more than 280 articles and chapters in books on plant population biology, cytology, ecology, evolution and taxonomy. *Leisure interest:* sailing. *Address:* Harvard University, Herbaria 321, 22 Divinity Avenue, Cambridge, MA 02138, USA (office). *Telephone:* (617) 495-4302 (office). *Fax:* (617) 495-9484 (office). *E-mail:* solbrig@fas.harvard.edu (office). *Website:* environment .harvard.edu (office); www.oeb.harvard.edu/faculty/solbrig (office).

SOLDI SOLDI, Rear-Adm. Héctor; Peruvian international organization official and fmr naval officer; ed Escuela Naval del Perú, Universidad Católica del Perú, Naval Postgraduate School, Monterey, Calif.; took part in Australian expedition to Antarctica as mem. scientific panel 1982; Peruvian rep. on Jacques Cousteau's expedition to Amazon on board ship Calypso 1982; Chief scientist for oceanography programme, first Peruvian expedition to Antarctica 1988, second expedition 1989; Head, Oceanography Dept, Peruvian Navy Directorate of Hydrography and Navigation, Lima 1985–90, Head, Dept of Environment 1992–93, Technical Dir 1994–97, Deputy Dir of Hydrography and Navigation 1998, Dir 2000–01; Commdr, Oceanographic research vessel Humboldt, Instituto del Mar de Peru 1990–91; Exec. Dir 12th Peruvian expedition to Antarctica 2000; Dir Escuela Naval del Perú (Peruvian Naval Acad.) 2002; Peruvian Naval Attaché to OAS and Head of Peruvian Del. to Inter-American Defense Bd, Washington, DC 2003–04; mem. Advisory Cttee, Ministry of Foreign Affairs 2005–09; Vice Chair. Intergovernmental Cttee, Global Oceans Observing System of Intergovernmental Oceanographic Comm. 2007–09; Pres. Multisectoral Comm., Nat. Focal Point Action Plan for Protection of Marine and Coastal Areas of S Pacific 2006–09; Pres. Nat. Cttee for Study of El Niño 2006–09; Chair. Instituto del Mar del Peru 2006–09; Sec.-Gen., Perm. Comm. for S Pacific, Ecuador 2010–14; Vice-Minister of Fisheries and Agric. 2016–18.

SOLH HAMADEH, Leila; Lebanese foundation executive; *Vice-President, Alwaleed Bin Talal Humanitarian Foundation;* b. Beirut; d. of Riad Al-Solh; m. Majed Hamadeh; ed St Joseph Univ., Beirut; Vice-Pres. Alwaleed Bin Talal Humanitarian Foundation 2003–; Minister of Industry 2004; Union des Français de l'Etranger Order of Cedars of Lebanon 2009, Légion d'honneur 2011; Dr hc (Lebanese American Univ.) 2006, (Notre Dame) 2009, (Acad. française, Hagazian Univ. Service Shield); Arab Women Medal, Arab Women Org. 2006, Pontifical Medal from Pope Benedict XVI 2008, Catholicos of All Armenians Gold Medal 2008, High Recognition Award, Arab Tender Forum, Abu Dhabi 2008, Vermeil Medal, St Joseph Univ. 2008, Woman of the Year 2008, Arab League Hon. Trophy 2008. *Publications include:* Un Liban à retrouver (A Return to Lebanon) 2008, Les élections de 2009, Les enjeux culturels (2009 Elections, Cultural Issues) 2009. *Address:* Alwaleed Bin Talal Humanitarian Foundation, Osaily Building, 1st Floor, Riad El-Solh Square, Beirut, Lebanon (office). *Telephone:* (1) 966966 (office). *Fax:* (1) 966966 (office). *E-mail:* general@alwaleedphilanthropies.org (office). *Website:* www.alwaleedphilanthropies.org (office).

SOLHEIM, Erik, BA; Norwegian politician and UN official; b. 18 Jan. 1955, Oslo; m.; four c.; ed Univ. of Oslo; mem. Socialist Left Party (Sosialistisk Venstreparti—SV), Leader Socialist Youth League 1977–80, Party Sec. Socialist Left Party 1981–85, mem. Cen. Exec. Cttee 1985–87, Leader of Socialist Left Party 1987–97; mem. Storting (Parl.) for Sør-Trøndelag Co. 1989–93, for Oslo 1993–2001; Sr Adviser, Ministry of Foreign Affairs 2000–05; Minister of Int. Devt 2005–07, of the Environment and Int. Devt 2007–12; Chair Devt Assistance Cttee, OECD 2013–16; Exec. Dir UN Environment Programme (UNEP) 2016–18 (resgnd); mem. Norwegian Asscn for the Disabled 1985–87; Observer at UN Conf. on Environment and Devt 1992, 1997, UN Conf. on Population and Devt 1995.

SOLIH, Ibrahim Mohamed, (Ibu); Maldivian politician; *President;* b. 4 May 1964, Hinnavaru Island, Lhaviyani Atoll; m. Fazna Ahmed; one d., one s.; mem. People's Majlis (Parl.) (Hinnavaru Constituency) 1994–, Parl. Group Leader 2011–; Founding mem. Maldivian Democreatic Party 2003; led Maldives Political Reform Movement 2003–08; Pres. of the Maldives 2018–. *Address:* Office of the President, Boduthakurufaanu Magu, Malé 20-113, The Maldives (office). *Telephone:* 3320701 (office). *Fax:* 3325500 (office). *E-mail:* info@presidencymaldives .gov.mv (office). *Website:* www.presidencymaldives.gov.mv.

SOLIS, Hilda Lucia, BA, MA; American politician and fmr government official; b. 20 Oct. 1957, Los Angeles, Calif.; d. of Raul Solis and Juana Solis; m. Sam H. Sayyad 1982; ed California State Polytechnic Univ., Univ. of Southern California; interpreter, US Immigration and Naturalization Service, LA 1977–79; Ed.-in-Chief Office of Hispanic Affairs, White House, Washington, DC 1980–81; Man. Analyst, Civil Rights Div., Office of Man. and Budget 1981–82; Field Rep. Office of Assemblyman Art Torres, LA 1982; Dir Calif. Student Opportunity and Access Program 1982; mem. Rio Hondo Community Coll. Bd of Trustees 1985; mem. Calif. State Ass. for 57th Dist 1992–94; mem. Calif. State Senate from 24th Dist 1994–2000; mem. US House of Reps from 32nd Dist 2001–08, mem. Resources Cttee, Energy and Commerce Cttee (Vice-Chair. Environment and Hazardous Materials Sub cttee), Select Cttee on Energy Independence and Global Warming; Co-Vice Chair. Democratic Steering and Policy Cttee, Sr Whip and Regional Whip for Southern California; Chair. Congressional Hispanic Caucus Task Force on Health and the Environment; mem. Comm. on Security and Cooperation in Europe

2007–08, Vice Chair. Gen. Cttee on Democracy, Human Rights and Humanitarian Questions; US Sec. of Labor, Washington, DC 2009–13; Democrat; Meritorious Service Award, US Dept of Defense 1981, Profile in Courage Award, John F. Kennedy Library Foundation 2000.

SOLÍS, Ottón, MA; Costa Rican academic and politician; b. 31 May 1954; m. Shirley Sanchez 1994; four c.; ed Univ. of Costa Rica, Univ. of Manchester, UK; has taught at Univs of Manchester and Reading, UK, Costa Rican univs, UN Univ. for Peace; Pres. Interamerican Econ. and Social Council, OAS 1987–88; Researcher Sustainable Devt Research Centre, Univ. of Costa Rica 2000; fmr Economist Cen. Bank of Costa Rica, Ministry of Planning and Econ. Policy; fmr Consultant ECLA, UNDP, SIDA; Founding Pres. Citizens Action Party (Partido Acción Ciudadana, PAC) 2000, unsuccessful presidential cand. 2006, 2010; apptd Bacardi Family Eminent Scholar, Center for Latin American Studies, Univ. of Florida 2008; mem. Legis. Ass. 2014–; mem. Univ. Bd Open Univ. of Costa Rica 1990–93; mem. Special Cttee, La Amistad Park Trust Fund 1999, Cttee of Experts on Public Admin, UN 2002; mem. Team, Millennium Ecosystem Assessment 2001. *Address:* Legislative Assembly, Avenida Central y primera entre calles 15 y 17, San José, Costa Rica (office). *Website:* www.asamblea.go.cr (office).

SOLÍS RIVERA, Luis Guillermo, MA; Costa Rican politician and fmr head of state; b. 25 April 1958, San José; s. of Freddy Solís Avendaño and Vivienne Rivera Allen; m. María Mercedes Peñas Domingo; six c.; ed Univ. of Costa Rica, Tulane Univ., USA; Assoc. Prof., Univ. of Costa Rica 1981–87; Fulbright Scholar, Univ. of Michigan 1983–85; Chief of Staff, Ministry of Foreign Affairs 1986–90, Amb. for Central American Affairs 1994–98; Coordinator, Center for Admin of Justice, also Researcher, Latin American and Caribbean Center, Florida Int. Univ. 1999; columnist, La República (daily newspaper) 1990s; Pres. of Costa Rica 2014–18; fmr mem. Costa Rican dels to UN, OAS, EU and several other int. bodies; Consultant to UNDP; mem. Editorial Bd Foreign Affairs, Global Governance, Espacios; mem. Partido Liberación Nacional (PLN) 1977–2005, Dir of Int. Relations, Sec.-Gen. 2002–03; mem. Partido Acción Ciudadana (PAC) 2009–. *Publications:* numerous essays and books on nat. and int. affairs.

SOLÍZ CARRIÓN, Doris; Ecuadorean sociologist, teacher and politician; *Executive Secretary, Alianza País (Patria Altiva i Soberana);* b. Cuenca; two s.; fmr Exec. Dir Service for an Alternative Devt of the South; Deputy Mayor of Cuenca 2000–02; Minister of Tourism 2003, Minister of Nat. and Cultural Heritage 2008–09, Minister/Head, Secr. of Peoples, Social Movts and Citizen Participation 2009–10, Minister of Policy Coordination 2011, Minister for Econ. and Social Inclusion 2012–14; Exec. Sec. Alianza País (Patria Altiva i Soberana) 2014–; mem. Faculty, Univ. of Cuenca, f. Gender Studies and Tourism programmes; Premio Valdivia, Nat. Congress 2001. *Address:* Alianza País (Patria Altiva i Soberana), Avda Los Shyris N34-368 y Portugal, Quito, Ecuador (office). *Telephone:* (2) 224-3299 (office). *Fax:* (2) 600-1029 (office). *E-mail:* comunicacion@35pais.com.ec (office). *Website:* www.alianzapais.com.ec (office).

SOLLERS, Philippe, (pseudonym of Philippe Joyaux); French author and critic; b. 28 Nov. 1936, Bordeaux; s. of Octave Joyaux and Marcelle Molinié; m. Julia Kristeva 1967; one s.; ed Lycées Montesquieu and Montaigne, Bordeaux and Ecole Sainte-Geneviève, Versailles; co-f. and ran avant garde journal Tel Quel (along with writer and art critic Marcelin Pleynet) 1960–82; Dir L'Infini (review) 1983–; mem. reading Cttee Editions Gallimard 1990–, Asscn of French Museums 1998–; Chevalier, Légion d'honneur, Officier, Ordre nat. du Mérite, Officier des Arts et des Lettres; Prix Médicis 1961, Grand Prix du Roman de la Ville de Paris 1988, Prix Paul-Morand (Académie française) 1992, Prix littéraire de la fondation Prince Pierre de Monaco 2006. *Publications include:* novels: Une Curieuse Solitude 1958, Le Parc 1961, Drame 1965, Nombres, Lois 1972, H 1973, Paradis, Vision à New York 1981, Femmes 1983, Portrait du joueur 1985, Paradis 2 1986, Le Coeur absolu 1987, Les Surprises de Fragonard 1987, Les Folies françaises 1988, Le Lys d'or 1989, Carnet de nuit 1989, La Fête à Venise 1991, Le Secret 1993, Venise Éternelle 1993, La Guerre du Goût 1994, Femmes, Mythologies (co-author) 1994, Les Passions de Francis Bacon 1996, Studio 1997, L'Année du Tigre, Journal de l'année 1998, 1999, L'Oeil de Proust, les dessins de Marcel Proust 1999, Passion fixe 2000, La Divine Comédie 2000, L'Etoile des amants 2002, Illuminations à travers les textes sacrés 2003, Le Saint-Ane 2004, Logique de la fiction 2006, Une Vie Divine 2007, Un vrai roman: Mémoires 2007, Les Voyageurs du temps 2009, Trésor d'Amour 2011, L'Éclaircie 2012, Portraits de femmes 2013, L'École du Mystère 2015; essays: L'Intermédiaire 1963, Logiques 1968, L'Écriture et l'Expérience des Limites 1968 (published as Writing and the Experience of Limits 1982), Sur le Matérialisme 1974, Théorie des Exceptions 1985, De Kooning, vite 1988, Improvisations 1991, Sade contre l'Être suprême 1996, Les passions de Francis Bacon 1996, Picasso, le héros 1996, La Guerre du Goût 1994, Casanova l'admirable (Prix Elsa-Morante 1999) 1998, Francesca Woodman 1998, Francis Ponge 2001, Éloge de l'Infini 2001, Mystérieux Mozart 2001, Liberté du XVIIIème (Extract from La Guerre du Goût) 2002, Dictionnaire amoureux de Venise 2004, Poker 2005, Fleurs 2006, Guerres secrètes 2007, Vers le Paradis (with DVD) 2010, Discours Parfait 2010, Fugues 2012. *Address:* L'Infini, 5 rue Gaston-Gallimard, 75007 Paris, France (office). *Website:* www.philippesollers.net.

SOLOMIN, Yuri Mefod'yevich; Russian actor and theatre director; *Artistic Director, Maly Drama Theatre (National Theatre of Russia);* b. 18 June 1935, Chita; s. of Mefody Solomin and Zinaida Ryabtseva; m. Olga Nikolayevna Solomina; one d.; ed Shchepkin Higher School of Theatre Art; actor Maly Drama Theatre 1959–; Artistic Dir 1988–; teacher, then Prof. Shchepkin Theatre Coll. 1960–; Minister of Culture of Russian Fed. 1990–92; Pres. Asscn of Russian Drama Theatres; mem. Int. Acad. of Creative Arts; corresp. mem. Russian Acad. of Educ.; master-classes in USA, Japan, S Korea; Order For Service to Motherland (Fourth and Third Class), Order Friendship of Peoples, Order of Russian Orthodox Church, Order for Contrib. to Int. Culture (Japan), Order of the Rising Sun, 3rd class (Japan) 2011; State Prize of Russian Fed., Prize Golden Aries, A. D. Popov Gold Medal, USSR Peoples' Artist, People's Artist of Russia and Kyrghyzia, Int. K.S. Stanislavsky Prize. *Film roles include:* Sleepless Night, Adjutant of His Highness, Dersu Ursala, Blockade, Ordinary Miracle, Dreams of Russia, There was Evening, There was Morning, Walking Through the Torments (serial), The Bat, The Farewell in June, Penitential Love, Native Land Waits, Moscow's Saga. *Plays include:* Inspector, Tsar Fedor Ioannovich, The Deep, Uncle Vanya, Cyrano de Bergerac, Seagull, Lady Windermere's Fan, Alive Corps. *Plays produced:* Forest (produced in Bulgaria and Russia), Perfidy and Love, Misfortune from Wit, Three Sisters, A Mysterious Box (vaudeville). *Publications:* From Adjutant to His Highness. *Leisure interest:* dogs and cats. *Address:* State Academic Maly Theatre of Russia, Teatralnaya pl. 1/6, Moscow, Russia (office). *Telephone:* (495) 925-98-68 (office). *Fax:* (495) 925-54-36 (office); (495) 921-03-50 (office). *E-mail:* theatre@maly.ru (office). *Website:* www.maly.ru (office).

SOLOMON, Edward I., BS, MA, PhD; American chemist and academic; *Monroe E. Spaght Professor of Chemistry and Professor of S.L.A.C. Photon Science, Stanford University;* b. 20 Oct. 1946, New York; s. of Mordecai L. Solomon and Sally S. Solomon; m. Darlene J. Spira 1984; one s. one d.; ed Rensselaer Polytechnic Inst., Princeton Univ.; Research Assoc., Princeton Univ., New Jersey 1972–73; Postdoctoral Fellow, H.C. Ørsted Inst. 1973–74, Calif. Inst. of Tech. 1974–75; Asst Prof., MIT 1975–79, Assoc. Prof. 1979–81, Prof. 1981–82; Prof., Stanford Univ. 1982–, Spaght Prof. of Chem. 1991–, also Prof. of S.L.A.C. Photon Science; Invited Prof., Univ. of Paris, Tokyo Inst. of Tech., Tata Inst., India, Xiamen Univ., China, La Plata Univ., Argentina; First Glen Seaborg and other lectureships; Fellow, AAAS, American Acad. of Arts and Sciences, Japan Soc. for Promotion of Science; NIH Merit Award, Dean's Award for Distinguished Teaching 1990, Westinghouse Foundation Nat. Talent Search Award, Remsen Award 1994, Wheland Medal 2000, Centenary Medal and Lectureship, Royal Soc., UK 2003, ACS Award in Inorganic Chemistry 2001, Bailar Medal, Univ. of Illinois 2007, Chakravorty Award, Chemical Research Soc., India 2008. *Publications include:* three books; over 320 papers in scientific journals. *Leisure interests:* tennis, running, gourmet dining, int. travel. *Address:* Stanford University, Department of Chemistry, 333 Campus Drive, Mudd Building, Room 121, Stanford, CA 94305-4401, USA. *Telephone:* (650) 723-9104 (office). *Fax:* (650) 725-0259 (office). *E-mail:* Edward.Solomon@stanford.edu (office). *Website:* chemistry.stanford.edu (office); web.stanford.edu/group/solomon/home (office).

SOLOMON, Sir Harry, Kt; British business executive; b. 20 March 1937, Middlesbrough, England; s. of Jacob Solomon and Belle Solomon; m. Judith D. Manuel 1962; one s. two d.; ed St Alban's School and Law Soc. School of Law; qualified solicitor 1960; in pvt. practice 1960–75; Man. Dir Hillsdown Holdings PLC 1975–84, Jt Chair. 1984–87, Chair. 1987–93, Dir (non-exec.) 1993–97; Chair. Harveys Holdings PLC 1994–2000; Co-founder Solomon Taylor & Shaw; Co-Founder and Vice-Chair. Portland Trust; Chair. UJIA Ashdown Bd; mem. Bd of Dirs Princedale Group PLC 1993–2000, Charterhouse European Holding Ltd 1993–2001, Frogmore Estates PLC 1993–2001, US Industries Inc. (now Jacuzzi Brands Inc.) 1995–2004, Falkland Islands Holdings PLC 1999–2009, Consolidated Land Investments Ltd 2000–09, Westcity Plc 2007–09, Portland Capital 2007–09, Monitor/Quest Ltd 2008–; Trustee National Life; Hon. FRCP; Lifetime Achievement Award, British–Israeli Business Awards 2015. *Leisure interests:* jogging, tennis, theatre, collector of historical autographed letters. *Address:* Hillsdown House, 32 Hampstead High Street, London, NW3 1QD, England (office). *Telephone:* (20) 7431-7739 (office). *Fax:* (20) 7431-7740 (office). *E-mail:* harry@heathside.co.uk (office).

SOLOMONT, Alan D., BA, BS; American business executive, university administrator and fmr diplomatist; *Pierre and Pamela Omidayar Dean, Jonathan M. Tisch College of Citizenship and Public Service, Tufts University;* b. 1957, Boston, Mass; m. Susan Lewis; two d.; ed Tufts Univ., Univ. of Massachusetts, Lowell; Founder and CEO ADS Group (sold co. in 1996); Chair. Solomont Bailis Ventures 1998–; Co-founder HouseWorks; Founder and Man. Dir Angel Healthcare Investors; mem. Bd of Dirs Corpn for Nat. and Community Service 2000–09 (Chair. 2009), Boston Private Bank & Trust Co., Boston Medical Center, New Israel Fund, Israel Policy Forum, Univ. of Lowell, Univ. of Massachusetts, John F. Kennedy Presidential Library Foundation, WGBH Educational Foundation; Amb. to Spain (also accred to Andorra) 2010–13; Finance Chair. Democratic Nat. Cttee 1997–98; Trustee, Tufts Univ. 1999–2009, Pierre and Pamela Omidayar Dean, Jonathan M. Tisch Coll. of Citizenship and Public Service 2014–; Chair. Combined Jewish Philanthropies of Greater Boston and Hebrew Sr Life. *Address:* Jonathan M. Tisch College of Citizenship and Public Service, Lincoln Filene Hall, Tufts University, Medford, MA 02155, USA. *Telephone:* (617) 627-3453. *Fax:* (617) 627-3401. *E-mail:* activecitizen@tufts.edu. *Website:* activecitizen.tufts.edu/solomont.

SOLOVYEV, Sergey Aleksandrovich; Russian film director and scriptwriter; b. 25 Aug. 1944, Kem, Karelia; m. Tatyana Drubich (divorced); ed All-Union Inst. of Cinematography with Leningrad TV 1960–69; film dir Mosfilm Studio 1969–, Artistic Dir Krug Film Union 1987–; Sec., USSR Union of Cinematographers 1986–90; Chair. Moscow Union of Cinematographers 1990–97; Co-Chair. Russian Union of Cinematographers 1990–92; Prof., All-Russian Inst. of Cinematography; debut as scriptwriter Look into the Face 1966, as film dir Family Happiness; worked as stage dir in Maly Theatre (Uncle Vanya) and Taganka Theatre (The Seagull). *Films include:* Yegor Bulychev and Others 1971, Station Inspector 1972, A Hundred Days After Childhood 1975 (Silver Bear, Berlin, Prize of All-Union Festival, Tunes of A White Night 1977), Rescuer 1980, Direct Heir 1982, Strange, White and Speckled 1986, Assa 1987, Black Rose: an Emblem of Sadness, Red Rose: an Emblem of Love 1989, The House Under the Starry Sky 1991, Three Sisters 1994, The Tender Age 2001, O lyubvi 2004, 2-Assa-2 2008, Odnoklassniki 2010, Sneakers 2016, Dom pod zvyozdnym nebom 2016. *Address:* Akademika Pilyugina, 117393 Moscow, str. 8, korp. 1, Apt. 330, Russia (home). *Telephone:* (495) 132-36-95 (home).

SOLOW, Robert Merton, PhD; American economist and academic; *Institute Professor Emeritus, Massachusetts Institute of Technology;* b. 23 Aug. 1924, Brooklyn, New York; s. of Milton Solow and Hannah Solow; m. Barbara Lewis 1945; two s. one d.; ed Harvard Univ.; Asst Prof. of Statistics, Mass. Inst. of Technology 1950–53, Assoc. Prof. of Econs 1954–57, Prof. of Econs 1958–73, Inst. Prof. 1973–95, Inst. Prof. Emer. 1995–; W. Edwards Deming Prof., New York Univ. 1996; Sr Economist, Council of Econ. Advisors 1961–62; Eastman Visiting Prof., Univ. of Oxford, UK 1968–69; Killian Prize Lecturer, MIT 1978; Geary Lecturer, Univ. of Dublin, Ireland 1980; Overseas Fellow, Churchill Coll., Cambridge 1984; Mitsui Lecturer, Birmingham 1985; Nobel Memorial Lecture, Stockholm 1987 and numerous others in int. academic insts; mem. Nat. Comm. on Tech., Automation and Econ. Progress 1964–65, Presidential Comm. on Income Maintenance 1968–69; mem. Bd of Dirs Fed. Reserve Bank of Boston 1975–81, Chair. 1979–81; Fellow, Center for Advanced Study in Behavioral Sciences 1957–58,

Trustee 1982–95; Vice-Pres. American Econ. Asscn 1968, Pres. 1979, Vice-Pres. AAAS 1970; Pres. Econometric Soc. 1964; Trustee Woods Hole Oceanographic Inst. 1988–, Alfred P. Sloan Foundation 1992–, Resources for the Future 1994–96, Urban Inst. 1994–, German Marshall Fund of US 1994–; Pres. Int. Econ. Asscn 1999–2002; mem. Nat. Science Bd 1995–2000; Fellow American Acad. of Arts and Sciences, mem. of Council, NAS 1977–80, mem. 1972–; Corresp. mem. British Acad.; mem. American Philosophical Soc.; Fellow, Acad. dei Lincei (Rome); Foundation Fellow, Russell Sage Foundation 2000–; Orden pour le mérite, Germany 1995; Hon. LLD (Chicago) 1967, (Brown) 1972, (Lehigh) 1977, (Wesleyan) 1982; Hon. LittD (Williams Coll.) 1974, (Rensselaer Polytechnic Inst.) 2003; Dr hc (Paris) 1975, (Geneva) 1982, (Conservatoire Nat. des Arts et Métiers, Paris) 1994, (Buenos Aires) 1999, (Pompeii Fabra, Barcelona) 2008; Hon. DLitt (Warwick) 1976, (Colgate) 1990, (Glasgow) 1992, (Harvard) 1992; Hon. ScD (Tulane) 1983; Hon. DScS (Yale) 1986, (Univ. of Mass., Boston) 1989, (Helsinki) 1990, (Boston Coll.) 1990, (Chile) 1992, (Rutgers Univ.) 1994; Hon. DSc in Business Admin. (Bryant Coll.) 1988; Hon. DEng (Colorado School of Mines) 1996; Hon. DHumLitt (New York) 2006; David A. Wells Prize, Harvard Univ. 1951, John Bates Clark Medal, American Econ. Asscn 1961, Marshall Lecturer, Univ. of Cambridge, UK 1963–64, De Vries Lecturer, Rotterdam 1963, Wicksell Lecturer, Stockholm 1964, Killian Award, MIT 1977, Seidman Award in Political Econ. 1983, Nobel Prize for Econs 1987, Nat. Medal of Science 2000, Presidential Medal of Freedom 2014. *Publications include:* Linear Programming and Economic Analysis 1958, Capital Theory and the Rate of Return 1963, Sources of Unemployment in the United States 1964, Price Expectations and the Behavior of the Price Level 1970, Growth Theory: An Exposition 1970, The Labor Market as a Social Institution 1989, Learning from "Learning by Doing" 1994, A Critical Essay On Modern Macroeconomic Theory (with Frank Hahn) 1995, Work and Welfare 1998, Inflation, Unemployment and Monetary Policy (with John B. Taylor) 1998; numerous journal articles. *Address:* 1010 Waltham Street, Apt. 328, Lexington, MA 02421-8057, USA (home). *Telephone:* (781) 538-5412 (home).

SOLSO, Theodore Matthew (Tim), BS, MBA; American automotive industry executive; *Independent Lead Director, General Motors Company;* b. 5 March 1947, Spokane, Wash.; s. of Virgil Edward Solso and Dorothy Jane Solso (née Burger); m. Denny Solso; three c.; ed DePauw Univ., Harvard Business School; Asst to Vice-Pres. of Personnel, Cummins Engine Co., Inc. 1971–72, Employment Dir Holset Engineering Co., Ltd (UK subsidiary) 1972–74, Dir of Devt and Training, Holset Engineering Co. 1974–77, Exec. Dir of Personnel, Cummins Engine Co. 1977–80, Vice-Pres. and Man. Dir Holset Engineering Co. 1980–84, Vice-Pres. of Special Engine Markets, Cummins Engine Co. 1984–86, Vice-Pres. of Marketing 1986–88, Vice-Pres. and Gen. Man. of Engine Business 1988–92, Exec. Vice-Pres. of Operations 1992–94, Exec. Vice-Pres. and COO 1994–95, Pres. and COO 1995–2000, Chair. and CEO Cummins Engine Co. 2000–11 (retd); Ind. Dir, General Motors Co. 2012–, Chair. (non-exec.) 2014–16, Ind. Lead Dir 2016–; Lead Dir, Ball Corpn. *Address:* General Motors Company, PO Box 33170, Detroit, MI 48232-5170, USA (office). *Telephone:* (313) 556-5000 (office). *E-mail:* info@gm.com (office). *Website:* www.gm.com (office).

SOLT, Pál; Hungarian judge; b. 3 Oct. 1937, Szentendre; m.; one c.; ed Univ. of Eötvös Lóránd, Budapest; Asst Court Clerk, Cen. Dist Court of Pest 1960–63, Judge 1964–66; Head, Secr. of Supreme Court of Justice 1966–71; Asst, Legal Dept, Secr. of Ministry of Finance 1971–80; Judge, Supreme Court of Justice 1980–87; mem. Constitutional Court 1989–90; Pres. Supreme Court of Justice 1990–2002; Pres. Nat. Council of Justice 1997–2002; Head, Hungarian Judicial Acad. 2006–11; Hon. LLD (San Beda Coll. of Law, Manila) 2001.

SOLTANI, Bouguerra, (Abou Jarra), LèsL, DESS, PhD; Algerian academic and politician; b. 12 Jan. 1954, Chréa; m. Nedjwa Soltani; five c.; ed Constantine Univ.; Lecturer, Faculty of Humanities, Constantine Univ. 1980–94, Dept of Communications, Emir AbdelKader Univ. 1990–94; Ed.-in-Chief Al Tadhamoun magazine 1990–94; Chair. Consultative Cttee Hamas (now Mouvement de la société pour la paix–MSP) 1992–93, Pres. MSP 2003–13; Sec. of State in charge of fishing 1992–93; mem. Nat. People's Ass. for Tébessa 1998–; Minister of Small and Medium-sized Enterprises and Handicrafts 1998–2000, of Labour and Social Security 2000–01; fmr Minister of State; Pres. Harakat Mudjtamaa Silm (Mouvement de la soc. pour la paix) 2010–13. *Publications:* novel: La vache des orphelins 1970; poetry: L'épée de Al Hajjaj, Regards sur le liens entre le bien et le mal, Roses et Epines; essays: Feuillets Islamique 1979–89, Les écorces de la confrontation 1997, Les racines de la confrontation 1999, L'Algérie nouvelle-L'avancée vers la démocratie. *Address:* c/o Mouvement de la société pour la paix, 63 rue Ali Haddad, Algiers, Algeria (office).

SOLYMAR, László, MA, PhD, FRS, FIEE; British (b. Hungarian) engineer and academic; b. 24 Jan. 1930, Budapest, Hungary; s. of Pál Solymar and Aranka Gold; m. Marianne Klopfer 1955; two d.; ed Tech. Univ., Budapest, Hungarian Acad. of Sciences; Lecturer, Tech. Univ., Budapest 1952–53; research engineer, Research Inst. for Telecommunications, Budapest 1953–56, Standard Telecommunications Labs Ltd, Harlow, Essex 1956–65; Lecturer, Dept of Eng Science, Univ. of Oxford 1966–86, Fellow Brasenose Coll. 1966–86, Donald Pollock Reader in Eng Science 1986–92, Fellow Hertford Coll. 1986–, Prof. of Applied Electromagnetism 1992–97, Leverhulme Emer. Fellow 1997–2001, now Prof. Emer.; Visiting Prof., Physics Lab., Ecole Normale Supérieure, Univ. of Paris 1965–66, Tech. Univ. of Denmark 1972–73, Dept of Physics, Univ. of Osnabrück 1987, Optical Inst., Tech. Univ., Berlin 1990, Dept of Materials, Autonomous Univ. of Madrid 1993, 1995, Tech. Univ., Budapest 1994, Dept of Electrical and Electronic Eng, Imperial Coll. London 2003–18; consultant Metaboards Ltd 2017–; Faraday Medal, IEE 1992. *Plays:* The Rhineland War 1936, Portrait of a Genius. *Radio:* plays: Anaxagoras, Archimedes, Hypatia (with John Wain). *Publications:* The Rhineland War: 1936: The Way it Might Have Happened 2012; a book on the history of communications; various research and text books; several hundred papers in learned journals in the field of engineering and physics. *Leisure interests:* history, bridge, chess, swimming. *Address:* 62 Hurst Rise Road, Oxford, OX2 9HQ, England (home). *E-mail:* laszlo.solymar@hertford.ox.ac.uk (office).

SÓLYOM, László, LLD; Hungarian academic, judge, politician and fmr head of state; b. 3 Jan. 1942, Pécs; m. Erzsébet Nagy; one s. one d.; ed Univ. of Pécs, Friedrich Schiller Univ., Jena, Hungarian Acad. of Sciences; Lecturer in Civil Law, Univ. of Jena 1966–69; Research Fellow, Hungarian Acad. of Sciences 1969–82; Prof. of Law, Univ. of Budapest 1982–2002, Catholic Univ. of Budapest 1996–2012, Univ. of Cologne 1999–2000; Pres. Constitutional Court 1990–98; legal adviser to environmental groups and other civic movts 1982–89; Pres. of Hungary 2005–10; mem. Int. Comm. of Jurists, Geneva 1994–2001, scientific council, Wissenschaftskolleg zu Berlin Inst. for Advanced Study, Berlin 1995–2001, European Comm. for Democracy Through Law (The Venice Comm.) 1998–2005; Corresp. mem. Hungarian Acad. of Sciences 2001, Full mem. 2013; Grand Cross of Merit with Star (Germany) 1998; Grand Cross of Merit (Hungary) 1999; Hon. DJur (Cologne) 1999, (Frankfurt/Main) 2006, (Seoul) 2009; Humboldt Research Award 1998, Nagy Imre Prize (Hungary) 2003. *Publications:* The Decline of Civil Law Liability 1980, Die Persönlichkeitsrechte: Eine vergleichend-historische Studie über ihre Grundlagen 1984, Verfassungsgerichtsbarkeit in Ungarn: Analysen und Entscheidungssammlung 1990–93 (with Georg Brunner) 1995, Constitutional Judiciary in a New Democracy: The Hungarian Constitutional Court (with Georg Brunner) 2000, The Beginnings of Constitutional Justice in Hungary (in Hungarian) 2001, The Role of Constitutional Courts in the Transition to Democracy, 18(1) Int. Sociology 2003, Political Parties and Trade Unions in the Constitution (in Hungarian) 2004, Marks of a Presidency (in Hungarian) 2010, Worte des Hörers, in M.Stolleis (ed.), Herzkammern der Republik 2011, The Separation of Powers is Integral to the Fabric of Democracy, 7 Journal of Parliamentary and Political Law 2013, Normenhierarchie in der Verfassung und verfassungswidrige Verfassungsänderungen, Jahrbuch für Ostrecht 1/2014, The Rise and Decline of Constitutional Culture in Hungary, in A. von Bogdandy and P. Sonnevend (eds), Constitutional Crisis in the European Constitutional Area 2014, Das ungarische Verfassungsgericht, in von Bogdandy, Grabenwarter, Huber (eds), Handbuch Ius Publicum Europaeum VI 2015. *Address:* c/o Office of the former President, 1118 Budapest, Kelenhegyi út 32, Hungary.

SOM, Peter; American fashion designer; ed Connecticut Coll., Parsons School of Design, New York; apprenticed with Michael Kors and Calvin Klein at Parson's School of Design, then worked Bill Blass design room; debut at Seventh on Sixth in Bryant Park tents with Spring 2001 Collection; returned to Bill Blass as Creative Dir Women's Collection 2007–08; consultant, Tommy Hilfiger 2009–12; Designer, Blue Collection, Les Copains Group 2014–; Guest Designer, Kohl's DesigNation series 2014–; mem. Council of Fashion Designers of America (CFDA); CFDA Scholarship Competition winner 1997, Parsons Gold Thimble for his work in the school's Designer Critic program, Lord & Taylor's Dress Competition winner, Ecco Domani Fashion Award 2002, Designer of the Year Award, Marymount Univ. 2009. *Address:* Peter Som, Inc., 611 Broadway, Suite 828, New York, NY 10012, USA (office). *Telephone:* (212) 221-5991 (office). *Fax:* (917) 210-3386 (office). *E-mail:* info@petersom.com (office). *Website:* www.petersom.com (office).

SOMARE, Rt Hon. Sir Michael Thomas, PC, CH, GCMG, KStJ, KCMG; Papua New Guinea politician; b. 9 April 1936, Rabaul, East New Britain Prov.; s. of Sana Ludwig Somare and Painari Betha; m. Veronica Bula Kaiap 1965; three s. two d.; ed Sogeri Secondary School, Admin. Coll.; teacher various schools 1956–64; Asst Area Educ. Officer, Madang 1962–63; Broadcasts Officer, Dept of Information and Extension Services, Wewak 1963–66, radio broadcaster and journalist 1966–67; mem. House of Ass. for East Sepik Regional 1968–2012; Parl. Leader Pangu Party 1968–88; Deputy Chair. Exec. Council 1972–73, Chair. 1973–75; Chief Minister Papua New Guinea 1974–75, Prime Minister 1975–80, 1982–85, 2002–11; Minister for Nat. Resources 1976–77, for Public Service Comm. and Nat. Planning 1977–80; Acting Minister for Police 1978–80; Leader of the Opposition 1980–82; Minister of Foreign Affairs 1988–94, 2000–01, 2006–07, also of Bougainville Affairs 2000–01, of Defence (acting) 2007, of Autonomy and Autonomous Regions 2007, for Correctional Services (acting); Gov. E Sepik Prov. 1995; Chair. Bd of Trustees, PNG; mem. Second Select Cttee on Constitutional Devt 1968–72, Australian Broadcasting Comm. Advisory Cttee; mem. Nat. Alliance Party; Ancient Order of Sikatuna, Title of Rajah (Philippines) 1976, Grand Cross of Equestrian Order of St Gregory the Great 1993, Grand Companion of the Order of Logohu, Companion, Order of Fiji; six hon. degrees; Queen's Silver Jubilee Medal 1977, Pacific Man of the Year Award 1983. *Publication:* Sana: An Autobiography. *Leisure interests:* reading, golf, soccer, cricket, fishing. *Address:* Karan, Murik Lakes, East Sepik, Papua New Guinea (home).

SOMAVÍA, Juan O.; Chilean lawyer, diplomatist and international organization official; b. 21 April 1941; m. Adriana Santa Cruz; two c.; ed Catholic Univ. of Chile, Univ. of Paris, France; various posts in Ministry of Foreign Relations; Founder and Exec. Dir Latin American Inst. for Transnational Studies, Mexico; Co-ordinator Third World Forum; mem. Bd of Dirs and Vice-Pres. for Latin America of Inter-Press Service 1976–87; Sec.-Gen. South American Peace Comm. 1987; Pres. International Comm. of Chilean opposition No Campaign for Referendum 1988–89; Perm. Rep. to UN, New York 1990–99; Dir-Gen. ILO 1999–2012; fmr consultant to GATT and UNDP; mem. Bd of Dirs International Foundation for Devt Alternatives; mem. MacBride Comm. on communication problems; Laurea hc (Univ. of Turin) 2001; Dr hc (Connecticut Coll.) 1994, (Catholic Univ. of Lima) 1999, (Univ. of Paris I, Panthéon-Sorbonne) 2003, (Univ. of Coimbra) 2009, (Univ. of Kassel) 2009; Leonidas Proaño Prize, Latin American Human Rights Asscn for contrib. to peace and regional security. *Address:* c/o International Labour Organization, 4 route des Morillons, 1211 Geneva 22, Switzerland. *E-mail:* ilo@ilo.org.

SOMCHAI, Wongsawat, BL, MPA; Thai judge and politician; b. 31 Aug. 1947; m.; ed Thammasat Univ., Nat. Defence Coll. of Thailand, Nat. Inst. of Devt Admin; Asst Judge, Ministry of Justice 1974–75, Judge 1975–76; Judge, Chiangmai-Kwaeng Court 1976–77, Chiangmai Court 1977–83, Chiangrai Court 1983–86; Chief Justice, Pang-nga Court 1986–87, Rayong Juvenile Court 1987–88, Chonburi Court 1988–89, Nonthaburi Court 1989–90, Thonburi Criminal Court 1990–93; Justice, Court of Appeal Region II 1993–97, Chief Justice 1997–98; Deputy Perm. Sec., Ministry of Justice 1998–99, Perm. Sec. 1999–2006; Perm. Sec., Ministry of Labour March–Sept. 2006; mem. House of Reps 2007–08; Deputy Leader People Power Party 2007–08; Minister of Educ. Feb.–Sept. 2008; Prime Minister of Thailand 2008, also Minister of Defence; banned by Constitutional Court from holding public office for five years in 2008, Court also dissolved People Power Party after finding it committed electoral fraud; Kt Commdr, Most Noble Order of the Crown of Thailand (second class) 1980, (first class) 1986, (special class) 1992, Most Exalted Order of the White Elephant (second class) 1984, (first class) 1989, (special class) 1997; Chakrabarti Mala Medal 1999.

SOMDY, Douangdy; Laotian economist and politician; *Minister of Finance;* b. 1952, Savannakhet Prov.; ed Int. Admin. Inst., Paris, Donetsk Nat. Univ., Ukraine; Tech. Officer, Dept of Gen. Planning, State Planning Cttee 1983–93, Dir Gen., Dept of Gen. Planning, State Planning Cttee 1999–2002, Vice-Pres. Planning and Co-operation Cttee 2002–03; Vice-Minister of Finance 2003–07, Minister of Finance 2007–11, 2016–, of Planning and Investment 2011–16, Deputy Prime Minister 2016–; fmr Vice-Chair. and Standing Mem. Poverty Reduction Fund Admin. Bd. *Address:* Ministry of Finance, 23 rue Singha, Ban Phonxay, BP 24, Vientiane, Laos (office). *Telephone:* (21) 900943 (office). *Fax:* (21) 900943 (office). *E-mail:* ict@mof.gov.la (office). *Website:* www.mof.gov.la (office).

SOMERVILLE, Christopher Roland, BSc, PhD, FRS, FRSC, FAAS; American (b. Canadian) biochemist and academic; *Philomathia Professor of Alternative Energy and Director, Energy Biosciences Institute (EBI), University of California, Berkeley;* b. 11 Oct. 1947; ed Univ. of Alberta; naturalized US citizen 1995; Research Assoc., Dept of Agronomy, Univ. of Illinois 1978–81; Asst Prof., Dept of Genetics, Univ. of Alberta 1981; Assoc. Prof., Dept of Botany and Plant Pathology, Michigan State Univ. (MSU) and MSU-DOE Plant Research Lab. 1982–86, Prof. 1986–93; Prof. of Biological Sciences, Stanford Univ. 1994–2007, Dir Dept of Plant Biology, Carnegie Inst. of Washington 1994–2007; Prof. of Plant and Microbial Biology, Univ. of California, Berkeley 2007–, Dir Energy Biosciences Inst. 2007–; Visiting Prof., Univ. of Glasgow, UK 1998–; Ed., Current Opinion in Plant Science 1997–2000; mem. numerous editorial Bds, advisory panels for NSF, NIH, US Dept of Agric. and other agencies and insts; consultant to numerous cos, including Unilever, DuPont, Monsanto, Eli Lilly, Pioneer, Dow, Mendel, Biotechnology, LS9; mem. Academia Europaea 2002, NAS 1996; Fellow, AAAS 2006; Hon. DSc (Queens) 1993, (Alberta) 1997, (Wageningen) 1998, (Guelph) 2006; NSF Young Presidential Investigator Award 1984, Schull Award, American Soc. of Plant Biologists 1987, MSU Distinguished Faculty Award 1992, Alexander von Humboldt US Sr Scientist Award 1992, Gibbs Medal, American Soc. of Plant Physiology 1993, Kumho Award Kumho Cultural Foundation 2001, Hopkins Award and Memorial Lecturer, Biochemical Soc. 2004, Mendel Medal, Genetics Soc. 2004, Balzan Prize, Int. Balzan Foundation (co-recipient) 2006, ACS Sterling B. Hendricks Memorial Lectureship Award 2010, Presidential Green Chemistry Award 2010. *Achievements include:* pioneered the use of the small mustard plant, *Arabidopsis thaliana,* as model species for plant molecular genetics. *Publications include:* Biochemistry and Molecular Biology of Membrane and Storage Lipids of Plants (co-ed.) 1993, Arabidopsis (co-ed.) 1994, The Arabidopsis Book (co-ed.) 2002, Feedstocks for Lignocellulosic Biofuels (co-ed.) 2010; numerous papers in professional journals on plant genomics, embryo devt and the synthesis of structural and storage components of plant cells. *Address:* University of California, Energy Biosciences Building, 2151 Berkeley Way, Berkeley, CA 94720 (office); 161 Avenida Drive, Berkeley, CA 94708, USA (home). *Telephone:* (510) 643-6265 (office); (510) 642-1487 (Lab) (office). *Fax:* (510) 642-4995 (office). *E-mail:* crs@berkeley.edu (office). *Website:* www.energybiosciencesinstitute.org (office); plantbio.berkeley.edu (office).

SOMERVILLE, Jane, MD, FRCP, FESC, FACC; British cardiologist and academic; *Professor Emeritus of Cardiology, Imperial College London;* b. (Jane Platnauer), 24 Jan. 1933, London; d. of Joseph Platnauer and Pearl Anne Backler; m. Walter Somerville (deceased); three s. one d.; ed Hill Crest Boys School, Wales, Queen's Coll., London, Guy's Hosp., London; est. Grown-Up Congenital Heart Disease (GUCH) Unit, Nat. Heart Hosp. (first specialist GUCH service in UK, led to new discipline in cardiology) 1975; Prof. of Cardiology, GUCH, Middlesex Hosp. and Univ. Coll. Hosp., London 1997–2002; Prof. Emer. of Cardiology, Imperial Coll. London; Chair. Council, Queen's Coll., Harley Street, London 2000–06; Consultant Cardiologist, Mater Dei Hosp., Malta; f. ESC Working Group, GUCH Patients' Asscn UK, World Congress of Pediatric Cardiology 1980; Fellow, European Soc. of Cardiology (ESC), American Coll. of Cardiology; Gold Medal, European Soc. of Cardiology 2008, Distinguished Service Award, American Coll. of Cardiology 2009, awarded LEGEND status of cardiovascular diseases, European Soc. of Cardiology 2007, American Coll. of Cardiology 2012; numerous int. guest lectures. *Publications include:* 300 papers in medical journals. *Leisure interests:* collecting glass, Edwardian silver, mustard pots etc., opera, gardening, wild flowers. *Address:* 81–83 Harley Street, London, W1G 8PP, England (office). *Telephone:* (20) 7262-2144 (office). *Fax:* (20) 7724-5840 (office). *E-mail:* trout@janesomerville.net.

SOMMARUGA, Cornelio, LLD; Swiss diplomatist and international organization official; *Chair, Geneva International Centre for Humanitarian Demining;* b. 29 Dec. 1932, Rome, Italy; s. of Carlo Sommaruga and Anna-Maria Valagussa; m. Ornella Marzorati 1957; two s. four d.; ed Rome, Paris, Univ. of Zürich; bank trainee, Zürich 1957–59; joined Diplomatic Service 1960; Attaché, Swiss Embassy, The Hague 1961; Sec., Swiss Embassy, Bonn 1962–64, Rome 1965–68; Deputy Head of Del. to EFTA, GATT and UNCTAD, Geneva 1969–73; Asst Sec.-Gen. EFTA 1973–75; Minister Plenipotentiary, Div. of Commerce, Fed. Dept of Public Economy, Berne 1976, Amb. 1977; del. to Fed. Council for Trade Agreements 1980–84; State Sec. for External Econ. Affairs 1984–86; Pres. ICRC 1987–99; Pres., UN Econ. Comm. for Europe 1977–78; Pres. Initiatives of Change Int., Caux 2000; Chair. J. P. Morgan (Suisse) SA, Geneva 2000–03 (mem. Bd 2003–), Geneva Int. Centre for Humanitarian Demining 2000, Karl Popper Foundation 2000; mem. Panel on UN Peace Operations, Int. Comm. on Intervention and State Sovereignty; Hon. mem. ICRC 2000; Commdr, Légion d'honneur; several other state honours from Italy, Belgium, The Holy See, Luxembourg, Lithuania, Iceland, Sweden; Hon. MD; Dr hc (Fribourg) 1985, (Minho) 1990, (Nice-Sophia Antipolis, Seoul Nat. Univ.) 1992; (Bologna) 1991, (Geneva) 1997, (Webster, St Louis) 1998; North-South Prize of the Council of Europe 2001; numerous awards from Red Cross Socs. *Address:* 7 bis, avenue de la Paix, 1202 Geneva, Switzerland (office); 16 chemin des Crêts-de-Champel, 1206 Geneva, Switzerland (home). *Telephone:* (22) 906-16-97 (office); (22) 347-45-52 (home). *Fax:* (22) 906-16-90 (office); (22) 347-45-55 (home). *E-mail:* c.sommaruga@gichd.org (office); cornelio.sommaruga@bluewin.ch (home). *Website:* www.gichd.ch (office); www.chaux.ch.

SOMMARUGA, Simonetta; Swiss politician; *Vice-President and Head, Federal Department of Justice and Police;* b. 14 May 1960, Sins, Aargau; m. Lukas Hartmann; ed Conservatoire de Lucerne, Conservatoire de Fribourg, Fribourg Univ.; early career as concert pianist; mem. Grosser Rat (Great Council) of Bern (Social Democrat) 1981–90; Dir Swiss Consumer Protection Foundation 1993–2000, Pres. 2000–10; local councillor, Köniz 1997–2005; mem. Nationalrat (Nat. Council) 1999–2003; Rep. for Bern, Ständerat (Council of States) 2003–10; Pres. SWISSAID 2003–08; mem. SDP 1986–; mem. Fed. Council 2010–, Head, Fed. Dept of Justice and Police 2010–; Vice-Pres., Swiss Confed. 2014–15, 2019, Pres. 2015; Dir Concret AG 2010–; mem. Fondation Slow Food Suisse 2009–, Fondation Bärenpark Bern 2009–. *Leisure interests:* playing the piano, gardening, reading, walking. *Address:* Federal Department of Justice and Police, Bundeshaus West, 3003 Bern, Switzerland (office). *Telephone:* 584622111 (office). *Fax:* 584627832 (office). *E-mail:* info@gs-ejpd.admin.ch (office). *Website:* www.ejpd.admin.ch (office); www.sommaruga.ch.

SOMMER, Alfred, MD, MHS; American epidemiologist and academic; *University Distinguished Professor and Dean Emeritus, Bloomberg School of Public Health, Johns Hopkins University;* b. 2 Oct. 1942, New York, NY; m. Jill Sommer; one s. one d.; ed Union Coll., Schenectady, NY, Harvard Medical School, Hopkins School of Public Health; Medical Intern and Resident, Beth Israel Hosp., Harvard Univ., Boston, Mass 1967–69; Attending Physician, Grady Memorial Hosp., Atlanta, Ga 1969–70; Fellow in Epidemiology, Johns Hopkins School of Hygiene and Public Health, Baltimore, Md 1972–73, Resident and Fellow in Ophthalmology, Wilmer Eye Inst. 1973–76, Instructor in Ophthalmology 1976–80, Active Staff, Ophthalmology 1980–, Asst Prof., Ophthalmology, Epidemiology, and Int. Health 1980–81, Assoc. Prof. 1981–85, Prof. 1985–, Prof. of Ophthalmology, Wilmer Eye Inst., Founding Dir Dana Center for Preventive Ophthalmology 1980–90, Dean, Johns Hopkins School of Hygiene and Public Health (now Bloomberg School of Public Health) 1990–2005, Dean Emer. 2005–, Univ. Distinguished Prof.; Visiting Prof. of Ophthalmology, Univ. of Padjadjaran; Dir Nutritional Blindness Prevention Research Program, Bandung, Indonesia 1976–79; Surgeon, Cicendo Eye Hosp., Bandung 1976–79; Visiting Fellow, Inst. of Ophthalmology, Univ. of London, UK 1979–80; Dir WHO Collaborating Center for the Prevention of Blindness 1980–90; Medical Adviser, Helen Keller Int., New York 1980–; Consulting Ophthalmologist, Loch Raven Veterans' Admin Hosp., Baltimore 1981–93; Corp. Dir Becton Dickenson & Co. 1998–, T. Rowe Price Group; Chair. Albert and Mary Lasker Foundation 2007–; Vice-Pres. Int. Council of Ophthalmology Foundation 2002–; mem. Bd of Dirs Int. Trachoma Initiative 2003–09 (also Trustee), Exec. Cttee Acad. for Educational Devt 1997–2007 (also Trustee); Chair. Advisory Bd Epidemiologic Reviews 1990–2005, Bd of Overseers American Journal of Epidemiology 1990–2005, Editorial Advisory Bd EyeNet Magazine 1999–; Editorial positions, American Journal of Ophthalmology, Archives Ophthalmology, American Journal of Epidemiology, Ophthalmology (TAAOO), New England Journal of Medicine, American Journal of Clinical Nutrition, Investigative Ophthalmology and Visual Science, Experimental Eye Research, American Journal of Public Health, Current Eye Research Journal of the American Medical Asscn, Milbank Quarterly, Journal of the Royal Soc. of Medicine, Current Issues in Public Health, 1993–; mem. Royal Soc. of Medicine (UK) 1979, Asscn for Research in Vision and Ophthalmology 1981, Soc. for Epidemiologic Research 1981, American Public Health Asscn 1982, American Ophthalmological Soc. 1983, American Glaucoma Soc. 1988, American Inst. of Nutrition/FASEB 1989, American Soc. for Clinical Nutrition 1989, Inst. of Medicine 1992, Academia Ophthalmologica Internationalis 1997, NAS 2001, Int. Council of Ophthalmology 2002, Nat. Acad. of Medicine; Trustee Foundation of the Int. Council of Ophthalmology; Fellow, American Acad. of Ophthalmology 1978, American Coll. of Preventive Medicine 1982; at forefront of research into vitamin A deficiency and blindness prevention; Hon. Prof. of Ophthalmology, Peking Union Medical College, Beijing 1993; Hon. Prof. of Public Health, Sun Yat-sen Univ. of Medical Sciences, People's Repub. of China, 1998; First Hon. Prof., King Carlos III Nat. Inst. of Health, School of Public Health, Madrid; numerous awards, including Helen Keller Blindness Prevention Award 1980, Charles A. Dana Award for Pioneering Achievements in Health 1988, Distinguished Service Award for Contribs to Vision Care, American Public Health Asscn 1988, Award for Distinguished Contribs to World Ophthalmology, XXIVth Int. Congress of Ophthalmology, Int. Fed. of Ophthalmological Societies 1990, ACAM Achievement Award in Preventive Medicine 1990, Gold Medal for Contribs to World Ophthalmology, Saudi Ophthalmological Soc. 1991, Scripps Insts of Medicine and Science 1992, Joseph E. Smadel Award, Infectious Diseases Soc. of America 1992, 1st Recipient, Gesellschaft für angewandte Vitaminforschung Prize (Germany) 1995, Albert Lasker Award for Clinical Medical Research 1997, Helmut Horten Medical Research Award 1997, Prince Mahidol Award for Int. Contribs to Medicine and Public Health (Thailand) 1997, Int. Gold Medal for Contribs to Ophthalmology, Singapore Nat. Eye Centre 1997, Int. Blindness Prevention Award, American Acad. of Ophthalmology 1998, E.H. Christopherson Award, American Acad. of Pediatrics 2000, Gold Jose Rizal Medal, Asia Pacific Acad. of Ophthalmology 2001, Bristol-Myers Squibb/Mead Johnson Award for Distinguished Achievement in Nutrition Research 2001, Danone Int. Prize for Nutrition 2001, George Gehrmann Lecturer, American Coll. of Occupational and Environmental Medicine, Baltimore 2002, Sir John Wilson Lecturer, Int. Congress of Ophthalmology, Sydney 2002, Pollin Prize in Pediatric Research 2004, Helen Keller Prize for Vision Research 2005, Gonin Medal 2006, Thomas Francis Medal in Public Health, Univ. of Michigan 2010, Laureate Award, American Acad. of Ophthalmology 2011, Ophthalmology Hall of Fame, American Soc. of Cataract and Refractive Surgery 2011, Danone Prize 2013. *Publications include:* Field Guide to the Detection and Control of Xerophthalmia 1978, Epidemiology and Statistics for the Ophthalmologist 1980, Nutritional Blindness: Xerophthalmia and Keratomalacia 1982, Periodic, Large Oral Doses of Vitamin A for the Prevention of Vitamin A Deficiency and Xerophthalmia (co-author) 1984, Vitamin A Deficiency: Health, Survival, and Vision (co-author) 1996, Getting What We Deserve: Health and Medical Care in America 2009, 10 Lessons in Public Health 2013; more than 80 book chapters and reviews and more than 250 articles in scientific journals. *Address:* Johns Hopkins Bloomberg School of Public Health, Suite E6527, 615 N Wolfe Street, Baltimore, MD 21205-2179, USA (office). *Telephone:* (410) 502-4167 (office). *Fax:* (410) 502-4169 (office). *E-mail:* asommer@jhu.edu (office). *Website:* www.jhsph.edu (office).

SOMMER, Elke; German actress and painter; b. (Elke Schletz), 5 Nov. 1940, Berlin; d. of Friedrich Schletz and Renate Schletz; m. Wolf Walther 1993; first film, L'Amico del Giaguaro 1958; since then has made more than 70 films including The

Prize, The Victors, Shot in the Dark, The Oscar, Himmelsheim, Neat and Tidy, Severed Ties; hosted TV show Painting with Elke (PBS) 1985; Golden Globe Award 1965, Jefferson Award, Merit of Achievement Award 1990. *Leisure interests:* riding, art. *Address:* 540 N Beverly Glen Boulevard West, Los Angeles, CA 90024, USA. *Telephone:* (310) 724-8990. *Fax:* (310) 724-8993. *E-mail:* elkesommer@elkesommeronline.com. *Website:* www.elkesommeronline.com.

SOMMER, Ron; German business executive; *Chairman, Mobile TeleSystems OJSC;* b. 1949, Haifa, Israel; ed Univ. of Vienna, Austria; began career with Nixdorf Group in New York, Paris and Paderborn, Germany; Man. Sony Deutschland 1980, Chair. 1986; Pres., CEO Sony USA 1990; Pres., CEO Sony Europe 1993; CEO Deutsche Telekom AG 1995–2002; Chair. Mobile TeleSystems OJSC 2009–; mem. Bd of Dirs Tata Consultancy Services, Munich Reinsurance, AFK Sistema, Motorola Inc. 2004–09; fmr mem. Bd of Dirs Muenchener Rueckversicherung, Weather Industries (now Wind Telecom SpA); mem. Int. Advisory Bd Blackstone Group –2012; mem. Supervisory Bd Celanese AG 2004–06. *Address:* Mobile TeleSystems OJSC, 109147 Moscow, Bldg. 2, 5 Vorontsovskaya Street, Russia (office). *Website:* www.mtsgsm.com (office).

SOMMER, Theo, DPhil; German journalist; b. 10 June 1930, Constance; s. of Theo Sommer and Else Sommer; m. 1st Elda Tsilenis 1952; two s.; m. 2nd Heide Grenz 1976; two s.; m. 3rd Sabine Grewe 1989; one d.; ed Univ of Tübingen, Univ of Chicago and Harvard Univ., USA; Local Ed. Schwäbisch-Gmünd 1952–54; Foreign Ed. Die Zeit 1958, Deputy Ed. 1968, Ed.-in-Chief 1973–92, Publr 1992, Ed.-at-Large 2000–14; Lecturer in Int. Relations, Univ. of Hamburg 1967–70; Chief of Planning Staff, Ministry of Defence 1969–70; mem. Deutsche Gesellschaft für Auswärtige Politik; mem. Council IISS 1963–76, 1978–87, German Armed Forces Structure Comm. 1970–72, Int. Comm. on the Balkans 1995–96, Ind. Int. Comm. on the Balkans 1999–2000; Deputy Chair. Comm. on the Future on the Bundeswehr 1999–2000; Chair. Comm. Investigating Effects of DU Ammunitions, Radar and Asbestos on German Armed Forces 2002; mem. Indo-German Consultative Group 1992 (apptd Co-Chair. 1996), German-Japanese Dialogue Forum 1993; mem. Bd Deutsche Welthungerhilfe 1992–2004, Max-Bauer Preis 1992–2004, German-Turkish Foundation 1998; mem. German Foreign Policy Asscn, IISS, Königswinter Conf., Advisory Council, Mil. History Inst., German Asscn for Asian Studies (Chair. 2003–07); Contributing Ed. Newsweek Int. 1968–90; mem. PEN Germany 2000–; regular contrib. to American, British, Japanese and Korean publs; commentator German TV, radio and moderator of monthly programmes; Hon. mem. Asscn of Anciens, NATO Defense Coll. 1971, Trilateral Comm. 1993, Hon. Senator, Helmut-Schmidt-Universität 2012; Fed. Order of Merit (First Class) 1998, Gold Honor Cross, German Armed Forces 2002; Hon. LLD (Univ. of Maryland, USA) 1982; Theoder-Wolf Prize 1966, Int. Communications Award, People's Repub. of China 1991, Columbus Prize 1993. *Publications:* Deutschland und Japan zwischen den Mächten (Germany and Japan Between the Powers) 1935–40 1962, Vom Antikominternpakt zum Dreimächte-pakt 1962, Reise in ein fernes Land 1964, Ed. Denken an Deutschland 1966, Ed. Schweden-Report 1974, Die chinesische Karte (The Chinese Card) 1979, Allianz in Umbruch (Alliance in Disarray) 1982, Blick zurück in die Zukunft (Look Back into the Future) 1984, Reise ins andere Deutschland (Journey to the Other Germany) 1986, Europa im 21 Jahrhundert 1989, Geschichte der Bonner Republik 1949–99 1999, Der Zukunft entgegen (Toward the Future) 1999, Phoenix Europe, The European Union: Its Progress, Problems and Prospects 2000, Hamburg 2004, 1945: Biographie eines Jahres 2005, Unser Schmidt: Der Staatsmann und der Publizist 2010, Diese NATO hat ausgedient: Das Bündnis muss europäischer werden Ein Standpunkt 2012. *Address:* 17 Zabelweg, 22359 Hamburg, Germany (home). *Telephone:* (40) 6037300 (home). *Fax:* (40) 6030044 (home). *E-mail:* sommer@zeit.de (office); tsommer01@aol.com. *Website:* www.theosommer.de.

SOMOGYI, Peter, PhD, FRS, FMedSci, FHAS; Hungarian/British professor of neurobiology; *Professor of Neurobiology, University of Oxford;* b. 27 Feb. 1950, Szentendre; m.; three c.; ed Loránd Eötvös Univ., Budapest; Junior Research Fellow, Hungarian Acad. of Sciences, 1st Dept of Anatomy, Semmelweis Univ. Medical School, Budapest 1975–76, Research Fellow 1976–83; apptd Assoc. Dir MRC Anatomical Neuropharmacology Unit, Dept of Pharmacology, Univ. of Oxford, UK 1985, Co-Dir Anatomical Neuropharmacology Unit 1995–98, Dir 1998–2016, Prof. of Neurobiology, Univ. of Oxford 1996–, Nicholas Kurti Sr Research Fellow, Brasenose Coll., Oxford 2004–; Sr Research Fellow, Dept of Human Physiology, Flinders Medical School, South Australia 1983–85; Distinguished Visiting Prof., Kyoto Univ., Japan 1998; Visiting Prof., Nat. Inst. of Physiological Sciences, Okazaki, Japan 2002; mem. Editorial Bd Neuroscience 1978–, Journal of Neurocytology 1987–89, Journal of Chemical Neuroanatomy 1988–2005, European Journal of Neuroscience 1988– (Receiving Ed. 1996–99), Experimental Brain Research 1989–, Cerebral Cortex 1990–, Journal Hirnforschung 1992–, Journal of Neuroscience 1995–2001, Hippocampus 2003–, Brain Structure and Function 2007–, Journal of Experimental Neuroscience 2008–; Assoc. of the Neuroscience Research Program, The Neuroscience Inst., San Diego, USA 2008–; Adjunct Prof., Medical Univ., Vienna 2016; Fellow, Medical Acad. Science, London, Hungarian Acad. Science, Royal Soc., London, Acad. Europea, German Nat. Acad. Science, Member Cell Types & Connections Advisory Council, Allen Inst. Brain Research; Commander's Cross Order of Merit of Hungary 2012; Dr hc (József Attila Univ., Szeged) 1990, (Loránd Eötvös Univ.) 2013, (Univ. of Zuirich) 2014; M. Lenhossek Prize, Asscn of Hungarian Anatomists and Embryologists 1982, Charles Judson Herrick Award, Asscn of American Anatomists 1984, Moruzzi Lecturer, European Neuroscience Asscn, Stockholm 1990, Krieg Cortical Discoverer Award, Cajal Club, American Anatomical Soc. 1991, Julian Tobias Memorial Lecture, Univ. of Chicago 1995, Yngve Zotterman Prize, Swedish Physiological Soc. 1995, Jerzy Olszewski Lecture, Montreal Neurological Inst. 2001, Janos Szentagothai Memorial Lecture, Budapest 2002, Wenner-Gren Foundation Distinguished Lecturer, Sweden 2003, Segerfalk Award Lecture, Lund, Sweden 2003, Special Plenary Lecture, 16th IFAA Conference, Kyoto, Japan 2004, Palay Award 2004, 2010, 1st Janos Szentagothai Memorial Lecture, Univ. of California, Irvine 2005, Quastel Lecure, Otto Loewi Conf., Eilat, Israel 2006, Servier Conf. Lecture, Neuroscience Research Centre, Univ. of Montreal 2006, János Arany Medal, Hungarian Acad. of Sciences, Presidential Cttee for Contribution to Hungarian Science from Abroad 2006, István Báthory Award, Hungarian Nat. Council of Transylvania 2006, The IBRO Lecture, Univ. of Debrecen, Hungary 2008, The 1st Hans Kosterlitz Lecture, Univ. of Aberdeen, Scotland 2008, Feldberg Prize and Lectures, Feldberg Foundation, London 2009, Palay Award 2004 2010, Grete Lundbeck European Brain Research Foundation Brain Prize 2011. *Address:* Department of Pharmacology, University of Oxford, Mansfield Road, Oxford, OX1 3QT, England (office). *Telephone:* (1865) 271898 (office). *E-mail:* peter.somogyi@pharm.ox.ac.uk (office). *Website:* pharm.ox.ac.uk (office).

SOMORJAI, Gabor Arpad, PhD, FAAS; American (b. Hungarian) chemist and academic; *Professor of Chemistry, University of California, Berkeley;* b. 4 May 1935, Budapest, Hungary; s. of Charles Somorjai and Livia Ormos; m. Judith Kaldor 1957; one s. one d.; ed Tech. Univ., Budapest, Univ. of California, Berkeley; mem. research staff, IBM, NY 1960–64; at Faculty, Dept of Chem., Univ. of California, Berkeley 1964–, Asst Prof. 1964–67, Assoc. Prof. 1967–72, Prof. 1972–; Faculty Sr Scientist, Materials Science Div. and Dir Surface Science and Catalysis Program, Lawrence Berkeley Lab., Berkeley, Calif. 1964–; Univ. Prof., Univ. of California System 2002–; numerous awards and visiting professorships in USA and UK, including Visiting Fellow, Emmanuel Coll. Cambridge 1969; mem. NAS 1979, ACS (Fellow 2009), American Physical Soc., American Acad. of Arts and Sciences 1983; Hon. mem. Hungarian Acad. of Sciences 1990, Chemical Soc. of Japan 2009; Hon. Fellow, Cardiff Univ. 2006; Dr hc (Tech. Univ., Budapest) 1989, (Univ. Pierre et Marie Curie) 1990, (Univ. Libre de Bruxelles) 1992, (Ferrara) 1998, József Attila Univ., Hungary) 1999 (Royal Inst. of Tech., Stockholm) 2000, (Manchester) 2001, (ETH Zurich) 2003, (Inst. of Chem., Chinese Acad. of Sciences—ICCAS) 2007, (Northwestern Univ.) 2010; Emmett Award American Catalysis Soc. 1977, ACS Colloid and Surface Chem. Award 1981, Centenary Lecturer, Royal Soc. of Chem., UK 1983, ACS Peter Debye Award 1989, ACS Adamson Surface Chemistry Award 1994, Hinshelwood Lecturer, Univ. of Oxford 1994, Linnett Lecturer, Univ. of Cambridge 1994, Von Hippel Award, Materials Research Soc. 1997, Wolf Prize 1998, ACS Catalysis Award 2000, Pauling Medal, Hungarian Acad. of Sciences 2000, Nat. Medal of Science 2002, Cotton Award 2003, Remsen Award, Maryland Section of ACS 2006, Langmuir Prize, American Physical Soc. 2007, Priestley Medal 2008, Miller Sr Fellow 2009, BBVA Frontiers of Knowledge Award in Basic Science 2010, ENI New Frontiers of Hydrocarbons Prize 2010, Honda Prize 2010, NAS Award in Chemical Sciences 2013, William H. Nichols Medal, New York Section, ACS. *Publications:* Principles of Surface Chemistry 1972, Chemistry in Two Dimensions 1981, Introduction to Surface Chemistry and Catalysis 1994, serves editorial bds of numerous scientific publs, more than 1,200 publs in major scientific journals. *Leisure interests:* swimming, walking. *Address:* Department of Chemistry, D58 Hildebrand, University of California, Berkeley, Berkeley, CA 94720-1460 (office); 665 San Luis Road, Berkeley, CA 94707, USA (home). *Telephone:* (510) 642-4053 (office). *Fax:* (510) 643-9668 (office). *E-mail:* somorjai@berkeley.edu (home). *Website:* www.cchem.berkeley.edu/gasgrp (office); chem.berkeley.edu/faculty/somorjai (office).

SOMPONG, Amornvivat, BBA, MA; Thai politician; b. 3 July 1941, Bangkok; m.; ed Curry Coll., Milton, Mass, USA, Chiangmai Univ.; mem. Parl. for Chonburi Prov. 1986–89, for Chiangmai Prov. 1992–93, 1994–96, 1999–2000, Vice-Chair. Industry Cttee 1988–89; Deputy Minister of Agric. and Cooperatives 1990–91, Minister of Industry 1992–93, of Labour and Social Welfare 1994–95, 1997, Minister to Prime Minister's Office 1996, Deputy Minister of Transport and Communications 1997, Minister of Justice 2008, Deputy Prime Minister and Minister of Foreign Affairs 2008; adviser to Prime Minister 2001–05; mem. Exec. Cttee, Nat. Democracy Party 1981–82, Deputy Sec.-Gen. 1983–84, Sec.-Gen. 1984–88; Sec.-Gen. Ruam Thai Party 1988–89; Deputy Leader, Unity Party 1988–89; Deputy Leader, Chart Pathana Party 1992–93, then mem. People's Power Party 1998–2008 (party dissolved), Election Dir Pheu Thai party 2016–. *Address:* Puea Thai (For Thais), 1770 Thanon Phetchaburi, Bangkapi, Huay Kwang, Bangkok 10310, Thailand (office). *Website:* www.ptp.or.th (office).

SOMSAVAT, Lengsavat; Laotian politician; b. 16 June 1945, Luangphrabang; m. Bounkongmany Lengsavad; one s. two d.; ed Nat. Org. for the Study of Policy and Admin; combatant in North Laos 1961–64; Officer, Cabinet of the Lao People's Revolutionary Party (LPRP) Cen. Cttee 1964–76, Head of Secr. 1975–82; Deputy Chief, Council of Ministers 1982–88; fmr Deputy Minister; First Vice-Chair. LPRP History Research Comm. 1982–88, Chief of the Cabinet of LPRP and Cabinet of Ministers 1991–93; Amb. to Bulgaria 1989–91, Minister of Foreign Affairs 1993–2006; Deputy Prime Minister 1998–2017; Chair. Vientiane Cttee for Flood Control; Hon. Dr rer. pol (Ramkhamheang Univ., Thailand) 2000; Medal of Liberty Issara, Medal of Labour, Anti-Imperialist Cross, Revolutionary Medal, People's Repub. of Korea, Medal of Friendship Govts of Cuba and Bulgaria. *Leisure interests:* reading, golf, singing.

SON, Kil-seung, BA; South Korean business executive; b. 1941; ed Seoul Nat. Univ.; joined Sunkyong Textiles Corpn (renamed SK Corpn) 1965, various Exec. Man. positions in Office of Corp. Man. and Planning, Group Pres. 1991, Pres. Daehan Telecom –1998, Chair. and CEO SK Corpn 1998–2003 (resgnd after conviction for accounting irregularities), also fmr Chair. and CEO SK Telecom (now Hon. Chair.), SK Shipping; fmr Chair. Korean Business Council for the Arts, Korean Business Messena Asscn; fmr Chair. Fed. of Korean Industries (FKI); mem. Bd of Dirs Forum Council; Hon. Citizen of China Award 2001, CEO of Korea Award, Korean Chamber of Commerce and Industry (KCCI) 2002, 2003, Korean Man. Award, Top Business Man. of Korea Award, KCCI.

SON, Masayoshi, BA (Econ); Japanese business executive; *Chairman and CEO, SoftBank Group Corporation;* b. 11 Aug. 1957, Tosu, Saga Pref.; m.; one s. one d.; ed Univ. of California, Berkeley, USA; f. SoftBank Corpn Japan (later SoftBank Corpn, then SoftBank Group Corpn from 2015) 1981, Chair. 1983–86, Chair. and CEO 1986–, serves in various capacities with SoftBank's portfolio of cos, including Pres. and CEO Yahoo Japan Corpn (jt venture between SoftBank and Yahoo! Inc.) 1996, Chair. 1996–, Pres. BB Technologies Corpn (currently SoftBank BB Corpn) 2001–, Chair. and CEO SoftBank BB Corpn 2004–, Chair. Japan Telecom Co. Ltd (currently SoftBank Telecom Corpn) 2004–, and CEO 2006–, Chair., Pres. and CEO Vodafone K.K. (currently SoftBank Mobile Corpn) 2006–07, Chair. and CEO 2007–, Chair. Sprint Corpn (following acquisition of majority stake by SoftBank) 2013–, Dir, Yahoo Japan Corpn 2015–, Rep. Dir, SoftBank Group International GK 2016–, acquired ARM Holdings plc semiconductor and software design co. 2016; fmr Chair. Broadband Asscn in Japan, Great East Japan Earthquake Recovery Initiative Foundation; Dir, Yahoo Japan Corpn 2015–. *Address:* SoftBank Group Corporation, 1-9-1 Higashi-shimbashi, Minato-ku, Tokyo 105-

7303, Japan (office); Sprint Corporation, 6200 Sprint Parkway, Overland Park, KS 66251, USA (office). *Telephone:* (3) 6889-2000 (Tokyo) (office); (703) 433-4000 (Overland Park) (office). *E-mail:* info@softbank.jp (office); boardinquiries@sprint.com (office). *Website:* www.softbank.jp/en/corp (office); www.sprint.com (office).

SONDAKH, Peter; Indonesian business executive; *Chairman, PT Rajawali Corporation;* b. 1953, N Sulawesi; m. Eve Sondakh; three c.; joined family business (trading in coconut oil and timber) 1971, took over after death of father 1975; f. PT Rajawali Corpn (conglomerate) 1984, interests include cement, cigarettes, hotels, telecommunications, mining, plantations, retail and transportation; associated cos include PT Semen Gresik, PT Bentoel International, PT Excelcomindo Pratama; cos est. Taksi Express 1989, Lombok Tourism Devt Corpn 1989, Bank Pos 1989 (now merged with Bank Danamon Indonesia). *Address:* Office of the Chairman, PT Rajawali Corporation, Jl Mega Kuningan, Lot 5.1, Menara Rajawali Lt 27-28, Kuningan Timur, Setia Budi, Jakarta 12950, Indonesia (office). *Telephone:* (21) 5760808 (office). *Fax:* (21) 5761588 (office). *Website:* www.rajawali.com (office).

SONDHEIM, Stephen Joshua, BA; American composer and lyricist; b. 22 March 1930, New York, NY; s. of Herbert Sondheim and Janet Fox; ed George School, Newtown, Pa, Williams Coll., private instruction; Pres. Dramatists' Guild 1973–81, Council mem. 1981–; Visiting Prof. of Drama and Musical Theatre, Univ. of Oxford, UK Jan.–June 1990; mem. American Acad. and Inst. of Arts and Letters 1983–, American Theater Hall of Fame 2014–; Antoinette Perry Awards for Company 1971, Follies 1972, A Little Night Music 1973, Sweeney Todd 1979; Drama Critics' Awards 1971, 1972, 1973, 1976, 1979; Evening Standard Drama Award 1996; Grammy Awards 1984, 1986; Nat. Medal of Arts 1997, Praemium Imperial 2000, Special Tony Award for Lifetime Achievement in the Theatre 2008, Presidential Medal of Freedom 2015. *Compositions include:* television: Topper (co-author) 1953, Evening Primrose (music and lyrics) 1967; lyrics: West Side Story 1957, Gypsy 1959, Do I Hear a Waltz? 1965, Candide 1973; music and lyrics: A Funny Thing Happened on the Way to the Forum 1962, Anyone Can Whistle 1964, Evening Primrose 1966, Company 1970, Follies 1971, A Little Night Music 1973, The Frogs 1974, Pacific Overtures 1976, Sweeney Todd 1978, Merrily We Roll Along 1981, Sunday in the Park with George 1984, Into the Woods (Drama Critics' Circle Award 1988) 1986, Assassins 1990, Passion 1994, Bounce 2003 (renamed Road Show 2008); anthologies: Side by Side by Sondheim 1976, Marry Me a Little 1980, You're Gonna Love Tomorrow 1983, Putting It Together 1993; screenplays: (with Anthony Perkins) The Last of Sheila 1973, Birdcage 1996, Getting Away with Murder 1996; film scores: Stavisky 1974, Reds 1981, Dick Tracy 1989; incidental music: The Girls of Summer 1956, Invitation to a March 1961, Twigs 1971, Company: A Musical 2007, Sweeney Todd 2007, Into the Woods 2014. *Publications:* Finishing the Hat 2010, Look, I Made a Hat: Collected Lyrics (1981–2011) 2011. *Address:* c/o John Breglio, 1285 Avenue of the Americas, New York, NY 10019, USA (office).

SONENBERG, Nahum, BSc, MSc, PhD, FRSC; Israeli biochemist and academic; *James McGill Professor, Department of Biochemistry, McGill University;* m.; two d.; ed Tel-Aviv Univ., Weizman Inst. of Science; early research position at Roche Inst. of Molecular Biology, NJ, USA; joined faculty at McGill Univ., Montreal, Canada 1979, currently James McGill Prof., Dept of Biochemistry, also Dir Sonenberg Lab.; Int. Research Scholar, Howard Hughes Medical Inst.; Distinguished Scientist, Canadian Insts of Health Research; Robert L. Noble Prize, Nat. Cancer Inst. of Canada 2002, Killiam Prize for Health Sciences 2005, Wolf Prize in Medicine (co-recipient) 2014. *Publications:* numerous papers in scientific and medical journals. *Address:* Goodman Cancer Centre, McGill University, 1160 Pine Avenue West, Room 614, Montreal, QC H3A 1A3, Canada (office). *Telephone:* (514) 398-7274 (office); (514) 398-7275 (Lab.) (office). *Fax:* (514) 398-1287 (office). *E-mail:* nahum.sonenberg@mcgill.ca (office). *Website:* www.med.mcgill.ca/nahum (office).

SONG, Baorui; Chinese politician; b. Dec. 1937, Shunyi Dist, Beijing; ed Tsinghua Univ., Beijing; joined CCP 1958; fmr Deputy Dir, Chief Engineer China Welding Rod Plant, Dir China Welding Rod Plant Inst. 1975–82; Man. China Welding Materials Manufacture Co. 1982–83; Deputy Sec. then Sec. CCP Zigong City Cttee 1983–86; fmr mem. Standing Cttee CCP Sichuan Prov. Cttee; Chair. Sichuan Prov. Comm. for Restructuring the Economy 1986–89, Exec. Deputy Sec. CCP Sichuan Prov. Cttee 1989–99; Gov. Sichuan Prov. 1996–99; Deputy Dir State Comm. for Restructuring Economy 2001–; Deputy Dir-Gen. CPPCC Sub-cttee for Handling Proposals 2003–; Alt. mem. 14th CCP Cen. Cttee 1992–97, mem. 15th CCP Cen. Cttee 1997–2002; Deputy 8th NPC. *Address:* Subcommittee for Handling Proposals, CPPCC, Beijing, People's Republic of China (office).

SONG, Fatang; Chinese politician; b. Dec. 1940, Tancheng, Shandong Prov.; ed Qufu Teachers' Univ.; joined CCP 1961; Cadre, Supervision Cttee, CCP Shandong Prov. Cttee 1964; Sec., Org. Dept, CCP Revolutionary Cttee, Shandong Prov. 1967; Deputy Div. Chief, Org. Dept, CCP Shandong Prov. Cttee 1973; Deputy Sec. CCP Tai'an Co. Cttee, Deputy Sec. CCP Tai'an Municipal Cttee, Shandong Prov. 1979–84, Sec. 1984, Mayor of Taian 1985–89; Vice-Gov. Shandong Prov. 1989–2000; Deputy Sec. CCP Shandong Prov. Cttee 1998–99; Deputy Gov., then Gov. Heilongjiang Prov. 2000–03; Sec. CCP Heilongjiang Prov. Cttee 2003–; Chair. Standing Cttee Heilongjiang Prov. People's Congress 2003–05; Alt. mem. 15th CCP Cen. Cttee 1997–2002, mem. 16th CCP Cen. Cttee 2002–07; Deputy, 9th NPC 1998–2003; apptd Vice-Chair. Education, Science, Culture and Public Health Cttee, NPC 2005.

SONG, Jian, DSc; Chinese state official and academic; b. 29 Dec. 1931, Rongcheng Co., Shandong Prov.; s. of Song Zengjin and Jiang Yuxian; m. Wang Yusheng 1961; one s. one d.; ed Harbin Tech. Univ., Beijing Foreign Languages Inst., Bauman Eng Inst., Moscow and Moscow Univ., USSR; joined CCP 1947; Dir and Head, Lab. of Cybernetics, Inst. of Math., Acad. Sinica 1960–70; Dir Guided Missile Control Lab., 7th Ministry of Machine Bldg Industry 1962–70; Head, Chief Scientist, Space Science Div., Acad. of Space Tech. 1971–78, Vice-Pres., Deputy Science Dir, Acad. of Space Tech. 1978–81; Vice-Minister and Chief Eng Scientist, Ministry of Astronautics 1981–84; Researcher, China Aviation Industry Corpn; Research Prof., Beijing Inst. of Information and Control 1983–; Visiting Prof., MIT, Harvard, Univ. of Minn. 1980; Prof., Tsinghua Univ., Fudan Univ., Harbin Univ. of Tech. 1986–; Chair. State Science and Tech. Comm. 1984–98; State Councillor 1986–98, Chair. Environmental Protection Cttee; Vice-Chair. Three Gorges Project Construction Cttee; Head, State Leading Group for Man. of Intellectual Property Rights; mem. State Steering Group of Science, Tech. and Educ. 1998; Vice-Chair. State Academic Degrees Cttee 1999; Vice-Pres. China Soc. of Demographic Science 1982–86; Assoc. Chief Ed. System & Control Letters 1983–85; Chief Ed. Automatic Control & System Eng, Encyclopaedia of China 1983–; mem. Ed. Bd Encyclopaedia of China 1984–; Council mem. Int. Fed. of Automatic Control 1984–87; Vice-Pres. China System Eng Soc. 1985–87; Vice-Chair. Chinese People's Political Consultative Conf. 1998–; Pres. China-Japan Friendship Asscn 1998–; Alt. mem. 12th CCP Cen. Cttee 1982–87, mem. 13th CCP Cen. Cttee 1987–92, 14th CCP Cen. Cttee 1992–97, 15th CCP Cen. Cttee 1997–2002; Vice-Chair. 9th CPPCC Nat. Cttee 1998–2003; mem. Chinese Acad. of Sciences 1991–, Chinese Acad. of Eng 1994– (Pres. 1998–2002); Foreign mem. Russian Acad. of Sciences 1994, Royal Swedish Acad. of Eng Sciences 1994, Nat. Acad. of Eng, USA 2000, Argentine Acad. of Eng 2001, Yugoslav Acad. of Eng 2002; Corresp. mem. Nat. Acad. of Eng of Mexico 1985; Hon. Distinguished Visiting Prof. Washington Univ. 1986–; Hon. Pres. Chinese Asscn of Environmental Protection; Hon. DHumLitt (Houston) 1996; Nat. Natural Sciences Award, Nat. Award for Advancements in Science and Tech. 1987, Albert Einstein Award 1987, Int. Asscn for Mathematics 1987 and numerous other nat. and int. awards. *Publications:* Reference Frames in Space Flight 1963, Engineering Cybernetics (co-author) 1980, China's Population: Problems and Prospects 1981, Recent Development in Control Theory and Its Applications 1984, Population Projections and Control 1981, Population Control Theory 1985, Population Control in China: Theory and Applications 1985, Population System Control 1988, Science and Technology and Social System 1988; numerous articles. *Leisure interest:* swimming. *Address:* National Committee of Chinese People's Political Consultative Conference, 23 Taipingqiao Street, Beijing, People's Republic of China (office).

SONG, Lin, BEng; Chinese business executive; b. 3 Feb. 1963, Shanghai; ed Tongji Univ., Shanghai; joined China Resources Holdings Co. 1985, held Sr exec. positions at China Resources Enterprise Ltd, China Resources Power Holdings Co. Ltd, China Resources Land Ltd, China Resources Cement Holdings Ltd, China Resources Logic Ltd (now China Resources Gas Group Ltd), China Resources Capital Holdings Co. Ltd, fmr Chair. and Gen. Man. China Resources Devt and Investment Co. Ltd, mem. Bd of Dirs and Chair. China Resources (Holdings) Co. Ltd 2008–14, Chair. China Resources Nat. Corpn 2008–14; Deputy Chair. China Vanke Co. Ltd; Ind. Dir (non-exec.) Geely Automobile Holdings Ltd 2004–, The Bank of East Asia (China) Ltd. *Address:* China Resources (Holdings) Co. Ltd, Floor 49, CRC Building, 26 Harbour Road, Wanchai, Hong Kong Special Administrative Region, People's Republic of China (office). *Telephone:* 28797888 (office). *Fax:* 28275774 (office). *Website:* www.crc.com.hk (office).

SONG, Ping; Chinese politician (retd) and party official; b. 24 April 1917, Juxian Co., Shandong Prov.; m. Chen Shunyao; one s.; ed Inst. Marxism-Leninism, Yan'an, Tsinghua Univ.; joined CCP 1937; Vice-Minister, Labour 1953; Vice-Chair. State Planning Comm. 1957–63; Sec. CCP Gansu and Vice-Chair. Gansu Revolutionary Cttee 1972, First Sec. CCP Gansu, Chair. Gansu Revolutionary Cttee, Second Political Commissar, PLA Lanzhou Mil. Region and First Political Commissar, Gansu Mil. Dist, PLA 1977–80; First Vice-Chair. State Planning Comm. 1981–83; Minister in charge of State Planning Comm. 1983–87; Chair. Family Planning Asscn 1990–; Deputy Sec.-Gen., First Session of the 7th NPC March 1988; Deputy Dir Leading Group for Co-ordinating Nat. Scientific Work 1983; State Councillor 1983–88; Vice-Chair. Environmental Protection Cttee State Council 1984–87, Nat. Agric. Zoning Cttee 1983–; Deputy Head Leading Group for Scientific Work, State Council 1983–92; Head Leading Group for Econ. Information Man., State Council 1986–92; Head Org. Dept Cen. Cttee CCP 1988–90; visited Pakistan 1991; mem. 11th Cen. Cttee CCP 1977, 12th Cen. Cttee CCP 1982–87, Political Bureau 1987–92, 13th Cen. Cttee (mem. Standing Cttee 1989–92); mem. Presidium 14th CCP Nat. Congress 1992; Hon. Pres. Chinese Asscn for Promotion of the Population Culture; Hon. Dir-in-Chief China Welfare Fund for the Handicapped; Hon. Adviser 'Happiness Project' Org. *Address:* Central Committee of CCP, Zhang Nan Hai, Beijing, People's Republic of China.

SONG, Ruixiang; Chinese politician; b. 1939, Jintan Co., Jiangsu Prov.; joined CCP 1959; Gov. of Qinghai Prov. 1985–93; Minister of Geology and Mineral Resources 1993–98, Party Group Sec. Ministry of Geology and Mineral Resources; Chair. Nat. Mineral Reserves Comm. 1995–96; Vice-Chair. Nat. Mineral Resources Cttee 1996–98; Deputy Dir State Gen. Admin. of Environment Protection 1998–2003; Dir China Seismological Bureau 2003–04; mem. 15th CCP Cen. Cttee 1997–2002; Del., 13th CCP Nat. Congress 1987–92. *Address:* c/o China Seismological Bureau, Beijing, People's Republic of China (office).

SONG, Sang-hyun, LLM, JSD; South Korean professor of law and judge (retd); b. 21 Dec. 1941, Seoul; m.; one s. one d.; ed Seoul Nat. Univ., Tulane Law School, New Orleans and Cornell Law School, Ithaca, NY, USA, Univ. of Cambridge, UK; called to the Bar, Repub. of Korea 1964; Mil. Prosecutor then Judge, Judge Advocate Office, Korean Armed Forces 1964–67; Attorney Haight, Gardner, Poor & Havens, New York 1970–72; Prof. of Law, Seoul Nat. Univ. 1972–2007, Dean Law School 1996–98; Lecturer in Law, Nat. Police Coll., Seoul 1983–2003; Vice-Pres. UNICEF Korea 1998–2012; Judge (Appeals Div.), Int. Criminal Court (ICC), The Hague, Netherlands 2003–15, Pres. ICC 2009–15 (retd); Pres. Korea Childhood Leukemia Foundation 1999–2009; has lectured at Univ. of Melbourne Law School, Harvard Law School and New York Univ.; Nat. Decoration of 2nd Highest Order (Moran), Govt of Repub. of Korea 1997, Nat. Decoration of the Highest Order (Mugunghwa), Govt of Repub. of Korea 2011; Most Distinguished Alumni Medal, Cornell Univ. 1994, Legal Culture Award, Korean Fed. Bar Asscn 1998. *Publications:* books: Introduction to the Law and Legal System of Korea 1983, An Introduction to Law and Economics 1983, Korean Law in the Global Economy 1996, The Korean Civil Procedure 2004; numerous articles in professional journals. *Address:* c/o International Criminal Court, PO Box 19519, 2500 CM The Hague, Netherlands (office).

SONG, Shuguang, MEcon; Chinese insurance industry executive; *Chairman of the Board of Supervisors, Bank of Communications;* b. Feb. 1961; ed Jilin Univ.; with China Nat. Planning Comm. 1985–93; with People's Insurance Co. of China 1993–98; Head of Finance and Accounting Dept, China Insurance Regulatory Comm. 1998–2000; with China Taiping Insurance Group (fmrly China Insurance Group) 2000–14, Chair. Taiping Life Insurance Co. Ltd 2004–08, 2010–11, Vice-Chair. and Gen. Man. China Taiping Insurance Group Ltd (China Taiping Insurance Group Ltd (HK)) 2008–14, Vice-Chair. China Taiping Insurance

Holdings Co. Ltd (Taiping Holdings) 2008–14, Vice-Chair. and Pres. Taiping Holdings 2013–14; joined Bank of Communications March 2014, Chair. Bd of Supervisors June 2014–. *Address:* Bank of Communications, 188 Yinchengzhong Road, Shanghai 200120, People's Republic of China (office). *Telephone:* (21) 95559 (office). *E-mail:* 95559@bankcomm.com (office). *Website:* www.bankcomm.com (office).

SONG, Adm. (retd) Young-moo; South Korean politician and fmr naval officer; *Minister of National Defence;* b. 1949; ed Kyungnam Univ., Korea Naval Acad.; more than 20 years in navy, including as Commdr, Repub. of Korea First Fleet 2000, Gen. Man., Navy HQ 2002, Deputy Chief of Naval Operations for Planning and Man. 2003, Chief, Directorate of Logistics and Personnel of Jt Chiefs of Staff 2005, Chief of Naval Operations 2006–08, Chief, Directorate of Strategic Planning 2011; Security Adviser to Pres. Moon Jae-in during presidential campaigns 2012, 2017; Minister of Nat. Defence 2017–; fmr Prof., Dept of Mil. Science, Konyang Univ. *Address:* Ministry of National Defence, 22 Itaewon-ro, Yeongsan-gu, Seoul 04383, Republic of Korea (office). *Telephone:* (2) 748-1111 (office). *Fax:* (2) 703-3109 (office). *E-mail:* cyber@mnd.go.kr (office). *Website:* www.mnd.go.kr (office).

SONG, Yufang; Chinese business executive; fmr Chair. China Railway Materials Commercial Corpn (now China Railway Materials Co. Ltd).

SONG, Zhaosu; Chinese politician; b. March 1941, Nanyang, He'nan Prov.; ed Zhengzhou Univ.; joined CCP 1965; Section Chief, Org. Dept, CCP Zhoukou Prefectural Cttee, He'nan Prov., later Deputy Sec. Zhoukou Prefectural Cttee; Deputy Sec. CCP Shangshui Co. Cttee, He'nan Prov.; Magistrate, Shangshui Co. (Dist) People's Court, He'nan Prov.; Sec. CCP Taikang Co. Cttee, He'nan Prov.; Sec. CCP Xuchang Prefectural Cttee, He'nan Prov.; Vice-Gov. He'nan Prov. 1988; Deputy Sec. CCP He'nan Prov. Cttee 1993–98, Sec. Political Science and Law Cttee; Acting Gov. Gansu Prov. 1998–99, Gov. 1999–2001; Deputy Sec. CCP Gansu Prov. Cttee 1998–2001, Sec. 2001–03; Chair. Standing Cttee, Gansu Prov. People's Congress 2003–04; Alt. mem. 15th CCP Cen. Cttee 1997–2002, mem. 16th CCP Cen. Cttee 2002–07; Vice-Chair. Environment and Resources Protection Cttee of NPC 2003. *Address:* Environment and Resources Protection Committee, National People's Congress, Beijing, People's Republic of China (office).

SONG, Zhe, MA; Chinese diplomatist; b. April 1960; m.; one d.; Attaché, Third Sec., People's Inst. of Foreign Affairs 1983–88, Third, later Second Sec., Embassy in London 1988–92, Counsellor 2000–01, Second Sec., Deputy Dir, First Sec., Dir, Western European Dept, Ministry of Foreign Affairs 1992–2000, Counsellor 2001–02, Deputy Dir-Gen. 2002–03; Dir-Gen., Gen. Office of State Council 2003–08; Amb. and Perm. Rep. to EU, Brussels 2008–12. *Address:* Ministry of Foreign Affairs, 2 Chao Yang Men, Nan Dajie, Chao Yang Qu, Beijing 100701, People's Republic of China (office). *Telephone:* (10) 65961114 (office). *Fax:* (10) 65962146 (office). *E-mail:* webmaster@mfa.gov.cn (office). *Website:* www.fmprc.gov.cn (office).

SONG, Zhiping; Chinese business executive; *President, World Cement Association;* worked as Factory Dir Beixin New Building Materials Plant, held several positions with Beijing New Building Materials (Group) Co. Ltd including Deputy Dir, Sec. of Party Cttee and Gen. Man. 1987–97, Chair. 1997–2002, fmr Gen. Man. and Deputy Sec. Party Cttee, China Nat. Building Materials Group Corpn, Chair. and Dir 2005–2018; Chair. and Exec. Dir China Nat. Pharmaceutical Group 2009–14; Pres. World Cement Asscn 2017–; Chair. China United 2003–05, China Enterprise & Devt Research Asscn; Chair. Bd China Fed. of Industrial Econs; Vice Pres. China Building Materials Industry Asscn, China Enterprise Confederation, China's Listed Cos. Asscn, China Logistics Alliance Network, China Capital Entrepreneurs' Club; Prof., Nat. School of Devt, Chinese Business Exec. Acad. *Address:* World Cement Association, New Broad Street House, 35 New Broad Street, London EC2M 1NH, England (office). *Telephone:* (33) 3939-8083 (office); ((77) 1492-8358 (office). *E-mail:* info@worldcementassociation.org (office). *Website:* www.worldcementassociation.or (office).

SONGWE, Vera, BA, MA, PhD; Cameroonian economist, international banker and UN official; *Executive Secretary, UN Economic Commission for Africa;* b. 1968, Bamenda; ed Our Lady of Lourdes Coll., Bamenda, Univ. of Michigan, Centre for Operations Research and Econometrics, Univ. Catholique de Louvain; joined World Bank as Young Professional 1998, becoming Lead Country Sector Coordinator and Sr Economist, Philippines 2005–08, Adviser to Man. Dir for Africa, Europe and Central Asia and South Asia Regions 2008–11, Country Dir for Senegal, Cape Verde, The Gambia, Guinea Bissau and Mauritania 2012–15; Sr Fellow, Brookings Inst. Global Devt and Africa Growth Initiative 2011–; Regional Dir for West and Central Africa, Int. Finance Corpn (IFC) 2015–17; Exec. Sec., UN Econ. Comm. for Africa 2017–. *Address:* Economic Commission for Africa, Menelik II Ave, POB 3001, Addis Ababa, Ethiopia (office). *Telephone:* (11) 5445000 (office). *Fax:* (11) 5514416 (office). *E-mail:* ecainfo@uneca.org (office). *Website:* www.uneca.org (office).

SONI, Rebecca; American swimmer; b. 18 March 1987, Freehold Borough, New Jersey; d. of Péter Sőni and Kinga Sőni; ed West Windsor-Plainsboro High School North, Plainsboro Township, New Jersey, Annenberg School for Communication, Univ. of Southern California; originally a gymnast, began swimming aged ten; six-time NCAA Champion 2006–09; 11-time All-American 2006–09; Summer Universiade, Izmir 2005: gold medal, 4×100m medley, silver medal, 100m breaststroke, 200m breaststroke; Olympic Games, Beijing 2008: gold medal, 200m breaststroke, silver medal, 100m breaststroke, 4×100m medley; World Championships (long course), Rome 2009: gold medal, 100m breaststroke, silver medal, 50m breaststroke, Shanghai 2011: gold medal, 100m breaststroke, 200m breaststroke, 4×100m medley, bronze medal, 50m breaststroke; World Championships (short course), Dubai 2010: gold medal, 50m breaststroke, 100m breaststroke, 200m breaststroke, silver medal, 4×100m medley; Pan Pacific Championships, Irvine 2010: gold medal, 100m breaststroke, 200m breaststroke, 4×100m medley; Olympic Games, London 2012: gold medal, 200m breaststroke, 4×100m medley relay (with Missy Franklin, Dana Vollmer, and Allison Schmitt), silver medal, 100m breaststroke; swims for Trojan Swim Club and Univ. of Southern California Trojans; coach: Dave Salo; spokeswoman for UN Foundation's Girl Up campaign 2010–; World Swimmer of the Year, Swimming World magazine 2010, 2011, American Swimmer of the Year, Swimming World magazine 2009, 2010, 2011. *Address:* c/o Wasserman Media Group, 10960 Wilshire Blvd, Suite 2200, Los Angeles, CA 90024, USA (office). *E-mail:* info@wmgllc.com (office). *Website:* www.rebsoni.com.

SONN, Franklin Abraham; South African diplomatist and academic; b. 11 Oct. 1939, Vosburg Dist; s. of Pieter (Pat) Sonn and Magdalene Klein; m.; two c.; ed UNISA and Univ. of Western Cape; fmr Rector, Peninsula Technikon; fmr Chair. Comm. of Technikon Prins, Chair. Western Cape Foundation for Community Work, Mobil Foundation of S Africa, Inst. for Distance Educ.; Chair. Bd Trustees, Die Suid-Afrikaan Magazine, Nat. Educ. and Training Forum 1994; Vice-Chair. Urban Foundation; Dir Metropolitan M-Net 1994; mem. Bd Corp. Africa; Vice-Pres. Jt Council of Teachers Asscn of S Africa; Amb. to USA 1995–98; Chancellor Univ. of the Free State 2002–09; Grand Counsellor, Order of the Baobab in Silver. *Publications include:* A Decade of Struggle 1986; numerous papers and official documents. *Leisure interests:* reading, walking, mountaineering, squash.

SONNENFELD, Barry; American cinematographer, film director and film producer; b. 1 April 1953, New York. *Films as cinematographer include:* Blood Simple 1984, Compromising Positions 1985, Three O'Clock High 1987, Raising Arizona 1987, Throw Momma from the Train 1987, Big 1988, When Harry Met Sally 1989, Miller's Crossing 1990, Misery 1990. *Films directed include:* The Addams Family 1991, For Love or Money 1993, Addams Family Values 1993, Get Shorty 1995, Men in Black 1997, Wild Wild West 1999, Big Trouble 2002, Men in Black II 2002, RV 2006, Men in Black III 2012, Nine Lives 2016. *Films produced include:* Get Shorty 1995, Out of Sight 1998, Wild Wild West 1999, The Crew 2000, Big Trouble 2002, The Ladykillers 2004, Lemony Snicket's A Series of Unfortunate Events 2004, Enchanted 2007, Space Chimps 2008. *Television includes:* Out of Step 1984 (Emmy Award for best cinematography 1984), Fantasy Island 1998, Secret Agent Man 2000, The Crew 2000, The Tick 2001, Karen Sisco 2003, Pushing Daisies 2007–09, A Series of Unfortunate Events 2017–.

SONO, Kiyoshi; Japanese banking executive; *Representative Corporate Executive Officer and Chairman, Mitsubishi UFJ Financial Group, Inc.;* Exec. Officer, UFJ Bank 2004–05, Exec. Officer, Bank of Tokyo-Mitsubishi UFJ Jan.–May 2006, Man. Exec. Officer and Group Head, Osaka Corp. Banking Group, Bank of Tokyo-Mitsubishi UFJ Ltd, Mitsubishi UFJ Financial Group, Inc. from 2006, Sr Man. Exec. Officer, Bank of Tokyo-Mitsubishi UFJ Ltd, Deputy Pres. and CEO Corp. Banking Business Unit, Bank of Tokyo-Mitsubishi UFJ Ltd 2012–14, Rep. Dir and Chair. Mitsubishi UFJ Financial Group, Inc. (MUFG) 2014–15, Dir, Rep. Corp. Exec. Officer and Chair. MUFG 2015–. *Address:* Mitsubishi UFJ Financial Group, Inc., 7-1, Marunouchi 2-chome, Chiyoda-ku, Tokyo 100-8330, Japan (office). *Telephone:* (3) 3240-8111 (office). *Fax:* (3) 3240-8203 (office). *E-mail:* info@mufg.jp (office). *Website:* www.mufg.jp (office).

SONOKROT, Mazen, BEng; Palestinian business executive and fmr government minister; *Chairman and CEO, Sinokrot Global Group;* b. 30 Nov. 1954, Jerusalem; s. of Mohammad Tawfique Sonokrot and Fatimah Sonokrot; four s.; ed Univ. of Nottingham, UK; Chair. and CEO Sinokrot Global Group 1982–; Regional Dir Arab Food Industries Fed., Arab League 1982–97; Founder and fmr Chair. Palestinian Food Industries Asscn; Chair. Palestinian Fed. of Industries, Universal Group for Eng and Consulting, Industrial Modernization Center; Minister of Nat. Economy 2005–06; Chair. Palestinian Investment Promotion Agency, Palestinian Industrial Estates and Free Zones Area, Palestinian Standards Inst.; Sec. Pvt. Sector Coordinating Council; mem. Bd and Head, Investment Cttee, Palestine Investment Fund; mem. Palestinian Businessmen Asscn, Bd of Palestinian Economic Task Force, Bd Nat. Reform Cttee, Public-Pvt. Jt Econ. Cttee, Bd of Registry and Sanction, Ministry of Higher Educ.; mem. Higher Council of High Council for Tech. and Vocational Educ.; Assoc. mem. of all cttees in charge of formulating laws and legislation relating to the Palestinian economy; rep. of Palestinian pvt. sector in many local, regional and int. activities; contrib. to econ. trade agreements between Palestinian National Authority and USA, EU, Turkey, Arab and EFTA countries. *Address:* Sinokrot Global Group, PO 1410, Betuniah, Industrial Zone, Ramallah, Palestinian Autonomous Area (office). *Telephone:* (2) 2955701 (office). *Fax:* (2) 2955702 (office). *Website:* www.sinokrot.com (office).

SONOMPIL, Mishigiyn; Mongolian politician; b. 27 Jan. 1965; m.; two c.; fmr Commdr mil. unit; Dir Zaluu Mongol Corpn 1991–2004; mem. Democratic Party –2006 (expelled from party); co-f. National New Party 2006; mem. Parl. 2004–; Minister of Defence 2006–07.

SONOWAL, Sarbananda, LLB; Indian politician; *Chief Minister of Assam;* b. 31 Oct. 1962, Molokgaon, Dibrugarh Dist, Assam; s. of Jibeswar and Dineswari Sonowal; ed Dibrugarh Univ., Gauhati Univ.; Pres., All Assam Students Union 1992–99; joined Asom Gana Parishad 2001; mem. Assam Legis. Ass. from Moran constituency 2001–04, from Majuli 2016–; mem., Lok Sabha (lower house of parl.) for Dibrugarh 2004–09, for Lakhimpur 2014–16; Minister of State for Entrepreneurship and Skill Devt May–Nov. 2014; Union Minister for Sports and Youth Affairs 2014–16; Chief Minister of Assam 2016–; mem. Bharatiya Janata Party (BJP), mem. Nat. Exec. 2011, BJP Assam State Pres. 2012–14. *Leisure interests:* football, cricket and badminton. *Address:* Office of the Chief Minister, Government of Assam, Janata Bhavan, Guwahati 781 006, India (office). *Telephone:* (361) 2266188 (office). *Fax:* (361) 2262069 (office). *E-mail:* asmgovt@asm.nic.in (office). *Website:* assam.gov.in (office).

SOOMER, June, PhD; Saint Lucia academic and international organization official; *Secretary-General, Association of Caribbean States;* ed Univ. of the West Indies; fmr Lecturer in History, Univ. of the West Indies, Univ. of N Carolina (Wilmington), Univ. of North Carolina Central; fmr Visiting Lecturer, Univ. of San Francisco; with Human Resource Devt and Strategic Planning Dept, Eastern Caribbean Central Bank 1996–2006; Amb. to CARICOM and Org. of Eastern Caribbean States –2016; Sec.-Gen. Asscn of Caribbean States 2016–; Elsa Goveia Award for History, Univ. of the West Indies. *Address:* Association of Caribbean States, 5–7 Sweet Briar Road, St Clair, POB 660, Port of Spain, Trinidad and Tobago (office). *Telephone:* 622-9575 (office). *Fax:* 622-1653 (office). *E-mail:* communications@acs-aec.org (office). *Website:* www.acs-aec.org (office).

SOOMRO, Mohammad Mian, BSc, MSc; Pakistani banker and politician; b. 19 Aug. 1950, Karachi, Sindh; s. of Ahmed Mian Soomro and Moula Bux Soomro; ed Forman Christian Coll., Lahore, Punjab Univ., Northrop Univ., USA; Head of

Soomro tribe; mem. Pakistan Muslim League (PML); held various positions in nat. and int. orgs, including Bank of America; fmr Gen. Man. and CEO Int. Bank of Yemen, Faysal Islamic Bank of Bahrain, Muslim Commercial Bank, Agriculture Devt Bank of Pakistan, Fed. Bank of Cooperatives, Nat. Bank of Pakistan; Chair. Pakistan Banks Asscn 1997–2000; Gov. of Sindh 2000–02 (resgnd); elected mem. Senate 2003, Chair. of Senate 2003–07, 2008–09, Chair. Finance Cttee; caretaker Prime Minister Nov. 2007–March 08; Interim Pres. of Pakistan (following resignation of Pres. Pervez Musharraf) 18 Aug.–9 Sept. 2008; mem. Governing Council Inst. of Bankers in Pakistan 1997–2000; mem. Bd of Dirs Shell Pakistan Ltd, Pakistan Int. Airlines Corpn, Pakistan Refinery Ltd (Shell Petroleum Jt Venture), Pak Arab Refinery, Pak Arab Fertilizer, Bank Al-Jazira (Jeddah, Saudi Arabia), Nat. Investment Trust, Investment Co-operation of Pakistan, Nat. Discounting Services Ltd, Nat. Exchange Co. (Abu Dhabi), Nat. Bank Modaraba Man. Co. Ltd, First Women Bank Ltd, Consolidated Leasing Co., Nat. Construction Co., Pakistan Tourism Devt Corpn (all 1997–2000); mem. Bd of Govs Univ. of Management and Technology (UMT); Trustee ILM Trust.

SOONG, James Chu-yul, PhD; Taiwanese politician; *Chairman, People First Party (PFP);* b. 16 March 1942, Hunan; m. Viola Chen; one s. one d.; ed Nat. Chengchi Univ., Taipei and Univ. of Calif., Berkeley, Catholic Univ. of America, Georgetown Univ., Washington, DC, USA; Sec. Exec. Yuan, Taiwan 1974–77; Deputy Dir-Gen. Govt Information Office 1977–79; Assoc. Prof., Nat. Taiwan Univ. 1975–79; Research Fellow, Inst. of Int. Relations, Nat. Chengchi Univ. 1974–; Personal Sec. to the Pres. 1978–89; Dir-Gen. Govt Information Office, Govt Spokesman 1979–84; mem. Cen. Cttee Kuomintang (KMT) 1981–2000, Dir-Gen. Dept of Cultural Affairs, KMT 1984–87; Deputy Sec.-Gen., KMT Cen. Cttee 1987–89, Sec.-Gen. 1989–93; mem. Cen. Standing Cttee 1988–2000; Gov., Taiwan Prov. Govt 1993–98; unsuccessful presidential cand. (ind.) 2000, then f. People First Party (PFP), Chair. 2000–; unsuccessful vice presidential cand. (PFP) 2004, 2012, 2016; Man. Dir China TV Co. 1984–93, Taiwan TV Enterprise 1984–93; Chair. Hua-hsia Investment Corpn; Distinguished Visiting Fellow Inst. of East Asian Studies, Univ. of Calif. 1999; Eisenhower Fellowship 1982; several decorations. *Publications:* A Manual for Academic Writers, How to Write Academic Papers, Politics and Public Opinions in the United States, Keep Free China Free. *Address:* People First Party, 1/F, 63 Chang-an East Road, Sec. 2, Taipei 10455, Taiwan (office). *Telephone:* (2) 25068555 (office). *Website:* www.pfp.org.tw (office).

SOPE, Barak; Ni-Vanuatu politician and diplomatist; *Chairman, Melanesian Progressive Party;* leading mem. Vanuaaku Pati (VP), Roving Amb.; mem. govts 1980–87; defected from VP, f. Melanesian Progressive Party 1987, Chair. 1987–; mem. coalition govts 1993–96; Prime Minister of Vanuatu 1999–2001 (resgnd); convicted of forgery and sentenced to three years in prison 2002, pardoned in 2003; Minister of Foreign Affairs 2004, of Agric., Quarantine, Forestry and Fisheries 2004–06. *Address:* Melanesian Progressive Pati, PO Box 39, Port Vila, Vanuatu (office). *Telephone:* 23485 (office). *Fax:* 23315 (office).

SOPHUSSON, Friðrik; Icelandic lawyer, politician and business executive; *Chairman, Íslandsbanki;* b. 18 Oct. 1943, Reykjavik; m. Dr Sigridur Duna Kristmundsdottir 1990; one d. (and five c. from first m.); ed Reykjavik Higher Secondary Grammar School and Univ. of Iceland; lawyer, part-time teacher Hlídaskóli School, Reykjavik 1963–67; Man. Icelandic Man. Asscn 1972–78; MP for Reykjavik 1978–98; Minister of Industry and Energy 1987–88, of Finance 1991–98; Man. Dir Landsvirkjun (Nat. Power Co.) 1999–2009; Chair. Íslandsbanki 2010–; mem. Radio Council Icelandic State Broadcasting Service 1975–78; Nat. Research Council and Exec. Cttee of State Hosps 1984–87; Cen. Cttee Independence Party 1969–77, 1981–99, Vice-Chair. 1981–89, 1991–99; Pres. Independence Party's Youth Fed. 1973–77; mem. Bd of Dirs Nat. Bank of Iceland 1990–92, Icelandic Church Aid 1990–92, Enex 2001–06, Pharmaco 2002–03, Samorka (Fed. of Electricity and Waterworks) 2001–09, Icelandic Int. Chamber of Commerce 2001–09, Nordel 2001–03, Icelandic Chamber of Commerce 2002–09. *Address:* Íslandsbanki, Kirkjusandur 2, 105, Reykjavik (office); Bjarkargata 10, 101 Reykjavik, Iceland (home). *E-mail:* islandsbanki@islandsbanki.is (office). *Website:* www.islandsbanki.is (office).

SOPOANGA, Saufatu, OBE; Tuvaluan politician and organization official; *Secretary-General, Tuvalu Red Cross Society;* elected mem. Parl., fmr Special Ministerial Adviser, Ministry of Works, Communication and Transport, fmr Minister of Finance, Prime Minister of Tuvalu and Minister of Foreign Affairs and Labour 2002–04, Deputy Prime Minister and Minister of Works and Energy and of Communications and Transport 2004–06; currently Sec.-Gen. Tuvalu Red Cross Soc. *Address:* Tuvalu Red Cross Society, PO Box 14, Funafuti, Tuvalu (office). *E-mail:* redcrosstuvalu@gmail.com (office).

SOPONRONNARIT, Somchart, PhD; Thai scientist and academic; *Professor of Energy Technology, King Mongkut's University of Technology Thonburi;* b. 27 May 1952; m.; one s. two d.; Lecturer, King Mongkut's Univ. of Tech., Thonburi Campus 1982–83, Asst Prof. 1983–86, Assoc. Prof. 1986–92, Prof. 1992–98, Prof. of Energy Technology (level 11) 1998–, Vice-Pres. for Research and Foreign Relations 1992–95, Dean, School of Energy and Materials 1995–96; Acting Dean, Faculty of Engineering, Mahasarakham Univ. 2001–06; Acting Pres. Shinawatra Univ. (SIU) July–Dec. 2008, apptd Pres. SIU 2009; mem. Academic Review Cttee, Sirindhorn Int. Inst. of Tech., Thammasat Univ.; mem. Asian Inst. of Tech.; Fellow, Royal Inst. of Thailand 1998; UNESCO Science Prize 2003. *Publications:* Drying Grains and Some Types of Foods (seventh edn, in Thai) 1997; book chapters, research reports and more than 150 scientific papers in professional journals on thermal processes such as thermal application of solar energy, drying and storage of foods and cereal grains. *Address:* School of Energy, Environment and Materials, King Mongkut's University of Technology, Thonburi Campus, Suksawat 48 Road, Bangkok 10140 (office); 128 Asadang Road, Bangkok 10200, Thailand (home). *Telephone:* (2) 4708624 (office); (2) 4270039 (ext. 8624) (office); (2) 263838 (home). *Fax:* (2) 4279062 (office). *E-mail:* somchart.sop@kmutt.ac.th (office). *Website:* www2.kmutt.ac.th (office).

SORABJI, Sir Richard Rustom Kharsedji, Kt, CBE, BPhil, MA, FBA; British historian and academic; *Cyprus Global Distinguished Professor in the History and Theory of Justice, New York University;* b. 8 Nov. 1934, Brighton, Sussex, England; s. of Prof. Richard Kakushru Sorabji and Mary Katherine Sorabji (née Monkhouse); m. Margaret Anne Catherine Taster 1958; one s. two d.; ed Charterhouse School, Pembroke Coll., Oxford; Assoc. Prof., Sage School of Philosophy, Cornell Univ., USA 1962–69; joined Dept of Philosophy, King's Coll., London 1970, Prof. of Ancient Philosophy 1981–2000, British Acad./Wolfson Research Prof. 1996–99, Prof. Emer. 1999–, Designer and First Dir King's Coll. Centre for Philosophical Studies 1989–91; Gresham Prof. of Rhetoric and mem. Sr Common Room, Pembroke Coll., Oxford 2000–03; Supernumerary Fellow, Wolfson Coll. Oxford 1996, now Hon. Fellow; Ranieri Distinguished Visiting Scholar, New York Univ. 2000–03, Cyprus Global Distinguished Prof. in the History and Theory of Justice 2008–; Adjunct Prof., Philosophy Dept, Univ. of Texas 2000–; Visiting Prof., CUNY 2004–07; Pres. Aristotelian Soc. 1985–86; Founder and organizer of int. project to translate ancient commentators on Aristotle in 50 vols 1985–; Dir Inst. of Classical Studies, London Univ. 1991–96; Foreign Hon. mem. American Acad. of Arts and Sciences 1997–. *Publications:* Aristotle on Memory 1972, Necessity, Cause and Blame 1980, Time, Creation and the Continuum 1983, Matter, Space and Motion 1988, Animal Minds and Human Morals 1993, Emotion and Peace of Mind 2001, Self: Ancient and Modern Insights about Individuality, Life and Death 2006, The Ethics of War: Shared Problems in Different Traditions (co-ed.) 2006, Greek and Roman Philosophy 100 BC to 200 AD (co-ed.) 2007, Opening Doors: The Untold Story of Cornelia Sorabji 2010, The Stoics and Gandhi: Modern Experiments on Ancient Values 2012, Perception, Conscience and Will in Ancient Philosophy (Variorum Collected Studies Series: CS 1030) 2013; ed. numerous vols on commentators on Aristotle; 73 articles and two poems. *Leisure interests:* archaeology, architecture. *Address:* Wolfson College, University of Oxford, Oxford, OX2 6UD (office); c/o Department of Philosophy, King's College London, Strand, London, WC2R 2LS, England (office); Graduate School of Arts and Science, New York University, 6 Washington Square North, New York, NY 10003, USA (office). *Telephone:* (1865) 274100 (Oxford) (office). *Fax:* (1865) 274125 (Oxford) (office). *E-mail:* richard.sorabji@philosophy.oxford.ac.uk (office). *Website:* www.richardsorabji.co.uk (office).

SOREN, Hemant; Indian politician and government official; b. 10 Aug. 1975, Nemara, Ramgarh Dist, Bihar; s. of Shibu Soren and Roopi Soren; m. Kalpana Soren; two s.; mem. Rajya Sabha (Jharkhand Mukti Morcha party) 2009–10; Chief Minister of Jharkhand 2013–14; Leader, Jharkhand Mukti Morcha 2015–. *Address:* Jharkhand Mukti Morcha, Bariatu Road, Ranchi 834 009, India (office). *Telephone:* (651) 2542990 (office). *Fax:* (651) 6453012 (office). *Website:* www.jharkhandmuktimorcha.org (office).

SOREN, Shibu; Indian politician; b. 11 Jan. 1944, Nemra village, Hazaribagh Dist, Jharkhand; s. of Shobaran Soren; m. Rupi Devi; three s. (one deceased) one d.; ed Gola High School; Gen. Sec., Jharkhand Mukti Morcha 1971–85, Pres. 1986; mem. Lok Sabha (Parl.) 1980–96, 2002–04, 2009–, mem. Cttee on Coal and Steel 2009, Jt Cttee on Salaries and Allowances of MPs 2009, Standing Cttee on Food, Consumer Affairs and Public Distribution 2014–, Consultative Cttee, Ministry of Steel and Mines 2014–; mem. Rajya Sabha (Parl.) 2001–02; Minister of Coal May–July 2004 (resgnd), reinstated 2006; Chief Minister of Jharkhand 2005, Aug. 2008–Jan. 2009, Dec. 2009–10; sentenced to life imprisonment on abduction and murder charges 2006, acquitted 2007. *Leisure interests:* archery, travelling, indoor games. *Address:* Lok Sabha, Parliament House Annexe, New Delhi 110 001 (office); 14, Sector 1-C, P.O. Ram Mandir, Bokaro Steel City 827 001, Jharkhand, India. *Telephone:* (11) 23017465 (office). *Fax:* (11) 23792107 (office). *E-mail:* shisoren@sansad.nic.in (office). *Website:* loksabha.nic.in (office).

SÓRENSEN, Jórgen Haugen; Danish sculptor; b. 3 Oct. 1934; ed Coll. of Art and Design, Copenhagen; began as apprentice plasterer and potter; debut in Charlottenborg's Spring Exhbn 1953; exhbns at Museum of Modern Art New York, Yorks. Sculpture Park; works in collections in Denmark, England, Italy, Slovenia, Turkey, Olympic Sculpture Park, Seoul; Dir film JHS late 1960s; Prix de la Critique for JHS, Paris Biennale 1963, Eckersberg Medal 1969, Thorvaldsen Medal 1979. *Address:* Galleri Veggerby, Ny Østergade 34, 1101 København K, Denmark. *E-mail:* haugensorensen@FJRN-DETTEhotmail.com. *Website:* www.haugen-sorensen.dk.

SØRENSEN, Peter Ingemann Moesgaard, BA, MLaw; Danish lawyer and diplomatist; *Head of Delegation to United Nations Office and Other International Organisations in Geneva, European Union;* b. 1967; m.; two c.; ed Århus Univ.; worked as lawyer in Denmark and served as officer in Danish Army; appointments have included Political/Legal Advisor to UN Special Envoy to the Balkans and Head of Political Affairs, OSCE Mission to Croatia; Legal Adviser to High Rep., Sarajevo, Bosnia & Herzegovina and European Community Monitor Mission, Sarajevo 1996–97; Sr Adviser to Special Rep. of UN Sec.-Gen. as well as to Deputy SRSG and Head of UNMIK EU Pillar IV, Kosovo 2001; Deputy Head of UNMIK EU Pillar IV and Dir of European Office 2002–06; EU High Rep.'s Personal Rep. in Belgrade, Serbia 2009–11; served as Head of EU Del. in Skopje, Former Yuguslav Repub. of Macedonia; Head of EU Del. and EU Special Rep. to Bosnia and Herzegovina 2011–14; Head of EU Del. to UN and other Int. Orgs in Geneva 2014–. *Address:* Delegation of the European Union to the United Nations and Other International Organisations in Geneva, Rue du Grand-Pré 64, 1211 Geneva, Switzerland (office). *Telephone:* (22) 9197400 (office). *Fax:* (22) 7342236 (office). *E-mail:* delegation-geneva-un@eeas.europa.eu (office). *Website:* www.eeas.europa.eu/delegations/un_geneva (office).

SORENSON, Arne M.; American lawyer and business executive; *President and CEO, Marriott International, Inc.;* b. 1959, Tokyo, Japan; m.; four c.; ed Luther Coll., Univ. of Minnesota Law School; Partner, Latham & Watkins (law firm), Washington, DC –1996, specialized in mergers and acquisitions litigation; joined Marriott International, Inc. (operates and franchises hotels and licenses vacation ownership resorts) 1996, later Exec. Vice-Pres., Chief Financial Officer and Pres. Continental European Lodging, mem. Bd of Dirs 2011–, Pres. and COO Marriott International, Inc. –2012, Pres. and CEO 2012–, Chair. Marriott's Global Diversity and Inclusion Council, mem. Cttee for Excellence, co-f. Marriott's Global Sustainability Council 2007; mem. Bd of Dirs Brand USA; mem. Bd of Regents, Luther Coll.; mem. Pres.'s Export Council. *Address:* Marriott International, Inc., Corporate Headquarters, 10400 Fernwood Road, Bethesda, MD 20817, USA (office). *Telephone:* (301) 380-3000 (office); (301) 380-7770 (office). *Fax:* (301) 380-3969 (office). *E-mail:* info@marriott.com (office). *Website:* www.marriott.com (office).

SORENSTAM, Annika; Swedish professional golfer (retd); b. 9 Oct. 1970, Stockholm; d. of Tom Sorenstam and Gunilla Sorenstam; m. David Esch; ed Univ. of Arizona, USA; World Amateur Champion 1992; 72 career wins on LPGA tour including 10 major championships; victories include US Women's Open 1995, 1996, Safeway Classic 2003, Mizuno Classic 2003, LPGA Championship 2003, 2004, 2005, Women's British Open 2003, Kraft Nabisco Championship 2005; played on eight European Solheim Cup teams; first woman to shoot 59 in an LPGA Tour tournament 2001; first woman to win US $13 million in golf prize money, is LPGA career earnings leader with more than US$22 million; finished first on LPGA money list 2001–05 and eight times overall; first woman for 58 years to participate in a men's professional tour event, Bank of America Colonial Tournament, Fort Worth, Tex., May 2003; first int. player to be inducted into World Golf Hall of Fame, St Augustine, USA 2003; announced retirement 2008; f. Annika Course Design, ANNIKA Academy; Rookie of the Year 1994, Sports Personality of the Year, Sweden 1995, Vare Trophy Award 1995, 1996, 1998, 2001, 2002, Rolex Player of the Year Award 1995, 1997, 1998, 2001–05; Patty Berg Award 2003, Jerring Prize 2004; inducted into LPGA Hall of Fame 2003. *Leisure interests:* sports, music, cooking, skiing. *Address:* c/o Annika Sorenstam, IMG Center, Suite 100, 1360 East 9th Street, Cleveland, OH 44114, USA; c/o IMG Stureplan, 4C, 114 35 Stockholm, Sweden. *Website:* www.annikasorenstam.com; www.theannikaacademy.com.

SORI-COULIBALY, Rosine; Burkinabè economist, politician and fmr UN official; *Minister of the Economy and Finance;* b. 1958; m.; two c.; ed Univ. Cheikh Anta Diop, Dakar, Senegal, UN Inst. for Econ. Devt and Planning; fmr Lecturer, Nat. School of Admin; fmr Consultant Economist, UN Dept of Econ. and Social Affairs; Econ. Advisor, Ministry of Econ., Planning and Devt 1982–91; Nat. Coordinator, ILO project covering women in informal sector 1991–92; Advisor, CIDA Small and Medium Enterprises Project 1992–95; held several positions with UN including Sr Economist, UNDP in Burundi and Benin 1995–2002, Deputy Resident Rep. in Mauritania 2002–06, UN Resident Coordinator and Resident Rep. in Togo 2006–11, Deputy Special Rep. of the Sec.-Gen., Resident Coordinator and Resident Rep., UN Office in Burundi 2011–15; Minister of the Economy and Finance 2016–; mem. Social and Econ. Council and other women's and human rights orgs; Chevalier, Ordre Nat. du Burkina Faso. *Address:* Ministry of the Economy and Finance, 395 avenue Ho Chi Minh, 01 BP 7008, Ouagadougou 01, Burkina Faso (office). *Telephone:* 50-32-42-11 (office). *Fax:* 50-31-27-15 (office). *E-mail:* webmaster@finances.gov.bf (office). *Website:* www.finances.gov.bf (office).

SORINAS BALFEGÓ, Mateo, MSc; Spanish teacher and international organization executive; b. 13 March 1946, Tarragona; m.; two c.; ed Universidad Complutense, Madrid; Deputy Dir Boarding School, Universidad Laboral de Alcalá de Henares, Madrid 1967–69; teacher, Agüimes High School, Las Palmas, Gran Canaria 1969–70; mil. service 1970–71; teacher, Isabel de España High School, Las Palmas 1971–77, Pérez Galdós High School, Las Palmas 1977–78; Co-Sec., Cttee on Environment, Regional Planning and Local Authorities, Council of Europe 1978–86, Sec., Cttee on Migration, Refugees and Demography 1986–92, Sec. Political Affairs Cttee 1992–94, Political Counsellor, Pvt. Office of the Pres. 1992–96, Head of Cen. Div. 1994–97, Dir Political and Legal Affairs Dept 1997–2002, Dir-Gen. 2002–06, Sec.-Gen. Parl. Ass. 2006–11; mem. Nat. Cttee of Juventud Estudiante Católica (Young Catholic Students), Madrid 1963–67, Governing Bd Professional Asscn of Teachers on Sciences and Humanities, Las Palmas 1974–78; Orden del Mérito Civil: Cruz de Caballero 1988, Encomienda 1995, Cavaliere Grand'Ufficiale, Ordine di Sant'Agata (San Marino) 2007.

SORIOT, Pascal, DrVetMed, MBA; French business executive; *Executive Director and CEO, AstraZeneca PLC;* b. 23 May 1959; m.; two c.; ed École Nationale Vétérinaire, Maisons-Alfort, École des Hautes Études Commerciales – Institut Supérieur des Affaires; Financial Controller for the Asia-Pacific region, Roussel Uclaf 1986, held various management positions in finance and marketing at cos that later formed part of Sanofi-Aventis, Dist Sales Man., Roussel New Zealand 1987–89, Sales and Marketing Man., Roussel Australia from 1989, later Gen. Man., Div. Global Marketing Dir, Roussel Uclaf Pharmaceuticals 1994–96, Gen. Man. Hoechst Marion Roussel Australia 1996–97, Regional Vice-Pres., Asia Pacific, Hoechst Marion Roussel Tokyo 1997–2000, Sr Vice-Pres. and Head of Global Marketing and Medical Affairs, Aventis Bridgewater (USA) 2000–02, COO 2002–04, Sr Vice-Pres. Commercial Operations, USA 2004–06, Head of Strategic Marketing Pharma Div., Roche AG March–Dec. 2006, Head of Commercial Operations 2007–09, led successful merger with Genentech, San Francisco, CEO Genentech 2009–10, COO Pharmaceuticals Div., Roche AG 2010–12; Exec. Dir and CEO AstraZeneca PLC 2012–; Dir, Chugai Pharmaceutical Co. Ltd –2012. *Address:* AstraZeneca PLC, 2 Kingdom Street, London, W2 6BD, England (office). *Telephone:* (20) 7604-8000 (office). *E-mail:* info@astrazeneca.com (office). *Website:* www.astrazeneca.com (office).

SORKIN, Ihor Vyacheslavovych; Ukrainian central banker; b. 3 March 1967, Donetsk; m.; one s.; ed Baku Higher Combined-Arms Command School, Azerbaijan SSR, Donetsk State Univ., Donetsk Nat. Univ.; served in Soviet Army 1988–92, Nat. Guard of Ukraine 1992–96, successively, commdr landing assault platoon, reconnaissance bn and regimental intelligence chief of Nat. Guard; joined Nat. Bank of Ukraine 1996, successively, Economist of 1st Category, Leading Economist, Chief Economist, Head of Sector, Deputy Head of Dept, Head of Banking Supervision Dept in Office of Nat. Bank of Ukraine in Donetsk Oblast 2001–10, Deputy Gov. Nat. Bank of Ukraine 2010–11, 3rd ranking civil servant 2011, Acting Gov. 2012–13, Gov. 2013–14 (dismissed); mem. Nat. Security and Defence Council of Ukraine 2013; Merited Economist of Ukraine 2011.

SORO, Guillaume Kigbafori; Côte d'Ivoirian politician and fmr rebel leader; b. 8 May 1972, Diawala; two c.; ed univ. studies in France; Leader, Ivorian Students' Fed. 1995–98; fmr Sec.-Gen. Mouvement patriotique de Côte d'Ivoire (MPCI); Leader, New Forces Rebels 2000–, led rebellion against Pres. Laurent Gbagbo that triggered Civil War 2002, controlled Northern Prov. of Côte d'Ivoire 2002; Minister of State for Communications 2003–05, of Reconstruction and Reinsertion 2005–07; Prime Minister 2007–12 (resgnd), also Minister of Defence –2012 (resgnd); mem. Nat. Ass. 2012–, Pres. 2012–19; Grand Officier, Ordre National de Côte d'Ivoire 2011, Grand Croix, Ordre National du Mérite du Sénégal 2013. *Publication:* Pourquoi je suis devenu un rebelle 2005. *Address:* c/o Office of the President, National Assembly, 01 BP 1381, Abidjan 01, Côte d'Ivoire (office). *Website:* www.guillaumesoro.ci.

SOROKIN, Vladimir Georgiyevich; Russian author, screenwriter, dramatist, librettist and painter; b. 7 Aug. 1955, Bykovo, Moscow Region; m. Irina Igorevna Sorokina; two d.; ed Moscow Inst. of Oil and Gas; worked as artist and writer in Moscow underground; not published in USSR until 1987; mem. Russian PEN Centre 1993–, German Acad. of Language and Literature 2013–; scholarship of Deutsche Akademische Austauschung Dienst 1992; Andrey Beliy Prize 2003, Liberty Prize, USA 2005, Maxim Gorky Prize 2010. *Plays:* wrote 12 plays 1986–2009. *Screenplays include:* Moskva 1995, Kopejka 1997, The Four 2000, Cashfire 2002, The Thing 2003, Exit 2004, The Target 2010. *Libretto:* opera 'The Children of Rosenthal' by Leonid Desyatnikov (performed at Bolshoi Theatre, Moscow) 2005. *Publications include:* Thirties Love of Marina 1982–84, The Queue (novel) 1983, The Norm 1984, Obelisk (short stories) 1980–84, Roman 1989, Four Stout Hearts (novel) 1991, Blue Lard 1999, The Feast 2001, The Ice (novel) 2002, Bro 2004, Trilogy 2005, Den' oprichnika 2006, Zaplyv 2006, Saharniy Kreml 2008, Day of the Oprichnik (trans.) 2011, Telluriya 2013, The Blizzard (novel) 2016. *Leisure interests:* chess, cooking, table tennis. *Address:* 119333 Moscow, ul. Gubkina, d4 kv 47, Russia (home). *Telephone:* (499) 135-90-76 (home). *E-mail:* sornorma@mtu-net.ru (home). *Website:* www.srkn.ru (home).

SOROS, George; American (b. Hungarian) investment banker and philanthropist; *Chairman, Soros Fund Management LLC;* b. 12 Aug. 1930, Budapest; m. 1st Annaliese Witschak 1960 (divorced 1983); m. 2nd Susan Weber 1983 (divorced 2005); m. 3rd Tamiko Bolton 2013; five c.; ed London School of Econs; moved to England 1947; with Singer & Friedlander (merchant bankers), London; moved to New York 1956; est. pvt. mutual fund, Quantum Fund, registered in Curaçao 1969; since 1991 has created other funds, including Quasar Int., Quota, Quantum Emerging Growth Fund (merged with Quantum Fund to form Quantum Endowment Fund 2000), Quantum Realty Trust; Pres. and Chair. Soros Fund Man. LLC, New York 1973–; philanthropist since 1979, provided funds to help black students attend Cape Town Univ., SA; Founder and Chair. Open Soc. Foundations 1979–, Soros Foundation, Cen. European Univ., Budapest 1992; f. Global Power Investments 1994; Dr hc (New School for Social Research, Univ. of Oxford), (Budapest Univ. of Econs), (Yale Univ.); Laurea hc (Univ. of Bologna) 1995. *Publications include:* The Alchemy of Finance 1987, Opening the Soviet System 1990, Underwriting Democracy 1991, Soros on Soros–Staying Ahead of the Curve (jtly) 1995, The Crisis of Global Capitalism–Open Society Engendered 1998, Open Society–Reforming Global Capitalism 2000, George Soros on Globalization 2002, The Bubble of American Supremacy–Correcting the Misuse of American Power 2004, Soros on Freedom 2006, Soros Lectures 2010, The Tragedy of the European Union: Disintegration or Revival? 2014; numerous essays on politics, soc. and econs in major int. newspapers and magazines. *Address:* Soros Fund Management LLC, 250 West 55th Street, 27th Floor, New York, NY 10019 (office); Open Society Institute, 224 West 57th Street, New York, NY 10019, USA. *Telephone:* (212) 548-0600. *Fax:* (212) 548-4600. *Website:* www.opensocietyfoundations.org; www.georgesoros.com; www.soros.org.

SOROUSH, Abdolkarim, BSc; Iranian academic; *Researcher, Institute for Iranian Contemporary Historical Studies;* b. (Hosein Haj Faraj Dabbagh), 1945, Tehran; ed Mortazavi High School, Alavi High School, Univ. of London and Chelsea Coll., London, UK; studied pharmacy and passed nat. entrance exams; left for London following graduation to continue studies; returned to Iran in 1979, and published book Knowledge and Value (Danesh va Arzesh); apptd Dir Islamic Culture Group, Teacher Training Coll., Tehran 1979; mem. Cultural Revolution Inst. 1980–83 (resgnd); Researcher, Inst. for Cultural Research and Studies (now the Inst. for Iranian Contemporary Historical Studies) 1983–; adviser to govt bodies; became more critical of political role played by Iranian clergy 1990s; co-founder monthly magazine Kiyan, and published his most controversial articles on religious pluralism, hermeneutics, tolerance, clericalism etc., magazine suppressed by direct order of supreme leader of Islamic Repub. 1998; more than 1,000 audio tapes of his speeches on various social, political, religious and literary subjects circulated world-wided, became subject to harassment and state censorship; Visiting Prof. teaching Islam and Democracy, Quranic Studies and Philosophy of Islamic Law, Harvard Univ., USA 2000–; Scholar-in-Residence, Yale Univ., USA; taught Islamic Political Philosophy at Princeton Univ. 2002–03; Visiting Scholar, Wissenschaftkolleg, Berlin, Germany 2003–04, Univ. of Maryland, College Park; Erasmus Prize 2004. *Publications include:* Dialectical Antagonism (in Persian) 1978, Philosophy of History (in Persian) 1978, The Restless Nature of the Universe (in Persian and Turkish) 1980, Sagaciousness, Intellectualism and Pietism (in Persian) 1991, What is Science, What is Philosophy (in Persian) (11th edn) 1992, Satanic Ideology (in Persian) (fifth edn) 1994, Wisdom and Livelihood: A Commentary on Imam Ali's Letter to Imam Hasan (in Persian) (second edn) 1994, Sturdier than Ideology (in Persian) 1994, Knowledge and Value (in Persian), Lectures in the Philosophy of Social Sciences: Hermeneutics in Social Sciences (in Persian) 1995, The Tale of the Lords of Sagacity (in Persian) (third edn) 1996, The Evolution and Devolution of Religious Knowledge in: Kurzman, Ch. (ed.), Intellectualism and Religious Conviction (in Persian), The World We Live (in Persian and Turkish), The Tale of Love and Servitude (in Persian), The Definitive Edition of Rumi's Mathnavi (in Persian) 1996, Tolerance and Governance (in Persian) 1997, Liberal Islam 1998, Straight Paths, An Essay on Religious Pluralism (in Persian) 1998, Political Letters (two vols) (in Persian) 1999, Expansion of Prophetic Experience (in Persian) 1999, Reason, Freedom and Democracy in Islam, Essential Writings of Adbolkarim Soroush (translated, ed with a critical introduction by M. Sadri and A. Sadri) 2000. *Address:* The Institute for Iranian Contemporary Historical Studies, PO Box 19395-1975, 128 Fayyazi (Fereshteh) Avenue, Elahieh, Tehran 19649, Iran (office). *Telephone:* (21) 22604037 (office); (21) 22003490 (office). *Fax:* (21) 2262096 (office). *E-mail:* info@drsoroush.com; info@iichs.org (office). *Website:* www.iichs.ir (office); www.drsoroush.com.

SORRELL, Lady Frances Mary, FRSA, FCSD; British design consultant; *Co-Chairman, The Sorrell Foundation;* b. (Frances Newell), 19 Jan. 1947, Surrey, England; d. of Alexander C. Newell and Julie S. Newell; m. Sir John William Sorrell 1974; two s. one d.; Founder and Chair. Newell & Sorrell (identity and design consultants, merged with Interbrand 1997) 1976–97, apptd Group Creative

Dir Interbrand Newell and Sorrell 1997; Chair. City & Guilds Nat. Advisory Cttee on Art, Craft and Design 1994–96, mem. Colour Group 1996–, City & Guilds Sr Awards Cttee 1996–; Co-founder and Co-Chair. The Sorrell Foundation 1999–; Visiting Prof., Univ. of the Arts, London; Fellow, Hereford Coll. of Arts 2011; Chancellor, Univ. of Westminster 2015–; mem. Bd of Dirs Royal Acad. Enterprises 1996–99; mem. Designers and Art Directors Asscn; mem. Exec. Cttee Mencap Blue Sky Appeal 1996–98, Advisory Bd of Nat. Museum of Photography, Film and TV; Hon. Fellow, Univ. Coll. Falmouth, RIBA; Dr hc (Open Univ.) 2010, (Univ. for the Creative Arts) 2015; 11 DBA Design Effectiveness Awards, five Silver D&ADs, five Clios, one Grand Award for British Airways Corp. Identity and five Gold Awards in New York Festivals, two Art Directors' Club of Europe Awards. *Publication:* joinedupdesignforschools (with Sir John Sorrell) 2005. *Leisure interests:* art, travel, gardening. *Address:* The Sorrell Foundation, Somerset House, The Strand, London, WC2R 1LA, England (office). *Website:* www.thesorrellfoundation.com (office).

SORRELL, Sir John William, Kt, CBE, FCSD, FRSA; British designer; *Co-Founder and Chairman, The Sorrell Foundation;* b. 28 Feb. 1945, London; s. of John William Sorrell and Elizabeth Jane Sorrell (née Taylor); m. Frances Mary Newell 1974; two s. one d.; ed Hornsey Coll. of Art; Designer, Maine Wolff & Partners 1964; Partner, Goodwin Sorrell 1964–71; Design Man. Wolff Olins 1971–76; Founder and Co-Chair. Newell and Sorrell 1976–97, Chair. Newell and Sorrell (now Interbrand Newell and Sorrell) 1983–2000; Vice-Pres. Chartered Soc. of Designers 1989–92; Chair. DBA 1990–92, Design Council 1994–2000; mem. British Rail Architecture and Design Panel 1991–93, RSA Design Advisory Group 1991–93, D & AD Strategic Planning Soc., Inst. of Design, New Millennium Experience Co. Creative Review Group 1998–2000 (and 'Godparent' for Identity Zone), Panel 2000, Dept of Trade & Industry's Encouraging Competitiveness Working Party 1998; Co-Founder and Chair. The Sorrell Foundation 1999–; Chair. Court of Govs, Univ. of the Arts London 2013–; Chair. NHS London Design Advisory Group 2000–, Comm. for Architecture and the Built Environment 2004–09, London Design Festival; Co-Chair. British Abroad Task Force 2000–; Gov. Design Dimension 1991–93; Trustee, Victoria and Albert Museum 2011–; hon. mem. Romanian Design Centre, Hon. FRIBA 2002–, Hon. Fellow, Royal Acad. of Eng 2009–; Hon. DDesign (De Montfort) 1997; Dr hc (London Inst.) 1999; RSA's Bicentenary Medal 1998, D&AD Pres.'s Award 2008. *Publications:* Secret of Design Effectiveness 1995, Utopian Nights 1996, Utopian Papers 1996–, Creative Island 2002. *Leisure interests:* arboriculture, Arsenal Football Club, art, film. *Address:* The Sorrell Foundation, Somerset House, Strand, London WC2R 1LA, England (office). *Telephone:* (20) 7845-5860 (office). *Fax:* (20) 7845-5872 (office). *E-mail:* info@thesorrellfoundation.com (office). *Website:* www.thesorrellfoundation.com (office).

SORRELL, Sir Martin Stuart, Kt, MA, MBA; British advertising executive; b. 14 Feb. 1945, London; ed Christ's Coll., Cambridge, Harvard Business School, USA; consultant, Glendinning Assocs, Westport, Conn. 1968–69; Vice-Pres. Mark McCormack Org. 1970–74; Dir James Gulliver Assocs. 1975–77; Group Financial Dir Saatchi and Saatchi Co. PLC 1977–84; Founder and Group Chief Exec. WPP PLC 1986–2018; Equity Analyst, Morgan Stanley Research Div.; Chair. Int. Business Leaders Advisory Council (IBLAC) Shanghai, Int. Business Advisory Council (IBAC) London, IBAC Rome, IBAC Jerusalem; mem. Advisory Bd Int. Grad. School of Man., Univ. of Navarra 1989–, Judge Inst. for Man. Studies, Univ. of Cambridge 1990–, IBM 1997–, ATP 2001–, Bowmark Capital LLP, Globant SA, Sistemas Globales SA, Stanhope Capital LLP; mem. Bd Dirs of Assocs, Harvard Business School 1998–, Bd Dean's Advisors 1998–; mem. Bd Dirs Storehouse PLC 1994–97, Colefax & Fowler Group PLC 1997–2003, Formula One 2006–, Alpha Topco 2006–, Alcoa Inc. 2012–, Sorrell Capital, Bloomberg Philanthropies, Nat. Deaf Children's Soc.; FCO Amb. for British Business 1997–99, mem. Panel 2000 2000–; mem. Council for Excellence in Man. and Leadership; mem. Bd and Cttee Special Olympics 2000–, Corp. Advisory Group, Tate Gallery 2000–, Bd Nat. Asscn of Securities Dealers Automated Quotation System (NASDAQ) 2001–; Advisory Bd IESE, Spain, Russian Museum, St Petersburg; mem. Dean's Advisory Council, Boston Univ., Indian School of Business 1998–; Chair. Int. Advisory Bd, British-American Business Council; Special Adviser, Aimia Coalition Loyalty UK Ltd; Deputy Chair. and Gov. London Business School 1990–; Trustee Cambridge Foundation, Royal Coll. of Art Foundation; Patron Cambridge Alumni in Man., Queen Charlotte's Appeal at Hammersmith Hosp.; Hon. DBA (London Guildhall Univ.) 2001; Alumni Achievement Award, Harvard Business School 2007. *Leisure interests:* family, skiing, cricket. *Address:* c/o WPP, 27 Farm Street, London, W1J 5RJ, England.

SORRENTINO, Paolo; Italian film director and screenwriter; b. 31 May 1970, Naples; m. Daniela D'Antonio; two c.; writer for various TV programmes including several episodes of The Team 2000; also directed TV commercials; mem. jury, Locarno Int. Film Festival 2008; Pres. jury, Turin Film Festival 2012. *Films include:* A Paradise (Un paradiso, short) 1994, Love has No Boundaries (L'amore non ha confini, short) 1998, One Man Up (L'uomo in più) 2001 (Nastro D'Argento for Best Young Dir), The Consequences of Love (Le conseguenze dell'amore) 2004, The Family Friend (L'amico di famiglia) 2006, Il divo 2008 (Jury Prize, Cannes Film Festival 2008, Italian Golden Globe for Best Screenplay 2009), The Slow Game (La partita lenta) 2009 (Raindance Festival Audience Award 2009), This Must Be the Place 2011, The Great Beauty (La grande bellezza) (BAFTA Award for Best Film not in the English Language 2014) 2013. *Publication:* Hanno tutti ragione (novel) 2010. *Address:* c/o Susan Norget Film Publicity, 198 Sixth Avenue, Suite 1, New York, NY 10013, USA (office). *Telephone:* (212) 431-0090 (office). *E-mail:* susan@norget.com (office). *Website:* www.norget.com (office).

SORU, Renato; Italian business executive and politician; b. 26 Aug. 1957, Sanluri, Sardinia; ed Bocconi Univ., Milan; fmr derivatives trader; Founder, Chair. and CEO Tiscali internet service provider (ISP) 1998–2004, bought six small telecoms cos and ISPs in Germany, France, Switzerland, Belgium and Czech Repub.; Pres. Sardinia Region (Partito Democratico Sardo) with centre-left coalition 2004–08 (resgnd); elected MEP 2014; apptd Sec., Partito Democratico in Sardegna 2014; sentenced to three years in prison for tax evasion 2016. *Website:* www.renatosoru.eu.

SORVINO, Mira, AB; American actress; b. 28 Sept. 1968; d. of Paul Sorvino; m. Christopher Backus 2004; two s. two d.; ed Harvard Univ. *Films include:* Amongst Friends 1993 (also assoc. producer), The Second Greatest Story Ever Told 1993, Quiz Show 1994, Parallel Lives 1994, Barcelona 1994, Tarantella 1995, Sweet Nothing 1995, Mighty Aphrodite (Acad. Award Best Supporting Actress 1996) 1995, The Dutch Master 1995, Blue in the Face 1995, Beautiful Girls 1996, Norma Jean and Marilyn 1996, Jake's Women 1996, Romy and Michele's High School Reunion 1997, The Replacement Killers 1997, Mimic 1997, Summer of Sam 1999, At First Sight 1999, Joan of Arc: The Virgin Warrior 2000, Lisa Picard is Famous 2001, The Great Gatsby 2001, The Triumph of Love 2001, Wisegirls 2002, The Grey Zone 2002, Gods and Generals 2003, The Final Cut 2004, Leningrad 2007, Reservation Road 2007, The Presence 2010, Jeremy Fink and the Meaning of Life 2011, Angels Crest 2011, Union Square 2011, Perfect Sisters 2012, The Trouble with Cali 2012, Smitty 2012, Trade of Innocents 2012, Space Warriors 2013, Do You Believe? 2015, Quitters 2015, Exposed 2016, Look Away 2018. *Television includes:* The Great Gatsby 2000, Human Trafficking 2005, Covert One: The Hades Factor 2006, The Last Templar 2009, Finding Mrs. Claus (film) 2012, Trooper 2013, Falling Skies 2014–15, Intruders 2014, Stalker 2015, Condor 2018, Modern Family 2018. *Address:* c/o Michelle Stern, William Morris Endeavor, 1325 Avenue of the Americas, New York, NY 10019, USA.

SOSRODJOJO, Soegiharto; Indonesian business executive (retd); b. 1930; m.; five c.; f. Rekso Group 1950s (conglomerate with interests in tea and beverages, property, plantation, printing and packaging, wellness and food), subsidiary cos include Sinar Sosro, Gunung Slamat, Agropangan, among others. *Address:* c/o Rekso International, Graha Rekso Building, 10th Floor, Jl. Bulevar Artha Gading Kav A1, Sentra Bisnis, Artha Gading Kelapa Gading, Jakarta Utara 14240, Indonesia (office). *Telephone:* (21) 45856222 (office). *Fax:* (21) 45856201 (office). *E-mail:* info@reksointernational.com (office). *Website:* www.reksointernational.com (office).

SOTO ESTIGARRIBIA, Gen. Bernardino, PhD; Paraguayan army officer and government official; *Minister of National Defence;* b. 20 May 1952, Coronel Oviedo; ed Mariscal Francisco Solano López Mil. Acad.; fmr Instructor, US Army School of the Americas, USA; held numerous post in army, including Head of Operations, 6th Infantry Div., Head of Operations Div. Staff, Jt Commdr, 16th Infantry Regt, eventually becoming Commdr of Armed Forces; fmr Mil. Attaché, Embassy in Brazil; fmr Head of Mil. Cabinet of Presidency; took part in service comms in Brazil, Chile, Taiwan, Ecuador and USA; attained rank of Gen. 2007; Minister of Nat. Defence 2013–15, 2018–; Grand Cross, Order of Mariscal José Félix Estigarribia; numerous awards including Infantry Medal of Honour, Paraguayan Army Medal, Bernardo O'Higgins Medal (Chile), Medalla del Pacificador (Brazil), Medal of the Spanish Army. *Address:* Ministry of National Defence, Avda Mariscal López, esq. Vicepresidente Sánchez y 22 de Septiembre, Asunción, Paraguay (office). *Telephone:* (21) 21-0052 (office). *Fax:* (21) 21-1815 (office). *E-mail:* ministro@mdn.gov.py (office). *Website:* www.mdn.gov.py (office).

SOTOMAYOR, Sonia, BA, JD; American lawyer, academic and judge; *Associate Justice, Supreme Court;* b. 25 June 1954, Bronx, New York; m. Kevin E. Noonan 1976 (divorced 1983); ed Blessed Sacrament School, Cardinal Spellman High School, New York, Princeton Univ., Yale Law School; born to Puerto Rican family that had moved to New York during World War II; Ed. Yale Law Journal and Man. Ed. Yale Studies in World Public Order; Asst Dist Attorney, New York Co. Dist Attorney's Office, Manhattan 1979–84; Assoc., Pavia & Harcourt (law firm), New York 1984–87, Partner 1988–92; Judge, US Dist Court, Southern Dist of NY (youngest mem. of court) 1992–98, Judge, US Court of Appeals for the Second Circuit (first Hispanic woman to serve on court) 1998–2009, Assoc. Justice, US Supreme Court 2009–; Adjunct Prof., New York Univ. Law School 1998–2007; Lecturer-in-Law, Columbia Univ. Law School 1999–; mem. ABA, New York Women's Bar Asscn, Puerto Rican Bar Asscn, Hispanic Nat. Bar Asscn, Asscn of Judges of Hispanic Heritage, Nat. Council of La Raza; fmr mem. Second Circuit Task Force on Gender, Racial and Ethnic Fairness in the Courts; fmr mem. Bd of Dirs New York Mortgage Agency, New York City Campaign Finance Bd, Puerto Rican Legal Defense and Educ. Fund; Hon. LLD (Herbert H. Hehman Coll.) 1999, Hon. JD (Princeton Univ.) 2001, (Brooklyn Law School) 2001, Hon. DJur (Northeastern Univ. School of Law) 2007, (St Lawrence Univ.) 2010, (Howard Univ.) 2010, Dr hc (Hofstra Univ.) 2006, (New York Univ.) 2012, (Yale Univ.) 2013, (Univ. of Michigan) 2017; M. Taylor Pyne Prize (co-recipient), Princeton Univ., Arabella Babb Mansfield Award, Nat. Asscn of Women Lawyers 2000, Katharine Hepburn Medal 2015. *Publications:* My Beloved World (autobiog.) 2013, Turning Pages: My Life Story 2018. *Address:* Supreme Court of the United States, 1 First Street, NE, Washington, DC 20543, USA (office). *Telephone:* (202) 479-3000 (office); (202) 479-3011 (Clerk's Office) (office); (202) 479-3211 (Public Information Office) (office). *E-mail:* info@supremecourt.gov (office). *Website:* www.supremecourt.gov (office).

SOUFLIAS, Georgios Ath.; Greek civil engineer and politician; b. 1941, Larisa; m. Marianna Koraka; two d.; civil engineer, Larisa 1966–74; mem. Parl. 1974–2000, Parl. Rep. of Nea Demokratia (New Democracy party) 1993–96, mem. Perm. Parl. Cttees of Foreign Affairs and Defence, Nat. Economy, Educ. and the Amendment of the Constitution 1993–2000, re-elected as Deputy at Large with Nea Demokratia 2004–; Deputy Minister of Interior Affairs 1977–80, of Nat. Economy 1980–81; Minister of Nat. Economy 1989; represented Nea Demokratia in tripartite cttee in charge of memorandum of co-operation that led to 'Ecumenical Govt' of Mr X. Zolotas 1989; Minister of Finance 1989–90, of Nat. Economy 1990, of Educ. 1991–93; cand. for presidency of Nea Demokratia 1997; expelled from Nea Demokratia Feb. 1998, returned to party on invitation of Pres. of Nea Demokratia during its Fifth Congress 2001, Head of Secr. of Political Planning and Program 2001–04; Minister for the Environment, Physical Planning and Public Works 2004–09; Prof. Emer. of Human Studies, Greek Coll., Boston, USA 1993.

SOULAGES, Pierre; French painter, engraver and sculptor; b. 24 Dec. 1919, Rodez, Aveyron; m. Colette Llaurens 1942; ed Lycée de Rodez; exhibited abstract painting from 1947, in Salon des Surindépendants, Salon de Mai et Réalités Nouvelles; exhibited at int. festivals, including Documenta, Kassel, Biennales of Venice and São Paulo and the itinerary of the Guggenheim Collection, Carnegie Inst., Pittsburgh, The New Decade at Museum of Modern Art, New York, Tate Gallery, London, etc.; also décors for theatres and ballet, and lithographs and engravings; works in Museums of Modern Art, Paris and New York, Tate Gallery, London, Guggenheim Museum, New York, Phillips Gallery, Washington, Museum of Modern Art, Rio de Janeiro, L'Ermitage, St Petersburg, museums in many American cities, in Europe, Australia and Japan; produced 104 stained glass windows for the Romanesque Abbey church Sainte-Foy in Conques, Aveyron 1987–94; first living artist invited to exhibit at the state Hermitage Museum, St Petersburg and later with Tretyakov Gallery, Moscow 2001; Le Musée Soulages (Soulages Museum), Rodez, open to the public 2014; Hon. mem. American Acad. of Arts and Letters 1979; Commdr, then Grand Officier, Légion d'honneur; Grand Officier des Arts et des Lettres; Grand Croix, Ordre nat. du Mérite; Austrian Decoration for Science and Art 2005, Grand'Croix 2015; Grand Prix, Tokyo Biennale 1957, Carnegie Prize, Pittsburgh, USA 1964, Grand Prix des Arts de la Ville de Paris 1975, Rembrandt Prize, Germany, 1976, Prix Nat. de Peinture, Paris 1986, Praemium Imperiale, Tokyo 1992, VII Premio Internacional Julio González, Valencia 2007, Prix Georges Pompidou, Paris 2007. *Publication:* subject of book 'Soulages, l'œuvre complet: Peintures' by Pierre. Encrevé (four vols). *Address:* 12 rue Monge, 75005 Paris, France (home). *Fax:* 1-43-26-88-36 (office). *E-mail:* sec .soulages@wanadoo.fr (office). *Website:* musee-soulages.grand-rodez.com/museum -soulages; www.pierre-soulages.com.

SOULEZ-LARIVIÈRE, Daniel Joseph; French lawyer and writer; *Partner, Soulez Larivière & Associés;* b. 19 March 1942, Angers (Maine-et-Loire); s. of Furcy Soulez-Larivière and Suzanne Soulez-Larivière (née Larivière); m. Mathilde-Mahaut Nobecourt 1988; one s. with Michèle Abbaye; ed Lycée Janson-de-Sailly, Collège Stanislas, Garden City High School, New York, USA, Faculty of Law, Paris and Institut d'Etudes Politiques; lawyer in Paris 1965–; Chargé de mission, Ministry of Equipment and Housing 1966–67; f. Soulez Larivière & Associés 1969; Second Sec., Conférence du stage 1969; mem. Conseil de l'Ordre 1988–90; mem. Consultative Comm. for Revision of Constitution 1992–93; mem. Advisory Bd Centre de prospective de la gendarmerie; Municipal Counsellor for Chambellay 1995–; mem. Soc. of French Jurists; Chevalier, Légion d'honneur, Ordre nat. du Mérite. *Publications include:* L'avocature 1982, Les juges dans la balance 1987, La réforme des professions juridiques et judiciaires, vingt propositions 1988, Justice pour la justice 1990, Du cirque médiatico-judiciaire et des moyens d'en sortir 1993, Paroles d'avocat 1994, Grand soir pour la justice 1997, Dans l'engrenage de la justice 1998, Lettres à un jeune avocat 1999, La justice à l'épreuve (with Jean-Marie Coulon) 2002, Notre justice 2002, Le temps des Victimes (co-author) 2007, Deals de justice (co-author) 2013, La transparence et la vertu 2014, Face aux juges 2017. *Leisure interest:* hunting. *Address:* Soulez Larivière & Associés, 22 avenue de la Grande Armée, 75017 Paris Cedex 17 (office); 6 rue des Fougères, 92140 Clamart (home); le Prieuré, 49220 Chambellay, France (home). *Telephone:* 1-47-63-37-22 (office); 1-45-34-56-50 (home). *Fax:* 1-42-67-83-05 (office); 1-46-26-23-65 (office). *E-mail:* dsl@soulezlariviere.com (office). *Website:* www.soulezlariviere.com (office).

SOUMAHORO, Amadou; Côte d'Ivoirian politician; *President of the National Assembly;* ed Institut des Relations Économiques Internationales de Paris, Université d'Abidjan; Head of Dept of Organisations Economiques Internationales, Ministry of Commerce 1981–86, Minister of Commerce 2003–05; Deputy Dir Foreign Trade 1986–89, Minister of Foreign Trade 2002–03; Chief Nat. Negotiator, Int. Trade Orgs 1986–89; Perm. Sec. Coordination Cttee of Parti Démocratique de la Côte d'Ivoire—Rassemblement Démocratique Africain (PDCI-RDA) activities, Dept of Séguéla 1986–90, mem. Secr. of Presidency of Congress, PDCI-RDA 1990, Political Bureau 1990–93, Municipal Council of Séguéla commune 1991–94; Founder mem. Rassemblement des républicains (Rally of the Republicans-RDR) 1994 (Pres. Exec. Bd 2015–17), then Acting Deputy Gen. Sec. 1999, 2006, 2011–17, Nat. Sec. in charge of Worodougou 2002–06, Head of del., Rassemblement des Houphouëtistes pour la Démocratie et la Paix (RHDP) 2007–10 (Chair. Exec. Bd 2015–17); Deputy Gen. Sec. for Training 1994–96; Nat. Sec. in charge of trade 1996–99; Mayor of Séguéla 1996–2013; Pres. Inter-African Org. of Cocoa 2004–05; 1st Vice-Pres., Independent Electoral Comm. 2010–11; Deputy of Dist of Séguéla sub-pref. and Bobi-Diarabana commune 2011; Special Adviser to the Pres. in charge of Political Affairs 2011–17, Minister 2018–19; Pres. Nat. Ass. 2019–; Founder Dir Sigui Lolo football div. 1998; Regional campaign dir to presidential candidate Alassane Ouattara, Denguélé, Bafing, Worodougou 2008–10; mem. Comm. Consultative Constitutionnelle et électorale 1999–2000. *Address:* Office of the President, National Assembly, 01 BP 1381, Abidjan 01, Côte d'Ivoire (office). *Telephone:* 20-20-96-48 (office). *Fax:* 20-20-82-33 (office). *E-mail:* infos@assnat.ci (office). *Website:* www.assnat.ci (office).

SOUMARÉ, Cheikh Hadjibou; Senegalese politician; b. 1951, Dakar; ed Ecole Nationale d'Administration et de Magistrature, Univ. of Dakar; served as municipal tax officer Kaolack, Sédhiou and Bambey 1981–85; Head Statistics Div., State Treasury 1985–90; Provisional Admin. Bank of Credit and Commerce Int., Senegal 1991–95; adviser to Minister for Finance 1995–96; Dir of the Budget 1996–2000; Dir-Gen. of Finance 2000–01; Deputy Minister for the Budget 2001–07; Prime Minister 2007–09 (resgnd); Pres., Comm. of the Union Economique et Monétaire Ouest Africaine (UEMOA) 2012–16 (resgnd).

SOURAPHIEL, HE Cardinal Berhaneyesus Demerew; Ethiopian ecclesiastic; *Archbishop of Addis Ababa (Ethiopian);* b. 14 July 1948, Tchela Claka, nr Harar; ed Makanissa Major Seminary, Pontifical Gregorian Univ., Italy; ordained priest of Congregation of the Mission (also known as the Lazarists or Vincentians) 1976; Prov. Superior of Lazarists in Addis Ababa 1990; Prefect of Apostolic Vicariate of Jimma-Bonga 1994–97; Apostolic Admin. of Addis Ababa (Ethiopian) 1997–99; consecrated Titular Bishop of Bita 1998; Archbishop of Addis Ababa (Ethiopian) 1999–; Chair. Asscn of Mem. Episcopal Confs in Eastern Africa 2014–; cr. Cardinal (Cardinal-Priest of San Romano Martire) 2015. *Address:* Catholic Archbishop's House, PO Box 21903, Addis Ababa, Ethiopia (office). *Telephone:* (11) 1111667 (office). *Fax:* (11) 1551348 (office).

SOUSA, Manuel Inocêncio, MSc; Cabo Verde politician; b. 1951; ed IST, Lisbon, Portugal, IHE, Delft, Netherlands; fmr Minister of the Communities; Minister of Foreign Affairs, Co-operation and Communities 2001–02; Sr Minister of Infrastructure and Transport (later Minister of State and of Infrastructure, Transport and the Sea) 2002–11; unsuccessful cand. in presidential election Aug. 2011; mem. Partido Africano da Independência de Cabo (PAICV—African Independence Party of Cabo Verde). *Address:* c/o Partido Africano da Independência de Cabo Verde, Av. Amílcar Cabral, CP 22, Praia, Santiago (office); CP 376, Santo Vicente, Cabo Verde (home). *Telephone:* (261) 9249 (home). *E-mail:* inocenciosousa@hotmail.com (home).

SOUSA, Lt Col Óscar Sacramento e; São Tomé and Príncipe politician; *Minister of Defence and Internal Administration;* b. 1951; fmr Minister of Agric.; Vice-Pres., Chamber of Commerce 2002; Minister of Nat. Defence 2003–08, 2012–14, 2015–16, of Foreign Affairs 2004, 2006, of Internal Order 2012–14, of Defence and Internal Administration 2018–; mem. Movimento Democrático Força da Mudança. *Address:* Ministry of Defence and Internal Administration, Av. 12 de Julho, CP 427, São Tomé, São Tomé and Príncipe (office). *Telephone:* 2222041 (office). *E-mail:* midefesa@cstome.net (office).

SOUTER, Sir Brian, Kt; British business executive; *CEO, Stagecoach Group PLC;* b. 1954; s. of Iain Souter and Catherine Souter; m. Elizabeth McGoldrick 1988; three s. one d.; ed Univs of Dundee and Strathclyde; fmrly trainee accountant; f. Stagecoach Selkent bus co. with sister Ann Gloag, Chair. Stagecoach Group PLC 1980–2002, CEO 2002–, firm now operates South West Trains including South Western and East Midlands Trains; fmr Chair. ScotAirways Group Ltd; f. Souter Charitable Trust; Businessman of the Year, Insider Elite Awards 2004. *Address:* Stagecoach Group PLC, 10 Dunkeld Road, Perth, PH1 5TW, Scotland (office). *Telephone:* (1738) 442111 (office). *Fax:* (1738) 443076 (office). *E-mail:* info@stagecoachgroup.com (office). *Website:* www.stagecoachgroup .com (office); www.briansouter.com.

SOUTER, David Hackett, AB, MA, LLB; American lawyer and judge; b. 17 Sept. 1939, Melrose, Mass; s. of Joseph A. Souter and Helen A. Hackett; ed Harvard Univ., Univ. of Oxford, UK, Harvard Univ. Law School; admitted to NH Bar 1967; Assoc., Orr & Reno, Concord 1966–68; Asst Attorney-Gen. of NH 1968–71, Deputy Attorney-Gen. 1971–76, Attorney-Gen. 1976–78; Assoc. Justice, NH Superior Court 1978–83, NH Supreme Court 1983–90; Judge US Court of Appeals, 1st Circuit 1990; Assoc. Justice US Supreme Court, Washington, DC 1990–2009; now regularly sits by designation on US Court of Appeals for First Circuit, Boston; mem. ABA, NH Bar Asscn; Trustee, Concord Hosp. 1972–85, NH Historical Soc. 1976–85; Fellow, American Acad. of Arts and Sciences. *Publication:* Traditional Republican on the Rehnquist Court 2005. *Address:* John Joseph Moakley US Courthouse, One Courthouse Way, Boston, MA 02210, USA.

SOUTHERN, Sir Edwin Mellor, Kt, FRS; British molecular biologist and academic; *Founder, Chairman and Chief Scientific Officer, Oxford Gene Technology;* b. 1938; initiated some of the earliest DNA sequencing at MRC Mammalian Genome Unit, Edinburgh 1967–79; Assoc. Dir MRC Clinical and Population Cytogenetics Unit, where in 1979 he est. first project to map human genome using molecular methods; Whitley Prof. of Biochemistry, Univ. of Oxford 1985–2009, Prof. Emer. 2009–, Fellow, Trinity Coll.; Founder, Chair. and Chief Scientific Officer, Oxford Gene Technology 1995; Founder and Chair. The Kirkhouse Trust (charity); Founder Edina Trust; Gairdner Foundation Int. Award 1990, Royal Medal, Royal Soc. of London 1998, Lasker Prize for Clinical Medical Research (co-recipient) 2005, Asscn of Biomolecular Resource Facilities Award 2005. *Inventions include:* the Southern Blot, now a common laboratory procedure used in DNA analysis for genetic fingerprinting and paternity testing. *Publications:* numerous articles in professional journals. *Address:* Oxford Gene Technology, The Hirsch Building, Begbroke Science Park, Begbroke Hill, Woodstock Road, Begbroke, OX5 1PF (office); Department of Biochemistry, University of Oxford, South Parks Road, Oxford, OX1 3QU, England (office). *Telephone:* (1865) 856800 (Begbroke) (office); (1865) 613200 (Oxford) (office). *Fax:* (1865) 613201 (Oxford) (office). *E-mail:* contact@ogt.co.uk (office); ed.southern@bioch.ox.ac.uk/~southern (office). *Website:* www.ogt.co.uk (office); www.bioch.ox.ac.uk (office).

SOUTO DE MOURA, Eduardo Elísio Machado; Portuguese architect; b. 25 July 1952, Porto; s. of José Alberto Souto de Moura and Maria Teresa Ramos Machado; m. Luisa Penha; three d.; ed School of Fine Arts, Univ. of Porto; worked in Atelier Alvaro Siza (architectural firm) 1975–79; worked for Serviço Ambulatorio de Apojo local (interdisciplinary group est. to address Portugal's shortage of affordable housing); f. Atelier Souto Moura Arquitectos Lda, Porto 1980; Asst Prof., Univ. of Porto 1981–90, later Prof.; Visiting Prof. at architectural schools of Geneva, Paris-Belleville, Harvard Univ., Dublin, ETH Zurich, Lausanne; mem. Acad. of Arts Architecture Section, Berlin 2010; awards include António de Almeida Foundation Prize 1980, Prémio Pessoa 1998, Academie d'Architecture de France Architecture Medal 2010, Pritzker Prize 2011, Wolf Prize 2013. *Works include:* more than 60 projects throughout Europe including Nevogilde houses, Porto 1983–88, Holiday home, Quinta do Lago, Algarve 1984–89, Univ. of Aveiro Dept of Geosciences bldg 1990–94, Burgo Empreendimento (office buildings), Porto 1991, conversion of Porto customs building to create the Museum of Transports and Communications 1993–2002, private house, Bom Jesus 1994, Trindade station, Porto Metro 1997, Knowledge of the Seas Pavilion, Expo 98, Lisbon, Casa del Cinema Manoel de Oliveira, Porto 1998–2002, Portugal Pavilion at Expo 2000, Hanover, Centro de Arte Contemporânea, Bragança 2002–08, Braga Municipal Stadium 2003, Serpentine Gallery Pavilion, London (with Alvaro Siza) 2005, Casa das Historias Paula Rego, Cascais 2005–09, Burgo Tower, Porto 2007. *Address:* Atelier Souto Moura Arquitectos Lda, Calçada do Ouro 1, 4150 Porto, Portugal (office).

SOVALENI, Siaosi 'Ofakivahafolau, MSc, MBA; Tongan IT specialist and politician; b. 28 Feb. 1970, Ngele'ia, Tongatapu; ed Auckland Univ., Oxford Univ., Univ. of the South Pacific, Suva; Dir of Information Tech., Ministry of Finance 1996–2002, Deputy Sec. for Finance (Corp. Services) 2002–05; ICT Advisor, Pacific Islands Applied Geoscience Comm., Fiji 2005–10; Man., Pacific ICT Outreach Programme, Secr. of the Pacific Community, Suva Regional Office, Fiji 2010–13; Deputy Team Leader, Strategic Program for Climate Resilience, Asian Devt Bank Feb.–April 2013; CEO of Public Enterprises, Ministry of Public Enterprises 2013–14; mem. Legis. Ass. for Tongatapu No. 3 constituency 2014–; Deputy Prime Minister, Minister of Foreign Affairs and Minister of Environment, Energy, Climate Change, Disaster Man., Meteorology, Information and Communications 2015–17; fmr Chair. Bd of Dirs Tonga Investment Ltd, Shipping Corpn of Polynesia Ltd; fmr mem. Bd of Dirs Tonga Cable Ltd, Seastar Ltd, Pacific Computer Emergency Response Team, Pacific Chapter of the Internet Soc. (PICISOC), Asia Pacific Telecentre Network; mem. Regional ICT for Educ. Working Group, UNESCAP Expert Group; mem. NZ Inst. of IT Professionals.

SOVERN, Michael Ira, BA, LLD, DPhil; American legal scholar, academic and fmr university president; *President Emeritus and Chancellor Kent Professor of Law, Columbia University;* b. 1 Dec. 1931, New York; m. 2nd Eleanor Lean 1963 (divorced 1974); m. 3rd Joan Wit 1974 (died 1993); m. 4th Patricia Walsh 1995; two s. one d. from first m.; one d. from second m.; ed Columbia Coll., Columbia School of Law; called to the Bar 1956; Asst Prof., then Assoc. Prof. of Law, Univ. Minnesota Law School 1955–58; joined Faculty, Columbia Law School 1957, apptd Prof. of Law 1960, Dean, Law School 1970–79, Chancellor Kent Prof. in Law 1977–, Univ. Provost 1979–80, Pres. Columbia Univ. 1980–93, now Pres. Emer.; Chair. Japan Soc. 1993–2004, American Acad., Rome 1993–2005, nat. advisory council Freedom Forum Media Studies Center 1993–2001, Sotheby's 2000–12; Pres. Schubert Foundation 1996–, also Dir Schubert Org.; mem. Bd of Dirs Comcast Corpn 2002–11, Chemical Bank 1981–96; fmr mem. Bd of Dirs AT&T, GNY Insurance Group, Orion Pictures Corpn, Asian Cultural Corpn; Fellow, American Acad. of Arts and Sciences; mem. American Law Inst.; Hon. DPhil (Tel-Aviv), Hon. LLD (Columbia) 1980; Commendatore, Order of Merit (Italy) 1991, Order of the Rising Sun, Gold and Silver Star (Japan) 2004; Alexander Hamilton Medal, Columbia Coll. 1993, Citizens Union Civic Leadership Award 1993, Columbia Law School Medal for Excellence 1997, Town Hall Friend of the Arts Award 2001, Centennial Medal, American Acad. in Rome 2006, Lawrence A. Wien Prize for Social Responsibility 2010. *Publications include:* Legal Restraints on Racial Discrimination in Employment 1966, Law and Poverty 1969, Of Boundless Domains 1994, An Improbable Life: My Sixty Years At Columbia and Other Adventures 2014. *Address:* School of Law, Columbia University, 435 West 116th Street, Jerome Greene Hall, Room 644, New York, NY 10027, USA (office). *Telephone:* (212) 854-7848 (office). *E-mail:* msovern@law.columbia.edu (office). *Website:* www.law.columbia.edu (office).

SØVNDAL, Villy; Danish politician; b. 4 April 1952, Linde; s. of Peter Søvndal and Agnes Søvndal; m. Heidi Perto Søvndal; three c.; ed Kolding Coll. of Educ.; teacher, Kolding school system 1980–92; mem. Kolding City Council 1982–94; mem. Folketing (Parl.) for Vejle County constituency 1994–2007, for Copenhagen greater constituency 2007–13; mem. Socialistisk Folkeparti (Socialist People's Party), Party Chair. 2005–12; Minister for Foreign Affairs 2011–13. *Publication:* Villys verden (Villy's World) 2008. *Address:* c/o Socialistisk Folkeparti (SF) (Socialist People's Party), Christiansborg, 1240 Copenhagen K, Denmark.

SOW, Sadio Lamine; Malian journalist and politician; b. 9 Aug. 1952, Kayes; m.; three c.; ed Université de Paris X Nanterre; began career as journalist with Jeune Afrique early 1980s; 30 years in Burkina Faso, becoming Special Adviser to Pres. Blaise Compaoré; Minister of Foreign Affairs and Int. Co-operation 2012–13, Special Advisor to the Prime Minister with rank of Minister. *Address:* c/o Ministry of Foreign Affairs, African Integration and International Co-operation, Koulouba, Bamako, Mali.

SOWRY, Hon. Roger; New Zealand fmr politician; b. 1958, Palmerston North; m. Shirley Sowry; four c.; ed Victoria Univ. of Wellington; fmr Distribution Man., R. Hannah & Co.; Nat. Party MP 1990–2005, apptd Jr Whip, then Sr Govt Whip 1994–96, Leader of the House 1998–99, Chair. Health Select Cttee 1993–96, apptd mem. Commerce Select Cttee 2003; Minister of Social Welfare, Minister in Charge of War Pensions, Assoc. Minister of Health 1996–98 and Minister in Charge of Social Services, Work, Income, Welfare, Housing, Employment and Leader of the House 1998–2000; Deputy Divisional Chair. Wellington Young Nationals 1979–80, Electorate Chair. Pencarrow 1982–86, Divisional Councillor 1985–96, Deputy Chair. Wellington Div. 1988–90, Wellington Rep. on NZ Nat. Exec. 1989–90; Deputy Leader Nat. Party 2001–03, Spokesman on Energy and Labour and Industrial Relations 2003; CEO Arthritis New Zealand 2005–08; Consultant, Saunders Unsworth (govt relations consultancy), Wellington 2008–; Chair. Weltec and Whitireia Polytechnic Councils, Teamtalk; mem. Electricity Authority. *Address:* Saunders Unsworth, Level 4, Solnet House, 70 The Terrace, Wellington 6011, New Zealand (office). *Telephone:* (4) 914-1754 (office). *E-mail:* roger.sowry@sul.co.nz (office). *Website:* www.sul.co.nz (office).

SOYINKA, Akinwande Oluwole (Wole), BA; Nigerian playwright and academic; *Professor in Residence, Marymount Institute for Faith, Culture, and the Arts, Loyola Marymount University;* b. 13 July 1934, Abeokuta; s. of Ayo Soyinka and Eniola Soyinka; m.; several c.; ed Univ. of Ibadan, Nigeria and Univ. of Leeds, UK; worked at Royal Court Theatre, London; Research Fellow in Drama, Univ. of Ibadan 1960–61; Lecturer in English, Univ. of Ife 1962–63; Sr Lecturer in English, Univ. of Lagos 1965–67; political prisoner 1967–69; Artistic Dir and Head, Dept of Theatre Arts, Univ. of Ibadan 1969–72; Research Prof. in Dramatic Literature, Univ. of Ife 1972, Prof. of Comparative Literature and Head of Dept of Dramatic Arts 1976–85; Goldwin Smith Prof. of Africana Studies and Theatre, Cornell Univ. 1988–92; passport seized Sept. 1994, living in France; charged with treason March 1997 in absentia; Woodruff Prof. Emer. of the Arts, Emory Univ., Atlanta 2004–; Prof. Emer. of Comparative Literature, Obafemi Awolowo Univ. 2007–; Prof. in Residence, Loyola Marymount Univ. 2007–; Founder and Chair. The Democratic Front for a People's Federation 2010–; Ed. Ch'Indaba (fmrly Transition) Accra; Artistic Dir Orisun Theatre, 1960 Masks; Literary Ed. Orisun Acting Editions; Pres. Int. Theatre Inst. 1986–; Fellow, Churchill Coll. Cambridge 1973–74; mem. American Acad. of Arts and Letters, Int. Theatre Inst., Union of Writers of the African Peoples, Nat. Liberation Council of Nigeria; Fellow, Ghana Asscn of Writers, Pan-African Writers Asscn; Commdr, Légion d'honneur; Commdr, Fed. Repub. of Nigeria 1986; Commdr, Order of Merit (Italy) 1990; Hon. DLitt (Leeds) 1973, (Yale) 1981, (Morehouse), (Paul Valéry), (Bayreuth), (Ibadan), (Harvard); Hon. DScS (Edin.) 1977; Rockefeller Foundation Grant 1960, John Whiting Drama Prize 1966, Prisoner of Conscience Award, Amnesty Int., Jock Campbell-New Statesman Literary Award 1969, Nobel Prize for Literature 1986, George Benson Medal, RSL 1990, Writers Guild Lifetime Achievement Award 1996, Distinguished Scholar-in-Residence, New York Univ. 1999, Europe Theatre Prize 2017, Premio FriulAdria 2017, and numerous other awards. *Plays:* The Invention 1955, The Lion and the Jewel 1959, The Swamp Dwellers 1959, A Dance of the Forests 1960, The Trials of Brother Jero 1961, The Strong Breed 1962, The Road 1964, Kongi's Harvest 1965, Madmen and Specialists 1971, Before the Blackout 1971, Jero's Metamorphosis 1973, Camwood on the Leaves 1973, The Bacchae of Euripides 1974, Death and the King's Horsemen 1975, Opera Wonyosi 1978, A Play of Giants 1984, Six Plays 1984, Requiem for a Futurologist 1985, From Zia, with Love 1991, A Scourge of Hyacinths (radio play) 1992, The Beatification of Area Boy 1995, King Baabu 2003. *Radio:* BBC Reith Lectures 2004. *Publications:* novels: The Interpreters 1964, The Forest of a Thousand Daemons (trans.), Season of Anomy 1973; poetry: Idanre and Other Poems 1967, Poems from Prison 1969, A Shuttle in the Crypt 1972, Poems of Black Africa (ed.) 1975, Ogun Abibman 1977, Mandela's Earth and Other Poems 1988, Samarkand and Other Markets I Have Known 2002; non-fiction: The Man Died (prison memoirs) 1972, Myth, Literature and the African World (lectures) 1972, Aké, The Years of Childhood (autobiog.) 1982, Art, Dialogue and Outrage 1988, Isara: A Voyage Round Essay 1990, Continuity and Amnesia 1991, Ibadan: The Pentelemes Years (memoir) 1994, The Open Sore of a Continent, A Personal Narrative of the Nigerian Crisis 1996, The Burden of Memory, The Muse of Forgiveness 1999, Conversations with Wole Soyinka 2001, You Must Set Forth at Dawn: A Memoir 2006. *Address:* Marymount Institute for Faith, Culture, and the Arts, Loyola Marymount University, 1 LMU Drive, Los Angeles, CA 90045, USA. *Website:* academics.lmu.edu/marymount; www.facebook.com/pages/Wole-Soyinka/23524573801.

SPACEK, Mary Elizabeth (Sissy); American actress; b. 25 Dec. 1949, Quitman, Tex.; d. of Edwin A. Spacek and Virginia Spacek; m. Jack Fisk 1974; two d.; ed Lee Strasberg Theater Inst. *Films:* Prime Cut 1972, Ginger in the Morning 1972, Badlands 1974, Carrie (Best Actress Nat. Soc. Film Critics) 1976, Three Women (Best Supporting Actress New York Film Critics) 1977, Welcome to LA 1977, Heart Beat 1980, Coal Miner's Daughter (Acad. Award for Best Actress, Best Actress New York and Los Angeles Film Critics, Foreign Press Asscn, Nat. Soc. Film Critics) 1980, Raggedy Man 1981, Missing 1982, The River 1984, Marie 1985, Violets are Blue 1986, Crimes of the Heart 1986, 'night Mother 1986, JFK 1991, The Long Walk Home, The Plastic Nightmare, Hard Promises 1992, Trading Mom 1994, The Grass Harp 1995, Streets of Laredo 1995, If These Walls Could Talk 1996, Affliction 1998, Blast From the Past 1999, In the Bedroom (Golden Globe for Best Actress 2002) 2001, Verna: USO Girl 2002, Tuck Everlasting 2002, Last Call 2003, A Home at the End of the World 2004, An American Haunting 2005, The Ring II 2005, Nine Lives 2005, Summer Running: The Race to Cure Breast Cancer 2005, North Country 2005, Gray Matters 2007, Hot Rod 2007, Lake City 2008, Four Christmases 2008, Get Low 2009, The Help 2011, Deadfall 2012. *Television:* The Girls of Huntington House 1973, The Migrants 1973, Katherine 1975, Verna, USO Girl 1978, A Private Matter (film) 1992, A Place for Annie (film) 1994, The Good Old Boys (film) 1995, Pictures of Hollis Woods (film) 2007, Gimme Shelter (film) 2010, Big Love (series) 2010, Bloodline (series) 2015. *Music includes:* Album of the Year Award (Country Music Asscn) for Coal Miner's Daughter 1980. *Publication:* My Extraordinary Ordinary Life (autobiog.) 2012. *Address:* c/o Steve Tellez, CAA, 2000 Avenue of the Stars, Beverly Hills, CA 90067, USA.

SPACEY, Kevin; American actor and theatre director; b. 26 July 1959, South Orange, NJ; ed Chatsworth High School, Los Angeles, Juilliard Drama School, New York; stage debut in Henry IV, Part I; Broadway debut in Ghosts 1982; mem. Bd of Trustees, Old Vic Theatre, London, Artistic Dir 2003–15, directed two and appeared in nine productions; Co-Dir The Bridge Project (theatre co. est. with Sam Mendes at Old Vic Theatre, London and Brooklyn Acad. of Arts, New York) 2007–12; Cameron Mackintosh Visiting Prof. of Contemporary Theatre, St Catherine's Coll., Oxford 2008–09; Hon. CBE 2010; Dr hc (London South Bank Univ.) 2005; Evening Standard Special Theatre Award 2008, Special Award, Olivier Awards 2015. *Theatre includes:* Hurlyburly 1985, Long Day's Journey into Night, London 1986, Yonkers, New York (Tony Award), The Iceman Cometh, London 1998, National Anthems (Old Vic) 2005, Richard II (Old Vic) 2005, The Philadelphia Story (Old Vic) 2006, A Moon for the Misbegotten (Old Vic and Broadway) 2007, Speed the Plow (Old Vic) 2007. *Films include:* Working Girl 1988, See No Evil, Hear No Evil 1989, Dad 1989, Henry and June 1990, Glengarry Glen Ross 1992, Consenting Adults 1992, Hostile Hostages 1994, Outbreak 1995, The Usual Suspects (Acad. Award for Best Supporting Actor) 1995, Se7en 1995, Looking for Richard 1996, A Time to Kill 1996, Los Angeles Confidential 1997, Midnight in the Garden of Good and Evil 1997, American Beauty (Acad. Award for Best Actor) 1999, Pay it Forward 2000, The Shipping News 2001, K-PAX 2001, The Life of David Gale 2003, Beyond the Sea (also dir) 2004, Superman Returns 2006, Fred Claus 2007, 21 2008, Recount 2008, Telstar 2008, Shrink 2009, Moon (voice) 2009, The Men Who Stare at Goats 2009, Father of Invention 2010, Casino Jack 2010, Margin Call 2011, Horrible Bosses 2011, Inseparable 2011, Horrible Bosses 2 2014; dir Albino Alligator 1997. *Television includes:* Wiseguy 1988, House of Cards (series) (Golden Globe Award for Best Actor in a TV Drama 2015, Outstanding Performance by a Male Actor in a Drama Series, Screen Actors Guild 2015, Screen Actors Guild Award for Outstanding Performance by a Male Actor in a Drama Series 2016) 2013–17. *Address:* c/o Polaris PR, 8135 West Fourth Street, Second Floor, Los Angeles, CA 90048, USA (office).

SPADER, James Todd; American actor; b. 7 Feb. 1960, Boston, Mass; ed Phillips Acad. *Films include:* Endless Love 1981, The New Kids 1985, Pretty in Pink 1986, Baby Boom 1987, Less Than Zero 1987, Mannequin 1987, Jack's Back 1988, The Rachel Papers 1989, Sex, Lies and Videotape 1989, Bad Influence 1990, The Music of Chance 1993, Dream Lover 1994, Wolf 1994, Stargate 1994, Two Days in the Valley 1996, Crash 1997, Keys to Tulsa 1997, Critical Care 1997, Curtain Call 1998, Supernova 1998, Slow Burn 1999, Curtain Call 1999, Secretary 2002, I Witness 2003, Alien Hunter 2003, Shadow of Fear 2004, Shorts 2009, Lincoln 2012, The Homesman 2014, Avengers: Age of Ultron 2015. *Television includes:* The Pentagon Papers 2003, The Practice (series) 2003–04, (Emmy Award for Outstanding Lead Actor in a Drama Series 2004), Boston Legal (series) (Emmy Award for Outstanding Lead Actor in a Drama Series 2005, 2007) 2004–08, The Office (series) 2011–12, The Blacklist (series) 2013–15. *Address:* c/o ICM, 8942 Wilshire Boulevard, Beverly Hills, CA 90211, USA.

SPALDING, Alistair, CBE; British theatre executive; *Artistic Director and CEO, Sadler's Wells;* b. 25 Aug. 1957, Stotfold, Herts., England; programmer of film, classical music and visual arts, Hawth Theatre, Crawley 1988–94; Head of Dance and Performance, South Bank Centre, London 1994–2000; Dir of Programming, Sadler's Wells, London 2000–03, Interim Artistic Dir 2003–04, Artistic Dir and CEO 2004– 2004–; External Advisor, Validation Bd for Laban Centre degree courses, City Univ., London; Chair. Dance UK; mem. Advisory Panel, Arts Council of England Dance 1995–2003, Nat. mem. Arts Council of England Bd 2009–; Chevalier des Artes et des Lettres 2005; De Valois Award for Outstanding

Achievement, Critics' Circle Dance Awards 2010. *Address:* Sadler's Wells, Rosebery Avenue, London, EC1R 4TN, England (office). *Telephone:* (20) 7863-8198 (office). *Fax:* (20) 7863-8016 (office). *E-mail:* reception@sadlerswells.com (home). *Website:* www.sadlerswells.com (office).

SPALL, Timothy, OBE, FRSA; British actor; b. 27 Feb. 1957, Battersea, London, England; s. of Joseph L. Spall and Sylvia Spall (née Leonard); m.; one s. two d.; ed Battersea Co. Comprehensive, Kingsway and Princeton Coll. of Further Ed., Royal Acad. of Dramatic Art, London; auditioned for and gained a place with Nat. Youth Theatre; portrayed title roles in Macbeth and Othello at RADA; joined RSC 1979. *Plays include:* Merry Wives of Windsor, Nicholas Nickleby, The Three Sisters, The Knight of the Burning Pestle (RSC 1978–81), St Joan 1985, Mandragola 1985, Le Bourgeois Gentilhomme 1993, A Midsummer Night's Dream 1994 (Royal Nat. Theatre), This is a Chair 1996 (Royal Court). *Films include:* Quadrophenia 1978, Gothic 1986, The Sheltering Sky 1989, Life is Sweet 1990, Secrets and Lies 1996, The Wisdom of Crocodiles 1998, Still Crazy 1998, Topsy Turvy 1999, Clandestine Marriage 1999, Love's Labour's Lost 2000, Intimacy 2001, Lucky Break 2001, Rock Star 2001, Vanilla Sky 2001, All or Nothing 2002, Nicholas Nickleby 2002, Gettin' Square 2003, The Last Samurai 2003, Harry Potter and the Prisoner of Azkaban 2004, Lemony Snickett's A Series of Unfortunate Events 2004, Harry Potter and the Goblet of Fire 2005, Pierrepoint 2005, Enchanted 2007, Sweeney Todd 2007, Death Defying Acts 2007, Apaloosa 2008, The Damned United 2009, Harry Potter and the Half Blood Prince 2009, Heartless 2009, Desert Flower 2009, From Time to Time 2009, Alice in Wonderland (voice) 2010, Re-Uniting the Rubins 2010, Wake Wood 2010, My Angel 2010, Jackboots on Whitehall (voice) 2010, Harry Potter and the Deathly Hallows: Part I 2010, The King's Speech 2010, Harry Potter and the Deathly Hallows: Part 2 2011, My Angel 2011, Comes a Bright Day 2012, Sofia 2012, Upside Down 2012, Ginger & Rosa 2012, The Rise 2012, Love Bite 2012, The Love Punch 2013, Mr. Turner (Award for Best Actor, Cannes Film Festival 2014, Best Actor, US Nat. Soc. of Film Critics 2014, British Actor of the Year, London Critics' Circle 2015) 2014, Sucker 2015, The Journey 2016, Denial 2016, The Party 2017, Finding Your Feet 2017, The Changeover 2017. *Television includes:* The Brylcream Boys 1978, Auf Wiedersehen Pet 1983, 1985, Roots 1993, Frank Stubbs Promotes 1994, 1995, Outside Edge 1994, 1995, Neville's Island 1997, Our Mutual Friend 1997, Shooting the Past 1999, The Thing About Vince 2000, Vacuuming Completely Nude in Paradise 2001, Perfect Strangers 2001, Auf Wiedersehen Pet (third series) 2002, My House in Umbria 2003, Cherished 2005, Mr Harvey Lights a Candle 2005, Mysterious Creatures 2006, A Room with a View 2007, The Street 2006–09, Oliver Twist 2007, Gunrush 2009, The Fattest Man in Britain 2009, 10 Minute Tales (Deep & Crisp & Even) 2009, The Syndicate (series) 2012, Blandings (series) 2013–14, Cider with Rosie (film) 2015, The Enfield Haunting (mini-series) 2015. *Leisure interests:* boating, drinking fine wines, reading. *Address:* c/o Markham & Froggatt, 4 Windmill Street, London, W1P 1HF, England (office); c/o Hofflund Palone, Suite 420, 9465 Wilshire Blvd, Beverley Hills, CA 90212, USA (office). *Telephone:* (20) 7636-4412 (London) (office); (310) 859-1971 (Beverley Hills) (office). *Fax:* (20) 7637-5233 (London) (office); (20) 8699-1657 (London) (office). *E-mail:* admin@markhamfroggatt.co.uk (office). *Website:* www.markhamfroggatt.com (office).

SPANIER, Graham B., BS, MS, PhD; American sociologist, academic and fmr university administrator; b. 18 July 1948; m. Sandra Spanier (neé Whipple) 1971; one s. one d.; ed Iowa State Univ., Northwestern Univ.; Prof. and Assoc. Dean, Pennsylvania State Univ. 1973–82, Pres. 1995–2011; Vice-Provost for Undergraduate Studies, State Univ. of New York at Stony Brook 1982–86; Provost and Vice-Pres. for Academic Affairs, Oregon State Univ. 1986–91; Chancellor Univ. of Nebraska 1991–95; fmr Chair. Nat. Asscn of State Univs and Land-Grant Colls (Co-Chair. Cttee on Higher Educ. and the Entertainment Industry), Nat. Security Higher Educ. Advisory Bd (mem. Nat. Counterintelligence Working Group), Big Ten Conference Council of Pres./Chancellors; Vice-Chair. Worldwide Univs Network; fmr Chair. Christian Children's Fund; fmr Pres. Nat. Council of Family Relations; mem. Bd of Dirs Jr Achievement Int. *Publications include:* ten books and more than 100 scholarly publs. *Leisure interests:* magic, music, racquetball.

SPANTA, Rangin Dadfar, PhD; Afghan academic and government official; b. 15 Dec. 1953, Herat prov.; m.; one c. one s. one d.; ed Kabul Univ., Aachen Univ., Germany; began living in Germany 1982; Prof., Inst. of Political Science, Tech. Univ. of Aachen 1992–2005, Dir Third World Studies Inst.; returned to Afghanistan to teach at Kabul Univ. 2005; Spokesperson, Alliance for Democracy; adviser to Pres. on int. affairs 2005, Minister of Foreign Affairs 2006–10, Nat. Security Adviser 2010–14.

SPAR, Debora L., BS, AM, PhD; American political scientist, academic and college administrator; m. Miltos Catomeris; two s. one d.; ed Georgetown and Harvard Univs; Grad. Assoc., Center for Int. Affairs, Harvard Univ. 1987–88, Crump Fellow, Energy and Environmental Policy Center, Kennedy School of Govt 1988, Research Fellow, Center for Business and Govt 1990, Asst Prof. of Business, Govt and Competition, Harvard Business School 1991–95, Assoc. Prof. 1995–99, Prof. 1999–2004, Chair. Business, Govt and the Int. Economy Unit, Sr Assoc. Dean, Recruiting 2004–05, Sr Assoc. Dean, Dir Div. of Research and Faculty Devt 2005–07, Spangler Family Prof., Harvard Business School 2005–08; Asst Prof., Dept of Political Science, Univ. of Toronto 1990–91; Pres. Barnard Coll. 2008–17, Lincoln Center for the Performing Arts 2017–18; Karl W. Deutsch Guest Prof., Wissenschaftszentrum, Berlin 2000; mem. Harvard Univ. Cttee on Human Rights 1995, Chair. 2006–07; mem. Exec. Cttee, Weatherhead Center for Int. Affairs, Harvard Univ. 1995–, Cttee on African Studies, Harvard Univ. 2002–, Policy Advisory Cttee, Center for Int. Devt 2005–, Advisory Cttee on Honorary Degrees 2006–, Embryonic Stem Cell Research Org. 2006–, Policy Cttee, David Rockefeller Center for Latin American Studies, Harvard Univ. 1997–2002; Chair. Making Markets Work (exec. educ. programme for African officials) 2002–; mem. Bd Newton Schools Foundation 2002–04, Bd of Overseers, Newton Wellesley Hosp. 2007–; mem. Bd of Dirs Goldman Sachs 2011–; Univ. English Medal, Georgetown Univ. 1984, Dean's Citation, School of Foreign Service, Georgetown Univ. 1984, J. Raymond Trainor Citation for Excellence in the Study of Govt, School of Foreign Service, Georgetown Univ. 1984, DACOR Fellow 1984–86, Certificates of Distinction in Teaching, Harvard Coll. 1987–89, Distinguished Teaching Fellow Award, Govt Dept, Harvard Univ. 1988, Helen Dwight Reid Award, Best Doctoral Dissertation in Int. Relations, American Political Science Asscn 1991, Student Asscn Faculty Award for Outstanding Teaching, Harvard Business School 2000, Robert F. Greenhill Award for Outstanding Service, Harvard Business School 2005. *Publications:* Beyond Globalism: Remaking American Foreign Economic Policy (with Raymond Vernon) 1988, Iron Triangles and Revolving Doors: Cases in U.S. Foreign Economic Policymaking (with Raymond Vernon and Glenn Tobin) 1991, The Cooperative Edge: The Internal Politics of International Cartels 1994, Ruling the Waves: Cycles of Discovery, Chaos and Wealth from the Compass to the Internet 2001 (simultaneously published as Pirates, Prophets and Pioneers: Business and Politics Along the Technological Frontier, London 2001), Managing International Trade and Investment 2003, The Baby Business: How Money, Science, and Politics Drive the Commerce of Conception 2006; numerous book chapters and articles on the economics of the human fertility industry and the evolution of the Internet. *Address:* c/o Office of the President, Lincoln Center for the Performing Arts, 70 Lincoln Center Plaza, 9th Floor, New York, NY 10023, USA (office).

SPARGO, Peter Ernest, BSc, MSc, Cert. Ed. (Cantab.), FRSSAf; South African academic; *Associate Professor Emeritus, University of Cape Town;* b. 7 June 1937, Johannesburg; s. of Alfred Hugh Spargo and Lilias McCall Spargo (née Fisher); m. Celia Rosamunde Key 1964; four d.; ed Jeppe High School, Univ. of the Witwatersrand, Johannesburg, Magdalene Coll. Cambridge, UK; Science Teacher, Jeppe High School, Johannesburg 1961–63; Lecturer in Science Educ., Johannesburg Coll. of Educ. 1964–71; Science Educ. Planner, Pretoria 1972–75; School of Educ., Univ. of Cape Town 1976–97, Dir Science Educ. Unit 1980–97, Hon. Research Assoc., Dept of Physics 1999–2012, Assoc. Prof. Emer. 2012–; Nat. Chair. SA Asscn of Teachers of Physical Science 1975–82; Trustee and Dir S African Science Educ. Project 1977–2008; Educ. Consultant to Shell Oil Co. (SA) 1977–89, Rössing Uranium Co. (Namibia) 1982–90; Nat. Pres. Fed. of Science and Math. Teachers Asscns of SA 1977–79, 1984–85; Gen. Sec. Royal Soc. of South Africa 1986–89, Fellow; Hon. Nat. Pres. South African Spelaeological Asscn 1996–; Medal of Honour, Fed. of Science and Math. Teachers Asscns of South Africa 1981. *Publications include:* numerous publs in the fields of science education, history of science and technology, author of science textbooks. *Leisure interests:* walking, reading, gardening. *Address:* PO Box 211, Rondebosch 7701; 10 Lochiel Road, Rondebosch, Cape Town, South Africa (home). *Telephone:* (21) 6864289 (home). *Fax:* (21) 5105979 (office). *E-mail:* peter@spargo.wcape.school.za.

SPARKS, Sir Robert Stephen John, Kt, CBE, PhD, FRS; British geologist, volcanologist and academic; *Channing Willis Professor of Geology, Department of Earth Sciences, University of Bristol;* b. 15 May 1949, Harpenden, Herts.; s. of Kenneth Grenfell Sparks and Ruth Joan Rugman; m. Ann Elizabeth Talbot 1971; two s.; ed Imperial Coll., London; Fellow of Royal Comm. of Exhbn of 1851, Univ. of Lancaster 1974–76; NATO Post-doctoral Fellow, Univ. of Rhode Island, USA 1976–78; Lecturer, Univ. of Cambridge 1978–89, Fellow, Trinity Hall Cambridge 1980–89; Prof. of Geology, Univ. of Bristol 1989–, Channing Willis Prof. of Geology 1990–; Chief Scientist, Montserrat Volcano Observatory 1997–99; Prof. of Earth Sciences, Nat. Environment Research Council 1998–; Pres. Geological Soc. of London 1994–96, Int. Asscn of Volcanology and Chem. of Earth's Interior 1999–, VGP Section, American Geophysical Union 2008–12; Chair. of Environmental Sciences, Research Assessment Exercise 2008, Advisory Cttee on Math. Educ. UK 2012–15; Dir Bristol Environmental Risk Research Centre (BRISK) 2008–11; European Research Council Advanced Researcher 2009–14; Fellow, American Geophysical Union 1998; Board of Trustees, Natural History Museum London 2015–; Hon. DSc (Lancaster) 2000; Dr hc (Univ. Blaise Pascal) 1999, (Univ. of Paris) 2003; Bakerian Lecture, Royal Soc. 2000; Bigsby Medal, Geological Soc. of London, Murchison Medal, Geological Soc. of London 1998, Arthur Day Medal, Geology Soc. of America 2000, Royal Soc. Wolfson Merit Award 2002, Arthur Holmes Medal, European Union of Geosciences 2004, Chiba Univ. Science Prize, Japan 2006, Thorarinsson Medal 2008, Wollaston Medal 2011, Vetlesen Prize 2015. *Publications:* Volcanic Plumes 1997; more than 450 scientific articles and papers on volcanology (especially physics of volcanic eruptions), fluid mechanics, petrology and other geological topics Over 39,000 citations. *Leisure interests:* music, travel, family, sports. *Address:* Department of Earth Sciences, Wills Memorial Building, Room G17, Queen's Road, Bristol University, Bristol, BS8 1RJ (office); Walnut Cottage, 19 Brinsea Road, Congresbury, Bristol, BS49 5JF, England (home). *Telephone:* (117) 9545419 (office); (1934) 834306 (home). *Fax:* (117) 9253385 (office). *E-mail:* steve.sparks@bristol.ac.uk (office). *Website:* gfd.gly.bris.ac.uk (office); www.gly.bris.ac.uk/www/admin/personnel/RSJS.html (office).

SPASOVSKI, Oliver; Macedonian politician; *Deputy Prime Minister and Minister of Internal Affairs;* b. 21 Oct. 1976, Kumanovo, Socialist Repub. of Macedonia, Socialist Fed. Repub. of Yugoslavia; ed Faculty of Law Iustinianus Primus, SS Cyril and Methodius Univ., Skopje; mem. Socijaldemokratski Sojuz na Makedonija (Social Democratic Alliance of Macedonia); mem. Sobranie (Ass.), mem. Legis. Cttee, Cttee on Defence and Security, Deputy mem. Cttee on Rules of Procedure and Mandatory and Immunity Issues, Cttee on Constitutional Issues, mem. Del. to Parl. Cttee for Stabilization and Asscn, Inter-Community Relations Cttee, Parl. Group for Co-operation with Parl. of People's Repub. of China; Minister of Internal Affairs 2015–16, 2017–, Deputy Prime Minister 2017–. *Address:* Ministry of Internal Affairs, 1000 Skopje, Dimče Mirčev bb, North Macedonia (office). *Telephone:* (2) 3117222 (office). *Fax:* (2) 3112468 (office). *E-mail:* kontakt@moi.gov.mk (office); o.spasovski@sobranie.mk (office). *Website:* www.mvr.gov.mk (office).

SPASSKIY, Nikolay Nikolayevich, DPolSc; Russian diplomatist and government official; *Deputy CEO for International Relations, Rosatom;* b. 10 Aug. 1961, Sevastopol; s. of Nikolay Spasskiy and Rimma Spasskaya; m. Angela Maria Catalano; one d.; ed Moscow Inst. of Int. Relations; with USSR (later Russian) Ministry of Foreign Affairs 1983–; Deputy Head, First Deputy, Dept of N America 1992–94; Dir 1994–97; mem. Advisory Council, Ministry of Foreign Affairs 1995; Amb. to Italy (also accred to San Marino) 1997–2004; Deputy Sec., Nat. Security Council 2004–06, Deputy Head, Fed. Agency for Atomic Energy 2006–08; Deputy CEO for Int. Relations, Rosatom (state nuclear energy corpn) 2008–. *Publications:* La Fine del Mondo e Altri Racconti Romani 1999, Il Complotto 2000, Il Bizantino 2002, Le Reliquie di San Cirillo 2004. *Leisure interests:* art, travel. *Address:* Rosatom, 119017 Moscow, Bolshaya Ordynka str. 24, Russia (office). *Telephone:* (499) 949-24-05 (office). *Fax:* (495) 951-68-58 (office). *E-mail:* info@rosatom.ru (office). *Website:* www.rosatom.ru/en/about/governance/managementboard/spasskiy.html (office).

SPASSKY, Boris Vasiliyevich; French/Russian chess player and journalist; b. 30 Jan. 1937, Leningrad (now St Petersburg); m. 1st Marina Shcherbacheva; m. 2nd; m. 3rd; ed Faculty of Journalism, Leningrad State Univ.; in Leningrad Section of Voluntary Sport Soc., Trud 1959–61; Trainer, Leningrad Section of Voluntary Sport Soc., Locomotiv 1964–79; played in numerous individual and command int. chess tournaments; USSR Grandmaster, Int. Grandmaster and World Chess Student Champion 1956, USSR Chess Champion 1962, World Chess Champion 1969–72 (when lost to Bobby Fischer); left USSR 1976; lost to Bobby Fischer in Yugoslavia 1992; works as a chess journalist; involved with World Chess Network; Hon. Pres. Kilkenny Chess Club, Ireland; several decorations including Honoured Master of the Sport 1965. *Website:* www.worldchessnetwork.com.

SPASSKY, Igor Dmitriyevich, DrTechSc; Russian engineer and academic; b. 2 Aug. 1926, Noginsk, Moscow Region; m.; one s. one d.; ed Dzerdjinsky Higher Naval Eng Coll.; service in Black Sea marine forces 1949–50; worked in enterprises of Ministry of Vessel Construction, Leningrad (now St Petersburg) 1950–; Head of Sector, Cen. Design Bureau for Marine Eng (RUBIN), then Deputy Chief Designer, Head and Chief Designer 1974–2007, now Chief of Research Activities; Scientific and Tech. Leader of Kursk submarine recovery project; USSR Peoples' Deputy 1990–91; mem. USSR (now Russian) Acad. of Sciences 1987–; Hon. Citizen of St Petersburg 2002; Red Banner of Labour 1963, Order of Lenin 1970, 1978, Orders of October Revolution 1986, Order of Merit for Services to the Motherland 2002; 16 medals; Lenin Prize 1965, Hero of Socialist Labour 1978, USSR State Prize 1983. *Publications:* ed. and contrib.: The Kurst 2000, Five Colours of Time, Submarines of the Tzarist Navy, History of National Shipbuilding (five vols), Submarines of Russia (three vols), Submarine Deisgn (collection of articles); more than 100 scientific works on designing atomic submarines, tech. of machine construction, construction mechanics, reliability and special energetics; articles in magazines Shipbuilding, Military Parade, Naval History, USA Naval Institute Proceedings. *Leisure interest:* fishing. *Address:* Central Design Bureau for Marine Engineering (RUBIN), 191119 St Petersburg, Marata str. 90, Russia (office). *Telephone:* (812) 113-51-32 (office). *Fax:* (812) 113-31-15 (office). *E-mail:* neptun@ckb-rubin.spb.su (office). *Website:* www.ckb-rubin.com (office).

SPAULDING, Winston, QC; Jamaican lawyer and fmr politician; b. 26 Aug. 1939; m.; five c.; called to the Bar, Inner Temple, London 1966; worked briefly in Jamaican and British civil service and practised law in the Bahamas; subsequently established legal practice in Jamaica; fmr mem. Nat. Exec. People's Nat. Party; Deputy Leader Jamaica Labour Party 1977–83; Senator and Opposition Spokesman on Security and Justice 1977–80; MP for Cen. St James 1980–83 and for SE St Andrew 1983–89; Minister of Nat. Security and Justice and Attorney-Gen. 1980–86; Chair. Defence Bd 1980–86, Legislation Cttee 1980–86, Statute Law Commrs under the Law Revision Act 1980–86; mem. Council of Legal Educ. 1980–86; Founder-mem. Jamaica Council for Human Rights; Founder and First Chair. Human Rights Bureau of Jamaica Labour Party; as Minister of Justice initiated review of Gun Court Act which included abolition of mandatory life sentence; as Minister of Security initiated establishment of Police Staff Coll. *Address:* 21 Balmoral Avenue, Kingston 10, Jamaica (office). *Telephone:* 9298601. *Fax:* 9296196.

SPEARMAN, Thomas David, PhD, MRIA; Irish mathematician, academic and fmr university pro-chancellor; b. 25 March 1937, Dublin; s. of Thomas Spearman and Elizabeth Leadbeater; m. Juanita Smale 1961; one s. two d.; ed Greenlanes and Mountjoy Schools, Dublin, Trinity Coll., Dublin and St John's Coll., Cambridge, UK; Research Fellow, Univ. Coll. London 1960–61; Research Assoc., Univ. of Illinois, USA 1962–64; Lecturer in Theoretical Physics, Univ. of Durham, UK 1964–66; Univ. Prof. of Natural Philosophy, Trinity Coll. Dublin 1966–97, Fellow 1969–94; Sr Fellow 1994–97 (Fellow Emer. 1997–), Bursar 1974–77, Vice-Provost 1991–97, Pro-Chancellor Univ. of Dublin 2009–12; Prof. Associé, Univ. of Montpellier, France 1985–; Chair. Trustee Savings Bank, Dublin 1989–92; mem. Council, European Physical Soc. 1979–82; mem. European Space Science Cttee 1984–89; Vice-Pres. European Science Foundation 1983–89; Treas. Royal Irish Acad. 1980–88, Pres. 1999–2002; mem. Academia Europaea, Treas. 1989–2000; mem. European Science and Tech. Ass. 1994–98; mem. Bd Nat. Gallery of Ireland 1999–2002; mem. Governing Council European Science Foundation 2000–02; Chair. European Acads Science Advisory Council 2004–07. *Publications include:* Elementary Particle Theory (with A. D. Martin) 1970; numerous papers and articles on aspects of elementary particle physics, inverse problems and history of science. *Leisure interests:* walking, gardening, reading, listening to music, looking at pictures. *Address:* House No. 25, Trinity College, Dublin 2, Ireland (office). *Telephone:* (1) 8962360 (office). *E-mail:* david.spearman@tcd.ie (office).

SPEARS, Britney Jean; American singer and entertainer; b. 2 Dec. 1981, McComb, Miss.; m. Kevin Federline 2004 (divorced 2007); two s.; raised in Kentwood, La; began performing as a child, landing acting roles in stage productions and TV shows; signed with Jive Records 1997, released debut album Baby One More Time 1999 (best-selling album by a teenage solo artist); presenter, Mickey Mouse Club; numerous tours, radio and TV appearances; judge, The X Factor (USA) 2012; Owner, southern grill restaurant, Nyla; f. The Britney Spears Foundation; MTV Europe Music Awards for Best Female Artist 1999, 2004, for Best Song (for Baby One More Time) 1999, Best Breakthrough Act 1999, Best Pop Act 1999, several MTV Video Music Awards 1999, and Best Female Pop Vocal Performance 2000, Billboard Music Award 2000, American Music Award for Favourite New Artist 2000, Grammy Award for Best Dance Recording (for Toxic) 2005, MTV Video Music Award for Best Female Video (for Piece of Me) 2008, Best Celebrity Fragrance For Women, Cosmopolitan Fragrance Awards 2010, Best Celebrity Fragrance For Women – Readers' Award, Cosmopolitan Fragrance Awards 2011, Billboard Millennium Award 2016, People's Choice Awards for Favorite Female Artist, for Favourite Pop Artist 2017. *Films:* Longshot (cameo) 2000, Austin Powers in Goldmember (cameo) 2002, Crossroads 2002, Fahrenheit 9/11 (cameo) 2004. *Recordings include:* albums: Baby One More Time 1999, Oops! I Did It Again 2000, Britney 2001, In The Zone 2003, My Prerogative 2004, Blackout 2007, Circus 2008, Femme Fatale 2011, Britney Jean 2013, Glory 2016. *Website:* www.britneyspears.com (office); www.britney.com.

SPECTOR, Jason A., BA, MD, FACS; American clinician, medical researcher and academic; *Associate Professor of Surgery, Weill Cornell Medical College;* b. New York; ed Cornell Univ., New York Univ. School of Medicine; postdoctoral research fellowship, Lab. of Developmental Biology Repair, NYU Medical Center; Adjunct Asst Prof. of Surgery, Weill Cornell Medical Coll. 2006, Asst Prof. of Surgery 2006–11, Assoc. Prof. of Surgery (Plastic Surgery) 2011–, Assoc. Prof. of Otolaryngology 2013–, Dir and Prin. Investigator, Lab. for Bioregenerative Medicine and Surgery, Weill Cornell Medical Center; mem. Editorial Bd, Aesthetic Plastic Surgery; Moderator, Emerging Technologies Section, American Surgical Congress 2011; mem. American Soc. of Plastic Surgeons, American Coll. of Surgeons, Soc. of Univ. Surgeons, American Asscn for Academic Surgery, Plastic Surgery Research Council; Valentine Mott Award, New York Univ. School of Medicine 1996, Best Resident Research Presentation, Northeastern Soc. of Plastic Surgeons 1999, Best Research Presentation, New York Regional Soc. of Plastic Surgeons' Residents Competition 2003, Academic Scholar, American Asscn of Plastic Surgeons 2009, Nat. Endowment for Plastic Surgery Award 2011, World Technology Award (Health and Medicine) (co-recipient) 2013. *Publications:* three book chapters and more than 100 papers in professional journals; holds two patents. *Address:* Weill Cornell Medical College, Cornell University, 1300 York Avenue, New York, NY 10065 (office); NewYork-Presbyterian Hospital, 525 East 68th Street, Starr 8, New York, NY 10065, USA (office). *Telephone:* (212) 746-4532 (office). *Fax:* (212) 746-8952 (office). *E-mail:* jas2037@med.cornell.edu (office). *Website:* weillcornell.org/jaspector (office); nyp.org/physician/jaspector (office).

SPEHAR, Elizabeth, BA, MA; Canadian UN official; *Secretary-General's Special Representative and Head, Peacekeeping Force in Cyprus, United Nations;* b. Port Arthur, Ont.; one d.; ed Queen's Univ., Carleton Univ. Norman Paterson School of Int. Affairs, Univ. of Pau, France; began career with a variety of insts, including MATCH International, Ottawa, UNDP, Cape Verde, and several consultancies with Int. Devt and Research Centre and Canadian Int. Devt Agency; Head of Americas Programme, Int. Centre for Human Rights and Democratic Devt, Montreal 1990–94; 12 years as sr official with OAS, including as Exec. Co-ordinator, Unit for Promotion of Democracy at OAS HQ, Washington, DC 1995–2004, Dir, OAS Electoral Support Program, Port-au-Prince, Haiti 2005–06, Dir, Dept for Promotion of Democracy, OAS Secr. for Political Affairs 2006–07; Interim Special Rep. of UN Sec.-Gen. and Head of UN Peacekeeping Force in Cyprus (UNFICYP) 2008, Dir, Americas and Europe Div., Dept of Political Affairs, UN Secr. 2007–09, Dir Europe Div. 2009–15, Dir Policy and Mediation Div. 2015–16, also Chair. UN Democracy Fund's Programme Consultative Group, Chair. Exec. Cttee on Peace and Security InterAgency Working Group on Democracy, UN Sec.-Gen.'s Special Rep. and Head, UNFICYP 2016–. *Address:* Office of the Secretary-General, United Nations, New York, NY 10017, USA (office). *Telephone:* (212) 963-1234 (office). *Fax:* (212) 963-4879 (office). *Website:* unficyp.unmissions.org (office).

SPEIRN, Sterling K., BSc, DIur; American lawyer and foundation executive; *Advisor, Stupski Foundation;* b. 7 Feb. 1948, Detroit, Mich.; m. Diana Aviv 2005; two s. (from previous m.); ed Stanford Univ., Univ. of Michigan Law School; taught high school in Cleveland, Ohio; law clerk, US Dept of Interior, Washington, DC; led Apple Computer's nat. computer grants program 1986–90; joined Peninsula Community Foundation, San Mateo, Calif. 1990, Pres. and Chief Exec. 1992–2005; Pres. and CEO W.K.Kellogg Foundation, Battle Creek, Mich. 2006–13; Pres. Stupski Foundation 2014–15, Advisor 2015–; fmr Chair. League of Calif. Community Foundations; Co-Chair. Nat. D5 coalition on Diversity in Philanthropy Project; mem. Bd of Advisors Pacific Community Ventures, Global Philanthropy Forum; mem. Bd of Dirs Northern California Grantmakers. *Address:* Stupski Foundation, 90 New Montgomery Street, Suite 315 San Francisco, CA 94105, USA (office). *Telephone:* (415) 655-4400 (office). *Fax:* (415) 655-4401 (office). *E-mail:* info@stupski.org (office). *Website:* www.stupski.org (office).

SPELMAN, Rt Hon. Dame Caroline Alice, DBE, PC, BA (Hons); British politician; b. (Caroline Alice Cormack), 4 May 1958, Bishop's Stortford, Herts.; m. Mark Spelman 1987; two s. one d.; ed Herts and Essex Grammar School for Girls (now Hertfordshire and Essex High School), Bishop's Stortford, Queen Mary Coll., London; Sugar Beet Commodity Sec., Nat. Farmers Union 1981–84; Deputy Dir Int. Confed. of European Beetgrowers, Paris 1984–89; Research Fellow, Centre for European Agricultural Studies (part of Univ. of Kent and since 2000 known as Centre for European Agri-Environmental Econs) 1989–93; Dir, Spelman, Cormack & Assocs, Food and Biotechnology Consultancy, Dorridge, W Midlands 1989–2009; contested Bassetlaw constituency, Notts. 1992; MP (Conservative) for Meriden, W Midlands 1997–2010, for Meriden (revised boundary) 2010–, mem. Science and Tech. Select Cttee 1997–98, Environmental Audit Select Cttee 2013–15, Parl. Jt Cttee on Slavery 2014–15, Opposition Whip 1998–99, Bd mem. Parl. Office of Science and Tech. 1997–2001, Opposition Spokesperson for Health 1999–2001, for Women's Issues 1999–2001, Shadow Sec. of State for Int. Devt 2001–03, Shadow Minister for Women 2001–04, Shadow Sec. of State for Environment 2003–04, for Local and Devolved Govt Affairs 2004–05, Shadow Office of Deputy Prime Minister/Communities and Local Govt 2005–07, 2009–10; Chair. Conservative Party 2007–09; Sec. of State for Environment, Food and Rural Affairs 2010–12; Amb. for Tearfund 2013–; 2nd Estates Church Commr 2015–; mem. Agricultural and Fisheries Council, Council of the EU 2010–12. *Address:* House of Commons, Westminster, London, SW1A 0AA (office); Constituency Office, 631 Warwick Road, Solihull, B91 1AR, England (home). *Telephone:* (20) 7219-4189 (London) (office); (121) 711-7029 (Solihull) (office). *E-mail:* caroline.spelman@parliament.uk (office). *Website:* www.carolinespelman.com.

SPENCE, A. Michael, BA, BA, MA, PhD; American economist and academic; *Philip H. Knight Professor and Dean, Emeritus, Graduate School of Business, Stanford University;* ed Princeton Univ., Univ. of Oxford, UK, Harvard Univ.; Assoc. Prof., Harvard Univ. 1973–75, Chair. Advisory Cttee on Shareholder Responsibility 1978–79, Prof. 1979–86, Chair. Project in Industry and Competitive Analysis 1980–85, Chair. Business Econs PhD Program 1981–83, Chair. Dept of Econs 1983–84, Dean of Faculty 1984–90; Philip H. Knight Prof., Stanford Univ. 1990–2000, Dean 1990–99, Prof. and Dean Emer. 2000–; Sr Fellow, Hoover Inst.; Partner, Oak Hill Capital Partners, Menlo Park, Calif. from 1999; Chair. Nat. Research Council Bd on Science, Tech. and Econ. Policy 1991–97, Comm. on Growth and Devt 2006–; mem. Bd of Dirs, General Mills, Inc., Nike, Inc.

1995–2004, Siebel Systems, Inc. 1995–2004, Exult, Inc. 1999–2004, Blue Martini Software, Torstar, ITI Educ.; mem. American Econ. Asscn; Fellow, AAAS, Econometric Soc.; Rhodes Scholar, Oxford 1966, Danforth Fellow 1966, David A. Wells Prize for outstanding doctoral dissertation, Harvard Univ. 1972, J.K. Galbraith Prize for Excellence in Teaching 1978, John Bates Clark Medal, American Econ. Asscn 1981, Nobel Memorial Prize in Econ. Sciences (co-recipient) 2001, and numerous other awards and prizes. *Publications:* Creating and Capturing Value: Perspectives and Cases on Electronic Commerce (co-author) 2002, Leadership and Growth (co-author) 2010, The Next Convergence: The Future of Economic Growth in a Multispeed World 2012; numerous articles in professional journals. *Address:* Graduate School of Business, 518 Memorial Way, Stanford University, Stanford, CA 94305-5015, USA (office). *Telephone:* (917) 678-1920 (New York). *E-mail:* premadvisory@worldbank.org. *Website:* www.gsb .stanford.edu/faculty-research/faculty/michael-spence (office); www .growthcommission.org.

SPENCE, Jonathan Dermot, PhD, CMG; American historian, academic and writer; *Sterling Professor Emeritus of History, Yale University;* b. 11 Aug. 1936, Surrey, England; s. of Dermot Spence and Muriel Crailsham; m. 1st Helen Alexander 1962 (divorced 1993); two s.; m. 2nd Chin Annping 1993; ed Univ. of Cambridge, UK and Yale Univ.; Asst Prof. of History, Yale Univ. 1966–71, Prof. 1971–93, Sterling Prof. of History 1993–2008, Sterling Prof. of History Emer. 2008–; Visiting Prof., Univ. of Beijing 1987; Pres. American Historial Asscn 2004–05; mem. Bd of Govs Yale Univ. Press 1988–; mem. American Acad. of Arts and Sciences, American Philosophical Soc.; Guggenheim Fellow 1979–80; MacArthur Fellow 1987–92; Hon. LHD (Knox Coll.) 1984, (New Haven) 1989; Hon. LittD (Wheeling Coll.) 1985, (Chinese Univ. of Hong Kong) 1996, (Gettysburg) Coll. 1996, (Union Coll.) 2000, (Beloit Coll.) 2000, (Conn. Coll.) 2000; William C. DeVane Medal, Yale Chapter of Phi Beta Kappa 1978, Los Angeles Times History Prize 1982, Vursell Prize, American Acad. and Inst. of Arts and Letters 1983, Comisso Prize (Italy) 1987; Gelber Literary Prize (Canada) 1991, Jefferson Lecturer in the Humanities, Nat. Endowment for the Humanities 2010. *Publications include:* Ts'Ao Yin and The K'Ang-Hsi Emperor 1966, To Change China 1969, Emperor of China 1974, The Death of Woman Wang 1978, The Gate of Heavenly Peace 1981, The Memory Palace of Matteo Ricci 1984, The Question of Hu 1988, The Search for Modern China 1990, Chinese Roundabout 1992, God's Chinese Son 1996, The Chan's Great Continent 1998, Mao Zedong 1999, Treason by the Book 2002, Return to Dragon Mountain: Memories of a Late Ming Man 2007. *Address:* 691 Forest Road, New Haven, CT 06515, USA (home). *E-mail:* jonathan.spence@yale.edu (office).

SPENCE, Rev. Michael James, BA (Hons), LLB (Hons), DPhil, AC; Australian academic and university administrator; *Vice-Chancellor and Principal, University of Sydney;* b. 10 Jan. 1962, Sydney, NSW; m. 1st Beth Spence (died 2012); five c.; m. 2nd Jenny Ihn 2015; two c.; ed Univ. of Sydney, Univ. of Oxford, UK; began career as lawyer with Mallesons Stephens Jacques, Sydney; lectured in Law at Univ. of Sydney –1988, Vice-Chancellor and Prin., Univ. of Sydney 2008–; also worked for Australian Copyright Council; Fellow, St Catherine's Coll., Oxford and Lecturer, Univ. of Oxford 1992, becoming Head of Social Sciences Div.; trained for priesthood at St Stephen's House, Oxford. *Address:* Office of the Vice-Chancellor, University of Sydney, Sydney, NSW 2006, Australia (office). *Telephone:* (2) 9351-6980 (office). *E-mail:* vice.chancellor@sydney.edu.au (office). *Website:* sydney.edu.au/about/ leadership/vice-chancellor.shtml (office).

SPENCER, (Winston) Baldwin; Antigua and Barbuda politician and trade union official; b. 8 Oct. 1948; m. Jacklyn Spencer; one s. one d.; Leader United Progressive Party; MP (UPP) for St John's Rural West constituency 1989–; fmr Leader of the Opposition; Prime Minister of Antigua and Barbuda 2004–14, also Minister of Foreign Affairs 2005–14. *Leisure interests:* football, cricket, basketball, listening to steel band music, reading, dancing. *Address:* United Progressive Party, Nevis Street, St John's (office); Cooks Estate, St John's, Antigua (home). *Telephone:* 461-4657 (home). *Fax:* 562-1065 (home). *E-mail:* upp@candw.ag (office). *Website:* www.antiguabarbuda.net/pmo (office); www.uppantigua.com (office).

SPENCER, Elizabeth, AB, MA; American writer; b. 19 July 1921, Carrollton, Miss.; d. of James L. Spencer and Mary James McCain; m. John A. B. Rusher 1956 (died 1998); ed Belhaven Coll. and Vanderbilt Univ.; Instructor in English, Northwest Junior Coll. 1943–44, Ward-Belmont School, Nashville, Tenn. 1944–45; reporter, Nashville Tennessean newspaper 1945–46; Instructor in English and Creative Writing, Univ. of Mississippi 1948–51, 1952–53; mem. graduate writing program, Concordia Univ., Montreal, Quebec, Canada Writer-in-Residence, then Adjunct Prof. 1976–86; Visiting Prof. of Creative Writing, Univ. of North Carolina 1986–92; Writer-in-Residence, Bryn Mawr Coll. 1962, Univ. of North Carolina 1969, Hollins Coll. 1972; Vice-Chancellor, Fellowship of Southern Writers 1993–97; mem. American Acad. of Arts and Letters; Hon. LittD (Southwestern Univ., Memphis) 1968, (Concordia Univ.) 1987, (Univ. of the South) 1992, (Univ. of North Carolina) 1998, (Belhaven Coll.) 1999; Recognition Award, American Acad. of Arts and Letters 1952, Guggenheim Foundation Fellow 1953, Rosenthal Foundation Award, American Acad. of Arts and Letters 1957, McGraw-Hill Fiction Award 1960, Award of Merit for short story, American Acad. of Arts and Letters 1983, Salem Award for Literature 1992, John Dos Passos Award for Fiction 1992, North Carolina Gov.'s Award for Literature 1994, Fortner Award for Literature 1998, Mississippi State Library Asscn Award for Non-fiction 1999, Thomas Wolfe Award, Univ. of North Carolina 2002, inducted into North Carolina Hall of Fame 2002, William Faulkner Award for Literary Excellence 2002, Gov.'s Award for Achievement in Literature, Mississippi Arts Comm. 2006, PEN/Malamud Award for Short Fiction 2007, Lifetime Achievement Award, Mississippi Acad. of Arts and Letters 2009, Sidney Lanier Award for Southern Literature 2014, Rea Award for the Short Story 2014. *Film:* Light in the Piazza 1962. *Plays:* For Lease or Sale 1989, The Light in the Piazza (musical drama) 2006. *Publications:* Fire in the Morning 1948, This Crooked Way 1952, The Voice at the Back Door 1956, The Light in the Piazza 1960, Knights and Dragons 1965, No Place for an Angel 1967, Ship Island and Other Stories 1968, The Snare 1972, The Stories of Elizabeth Spencer 1981, Marilee 1981, The Salt Line 1984, Jack of Diamonds and Other Stories 1988, For Lease or Sale (play) 1989, On the Gulf 1991, The Night Travellers 1991, Landscapes of the Heart (memoir) 1998, The Southern Woman: New and Selected Fiction 2000, Starting Over (short stories) 2014; contrib. short stories in magazines

and collections. *Leisure interests:* movies, theatre, travel. *Address:* 402 Longleaf Drive, Chapel Hill, NC 27517, USA (home). *Telephone:* (919) 929-2115 (home). *E-mail:* elizabeth0222@earthlink.net. *Website:* www.elizabethspencerwriter.com.

SPENCER, Octavia L., BS; American actress; b. 25 May 1970, Montgomery, Ala; ed Auburn Univ. *Films include:* A Time to Kill 1996, The Sixth Man 1997, Sparkler 1997, Never Been Kissed 1999, Live Virgin 1999, Being John Malkovich 1999, Blue Streak 1999, Everything Put Together 2000, What Planet Are You From? 2000, Big Momma's House 2000, Four Dogs Playing Poker 2000, The Journeyman 2001, The Sky Is Falling 2001, Spider-Man 2002, Legally Blonde 2: Red, White & Blonde 2003 S.W.A.T. 2003, Sol Goode 2003, Bad Santa 2003, Win a Date with Tad Hamilton! 2004, Breakin' All the Rules 2004, Coach Carter 2005, Pretty Persuasion 2005, Marilyn Hotchkiss' Ballroom Dancing & Charm School 2005, Miss Congeniality 2: Armed and Fabulous 2005, Beauty Shop 2005, Wannabe 2005, Pulse 2006, The Nines 2007, Next of Kin 2008, Pretty Ugly People 2008, Seven Pounds 2008, Love at First Hiccup 2009, Drag Me to Hell 2009, Jesus People: The Movie 2009, The Soloist 2009, Just Peck 2009, Halloween II 2009, Herpes Boy 2009, Small Town Saturday Night 2010, Dinner for Schmucks 2010, Peep World 2010, Girls! Girls! Girls! 2011, Flypaper 2011, The Help (Golden Globe Award for Best Supporting Actress 2012) 2011, Smashed 2012, The Trials and Tribulations of a Trailer Trash Housewife 2012, Lost on Purpose 2012, Snowpiercer 2013, Get On Up 2014, Black or White 2015, The Divergent Series: Insurgent 2015, Fathers and Daughters 2015, Car Dogs 2016, Allegiant 2016, The Great Gilly Hopkins 2016, Zootropolis (voice) 2016, The Free World 2016, Bad Santa 2 2016, Hidden Figures 2016. *Television includes:* Lansky (film) 1999, Missing Pieces (film) 2000, Follow the Stars Home (film) 2001, Little John (film) 2002, Titus (series) 2001-02, NYPD Blue (series) 2002-05, LAX (series) 2004-05, Ugly Betty (series) 2007, Halfway Home (series) 2007, The Minor Accomplishments of Jackie Woodman (series) 2006-07, Raising the Bar (series) 2009, The Looney Tunes Show (series, voice) 2011, Family Practice (film) 2011, Call Me Crazy: A Five Film (film) 2013, Mom (series) 2013–15, Red Band Society (series) 2014–15, Drunk History (series) 2015. *Address:* c/o TalentWorks, 3500 West Olive Avenue, Suite 1400, Burbank, CA 91505, USA (office). *E-mail:* info@talentworks (office). *Website:* www.talentworks.com (office).

SPERBER, Dan; French social sciences researcher; *Researcher, Institut Jean Nicod;* b. 20 June 1942, Cagnes; s. of Manes Sperber; ed Univ. of Paris (Sorbonne), Univ. of Oxford, UK; joined CNRS as Researcher 1965, apptd Dir of Research 1983, then Research Prof. and Researcher, Institut Jean Nicod, now Dir of Research Emer.; Co-f. EURO-EDU Asscn; Visiting Prof., LSE, Van Leer Inst., Jerusalem, Inst. for Advanced Study, Princeton Univ., Univ. of Michigan, Duxx School, Univ. of Hong Kong, Univ. of Cambridge, Univ. of Bologna; Annual Fellow, Templeton Research Lectures, Vanderbilt Univ. 2007–08; Corresp. Fellow, British Acad.; Foreign hon. mem. American Acad. of Arts and Sciences; mem. Academia Europaea; Rivers Memorial Medal, Royal Anthropological Inst. 1991, Claude Lévi-Strauss Prize 2009. *Publications include:* Rethinking Symbolism 1975, On Anthropological Knowledge 1982, Relevance: Communication and Cognition (with Deirdre Wilson) 1986, Explaining Culture 1996. *Address:* Institut Jean Nicod (EHESS/CNRS), 1bis av. Lowendal, 75007 Paris, France. *Telephone:* 1-53-59-32-89 (office). *E-mail:* dan@sperber.com (home). *Website:* www.institutnicod.org (office); www.dan.sperber.fr.

SPERGEL, David Nathaniel, AB, MA, PhD; American astrophysicist and academic; *Professor of Astrophysical Sciences and Chairman, Department of Astrophysical Sciences, Princeton University;* b. 25 March 1961, Rochester, NY; ed John Glenn High School, Huntington, NY, Princeton and Harvard Univs; Visiting Scholar, Univ. of Oxford, UK 1983; Asst Prof., Princeton Univ. 1987–92, Assoc. Prof. 1992–97, Prof. 1997–2007, Charles A. Young Prof. of Astronomy on the Class of 1897 Foundation, Prof. of Astrophysical Sciences 2007–, Chair. Dept of Astrophysical Sciences 2006–, also Assoc. Faculty in Physics and Dept of Mechanical and Aerospace Eng; mem. Inst. for Advanced Study, Princeton, NJ, Keck Distinguished Visiting Prof. 2000–01; Co-founder and Prin. Investigator, Inst. for Physics and Math. of Universe, Univ. of Tokyo, Japan 2007–; Co-Chair. NAS Cttee on Astronomy and Astrophysics, NASA Science Definition Team for NRO 2.4m telescope; fmr Chair. NAS ASTRO 2010 Panel on Cosmology and Fundamental Physics, KITP Advisory Bd, NASA Astrophysics Subcommittee and numerous reviews; mem. NAS 2008; Fellow, American Acad. of Arts and Sciences 2012; Alfred P. Sloan Research Fellow 1988, NSF Presidential Young Investigator Award 1988, Helen B. Warner Prize, American Astronomical Soc. 1994, John T. and Helen D. MacArthur Fellowship 2001, Shaw Prize in Astronomy (co-recipient) 2010, Gruber Prize (as part of WMAP team) 2012, Pres.'s Distinguished Teaching Award 2013. *Publications:* more than 260 papers in peer-reviewed journals. *Address:* Astrophysical Sciences, 113 Peyton Hall, Princeton, NJ 08544, USA (office). *Telephone:* (609) 258-3589 (office). *Fax:* (609) 258-1020 (office). *E-mail:* dns@astro.princeton.edu (office). *Website:* www.princeton.edu/astro (office); www .astro.princeton.edu/~dns (office).

SPERLICH, Peter Werner, PhD; American political scientist, academic and legal consultant; *Professor Emeritus of Political Science and Law, University of California, Berkeley;* b. 27 June 1934, Breslau, Germany (now Wrocław, Poland); s. of Max Otto and Anneliese Gertrud Sperlich (née Greulich); ed Minnesota State Univ. at Mankato, Univ. of Michigan at Ann Arbor; arrived in USA 1956, naturalized 1961; joined Faculty of Univ. of California, Berkeley 1963, apptd Prof. of Political Science 1963, apptd Prof. in Law School 1980, now Prof. Emer.; has served as consultant to courts and law firms; cited by US Supreme Court and various state courts; Social Science Research Council Fellow 1966, Ford Foundation Fellow 1968; mem. American Legal Studies Asscn, Law and Soc. Asscn, Nat. Asscn for Dispute Resolution, Int. Soc. of Political Psychology, Soc. for Psychological Study of Social Issues, American, Int. and Western Political Science Asscns, Conf. Group on German Politics; research on law and politics in USA, Germany, Austria, Denmark, the Netherlands, Switzerland, the UK, Canada, Mexico, the USSR, Japan, Thailand, Hong Kong. *Publications:* Conflict and Harmony in Human Affairs 1971, Single Family Defaults and Foreclosures 1975, Trade Rules and Industry Practices 1976, Over-the-Counter Drug Advertisements 1977, Residing in a Mobile Home 1977, An Evaluation of the Emergency School Aid Act Nonprofit Organization 1978, Rotten Foundations – The Conceptual Basis of the Marxist-Leninist Regimes of East Germany and Other Countries of the Soviet

Bloc 2002, Oppression and Scarcity – The History and Institutional Structure of the Marxist-Leninist Government of East Germany and Some Perspectives on Life in a Socialist System 2006, The East German Social Courts – Law and Popular Justice in a Marxist-Leninist Society 2007; numerous articles, including Easter Explained, in Free Inquiry Feb. 2012. *Address:* Department of Political Science, University of California, 581 Barrows Hall, Berkeley, CA 94720 (office); 35503 Vista del Luna, Rancho Mirage, CA 92270, USA (home). *Telephone:* (760) 770-0899 (office). *E-mail:* pws1934@gmail.com (home); pws34@yahoo.com.

SPERLING, Gene B., BA, JD; American lawyer, economist and government official; *President, Sperling Economic Strategies;* b. 24 Dec. 1958, Ann Arbor, Mich.; m. Allison Abner; two c.; ed Univ. of Minnesota, Yale Law School, Wharton School, Univ. of Pennsylvania; worked for New York Gov. Mario Cuomo 1990s; adviser to Pres. Bill Clinton 1993–2001; Deputy Dir Nat. Econ. Council 1993–96, Dir 1996–2000, 2011–14; Chief Econ. Advisor to Hillary Clinton during her presidential campaign 2008; Counsellor to US Treasury Sec. Tim Geithner 2009–11; f. Sperling Economic Strategies, Consultant, Pacific Investment Management Company, LLC 2015–; Sr Advisor, Renovate America 2015–; Visiting Fellow, Brookings Inst.; contributing ed. and columnist, Bloomberg News; Sr Fellow, Center for American Progress; consultant and contributing writer for NBC's The West Wing (TV series); mem. Council on Foreign Relations 2000–, Sr Fellow for Econ. Policy and Dir Center on Universal Educ.; mem. Bd of Dirs Ripple Labs 2015–; elected mem. Bd of Govs Philadelphia Stock Exchange 2002; fmr advisor to Goldman Sachs. *Publications include:* The Pro-Growth Progressive: An Economic Strategy for Shared Prosperity 2006, What Works In Girls' Education? (co-author) 2007; articles on universal education in Foreign Affairs, The New York Times, The Washington Post, The Los Angeles Times, The Financial Times. *Address:* c/o Pacific Investment Management Company, LLC (PIMCO), 1633 Broadway, New York, NY 10019, USA.

SPETH, James Gustave (Gus), BA, MLitt, JD; American lawyer, scientist and academic; *Co-Founder, New Economy Law Center, Vermont Law School;* b. 4 March 1942, Orangeburg, South Carolina; s. of James Gustave and Amelia St Clair Albergotti; m. Caroline Cameron Council 1964; two s. one d.; ed Yale Univ., Univ. of Oxford, UK (Rhodes Scholar); barrister, Washington, DC 1969, Clerk, Supreme Court 1969–70; Sr Staff Attorney, Nat. Resources Defence Council, Washington, DC 1977–79, mem. Bd of Dirs 1981–82, now Trustee; Chair. Council for Environmental Quality 1977–79; Prof. of Law, Georgetown Univ. 1981–82; Pres. and Founder World Resources Inst. 1982–93; joined UNDP 1982, Admin. 1993–99; Carl W. Knobloch, Jr Dean of the School of Forestry and Environmental Studies and Sara Shallenberger Brown Prof. in the Practice of Environmental Policy, Yale Univ. 1999–2009; Co-Founder, New Economy Law Center, Vermont Law School 2009–; Founder and Trustee Emer., World Resources Inst.; mem. Bd of Dirs Center for Humans and Nature, World Resources Inst., Population Action International; Trustee, Rockefeller Brothers Fund; mem. India Council for Sustainable Devt; Hon. DIur (Clark Univ.) 1995, Vermont Law School 2005; Hon. Master of Philosophy (Coll. of the Atlantic) 2001; Hon. DS (Middlebury Coll.) 2007; Hon. DHumLitt (Univ. of South Carolina 2008); Resource Defense Award, Nat. Wildlife Fed. 1975, Nat. Leadership Award, Keystone Center 1991, Barbara Swain Award, Nat. Resources Council of America 1992, Special Recognition Award, Soc. for Int. Devt 1997, Special Leadership Award, Alliance for UN Sustainable Devt Programs 1998, Lifetime Achievement Award, Environmental Law Inst. 1999, Blue Planet Prize 2002, Global Environmental Award, Int. Asscn for Impact Assessment 2005, DeVane Lecturer, Yale Univ. 2007. *Publications include:* Worlds Apart: Globalization and the Environment 2003, Red Sky at Morning: America and the Crisis of the Global Environment 2004, Global Environmental Governance (with Peter Haas) 2006, The Bridge at the Edge of the World: Capitalism, the Environment, and Crossing from Crisis to Sustainability 2008, Angels by the River (memoir) 2014. *Address:* Vermont Law School, 164 Chelsea Street, PO Box 96, South Royalton, VT 05068 (office); 986 Forest Road, New Haven, CT 06515, USA (home). *Telephone:* (802) 831-1192 (office). *E-mail:* GSPETH@vermontlaw.edu (office). *Website:* www.vermontlaw.edu (office).

SPICER, Sean Michael, BA, MA; American political adviser and government official; b. 23 Sept. 1971, Barrington, Rhode Island; s. of Michael Spicer and Kathryn Spicer (née Grossman); m. Rebecca Spicer; two c.; ed Connecticut Coll., Naval War Coll.; joined USN Reserves 1999 (attained rank of Commdr); Dir of Incumbent Retention, Nat. Republican Congressional Cttee 2000–02; Communications Dir, House of Reps Budget Cttee 2002–05; Communications Dir, Republican Conf., House of Reps 2005–06; Asst US Trade Rep. for Media, The White House 2006–09; Partner, Endeavour Global Strategies 2009–11; Communications Dir, Republican Nat. Cttee 2011–, Chief Strategist 2015–; White House Press Sec. and Dir of Communications Jan.–Aug. 2017.

ŠPIDLA, Vladimír, PhDr; Czech think-tank director and fmr politician; b. 22 April 1951, Prague; s. of Václav Špidla and Dagmar Špidlová; m. 1st; two s.; m. 2nd Viktorie Špidlová; one s. one d.; ed Charles Univ., Prague; fmr archaeologist, worker at historical monuments, sawmill, dairy and livestock industry; Vice-Pres. for Educ., Health Service, Social Affairs and Culture, Dist Cttee, Jindřichův Hradec 1990–91; Dir Labour Office, Jindřichův Hradec 1991–96; mem. Chamber of Deputies 1996–2004; Deputy Prime Minister and Minister of Labour and Social Affairs 1998–2002; Prime Minister of the Czech Repub. 2002–04 (resgnd); EU Commr for Employment, Social Affairs and Equal Opportunities 2004–10; Pres. Masaryk Democratic Academy (Masarykova demokratická akademie) (think-tank) 2011; Founding mem. Czech Social Democratic Party Br. in S Bohemia 1989, joined party leadership 1992, Vice-Chair. 1997–2001, Chair. 2001–04; Chief Adviser to Prime Minister 2014–17. *Leisure interests:* jogging, poetry, sports in nature, cross-country running, history and prehistory. *Address:* Hybernská 1033/7, 110 00 Prague 1, Czech Republic (office). *E-mail:* kontakt@vladimirspidla.cz (office). *Website:* www.vladimirspidla.cz (office).

SPIEGLER, Marc, MJ; American/French journalist; *Global Director, Art Basel;* b. 1968, Chicago, IL; m.; ed Haverford Coll., Northwestern Univ.; Research Assoc. Daniel Yankelovich Group 1990–92; Sr Ed., NewCity Chicago 1994–96, Chicago Magazine 1996–98; worked as a journalist in Chicago; moved to Switzerland 1998, freelance art journalist and columnist writing for magazines and newspapers including The Art Newspaper, Monopol, Art and Auction Magazine, ARTnews Magazine, Artworld Salon, Neue Zürcher Zeitung, New York Magazine; Dir of Strategy and Devt, Art Basel 2007–08, Co-Dir 2008–12, Global Dir 2012–. *Address:* Art Basel, c/o MCH Swiss Exhibition (Basel) Ltd, Messeplatz 10, 4005 Basel, Switzerland (office). *Telephone:* (58) 2062728 (office). *E-mail:* infoinfo@mch-group.com (office); homepage@marcspiegler.com. *Website:* www.artbasel.com (office); www.mch-group.com (office); www.marcspiegler.com.

SPIELBERG, Steven, BA; American film director and producer; *Chairman and CEO, Amblin Partners;* b. 18 Dec. 1947, Cincinnati, Ohio; s. of Arnold Spielberg and Leah Spielberg (née Posner); m. 1st Amy Irving 1985 (divorced 1989); two s.; m. 2nd Kate Capshaw; two d. (one adopted); ed California State Coll., Long Beach; won film contest with war film Escape to Nowhere 1961; dir episodes of TV series, including Night Gallery, Marcus Welby, MD, Columbo; directed 20-minute short Amblin'; dir TV films Duel 1971, Something Evil 1972; Co-founder and Partner, Dreamworks SKG 1995–2005; f. USC Shoah Foundation 1994; Co-founder and Chair. Emer. Starlight Foundation; Artistic Adviser, 2008 Olympic Games in Beijing 2007–08 (resgnd); Chair. Amblin Partners 2015–, CEO 2017–; Hon. KBE (UK), Grosses Bundesverdienstkreuz 1998, Knight Grand Cross, Order of Merit of the Italian Repub. 2003, Legion d'honneur 2004; Dr hc (Univ. of Southern California) 1994, Hon. DLitt (Sussex) 1997; Directors Guild of America Award Fellowship 1986, Irving G. Thalberg Award 1987, Golden Lion Award (Venice Film Festival) 1993, BAFTA Award 1994, Acad. Award for Schindler's List 1994, David Lean (BAFTA), John Huston Award for Artists Rights 1995, American Film Inst. Lifetime Achievement Award 1995, James Smithson Bicentennial Medal 1999, Lifetime Achievement Award, Dir's Guild of America 1999, Britannia Award 2000, Lifetime Achievement Award, David di Donatello Awards 2004, Kennedy Center Honor 2006, Golden Globe Cecil B. DeMille Award 2009, Philadelphia Liberty Medal 2009, Presidential Medal of Freedom 2015. *Films directed include:* The Sugarland Express 1974, Jaws 1975, Close Encounters of the Third Kind 1977, 1941 1979, Indiana Jones and the Raiders of the Lost Ark 1981, E.T.: The Extra-Terrestrial 1982, Twilight Zone: The Movie (segment 2) 1983, Indiana Jones and the Temple of Doom 1984, The Color Purple (also producer) 1985, Empire of the Sun 1987, Indiana Jones and the Last Crusade 1989, always 1989, The Visionary (video) (segment 'Par for the Course') 1990, Hook 1991, Jurassic Park 1993, Schindler's List 1993 (Acad. Award for Best Dir 1994, Golden Globe for Best Dir 1994), The Lost World: Jurassic Park 1997, Amistad 1997, Saving Private Ryan 1998 (Acad. Award for Best Dir 1999), The Unfinished Journey (documentary short) 1999, AI: Artificial Intelligence 2001, Minority Report 2002, Catch Me If You Can 2002, The Terminal 2004, War of the Worlds 2005, Munich 2005, Indiana Jones and the Kingdom of the Crystal Skull 2008, A Timeless Call (documentary short) 2008, The Adventures of Tintin: Secret of the Unicorn (also producer) (Golden Globe Award for Best Animated Feature Film 2012) 2011, War Horse (also producer) 2011, Lincoln (also producer) 2012, Bridge of Spies (also producer) 2015. *Films produced include:* I Wanna Hold Your Hand 1978, Poltergeist (co-writer) 1982, Gremlins 1984, Young Sherlock Holmes (exec. producer) 1985, Back to the Future (co-exec. producer), The Goonies (writer and exec. producer) 1986, Batteries Not Included (exec. producer) 1986, The Money Pit (co-produced) 1986, An American Tail (co-exec. producer) 1986, Always 1989, Gremlins II (exec. producer), Dad (exec. producer), Joe versus the Volcano (exec. producer), Cape Fear (co-exec. producer) 1992, Casper 1995, Twister 1996, Deep Impact 1998, Eyes of the Holocaust (documentary) 2000, Shrek (uncredited) 2001, Evolution (uncredited) 2001, Jurassic Park III 2001, Men in Black II 2002, The Legend of Zorro 2005, Memoirs of a Geisha 2005, Monster House 2006, Spell Your Name (documentary) 2006, Flags of Our Fathers 2006, Letters from Iwo Jima 2006, Eagle Eye 2008, Transformers: Revenge of the Fallen 2009, The Lovely Bones 2009, Hereafter 2010, True Grit 2010, Super 8 2011, Transformers: Dark of the Moon 2011, Cowboys & Aliens 2011, Real Steel 2011, Transformers: The Ride – 3D 2011, War Horse 2011, Men in Black III 2012, Delivery Man 2013, Jurassic World 2015, Transformers: The Last Knight 2017. *Television includes:* Night Gallery (series) 1969–71, Marcus Welby, M.D. (series) 1970, The Name of the Game (series) 1971, The Psychiatrist (series) 1971, Columbo (series) 1971, Owen Marshall: Counselor at Law (series) 1971, Duel (film) 1971, Something Evil (film) 1972, Savage (film) 1973, Strokes of Genius (mini-series) (introductory segments, uncredited) 1984, Amazing Stories (series) 1985, Some Mother's Son 1996, Band of Brothers (mini-series) 2001, Semper Fi 2000, We Stand Alone Together (documentary) 2001, Broken Silence (mini-series documentary) 2002, Taken (mini-series) 2002, Burma Bridge Busters (documentary) 2003, Dan Finnerty & the Dan Band: I Am Woman (film) 2005, Into the West (mini-series) 2005, On the Lot (series) 2007, United States of Tara (series) 2009–11, The Pacific (mini-series) 2010, Locke & Key (film) (also exec. producer) 2011, Rising: Rebuilding Ground Zero (series documentary) 2011, Falling Skies (series) 2011, Terra Nova (series) 2011, Smash (series) 2012–13, The River (series) 2012, Smash (series) 2012–13, Under the Dome (series) 2013–15, Extant (series) 2014–15, Public Morals (series) 2015, Bull (series) 2016–17. *Publication:* Close Encounters of the Third Kind (with Patrick Mann). *Address:* c/o Creative Artists Agency, 2000 Avenue of the Stars, Los Angeles, CA 90067, USA (office). *Telephone:* (424) 288-2000 (office). *Fax:* (424) 288-2900 (office). *Website:* www.caa.com (office); www.amblinpartners.com.

SPIELMAN, Daniel Alan, BA, PhD; American computer scientist and academic; *Sterling Professor of Computer Science, Yale University;* b. March 1970, Philadelphia, PA; ed Yale Univ., Massachusetts Inst. of Tech.; NSF Math. Sciences Postdoctoral Researcher, Div. of Computer Science, Univ. of California 1995–96; Asst Prof. of Applied Math., MIT 1996–2002, Assoc. Prof. 2002–05; Sterling Prof. of Computer Science, Yale Univ. 2005–, Chair. and Prof. of Statistics and Data Science 2005–, Prof. of Math. and Applied Math. 2005–; Assoc. Ed. SIAM Journal on Discrete Mathematics 2009–12; mem. Gödel Prize Cttee 2012–14; mem. Editorial Bd, Theory of Computing; mem. Connecticut Acad. of Science and Eng 2012, NAS 2017–; Fellow, Asscn for Computing Machinery (ACM) 2010; Best Student Paper at 26th ACM Symposium on Theory of Computing 1994, at 27th ACM Symposium on Theory of Computing 1995, MIT Lab. for Computer Science Thesis Award 1995, ACM Doctoral Dissertation Award 1995, NSF Career Award 1997, Alfred P. Sloan Foundation Research Fellowship 1998, Invited Speaker, Int. Congress of Mathematicians 2002, 2010, 2014, IEEE Information Theory Soc. Paper Award 2002, Gödel Prize, ACM and European Asscn for Theoretical Computer Science 2008, 2015, Fulkerson Prize, American Math. Soc. and Math. Programming Soc. 2009, Rolf Nevanlinna Prize, Int. Math. Union 2010, Best Paper at 43rd ACM Symposium on Theory of Computing 2011, Best Paper at 25th Conf.

on Learning Theory 2012, Simons Investigator 2012, MacArthur Fellowship 2012, Yale Science and Eng Asscn Award for Advancement of Basic and Applied Science 2013, Best Paper at 54th Annual IEEE Symposium on Foundations of Computer Science 2013, George Pólya Prize in Math. SIAM 2014. *Publications:* numerous papers in professional journals; five US patents. *Address:* Yale Institute for Network Science, PO Box 208263, 17 Hillhouse Ave, Room 340, New Haven, CT 06520-8263, USA (office). *Telephone:* (203) 436-1264 (office). *Fax:* (203) 432-0593 (office). *E-mail:* spielman@cs.yale.edu (office). *Website:* www.cs.yale.edu (office); www.cs.yale.edu/homes/spielman (office).

SPIELVOGEL, Carl, BA; American advertising executive; b. 27 Dec. 1928, New York City; s. of Joseph Spielvogel and Sadie Spielvogel (née Tellerman); m. Barbara Lee Diamonstein 1981; two s. one d.; ed Baruch Coll.; reporter and columnist, New York Times 1950–60; with McCann Erickson, Inc., Interpublic Group of Cos, Inc., New York City 1960–74; Vice-Chair., Chair. Exec. Cttee and Dir Interpublic Group of Cos, Inc. 1974–80; Chair. and CEO Backer & Spielvogel Inc. 1980–87, Backer Spielvogel Bates Worldwide Inc. New York 1987–94; Chair., CEO United Auto Group 1994–97, Consultant –2000; Amb. to the Slovak Repub. 2000–01; Chair. and CEO Carl Spielvogel Assocs Inc., New York 2001–14; mem. Bd of Dirs Apollo Investors Inc., Data Broadcasting Corpn (now Interactive Data Corpn) 1996–2000, 2001–, Asia Soc., Columbia Univ. Institute for Study of Europe; fmr mem. Bd of Dirs Hasbro Inc., Barney's Inc.; Chair. Cttee Div., WNET-Public Broadcasting, Business Cttee; Trustee, State Univ. of New York 2008–, Metropolitan Museum of Art, Lincoln Center for the Performing Arts; fmr Trustee Mount Sinai Hosp., Philharmonic Symphony Soc. of New York; mem. Council on Foreign Relations; mem. Exec. Cttee Council of American Ambs; fmr Fellow, John F. Kennedy School of Govt, Harvard Univ.

SPIERKEL, Gregory M. E., BA, MBA; American electronics industry executive; ed Carleton Univ., Canada, Georgetown Univ., Institut Européen d'Admin des Affaires (INSEAD), France; Man. Dir Mitel Telecom, UK 1986–89, Gen. Man. for Far East, Hong Kong 1989–90, Pres. Mitel Inc., USA 1992–96, Vice-Pres. Global Sales and Marketing 1996–97; Pres. Ingram Micro Asia-Pacific 1997–99, Exec. Vice-Pres. Ingram Micro Inc. and Pres. Ingram Micro Europe 1999–2004, Corp. Pres. Ingram Micro Inc. 2004–05, CEO 2005–12; mem. Bd Dirs PACCAR Inc. 2008–, MGM Resorts International 2013–, Schneider Electric (Paris) 2014–; mem. Dean's Advisory Bd School of Business, Univ. of California, Irvine; mem. Bd of Counselors, George L. Argyros School of Business, Chapman Univ., Orange, Calif.

SPIERS, Hon. Ronald Ian, BA, MPA; American diplomatist (retd); b. 9 July 1925, Orange, NJ; s. of Tomas Hoskins Spiers and Blanca Spiers (née De Ponthier); m. Patience Baker 1949; one s. three d.; ed Dartmouth Coll., Princeton Univ.; USN 1943–46; mem. US Del. to UN 1955–58; Dir Disarmament Affairs, State Dept, Washington 1958–62, NATO Affairs 1962–66; Political Counsellor, Embassy in London 1966–69, Minister 1974–77; Asst Sec. of State for Political-Mil. Affairs 1969–73; Amb. to the Bahamas 1973–74, to Turkey 1977–80; Asst Sec. for Intelligence and Research, Dept of State 1980–81; Amb. to Pakistan 1981–83; Under-Sec. for Man., Dept of State 1983–89; Under-Sec.-Gen. for Political and Gen. Ass. Affairs, UN, New York 1989–92; apptd consultant to State Dept 1992; mem. Council on Foreign Relations; Fellow, Nat. Acad. of Public Admin., American Acad. of Diplomacy; Presidential Distinguished Service Award 1984, 1986, Presidentially conferred with Rank of Career Amb. 1984, Woodrow Wilson Fellowship, Princeton Univ. *Leisure interests:* gardening, furniture making, classical music, opera. *Address:* 5 Timber Lane, Apt 312, Exeter, NH 03833, USA. *Telephone:* (603) 658-7069. *E-mail:* spiersronald1@gmail.com.

SPILIOTOPOULOS, Spilios P., LLM, MPhil; Greek politician and fmr air force pilot; b. 31 Oct. 1946, Pyrgos; m. Maria Tsouni; one d.; ed Univ. of Athens, Hellenic Air Force Acad., Inst. of S Florida, USA; mil. service with air force, becoming Aide de Camp to Pres. Constantine Caramanlis 1980–85, retd from air force with rank of Lt-Col; mem. Parl. (Nea Demokratia Party, NDP) for Achaia Dist 1989–2007; Deputy Minister for Nat. Defence 1992–93, also Deputy Sec.-Gen., NPD Parl. Ass. and mem. Educational Affairs Parl. Cttee, Foreign Affairs and Defence Parl. Cttee, Inter-parl. Cttee of Greece-Cyprus, Minister of Nat. Defence 2004–06, Chair. NDP Nat. Defence Cttee, NDP Political Council; fmr Dir Foundation of Political Studies and Educ.; fmr Head, Greek Del. to N Atlantic Ass. and mem. Political Cttee; fmr mem. Ass. WEU, OSCE, Org. for Black Sea Econ. Co-operation, Special Mediterranean Group; Grand Decoration of Honour in Silver (Austria), Commdr, Order of Merit (Cyprus, Egypt, Italy), Chevalier, Légion d'honneur, Commdr, Order of Merit and Golden Cross of Honour (Greece), Commdr, Mil. Order of Aviz (Portugal); First Air Acad. Graduation Award. *Publication:* Responsibilities of the National Air Carrier 1985; several articles. *Leisure interests:* sailing, sports, music. *Address:* 18 Dimikritoy str., 10673, Athens, Greece. *E-mail:* info@e-spilios.gr. *Website:* www.e-spilios.gr.

SPINDELEGGER, Michael, Dr iur.; Austrian politician; b. 21 Dec. 1959, Mödling; m.; two c.; ed Univ. of Vienna; Asst Lecturer and Researcher, Inst. of Criminal Law, Univ. of Vienna 1982–83; Judges' Asst at several Courts of Law in Vienna 1983–84; civil servant, Fed. State Lower Austria 1984–87; mem. Cabinet of the Minister of Defence 1987–90; employed within the Secr. of the Bd, Strategic Man., GiroCredit (Austrian bank) 1993–94; speaker on European Relations, Employees' Asscn of the Austrian People's Party (ÖAAB) 1989–91, apptd Deputy Head ÖAAB 1991; mem. Fed. Chamber, Austrian Parl. 1992–93; mem. Nat. Ass. 1993–95; MEP (ÖVP-EVP), mem. of Parl. Cttee on Econs, Currency Issues and Industrial Policy, Deputy mem. Cttee for Social Issues and Employment 1995–96; ÖAAB Speaker on Foreign Affairs and Head of Parl. Cttee on Foreign Affairs 1996–2006; apptd Chair. NÖAAB (ÖAAB of Lower Austria) 1998; mem. Parl. Ass., Council of Europe 2000–07; Deputy Parl. Group Leader of the Austrian Peoples Party 2000–06; Head of the Austrian Del. to the Parl. Ass. of the Council of Europe 2002–06; Second Pres. Austrian Nat. Council 2006–08; Fed. Minister for European and Int. Affairs 2008–13, Vice-Chancellor 2011–14, Fed. Minister for Finance 2013–14; Leader, Austrian People's Party 2011–14; Grand Decoration of Honour in Silver with Star 2004, Grand Decoration of Honour in Gold with Sash 2011. *Address:* c/o Federal Ministry of Finance, Johannesgasse 5, 1010 Vienna, Austria. *E-mail:* buergerservice@bmf.gv.at.

SPINETTA, Jean-Cyril, LLB, BSc; French airline executive; *Honorary Chairman, Air France-KLM Group;* b. 4 Oct. 1943, Paris; s. of Adrien Spinetta and Antoinette Brignoll; m. Nicole Spinetta (née Ricquebourg); two s. two d.; ed Lycée Hoche, Versailles, Faculty of Law, Univ. of Paris, Institut d'études politiques (Sciences Po), Ecole nationale d'admin, Paris; teacher 1961–70; with Ecole nationale d'admin 1970–72; entered French civil service 1972, Head of Investments and Planning Dept, Ministry of Educ. 1972–76, seconded to Conseil d'Etat as Auditor 1976–78; served as Govt's Gen. Secr. 1978–81; Head of Information Dept, Office of Prime Minister Pierre Mauroy 1981–83; Dir, Ministry of Educ. 1983–84; Chief of Staff for Michel Delebarre 1984–90; successively Minister of Labour and Vocational Training, Minister of Social Affairs and Employment and Minister of Planning and Devt, Housing and Transport; joined Air Inter 1990, Pres. and CEO 1990–93; advisory posts to Pres. of France (including industrial matters) 1993–95; Admin. in charge of Public Service 1995–96; joined staff of Edith Cresson, European Commr for Science, Research and Educ. 1996–97; Chair. and CEO Air France SA 1997–2008, Chair. 2009–11, Chair. and CEO Air France-KLM Group 2004–08, 2011–13, Chair. 2009–11, Hon. Chair. 2013–; Chair. Asscn European Airlines 2001–, Scientific Council, Inst. of Public Admin and Econ. Devt 2002–, Bd of Govs IATA 2004–05; Chair. Supervisory Bd Areva SA 2009–13; Dir (non-exec.) CNES 2002–, Unilever PLC and Unilever NV 2006–07; mem. Bd of Dirs Saint-Gobain 2005–13, Alcatel Lucent 2006–16, Alitalia-Linee Aeree Italiane SpA –2007, GDF Suez 2008, Le Monde Entreprises, Gaz de France SA; Officier, Ordre des Palmes Académiques; Commdr, Ordre nat. du Mérite, Légion d'honneur; Commdr, Order of Orange-Nassau (Netherlands). *Leisure interests:* tennis, skiing. *Address:* Groupe Air France, 45 rue de Paris, 95747 Roissy CDG Cedex, France (office). *Telephone:* 1-41-56-61-65 (office). *Fax:* 1-41-56-61-59 (office). *E-mail:* mail .airfranceklmfinance@airfrance.fr (office). *Website:* www.airfrance.com (office).

ŠPIRIĆ, Nikola, PhD; Bosnia and Herzegovina professor of economics and politician; b. 4 Sept. 1956, Drvar; m.; two c.; ed Univ. of Sarajevo; fmr Pres. Democratic Party for Banja Luka and Krajina; currently mem. Alliance of Ind. Social Democrats (SNSD); Prof. of Econs, Univ. of Banja Luka 1992–; mem. Parl. in House of Reps of Parl. Ass. of Bosnia and Herzegovina 1999–2000; Deputy Minister of Human Rights and Refugees, Council of Ministers of Bosnia and Herzegovina 2000; Chair. House of Peoples of Parl. Ass. of Bosnia and Herzegovina 2001–02; Chair./Deputy Chair. House of Reps 2002–06; Chair. State Council of Ministers (Prime Minister) Jan.–Nov. 2007 (resgnd), Dec. 2007–12; Minister of Finance and the Treasury 2012–15. *Address:* c/o Ministry of Finance and the Treasury, 71000 Sarajevo, trg Bosne i Hercegovine 1, Bosnia and Herzegovina.

SPIRIN, Aleksandr Sergeyevich, PhD, DSc; Russian biochemist and molecular biologist; b. 4 Sept. 1931, Kaliningrad (now Korolev), Moscow Region; s. of Sergey Stepanovitch Spirin and Elena Abramovna Spirina (née Kalabekova); m. Tatiana Nikolayevna Fokina; ed Moscow State Univ.; mem. staff, Bakh Inst. of Biochemistry 1958–62, Head of Lab. 1962–73; Prof., Moscow State Univ. 1964–92, Prof. Emer. 1992–, Prof. and Chair of Molecular Biology 1973–; Head of Lab. of Protein Biosynthesis Mechanisms, Inst. of Protein Research 1967, Dir Inst. 1967–2001; Chair. Bd Pushchino Scientific Centre 1990–2000; Corresp. mem. USSR (now Russian) Acad. of Sciences 1966–70, mem. 1970–, mem. Presidium 1988–2001, Adviser Presidium 2001–; mem. Deutsche Akad. der Naturforscher Leopoldina (now German Nat. Acad. of Sciences) 1974, Czechoslovak Acad. of Sciences 1988, Academia Europaea 1990, European Molecular Biology Org. 1991, Royal Physiographic Soc. (Lund) 1996, American Philosophical Soc. 1997, AAAS 1997, American Soc. for Biochemistry and Molecular Biology 2003; Two Orders of Lenin and other decorations; Dr hc (Granada) 1972, (Toulouse) 1999; Sir Hans Krebs Medal 1969, Lenin Prize 1976, State Prize of the USSR for Science 1988, Ovchinnikov Prize, Russian Acad. of Science 1992, Karpinskij Prize of FVS for Achievements in Science (Hamburg) 1992, State Prize of Russian Fed. for Science 2000, Belozersky Prize, Russian Acad. of Sciences 2000, Big Gold Lomonosov Medal, Russian Acad. of Sciences 2001, Science Prize, Russian Ind. Charity Foundation 'Triumph' 2005. *Publications include:* Macromolecular Structure of Ribonucleic Acids 1964, The Ribosome 1969, Ribosome Structure and Protein Biosynthesis 1986, Ribosomes 1999, Cell-Free Translation Systems (ed.) 2002. *Leisure interests:* hunting, breeding cats. *Address:* Institute of Protein Research, Russian Academy of Sciences, 142290 Pushchino, Moscow Region, Russia (office). *Telephone:* (495) 632-78-71 (office); (499) 137-39-20 (home). *Fax:* (495) 632-78-71 (office). *E-mail:* spirin@vega.protres.ru (office). *Website:* www.protres.ru (office); spirin.protres.ru (office).

SPITLER, Kenneth F., BA; American business executive (retd); b. 1949; ed Univ. of Tulsa; Pres. White Swan Food Service 1973–83; joined SYSCO Corpn 1986, Exec. Vice-Pres., Dallas 1986–92, Pres., Detroit 1992–95, Pres. and CEO, Houston 1995–2000, Sr Vice-Pres. of Operations, NE Region 2000–02, Exec. Vice-Pres. Redistribution and NE Region 2002–02, Exec. Vice-Pres. Foodservice Operations 2002–05, Exec. Vice-Pres. and Pres. N American Foodservice Operations 2005–07, Pres. and CEO 2007–09, Vice-Chair., Pres. and COO 2009–10; Exec. Advisor, Grocer's Supply 2013–14.

SPITZ, Lewis, MB ChB, PhD, FRCS, FRCSE; British paediatric surgeon and academic; *Nuffield Professor Emeritus of Paediatric Surgery, Institute of Child Health, University College London;* b. 25 Aug. 1939, Pretoria, S Africa; s. of Woolf Spitz and Selma Spitz; m.; one s. one d.; ed Univ. of Pretoria, Univ. of the Witwatersrand; Consultant Paediatric Surgeon, Sheffield 1974–79; Nuffield Prof. of Paediatric Surgery, Inst. of Child Health, University Coll. London 1979–2004, Nuffield Prof. Emer. of Paediatric Surgery 2004–; Consultant Paediatric Surgeon, Great Ormond St Hosp. for Children, London 1979–2006; Hunterian Prof., Royal Coll. of Surgeons (England) 2001–02; Hon. Fellow, Inst. of Child Health, American Acad. of Pediatrics, Royal Coll. of Surgeons in Ireland, Coll. of Medicine, SA, Royal Coll. of Paediatrics and Child Health, American Coll. of Surgeons; Hon. MD (Sheffield) 2002, (Univ. of the Witwatersrand, South Africa) 2008; James Spence Medal, Royal Coll. of Paediatrics 2004, Clement-Price Thomas Award, Royal Coll. of Surgeons (England) 2004, Denis Browne Gold Medal, British Asscn of Paediatric Surgeons 2004, Rehbein Medal, German Asscn of Pediatric Surgeons, Rehbein Medal, European Asscn of Pediatric Surgeons, Ladd Medal, American Acad. of Pediatrics, Sulama Medal, Rickham Medal. *Publications:* Paediatric Surgical Diagnosis (co-ed.) 1981, Pediatric Surgery (co-ed.) 1995 (revised edn 2013), Great Ormond Street (co-ed.) 2007, Handbook of Paediatrics and Child Health: Papers on Oesophageal Atresia and Replacement and Conjoined Twins, Neonatal Surgery, Psychological Effects of Neonatal Surgery (co-ed., revised edn) 2016. *Leisure* *interests:* sport, books, food, drink, theatre. *Address:* Institute of Child Health, 30 Guilford Street, London, WC1N 1EH (office); Flat 2 Roseneath Mansions, Woodside Square, 59 Woodside Avenue, London, N10 3JA, England (home). *Telephone:* (20) 8444-9985 (home). *E-mail:* l.spitz@ucl.ac.uk (office).

SPITZ, Mark (Andrew); American fmr swimmer; b. 10 Feb. 1950, Modesto, Calif.; s. of Arnold Spitz; m. Suzy Weiner; two s.; ed Indiana Univ.; won two gold medals in the team relay races (4×100m and 4×200m), Olympic Games, Mexico City 1968; became first athlete to win seven gold medals in a single Olympic Games, Munich 1972, in the 100m and 200m freestyle, 100m and 200m butterfly and as a team mem. of the 4×100m relay, 4×200m relay and 4×100m medley relay (all world records); unsuccessful comeback 1991; corporate spokesman, TV broadcaster, real-estate co. owner, now works as stock broker; mem. Int. Swimming Hall of Fame Selection Cttee; World Swimmer of the Year 1969, 1971, 1972, James E. Sullivan Award (for America's Outstanding Amateur Athlete) 1971, Associated Press Male Athlete of the Year 1972, Athlete of the Century (Water Sports) 1999; mem. Laureus World Sports Acad. *Leisure interests:* sailing, travel. *Address:* Premier Management Group, LLC, 200 Merry Hill Drive, Cary, NC 27511, USA (office). *Website:* www.markspitzusa.com.

SPITZER, Eliot Laurence, BA, JD; American lawyer, broadcaster, fmr government official and fmr politician; b. 10 June 1959, New York; s. of Bernard Spitzer; m. Silda Spitzer (née Wall) (divorced 2014); three d.; ed Princeton Univ. and Harvard Law School; fmr Ed. Harvard Law Review; Law Clerk for Hon. Robert W. Sweet, US Dist Court, Southern Dist of New York 1984–85; Assoc. Paul Weiss, Rifkind, Wharton & Garrison 1985–86; Asst Dist Attorney, Manhattan 1986–92, Chief Labor Racketeering Unit 1991–92; Assoc. Skadden, Arps, Slate, Meagher & Flom 1992–94; Pnr, Constantine & Partners 1994–98; Attorney-Gen. of State of New York 1999–2007; columnist, Slate (online magazine) 2008–; Gov. of New York 2007–08 (resgnd); adjunct faculty mem. CUNY 2009–; Host, CNN's In the Arena (fmrly Parker Spitzer) 2010–11; Host, Viewpoint with Eliot Spitzer (Currrent TV) 2012–13; unsuccessful cand. for New York City Comptroller 2013; Head, real estate agency Spitzer Engineering LLC (upon death of his father), New York 2014–; mem. Bd of Dirs TipRanks Ltd; Democrat; Paul H. Douglas Ethics in Govt Award, Univ. of Illinois 2004, Jacob J. Javits Public Service Award, American Psychiatric Asscn 2005. *Address:* Spitzer Engineering LLC, 730 5th Avenue, Suite 2202, New York, NY 10019-4105, USA (office).

SPIVAK, Gayatri Chakravorty, MA, PhD; Indian literary theorist, academic and rural literacy and ecological agriculture activist; *University Professor, Columbia University;* b. 24 Feb. 1942, Kolkata; d. of Pares Chandra Chakravorty and Sivani Chakravorty; m. 1st Talbot Spivak (divorced); m. 2nd Basudeb Chatterji (divorced); ed Univ. of Calcutta, Univ. of Cambridge, Cornell Univ.; Asst Prof., then Prof. of Comparative Literature, Iowa Univ. 1965–77; Prof., Univ. of Texas 1978–83; Longstreet Prof. of English, Emory Univ. 1983–86; Andrew W. Mellon Prof. of English, Univ. of Pittsburgh 1986–91; Avalon Foundation Prof. in the Humanities, Columbia Univ., New York 1991–2007, Univ. Prof. 2007–, Dir Inst. for Comparative Literature and Soc. 2002–08; Visiting Prof., Brown Univ., Univ. of Texas, Univ. of California, Santa Cruz, Berkeley, Irvine, Université Paul Valery, Jawaharlal Nehru Univ., Stanford Univ., Univ. of British Columbia, Goethe Inst., Frankfurt, Riydah Univ.; Y.K. Pao Distinguished Visiting Prof. in Cultural Studies, Hong Kong Univ. of Science and Tech. 2001; translated the work of French philosopher Jacques Derrida 1976, Bengali writer Mahasweta Devi 2003; Distinguished Faculty Fellow, Maharaja Sayajirao Univ. of Baroda, India; fmr Fellow, Nat. Humanities Inst., Center for the Humanities at Wesleyan, Humanities Research Center, ANU, Canberra, Australia, Centre for the Study of the Social Sciences, Kolkata, Davis Center for Historial Studies, Princeton Univ., Rockefeller Foundation, Bellagio, Guggenheim Foundation; mem. Editorial Bd Cultural Critique, Diaspora, ARIEL, Re-thinking Marxism, Public Culture, Parallax, Interventions, etc.; mem. Global Agenda Council on Values, World Econ. Forum; Chevalier de l'Ordre des Arts et des Lettres 2016; Hon. PhD (Univ. of Toronto) 2000, (Univ. of London) 2003, Hon. DH (Oberlin Coll.) 2008, (Yale) 2015, Dr hc (Univ. Roveri) 2011, (Rabindra Bharati) 2012, (Univ. Nacional de San Martin) 2013, (Paris VIII) 2014, (Univ. de Chile) 2016, Hon. DLitt (St Andrews) 2014, (Ghana-Legon) 2015; India 1997, Kyoto Prize in Thought and Ethics 2012, Padma Bhushan 2013, Lifetime Scholarly Achievement Award, Modern Language Asscn 2018, Guggenheim Fellowship, Sahitya Akademi Translation Prize. *Publications include:* Myself I Must Remake: The Life and Poetry of W. B. Yeats 1974, Of Grammatology (trans. of Jacques Derrida) 1976, In Other Worlds: Essays in Cultural Politics 1987, Selected Subaltern Studies (co-ed.) 1988, The Post-Colonial Critic: Interviews, Strategies, Dialogues 1990, Outside in the Teaching Machine 1993, The Spivak Reader 1996, Don't Call Me Post-Colonial: From Kant to Kawakubo 1998, A Critique of Post-Colonial Reason: Toward a History of the Vanishing Present 1999, Death of a Discipline 2003, Other Asias 2005, An Aesthetic Education in the Era of Globalization 2012, Readings 2014, Du Bois and the General Strike; chapters in books and articles in professional journals. *Address:* 602 Philosophy Hall, MC 4927, Columbia University, New York, NY 10027, USA (office). *Telephone:* (212) 870-2781 (office). *E-mail:* gcspiv@gmail.com (office). *Website:* www.columbia.edu/cu/english (office).

SPIVAKOV, Vladimir Teodorovich; Russian violinist and conductor; *Artistic Director and Principal Conductor, National Philharmonic of Russia;* b. 12 Sept. 1944, Ufa, Bashkortostan; m. Satinik Saakyants; three d.; ed Moscow State Conservatory, postgraduate with Yury Yankelevich; studied violin since age of six with B. Kroger in Leningrad; Founder and Conductor, Chamber Orchestra Virtuosi of Moscow 1979–; Founder and Artistic Dir Music Festival in Colmar, France 1989–; Artistic Dir and Chief Conductor, Russian Nat. Symphony Orchestra 1999–2002; Founder, Artistic Dir and Prin. Conductor, Nat. Philharmonic of Russia 2003–; Artistic Dir and Prin. Conductor, Moscow Virtuosi Chamber Orchestra; guest conductor of several orchestras including Chicago Symphony Orchestra, LA Philharmonic, London Symphony Orchestra, English and Scottish Chamber Orchestras; Pres. Moscow Performing Arts Centre 2003–, Sarasate Violin Contest, Spain; f. Spivakov Foundation 1994; apptd UNESCO Artist for Peace 2006; Order of Peoples' Friendship 1993, Order for Merits of Grade III (Ukraine) 1996, Officier, Ordre des Arts et des Lettres 1999, St Mesrop Mashtots Order (Armenia) 1999, Order for Services To Fatherland, Grade III 1999, Chevalier, Légion d'Honneur 2000, Officier, Légion d'Honneur 2010, Commdr, Star of Italy 2012, Order of Saint Prince Daniel of Moscow, 1st class 2014, Order of St Nino (Georgia) 2014; Dr hc (Moscow Lomonosov Univ.) 2002; First Prize Montreal Competition, Marguerite Long St Jacques Thibaud Competition, Paris, Niccolo Paganini Int. Violin Competition, Genoa, Int. Tchaikovsky Competition, Moscow; USSR State Prize 1989, USSR People's Artist of USSR 1989, Triumph Prize, Nat. Cultural Heritage Award, Russia's Artist of the Year 2002, with Alexander Solzhenitsyn and Leonid Roshal chosen Russian of the Year in Russia Without Borders programme 2005, Liberty Prize 2007, State Prize of Russia 2012, Int. Award Zvezda Chernobyl 2013, People's Artist of the Repub. of Dagestan, Kabardino-Balkaria 2013, People's Artist of the Repub. of Bashkortostan 2014. *Recordings include:* more than 20 CDs on Capriccio, RCA Victor Red Seal and BMG Classics including works by Brahms, Berg, Chausson, Franck, Prokoviev, Ravel, Tchaikovsky, Richard Strauss, Schubert, Sibelius, Shostakovich. *Leisure interest:* collecting paintings. *Address:* Columbia Artists Management, 1790 Broadway, New York, NY 10019, USA (office); National Philharmonic of Russia, Moscow 115054, Office 208, 52/8 Kosmodamianskaya Embankment, Russia; Vspolny per. 17, Apt 14, Moscow, Russia. *Telephone:* (495) 290-23-24 (Moscow); (495) 730-1367 (Nat. Philharmonic). *Fax:* (495) 730-3778 (Nat. Philharmonic). *E-mail:* info@spivakovmusic.com. *Website:* www.nfor.ru/eng; www.mvco.ru/en; www.vladimirspivakov.com; spivakov.ru.

SPOERRI, Philip, PhD; Swiss lawyer and international organization official; b. 1963, Zurich; m.; one s.; ed Göttingen, Munich and Bielefeld Univs, Geneva Univ., Switzerland; worked as lawyer in pvt. firm in Munich; began career with ICRC in 1994, carried out first mission for ICRC in Israel (Occupied Territories), continued with missions in Kuwait and Yemen, Afghanistan and Democratic Repub. of Congo, headed legal advisers to Dept of Operations, Geneva, returned to Afghanistan as Head of Del. 2004–06, Dir for Int. Law and Co-operation within the Movt 2006–14. *Address:* c/o International Committee of the Red Cross, 19 Avenue de la Paix, 1202 Geneva, Switzerland. *E-mail:* press.gva@icrc.org.

SPOGLI, Ronald P., AB, MBA; American investment banker and fmr diplomatist; *Partner and CEO, Freeman Spogli & Co.;* b. 1948, Los Angeles, Calif.; m. Georgia Spogli; one d. one step-s.; ed Stanford Univ., Harvard Business School; Researcher, Stanford Univ. based in Milan, Italy 1972–73; fmr Man. Dir Investment Banking Div. Dean Witter Reynolds Inc.; Co-founder and Partner, Freeman Spogli & Co. (pvt. equity firm) 1983–2005, 2009–, now also CEO; Amb. to Italy 2005–09 (also accred to San Marino 2006–09); apptd to US State Dept's Fulbright Foreign Scholarship Bd 2002; mem. Bd of Visitors, Stanford Univ.'s Inst. for Int. Studies 2000–; mem. Bd AFC Enterprises, Regents Bancshares, Winebow. *Address:* Freeman Spogli & Co., 11100 Santa Monica Blvd, Suite 1900, Los Angeles, CA 90025, USA (office). *Telephone:* (310) 444-1822 (office). *Fax:* (310) 444-1870 (office). *E-mail:* IR@freemanspogli.com (office). *Website:* www.freemanspogli.com (office).

SPONG, Rt Rev. John Shelby, AB, MDiv; American ecclesiastic and writer; b. 16 June 1931, Charlotte, NC; s. of John Shelby Spong and Doolie Griffith Spong; m. 1st Joan Lydia Ketner 1952 (died 1988); three d.; m. 2nd Christine Mary Bridger 1990; ed Univ. of North Carolina, Virginia Theological Seminary; Rector, St Joseph's, Durham, NC 1955–57, Calvary Church, Tarboro, NC 1957–65, St John's Church, Lynchburg, Va 1965–69, St Paul's Church, Richmond, Va 1969–76, Bishop, Diocese of Newark, NJ 1976–2000; Pres. NJ Council of Churches; Quatercentenary Fellow, Emmanuel Coll. Cambridge, UK 1992; William Belden Noble Lecturer, Harvard Univ. 2000; Visiting Lecturer, Univ. of The Pacific, Stockton, Calif. 2003; mem. Faculty, Grad. Theological Union, Berkeley, Calif.; columnist, Beliefnet.com 1999–2000, AgoraMedia 2002–, Waterfront Media 2002–; Hon. DD (Virginia Theological Seminary), (St Paul's Coll.); Hon. DHL (Muhlenberg Coll.), (Holmes Inst., Chicago) 2004, (Univ. of North Carolina) 2007, (Lehigh Univ.) 2007, (Drew Univ.) 2010; David Frederick Strauss Award, Jesus Seminar 1999, Humanist of the Year, New York City 1999, John A. T, Robinson Award 2004, portrait hung in Hall of Honor in Martin Luther King Chapel, Morehead Coll. for leadership in breaking the oppression of homosexual people 2010. *Radio:* play-by-play sportscaster in Tarboro, NC and Lynchburg, Va 1960–65. *Publications include:* Honest Prayer 1973, This Hebrew Lord 1974, 1988, Dialogue: In Search of Jewish-Christian Understanding 1975, Christpower 1975, Life Approaches Death: A Dialogue on Medical Ethics 1976, The Living Commandments 1977, The Easter Moment 1980, Into the Whirlwind 1983, Beyond Moralism 1986, Consciousness and Survival 1987, Living in Sin? 1988, Rescuing the Bible from Fundamentalism 1991, Born of a Woman – A Bishop Rethinks the Virgin Birth and the Place of Women in a Male-Dominated Church 1992, Resurrection: Myth or Reality? 1994, Liberating the Gospels: Reading the Bible with Jewish Eyes 1996, Why Christianity Must Change or Die: A Bishop Speaks to Believers in Exile 1998, Here I Stand: My Struggle for a Christianity of Integrity, Love and Equality 2000, The Bishop's Voice 1999, A New Christianity for a New World 2001, Crossroads – The Sins of Scripture 2005, Eternal Life: A New Vision beyond Religion, Beyond Theism, Beyond Heaven and Hell 2009, Re-Claiming the Bible for a Non-Religious World 2011, The Fourth Gospel: Tales of a Jewish Mystic 2013, The Birth of Jesus 2014, Biblical Literalism: A Gentile Heresy 2016. *Leisure interests:* hiking, reading. *Address:* c/o Julie Rae Mitchell, HarperSanFrancisco, 353 Sacramento Street, Suite 500, San Francisco, CA 94111, USA (office); 24 Puddingstone Road, Morris Plains, NJ 07950, USA (home). *Telephone:* (973) 538-9825 (home). *Fax:* (973) 540-9584 (home). *E-mail:* johnsspong@aol.com (home); cmsctm@aol.com (home). *Website:* www.johnshelbyspong.com.

SPONHEIM, Lars, MSc; Norwegian politician; b. 23 May 1957, Halden; m.; three c.; consultant 1981–84; teacher, Statens Gartnerskule Hjeltnes 1984–88, Prin. 1992–; mem. local council, Ulvik Municipality 1984–95, Mayor 1988–91; mem. County Council, Hordaland Co. 1992–93; Dir of Agric., Ulvik and Granvin Municipalities 1993; mem. Parl. for Hordaland Co. to Storting (Parl.) 1993–2009, mem. Parl. Finance Cttee; Leader Venstre (Liberal) Party 1996–2010; Minister of Trade and Industry 1997–2000; Minister of Food and Agric. 2001–05; County Gov. of Hordaland 2010–16.

SPRING, Richard (Dick), BA, BL; Irish business executive and fmr politician; *Deputy Chairman, Fexco Ltd;* b. 29 Aug. 1950, Tralee, Co. Kerry; s. of Dan Spring and Anna Laide; m. Kristi Lee Hutcheson 1977; two s. one d.; ed Mount St Joseph Çoll., Roscrea, Co. Tipperary, Trinity Coll. Dublin, King's Inns, Dublin; mem. Dáil Éireann (House of Reps) for Kerry North 1981–2002; Leader of Labour Party

1982–97; Tanaiste (Deputy Prime Minister) 1982–87, also Minister for the Environment 1982–83, for Energy 1983–87, Tanaiste and Minister for Foreign Affairs 1993–97; Chair. Gulliver Ireland; Deputy Chair. Fexco 2002–, also mem. Bd of Dirs; Chair. Industrial Development Ireland 2002–, Altobridge Ltd, Airtel ATN; chair. or dir numerous public and pvt. cos; mem. Bd of Dirs AIB Group, UK PLC 2009, Allied Irish Banks, PLC 2009–14, Quintessential Brands Ireland 2016–, Realta (Irish Global HIV/AIDS Foundation), Eircom Ltd, Alder Capital Ltd; fmr Irish rugby union int.; Assoc. Fellow, Kennedy School of Govt, Harvard Univ. 1998–; Fellow, Salzburg Seminar 1998; mem. Council on Foreign Relations; Dr hc (Hartwick Coll., New York) 1998, (Misericordia Coll., Pennsylvania) 1999. *Leisure interests:* sport, reading, golf, swimming. *Address:* Fexco Ltd, 12 Ely Place, Dublin 2 (office); Fexco Ltd, Iveragh Road, Killorglin, Ireland (office). *Telephone:* (1) 6611800 (Dublin) (office); (66) 9761258 (Killorglin) (office); (87) 2391200 (mobile) (home). *E-mail:* dspring@fexco.com (office). *Website:* www.fexco.com (office).

SPRINGER, Timothy Alan, BA, PhD; American immunologist and academic; *Latham Family Professor of Pathology, Harvard Medical School;* b. 23 Feb. 1948, Fort Benning, Ga; ed Univ. of California, Berkeley, Harvard Univ.; Biochemistry 10 Teaching Asst, Harvard Univ. 1972–74, Biochemistry 111 Teaching Asst 1974–75; NIH Research Fellow, Univ. of Cambridge, UK and MRC Lab. of Molecular Biology, Cambridge 1976–77; Asst Prof., Harvard Medical School 1977–83, Assoc. Prof. 1983–89, Latham Family Prof. of Pathology 1989–, Prof. of Biological Chemistry and Molecular Pharmacology 2011–, Prof. of Medicine, Boston Children's Hospital 2011–, Sr Investigator, Program in Cellular and Molecular Medicine 2012–, mem. Faculty Council, Harvard Univ. 1996–; Chief of Lab. of Membrane Immunochemistry, Dana Farber Cancer Inst. 1981–88; Vice-Pres. Center for Blood Research 1988–92; Councillor, Int. Leukocyte Workshop 1989–; mem. Scientific Review Bd, Howard Hughes Medical Inst. 1996–2000; Overseer, Bd of Overseers, CBR Inst. for Biomedical Research, Inc. 2002–; Visiting Prof., Univ. of Michigan 1990; Wellcome Visiting Prof., Wayne State Univ. 1997; consultant, Boehringer-Ingelheim 1989–95, LeukoSite, Inc. (Founder and Chair. Scientific Advisory Bd) 1992–99, Scientific Advisory Bd, Molecular Applications Group, Inc. 1997–, Millennium Pharmaceuticals 1999–2001, Sunesis Pharmaceuticals 2003–; Scientific Advisor, Canadian Vaccines and Immunotherapeutics Network 2001; Assoc. Ed. Journal of Immunology 1981–85, Molecular Biology of the Cell 1992–96; Advisory Ed. Journal of Experimental Medicine 1985–95; mem. Editorial Bd, Hybridoma 1981–, Regional Immunology 1988–, Cellular Immunology 1988–93, Journal of Clinical Immunology 1988–92, New Biologist 1989–92, Cell Regulation (Molecular Biology of the Cell) 1989–92, Immunological Reviews 1996–2001; mem. American Asscn of Immunologists 1979– (mem. Nomination Cttee 1993), Reticuloendothelial Soc. 1981–94 (Membership Chair. 1986, Chair. Program Cttee 1989), American Soc. of Biological Chemists 1982–, American Asscn of Pathologists 1989–, Soc. for Leukocyte Biology 1995–, NAS 1996– (Chair. Section 29, Biophysics and Computational Biology 2004–07); Fellow, American Acad. of Arts and Sciences 2001–; Dr hc (Aarhus Univ., Denmark) 2011; Hon. Prof., Fudan Univ. Shanghai, China 2004, College of Life Sciences, Nankai Univ., Tianjin, China 2006, Shanghai JiaoTong Univ. 2007; Nat. Merit Scholar 1966, Biochemistry Departmental Citation (awarded to most outstanding grad.) 1971, American Cancer Soc. Jr Faculty Research Award 1981, American Cancer Soc. Faculty Research Award 1984, NIH MERIT Grant Award 1988, 2004, Distinguished Lectureship, Vanderbilt School of Medicine 1992, American Heart Asscn Basic Research Prize 1993, Royal Soc. of Medicine Medal and Visiting Prof., UK 1994, William B. Coley Medal for Distinguished Research in Fundamental Immunology, Cancer Research Inst. 1995, Marie T. Bonazinga Award for Excellence in Leukocyte Biology Research, Soc. for Leukocyte Biology 1995, Crafoord Prize in Polyarthritis, Royal Swedish Acad. of Sciences (co-recipient) 2004, Fellowship, John Simon Guggenheim Memorial Foundation 2004, Henry M. Stratton Medal, American Soc. of Hematology 2014. *Publications include:* numerous scientific papers in professional journals on adhesion receptors of the immune system. *Address:* Harvard Medical School, Boston Children's Hospital, 3 Blackfan Circle, CLSB, Room 3103, Boston, MA 02115, USA (office). *Telephone:* (617) 713-8200 (office). *Fax:* (617) 713-8232 (office). *E-mail:* timothy.springer@childrens.harvard.edu (office). *Website:* www.hms.harvard.edu (office).

SPRINGSTEEN, Bruce; American singer, songwriter and musician (guitar); b. 23 Sept. 1949, Freehold, NJ; s. of Douglas Springsteen and Adele Springsteen; m. 1st Julianne Phillips 1985 (divorced 1990); m. 2nd Patti Scialfa 1991; two s. one d.; ed community coll.; performed in New York and NJ nightclubs; solo artist 1972–; numerous tours of USA and Europe; formed backing group the E-Street Band 1974; Grammy Award for Best Male Vocalist 1984, 1987, for Best Rock Performance by a Duo (jtly) 2004, BRIT Award for Best Int. Solo Artist 1986, Acad. Award for Best Original Song in a Film (for Streets of Philadelphia) 1994, MTV Best Video from a Film Award (for Streets of Philadelphia) 1994, Grammy Awards for Best Solo Rock Vocal Performance (for Devils & Dust) 2006, (for Radio Nowhere) 2008, (for Working on a Dream) 2010, for Best Rock Instrumental Performance (for Once Upon a Time in the West) 2008, for Best Rock Song (for Radio Nowhere) 2008, (for Girls in Their Summer Clothes) 2009, Golden Globe Award for Best Original Song (for The Wrestler) 2009, Kennedy Center Honor 2009, Presidential Medal of Freedom 2016. *Recordings include:* albums: Greetings from Asbury Park, New Jersey 1973, The Wild, The Innocent And The E-Street Shuffle 1973, Born To Run 1975, Darkness On The Edge Of Town 1978, The River 1980, Nebraska 1982, Born In The USA 1984, Bruce Springsteen And The E Street Band Live 1975–85 1986, Tunnel Of Love 1987, Chimes of Freedom 1988, Human Touch 1992, Lucky Town 1992, The Ghost Of Tom Joad 1995, The Rising (Grammy Award for Best Rock Album 2003) 2002, Roll Of The Dice 2003, Devils & Dust 2005, We Shall Overcome: The Seeger Sessions (Grammy Award for Best Traditional Folk Album 2007) 2006, Magic 2007, Working on a Dream 2009, Wrecking Ball 2012, High Hopes 2014, Springsteen on Broadway 2018, Western Stars 2019. *Publications:* Born to Run (autobiography) 2016. *Address:* Premier Talent Agency, 3 East 54th Street, New York, NY 10022, USA (office). *Website:* www.brucespringsteen.net.

SPRÜTH, Monika Ilse Gabriele; German art gallery owner; b. 18 May 1949, Memmingen; d. of Gerhard Merfort and Hannelore Sprüth; one s. one d.; ed Rheinisch-Westfälische Technische Hochschule, Aachen; Diplom Ingenieur, Stadtplanungsamt Oberhausen 1975–79; Teacher of construction, Maths and Art, Fachhochschule für Bauwesen, Cologne 1981–83; co-owner (with Philomene Magers) of Sprüth Magers galleries for contemporary art; opened gallery in Cologne 1983, London 2003, Berlin 2008, Los Angeles 2016, Hong Kong 2016. *Publications include:* Peter Fischli und David Weiss. Stiller Nachmittag 1985, Eau de Cologne Nr.1 (co-ed.) 1985, Eau de Cologne Nr.2 (co-ed.) 1987, Eau de Cologne Nr.3 (co(ed.) 1989, Das Licht von der anderen Seite II (co(ed.) 1988, Ed Ruscha, Gunpowder and Stains (co-ed.) 2000, Frances Scholz. Ich geb der Welt die Abstraktion zurück (co-ed.) 2008. *Leisure interest:* soccer. *Address:* Sprüth Magers Berlin, Oranienburger Straße 18, 10178 Berlin, Germany (office); Sprüth Magers London, 7A Grafton Street, London, W1S 4EJ, England (office); Sprüth Magers Los Angeles, 5900 Wilshire Blvd, Los Angeles, CA 90036, USA (office). *Telephone:* (30) 28884030 (Berlin) (office); (20) 7408-1613 (London) (office); (323) 634-0600 (LA) (office). *Fax:* (30) 288840352 (Berlin) (office); (20) 7499-4531 (London) (office); (323) 634-0602 (LA) (office). *E-mail:* info@spruethmagers.com (office). *Website:* www.spruethmagers.com (office).

SPUDICH, James A., BS, PhD; American biochemist and academic; *Douglass M. and Nola Leishman Professor of Cardiovascular Disease, Stanford University;* b. Benld, Ill.; m. Annamma (Anna) Spudich; two d.; ed Univ. of Illinois, Stanford Univ., Univ. of Cambridge, UK; Asst Prof., Dept of Biochemistry and Biophysics, Univ. of California, San Francisco 1971–74, Assoc. Prof. 1974–76, Prof. 1976–77; Prof., Dept of Structural Biology, Stanford Univ. School of Medicine 1977–92, Chair. 1979–84, Prof., Dept of Developmental Biology 1989–2011, Prof., Dept of Biochemistry 1992–, Chair. 1994–98, Douglass M. and Nola Leishman Prof. of Cardiovascular Disease 1987–, Co-founder and first Dir Interdisciplinary Program in Bioengineering, Biomedicine and Biosciences – Bio-X Stanford Univ. 1998–2002; Adjunct Faculty mem., Nat. Centre for Biological Sciences, Tata Inst. of Fundamental Research, Bangalore, India 2005–; Monitoring Ed., Proceedings of the National Academy of Sciences, USA 2000–; Ed. Cell 2009–; Co-founder Cytokinetics Inc., San Francisco; Pres. American Soc. for Cell Biology 1989; mem. NAS 1991; External Scientific mem. Max Planck Inst. for Biochemistry, Martinsried, Germany; Fellow, American Academy of Arts and Sciences 1997, AAAS 2001; Newhouse Foundation Fellow 1965–67, Dreyfus Teaching and Research Scholar 1976–77, Guggenheim Fellow 1978, Basic Research Prize, American Heart Asscn 1991, Alexander von Humboldt Research Award 1991, NIH Merit Award 1991, Lifetime Research Career Award, Biophysical Soc. 1995, Lewis S. Rosenstiel Award for Outstanding Research Achievement in Field of Basic Medical Studies 1996, 1997 Repligen Award for Chem. of Biological Processes, ACS Div. of Biological Chem. 1996, Award for Outstanding Investigator in Field of Single Molecule Biology, Biophysics Soc. 2005, E.B. Wilson Medal, American Soc. for Cell Biology 2011, Albert Lasker Basic Medical Research Award (co-recipient) 2012. *Publications:* book chapters, reviews and more than 190 papers in professional journals. *Leisure interests:* flying small planes. *Address:* Spudich Lab, Department of Biochemistry, Beckman Center B405, Stanford, CA 94305-5307, USA (office). *Telephone:* (650) 723-7634 (office); (650) 723-6201 (office). *E-mail:* jspudich@stanford.edu (office). *Website:* med.stanford.edu/profiles/devbio/faculty/James_Spudich (office); spudlab.stanford.edu (office).

SPURDZIŅŠ, Oskars; Latvian economist, politician and business executive; *Chairman, SC VTU Valmiera;* b. 22 Aug. 1963, Aizpute; m.; two c.; ed Aizpute Secondary School, Univ. of Latvia; Chair. Deputies' Council and Bd Valmiera City Council 1990–94; consultant, Latvian Asscn of Local Self-Govts 1994; Adviser, Ministry of Finance 1994–96; Adviser, Admin of Local Govt Affairs 1996–97; Man. Municipal Projects, Latvian Environmental Investment Fund 1997–99; mem. Saeima (Parl., People's Party, TP) 1999–2002; Parl. Sec., Ministry of Educ. and Science 1999–2000, Ministry of Finance 2000–02, 2004–07; Project Man. Hipoteku Banka 2002–04; currently Chair. SC VTU Valmiera. *Address:* JSC VTU Valmiera, Brandeļi, Brandeļos, Kocēnu pagasts, Kocēnu novads, 4220, Latvia (office). *E-mail:* info@vtu-valmiera.lv (office). *Website:* vtu-valmiera.lv (office).

SPYROU, Nicholas M., PhD; British physicist and academic; *Professor Emeritus of Medical Physics, University of Surrey;* joined as Lecturer, Univ. of Surrey 1969, apptd Prof. of Radiation and Medical Physics and Chair. of Medical Physics, Prof. Emer. of Medical Physics 2008–, fmr Dir MSc Course in Medical Physics and BSc course in Physics with Medical Physics; mem. numerous int. cttees, including Int. Cttee of Activation Analysis, Nat. Health Group Knowledge Group-Network; Exec. mem. Biology and Medicine Div., American Nuclear Soc.; Hon. MD 1988; Hevesy Medal, Journal of Radioanalytical and Nuclear Chemistry 2005. *Publications:* more than 220 scientific publs. *Address:* Room 17BC04, Faculty of Engineering and Physical Sciences, University of Surrey, Guildford, GU2 7XH, England (office). *Telephone:* (1483) 686800 (office). *Fax:* (1483) 686781 (office). *E-mail:* n.spyrou@surrey.ac.uk (office). *Website:* www.surrey.ac.uk/physics (office).

SQUIRE, Air Chief Marshal Sir Peter (Ted), GCB, DFC, AFC, DL, DSc, FRAeS; British air force officer (retd); b. 7 Oct. 1945, Felixstowe, Suffolk; s. of Wing Commdr Frank Squire, DSO, DFC and Margaret Pascoe Squire (née Trump); m. Carolyn Joynson 1970; three s.; ed King's School, Bruton; with 20 Squadron, Singapore 1968–70, 4 FTS, Anglesey 1970–73, 3 (F) Squadron, Germany 1975–78; OC 1(F) Squadron 1981–83; Personal Staff Officer to Air Officer Commdg-in-Chief, Strike Command 1984–86; Station Commdr, RAF Cottesmore 1986–88; Dir Air Offensive 1989–91; SASO, RAF Strike Command 1991–93; Air Officer Commdg No. 1 Group 1993–94; ACAS 1994–96, DCDS (Programmes and Personnel), Ministry of Defence 1996–99; Air Officer Commdg-in-Chief, Strike Command and Commdr Allied Air Forces Northwestern Europe 1999–2000; Air ADC to HM The Queen 1999–2003; Chief of the Air Staff 2000–03; Commr Commonwealth War Graves Comm. 2003–08, Vice-Chair. 2005–08; Trustee, Imperial War Museum 2001–11 (Deputy Chair. 2004–06, Chair. 2006–11), American Air Museum in Britain 2002–15 (Pres. 2006–15); Sr Warden King's School, Bruton 2004–11; Pres. Air Training Corps (Devon and Somerset) 2011–, RAF Club 2013–. *Leisure interests:* golf, cricket, gardening. *Address:* c/o National Westminster Bank, 5 South Street, Wincanton, Somerset, BA9 9DJ, England.

SQUYRES, Steven W., BA, PhD; American astronomer and academic; *James A. Weeks Professor of Physical Sciences, Cornell University;* b. 1957, Wenonah, New Jersey; m. Mary Squyres; two d.; ed Gateway Regional High School, Woodbury Heights, New Jersey, Cornell Univ.; Postdoctoral Assoc. and Research Scientist at NASA Ames Research Center 1981–86; joined Faculty, Cornell Univ. 1986, apptd Goldwin Smith Prof. of Astronomy, then James A. Weeks Prof. of Physical Sciences; Assoc. of Voyager imaging science team 1978–81, radar investigator on

Magellan mission to Venus; mem. Mars Observer gamma-ray spectrometer flight investigation team; co-investigator on Russian Mars '96 mission; currently Scientific Prin. Investigator for Mars Exploration Rover Project; co-investigator on Mars Express mission 2003, Mars Reconnaissance Orbiter's High Resolution Imaging Science Experiment 2005; mem. Gamma-Ray Spectrometer Flight Investigation Team for Mars Odyssey mission, imaging team for Cassini mission to Saturn; fmr Chair. NASA Space Science Advisory Cttee; mem. NASA Advisory Council, Chair. 2011–; Fellow, American Acad. of Arts and Sciences; H.C. Urey Prize, Planetary Div. of American Astronomical Soc. 1987, Carl Sagan Memorial Award 2004, Space Science Award, American Inst. of Aeronautics and Astronautics 2004, World Tech. Award in Space, The World Tech. Network 2005, Wired Rave Award for Science 2005, Benjamin Franklin Medal in Earth and Environmental Science, Franklin Inst. 2007, Wernher von Braun Award, Nat. Space Soc. 2007, Carl Sagan Medal for Excellence in Communication in Planetary Science 2009, Mines Medal 2010, Eugene Shoemaker Memorial Award 2010, Whipple Award 2012. *Publications include:* Roving Mars: Spirit, Opportunity, and the Exploration of the Red Planet 2005; numerous scientific papers in professional journals on planetary sciences. *Address:* 428 Space Sciences Building, Cornell University, Ithaca, NY 14853, USA (office). *Telephone:* (607) 255-3508 (office). *Fax:* (607) 255-6918 (office). *E-mail:* squyres@astro.cornell.edu (office). *Website:* www.astro.cornell.edu (office).

ŠRAMKO, Ivan; Slovak banking executive, diplomatist and fmr central banker; *Chairman, Council for Budget Responsibility;* b. 3 Sept. 1957, Bratislava; m.; three c.; ed Univ. of Econs, Bratislava; worked in finance depts in several cos 1981–90; Deputy Dir VUB-ING Banking Co. 1990–91, Head, VUB-Credit Lyonnais joint venture task force 1991–92; Gen. Man., then Deputy Chair., then Chair., Istrobanka 1992–98; Man. Tatra Banka 1998–2000, mem. Bd of Dirs 2000–02; Deputy Gov. Nat. Bank of Slovakia (Národná banka Slovenska) 2002–04, Gov. 2005–10, Gov. IMF 2005–10; Alt. Gov. EBRD 2005–10, mem. Gen. Council of European Cen. Bank 2009–10; Amb. and Perm. Rep. to OECD, Paris 2010–11; Adviser on central and southeastern European operations, Intesa Sanpaolo SpA 2011–; Chair. Council for Budget Responsibility (ind. body est. to monitor and evaluate the fiscal performance of Slovak govt) 2012–; mem. Bd Slovak-Austrian Chamber of Commerce 1998; Chair. Man. Bd Univ. of Econs, Bratislava 2003–; European Central Banker of the Year, Banker magazine 2006, Central Bank Governor of the Year, Emerging Markets (newspaper) 2006, 2008. *Address:* Council for Budget Responsibility, Imricha Karvaša 1, 813 25 Bratislava, Slovakia (office). *Telephone:* (2) 5787-4959 (office). *Fax:* (2) 5787-1133 (office). *E-mail:* sekretariat@rrz.sk (office). *Website:* www.rozpoctovarada.sk (office).

SREEDHARAN, E.; Indian transport engineer; b. 12 June 1932, Palakkad, Kerala; ed Basel Evangelical Mission Higher Secondary School, Victoria Coll., Palghat, Govt Eng Coll., Kakinada; Lecturer in Civil Eng, Govt Polytechnic, Kozhikode; Apprentice, Bombay Port Trust; joined Indian Railways, Probationary Asst Engineer, Southern Railway 1954, eventually man. of numerous projects including implementation, planning and design for Kolkata Metro, retired 1990; Chair. and Man. Dir (on contract) Konkan Railway 1990; Man. Dir Delhi Metro Rail Corpn 1997–2012; Prin. Adviser, Kochi Metro Rail Project 2012–, Mass Rapid Transit Corpn 2019–; mem. Advisory Bd Foundation for Restoration of National Values; Chevalier de la Légion d'Honneur 2005; Hon. DSc (Indian Inst. of Tech., Delhi), Hon. DLit (Rajasthan Tech. Univ.) 2009; Railway Minister's Award 1963, Padma Shri 2001, Man of the Year, The Times of India 2002, Shri Om Prakash Bhasin Award 2002, Juror's Award, Confed. of Indian Industry 2002–03, One of Asia's Heroes, TIME magazine 2003, All India Man. Asscn Award 2003, Bharat Shiromani Award, Shiromani Inst., Chandigarh 2005, CNN-IBN Indian of the Year 2007 (Public Service) 2008, Padma Vibhushan 2008, Lal Bahadur Shastri Nat. Award 2008. *Leisure interests:* yoga, reading the Bhagavad Gita. *Website:* kochimetro.org.

SRINIVASAN, Krishnan, MA; Indian diplomatist, scholar and author; b. 15 Feb. 1937, Madras; s. of Capt. C. Srinivasan and Rukmani Chari; m. Brinda Srinivasan 1975; one s.; ed Bedford School, Christ Church, Oxford, UK; Chargé d'affaires, Libya 1969–71; High Commr in Zambia (also accred to Botswana) 1974–77, in Nigeria (also accred to Benin and Cameroon) 1980–82, in Bangladesh 1989–92; Amb. to Netherlands 1986–89; Perm. Sec. Foreign Ministry 1992–94, Foreign Sec. 1994–95; Deputy Sec.-Gen. (Political) Commonwealth 1995–2002; Visiting Fellow, Wolfson Coll., Cambridge 2002–05, Centre of Int. Studies, Cambridge 2002–05; Sr Fellow, Inst. of Commonwealth Studies, Univ. of London 2002–05; Visiting Prof., ASCI, Hyderabad 2004–; Fellow, Maulana Azad Inst. of Asian Studies, Calcutta 2006–15, Netherlands Inst. of Advanced Study 2003–04, Swedish Collegium for Advanced Studies 2008, 2012–13; columnist, The Telegraph, The Statesman, Kolkata; Hon. mem. Christ Church Sr Common Room 2004–16; Hind Ratna (India) 2001, Chevalier (Cameroon) 2007; Ramsden Sermon, Univ. of Oxford 2002, Rajiv Gandhi Memorial Lecturer, Hyderabad 2006, DC Pavate Memorial Lecturer, Dharwar 2010. *Publications include:* fiction: The Eccentric Effect 2001, The Ugly Ambassador 2003, Guesswork 2005, The Invisible African 2012, Ambassador Marco's Indian Instincts 2017; non-fiction: Tricks of the Trade 2000, The Rise, Decline and Future of the British Commonwealth 2005, The Jamdani Revolution 2008, Towards the New Horizon: World Order in the 21st Century 2009, Diplomatic Channels 2012, Europe in Emerging Asia 2015, Old Europe, New Asia 2015; numerous articles on int. affairs. *Leisure interests:* reading, music, watching sports. *Address:* Flat 8, Courtleigh, 126 Earls Court Road, London, W8 6QL, England.

SRINIVASAN, Mallika, MA, MBA; Indian business executive; *Chair and CEO, Tractors and Farm Equipment Limited;* b. 19 Nov. 1959; d. of A. Sivasailam; m. Venu Srinivasan; one s. one d.; ed Univ. of Madras, Univ. of Pennsylvania Wharton School of Business; joined Tractors and Farm Equipment Ltd (TAFE) as Gen. Man. 1986, worked in various positions, including as Exec. Asst to Chair. and Man. Dir, Gen. Man. (Planning and Coordination), Vice Pres. and Vice Chair., becoming Chair. and CEO 2011–; Chair. and Dir (non-exec.) Tata Global Beverages Ltd 2008–, The United Nilgiri Tea Estates Co. Ltd 2011–, AGCO Corpn 2011–, Tata Steel Ltd 2012–; Padma Shri 2014; named Ernst & Young Entrepreneur of the Year (Manufacturing) 2010. *Address:* Tractors and Farm Equipment Limited, 77, Nungambakkam High Road, Nungambakkam, Chennai 600 034, India (office).

Telephone: (44) 66919000 (office). *E-mail:* corporate@tafe.com (office). *Website:* www.tafe.com (office).

SRIPAVAN, Kanagasabapathy J.; Sri Lankan lawyer and judge (retd); b. 29 Feb. 1952, Jaffna; s. of Nadaraja Kanagasabapathy; ed Jaffna Hindu Coll., Sri Lanka Law Coll., Queen Mary and Westfield Coll., Univ. of London, UK; qualified as attorney 1976, practised law at Unofficial Bar of Sri Lanka 1977–78; acting State Counsel, Attorney-Gen. Dept 1978–79, permanent State Counsel 1979–89, Sr State Counsel 1989–96, Deputy Solicitor-Gen. 1996–2002, also functioned as Head of Court of Appeal Unit, Judge, Court of Appeal 2002–07, Pres. Court of Appeal 2007–08; apptd Judge, Supreme Court 2008 (also Pisne Justice), Chief Justice, Supreme Court 2015–17.

SSEKANDI, Edward Kiwanuka, LLB; Ugandan lawyer and politician; *Vice-President;* b. 19 Jan. 1943, Masaka Dist; m. Margret Ssekandi; four c.; ed Univ. of East Africa, Law Devt Centre, Kampala; Llecturer, Law Devt Centre 1973–78, Acting Dir 1978–79; Lead Counsel, Comm. of Inquiry into Violations of Human Rights 1986–93; del. to Constitutional Ass. (responsible for drafting new Ugandan constitution) 1994–95; elected MP for Bukoto Co. Cen. 1996, Deputy Speaker of Parl. 1996–2001, Speaker 2001–11; Vice-Pres. of Uganda 2011–; mem. Nat. Resistance Movt. *Address:* Office of the Vice-President, Parliament Bldg, POB 7168, Kampala, Uganda (office). *Telephone:* (41) 4258441 (office). *E-mail:* aak@statehouse.go.ug (office). *Website:* www.statehouse.go.ug (office).

SSEMOGERERE, Paul Kawanga, DipEd, MPA; Ugandan politician; b. 11 Feb. 1932, Bumangi Ssese Islands, Kalangala Dist; s. of Yozefu Kapere and Maria Lwiza Nakirya; m. Dr Germina N. Ssemogerere; one s. four d.; ed St Mary's Coll., Kisubu, Makerere Univ. and Syracuse Univ., USA; teacher 1959–60; elected mem. Parl. for Mengo North constituency 1961; served time in prison as political prisoner, then went into exile in USA; Leader Democratic Party (DP) 1977–2005; Leader of Opposition in Nat. Ass. 1981–85; Minister of Internal Affairs 1986–88, Second Deputy Prime Minister and Minister of Foreign Affairs 1988–94, of the Public Service 1994, of Regional Co-operation 1989; Chair. OAU Council of Ministers 1993–94; unsuccessful cand. in 1980 and 1996 Presidential elections; apptd mem. Bd of Migration Policy Group 1999; Hon. LHD (Alleghony Coll., USA) 1989. *Publications:* two book chapters on democracy and human rights in Africa. *Leisure interests:* seminars on politics and economics, eco-tourism, human rights advocacy, farming. *Address:* 401 Streicher Road, Cathedral Lubaga-Kampala, P.O. Box 548, Kampala, Uganda (home). *Telephone:* (41) 344155 (home). *E-mail:* ssemo2@africaonline.com (home).

SSENDAULA, Gerald; Ugandan politician (retd); b. 15 May 1943; mem. Bd of Govs African Capacity Building Foundation (ACBF); fmr Gov. Bank of Uganda; Minister of Finance, Planning and Econ. Devt 1998–2005; Sr Presidential Adviser on Financial Affairs 2005; Chair. Private Sector Foundation Uganda 2008–14; Chair. Uganda Revenue Authority 2010–16.

STABENOW, Deborah (Debbie) Ann, BS, MSW; American politician; *Senator from Michigan;* b. 29 April 1950, Gladwin, Mich.; d. of Robert Lee Greer and Anna Merle Greer (née Hallmark); one s. one d.; ed Michigan State Univ.; with Special Services, Lansing School Dist 1972–73; Co. Commr Ingham Co., Mason, Mich. 1975–78; mem. Mich. State House of Reps 1979–91; mem. State Senate 1991–94; mem. US House of Reps from 8th Mich. Dist 1997–2000; Senator from Mich. 2001–, Chair. Cttee on Agric., Nutrition, and Forestry 2011–15, mem. Cttee on Budget, on Energy and Natural Resources, on Finance; Founder Ingham Co. Women's Comm.; Co-founder Council Against Domestic Assault; mem. Democratic Business and Professional Club, Mich. Democratic Women's Political Caucus, Grance United Methodist Church (fmr lay preacher, Chair. Social Concerns Task Force, Sunday School Music teacher), Lansing Boys' Club, Professional Advisory Cttee Lansing Parents Without Partners, Advisory Cttee Center for Handicapped Affairs, Mich. Council Family and Divorce Mediation Advisory Bd, Nat. Council for Children's Rights, Big Brothers/Big Sisters Greater Lansing Advisory Bd, Mich. Child Study Asscn Bd Advisers, Mich. Women's Campaign Fund; mem. Nat. Asscn for the Advancement of Colored People (NAACP), Lansing Regional Chamber of Commerce; awards include Service to Children Award, Council for Prevention of Child Abuse and Neglect 1983, Outstanding Leadership Award, Nat. Council of Community Mental Health Centers 1983, Snyder-Kok Award, Mental Health Asscn Mich., Awareness Leader of the Year Award, Awareness Communications Team Developmentally Disabled 1984, Communicator of the Year Award, Woman in Communications 1984, Lawmaker of the Year Award, Nat. Child Support Enforcement Asscn 1985, Distinguished Service Award, Lansing Jaycees 1985, Distinguished Service in Govt Award, Retarded Citizens of Mich. 1986. *Address:* 731 Hart Senate Office Building, Washington, DC 20510 (office); 2709 South Deerfield Avenue, Lansing, MI 48911-1783, USA (home). *Telephone:* (202) 224-4822 (home). *Fax:* (202) 224-2066 (office). *E-mail:* senator@stabenow.senate.gov (office). *Website:* stabenow.senate.gov (office).

STADLER, Sergey Valentinovich; Russian violinist and conductor; b. 30 May 1962, Leningrad (now St Petersburg); s. of Valentin Raymundovich Stadler and Margarita Petrovna Stadler; m. Ilza Liepa (divorced); ed Leningrad State Conservatory, studied with Mikhail Vaiman, Boris Gutnikov in Leningrad Conservatory, with Leonid Kogan, Viktor Tretyakov in Moscow State Conservatory; has toured more than 50 countries since 1976; first performed music by Russian composers Rodion Shchedrin, Sergey Slonimsky, Boris Tishchenko and others; Prof., St. Petersburg State Conservatory 1984–89, fmr Artistic Dir and Chief Conductor N.A. Rimsky-Korsakov Saint-Petersburg State Conservatory of Opera and Ballet; began conducting 1996; Head of Competition Jury, Paganini Moscow Int. Violin Competition 2003–; Founder Hermitage Acad. of Music; apptd Chief Conductor, Symphony Orchestra of Russia 2007–; People's Artist of Russia, winner, Concertino Contest, Prague 1976, winner, Concours Long-Thibaud 1979, second prize, Sibelius Competition 1980, winner, Tchaikovsky Competition 1982.

STAEHELIN, Jenö C. A., Lic.Iur., LLM; Swiss lawyer and fmr diplomatist; b. 1940, Basel; ed Univ. of Berne, Harvard Univ. Law School, USA; called to the Bar, Zurich 1968; fmr Clerk, Zurich Court then pvt. law practice, Zurich 1968–69; joined Foreign Service 1969, overseas postings included at Embassies in Berne, Geneva and Stockholm 1969–71, Legal Adviser, Ministry of Foreign Affairs 1971–76, mem. Del. to OECD, Paris 1976–77; Vice-Pres. European Patent Office, Munich 1977–84; Minister and Deputy Dir for Int. Orgs, Ministry of Foreign

Affairs 1984–87, Amb. in charge of European and North American Affairs 1987–93, also Amb. to Holy See 1991–93, Amb. to Japan 1993–97, Perm. Observer to UN, New York 1997–2002, Perm. Rep. to UN 2002–04; Pres. UNICEF 2003–04; Chair. UN Mine Action Support Group 2004; Special Advisor to Swiss Foreign Minister 2004–05; Sr Advisor, Brock Capital LLP, New York; f. Dr. Jenö Staehelin Foundation; Dean of Mercator Fellowship on International Affairs, Switzerland 2011–; Founder and Pres. of the Jury, Geneva Challenge 2014–; mem. Bd of Dirs Kofi Annan Foundation 2007–, Schindler Holding Ltd 1980–2010; mem. Dean's Advisory Bd, Harvard Law School 1997–2010, Overseers' Visiting Cttee, Harvard Law School 2011–15, Centre for Humanitarian Dialogue 2006–12, ICRC 2006–10; Distinguished Fellow, Grad. Inst. of International and Development Studies (Institut de hautes études internationales et du développement). *Address:* Graduate Institute of International and Development Studies (Institut de hautes études internationales et du développement), Maison de la Paix, Chemin Eugène-Rigot 2, 1202 Geneva, Switzerland. *Website:* jstaehelin.com.

STAFF, Joel, BBA, MBA; American business executive; *Senior Advisor, TPH Partners;* ed Univ. of Texas, Texas A&M Univ.; began career with Baker Hughes Inc. (oil and gas industry supplier) 1976, served in various financial man. positions including Sr Vice-Pres. of parent co. and Pres. Drilling and Production Groups –1993; Chair., Pres. and CEO Nat. OilWell Inc. 1993–2001; joined Reliant Resources Inc. 2002, apptd mem. Bd of Dirs 2002, Interim Pres. Reliant Energy Retail Group, Chair. and CEO Reliant Resources 2003–07, Chair. 2007–08; Sr Advisor, TPH (Tudor, Pickering, Holt & Co.) Partners 2008–; Advisory Dir King Chapman & Broussard, Boys and Girls Club of Greater Houston; mem. Devt Bd Univ. of Tex. Health Science Center, Houston. *Address:* TPH Partners, Heritage Plaza, 1111 Bagby, Suite 4950, Houston, TX 77002, USA. *Telephone:* (715) 333-7107 (office). *Fax:* (713) 337-5354 (office). *E-mail:* info@tphpartners.com (office). *Website:* www.tphpartners.com (office).

STAFFORD, HE Cardinal James Francis; American ecclesiastic; b. 26 July 1932, Baltimore, Md; s. of F. Emmett Stafford and Mary Dorothy Stafford; ordained priest 1957; Auxiliary Bishop of Baltimore 1976–82; Bishop of Memphis 1982–86; Archbishop of Denver 1986–96, now Archbishop Emer.; cr. Cardinal (Cardinal-Deacon of Gesù Buon Pastore alla Montagnola) 1998–; Pres. Pontifical Council for the Laity 1998–2003; Major Penitentiary of Apostolic Penitentiary, Roman Curia 2003–09; Dr hc (Dominican School of Philosophy and Theology) 2009. *Address:* c/o Palazzo della Cancelleria, Piazza della Cancelleria, 1, 00186 Rome, Italy.

STAFFORD-CLARK, Max; British theatre director; *Artistic Director, Out of Joint Theatre Company;* b. 17 March 1941; s. of David Stafford-Clark and Dorothy Stafford-Clark; m. 1st Carole Hayman 1971; m. 2nd Ann Pennington 1981; one d.; m. 3rd Stella Feehily 2010; one d.; ed Felsted School, Riverdale Country Day School, New York and Trinity Coll. Dublin; Artistic Dir Traverse Theatre, Edin. 1968–70; Dir Traverse Workshop Co. 1970–74; Founder and Artistic Dir Joint Stock Theatre Group 1974–79, English Stage Co. at Royal Court Theatre 1979–93; Founder and Artistic Dir Out of Joint Theatre Co. 1993–; Visiting Prof., Royal Holloway and Bedford Coll., Univ. of London 1993–94; Maisie Glass Prof., Univ. of Sheffield 1995–96; Visiting Prof., Univ. of Herts. 1999–, Univ. of York 2002–; Hon. Fellow, Rose Bruford Coll. 1996; Hon. DLitt (Oxford Brookes) 2000, (Herts.) 2000, (Warwick) 2006; Special Award, Evening Standard Theatre Awards 2004, TMA Special Award for Individual Achievement 2010, The Critics' Circle Centenary Award for Services to the Arts in Britain 2013. *Principal productions:* Fanshen 1975, Top Girls 1982, Tom and Viv, Rat in the Skull, Serious Money, Our Country's Good, The Steward of Christendom, Shopping And Fucking, Blue Heart, Some Explicit Polaroids, Rita Sue and Bob Too/A State Affair 2000, A Laughing Matter 2002, The Permanent Way 2003, Talking to Terrorists 2005, The Overwhelming 2006, O Go My Man 2006, The Convicts Opera 2008, Mixed Up North 2009, The Big Fella, Bang Bang Bang 2010, This May Hurt a Bit, Pitcairn 2014, Crouch, Touch, Pause, Engage 2015, All That Fall 2015, A View from Islington North 2016. *Publications:* Letters to George 1989, Taking Stock 2007, Page to Stage, Our Country's Good 2011, Journal of the Plague Year 2014. *Address:* Out of Joint, 7 Thane Works, Thane Villas, London, N7 7NU, England (office). *Telephone:* (20) 7609-0207 (office). *E-mail:* ojo@outofjoint.co.uk (office). *Website:* www.outofjoint.co.uk (office).

STALEY, James (Jes) Edward, BS (Econ); American banker and business executive; *Group CEO, Barclays plc;* b. 27 Dec. 1956, Boston, Mass; s. of Paul R. Staley; m. Debbie Staley; two d.; ed Bowdoin Coll.; joined Morgan Guaranty Trust Co. of New York 1979, worked in Latin America Div. as Head of Corp. Finance for Brazil and Gen. Man. of Morgan Guaranty Trust Co. Brazilian brokerage firm 1980–89, Co-founding mem. J.P. Morgan's equities business, ran Equity Capital Market and Syndicate groups early 1990s, Head of Pvt. Banking Div. 1999–2001, CEO J.P. Morgan Asset Management 2001–09, Chief Exec. of the Investment Bank 2009–13; Man. Partner, BlueMountain Capital 2013–15; Group CEO Barclays plc 2015–; mem. Bd of Dirs UBS 2015–; mem. Bd, Robin Hood Foundation, Inst. of Int. Finance, US–China Business Council, American Museum of Natural History; mem. Bd of Trustees, Bowdoin Coll. 2007–. *Leisure interests:* sailing, spending time with children. *Address:* Barclays plc, One Churchill Place, Canary Wharf, London, E14 5HP, England (office); BlueMountain Capital Management LLC, 280 Park Avenue, 5th Floor E, New York, NY 10017, USA. *Telephone:* (20) 7116-1000 (London) (office). *Website:* www.barclays.com (office); www.bluemountaincapital.com (office).

STALLKAMP, Thomas J., BS, MBA; American business executive; b. 6 Sept. 1946, Bryn Mawr, Pa; ed Miami Univ.; joined professional supply training program, Ford Motor Co. 1972, worked in Procurement Dept –1980; joined Chrysler Corpn, Detroit (name changed to DaimlerChrysler Corpn, now officially FCA US LLC) 1980, held various man. positions including Pres., Chrysler Group 1998–2000, mem. Man. Bd, then Vice-Chair. 1999; Vice-Chair. and CEO MSX Int. 2000–04; Founder and Prin., Collaborative Management LLC (supply-chain consulting firm) 2004–10; Industrial Partner, Ripplewood Holdings LLC 2004–10; mem. Bd of Mans CEVA Holdings LLC 2014–; mem. Bd of Dirs Baxter Int. Inc. 2000–14, Visteon 2002–05, Borg Warner Automotive 2005–, Asahi TEC Corpn (fmr Co-Chair.) –2010, Smith Electric Vehicles Corpn 2011–; mem. Bd of Advisors, McDonough School of Business, Georgetown Univ.; Adjunct Prof. in Entrepreneurship, Babson Coll.; Trustee EntrepreneurShares Series Trust, Babson Coll. (now Trustee Emer.).

STALLONE, Sylvester Enzio; American actor and film director; b. 6 July 1946, New York; s. of Frank Stallone and Jacqueline Labofish; m. 1st Sasha Czach 1974 (divorced); two s.; m. 2nd Brigitte Nielsen 1985 (divorced 1987); m. 3rd Jennifer Flavin 1997; two d.; ed American Coll. of Switzerland, Univ. of Miami; f. White Eagle Co.; Dir Carolco Pictures Inc. 1987–; mem. Screen Actors Guild, Writers Guild, Directors Guild; Hon. mem. Stuntmans Asscn; Officier, Ordre des Arts et des Lettres; Hon. César 1992, Golden Apple Male Star of the Year 1997, Hollywood Film Festival Lifetime Achievement Award 2010. *Films include:* Lords of Flatbush 1973, Capone 1974, Rocky (Donatello Award Best Foreign Actor 1976) 1976, F.I.S.T. 1978, Paradise Alley 1978, Rocky II 1979, Nighthawks 1980, Escape to Victory 1980, Rocky III 1981, First Blood, Rambo 1984, Rocky IV 1985, Cobra 1986, Over the Top 1986, Rambo II 1986, Rambo III 1988, Lock Up 1989, Set Up 1990, Tango and Cash 1990, Rocky V 1990, Isobar 1991, Stop or My Mom Will Shoot 1991, Oscar 1991, Cliffhanger 1992, Demolition Man 1993, Judge Dredd 1994, The Specialist 1994, Assassins 1995, Firestorm 1996, Daylight 1996, Cop Land 1997, An Alan Smithee Film: Burn Hollywood Burn 1998, Get Carter 2000, Driven (also screenwriter and producer) 2001, D-Tox 2002, Avenging Angelo 2002, Shade 2003, Spy Kids 3-D: Game Over 2003, Rocky Balboa 2006; films directed: Paradise Alley 1978, Rocky II 1979, Rocky III 1982, Staying Alive 1983, Rocky IV 1985, Rocky Balboa 2006, Rambo 2008, The Expendables (also dir and writer) 2010, The Expendables 2 (also sreenwriter) 2012, Bullet to the Head 2012, Escape Plan 2013, Grudge Match 2013, The Expendables 3 2014, Reach Me 2014, Creed (Golden Globe Award for Best Actor in a Supporting Role in Motion Picture 2016) 2015. *Publications include:* Paradise Alley 1977, The Rocky Scrapbook 1997. *Website:* www.sylvesterstallone.com.

STALS, Christian Lodewyk, DComm; South African fmr central banker; b. 13 March 1935, Germiston; s. of Petrus J. Stals and Lilian Barnard; m. Hester Barnard 1958; three s. one d.; ed Afrikaans Hoër, Germiston and Univ. of Pretoria Extramural Div.; joined South African Reserve Bank as Clerk, Foreign Exchange Control Dept 1955, Gen. Man. 1975, Deputy Gov. 1976–81, apptd Sr Deputy Gov. 1981; Dir-Gen. Dept of Finance 1985; Special Econ. Adviser to Minister of Finance 1989; Gov. South African Reserve Bank 1989–99 (retd); Chancellor, Univ. of Pretoria 1997–2006; mem. Econ. Soc.; Fellow and Hon. Life Mem., Inst. of Bankers of South Africa; Hon. Prof. of Econs, Univ. of Pretoria and Rand Afrikaans Univ.; Grand Officer, Order of the Crown (Belgium) 1998; Dr hc (Univ. of Stellenbosch) 1995, (Rand Afrikaans Univ.) 1999, (Univ. of Port Elizabeth) 2000; State President's Decoration for Distinguished Service 1988, M.S. Louw Prize 1993, Prestige Award, Federasie van Suid-Afrikaanse Kultuurverenigings 1993, Central Banker of the Year Award, Euromoney magazine 1995. *Leisure interest:* golf.

STAMP, Terence; British actor; b. 22 July 1938, Bow, London; s. of Thomas Stamp and Ethel Esther Perrott; m. Elizabeth O'Rourke 2002 (divorced 2008); ed Plaistow Co. Grammar School, Webber–Douglas Dramatic Acad.; theatre work before film debut in Peter Ustinov's film adaptation of Herman Melville's novel Billy Budd 1962; Hon. Dr of Arts (Univ. of East London) 1993; Amhurst Webber Memorial Scholarship 1957. *Music:* The Airborne Symphony (narrator). *Theatre:* Dracula, The Lady from the Sea. *Films include:* Billy Budd (Golden Globe Award for New Star of the Year) 1962, Term of Trial 1962, The Collector 1965 (Best Actor, Cannes Film Festival), Modesty Blaise 1966, Far From the Madding Crowd 1967, Poor Cow 1967, Blue 1968, Theorem 1968, Tales of Mystery 1968, The Mind of Mr. Soames 1969, A Season in Hell 1971, Hu-man 1975, The Divine Creature 1976, Striptease 1977, Meetings With Remarkable Men 1978, Superman 1978, Superman II 1979 (Superman II: The Richard Donner Cut 2006), Death in the Vatican 1980, The Bloody Chamber 1982, The Hit 1984, Link 1985, Legal Eagles 1986, The Sicilian 1986, Wall Street 1988, Alien Nation 1988, Young Guns 1988, Prince of Shadows 1991, The Real McCoy 1992, The Adventures of Priscilla Queen of the Desert (Seattle Int. Film Festival Award for Best Actor) 1994, Limited Edition 1995, Tiré à part 1996, Bliss 1997, Love Walked In 1997, The Limey (Satellite Award for Best Actor) 1999, Star Wars: Episode I – The Phantom Menace 1999, Bowfinger 1999, Kiss the Sky 1999, Red Planet 2000, My Wife is an Actress 2000, Revelation 2001, Full Frontal 2002, My Boss's Daughter 2003, The Kiss 2003, The Haunted Mansion 2003, Dead Fish 2004, These Foolish Things 2004, Elektra 2005, Mr. & Mrs. Smith (scenes deleted) 2005, The Elder Scrolls IV: Oblivion (video game; voice) 2006, 9/11: The Twin Towers (narrator) 2006, September Dawn 2007, Wanted 2008, Get Smart 2008, Ultramarines: The Movie 2010, The Adjustment Bureau 2011, Song for Marion 2012, One Square Mile: London 2012, The Art of the Steal 2013, Big Eyes 2014. *Television includes:* Mindbender 1996, The Hunger–Anais 1997, Static Shock–Blast from the Past (voice) 2003, Smallville 2003–11. *Publications:* Stamp Album (memoirs, Vol. 1) 1988, Coming Attractions (memoirs, Vol. 2) 1988, Double Feature (memoirs, Vol. 3) 1989, The Night (novel) 1992, Stamp Collection Cookbook (jtly) 1997, The New Testament (audio book). *Leisure interest:* still tap dancing. *Address:* c/o Julia Charteris, United Agents LLP, 26 Lexington Street, London, W1F 0LE, England (office). *Telephone:* (20) 3214-0923 (office). *Fax:* (20) 3214-0801 (office). *E-mail:* jcharteris@unitedagents.co.uk (office). *Website:* unitedagents.co.uk (office); www.terencestamp.co.uk (office).

STAMPFER, Meir J., AB, MD, DrPH; American nutritionist, epidemiologist and academic; *Professor of Nutrition and Epidemiology and Chairman, Department of Epidemiology and Nutrition, T. H. Chan School of Public Health, Harvard University;* b. Lincoln, Neb.; ed Columbia Coll., New York Univ. School of Medicine, Harvard School of Public Health; Intern in Internal Medicine, Maimonides Hosp., Brooklyn, New York 1977–78; Resident, Community Medicine (Environmental), Mount Sinai School of Medicine, New York 1978–79; Resident, Preventive Medicine, Harvard School of Public Health (now T. H. Chan School of Public Health), Boston, Mass 1979–81, Instructor in Medicine, Harvard Medical School 1982–85, Teaching Fellow, Dept of Epidemiology, Harvard School of Public Health 1982–85, Asst Prof. of Medicine, Harvard Medical School 1985–93, Assoc. Prof. of Epidemiology, Harvard School of Public Health 1988–93, Prof. of Nutrition and Epidemiology 1993–, mem. Faculty, Div. of Biological Sciences 1989, Assoc. Prof. of Medicine, Harvard Medical School 1993–2001, Chair. Dept of Epidemiology, Harvard School of Public Health 2000–, mem. Dana-Farber/Harvard Cancer Center 2000–, Prof. of Medicine, Harvard Medical School 2001–; Assoc. Physician, Brigham and Women's Hosp., Boston 1982–91, Physician 1991–; Consultant

Physician, Veteran's Admin Hosp., Brockton, Mass 1984–85; Adjunct Prof., Karolinska Institutet, Stockholm, Sweden 2003–; Dozer Visiting Prof., Ben Gurion Univ., Israel; Assoc. Ed. American Journal of Epidemiology 1991–92, 1997, 2003–, Ed. 1992–97; mem. Editorial Bd American Fertility Society Menopause Publication 1992–94, Menopause (The Journal of the North American Menopause Soc.) 1993–, Journal of the American College Coll. of Nutrition 1994–, European Menopause Journal 1994–98, Journal of Womens Health 1998, American Journal of Medicine 1998; Tech. Reviewer, New England Journal of Medicine 1987–96; Int. Editorial Advisor, Journal of the British Menopause Society 2002–; mem. Soc. for Epidemiologic Research 1980–, Int. Soc. and Fed. of Cardiology, Council of Epidemiology and Prevention 1981–, American Epidemiological Soc. 1993–, American Asscn of Cancer Research 1999; Fellow, American Heart Asscn (Council of Epidemiology 1984, Council on Nutrition, Physical Activity and Metabolism 2003), American Coll. of Nutrition 1986; Jones Prize for Logic and Philosophy of Science, Columbia Univ. 1973, NIH Nat. Research Service Award 1979–82, Distinguished Alumnus Speaker, Maimonides Hosp. 1989, Duphar Lecturer, British Menopause Soc., UK 1994, Sr Investigator Award in Antioxidant Research, Comité Français de Coordination des Recherches sur l'Atherosclerose et le Cholesterol (France) 1994, Frost Award, American Public Health Asscn 2000. *Publications include:* more than 600 articles in medical journals on nutrition and chronic disease. *Address:* Department of Epidemiology, T. H. Chan School of Public Health, Channing Laboratory, 181 Longwood Avenue, Room 345, Boston, MA 02115, USA (office). *Telephone:* (617) 525-2749 (office). *E-mail:* mstampfe@hsph .harvard.edu (office). *Website:* www.hsph.harvard.edu (office).

STANCLIFFE, Rt Rev. David Staffurth, MA, DD, FRSCM; British ecclesiastic; *Fellow, St Chad's College, Durham University;* b. 1 Oct. 1942, Devizes, Wilts., England; s. of Very Rev. Michael Stancliffe and Barbara Tatlow; m. Sarah Smith 1965; one s. two d.; ed Westminster School, Trinity Coll., Oxford, Cuddesdon Theological Coll.; ordained deacon 1967, priest 1968; Asst Curate, St Bartholomew's, Armley, Leeds 1967–70; Chaplain, Clifton Coll. Bristol 1970–77; Canon Residentiary, Portsmouth Cathedral 1977–82, also Dir of Ordinands and Lay Ministry Adviser, Diocese of Portsmouth 1977–82; Vicar, St Thomas of Canterbury, Portsmouth and Provost of Portsmouth 1982–93; Bishop of Salisbury 1993–2010; mem. Gen. Synod 1985–2010, Liturgical Comm. 1986–2005 (Chair. 1993–2005), Cathedral's Fabric Comm. 1991–2001; Pres. Council, Marlborough Coll. 1994–2010; Pres. The Ecclesiological Soc. 2010–; Conductor The Westron Wynd 1971–77, Apparatus Musicus 1977–93, The Bishop's Consort 1993–, Fellow, Royal School of Church Music (Vice-Pres. 2005–), St Chad's Coll., Durham Univ. 2010–; Hon. Fellow, Guild of Church Musicians 2005; Hon. Fellow, Trinity Coll., Oxford 2003, Sarum Coll., Salisbury 2012; Hon. DLitt (Portsmouth) 1993. *Publications include:* Liturgy for a New Century 1990 (contrib.), The Identity of Anglican Worship 1991, Enriching the Christian Year 1992, Celebrating Common Prayer—Pocket Version 1994, The Sense of the Sacramental 1995, New Soundings 1997 (contrib.), Flagships of the Spirit 1998 (contrib.), The Pilgrim Prayer Book 2003 (second edn 2007), God's Pattern 2003, The Lion Companion to Church Architecture 2008, The Gospels in Art, Music and Literature 2013. *Leisure interests:* old music, travel, Italy. *Address:* Butts House, Stanhope, Co. Durham, DL13 2UQ, England (office). *Telephone:* (1388) 526912 (office). *E-mail:* d.s .stancliffe@durham.ac.uk (office).

STANCZYK, Janusz Józef, PhD; Polish diplomatist; b. 22 Jan. 1955, Tarnow; m.; two c.; ed Jagiellonian Univ., Kraków, Saint Louis Univ. and Univ. of Michigan, USA, Inst. of Legal Sciences, Polish Acad. of Sciences; Dir Legal and Treaties Dept, Foreign Ministry, Poland 1992–95, Dir Gen. for Legal Affairs 1995–97, Under-Sec. of State for Legal and Econ. Affairs and for relations with int. orgs (also responsible for ministry contact with nat. parl.) 1997–2000; mem. Del. UN Gen. Ass. 1992–96, 1998–2000; Perm. Rep. to UN, New York 2000–04; Deputy Minister for Foreign Affairs and Under-Sec. of State 2004–07; Amb. to Netherlands and Perm. Rep. OPCW 2007–12; Officer's Cross, Order of Polonia Restituta 2012. *Address:* Ministry of Foreign Affairs, 00-580 Warsaw, Al. Szucha 23, Poland (office). *Telephone:* (22) 5239201 (office). *Fax:* (22) 6257652 (office). *E-mail:* sm .sekretariat@msz.gov.pl (office). *Website:* www.msz.gov.pl (office).

STANDLEY, John T., BS; American business executive; *CEO, Rite Aid Corporation;* b. 20 April 1964, Los Angeles, Calif.; m.; two c.; ed Pepperdine Univ.; fmr Sr Vice-Pres. Smith's Food and Drug, Salt Lake City; fmr Chief Financial Officer (CFO) Smitty's Supervalu Inc., Phoenix; Sr Vice-Pres. and CFO Ralphs Grocery Co. 1996–98; Sr Vice-Pres. Fred Meyer, Inc., Portland, Ore. 1998–99; Exec. Vice-Pres. and CFO Fleming Co., Inc., Oklahoma City May–Dec. 1999; joined Rite Aid Corpn 1999, Sr Exec. Vice-Pres. and Chief Admin. Officer 2002, CFO 2003–05, Pres. and COO Rite Aid Corpn 2008–10, Pres. 2010–13, CEO 2010–, Chair. 2012–18; CEO Pathmark Stores 2005–07; Vice Chair. Nat. Asscn of Chain Drug Stores, Inc. (NACDS) 2013–14, apptd Chair. 2014; mem. Bd of Dirs, Pathmark Stores, Inc. 2005–07, SuperValu, Inc. 2013–15, CarMax, Inc. 2016–18. *Address:* Rite Aid Corpn, 30 Hunter Lane, Camp Hill, PA 17011, USA (office). *Telephone:* (717) 761-2633 (office). *E-mail:* contacttheboard@riteaid.com (office). *Website:* www.riteaid.com (office).

STANG, Peter J., BS, PhD; American chemist and academic; *Distinguished Professor of Chemistry, University of Utah;* b. 17 Nov. 1941, Nürnburg, Germany; m. Christine S. Stang; two d.; ed DePaul Univ., Univ. of California, Berkeley; NIH Postdoctoral Fellow, Princeton Univ. 1967–68; Dept Chair., Univ. of Utah 1989–95, Distinguished Prof. of Chem. 1992–, Dean, Coll. of Science 1997–2007; Assoc. Ed. Journal of the American Chemical Society 1982–99, Ed. 2002–; Ed.-in-Chief, Journal of Organic Chemistry 2000–01; mem. NAS 2000; Foreign mem. Chinese Acad. of Sciences 2006, Hungarian Acad. of Sciences 2007; Fellow, American Acad. of Arts and Sciences 2002; Hon. Prof., CAS Inst. of Chem., Beijing 2010, Zheijiang Univ. 2010, East China Normal Univ. 2010, East China Univ. of Science and Tech. 2010; Dr hc (Russian Acad. of Sciences), (Lomonosov Moscow State Univ.) 1992, (Technion-Israel Inst. of Tech.) 2014, (Texas A&M Univ.) 2016; Hon. DHumLitt (DePaul Univ.) 2015; A. von Humboldt Sr Scientist Award 1977, 1997, Lady Davis Fellowship, Haifa, Israel 1986, 1997, Fulbright Hays Sr Scholar, Zagreb, Croatia 1988, JSPS Fellowship 1995, 1998, ACS James Flack Norris Award in Physical Organic Chem. 1998, ACS George A. Olah Award in Hydrocarbon Chem. 2003, Linus Pauling Medal 2006, Fred Basolo Medal for Outstanding Research in Inorganic Chem. 2009, Paul G. Gassman Distinguished

Service Award, ACS Div. of Organic Chem. 2010, ACS F.A. Cotton Medal for Excellence in Chemical Research 2010, Nat. Medal of Science 2010, ACS Priestley Medal 2013, Award for Int. Scientific Cooperation of Chinese Acad. of Sciences 2016. *Publications include:* Metal-catalyzed Cross-Coupling Reactions 1997, Templated Organic Synthesis (co-ed.) 1999. *Address:* Department of Chemistry, University of Utah, 315 South 1400 East, Room 2020, Salt Lake City, UT 84112-0850, USA (office). *Telephone:* (801) 581-8329 (office). *E-mail:* stang@chem.utah .edu (office). *Website:* www.chem.utah.edu/directory/faculty/stang.html (office).

STANIKZAI, Mohammad Masoom, BA, MA; Afghan government official; *Director, National Directorate of Security;* b. 1958, Logar Prov.; ed Kabul Telecommunication Inst., Kabul Military Univ., Preston Univ., Pakistan, Univ. of Cambridge, UK; served for more than ten years in Afghan Army, including as Col, Qargha div.; Dir Agency for Rehabilitation and Energy Conservation 2001–02; Minister of Telecommunication, Information and Communications Tech. 2002–04; Sec., High Council for Peace and Reconciliation, also, Security Adviser to the Pres. 2010–14; Acting Minister of Defence 2015–16; Dir Nat. Directorate of Security 2016–. *Address:* National Directorate of Security, Kabul, Afghanistan (office).

STANISHEV, Sergey Dmitrievich, PhD; Bulgarian politician; *President, Party of European Socialists (PES);* b. 5 May 1966, Kherson, Ukrainian SSR; s. of Dimitar Stanishev and Dina Stanisheva; partner Elena Yoncheva 1994–2009; m. Monika Yosifova 2013; one s. one d. and one step-s. one step-d.; ed Moscow State Univ., Moscow School for Political Studies, London School of Econs, UK; freelance journalist 1994–95; acquired Bulgarian citizenship 1996; staff mem. Foreign Affairs Dept, Balgarska Sotsialisticheska Partiya (BSP—Bulgarian Socialist Party) 1995, Chief Foreign Policy and Int. Relations Dept 1996–2001, elected mem. BSP Supreme Council (Chair. 2001–14) and mem. Exec. Bureau 2000; mem. Bulgarian Nat. Ass. for Ruse (Roussé) constituency 2001–; mem. of the Presidency, Party of European Socialists (PES) 2002, Chair. PES Foreign Policy Network, Acting Pres. PES 2011–12, Pres. 2012–; Prime Minister of Bulgaria 2005–09; Vice-Pres. Socialist International 2012–; mem. European Parl. 2014–; voluntarily gave up his parl. immunity to be tried in court on a charge of losing seven classified documents while he was Prime Minister Oct. 2013, cleared of all charges Jan. 2017. *Publications:* more than 50 publs on foreign policy issues. *Leisure interests:* fitness, skiing, diving, motorcycling. *Address:* European Parliament, Rue Wiertz, Altiero Spinelli 11G154, 1047 Brussels (office); Party of European Socialists (PES), 10 rue Guimard, 1040 Brussels, Belgium (office). *Telephone:* (2) 548-90-80 (PES) (office). *Fax:* (2) 230-17-66 (PES) (office). *E-mail:* pes.president@pes.eu (office). *Website:* www.europarl.europa.eu (office); www.pes.eu/oc/en/about-us/the-party/ president (office).

STĂNIŞOARĂ, Mihai; Romanian engineer and politician; b. 11 June 1962, Craiova, Dolj co.; m. Codruţa-Mirela Stănişoară; one s. one d.; ed Polytechnic Inst. of Timisoara, Nat. Defence Coll., Higher Coll. of Nat. Security, NATO Defence Coll., Rome; worked as engineer at measurement and control devices factory 1986–89; Asst, Tech. Univ. of Timisoara 1988–90; design engineer, Centre of Appliances Research and Technological Eng 1989–90; Sec.-Gen., Chamber of Commerce and Industry, Mehedinti co. 1992–94, Chair. 1994–96; Sec. Gen. Ministry of Defence 2000; mem. Chamber of Deputies for Mehedinţi Co. 2000–08 (Democratic Party), Pres. Parl. Del. to OSCE Parl. Ass. 2000–04, mem. Foreign Policy Cttee 2000–04, Chair. Defence, Public Order and Nat. Security Cttee 2004–07; Vice-Pres. Parl. Del. to NATO Parl. Ass. 2004–07; Presidential adviser on Nat. Security 2007–08; mem. Senate (Democratic Liberal Party) for Mehedinţi Co. 2008–; Minister of Nat. Defence 2008–09. *Address:* Senate of Romania, 050711 Bucharest, Calea 13 Septembrie, nr 1–3, Sector 5, Romania (office). *Telephone:* (21) 414-1111 (office). *Fax:* (21) 315-6003 (office). *E-mail:* infopub@senat.ro (office). *Website:* www.senat.ro (office).

STANKEVIČIUS, Česlovas Vytautas; Lithuanian politician, engineer and diplomatist; b. 27 Feb. 1937, Vilkaviskis Region; s. of Jonas Stankevičius and Uršulė Dubickaitė; m. Jadvyga Litvinaitė 1962; two s.; ed Kaunas Polytechnic Inst.; engineer, Chief of Design, Chief Engineer, Kaunas Inst. of Urban Planning and Designing 1965–89; Chair. Kaunas Bd Sajūdis Movt 1989–90; elected Deputy and Vice-Pres. of Supreme Council, Repub. of Lithuania; signatory to March 11th Act on Re-establishment of Independence; Head official del. in negotiations with Russia 1990–93; Head, Lithuanian Parl. del. to N Atlantic Ass. 1991–92; mem. Seimas, Parl. 1996–2000, 2008–12, Deputy Chair. 2008–12; Minister of Defence 1996–2000; Amb. to Norway 2001–05; Adviser to the Minister of Foreign Affairs 2005–08; co-author projects on nat. security and defence concept of Lithuania 1996, Law on Defence Org. 1997, Lithuanian defence strategy 2000; Order of Gediminas 2000. *Publications:* Enhancing Security of Lithuania and Other Baltic States in 1992–94 (monograph), Negotiations with Russia on Troop Withdrawal 2002. *Leisure interests:* literature, the arts.

STANKOVIĆ, Zoran, BA MA PhD; Serbian pathologist and politician; *President of Coordination Body for Municipalities of Presevo, Bujanovac and Medvedja;* b. 9 Nov. 1954, Tegoviste, Vladicin Han Municipality; m. Marina Stanković; two d.; ed Univ. of Niš, Mil. Medical Acad.; head of garrison first aid station, Peč 1982–85; commissioned Medical Corps Lt 1983; specialized training 1985–88; Forensic Assessor 1987; pathologist 1988–90, Head of Tissue Culture Dept 1990–96, Pathology and Forensic Medicine Inst., Mil. Medical Acad.; extraordinarily commissioned Maj. 1991; mem. Vukovar Ad Hoc Group, ICRC 1992–93; extraordinarily commissioned Lt-Col 1993; mem. Comm. Expert on Tracing Missing Persons of Republika Srpska Govt 1994; Prof., Faculty of Medicine, Banja Luka 1994–95; apptd Visiting Prof. King's Coll., Cambridge 1995; apptd Prof. of Criminological Medicine, Belgrade Police Acad. 1996; Head of Forensic Medicine Inst., Pathology and Forensic Medicine Inst. 1996–2001; commissioned Col 1997; Expert Officer, Comm. on Humanitarian Issues and Missing Persons of Fed. Repub. of Yugoslavia Govt 1997; Expert Witness, The Hague Tribunal 1998; extraordinarily commissioned Maj.-Gen. 2001 (retd in rank, 2005); Head of Pathology and Forensic Medicine Inst., Mil. Medical Acad. 2001–02, Head of Mil. Medical Acad. 2002–05; Minister of Defence 2005–07, also mem. Council of Ministers, Minister of Health 2011–12; Pres. of the Cttee on Data Collection on Crimes Against Humanity and Int. Law of Fed. Repub. of Yugoslavia Govt 2002–03; mem. of Truth Comm. 2002; currently Pres. Coordination Body for Municipalities of Presevo, Bujanovac and Medvedja; Mil. Merits Medal 1988, "Bela Povelja" Award, Serbian Asscn of Doctors 1993, Public Health Service Org. Annual

Award 1993, Cvijiceva Medal 1999. *Publications:* author or co-author of over 40 scientific papers. *Address:* Office of the President of the Coordination Body, Bulevar Mihaila Pupina 2, 11070 Belgrade, Serbia (office). *E-mail:* kabinet@kt.gov.rs (office). *Website:* www.kt.gov.rs/en (office).

STANTON, Andrew, BFA; American film director, screenwriter and producer; b. 3 Dec. 1965, Rockport, Mass; m. Julie Stanton 1991; one s. one d.; ed Calif. Inst. of the Arts; worked as an animator for Kroyer Films; writer for animator Ralph Bakshi's Mighty Mouse, the New Adventure (Season 1); joined Pixar Animation Studios in 1990 as animator. *Films include:* Toy Story (screen writer) (co-recipient, Annie Award for Best Individual Achievement: Writing 1996) 1995, A Bug's Life (screen writer and co-dir) 1998, Toy Story 2 (screenwriter) (co-recipient, Annie Award for Outstanding Individual Achievement: Writing 2000) 1999, Monsters, Inc. (screenwriter and producer) (co-recipient, BAFTA Children's Award for Best Feature Film 2002) 2001, Finding Nemo (screenwriter and dir) (co-recipient, Annie Award for Outstanding Directing in an Animated Feature Production 2004, Acad. Award for Best Animated Feature 2004) 2003, The Incredibles (voice) 2004, Cars (voice) 2006, Ratatouille (exec. producer) 2007, WALL·E (screenwriter and dir) (co-recipient, BAFTA Children's Award for Best Feature Film 2008, Acad. Award for Best Animated Feature Film of the Year 2009, BAFTA Award for Best Animated Film 2009) 2008, Up (exec. producer) 2009, Toy Story 3 2010, John Carter (screenwriter and dir) 2012, Brave (exec. producer) 2012, Monsters University (exec. producer) 2013, Inside Out (exec. producer) 2015, The Good Dinosaur (exec. producer) 2015, Finding Dory (screenwriter and dir) 2016. *Television includes:* Mighty Mouse, the New Adventures (screen writer) 1987, Toy Story of Terror (TV movie) (screen writer and producer) 2013. *Address:* Pixar Animation Studios, 1200 Park Avenue Emeryville, CA 94608, USA (office). *Telephone:* (510) 922-3000 (office). *Fax:* (510) 922-3151 (office). *Website:* www.pixar.com (office).

STANTON, Katie Jacobs, BA, MA; American business executive; b. 1970, Peekskill, NY; m.; three c.; ed Rhodes Coll., Columbia Univ. School of Int. and Public Affairs; fmr producer for Yahoo! Finance; worked for Google Inc. on Google Moderator, Google Finance and Open Social initiative; Dir of Citizen Participation, The White House, Washington, DC 2009; Special Advisor to the Office of Innovation, US Dept of State Jan.–July 2010, launched Text Haiti (mobile donation campaign for American Red Cross following earthquake in Haiti); Vice-Pres., Int. Market Devt, Twitter Inc. 2010–14, Vice-Pres., Global Media 2014–16 (resgnd). *Website:* www.twitter.com (office).

STANZEL, Franz-Karl, DrPhil; Austrian academic; *Professor Emeritus of English, Karl-Franzens-Universität Graz;* b. 4 Aug. 1923, Molln; s. of Franz Stanzel and Luise Stanzel; m. Ina v. Navarini 1992; one d.; ed Univ. of Graz and Harvard Univ., USA; Lecturer in English, Karl-Franzens Univ. Graz 1949–50, 1951–57, Prof. of English 1962–93, Prof. Emer. 1993–, Dean, Faculty of Arts and Sciences 1967–68, Head, Dept of English 1962–78; Asst Prof., Univ. of Göttingen 1957–59; Prof., Univ. of Erlangen 1959–62; mem. Austrian Acad. 1972–2009; Bundesverdienstkreuz (Austria); Dr hc (Fribourg), (Marburg). *Publications include:* Typische Erzählsituationen im Roman 1955, Typische Formen des Romans 1964, Narrative Situations in the Novel 1969, Der literarische Aspekt unserer Vorstellungen vom Charakter fremder Völker 1974, Theorie des Erzählens 1979, A Theory of Narrative 1984, Englische und deutsche Kriegsdichtung, Sprachkunst 1987, Intimate Enemies (ed.) 1993, Europäer: Ein imagologischer Essay 1997, Europäischer Völkerspiegel (ed.) 1999, Unterwegs Erzähltheorie für Leser 2002, Telegonie-Fernzeugung. Macht und Magie der Imagination 2008, Welt als Text: Grundbegriffe der Interpretation 2011, Der Fall 'Laconia' und seine Folgen. Vergleich der BBC und ARD TV-Filme 2012, Verlust einer Jugend: Rückschau eines Neunzigjährigen auf Krieg und Gefangenschaft 2013, Die typischen Erzählsituationen 1955–2015: Erfolgeschichte einer Triade 2015. *Leisure interests:* cross-country skiing, gardening, travel, sculpture, stone-carvings. *Address:* Karl-Franzens-Universität Graz, Universitäts-platz 3, 8010 Graz (office); 511 Institut für Anglistik, Heinrichstrasse 36/II, 8010 Graz; Am Blumenhang 31/5, 8010 Graz, Austria (home). *Telephone:* (316) 380-2485 (office); (316) 47-55-56 (home). *E-mail:* franzkarl.stanzel@uni-graz.at (office). *Website:* www-gewi.uni-graz.at (office).

STANZEL, Volker, PhD; German fmr diplomatist and academic; *Visiting Professor of Government and Podlich Fellow, Claremont McKenna College;* b. 22 Sept. 1948, Frankfurt; ed Univ. of Frankfurt, Kyoto Univ., Japan, Univ. of Cologne; joined Foreign Service 1979, worked in Embassies in Rome, Tokyo, Aden, Beijing, Head of Press and Information Dept, Embassy in Beijing 1990–93, Head of Operation Centre, Foreign Office in Bonn 1993–95, Head of Dept for Non-Proliferation and Civilian Use of Nuclear Energy 1999–2001; Foreign Policy Advisor to SPD, Bundestag 1995–98; Visiting Fellow, German Marshall Fund, Washington, DC 1998–99; Dir for Asian and Pacific Affairs, Ministry of Foreign Affairs 2001–02, Dir-Gen. for Political Affairs 2002–04, Amb. to People's Repub. of China 2004–07, Political Dir, Ministry of Foreign Affairs 2007–09, Amb. to Japan 2009–13 (retd); Visiting Prof. of Govt and Podlich Fellow, Claremont McKenna Coll., Claremont, Calif., USA 2013–; mem. European Council on Foreign Relations; Sr Policy Fellow for China in Int. Affairs, Mercator Inst. for China Studies, Berlin; mem. Advisory Bd China programmes for the Robert Bosch Stiftung; mem. SPD 1966–2013; Hon. Prof., Zhengzhou Univ. 2006; Order of Merit of the FRG, First Class. *Publications:* Japan: Head of the Earth 1982, Winds of Change: East Asia's New Revolution 1997, A World of Warring States: China's Perception and Possibilities of Its International Role 1997, NATO after Enlargement 1998, Dealing with the Backwoods: New Problems in Transatlantic Relations 1999, Remembering and Forgetting: But Will the Past Forget About Us? 2001, China's Foreign Policy 2001, Germany's Defense at the Hindukush: The Experiment of Afghanistan 2005. *Address:* Claremont McKenna College, 385 East Eighth Street, Claremont, CA 91711, USA (office). *Telephone:* (909) 621-8244 (office). *Fax:* (909) 621-8579 (office). *E-mail:* athenaeum@cmc.edu (office). *Website:* www.claremontmckenna.edu (office).

STAPLE, George Warren, CB, QC; British lawyer; *Consultant, Clifford Chance LLP;* b. 13 Sept. 1940, Bristol; s. of Kenneth Staple and Betty Staple; m. Olivia Lowry 1968; two s. two d.; ed Haileybury; qualified as solicitor 1963; Assoc., Condon & Forsyth, New York 1963; Pnr, Clifford-Turner, later Clifford Chance 1967–92, 1997–2001, consultant to Clifford Chance LLP 2001–; Dir, Serious Fraud Office 1992–97; Legal Assessor, Disciplinary Cttee Stock Exchange 1978–92; Dept of Trade & Industry Insp., Consolidated Goldfields 1986, Aldermanbury Trust 1988; Chair., Authorization and Disciplinary Tribunals of Securities Asscn 1987–91, Securities and Futures Authority 1991–92; mem. Commercial Court Cttee 1977–92; mem. Council, Law Soc. 1986–2000; mem. Law Advisory Cttee of British Council 1998–2001; mem. Sr Salaries Review Body 2000–04; Chair., Review Bd for Govt Contracts 2002–09; Chair. Govs, Haileybury 2000–08; mem. Accountancy and Actuarial Disciplinary Tribunal; Gov., London Guildhall Univ. 1982–94; Fellow, Soc. for Advanced Legal Studies 1997; Trustee, Royal Humane Soc. 2007–, Romney Marsh Historic Churches Trust; Hon. QC 1997, Hon. Bencher, Inner Temple 2000. *Leisure interests:* cricket, hill walking, gardening. *Address:* Clifford Chance, 10 Upper Bank Street, London, E14 5JJ, England. *Telephone:* (20) 7006-1000. *Fax:* (20) 7006-5555. *Website:* www.cliffordchance.com (office).

STAPLETON, Craig Roberts, BA, MBA; American business executive and fmr diplomatist; *Senior Advisor, Stone Point Capital LLC;* b. 1945, Kansas City, Mo.; m. Dorothy Walker Stapleton; one s. one d.; ed Phillips Exeter Acad., Harvard Coll. and Harvard Business School; Pres. Marsh & McLennan Real Estate Advisors, New York 1982–2001; Partner with George W. Bush in ownership of Texas Rangers professional baseball team 1989–98; Conn. State Chair. for re-election campaign of Pres. George W. Bush 2004; Amb. to Czech Repub. 2001–04, to France 2005–09 (also accred to Monaco 2006–09); Sr Advisor, Stone Point Capital LLC, Greenwich, Conn. 2009–; Co-owner St Louis Cardinals professional baseball team 2009–; CEO SonomaWest Holdings 2010–11; f. Stapleton Acquisition Company, Denver; Pres. Vaclav Havel Foundation; mem. Bd of Dirs Abercrombie and Fitch, Carlile Bancshares, Inc., Flamel Technologies, C3 GP, LLC; fmr mem. Visiting Cttee for Harvard Coll. and Cttee on Univ. Resources, Bd Peace Corps; Trustee, George W. Bush Library and Foundation, 9/11 Memorial Foundation;, Mona Bismark Foundation, de Touqueville/United Way Foundation, Cen. Europe for Research and Grad. Educ., Asscn Francois-Xavier Bagnoud; fmr Trustee Brunswick School, Greenwich, Conn.; Hon. Citizen of Deauville, Chateauneuf du Pape, Rocamadour and Vienne, France; Commdr, Légion d'honneur 2009; Jan Masaryk Medal for service to the Czech Repub. *Publications:* Where Liberty Dwells, There is My Country 2009. *Address:* Stone Point Capital LLC, 20 Horseneck Lane, Greenwich, CT 06830-6327, USA (office). *Telephone:* (203) 862-2900 (office). *Fax:* (203) 625-8357 (office). *E-mail:* CRSTAPLETON45@gmail.com. *Website:* www.stonepoint.com (office).

STAPLETON, Nigel John, MA; British business executive; b. 1 Nov. 1946, London; s. of Frederick E J. Stapleton and Katie M. Tyson; m. Johanna Molhoek 1982; one s. one d.; ed Univ. of Cambridge; internal auditor, Unilever Ltd 1968–70; Group Man. Internal Audit, Unilever Ltd 1970–73, Sr Auditor 1973–75; Corp. Planning Man. BOCM Silcock 1975–77, Devt Dir 1977–80; Commercial mem. N American office, Unilever PLC 1980–83; Vice-Pres. Finance, Unilever US Inc. 1983–86; Finance Dir Reed Int. PLC, London 1986–96, Deputy Chair. 1994–97, Chair. 1997–99, CEO 1999, Deputy Chair., Chief Financial Officer, Reed Elsevier 1994–97, Co-Chair. 1996–98; Chair. Veronis, Suhler Int. Ltd 1999–2002; Chair. Uniq PLC 2000–06; Chair. Postal Services Comm. 2004–11; Chair. Mineworkers Pension Scheme 2008–, Coal Pension Trustees Ltd 2012–; mem. Bd of Dirs Axa UK PLC 2000–02, London Stock Exchange PLC 2001–10, JSC Kazpost 2008–14, Real Estate Fund Samruk Kazyna 2011–14, Samruk Kazyna JSC 2014–; Fellow, Chartered Inst. of Man. Accountants; Liveryman of the Worshipful Company of Stationers and Newspaper Makers; Hon. Fellow, Fitzwilliam Coll., Univ. of Cambridge 1997; Freedom of the City of London 1999. *Leisure interests:* gardening, classical music, opera, food and wine. *Address:* Mineworkers' Pension Scheme, Sutherland House, Russell Way, Crawley, RH10 1UH, England (office). *E-mail:* nigel.stapleton@btinternet.com. *Website:* www.mps-pension.org.uk (office).

STARACE, Francesco; Italian engineer and business executive; *CEO and General Manager, Enel SpA;* b. 1955, Rome; ed Milan Polytechnic Inst.; analyst for security of electronuclear plants at Nira Ansaldo 1981–82; several exec. man. positions in Italy, USA, Saudi Arabia, Egypt and UAE for Sae Sadelmi (part of General Electric group) 1982–87; worked for ABB and then Alstom Power Corpn 1987–2000, CEO ABB Combustion Engineering Italia 1997–98, Sr Vice-Pres. for Global and Turnkey Systems Sales for Gas Turbine Div. 1998–2000; joined Enel Group 2000, several sr man. positions, including Chief of Business Power 2002–05, Chief of Market Div. 2005–08, CEO and Gen. Man. Enel Green Power 2008–14, CEO and Gen. Man. Enel SpA 2014–; mem. Advisory Bd, UN Sustainable Energy 4 All initiative 2014–, Bd of Dirs, UN Global Compact 2015–; Co-Chair. Energy Utilities and Energy Technologies Community, World Econ. Forum 2016–. *Address:* Enel SpA, Viale Regina Margherita 137, 00198 Rome, Italy (office). *Telephone:* (06) 83057610 (office). *Fax:* (06) 83057954 (office). *E-mail:* francesco.starace@enel.com (office). *Website:* www.enel.com (office).

STARCK, Christian, DrIur; German legal scholar and academic; *Professor Emeritus of Public Law, University of Göttingen;* b. 9 Jan. 1937, Breslau; s. of Walter Starck and Ruth Hubrich; m. Brigitte Edelmann 1965; one s. two d.; ed Univs of Kiel, Freiburg and Würzburg; clerk, Fed. Constitutional Court 1964–67; Govt official 1968–69; Lecturer, Univ. of Würzburg 1969–71; Prof. of Public Law, Univ. of Göttingen 1971–, currently Prof. Emer.; Rector Univ. of Göttingen 1976–77; Judge, Constitutional Court of Lower Saxony 1991–2006; Ed. Studien und Materialen zur Verfassungsgerichtsbarkeit 1973–; co-Ed. Juristenzeitung 1978–2006, Staatswissenschaften und Staatspraxis 1990–98, Beiträge zum ausländischen und vergleichenden öffentlichen Recht 1989–, Zeitschrift für Staats- und Europawissenschaften 2003–05; mem. TV Bd Zweites Deutsches Fernsehen 1978–92; mem. Asscn of German Profs of Public Law 1969– (Exec. Cttee 1988, 1989, Pres. 1998, 1999), Exec. Cttee Int. Asscn of Constitutional Law 1981–2004, Exec. Cttee German Asscn of Comparative Law 1985–; Pres. Societas Juris Publici Europaei 2003–07; Visiting Prof., Paris I (Panthéon-Sorbonne) 1987; mem. Acad. of Sciences and Humanities in Göttingen 1982– (Pres. 2008–12); Corresp. mem. Real Academia de Jurisprudencia y Legislación, Madrid 2010–; Fellow Inst. for Advanced Study, Berlin 1990–91; Hon. Pres. Int. Asscn of Constitutional Law 2004, Hon. Pres. Societas Iuris Publici Europeei 2007–, Hon. mem. Acad. of Sciences of Repub. of Korea. *Publications include:* Der Gesetzesbegriff des Grundgesetzes 1970, Rundfunkfreiheit als Organisationsproblem 1973, Das Bundesverfassungsgericht im politischen Prozess 1976; Bundesverfassungsgericht und Grundgesetz (two vols) (ed.) 1976, Vom Grund des Grundgesetzes 1979, El Concepto de Ley en la Constitución Alemana 1979, La Constitution, cadre et mesure du droit 1994, Praxis der Verfassungsauslegung Vol. I 1994, Vol. II 2006, Die Verfassungen der neuen deutschen Länder 1994, Der demokratische Verfassungsstaat 1995, Constitutionalism, Universalism and Democracy – A Comparative Analysis (ed.) 1999, Freiheit und Institutionen 2002, Verfassungen 2009, Grundgesetz Kommentar, 6th edn, Vol. I–III 2010, Jurisdicción constitucional y derechos fundamentales 2011, Woher kommt das Recht? 2015. *Leisure interests:* architecture, literature, walking. *Address:* Schlegelweg 10, 37075 Göttingen, Germany (home). *Fax:* (551) 4882891 (home). *E-mail:* cstarck@gdwg .de (home). *Website:* www.jura.uni-goettingen.de/privat/c.starck.

STARCK, Philippe-Patrick; French designer; b. 18 Jan. 1949, Paris; s. of André Starck and Jacqueline Lanourisse; m. 1st Brigitte Laurent 1977 (deceased); two c.; m. 2nd Nori Vaccari-Starck; ed Inst. Notre-Dame de Sainte-Croix, Neuilly-sur-Seine, Ecole Nissim de Camondo, Paris; f. Starck Products 1979; Interior architecture: La Main-Bleue 1976, Les Bains-Douches 1978, pvt. apartments in Elysée Palace 1982, Le Café Costes 1984, La Cigale, Paris 1987, restaurants, housing and offices in Tokyo 1986–88, Royalton Hotel, New York 1988, Paramount Hotel, New York 1990, Teatriz Restaurant, Madrid 1990, Groningen Museum 1994, Peninsula Restaurant, Hong Kong 1994, Delano Hotel, Miami 1995, Theatron Restaurant, Mexico 1995, Mondrian Hotel, LA 1996, Asia de Cuba Restaurant, New York 1997, St Martin's Hotel, London 1999, Mikli glasses shop, Paris 1999, Restaurant BON, Paris 2000, Sanderson Hotel, London 2000, Hudson Hotel, New York 2000, Clift Hotel, San Francisco 2001, Miramar Hotel, Santa Barbara (in progress); architecture includes knife factory, Laguiole 1988, Nani Nani Bldg, Tokyo 1989, bldgs in USA, Japan, France, Spain, Ecole Nat. des Arts Décoratifs, Paris 1995, air traffic control tower for Bordeaux Airport 1997, incineration plant, Paris/Vitry (2004); cr. furniture for Pres. of the Repub. 1982, for French, Italian, Spanish, Japanese and Swiss cos; designed boats for Bénéteau, vases for Daum, luggage for Vuitton, toothbrush for Fluocaril, urban furniture for Jean-Claude Decaux, Olympic Flame 1992, children's toys, Aprilia scooters, etc.; Worldwide Artistic Dir Thomson Consumer Electronics Group 1993–96; Artistic Dir Eurostar train 2001; Prof., Domus Acad., Milan, Italy, Ecole des Arts Décoratifs de Paris; Artistic Dir Int. Design Yearbook; exhbns at Georges Pompidou Museum and Decorative Arts Museum, Paris, Villa Medici, Italy, Deutsches Museum, Munich, Kunstmuseum, Düsseldorf, Museum of Modern Art, Kyoto, Japan, Design Museum, London and in Switzerland and USA; Vanity Case Exhbn travelling around the world; Commdr des Arts et des Lettres 1998, Chevalier, Légion d'honneur 2000; numerous prizes, including Oscar du Luminaire 1980, three 1st prizes at Neocon, Chicago 1986, Delta de Plata, Barcelona 1986, Platinum Circle Award, Chicago 1987, Grand prix nat. de la Création Industrielle 1988; three awards for hotels in USA 1990, 1991, one for Hotel Paramount 1992, Disseny Barcelona 1995, Design-Zentrum Nordrhein Westfalen Award (Germany) for Duraint bathroom design 1995, Harvard Excellence in Design Award 1997, Prath Inst. Black Alumni Award 2001. *Leisure interest:* sailing. *Website:* www.starck.com.

STARKEY, David Robert, CBE, MA, PhD, FSA, FRHistS; British historian, academic and broadcaster; b. 3 Jan. 1945, Kendal; s. of Robert Starkey and Elsie Lyon; ed Kendal Grammar School, Fitzwilliam Coll., Cambridge; Research Fellow, Fitzwilliam Coll., Cambridge 1970–72, Visiting Fellow 1998–2001, Bye-Fellow 2001–06, Hon. Fellow 2006–; Lecturer in History, Dept of Int. History, LSE 1972–98; Visiting Vernon Prof. of Biography, Dartmouth Coll., NH, USA 1987, 1989; British Council Specialist Visitor, Australia 1989; mem. Editorial Bd History Today 1980–, Commemorative Plaques Working Group, English Heritage 1993–2006; Pres., Soc. for Court Studies 1995–2005; Patron, Tory Group for Homosexual Equality 1994–; Historical Adviser to Henry VIII Exhbn, Nat. Maritime Museum, Greenwich 1991; Guest Curator, Elizabeth I Exhbn, Nat. Maritime Museum 2003, Lost Faces – Identity and Discovery in Tudor Royal Portraiture Exhbn, Philip Mould Gallery 2006, Henry VIII: Man and Monarch Exhbn, British Library 2009; mem. Fitzwilliam Soc. (Pres. 2003–04); Hon. Assoc., Rationalist Press Asscn 1995–; Freeman, Worshipful Co. of Barbers 1992, Liveryman 1999; Hon. DLitt (Lancaster) 2004, (Kent) 2006; Medlicott Medal 2001. *Radio:* panellist, The Moral Maze (BBC Radio 4) 1992–2001, presenter, Talk Radio 1995–98. *Television:* presenter/writer, This Land of England (Channel 4) 1985, Henry VIII (Channel 4) (Indie Documentary Award 2002) 1998, Elizabeth (Channel 4) 2000, The Six Wives of Henry VIII (Channel 4) (New York Festival for int. TV programming and promotion silver medal) 2001, The Unknown Tudors (Channel 4) 2002, Re-Inventing the Royals 2002, Monarchy (Channel 4) 2004–07, Starkey's Last Word (More 4) 2006, Henry VIII: Mind of a Tyrant (Channel 4) 2009, Kate and William: Romance and the Royals 2011, The Churchills 2012, David Starkey's Music and Monarchy 2013. *Publications include:* This Land of England (with David Souden) 1985, The Reign of Henry VIII: Personalities and Politics 1985–86, Revolution Reassessed: Revisions in the History of Tudor Government and Administration (ed. with Christopher Coleman) 1986, The English Court from the Wars of the Roses to the Civil War (ed.) 1987, Rivals in Power: the Lives and Letters of the Great Tudor Dynasties (ed.) 1990, Henry VIII: A European Court in England 1991, The Inventory of Henry VIII, Vol. 1 (with Philip Ward) 1998, Elizabeth: Apprenticeship 2000 (WHSmith Award for Biog./ Autobiog. 2001), Six Wives: The Queens of Henry VIII 2003, Monarchy: The Early Kings 2004, The History of England: Jane Austen and Charles Dickens 2006, Monarchy: From the Middles Ages to Modernity 2006, Henry: Virtuous Prince 2008, Crown & Country 2010; numerous articles in learned journals. *Leisure interests:* decorating, gardening. *Address:* Fitzwilliam College, Cambridge, CB3 0DG, England (office). *Telephone:* (1223) 332000 (office). *Website:* www.fitz.cam.ac .uk (office).

STAROBINSKY, Aleksei A., MSc, PhD; Russian theoretical physicist and academic; *Principal Research Scientist, Landau Institute for Theoretical Physics;* b. 19 April 1948, Moscow; ed Moscow State Univ., Landau Inst. for Theoretical Physics, USSR (now Russian) Acad. of Sciences; Research Scientist, Sr Research Scientist, Landau Inst. for Theoretical Physics 1975–90, Science Sec. 1987–90, Head of Dept of Gravity and Cosmology and Leading Research Scientist 1990–97, Prin. Research Scientist 1997–, Co-Dir USSR-USA Summer Program for Young Investigators in Cosmology 1990, 1991, Deputy Dir of Inst. 1999–2003; Visiting Prof., Ecole Normale Superieure, Paris March–Sept. 1991, Yukawa Inst. for Theoretical Physics, Kyoto Univ., Japan 1993–94, Research Centre for Early Universe, Univ. of Tokyo, Japan 2000–01, Institut Henry Poincaré, CNRS, Paris Sept.–Dec. 2006, Yukawa Inst. for Theoretical Physics, Kyoto Univ. March–June 2007; mem. Int. Cttee on Gen. Relativity and Gravitation 1989–97, IUPAP Rep. 2004–10; mem. Astronomy Panel, Long-Term Research Grants Program, Int. Science Foundation 1993–94; mem. Editorial Bd, General Relativity and Gravitation 1989–97, JETP Letters (Russia) 1991–, Astronomy Letters (Russia) 1992–, International Journal of Modern Physics D 1992–, Classical and Quantum Gravity 1993–96, Gravitation and Cosmology (Russia) 1994–, Physical Review D 2001–03, Journal of Cosmology and Astroparticle Physics 2002–; mem. New York Acad. of Sciences 1995; Corresp. mem. Russian Acad. of Science 1997; Russian State Distinguished Scientific Fellowship 1994–97, A.A. Friedmann Prize for Research in Field of Gravity and Cosmology, Russian Acad. of Sciences 1996, Prize of Int. Academic Publishing Co. Nauka/Interperiodica for best work of the year published in its journals 2004, Klein Medal, Stockholm Univ., Tomalla Prize, Tomalla Foundation for Gravity Research, Switzerland (co-recipient), Amaldi Medal, Italian Soc. for Gen. Relativity and Gravitational Physics (co-recipient), Cosmology Prize, Peter Gruber Foundation (co-recipient) 2013. *Achievements include:* developed first working model of inflation and calculated the generation of gravitational waves during inflation 1979. *Publications:* more than 230 papers in professional journals. *Address:* Landau Institute for Theoretical Physics, 142432 Moscow Region, Chernogolovka, Akademika Semenova av., 1-A, Russia (office). *Telephone:* (495) 702-93-17 (office). *Fax:* (495) 702-93-17 (office). *E-mail:* office@itp .ac.ru (office). *Website:* www.itp.ac.ru (office).

STARODUBOV, Vladimir Ivanovich; Russian surgeon, academic and government official; *Vice-President, Russian Academy of Medical Sciences;* b. 17 May 1950, Kosobrodsk, Kurgan Region; m.; two d.; ed Sverdlovsk State Medical Inst.; surgeon, Head, Surgery Dept, Nizhny Tagil Hosp., Sverdlovsk Region 1973–77; Asst, Chair of Surgery, Sverdlovsk State Inst. of Medicine 1977–80; Chief, Sverdlovsk town clinic 1980–81; instructor, Sverdlovsk Regional CP Cttee 1981–87; Deputy Head, Sverdlovsk Regional Dept of Public Health 1987–88; First Deputy Head, Main Dept of Public Health, Sverdlovsk, Regional Soviet 1988–89; Head, Main Dept of Treatment and Prophylactics, Ministry of Public Health RSFSR 1989–90; Deputy Minister of Public Health Russian Fed. 1990–94; Head, Prof., Chair of Econs of Man., Russian Medical Univ. 1994–96; Deputy Minister of Public Health and Medical Industry 1996–98, Minister of Public Health 1998–99, First Deputy Minister of Public Health 2004; Dir Central Scientific Research Inst., Organisation and Informatisation of Public Health, Ministry of Public Health 1999–2004, 2007–; Deputy Minister of Health and Social Devt 2005, (acting Minister of Health and Social Devt 2007); Vice-Pres. Russian Acad. of Medical Sciences 2011–; Rep. of the Russian Fed. to WHO 1999–2001, 2004; Prof., Russian State Medical Univ. 1999–; Ed. Physician and Information Technology, Health Care Manager 2003–; mem. Russian Acad. Medical Sciences 2004; Honored Physician, Russian Federation 1999. *Publications:* articles: Methodological basics and mechanisms for health care quality assurance, (with O. Shchepin, A. Lindenbraten, G. Galanova) Moscow Medicine 2002, Clinical Management: theory and practice (with T. Lugovkina) 2003, Epidermilogy of tuberculosis (with I. Son, V. Litvinov, P. Seltsovsky) 2003, Health of Russian Population in social context of 1990s: problems and perspectives (ed with Y. Mikhailova, A. Ivanova) 2003; more than 250 publications. *Address:* 117587 Moscow, 9 Kirovogradskaya str., block 2 Apartment 169, Russia (home). *Telephone:* (495) 315-39-26 (home).

STAROSTENKO, Vladimir Ivanovich; Russian transport official; *President, JSC Russian Railways;* b. 2 Sept. 1948, Tatarsk, Novosibirsk Region; m.; one s.; ed Tomsk Higher School of Railway Transport, Novosibirsk Inst. of Railway Eng; mem. of station staff, Tatarskaya W Siberian railway 1966–79, Station Man. 1970–75, inspector, Omsk Div. 1975–80, Station Man. Karbyshevo 1980–83, Head of Div. of Cargo, then Head of Div. of Transportation, Omsk Div. 1983–88, First Deputy Head of Omsk Div. 1988–90, Head of Novosibirsk Div. 1990–95, Deputy Head of West Siberian Railway 1995–96, Head 1997–99, Sept. 1999; Head of Kemerovo Railway 1996–97; Minister of Railways May–Sept. 1999; 2003, First Vice-Pres. JSC Russian Railways 2003–05, Pres. 2005–; Chair. Comm. on Transport and Transport Infrastructure, GEFCO; Chair. Bd of Trustees Centre of Nat. Glory of Russia, Foundation of St Andrew the First, Governance and Problem Analysis Centre at Social Sciences Div., Russian Acad. of Sciences (also Scientific Dir), Child Welfare Foundation Spread Your Wings; Founding Pres. World Public Forum Dialogue of Civilizations; Pres. Int. Union of Railways; Co-Pres. Asscn for Franco-Russian Dialogue; mem. Faculty of Political Science, Moscow State Univ.; Visiting Prof., Stockholm School of Econs; mem. Bd of Dirs Russian Union of Industrialists and Entrepreneurs; Trustee Russian World; the Chairman of the Board, GEFCO; Dr hc (Diplomatic Acad. of the Russian Foreign Ministry)nt of the International Union of Railways (UIC). *Address:* JSC Russian Railways, 107174 Moscow, Novaya Basmannaya Street, 2, Russia (office). *Website:* eng.rzd.ru (office).

STARR, Albert, MD; American cardiovascular surgeon and academic; b. 1 June 1926, New York, NY; ed Columbia Coll. (now Columbia Univ.), Columbia Coll. of Physicians and Surgeons; completed internship at Johns Hopkins Hosp. and residency in gen. and thoracic surgery at Bellevue and Presbyterian Hosps of Columbia Univ.; Asst in Surgery, Columbia Univ. –1957; joined Univ. of Oregon Medical School (now Oregon Health and Science Univ.—OHSU), led heart surgery program 1957–64, led joint cardiac surgery program for OHSU and Providence St Vincent Medical Center 1964–89, then moved to Providence, Medical Dir Providence Heart and Vascular Inst. 1989–2011, now Medical Dir Emer., Special Advisor to OHSU Dean of Medicine and OHSU Pres. 2011–; Chair Holder, Albert Starr Academic Center for Cardiac Surgery; mem. Starr-Wood Cardiac Group of Portland; Dr hc (Columbia Univ.), (Univ. of London), (Reed Coll.), (Lewis and Clark Coll.), (American Coll. of Surgeons); Int. Heart Pioneer Award, Soc. de Chirurgie Thoracique Cardio-Vasculaire de Langue Francaise 2000, Albert Lasker Award for Clinical Medical Research, Lasker Foundation (co-recipient) 2007. *Achievements include:* co-inventor of first artificial heart valve (Starr heart valve), which he successfully implanted in 1960. *Publications:* numerous papers in professional journals. *Address:* Starr Wood Group, Suite 240, 9155 S.W. Barnes Road, Portland, OR 97225-6625, USA (office). *Telephone:* (503) 296-4027 (office). *Fax:* (503) 216-2488 (office). *E-mail:* astarr@starrwood.com (office). *Website:* www .starrwood.com (office); www.providence.org (office).

STARR, Gregory B., BSc, MSc; American international organization official; b. 3 Feb. 1953; m.; two c.; ed George Washington Univ.; Sr Regional Security Officer, Embassy in Tel-Aviv 1997–2000; also served as Regional Security Officer at embassies in Tunis, Dakar and Kinshasa; Dir Office of Physical Security Programs, Dept of State, Washington, DC 2000–04, Deputy Asst Sec. of State for Countermeasures 2004–07, Acting Asst Sec. for Diplomatic Security and Acting Dir of Office of Foreign Missions 2007–08, Dir Diplomatic Security Service and Prin. Deputy Asst Sec. for Diplomatic Security 2008–09, 2013–17; Under-Sec.-Gen. for Safety and Security, UN 2009–13.

STARR, Kenneth Winston, BA, MA, JD; American lawyer, academic and fmr university administrator; *Louise L. Morrison Chair of Constitutional Law, Law School, Baylor University;* b. 21 July 1946, Vernon, Tex.; s. of W.D. Starr and Vannie M. Starr (née Trimble); m. Alice J. Mendell 1970; one s. two d.; ed George Washington, Brown and Duke Univs; law clerk, Court of Appeals (5th Circuit), Miami 1973–74, Supreme Court 1975–77; Assoc. Gibson, Dunn & Crutcher, Los Angeles 1974–75, Assoc. Partner, 1977–81; counsellor to Attorney-Gen., US Justice Dept, Washington, DC 1981–83, Solicitor Gen. 1989–93; Judge, Court of Appeals (DC Circuit) 1983; Partner, Kirkland & Ellis, Washington, DC 1993–2004; apptd ind. counsel for Whitewater Investigation 1994; Prof. and Dean, Pepperdine Univ. School of Law 2004–10; Pres. Baylor Univ. 2010–16, Chancellor 2013–16 (resgnd), currently Louise L. Morrison Chair of Constitutional Law, Baylor Law School; Pres. Southern Univs Conf.; mem. Bd of Dirs Nat. Asscn of Ind. Colls and Univs; mem. Bd of Trustees, Baylor Coll. of Medicine, Baylor Scott & White Health. *Publications include:* First Among Equals: The Supreme Court in American Life 2002; contrib. articles to legal journals. *Address:* Baylor Law School, Sheila and Walter Umphrey Law Center, 1114 South University Parks Drive, One Bear Place, #97288, Waco, TX 76798, USA (office). *Website:* www.baylor.edu/law (office).

STARR, Sir Ringo, MBE; British musician (drums); b. (Richard Starkey), 7 July 1940, Dingle, Liverpool; m. 1st Maureen Cox 1965 (divorced 1975); two s. one d.; m. 2nd Barbara Bach 1981; ed Dingle Vale Secondary Modern School; fmrly an apprentice engineer; played with Rory Storme and The Hurricanes 1959–62; mem. The Beatles 1962–70; numerous performances and tours world-wide; attended Transcendental Meditation Course at Maharishi's Acad., Rishikesh, India Feb. 1968; formed Apple Corps Ltd, parent org. of The Beatles Group of Companies 1968; solo artist 1969–; BPI Award for Best British Group 1977, Lifetime of Peace and Love Award, David Lynch Foundation 2014. *Film appearances include:* with The Beatles: A Hard Day's Night 1964, Help! 1965, Magical Mystery Tour (TV film) 1967, Yellow Submarine (animated film) 1968, Let it Be 1970; solo: Candy 1968, The Magic Christian 1969, 200 Motels 1971, Blindman 1971, That'll be the Day 1973, Born to Boogie (also dir and producer) 1974, Son of Dracula (also producer) 1975, Lisztomania 1975, Ringo Stars 1976, Caveman 1981, The Cooler 1982, Give My Regards to Broad Street 1984. *Television:* narrator of Thomas the Tank Engine (children's programme) 1980s. *Recordings include:* albums: with The Beatles: Please, Please Me 1963, Introducing... The Beatles 1963, With The Beatles 1963, Meet The Beatles! 1964, A Hard Day's Night 1964, Something New 1964, Beatles For Sale 1965, Help! 1965, Rubber Soul 1966, Yesterday... And Today 1966, Revolver 1966, Sgt. Pepper's Lonely Hearts Club Band (BPI Award for Best British Album) 1967, Magical Mystery Tour 1967, The Beatles (White Album) 1968, Yellow Submarine 1969, Abbey Road 1969, Let It Be 1970, At The Beeb 1994, 1 2000; solo: Sentimental Journey 1969, Beaucoups Of Blues 1970, Ringo 1973, Goodnight Vienna 1974, Blasts From Your Past 1975, Ringo's Rotogravure 1976, Ringo The 4th 1977, Bad Boy 1977, Stop And Smell The Roses 1981, Old Wave 1983, All-Starr Band 1990, Time Takes Time 1992, Live From Montreaux 1994, Vertical Man 1998, I Wanna Be Santa Claus 1999, Ringo Starr & His All-Star Band: The Anthology 2001, King Biscuit Flower Hour 2002, Ringorama 2003, Anthology... So Far 2004, Choose Love 2005, Liverpool 8 2008, Y Not 2010, Ringo 2012 2012, Icon 2014, Postcards from Paradise 2015, Give More Love 2017. *Address:* c/o Elizabeth Freund, Beautiful Day Media & Management LLC, 128 Coffey Street, 1R, Brooklyn, NY 11231, USA (office). *E-mail:* elizabeth@beautifuldaymedia.com (office). *Website:* www.beautifuldaymedia.com (office); www.ringostarr.com.

STARSKI, Allan Mieczysław; Polish production designer; b. 1 Jan. 1943, Warsaw; m.; ed Fine Art Acad., Warsaw; mem. Acad. of Motion Picture Arts and Sciences, Polish Film Asscn; Gdańsk Film Festival Award 1979, Los Angeles Critics' Asscn Award, Polish Film Award for Polish Eagles 2000. *Films include:* The Shadow Line 1976, Man of Marble 1977, The Young Ladies of Wilko 1979, The Conductor 1979, Man of Iron 1981, Danton 1982, Eine Liebe in Deutschland 1983, Escape From Sobibor 1986, Korczak 1990, Europa, Europa 1990, Daens 1992, Papierowe malzenstwo (Paper Marriage) 1992, Schindler's List (Acad. Award 1994) 1993, Wielki tydzien (Holy Week) 1995, Historie milosne (Love Stories) 1997, Washington Square 1997, Pan Tadeusz (Pan Tadeusz: The Last Foray in Lithuania) 1999, Prawo ojca 2000, The Body 2000, The Pianist 2002, The I Inside 2003, EuroTrip 2004, Oliver Twist 2005, Hannibal Rising 2007, Aftermath 20121939 Battle of Westerplatte 2013, The Cut 2014. *Leisure interests:* cinema, ice skating.

STARZEWSKI, Tomasz; British/Polish fashion designer; b. 1961, London; ed St Martin's School of Design, London; began career designing eveningwear for royals and celebrities 1981; built up large business with distribution over UK, USA and Middle East; collections shown around the world as part of British Collections, group he f. in 1987; opened his first ready-to-wear boutique on Old Brompton Road, London 1989; opened House of Tomasz Starzewski, London 1991; American debut, New York 1999. *Address:* 229 Ebury Street, London, SW1W 8UT, England (office). *Telephone:* (20) 7730-5559 (office). *Fax:* (20) 7730-5977 (office). *E-mail:* info@starzewski.com (office). *Website:* www.starzewski.com (office).

STASHEVSKYI, Stanislav Telisforovych; Ukrainian politician and electrical engineer; b. 1943, Mar'yanivka, Vasylkivsky dist, Kiev region; ed Kiev Polytechnic Inst.; mil. service 1962–65; electrician, Specialized Planning Dept, Kyivelectromontazh Trust of Kyivmiskbud 1962, then Repairman, Foreman, Sr Foreman, Chief Engineer, Head of Dept 1965–79, then Deputy Head of co. and Chief Engineer 1979–87; Deputy Head, Holovkyivmiskbud 1987–92; First Vice-Pres. Kyivmiskbud Corpn (later Kyivmiskbud Holding Co.) 1992–96; First Deputy Head, Kyiv City Admin 1996–2001, Minister of Fuel and Energy 2001; Deputy,

Verkhovna Rada (Parl.) 2002–05, Chair. Foreign Relations Cttee, Co-Chair. Inter-Parl. Comm. for Cooperation between Verkhovna Rada and Ass. of Russian Fed., Head of Verkhovna Rada Perm. Del. to GUAM Parl. Ass., Chair. GUAM Parl. Ass. Cttee on Political and Legal Issues; mem. Ukraine-EU Co-operation Cttee, Deputy Chair., Exec. Cttee of Nat. Parl. Group of Ukraine at Inter-Parl. Union 2002–05; First Deputy Prime Minister 2005–06; apptd Ukraine's rep. to CIS Economic Council 2006; Chargé d'affaires of the Embassy of Ukraine in Canberra, fmr mem. Kiev City Council and Nat. Political Council; Head of Pechersk Regional Org.; mem. Our Ukraine Party; I, II, and III Class Orders of Merit, II and III Class Orders of St Prince Volodymyr the Great, Arhistratig Michael Order; Diploma of the Verkhovna Rada. *Leisure interests:* riding, tennis.

STASSE, François; French civil servant and economist; *Senior Member, Council of State;* b. 11 Jan. 1948, Neuilly-sur-Seine; s. of Roger Stasse and Christiane Stasse (née Deveaux); m. Nathalie Duhamel 1978; ed Inst. of Political Studies, Paris; with Ministry of Industry 1972–73; joined Gen. Bd of Planning 1974, Dir Commr's Office 1979–81; Tech. Adviser to Pres. of Rep. on Econs and Finance 1981–84; Counsel Council of State 1984, Sr mem. 1996–; Dir State Hosp. Paris 1989–93; Dir-Gen. Bibliothèque nationale de France 1998–2001. *Publications include:* La Morale de l'histoire 1994, La Véritable Histoire de la Grande Bibliotheque 2002, L'Heritage de Mendés France 2004; numerous articles in journals. *Address:* Conseil d'Etat, place du Palais Royal, 75100 Paris, France (office).

STAUDINGER, Ulrich; German publisher; b. 30 May 1935, Berlin; s. of Dr Wilhelm Staudinger and Elfriede Poth; m. Irmengard Ehrenwirth 1960 (died 1989); one s. two d.; ed Volksschule and Realgymnasium; publishing training 1954–57; Lingenbrinck Barsortiment, Hamburg 1957–58; Publicity and Sales, Ensslin & Laiblin, Jugendbuchverlag, Reutlingen 1958–59; Production, Carl Hanser Verlag, Munich 1959–60; Dawson & Sons, London 1960; Franz Ehrenwirth Verlag, Munich 1960; Partner, Ehrenwirth Verlag, Munich 1964–76; responsible for purchase of Franz Schneekluth Verlag KG, Darmstadt by Ehrenwirth Verlag 1967; purchased Schneekluth 1976, sold to Weltbild Verlag 1996; purchased Philosophia Verlag GmbH, Düsseldorf 1980; Perthes – Medaille des Börsenvereins des Deutschen Buchhandels e.V. Ehrenmitglied der Verwertungsgesellschaft Wort. *Address:* Philosophia Verlag GmbH, Gundelindenstraße 10, 80805 Munich, Germany (office). *Telephone:* (89) 299975 (office). *E-mail:* info@philosophiaverlag.com (office). *Website:* en.philosophiaverlag.com (office).

STAUNTON, Imelda Mary Philomena Bernadette, CBE, OBE; British actress; b. 9 Jan. 1956, Archway, London, England; d. of Joseph Staunton and Bridie McNicholas; m. Jim Carter 1983; one d.; ed La Sainte Union Convent, Highgate, London, RADA; repertory Exeter, Nottingham, York 1976–81; Olivier Award 1985, 1990, Screen Actors' Guild Award 1999. *Stage appearances include:* Guys and Dolls 1982, 1996, Beggar's Opera 1985, She Stoops to Conquer, A Chorus of Disapproval 1985 (Olivier Award, Best Supporting Actress), The Corn is Green 1985, Fair Maid of the West 1986, Wizard of Oz 1986, Uncle Vanya 1988, Into the Woods 1990, Phoenix (Olivier Award, Best Actress in a Musical) 1990, Life x 3 2000, There Came a Gypsy Riding 2007, Sweeney Todd (Olivier Award, Best Actress in a Musical) 2011–12, Gypsy (Olivier Award, Best Actress in a Musical 2016), Who's Afraid of Virginia Woolf? 2017, Follies 2017. *Films include:* Comrades 1987, Peter's Friends 1992, Much Ado About Nothing 1993, Deadly Advice 1994, Sense and Sensibility, Twelfth Night, Remember Me 1996, Shakespeare in Love 1998, Another Life 1999, Rat 1999, Crush 2000, Bright Young Things 2002, Virgin of Liverpool 2002, Blackball 2002, Family Business 2002, Vera Drake (Best Performance by an Actress, British Ind. Film Awards, Best Actress, European Film Awards, Los Angeles Film Critics' Asscn, New York Film Critics' Circle, Evening Standard British Film Awards 2005, Best Actress in a Leading Role, BAFTA Awards 2005) 2004, Nanny McPhee 2005, 3 & 3 2005, Freedom Writers 2007, Harry Potter and the Order of the Phoenix 2007, Where Have I Been All Your Life? 2007, Three and Out 2008, A Bunch of Amateurs 2008, Taking Woodstock 2009, Harry Potter and the Deathly Hallows 2010, Another Year 2010, The Awakening 2011, Arthur Christmas (voice) 2011, The Pirates! In an Adventure with Scientists! (voice) 2012, Pride 2014, Maleficent 2014, Paddington (voice) 2014, The Canterville Ghost (voice) 2016. *Television includes:* The Singing Detective 1986, Yellowbacks 1990, Sleeping Life, Roots, Up the Garden Path 1990, Antonia and Jane, David Copperfield 1999, Victoria Wood Xmas Special 2000, Murder 2001, Cambridge Spies 2002, Strange 2002, Fingersmith 2005, A Midsummer Night's Dream 2005, Little Britain 2005, My Family and Other Animals 2005, Cranford (series) 2007–09, Clay 2008, Big and Small 2008, Psychoville (series) 2010–11, Doctor Who (series) 2011, The Girl (film) 2012, Mouse and Mole at Christmas Time (film) (voice) 2013, That Day We Sang (film) 2014. *Address:* c/o ARG, 4 Great Portland Street, London, W1W 4PA, England.

STAVRAKIS, Charilaos G., BA, MBA; Cypriot banker and politician; b. 1956; ed Univ. of Cambridge, UK, Harvard Univ. Grad. School of Business Admin, USA; more than 25 years' experience in banking sector; undertook two-month consulting position at World Bank 1989; held various positions at Bank of Cyprus, including Head of Strategic Planning and Business Devt and Sr Man. of Treasury and Int. Services, Group Gen. Man. Int. Banking 1988–2004, Gen. Man. Cyprus Investment & Securities Corpn Ltd (CISCO) (investment banking arm of the Group) 2003–08; mem. Bd Dirs Cyprus Oil Refinery, Bank of Cyprus Australia, Bank of Cyprus (Channel Islands) Ltd, Bank of Cyprus (AEDAK), Bank of Cyprus Mutual Funds Ltd, BOC Ventures Ltd, CEO-Cyprus and Deputy Group CEO 2005–08, assumed additional duties involving man. of subsidiary cos of the Group: BOC Factors, Bank of Cyprus Finance Corpn, General Insurance of Cyprus, Eurolife, The Cyprus Investment and Securities Corpn Ltd (CISCO), BOC Mutual Funds Ltd, Bank of Cyprus UK and the setting up of banks in Russia and Ukraine; Chair. Electricity Authority Cyprus 2005–08, Cyprus Bankers Employers' Asscn 2005–08; Minister of Finance (Ind.) 2008–11; mem. Chartered Inst. of Bankers (ACIB) 1988.

STAVRESKI, Zoran, BA, MA; Macedonian economist and politician; b. 29 Oct. 1964, Ohrid; m.; one c.; ed Faculty of Econs, SS Cyril and Methodius Univ., Skopje; Researcher, Research Directorate, Cen. Bank of Repub. of Macedonia 1993–97, Dir of Research Directorate 1997–2000; Under-Sec., Ministry of Finance 2000–01; Advisor to Exec. Dir in the Netherlands Constituency, World Bank 2001–04, Consultant in Europe and Cen. Asia Poverty Reduction and Econ. Man. Unit

March–Aug. 2005, in Operational Policy and Country Services Units Sept. 2005–Feb. 2006, Sr Economist for Operational Policy and Country Services Units Feb.–Aug. 2006; Deputy Prime Minister, in charge of Econ. Affairs 2006–09, Deputy Prime Minister and Minister of Finance 2009–16 (resgnd); Chair. Annual Meetings of the World Bank and IMF for 2008. *Address:* c/o Ministry of Finance, 1000 Skopje, Mito Hadjivasilev Jasmin bb, North Macedonia.

STAVRIDIS, Adm. James G., PhD, MALD; American naval officer and international organization official; *Chairman, US Naval Institute;* b. South Florida; m. Laura Stavridis; two d.; ed US Naval Acad. (distinguished grad.), Nat. War Coll. (distinguished grad.), Fletcher School of Law and Diplomacy, Tufts Univ.; Surface Warfare Officer, commanded Destroyer USS Barry (DDG-52) 1993–95, completed UN and NATO deployment to Haiti and Bosnia, and combat cruise to the Arabian Gulf, commanded Destroyer Squadron 21 1998, deployed to Arabian Gulf, commanded Enterprise Carrier Strike Group 2002–04, conducted combat operations in Arabian Gulf in support of both Operation Iraqi Freedom and Operation Enduring Freedom, commanded US Southern Command in Miami focused on Latin America and the Caribbean 2006–09; Supreme Allied Commdr, Europe, NATO 2009–13; Chair. US Naval Inst. 2013–; Dean, Fletcher School of Law and Diplomacy, Tufts Univ. 2013–18; Dir Utilidata, Inc., PreVeil, LLC, American Water Works Co. March–Aug. 2018; Operating Exec., The Carlyle Group L.P. 2018–; Chair Bd of Counselors, McLarty Associates 2018–; currently, Chair. Int. Advisory Bd Northrop Grumman Corporation, Chief Int. Security Analyst, NBC News; mem. Defense and Intelligence Advisory Bd Thinklogical Inc. 2013–; mem. Governing Bd Indian School of Business; mem. Bd of Advisors DC Capital Partners, LLC; has served as a strategic and long-range planner on staffs of Chief of Naval Operations and Chair. of Jt Chiefs of Staff; also served as Exec. Asst to the Sec. of the Navy and as Sr Mil. Asst to the Sec. of Defense; Defense Distinguished Service Medal, Defense Superior Service Medal, five awards of the Legion of Merit; Gullion Prize, Fletcher School of Law and Diplomacy 1984, USS Barry won the Battenberg Cup as the top ship in the Atlantic Fleet under his command, John Paul Jones Award for Inspirational Leadership, Navy League 1998, Ellis Island Medal of Honor 2017. *Publications include:* The Accidental Admiral 2014, Sea Power: The History and Geopolitics of the World's Oceans 2017; author or co-author of several books on naval ship-handling and leadership, including Command at Sea, Destroyer Captain, Partnership for the Americas about Latin America. *Leisure interests:* squash, tennis, cycling. *Address:* US Naval Institute, 291 Wood Road, Annapolis, MD 21402, USA (office). *Telephone:* (410) 268-6110 (office). *Fax:* (410) 571-1703 (office). *E-mail:* customer@usni.org (office). *Website:* www.usni.org (office).

STAVROPOULOS, William S., BS, LLD (Hons), PhD; American chemical company executive (retd); *Chairman, Univar Inc.;* b. 12 May 1939, Bridgehampton; m. Linda Stavropoulos; one s. one d.; ed Fordham Univ., Univ. of Washington; research chemist, Pharmaceutical Research Div., Dow Chemical Co. 1967, Diagnostics Product Research Div. 1970, Research Man. 1973, Diagnostic Products Business Man. 1976, Business Man. for polyolefins 1977, Dir of Marketing, Dow USA Plastics Dept 1979, Commercial Vice-Pres. Dow Latin America 1980, Pres. 1984, Commercial Vice-Pres. Dow USA, Basics and Hydrocarbons 1985, Group Vice-Pres. 1987, Pres. Dow USA 1990, Vice-Pres. The Dow Chemical Co. 1990, apptd mem. Bd of Dirs 1990, Sr Vice-Pres. 1991, Pres. and COO 1993–95, Pres. and CEO 1995–2000, 2002–04, Chair. 2002–06 (retd), now Chair. Emer.; Advisory Partner, Clayton, Dubilier & Rice, LLC 2006–; fmr Chair. American Chemistry Council, Soc. of Chemical Industry, American Plastics Council; Chair. Univar Inc. 2010–; Pres. and Founder Michigan Baseball Foundation; Pres. Great Lakes Loons (minor league baseball team); mem. Bd of Dirs Teradata Corpn, Chemical Financial Corpn, Maersk Inc., Tyco International, Inc.; mem. Advisory Bd Metalmark Capital LLC; Trustee, Fidelity Equity and High Income Funds Bd; Dr hc (Northwood Univ.) 1998; Man of the Year Award, American Hellenic Education Progressive Association 1995, Man of the Year Award, Hellenic American Bankers Association 1997, Ellis Island Medal of Honor 1998, CEO of the Year, Kavaler Award 1999, Man of the Year Award, Hellenic American Chamber of Commerce 2000, Société de Chimie Industrielle's Palladium Medal Award 2001, Chemical Industry Medal Award, Soc. of Chemical Industry 2001, Best CEO in America, Chemicals/Commodity category, Institutional Investor magazine 1998, 2003, 2004, Soc. of Plastic Engineers Annual Business Man. Award 2003, Outstanding Business Leader Award, Junior Achievement of Central Michigan Business Hall of Fame 2005. *Address:* Univar Inc., 3075 Highland Parkway, #200, Downers Grove, IL 60515, USA (office). *Website:* www.univar.com (office).

STEAD, C(hristian) K(arlson), CBE, ONZ, MA, PhD, LittD, FRSL, FEA; New Zealand writer and academic; *New Zealand Poet Laureate;* b. 17 Oct. 1932, Auckland; s. of James Walter Ambrose Stead and Olive Ethel Stead (née Karlson); m. Kathleen Elizabeth Roberts 1955; one s. two d.; ed Mt Albert Grammar School, Auckland Univ. Coll. and Auckland Teachers' Coll., Univ. of Bristol, UK; Lecturer in English, Univ. of New England, NSW, Australia 1956–57; Michael Hiatt Baker Scholar, Univ. of Bristol 1957–59; Lecturer, Sr Lecturer, Assoc. Prof., Univ. of Auckland 1960–67, Prof. of English 1967–86, Prof. Emer. 1986–; writer 1986–; NZ Poet Laureate 2015–; Nuffield Fellow, Univ. of London 1965, Hon. Fellow, Univ. Coll. London 1977, Sr Visiting Fellow, St John's Coll., Oxford 1996–97; Chair. NZ Literary Fund Advisory Cttee 1972–75, NZ Authors' Fund Cttee 1989–91; mem. NZ PEN (Chair. Auckland br. 1986–89, Nat. Vice-Pres. 1988–90), Creative New Zealand 1999; Fellow, English Asscn; Hon. DLetters (Bristol) 2001; Katherine Mansfield Prize 1960, Jessie Mackay Award for Poetry 1972, Katherine Mansfield Menton Fellowship 1972, New Zealand Book Award for Poetry 1976, New Zealand Book Award for Fiction 1985, 1995, Queen Elizabeth II Arts Council Scholarship in Letters 1988–89, Queen's Medal for Services to NZ Literature 1990, King's Lynn Award for poetry 2001, Michael King Fellowship 2005–06, Bogliasco Fellowship in Literature 2007, 2011, Prime Minister's Award for Literary Achievement (for fiction) 2009, Sunday Times EFG Private Bank Short Story Award 2010, Hippocrates Prize for Poetry and Medicine 2010. *Film:* Sleeping Dogs 1977. *Publications:* fiction: Smith's Dream 1972, All Visitors Ashore 1984, The Death of the Body 1986, Sister Hollywood 1989, The End of the Century at the End of the World 1992, The Singing Whakapapa 1994, Villa Vittoria 1997, Talking about O'Dwyer 2000, The Secret History of Modernism 2002, Mansfield: a novel 2004, My Name Was Judas 2006, Risk 2012, The Necessary Angel 2017; poetry: Whether the Will is Free 1964, Crossing the Bar 1972, Quesada 1975, Walking Westward 1978, Geographies 1982, Poems of a Decade 1983, Paris 1984, Between 1986, Voices 1990, Straw into Gold 1997, The Right Thing 2000, Dog 2002, The Red Tram 2004, The Black River 2007, Collected Poems 1951–2006 (Montana Book Award 2009) 2008, The Yellow Buoy 2013, That Derrida Whom I Derided Died 2018; short story collections: Five for the Symbol 1981, The Blind Blonde with Candles in Her Hair 1998, The Name on the Door is not Mine, Stories New and Selected 2016; non-fiction: The New Poetic: Yeats to Eliot 1964, In the Glass Case: Essays on New Zealand Literature 1981, Pound Yeats Eliot and the Modernist Movement 1986, Answering to the Language: Essays on Modern Writers 1990, The Writer at Work 2000, Kin of Place: Essays on 20 New Zealand Writers 2002, Book Self: the reader as writer and the writer as critic 2008, Shelf Life: Reviews, Replies & Reminiscences 2016; editor: Oxford New Zealand Short Stories (2nd series) 1966, Measure for Measure, a Casebook 1971, Letters and Journals of Katherine Mansfield 1977, Collected Stories of Maurice Duggan 1981, The Faber Book of Contemporary South Pacific Stories 1994, Werner Forman's New Zealand 1994. *Leisure interests:* music, politics, swimming. *Address:* 37 Tohunga Crescent, Parnell, Auckland 1052, New Zealand (home). *Telephone:* (9) 379-9420 (home). *E-mail:* ckstead1@xtra.co.nz (home). *Website:* www.otago.ac.nz/library/exhibitions/poet_laureate/pl_temata.html.

STEADMAN, Alison, OBE; British actress; b. 26 Aug. 1946, Liverpool, Merseyside, England; d. of George Percival Steadman and Marjorie Evans; m. Mike Leigh (q.v.) (divorced 2001); two s.; partner Michael Elwyn; ed East 15 drama school, Loughton, Essex; began career in repertory theatre in Lincoln, Bolton, Liverpool, Worcester and Nottingham; Hon. Fellow, John Moores Univ., Liverpool; Hon. MA (East London); Hon. DLit (Liverpool) 2008; Dr hc (Essex) 2003; Evening Standard Best Actress Award 1977, Olivier Award for Best Actress 1993. *Stage appearances include:* Beverley in Abigail's Party, Mae-Sister Woman in Cat on a Hot Tin Roof, Nat. Theatre (NT) 1988, Uncle Vanya, Mari Hoff in The Rise and Fall of Little Voice, NT, David Edgar's Maydays, RSC, Tartuffe, RSC 1983, Joking Apart, Kafka's Dick, Royal Court, Marvin's Room 1993, The Plotters of Cabbage Patch Corner, The Provok'd Wife, Old Vic 1997, When We Are Married, Chichester and Savoy Theatres, The Memory of Water, Vaudeville Theatre, Entertaining Mr Sloane, Arts Theatre, The Woman Who Cooked Her Husband, New Ambassador Theatre, Losing Louis, Hampstead Theatre and Trafalgar Studios, London, Enjoy, UK tour and Gielgud Theatre, London, Blithe Spirit UK tour and Apollo Theatre, London 2010–11. *Films include:* Champions 1984, A Private Function 1984, Coming Through 1985, Clockwise 1986, Stormy Monday 1988, The Adventures of Baron Munchausen 1988, Wilt 1989, Shirley Valentine 1989, Life is Sweet 1990, Blame It On the Bellboy 1992, Secrets and Lies 1996, Topsy-Turvy 1999, Chunky Monkey 2001, Happy Now 2001, D.I.Y. Hard 2002, The Life and Death of Peter Sellers 2004, The Housewife 2005, Confetti 2006, Dead Rich 2006, Second Chance (short) 2009, French Exchange (short) 2011, The Day My Nan Died (short) 2012, (Notes) (short) 2012, Peterman 2014, Burn Burn Burn 2015. *Radio includes:* Bette in Cousin Bette, Beyond Black 2009, My Mad Grandad 2009, Clarissa 2010, Miss Pross in Tale of Two Cities (BBC Radio 4) 2011. *Television includes:* Hard Labour 1973, Frost's Weekly (series) 1973, Girl 1974, The Wackers (series) 1975, Tarbuck and All That! (series) 1975, Through the Night 1975, Nuts in May 1976, Esther Waters 1977, Abigail's Party 1977, The Tartuffe or Imposter 1983, P'tang Yang Kipperbang 1984, Number One 1985, The Singing Detective (series) 1986, The Short and Curlies 1987, Virtuoso 1988, Monster Maker 1989, A Small Mourning 1989, The Finding 1990, Newshounds 1990, Gone to the Dogs (series) 1991, Selling Hitler (series) 1991, Gone to Seed (series) 1992, The Wimbledon Poisoner (series) 1994, Pride and Prejudice (series) 1995, The Snow Queen's Revenge (voice) 1996, No Bananas (series) 1996, Cold Lazarus (series) 1996, Karaoke (series) 1996, The Ugly Duckling (voice) 1997, The Missing Postman 1997, Crapston Villas (series, voice) 1998, Stressed Eric (series, voice) 1998, Santa's Last Christmas (voice) 1999, Let Them Eat Cake (series) 1999, Jack and the Beanstalk (voice) 2000, Fat Friends (series 1–4) 2000, Hans Christian Andersen: My Life as a Fairy Tale 2001, Adrian Mole: The Cappuccino Years 2001, Dalziel and Pascoe 2002, 2004, Comic Relief 2003: The Big Hair Do 2003, The Worst Week of My Life (series) 2004–06, Bosom Pals (voice) 2004, Twisted Tales – Fruitcake of the Living Dead 2005, Who Gets the Dog? 2006, The Worst Christmas of My Life 2006, The Last Detective (series) 2007, Marple: Ordeal by Innocence (film) 2007, The Dinner Party (film) 2007, Fanny Hill (series) 2007, Who Gets the Dog? (film) 2007, The Omid Djalili Show (series) 2007, Gavin & Stacey (Series 1, 2 and 3) 2007–10, Gavin & Stacey Christmas Special 2008, Come Rain Come Shine (ITV drama) 2010, All Roads Lead Home (BBC) 2011, Playhouse Presents (series) – King of the Teds 2012, A Civil Arrangement (film) 2012, Inspector George Gently (series) 2012, Little Crackers (series) 2012, Lewis (series) – Intelligent Design 2013, The Syndicate (series) 2013, Love & Marriage (series) 2013, Boomers (series) 2014–16, Hold the Sunset (series) 2018, Care (film) 2018. *Address:* c/o Sue Latimer, Artists Rights Group Ltd, 4 Great Portland Street, London, W1W 8PA, England (office). *Telephone:* (20) 7436-6400 (office). *Fax:* (20) 7436-6700 (office). *E-mail:* info@argtalent.com (office). *Website:* www.argtalent.com (office).

STEADMAN, Ralph Idris; British cartoonist, writer and illustrator; b. 15 May 1936, Wallesey, Liverpool; s. of Raphael Steadman and Gwendoline Steadman; m. 1st Sheila Thwaite 1959 (divorced 1971); two s. two d.; m. 2nd Anna Deverson 1972; one d.; ed London School of Printing and Graphic Arts; with de Havilland Aircraft Co. 1952; cartoonist, Kemsley (Thomson) Newspapers 1956–59; freelance for Punch, Private Eye, Daily Telegraph during 1960s; political cartoonist, New Statesman 1978–80; designed set of stamps depicting Halley's Comet 1986; Artist-in-Residence, Leviathan (series of films, BBC 2) 1999; designer of set and costumes, The Crucible, Royal Ballet 2000; Hon. DLitt (Kent) 1995; Designers and Art Dirs Asscn Gold Award 1977, Silver Award 1977, Lifetime Achievement Award – Milton Caniff Award, Nat. Cartoonists Soc. (USA) 2005. *Written and illustrated:* Alice in Wonderland 1967, Alice Through the Looking Glass 1972, Sigmund Freud 1979, A Leg in the Wind and Other Canine Curses 1982, I, Leonardo 1983, That's My Dad 1986, The Big I Am 1988, No Room to Swing a Cat 1989, Near the Bone 1990, Tales of Weirrd 1990, Still Life with Bottle, Whisky According to Ralph Steadman 1994, Jones of Colorado 1998, Gonzo: The Art 1998, little.com 2000, The Joke's Over 2006. *Illustrator:* numerous books from 1961, including Friendship 1990 (in aid of John McCarthy), Adrian Mitchell, Heart on the Left, Poems 1953–84 1997, Roald Dahl, The Mildenhall Treasure 1999, Doodaa: The Balletic

Art of Gavin Twinge 2002. *Publications include:* Jelly Book 1968, Still Life with Raspberry: collected drawings 1969, The Little Red Computer 1970, Dogs Bodies 1971, Bumper to Bumper Book 1973, Two Donkeys and the Bridge 1974, Flowers for the Moon 1974, The Watchdog and the Lazy Dog 1974, America: drawings 1975, America: collected drawings 1977 (r.e. Scar Strangled Banger 1987), Between the Eyes 1984, Paranoids 1986, The Grapes of Ralph 1992, Teddy Where Are You? 1994, Sigmund Freud 1997, Untrodden Grapes 2005, Bruised Memories: Gonzo, Hunter Thompson and Me 2006, The Joke's Over 2007, The Devil's Dictionary (with Ambrose Bierce) 2008, Ralph Steadman's Book of Dogs 2011, Ralph Steadman's Book of Cats 2012, Ralph Steadman's Book of Extinct Boids 2012. *Leisure interests:* gardening, sheep husbandry, fishing, guitar, trumpet. *Address:* c/o Nat Sobel, Sobel Weber Associates, Inc., 146 East 19th Street, New York, NY 10003-2404, USA (office). *Telephone:* (212) 420-8585 (office). *Website:* www.sobelweber.com (office); www.ralphsteadman.com.

STEBBINS, Donald J., BSc, MBA; American business executive; b. 1958; ed Miami Univ., Univ. of Michigan; fmrly with Bankers Trust Co. and Citibank; joined Lear Corpn as Vice-Pres. Treas. 1992, then Sr Vice-Pres. Chief Financial Officer 1997, then COO Americas, Co-COO Europe, Asia and Africa; Pres. and COO Visteon Corpn 2005–08, Pres. and CEO 2008–12; mem. Bd of Dirs WABCO Holdings Inc., ITT Corpn 2012–, Allied Specialty Vehicles 2013–; mem. Business Advisory Council, Miami Univ.; Trustee Detroit Country Day School; mem. Business Leaders for Mich.

STEBBINS, Paul H.; American business executive; *Chairman Emeritus, World Fuel Services Corporation;* ed Georgetown Univ.; co-f., with Michael Kasbar, Trans-Tec Services, Inc. (global marine fuel services co.), acquired by World Fuel 1995, Exec. and Dir of World Fuel Services Corpn 1995–, Exec. Vice-Pres. and Pres. of marine segment 1995–2000, Pres. and COO World Fuel Services Corpn 2000–02, Exec. Chair. 2002–14, Chair. Emer. 2014–; mem. Bd of Dirs, First Solar, Inc.; mem. Business Round Table; mem. Bd of Trustees, New World Symphony. *Address:* World Fuel Services Corporation, 9800 NW 41st Street, Suite 400, Miami, FL 33178, USA (office). *Telephone:* (305) 428-8000 (office). *E-mail:* info@wfscorp.com (office). *Website:* www.wfscorp.com (office).

STEEDS, John Wickham, PhD, FRS, FInstP; British physicist and academic; *Professor Emeritus of Physics, University of Bristol;* b. 9 Feb. 1940, London; s. of John Henry William Steeds and Ethel Amelia Steeds (née Tyler); m. Diana Mary Kettlewell 1969; two d.; ed Haberdashers' Aske's School, Univ. Coll. London, Univ. of Cambridge; Mullard Research Fellow, Selwyn Coll. Cambridge 1964–67; Lecturer, Physics Dept, Univ. of Bristol 1967–77, Reader 1977–85, Prof. of Electron Microscopy 1985–2007, Head of Dept 2001–05, Henry Overton Wills Prof. of Physics 2002–07, Prof. Emer. 2007–; fmr mem. Council European Pole Univ. of Lille; Chair. Emersons Innovations Ltd; Gov. Univ. Hospitals Bristol 2010–16; Holweck Medal (Soc. Française de Physique and Inst. of Physics) 1996, Gjonnes Medal, Int. Union of Crystallography 2004. *Publications:* Introduction to Anistropic Elasticity Theory of Dislocations 1973, Electron Diffraction of Phases in Alloys (with J. F. Mansfield) 1984, Thin Film Diamond (co-ed.) 1994. *Leisure interest:* tennis. *Address:* H.H. Wills Physics Laboratory, Room 3.20, Royal Fort Tyndall Avenue, University of Bristol, Bristol, BS8 1TL, England (office). *Telephone:* (117) 928-8730 (office); (117) 973-2183 (home). *Fax:* (117) 925-5624 (office). *E-mail:* J.W.Steeds@bristol.ac.uk (office). *Website:* www.phy.bris.ac.uk (office).

STEEL, Danielle Fernande Schüelein; American writer; b. 14 Aug. 1950, New York; d. of John Steel and Norma Schüelein-Steel (née Stone); m. 2nd Bill Toth 1977; m. 3rd John A. Traina Jr; four s. five d.; ed Lycée Français, Parsons School of Design, New York, Univ. of New York; worked as public relations and advertising exec., Manhattan, New York; published first novel 1973, then wrote advertising copy and poems for women's magazines; wrote first bestseller, The Promise 1979; Officier, Ordre des Arts et des Lettres. *Publications:* Going Home 1973, Passion's Promise 1977, Now and Forever 1978, Season of Passion 1978, The Promise 1979, Summer's End 1980, The Ring 1980, To Love Again 1981, Palomino 1981, Loving 1981, Remembrance 1981, Love: Poems 1981, A Perfect Stranger 1982, Once in a Lifetime 1982, Crossings 1982, Thurston House 1983, Changes 1983, Full Circle 1984, Having a Baby (contrib., non-fiction) 1984, Family Album 1985, Secrets 1985, Wanderlust 1986, Fine Things 1987, Kaleidoscope 1987, Zoya 1988, Star 1989, Daddy 1989, Heartbeat 1991, Message from Nam 1991, No Greater Love 1991, Jewels 1992, Mixed Blessings 1992, Vanished 1993, Accident 1994, The Gift 1994, Wings 1995, Lightning 1995, Five Days in Paris 1995, Malice 1995, Silent Honor 1996, The Ranch 1996, The Ghost 1997, Special Delivery 1997, His Bright Light (non-fiction) 1998, The Long Road Home 1998, The Klone and I 1998, Mirror Image 1998, Bittersweet 1999, Granny Dan 1999, Irresistible Forces 1999, The Wedding 2000, The House on Hope Street 2000, Journey 2000, Leap of Faith 2001, The Kiss 2001, Lone Eagle 2001, The Cottage 2002, Sunset in San Tropez 2002, Answered Prayers 2002, Dating Game 2003, Johnny Angel 2003, Safe Harbour 2003, Echoes 2004, Toxic Bachelors 2005, The House 2006, Impossible 2006, Miracle 2006, Coming Out 2006, HRH 2006, Bungalow 2 2007, Amazing Grace 2007, Sisters 2007, Honor Thyself 2008, A Good Woman 2008, Rogue 2008, One Day at a Time 2009, Summer's End 2009, Matters of the Heart 2009, Southern Lights 2009, Big Girl 2010, Family Ties 2010, Legacy 2010, Happy Birthday 2011, Hotel Vendome 2011, Betrayal 2012, Friends Forever 2012, A Perfect Life 2014, Pretty Minnie in Paris 2014, Pegasus 2014, Prodigal Son 2015, Country 2015, Undercover 2015, Precious Gifts 2015, Blue 2016, Property of a Noblewoman 2016, The Apartment 2016, Magic 2016, Rushing Waters 2016, The Award 2016, The Mistress 2017, Dangerous Games 2017, Against All Odds 2017, The Duchess 2017; eight children's books, one book of poetry. *Leisure interest:* my children. *Address:* c/o Random House Publicity Department, 1745 Broadway, New York, NY 10019 (office); PO Box 1637, New York, NY 10156, USA (home). *E-mail:* atrandompublicity@randomhouse.com (office). *Website:* daniellesteel.com.

STEEL, Robert (Bob) K., BA, MBA; American banking executive and fmr government official; *Partner and CEO, Perella Weinberg Partners;* b. 3 Aug. 1951; m. Gillian Steel; three d.; ed Duke Univ., Univ. of Chicago; joined Goldman Sachs 1976, held several exec. positions including first as individual and institutional salesperson, then Man. Dir and Co-head of Equity Sales and Trading, Partner, Head of Equities Div., New York, Co-Chief Operating Officer, Equities Div., Man. Dir and Head of Equities Div., Goldman Sachs Equities Europe 1988–94, Vice-Chair., Co-head of Equities Div. and Fixed Income 1998–2001, Head of Equities Div. 2001–02, Vice-Chair. 2002–04, Advisory Dir and Chair. (non-exec.) Securities 2004–06; Sr Fellow, John F. Kennedy School of Govt, Harvard Univ. 2004–06; Under-Sec. for Domestic Finance, US Dept of the Treasury, Washington, DC 2006–08; Pres. and CEO Wachovia Corpn 2008–10; Partner and CEO Perella Weinberg Partners 2014–; Chair. Bd of Trustees, Duke Univ.; fmr mem. Bd of Dirs Barclays Bank PLC, Barclays PLC. *Address:* Perella Weinberg Partners, 767 Fifth Avenue, New York, NY 10153, USA (office). *Telephone:* (212) 287-3200 (office). *Fax:* (212) 287-3201 (office). *Website:* www.pwpartners.com (office).

STEEL OF AIKWOOD, Baron (Life Peer), cr. 1997, of Ettrick Forest in the Scottish Borders; **David Martin Scott Steel,** KT, KBE, PC, MA, LLB, DL; Scottish politician, journalist and broadcaster; b. 31 March 1938, Kirkcaldy, Fife, Scotland; s. of Very Rev. Dr David Steel; m. Judith Mary MacGregor 1962; two s. one d.; ed Prince of Wales School, Nairobi, Kenya, George Watson's Coll. and Univ. of Edinburgh; Pres., Edin. Univ. Liberals 1959; Past Pres., Students' Rep. Council 1960; Asst Sec., Scottish Liberal Party 1962–64; MP for Roxburgh, Selkirk and Peebles 1965–83, for Tweeddale, Ettrick and Lauderdale 1983–97; Scottish Liberal Whip 1967–70, Liberal Chief Whip 1970–75; Leader of Liberal Party 1976–88; Co-Founder, Social and Liberal Democrats 1988; Vice-Pres., Liberal Int. 1978–93, Pres. 1994–96; mem. Parl. del. to UN Gen. Ass. 1967; Sponsor, Pvt. Member's Bill to reform law on abortion 1966–67; Pres., Anti-Apartheid Movt of UK 1966–69; Chair., Shelter, Scotland 1969–73, Countryside Movt 1995–97; BBC TV Interviewer in Scotland 1964–65; Presenter of weekly religious programme for Scottish TV 1966–67, for Granada 1969, for BBC 1971–76; Dir, Border TV 1991–99; Rector, Univ. of Edin. 1982–85; MSP 1999–2003, Presiding Officer of Scottish Parl. 1999–2003; Chubb Fellow, Yale Univ., USA 1987; fmr DL Ettrick and Lauderdale and Roxburghshire; Freedom of Tweeddale 1989, of Ettrick and Lauderdale 1990, Hon. FRCOG 2014; Grand Cross, Order of Merit (Germany), Chevalier, Légion d'honneur; Dr hc (Stirling) 1991, (Heriot Watt) 1996; Hon. DLitt (Buckingham) 1994; Hon. LLD (Edin.) 1997, (Strathclyde) 2000, (Aberdeen) 2001, (St Andrews) 2003, (Glasgow Caledonian) 2004, (Brunel) 2010, Hon. DUniv (Open Univ.) 2001; Bronze Medal London-Cape Town Classic Car Rally 1998. *Publications include:* Boost for the Borders 1964, No Entry 1969, A House Divided 1980, Border Country 1985, Partners in One Nation 1985, The Time Has Come (with David Owen) 1987, Mary Stuart's Scotland (with Judy Steel) 1987, Against Goliath (autobiography) 1989. *Leisure interests:* angling, classic cars. *Address:* House of Lords, Westminster, London, SW1A 0PW, England (office); Ettrick Lodge, Selkirk, TD7 4LE, Scotland (home). *Telephone:* (20) 7219-4433 (office). *E-mail:* steeld@parliament.uk (office).

STEELE, Nickolas; Grenadian business executive and politician; *Minister for Health, Social Security and International Business;* ed Northeastern Univ., USA; Owner, Steele's Auto Supplies Co. Ltd; fmr Shadow Minister of Trade and Investment; MP for Town of St George's 2013–; Minister of Foreign Affairs and Int. Business 2013–14; Minister of Health and Social Security 2014–, also responsible for Int. Business 2016–; organizer and country head, Caribbean Canada Emerging Leaders Org.; mem. numerous public bodies including Grenada Bd of Tourism, Grenada Chamber of Industry and Commerce, Westmorland School, Nat. Emergency Relief Org. (NERO); mem. New Nat. Party (NNP). *Address:* Ministry of Health, Social Security and International Business, Ministerial Complex, Botanical Gardens, Tanteen, St George's, Grenada (office). *Telephone:* 440-2649 (office). *Fax:* 440-4127 (office). *E-mail:* min-healthgrenada@spiceisle.com (office). *Website:* www.health.gov.gd.

STEELE, Tommy, OBE; British actor and singer; b. (Thomas Hicks), 17 Dec. 1936, Bermondsey, London; s. of Thomas Walter Hicks and Elizabeth Ellen Bennett; m. Ann Donoughue 1960; one d.; ed Bacon's School for Boys, Bermondsey; entered Merchant Navy 1952; first stage appearance Empire Theatre, Sunderland 1956, London debut 1957; roles include Buttons (Cinderella), London 1958/59, Tony Lumpkin (She Stoops to Conquer) 1960, Arthur Kipps (Half A Sixpence) 1963/64, New York 1965/66, Truffaldino (The Servant of Two Masters) 1968, title role in Hans Andersen, London 1974/75, 1977/78, 1981, Don Lockwood (Singin' in the Rain), London (also dir) 1983–85, 1989 Some Like it Hot (also dir) 1991, What a Show! 1995; film debut in Kill Me Tomorrow 1956; sculpted tribute to the Beatles' Eleanor Rigby 1982; Hon. DLitt (South Bank) 1998. *Films include:* The Tommy Steele Story, The Duke Wore Jeans 1957, Tommy the Toreador 1959, Light Up the Sky 1963, Its All Happening 1966, The Happiest Millionaire 1967, Half A Sixpence, Finian's Rainbow 1968, Where's Jack 1971; TV debut in Off the Record 1956, cabaret debut, Caesar's Palace, Las Vegas 1974; composed and recorded musical autobiog. My Life, My Song 1974. *Live performances include:* An Evening with Tommy Steele 1979, Tommy Steele in Concert 1998, lead role in Bill Kenwright's stage production of Scrooge (UK tour) 2003–04; Quincy's Quest (TV) 1979. *Publications include:* Hans Andersen (co-author, stage version), Quincy 1981, The Final Run 1983, Bermondsey Boy (autobiog.) 2006. *Leisure interests:* tennis, painting, sculpture. *Address:* c/o Laurie Mansfield, International Artistes, Suite 17, Adam House, 7–10 Adam Street, London, WC2N 6AA, England (office). *Telephone:* (20) 7520-9411 (office). *E-mail:* info@lauriemansfield.co.uk (office). *Website:* www.lauriemansfield.co.uk (office).

STEELE-PERKINS, Christopher Horace, BSc; British photographer; b. 28 July 1947, Burma; s. of Alfred Steele-Perkins and Mary Lloyd; m. 1st Jacqueline de Gier 1984 (divorced 1999); two s.; m. 2nd Miyako Yamada 1999; ed Christ's Hospital, Horsham, Sussex, Univ. of Newcastle; mem. Exit Group, London 1974–82; Assoc. Viva Agency, Paris 1976–79; mem. Photography Cttee, Arts Council of GB 1977–79; mem. Magnum Photos 1983–, Pres. 1996–98; Visiting Prof., Mushishino Art Univ., Tokyo 2000; World Press Oskar Barnack 1988, Tom Hopkinson Award for Photo-journalism 1988, Robert Capa Gold Medal 1989, Cooperative Award, One World Award (both for film Dying for Publicity) 1994, Naçion-Premier Photojournalism Award, World Press Daily Life First 2000. *Television films:* Dying for Publicity 1993, Afghan Taliban 1995. *Publications:* The Teds 1979, About 70 Photographs 1980, Survival Programmes 1982, Beirut: Frontline Story 1982, The Pleasure Principle 1989, St Thomas' Hospital 1992, Afghanistan 2000, Fuji 2002, Echoes 2004, England, My England 2009, Fading Light: Portraits of Centenarians 2012. *Leisure interests:* boxing, chess, photography, film, music, literature. *Address:* 49 St Francis Road, London, SE22 8DE; Magnum Photos, 63 Gee Street, London, EC1V 3RS, England (office). *Telephone:*

(20) 7490-1771 (office); (20) 8693-1114. *E-mail:* chrissteeleperkins@hotmail.com. *Website:* www.magnumphotos.com; chrissteeleperkins.com.

STEENBURGEN, Mary; American film actress; b. 8 Feb. 1953, Newport, Ariz.; m. 1st Malcolm McDowell 1980 (divorced); one s. one d.; m. 2nd Ted Danson (q.v.) 1995; ed Neighborhood Playhouse. *Films include:* Goin' South 1978, Time After Time 1979, Melvin and Howard (Acad. Award for Best Supporting Actress) 1980, Ragtime 1981, A Midsummer Night's Sex Comedy 1982, Romantic Comedy 1983, Cross Creek 1983, Sanford Meisner – The Theatre's Best Kept Secret 1984, One Magic Christmas 1985, Dead of Winter 1987, End of the Line (also exec. producer) 1987, The Whales of August 1987, The Attic: The Hiding of Anne Frank 1988, Parenthood 1989, Back to the Future Part III 1989, Miss Firecracker 1989, The Long Walk Home 1990, The Butcher's Wife 1991, What's Eating Gilbert Grape 1993, Philadelphia 1993, Pontiac Moon 1994, Clifford 1994, It Runs in the Family 1994, My Family, Powder, The Grass Harp, Nixon, About Sarah 1995, Picnic (TV) 2000, Wish You Were Dead 2001, The Trumpet of the Swan 2001, Sunshine State 2002, Life as a House 2001, Nobody's Baby 2002, Casa de Los Babys 2003, Elf 2003, Hope Springs 2003, Marilyn Hotchkiss Ballroom Dancing & Charm School 2005, Inland Empire 2006, The Dead Girl 2006, Elvis and Anabelle 2007, Nobel Son 2007, Numb 2007, The Brave One 2007, Honeydripper 2007, Step Brothers 2008, Four Christmases 2008, In the Electric Mist 2009, The Proposal 2009, Did You Hear About the Morgans? 2009, Dirty Girl 2010, The Help 2011, Last Vegas 2013, Brahmin Bulls 2013, Song One 2014, A Walk in the Woods 2015, Book Club 2018. *Television includes:* Joan of Arcadia (series) 2003–05, Curb Your Enthusiasm 2000–09, Robot Chicken 2011, Bored to Death 2011, Wilfred 2011–12, 30 Rock 2012, Wilfred (series) 2011–13, Justified (series) 2014–15, The Last Man on Earth (series) 2015, Orange Is the New Black (series) 2015–17. *Theatre appearances include:* Holiday (Old Vic, London) 1987, Candida (Broadway) 1993. *Address:* c/o Gersh Agency, 9465 Wilshire Blvd, 6th Floor, Beverly Hills, CA 90212, USA.

STEENLAND, Douglas M., BA, JD; American lawyer and business executive; *Chairman, American International Group (AIG), Inc.;* ed Calvin Coll., Nat. Law Center at George Washington Univ.; fmr Sr Partner, Verner, Liipfert, Bernhard, McPherson & Hand (now part of Piper Rudnick, Washington, DC); also served in Office of Gen. Counsel, US Dept of Transportation; Vice-Pres. and Deputy Gen. Counsel, Northwest Airlines Corpn 1991–94, Sr Vice-Pres. and Gen. Counsel 1994–99, Exec. Vice-Pres. and Chief Corp. Officer 1999–2004, Pres. and CEO 2004–08 (airline merged with Delta Air Lines); Chair. (non-exec.) Performance Food Group 2010–; Chair. (non-exec.) International Lease Finance Corpn –2012; Vice-Chair. Travelport Worldwide Ltd 2011–13, Chair. 2013–; Chair. (non-exec.), American International Group, Inc. 2015–; Exec. Advisor, The Blackstone Group; mem. Bd of Dirs, MAIR Holdings, Inc. 1999–2003, 2004–05, Mesaba Holdings, Inc. 1999–, Northwest Airlines Corpn 2001–08, Delta Airlines 2008–11, Chrysler Group LLC 2009–14, Old Carco LLC 2009–, Digital River Inc. 2009–15; Pres. Bd of Dirs, Air Transport Asscn; mem. Bd, IATA; Chair. Guthrie Theater; mem. Bd of Dirs, Minnesota Orchestra, Greater Twin Cities United Way. *Address:* American International Group, Inc., 70 Pine Street, New York, NY 10270, USA (office). *Telephone:* (212) 770-7000 (office). *Fax:* (212) 509-9705 (office). *Website:* www.aigcorporate.com (office).

ŞTEFAN, Viorel, PhD; Romanian economist and politician; b. 26 July 1954, Mitoc, Botoşani county; m.; three c.; ed Univ. Alexandru Ioan Cuza; Economist, Enterprise NAVROM Galati River Navigation 1980–87, Man. 1987–91, CEO 1991–96, Pres. 1996–2002; mem. Senatul (upper house of parl.) 1996–2008, Chair. Bd of Finance Budget 2000–04, Deputy Chair., Finance Cttee 2004–08; mem. Camera Deputaţilor (lower house of parl.) 2008–; Minister of Public Finance Jan.–June 2017; Pres. Naval Transport Employers' Asscn 1992–98, Romanian River Shipowners and Operators Asscn 1995–2008; mem. Partidul Social Democrat 1993–; Kt, Nat. Order For Merit.

STEFANELLI, Lorella; San Marino lawyer and politician; b. 20 Feb. 1959; m. Silvano Di Mario; one s. one d.; ed Univ. of Bologna; Dir Ufficio Segreteria Istituzionale 1978–91; legal practise 1991–94; law teacher, Scuola Secondaria Superiore 1991–94; with Demographic and Electoral Services Dept, Ufficio di Stato Civile 1994; Co-ordinator, Ministry of Health 2003; Dir, Public Finance Directorate 2004–07; Co-ordinator, Ministry of Employment 2010–12; mem. Consiglio Grande e Generale (Parl.) (Ind.) 2012–, mem. Parl. Comm. of Inquiry into Cassa di Risparmio affair; Co-Capt.-Regent (jt head of state) 2015–16; Head, del. to Council of Europe Parl. Ass. *Address:* Palazzo pubblico, Piazza della Libertà, 47890 San Marino (office). *Telephone:* (549) 882286 (office). *Website:* www.reggenzadellarepubblica.sm (office).

ŞTEFĂNESCU, I. Ştefan, PhD; Romanian historian and academic; b. 24 May 1929, Goicea, Dolj Co.; s. of Ion Ştefănescu and Dumitra Ştefănescu; m. Teodora Ştefănescu 1958; one s. one d.; ed Coll. of History, Bucharest Univ. Lomonosov Univ. Moscow; researcher in history 1951–65; Head, Romanian Medieval History Dept of the N Iorga Inst. of History of the Romanian Acad. 1965–66, Deputy Dir 1966–70, Dir 1970–90; Dean of the Coll. of History and Philosophy, Bucharest Univ. 1977–85; Deputy, Nat. Ass. 1975–80, 1985–90; mem. Romanian Acad. of Social and Political Sciences 1970–90; corresp. mem. Romanian Academy 1974, mem. 1992; mem. Romanian Soc. for Historical Sciences (on main Bd), Int. Comm. for Hist. of State Ass., Comm. int. des études slaves; Vice-Chair. of the Nat. Cttee of Historical Sciences; Chair. of the Dept of History and Archaeology, Romanian Acad. of Social and Political Sciences 1970–90; mem. European Acad. of History 1981–; Order of Scientific Merit 1966, Star of the Repub. 1971; Prize of the Romanian Acad. 1967, Romanian Acad. Silver Medal 2003. *Works include:* The History of the Romanian People 1970, Medieval Wallachia from Basarab I the Founder until Michael the Brave, 1970, History of Dobrudja, Vol. III (with I. Barnea) 1971, Demography – a Dimension of History 1974, Encyclopedia of Romanian Historiography 1978, The Romanian Nation 1984, The Beginnings of Romanian Principalities 1991, The Romanian Principalities in the 14th–16th Centuries 1992, Romania's Economic History (co-author) 1994, History of the Romanians in the 17th Century 1996, Romania: Historical-Geographic Atlas (co-author) 1996, The Illustrated History of Craiova (co-author) 1996, The Romanian Principalities in the Eighteenth Century 1998, Studies of Economic History and History of Economic Thought (co-author) 1998, A History of the Romanians (Medieval History), Vol. III (co-author), Vol. IV (Ed.) 2001, Romania: Historical Landmarks (co-author) 2004. *Address:* 214 Calea Victoriei, Apt. 44, 010098 Bucharest, Romania (home). *Telephone:* (1) 6593932 (home).

STEFANIUK, Franciszek Jerzy; Polish farmer, economist and politician; b. 4 June 1944, Drelów, Biała Podlaska Prov.; m.; five c.; ed Economic Tech. School, Międzyrzec Podlaski; manages own farm; Chair. Cooperative of Agricultural Circles, Drelów 1978–82; mem. United Peasant Party (ZSL) 1963–89, Polish Peasant Party (Polskie Stronnictwo Ludowe—PSL) 1989–, Chair. Party Commune Cttee, Drelów 1982–89; Chair. Party Voivodship Cttee, Biała Podlaska 1990–98, Vice-Chair. Bd Supreme Exec. Cttee 1992–97, Chair. Supervisory Bd PSL 2000–; Deputy to Sejm (Parl.) 1989–2015, Deputy Chair. PSL Parl. Caucus 1991–93, Vice-Marshal (Deputy Speaker) Sejm 1997–2001. *Leisure interests:* folklore, folk poetry, bee-keeping.

STEFANOVIĆ, Nebojša, MEconSc, PhD; Serbian business executive and politician; *Deputy Prime Minister and Minister of Internal Affairs;* b. 20 Nov. 1976, Belgrade, Socialist Repub. of Serbia, Socialist Fed. Repub. of Yugoslavia; m. Ana Filipović; one d.; ed Gymnasium No. 9, Belgrade, Faculty of Business Studies, Megatrend Univ., Belgrade; worked in various pvt. firms, including computer equipment distribution and marketing; Marketing Dir, Intersped JSC 2004–08; Councillor, Belgrade City Ass. 2004–08, 2012–; Financial Man., Jabuka JSC 2008; mem. Srpska Radikalna Stranka (Serbian Radical Party) –2008, left to found Srpska Napredna Stranka (Serbian Progressive Party) 2008–, mem. Presidency, Vice-Pres. Main Bd and Pres. Belgrade City Bd; Deputy in Nat. Ass. of Serbia 2007–, Chair. Cttee on Trade and Tourism 2007–08, Pres. (Speaker), Nat. Ass. of Serbia 2012–14; Minister of Internal Affairs 2014–, Deputy Prime Minister 2016–. *Address:* Ministry of Internal Affairs, 11070 Belgrade, bul. Mihaila Pupina 2, Serbia (office). *Telephone:* (11) 3062000 (office). *Fax:* (11) 3114650 (office). *E-mail:* info@mup.gov.rs (office). *Website:* www.mup.gov.rs (office).

STEFFEN, Will, PhD; Australian environmental scientist and academic; *Professor Emeritus, Fenner School of Environment and Society, Australian National University;* ed Univ. of Florida, USA; began career as research chemist; fmr Researcher, Div. of Environmental Mechanics, CSIRO, Canberra; Exec. Dir Int. Geosphere-Biosphere Programme, Stockholm, Sweden 1998–2004; Visiting Fellow, Bureau of Rural Sciences, Dept of Agric., Fisheries and Forestry 2004–05; Dir Fenner School of Environment and Soc., also Pro Vice-Chancellor (Research), ANU, then Exec. Dir ANU Climate Change Inst. 2008–12, now Climate Councillor and Prof. Emer.; mem. Multi-Party Climate Change Committee 2010–11, Climate Commr 2011–13; Co-Dir Canberra Urban and Regional Futures (CURF) initiative; Science Adviser to Australian Dept of Climate 2004–11. *Address:* Climate Change Institute, Australian National University, Building 141, Linnaeus Way, Canberra, ACT 2601, Australia (office). *Telephone:* (2) 6125-6599 (office). *E-mail:* will.steffen@anu.edu.au (office). *Website:* climate.anu.edu.au (office).

STEFFENSEN, Anne Hedensted, MSc, MPol; Danish diplomatist; *Administrative Director/Director General, Danish Shipowners Association;* b. 14 Nov. 1963, Aalborg; d. of Palle H. Steffensen and Tove Steffensen; m. Lars Lundorf Nielsen 1989; three d.; ed Univ. of Aarhus, London School of Econs, UK, Univ. of Oslo, Norway; joined Danish Foreign Service 1990, Head of Section, Ministry of Foreign Affairs 1990–92, Deputy Head of Commercial Section, Embassy in London 1992–95, Head of Section, Secr. for Foreign Trade, Ministry of Foreign Affairs 1995–96, Head of Section 1996–98, Deputy Consul Gen., Consulate Gen. in New York 1998–2000, Chief Consultant, Financial Dept, Ministry of Foreign Affairs 2000–01, Head of Dept, Bilateral Relations and Project Export, Danish Trade Council 2001–03, Head of Dept, Secr., Danish Trade Council 2003–04, Under-Sec. for Foreign Trade and Investment, Amb., Ministry of Foreign Affairs 2004–06, State Sec., Head of the Trade Council, Amb. 2006–09, mem. Sr Man. Group and State Sec. for Trade and Corp. Affairs 2009–11, Amb. to UK 2011–13; Admin. Dir/Dir Gen., The Danish Shipowners Asscn 2013–; mem. Nordic Project Fund (NOPEF) 2001–03, Export Credit Fund (EKF) 2004–, The Industrialisation Fund for Developing Countries 2005–06, The Investment Fund for Central and Eastern Europe 2005–06, The Marketing Denmark Fund 2007–, The Climate Consortium 2010–; Kt, Order of the Dannebrog (First Degree) 2008. *Leisure interests:* contemporary literature, running, walking, cycling, good food. *Address:* The Danish Shipowners Association, Amaliegade 33, 1256 Copenhagen, Denmark (office). *Telephone:* 33-11-40-88 (office). *E-mail:* info@shipowners.dk (office). *Website:* www.shipowners.dk (office).

STEFFLER, John Earl, BA, MA; Canadian poet, writer and academic; b. 13 Nov. 1947, Toronto, Ont.; one s. one d.; ed Univ. of Toronto, Univ. of Guelph; Prof. of English, Sir Wilfred Grenfell Coll., Memorial Univ. of Newfoundland, Corner Brook Campus 1975–2005 (retd); Parl. Poet Laureate 2006–08; Scholar-in-Residence, Concordia Univ. 2007; mem. League of Canadian Poets, PEN, Writers' Alliance of Newfoundland and Labrador; Newfoundland Arts Council Artist of the Year Award 1992, Joseph S. Stauffer Prize 1993, Newfoundland and Labrador Poetry Award 1998, 2003. *Publications include:* An Explanation of Yellow 1980, The Grey Islands 1985, The Wreckage of Play 1988, The Afterlife of George Cartwright (novel) (Smithbooks/Books in Canada First Novel Award 1992, Thomas Raddall Atlantic Fiction Award 1992) 1991, That Night We Were Ravenous (poems) (Atlantic Poetry Award) 1998, Helix 2003, Lookout 2010; contrib. to journals and periodicals. *Address:* c/o McClelland & Stewart Ltd, 75 Sherbourne Street, 5th Floor, Toronto, ON M5A 2P9, Canada.

ŠTEFKA, Army Gen. Pavel; Czech army general; b. 15 Sept. 1954, Ruda nad Modravou; s. of Ludevít Štefka and Irena Štefka; m. Jirina Štefka; three d.; ed Mil. Coll., Vyskov, Mil. Acad., Warsaw, European Business School, Prague and American Nat. War Coll., Washington DC, USA; Chief of Staff of motorized bn, then Deputy Chief of Staff of motorized Regt, E Mil. Dist; Chief of Staff, later Commdr of motorized regt, Bratislava; Chief of Operations in an armoured div.; tutor, Mil. Acad., Brno 1991–94; Commdr 6th Mechanized Brigade, Brno 1994; Deputy Commdr 2nd Army Corps and Chief of Staff, HQ Ground Forces, Olomouc 1994–98; Chief of Operations Section of the Gen. Staff, Army of Czech Repub. 1998–99, Chief of the Gen. Staff of the Armed Forces of Czech Repub. 2002–07, Chief of the Gen. Staff of the Army 2007; rank of Maj. Gen. 2002, temporary rank of Lt Gen. 2002, Lt Gen. 2003, Gen. of the Army 2006; Cross of Merit of Minister of Defence, I, II, III Degree, Medal for Service to the Nation, NATO Medal for Service for Peace and Freedom, Commemorative Medal of Minister of Defence (Slovakia),

Silver Medal of Polish Army, Commemorative Medal of Auxiliary Tech. Bns, Hon. Remembrance Badge of Fifty Years of NATO, Order of the Legion of Merit (USA), Chevalier, Légion d'honneur, Gold Medal of the Polish Army, Pro Memoria Medal (Poland), Mil. Order of Heroism, Degree Velkodůstojník (Romania), Cross of Mil. Police. *Leisure interests:* sport, film, travel. *Address:* c/o Ministry of Defence, Tychonova 1, 160 01 Prague 6, Czech Republic (office). *Telephone:* (973) 201111 (office). *Fax:* (973) 200149 (office). *E-mail:* stefkap@army.cz (office). *Website:* www.army.cz/scripts/detail.php?id=5002 (office).

STEHELIN, Dominique Jean Bernard, PhD; French research scientist; *Director Emeritus of Research, Institute of Biology, Centre national de la recherche scientifique (CNRS);* b. 4 Sept. 1943, Thoisy; s. of Robert Stehelin and Berthe Zimmermann; m. 1st Liliane Fachan 1969 (divorced 1975); one d.; m. 2nd Monique Braun 2001; ed Lycée Fustel, Strasbourg and Univ. Louis Pasteur, Strasbourg; Perm. Researcher, sponsored by CNRS, at Louis Pasteur Univ. 1969–71; Post-doctoral studies at Institut de la Recherche Scientifique sur le Cancer with Dr A. Lwoff, Villejuif 1970–71; Visiting Scientist with J. M. Bishop at Univ. of Calif. Medical Center, San Francisco, USA 1972–75; Head of Molecular Oncology Research Unit, Institut Pasteur, Lille 1979–84, Prof. 1984–; apptd Dir of Research CNRS 1985, now Dir Emer.; Founding Dir CNRS Inst. of Biology, Lille 1994–2000; Corresp. mem. Acad. of Sciences 1990–; mem. American Soc. of Microbiology, European Molecular Biology Org., Editorial Bd Oncogene; Foreign mem. Royal Acad. of Medicine of Belgium; Chevalier, Ordre nat. du Mérite; Officier, Légion d'honneur; Grand Prix, Acad. des Sciences 1975, Louis Jeantet Award (Medicine), Geneva 1987 and four other awards. *Publications:* more than 300 int. publs on cancer research (cancer genes, retrovirus, angiogenesis). *Leisure interests:* skiing, diving, music. *Address:* CNRS Institut de Biologie, 1 rue Calmette, 59021 Lille (office); 36 rue Jacquemars Gielée, 59800 Lille, France (home). *E-mail:* dominique.stehelin@ibl.fr (office). *Website:* www.ibl.fr (office).

STEICHEN, René, DenD; Luxembourg business executive and fmr politician; *Chairman, LuxConnect SA;* b. 27 Nov. 1942; m.; three c.; ed Lycée Classique, Diekirch, Cours Supérieurs, Luxembourg, Faculties of Law, Aix-en-Provence and Paris and Inst. d'Etudes Politiques, Paris; lawyer, Diekirch 1969–84; mem. Diekirch Town Council 1969, Mayor 1974–84; Christian Social Deputy in Parl. 1979; Sec. of State for Agric. and Viticulture 1984, of Agric., Viticulture and Rural Devt and Minister-Del. for Cultural Research and Scientific Research 1989–93; Commr for Agric. and Rural Devt, EC 1993–95; Chair. Soc. Européenne des Satellites 1996–2000, SES Global 2001–07; currently Chair. LuxConnect SA and Attorney-at-Law, Court of Luxembourg. *Address:* LuxConnect SA, 4, rue A. Graham Bell, 3235 Bettembourg (office); 30 Rue Marie-Adelaide, Luxembourg 2128, Luxembourg (office). *Telephone:* 276-16-81 (LuxConnect) (office); 274-49-967 (office). *Fax:* 276-16-899 (LuxConnect) (office). *E-mail:* info@luxconnect.lu (office). *Website:* www.luxconnect.lu (office); luxembourg.public.lu (office).

STEIDEL, Charles (Chuck), AB, PhD; American astronomer and academic; *Lee A. DuBridge Professor of Astronomy, California Institute of Technology;* b. 14 Oct. 1962, Ithaca, NY; ed Princeton Univ., California Inst. of Tech.; Hubble Fellow, Univ. of California, Berkeley 1990–93; Asst Prof. of Physics, MIT 1993–95; Asst Prof. of Astronomy, California Inst. of Tech. 1995–97, Assoc. Prof. of Astronomy 1997–98, Prof. of Astronomy 1998–2004, Lee A. DuBridge Prof. of Astronomy 2004–; Tinsley Visiting Prof., Univ. of Texas 2010; mem. NAS 2006; Alfred P. Sloan Foundation Fellowship 1994–96, NSF Young Investigator Award 1994–99, ASCIT Undergraduate Teaching Award, California Inst. of Tech. 1997, Helen B. Warner Prize, American Astronomical Soc. 1997, David and Lucile Packard Foundation Fellowship 1997–2002, Lyman Spitzer Lecturer, Princeton Univ. 2001, MacArthur Fellowship 2002–07, Sackler Lecturer, Leiden Observatory (Netherlands) 2006, Medal of Institut d'Astrophysique, Paris 2008, Mohler Prize Lecturer, Univ. of Michigan 2009, Cosmology Prize, Gruber Foundation 2010. *Publications:* numerous papers in professional journals. *Address:* 252 Center for Astrophysics, Caltech 249-17, Pasadena, CA 91125, USA (office). *Telephone:* (626) 395-4168 (office). *E-mail:* ccs@astro.caltech.edu (office). *Website:* www.astro.caltech.edu/~ccs (office).

STEIGER, Paul E., BA; American journalist and editor; *Executive Chairman, ProPublica;* b. 15 Aug. 1942, Bronx, New York; ed Yale Univ.; staff writer, Los Angeles Times 1968, Econ. Corresp., Washington, DC Bureau 1971–78, apptd Business Ed. 1978; with Wall Street Journal, reporter for San Francisco Bureau 1966–68, Asst Man. Ed. 1983–85, Deputy Man. Ed. 1985–91, Man. Ed. 1991–2007, Ed.-at-Large 2007–, also Vice-Pres. Dow Jones & Co.; Ed.-in-Chief, Pres. and CEO ProPublica (ind. non-profit newsroom) 2008–12, Exec. Chair. 2013–; Chair. Committee to Protect Journalists; mem. Reporters Cttee for Freedom of the Press (mem. Steering Cttee); Trustee, John S. and James L. Knight Foundation; mem. Pulitzer Prize Bd 1998–2007 (Chair. 2007), Columbia Grad. School of Journalism Bd of Visitors; Poynter Fellow, Yale Univ. 2001–02; George Beveridge Ed. of the Year Award 2001, American Soc. of Newspaper Eds Leadership Award 2002, Gerald Loeb Award 2002, John Hancock Award 2002, Columbia Journalism Award 2002, Goldsmith Career Award for Excellence in Journalism, Harvard Univ. Joan Shorenstein Center on Press, Politics and Public Policy 2008. *Publications include:* The '70s Crash and How to Survive It 1970. *Address:* ProPublica, One Exchange Plaza, 55 Broadway, 23rd Floor, New York, NY 10006, USA (office). *Telephone:* (212) 514-5250 (office). *E-mail:* info@propublica.org (office). *Website:* www.propublica.org (office).

STEILMANN, Britta; German retail executive; *Founder, Britta Steilmann Design;* b. 1966, Wattenscheid; d. of Prof. Klaus Steilmann; one d.; Marketing and Product Man. Klaus Steilmann GmbH & Co. KG 1987–89, Chief Exec., Environment and Communications Dept 1993–96, Chair. Bd Dirs and CEO 2001–03; opened internet shop and launched website for services including living and interior design www.brittasteilmann.com 2003; f. B.S.S.D. GmbH & Co. KG 1992; Man. SG Wattenscheid 09 professional soccer team 1995; mem. Factor 10 Club, 100 Global Leaders for Tomorrow, World Econ. Forum, Innovation in Deutschland, Curator's Bd Fachhochschule für Technik und Wirtschaft Coll., Dresden Cultural Foundation, Curator's Bd Art of Nature, Bd German Fashion Institute DMI; Patron and Consultant, Big Sisters, AIESEC Meets EXPO 2000; Bundesverdienstkreuz; Capital Magazine Man. of the Year 1993, World-Wide Fund for Nature Eco-Manager of the Year 1993, Forbes Magazine Jr Man. of the Year 1994, Bavarian Communication Assen Ecology and Communication First Prize 1995. *Publication:* Millenium Moral. *Leisure interests:* hiking, horseback riding. *Address:* B.S.S.D. GmbH & Co. KG, Britta Steilmann | Design, Postfach 101011, 40839 Ratingen, Germany (office). *Telephone:* (2102) 875-0 (office). *Fax:* (2102) 87525 (office). *E-mail:* britta.steilmann@bssd.com (office); britta.steilmann@brittasteilmann.com (office). *Website:* www.brittasteilmann.com (office).

STEIN BARILLAS, Eduardo; Guatemalan politician; b. 20 Oct. 1945; m. Myrna Coronado; five d.; ed Univ. of St. Louis, Northwestern Univ., USA; teaching positions at Universidad Rafael Landívar, Guatemala 1971–72, Universidad Centroamericana José Simeón Cañas, El Salvador 1972–80), Florida State Univ. Panama campus 1985–87; Resident Rep., Int. Org. for Migration (IOM), Panama 1993–95; Minister of Foreign Affairs 1996–2000; Vice-Pres. of Guatemala 2004–08; fmr Pres. Foundation of the Americas, Washington, DC; apptd by OAS to Head of Electoral Observation Mission, Presidential Elections in Peru 2000, resgnd, then returned as Head of Electoral Observation Mission 2001; presided over Honduras Truth and Reconciliation Commission 2010–11; consultant to IOM, Guatemala and UNDP, Panama; coordinates Central American Network and Advocacy Thought Centers (laRED); mem. Bd of Dirs Inter-American Dialogue, Global Centre for Pluralism, Heifer International; mem. Global Leadership Foundation, Int. Crisis Group, Asociación de Investigación y Estudios Sociales; fmr mem. UN Int. Comm. on Intervention and State Sovereignty 2001.

STEINBERG, Donald K., BA, M.Econ., MA; American diplomatist and international organization official; *Deputy President (Policy), International Crisis Group;* b. 25 March 1953, Los Angeles, Calif.; s. of Warren Linnington and Beatrice Blass; ed Reed Coll., Univ. of Toronto, Canada, Columbia Univ.; joined Foreign Service, rising to rank of Minister-Counselor, postings in Brazil, Malaysia, Mauritius and Cen. African Repub.; acting Chief Textile Negotiator, Office of US Trade Rep. 1988–89; first Dir House Task Force on Trade and Competitiveness 1989, Sr Policy Adviser for Foreign Affairs and Defense to Leader of House of Reps 1989–90; Officer-in-Charge and Counselor for Econ. and Commercial Affairs, US Embassy, Pretoria 1990–93; Deputy Press Sec. for Nat. Security Affairs, White House 1993; Special Asst to fmr Pres. Clinton for W African Affairs and Sr Dir for African Affairs, Sr Dir for Public Affairs, Nat. Security Council; Amb. to Angola 1995–98; Special Haiti Coordinator, Dept of State 1999–2001, Special Rep. of Pres. and Sec. of State for Global Humanitarian Demining 1998, Deputy Asst Sec. of State for Population, Refugees and Migration 2000–01, Prin. Deputy Dir for Policy Planning 2001–03, Dir Jt Policy Council 2003–05; Sr Fellow, Jennings Randolph Fellowship Program, US Inst. of Peace 2004–05; Vice Pres. for Multilateral Affairs and Dir, New York office, Int. Crisis Group 2005, Deputy Pres. (Policy); Pulitzer Fellowship and fellowships from American Political Science Assen, Univ. of Toronto, Uma Chapman Fox Foundation and US Dept of State; Presidential Meritorious Honor Award 1994, Hough Award for Excellence in Print, three Superior Honor Awards, Distinguished Service Award 2002, Hunt Award for Advancing Women's Role in Policy Formation 2003. *Publications include:* many publs on US trade policies, Africa, landmines and the role of Congress in foreign affairs. *Address:* c/o International Crisis Group, 149 Avenue Louise, Level 24, 1050 Brussels, Belgium (office). *Telephone:* (2) 502-90-38 (office). *Fax:* (2) 502-50-38 (office). *Website:* www.crisisgroup.org (office).

STEINBERGER, Jack, PhD; American/Swiss physicist; b. 25 May 1921, Germany; s. of Ludwig Steinberger and Bertha Steinberger (née May); m. 1st Joan Beauregard 1943; m. 2nd Cynthia Eve Alff 1962; three s. one d.; ed Univ. of Chicago; Visiting mem., Inst. of Advanced Study, Princeton 1948–49; Research Asst, Univ. of Calif., Berkeley 1949–50; Prof., Columbia Univ., New York 1950–71, Higgins Prof. 1967–71; staff mem., CERN 1968–; mem. NAS 1967–2002, Heidelberg Acad. of Sciences 1967–, American Acad. of Arts and Sciences 1969–, Acad. Nazionale dei Lincei 1997; Hon. Prof., Univ. of Heidelberg 1968; Hon. DLitt (Glasgow) 1990, Dr hc (IU Inst. of Tech., Dortmund, Columbia, Barcelona, Univ. Blaise Pascal); Nobel Prize in Physics (jtly) 1988, Pres.'s Science Medal, USA 1988, Mateuzzi Medal, Società Italiana delle Scienze 1991. *Publications include:* Muon Decay 1949, Pi Zero Meson 1950, Spin of Pion 1951, Parity of Pion 1954, 1959, Σ° Hyperon 1957, Properties of 'Strange Particles' 1957–64, Two Neutrinos 1962, CP Violating Effects in K° Decay 1966–74, High Energy Neutrino Physics 1975–83, Preparation of Lep Detector 1981, 3 Families of Matter 1989, Electroweak physics experiments 1989–97. *Leisure interests:* mountaineering, flute, cruising. *Address:* CERN, 1211 Geneva 23 (office); 25 chemin des Merles, 1213 Onex, Geneva, Switzerland (home). *Telephone:* (22) 7678125 (office); (22) 7934612 (home). *Fax:* (22) 7679425 (office).

STEINBRUCH, Benjamin; Brazilian business executive; *Chairman and CEO, Companhia Siderúrgica Nacional ADS;* b. 28 June 1953, Rio de Janeiro; s. of Mendel Steinbruch and Dorothéa Steinbruch; m. Carolina Steinbruch; four c.; ed Getulio Vargas Business Foundation; started work at Vicunha Siderurgia (family textiles and telecoms conglomerate) 1983, now Supt Officer; Chair. Companhia Siderúrgica Nacional ADS (steel producer) 1995–, CEO 2002–; Pres. Companhia Vale do Rio Doce (iron ore co.) 1997–2011; First Vice-Pres. Fiesp (Federação das Indústrias do Estado de São Paulo) 2004–, also mem. Superior Strategic Bd; regular columnist for Folha de São Paulo (newspaper); Vice-Pres., Treasury, Albert Einstein Soc. 2001–04; Admin. Emer., Regional Admin. Council of São Paulo 1997; mem. Superior Council for Infrastructure 2006–. *Leisure interests:* racehorse training. *Address:* Companhia Siderúrgica Nacional, Avenida Brigadeiro Faria Lima, 3400, 20° Andar, Itaim Bibi, 04538-132 São Paulo, Brazil (office). *Telephone:* (11) 3049-7591 (office). *E-mail:* invrel@csn.com.br (office). *Website:* www.csn.com.br (office).

STEINBRÜCK, Peer; German politician; b. 10 Jan. 1947, Hamburg; m.; three c.; ed Christian-Albrechts-Univ. zu Kiel; worked for Fed. Ministry of Planning 1974–76, Fed. Ministry of Research and Tech. 1976–77, Personal Asst to Minister 1977; mem. SPD Party; Chief of Staff for Minister-Pres., State of Nordrhein-Westfalen 1986–90; State Sec., Ministry of Natural Conservation, Environmental Protection and Regional Devt, State of Schleswig-Holstein 1990–92, State Sec., Ministry of Econs, Tech. and Transport 1992–93, State Minister of Econs, Tech. and Transport 1993–98; State Minister of Econs, Small Businesses, Tech. and Transport, State of Nordrhein-Westfalen 1998–2000, State Finance Minister 2000–02, Minister-Pres. 2002–05; Fed. Minister of Finance 2005–09; mem. Bundestag 2009–; Chair. Bd of Supervisory Dirs, KfW Bankengruppe 2009.

Address: Bundestag, 11011 Berlin, Germany (office). *Telephone:* (30) 22771340 (office). *E-mail:* peer.steinbrueck@bundestag.de (office). *Website:* www.peer -steinbrueck.de (office).

STEINEM, Gloria, BA; American writer, journalist and editor; *Consulting Editor, Ms Magazine;* b. 25 March 1934, Toledo, Ohio; d. of Leo Steinem and Ruth Steinem (née Nuneviller); m. David Bale 2000; ed Smith Coll.; Chester Bowles Asian Fellow, India 1957–58; Co-Dir, Dir Ind. Research Service, Cambridge, Mass. and New York 1959–60; editorial asst, contributing, ed., freelance writer for various nat. and New York publs 1960–; Co-founder New York Magazine, contrib. 1968–72; Co-founder Ms Magazine 1972 (Ed. 1971–87, columnist 1980–87, Consulting Ed. 1987–); feminist lecturer 1969–; active various civil rights and peace campaigns including United Farmworkers, Vietnam War Tax Protest, Cttee for the Legal Defense of Angela Davis and political campaigns of Adlai Stevenson, Robert Kennedy, Eugene McCarthy, Shirley Chisholm, George McGovern; Co-founder and Chair Bd Women's Action Alliance 1970–; Convenor, mem. Nat. Advisory Cttee Nat. Women's Political Caucus 1971–; Co-Founder and Pres. Bd of Dirs Ms Foundation for Women 1972–; Founding mem. Coalition of Labor Union Women; Woodrow Wilson Int. Center for Scholars Fellow 1977, Women's Media Center 2004; mem. advisory bd Feminist.com; Penney-Missouri Journalism Award 1970, Ohio Gov.'s Award for Journalism 1972, named Woman of the Year, McCall's Magazine 1972, Missouri Honor Medal for Distinguished Service in Journalism 2004. *Publications include:* The Thousand Indias 1957, The Beach Book 1963, Outrageous Acts and Everyday Rebellions 1983, Marilyn 1986, Revolution From Within: A Book of Self-Esteem 1992, Moving Beyond Words 1994, Doing Sixty and Seventy 2006, My Life on the Road 2015; contribs to various anthologies. *Address:* PO Box 25431, Brooklyn, NY 11202-5431, USA (office). *Website:* www .gloriasteinem.com.

STEINEMANN, Jürgen B.; German business executive; *Chairman of the Supervisory Board, METRO AG;* b. 1958; ed European Business School in Wiesbaden, London, UK and Paris, France; held various sr positions with fmr Eridania Beghin-Say Group, later with corp. planning and strategy unit at head office in Paris 1990–98; CEO Loders Croklaan (Unilever subsidiary) 1999–2001; mem. Exec. Bd, Nutreco and COO 2001–09; CEO Barry Callebaut AG, Zurich, Switzerland 2009–15, mem. Bd of Dirs and Vice-Chair. 2014–; Chair. Supervisory Bd, METRO AG 2016–; mem. Supervisory Bd, Ewald Dörken AG, Big Dutchman AG; mem. Bd of Dirs Lonza Group AG, Basel, Switzerland 2014–. *Address:* METRO AG, Schlüterstrasse 1, 40235 Düsseldorf, Germany (office). *Telephone:* (211) 68860 (office). *E-mail:* kontakt@metro.de (office). *Website:* www.metrogroup .de (office).

STEINER, Achim, BA, MA; German/Brazilian international organization executive; *Administrator, United Nations Development Programme (UNDP);* b. 17 May 1961, Brazil; s. of Roland Steiner and Helga Steiner; m. Liz Rihoy; ed Univs of Oxford and London, UK, German Devt Inst., Berlin, Harvard Business School, USA; Sr Policy Adviser, Global Policy Unit, Int. Union for the Conservation of Nature and Natural Resources (IUCN—The World Conservation Union), Washington, DC mid-1990s, worked in SE Asia as Chief Tech. Adviser on a programme for sustainable man. of Mekong River watersheds and community-based natural resources man., worked in IUCN's Southern Africa Regional Office, Dir-Gen. IUCN 2001–06; Sec.-Gen. World Comm. on Dams, based in SA 1998–2001; UN Under-Sec.-Gen. and Exec. Dir UNEP 2006–16, also Dir-Gen. UNON (UN Office at Nairobi); Dir Oxford Martin School 2016–17; Admin., UNDP 2017–; Founding mem. Institut du developpement durable et des relations internationales (France); mem. several int. advisory bds including China Council for Inst. Cooperation on Environment and Devt, Environmental Advisory Council (ENVAC) of EBRD, UN Sec.-Gen.'s Advisory Council for the Global Compact, Int. Advisory Cttee of Global Environmental Action (Japan), Bd of Global Public Policy Inst. (Germany); Bruno H. Schubert-Stiftung Award, Steiger Award for Environment 2007, Tallberg Award for Environmental Leadership 2010. *Address:* Office of the Administrator, United Nations Development Programme, One United Nations Plaza, New York, NY 10017, USA (office). *Telephone:* (212) 906-5300 (office). *Fax:* (212) 906-5364 (office). *E-mail:* hq@undp.org (office). *Website:* www.undp.org.

STEINER, David P., BA, LLB, JD; American lawyer and business executive; *President and CEO, Waste Management Inc.;* ed Louisiana State Univ., Univ. of California, Los Angeles; began legal career with Jones, Walker, Waechter, Poitevent, Carrere & Denegre, New Orleans, La; fmr Assoc. Gibson, Dunn & Crutcher, San Jose, Calif.; Assoc. Phelps Dunbar, New Orleans –2000; Vice-Pres. and Deputy Gen. Counsel, Waste Man. Inc., Houston 2000–01, Sr Vice-Pres., Gen. Counsel and Corp. Sec. 2001–03, Exec. Vice-Pres. and Chief Financial Officer 2003–04, Pres. and CEO and mem. Bd of Dirs 2004–; mem. Bd of Dirs Tyco Electronics Corp., FedEx Corp.; mem. Los Angeles and Calif. Bar Asscns. *Address:* Waste Management Inc., 1001 Fannin Street, Suite 4000, Houston, TX 77002, USA (office). *Telephone:* (713) 512-6200 (office). *Fax:* (713) 512-6299 (office). *Website:* www.wm.com (office).

STEINER, (Francis) George, DPhil, FBA, FRSL; American (b. French) writer and scholar; b. 23 April 1929, Paris, France; s. of Frederick George Steiner and Else Steiner (née Franzos); m. Zara Shakow 1955; one s. one d.; ed Univ. of Paris, France, Univ. of Chicago, Harvard Univ. and Balliol Coll., Oxford, UK; mem. editorial staff, The Economist, London 1952–56; Fellow, Inst. for Advanced Study, Princeton 1956–58; Gauss Lecturer, Princeton Univ. 1959–60; Fellow and Dir of English Studies, Churchill Coll., Cambridge 1961–69, Extraordinary Fellow 1969–, Pensioner Fellow 1996–; Albert Schweitzer Visiting Prof., New York Univ. 1966–67; Visiting Prof., Yale Univ. 1970–71; Prof. of English and Comparative Literature, Univ. of Geneva 1974–94, Prof. Emer. 1994–; Visiting Prof., Collège de France 1992; First Lord Weidenfeld Visiting Prof. of Comparative Literature, Univ. of Oxford 1994–95; Charles Eliot Norton Prof. of Poetry, Harvard Univ. 2001–02; Pres. The English Asscn 1975–76; Corresp. mem. German Acad., Harvard Club, New York; Hon. mem. American Acad. of Arts and Sciences 1989; Hon. RA (London) 2004; Hon. Fellow, Balliol Coll., Oxford, St Anne's Coll., Oxford; Chevalier, Légion d'honneur, Commdr, Ordre des Arts et des Lettres 2001; Hon. DLitt (East Anglia) 1976, (Louvain) 1979, (Bristol) 1989, (Glasgow, Liège) 1990, (Ulster) 1993, (Kenyon Coll., USA) 1995, (Trinity Coll. Dublin) 1995, (Rome) 1998, (Sorbonne) 1998, (Salamanca) 2002, (Athens) 2004, (London) 2006, (Bologna) 2006; Dr hc (Lisbon) 2009; O. Henry Award 1958, Jewish Chronicle Book Award 1968,

Zabel Prize of Nat. Inst. of Arts and Letters 1970, Le Prix du Souvenir 1974, Massey Lecturer 1974, Ransom Memorial Lecturer 1976, King Albert Medal of the Royal Belgian Acad. 1982, F.D. Maurice Lecturer, Univ. of London 1984, Leslie Stephen Lecturer, Univ. of Cambridge 1985, Robertson Lecturer, Courtauld Inst., London 1985, W.P. Ker Lecturer, Univ. of Glasgow 1986, Page-Barbour Lecturer, Univ. of Virginia 1987, Gifford Lecturer 1990, Priestley Lecturer, Univ. of Toronto 1995, Prince of Asturias Prize 2001, 2002, Alfonso Reyes Prize (Mexico) 2007. *Publications include:* Tolstoy or Dostoevsky: An Essay in the Old Criticism 1958, The Death of Tragedy 1960, Homer: A Collection of Critical Essays (co-ed. with Robert Flagles) 1962, Anno Domini: Three Stories 1964, The Penguin Book of Modern Verse Translation (ed.) 1966, Language and Silence 1967, Extraterritorial 1971, In Bluebeard's Castle: Some Notes Towards the Re-Definition of Culture 1971, The Sporting Scene: White Knights in Reykjavík 1973, Fields of Force 1974, A Nostalgia for the Absolute (Massey Lectures) 1974, After Babel: Aspects of Language and Translation 1975, Heidegger 1978, On Difficulty and Other Essays 1978, The Portage to San Cristóbal of A.H. 1981, Antigones 1984, George Steiner: A Reader 1984, Real Presences: Is There Anything in What We Say? 1989, Proofs and Three Parables 1992, The Deeps of the Sea 1996, Homer in English 1996, No Passion Spent 1996, Errata: An Examined Life 1998, Grammars of Creation 2001, Lessons of the Masters: The Charles Eliot Morton Lectures 2001–2002 2004, My Unwritten Books 2008, The Poetry of Thought 2012. *Leisure interests:* chess, music, mountain walking. *Address:* 32 Barrow Road, Cambridge, CB2 8AS, England (home).

STEINER, Michael; German diplomatist, fmr government official and fmr UN official; b. 28 Nov. 1949, Munich, Bavaria; m. Eliese Steiner; ed Univ. of Munich Law School, Univ. of Paris, France; Scientific Asst, Inst. of Int. Law, Univ. of Munich 1978–81; joined Diplomatic Service 1981, Counsellor for Econ. Collaboration, Embassy in Kinshasa 1983, with Int. Law Div., Ministry of Foreign Affairs 1983–86, Political Counsellor, Perm. Mission to UN, New York 1986–89, Political Counsellor, Embassy in Prague 1989–91, Head of Office for German Humanitarian Aid, Zagreb 1991–92, Head of Office of German Humanitarian Aid, Zagreb, Croatia 1991–92, Head of Labour Unit for Multilateral Efforts for Peace, Ministry of Foreign Affairs 1992–94, Head of Special Task Force for Peace Efforts in Bosnia and Herzegovina and Nat. Rep. at Int. Contact Group on the Balkans 1994–95, Contrib. Dayton Peace Talks 1995, Prin. Deputy High Rep. in Sarajevo 1996–97, Amb. to Czech Repub. 1998; Foreign Policy and Security Adviser to Chancellor 1998–2001; Special Rep. for Kosovo and Head of UN Interim Admin. Mission in Kosovo (UNMIK) 2002–03; Perm. Rep. to UN and Int. Orgs, Geneva 2003–07; Pres. Governing Council of UN Compensation Comm. for Iraq 2004; Amb. to Italy (also accred to San Marino) 2007–10, Amb. and Special Rep. to Afghanistan and Pakistan 2010–12, Amb. to India 2012–15; Officer's Cross, Order of Merit. *Address:* Federal Ministry of Foreign Affairs, 11013 Berlin, Germany (office). *Telephone:* (30) 18170-0 (office). *Fax:* (30) 18173402 (office). *E-mail:* poststelle@auswaertiges -amt.de (office). *Website:* www.auswaertiges-amt.de (office).

STEINER, Sylvia Helena de Figueiredo, LLM; Brazilian judge; *Judge, Pre-Trial Division, International Criminal Court;* b. 19 Jan. 1953, São Paulo; m. (divorced); ed Univ. of São Paulo, Univ. of Brasilia; lawyer –1982; mem. Fed. Public Ministry 1982–95; fmr mem. and Vice-Pres. Penitentiary Council of São Paulo; Fed. Judge Regional, Court of Appeal of São Paulo 1995–2003; Judge, Pre-Trial Div., Int. Criminal Court (ICC) 2003–; mem. Brazilian Del. to Preparatory Comm. of ICC 1999–2001, to Experts' Conf. on Implementation of Humanitarian Law 2001, to Meeting on Implementation of ICC Statute 2001, to First Ass. of State Parties of ICC 2002; Founding Assoc. mem. Brazilian Inst. of Criminal Sciences; Deputy Dir Brazilian Criminal Sciences Journal; mem. Admin. Council Asscn of Judges for Democracy, Exec. Council Brazilian Section of Int. Legal Comm., São Paulo Comm. for Peace and Justice; guest lecturer at numerous orgs, univs and insts. *Publications include:* A convenção americana sobre direitos humanos e sua integração ao processo penal brasileiro 2000; articles in professional journals. *Address:* International Criminal Court, PO Box 19519, 2500 CM The Hague, The Netherlands (office); Rua Estado de Israel, No. 181, Apt. 13, Vila Mariana, CEP 04022-000, São Paulo, Brazil (home). *Telephone:* (70) 515-85-15 (office); (11) 3311-4412 (home). *Fax:* (70) 515-85-55 (office); (11) 5572-3897 (home). *E-mail:* pio@icc -cpi.int (office); sylstein@uol.com.br (home); ssteiner@trf3.gov.br (home). *Website:* www.icp-cpi.int (office).

STEINFELD, Hailee; American actress and singer; b. 11 Dec. 1996, Los Angeles, Calif.; d. of Peter Steinfeld and Cheri Steinfeld; began acting at age eight; early supporting roles in several TV series and commercials; MTV Europe Music Awards For Best Push Act 2017. *Television includes:* Back to You 2007, Summer Camp 2010, Sons of Tucson 2010. *Films include:* She's a Fox 2009, True Grit (Alliance of Women Film Journalists Award for Best Supporting Actress, Austin Film Critics Asscn Award for Best Supporting Actress, Broadcast Film Critics Asscn Award for Best Young Performer, Central Ohio Film Critics Asscn Award for Best Supporting Actress, Chicago Film Critics Asscn Award for Best Supporting Actress, Houston Film Critics Soc. Award for Best Supporting Actress, Indiana Film Journalists Asscn Award for Best Supporting Actress, Kansas City Film Critics Circle Award for Best Supporting Actress, Online Film Critics Soc. Award for Best Supporting Actress, Southeastern Film Critics Asscn Award for Best Supporting Actress) 2010, Hateship Loveship 2013, Romeo & Juliet 2013, Ender's Game 2013, 3 Days to Kill 2014, The Homesman 2014, The Keeping Room 2014, Ten Thousand Saints 2015, Pitch Perfect 2 2015, Barely Lethal 2015, Term Life 2016, The Edge of Seventeen 2016, Pitch Perfect 3 2017. *Recordings include:* Haiz 2015; single: Let Me Go 2017. *Address:* Creative Artists Agency, 2000 Avenue of the Stars, Los Angeles, CA 90067, USA (office). *Website:* touring.caa.com (office); www .haileesteinfeldofficial.com.

STEINHAFEL, Gregg W., BA, MBA; American business executive; b. Milwaukee, Wis.; m.; three c.; ed Carroll Coll., Kellogg Grad. School of Man., Northwestern Univ.; began career at Target as merchandising trainee 1979, has held various man. positions, Exec. Vice-Pres. of Merchandising, Target Stores, Inc. (subsidiary of Target Corpn) 1994–99, Pres. 1999–2014, mem. Bd of Dirs Target Corpn 2007–14, CEO 2008–14, Chair. 2009–14 (resgnd); mem. Bd of Dirs The Toro Co. 1999–; mem. or fmr mem. Bd The Retail Industry Leaders Asscn, TreeHouse (Minnesota-based non-profit org.), Business Roundtable, Minnesota Business Partnership, Council for the Smithsonian Nat. Museum of African American

History and Culture 2010–. *Address:* The Toro Company, 8111 Lyndale Avenue South, Bloomington, MN 55420-1196, USA (office). *Telephone:* (952) 888-8801 (office). *E-mail:* companyinfo@thetorocompany.com (office). *Website:* www.thetorocompany.com (office).

STEINHOFF, Janusz Wojciech, DTech; Polish politician; b. 24 Oct. 1946, Gliwice; m.; one d.; ed Silesian Tech. Univ., Gliwice; with Coal Industry Construction and Mechanization Plants, Gliwice 1974–75; Mining Dept Silesian Tech. Univ., Gliwice 1976–89, 1994–97; Chair. Higher Mining Office 1990–94; adviser, State Hard Coal Agency 1994–95; Vice-Chair. Regional Chamber of Commerce, Katowice 1996–97; Minister of the Economy 1997–2001, also Deputy Prime Minister; Co-Founder Solidarity Trade Union, Silesian Tech. Univ. 1980; underground Solidarity activist during martial law 1981–89; Solidarity expert on mining and protection of environment during Round Table debates, 1989; Deputy to Sejm (Parl.) 1989–93, 1997–2001; mem. Presidium Citizens Parl. Caucus (OKP) 1989–91; mem. Solidarity Election Action (AWS) Parl. Caucus 1997–2001; author of AWS programme for restructuring the mining sector; Co-Founder and Vice-Leader Christian Democratic Party; Co-founder and Leader, Centre Party (Partia Centrum) 2004–08; apptd mem. Narodowa Rada Rozwoju (Nat. Devt Council) 2010.

STEINITZ, Yuval, BA, MA, PhD; Israeli academic and politician; *Minister of National Infrastructure, Energy and Water Resources;* b. 10 April 1958; m.; three c.; ed Hebrew Univ., Jerusalem, Tel-Aviv Univ.; mil. serviced in Golani Brigade, reservist in Alexandroni Brigade; fmr mem. Peace Now movt; Prof. of Philosophy, Haifa Univ. –1999; mem. Knesset (Likud Party) 1999–, Chair. Sub-Cttee for Defence, Planning and Policy 1999–2003, Sub-Cttee for Intelligence and Secret Services 2003–06, Cttee for Examination of Intelligence Services Following the War in Iraq 2003–06, Co-Chair. Jt Security Cttee between Knesset and US Congress 2003–, Sub-Cttee for State of Alert and Field Security 2006–, Sub-Cttee on Intelligence and Secret Services 2006–, mem. Foreign Affairs and Defence Cttee 1993– (Chair. 2003–06), Constitution Law and Courts Cttee 1999–2003; Minister of Finance 2009–13, of Intelligence, of Int. Relations and of Strategic Affairs 2013–15, Minister of National Infrastructure, Energy and Water Resources 2015–; Pres. Asscn for the Public's Right to Know 1999–2004. *Publications:* Invitation to Philosophy 1994, In Defense of Metaphysics 1995; articles in Israeli and int. academic journals. *Address:* Ministry of National Infrastructure, Energy and Water, POB 33541, Haifa 31334 (office); Knesset, Kiryat Ben-Gurion, Jerusalem 91008, Israel (office). *Telephone:* 2-8644024 (Haifa) (office); 2-6496115 (Knesset) (office). *Fax:* 4-8660189 (Haifa) (office); 2-6496579 (Knesset) (office). *E-mail:* pniot@energy.gov.il (office); ysteinitz@knesset.gov.il (office). *Website:* www.energy.gov.il (office); www.knesset.gov.il (office).

STEINKÜHLER, Franz; German trade union official; b. 20 May 1937, Würzburg; m.; one c.; trained as toolmaker and became Chief of Production Planning 1951–60; joined IG Metall 1951, mem. Youth Group 1952, Chair. Youth Del. 1953, numerous local exec. positions 1953–63, Sec. Regional Exec. Bd, Stuttgart 1963–72, Dir Stuttgart Region 1972–83, Vice-Pres. IG Metall 1983–86, Pres. 1986–93; Pres. Int. Metalworkers' Fed. June 1987; mem. SPD 1951, Vice-Pres. in Baden-Württemberg 1975–83, mem. Programme Cttee of Exec. Bd 1984; Workers' Rep. VW-AG, Wolfsburg Mannesmann AG, Supervisory Bd, Daimler Benz AG Supervisory Bd –1993, Thyssen AG; fmr Deputy Chair. Supervisory Bd Volkswagen AG; mem. State Tribunal of Baden-Württemberg 1983; currently business consultant; Hon. Senator Univ. of Konstanz 1983.

STEINMEIER, Frank-Walter; German politician and lawyer; *President;* b. 5 Jan. 1956, Detmold (Dist of Lippe); m.; one d.; ed secondary school in Blomberg, Justus Liebig Univ., Giessen; mil. service 1974–76; legal training in Frankfurt and Giessen 1983–86; Academic Asst to Chair of Public Law and Political Science, Dept of Law, Univ. of Giessen 1986–91; Desk Officer for Media Law and Policy, State Chancellery of Lower Saxony 1991, Chief-of-Staff, Office of the Minister-Pres., State of Lower Saxony 1993–94, Head of Directorate for Policy Guidelines, Inter-departmental Coordination and Planning 1994–96, State Sec. and Chief-of-Staff, Lower Saxony State Chancellery 1996–98; State Sec., Federal Chancellery and Commr for the Intelligence Services 1998–99, Fed. Chancellery Chief-of-Staff 1999–2005; Fed. Minister for Foreign Affairs 2005–09, 2013–17, Vice-Chancellor 2007–09; Pres. of Germany 2017–; Chair.-in-Office OSCE 2016; mem. Sozialdemokratische Partei Deutschlands (SPD—Social Democratic Party), Chair. SPD Parl. Group (Leader of the Opposition) 2009–13; Pres. European Council 2007. *Address:* Office of Federal President, Bundespräsidialamt, Spreeweg 1, 10557 Berlin, Germany (office). *Telephone:* (30) 20000 (office). *Fax:* (30) 20001999 (office). *E-mail:* bundespraesidialamt@bpra.bund.de (office). *Website:* www.bundespraesident.de (office).

STEINMETZ, Pierre; French lawyer and politician; b. 23 Jan. 1943, Sainte-Colombe (Rhône); s. of Emile Steinmetz and Marguerite Frossard; m. Daniele Sebi 1968; two s.; ed Ecole Nationale d'Administration, Institut d'études politiques de Paris; Civil Admin. second class, Ministry of Depts and Territories Overseas, also with Ministry of Public Health and Social Security 1970; Dir Office of High Commr in Noumea 1972; Chargé de mission, Gen. Secretariat 1975; Special Adviser in cabinet of Prime Minister Raymond Barre 1979–82; Special Adviser, Ministry of Urban Devt and Housing 1982; Chief, Office of the Sec.-Gen. of City of Paris 1982–87; Dir Econ. and Social Devt, Regional Council of Ile-de-France 1987; apptd to assess situation and restore dialogue in New Caledonia 1988; Prefect of Haute-Marne 1988; Chief, Office of Minister of Int. Cooperation and Devt 1989–91; Prefect of Pyrenees-Orientales 1992, of Haute-Savoie 1993, of Reunion 1994; Dir Cabinet for Minister of Public Service, Reform of the State and Decentralization 1995; Prefect of Burgundy region, of defence zone of Central East, of Côte d'Or 1996, of Poitou-Charentes, of La Vienne 1997; Dir Nat. Gendarmerie 2000–02; Chief of Staff, Prime Minister's Office 2002–03; mem. Conseil Constitutionnel 2004–13; Commdr, Légion d'honneur 2011, Officier de l'ordre national du Mérite. *Leisure interests:* tennis, skiing.

STEINNES, Eiliv, DPhil; Norwegian environmental scientist and academic; *Professor Emeritus of Environmental Science, Norwegian University of Science and Technology;* b. 21 Sept. 1938, Elverum; s. of Eirik Steinnes and Aslaug Steinnes; m. Randi Surdal 1962; three d.; ed Univ. of Oslo; scientist, Norwegian Inst. for Atomic Energy 1964–68, Research leader 1969–79; Prof. of Environmental Science, Univ. of Trondheim Coll. of Arts and Science (now Norwegian Univ. of Science and Tech.) 1980–2008, Prof. Emer. 2008–, Rector 1984–90; mem. Norwegian Acad. of Tech. Sciences, Norwegian Acad. of Science and Letters, Royal Norwegian Soc. of Science and Letters; Hon. Prof., Univ. of Iasi, Romania 2000; Dr hc (Moldova State Univ.) 2002, (Joint Inst. for Nuclear Research, Dubna, Russia) 2005; Hevesy Medal (co-recipient) 2001, Guldberg-Waage Medal 2009. *Publications:* three books and more than 700 scientific papers. *Leisure interests:* outdoor life, in particular cross-country skiing and mountain tours. *Address:* Department of Chemistry, Norwegian University of Science and Technology, 7491 Trondheim (office); Sloreåsen 17A, 1257 Oslo, Norway (home). *Telephone:* 73-59-62-37 (office); 22-75-43-20 (home). *E-mail:* eiliv.steinnes@ntnu.no (office). *Website:* www.chem.ntnu.no/english (office).

STEITZ, Joan Argetsinger, BS, PhD, FRSE; American biophysicist, biochemist and academic; *Sterling Professor of Molecular Biophysics and Biochemistry, School of Medicine, Yale University;* b. (Joan Elaine Argetsinger), 26 Jan. 1941, Minneapolis; d. of Glenn Argetsinger and Elaine Argetsinger; m. Thomas A. Steitz; ed Antioch Coll., Harvard Univ.; NSF and Jane Coffin Childs Postdoctoral Fellowships, MRC Lab. of Molecular Biology, Cambridge, UK 1967–70; joined faculty, Yale Univ., New Haven, Conn. in 1970, currently Sterling Prof. of Molecular Biophysics and Biochemistry, School of Medicine, also Investigator, Howard Hughes Medical Inst. 1986–, and Dir Molecular Genetics Program, Boyer Center for Molecular Medicine; mem. Jury of 2004 L'Oréal USA Fellowships 2002, 2004; mem. American Acad. of Arts and Sciences 1982, NAS 1983, American Philosophical Soc. 1992; Fellow, American Acad. of Microbiology, Academia Europaea 2002, Royal Soc. 2014; Hon. Fellow New York Acad. of Medicine 2009; Hon. ScD (Lawrence Univ.) 1982, (Univ. of Rochester School of Medicine) 1984, (Mount Sinai School of Medicine) 1988, (Bates Coll.) 1990, (Trinity Coll.) 1992, (Harvard Univ.) 1992, (Brandeis Univ.) 2002, (Brown Univ.) 2003, (Princeton Univ.) 2003, (Watson School of Biological Sciences, Cold Spring Harbor Lab.) 2004, (Paul Sabatier Univ., France) 2005, (Univ. of British Columbia) 2005, (Clarkson Univ.) 2009, (Albany Medical Coll.) 2010, (Columbia Univ.) 2011, (Univ. of Buenos Aires) 2011, (Rockefeller Univ.) 2012, (Univ. of Oxford) 2017, (Univ. of Conn.) 2017; Passano Foundation Young Scientist Award 1975, Eli Lilly Award in Biological Chemistry 1976, US Steel Foundation Award in Molecular Biology 1982, Lee Hawley, Sr Award for Arthritis Research 1983, Nat. Medal of Science 1986, Radcliffe Grad. Soc. Medal for Distinguished Achievement 1987, Dickson Prize for Science, Carnegie-Mellon Univ. 1988, Warren Triennial Prize 1989, Christopher Columbus Discovery Award in Biomedical Research 1992, first Weizmann Women and Science Award 1994, City of Medicine Award 1996, Novartis Drew Award in Biomedical Research 1999, L'Oréal-UNESCO For Women in Science Award 2001, Lewis S. Rosensteil Award 2002, FASEB Excellence in Science Award 2003, Howard Taylor Ricketts Award, Univ. of Chicago 2004, Caledonian Research Foundation Prize Lectureship 2004, RNA Soc. Lifetime Achievement Award 2004, American Society for Cell Biology E.B. Wilson Medal 2005, Rosalind E. Franklin Award 2006, Gairdner Foundation Int. Award 2006, Albany Medical Center Prize in Medicine and Biomedical Research 2008, New York Acad. of Medicine Medal for Distinguished Contributions in Biomedical Science 2008, British Biochemical Soc. Harden Jubilee Medal 2009, Robert J. and Claire Pasarow Foundation Annual Medical Research Award for Extraordinary Achievement in Cancer Research 2011, Pearl Meister Greengard Prize 2012, Joseph Priestley Award, Dickinson Coll. 2013, Vanderbilt Prize in Biomedical Science 2013, American Acad. of Microbiology EMD Millipore Alice C. Evans Award 2013, Institut de France La grande médaille de l'Académie des sciences 2013, Yale University Postdoctoral Mentoring Prize 2014, American Chemical Soc. Biopolymers Murray Goodman Memorial Prize 2015, American Soc. of Biochemistry and Molecular Biology Herbert Tabor Award 2015, Conn. Acad. of Science and Engineering Medal of Science 2015, Hope Funds for Cancer Research Basic Science Award 2015, Mass General Hospital Jonathan Kraft Prize for Excellence in Cancer Research 2016, Yale Univ. William Clyde DeVane Award for Teaching Excellence 2016, Luminary Award, World Affairs Council, Conn. 2018, Lasker-Koshland Award for Special Achievement in Medical Science 2018. *Publications:* Molecular Biology of the Gene (Vol. II, 4th edn) (co-author) 1987; numerous articles on molecular genetics, especially RNA structure and function. *Address:* Howard Hughes Medical Institute, Yale University, BCMM 136E, 295 Congress Avenue, PO Box 9812, New Haven, CT 06536-0812, USA (office). *Telephone:* (203) 737-4418 (office). *Fax:* (203) 624-8213 (office). *E-mail:* joan.steitz@yale.edu (office). *Website:* www.mbb.yale.edu/faculty/pages/steitzj.html (office).

STELLA, HE Cardinal Beniamino; Italian ecclesiastic and diplomatist; *Prefect of the Congregation for the Clergy;* b. 18 Aug. 1941, Pieve di Soligo, Treviso; ordained priest, Archdiocese of Vittorio Veneto 1966; entered diplomatic service of the Holy See 1970; consecrated Titular Archbishop of Midila 1987; Official of the Roman Curia 1987–; Apostolic Pro-Nuncio to Repub. of the Congo 1987–92, Apostolic Nuncio to Cuba 1992–99, to Colombia 1999–2007; Pres. Pontifical Ecclesiastical Acad. 2007–13; Prefect of the Congregation for the Clergy 2013–; cr. Cardinal (Cardinal-Deacon of Santi Cosma e Damiano) 2014–; mem. Congregation for Catholic Educ. 2013, Congregation for Bishop 2013–. *Address:* Congregation for the Clergy, Palazzo delle Congregazioni, Piazza Pio XII 3, 00193 Rome, Italy (office). *Telephone:* (06) 69884151 (office). *Fax:* (06) 69884845 (office). *Website:* www.clerus.org (office).

STELLA, Frank, MA; American painter and sculptor; b. 12 May 1936, Malden; m. Barbara Rose 1961 (divorced 1969); m. Harriet McGurk 1978; ed Princeton Univ.; Charles Eliot Norton Prof. of Poetry, Harvard Univ. 1983; Ordre des Arts et des Lettres 1989; Dr hc (Univ. of Jena) 1996; American Art Award 1985, Barnard Medal of Distinction 1992, Nat. Medal of Arts 2010, Lifetime Achievement Award in Contemporary Sculpture, Int. Sculpture Center 2011. *Address:* Frank Stella Studio, 453 17K Rock Tavern, New York, NY 12575, USA (office). *Telephone:* (212) 957-1600 (office).

STELLE, Kellogg Sheffield, PhD, FInstP; American physicist and academic; *Professor of Physics, Imperial College London;* b. 11 March 1948, Washington, DC; s. of Charles C. Stelle and Jane E. Kellogg; ed Phillips Acad. Andover, Mass., Harvard Coll. and Brandeis Univ.; Field Observer, Bartol Research Foundation, S Pole, Antarctica 1970–72; Lecturer in Math., King's Coll. London 1977–78; Research Fellow, Imperial Coll. London 1978–80, Advanced Fellow 1982–87,

Lecturer in Physics 1987–88, Reader 1988–95, Prof. 1995–, Head of Theoretical Physics Group 2002–07; mem. Inst. for Advanced Study, Princeton, NJ 1986; Scientific Assoc., CERN, Geneva 1980–81, 1987, 1997–98; Programme Dir Institut Henri Poincaré, Paris 2000–01; Humboldt Visiting Prof., Albert Einstein Inst., Potsdam 2007–08; Ed. Classical and Quantum Gravity 1984–93; mem. London Math. Soc., AAAS, Fed. of American Scientists, Campaign for Science and Eng; Fellow, American Physical Soc.; Humboldt Research Award, Alexander von Humboldt Foundation 2006. *Publications:* numerous articles in scientific journals. *Address:* The Blackett Laboratory, Imperial College, H/519 Huxley Building, South Kensington Campus, Prince Consort Road, London, SW7 2AZ, England (office). *Telephone:* (20) 7594-7826 (office). *E-mail:* k.stelle@imperial.ac.uk (office). *Website:* www3.imperial.ac.uk/people/k.stelle (office).

STELMACH, Edward (Ed) Michael; Canadian politician; b. 11 May 1951, Andrew, Alberta; m. Marie Stelmach 1973; four c.; ed Univ. of Alberta; took over family farm and homestead near Vegreville, Alberta; elected Lamont Co. Council 1986, apptd Reeve 1987; fmr Chair. Vegreville Health Unit Bd and mem. Archer Memorial Hosp. and Lamont Auxiliary Hosp. and Nursing Home Bds; MLA for Vegreville-Viking (now Fort Saskatchewan-Vegreville) 1993–2011, Deputy Whip, then Govt Caucus Whip 1995–97, Minister of Agric. 1997–99, of Infrastructure 1999–2001, of Transportation 2001–04, of Int. and Intergovernmental Affairs 2004–06; Leader, Progressive Conservative Party of Alberta 2006–11; Premier of Alberta 2006–11 (resgnd); fmr Chair. Alberta Agric. Research Inst.; fmr Leader Andrew 4-H Beef Club; fmr Pres. Lamont and District 4-H.

STELMAKH, Volodymyr, PhD; Ukrainian economist and fmr central banker; *Chairman of the Supervisory Board CB PrivatBank PJSC;* b. 18 Jan. 1939; joined Nat. Bank of Ukraine 1992, First Vice-Gov. 1993–2000, Gov. 2000–02, 2004–10; Chair. Supervisory Bd CB PrivatBank PJSC 2015–; Hero of Ukraine 2007, Order of Yaroslav the Wise 2010. *Address:* CB PrivatBank PJSC, 50 Naberezhna Peremogy Street, Dnipropetrovsk 49094, Ukraine (office). *Website:* en.privatbank .ua (office).

STEMPLOWSKI, Ryszard Marian, MJ, PhD, DHabil (Hist); Polish academic, lawyer, historian and diplomatist; *Professor Emeritus of History and Politics, Jagiellonian University;* b. 25 March 1939, Wygoda-Witwica; s. of Kazimierz Stemplowski and Eugenia Białecka; m. Irena Zasłona 1975; two d.; ed Tech. Lycée, Bydgoszcz, Dept of Ecological Eng, Wrocław Univ. of Tech., Dept of Law, Wrocław Univ., Inst. of History, Polish Acad. of Sciences, Warsaw; Research Fellow, Inst. of History, Polish Acad. of Sciences 1973–90; Chief, Chancellery of Sejm (Parl.) 1990–93; Amb. to UK 1994–99; Dir Polish Inst. of Int. Affairs 1999–2004; Prof., Warsaw School of Econs 2001–04; Prof. of History and Politics, Jagiellonian Univ. 2005–10, now Prof. Emer.; Prof., Inst. of Political Science, Akademia Ignatianum 2010–16; Ed. Polish Diplomatic Review 2000–04; Co-founder and mem. Polish Soc. of Studies of Latin America 1978–; Visiting Fellow, St Antony's Coll. Oxford 1974; Alexander von Humboldt Research Fellow, Univ. of Cologne 1981–82; mem. Polish Historical Soc. 1975– (Sec.-Gen. 1976–78), Academia Europaea 2013; Gran Croce di Merito del Ordine Constantiniano di S. Giorgio 1997; Kt, Order of Polonia Restituta 2000; Interfaith Gold Medallion Peace Through Dialogue, Int. Council of Christians and Jews 1999. *Publications include:* more than 200 articles; 25 books, including (in Polish) Argentina and the Rivalries among the United States, United Kingdom and Germany 1930–46 1975 (second edn 2014), State Socialism in the Actually Existing Capitalism: Chile 1932 1996 (second edn 2013), An Introduction to the Polish Foreign Policy Analysis (two vols) 2006 (third edn 2015), Philosophical Foundations of Integration of European States in the 20th and 21st Centuries 2012, Poles, Ruthenians, Ukrainians, Argentines in Misiones (Argentina) 1892–2009 2011 (second edn 2013), The Polish Students' Association under State Socialism 1950-1973 (English edn: On the State of Latin American States – Approaching the Bicentenary 2009), Europe – Latin America: Looking at Each Other 2010, The Conduct and Analysis of Public Policy 2013, Political Cultures of Our Times: A European-Latin-Americanist Sketch 2016, Contemporary Diplomatic Culture (ed) 2017. *Leisure interests:* music, cosmology, poetry in translation. *Address:* ul. Sulkowskiego 4 M. 3, 01-602, Warsaw, Poland (home). *Telephone:* 50-9928193 (mobile) (home). *E-mail:* ryszard@stemplowski.pl (home). *Website:* www .stemplowski.pl.

STENBÄCK, Pär Olav Mikael, MPolSci; Finnish international administrator and fmr politician; b. 12 Aug. 1941, Porvoo (Borgå); s. of Arne Mikael Stenbäck and Rakel Stenbäck (née Granholm); m. Liv Sissel Lund 1970; two s.; ed Helsinki Univ.; Ed. with Finnish Broadcasting Co. 1962–68; Chair. Svensk Ungdom (youth org. of Swedish People's Party of Finland) 1967–70; mem. Parl. 1970–85; Chair. Swedish People's Party 1977–85; Minister of Educ. 1979–82, of Foreign Affairs 1982–83; Man. Dir Hanaholmen Swedish-Finnish Culture Centre 1974–85; Sec.-Gen. Finnish Red Cross 1985–88, Pres. 1996–99; Sec.-Gen. Int. Fed. (fmrly League) of Red Cross and Red Crescent Socs, Geneva 1988–92; Sec.-Gen. Nordic Council of Ministers, Copenhagen 1992–96; mem. Esbo City Council 2005–08; Pres. Foundation for Swedish Culture in Finland 1996–2002; Chair. Norwegian-Swedish Comm. preparing new Reindeer Grazing Convention 1998–2001, Finnish Children and Youth Foundation 2001–16, Finnish-Swedish Cultural Foundation 2005–10; Pres. European Cultural Parl. 2001–; Vice-Pres. for Europe, Int. Youth Foundation, USA 1996–2005; mem. Bd of Dirs International Crisis Group 1995–, Mehiläinen Pvt. Hosp. Corpn 2001–06, Deutsche Kinder- und Jugendstiftung 2001–11, ICTI-Care Foundation 2008–; Vice-Chair. UWC Int. Council 2013–; Monitor, Int. Red Cross and Red Crescent Movt (Israel/Palestine) 2007–13, mem. Standing Comm. of Int. Red Cross and Red Crescent Movt 2011–15; numerous other professional appointments; Hon. Minister (Finland) 1999; Grand Cross, Royal Order of Northern Star (Sweden), Grand Cross of the Falcon (Iceland), Grand Cross St Olav (Norway), Grand Cross of Dannebrog (Denmark), Commdr of the Order of the Lion, Commdr (First Class), White Rose (Finland), Grand Cross of Santa Miranda (Venezuela) and numerous other foreign and Red Cross decorations; Dr hc (Petrozavodsk State Univ.) 2000; Helsinki Univ. Medal, Henri Dunant Medal 2009. *Publications:* Vision och verklighet (Vision and Reality) 2003, När världen öppnade sig (When the World Opened Up) 2007, Kriser och katastrofer (Crises and Disasters, memoir) 2009 (edns in Swedish and Finnish). *Leisure interests:* literature, fishing, history, African colonial stamps. *Address:* Hirbölebågen 15, 02160 Esbo, Finland. *Telephone:* 50-5252060 (mobile). *Fax:* (9) 4128725. *E-mail:* par@stenback.fi. *Website:* www.stenback.fi.

STENBECK, Cristina, BSc; Swedish business executive; *Chairman, Investment AB Kinnevik;* b. 1977; d. of Jan Stenbeck; m. Alexander Fitzgibbons; three d.; ed Georgetown Univ., USA; worked for Polo Ralph Lauren, New York, USA for two years; mem. Bd Invik & Co. AB 1997–, Vice-Chair. Invik & Co. AB and Industriförvaltnings AB Kinnevik 2003–07, Chair. 2007–, cos merged to form Investment AB Kinnevik 2003; mem. Bd of Dirs Metro International SA, Millicom International Cellular SA, Modern Times Group MTG AB, Tele2, Transcom WorldWide SA, Emesco AB. *Address:* Investment AB Kinnevik, PO Box 2094, 103 13 Stockholm, Sweden (office). *Telephone:* (8) 56200000 (office). *Fax:* (8) 203774 (office). *E-mail:* info@kinnevik.se (office). *Website:* www.kinnevik.se (office).

STENFLO, Jan Olof, MS, PhD; Swedish/Swiss astronomer; b. 10 Nov. 1942, Sweden; s. of Carl Stenflo and Signe Rödén; m. Joyce E. Tucker 1971; two s.; ed Univ. of Lund; Asst Prof., Univ. of Lund 1969–75; Research Scientist, Swedish Natural Science Research Council 1975–80; Prof. of Astronomy, ETH, Zürich and Univ. of Zürich 1980–2007, Dir Inst. of Astronomy, ETH 1980–2006; Pres. LEST Foundation 1983–97; mem. Royal Swedish Acad. of Sciences, Norwegian Acad. of Science and Letters, Royal Physiographic Soc. Lund; Edlund Prize, Royal Swedish Acad. of Sciences 1974, Minor planet named 70737 Stenflo 2007, Prix Janssen, Soc. Astronomique de France 2008, G.G. Stokes Award, SPIE 2012. *Publications:* Solar Magnetic Fields 1994; more than 300 scientific papers on astronomy in int. journals. *Leisure interests:* classical music, mountain hiking. *Address:* Institute for Particle Physics and Astrophysics (ETH), 8093 Zürich, Switzerland (office). *E-mail:* stenflo@astro.phys.ethz.ch (office). *Website:* www.ipa.phys.ethz.ch (office).

STENGEL, Richard, BA; American editor and government official; *Under Secretary of State for Public Diplomacy and Public Affairs;* b. 2 May 1955, New York; m. Mary Pfaff; two c.; ed Princeton Univ., Christ Church Coll., Oxford, UK; worked for MSNBC TV; staff writer, Time magazine, New York 1981–83, Assoc. Ed. 1984–88, sr writer and essayist 1989–98; Ferris Prof. of Journalism, Princeton Univ. 1998–99; Sr Advisor and chief speechwriter for presidential candidate Bill Bradley 1999; Man. Ed., Time.com 2000, Cultural Ed., Time magazine, then Nat. Ed. and Asst Man. Ed. –2004; Pres. and CEO, Nat. Constitutional Center, Philadelphia 2004–06; Man. Ed., Time magazine 2006–13; UnderSec. of State for Public Diplomacy and Public Affairs, US State Dept 2014–. *Film:* Mandela (producer, documentary) 1995. *Publications include:* January Sun: One Day, Three Lives, a South African Town 1990, Long Walk to Freedom (with Nelson Mandela) 1993, You're Too Kind: A Brief History of Flattery 2000, Mandela's Way: Fifteen Lessons on Life, Love and Courage 2010; contrib. articles to The New Yorker, The New Republic, New York Times and others. *Address:* Department of State, 2201 C Street, NW, Washington, DC 20520, USA (office). *Telephone:* (202) 647-4000 (office). *Fax:* (202) 647-6738 (office). *Website:* www.state.gov (office).

STENLUND, Bengt Gustav Verner, MSc (Eng), DTech; Finnish professor of polymer technology (retd); b. 17 Aug. 1939, Kristinestad; s. of Gustav Stenlund and Linda Hofman; m. Kerstin Ottosson 1964; one s.; Research Assoc. The Finnish Pulp and Paper Research Inst. 1965–77; Acting Prof. of Polymer Tech., Åbo Akad. 1977–79, Prof. 1979–2002, Dean. Faculty of Chemical Eng 1982–85, Vice-Rector 1985–88, Rector 1988–97; mem. Research Council of Tech. Finish Acad. of Sciences 1983–85, Chair. and Bd mem. 1986–88; Chair. Finnish Rectors' Council 1990–92; Chair. LC Working Group on EC Research Policy 1993–95; Chair. Steering Group, Baltic Univ. Programme 1995–98; Head of Lab. of Polymer Tech. 1997–2002; mem. Scientific Del. of Finnish Chemical Industry 1985–90; mem. Bd Nordic Foundation of Tech. 1987–90; mem. Steering Cttee Finnish Centres of Expertise 1996–98; mem. Bd CRE 1994–98; Chair. Swedish Acad. of Eng of Finland 2001–04, Evaluation Cttee The Bank of Sweden Tercentenary Foundation 2002–04; mem. European Univ. Evaluation Team 1998, Int. Selection Cttee, The Millenium Tech. Prize 2003–06, Int. Expert Cttee of Vinnova, Sweden 2006, Bd Resource Centre of Math., Science and Tech. 2006; mem. European Science and Tech. Asscn 1994–97, Finnish Acad. of Eng, Finnish Soc. of Science and Letters, Royal Swedish Acad. of Eng, ACS 1997–2001, Japanese Inst. of Finland 1997–2002; Hon. mem. Swedish Acad. of Eng Sciences of Finland; Commdr, Order of the White Rose of Finland; Hon. DTech (Karlstad) 2000. *Publications:* Gel Chromatography of Lignosulfonates 1970; about 50 publs about natural and synthetic polymers. *Leisure interests:* art, society activities, grandchildren. *Address:* Peltolantie 6 B 61, 20700 Åbo (home); Åbo Akademi University, Biskopsgatan 8, 20500 Åbo, Finland (office). *Telephone:* (400) 521556 (home). *E-mail:* bengt.stenlund@abo.fi (office). *Website:* www.abo.fi/fak/tkf (office).

STEPANIUC, Victor, DHist; Moldovan politician; b. 13 July 1958, Ialoveni; m.; three c.; ed State Univ. of Moldova, Free Int. Univ. of Moldova; teacher of Russian language and literature, Hansca Village School, Ialoveni 1975–86, Dir of School 1986–96; mem. Parl. 1996–, mem. Juridical Comm. on Nominations and Immunities 1996–98, Chair. Parl. Comm. for Youth, Sport and Tourism 1998–2001, for Culture, Science, Educ., Sport, Tourism and Media 2005–08, Chair. CP Parl. Group 1998–2005, mem. Perm. Bureau 1998–; Deputy Prime Minister of Moldova 2008–09. *Address:* Parliament (Parlamentul), 2073 Chişinău, bd. Ştefan cel Mare şi Sfânt 105, Moldova (office). *Telephone:* (22) 26-82-44 (office). *Fax:* (22) 23-30-12 (office). *E-mail:* inform@parlament.md (office). *Website:* www .parlament.md (office).

STEPANKOV, Valentin Georgievich; Russian lawyer; b. 17 Sept. 1951, Perm; s. of Georgii Vassilyevich Stepankov and Antonina Andreyevna Klopova; m. 2nd Irina Vasilevna Martynova 2000; one s. from first m.; ed Perm State Univ.; investigator, Office of Public Prosecutor, Sverdlovsk Dist 1975–76, Perm Region 1976–77; Public Prosecutor of town of Gubakh Perm Region 1977–81; instructor, Div. of Regional Cttee of CPSU 1981–83; Public Prosecutor of Perm 1983–87; Deputy-Dir Investigation Dept Office of Public Prosecutor of USSR 1987–88; Public Prosecutor of Khabarovsk Region 1986–90; First Deputy Public Prosecutor of RSFSR 1990–91; Procurator-Gen. of Russia 1991–93; Deputy Head of Admin., Perm Region 1994–96; mem. State Duma (Parl.) 1996–99; Deputy Rep. of Russian Pres. to Volga Fed. Dist 2000; Deputy Sec. Security Council of Russia 2003; Deputy Minister of Natural Resources 2004–06; mem. Bd of Dirs Permskiye Motory (Perm Engines) 1999–2000; Honoured Lawyer of Russian Fed. 2001–. *Publications:* monograph on Kremlin conspiracy and numerous articles. *Leisure interests:* painting, reading, walks in the forest.

STEPANOV, Petr Petrovich; Moldovan (b. Russian) politician; b. 2 Jan. 1959, Sankino village, Krasnochetaiskii region, Chuvash Autonomous Okrug, USSR; m.; two c.; ed Superior Tech. School 'A.D. Baumann', Moscow, VUZ Inst. of Higher Educ.; worked as engineer at natural gas compression stations in city of Surgut, Tyumen Oblast, transferred to Yamalo-Nenets Autonomous Okrug 1982–85, Head of gas compression station 1985–87; worked at Petr Stepanov man. co. providing gas from Tiraspol 1987–96, held positions of engineer in charge of checking tech. condition of the pipes; Gen. Man. Tiraspoltransgaz 1996–2005, CEO Tiraspoltransgaz-Pridnestrovie 2005–07; Minister of Industry of self-proclaimed 'Transnistrian Moldovan Republic' 2007–12; Chair. of the Govt, 'Transnistrian Moldovan Republic' 2012–13; Order of Honour, Order 'Labour Glory', Order 'For Merit' Grade II, Medal 'for hard work' and other medals of anniversary of breakaway Repub. of Transnistria; Gold Reserve 2000, Man of the Year 2003.

STEPASHIN, Col Gen. Sergey Vadimovich, CandHist, LLD; Russian security official; b. 2 March 1952, Lüshunkou, China; m.; one s.; ed Higher Political Coll., USSR Ministry of Internal Affairs, Mil. Acad., Financial Acad. under Russian Fed. Govt; service in Interior Forces 1973–90; Lecturer, Higher Political Coll., Leningrad 1981–90; Deputy to RSFSR Supreme Soviet 1990–93; after attempted coup Aug. 1991 Head of Cttee on Defence and Security of the Russian Fed. Supreme Soviet; author programme of reorganization of state security system; Chief, Leningrad Fed. Security Agency; Admin. and Deputy Chair. Russian Fed. Security Agency 1991–92; First Deputy Dir Fed. Counter-Intelligence Service (later Fed. Security Service) 1993–94, Dir 1994–95; Head of Admin, Dept of Govt 1995–97; Minister of Justice 1997–98, of Internal Affairs 1998–99; First Deputy Chair. of Govt April–May 1999, Chair. of Govt (Prime Minister) May–Aug. 1999; Chair. Exec. Council of Russia and Belarus Union May–Aug. 1999; joined Yabloko Movt 1999; mem. State Duma (Parl.) 1999–2000; Chair. Accounts Chamber of Russian Fed. 2000–13; Pres. European Org. of Supreme Audit Insts (EUROSAI) 2002–14; Head of Imperial Orthodox Palestine Soc. 2007–; Hon. Citizen of Murom 2006; Hon. Prof., Russian Fed. State Counsellor of Justice; Dr hc (Diplomatic Acad. of Russia) 2011; Order of Saint Nicholas the Wonderworker, 1st class (Russian Imperial House); Order of the Commonwealth (CIS Interparliamentary Assembly); Medal For Distinguished Service to the Public Order, Medal For Distinction in Military Service, 1st and 2nd classes, Commander 1st Class of the Order of the Polar Star (Sweden); Order of Fortitude 1998; Order of Merit for the Fatherland, Third Degree 2002, Third Class 2007, First Class 2012; Commdr, Légion d'honneur 2005; Order of Diplomatic Service Merit, First Class (South Korea) 2004; Honour of the State Duma of the Russian Fed. 2006; Order of St Seraphim of Sarov (Russian Orthodox Church), Second Class 2006, First Class 2009; Diploma of the Government of the Russian Federation 2006. *Publication:* Personal and Social Security (Political and Legal Issues) 1994. *Leisure interests:* sports, literature, theatre. *Address:* c/o Accounts Chamber of the Russian Federation, 119992 Moscow, Zubovskaya Str. 2, Russia. *E-mail:* info@ach.gov.ru.

STEPHANOPOULOS, George Robert, AB,MA; American broadcast journalist and fmr government official; *Chief Anchor, Good Morning America, ABC News;* b. 10 Feb. 1961, Fall River, Mass.; s. of Robert Stephanopoulos and Nikki C. Stephanopoulos; m. Alexandra Wentworth 2001; two d.; ed Columbia Univ., Univ. of Oxford, UK (Rhodes Scholar); fmrly admin. asst to US Rep. Edward Feighan, Washington, DC; Deputy Communications Dir, Dukakis-Bentsen Presidential Campaign 1988; fmr Exec. Floor Man. to US Rep. Richard Gephardt (later House Majority Leader); Sr Advisor to Pres. of USA 1993–96; Communications Dir, Clinton-Gore Presidential Campaign 1992; Communications Dir, The White House 1992–96, also Sr Advisor for Policy and Strategy; Visiting Prof. of Political Science, School of Int. and Public Affairs, Columbia Univ. 2001–02; contrib. and corresp., ABC News 1997–2002, Host and Chief Political Analyst, This Week with George Stephanopoulos (public affairs TV programme) 2002–09, Chief Political Corresp., ABC News 2005–, Co-anchor, Good Morning America 2009–, Chief Anchor 2014–; mem. Bd of Dirs; Hon. DJur (St John's Univ.) 2007; Medal of Excellence, Columbia Univ. 1993, Walter Cronkite Award for Excellence in TV Political Journalism, Annenberg School of Journalism, Univ. of Southern California, 2007, 2009. *Publication:* All Too Human: A Political Education 1999. *Address:* Good Morning America, ABC News, 47 West 66th Street, New York, NY 10023, USA (office). *Website:* abcnews.go.com/author/george_stephanopoulos (office).

STEPHEN, Marcus; Nauruan politician, fmr head of state and fmr weightlifter; b. 1 Oct. 1969; s. of Lawrence Stephen and Sunshine Stephen; m. Amanda Stephen; one s. two d.; ed St Bede's Coll. and Royal Melbourne Inst. of Tech., Australia; participated as weightlifter for Samoa at Olympic Games, Barcelona 1992, for Nauru at Olympic Games, Atlanta 1996, Sydney 2000; in Commonwealth Games won one gold and two silver medals at Auckland 1990, three gold medals in Victoria 1994, three gold medals in Kuala Lumpur 1998, three silver medals at Manchester 2002; retd from sport in 2002; mem. Parl. from Ewa and Anetan 2003–07, held positions of Minister of Finance, for Sport, Telecommunications and Transport; Pres. of Nauru 2007–11 (resgnd); Rep. at Int. Whaling Comm. 2005; Pres. Nauru Olympic Cttee 2009–.

STEPHEN, Baron (Life Peer), cr. 2011, of Lower Deeside in the City of Aberdeen; **Nicol Stephen,** LLB; British politician and business executive; b. 23 March 1960, Aberdeen, Scotland; ed Robert Gordon's Coll., Aberdeen, Univs of Aberdeen and Edinburgh; Dip. Legal Practice 1981; trainee solicitor, C & P H Chalmers 1981–83; Solicitor, Milne & Mackinnon 1983–88; Sr Man., Touche Ross Corp. Finance 1988–91; Dir, Glassbox Ltd 1992–99; Councillor, Grampian Regional Council 1982–92; contested Kincardine and Deeside in gen. elections 1987, 1992; MP for Kincardine and Deeside 1991–92; Scottish Liberal Democrat Spokesperson for Health 1995–97; contested Aberdeen South 1997; MSP (Liberal Democrat) 1999–2011, Party Spokesperson for Educ. and Heritage, Team Leader; held several Ministerial posts, including Deputy First Minister of Scotland 2005–07; Leader of Scottish Liberal Democrats 2005–08; mem. Cttee of the Regions 2002–05, Alt. mem. 2010–; mem. (Liberal Democrat) House of Lords 2011–; Dir, Renewable Energy Ventures Ltd, Grampian Youth Orchestra. *Address:* House of Lords, Westminster, London, SW1A 0PW, England (office). *Telephone:* (20) 7219-2964 (office). *Fax:* (20) 7219-5979 (office). *E-mail:* stephenn@parliament.uk (office).

STEPHENS, Toby; British actor; b. 21 April 1969, London; s. of Sir Robert Stephens and Dame Maggie Smith; m. Anna-Louise Plowman 2001; three d.; ed London Acad. of Music and Dramatic Art. *Plays include:* Measure for Measure (RSC), A Midsummer Night's Dream (RSC), Unfinished Business (playing Young Beamish, RSC), Wallenstein (RSC), All's Well That Ends Well (playing Bertram, RSC), Anthony and Cleopatra (playing Pompey, RSC), Coriolanus (playing Coriolanus, RSC) (Sir John Gielgud Award for Best Actor 1994, Ian Charlson Award 1995), Britannicus, Phedre (Almedia & Brooklyn Acad., New York), A Streetcar Named Desire (The Haymarket), Tartuffe (playing Damis, Playhouse Theatre), Ring Around the Moon (Lincoln Center Theater, New York) 1999, Betrayal (Donmar Warehouse, London) 2007, The Country Wife 2007, The Real Thing 2010, Private Lives 2012, 2013. *Films include:* Orlando 1992, Twelfth Night 1996, Sunset Heights 1997, Photographic Fairies 1997, Cousin Bette 1998, Onegin 1999, The Announcement 2000, Space Cowboys 2000, Possession 2002, James Bond: Die Another Day 2002, Terkel in Trouble (voice) 2004, The Rising Ballad of Mangal Pandey 2005, Midsummer Dream (voice) 2005, Severance 2006, Dark Corners 2006, One Day 2007, Believe 2013, All Things to All Men 2013, The Machine 2013, The Journey 2016. *Television:* The Camomile Lawn 1992, Tenant of Wildfell Hall 1996, The Great Gatsby 2000, Perfect Strangers 2001, Napoléon 2002, Cambridge Spies 2003, Poirot (episode, Five Little Pigs) 2003, London 2004, The Queen's Sister 2005, The Best Man 2005, Sharpe's Challenge 2006, Jane Eyre (miniseries) 2006, Robin Hood (series), Strike Back 2010, Vexed 2010, 2012, Lewis 2012, Black Sails 2014–. *Address:* c/o Olivia Homan, United Agents, 12–26 Lexington Street, London, W1F 0LE, England (office). *Telephone:* (20) 3214-0800 (office). *Fax:* (20) 3214-0802 (office). *E-mail:* ohoman@unitedagents.co.uk (office); acarrington@unitedagents.co.uk (office). *Website:* www.unitedagents.co.uk (office).

STEPHENSON, Barbara J., BA, MA, PhD; American diplomatist; *President, American Foreign Service Association;* b. Fla; m. Matthew Furbush; two c.; ed Univ. of Florida; career mem. Sr Foreign Service, joined Foreign Service 1985, served as Political and Econ. Officer, Embassy in Panama City, later Prin. Officer, Belfast, NI, Desk Officer for the UK, Political-Military Officer, Embassy in South Africa, Political Officer, Embassy in The Hague and Embassy in San Salvador, served as Special Asst to Under Secretaries for Political Affairs Peter Tarnoff and Tom Pickering, covering European affairs, Consul Gen. and Chief of Mission in Curacao 1998–2001, Consul Gen. in Belfast 2001–04, Dir for Planning, Office of the Coordinator for Reconstruction and Stabilization –2006, Deputy Sr Advisor to the Sec. and Deputy Coordinator for Iraq 2006–08, Amb. to Panama 2008–10, Deputy Chief of Mission and Chargé d'affaires, Embassy in London 2010–13, Dean, Leadership and Man. School, Foreign Service Inst. 2013–15; Pres. American Foreign Service Asscn 2015–; Distinguished Honor Award, Dept of State. *Address:* American Foreign Service Association, 2101 E Street, NW, Washington, DC 20037, USA (office). *Telephone:* (202) 338-4045 (office). *Fax:* (202) 338-6820 (office). *E-mail:* member@afsa.org (office). *Website:* www.afsa.org (office).

STEPHENSON, Hugh; British journalist and academic; b. 18 July 1938, Simla, India; s. of Sir Hugh Stephenson and Lady Stephenson; m. 1st Auriol Stevens 1962 (divorced 1987); two s. one d.; m. 2nd Diana Eden 1990; ed New Coll. Oxford, Univ. of California, Berkeley, USA; served in diplomatic service in London and Bonn 1964–68; with The Times, London 1969–81, Ed., The Times Business News 1971–81; Ed. The New Statesman 1982–86; Prof. of Journalism, City Univ. 1986–2003, Prof. Emer. 2003–; Dir History Today Ltd 1981–2014; Dir European Journalism Centre, Maastricht 1992–2008, Chair. 1995–2002; currently crossword ed., The Guardian newspaper. *Publications include:* The Coming Clash 1972, Mrs. Thatcher's First Year 1980, Claret and Chips 1982, Libel and the Media (with others) 1997, Secrets of the Setters 2005, also various series of crosswords collections. *E-mail:* hugh.stephenson@theguardian.com (office).

STEPHENSON, Randall L., BS, MAcc; American telecommunications executive; *Chairman and CEO, AT&T Inc.;* b. 22 April 1960, Oklahoma City; m. Lenise H. Stephenson; ed Central State Univ., Okla, Univ. of Oklahoma; began career with Southwestern Bell Telephone, Oklahoma City (later SBC) 1982, various man. roles in finance, becoming Dir of Finance SBC Int., Mexico City 1992–96, Controller SBC Communications, San Antonio 1996–97, Sr Exec. Vice-Pres. and Chief Financial Officer 2001–04, COO SBC Communications Inc. 2004–05, COO AT&T Inc. (following merger of SBC and AT&T Corpn 2005) 2005–07, mem. Bd of Dirs, AT&T Inc. 2005–, Chair. and CEO 2007–; Dir Cingular Wireless 2001–06, Chair. 2003–04; Dir Emerson Electric Co. 2006–; Chair. United Way of Metropolitan Dallas Campaign 2011; mem. Nat. Exec. Bd, Boy Scouts of America. *Address:* AT&T Inc., 208 South Akard Street, Dallas, TX 75202, USA (office). *Telephone:* (210) 821-4105 (office). *Fax:* (210) 351-2071 (office). *E-mail:* info@att.com (office). *Website:* www.att.com (office).

STEPHENSON, Thomas F., AB, MBA, JD; American business executive and diplomatist; b. 1942, Wilmington, Del.; m. Barbara Stephenson; four c.; ed Harvard Coll., Harvard Business School, Boston Coll. Law School; fmr securities analyst, Fidelity Management Co., helped found Fidelity Ventures, Pres. Fidelity Ventures 1977–87; Partner, Sequoia Capital (Silicon Valley venture capital co.) 1987–2006; Amb. to Portugal 2007–09; mem. Diplomatic Council on Energy Security, Securing America's Future Energy; mem. Bd of Overseers and Exec. Cttee, Harvard Univ.; fmr mem. Exec. Cttee of Bd of Overseers of Hoover Inst., Stanford Univ., Bd of Advisors of Stanford Inst. for Econ. Policy Research, Bd of Dirs of Conservation Int., Wilson Center Council; fmr Corp. Fund Vice-Chair. The Kennedy Center; fmr mem. bds and cttees Tufts New England Medical Center, Boston. *Address:* c/o Securing America's Future Energy, 1111 19th Street, NW, Suite 406, Washington, DC 20036, USA.

STERIU, Valeriu Andrei, PhD; Romanian engineer and politician; *Leader, Uniunea Naţională pentru Progresul României (UNPR—National Union for the Progress of Romania);* b. 24 Sept. 1965, Bucharest; m.; two c.; Sec. of State for issues of European integration and int. trade, Ministry of Agric. 2001–05; Senator (Social Democratic Party) 2004–08; mem. Chamber of Deputies (PSD) for 12 Calarasi, uninominal Coll. No. 2 2008–09, (Uniunea Naţională pentru Progresul României (UNPR—Nat. Union for the Progress of Romania)) 2009–, mem. Cttee for Agric., Forestry, Food Industry and Specific Services; Leader, UNPR 2016–, mem. Politburo Standing Cttee. *Address:* Uniunea Naţională pentru Progresul României (National Union for the Progress of Romania), 011413 Bucharest 1, Str. Gheorghe Bratianu 7, Romania (office). *Telephone:* (31) 4327774 (office). *Fax:* (31)

4327774 (office). *E-mail:* secretariat@unpr.eu (office). *Website:* www.unpr.eu (office).

STERLING, Sir Michael John Howard, Kt, PhD, DEng, FIEE, FInstMC, FCMI, FREng; British engineer, academic and university vice-chancellor (retd); *Chairman, Science and Technology Facilities Council;* b. 9 Feb. 1946, Paddock Wood, Kent, England; s. of Richard Howard Sterling and Joan Valeria Sterling (née Skinner); m. Wendy Karla Anstead 1969; two s.; ed Hampton Grammar School, Middx, Univ. of Sheffield; student apprentice, AEI 1964–68; GEC Research Engineer 1968–71; Lecturer in Control Eng, Univ. of Sheffield 1971–78, Sr Lecturer 1978–80; Prof. of Eng, Univ. of Durham 1980–90; Vice-Chancellor and Prin., Brunel Univ. 1990–2001; Vice-Chancellor, Univ. of Birmingham 2001–09; mem. Council IEE 1991–93, Vice-Pres. 1997–2001, Deputy Pres. 2001–02, Pres. 2002–03; Chair. Higher Educ. Statistics Agency 1992–2003, Higher Educ. Funding Council Steering Cttee on Performance Indicators 1992–95 (mem. Quality Assessment Cttee 1992–95), WASMACS Ltd 1994–, MidMAN 2001; Pres. Inst. of Electrical Engineers 2002–03; Chair. Russell Group 2003–06, STEMNET 2006–11, Science and Tech. Facilities Council 2009–, DECC/IET Transmission Costing Group 2011–12; apptd by China to be an Academic Grand Master to lead a national '111' R&D five-year project in smart grid technology 2014–, based at Hohai Univ., Nanjing; Chair. OCEPS Ltd 1990–2015; Dir COBUILD Ltd 2001–09, UCAS 2001–09, Universitas 21 2001–09; mem. Science and Eng Research Council Eng Bd 1989–92, Electricity Research Council 1987–89, Royal Acad. of Eng Standing Cttee for Educ., Training and Competence to Practise 1993–97, Cttee 2 for Int. Co-operation in Higher Educ., British Council 1991–96, AWM Broadband Steering Group 2002–10, Bd WMHEA 2001–09; Fellow, Inst. of Measurement and Control (Pres. 1988, Council mem. 1983–91), Royal Acad. of Engineering; mem. West Midlands Regional Development Agency 2002–09, Prime Minister's Council for Science and Technology 2003–13, DECC Science Review Panel 2011–12, Foresight Lead Expert Group on Manufacturing 2012–14, MoD Science Capability review 2015; Pres. Elmhurst School for Dance 2002–09; Trustee, Barber Inst. of Fine Art 2001–09; Gov. Burnham Grammar School 1990–2001, Hampton School 1991–2001 (Chair. of Govs 1997–2001); consultant Global Energy Interconnection & Develpoment Organisation GEIDCO Beijing China 2017–; Freeman City of London 1996, Liveryman Worshipful Co. of Engineers 1998; Hon. DEng (Sheffield) 1995, (Brunel Univ.) 2008, (Univ. of Birmingham) 2013; Hon. DUniv (Tashkent, Uzbekistan) 1999, (West Bohemia, Czech Repub.) 2001; Inst. of Measurement and Control ICI Prize 1980, IEE Hartree Premium 1985, Commemorative Medal 2000. *Publications:* Power Systems Control 1978; over 200 tech. papers and book contribs. *Leisure interests:* gardening, DIY, computers, model eng. *Address:* Science and Technology Facilities Council, Polaris House, North Star Avenue, Swindon, SN2 1SZ, England (office). *Telephone:* (1793) 442-000 (office). *E-mail:* enquiries@stfc.ac.uk (office). *Website:* www.stfc.ac.uk (office).

STERLING OF PLAISTOW, Baron (Life Peer), cr. 1990, of Pall Mall in the City of Westminster; **Jeffrey Maurice Sterling,** GCVO, CBE; British business executive; b. 27 Dec. 1934, London; s. of Harry Sterling and Alice Sterling; m. Dorothy Ann Smith 1985; one d.; ed Reigate Grammar School, Preston Manor County School and Guildhall School of Music, London; Paul Schweder & Co. (Stock Exchange) 1955-57; G. Eberstadt & Co. 1957–62; Financial Dir General Guarantee Corpn 1962–64; Man. Dir Gula Investments Ltd 1964–69; Chair. Sterling Guarantee Trust PLC 1969–85 (merged with P&O 1985), P&O Steam Navigation Co. 1983, P&O Asia 1992, P&O Princess Cruises 2000–03, now Life Pres.; Special Adviser to Sec. of State for Industry 1982–83, to Sec. of State for Trade and Industry 1983–90; mem. British Airways Bd 1979–82; mem. Exec., World Org. for Rehabilitation by Training Union 1966–, Chair. Org. Cttee 1969–73, Chair. ORT Tech. Services 1974, Vice-Pres. British ORT 1978; Pres. Gen. Council of British Shipping 1990–91, EC Shipowners' Asscns 1992–94; Deputy Chair. and Hon. Treasurer London Celebrations Cttee Queen's Silver Jubilee 1975–83; Chair. Young Vic Co. 1975–83; f. Motability (charity) 1977, Vice-Chair. and Chair. of Exec. 1977–94, Chair. 1994–; Chair. of the Govs Royal Ballet School 1983–99; Chair. Queen's Golden Jubilee Weekend Trust 2001–02; Fellow, ISVA 1995; Gov. Royal Ballet 1986–99; Hon. Capt. RNR 1991–; Elder Brother Trinity House 1991; Hon mem. Royal Inst. of Chartered Surveyors 1993; Freeman City of London; Hon. Fellow, Inst. of Marine Engineers 1991, Inst. of Chartered Shipbrokers 1992, Royal Inst. of Chartered Shipbrokers 1992, Royal Inst. of Naval Architects 1997; KStJ 1998; Hon. DBA (Nottingham Trent) 1995; Hon. DCL (Durham) 1996. *Leisure interests:* music, swimming, tennis. *Address:* House of Lords, London, SW1A 0PW, England. *Telephone:* (20) 7219-4819. *Website:* www.motability.co.uk.

STERN, Ernest, MA, PhD; American economist and academic; *Partner Emeritus, The Rohatyn Group;* b. 25 Aug. 1933, Frankfurt, Germany; s. of Henry Stern; m. Zina Gold 1957; ed Queens Coll., New York and Fletcher School of Law and Diplomacy, Tufts Univ.; Economist, US Dept of Commerce 1957–59; Program Economist, USAID 1959–63; Instructor, Middle East Tech. Univ. 1960–61; Economist, Office of Pakistan Affairs, USAID 1963–64, Officer in Charge of Pakistan Affairs 1964–64, Asst Dir for Devt Policy USAID India 1965–67, Deputy Dir USAID Pakistan 1967–68, Deputy Staff Dir Comm. on Int. Devt (Pearson Comm.) 1968–69; Lecturer, Woodrow Wilson School of Public and Int. Affairs, Princeton, New Jersey 1971; Sr Staff mem. Council on Int. Econ. Policy, The White House 1971; joined World Bank 1972, various posts including Deputy Chair. Econ. Cttee, Sr Advisor on Devt Policy, Dir Devt Policy, then Vice-Pres. S Asia until 1978, Vice-Pres. Operations, World Bank July 1978, Sr Vice-Pres., Operations 1980–87, Sr Vice-Pres., Finance 1987, Man. Dir 1991–95 (retd); Man. Dir JP Morgan Chase 1995; Partner and Sr Advisor, The Rohatyn Group, New York, now Partner Emer. and mem. Bd of Partners; currently Sr Advisor, Pro Mujer Inc.; mem. Bd of Advisors, Inst. for Int. Econs, Washington, DC; mem. Bd of Overseers, Int. Center for Econ. Growth, Calif.; fmr mem. Bd of Dirs Center for Global Devt, US-Russian Business Council, Commonfund; mem. Council on Foreign Relations, Group of Thirty Consultative Group on Int. Econ. and Monetary Affairs, Inc. (G-30), Washington, DC; William A. Jump Memorial Foundation Meritorious Award 1964, 1966. *Address:* TRG Management LP, 280 Park Avenue, 30th Floor West, New York, NY 10017, USA (office). *Telephone:* (212) 984-2900 (office). *E-mail:* TRG@rohatyngroup.com (office). *Website:* www.rohatyngroup.com/stern (office).

STERN, Howard Allan, BA; American radio broadcaster, television host, author, actor and photographer; b. 12 Jan. 1954, Jackson Heights, Queens, New York; s. of Ben Stern and Rae Stern; m. 1st Alison Berns 1978 (divorced 2001); three d.; m. 2nd Beth Ostrosky 2008; ed Boston Univ.; disc jockey with WRNW, Briarcliff Manor, NY 1976–78, WCCC, Hartford, Conn. 1978–79, WWWW, Detroit 1979–80, WWDC, Washington, DC 1980–82, WNBC, New York 1982–85, WXRK, New York 1985–2005; syndicated in several other radio markets with Clear Channel 1986, with Infinity Broadcasting Corpn 1998–2005; The Howard Stern Show, Sirius XM Radio 2006–; judge on TV talent show America's Got Talent (replaced Piers Morgan) 2012–15; partnership with Whalerock Industries 2015; Libertarian cand. for Gov. of NY 1994. *Television includes:* Petey Greene's Washington 1981, Late Night with David Letterman 1984–93, Nightlife 1987, The New Hollywood Squares 1988, The Howard Stern Show (WOR-TV) 1990–92, 1992 MTV Video Music Awards 1992, The Howard Stern 'Interview' 1992–93, The Larry Sanders Show 1993, The Jon Stewart Show 1993, Howard Stern 1994–2005, Saturday Night Live 1997, The Magic Hour 1998, The Roseanne Show 1998, The Howard Stern Radio Show 1998–2001, The Concert for New York City 2001, Extra 2004, Howard TV 2005–13, Piers Morgan Tonight 2011, The Daily Show with Jon Stewart 2011, Late Show with David Letterman 2011, America's Got Talent (judge) 2012–15; as producer: Son of the Beach (also writer) 2000, Doomsday (also writer) 2002, Howard Stern: The High School Years 2003. *Radio:* The Howard Stern Radio Show 1998–2001. *Recordings include:* 50 Ways to Rank Your Mother 1982, Crucified by the FCC 1991, Private Parts: The Album 1997. *Publications:* Private Parts 1993, Miss America 1995, Howard Stern Comes Again 2019. *Address:* c/o Don Buchwald & Associates, 10 East 44th Street, New York, NY 10017, USA (office). *Website:* www.howardstern.com.

STERN, Jacques; French engineer, business executive and fmr academic; b. 21 March 1932, Paris; m. Janine Riemer 1956; three s.; ed Ecole Polytechnique, Ecole Nationale supérieure de l'Aéronautique, Harvard Univ., USA, Institut des Hautes Etudes de la Defense Nationale; in charge of design and devt of French Air Defence computer system (STRIDA), French Air Force 1958–64; Founder and Pres. Soc. d'Etudes des Systèmes d'Automation (SESA) 1964; apptd Chair. and CEO Bull 1982, Chair. Honeywell Bull Inc. 1987, Hon. Pres. Bull 1989–; Founder and Pres. Sycomore 1989–; Founder, Stern Systèmes d'information 1998–; Founder and Pres. Synesys 1998–2001; Vice-Pres. Fyssen Foundation 1994; mem. Bd of Dirs Planet Finance, Air France, Thomson Group; Bd mem. Ecole Polytechnique, Fondation des Sciences Politiques et Sociales (representing Prime Minister), Conseil Perfectionnement de l'ENST; mem. Comité Consultatif Banque de France, Comité Nat. Evaluation de la Recherche; Prof., various univs and eng schools; Hon. mem. Acad. des Technologies; Officier, Ordre nat. du Mérite, Chevalier, Légion d'honneur. *Publications include:* several tech. books. *Address:* 1 rue Le Notre, 75016 Paris, France (home). *Telephone:* 1-45-27-35-11 (office). *E-mail:* jj.stern@free.fr (home).

STERN, Klaus, DrIur; German legal scholar, academic and judge; *Professor Emeritus, Institute für öffentliches Recht und Verwaltungslehre, University of Cologne;* b. 11 Jan. 1932, Nuremberg; m. Helga Stern 1976; ed Humanistisches Gymnasium, Nuremberg and Univs of Erlangen and Munich; Dozent, Univ. of Munich 1961; Prof., Free Univ. of Berlin 1962–66; apptd Prof. and Dir Inst. für öffentliches Recht und Verwaltungslehre, Univ. of Cologne 1966, apptd Inst. of Broadcasting Law 1968, Dean of Law Faculty 1969–71, Rector, Univ. of Cologne 1971–73, Pro-Rector 1973–75, now Prof. Emer.; Judge, Constitutional Court, Nordrhein-Westfalen 1976–2000; Head of Studies, Verwaltungs- und Wirtschaft-sakademie, Düsseldorf 1966–; Chair. Asscn of German Constitutional Law Profs 1978–80; mem. Comm. of Bundestag for reform of the German constitution 1971–76; mem. Standing Cttee of German Law Conference 1972–84; mem. Comm. of Landtag North-Rhine-Westfalia negotiating questioins on law of mems of Parl. 2001–02; mem. Rheinland-Westfalische Akad. der Wissenschaften 1978–; Hon. mem. Japan Acad. 2006–; Dr hc (Univ. of Breslau, Poland) 1987, (Fed. Univ. Ceara of Fortaleza, Brazil) 1991, (Univ. of Verona) 2005; Grosses Bundesverdienstkreuz 1989, Austrian Ehrenkreuz for Research and Art 1998, Verdienstorden, NRW 2000, Verdienstorden, City of Düsseldorf 2002. *Publications:* Staatsrecht der Bundesrepublik Deutschland (four vols); many other books and articles on constitutional and admin. law. *Address:* Institut für Rundfunkrecht an der Universität zu Köln, Aachener Straße 197–199, 50931 Cologne (office); Institut für öffentliches Recht und Verwaltungslehre, Universität zu Köln, Albertus-Magnus-Platz, 50931 Cologne, Germany. *Telephone:* (221) 9415465 (office). *Fax:* (221) 9415466 (office). *E-mail:* klaus.stern@uni-koeln.de (office); mail@klaus-stern.net. *Website:* www.jura.uni-koeln.de (office); www.klaus-stern.net.

STERN, Robert Arthur Morton, BA, MArch, FAIA; American architect and academic; b. 23 May 1939, New York; s. of Sidney Stern and Sonya Stern (née Cohen); m. Lynn G. Solinger 1966 (divorced 1977); one s.; ed Columbia and Yale Univs; Program Dir Architectural League New York 1965–66; designer, Richard Meier, architect, New York 1966; consultant Small Parks Program, Dept of Parks, New York 1966–70; urban designer, Housing and Devt Admin. New York 1967–70; partner Robert AM Stern & John S. Hagmann, Architects, New York 1969–77, Prin. Robert AM Stern Architects 1977–89, Sr Partner 1989–; lecturer to Prof. of Architecture, Columbia Univ. 1970–72, Prof. 1982–98; Dean, School of Architecture, Yale Univ. 1998–2016; Acting Dir Historical Preservation Program, Columbia Univ. School of Architecture 1991–98; mem. Bd of Regents American Architecture Foundation 1989–91, Bd of Dirs Chicago Inst. for Architecture and Urbanism 1990–93, Bd of Dirs Preservation League of New York, Exec. Cttee, Architectural League of New York 1977– (Pres. 1973–77); Dir (non-exec.) Walt Disney Co. 1992–2003; numerous awards including AIA Nat. Honor Award 1980, 1985, 1990, President's Medal, Architectural League of New York 2002, Vincent Scully Prize, Nat. Building Museum 2008, Richard H. Driehaus Prize for Classical Architecture 2011. *Television includes:* host, Pride of Place: Building the American Dream documentary series on PBS 1986. *Publications include:* New Directions in American Architecture 1969, George Howe: Toward a Modern American Architecture 1975, Modern Classicism, 1988, New York 1960 (with Thomas Mellins and David Fishman) 1995, The Philip Johnson Tapes: Interviews by Robert A.M. Stern 2008, Architecture on the Edge of Postmodernism: Collected Essays 1964–1988 2009, Robert A.M. Stern: On Campus 2010, Tradition and Invention in Architecture: Conversations and Essays 2011, Paradise Planned: The Garden Suburb and the Modern City 2013, The American Houses by Robert A. M. Stern Architects 2015, Pedagogy and Place: 100 Years of Architecture Education at Yale 2016, The New Residential Colleges at Yale: A Conversation Across Time 2017, Open Studio:

The Work of Robert A.M. Stern Architects 2018; also co-authored series New York 1880, New York 1900, New York 1930, New York 1960, New York 2020. *Address:* Robert A.M. Stern Architects LLP, One Park Avenue, New York, NY 10016, USA (office). *Telephone:* (212) 967-5100 (office). *Fax:* (212) 967-5588 (office). *Website:* www.ramsa.com (office).

STERN OF BRENTFORD, Baron (Life Peer), cr. 2007, of Elsted in the County of West Sussex and of Wimbledon in the London Borough of Merton; **Nicholas Herbert Stern,** CH PhD; British economist, academic and fmr government official; *IG Patel Chair in Economics and Government, London School of Economics;* b. 1946, London; m. Susan Stern; three c.; ed Latymer Upper School, Peterhouse Coll., Univ. of Cambridge; taught at Univ. of Oxford, Univ. of Warwick, LSE, Univ. of Paris (Sorbonne), MIT; Chief Economist, EBRD 1993–99; Sr Vice-Pres. and Chief Economist, World Bank 2000–03; Second Perm. Sec., Man. Dir, Budget and Public Finances, Treasury of the UK 2003–04, Head of Govt Econ. Service 2003–07 (retd); commissioned to compile Stern Review on the Econs of Climate Change 2005, published 2006; IG Patel Chair in Econs and Govt, LSE 2007–, also Dir India Observatory, Chair. Asia Research Centre, Grantham Research Inst. on Climate Change and the Environment, Centre for Climate Change Econs and Policy; Deputy Chair. Bd of Trustees, British Museum; Pres. The British Acad.; Fellow, Econometrics Soc.; mem. Int. Advisory Panel, Global Carbon Capture and Storage Inst., Australia; mem. Int. Advisory Bd Abengoa SA; Hon. Fellow, American Acad. of Arts and Sciences; Hon. DSc (Warwick) 2006. *Publications:* Palanpur: The Economy of an Indian Village (with C. J. Bliss) 1982, The Theory and Practice of Tax Reform in Developing Countries (with E. Ahmad) 1991, A Strategy for Development 2002. *Leisure interests:* reading, travelling, watching Wimbledon Football Club. *Address:* House of Lords, London, SW1A 0PW; Asia Research Centre, 10th Floor, Tower 2, London School of Economics, Houghton Street, London, WC2A 2AE, England. *Telephone:* (20) 7219-5353 (House of Lords). *Fax:* (20) 7107-5285. *E-mail:* arc@lse.ac.uk. *Website:* www.lse.ac.uk/collections/IndiaObservatory (office); www.lse.ac.uk/collections/asiaResearchCentre.

STERNBERG, Robert Jeffrey, BA, PhD; American psychologist, writer, editor and academic; *Professor of Human Development, College of Human Ecology, Cornell University;* b. 8 Dec. 1949, Newark, NJ; m. 2nd Karin Sternberg; two s. three d.; ed Yale Univ., Stanford Univ.; Asst Prof., Yale Univ. 1975–80, Assoc. Prof. 1980–83, Prof. 1983–86, IBM Prof. of Psychology and Education 1986–2005, Dir Center for Psychology of Abilities, Competencies and Expertise 2000–05; Dean, School of Arts and Sciences, Tufts Univ. 2005–10, Dir Center for the Psychology of Abilities, Competencies and Expertise 2006–10; Provost and Sr Vice-Pres., Oklahama State Univ. 2010–13, also served as Regents Prof. of Psychology and Education and George Kaiser Family Foundation Chair of Ethical Leadership; Pres. and Prof. of Psychology and Education, Univ. of Wyoming 2013; Prof. of Human Development, Coll. of Human Ecology, Cornell Univ. 2014–; Distinguished Assoc., The Psychometrics Centre, Univ. of Cambridge; Assoc. Ed. Perspectives on Psychological Science –2015, Ed. 2015–; Ed. Psychological Bulletin 1991–96, Contemporary Psychology 1999; Ed.-in-Chief, Educational Psychology Series, Lawrence Erlbaum Assocs 1996–; Pres. Federation of Asscns in Behavioral and Brain Sciences 2012–13; Treasurer, Asscn of American Colls and Univs 2011–13; mem. American Acad. of Arts and Sciences, AAAS, Nat. Acad. of Education 2011–, American Educational Research Asscn, American Psychological Soc., International Council of Psychologists, National Asscn for Gifted Children, Psychonomic Soc., Soc. for Research in Child Development, Soc. of Multivariate Experimental Psychology, American Psychological Asscn (Pres. 2003), Eastern Psychological Asscn (Pres. 2007–08), International Asscn for Cognitive Education and Psychology (Pres. 2009–11); Hon. Prof., Univ. of Heidelberg; Dr hc (Complutense Univ., Madrid) 1994, (Univ. of Paris V, France) 2000, (Univ. of Cyprus) 2000, (Univ. of Leuven, Belgium) 2001, (Constantine the Philosopher Univ., Slovakia), 2004, (Durham Univ., UK) 2006, (St Petersburg State Univ., Russia) 2006, (Tilburg Univ.) 2007, (Ricardo Palma Univ., Peru) 2008, Eureka Coll.) 2008, (Univ. of Connecticut) 2009, (De la Salle Univ., Philippines) 2011, (Univ. of Huelva, Spain) 2012; Distinguished Scholar Award, Nat. Asscn for Gifted Children 1985, Outstanding Book Award, American Educational Research Asscn 1987, Sylvia Scribner Award 1996, Guggenheim Fellowship 1985–86, Award for Excellence, Mensa Educ. and Research Foundation 1989, G. Stanley Hall Distinguished Lecturer, American Psychological Asscn 1997, E.L. Thorndike Award for Career Achievement in Educational Psychology 2003, Farnsworth Award, American Psychological Asscn 2003, Arthur W. Staats Award, American Psychological Foundation and Soc. for Gen. Psychology 2003, Anton Jurovsky Award, Slovak Psychological Soc. 2004, Arnheim Award, American Psychological Asscn 2005, Interamerican Psychologist Award, Interamerican Soc. of Psychology 2005, E. Paul Torrance Award, Nat. Asscn for Gifted Children 2006, Sir Francis Galton Award, Int. Asscn of Empirical Aesthetics 2008, Presidential Award for Distinguished Lifetime Contribs to the Public Understanding of Psychology, American Psychological Asscn Div. of Media Psychology 2008, Distinguished Service Award, Int. Asscn for Cognitive Educ. and Psychology 2011, William James Award, Asscn for Psychological Science 2017, Ernest Hilgard Award, American Psychological Asscn Div. 1 2017. *Publications include:* Intelligence, Information Processing, and Analogical Reasoning: The Componential Analysis of Human Abilities 1977, Beyond IQ: A Triarchic Theory of Human Intelligence 1985, Intelligence Applied: Understanding and Increasing Your Intellectual Skills 1986, What is Intelligence? (co-author) 1986, The Psychologist's Companion (second edn) 1988, The Triangle of Love 1988, The Triarchic Mind: A New Theory of Human Intelligence 1988, Metaphors of Mind: Conceptions of the Nature of Intelligence 1990, Love the Way You Want It 1991, Tacit Knowledge Inventory for Managers (co-author) 1991, For Whom Does the Bell Curve Toll?: It Tolls for You 1995, In Search of the Human Mind 1995, Defying the Crowd: Cultivating Creativity in a Culture of Conformity (co-author) 1995, Off Track: When Poor Readers Become Learning Disabled (co-author) 1996, Cognitive Psychology 1996, Successful Intelligence 1996, Introduction to Psychology 1997, Pathways to Psychology 1997, Thinking Styles 1997, Successful Intelligence 1997, Cupid's Arrow: The Course of Love Through Time 1998, Love is a Story 1998, Perspectives on Learning Disabilities: Biological, Cognitive, Contextual (co-author) 1999, Our Labeled Children: What Every Parent and Teacher Needs to Know About Learning Disabilities (co-author) 1999, Teaching for Successful Intelligence (co-author) 2000, Psychology: In Search of the Human Mind 2001, Educational Psychology (co-author) 2001, Dynamic Testing (co-author) 2002, Psychology 101½: The Unspoken Rules for Success in Academia 2004, The Nature of Leadership 2004, A Brief History of Intelligence 2004, Wisdom, Intelligence and Creativity Synthesized 2007, The Nature of Hate (co-author) 2008, College Admissions for the 21st Century 2010, Explorations of the Nature of Giftedness (co-author) 2011, What Universities Can Be 2016; other: ed. of numerous books; contribs: numerous scholarly books and journals. *Address:* Department of Human Development, Cornell University, 116 Reservoir Avenue, B44 Martha Van Rensselaer Hall, Ithaca, NY 14853-4401, USA (office). *Telephone:* (607) 882-0001 (office). *E-mail:* rjs487@cornell.edu (office). *Website:* www.human.cornell.edu/bio.cfm?netid=rjs487 (office); www.robertjsternberg.com.

STERNBERG, Seymour (Sy) G.; American insurance executive; b. 24 June 1943, New York, NY; s. of Max Sternberg and Mollie Sternberg; m. 1st Roslyn Jacobowitz 1965 (divorced); two c.; m. 2nd Laurette Zolty 1980; one s.; Sr Vice-Pres. Insurance Dept, New York Life Insurance Co. 1989–91, Exec. Vice-Pres. and Vice-Chair. Bd 1991–95, Pres. and COO 1995–97, Chair. and CEO 1997–2001, Chair., Pres. and CEO 2001–03, Chair. and CEO 2003–08, Chair. 2008–09 (retd); Partner and mem. New York City Partnership and Chamber of Commerce, Co-Chair. Breakthrough for Learning Initiative; Vice-Chair. Kennedy Center Corp. Fund; US Rep. to Asia-Pacific Econ. Co-operation Business Advisory Council 1999–2002; Chair. Bd of Trustees, Northeastern Univ. 2008–; mem. Bd Dirs, Express Scripts Inc. from 1992, CIT Group Inc. 2005–16; mem. The Business Roundtable, Lincoln Center Consolidated Corp. Fund Leadership Cttee, Bd Govs United Way of Tri-State; mem. Bd Trustees Big Brothers and Big Sisters of New York City; Hon. DrIng (Polytechnic Univ.) 2006, Hon. DHumLitt (City Coll. of New York) 2010; New Yorker for New York Award, Citizens Cttee of New York 2001. *Leisure interests:* stamp collecting, tennis.

STETTER, Karl Otto, Dr rer. nat (habil.); German microbiologist and academic; *Professor Emeritus, University of Regensburg;* b. 16 July 1941, Munich, Bavaria; one s.; ed Staatliche Luitpold-Oberrealschule, Munich, Technical Univ., Munich, Ludwig Maximilians Univ., Munich; Postdoctoral Fellow, Dept of Molecular Biology, Max Planck Inst. for Biochemistry, Martinsried 1973–75; Lecturer, Botanical Inst. 1975–77; Asst Prof. ('Privatdozent' and 'Oberassistent'), Faculty of Biology, Ludwig Maximilians Univ., Munich 1977–80; Prof. of Microbiology and Head of Dept of Microbiology ('Ordinarius') and Archaeencenter, Univ. of Regensburg 1980–2002, Prof. Emer. 2002–; mem. (Prof. Above Scale) Dept of Microbiology and Molecular Genetics and Inst. of Geophysics and Planetary Science, Faculty of Life Sciences, UCLA, USA 1989–; Co-founder DIVERSA Corpn, San Diego, Calif., USA 1994 (merged with Celunol to form Verenium Corpn 2007); mem. Editorial Bd Systematic and Applied Microbiology 1992–, Extremophiles – Microbial Life Under Extreme Conditions 1996–, Geobiology 2000–; mem. Gesellschaft für Biologische Chemie 1970–, American Soc. of Microbiology 1974–, Deutsche Gesellschaft für Hygiene und Mikrobiologie 1979–, German Univ. Soc. 1981–, Int. Cttee on Environmental Biogeochemistry (ISEB) 1984–, Vereinigung für Allgemeine und Angewandte Mikrobiologie 1986–, Soc. of German Scientists and Physicians 1986–, Int. Cttee on Systematic Bacteriology 1986–, Int. Inst. of Biotechnology 1992–, Gesellschaft Deutscher Chemiker 1994–, Deutsche Akad. der Naturforscher Leopoldina, 1995–, Int. Soc. for the Study of the Origin of Life 1996–, Royal Netherlands Acad. of Arts and Sciences 1999–, Bayerische Akad. der Wissenschaften 2002–; Hon. mem. Botanical Soc. of Regensburg 2001; Annual Award, German Soc. of Hygiene and Microbiology 1985, Gottfried Wilhelm Leibniz Award, German Science Foundation (Highest German Award for Research Excellence) 1988, Medal Lecture, Int. Inst. of Biotechnology 1994, Bergey Medal, Bergey's Manual Trust 1999, Leeuwenhoek Medal, Royal Netherlands Acad. of Arts and Sciences (in recognition for the most influential work in microbiology in the previous decade) 2003; approx. 330 invited lectures 1987–2007. *Major discovery: Nanoarchaeum equitans*, an archaeal microorganism containing world's smallest known genome, discovered in hydrothermal vent off coast of Iceland 2002. *Television:* contrib. to and appearance in more than 30 nat. and int. films and documentaries, including Life is Impossible (BBC TV Horizon, UK) 1993, The Secret of Life – The Immortal Thread (WGBH, USA) 1993, The Origin of Life (ARTE, France and Germany) 1994, Planet of Ocean (NHK TV, Japan) 1998, Intimate Strangers (PBS, USA) 1999, Die Jagd nach den Feürzwergen (Hunting the Fire Dwarfs; ZDF, Germany) 2001. *Publications:* author or co-author of more than 330 scientific publs. *Address:* Lehrstuhl für Mikrobiologie, Universität Regensburg, Universitätstraße 31, 93343 Regensburg, Germany (office). *Telephone:* (941) 943-1821 (office); (941) 943-3161 (office); (89) 68096548 (home). *Fax:* (941) 943-3243 (office); (89) 68096580 (home). *E-mail:* karl.stetter@biologie.uni-regensburg.de (office). *Website:* www.biologie.uni-regensburg.de/Mikrobio/Stetter (office).

STEVENS, Anne L., BEng; American business executive; b. Reading, Pa; ed Drexel Univ., Rutgers Univ.; held various eng, mfg and marketing positions at Exxon Chemical Co.; marketing specialist in Plastic Products Div., Vehicle Exterior Systems, Ford Motor Co. 1990–92, Man. Quality Services Dept, Saline, Mich. 1992–95, Mfg Man., Plastic and Trim Products Operations 1995, Plant Man., Enfield Plant, UK (Ford's first female plant man. in Europe) 1995–97, Asst Vehicle Line Dir Small Car Vehicle Centre, Ford Automotive Operations, Dunton, UK 1997–99, Dir Mfg Business Office for Ford in N America 1999–2001, Exec. Dir Vehicle Operations in N America 2000–01, Vice-Pres. N America Ass. Operations 2001, Vice-Pres. N America Vehicle Operations 2001–03, Group Vice-Pres. Canada, Mexico and S America 2003–06, Exec. Vice-Pres. and COO The Americas 2006 (retd); Chair., Pres. and CEO Carpenter Technology Corpn, Reading, Pa 2006–09; Chair. and Prin., SA IT Services, Atlanta, Ga 2011–14 (retd); mem. Bd of Dirs Lockheed Martin 2002–, Anglo American plc 2012–, XL Group plc 2014–; mem. Advisory Bd Mexico Inst. of the Woodrow Wilson Int. Center for Scholars, Graduate Business Program at Northwestern Univ.; mem. Exec. Advisory Bd Juran Center for Leadership in Quality, Univ. of Minnesota; mem. Shingo Prize Bd of Govs; mem. Council of the Americas, Nat. Acad. of Eng 2004; Trustee, Drexel Univ., Women's Automotive Asscn Int; Dr hc (Central Michigan Univ.); Shingo Leadership Award 2000, Soc. of Mfg Engineers Eli Whitney Award 2003, Automotive Hall of Fame Distinguished Service Citation 2003. *Leisure interest:* car racing.

STEVENS, Cat (see ISLAM, Yusuf).

STEVENS, Glenn, BEcons, MA; Australian economist and central banker; *Independent Director, Macquarie Group;* b. 23 Jan. 1958, Sydney; m.; two c.; ed Univ. of Sydney, Univ. of Western Ont., Canada; joined Research Dept, Reserve Bank of Australia 1980, Head, Econ. Analysis Dept 1992–95, Head, Int. Dept 1995–96, Asst Gov. (Econ.) 1996–2001, Deputy Gov. 2001–06, Gov. 2006–16, also Chair. Payments System Bd; Chair. Council of Financial Regulators, Foundation for Children; Visiting Scholar, Fed. Reserve Bank of San Francisco 1990; mem. Bd of Dirs Anika Foundation, Lowy Inst.; Ind. Dir Macquarie Group 2017–, Macquarie Bank 2017–; fmr mem. Advisory Bd Melbourne Inst. for Applied Econ. and Social Research, Hong Kong Inst. for Monetary Research. *Publications include:* numerous articles on monetary policy and other econ. matters. *Address:* Macquarie Group, 50 Martin Place, Sydney, NSW 2000, Australia (office). *Telephone:* (2) 6601-0888 (office); (2) 8232-3333 (office). *E-mail:* foundation@ macquarie.com (office). *Website:* www.macquarie.com (office).

STEVENS, John Paul, AB JD; American lawyer and judge (retd); b. 20 April 1920, Chicago, Ill.; s. of Ernest James Stevens and Elizabeth Street; m. 1st Elizabeth Jane Sheeren 1942; one s. three d.; m. 2nd Maryan Mulholland Simon 1979; ed Univ. of Chicago, Northwestern Univ. School of Law; served USN (awarded Bronze Star Medal) 1942–45; Co-Ed. of Law Review, Northwestern Univ. School of Law 1947; Law Clerk to Supreme Court Justice Wiley Rutledge 1947; with Poppenhusen, Johnston, Thompson and Raymond (law firm) 1948–51, 1952; Pnr, Rothschild, Stevens, Barry and Myers 1952–70; Circuit Judge, Seventh Circuit Court of Appeals 1970–75; Assoc. Justice, US Supreme Court 1975–2010 (retd); Assoc. Counsel, Monopoly Power Sub-Cttee of US House of Reps Judiciary Cttee 1951; mem. Attorney Gen.'s Nat. Cttee on Antitrust Laws 1953–55; part-time teacher, Northwestern Univ. School of Law, later Univ. of Chicago Law School 1952–56; admitted to Ill. Bar 1949, to US Supreme Court 1954; mem. American Law Inst.; Presidential Medal of Freedom 2012. *Publications:* Five Chiefs: A Supreme Court Memoir 2011, Six Amendments: How and Why We Should Change the Constitution 2014; numerous articles on commercial monopoly affairs.

STEVENS, Robert Bocking, BA, MA, DCL, LLM; British lawyer and academic; *Senior Of Counsel, Covington & Burling LLP;* b. 8 June 1933; s. of John S. Stevens and Enid Dorothy Bocking Stevens; m. 1st Rosemary Wallace 1961 (divorced 1983); m. 2nd Katherine Booth 1985; one s. two d.; ed Keble Coll. Oxford and Yale Univ., USA; mem. Essex Court Chambers, Lincoln's Inn Fields 1965–, Midland Circuit 1962–76; Asst Prof. of Law, Yale Univ., USA 1959–61, Assoc. Prof. 1961–65, Prof. 1965–76, Fellow, Jonathan Edwards Coll. 1963–76; Prof. of Law and Adjunct Prof. of History, Tulane Univ. 1976–78; Provost 1976–78; Pres. Haverford Coll. 1978–87; Prof. of History, Univ. of California, Santa Cruz 1987–93, Chancellor 1987–91; apptd Counsel, Covington & Burling LLP (law firm) 1991, now Sr Of Counsel; mem. Council, Justice (UK Br., Int. Comm. of Jurists 1992–98; Master, Pembroke Coll., Oxford 1993–2001; Chair. Sulgrave Manor (Home of Washington Family) Bd 2002–; Bencher, Gray's Inn 1999; Hon. Fellow, Keble Coll., Oxford 1983, Pembroke Coll., Oxford 2001; several hon. degrees. *Publications include:* Law and Politics: The House of Lords as a Judicial Body 1800–1976 1978, The American Law School: Legal Education in America 1850–1980 1983, The Independence of the Judiciary: The View from the Lord Chancellor's Office 1993, The English Judges 2002, From University to Uni 2004; co-author and ed. of other books on law, history and welfare; articles and monographs. *Leisure interests:* politics, history, talking, claret. *Address:* Covington & Burling, 265 Strand, London, WC2R 1BH (office); 19 Burgess Meade, Oxford, OX2 6XP, England (home). *Telephone:* (20) 7067-2038 (office); (1865) 558420 (home). *Fax:* (20) 7067-2222 (office); (1865) 558420 (home). *E-mail:* rstevens@cov.com (office). *Website:* www.cov.com (office).

STEVENS, Robert J., MEng, MBA; American business executive; b. 1951, McKeesport, Pa; ed Slippery Rock Univ., Polytechnic Univ. of New York, Columbia Univ. (Fairchild Fellowship), Dept of Defense Systems Man. Coll.; served in US Marine Corps; various man. positions in program man., finance, mfg and operations, Loral Systems Mfg Co., Vice-Pres. and Chief Financial Officer –1988, Gen. Man. 1988–93; Exec. Vice-Pres. and Chief Financial Officer, Lockheed Martin Air Traffic Man. 1993–96, Pres. Lockheed Martin Air Traffic Man. 1996–98, Pres. and COO Lockheed Martin Energy and Environment Sector 1998–99, Vice-Pres. Strategic Devt Org., Lockheed Martin Corpn 1998–99, Chief Financial Officer 1999–2001, Pres. and COO 2001–04, Pres. and CEO 2004–10, Chair. 2005–12, CEO 2010–12, Exec. Chair. Jan.–Dec. 2013; Lead Dir Monsanto Co.; mem. Bd of Dirs Congressional Medal of Honor Foundation, US Steel Corpn, Marine Corps Scholarship Foundation, Brent Scowcroft Center, Int. Security at the Atlantic Council; mem. US Pres. Bush's Comm. to examine the Future of the US Aerospace Industry 2001–02; mem. Int. Advisory Bd Atlantic Council, British-American Business Council, Council on Foreign Relations; mem. Bd of Govs Aerospace Industries Asscn; apptd by Pres. Obama to the Advisory Cttee for Trade Policy and Negotiations 2012; Fellow, American Astronautical Soc., AIAA (Hon. Fellow 2012), Royal Aeronautical Soc., Int. Acad. of Astronautics; Distinguished Alumni Award, Slippery Rock Univ., Exec. of the Year, Nat. Man. Asscn 2004, Industry Executive of the Year, Government Computer News, Private Sector Council Leadership Award, Partnership for Public Service, Globe and Anchor Award, Marine Corps Scholarship Foundation, inaugural LeJeune Recognition for Exemplary Leadership, Marine Corps Heritage Foundation 2010, James Forrestal Industry Leadership Award, Nat. Defense Industrial Asscn 2011, Hispanic Engineer Nat. Achievement Awards Corporation's Chairman's Award 2012, Wright Brothers Memorial Trophy, Nat. Aeronautic Asscn 2012, Circle of Honor Award, Congressional Medal of Honor Foundation 2013, Semper Fidelis Award, Marine Corps Scholarship Foundation 2013, Adm. of the Navy George Dewey Award, Naval Order of the US 2017.

STEVENS OF KIRKWHELPINGTON, Baron (Life Peer), cr. 2005, of Kirkwhelpington in the County of Northumberland; **John Arthur Stevens,** QPM, MPhil, LLB, CIMgt, FRSA, DL; British police officer (retd) and business executive; *Chairman, Quest Limited;* b. 21 Oct. 1942; s. of C. J. Stevens and S. Stevens; m.; two s. one d.; ed St Lawrence Coll., Ramsgate, Univ. of Leicester, Univ. of Southampton; mem. Metropolitan Police 1963–83, staff Police Staff Coll. 1983–84, Deputy Commr 1998–99, Commr 2000–05 (retd); Asst Chief Constable of Hants. Constabulary 1986–89, Deputy Chief Constable of Cambs. Constabulary 1989–91;

Chief Constable of Northumbria 1991–96; HM Inspector of Constabulary 1996–98; currently Chair. Quest Ltd (pvt. security co.); has chaired numerous enquiries including Stevens Enquiry on NI 1989–2003, Operation Paget into deaths of Diana, Princess of Wales and Dodi Fayed 2003–06, inquiry into football corruption 2006; Dir (non-exec.) BAA 2007–; Adviser, Forensic Science Service; Visiting Prof., Univ. of Cambridge 1984–85, City Univ. of New York 1984–85; Chancellor, Univ. of Northumbria 2005–; Visiting Lecturer, Int. Crime Prevention Centre, Canada 1998; Adviser to Prime Minister of Romania 2002–; patron, various charities in Romania and London; DL Greater London 2001; Hon. Fellow, Wolfson Coll. Cambridge 2000; KStJ; Hon. LLD (Leicester) 2000; Hon. DCL (Northumbria) 2001. *Leisure interests:* flying, rugby, walking, cricket, charity work. *Address:* House of Lords, London, SW1A 0PW; Quest Limited, 1 Duke Street, London, W1U 3EA, England (office). *Telephone:* (20) 7224-4004 (office). *Fax:* (20) 7387-7994 (office). *E-mail:* info@quest.co.uk (office). *Website:* www.quest.co.uk (office).

STEVENS OF LUDGATE, Baron (Life Peer), cr. 1987, of Ludgate in the City of London; **David Robert Stevens,** MA; British business executive; b. 26 May 1936; s. of (Arthur) Edwin Stevens; m. 1st Patricia Rose (divorced 1971); one s. one d.; m. 2nd Melissa Milicevich 1977 (died 1989); m. 3rd Meriza Giori 1990; ed Stowe School and Sidney Sussex Coll. Cambridge; man. trainee, Elliott Automation 1959; Dir Hill Samuel Securities 1959–68, Drayton Group 1968–74; Chair. City & Foreign (now Alexander Proudfoot PLC) 1976–95, Drayton Far East 1976–93, English & Int. 1976–79, Consolidated Venture (fmrly Montagu Boston) 1979–93, Drayton Consolidated 1980–92, Drayton Japan 1980–93, Econ. Devt Cttee for Civil Eng 1984–86; Dir United News & Media PLC (fmrly United Newspapers PLC) 1974–99, Chair. 1981–99; CEO INVESCO MIM 1980–87, Deputy Chair. 1987–89, Chair. 1989–93; Chair. MIM Britannia Ltd (fmrly Montagu Investment Man. Ltd) 1980–92 (CEO 1980–87), Express Newspapers 1985–99, PNC Telecom (fmrly Personal Number Co.) 1998–. *Leisure interests:* golf, gardening. *Address:* House of Lords, London, SW1A 0PW, England.

STEVENSON, Hon. Adlai E., III; American lawyer, investment banker and fmr politician; *Co-Chairman, HuaMei Capital Company, Inc.;* b. 10 Oct. 1930, Chicago, Ill.; s. of Adlai Stevenson II (fmr Gov. of Illinois, presidential candidate and Amb. to UN); great-grandson of Adlai E. Stevenson (Vice-Pres. of USA 1893–97); m. Nancy L. Anderson 1955; two s. two d.; ed Milton Acad., Mass. and Harvard Univ.; law clerk to a justice of Ill. Supreme Court 1957; joined Chicago law firm of Mayer, Brown and Platt 1958–66, pnr 1966–67, 1981–83, of Counsel 1983–91; elected to Ill. House of Reps. 1964; State Treas. of Ill. 1966–70; Senator from Illinois 1970–81; Democratic Cand. for Gov. of Ill. 1982, 1986; Chair. SC&M Int. Ltd (now SC&M Investment Man. Corpn) 1991–95, Pres. 1995–98, Chair. 1998–; Co-founder and Co-Chair. Huamei Capital Co., Inc. 2005–; Co-Chair. Stevenson, Melamed & Assocs; mem. Bd of Dirs Stonewater Control Systems Inc.; Advisor, Jane Capital Partners; Order of the Sacred Treasure, Gold and Silver Stars (Japan); numerous awards, hon. degrees and directorships. *Address:* HuaMei Capital Company, Inc., 71 South Wacker Drive, Suite 2760, Chicago, IL 60606 (office); 4302 South Blandings Road, Hanover, IL 61041, USA (home). *Telephone:* (312) 957-4260 (office). *Fax:* (312) 957-4261 (office). *E-mail:* info@huameicapital.com (office). *Website:* www.huameicapital.com (office).

STEVENSON, Juliet, CBE; British actress; b. 30 Oct. 1956; d. of Michael Guy Stevens and Virginia Ruth Marshall; one s. one d. two step-s.; ed Hurst Lodge School, Berks., St Catherine's School, Surrey, Royal Acad. of Dramatic Art; with RSC (now Assoc. Artist), Royal Nat. Theatre, Royal Court Theatre, film, TV, radio, audiobooks; Bancroft Gold Medal, Royal Acad. of Dramatic Art 1977, Time Out Award for Best Actress 1991, Evening Standard Film Award for Best Actress 1992, Lawrence Olivier Theatre Award for Best Actress 1992. *Plays include:* Measure for Measure 1978, Henry IV Parts 1 and 2 1980, A Midsummer Night's Dream 1981, The Witch of Edmonton 1981, Breaking the Silence 1984, As You Like It 1985, Troilus and Cressida 1985, Les Liaisons Dangereuses 1986 (all for RSC), Not I, Footfalls Money, Burn This (West End) 1990, Death and the Maiden (Royal Court and West End) (Olivier Award 1992) 1991, The Duchess of Malfi (Greenwich Theatre and West End) 1995, Yerma 1987, Hedda Gabler 1989, The Caucasian Chalk Circle 1997, The Country (Royal Court) 2000, Private Lives 1999, The Seagull (Nat. Theatre) 2006, Other Worlds, A Little Night Music (New York City Opera), Duet for One 2009, The Heretic (Royal Court Theatre) 2011, Happy Days (Young Vic) 2014–15, Mary Stuart (Almeida Theatre) 2016–17, Hamlet (Almeida and Harold Pinter Theatre) 2017. *Films include:* Drowning by Numbers, Ladder of Swords, Truly Madly Deeply, The Trial, The Secret Rapture, Emma, The Search for John Gissing, Who Dealt?, Beckett's Play, Bend It Like Beckham, Food of Love, Nicholas Nickleby, Mona Lisa Smile, Being Julia, Pierrepoint 2006, Breaking and Entering 2006, When Did You Last See Your Father? 2007, Dustbin Baby 2008, The Secret of Moonacre 2008, Desert Flower 2009, Shell Shock 2009, Diana 2013, The Letters 2014. *Radio includes:* To the Lighthouse, Volcano, Albertina, House of Correction, Hang Up, Cigarettes and Chocolate, A Little Like Drowning, Victory, The Pallisers, Mary Poppins, The Lovers of Viorne. *Television includes:* Miss Marple, Hear the Silence, The Road From Coorain, Play (Beckett), Trial by Fire, Cider with Rosie, Stone Scissors Paper, The Politician's Wife, A Doll's House (Nora), Life Story, Antigone, The March, Maybury, Thomas and Ruth, Aimée, The Mallens, Living With Dinosaurs, The Hour (series) 2011, White Heat (series) 2012, The Village (series) 2013–14, Atlantis 2013–15, The Enfield Hunting 2015, One of Us 2016; wrote and fronted BBC documentary Great Journeys. *Publications:* Clamorous Voices (jtly) 1988, Shall I See You Again? (jtly), Players of Shakespeare (jtly). *Leisure interests:* piano, travelling, gardening, reading, tennis. *Address:* c/o Markham and Froggatt Ltd, Julian House, 4 Windmill Street, London, W1P 1HF, England.

STEVENSON OF BALMACARA, Baron, (Life Peer), cr. 2010, of Little Missenden in the County of Buckinghamshire; **Robert Wilfrid (Wilf) Stevenson,** MA, FCCA; British public affairs consultant; b. 19 April 1947, Lochalsh, Ross-shire, Scotland; s. of James Stevenson and Elizabeth Macrae; m. 1st Jennifer Grace Antonio 1972 (divorced 1979); m. 2nd Elizabeth Ann Minogue 1991; one s. two d.; ed Edinburgh Acad., Univ. Coll., Oxford, Napier Coll., Edinburgh; Research Officer, Univ. of Edinburgh Students Asscn 1970–74; Sec. and Acad. Registrar, Napier Polytechnic, Edinburgh 1974–87; Deputy Dir BFI 1987–88, Dir 1988–97; Dir The Smith Inst. 1997–2008; Sr Policy Adviser to the Prime Minister 2008–10; mem. (Labour), House of Lords 2010–, Opposition Whip 2011–, Opposition

Spokesperson for Business, Enterprise and Industrial Strategy 2011–16, Culture, Media and Sport 2011–16, Educ. 2016, Int. Trade 2016–; Hon. DArts (Napier Univ., Edinburgh) 2008. *Publications:* Gordon Brown Speeches 1997–2006 (ed.) 2006, Moving Britain Forward (ed.) 2006, The Change We Choose (ed.) 2010. *Leisure interests:* cinema, bee keeping. *Address:* House of Lords, Westminster, London, SW1A 0PW (office); Missenden House, Little Missenden, Amersham, Bucks., HP7 0RD, England (home). *Telephone:* (20) 7219-8194 (office); (1494) 890689 (home). *E-mail:* stevensonw@parliament.uk (office); wilf@wilfstevenson.co .uk (home). *Website:* www.parliament.uk/biographies/lords/lord-stevenson-of -balmacara/4175 (office).

STEVENSON OF CODDENHAM, Baron (Life Peer), cr. 1999, of Coddenham in the County of Suffolk; **Henry Dennistoun Stevenson,** Kt, CBE; British business executive and business consultant; b. 19 July 1945, Edinburgh, Scotland; s. of Alexander James Stevenson and Sylvia Florence Stevenson (née Ingleby); m. Charlotte Susan Stevenson (née Vanneck); four s.; ed Glenalmond School and King's Coll., Cambridge; Chair. SRU Group of cos 1972–96; Chair. GPA, then AerFi, Group 1993–2000; Chair. Pearson plc 1997–2005 (Dir 1986–97); Dir, Halifax plc 1999–2009; Chair. HBOS plc 2001–09; Gov., Bank of Scotland 2006–09; Dir, British Technology Group 1979–89, Tyne Tees TV 1982–87, Manpower Inc. (fmrly Blue Arrow) 1988–2006, Thames Television plc 1991–93, J. Rothschild Assurance plc 1991–97, J. Rothschild Assurance Holdings plc 1991–99, English Partnerships 1993–99, BSkyB Group plc 1994–2000, Lazard Bros 1997–2000, Whitehall Trust Ltd 1997–2004, St James's Place Capital 1997–2002 (Hon. Pres. 2002–04), Economist Newspapers 1998–2011, Western Union Co. 2006–12, Loudwater Investment Partners Ltd 2007–12, Culture and Sport Glasgow 2007–09, Cloaca Maxima Ltd 2010–13, Waterstones Holdings Ltd 2011–; Chair. of Trustees, Tate Gallery 1989–98, Inter Mediate 2011–; Chair. Newton Aycliffe and Peterlee New Town Devt Corpn 1971–80, Intermediate Technology Devt Group 1983–90; Dir, Nat. Building Agency 1977–81, LDDC 1981–88; mem. (Crossbench), House of Lords 1999–, Chair. Appointments Comm. 2000–09, Arts and Media Honours Cttee 2008–12, mem. Works of Art Cttee 2009–; Chair. Govt working party on role of voluntary movements and youth in the environmtent 1971, '50 Million Volunteers' (HMSO), Ind. Advisory Cttee on Pop Festivals 1972–76, 'Pop Festivals, Report and Code of Practice' (HMSO), Advisory on Agricultural Marketing to Minister of Agric. 1979–83, Special Advisory to Prime Minister and Sec. of State for Educ. on use of IT in Educ. 1997–2000; mem. Panel on Takeovers and Mergers 1992–2000, Bd British Council 1996–2003, Standards Cttee, Westminster City Council 2008–12; Chair. NAYC 1973–81, Sinfonia 21 (fmrly Docklands Sinfonietta) 1989–99, Aldeburgh Music (fmrly Aldeburgh Productions) 2000–12; Pres. Aldeburgh Music 2012–; MQ, Transforming Mental Health 2010–; Dir, Glyndebourne Productions 1998–, London Music Masters 2011–, Inst. for Govt 2008–13; Trustee, Tate Gallery Foundation 1998–, Horse's Mouth 2006–; mem. Admin. Council, Royal Jubilee Trusts 1978–80; Chancellor, Univ. of the Arts London (fmrly London Inst.) 2000–10; Gov., LSE 1995–99, London Business School 1999–2002; DL, Suffolk 2008. *Publication:* Information and Communications Technology in UK Schools (The Stevenson Report) 1997. *Address:* House of Lords, Westminster, London, SW1A 0PW, England.

STEWART, Alec James, OBE; British fmr professional cricketer; *Director of Cricket, Surrey County Cricket Club;* b. 8 April 1963, Merton, London; s. of Michael James Stewart (fmr Surrey Capt. and Test player) and Sheila Stewart; m. Lynn Blades 1991; one s. one d.; ed Tiffin Boys' School, Kingston upon Thames; right-hand opening batsman; wicket-keeper; Surrey 1981–2003 (Capt. 1992–97); played in 133 Tests for England 1990–2003, 14 as Capt. 1993 (deputized), 1998–99, scoring 8,463 runs (average 39.54, highest score 190) including 15 hundreds; played in 170 One-Day Ints, scored 4,677 runs (average 31.60, highest score 116) including four hundreds; played in 447 First-class matches, scored 26,165 runs (average 40.06, highest score 271 not out) including 48 hundreds; held 11 catches, equalling world first-class record, for Surrey vs Leicestershire, Leicester 19–22 Aug. 1989; toured Australia 1990–91, 1994–95, 1998–99 (Capt.); overtook record (118 Tests) of Graham Gooch to become England's most-capped cricketer, Lords July 2002; retd 2003; Dir of Cricket, Surrey County Cricket Club 2003–, rejoined Surrey as mem. coaching staff specializing in batting, wicket keeping and mentoring 2009–; Founding Dir Arundel Promotions, with specific responsibility for player man. and representation 2004–; cricket columnist, Daily Mirror; Wisden Cricketer of the Year 1993. *Publications:* Alec Stewart: A Captain's Diary (co-author) 1999, Playing for Keeps 2003. *Leisure interests:* Chelsea Football Club, spending time with his family. *Address:* Surrey County Cricket Club, The Kia Oval, Kennington, London, SE11 5SS, England (office). *Telephone:* (844) 375-1845 (office). *E-mail:* enquiries@surreycricket.com (office). *Website:* www.kiaoval.com (office).

STEWART, Sir Brian John, Kt, CBE, MSc, CA; British business executive; b. 9 April 1945, Stirling, Scotland; s. of Ian M. Stewart and Christina McIntyre; m. Seonaid Duncan 1971; two s. one d.; ed Perth Acad., Edinburgh Univ.; joined Scottish & Newcastle Breweries (now Scottish and Newcastle PLC) 1976, Corp. Devt Dir 1985–88, Group Finance Dir 1988–91, Group Chief Exec. 1991–2000, Deputy Chair. 1997–2000, Exec. Chair. 2000–03, Chair. (non-exec.) 2003–08 (after acquisition of Scottish & Newcastle by a consortium of Carlsberg and Heineken); Chair. Miller Group PLC 2009–12; Chair. C&C Group plc 2010–18; mem. Bd of Dirs (non-exec.) Booker 1993–99, Baltic Beverages Holding, Standard Life Assurance Co. 1993–2007 (Chair. 2003–07). *Leisure interests:* skiing, golf.

STEWART, Colin; Candian diplomatist and UN official; *Special Representative and Chief of Mission, United Nations Mission for the Referendum in Western Sahara (MINURSO);* b. 1961; ed Laval Univ., Canada; Diplomatic and Foreign Service Officer 1990–97; worked for UN Mission in East Timor (UNAMET), UN Transitional Admin. in East Timor (UNTAET), UN Mission of Support in East Timor (UNMISET) 1999–2004, Acting Chief of Staff of Political Affairs, UN Integrated Mission in Timor-Leste (UNMIT) 2007–09, Deputy Dir and Chief of Staff UN Office at African Union (UNOAU), Addis Ababa 2011–16, Special Rep. for Western Sahara and Chief of Mission, UN Mission for Referendum in Western Sahara (MINURSO) 2017–; Rep. of The Carter Center in West Bank and Gaza, and Democratic Repub. of Congo 2004–06. *Address:* Department of Peacekeeping Operations, Room S-3727B, United Nations, New York, NY 10017, USA (office).

Telephone: (212) 963-8077 (office). *Fax:* (212) 963-9222 (office). *Website:* www .peacekeeping.un.org (office).

STEWART, David (Dave) A.; British musician (guitar, keyboards) and song-writer; b. 9 Sept. 1952, Sunderland; m. 1st Pam Stewart (divorced); m. 2nd Siobhan Fahey 1987 (divorced); two s.; m. 3rd Anoushka Fisz 2001; two d.; fmr mem. Harrison and Stewart (with Brian Harrison); Founder-mem. Longdancer 1973; Founder-mem. The Catch 1977, later renamed The Tourists 1979–80; Founder-mem. Eurythmics (with Annie Lennox) 1980–89, 1999–; solo artist 1990–; Founder-mem. The Spiritual Cowboys 1990–92; mem. Vegas 1992–93; f. record label Anxious Records 1988; Founder, Dave Stewart Entertainment, Weapons of Mass Entertainment; produces and directs films, including computer-enhanced films; writes film soundtracks; owner of recording studio, The Church 1992; producer and session musician for artists, including Mick Jagger, Bob Dylan, Tom Petty, Daryl Hall, Bob Geldof, Boris Grebenshikov, Sinead O'Connor, Feargal Sharkey; Hon. DMus (Westminster) 1998; Ivor Novello Award for Songwriter of the Year (for Sweet Dreams, with Annie Lennox) 1984, MTV Music Award for Best New Artist Video (for Sweet Dreams (Are Made Of This)) 1984, Ivor Novello Award for Best Song (for It's Alright (Baby's Coming Back), with Annie Lennox) 1987, Grammy Award for Best Rock Performance (for Missionary Man) 1987, BRIT Awards for Best Producer 1986, 1987, 1990, for Oustanding Contribution 1999, Golden Globe Award for Best Original Song (with Mick Jagger, for Old Habits Die Hard, from the film Alfie) 2005. *Compositions for film and television:* Rooftops 1989, De Kassière (with Candy Dulfer) 1989, Jute City (BBC1) 1991, GFI (TV series, with Gerry Anderson) 1992, No Worries 1993, The Ref 1994, Showgirls 1995, Beautiful Girls 1996, Crimetime 1996, Cookie's Fortune 1999, Honest 2000, Le Pont du trieur 2000, Chaos 2002, Around the World in 80 Days 2004, Alfie 2004; contrib. songs to numerous other films. *Film directed:* Honest 2000. *Television:* Malibu Country (co-creator) 2012. *Stage musicals:* as composer: Barbarella 2004, Ghost: the Musical 2011. *Recordings include:* albums: with The Tourists: The Tourists 1979, Reality Affect 1979, Luminous Basement 1980; with Eurythmics: In The Garden 1981, Sweet Dreams 1982, Touch 1983, Be Yourself Tonight 1985, Revenge 1986, Savage 1987, We Too Are One 1989, Eurythmics Live 1983–89 1992, Peace 1999; with The Spiritual Cowboys: Dave Stewart And The Spiritual Cowboys 1990; with Vegas: Vegas 1992; solo: Greetings From The Gutter 1994, The Blackbird Diaries 2011, The Ringmaster General 2012, Lucky Numbers 2013; with SuperHeavy: SuperHeavy 2009. *Publication:* Sweet Dreams Are Made of This: A Life In Music 2016. *Address:* Dave Stewart Entertainment, 10153 Riverside Drive, Suite 769, Toluca Lake, CA 91602, USA (office). *Telephone:* (818) 760-1144 (office). *Fax:* (323) 871-8132 (office). *E-mail:* info@davestewartent .com (office). *Website:* www.davestewartent.com (office); www.davestewart.com; www.eurythmics.com.

STEWART, Donald Alexander, BA, FIA, FCIA; British insurance industry executive; b. 1946, Glasgow, Scotland; ed Univ. of Glasgow, Harvard Business School, USA; joined Sun Life Financial, London 1969–74, Head of Canadian Pension Div., Toronto, Canada 1980–86, Head Project Team to Est. Mutual Fund Operation 1986, Pres. Spectrum Investments (mutual funds) 1986–87, Head of Information Tech., Sun Life Financial 1987–92, Chair. and CEO Sun Life Financial Trust 1992–95, Sr Vice-Pres. and Chief Actuary 1995–96, Pres. and COO 1996–98, Pres. and CEO Sun Life Insurance Co. of Canada 1998–99, Chair. and CEO 1999–2000, Chair. and CEO Sun Life Financial Inc. 2000–05, CEO 2005–11 (retd), Chair. and CEO Sun Life Assurance Co. of Canada 2000, also Chair. Sun Life Insurance and Annuity Co. of NY; benefits consultant, William M. Mercer, Toronto 1974–80; mem. Bd of Dirs MFS Investment Man., Novelis Inc. 2007–, Canadian Life and Health Insurance Asscn, The Geneva Asscn (think tank); Chair. Canada's Nat. Task Force on Financial Literacy 2009–, Birla Sun Life Asset Management Co. Ltd, Mumbai; fmr Chair. Canadian Life and Health Insurance Association; fmr Vice-Chair. International Insurance Soc.; fmr Dir American Council of Life Insurers; Chair. Federal-Provincial Nominating Cttee, Canada Pension Plan Investment Bd, Canada-India Business Council; Dir Birla Sun Life Insurance Co., Mumbai, Sun Life Everbright, Beijing; mem. Dean's Advisory Council, Schulich School of Business, Toronto; Dr hc (York Univ.) 2012; Int. Exec. of the Year, Canadian Chamber of Commerce 2007, Lifetime Achieve-ment Award, Canada-India Business Council 2011.

STEWART, John M.; British banker; joined Woolwich 1977, served in numerous exec. positions, Group Operations Dir 1995–96, CEO 1996–2000, Deputy Group CEO Barclays Bank (after acquisition of Woolwich by Barclays) 2000–03; CEO and Prin. Bd mem. Nat. Australia Group Europe 2003–04, Man. Dir and Group CEO Nat. Australia Bank Ltd 2004–08; Chair. Legal & General Group Plc 2010–16; Dir (non-exec.), Telstra Corpn; mem. Scottish Enterprise's Int. Advisory Bd, Court of the Bank of England, Australian Fed. Attorney Gen.'s Business-Govt Advisory Group on Nat. Security; fmr mem. Australian Prime Minister's Task Group on Emissions Trading; Assoc. Chartered Insurance Inst. *Address:* c/o Legal & General Group Plc, One Coleman Street, London, EC2R 5AA, England. *E-mail:* info@ legalandgeneralgroup.com.

STEWART, Sir John Young (Jackie), Kt, OBE; British fmr racing driver; b. 11 June 1939, Milton, West Dunbartonshire, Scotland; s. of Robert Paul Stewart and Jean Clark Young; m. Helen McGregor 1962; two s.; ed Dumbarton Acad.; mem. British Clay Pigeon Shooting Team 1956–62; first raced 1961; competed in four meetings driving for Barry Filer, Glasgow 1961–62; drove for Ecurie Ecosse and other private entrants, winning 14 out of 23 starts 1963, 28 wins out of 53 starts 1964; drove Formula 1 for British Racing Motors (BRM) 1965–67, for Ken Tyrrell 1968–73; has won Australian, New Zealand, Swedish, Mediterranean, Japanese and many other non-championship major int. Grands Prix; set new world record by winning his 26th World Championship Grand Prix (Zandvoort) 1973, 27th (Nürburgring) 1973; third in World Championship 1965, 2nd in 1968 and 1972, World Champion 1969, 1971, 1973; retd 1973; involved with son, Paul, in operation of Paul Stewart Racing and Stewart Grand Prix, a Formula One team cr. 1996, sold to Ford Motor Co. in 1999 who ran the operation as Jaguar Racing from start of 2000 season; Chair. and CEO Jaguar Racing 1999–2000; Vice-Pres. British Dyslexia Asscn 1998–; Pres. British Racing Drivers' Club 2000–06; RBS Global Amb. 2004–12; Pres. Dyslexia Scotland 2004–; Chair. Race Against Dementia 2015–; Freedom of West 2009; Hon. Prof., Univ. of Stirling 1998; Hon. Dr Aut. Eng (Lawrence Inst. of Tech., USA) 1986; Dr hc (Glasgow Caledonian) 1993, (Stirling

Univ.) 2001, (Edinburgh Univ.) 2006; Hon. DEng (Heriot-Watt Univ.) 1996, (Glasgow Univ.) 2001; Hon. DSc (St Andrews Univ.) 2008; British Automobile Racing Club Gold Medal 1971, 1973, Daily Express Sportsman of the Year 1971, 1973, BBC Sports Personality of the Year 1973, Scottish Sportsman of the Year 1973, Sports Illustrated American Sportsman of the Year 1973, World Sportsman of the Year 1973, ABC Sports Personality of the Year 1973, Seagrove Trophy 1973, 1999. *Film:* Weekend of a Champion 1972. *Publications:* World Champion (with Eric Dymock) 1970, Faster! (with Peter Manso) 1972, On the Road 1983, Jackie Stewart's Principles of Performance Driving (with Alan Henry) 1986, The Jackie Stewart Book of Shooting 1991, Winning is Not Enough (auto-biog.) 2007. *Leisure interests:* shooting (clay pigeon champion). *Telephone:* (1296) 620913 (office). *Website:* www.raceagainstdementia.com (office).

STEWART, Jon; American comedian, actor, writer and producer; b. (Jonathan Stuart Leibowitz), 28 Nov. 1962, New York City; m. Tracey McShane 2000; one s. one d.; ed Coll. of William and Mary; numerous early jobs, including contingency planner for New Jersey Dept of Human Services, contract admin. for CUNY, puppeteer for children with disabilities, and bartender at local Franklin Corner Tavern, stand-up comedian; moved to New York City 1986; began hosting TV network Comedy Central's Short Attention Span Theater 1989; hosted You Wrote It, You Watch It on MTV 1992; appeared several times in HBO's The Larry Sanders Show 1992–2001; host, The Jon Stewart Show on MTV (first talk show on that network) 1993–95; host, Comedy Central's The Daily Show with Jon Stewart 1999–2015; host, Acad. Awards ceremony 2006, 2008; Hon. DArts (Coll. of William and Mary) 2004; Peabody Awards for coverage of 2000 and 2004 US presidential elections on The Daily Show, keynote speaker at Commencement Ceremony, Princeton Univ. 2004, recipient of 11 Emmy Awards. *Films include:* Mixed Nuts 1994, Wishful Thinking 1997, Half Baked 1998, The Faculty 1998, Playing by Heart 1999, Big Daddy 1999, The Office Party 2000, Jay and Silent Bob Strike Back 2001, Death to Smoochy 2002, Rosewater (writer and dir) 2014. *Television includes:* as writer: The Sweet Life (series) 1989, The Jon Stewart Show (series) 1993, The Daily Show (series) (also co-exec. producer) (Primetime Emmy Award for Outstanding Writing for a Variety Series and Outstanding Variety Talk Series 2015) 1996–2015; Since You've Been Gone 1998, The Colbert Report (series) (exec. producer) 2005–14. *Recordings include:* The Daily Show with Jon Stewart Presents Earth (The Audiobook) (Grammy Award for Best Spoken Word Album 2011) 2010. *Publications include:* The Daily Show with Jon Stewart Presents America (The Book): A Citizen's Guide to Democracy Inaction 2004, Earth (The Book): A Visitor's Guide to the Human Race 2010. *Address:* Comedy Partners, 1175 Broadway, 10th Floor, New York, NY 10019, USA (office). *Telephone:* (212) 767-8600 (office). *Fax:* (212) 767-8592 (office).

STEWART, Kirstine; Canadian media executive; *President, TribalScale;* b. 1968, Toronto, Ont.; m. 1st Ken Layfield (divorced); two d.; m. 2nd Zaib Shaikh 2011; ed Univ. of Toronto, Global Leadership in the 21st Century Program, Kennedy School of Govt, Harvard Univ., USA; worked as receptionist at Paragon Entertainment following graduation 1988, rose to become Pres. of Distribution; fmr Gen. Man. and Vice-Pres. Programming Trio/Newsworld International (CBC/Power Corpn jt venture); later joined US-based Hallmark Entertainment as Sr Vice-Pres. of Programming; Sr Vice-Pres. Programming, Alliance Atlantis Communications 2003–06; joined CBC as Gen. Man., Television 2006, Exec. Dir of Network Programming, CBC Television 2006–10, Exec. Vice-Pres. of English Services, CBC (first woman) 2010–13; Man. Dir Twitter Canada, Toronto 2013–, then Vice-Pres. for Media, N America –2016; Chief Strategy Officer, Diply 2016–17; Pres. TribalScale 2018–; mem. Forum of Young Global Leaders, selected to advise World Econ. Forum; Founding Bd mem. Culture Days; mem. Bd Banff Television and Film Festival, White Knights, Amfar; named Canadian Women in Communications Woman of the Year 2010, her role recognized by Marketing Magazine in naming CBC Media Player of the Year 2009, Gala Co-Chair. Canadian Centre for Diversity 2012, Gala Co-Chair. Writers' Trust 2012. *Address:* TribalScale, 200 Wellington Street West, Suite 900, Toronto, ON M5V 3C7, Canada (office). *Telephone:* (416) 800-0918. *E-mail:* contact@tribalscale.com. *Website:* www.tribalscale.com (office).

STEWART, Martha Helen Kostyra, BA; American editor, writer and business executive; b. 3 Aug. 1941, Jersey City, NJ; d. of Edward Kostyra and Martha Kostyra (née Ruszkowski); m. Andy Stewart 1961 (divorced 1989); one d.; ed Barnard Univ.; fmr model, stockbroker, caterer; Owner and Ed.-in-Chief Martha Stewart Living magazine 1990–; Founder, Chair. and CEO Martha Stewart Living Omnimedia 1997–2003, mem. Bd –2004, Founding Editorial Dir (non-exec.) March 2004–, co. acquired by Sequential Brands 2015; also appears in cooking feature on NBC's Today Show; mem. Bd NY Stock Exchange June–Oct. 2002; mem. Bd Revlon Inc. –2004; under investigation for alleged insider trading June 2002, found guilty of conspiracy, making false statements and obstruction of justice March 2004, sentenced to prison and released March 2005. *Television:* host of TV show Martha 2005–10, Everyday Food 2008–09, Martha Bakes 2011–15, starred in The Apprentice: Martha Stewart 2005, numerous other appearances. *Publications include:* (with Elizabeth Hawes) Entertaining 1982, Weddings 1987; (as sole author) Martha Stewart's Hors d'Oeuvres: The Creation and Presentation of Fabulous Finger Food 1984, Martha Stewart's Pies and Tarts 1985, Martha Stewart's Quick Cook Menus 1988, The Wedding Planner 1988, Martha Stewart's Gardening: Month by Month 1991, Martha Stewart's New Old House: Restoration, Renovation, Decoration 1992, Martha Stewart's Christmas 1993, Martha Stewart's Menus for Entertaining 1994, Holidays 1994, The Martha Rules 2005, Martha Stewart's Homekeeping Handbook 2006, Martha Stewart's Dinner at Home 2009. *Leisure interests:* avid animal lover, pets include champion show Chow Chow dogs, French Bulldogs, Himalayan cats and Friesian horses. *Address:* Martha Stewart Living Omnimedia, 11 West 42nd Street, 25th Floor, New York, NY 10036 (office); Martha Stewart, 19 Newton Toke, Suite 6, Westport, CT 06880; 10 Saugatuck Avenue, Westport, CT 06880, USA (home); c/o Susan Magrino Agency, 40 West 57th Street, 31st Floor, New York, NY 10019. *Telephone:* (212) 827-8000 (office). *Fax:* (212) 827-8204 (office). *Website:* www.marthastewart.com (office); www.themarthablog.com.

STEWART, Sir Patrick, OBE; British actor and producer; *Professor of Performing Arts, University of Huddersfield;* b. 13 July 1940, Mirfield, W Yorks.; s. of Alfred Stewart and Gladys Stewart; m. 1st Sheila Falconer 1966; one s. one d.; m. 2nd Wendy Neuss 2002 (divorced); m. 3rd Sunny Ozell 2013; ed Bristol Old Vic Theatre School; mem. various local drama groups from about age 12; left school at 15 to work as jr reporter on local newspaper; acting experience with various repertory cos; spent year as furniture salesman, saving cash to attend drama school 1957; professional debut in Repertory in Lincoln 1959; performed at Manchester Library Theatre and toured around the world with Old Vic Co. early 1960s; joined RSC 1966, Assoc. Artist 1967–87; spell with Royal Nat. Theatre in mid-1980s; went to Los Angeles to star in Star Trek: The Next Generation, playing role of Capt. Jean-Luc Picard 1987–94; Founding Dir ACTER (A Centre for Theatre Educ. and Research); Dir Flying Freehold Productions, Paramount Studios, Los Angeles 1998–; Cameron Mackintosh Visiting Prof. of Contemporary Theatre, St Catherine's Coll. Oxford 2007–08, now Fellow Emer.; Chancellor, Univ. of Huddersfield 2004–, Prof. of Performing Arts 2008–. *Films include:* Hedda 1975, Excalibur 1981, Dune 1984, Lady Jane 1986, LA Story 1991, Robin Hood – Men in Tights 1993, Gunmen 1994, Jeffrey 1995, Star Trek: First Contact 1996, Conspiracy Theory 1997, Masterminds 1997, Moby Dick 1998, Dad Savage 1998, Star Trek: Insurrection 1999, X-Men 2000, Star Trek: Nemesis 2002, X-Men: X2 2003, Boo, Zino and the Snurks (voice) 2004, Chicken Little (voice) 2005, Bambi II (voice) 2006, X-Men: The Last Stand 2006, TMNT (voice) 2007, X-Men Origins: Wolverine (uncredited) 2009, Castlevania: Lords of Shadow (voice) 2010, Match 2012, Ted (voice, narrator) 2012, Hunting Elephants 2013, The Wolverine 2013, X-Men: Days of Future Past 2014, Match 2014, Green Room 2015, Logan 2016. *Theatre includes:* Antony and Cleopatra (Olivier Award, Soc. of West End Theatre Award) 1979, 2006, Henry IV 1984, Who's Afraid of Virginia Woolf (London Fringe Award) 1987, A Christmas Carol (Drama Desk Award, Olivier Award 1992) 1988–1996, The Tempest 1995, Othello 1997, The Ride Down Mount Morgan 1998, The Master Builder 2003, A Christmas Carol 2005, Macbeth (London Evening Standard Award for Best Actor 2007) 2007, Waiting for Godot 2009, Bingo: Scenes of Money and Death 2010, A Life in the Theatre 2010, The Merchant of Venice 2011, The Improvised Shakespeare Co. 2013. *Television includes:* Star Trek: The Next Generation, The Mozart Inquest, Maybury, I Claudius, Tinker, Tailor, Soldier, Spy, Smiley's People, The Lion in Winter 2003, Mysterious Island 2005, The Snow Queen (voice) 2005, Family Guy (voice14) 2005–07, Eleventh Hour 2006, American Dad! (voice) 2005–14, Hamlet (as Claudius/Ghost) 2009, Macbeth 2011, Richard II 2012, Blunt Talk (series) 2015–16. *Music:* narrative on Peter and the Wolf (Grammy Award) 1996. *Address:* c/o Independent Talent Agency, Oxford House, 76 Oxford Street, London, W1B 1DS, England. *Telephone:* (20) 7231-1964; (20) 7636-6565.

STEWART, Sir Roderick (Rod) David, Kt, CBE; British singer; b. 10 Jan. 1945, London, England; m. 1st Alana Collins 1979 (divorced 1984), one s. one d.; one d. with Kelly Emberg; m. 2nd Rachel Hunter 1990 (divorced), one d. one s.; m. 3rd Penny Lancaster 2007, two s.; singer with Steampacket, Shotgun Express, Jeff Beck Group 1968–69, Faces 1969–75; solo artist 1971–; Rolling Stone Magazine Rock Star of the Year 1971, British Rock and Pop Award for Lifetime Achievement 1992, BRIT Lifetime Achievement Award 1993. *Recordings include:* albums: two with Jeff Beck, four with Faces; solo: Every Picture Tells a Story 1971, Never a Dull Moment 1972, Atlantic Crossing 1975, A Night On The Town 1976, Foot Lose and Fancy Free 1977, Blondes Have More Fun 1978, Foolish Behaviour 1980, Tonight I'm Yours 1981, Camouflage 1984, Love Touch 1986, Out of Order 1988, The Best Of 1989, Downtown Train 1990, Vagabond Heart 1991, Lead Vocalist 1992, Unplugged… and Seated 1993, A Spanner In The Works 1995, When We Were the New Boys 1998, Human 2000, It Had To Be You… The Great American Songbook 2002, The Story So Far: The Best of Rod Stewart 2003, Thanks for the Memory 2005, Still the Same 2006, Some Guys Have All the Luck 2008, Songbook 2009, Merry Christmas, Baby 2012, Time 2013, Another Country 2015, Blood Red Roses 2018. *Publication:* Rod: The Autobiography 2012. *Website:* www.rodstewart.com.

STEWART, Roderick (Rory) James Nugent, OBE, FRSL, FRSGS, BA, MA; British diplomatist, writer and politician; *Secretary of State for International Development;* b. 3 Jan. 1972, Hong Kong; s. of Brian Stewart and Sally Stewart; m. Shoshana Clark; two c.; ed Eton Coll., Balliol Coll., Oxford; served in British Army; fmr Desk Officer (Japan and Korea), FCO, London; fmr Second Sec. (Political/Econ.), Embassy in Jakarta, Indonesia; fmr UK Rep. in Montenegro –2000; walked from Turkey to Bangladesh 2000–02, crossing Iran, Afghanistan, Pakistan, India and Nepal; Deputy Governorate Co-ordinator (Amara/Maysan) and Sr Adviser and Deputy Governorate Co-ordinator (Nasiriyah/Dhi Qar), for the Coalition Provisional Authority, Maysan Prov., Iraq 2003–04; Fellow, The Carr Center for Human Rights Policy, Harvard Univ., USA 2004–05, Ryan Family Prof. of Human Rights 2009–, Dir The Carr Center for Human Rights Policy 2009–; CEO Turquoise Mountain Foundation, Afghanistan 2006–08; MP (Conservative) for Penrith and The Border 2010–; mem. Foreign Affairs Cttee 2010–15, Chair. Defence Select Cttee 2014–15; Parl. Under-Sec., Dept for Environment, Food and Rural Affairs 2015–16, Minister of State for Int. Devt 2016–18, Minister of State for Africa 2017–18, Minister of State for Prisons Jan.–May 2019, Sec. of State for Int. Devt 2019–; Royal Scottish Geographical Soc. Livingstone Medal 2009, Royal Geographical Soc. Ness Award 2018. *Publications:* The Places in Between (Royal Soc. of Literature Ondaatje Prize 2005, Premio de Literatura de Viaje Caminos del Cid) 2004, The Prince of the Marshes and Other Occupational Hazards of a Year in Iraq 2006, Can Intervention Work? (with Gerald Knaus) 2011, The Marches: Border Walks with My Father (Hunter Davies Lakeland Book of the Year) 2016; contrib. to Granta, LRB, New York Times Magazine. *Address:* Department for International Development, 22 Whitehall, London, SW1A 2EG (office); House of Commons, Westminster, London, SW1A 0AA, England (office). *Telephone:* (20) 7023-0000 (DFID) (office); (20) 7219-7127 (office). *Fax:* (20) 7023-0012 (DFID) (office). *E-mail:* enquiry@dfid.gov.uk (office); rory.stewart.mp@parliament.uk (office); rory@rorystewart.co.uk (office). *Website:* www.gov.uk/government/organisations/department-for-international-development (office); www.parliament.uk/biographies/commons/rory-stewart/4137 (office); www.rorystewart.co.uk.

STEWART, S. Jay, BS, MBA; American business executive (retd); b. 18 Sept. 1938; s. of Virgil Harvey Stewart and Lena Rivers Repair; m. Judith Daniels 1961; one s. two d.; ed Univ. of West Virginia, Univ. of Cincinnati; Eng Marketing and Mfg, Monsanto Corpn 1961–73; Dir of Devt, Dir of Marketing, Gen. Man. Ventron Div., Thiokol Corpn 1973–79, Pres. Dynachem Div. 1979–82, Group Vice-Pres. for

Chemicals 1982; Pres. Thiokol Chemical Div., Morton Thiokol, Inc. 1982–83, Group Vice-Pres. Chemicals 1983–86, Pres., COO and Dir 1986–89; Pres., COO and Dir Morton Int. Inc. 1986–94, Chair. and CEO 1994–99 (Morton Int. acquired by Rohm and Haas Co. 1999); Chair. Autoliv, Inc. 2001–07; mem. Bd of Dirs KapStone Paper and Packaging Corpn 2010–14, HSBC North America Holdings Inc.; mem. Advisory Bd Nat. Foundation for History of Chem. 1991–; mem. ACS, AIChE, Commercial Devt Asscn; Distinguished Alumnus Award, Univ. of Cincinnati 1984.

STICH, Michael; German business executive and professional tennis player (retd); b. 18 Oct. 1968, Pinneberg; m. 1st Jessica Stockmann 1992 (divorced 2003); m. 2nd Alexandra Rikowski 2005; ed studied history of art; Nat. Jr Champion 1986; turned professional 1988; semi-finalist, French Open 1990; mem. W German Davis Cup Team 1990; won first professional title, Memphis 1990; winner, Men's Singles Championship, Wimbledon 1991; Men's Doubles (with John McEnroe q.v.) 1992; won ATP World Championship 1993; retd 1997; won 28 professional titles; apptd UN Amb. 1999; German Davis Cup team Capt. Oct. 2001–Sept. 2002; mem. Senior tour; CEO Hanseatik Rückenzentrum, Michael Stich Foundation; Tournament Dir, German Tennis Open, Hamburg and NORD/LB Braunschweig; commentator, BBC and Eurosport. *Television:* game show (PRO 7) 2000. *Leisure interests:* golf, horses, sports, painting. *Address:* Magdalenstr. 42–43B, 20148 Hamburg, Germany.

STICH, Stephen Peter, PhD; American professor of philosophy and cognitive science; *Board of Governors Distinguished Professor, Rutgers University;* b. 9 May 1943, New York, NY; s. of Samuel J. Stich and Sylvia L. Stich; m. Judith Ann Gagnon 1971; one s. one d.; ed Univ. of Pennsylvania, Princeton Univ.; mem. staff, Univs of Michigan 1968–78, Maryland 1978–86, California, San Diego 1986–89; apptd Prof. of Philosophy and Cognitive Science, Rutgers Univ. 1989–98, Bd of Govs Distinguished Prof. 1998–, Dir Research Group on Evolution and Higher Cognition; Adjunct Prof., CUNY Grad. Center 1994–97; Pres. Soc. for Philosophy and Psychology 1982–83; Fulbright Sr Research Scholar 1978–79; Fellow, Center for Advanced Study in the Behavioral Sciences 1983–84; Visiting Fellow, Research School of Social Sciences, ANU 1992; Erskine Fellow, Canterbury Univ., Christchurch, NZ 1996, 2018; Clark-Way-Harrison Distinguished Visiting Prof., Dept of Philosophy, Washington Univ. in St Louis 2007; Fellow, American Acad. of Arts and Sciences 2009; Hon. Prof. of Philosophy, Univ. of Sheffield 2005–; Jean Nicod Prize, Institut Jean Nicod, Paris 2007, Gittler Award for Outstanding Scholarly Contribution in the Philosophy of the Social Sciences, American Philosophical Asscn 2008, Lebowitz Prize for Philosophical Achievement and Contrib., Phi Beta Kappa Soc. in conjunction with American Philosophical Asscn. *Publications include:* From Folk Psychology to Cognitive Science 1983, The Fragmentation of Reason 1990, Philosophy and Connectionist Theory (co-author) 1991, Deconstructing The Mind 1996, Mindreading (co-author) 2003, Collected Papers, vol. 1, Mind and Language 2011, Collected Papers vol. 2, Knowledge, Rationality and Morality 2012. *Address:* Rutgers University, Department of Philosophy, 106 Somerset Street, 518, New Brunswick, NJ 08901 (office); 55 Liberty Street, Apt 8-A, New York, NY 10005, USA (home). *Telephone:* (732) 932-9861 (office). *Fax:* (732) 932-8617 (office). *E-mail:* stich@philosophy.rutgers.edu (office); stich.steve@gmail.com (home). *Website:* www.philosophy.rutgers.edu/people/faculty/635-stich-stephen (office).

STIELER, Frank, DrJur; German lawyer and business executive; *CEO, KraussMaffei Group GmbH;* b. 13 Dec. 1958, Frankfurt; m.; five c.; ed Johann Wolfgang Goethe Univ., Frankfurt; lawyer in Frankfurt 1984; held various positions with Lurgi AG, including Chief Financial Officer Lurgi Energie and Umwelt GmbH 1994–97 and CEO Lurgi Bamag GmbH 1997–99; Sr Vice-Pres., Azurix (subsidiary of Enron), Houston, USA 1999–2001; moved to Siemens 2001, responsible for Industrial Application div., Power Generation Group, CEO Siemens Oil & Gas Div. 2008–11; mem. Exec. Bd Hochtief AG 2009–12, Chair. and CEO 2011–12; CEO and mem. Exec. Bd KraussMaffei Group GmbH 2015–; mem. Bd of Dirs CIMIC Group Ltd 2011–12; mem. Advisory Bd NRW.BANK 2012. *Address:* KraussMaffei Group GmbH, Krauss-Maffei-Strasse 2, Munich 80997, Germany (office). *Telephone:* (89) 88990 (office). *Fax:* (89) 88992206 (office). *Website:* www.kraussmaffeigroup.com (office).

STIER, Davor Ivo; Croatian diplomatist and politician; b. 6 Jan. 1972, Buenos Aires, Argentina; m.; three c.; ed Pontifical Catholic Univ. of Argentina, Inst. of World Politics, Washington, DC, USA; fmr Corresp., Radio America and El Cronista (Argentine daily); joined Croatian Ministry of Foreign and European Affairs 1996, roles include positions with Dept of Protocol, Dept for N America, Dept of Int. Security, with Office of Chief Negotiator for EU accession negotiations 1996–2011, at Embassy in Washington, DC 1998–2002, Perm. Mission to NATO, Brussels 2003–08, Adviser on foreign policy to Prime Minister Ivo Sanader 2009; mem. Sabor (Parl.) 2011–13, 2016–, Vice-Pres. Parl. Cttee on Foreign Affairs, mem. Cttee for European Integration, mem. Del. to NATO Parl. Ass.; mem. European Parl. 2013–16, Full mem. Cttee on Foreign Affairs 2013–14, Substitute mem. Cttee on Civil Liberties, Justice and Domestic Policy 2013–14; Deputy Prime Minister and Minister of Foreign and European Affairs 2016–17 (resgnd); mem. European People's Party 2013–16, fmr Chair. and mem. Cen. Cttee; mem. Hrvatska Demokratska Zajednica (HDZ—Croatian Democratic Union) 1995–; Order of Duke Branimir. *Publication:* New Paradigm Croatia: view of social integration and development 2015. *Address:* Hrvatska Demokratska Zajednica, 10000 Zagreb, trg Žrtava fašizma 4, Croatia (office). *Telephone:* (1) 4553000 (office). *Fax:* (1) 4552600 (office). *E-mail:* hdz@hdz.hr (office). *Website:* www.hdz.hr (office).

STIGLITZ, Joseph Eugene, PhD, FBA; American economist and academic; *Professor of Finance and Economics, Graduate School of Business, Columbia University;* b. 9 Feb. 1943, Gary, Ind.; s. of Nathaniel D. Stiglitz and Charlotte Fishman; m. 1st 1978; two s. two d.; m. 2nd Anya Schiffrin 2004; ed Amherst Coll., Mass. Inst. of Tech. and Univ. of Cambridge (Fulbright Scholar); Prof. of Econs, Cowles Foundation, Yale Univ. 1970–74; Visiting Fellow, St Catherine's Coll. Oxford 1973–74; Prof. of Econs, Stanford Univ. 1974–76, Sr Fellow, Hoover Inst. 1988–2001, Joan Kenney Prof. of Econs 1992–2001; Drummond Prof. of Political Econ., Univ. of Oxford 1976–79; Oskar Morgenstern Distinguished Fellow, Inst. of Advanced Studies, Princeton 1978–79; Prof. of Econs, Princeton Univ. 1979–88; Stern Visiting Prof., Columbia Univ. 2000, Prof. of Finance and Econs, Grad. School of Business 2000, Co-Founder and Pres. Initiative for Policy Dialogue 2000–, Univ. Prof. 2000–, Chair. Cttee on Global Thought 2006–; mem. Pres.'s Council of Econ. Advisers 1993–95, Chair. (mem. of cabinet) 1995–97; Special Adviser to Pres. of World Bank, Sr Vice-Pres. and Chief Economist 1997–2000; Chair. Man. Bd and Dir Grad. Summer Programs, Brooks World Poverty Inst., Univ. of Manchester 2006–; Special Adviser, Bell Communications Research, numerous consultancies in public and pvt. sector; Sr Fellow, Brookings Inst. 2000; Fellow, American Acad. of Arts and Sciences, NAS, Econometric Soc., American Philosophical Soc., Inst. for Policy Research (Sr Fellow 1991–93); Hon. DHL (Amherst Coll.) 1974; Dr hc (Univ. of Leuven, Ben Gurion Univ.), (Oxford) 2004; Guggenheim Fellow 1969–70, John Bates Clark Award, American Econ. Asscn 1979, Int. Prize, Accad. dei Lincei, Rome 1988, UAP Scientific Prize, Paris 1989, Nobel Prize in Econs (jt recipient) 2001. *Film appearance:* Four Horseman (documentary) 2012. *Publications include:* Principles of Economics 1997, Globalization and its Discontents, Economics of the Public Sector 2000, Rethinking the East Asia Miracle (co-ed.) 2001, The Roaring Nineties 2003, Fair Trade for All (co-author), 2005, Making Globalization Work 2006, The Three Trillion Dollar War: The True Cost of the Iraq Conflict (co-author) 2008, Freefall: America, Free Markets and the Sinking of the World Economy 2010, The Price of Inequality: The Avoidable Causes and Invisible Costs of Inequality 2012, Creating a learning society: a new approach to growth, development, and social progress (co–author) 2014; other books and more than 300 papers in learned journals. *Address:* Uris Hall, Room 814, Columbia University, 3022 Broadway, New York, NY 10027, USA (office). *Telephone:* (212) 854-1481 (office). *Fax:* (212) 662-8474 (office). *E-mail:* jes322@columbia.edu (office). *Website:* www.josephstiglitz.com.

STIHL, Hans Peter; German business executive; *Honorary Chairman, Stihl Holding AG & Co;* b. 18 April 1932, Stuttgart; s. of Andreas Stihl and Maria Giersch; m.; ed Technische Hochschule, Stuttgart; joined Managing Board of father's company Stihl 1960, mem. Management Board 1966 with responsibility for the Development, Production and Purchasing departments, following his father's death in 1973, he assumed the management as Chair. 1973–2002, Chair. Advisory Bd Stihl Holding AF & Co. KG and Chair. Supervisory Bd Stihl AG 2002–12, now Hon. Chair.; Pres. Deutsche Industrie und Handelstag, Bonn 1988–2000, Hon. Pres. 2001–; Vice-Pres. Inst. of German Economy, Cologne 1983–88, Treas. 1983–88; Pres. IHK Stuttgart 1990–2001, Hon. Pres. 2001–; Hon. Consul-Gen. of Singapore, Stuttgart 2006–; mem. Man. Bd Verein Deutscher Maschinen- und Anlagenbau (VDMA) –1988; Hon. Consul-Gen. of Singapore 2002–; Grand Cross with Star for Distinguished Service of the Order of Merit of FRG 2002; Hanns Martin Schleyer Award 2003, Lifetime Achievement Award, Service Dealer Heritage Awards. *Address:* Stihl Holding AG & Co., Badstr. 115, 71336 Dieburg; Consulate-General of Singapore, Badstrasse 98, 71336 Waiblingen, Germany. *E-mail:* hans.peter.stihl@stihl.de.

STILLER, Ben; American actor and film director; b. 30 Nov. 1965, New York; s. of Jerry Stiller and Ann Meara; m. Christine Taylor; two c.; ed Univ. of California, Los Angeles. *Films include:* Empire of the Sun 1988, Reality Bites (also dir) 1994, Happy Gilmore 1996, Flirting with Disaster 1996, The Cable Guy (also Dir) 1996, Zero Effect 1998, Your Friends and Neighbors 1998, There's Something About Mary 1998, Permanent Midnight 1998, Mystery Men 1999, Black and White 1999, Meet the Parents 2000, Keeping the Faith 2000, Zoolander (also dir) 2001, The Royal Tenenbaums 2001, Duplex 2003, Nobody Knows Anything 2003, Along Came Polly 2004, Starsky & Hutch 2004, Envy 2004, Dodgeball 2004, Anchorman 2004, Meet the Fockers 2004, Madagascar (voice) 2005, Danny Roane: First Time Director 2006, School for Scoundrels 2006, Tenacious D: The Pick of Destiny 2006, Night at the Museum 2006, The Heartbreak Kid 2007, Tropic Thunder (also dir) 2008, Madagascar: Escape 2 Africa (voice) 2008, Night at the Museum: Battle of the Smithsonian 2009, The Marc Pease Experience 2009, Greenberg 2010, Little Fockers 2010, Tower Heist 2011, Madagascar 3: Europe's Most Wanted (voice) 2012, The Watch 2012, The Secret Life of Walter Mitty 2013, While We're Young 2014, Night at the Museum: Secret of the Tomb 2014, Zoolander 2 2016. *Television includes:* The Ben Stiller Show (Emmy Award) 1990–93, Heat Vision and Jack 1999, Freaks and Geeks 2000, Arrested Development 2005–13, Phineas and Ferb 2010, Burning Love (series) 2012–13. *Address:* William Morris Endeavor Entertainment, 9601 Wilshire Blvd, Beverly Hills, CA 90210, USA (office).

STINCO, Antoine; French architect; b. 9 Jan. 1934, Tunis, Tunisia; ed Ecole Nationale Supérieure des Beaux-Arts, Paris (studio of Edouard Albert-Paul Herbe, Jean Prouvé); worked on light and mobile architecture and particularly on inflated structures; exhibited inflated structure in ARC (Museum of Modern Arts of Paris) 1968; participated with GAU (Urban Architecture Group) in renewal of urban architecture in France 1974; est. own architectural firm 1984; fashion design artist with Christiane Bailly Assocs 1970–90; taught in Sculpture Dept at Beaux-Art, Paris 1993–99. *Major works include:* Jeu de paume, Nat. Gallery, Jardin de Tuileries, Paris 1991, Musée du Louvre, Paris, six kiosks in Jardin de Tuileries 1995–97, Ecole du Louvre and Aile de Flore, Louvre Museum 1997–98, Musée d'art moderne et contemporain Les Abattoirs, Toulouse (with R. Papillault) 2000, Musée des Beaux Arts, Angers 2003, MC2 Arts Centre extension, Maison de la Culture, Grenoble 2004, Le Théâtre nat. de Bretagne 2008. *Publications:* Le Territoire de L'Architecture – Suivi de Vingt-Quatre Projets et Realisations (with Vittorio Gregotti) 1982, Les Abattoirs, Histoires et Transformation 2000. *Address:* SA Antoine Stinco, 73 boulevard de Sebastopol, 75002 Paris, France (office). *Telephone:* 1-45-08-18-66 (office). *E-mail:* stinco.antoine@neuf.fr. *Website:* www.stinco.fr (office).

STING, CBE; British singer, musician (bass guitar), songwriter and actor; b. (Gordon Matthew Thomas Sumner), 2 Oct. 1951, Wallsend, Newcastle upon Tyne; s. of Ernest Sumner and Audrey Sumner (née Cowell); m. 1st Frances Tomelty 1976 (divorced 1984); one s. one d.; m. 2nd Trudie Styler 1992; two s. two d.; ed St Cuthbert's High School, Newcastle upon Tyne, Univ. of Warwick, Coventry, Northern Counties Coll. of Educ.; worked as bus conductor, construction labourer and tax officer –1971; primary school teacher, St Paul's First School, Cramlington, Newcastle 1975–77; played with local jazz bands, including Phoenix Jazzmen, the Newcastle Big Band, and Last Exit; mem., with Stewart Copeland and Henry Padovani (replaced by Andy Summers), and lead singer of rock group, The Police 1977–84, re-formed to tour 2007–08; solo artist 1985–; numerous tours, TV and radio broadcasts in Europe and USA; Chevalier, Ordre des Arts et Lettres 2007; Hon. DMus (Northumbria) 1992; numerous awards, including Ivor Novello

Awards for Best Song (for They Dance Alone) 1989, four BMI songwriting awards 1998, BMI Award for Int. Achievement 2002, BRIT Award for Best Male Artist 1994, for Outstanding Contribution to Music 2002, Emmy Award for Best Performance (Sting in Tuscany... All This Time) 2002, 14 Grammy Awards (with The Police and solo), Grammy Award for Best Pop Collaboration with Vocals (for Whenever I Say Your Name, with Mary J. Blige) 2004, MusiCares Foundation Person of the Year 2003, Billboard Music Century Award for Creative Achievement 2003, Kennedy Center Honor 2014. *Stage appearance:* The Threepenny Opera (Broadway) 1989, Twin Spirits 2009. *Play:* The Last Ship, writer and producer 2013, actor 2014. *Film appearances include:* Quadrophenia 1979, Radio On 1980, Artemis 81 (BBC TV) 1981, Brimstone and Treacle 1982, Dune 1984, The Bride 1985, Plenty 1985, Bring on the Night 1985, Giulia and Giulia 1987, The Adventures of Baron Munchausen 1988, Stormy Monday 1988, The Grotesque 1995, Lock, Stock and Two Smoking Barrels 1998, The Tulse Luper Suitcases: The Moab Story 2003, Bee Movie 2007. *Recordings include:* albums: with the Police: Outlandos D'Amour 1977, Regatta De Blanc 1979, Zenyatta Mondatta 1980, Ghost In The Machine 1981, Synchronicity 1983, Every Breath You Take: The Classics 1995, Sting & The Police—The Very Best Of 1997, 2002, The Police 2007; solo: The Dream of The Blue Turtles 1985, Bring On The Night 1986, Nothing Like The Sun 1987, The Soul Cages 1991, Ten Summoner's Tales 1994, Mercury Falling 1996, Brand New Day 1999, All This Time 2001, Sacred Love 2003, Songs of Love 2003, My Funny Valentine 2005, Songs From The Labyrinth 2007, Songs for Tibet - The Art of Peace 2008, If On a Winter's Night 2009, Symphonicities 2010, The Last Ship 2013, 57th & 9th 2016, Sting - The Studio Collection 2016, 44/876 (with Shaggy) 2018. *Publications:* Jungle Stories: The Fight for the Amazon 1989, Escape Artist (memoir) 2003. *Address:* Kathryn Schenker Associates, 1776 Broadway, 12th Floor, New York, NY 10019, USA (office); c/o Publicity Department, Polydor Records, 72 Black Lane, London, W6, England (office). *Website:* www.sting.com.

STINGEL, Rudolf; Italian artist; b. 1956 , Merano. *Address:* c/o Gagosian Gallery, 821, Park Avenue, New York, NY 10021, USA. *Telephone:* (212) 796-1228. *E-mail:* parkand75@gagosian.com. *Website:* www.gagosian.com.

STINSON, William W.; Canadian insurance industry executive; *Chairman, Westshore Terminals Investment Corporation;* CEO Canadian Pacific Ltd 1985–96; apptd mem. Bd of Dirs Sun Life Financial Inc. 1985, Lead Dir 1999–2003, Chair. (non-exec.) Sun Life Financial Inc. and Sun Life Assurance Co. 2003–05 (retd); Chair. Westshore Terminals Investment Corpn 2011–; mem. Bd of Dirs Grant Forest Products Inc. 2003–, Canfor Corpn; fmr mem. Bd of Dirs CHC Helecopter Corpn; Trustee Fording Canadian Coal Trust. *Address:* Westshore Terminals Investment Corporation, 1067 Cordova Street West, Vancouver, BC V6C 1C7, Canada (office). *Telephone:* (604) 946-4491 (office). *Website:* www.westshore.com (office).

STIPE, (John) Michael; American musician and songwriter; b. 1 April 1960, Decatur, Ga; ed Univ. of Georgia; Founder mem. and lead singer, R.E.M. 1980–2011; Owner, C-00 (film co.) and Single Cell Pictures 1987–; Owner, Grit vegetarian restaurant, Athens, Ga; numerous MTV Music Video Awards, Earth Day Award 1990, Billboard Award for Best Modern Rock Artist 1991, BRIT Awards for Best Int. Group 1992, 1993, 1995, Grammy Awards for Best Pop Performance, Best Music Video 1992, Atlanta Music Awards for Act of the Year, Video of the Year 1992, IRMA Award for Int. Band of the Year 1993, Rolling Stone Critics Award for Best Band 1993. *Films:* as composer: The Cold Lands 2014. *Recordings include:* albums: Chronic Town 1982, Murmur 1983, Reckoning 1984, Fables Of The Reconstruction 1985, Life's Rich Pageant 1986, Dead Letter Office 1987, Document 1987, Eponymous 1988, Green 1988, Out Of Time (Billboard Award for Best World Album, Q Award for Best Album) 1991, Automatic For The People (Grammy Award for Best Alternative Music Album, Atlanta Music Award for Rock Album, Q Award for Best Album, Rolling Stone Critics Award for Best Album 1993) 1992, Monster 1994, New Adventures In Hi-Fi 1996, Up 1998, Star Profiles 1999, Reveal 2001, Bad Day Pt 1 and 2 2003, Glastonbury 1999 2003, Around The Sun 2004, Accelerate 2008, Collapse into Now 2011. *E-mail:* admin@michaelstipe.com. *Website:* www.michaelstipe.com; www.remhq.com.

STIPRAIS, Eduards; Latvian diplomatist, government official and economist; *Head of EU Delegation, Uzbekistan;* b. 19 Feb. 1969, Rīga; m. Zanda Grauze; one d.; ed Univ. of Latvia; mil. service 1988–89; trainee, Ministry of Social Maintenance May–July 1991, Dept of Foreign Econ. Relations, Council of Ministers 1991–92; Desk Officer, Ministry of Foreign Trade 1992–93; EC Desk Officer, Ministry of Foreign Affairs 1993, Head EC/EFTA Relations Div. 1993–94, Deputy Dir Dept of Int. Econ. Relations 1994–95, Sec. Latvian del. for the negotiations on the Agreement on Free Trade and Trade Related Matters with the EU 1993–94, for the negotiations on the Europe Agreement 1994–95, Advisor on Secondment to OECD/EU SIGMA Programme, Paris 1995, Second Sec., Latvian Mission to the EU, Brussels March–Oct. 1995, First Sec. 1995–98, Head, task force for preparation of EU accession negotiations 1998–99, Deputy Chief Negotiator EU accession negotiations 1999–2003, Deputy Head 2003–04, Deputy Perm. Rep. 2004, Perm. Rep. 2004–07; Head of Chancery of Pres. of Latvia 2007–08; Amb. and Dir Gen. for Bilateral Relations, Ministry of Foreign Affairs 2009; Amb. to UK 2009–13; Under-Sec. of State and Political Dir, Ministry of Foreign Affairs 2013–16; Head of EU Del. to Uzbekistan 2016–; mem. Latvian European Movt; Officer, Order of Three Stars (Fourth Class) 2004; Kt, Order of Merits (Second Class) (Ukraine) 2009; Grand Officer, Royal Norwegian Order of Merit (Second Class) 2015; Officier, Ordre nat. du Mérite 2015; State Sec.'s Award, Ministry of Foreign Affairs 2000, Silver Award of Honour, Ministry of Interior 2003, Certificate of Recognition, Cabinet of Ministers 2003, 2015. *Address:* Delegation of the EU to Uzbekistan, International Business Centre, 107 B, Amir Temur Street, 15th Floor, 100 084 Tashkent, Uzbekistan (office). *Telephone:* (71) 120-16-01 (office). *E-mail:* delegation-uzbekistan@eeas.europa.eu (office). *Website:* www.eeas.europa.eu (office).

STIRLING, Sir Angus Duncan Aeneas, Kt; British arts administrator; b. 10 Dec. 1933, London; s. of Duncan Alexander Stirling and Lady Marjorie Stirling; m. Armyne Morar Helen Schofield 1959; one s. two d.; ed Eton Coll., Trinity Coll., Cambridge, Univ. of London; mem. staff, Christie, Manson & Woods Ltd 1954–57, Lazard Bros. and Co. Ltd 1957–66; Asst Dir Paul Mellon Foundation for British Art 1966–69, Jt Dir 1969–70; Deputy Sec.-Gen. Arts Council of GB 1971–79; Deputy Dir-Gen. The Nat. Trust 1979–83, Dir-Gen. 1983–95; Sr Policy Adviser Nat. Heritage Memorial Fund 1996–97; Dir Royal Opera House, Covent Garden 1979–96, Chair. 1991–96, Chair. Friends of Covent Garden 1981–91, mem. of Bd of Dirs Royal Ballet Bd 1979–96, Gov. 1988–96, Deputy Chair. 1989–91; Chair. Greenwich Foundation for Royal Naval Coll. 1996–2003, Policy Cttee, Council for Protection of Rural England 1996–2001, Jt Nature Conservation Cttee 1997–2002; mem. Crafts Council 1980–85, Council of Man. Byam Shaw School of Art 1965–89, Advisory Council London Symphony Orchestra 1979–, Bd of Govs Live Music Now 1982–89, Govt Task Force on Tourism and the Environment 1991, Court of the Fishmongers' Co. 1991– (Prime Warden 2004–05), ICOMOS UK Tourism Cttee 1993–2003 (Chair. IUCN/ICOMOS UK Liaison Cttee 2003–07), Council Royal School of Church Music 1996–98, Bd of Govs Gresham School 1999–2007, Fabric Advisory Cttee, Wells Cathedral 2001–, Council, Kensington Soc. 2002–, City & Guilds of London Art School 2003–10; mem. Bd of Dirs Courtauld Inst. of Art 1981–83, 2002–14, currently Trustee; Trustee, Theatres Trust 1983–91, Heritage of London Trust 1983–95, Samuel Courtauld Trust 1984–, World Monuments Fund UK 1996–2008, Stowe House Preservation Trust 1998–2012; Vice-Patron Almshouses Asscn 1998–2009; Pres. Friends of Holland Park 2003–, Kensington and Chelsea Nat. Asscn of Decorative and Fine Arts Socs 2008–15; Hon. Fellow, Trinity Coll. of Music 2004, Courtauld Inst. of Art 2015; Hon. DLitt (Univ. of Leicester) 1995, (Univ. of Greenwich) 2002. *Leisure interests:* music, travel, walking, painting. *Address:* 30 Upper Addison Gardens, London, W14 8AJ, England (home). *E-mail:* angusstirling@me.com. *Website:* www.angusstirling.co.uk.

STIRN, Olivier, LenD; French politician; b. 24 Feb. 1936, Boulogne-Billancourt; s. of Alexandre Stirn and Geneviève Dreyfus; m. Evelyn Toledano 1989; one s. one d. (and two s. from previous m.); ed Univ. of Paris, Institut de Sciences Politiques; Chief of Cabinet for Prefect of La Meuse 1961–64, Chargé de mission 1964; Chief of Cabinet for Minister of State in charge of Overseas Depts and Territories 1964, for Sec. of State for Foreign Affairs 1966–67, for Sec. of State for Social Affairs 1967–68; Deputy for Calvados 1968–73, 1981–86 (Gen. Councillor 1970–88, 1994–2001), for Manche 1986–88; Councillor Gen., Mayor of Vire 1971; Pres., Urban Community of Cherbourg 1989–90; Sec. of State for Parl. Relations 1973–74, for Overseas Territories 1974–78, for Foreign Affairs 1978–81, for Defence 1980–81; Minister Del. for Overseas Territories May–June 1988, Minister Del. attached to Minister of Industry and Territorial Devt 1988–89, to Minister of Industry, Territorial Devt and Tourism (with special responsibility for Tourism) 1989–90; apptd Chair. Dialogue 2000 1988; Amb. to Council of Europe, Strasbourg 1991–93; Consultant to Rothschild & Cie 1998–2001; Editorial Dir Editions du Félin 2005; apptd Exec. Adviser, Union pour un Mouvement Populaire (UMP) 2004, nat. dir for diversity 2010; Adviser to the Pres. for Union pour la Méditerranée 2009–10; Founder, Mouvement des sociaux-libéraux 1977; Vice-Pres., Parti radical socialiste 1977; Co-founder, Carrefour social-démocrate 1977; Founder and Pres., Union centriste et républicaine 1984; Nat. Del., Parti socialiste 1986; Hon. Pres. Union pour la diversité républicaine; Chevalier, Légion d'honneur 1993, and numerous other decorations. *Publications include:* Le piège (with Bernard Stasi and J. P. Soisson) 1973, Une certaine idée du centre 1985, Tourisme: chance pour l'économie, risque pour les sociétés?, Mes Présidents: 50 ans au service de la 5e Republique 2004. *Leisure interests:* tennis, golf, history. *Address:* 14 Avenue Pierre 1er de Serbie, 75116 Paris, France (home). *Telephone:* 1-47-20-41-57 (home). *Fax:* 1-47-20-41-93 (home). *E-mail:* evestirn.sic@free.fr.

STIRRUP, Baron (Life Peer), cr. 2011, of Marylebone in the City of Westminster; **Graham Eric (Jock) Stirrup,** Kt, KG, GCB, AFC, ADC, DSc, FRAeS, FCMI, RAF; British air force officer; b. 4 Dec. 1949; s. of William Hamilton Stirrup and Jacqueline Brenda Stirrup (née Coulson); m. Mary Alexandra Elliot 1976; one s.; ed Merchant Taylors' School, Northwood, RAF Coll., Cranwell, Jt Service Defence Coll., Royal Coll. of Defence Studies; qualified flying instructor 1971–73; loan service, Sultan of Oman's Air Force 1973–75; fighter reconnaissance pilot 1976–78; exchange pilot, USAF 1978–81; Flight Commdr 1982–84; Officer Commdr No. II (Army Co-operation) Squadron 1985–87; Dir Air Force Plans and Programmes, Ministry of Defence 1994–97; Air Officer Commdr No. 1 Group 1997–98; Asst Chief of Air Staff 1998–2000; Deputy C-in-C, Stike Commdr, Commdr NATO Combined Air Operations Centre 9 and Dir European Air Group 2000–02; Deputy Chief of Defence Staff (Equipment Capability) 2002–03; Chief of Air Staff 2003–06, Chief of Defence Staff 2006–10 (retd); rank of Marshal of the RAF; mem. (Crossbench), House of Lords 2011–; mem. Soc. of Kts of the Round Table; Hon. Col, 73 Engineer Regt (Volunteers) 2002–08; Air ADC to HM The Queen; Omani As Samood Medal (Endurance Medal); Omani Gen. Service Medal (Sultan Qaboos); Queen Elizabeth II Golden Jubilee Medal 2002; Hon. DSc (Cranfield Univ.). *Leisure interests:* golf, music, theatre, history. *Address:* House of Lords, Westminster, London, SW1A 0PW, England (office). *Telephone:* (20) 7219-5353 (office).

STITT, Kevin, BS; American business executive and politician; *Governor of Oklahoma;* b. 28 Dec. 1972, Milton, Fla; m. Sarah Hazen 1998; six c.; founder, Chair. and CEO Gateway Mortgage Group 2000–18; Gov. of Okla 2019–. *Address:* Office of the Governor, 212 State Capitol Building, 2300 N Lincoln Blvd, Room 212, Oklahoma City, OK 73105, USA (office). *E-mail:* governorstitt.info@gov.ok.gov (office). *Website:* www.ok.gov/governorstitt (office).

STITZER, H. Todd; American business executive; *Chairman, Signet Jewelers Ltd;* m. Marenda Stitzer; two c.; ed Harvard and Columbia Univs; Asst Gen. Counsel, Cadbury Schweppes Beverages N America 1983, Vice-Pres. and Gen. Counsel, Worldwide Beverages Stream 1988, Group Devt Dir responsible for Strategic Planning and External Devt, UK 1991–93, Vice-Pres. Marketing and Strategic Planning N America 1993–95, COO N America 1995–97; Pres. and CEO Dr Pepper/Seven Up 1997–2000; Chief Strategy Officer, Cadbury Schweppes (now Cadbury plc) 2000–02, Deputy CEO 2002–03, CEO 2003–10; Chair. Signet Jewelers Ltd 2012–; mem. Bd of Dirs Massachusetts Mutual Life Insurance Company, Diageo plc 2004–13; mem. Bd of Trustees Business in the Community 2008–. *Address:* Signet Jewelers Ltd, Clarendon House, 2 Church Street, Hamilton HM11, Bermuda (office). *Website:* www.signetjewelers.com (office).

STOCK, Carlos Olímpio; São Tomé and Príncipe lawyer and politician; fmr Dir Studies and Documentation Office, Ministry of Justice; Minister of Defence and Public Security 2010–12, 2014–17; mem. Acção Democrática Independente (ADI), lawyer for the party 2012–.

STOCKING, Dame Barbara, DBE; British charity administrator; b. 28 July 1951, Rugby, Warwicks.; m. John MacInnes; two s.; fmr regional dir in the Nat. Health Service (NHS); Chief Exec. Oxfam GB (first woman) 2001–13; Vice-Chair. Steering Cttee for Humanitarian Response (alliance made up of CEOs of nine humanitarian networks or agencies (Care International, Caritas Internationalis, International Cttee of the Red Cross, Int. Fed. of Red Cross and Red Crescent Socs, Int. Save the Children Alliance, Lutheran World Fed., Oxfam, WCC and World Vision International).

STOCKTON, 2nd Earl of; **Alexander Daniel Alan Macmillan,** FBIM, FRSA; British publisher, farmer and politician; *District Councillor, South Bucks District Council;* b. 10 Oct. 1943, Oswestry; s. of Maurice Victor Macmillan (Viscount Macmillan of Ovenden) and Dame Katherine Macmillan (Viscountess Macmillan of Ovenden), DBE; grandson of the late 1st Earl of Stockton (fmrly, as Harold Macmillan, Prime Minister of UK 1957–63); m. 1st Hélène Birgitte Hamilton 1970 (divorced 1991); one s. two d.; m. 2nd Miranda Elizabeth Louise Nultall 1995 (divorced 2010); ed Eton Coll. and Paris and Strathclyde Univs; Sub-Ed., Glasgow Herald 1963–65; Reporter, Daily Telegraph 1965–67, Foreign Corresp. 1967–68, Chief European Corresp., Sunday Telegraph 1968–70; Dir, Birch Grove Estates Ltd 1969–86, Chair. 1983–89; Dir, Macmillan and Co. Ltd 1970–76, Deputy Chair. 1976–80, Chair. 1984–90, Pres. 1990–; Chair., Macmillan Publrs Ltd 1980–90 (Pres. 1990–), St Martin's Press, New York 1983–88 (Dir 1974–90), Sidgwick and Jackson 1989–90; mem. MEP (Conservative) for SW of England 1999–2004, Vice Pres. (Defence), European Parl. Foreign Affairs Cttee 2000–04, mem. Convention on the Future of Europe (Rep. of European Peoples' Party) 2003–04; District Councillor, South Bucks. District Council 2011–; Chair., Cen. London Training & Enterprise Council 1990–95; Pres., Ludwig von Mises Institut UZW 2005–; Dir, Book Trade Benevolent Soc. 1976–88, Chair., Bookrest Appeal 1978–86; Dir, United British Artists Ltd 1984–90 (Chair. 1985–90); mem. Lindemann Fellowship Cttee 1979– (Chair. 1983–), British Inst. of Man. 1981–, Council of Publrs Asscn 1985–88, Carlton Club Political Cttee 1975–88 (Chair. 1984); Gov., Archbishop Tenison's School 1979–86, Merchant Taylor's School 1980–82, 1990–, English Speaking Union 1980–84, 1986–93; Liveryman, Worshipful Co. of Merchant Taylors 1972, Court Asst 1987, Master 1991–92; Liveryman, Worshipful Co. of Stationers 1973, Court Asst 1989; Hon. DLitt (De Montfort) 1993, (Westminster) 1995; Hon. DUniv (Strathclyde) 1993; Schumann Medal 2004. *Leisure interests:* fishing, aviation. *Address:* The Priory, Denham Village, Bucks., UB9 5AS, England (home). *Telephone:* (1895) 834181 (home). *E-mail:* thepriory@dbac.co.uk (home).

STODDART, Brian, BA, MA, PhD; New Zealand university administrator; ed Univ. of Canterbury, Univ. of Western Australia; fmr Pro Vice-Chancellor (Asia), RMIT Univ., Dir of Int. Programmes, RMIT Univ., Pro Vice-Chancellor (Research and Int.), Univ. of New England, Pro Vice-Chancellor (Int.), Victoria Univ., Acting Deputy Vice-Chancellor, Victoria Univ.; joined La Trobe Univ. as Deputy Vice-Chancellor (Research) 2004, Vice-Chancellor and Pres. 2005–06 (resgnd), now Prof. Emer.; currently Distinguished Fellow, Australia India Inst., Univ. of Melbourne; mem. Australian Vice-Chancellors' Cttee (AVCC); fmr mem. numerous editorial bds including Journal of Sport and Social Issues, Australian Soc. for Sports History; Australia-New Zealand Foundation Award. *Publications include:* Cricket and Empire: the 1932–33 Bodyline Tour of Australia (co-author) 1984, Saturday Afternoon Fever: Sport in the Australian Culture 1986, Liberation Cricket: Caribbean Cricket Culture 1995, The A–Z of Australian Cricketers 1997, The Imperial Game: Cricket, Culture and Society 1998, Soundings in Modern Sports Culture 2006, Sport, Culture and History: Region, Nation and Globe 2008, Land, Water, Language and Politics in Andhra: Regional Evolution in India Since 1850 2011; contribs to Sport Report, Pro News, World of Cricket, Action, The Australian, Sunday Herald, The Age, numerous articles in refereed journals and collections. *E-mail:* b.stoddart@bigpond.com. *Website:* professorbrianstoddart .com.

STODDART, Sir James Fraser, Kt, PhD, DSc, FRS; British chemist and academic; *Board of Trustees Professor of Chemistry, Northwestern University;* b. 24 May 1942, Edinburgh, Scotland; s. of Thomas Fraser Stoddart and Jane Spalding Hislop Fortune; two c.; ed Univ. of Edinburgh; NRC Postdoctoral Fellow, Queens' Univ., Kingston, Ont., Canada 1967–70; ICI Research Fellow, Univ. of Sheffield 1970, Lecturer in Chem. 1970–78, Reader 1981–90; Researcher, ICI Corp. Lab., Runcorn 1978–81; Prof. of Organic Chem., Univ. of Birmingham 1990–97, Head of School of Chem. 1993–97; Winstein Chair, Dept of Chem. and Biochemistry, UCLA 1997–2003, Dir California NanoSystems Inst. 2002–07, Fred Kavli Chair in NanoSystems Sciences, UCLA 2003–08; Bd of Trustees Prof. of Chem., Northwestern Univ. 2008–; visiting prof. at numerous int. univs, including as Carnegie Centenary Visiting Prof., Scottish Univs 2005, World Class Univ. Faculty, Korea Inst. of Science and Tech. 2011, 2012; mem. Editorial Bd Crystal Growth and Design, Journal of Organic Chemistry, Organic Letters, Angewandte Chemie, Chemistry-A European Journal, Synthesis, Bioorganic Chemistry Reviews; Pres. Chemical Section, BAAS 1996; mem. American Acad. of Arts and Sciences 2012, NAS 2014; Fellow, German Acad. of Natural Sciences Leopoldina 1999, AAAS 2005; Hon. Prof., East China Univ. 2005, Jilin Univ. 2012, Univ. of Nottingham 2015; Hon. FRSE 2008; Hon. FRSC 2011; hon. lecturer at numerous int. univs; Hon. DSc (Birmingham) 2005, (Twente) 2006, (Sheffield) 2008, (Trinity Coll. Dublin) 2009, (St Andrews) 2010; numerous awards, including Univ. of Edinburgh Hope Prize in Chem. 1964, Humboldt Fellowship 1998, Izatt-Christensen Award 1993, ACS Cope Scholar Award 1999, UCLA Herbert Newby McCoy Award 2000, Nagoya Gold Medal 2004, Nagoya Gold Medal in Organic Chemistry 2005, Univ. of Edinburgh Alumnus of the Year 2005, AAAS Fellowship 2005, King Faisal Int. Prize in Science 2007, Albert Einstein World Award in Science 2007, Tetrahedron Prize for Creativity 2007, Feynman Prize in Nanotechnology 2007, ACS Arthur C. Cope Award 2008, Davy Medal, Royal Soc. 2008, Royal Medal, Royal Soc. of Edinburgh 2010, Int. Soc. for Nanoscale Science, Computation, and Eng Award, Foundations of Nanoscience (FNANO) 2010, Undergraduate Chem. Council Teacher of the Year, Northwestern Univ. 2011, Distinguished Citizen Award, Illinois St Andrews Soc. 2012, RSC Centenary Prize 2014, Nobel Prize in Chem. (co-recipient with Jean-Pierre Sauvage and Bernard Feringa) 2016. *Publications include:* more than 1,100 publs in scientific journals. *Address:* Department of Chemistry, Northwestern University, 2145 Sheridan Road, Evanston, IL 60208-3113, USA (office). *Telephone:* (847) 491-3793 (office). *Fax:* (847) 491-1009 (office). *E-mail:* stoddart@northwestern.edu (office). *Website:* stoddart.northwestern.edu (office).

STOIBER, Edmund Rüdiger, DJur; German lawyer and politician; b. 1941, Oberaudorf; m. Karin Stoiber; one s. two d.; ed Ignaz-Günther-Gymnasium, Rosenheim, Univs of Munich and Regensburg, Hochschule für Politische Wissenschaft; personal counsellor to Bavarian State Minister for Devt 1972–74, Dir of Ministerial Office 1974; entered Bavarian Parl. 1974; admitted solicitor 1978; Gen. Sec. Christian Social Union (CSU) 1978–83, Chair. CSU 1999–2007, Hon. Chair. 2007–; Campaign Man. for Franz Josef Strauss, Fed. Elections 1980; State Sec. and Dir Bavarian State Chancellery 1982–86, State Minister and Dir 1986–88; Bavarian State Minister for Internal Affairs 1988–93, Minister-Pres. of Bavaria 1993–2007; Chair, EU High Level Group of Independent Stakeholders on Admin. Burdens 2007–12; cand. in Chancellery elections 2002; Co-Chair. Advisory Bd Bayern Munich (football team); Bayerischer Verdienstorden 1984; Karl-Valentin-Orden 1996; Grand Order of King Dmitar Zvonimir 1996; Grand Cross, Order of the Star of Romania 1999; Grosses Bundesverdienstkreuz mit Stern und Schulterband 1999; Commdr, Légion d'honneur 2002; Officier, Ordre nat. du Québec 2003; Grosskreuz des Verdienstordens der Bundesrepublik Deutschland 2004; Grand Decoration of Honour in Gold with Sash for Services to the Repub. of Austria 2005; Grand Cross, Order of Merit of the Italian Repub. 2006; Large Gold Medal of the Prov. of Upper Austria 2007; Verdienstorden des Landes Baden-Württemberg 2009; hon. degree from Sogang Univ. 2007; Steiger Award 2008. *Publications:* Politik aus Bayern 1976, Der Hausfriedensbruch im Licht akt. Probleme 1984. *Leisure interests:* skiing, football. *Address:* Wagmüllerstraße 23, 80538 Munich, Germany. *E-mail:* info@stoiber.de. *Website:* www.stoiber.de.

STOKES, Kerry Matthew, AC, FAIM; Australian business executive; *Chairman, Seven Network Ltd;* b. 13 Sept. 1940, Vic.; s. of M. P. Stokes; m. 2nd Christine Simpson 2003; two s.; ed St George's CBC, Western Australia Tech. Coll.; Chair. Australian Capital Equity Pty Ltd (Dir 1981–), Austrim Ltd, Golden West Network (TV), Westrac Equipment Pty Ltd; Chair. Canberra Theatre Trust 1981–86, Dir 1989–91; Chair. Art Gallery Foundation, WA 1989–91; Chair. The Fed. Capital Press Pty Ltd (Canberra Times), Seven Network Ltd 1995–, Chair. Seven Network Ltd 1995–99, Exec. Chair. 1999–; Dir 1989–91; Pres. Appeal Campaign for Inst. for Child Health Research; Founder-mem. Council Nat. Gallery of Australia, Chair. 1996–2000; Hon. Life Mem. RSL Australia 1993–, Hon. Fellow, Murdoch Univ. 2000; WA Citizen of the Year Award 1994, Centenary Medal 2003, Western Australia's Australian of the Year 2012. *Publications:* Boyer Lectures (Advance Australia Where) 1994, Andrew Olle Memorial Lecture 2001. *Leisure interests:* photography, sailing, scuba diving. *Address:* Seven Network Ltd, Wharf 17, Pirrama Road, Pyrmont, NSW 2009 (office); c/o Australian Capital Equity Pty Ltd, Level 3, 30 Kings Park Road, West Perth, WA 6005, Australia. *Telephone:* (2) 87777102 (office). *Fax:* (2) 87777149 (office). *Website:* www.yahoo!7.com.au (office).

STOKES, Patrick T., BS, MBA; American business executive; b. 11 Aug. 1942, Washington, DC; m. Anna-Kristina Stokes; ed Boston Coll., Columbia Univ.; Financial Analyst, Shell Oil Co. 1966–67; began career in corp. planning, Anheuser-Busch 1969, held various positions including mem. Policy Cttee 1974, Vice-Pres. Raw Materials Acquisition 1976–81, Vice-Pres. and Group Exec. 1981–86, COO Campbell Taggert Inc. (subsidiary), Dallas 1986–90, CEO 1990–2002; Sr Exec. Vice-Pres. Anheuser-Busch Cos Inc. 2000–02, Pres. and CEO 2002–06, Chair. 2006–08, Pres. Anheuser-Busch Int. Inc. 1990–99; mem. Bd of Dirs U.S. BanCorp 1992–, Lead Ind. Dir 2011–; Trustee Boston Coll.

STOL, Marten; Dutch academic; *Professor Emeritus of Akkadian (Assyriology), Ugaritic and History of Ancient Near East, Free University of Amsterdam;* b. 10 Nov. 1940, Oldekerk; m. Rose C. van Wyngaarden 1968; one s. one d.; ed Gymnasium, Middelburg and Univ. of Leiden; Research Assoc., Univ. Leiden 1968–70, Asst Prof. 1970–82; Research Assoc., Chicago Assyrian Dictionary, Oriental Inst., Univ. of Chicago 1973–74; Prof. of Akkadian (Assyriology), Ugaritic and History of Ancient Near East, Free Univ. Amsterdam 1983–2005, Prof. Emer. 2005–; Sr Researcher, Nederlands Instituut voor het Nabije Oosten, Leiden 2006–; Gen. Sec., Soc. Ex Oriente Lux 1973–99; mem. Royal Netherlands Acad.; Hon. mem., American Oriental Soc. 1999, Ex Oriente Lux 2003. *Publications:* Studies in Old Babylonian History 1976, On Trees, Mountains and Millstones in the Ancient Near East 1979, Letters from Yale 1981, Letters from Collections in Philadelphia, Chicago and Berkeley 1986, Epilepsy in Babylonia 1993, Langs's Heeren wegen 1997, Birth in Babylonia and the Bible 2000, Die Altbabylonische Zeit 2004, Vrouwen van Babylon 2012. *Address:* Heivlinder 27, 2317 JS Leiden, Netherlands.

STOLER, Andrew L., BS, MBA; American/Australian international organization official and academic; b. 20 Aug. 1951; ed George Washington Univ., Georgetown Univ.'s School of Foreign Service; with Office of Int. Trade Policy, US Dept of Commerce, Washington, DC 1975–79; Dir for Canada, Australia and NZ, US Trade Rep. Office 1980–81, MTN Codes Co-ordinator, Geneva 1982–87, Deputy Asst US Trade Rep. for Europe and the Mediterranean, Washington, DC 1988–89, Deputy Chief of Mission, Geneva 1989–99 (concurrently Deputy Perm. Rep. to WTO); Deputy Dir-Gen. WTO 1999–2002; Exec. Dir Inst. for Int. Trade, Univ. of Adelaide, Australia 2002–11, also Adjunct Prof. of Int. Trade; mem. Int. Academic Advisory Bd United States Studies Centre, Univ. of Sydney; mem. Aid Advisory Council (Australia) 2004–, Advisory Cttee of Shanghai WTO Affairs Consultation Centre; Sr Advisor, Shenzhen WTO Affairs Centre; Assoc. Commr, Australian Productivity Comm. 2009–10. *Address:* United States Studies Centre, Institute Building (H03), City Rd, University of Sydney, Sydney, NSW 2006, Australia (office). *Telephone:* 41-2586063 (mobile). *E-mail:* andrewlstoler@gmail.com. *Website:* ussc .edu.au/ (office).

STOLKER, Carel J. J. M., PhD; Dutch judge, academic and university administrator; *Rector Magnificus and President, University of Leiden;* b. 23 June 1954, Leiden; ed Univ. of Leiden; taught liability law at Hastings School of Law, Univ. of California, San Francisco, USA; published regularly on issues relating to liability law, in co-operation with Hastings' colleague David Levine; mem. Faculty, Civil Law Dept, Univ. of Leiden, Vice-Dean for Research 2000–05, Dean of the Law School 2005–11, Rector Magnificus and Pres. Univ. of Leiden 2013–; mem. Chief Editorial Staff, Tekst & Commentaar series; Ed.-in-Chief Onrechtmatige Daad (Negligence); has served in numerous public posts, including as mem. of two nat. audit cttees of the Dutch Judiciary 2005, Co-Chair. 2010; Deputy Judge, Court of

Haarlem; Deputy Justice, Court of Appeal of 's-Hertogenbosch; mem. Bd of Govs, Research Foundation – Flanders 2011–16; mem. Koninklijke Hollandsche Maatschappij der Wetenschappen 2016; mem. Supervisory Bd, Nat. Museum of World Cultures. *Publications include:* dissertation (published as a book) on the liability of medical doctors, in particular in wrongful birth cases 1988, a study on medical liability crisis in USA 1989, Legal Journals: In pursuit of a more scientific approach 2005, Rethinking the law school - Education, research, outreach and governance 2014, vol. on Dutch Civil Code (ed.); numerous publs on private law and comparative law. *Address:* Office of the Rektor, A.2.05, The Old Library, University of Leiden, Rapenburg 70, PO Box 9500, 2311 EZ Leiden, Netherlands (office). *Telephone:* (71) 527-31-43 (office). *E-mail:* cjjmstolker@cvb.leidenuniv.nl (office). *Website:* www.leidenuniv.nl (office).

STOLL, Jean-François; French civil servant; *General Administrator of Public Finances;* b. 19 Jan. 1950, Isle-Adam; m. Noëlle Nicolas 1976; four c.; ed Institut des études politiques, Paris, Ecole nat. d'admin; joined Ministry of the Economy, Commercial Attaché, Embassy in Jakarta 1982–84, Tech. Adviser 1982–86, Commercial Adviser, Embassy in Mexico 1987–90, Tech. Adviser for Int. Affairs, Office of the Prime Minister 1990–93, Head of Service for Promotion of External Trade 1993–98, Dir External Econ. Relations Dept 1998–2003; Head, Gen. Treasury Office (Seine-Saint-Denis departement) 2003–11, (Yvelines departement) 2011–14; Gen. Admin. of Public Finances, Ministry of the Economy and Finance; Dir, Electricité de France (EDF) 1999–2003; Chevalier, Ordre nat. du Mérite. *Address:* Ministry of the Economy and Finance, 139 rue de Bercy, 75572 Paris Cedex 12 (office); 6 rue d'Ulm, 75005 Paris, France (home). *Telephone:* 1-40-04-04-04 (office); 1-48-96-60-01 (home). *E-mail:* mediateur@economie.gouv.fr (office). *Website:* www.economie.gouv.fr (office).

STOLL, Kara Farnandez, BSc, JD; American judge; *Judge, US Court of Appeals for the Federal Circuit;* b. (Kara Ann Farnandez), 1968, Wilmington, Del.; m. Thomas Stoll; three c.; ed Michigan State Univ., Georgetown Univ. Law School; Patent Examiner, US Patent and Trademark Office 1991–97; Law Clerk to Judge Alvin Schall, US Court of Appeals for the Fed. Circuit 1997–98; Assoc., Finnegan, Henderson, Farabow, Garrett & Dunner (law firm) 1998–2006, Partner 2006–15; Adjunct Prof., Howard Univ. School of Law 2004–08, George Mason Univ. Law School 2008–15; Judge, US Court of Appeals for the Fed. Circuit 2015–; mem. Fed. Circuit Bar Asscn (Vice-Chair., Rules Cttee 2012–13, Co-Chair. 2013–15). *Address:* United States Court of Appeals for the Federal Circuit, 717 Madison Place, NW, Washington, DC 20439, USA (office). *Telephone:* (202) 275-8000 (office). *Website:* www.cafc.uscourts.gov (office).

STOLOJAN, Theodor Dumitru, PhD, DEcon; Romanian economist and politician; b. 24 Oct. 1943, Tîrgoviste; s. of Theodor Stolojan and Nadejda Stolojan; m. Elena Stolojan; one s. one d.; ed Acad. of Econ. Studies, Coll. of Finances, Credit and Accountancy, Bucharest; worked as economist, Ministry of the Food Industry 1966–72; first as economist and then as Chief of Division, State Budget Dept, Ministry of Finance 1972–82, then Deputy Dir, Dir of Dept Foreign Currencies and Int. Financial Relations 1982–87, Gen. Insp. Dept of State Revenues 1988–89, First Deputy Minister of Finance 1989–90, Minister of Finance 1990–91; Pres. of Nat. Agency of Privatization 1991; Prime Minister of Romania 1991–92; Economist, later Sr Economist, IBRD 1993–98; Pres. Tofan Corporated Finance 1999–2000; Partner, Strategic Consulting Ltd; Prof., Univ. of Transylvania, Brașov 2002–12; Pres. Nat. Liberal Party 2002–04; Adviser to the Pres. 2004–06; Co-founder and Chair. Liberal Democratic Party (Partidul Liberal Democrat) 2006–07, First Vice-Chair. 2008–11, apptd mem. Nat. Exec. 2012 (party absorbed by Partidul Național Liberal (National Liberal Party) 2014); MEP 2007–; mem. European People's Party (Christian Democrats) and European Democrats; apptd Prime Minister by Pres. of Romania 10 Dec. 2008, withdrew acceptance 15 Dec.; mem. Bd of Dirs Romanian-American Investment Fund, Bucharest; mem. Int. Inst. of Public Finance 1978–; Dr hc (Valahia Univ.) 2012. *Publications include:* Integration and European Fiscal Policy 2002; numerous studies. *Leisure interests:* skiing, travelling in mountains, jogging. *Address:* European Parliament, Bât. Willy Brandt 04M121, 60, rue Wiertz, 1047 Brussels, Belgium (office); Aurel Vlaicu 42-44, Apt 3, Sector 2, Bucharest, Romania. *Telephone:* (2) 284-56-70 (office). *Fax:* (2) 284-96-70 (office). *Website:* www.europarl.europa.eu (office).

STOLPE, Manfred; German politician; b. 16 May 1936, Stettin, Germany (now Szczecin, Poland); m. Ingrid Ehrhardt; one d.; legal studies in Jena and Berlin; fmrly in charge of organizational work of Protestant Church in East Germany; Consistorial Pres. Berlin-Brandenburg Church 1982–90; joined SPD 1990; Minister-Pres. of Brandenburg 1990–2002; Fed. Minister of Transport, Building and Housing 2002–05; Order of Merit of the State of Brandenburg 2006; Dr hc (Univ. of Dokkyo, Japan) 1989, (Ernst-Moritz-Arndt Univ., Greifswald) 1989, (Univ. of Zürich) 1991, (Univ. of Szczecin) 1996; Carlo-Schmid Prize 1991, Europäischer Kulturpreis für Politik 2012. *Website:* manfred-stolpe.de.

STOLPER, Edward M., AB, MPhil, PhD; American geologist, academic and university administrator; *William E. Leonhard Professor of Geology, California Institute of Technology;* b. 16 Dec. 1952; m. 1973; ed Harvard Coll., Univ. of Edinburgh, UK, Harvard Univ.; Asst Prof. of Geology, California Inst. of Tech. 1979–82, Assoc. Prof. 1982–83, apptd Prof. 1983, named William E. Leonhard Prof. of Geology 1990, Chair. Div. of Geological and Planetary Sciences 1994–2004, Interim Provost 2004, Provost 2007–17, Interim Pres. 2013–14; Scholar, Carl and Shirley Larson Provostial Chair 2013–17, QRI (Quantum Resevoir Impact); Bateman Visiting Scholar, Yale Univ. 1988, 2005; Miller Visiting Research Prof., Univ. of California, Berkeley 1990; Fellow, American Acad. of Arts and Sciences, Geological Soc. of America, Geochemical Soc., European Asscn for Geochemistry, Mineralogical Soc. of America, American Geophysical Union, Meteoritical Soc.; mem. NAS, Mineralogical Soc. of America, Academia Europaea, Royal Soc. of London; Dr hc (Univ. of Edinburgh) 2008, (Hebrew Univ. of Jerusalem) 2012; Newcomb Cleveland Prize, American AAAS 1984, F.W. Clarke Medal, Geochemical Soc. 1985, James B. Macelwane Award, American Geophysical Union 1986, Arthur Holmes Medal, European Union of Geosciences 1997, Arthur L. Day Medal, Geological Soc. of America 2004, V.M. Goldschmidt Medal, Geochemical Soc. 2012. *Publications:* numerous papers in professional journals on the origin and evolution of igneous rocks on the earth and other planets. *Address:* California Institute of Technology, 1200 East California Blvd, Pasadena, CA 91125, USA (office). *E-mail:* ems@caltech.edu (office). *Website:* www.gps.caltech.edu (office).

STOLTE, Dieter; German business executive, newspaper publisher and academic; b. 18 Sept. 1934, Cologne; ed Univs of Tübingen and Mainz; Head of Science Dept, Saarländischer Rundfunk 1961–62; Personal adviser to Dir-Gen. of Zweites Deutsches Fernsehen (ZDF) 1962, Controller, Programme Planning Dept 1967, Programming Dir 1976–82, Dir-Gen. ZDF March 1982–2002; Publisher, Die Welt and Berliner Morgenpost (newspapers) 2002–05; mem. Supervisory Bd Ströer Out-of-Home Media AG, Cologne 2002–, Chair. 2011–14; Dir and Deputy Dir Gen., Südwestfunk 1973; fmr Prof., Univ. of Music and Presentation Arts, Hamburg; mem. Admin. Council, German Press Agency (dpa), Hamburg, European Broadcasting Union (EBU); Chair. Admin. Council TransTel, Cologne; Chair. DeutschlandRadio, Cologne; mem. Bd of Dirs Axel Springer Foundation 2004–; mem. Int. Broadcast Inst., London; mem. Council, Nat. Acad. of TV Arts, New York, Int. Acad. of Arts and Sciences, New York; Hon. Citizen of State of Tenn., USA; Bundesverdienstkreuz, Officer's Cross, Golden Order of Merit (Austria), Bavarian Order of Merit; Int. Emmy Directorate Award 1997, Köckritz Prize 1999, Verdienstorden, Berlin 1999, Robert Geissendorfer Prize 2001. *Publications:* ed. and co-author of several books on programme concepts and function of television, etc.; several essays on subjects relating to the philosophy of culture and the science of communication.

STOLTENBERG, Jens; Norwegian politician and international organization official; *Secretary-General, NATO;* b. 16 March 1959, Oslo; m. Ingrid Schulerud; one s. one d.; ed Univ. of Oslo; journalist, Arbeiderbladet (nat. daily) 1979–81; Information Sec., Oslo Labour Party 1981; Exec. Officer, Statistics Norway 1989–90; Lecturer in Econs, Univ. of Oslo 1989–90; mem. Cen. Bd, Labour Youth League (AUF) 1979–89, Leader, AUF 1985–89; Vice-Pres. Int. Union of Socialist Youth 1985–89; mem. Cen. Bd, Norwegian Labour Party (Arbeiderpartiet) 1985–, Leader Oslo Labour Party 1990–92, Deputy Leader Labour Party 1992–2002, Leader 2002–14; Deputy mem. Storting (Parl.) 1989–93, mem. for Oslo 1993–2014, mem. Standing Cttee Social Afairs 1991–93, on Oil and Energy Affairs 1997–2000, on Foreign Affairs 2001–05; Sec., Ministry of Environment 1990–91; Minister of Trade and Energy 1993–96, of Finance 1996–97; Prime Minister of Norway 2000–01, 2005–13; Sec.-Gen. NATO, Brussels Oct. 2014–; Chair. North Atlantic Council 2014–; Head, Govt Comm. on Male Roles 1986; mem. Norwegian Defence Comm. 1990–92; mem. Bd Global Vaccine Fund 2001–05; apptd UN Special Envoy on Climate Change 2013. *Address:* Office of the Secretary-General, North Atlantic Treaty Organisation, Blvd Léopold III, 1110 Brussels, Belgium (office). *Telephone:* (2) 707-41-11 (office). *Fax:* (2) 707-45-79 (office). *E-mail:* natodoc@hq.nato.int (office). *Website:* www.nato.int/cps/en/natohq/who_is_who_49999.htm? (office).

STONE, (Isaac) 'Biz'; American internet company executive; *Co-founder, Twitter Inc.;* b. 10 March 1974; m. Livia Stone; ed Wellesley High School, Mass, Northeastern Univ., Univ. of Massachusetts; Designer, Little, Brown and Co. 1994–97; Creative Dir Xanga Inc. 1999–2001; Sr Specialist, Google Inc. 2003–05; Dir Community Odeo Inc. 2005–06; Co-founder (with Jack Dorsey) Obvious Corpn 2006 (spun off Twitter Inc. 2006), Chief Creative Officer 2011–13, Twitter Inc. 2007, Creative Dir 2007; Co-founder and Chief Creative Officer, Medium.com 2011–13; Co-founder and CEO Jelly Industries, Inc. 2013–; strategic adviser for social impact, Huffington Post 2011–; Hon. DIur (Babson Coll.); Innovation Award, Int. Center for Journalists 2010, Innovation Award, The Economist magazine 2014. *Publications include:* Blogging: Genius Strategies for Instant Web Content 2002, Who Let the Blogs Out? 2004, Things A Little Bird Told Me 2014. *Address:* Twitter Inc., 1355 Market Street Suite 900, San Francisco, CA 94103, USA (office). *Telephone:* (415) 896-2008 (office). *Website:* twitter.com (office); www.bizstone.com (office); super.me (office); www.jelly.co (office).

STONE, Emily (Emma) Jean; American actress; b. 6 Nov. 1988, Scottsdale, Ariz.; d. of Jeff Stone and Krista Stone (née Yeager); first stage appearances with Valley Youth Theatre, Phoenix, Ariz. *Films include:* Superbad 2007, The Rocker 2008, The House Bunny 2008, Ghosts of Girlfriends Past 2009, Paper Man 2009, Zombieland 2009, Marmaduke 2010, Easy A (MTV Movie Awards Best Comedic Performance 2011) 2010, Friends with Benefits 2011, Crazy, Stupid, Love 2011, The Help 2011, The Amazing Spider-Man 2012, Gangster Squad 2013, Movie 43 2013, The Croods 2013, The Amazing Spider-Man 2 2014, Magic in the Moonlight 2014, Birdman (Boston Soc. of Film Critics Awards Best Supporting Actress 2014) 2014, Irrational Man 2015, Aloha 2015, La La Land (SAG Award for Outstanding Performance by a Female Actor in a Leading Role 2017, Australian Acad. of Cinema and Television Arts 2017, BAFTA Award for Best Actress 2017, Acad. Award for Best Actress 2017) 2016, Battle of the Sexes 2017, The Favourite (North Texas Film Critics Asscn Award for Best Supporting Actress 2018) 2018. *Address:* Anonymous Content, 3532 Hayden Avenue, Culver City, Los Angeles, CA 90232, USA (office). *Telephone:* (310) 558-6000 (office). *Fax:* (310) 558-2724 (office). *Website:* www.anonymouscontent.com (office).

STONE, John Owen, BA (Hons), BSc (Hons); Australian politician, financial executive, public servant and columnist; b. 31 Jan. 1929, Perth, WA; s. of Horace Stone and Eva Stone (née Hunt); m. Nancy Hardwick 1954; four s. one d.; ed Univ. of Western Australia and New Coll., Oxford, UK; Rhodes Scholar 1951; Asst to Australian Treasury Rep. in London 1954–56, Australian Treasury Rep. in London 1958–61; in Research and Information Div., Gen. Financial and Econ. Policy Br., Dept of Treasury, Canberra 1956–57, in Home Finance Div. 1961–62, Asst Sec. Econ. and Financial Surveys Div. 1962–66; Exec. Dir for Australia, New Zealand and South Africa, IMF and IBRD 1967–70, for Swaziland and Lesotho, IMF 1969–70; First Asst Sec., Revenue, Loans and Investment Div., Treasury 1971; Sec., Australian Loan Council; Sec., Australian Nat. Debt Comm. 1971; Deputy Sec. (Econ.), Treasury 1971–76, Deputy Sec. Treasury 1976–78, Sec. 1979–84; Prof., Centre of Policy Studies, Monash Univ., Melbourne 1984; consultant, Potter Partners, Stockbrokers 1985–87; weekly columnist, Melbourne Herald, Sydney Morning Herald 1985–87, The Australian 1987–89, Sunday Telegraph 1989, The Australian Financial Review 1990–98, Adelaide Review 1998–2003; regular contrib. to National Observer quarterly 2002–09, Quadrant Magazine 1985–2017, Spectator Australia Magazine 2015–; Ed. and Publr Proceedings of The Samuel Griffith Soc. 1992–2010; Dir Sperry (Australia) Ltd 1985–87, Peko-Wallsend Ltd 1986–87; Chair. J.T. Campbell & Co. Ltd 1994–96; Senator for Queensland, Leader of Nat. Party in the Senate and Shadow Minister for Finance 1987–90; mem. Defence Efficiency Review 1996–97; Sr Fellow, Inst. of Public Affairs, Melbourne 1985–87, 1990–95; Fellow, Acad. of the Social Sciences of

Australia 1976–81 (resgnd); mem. Mont Pelerin Soc. 2008–; James Webb Medley Prize, Univ. of Oxford 1953. *Publications include:* Upholding the Australian Constitution, in Proceedings of the Samuel Griffith Society (Vols 1–21) 1992–2009 (Ed. and Publr), four chapters in The Howard Era 2009. *Leisure interests:* reading, wine and food. *Address:* 17 Fitzsimmons Avenue, Lane Cove, NSW 2066, Australia. *Telephone:* (2) 9428-1311. *E-mail:* j_o_stone@bigpond.com.

STONE, Matthew (Matt) Richard; American screenwriter, film director and producer; b. 26 May 1971, Houston, Tex.; s. of Gerald Whitney Stone, Jr and Sheila Lois Belasco; m. Angela Howard; one s.; collaborated with Trey Parker on short animation, Jesus vs Frosty 1992, later remade as animated Christmas card for FoxLab, titled The Spirit of Christmas 1995; Co-creator and Exec. Producer, South Park animation (with Trey Parker) 1997–, and other films and TV series. *Films include:* Jesus vs Frosty (writer, dir) 1992, Your Studio and You (writer) 1995, The Spirit of Christmas (writer, dir) 1995, Alferd Packer: The Musical (aka Cannibal! The Musical) (writer, producer) 1996, Orgazmo (writer, dir, producer) 1997, South Park: Bigger Longer & Uncut (writer, producer) (Los Angeles Film Critics Award, New York Film Critics Award, MTV Movie Award) 1999, How's Your News? (exec. producer) 1999, Team America: World Police (writer, producer) 2004. *Television includes:* South Park (series writer, dir, producer) 1997–, That's My Bush! (series writer, producer) 2001, Kenny vs. Spenny (producer) 2007. *Film appearances include:* BASEketball 1998, provides voices for many characters in his animation films and television series. *Recordings include:* albums: Chef Aid: The South Park Album, South Park: Bigger, Longer and Uncut (soundtrack), Mr Hankey's Christmas Classics, Timmy and the Lords of the Underworld, The Book of Mormon (Grammy Award for Best Musical Theater Album 2012) 2011. *Play:* The Book of Mormon (Tony Award for Best Musical 2011, WhatsOnStage Award for Best New Musical 2014, Olivier Award for Best New Musical 2014) 2011. *Address:* c/o Paramount Studios, 5555 Melrose Avenue, Hollywood, CA 90038, USA. *E-mail:* news@southparkstudios.com. *Website:* www.southparkstudios.com.

STONE, Norman, MA; British historian, writer and academic; *Professor of International Relations and Director, Center for Russian Studies, Bilkent University;* b. 8 March 1941, Glasgow; s. of Norman Stone and Mary Robertson Stone (née Pettigrew); m. 1st Marie-Nicole Aubry 1966 (dissolved 1977); two s.; m. 2nd Christine Booker (née Verity) 1982; one s.; ed Glasgow Acad. and Gonville & Caius Coll., Cambridge; research student, Christ's Coll., Cambridge attached to Austrian and Hungarian insts 1962–65; Research Fellow, Gonville & Caius Coll. 1965–67; Asst Lecturer, Faculty of History, Univ. of Cambridge 1967–72, lecturer in History (Russian) 1973–84; Fellow, Jesus Coll., Cambridge and Dir of Studies in History 1971–79; Fellow, Trinity Coll. Cambridge 1979–84; Prof. of Modern History, Univ. of Oxford and Fellow, Worcester Coll. Oxford 1984–97; Prof. of Int. Relations, Bilkent Univ., Turkey 1997–, also Dir Center for Russian Studies; Order of Merit (Poland) 1993; Wolfson Prize 1976. *Publications:* The Eastern Front 1914–17 1976, Hitler 1980, Europe Transformed 1878–1919 1982, Czechoslovakia: Crossroads and Crises (Ed.) 1989, The Other Russia (with Michael Glenny) 1990, World War One 2009, The Atlantic and Its Enemies: A Personal History of the Cold War 2010, World War Two: A Short History 2013; numerous articles. *Leisure interests:* music, Eastern Europe, languages, Turkey. *Address:* Center for Russian Studies, Department of International Relations, Bilkent University, 06800 Bilkent, Ankara, Turkey (office); 22 St Margaret's Road, Oxford, OX2 6RX, England (home). *Telephone:* (312) 2901249 (Turkey) (office); (1865) 439481 (home). *Fax:* (312) 2664326 (Oxford) (office). *E-mail:* CRS@bilkent.edu.tr (office). *Website:* crs .bilkent.edu.tr (office).

STONE, Oliver, BFA; American film director, producer and screenwriter; b. 15 Sept. 1946, New York; s. of Louis Stone and Jacqueline Goddet; m. 1st Najwa Sarkis (divorced); m. 2nd Elizabeth Stone (divorced); m. 3rd Sun-jung Jung 1996; three c.; ed Yale Univ. and New York Univ. Film School; teacher, Cholon, Viet Nam 1965–66; US Merchant Marine 1966, served in US Army, Viet Nam 1967–68; Légion d'Honneur 2004; Extraordinary Contribution to Filmmaking Award, Austin Film Festival 2007, Donostia Award 2012, Lifetime Achievement Award, Sarajevo Film Festival 2017. *Films include:* as writer: Midnight Express (Acad. Award for best screenplay adapted from another medium) 1978, Conan the Barbarian 1982, Scarface 1983; as writer and dir: Seizure 1973, The Hand 1981, Year of the Dragon (with Michael Cimino) 1985, Salvador (co-writer) 1986, Platoon (Acad. Award for Best Film and Best Dir) 1986, Wall Street 1987, Talk Radio (co-writer) 1988, Born on the Fourth of July (Acad. Award for Best Dir 1990) 1989, No One Here Gets Out Alive 1990, The Doors 1991, JFK 1991, Heaven and Earth 1993, Natural Born Killers 1994, Nixon 1995, A Child's Night Dream 1997, U-Turn 1998, Saviour 1998; as producer: Reversal of Fortune, Iron Maze, South Central, Zebrahead, Wild Palms (TV series) 1993, New Age 1994, The People vs Larry Flynt; as writer, dir and producer: Any Given Sunday 2000, Comandante (documentary) 2003, Alexander 2004, World Trade Center 2006, W. 2008, South of the Border 2009, Wall Street: Money Never Sleeps 2010, Savages 2012. *Television includes:* The Untold History of the United States (series documentary) 2012–13. *Address:* Ixtlan Productions, 12233 West Olympic Blvd, Suite 322, Los Angeles, CA 90064, USA (office). *Telephone:* (310) 826-7080 (office). *Fax:* (310) 826-7090 (office). *Website:* www.oliverstone.com.

STONE, Roger W., BS (Econ); American business executive; *Executive Chairman, KapStone Paper and Packaging Corporation;* b. 16 Feb. 1935, Chicago, Ill.; s. of Marvin Stone and Anita Masover; m. Susan Kessert 1955; three d.; ed Wharton School of Finance, Univ. of Pennsylvania; joined Stone Container Corpn 1957, Vice-Pres. Gen. Man. Container Div. 1970–75, Pres. and COO 1975–79, Pres., CEO 1979–98, Chair. 1983–98, Pres., CEO Smurfit Stone Container Corpn 1998–99; Chair. and CEO Box USA Group, Inc. 2000–04; Man. Stone-Kaplan Investments, LLC (pvt. investment co.) 2004–07; Chair. and CEO KapStone Paper and Packaging Corpn, Northbrook, Ill. 2005–16, Exec. Chair. 2017–; mem. Bd of Dirs McDonalds Corpn, Autoliv, Inc.; fmr mem. Bd of Dirs Morton Int., Option Care Inc.; mem. Advisory Council for Econ. Devt. *Leisure interest:* golf. *Address:* KapStone Paper and Packaging Corporation, 1101 Skokie Blvd, Suite 300, Northbrook, IL 60062-4124, USA (office). *Telephone:* (847) 239-8800 (office). *Fax:* (847) 205-7551 (office). *E-mail:* information@kapstonepaper.com (office). *Website:* www.kapstonepaper.com (office).

STONE, Sharon; American actress; b. 10 March 1958, Meadville, Pa; m. 1st George Englund Jr; m. 2nd Michael Greenburg 1984 (divorced 1987); m. 3rd Phil Bronstein 1998 (divorced 2004); three adopted s.; ed high school in Pennsylvania and Edinboro Coll.; Chevalier, Ordre des Arts et Lettres. *Films include:* Above the Law, Action Jackson, King Solomon's Mines, Allan Quatermain and the Lost City of Gold, Irreconcilable Differences, Deadly Blessing, Personal Choice, Basic Instinct, Diary of a Hit Man, Where Sleeping Dogs Lie, Sliver, Intersection, The Specialist, The Quick and the Dead, Casino, Last Dance, Diabolique 1996, Sphere, The Mighty 1999, The Muse 1999, Simpatico 1999, Gloria 1999, Beautiful Joe 2000, Cold Creek Manor 2003, A Different Loyalty 2004, Catwoman 2004, Jiminy Glick in La La Wood 2004, Broken Flowers 2005, Alpha Dog 2006, Basic Instinct 2 2006, Bobby 2006, If I Had Known I Was a Genius 2007, When a Man Falls in the Forest 2007, Democrazy 2007, The Year of Getting to Know Us 2008, Five Dollars a Day 2008, Streets of Blood 2009, The Burma Conspiracy 2011, The Mule 2012, Lovelace 2013, Fading Gigolo 2013, Mothers and Daughters 2014, Life on the line 2016, Running Wild 2017. *Television appearances include:* Bay City Blues (series), Tears in the Rain (film), War and Remembrance (mini-series), Calendar Girl Murders (film), The Vegas Strip Wars (film), Huff (series) 2006, Law & Order: Special Victims Unit (series) 2010, Agents Series 2014. *Address:* William Morris Endeavour, 1 William Morris Place, Beverly Hills, CA 90212; c/o Guy McElwaine, PO Box 7304, North Hollywood, CA 91603, USA.

STONEBRAKER, Michael R., BS, MS, PhD; American computer scientist and academic; *Adjunct Professor, Computer Science and Artificial Intelligence Laboratory, Massachusetts Institute of Technology;* b. 11 Oct. 1943, Milton, NH; m. Beth Stonebraker; ed Princeton Univ., Univ. of Michigan; Asst Prof. of Computer Science, Univ. of California, Berkeley 1971–76, Assoc. Prof. 1976–81, Prof. 1981–99 (retd); Adjunct Prof., MIT Computer Science and Artificial Intelligence Lab. 2001–, Co-founder and Co-Dir Intel Science and Tech. Center for Big Data; fmr Chief Tech. Officer, Informix; Founder of several database cos, including Ingres, Illustra, Cohera, StreamBase Systems, Vertica, VoltDB, Tamr and Paradigm4; mem. Nat. Acad. of Eng 1997; Fellow, Asscn for Computing Machinery (ACM) 1994; Software System Award (co-recipient), inaugural SIGMOD Edgar F. Codd Innovations Award, IEEE John von Neumann Medal, ACM A.M. Turing Award 2014. *Achievements include:* developed Ingres and Postgres relational database systems. *Publications:* Readings in Database Systems (co-ed.); numerous papers in professional journals. *Address:* Room 32-G922, MIT Computer Science and Artificial Intelligence Laboratory, The Stata Center, Building 32, 32 Vassar Street, Cambridge, MA 02139, USA (office). *Telephone:* (617) 253-3538 (office). *Fax:* (617) 258-8682 (office). *E-mail:* stonebraker@csail.mit.edu (office). *Website:* www .csail.mit.edu (office).

STONECIPHER, Harry Curtis, BS; American aircraft industry executive (retd); b. 16 May 1936, Scott Co., Tenn.; m. Joan Stonecipher 1954; two c.; ed Tennessee Polytechnic Inst.; with General Electric 1960–61, 1962–86, Martin Aircraft Co. 1961–62; Exec. Vice-Pres. Sundstrand Corpn 1987, Pres. and COO 1987–88, Pres. and CEO 1988–94, Chair. 1991–94; Pres. and CEO McDonnell-Douglas Corpn, St Louis 1994–97; apptd Pres. and CEO Boeing Co., Seattle 1997, COO Boeing Corpn (later Boeing Co.) 1997–2002, Pres. and CEO 1997–2002, 2003–05 (resgnd); fmr mem. Bd of Dirs Milacron, Inc.; Fellow, Royal Aeronautical Soc.; John R. Allison Award 1996, Rear Adm. John J. Bergen Leadership Medal Nay League 1996.

STONEHAM OF DROXFORD, Baron (Life Peer), cr. 2011, of the Meon Valley in the County of Hampshire; **Ben Stoneham,** BA, MA; British political activist, fmr company director, fmr newspaper director and fmr manager; *Chief Whip of the Liberal Democrats, House of Lords;* b. 24 April 1948, Tunbridge Wells, Kent; s. of Maj. B.J.R. Stoneham and Mrs B.M. Stoneham; m. Anne Kristine Mackintosh 1975; two s., one d.; ed Christ's Coll., Univ. of Cambridge, Univ. of Warwick, London Business School; Dir and Man. Dir Portsmouth and Sunderland Newspapers Ltd 1987–89; Group Production Dir and Personnel Dir News International 2000–03; Operations Dir, Liberal Democrat HQ 2003–10, Spokesperson for Business, Innovation and Skills 2015–; Chair. Portsmouth Harbour Renaissance Ltd 1996–2005, First Wessex Housing Group 2004–11, Housing & Care 21 2011–18; Chief Whip of the Liberal Democrats, House of Lords 2016–; fmr mem. House of Lords Select Cttee on Legacy of Olympics and Para-Olympics; Dir Thames Gateway Thurrock Urban Devt Corpn 2004–10. *Leisure interests:* gardening, sport, war history. *Address:* House of Lords, Westminster, London, SW1A 0PW, England (home). *Telephone:* (20) 7219-3000 (home). *E-mail:* stonehamb@parliament.uk (home).

STONESIFER, Patricia Q. (Patty), BA; American foundation executive; *President and CEO, Martha's Table;* b. 1956, Indianapolis, Ind.; m. 2nd Michael Kinsley; two c. (from previous m.); ed Indiana Univ.; several sr man. positions with Microsoft Corpn 1988–96, most recently Sr Vice-Pres. Interactive Media Div.; man. consultant 1996–97; Pres. and Chair. Gates Learning Foundation 1997–99, Pres. and Co-Chair. Bill and Melinda Gates Foundation 1999–2006, CEO 2006–08; apptd mem. Bd of Dirs Amazon.com 1997, Viacom 2000; mem. Bd The Vaccine Fund; mem. Bd of Regents Smithsonian Inst., Washington, DC, Chair. 2009–12; Pres. and CEO Martha's Table (non-profit), Washington, DC 2013–; apptd Chair. White House Council on Community Solutions 2010; fmr mem. US Del. to UN Gen. Ass. Special Session on AIDS; mem. American Acad. of Arts and Sciences, Council on Foreign Relations; Dr hc (Indiana Univ.) 2007, (Tufts Univ.) 2009. *Address:* Martha's Table Headquarters, 2114 14th Street, NW, Washington, DC 20009, USA (office). *E-mail:* info@marthastable.org (office). *Website:* marthastable.org (office).

STOPFORD, Michael, MA; American (b. British) public relations executive, fmr diplomatist and fmr UN official; *Assistant Vice-Chancellor for International Affairs, University of Nebraska, Kearney;* b. 22 June 1953, London, England; s. of Edward Stopford and Patricia Carrick; m. Susan Navrat; two s. one d.; ed Oxford Univ., UK; fmr mem. HM Diplomatic Service, served at Perm. Mission to UN, New York, Second Sec. and Press Attaché, Embassy in Vienna; Assoc. then Second Officer, Exec. Office of Sec.-Gen. of UN 1979–83, Special Projects Officer, Dept of Public Information 1983–87, Chef de Cabinet to Dir-Gen., UN Office in Geneva and Under-Sec.-Gen. for Human Rights 1987–91, Chef de Cabinet to Exec. Del. of Sec.-Gen. for Inter-Agency Humanitarian Programme in Iraq, Kuwait and Iraq–Turkey and Iraq–Iran border areas 1991–92, with Dept for Humanitarian Affairs 1992, Special Asst to UnderSec.-Gen. for Public Information, Dept of Public Information, UN, New York 1992, Dir UN Information Center, Washington, DC, 1992–95; Chief of Media and Public Relations, Int. Financial Corpn 1996–97; Sr

Asst to Pres. for Int. Affairs, American Univ., Washington, DC 1997; Sr Issues Adviser, Exxon Mobil Corpn, USA 2000–01; Head of Global Public Affairs and Govt Relations, Syngenta International AG, Basel, Switzerland 2002–06; Group Dir, Corp. Reputation, The Coca-Cola Company, Atlanta, Ga 2006–08; Deputy Asst Sec.-Gen., Strategic Communications Services, Public Diplomacy, NATO 2008–11; Global Corp. Strategist, Weber Shandwick, Washington, DC 2011–15; Asst Vice-Chancellor for Int. Affairs, Univ. of Nebraska, Kearney 2015–; mem. Bd of Dirs Josef Korbel School of Int. Studies, Univ. of Denver; Hon. LLD (New England Coll.) 1998. *Publication:* The UN and Global Intervention: Delusions of Grandeur (co-author) 1997. *Leisure interests:* opera, art, sailing, skiing. *Address:* International Education, University of Nebraska, 905 West 25th Street, Kearney, NE 68849 (office); 723 Rock Springs Court, NE, Atlanta, GA 30306-2328, USA (home). *Telephone:* (308) 865-8441 (office). *E-mail:* stopfordmj@unk.edu (office); m.stopford@gmx.ch. *Website:* www.unk.edu/international (office).

STOPPARD, Sir Tom, Kt, OM, CBE, FRSL; British writer; b. (Thomas Straussler), 3 July 1937, Zlin, Czechoslovakia; s. of Dr Eugene Straussler and Martha Straussler; step-s. of Kenneth Stoppard; m. 1st Jose Ingle 1965 (divorced 1972); two s.; m. 2nd Dr Miriam Moore-Robinson 1972 (divorced 1992); two s.; m. 3rd Sabrina Guinness 2014; ed Pocklington Grammar School, Yorks.; journalist, Bristol 1954–60, freelance journalist, London 1960–64; mem. Cttee of the Free World 1981–; mem. Royal Nat. Theatre Bd 1989–; Pres. London Library 2002; Fellow, RSL 1972; Hon Fellow, British Acad. 2017; Hon MLitt (Bristol), (Brunel); Hon. LittD (Leeds) 1979, (Sussex) 1980, (Warwick) 1981, (London) 1982, (Yale) 2000, (Cambridge) 2000, (Oxford) 2013; Dr hc (Kenyon Coll.) 1984, (York) 1984; John Whiting Award, Arts Council 1967, Italia Prize (radio drama) 1968, New York Drama Critics Best Play Award 1968, Antoinette Perry Awards (Tony Awards) 1968, 1976, 2007, Evening Standard Awards 1967, 1972, 1974, 1978, 1982, 1993, 1997, 2006, Sony Award 1991, Olivier Award 1993, inducted into American Theatre Hall of Fame 1999, Dan David Prize 2008, Sunday Times Award for Literary Excellence 2008, Praemium Imperiale 2009, PEN Pinter Prize 2013, Laurel Award for Screenwriting Achievement 2013, PEN/Allen Foundation Literary Service Award 2015, America Award in Literature 2017, David Cohen Prize 2017. *Plays:* Rosencrantz and Guildenstern are Dead 1967, The Real Inspector Hound 1968, Enter a Free Man 1968, After Magritte 1970, Dogg's Our Pet 1972, Jumpers 1972, Travesties 1975, Dirty Linen 1976, New-Found-Land 1976, Every Good Boy Deserves Favour (with music by André Previn), 1978, Night and Day 1978, Dogg's Hamlet, Cahoots Macbeth 1979, Undiscovered Country 1980, On the Razzle 1981, The Real Thing 1982, Rough Crossing 1984, Dalliance (adaption of Schnitzler's Liebelei) 1986, Hapgood 1988, Arcadia (Evening Standard Award for Best Play) 1993, Indian Ink 1995, The Invention of Love 1997, The Seagull (trans. 1997), The Coast of Utopia (trilogy: Part One: Voyage, Part Two: Shipwreck, Part Three: Salvage) (Tony Award for Best Play 2007) 2002, Rock 'N' Roll (London Critics' Circle Award for Best New Play) 2006, The Hard Problem 2015. *Screenplays:* The Romantic Englishwoman (co-author) 1975, Despair 1977; film scripts: The Human Factor 1979, Brazil (with Terry Gilliam and Charles McKeown) 1984, Crown 1987, Empire of the Sun 1987, Rosencrantz and Guildenstern are Dead (also dir) 1989, The Russia House 1989, Billy Bathgate 1990, Shakespeare in Love (co-author) 1998 (jt winner Acad. Award for Best Original Screenplay 1999), Enigma 2001, Anna Karenina 2012. *Radio plays:* The Dissolution of Dominic Boot 1964, M is for Moon among Other Things 1964, Albert's Bridge 1967, If You're Glad I'll be Frank 1968, Where are They Now? 1970, Artist Descending a Staircase 1972, The Dog It Was That Died 1983, In the Native State 1991, On Dover Beach 2007, Darkside 2013. *Television plays:* Professional Foul 1977, Squaring the Circle 1984, The Television Plays 1965–84 1993, Parade's End 2012. *Publications include:* Lord Malquist and Mr Moon (novel) 1966, Introduction 2 (short stories) 1963, The Plays for Radio 1964–91 (radio plays) 1994. *Address:* c/o United Agents Ltd, 12–26 Lexington Street, London, W1F 0LE, England (office). *Telephone:* (20) 3214-0800 (office). *Fax:* (20) 3214-0801 (office). *E-mail:* info@unitedagents.co.uk (office). *Website:* www.unitedagents.co.uk (office).

STORARO, Vittorio; Italian cinematographer; b. 24 June 1940, Rome; ed Centro Sperimentale; mem. Italian Asscn of Cinematographers 1971–, Vice-Pres. 1977–78, Pres. 1988–90; mem. Acad. of Motion Picture Arts and Sciences 1980–, American Soc. of Cinematographers 1988–, European Acad. of Motion Picture Arts and Sciences 1999–; teacher, Acad. of Motion Picture Arts and Sciences of Image, L'Aquila, Italy 1994; Lifetime Achievement Award, American Soc. of Cinematographers 2001, Coolidge Award 2005. *Films include:* Giovinezza, Giovinezza 1968, Delitto al Circolo del Tennis, La Strategia del Rango 1969, Il Conformista, L'Eneide 1970, Addio Fratello Crudele 1971, Giornata Nera per l'Ariete 1971, Orlando Furioso 1971, Last Tango in Paris 1972, Bleu Gang..., Malizia 1972, Giordano Bruno 1973, Le Orme 1974, Novecento 1974, Scandalo 1975, Agatha, La Luna 1978, Apocalypse Now (Acad. Award for Best Cinematography 1980) 1979, Reds (Acad. Award for Best Cinematography 1981) 1982, Tarzan, the Ape Man 1980, One from the Heart 1981, Wagner 1982, Ladyhawke 1983, The Last Emperor (Acad. Award for Best Cinematography 1988) 1987, Tucker: The Man and His Dream 1988, New York Stories (Life Without Zoe) 1989, Dick Tracy 1990, The Sheltering Sky 1990, Tosca (TV) 1992, Little Buddha 1993, Roma!, Imago Urbis, Flamenco (de Carlos Saura) 1995, Taxi 1996, Tango, no me dejes nunca (Cannes Film Festival Award) 1998, Bulworth 1998, Goya en Burdeos (Goya in Bordeaux) 1999, Mirka 2000, Picking up the Pieces 2000, La Traviata (TV) 2000, Zapata: El sueño del héroe 2004, Exorcist: The Beginning 2004, Dominion: Prequel to the Exorcist 2005, I, Don Giovanni 2009, L'imbroglio nel lenzuolo 2010, Muhammad: The Messenger of God 2015, Café Society 2016. *E-mail:* vittorio@storarovittorio .com. *Website:* storarovittorio.com.

STORCH, Marcus, MSc; Swedish business executive; b. 28 July 1942, Stockholm; s. of Hilel Storch and Anna Storch; m. Gunilla Berglund 1972; one d.; ed Royal Inst. of Tech., Stockholm; Dept Head, AGA AB, Welding 1968–72, Pres. Welding Div. AGA AB 1972–75, Pres. Gas Div. 1975–81, Exec. Vice-Pres. AGA AB 1978–81, Pres. and CEO 1981–96; Chair. Nobel Foundation 2005–13; Vice-Chair. A. Johnson AB 1997, AXFOOD AB 2000, Mekonomen 2008–15 (mem. Bd of Dirs 2006–15); mem. Bd Nordstjernan AB 1997, NCC AB 1998–12, Oresund AB, Axel and Margaret Ax:son Johnson Foundation; Hon. Dr Med. (Karolinska Institutet). *Address:* Linnégatan 8, 114 47 Stockholm, Sweden (office). *Telephone:* (8) 679-97-00 (office). *E-mail:* storch@telia.com (office).

STØRE, Jonas Gahr, BSc; Norwegian politician and diplomatist; *Leader, Arbeiderparti (Norwegian Labour Party);* b. 25 Aug. 1960; m.; three c.; ed Royal Norwegian Naval Acad., Institut d'Etudes Politiques de Paris, France; Teaching Fellow, Harvard Law School, USA 1986; Researcher, Norwegian School of Man. 1986–89; Special Adviser, Office of the Prime Minister 1989–95, Dir-Gen., Int. Dept 1995–98, State Sec. and Chief of Staff 2000–01; Perm. Rep. to UN, Geneva 1998; Chief of Staff, WHO 1998–2000; Working Chair., ECON Analysis 2002–03; Sec.-Gen., Norwegian Red Cross 2003–05; Minister of Foreign Affairs 2005–12, of Health and Care Services 2012–13; mem. Arbeiderparti (Norwegian Labour Party), Leader 2014–. *Address:* Arbeiderpartiet, Youngstorget 2A, 5th Floor, Oslo, PO Box 8743, 0028 Oslo, Norway (office). *Telephone:* 24-14-40-00 (office). *Fax:* 24-14-40-01 (office). *E-mail:* post@arbeiderpartiet.no (office). *Website:* www .arbeiderpartiet.no (office).

STOREY, Baron (Life Peer), cr. 2011, of Childwall in the City of Liverpool; **Mike Storey,** OBE, CBE, BEd (Hons); British head teacher and politician; m.; one d.; ed St Katharine's Coll., Liverpool, Chester Coll.; fmr Head Teacher, Plantation Primary School, Halewood, Knowsley; Councillor (Liberal Democrat) for Wavetree Ward, South Cen. Dist, Liverpool City Council 1973–2011, became youngest Chair. of Educ. in history of Liverpool 1980–83, Deputy Leader of Council 1980–83, Leader 1998–2005, involved in Liverpool's successful bid to become European Capital of Culture 2008; Lord Mayor of Liverpool 2010; mem. (Liberal Democrat), House of Lords 2011–; Co-Chair. Liberal Democrat PPC on Educ., Families and Young People 2013–. *Address:* House of Lords, Westminster, London, SW1A 0PW, England (office). *Telephone:* (151) 722-6847 (home); (20) 7219-1972 (office). *E-mail:* storeym@parliament.uk (office).

STORM, Kornelis (Kees), MA, CPA; Dutch business executive; *Chairman of the Supervisory Board, KLM NV;* b. 12 June 1942, Amsterdam; m.; two c.; ed Univ. of Rotterdam; chartered accountant, Moret & Limperg 1970–76; mem. Exec. Bd Kon. Scholten-Honig NV 1976–78, AGO 1978–83; mem. Exec. Bd, AEGON NV 1983–93, Chair. 1993–2002, currently mem. Supervisory Bd; Chair. Supervisory Bd KLM NV, PON Holding BV; mem. Bd of Dirs, Unilever NV, Baxter International; Ind. Dir, Anheuser-Busch InBev, Chair. 2012–15. *Publication:* Management With a Smile. *Address:* c/o Supervisory Board, AEGON NV, Aegonplein 50, PO Box 202, 2501 The Hague (office); Zwaluwenweg 2, 2111 HC Aerdenhout, Netherlands (home). *Telephone:* (70) 3448287 (office); (23) 5242619 (home). *Fax:* (70) 3448593 (office); (23) 5248076 (home). *E-mail:* kees.storm@aegon.com (office). *Website:* www .aegon.com (office).

STÖRMER, Horst Ludwig, PhD; German physicist and academic; *Professor Emeritus of Applied Physics and I. I. Rabi Professor Emeritus of Physics, Columbia University;* b. 6 April 1949, Frankfurt am Main; s. of Karl-Ludwig Stormer and Marie Ihrig; m. Dominique A. Parchet 1982; ed Goethe Univ., Frankfurt, Univ. of Stuttgart; with tech. staff, AT&T Bell Labs (now part of Lucent Technologies) 1977–83, head of Dept 1983–91, Dir Physics Research Lab. 1991–97, then Adjunct Physics Dir (part-time); Prof. of Physics and Applied Physics, Columbia Univ. 1998–2006, I. I. Rabi Prof. of Physics and Prof. of Applied Physics 2006–11, Prof. Emer. of Applied Physics and I.I. Rabi Prof. Emer. of Physics 2011–; Fellow, American Physics Soc., American Acad. of Arts and Sciences; Officier, Légion d'honneur 1999; Buckley Prize, American Physics Soc. 1984, Otto Klug Prize, Germany 1985, Nobel Prize in Physics (jtly) 1998, New York City Mayor's Award 2000. *Address:* Department of Physics, Columbia University, 922 Schapiro CEPSR, MC 5206, New York, NY 10027, USA (office). *Telephone:* (212) 854-3279 (office). *E-mail:* horst@phys.columbia.edu (office). *Website:* www.ap.columbia.edu (office).

STORR, Robert, BA, MFA; American writer, critic, curator and academic; *Professor of Painting/Printmaking and Dean of the School of Art, Yale University;* b. 1949; ed Swarthmore Coll., School of the Art Inst. of Chicago, and studies in Europe and Mexico; Curator of Painting and Sculpture, Museum of Modern Art (MOMA), New York 1990–98, Sr Curator of Contemporary Art 1999–2002; Rosalee Solow Prof. of Modern Art, Inst. of Fine Arts, New York Univ. 2002–06; fmr mem. Faculty, Center for Curatorial Studies, Bard Coll.; Prof. of Painting/Printmaking and Dean of the School of Art, Yale Univ. 2006–, apptd Stavros Niarchos Foundation Dean 2014; also currently Consulting Curator of Modern and Contemporary Art, Philadelphia Museum of Art; Visual Arts Dir Venice Biennale 2005–07, Curator 2007; Visiting Artist, Critic and Lecturer, Univ. of Pennsylvania, Ruskin School of Drawing, Oxford, UK, School of the Art Inst. of Chicago, Rhode Island School of Design, RCA, London, UK, Grad. Painting Program, Hunter Coll.; Grad. School and Univ. Center, CUNY, Harvard Univ.; Contributing Ed. Art in America, Grand Street; mem. Editorial Bd Art Journal 1985–95; Chevalier des Arts et des Lettres 2000; Dr hc (School of the Art Institute of Chicago), (Maine Coll. of Art), (Swarthmore Coll.); First Prize, American Inst. of Commemorative Art 2002, American Chapter of Int. Asscn of Art Critics Award, AICA Award for Distinguished Contribution to the Field of Art Criticism, ICI Agnes Gund Curatorial Award, Lawrence A. Fleischman Award for Scholarly Excellence in the Field of American Art History, Smithsonian Institution's Archives of American Art. *Publications include:* prin. author or ed. of 35 books and monographs, including Philip Guston 1986, Modern Art Despite Modernism 2000, Gerhard Richter: October 18, 1977 2000, Gerhard Richter: 40 Years of Painting 2002, Louise Bourgeois 2003, Touching Down Lightly 2005, Think with the Senses, Feel with the Mind: Art in the Present Tense 2007, Gerhardt Richter: The Cage Paintings 2009, Selections from the Private Collection of Robert Rauschenberg 2012, How to Look: Ad Reinhardt Art Comics 2013; author of essays for exhbn catalogues and books on Louise Bourgeois, Chuck Close, Felix Gonzalez-Torres, Philip Guston, David Hammons, Eva Hesse, Ilya Kabakov, Alex Katz, Ellsworth Kelly, Steve McQueen, Elizabeth Murray, Bruce Nauman, Jim Nutt, Raymond Pettibon, Martin Puryear, Susan Rothenberg, Peter Saul, and Nancy Spero, among others; other publs include articles, interviews, and exhbn reviews for Art in America, Art/Press, Paris, Artforum, Grand Street, Parkett, The Art Journal, Washington Post BookWorld, and other journals and newspapers. *Address:* Yale University School of Art, 1156 Chapel Street, POB 208339, New Haven, CT 06520-8339, USA (office). *Telephone:* (203) 432-2600 (office). *Website:* art.yale.edu/ RobertStorr (office).

STOTHARD, Sir Peter M., Kt, MA; British writer, classicist, journalist and critic; b. 28 Feb. 1951, Chelmsford, Essex, England; s. of Wilfred Stothard and

Patricia Savage; m. Sally Ceris Emerson 1980; one s. one d.; ed Brentwood School, Essex and Trinity Coll., Oxford; journalist, BBC 1974–77; business and political writer, Sunday Times 1979–80; Features Ed. and leader writer, The Times 1980–85; Deputy Ed. The Times 1985–92, US Ed. 1989–92, Ed. 1992–2002; Ed. The Times Literary Supplement 2002–16; Chair. of judging panel for Man Booker Prize 2012; Pres. Classical Asscn –2012; Trustee, Nat. Portrait Gallery 2017; Hon. Fellow, Trinity Coll. Oxford 2000–; Pres.'s Medal, British Acad. 2013. *Publications:* Thirty Days: A Month at the Heart of Blair's War 2003, On the Spartacus Road: A Spectacular Journey through Ancient Italy 2010, Alexandria: The Last Nights of Cleopatra 2013, The Senecans: Four Men and Margaret Thatcher 2016. *Leisure interests:* ancient and modern literature. *Telephone:* 7774-617820 (mobile) (office). *E-mail:* peter.stothard@gmail.com.

STOURNARAS, Yannis, BEcons, MPhil, DPhil; Greek economist, academic and government official; *Governor, Bank of Greece;* b. 10 Dec. 1956, Athens; ed Univ. of Athens, Univ. of Oxford, UK; Research Fellow and Lecturer, St Catherine's Coll., Oxford 1982–86, worked at Oxford Inst. for Energy Studies; mil. service 1986; Special Adviser to Ministry of Economy and Finance on Public Enterprises and Incomes Policy 1986–89, to Bank of Greece on Monetary Policy 1989–94; represented Bank of Greece as alt. mem. in Meetings of the Govs of EU Cen. Banks; Prof. of Econs, Dept of Econs, Univ. of Athens 1989–, teaches Macroeconomics and Econ. Policy; Chair. Council of Econ. Advisors, Ministry of Economy and Finance 1994–2000; represented Ministry of Economy and Finance at Monetary Cttee (now Econ. and Financial Cttee) of the EU; participated in negotiations for Greek entry into Econ. and Monetary Union; responsible for consultations with int. orgs including IMF, EC and OECD; Vice-Chair. Public Gas Corpn 1994–97; mem. Bd of Dirs, Public Debt Man. Office 1998–2000; Chair. and CEO Emporiki Bank 2000–04; Vice-Chair. Asscn of Greek Banks 2000–04; Man. Dir Kappa Securities 2005–08; Dir Gen. Foundation for Econ. and Industrial Research (IOBE) 2008–; Minister for Devt, Competitiveness and Shipping in caretaker govt of Panagiotis Pikrammenos May–June 2012; Minister of Finance (following formation of coalition govt between Nea Demokratia (New Democracy), Panellinio Socialistikio Kinima (PASOK—Panhellenic Socialist Movt) and Dimokratiki Aristera (DIMAR—Democratic Left) July 2012–14; Gov. Bank of Greece 2014–; Trustee, Gennadius Library 2005–. *Publications:* articles in academic journals on macroeconomics, optimum taxation theory, public debt dynamics, Economic and Monetary Union, energy economics, monetary policy, distortions of financial systems. *Address:* Bank of Greece, Leoforos E. Venizelos 21, 102 50 Athens (office); Department of Economics, School of Law, Economics and Political Sciences, University of Athens, Odos Pesmazoglou 8, 10509 Athens, Greece. *Telephone:* (210) 3201111 (office); (210) 3243525. *Fax:* (210) 3232239 (office); (210) 3228538. *E-mail:* sec.secretariat@bankofgreece.gr (office); ystourn@econ.uoa.gr. *Website:* www.bankofgreece.gr (office); www.econ.uoa.gr.

STOWE, Madeleine; American actress; b. 18 Aug. 1958, Los Angeles; d. of Robert Stone and Mireya Mora; m. Brian Benben 1986; one d.; ed Univ. of Southern California; began acting career at Solari Theatre, Beverly Hills; appeared in TV series The Gangster Chronicles, mini-series Beulah Land and TV films The Nativity, The Deerslayer, Amazons, Blood and Orchids. *Films include:* Stakeout 1987, Tropical Snow 1989, Worth Winning 1989, Revenge 1990, The Two Jakes 1990, Closet Land 1991, Unlawful Entry 1992, The Last of the Mohicans 1992, Short Cuts 1993, Blink 1994, China Moon 1994, Twelve Monkeys 1995, Playing by Heart 1998, The Proposition 1998, The General's Daughter 1999, Imposter 2001, We Were Soldiers 2002, Avenging Angelo 2002, Octane 2003. *Television includes:* The Magnificent Ambersons 2002, Saving Milly 2005, Raines (series) 2007, The Christmas Hope (film) 2009, Revenge (series) 2011–15. *Address:* c/o David Schiff, UTA, 9560 Wilshire Boulevard, Suite 500, Beverly Hills, CA 90212, USA.

STOWELL OF BEESTON, Baroness (Life Peer), cr. 2011, of Beeston in the County of Nottinghamshire; **Tina Wendy Stowell,** MBE; British politician, fmr civil servant and fmr media executive; b. 2 July 1967, Beeston, Notts., England; ed Chilwell Comprehensive, Broxtowe Coll. of Further Educ.; worked at Ministry of Defence 1986–88, Embassy in Washington, DC 1988–91, Press Office, No. 10 Downing Street 1991–96; various commercial sector positions at cos including for Sir David Frost at Paradine Productions and at Granada Media 1996–98; Deputy Chief of Staff to William Hague as Leader of HM Opposition and Leader of Conservative Party 1998–2001; Deputy Sec., BBC 2001–03, Head of Communications for BBC Trust 2003–08, Head of Corp. Affairs, BBC 2008–10; communications consultant and fmr Chair. Tina Stowell Assocs 2010–11; mem. (Conservative), House of Lords 2011–; Govt Whip in the House of Lords and Baroness-in-Waiting to HM The Queen 2011–14; Jr Minister (Parl. Under-Sec.), Dept for Communities and Local Govt 2013–14; Leader of the House of Lords and Lord Privy Seal 2014–16; Spectator's Peer of the Year 2013, Stonewall's Politician of the Year 2013, PinkNews' Politician of the Year 2013. *Address:* House of Lords, Westminster, London, SW1A 0PW, England (office). *Telephone:* (20) 7219-5353 (office). *E-mail:* stowellt@parliament.uk (office). *Website:* www.parliament.uk/biographies/lords/baroness-stowell-of-beeston/4205 (office); www.tinastowell.co.uk.

STOYANOV, Petar Stefanov; Bulgarian lawyer and fmr head of state; b. 25 May 1952, Plovdiv; m. Antonina Stoyanova; one s. one d.; ed St Kliment Ohridski Univ. of Sofia; divorce lawyer 1978–90; became active in politics 1989; mem. Union of Democratic Forces (UDF), Spokesman in Plovdiv 1990, Pres. UDF Legal Council 1993, Deputy Chair. UDF responsible for domestic policy 1995, Chair. 2005–07 (resgnd), mem. Nat. Exec. Council; Deputy Minister of Justice 1992–93; mem. Parl. 1994–96, 2005–07, Chair. UDF Parl. Group Parl. Comm. on Youth, Sports, and Tourism; presidential cand. 1996; Pres. of Bulgaria 1997–2002; Special Envoy for Moldova of OSCE Chair-in-Office 2004; Pres. Centre for Global Dialogue and Co-operation, Geneva and Vienna 2009–; Grand Cross (First Class), Order of the White Double Cross (Slovakia) 1997; Grand Cross with Sash, Order of the Star of Romania 1998; Grand Star of the Decoration of Honour for Services to the Repub. of Austria 1999; Kt, Order of the Elephant (Denmark) 2000. *Address:* Centre for Global Dialogue and Co-operation, Mahlerstraße 12/6/3.6.1, Palais Corso, 1010 Vienna, Austria (office); Blvd V. Levski 54, 1000 Sofia, Bulgaria. *Telephone:* (1) 8900549 (Vienna) (office); (2) 986-59-19 (Sofia); 888-80-10-92 (mobile) (office). *Fax:* (1) 8900549 (Vienna) (office); (2) 988-40-47 (Sofia). *E-mail:* office@petarstoyanov

.com; office@cgdc.eu (office). *Website:* www.cgdc.eu (office); www.petarstoyanov.com/en.

STRAARUP, Peter, BCom; Danish banking executive; b. 19 July 1951; m. Rickie Retchin; two c.; joined Den Danske Bank 1968, Arbitrage Dealer 1975; Loan Admin Man. Scandinavian Bank Ltd, London 1976–77; Vice-Pres. Den Danske Bank 1977–81, Rep. Houston Rep. Office 1981–83, Head of Foreign Banking Relations, Copenhagen 1983, Gen. Man. Singapore Br. 1984–85, New York 1985–86, mem. Exec. Bd, Copenhagen 1986, CEO, Chair. Exec. Bd and Chair. Exec. Cttee Danske Bank Group 1998–2012; Chair. Forsikringsselskabet Danica, Skadeforsikringsaktieselskab af 1999, Danica Pension, Livsforsikringsaktieselskab, Danica Liv III, Livsforsikringsaktieselskab, Danica Pension I, Livsforsikringsaktieselskab, DDB Invest AB; mem. Bd of Dirs Denmark-America Foundation; mem. Int. Monetary Conf., Institut Int. d'Etudes Bancaires.

STRÅBERG, Hans, MSE; Swedish business executive; *Chairman, Atlas Copco AB;* b. 22 Feb. 1957, Västervik; m.; two c.; ed Chalmers Univ. of Technology, Gothenborg; early position as Asst to Scientific Counsellor, Swedish Embassy in Washington, DC; joined AB Electrolux 1983, held various exec. positions including Exec. Vice-Pres. of Operations at American subsidiary Frigidaire Home Appliances –1998, Exec. Vice-Pres. Electrolux Group and Pres. Floor Care and Light Appliances Business Sector 1998, Pres. and CEO 2002–10; Chair. Atlas Copco AB 2014–; mem. Bd of Dirs Stora Enso Oyj 2009–, Investor AB 2011–, Mellby Gård AB, Nederman Holding AB, Roxtec AB (Chair.) CTEK AB (Chair.), Nikkarit Holding AB (Chair.), Orchid Orthopedics Inc. (Chair.), Asscn of Swedish Eng Industries; mem. Royal Swedish Acad. of Eng Sciences (IVA). *Leisure interests:* tennis, hunting, cars, family. *Address:* Atlas Copco AB, 105 23 Stockholm, Sweden (office). *Website:* www.atlascopco.com (office).

STRACHAN, Sir Ian Charles, Kt, MA, MPA; British business executive; b. 7 April 1943, Oldham; s. of Dr Charles Strachan and Margaret Craig; m. 1st Diane Shafer 1967 (divorced 1987); one d.; m. 2nd Margaret Auchincloss 1987; one step-s. one step-d.; ed Fettes Coll. Edinburgh, Christ's Coll., Cambridge and Princeton and Harvard Univs, USA; Assoc., Ford Foundation, Malaysia 1967–69; various positions in Exxon Corpn 1970–86; Sr Vice-Pres. and Chief Financial Officer, Johnson & Higgins, New York 1986–87; Finance Dir RTZ Corpn PLC (now Rio Tinto) 1987–91, Deputy Chief Exec. 1991–95; Man. Dir BTR PLC July–Dec. 1995, Chief Exec. 1996–99; Deputy Chair. Invensys PLC 1999–2000; Chair. Instinet Group LLC 2003–05; mem. Bd of Dirs (non-exec.) Transocean Inc. 2000–, Johnson Matthey PLC, Xstrata PLC 2003–, Rolls-Royce Group PLC, Commercial Union 1992–95, Thomson-Reuters PLC 2000–. *Leisure interests:* tennis, golf, reading, oriental antiques.

STRACHE, Heinz-Christian; Austrian politician; *Vice-Chancellor;* b. 12 June 1969, Vienna; divorced; two c.; trained as a dental technician; Chair. Freiheitliche Partei Österreichs (FPÖ—Die Freiheitlichen) (Freedom Party) 2005–; mem. Nationalist 2006–, Chair. Parl. Group of FPÖ; Vice-Chancellor 2017–, Fed. Minister for Public Service and Sports 2018–. *Address:* Federal Ministry of Public Service and Sports, Minoritenpl. 3, 1010 Vienna (office); Freiheitliche Partei Österreichs (Die Freiheitlichen), Friedrich–Schmidt Pl. 4, 1080 Vienna, Austria (office). *Telephone:* (1) 531-15-0 (office). *E-mail:* heinz-christian.strache@parlament.gv.at (office); hc.strache@fpoe.at (office); buergerservice@bmoeds.gv.at. *Website:* www.parlament.gv.at (office); www.fpoe.at (office); www.bmoeds.gv.at.

STRAHL, Charles (Chuck); Canadian politician (retd); b. 1957, British Columbia; m. Deb Strahl 1975; four c.; ed Trinity Western Univ.; fmr partner in road construction and logging contracting firm; elected MP 1993 as Reform Party mem., re-elected 1997 (Reform Party), 2000 (Canadian Alliance), 2004, 2006 (Conservative Party), represented constituencies of Fraser Valley East 1993–97, Fraser Valley 1997–2004, Chilliwack—Fraser Canyon 2004–11; fmr Official Opposition Whip and House Leader; Deputy Speaker of House and Chair., Cttees of the Whole 2004; Minister of Agric. and Agri-Food and Minister for Canadian Wheat Bd 2006–07, of Indian Affairs and Northern Devt and Federal Interlocutor for Métis and Non-Status Indians 2007–10, of Transport, Infrastructure and Communities 2010–11 (retd); f. Chuck Strahl Consulting. *Address:* Chuck Strahl Consulting, 5100 Farnham Road, Chilliwack, BC V4Z 1E7, Canada. *Website:* www.chuckstrahl.com (home).

STRAHLMAN, Ellen, MD, MHSc; American ophthalmologist and pharmaceutical industry executive; *Chief Medical Officer and Senior Vice-President, Research & Development, BD (Becton, Dickinson and Company);* ed Harvard Univ., Johns Hopkins Univ. School of Medicine, Bloomberg School of Public Health; fmr CEO Virogen Ltd; fmr Chief Medical Officer and Global Head of Research and Devt, Bausch & Lomb; fmr Sr Medical Officer, Nat. Eye Inst., NIH; fmrly held sr positions at Merck and Novartis; Vice-Pres. of Licensing and Worldwide Business Devt, Pfizer –2008; Chief Medical Officer, GlaxoSmithKline North American Pharmaceuticals 2008–13, also Global Head, Neglected Tropical Diseases; Chief Medical Officer and Sr Vice-Pres., Research and Devt, BD (Becton, Dickinson and Co.) 2013–; mem. Bd of Dirs Syncona Partners LLP; mem. Columbia Univ. Medical and Science Tech. Council; Bd mem. Foundation of American Acad. of Ophthalmology; mem. Health Advisory Bd Johns Hopkins Bloomberg School of Public Health. *Address:* BD (Becton, Dickinson and Company), 1 Becton Drive, Franklin Lakes, NJ 07417, USA (office). *Telephone:* (201) 847-6800 (office). *Website:* www.bd.com (office).

STRAKER, Sir Louis, BA, MA, KCMG; Saint Vincent and the Grenadines politician; *Minister of Foreign Affairs, Foreign Trade and Consumer Affairs;* b. 23 Feb. 1944, Layou; ed Hunter Coll., City Univ. of New York, Long Island Univ., USA; 25 years with Chemical Bank of New York (now Chase Manhattan); MP for Central Leeward Constituency 1994–; Deputy Prime Minister of Saint Vincent and the Grenadines, Minister of Foreign Affairs, Commerce and Trade 2001–05, Deputy Prime Minister and Minister of Transport, Works and Housing May–Dec. 2005; Deputy Prime Minister 2005–10, 2015–, Minister of Foreign Affairs, Commerce and Trade 2005–10, 2015–; mem. Unity Labour Party. *Address:* Ministry of Foreign Affairs, Foreign Trade and Consumer Affairs, Administrative Building, 3rd Floor, Bay Street, Kingstown, St Vincent and the Grenadines (office). *Telephone:* 456-2060 (office). *Fax:* 456-2610 (office). *E-mail:* office.foreignaffairs@mail.gov.vc (office). *Website:* www.foreign.gov.vc (office).

STRANGE, Curtis Northrop; American professional golfer; b. 30 Jan. 1955, Norfolk, Va; s. of Thomas Wright Strange, Jr and Nancy Neal; m. Sarah Jones; two s.; ed Wake Forest Univ.; turned professional 1976; won Pensacola Open 1979, Sammy Davis Jr Greater Hartford Open 1983, LaJel Classic 1984, Honda Classic, Panasonic-Las Vegas Int. 1985, Canadian Open 1985, Houston Open 1986, Canadian Open, Fed. Express-St Jude Classic, NEC Series of Golf 1987, Sandway Cove Classic, Australia 1988, Ind. Insurance Agent Open, Memorial Tournament, US Open, Nabisco Championships 1988, US Open, Palm Meadows Cup, Australia 1989, Holden Classic, Australia 1993; mem. PGA Tour Charity Team, Michelob Championship, Kingsmill 1996; Capt. US Ryder Cup Team 2002 after playing on five Ryder Cup Teams; golf analyst for ABC Sports 1997–2004; Champions Tour 2005–; Golfer of the Year 1986, 1987, inducted into Virginia Sports Hall of Fame 2004, World Golf Hall of Fame 2007, Hampton Roads Sports Hall of Fame 2009. *Leisure interests:* hunting, fishing, Harley-Davidson motorcycles.

STRANGE, Luther Johnson, III, BA, JD; American lawyer and politician; b. 1 March 1953, Birmingham, Ala; m. Melissa Strange; two s.; ed Tulane Univ. Law School; lawyer with Sonat Offshore (subsidiary of Sonat, Inc., natural gas utility) 1980–85, Head, Sonat Office in Washington, DC 1985–94; registered lobbyist for Sonat and Transocean Offshore Drilling Co., Washington, DC 1980s and 1990s; admitted to Alabama Bar 1981; fmr Partner, Bradley Arant Boult Cummings LLP; f. Strange LLC (law firm), Birmingham, Ala; Attorney Gen. of Alabama 2011–17; Senator from Alabama 2017–18; mem. Republican Attorneys Gen. Asscn (Chair. 2016–17); Republican. *Address:* c/o G-12 Dirksen Senate Office Building, Washington, DC 20510, USA (office).

STRANGFELD, John R., Jr, BS, MBA; American business executive; *Chairman and CEO, Prudential Financial, Inc.;* b. 27 Dec. 1953; m. Mary Kay Strangfeld; ed Susquehanna Univ., Darden School of Business, Univ. of Virginia; joined Prudential 1977, served in various exec. positions, including Chair. PRICOA Capital Group, London, UK 1989–95, Sr Man. Dir, Pvt. Asset Man. Group 1995–98, CEO Prudential Investment Man. of Prudential Insurance 1998–2002, Chair. and CEO Prudential Securities (renamed Prudential Equity Group LLC) 2000, Exec. Vice-Pres. Prudential Financial 2001–02, Vice-Chair. Prudential Financial, Inc. 2002–07, Pres. and CEO 2007–08, mem. Bd Dirs, Chair. and CEO 2008–; mem. Bd of Mans Wachovia Securities Financial Holdings LLC (jt venture of Prudential and Wachovia) 2003–; mem. Financial Services Forum, Financial Services Roundtable, Business Roundtable, Geneva Asscn, American Council of Life Insurers; mem. Exec. Cttee of the Bd of Dirs New Jersey Performing Arts Center, Newark; Vice-Chair. Bd of Trustees, Susquehanna Univ.; Pres. Bd of Trustees, Darden Foundation, Univ. of Virginia. *Address:* Prudential Financial, Inc., 751 Broad Street, Newark, NJ 07102-3777, USA (office). *Telephone:* (973) 802-6000 (office). *Fax:* (973) 802-4479 (office). *E-mail:* info@prudential.com (office). *Website:* www.prudential.com (office).

STRASBURGER, Baron (Life Peer), cr. 2011, of Langridge in the County of Somerset; **Paul Strasburger;** British business executive and philanthropist; m. Evelyn S. Strasburger; f. Safe Estates Services Ltd; mem. Bd of Dirs 12 Queen's Parade Management Company Ltd, 7 Southcot Place Ltd, 14 Cavendish Crescent (Bath) Ltd, Reside Bath Ltd (residential letting agency); mem. Liberal Democrat party. *Address:* House of Lords, Westminster, London, SW1A 0PW, England (office). *Telephone:* (20) 7219-5081 (office). *E-mail:* strasburgerp@parliament.uk.

STRATAN, Cosmina; Romanian actress and journalist; b. 20 Oct. 1984, Iaşi; ed Nat. Univ. of Acting and Cinematography; worked as a journalist for Antena 3. *Theatre includes:* Lear (Shakespeare) 2012. *Films include:* Beyond the Hills (Best Actress Award (jtly with Cristina Flutur), Cannes Film Festival) 2012, Prologen (short) 2015. *Television includes:* Cinema 3 (series) 2012, Rămâi cu mine (series) 2013–14. *Address:* Das Imperium Talent Agency, Mitte, 10119 Berlin, Germany (office). *Telephone:* (30) 28879520 (office); (151) 19324297 (office). *E-mail:* manuel@dasimperium.com (office). *Website:* www.dasimperium.com/de/actor/3223 (office).

STRATHAIRN, David Russell; American actor; b. 26 Jan. 1949, San Francisco, Calif.; s. of Thomas Scott Strathairn, Jr and Mary Frances Strathairn (née Frazier); m. Logan Goodma 1980; two s.; ed Redwood High School, Larkspur, Calif., Williams Coll.; studied clowning at the Ringling Brothers and Barnum & Bailey Clown Coll., Venice, Fla; worked briefly as a clown in a travelling circus. *Theatre includes:* has performed several roles in stage plays by Harold Pinter, including two consecutive New York Classic Stage Co. (CSC) productions of The Birthday Party 1988, 1989 and dual roles of Prison Officer and Prisoner in Mountain Language 1989; workshop production of A House Divided by W. Stuart McDowell at The Players 1989; Kerner in Tom Stoppard's Hapgood 1994; Devlin in Pinter's Ashes to Ashes in New York premiere by the Roundabout Theatre Co. 1999. *Films include:* Return of the Secaucus Seven 1979, Lovesick 1983, Enormous Changes at the Last Minute 1983, Silkwood, Iceman 1984, The Brother from Another Planet 1984, When Nature Calls 1985, At Close Range 1986, Matewan 1987, Nicky and Gino 1988, Stars and Bars 1988, Call Me 1988, Eight Men Out 1988, The Feud 1989, Memphis Belle 1990, City of Hope 1991, Big Girls Don't Cry… They Get Even 1992, A League of Their Own 1992, Bob Roberts 1992, Sneakers 1992, Passion Fish 1992, Stand Off 1993, Lost in Yonkers 1993, The River Wild 1994, Losing Isaiah 1995, Dolores Claiborne 1995, Home for the Holidays 1995, Mother Night 1996, Song of Hiawatha 1997, L.A. Confidential 1997, Bad Manners 1997, The Climb 1998, With Friends Like These… 1998, Simon Birch 1998, Meschugge 1998, A Midsummer Night's Dream 1999, Limbo 1999, A Map of the World 1999, A Good Baby 2000, Harrison's Flowers 2000, The Victim (short) 2001, Ball in the House 2001, Speakeasy 2002, Blue Car 2002, The Root 2003, Twisted 2004, Missing in America 2005, Good Night, and Good Luck (Best Actor, Venice Int. Film Festival 2005) 2005, The Notorious Bettie Page 2005, Steel Toes 2006, The Shovel (short) 2006, Heavens Fall 2006, The Sensation of Sight 2006, We Are Marshall 2006, Fracture 2007, Racing Daylight 2007, My Blueberry Nights 2007, The Bourne Ultimatum 2007, Matters of Life and Death (short) 2007, The Spiderwick Chronicles 2008, Kisses Over Babylon (short) 2009, Cold Souls 2009, The Uninvited 2009, Howl 2010, The Tempest 2010, The Whistleblower 2010, No God, No Master 2012, The Bourne Legacy 2012, Lincoln 2012, Maladies 2013, Godzilla 2014, The Second Best Exotic Marigold Hotel 2015, Louder Than Bombs 2015, American Pastoral 2016, November Criminals 2017, An Interview with God 2018. *Television includes:* Miami Vice (series) – Out Where the Buses Don't Run 1985, Broken Vows (film) 1987, Spenser: For Hire (series) – One for My Daughter 1987, Another World (series) 1987, The Days and Nights of Molly Dodd (series) 1988–91, The Equalizer (series) – Sea of Fire 1988, Day One (film) 1989, Wiseguy (series) 1990, Heat Wave (film) 1990, Judgment (film) 1990, Son of the Morning Star (film) 1991, Without Warning: The James Brady Story (film) 1991, Lethal Innocence (film) 1991, O Pioneers! (film) 1992, The American Clock (film) 1993, American Masters (series documentary) (narrator) 1993–2005, Beyond the Call (film) 1996, In the Gloaming (film) 1997, Evidence of Blood (film) 1998, Freedom Song (film) 2000, The Miracle Worker (film) 2000, Big Apple (series) 2001, Lathe of Heaven (film) 2002, Master Spy: The Robert Hanssen Story (film) 2002, Paradise (film) 2004, The Sopranos (series) 2004, Take 3 (film) 2006, The Supreme Court (series) (narrator) 2007, Monk (series) – Mr. Monk and the Genius 2008, The American Experience (series documentary) – The Trials of J. Robert Oppenheimer 2009, Matadors (film) 2010, Temple Grandin (film) (Outstanding Supporting Actor in a Miniseries or a Movie, Acad. of Television Arts and Sciences 2010) 2010, House (series) – Lockdown 2010, Alphas (series) 2011–12, Hemingway & Gellhorn (film) 2012, Clementine 2014, Great Decisions 2014–18, The Blacklist 2015–16, Z: The Beginning of Everything 2015–17, Billions 2017–18, McMafia 2018, The Expanse 2018. *Address:* c/o Celebrity Talent International, PO Box 2240, Carlsbad, CA 92018, USA (office).

STRATHCLYDE, 2nd Baron, cr. 1955; **Rt Hon. Thomas Galloway Dunlop du Roy de Blicquy Galbraith,** PC; British politician; b. 22 Feb. 1960, Glasgow, Scotland; s. of The Hon. Sir Thomas (Tam) Galbraith, KBE and Simone Galbraith (née du Roy de Blicquy); m. Jane Skinner 1992; three d.; ed Sussex House, London, Wellington Coll., Univs of East Anglia and Aix-en-Provence; insurance broker, Bain Clarkson Ltd (fmrly Bain Dawes) 1982–88; Conservative cand. in European Election, Merseyside E 1984; Govt Whip, House of Lords 1988–89; Govt Spokesman for Dept of Trade and Industry 1988–89, Parl. Under-Sec. of State Dept of Employment (Tourism) 1989–90, Dept of Environment July–Sept. 1990, 1992, Scottish Office 1990–92; Minister for Agric., Fisheries, Highlands and Islands 1990–92; Chief Govt Whip 1994–97, Opposition Chief Whip 1997–98, Deputy Speaker 1997–98, Leader of the Opposition 1998–2010, Leader of the House of Lords 2010–13; Chancellor of the Duchy of Lancaster 2010–13; Dir, Auchendrane Estates Ltd; Gov., Wellington Coll., Berks. *Address:* House of Lords, Westminster, London, SW1A 0PW, England (office). *Telephone:* (20) 7219-5353 (office). *Fax:* (20) 7219-3051 (office).

STRAUB, Elek, BEng; Hungarian business executive; *Managing Partner and Chairman, Day One Capital Venture Capital Fund Management Ltd;* b. 1944; ed Budapest Tech. Univ.; Head of Information Tech. Dept, Ministry of Labour 1970–80; Head of Information Tech. Div. and later Vice-Pres., Cen. Statistical Office 1980–90, also Govt Adviser, Information Tech. Devt Cttee; Gen. Man. IBM Hungary 1990–95; CEO Matáv 1995–2005, mem. Bd 1995–2005, Chair. 1996–2000, Chair. Man. Cttee 2000–05, (Matáv renamed Magyar Telekom 2005), Chair. and CEO Magyar Telekom 2005–06 (resgnd); Man. Partner and Chair. Day One Capital Venture Capital Fund Management Ltd, Budapest 2010–; Pres. Hungarian Yachting Asscn 2005–12; Chair. German-Hungarian Chamber of Commerce 2004–06; mem. Bd of Dirs Graphisoft SE; 1st Class Cross of Distinction of Order (FRG) 2004, Order of Merit of Republic of Hungary, Officer's Cross 2004. *Address:* Day One Capital Venture Capital Fund Management Ltd, 1123 Budapest, Alkotás utca 53, Hungary MOM Park Building B, 5th floor, Hungary (office). *E-mail:* info@dayonecapital.com (office). *Website:* www.dayonecapital.com (office).

STRAUJUMA, Laimdota; Latvian economist, politician and government official; b. 24 Feb. 1951; ed Univ. of Latvia; Deputy Dir, Latvian Agricultural Consulting and Educational Support Centre 1993–97, Dir 1997–98; Deputy State Sec., Ministry of Agric. 1999–2000, State Sec. 2000–06, 2007–10; mem. Bd, Latvijas Hipotēku un zemes banka 2002–07; Deputy State Sec., Ministry of the Environment and Regional Devt 2010–11; mem. Tautas Partija (People's Party) 1998–2014, Vienotība (Unity) 2014–; Minister of Agric. 2011–14; Prime Minister of Latvia 2014–16 (resgnd); mem. Latvian Acad. of Sciences. *Address:* Saeima, Jēkaba iela 11, Rīga 1811, Latvia (office). *Telephone:* 6708-7321 (office). *Fax:* 6708-7100 (office). *E-mail:* info@saeima.lv (office). *Website:* www.saeima.lv (office).

STRAUME, Janis; Latvian physician and politician; b. 1962, Sigulda; m.; one s. two d.; ed Rīga State Medical Inst.; physician, Riga City clinic, endoscopist, Latvian Diagnostics Centre 1986–90; mem. Latvian Human Rights Group Helsinki 86 (Rīga Chapter), Latvian Nat. Independence Movt, Citizen's Congress of Latvian Repub., Union of 18th Nov.; mem. Saeima 1990–2006, Chair. (Speaker) 1998–2002, Deputy Chair. 2002–06, mem. Foreign Affairs Cttee, Nat. Security Cttee; Chair. Union for Fatherland and Freedom Faction (LNNK) 1998–2002, For Fatherland and Freedom Union/Latvian Nat. Independence Movt (TB/LNNK) 2002–06.

STRAUSS, Andrew John, OBE, MBE; British (b. South African) fmr professional cricketer; b. 2 March 1977, Johannesburg, Transvaal, South Africa; m. Ruth McDonald 2003 (died 2018); one s. one d.; ed Caulfield Grammar School, Melbourne, Australia, Caldicott School, Radley Coll., Hatfield Coll., Durham Univ.; moved to England aged six; left-handed opening batsman; left-arm medium bowler; played for Durham Univ. cricket team and Middx second XI; played for Middx 1998–2012 (Capt. 2002–04), MCC 2002, Northern Dists 2007–08, England 2004–12 (Test Capt. 2006 (deputized), 2009–12, ODI Capt. –2011); First-class debut: 1998; Test debut: England v New Zealand, Lord's 20–24 May 2004; One-Day Int. (ODI) debut: Sri Lanka v England at Dambulla 18 Nov. 2003; T20I debut: England v Australia, Southampton 13 June 2005; played in 100 Tests and scored 7,037 runs (21 centuries and 27 fifties), highest score 177, average 40.91; ODIs: 127 matches, scored 4,205 runs, average 35.63, highest score 158; First-class: 241 matches, 17,046 runs, average 42.72, highest score 241 not out; first England batsman to score two centuries in a Test in India 2008; only second England capt. in two decades to regain the Ashes 2009; Capt. England Ashes-winning Test team 2009, 2010–11; set record for most catches (121) by an outfield player for England Aug. 2012, later surpassed by Alastair Cook; announced retirement from all forms of the game 29 Aug. 2012; commentator, Sky TV cricket 2013–15; Dir of England Cricket 2015–18; Pres. Primary Club Juniors (charity that helps fund blind cricket). *Address:* c/o England and Wales Cricket Board, Lord's Cricket Ground, London, NW8 8QZ, England (office). *Telephone:* (20) 7432-1200 (office). *Fax:* (20) 7286-5583 (office). *Website:* www.ecb.co.uk (office).

STRAUSS, Botho; German playwright and novelist; b. 2 Dec. 1944, Naumburg; s. of Eduard Strauss; ed Cologne and Munich; moved with family to Remscheid, Ruhr region; ed. and critic, Theater Heute periodical 1967–70; dramaturg, Schaubühne Theater, West Berlin 1970–75; mem. PEN; Schiller Prize Baden-Württemberg 1977, Literaturpreis, Bayerische Akademie der Schönen Künste 1981, Mülheimer Drama Prize 1982, Jean Paul Prize 1987, Georg Büchner Prize 1989, Berlin Theatre Prize 1993, Lessing Prize 2001, Schiller Memorial Prize 2007. *Plays include:* Die Hypochonder (first play, 1971, winner Hannover Dramaturgie Award), Trilogie des Wiedersehens 1976, Gross und Klein 1978, Kalldeway Farce 1981, Der Park 1983, Das Gleichgewicht 1994, Theaterstücke in zwei Banden 1994. *Publications:* Bekannte Gesichter, gemischte Gefühle (jtly) 1974, Die Widmung (novel) 1979, Rumor (novel) 1980, Paare, Passanten (novel) 1981, Der Junge Mann (novel) 1984, Diese Erinnerung an einen, der nur einen Tag zu Gast War 1985, Die Fremdenführerin 1986, Niemand Anderes (novel) 1987, Besucher 1988, Kongress: Die Kette der Demütigungen 1989, Beginnlosigkeit. Reflexionen 1992, Anschwellender 1993, Wohnen Dammern Lügen 1994, Die Fehler des Kopisten 1997, Das Partikular 2000, Der Narr und seine Frau heute abend in Pancomedia 2001, Die Nacht mit Alice, als Julia ums Haus schlich 2003, Der Untenstehende auf Zehenspitzen 2004, Mikado 2006, Herkunft 2014, Allein mit allen: Gedankenbuch 2014, Oniritti Höhlenbilder 2016, Sieben Nächte 2017, Der Fortführer 2018. *Address:* c/o Rowohlt Verlag, Hamburger Straße 17, 21465 Reinbek, Germany.

STRAUSS-KAHN, Dominique Gaston André; French economist, lawyer, politician and international organization executive; b. 25 April 1949, Neuilly-sur-Seine; s. of Gilbert Strauss-Kahn and Jacqueline Fellus; m. 3rd Anne Sinclair 1991; one s. three d. from fmr marriages; ed Paris Inst. for Political Studies, École des Hautes Études Commerciales; Lecturer, Univ. of Nancy II 1977–80; Scientific Counsellor Nat. Inst. of Statistics and Econ. Studies (INSEE) 1978–80; Dir Cerepi (CNRS) 1980–; Prof., Univ. of Paris-X Nanterre 1981; Chief of Financial Services Commissariat Gen., Plan, Asst Commr Plan 1984–86; elected Socialist Deputy Val-d'Oise 1988–91, 1997, 2001–02; Pres. of Comm. on Finances, Assemblée Nationale 1988, Minister Del. of Industry and Foreign Trade to the Minister of State, Minister of the Economy, Finance and Budget 1991–92; Minister of Industry and Foreign Commerce under Minister of Economy, Finance and Budget 1992–93, Minister of Economy, Finance and Industry 1997–99; mem. Socialist Party Cttee of Dirs 1983, Nat. Sec. 1984–89, mem. Socialist Party Bureau 1995; Mayor of City of Sorcelles (Val d'Oise) 1995–97; apptd First Deputy Mayor 1997; Chair. Scientific Cttee Jean-Jaurès Foundation 2000; Special Councellor to Sec.-Gen. OECD 2000; Visiting Prof., Stanford Univ., USA 2000–01; fmr Dir of Research, Paris Inst. of Political Studies and Prof. of Econs; fmr Prof., École des Hautes Études Commerciales (HEC School of Man.); Co-founder À gauche en Europe (think-tank) 2003; Chair. Exec. Bd and Man. Dir IMF 2007–11 (resgnd); unsuccessful cand. for Socialist Party nomination in presidential election 2007; Head of Bilderberg Group 2010; mem. Supervisory Bd Bank Credit-Dnepr, Ukraine 2016–. *Publications include:* Inflation et partage des surplus: le cas des ménages (co-author) 1975, La richesse des Français 1977, Économie de la famille et accumulation patrimoniale 1977, L'epargne et la retraite 1982, Pierre Bérégovoy: une volonté de réforme au service de l'économie 1984–1993 2000, La Flamme et la Cendre 2002, Pour l'égalité réelle: Eléments pour un réformisme radical 2004, Lettre ouverte aux enfants d'Europe 2004, DVD pour le Oui à la constitution 2005, 365 jours, journal contre le renoncement 2006. *Leisure interests:* piano, cinema, skiing, rugby.

STRAUSS-LAHAT, Ofra, LLB; Israeli business executive; *Chairperson, Strauss Group;* b. 22 Aug. 1960; ed Tel-Aviv Univ.; began career in int. marketing services and training programme at Estée Lauder, USA, Area and Marketing Man. 1987–89; joined family-owned Strauss Ice-cream Co. 1989, Organized Market Man., Strauss Sales Div. 1989–90, Marketing Man. 1991–93, Gen. Man. Strauss Salads 1993–95, Deputy Pres. and CEO 1996–2001, Chair. 2001–04, Chair. Strauss Group 2004–; Chair. Ametz Lochem 1992–97; mem. Supervisory Bd Numico NV 2006–; Chair. Donations Apparatus, WIZO Israel 1995; Co-Chair. Israel, United Jewish Communities Gen. Ass.; mem. Bd of Trustees, The Jewish Agency for Israel, Chair. Babayit Beyachad project 2005. *Address:* Strauss Group, 84 Arlozorov Street, PO Box 19, 52100 Ramat Gan (office); 49 Hasivim Street, PO Box 194, 49517 Petach Tikva, Israel (office). *Telephone:* (3) 6752111 (office). *Fax:* (3) 6752366 (office). *E-mail:* peril@elite.co.il (office); Service@Strauss-Group.com (office). *Website:* www.elite.co.il (office).

STRAW, John (Jack) Whitaker; British lawyer and politician; b. 3 Aug. 1946, Buckhurst Hill, Essex, England; s. of Walter A. W. Straw and Joan S. Straw; m. 1st Anthea L. Weston 1968 (divorced 1978); one d. (deceased); m. 2nd Alice E. Perkins 1978; one s. one d.; ed Brentwood School, Univ. of Essex and Univ. of Leeds School of Law; Pres. Nat. Union of Students 1969–71; mem. Islington Borough Council 1971–78, Inner London Educ. Authority 1971–74 (Deputy Leader 1973–74); called to Bar, Inner Temple 1972, Bencher 1997, practised as barrister 1972–74; special adviser to Sec. of State for Social Services 1974–76, to Sec. of State for Environment 1976–77; on staff of Granada TV (World in Action) 1977–79; MP for Blackburn 1979–2015; Opposition Treasury Spokesman 1980–83, Environment 1983–87; mem. Parl. Cttee of Labour Party (Shadow Cabinet) 1987–97; Shadow Sec. of State for Educ. 1987–92, for the Environment (Local Govt) 1992–94; Shadow Home Sec. 1994–97; Home Sec. 1997–2001; Sec. of State for Foreign and Commonwealth Affairs 2001–06; Leader of the House of Commons and Lord Privy Seal 2006–07; Lord Chancellor and Sec. of State for Justice 2007–10; mem. Council, Inst. for Fiscal Studies 1983–2000, Lancaster Univ. 1989–92; Vice-Pres. Asscn of District Councils; Visiting Fellow, Nuffield Coll. Oxford 1990–98; Visiting Prof., Univ. Coll. London 2011–; Gov. Blackburn Coll. 1990–, Pimlico School 1994–2000 (Chair. 1995–98); Fellow, Royal Statistical Soc. 1995; Labour; Hon. LLD (Leeds) 1999, (Brunel) 2007. *Publications:* Policy and Ideology 1993, Last Man Standing 2012; contribs to pamphlets, newspaper articles. *Leisure interests:* walking, cooking puddings, music. *E-mail:* jack.straw@blackburnlabour.org.

STREEP, Meryl (Mary Louise), AB, MFA; American actress; b. 22 June 1949, Summit, NJ; d. of Harry Streep, Jr and Mary W. Streep; partner John Cazale 1976 (died 1978); m. Donald J. Gummer 1978; one s. three d.; ed Vassar Coll., Yale School of Drama, singing studies with Estelle Liebling; professional acting debut in New York in The Playboy of Seville at Cubiculo Theatre 1971; Broadway debut in New York in Trelawny of the Wells at Vivian Beaumont Theater, Lincoln Center 1975; appeared in 27 Wagons Full of Cotton, New York 1976; took part in Henry V and Measure for Measure at New York Shakespeare Festival 1976; also acted in Happy End (musical), The Taming of the Shrew, Wonderland (musical), Taken in Marriage and numerous other plays; Hon. mem. American Acad. of Arts and Letters 2010; Officer, Ordre des Arts et des Lettres 2000, Commdr, Ordre des Arts et des Lettres 2003; Dr hc (Dartmouth) 1981, (Yale) 1983, (Lafayette) 1985; Hon. DFA (Princeton) 2009; Hon. Dr of Arts (Harvard) 2010; People's Choice Award for Favorite Motion Picture Actress 1984–90, Favorite All-Around Female Entertainer 1986, World-Favorite Motion Picture Actress 1990, Aftonbladet TV Prize for Best Foreign TV Personality – Female (Bästa utländska kvinna) 1987, received a star on the Hollywood Walk of Fame 1998, Women in Film Crystal Award 1998, Bette Davis Lifetime Achievement Award 1998, Special Award, Berlin Int. Film Festival 1999, Hon. César Award, Acad. des Arts et Techniques du Cinéma 2003, American Film Inst. Lifetime Achievement Award 2004, Stanislavsky Award, Moscow Int. Film Festival 2004, 27 May 2004 proclaimed 'Meryl Streep Day' by Manhattan Borough Pres. C. Virginia Fields 2004, inducted into New Jersey Hall of Fame 2008, Honoree, 34th Annual Kennedy Center Honors 2011, Hon. Golden Bear, Berlin Int. Film Festival 2012, Presidential Medal of Freedom 2014, Cecil B. DeMille Award, Golden Globe Awards, Hollywood Foreign Press Asscn 2017. *Plays include:* The Playboy of Seville 1971, Trelawny of the Wells 1975, Measure for Measure 1976, 27 Wagons Full of Cotton 1976, A Memory of Two Mondays 1976, Alice in Concert 1978, 1980–81, The Seagull 2001, Mother Courage and her Children 2006, Soho Rep Spring Gala 2007. *Films include:* Julia 1976, The Deer Hunter (Best Supporting Actress Award from Nat. Soc. of Film Critics) 1978, Manhattan 1979, The Seduction of Joe Tynan (New York Film Critics Circle Award for Best Supporting Actress) 1979, The Senator 1979, Kramer vs. Kramer (New York Film Critics Circle Award for Best Supporting Actress 1979, Acad. Award for Best Supporting Actress 1980, Golden Globe Award for Best Motion Picture Actress in a Supporting Role 1980) 1979, The French Lieutenant's Woman 1981 (BAFTA Film Award for Best Actress 1982), Sophie's Choice (New York Film Critics Circle Award for Best Actress 1982, Acad. Award for Best Actress in a Leading Role 1983, Golden Globe Award for Best Actress in a Motion Picture – Drama 1983) 1982, Still of the Night 1982, Silkwood 1983, Plenty 1984, Falling in Love 1984, Out of Africa 1985, Heartburn 1985, Ironweed 1987, A Cry in the Dark (Best Actress Award, New York Critics 1988, Cannes 1989) 1988, Evil Angels (Best Actress, Cannes Film Festival 1989) 1988, The Lives and Loves of a She Devil 1989, Hollywood and Me 1989, Postcards from the Edge 1991, Defending Your Life 1991, Death Becomes Her 1992, The House of the Spirits, The River Wild 1994, The Bridges of Madison County 1995, Before and After, Marvin's Room, One True Thing 1998, Dancing at Lughnasa 1999, Music of the Heart 1999, The Hours 2002 (Silver Berlin Bear Award for Best Actress with Nicole Kidman and Julianne Moore), Adaptation (Golden Globe for Best Supporting Actress 2003) 2002, The Manchurian Candidate 2004, Lemony Snicket's A Series of Unfortunate Events 2004, Prime 2005, The Ant Bully (voice) 2006, The Devil Wears Prada (Golden Globe for Best Actress Musical or Comedy 2007) 2006, A Prairie Home Companion (Best Supporting Actress Nat. Soc. of Film Critics 2007, Best Actress, London Film Critics' Circle Awards 2007) 2006, Evening 2007, Rendition 2007, Lions for Lambs 2007, Mamma Mia! 2008, Doubt 2008, Julie and Julia (Golden Globe for Best Performance by an Actress in a Motion Picture—Comedy or Musical 2010) 2009, Fantastic Mr Fox (voice) 2009, It's Complicated 2009, Higglety Pigglety Pop! or There Must Be More to Life (video short) (voice) 2010, The Iron Lady (Golden Globe Award for Best Performance by an Actress in a Motion Picture – Drama 2012, BAFTA Film Award for Leading Actress 2012, Australian Acad. of Cinema and Television Arts Int. Award 2011, Acad. Award for Best Performance by an Actress in a Leading Role 2012) 2011, Hope Springs 2012, To the Arctic 3D (documentary) (narrator) 2012, August: Osage County 2013, The Homesman 2014, Into the Woods 2014, Ricki and the Flash 2015, Suffragette 2015, Florence Foster Jenkins 2016, The Post 2017. *Television includes:* The Deadliest Season 1977, Holocaust (Emmy Award) 1978, Uncommon Women 1979, Velveteen Rabbit, First Do No Harm 1997, Angels in America (Golden Globe for Best Actress in a Miniseries or TV Movie 2004, Screen Actors Guild Award for Best Actress in a Miniseries 2004, Emmy Award for Outstanding Lead Actress in a Miniseries or Movie 2004) 2003, Web Therapy (series) 2012. *Leisure interests:* peace and anti-nuclear causes, gardening, skiing, raising family, visiting art galleries and museums. *Address:* c/o Kevin S. Huvane, Creative Artists Agency, 2000 Avenue of the Stars, Los Angeles, CA 90067, USA (office). *Telephone:* (424) 288-2000 (office). *Fax:* (424) 288-2900 (office). *Website:* www.caa.com (office).

STREET, Hon. Anthony Austin; Australian business executive and fmr politician; b. 8 Feb. 1926, Melbourne, Vic.; s. of Brig. the Hon. Geoffrey Austin Street, MC and Evora Francis Street (née Currie); m. Valerie Erica Rickard 1951; three s.; ed Melbourne Grammar; Royal Australian Navy; primary producer; mem. for Corangamite, House of Reps 1966–84; Sec. Govt Mems Defence and Wool Cttees 1967–71; mem. Jt Parl. Cttee on Foreign Affairs 1969; Chair. Fed. Rural Cttee of Liberal Party 1970–74; mem. Fed. Exec. Council 1971–; Asst Minister for Labour and Nat. Service 1971–72; mem. Liberal Party Shadow Cabinet for Social Security, Health and Welfare 1973, for Primary Industry, Shipping and Transport 1973–74, for Science and Tech. and ACT 1974–75, for Labour 1975; Minister for Labour and Immigration Nov.–Dec. 1975; Minister Assisting the Prime Minister in Public Service Matters 1975–77; Minister for Employment and Industrial Relations 1975–78, for Industrial Relations 1978–80, for Foreign Affairs 1980–83; resgnd from Parl. 1984; now Man. and Co. Dir. *Leisure interests:* flying, cricket, golf, tennis. *Address:* 153 The Terrace, Ocean Grove, Vic. 3226, Australia (home).

STREET-PORTER, Janet, CBE, FRTS; British writer, broadcaster and fmr newspaper editor; b. (Janet Bull), 27 Dec. 1946, London, England; m. 1st Tim Street-Porter 1967 (divorced 1975); m. 2nd A. M. M. Elliott 1976 (divorced 1978); m. 3rd Frank Cvitanovich (divorced 1988, died 1995); ed Lady Margaret Grammar School and Architectural Asscn; columnist, Petticoat Magazine 1968, Daily Mail 1969–71, Evening Standard 1971–73; own show, LBC Radio 1973; presenter of youth programmes, late night talk shows and factual series, London Weekend Television 1975–83; Head of Youth and Entertainment Features, BBC TV 1988–94, Head of Ind. Production for Entertainment 1994; Head of Live TV,

Mirror Group TV 1994–95; Ed. The Independent on Sunday 1999–2001, apptd Ed.-at-Large 2002; presenter, Bloomberg TV 2001–05; currently columnist, Daily Mail. also writes celebrity interviews monthly for Marie Claire magazine; Pres. Ramblers Assn 1994–97 (now Vice-Pres.); Pres. Globetrotters Club; Trustee, Science Museum 2008; Assoc. RIBA; Patron Clerkenwell Green Association, Inst. of Contemporary Arts; Prix Italia 1992, BAFTA Award for Originality 1988, European Cedefop Award (twice), Food and Farming Industry Award 2008. *Theatre includes:* wrote and presented one-woman show All The Rage at Edinburgh Festival 2003, UK tour 2004–05. *Television includes:* as series presenter: London Weekend Show 1975–79, Saturday Night People 1978–80, Six O'Clock Show 1982–83, Design Awards, Travels with Pevsner, Coast to Coast, The Midnight Hour, As The Crow Flies (series), Cathedral Calls, J'Accuse, The Internet, Men Talking, Demolition, The F Word, A Taste of Britain (with Brian Turner) 2014–; presented two series on teaching and nursing for Channel 5 and various documentaries for Sky, The Genius of British Art, Channel 4 2009; writer and producer: The Vampire (opera for BBC 2); as producer: Network 7 (co-producer, Channel 4) 1987; numerous other appearances, including Have I Got News for You, QI, Call Me a Cabbie, So You Think You Can Teach, Celebrity MasterChef 2013, Loose Women 2013–. *Publications:* Scandal 1980, The British Teapot 1981, Coast to Coast 1998, As the Crow Flies 1999, Baggage – My Childhood 2004, Fall Out 2006, Life's too F***ing Short 2008, Don't Let the B*****ds Get You Down 2009. *Leisure interests:* walking, modern art. *Address:* c/o Rosemary Scoular, United Agents, 12–26 Lexington Street, London, W1P 0LE, England (office). *Telephone:* (20) 3214-0893 (office). *E-mail:* rscoular@unitedagents.co.uk (office). *Website:* www.janetstreetporter.com.

STREETER, Stephanie A.; American business executive; b. 19 Sept. 1957; m. Ed Streeter; one s. one d. (twins); ed Stanford Univ.; worked in product devt, market analysis and sales man. for several software and office equipment cos; spent 14 years with Avery Dennison Corpn in a variety of product and business man. positions, including as Group Vice-Pres. of Worldwide Office Products 1996–2000; Pres. and COO Banta Corpn (printing and supply chain man. services) 2001–02, Pres. and CEO 2002–07, Chair. 2004–07 (until its acquisition by R.R. Donnelley & Sons); CEO Libbey Inc. (manufacturer of glassware and tableware) 2011–16; mem. Bd of Dirs US Olympic Cttee 2004–09, Acting CEO 2009–10; mem. Bd of Dirs Kohl's Corpn (Chair. Audit Cttee, mem. Nominating and Governance Cttee) 2007–, Goodyear Tire and Rubber Co. 2008–, Western Digital Corpn (mem. Audit Cttee) 2018–, Olin Corpn 2018–, Green Bay Packers (professional football team), Catalyst. *Address:* c/o Libbey Inc., 300 Madison Avenue, Toledo, OH 43604, USA.

STREIFF, Christian; French aerospace industry executive; *Vice-Chairman, Safran SA;* b. 21 Sept. 1954, Sarrebourg; m.; three c.; ed Ecole Nationale Supérieure de Mines, Paris; joined Saint-Gobain Group 1979, served in various mfg positions and as Corp. Planning Man., Gen. Man. Gevetex GmbH 1988–91, Gen. Man. Vetrerie Italaine SpA, Italy 1991–94, CEO Saint-Gobain Emballage 1994–97, Pres. Pipe Div. and Chair. and CEO Pont-a-Mousson SA 1997–2001, Sr Vice-Pres. Saint-Gobain Group and Pres. Abrasives and Ceramics and Plastics Div. 2001–03, Deputy CEO Saint-Gobain Group 2003–05; Pres. and CEO Airbus S.A.S. July–Oct. 2006 (resgnd); Special Advisor, reporting to Chair. Man. Bd PSA Peugeot Citroën SA 2006–07, Chair. Man. Bd 2007–09; Vice-Chair. Safran SA 2013–; Dir (non-exec.) Thyssen-Krupp AG 2005–, Continental AG 2005–09, Finmeccanica SpA 2011–13, Credit Agricole SA 2011–16; fmr mem. Supervisory Bd Prysmian SpA (Italy). *Publication:* J'étais un homme pressé 2014. *Address:* Safran SA, 2 boulevard du Général Martial-Valin, 75724 Paris Cedex 15, France (office). *Telephone:* 1-40-60-80-80 (office). *Fax:* 1-40-60-81-02 (office). *E-mail:* info@safran-group.com (office). *Website:* www.safran-group.com (office).

STREISAND, Barbra Joan; American singer and actress; b. 24 April 1942, Brooklyn, New York; d. of Emanuel Streisand and Diana Streisand (née Rosen); m. 1st Elliot Gould 1963 (divorced 1971); one s.; m. 2nd James Brolin 1998; ed Erasmus Hall High School; nightclub debut at Bon Soir 1961; appeared in off-Broadway revue Another Evening with Harry Stoones 1961; appeared at Caucus Club, Detroit and Blue Angel, New York 1961; played in musical comedy I Can Get It for You Wholesale 1962; began recording career with Columbia records 1963; appeared in musical play Funny Girl, New York 1964, London 1966; TV programme My Name is Barbra shown in England, Holland, Australia, Sweden, Bermuda and the Philippines, winning five Emmy awards; second programme Color Me Barbra also shown abroad; numerous concert and nightclub appearances; f. Barwood Films (film production co.) 1972; f. Streisand Foundation; Commdr des Arts et Lettres 1984; Dr hc (Hebrew Univ. of Jerusalem) 2013; New York, Critics Best Supporting Actress Award 1962, Grammy Awards for Best Female Pop Vocalist 1963, 1964, 1965, 1977, 1986, London Critics' Musical Award 1966, American Guild of Variety Artists' Entertainer of the Year Award 1970, Nat. Medal of Arts, Emmy Award for Best Individual Performance in a Music or Variety Programme (for Barbra Streisand: Timeless) 2001, American Film Inst. Lifetime Achievement Award 2001, Kennedy Center Honor 2008, Chaplin Award, Film Soc. of Lincoln Center 2013, Presidential Medal of Freedom 2015, Sherry Lansing Leadership Award 2015. *Recordings include:* albums: The Barbra Streisand Album 1963, The Second Barbra Streisand Album 1963, The Third Album 1964, My Name Is Barbra 1965, People 1965, Color Me Barbra 1966, Je m'appelle Barbra 1967, Barbra Streisand: A Happening In Central Park 1968, What About Me? 1969, Stoney End 1970, Barbra Joan Streisand 1972, Classical Barbra 1974, The Way We Were 1974, Lazy Afternoon 1975, A Star Is Born 1976, Superman 1977, Songbird, 1978, Wet 1979, Guilty (with Barry Gibb) 1980, Memories 1981, Emotion 1984, The Broadway Album 1986, One Voice 1986, Til I Loved You 1989, Just For The Record 1991, Butterfly 1992, Back To Broadway 1993, Barbra Streisand – The Concert 1994, The Concert – Highlights 1995, Mirror Has Two Faces 1996, Higher Ground 1997, A Love Like Ours 1999, Timeless 2000, Christmas Memories 2001, The Essential Barbra Streisand 2002, Duets 2002, The Movie Album 2003, Guilty Pleasures 2005, Love is the Answer 2009, One Night Only 2010, What Matters Most 2011, Release Me 2012, Partners 2014, Encore: Movie Partners Sing Broadway 2016, Walls 2018; soundtracks include: Funny Girl 1968, Yentl 1983, Nuts 1987, The Prince of Tides 1991. *Films include:* Funny Girl (Acad. Award (Oscar) 1968) 1968, Hello Dolly 1969, On a Clear Day You Can See Forever 1969, The Owl and the Pussycat 1971, What's up Doc? 1972, Up the Sandbox 1973, The Way We Were 1973, For Pete's Sake 1974, Funny Lady 1975, A Star is Born 1977, Yentl 1983 (also dir and producer), Nuts 1987, Sing 1989, Prince of Tides 1990 (also dir, co-producer), The Mirror Has Two Faces (also dir) 1996, Meet the Fockers 2004. *Address:* Martin Erlichman Associates, 5670 Wilshire Boulevard, Suite 2400, Los Angeles, CA 90036, USA (office); Barwood Films, 40 West 57th Street, #18, New York, NY 10019, USA (office). *Telephone:* (212) 762-7191 (office). *Website:* www.barbrastreisand.com.

STREISSLER, Erich W., DrIur; Austrian economist and academic; *Professor Emeritus of Economics, Econometrics and Economic History, University of Vienna;* b. 8 April 1933, Vienna; s. of Albert Streissler and Erna Leithe; m. Monika Ruppe 1961; two s. (one deceased) three d.; ed Vienna Law School, Univ. of Vienna, Univ. of Oxford, UK, Hamilton Coll., New York, USA; studied also in France and Spain; Prof. of Statistics and Econometrics, Univ. of Freiburg Br., Germany 1962–68, twice Dean of Law and Social Science Faculty 1965–67; Prof., Univ. of Vienna 1968, now Prof. Emer., Dean of Law and Social Science Faculty 1973–74; apptd Vice-Pres. Austrian Inst. of Econ. Research 1990; Distinguished Austrian Visiting Prof., Stanford Univ., USA 1983; Pres. Austrian Econs Assn 1988–94, Pres. Confed. of European Econ. Asscns 1990–91; mem. Bd of Control, Vienna Stock Exchange 1990–98; Treas. Int. Econ. Assn 1992–99; mem. Austrian Acad. of Sciences; Hon. mem. Hungarian Acad. of Sciences, Bavarian Acad. of Sciences; various science prizes. *Publications:* numerous articles in scientific journals on econ. growth, distribution, monetary matters, analysis of econ. systems and especially on the history of thought in econs. *Leisure interests:* hiking, history. *Address:* 18 Khevenhuellerstrasse 15, 1180 Vienna, Austria (home). *Telephone:* 44-05-770 (home).

STREITWIESER, Andrew, Jr, AB, MA, PhD; American chemist and academic; *Professor Emeritus of Chemistry, University of California, Berkeley;* b. 23 June 1927, Buffalo, New York; s. of Andrew Streitwieser and Sophie Streitwieser; m. 1st Mary Ann Good 1950 (died 1965); m. 2nd Suzanne Cope 1967 (died 2006); m. 3rd Joyce Hessel 2007; one s. one d.; ed Stuyvesant High School, Columbia Univ.; Atomic Energy Comm. Postdoctoral Fellow, MIT 1951–52; Instructor in Chem., Univ. of Calif., Berkeley 1952–54, Asst Prof. 1954–59, Assoc. Prof. 1959–63, Prof. of Chem. 1963, Prof. Emer. 1993–, Prof. Grad. School 1995–98; consultant to chemical industry 1957–; Guggenheim Fellow 1969; mem. NAS, American Acad. of Arts and Sciences, Bavarian Acad. of Sciences; ACS awards: Calif. Section 1964, Award in Petroleum Chem. 1967; Humboldt Sr Scientist Award (Bonn) 1976, Humboldt Award (Bonn) 1979, Norris Award in Physical Organic Chem. 1982, Cope Scholar Award 1989, Sr Scientist Mentor, Camille and Henry Dreyfus Foundation 2008, Roger Adams Award in Organic Chem. 2009. *Publications include:* Molecular Orbital Theory for Organic Chemists 1961, Solvolytic Displacement Reactions 1962, Supplemental Tables of Molecular Orbital Calculations (with J. I. Brauman) Vols I and II 1965, Progress in Physical Organic Chemistry (co-ed.) Vols I–XI 1963–74, Dictionary of π-Electron Calculations (with C. A. Coulson) 1965, Orbital and Electron Density Diagrams (with P. H. Owens) 1973, Introduction to Organic Chemistry (with C. H. Heathcock) 1976, 1981, 1985, (also with E. L. Kosower) 1992, Solutions Manual and Study Guide for Introduction to Organic Chemistry (with C. H. Heathcock and P. A. Bartlett) 1985 (third edn), A Lifetime of Synergy with Theory and Experiment 1996. *Leisure interests:* music (especially opera), wine, photography. *Address:* 325B Lewis, Department of Chemistry, University of California, Berkeley, CA 94720-1960 (office); 1160 Miller Avenue, Berkeley, CA 94708, USA. *Telephone:* (510) 841-6877 (office); (510) 642-2204 (home). *E-mail:* astreit@berkeley.edu (office). *Website:* chemistry.berkeley.edu (office).

STRELEȚ, Valeriu; Moldovan politician; b. 8 March 1970, Țareuca, Rezina dist, Moldovan SSR, USSR; m.; four c.; ed State Univ. of Moldova, Acad. of Econ. Studies of Moldova, European Inst. of Political Studies; Prof. of Political Science and History of Culture, Romanian-French School 'Gh. Asachi', Chișinău 1993–94; Head of Advertising for privatization investment fund CAIS 1994–95; Dir, FPC Bioagrochem SRL 1996–2003; Gen. Dir, Bioprotect SRL 2003–09; Pres. and later mem. of local network in Moldova, UN Global Compact on Corp. Social Responsibility 2006–09; Pres. Liga Naţională a Tineretului (Nat. Youth League of Moldova) 1994–2001; on list in parl. elections, Blocul Social Democrat (Bloc of Social Democrats) 1994; on list in parl. elections, Electoral Bloc 'Plai Natal' (Native Realm) 2001; Sec.-Gen. Partidul Social-Liberal (Social Liberal Party) 2001–02; Vice-Pres. 2002–07; mem. Partidul Liberal Democrat din Moldova (PLDM—Liberal Democratic Party of Moldova), Vice-Pres. 2007–, Acting Pres. 2015–16; mem. Parl. (PLDM) 2009–, Pres. Liberal Democratic faction 2011–; Prime Minister of Moldova July–Oct. 2015; mem. Alianţa pentru Integrare Europeană (Alliance for European Integration) 2009–13, 2013–15, 2015–. *Address:* Parliament (Parlamentul), 2073 Chișinău, bd. Ștefan cel Mare și Sfânt 105, Moldova (office). *Telephone:* (22) 26-82-44 (office). *Fax:* (22) 23-30-12 (office). *E-mail:* inform@parlament.md (office). *Website:* www.parlament.md (office).

STREPPEL, J. B. M. (Joseph Bonifatius Maria); Dutch business executive; ed Tilburg Univ.; CEO Labouchere 1991–95; CEO FGH Bank 1995; Chief Financial Officer AEGON NV 1998–2009; apptd mem. Supervisory Bd Royal KPN 2003, Chair. 2010–15; mem. Supervisory Bd Van Lanschot NV; mem. Cttee of Listed Cos of Euronext (Amsterdam); Chair. Shareholders Communication Channel, Monitoring Cttee Corp. Governance Code, Duisenberg School of Finance, Holland Financial Centre.

STRETTON, James, BA, MBE; British business executive; b. 16 Dec. 1943, Peterborough, Cambs.; m. Isobel Christine Robertson 1968; two d.; ed Laxton Grammar School, Oundle, Worcester Coll., Oxford; Deputy Man. Dir Standard Life Assurance Co. 1988–94, Chief Exec. UK Operations 1994–2001; Dir Bank of England 1998–2003, Chair. Bank of England Pension Trustee Co. 2001–04; fmr Chair. The Wise Group; mem. Scottish Business Forum 1998–99, Court of Univ. of Edinburgh 1996–2002 (apptd Rector's Assessor 2003), Franchise Bd of Lloyds 2002–09 (Chair. Lloyd's Pension Scheme Trustees) 2010–14; fmr Disciplinary Bd of Actuarial Profession; Dir Edinburgh Int. Festival Ltd 1997–2004; Trustee, Lamp of Lothian Collegiate Trust 2003–; Chair. Lammermuir Festival 2010. *Address:* 15 Letham Mains, Haddington, East Lothian, EH41 4NW, Scotland.

STRICKER, Steven (Steve) Charles; American professional golfer; b. 23 Feb. 1967, Edgerton, Wis.; m. Nicki Stricker; two d.; ed Univ. of Illinois; grew up playing golf at Lake Ripley Country Club and Edgerton Towne Country Club; turned professional 1990; began career on Canadian Professional Golf Tour, won two tournaments; first joined PGA Tour 1994; has won eleven tournaments on PGA Tour including WGC-Accenture Match Play Championship 2001 and two FedEx Cup playoff events; winner The Barclays 2007, Crowne Plaza Invitational at Colonial 2009, John Deere Classic 2009, 2010, 2011, Deutsche Bank Championship 2009, Northern Trust Open 2010, Memorial Tournament 2011, Hyundai Tournament of Champions 2012; other wins include Wisconsin State Open (as an amateur) 1987, Victoria Open (Canada) 1990, Wisconsin State Open 1990, 1991, 1998, 2000, Canadian PGA Championship 1993, The Shark Shootout (with Jerry Kelly) 2009; results in major championships: tied for fifth at US Open 1998, second at PGA Championship 1998, fifth at US Open 1999, tied for tenth at US Masters 2001, tied for sixth at US Open 2006, tied for seventh at PGA Championship 2006, tied for eighth at British Open 2007, tied for seventh 2008, tied for sixth at US Masters 2009; mem. US team at Dunhill Cup 1996 (winners), US team at Presidents Cup 1996 (winners), 2007 (winners), 2009, 2011, 2013 (winners), US team at Ryder Cup 2008 (winners), 2010, 2012, CVS Caremark Charity Classic (with Bo Van Pelt) 2013, 2014; Partner, Steve Stricker American Family Insurance Foundation; inducted into Wisconsin State Golf Asscn Hall of Fame 2007, Payne Stewart Award 2012. *Address:* c/o Mario Tiziani, 825 South Waukegan Road, Suite, A8-107, Lake Forest, IL 60045, USA (office). *Telephone:* (612) 819-1304 (office). *E-mail:* mario@1degreemanagement.com (office); strickeramfamfoundation@amfam.com. *Website:* www.1degreemanagement.com (office); www.stevestrickergolf.com; www.strickerfoundation.org.

STRICKLAND, Donna, BEng, PhD; Canadian physicist; *Associate Professor, University of Waterloo;* b. 27 May 1959, Guelph, Ont.; d. of Lloyd Strickland and Edith J. Strickland (née Ranney); m. Douglas Dykaar; two c.; ed McMaster Univ., Univ. of Rochester; Research Assoc., Nat. Research Council of Canada 1988–91; worked in laser div., Lawrence Livermore Nat. Lab. 1991–92; mem. technical staff, Princeton Univ. Advanced Tech. Center for Photonics and Opto-electronic Materials 1992–97; Asst Prof., Univ. of Waterloo 1997, currently Assoc. Prof.; known for groundbreaking inventions in the field of laser physics and research on generating high-intensity, ultra-short optical pulses; Fellow, The Optical Soc. 2008 (Vice Pres. 2011, Pres. 2013); Premier's Research Excellence Award 1999, Cottrell Scholars Award from Research Corpn 2000, Nobel Prize in Physics (jtly with Gérard Mourou) 2018. *Address:* Department of Physics and Astronomy, University of Waterloo, 200 University Avenue, West Waterloo, Ont. N2L 3G1, Canada (office). *Telephone:* (519) 888-4567 (ext. 32724) (office). *Fax:* (519) 746-8115 (office). *Website:* uwaterloo.ca/physics-astronomy/people-profiles/donna-strickland (office).

STRICKLAND, John Estmond, MA, JP; British business executive; *Chairman, Octopus Holdings Ltd;* b. 23 Oct. 1939; s. of William F. Strickland and Nora N. Strickland; m. Anthea Granville-Lewis 1963; three s.; ed Jesus Coll., Univ. of Cambridge; early positions with IBM in UK and Control Data in USA; Asst Gen. Man. TSV, Hongkong and Shanghai Banking Corpn 1980–82, Gen. Man. TSV 1983–88, Exec. Dir Services 1989–96, Chair. 1996–99; Dir HSBC Holdings PLC 1988, Marine Midland Bank 1991–96, Midland Bank PLC 1993–96; Chair. Hongkong Bank Malaysia Berhad 1996–98; Vice-Chair. Hang Seng Bank Ltd 1996; Chair. Octopus Holdings Ltd 2011–; Chair. Hong Kong Cyberport Management Co. Ltd 2003–10; Pres. Outward Bound Trust of Hong Kong; mem. Bd of Dirs Airport Authority Hong Kong, Hong Kong Exchanges and Clearing Ltd 2000–, Esquel Enterprises Ltd 2001–; mem. Council Outward Bound Trust of Hong Kong; Hon. Fellow, Univ. of Hong Kong 2000, Hong Kong Computer Soc., Hong Kong Inst. of Bankers, Hong Kong Man. Asscn; Dr hc (City Univ. of Hong Kong), (Hong Kong Polytechnic Univ.). *Leisure interests:* mountaineering, reading. *Address:* Octopus Cards Limited, 46/F, Manhattan Place, 23 Wang Tai Road, Kowloon Bay, Kowloon, Hong Kong Special Administrative Region, People's Republic of China (office). *Website:* www.octopus.com.hk (office).

STRICKLAND, Theodore (Ted), BA, MA, PhD, MDiv; American psychologist and fmr politician; b. 4 Aug. 1941, Lucasville, Ohio; s. of Orville Strickland and Carrie Strickland; m. Frances Smith; ed Asbury Coll., Wilmore, Ky, Univ. of Kentucky, Lexington, Asbury Theological Seminary; Consulting Psychologist, Southern Ohio Correctional Facility 1985–92, 1994–96; Dir of Social Services, Kentucky Methodist Home (children's home); Asst Prof. of Psychology, Shawnee State Univ., Portsmouth, Ohio 1988–92, 1994–96; also served as United Methodist Minister; briefly Assoc. Pastor, Wesley United Methodist Church (now Cornerstone United Methodist Church), Portsmouth; cand. for 6th Congressional Dist of Ohio 1976, 1978, 1980; mem. US House of Reps for 6th Congressional Dist of Ohio 1993–95, 1997–2007; Gov. of Ohio 2007–11; mem. Govs Council, Health Project, Bipartisan Policy Center, Washington, DC 2011; Spring 2012 Resident Fellow, Inst. of Politics, Harvard Univ.; Co-Chair. Appalachian Regional Comm. 2009; Chair. Midwest Govs Asscn 2010; Pres. Center for American Progress Action Fund 2014; mem. Governors Council, Bipartisan Policy Center 2013–; mem. American Psychological Asscn, Ohio Psychological Asscn; Democrat; Outstanding Psychologist Award, Nat. Alliance for the Mentally Ill (co-recipient) 2004. *Website:* www.tedstrickland.com.

STRINA, Luisa; Brazilian gallery owner, art dealer and collector; art dealer 1970–; f. Galeria Luisa Strina, São Paulo 1974; first Latin-American gallery invited to participate in Basel Art Fair 1992. *Address:* Galeria Luisa Strina, Rua Padre João Manuel 755, Cerqueira César, São Paulo, 01411-001 Brazil (office). *Telephone:* (11) 3088-2471 (office). *Fax:* (11) 3064-6391 (office). *E-mail:* info@galerialuisastrina.com.br (office). *Website:* www.galerialuisastrina.com.br (office).

STRINGER, Sir Howard, Kt, MA; American/British electronics industry executive and broadcasting executive; b. 19 Feb. 1942, Cardiff, Wales; s. of Harry Stringer and Marjorie Mary Pook; m. Jennifer A. Kinmond Patterson 1978; two c.; ed Oundle School, Northants., Merton Coll., Oxford; emigrated to USA 1965; served with US Army in Viet Nam 1965–67; researcher and producer, CBS News 1967–76; Exec. Producer, CBS Reports 1976–81, CBS Evening News 1981–84; naturalized US citizen 1985; Exec. Vice-Pres. CBS News 1984–86, Pres. 1986–88; Pres. CBS Broadcast Group 1988–95; Chair. and CEO Tele-TV 1995–97; Pres. Sony Corpn of America 1997, Chair. and CEO 1998–2012, Pres. and CEO Sony Corpn 2005–12, Chair. 2005–12, Chair. of the Bd of Sony Corpn 2012–13; Vice-Chair. American Film Inst. –1999, Chair. Bd of Trustees 1999–; non-exec. mem. Exec. Bd, BBC 2014–; Chair. of the School Bd, Said Business School, Univ. of Oxford 2013–; Chair. Bd of Advisors, New York Presbyterian Ophthalmology Center 2012–; mem. Bd of Dirs TalkTalk Telecom Group 2012–, Time Inc. 2014–; Gov. Motion Picture and TV Fund Foundation; Trustee, Presbyterian Hosp., Museum of TV and Radio; Hon. Fellow, Merton Coll., Oxford 2000, Royal Welsh Coll. of Music and Drama 2001; US Army Commendation Medal; Dr hc (Univ. of Glamorgan, Univ. of the Arts, London); nine Emmy Awards for: The Rockefellers, The Palestinians, A Tale of Two Irelands, The Defense of the United States, The Boat People, The Boston Goes to China, The Fire Next Door, and The CIA's Secret Army 1974–76; First Amendment Leadership Award, Radio and Television News Dirs Foundation 1996, inducted into Broadcasting and Cable Hall of Fame 1996, Steven J. Ross Humanitarian Award, UJA-Fed. of New York 1999, inducted into Royal Television Soc.'s Welsh Hall of Fame 1999, Visionary Award for Innovative Leadership in Media and Entertainment, Museum of Television and Radio 2007, honoured by Lincoln Center, Big Brothers Big Sisters and New York Hall of Science. *Television includes:* CBS Reports (exec. producer) 1976–81, CBS Evening News with Dan Rather (exec. producer) 1981–84.

STROE, Radu; Romanian engineer and politician; b. 31 Aug. 1949, Iaşi Co.; m. Victoria Stroe (divorced); ed Civilian Marine Inst., Constanţa, Univ. of Law, Bucharest; marine and naval officer in merchant fleet, Navrom, Constanţa 1972–74; Chief Engineer III with Dept of Naval Transportation, Ministry of Transport and Communications 1974–85; Chief Engineer, Admin of Danube-Bucharest Canal 1986–90; Gen. Dir, Ministry of Transport 1991–93, Minister's Counsellor 1993–94, Chief Engineer 1994–97; Deputy Sec.-Gen. and Sec.-Gen. of the Govt 1997–2000; mem. Nat. Liberal Party; mem. Camera Deputaţilor (Chamber of Deputies) for Maramureş Co. 2001–04, for Bucharest 2010–; Minister for Co-ordinating the Gen. Secr. of Govt 2005–08; mem. Senate for Maramureş Co. and Pres. Parl. Comm. for Overseeing and Controlling the Romanian Intelligence Service 2005–08; Project Man., Frontal Communication SRL 2009–10; Minister-Del. for Admin, Ministry of Admin and Interior Aug.–Dec. 2012; Minister of Internal Affairs Dec. 2012–14; Officer, Order 'Star of Romania'. *Address:* c/o Ministry of Internal Affairs, 010086 Bucharest 1, Piaţa Revoluţiei 1A, Romania. *E-mail:* petitii@mai.gov.ro.

STROHAL, Christian, DrIur; Austrian diplomatist and international organization executive; *Permanent Representative, Organization for Security and Co-operation in Europe;* b. 1 May 1951, Vienna; m.; three c.; ed schools in Vienna, studies in law, econs and int. relations in Vienna, London and Geneva; with Ministry for Foreign Affairs (MFA) since 1976, postings to London, Geneva and Deputy Head of Mission to Rabat 1981–85, Head of Human Rights Office, MFA, Minister and Deputy Perm. Rep., Austrian Mission to UN and int. orgs, Geneva 1988–92, Amb. and Special Rep. for World Conf. on Human Rights 1992–93, Dir for Human Rights, Int. Humanitarian Law, and Minority and Gender Issues, MFA 1994–2000, Amb. to Luxembourg 2000–03, Amb. and Dir Office for Democratic Insts and Human Rights, OSCE 2003–08, Perm. Rep. to UN, Geneva 2008–13, to OSCE, Vienna 2013–, Special Rep., Austria's OSCE Chairmanship 2017–; del. to numerous int. confs in framework of UN, Council of Europe and OSCE; Vice-Chair. UN Comm. on Human Rights 1997–98, UN Human Rights Council 2011–12; Pres. Governing Council, UN Security Council Compensation Comm. 2009–10, Governing Bodies, Int. Org. for Migration 2011–12, lecturer at various insts; Felix Ermacora Prize for Human Rights, Pro merito Medal, Venice Comm. *Publications:* several publs on int. human rights issues. *Address:* Permanent Mission of Austria to the OSCE, Federal Ministry for Foreign Affairs, Minoritenplatz 8, 1014, Vienna (office); Ministry for European and International Affairs, Minoritenplatz 8, 1014 Vienna, Austria (office). *Telephone:* (5) 011-50-0 (office). *Fax:* (5) 011-59-0 (office). *E-mail:* christian.strohal@bmeia.gv.at (office). *Website:* www.bmeia.gv.at (office).

STRØM-ERICHSEN, Anne-Grete; Norwegian computer engineer and politician; b. 21 Oct. 1949, Bergen; m.; two c.; mem., Bergen City Council 1991–2005, mem. Exec. Bd 1991–2000, Deputy Mayor, City of Bergen 1998–99, Mayor 1999–2000, Chief Commr, City of Bergen 2000–03, Commr 2003–, Councillor and Chair., Standing Cttee on Environmental Affairs and Urban Devt, City of Bergen 2003–05; Deputy Leader, Labour Party in Bergen 1992, Leader, Hordaland Labour Party 1997–99, mem. Det norske Arbeiderparti (Norwegian Labour Party) Cen. Council 2002–07; Minister of Defence 2005–09, 2012–13, Minister of Health and Care Services 2009–12. *Address:* c/o Ministry of Defence, Glacisgt. 1, 0150 Oslo, Norway (office).

STRÖMHOLM, Stig Fredrik, LLD, DJur; Swedish university vice-chancellor (retd); b. 16 Sept. 1931, Boden; s. of Major Frederik Strömholm and Gerda Jansson; m. Gunilla M. Forslund 1958; one s. two d.; ed Univ. of Uppsala, Univ. of Cambridge, UK, Univ. of Munich, Germany; clerk, Southern Dist Court of Uppsala 1958–60; Jr Judge, Stockholm Court of Appeal 1961; Asst Prof. of Comparative Law, Uppsala Univ. 1966, Prof. of Jurisprudence 1969, Dean, Faculty of Law 1973–79, Deputy Vice-Chancellor 1978–89, Vice-Chancellor 1989–97; Pres. Royal Swedish Acad. of Letters, History and Antiquities 1985–93, Academia Europaea, London 1997–2002; mem. several Swedish and foreign acads; Orden pour le Mérite (FRG) and other decorations; Dr hc from several Swedish and foreign univs; several awards including Royal Norwegian Soc. of Sciences and Letters Gunnerus Medal 1997, Swedish Acad. Royal Prize 2001. *Publications include:* 25 vols of legal science including Le droit moral de l'auteur, three vols 1967–73, A Short History of Legal Thinking in the West 1985; some 20 vols of criticism and fiction. *Leisure interests:* reading, travelling. *Address:* Flogstavägen 5CI, 752 73 Uppsala, Sweden (home). *Telephone:* (18) 515045 (home). *E-mail:* gunnila.stromholm@telia.com.

STROMINGER, Jack L., MD; American physician, biochemist and academic; *Higgins Professor of Biochemistry, Department of Molecular and Cellular Biology, Harvard University;* b. 7 Aug. 1925, New York; m.; four c.; ed Harvard and Yale Univs; Intern, Barnes Hosp., St Louis 1948–49; Research Fellow, American Coll. of Physicians, Dept of Pharmacology, Washington Univ. School of Medicine, St Louis 1949–50, Research Asst 1950–51; Sr Asst Surgeon, Public Health Service, Nat. Inst. of Arthritis and Metabolic Diseases, Bethesda 1951–54; leave of absence, Carlsberg Laboratory, Copenhagen, Denmark and Molteno Inst., Cambridge Univ., England, Commonwealth Fund Fellow 1955; Asst Prof. of Pharmacology, Dept of Pharmacology, Washington Univ. School of Medicine, Markel Scholar in Medical Science 1958–60, Prof., 1960–61, Forsyth Faculty Fellow 1960, Prof. of Pharmacology and Microbiology, Depts of Pharmacology and Microbiology 1961–64; Prof. of Pharmacology and Chemical Microbiology, Univ. of Wis. Medical School, Madison, Chair. Dept of Pharmacology, mem. Univ. Cttee on Molecular Biology 1964–68; Prof. of Biochemistry, Dept of Biochemistry and Molecular

Biology, Harvard Univ., Cambridge, Mass. 1968–83, Chair. Dept of Biochemistry and Molecular Biology 1970–73, Higgins Prof. of Biochemistry 1983–, Dir of Basic Sciences, Sidney Farber Cancer Center 1974–77; Head of Tumor Virology Div., Dana–Farber Cancer Inst., Boston 1977–; mem. Steering Cttee Biomedical Sciences Scientific Working Group, WHO; mem. NAS 1970–, American Acad. of Arts and Sciences, Nat. Inst. of Medicine 1975–, AAAS, American Soc. of Biological Chemists, of Microbiologists, of Pharmacology and Experimental Therapeutics, American Asscn of Immunologists, ACS; Hon. DSc (Trinity Coll., Dublin) 1975; Guggenheim Fellowship 1974–75, John J. Abel Award in Pharmacology 1960, Paul-Lewis Laboratories Award in Enzyme Chem. 1962, NAS Award in Microbiology in Honour of Selman Waxman 1968, Rose Payne Award, American Soc. for Histocompatibility and Immunogenetics 1986, Pasteur Medal 1990, Albert Lasker Award for Basic Medical Research 1995, Paul Ehrlich Prize 1996, Klemperer Award, New York Acad. of Medicine 1999, Japan Prize, Science and Technology Foundation of Japan 1999. *Address:* Dana-Farber Cancer Institute, 44 Binney Street, Dana 1410, Boston, MA 02115; Department of Molecular and Cell Biology, Harvard University, Room 407, 7 Divinity Avenue, Cambridge, MA 02138, USA (office). *Telephone:* (617) 632-3083 (office). *Fax:* (617) 632-2662. *E-mail:* jlstrom@ fas.harvard.edu (office). *Website:* www.mcb.harvard.edu/Faculty/Strominger.html (office); www.people.fas.harvard.edu/%7Ejlstrom (office).

STRONACH, Hon. Belinda C., PC; Canadian politician and business executive; b. 2 May 1966, Newmarket, Ont.; d. of Frank Stronach; two c.; ed York Univ.; joined family-owned Magna Int. Inc. (automotive components supplier) 1988, mem. Bd of Dirs 1988–, held various sr positions including Vice-Pres. 1995–98, Exec. Vice-Pres. 1998–2001, CEO 2001–02, Pres. and CEO 2002–04, Exec. Vice-Chair. 2006–2010; resgnd from Magna in 2004 to run for leadership of Conservative Party of Canada, which she lost, also resgnd as Chair. Bd of Dirs Decoma Int. Inc., Tesma Int. Inc.; MP (Conservative) for Newmarket-Aurora and trade critic 2004–05, MP (Liberal) May 2005–08; Minister of Human Resources and Skills Devt and Minister responsible for Democratic Renewal 2005–06; Critic for Competitiveness and the New Economy 2006–07, Chair. Women's Caucus 2006–07; Founder and Chair. Belinda Stronach Foundation 2008–; Co-founder (with Rick Mercer) Spread the Net (now a programme of Plan Canada) 2007; fmr mem. Bd of Dirs Intier Automotive Inc.; Founding mem. Canadian Automotive Partnership Council; Dir Yves Landry Technological Endowment Fund, US Chamber of Commerce 2003; mem. Dean's Council, John F. Kennedy School of Govt, Harvard Univ., Dean's Advisory Council, Joseph L. Rotman School of Man., Univ. of Toronto; mem. Ont. Task Force on Productivity, Competitiveness and Econ. Progress; Hon. LLD (McMaster Univ.) 2003, Dr hc (Brock Univ.) 2009; Paul Harris Award 2008. *Address:* The Belinda Stronach Foundation, 150 Bloor Street West, Toronto, ON M5S 2X9, Canada (office). *Telephone:* (416) 531-1919 (office). *Fax:* (416) 531-1918 (office). *E-mail:* info@tbsf.ca (office). *Website:* belindastronach .com (office).

STRONACH, Frank, CM; Austrian/Canadian automotive industry executive and politician; *Founder and Honorary Chairman, Magna International Inc.;* b. (Franz Strohsack), 6 Sept. 1932, Kleinsemmering, Styria, Austria; m. Elfriede Sallmutter; one s. one d. Belinda C. Stronach (q.v.); tool and die apprentice in Weiz, Austria; emigrated to Montreal, Canada 1954; various jobs including machinist, dishwasher and golf course asst, Kitchener and Toronto, Ont. 1954–57; Co-founder (with Tony Czapka) Multimatic Investments Ltd 1957, merged with Magna Electronics Co. Ltd 1969, renamed Magna International Inc. 1973, Chair. 1969–2011, Hon. Chair. 2011–; cand. for Liberal Party, Fed. Elections 1988; Pnr, Stronach & Co. (consulting firm); Owner Magna Entertainment Corpn specializing in horse-racing entertainment and owns and operates several US racetracks; entered Austrian politics, founding Stronach Inst. 2011, campaigned against the euro, f. Team Stronach for Austria political party 2012, mem. Nationalrat 2013–14 (resgnd). Hon. Prof. of Practical Business Man., Graz Univ. of Tech. 2004; Hon. PhD (Haifa Univ.), Hon. LLD (Univ. Coll. of Cape Breton), Hon. DComm (St Mary's Univ., Halifax), Hon. DEng (Kettering Univ.) 1997; inducted into Canadian Business Hall of Fame 1996, Business Leader of the Year Award, Richard Ivey School of Business 1997, Entrepreneur of the Year Award, Univ. of Michigan 1998, Sovereign Award for Outstanding Owner nine times, Eclipse Award for Outstanding Owner 1998, 1999, 2000, Eclipse Award for Outstanding Breeder 2000, 2004, 2005, 2006, Entrepreneur of the Year Lifetime Achievement Award, Ernst & Young 2000, 2001, Canadian Int. Exec. of the Year, Canadian Council for Int. Business 2002, Gold Medal for meritorious service from Austria 2002, Person of the Year Award, Yves Landry Foundation 2004, B'nai Brith Canada Award of Merit 2005. *Leisure interest:* thoroughbred horse breeding. *Address:* Magna International Inc., 337 Magna Drive, Aurora, ON L4G 7K1, Canada (office).

STRONG, David F., PhD, FRSC; Canadian geologist, academic, publisher and fmr university president; *Chairman, Canadian Science Publishing;* b. 26 Feb. 1944, Botwood, Newfoundland; m. Lynda Joan Marshall; two d.; ed Memorial Univ. of Newfoundland, Lehigh Univ., Pa, USA, Univ. of Edinburgh, Scotland; Asst Prof., Dept of Geology, Memorial Univ. of Newfoundland 1970–72, Assoc. Prof. 1972–74, Acting Head of Dept 1974–75, Prof., Dept of Earth Sciences 1974–90, Univ. Research Prof. 1985–90, Special Adviser to Pres. 1986–87, Vice-Pres. (Academic) 1987–90; W.F. James Prof. of Pure and Applied Sciences, St Francis Xavier Univ., Nova Scotia 1981–82; Pres. and Vice-Chancellor Univ. of Vic. 1990–2000, Pres. Emer. 2000–; Founding Pres. Vice-Chancellor, Univ. Canada West 2002–08; Visiting Prof., Université de Montpellier, France 1976–77; mem. Bd of Dirs Artisanal Gold Council, Puddle Pond Resources Inc. 2012–; Chair. Canadian Science Publishing 2010–; Assoc. Ed. Canadian Journal of Earth Sciences 1977–83, Transactions of the Royal Soc. of Edinburgh 1980–; Chair. Natural Sciences and Eng Research Council of Canada 1983–86, mem. 1982–88; mem. Research Council, Canadian Inst. of Advanced Research 1986–, Newfoundland and Labrador Advisory Council on Science and Tech. 1988–, Governing Council, Nat. Research Council of Canada 1999– (mem. Exec. Cttee 2002–); Fellow, Geological Asscn of Canada, Geological Soc. of America, Soc. of Econ. Geologists; mem. Canadian Inst. of Mining and Metallurgy, Mineralogical Asscn of Canada; Univ. of Edin. Swiney Lecturer 1981; Hon. Fellow Geological Asscn of Canada; Hon. DSc (Memorial Univ., Newfoundland) 1990; Hon. LLD (St Francis Xavier Univ.) 1992; APICS Young Scientist Award (now the Frazer Medal) 1973, Foreign Exchange Fellowships to Japan 1976, to France 1976–77, Canadian Inst. of Mining and Metallurgy Distinguished Service Award 1979, Geological

Asscn of Canada Past Pres.'s Medal 1980. *Publications:* about 200 scientific and technical papers. *Leisure interests:* reading, music, gardening. *Address:* Canadian Science Publishing, 65 Auriga Drive, Suite 203, Ottawa, ON K2E 7W6, Canada (office). *Website:* www.cdnsciencepub.com (office).

STRONG, Liam (Gerald Porter), BA; British business executive; *CEO Cerberus European Capital Advisors, LLP and Head, Operations Europe, Cerberus Capital Management, LP;* b. 6 Jan. 1945, Enniskillen, Northern Ireland; s. of Gerald James Strong and Geraldine Crozier Strong; m. Jacqueline Gray 1970; one s. one d.; ed Trinity Coll., Dublin; joined Procter & Gamble, Newcastle-upon-Tyne 1967–71; Household Man., Reckitt & Colman 1971, moved to Corp. Planning Unit, London 1973, Marketing and Sales Dir, then Gen. Man. Reckitt & Colman 1975–80, Vice-Pres. Sunset Designs, Calif., USA 1980–82, Head Int. Pharmaceuticals Div., Reckitt & Colman 1982–86, Pres. Durkee French, USA 1986–89; Dir of Marketing, British Airways 1989–90, Dir Marketing and Operations 1990–91; Chief Exec. Sears PLC 1991–97; CEO Worldcom International 1997–2001; Pres. CEO Teleglobe International Holdings Ltd. 2003–06; joined Cerberus Capital Man. LP 2006, currently CEO Cerberus European Capital Advisors, LLP and Head of Cerberus Operations Europe; also currently Chair. (non-exec.) Virtual IT Ltd; mem. Bd of Dirs AerCap Holding 2006–, Focus Ltd, Torex Ltd; mem. Bd of Govs Ashridge Business School; Chair. UK Prime Minister's Industry Advisory Group, UK Advisory Bd on Telecom Security 2002–05. *Leisure interests:* reading, shooting, opera. *Address:* Cerberus European Capital Advisors, LLP. 84 Grosvenor Street, London, W1K 3JZ, England (office). *Telephone:* (20) 7647-6000 (office). *E-mail:* info@cerberuscapital.com (office). *Website:* www.cerberuscapital.com (office).

STRONG, Sir Roy Colin, Kt, CH, PhD, FSA, FRSL; English historian, writer and fmr museum director; b. 23 Aug. 1935, London, England; s. of George Edward Clement Strong and Mabel Ada Smart; m. Julia Trevelyan Oman 1971 (died 2003); ed Queen Mary Coll., Univ. of London and Warburg Inst.; Asst Keeper, Nat. Portrait Gallery, London 1959–67, Dir 1967–73; Dir Victoria and Albert Museum, London 1974–87; Vice-Chair., South Bank Bd (now South Bank Centre) 1985–90; Dir Oman Productions Ltd, Nordstern Fine Art Insurance 1988–2001; organizer of exhbns including The Elizabethan Image (Tate Gallery) 1969, The Destruction of the Country House (Victoria and Albert Museum) 1974, Artists of the Tudor Court (Victoria and Albert Museum) 1983; mem. Arts Council of GB 1983–87 (Chair. Arts Panel 1983–87), Council, RCA 1979–87; Pres. Garden History Soc. 2000–06; High Bailiff and Searcher of Sanctuary of Westminster Abbey 2000; Patron, Pallant House, Chichester 1986–; Fellow, Queen Mary Coll., Univ. of London, Royal Soc. of Literature 1999; Hon. MA (Worcester) 2004; Hon. DLitt (Leeds) 1983, (Keele) 1984; Shakespeare Prize, FVS Foundation, Hamburg 1980, President's Award, Royal Photographic Soc. of GB 2003. *Radio includes:* numerous series. *Television includes:* Royal Gardens (series) 1992, The Diets Time Forgot (series) 2008, Visions of England 2010. *Publications include:* Portraits of Queen Elizabeth I 1963, Leicester's Triumph (with J. A. Van Dorsten) 1964, Holbein and Henry VIII 1967, Tudor and Jacobean Portraits 1969, The English Icon: Elizabethan and Jacobean Portraiture 1969, Elizabeth R (with Julia Trevelyan Oman) 1971, Van Dyck: Charles I on Horseback 1972, Inigo Jones: The Theatre of the Stuart Court (with S. Orgel) 1972, Mary Queen of Scots (with Julia Trevelyan Oman) 1972, Splendour at Court: Renaissance Spectacle and The Theatre of Power 1973, An Early Victorian Album (with Colin Ford) 1974, Nicholas Hilliard 1975, The Cult of Elizabeth: Elizabethan Portraiture and Pageantry 1977, And When Did You Last See Your Father? The Victorian Painter and British History 1978, The Renaissance Garden in England 1979, Britannia Triumphans, Inigo Jones, Rubens and Whitehall Palace 1980, Holbein 1980, The English Miniature (with J. Murdoch, J. Murrell and P. Noon) 1981, The English Year (with Julia Trevelyan Oman) 1982, The English Renaissance Miniature 1983, Artists of the Tudor Court (with J. Murrell) 1983, Glyndebourne, A Celebration (contrib.) 1984, Art and Power, Renaissance Festivals 1450–1650 1984, Strong Points 1985, Henry Prince of Wales and England's Lost Renaissance 1986, C.V. Wedgwood Festschrift (contrib.) 1986, Creating Small Gardens 1986, Gloriana, Portraits of Queen Elizabeth I 1987, The Small Garden Designers Handbook 1987, Cecil Beaton: the Royal Portraits 1988, Creating Small Formal Gardens 1989, Lost Treasures of Britain 1990, A Celebration of Gardens 1991, Small Period Gardens 1992, Royal Gardens 1992, Versace Theatre 1992, William Larkin 1994, A Country Life 1994, Successful Small Gardens 1994, The Tudor and Stuart Monarchy 1995, The Story of Britain 1996, The English Arcadia 1996, Country Life 1897–1997 1997, The Roy Strong Diaries 1967–1987 1997, On Happiness 1997, The Tudor and Stuart Monarchy 1998, The Spirit of Britain 1999, Garden Party 2000, The Artist and the Garden 2000, Ornament in the Small Garden 2001, Feast – A History of Grand Eating 2002, The Laskett – The Story of a Garden 2003, Coronation: A History of Kingship and the British Monarchy 2005, Passions Past and Present 2005, A Little History of the English Country Church 2007, Visions of England 2011, Remaking a Garden – The Laskett Transformed 2014; numerous articles in newspapers and periodicals. *Leisure interests:* gardening, cooking, weight training. *Address:* The Laskett, Much Birch, Hereford, Herefords., HR2 8HZ, England. *E-mail:* strong@ereal.net. *Website:* www.thelaskettgardens.co.uk.

STROPNICKÝ, Martin; Czech actor, theatre director, diplomatist and politician; b. 19 Dec. 1956, Prague, Czechoslovak Repub. (now Czech Repub.); ed Theatre Faculty of Acad. of Performing Arts, Prague, Diplomatic Acad., Vienna, Austria; worked at Prague Municipal Theatres and Vinohrady Theatre 1980–90; worked at Ministry of Foreign Affairs from 1990, Amb. to Portugal 1993–94, to Italy 1994–97, to the Holy See 1999–2002; mem. caretaker govt as Minister of Culture 1998; Artistic Dir, Vinohrady Theatre 2003–12; mem. Akce Nespokojených Občanů (ANO—YES-Action of Dissatisfied Citizens), later renamed Ano (Yes), Vice-Chair. 2017–; mem. Parl. (Ano) for Prague 2013–; Minister of Defence 2014–17, of Foreign Affairs 2017–18, also Deputy Prime Minister 2017–18. *Address:* Ministry of Foreign Affairs, Loretánská nám. 101/5, 118 00 Prague 1, Czech Republic (office). *Telephone:* (2) 24181111 (office). *Fax:* (2) 24182048 (office). *E-mail:* epodatelna@ mzv.cz (office). *Website:* www.mzv.cz (office).

STROSSEN, Nadine, BA, JD; American lawyer and academic; *Assistant Professor of Clinical Law, New York Law School;* b. 18 Aug. 1950, Jersey City, NJ; d. of Woodrow John Strossen and Sylvia Strossen; m. Eli Michael Noam 1980; ed Harvard Law School, Radcliffe Coll.; Assoc. Attorney, Sullivan & Cromwell 1978–83; Partner, Harvis & Zeichner 1983–84; mem. Nat. Bd of Dirs American

Civil Liberties Union 1983–, Pres. 1991–2008, mem. Advisory Cttee on Reproductive Freedom Project 1983–, Nat. Exec. Cttee 1985–, Nat. Gen. Council 1986–91; Asst Prof. of Clinical Law, New York Law School 1989–; Adjunct Prof. Grad. School of Business Univ. of Columbia 1990–; mem. Exec. Cttee Human Rights Watch 1989–91; mem. Bd Dirs Coalition to Free Soviet Jewry 1984–; mem. Asia Watch 1987–, Vice-Chair. 1989–91; mem. Nat. Coalition Against Censorship 1988, Middle East Watch 1989–91, The Fund for Free Expression 1990–; mem. Steering Cttee New York Legal Council for Soviet Jewry 1987–. *Publications include:* Regulating Campus Hate Speech – A Modest Proposal? 1990, Recent US and International Judicial Protection of Individuals Rights: A Comparative Legal Process Analysis and Proposed Synthesis 1990, In Defense of Pornography: Free Speech and the Fight for Women's Rights 1995, numerous articles in professional journals. *Leisure interests:* singing, skiing, travel. *Address:* New York Law School, 57 Worth Street, New York, NY 10013-2960 (office); 450 Riverside Drive, #51, New York, NY 10027, USA (home). *Telephone:* (212) 431-2375 (office). *Fax:* (212) 431-1992 (office). *E-mail:* nadine.strossen@nyls.edu (office). *Website:* www.nyls.edu (office).

STROTHOTTE, Willy; German mining industry executive; b. 23 April 1944; apprentice Frank & Schulte 1961–64; joined C Tennant 1966; various positions trading in metals and minerals in Germany, Belgium and USA 1961–78; joined Glencore International 1978, becoming Head of Metals and Minerals 1984–93, CEO 1993–94, Chair. and CEO 1994–2001, fmr Chair. Glencore International AG, also Chair. Xstrata AG 1994–2002, Xstrata plc 2002–13 (merged with Glencore International plc to form Glencore Xstrata plc May 2013, now called Glencore plc); mem. Bd of Dirs Century Aluminium Corpn, Minara Resources Ltd 2000–, KKR Financial Holdings LLC 2007–. *Address:* c/o Glencore plc, Baarermattstrasse 3, 6340 Baar, Switzerland. *E-mail:* info@glencore.com.

STROUT, Elizabeth; American writer; b. Portland, Me; m. James Tierney; one d.; ed Bates Coll., Syracuse Univ. Coll. of Law; fmr mem. Faculty, Bard Coll., Warren Wilson Coll., Manhattan Community, Queens Univ. of Charlotte; Dr hc (Bates Coll.) 2010. *Publications include:* Amy and Isabelle (Los Angeles Times Art Siedenbaum Award for First Fiction, Chicago Tribune Heartland Prize) 1998, Abide With Me 2006, Olive Kitteridge (short stories) (Pulitzer Prize for Fiction 2009, Premio Bancarella Prize 2010) 2008, The Burgess Boys 2013, My Name Is Lucy Barton: A Novel 2015, Anything is Possible 2017. *Website:* elizabethstrout .com.

STROYEV, Yegor Semyonovich, DEcons; Russian politician; b. 25 Feb. 1937, Stroyevo, Khotynetsky, Orel Region; s. of Semyon Fedorovich Stroyev and Anna Ivanovna Stroyeva; m. Nina Semvyovna Stroyeva; one d.; ed I.V. Michurin Horticultural Inst., Acad. of Social Sciences, Moscow; mem CPSU 1958–91; worked at Progress collective farm, Khotynetsky Dist; Sec. Khotynetsky CPSU Dist Cttee, Chair. Exec. Cttee Pokrovsky Dist Soviet of People's Deputies, First Sec. Pokrovsky CPSU Dist Cttee, Sec., First Sec. Orel CPSU Regional Cttee 1985–89; Sec. CPSU Cen. Cttee 1989–91; mem. Politburo of CPSU Cen. Cttee 1990–91; resgnd after Aug. coup d'état; Head of Admin. Orel Oblast 1993–2009; fmr People's Deputy of USSR; mem. Council of Fed. Ass. of Russian Fed. 1995–2001, Chair. 1996–2001, Hon. Chair. 2001–; Chair. Council of Inter-parl. Ass. of CIS Mem. States 1996–; Dir All-Russia Scientific Research Inst. of Fruit Crop Breeding 1991–93; Academician, Russian Acad. of Agricultural Sciences; Hon. mem. Russian Acad. of Literature; Order of the Oct. Revolution 1973, Order of the Red Banner of Labour 1987, Order of St Prince Vladimir 1997 and other awards. *Publications include:* Methodology and Practices of Agrarian Restructuring 1994, To Give a Chance to the Peasant 1995, Land Issue 1999, Self-determination of Russia and Global Modernization 2001, In A Rapid River 2003, Agricultural Complex of Russian Chernozem Land 2003. *Leisure interest:* recreation in the countryside.

STRUBE, Jürgen Friedrich, DJur; German business executive; *Honorary Chairman of the Supervisory Board, BASF SE;* b. 1939, Bochum; m.; one d.; ed Univs of Freiburg, Geneva, Switzerland and Munich; joined BASF 1969, several posts, then with BASF Brasileira SA, São Paulo 1974–85, Head, Glasurit do Brasil Ltda 1980–, Head, Brazil Regional Div. 1982–, in charge of Information Systems and Fibres Operating Divs. and Regional Divs in N America 1985–88, of Foams, Polyolefins and PVC and Information Systems Operating Divs and Brazil and Latin American Regional Divs 1988–90, mem. Bd Exec. Dirs BASF AG, Ludwigshafen, Germany 1985–, Chair. 1990–2003, Chair. Supervisory Bd BASF AG (renamed BASF SE Jan. 2008) 2003–09, Hon. Chair. 2009–; Chair. Supervisory Bd Fuchs Petrolub AG 2003–11; mem. Supervisory Bd Allianz Deutschland AG, BMW Group 2001–10 (currently Deputy Chair.), Bertelsmann AG (Deputy Chair. 2004–), Commerzbank AG –2008, Hapag-Lloyd AG, Linde AG –2008; Pres. Asscn of Chemical Industry (VCI) 1996–97, UNICE 2003–; mem. Int. Advisory Cttee New York Stock Exchange Euronext, Inc.; mem. Econ. Advisory Bd RWE AG; Hon. Senator, Deutsche Hochschule für Verwaltungswissenschaften, Speyer 1997, Hon. Prof. 1999; Hon. Senator, Univ. of Mannheim 1998, Univ. of Heidelberg 2003; Bundesverdienstkreuz, 1st Class 2000, Großes Bundesverdienstkreuz 2013; Dr hc (Univ. of Maryland) 1995, (European Business School, Oestrich-Winkel) 2003; Centenary Medal, Soc. of Chemical Industry 1999, John J. McCloy Award, American Council on Germany 2001, Rhine-Neckar Regional Award 2003, Medal of Merit (Rhineland-Palatinate) 2003, Int. Palladium Medal Award, Soc. de Chimie Industrielle (American Section) 2005, Hanns Martin Schleyer Prize 2011.

STRUZIK, Adam; Polish physician and politician; *Marshal of Mazowieckie Voivodeship;* b. 1 Jan. 1957, Kutno; m.; one s. one d.; ed Medical Acad., Łódź, Univ. of Warsaw; Councillor, Municipal Council of Duninów 1986–90, City and Commune of Gąbin 1990; Dir Voivodeships Jt Hosp. in Płock 1990–97; Marshal (Speaker) of Nat. Regional Council of Territorial Self-Govt 1994–98; Councillor, Regional Council of Mazowieckie Voivodeship 1998–, Marshal of Mazovian Voivodeship 2001–; mem. Solidarity Trade Union 1980–; mem. Polish Peasant Party (PSL) 1989–, Exec. Council; Senator (Płock Voivodeship) 1991–2001, Marshal of Senate 1993–97; Vice-Pres. Nat. Ass. that adopted Constitution of Repub. of Poland 1997; Pres. Council of Mazovian Sickness Foundation 1999–2001, Council for Nat. Asscn of Sickness Foundations 1999–2001; Co-founder Aid Foundation for Voivodeship Hosp., Płock; mem. Programming Bd TVP SA; mem. supreme authorities of govt coalition party (PSL) 2007–, Cttee on Devt (DEVE), Cttee of The Regions, RELEX Cttee; mem. Polish Hunting Asscn, Płock Scientific Soc., Polish Haematology Soc.; Grand Officier de L'Ordre National du Merite (France) 1996, Commdr's Cross, Order of Leopold (Belgium) 2009, Kt's Cross, Orderu Odrodzenia Polski 2004, Officer's Cross, Orderu Odrodzenia Polski 2010. *Leisure interests:* politics, literature, tourism. *Address:* Office of the Marshal, Mazowieckie Voivodeshi, ul. Jagiellońska 26, 03-719 Warsaw, Poland (office). *Telephone:* (22) 5907804 (office). *Fax:* (22) 5907875 (office). *E-mail:* a.struzik@mazovia.pl (office). *Website:* www.mazovia.pl (office).

STRZEMBOSZ, Adam Justyn, DrIur; Polish lawyer, judge and government official; b. 11 Nov. 1930, Warsaw; s. of Adam Strzembosz and Zofia Strzembosz (née Gadomska); m. Zofia Strzembosz 1957; two s. two d.; ed Jagiellonian Univ., Cracow, Warsaw Univ.; legal adviser, Ministry of Labour and Social Security 1953–56; judge, Co. Court 1956–68, Prov. Court 1968–81; researcher, Research Inst. of Judicial Law 1974–81; Head of Solidarity Group, Ministry of Justice 1980–81; Asst Prof. and Head of Dept of Penal Law, Catholic Univ. of Lublin 1982–89, Prof. 1986–; Vice-Minister of Justice 1989–90; Judge and First Pres. Supreme Court 1990–98 (retd); Head of Tribunal of State 1990–98; mem. Bd Solidarity Mazowsze Region 1980; Del. to 1st Solidarity Conf., Jt Leader Appeal Comm., Gdańsk Oliwa 1981; Co-Founder Soc. for Promotion and Propagation of Sciences; mem. Catholic Univ. of Lublin Scientific Asscn, Penal Law Asscn; Hon. Citizen of the City of Warsaw 2016; Grand Cross, Order Odrodzenia Polski 2008, Knightly Order of St Gregory the Great (Holy See) 2010, Order Orła Białego 2012. *Publications:* six books and more than over 200 treatises and articles. *Leisure interests:* cycling, literature. *Address:* ul. Stanisława Augusta 73 m.20, 03-846 Warsaw, Poland (home).

STUART, Freundel Jerome, BA, LLB, LLM, QC, PC; Barbadian lawyer and politician (resgnd); b. 27 April 1951, St Philip; ed Univ. of the West Indies; practising attorney 1984–; mem. House of Ass. (Parl.) for St Philip South 1994–99, for St Michael South 2008–; Senator 2003–07; fmr Attorney-Gen. and Minister of Home Affairs; Acting Prime Minister of Barbados May–Oct. 2010, Prime Minister 2010–18; mem. Democratic Labour Party, fmr Leader; resgnd from politics May 2018; Order of Roraima (Guyana) 2016. *Address:* c/o Democratic Labour Party, 'Kennington', George St, Belleville, St Michael, Barbados (office). *Telephone:* 429-3104 (office). *Fax:* 427-0548 (office). *Website:* www.dlpbarbados.org (office).

STUBB, Cai-Göran Alexander, BA, MA, PhD; Finnish journalist, politician and academic; *Vice-President, European Investment Bank (EIB);* b. 1 April 1968, Espoo; m. Suzanne Innes-Stubb; one s. one d.; ed Mainland High School, Daytona Beach, Fla, USA, Gymnasiet Lärkan, Helsinki, Furman Univ. (golf scholarship), USA, Univ. of Paris (Sorbonne), Coll. of Europe, Belgium, London School of Econs, UK; mil. service; researcher, Ministry of Foreign Affairs 1995–97, Finnish Acad. 1997–99; columnist for various newspapers, including APU, Ilta-Sanomat, Blue Wings, various papers in Suomen Lehtiyhtymä group, Nykypäivä and Hufvudstadsbladet 1997–; special researcher, Finland's representation to EU, Brussels 1999–2001; Prof., Coll. of Europe, Brussels 2000–07; adviser to Pres. of EC 2001–03, mem. Comm. Task Force on European Convention; mem. Finland's representation to EU as a special expert and to intergovernmental negotiations for European Constitution 2003–04; mem. European Parl. (European People's Party) 2004–08; Minister for Foreign Affairs 2008–11, for European Affairs and Foreign Trade 2011–14, Prime Minister 2014–15, Minister of Finance 2015–16; Vice-Pres. and mem. Management Cttee, European Investment Bank (EIB) 2017–; mem. (Nat. Coalition) Eduskunta (Parl.) for Uusimaa 2011–17; mem. Nat. Coalition Party, Chair. 2014–16. *Publications:* 11 books about the EU; several articles in academic journals. *Address:* European Investment Bank, 98-100 boulevard Konrad Adenauer, Luxembourg-Ville, Luxembourg (office). *Telephone:* 43 79 1 (office). *E-mail:* alexander.stubb@parliament.fi (office). *Website:* www.eib.org; www.alexstubb.com.

STUBBE, JoAnne, BS, PhD; American chemist and academic; *Novartis Professor Emeritus of Chemistry and Professor Emeritus of Biology, Massachusetts Institute of Technology;* b. Champagne, Ill.; ed Univ. of Pennsylvania, Univ. of California, Berkeley; Postdoctoral Researcher, UCLA 1971–72; Asst Prof., Dept of Chem., Williams Coll. 1972–77; Asst Prof., Dept of Pharmacology, Yale Univ. 1977–80; Asst Prof., Dept of Biochemistry, Univ. of Wisconsin 1980–87; apptd Prof., Dept of Chem., MIT 1987, currently Novartis Prof. Emer. of Chem. and Prof. Emer. of Biology; mem. NAS 1992; Fellow, American Acad. of Arts and Sciences 1991, American Philosophical Soc.; Hon. DSc (Harvard) 2013; Myron L. Bender and Muriel S. Bender Distinguished Summer Lecturer, Northwestern Univ. 1992, ACS F.A. Cotton Medal for Excellence in Chemical Research 1998, NSF Nat. Medal of Science 2009, ACS Nakanishi Prize 2009, Benjamin Franklin Medal in Chem. 2010, Welch Award in Chem. (co-recipient) 2010, Killian Faculty Achievement Award, MIT 2012, Remsen Award, American Chemical Soc. 2015, Pearl Meister Greengard Prize 2017. *Publications:* numerous papers in professional journals. *Address:* Room 56-579, Department of Chemistry, Massachusetts Institute of Technology, 77 Massachusetts Avenue, Cambridge, MA 02139, USA (office). *Telephone:* (617) 253-1814 (office). *E-mail:* stubbe@mit.edu (office). *Website:* chemistry.mit.edu (office); biology.mit.edu/people/joanne_stubbe (office).

STUBBS, Imogen Mary, MA; British actress; b. 20 Feb. 1961, Rothbury; d. of Robin Stubbs and Heather McCracken; m. Trevor Nunn (q.v.) 1994; one s. one d.; ed St Paul's Girls School, London, Exeter Coll., Oxford, Royal Acad. of Dramatic Art; Gold Medal, Chicago Film Festival. *Plays as actress:* appeared with RSC in The Rover, Two Noble Kinsmen, Richard II 1987–88, Othello 1991, Heartbreak House 1992, St Joan 1994, Twelfth Night 1996, Blast from the Past 1998, Betrayal 1998, The Relapse 2001, Three Sisters 2002, Fallujah 2007, Alphabetical Order 2009, The Glass Menagerie 2010, Private Lives 2011, Little Eyolf 2011. *Play as author:* We Happy Few (Gielgud Theatre, London) 2004, Strangers on a Train 2013, Little Revolution 2014, The Hyperchondriac 2014, Communicating Doors 2015, Things I Know to be True 2016. *Television appearances include:* The Browning Version 1985, The Rainbow 1988, Fellow Traveller 1989, Pasternak 1990, Othello 1990, Relatively Speaking 1990, Sandra, c'est la vie 1993, Anna Lee (series) 1993, Mothertime 1997, Blind Ambition 2000, Big Kids (series) 2000, So What Now? 2001, Marple: The Moving Finger 2006, Brief Encounters 2006, New Tricks 2009, The Adventures of Daniel 2010, Injustice (mini-series) 2011. *Films:* Privileged 1982, Nanou 1986, A Summer Story 1988, Deadline 1988, Erik the Viking 1989, True Colors 1991, The Wanderer (voice) 1991, A Pin for the Butterfly 1994, Jack and Sarah 1995, Sense and Sensibility 1995, Twelfth Night: Or What

You Will 1996, Collusion 2003, Dead Cool 2004. *Leisure interests:* writing, skiing, collecting junk. *Address:* c/o Nick Hern Books Ltd, The Glasshouse, 49a Goldhawk Road, London, W12 8QP, England.

STUDER, Cheryl; American singer (soprano); *Professor of Voice, Hochschule für Musik, Würzburg;* b. (Cheryl Lynn Studer), 24 Oct. 1955, Midland, Mich.; m. 3rd Michalis Doukakis; two d. (by previous m.); ed Interlochen Arts Acad., Oberlin Coll., Univ. of Tennessee, Hochschule für Musik, Vienna; studied singing with Gwendolyn Pike, at Berkshire Music Centre, at Tanglewood with Phyllis Curtin and at Hochschule für Musik, Vienna with Hans Hotter; Fellow, Tanglewood Berkshire Music Center 1975–77; engaged for concert series with Boston Symphony Orchestra by Seiji Ozawa 1979; opera debut as First Lady in The Magic Flute, Munich 1980–82; with Darmstadt State Theatre, Germany 1982–84, Deutsche Oper, Berlin 1984–86; US debut as Micaela in Carmen, Lyric Opera of Chicago 1984; debut at Bayreuth 1985, Royal Opera House, Covent Garden 1987, Metropolitan Opera, New York 1988; debut as Adelaide in Arabella, Hamburg State Opera 2014, as Madame de Croissy in Dialogues des Carmelites, Stadttheater Klagenfurt 2015; sings wide variety of roles, especially Wagner, Verdi, Mozart and Strauss; professional stage directing debut with Bavarian Chamber Opera Company with Il barbiere di Siviglia from Rossini 2010; Prof. of Voice, Hochschule für Musik Würzburg 2003–; Chair., Maria Callas Grand Prix Int. Voice Competition; Hon. Prof., Beijing Central Conservatory; Int. Music Award 1993, Vocalist of the Year (USA) 1994, Terras Sem Sombre 2011, Ovation Award 2012, Furtwängler Preis; numerous awards for recordings including Grand Prix du Disque - Prix Maria Callas, Orphée d'Or, Cannes Classical Award and two Grammys. *Address:* Hochschule für Musik, Hofstallstrasse 6–8, 97070 Würzburg, Germany (office). *E-mail:* studouk@aol.com (office). *Website:* www.hfm-wuerzburg .de (office); www.cherylstuder.com.

STUHR, Jerzy; Polish actor, film director and academic; b. 18 April 1947, Kraków; s. of Tadeusz Stuhr and Maria Stuhr; m. 1971; one s. one d.; ed Jagiellonian Univ. and Ludwik Solski State School of Drama, Kraków; main theatrical roles at Stary Theatre, Kraków with Andrzej Wajda, notably Hamlet 1982, Dostoevsky's The Possessed and Crime and Punishment 1984, P. Süskind's Double Bass (actor and dir) 1985–, Le Bourgeois Gentilhomme 1993, Harold Pinter's Ashes to Ashes 1996, Merry Wives of Windsor (dir) 1998; dir, actor and teacher, Italy 1980–; Rector, Ludwik Solski State School of Drama, Kraków 1990–97, 2002–08, Lecturer 1998–; Lecturer, Faculty of Radio and Television, Silesia Univ. 1998–; mem. European Film Acad. 1998–; Chief Judge, Odessa International Film Festival 2011; Co-founder (with wife) Stowarzyszenie Unicorn (cancer patient support org.) 1999; Dr hc (Silesia Univ.); Best Actor, Chicago Festival 1978, Premio della Critica Teatrale 1982, Premio Fipresci for Love Stories, Venice Film Festival 1997, Grand Prix for Love Stories, Polish Film Festival, Gdynia 1997, Nastro d'Argento 1997, Big Anima Special Jury Prize, Karlovy Vary 2000, Emerging Master, Int. Film Festival, Seattle 2001. *Films as actor include:* Zycie za zycie (Life for Life) 1991, Uprowadzenie Agaty (Hijacking of Agata) 1993, Decalogue X, Three Colours – White 1994, Spis cudzoloznic (List of Lovers) 1995, Matka swojej matki 1996, Historie milosne (Love Stories) 1997, Kiler 1997, Kilerów 2-óch 1999, Tydzien z zycia mezczyzny (A Week in the Life of a Man) 1999, Down House 2000, La Vita altrui 2000, Duze zwierze (Big Animal) 2000, Weiser 2001, Show 2003, Pogoda na jutro (Tomorrow's Weather) 2003, Persona non grata 2005, Doskonale popoludnie 2005, Il Caimano 2006, The Making of Parts 2006, Korowód 2007, Habemus Papa 2011, Obywatel 2014, My Italy 2016. *Films directed include:* Spis cudzoloznic (List of Lovers) (also screenwriter) 1995, Historie milosne (Love Stories) (also screenwriter) 1997, Tydzien z zycia mezczyzny (A Week in the Life of a Man) (also screenwriter) 1999, Duze zwierze (Big Animal) 2000, Pogoda na jutro (Tomorrow's Weather) (also screenwriter) 2003, Korowód (also screenwriter) 2007, We Have a Pope 2011. *Publications include:* Heart Illness, or My Life in Art (autobiography) 1992, Big Animal 2000, True Pretender 2000. *Leisure interests:* literature, sport. *Address:* Stowarzyszenie Unicorn, ul. Zielony Dół 4, 30-228 Kraków, Poland. *E-mail:* unicorn@unicorn.org .pl. *Website:* unicorn.org.pl.

STUIVER, Minze, PhD; American geologist and academic; *Professor Emeritus, Department of Earth and Space Sciences, University of Washington;* b. 25 Oct. 1929, Vlagtwedde, Netherlands; s. of Albert Stuiver; ed Univ. of Groningen; Research Assoc., Yale Univ. 1959–62; Sr Research Assoc. and Dir Radiocarbon Lab. 1962–69; Prof. of Geological Sciences and Zoology, Univ. of Washington, Seattle 1969–82, Prof. of Geological Sciences and Quaternary Sciences 1982–98, now Prof. Emer., Dir Quaternary Isotope Lab. 1972–98; Ed. Radiocarbon 1976–88; mem. Geological Soc. of America, American Quaternary Asscn; Alexander von Humboldt Sr Scientist, FRG 1983; Hon. DSc (Queen's Univ., Belfast) 2009; Pomerance Award, Archaeological Inst. of America 1993, Distinguished Career Award in Quaternary Science, AMQUA 2000, Penrose Medal, Geological Soc. of America 2005. *Achievements include:* second-most-cited scientist in the field of Geosciences in 1990s, Incites. *Address:* University of Washington, Department of Earth and Space Sciences, 4000 15th Ave NE, Seattle, WA 98195, USA (office). *Fax:* (206) 543-0489 (office). *E-mail:* minze@uw.edu (office). *Website:* depts .washington.edu/qil (office).

STUMP, Nicholas (Nick) Withrington, BAppSc, MAppSc, FAusIMM; Australian business executive; *Chairman, Aurukun Bauxite Development Pty Ltd;* b. 16 Dec. 1941, Adelaide, S Australia; s. of Stanley Withrington and Dorothy Ellen; m. Alison Goode 1966; one s. two d.; ed Scotch Coll. Adelaide, Unley High School, Univ. of Adelaide and S Australian Inst. of Tech.; worked for CRA Group (now Rio Tinto) 1970–95, held several tech. and operating man. positions with Zinc Corpn Broken Hill 1970–77, transferred to Mary Kathleen Uranium Ltd (CRA subsidiary) 1977, Man. Planning and Evaluation, CRA Group, Melbourne 1980, Gen. Man. CRA's Sulphide Corpn zinc smelter, Cockle Creek, NSW 1983–85, Man. Dir Comalco Rolled Products, Sydney 1985–87, apptd Pres. Commonwealth Aluminum Corpn Ltd USA (CRA subsidiary) 1988, CEO Comalco Ltd and Group Exec. CRA Ltd 1991–95; CEO MIM Holdings Ltd 1995–2001; apptd Chair. GroundProbe Pty Ltd; currently Chair. Aurukun Bauxite Development Pty Ltd; fmr Chair. Sustainable Minerals Inst., Univ. of Queensland; mem. Bd of Dirs John Holland Group Pty Ltd, Ludowici Ltd, Australia 21 Ltd; mem. Senate, Univ. of Queensland 1996–; Pres. Minerals Council of Australia 1997–99 (mem. 1995–); Vice-Pres. Queensland Mining Council Ltd 1995; Fellow, Australasian Inst. of Mining and Metallurgy; Dr hc (Univ. of Queensland) 2009; Arthur F. Taggart Award, American Inst. of Mining Engineers (co-recipient) 1975. *Leisure interests:* cruising and offshore yacht racing. *Address:* Aurukun Bauxite Development Pty Ltd, ACN 169 710 249, PO Box 427, Cranebrook, NSW 2749, Australia (office). *E-mail:* enquire@abdmining.com.au (office). *Website:* abdmining.com.au (office).

STUMPF, John G., BA, MBA; American banker; b. 15 Sept. 1953, Pierz, Minn.; ed St Cloud State Univ., Univ. of Minnesota; joined Norwest Corpn 1982, served in numerous exec. positions including Sr Vice-Pres. and Chief Credit Officer, Norwest Bank NA, Minneapolis 1982–89, Exec. Vice-Pres. Southwestern Banking 1989–91, Regional Pres. Norwest Banks Colo/Ariz. 1991–94, Regional Pres. Norwest Banks Texas 1994–98, Head of Southwestern Banking Group (after merger of Norwest Corpn and Wells Fargo & Co.) 1998–2000, Head of Western Banking Group 2000–02, Group Exec. Vice-Pres. of Community Banking 2002–05, Pres. Wells Fargo & Co. 2005–15, CEO 2007–16, Chair. 2010–16 (retd); Advisor, Federal Reserve Bank of San Francisco Jan.–Sept. 2016; elected Chair. Visa USA 2005; mem. Bd of Dirs The Clearing House (Chair.), Financial Services Roundtable, Target Corpn 2010–, Chevron Corpn 2010–; mem. California Business Roundtable; Trustee, San Francisco Museum of Modern Art.

STURGEON, Nicola, LLB (Hons); British lawyer and politician; *First Minister of Scotland;* b. 19 July 1970, Irvine, North Ayrshire, Scotland; m. Peter Murrell; ed Greenwood Acad., Irvine, Univ. of Glasgow; solicitor, Drumchapel Law Centre, Glasgow 1997–99; MSP (Scottish Nat. Party—SNP) for Glasgow 1999–2007, for Glasgow Govan 2007–11, for Glasgow Southside 2011–, Leader of SNP in the Scottish Parl. 2004–07; Vice-Convenor of SNP 1999–2004, Deputy Leader of SNP 2004–14, Leader 2014–; Deputy First Minister of Scotland 2007–14, First Minister 2014–; Cabinet Sec. for Health and Wellbeing 2007–12, for Infrastructure, Investment and Cities 2012–14, also for Parl. and Govt Strategy 2012; Donald Dewar Debater of the Year Award 2004, 2008, Scottish Politician of the Year Award 2008, 2012, 2014, 2015. *Leisure interest:* reading. *Address:* St Andrew's House, Regent Road, Edinburgh, EH1 3DG (office); The Scottish Parliament, Holyrood, Edinburgh, EH99 1SP, Scotland (office). *Telephone:* (300) 244-4000 (office); (141) 424-1174 (Glasgow) (office). *Fax:* (13) 9779-5001 (office). *E-mail:* firstminister@gov.scot (office). *Website:* www.gov.scot (office); www.firstminister .gov.scot (home).

STURLA BERHOUET, HE Cardinal Daniel Fernando, LicenTheol, SDB; Uruguayan ecclesiastic and academic; *Archbishop of Montevideo;* b. 4 July 1959, Montevideo; ed John XXIII Inst., Michael Rua Inst., Bishop Mariano Soler Theological Inst. of Uruguay; professed as mem. Salesians of Don Bosco (SDB) 1980, ordained priest 1987; served as Vicar of Salesian Novitiate and Post-Novitiate, Dir of Salesian Aspirantate, Master of Novices, Dir of John XXIII Pre-univ. Inst., and Prof. of Church History; Salesian Prov. for Uruguay 2008–11; Pres. Conf. of Religious of Uruguay 2008–, in charge of Depts of Missions and of the Laity; Auxiliary Bishop of Montevideo 2011–14; consecrated Titular Bishop of Phelbes 2012–14; Archbishop of Montevideo 2014–; cr. Cardinal (Cardinal-Priest of Santa Galla) 2015. *Publications include:* ¿Santa o de Turismo? La secularización en el Uruguay 2010, Mi vivir es Cristo, Biografía y textos del P. Arturo Mossman Gros, padre y amestro espiritual 1888–1964 2015, Carta pastoral 'Transparencia de Evangelio' 2015. *Address:* Calle Treinta y Tres 1368, Casilla de Correo entral 356, 11000 Montevideo, Uruguay (office). *Telephone:* (2) 915-8127 (office); (2) 915-8879 (office). *Fax:* (2) 915-8926 (office). *E-mail:* info@arquidiocesis.net (office); dfsturla2gmail.com. *Website:* www.arquidiocesis.net (office).

STURRIDGE, Charles, BA; British director, writer and producer; b. 24 June 1951, London, England; s. of Jerome Sturridge and Alyson Sturridge (née Burke); m. Phoebe Nicholls; three c.; ed Univ. Coll., Oxford; fmr mem. Nat. Youth Theatre; fmr Pres. Oxford Univ. Dramatic Soc.; worked as actor and theatre dir; debut as professional dir in musical version of Hard Times, Belgrade Theatre, Coventry; joined Granada TV 1974; freelance dir/writer/producer 1979–; Chair. Directors UK 2008–15; numerous awards for feature films and TV documentaries. *Theatre includes:* Dir and Co-writer Hard Times, Belgrade Theatre, Coventry 1974; Dir own trans. (with Tania Alexander) of The Seagull, Queens Theatre, London 1985, Endgame, Gate Theatre/Barbican 2006; trans. (with Tania Alexander) of Uncle Vanya. *Films include:* Runners 1982, Contrib. Dir to Aria (La Vergine degli angeli from La Forza del Destino) 1987, A Handful of Dust (writer/dir) 1988, Where Angels Fear to Tread (writer/dir) 1991, Fairytale – A True Story (BAFTA Best Children's Film 1998) 1997, Lassie 2005 (writer/dir), The Scapegoat (writer/dir) 2012. *Television documentaries and dramas include:* Coronation Street, World In Action, Brideshead Revisited (17 awards including BAFTA award for Best Series, two American Golden Globe awards, Grand Award of New York Film and TV Festival), Soft Targets (BBC 1) 1982, The Storyteller 1988, Gulliver's Travels 1996 (12 int. awards, including Humanitas Prize and five US Primetime Emmys), A Foreign Field, Longitude (writer/dir, Channel 4) 2000 (five BAFTA Awards including Best Series), Shackleton (writer/dir, Channel 4) (BAFTA Award for Best Series and two Emmy Awards), Ohio Impromptu (Beckett on Film, Channel 4) (LWT South Bank Award for Best TV Drama), No. 1 Ladies Detective Agency (Mirage/BBC/HBO/Weinstein Co.) 2009, The Road to Coronation Street (ITV/BBC 4) (BAFTA and RTS Awards for Best Single Drama, New York Film and TV Festival Gold Medal) 2010, Astonish Me (WWF) 2010, Dates (series) 2013, The Ends of The Earth 2013, Da Vinci's Demons (series) 2014, Churchill's Secret 2016 (ITV). *Address:* c/o Independent Talent Group Ltd, Oxford House, 76 Oxford Street, London, W1D 1BS, England (office). *Telephone:* (20) 7636-6565 (office). *Fax:* (20) 7323-0101 (office). *E-mail:* info@independenttalent.com (office). *Website:* www .independenttalent.com (office).

STURUA, Robert Robertovich; Georgian theatre director; *Artistic Director, Shota Rustaveli Professional State Drama Theatre;* b. 31 July 1938, Tbilisi; s. of Robert Ivanovich Sturua; m. Dudana Kveselava 1968; two s.; ed Shota Rustaveli Theatre and Film, Georgian State Inst.; joined Rustaveli Theatre, Tbilisi 1962, Dir 1979–80, Artistic Dir 1982–2011; Artistic Dir, Shota Rustaveli Professional State Drama Theatre 2013–; first Guest Dir at Saarbrücken State Theatre; has staged over 100 productions, including operas; Hon. Citizen of Tbilisi 1996; Order of Merit (Georgia) 1998, Order of Friendship (Russian Fed.) 2008; Albert Schweiter Prize, Germany 1975, Honoured Art Worker of Georgian Soviet Repub. 1976, Kote Marjanishvili Award (for the production "Kvarkvare" by P. Kakabadze) 1976, State Award of USSR (for "The Caucasian Chalk Circle" by B. Brecht) 1979,

People's Artist of Georgia 1980, The English Critic's Prize 1980, The Italian Critics' Prize 1981, Shota Rustaveli Prize for Richard III 1981, People's Artist of the USSR 1982, Prize of the State Univ. of Argentina 1988, The Shakespeare's International Society included the production of Hamlet at the Riverside Studio on its list of the ten best productions of Hamlet of the 20th century 1992, State Prize of Georgia 1996, Grand Prize at Rustavi Festival "Golden Mask" for Macbeth 1996, Mikheil Tumanishvili Prize 1997, Georgian Theatre Soc. Prize for The Best Production of the Year/Best Stage Directing for The Snake Lady 1998, Gold Medal at Rustavi Festival "Golden Mask" 1998, Chaplin Club Award and Grand Prize at Russian Festival "Baltic House" for the production of What if the Wet Lilac is Wet 1998, Alexandre Kazbegi Prize 1999, State Prize of the Russian Fed. 1999, Gold Medal at Rustavi Festival "Gold Mask" 2000, "Patriarch of the Theatre", VI Ceremony of Awarding the Theatre Prize "Chaika" (Seagull) 2001, Stanislavski Int. Prize for contributing to the development of the theatrical art, Moscow 2002, Polikarpe Kakabadze Prize 2002, Prize "Zolotaya Moskva" (Golden Moscow) for the production of Sior Todero Brontolon at Theatre Satiricon 2003, Grand Prize for Hamlet at the Rustavi Festival 2003, Best Stage Dir for the production of The Styx, Faces magazine 2005, Grand Prize, Eighth Int. Theatre Festival "Baltic House" 2006, Sergo Parajanov Int. Prize 2006, Asscn of Theatre Historians and Critics of Argentina acknowledged the San Martine Theatre production of The Resistable Rise of Arturo Ui as the best in 7 nominations 2006, Giorgi Tovstonogov Prize, St Petersburg br. of the Theatrical Artists' Union of the Russian Fed. 2009, Special Prize of the Journalists' Int. Fund "Gold Pen" 2009, Ilia Chavchavadze Medal 2009, "Hit of the Season" (The Tempest", Theatre "ET CETERA", Russian Theatre Soc. Award) 2012 Grand Prize ("Hunting Season", best productions of 2010–11) 2012, Theatre Prize "Duruji" for Best Direction "Hunting Season" 2012, "Golden Mask" (Zolotaya Maska) 2013, Special Prize from His Holiness Beatitude Ilia II, Archbishop of Mtskheta-Tbilisi and Catholicos-Patriarch of All Georgia on his 75th birthday 2013. *Theatre productions:* Rustaveli Theatre: The Third Desire (V. Blazek) 1963, Before the Supper (V. Rozov, Georgian version by G. Charkviani) 1963, The Accusation (R. Sturua, G. Kavtaradze) 1964, The Trial of Salem (Miller, original title The Crucible) 1964, Marie-Octobre (J. Rober) 1965, The Sunny Night (N. Dumbadze) 1965, Khanuma (A. Tsagareli) 1969, The Good Woman of Sezuan (Brecht) 1969, 1993, The Stepmother of Samanishvili (D. Kldiashvili) 1969, The Georgian Poetry Evening 1970, The Children of the World (S. Jgenti) 1970, Salamura (A. Sulakauri) 1971, Medea (Anouilh) 1971, Our Melodies (G. Kancheli) 1972, Doctor Stockman (Enemy of Society) (Ibsen) 1973, The Verdict (N. Dumbadze) 1973, The Chairman of Raikom (R. Tabukashvili) 1974, Kvarkvare (P. Kakabadze) 1974, The Betrayal (A. Sumbatashvili) 1976, The Caucasian Chalk Circle (Brecht) 1975, The Beginning (A. Gellman) 1981, The Dragon (E. Schwartz) 1976, Grandmother, Iliko, Ilarion and Myself (N. Dumbadze) 1977, The Contemporary Man (E. Gabrilovich, I. Reisman) 1977, Richard III (Shakespeare) 1979, The Role for the Young Actress (T. Chiladze) 1980, Blue Horses on the Red Grass (M. Shatrov) 1980, Variations on Contemporary Theme (R. Sturua, L. Popkadze, A. Varsimashvili) 1981, The Charm of Amherst (W. Luis) 1981, Funerals in California (R. Ibraginbekov) 1983, From 3 till 6 (A. Chkhaidze) 1984, The Day of Hundred Ergasterum (M. Kveselava) 1985, The Concert for Two Violins Accompanied by Oriental Instruments (R. Sturua, A. Chichinadze) 1987, King Lear (Shakespeare) 1987, The Mother of God (liturgy, composer G. Kancheli) 1989, The Dialogues for the Play in Two Acts (D. Turashvili) 1990, Life is a Dream (P. Calderon) 1992, Gospel According to Jacob (R. Sturua) 1994, Macbeth (Shakespeare) 1995, Lamara (G. Robakidze) 1996, Does It Matter if Wet Lilac Is Wet (L. Tabukashvili, co-dir D. Khinikadze) 1997, The Serpent-Woman (C. Gozzi, co-dir D. Sakvarelidze) 1998, The Day of Meeting (T. Chiladze, co-dir G. Tavadze) 1999, Is He Human?! (I. Chavchavadze) 2000, Twelfth Night or What You Will (Shakespeare) 2001, Hamlet (Shakespeare) 2001, Waiting for Godot (Beckett) 2003, The Styx (G. Kancheli) 2003, Soldier, Love, Bodyguard and... the President (L. Bugadze) 2005, The Misfortune of Darispan (D. Kldaishvili) 2006, Sweet, Sad Scent of Vanilla (I. Samsonadze) 2006, The Mask of Foe (A. Nothomb, original title La cosmetique de l'ennemi) 2007, Twelve Angry Man (R. Rose) 2007, Birdie Died in Glen (T. Chiladze) 2007, Play Strindberg (F. Dürrenmatt) 2008, Biederman and the Fire Raisers (M. Frisch) 2009, The Star-Child (O. Wilde) 2010, The Hunting Season (T. Chiladze) 2011, Maria Callas (Terrence McNally) 2013, The Prince and the Pauper (Mark Twain) 2013, Julius Caesar (Shakespeare) 2015, Ordered Disorder (B. Brecht) 2016, Somewhere over the Rainbow (L. Tabukashvili) 2017, Vano and Niko (E. Akhvlediani) 2018; overseas: The Stepmother of Samanishvili D. Kldiashvili, The Saarbrucken Municipal Theatre 1974, The Wild Money (A. Ostrovsky), Schauspielhaus, Düsseldorf 1977, As You Like It (Shakespeare), Schauspielhaus, Düsseldorf 1980, Electra (Sophocles), Theatre Athenaeum, Festival of Ancient Greek Drama, Athens 1986, The Brest Piece (M. Shatrov), Vakhtangov Theatre, Moscow 1987, Mother Courage (Brecht), Cervantes Nat. Theatre, Buenos Aires 1988, Oedipus Rex (Sophocles), Theatre Athenaeum, Festival of Ancient Greek Drama, Athens 1989, Tartuffe (Molière), Habima Theatre, Tel-Aviv 1989, Three Sisters (Chekhov), Queen's Theatre, London 1990, Eugene Onegin (Tschaikhovsky), Teatro Communale di Bologna 1991, The Comedy of Errors (Shakespeare), Nat. Theatre, Helsinki 1991, Hamlet (Shakespeare), Riverside Studios, London 1992, Antigone (Sophocles), Istanbul Municipal Theatre 1994, The Seagull (Chekhov), The London King Theatre 1995, Mouth Open (Hanoch Levin), Tel-Aviv Chamber Theatre 1995, Measure for Measure (Shakespeare), Nat. Theatre, Helsinki 1995, The Visions of Simone Machard (Brecht), Alvares Theatre, Argentina 1997, Hamlet (Shakespeare), The Satirikon Theatre, Moscow 1998, Coriolanus (Shakespeare), Irodio Theatre, Acropolis, Athens 1999, The Merchant of Venice (Shakespeare), Moscow Theatre Et Cetera 1999, The Merchant of Venice (Shakespeare), Moscow Theatre Et Cetera 2000, Twelfth Night or What You Will (Shakespeare), Ivan Vazov Nat. Theatre, Sofia 2001, Signor Todero (Goldoni), Satirikon Theatre, Moscow 2002, Krapp's Last Tape (Beckett), Et Cetera Theatre, Moscow 2002, Oedipus Rex (Sophocles), Kiev 2003, Hamlet (Shakespeare), State Theatre, Ankara 2004, Romeo and Juliet (Shakespeare), Pushkin Theatre, Moscow 2004, The Resistible Raise of Arturo Ui (Brecht), President Alvares Theatre, Buenos Aires 2005, King Lear (Shakespeare), Chamber Theatre, Israel 2006, The Tempest (Shakespeare), Theatre Et Cetera, Moscow 2010, The Taming of the Shrew (Shakespeare), Athens 2011, You have found a good place for feeding dogs (Tarik Noui), Theatre Et Cetera, Moscow 2012, The Comedy of Errors (Shakespeare), Theatre Et Cetera, Moscow 2013, Mourning Becomes Electra (O'Neill), Teatro San Martín, Buenos Aires 2014. *Opera productions:* And it was on eighth year, Tbilisi State Opera, 1983, Music for the Living (G. Kancheli, libretto R. Sturua), Tbilisi State Opera 1984, Barbale (V. Dolidze, interpreted by V. Kakhidze, libretto R. Sturua and D. Akhobadze) 1986, Eugene Onegin (Tschaikhovsky), Teatro Communale di Bologna, Italy 1990, Othello (Verdi), Tbilisi State Opera 1991, Angel of Fire (Prokofiev), Tbilisi State Opera 1990, Carmen (Bizet), Tbilisi State Opera 1992, The Visions of Ivan the Terrible (S. Solimski), Samara State Academic Opera Theatre, conductor M. Rostropovich (world premiere) 1999, Music for the Living (G. Kancheli, libretto R. Sturua), Tbilisi State Opera 1999, Lady in the Dark, Teatro dell'Opera di Roma (Costanzi Theatre), Italy 2002, Mazeppa (Tchaikovsky), Bolshoi Theatre, Moscow 2004. *Address:* Shota Rustaveli Theatre, Tbilisi, Georgia (office). *E-mail:* info@rustavelitheatre.ge (office). *Website:* www.rustavelitheatre.ge (office).

STURZA, Eugen; Moldovan politician; *Minister of Defence;* b. 15 Dec. 1984; m. Anastasia Sturza 2012; one c.; ed Acad. of Econ. Studies of Moldova; Chief Advisor to Prime Minister 2009–13, Chef de cabinet of Prime Minister 2013–15; Moderator, Public Admin Reform, Inst. for European Policies and Reforms 2015–17; Minister of Defence 2017–; mem. Partidul Popular European din Moldova (European People's Party of Moldova), currently Deputy Chair. *Address:* Ministry of Defence, 2021 Chişinău, şos. Hînceşti 84, Moldova (office). *Telephone:* (22) 25-20-09 (office). *E-mail:* ministru@army.md (office). *Website:* www.army.md (office).

STURZA, Ion; Moldovan business executive and politician; b. 9 May 1960, Pîrjolteni; m. Stela Sturza; two c.; ed Moldova State Univ.; began career as Deputy Dir-Gen., Foreign Trade Soc. of Moldavian SSR (MOLDEX); f. Incon Co. (canned food and beverage production jt-stock co.), Chişinău 1991; fmr Pres. FinComBank, Chişinău, Chair. Bank Steering Bd 1996; fmr Presiding Dir-Gen., ROMPETROL MOLDOVA (Romanian oil co.); elected mem. Parlamentul (Parl.) 1998; Deputy Prime Minister and Minister of the Economy 1998–99; Prime Minister Feb.–Nov. 1999, Prime Minister-desig. Dec. 2015–Jan. 2016 (renounced mandate after parl. failed to confirm his nomination); f. Fribourg Capital (pvt. equity and venture capital fund) 2009; fmr mem. Democratic Party of Moldova, Deputy Chair. –2001. *Address:* Fribourg Capital, Chişinău 2012, 64 Sciusev St., Moldova.

STURZENEGGER, Federico, PhD (Econs); Argentine economist, academic and central banker; b. 11 Feb. 1966, Rufino; s. of Adolfo Sturzenegger; ed Nat. Univ. of La Plata, Massachusetts Inst. of Tech., USA; Asst Prof., UCLA 1991–95; Chief Economist, Yacimientos Petrolíferos Fiscales 1995–98; Dean, Business School, Torcuato di Tella Univ. 1998–2000, 2002–05; Sec., Political Economy, Argentina 2001–02; Visiting Prof., John F. Kennedy School of Govt, Harvard Univ. 2005–07; Pres. Banco Ciudad 2008–13 (resgnd); mem. Chamber of Deputies 2013–15; Pres. Banco Central de la República Argentina 2015–18; fmr consultant to World Bank, Cen. Bank of Ukraine, IMF, Foundation for Latin American Research, IDB, Nat. Bank of Switzerland, BIS, UNDP, Bank of England, Global Devt Network, Japanese Bank for Int. Cooperation; Hon. Professor, Ecole des Hautes Etudes Commerciales 2016; Young Global Leader, World Economic Forum 2005, Konex Prize 2006. *Publications include:* The Political Economy of Reform 1998, Coordinación de Políticas Macroeconómicas en el Mercosur 2000, Dollarization 2003, La economía de los Argentinos 2005, El país que queremos 2006, Debt Defaults and Lessons from a Decade of Crisis 2006, The Natural Resources Trap 2010; numerous research papers. *Address:* c/o Banco Central de la República Argentina, Reconquista 266, C1003ABF Buenos Aires, Argentina.

STÜTZLE, Walther K. A., Dr rer. pol; German journalist; *Senior Distinguished Fellow, Stiftung Wissenschaft und Politik;* b. 29 Nov. 1941, Westerland-Sylt; s. of Moritz Stützle and Annemarie Ruge; m. Dr H. Kauper 1966; two s. two d.; ed Westerland High School and Univs of Berlin, Bordeaux and Hamburg; Researcher, IISS, London 1967–68, Foreign Policy Inst. Bonn 1968–69; Desk Officer, Ministry of Defence, Planning Staff, Bonn 1969–72, Pvt. Sec. and Chef de Cabinet, 1973–76, Head, Planning Staff, Under-Sec. of Defence, Plans and Policy 1976–82; mem. editorial staff, Stuttgarter Zeitung 1983–86; Dir Stockholm Int. Peace Research Inst. (SIPRI) 1986–91; Ed.-in-Chief Der Tagesspiegel 1994–98; Perm. Sec., Ministry of Defence 1998–2002, Visiting Prof., Potsdam Univ. 2004–; Sr Distinguished Fellow, German Inst. for Int. and Security Affairs 2004–. *Publications include:* Europe's Future: Europe's Choices (co-author) 1967, Adenauer und Kennedy in der Berlinkrise 1961–62 1972, Politik und Kräftverhältnis 1983, ABM Treaty: To Defend or Not to Defend 1987, SIPRI Yearbook (ed.) 1986–90, From Alliance to Coalition: The Future of Transatlantic Relations (contributor) 2004. *Leisure interests:* history, reading, sailing, mountain walking. *Address:* Stiftung Wissenschaft und Politik, Deutsches Institut für Internationale Politik und Sicherheit, Ludwigkirchplatz 3-4, 10719 Berlin, Germany (office). *Telephone:* (30) 880070 (office). *Fax:* (30) 88007100 (office). *E-mail:* walther.stuetzle@swp-berlin.org (office). *Website:* www.swp-berlin.org (office).

STYLIANIDES, Christos; Cypriot dental surgeon, politician and EU official; *Commissioner for Humanitarian Aid and Crisis Management, European Commission;* b. 26 June 1958, Nicosia; ed Aristotle Univ. of Thessaloniki, Panteion Univ., Greece, JFK School of Govt, Harvard Univ., USA; Govt Spokesperson 1998–99, 2013–14; mem. Parl. (Democratic Rally) 2006–13, mem. Cttee on European Affairs, Cttee on Internal Affairs, Cttee on Employment and Social Affairs 2006–11, mem. OSCE Parl. Ass. 2006–11, Vice-Chair. Cttee on Foreign and European Affairs 2011–13; mem. European Parl. (Group of the European People's Party (Christian Democrats) 2014–, mem. Cttee on Budgets, Substitute mem. Cttee on Industry, Research and Energy, mem. Del. for Relations with USA, Substitute mem. Del. for Relations with Israel and of Del. to Parl. Ass. of the Union for the Mediterranean; Commr for Humanitarian Aid and Crisis Man., European Comm. (EC), Brussels Nov. 2014–; Council mem. European Council on Foreign Relations; mem. Parl. Forum on Small Arms and Light Weapons; co-f. Movt for Political Modernization and Reform 1995. *Address:* Humanitarian Aid and Crisis Management, European Commission, 200 Rue de la Loi/Wetstraat 200, 1049 Brussels, Belgium (office). *Telephone:* (2) 299-11-11 (office). *E-mail:* christos.stylianides@europarl.europa.eu (office). *Website:* ec.europa.eu/echo/_en (office).

STYLIANIDIS, Evripidis, PhD; Greek lawyer and politician; b. 8 April 1966, Maroneia, nr Komotini, Rhodope Pref. of Thrace; m. Stergioula Papachristou; three c.; ed Democritus Univ. of Thrace, Komotini, Univ. of Hamburg, Germany; worked at Gen. Consulate in Hamburg, Germany 1991–94; served in Artillery Corps of the Hellenic Army 1994–95; adviser to Pres. of New Democracy party on youth affairs and cultural diplomacy 1995–96; Fellow, European Public Law

Centre 1997–98, Researcher 1997–2000; taught in Master's degree programme in public law at Law School of Nat. and Capodistrian Univ. of Athens 1997–98; first entered politics with New Democracy (Nea Demokratia) as mem. European Parl. nominee 1994; ran for Parl. 1996; elected mem. Hellenic Parl. for Rhodope Pref. 2000–; New Democracy's Alt. Co-ordinator for Foreign Affairs 2001–04; fmr mem. NATO Parl. Ass. and Vice-Pres. Greece-Brazil and Greece-Germany and mem. Greece-Russia Parl. Friendship Cttees; Minister for Nat. Educ. and Religious Affairs 2007–09, for Transport and Communications Jan.–Oct. 2009; Minister for the Interior following formation of coalition govt with Panhellenic Socialist Movt (PASOK) and Democratic Left (Dimokratiki Aristera) 2012–13; Parl. Cand. 2015. *Address:* 4 Nireidon str. Pagrati, 11634 Athens (office); New Democracy (Nea Demokratia), Piraeus 62, Moschato, 183 46 Athens, Greece (office). *Telephone:* (210) 7297223 (office); (210) 9444000 (New Democracy) (office). *Fax:* (210) 7258853 (office). *E-mail:* stylianidis@e-stylianidis.gr; ndpress@nd.gr (office). *Website:* www.e-stylianidis.gr; www.nd.gr (office).

STYMIEST, Barbara, HBA, MBA, FCA; Canadian business executive and fmr banking executive; *Chairman, Canadian Institute for Advanced Research;* ed Richard Ivey School of Business, Univ. of Western Ontario; started career as partner at Ernst & Young; Exec. Vice-Pres. and Chief Financial Officer Investment Banking Div., Bank of Montreal –2000; CEO (first woman) TSX (Toronto Stock Exchange) Group 2000–05; COO RBC (Royal Bank of Canada) Financial Group 2004–11 (retd); mem. Bd of Dirs Research In Motion Ltd 2007– (name changed to BlackBerry 2013), Chair. 2012–13; Chair. Canadian Inst. for Advanced Research 2014–; Dir, George Weston Ltd, Sun Life Financial Inc., University Health Network, Canadian Inst. for Advanced Research; mem. or fmr mem. Royal Ont. Museum, Toronto Rehabilitation Inst. Foundation, Hincks-Dellcrest Children's Centre, United Way Campaign Cabinet; Fellow, Inst. of Chartered Accountants of Ont. *Address:* Canadian Institute for Advanced Research, MaRS Centre, West Tower 661 University Avenue, Suite 505, Toronto, ON M5G 1M1, Canada (office). *Telephone:* (416) 971-4251 (office). *Website:* www.cifar.ca (office).

SU, C(hi) Y(i); Taiwanese business executive; *Chairman, Formosa Oil (Asia Pacific) Corporation;* Dir, Formosa Petrochemical Corpn, Pres. –2011, Chair. Formosa Oil (Asia Pacific) Corpn; Dir Nat. Petroleum Corpn. *Address:* Formosa Petrochemical Corporation, 1-1, Formosa Plastics Group Industrial Zone, Mailiao, Yunlin (office); Formosa Oil (Asia Pacific) Corporation, Second Floor 6, 54 Sector 4, Minsheng East Road, Songshan District, Taipei 10574, Taiwan (office). *Telephone:* (2) 27122211 (Yunlin) (office); (2) 87129988 (Taipei) (office). *Fax:* (2) 87128050 (Yunlin) (office); (2) 87705283 (Taipei) (office). *E-mail:* fpccpre@fpcc.com.tw (office). *Website:* www.fpcc.com.tw (office); www.fpg.com.tw (office).

SU, Chi, PhD; Taiwanese government official and academic; *Chairman, Taipei Forum;* b. 1 Oct. 1949, Taichung; s. of Chan-Wu Su and Kuo-Yin Ni; m. Chen Yue-ching (Grace Chen); one s. one d.; ed Nat. Chengchi Univ., Johns Hopkins and Columbia Univs, USA; Assoc. Prof., Dept of Diplomacy, Nat. Chengchi Univ. 1984–90, Prof. 1990–, Deputy Dir Inst. of Int. Relations 1990–93; Sec. Gen., Office of the Univ. Pres. 1989–90; mem. Exec., Yuan Research, Devt and Evaluation Comm. 1990–94; Sec.-Gen., China Political Science Asscn 1990–91; Deputy Dir, Kuomintang Cen. Cttee, Dept of Mainland Affairs 1992–93; Vice-Chair Exec., Yuan Mainland Affairs Council 1993–96; Dir-Gen., Govt Information Office 1996–97; mem. Exec., Yuan Minister of State 1997; Nat. Policy Adviser to Pres. of Repub. 1997, Deputy Sec.-Gen. to Pres. 1997–99; Chair., Mainland Affairs Council 1999; Prof., Inst. of China Studies, Tamkang Univ. and Convener, Nat. Security Div., Nat. Policy Foundation 2000–05; Legislator 2005–08; Sec.-Gen. Nat. Security Council 2008–10 (resgnd); Chair. Taipei Forum 2011–. *Publications:* The Normalization of Sino-Soviet Relations, Taiwan's Relations with Mainland China: A Tail Wagging Two Dogs; over 20 papers and articles. *Address:* Taipai Forum, 12–2 Fl., No. 510, Sec. 5, Zhang-Xiao East Road, Taipei 11077, Taiwan (office). *Telephone:* (2) 2726-0855 (office). *Fax:* (2) 2726-0857 (office). *E-mail:* suchi1949@taipeiforum.org.tw (office). *Website:* www.taipeiforum.org.tw (office).

SU, Guaning, BSc, MS, PhD; Singaporean engineer and university administrator; *President Emeritus, Nanyang Technological University;* ed Univ. of Alberta, Canada, California Inst. of Tech., Stanford Univ., Harvard Business School, USA; began career as Research and Devt Engineer, Ministry of Defence; CEO Defence Science and Tech. Agency 2000–02; Pres. Nanyang Tech. Univ. 2003–11, Pres. Emer. 2011–; Adviser, Bitwave Pte Ltd; Dir Singapore Cable Vision, DSO Nat. Labs, Agency for Science, Tech. and Research, Biomedical Research Council; mem. Science and Eng Research Council, Nat. Science and Tech. Bd 1991–2001; Founding Bd mem. Nat. Science and Tech. Bd, Deputy Chair. 1998–2000; mem. External Advisory Bd, Dept of Electrical and Systems Eng, Washington Univ. in St. Louis; mem. Bd of Trustees, Singapore Nat. Research Foundation, Business China; Founder Chair. Global Alliance of Technological Univs 2009; Fellow, Inst. of Engineers, Singapore (Pres. 1994–96); Chevalier, Legion d'Honneur 2005; Public Admin Medal (Silver) 1989, Public Service Medal 1997, Public Admin Medal (Gold) 1998, Long Service Medal 1998, IES/IEEE Joint Medal of Excellence 2002, ASEAN Eng Award 2002, Nat. Science and Tech. Medal 2003, Friendship Award, State Council China 2011, Fed. of Eng Insts of the Asia Pacific Engineer of the Year 2011, Guangdong Friendship Award 2012, Defence Tech. Medal (Outstanding Service) 2015. *Address:* Nanyang Technological University, Nanyang Avenue, Singapore, 639798, Singapore (office). *Telephone:* 6790-4769 (office). *Fax:* 6791-8494 (office). *E-mail:* ntu@edu.sg (office). *Website:* www.ntu.edu.sg (office).

SU, Jain-rong, BA, MA; Taiwanese politician; *Minister of Finance;* b. Nov. 1961; ed Nat. Chung Hsing Univ., Pennsylvania State Univ.; Prof., Dept of Public Finance, Nat. Taipei Univ. 2000–, also Dean of Academic Affairs 2006–08, Dean, Coll. of Public Affairs 2012–14; Commr, Dept of Finance, Taipei City Govt 2014–16; Man. Dir Bank of Taiwan 2016; Deputy Minister of Finance 2016–18, Minister of Finance 2018–; Dir Fubon Financial Holding Co. Ltd –2016. *Address:* Ministry of Finance, 2 Ai Kuo West Rd, Taipei 10066, Taiwan (office). *Telephone:* (2) 23228000 (office). *Fax:* (2) 23568774 (office). *E-mail:* service_mof@ekera.com.tw (office). *Website:* www.mof.gov.tw (office).

SU, Rong; Chinese politician; b. Oct. 1948, Taonan, Jilin Prov.; ed Jilin Univ.; joined CCP 1970; Deputy Sec., later Sec. CCP Party Cttee, Najin Commune, Tao'an Co., Jilin Prov. 1974, Sec. Najin Commune 1975, Lingxia Commune 1975; Deputy Sec. CCP Tao'an Co. Cttee 1980; Sec. CCP Fuyu Co. Cttee, Jilin Prov. 1983; mem. Standing Cttee, CCP Baicheng Prefectural Cttee, Jilin Prov. 1983, Deputy Sec. CCP Baicheng Prefectural Cttee 1985–87, Commr Prefectural Admin. Office 1985, Sec. CCP Baicheng Prefectural Cttee 1987; Sec. CCP Siping City Cttee, Jilin Prov. 1989, Chair. Standing Cttee, Siping City People's Congress 1990; mem. Standing Cttee, CCP Jilin Prov. Cttee 1992–93, Sec.-Gen. Jilin Prov. Cttee 1992–93, Deputy Sec. 1996–2001; Sec. Yanbian Korean Autonomous Prefecture Cttee 1995–97, Qinghai Prov. Cttee 2001–03 (mem. Standing Cttee 2001–03), CCP Gansu Prov. Cttee 2003–06; Chair. Standing Cttee, Gansu Prov. People's Congress 2004–06; Exec. Vice-Pres. CCP Cen. Cttee Party School 2006–07; Alt. mem. 14th CCP Cen. Cttee 1992–97, 15th CCP Cen. Cttee 1997–2002, mem. 16th CCP Cen. Cttee 2002–07, 17th CCP Cen. Cttee 2007–; Sec. CCP Jianqxi Prov. Cttee 2007–13; arrested on corruption charges 2014.

SU, Shulin, BSc, MSc; Chinese government official, petroleum engineer and business executive; b. March 1962, Dong'e Co., Shandong Prov.; ed Daqing Petroleum Inst., Harbin Inst. of Tech.; sr engineer with experience in China's oil and gas industry; Deputy Dir, later Dir Petroleum Admin, Daqing, Heilongjiang Prov. 1998–99; Vice-Pres. and Gen. Man. and Chair. PetroChina Co. Ltd, Daqing Oilfield Co. Ltd, Daqing 1999–2003, Dir, PetroChina Co. Ltd 2002–06; Chair. China Petrochemical Corpn (Sinopec Group) 2007–11, Sec. Party Cttee 2007–11; Deputy Sec., CCP, Prov. Cttee Fujian Prov. 2011; Acting Gov., then Vice-Gov., then Gov. People's Govt, Fujian Prov. 2011–15; Sec. Leading Party Group, CCP, People's Govt, Fujian Prov. 2011–; Alt. mem. 16th CCP Cen. Cttee 2002–07, 17th CCP Cen. Cttee 2007–12, mem. 18th CCP Cen. Cttee 2012–; sentenced to 16 years in prison Jan. 2018. *Address:* General Office of Fujian Provincial People's Government, Fuzhou, Fujian Province, People's Republic of China (office).

SU, Shuyang, (Su Yang, Yu Pingfu); Chinese writer; b. 1938, Baoding, Hebei Prov.; ed Renmin Univ.; fmr teaching asst, Dept of CCP History, Renmin Univ.; Lecturer, Beijing Teachers' Coll.; worker, Baoding Voltage Transformer Factory; Lecturer, Beijing Coll. of Chinese Medicine; currently playwright, Beijing Film Studio; Vice-Chair. China Film Asscn; mem. Bd of Dirs Chinese Writers Asscn; Nat. Book Award, Best Works Award, China Books Award, Huabiao Award, Splendor Award, Golden Rooster Award, Nat. Short Stories Award, Nat. Prose Award, Nat. Literature Prize. *Publications include:* Song of Loyal Hearts (play), Wedding, Masquerade, The Death of Lao She, The Moon Goddess, I Am a Zero, Big Family Matter, Flying Moth, Taiping Lake, Sunset Boulevard: Selected Screenplays by Su Shuyang, Homeland (novel), About Love (poetry), A Reader on China 2007, A Reader on Tibet 2009, China: Insight Traditions and Culture 2010, China: Insight Traditions and Culture (Youth Edition) 2011. *Address:* Chinese Writers Association, No.25, East Tucheng Road, Chaoyang District, Beijing 100013, People's Republic of China.

SU, Tong; Chinese writer; b. (Tong Zhonggui), 23 Jan. 1963, Suzhou, Jiangsu Prov.; ed Beijing Normal Univ.; fmrly Lecturer, Nanjing Acad. of Arts; Ed. Zhongshan Magazine; Writer-in-Residence, Univ. of Iowa Int. Writing Program 2001; mem. Jiangsu Provincial Writers' Asscn. *Publications include:* (titles in translation) The Eighth Is a Bronze Sculpture, The Escape of 1934, The Mournful Dance, The Lives of Women, Wives and Concubines 1990, Raise the Red Lantern (three novellas) 1991, Blush 1994, Rice 1995, Jasmine Woman 2004, My Life as an Emperor 2006, Binu – The Myth of Meng Jiang Nu 2007, The Boat to Redemption (Man Asian Literary Prize) 2009, Tattoo: Three Novellas 2010. *Address:* c/o Canongate Books, 14 High Street, Edinburgh, EH1 1TE, Scotland (office).

SU, Tseng-chang; Taiwanese lawyer and politician; *Premier;* b. 28 July 1947, Pingtung; m. Su Jan Shiow-ling; three d.; ed Nat. Taiwan Univ.; practised as lawyer 1973–83; joined Taipei Jr Chamber 1973, Pres. 1978; Vice-Pres. Jr Chamber International Taiwan 1979; elected mem. Taiwan Prov. Ass. 1981; Magistrate, Pingtung Co. 1989–94, Taipei Co. 1997–2004; Sec.-Gen. Office of the Pres. 2004–05; Premier of Taiwan 2006–07, 2019–; Sec.-Gen. Democratic Progressive Party, Chair. 2005, 2012–14; unsuccessful cand. for Vice-Pres. of Taiwan 2008, for Mayor of Taipei 2010; Most Outstanding Chapter in Asia Award 1978, Outstanding LOM Pres. of the World Award 1978. *Address:* Executive Yuan, No.1, Sec. 1, Zhongxiao E. Road, Zhongzheng District, Taipei 10058, Taiwan (office). *Telephone:* (2) 33566500 (office). *Fax:* (2) 33566920 (office). *Website:* www.ey.gov.tw (office).

SUALAUVI, II, HH Tuimaleali'ifano Va'aletoa, LLB; lawyer, lay preacher and head of state; b. 29 April 1947; m. HH Masiofo Fa'amausili Leinafo; ed Malua Theological Coll., Australian Nat. Univ.; fmr Secondary School Teacher; Police Officer in New Zealand for three years; fmr Prin. State Solicitor, Office of the Attorney-Gen.; fmr Public Trustee, Barrister and Solicitor in Supreme Court of Samoa; lay preacher for village of Matautu Falelatai; mem. Council of Deputies 1993–2001, 2004–; Tui A'ana Tuimaleali'ifano (paramount chief) 1977–; Head of State (O le Ao o le Malo) of Samoa 2017–. *Address:* Government House, Vailima, Apia, Samoa (office). *Website:* www.govt.ws (office).

SUÁREZ COPPEL, Juan José, BA, PhD; Mexican business executive, economist and academic; b. 1959; ed Instituto Tecnológico Autónomo de México (ITAM), Univ. of Chicago, USA; fmr Prof. of Econs, ITAM, Univ. Autónoma de Barcelona, Spain, Brown Univ., USA; Co-Head, Equity Derivatives Trading, Banamex 1995–97; Corp. Treas., Grupo Televisa 1997–2000; Chief of Staff to Sec. of Finance and Public Credit 2000–01; Dir of Derivatives Trading Desk, Banco Nacional de México SA (Banamex) 2001; Chief Financial Officer, Petróleos Mexicanos (PEMEX) 2001–06, Dir-Gen. 2009–12, apptd Chair. PEMEX Exploration & Production, 2009, PEMEX-Refining 2009; Chief Financial Officer, Grupo Modelo –2009; Dir, El Cid Resorts, Jacobs Engineering Group Inc. 2013–; fmr Dir I.I.I. Servicios SA de CV, Instalaciones Inmobiliarias para Industrias SA de CV, Mexicana de Lubricantes SA de CV, Instituto Mexicano del Petróleo. *Address:* c/o Corporate Secretary, Jacobs Engineering Group Inc., 155 North Lake Avenue 91101, PO Box 7084, Pasadena, CA 91109-7084, USA. *Telephone:* (877) 522-6272 (office). *E-mail:* presiding.director@jacobs.com (office). *Website:* www.jacobs.com (office).

SUÁREZ INDA, HE Cardinal Alberto; Mexican ecclesiastic; *Archbishop of Morelia;* b. 30 Jan. 1939, Celaya, Guanajuato; ed diocesan seminary of Morelia, Latin American Pius Coll., Pontifical Gregorian Univ., Rome; ordained priest, Archdiocese of Morelia, Michoacán 1964; consecrated Bishop of Tacámbaro, Michoacán 1985–95; Archbishop of Morelia 1995–; cr. Cardinal (Cardinal-Priest of

San Policarpo) 2015. *Address:* Costado Catedral, Frente Avenida Madero Pte. s/n, Apartado 17, 58000 Morelia, Michoacán, Mexico (office). *Telephone:* (4) 312-0523 (office); (4) 312-3738 (office). *Fax:* (4) 312-3744 (office). *E-mail:* info@arquimorelia.org.mx (office). *Website:* www.arquimorelia.org.mx (office).

SUÁREZ PERTIERRA, Gustavo, LLD; Spanish academic and fmr politician; *President, UNICEF Spanish Committee;* b. 1949, Cudillero, Oviedo; m.; one s. one d.; ed Univs of Oviedo, Valladolid and Munich; Prof. in Canon Law, Complutense Univ., Madrid 1978, also sometime Vice-Dean of Law, Sec.-Gen. and mem. Academic Council of Human Rights Inst.; Dir-Gen. of Religious Matters, Ministry of Justice and Pres. of Advisory Comm. on Religious Freedom 1982; Deputy Sec., Ministry of Defence 1984; Sec. of State for Mil. Admin. 1990–93; Minister of Educ. and Science 1993–95, of Defence 1995–96; Pres. Parl. Comm. for Public Admin. 1996–2000; Prof., Universidad Nacional de Educación a Distancia 2000; Dir Instituto Universitario Gen. Gutiérrez Mellado 2001–05; Chair. Real Instituto Elcano (research inst.), Madrid 2002–12; Trustee UNICEF Spanish Cttee 2012–17 (Pres. 2018–). *Address:* UNICEF Spanish Committee, Mauricio Legendre, 36, 28046 Madrid, Spain (office). *Telephone:* (91) 3789555 (office). *E-mail:* unicef@unicef.es (office). *Website:* www.unicef.es (office).

SUBAEY, Ahmed A. Al-; Saudi Arabian oil industry executive; *Vice-President of Marketing and Supply, Saudi Aramco;* fmr Pres. and CEO Saudi Petroleum International Inc. (US subsidiary of Saudi Aramco), fmr Pres. Saudi Petroleum Ltd (Japanese unit of Saudi Aramco); CEO S-Oil Corpn (jt venture between Saudi Arabia's state-run oil co. and Hanjin Group) 2008–12; apptd Exec. Dir for Marketing, Saudi Aramco 2012, Vice-Pres. of Marketing and Supply 2016–; mem. Bd of Dirs National Shipping Company of Saudi Arabia (Bahri). *Address:* Saudi Aramco, PO Box 5000, Dhahran 31311, Saudi Arabia (office). *E-mail:* webmaster2@aramco.com (office). *Website:* www.saudiaramco.com (office).

SUBAIHI, Maj.-Gen. Mahmud al-; Yemeni army officer and government official; b. 22 July 1956; ed Aden Mil. Coll.; Dir of Cabinet, Ministry of Defence 1976–78; fmr Commdr Anad base and Anad Axis, Lahij governorate, Southern Yemen; Commdr Fourth Mil. Region 2013–14; Minister of Defence 2014–15, 2016–18, Acting Minister of Defence (in Revolutionary Cttee declared Feb. 2015) 2015–16; defected to side of Aden-based govt 7 March 2015, captured by rebels 25 March 2015.

SUBBA ROW, Raman, CBE, MA; British company director, public relations consultant and fmr cricketer; b. 29 Jan. 1932, Streatham, London, England; s. of Panguluri Venkata Subba Row and Doris Pinner; m. Anne Harrison 1960; two s. one d.; ed Whitgift School, Croydon and Trinity Hall, Cambridge; Pilot Officer, RAF 1956–58; left-hand opening batsman; played for Univ. of Cambridge 1951–53, Surrey 1953–54, Northants. 1955–61 (Capt. 1958–61); Test debut: England v NZ, Manchester 24–29 July 1958; played in 13 Tests for England 1958–61, scored 984 runs (average 46.85, highest score 137) including three hundreds; toured Australia 1958–59; played in 260 First-class matches, scored 14,182 runs (average 41.46, highest score 300) including 30 hundreds; Assoc. Dir W.S. Crawford Ltd 1963–69; Man. Dir Management Public Relations Ltd 1969–92; Chair. Surrey Co. Cricket Club 1974–79, Test and County Cricket Bd 1985–90; Int. Cricket Council (ICC) referee (41 Tests, 119 One-Day Ints) 1992–2001; apptd to work with ICC on reform of int. umpiring and refereeing panels; mem. Inst. of Dirs; Wisden Cricketer of the Year 1961. *Leisure interests:* golf, sports generally. *Address:* Leeward, 13 Manor Way, South Croydon, Surrey, CR2 7BT, England (home). *Telephone:* (20) 8688-2991 (home). *Fax:* (20) 8688-2991 (home).

SUBBARAO, Duvvuri, BSc (Hons), MSc, MS (Econs), PhD; Indian economist and fmr central banker; b. 11 Aug. 1949, Eluru, AP; m. Urmila Rao; two s.; ed Indian Inst. of Tech., Kharagpur, Indian Inst. of Tech., Kanpur, Ohio State Univ., USA, Andhra Univ.; came top in All India Civil Service examination for entry into Indian Admin. Service and Indian Foreign Service 1972; Humphrey Fellow, MIT, USA 1982–83; Jt Sec., Dept of Econ. Affairs 1988–93; Finance Sec., Govt of AP 1993–98; Lead Economist, World Bank 1999–2004; Sec. to Prime Minister's Econ. Advisory Council 2005–07; Finance Sec., Ministry of Finance 2007–08; Gov. Reserve Bank of India 2008–13. *Publications include:* has written extensively on issues in public finance, decentralization and political economy of reforms. *Address:* c/o Reserve Bank of India, Central Office, Shahid Bhagat Singh Road, POB 10007, Mumbai 400 001, India.

SUBOTNICK, Morton Leon, MA; American composer and academic; b. 14 April 1933, Los Angeles, Calif.; s. of Jack Jacob Subotnick and Rose Luckerman; m. 1st Linn Pottle 1953 (divorced 1971); one s. one d.; m. 2nd Doreen Nelson 1976 (divorced 1977); m. 3rd Joan La Barbara 1979; one s.; ed Univ. of Denver, Mills Coll.; Co-founder San Francisco Tape Music Center 1961–65; fmr Music Dir Ann Halprin's Dance Co. and San Francisco Actors' Workshop, fmr Music Dir Lincoln Center Repertory Theatre; Dir of electronic music at original Electric Circus, St Mark's Place, New York 1967–68; Artist-in-Residence, New York Univ. School of the Arts 1966–69; apptd Co-Dir Center for Experiments in Art, Information and Tech., California Inst. of Arts, Valencia 1969, also Co-Chair. Composition Dept; Visiting Prof. in Composition, Univ. of Maryland 1968, Univ. of Pittsburgh 1969, Yale Univ. 1982, 1983; Composer-in-Residence DAAD, West Berlin 1981, MIT 1986; Brandeis Award for Music 1983, American Acad. of Arts and Letters Composer Award, SEAMUS Lifetime Achievement Award 1998, ASCAP John Cage Award, ACO Lifetime Achievement Award. *Compositions include:* Silver Apples of the Moon, The Wild Bull, Trembling, The Double Life of Amphibians, The Key to Songs, Return: The Triumph of Reason (electronic composition in honour of the return of Halley's Comet) 1986, In Two Worlds 1987–88, And The Butterflies Begin to Sing 1988, A Desert Flowers 1989, All my Hummingbirds have Alibis, Jacob's Room (opera) 1993, Making Music 1996, Intimate Immensity 1997, Echoes from the Silent Call of Girona 1998, Then Now and Forever 2008, Jacob's Room Opera 2010, From Silver Apples of the Moon to A Sky of Cloudless Sulphur 2009–13. *Address:* 25 Minetta Lane, Apt 4B, New York, NY 10012, USA. *E-mail:* morts@creatingmusic.com. *Website:* www.mortonsubotnick.com.

SUCHET, David, CBE, OBE; British actor; b. 2 May 1946, London, England; s. of Jack Suchet and Joan Suchet (née Jarché); m. Sheila Ferris 1976; one s. one d.; ed Wellington School, Somerset, London Acad. of Music and Dramatic Art; fmr mem. Nat. Youth Theatre, Chester Repertory Co.; joined RSC 1973; Assoc. Artist, Birmingham Rep., Connaught Theatre, Worthing, Northcott Theatre, Exeter, Liverpool Rep., Chichester Festival Theatre, Theatre Royal, Bath; Visiting Prof. of Theatre, Univ. of Neb., USA 1975; mem. Fight Dirs Asscn; Freedom of the City of London 2009; hon. degree from Univ. of Kent, Canterbury 2010; awards for Salieri in Amadeus 2000, Melmotte in The Way We Live Now 2002, Maxwell 2009. *Roles for RSC include:* Tybalt in Romeo and Juliet 1973, Orlando in As You Like It 1973, Tranio in Taming of the Shrew 1973, Zamislov in Summerfolk 1974, 1975, Wilmer in Comrades 1974, The Fool in King Lear 1974, 1975, Pisanio in Cymbeline 1974, Hubert in King John, Ferdinand King of Navarre in Love's Labour's Lost 1975, Shylock in The Merchant of Venice 1978, Grumio in Taming of the Shrew 1978, Sir Nathaniel in Love's Labour's Lost 1978, Glougauer in Once in a Lifetime 1978, Caliban in The Tempest 1978, Sextus Pompey in Antony and Cleopatra 1978, Angelo in Measure for Measure 1979, Iago in Othello, Every Good Boy Deserves Favour, Bolingbroke in Richard II 1981, Achilles in Troilus and Cressida, Mercutio in Romeo and Juliet, Iago in Othello 1985. *Other stage roles include:* Lucio in Measure for Measure 1977, Thomas Gilthead in The Devil is an Ass 1977, The Kreutzer Sonata 1978, Tsaravitch and George Wochner in Laughter! 1978, Joe Green in Separation 1987, This Story of Yours, Litvanoy in The Wedding Feast, Estragon in Waiting for Godot, John Aubrey in Brief Lives, Mole in Toad of Toad Hall, Timon in Timon of Athens 1991, John in Oleanna (Variety Club Best Actor Award 1994) 1993, Sid Field in What a Performance 1994, George in Who's Afraid of Virginia Woolf? (Critic's Circle Best Actor Award 1997) 1996, Salieri in Amadeus (Variety Club Best Actor Award 1998, South Bank Award and Backstage Theatre Award 2000) 1998–2000, Gregor Antonescu in Man and Boy, Duchess Theatre, London 2005, Once in a Lifetime, Royal Nat. Theatre 2006, All My Sons, Apollo Theatre, London (Best Actor, Olivier Awards, Critics' Circle Award) 2010, Long Day's Journey into Night, London 2012. *Films include:* Tale of Two Cities 1978, Schiele in Prison 1980, The Missionary 1982, Hunchback of Notre Dame 1982, Red Monarch (Best Actor, Marseilles Film Festival 1983) 1983, Trenchcoat 1983, Greystoke: The Legend of Tarzan, Lord of the Apes 1984, Little Drummer Girl 1984, Song for Europe (video title Cry for Justice) (Best Actor, Royal TV Soc. Performance Awards 1986) 1985, Thirteen to Dinner 1985, Falcon and the Snowman 1985, Gulag 1985, Iron Eagle 1986, Murrow 1986, Big Foot and The Hendersons 1986, Stress (Best Actor Award, British Industry/Scientific Film Asscn 1986) 1986, Crime of Honor 1987, The Last Innocent Man 1987, A World Apart 1988, To Kill a Priest (also known as Popielusko) 1988, The Lucona Affair, When the Whales Came 1990, Executive Decision 1995, Deadly Voyage 1995, Sunday 1996, A Perfect Murder 1997, RKO 1999, Sabotage 1999, Live From Baghdad 2002, The In-Laws 2003, Foolproof 2003, Flood 2006, Flushed Away (voice) 2006, Flood 2007, The Bank Job 2008, Act of God 2009, Effie 2010. *Work for radio includes:* The Kreutzer Sonata (one-man show) (Best Radio Actor of the Year 1979), Shylock in The Merchant of Venice, Bolingbroke in Richard II, First Night Impression, Rosenberg in the Trenches, Chimes at Midnight, The Isaac Babel Stories, Super Cannes (Book at Bedtime) and numerous other parts. *Television includes:* role of Hercule Poirot in dramatization of 65 Agatha Christie Poirot novels (for LWT) Series 1989–, 100th Anniversary Special: The Mysterious Affair at Styles 1990, Oppenheimer 1978, Being Normal, Saigon – the Last Days, Time to Die, The Life of Freud (Best Actor, Royal TV Soc. Performance Awards 1986), Blott on the Landscape (Best Actor, Royal TV Soc. Performance Awards 1986), Oxbridge Blues 1986, Playing Shakespeare 1983, Master of the Game 1984, Reilly – Ace of Spies 1984, Mussolini: The Untold Story 1985, James Joyce's Ulysses, Cause Célèbre 1988, The Life of Agatha Christie 1990, Once in a Lifetime, Bingo, Long Ago and Far Away 1989, Days of Majesty 1994, Fighting Fund (episode of The Protectors), Separation 1990, Secret Agent, Kings and Castles, Nobody Here but Us Chickens 1989, The Cruel Train, The Curious 1994, Moses 1995, Solomon 1997, See Saw 1997, The Way We Live Now 2001, National Crime Squad 2001–02, The First Lady 2003, Henry VIII 2003, Space Odyssey (voice) 2004, A Bear Named Winnie 2004, Dracula (film) 2006, Maxwell (film) 2007, Diverted (film) 2009, Going Postal (film) 2010, Hidden (series) 2011, Richard II (film) 2012 In The Footsteps of St Paul (documentary) 2012. *Achievements include:* brown belt in Aikido; a First Master of Japanese Samurai. *Publications:* essays in Players of Shakespeare 1985. *Leisure interests:* photography, clarinet, ornithology, theology, boating on inland waterways. *Address:* c/o Ken McReddie Associates Ltd, 36–40 Glasshouse Street, London, W1B 5DL, England (office). *Telephone:* (20) 7439-1456 (office). *Fax:* (20) 7734-6530 (office). *E-mail:* email@kenmcreddie.com (office).

SUCHOCKA, Hanna, DrIur; Polish lawyer, politician and diplomatist; b. 3 April 1946, Pleszew; ed Adam Mickiewicz Univ.; scientific worker, Dept of Constitutional Law, Adam Mickiewicz Univ., Poznań 1968–69, 1972–90, Catholic Univ., Lublin 1988–92, Polish Acad. of Science 1990–; mem. Democratic Party (SD) 1969–84, Democratic Union 1991–94, Freedom Union 1994–; Deputy to Sejm (Parl.) 1980–85, 1989–2001; mem. Civic Parl. Caucus 1989–91, mem. Democratic Union Parl. Caucus (now Freedom Union) 1991–, Deputy Chair. Parl. Legis. Cttee 1989–92; Chair. Council of Ministers (Prime Minister) 1992–93; Minister of Justice and Attorney-Gen. 1997–99; mem. Pontifical Acad. of Social Sciences, Rome 1994; Amb. to the Holy See 2001–13; Dr hc (Oklahoma); Max Schmidtheiny Prize 1994, Foyer Prize 2004. *Publications:* author of reports and articles for professional publs and int. confs.

SUDAN, Madhu, PhD; American (b. Indian) mathematician and academic; *Gordon McKay Professor, John A. Paulson School of Engineering and Applied Sciences, Harvard University;* b. 12 Sept. 1966; ed Indian Inst. of Tech. and Univ. of California, Berkeley, USA; student researcher, IBM Almaden Research Center 1990, mem. Research Staff, Math. Sciences Dept, IBM Thomas J. Watson Research Center, Yorktown Heights, NY 1992–97; Assoc. Prof., Dept of Electrical Eng and Computer Science, MIT 1997–2002, Prof. 2003–05, Fujitsu Chair Prof. 2005– (on leave since 2009), Adjunct Prof., MIT EECS 2011–15, mem. Computer Science and AI Lab. (CSAIL), Theory of Computing (TOC) Group, CSAIL, Algorithms, Complexity, and Cryptography and Information Security subgroups, TOC; Prin. Researcher, Microsoft Research 2009–15; Gordon McKay Prof., John A. Paulson School of Eng and Applied Sciences, Harvard Univ. 2015–; Fellow, Radcliffe Inst. for Advanced Study 2003–04; Ed. Society for Industrial and Applied Math. (SIAM) Journal on Discrete Mathematics 1997–, SIAM Journal on Computing 2000–03, Information and Computation 2000–03; Guest Ed. Journal of Computer and System Sciences (special issue devoted to papers from Complexity 2001) 2001–02; Ed.-in-chief Foundations and Trends in Theoretical 2004–; mem. Asscn for Computing Machinery, IEEE, Society for Industrial and Applied Math., American

Math. Soc.; Sakrison Memorial Award for PhD Thesis, Dept of Electrical Eng and Computer Science, Univ. of California, Berkeley 1993, ACM Doctoral Dissertation Award 1993, Sloan Foundation Fellowship 1998, NSF Career Award 1999, Information Theory Paper Award 2000, Gödel Prize 2001, Nevanlinna Prize 2002. *Publications include:* Efficient Checking of Polynomials and Proofs and the Hardness of Approximation Problems 1996, Complexity Classiffications of Boolean Constraint Satisfaction Problems (co-author) 2001; more than 90 articles in scientific journals on theoretical computer science, algorithms, computational complexity, optimization and coding theory. *Address:* 339 Maxwell Dworkin, 33 Oxford Street, Cambridge, MA 02138, USA (office). *E-mail:* madhu@cs.harvard.edu (office). *Website:* www.seas.harvard.edu (office).

SUDARSONO, Juwono, MS, PhD; Indonesian government official, diplomatist and academic; *Professor Emeritus, Department of International Relations, University of Indonesia;* b. 5 March 1942; m.; two s. one d.; ed Univ. of Indonesia, Univ. of California, Berkeley, USA, London School of Econs, UK; Visiting Prof., Columbia Univ. 1986–87; Dean of Social and Political Science, Univ. of Indonesia 1988–94, later Prof. Emer., Dept of Int. Relations; Vice-Gov. Indonesian Defence Coll. 1995–98; apptd Minister of Environment 1998, then Minister of Educ.; served as first civilian Minister of Defence 1999; returned to Univ. of Indonesia teaching part-time; fmr Commr Strategic Intelligence; Amb. to UK and Repub. of Ireland 2003–04; Minister of Defence 2004–09. *Address:* University of Indonesia, New Campus UI Depok, West Java 16424, Indonesia (office). *Telephone:* (21) 7867222 (office). *E-mail:* humas-ui@ui.ac.id (office). *Website:* www.ui.ac.id (office).

SÜDHOF, Thomas Christian, MD; German/American neuroscientist and academic; *Avram Goldstein Professor in the School of Medicine and Professor, by courtesy, of Neurology and of Psychiatry and Behavioral Sciences, Stanford University;* b. 22 Dec. 1955, Göttingen; m. Lu Chen; ed Univ. of Göttingen, Harvard Univ., USA; Postdoctoral Researcher, Max Planck Inst. for Biophysical Chemistry, Göttingen –1982; Postdoctoral Fellow, Univ. of Texas SW Medical Center, Dallas 1983, headed own lab. 1986–2008, Prof., Faculty for Molecular Genetics 1991–2008, Gill Distinguished Chair. 1995–2008, Chair. Grad. Program in Neuroscience 1999–2001, Lloyd B. Sands Distinguished Chair. in Neuroscience 1997–2008, Dir Center for Basic Neuroscience 1997–2006, Adjunct Prof. of Neuroscience 2008–; Investigator, Howard Hughes Medical Inst. 1986–89; Scientific mem. and Dir, Max Planck Inst. for Experimental Medicine, Göttingen 1995–98; moved to Stanford Univ. 2008, currently Avram Goldstein Prof. in the School of Medicine and Prof., by courtesy, of Neurology and of Psychiatry and Behavioral Sciences; mem. numerous Editorial Bds including Journal of Molecular Neuro-science 2000–, European Journal of Neuro-science 2001–, PLOS Biology 2017–; mem. Bd of Dirs Sanofi Inc. 2016–; mem. Scientific Advisory Bd Elysium Inc. 2014–, Simcere Therapeutics 2016–, C-Bridge Investment Corp. 2017–, Berlin Insts. of Health, Beihang Univ., Beijing, Abide Therapeutics; mem. NAS 2002, Inst. of Medicine 2007, American Acad. of Arts and Sciences 2010, Shemyakin-Ovchinnikov Inst. for Bio-organic Chemistry, Moscow 2013–, Deutsche Akademie der Naturforscher Leopoldina 2015; Foreign mem. Royal Soc. of London for Improving Natural Knowledge 2017; Albert Einstein Hon. Prof., Chinese Acad. of Sciences, Beijing 2010; Grosses Bundesverdienstkreuz mit Stern der Bundesrepublik Deutschland 2016; W. Alden Spencer Award, Columbia Univ. (jtly with Richard Scheller) 1993, Wilhelm Feldberg Award 1994, US Nat. Acad. Award in Molecular Biology (jtly with Richard Scheller) 1997, Ulf von Euler Lecture Award, Karolinska Institutet, MetLife Award in Alzheimer's Disease Research (jtly with Roberto Malinow), Bristol-Myers Squibb Award for Distinguished Achievement in Neuroscience Research 2004, Bernhard Katz Award, Biophysical Soc. (jtly with Reinhard Jahn), Passano Foundation Award 2008, Kavli Prize in Neuroscience, Kavli Foundation 2010, Lasker DeBakey Basic Medical Research Award, Albert and Mary Lasker Foundation 2013, Nobel Prize in Physiology or Medicine (jtly with James Rothman and Randy Schekman) 2013, CINP Pioneer Award (jtly with Solomon Snyder and Julien Mendlewicz), Grande Médaille de la Ville de Paris (jtly with James Rothman and Randy Schekman) 2014. *Publications include:* Synapses (co-Ed. with W. Maxwell Cowan and Charles F. Stevens) 2000, Pharmacology of Neurotransmitter Release (co-Ed. with Klaus Starke) 2008, The Synapse (co-Ed. with Morgan Sheng and Bernardo Sabatini) 2012. *Address:* Stanford University School of Medicine, Department of Molecular and Cellular Physiology, Beckman Center, Room G1021, 265 Campus Drive, Stanford, CA 94305-5453, USA (office). *Telephone:* (650) 721-1418 (office). *Fax:* (650) 498-4585 (office). *E-mail:* tcs1@stanford.edu (office). *Website:* med.stanford.edu/profiles/neuroscience/researcher/Thomas_Sudhof (office).

SUDJIC, Deyan, OBE; British architecture critic and arts administrator; *Director, The Design Museum;* b. 6 Sept. 1952, London; s. of Miša J. Sudjic and Ceja Sudjic (née Pavlovic); m. Sarah Miller; one d.; ed Univ. of Edin.; chose not to practise as an architect; Architecture Corresp., Sunday Times 1980–85; fmr Critic, London Daily News;Critic, Sunday Correspondent 1989–90; Architecture Critic, The Guardian 1991–97; Visiting Prof. of Design Theory and History, Hochschule für Angewandte Kunst, Vienna 1993–97; Dir Glasgow 1999 UK City of Architecture and Design; Ed. Domus Magazine 2000–04; Architecture Critic, The Observer 2000–; Dir 8th Venice Architectural Biennale 2002; Dir The Design Museum, London 2006–; Visiting Prof. of Design, Royal Coll. of Art; Founding Ed. Blueprint magazine 1983–96, later Editorial Dir; f. Tate and Eye magazines; Dr hc (Univ. for the Creative Arts). *Publications include:* Cult Objects 1985, New British Architecture: The Design of Richard Rogers, Norman Foster and James Stirling 1986, Rei Kawakubo: A Monograph of the Japanese Fashion Designer 1990, Cult Heroes: An Investigation of the Mechanics of Celebrity 1990, The Hundred Mile City: A Study of the Rapidly Evolving Modern City 1992, The Architecture of Richard Rogers 1995, The Architecture of Erick van Egeraat 1997, Ron Arad: A Monograph 1999, John Pawson Works 2000, Architecture and Democracy 2001, The Edifice Complex: How the Rich and Powerful Shape the World 2005, The Language of Things 2008, Norman Foster: A Life in Architecture 2010, Shiro Kuramata 2013, B is for Bauhaus: An A-Z of the Modern World 2014. *Address:* The Design Museum, Shad Thames, London, SE1 2YD, England (office). *Telephone:* (20) 7940-8790 (office). *E-mail:* info@designmuseum.org (office). *Website:* designmuseum.org (office).

SUDO, Fumio; Japanese steel industry executive; *Chairman, Tokyo Electric Power Company (TEPCO), Inc.;* b. 3 March 1941; ed Hokkaido Univ.; joined Kawasaki Steel Corpn 1964, Gen. Man., Steelmaking, Mizushima 1988, mem. Bd of Dirs 1994–, Exec. Officer 1994–2000, Exec. Vice-Pres. 2001, Pres. and CEO 2001–03, Pres. and CEO JFE Steel Corpn 2003–05, mem. Bd of Dirs JFE Holdings Inc. (following merger of Kawasaki Steel Corpn with Nihon Kōkan Kabushiki-gaisha) 2002–10, Pres. and CEO 2005–10, Consultant 2010–, Pres. Nihon Keizai Shimbun (now called The Nikkei) of JFE Holdings, Inc. 2005–08, Chair. JFE 21st Century Foundation; mem. Bd of Govs and Chair. Nippon Hoso Kyokai 2011–12; Chair. Tokyo Electric Power Co. (TEPCO), Inc. 2014–; Dir, LIXIL Group Corpn 2010–; External Dir, Takeda Pharmaceuticals International, Inc. 2011–; Dir (non-exec.), Takeda Pharmaceutical Co. Ltd 2011–; Outside Dir, Taisei Corpn 2011–. *Address:* Tokyo Electric Power Co., Inc., 1-1-3 Uchisaiwai-cho, Chiyoda-ku, Tokyo 100-8560, Japan (office). *Telephone:* (3) 4216-1111 (office). *Fax:* (3) 4216-2539 (office). *E-mail:* info@tepco.co.jp (office). *Website:* www.tepco.co.jp (office).

SUEBWONGLEE, Surapong; Thai physician and politician; fmr Communist rebel; trained as a medical doctor before entering politics; fmr mem. Thai Rak Thai party; Govt Spokesman 2005; Minister of Information and Communications Tech. –2006 (Govt of Prime Minister Thaksin Sinawatra deposed in mil. coup Sept. 2006); Sec.-Gen. People's Power Party 2007–08 (party dissolved by Constitutional Court); Deputy Prime Minister and Minister of Finance Sept. 2008; to face trial for abuse of power 2011, sentenced to one-year suspended prison term 2016.

SUEMATSU, Yasuharu, BS, PhD; Japanese electrical engineer and academic; *Honorary Professor, Tokyo Institute of Technology;* b. 22 Sept. 1932; ed Tokyo Inst. of Tech.; Assoc. Prof., Tokyo Inst. of Tech. 1961–73, Prof. 1973, now Emer., Pres. 1989–95, Hon. Prof. 2011–; Dir Gen. Nat. Inst. for Advanced Interdisciplinary Research 1995–97; Pres. Kochi Univ. of Tech. 1997–2001; Dir Gen. Nat. Inst. of Informatics 2001–05, Adviser 2005–09; Valdemar Poulsen Gold Medal 1983, Prime Minister's Award for Communication Achievement 1983, David Sarnoff Award 1986, Toray Science and Tech. Prize 1989, John Tyndall Award 1994, C&C Prize 1994, Medal with Purple Ribbon 1996, Eduard Rhein Basic Research Prize 1997, IEEE James H. Mulligan, Jr Educ. Medal 2003, Person of Cultural Merits 2003, Japan Prize (co-recipient) 2014. *Publications:* numerous papers in professional journals. *Address:* Center for Public Affairs and Communications, Tokyo Institute of Technology, 2-12-1 Ookayama, Meguro-ku, Tokyo 152-8550, Japan (office). *Telephone:* (3) 5734-2975 (office). *E-mail:* media@jim.titech.ac.jp (office); pr@jim.titech.ac.jp (office). *Website:* www.titech.ac.jp/english (office).

SUGA, Yoshihide, LLB; Japanese politician; *Chief Cabinet Secretary;* b. 6 Dec. 1948, Akita Pref.; ed Hosei Univ.; Sec. to Rep. Hikosaburo Okonogi 1975, Sec. to Minister for Int. Trade and Industry 1984–87; mem. Yokohama City Council 1987; mem. House of Reps 1996–, Parl. Sec. for Land, Infrastructure and Transport 2002–03, for Int. Trade and Industry 2003–04; Deputy Sec.-Gen. LDP 2001–, Chair. Diet Affairs Cttee 2004, Sr Vice-Minister for Internal Affairs and Communications 2005–06, Minister of Internal Affairs and Communications and Minister of State for Privatization of Postal Services 2006–07; Chief Cabinet Sec. 2012–, also Minister in charge of Alleviating the Burden of the Bases in Okinawa. *Address:* Cabinet Office, 1-6-1, Nagata-cho, Chiyoda-ku, Tokyo 100-8968 (office); Liberal-Democratic Party (Jiyu-Minshuto), 1-11-23, Nagata-cho, Chiyoda-ku, Tokyo 100-8910, Japan (office). *Telephone:* (3) 5253-2111 (office); (3) 3581-6211 (office). *E-mail:* koho@ldp.jimin.or.jp (office). *Website:* www.cao.go.jp (office); www.jimin.jp (office); www.sugayoshihide.gr.jp.

SUGAR, Baron (Life Peer), cr. 2009, of Clapton in the London Borough of Hackney; **Alan Michael Sugar;** British business executive and government official; b. 24 March 1947, London, England; s. of Nathan Sugar and Fay Sugar; m. Ann Simons 1968; two s. one d.; ed Brooke House School, London; Chair. and Man. Dir Amstrad PLC 1968–97, CEO –1993, Chair. 1997–2001, Chair. and CEO 2001–07; Chair. Amshold Group Ltd, Amshold International Ltd, Amstar Entertainment Ltd, Amsprop London Ltd, Amsvest Ltd; Owner and Chair. Tottenham Hotspur PLC 1991–2001; Chair. Viglen PLC 1997–2009; mem. Bd of Dirs Aventom Ltd, Tropic Skin Care Ltd, Hyper Recruitment Solutions Ltd, Dr Leah Ltd, Amstar Media Ltd; Govt Enterprise Champion 2009–10; Trustee, Alan Sugar Foundation; Empire Partner, The Hackney Empire (charity); Hon. DSc (City Univ.) 1988; Hon. Fellow, City and Guilds of London Inst. *Television includes:* host of The Apprentice (BBC) 2005–, Young Apprentice (Junior Apprentice in series 1) (BBC) (BAFTA Award for Best Reality & Constructed Factual 2012) 2010–. *Publications include:* The Apprentice Revisited 2006, What You See is What You Get: My Autobiography 2010. *Leisure interest:* tennis. *Address:* House of Lords, Westminster, London, SW1A 0PW, England (office). *Telephone:* (20) 7219-5353 (office). *Fax:* (20) 7219-5979 (office).

SUGAR, Ronald D., BEng, MSc, PhD; American business executive; b. 30 July 1948, Toronto, Ont., Canada; m. Valerie Sugar; two c.; ed Univ. of California, Los Angeles, Stanford Univ., Univ. of Pennsylvania, Harvard Univ.; began career in tech. and man. positions at Hughes Aircraft Co., Argosystems Inc. and The Aerospace Corpn 1970s; joined TRW Aerospace and Information Systems 1970s, held various sr positions including Vice-Pres. Space Communications Div., Chief Financial Officer, Exec. Vice-Pres., Gen. Man. Global Automotive Electronics –1990s; Pres. and COO Litton Industries 2000–01, Pres. and COO Northrup Grumman Corpn (following acquisition of Litton by Northrup 2001) 2001–03, Chair., Pres. and CEO 2003–06, Chair. and CEO 2006–10 (retd), now Sr Advisor; mem. Bd Dirs Chevron Corpn 2005– (Lead Dir 2015–), Air Lease Corpn, Apple Inc. 2010–, Amgen Inc.; apptd by Pres. of USA to Nat. Security Telecommunications Advisory Cttee; Sr Advisor, Ares Management LLC, Bain & Company; fmr Gov. Aerospace Industries Asscn; Nat. Fundraising Chair. Pearl Harbor Memorial Fund; fmr Chair. Aerospace Industries Asscn; Nat. Trustee Boys & Girls Clubs of America; Trustee, Cleveland Inst. of Music, Nat. Defense Industrial Asscn, Univ. of Southern California; Fellow, AIAA; FRAeS; mem. Nat. Acad. of Eng; Engineering Alumnus of the Year, UCLA 1996, Daniel J. Epstein Eng Man. Award, Univ. of Southern Calif. 2003, Semper Fidelis Award, Marine Corps Foundation, John R. Alison Leadership to Nat. Defense Award, Air Force Asscn, Eisenhower Distinguished Citizen Award, Army Distaff Foundation.

SUGISAKI, Shigemitsu; Japanese financial industry executive, international organization official and fmr civil servant; *Vice-Chairman, Goldman Sachs Japan Company, Ltd;* b. 1941, Tokyo; ed Univ. of Tokyo, Columbia Univ., USA; positions with Ministry of Finance 1964–76, 1979–94 including mem. Minister's Secr.,

Deputy Vice-Minister of Finance for Int. Affairs 1990–91, Deputy Dir-Gen. Int. Finance Bureau 1991–92, Commr Tokyo Regional Taxation Bureau 1992–93, Sec.-Gen. Exec. Bureau Securities and Exchange Surveillance Comm. 1993–94; Personal Asst to Pres. Asian Devt Bank 1976–79; Special Adviser to Man. Dir IMF 1994–97, Deputy Man. Dir 1997–2004; Chair. Sompo Japan Research Inst.; Vice-Chair. Goldman Sachs Japan Co. Ltd 2006–. *Address:* Goldman Sachs Japan Co. Ltd, Roppongi Hills, Mori Tower, Level 43-48, 10-1, Roppongi 6-chome, Minato-ku, Tokyo 106-6147, Japan (office). *Telephone:* (3) 6437-1000 (office). *Website:* www2.goldmansachs.com/japan (office).

SUGIYAMA, Shinsuke J.; Japanese diplomatist; *Ambassador to*USA;b. 14 May 1953; m. Yoko E. Sugiyama; s. one d.; ed Waseda Univ., Univ. of Oxford; fmr Prof. of Int. Law at Waseda Univ.; Pvt. Sec. to the Vice-Minister for Foreign Affairs 1993–95, Dir, UN Policy Div., Foreign Policy Bureau 1995, Dir, Treaties Div., Treaties Bureau 1998; Minister, Embassy of Japan, South Korea 2000–04; Deputy Chief of Mission, Egypt 2004–05; Deputy Dir-Gen., Middle Eastern and African Affairs Bureau, Ministry of Foreign Affairs 2005, Asian and Oceanian Affairs Bureau 2011, Deputy Dir-Gen., Int. Cooperation Bureau 2006, Amb. to Dir-Gen. for Global Issues 2008–11; Deputy Minister for Foreign Affairs 2013–16, Vice-Minister for Foreign Affairs 2016–18; Amb. to USA 2018–. *Publications include:* written and edited numerous articles and books on int. law. *Address:* Embassy of Japan, 2520 Massachusetts Ave, NW, Washington, DC 20008, USA (office). *Telephone:* (202) 238-6700 (office). *Fax:* (202) 328-2187 (office). *E-mail:* jicc@ws.mofa.go.jp (office). *Website:* www.us.emb-japan.go.jp (office).

SUH, Kyung-bae, MBA; South Korean business executive; *Chairman and CEO, AmorePacific Group;* b. 1963; s. of Suh Sung-whan; m.; two c.; ed Cornell Univ., USA; joined family business AmorePacific Corpn (cosmetics co.) 1980s, Pres. and CEO 1997, now Chair. and CEO, AmorePacific Group; Korea's Best CEO, Ernst & Young 2010, named Forbes Asian Businessman of the Year 2015. *Address:* AmorePacific Corpn, 100 Cheonggyecheon-ro, Jung-gu, Seoul 100-230, Republic of Korea (office). *Telephone:* (2) 709-5000 (office). *Fax:* (2) 709-5000 (office). *Website:* www.amorepacific.com (office).

SUH, Kyung-suk; South Korean business executive; *Vice-Chairman (Senior Advisor), GS Holdings Corporation;* began career in Ministry of Finance, Man. Ulsan Tax Office 1971–75, Sr Officer, Ministry of Finance 1975–89, Vice-Dir Tax Court 1989–90; Financial Commr, Embassy in Japan 1990–91; moved to LG Group as Finance Advisor to Chair. of LG Group 1991–92, Vice-Pres. 1992–94, Sr Vice-Pres. 1994–96, Exec. Vice-Pres. LG Strategic Business Devt Dept 1996, Exec. Vice-Pres. LG Investment Trust 1996–97, Pres. and CEO LG Investment Trust 1997–98, Pres. and CEO LG Capital 1998–2000, Pres. and CEO Kukdong City Gas 2000–01, Pres. and CEO LG Investment Securities 2001–04, mem. Exec. Bd, Pres. and CEO GS Holdings (spun off from LG Group in 2004) 2004–14, Vice-Chair. (Sr Advisor) 2014–. *Address:* GS Holdings Corpn, 23 F, GS Tower, 679 Yoksam Dong, Gangnam Gu, Seoul, South Korea (office). *Telephone:* (2) 2005-1114 (office). *Fax:* (2) 2005-8181 (office). *E-mail:* info@gsholdings.com (office). *Website:* www.gsholdings.com (office); www.gs.co.kr (office).

SUHAIBI, Noman Taher as-; Yemeni politician; b. 1965, Al-Sadda, Ibb; ed San'a Univ.; Dir Gen. Office of the Prime Interest 1995–2001; Deputy Chair. Tax Authority 2001–05, Chair. 2005–07; Minister of Finance 2007–11. *Address:* c/o Ministry of Finance, PO Box 190, San'a, Yemeni. *E-mail:* support@mofyemen.net.

SUHL, Harry, PhD; American physicist and academic; *Professor Emeritus of Physics, University of California, San Diego;* b. 18 Oct. 1922, Leipzig, Germany; s. of Bernhard Suhl and Klara Bergwerk; m. 1949 (deceased); ed Univ. Coll., Cardiff and Oriel Coll., Oxford, UK; Temp. Experimental Officer, Admiralty, London 1943–46; Tech. Staff, Bell Labs, NJ 1948–60; Prof. of Physics, Univ. of California, San Diego 1961, now Prof. Emer. Inst. for Pure and Applied Physical Sciences; Consultant, Aerospace Corpn 1961–, Exxon Research and Eng, NJ 1977–; Co-Ed. Magnetism 1961–74; Solid State Communications 1961–; Nat. Science Foundation Fellow 1971; Alexander V. Humboldt Sr Fellow 1991; Fellow, American Physics Soc., NAS, American Acad. of Arts and Sciences; Guggenheim Fellow 1968–69. *Publication:* Magnetism – A Treatise on Modern Theory and Materials (with G.T. Rado) 1966. *Address:* Physics Department, University of California, San Diego, 9500 Gilman Drive, La Jolla, CA 92093, USA (office). *Telephone:* (619) 534-4748 (office). *Fax:* (619) 534-0173 (office). *E-mail:* suhl@physics.ucsd.edu (office). *Website:* ipaps.ucsd.edu (office).

SUI, Anna; American fashion designer; *Founder and Designer, Anna Sui Corporation;* b. 4 Aug. 1955, Dearborn, Mich.; d. of Paul Sui and Grace Sui; ed Parsons School of Design, New York; Founder and Designer, Anna Sui Corpn 1988–; launched first collection 1991; established reputation with 'baby-doll' collection 1993; designer Sui Anna Sui 1995–; launched new line of special-occasion gowns 1997; CFDA Perry Ellis Award for New Fashion Talent 1993, Geoffrey Beene Lifetime Achievement Award 2009. *Address:* c/o KCD Inc., 450 West 15th Street, Suite 604, New York, NY 10011; Anna Sui Corporation, 275 West 39th Street, Floor 9, New York, NY 10018 (office); 113 Green Street, New York, NY 10012, USA (office). *Telephone:* (212) 768-1951 (office). *E-mail:* contactus@annasui.com. *Website:* www.annasui.com.

SUI, Gen. Yongju; Chinese army officer; b. Nov. 1932, Dalian City; engaged in secret communist activities while still at school as mem. New Democratic Youth; joined CCP 1950, PLA 1950; Clerk Luda Garrison Command responsible for Communist Youth League work; Sec. Political Office Public Security Militia Luda Border Defence Regt 1953; Co. Political Guidance Officer Eng Regt Second Artillery, Regt Org. Section Chief, Div. Chief Political Dept 1969, Political Commissar, Dir Base Political Dept, Asst Political Commissar, Base Political Commissar; elected. mil. rep. 7th NPC 1988; selected as activist to study Mao's works 1968; trained Second Artillery Eng Acad. 1985, Dir Political Office Second Artillery 1988; Second Asst Political Commissar, Second Artillery 1985–92, apptd Political Commissar 1992; mem. Cen. Comm. for Disciplinary Inspection; rank of Maj.-Gen. 1988, Lt-Gen. 1990, Gen. 1996; Del., 15th CCP Nat. Congress 1997–2002; mem. 9th Standing Cttee of NPC 1998–2003.

ŠUICA, Dubravka, BA; Croatian teacher and politician; *Vice-President, Croatian Democratic Union;* b. 20 May 1957, Dubrovnik; m. Capt. Stijepo Šuica; one d.; ed Univ. of Zagreb, Univ. of Buffalo, USA; taught English and German in Lapad Elementary School, Dubrovnik 1981–88, Centar za odgoj i usmjereno obrazovanje High School, Dubrovnik 1988–90; Prof. of English and German, Luka Sorkočević School of Arts, Dubrovnik 1990–92; Asst, Maritime Faculty, Dubrovnik 1992–94; Prof. of English, Polytechnic of Dubrovnik 1994–2000; Prin. Gimnazija Dubrovnik Classical Academic High School 1996–2000; Prof. of German, American Coll. of Man. and Tech., Dubrovnik 1998–2000; mem. Exec. Bd Municipality of Dubrovnik in charge of educ. 1991–93; Mayor of Dubrovnik 2001–09; mem. Croatian Democratic Union (HDZ) 1990–, Pres. City Cttee and mem. HDZ's Cen. Cttee 1998–, Vice-Pres. HDZ 2012–; mem. Croatian Parl. 2000–11, mem. Inter-Parl. Cooperation Cttee 2000–04, Cttee on Local and Regional Self-Govt 2000–04, Deputy mem. Del. in OSCE Parl. Ass. 2000–04, Pres. Cttee for Family, Youth and Sport 2000–04; mem. European Parl. (EPP) 2013–; Pres. Croatian Del. to Congress of Local and Regional Authorities of Council of Europe (CLRAE) 2004, First Vice-Pres. Chamber of Local Authorities of CLRAE 2004; Councillor, Dubrovnik-Neretva Co. Ass. 1997–2001, 2006–09; mem. Bd Union of Asscn of Towns of Repub. of Croatia 2002, European Asscn of Historic Towns and Regions 2004, Union of Asscn of Towns and Asscn of Municipalities of Repub. of Croatia 2005; Kt, Order of European Wine Kts 2005, Croatian Kts' Consulate–Order of European Wine Kts 2005; named Croatia's Mayor of the Year 2005, 'Tourist Flower – Quality for Croatia' Award 2005, named one of Top 10 World Mayors 2006, World Mayor Award, City Mayors 2006. *Address:* European Parliament, 60 Rue Wiertz, Altiero Spinelli 04F259, 1047 Brussels, Belgium (office); 20000 Dubrovnik, Ante Topića Mimare 6, Croatia (home). *Telephone:* (2) 0321044 (home). *Fax:* (2) 0322102 (home). *E-mail:* info@dubravka-suica.com (home).

SUISSA, Eliyahu (Eli); Israeli politician and fmr army officer; b. 1956, Afula, Morocco; m.; four c.; career officer in Israel Defense Forces (IDF) and Army Chaplain of IDF Northern Command; Dist Commr (Jerusalem), Ministry of the Interior 1986–96, Minister of the Interior and of Religious Affairs 1996–99; mem. Knesset (Shas) 1999–2003; Minister of Nat. Infrastructure 1999–2000 (resgnd), Minister without Portfolio, responsible for Jerusalem Affairs 2001–03.

SUKARNOPUTRI, Megawati (see MEGAWATI, Sukarnoputri).

ŠUKER, Ivan, DiplEcon; Croatian politician and economist; b. 12 Nov. 1957, Livno; m. Andrea Šuker; one s. one d.; ed Univ. of Zagreb; Chief Accountant, City Council, Velika Gorica 1984–86, Financial Dir 1986–90, Head of Fiscal Office 1990–2000, Deputy Mayor 1990–91, Chief of Gen. Staff, Velika Gorica (during war) 1991–92; mem. City Council, Zagreb 1993–97, Deputy Mayor 1997–2000; elected to Sabor (Parl.) for Croatian Democratic Union (Hrvatska demokratska zajednica—HDZ) 2000–, mem. Finance and Budget Cttee, Pres. HDZ, Velika Gorica 2000–03, mem. HDZ Nat. Bureau 2000–, Deputy Chair. HDZ 2002–; Minister of Finance 2003–10, Deputy Prime Minister 2009–10; fmr Chair. Croatian Basketball Asscn. *Leisure interest:* basketball. *Address:* c/o Ministry of Finance, 10000 Zagreb, ul. Katančićeva 5, Croatia.

SUKHEE, Sukhbold, MBA; Mongolian diplomatist; *Permanent Representative to United Nations;* b. 30 Oct. 1976, Orhontuul soum, Selenge Province; ed Univ. of Int. Relations, Clengendeal Inst. of Int. Relations, Netherland, Victoria Univ., Melbourne; Attaché, Dept of Int. Org., Ministry of Foreign Affairs 1999, for Dept of Legal and Consular Affairs 2000–04, Third Sec. Dept of Law and Treaty 2006–07, Acting Dir 2012, Second Sec., Perm. Mission to UN 2007–10, Deputy Dir Dept of Public Admin and Man. 2010–12, Dir 2012–15; Amb. and Perm. Rep. to UN 2015–; mem. Exec. Bd Mongolian Cricket Asscn 2006–; mem. Bd of Dirs MGIMO-Mongol 2012–. *Address:* Permanent Missions of Mongolia, 6 E 77th Street, New York, NY 10075, USA.

SUKMA, Rizal, PhD; Indonesian academic and diplomatist; *Ambassador to UK;* ed London School of Econs, UK; Sec., Int. Relations Bureau, Cen. Exec. Bd of Muhammadiyah; Visiting Lecturer, Postgraduate Faculty, Univ. of Indonesia; Dir of Studies, Centre for Strategic and Int. Studies, Jakarta –2015; Amb. to UK and Perm. Rep. to IMO London 2015–; mem. Bd, Syafii Maarif Inst. for Culture and Humanity; Visiting Lecturer, Dept of Int. Relations, Muhammadiyah Univ., Malang; mem. Nat. Cttee on Strategic Defence Review, Ministry of Defence. *Publications:* Human Security and Political Stability: Should There Be a Tension? 2001; numerous articles, papers and reports. *Address:* Embassy of Indonesia, 38 Grosvenor Square, London, W1X 2HW, England (office). *Telephone:* (20) 7499-7661 (office). *Fax:* (20) 7491-4993 (office). *E-mail:* kbri@btconnect.com (office). *Website:* www.indonesianembassy.org.uk (office).

ŠUKYS, Raimondas, DCL; Lithuanian lawyer and politician; b. 27 Oct. 1966, Šiauliai; m. Adelė Šukys; one s. one d.; ed Janonio Secondary School (now J. Janonio Gymnasium), Šiauliai, Vilnius State Univ. (now Vilnius Univ.); mil. service 1985–87; lawyer, Šiauliu kraštas (daily newspaper) 1991–92; lawyer, Verslo raktas (advisory co.) 1992–94; asst, Civil Law and Civil Process Dept, Law Faculty, Vilnius Univ. 1992–2004; referent, Fraction of Lithuanian Democratic Working Party (LDDP) 1993–94; adviser, Seimas (Parl.) Comm. on Econ. Crime Investigation 1994–97; mem. Lithuanian Liberal Party 1997–2003, Liberal and Centre Union 2003–14; mem. election HQ of cand. for presidency, Valdas Adamkus 1997; solicitor, UAB BNA group 1998–99; adviser for civil law, Legal Dept, Office of the Govt 1999–2000; mem. Seimas (Lithuanian Liberal Party) for Fabijoniškes Election Dist No. 5, mem. Cttee on Legal Affairs 2000–04, re-elected to Seimas for Liberal and Centre Union 2004; Attorney of Pres. Valdas Adamkus for elections 2004; Minister of the Interior 2006–07, of Health 2010–12; Adviser to the Minister of Justice 2012–13; Seimas Ombudsman 2013–18; Dir of Customer Service Dept, Šiauliai City Employment Service 2019–; mem. Vilnius City Bd 2002–03; Grand Cross, Order of the Lithuanian Grand Duke Gediminas, Order of the Cross of Terra Mariana (Estonia), 3rd Class, Grand Cross, Order of Prince Henry (Portugal). *Leisure interests:* gardening, literature, music, fishing.

SULAIMAN, Lama al-, BSc, MSc, PhD; Saudi Arabian business executive; *Vice-President, Jeddah Chamber of Commerce and Industry;* b. 11 Sept. 1966, Beirut, Lebanon; m.; four c.; ed King Abdulaziz Univ., King's Coll., Univ. of London; Consultant (part-time), Nutrition Laboratory, King Fahad Research Centre, King Abdulaziz Univ. Hospital 1990–2002; Owner, Chamelle Health Club for Women, Jeddah 2000–; Deputy Chair. Jeddah Chamber of Commerce and Industry 2005–, also Vice-Pres.; Pres. Al-Sayedah Khadija Bint Khouaylid Center for Business Women 2005–; mem. ILO Saudi Delegation and Head of Saudi Arabia's Employees Delegation representing the private sector 2009–; mem. Bd of Dirs Rolaco

Holdings, Luxembourg 2000–, Saudi Inst. for Health Services 2005–, Saudi French Business Council 2007–, Sa'afa Soc. to fight corruption and encourage transparency 2009–, Advisory Honorary Board Bylaws of Effat Univ. 2012–; mem. Bd of Trustees Jeddah Social and Economic Circle 2004; mem. Young Arab Leaders 2003–09. *Address:* Jeddah Chamber of Commerce and Industry, King Khalid Street, Ghurfa Building, PO Box 9549, Jeddah, 21423, Saudi Arabia (office). *Telephone:* (2) 6518028 (office); (2) 6534280 (home). *Fax:* (2) 6601802 (home); (2) 6674335. *E-mail:* info@jcci.org.sa (office); nutrilama@yahoo.co.uk (home). *Website:* www.jcci.org.sa/jcci/en (office).

SULAYEM, Sultan Ahmed bin, BS; United Arab Emirates business executive; *Group Chairman and CEO, DP World;* b. 1955; ed Temple Univ., USA; began career as customs inspector, Dubai Port late 1970s; Chair. Jebel Ali Free Zone 1985; Chair. and Man. Dir Dubai Ports Authority 1991; f. Nakheel (property developer), Chair. –2010; Chair. Dubai World (holding co. for govt investments) –2010; Group Chair. and CEO DP World (operates more than 60 container-handling terminals across six continents) 2007–; mem. Bd Dubai Exec. Council; Chair. Tejari.com; f. Istithmar (pvt. equity fund); Dir Investment Corpn of Dubai –2009, Seven Tides International; Chair. UAE Br., Chartered Inst. of Logistics and Transport; mem. World Export Processing Zones Asscn; Assoc. mem. French Business Council; Dr hc (Middlesex Univ., Dubai) 2008; Arabian Hotel Investment Conf. Leadership Award 2008, named by World Econ. Forum as Global Leader for Tomorrow. *Leisure interests:* endurance racing, deep-sea diving. *Address:* DP World, 5th Floor, JAFZA 17, Jebel Ali Free Zone, PO Box 17000, Dubai, United Arab Emirates (office). *Telephone:* (4) 8811110 (office). *Fax:* (4) 8811331 (office). *E-mail:* info@dpworld.com (office). *Website:* www.dpworld.com (office).

SULEIMAN, Mohamud Hassan; Somali politician; Minister of Finance and the Treasury 2012–14. *Address:* Ministry of Finance and the Treasury, 1 Villa Somalia, 2525 Mogadishu, Somalia (office). *Telephone:* (5) 404240 (office). *Website:* www.mof.somaligov.net (office).

SULEMAN, Rao Qamar, MA; Pakistani air force officer; b. 1954, Okara, Okara Dist, Punjab Prov.; ed Pakistan Air Force Public School, Sargodha (belonged to 17th entry, 851-Sabre House), Flying Instructors' School, Combat Commanders' School, PAF Air War Coll., Faisal, Nat. Defence Coll., Islamabad; joined Pakistan Air Force (PAF) Acad., Risalpur 1972, commissioned in PAF as fighter pilot in 59th GD(P) Course 1975, has commanded No. 15 Squadron, No. 31 (Fighter) Wing at Samungli, PAF Base, Peshawar and Southern Air Command, also served in UAE Air Force on deputation, directed staff at PAF Air War Coll., later served as Commdt there, Deputy Dir at Operations Br., Asst Chief of Staff (Plans), Asst Chief of Air Staff (Evaluation), Deputy Insp. Gen. of PAF at Air HQ, sr staff appointments include Dir-Gen. Air Force Strategic Command and Deputy Chief of Air Staff (Operations) at Air HQ, Islamabad, promoted to Air Vice-Marshal 2003, to Air Marshal 2007, Chief of the Air Staff 2009–12; Tamgha-e-Imtiaz (Mil.), Sitara-e-Basalat Sitara-e-Imtiaz (Mil.), Hilal-e-Imtiaz (Mil.), Nishan-e-Imtiaz (Mil.).

SULEYMENOV, Olzhas Omarovich; Kazakhstani politician, diplomatist and writer; b. 18 May 1936; ed Kazak State Univ., Maxim Gorky Inst. of Literature in Moscow; mem. CPSU 1989–90; debut as writer in 1960; Ed.-in-Chief Studio Kazakhfilm 1962–71; head of div. Prostor (magazine) 1971–; Sec. Bd Kazakh Writers' Union 1971–; Chair. Kazakh Cttee on relations with writers of Asia and Africa 1980–; actively participates in ecological movt, actions of protest against nuclear tests in Semipalatinsk since late 1980s; Deputy to USSR Supreme Soviet 1984–89; People's Deputy, mem. USSR Supreme Soviet 1989–91; Founder and Leader of People's Progress Party of Kazakhstan 1992–95; Amb. to Italy 1995–2001; Amb. and Perm. Del. to UNESCO, Paris 2001–13; USSR Komsomol Prize, State Abai Prize of Kazakh SSR. *Publications:* poetry collections, including Argamaki 1961, Sunny Nights 1962, The Night of Paris 1963, The Kind Time of the Sunrise 1964, The Year of Monkey 1967, Above White Rivers 1970, Each Day – Morning 1973, Repeating in the Noon 1973, A Round Star 1975, Definition of a Bank 1976, Tiurki v Doistorii: o proiskhzhdenii drevnetiurkskikh iazykov i pis'mennostei 2002 and others. *Address:* Ministry of Foreign Affairs, 010000 Nur-Sultan, D. Kunaev kosh. 31, Kazakhstan (office). *Telephone:* (7172) 72-05-18 (office). *Fax:* (7172) 72-05-16 (office). *E-mail:* mfa@mfa.kz (office). *Website:* www .mfa.kz (office).

SULÍK, Richard; Slovak economist, business executive and politician; *Chairman, Sloboda a Solidarita (Freedom and Solidarity);* b. 22 Jan. 1968, Bratislava, Slovak Socialist Repub., Czechoslovak Socialist Repub.; four c.; ed Ludwig Maximilian Univ., Germany, Univ. of Econs, Bratislava; emigrated with parents to Pforzheim, FRG 1980; returned to Czechoslovakia 1991; f. co. FaxCOPY; Special Adviser to Minister of Finance Ivan Miklos *c.* 2003 whom he convinced to take his masters thesis as a blueprint for the 2004 Slovak tax reform, remained on Advisory Bd of the Ministry; CEO of municipal waste disposal co. 2004–06; returned as Special Adviser to Ministry of Finance under Ján Počiatek; Founder and Chair. Sloboda a Solidarita (Freedom and Solidarity) 2009–; mem. Nat. Council of the Slovak Repub. (Národná rada Slovenskej republiky) 2010–, Chair. (Speaker) 2010–11; mem. European Parl. 2014–19. *Address:* National Council of the Slovak Republic (Národná rada Slovenskej republiky), nam. Alexandra Dubčeka 1, 812 80 Bratislava (office); Sloboda a Solidarita, Priemyselná 8, 821 09 Bratislava, Slovakia (office). *Telephone:* (2) 5972-1111 (Nat. Council) (office); (2) 5245-4089 (Party) (office). *Fax:* (2) 5441-9529 (Nat. Council) (office). *E-mail:* richard@sulik.sk (office); sas@sas.sk (home). *Website:* www.sulik.sk (office); www.sas.sk (office); richardsulik.blog.sme.sk; web.sulik.sk.

SULLIVAN, Andrew, PhD; British journalist; b. 20 Aug. 1963, Godstone, Surrey; pnr Aaron Tone; ed Magdalen Coll., Oxford, Kennedy School of Govt, Harvard Univ., USA; intern, Centre For Policy Studies, London; intern, New Republic magazine 1986, returned to Harvard and taught in Govt Dept 1987, returned as Assoc. Ed. New Republic 1987, Deputy Ed. 1990, Acting Ed. 1991, Ed. 1991–96; contributing writer and columnist, New York Times Magazine, contrib. New York Times Book Review –2002; weekly columnist for Sunday Times of London; est. andrewsullivan.com's Daily Dish blog 2000 at Time magazine, moved to TheAtlantic.com 2007–11, with Daily Beast 2011–13, est. Dish Publishing LLC to offer subscription service, announced he would cease blogging 2015. *Publications include:* Virtually Normal: An Argument About Homosexuality 1995, Love

Undetectable: Notes on Friendship, Sex, and Survival 1999, The Conservative Soul 2006, Intimations Pursued: The Voice of Practice in the Conversation of Michael Oakeshott 2007; as ed.: Same-Sex Marriage Pro & Con: A Reader 1997 (2nd edition 2004). *Website:* dish.andrewsullivan.com.

SULLIVAN, Dennis Parnell, BA, PhD; American mathematician and academic; *Albert Einstein Chair in Science, City University of New York;* b. 12 Feb. 1941, Port Huron, Mich.; three s. two d.; ed Rice and Princeton Univs; NATO Fellow, Univ. of Warwick, UK 1966; Miller Fellow, Univ. of California, Berkeley 1967–69; Sloan Fellow of Math., MIT 1969–72, Prof. of Math. 1972–73; Prof. Perm., Institut des Hautes Etudes Scientifiques, Paris, France 1973–96; Albert Einstein Chair in Science, Queens Coll. and Grad. School, CUNY, New York 1981–; concurrently Distinguished Prof. of Math., State Univ. of New York at Stony Brook; fmr Vice-Pres. American Math. Soc.; mem. NAS, New York Acad. of Sciences; Fellow, AAAS, American Acad. of Arts and Sciences 1991, American Math. Soc. 2012; Dr hc (Warwick) 1984; Oswald Veblen Prize in Geometry 1971, Elie Cartan Prix en Géométrie, French Acad. of Sciences 1981, King Faisal Int. Prize of Science 1994, New York City Mayor's Award for Excellence in Science and Tech. 1997, Nat. Medal of Science 2004, Steele Prize, American Math. Soc. 2006, Wolf Prize in Math. 2010. *Publications:* several papers in math. journals. *Leisure interest:* people. *Address:* Mathematics PhD Program, City University of New York, The Graduate Center, 365 Fifth Avenue, Room 4214-12, New York, NY 10016-4309 (office); Mathematics Department, 5-114 Mathematics Building, SUNY, Stony Brook, NY 11794-3651, USA. *Telephone:* (212) 817-8578 (office); (631) 632-8359 (Stony Brook). *Fax:* (212) 817-1527; (631) 632-7631 (Stony Brook). *E-mail:* dsullivan@gc.cuny.edu (office); dennis@math.sunysb.edu (office). *Website:* www.gc .cuny.edu/Page-Elements/Academics-Research-Centers-Initiatives/Doctoral -Programs/Mathematics/Faculty-Bios/Dennis-Sullivan (office); www.math.sunysb .edu (office).

SULLIVAN, Louis Wade, BS, MD; American physician, academic and fmr government official; *President Emeritus, School of Medicine, Morehouse College;* b. 3 Nov. 1933, Atlanta, Ga; s. of Walter Wade Sullivan and Lubirda Elizabeth Sullivan (née Priester); m. Eve Williamson 1955; three c.; ed Morehouse Coll., Boston Univ.; Intern, New York Hosp.-Cornell Medical Centre, New York 1958–59, resident in internal medicine 1959–60; Fellow in Pathology, Mass. Gen. Hosp., Boston 1960–61; Research Fellow, Thorndike Memorial Lab., Harvard Medical School, Boston 1961–63, Instructor of Medicine 1963–64; Asst Prof. Medicine, New Jersey Coll. of Medicine 1964–66; Co-Dir Haematology, Boston Univ. Medical Centre 1966, Assoc. Prof. 1968–74, Prof. of Medicine and Physiology 1974–75; Dir of Hematology, Boston City Hosp.; Founder and Dean, School of Medicine, Morehouse Coll. 1975–89, Pres. 1981–89, 1993–2002, Pres. Emer. 2002–; Sec., US Health and Human Services Admin., Washington, DC 1989–93; Chair. Nat. Health Museum, Atlanta, Ga, Sullivan Alliance to Transform America's Health Professions; Chair. President's Commission on Historically Black Colleges and Universities 2002–09; Co-Chair. President's Commission on HIV and AIDS 2001–06; mem. Bd of Dirs Henry Schein, United Therapeutics, Emergent Biosolutions, BioSante Pharmaceuticals; fmr mem. Bd of Dirs General Motors, 3M, Bristol Myers Squibb, CIGNA, Household International (now HBSC), Equifax; mem. Sickle Cell Anaemia Advisory Cttee, NIH 1974–75, Medical Advisory Bd, Nat. Leukemia Asscn 1968–70, (Chair. 1970); mem. American Soc. of Hematology, American Soc. of Clinical Investigation, Inst. of Medicine; Founding Pres. Asscn of Minority Health Professions Schools; Trustee, Grady Hospital Corporation 2008–; more than 60 hon. degrees. *Publications include:* The Morehouse Mystique: Becoming a Doctor at the Nation's Newest African American Medical School (with Marybeth Gasman) 2012, Breaking Ground: My Life in Medicine 2014; numerous papers in professional journals.

SULLIVAN, Martin J., OBE; British insurance executive and business executive; b. 1955; m.; two d.; joined Finance Dept, American Int. Underwriters (AIU), part of American Int. Group (AIG) 1971, with Property Dept 1974, Property Man. UK 1983, later Regional Property Man. UK/Ireland, Man. AIU London and Regional Marketing Man. UK/Ireland 1988, Asst Man. Dir AIG Europe (UK) Ltd 1989, COO 1991, Pres. UK/Ireland Div., AIU and Man. Dir AIG Europe (UK) Ltd 1993, Sr Vice-Pres., Foreign Gen. Insurance 1996, Exec. Vice-Pres. 1998, COO AIU New York 1996, Pres. 1997, mem. Bd AIG Inc. 2002–08, Vice-Chair. and Co-COO AIG Inc. 2002–05, Pres. and CEO AIG Inc. 2005–08; fmr Pres. British American Business, Inc.; Deputy Chair. Willis Group Holdings PLC, Chair. and CEO Willis Global Solutions, London 2010–13; Dir International Insurance Soc., Geneva Asscn, Young Audiences Inc., Friends of London Youth Inc.; mem. Bd of Dirs Transatlantic Holdings (apptd Chair. 2006), Navigators Underwriting Agency Ltd 2015–; mem. Business Advisory Cttee, St George's Soc., British Memorial Garden Trust; mem. Bd of Trustees, American Assocs of the Royal Acad. Trust; assoc. mem. Chartered Insurance Inst.; mem. Chartered Man. Inst.; Fellow, Inst. of Leadership and Man.; Dr hc (Hofstra Univ.) 2008; The American Ireland Fund Leadership Award 2007.

SULLIVAN, Michael J., BSc, JD; American lawyer, diplomatist and fmr politician; *Partner, Lewis Roca Rothgerber LLP;* b. 22 Sept. 1939, Omaha, Neb.; s. of Joseph B. Sullivan and Margaret Hamilton; m. Jane Metzler 1961; one s. two d.; ed Univ. of Wyoming; Assoc., Brown, Drew, Apostolos, Barton & Massey (law firm), Casper, Wyo. 1964–67, apptd Partner 1967; Gov. of Wyo. 1987–95; Amb. to Ireland 1998–2001; Partner, Rothgerber Johnson & Lyons LLP (now Lewis Roca Rothgerber LLP) 2001–; fmr Fellow, Inst. of Politics, Kennedy School of Govt, Harvard Univ.; mem. Univ. of Wyoming Coll. of Law Dean's Advisory Bd; Chair. Interstate Oil and Gas Compact Comm. 1990, Western Govs Asscn 1992–93; mem. ABA; Democrat; Distinguished Service Medal, Wyoming National Guard, Univ. of Wyoming Coll. of Law Outstanding Alumnus Award, Wyoming Heritage Soc. Award of Merit, inducted into Univ. of Wyoming Coll. of Engineering Hall of Fame, Winston Howard Distinguished Lecturer, Wyoming State Bar President's Award 2013, Citizen of the West, National Western Stock Show 2016. *Leisure interests:* jogging, tennis, golf, fly-fishing, reading. *Address:* Lewis Roca Rothgerber LLP, 123 West First Street, Suite 200, Casper, WY 82601, USA (office). *E-mail:* msullivan@rothgerber.com (office). *Website:* www.1rrlaw.com (office).

SULLIVAN, Teresa A., PhD; American sociologist, academic and university administrator; *President, University of Virginia;* m. Douglas Laycock; two s.; ed St Joseph's High School, Jackson, Miss., James Madison Coll. at Michigan State

Univ., Univ. of Chicago; Summer Research Assoc., Survey Research Laboratory, Univ. of Illinois, Urbana 1970; Admin. Intern, Office of the President, Michigan State Univ. 1970–71; Instructor to Asst Prof. of Sociology, Population Research Center, Univ. of Texas at Austin 1975–76, Faculty Research Assoc., Population Research Center 1981, Assoc. Prof. of Sociology 1981–87, Training Dir Population Research Center 1982–87, Dir of Women's Studies 1985–87, Prof. of Sociology 1987–2006, Prof. of Law 1988–2006, Asst Chair. Dept of Sociology 1988–89, Assoc. Dean, Office of Grad. Studies 1989–90, 1992–95, Chair. Dept of Sociology 1990–92, Vice-Provost, Office of the Exec. Vice-Pres. and Provost Univ. of Texas at Austin 1994–95, Vice-Pres. and Grad. Dean 1995–2003, Exec. Vice-Chancellor for Academic Affairs 2002–06, Prof. Emer. of Sociology and Law 2006–10; Asst Prof. of Sociology and the Coll., Faculty Research Assoc., Population Research Center, Univ. of Chicago 1977–81; Prof. of Sociology, Provost and Exec. Vice-Pres. for Academic Affairs, Univ. of Michigan, Ann Arbor 2006–10; George M. Kaufman Presidential Prof. of Sociology and Pres. Univ. of Virginia 2010–18 (resgnd then reinstated June 2012); Research Fellow, East-West Population Inst., Honolulu, HI 1986; Visiting Scholar, Population Studies Center, Univ. of Michigan 1990; Faculty mem., Man. Devt Seminar, Univ. of Chicago Grad. School of Business, Vail, Colo Summers 1991–93; fmr Chair. US Census Advisory Cttee; Fellow, AAAS 1995; mem. Sociological Research Asscn 1990, Philosophical Soc. of Texas 1997; General Mills Scholarship 1967–68, Michigan State Univ. Merit Scholar 1967–70, Presidential Fellow, Michigan State Univ. 1970–71 (Carnegie Foundation), Maria Leonard Honor Fellow, Nat. Alpha Lambda Delta 1971–72, Sparks Memorial Honor Fellow, Nat. Phi Kappa Phi 1971–72, NSF Grad. Fellow 1971–74, Liberal Arts Council Teaching Excellence Award 1985, Dean's Merit Award for Community Service 1985, UtmosT Magazine 'Ten Best Professors' Poll 1987, Pres.'s Associates Teaching Excellence Award 1989–90, Faculty Fellowship in Law, Cox & Smith, Inc. 1991–94, 1995–2006, UtmosT Magazine 'Best Professor Hall of Fame' 1992, Students' Asscn Teaching Excellence Award 1992, Distinguished Scholarly Publ. Award, American Sociological Asscn 1992, Distinguished Scholarly Paper Award, Southwestern Sociological Asscn 1993, Leadership Texas, Class of 1994, Faculty Fellowship in Law, Locke, Harrell, Raine, Purcell 1994–95, Fellow, Woodrow Wilson Foundation Award for Innovation in Grad. Educ. 2000, Sister Agnes McPhee Award for contribs to educ. 2002, Distinguished Alumna Award, James Madison Coll. 2004. *Publications:* Marginal Workers, Marginal Jobs: The Underutilized American Worker 1978, Young Catholics in the United States and Canada (co-author) 1981, The Dilemma of American Immigration: Beyond the Golden Door (co-author) 1983, Underemployment, in International Journal of Sociology and Social Policy (special issue) (ed.) 1987, As We Forgive Our Debtors: Bankruptcy and Consumer Credit in America (co-author) (ABA Silver Gavel Award 1990) 1989, The Social Organization of Work (co-author) 1990 (fifth edn 2012), Instructor's Manual to Accompany Hodson and Sullivan's Social Organization of Work 1995, The Fragile Middle Class: Americans in Debt (co-author) (Writing Award, American Coll. of Financial Services Lawyers 2000) 2000, Instructor's Manual with Test Bank for Hodson and Sullivan's The Social Organization of Work (third edn 2002), Instructor's Resource Manual with Test Bank for Hodson and Sullivan's The Social Organization of Work (fourth edn 2008); more than 80 scholarly articles and chapters on social demography, especially labour force and ethnic groups, sociology of cultural insts (science, educ., law, religion). *Address:* Office of the President, University of Virginia, Madison Hall, PO Box 400224, Charlottesville, VA 22904-4224, USA (office). *Telephone:* (434) 924-3337 (office). *Fax:* (434) 924-3792 (office). *E-mail:* jbg@virginia.edu (office). *Website:* www.virginia.edu/president (office).

SULTAN, Donald Keith, BFA, MFA; American painter, printmaker and sculptor; b. 5 May 1951, Asheville, North Carolina; s. of Norman Sultan and Phyllis Sultan; m. Susan Reynolds 1978; one s. one d.; ed Univ. of North Carolina, Art Inst. of Chicago; work in numerous collections, including Art Inst. of Chicago, Hirsh Museum and Sculpture Garden, Washington, DC, Metropolitan Museum of Art, New York, Museum of Fine Arts, Boston, Museum of Modern Art, New York, Solomon R. Guggenheim Museum, New York, Walker Art Center, Minneapolis, Bibliothèque Nationale, Paris 1992; Public Service Grant, New York State 1978–79, Nat. Endowments for the Arts 1980–81; Dr hc (Corcoran School of Art, Washington, DC) 2000, (New York Acad. of Art) 2002, (Univ. of North Carolina) 2007; North Carolina Award 2010, Lifetime Achievement Award, Houston Fine Art Fair 2011. *E-mail:* sultanstudio@gmail.com. *Website:* www.donaldsultanstudio.com.

SULTANOV, Baqıt Turlıhanulı; Kazakhstani economist and politician; *Mayor of Astana;* b. 29 Nov. 1971; m. Regina Sultanova; two s. one d.; ed Kazakh Nat. Tech. Univ.; several years with Ministry of Finance, including as Deputy Dir, Budget Dept 1997, Dir, Public Procurement Dept 1998, Deputy Dir, Dept of the Treasury 1999, Dir of State Budget 2002, Dir, Dept of Fiscal Policy and Planning, Ministry of Econ. Affairs and Budget Planning 2002–03, Deputy Minister of Economy and Budget Planning 2003–06, Chair. Statistical Agency 2006–07, Deputy Minister of Finance Jan.–Aug. 2007, Minister of Econ. Affairs and Budget Planning 2007–10, Asst to Pres. 2010, Deputy Head, Admin of the Pres. 2012–13, Deputy Prime Minister and Minister of Finance 2013–14, Minister of Finance 2014–18; Akim (Mayor) of Astana 2018–; Order of Kurmet (Honour); Astana 10 Year Anniversary Medal. *Address:* Office of the Mayor, 010000 Nur-Sultan, Beibitshilik Street 11, Kazakhstan (office). *Website:* astana.gov.kz (office).

SULTANOV, Marat Abdyrazakovich; Kyrgyzstani politician; b. 5 Dec. 1960, Frunze (Bishkek); m.; two d.; ed Moscow State Univ.; Prof., Kyrgyz Nat. Univ. 1987–92; Deputy Chair. Nat. Bank of the Kyrgyz Repub. (Kyrgyz Respublikasynyn Uluttuk Banky) 1992–94, Chair. 1994–98; Minister of Finance Jan.–June 1999, 2009–10; mem. Parl. 2000–, Speaker, Zhogorku Kenesh (Supreme Council) 2006–09; Head, Defence and Security Dept in Presidential Admin 2004.

SULZBERGER, Arthur Ochs, Jr, BA; American newspaper publisher; *Chairman, The New York Times Company;* b. 22 Sept. 1951, Mount Kisco, NY; s. of Arthur Ochs Sulzberger and Barbara Winslow Grant; m. Gail Gregg 1975; one s. one d.; ed Tufts Univ., Harvard Univ. Business School; reporter, The Raleigh Times, N Carolina 1974–76; corresp., Associated Press, London, UK 1976–78; Washington, DC bureau corresp., The New York Times 1978–81, city hall reporter 1981, Asst Metro Ed. 1981–82, Group Man., Advertising Dept 1983–84, Sr Analyst, Corp. Planning 1985, Production Co-ordinator 1985–87, Asst Publr 1987–88,

Deputy Publr 1988–92, Publr 1992–, Chair. The New York Times Co. 1997–; mem. Bd New York City Outward Bound Center; RIT Isaiah Thomas Award in Publishing 2003, Nat. Book Award 'Literarian Award for Outstanding Service to the American Literary Community' 2012. *Address:* The New York Times Company, 620 Eighth Avenue, New York, NY 10018, USA (office). *Telephone:* (212) 556-1234 (office). *E-mail:* publisher@nytimes.com (office). *Website:* www.nytco.com (office).

SUMAH, Adikalie Foday, LLM; Sierra Leonean lawyer and diplomatist; *Permanent Mission of United Nations;* b. 23 May 1960; m.; three c.; ed Univ. of East London; Assoc. Solicitor and Legal Rep., Markandan & Co. Solicitors, London 1997–2002; Researcher, Office of Nat. Statistics, Dept of Registrar-Gen., London 2003–04; Admin. Officer, Dept for Constitutional Affairs in Asylum and Immigration Tribunal Div. 2005–07; Amb. to Guinea, to Mali, to Niger 2009–16, Dean Diplomatic Corps, Guinea 2012–16, African and Econ. Community of West African States (ECOWAS) Diplomatic Groups 2012–16; Perm. Rep. to UN 2016–. *Address:* Permanent Mission of Sierra Leone, 336 E 45th Street, 6th Floor, New York, NY 10017, USA (office). *Telephone:* (212) 688-1656 (office). *Fax:* (212) 688-4924 (office). *E-mail:* sierraleone@un.int (office).

SUMAIDA'IE, Samir Shakir Mahmood, BSc; Iraqi business executive and diplomatist; b. 1944, Baghdad; m.; five c.; ed Durham Univ., UK; left Iraq after Saddam Hussein seized power 1973; Middle East Man., Nixdorf Computers, Paderborn, Germany 1973–74; Middle East Man., Logica Ltd, London 1974–78; Man. Dir Tenda Ltd, London 1978–82; Man. Dir Turath Ltd, London 1982–90; Man. Dir Samir Design Ltd, London 1991–96; Man. Dir China Business Int., Beijing 1996–2003; returned to Baghdad and was apptd mem. Iraq Governing Council July 2003; Minister of the Interior April–Aug. 2004; Perm. Rep. to UN, New York 2004–06, Amb. to USA 2006–11; participant, Beirut and Vienna Opposition Confs 1991, NY Iraqi Opposition Conf. 1992; Co-founder, manifesto, Democratic Party of Iraq 1993; mem. Governing Council of Iraq 2003, fmr Chair. Media Cttee, Cttee on Provs, fmr Deputy Chair. Foreign Affairs Cttee, fmr mem. Security, Finance and Public Service Cttees. *Publication:* The Night of the Long Lament: A Day in the Life of an Iraqi Dissident, Ahmed Al-Habboubi (trans). *Leisure interests:* writing Arabic poetry in classical form, calligraphy and design in the Islamic decorative medium. *Address:* c/o Ministry of Foreign Affairs, opp. State Org. for Roads and Bridges, Karradat Mariam, Baghdad, Iraq (office).

SUMAYE, Frederick; Tanzanian politician; b. 29 May 1950, Hanang Dist, Arusah; ed Egerton Coll., Kenya, Edward S. Mason Program, Kennedy School of Govt, Harvard Univ., USA; Tutor, MATI–Nyegezi 1973–76; Eng Section Man. Kilombero Sugar Co. 1976–80; Head of Rural Energy Dept, CARMATEC 1980–82; mem. Parl. (Chama Cha Mapinduzi,) for Hanang constituency 1985–2005; Deputy Minister of Agric. 1987–94, Minister of Agric. 1995; Prime Minister of Tanzania 1995–2005; mem. Cen. Cttee, Chama Cha Mapinduzi (Party for Democracy and Progress) –2007; mem. Bd of Dirs Nyanya Project. *Address:* c/o Chama Cha Mapinduzi, (Revolutionary Party of Tanzania), Kuu Street, POB 50, Dodoma, Tanzania. *E-mail:* katibumkuu@ccmtz.org. *Website:* www.ccmtz.org.

SUMI, Shuzo, BEng; Japanese insurance executive; *Chairman and Representative Director, Tokio Marine Holdings, Inc.;* b. 11 July 1947; ed Waseda Univ.; joined Tokio Marine 1970, Dir and Chief Rep., Overseas Div. of Tokio Marine, London, UK 2000–01, Dir, Gen. Man. and Chief Rep., Overseas Div. of Tokio Marine, London 2001–02, Man. Dir Tokio Marine 2002–04, Man. Dir Tokio Marine & Nichido 2004–05, Sr Man. Dir June–Dec. 2005, Sr Man. Dir and Gen. Man. Drastic Reform Promotion Dept, Tokio Marine & Nichido 2005–06, Sr Man. Dir Tokio Marine & Nichido 2006–07, Pres. and Rep. Dir Tokio Marine & Nichido 2007–13, Chair. and Rep. Dir 2013–, Pres. and Rep. Dir Tokio Marine Holdings, Inc. 2007–13, Chair. and Rep. Dir 2013–. *Address:* Tokio Marine Nichido Building Shinkan, 1-2-1 Marunouchi, Chiyoda-ku, Tokyo, 100-0005, Japan (office). *Telephone:* (3) 6212-3333 (office). *E-mail:* ir@tokiomarinehd.com (office). *Website:* www.tokiomarinehd.com (office).

SUMMERS, Lawrence H., PhD; American economist, academic, fmr government official and fmr university administrator; *Charles W. Eliot University Professor and President Emeritus, Harvard University;* b. 30 Nov. 1954, New Haven, Conn.; s. of Dr Robert Summers and Anita Summers; one s. two d.; ed Massachusetts Inst. of Tech. and Harvard Univ.; domestic policy economist, US Council of Econ. Advisers 1982–83; Prof. of Econs Harvard Univ. 1983–93, 2002, Nathaniel Ropes Prof. of Political Economy 1987, Pres. Harvard Univ. 2002–06, Charles W. Eliot Univ. Prof. and Pres. Emer. 2006–, Dir Mossavar-Rhomani Center for Business and Govt; Chief Economist and Vice-Pres. of Devt Econs IBRD 1991–93; fmr Econ. Adviser to Pres. Bill Clinton; Treasury Under-Sec. for Int. Affairs 1993–95; Deputy Treasury Sec. 1995–99; Sec. of Treasury 1999–2001; Arthur Okun Distinguished Fellow in Econs, Globalization and Governance, Brookings Inst. 2001–02; Dir Nat. Econ. Council, The White House, Washington, DC 2009–10; Fellow, American Acad. of Arts and Sciences; mem. NAS 2002–; mem. Bd of Dirs Square 2011–, Lending Club 2012–18; Chair. Citizen Schools, Center for Global Devt; Hon. DJur (Harvard) 2007; Alan T. Waterman Award, Nat. Science Foundation 1987, John Bates Clark Medal 1993, Alexander Hamilton Medal 2001. *Publications include:* Understanding Unemployment 1990, Reform in Eastern Europe (co-author) 1993, numerous articles. *Leisure interests:* skiing, tennis. *Address:* Department of Economics, Harvard University, Littauer Center 242, 1875 Cambridge Street, Cambridge, MA 02138, USA. *Telephone:* (617) 495-0436 (office). *Fax:* (617) 495-8550 (office). *E-mail:* lawrence_summers@harvard.edu (office). *Website:* www.economics.harvard.edu (office). larrysummers.com.

SUMNER, Gordon Matthew (see STING).

SUMPTION, Jonathan Philip Chadwick, OBE, MA; British judge and author; *Judge of the Supreme Court of the United Kingdom;* b. 9 Dec. 1948, London; s. of A. J. Sumption and H. Sumption; m. Teresa Mary Whelan 1971; one s. two d.; ed Eton Coll., Magdalen Coll., Oxford; Fellow in History, Magdalen Coll., Oxford 1971–75; called to Bar (Inner Temple) 1975; Recorder 1993–2001; Judge of Courts of Appeal of Guernsey and Jersey 1995–2011; mem. Brick Court Chambers; Judge, Supreme Court of the UK 2011–; Gov. RAM. *Publications include:* Pilgrimage: An Image of Medieval Religion 1975, The Albigensian Crusade 1979, The Hundred Years War (Vol. 1) 1989, (Vol. 2) 1999, (Vol. 3) 2012, (Vol. 4) 2015. *Leisure interests:* music, history. *Address:* Supreme Court, Parliament Square, London, SW1P 3BD,

England (office). *Telephone:* (20) 7960-1500 (office). *Fax:* (20) 7960-1901 (office). *Website:* www.supremecourt.gov.uk (office).

SUN, Chunlan; Chinese party official and fmr trade union official; *Vice Premier;* b. 1950, Hebei Prov.; ed Anshan Industrial Tech. Acad.; joined CCP 1973; began career at Anshan Clock Factory; leading positions in provincial women's fed., provincial and nat. trade unions including Chair., Liaoning Provincial Fed. of Trade Unions 1994, Vice-Chair., All-China Fed. of Trade Unions 2005–09; Mayor, Dalian City, Liaoning Prov. 2001–05; Sec., Fujian CCP Provincial Cttee 2009–12, Chair. Cttee, Fujian Provincial People's Congress 2010–12; Sec., Tianjin Municipal CCP Cttee (only female provincial-level party chief in China) 2012–14; Head, United Front Work Dept, CCP Cen. Cttee 2014–17; mem. State Council 2018–; Vice Premier 2018–; alt. mem. 15th CCP Cen. Cttee 1997–2002, 16th CCP Cen. Cttee 2002–07, mem. 17th CCP Cen. Cttee 2007–12, 18th CCP Cen. Cttee 2012–17, also mem. 18th CCP Cen. Cttee Politburo 2012–17; mem. 19th CCP Cen. Cttee 2017–, also mem. 19th CCP Cen. Cttee Politburo 2017–. *Address:* State Council, 22 Xi'anmen Avenue, Beijing, People's Republic of China (office). *Telephone:* (10) 66036884 (office).

SUN, Honglie, BSc, MSc; Chinese agronomist; b. 2 Jan. 1932, Puyang, Henan Prov.; m. Wu Huanning 1956; one s. one d.; ed Beijing Agricultural Univ., Shenyang Inst. of Forestry and Soil Science, Chinese Acad. of Sciences; Research Fellow, Comm. for Integrated Survey of Natural Resources (Chinese Acad. of Sciences) 1961–, Dir 1983; Head Multi-disciplinary Expedition of Qinghai-Tibet Plateau 1973; Visiting Scholar, Inst. of Alpine and Arctic Research, Colorado Univ. 1981–82; Vice-Pres. Chinese Acad. of Sciences 1984–92; Vice-Pres. International Council of Scientific Unions 1993–96. Chair. Academic Cttee of Antarctic Research of China 1986; Chair. Nat. Cttee of China for MAB, UNESCO; Vice-Chair. Int. Mountain Soc., State Antarctic Cttee; apptd a Vice-Pres. Social Devt Science Soc. 1992; Dir Cttee for Comprehensive Survey of Natural Resources; Fellow, Third World Acad. of Sciences 1987; mem. Gen. Cttee of ICSU 1990; mem. Div. of Earth Sciences, Chinese Acad. of Sciences 1992–, mem. 4th Presidium of Depts 2000; mem. Standing Cttee of 8th Nat. People's Congress 1993; mem. Credentials Cttee, Environmental and Resources Protection Cttee; mem. 21st Century Cttee for China-Japan Friendship; Special Prize, Chinese Acad. of Sciences 1986, First Prize, State Natural Sciences Awards 1987, Chen Jiagen Prize 1989. *Publications include:* The Soil of Heilongjiang River Valley 1960, The Land Resources Assessment of North-East China, Inner Mongolia and West China 1966, The Soils of Tibet 1970, Land Types of Qinghai-Tibet Plateau and the Principles of Agricultural Assessment 1980, Land Resources and Agricultural Utilization in Tibet Autonomous Region, Mountain Research and Development 1983, Integrated Scientific Survey on Tibetan Plateau (series) 1983–89. *Leisure interest:* photography. *Address:* Chinese Academy of Sciences, 52 Sanlihe Road, Beijing 100864, People's Republic of China (office).

SUN, Hongshui; Chinese business executive; *President, Power Construction Corporation of China (PowerChina);* served successively at Sinohydro Group Ltd as Deputy Gen. Man., Exec. Vice-Pres., Pres. and mem. Exec. Bd, and as Gen. Man. and Deputy Party Sec.; has served successively at Power Construction Corpn of China Ltd as Vice-Pres., as Gen. Man., now Dir and Pres. *Address:* Power Construction Corporation of China, No. 7 & 8 Building, Beijing Xiyuan Hotel, 1 Sanlihe Road, Haidian District, Beijing 100040, People's Republic of China (office). *Telephone:* (10) 58382266 (office); (10) 88358715 (office). *Fax:* (10) 58382888 (office). *E-mail:* infocenter@powerchin.com (office). *Website:* www.powerchina.cn (office); en.powerchina.cn (office).

SUN, Jiadong; Chinese scientist; b. 7 April 1948, Fuxian, Liaoning Prov.; ed Harbin Univ. of Tech., USSR Ruchkovski Air Force Eng Inst.; Dir of Design Section, Vice-Dir Overall Design Dept, No. 5 Research Inst. of Ministry of Defence; Vice-Pres. No. 5 Research Inst. of Seventh Ministry of Machine Bldg Industry; Pres. Chinese Space Tech. Research Inst.; Dir Science and Tech. Cttee, Chief Engineer, fmr Vice-Minister of Ministry of Aerospace Industry; fmr Researcher, Sr Science and Tech. Adviser, China Aviation Industry Corpn; Chief Designer, Chinese Lunar Exploration Program 2003–; Fellow, Chinese Acad. of Sciences; mem. International Acad. of Astronautics; Meritorious Service Medal, CCP Cen. Cttee, Ho Leung Ho Lee Foundation Science and Tech. Award 1996, State Council and Cen. Mil. Comm. 1999, Nat. Science and Tech. Award 2009. *Achievements include:* instrumental in devt of China's first atomic bomb and hydrogen bomb; presided over the overall design of China's first medium-range missile, first satellite and first telecommunications satellite. *Address:* Chinese Academy of Sciences, 52 Sanlihe Road, Beijing 100864, People's Republic of China. *Website:* www.clep.org.cn.

SUN, Jiazheng; Chinese politician; b. March 1944, Siyang, Jiangsu Prov.; ed Nanjing Univ., May 7th Cadre School, Jilin Prov.; joined CCP 1966; sent to do manual labour, Liuhe Co., Jilin Prov.; fmr Deputy Head, Chinese People's Armed Police Force, Fanji Commune; Deputy Head, Work Group, CCP Revolutionary Cttee, Liuhe Co. 1971; Sec. Liuhe Co. Cttee CCP Communist Youth League of China 1971; Sec. CCP Party Cttee, Ma'an Commune, Liuhe Co. 1971, mem. Standing Cttee CCP Liuhe Co. Cttee 1975; Vice-Chair. CCP Revolutionary Cttee, Liuhe Co. 1975; Sec. Jiangsu Prov. Cttee CCP Communist Youth League of China 1978; mem. Standing Cttee CCP Jiangsu Prov. Cttee 1983–89, Sec.-Gen. Jiangsu Prov. Cttee 1983–89, Head, Publicity Dept 1988; Sec. CCP Xuzhou City Cttee, Jiangsu Prov. 1984–86; Minister of Radio, Film and TV 1984–88; Minister of Culture 1998–2007; Pres. China Fed. of Literary and Art Circles 2006–16; Alt. mem. 12th CCP Cen. Cttee 1982–87, 13th CCP Cen. Cttee 1987–92, 14th CCP Cen. Cttee 1992–97, mem. 15th CCP Cen. Cttee 1997–2002, 16th CCP Cen. Cttee 2002–07; Vice-Chair. 11th CPPCC Nat. Cttee 2008–13; Hon. Chair. Bd of Dirs Beijing Film Coll.

SUN, Laiyan, PhD; Chinese engineer; *Chairman, Supervision and Administration Commission, Ministry of Supervision;* b. Oct. 1957, Beijing; m.; one d.; ed Xian Communication Univ., Univ. de Paris, France; Eng Team Leader/Deputy Div. Dir Beijing Inst. of Satellite Environment Eng 1982–87, Acting Deputy Dir, later Dir, Prof. 1993–99; Vice Admin. China Nat. Space Admin (CNSA) 1999–2004, Admin. 2004–10; Sec.-Gen. Comm. of Science, Tech. and Industry for Nat. Defence (COSTIND) 2001–04, Vice Minister 2004–08, Dir COSTIND State Aerospace Industry Bureau 2008–10; Chair. Supervision and Admin Comm., Ministry of

Supervision 2010–; numerous ministerial and nat. awards. *Address:* Supervision and Administration Commission, Ministry of Supervision, 4 Zaojunmiao, Haidian Qu, Beijing 100081, People's Republic of China (office). *Telephone:* (10) 62114181 (office). *Fax:* (10) 62217692 (office). *Website:* www.mos.gov.cn (office).

SUN, Li; Chinese engineer and business executive; *President and General Manager, China National Aviation Fuel Group Corporation;* ed Tsinghua Univ., Capital Univ. of Econs and Business, Beijing, Party School of Cen. Cttee of CCP, corp. man. training with IBM, ENSPM (France), ICI (UK); joined Liaoyang Petrochemical & Fibre Co. 1975, promoted several times until Deputy Gen. Man. –1998; Deputy Dir Refinery Dept, China Nat. Petroleum Corpn 1998–99; Gen. Man. PetroChina Lanzhou Petrochemical Co. 1999–2002; Gen. Man. PetroChina Chemical and Sales Co. 2002–05; Deputy Pres. China Nat. Aviation Fuel (CNAF) Group Corpn (fmrly China Aviation Oil Holding Co.) 2005–07, Pres. and Gen. Man. 2007–, Chair. CNAF Corpn Ltd and CNAF Land Oil Co. Ltd; mem. Bd of Dirs and Deputy Chair. (non-exec.) China Aviation Oil Singapore Corpn Ltd 2007–10, Chair. (non-exec.) 2010–15. *Address:* China National Aviation Fuel Group Corporation, 2 Madian Road, Haidan District, Beijing 100088, People's Republic of China (office). *Telephone:* (10) 59890000 (office). *E-mail:* info@cnaf.com (office). *Website:* www.cnaf.com (office).

SUN, Mingbo, PhD, MBA; Chinese business executive; *Chairman, Tsingtao Brewery Group;* b. Dec. 1956; ed Tongji Univ., Fudan Univ., Washington Univ., St Louis, USA; following graduation assigned to Shandong Xintai Xingtai Brewery, becoming Brewery Technician, Workshop Dir, Deputy Dir; transferred to Tsingtao Brewery 1993, positions included Deputy Factory Man., Chief Engineer, Asst to Gen. Man., Vice-Chief Engineer, Exec. Vice-Pres., Pres., Tsingtao Brewery Group Co. Ltd 2008–12, Chair. 2012–. *Address:* Tsingtao Brewery Group, Tsingtao Beer Tower, May 4th Square, Hong Kong Road, Qingdao 266071, People's Republic of China (office). *Telephone:* (532) 571-1119 (office). *Fax:* (532) 85713240 (office). *Website:* www.tsingtaobeer.com (office).

SUN, Wenjie; Chinese engineer and construction industry executive; ed Tongji Univ.; joined China State Construction Engineering Corpn (CSCEC) 1968, posted to Hong Kong 1981, Vice-Pres. CSCEC an Chair. China Overseas Holdings Ltd 1997–2001, Pres. CSCEC 2001–09, Chair. 2009–10, also Deputy Sec. Leading Party Mems' Group; Vice-Pres. Hong Kong Construction Asscn Ltd, Hong Kong Chinese Enterprises Asscn; Rep. 15th and 16th CCP Cen. Cttees; Hon. LLD (Warwick), (Cantab.); Nat. Outstanding Award, State Council 1995. *Address:* c/o China State Construction Engineering Corporation, CSCEC Mansion, 15 Sanlihe Road, Haidian District, Beijing 100037, People's Republic of China. *E-mail:* info@cscec.com.

SUN, Wensheng; Chinese government official; b. Feb. 1942, Weihai City, Shandong Prov.; ed Shandong Metallurgical Inst. and CCP Cen. Cttee Cen. Party School; joined CCP 1966; workshop dir, Zhuzhou Smeltery 1963–81, Deputy Dir 1981–83; Sec. CCP Zhuzhou City Cttee 1983; Vice-Dir Org. Dept CCP Hunan Prov. Cttee, CCP 1984, Dir 1985, Vice-Sec. 1989; Vice-Sec. CCP Shanxi Prov. Cttee, Vice-Gov., Acting Gov. of Shanxi Prov. 1993–94, Gov. 1994–98; Vice-Minister of Land and Resources 1999–2003, Minister of Land and Resources 2003–07; Deputy Sec., CCP Leading Party Group, Ministry of Land and Resources 1999–2003, Sec. 2003; mem. Cen. Comm. for Discipline Inspection, CCP Cen. Cttee 2002–; Alt. mem. 12th CCP Cen. Cttee 1982–87, 13th CCP Cen. Cttee 1987–92, mem. 14th CCP Cen. Cttee 1992–97, 15th CCP Cen. Cttee 1997–2002.

SUN, Yafang; Chinese business executive and fmr government official; *Chairwoman, Huawei Investment & Holding Company Limited;* b. 1955; ed Chengdu Univ. of Electronic Science and Tech., Harvard Business School, USA; worked as a technician at state-owned Xinxiang Liaoyuan Radio Factory 1982–83, teacher at China Research Inst. of Radio Wave Propagation 1983–85, engineer at Beijing Research Inst. of Information Tech. 1985–89; joined Huawei 1989 Co-founder Huawei Technologies 1992, has held several exec.-level positions, including Pres. of Marketing and Sales, Pres. of Human Resources, Pres. of Strategy and Marketing Cttee, Pres. Huawei Univ., Chair. Huawei Investment & Holding Co. Ltd 1999–. *Address:* Huawei Investment & Holding Co. Ltd, Huawei Industrial Base, Shenzhen 518129, People's Republic of China (office). *Telephone:* (755) 28780808 (office). *E-mail:* hwtech@huawei.com (office). *Website:* www.huawei.com (office).

SUN, Yang; Chinese swimmer; b. 1 Dec. 1991, Hangzhou, Zhejiang; ed Hangzhou Chenjinglun Sports School, Zhejiang Univ.; mem. Zhejiang Prov. Sports Team 2003–, Nat. Team 2006–; winner, 400m, 1500m freestyle, Nat. Winter Championships 2006, 10km freestyle, Nat. Marathon Swimming Tournament 2006, 1500m freestyle, Nat. Championships 2007, 1500m freestyle, Nat. Intercity Games 2007; runner-up, 400m, 1500m freestyle, Nat. Champions Tournament 2007; competed for China at Beijing Olympics 2008; World Championships (long course): Rome 2009: bronze medal, 1500m freestyle; Shanghai 2011: gold medal, 800m freestyle, 1500m freestyle, silver medal, 400m freestyle, bronze medal, 4×200m freestyle; Barcelona 2013: gold medal, 400m freestyle, 800m freestyle, 1500m freestyle; Kazan 2015: gold medal, 400m freestyle, 800m freestyle, silver medal, 200m freestyle; Budapest 2017: gold medal, 200m freestyle, 400m freestyle; Asian Games: Guangzhou 2010: gold medal, 1500m freestyle, 4×200m freestyle, silver medal, 200m freestyle, 400m freestyle; Incheon 2014: gold medal, 400m freestyle, 1500m freestyle, silver medal 200m freestyle, gold medal 4×100m freestyle relay; Jakarta 2018: gold medal, 200m freestyle, 400m freestyle, 800m freestyle, 1500m freestyle, silver medal, 4×100m freestyle relay, 4×200m freestyle relay; Olympic Games: London 2012: gold medal, 400m freestyle, 1500m freestyle, silver medal, 200m freestyle, bronze medal, 4×200m freestyle; Rio de Janeiro 2016: gold medal 200m freestyle, silver medal 400m freestyle; World Championship (short course): Beijing 2014: gold medal, 400m freestyle; coach: Zhu Zhigen; first swimmer to win Olympic gold medals in 200m, 400m and 1500m freestyle; named the Rookie of the Year at CCTV Sports Awards 2010, Pacific Rim Swimmer of the Year 2011, Laureus Chinese Sportsman of the Year Award 2017. *Leisure interests:* basketball, music. *Address:* Chinese Swimming Association, Beijing, People's Republic of China. *Website:* swimming.sport.org.cn.

SUN, Ying; Chinese academic and politician; b. Nov. 1936, Tianjin, Baodi Co.; ed Shanxi Teachers' Coll. 1958; joined CCP 1956; fmr Deputy Sec. CCP Communist Youth League of China, Shanxi Univ.; fmr Dir Political Dept, Taiyuan Eng Inst.,

Shanxi Prov.; fmr Deputy Sec. Shanxi Prov. Cttee CCP Communist Youth League of China; fmr Vice-Chair. Shanxi Prov. Science and Tech. Asscn; fmr mem. Standing Cttee CCP Shanxi Prov. Cttee; Deputy Sec. CCP Taiyuan City Cttee, Sec. 1985; Deputy Sec. CCP Gansu Prov. Cttee 1988–98, Sec. 1998–2001, Standing Cttee CCP Gansu Prov. Cttee 1998–2001; Vice-Gov. Gansu Prov. 1996–97, Gov. 1997–98; apptd Dir Party History Research Centre of CCP Cen. Cttee 2001; mem. 15th CCP Cen. Cttee 1997–2002; Deputy, 9th NPC 2002–03.

SUN, Zhengcai, DAgric; Chinese agricultural scientist and politician; b. Sept. 1963, Rongcheng Co., Shandong Province; joined CCP 1988; began career as researcher in agricultural science, Beijing; Head, Shunyi Dist People's Govt, Beijing 2002–06, also Sec.-Gen., Beijing Municipality CCP Cttee 2002–06; Minister of Agric. 2006–09, also Sec., CCP Leading Party Group 2006–09; Sec., Jilin CCP Provincial Cttee 2009–12; Chair. Standing Cttee, Jilin Provincial People's Congress 2010–12; Sec., Chongqing Municipal CCP Cttee 2012–17; mem. 17th CCP Cen. Cttee 2007–12, 18th CCP Cen. Cttee 2012–17, also mem. 18th CCP Cen. Cttee Politburo 2012–17; expelled from CCP for 'serious discipline violations' Sept. 2017; charged with bribery Feb. 2018.

SUN, Zhenyu; Chinese economist, government official and diplomatist; b. 1946, Fengrun, Hebei Prov.; ed Beijing Foreign Languages Inst.; joined Ministry of Foreign Trade 1973, served as Deputy Dir, Dir and Deputy Dir-Gen. Regional Policy Dept; fmr Vice-Pres. China Nat. Cereals, Oils and Foodstuffs Import and Export Corpn 1985–90; Dir-Gen., Dept of American and Oceanic Affairs, Ministry of Foreign Trade and Econ. Cooperation 1990–94, Vice-Minister 1994–2002, Amb. and Perm. Rep. to WTO, Lausanne, Switzerland 2002–10; currently Chair. China Soc. for World Trade Organization Studies. *Publications:* Decision Making in the WTO 2004, Multilateralism and Regionalism 2005, China's Performance in the WTO 2007. *Address:* Ministry of Foreign Affairs, 2 Chaoyangmen, Nan Dajie, Chao Yang Qu, Beijing 100701, People's Republic of China (office). *Telephone:* (10) 65961114 (office). *Fax:* (10) 65962146 (office). *E-mail:* webmaster@mfa.gov.cn (office). *Website:* www.fmprc.gov.cn (office).

SUNDERLAND, Sir John Michael, Kt, MA, FRSA; British business executive; *Chairman, Merlin Entertainments Group Ltd;* b. 24 Aug. 1945, Oxford; m.; three d. one s.; ed King Edward VII School, Lytham, Lancs., Queen's Coll., Univ. of St Andrews, Scotland; joined Cadbury Ltd 1968, apptd. mem. Bd Cadbury Ireland 1978, Cadbury Schweppes SA 1981, Marketing Dir, then Man. Dir Schweppes Ltd UK 1983, Founding Dir Coca-Cola & Schweppes Beverages 1987, Man. Dir Trebor Bassett 1989, Cadbury Schweppes Confectionery and Cadbury Schweppes Main Bd Dir 1993, Group CEO Cadbury Schweppes PLC (now Cadbury PLC) 1996–2003, Chair. 2003–08; Chair. Merlin Entertainments Group 2009–; Deputy Pres. CBI 2003, 2007, Pres. 2004–06; mem. Bd of Dirs Financial Reporting Council 2004–11; Dir (non-exec.) Barclays Bank PLC 2005–15, AFC Energy PLC 2012–15; Adviser, CVC Capital Partners (pvt. equity firm), London; mem. Advisory Bd Trinsum Group (fmrly Marakon and IFL); Asscn mem., BUPA; Fellow, RAM; Gov. Court of Henley Man. Coll., Univ. of Reading; Pres. Food and Drink Fed. 2002–04, Inc. Soc. of British Advertisers 2002–05, Confed. of British Industry 2004–06, Chartered Man. Inst. 2007–08; Chancellor, Aston Univ. 2011–; Hon. LLD St Andrews Univ. 2007, Hon. DLitt Aston Univ. 2011. *Leisure interests:* sport, history, theatre. *Address:* Merlin Entertainments Group Ltd, 3 Market Close, Poole, BH15 1NQ, England (office). *Telephone:* (1202) 666900 (office). *E-mail:* enquiries@merlinentertainments.biz (office). *Website:* www.merlinentertainments.biz (office).

SUNDQUIST, Donald (Don) Kenneth, BA; American business executive and fmr politician; *Founding Partner, Sundquist Group;* b. 15 March 1936, Moline, Ill.; s. of Kenneth Sundquist and Louise Rohren; m. Martha Swanson 1959; one s. two d.; ed Augustana Coll. Rock Island, Ill.; Div. Man. Josten's Inc. 1961–72; Chair. Young Republicans 1971–73, Shelby County Republican Party 1975–77; Exec. Vice-Pres. Graphic Sales of America, Memphis 1973, Pres. 1973–82; mem. US House of Reps from 7th Tenn. Dist 1983–95; Gov. of Tennessee 1995–2003; Founding Partner, Sundquist Anthony LLC (now Sundquist Group), Washington, DC 2004–; Chair. Medicaid Advisory Comm., US Dept of Health and Human Services 2005–06; Founding mem. and Hon. Co-Chair. Japan-America Soc. of Tenn.; Republican. *Leisure interests:* golf, reading. *Address:* Sundquist Group, 51 Louisiana Avenue, NW, Washington, DC 20001, USA (office). *Telephone:* (202) 347-3900 (office). *Fax:* (202) 347-4448 (office). *E-mail:* dh@sundquistgroup.com (office). *Website:* sundquistgroup.com (office).

SUNDQVIST, Ulf Ludvig, MPolSc; Finnish business consultant and fmr politician; b. 22 Feb. 1945, Sipoo; s. of Karl Eric Sundqvist and Helga Linnea Lönnkvist; m. Eine Kristiina Joki 1969; one s. one d.; ed Helsinki Univ.; Asst Lecturer, Faculty of Political Science, Helsinki Univ. 1968–70; mem. Parl. 1970–83; Minister of Educ. 1972–75, of Trade and Industry 1979–81; Gen. Sec. Finnish Social Democratic Party 1975–81, Chair. 1991–93; apptd mem. Supervisory Bd Neste Ltd 1970, Chair. 1976–94; Deputy Chief Gen. Man. STS-Bank Ltd 1981, Chief Gen. Man. 1982–91, mem. Bd 1992–94; f. Navinor Oy (consultancy), Helsinki 1995; fmr Sr Assoc., Business Environment Europe SA, Brussels; Sr Advisor, Klaraberg Business Advisors 2002–06, Nordic Rothschild 2006–, Kreab Gavin Anderson 2010–; Hon. PhD (Kuopio). *Leisure interests:* music, literature. *Address:* Navinor Oy, Niittaajankatu 1, 00810 Helsinki, Finland (office).

SUNG, Joseph J. Y., MB BS, PhD, MD, FRCPE, FRACP; Hong Kong medical scientist, academic and university administrator; *Vice-Chancellor and President, The Chinese University of Hong Kong;* ed Univ. of Hong Kong, Univ. of Calgary, Canada, Chinese Univ. of Hong Kong; Medical Officer, Prince of Wales Hosp. 1985–92; Lecturer, Dept of Medicine, Shaw Coll. 1992–98, Chair. Dept of Medicine and Therapeutics 1999–2010, Assoc. Dean (Clinical), Faculty of Medicine 2002–04, Assoc. Dean (Gen. Affairs) 2004–09, Head of Shaw Coll. 2008–10; Prof. of Medicine and Therapeutics, Chinese Univ. of Hong Kong 1998–, Mok Hing Yiu Prof. of Medicine 2007–, Vice-Chancellor and Pres. 2010–; Chair. Worldwide Univs Network 2016–; mem. Medical Council of Hong Kong 2007, Research Council, Food and Health Bureau, Hong Kong Special Admin. Region (HKSAR) 2007; Academician, Chinese Acad. of Eng 2011; Fellow, Royal Coll. of Glasgow, Royal Coll. of London, Royal Coll. of Thailand, American Coll. of Gastroenterology, American Gastroenterological Asscn, Hong Kong Coll. of Physicians, Hong Kong Acad. of Medicine; JP, HKSAR Govt 2012; Hon. Prof., Li Ka Shing Faculty of Medicine, Univ. of Hong Kong 2007–09; Hon. mem. American Soc. for Gastrointestinal Endoscopy; Outstanding Staff and Team Award, Hosp. Authority 1998, Eminent Scientist of the Year, Int. Research Promotion Council 2003, Vice-Chancellor's Exemplary Teaching Award, CUHK 2003, Silver Bauhinia Star, HKSAR Govt 2004, Cheung Kong Achievement Award, Ministry of Educ., People's Repub. of China (PRC) and Li Ka Shing Foundation 2006, The Most Outstanding Contrib. Award (Clinical Therapeutics), Food and Health Bureau, HKSAR Govt 2007, State Scientific and Technological Progress Award, Second-Class Award, Nat. Office for Science and Tech. Awards, PRC 2007, Marshall and Warren Lecture Award 2009, Endoscopy Award, German Soc. of Gastroenterology 2009, Ho Leung Ho Lee Advancement Prize, The Ho Leung Ho Lee Foundation 2011, World Outstanding Chinese Award 2013, State Natural Sciences Award, State Council 2016. *Publications:* numerous papers in professional journals on intestinal bleeding, *Helicobacter pylori*, peptic ulcer, hepatitis B and colorectal cancer. *Address:* Office of the Vice-Chancellor, 1/F, Room 101, University Administration Building, The Chinese University of Hong Kong, Shatin, NT, Hong Kong Special Administrative Region, People's Republic of China (office). *Telephone:* 3943-8600 (office). *Fax:* 2603-7301 (office). *E-mail:* js_vcoffice@cuhk.edu.hk (office). *Website:* www.cuhk.edu.hk (office).

SUNGURLU, Mahmut Oltan; Turkish lawyer and politician; b. 1936, Gümüşhane; m.; one c.; ed Bursa Lycée, Istanbul Univ.; began practising law in Gümüşhane in 1963; f. Anavatan Partisi (Motherland Party) prov. org. in Gümüşhane 1983; mem. Parl. for Gümüşhane 1983–99; Minister of Justice 1986–87, 1987–88, 1989–92, 1997–98; Deputy Chair. Anavatan Partisi (Motherland Party) June 1988; Chair. Bd of Trustees Istanbul Şehir Univ.

SUNUNU, Christopher (Chris) T., BS; American engineer, business executive and politician; *Governor of New Hampshire;* b. 5 Nov. 1974, Salem, New Hampshire; s. of John H. Sununu (fmr Gov. of New Hampshire) and Nancy Sununu (née Hayes); m. Valerie Sununu; three c.; ed Massachusetts Inst. of Tech.; worked for 10 years as environmental engineer, including as Project Engineer, Tait Engineering, Foster Wheeler, ECS and SCA; Sr Environmental Engineer, LFR, Inc. 2006–07; Owner and Dir Sununu Enterprises (family business and strategic consulting group) 2006–10; CEO Waterville Valley Resort 2010–; mem. New Hampshire Exec. Council from 3rd Dist 2011–; Gov. of New Hampshire 2017–; Republican. *Leisure interests:* skiing, rugby. *Address:* Office of the Governor, State House, 107 North Main Street, Concord, NH 03301, USA (office). *Telephone:* (603) 271-2121 (office). *Fax:* (603) 271-7640 (office). *Website:* www.governor.nh.gov (office); chrissununu.com (office).

SUNUNU, John E., MS, MBA; American business executive and fmr politician; *Senior Policy Advisor, Akin Gump Strauss Hauer & Feld LLP;* b. 10 Sept. 1964, Salem, NH; s. of John H. Sununu; m. Kitty Sununu; three c.; ed Salem High School, Massachusetts Inst. of Technology and Harvard Grad. School of Business; worked for REMEC, Inc. 1987; man. and operations specialist with Pittiglio, Rabin Todd & McGrath 1990–92; Chief Financial Officer and Dir of Operations Teletrol Systems, Inc. 1992–96; mem. US House of Reps for First Congressional Dist, NH 1996–2002, mem. Commerce, Science, and Transportation Cttee, Finance Cttee, Homeland Security and Governmental Affairs Cttee, Jt Econ. Cttee; Senator from New Hampshire 2003–09; Sr Policy Advisor, Akin Gump Strauss Hauer & Feld LLP 2010–; mem. Bd of Dirs Time Warner Cable Inc. 2009–, Boston Scientific Inc.; mem. Bd of Mans ConvergEx Holdings. *Address:* Akin Gump Strauss Hauer & Feld LLP, Robert S. Strauss Building 1333 New Hampshire Avenue, NW, Washington, DC 20036-1564, USA (office). *Telephone:* (202) 887-4140 (office). *Fax:* (202) 887-4288 (office). *E-mail:* jsununu@akingump.com (office). *Website:* www.akingump.com (office).

SUNUNU, John H., PhD; American business consultant and fmr politician; *President, JHS Associates, Ltd;* b. 2 July 1939, Havana, Cuba; m. Nancy Hayes 1958; five s. including John E. Sununu; three d.; ed Massachusetts Inst. of Tech.; Founder and Chief Engineer, Astro Dynamics 1960–65; Pres. JHS Engineering Co. and Thermal Research Inc., Salem, NH 1965–82; Assoc. Prof. of Mechanical Eng, Tufts Univ. 1966–82, Assoc. Dean, Coll. of Eng 1968–73; mem. NH House of Reps 1973–74, Govt Energy Council; Chair. Govt Council on NH Future 1977–78; mem. Govt Advisory Cttee on Science and Tech. 1977–78; Gov. of NH 1983–89; Chair. coalition of NE Govs 1985–86; White House Chief of Staff, Washington, DC 1989–91, Counsellor to the Pres. 1991–92; Chair. Task Force on Tech.; Pres. JHS Assoc. Ltd 1992–; host, Crossfire (CNN nightly news/public affairs discussion programme) 1992–98; fmr Partner, Trinity Int. Partners; Vice-Chair. Alliance for Acid Rain Control; Chair. Emer. NH Republican Party GOP; mem. Hon. Council of Advisors, US-Azerbaijan Chamber of Commerce; fmr Chair. Republican Gov.'s Asscn, New England Gov.'s Asscn; Vice-Chair. Advisory Comm. on Intergovernmental Relations; mem. Advisory Bd, Technology and Policy Program, MIT 1984–89; mem. Bd of Dirs North American Galvanizing & Coatings Inc. (fmrly Kinark Corpn) 1996–2010, Anglo Asian Mining PLC 2006–, Hampton Financial Corpn 2016–. *Address:* JHS Associates Ltd, 49 Linden Road, Hampton Falls, NH 03844 (office); JHS Associates Ltd, 815 Connecticut Avenue, NW, Suite 1200, Washington, DC 20006, USA (office). *Telephone:* (603) 890-1630 (office). *Fax:* (603) 890-1634 (office). *Website:* www.jhsassociates.com (office).

SUNYAEV, Rashid Alievich; Russian astrophysicist and research institute director; *Chief Scientist, Space Research Institute, Russian Academy of Sciences;* b. 1 March 1943, Tashkent; m.; three s. one d.; ed Moscow Inst. of Physics and Tech.; Jr Researcher, Inst. of Applied Math., USSR (now Russian) Acad. of Sciences 1968–71, Sr Researcher 1971–74, Head of Lab. of Theoretical Astrophysics, Space Research Inst. 1974–82, Head of Dept of High Energy Astrophysics 1982–2002, Chief Scientist 1992–, Corresp. mem. USSR (now Russian) Acad. of Sciences 1984, mem. 1992; Prof., Moscow Inst. of Physics and Tech. 1975–2001; Scientific mem. Max Planck Inst. for Astrophysics, Garching, Germany 1995–, Dir 1996–; Adjunct Prof., Columbia Univ., USA; Maureen and John Hendricks Visiting Prof., Inst. for Advanced Study, Princeton, NJ, USA 2010–; Scientific Head, Int. Orbital Observatory ROENTGEN on complex space station Mir, Orbital Observatory GRANAT; Vice-Pres. COSPAR (ICSU Cttee on Space Research) 1986–94; Ed.-in-Chief, Astronomy Letters 1985, Astrophysics and Space Physics Reviews 1979–2005; mem. Editorial Bd, Space Science Reviews 1988–2007; mem. Advisory Bd on Astrophysics and Space Physics, Springer (previously Kluwer) Scientific Publrs 1995–; mem. Int. Astronomical Union 1968, European Acad. of Sciences,

Int. Acad. of Astronautics, European Astronomical Soc. 1991 (Vice-Pres. 1991–93), American Physical Soc. 1993, German Acad. of Natural Scientists Leopoldina 2003; Foreign Assoc. NAS 1991, American Acad. of Arts and Sciences 1992; Scientific mem. Max-Planck Soc. 1995; Foreign mem. Royal Netherlands Acad. of Arts and Sciences 2004, Royal Soc. 2009; Int. mem. American Philosophical Soc. 2007; Foreign Fellow, Royal Astronomical Soc. 1993; Hon. mem. American Astronomical Soc. 1992; Bundesverdienstkreuz 2010; Bruno Rossi Prize 1988, Bruce Medal 2000, State Prize of Russian Fed. 2000, Alexander Friedman Prize, Russian Acad. of Sciences 2002, Dannie Heineman Prize for Astrophysics 2003, Gruber Prize in Cosmology 2003, Int. Astronomical Union Gold Medal for Cosmology, Crafoord Prize (jtly) 2008, Henry Norris Russell Award, American Astronomical Soc. 2008, Karl Schwarzschild Medal, German Astronomische Gesellschaft 2008, King Faisal Int. Prize for Science (Physics) and Gold Medal (co-recipient) 2009, Antoinette de Vaucouleurs Medal, Univ. of Texas, Austin 2009, Kyoto Prize and Gold Medal, Inamori Foundation (co-recipient) 2011, Benjamin Franklin Medal in Physics, Franklin Inst. 2012. *Publications include:* Black Holes in Double Systems 1973, Observation of Relict Irradiation as Method of Studying the Nature of X-ray Irradiation of Galaxy Clusters 1973, Comptonization of X-ray Irradiation in Plasma Clouds: characteristic spectra 1980; numerous articles. *Address:* Space Research Institute, Russian Academy of Sciences, 117997 Moscow, Profsoyuznaya Street 84/32, Russia (office); Room 130, Max-Planck-Institut für Astrophysik, Karl-Schwarzschild-Str. 1, 85748 Garching, Germany (office). *Telephone:* (495) 333-33-73 (office); (89) 300002244 (office); (495) 331-38-05 (home). *Fax:* (495) 233-53-77; (89) 300002899 (office). *E-mail:* rs@star.iki.rssi.ru (office); sunyaev@mpa-garching.mpg.de (office); iki@cosmos.ru. *Website:* arc.iki.rssi.ru/eng/index.htm (office).

SUNYÉ, Gilbert Saboya, BEcons; Andorran economist and politician; *Minister of Economy, Competitiveness and Innovation;* b. 1966, Andorra la Vella; ed Univ. of Social Sciences, Toulouse, France; began career in banking sector, as CEO, Asset Management BIBM UAA, later Deputy Dir-Gen. of BIBM responsible for Private Banking and Asset Man. 1991–2009; f. Savoy AlfaQuest Advisors (ind. financial consultancy) 2010; Minister of Foreign Affairs 2011–17, Minister of Economy, Competitiveness and Innovation 2017—; Acting Prime Minister March–April 2015; Dir-Gen. Agrupament Nacional Democràtic (AND) 1994–97, also Pres. Parl. Econ. Comm.; Founding mem. Partit Demòcrata 2002, Nou Centre 2008; currently mem. Bd of Man. Partit Reformista d'Andorra. *Leisure interests:* music, reading, travel, football, computer technology. *Address:* Ministry of Economy, Competitiveness and Innovation, Carrer Prat de la Creu 62–64, Edif. Administratiu, Andorra la Vella AD500, Andorra (office). *Telephone:* 875700 (office).

SUOMINEN, Ilkka Olavi, MPolSci; Finnish business executive and fmr politician; b. 8 April 1939, Nakkila; s. of Leo Suominen and Anna Suominen; m. Riitta Suhonen 1977; one s. two d.; Dept Head, J.W. Suominen Oy 1960–72, Deputy Man. Dir 1972–74, Man. Dir 1975–79, mem. Man. Bd; mem. Parl. 1970–75, 1983–94; Leader Nat. Coalition Party 1979–91; Vice-Chair. European Democrat Union 1986–93; Speaker of Parl. 1987, 1991–96; Minister of Trade and Industry 1987–91; Pres. CSCE Parl. Ass. 1992–94; mem. European Parl. 1999–2004; Chair. Admin. Bd Oy Alko AB 1980–88, 1991–94, Gen. Man. 1994; Chair. Bd of Dirs ICL Data (Finland) 1992–96; Vice-Chair. Confed. of Finnish Industries 1978–79; Pres. Finnish Biathlon Asscn 1998–2003; Chevalier, Ordre nat. du Mérite 1983; Commdr, Order of Lion 1986, Grand Cross 1993; Grand Cross, Order of Merit (Hungary) 1992; Grand Cross, Order of Merit (Norway) 1993; Grand Cross, Order of Merit (Italy) 1993; Dr hc (Tampere Univ. of Technology) 1992. *Leisure interests:* hunting, fishing. *Address:* Ruoholahdenkatu 6 A 15, 00180 Helsinki, Finland (home). *Telephone:* 405066145 (mobile) (home). *E-mail:* ilkka@suominen.net (home).

SUOOD, Husnu, LLB, LLM; Maldivian lawyer and politician; *Senior Partner, Suood & Anwar LLP;* b. 12 Jan. 1967; m. Nuzha Abdul Bari; ed Int. Islamic Univ., Malaysia, Univ. of Queensland, Australia; Asst to Attorney-Gen. 1988–94, State Attorney at Attorney-Gen.'s Office 1994–97; Chief Judge of Civil Court, Malé 1997–99; Pnr, Muizzu Suood and Co. (law firm), Malé 1999–2009, Man. Pnr 2008–09; Attorney Gen. 2009–10; Chair. Nat. Law Reform Comm. 2009–10; currently Sr Pnr, Suood & Anwar LLP (law firm); mem. Maldives Law Comm. 1994–2002; lecturer in business law and Maldives legal system at Faculty of Man. and Computing and Faculty of Sharia Law, Maldives Coll. of Higher Educ. and Inst. of Islamic Studies, Malé; mem. Human Rights Comm. of the Maldives; mem. Maldivian Democratic Party; Nat. Award of Excellence for Outstanding Services in the field of law/legal services 2011. *Publications:* International Human Rights 2004, Our Rights – Our Nation 2006, The Maldivian Legal System 2007, Understanding Maldivian Company Law 2009, The Maldivian Legal System 2014, Understanding Maldivian Law of Contract 2015, Law and Society 2015. *Address:* Suood & Anwar LLP, Level 2, Orchid Maage Ameer Ahmed Magu, Malé 20095, The Maldives (office). *Telephone:* 3344-911 (office). *E-mail:* suood@suoodanwar.com (office). *Website:* www.suoodanwar.com (office).

SUPANDJI, Hendarman; Indonesian lawyer and government official; b. 6 Jan. 1947, Klaten, Cen. Java; ed Univ. of Diponegoro; began career with Dist Prosecutor's Office, Cen. Jakarta 1979–81; with Cen. Intelligence Operation, Office of the Attorney-Gen. 1982–83, Prosecutor's Attaché, Embassy in Bangkok 1990–95, Civil and State Admin Asst, Chief's Prosecutor Office, Palembang 1996–97, Staff Expert Adviser to Attorney-Gen. 1998, Head of Financial Bureau, Attorney-Gen.'s Office 1998–2002, Chief Prosecutor in Yogyakarta and Sec. to Deputy Attorney for Supervision 2002–04, Head of Corruption Eradication Team 2005, Deputy Attorney-Gen. for Special Crimes 2005–07, Attorney-Gen. 2007–10; Head of Badan Pertanahan Nasional (Nat. Land Agency) 2012–14; Dr hc (Diponegoro) 2009.

SUPHAMONGKHON, Kantathi, MA, PhD; Thai government official and academic; *Senior Fellow, Asia Institute, University of California, Los Angeles;* b. 3 April 1952; m.; ed Univ. of California, Los Angeles, Univ. of Southern California, American Univ., USA; fmr Prof. of Law and Int. Relations; joined Ministry of Foreign Affairs 1984, with Perm. Mission to UN, New York 1988–92, Adviser on Foreign Affairs to Speaker of House of Reps 1992, Dir Policy and Planning Div., Ministry of Foreign Affairs 1993–94; mem. Parl. 2001–05, mem. Cttee on Foreign Affairs, Cttee on Tourism, House of Reps; Adviser on Foreign Affairs to Prime Minister 1996; Trade Rep. of Thailand 2001–05; Adviser to Minister of Industry;

Special Envoy of the Prime Minister; Adviser on Foreign Affairs to Minister of Foreign Affairs; Minister of Foreign Affairs 2005–06; Univ. of California Regents' Prof., UCLA, USA 2007–09, currently Sr Fellow, Asia Inst. and Burkle Center for International Relations, Visiting Professor of Law and Diplomacy; fmr Chair. Human Security Network, Kanta Enterprise International; fmr Dir Post Publishing Public Co.; Kt Grand Cordon (Special Class) of the Most Noble Order of the Crown of Thailand. *Address:* Asia Institute, 11359 Bunche Hall, Los Angeles, CA 90095-1487, USA (office). *Telephone:* (310) 825-0007 (office). *Fax:* (310) 206-3555 (office). *E-mail:* Kantathi@ucla.edu (office). *Website:* www.international.ucla.edu/asia (office); www.kantagroup.com.

SUPPLE, Barry Emanuel, CBE, PhD, FRHistS, FBA; British economic historian and academic; b. 27 Oct. 1930, London; s. of Solomon Supple and Rose Supple; m. 1st Sonia Caller 1958; two s. one d.; m. 2nd Virginia McNay 2003; ed Hackney Downs Grammar School, LSE and Christ's Coll. Cambridge; Asst Prof. of Business History, Grad. School of Business Admin., Harvard Univ., USA 1955–60; Assoc. Prof. of Econ. History, McGill Univ. 1960–62; Lecturer in Econ. and Social History, Univ. of Sussex, Reader, then Prof. 1962–78, Dean, School of Social Sciences 1965–68, Pro-Vice-Chancellor (Arts and Social Studies) 1968–72, Pro-Vice-Chancellor 1978; Reader in Recent Social and Econ. History, Univ. of Oxford 1978–81, Professorial Fellow, Nuffield Coll. 1978–81; Prof. of Econ. History Univ. of Cambridge 1981–93, Prof. Emer. 1993–, Professorial Fellow, Christ's Coll. 1981–83, Hon. Fellow 1984; Master of St Catharine's Coll., Cambridge 1984–93, Hon. Fellow 1993; Dir Leverhulme Trust 1993–2001; Pres. Econ. History Soc. 1992–95, Foreign Sec. British Acad. 1995–99; mem. Social Science Fellowship Cttee, Nuffield Foundation 1974–94; Co-Ed. Econ. History Review 1973–82; Academic Consultant, Lisbet Rausing Charitable Fund (renamed Arcadia) 2001–07; Hon. Fellow, Worcester Coll., Oxford 1986; Hon. FRAM 2001; Hon. DLitt (Sussex) 1998, (Leicester) 1999, (Warwick) 2000, (Bristol) 2001. *Publications include:* Commercial Crisis and Change in England, 1600–42, 1959, The Experience of Economic Growth (ed.) 1963, Boston Capitalists and Western Railroads 1967, The Royal Exchange Assurance: a history of British insurance 1720–1970, 1970, Essays in Business History (ed.) 1977, History of the British Coal Industry, Vol. IV (1914–46), The Political Economy of Decline 1987, The State and Economic Knowledge: the American and British Experience (ed.) 1990, The Rise of Big Business (ed.) 1992, Doors Open 2008, Six Days in Poland 2010, It Will Go Away: A Memoir of the Solovitch Family 1911–2013 2013, articles and reviews in learned journals. *Leisure interests:* tennis, photography. *Address:* 3 Scotts Gardens, Whittlesford, Cambridge, CB22 4NR, England (home). *Telephone:* (1223) 830606 (home). *E-mail:* barrysupple@gmail.com (home).

SUR, Pierre-Olivier, BA; French lawyer; b. 19 July 1963, Paris; s. of Bernard Sur and Marie-Claude Pellerin; two d.; ed Lycée Montaigne, Paris, Univs of Paris IV-Sorbonne and Paris II-Panthéon Assas, Inst. of Political Studies (IEP), Paris; attorney, Court of Appeal, Paris 1985–, Bar Phnom Penh, Cambodia 2008; Sec. Conférence du stage 1990; Prof., IEP 2001–, mem. Bd 1997–2000, Dauphin 2012–13; Pres. of the Paris Bar 2014–, mem. Ethics Cttee 2001–09; Dir Victims Guarantee Fund 2002–10, Nat. Inst. of Advanced Studies of Safety and Justice 2010–; Judicial Observer to Sarajevo 1994; mem. Cercle du Bois de Boulogne (clay pigeon shooting), Compagnia della vela de Venise; Chevalier, Légion d'honneur, Ordre nat. du Mérite. *Publications:* Droit pénal général (co-author) 1997, Nul n'est censé ignorer la loi 2004, Dans les yeux du bourreau 2010. *Leisure interests:* tennis, sailing. *Address:* SCP Fischer, Tandeau de Marsac, Sur & associés, 67 boulevard Malesherbes, 75008 Paris, France (office). *E-mail:* posur@ftms-a.com (office).

SURANCHIYEV, Abdulda Shergaziyevich; Kyrgyzstani politician; b. 1950, Tuzovka village, Yssyk-Atin dist, Chui Oblast; ed Kyrgyz State Univ.; rank of Police Maj. Gen.; Insp. of Correctional Labour Insts, Ministry of Internal Affairs, Kyrgyz SSR 1970–71; Investigator in internal affairs section of Djet-Oguz Dist Exec. Cttee, Yssyk-Kul Oblast 1973; served in interior forces of USSR Ministry of Internal Affairs 1973–76, Insp., Deputy Head of Criminal Investigation Dept of Internal Affairs section, Sverdlovsk Dist Exec. Cttee, Frunze City (now Bishkek) 1976–81; Sr Insp., Head of Dept, Criminal Investigation Dept of Internal Affairs, Frunze City Exec. Cttee 1981–85; Deputy Head of Internal Affairs section, Pervomai Dist, Frunze City Exec. Cttee 1985–89; Head of Criminal Investigations Section, Ministry of Internal Affairs, Kyrgyz SSR and Kyrgyz Repub. 1989–93; Deputy Head of Criminal Investigations Dept, Ministry of Internal Affairs 1993; Head of Internal Affairs Section, Pervomai Dist, Bishkek City 1993–96; Head of Internal Affairs Section, Bishkek City 1996–2002; Deputy Minister of Internal Affairs 2002–05; worked for Ministry of Internal Affairs 2005–08, Deputy Head of Section for Defence and Security of the Admin of the Pres. 2008; transferred to mil. reserve 2009; Acting Minister of Internal Affairs 2013–14; mem. Kyrgyzstandyn Sotsial-Demokratiyalyk Partiyasy (KSDP—Social Democratic Party of Kyrgyzstan); 'Dank' Medal. *Address:* c/o Ministry of Internal Affairs, 720040 Bishkek, Frunze 469; Kyrgyzstandyn Sotsial-Demokratiyalyk Partiyasy, 720000 Bishkek, Shabdan Batyr 46D, Kyrgyzstan (office). *Telephone:* (312) 53-16-84 (office). *Fax:* (312) 53-16-87 (office). *E-mail:* sdpkkenesh@gmail.com (office). *Website:* www.sdpk.kg (office).

SURANI, Azim, CBE, PhD, FRS, FMedSci; British biologist and academic; *Director of Germline and Epigenomics Research, The Wellcome Trust/Cancer Research UK Gurdon Institute, University of Cambridge;* b. 13 Jan. 1945, Kisumu, Kenya; s. of Habib Surani and Sherbanu Surani; m.; two d.; ed Univs of Cambridge; Mary Marshall and Arthur Walton Prof. of Physiology and Reproduction, The Wellcome Trust/Cancer Research UK Gurdon Inst. of Cancer and Developmental Biology, Univ. of Cambridge 1992–, Dir of Germline and Epigenomics Research 2013–, also mem. Dept of Physiology, Devt and Neuroscience; Gabor Award 2001, Rosenstiel Award 2006, Royal Medal, Royal Soc. 2010, Gairdner Foundation Int. Award 2018. *Publications:* numerous papers on embryonic devt, genomic imprinting, specification of germ cells, epigenetic reprogramming, and pluripotent stem cells. *Leisure interests:* reading, hiking, music. *Address:* The Wellcome Trust/Cancer Research UK Gurdon Institute, Henry Wellcome Building of Cancer and Developmental Biology, University of Cambridge, Tennis Court Road, Cambridge, CB2 1QN, England (office). *Telephone:* (1223) 334136 (office). *E-mail:* a.surani@gurdon.cam.ac.uk (office). *Website:* www.gurdon.cam.ac.uk/research/surani (office); www.stemcells.cam.ac.uk/researchers/principal-investigators/azim-surani (office).

SURÁNYI, György, PhD, DEcon; Hungarian economist, banking executive and academic; *Professor of Finance, Corvinus University;* b. 3 Jan. 1954, Budapest; m.; two c.; ed Univ. of Economics, Budapest, Hungarian Acad. of Sciences; Research Fellow and Head of Dept, Financial Research Inst., Budapest 1977–86; consultant, World Bank, Washington, DC 1986–87; Counsellor to Deputy Prime Minister, Council of Ministers 1988–89; Sec. of State, Nat. Planning Office 1989–90; Pres. Nat. Bank of Hungary 1990–91; co-CEO Cen. European Int. Bank Ltd 1992–95, Chair. 2001; Pres. Nat. Bank of Hungary 1995–2001; Head of CEE Region, IntesaSanpaolo Group, Italy 2001–14; Pres. Supervisory Bd Privredna Banka, Zagreb 2001–14, VUB, Bratislava 2001–14, Intesa Beograd 2006–13; Pres. Bd of Dirs CIB Bank, Budapest 2001–14; currently Prof. of Finance, Corvinus Univ. of Economics, Central European Univ., Budapest; fmr mem. Bd of Dirs Bruegel (econ. research inst.), EastWest Inst., New York; mem. PCG Principles Consultative Group; mem. Int. Advisory Bd Brandeis Univ.; Global Leader for Tomorrow, World Econ. Forum 1993, Leadership in Econ. Transition, EastWest Inst., New York 2001, Euromoney Award, Central Banker of CEE 1996, Global Finance Award, Top Central Banker 1997, 1998, 1999. *Publications:* author of several articles and books on monetary and financial issues. *Address:* Kikelet u. 17/a, 1125 Budapest, Hungary (office). *Telephone:* (30) 222-1516 (office). *E-mail:* gyorgysuranyi@gmail.com (office).

SURAPONG, Tovichakchaikul, BA, MA, PhD; Thai politician; b. 1 May 1953; ed Khon Kaen Univ., Youngstown State Univ., Univ. of Akron, USA; mem. House of Reps 1996–2000; Chair. Standing Cttee on Monetary Affairs, Finance, Banking and Financial Insts 2000; Minister of Foreign Affairs 2011–14; mem. Puea Thai; Kt Grand Cross (First Class), Most Noble Order of Crown of Thailand. *Address:* c/o Ministry of Foreign Affairs, 443 Sri Ayudhya Road, Bangkok 10400, Thailand (office).

SURDO BONETTI, Vittorio Claudio; Italian fmr diplomatist and business executive; b. 22 Nov. 1943, Suq al-Juma, Tripoli, Libya; m. Roya Mirtolouei Surdo; ed Univ. of Rome; joined diplomatic service in Directorate Gen. for Cultural Relations 1970, Sec. of Legation 1970, transferred to Directorate Gen. of Personnel 1972–73, posted to Cairo 1973, First Sec. 1974–76, First Deputy Consul, Embassy in Paris 1976–78, Head of Secr., Directorate Gen. for Cultural Co-operation, Science and Tech., Ministry of Foreign Affairs 1978–80, Counsellor 1980, Counsellor, Embassy in Tehran 1981–84, First Counsellor 1984–85, First Counsellor, Embassy in Bonn 1985–89, reported to Dir Gen. for Political Affairs, Ministry of Foreign Affairs 1989–90, Deputy Head of Press and Information Service 1990–91, Head of Office of Directorate Gen. for Political Affairs 1991–92, Amb. to Ukraine 1992–96, Deputy Dir Gen. for Cultural Relations, Ministry of Foreign Affairs 1996–97, Head of Special Diplomatic Del. to Albania June–Dec. 1997, Chief of Office of Sec. Gen., Ministry of Foreign Affairs 1997–98, rank of Envoy Extraordinary and Minister Plenipotentiary 1st Class 1998, Amb. to Turkey 1999–2004, Dir Gen. for Personnel, Ministry of Foreign Affairs 2004–06, Amb. to Russia (also accred to Turkmenistan) 2006–10; Adviser, Enel Group 2012–; Dir for External Relations and Communication, Lukoil Italy 2013–; Commendatore dell'Ordine al merito della Repubblica italiana 1995, Grande Ufficiale 2004, Cavaliere 2010, Order of Friendship (Russia) 2010. *Address:* Enel SpA, Viale Regina Margherita 137, 00198 Rome, Italy.

SUREAU, Claude, LèsSc, MD; French obstetrician and gynaecologist; b. 27 Sept. 1927, Paris; s. of Maurice Sureau and Rita Jullian; m. Janine Murset 1956; one s. two d.; ed Paris Univ., Columbia Presbyterian Medical Center; Asst Prof., Paris Univ. 1956–61, Assoc. Prof. 1961–74; Prof. and Chair., Dept of Obstetrics and Gynaecology, St Vincent de Paul Hosp., Paris 1974–76, Univ. Clinique Baudelocque 1976–89; Pres., Int. Fed. of Obstetricians and Gynaecologists 1982–85, Pres., Standing Cttee on Ethical Aspects of Human Reproduction 1985–94; Pres. European Asscn of Gynaecology and Obstetrics 1988–91; Dir Unit 262, Physiology and Physiopathology of Reproduction, Nat. Inst. of Health and Medical Research 1983–90; Active Staff mem. American Hosp. of Paris 1989–93, Chief of Gynaecological Unit 1990–93, Medical Dir American Hosp. of Paris 1994–95; Pres. Theramex Inst. 1996–2008; mem. Nat. Acad. of Medicine of France 1978–, Vice-Pres. 1999, Pres. 2000; Vice-Pres. Observatory of the Precautionary Principle 2007; mem. High Council on Population and Family 1996–2003, Nat. Ethics Advisory Cttee 2005–; Commdr Ordre nat. du Mérite 1996, Légion d'honneur. *Publications:* Le danger de naître 1978, Ethical Dilemmas in Assisted Reproduction 1996, Alice au pays des clones 1999; Co-ed.: Clinical Perinatology 1980, Immunologie de la réproduction humaine 1983, Aux débuts de la vie 1990, Ethical Aspects of Human Reproduction 1995, Ethical Problems in Obstetrics and Gynaecology 2000, Fallait-il tuer l'enfant Foucault? et Humanisme médical 2003, Son nom est personne 2005, Contemporary Ethical Dilemmas in Assisted Reproduction, l'Erreur médicale et De la sanction à la prévention de l'erreur médicale 2006. *Address:* 16 rue d'Aubigny, 75017 Paris, France (home).

SURESH, Subra, MS, ScD; Indian/American engineer, materials scientist, academic and university administrator; *President, Nanyang Technological University;* b. 30 May 1956; m. Mary Delmar 1986; two d.; ed Indian Inst. of Tech., Madras, Iowa State Univ., Massachusetts Inst. of Tech.; Postdoctoral Researcher, Univ. of California, Berkeley and Lawrence Berkeley Lab. 1981–83; Asst Prof. of Eng, Brown Univ. 1983–89, Prof. 1989–93; R.P. Simmons Prof. of Materials Science and Eng, MIT 1993, Head of Dept of Materials Science and Engineering 2000–06, Ford Prof. of Eng 2002–10, later Vannevar Bush Prof. of Eng, Dean, School of Eng 2007–10; Dir NSF 2010–13; Pres. Carnegie Mellon Univ. 2013–17, Nanyang Technological Univ., Singapore 2018–; Clark B. Millikan Endowed Chair for Visiting Professorship, California Inst. of Tech. 1999–2000; Founding Chair, Program on Advanced Materials, Singapore-MIT Alliance; Founding Dir Global Enterprise for Micromechanics and Molecular Medicine; mem. NAS, Nat. Acad. of Eng 2002, American Acad. of Arts and Sciences 2004, Indian Nat. Acad. of Eng 2004, German Nat. Acad. of Sciences 2007, Spanish Royal Acad. of Sciences, Spanish Royal Acad. of Eng, Royal Swedish Acad. of Eng Sciences, Acad. of Sciences of the Developing World, Indian Acad. of Sciences, Chinese Acad. of Sciences, French Acad. of Sciences; mem. Bd of Dirs Battelle 2014–, Allegheny Conf. on Community Devt Pittsburgh Symphony Orchestra; elected a fellow or hon. mem. of all the major materials research societies in USA and India; Dr hc (Sweden Royal Inst. of Tech. and univs in USA, Switzerland, Spain, China and India); selected by Technology Review magazine as a top-ten researcher whose research "will have a significant impact on business, medicine or culture" 2006, Acta Materialia Gold Medal 2006, European Materials Medal, Fed. of European Materials Socs 2007, Eringen Medal, Soc. of Eng Science 2008, Gen. Pres.'s Gold Medal, Indian Nat. Science Congress 2011, Padma Shri Award 2011, Nadai Medal 2011, ASME Timoshenko Medal 2012, R.F. Mehl Award, Minerals, Metals and Materials Soc. 2012, Benjamin Franklin Medal in Mechanical Eng and Materials Science 2013, IRI Medal 2015. *Publications:* Fatigue of Materials 1991, Fundamentals of Functionally Graded Materials (co-author) 1998, Thin Film Materials: Stress, Surface Evolution and Failure (co-author) 2003. *Address:* Nanyang Technological University, 50 Nanyang Avenue, Singapore 639798, Singapore (office). *Telephone:* (65) 67911744 (office). *Website:* www.ntu.edu.sg (office).

SURI, Navdeep Singh, MA (Econ); Indian diplomatist and writer; *Ambassador to United Arab Emirates;* b. 1959, Amritsar, Punjab; s. of Kulwant Singh and Attarjit Singh; grandson of Punjabi novelist and poet Nanak Singh; m. Mani Suri; two d.; ed St Francis School, Amritsar, Guru Nanak Dev Univ., Amritsar; joined Foreign Service 1983, served in missions in Cairo, Damascus, Washington, DC, Dar es Salaam and London and as Consul Gen. in Johannesburg, headed West Africa Div., Ministry of External Affairs, Jt Sec. (Public Diplomacy) 2010–12, Amb. to Egypt (also accred to the Arab League) 2012–15, High Commr to Australia 2015–16, Amb. to UAE 2016–; two awards for innovative use of social media in public diplomacy. *Publications include:* has written on India's Africa policy, on public diplomacy and on the IT outsourcing industry; English translations of his grandfather's Punjabi novels. *Address:* Embassy of India, POB 4090, Abu Dhabi, United Arab Emirates (office). *Telephone:* (2) 4492700 (office). *Fax:* (2) 4444685 (office). *E-mail:* ambassador@indembassyuae.org (office). *Website:* www.indembassyuae.org (office).

SURJÁN, László, MD, PhD; Hungarian physician and politician; b. 7 Sept. 1941, Kolozsvár (now Cluj, Romania); s. of László Surján and Margit Surján (née Göttinger); m. Zsófia Stverteczky 1966; one s. two d.; ed Roman Catholic Theologic Acad. Semmelweis Univ. Medical School, Budapest; Lecturer, Semmelweis Medical Univ. 1969–70, Post-grad. Medical School 1970–90; joined Hungarian Christian Democratic Party (Chair. 1990–95); elected mem. Hungarian Parl. (Magyar Polgári Szövetség—Fidesz) 1990, Pres. Employment and Labour Affairs Cttee of Parl. 1994–98, Vice-Chair. Foreign Affairs Cttee 1998–2002, Deputy Speaker 2000–01; Minister of Welfare 1990–94; Head, Hungarian Del. to Parl. Ass. of Council of Europe and Vice-Chair. Foreign Affairs Cttee 1998–2004; mem. European Parl. (Group of the European People's Party—Christian Democrats and European Democrats) 2004–14; Chair. WHO Regional Cttee for Europe 1992–93; Vice-Chair. European Union of Christian Democrats 1992–99; mem. numerous socs. *Publications:* author of 48 scientific publs.

SURKIS, Grigoriy; Ukrainian politician, business executive and international organization executive; *Honorary President, Football Federation of Ukraine;* b. 4 Sept. 1949, Odessa; m.; one s. one d.; ed Kyiv Technological Inst. of Food Industry; worked for Trest Kievzhilstroymontazh 1974–88; held exec. positions with Kiev City Council 1988–91; Pres. Slavutich (holding co.) 1993–98; Owner, Dynamo Kiev Football Club, Pres. 1993–98; Pres. Professional Football League and Vice-Pres. Football Fed. of Ukraine 1996–2000, Pres. 2000–12, Hon. Pres. 2012–; mem. Parl. 1998–2006; mem. UEFA Professional Football Cttee 2002–04, mem. UEFA Exec. Cttee 2004–, Vice-Pres. UEFA 2013–; mem. FIFA Nat. Asscns Cttee; Amb. to Council of Europe for Sport; mem. Nat. Olympic Cttee of Ukraine; mem. Bd of Trustees Jewish Confed. of Ukraine; Order of Merit (Third Degree) 1996, (Second Degree) 1999, (First Degree) 2004, Commdr, Order of the Italian Repub., Order of Prince Yaroslav Mudry The Wise (Fifth Degree) 2006), Order of Ukrainian Orthodox Church 'Apostale Prince Volodymyr' (First Degree) 2006, (Fourth Degree) 2012; Businessman of the Year 1996, 1998, Man of the Year 1997. *Leisure interest:* fitness. *Address:* Football Federation of Ukraine, 7-A Laboratornyi provulok, PO Box 293, Kiev 03150, Ukraine (office). *Telephone:* (44) 521-05-21 (office). *Fax:* (44) 521-05-50 (office). *E-mail:* info@ffu.org.ua (office). *Website:* www.ffu.org.ua (office).

SURKOV, Vladislav Yuryevich, MSc; Russian business executive and government official; *Aide to the President;* b. (Aslambek Dudayev), 21 Sept. 1964, Solntsevo, Lipetsk Oblast, Russian SFSR, USSR; s. of Andarbek (Yuriy) Danilbekovich Dudayev and Zinaida Antonovna Surkova; m. 1st Yuliya Vishnevskaya; one s.; m. 2nd Natalya Dubovitskaya 1998; two c.; ed Moscow Inst. of Steel and Alloys, Moscow Inst. of Culture, Moscow Int. Univ.; name changed to Vladislav Surkov 1969; army service 1983–85; Dir Metapress Agency (communications) 1990–92; Head of Advertising Dept Menatep Credit and Financial Enterprises Asscn (later Menatep Bank) 1992–94, Deputy Head of Client Services Dept 1992–94, Deputy Head of Public Relations Dept 1994–96, Vice-Pres. State Orgs Relations Dept 1996–97, mem. Bd of Dirs 1996–97; Deputy Head, Head of Public Relations, Rosprom 1996–97; First Deputy Council Chair. Commercial Innovation Bank Alfa Bank 1996–97; First Deputy Dir-Gen., then Public Relations Dir Public Russian TV (ORT) 1998, First Sec., Supervisory Bd 1998–99; Aide to Chief of Staff, Presidential Admin 1999, Deputy Chief of Staff, Presidential Admin 1999–2008, Aide to the Pres. 2004–08, 2013–, First Deputy Chief of Staff, Presidential Admin 2008–11; Deputy Chair. of the Govt (in charge of econ. modernization), Head of the Govt Admin 2011–13 (resgnd); placed under exec. sanctions by USA March 2014; State Councillor of the Russian Fed. (First Class), Order of Merit for the Fatherland (Third Class) 2003, Gratitude of the Pres. of the Russian Fed. 2003, 2004, 2010, Medal of P.A. Stolypin (Second Class) 2011; Diploma of the Cen. Election Comm. of the Russian Fed. 2008. *Leisure interests:* playing the guitar, writing music. *Address:* Office of the President, 103132 Moscow, Staraya pl. 4, Russian Federation (office). *Telephone:* (495) 925-35-81 (office). *Fax:* (495) 206-07-66 (office). *Website:* en.kremlin.ru/catalog/persons/2 (office).

SURLYK, Finn C., Cand. scient., PhD, Dr scient.; Danish geologist and academic; *Professor, Department of Geoscience and Natural Resource Management, University of Copenhagen;* b. 17 March 1943, Copenhagen; s. of C. Surlyk and K. Surlyk; m. Nanna Noe-Nygaard; two s.; Asst Prof., Univ. of Copenhagen 1968–69, Assoc. Prof. 1971–80, Research Prof., Dept of Geography and Geology 1984–89, Prof. (Geology of Sedimentary Basins) 1989, currently Prof., Dept of Geoscience and Natural Resource Man.; Head, Dept of Petroleum Geology, Geological Survey of Greenland, Copenhagen 1981–84; Chair. Danish Nat. Cttee of Geology 1976–86;

Gen. Sec. Int. Asscn of Sedimentologists 1986–90, Pres. 1990–94; Sec. Subcommission on Cretaceous Stratigraphy, Int. Union of Geological Sciences 2005–10; mem. Bd Govs, Geological Survey of Denmark 1979–81, Geological Survey of Denmark and Greenland 1988–91, 1991–94; mem. Cttee for Petroleum-Related Research, Ministry of Energy 1986–90, Danish Natural Science Research Council 1992–98; mem. Sedimentary and Geochemical Processes Panel, Ocean Drilling Programme/ JOIDES Resolution (Jt Oceanographic Insts for Deep Earth Sampling) 1991–98, European Science Foundation Man. Cttee for the Ocean Drilling Programme (EMCO), Bd of Dansk Ekspeditionsfond (Galathea 3); Ed.-in-Chief Palaeogeography, Palaeoclimatology, Palaeoecology; Head of FNU-sponsored Cretaceous Research Centre, SedBas PhD School (Geology of Sedimentary Basins); Co-convenor of six int. congresses and symposia; mem. scientific evaluation cttees in Norway, Sweden, France, Portugal, UK, USA; reviewer for the research councils in Norway, Sweden, Finland, Portugal, UK, USA, Canada, the Netherlands; reviewer for numerous scientific journals; participant or leader of more than 20 expeditions to East and North Greenland; participant in the Galathea 3 expedition as a scientist on one leg and as cruise leader on two legs; field work in Denmark, Faroe Islands, Norway, Sweden, Germany, Poland, France, UK, Ireland, Switzerland, Croatia, Italy, Spain, Portugal, Greece, Tunisia, Australia, USA, Canada; mem. Royal Danish Acad. of Arts and Letters 1986; Hon. Fellow, Geological Soc. of London 1991; Kt of the Dannebrog 2001, (First Degree) 2012; Gold Medal, Univ. of Copenhagen 1969, Recipient First Jubilee Prize, Danish Nat. Oil and Gas Co., Danmarks Geologipris 2003, Steno Medal. *Television:* Magasinprogram 2008. *Publications:* about 200 papers, particularly on the geology of Greenland. *Leisure interests:* jazz, bass-playing, outdoor life. *Address:* Department of Geoscience and Natural Resource Management, University of Copenhagen, Øster Voldgade 10, 1350 Copenhagen K (office); Islandsvej 11, 2800 Lyngby, Denmark (home). *Telephone:* 35-32-24-53 (office); 21-65-35-25 (home). *E-mail:* finns@ignl.ku.dk (office). *Website:* geo.ku.dk (office).

SURMA, John P., Jr, BS; American business executive; *Chairman, Federal Reserve Bank of Cleveland;* b. 25 May 1954, Pittsburgh, Pa; m. Becky Surma; ed Pennsylvania State Univ.; joined Price Waterhouse LLP 1976–81, Man. 1981–85, Sr Man. 1985–87, Partner 1987–97; Exec. Staff Asst to Vice-Chair. Fed. Reserve Bd (as part of Pres.'s Exec. Exchange Program) 1983; Sr Vice-Pres. Finance and Accounting, Marathon Oil Co. 1997, Pres. Speedway SuperAmerica LLC 1998–2000, Sr Vice-Pres. Supply and Transportation, Marathon Ashland Petroleum LLC 2000, Pres. 2001; Vice-Chair. and Chief Financial Officer, United States Steel Corpn 2002–03, Pres. and COO 2003–04, Pres. and CEO 2004–06, Chair. and CEO 2006–13 (retd); Deputy-Chair. Federal Reserve Bank of Cleveland 2015–16, Chair. 2017–; Chair. National Safety Council 2015–; Chair. International Iron and Steel Inst. 2006–07; Vice-Chair. 2007–13; mem. Bd of Dirs Marathon Petroleum Corporation, Ingersoll-Rand plc 2012–, MPLX GP LLC, Concho Resources Inc. 2014–, Univ. of Pittsburgh Medical Center; fmr mem. Bd of Dirs American Iron and Steel Inst. (fmr Chair. and Vice-Chair.), Bank of New York, Mellon Corpn, Calgon Carbon Corpn, Nat. Asscn of Mfrs, International Iron and Steel Inst., Allegheny Conf. on Community Devt (also mem. Exec. Cttee), Nat. Petroleum Council; fmr Chair. Allegheny County (Pa) Parks Foundation; mem. Bd of Visitors, Univ. of Pittsburgh Katz Grad. School of Business; mem. Bd of Trustees, Pennylvania State Univ. 2007–13 (Vice-Chair. 2010–11); mem. Smeal Coll. of Business's Bd of Visitors; mem. American Inst. of CPAs; Hon. mem. Nat. Soc. of Black Engineers 2006; Elbert Gary Medal, American Iron and Steel Inst. 2006. *Address:* Federal Reserve Bank of Cleveland, One Oxford Centre, Suite 3000, 301 Grant Street, Pittsburgh, PA 15219, USA (office). *Telephone:* (216) 579-2000 (office). *Website:* www.clevelandfed.org (office).

SURTY, Mohamed Enver, BA, LLM; South African lawyer and politician; *Deputy Minister of Basic Education;* b. 15 Aug. 1953; m.; ed Univ. of Durban-Westville, Univ. of South Africa, Univ. of Western Cape; cand. attorney, Johannesburg 1975, gen. practitioner and human rights lawyer, Rustenburg 1977–94; Prov. and Programming Whip for NW Prov. 1994–99; mem. Senate, then Nat. Council of Provs 1994–2004, Chief Whip 1999–2004; mem. Man. Cttee, Constitutional Ass., negotiator for African Nat. Congress (ANC) on the Bill of Rights 1994–96, observer mem. ANC Nat. Exec. Council 1999–2007; Deputy Minister of Educ. 2003–04; Minister of Justice and Constitutional Devt 2008–09; Deputy Minister of Basic Educ. 2009–. *Leisure interests:* soccer, cricket, squash reading. *Address:* Ministry of Basic Education, Sol Plaatje House, 123 Schoeman Street, Private Bag X603, Pretoria 0002, South Africa (office). *Telephone:* (12) 3125501 (office). *Fax:* (12) 3235989 (office). *Website:* www.education.gov.za (office).

SURUMA, Ezra, PhD, MA, BSc; Ugandan economist; *Chancellor, Makerere University;* b. 11 Nov. 1945; s. of Sulimani Balirenwa and Esiteri; m. Specioza Suruma; four s.; ed Fordham Univ., Univ. of Conn.; previous positions include Dir of Econ. Affairs, Movement Secr., Chair. and Man. Dir, Uganda Commercial Bank, Deputy Gov. and Dir of Research, Bank of Uganda; Minister of Finance, Planning and Econ. Devt 2005–09; Sr Adviser to Pres. of Uganda on Finance and Economic Planning 2009–16; Chancellor, Makerere Univ. 2016–; Visiting Fellow, Brookings Inst., Washington, DC 2010. *Leisure interests:* tennis, music. *Address:* Makerere University, Wandegeya, Makerere, PO Box 7062, Kampala, Uganda (office). *Telephone:* (41) 4542803 (office). *Website:* www.mak.ac.ug (office).

SURUR, Ahmad Fathi, BSc, MA, LLM, PhD; Egyptian politician and academic; b. 9 July 1932, Kena; s. of Mostafa Kamel Surur and Fatma Ali Hassan; m. Zeinab El-Housseiny; one s. two d.; ed Cairo Univ., Univ. of Mich; Deputy Attorney Gen. 1953–59; Prof. of Criminal Law, Cairo Univ. 1959–, Head of Dept 1978–83, Dean of Faculty of Law 1983–85, Vice-Rector Cairo Univ. 1985–86; Chair. Supreme Council of Univs 1986–90; Cultural Attaché, Embassy in Switzerland 1964, Cultural Counsellor, Embassy in France 1965–67; Minister of Educ. 1986–90; Mem. Majlis Ash-sha'ab (People's Ass.) 1987–, Speaker 1990–2011; mem. Political Bureau Nat. Democratic Party 1990–; Pres. Union of African Parls 1990–91; Pres. Inter-parl. Union 1994–97; Pres. Arab Parl. Union 1998–2000; Pres. Union of Islamic Parls. 2000–; Chair. Egyptian Soc. for Criminal Law 1989–, Egyptian Soc. of Francophone affiliated Jurists 1992–, Int. Inst. for Law in the totally or partially Francophone countries, Paris 1994–, Conf. of Euro-Mediterranean Speakers, Alexandria 2000–; Vice Chair. Int. Soc. for Criminal Law, Paris 1989–; Hon. Chair. Inst. for Higher Studies in Criminal Science, Sicily 2000–; Dr hc (Constantin Univ., USA) 2001; Sciences and Art Medal 1964, 1983, Highest Homala Decoration of Alawi Throne, Morocco 1987, Ordre de la Pleiade, Assemblée Internationale des Parlementaires des Francophones 1992; Highest Distinction Award in Social Sciences 1993. *Publications:* Theory of Nullity 1959, Offences Against Public Interest 1963, Penal Law (parts I and II) 1980, Criminal Procedures Law 1993, Constitutional Legality and Human Rights 1995, Constitutional Protection of Rights and Liberties 2000, Criminal Constitutional Law 2001.

SUSMAN, Louis B., BA, LLB; American lawyer, diplomatist and investment banking executive; *Chairman, DJE Holdings;* b. 19 Nov. 1938, Chicago, Ill.; m. Marjorie Sachs; two c.; ed Univ. of Michigan, Washington Univ., St Louis; practised law in St Louis, Mo. for 27 years, Sr Partner, Thompson & Mitchell law firm 1981–89; served in leadership positions with Salomon Brothers 1989–98; Chair. N American Customer Cttee, Citibank and Citigroup Inc. 1998–2000, Vice-Chair. Citigroup Global Markets, Chicago 2000–09 (retd); Amb. to UK 2009–13; Chair. DJE Holdings 2013–, CBI Holdings, L.P. (subsidiary of BDT Capital Partners); Special Adviser, BDT Capital Partners 2013–, Henry Crown & Co. 2013–, Perella Weinberg Partners LP. 2018–; mem. Democratic Nat. Cttee 1972–82; Nat. Finance Chair. John Kerry for Pres. 2003–04; Co-Chair. Finance Cttee Bill Bradley for Pres. 1999–2000; Finance Chair. (Mo.) Dick Gephardt for Pres. 1998; Chair. Bd Fait Accompli; Chair. Chicago Architecture Biennial; Vice-Chair. Chicago Council on Global Affairs; Dir US Can Corp. 1998–, Drury Industries Inc., Drury Devt Corpn, Armstrong Energy Inc. 2017–; Chair. (non-exec.) Edelman; mem. Bd of Dirs and Man. Cttee St Louis Cardinals professional baseball team 1975–89; mem. Chair.'s Circle of the Chicago Council on Global Affairs; mem. Bd Art Inst. of Chicago, Northwestern Children's Memorial Hosp.; mem. US Advisory Comm. on Public Diplomacy 1988; mem. Sec. of State's Foreign Affairs Policy Bd 2012–17, Bd Lurie Children's Hospital, Edward M. Kennedy Inst., Advisory Bd Atlas Merchant Capital, Holdingham Int., Council of American Ambs., Int. Council Whitney R. Harris World Law Inst., Washington Univ.; fmr Dir Center for Nat. Policy, Washington, DC; mem. Bd of Trustees, Woodrow Wilson Int. Center for Scholars 2017–; Life Trustee, The Art Inst. of Chicago; Hon. DHumLitt (Connecticut Coll.) 2012. *Address:* DJE Holdings/Edelman, 200 East Randolph Street, 63rd Floor, Chicago, IL 60601, USA (office). *Website:* www .edelman.com (office).

SUŠNIK, Janez; Slovenian transport industry executive and government official; b. 18 Sept. 1942, Golnik; m.; two c.; ed Tech. Coll., Ljubljana; Pres. Admin. Bd Alpe Tour (forwarding agency) –2001; Asst Man. Viator–Vektor (forwarding agency) 2002; Pres. Nat. Council of Slovenia 2002–08; apptd Pres. Adria Kombi (intermodal transport co.), Ljubljana 2008; mem. Exec. Cttee Chamber of Commerce and Industry of Slovenia (CCIS), Transport Section 1995–2003, Exec. Cttee Regional Chamber for Gorenska Region at CCIS 1995–2003; apptd Chair. Supervisory Bd Adtla Kaubl (nat. authority for combining traffic) 1990, Supervisory Bd Automehaniza (road enterprise) 1998–2002; fmr Pres. Regional Fed. of Pensioners Gorenjska, Vice-Pres. ZDUS (fed. of asscns of pensioners) 2015–; First Prize, Dance Contest, Bled 1959, Silver Plaquette of Community Kranw 1982, Praise of the Fed. Traffic Ministry of Yugoslavia 1984, Acknowledgement of the Presidency of the Yugoslav Repub. Traffic Agency 1988. *Leisure interests:* cycling, skiing, swimming, mountaineering, reading. *Website:* www.zdus-zveza.si (office).

SUSSKIND, Leonard, BS, PhD; American physicist and academic; *Felix Bloch Professor of Physics, Stanford University;* b. 20 May 1940, South Bronx, New York; m. 1st 1960; four c.; m. 2nd Anne Warren; ed City Coll. of New York, Cornell Univ.; began working as a plumber aged 16; NSF Post-doctoral Fellow, Cornell Univ. 1965–66; Asst Prof. of Physics, Belfer Grad. School of Science, Yeshiva Univ., New York 1966–68, Assoc. Prof. of Physics 1968–70, Prof. of Physics 1970–79; Prof. of Physics, Tel-Aviv Univ., Israel 1971–72; Prof. of Physics, Stanford Univ., 1979–2000, Felix Bloch Prof. of Physics 2000–, Dir Stanford Inst. for Theoretical Physics 2009–; Assoc. Faculty mem. Perimeter Inst. for Theoretical Physics, Waterloo, Ont., Canada 2007; Distinguished Prof., Korea Inst. for Advanced Study; mem. NAS, American Acad. of Arts and Sciences; Pregel Award, New York Acad. of Science 1975, Loeb Lecturer, Harvard Univ. 1976, J.J. Sakurai Prize in Theoretical Particle Physics 1997. *Achievements include:* regarded as one of the fathers of string theory for his early contributions to the string theory model of particle physics; one of at least three physicists who independently discovered, during or around 1970, that Veneziano dual resonance model of strong interactions could be described by a quantum mechanical model of strings. *Publications include:* The Cosmic Landscape: String Theory and the Illusion of Intelligent Design 2005, The Black Hole War 2008, The Theoretical Minimum: What You Need to Know to Start Doing Physics 2014, Quantum Mechanics: The Theoretical Minimum 2015; numerous scientific papers in professional journals on models of internal structure of hadrons, gauge theories, quark confinement, symmetry breaking, instantons, quantum statistical mechanics, baryon production in the universe, model for fermion masses, gravity in lower dimensions and quantum cosmology. *Address:* Stanford University, Room 388, Varian Physics Building, 382 Via Pueblo Mall, Stanford, CA 94305-4060, USA (office). *Telephone:* (650) 723-2686 (office). *Fax:* (650) 723-9389 (office). *E-mail:* susskind@stanford.edu (office). *Website:* www.stanford.edu/dept/physics (office); www.theoreticalminimum.com.

SÜSSMUTH, Rita, DPhil; German politician; *President, German Adult Education Association;* b. (Rita Kicknuth), 17 Feb. 1937, Wuppertal; m. Prof. Hans Süssmuth; one d.; ed Univs of Münster, Tübingen and Paris; Prof. and Scientific Adviser, Int. Comparative Educ. Science, Ruhr-Universität, Bochum 1969–71, Full Prof. of Educ. 1971–80; mem. Scientific Advisory Cttee on Family Affairs, Fed. Ministry for Youth, Family Affairs and Health 1971–85; Prof. of Educ., Univ. of Dortmund 1973; joined CDU 1981, Chair. Fed. Cttee Family Policy of the CDU 1983, mem. CDU Bd 1987–98, Fed. Chair. Women's Union of CDU 1986–2001; Dir Research Inst. Frau und Gesellschaft (Woman and Soc.), Hanover 1982–85; mem. 3rd Comm. on Family Affairs; Head of 7th Comm. on Youth; Fed. Minister for Family Affairs, Youth and Health 1985–88; Fed. Minister for Youth, Family Affairs, Women and Health 1986–88; Pres. German Fed. Parl. 1988–98; mem. Bundestag representing Göttingen 1987–2002; Pres. European Movt Germany; apptd Vice-Pres. German Asscn of Adult Educ. Centres 1997 (now German Adult Educ. Asscn), Pres. 1988–; mem. Advisory Council, Bertelsmann Stiftung 1997–; Vice-Pres. Parl. Asscn of OSCE 2000–03, Chair. Kosovo Democracy Team of OSCE 2000–02; Chair. Ind. Comm. on Migration to Germany 2000–01; Chair. Ind. Council of Experts on Immigration and Integration 2002–; Pres. SRH Hochschule

Berlin 2006, Deutsche Polen-Institut 2006–; Steering Cttee on Intercultural Conflict and Societal Integration, Social Science Research Centre, Berlin 2004; mem. UN Comm. on Int. Migration 2004–05; mem. Bd of Dirs Inst. for East–West Studies (IEWS) 1990–, Int. Youth Fed. 1991–; mem. Advisory Bd German Foundation for World Population; mem. Presidium, Deutschen Gesellschaft für Auswärtige Politik (DGAP) 1991–; mem. Bd of Trustees, Aspen Inst., Berlin 1989–; mem. Bd Genshagen Foundation 2009–; Hon. Prof., Univ. of Göttingen 2003–; Hon. mem. Deutsche AIDS-Hilfe 2016; Verdienstorden des Landes Nordrhein-Westfalen 2011, Brandenburg 2016; Dr hc (Hildesheim) 1988, (Bochum) 1990, (Veliko Tărnovo, Czech Repub.) 1994, (Timişoara, Romania) 1995, (Sorbonne Nouvelle) 1996, (Johns Hopkins) 1998, (Ben Gurion, Israel) 1998, (Univ of Augsburg) 2002, (Univ of Rzeszów) 2018; UNESCO Avicenna-Gold-Medaille 1997, Magnus Hirschfeld Medal 2006, Theodor Heuss Prize 2007, Viadrina Prize, Europa-Universität Viadrina 2008, Edith Stein Prize 2013, Reinhard Mohn Prize 2015, Winfried Prize 2015, Dorothea Schlözer Medal, Univ of Göttingen, Humanism Prize 2018. *Publications include:* Frauen: Der Resignation keine Chance 1985, Aids: Wege aus der Angst 1987, Kämpfen und Bewegen: Frauenreden 1989, Wenn der Zeit der Rhythmus ändert 1991, Die planlosen Eliten (jtly) 1993, Wer nicht kämpft, hat schon verloren 2000, Mut zur Macht in Frauenhand, Migration und Integration: Testfall für unsere Gesellschaft 2006, Dennoch: Der Mensch geht vor. Für eine Umkehr in Politik und Gesellschaft 2007, Bildung als globale Herausforderung. Zwei Statements: ein Gespräch (with Hermann Glaser) 2007, Das Gift des Politischen: Gedanken und Erinnerungen 2015. *Leisure interest:* tennis. *Address:* German Adult Education Association, Obere Wilhelmstraße 32, 53225 Bonn, Germany (office). *Telephone:* (228) 97569 (office). *Fax:* (228) 97555 (office). *E-mail:* info@dvv-international.de (office). *Website:* www.rita-suessmuth.de.

ŠUŠTERŠIČ, Janez, PhD; Slovenian economist, academic and politician; *Vice-President, Civic List;* b. 29 Dec. 1966, Ljubljana; ed Univ. of Ljubljana, Univ. of Zurich, Switzerland; Dir Office for Macroeconomic Analyses and Devt 2001–07; Founding mem. Slovenian Econ. Forum 2003; Vice-Pres. Econ. Policy Cttee, EU Council (Ecofin) 2005–07; Prof., Faculty of Man., Univ. of Primorska and School of Advanced Social Studies, Nova Gorica; Assoc. Prof. of Econs, Faculty of Man., Univ. of Primorska, Koper; fmr Visiting Lecturer, Int. School of Business and Social Studies, Celje; Vice-Chair. Econ. Policy Cttee, ECOFIN 2005–07; fmr Vice-Chair. Govt's Reforms Cttee; Nat. Lisbon Strategy Co-ordinator; mem. Gregor Virant's Civic List (renamed Civic List April 2012), Vice-Pres. 2011–; Minister of Finance 2012–13. *Address:* Civic List (Državljanska lista), 1000 Ljubljana, Ukmarjeva ulica 2, Slovenia (office). *Telephone:* (51) 352467 (office). *E-mail:* info@d-l.si (office). *Website:* www.d-l.si (office).

ŠUTANOVAC, Dragan; Serbian politician; *President, Demokratska Stranka (DS—Democratic Party);* b. 24 July 1968, Belgrade; m. Marija Šutanovac; two s.; ed Faculty of Mechanical Eng, Univ. of Belgrade, US-German Marshall Center for Security Studies, Garmisch-Partenkirchen, Germany; Deputy, Belgrade City Ass. 2000–; Special Adviser, Ministry of Internal Affairs 2000–01; mem. Nat. Ass. (Parl.) April–May 2000, Pres. Parl. Cttee for Defence and Security 2002–03; Deputy Minister of the Interior 2001–06; Minister of Defence 2007–12; mem. Demokratska stranka (DS—Democratic Party) 1997–, Vice-Pres. 2010–16, Pres. 2016–; mem. Municipal Bd, Rakovica, Belgrade. *Address:* Demokratska Stranka, 11000 Belgrade, Terazije 3/IV, Serbia (office). *Telephone:* (11) 3443003 (office). *Fax:* (11) 2444864 (office). *E-mail:* info@ds.org.rs (office). *Website:* www.ds.org.rs (office).

SUTANTO, Harjo; Indonesian business executive (retd); b. 1926; m.; four c.; co-f. Wings Group (consumer products co.), Surabaya 1948, now retd; fmrly controlled PT Bank Ekonomi. *Address:* c/o Wings Group, Kawasan Perluasan Utara, PT JIEP, Jalan Tipar Cakung Kav F 5-7, Jakarta 13910, Indonesia (office). *Telephone:* (21) 4602696 (office). *Fax:* (21) 4603494, (office). *Website:* www.wingscorp.com (office).

SUTCLIFFE, James (Jim) H., BSc, FIA; British business executive; *Chairman, Sun Life Financial Inc.;* b. 20 April 1964, Blantyre, Malawi; ed Univ. of Cape Town, South Africa; joined Prudential plc as an actuary 1976, went on to hold several exec. roles in UK and US subsidiaries, including CEO Prudential UK 1994–97; Exec. Dir and Deputy Chair. Liberty International Holdings plc 1998–99, joined Old Mutual plc 2000, Group CEO –2008; mem. Bd of Dirs Sun Life Financial Inc. 2009–, Chair. Sun Life Financial and Sun Life Assurance 2011–; Deputy Chair. Watchstone Group (fmrly Quindell) 2015–; mem. UK Financial Reporting Council 2009–15 (resgnd), Chair. Codes and Standards Cttee 2012–15, fmr Chair. Bd for Actuarial Standards; Chair. FxPro Financial Services Ltd 2010–, Instratus Ltd 2013–; mem. Bd of Dirs Lonmin plc 2007–, Nedcor Ltd 2001–08, BaxterBruce Ltd, STANLIB Ltd, Gunn Agri Partners Pty Ltd, Liberty Group 2009–; Fellow, UK Inst. of Actuaries; Adviser, CVC Capital Partners Ltd 2009–; Trustee, Buffelshoek Trust, The Nelson Mandela Legacy Trust (UK) 2005–08, Friends Of Michael Sobell House 2009–. *Address:* Sun Life Financial Inc., 150 King Street West, Toronto, ON M5H 1J9, Canada (office). *Telephone:* (416) 979-9966 (office). *Fax:* (416) 597-9108 (office). *E-mail:* boarddirectors@sunlife.com (office). *Website:* www.sunlife.com (office).

SUTHERLAND, Donald McNichol, OC; Canadian actor; b. 17 July 1935, St John, NB; s. of Frederick McLae Sutherland and Dorothy Isabel Sutherland (née McNichol); m. 1st Lois May Hardwick 1959; m. 2nd Shirley Jean Douglas 1966 (divorced); one s. Kiefer Sutherland (q.v.) one d.; m. 3rd Francine Racette 1971; three s.; ed Bridgewater High School, NS, Univ. of Toronto; appeared on TV (BBC and ITV) in Hamlet, Man in a Suitcase, The Saint, Gideon's Way, The Avengers, Flight into Danger, Rose Tattoo, March to the Sea, Lee Harvey Oswald, Court Martial, Death of Bessie Smith, Max Dugan Returns, Crackers, Louis Malle, The Disappearance; Pres. McNichol Pictures Inc.; Officier, Ordre des Arts et des Lettres; Hon. PhD; Honorary Oscar For Lifetime Achievements 2017. *Plays:* Lolita (Broadway) 1981, Enigmatic Variations 2000. *Films include:* The World Ten Times Over 1963, Castle of the Living Dead 1964, Dr Terror's House of Horrors 1965, Fanatic 1965, The Bedford Incident 1965, Promise Her Anything 1966, The Dirty Dozen 1967, Billion Dollar Brain 1967, Oedipus Rex 1968, Interlude 1968, Joanna 1968, The Split 1968, Start the Revolution Without Me 1969, Act of the Heart 1970, M*A*S*H* 1970, Kelly's Heroes 1970, Little Murders 1970, Alex in Wonderland 1971, Klute 1971, Johnny Got His Gun (as Christ) 1971, Steelyard Blues 1972, Lady Ice 1972, Alien Thunder 1973, Don't Look Now 1973, S*P*Y*S* 1974, The Day of the Locust 1975, 1900 1976, Casanova (Fellini) 1976, The Eagle Has Landed 1977, The Great Train Robbery 1978, Blood Relatives 1978, Bear Island 1979, Ordinary People 1980, Lolita 1981, Eye of the Needle 1981, Threshold 1982, Winter of Our Discontent, Ordeal by Innocence 1984, Revolution 1985, Gauguin 1986, The Wolf at the Door 1987, A Dry White Season 1988, Bethune: The Making of a Hero 1989, Lock Up 1989, Apprentice to Murder 1989, Lost Angels 1989, The Railway Station-man 1991, Scream from Stone 1991, Faithful 1991, JFK 1991, Backdraft, Agaguk, Buffy the Vampire Slayer, Shadow of the Wolf 1993, Benefit of the Doubt, Younger and Younger 1993, Six Degrees of Separation 1993, The Puppet Masters, Disclosure, Outbreak, Hollow Point, The Shadow Conspiracy, A Time to Kill, Virus 1999, Instinct 1999, Toscano 1999, The Art of War 2000, Panic 2000, Space Cowboys 2000, Uprising 2001, The Big Herst 2001, Final Fantasy: The Spirits Within 2001, Big Shot's Funeral 2001, Five Moons Plaza 2003, Italian Job 2003, Baltic Storm 2003, Cold Mountain 2003, Aurora Borealis 2005, Fierce People 2005, Pride and Prejudice 2005, Land of the Blind 2005, An American Haunting 2005, Ask the Dust 2006, Sleepwalkers 2007, Reign Over Me 2007, Puffball 2007, Fool's Gold 2008, Astro Boy (voice) 2009, The Con Artist 2010, The Mechanic 2011, The Hunger Games 2012, Sofia 2012, Dawn Rider 2012, The Best Offer 2013, Jappeloup 2013, The Hunger Games: Catching Fire 2013, The Calling 2014, The Hunger Games: Mockingjay - Part 1 2014, Forsaken 2015, The Hunger Games: Mockingjay - Part 2 2015, Milton's Secret 2016, The Leisure Seeker 2017, Basmati Blues 2017. *Television includes:* Hamlet, Man in a Suitcase, The Saint, Gideon's Way, The Avengers, Flight into Danger, Rose Tattoo, March to the Sea, Lee Harvey Oswald, Court Martial, Death of Bessie Smith, Max Dugan Returns, Crackers, Louis Malle, The Disappearance, The Path To War (Golden Globe for Best Supporting Actor in a TV series or TV movie 2003) 2002, Salem's Lot 2004, Human Trafficking 2005, Commander in Chief (series) 2005–06, Land of the Blind 2006, Dirty Sexy Money 2007–09, The Pillars of the Earth (mini-series) 2010, Crossing Lines (series) 2013–15. *Leisure interests:* sailing, baseball, Montreal.

SUTHERLAND, Grant Robert, AC, PhD, DSc, FRS, FAA; Australian geneticist and academic; *Geneticist Emeritus, Women's and Children's Hospital, Adelaide;* b. 2 June 1945, Bairnsdale, Vic.; s. of John Sutherland and Hazel Wilson Mason McClelland; m. Elizabeth Dougan 1979; one s. one d.; ed Numurkah High School, Univ. of Melbourne and Univ. of Edinburgh, UK; Dir Dept of Cytogenetics and Molecular Genetics, Women's and Children's Hosp., Adelaide 1975–2002, Foundation Research Fellow 2002–07, Geneticist Emer. 2007–; Affiliate Prof., School of Molecular and Biomedical Science, Univ. of Adelaide 1996–2017, Emer. Prof. 2017–; Int. Research Scholar, Howard Hughes Medical Inst., Bethesda, Md, USA 1993–97; Pres. Human Genetics Soc. of Australasia 1989–91, Human Genome Org. 1996–97; Co-founder and Co-Chair., Scientific Advisory Bd of Bionomics Ltd; mem. Bd of Dirs Thesan PLC, Beef CRC Ltd; Hon. Fellow, Royal Coll. of Pathologists of Australasia 1994; Hon. mem. European Cytogenetics Asscn 2005; Hon. MD (Adelaide) 2013; Australia Prize in Molecular Genetics (co-recipient) 1998, Nat. Australia Day Council Australian Achiever Award 2001, Ramaciotti Medal for Excellence in Biomedical Research 2001, Thompson ISI Australian Citation Laureate 2004, Major Lecture, Annual Scientific Meeting of Human Genetics Soc. of Australasia (named Grant Sutherland Lecture 2005–) 2005, listed among NHMRC High Achievers in Health and Medical Research 2013. *Publications:* two books and more than 480 papers in medical and scientific journals on human genetics. *Leisure interest:* gardening, reading. *Address:* Women's and Children's Hospital, Adelaide, SA 5006 (office); PO Box 1635, Victor Harbor, SA 5211, Australia (home). *Telephone:* 41-8548022 (mobile) (home). *E-mail:* grant.sutherland@adelaide.edu.au (office). *Website:* www.adelaide.edu.au/mbs (office); www.wch.sa.gov.au (office).

SUTHERLAND, Ivan Edward, BSc, MSc, PhD; American electrical engineer, computer scientist and academic; *Visiting Scientist, Electrical and Computer Engineering Department, Portland State University;* b. 16 May 1938, Hastings, Neb.; m. Marly Roncken 2006; one s. one d.; ed Scarsdale High School, NY, Carnegie Inst. of Tech. (now Carnegie Mellon Univ.), California Inst. of Tech., Massachusetts Inst. of Tech.; commissioned as First Lt in US Army, served as electrical engineer at Nat. Security Agency 1963–64, then as researcher at Defense Advanced Research Projects Agency 1964–65; Assoc. Prof. of Electrical Eng, Harvard Univ. 1965–68; Prof. of Computer Science, Univ. of Utah 1968–74; Fletcher Jones Prof. of Computer Science, California Inst. of Tech. 1974–81; Visiting Scientist, Robotics Inst., Carnegie-Mellon Univ. 1980–84; Visiting Scholar, Computer Science Div., Univ. of California, Berkeley 2005–08; co-f. (with David C. Evans) Evans & Sutherland, Salt Lake City, Utah 1968, Vice-Pres. and Chief Scientist 1968–94; also worked as consultant for RAND Corpn 1976–80; Founder and Gen. Partner, Chair. Bd of Advisors, Advanced Tech. Ventures 1980–2008; co-f. Sutherland, Sproull & Assoc. 1980, Vice-Pres. and Tech. Dir 1980–91, acquired by Sun Microsystems, Inc. and formed core of Sun Microsystems Labs 1990, Vice-Pres. and Fellow 1991–2009; Visiting Scientist, Electrical and Computer Eng Dept, Portland State Univ. 2009–, co-f. Asynchronous Research Center, Maseeh Coll. of Eng and Computer Science 2009–; Consultant (part-time), Oracle Laboratory 2009–, ForrestHunt Inc. 2012–; mem. Nat. Acad. of Eng 1972, NAS 1978; fmrly mem. bd of dirs to several public and pvt. cos. including Newmarket Venture Capital Ltd, Tartan Labs; Fellow, Asscn for Computing Machinery (ACM) 1994, Computer History Museum 2005; first Zworykin Award, Nat. Acad. of Eng 1972, IEEE Emanuel R. Piore Award 1986, Leadership Award, Computerworld Honors Program 1987, A.M. Turing Award 1988, ACM Software System Award 1993, EFF Pioneer Award, Electronic Frontier Foundation 1994, Certificate of Merit, The Franklin Inst. 1996, Smithsonian Computer World Award 1996, IEEE John von Neumann Medal 1998, R&D 100 Award (team) 2004, Kyoto Prize in Advanced Tech. (co-recipient) 2012, Proto Awards, Virtual Reality Soc. 2015, inducted into Nat. Inventor's Hall of Fame 2016. *Publications:* SketchPad (software); more than 60 patents. *Address:* Asynchronous Research Center, Maseeh College of Engineering and Computer Science, Portland State University, PO Box 751, 1900 SW Fourth Avenue, Suite 105, Portland, OR 97201, USA (office). *Telephone:* (310) 963-0603 (office). *E-mail:* marly.roncken@gmail.com (office); ies@pdx.edu (office). *Website:* www.pdx.edu (office).

SUTHERLAND, John Andrew, PhD, FRSL; British academic and writer; *Lord Northcliffe Professor of Modern English Literature Emeritus, University College London;* b. 9 Oct. 1938; s. of Jack Sutherland and Elizabeth Sutherland (née

Salter); m. Guilland Watt 1967; one s.; ed Colchester Royal Grammar School, Univs of Leicester and Edinburgh; nat. service, 2nd Lt, Suffolk Regt 1958–60; Lecturer in English, Univ. of Edin. 1965–72; Lecturer in English, Univ. Coll. London 1972–84, Lord Northcliffe Prof. of Modern English Literature 1992–2004, Prof. Emer. 2004–; columnist, The Guardian; Hon. DLitt (Leicester) 1998. *Publications include:* Thackeray at Work 1974, Victorian Novelists and Publishers 1976, Fiction and the Fiction Industry 1978, Bestsellers 1980, Offensive Literature 1982, The Longman Companion to Victorian Fiction 1989, Mrs Humphry Ward 1992, The Life of Walter Scott: A Critical Biography 1995, Victorian Fiction: Writers, Publishers, Readers 1995, Is Heathcliffe a Murderer? 1996, Can Jane Eyre be Happy? 1997, Where Was Rebecca Shot? 1998, Who Betrays Elizabeth Bennet? 1999, Henry V, War Criminal? 1999, Last Drink to LA 2000, The Literary Detective 2000, Literary Lives 2001, Reading the Decades 2002, Stephen Spender: The Authorised Biography 2004, How to Read a Novel: A User's Guide 2006, Bestsellers: A Very Short Introduction 2007, Curiosities of Literature 2008, Magic Moments 2008, Love, Sex, Death and Words (with Stephen Fender) 2010, Lives of the Novelists: A History of Fiction in 294 Lives 2012, A Little History of Literature 2013, How to be Well Read: A guide to 500 great novels and a handful of literary curiosities 2014, Literary Landscapes: Charting the Worlds of Classic Literature (Ed., 2018). *Leisure interest:* walking. *Address:* c/o Department of English, University College London, Gower Street, London, WC1E 6BT, England (office). *E-mail:* j.sutherland@ucl.ac.uk (office).

SUTHERLAND, John D., DPhil, FRS; British chemist, molecular biologist and academic; *Group Leader, MRC Laboratory of Molecular Biology, Cambridge;* ed Univ. of Oxford; fmr Kennedy Scholar, Harvard Univ., USA; fmr Jr Research Fellow, Univ. of Oxford, then Univ. Lecturer in Organic Chem.; Prof. of Biological Chem., Univ. of Manchester 1998–2010; Group Leader, Protein and Nucleic Acid Chem. Div., MRC Lab. of Molecular Biology, Cambridge 2010–; Max Tishler Prize Lectureship, Harvard Univ. 2009, co-winner, Origin of Life Challenge 2012, Darwin Medal, Royal Soc. 2014. *Publications:* numerous papers in professional journals on the chemistry associated with the origin of life. *Address:* MRC Laboratory of Molecular Biology, Francis Crick Avenue, Cambridge Biomedical Campus, Cambridge, CB2 0QH, England (office). *Telephone:* (1223) 267165 (office). *Fax:* (1223) 268300 (office). *E-mail:* johns@mrc-lmb.cam.ac.uk (office). *Website:* www2.mrc-lmb.cam.ac.uk/group-leaders/n-to-s/john-sutherland (office).

SUTHERLAND, Kiefer; American actor; b. 21 Dec. 1966, London, England; s. of Donald Sutherland (q.v.) and Shirley Douglas; m. 1st Camelia Kath 1987 (divorced 1990); two d.; m. 2nd Kelly Winn 1996 (divorced 2008); two step-s.; debut with LA Odyssey Theatre in Throne of Straw aged 9. *Films include:* Max Dugan Returns 1983, The Bay Boy 1984, At Close Range 1986, Crazy Moon 1986, Stand By Me 1986, The Lost Boys 1987, The Killing Time 1987, Promised Land 1987, Bright Lights, Big City 1988, Young Guns 1988, Renegades 1989, Chicago Joe and the Showgirl 1990, Flashback 1990, Flatliners 1990, The Nutcracker Prince (voice) 1990, Young Guns II 1990, Article 99 1991, Twin Peaks: Fire Walk With Me 1992, A Few Good Men 1992, The Vanishing 1993, The Three Musketeers, The Cowboy Way, Teresa's Tattoo, Eye for an Eye, A Time to Kill 1996, Truth or Consequences NM (also Dir) 1997, Dark City 1997, Ground Control 1998, The Breakup 1998, Woman Wanted 1999, The Red Dove 1999, Hearts and Bones 1999, Beat 2000, Picking up the Pieces 2000, The Right Temptation 2000, Cowboy Up 2001, To End All Wars 2001, Desert Saints 2002, Dead Heat 2002, Behind the Red Door 2002, Phone Booth 2002, Paradise Found 2003, Taking Lives 2004, Jiminy Glick in La La Wood 2004, River Queen 2005, The Sentinel 2006, Mirrors 2008, Marmaduke (voice) 2010, The Reluctant Fundamentalist 2012, Pompeii 2014, Twin Peaks: The Missing Pieces 2014, Forsaken 2015, Zoolander 2 2016. *Television appearances include:* Amazing Stories, Trapped in Silence, Brotherhood of Justice, Last Light (also Dir), 24 (Golden Globe for Best Actor in a TV Series 2002, Screen Actors Guild Best Actor in a Drama Series Award 2004, 2006) 2001–10, Touch (series) 2012–13, 24: Live Another Day (mini-series) 2014, Marked (film) 2014, 24: Live Another Day (mini-series) 2014. *Address:* c/o Creative Artists Agency, 2000 Avenue of the Stars, Los Angeles, CA 90607, USA.

SUTHERLAND, Dame Veronica Evelyn, DBE, MA; British college president and fmr diplomatist; *Pro-Chancellor, University of Southampton;* b. 25 April 1939, York, Yorks., England; d. of Lt-Col Maurice G. Beckett and Constance M. Cavenagh-Mainwaring; m. Alex J. Sutherland 1981; ed Royal School, Bath, Univs of London and Southampton; joined diplomatic service 1965, Second Sec., then First Sec. Embassy in Copenhagen 1967–70, Embassy in New Delhi 1975–78; with FCO 1970–75, 1978–80, Counsellor 1981, 1984–87, Asst Under-Sec. of State (Personnel) 1990–95; Perm. Del. to UNESCO 1981–84; Amb. to Côte d'Ivoire 1987–90, to Ireland 1995–99; Deputy Sec.-Gen. of the Commonwealth 1999–2001; Pres. Lucy Cavendish Coll., Cambridge 2001–08; Chair. Airey Neave Trust 2001–11; Pro-Chancellor, Univ. of Southampton 2018–; Trustee, Relate Cambridge 2015–; Hon. LLD (Trinity Coll., Dublin) 1998. *Leisure interest:* painting.

SUTLEY, Nancy, BA, MA; American government official; *Chief Sustainability and Economic Development Officer, Los Angeles Department of Water and Power;* b. 20 April 1962, New York City; ed Cornell Univ., Kennedy School of Govt, Harvard Univ.; fmr Special Asst to Admin. US Environmental Protection Agency (EPA), Washington, DC; Deputy Sec. for Policy and Intergovernmental Relations, Calif. Environmental Protection Agency 1999–2003; Energy Adviser to Calif. Gov. Gray Davis 1999–2003; Deputy Mayor for Energy and Environment, Los Angeles; mem. Calif. State Water Resources Control Bd 2003–05; mem. Bd Metropolitan Water Dist of Southern Calif.; Chair. White House Council on Environmental Quality, Washington, DC 2009–14; Chief Sustainability and Econ. Devt Officer, Los Angeles Dept of Water and Power 2014–; mem. Bd of Dirs Climate Action Reserve 2015–. *Address:* Los Angeles Department of Water and Power, PO Box 51111, Los Angeles, CA 90051-0100, USA (office). *Website:* www.ladwp.com (office).

SUTRISNO, Gen. (retd) Try; Indonesian army officer (retd) and politician; b. 15 Nov. 1935; s. of Subandi Sutrisno and Mardiyah Sutrisno; m. Tuti Sutiawati; seven c.; early career as mil. engineer; ADC to Pres. 1974–78; Army Chief of Staff 1986–88; Commdr of the Armed Forces 1988–93; Vice-Pres. of Indonesia 1993–97; left Golkar Party to join Justice and Unity Party 1998; mem. Indonesian-Malaysian Eminent Persons Group (est. by govts of Indonesia and Malaysia to advise on jt issues) 2008–.

SUTTER, Joos, Lic. oec. HSG; Swiss business executive; *CEO, Coop Genossenschaft;* b. 13 April 1964, Versam; m.; three c.; ed Univ. of St Gallen; Auditor, PricewaterhouseCoopers, Zurich 1991–96; Interim Head of Finance/Services Business Unit, Coop Genossenschaft 1991–96, Head of Retail Business Unit 2011–, Chair. Exec. Cttee 2011, CEO 2011–; Head of Finances, Import Parfümerien AG, Zurich 1996–99; Head of Finances and Sales, Interdiscount AG, Jegenstorf 2005–09; Dir, Coop Vitality AG, Berne, Coop ITS-Travel AG, Wollerau (Chair.), Coopernic SCRL, Brussels, Palink UAB, Lithuania/Palink SIA (Latvia), Marché Restaurants Schweiz AG. *Address:* Coop Genossenschaft, Thiersteinerallee 12, Postfach 2550, 4002 Basel, Switzerland (office). *Telephone:* (61) 3366666 (office). *Fax:* (61) 3366040 (office). *E-mail:* impressum@coop.ch (office). *Website:* www.coop.ch (office).

SUTTON, Cecilia (Cece) Stewart, BA, MBA; American banking executive; *President, US Consumer and Commercial Banking, Citigroup Inc.;* b. 1956, Charlotte, North Carolina; two c.; ed Univ. of South Carolina, Winthrop Univ.; joined First Union Corpn 1978, Br. Man., Raleigh, N Carolina 1984–86, Consumer Banking Man., Greenville, S Carolina 1986–89, Consumer Bank Training Dir Charlotte, N Carolina 1988–89, Area Exec. Rock Hill, S Carolina 1989–92, 1993–95, Head of S Carolina Gen. Banking Group, Greenville 1992–93, Exec. Vice-Pres. 2001; Exec. Vice-Pres. and Head of Retail and Small Business Banking, Wachovia Corpn (following merger with First Union Corpn), Charlotte 2001–08; Pres. Retail Banking Group, Morgan Stanley, New York 2008–10; Pres. US Consumer and Commercial Banking, Citigroup Inc. 2011–; Chair. Consumers Bankers Asscn 2006–; mem. Bd of Dirs United States Cellular Corpn 2013–. *Address:* Citigroup Inc., 399 Park Avenue, New York, NY 10022, USA (office). *Telephone:* (212) 559-1000 (office). *Website:* www.citigroup.com (office).

SUTTON, Henry (see Slavitt, David Rytman).

SUTTON, Philip John, RA; British artist; b. 20 Oct. 1928, Poole, Dorset, England; s. of L. L. Sutton and Anne Sutton; m. Heather Cooke 1954; one s. three d.; ed Slade School of Fine Art and Univ. Coll., London; Lecturer, Slade School of Fine Art, Univ. Coll. 1954–; Artist-in-Residence, Fulham Pottery 1987–; solo exhbns bi-annually at Roland Browse & Delbanco and Browse & Darby 1956–84; Leeds City Art Gallery retrospective 1960; travelled in Australia and Fiji painting landscapes 1963–64; retrospective exhbn, Diploma Gallery, Royal Acad. 1977; toured Israel with 10 British artists 1979; visited Australia 1980; designed Post Office Greeting Stamps 1989; moved to Manorbier, Wales 1989; worked on ceramics with Jean-Paul Landreau in Wales and visited Italy painting watercolours 1990. *Publications:* Philip Sutton RA – His Family & His Friends 1998, Philip Sutton – Life and Art & Work 2008, Philip Sutton – An Artist's View 2009. *Leisure interests:* swimming, running. *Address:* The Studio, 3 Barrack Street, Bridport, Dorset, DT6 3LX (office); 7 Riverside Court, South Walk, Bridport, Dorset, DT6 3XB, England (home). *Telephone:* (1308) 422798 (office); (1308) 421802 (home). *E-mail:* office.psuttonra@gmail.com (office); suttoncooke@gmail.com (home). *Website:* philipsuttonra.com.

SUWAIDI, Sultan bin Nasser as-, BS; United Arab Emirates fmr central banker and business executive; joined Abu Dhabi Investment Authority 1978, later Deputy Dir –1982; Gen. Man. Abu Dhabi Investment Co. 1982–84; Gen. Man. Gulf International Bank, Bahrain 1984–85; Man. Dir and CEO Abu Dhabi Commercial Bank 1985–91; Gov. Cen. Bank of the UAE 1991–2014; Central Bank Gov. of the Year Award 2006. *Address:* c/o Central Bank of the United Arab Emirates, PO Box 854, Abu Dhabi, United Arab Emirates (office).

SUWANNATHAT, Air Chief Marshall Sukampol; Thai politician and fmr air force officer; ed Armed Forces Academies Preparatory School; several years' service in Royal Thai Air Force, including fmr F5 jet pilot, fmr Asst Chief of Staff of Royal Thai Air Force, Insp.-Gen., Ministry of Defence –2011; Minister of Transport 2011–12, of Defence 2012–13. *Address:* c/o Ministry of Defence, Thanon Sanam Chai, Bangkok 10200, Thailand.

SUZMAN, Dame Janet, DBE, BA; South African/British actress and director; b. 9 Feb. 1939, Johannesburg, South Africa; d. of Saul Suzman and Betty Sonnenberg; m. Trevor Nunn (q.v.) 1969 (divorced 1986); one s.; ed Kingsmead Coll., Univ. of the Witwatersrand, London Acad. of Music and Dramatic Art; moved to UK 1960; The Spencer Memorial Lecture, Harvard Univ. 1987; The Tanner Lectures, Brasenose Coll., Oxford 1995, The Drapers Lecture, Queen Mary and Westfield Coll., Univ. of London 1996, The Morell Lecture, Univ. of York 1999; Pres. Shakespeare's Birthday Celebrations 2010–11; Vice-Pres. London Acad. of Music and Dramatic Art; Life Fellow, Shakespeare Asscn of Great Britain; Hon. Assoc. Artist RSC; Hon. Patron the Market Theatre, The Baxter Theatre, Cape Town; Hon. Lecturer in the Shakespeare Inst., Stratford, Univ. of Birmingham; Hon. Fellow, School of Arts Univ. of Liverpool; Queen's Silver Jubilee Medal 1977; Hon. MA (Open Univ.) 1984; Hon. DLit (Warwick) 1990, (Leicester) 1992, (Queen Mary and Westfield Coll.) 1997, (Southampton) 2002, (Middlesex) 2003, (Kingston) 2006, (Cape Town) 2010, (Liverpool John Moore's Univ.) 2011, (Buckingham) 2014, (Edge Hill) 2015; Best Actress, Evening Standard Drama Award 1973, 1976, Plays and Players Award 1976, Best Production Award, Liverpool Echo 1993, Barclays TMA Award for Best Dir 1997, Best Dir Award, Liverpool Echo 2010, The Pragnell Prize for Services to Shakespeare 2011. *Roles for RSC and West End include:* Lady Anne, La Pucelle, Lady Percy, Luciana, Ophelia, Beatrice, Rosalind 1962–70, Lulu in The Birthday Party 1963–64, Portia, Rosalind (RSC) 1965, Carmen in The Balcony, She Stoops to Conquer (Oxford Playhouse) 1966, Katharina, Celia, Berinthia in The Relapse 1967, Cleopatra and Lavinia (RSC) 1972–73, Hester in Hello and Goodbye (Kings Head) 1973, Masha in Three Sisters (Cambridge Theatre) 1976, The Death of Bessie Smith (Market Theatre, Johannesburg) 1976, Shen Te in The Good Woman of Setzuan (Tyneside Theatre Co.) 1976, at Royal Court Theatre 1977; Hedda Gabler (Duke of York's Theatre) 1977, Duchess of Malfi 1978, The Greeks (Aldwych) 1980, Boesman and Lena (Hampstead) 1984, Vassa (Greenwich Theatre) 1985, Andromache (Old Vic) 1987, Another Time (Wyndhams) 1989–90, Hippolytus (Almeida) 1991, The Sisters Rosensweig (Old Vic) 1994, The Retreat from Moscow (Chichester) 1999, The Free State (Birmingham Repertory and tour) 2000, The Hollow Crown (tour of Far East) 2003, Whose Life is it Anyway (Comedy) 2005, Frobishers Gold (The Shaw) 2006, Volumnia in Coriolanus (RSC) 2007, The Dream of the Dog (Finborough Theatre, Trafalgar Studios) 2010, Solomon and Marion (Baxter Theatre) 2011. *Plays* *directed:* Othello, (Market Theatre, Johannesburg) 1987, Othello (Channel Four) 1988, A Dream of People (The Pit) 1990, The Cruel Grasp (Edinburgh Festival) 1991, No Flies on Mr. Hunter (Chelsea Centre) 1992, Death of a Salesman (Theatr Clwyd) 1993, The Deep Blue Sea (Theatr Clwyd) 1996, The Good Woman of Sharkville (Market Theatre, Johannesburg) 1996 and UK tour 1997, The Cherry Orchard (Birmingham Rep.) 1997, The Snow Palace (tour 1998) and Tricycle Theatre 1998, The Free State – A South African Response to The Cherry Orchard (Birmingham Repertory) and UK tour 2000, The Guardsman 2000, Measure for Measure (Guildhall) 2004, Hamlet (Grahamstown Festival and The Complete Works Festival, Stratford-on-Avon) 2006, Master Harold and the Boys (LAMDA) 2009, Antony and Cleopatra (Liverpool Playhouse) (Liverpool Echo Best Production Award 2010) 2010, Antony and Cleopatra (Chichester Festival Theatre) 2012, Much Ado About Nothing (LAMDA) 2012. *Film appearances:* A Day in the Death of Joe Egg 1970, Nicholas and Alexandra 1971, Nijinsky 1978, The Black Windmill 1979, The House on Garibaldi Street 1979, Priest of Love 1981, The Draughtsman's Contract 1981, E la Nave Va 1982, A Dry White Season 1988, Nuns on the Run 1990, Leon the Pig-Farmer 1992, Max 2001, Fairy Story 2002, Felix 2013. *Radio:* Latest: Miss Haversham, Mrs. Klein, Life and Fate. *Television includes:* The Family Reunion 1967, Saint Joan 1968, The Three Sisters 1969, Macbeth 1970, Hedda Gabler 1972, Twelfth Night 1973, Shakespeare or Bust 1973, Antony and Cleopatra (RSC) 1974, Miss Nightingale, Clayhanger (serial) 1975–76, Robin Hood (CBS TV) 1983, Mountbatten: The Last Viceroy 1985, The Singing Detective 1986, The Miser 1987, Revolutionary Witness 1989, Masterclass on Shakespearian Comedy 1990, Masterclass from Haymarket Theatre (Sky TV) 2001, White Clouds (BBC) 2002, Hiroshima (movie) 2005, Trial & Retribution (series) 2006, The Colour of Magic (film) 2008, Midsomer Murders (series) – The Sword of Guillaume 2010, Tinga Tinga Tales (series) (voice of Ostrich) 2011, Sinbad (series) 2012, Labyrinth (series) 2012, Moominland Tales: The Life of Tove Jansson (film) 2012. *Publications:* Hedda Gabler: The Play in Performance 1980, Acting with Shakespeare: Three Comedies 1996, The Free State 2000 (republished 2011), A Commentary on Antony and Cleopatra 2001, Not Hamlet 2012, Antony and Cleopatra (ed.) 2012. *Leisure interests:* not climbing Everest or rowing the Atlantic. *Address:* c/o Steve Kenis and Co., 95 Barkston Gardens, London, SW5 0EU, England (office). *Telephone:* (20) 7434-9055 (office). *Fax:* (20) 7287-6328 (office). *E-mail:* sk@sknco.com (office).

SUZUKI, Akira, PhD; Japanese chemist and academic; *Professor Emeritus, Hokkaido University;* b. 12 Sept. 1930, Mukawa, Hokkaido; ed Hokkaido Univ., Sapporo; apptd Asst Prof., Dept of Chemical Process Eng, Faculty of Eng, Hokkaido Univ. 1961, Prof., Dept of Applied Chem. 1973–94, Prof. Emer. 1994–, Distinguished Prof., Graduate School of Eng 2006, Catalysis Research Center 2010, Univ. Prof. 2015; Prof., Okayama Univ. of Science 1994–95, Univ. of Science and the Arts 1995–2002; postdoctoral research with Herbert Charles Brown at Purdue Univ., USA 1963–65; Prof. Emer., Xi'an Jiaotong Univ. 2014–; Vice-Pres., Dir and Editorial mem. Chemical Soc. of Japan; Dir and Pres. Soc. of Synthetic Organic Chemistry; mem. American Chemical Soc., The Japan Acad. 2011; Fellow, Royal Soc. of Chemistry (UK) 2009, Hon. Fellow 2012; Hon. mem. Argentine Organic Chemistry Soc. 2001, Soc. of Synthetic Organic Chemistry 2005, The Chemical Soc. of Japan 2005, Catalysis Soc. of Japan 2012, Hon. Prof. Shanghai Inst. of Organic Chemistry, Chinese Acad. of Sciences 2006; Person of Cultural Merit 2010, Order of Culture 2010; Weissberger-Williams Lectureship Award 1986, Korean Chemical Soc. Award 1987, Chemical Soc. of Japan Award 1989, DowElanco Lectureship Award 1995, Weissberger-Williams Lectureship Award 2001, Distinguished Lecturer Award, Queens Univ. 2001, The H.C. Brown Lecture Award 2000, Japan Acad. Prize 2003, Synthetic Organic Chemistry Japan Special Award 2004, Karrer Gold Medal, Zürich Univ. 2009, Nobel Prize in Chem. (jtly with Richard Heck and Ei-ichi Negishi) "for palladium-catalyzed cross couplings in organic synthesis" 2010, H.C. Brown Award for Creative Research in Synthetic Methods 2011. *Achievements include:* first published the Suzuki reaction, the organic reaction of an aryl- or vinyl-boronic acid with an aryl- or vinyl-halide catalysed by a palladium(0) complex 1979. *Publications:* numerous papers in professional journals. *Address:* Faculty and Graduate School of Engineering, Hokkaido University, Kita 13, Nishi 8, Kita-ku, Sapporo 060-8628, Hokkaido, Japan (office). *E-mail:* info@eng.hokudai.ac.jp (office). *Website:* www.eng.hokudai.ac.jp (office).

SUZUKI, Atsuto, PhD; Japanese physicist, university administrator and academic; *President, Iwate Prefectural University;* b. 1946; ed Univ. of Niigata, Tohoku Univ.; Prof., Tohoku Univ. from 1993, now Emer., carried out research at Japanese Super-Kamiokande experiment (Neutrino Detector), Vice-Pres. Tohoku Univ., Dir Research Center for Neutrino Science 1998–, also organized KamLAND experiments for observing neutrinos; Dir Gen. High Energy Accelerator Research Org. (KEK), Japan 2006–15; Pres. Iwate Prefectural Univ. 2015–; Foreign mem. Russian Acad. of Sciences 2011; Medal of Honor with Purple Ribbon, Japanese Govt 2005, Japan Acad. Prize 2006, Bruno-Pontecorvo Prize 2006, Breakthrough Prize in Fundamental Physics (co-recipient) 2016. *Achievements include:* first observation of geologically produced neutrinos by radiogenic material decays deep inside the earth. *Publications:* numerous papers in professional journals. *Address:* Iwate Prefectural University, 152-52 Sugo, Takizawa-shi, Iwate-ken 020-0193, Japan (office). *Telephone:* (19) 694-2000 (office). *Fax:* (19) 694-2001 (office). *E-mail:* kyoumu@ml.iwate-pu.ac.jp (office). *Website:* www.iwate-pu.ac.jp/universityguide/president2.html (office).

SUZUKI, David Takayoshi, OC, BA, PhD; Canadian broadcaster, geneticist and academic; *Chairman, David Suzuki Foundation;* b. 24 March 1936, Vancouver, BC; s. of Kaoru Carr Suzuki; m. 2nd Tara Cullis; two c.; ed Amherst Coll. and Univ. of Chicago, USA; Biologist, Dept of Lands & Forests, Sudbury, Ont. 1958; Teaching Asst, Dept of Biology, Amherst Coll. 1957–58; Research Asst for Dr W. K. Baker, Univ. of Chicago 1958–59, Teaching Asst, Dept of Zoology, Univ. of Chicago 1959–61; Asst Prof., Dept of Genetics, Univ. of Alberta 1962–63; Asst Prof., Dept of Zoology, Univ. of BC 1963–65, Assoc. Prof. 1965–69, Prof. 1969–93, Prof. Emer. 2001–; Visiting Prof., Univ. of Calif., Berkeley 1966, 1969, 1976, 1977, Univ. of Puerto Rico 1972, Univ. of Toronto 1978; f. David Suzuki Foundation 1990, now Chair.; Fellow, Royal Soc. of Canada 1978–84, AAAS 1980–; has produced and hosted numerous CBC and other TV series and specials on science topics; Order of BC 1995; Hon. LLD (Univ. of Prince Edward Island) 1974, (Trent Univ.) 1981, (Univ. of Calgary) 1986, (Queen's Univ.) 1987; Hon. DSc (Univ. of Windsor) 1979,

(Acadia Univ.) 1979, (Lakehead Univ.) 1986, (McMaster Univ.) 1987, (Carleton Univ.) 1987, (Amherst Coll.) 1988, (Griffith Univ.) 1997, (Whitman Coll.) 1999, (York Univ.) 2005, (UQAM) 2005, (Flinders Univ.) 2006, (Univ. of Montreal) 2007, (Univ. of Western Ont.) 2007; Hon. DHL (Governors State Univ.) 1986; Hon. DDL (Open Univ., Canada) 1998, (Simon Fraser Univ.) 2001; Hon. Doctor of Environmental Science (Unity Coll.) 2000; Hon. Doctor of Communication (Ryerson Univ.) 2007; numerous awards including Oustanding Japanese-Canadian of the Year Award 1972, Broadcaster of the Year, Canadian Broadcasters League 1976, Sanford Fleming Medal, Royal Canadian Inst. 1981, Japan Times Prize 1983, Medal of Honor, Canadian Asscn 1984, Gold Medal Award, Biological Council of Canada 1986, UNESCO Kalinga Prize 1986, Wiegand Award for Canadian Excellence, Univ. of Waterloo 1990, Lifetime Achievement Award, Univ. of BC Alumni 2000, John Drainie Award for Excellence in Broadcast Journalism 2002, Queen Elizabeth II Golden Jubilee Medal 2002, Lindbergh Award 2004, voted one of 10 Greatest Canadians by CBC viewers 2004, Bradford Washburn 2006, Right Livelihood Award 2009. *Radio includes:* Quirks and Quarks 1974–79, It's a Matter of Survival 1989. *Television includes:* Science Magazine 1974–79, Suzuki on Science 1979, The Nature of Things 1979–, A Planet for the Taking (UNEP Medal) 1985, From Naked Ape to Superspecies. *Publications:* more than 45 books, including An Introduction to Genetic Analysis (with A. F. Griffiths) 1976, The Japan We Never Knew 1996, The Sacred Balance: Rediscovering Our Place in Nature (with A. McConnell) 1997, A Glimpse of Canada's Future 1997, Tree Suitcase 1998, Earth Time 1998, From Naked Ape to Superspecies 1999, You Are the Earth 1999, Eco-Fun 2000, Good News for a Change 2001, When the Wild Comes Leaping Up 2002, Genetics – A Beginner's Guide (co-author) 2002, Sacred Balance – A Visual Celebration 2002, The Salmon Forest 2002, David Suzuki Reader 2003, Tree – A Life Story 2004, Grassroots Rising 2006, David Suzuki: The Autobiography (British Columbia Booksellers' Choice Award in Honour of Bill Duthie 2007) 2006. *Address:* c/o Elois Yaxley, David Suzuki Foundation, Suite 219, 2211 West 4th Avenue, Vancouver, BC V6K 4S2, Canada (office). *Telephone:* (604) 732-4228 (office). *Fax:* (604) 730-9672 (office). *Website:* www.davidsuzuki.org (office).

SUZUKI, Hisahito; Japanese business executive; *Representative Director and Chairman, MS&AD Insurance Group Holdings, Inc.;* b. 15 Sept. 1950; joined Dai-Tokyo Fire & Marine Insurance Co. Ltd (Dai-Tokyo) 1973, Exec. Officer and Gen. Man. Merger Preparation Dept, Dai-Tokyo 2000–01, Exec. Officer and Gen. Man. Corp. Planning Dept, Aioi Insurance Co. Ltd (Aioi) 2001–02, Man. Exec. Officer, Aioi April–June 2002, Man. Dir Aioi 2002–03, Sr Man. Exec. Officer, Aioi Life Insurance Co. Ltd (Aioi Life) May–June 2003, Dir and Vice-Pres., Aioi Life 2003–04, Sr Man. Exec. Officer, Aioi March–June 2004, Sr Man. Dir Aioi 2004–08, Dir and Sr Man. Exec. Officer, Aioi 2008–10, Dir and Pres. Aioi 2010, Rep. Dir and Exec. Officer, MS&AD Insurance Group Holdings, Inc. 2010–14, Dir and Pres., Aioi Nissay Dowa Insurance Co. Ltd 2010–14, Rep. Dir and Chair. MS&AD Insurance Group Holdings, Inc. 2014–. *Address:* MS&AD Insurance Group Holdings, Inc., Yaesu First Financial Building, Yaesu 1-3-7, Chuo-ku, Tokyo 103-0028, Japan (office). *Telephone:* (3) 6202-5268 (office). *Fax:* (3) 6202-6882 (office). *E-mail:* info@ms-ad-hd.com (office). *Website:* www.ms-ad-hd.com (office).

SUZUKI, Ichiro; Japanese professional baseball player; b. 22 Oct. 1973, Kasugai; m. Yumiko Suzuki; ed Aikoudai Meiden, Aichi Pref.; outfielder; with Japanese Pacific League team Orix Blue Wave 1994–2000; set Japanese records for continuous games and batting average; signed with Seattle Mariners Nov. 2000–2012, traded to New York Yankees 2012–14, Miami Marlins 2015–; set American League record for singles (190) in a season 2001; American League batting champion 2001, 2004; set major league record for hits (262) 2004; Matsutaro Shoriki Award 1994–95, 2004, American League Most Valuable Player 2001, American League Rookie of the Year 2001, Gold Glove Award 2001–10, Commissioner's Historic Achievement Award 2005. *Address:* Miami Marlins, Marlins Park, 501 Marlins Way (NW 16th Avenue), Miami, FL 33125, USA. *Website:* miami.marlins.mlb.com.

SUZUKI, Kunio; Japanese business executive; b. 27 Aug. 1939; joined Osaka Shosen Kaisha 1962 (renamed Mitsui OSK Lines Ltd 1964), Gen. Man. Tanker Div. 1988–91, Dir and Gen. Man. Tanker Div. 1991–93, Dir 1993–94, Man. Dir 1994–95, apptd Rep. Dir 1995, Sr Man. Dir 1995–98, Vice-Pres. 1998–2000, Pres. 2000–04, Chair. and CEO Mitsui OSK Lines Ltd 2004–06, Chair. 2006–10, Counselor 2010–; Chair. Japanese Shipowners' Asscn; mem. Bd of Dirs Dah Sing Financial Holdings Ltd 2003, Teijin Ltd.

SUZUKI, Nobuya, BSc; Japanese insurance company executive; *Chairman and Representative Director, Meiji Yasuda Life Insurance Company;* b. 1955; ed Kyoto Univ.; joined Meiji Yasuda Life Insurance Co. 1979, Gen. Man. Yamagata Regional Office 1999–2001, Gen. Man. Strategic Research Office 2001–04, Gen. Man. Risk Man. Control Dept 2004–06, Gen. Man. Product Devt Dept 2006–08, Exec. Officer and Gen. Man. Product Devt Dept 2008–10, Man. Exec. Officer 2010–13, Chair. and Rep. Dir 2013–. *Address:* Meiji Yasuda Life Insurance Co., 1-1, Marunouchi 2-chome, Chiyoda-ku, Tokyo 100-0005, Japan (office). *Telephone:* (3) 3283-8293 (office). *Fax:* (3) 3215-8123 (office). *E-mail:* info@meijiyasuda.co.jp (office). *Website:* www.meijiyasuda.co.jp (office).

SUZUKI, Osamu; Japanese business executive; *Chairman and CEO, Suzuki Motor Corporation;* b. 30 Jan. 1930, Gero, Gifu; s. of Shunzo Suzuki and Toshiko Suzuki; m. Shoko Suzuki 1958; two s. one d.; ed Chuo Univ.; joined Suzuki Motor Co. Ltd 1958, Dir 1963–66, Jr Man. Dir 1967–72, Sr Man. Dir 1973–77, Pres. and CEO 1978–2000 (name changed to Suzuki Motor Corpn 1990), Chair. and CEO 2000–, Pres. and COO 2008–15; Exec. Officer, Narita Int. Airport Corpn; Exec. Officer, later Man. Dir Exec. Officer Mitsui OSK Lines Ltd –2005, Man. Dir MOL (Asia) Ltd –2005, Pres. and CEO MOL (America) Inc. (subsidiary of Mitsui Osk Lines Ltd) 2005–08; fmr Gen. Man. Keihanshin region of Daito Trust Construction Co. Ltd; Dir (non-exec.) Maruti Suzuki India Ltd; Chair. Suzuki Foundation; Dir, Yamada Corpn 2010–; Sitara-i-Pakistan (Pakistan) 1985, Medal of Honour with Blue Ribbon 1987, Mil. Cross of Order of Repub. of Hungary 1993, Middle Cross with Star Order of Merit (Hungary) 2004, Padma Bhushan (India) 2007. *Leisure interest:* golf. *Address:* Suzuki Motor Corpn, 300 Takatsuka-cho, Minami-ku, Hamamatsu-shi, Shizuoka 432-8611, Japan (office). *Telephone:* (53) 440-2023 (office). *Fax:* (53) 440-2776 (office). *E-mail:* info@suzuki.co.jp (office). *Website:* www.globalsuzuki.com (office); www.suzuki.co.jp (office).

SUZUKI, Tadashi; Japanese theatre director and producer; *Artistic Director, Suzuki Company of Toga;* b. 20 June 1939, Shimizu City; m. Hiroko Takeuchi 1969; one s.; ed Kitazono High School and Waseda Univ.; f. Waseda Sho-Gekijo 1966; apptd. Artistic Dir Iwanami Hall 1974; built Toga Theatre, Toga Village, Toyama Pref. 1976; Guest Prof. at Juilliard School, Univ. of Wis. (Milwaukee), Univ. of Calif. (San Diego), Univ. of Del., Central Acad. of Drama (Beijing), Shanghai Theatre Acad. and others; founded Japan Performing Arts Center 1982–99; began annual Toga Int. Arts Festival 1982, Toga Int. Actor Training Programme 1983; Artistic Dir Acting Co. Mito (ACM) Theatre 1989–94; Gen. Artistic Dir Shizuoka Performing Arts Center 1995–2007; Artistic Dir Suzuki Co. of Toga; Chair. Japan Performing Arts Foundation 2000–10; mem. Int. Cttee Theatre Olympics 1994; several awards for services to the arts. *Work includes:* own texts On the Dramatic Passions I 1969, II 1970, III 1970, Night and Clock 1975, Greek tragedies and plays by Chekhov and Shakespeare, adaptations of Edmond Rostand's Cyrano de Bergerac, Yukio Mishima's Madame de Sade and Junichiro Tanizaki's Okuni to Gohei. *Publications:* The Sum of the Internal Angles 1973, Dramatic Language 1977, On the Dramatic Passions 1977, Horizon of Deception 1980, Force that Crosses the Border 1984, The Way of Acting 1986, What Theatre Is 1988, The Way of Directing 1994, Dramatic Language II 1999, The Sum of the Internal Angles II 2003. *Leisure interest:* collecting costumes (especially hats). *Address:* Japan Performing Arts Foundation, 3-19-17-402, Takanawa, Minato-ku, Tokyo 108-0074, Japan (office). *Telephone:* (3) 3445-8010 (office). *Fax:* (3) 3445-8012 (office). *E-mail:* engekijin@jpaf.or.jp (office). *Website:* www.jpaf.or.jp (office); www.scot-suzukicompany.com (office).

SUZUKI, Toshifumi; Japanese retail executive; b. 1933; opened first convenience store (konbini) 1974; fmr labour union leader; f. Seven-Eleven Japan Co. (imported name and concept from US to Japan 1970s); Pres. Ito Yokado Co. Ltd (supermarket chain) 2000–03, Chair. and CEO 2003–05, Chair. and CEO Seven & i Holdings Co. Ltd (holding co. of Ito Yokado, Seven Eleven Japan, Denny's Japan and other operating cos) 2005–16, Chair. 7-Eleven Inc. (after acquisition by Seven & i Holdings) 2005–16 (resgnd); Pres. Keiranden Cttee on Distribution from 2000. *Address:* c/o Seven & i Holdings Co. Ltd, 8-8 Nibancho, Chiyoda-ku, Tokyo 102-8455, Japan. *E-mail:* info@7andi.com.

SUZUKI, Tsuneo; Japanese politician; b. 10 Feb. 1941; ed Faculty of Political Science and Econs, Waseda Univ.; mem. House of Reps (Kanagawa Pref. 1st Dist, then 7th Dist) 1986–; joined LDP 1986, Dir Environment Div., LDP 1997, Deputy Chair. Research Comm. on the Educ. System 1998, Research Comm. on Fundamental Environmental Issues 1999, Policy Research Council 2000–01, Vice-Chair. Party Org. HQ 2001, Chair. Special Cttee on Foreign Students 2001–03, Deputy Chair. Diet Affairs Cttee 2003–04, Chair. Cttee on Nat. Capital Area 2004–05, Dir-Gen. Information Research Bureau 2006–07, Chair. Special Cttee on Public Safety 2007; Parl. Sec. of Educ. 1992–96, of Environment 1996–97; Chair. Cttee on Educ., House of Reps 1999, Special Cttee on Political Ethics and Election Law 2005, Cttee on Disasters 2007–08; Sr State Sec. for Educ., Science, Sports and Culture 2000; Minister of Educ., Culture, Sports, Science and Tech. 2008–10. *Address:* House of Representatives, 1-7-1 Nagatacho, Chiyoda-ku, Tokyo 100-0014, Japan (office). *Telephone:* (3) 3581-3111 (office). *E-mail:* webmaster@shugiin.go.jp (office). *Website:* www.shugiin.go.jp/internet/index.nsf/html/index_e.htm (office).

SUZUKI, Yoichi, LLB; Japanese diplomatist; ed Univ. of Hitotsubashi, Tokyo, Ecole nat. d'Admin, Paris; joined diplomatic service 1975, Deputy Perm. Rep. to WTO, Geneva 1997–2003, chaired Agric. Cttee of WTO and OECD Trade Cttee, mem. of special group for the settlement of disputes in WTO, Deputy Dir Gen. for Econ. Affairs, Ministry of Foreign Affairs 2003–05, Consul Gen. in Boston, Mass 2005–09, Dir Gen. for Econ. Affairs and Deputy Japanese Foreign Sherpa for the G8 2009–10, Amb. to Singapore 2010–13, to France 2013–16; Japanese Govt Rep. for Free Trade and Econ. Partnership Agreement Negotiations; taught at Inst. of Oriental Languages and Civilizations. *Publications:* numerous articles in Gaiko Forum journal on int. trade negotiations. *Address:* c/o Ministry of Foreign Affairs, 2-2-1, Kasumigaseki, Chiyoda-ku, Tokyo 100-8919, Japan (office). *Telephone:* (3) 3580-3311 (office).

SUZUKI, Yoichiro, BSc, MSc, PhD; Japanese physicist, research institute director and academic; b. 14 Dec. 1949; m.; ed Kyoto Univ.; Research Assoc., Dept of Physics, Brown Univ., USA 1979–81, Research Asst Prof., Dept of Physics 1981; Research Assoc., Dept of Physics, Osaka Univ. 1981–89; Assoc. Prof., Inst. for Cosmic Ray Research, Univ. of Tokyo 1989–96, Prof., Kamioka Observatory, Inst. for Cosmic Ray Research 1996–, Dir Kamioka Observatory 2002–04, Adviser to Pres. of Univ. of Tokyo 2003–04, Dir Inst. for Cosmic Ray Research 2004–08; Spokesperson for Super-Kamiokande Collaboration; Asahi Prize (co-recipient) 1999, Nishina Memorial Prize 2001, Breakthrough Prize in Fundamental Physics (co-recipient) 2016. *Achievements include:* discovery of neutrino mass. *Publications:* numerous papers in professional journals. *Address:* Kamioka Observatory, Institute for Cosmic Ray Research, University of Tokyo, Higashi-Mozumi, Kamioka 506-1205, Hida Gifu, Japan (office). *E-mail:* suzuki@icrr.u-tokyo.ac.jp (office). *Website:* www.icrr.u-tokyo.ac.jp (office).

SUZUMURA, Kotaro, BA, MA, PhD; Japanese economist and academic; *Professor Emeritus of Public Economics, Institute of Economic Research, Hitotsubashi University;* b. 7 Jan. 1944, Tokoname, Aichi Pref.; s. of Hidetaro Suzumura and Sumie Suzumura; m. Akiko Suzumura; three d.; ed Hitotsubashi Univ.; Lecturer, Dept of Econs, Hitotsubashi Univ. 1971–73, apptd Prof. of Public Econs, Inst. of Econ. Research, Hitotsubashi Univ. 1984, now Prof. Emer.; Assoc. Prof., Inst. of Econ. Research, Kyoto Univ. 1973–82; Lecturer, LSE 1974–76; Visiting Assoc. Prof. of Econs, Stanford Univ. 1979–80; Visiting Fellow, Dept of Econs, Univ. of Pennsylvania 1987, All Souls Coll., Oxford, UK 1988; Dir-Gen. Tokyo Centre for Econ. Research 1990–92; Pres. Japanese Econ. Asscn 1999–2000, Soc. for Social Change and Welfare 2000–01; Chair. Far Eastern Standing Cttee, Econometric Soc. 1995–2000, Fellow 1990–, mem. Council 1995–2000; Ed.-in-Chief Japanese Economic Review 1995–97; Vice Pres. Science Council of Japan 2006–11; mem. Council Soc. for Social Choice and Welfare, Science Council of Japan 2000–03, mem. The Japan Acad.; Lifetime Fellow, Int. Econ. Asscn 2017–; Order of the Sacred Treasure 2017; Medal with Purple Ribbon 2004, Japan Acad. Prize 2006. *Publications include:* Rational Choice, Collective Decisions and Social Welfare (Nikkei Econs Book Prize 1984) 1983, The Economic Analysis of Industrial Policy (Nikkei Econs Book Prize 1988) 1988, Competition, Commitment and

Welfare 1995, Social Choice Re-examined (co-ed. two vols) 1996, 1997, Development Strategy and Management of the Market Economy (jtly) 1997, Handbook of Social Choice and Welfare vol. I (co-ed.) 2002, Choice, Preferences, and Procedures: A Rational Choice Theoretic Approach 2016. *Leisure interests:* reading novels. *Address:* Institute of Economic Research, Hitotsubashi University, Naka 2–1, Kunitachi, Tokyo 186-8603 (office); 1-29-3 Asagaya Minami, Suginami-ku, Tokyo, Japan (home). *Telephone:* (42) 580-8353 (office); (3) 3311-5110 (home). *Fax:* (42) 580-8353 (office); (3) 3311-5110 (home). *E-mail:* suzumura@ier.hit-u.ac.jp (office). *Website:* www.ier.hit-u.ac.jp (office).

SVANBERG, Carl-Henric, BSc, MSc; Swedish business executive; *Chairman, AB Volvo;* b. 29 May 1952, Porjus; m. Agneta Svanberg 1983; three c.; ed Univ. of Uppsala, Linköping Inst. of Tech.; fmr ice hockey player with IF Björklöven, Umeå; various foreign assignments in project exports, Asea Brown Boveri 1977–85; joined Securitas (security co.) 1986, Exec. Vice-Pres. 1990–94; Pres. and CEO Assa Abloy Group 1994–2003, Deputy Chair. 2003–; Dir (non-exec.) Telefonaktiebolaget L.M. Ericsson 2003–12, Pres. and CEO 2003–09, Chair. Sony Ericsson Mobile Communications AB 2003–09; Dir (non-exec.) BP plc 2009–, Chair. 2010–18, Chair. Chair.'s Cttee, Nomination Cttee; Chair. AB Volvo 2012–; Chair. European Round Table of Industrialists 2018–; mem. Bd Dirs Melker Schörling AB; mem. Bd Confed. of Swedish Enterprise, Bd Univ. of Uppsala, Steering Cttee Global Alliance for Information and Communication Technologies and Devt, External Advisory Bd, Earth Inst. at Columbia Univ., Bd of Djurgårdens IF Hockey; mem. Advisory Bd, Harvard Kennedy School; Dr hc (Linköping Univ.) 2006, (Luleå Univ. of Tech.); King of Sweden's Medal. *Leisure interests:* sailing, working with Boy Scouts. *Address:* AB Volvo, 405 08 Gothenburg, Sweden (office). *Telephone:* (31) 660000 (office). *Fax:* (31) 545772 (office). *Website:* www.volvogroup.com (office).

SVANHOLM, Poul Johan, LLB; Danish banker and business executive; b. 7 June 1933, Aalborg; s. of Poul Svanholm and Gerda Svanholm (née Stougaard); m. Lise Andersen 1957; one s. one d.; ed Univ. of Copenhagen; Pres. Vingaarden, Odense 1962–72; Pres. Carlsberg A/S, Copenhagen 1972–82, CEO Carlsberg Group 1982–96; Chair. Danske Bank 1983–2003; mem. Bd D/S Svendborg (A.P. Moeller Group) 1978–2003, Vice-Chair. A.P. Moeller-Maersk A/S from 2003; mem. European Advisory Cttee to New York Stock Exchange 1986–2005; Chair. Thomas B. Thrige Foundation 1979–2008; Grand Cross of Order of Dannebrog 1997, Hon. CBE 1997. *Leisure interest:* Ravnborg Estate. *Address:* 15 Helleruplund Allé, 2900 Hellerup, Denmark (home). *Telephone:* 39-62-23-45 (home). *Fax:* 39-62-75-46 (home). *E-mail:* poul.svanholm@privat.dk (home).

SVANIDZE, Nikolay Karlovich; Russian historian and broadcast journalist; b. 2 April 1955, Moscow; m. Marina Svanidze; one s.; ed Moscow State Univ.; Researcher, Inst. of USA and Canada, USSR (now Russian) Acad. of Sciences 1978–91; on staff, Russian TV 1992–, commentator, Vesti 1991–94, host, Zerkalo 1996–2007, Deputy Dir of Information Programmes and Head of Studio Information and Analytical Programmes 1996–97; Deputy Chair., then Chair. All Russian State TV and Radio Co. 1996–98; mem. Civic Chamber 2005–; Teffi Prize, Russian Acad. of TV. *Publication:* Medvedev 2008. *Address:* Civic Chamber of the Russian Federation, Moscow 125993, 7/1, Miusskaya sq., Russia. *Website:* www.oprf.ru/en.

ŠVANKMAJER, Jan; Czech stage designer and film director; b. 4 Sept. 1934, Prague; m. Eva Svankmajerová 1960; one s. one d.; ed Theatrical Acad. of Performing Arts, Prague 1954–58; freelance artist 1958–; numerous drawings, graphic sheets, collages, stage sets and (with his wife) art pottery; Prix Special ASIFA 1990, Award for Lifetime Work UK 1995, Freedom Prize (Berlin) 2001, Czech Lion Prize 2002. *Films directed include:* Dimensions of Dialogue 1982, Down to the Cellar 1982, The Pendulum, The Pit and Hope 1983, Alice 1987, Virile Games 1988, Another Kind of Love 1988, Meat Love 1988, Darkness-Lightness-Darkness 1989, The Death of Stalinism in Bohemia 1990, Food 1992, The Faust Lesson 1994, Conspirators of Pleasure 1996, Otesánek (Little Otik) (Czech Lion) 2001, Lunacy 2005, Surviving Life 2010, Insect 2018. *Publications:* Hmat a imaginace 1994, Animus Anima Animation (co-author) 1998, Power of Imagination 2001, Transmutation of the Senses 2004. *Address:* Athanor Lld, Film Production Company, Jaromir Kallista & Jan Svankmajer, U 5.baterie 21/1034, 162 00 Prague 6, Czech Republic (office). *Telephone:* (2) 33322905 (office). *Fax:* (2) 24313383 (office). *E-mail:* athanor@nextra.cz (office). *Website:* www.athanor.cz (office).

SVARTVIK, Jan, PhD; Swedish academic; *Professor Emeritus of English, Lund University;* b. 18 Aug. 1931, Torsby; s. of Gustaf Svartvik and Sigrid Svartvik; m. Gunilla Berner 1958; two s. one d.; ed Uppsala Univ.; Research Asst and Asst Dir Survey of English Usage, Univ. Coll. London 1961–65; Lecturer, Univ. of Gothenburg 1965–70; Prof. of English, Lund Univ. 1970–95, now Prof. Emer.; Visiting Prof., Brown Univ., USA 1969; Pres. Asscn Int. de Linguistique Appliquée 1981–84; Chair. Org. Cttee, Nobel Symposium on Corpus Linguistics 1991; Chair. Steering Cttee for Evaluation of Linguistics in Sweden 1990–92; mem. Royal Acad. of Letters, History and Antiquities, Royal Swedish Acad. of Sciences, Academia Europaea, Societas Scientarum Fennica; Dr hc (Bergen) 1996, (Masaryk Univ.) 1998, (Helsinki) 2000. *Publications:* On Voice in the English Verb 1966, The Evans Statements 1968, A Grammar of Contemporary English (co-author) 1972, A Comprehensive Grammar of the English Language (co-author) 1985, The London-Lund Corpus of Spoken English: Description and Research 1990, Directions in Corpus Linguistics: Proceedings of Nobel Symposium 82 1992 (ed.), Words, Proceedings (ed.) 1996, Engelska – ösprak världsspråk, trendspråk (August Prize for Swedish Non-fiction Book of the Year) 1999, Handbok i engelska (co-author) 2001, Politikens bog om engelsk 2001, A Communicative Grammar of English 2002, English: One Tongue, Many Voices (co-author) 2006. *Address:* Tumlaregränden 7, 22651 Lund, Sweden.

SVEDBERG, Bjoern, MSc; Swedish business executive; b. 4 July 1937, Stockholm; s. of Inge Svedberg and Anna-Lisa Svedberg; m. Gunnel Nilsson 1960; four c.; ed Royal Inst. of Tech., Stockholm and Man. Devt Inst., Univ. of Lausanne; Man. Eng Telephone Exchange Div., L.M. Ericsson Telephone Co. 1972–76, Sr Vice-Pres. of Research and Devt 1976–77, Pres. 1977–90, Chair. 1990; apptd Chair. Nefab AB 1999; Chair. Mo och Domsjo AB 1991–92; mem. Bd of Dirs AB Volvo 1994, ABB Ltd –1999, Stora AB, Investor 1998–2007, Prêt à Porter AB; mem. Royal Swedish Acad. of Eng Sciences (fmr Chair.); fmr Pres. Canada/Sweden Business Asscn; fmr mem. Bd Fed. of Swedish Industry.

SVEDMAN, Sven-Erik, MBA; Norwegian diplomatist; b. 13 Oct. 1946; m. Gunilla Svedman; three c.; ed Lund Univ., Sweden; with Ministry of Foreign Affairs, Oslo 1973–76, Attaché, Embassy in Reykjavik 1976–78, Embassy Sec., Norwegian Del. to OECD, Paris 1978–81, Ministry of Foreign Affairs 1981–82, World Bank, Washington, DC 1982–84, Embassy Sec. (Political Affairs), Embassy in Bonn 1984–88, Political Adviser, Ministry of Foreign Affairs 1988–89, Sec. of State, Ministry of Foreign Affairs 1989–90, Minister and Deputy Amb., Embassy in Washington, DC 1990–94, Amb. to Israel 1994–97, Man. Dir, Oil & Gas 1997–99, Dir Gen., Ministry of Foreign Affairs 1999–2003, Amb. to France (also Perm. Rep. to UNESCO) 2003–05, Perm. Sec. Gen., Ministry of Foreign Affairs 2005–07, Amb. to Germany 2007–14, Chief Economist, Ministry of Foreign Affairs 2014–15; Pres. EFTA Surveillance Authority 2014–18; Commdr, Royal Norwegian Order of Merit 2000, Grand Officer, Order of St Olav 2005, Commdr de la Légion d'honneur 2003, Italian, Spanish and German Grand Cross.

SVENSSON, Åke, MSc; Swedish business executive; *Chairman, Swedavia AB;* b. 1952; joined Saab Group 1976, held several exec. positions including Project Man., Gen. Man. Saab Aerosystems, Gen. Man. Future Products and Tech., Sr Vice-Pres. Saab Aerospace 2000–03, Pres. and CEO Saab AB 2003–10; Chair. Swedavia AB 2016–; mem. Bd of Dirs Parker Hannifin Corpn, Business Sweden, ICC Sverige, Vetenskap & Allmänhet; Pres. Teknikföretagen (Asscn of Swedish Eng Industries) 2010–; apptd Chair. AeroSpace and Defence Industries Asscn of Europe 2007; mem. Royal Swedish Acad. of War Sciences. *Address:* Swedavia AB, 190 45 Stockholm-Arlanda, Sweden (office). *E-mail:* info@swedavia.se (office). *Website:* https://www.swedavia.se/om-swedavia/kontakt/ (office).

SVĚRÁK, Jan; Czech film director; b. 6 Feb. 1965, Žatec; m.; three c.; ed Film Acad. of Arts; partner in film production co. Luxor 1996; Co. Biograf Jan Svěrák Pictures 1996–; mem. Acad. of Motion Picture Arts and Sciences, Czech Film Acad.; numerous awards including Acad. Award for best foreign student film 1989, Czech Lion Awards for Direction 1996, 1997, 2001, Time for Peace Prize 1997. *Film roles:* Kulový blesk (Ball Lightning) (uncredited) 1978, Nejistá sezóna (An Uncertain Season) 1988, Valka barev 1993, Rebelové (The Rebels) 2001, Tmavomodrý svet (Dark World Blue) (uncredited) 2001, Román pro zeny 2005. *Films directed include:* Sbohem, nadrazicko 1984, Vsak su vinar 1985, Ropáci (Oil Gobblers) 1988, Obecná skola (The Elementary School) 1991, Akumulátor 1 1994, Jizda (The Ride) 1994, Kolya (Golden Globe Award, Acad. Award and Czech Lion Award) 1996, Tmavomodrý svet (Dark World Blue) 2001, Tatínek (video) 2004, Vratné lahve 2007, Kuky se vrací 2010, Three Brothers 2014. *Leisure interest:* painting. *Address:* PO Box 33, 155 00 Prague 515, Czech Republic. *E-mail:* biograf@sverak.cz. *Website:* www.sverak.cz.

SVERDLOV, Yevgeny Davidovich; Russian biochemist; *Councillor, Institute of Molecular Genetics, Russian Academy of Sciences;* b. 16 Nov. 1938, Dnepropetrovsk, Ukrainian SSR; ed Moscow State Univ.; Sr Lab., Jr, Sr Researcher, Inst. of Bio-organic Chem. 1965–88; Dir, then Scientific Dir, then Councillor, Inst. of Molecular Genetics, USSR (now Russian) Acad. of Sciences 1988–; Ed.-in-Chief Molekulyarnaya Genetika, Mikrobiologiya i Virusologiya (Molecular Genetics, Microbiology and Virology); mem. Scientific Council of Biotechnology, Russian Acad. of Sciences; Corresp. mem. USSR (now Russian) Acad. of Sciences 1984, mem. 1994; mem. Russian Acad. of Agricultural Sciences 1994, German Acad. of Sciences Leopoldina, Academia Europaea; Lenin Prize, USSR State Prize, Russian Federation National Award (for Science and Technology) 2015. *Publications include:* Organic Chemistry of Nucleic Acids 1970; more than 300 scientific articles. *Address:* Institute of Molecular Genetics, 123182 Moscow 2, Kurchatov Square, Russia (office). *Telephone:* (499) 196-00-00 (office). *Fax:* (499) 196-02-21 (office). *E-mail:* img@img.ras.ru (office); edsverd@gmail.com.

SVILANOVIČ, Goran, LLM, PhD; Serbian politician and lawyer; b. 22 Oct. 1963, Gnjilane, Kosovo; s. of Tihomir Svilanović and Stavrula Svilanović; m.; two c.; ed Belgrade Univ., Inst. of Law, Strasbourg, Saarbrücken Univ., European Univ. of Peace, Austria; worked as Asst Researcher, Belgrade Univ. 1986–98, discharged following protest against controversial univ. law 1998; collaborator with Yugoslavian Forum on Human Rights 1989–93; head of telephone service for rescue of victims of nat., ethnic, religious and other discrimination, Centre for Anti-war Action 1993–97; Chair. Council on Human Rights 1996–98; Official Rep. of Civic Alliance of Serbia (Građanski savez Srbije—GSS) 1997, Vice-Pres. 1998, Pres. 1999, left party 2004; Fed. Minister of Foreign Affairs 2000–04; mem. Parl. (nominated for Democratic Party) 2004–; Chair. Working Table I, Stability Pact for South Eastern Europe 2004–08; Co-ordinator of Econ. and Environmental Activities, OSCE 2008–14; Sec. Gen., Regional Cooperation Council 2013–18; mem. Int. Comm. on the Balkans 2004–06, Belgrade Centre for Human Rights 2004–08. *Publications:* Civil and Civil Process Law; books and numerous articles on the situation of refugees and problems of citizenship. *Address:* c/o Office of the Secretary General, Regional Cooperation Council Secretariat, 71000 Sarajevo, Hercegovine 1/V, Bosnia and Herzegovina.

SVINAROV, Nikolai Avramov, LLB; Bulgarian lawyer and politician; b. 6 May 1958, Shuman; m.; two d.; ed Univ. of Sofia St Kliment Ohridsky; lawyer practising penal law, Turgoviste 1984–85, civil and commercial law, Sofia 1985–2001; mem. Council, Lawyer's League, Sofia 1992–96; mem. and Chief Sec., Supreme Lawyer's Council 1998–2001; apptd mem. Parl., 39th Nat. Ass. (Nat. Movt Simeon the Second) 2001, Chair. Bulgarian New Democracy Parl. Group 2007–09; Minister of Defence 2001–05.

SVOBODA, Cyril, JUDr; Czech politician, lawyer and academic; b. 25 Nov. 1956, Prague; m. Věnceslava Svoboda; four s.; ed Charles Univ., Prague, Pan American Inst. for Int. Studies, Notre Dame Univ., USA; legal officer, Transgas 1980–93; Adviser to Deputy Prime Minister for Human Rights, Restitution and Relations Between the State and the Church 1990–92; Deputy Chair. Legis. Council, Czech Govt 1992–98; mem. Parl. for Prague 1998–2010, Chair. Petition Cttee 1998–2002; Deputy Minister of Justice 1992–96, Deputy Minister of Foreign Affairs for issues related to accession to the EU 1996–98, Minister of the Interior Jan.–July 1998, Deputy Prime Minister and Minister of Foreign Affairs 2002–04, Minister of Foreign Affairs 2002–06; apptd Chair. Govt Legis. Council 2007; joined Christian Democratic Union-Czecheslovak People's Party (KDU-ČSL) 1995, First Deputy Chair. 1999–2001, Chair. 2001–03, 2009–10, Deputy Chair. 2003–06, Leader of Coalition of Four Jan.–March 2001; mem. European Comm. for Democracy through Law 1994, Deputy Chair. 1997; Chair. Cttee for the Rules of Procedure and Immunity of the Parl. Ass., Council of Europe 2001; f. Diplomatic Acad., Prague 2011, currently Man. Dir; mem. Faculty, CEVRO Inst.; mem. Bd Advisors, Global Panel Foundation; Grosses Verdienstkreuz mit Stern und Schulterband (Germany) 2008. *Publications include:* Annotations on the Constitution of the Czech Republic (co-author), The Act on Out-of-Court Rehabilitation in Questions and Answers; numerous articles and studies on legislation and foreign policy. *Leisure interests:* literature, sport (running, skiing, swimming, cycling). *Address:* CEVRO Institute, z.ú., Jungmann 17, 110 00 Prague 1, Czech Republic (office). *Telephone:* (2) 21506777 (office). *E-mail:* cyril.svoboda@vsci.cz (office). *Website:* cevroinstitut.cz (office).

SVOBODA, Jiří, MgA; Czech film director and academic; *Professor, University of Finance and Administration;* b. 5 May 1945, Kladno; s. of Dr Jiří Svoboda and Bozena Svobodova (née Procházková); m. Milena Niznanska 1973; two d.; ed Film Acad. of Performing Arts, Prague (FAMU); studied drama at Acad. of Performing Arts, Prague, expelled for political reasons 1963; worked as warehouseman and driver 1963–66; dir and scriptwriter, Film Studios Barrandov 1971–93; freelance film dir and scriptwriter 1994–; mem. CP of Czechoslovakia 1975–90; Deputy Chair. Film Union of Czech Artists 1987–90; Chair. CP of the Czechlands and Moravia 1990–93; Deputy to House of Nations, Fed. Ass. of CSFR 1990–92; seriously wounded in attempt on his life Dec. 1992; Sr Lecturer, Acad. of Performing Arts; Prof., Film and TV and New Media, Univ. of Finance and Admin (VSFS) 2009–, Univ. of J.A. Komensky 2011–; mem. European Film Acad., Czech Film and TV Acad., Franz Kafka Soc.; Merited Artist 1986; Grand Prize Karlovy Vary 1982, San Remo 1982, Jury Prize Cannes 1983, Prix CIRCOM 2009, Grand Prix CIRCOM 2010. *Films include:* (as dir or scriptwriter): Hostage 1975, A Mirror for Christine 1975, House on the Embankment 1976, The Break Time 1977, The Blue Planet 1979, Girl with a Shell 1980, The Chain 1981, A Meeting with Shadows 1982, The End of the Lonely Berhof Farmstead 1983, The Lancet, Please 1985, Papilio 1986, The World Knows Nothing 1987, A Curse on the Hajnůs' House 1988, Only About Family Orders (about political trials in 1950s) 1989, Bolt from the Blue 2004, Sametoví vrazi 2005, The Wave 2007, Irreversible Man 2009, Dominant Women 2010, Poslední cyklista 2014, Jan Hus 2015. *Television:* wrote and directed more than 25 TV films and plays and part of series 10 Centuries of Architecture 1999–2000, Blow Up 2001, (Udelení milosti se zamítá) The Act of Grace is Disproved 2002, The Visionary 2003, Billow (Parts 1–3) 2005, Rainbow of God 2007, The Irredeemable Man 2009, Pretty Women and Monster 2010, Domina 2010, Last Rowd 2014, Jan Hus 2015, Alois Rasin – First Minister of Finance CR 2017. *Publications:* Killers from the Velvet (novel), Rašín (with Marca Arichteva) 2018. *Leisure interests:* philosophy, political theory, literature. *Address:* Perlitova 19B, 140 00 Prague 4, Czech Republic (home). *Telephone:* 77-7211324 (mobile) (home). *E-mail:* jiri@jiri-svoboda.cz (home). *Website:* www.ujak.cz (office); www.svobodajiri.euweb.cz (home).

SWAGER, Timothy M., BS, PhD; American chemist and academic; *John D. MacArthur Professor of Chemistry, Massachusetts Institute of Technology;* b. 1 July 1961, Sheridan, Mont.; m.; two c.; ed California Inst. of Tech., Montana State Univ.; IBM Graduate Fellow 1984–87; Asst Prof. of Chem., Univ. of Pennsylvania 1990–96, Prof. 1996; Prof. of Chem., MIT 1996–2005, John D. MacArthur Prof. of Chemistry 2005–, Assoc. Dir Inst. for Soldier Nanotechnologies 2002–05, Head, Dept of Chem. 2005–10; Founder, Iptyx Corpn 2003–09, Dynupol Inc., 2009–; Clare Hall Visiting Fellow, Univ. of Cambridge, UK 2005; has served on panels for Nat. Research Council, Defense Science Bd, Nat. Science Foundation, US Senate Commerce Cttee; mem. Science Advisory Bd, ICx Technologies, Nomadics Inc., Collegium Pharmaceutical Inc., Plextronics Inc., Nano-C Inc.; Assoc. Ed. Synfacts 2005–; mem. Editorial Advisory Bd Accounts of Chemical Research, Journal of Polymer Science, Supramolecular Chemistry, Advanced Synthesis & Catalysis, Journal of Supramolecular Chemistry, Journal of Materials Chemistry; Alfred P. Sloan Research Fellow 1994–96; Fellow, American Acad. of Arts and Sciences 2006–; mem. American Academy of Arts and Sciences 2006–, NAS 2008–; Dr hc (Montana State Univ.) 2008; Merck Index Undergraduate Chem. Award 1983, Most Outstanding Senior Chem. Major, American Inst. of Chemists 1983, Herbert Newby McCoy Award For Outstanding Graduate Research, California Inst. of Tech. 1988, Office of Naval Research Young Investigator 1992–95, DuPont Young Faculty Award 1993–96, ACS Philadelphia Section Award 1996, Union Carbide Innovation Recognition Award 1998, ACS Cope Scholar Award 2000, Vladimir Karapetoff Award, MIT 2000, Carl S. Marvel Creative Polymer Chem. Award, ACS-Polymer Div. 2005, Christopher Columbus Foundation Homeland Security Award 2005, Lemelson-MIT Award for Inventorship 2007. *Publications include:* more than 200 publs in scientific books and journals. *Address:* Massachusetts Institute of Technology, Department of Chemistry, Bldg. 18-597, Cambridge, MA 02139, USA (office). *Telephone:* (617) 253-4423 (office). *Fax:* (617) 253-7929 (office). *E-mail:* tswager@mit.edu (office). *Website:* www.swagergroup.mit.edu (office); www.chemistry.mit.edu (office).

SWAMINATHAN, Soumya, MBBS, MD; Indian paediatrician and international organization official; *Chief Scientist, World Health Organization;* d. of M. S. Swaminathan and Mina Swaminathan; ed Armed Forces Medical Coll., Pune, All India Inst. of Medical Sciences, Delhi; Fellowship in Neonatology and Pediatric Pulmonology, Children's Hosp. of Los Angeles, Univ. of S California 1987–89; Research Fellow (Registrar), Dept of Paediatric Respiratory Diseases, Univ. of Leicester, UK 1989–90; fmr Adjunct Assoc. Clinical Prof., Dept of Public Health and Family Medicine, Tufts Univ. School of Medicine; joined Nat. Inst. for Research in Tuberculosis, Chennai as Research Scientist 1992, becoming Dir 2012; Coordinator, UNICEF/UNDP/World Bank/WHO Special Programme for Research and Training in Tropical Diseases, Geneva 2009–11; Dir-Gen., Indian Council of Medical Research 2015; Sec., Dept of Health Research, Govt of India 2015; Deputy Dir-Gen. of Programmes, WHO 2017–19, Chief Scientist 2019–; mem. numerous WHO and global advisory bodies and cttees, including WHO Expert Panel to Review Global Strategy and Plan of Action on Public Health, Innovation and Intellectual Property, Strategic and Technical Advisory Group of WHO Global TB Dept, Co-Chair., Lancet Comm. on TB; Fellow, Indian Nat. Science Acad., Indian Acad. of Sciences, Indian Acad. of Pediatrics; Indian Council of Medical Research Kshanika Oration Award 2008, Tamil Nadu Science and Tech. Award 2012. *Publications:* more than 250 peer-reviewed publications. *Address:* World Health Organization (WHO), 20 ave Appia, 1211 Geneva 27, Switzerland (office).

Telephone: 227912111 (office). *Fax:* 227913111 (office). *E-mail:* info@who.int (office). *Website:* www.who.int (office).

SWAN, Sir John William David, KBE, BA, JP; Bermudian business executive; *Chairman, Swan Group of Companies;* b. 3 July 1935; s. of John Nicholas and Margaret Swan; m. Jacqueline Roberts 1965; one s. two d.; ed Cen. School and Howard Acad., Bermuda and W. Virginia Wesleyan Coll.; Real Estate Salesman with Rego Ltd 1960–62; Founder, CEO and Chair. John W Swan Ltd 1962–, Chair. Swan Group of Cos 1996–; mem. Parl. (United Bermuda Party) 1972–95, Minister for Marine and Air Services, Labour and Immigration 1977–78, Home Affairs 1978–82, Premier of Bermuda 1982–95; fmr Parl. Sec. for Finance, Chair. Bermuda Hosp. Bd, Chair. Dept of Civil Aviation; mem. Chief Execs Org. and World Business Council; mem. and Fellow, Senate, Jr Chamber Int. 1992; Eminent Professional Mem. Royal Inst. of Chartered Surveyors 2006–; Trustee Bermuda Inst. of Ocean Sciences; Hon. Freeman City of London 1985; Hon. LLD (Tampa Univ.) 1986, (W Va Wesleyan Coll.) 1987, (Atlantic Union Coll., Mass.) 1991; St Paul's Anniversary Citation 1969, Outstanding Young Man of the Year 1969, Int. Medal of Excellence (first recipient), Poor Richard Club of Phila 1987 and other awards. *Leisure interests:* tennis, sailing, reading. *Address:* Swan Building, 26 Victoria Street, Hamilton, HM12 (home); 11 Grape Bay Drive, Paget PG06, Bermuda (home). *Telephone:* (441) 295-1785 (office); (441) 236-1303 (home). *Fax:* (441) 295-6270 (office); (441) 236-7935 (home). *E-mail:* sirjohn@challengerbanks.bm (office). *Website:* sirjohnswan.webs.com.

SWAN, Wayne Maxwell, BA; Australian academic and politician; b. 30 June 1954, Nambour, Queensland; m. 2nd Kim Swan; one s. two d.; ed Nambour State High School, Univ. of Queensland; Lecturer in Public Admin, Queensland Inst. of Tech. 1976–77, 1981–82, 1985–88; Policy Analyst, Office of Youth Affairs 1978; adviser to Leader of the Opposition, Bill Hayden 1978–80, to Fed. Labor Ministers, Mick Young and Kim Beazley 1983, to Minister for Foreign Affairs, Bill Hayden 1984; mem. Australian Labor Party (ALP) Admin. Cttee (Queensland) 1984–90, Del., ALP Nat. Conf. 1986, 1988, 1990, Campaign Dir 1989–, State Sec. Queensland Br. of ALP 1991–93, Deputy Leader of ALP 2010–13, Nat. Pres. 2018–; Treas. and Labor MP for Lilley, Brisbane 1993–96, 1998–; Shadow Minister for Family and Community Services 1998–2000, 2001–04, Man. of Opposition Business in the House 2001–03; Shadow Treas. 2004–07; Treas. of Australia 2007–13; Deputy Prime Minister 2010–13. *Publication:* Postcode: The Splintering of a Nation 2005. *Address:* Australian Labor Party, 5/9 Sydney Ave, Barton, ACT 2600, Australia (office). *Telephone:* (2) 6120-0800 (office). *Fax:* (2) 6120-0801 (office). *E-mail:* info@cbr.alp.org.au (office). *Website:* www.alp.org.au (office).

SWANK, Hilary; American actress; b. 30 July 1974, Bellingham, Wash.; m. Chad Lowe 1997 (divorced 2007); m. Philip Schneider 2018. *Films include:* Buffy the Vampire Slayer 1992, The Next Karate Kid 1994, Sometimes They Came Back... Again 1996, Heartwood 1997, Boys Don't Cry (numerous awards including Acad. Award for Best Actress, Boston Soc. of Film Critics Award for Best Actress, Chicago Film Critics Asscn Award for Best Actress, Las Vegas Film Critics Soc. Award for Best Actress, Golden Globe Award for Best Actress) 1999, The Gift 2000, Affair of the Necklace 2000, Insomnia 2002, The Core 2003, 11:14 2003, Red Dust 2004, Million Dollar Baby (Best Dramatic Actress, Golden Globe Awards 2005, Best Actress, Screen Actors Guild Awards 2005, Acad. Award for Best Actress 2005) 2004, Black Dahlia 2006, Freedom Writers 2007, The Reaping 2007, P.S. I Love You 2007, Birds of America 2008, Amelia (Hollywood Film Festival Best Actress) 2009, Conviction 2010, The Resident 2011, New Year's Eve 2011, The Homesman 2014, You're Not You 2014, Lauda: The Untold Story 2015, Spark (voice) 2016, Logan Lucky 2017, 55 Steps 2017, What They Had (also, Exec. Producer) 2018. *Television includes:* Growing Pains 1991–92, Camp Wilder 1992–93, Cries Unheard: The Donna Yaklich Story (TV Movie) 1994, Terror in the Family (TV Movie) 1996, Beverly Hills, 90210 1997–98, Leaving LA 1997, Iron Jawed Angels (TV Movie) 2004, Mary and Martha (TV Movie) 2013, Trust 2018.

SWANN, Kathryn (Kate) Elizabeth, BSc; British business executive; *CEO, SSP Group;* ed Univ. of Bradford; fmrly in retail marketing, Tesco Plc, Coca-Cola Schweppes, Homepride Foods and Dixons Stores Group; fmr Marketing Dir Currys PLC; Marketing Dir then Man. Dir Homebase, J Sainsbury PLC –2000; Man. Dir Argos PLC 2000–03; CEO WH Smith PLC 2003–13; CEO SSP Group 2013–; Chancellor Bradford Univ. 2016–; Dir (non-exec.) Lambert Howarth Group PLC 2000–06, The British Land Co. PLC 2006–, England Hockey 2016–; Dr hc (Bradford) 2007. *Address:* 169 Euston Road, London, NW1 2AE, England (office). *Telephone:* (20) 3714-5243 (office). *Website:* www.foodtravelexperts.com (office).

SWANNELL, Robert William Ashburnham, CBE; British lawyer, chartered accountant and business executive; *Chairman, UK Government Investments Limited;* ed Rugby School; with Schroders investment bank (acquired by Citigroup 2000) 1977–2010, later Chair. Citigroup 2007–10, Vice-Chair. CitiEurope –2008; Chair. HMV 2009–11, Dir (non-exec.) –2011; Dir (non-exec.) Marks & Spencer 2010–, Chair. 2011–17; Chair. Governing Body, Rugby School; Sr Ind. Dir The British Land Company plc 1999–2010, 3i Group plc –2010; currently Chair. UK Govt Investments Ltd 2015–; fmr Dir and Trustee Career Academies UK 2003–10; fmr mem. Regulatory Decisions Cttee of FSA, Industrial Advisory Bd of BIS (Dept for Business, Innovation and Skills); Dir and Trustee, Career Academies UK 2003–10. *Address:* UK Govt Investments, 1 Victoria Street, London, SW1A 0ET, England (office). *E-mail:* enquiries@ukgi.gov.uk (office). *Website:* www.gov.uk/government/organisations/uk-government-investments (office).

SWANSON, William H., BEng, FRAeS; American business executive; b. 1949, Calif.; m. Cheryl Swanson; ed Calif. Polytechnic State Univ., Golden Gate Univ.; joined Raytheon Co. 1972, various man. positions including Exec. Vice-Pres. and Chair. and CEO Raytheon Systems Co. 1998–2000, Exec. Vice-Pres. and Pres. Electronic Systems Div. 2000–02, Pres. 2002–03, Pres., Dir and CEO Raytheon Co. 2003–04, Chair. and CEO 2004–14; Chair. Emer. Massachusetts Competitive Partnership; Vice-Chair. Emer. Bd of Dirs John F. Kennedy Library Foundation; mem. Bd; mem. Advisory Council Calif. Polytechnic State Univ. School of Eng (also Chair. of Bd), Bd of Regents Pepperdine Univ., Bd of Visitors Graziadio School of Business and Man., CIA Officers Memorial Foundation Bd of Advisors, Pres.'s Nat. Security Telecommunications Advisory Cttee, Bd of Regents Pepperdine Univ.; mem. Bd Dirs Cal Poly Foundation, John F. Kennedy Library Foundation, Bd Govs' Exec. Cttee, Aerospace Industries Asscn; mem. Defense Business Bd 2015–;

mem. Bd NextEra Energy, Inc., Resilient, Rapid Focus Security, Inc., RapidSOS, TJX Companies, Inc., Congressional Medal of Honor Foundation; Vice-Chair. Business-Higher Educ. Forum, Co-Chair. Securing America's Leadership in Science, Tech., Eng and Math. Initiative; mem. Editorial Advisory Bd The Journal of Electronic Defense; mem. Nat. Defense Industrial Asscn, Asscn of the United States Army, the Navy League, Air Force Asscn; Trustee, Asscn of the US Army; Fellow, AIAA; Hon. Chair. MATHCOUNTS®; Hon. LLD (Pepperdine Univ.) 2002, Hon. DrSc (California Polytechnic State Univ.); Outstanding Industrial Eng Grad. 1972, Hon. Alumnus Award, Calif. Polytechnic State Univ. School of Eng 1991, Semper Fidelis Award, Marine Corps Scholarship Foundation, Aviation Week & Space Technology Laurel Award for "significant contributions" to the field of aeronautics/propulsion, named "California Manufacturer of the Year" by California Manufacturing & Tech. Asscn, Navy League Fleet Adm. Chester W. Nimitz Award, NDIA James Forrestal Industry Leadership Award, John W. Dixon Award, Asscn of the United States Army, Diversity Best Practices CEO Diversity Leadership Award, Inst. of Industrial Engineers' Captains of Industry Award, Six Sigma Premier Leader Award, Int. Soc. of Six Sigma Professionals, Woodrow Wilson Award for Corp. Citizenship, Kennedy Greenway Vision Award. *Address:* c/o Raytheon Co., 870 Winter Street, Waltham, MA 02451-1449, USA.

SWARAJ, Sushma, BA, LLB; Indian politician; *Minister of External Affairs and of Overseas Indian Affairs;* b. 14 Feb. 1952, Ambala Cantonment; d. of Hardev Sharma and Shrimati Laxmi Devi; m. Swaraj Kaushal 1975; one d.; ed Sanatan Dharma Coll., Ambala Cantonment, Punjab Univ., Chandigarh; Advocate, Supreme Court of India 1973–; mem. (Janata Party) Haryana Legis. Ass. 1977–82, (Bharatiya Janata Party–BJP) 1987–90; All-India Sec. BJP 1985–87, 1990–92, All-India Gen. Sec. and Official Spokesperson 1992–96; Cabinet Minister 1977–78; Minister for Educ. 1987–89; mem. Parl. (Rajya Sabha) 1990–96, 2000–, Chair. Cttee on Petitions 1994–96; mem. Parl. (Lok Sabha) for S Delhi 1996–98, 1998–2000, for Vidisha 2009–, Leader of the Opposition 2009–14; mem. Delhi Legis. Ass. 1998; Chief Minister of Delhi 1998; Minister of Information and Broadcasting 1996–98, 2000–03, with additional charge of Ministry of Communications 1998, Minister of Health and Family Welfare and of Parl. Affairs 2003–04, Minister of External Affairs and of Overseas Indian Affairs 2014–; Head of BJP 2009 poll campaign cttee. *Address:* Ministry of External Affairs, South Block, New Delhi 110 011 (office); C-7, Civil Lines, Prof. Colony, Bhopal, India (home). *Telephone:* (11) 23011127 (office). *Fax:* (11) 23013254 (office). *E-mail:* eam@mea.gov.in (office). *Website:* www.mea.gov.in (office).

SWARUP, Vikas, BA; Indian diplomatist and writer; *High Commissioner to Canada;* b. 1961, Allahabad; m. Aparna Swarup; two s.; ed Allahabad Univ.; joined Indian Foreign Service 1986, posted to Turkey 1987–90, to USA 1993–97, to Ethiopia 1997–2000, to UK 2000–03, Deputy High Commr, Pretoria, South Africa 2006–09; Consul Gen. to Osaka-Kobe, Japan 2009–13, Jt Sec., Ministry of External Affairs 2013–15, Spokesperson 2015–17; High Commr to Canada 2017–; Dr hc (Univ. of South Africa) 2010; Lifetime Achievement Award, US-India Business Council 2009. *Publications include:* Q&A (film version as Slumdog Millionaire) (Boeke Prize, South Africa) 2006, Six Suspects 2008, The Accidental Apprentice 2013; contrib.: The Children's Hours: Stories of Childhood 2009, various newspaper articles. *Leisure interests:* reading, listening to music, playing cricket, tennis, table tennis. *Address:* High Commission of India, 10, Springfield Road, Ottawa, ON K1M 1C9, Canada (office); c/o Peter Buckman, The Ampersand Agency, Ryman's Cottages, Little Tew, Oxon., OX7 4JJ, England (office). *Telephone:* (613) 744-3751 (office); (1608) 683677 (office). *Fax:* (613) 744-3033 (office). *E-mail:* hc.ottawa@mea.gov.in (office); info@theampersandagency.co.uk (office). *Website:* www.theampersandagency.co.uk (office).

SWEDISH, Joseph R., BA, MA; American business executive; *Chairman, President and CEO, Anthem Inc.;* ed Univ. of North Carolina, Charlotte, Duke Univ.; has worked in health care industry since early 1970s; has served as CEO for a range of major health systems since 1989; Pres. and CEO Trinity Health Corpn 2004–13; Pres. and CEO WellPoint, Inc. (renamed Anthem Inc. 2014) 2013–, Chair. 2015–; mem. Bd of Dirs, Blue Cross Blue Shield Asscn, Nat. Inst. for Health Care Man., America's Health Insurance Plans; mem. Bd of Trustees, AHA Health Research and Educational Trust; previously held board and advisory positions with Coventry Health Care, Inc., RehabCare Group, Inc., Cross Country, Inc., American Hosp. Asscn, Catholic Health Asscn, Nat. Quality Forum, Loyola Univ., Chicago. *Address:* Anthem, Inc., 120 Monument Circle, Indianapolis, IN 46204, USA (office). *Telephone:* (317) 532-6000 (office). *Fax:* (317) 488-6028 (office). *E-mail:* boardofdirectors@antheminc.com (office). *Website:* www.antheminc.com (office).

SWEENEY, Anne Mary, BA, EdM; American media executive; b. 4 Nov. 1957, Kingston, NY; m. Philip Miller; two c.; ed The Coll. of New Rochelle, NY and Harvard Univ.; various exec. positions at Nickelodeon/Nick at Nite 1981–93, most recently Sr Vice-Pres. Program Enterprises; Chair. and CEO FX Networks Inc. 1993–96; Pres. Disney Channel and Exec. Vice-Pres. Disney/ABC Cable Networks, The Walt Disney Co. 1996–2000, Pres. ABC Cable Networks Group and Disney Channel Worldwide 2000–04, Co-Chair. Media Networks and Pres. Disney-ABC Television, The Walt Disney Co. 2004–14; mem. Bd of Dirs Lifetime Television, The Museum of Radio & Television, Special Olympics, Women in Cable and Telecommunications, Walter Kaitz Foundation; Hon. Chair. Cable Positive; Women in Cable Exec. of the Year 1994, American Women in Radio and Television STAR Award 1995, inducted into American Advertising Fed.'s Advertising Hall of Achievement 1996, Women in Cable Woman of the Year 1997, Women in Cable Advocate Leader Award, Southern Calif. Chapter 1998, Women in Film's Lucy Award 2002, Cable Television Public Affairs Asscn's Pres.'s Award 2004, New York Women in Film & Television Muse Award 2004, named by The Hollywood Reporter "The Most Powerful Woman in Entertainment", inducted into the Broadcasting & Cable Hall of Fame 2005.

SWEENEY, John Joseph, BSc; American trade union official; *President Emeritus, American Federation of Labor-Congress of Industrial Organizations;* b. 5 May 1934, Bronx, New York; s. of John Sweeney and Patricia Sweeney; m. Maureen Power; one s. one d.; ed Iona Coll.; researcher, Int. Ladies Garment Workers Union; Contract Dir Building Service Employees Int. Union (later Service Employees Int. Union) New York City Local 32B 1960–80, Pres. 1980; Vice-Pres. AFL-CIO (American Fed. of Labor-Congress of Industrial Orgs) 1980–95, Pres.

1995–2009 (retd), Pres. Emer. 2009–; Dr hc (Georgetown Univ.), (Oberlin Coll.), (Univ. of Massachusetts at Amherst), (Univ. of Baltimore), (Catholic Univ. Law School), (Univ. of Toledo Coll. of Law); Presidential Medal of Freedom 2010. *Publication includes:* America Needs a Raise 1996. *Leisure interests:* golf, bowling. *Address:* c/o AFL-CIO, 815 16th Street, NW, Washington, DC 20006, USA.

SWEENEY, Ed, CBE, BA, MSc; British business executive and economist; b. 6 Aug. 1954; s. of William and Louise; ed Univ. of Warwick, London School of Econs; Research Officer Nat. Union of Bank Employees (NUBE) 1977, various roles in finance, becoming Deputy Gen. Sec. Banking Insurance and Finance Union (BIFU) 1991–96, Gen. Sec. 1996–2000, Gen. Sec. UNIFI 2000–04, Deputy Gen. Sec. Amicus (following merger) 2004–07; Chair. Advisory, Conciliation and Arbitration Service (ACAS) 2007–14; mem. TUC Gen. Council, TUC Exec. Cttee; Chair. TUC Int. Devt Group; Jt Chair. DfID/TUC Forum; mem. TUC Superannuation Cttee, TUC Learning and Skills Task Group; TUC Skills for Life Advocate; mem. Trade Union Sustainable Devt Cttee; mem. Council Inst. of Employment Rights; mem. British Del. to WTO Ministerial Confs 2001, 2003; Reviewer on Occupational Pensions De-Regulation Review; Visiting Prof., Leeds Business School.

SWENSEN, Joseph Anton; American conductor, composer and violinist; *Principal Guest Conductor, Orquesta Ciudad de Granada;* b. 4 Aug. 1960, New York, NY; m. 2nd Kristina Algot-Sörensen; three s. (one from previous m.); partner Victoria Eisen; ed Juilliard School; Prin. Guest Conductor, Stockholm Chamber Orchestra 1994–97, Lahti Symphony Orchestra 1995–2000; Prin. Conductor, Scottish Chamber Orchestra (SCO) 1996–2005, Conductor Emer. 2005–; Prin. Guest Conductor, BBC Nat. Orchestra of Wales 2000–03; Prin. Conductor, Malmö Opera och Musiktheater 2006–11; Prin. Guest Conductor and Artistic Advisor, Ensemble Orchestral de Paris 2009–12; Co-founder (with Victoria Eisen) and Dir Habitat4Music (non-profit org.) 2012–; Prin. Guest Conductor, Orquesta Ciudad de Granada 2015–; Artistic Partner, Northwest Sinfonietta; toured Japan with SCO 1995, USA 1999; debut at Edinburgh Int. Festival with SCO 1998; cycle of Beethoven performances to mark 25th anniversary of SCO 1999; conducted new production of The Marriage of Figaro at the Royal Danish Opera 1999; Guest Conductor with City of Birmingham Symphony, Finnish Radio Symphony, Hallé Orchestra, Orchestra Nat. du Capitole de Toulouse; Starling Prof. of Violin, Indiana Univ. Jacobs School of Music 2013–; mem. KahaneSwensenBrey Trio; Dr hc (St Andrew's, Scotland) 2001; Leventritt Foundation Scholarship 1978, Avery Fisher Career Grant 1982. *Recordings include:* Mendelssohn, Sibelius, Brahms, Prokofiev, Dvořák. *Address:* Victoria Rowsell Artist Management Ltd, 34 Addington Square, London, SE5 7LB, England (office). *Telephone:* (20) 7701-3219 (office). (812) 855-9846 (Indiana Univ.). *Fax:* (20) 7701-3219 (office). *E-mail:* management@victoriarowsell.co.uk (office), jswensen@indiana.edu. *Website:* www .victoriarowsell.co.uk (office); music.indiana.edu/departments/academic/strings/ index.shtm; www.josephswensen.com; www.orquestaciudadgranada.es.

SWETT, Richard Nelson, BA, FAIA; American architect, business consultant, diplomatist and fmr politician; *CEO, Climate PROSPERITY Enterprise Solutions, LLC;* b. 1 May 1957, Lower Merion, Pa; s. of Philip Eugene Swett Sr and Ann Parkhurst Swett; m. Yvonne Katrina Lantos 1980; three s. four d.; ed Yale Univ.; licensed architect in several states; has worked in real estate devt, alternative energy devt, energy conservation, industrial devt and export promotion; mem. US House of Reps from 2nd Congressional Dist of NH 1990–95; Amb. to Denmark 1998–2001; fmr Sr Counselor, APCO Worldwide Inc.; fmr Pres. Swett Assocs Inc.; Co-founder and CEO Climate PROSPERITY Enterprise Solutions, LLC 2011–; mem. Board of Advisors, H.C. Andersen Foundation; mem. Bd of Peers overseeing design quality issues for US Gen. Services Admin for US Govt bldg portfolio; Founding mem. Advisory Bd European Center of Calif. 2001–06; mem. Bd Sunrise Capital Partners 2001–04, CATCH (Concord Area Trust for Community Housing); fmr State Chair. US Olympic Cttee 2001; Fellow, AIA; Sr Fellow, Design Futures Council; Grand-Croix, Order of the Dannebrog (Denmark) 2001; Hon. LLD (Franklin Pierce Coll.) and several other hon. degrees; President's Award, AIA 1992, 1994, Arnold W. Brunner Award, NY AIA 2001. *Publications include:* A Nation Reconstructed, A Quest to Make Cities All That They Can Be (co-author), Leadership by Design: Creating an Architecture of Trust. *Leisure interests:* tennis, reading, piano, sailing, skiing, running, basketball, golf, painting, travel, family. *Address:* CPES, 5 South State Street, Suite 1, Concord, NH 03301 (office); 1 Putney Road, Bow, NH 03304, USA (home). *Telephone:* (603) 226-1072 (office). *Fax:* (603) 226-1071 (office). *E-mail:* admin@climateprosperitysolutions.com (office). *Website:* www.climateprosperitysolutions.com (office).

ŚWIĘCICKI, Marcin, DEconSc; Polish politician and economist; *President, European Movement Forum;* b. 17 April 1947, Warsaw; s. of Andrzej Święcicki and Jadwiga Święcicka; m. Joanna Szyr 1969; three s. one d.; ed Univ. of Warsaw; Asst. Econ. Sciences Inst., Warsaw Univ. 1971–72; Councillor, then Chief Specialist in Planning Comm. attached to the Council of Ministers 1972–82; Dir for study and analysis matters 1982–87, Gen. Sec. of Consultative Econ. Council 1987–89; Deputy to Sejm (Parl.) 1989–91, 1993–96, 2011–; Minister for Foreign Econ. Co-operation 1989–91; Deputy Chair. Sejm Cttee on Foreign Econ. Relations 1993–95; Mayor of Warsaw 1994–99; Under-Sec. of State, Ministry of the Economy 1999, mem. Negotiating Team, Polish Accession to EU 1999–2000; mem. PZPR 1974–90, PZPR Cen. Cttee 1989–90, Sec. PZPR Cen. Cttee Aug.–Sept. 1989; Co-Chair. Govt and Territorial Self-Govt Jt Comm. 1994–99; Adviser to Lithuanian Govt 1993, Adviser to Pres. of Lithuania 1999–2000; Dir UNDP Blue Ribbon Analytical and Advisory Centre, Kyiv, Ukraine 2007–11; Co-Founder Tax Reform Movt 1993, Cen. European Forum 1995; Pres. Union of Polish Metropolises 1994–99; Co-Founder Consensus Dialogue Group 1986–90, mem. Secr. 1986–89; Co-Founder and Treas. Polish Asscn for the Club of Rome 1987–91; scientific worker, Inst. of Econ. Sciences, Polish Acad. of Sciences 1991–93; Co-ordinator, OSCE Econ. and Environmental Activities 2002–05; Co-Founder and Pres. European Movement Forum 2011–; mem. Democratic Union (now Freedom Union) 1991–2009 (mem. Council, Warsaw br. 1991–93, mem. Nat. Council 1993–2009; Co-Founder and Vice-Pres. Polish Fulbright Alumni Asscn 1993–96; Pres. Polish Cttee of Support for Museum of the History of Polish Jews (POLIN) 1997–; mem. Polish Econ. Soc. 1978–; Fellowship, George Washington Univ. 1975–76; Sr Fulbright Fellowship Harvard Univ. 1984–85; Hon. mem. Union of Warsaw Uprising Veterans (Związek Powstańców Warszawskich); Officer's Cross

of the Order of Polonia Restituta 2011, Gold and Bronze Cross of Merit; Bronze Medal in long jump, European Jr Athletic Championship, Odessa 1966, Labour and Wages Comm. Award 1971, Award of Chair. of Radio and TV Cttee 1988, Daily Trybuna Ludu Award 1989. *Publications include:* Perspektywiczne programowanie problemowe w Polsce 1978, Revolution in Social Sciences and Future Studies Movement 1978, Rozwój sytuacji i polityki gospodarczej (Ed.) 1985, Reforma własnościowa 1989, The Economy of Ukraine (with Stanisław Wellisz) 1993, Demographic and Financial Preconditions for Pension Reform in Ukraine 2010, On Federal European Union 2014. *Leisure interests:* mountain hiking, jogging, volleyball, political books, memoirs, essays. *Address:* Sejm (Assembly), 00-902 Warsaw, ul. Wiejska 4/6/8 (office); European Movement Forum, 00540 Warsaw, Al. Ujazdowskie 37 ap. 5 (office); Węgrzyna 29, 00-769 Warsaw, Poland (home). *Telephone:* (22) 6927227 (office). *Fax:* (22) 6927726 (office). *E-mail:* Marcin .Swiecicki@sejm.pl (office); www.rucheuropejski.eu (office). *Website:* www.sejm .gov.pl (office); www.swiecicki.pl; www.europeanmovement.eu (office).

SWIFT, Graham Colin, FRSL; British writer; b. 4 May 1949, London; s. of Lionel Allan Stanley Swift and Sheila Irene Swift (née Bourne); ed Dulwich Coll., Queens' Coll., Cambridge, Univ. of York; Hon. Fellow, Queens' Coll., Cambridge 2005; Hon. LittD (East Anglia) 1998; Hon. DUniv (York) 1998; Hon. DLit (London) 2003, (Sussex) 2015; Prix du meilleur livre étranger (France) 1994. *Publications include:* novels: The Sweet Shop Owner 1980, Shuttlecock 1981, Waterland (Geoffrey Faber Memorial Prize, Guardian Fiction Prize, RSL Winifred Holtby Award 1983, Premio Grinzane Cavour (Italy) 1987) 1983, Out of This World 1988, Ever After 1992, Last Orders (Booker Prize 1996, James Tait Black Memorial Prize 1996) 1996, The Light of Day 2003, Tomorrow 2007, Wish You Were Here 2011, Mothering Sunday: A Romance (Hawthornden Prize 2017) 2016; short stories: Learning to Swim and Other Stories 1982, England and Other Stories 2014; anthology: The Magic Wheel (co-ed. with David Profumo) 1986; non-fiction: Making an Elephant: Writing from Within 2009. *Leisure interest:* fishing. *Address:* AP Watt at United Agents LLP, 12–26 Lexington Street, London, W1F 0LE, England (office). *Telephone:* (20) 3214-0800 (office). *Fax:* (20) 3214-0801 (office). *E-mail:* info@unitedagents.co.uk (office). *Website:* www.apwatt.co.uk (office).

SWIFT, Taylor Alison; American singer and songwriter; b. 13 Dec. 1989, Wyomissing, Pa; d. of Scott Swift and Andrea Swift; began songwriting 2001; solo artist 2006–; CMA Horizon Award 2007, CMT Award for Female Video of the Year 2008, Acad. of Country Music Awards for Best New Female Vocalist 2008, for Entertainer of the Year 2011, 2012, for Video of the Year (for Highway Don't Care) 2014, CMA Awards for Female Vocalist of the Year 2009, for Entertainer of the Year 2009, 2011, for Music Video of the Year 2009, for Int. Artist Achievement 2009, American Music Awards for Artist of the Year 2009, 2013, for Favorite Female Artist 2009, for Favorite Pop/Rock Female Artist 2009, 2013, for Favorite Adult Contemporary Artist 2009, 2015, for Favorite Country Female Artist 2013, for Musical Event of the Year (for Highway Don't Care) 2013, for Song of the Year (for Blank Space) 2015, American Music Dick Clark Award for Excellence 2014, CMA Pinnacle Award 2013, Grammy Awards for Best Female Country Vocal Performance (for White Horse) 2010, for Best Country Song (for White Horse) 2010, for Country Solo Performance (for Mean) 2012, for Country Song (for Mean) 2012, for Best Song Written for Visual Media (for Safe & Sound) 2013, Woman of the Year, Billboard magazine 2011, 2014, MTV Europe Music Awards for Best Female 2012, for Best Live Act 2012, for Best Look 2012, for Best US Act 2015, for Best Song (Bad Blood) (with Kendrick Lamar) 2015, Billboard Music Awards for Top Artist 2013, 2015, for Top Female Artist 2013, 2015, for Top Country Artist 2013, for Top Billboard 200 Artist 2013, 2015, for Top Digital Songs Artist 2013, 2015, for Top Country Song (for We Are Never Ever Getting Back Together) 2013, for Top Streaming Song (Video) 2015, for Chart Achievement 2015, for Top Touring Artist 2016, American Country Award for Single of the Year: Vocal Collaboration (for Highway Don't Care) 2013, for Worldwide Artist of the Year 2013, MTV Video Music Awards for Best Female Video (for I Knew You Were Trouble) 2013, for Video of the Year and Best Collaboration (for Bad Blood) 2015, for Best Female Video and Best Pop Video (both for Blank Space) 2015, for Best Collaboration (for I Don't Wanna Live Forever) 2017, BRIT Award for Best Int. Female Solo Artist 2015, 50th Anniversary Milestone Award, Acad. of Country Music Awards 2015, Primetime Emmy Award for Outstanding Creative Achievement In Interactive Media (for AMEX Unstaged: Taylor Swift Experience) 2015, Q Award for Best Live Act 2018. *Recordings include:* albums: Taylor Swift 2006, Sound of the Season 2007, Fearless (Acad. of Country Music Award for Best Album 2009, CMA Award for Album of the Year 2009, American Music Award for Favorite Country Album 2009, Grammy Award for Album of the Year 2010, Grammy Award for Best Country Album 2010) 2008, Speak Now 2010, Red (Billboard Music Awards for Top Billboard 200 Album 2013, for Top Country Album 2013, American Music Award for Favorite Country Album 2013) 2012, 1989 (American Music Award for Favorite Pop/Rock Album 2015, Grammy Awards for Album of the Year 2016, for Best Pop Album 2016) 2014, Reputation 2017. *Film appearances:* Valentine's Day 2010, Dr Seuss' The Lorax (voice) 2012, The Giver 2014. *Address:* c/o Big Machine Records, 1219 16th Avenue South, Nashville, TN 37212, USA. *Website:* www .bigmachinerecords.com; www.taylorswift.com.

SWINBURNE, Richard Granville, MA, BPhil, FBA; British academic; *Nolloth Professor Emeritus of the Philosophy of the Christian Religion, University of Oxford;* b. 26 Dec. 1934, Smethwick, West Midlands; s. of William H. Swinburne and Gladys E. Swinburne; m. Monica Holmstrom 1960 (separated 1985); two d.; ed Univ. of Oxford; Fereday Fellow, St John's Coll., Oxford 1958–61; Leverhulme Research Fellow in History and Philosophy of Science, Univ. of Leeds 1961–63; Lecturer in Philosophy, Univ. of Hull 1963–72; Prof. of Philosophy, Univ. of Keele 1972–84; Nolloth Prof. of the Philosophy of the Christian Religion, Univ. of Oxford 1985–2002, Prof. Emer. 2002–; Visiting Assoc. Prof., Univ. of Maryland 1969–70; Visiting Prof., Syracuse Univ. 1987, Univ. of Rome 2002, Catholic Univ. of Lublin 2002, Yale Univ. 2003, St Louis Univ. 2003; Dr hc (Catholic Univ. of Lublin) 2015, ('Dimitrie Cantemir' Christian Univ., Bucharest) 2016, (Int. Philosophical Acad. of Liechtenstein) 2017. *Publications:* Space and Time 1968 (second edn) 1981, The Concept of Miracle 1971, An Introduction to Confirmation Theory 1973, The Coherence of Theism 1977 (revised edn 1993, second edn 2016), The Existence of God 1979 (second edn 2004), Faith and Reason 1981 (second edn 2005), Personal Identity (with S. Shoemaker) 1984, The Evolution of the Soul 1986 (revised edn 1997), Responsibility and Atonement 1989, Revelation 1991 (second edn 2007),

The Christian God 1994, Is There a God? 1996 (revised edn 2010), Providence and the Problem of Evil 1998, Epistemic Justification 2001, The Resurrection of God Incarnate 2003, Was Jesus God? 2008, Mind, Brain, & Free Will 2013, Are We Bodies or Souls 2019. *Address:* 50 Butler Close, Oxford, OX2 6JG, England (home). *Telephone:* (1865) 514406 (home). *E-mail:* richard.swinburne@oriel.ox.ac.uk (office). *Website:* users.ox.ac.uk/~orie0087/ (office).

SWING, William Lacy, BA, BD; American diplomatist and international organization official; b. 11 Sept. 1934, Lexington, N Carolina; s. of Baxter D. Swing and Mary F. Swing (née Barbee); m. Yuen Cheong 1993; one s. one d. (from previous m.); ed Catawba Coll., Yale Univ., Tübingen Univ., Harvard Univ.; Vice-Consul, Port Elizabeth, S Africa 1963–66; int. economist, Bureau of Econ. Affairs, Dept of State 1966–68; Consul, Hamburg 1968–72; Desk Officer for FRG, Dept of State 1972–74; Deputy Chief of Mission, Embassy in Bangui, Cen. African Repub. 1974–76; Sr Fellow, Center for Int. Affairs, Harvard Univ. 1976–77; Deputy Dir, Office of Cen. African Affairs, Dept of State 1977–79; Amb. to Repub. of the Congo 1979–81, to Liberia 1981–85, to S Africa 1989–92, to Nigeria 1992–93, to Haiti 1993–98, to Democratic Repub. of the Congo 1998–2001; Dir Office of Foreign Service Assignments and Career Devt 1985–87; Deputy Asst Sec. for Personnel 1987–89; Special Rep. of UN Sec.-Gen. for Western Sahara 2001–03, Democratic Repub. of the Congo 2003–08; Dir-Gen. Int. Org. for Migration 2008–18; mem. American Acad. of Diplomacy; Fellow, Harvard Univ., Oxford Univ.; Hon. Fellow, Univ. of Oxford 2013; Hon. LLD (Catawba Coll.) 1980; Hon. DHumLitt (Hofstra) 1994; Presidential Distinguished Service Award 1985; Distinguished Honor Award 1994, Award for Valor 1995, Presidential Meritorious Service Award 1987, 1990, 1994, 1998, Presidential Certificate of Commendation 1998, Award for Lifetime Contribs to American Diplomacy, American Foreign Service Asscn 2012. *Publications:* Education for Decision 1963, U.S. Policy Towards South Africa: Dilemmas and Priorities 1977, Liberia: The Road to Recovery 1982, Haiti: In Physical Contact with History 1994; book chapter in Challenges of Peace Implementation 2004. *Leisure interests:* tennis, squash, golf. *Address:* c/o International Organization for Migration, 17 route des Morillons, CP 17, 1211 Geneva 19, Switzerland.

SWINNEY, John Ramsay, MA; Scottish politician and management specialist; *Deputy First Minister and Cabinet Secretary for Education and Skills;* b. 13 April 1964, Edin., Scotland; s. of Kenneth Swinney and Nancy Swinney (née Hunter); m. 1st Lorna Ann King 1991 (divorced 1998); one s. one d.; m. 2nd Elizabeth Quigley 2003; one s.; ed Univ. of Edinburgh; Sr Man. Consultant, Devt Options Ltd 1988–92; Strategic Planning Prin., Scottish Amicable 1992–97; MP (Scottish Nat. Party—SNP) for N Tayside 1997–2001; MSP (SNP) for N Tayside 1999–2011, for Perthshire N 2011–; Leader of the Opposition 2000–04, Convener, Enterprise and Lifelong Learning Cttee 1999–2000, Convener, European and External Relations Cttee 2004–05; Nat. Sec. SNP 1986–92, Vice-Convener for Publicity 1992–97, Treasury Spokesperson 1995–2000, Sr Vice-Convener (Deputy Leader) 1998–2000, Nat. Convener (Leader) 2000–04; Shadow Minister for Finance and Public Services 2005–07; Deputy First Minister of Scotland 2014–; Cabinet Sec. for Finance and Sustainable Growth 2007–14, for Finance, Constitution and Economy 2014–16, for Educ. and Skills 2016–. *Leisure interests:* hill walking, cycling, running. *Address:* T4 23, The Scottish Parliament, Edinburgh, EH99 1SP, Scotland. *Telephone:* (131) 348-5717. *Fax:* (131) 348-5946; (1250) 876991 (constituency). *E-mail:* John.Swinney.msp@parliament.scot (office). *Website:* johnswinneymsp.com; www.johnswinney.scot.

SWINTON, Tilda, BA (Hons); British actress; b. (Katherine Mathilda Swinton), 5 Nov. 1960, London; d. of Maj.-Gen. Sir John Swinton and Judith Balfour, Lady Swinton (née Killen); partner John Byrne 1989–2005; two c. (twins); partner Sandro Kopp 2004–; ed Queen's Gate School, London, West Heath Girls' School, Fettes Coll., New Hall, Cambridge; known for both arthouse and mainstream films; mem. Jury, 38th Berlin Int. Film Festival 1988; performance art appearance sleeping in a glass case, Serpentine Gallery, London 1996; f. Ballerina Ballroom Cinema Of Dreams film festival 2008; Dr hc (Royal Scottish Acad. of Music and Drama, Glasgow) 2006; Saturn Award for Best Film Supporting Actress 2017. *Films:* Caravaggio 1986, Egomania – Insel ohne Hoffnung 1986, Aria 1987, Friendship's Death 1987, Das andere Ende der Welt 1988, Degrees of Blindness 1988, L'ispirazione (short) 1988, The Last of England 1988, War Requiem 1989, Play Me Something 1989, The Garden 1990, Edward II 1991, The Party: Nature Morte 1991, Orlando 1992, Wittgenstein 1993, Blue (voice) 1993, Remembrance of Things Fast: True Stories Visual Lies 1994, Female Perversions 1996, Conceiving Ada 1997, Love is the Devil: Study for a Portrait of Francis Bacon 1998, The War Zone 1999, The Protagonists 1999, The Beach 2000, Possible Worlds 2000, The Deep End 2001, Vanilla Sky 2001, Teknolust 2002, Adaptation 2003, Young Adam (Scottish BAFTA Award for Best Actress 2004) 2003, The Statement 2003, Thumbsucker 2004, Broken Flowers 2005, Constantine 2005, Absent Presence (short) 2005, The Chronicles of Narnia: The Lion, the Witch and the Wardrobe 2005, Stephanie Daley 2006, Deep Water (voice) 2006, The Man from London 2007, Sleepwalkers 2007, Michael Clayton (Acad. Award for Best Supporting Actress 2008) 2007, Burn After Reading 2008, The Chronicles of Narnia: Prince Caspian 2008, Julia 2008, The Curious Case of Benjamin Button 2008, The Limits of Control 2009, Io Sono l'Amore (I Am Love) 2009, The Chronicles of Narnia: The Voyage of the Dawn Treader 2010, We Need to Talk about Kevin (several awards for Best Actress including Austin Film Critics Asscn Award, European Film Award, Houston Film Critics Award, Nat. Bd of Review Award, Online Film Critics Soc. Award, San Francisco Film Critics Circle Award) 2011, Genevieve Goes Boating (video short) (narrator) 2011, Moonrise Kingdom 2012, Snowpiercer 2013, Only Lovers Left Alive 2013, The Zero Theorem 2013, The Grand Budapest Hotel 2014, Trainwreck 2015, A Bigger Splash 2015, Hail, Caesar! 2016, Doctor Strange 2016, Okja 2017, War Machine 2017, Isle of Dogs 2018, Suspiria 2018, The Souvenir 2019, The Personal History of David Copperfield 2019, The Dead Don't Die 2019. *Television:* Zastrozzi: A Romance (mini-series) 1986, Your Cheatin' Heart (series) 1990, Screenplay (series) – Man to Man: Another Night of Rubbish on the Telly 1992, Shakespeare: The Animated Tales (series)—Hamlet 1992, Das offene Universum (film) 1993, The Somme (film) 2005, Getting On (series) 2012. *Address:* c/o Christian Hodell, Hamilton Hodell Ltd, 20 Golden Square, London, W1F 9JL, England (office). *Telephone:* (20) 7636-1221 (office). *Fax:* (20) 7636-1226 (office). *E-mail:* info@hamiltonhodell.co.uk (office). *Website:* www.hamiltonhodell.co.uk (office).

SWITKOWSKI, Zygmunt (Ziggy) Edward, AO, BSc, PhD; Australian (b. German) scientist and business executive; *Chairman, NBN Company Ltd;* b. 21 June 1948, Rheine, Germany; m. Jadzia Teresa 1970; one s. one d.; ed St Bernardo's Coll., Univ. of Melbourne; Sr Research Scientist, Eastman Kodak Co., New York 1978–80, Man. Research and Devt 1980–82, Sales Man. 1982–83, Marketing Man. Consumer Products 1983–85, Dir Business Planning 1985–88; Deputy Man. Dir Kodak (Australasia) Ltd 1988–92, Chair., Man. Dir 1992–96; Dir Amcor Ltd 1995–99; Chair., Acting CEO Optus Vision Pty Ltd 1996–97, CEO Optus Communications Pty Ltd 1996–97; Group Man. Dir Business Int. Div. Telstra Corpn Ltd 1997–99, CEO 1999–2004 (resgnd); Chair. Australian Nuclear Science and Tech. Org. 2007–10; Chair. Suncorp Group 2011–, NBN Co Ltd (broadband network) 2013–; Chair. Opera Australia 2008–; Chancellor Royal Melbourne Inst. of Tech. 2011–; mem. Bd of Dirs Tabcorp Holdings Ltd 2006–, Oil Search Ltd 2010–, Healthscope Ltd 2016–; fmr Chair. Australian Quality Council; Fellow, Australian Inst. of Co. Dirs; mem. Australian Acad. of Science, Business Council of Australia. *Address:* NBN Company Ltd, 360 Elizabeth Street, Level 40, Melbourne, Vic 3000, Australia (office). *Website:* www1.nbnco.com.au (office).

SY, Elhadj Amadou Gueye As; Senegalese international organization official; *Secretary-General, International Federation of Red Cross and Red Crescent Societies;* ed Dakar Univ., Ecole Normale Superieure de Dakar, Univ. of Graz, and Vienna Diplomatic Acad., Austria; Dir of Health Programmes, ENDA Tiers Monde (Environment and Devt Action in the Third World), Dakar 1988–97; Co-founder, Int. Council of AIDS Service Orgs and Dir of its African Chapter, Dakar; fmr Dir, UNAIDS New York Liaison Office and Team Leader for UNAIDS Inter-country Team for Eastern and Southern Africa; fmr Dir Operational Partnerships and Country Support and Regional Dir for Africa, Global Fund to Fight AIDS, Tuberculosis and Malaria; Dir, HIV/AIDS Group, Bureau for Devt Policy, UNDP 2005–07; Chair., Open Society Initiative for W Africa 2007–10; UNICEF Regional Dir for Eastern and Southern Africa 2009–14; Sec.-Gen., Int. Fed. of Red Cross and Red Crescent Socs 2014–. *Address:* International Federation of Red Cross and Red Crescent Societies, PO Box 303, 1211 Geneva 19, Switzerland (office). *Telephone:* 227304222 (office). *Fax:* 227330395 (office). *Website:* www.ifrc.org (office).

SY, Moumina Chériff; Burkinabè politician and fmr journalist; *Minister of State, Minister of National Defence and War Veterans;* b. 17 May 1960, Néma, Mauritania; s. of Baba Sy; fmr Ed., Bendré (weekly newspaper); Pres. Nat. Transitional Council 2014–15; Acting Pres. of Burkina Faso 1–23 Sept. 2015; Minister of State, Minister of Nat. Defence and War Veterans 2019–. *Address:* Ministry of National Defence and War Veterans, 01 BP 496, Ouagadougou 01, Burkina Faso (office). *Telephone:* 25-50-72-14 (office). *Fax:* 25-31-36-10 (home). *Website:* www.defense.gov.bf (office).

SY-COSON, Teresita T., AB-BSc; Philippine retail executive; *Advisor to the Board, SM Prime Holdings Inc.;* b. 19 Oct. 1950, Manila; d. of Henry Sy, Sr; m. Louis Coson (died 2003); three c.; ed Assumption Coll.; Pres. Shoemart 1990, mem. Bd of Dirs and Exec. Vice-Pres. SM Prime Holdings Inc. 1994, Advisor 2008–, Vice-Chair. Investments Corpn (SM Group's holding co.); Chair. BDO Unibank, Inc. 2013–; fmr Chair. and Chief Exec. Banco de Oro Universal, Chair. Banco de Oro Unibank, Inc. –2005, (following merger with Equitable PCI Bank) 2007–, Vice-Chair. June–July 2007; Dir and Exec. Vice-Pres. First Asia Realty Devt Corpn; Pres. SM Mart, Inc.; Pres. and Chair. ShoeMart, Inc., Supervalue, Inc.; Chair. BDO Realty Corpn, BDO Leasing & Finance, Inc. (Dir 2005–); Vice-Chair. Generali Pilipinas Holding Co., Inc., Equitable PCI Bank 2006–; Dir, Multi-Realty Devt Corpn, Supervalue, Inc., Asia-Pacific Computer Tech. Center, Inc., BDO Capital Insurance Brokers, Inc., SM Keppel Land, Inc., PCI Leasing & Finance, Inc. 2005–, PCI Capital Corpn, Equitable Card Network, Inc., Equitable Savings Bank, Inc., EBC Investments, Inc., and other pvt. insts; Ind. Dir, Philippine Long Distance Telephone Co. 2004–06; mem. APEC Business Advisory Council; Trustee and Treas. SM Foundation Inc. 2003–; Excellence in Retail Banking Award, The Asian Banker 2004, Best Retail Banker of the Year, The Asian Banker 2012, President's Award, Philippine Retailers Asscn 2014, Asia's Best CEO (jtly), Corporate Governance Asia 2015. *Leisure interest:* reading business books. *Address:* SM Prime Holdings Inc., Building A, SM Corporate Offices, J.W. Diokno Blvd, Mall of Asia Complex, Pasay City 1300, Philippines (office). *Telephone:* (632) 831-1000 (office). *Fax:* (632) 833-8991 (office). *E-mail:* info@smprime.com (office). *Website:* www.smprime.com (office).

SYAL, Meera, CBE, MBE, BA, FRSL; British comedian, writer and actress; b. 27 June 1963, Wolverhampton, West Midlands, England; d. of Surendra Syal and Surrinder Syal (née Uppal); m. 1st Shekhar Bhatia 1989 (divorced 2002); one d.; m. 2nd Sanjeev Bhaskar 2005; one s.; ed Queen Mary's High School for Girls, Walsall, Univ. of Manchester; actress in one-woman comedy One of Us after graduation (Nat. Student Drama Award); fmr actress Royal Court Theatre, London; writer of screenplays and novels; actress and comedian in theatre, film and on TV; contrib. to The Guardian newspaper; Visiting Prof. of Contemporary Theatre, St Catherine's Coll., Oxford 2011–12; hon. degrees from SOAS and Univ. of Roehampton; Scottish Critics Award for Most Promising Performer 1984, Woman of the Year in the Performing Arts, Cosmopolitan Magazine 1994, Chair.'s Award, Asian Women of Achievement Awards 2002, Women in Film and TV Creative Originality Award 2002, Nazia Hassan Foundation Award 2003, listed in The Observer as one of the 50 funniest acts in British comedy 2003. *Theatre includes:* Serious Money (London and Broadway, New York) 1987, Stitch 1990, Peer Gynt 1990, Bombay Dreams (story to musical) 2002, Rafta Rafta (Royal Nat. Theatre) 2007, Shirley Valentine 2010, The Killing of Sister George 2011, Much Ado About Nothing 2012. *Films include:* Sammie and Rosie Get Laid 1987, A Nice Arrangement, It's Not Unusual, Beautiful Thing 1996, Girls' Night 1997, Jhoom Barabar Jhoom 2007, Mad Sad & Bad 2009. *Radio includes:* Masala FM 1996, Legal Affairs 1996, Goodness Gracious Me 1996–98, The World as We Know It 1999, Woman's Hour Drama: A Small Town Murder 2010, My Teenage Diary (BBC Radio 4) 2011. *Television includes:* The Secret Diary of Adrian Mole 1985, Tandoori Nights 1985, The Real McCoy (five series) 1990–95, My Sister Wife (BBC series) 1992, Have I Got News For You 1992, 1993, 1999, Sean's Show 1993, The Brain Drain 1993, Absolutely Fabulous 1995, Soldier Soldier 1995, Degrees of Error 1995, Band of Gold 1995, Drop the Dead Donkey 1996, Ruby 1997, Keeping Mum (BBC sitcom) 1997–98, The Book Quiz 1998, Goodness Gracious Me (first UK Asian TV comedy sketch show; co-writer) 1998–2000, Room 101 1999, The

Strangerers 2000, The Kumars at No. 42 2002–06, Who Do You Think You Are? (BBC 1) 2004, Bad Girls (series) 2004, Life Isn't All Ha Ha Hee Hee 2005, Jekyll 2007, Beautiful People 2008–09, Holby City 2009, Horrible Histories (children's series) 2010, Uncle Santa (Little Crackers series) 2010, Doctor Who 2010, The Jury 2011, Hunted 2012, The Kumars 2014, Broadchurch 2015. *Written works include:* One of Us (play) 1983, A Nice Arrangement (short TV film) 1991, My Sister Wife (TV film; Best TV Drama Award, Comm. for Racial Equality, Awards for Best Actress and Best Screenplay, Asian Film Acad. 1993) 1992, The Oppressed Minorities Big Fun Show (play) 1992, Bhaji on the Beach (film) 1994, Anita and Me (novel and adapted for TV) (Betty Trask Award) 1996, Goodness Gracious Me (comedy sketch TV show; co-writer) 1999, Life Isn't All Ha Ha Hee Hee (novel) 1999, Bollywood Carmen Live (screenplay) 2013, The House of Hidden Mothers (novel) 2015. *Leisure interests:* singing in jazz quintet, netball. *Address:* c/o Rochelle Stevens, 2 Terretts Place, Islington, London, N1 1QZ, England (office). *Telephone:* (20) 7359-3900 (office).

SYBERBERG, Hans-Jürgen, DrPhil; German film director, film producer, theatre director and writer; b. 8 Dec. 1935, Nossendorf, Pomerania; m.; ed studies in literature and history of art at Munich; made over 80 short TV films 1963–65; later work includes documentaries, feature films and theatre; several Bundesfilm-preise and other awards including Bayerischer Filmpreis. *Films include:* Fritz Kortner Rehearses Schiller's Intrigue and Love 1965, Shylock Monolog 1966, The Counts Pocci 1967, How Much Earth Does a Man Need 1968, Sexbusiness Made in Passing 1969, San Domingo 1970, After My Last Removal (Brecht) 1971, Ludwig—Requiem for a Virgin King 1972, Ludwig's Cook 1972, Karl May—In Search of Paradise Lost 1974, The Confessions of Winifred Wagner 1975, Hitler, A Film from Germany 1977, Parsifal (Kritiker Preis, Berlin 1983) 1982, Die Nacht 1984, Edith Clever liest Joyce-Molly 1985, Fräulein Else 1987, Penthesilea 1988, Marquise von O 1990, Ein Traum, was sonst? 1994, Höhle der Erinnerung 1997. *Plays include:* (in collaboration with E. Clever) Die Nacht 1984, Penthesilea 1988, Die Marquise von O... 1989, Ein Traum, was sonst? 1990. *Publications include:* The Film as the Music of the Future 1975, Syberbergs Filmbuch 1976, Die Kunst als Rettung aus der deutschen Misere (essay) 1978, Die freudlose Gesellschaft 1981, Der Wald steht schwarz und schweiget 1984, VomUnglück und Glück der Kunst in Deutschland nach dem letzten Kriege 1990, Der verlorene Auftrag 1994. *Address:* Genter Strasse 15A, 80805 Munich, Germany. *Telephone:* (89) 3614882. *Fax:* (89) 3614905. *E-mail:* film@syberberg.de; hjs@syberberg.de. *Website:* www.syberberg.de.

SYCHOV, Alyaksandr; Belarusian diplomatist; b. 19 Sept. 1951, Gomel, Byelorussian SSR; m. Natalia Vedmedenko 1976; one s. one d.; ed Moscow State Inst. of Int. Relations; Third then Second Sec., Ministry of Foreign Affairs 1979–84; Del. Perm. Mission of the Repub. of Belarus to UN office and other int. orgs, Geneva 1984–90; Head Dept of Foreign Econ. Relations, Ministry of Foreign Affairs 1991–92, Deputy Minister for Foreign Affairs 1992–94; Perm. Rep. to UN, New York 1994–2000; Deputy Minister of Foreign Affairs 2000–05; Amb. to Austria 2005–11, also Perm. Rep. to OSCE, JCG, OSCC and other int. orgs in Vienna; Chair. First Cttee of the 51st session of the UN Gen. Ass., 19th Special Session 1996–97; Vice-Pres. ECOSOC 1998–99. *Publications:* numerous articles on Belarus foreign policy and int. affairs. *Leisure interests:* art, opera, tennis, soccer.

SYDOW, Max von; French (b. Swedish) actor; b. 10 April 1929, Lund, Sweden; s. of Carl W. von Sydow and Greta Rappe; m. 1st Kerstin Olin 1951 (divorced 1979); two s.; m. 2nd Catherine Brelet 1997; two s.; ed Royal Dramatic Theatre School, Stockholm; Norrköping-Linköping Theatre 1951–53, Hälsingborg Theatre 1953–55, Malmö Theatre 1955–60, Royal Dramatic Theatre, Stockholm 1960–74, 1988–94; film work in Sweden 1949–95; int. productions 1962–; Commdr Ordre des Arts et Lettres; Golden Beetle Award for Best Actor 1987, 1996, for Best Dir 1988, Litteris et Artibus (medal) 1978 (Sweden). *Plays acted in include:* Peer Gynt, Henry IV (Pirandello), The Tempest, Le misanthrope, Faust, Ett Drömspel, La valse des toréadors, Les sequestrés d'Altona, After the Fall, The Wild Duck, The Night of the Tribades 1977, Duet for One 1981, The Tempest 1988, Swedenhielms 1990, And Give Us the Shadows 1991, The Ghost Sonata 1994. *Films include:* Bara en mor (Only a Mother) 1949, Fröken Julie (Miss Julie) 1951, Ingen mans kvinna 1953, Rätten att älska 1956, Det sjunde inseglet (The Seventh Seal) 1957, Smultronstället (Wild Strawberries) 1957, Prästen i Uddarbo 1957, Nära livet (So Close to Life) 1958, Spion 503 1958, Ansiktet (The Face) 1958, Jungfrukällan (The Virgin Spring) 1960, Bröllopsdagen (The Wedding Day) 1960, Såsom i en spegel (Through a Glass Darkly) 1961, Nils Holgerssons underbara resa (Wonderful Adventures of Nils) 1962, Älskarinnan (The Mistress) 1962, Nattvardsgästerna (Winter Light) 1963, The Greatest Story Ever Told 1965, 4 × 4 1965, The Reward 1965, Hawaii 1966, The Quiller Memorandum 1966, Här har du ditt liv (This Is Your Life) 1966, Vargtimmen (Hour of the Wolf) 1968, Svarta palmkronor (Black Palm Trees) 1968, Skammen (Shame) 1968, Made in Sweden 1969, En passion (A Passion) 1969, The Kremlin Letter 1970, The Night Visitor 1971, Utvandrarna (The Emigrants) 1971, Beröringen (The Touch) 1971, Äppelkriget (The Apple War) 1971, Embassy 1972, Nybyggarna (The New Land) 1972, The Exorcist 1973, Steppenwolf 1974, Cuore di cane (Dog's Heart) 1975, Ägget är löst! (Egg! Egg! A Hardboiled Story) 1975, Trompe-l'oeil 1975, Three Days of the Condor 1975, The Ultimate Warrior 1975, Cadaveri eccellenti (aka Illustrious Corpses) 1976, Foxtrot (aka The Far Side of Paradise) 1976, Il deserto dei Tartari (The Desert of the Tartars) 1976, Voyage of the Damned 1976, Gran bollito (aka Black Journal) 1977, Exorcist II: The Heretic 1977, March or Die 1977, Brass Target 1978, Hurricane 1979, Bugie bianche (aka Footloose, and Venetian Lies) 1980, La mort en direct (Death Watch) 1980, Flash Gordon 1980, Victory 1981, Jugando con la muerte (aka Hit Man, USA) 1982, Conan the Barbarian 1982, Ingenjör Andrées luftfärd (The Flight of the Eagle) 1982, Le cercle des passions (aka Circle of Passions), The Adventures of Bob & Doug McKenzie: Strange Brew 1983, Never Say Never Again 1983, A Soldier's Tale 1984, The Ice Pirates 1984, Dreamscape 1984, Dune 1984, Code Name: Emerald (aka Deep Cover, USA TV title) 1985, Il pentito (The Repenter) 1985, The Second Victory 1986, Hannah and Her Sisters 1986, Oviri (The Wolf at the Door) 1986, Duet for One 1986, Pelle erobreren (Pelle the Conqueror) (Bodil Award Best Actor, European Film Award for Best Actor, Guldbagge Award Best Actor, Robert Festival Best Actor) 1987, Una vita scellerata (A Violent Life) 1990, Father 1990, Awakenings 1990, Mio caro dottor Gräsler (aka The Bachelor, USA) 1991, A Kiss Before Dying 1991, Europa (voice) 1991, Bis ans

Ende der Welt (Until the End of the World) 1991, Oxen 1991, Den goda viljan (The Best Intentions) 1992, Dotkniecie reki (The Silent Touch) 1992, Morfars resa (Grandpa's Journey) 1993, Needful Things 1993, Time Is Money 1994, Dypets ensomhet (Depth Solitude) 1995, Judge Dredd 1995, Truck Stop 1996, Hamsun (Swedish Guldbagge Award for Best Actor 1997) 1996, Jerusalem 1996, What Dreams May Come 1998, Snow Falling on Cedars 1999, Non ho sonno (aka Sleepless, USA) 2001, Vercingétorix 2001, Intacto (Intact) 2001, Les amants de Mogador 2002, Minority Report 2002, Heidi 2005, Le Scaphandre et le papillon 2007, Rush Hour 3 2007, Emotional Arithmetic 2007, The Diving Bell and the Butterfly 2007, Shutter Island 2010, Truth & Treason 2011, Extremely Loud & Incredibly Close 2011, Branded 2012, The Letters 2014, Star Wars: The Force Awakens 2015; Dir: Katinka 1988. *Television includes:* Herr Sleeman kommer 1957, Rabies 1958, The Diary of Anne Frank 1967, I havsbandet (mini-series) 1971, Kvartetten som sprängdes (mini-series) 1973, Le dernier civil 1983, Samson and Delilah 1984, Quo Vadis? (mini-series) 1985, The Last Place on Earth (mini-series) 1985, Kojak: The Belarus File 1985, Christopher Columbus (mini-series) 1985, Gösta Berlings saga (mini-series, segments 1–3) 1986, Red King, White Knight 1989, Hiroshima: Out of the Ashes 1990, Den goda viljan (mini-series) 1991, Och ge oss skuggorna 1993, Onkel Vanja 1994, A che punto è la notte 1995, Citizen X 1995, Radetzkymarsch (mini-series Radetzky March) 1995, Samson and Delilah (voice, uncredited) 1996, Enskilda samtal (Private Conversations) 1996, Profiler (series) 1997, Hostile Waters 1997, La principessa e il povero (The Princess and the Pauper) 1997, Solomon 1997, Nuremberg (mini-series) 2000, La fuga degli innocenti (Hidden Children: The Flight of the Innocents) (mini-series) 2004, Ring of the Nibelungs 2004, L'Inchiesta 2007, The Tudors 2009. *Publication:* Loppcirkus (with Elisabeth Sörenson) 1989. *Leisure interests:* nautical history, environment preservation, Baroque music. *Address:* c/o Diamond Management, 31 Percy Street, London, W1T 2DD, England (office); c/o Agence Anne Alvares Correa, 18 rue Troyon, 75017 Paris, France (office).

SYKES, Lynn R., PhD; American geologist and academic; *Higgins Professor Emeritus of Earth and Environmental Sciences, Lamont-Doherty Geological Observatory, Columbia University;* b. 16 April 1937, Pittsburgh, Pa; s. of Lloyd A. Sykes and Margaret Woodburn Sykes; m. 1st Meredith Henschkel (divorced); m. 2nd Katherine Flanz 1986 (died 1996); m. 3rd Kathleen Mahoney 1998; ed Massachusetts Inst. of Tech., Columbia Univ.; Research Asst, Lamont-Doherty Geological Observatory, Columbia Univ. 1961–64, Research Assoc. 1964–66, Adjunct Asst Prof. of Geology 1966–68, Head of Seismology Group 1973–83, apptd Higgins Prof. of Earth and Environmental Sciences 1978, now Prof. Emer.; mem. US Negotiating Team, Threshold Test Ban Treaty, Moscow 1974; Chair. Nat. Earthquake Prediction Evaluation Council 1984–88; mem. Seismic Verification Advisory Panel, US Congress, Office Technology Assessment 1986–87; mem. NAS, American Acad. of Arts and Sciences, Geological Soc. of London, Arms Control Asscn; Fellow, American Geophysical Union, Geological Soc. of America, Royal Astronomical Soc., AAAS; Walter H. Bucher Medal of American Geophysical Union for original contribs. to basic knowledge of earth's crust 1975, Public Service Award, Fed. of American Scientists 1986, John Wesley Powell Award, US Geological Survey 1990, Vetleson Award for devt and testing of plate tectonics 2000. *Publications include:* more than 135 papers in scientific journals. *Leisure interests:* hiking, canoeing, opera, travel. *Address:* Lamont-Doherty Earth Observatory, Columbia University, PO Box 1000, 202D Seismology Building, 61 Route 9W, Palisades, NY 10964-8000 (office); 100 Washington Spring Road, Palisades, NY 10964-8000, USA. *Telephone:* (845) 365-8880 (office). *Fax:* (845) 365-8150 (office). *E-mail:* sykes@ldeo.columbia.edu (office). *Website:* www.ldeo.columbia.edu (office).

SYKES, Sir Richard (Brook), Kt, PhD, DSc, FRS, FMedSci; British research microbiologist, business executive and university administrator; *Chairman, Board of Trustees, The Royal Institution of Great Britain;* b. 7 Aug. 1942, Huddersfield, Yorks.; s. of Eric Sykes and Muriel Mary Sykes; m. Janet Mary Norman 1969; one s. one d.; ed Queen Elizabeth Coll., London, Bristol Univ., London Univ.; Head of Antibiotic Research Unit, Glaxo Research Ltd 1972–77; Asst Dir, Dept of Microbiology, Squibb Inst. for Medical Research, Princeton 1977, Dir of Micro-biology 1979, Vice-Pres. Infectious and Metabolic Diseases 1983–86; Deputy Chief Exec., Glaxo Group Research Ltd 1986, Group Research and Devt Dir, Glaxo PLC and Chair. and Chief Exec., Glaxo Group Research Ltd 1987, Deputy Chair. and Chief Exec., Glaxo PLC 1993, Chair., Glaxo Wellcome PLC 1997–2001, CEO 1997; Chair. (non-exec.), GlaxoSmithKline 2001–02; Chair., Metabometrix Ltd 2004–, Merlion Pharmaceuticals Pte Ltd 2005–, Omnicyte Ltd 2006–, Circassia Ltd 2007–12, NHS London 2008–10, NetScientific PLC; Rector, Imperial Coll. of Science, Tech. and Medicine 2001–08; Visiting Prof., King's Coll., London and Univ. of Bristol; Pres., British Asscn for the Advancement of Science 1998–99; mem. Bd of Dirs (non-exec.), Rio Tinto PLC 1997–2008, Lonza Group Ltd 2003–12, Imperial Coll. Healthcare NHS Trust 2007–, Eurasian Natural Resources Corpn 2007–; Chair., UK Stem Cell Foundation 2005–; mem. Council for Science and Tech. 1993–2002; Chair., Bd of Trustees, The Royal Institution of Great Britain 2010–; mem. Bd of Trustees Nat. History Museum 1996–2005, Bd Higher Educ. Funding Council for England 2002–, UK India Business Council 2007–; Chancellor, Brunel Univ. 2013–; mem. Int. Advisory Bd A*Star Biomedical Research Council, Singapore; Fellow, Imperial Coll. School of Medicine, King's Coll. London; Fleming Fellow, Lincoln Coll., Oxford 1992; Hon. mem. Nat. Acad. of Medicine, Brazil; Hon. Fellow, Royal Coll. of Physicians, Royal Acad. of Eng, Royal Soc. of Chemistry, Royal Coll. of Pathologists, Univ. of Wales, Cardiff, Univ. of Central Lancashire, Royal Pharmaceutical Soc.; Hon. FRSC; Hon. Citizen of Singapore 2004; Companion of the Most Admirable Order of Direkgunabhom (Thailand) 2006; Hon. DPharm (Madrid) 1993, Hon. DSc (Brunel, Hull, Herts.) 1994, (Bristol, Newcastle) 1995, (Huddersfield, Westminster) 1996, (Leeds) 1997, (Edin., Strathclyde) 1998, (Cranfield, Leicester, Sheffield, Warwick) 1999, Hon. MD (Birmingham) 1995, Hon. LLD (Nottingham) 1997, Dr hc (Sheffield Hallam, Surrey); Hamao Umezawa Memorial Award (Int. Soc. of Chemotherapy) 1999, Singapore Nat. Day Public Service Star Award 1999. *Leisure interests:* tennis, swimming, opera, skiing. *Address:* The Royal Institution of Great Britain, 21 Ablemarle Street, London, W1S 4BS (office); Flat 11, Hale House, 34 De Vere Gardens, London W8 5AQ, England (home). *Telephone:* (20) 7409-2992 (office). *E-mail:* ri@ri.ac.uk (office). *Website:* www.rigb.org (office).

SYMON, Lindsay, CBE, TD, MB, ChB, FRCS, FRCSE; British professor of neurological surgery; b. 4 Nov. 1929, Aberdeen, Scotland; s. of William L. Symon and Isabel Symon; m. Pauline Barbara Rowland 1954; one s. two d.; ed Aberdeen Grammar School and Univ. of Aberdeen; House Physician/Surgeon, Aberdeen Royal Infirmary 1952–53, Surgical Registrar 1956–58; Clinical Officer/Jr Specialist in Surgery, British troops in Austria 1953–55; Clinical Research Fellow, MRC 1958–61; Major in charge, No. 2 Mobile Neurosurgical Team, TA, RAMC 1960–68; Rockefeller Travelling Fellow, Wayne State Univ., Detroit, Mich., USA 1961–62; Sr Registrar, Neurosurgery, Nat. Hosps 1962–65, Consultant Neurosurgeon 1965–78, Prof. of Neurological Surgery and Sr Surgeon 1978–95; mem. External Staff MRC 1965–78; Hon. Consultant Neurosurgeon, St Thomas's Hosp., London 1973–95, Hammersmith Hosp., London 1978–95, Royal Nat. Throat, Nose and Ear Hosp. 1979–95, The Italian Hosp. 1981–89; Adjunct Prof., Dept of Surgery, Southwestern Medical School, Dallas, Tex. 1982–95; Civilian Adviser in Neurosurgery, RN 1979–95; Pres. World Fed. of Neurosurgical Socs 1979–93, Hon. Pres. 1993–; Pres. Harveian Soc., London 1997–98, Trustee 1999–; mem. Ukrainian Acad. of Science 1992–; Hon. Sr Fellow, American Neurological Asscn 1982, Hon. FACS 1994, Hon. mem. Soc. of Neurological Surgeons; Olivecrona Lecturer, Karolinska Inst., Sweden 1980, Jamieson Medal, Australasian Neurosurgical Soc. 1982, John Hunter Medal, Royal Coll. of Surgeons 1985, Mayfield/Aring Lecturer, Univ. 1990, Joachim Zulch Prize, Max Planck Inst. 1993, Otfrid Förster Medal, German Soc. Neurosurgery 1998, Medal of Honour, Soc. of British Neurological Surgeons 2008, Samii Medal of Honour, World Fed. of Neurological Socs 2013. *Publications include:* texts on cerebrovascular surgery, physiology of the cerebral circulation, surgery of acoustic neuroma, general neurosurgical topics. *Leisure interests:* golf, prehistory. *Address:* Maple Lodge, Rivar Road, Shalbourne, nr Marlborough, Wilts., SN8 3QE, England (home). *Telephone:* (1672) 870501 (home). *Fax:* (1672) 870501 (home). *E-mail:* lindsaysymon@tiscali.co.uk.

SYMONENKO, Petro Mykolayovych; Ukrainian politician; *First Secretary of Central Committee, Komunistychna Partiya Ukrainy (Communist Party of Ukraine);* b. 1 Aug. 1952, Donetsk, Ukrainian SSR, USSR; m. 1st Svitlana; two s.; m. 2nd Oksana Vashchenko; one d.; ed Donetsk State Polytechnical Inst. and Kyiv Inst. of Political Science and Social Admin; joined Komsomol 1975; joined CPSU 1978, fmr Deputy Sec. Donetsk regional CP Cttee; Deputy Dir Ukrvuhlemash machine-building co. 1991–93; First Sec. Cen. Cttee of Komunistychna Partiya Ukrainy (KPU—Communist Party of Ukraine) 1993–(party banned from participating in elections Dec. 2015, ban appealed to European Court of Human Rights Jan. 2016); mem. Verkhovna Rada (Parl.) 1994–2014, Chair. CP Parl. faction; mem. Parl. Ass. of the Council of Europe from 1997; unsuccessful cand. in presidential elections 1999, 2004, 2010, 2014 (withdrew). *Address:* Komunistychna Partiya Ukrainy (Communist Party of Ukraine), 04070 Kyiv, vul. Borysohlibska 7, Ukraine (office). *Telephone:* (44) 238-93-76 (office). *E-mail:* kpu1993@gmail.com (office). *Website:* www.kpu.ua (office).

SYMONETTE, Theodore Brent; Bahamian barrister, real estate developer and politician; b. 2 Dec. 1954, Nassau; s. of Sir Roland Symonette and Lady Margaret Symonette; m. Robin Mactaggart; one s. two d.; ed St Andrew's School, Nassau, Leys School, Cambridge, Brunel Univ., UK; called to Bahamas Bar 1978; fmr Senator; mem. House of Ass. for St Anne; fmr Minister of Tourism; fmr Attorney-Gen.; mem. and fmr Deputy Leader, Free Nat. Movt; Deputy Prime Minister and Minister of Foreign Affairs 2007–12, also responsible for Immigration 2008–12; fmr Chair. Hotel Corpn, Airport Authority, Public Accounts Cttee.

SYMONS OF VERNHAM DEAN, Baroness (Life Peer), cr. 1996, of Vernham Dean in the County of Hampshire; **Elizabeth Conway Symons,** MA, FRSA; British politician; b. 14 April 1951; d. of Ernest Vize Symons and Elizabeth Megan Symons (née Jenkins); partner Philip Alan Bassett; one s.; ed Putney High School for Girls, Girton Coll., Cambridge; Admin. Trainee, Dept of the Environment 1974–77; Asst Sec., Inland Revenue Staff Fed. 1977–88, Deputy Gen. Sec. 1988–89; Gen. Sec., Asscn of First Div. Civil Servants 1989–96; Parl. Under-Sec. of State, FCO 1997–99; Minister of Defence Procurement, Ministry of Defence 1999–2001; apptd Minister of State (Minister for Trade), FCO and Dept of Trade and Industry 2001; Deputy Leader of House of Lords 2001–05; Minister of State for the Middle East, FCO and Dept of Trade and Industry 2003–05; Chair. Arab British Chamber of Commerce, Saudi British Joint Business Council, British Egyptian Soc., Britain Azerbaijan Business Council; mem. Bd of Dirs Manchester Airports Group plc, British Expertise, Egyptian British Business Council; Int. Consultant, DLA Piper, CCC UK, Blenheim Capital Services Ltd; mem. British Tunisian Business Council; mem. Advisory Bd PGI Protection Group International; mem. Gen. Council, TUC 1989–96, Council, RIPA 1989–97, Exec. Council, Campaign for Freedom of Information 1989–97, Hansard Soc. Council 1992–97, Advisory Council, Civil Service Coll. 1992–97, Council, Industrial Soc. 1994–97, Council, Open Univ. 1994–97; Employment Appeal Tribunal 1995, Equal Opportunities Comm. 1995–97; Exec. mem. Involvement and Participation Asscn 1992; Gov. Polytechnic of N London 1989–94, London Business School 1993–97; Trustee, Inst. for Public Policy Research 1993; Hon. Assoc. Nat. Council of Women 1989. *Leisure interests:* gardening, reading. *Address:* House of Lords, Westminster, London, SW1A 0PW, England (office). *Telephone:* (20) 7219-5353 (office). *Fax:* (20) 7219-5979 (office).

SYMS, Sylvia, OBE; British actress and director; b. 6 Jan. 1934, London; m. Alan Edney 1957 (divorced 1989); one s. one d.; ed Royal Acad. of Dramatic Art; Founder-mem. and Artistic Dir Arbela Production Co.; numerous lectures, including Dodo White McLarty Memorial Lecture 1986; mem. The Actors' Centre 1986–91, Arts Council Drama Panel 1991–96, Council for RADA 1992–2010; Variety Club Best Actress in Films Award 1958, Ondas Award for Most Popular Foreign Actress (Spain) 1966, Manchester Evening News Best Actress Award. *Theatre includes:* Dance of Death, Much Ado About Nothing, An Ideal Husband, Ghosts, Entertaining Mr. Sloane (Best Actress Award, Manchester Evening News) 1985, Who's Afraid of Virgina Woolf? 1989, The Floating Lightbulb 1990, Antony and Cleopatra 1991, For Services Rendered 1993, Funny Money 1996, Ugly Rumours 1998, Mothers and Daughters 1999–2003, Love Lust 2003, We All Make Mistakes 2003. *Films include:* Ice Cold in Alex 1953, The Birthday Present 1956, The World of Suzie Wong 1961, Run Wild Run Free 1969, The Tamarind Seed 1974, Chorus of Disapproval 1988, Shirley Valentine 1989, Shining Through 1991, Dirty Weekend 1992, Staggered 1994, Food for Love 1996, Mavis and the Mermaid 1999, Deep Down 2001, What a Girl Wants 2002, I'll Sleep When I'm Dead 2003,

The Queen 2006, Is There Anybody There? 2008, Bunny and the Bull 2009, Booked Out 2012, Run for Your Wife 2012. *Television includes:* Love Story 1964, The Saint 1967, My Good Woman 1972–73, Nancy Astor 1982, Ruth Rendell Mysteries 1989, Dr. Who 1989–90, May to December 1989–90, The Last Days of Margaret Thatcher 1991, Natural Lies, Mulberry, Peak Practice, Ruth Randell Mysteries 1993, 1997–98, Ghost Hour 1995, Heartbeat 1998, At Home with the Braithwaites 2000–03, The Jury 2002, Where the Heart Is 2003, Born and Bread 2003, The Poseidon Adventure 2005, Child of Mine 2005, Eastenders 2007–10, Bouquet of Barbed Wire (mni-series) 2010. *Radio includes:* Little Dorrit, Danger in the Village, Post Mortems, Joe Orton, Love Story, The Change 2001, 2003. *Plays and television directed:* Better in My Dreams 1988, The Price 1991, Natural Lies 1991–92. *Leisure interests:* gardening, dogs. *Address:* c/o Brown & Simcocks, 1 Bridge House Court, 109 Blackfriars Road, London, SE1 8HW, England (office). *Telephone:* (20) 7928-1229 (office). *Fax:* (20) 7928-1909 (office). *E-mail:* barryandcarrig@lingone.net (office); sylviasymsedney@aol.com (home). *Website:* www.sylviasyms.co.uk (home).

SYRON, Richard (Dick) Francis, PhD; American economist, banking executive and academic; b. 25 Oct. 1943, Boston, Mass; s. of Dominick Syron and Elizabeth Syron (née McGuire); m. Margaret Mary Garatoni 1972; one s. one d.; ed Boston Coll., Tufts Univ.; Deputy Dir Commonwealth of Mass 1973–74; Vice-Pres. and Economist Fed. Reserve Bank of Boston 1974–82, Sr Vice-Pres. and Econ. Adviser 1982–85, Pres. and CEO 1989–94; Exec. Asst to US Sec. of Treasury, Washington, DC 1979–80, Deputy Asst to Sec. for Econ. Policy 1980–81; Asst to Chair. Volcker, Fed. Reserve System, Washington, DC 1981–82; Pres. Fed. Home Loan Bank of Boston 1986–88; Chair. American Stock Exchange 1994–99; Chair. and CEO Thermo Electron, Mass. 1999–2002; Chair. and CEO Freddie Mac (Fed. Home Loan Mortgage Corpn), Washington, DC 2003–08; Adjunct Prof. of Finance, Carroll School of Management, Boston College; mem. Bd of Dirs Genzyme Corpn 2006–; Trustee, Boston Coll., Woods Hole Oceanographic Inst.

SYRYJCZYK, Tadeusz Andrzej, DTech; Polish politician and consultant; b. 9 Feb. 1948, Kraków; m. Barbara Syryjczyk; ed AGH Univ. of Science and Tech., Kraków; Lecturer, AGH Univ. of Science and Tech. y, Kraków 1971–89; mem. Solidarity Trade Union 1980–89; interned during state of martial law 1981–82; mem. Presidium Małopolska Region 1981; mem. regional authorities in Kraków 1982–84; with ABAKS, Kraków 1987–89; Minister of Industry 1989–91; Chief of Prime Minister's team of advisers and Under-Sec. of State in Council of Ministers 1992–93; Minister of Transport and Maritime Economy 1998–2000; Deputy to Sejm (Parl.) 1991–2001; Dir for Poland, EBRD, London 2003–07; apptd Sr Expert, Transport Consultants Group TOR Ltd 2007; mem. Democratic Union Parl. Caucus 1991–94, Freedom Union Parl. Caucus 1994–2001, Chair. 1997–98; mem. Democratic Union 1991–94; mem. Freedom Union 1994–2001, Nat. Council and Regional Council, Kraków 1983–2001; Vice-Pres. Freedom Union 1995–2001; Co-founder Cracow Industrial Soc., Kraków 1987, Pres. 1990–; mem. Polish Tourist Country-Lovers Asscn, Polish Informatics Soc. *Publications:* papers on automatics and informatics, articles in nat. magazines. *Leisure interest:* tourism, mountaineering. *E-mail:* tadeusz@syryjczyk.krakow.pl. *Website:* www.syryjczyk.krakow.pl.

SYSTROM, Kevin, BS; American software engineer; b. 30 Dec. 1983, Holliston, Mass; s. of Douglas Systrom and Diane Systrom; m. Nicole Systrom 2015; one d.; ed Stanford Univ.; internship at Odeo (search website) Jun.–Sept. 2005; joined Google, Inc. 2006, worked as an Assoc. on Gmail, Google Reader and other products, with Corporate Devt team –2009; Product Man., nextstop.com (destinations' recommendation website) 2009–10; co-f. Burbn (HTML5-based location-sharing service) 2010; co-f. Instagram (photo-sharing service) 2010, CEO –2018; mem. Bd of Dirs Walmart Inc. 2014–18; listed in Forbes' 30 under 30 in Social/Mobile 2014. *Leisure interests:* food, golf, skiing. *Address:* c/o Instagram, 181 South Park Street, Suite 2, San Francisco, CA 94107, USA.

SYSUYEV, Oleg Nikolayevich; Russian banker and fmr politician; *First Deputy Chairman, Alfa-Bank;* b. 23 March 1953, Kuybyshev (now Samara); m.; one s. one d.; ed Kuybyshev Moscow Aviation Inst.; Master, Head of Tech. Div., engineer and Sec., CP Cttee at Kuibyshev aviation team 1976–87; Sec., Krasnoglinsk Dist CP Cttee of Kuybyshev 1987–91; del. to 18th CP Congress; Head of Samara Admin. 1991–94; Mayor of Samara 1994–97; participant in Russia Our Home movt; Co-Chair. Union of Mayors of Russian Towns 1995–97; Deputy Head of Russian Govt, Minister of Labour and Social Devt 1997–98; Co-ordinator, Russian Comm. on Regulation of Trade-Social Relations 1997–98; First Deputy Head of Admin. of Pres. Yeltsin 1998–99; First Deputy Chair. Alfa-Bank 1999–; Pres. Congress of Municipalities of Russia 2000; mem. Presidential Council for Local Govt; Deputy Chair. Presidential Cttee for Literature and the Arts; Chair. Life-Line Charity Foundation. *Leisure interests:* playing guitar, piano, violin. *Address:* Alfa-Bank, 107078 Moscow, 27 Kalanchevskaya Str., Russia (office). *Telephone:* (495) 620-91-91 (office). *E-mail:* mail@alfabank.ru (office). *Website:* www.alfabank.com (office).

SZABO, Gabriela; Romanian professional athlete (retd) and government official; b. 14 Nov. 1975, Bistrita; m. Gyonyossy Zsolt 1999; fmr indoor European record-holder and outdoor World record-holder in 5,000m; silver medal, 1,500m, Olympic Games, Atlanta 1996; world's fastest at 1,500m, one mile, 2,000m, 3,000m and 5,000m 1998; gold medal, 5,000m Olympic Games, Sydney 2000, bronze medal, 1,500m, Sydney 2000; set new world records for indoor 5,000m in Feb. 1999, 3,000m Birmingham, England, Feb. 2001; gold medal, 1,500m World Championships 2001; silver medal, European Championships 5,000m 1998, 1,500m 2002; retd 2005; fmr Vice-Pres. Romanian Athletics Fed.; Minister of Youth and Sports 2014–15; European Athlete of the Year 1999, IAAF Athlete of the Year 1999. *Address:* c/o Ministry of Youth and Sports, 020954, Str. Vasile Conta 16, Bucharest, Romania (office). *Website:* www.gabiszabo.com.

SZABÓ, István, DLA; Hungarian film director, writer and academic; b. 18 Feb. 1938, Budapest; s. of Dr István Szabó and Mária Vita; m. Vera Gyürey; ed Budapest Acad. of Theatre and Film Arts; started as mem. Balázs B. Studio, Budapest; leading mem. Hungarian Film Studios; Tutor, Coll. of Theatre and Film Arts, Budapest, Univ. of Vienna, Max Reinhardt Seminar; mem. Acad. of Motion Picture Arts and Sciences, Akad. der Künste, Berlin; Béla Balázs Prize 1967, Kossuth Prize 1975. *Productions:* short films: Concert (Prix de Cannes) 1961, Variations upon a Theme 1961, Te (You) (Grand Prix de Tours) 1963, Budapest, amiért szeretem (Budapest, Why I Love It) 1971; series: Álom a házról (Dream

About the House) (Main Prize of Oberhausen) 1971; documentaries: Kegyelet (Piety) 1967, Várostérkép (City Map) (Grand Prix of Oberhausen) 1977, Steadying the Boat 1996; TV plays: Osbemutató (Première) 1974, Katzenspiel (Cat Play) 1982, Bali 1983; TV films: Der grüne Vogel (The Green Bird) 1979, Offenbach 1995; full-length films: Álmodozások kora (The Age of Day-Dreaming) (Silver Prix, Locarno) 1964, Apa (Father) (Grand Prix, Moscow) 1966, Szerelmesfilm (A Film of Love) 1970, Tüzoltó utca 25 (No. 25 Fireman's Street) (Grand Prix of Locarno) 1973, Budapesti mesék (Budapest Tales) 1976, Bizalom (Confidence) (Silver Bear of Berlin 1981) 1979, Mephisto (Acad. Award 1982, David di Donatello Prize (Italy), Italian Critics' Prize, Critics' Prize, UK) 1981, Colonel Redl (BAFTA Award 1986, Best West German Film—Golden Band) 1985, Hanussen 1988, Meeting Venus 1990, Sweet Emma, Dear Böbe (Silver Bear of Berlin, European Acad. Award for Best Screenplay) 1991, Steadying the Boat (BBC) 1996, Sunshine (European Acad. Award for Best Screenplay, Canadian Acad. Award for Best Film) 1999, Taking Sides 2001, Being Julia 2003, Relatives 2005, The Door 2011; operas: Tannhäuser, Paris 1987, Boris Godunov, Leipzig 1993, Il Trovatore, Vienna 1993, The Three Sisters, Budapest 2000 (also Kassel 2002). *Address:* 1132 Budapest, Váci-6, Hungary (home). *Telephone:* (1) 340-5559 (home). *Fax:* (1) 340-5559 (home). *E-mail:* islfilm@t-online.hu.

SZABÓ, Miklós, PhD, DSc; Hungarian archaeologist and academic; b. 3 July 1940, Szombathely; s. of Dezső Szabó and Irén Süle; m. Ágnes Molnár; three s.; ed Eötvös Loránd Univ. of Arts and Sciences (ELTE); with Dept of Archaeology, Hungarian Nat. Museum 1963–66; with Dept of Antiquities Museum of Fine Arts 1966–85, Deputy Dir Gen. 1985–87; Asst Prof., Dept of Classical Archaeology of ELTE 1983–89, Prof. and Head of Dept 1989, Gen. Vice-Rector 1991–93, Rector 1993–99, Dir Archaeological Inst.; research into Ancient Greek and Celtic archaeology, involved in excavations in Greece by the French Inst. of Archaeology in Athens 1970–78; in France 1978, led the Hungarian excavation expedition in Bibracte, France 1988–; Visiting Prof., Univ. of Paris (Sorbonne) 1980–81, Ecole normale supérieure, Paris 1985, Coll. de France 1989, 2000–01, Univ. of Burgundy 2003; Pres. Archaeological Cttee Hungarian Acad. of Sciences 1994; Corresp. mem. Hungarian Acad. of Sciences 1995 (mem. 2001–), German Archaeological Inst. 1977–, Royal Acad. of Barcelona 1997–, Acad. française 2002–; Ed. Dissertationes Pannonicae; mem. Editorial Bd Acta Archaeologica and Études Celtiques; Hon. mem. Greek Archaeological Soc. 1998; Chevalier, Ordre nat. du Mérite 1995, Commdr, Légion d'honneur 2001, Ordre des Arts et Lettres 2001; Dr hc (Burgundy) 1997, (Dijon) 1997, (Bologna) 1999; Kuzsinszky Medal 1984, Collège de France Medal 1989, Rómer Flóris Commemorative Medal 1990, City of Dijon Commemorative Medal 1991. *Publications include:* The Celtic Heritage in Hungary 1971, Hellász fénykora (The Golden Age of Greece) 1972, Világtörténelem képekben I, (World History in Pictures I, co-author) 1972, A keleti kelta művészet (Eastern Celtic Art, co-author) 1974, Les Celtes (co-author) 1978, Les Celtes en Pannonie. Contribution à l'histoire de la civilisation celtique dans la cuvette des Karpates 1988, I Celti (co-author) 1991, Les Celtes de l'Est: Le second âge du fer dans la cuvette des Karpates 1992, Decorated Weapons of the La Tène Iron Age in the Carpathian Basin (co-author) 1992, Archaic Terracottas of Boeotia 1994, Storia d'Europa II (co-author) 1994, A la frontière entre l'Est et l'Ouest (co-author) 1998, Prähistorische Goldschätze im Ungarischen National-museum (co-author) 1999, Trésors préhistoriques de Hongrie (co-author) 2001, Celtes de Hongrie (co-author) 2001, Celtas y Vettones (co-author) 2001.

SZAŁAMACHA, Paweł Włodzimierz, MPA; Polish lawyer and politician; b. 24 Jan. 1969, Gorzow Wielkopolski; m. Beata Chomątowska; ed Adam Mickiewicz Univ., Poznań, Coll. of Europe, Bruges, Belgium, John F. Kennedy School of Govt, Harvard Univ., USA; worked at Clifford Chance law firm, Warsaw 1994–2004; licensed as legal adviser at Dist Chamber of Legal Advisers, Poznań 1998; expert at Adam Smith Centre; Co-founder Sobieski Inst., mem. Bd 2003–05, Chair. 2008–11; Undersecretary of State, Ministry of the Treasury 2005–06, Sec. of State 2006–07; mem. Nat. Devt Council 2010–; mem. Sejm (Parl.) as non-party cand. on behalf of Prawo i Sprawiedliwość (PiS—Law and Justice) 2011–14, re-elected for Dist of Poznań 2015–; Minister of Finance 2015–16; Commdr, Order of the Star of Italian Solidarity 2006. *Publications include:* Rzeczpospolita – pierwsza odsłona (Republic – the first part) 2009; contrib. to MPP, Rzeczpospolita, Najwyższym CZASIE!, Gazecie Polskiej. *Address:* c/o Ministry of Finance, 00-916 Warsaw, ul. Świętokrzyska 12, Poland. *E-mail:* kancelaria@mofnet.gov.pl.

SZCZUREK, Mateusz, DEcon, MEconSc, PhD; Polish economist and fmr government official; b. 11 Aug. 1975; m.; five c.; ed Univ. of Warsaw, Univ. of Sussex, UK, Int. Centre for Money and Banking Studies, Geneva and London, Columbia Univ., USA; Economist with ING Barings 1997–2011, becoming Chief Economist, ING Bank Slaski; Lecturer in Econs, School of Econs, Warsaw, Univ. of Sussex, Goethe Business School, Frankfurt; Minister of Finance 2013–15; mem. Asscn of Polish Economists; named by Emerging Markets magazine as Finance Minister of the Year, Cen. & Eastern Europe 2014, named by The Banker magazine as European Finance Minister of the Year 2015. *Leisure interests:* photography, cycling.

SZÉKELY, Gábor, MA; Hungarian theatre director and academic; *Faculty Director, University of Drama, Film and Television, Budapest;* b. 26 May 1944, Jászberény; s. of Árpád Székely and Irma Csuka; m. Erika Székely 1967; one s. two d.; ed Könyves Kalmán Grammar School, Budapest, Budapest Acad. of Dramatic and Cinematic Art; Asst Dir, Szolnoki Szigligeti Theatre 1968–71, Prin. Dir 1971–72, Theatre Man. and Prin. Dir 1972–78; Prin. Dir Budapest Nat. Theatre 1978–82, apptd Theatre Man. 1982; Theatre Man. Budapest Katona József Theatre 1982–89; teacher of dramatic art and theatre direction, Acad. of Dramatic and Cinematic Art 1972–, apptd Head, Theatre Dirs' Faculty 1990; has directed in Novi Sad, Stuttgart, Prague Nat. Theatre; invited to direct at Deutsches Theater, Berlin, Comédie Française, Paris 1991, Helsinki City Theatre 1993; Dir Új Szinház Theatre 1993–97; univ. prof. 1991–; guest teacher, Paris Acad. of Dramatic and Cinematic Art 1993; Rector Univ. of Drama, Film and TV, Budapest 2001–06, Faculty Dir 2007–; Dr hc (Tirgu Mures Univ.); Jászai Mari Prize, Merited Artist, Outstanding Artist, Kossuth Prize, critics' prize for best theatre performance and best theatre direction, several times. *Plays directed include:* As You Like It, Troilus and Cressida, Timon of Athens (Shakespeare), Georges Dandin, L'impromptu de Versailles, Don Juan (Molière), The Death of Tarelkin (Kobilin), The Death of Danton, Woyzeck (Büchner); guest performances abroad with Budapest Nat. and Katona József theatres (among others): Cat's Play (Orkény), Family Toth (Orkény), Moscow, Bucharest, Prague, Helsinki; Catullus (Fust), Vienna, Paris (Odeon), Zürich; Le Misanthrope (Molière), Moscow; Coriolanus (Shakespeare), Berlin; The Escape (Bulgakov), Prague. *Leisure interests:* architecture, fine arts. *Address:* Jókai u. 36. II/12, 1066 Budapest, Hungary. *Telephone:* (1) 332-4284.

SZEKERES, Imre, PhD; Hungarian engineer and politician; b. 9 Sept. 1950, Szolnok; m.; two c.; ed Veszprém Univ. of Chemical Eng; sec. of communist youth org. at Univ.; Asst Lecturer, Cybernetics Inst., Veszprém Univ. 1974–77; mem. Veszprém City Council 1986, later Deputy Chair. responsible for culture and finances; co-f. Reformkömök movt; Chair. Hungarian Socialist Party (Magyar Szocialista Párty—MSzP) Org. in Veszprém Co. 1989, headed electoral list during first parl. elections 1990, Nat. Sec. 1990, Vice-Chair. 1990–2004, Deputy Chair. 2004–, electoral campaign chief 1994; mem. Parl. for Jászapáti 1994–2002, 2006–, for co. party list of Jász-Nagykun-Szolnok Co. 2002–06, Head, HSP parl. group 1994–98; Chair. Parl. Budget and Finance Cttee 1998–2002; Political State Sec., Cabinet of Prime Minister 2002–04; Minister of Defence 2006–10; Pres. Hungarian Triathlon Asscn 2003–; mem. Jász Asscn ('The people of Jászság Asscn') and other social orgs of Jászság (geographical region of Hungary); Freeman of Jászapáti. *Leisure interest:* triathalon. *Address:* Hungarian Socialist Party, 1066 Budapest, Jókai u. 6, Hungary (office). *Telephone:* (1) 459-7200 (office). *Fax:* (1) 210-0081 (office). *Website:* www.mszp.hu (office).

SZEMERÉDI, Endre, PhD; Hungarian/American mathematician, computer scientist and academic; *State of New Jersey Professor of Computer Science, Rutgers University;* b. 21 Aug. 1940, Budapest, Hungary; m.; five c.; ed Eötvös Loránd Univ., Moscow State Univ., USSR; Visiting Prof., Stanford Univ. 1974, McGill Univ., Canada 1980, Univ. of South Carolina 1981–83, Univ. of Chicago 1985–86; State of New Jersey Prof. of Computer Science, Rutgers Univ. 1986–; Perm. Research Fellow, Rényi Inst. of Math., Budapest, also Prof. Emer.; mem. Inst. for Advanced Study, Princeton, NJ; Fairchild Distinguished Scholar, California Inst. of Tech. 1987–88; Eisenbud Prof., MSRI Berkeley 2008; Aisenstadt Chair, CRM, Univ. of Montreal; Corresp. mem. Hungarian Acad. of Sciences 1982, 1987; mem. NAS 2010; Dr hc (Charles Univ., Prague); Grünwald Prize 1967, 1968, Rényi Prize 1973, Pólya Prize for Achievement in Applied Math., Soc. for Industrial and Applied Math. 1975, Prize of Hungarian Acad. of Sciences 1979, Leroy P. Steele Prize for Seminal Contrib. to Research, American Math. Soc. 2008, Rolf Schock Prize in Math. 2008, Abel Prize, Norwegian Acad. of Science and Letters 2012. *Achievements include:* his proof of an old conjecture of Paul Erdős and Paul Turán 1975 (now known as Szemerédi's theorem). *Publications:* more than 200 papers in professional journals on discrete mathematics, theoretical computer science, arithmetic combinatorics and discrete geometry. *E-mail:* szemered@cs.rutgers.edu (office).

SZENES, Gen. (retd) Zoltán, MSc, PhD, CSc; Hungarian army officer (retd) and academic; *Professor and Director of International Security and Defence Studies, Faculty of International and European Studies, National University of Public Service;* b. 23 July 1951, Köcsk; m. Dr Ibolya Gáspár; one d.; ed Mil. Tech. Acad., Budapest, War Coll. of Logistics and Transportation, Leningrad (now St Petersburg), Russia, Hungarian Acad. of Science, Budapest Univ. of Econs, Royal Coll. of Defence Studies, London, UK; joined Hungarian People's Army 1969, assigned to 25th Tank Regt, Tata 1973–74; staff officer, 11th Tank Div. 1974–75; Chief of Staff for Logistics, 9th Mechanized Div., Kaposvár 1979–82; Sr Lecturer, Assoc. Prof. and Head of Logistics Dept, Zrínyi Miklós War Coll., Budapest 1986–91, then Prof., Zrínyi Miklós Nat. Defence Univ. 2009–11, then Prof. at Nat. Univ. of Public Service (NUPS, through merger with Police Acad. and Faculty of Public Admin of Corvinus Univ. of Budapest) 2011–, currently Prof. and Dir of Int. Security and Defence Studies, Faculty of Int. and European Studies; Chief of Supply Services of Defence Command 1991–94; Fellow, Royal Coll. of Defence Studies, London 1995; Head of Educ. and Science Dept, Ministry of Defence 1996–98; Mil. Rep. to NATO and WEU, Brussels, Belgium 1998–99; ACOS Logistics, AFSOUTH HQ, Naples, Italy 1999–2002; Dir of Defence Staff 2002–03, Chief of Defence 2003–05; apptd Maj.-Gen. 2002, Lt-Gen. 2003, Gen. (retd) 2008; Visiting Prof., Baltic Defence Coll., Tartu, Estonia 2006–14; Guest Lecturer, NATO Defence Coll. 2005, 2009–11; Chair. Mil. Science Cttee, Hungarian Acad. of Sciences 2008–14; Pres. Budapesti Honvéd Sport Club 2003–10; mem. Hungarian Logistics Asscn 1991–2005, Hungarian Mil. Science Asscn 1991–, IISS, London 1995–2005, Hungarian UN Asscn 2015–; Cross of the Legion of Honour (Officer Grade) 2004, Commdr's Cross, Order of Merit (Mil. Div.) 2004; Meritorious Service Award, Tanárky Sándor Price Award, Hungarian Asscn of Mil. Sciences, Budapest, Hungarian NATO Enlargement Medal, NATO KFOR and SFOR Medals, Officer Service Medal (First Class), Andrássy Gyula Price Award, Ministry of Defence 2001, NATO Service Award for the Period 1998–2002 2004, Medal of Merit, Baltic Defence Coll. 2009, Defence Service Award (First Class) 2010, Memorial Military Science Medal 2018, NUPS, Apáczai Csere János Price, Ministry of Human Resources 2018. *Publications:* The Implications of NATO for Civil-Military Relations in Hungary 2001, Future of NATO (in Academic and Applied Research in Military Science journal) 2005, The Effects of Peacekeeping on the HDF (in Peacekeeping Today and Tomorrow) 2006, Ten Years in NATO (with Peter Tálas) 2009, On the Hungarian Military Science (article) in Military Science Quarterly 2011, 1, UN Peacekeeping NUPS 2013, Wales Summit in Military Science Quarterly, Issue 4 2014, Forward Military Presence (in Military Science Quarterly, Issue 2) 2016, NATO 4.0. and Hungary (co-author) 2019. *Leisure interests:* travelling, reading, fitness. *Address:* National University of Public Service, Faculty of International and European Studies, 1083 Budapest, Ludovika tér 2, Hungary (office). *Telephone:* (1) 432-9000 (office); (1) 432-20802 (office); 30-2428914 (mobile). *Fax:* (1) 432-9331 (office). *E-mail:* szenes.zoltan@uni-nke.hu (office); szenes@hotmail.com (home). *Website:* www.uni-nke.hu (office).

SZENTIVÁNYI, Gábor; Hungarian economist and diplomatist; *Ambassador for Nordic-Baltic Issues;* b. 9 Oct. 1952, Vaskút; s. of József Szentiványi and Ilona Fejes; m. Gabriella Gönczi; one s. one d.; ed Univ. of Econ. Sciences, Budapest; joined Foreign Service 1975, positions in Baghdad 1976–81, Washington, DC 1986–91; mem. staff Protocol Dept, Ministry of Foreign Affairs 1982–85, Spokesman and Dir-Gen. for Press and Int. Information Dept 1994–97, Deputy State Sec. 2002–04, State Sec. and Political Dir 2007–09; Amb. to UK 1997–2002, to the Netherlands 2004–07, to Sweden 2009–13; Amb. for Nordic-Baltic Issues 2013–;

Man. Dir Burson-Marsteller's Budapest office 1991–94; mem. Hungarian Foreign Affairs Soc., Hungarian Atlantic Council; Freeman, City of London, UK 2000; Hon. GCVO, Officer, Order of Prince Henry the Navigator 1982, Grand Cross of Merit (Chile) 2002, Middle Cross of the Order of Merit 2004, Kt Grand Cross, Order of Oranje-Nassau (Netherlands) 2007. *Leisure interests:* boating, reading. *Address:* Ministry of Foreign Affairs, Bem rkp. 47, 1027 Budapest, Hungary (office). *Telephone:* (1) 458-1545 (office). *Fax:* (1) 214-8059 (office). *E-mail:* gszentivanyi@mfa.gov.hu (office). *Website:* www.kormany.hu/en/ministry-of-foreign-affairs (office).

SZIJJÁRTÓ, Péter, BA, MA; Hungarian economist and politician; *Minister of Foreign Affairs and Trade;* b. 30 Oct. 1978, Komárom; m. Szilvia Szijjártó 2009; ed Czuczor Gergely Benedictine Secondary Grammar School, Győr, Budapest Univ. of Econ. Sciences and Public Admin (now Corvinus Univ. of Budapest); elected mem. Municipal Ass. of Győr 1998, 2006–10, served as Vice-Chair. Educ., Culture and Sports Cttee; mem. Fidesz – Magyar Polgári Szövetség (Fidesz – Hungarian Civic Alliance) 1998–, Co-founder Fidelitas (youth org. of Fidesz) in Győr, Vice-Pres. 2001, Pres. 2005–09, mem. Fidesz Nat. Bd, Leader of Győr br. of Fidesz, Communications Dir and Spokesman for Fidesz 2006–10, Chief of Staff of the party Pres. 2009–10; Spokesman of Prime Minister Viktor Orbán 2010–12, headed Prime Ministerial staff in charge of press, int. and organizational affairs; mem. Nat. Ass. 2002–, Vice-Chair. Cttee on Youth and Sport Affairs 2004–06, Deputy Faction Leader of Fidesz and Chair. Budget Cttee; State Sec. for Foreign Affairs and External Econ. Relations of the Prime Minister's Office 2010–12; Govt Commr for Hungarian-Russian Relations and Hungarian-Chinese Bilateral Relations 2013–14; Deputy Minister of Foreign Affairs and Trade and Parl. State Sec. of the Ministry of Foreign Affairs and Trade 2012–14, Minister of Foreign Affairs and Trade 2014–. *Address:* Ministry of Foreign Affairs and Trade, 1027 Budapest, Bem rakpart 47, Hungary (office). *Telephone:* (1) 458-1178 (office). *Fax:* (1) 375-3766 (office). *E-mail:* konz@mfa.gov.hu (office). *Website:* www.kormany.hu/en/ministry-of-foreign-affairs-and-trade (office).

SZILI, Katalin, DJur; Hungarian lawyer, political scientist and politician; b. 13 May 1956, Barcs; m. Miklós Molnár 1977; two c. of friends who died in an accident; ed Nagy Lajos Grammar School, Pécs, Janus Pannonius, Univ. of Pécs, Eötvös Loránd Univ., Budapest; Counsellor of Tutelage Affairs, then Head of Section, Pécs City Council 1981–85; legal counsellor, Water Directorate, South Transdanubian Region, then Admin. Head of Dept, then Leader of Authority Dept of Environment and Water Directorate, then of Environment Supervisory Authority 1985–92; mem. of Local Govt of Pécs 1992–94; expert, Parl. Group of Hungarian Socialist Party (MSZP) 1993–94; Political Sec. of State, Ministry for Environment and Regional Devt 1994–98; mem. MSZP 1989–, Baranya Co. Pres. of MSZP 1997–2001, Pres. Nat. Women's Asscn of MSZP 1998–2000, Nat. Vice-Pres. MSZP 2000–; mem. Gen. Ass. of Co. of Baranya 1998–99; mem. (MSZP) Hungarian Nat. Ass. for Pécs 1994–2010, Ind. mem. 2010–, Deputy Speaker 1998–2002, Speaker 2002–09, mem. Cttee on Sustainable Devt 2010– (Chair. 2013–), Vice-Chair. Parl. Cttee of Nat. Cohesion 2011–13, Chair. Sub-cttee on Autonomy 2012–, Chair. Community of Social Justice 2013–; nominated as cand. for presidential election 2005; Chair. Global Centre for ICT in Parl. 2008–09, Forum of Hungarian Reps from the Carpathian Basin 2002–09, Nat. Council for Sustainable Devt 2008 (Hon. Chair. 2009–); Founder and Chair. Forum of Nat. and Ethnic Minorities in Hungary 2009; Founder Social Union Party 2010; Hon. Assoc. Prof., Univ. of Pécs 2008; Hon. Citizen of Barcs, Dejtár, Kazincbarcika, Kővágószőlős and Szügy; Grand Cross of Belgium 2003, Grand Cross, Order of Merit (Germany) 2004, Commdr, Légion d'honneur 2005, Grand Gold Service Medal with Ribbon (Austria), Congressional Great Cross of Peru 2005, Commdr's Cross, Order of Merit with Star (Poland) 2006, Order of Merit (Mongolia) 2006, Hon. Certificate and Hon. Medal of the Bulgarian Pres. 2007, Spanish Legion of Honour Grand Cross 2007, Grand Officer, Order of the Star of Italian Solidarity 2009, Order of White Rose (Finland) 2012; Dr hc (L.N. Gumilev Eurasian Univ., Kazakhstan) 2007; Appreciative Title of the Chamber 'Pro economy of Baranya' 1998, 18 Trees in the Yad Vashem Memorial Park, Israel 2005, Medal of Honour, Asscn of Displaced Persons for achievements in human rights issues 2007, Pro Urbe Award, Tirgu-Mures (Romania) 2008, Báthory Award, Hungarian Nat. Council of Transylvania 2008, Tolerance Award, Ass. of the Autonomous Prov. of Vojvodina 2009. *Leisure interests:* environmental protection, minority issues. *Address:* Országgyülés (National Assembly), 1054 Budapest, rkp. 19, Hungary (office). *Telephone:* (1) 441-4000 (office); (1) 441-5012 (office). *Fax:* (1) 441-5010 (office). *E-mail:* katalin.szili@parlament.hu (office). *Website:* www.parlament.hu (office); www.szilikatalin.hu.

SZINETÁR, Miklós; Hungarian theatre and film director; b. 8 Feb. 1932, Budapest; m. Ildikó Hámori, one s. one d.; ed High School of Dramatic Art; Producer, Budapest Operetta Theatre, then Chief Producer 1953–60; Chief Producer, Hungarian TV, Artistic Dir then Chief Artistic Dir 1962, Deputy Chair. of Hungarian TV 1979–90; Man. Dir Budapest Operetta Theatre 1993–96; Chief Man. Dir Hungarian State Opera House 1996–2001, apptd Gen. Dir 2002; Golden Nympha, Monte Carlo 1970, Best Director, Prague TV Festival 1976–79, Silver Asterix, Trieste 1980, Pro urbe Budapest 2001. *Films include:* Délibáb minden mennyiségben 1961, Janos Háry 1965, Baleset 1967, Csárdás Fürstine (The Csardas Princess, UK) (also adaptation) 1971, Az erőd (The Fortress) (also screenwriter) 1979. *Television:* Éjszakai repülés 1963, Halálnak halála 1969, Az ember tragédiája (The Tragedy of the Man, USA) 1969, Igéző 1969, Rózsa Sándor (mini-series) 1979, A Kékszakállú herceg vára (Bluebeard's Castle) 1981, Der Kronprinz 1988, Così fan Tutte, Fidelio, The Barber of Seville, The Life of Franz Liszt. *Publications:* Kalandsaim 1987, Igy Kell Ezt 2003. *Address:* Bethlen Gábor u. 16, 2011 Budakalász, Hungary (home). *Telephone:* (36) 26343000 (home). *Fax:* (36) 26540380 (home). *E-mail:* szini1@axelero.hu.

SZŐNYI, Erzsébet; Hungarian musician; b. 25 April 1924; d. of Jenő Szőnyi and Erzsébet Piszanoff; m. Dr Lajos Gémes 1948; two s.; ed Music Acad., Budapest and Paris Conservatoire, France; teacher of music at a Budapest grammar school 1945–48, Music Acad., Budapest 1948–; leading Prof. of Music Acad. 1960–81; Vice-Pres. Int. Soc. for Music Educ. 1970–74; Co-Chair. Hungarian Kodály Soc. 1978–2003, Chair. 2007–, Co-Chair. Bárdos Soc. 1988–, Forum of Hungarian Musicians 1995–; Hon. Pres. Hungarian Choir Asscn 1990–; Gen. adviser on methodology, Int. Kodály Soc. 1979–; mem. Chopin Soc. of Warsaw, Liszt Soc. of Hungary; mem. Hungarian Acad. of Art 1992–, Hungarian Composers' Soc. 1999–; Dr hc (Duquesne Univ., Pittsburgh) 2006; Erkel Prize 1959, Hungarian Repub. Medal 1993, Apácai Csere János Prize 1994, Bartók-Pásztory Prize 1995, 2004, Prize for Artistic Excellence 2000, Zoltán Kodály Prize 2001, Hungarian Heritage Prize 2004, Hungarian Choir Asscn Medal 2004, Kossuth Prize 2006, Prima Prize 2011, Artist of the Nation 2014. *Compositions include:* Concerto for Organ and Orchestra; symphonic works: Musica Festiva, Divertimento 1 and 2, Prelude and Fugue, Three Ideas in Four Movements; operas: Tragedy of Firenze, A Gay Lament, Break in Transmission, Elfrida (madrigal opera) 1987–, several children's operas; chamber music, oratorios, vocal compositions, etc. *Publications:* Methods of Musical Reading and Writing, Kodály's Principles in Practice, Travels in Five Continents, Twentieth-Century Musical Methods. *Leisure interests:* gardening, cooking. *Address:* Attila-út 4, 1013 Budapest I (office); Ormódi-utca 13, 1124 Budapest XII, Hungary (home). *Telephone:* (1) 375-0052 (office); (1) 356-7329 (home).

SZOSTAK, Jack William, BS, PhD; Canadian/American molecular biologist and academic; *Professor of Genetics, Harvard Medical School;* b. 9 Nov. 1952, London, England; ed McGill Univ., Canada, Cornell Univ.; Asst Prof., Sidney Farber Cancer Inst. and Dept of Biological Chemistry, Harvard Medical School 1979–83, Assoc. Prof., Dana Farber Cancer Inst. and Dept of Biological Chem. 1983–84, Assoc. Prof., Dept of Genetics 1984–87, Prof. 1988–, Prof. of Chem. and Chemical Biology, Harvard Univ.; Assoc. Molecular Biologist, Dept of Molecular Biology, Massachusetts Gen. Hosp. 1984–87, Molecular Biologist 1988–, Alex A. Rich Distinguished Investigator 2000–; Investigator, Howard Hughes Medical Inst. 1998–; Co-Chair. Nat. Research Council Cttee on the Origin and Evolution of Life 2003–; mem. NAS 1998–; Fellow, New York Acad. of Sciences 1999–; mem. Editorial Bd Chemistry and Biology 1994–; Penhallow Prize in Botany, McGill Univ. 1972, NAS Award in Molecular Biology 1994, Louis Vuitton-Moet Hennesey 'Vinci of Excellence' Award 1996, Hans Sigrist Prize, Univ. of Bern, Switzerland 1997, Genetics Soc. of America Medal 2000, ACS Harrison Howe Award 2003, Albert Lasker Award for Basic Medical Research (with Elizabeth Blackburn and Carol Greider) 2006, Dr H.P. Heineken Prize for Biochemistry and Biophysics 2008, Nobel Prize in Physiology or Medicine (with Elizabeth Blackburn and Carol Greider) 2009, Oparin Medal 2011. *Publications:* more than 170 papers in scientific journals. *Address:* Szostak Lab, CCIB 7215, Simches Research Center, 185 Cambridge Street, Boston, MA 02114 (office); Department of Molecular Biology, Massachusetts General Hospital, Wellman 9, Fruit Street, Boston, MA 02114, USA (office). *Telephone:* (617) 726-5102 (Lab.) (office); (617) 726-5981 (Hosp.) (office). *Fax:* (617) 643-3328 (Lab.) (office); (617) 726-6893 (Hosp.) (office). *E-mail:* szostak@molbio.mgh.harvard.edu (office). *Website:* molbio.mgh.harvard.edu/szostakweb (office).

SZOSTEK, Andrzej Ryszard, BPhil; Polish ecclesiastic and academic; b. 9 Nov. 1945, Grudziądz; ed Catholic Univ. of Lublin; ordained priest 1974; with Dept of Ethics, Catholic Univ. of Lublin 1970–04, scientific worker 1971–04, Extraordinary Prof. 1992–99, Ordinary Prof. of Ethics and Philosophy 2000–04, Head of Dept of Ethics, mem. man. team Inst. of John Paul II 1983–98, Pro-Rector 1992–98, Rector 1998–2004; Lecturer, Superior Monastic House, Lublin 1987–90; Provincial Councillor Marians 1987–93; mem. Cttee of Formation of Marians 1975–90, Scientific Soc., Catholic Univ. of Lublin 1980–, Polish Philosophical Soc., Lublin 1982, Int. Cttee of Theology, Vatican Congregation of Religious Studies 1992–98, Lublin Scientific Soc. 1998–2001 (Distinguished mem. 2001–), Pontificia Academia Pro Vita 2001–, Polskiej Akademii Umiejętności; Hon. Fellow, St Mary's Coll., London 2000; Order of Merit 2001, Palmes Académiques 2001, Krzyż Kawalerski, Orderu Odrodzenia Polski 2005, Krzyżem Oficerskim, Orderu Odrodzenia Polski 2013; Medal, Comm. of Nat. Educ. 2001, Brązowe Odznaczenie, Za załugi w obronności kraju 2002, Honorowe Odznaczenie (Premium Honorificum) Lubelskiego Towarzystwa Naukowego 2003, Nagroda naukowa im Wł, Pietrzaka 2003, Nagroda Rektora KUL I stopnia 2005, Wyróżnienie Lubelskiego Towarzystwa Naukowego Resolutio pro Laude Academica 2005. *Publications include:* Rules and Exceptions – Philosophical Aspects of the Discussion about Absolute Norms in Contemporary Theology 1980, Nature–Reason–Freedom. Philosophical Analysis of the Concept of Creative Intellect in Contemporary Moral Theology 1989, Talks on Ethics 1993, On Dignity, Truth and Love 1995 and numerous other publs. *Leisure interests:* mountaineering, music, chess.

SZUMOWSKA, Małgorzata; Polish film director, screenwriter and producer; b. 26 Feb. 1973, Kraków; d. of Maciej Szumowski and Dorota Terakowska; one s. with Jacek Drosio; m. Mateusz Kosciukiewicz 2012; one d.; ed Jagiellonian Univ., Łódź Film School; mem. European Film Acad. 2001. *Films include:* Cisza (documentary short) 1998, Siedem lekcji milosci (documentary short) 1999, Happy Man 2000, Dokument...? (documentary short) 2001, Visions of Europe (segment 'Crossroad) 2004, Stranger 2004, Mój tata Maciek (documentary) 2005, Solidarnosc, Solidarnosc... (segment 'Father') 2005, Nothing to be Scared of (documentary short) 2007, 33 Scenes from Life (as Malgosia Szumowska) 2008, Elles (as Malgoska Szumowska) 2011, In the Name of 2013, Body (Silver Bear for Best Dir (shared with Radu Jude), Berlin Int. Film Festival) 2015. *Address:* c/o Memento Films International, 9 cité Paradis, 75010 Paris, France. *Telephone:* 1-53-34-90-20. *Fax:* 1-42-47-11-24. *E-mail:* festival@memento-films.com. *Website:* www.memento-films.com.

SZŰRÖS, Mátyás, PhD; Hungarian politician and diplomatist; b. 11 Sept. 1933, Püspökladány; ed Moscow Univ. Inst. of Int. Relations, Budapest Univ. of Econ. Sciences; on staff of Foreign Ministry 1959–65; staff mem. HSWP 1965–74, Deputy Leader Foreign Dept HSWP Cen. Cttee 1974–75, Head 1982–83; Amb. to GDR 1975–78, to USSR 1978–82; mem. Cen. Cttee HSWP 1978, Secr. 1983–89; mem. Parl. 1985–2002, Chair. Foreign Relations Parl. Cttee 1985–89, Pres. of Parl. March–Oct. 1989, Acting Pres. 1989–90, Deputy Speaker 1990–94; Chair. Hungarian Group of IPU 1989–90, 1994–2002, mem. Exec. Cttee IPU 1994–96; Gen. Pres. SDP 2003–05; Chair. Ópusztaszer Historical Commemorative Cttee 1989–98, Bd Trustees Illyés Foundation 1994–99, Trustee 1999–; mem. Council of Hundreds (World Fed. of Hungarians) 1997–; Freeman of Püspökladány 1996, of Beregszász 1997; Bocskai Award 1996. *Publications:* Hazánk és a nagyvilág (Homeland and World) 1985, Hazánk és Európa (Homeland and Europe) 1987, Magyarságról-Külpolitikáról (On Being Hungarian and on Foreign Policy) 1989, Cselekvő politikával a magyarságért-Politikai portré (1988–96) (Active policy for

Hungary, portrait of a politician) 1996, Köztársaság született harangszavú délben (1989. október 23) (The Republic Was Born and the Bells Rang at Noon, 23 October 1989) 1999, National Politics and Joining. Questions of Integration 2001, Hoggan tovább a rögős utakon (How Much Marching Further on the Thorny Way) 2003.

SZYDŁO, Beata Maria; Polish politician; *Deputy Prime Minister;* b. (Beata Maria Kusińska), 15 April 1963, Oświęcim; m. Edward Szydło; two s.; ed Jagiellonian Univ., Kraków, Warsaw School of Econs, Kraków Univ. of Econs; raised nr Brzeszcze; Asst at Museum of History of Kraków City, then Head of Dept at Cultural Centre in Libiąż 1987–95; Dir of Cultural Centre in Brzeszcze 1997–98; mem. Prawo i Sprawiedliwość (PiS—Law and Justice), currently Vice-Chair.; Dist Councillor in Oświęcim for Akcji Wyborczej Solidarność (Solidarity Electoral Action) 1998–2002; Mayor of Brzeszcze 1998–2005; participated in Int. Visitor Leadership Program 2004; mem. (PiS), Sejm (Parl.) for 12 Chrzanów 2005–; Prime Minister 2015–17; Deputy Prime Minister 2017–. *Address:* Prawo i Sprawiedliwość (Law and Justice), 02-018 Warsaw, ul. Nowogrodzka 84/86, Poland (office). *Telephone:* (22) 6215035. *Fax:* (22) 6216767. *E-mail:* biuro@pis.org.pl. *Website:* www.pis.org.pl.

SZYMANCZYK, Michael E., BS; American business executive (retd); b. 1949; ed Indiana Univ.; joined Proctor & Gamble 1971, served in several sales and marketing positions –1987; Vice-Pres. of Sales, Kraft Inc. 1987–88, Vice-Pres. Retail Operations 1988, Sr Vice-Pres. Swift-Eckrich Inc. 1989; Sr Vice-Pres. of Sales, Philip Morris USA, New York 1990–97, COO July-Nov. 1997, Pres. and CEO 1997–2008, Chair. 2002–08, Chair. and CEO Altria Group Inc. (parent co.) 2008–12; mem. Bd of Dirs Duke Realty, Dominion 2012–; mem. Bd of Trustees Univ. of Richmond, Virginia Commonwealth Univ. School of Eng Foundation, United Negro Coll. Fund, Richmond Performing Arts Center; fmr Chair. and current mem. Dean's Advisory Council for Indiana Univ. Kelley School of Business; fmr mem. Bd Futures for Children.

SZYMCZYK, Adam; Polish gallery curator; *Artistic Director, documenta 14, Athens and Kessel;* b. 1970, Piotrków Trybunalski; ed Univ. of Warsaw; Co-founder and Curator, Foksal Gallery Foundation, Warsaw 1997–2003; Dir and Chief Curator Kunsthalle Basel 2003–14; co-curated, with Elena Filipovic, When Things Cast No Shadow, 5th Berlin Biennale for Contemporary Art 2008; currently Artistic Dir documenta 14, Athens and Kessel 2017; Walter Hopps Award for Curatorial Achievement 2011. *Publications include:* numerous exhbn catalogues; contrib. to Parkett, Frieze, Flash Art, Fluid, Kunstbulletin, Spike. *Address:* c/o Andrea Linnenkohl, documenta 14, Friedrichsplatz 18, 34117 Kessel, Germany (office). *Telephone:* (561) 707270 (office). *Fax:* (561) 7072739 (office). *E-mail:* office@documenta.de (office); linnenkohl@documenta.de (office). *Website:* www.documenta14.de (office).

T

TAALAS, Petteri, PhD; Finnish meteorologist and international organization official; *Secretary-General, World Meteorological Organization;* b. 3 July 1961, Helsinki; m.; five c.; ed Univ. of Helsinki, Helsinki School of Econs, Leonardo da Vinci Univ., France, Finnish Naval Acad.; served as weather technician at several airports 1983–86; Scientist, Air Quality Dept, Finnish Meteorological Inst. 1986–89, Sr Scientist, Weather Dept 1989–96, Head of Research, Meteorological Research Dept 1996–2001, Prof. and Dir-Gen., Finnish Meteorological Inst. 2002–15; Dir, Devt and Regional Activities Dept, WMO 2005–07, mem. WMO Exec. Council 2008–15, Sec.-Gen., WMO 2016–; Dean, Kuopio Univ. 1997; Vice-Chair., EC Cttee for Atmospheric Sciences 1995–2003; Chair. Council, European Org. for the Exploitation of Meteorological Satellites (EUMETSAT) 2003–05, 2010–14, Vice-Chair. 2007–09; Chair., Finnish Intergovernmental Panel on Climate Change Council 2008–15; Chair., Univ. of Eastern Finland 2009–15; mem. Advisory Bd, Fortum Energy Co. 2011–16; mem. Finnish Space Bd 2003–12, Finnish Arctic Bd 2009–15; mem. Finnish Acad. of Science and Letters 2009–. *Publications include:* more than 50 peer-reviewed papers on satellite technology, global change, climate and atmospheric chemistry. *Address:* Office of the Secretary-General, World Meteorological Organization, 7bis, avenue de la Paix, Case postale 2300, 1211 Geneva 2, Switzerland (office). *Telephone:* 227308111 (office). *Fax:* 227308181 (office). *E-mail:* wmo@wmo.int (office). *Website:* www.wmo.int (office).

TABACHNYK, Dmytro Volodimirovych, DS; Ukrainian politician and historian; b. 26 Nov. 1964, Kiev; s. of Volodomir Igorovich Tabachnyk and Alla Viktorovna Tabachnyk; m. Tetyana Evgenyovna Nazarova; ed Kiev State Univ.; fmr copyist, then restorer, Cen. State Archives of Cinematography, Documents of Ukraine; jr researcher, Inst. of History of Ukraine, Ukrainian Acad. of Sciences, leading researcher, Inst. of Politology 1997–; Deputy, Kiev City Soviet 1990–94; Deputy Head Kiev City Exec. Comsomol Cttee 1991–92; Head of Press Service, Cabinet of Ministers 1992–93; First Deputy Head, State Cttee on Publishing, Polygraphy and Book Trade 1993–94; Head of Admin., Presidency 1994–96, Counsellor 1997–98, Head, Constitution Comm. 1994–96; People's Deputy of Ukraine of III, IV Convocations 1998–2003, Deputy of Verkhovna Rada (Party of the Regions), Crimean Autonomous Repub. 2006; Vice-Prime Minister of Ukraine 2002–05, responsible for Humanitarian Issues 2006–07; elected mem. Verkhovna Rada (Parl.) 2007; Minister of Educ. and Science and Youth and Sports 2010–14; Dir Nat. Expert Inst. of Ukraine 2005; Prof., Ukrainian Acad. of State Man. 1995; Corresp. mem. Acad. of Juridical Sciences; currently in exile in Israel. *Publications:* over 400 papers. *Leisure interests:* collecting art, theatre, books.

TABAI, Ieremia T., CMG; I-Kiribati international organization official and fmr head of state; b. 1950, Nonouti; m.; two c.; ed King George V School, Tarawa, St Andrew's Coll., Christchurch, NZ, Victoria Univ., Wellington, NZ; mem. Gilbert Islands (later Kiribati) House of Ass. 1974–91; fmr Leader of the Opposition; Chief Minister of the Gilbert Islands 1978–79, also Minister of Local Govt; Pres. of Kiribati and Minister of Foreign Affairs (fmrly Gilbert Islands) 1979–91; Sec.-Gen. South Pacific Forum 1991–98; Chair. Commonwealth Observer Group 2001; Co-Owner New Star newspaper; Hon. LLD (Vic. Univ. of Wellington).

TABAKOVIĆ, Jorgovanka, MA, PhD; Serbian economist, politician and central banker; *Governor, National Bank of Serbia;* b. 21 March 1960, Vučitrn; widowed; three c.; ed Univ. of Priština; began career as econs teacher, Secondary Econs School, Priština 1981–89; Financial Dir, Grmija trading co. 1990–92; Gen. Man. Prištinska banka AD 1992; various posts in domestic banking –1999; mem. Nat. Ass. (parl.) (Serbian Radical Party) 1993–2000, (Serbian Progressive Party) 2008–12, May–Aug. 2012; Minister of Econ. and Ownership Transformation 1998–2000; joined Telekom Srbija (telecoms co.) 1999, Gen. Man., Logistics Dept 2005–08; Lecturer, Faculty of Man., Univ. of Novi Sad 2006–07; Gov. Nat. Bank of Serbia (central bank) 2012–; mem. Serbian Progressive Party 2008–, Vice-Pres. 2012–. *Publications:* several studies on privatization and financial markets. *Address:* Office of the Governor, National Bank of Serbia, 11000 Belgrade, Kralja Petra 12, POB 1010, Serbia (office). *Telephone:* (11) 3027194 (office). *Fax:* (11) 3027394 (office). *E-mail:* kabinet@nbs.rs (office). *Website:* www.nbs.rs (office).

TABINAMAN, John; Papua New Guinea politician; *Minister for Lands, Physical Planning, Environment and Conservation;* mem. Regional House of Reps from Mahari 2005–; Vice-Pres. Autonomous Bougainville Govt (ABG) 2007–09, additional ministerial portfolios for Public Service, Planning and Implementation and Peace and Autonomy 2007–, Acting Pres. ABG 2008–09, Minister for Lands, Physical Planning, Environment and Conservation 2015–. *Address:* Ministry of Lands, Physical Planning, Environment and Conservation, Autonomous Bougainville Government, House of Representatives, PO Box 322, Buka, Autonomous Region of Bougainville, Papua New Guinea (office). *Website:* www.abg.gov.pg (office).

TABONA, Joseph Zammit, FCA; Maltese diplomatist, government official, accountant and business executive; *Prime Minister's Special Envoy for Business Promotion;* m. Susan Lee Watson; one s. one d.; qualified as chartered accountant, Turquand, Youngs & Co., London, UK 1971, became partner of local br. 1972; Sr Partner, PricewaterhouseCoopers –2000 (retd); holds warrant to practise as a Certified Public Accountant; Chair. Malta Accountancy Bd 2001–09; High Commr to UK 2009–13; Prime Minister's Special Envoy for Business Promotion 2013–; fmr Chair. Malta Stock Exchange, FinanceMalta, Viset Malta plc; Pres. Malta Fed. of Industry, merged three govt agencies to create Malta Enterprise; Commr Shanghai Expo 2010; Chair. Malta Jaguar Enthusiasts' Club; an organiser of the annual Valletta Grand Prix for historical and classic cars; Fellow, Malta Inst. of Accountants; Fellow mem. Inst. of Taxation; Kt of Malta. *Address:* Office of the Prime Minister, Auberge de Castille, Valletta, VLT 2000, Malta (office). *E-mail:* joseph.muscat@gov.mt (office).

TÁBORA, (Isabel) Rocío, BA, MA; Honduran writer and government official; *Secretary of Finance;* ed Univ. Nacional Autónoma de Honduras, Univ. Academia de Humanismo Cristiano, Santiago; Democratic Governance Coordinator, UNDP 2008–11; Under-Sec. of State in Office of the Pres. 2002–06, Dir of Technical Support Unit, Presidential Secr. 2011–13; long career in Secr. (Ministry) of Finance, including as Dir of Planning, Budget and Public Investment 2014–15, Under-Sec. of Credit and Public Investment 2014–18, Sec. (Minister) of Finance (first female) 2018–. *Publications:* numerous publs on political and social issues, and several literary works, including Cosas que rozan (short stories), Guardarropa (poetry collection), Con olor a especies vengo . . . Crónica brevísima de un viaje a Marruecos (travel narrative) 2012. *Address:* Secretariat of Finance, Edif. SEFIN, Avda Cervantes, Barrio El Jazmín, Tegucigalpa, Honduras (office). *Telephone:* 2222-0112 (office). *Fax:* 2238-2309 (office). *E-mail:* sgeneral@sefin.gob.hn (office). *Website:* www.sefin.gob.hn (office).

TÁBORA MUÑOZ, Marlón Ramssés, Dr Ciencias Administrativas; Honduran central banker and diplomat; *Ambassador to USA ;* ed Universidad Católica de Honduras; fmr Chair. Honduran Nat. Telecommunications Comm.; fmr Head of Finance Unit and Asst Pres., Inversiones La Paz; fmr Alt. Gov. Central American Bank for Econ. Integration; fmr Project Engineer, Honduran Telecommunications Co.; mem. Bd of Exec. Dirs Interamerican Devt Bank 2010–13; Pres. Banco Central de Honduras 2014–16, also Head of Econ. Cabinet; Exec. Dir for Cen. America 2015–17; Amb. to USA 2017–. *Address:* Banco Central de Honduras, Avda Juan Ramón Molina, 7a Avda y 1a Calle, Apdo 3165, Tegulcigalpa, Honduras (office). *Telephone:* 2237-2270 (office). *Fax:* 2237-187 (office). *E-mail:* Carlos.Espinoza@bch.hn (office). *Website:* www.bch.hn (office).

TABUNSCIC, Gheorghe, PhD; Moldovan politician; b. 1 Jan. 1949, Copciac; m.; two c.; ed Chişinău Agricultural Inst.; agronomist and Vice-Chair. Victory collective farm, Taraclia rayon 1962–75; fmr Leader, Moldovan CP Comrat Br., advocate for autonomy of Gagauz region; elected Başkan (Gov.) of Gagauz-Yeri following autonomy 1995–99, re-elected 2002–06.

TACHA, Deanell Reece, JD; American lawyer, federal judge and university administrator; *School of Law Dean Emeritus, Pepperdine University;* b. 26 Jan. 1946, Goodland, Kan.; ed Univ of Kansas, Univ of Michigan Law School; Special Asst to US Sec. of Labor, Washington, DC 1971–72; Assoc. Hogan and Hartson (law firm) 1973, Thomas J. Pitner 1973–74; Dir Douglas Co. Legal Aid Clinic, Lawrence, Kan. 1974–77; Assoc. Prof. of Law Univ. of Kansas 1974–77, Prof. 1977–85, Assoc. Dean 1977–79, Assoc. Vice-Chancellor 1979–81, Vice-Chancellor 1981–85; Judge US Court of Appeals, 10th Circuit 1985–2001, 2007–11, Chief Judge 2001–07; Duane and Kelly Roberts Dean of Law, School of Law, Pepperdine Univ. 2011–16, then Dean Emer., Prof. of Law 2011–; mem., US Sentencing Comm. 1994–98. *Address:* School of Law, Pepperdine University, 24255 Pacific Coast Highway, Malibu, CA 90263, USA (office). *Telephone:* (310) 506-4676 (office). *E-mail:* deannell_tacha@pepperdine.edu. *Website:* law.pepperdine.edu (office).

TADDZHUDDIN, Talgat Safich; Russian (Tartar) ecclesiastic; b. 12 Oct. 1948, Kazan, Tatarstan, Russia; m.; five c.; ed El-Azkhar Theological Univ., Cairo; First Imam-Khatyb, mufti and Chair. of Sacred Bd Mosque El-Mardjani; Chair. Dept of Int. Relations of Muslim Orgs of the USSR 1990; Supreme Mufti of Russia and European countries of CIS; awarded the sacred title Sheik-iul-Islam; Official Rep. of Muslims of Russia to maj. foreign and public Muslim orgs., Org. of Islam Confed., UNESCO, European League of Muslims; Head, Central Spiritual Directorate of Russian Muslims 1992–2015; Order of Friendship 1998, Order of Honour 2009. *Publications:* The Wild East 1999, Limit of Rationality 1998, and numerous scientific works on political and religious culture. *Leisure interest:* foreign languages. *Address:* 129090 Moscow, Vypolzov per. 7, Russia (office). *Telephone:* (495) 281-49-04 (office).

TADIĆ, Boris; Serbian politician, psychologist and fmr head of state; *President, Socijaldemokratska Stranka (SDP—Social Democratic Party);* b. 15 Jan. 1958, Sarajevo, Bosnia and Herzegovina; s. of Ljuba Tadić and Nevenka Tadić; m. 1st Veselinka Zastavniković 1980 (divorced 1996); m. 2nd Tatjana Rodić; two d.; ed Univ. of Belgrade; convicted for student political activities; several positions as prof. of psychology, army clinical psychologist, researcher on devt and social psychology projects; Prof. of Politics and Advertising, Univ. for Drama and Arts, Belgrade 2003; Founder and Dir Centre for the Devt of Democracy and Political Skills 1997–2002; mem. Democratic Party 1990–2014, later Sec. of Gen. Cttee, Vice-Pres. Exec. Bd, Acting Pres. Exec. Bd, Vice-Pres. of Demokratska Stranka (DS—Democratic Party) 2000–04, Pres. 2004–12, Hon. Pres. 2012–14 (resgnd); Founder-mem. and Pres., Nova Demokratska Stranka (NDS—New Democratic Party), later renamed Socijaldemokratska Stranka (SDP—Social Democratic Party) 2014–; Rep. to Nat. Ass. 1996–97; mem. Council for Science and Tech.; Rep. in Council of Fed. Ass. 2000; Minister of Telecommunications, Fed. Repub. of Yugoslavia 2002–03; Minister of Defence, Council of Ministers of Serbia and Montenegro 2003–04; elected Rep. to Ass. of Serbia and Montenegro 2003, Acting Head of Group of Democratic Party Reps; Pres. of Serbia 2004–12 (resgnd); mem. Bd for Defence and Security; first Pres. Comm. for the Supervision of Security Service; Order of Republika Srpska 2012; Dr hc (Dimitrie Cantemir Christian Univ., Bucharest, Romania) 2009; European Prize for Political Culture, Ringier Group, Zurich 2007, Medal For the Contrib. to the Victory of Russian Fed. 2008, The Courage of Perseverance Quadriga Award, Werkstatt Deutschland, Berlin 2008, Golden Keys of the City of Madrid 2009, Steiger Award of Rhine-Ruhr 2010, North-South Prize of the Council of Europe 2011, Ilyas Afandiyev Int. Prize (Azerbaijan) 2012. *Address:* Socijaldemokratska Stranka, 11000 Belgrade, Vatroslava Jagića 5, Serbia (office). *Telephone:* (11) 4141000 (office). *E-mail:* sekretarijat@sds-org.rs (office). *Website:* www.sds-org.rs (office).

TADLAOUI, Mohammed, BSc; Moroccan engineer; *President, Socoplan;* b. 1939, Meknès; m.; two s. one d.; ed Imperial Coll. London and Inst. of Civil Engineers, UK, Sorbonne, Paris; research engineer, UK 1963, project engineer Arup and Partners 1966; consulting engineer Morocco 1973; Founder, Pres. and Gen. Dir Socoplan (consulting engineers) 1975–; co-founder and mem. Moroccan Fed. of Consulting Engineers (FMCI) 1976–; Gen. Sec. Ismailia Asscn of Micro Credit; Founding mem. Regional Asscn Grande Ismailia, Meknès; mem. Moroccan Nat. Fed. of Micro-Credit. *Leisure interests:* swimming, tennis, history, literature. *Address:* Socoplan, Residence Royale, av. Moulay Slimane, Rabat 10000, Morocco (office). *Telephone:* (7) 721020 (office). *Fax:* (7) 735663 (office). *E-mail:* socoplan@gmail.com (office).

TAFAJ, Myqerem, BA, MSc, PhD; Albanian politician and academic; b. 14 Nov. 1957, Diber; ed Agricultural Univ. of Tirana, Univ. of Hohenheim, Stuttgart, Germany; Asst, Agricultural Univ. of Tirana 1982–88, Lecturer 1989–91, Prof. 1997–, expert in fields of systems of educ., educational legislation, governance and man., curriculum devt, higher educ.; fellowship from German Foundation for Int. Devt 1990; Lecturer, Univ. of Stuttgart-Hohenheim 1999–2005, Guest Scientist (under auspices of the Alexander von Humboldt Foundation); Dir-Gen. of Science, Ministry of Higher Educ. 1996–97, Minister of Higher Educ. and Science March–July 1997; Educ. and Science Adviser to the Prime Minister 2005–09; mem. Democratic Party 1991, mem. Cttee, Political Orientation 2005; mem. Democratic Party of Albania 2005–; Sec.-Gen. Council of Ministers 2006–07; mem. Parl. for Tirana Dist 2009–; Minister of Educ. and Science 2009–13; Deputy Prime Minister April–Sept. 2013; Chair. Group of Experts on Reform of Science. *Address:* Kuvendi Popullor, Bulevardi Dëshmorët e Kombit 4, Tirana, Albania (office). *E-mail:* tafaj@uni-hohenheim.de (office); info@parlament.al. *Website:* www.parlament.al (office).

TAFIDA, Dalhatu Sarki, MBBS, MRCP; Nigerian physician, politician and diplomatist; b. 24 Nov. 1940, Zaria, Kaduna State; m. Salamatu Ndana Tafida; nine c.; ed Middle School, Zaria, Barewa Coll., Zaria, Govt Coll., Keffi, Coll. of Medicine, Univ. of Lagos, Royal Victoria Infirmary, Newcastle upon Tyne and Univ. of Liverpool, UK, Johns Hopkins Univ., USA; House Officer, Ahmadu Bello Univ. 1967–68, Sr House Officer 1968–69, Registrar from 1969–70; Clinical Asst in Medicine, Royal Victoria Infirmary, Newcastle upon Tyne 1970–71; Sr Registrar in Medicine, Katsina Specialist Hosp. 1972–73; Consultant Physician, Ministry of Health, Kaduna State 1973–76; Perm. Sec., Ministry of Health, Kaduna 1976–80; Chief Physician to Pres. of Nigeria 1980–83; Commr for Health, Agric. and Educ., Kaduna State 1984–87; Pro-Chancellor Univ. of Agriculture, Makurdi 1989–91; Fed. Minister of Health 1993–95; represented Kaduna North in Senate 2003–07, Senate Majority Leader 2003–07; High Commr to UK 2008–15; Vice-Pres. 28th Ass. of IMO 2013; Founding mem. Peoples Democratic Party (PDP) 1998, resgnd from PDP 2016; Dir-Gen. Jonathan/Sambo Presidential (Nigeria) Campaign Org. 2010–11; Fellow, Nigerian Medical Coll. of Physicians 1975, West African Coll. of Physicians 1975; conferred with traditional title of Tafidan Zazzau 1995; Order of the Fed. Rep. 1983, Commdr 2011. *Leisure interests:* Scrabble, table tennis.

TAFT, Robert (Bob) Alphonso II, BA, MA, JD; American politician and academic; b. 8 Jan. 1942; s. of Robert Taft Jr, fmr Senator from Ohio, grand-s. of Robert Taft (fmr Senator from Ohio), great grand-s. of William Howard Taft (fmr US Pres.); m. Hope Taft; one d.; ed Yale Univ, Princeton Univ, Univ of Cincinnati Law School; served as volunteer teacher for US Peace Corps in East Africa; mem. Ohio House of Reps 1976–80; Commr Hamilton Co., Ohio 1981–90; Sec. of State of Ohio 1990–99; Gov. of Ohio 1999–2007; Distinguished Research Assoc., Univ. of Dayton, School of Education and Health Sciences 2007–; mem. Bd of Dirs Alliance for the Great Lakes 2008–. *Address:* School of Education and Health Sciences, Fitz Hall 618, 300 College Park, Dayton, OH 45469, USA (office). *Website:* www.udayton.edu/education (office).

TAGAREV, Todor, MSc, PhD, ACSC (Distinguished Grad.); Bulgarian researcher and fmr government official; *Director, Centre for Security and Defence Management;* b. 18 April 1960, Stamboliyski; m. Petya Tagareva; two s. one d.; ed Air Force Acad., Dolna Mitropolia, NE Zhukovsky Air Force Eng Acad., Moscow, Russia, US Air Command and Staff Coll., Air Univ., Alabama, USA; 12 years of field, teaching and man. experience in Bulgarian Air Force; Researcher, Bulgarian Acad. of Sciences Inst. of Control and Systems Research 1994–97 and Space Research Inst. 1997–98; Head, Information Technologies for Security Dept, Inst. of Information and Communication Technologies 2008, Prof. 2014–16, Dir, Centre for Security and Defence Management 2013–; Sr Research Assoc., Inst. for Security and Int. Studies 1995–; Dir Defence Planning Directorate, Ministry of Defence 1998–2001, also Dir Armaments Policy Directorate and Nat. Armaments Dir May–Sept. 2001, Adviser to Minister of Defence 2009–10, Minister of Defence (in caretaker govt) March–May 2013; Head of Security and Defence Man. Dept, G.S. Rakovski Nat. Defence Acad., Sofia 2004–08; mem. NATO Research and Tech. Bd and Nat. Rep. to System Analysis and Studies Panel 2005–08. *Publications include:* Building Integrity and Reducing Corruption in Defence: A Compendium of Best Practices (ed. and lead author). *Address:* Centre for Security and Defence Management, Institute of Information and Communication Technologies, G. Bonchev Street, Bl. 25-A, 1113 Sofia, Bulgaria (office). *Telephone:* (2) 979-67-47 (office). *Fax:* (2) 870-72-73 (office). *E-mail:* tagarev@bas.bg (office). *Website:* it4sec.org/content/csdm (office); www.iict.bas.bg.

TAGAYEV, Aitibai Sultanovich; Kyrgyzstani economist and politician; b. 30 April 1958, Naukat Dist, Osh Oblast; m.; three s.; ed Kyrgyz State Univ.; started career at Chapayev Collective Farm, Naukat Dist, Osh Oblast 1974; Deputy Head Accountant, Construction Materials Factory, Kyzylkiya town 1981, becoming Head Accountant and Deputy Dir of Financial and Econ. Questions; Deputy Dir for Commercial Matters, Nur KM Building Materials Co., Kyzylkiya town, Batken Oblast 1993–94, Man. Dir 1994–98, Asst Chair., later Chair. 1998–2005; Deputy, Zhogorku Kenesh (Parl.) 2005–, mem. Econs, Budget and Finance Cttee 2005–, Chair. Zhogorku Kenesh (Speaker) 2008–09; mem. Bright Road People's Party (Ak Zhol) 2007–; Hon. Scholar of the Kyrgyz Repub. 2003. *Address:* Zhogorku Kenesh, 720053 Bishkek, ul. Abdymomunov 207, Kyrgyzstan (office). *E-mail:* zs@kenesh.gov.kg (office). *Website:* www.kenesh.kg (office).

TAGLE, HE Cardinal Luis Antonio Gokim, BA, MA, STD; Philippine ecclesiastic and academic; *Archbishop of Manila;* b. 21 June 1957, Manila; s. of Manuel Topacio Tagle and Milagros Gokim; ed St Andrew's School, Parañaque, San José Seminary, Ateneo de Manila Univ., Loyola School of Theology, Catholic Univ. of America, doctrinal courses at Inst. of Pope Paul VI Univ.; ordained priest, Archdiocese of Imus 1982; Parochial Vicar of San Agustín Parish – Méndez-Núñez, Cavite 1982–83, Spiritual Dir 1982–83; Rector diocesan seminary of Imus 1983–85; studies in Rome 1985–92; Episcopal Vicar for Religious 1993–95; Parish Priest and Rector of Nuestra Señora del Pilar Cathedral-Parish, Imus 1998–2001; taught Theology at San Carlos Seminary 1982–85 and Divine Word Seminary, Tagaytay, Cavite; mem. Int. Theological Comm. 1997–2002; mem. Editorial Bd History of Vatican II project led by Alberto Melloni, Bologna 1995–2001; Bishop of

Imus 2001–11; Archbishop of Manila 2011–; cr. Cardinal (Cardinal-Priest of San Felice da Cantalice a Centocelle) 2012; Chair. Episcopal Comm. on Doctrine of Faith of the Philippines 2003–; mem. Congregation for Catholic Educ. 2012–; named a Synod Father for 13th Ordinary Gen. Ass. of Synod of Bishops on New Evangelization 2012; mem. Presidential Cttee of Pontifical Council for the Family 2013–, Pontifical Council for Pastoral Care of Migrants and Itinerants 2013–; Prof. of Dogmatic Synthesis, Grad. School of Theology, San Carlos Seminary, Archdiocesan Major Seminary of Manila; Assoc. Prof. of Systematic Theology, Loyola School of Theology, Ateneo de Manila Univ.; Order of the Holy Sepulchre; Hon. DHumLitt (San Beda Coll.) 2012, (De La Salle Univ.) 2013, (Xavier Univ.-Ateneo de Cagayan) 2013, (Univ. of Santo Tomas) 2013, (Holy Angel Univ.) 2013, (Fordham Univ.) 2014, (Catholic Univ. of America) 2014, (La Salle Univ.) 2015, (Far Eastern Univ.); Hon. DTheol (Catholic Theological Union) 2015; Outstanding Manilan 2013, Fides Award 2015. *Television:* presenter, The Word Exposed; co-presenter, Kape't Pandasal (Coffee and Prayer) (ABS-CBN). *Address:* 121 Arzobispo Street, Intramuros, PO Box 132, 1099 Manila, Philippines (office). *Telephone:* (2) 521-6501 (office). *Fax:* (2) 527-3955 (office). *Website:* www.rcam.org (office).

TAGLIAVINI, Heidi, PhD; Swiss diplomatist and international organization official; b. 1950, Basel; ed Univ. of Geneva; joined Diplomatic Service 1982, mem. first OSCE Assistance Group to Chechnya 1995, worked in Directorate of Political Affairs, Head of Human Rights and Humanitarian Policy 1999, mem. staff, Embassy in The Hague, Netherlands, Deputy Head of Mission, Embassy in Moscow 1996, Deputy Head of UN Observer Mission in Georgia (UNOMIG) 1998–99, Personal Rep. of OSCE and Chair.-in-Office for the Caucasus 2000–01, Amb. to Bosnia and Herzegovina 2001–02, Special Rep. of UN Sec.-Gen. for Georgia and Head of Mission 2002–06, Deputy Head of Directorate of Political Affairs, Department of Foreign Affairs 2006, led EU investigation into 2008 South Ossetia war between Russia and Georgia 2008–09, led OSCE observation mission during Ukrainian presidential elections 2010, mem. ICRC Ass. 2012–, mem. Ass. Council 2014–, Special Rep. of OSCE Chair.-in-Office in Ukraine and mem. Trilateral Contact Group on Ukraine 2014–15; Dr hc (Franklin Univ. Switzerland) 2016; OSCE Award 2015. *Publications include:* Defence of the Future: The Caucasus in the Search for Peace (co-ed with F. Duve). *Address:* International Committee of the Red Cross (ICRC), 19 ave de la Paix, 1202 Geneva, Switzerland (office). *Telephone:* 227346001 (office). *Fax:* 227332057 (office). *E-mail:* press.gva@icrc.org (office). *Website:* www.icrc.org (office).

TAGORE, Sharmila; Indian actress; b. 8 Dec. 1946, Hyderabad; d. of Gitindranath Tagore; m. Mansoor Ali Khan Pataudi (died 2011) 1969; three c.; began career as actress 1959; Chair. Cen. Bd of Film Certification 2004–11; UNICEF Goodwill Amb. 2005–; Ordre des Arts et des Lettres 2004; Filmfare Lifetime Achievement Award 1997, Star Screen Lifetime Achievement Award 2002, Lifetime Achievement Nat. Award, Journalist Asscn of India 2007. *Films include:* Apur Sansar 1959, Devi 1960, Nirjan Saikatey 1963, Kashmir Ki Kali 1964, Waqt 1965, Devar 1966, Nayak 1966, An Evening in Paris 1967, Aradhana (Filmfare Best Actress Award) 1969, Aranyer Din Ratri 1970, Seemabaddha 1971, Chhoti Bahu 1971, Amar Prem 1972, Daag 1973, Aa Gale Lag Jaa 1973, Chupke Chupke 1975, Mausam (Nat. Film Award for Best Actress) 1975, Amanush 1977, Desh Premee 1982, Sunny 1984, Mississippi Masala 1991, Aashiq Awara 1993, Mann 1999, Dhadkan 2000, Shubho Mahurat 2003, Abar Aranye (Best Supporting Actress) 2004, Viruddh: Family Comes First 2005, Eklavya: The Royal Guard 2006, Fool and Final 2007, Tasveer 8*10 2008, Morning Walk 2009.

TAHA, Ali Osman Mohamed; Sudanese politician; b. 1 Jan. 1944, Khartoum; m. Fatima al-Amin; ed Univ. of Khartoum; mem. Khartoum Univ. Student Union (Kusu) 1966–71, Pres. 1969–70; organizer sha'ban movement 1973; in judiciary 1972–76; Minister of Social Planning 1973; Minister of Foreign Affairs 1996–98; First Vice-Pres. of Sudan 1998–2005; Second Vice-Pres. 2005–11, First Vice-Pres. 2011–13. *Address:* National Congress Party, Khartoum, Sudan (office). *Website:* www.ncp-sd.org (office).

TAHA, Hissène Brahim; Chadian diplomatist and politician; b. 1 Nov. 1951, Abéché; m.; six c.; ed Inst. Nat. des Langues et Civilisations Orientales, Paris; Counsellor, Ministry of Foreign Affairs (MFA) 1979–82, Head of Div., MFA Directorate of Econ. and Affairs 1982, Head of Europe-America Div., MFA Directorate of Public Affairs and Int. Orgs 1989–90, Dir of Cabinet of Minister of Foreign Affairs 1990–91, Counsellor, Embassy in Riyadh 1991–2001, Amb. to Taiwan 2001–06, to France 2007–17; Minister of External Relations and African Integration Feb.–Dec. 2017; Kt, Nat. Order of Chad.

TAHER, Nahed, BS, MA, MSc, PhD; Saudi Arabian banker and economist; *CEO, Gulf One Investment Bank;* ed King Abdulaziz Univ., Jeddah, Lancaster Univ., UK; Co-owner and Financial Advisor, Bullhide Liner (polyurethane coating) franchise, Jeddah 1987–97; Financial Advisor, Minara (support services co.), Jeddah 1993–2002; Lecturer, later Asst Prof. of Econs and Head of Accounting Dept, King Abdulaziz Univ.; Sr Strategic Economist and Chair. Portfolio Man. Cttee, Nat. Commercial Bank, Jeddah (first woman to hold such a position in a bank in Saudi Arabia) 2002–05; Founder and CEO Gulf One Investment Bank, Bahrain (first Saudi woman to head a bank in Gulf region) 2005–; consultant to Saudi Cultural Summit; mem. Saudi Econ. Asscn, Center for Strategic Studies of Mekkah Emirate, Businesswomen's Cttee of Jeddah Chamber of Commerce, Saudi Cttee of Eisenhower Fellowship; mem. Bd Int. Inst. for Man. Devt (Switzerland) (first mem. from Middle East) 2008–, Advisory Bd King Abdulaziz Univ. 2010–; Businesswoman of the Year Award (Saudi Arabia) 2007, Professorship Award, Lancaster Univ. 2011. *Address:* Gulf One Investment Bank BSC, Bahrain Financial Harbour, West Tower, Level 15, PO Box 11172, Manama, Bahrain (office). *Telephone:* 17102555 (office). *Fax:* 17100063 (office). *E-mail:* info@gulf1bank.com (office). *Website:* www.gulf1bank.com (office).

TAHIJA, George Santosa, BSc, MBA; Indonesian business executive; *President Director, PT Austindo Nusantara Jaya;* b. 1958; s. of Julius Tahija and Jean Tahija; brother of Sjakon George Tahija; ed Trisakti Univ., Jakarta, Darden School, Univ. of Virginia, USA; Pres. Dir PT Austindo Nusantara Jaya and CEO Austindo Group; Commr Freeport Indonesia; Dir Arc Exploration 1998–2014, Advisor 2014–; Founder and Chair. Coral Triangle Center; Advisor, Indonesia Mining Asscn; mem. Founding Bd PSKD Mandiri School; mem. Advisory Bd The

Nature Conservancy Indonesia Chapter; mem. Bd of Supervisors, Endeavor Indonesia; mem. Bd of Trustees Asia Business Council, Darden School, Univ. of Virginia, United States Indonesia Soc. (USINDO); mem. Plenary Cttee Trisakti Univ. Foundation; mem. Bd of Govs Indonesia Netherlands Asscn. *Achievements include:* has summited Mount Kilimanjaro, Tanzania, Carstensz Pyramid, Indonesia, Mount Elbrus, Russia. *Publications:* A Walk In the Clouds 2005, Land of Water 2006. *Address:* PT Austindo Nusantara Jaya, Graha Irama, 3rd Floor, Jl.H.R.Rasuna Said Kav. 1-2, Jakarta 12950, Indonesia (office). *Telephone:* (21) 5261415 (office). *Fax:* (21) 5261416 (office). *E-mail:* contact@austindogroup.com (office). *Website:* www.austindogroup.com (office).

TAHIJA, Sjakon George, MD; Indonesian ophthalmologist, eye surgeon and business executive; *Medical Director, Klinik Mata Nusantara;* b. 1953; s. of Julius Tahija and Jean Tahija; brother of George Santosa Tahija; ed Univ. of Indonesia, Lions Eye Inst., Perth, Australia, Univ. of Wisconsin, USA; mem. Bd of Commrs PT Austindo Nusantara Jaya 1986–, Pres. Dir PT Austindo Nusantara Jaya Healthcare Services Div.; Medical Dir and Vitreoretinal Consultant, Klinik Mata Nusantara; mem. European Soc. of Cataract and Refractive Surgeons, American Acad. of Ophthalmology, Indonesian Ophthalmologists Asscn. *Publications:* numerous publications in the field of ophthalmology. *Address:* PT Austindo Nusantara Jaya, Graha Irama, 3rd Floor, Jl.H.R.Rasuna Said Kav. 1–2, Jakarta 12950, Indonesia (office). *Telephone:* (21) 5261415 (office). *Fax:* (21) 5261416 (office). *E-mail:* contact@austindogroup.com (office). *Website:* www.austindogroup.com (office).

TAHIRI, Saimir, MPL; Albanian lawyer and politician; b. 30 Oct. 1979, Tirana; ed Faculty of Law, Univ. of Tirana; External Lecturer, Faculty of Law, Univ. of Tirana 2006–08 and in several other higher educational insts; practising lawyer 2008–; mem. Partia Socialiste e Shqipërisë (PSSh—Socialist Party of Albania); mem. (PSSh) Parl. for Tirana Dist 2009–18, Deputy Chair. Parl. Group, mem. Cttee on Legal Affairs, Public Admin and Human Rights 2009–13; Acting Pres. Socialist Party of Tirana 2011; Minister of the Interior 2013–17. *Address:* Partia Socialiste e Shqipërisë (Albanian Socialist Party), Sheshi Austria 91, 1001 Tirana (office). *Telephone:* (4) 2229428 (office). *E-mail:* info@ps.al (office). *Website:* www.ps.al (office).

TAIANA, Jorge; Argentine academic, politician and diplomatist; b. 31 May 1950, Buenos Aires; m.; three c.; ed Bachiller Colegio Nacional, Univ. of Buenos Aires; Adjunct Prof., Univ. of Buenos Aires 1985–91; Titular Prof., Univ. of Lomas de Zamora 1987; Prof., Univ. Rafael Landívar, Guatemala 1994; Titular Prof., Nat. Univ. of Quilmes 1995–2001; Head of Cabinet, Ministry of Education 1973–74, Under-Sec., Ministry of Economy 1974–75; Regional Dir Servicio Universitario Mundial (NGO) 1986–89; adviser to Foreign Affairs Cttee, Chamber of Deputies 1987–89; Under-Sec. for Foreign Policy, Ministry of Foreign Affairs 1989–90, Dir Int. Orgs 1990–91; Amb. to Guatemala and Belize 1992–96; Exec.–Sec. Inter-American Comm. on Human Rights, OAS 1996–2001; Sec. for Human Rights, Govt of Buenos Aires Prov. 2002–03; Vice-Minister of Foreign Affairs 2003–05, Minister of Foreign Affairs, Int. Trade and Worship 2005–10; mem. Buenos Aires City Legislature 2013–; mem. Frente para la Victoria (Front for Victory); Grand Cross, Order of Quetza (Guatemala) 1996, Order of El Sol del Peru (Peru) 2003, Order of Antonio José de Irisarri (Guatemala) 2003, Order of Baron de Rio Branco (Brazil) 2005, Officer, Order of Wissam Al Alaoui (Morocco) 2004. *Publications:* author of several publications on human rights and labour movements. *E-mail:* correo@legislatura.gov.ar. *Website:* www.legislatura.gov.ar.

TAIBU, Tatenda; Zimbabwean professional cricketer (retd); b. 14 May 1983, Harare; ed Churchill Boys High School; wicketkeeper; right-handed batsman; right-arm off-break/right-arm medium pace bowler; plays for Mashonaland 2000–05, Zimbabwe 2001– (Capt. 2003/04–05), Cape Cobras 2005–06, Namibia 2006–07 (List A Capt. 2006), Kolkata Knight Riders 2008–, Mashonaland A, Mountaineers Franchise Team, Northerns (Zimbabwe), Africa XI; First-class debut: 1999/2000; Test debut: Zimbabwe v West Indies, Bulawayo 19–22 July 2001; One-Day Int. (ODI) debut: Zimbabwe v West Indies, Harare 23 June 2001; T20I debut: Australia v Zimbabwe, Cape Town 12 Sept. 2007; moved to UK, served as player-coach-development-officer, for Hightown St Mary's, Liverpool; convener of selectors and development officer, Zimbabwe Cricket 2016–. *Achievements include:* became youngest Test capt. in history when given Zimbabwean captaincy April 2004. *Address:* Zimbabwe Cricket, Head Office, 28 Maiden Drive, Highlands, PO Box 2739, Harare, Zimbabwe.

TAILLANDIER, François Antoine Georges, MA; French writer; b. 20 June 1955, Chamalières; s. of Henri Taillandier and Denise Ducher; three c.; teacher 1980–83; full-time writer 1984–, also contrib. Le Figaro (newspaper), La Montagne (newspaper), L'Humanité (newspaper), L'Atelier du Roman (periodical); Admin., Soc. des Gens de Lettres de France; Prix Roger Nimier 1992, Acad. française Prix de la critique 1997. *Publications include:* fiction: Personnages de la rue du Couteau 1984, Tott 1985, Benoît ou les contemporains obscurs 1986, Les Clandestins (Prix Jean-Freustié 1991) 1990, Les Nuits Racine 1992, Fan et le jouet qui n'existe pas (with Charles Barat) 1993, Mémoires de Monte-Cristo 1994, Des hommes qui s'éloignent 1997, Anielka (Grand Prix du roman de l'Académie française 1999) 1999, Le cas Gentile 2001, La Grande Intrigue: Vol. 1 Option Paradis 2005, Vol. 2 Telling 2006, Il n'y a personne dans les tombes 2007; non-fiction: Tous les secrets de l'avenir 1996, Aragon 1997, Journal de Marseille 1999, N6, la route de l'Italie 1999, Les Parents lâcheurs 2001, Borges, une restitution du monde 2002, Pour ou contre Jacques Chirac (with Joseph Macé-Scaron) 2002, Un Autre langue 2004, Balzac (biography) 2005, L'Épopée de Compostelle 2006, La Langue française au défi 2009, Le Père Dutourd 2011, L'Écriture du monde 2013, La croix et le croissant 2014, Solstice 2015, Edmond Rostand: l'homme qui voulait bien faire 2018.

TAILLEFER, Louis, PhD, FRSC; Canadian quantum physicist and academic; *Professor of Physics and Canada Research Chair in Quantum Materials, University of Sherbrooke;* ed Univ. of Cambridge, UK; Post-doctoral Fellow, Univ. of Cambridge; later worked at CNRS, Grenoble, France; Research Fellow, Alfred P. Sloan Foundation 1993–97; Prof. of Physics, McGill Univ. –2002, Univ. of Toronto –2002; Prof. of Physics and Canada Research Chair in Quantum Materials, Univ. of Sherbrooke 2002–, Sr Fellow and Dir Quantum Materials programme, Canadian Inst. for Advanced Research (CIFAR); Fellow, American Physical Soc. 2003; Officière, Ordre nat. du Québec 2012; numerous awards, including Prix Urgel-Archambault, Asscn francophone pour le savoir 1998, E.W.R. Steacie Memorial Fellowship, Natural Sciences and Eng Research Council of Canada 1998–2000, Herzberg Medal, Canadian Asscn of Physicists (CAP) 1998, Premier's Research Excellence Award, Govt of Ontario 2000–03, Scientist of the Year, Radio-Canada 2002, Canada Research Chair (Level I) 2002–09, Prix Marie-Victorin, Govt of Québec (youngest recipient) 2003, CAP Brockhouse Medal 2003, CAP Medal of Achievement 2008, Institutional Prize for Research and Creation, Univ. of Sherbrooke 2012, Killam Prize (co-recipient), Canada Council for the Arts 2012, Diamond Jubilee Medal 2013. *Publications:* numerous papers in professional journals. *Address:* Local D2-1084-2, Département de physique, Faculté des sciences, 2500 boulevard Université, Sherbrooke, PQ J1K 2R1 (office); Canadian Institute for Advanced Research, 180 Dundas Street West, Suite 1400, Toronto, ON M5G 1Z8, Canada (office). *Telephone:* (819) 821-8000 (ext. 62051) (Sherbrooke) (office); (416) 971-4251 (Toronto) (office). *Fax:* (819) 821-8046 (Sherbrooke) (office); (416) 971-6169 (Toronto) (office). *E-mail:* louis.taillefer@usherbrooke.ca (office). *Website:* www.physique.usherbrooke.ca/taillefer (office); www.cifar.ca/louis-taillefer (office).

TAILLIBERT, Roger René; French architect; b. 21 Jan. 1926, Châtres-sur-Cher; s. of Gaston Taillibert and Melina Benoit; m. Béatrice Pfister 1965; one d.; ed school in Châtres sur Cher, École Nat. des Beaux-Arts, Paris; own practice 1969–; Chief Architect, Public Buildings for Govt 1967, civil buildings and nat. palaces; Curator Grand Palais 1977–82, Palais de Chaillot 1983–86; Chair. Taillibert International Sarl, Taillibert Gulf International (UAE), TGE, Doha 2007–; mem. Acad. des Beaux-Arts (Pres. 2005, 2010–), Inst. de France, Acad. d'Architecture 2000, Acad. des Sports, des Arts de la Rue, New Thinking group, RSA; Commdr, Légion d'honneur 1983, Ordre nat. du Mérite 1983, des Arts et des Lettres 1983, des Palmes Académiques 1983, Ordre du Mérite pour le Commerce et l'Industrie 2000; Ecole Nat. Supérieure des Beaux-Arts, Diplôme d'Architecture (DPLG) décerné par le Gouvernement Français 1955; Médaille d'argent décerné par l'Acad. d'Architecture pour ses recherches et ses applications pratiques 1971, Grand Médaille du Sport 1972, Prix Nat. des Arts et de la Littérature 1973, Prix Européen 1973, Médaille d'or de la Créatvitié Architecturale 1973, Grand Prix Cembureau 1974–76, Médaille des Structures 1976, Grand Prix Nat. d'Architecture 1976, Premier Prix Nat. d'Architecture 1977, Grand Prix des Arts, Canada 1977, Prix Elphège Baude 1977, Médaille de l'Acad. Nat. des Sports, Italie 1977, Grand Prix du Rayonnement Français 1982, Laureat du Prix Européen d'Architecture Métallique 2000, Médaille de Vermeil de la Ville de Paris 2000, Médaille d'Or du Sport 2000, Grand Prix of Europe Timber Structures, IAKS Award 2007, Int. Architecture Award 2012. *Main works:* numerous including: sporting facilities: Deauville Swimming-Pool 1966, Parc des Princes Stadium Paris 1972, Olympic Complex, Montréal, Canada 1976, Olympic Complex, Lille, France 1977–81, Sporting and cultural facilities at Kirchberg Luxembourg 1984, Khalifa Stadium, Qatar 2002, Bamenda Stadium Cameroon, Ice Skating-Ring, Abu Dhabi, Stadia for Soccer World Cup 2006, Morocco, velodromes at Bordeaux 1987, Poitiers 1997, Vannes 2001, Astana (Kazasthan) 2004; also: Nat. Geographic Centre, Amman, Jordan; Officers' Club, Abu Dhabi, UAE; sports complex, Baghdad, Guests' Palace, Bahrain, univ. bldgs, Sousse, Gabès, Tunisia, sports and golf club houses, Yamoussoukro and Abidjan, 'La Riviera' Hotel and Leisure Complex, Côte d'Ivoire; in France: secondary schools in Tours, Vauréal, Dreux, Argenton sur Creuse, School of Pharmacy, Toulouse, Coca-Cola plant, Grigny, pharmaceutical lab. P. Fabre, Castres, DAF plant, Survilliers, skiing and mountaineering nat. school, Chamonix, Nat. Inst. for Sports and Physical Educ., Paris, pre-Olympic centre, Font-Romeu, nuclear plants Penly and Civaux, Thomson CSF (now EADS – Elancourt/France), Pierre Centre, St Julien en Genevoix, swimming complex at Nogent-sur-Oise 1995, Lycée Raspail, Paris 1995, Commercial and residential complex, St-Quentin-en-Yvelines 1995, Pierre Fabre Lab., Lavaur, 'Les Pyramides' Sport and Leisure Complex, Port-Marly, La Porte Océane, La Rochelle, Aspire, Pierre Fabre Canceropole, Toulouse, Crèche in Montauban, 'Besselue' Villas, La Rochelle; studies for projects in Iraq and Lebanon; feasibility studies for projects in Argentina and Uruguay (hotels, sports facilities, leisure parks, etc.); armed forces Officers' club (Abu Dhabi/UAE), Mercure Grand Hotel, Jebel Hafeet, Al ain (UAE), 'd'Coque' Nat. Sports and Cultural Complex (Luxembourg), Silhouette Tower and Conf. Centre, Doha (Qatar), New Baniyas Stadium (UAE), Coca-Cola extension, Aspire Acad. extension. *Publications:* Montréal – Jeux Olympiques 1976, Construire l'avenir 1977, Roger Taillibert (autobiog.) 1978, Taillibert Architect I and II 1985 1997, Transluscent City 2000, Notre Cher Stade Olympique 2005, Roger Taillibert-Réalisations Vols 1 and 2 2006, Evasions Chromatiques/Roger Taillibert's Paintings 2007, Roger Taillibert: Constructions Vols 1 and 2 2008, Le Parc des Princes 2009, Roger Taillibert Architecte (in French and English) 2010, Entrée Principale 2010, Main Entrance '76' 2011, Montréal mythes et scandales (in French and English) 2011, Book of Sketches 2011, Le Parc Olympique de Montréal 2011; numerous articles and conference presentations for Acad. des Beaux-Arts/Institut de France and other publs. *Leisure interests:* painting, photography, music, sport (especially football). *E-mail:* rtaillibert-1@dial.oleane.com (office).

TAIPALE, Vappu Tuulikki, MD; Finnish politician and child psychiatrist; b. 1 May 1940, Vaasa; m. Ilkka Taipale 1965; two s. two d.; psychiatrist, Aurora Youth Polyclinic 1970–74; Paediatric Clinic 1975–79; Asst Prof. of Child Psychiatry, Kuopio Univ. 1980–83, Tampere Univ. 1983–; First Minister of Social Affairs and Health 1982–83, Second Minister 1983–84; Dir-Gen. Nat. Bd of Social Welfare 1984–90; Dir-Gen. Nat. Agency for Welfare and Health 1991–92, Nat. Research and Devt Centre for Welfare and Health 1992–2008; Co-Pres. Int. Physicians for the Prevention of Nuclear War 2008–12, Grandmaster, Gerontechnology 2014; Pres. Valli (Union for Senior Services), Helsinki 2007–16; Chair. COST A5 Ageing and Tech. Int. Soc. for Gerontechnology, EAG Key Action 6, EU 5th FP; mem. SDP, UNU Council 2001–07, Bd of Trustees, HelpAge International 2016–; Dr hc (Univ. of Vaasa) 1998, (Univ. of Jyväskylä) 2004, (Univ. of Helsinki) 2010. *Publications include:* Rauhan lapset 1982, Lasten mielenterveystyö 1992, Isoäitikirja 2002 (second edn 2017), Vanha ja vireä: Virkistyskirja vanhoille naisille 2011 (second edn 2017), Nuclear Exits (co-ed.) 2015. *E-mail:* vappu@vapputaipale.fi (home).

TAIT, Marion, CBE; British ballet mistress and dancer; *Assistant Director, Birmingham Royal Ballet;* b. 7 Oct. 1950, London, England; d. of Charles Tait and Betty Hooper; m. David Morse 1971; ed Royal Acad. of Dancing and Royal Ballet School; joined Royal Ballet School aged 15, graduating to Royal Ballet's touring co.

(later known as Sadler's Wells Royal Ballet, now Birmingham Royal Ballet), Prin. Dancer 1974, Ballet Mistress (to both co. and students) and still performs character roles 1995–, Asst Dir to David Bintley 2011–; prin. roles include Juliet, Elite Syncopations, Las Hermanas, The Invitation, Hobson's Choice, The Dream, The Burrow, Lizzie Borden in Fall River Legend and Hagar in Pillar of Fire; cr. numerous roles for Kenneth MacMillan and David Bintley; guest appearances world-wide; Dancer of the Year 1994, Evening Standard Ballet Award 1994, Critics' Circle Award with Desmond Kelly for TV programme Ballet Hoo!. *Leisure interest:* needlework, garden. *Address:* Birmingham Royal Ballet, Thorp Street, Birmingham, B5 4AU, England (office). *Telephone:* (121) 245-3500 (office). *Website:* www.brb.org.uk (office).

TAITTINGER, Anne-Claire, MA; French business executive; *President, Riffray SAS;* d. of Jean Taittinger and Corinne Deville; m.; two s.; ed Inst. d'Etudes Politiques de Paris and HEC (CPA Paris); fmr urban planner; fmrly held positions within several Soc. du Louvre cos, Head Soc. du Louvre 1997–2006, Pres. and CEO 2003–06; Chair. Bd Baccarat 1993–2005, Vice-Pres. 2005–06, mem. Bd of Dirs 2006–07; Chair. Exec. Bd Groupe Taittinger 2003–06; fmr Vice-Chair. and Man. Dir Deville SA, Compagnie Financiere Leblanc, ELM Leblanc; currently Pres. Riffray SAS; also currently CEO SAS DFT Immobilier; mem. Supervisory Bd Planet Finance; mem. Bd of Dirs Carrefour Group 2008–, Thales 2012–. *Address:* Riffray SAS, 2 rue Lord Byron, 75008 Paris, France (office). *E-mail:* anneclairetaittinger@free.fr (office).

TAJANI, Antonio; Italian journalist, politician and fmr EU official; *President, European Parliament;* b. 4 Aug. 1953, Rome; m.; two c.; ed La Sapienza Univ., Rome, Scuola di Guerra Aerea, Florence; fmr Officer in Italian Air Force; fmr Air Defence Controller and Head of Operations Room, 33rd Air Force Radar Centre; fmr professional and parl. journalist; Ed. Il Settimanale (weekly newspaper) 1982; Presenter, radio news programme, RAI Uno 1982; Head of Rome editorial office, Il Giornale (daily newspaper) 1983; co-f. Forza Italia 1993; mem. European Parl. 1994–2008, 2004–, Vice-Pres. 2014–17, Pres. 2017–; Vice-Pres., European People's Party 2002–, Head of Forza Italia European Parl. Del. 1999–2008; mem. Rome City Council 2001; Vice-Pres. EC and Commr for Transport 2008–10, Vice-Pres. EC and Commr for Industry and Entrepreneurship 2010–14; Order of Civil Merit, Officier, Légion d'honneur; Honours for the commitment for SMEs and EU integration, Spanish Royal Inst. of European Studies 2012, Innovadores Award 2014, Aragon Empresa Award 2014. *Address:* European Parliament, Bâtiment Altiero Spinelli, 05F243, 60 rue Wiertz, 1047 Brussels, Belgium (office). *E-mail:* tajani@antoniotajani.eu (office). *Website:* www.europarl.europa.eu (office); www.antoniotajani.it.

TAJIN, Marat Muhanbetkaziyevich, PhD; Kazakhstani politician and diplomatist; *First Deputy Head, Office of the President;* b. 8 April 1960, Aktubinsk; ed Almaty Inst. of Nat. Economy, Kazakh State Univ.; scientific researcher –1992; First Deputy Head, then Head of Internal Policy Dept, Deputy Chief of Presidential Apparatus, Head of Information and Analysis Center, Office of the Pres. 1992–94, State Adviser to Pres. 1994–95, Deputy Head, Admin of Pres. and Head, Analysis and Strategic Research Center 1995–99, Nat. Security Asst to Pres. 1999–2001, 2002, 2006–07, Sec., Security Council 1999–2001, Dec. 2001–Aug. 2002, April 2006–Jan. 2007, 2009–13, Chair. Nat. Security Cttee May–Dec. 2001, First Deputy Chief, Admin of Pres. 2002–06; Minister of Foreign Affairs 2007–09; Sec. of State 2013–14; Amb. to Russia 2014–17; First Deputy Head, Office of the Pres. 2017–; Order of Kurmet, Order of Barys. *Address:* Government House, Mangilik Yel, street 6, Nur-Sultan, Kazakhstan (office). *Fax:* (7172) 74-56-31 (office). *E-mail:* aprk@akorda.kz (office). *Website:* www.akorda.kz (office).

TAKÁCS-NAGY, Gábor; Hungarian/Swiss violinist and conductor; *Music Director, Verbier Festival Chamber Orchestra and Manchester Camerata;* b. 17 April 1956, Budapest, Hungary; s. of László Takács-Nagy and Matild Pataki; m. Lesley de Senger (née Townson) 1991; two d.; ed Béla Bartók Conservatory, Franz Liszt Music Acad. of Budapest; f. Takács String Quartet 1976, Takács Piano Trio 1996, Mikrokosmos String Quartet 1998, Camerata Bellerive 2005; concert tours from 1980 every year throughout Europe, every other year in Australia, USA, Japan, South America; Prof., Haute Ecole de Musique, Geneva 1997–; Music Dir Verbier Festival Chamber Orchestra 2007–, Weinberger Kammer Orchestra 2007–, MAV Symphony Orchestra, Budapest 2010–12, Manchester Camerata 2011–; Prin. Guest Conductor, Budapest Festival Orchestra 2012–; Prin. Artistic Partner, Irish Chamber Orchestra 2013–17; Hon. mem. RAM; First Prize Evian Competition 1977, Menuhin Competition (Portsmouth) 1981, Scholarship Award, Banff School of Fine Arts, Franz Liszt Prize 1983, Bartók-Pásztory Award 2017. *Leisure interests:* sport, theatre, hiking, reading. *Address:* Case postale 67, 1222 Vésenaz, Switzerland (home). *E-mail:* Lesley@bellerive-festival.ch (office); ldstn@hotmail.com (home). *Website:* www.bellerive-festival.ch; www.gabortakacsnagy.com.

TAKAHAGI, Mitsunori; Japanese business executive; *Executive Consultant, JX Holdings, Inc.;* b. 3 Dec. 1940, Kanagawa Pref.; ed Faculty of Law, Hitotsubashi Univ.; joined Nippon Mining Co. Ltd 1964, Gen. Man. Products Export Dept, Petroleum Group 1988–89, Gen. Man. Marketing Dept, Petroleum Group 1989–91, Deputy Gen. Man., Chita Oil Refinery, Japan Energy Corpn 1991–94 (Nippon Mining Co. merged with Kyodo Oil Co. in 1992 to create Nikko Kyodo, renamed Japan Energy Corpn 1993), Dir in charge of Industry Energy Dept 1994–96, Dir and Gen. Man. Osaka Br. Office 1996–98, Man. Dir and Gen. Man. Tokyo Br. Office 1998–99, Dir, Exec. Corp. Officer, Gen. Man. of Managerial Staff Group 1999–2001, Dir and Sr Exec. Corp. Officer 2001–02, Pres., Rep. Dir and Dir Nippon Mining Holdings, Inc. 2002–06, Pres. and CEO 2006–10, Pres., CEO and Rep. Dir JX Holdings, Inc. (following incorporation of Nippon Oil Corpn and Nippon Mining Holdings in JX Holdings, Inc. through a share transfer) 2010–12, Exec. Consultant 2012–. *Address:* JX Holdings, Inc., 2-6-3, Ote-machi, Chiyoda-ku, Tokyo 100-0004, Japan (office). *Telephone:* (3) 3502-1131 (office). *Fax:* (3) 3502-9352 (office). *E-mail:* info@hd.jx-group.co.jp (office). *Website:* www.hd.jx-group.co.jp (office).

TAKAHASHI, Genichirō; Japanese writer, critic and academic; b. 1 Jan. 1951, Onomichi, Hiroshima; ed Yokohama Nat. Univ.; participated in student movt 1960s and early 70s, imprisoned for six months; worked as labourer until 1981; novelist and essayist 1982–; currently Prof. of Literature, Meiji Gakuin Univ.;

Visiting Fellow, Donald Keene Center of Japanese Culture, Columbia Univ., USA 2002. *Publications include:* Sayonara Gyangutachi (Gunzō New Writers' Award) (first novel to be translated into English, as Sayonara, Gangsters 2004) 1982, Ōbaa za reinbō (Over the Rainbow) 1984, Oyogu Otoko (The Swimming Man) 1984, Jon Renon tai kaseijin (John Lennon Versus the Martians) 1985, Yūga de kanshōteki Nihon yakkyū (Japanese Baseball: Languid and Happy) (Mishima Yukio Award 1988) 1987, Penguin mura ni hi ga Ochite (Sundown in Penguin Town) 1989, Wakusei P-13 no himitsu (The Secret of Planet 13) 1990, Gosutobasutazu (Ghostbusters) 1997, Godzilla 2001, The Rise and Fall of Japanese Literature (Itoh Sei Literature Award) 2001, May Your Reign Last Forever and Ever 2002, Some Stories on Sex and Love 2005, Miyazawa Kenji's Greatest Hits 2005, Until The Day We Ride the Soul Train 2008, Battling Evil 2010, A Nuclear Reactor in Love 2011, Goodbye, Christopher Robin (Tanizaki Prize 2012) 2012, Ginga tetsudo no kanata ni 2013; numerous collections of essays including Bungaku ga konna ni wakatte ii kashira (Is it Okay to Understand Literature So Well?) 1989. *Address:* Faculty of International Studies, Meiji Gakuin University, 1-2-37 Shirokanedai, Minato-ku, Tokyo 108-8636, Japan.

TAKAHASHI, Hiroaki; Japanese energy industry executive; *Senior Advisor, Tohoku Electric Power Company, Inc.;* ed Tohoku Univ.; joined Tohoku Electric Power Co., Inc. 1963, served in various exec. positions, including Man. of Sec.'s Office, Man. Dir, Vice-Pres. and Chief Dir of Customer Service, Pres. and Rep. Dir –2010, Chair. and Rep. Dir 2010–15, Sr Advisor 2015–; Sr Exec. Officer, Micronics Japan Co. Ltd 2010–; mem. Bd of Dirs The Energy Conservation Centre, Japan, Japan Atomic Power Co. 2009–. *Address:* Tohoku Electric Power Company, Inc., 1-7-1 Honcho, Aoba-ku, Sendai, Miyagi 980-8550, Japan (office). *Telephone:* (22) 225-2111 (office). *Fax:* (22) 225-2550 (office). *Website:* www.tohoku-epco.co.jp (office).

TAKAHASHI, Kozo; Japanese business executive; joined Sharp Corpn 1980s, served as its Exec. Officer and Group Gen. Man. in Health and Environment Systems Group, served as part of man. team of Sharp Electronics Corpn's business-to-business group 1997–2001, Dir of Sharp Electronics Corpn 2010–, Chair. and CEO Sharp Electronics Corpn 2010–12, Group Gen. Man. North and South America Group 2010–12, Chief Officer of Products Business Group, Chief Products Officer of Sharp Corpn 2012–13, Exec. Vice-Pres. 2012–13, Chief Officer of Sales and Marketing 2012–13, Group Gen. Man. Global Business Group, Pres. Sharp Corpn 2013–16, CEO 2015–16.

TAKAHASI, Yutaka, BE, PhD; Japanese engineer and academic; *Professor Emeritus, Faculty of Engineering, University of Tokyo;* b. 28 Jan. 1927; ed Univ. of Tokyo; Lecturer, Faculty of Eng, Univ. of Tokyo 1955–61, Assoc. Prof. 1961–68, Prof. 1968–87, Prof. Emer. 1987–; Prof., Faculty of Eng, Shibaura Inst. of Tech. 1987–98; Sr Academic Adviser, United Nations Univ. 2000–10; mem. Soc. Franco Japonaise des Technique Industrielles, Asscn for Rainwater Storage and Infiltration Tech., Natural Environment Coexistence Tech. Asscn; Suprabal Gorakha Dakshin Bafu (Nepal) 1978; Chevalier des Palmes académiques 1981; Order of the Sacred Treasure (Second Class) 2007 Nat. Land Agency Achievement Award for Water Resources 1987, Meijimura Award 1994, Achievement Award, Japan Soc. of Civil Engineers 1998, Crystal Drop Award, Int. Water Resources Asscn 2000, Academic Award, Japanese Asscn of Groundwater Hydrology 2011, Japan Prize 2015. *Publications:* numerous papers in professional journals on resources, energy and social infrastructure. *Address:* Faculty of Engineering, University of Tokyo, 7-3-1 Hongo, Bunkyo, Tokyo, 113-8654, Japan (office). *Website:* www.t.u-tokyo.ac.jp (office).

TAKAICHI, Sanae; Japanese politician; b. 7 March 1961; m. Taku Yamamoto; ed Faculty of Business Admin, Kobe Univ.; with Matsushita Inst. of Govt and Man. 1984–87; Congressional Fellow and mem. staff of fmr US Congresswoman Patricia Schroeder, Washington, DC 1987–89; Lecturer, Nihon Jr Coll. of Econs 1989–93; mem. House of Reps (LDP) 1993–, Deputy Chair. LDP Research Comm. on Security 1997, Deputy Dir LDP Public Speeches Div. 1997, Deputy Dir LDP Comm. on Small and Medium Sized Enterprises 1997, Dir Nara 1st Election Dist Br. 1997, Acting Dir LDP Finance Div. 1997, Deputy Dir LDP Youth Div. 1997; State Sec. for Int. Trade and Industry 1998–2000, Chair. Cttee on Educ., Culture, Sports, Science and Tech. 2001, Chair. Sub-cttee on Fundamental and Organizational Role of Politics, Research Comm. on Constitution 2002, Deputy Chair. LDP Gen. Council 2002, Dir-Gen. LDP Information Research Bureau 2005–06; Sr Vice-Minister of Economy, Trade and Industry 2002–04; Minister of State for Okinawa and Northern Territories Affairs, Science and Tech. Policy, Innovation, Gender Equality, Social Affairs and Food Safety 2006–07, Minister of Internal Affairs and Communications 2014–17; Prof., Faculty of Econs, Kinki Univ. 2004–. *Address:* Liberal-Democratic Party (Jiyu-Minshuto), 1-11-23, Nagata-cho, Chiyoda-ku, Tokyo 100-8910, Japan (office). *Telephone:* (3) 3581-6211 (office). *Website:* www.jimin.jp (office); rep.sanae.gr.jp.

TAKAMATSU, Shin, PhD; Japanese architect; *Executive Director, Shin Takamatsu Architect and Associates;* b. 5 Aug. 1948, Shimane Pref.; s. of Toshio Takamatsu and Yuriko Takamatsu; m. Toshiko Hariguchi 1970; two d.; ed Kyoto Univ.; Prin. Architect, Shin Takamatsu Architects and Assocs, Kyoto 1980, Exec. Dir 2013–; Rep. Dir Takamatsu Planning Ltd 1988–; Prof., Graduate School of Eng, Kyoto Univ. 1997–2013, Prof. Emer. 2013–; mem. Nihon Kenchiku Gakai (Japan Architecture Inst.) 1989–, Japan Inst. of Architecture 1993–; Hon. mem. AIA 1995, Asscn of German Architects 1997; Japan Architects Asscn Prize 1984, Venice Biennale Prize 1985, Second Int. Interior Design Award 1987, Architectural Inst. of Japan Prize 1989, Grand Prize, Journal of Japanese Soc. of Commercial Space Designers 1989, Architectural Inst. of Japan Prize 1990, Kyoto Pref. Meritorious Cultural Service Award 1994, Art Encouragement Prize, Ministry of Educ. 1996, Public Architecture Prize 1998, Osaka Landscape Architecture Award 2011. *Publications:* Works-Shin Takamatsu 1984, Architecture and Nothingness 1996, To the Poetic Space 1998. *Leisure interests:* architecture, furniture design. *Address:* Shin Takamatsu Architects and Associates, 195 Jobodaiin-cho Takeda, Fushimi-ku, Kyoto 612, Japan. *Telephone:* (7) 5621-6002 (office). *Fax:* (7) 5621-6079 (office). *E-mail:* syntax@takamatsu.co.jp (office). *Website:* www.takamatsu.co.jp (office).

TAKASHIMA, Tatsuyoshi; Japanese advertising industry executive; joined Dentsu Inc. (advertising agency) 1966, has held several man. positions including Sr Man. Dir, Exec. Vice-Pres. –2007, Pres. and COO 2007–09, Rep. Dir 2007–11,

Pres. and CEO 2009–11, Chair., Pres. and CEO 2011–13; fmr Exec. Dir Japan Marketing Asscn; mem. Supervisory Bd Publicis Groupe SA 2008–12; mem. Bd of Dirs Tokyo Broadcasting System Holdings Inc. 2009–; mem. Foundation Bd, International Inst. for Man. Devt.

TAKASU, Yukio, LLB; Japanese diplomatist and UN official; *Special Adviser on Human Security, United Nations;* ed Univ. of Tokyo, Merton Coll., Oxford; First Sec., then Counsellor, Perm. Mission to UN, New York 1981–88, Dir Western Europe Div., Ministry of Foreign Affairs 1989–92, Deputy Chief of Mission, Embassy in Jakarta 1992–93, Asst Sec.-Gen. and Controller, UN, New York 1993–97, Amb. and Perm. Rep. to UN, New York 1997–2000, Dir-Gen. Multilateral Co-operation Dept, Ministry of Foreign Affairs 2000–01, Perm. Rep. to IAEA and UNIDO 2001–05, Amb. responsible for Human Security, Science and Tech. Co-operation, also Special Envoy for UN Reform 2005–06, Amb. and Perm. Rep. to UN, New York 2007–10, Special Adviser to the Sec.-Gen. on Human Security, UN 2011–12, 2017–, Under-Sec.-Gen. for Management, UN 2012–17; Prof., Nat. Grad. Inst. for Policy Studies; Visiting Fellow, Harvard Univ., USA 2006–07. *Address:* United Nations, 405 East 42nd Street, New York, NY 10017, USA (office). *Website:* www.un.org/humansecurity (office).

TAKEBE, Tsutomu; Japanese politician; *Special Adviser, Japan-Viet Nam Friendship Parliamentary Alliance;* b. 1 May 1941, Hokkaido Pref.; ed Waseda Univ.; elected to Hokkaido Ass. 1971; elected to House of Reps 1986; Vice-Minister, Hokkaido Devt Agency 1990–92, Vice-Minister, Ministry of Transport 1992–94, apptd Chair. Commerce and Industry Cttee 1996, Judicial Affairs Cttee 1999, Rules and Admin Cttee 2003; apptd Dir Transport Div., LDP 1994, Dir Cabinet Div. 1994, Deputy Sec.-Gen. 1998, Deputy Chair. Policy Research 2000, Chief Deputy Chair. Policy Research 2002, Sec.-Gen. 2004–06; currently Special Adviser, Japan-Viet Nam Friendship Parl. Alliance.

TAKEICHI, Masatoshi, MSc, PhD; Japanese cell biologist and academic; *Team Leader, RIKEN Centre for Developmental Biology;* b. 27 Nov. 1943, Nagoya; ed Nagoya and Kyoto Univs; Asst Prof., Dept of Biophysics, Faculty of Science, Kyoto Univ. 1970–78, Assoc. Prof. 1978–86, Prof. 1986–99, Head, Centre for Molecular and Developmental Biology 1993–98, Prof., Dept of Cell and Developmental Biology, Grad. School of Biostudies 1999–2002; Visiting Prof., Nat. Inst. for Basic Biology 1992–97; Dir RIKEN Centre for Developmental Biology, Kobe 2000–14, Team Leader 2015–; Assoc. Ed., Cell Structure and Function 1983–, Neuron 1988–2016, Molecular Biology of the Cell 1989–97, Development, Growth and Differentiation 1990–, Developmental Biology 1991–95 (mem. Editorial Bd 1995–), Developmental Cell 2001–; Reviewing Ed. Science 1996–99; mem. Advisory Bd, Development 1987–2003; mem. Editorial Bd, Differentiation 1988–, Current Opinion in Cell Biology 1989–, Cell 1991–94, Trends in Genetics 1994–2010, Genes and Development 1995–, Molecular and Cellular Neuroscience 1995–, Genes to Cells 1996–, Developmental Dynamics 1996–2002, Journal of Cell Biology 1998–2000, Journal of Neuroscience 1998–2003; mem. Japan Acad. 2000, Japanese Soc. of Developmental Biologists (Pres. 1999–), Japan Soc. for Cell Biology (Bd mem.), Molecular Biology Soc. of Japan, Japan Neuroscience Soc. 2001, Japanese Cancer Asscn (Bd mem. –2000), Japanese Soc. for Molecular Biology, American Soc. for Cell Biology, Int. Soc. of Developmental Biologists (Bd mem.); Foreign Assoc. NAS 2007; Assoc. mem. European Molecular Biology Org. (EMBO) 2009; Fellow, AAAS 2014; Special Prof., Nagoya Univ. 2010; Dr hc (Ghent Univ.) 2012; Toray Science and Tech. Grant 1984, Asahi Gakujyutsu Grant 1985, Naito Foundation Special Project Grant 1988–90, Tsukahara Nakaakira Award 1989, Chunichi Culture Award 1992, Dunham Lecturer, Harvard Medical School 1993, Osaka Science Award 1993, Keith Porter Lecturer, 33rd Annual Meeting of American Soc. of Cell Biology 1993, Asahi Award, Asahi Shimbun 1994, Jean Brachet Lecturer, 8th Congress of Int. Soc. of Differentiation 1994, Academic Prize, The Princess Takamatsuno-miya Cancer Research Foundation 1995, Japan Acad. Prize 1996, Uehara Award 1996, Ross Harrison Prize, Int. Soc. of Developmental Biologists 2001, Keio Medical Science Prize 2001, Person of Cultural Merits 2004, Japan Prize, Science and Tech. Foundation of Japan (co-recipient) 2005, Lecturer, Ceremony of the Kosho Hajime (Imperial New Year Lectures) 2011, Thomson Reuters Citation Laureate 2012, Meister Award, Japan Endocrine Soc. 2014. *Publications:* numerous articles in scientific journals. *Address:* RIKEN Centre for Developmental Biology, 2-2-3 Minatojima-minami-machi, Chuo-ku, Kobe 650-0047, Japan (office). *Telephone:* (78) 306-0111 (office). *Fax:* (78) 306-0101 (office). *E-mail:* takeichi@cdb.riken.jp (office). *Website:* www.cdb.riken.go.jp (office).

TAKENAKA, Heizo, PhD; Japanese economist, academic and government official; *Chairman, Pasona Group Inc.;* b. 3 March 1951; ed Hitotsubashi Univ. and Osaka Univ.; joined Japan Devt Bank 1973, Research Inst. of Capital Formation 1977; Visiting Scholar, Harvard Univ., USA 1981, Visiting Assoc. Prof. 1989; Visiting Scholar, Univ. of Pennsylvania 1981; Assoc. Prof., Faculty of Econs, Osaka Univ. 1987; Visiting Fellow, Inst. of Int. Econs 1989; Assoc. Prof., Faculty of Policy Man., Keio Univ. 1990, Prof., Faculty of Policy Man. 1996, 2006–, Dir Global Security Research Inst. 2001, 2004, 2006–; Minister of State for Econ. and Fiscal Policy 2001–05, for Information Tech. Policy 2001–02, for Financial Services Agency 2002–04, for Privatization of the Postal Services 2004–06, of Internal Affairs and Communications 2005–06; mem. House of Councillors, Diet, Tokyo 2004–05; Chair. Pasona Group Inc. 2009–; Dir The Tokyo Foundation (fmrly Global Foundation for Research and Scholarship) 1997, Exec. Dir 1998, Pres. 1999. *Publications:* in Japanese: The Economics of Business Investment 1984, The Macroeconomic Analysis of External Imbalances 1987, The Economics of US–Japan Friction 1991, The Globalization of the Japanese Economy and Corporate Investment 1993, Wealth of People 1994, The Economy in Which Fast Movers Win 1998; in English: Contemporary Japanese Economy and Economic Policy 1991; popular writing includes a cartoon book explaining economics. *Address:* Office of the Chairman, Pasona Group Inc., Otemachi 2-6-4 Chiyoda-ku, Tokyo 100-8228, Japan (office). *Website:* www.pasonagroup.co.jp/english (office); takenakaheizo.cocolog-nifty.com.

TAKENAKA, Kyoji; Japanese manufacturing industry executive; *Head, Robot Business Promotion Council;* b. 28 Nov. 1946; joined Fuji Heavy Industries Ltd 1969, Staff Gen. Man. Product Planning Office 1998–91, Staff Gen. Man. Product Planning Div. 1991–95, Project Gen. Man. Subara Devt and Eng Div. 1995–99, Vice-Pres., Project Gen. Man. of Product Planning Office and Gen. Man. Special Version Devt Dept 1999–2000, Vice-Pres., Sr Gen. Man. of Corp. Planning Div. and Gen. Man. Alliance Promotion Office 2000–01, Pres. and COO 2001–03, Pres. and CEO Fuji Heavy Industries Ltd 2003–06; currently Head of Robot Business Promotion Council, Japan Robot Asscn. *Address:* Robot Business Promotion Council, c/o Japan Robot Association, Kikaishinko Bldg., 3-5-8 Shiba-koen, Minato-ku, Tokyo 105-0011, Japan. *Telephone:* (3) 3434-2919. *Fax:* (3) 3578-1404. *Website:* www.jara.jp/e.

TAKESY, Asterio R.; Micronesian government official and diplomatist (retd) and banking executive; *Vice-President of Governmental Affairs for Neighboring Islands, Bank of Guam;* b. 25 May 1944, Chuuk (fmrly Truk) State; m. Justina Yangilmau; three d.; ed Xavier High School, Univ. of Guam, Univ. of New Mexico, USA; began career as an admin. asst in Chuuk Dist Educ. Dept, followed by stints in Trust Territory of the Pacific Islands HQ Information Office, Saipan, Northern Mariana Islands; also served as Chief Clerk in fmr Congress of the Micronesian House of Representatives; Asst Sec. for the Micronesia Constitutional Convention 1975; Exec. Dir Comm. on Future Political Association with the US 1975–79; served as the Rep. of Micronesia to USA (effectively Amb. though term not officially used) 1979–82; Deputy Sec. of Foreign Affairs 1982–89, Acting Sec. 1989–91; represented Western Namonwitto and Hall Islands of Chuuk State at Second Micronesia Constitutional Convention 1990; Sec. of Resources and Devt 1991–95, Sec. for Foreign Affairs 1995–97; Exec. Dir for the Jt Cttee on Compact Econ. Negotiations 1997–2000; Exec. Dir South Pacific Regional Environmental Program (SPREP), Apia, Samoa 2003–09; Sr Advisor, Conceptus Consultants Inc., Washington, DC 2009–11, Amb. to USA 2012–16; Vice-Pres. of Governmental Affairs for Neighboring Islands, Bank of Guam, Kolonia, Pohnpei 2016–. *Address:* Bank of Guam, Kolonia, Pohnpei FM 96941, Micronesia (office). *Website:* www.bankofguam.com (office).

TAKEYAMA, Minoru, BArch, MArch; Japanese architect and academic; *Principal, Minoru Takeyama architect & U/A;* b. 15 March 1934, Sapporo; ed Waseda Univ., Harvard Univ., USA; began career with Josep Lluis Sert, Mass, USA 1960–61, Harrison Abramovitz, New York 1961, Jorn Utzon, Arne Jacobsen and Henning Larsen, Copenhagen, Denmark 1962–64; returned to Japan and est. Minoru Takeyama architect & United Actions, Prin. 1965–, opened second office in Sapporo 1975; Prof. of Architecture, Musashino Art Univ., Tokyo 1975–, currently Prof. of Architectural and Urban Design; Visiting Prof., Royal Danish Acad. of Fine Arts, Copenhagen 1962–63, Univ. Manitoba 1979, Univ. of Hong Kong 1981, Nat. Univ. of Singapore 1983, Univ. of California, Berkeley 1997, 1978, 1979, 1986, Harvard Univ. 1987, Univ. of Illinois, Ubana-Champaign 1989–90, Tech. Univ. of Liberec, Czech Repub. 2006; mem. Architectural Inst. of Japan, Japan Inst. of Architects; Hon. Fellow, AIA 1993–, Hon. mem. Soc. of Czech Architects 2006–; Special Prize, First World Biennale of Architecture, Bulgaria 1981, Annual Design Award 1987, Int. Illumination Design Award 1992, Honour Award of Waterfront Design 1993, Tokyo Design Award 1993. *Buildings include:* Ichiban-kan, Number One Bldg 1969, Niban-kan, Number Two Bldg 1970, Hotel Beverley Tom, Hokkaido 1973, Atelier Indigo studio, Sapporo 1976, Nakamura Hospital, Sapporo 1978, Sweet Factory, Nara 1985, Renaissance Bldg, Kyoto 1986, Tokyo Port Terminal 1991, Crematorium, Cemetery and Memorial Complex, Yokohama 2001, Central Railway Station Complex, Seoul 2002; co-f. post-modernist group ARCHITEXT 1971. *Publications:* Blue Nirvana 1972, Autobiography of an Architect 1973, Street Semiology 1975, Meaning of Streets 1977, Language in Architecture 1983, Tokyo Urban Language 1984. *Address:* Minoru Takeyama architect & U/A, 4-6-26, Komaba Meguro-ku, Tokyo (office); Musashino Art University, 1-736 Ogawa-cho, Kodaira-shi, Tokyo 187-8505, Japan. *Telephone:* (3) 5790-6268 (office). *Fax:* (3) 5454-8531 (office). *E-mail:* info@m-take.com (office). *Website:* www.m-take.com (office); www.musabi.ac.jp.

TAKIZAKI, Takemitsu; Japanese business executive; *Chair, Keyence Corporation;* b. 10 June 1945; m.; f. Lead Electric Co. (mfr of electronic sensors) 1974, later renamed Keyence Corpn, becoming Pres. and Rep. Dir, Chair. and Rep. Dir 2000–. *Address:* Office of the Chairman, Keyence Corporation, 1-3-14 Higashi-nakajima, Higashi-Yodogawa, Osaka, Japan (office). *Telephone:* (6) 6379-1111 (office). *Website:* www.keyence.com (office).

TAKUMIYA, Osamu; Japanese health care industry executive; *Advisor, Mediceo Corporation;* Vice-Pres. Kuraya Sanseido Inc. 2001, Vice-Pres. and Exec. Dir of Sales 2003, Chair. and Rep. Dir Kuraya Sanseido Inc. (following separation of pharmaceutical distribution from purchasing businesses to form new Kuraya Sanseido Inc. and Mediceo Holdings Co. Ltd, as parts of Mediceo Group) 2004–09, Chair. and Rep. Dir Mediceo Corpn (after merger of several Mediceo Group cos) 2009–, Hon. Chair. –2016, Advisor 2016–. *Address:* Mediceo Corporation, 7-15 Yaesu 2-chome, Chuo-ku, Tokyo 104-8464, Japan (office). *Telephone:* (3) 3517-5800 (office). *Fax:* (3) 230-5566 (office). *E-mail:* staff@mediceo-gp.com (office). *Website:* www.mediceo.co.jp (office).

TAL, Hisham; Jordanian lawyer, judge and government official; *Chairman, Constitutional Court;* b. 1943, Irbid; ed Damascus Univ.; Judge, Court of Cassation and Higher Court of Justice 1991–94; Deputy Prime Minister and Minister of Political Devt and Parl. Affairs 2005; Pres. Legislation and Opinion Bureau 2009–10; Minister of Justice 2010–11; Pres. Higher Judicial Council and Court of Cassation 2012–17; Chair. Constitutional Court 2018–. *Address:* Tlaa al-Ali, 12 al-Hatimiah Street, Amman 11953, Jordan (office). *Telephone:* (6) 5505777 (office). *Fax:* (6) 5513248 (office). *E-mail:* info@cco.gov.jo (office). *Website:* www.cco.gov.jo (office).

TALAGI, Sir Toke Tufukia, KNZM, BAgric Sc; Niuean politician; *Premier;* b. 9 Jan. 1951, Alofi; s. of Sione Talagi and Pelenita Talagi; m. Emeline Fifitaloa Peleni; three c.; ed Nelson Coll., Massey Univ., New Zealand; elected to Nat. Ass. 1999; fmr Deputy Prime Minister, Minister of Educ.; Premier 2008–, also Chair. of Cabinet and Minister for Central and Commercial Agencies; Chair. Pacific Islands Forum 2008; Pres. Niue Rugby Union. *Leisure interest:* reading. *Address:* Office of the Premier, PO Box 40, Fale Fono, Alofi, Niue (office). *Telephone:* 4200 (office).

TALAL, Prince Walid bin, BSc, MA; Saudi Arabian business executive; *Founder and Chairman, Kingdom Holding Company;* b. 7 March 1955, Riyadh; s. of HRH Prince Talal bin Abd al-Aziz a-Sa'ud and Princess Mona as-Solh; nephew of HM King Abdullah bin Abd al-Aziz a Sa'ud; m. 1st Dalal bint Saud bin Abdul Aziz; one s. one d.; m. 4th Princess Ameerah al Taweel; ed Menlo Coll., Calif., Syracuse

Univ., NY, USA; began building investment portfolio 1979; Chair. United Saudi Bank 1988–99; Founder and Chair. Kingdom Holding Co. 1980– (now one of the largest and most diversified private investment cos in the world); investments in numerous int. cos, including Citigroup Inc., News Corpn, Euro Disney SCA, Planet Hollywood chain of restaurants, Apple Computers, Fairmont Hotels & Resorts, PepsiCo Inc., Procter & Gamble, Kodak, Motorola, Compaq Computer Group, Savoy Hotel, London, Twitter, Beijing Jingdong Trading Co. (Chinese online retailer) etc.; unveiled plans to construct the world's tallest building, Kingdom Tower in Jeddah 2011; also struck deal with Bloomberg to launch own news channel 2011; investments in Nigeria through Kingdom Zephyr Africa Management 2012; Hon. Citizen of 19 cities 1998–2009; numerous decorations, including Grand Officer, Nat. Cedar Medal (Lebanon) 2002, Nat. Order of the Lion (Senegal) 2003, Officer, Order of Orange Nassau (Netherlands) 2003, Hilal i Pakistan Medal 2006, Commdr, Légion d'honneur 2006, Grand Officer, Order of the Golden Heart (Philippines) 2007, Order of the Brilliant Star with Grand Cordon Medal (Taiwan) 2007, Pontifical Medal (Vatican) 2008; 20 hon. doctorates from univs in USA, UK, Bosnia and Herzegovina, Bulgaria, Central Africa Republic, Egypt, Ghana, Indonesia, Korea, Lebanon, Madagascar, Malaysia, Palestine, Philippines, Tunisia and Uganda; Presidential Medal, Univ. of New Haven, Conn., USA 1999, Vermeil Medal, St Joseph's Univ. (Lebanon) 2010. *Address:* Kingdom Holding Co., PO Box 1, Riyadh 11321, Saudi Arabia (office). *Telephone:* (1) 211-1111 (office). *Fax:* (1) 211-1112 (office). *E-mail:* media&info@kingdom.com.sa (office). *Website:* www.kingdom.com.sa (office); www.alwaleedfoundations.org.

TALAT, Mehmet Ali, MSc; Turkish-Cypriot politician; b. 6 July 1952, Kyrenia; m.; one s. one d.; ed Middle East Tech. Univ., Ankara, Eastern Mediterranean Univ., Famagusta; began career as self-employed electrical engineer; active in Turkish Cypriot orgs, Co-founder and first Chair. Cypriots Educ. and Youth Fed. (KÖGEF), Turkey; joined youth div. Republican Turkish Party (Cumhuriyetçi Türk Partisi, CTP), mem. CTP Party Council, and Cen. Exec. Cttee, also CTP Sec., becoming Chair. 1996–; Minister of Educ. and Culture 1994, later Minister of State and Deputy Prime Minister; mem. Parl. for Nicosia 1998–; Prime Minister of 'Turkish Repub. of Northern Cyprus' 2004–05, Pres. 2005–10. *Address:* Mersin Cad 9, Kyrenia, Turkish Republic of Northern Cyprus (home). *Telephone:* (392) 2293242 (home). *E-mail:* mat@defne.net.

TALBAKOV, Ismoil; Tajikistani economist and politician; *Chairman, Communist Party of Tajikistan;* b. 24 March 1955; m.; four c.; ed Tajik State Univ.; fmr officer in Soviet Army; mem. Majlisi Namoyandagon (Parl.); fmr Sec., Cen. Cttee, CP of Tajikistan, Chair. 2016–; unsuccessful cand. in presidential elections 2006, 2013. *Address:* Communist Party of Tajikistan, 734002 Dushanbe, Kuchai F. Niyazi 37, Tajikistan (office). *Telephone:* (372) 23-29-53 (office).

TALBOTT, Strobe; American journalist and fmr government official; b. 25 April 1946, Dayton, Ohio; s. of Nelson S. Talbott and Josephine Large; m. 1st Brooke Lloyd Shearer 1971 (died 2009); two s.; m. 2nd Barbara Lazear Ascher 2015; ed Hotchkiss School, Connecticut, Yale Univ. and Univ. of Oxford, UK; joined Time magazine, Diplomatic Corresp., White House Corresp., Eastern Europe Corresp., Washington Bureau Chief 1984–89, Ed.-at-Large 1989–94; Amb.-at-Large, US State Dept Feb.–Dec. 1993, Deputy Sec. of State 1994–2001; Pres. The Brookings Inst. 2002–17; Chair. Foreign Affairs Policy Bd, US State Dept 2011–17; Rhodes Scholar, Univ. of Oxford 1969; Dir Carnegie Endowment for Int. Peace; mem. Council on Foreign Relations; Fellow, American Acad. of Arts and Sciences 2009–; Dr hc (Monterey Inst., Trinity Coll., Georgetown Univ., Washington Univ. in St Louis, Fairfield Univ.). *Publications include:* Khrushchev Remembers 1970, Khrushchev Remembers: The Last Testament (jtly) 1974, Endgame: The Inside Story of Salt II 1979, Deadly Gambits: The Reagan Administration and the Stalemate in Nuclear Arms Control 1984, The Russians and Reagan 1984, Reagan and Gorbachev (jtly) 1987, The Master of the Game: Paul Nitze and the Nuclear Peace 1988, At the Highest Levels: The Inside Story of the End of the Cold War (jtly) 1993, The Age of Terror: America and The World After September 11 (co-ed.) 2001, The Russia Hand: A Memoir of Presidential Diplomacy 2002, Engaging India 2005, The Great Experiment 2008, Fast Forward: Ethics and Politics in the Age of Global Warming (with William Antholis) 2010.

TALENT, James (Jim) Matthes, BA, JD; American politician; *Distinguished Fellow, Heritage Foundation;* b. 18 Oct. 1956, Des Peres, Mo.; s. of Milton Talent and Marie Talent (née Matthes); m. Brenda Talent 1984; one s. two d.; ed Kirkwood High School, Washington Univ., St Louis and Univ. of Chicago Law School; clerk to Judge of US Court of Appeals 1982–83; mem. Mo. House of Reps 1984–92, later Minority Leader –1992; mem. US House of Reps from Second Dist, Mo. 1992–2000, later Asst Minority Leader, mem. Armed Services Cttee 1992–2000, Small Business Cttee 1992–2000 (Chair. 1997), Educ. Cttee; Senator from Missouri 2003–07; Distinguished Fellow, Heritage Foundation, Washington, DC 2007–; Vice-Chair. Comm. on Prevention of Weapons of Mass Destruction Proliferation and Terrorism 2008; mem. US-China Econ. and Security Review Comm.; Arnold J. Lien Prize for Most Outstanding Undergrad. in Political Science, Nat. Asscn of Women Business Owners' Nat. Public Policy Award (first male recipient), named Legislator of the Year by Dept of Missouri Veterans of Foreign Wars, Int. Franchise Asscn and Ind. Electrical Contractors, Vietnam Veterans of America's Lifetime Achievement Award 2000. *Address:* Heritage Foundation, 214 Massachusetts Ave, NE, Washington, DC 20002-4999 (office); 9433 Olive Blvd, St Louis, MO 63132, USA (home). *Telephone:* (314) 453-0344 (home). *Fax:* (314) 453-0805 (home). *E-mail:* staff@heritage.org (office). *Website:* www.heritage.org/about/staff/t/jim-talent (office).

TALIBOV, Vasif Yusif oğlu, PhD; Azerbaijani politician; *Chairman, Ali Mäclis (Supreme Assembly) of the Autonomous Republic of Naxçıvan;* b. 14 Jan. 1960, Aralig, Ilyich (now Şarur Dist), Naxçıvan ASSR, Azerbaijan SSR, USSR; s. of Yusif Talibov and Minaye Talibova; m. Sevil Sultanova; two s. one d.; ed Naxçıvan State Pedagogical Inst., Baku State Univ.; began career with Ilyich Dist (now Şarur Dist) Public Educ. Dept 1976; secondary school teacher, Damirchi, Ilyich Dist 1981–82; Cadre Inspector, Naxçıvan Knitted Goods Factory 1982; military service at Border Military Forces 1982–83; Head, Special Dept Sewing, Knitting and Carpetmaking Manufacturing Asscn 1983; Sr Asst, Ali Mäclis (Supreme Ass.) of Autonomous Repub. of Naxçıvan 1991–94, First Deputy of Prime Minister for Foreign Economic Relations 1994–95, Deputy (mem. Parl.) Ali Mäclis, Azerbaijan Repub. 1995–, Chair. Ali Mäclis 2005–; Founder-mem. Yeni Azärbaycan Partiyasi (YAP—New Azerbaijan Party); mem. Co-ordinating Council, Congress of Azerbaijanis Worldwide 2001–; Order of Glory of Azerbaijan Republic, Order of Honour of Georgia. *Address:* Ali Mäclis (Supreme Assembly) of the Autonomous Republic of Naxçıvan, 7000 Naxçıvan, H. Aliyev pr. 50, Azerbaijan (office). *Telephone:* (36) 544-01-18 (office). *E-mail:* xaricielaqeler@alimeclis.az (office). *Website:* www.alimeclis.az (office).

TALLAWY, Mervat Mehani Ahmed; Egyptian diplomatist and international organization official; *Director General, Arab Women Organization;* b. 1 Dec. 1937, Menya; d. of Mehani Tallawy and Soraya Abdel-Hamid; m. Dr Ali Abdel-Rahman Rahmy 1964; one d.; ed American Univ. Cairo, Inst. for Diplomatic Studies, Cairo and Grad. Inst. of Int. Studies, Switzerland, Harvard Law School, USA; joined Ministry of Foreign Affairs 1963, served in Geneva, New York and Caribbean countries, Vienna and Tokyo; Deputy Dir UN Inst. for Advancement of Women 1982–85; Amb. to Austria and Resident Rep. to IAEA, UNIDO and UN Centre for Social and Humanitarian Affairs 1988–91, Dir of Int. Econ. Dept, Ministry of Foreign Affairs 1991, Asst Minister for Int. Political and Econ. Affairs 1992–93, Amb. to Japan 1993–97; Minister of Insurance and Social Affairs 1997–99; Sec.-Gen. Nat. Council for Women 2000; UN Under-Sec.-Gen. and Exec. Dir UN Econ. and Social Comm. for Western Asia (ESCWA) 2000–07; Rapporteur-Gen. UN Conf. on Adoption of Int. Convention on Prevention of Illicit Drug Trafficking, Vienna 1988; Co-ordinator-Gen. for the Arab Econ. and Social Summit, Kuwait 2009; mem. UN Cttee on Elimination of Discrimination against Women (CEDAW) (Chair. 1990–92); Chair. UN Comm. on Status of Women 1991–93; Chair. workshop on Women and Violence leading to adoption of UN Declaration on Elimination of Violence Against Women, Vienna 1992; Chair. Working Group on Health, UN Int. Conf. for Advancement of Women, Beijing 1995; Head, Egyptian Del. to Multilateral Middle East Peace Talks Working Group on Econ. Regional Co-operation, Brussels 1992, Paris 1992, Rome 1993 and to Steering Cttee of Multilateral Middle East Talks, Tokyo 1994; Head, Egyptian Del. to UN World Conf. on Natural Disasters, Yokohama 1994; Del. to UN Environment Conf., Rio de Janeiro 1992; Head, Negotiation Group to UN Int. Conf. on Population and Devt, Cairo 1994; initiator of proposal leading to adoption of UN Declaration for Protection of Women and Children in Time of Armed Conflicts 1974; Founder-mem. Egyptian Social Democratic Party 2011; Chair. Egyptian Nat. Council of Women 2012; Head, Egyptian Del. to UN Comm. on Status of Women 2013; Dir-Gen. Arab Women Org. 2014–; mem. Cttee of Fifty for Drafting the New Constitution of Egypt 2013; mem. Club of Rome; Amb. of the Year (Austria) 1991, Nat. Order of the Cedar (Lebanon). *Leisure interests:* theatre, classical music, walking, reading, painting. *Address:* 8 El-Kamel Mohammed, El Zamalek, 11211 Cairo, Egypt. *Telephone:* (2) 735-8102. *Fax:* (2) 735-8102. *E-mail:* tallawy@hotmail.com.

TALMACI, Leonid; Moldovan economist and banker; *Chairman, BC Moldindconbank SA;* b. 26 April 1956, Reteni; m. Nina Talmaci 1977; one d.; ed Financial Banking Coll., Chişinău, Financial-Econ. Inst. Leningrad (now St Petersburg); Prin. Economist, Stroibank USSR 1984–88; Deputy Head Dept, Promstroibank USSR 1988, Chair. Energomash Bank 1988–91; Gov. Nat. Bank of Moldova 1991–2009 (resgnd); Deputy Chair. Russia Bank Asscn 1990–92; Pres. Asscn of Banks of Moldova 2013; Chair. BC Moldindconbank SA 2015–; Knight of the Order of the Republic 2001. *Address:* BC Moldindconbank SA, 2012 Chişinău, str. Armenească, 38, Moldova (office). *Telephone:* (22) 57-67-82 (office). *Fax:* (22) 27-91-95 (office). *Website:* www.micb.md (office).

TALMI, Igal, DrScNat; Israeli physicist and academic; *Professor Emeritus, Department of Particle Physics, Weizmann Institute of Science;* b. 31 Jan. 1925, Kiev, Ukraine; s. of Moshe Talmi and Lea Talmi (née Weinstein); m. Chana Talmi (née Kivelewitz) 1949; one s. one d.; ed Herzlia High School, Hebrew Univ. of Jerusalem and Swiss Fed. Inst. of Tech.; served in Israeli Defence Forces 1947–49; Research Fellow, Princeton Univ. 1952–54, Visiting Assoc. Prof. 1956–57, Visiting Prof. 1961–62, 1966–67; apptd Prof. of Physics, Weizmann Inst. of Science 1958, Prof. Emer. 1995–, Head, Dept of Nuclear Physics 1967–76, Dean Faculty of Physics 1970–84; mem. Israel Acad. of Sciences and Humanities 1963–, Chair. Div. of Sciences 1974–80; Weizmann Prize of the Tel-Aviv Municipality 1962, Israel Prize (with A. de Shalit) 1965, Rothschild Prize, 1971, Hans A. Bethe Prize, American Physical Soc. 2000, EMT Prize 2003. *Publications include:* Nuclear Shell Theory (with A. de Shalit) 1963, Simple Models of Complex Nuclei 1993, numerous publs on theoretical nuclear physics. *Leisure interest:* bird watching. *Address:* Department of Particle Physics, Weizmann Institute of Science, Rehovot 76100, Israel (office). *Telephone:* (8) 9342060 (office); (8) 9468166 (home). *Fax:* (8) 9344106 (office). *E-mail:* igal.talmi@weizmann.ac.il (office). *Website:* www.weizmann.ac.il/(office); www.weizmann.ac.il/physics/staff/Talmi.htm (office).

TALON, Patrice Guillaume Athanase; Benin business executive, politician and head of state; *President;* b. 1 May 1958, Ouidah; m. Claudine Gbénagnon; two c.; ed Univ. of Dakar, Senegal, Ecole Nat. de l'Aviation Civile, Paris, France; accepted for airline pilot training with Air Afrique but forced to give up after failing medical test; several years working in cotton industry; f. Société de Distribution Intercontinentale (providing agricultural inputs to cotton farmers), Benin 1985; Founder, Société de financement et de participation (major holding co. with subsidiaries in several countries in W Africa; financed electoral campaigns of Pres. Thomas Boni Yayi 2006, 2011; accused of masterminding plot to poison Boni Yayi 2012, fled to exile in France 2012; returned to Benin after receiving presidential pardon 2015; Pres. of Benin 2016–. *Address:* Office of the President, BP 1288, Cotonou, Benin (office). *Telephone:* 21-30-00-90 (office). *Fax:* 21-30-06-36 (office). *Website:* www.gouv.bj (office); patricetalon.com.

TALPES, Ioan, PhD; Romanian politician and fmr army officer; b. 24 Aug. 1944, Topleţ, Caraş-Severin Co.; m.; one c.; ed Faculty of History and Philosophy and School of Active Officers 'Nicolae Balcescu', Sibiu; scientific research mil. officer, Centre of Historical Studies and Researches and Mil. Theory of the Defence Ministry 1970–88; Ed.-in-Chief Mil. Publishing House 1988–90, Dir March–July 1990; worked for secret service –1989; Presidential Adviser, Romanian Presidency 1990–92; Dir Foreign Intelligence Service with ministerial rank 1994–97; Amb. to Bulgaria 1997–98; Chief Adviser on Security Matters to the Pres. and Head of Presidental Admin 2000–04, Minister of State responsible for Defence, European Integration and Justice and Head of Nat. Security Dept 2004; mem. Senatul (Senate) 2004–. *Publications:* numerous articles, studies and books published in

Romania and abroad. *Address:* Senatul, 050711 Bucharest 5, Calea 13 Septembrie 1–3, Romania (office). *Telephone:* (21) 4141111 (office). *Fax:* (21) 4012709 (office). *E-mail:* infopub@senat.ro (office). *Website:* www.senat.ro (office).

TALU, Umur E., BA; Turkish journalist; b. 7 Aug. 1957, Istanbul; s. of M. Muvakkar and G. Güzin; m. Şule Talu 1987; two d.; ed Galatasaray High School and Bosphorus Univ.; educ. specialist, Railway Workers' Union 1977–78; Int. Econ. Cooperation Sec. Union of Municipalities 1978–80; Econ. Corresp. Günaydin (newspaper) 1980–82; Chief, Econ. Dept Günes (newspaper) 1982–83; Ed. with Cumhuriyet (newspaper) 1983–85; Chief, Econ. Dept, Milliyet (newspaper) 1985–86, News Ed. 1986–87, 1988–92, Ed.-in-Chief 1992–94, columnist 1994; currently columnist, Gazete Haberturk; Ed. Hürriyet (newspaper) 1987–88; Freedom of the Press Award, Turkish Journalists' Asscn 1996. *Publications:* Social Democracy in Europe (co-author) 1985, Keynes (trans.) 1986, Mr Uguran's Post Office 1996. *Leisure interests:* sport, music, films. *Address:* c/o Gazete Haberturk, Abdülhakhamit Cad. No: 25, Beyoğlu, Istanbul, Turkey. *E-mail:* utalu@htgazete.com.tr. *Website:* www.haberturk.com/htyazar/umur-talu.

TALWAR, Rana Gurvirendra Singh, BA; Indian banker and investment industry executive; *Chairman, Sabre Capital Worldwide Inc.;* b. 22 March 1948; s. of R. S. Talwar and Veera Talwar; m. 1st Roop Som Dutt 1970 (divorced); one s. one d.; m. 2nd Renuka Singh 1995; one s.; ed Lawrence School, Sanawar, St Stephen's Coll., Delhi, Delhi Univ.; exec. trainee, Citibank 1969–70, numerous operational, corp. and institutional banking assignments, India 1970–76, Group Head for Treasury and Financial Inst. 1976, Regional Man. for Eastern India 1977, Group Head of Treasury and Financial Insts Group, Saudi American Bank, Jeddah 1978–80, Regional Consumer Business Man., Singapore, Malaysia, Indonesia, Thailand and India 1982–88, Div. Exec., Asia Pacific 1988–91, Exec. Vice-Pres. and Group Exec., Consumer Bank, Asia Pacific, Middle East and Eastern Europe 1991–95, Exec. Vice-Pres. Citicorp and Citibank, responsible for USA and Europe 1996–97; Group Exec. Dir Standard Chartered PLC 1997–98, CEO 1998–2001; Chair. Centurion Bank of Punjab 2004–08 (Centurion acquired by HDFC Bank Ltd); currently Co-Founder and Chair. Sabre Capital Worldwide Inc., London; mem. Bd of Dirs (non-exec.) Pearson PLC 2000–07, Fortis SA 2004–09, Schlumberger Ltd 2005–08; Patron Nat. Soc. for Prevention of Cruelty to Children 2005; mem. Governing Body London Business School; fmr mem. Indian School of Business. *Leisure interests:* bridge, golf, tennis, travel. *Address:* Sabre Capital Worldwide Inc., 2nd Floor, Berkeley Square House, Berkeley Square, London, W1J 6BD, England (office).

TAM, Yiu Chung, JP; Chinese government official; b. 15 Dec. 1949, Hong Kong; m. Lai Xiang Ming; two c.; ed Australian Nat. Univ., London School of Econs, UK; trade union officer; Vice-Chair. Hong Kong Fed. of Trade Unions; Chair. Employees' Retraining Bd, Elderly Comm., fmr mem. Preparatory Cttee for Hong Kong Special Admin. Region; mem. Exec. Council Hong Kong Special Admin. Region 1997–2002, Legis. Council Hong Kong Special Admin. Region 1998–; mem. Vocational Training Council, Standing Comm. on Civil Service Salaries and Conditions of Service, Ind. Comm. Against Corruption Complaints Cttee, Services Promotion Strategy Unit; fmr Vice-Chair. Democratic Alliance for Betterment of Hong Kong, Chair. 2007–15; currently mem., Legis. Council of Hong Kong Special Admin. Region; Hon. Life Fellow, Inst. of Commercial Man., UK; Gold Bauhinia Star. *Address:* 15F SUP Tower, 83 King's Road, North Point, Hong Kong Special Administrative Region, People's Republic of China (office). *Telephone:* 35281111 (office). *Fax:* 35821188 (office). *E-mail:* yctam@dab.org.hk (office). *Website:* www.yctam.org (office).

TAMAKOSHI, Ryosuke; Japanese banking executive; b. 10 July 1947; joined Sanwa Bank Ltd 1970, mem. Bd of Dirs 1997–2002, Sr Exec. Officer 1999–2000, Pres. 2000–01; Pres. United Calif. Bank 2001–02; Sr Exec. Officer UFJ Bank Ltd 2002, Deputy Pres. 2002–04, Head, Global Banking and Trading Div. 2003, Chair. 2004, Pres. and CEO UFJ Holdings Inc. 2004, Chair. UFJ Holdings Inc. and UFJ Bank Ltd 2004–05, Chair. Mitsubishi UFJ Financial Group (after merger with Mitubishi Tokyo Financial Group, Inc.) 2005–10, Deputy Chair. Bank of Tokyo-Mitsubishi UFJ Ltd 2006–08; Dir, Mitsubishi UFJ Financial Group, Inc. 2005–10, The Kansai Electric Power Co., Inc. 2006–, Morgan Stanley 2011–; Dir (non-exec.) Dah Sing Financial Holdings Ltd 2003–05. *Address:* c/o Mitsubishi UFJ Financial Group, Inc., 7-1, Marunouchi 2-Chome, Chiyoda-ku, Tokyo 100-8330, Japan. *E-mail:* info@mufg.jp.

TAMARÓN, Marqués de Santiago de Mora-Figueroa, 9th Marqués de Tamarón; Spanish diplomatist; b. 18 Oct. 1941, Jerez de la Frontera; s. of José de Mora-Figueroa, 8th Marqués de Tamarón, and the Marquesa de Tamarón (née Dagmar Williams); m. Isabelle de Yturbe 1966; one s. one d.; ed Univ. of Madrid and Escuela Diplomática; Lt, Spanish Marine Corps 1967; Sec., Embassy in Nouakchott 1968–70, Paris 1970–73; Banco del Noroeste 1974; Counsellor, Copenhagen 1975–80, Minister-Counsellor, Ottawa 1980–81, Pvt. Sec. to Minister of Foreign Affairs 1981–82, Head of Studies and Deputy Dir, Escuela Diplomática 1982–88; Dir Instituto de Cuestiones Internacionales y Política Exterior (INCIPE) 1988–96, Instituto Cervantes 1996–99; Amb. to UK 1999–2004; Vice-Pres., Spanish section, Hispano-American Cttee 2006–11; Amb. of Spain for Cultural Diplomacy 2012–17; mem. Trilateral Comm. 1989–96; Commdr, Order of Carlos III; Officier, Ordre nat. du Mérite; Commdr, Order of the Dannebrog; Commdr, Order of Merit (Germany); Gran Cruz Mérito Naval. *Publications:* Pólvora con Aguardiente 1983, El Guirigay Nacional 1988, Trampantojos 1990, El Siglo XX y otras Calamidades 1993, El Peso de la Lengua Española en el Mundo (co-author) 1995, El Rompimiento de Gloria 2003, El Avestruz, Tótem Utópico 2012, Entre líneas y a contracorriente, Bitácora 2008–2018 (vols. I, II and III) 2018. *Leisure interests:* philology, mountain walking, gardening. *Website:* www.marquesdetamaron.es.

TAMBAJANG, Aja Fatoumata Jallow, BA; Gambian politician; b. 22 Oct. 1949, Brikama; eight c.; ed Univ. of Nice Sophia Antipolis; fmr adviser on women's issues and children's affairs to Dawda Jawara (first Pres. of the Gambia); fmr Chair. Gambia Nat. Women's Council; fmr Consultant, UNDP; Minister of Health and Welfare 1994–95; Minister of Women's Affairs 2017–18; Vice-Pres. of the Gambia Nov. 2017–June 2018; mem. United Democratic Party (UDP) 2015–. *Address:* c/o Office of the Vice-President, State House, Banju, The Gambia (office).

TAMBO, Nomatemba, BA (Hons), LLB; South African diplomatist; *High Commissioner to United Kingdom;* d. of Oliver Reginald Tambo and Adelaide Tambo; ed Roehampton Inst., Univ. of London, UK, Univ. of the Witwatersrand, Johannesburg, Dept of Int. Relations and Co-operation; Consul Gen. in Hong Kong –2013, Amb. to Italy (also Perm. Rep. to Rome-based UN Agencies) 2013–18, High Commr to UK 2018–; Co-founder and Chair. South African Women's Chamber of Commerce, Hong Kong; Co-founding mem. Women in Capital Growth; Contributing Ed., Fair Lady Magazine; Chief Exec. Evening Star Manufacturing; Dir, Webnet Solutions, Resilient Income Property Fund; mem. Bd of Advisors, Bridging Gaps; mem. Int. Women's Forum; Trustee, Oliver & Adelaide Tambo Foundation. *Address:* South African High Commission, Trafalgar Square, London, WC2N 5DP, England (office). *Telephone:* (20) 7451-7299 (office). *Fax:* (20) 7839-5670 (office). *Website:* southafricahouseuk.com (office).

TAMBUNTING, Jesus P., OBE, BS; Philippine banking executive and diplomatist; *Chairman and CEO, Planters Development Bank;* b. 1937; m. Margarita Tambunting; four c.; ed Ateneo de Manila Univ., Culver Mil. Acad., Ind., Univ. of Maryland, USA; began career as asst cashier with Philippine bank, becoming Sr Vice-Pres. and Treas.; bought small thrift bank, Malolos, Bulacan; acquired Bulacan Devt Bank 1972, renamed Planters Devt Bank (Plantersbank) 1976 (now largest devt bank in Philippines), currently Chair. and CEO, also Chair. PlantersbankSME Solutions, Inc.; Chair. PDB-FMO Development Center; Amb. to UK (also accred to Ireland) 1993–98, also Perm. Rep. to IMO; Chair. Micro Enterprise Bank of the Philippines; Co-Chair. Philippine-British Business Council; Dir Philam Asset Management Inc., Globe Telecom, Philam Fund Inc., Philam Strategic Growth Fund Inc., Philam Bond Fund Inc., Philam Dollar Bond Fund Inc.; fmr Chair. Asscn of Devt Financing Insts in Asia and the Pacific; fmr Pres. Management Asscn of the Philippines, Chamber of Thrift Banks, Devt Bankers Asscn of the Philippines; mem. Bd of Trustees Philippine Business for Social Progress, Carlos P. Romulo Foundation; Knight, Equestrian Order of the Holy Sepulchre of Jerusalem (Vatican) 2004; Management Man of the Year, Management Asscn of Philippines 2003, Asian Bankers Asscn Lifetime Achievement Award 2005, Ernst & Young Philippines Entrepreneur of the Year 2009. *Address:* Planters Development Bank, Plantersbank Building, 314 Sen. Gil Puyat Avenue, Makati City, Philippines (office). *Telephone:* (2) 8847600 (office). *E-mail:* info@plantersbank.com.ph (office). *Website:* www.plantersbank.com.ph (office).

TAMEN, Pedro, LLB; Portuguese poet and translator; b. 1 Dec. 1934, Lisbon; s. of Mário Tamen and Emília Tamen; m. Maria da Graça Seabra Gomes 1975; two s. two d.; ed Lisbon Univ.; Dir Moraes Publishing House 1958–75; Pres. Portuguese PEN Club 1987–90, Vice-Pres. 1991–2002; Trustee, Calouste Gulbenkian Foundation, Lisbon 1975–2000; mem. Bd of Dirs Portuguese Asscn of Writers; D. Diniz Prize 1981, Grand Prix for Translation 1990, Critics Award 1993, INAPA Prize for Poetry 1993, Nicola Prize for Poetry 1998, Press Poetry Prize 2000, PEN Club Poetry Prize 2000, Inês de Castro Prize 2006, Luis Miguel Nava Prize 2006, Correntes de Escritas Prize 2007. *Publications include:* 12 books of poetry since 1958; Retábulo das Matérias (Collected Works) 2001, Analogia e Dedos (Prémio Literário Inês de Castro 2008) 2006, O Livro do Sapateiro (Poetry Prize, Portuguese Asscn of Writers 2011, Correntes de Escritas Prize 2011) 2010, Um Teatro às Escuras 2011. *Address:* Apartado 47, EC Palmela, 2951-901 Palmela, Portugal (home). *Telephone:* (21) 233-1144 (office). *Fax:* (21) 233-2203 (office). *E-mail:* ptamen@gmail.com. *Website:* www.arscives.com/pedrotamen.

TAMIM, Lt-Gen. Dahi Khalfan; United Arab Emirates police officer and government official; *Head of General Security for Emirate of Dubai;* b. 1 Oct. 1951; m.; two s. three d.; ed Royal Police Acad., Amman, Jordan; joined Dubai Police Force 1970, becoming Head of Financial and Admin. Affairs, Deputy Commdr-in-Chief 1979–80, Commdr-in-Chief 1980–2013; Head of Gen. Security, Emirate of Dubai 2013–; attained rank of Lt-Gen. 2004; rose to worldwide fame when he led the investigation into the assassination of Mahmoud al-Mabhouh, a Hamas operative killed by a hit squad in a hotel in Dubai 2010; mem. Dubai Exec. Cttee; Chair. Hamdan Bin Mohammed e-Univ. (fmrly e-TQM Coll.), Dubai; est. an orphanage in Dubai and launched the Khalfan School for teaching the Holy Quran; Service Order (First Class); Dubai Police Medal of Appreciation (First Class) twice, Dubai Police Distinguished Service Medal three times, Dubai Police Good Conduct Medal three times, Best Man. Dir Award in the public sector at the GCC level 1983, Nat. Security Medal (Saudi Arabia), Social Defence Medal, HH Ruler of Sharjah, UN Most Prominent Arab Figure Award in the field of Narcotics Control 2000, Middle East Regional Exec. CEO Personality Award 2004. *Address:* Dubai Police Headquarters, PO Box 1493, Dubai, United Arab Emirates (office). *Telephone:* (4) 269-2222 (office). *Fax:* (4) 217-1430 (office). *E-mail:* mail@dubaipolice.gov.ae (office). *Website:* www.dubaipolice.gov.ae (office).

TAMM, Ditlev, DJur, DPhil; Danish historian, academic and legal scholar; *Professor of Legal History, Faculty of Law, University of Copenhagen;* b. 7 March 1946, Copenhagen; s. of Henrik Tamm and Lizzie Knutzen; m. 1st Maria Pilar Lorenzo 1973 (separated 1987); two d.; m. 2nd Dean Pia Letto-Vanamo 2011; ed Univ. of Copenhagen and in Germany and France; Prof. of Legal History, Univ. of Copenhagen 1978–; mem. Royal Danish Acad., Academia Europea and several other Danish and int. scientific bds and cttees; Kt of Dannebrog 2004; Dr Jur hc (Univ. of Helsinki) 2000; A.S. Orsted Award 1974, Sarton Medal 2005. *Publications include:* Fra lovkyndighed til retsvidenskab 1976, Retsopgøret efter besaettelsen 1984, Roman Law 1997, Bournonville 2005, The Supreme Court of Denmark (co-author) 2015, Kulturarven og dens retlige beskyttelse 2016; several books and articles on Danish and European legal history, political history and cultural history. *Leisure interests:* languages, opera, bicycling. *Address:* Studiegården, Studiestraede 6, 1455 Copenhagen (office); Dantes Plads 3, 3, th, 1556 Copenhagen V, Denmark (home). *Telephone:* 35-32-31-67 (office); 39-29-93-92 (home). *Fax:* 35-32-32-05 (office). *E-mail:* ditlev.tamm@jur.ku.dk (office). *Website:* jur.ku.dk/english (office).

TAMURA, Norihisa; Japanese politician; b. 15 Dec. 1964, Mie Pref.; ed Chiba Univ.; started career at Nippon Doken Co. (construction co.), Tsu, Mie Pref. 1987; Sec. to MP Hajime Tamura 1994–96; mem. House of Reps (lower house of Parl.) for Mie Pref. Dist No. 4 (LDP) 1996–, Dir Cttee on Rules and Admin 2005, Cttee on Health, Labour and Welfare 2007, 2010 (Chair. 2008); Parl. Sec. of Health, Labour and Welfare 2002, of Educ., Culture, Sports, Science and Tech. 2003; Vice-Minister for Internal Affairs and Communication 2006; Minister of Health, Labour and

Welfare 2012–14; Deputy Sec.-Gen. LDP 2005, Acting Chair. Research Comm. on Social Security System 2007, Deputy Chair. Policy Research Council 2009, Dir Health, Labour and Welfare Div., Policy Research Council 2010. *Address:* House of Representatives, 1-7-1 Nagatacho, Chiyoda-ku, Tokyo 100-0014, Japan (office). *Telephone:* (3) 3581-3111 (office). *E-mail:* webmaster@shugiin.go.jp (office). *Website:* www.shugiin.go.jp/internet/index.nsf/html/index_e.htm (office).

TAN, Amy Ruth, MA, LHD; American writer; b. 19 Feb. 1952, Oakland, Calif.; d. of John Yuehhan and Daisy Ching Tan (née Tu); m. Louis M. DeMattei 1974; ed San José State Univ., Univ. of California, Berkeley, Dominican Coll.; specialist in language devt, Alameda Co. Asscn for Mentally Retarded 1976–80; Project Dir MORE, San Francisco 1980–81; freelance writer 1981–88; Best American Essays Award 1991, Marian McFadden Memorial Lecturer, Indianapolis-Marion Co. Public Library 1996. *Film:* The Joy Luck Club (screenwriter, producer) 1993. *Publications include:* The Joy Luck Club (Commonwealth Club and Bay Area Book Reviewers' Best Fiction Award 1990) 1989, The Kitchen God's Wife 1991, The Hundred Secret Senses 1995, The Bonesetter's Daughter 2000, Saving Fish from Drowning 2005, Rules for Virgins 2011, The Valley of Amazement 2013; for children: The Moon Lady 1992, The Chinese Siamese Cat 1994; non-fiction: The Opposite of Fate: A Book of Musings (autobiog.) 2003, Where the Past Begins: A Writer's Memoir 2017; numerous short stories and essays. *Address:* Steven Barclay Agency, 12 Western Avenue, Petaluma, CA 94952, USA (office). *E-mail:* Steven@BarclayAgency.com (office). *Website:* www.amytanauthor.com.

TAN, Andrew L., BS; Philippine real estate executive; *Chairman, Alliance Global Group Inc.;* b. 1952, Fujian Prov., People's Repub. of China; s. of Tan Ha; m.; four c.; ed Univ. of the East, Manila; f. Megaworld Corpn 1989, currently Chair., also Pres. Megaworld Foundation Inc.; Chair. and CEO Alliance Global Group Inc. 2006–18, Chair. 2018–; CEO and Pres. Yonghe King Brand 2007–; Pres. Richmonde Hotel Group Int. Ltd; Chair. Emperador Inc., Travellers Int. Hotel Group Inc.; Treas., Empire East Land Holdings Inc. 1994–98, Chair. 1994, currently Prin. Exec. Officer; Vice-Chair. and Treas. Golden Arches Devt Corpn; Co-owner Resort World Manila (casino); Chair. Dr. Andrew L. Tan Center for Tourism, Asian Inst. of Man. 2012–; mem. European and Philippine Chambers of Commerce; Order of Lakandula (rank of Bayani); Hon. DH (Univ. of the East); Quezon City Businessman of the Year 2004. *Address:* Alliance Global Group Inc., 7/F 1880 Eastwood Avenue, Eastwood City CyperPark, Bagumbayan, Quezon City 1110, Philippines (office). *Telephone:* (2) 7092038 (office). *Fax:* (2) 4210851 (office). *Website:* allianceglobalinc.com (office).

TAN, Chorh Chuan, MD, FRCP, FRCPE, FRACP, FACP, FRGS; Singaporean renal physician, academic and university administrator; ed Nat. Univ. of Singapore, Inst. of Molecular Medicine, Oxford, UK; fmr Commonwealth Medical Fellow and Wellcome Fellow, Univ. of Oxford, fmr Visiting Scholar, Wolfson Coll., Oxford; Dean of Nat. Univ. of Singapore (NUS) Faculty of Medicine 1997–2000, Provost of NUS, then Sr Deputy Pres. 2004–08, Pres. NUS 2008–17; Dir of Medical Services, Ministry of Health 2000–04, led public health response to the 2003 SARS epidemic; Chair. Nat. Univ. Health System; Deputy Chair. Agency for Science, Tech. and Research (A*STAR); helped establish Duke-NUS Grad. Medical School, in his capacity as Deputy Chair. Governing Bd NUS 2004–07, now Sr Advisor to Governing Bd; mem. Bd of Dirs Monetary Authority of Singapore; inaugural Chief Exec. Nat. Univ. Health System 2008; mem. World Econ. Forum's Global Univ. Leaders Forum 2008–, mem. World Econ. Forum's Science Advisory Cttee; Chair. Int. Alliance of Research Univs 2008–12; Fellow, Polish Acad. of Medicine, Singapore Nat. Acad. of Science 2016; Hon. MD (King's Coll. London); Hon. DSc (Duke Univ., USA, Loughborough Univ., UK); Dr John Yu Medal, George Inst. for Global Health (Australia), Albert Schweitzer Gold Medal, Polish Acad. of Medicine, Achievement Medal, Singapore Soc. of Nephrology, Singapore Youth Award 1996, Public Service Star for outstanding contribs to overcoming SARS in Singapore 2003, Public Admin Gold Medal 2004, Nat. Science and Tech. Medal 2008. *Publications:* numerous papers in professional journals.

TAN, Dun, MA; Chinese composer; b. 18 Aug. 1957, Si Mao, Hunan Prov.; s. of Tan Xiang Qiu and Fang Qun Ying; m. Jane Huang 1994; ed Cen. Conservatory of Music, Beijing, Columbia Univ., USA; violist, Beijing Opera Orchestra 1976–77; Vice-Pres. Cen. Conservatory of Music 1978–; works performed by major orchestras in China and at festivals world-wide; has conducted orchestras including Royal Concertgebouw, London Symphony, New York Philharmonic, Berlin Philharmonic, BBC Symphony and Filarmonica della Scala; four recordings of his major orchestral works, oriental instrumental music, chamber music and electronic music issued by China Nat. Recording Co.; orchestral piece commissioned by Inst. for Devt of Intercultural Relations Through the Arts, USA for Beijing Int. Music Festival 1988; Artistic Dir Fire Crossing Water Festival, Barbican Centre, London 2000; composed music for Olympic Games medal ceremonies, Beijing 2008; commissioned by Google/YouTube to compose internet Symphony Eroica; named UNESCO Goodwill Amb. 2013; Dean, Bard College Conservatory of Music 2019–; second place, Weber Int. Chamber Music Composition Competition, Dresden 1983, Suntory Prize 1992, Grawemeyer Award 1998, Musical America Composer of the Year 2003. *Film scores include:* Aktion K 1994, Nanjing 1937 1995, Fallen 1997, In the Name of the Emperor 1998, Wo hu cang long (Crouching Tiger Hidden Dragon) (Grammy Award 2001, Acad. Award 2001, British Acad. Film Award 2001, Classical BRIT Contemporary Music Award 2001) 2000, Ying xiong (Hero) 2002. *Compositions include:* orchestral works: Li Sao (symphony) 1979, Five Pieces in Human Accent for piano 1980, Feng Ya Song for string quartet 1982, Fu for two sopranos, bass and ensemble 1982, Piano Concerto 1983, Symphony in two movements 1985, On Taoism for orchestra 1985, Traces for piano 1989, Eight Colours for string quartet 1989, Silk Road for soprano and percussion 1989, Orchestral Theatre I: Xun 1990, Soundshape 1990, Silent Earth 1991, Elegy: Snow in June 1991, Jo-Ha-Kyu 1992, Death and Fire: Dialogue with Paul Klee 1992, Orchestral Theatre II: Re 1992, CAGE for piano 1993, Circle for four trios, conductor and audience 1993, The Pink 1993, Autumn Winds for instruments and conductor ad lib 1993, Memorial Nineteen for voice, piano and double paper 1993, Orchestral Theatre III: Red 1993, Yi concerto for cello 1994, Ghost Opera 1994, Marco Polo 1995, A Sinking Love 1995, Heaven, Earth, Mankind symphony for the 'Bian Zhong' bronze bells (composed in celebration of the Hong Kong handover) 1997, Concerto for Six 1997, Heaven Earth Mankind 1997, Peony Pavilion 1998, 2000 Today: A World Symphony for the Millennium: A

Musical Odyssey for the Ages 1999, Water Passion after St Matthew 2000, Crouching Tiger Concerto 2000, The Map concerto for cello, video and orchestra 2003, Eight Memories in Watercolor 2003, Secret Land: for Orchestra and 12 Violoncelli 2004, Tears of Nature 2012, Contrabass Concerto: Wolf Totem 2014, Passacaglia: Secret of Wind and Birds 2015; opera: Out of Beijing 1987, Nine Songs 1989, Marco Polo 1994, Peony Pavilion 1998, Tea 2002, Eight Memories in Watercolor 2003, The First Emperor (opera score, libretto co-writer) 2006. *Leisure interests:* painting in ink, calligraphy. *Address:* 367 West 19th Street, Suite A, New York, NY 10011, USA (office). *Telephone:* (212) 627-0410 (office). *Fax:* (917) 606-0247 (office). *E-mail:* tan_dun@hotmail.com (office). *Website:* tandun.com (office).

TAN, Kim, BSc, PhD; Malaysian biotechnology entrepreneur; *Chairman, Spring-Hill Management Ltd;* Chair. Spring Hill Man. Ltd, Fund Man. Spring Hill Bioventures Sdn Bhd, AsiaPrise Biotech Sdn Bhd, NCI Cancer Hospital, Research Expert Working Group for the Asia Pacific Economic Community (APEC) Life Science Forum, Transformational Business Network (TBN); advisor to many govt agencies in Asia on bio-tech.; mem. Bd of Dirs Active Capital Investment Trust; Fellow, Royal Society of Medicine. *Publications include:* Fighting Poverty through Enterprise (with Lord Brian Griffiths); over 40 scientific publs. *Website:* www .springhilluk.com (office).

TAN, Lucio C., BS; Philippine business executive; b. 17 July 1934, Amoy, Fujian province, China; m.; six c.; ed Far Eastern Univ., Manila; f. Fortune Tobacco 1966, f. Asian Breweries 1970s, acquired Allied Banking Corpn, Chair. 1977–99, Chair. and CEO Philippine Airlines Inc. 1995, acquired Philippine National Bank, other cos under Lucio Tan Group of Cos include Foremost Farms Inc., Shareholdings Inc. *Address:* Philippine Airlines Inc., PAL Corporate Communications Department, PAL Center, Ground Floor, Legazpi Street, Legaspi Village, Makati City, Metro Manila, 0750, The Philippines (office). *Website:* www.philippineairlines.com (office).

TAN, Melvyn, FRCM; British concert pianist; b. 13 Oct. 1956, Singapore; s. of Tan Keng Hian and Wong Sou Yuen; ed Anglo-Chinese School, Yehudi Menuhin School, Royal Coll. of Music; has been performing on concert stage since early 1980s; following graduation, performed on historical instruments, culminating in original recordings of Beethoven sonatas for EMI and a tour on Beethoven's own piano in Europe and UK; tours regularly and extensively in Europe, Australia, the Far East and USA; has performed in most major venues and music festivals world-wide; returned to Singapore after a self-imposed exile of nearly 32 years for a homecoming concert 2011, continues to visit Singapore regularly to perform and encourage young musical talent; Artist-in-Residence, Yong Siew Toh Conservatory of Music, Singapore 2012–15. *Recordings include:* Debussy Préludes 2005, Beethoven Complete Piano Concertos with London Classical Players under Sir Roger Norrington, Beethoven and Schubert piano works, Mozart Piano Concert K414, Beethoven Concerto No. 2 with London Chamber Orchestra directing from keyboard, Master and Pupil (works by Beethoven, Czerny and Liszt) 2016. *Television:* featured extensively on the BBC soundtrack of Pride and Prejudice with music by Carl Davis. *Leisure interests:* keeping fit, good cuisine and being able to visit places without having to perform. *Address:* c/o Mark Stephan Buhl Artists Management, Geylinggasse 1, 1130 Vienna, Austria (office). *E-mail:* chinglee@ culturelink.com.sg (office). *Website:* www.msbuhl.com (office); www.melvyntan .com.

TAN, Royston; Singaporean filmmaker; ed Temasek Polytechnic; ASEAN Dir of the Year Award 2001, Young Artist of the Year, Singapore Nat. Arts Council 2002, Asia's Most Promising Talents, Netpac Jury 2003. *Films include:* short films: Sons (Best Short Film, Singapore Int. Film Festival 2000) 1999, Hock hiap leong (Merit Award, Tampere Int. Film Festival) 2001, Mother (Voice Award, Singapore Shorts Film Festival) 2001, 24 Hours 2002, 4A Florence Close, AIDS documentary for Channel News Asia, Monkeylove 2005, Hotel Vladivostok 2006, After the Rain 2007, Little Note 2009; feature films: 15 (Netpac-Frespesci Award, Singapore Int. Film Festival) 2003, 4:30 2006, 881 2007, 12 Lotus 2008, 3688 2015. *Address:* c/o The Substation, 45 Armenian Street, 179936 Singapore (office).

TAN, Ruisong, BEng, MEng, PhD; Chinese aviation industry executive; *President, Aviation Industry Corporation of China (AVIC);* ed Beijing Univ. of Aeronautics and Astronautics, Harbin Eng Univ.; has held numerous positions in AVIC Harbin Dong'an Automotive Engine Manufacturing Co. Ltd since 1983, Vice-Pres. Aviation Industry Corpn of China (AVIC) II and Exec. Vice-Pres. AVIC 2004–12, Pres. AVIC 2012–. *Address:* Aviation Industry Corporation of China, PO Box 2399, AVIC Plaza, 128 Jianguo Road, Chaoyang District, Beijing 100022, People's Republic of China (office). *Telephone:* (10) 58356511 (office). *Fax:* (10) 58356516 (office). *E-mail:* overseascrm@avic.com (office). *Website:* www.avic.com .cn (office); www.avic2.com (office).

TAN, Tan Sri Dato' Seri Vincent; Malaysian entrepreneur; *Executive Chairman, Berjaya Corporation Berhad;* b. (Tan Chee Yioun), 1952; m.; 11 c.; family originated from Yongchun Pref., Fujian Prov., China; began career as McDonald's franchisee; acquired major controlling stake in share capital of Berjaya Kawat Berhad, fmr Chair. and CEO Berjaya Corpn Berhad –2012, Exec. Chair. 2017–, businesses include golfing, property, resorts and gambling; operates MiTV, pay-TV service in Malaysia launched 2005; acquired controlling share in Cardiff City Football Club 2010; co-owner 289-foot yacht, Asean Lady. *Leisure interest:* scuba diving. *Address:* Berjaya Corporation Berhad, Lot 13-01A, Level 13 (East Wing), Berjaya Times Square, No. 1 Jalan Imbi, 55100 Kuala Lumpur, Malaysia (office). *Telephone:* (3) 2149-1999 (office). *Fax:* (3) 2143-1685 (office). *E-mail:* info@berjaya .com (office). *Website:* www.berjaya.com (office).

TAN, Yuan Yuan; Chinese ballet dancer; b. 14 Feb. 1976, Shanghai; ed Shanghai Dancing School, John Cranko School, Stuttgart, Germany; enrolled Shanghai Dance School 1987; briefly studied in Stuttgart, Germany; joined San Francisco Ballet as a soloist 1995, promoted to Prin. Ballerina 1997; Guest Prin. Dancer, Hong Kong Ballet May 2008; Silver Medal, Jr Female Div., Second Int. Ballet Competition, Helsinki 1991, Gold Medal, Jr Female Div., 5th Int. Ballet Competition, Paris 1992, Gold Medal, Jr Female Classical Div. and Nijinsky Award, 1st Japan Int. Ballet and Modern Dance Competition 1993, MOVADO Award for Outstanding Contrib. to Arts and Culture in China 1998, World Journal Outstanding Youth Award 2003, The Bund magazine City of Heart award, Shanghai 2007. *Ballet roles:* Giselle in Giselle (Tomasson), Juliet in Romeo &

Juliet (Tomasson), Odette/Odile in Swan Lake (Tomasson), Kitri in Don Quixote (Tomasson/Possokhov), Nanna in Nanna's Lied (Tomasson), cr. role in 7 for Eight (Tomasson), Aurora, Lilac Fairy, and Enchanted Princess in The Sleeping Beauty (Tomasson), cr. lead role in Sylvia (Morris), Desdemona in Othello (Lubovitch), Sugar Plum Fairy and Snow Queen in Nutcracker (Christensen/Tomasson), cr. title role in Chi-Lin, cr. prin. role in Silver Ladders, cr. pas de deux in Pandora Dance, Schoenberg variation prin. in Criss-Cross, pas de deux and second movt prin. in Prism, pas de trois in Tuning Game, Prin. in Handel – a Celebration, Valses Poeticos, and Beads of Memory (Tomasson), second movt prin. in Symphony in C, Angel and Waltz Couple in Serenade, fourth movt prin. in Western Symphony, Prin. in Theme and Variations, Prin. and Soloist in Concerto Barocco, demi-soloist in Ballo Delia Regina, Aria II in Stravinsky Violin Concerto, Siren in Prodigal Son and Prin. in Bugaku, pas de deux in Emeralds, soloist in Rubies, Terpsichore in Apollo, second aria in Stravinsky Violin Concerto, and Prin. in Diamonds (Balanchine), Maninyas, La Cathedrale Engloutie, Spirit in Taiko, and cr. prin. role in Tu Tu (Welch), Thais Pas de Deux (Ashton), cr. role in Continuum and Polyphonia (Wheeldon), cr. role of Princess in Damned (Possokhov), cr. role in Study in Motion (Possokhov), The Waltz Project (Martins), Prin. in Raymonda, Act III (Nureyev after Petipa), Elite Syncopations (MacMillan), La Esmeralda pas de deux (Perrot), first and second pas de deux in Without Words (Duato), Italian Ballerina in Gala Performance (Tudor), Prin. in Etudes (Lander), Prin. and Soloist in Glass Pieces, Mauve and Pink in Dances at a Gathering, and first pas de deux in In the Night (Bobbins), Prin. in Paquita and Nikiya and third variation in La Bayadere, Act II (Makarova after Petipa), cr. prin. role in Magrittomania (Possokhov), Angelo (Adam), Grand Pas Classique (Gsovsky). *Address:* Hong Kong Ballet, G/F 60 Blue Pool Road, Happy Valley, Hong Kong Special Administrative Region, People's Republic of China (office). *Website:* www.hkballet.com (office).

TAN KENG YAM, Tony, PhD; Singaporean academic, banker, government official, business executive and fmr head of state; b. 7 Feb. 1940, Singapore; s. of Tan Seng Hwee and Lim Neo Swee; m. Mary Chee Bee Kiang 1964; three s. one d.; ed St Patrick's School, St Joseph's Inst., Univ. of Singapore, Mass. Inst. of Tech., USA and Univ. of Adelaide, Australia; Lecturer in Math., Univ. of Singapore 1967–69; Sub-Man. Overseas Chinese Banking Corpn 1969, Gen. Man. 1978; MP for Sembawang 1979–2006; Sr Minister of State (Educ.) 1979; Minister of Educ. 1980, concurrently Vice-Chancellor, Nat. Univ. of Singapore; Minister for Trade and Industry, concurrently Minister in charge of Nat. Univ. of Singapore and Nanyang Tech. Inst. 1981–83; Minister of Finance 1983–85, of Educ. and Health Jan.–April 1985, for Trade and Industry 1985–86, of Educ. 1985–91; Chair. People's Action Party Cen. Exec. Cttee 1993; Chair. and CEO Oversea-Chinese Banking Corpn Ltd 1992; Deputy Prime Minister of Singapore Aug. 1995–2005, concurrently Minister of Defence 1995–2003, Coordinating Minister for Security and Defence 2003–05; Pres. of Singapore 2011–17; Chair. Singapore Press Holdings Ltd 2005–11; Deputy Chair. and Exec. Dir Govt of Singapore Investment Corpn Pte Ltd (GIC); Chair. Nat. Research Foundation; Deputy Chair. Research, Innovation and Enterprise Council; Chair. Int. Academic Advisory Panel, Ministry of Educ; Hon. Fellow, Singapore Acad. of Medicine 2006; Hon. DSc (Loughborough Univ.) 1994; Hon. DrIur (Murdoch Univ.) 1995, (Univ. of Sheffield) 1998; Hon. DPhil (Univ. of Adelaide) 2014; Nat. Trades Union Congress Medal of Honour 1988, Eminent Alumni Award, NUS 2005, New York Foreign Policy Assn Medal 2011, inducted into Hon. Senate, Foundation Lindau Nobel Laureate Meetings 2012, Great Gold Medal, Comenius Univ. 2013, King Charles II Medal, Royal Soc. (UK) 2014. *Leisure interests:* swimming, golf and walking. *Address:* c/o Office of the President, The Istana, Orchard Road, Singapore 238823, Singapore (office).

TANAI, Shahnawaz; Afghan politician and fmr army general; *Leader, Da Afghanistan Da Solay Ghorzang Gond;* b. 1950, Dargai, Khost Prov.; m.; two s. one d.; apptd Chief of Mil. Intelligence 1978, served as Chief of Army Staff and Minister of Defence in Soviet-backed Democratic Repub. of Afghanistan 1988–90; led mil. coup against Pres. Mohammad Najibullah 1990, after failure of coup went into exile in Pakistan 1990–2005; returned to Afghanistan 2005 as Leader, Da Afghanistan Da Solay Ghorzang Gond (Afghanistan Peace Movt). *Address:* Da Afghanistan Da Solay Ghorzang Gond, Kolola Poshta (adjacent to Dost Hotel), Kabul, Afghanistan (office).

TANAKA, Hisao, BEcons; Japanese business executive; b. 20 Dec. 1950; ed Kobe Univ. of Commerce; joined Toshiba Corpn 1973, Sr Vice-Pres., Toshiba Information Equipment (Philippines) Corpn 1996–2000, Gen. Man. and Deputy Man. Dir Toshiba (UK) Co. Ltd 2000–01, Toshiba Information Systems (UK) Ltd 2001–02, Gen. Man., Procurement Div., Digital Media & Network Co. 2002–04, Gen. Man., Procurement Div., PC & Network Co. 2004–05, Chief Production Exec., PC & Network Co. 2005–06, Exec. Vice-Pres. and Chief Production Exec. April–June 2006, Officer, Corp. Vice-Pres., Exec. Vice-Pres. and Chief Production Exec. 2006–07, Exec. Officer, Vice-Pres., Man., Corp. Procurement Div. 2007–08, Exec. Officer, Corp. Sr Vice-Pres., Gen. Exec., Procurement Group 2008–09, Exec. Officer, Corp. Exec. Vice-Pres., Gen. Exec., Procurement & Logistics Group 2009–11, Dir, Rep. Exec. Officer, Corp. Sr Exec. Vice-Pres., Gen. Exec., Quality Div., Procurement & Logistics Group, Productivity & Environment Group 2011–12, Dir, Rep. Exec. Officer, Corp. Sr Exec. Vice-Pres., Gen. Exec., Strategic Planning & Communications Group, Procurement & Logistics Group, Productivity & Environment Group 2012–13, Dir, Rep. Exec. Officer, Pres. and CEO Toshiba Corpn 2013–15 (resgnd). *Address:* c/o Toshiba Corpn, 1-1, Shibaura 1-chome, Minato-ku, Tokyo 105-8001, Japan.

TANAKA, Koichi, BS; Japanese chemist and engineer; *Core Researcher and General Manager, Koichi Tanaka Laboratory of Advanced Science and Technology, Shimadzu Corporation;* b. 3 Aug. 1959, Toyama City; ed Tohoku Univ.; joined Cen. Research Lab., Shimadzu Corpn 1983, seconded to subsidiary Kratos Group PLC, UK 1992, joined R&D Dept of Analytical Instruments Div., Japan 1992, seconded to Shimadzu Research Lab. (Europe) Ltd, UK 1997, seconded to Kratos Group PLC, UK 1999, apptd Asst Man. Life Science Lab., Shimadzu Corpn, Kyoto 2002, Gen. Man. of Mass Spectrometry Research Lab. 2003, Core Researcher and Gen. Man. Koichi Tanaka Lab. of Advanced Science and Tech., Shimadzu Corpn 2010–; Encouragement Award, Mass Spectrometry Soc. of Japan 1989, Nobel Prize in Chemistry (co-recipient) 2002, Person of Cultural Merit, Japan 2002, Order of Culture, Japan 2003. *Address:* Shimadzu Corporation, 1 Nishinkokyo Kuwabaracho, Nakagyou-ku, Kyoto 604-8511, Japan (office). *Website:* www.shimadzu.com (office).

TANAKA, Makiko; Japanese politician; b. 14 Jan. 1944; d. of Kakuei Tanaka (fmr Prime Minister of Japan); m. Naoki Tanaka; ed Waseda Univ.; fmr Deputy Dir-Gen. LDP Int. Bureau; Minister of State, Dir-Gen. Science and Tech. Agency 1994–95; Ministry of Foreign Affairs 2001–02; mem. House of Reps for Nigata –2002 (resgnd), 2003–12, Chair., Cttee Education, Culture, Sports, Science and Technology 2009, Cttee Foreign Affairs 2011; Minister of Education, Culture, Sports, Science and Technology Oct.–Dec. 2012; mem. House Cttee on Health and Welfare; mem. Democratic Party of Japan 2009–. *Address:* Democratic Party of Japan, 1-11-1, Nagata-cho, Chiyoda-ku, Tokyo 100-0014, Japan (office). *Telephone:* (3) 3595-9988 (office). *Fax:* (3) 3595-9961 (office). *E-mail:* dpjenews@dpj.or.jp (office). *Website:* www.dpj.or.jp (office).

TANAKA, Naoki; Japanese politician; b. (Naoki Suzuki), 19 June 1940, Kanazawa, Ishikawa; m. Makiko Tanaka; mem. House of Reps 1983–96, House of Councillors from Niigata Pref. 1998–; Minister of Defence Jan.–June 2012; mem. Democratic Party of Japan. *Address:* Democratic Party of Japan, 1-11-1, Nagata-cho, Chiyoda-ku, Tokyo 100-0014, Japan (office). *Telephone:* (3) 3595-9988 (office). *Fax:* (3) 3595-9961 (office). *E-mail:* dpjenews@dpj.or.jp (office). *Website:* www.dpj.or.jp (office); www.naoki-tanaka.jp.

TANAKA, Nobuo, MBA; Japanese international organization official; *Global Associate for Energy, Security and Sustainability, Institute of Energy Economics;* b. 3 March 1950; m. Gloria Tanaka; two c.; ed Univ. of Tokyo, Case Western Reserve Univ., Ohio, USA; began career with Ministry of Economy, Trade and Industry (METI) 1973, held posts including Deputy Dir-Gen. Affairs Div., Machinery and Information Industries Bureau, Personnel Div., Dir of Int. Nuclear Energy Affairs, Natural Resources and Energy Agency, Dir for Industrial Finance Div. and Dir for Policy Planning and Coordination Div. 1995–98, Dir-Gen. Multilateral Trade System Dept 2002–04; Deputy Dir for Science, Tech. and Industry, OECD 1989–91, Dir for Science, Tech. and Industry 1991–95, 2004–07, also Head Steering Group of Centre for Entrepreneurship 2004–07; Minister for Energy, Trade and Industry, Embassy in Washington, DC 1998–2000; Exec. Vice-Pres. Research Inst. of Economy Trade and Industry, Japan 2000–02; Exec. Dir IEA 2007–11; Global Assoc. for Energy Security and Sustainability, Inst. of Energy Economics 2011–. *Address:* Institute of Energy Economics, Inui Kachidoki Building, 1-13-1 Kachidoki, Chuo-ku, Tokyo 104-0054, Japan (office). *Telephone:* (3) 5547-0222 (office). *Fax:* (3) 5547-0223 (office). *Website:* www.eneken.ieej.or.jp (office).

TANAKA, Takashi; Japanese business executive; *General Manager, Corporate & Marketing Communications Sector and President, KDDI Corporation;* b. 26 Feb. 1957; mem. Bd of Dirs, Assoc. Sr Vice-Pres., Gen. Man., Solution Business Sector, KDDI Corpn 2007–10, Assoc. Sr Vice-Pres., Solution Business, Consumer Business, and Product Devt Sector April–June 2010, Sr Vice-Pres. June–Dec. 2010, Pres. KDDI Corpn Dec. 2010–13, Gen. Man. Corp. & Marketing Communications Sector and Pres. KDDI Corpn 2013–. *Address:* KDDI Corpn, Garden Air Tower, 3-10-10, Iidabashi, Chiyoda-ku, Tokyo 102-8460, Japan (office). *Telephone:* (3) 6678-0692 (office). *Fax:* (3) 6678-0305 (office). *E-mail:* info@kddi.com (office). *Website:* www.kddi.com (office).

TANAKA, Tatsuya; Japanese business executive; *Representative Director, President and Corporate Executive Officer, Fujitsu Ltd;* b. Sept. 1956; served as a Sr Vice-Pres., then Sr Exec. Vice-Pres., Fujitsu Ltd and as Head of Asia Region, Corp. Vice-Pres., Fujitsu Ltd 2012–14, Corp. Sr Vice-Pres. 2014–16, Rep. Dir, Pres. and Corp. Exec. Officer 2016–, Dir, Fujitsu Laboratories Ltd. *Address:* Fujitsu Headquarters, Shiodome City Centre, 1-5-2 Higashi-Shimbashi, Minato-ku, Tokyo 105-7123, Japan (office). *Telephone:* (3) 6252-2220 (office). *Fax:* (3) 6252-2783 (office). *E-mail:* info@fujitsu.com (office). *Website:* www.fujitsu.com (office).

TANAKA, Yasuo; Japanese writer and politician; *Leader, New Party Nippon;* b. 12 April 1956, Tokyo; ed Univ. of Hitotsubashi; community activist, Kobe, following 1995 earthquake; elected first ind. Gov. of Nagano Pref. 2000–06; mem. House of Councillors for Hyogo 8th Dist 2006–12; Co-founded New Party Nippon (Shinto Nippon) 2005, Leader 2005–. *Publications:* Nantonaku Kurisutaru (Somehow Crystal, Bungei Prize) 1983. *Address:* New Party Nippon, 1-7-11, Hirakawa-cho, Chiyoda-ku, Tokyo 102-0093, Japan (office). *Telephone:* (3) 5213-0333 (office). *Fax:* (3) 5213-0888 (office). *Website:* www.love-nippon.com (office).

TANAKA, Yoshikazu, BL; Japanese business executive; *Founder and CEO, GREE Inc.;* b. 18 Feb. 1977, Mitaka-City, Tokyo; ed Nihon Univ.; worked at So-net Entertainment Corpn and Rakuten, Inc.; while at the latter, began developing SNS GREE in his spare time 2003, opened SNS GREE to the public as a personal website Feb. 2004; Founder, CEO, Pres. and Rep. Dir GREE, Inc. (social network service) Dec. 2004–, mem. Bd of Dirs GREE International, Inc.; selected as the World's Second-Youngest Self-Made Billionaire after Mark Zuckerberg 2010, youngest founder whose company is listed on the TSE first section 2010. *Address:* GREE, Inc., Roppongi Hills Mori Tower, 6-10-1 Roppongi, Minato-ku, Tokyo 106-6151, Japan (office). *E-mail:* pr@gree.co.jp (office); inquiry@gree-corp.com (office). *Website:* www.gree.jp (office); www.gree.co.jp/en (office); www.gree-corp.com (office).

TANASESCU, Mihai Nicolae; Romanian politician; b. 11 Jan. 1956, Bucharest; m.; two c.; ed Acad. of Econ. Studies, Bucharest, Int. Inst. for Public Admin, Paris, France, Int. Monetary Fund Inst., Vienna, Austria, Harvard Business School, USA; Head of Accounting Dept, ICRAL (Constructions, Repairs and Locative Admin Enterprise), Bucharest 1978–83; Exec., Dept for State Incomes, Ministry of Finance 1990–92, Dept for the State Budget 1992–93, Dept for Public Debt 1993–97; Alt. Exec. Chair. IBRD for group of 12 East European countries, Washington, DC 1997–2000; Minister of Public Finance 2000–04; mem. Man. Cttee European Investment Bank 2012–16; Commdr, Légion d'honneur 2002, Knight, Order of the Star of Romania 2002. *Publications:* scientific research papers on econs, financial analysis and forecasting in Romanian and foreign journals.

TANAYEV, Nikolai Timofeyevich; Kyrgyzstani politician; b. 5 Nov. 1945, Penza Oblast, Russia; ed Dzhambul Hydroengineering Inst. (Kazakh SSR); Head of Osh Regional Water Canal Directorate 1984; Head of Chuipromstroi (Chui Industrial Construction) Trust 1985; apptd Chair. State Agency on Architecture and Construction 2000; fmr First Deputy Prime Minister 2001; Head of Special Comm. investigating deaths of demonstrators shot by police March 2002; Acting Prime Minister of Kyrgyzstan May 2002, Prime Minister 2002–05.

TANDJA, Col (retd) Mamadou; Niger army officer (retd) and fmr head of state; b. 1938, Maine-Soroa; m.; 10 c.; participated in mil. junta that ousted Pres. Diori 1974, apptd mem. Supreme Mil. Council; Prefect of Maradi region 1976–79; Minister of the Interior 1979–81, 1990–91; Prefect of Tahoua region 1981–88; Amb. to Nigeria 1988–90; Chair. Mouvement national pour la société de développement—Nassara 1991; Pres. of Niger 1999–2010 (ousted in coup); fmr Chair. Econ. Community of West African States.

TANDJUNG, Akbar; Indonesian politician; b. 14 Aug. 1945, Sibolga, N Sumatera; m. R. A. Krissnina Maharani; four d.; ed Univ. of Indonesia; mem. Functional Devt Faction, House of Reps 1977–88, Deputy Chair. 1997–, Speaker House of Reps 1999–2004; State Minister for Youth and Sports 1988–93, for People's Housing 1993–98, for People's Housing and Settlement 1998, Minister State Sec. 1998; found guilty of embezzling state funds Sept. 2002, conviction dismissed Feb. 2004; mem. People's Consultative Ass. 1992–97; Chair. Cen. Bd Golkar Party 1998–2004; Mahaputra Adiprandana Star 1992, Kruis Award, Order van Oranje-Nassau (Netherlands) 1996, Star of the Repub. of Indonesia 1998. *Leisure interest:* swimming.

TANDON, Lalji; Indian politician; *Governor of Bihar;* b. 12 April 1935, Lucknow, Uttar Pradesh; s. of Shivnarayan Tandon and Annpurna Devi; m. Krishna Tandon 1958; three s.; mem. Uttar Pradesh State Legislative Council 1978–84, 1990–96, also Leader of House 1997–2002; mem. Uttar Pradesh Legislative Ass. 1996–2009, Leader of Opposition 2003–07; Minister of State, Power 1991–92, Urban Devt and Housing 1997, Urban Devt and Water Supply 1997–99, Urban Devt and Urban Poverty Alleviation 1999–2000, 2000–02, Housing, Finance, Urban Devt and Tourism 2002–03; elected to 15th Lok Sabha as MP for Lucknow 2009–14, apptd mem. Cttee on Estimates and Cttee on Railways 2009; Gov. of Bihar 2018–; currently mem. Bharatiya Janata Party (BJP); established numerous educational, social and cultural insts in Avadh, Uttar Pradesh. *Leisure interest:* cattle rearing. *Address:* Governor House, B.G. Camp, Patna, Bihar 800022, India (office); 64, Saundhi Tola Chowk, Lucknow, Uttar Pradesh, 226003, India (office). *Telephone:* (13) 42217626 (office). *E-mail:* governorbihar@nic.in (office). *Website:* www .governor.bih.nic.in (office).

TANG, Ching W., BS, PhD; American scientist and academic; *Doris Johns Cherry Professor of Chemical Engineering and Professor of Chemistry, University of Rochester;* b. 23 July 1947, Yuen Long, Hong Kong; ed Univ. of British Columbia, Canada, Cornell Univ.; joined Eastman Kodak as Research Scientist 1975, Sr Research Scientist 1981–90, Research Assoc. 1990–98, Sr Research Assoc. 1998–2003, Distinguished Fellow, Kodak Research Laboratories, Eastman Kodak Co. 2003; Doris Johns Cherry Prof. of Chemical Eng, Univ. of Rochester 1996–, jt appointments in Dept of Chem. and Dept of Physics and Astronomy, apptd Chair. Chemical Eng Dept 2011; currently Emer. Prof., Cornell Univ.; Chair. Prof., Dept of Electronic and Computer Eng, Hong Kong Univ. of Science and Tech., IAS Bank of East Asia Prof. 2013–; mem. Nat. Acad. of Eng 2006; Fellow, American Physical Soc. 1998, Soc. for Information Display 2002; Hon. Prof., Shanghai Univ. 2002, South China Univ. of Tech. 2002; Dr hc (Shanghai Univ., South China Univ. of Tech.); numerous awards, including Eastman Kodak Distinguished Inventor 1994, Eastman Kodak Team Achievement Award 1999, Eastman Kodak Innovation Award 2000, Jack Rajchman Prize, Soc. of Information Display 2001, ACS Carothers Award 2001, ACS Northeast Regional Innovation Award 2001, Rochester Law Asscn Inventor of the Year Award 2002, ACS Award for Team Innovation 2003, Humboldt Research Award 2005, Lifetime Achievement Award, Hajim School of Eng and Applied Sciences, Univ. of Rochester 2010, Wolf Prize in Chem. (co-recipient) 2011, Eduard Rhein Award 2013, Nick Holonyak Jr Award, The Optical Soc. 2014. *Achievements include:* recognized for invention of high-efficiency Organic Light Emitting Diodes (OLED). *Publications:* numerous papers in professional journals on chemical and condensed matter physics and, in particular, on organic electronics. *Address:* Department of Chemical Engineering, 101A Gavett Hall, RC 270166, University of Rochester, Rochester, NY 14627-0166, USA (office); School of Engineering, Room IA S2010, Hong Kong University of Science and Technology, Clear Water Bay, Kowloon, Hong Kong, People's Republic of China. *Telephone:* (585) 275-3552 (USA) (office); (852) 34692308 (China) (office). *Fax:* (585) 273-3237 (USA) (office); (852) 27196615 (China) (office). *E-mail:* chtang@che.rochester.edu (office); ching.tang@rochester.edu (office); chingtang@ ust.hk (office). *Website:* www.chem.rochester.edu/faculty/faculty.php?name=tang (office); www.seng.ust.hk (office).

TANG, Dengjie, MBA; Chinese engineer, business executive and government official; *Governor of Fujian Province;* b. June 1964, Jianhu Co., Jiangsu Prov.; ed Tongji Univ.; elected Vice-Mayor of Shanghai Municipality 2003; served successively as Head of Control Section and Man. of Industrial Eng Section of Production Project Dept, Shanghai Volkswagen Automotive Co. Ltd, Deputy Man. of Project and Devt Dept, Shanghai Automotive Industry General Co. (Group), Gen. Man. Shanghai ZF Steering Co. Ltd, Vice-Pres. Shanghai Automotive Industry Co. (Group), Deputy Party Sec. and Pres. Shanghai Electrical General Co. (Group), Deputy Party Sec. Shanghai Party Work Cttee for Industry and Dir of Shanghai Econ. Comm.; Chair. China South Industries Group Corpn 2012–; Vice Minister of Industry and Information Tech. 2017–; Administrator, China Nat. Space Admin 2017–, also Chair., China Atomic Energy Authority and Dir, State Admin for Science, Tech. and Industry for Nat. Defence 2017–; Gov. Fujian Prov. 2018–; Alt. mem. 19th CCP Cen. Cttee 2017–. *Address:* Office of the Governor, 35000 Fuzhou, People's Republic of China (office). *Website:* www.fkpg.gov.tw (office).

TANG, Gen. Fei; Taiwanese politician and air force officer (retd) and government official; b. 15 March 1932, Jiangsu; m. Chang, Ming-tsan; one s. two d.; ed Air Force Preparatory School, Chinese Air Force Acad.; air force pilot 1953–60, Operations Officer 1960–61, Flight Leader 1961–65, Squadron Commdr 1968–72, Asst Air Attaché, Embassy in USA 1972–75, Chief, Operations Section, 3rd Wing 1975–76, Group Commdr 1976–78, Mil. Attaché, Embassy in SA 1979–83, Wing Commdr 1983–84, C/S/Planning, GHQ, ROCAF 1984–85, Supt, Air Force Acad. 1985–86, Dir, Political Warfare Dept, GHQ, ROCAF 1986–89, CG, Combat Air Commdr 1989, Vice C-in-C ROCAF 1989–91, Insp.-Gen., MND 1991–92, C-in-C ROCAF

1992–95, Vice Chief of Gen. Staff (Exec.), MND 1995–98, Chief of Gen. Staff, MND 1998–99, Gen., ROCAF (retd); Minister of Defence 1999–2000; Premier of Taiwan May–Oct. 2000; Sr Adviser to Pres. 2000; Visiting Fellow, Hoover Inst., Stanford Univ. 2004.

TANG, Ignacio Milam; Equatorial Guinean politician and diplomatist; *Vice-President, in charge of Presidential Affairs;* b. 20 June 1940; Minister of Justice and Worship 1996–98, of Youth and Sports 1998–99; fmr Second Vice-Pres. Chamber of People's Reps 1999–2001; Deputy Prime Minister for the Civil Service and Admin Co-ordination 2001–03; Sec.-Gen. of the Presidency 2003–06; Amb. to Spain 2006–08; Prime Minister of Equatorial Guinea 2008–12; Vice-Pres., in charge of Presidential Affairs 2012–; mem. Democratic Party of Equatorial Guinea. *Address:* Office of the Vice-President, Malabo, Equatorial Guinea (office).

TANG, Jiaxuan; Chinese diplomatist; *President, China-Japan Friendship Association;* b. 17 Jan. 1938, Zhenjiang City, Jiangsu Prov.; ed Fudan Univ., Shanghai, Peking Univ.; intern, State Broadcasting Admin 1962; staff mem., Translation and Interpretation Dept, Ministry of Foreign Affairs 1964–70; mem. Council and Deputy Div. Chief Chinese People's Asscn for Friendship with Foreign Countries 1970–78; mem. Council Sino-Japanese Friendship Asscn 1970–78; joined CCP 1973; Second Sec., then First Sec. Embassy, Tokyo, Japan 1978–83, Minister-Counsellor 1988–91, Minister 1988–91; First Secretary, then Deputy Dir Asian Affairs Dept, Ministry of Foreign Affairs 1983–88; Asst to Minister of Foreign Affairs 1991–93, Vice-Minister 1993–98, Minister 1998–2003; State Councillor 2003–08; mem. 15th CCP Cen. Cttee 1997–2002, 16th CCP Cen. Cttee 2002–07; currently Pres. China-Japan Friendship Asscn. *Publication:* Heavy Storm & Gentle Breeze: A Memoir of China's Diplomacy 2011. *Address:* China-Japan Friendship Association, 1, Taijichang Avenue, Dongcheng District, Beijing 100740, People's Republic of China (office). *E-mail:* office@zryx.org.cn (office). *Website:* www.zryx.org.cn (office).

TANG, Shubei; Chinese government official; b. Jan. 1931, Shanghai; m. Liang Wenfeng; one s. one d.; joined CCP 1949; fmrly official Shanghai Fed. of Trade Unions; Ed., Head of Reporters Centre, Fujian Daily 1955; Chief, Editorial Dept, New Vietnamese-Chinese News 1955–57; Sec., then Deputy Dir, Dir China News Service 1957–69; Deputy Div. Chief Dept of Consular Affairs 1971–78; First Sec. Tokyo Embassy 1978–82; Div. Chief Dept of Consular Affairs 1982–83; Consul-Gen., San Francisco 1983–86; Amb. to USA 1986–88; Dir Office for Taiwan Affairs of Foreign Ministry 1988–89, Deputy Dir for Taiwan Affairs of State Council 1989–2000; Deputy Dir CCP Cen. Cttee Taiwan Affairs Office 1991–; Exec. Vice-Chair. Asscn for Relations Across the Taiwan Straits 1991–2000; Deputy Dir CPPCC Cen. Cttee Coordinating Cttee for Reunification of the Motherland 1993–98; mem. Standing Cttee 8th CPPCC Nat. Cttee 1993–98, 9th CPPCC Nat. Cttee 1998–2003, Vice-Chair. CPPCC Sub-cttee for Hong Kong, Macao and Taiwan Compatriots and Overseas Chinese 1998–2003; mem. Hong Kong Special Admin. Region Preparatory Cttee 1995–97. *Address:* Taiwan Affairs Office of the State Council, Beijing, People's Republic of China (office). *Telephone:* (10) 83551789 (office).

TANG, Gen. Tianbiao; Chinese army officer; b. Oct. 1940, Shimen Co., Hunan Prov.; ed Harbin Inst. of Mil. Eng, Inst. of PLA Engineer Corps, Propaganda and Theoretical Cadre Training Course of CCP Cen. Cttee Party School and Univ. of Nat. Defence; joined CCP 1961; held various posts in Guangzhou Mil. Region; Deputy Dir Propaganda Dept Guangzhou Mil. Region 1983; Deputy Office Head and Deputy Dir Cadre Dept of PLA Gen. Political Dept; Deputy Dir PLA Navy's Political Dept; Dir Cadre Dept of Gen. Political Dept; Deputy Dir Leading Group for the Placement of Demobilized Army Officers 1995–; Asst Dir PLA Gen. Political Dept 1993–95, Deputy Dir 1995–; rank of Lt-Gen. 1994, Gen. 2000; Deputy to 8th NPC 1993–98; mem. 15th CCP Cen. Cttee 1997–2002, 16th CCP Cen. Cttee 2002–07; Vice Chair. China Int. Culture Communication Centre (CICCC). *E-mail:* www.ciccc.org.cn (office).

TANG, Xiaowei; Chinese physicist; *Professor, Department of Physics, Zhejiang University;* b. 1 Oct. 1931, Wuxi Co., Jiangsu Prov.; ed Tsinghua Univ., Beijing; Researcher, Inst. of High Energy Physics (IHEP), Chinese Acad. of Sciences, later Prof. and Academician; currently Prof. and PhD Supervisor, Dept of Physics, Zhejiang Univ., also Dir Academic Cttee of Brain and Intelligence Research Center; Adjunct Prof., Peking Univ., Univ. of Science and Tech. of China (USTC); mem. Dept Math. and Physics, Academia Sinica 1985; Del. 12th and 13th CCP Nat. Congress; mem. Chinese Acad. of Sciences 1980–; Nat. Scientific Prize of China. *Publications:* author or co-author of more than 400 papers. *Address:* Department of Physics, Zijingang Campus, Zhejiang University, Hangzhou 310058, People's Republic of China (office). *Telephone:* (571) 87952388 (office). *E-mail:* fmrilab@zju .edu.cn (office). *Website:* physics.zju.edu.cn/pw/biox/tangxw_en.htm (office).

TANG, Yuanyou; Chinese business executive and party official; Man. Dir Henan Coal and Chemical Industry Group Co. Ltd; Mayor of Hebi City –2017; Dir Quality Supervision Bureau, Henan Prov. and Sec., CCP Group 2017–.

TANG YING YEN, Henry, JP, GBS; Hong Kong business executive and government official; b. 6 Sept. 1952, Jiangsu Province, Wuxi City; m. Lisa Kuo; one s. three d.; ed Univ. of Michigan, USA; Man. Dir Peninsula Knitters Ltd; Chair. Fed. of Hong Kong Industries 1995–2001; Dir Meadville Ltd; Hong Kong Affairs Adviser to Chinese Govt; mem. Legis. Council 1991–98; mem. Exec. Council, Hong Kong Special Admin. Region July 1997–2002, Sec. for Commerce, Industry and Technology July 2002–Aug. 2003, Financial Sec. Aug. 2003–07, Chief Sec. for Admin 2007–11 (resgnd); mem. Selection Cttee for First Govt of Hong Kong Special Admin. Region, CPPCC Shanghai Cttee, Hong Kong Trade Devt Council, Liberal Party; Dr hc (Hong Kong Polytechnic Univ.), Hon. DIur (City Univ. of Hong Kong); Young Industrialist Award 1989, Global Leader for Tomorrow, World Economic Forum 1993.

TANGARA, Mamadou, MA, MA, PhD; Gambian academic, politician and diplomatist; *Minister of Foreign Affairs;* b. 4 June 1965, Banjul; m. Saffiatou Tangara Samba; several c.; ed Université Catholique de Louvain, Belgium, Université de Limoges, France; fmr Ed.-in-Chief of La Lune (magazine for French learners); held various positions at Univ. of The Gambia, first as Lecturer 2002–08, then as Pres. and Chair. Univ. Governing Council 2008–; Co-ordinator Nat. Authorizing Office Support Unit for European Union-funded programmes and projects in The Gambia 2008–10; apptd by the Pres. as focal point on matters related to UNESCO Science Sector 2009; held various positions within Govt, serving as Minister for Fisheries, Water Resources and Nat. Ass. Matters, for Higher Educ., Research, Science and Tech., for Foreign Affairs, Int. Co-operation and Gambians Abroad 2010–13; Amb. and Perm. Rep. to UN, New York 2013–18; Minister of Foreign Affairs 2018–. *Address:* Ministry of Foreign Affairs, 4 Marina Parade, Banjul, The Gambia (office). *Telephone:* 4223577 (office); 4221730 (UDP) (office). *Fax:* 4227917 (office); 4224601 (UDP) (office). *E-mail:* info@mofa.gov.gm (office); info@udpgambia.org (office). *Website:* www.mofa.gov.gm (office).

TANGNEY, Lt-Gen. (retd) William Patrick, BA, MA; American army officer (retd) and business executive; *Senior Vice-President for Intelligence, Future Technologies, Inc.;* b. 7 Oct. 1945, Worcester, Mass.; ed The Citadel, Syracuse Univ., US Naval Coll.; joined US Army 1968, advanced to rank of Lt-Gen. 1998; Operational Staff Officer G-3 Training Div., US Army John F. Kennedy Center for Mil. Assistance, Fort Bragg 1972–74; Exec. Officer, 2nd Special Forces Bn, 7th Special Forces Group 1974, 5th Special Forces Group 1981–83; Deputy Asst Chief of Staff G-3 1983–85; Commdr 3rd Bn 5th Special Forces Group 1985–87; Chief of Special Forces, US Total Army Personnel Command, Alexandria, Va 1987–88; Commdr 10th Special Forces Group, Fort Devens, Mass. 1990–92; Commanding Gen. Special Operations, MacDill Air Force Base, Fla 1993–94; Deputy Commdg Gen., Chief of Staff, US Army Special Operations Command, Fort Bragg 1994–95; Commanding Gen. US Army Special Forces Command (Airborne), Fort Bragg 1995–97, US Army John F. Kennedy Special Warfare Center, Fort Bragg 1996–98; Deputy Commdr in Chief, Special Operations Command, MacDill Air Force Base, Fla 2000–02 (retd); currently Sr Vice-Pres. for Intelligence, Future Technologies, Inc.; Distinguished Service Medal, Defense Superior Service Medal (with Oak Leaf Cluster), Legion of Merit (with Oak Leaf Cluster), Bronze Star Medal with V Device, Bronze Star Medal (with 2 Oak Leaf Clusters), Defense Meritorious Service Medal. *Address:* Future Technologies, Inc., 12600 Fair Lakes Circle, Suite 200, Fairfax, VA 22033, USA (office). *Telephone:* (703) 278-0199 (office). *Fax:* (703) 385-0886 (office). *Website:* www.ftechi.com (office).

TANIGAKI, Sadakazu, LLB; Japanese lawyer and politician; b. 7 March 1945, Tokyo; ed Univ. of Tokyo; passed Nat. Bar Examination 1979; Attorney-at-Law 1984; mem. House of Reps (lower house of Parl.) for Kyoto No. 5 constituency (LDP) 1983–, Chair. Standing Cttee on Communications 1991, Standing Cttee on Rules and Admin 1995; Vice-Minister of Posts and Telecommunications 1988, of Defence 1990; Minister of State for Science and Tech. 1997, State Sec. for Finance 1998; Minister of State for Industrial Revitalization Corpn 2002; Minister of Finance 2003–06, of Land, Infrastructure and Transport 2008, of Justice 2012–14; Chair. Financial Reconstruction Comm. 2000, Nat. Public Safety Comm. 2002, Food Safety Comm. 2002; Vice-Chair. LDP Nat. Diet Cttee 1987, Dir-Gen. LDP Election Bureau 1996, Chair. Policy Research Council 2007, LDP Pres. 2009–12, Sec.-Gen. 2014–16. *Leisure interests:* mountaineering, cycling, wine tasting. *Address:* c/o Liberal Democratic Party, 1-11-23, Nagata-cho, Chiyoda-ku, Tokyo 100-8910, Japan.

TANIGUCHI, Yoshio; Japanese architect; *Principal, Taniguchi and Associates;* b. 17 Oct. 1937, Tokyo; ed Keio Univ., Tokyo, Grad. School of Design, Harvard Univ., USA; worked in studio of Kenzo Tange 1964–72; Prin. Taniguchi Associates, Tokyo 1979–; has taught architecture at Harvard Univ., UCLA, Univ. of Tokyo; Praemium Imperiale, Japan Art Asscn 2005. *Achievements include:* won competition to design expansion of Museum of Modern Art, New York 1998, completed 2004. *Address:* Taniguchi and Associates, 4-1-40 Toranomon, Minato-ku, Tokyo 105-8529, Japan. *Telephone:* (3) 3438-1506. *Fax:* (3) 3438-1248.

TANIN, Zahir, MD; Afghan journalist, physician and diplomatist; *Special Representative and Head, United Nations Interim Administration Mission in Kosovo (UNMIK);* b. 1 May 1956; m. Dr Zarghoona Sediq Tanin; two c.; ed Kabul Medical Univ.; began career as journalist in Kabul 1980; freelance writer in France 1992–93; fmr Ed.-in-Chief Afkbar-e-Haftah and Sabawoon Magazine; Research Fellow, Int. Relations Dept, LSE, England 1994–95; Producer, BBC World Service 1995–2000, Sr Producer 2000–01, Ed. Afghanistan and Cen. Asia (Persian Section) 2001–03, Persian/Pashto Section in Afghanistan 2003–06; Amb. and Perm. Rep. to UN, New York 2006–15, apptd Vice-Chair. Bureau on the Inalienable Rights of the Palestinian People 2006, Vice-Pres. 63rd Session of UN Gen. Ass. 2008–09, chaired several plenary meetings, including part of High Level Meeting on Interfaith and Intercultural Dialogue 2008, apptd Chair intergovernmental negotiations on Security Council reform on behalf of Pres. of Gen. Ass. 2009, Vice-Chair. Open Ended Working Group on the Question of Equitable Representation of and an Increase in Membership to the Security Council and Other Related Matters, Special Rep. and Head, UN Interim Administration Mission in Kosovo (UNMIK) 2015–. *Radio:* The Oral History of Afghanistan in the 20th Century (BBC). *Publications include:* The Communist Regime in Afghanistan (co-author), Afghanistan in the Twentieth Century. *Address:* United Nations Interim Administration Mission in Kosovo (UNMIK) Headquaters, Industrial Zone, 10 000 Pristina, Kosovo (office); United Nations Interim Administration Mission in Kosovo (UNMIK), Department of Peacekeeping Operations, Room S-3727-B, United Nations, New York, NY 10017, USA (office). *Telephone:* (38) 5046045900 (Pristina) (office); (212) 967-3104 (New York) (office). *Fax:* (38) 5046045406 (Pristina) (office). *E-mail:* office-srsg@un.org (office). *Website:* www.unmikonline .org (office).

TANIZAKI, Yasuaki; Japanese diplomatist; *Ambassador to Indonesia;* b. 20 Oct. 1951; ed Univ. of Tokyo, Univ. of Tübingen, Germany; joined Ministry of Foreign Affairs (MFA) 1975, Second Sec., Embassy in Vienna 1978–86, First Sec., Embassy in Manila 1986–88, First Sec., Embassy in Moscow, USSR 1988–98, Minister, Embassy in Berlin 1998–2001, Dir, Gen. Affairs Div., Minister's Secr., MFA 2001–02, Deputy Dir-Gen., European Affairs Bureau/Econ. Co-operation Bureau 2002–04, Asst Vice-Minister 2004–05, Dir-Gen., Consular Affairs Bureau 2005–08, Dir-Gen., European Affairs Bureau 2008–10, Amb. to Viet Nam 2010–13, Dir-Gen., Foreign Service Training Inst., MFA 2013–14, Amb. to Indonesia 2014–. *Address:* Embassy of Japan, Jalan M.H. Thamrin 24, Jakarta Pusat 10350, Indonesia (office). *Telephone:* (21) 31924308 (office). *Fax:* (21) 31925460 (office). *Website:* www.id.emb-japan.go.jp (office).

TANJUNG, Chairul, MBA; Indonesian business executive; *Founder and Chairman, CT Corporation;* b. 16 June 1962, Jakarta; m.; two c.; ed Univ. of Indonesia, Institut Pendidikan and Pengembangan Manajemen (Educ. and Man. Devt Inst.); Founder and Chair. Para Group (PT Para Inti Holtindo, now CT Corpn) 1987–); extensive business interests in banking, media, property, lifestyle and entertainment; Chair. Indonesia Forum Foundation, Nat. Kidney Foundation Indonesia; Dir Pacific Basin Econ. Council; mem. Bd of Dirs Indonesian Cttee for Humanitarian Program, Indonesian Red Cross, Jakarta Art Foundation; Cttee mem. Jakarta Initiative (The Company Restructuring Agency); fmr Chair. Badminton Asscn of Indonesia. *Address:* CT Corporation, Menara Bank Mega, 24th Floor. Jl. Kapt. P. Tendean Kav. 12–14 A, Jakarta 12790, Indonesia (office). *Telephone:* (21) 79175533 (office). *Fax:* (21) 79193300 (office). *Website:* www.ctcorpora.com (office).

TANKARD, Meryl; Australian choreographer, director and designer; b. 8 Sept. 1955, Darwin, NT; d. of (Mick) Clifford Tankard and Margot Tankard; m. Regis Lansac; ed Australian Ballet School, Australian Film Television and Radio School (Grad. Diploma in Directing); dancer with Australian Ballet Co. 1975–78; solo dancer with Pina Bausch Wuppertal Tanztheater, Germany 1978–84, Guest Performer and Choreographer 1984–89; Artistic Dir Meryl Tankard Co., Canberra 1989–92, Meryl Tankard Australian Dance Theatre 1993–99, freelance dir/ choreographer 1999–; Canberran of the Year 1992, Sidney Myer Performing Arts Award for Individual Achievement 1993, Victoria Green Room Awards 1993, 1994, Betty Pounder Award for Original Choreography 1994, 'Age' Performing Arts Award for Best Collaboration (Dance) 1995, Mobil Pegasus Award for Best Production 1997, Australian Dance Awards' Lifetime Achievement Award 2003, Centenary Medal Australia, Australia Council Fellowship, Australian Dance Awards outstanding achievement in choreography 2010. *Major works choreographed include:* Echo Point (Australia) 1984, 1990, Travelling Light (UK and Australia) 1986–87, Two Feet (Australia, NZ, Japan and Germany) 1988–94, VX 18504 (Australia) 1989–95, Court of Flora (Australia) 1990–93, Nuti & Kikimora (Italy, Indonesia, Australia, China and Germany) 1990–94, Chants of Marriage I and II (Australia) 1991–92, Furioso (Australia and overseas) 1993–99, O Let Me Weep (Australia) 1994, Aurora (Australia) 1994–96, Orphée et Eurydice (Australia) 1995–96, Possessed (Australia, France and Germany) 1995–99, The Deep End (Australia) 1996, Rasa 1996, Inuk 1997 (Australia, Germany), Bolero (France, USA, Hong Kong) 1999, The Beautiful Game (UK) 2000, Sydney Olympic Opening Ceremony 'Deep Sea Dreaming', Merryland (Netherlands, Switzerland, Germany) 2002, The Wild Swans (Australian Ballet) 2003, @North (Berlinballet, Berlin) 2004, Petrushka for Netherlands Dance Theatre I (Den Haag) 2004, Tarzan for Disney Productions 2006, Kaidan (Sydney Opera House) 2007, Inuk 2 (Sydney Dance Co.), The Oracle (Sydney Opera House) 2009. *Films:* Moth, Mad 2010. *Leisure interest:* designing. *Address:* PO Box 3129, Bellevue Hill, NSW 2023, Australia (office). *Telephone:* (2) 9300-6811 (office). *Fax:* (2) 9300-6811 (office). *E-mail:* meryltankard@iprimus.com.au (office). *Website:* www.meryltankard.com (office).

TANKSLEY, Steven D., BS, PhD; American agronomist, geneticist and academic; *CEO and Chief Scientific Officer, Natural Source Genetics;* b. 7 April 1954, Hattiesburg, Miss.; ed Colorado State Univ., Univ. of California, Davis; Research Asst, Univ. of California, Davis 1976–79, Postdoctoral Fellow 1979–81; Asst Prof., New Mexico State Univ., Las Cruces 1981–85; Assoc. Prof. of Plant Breeding, Cornell Univ. 1985–91, Prof. 1991–2010, then Liberty Hyde Bailey Prof. of Plant Breeding and Chair. Genomics Initiative Task Force, Prof. Emer. 2010–; Founder, CEO and Chief Scientific Officer, Natural Source Genetics 2006–; mem. NAS 1995; Foreign mem. Royal Soc. of London 2009; Alexander von Humboldt Foundation Award 1998, Martin Gibbs Medal, American Soc. of Plant Biologists 1999, Wolf Prize in Agric., Wolf Foundation (co-recipient) 2004, Kumho Int. Science Award Korea 2005, Rank Prize 2008, Japan Prize 2016. *Achievements include:* mem. of team of Cornell Univ. scientists who successfully cloned first gene for disease resistance in tomato, using technique known as map-based cloning developed for Human Genome Project 1993. *Publications include:* numerous scientific papers in professional journals. *Address:* Nature Source Genetics 33 Thornwood Drive, Suite 300, Ithaca, NY 14850 (office); Department of Plant Breeding and Genetics, Cornell University, Emerson Hall, Room 240, Ithaca, NY 14853, USA (office). *Telephone:* (607) 844-3442 (office). *Fax:* (607) 255-6683 (office). *E-mail:* sdt4@ cornell.edu (office). *Website:* plbrgen.cals.cornell.edu (office); www .naturesourcegenetics.com (office).

TANNER, Alain; Swiss film director; b. 6 Dec. 1929, Geneva. *Films include:* Charles Dead or Alive 1969, Salamander 1971, The Middle of the World, Jonah Who Will be 25 in the Year 2000 1976, Messidor 1979, Light Years Away (Special Jury Prize, Cannes Film Festival 1985) 1981, In the White City 1983, No Man's Land 1985, Une Flamme Dans Mon Coeur 1987, The Woman of Rose Hill 1989, The Man Who Lost His Shadow 1991, The Diary of Lady M 1993, Les Hommes du port 1995, Fourbi 1996, Requiem 1998, Jonas et Lila, à demain 1999, Fleurs de sang 2002, Paul s'en va 2004.

TANNER, Lindsay, BA, LLB, MA; Australian politician and academic; *Vice-Chancellor's Fellow and Adjunct Professor, Victoria University;* b. 26 April 1956, Orbost, Vic.; m. Andrea Tanner; two d.; ed Univ. of Melbourne; Articled Clerk and Solicitor, Holding Redlich 1982–85; Electorate Asst for Senator Barney Cooney 1985–87; Asst Sec., Federated Clerks Union, Vic. 1987–88, State Sec. 1988–93; MP (Australia Labor Party) for Melbourne 1993–2010, Shadow Minister for Transport 1996–98, for Finance and Consumer Affairs 1998, for Communications 2001–04, for Finance 2005–07, Minister for Finance and Deregulation 2007–10; Vice-Chancellor's Fellow and Adjunct Prof., Victoria Univ. 2010–, also Chair. Advisory Bd Mitchell Inst. for Health and Educ. Policy; Hon. Fellow, Chartered Inst. of Purchasing and Supply 2011. *Publications:* The Politics of Pollution (jt author) 1978, The Last Battle 1996, Open Australia 1999, Crowded Lives 2003; numerous articles in journals and newspapers. *Leisure interests:* reading, playing piano, sport. *Address:* Victoria University, POB 14428, Melbourne VIC 8001, Australia (office). *Telephone:* (3) 9919-4000 (office). *E-mail:* lindsay.tanner1@vu.edu.au (office). *Website:* www.vu.edu.au (office).

TANNER, Roger Ian, PhD, FRS, FAA; British engineer and academic; *P.N. Russell Professor of Mechanical Engineering, University of Sydney;* b. 25 July 1933, Wells, Somerset; s. of R. J. Tanner and E. Tanner; m. Elizabeth Bogen 1957; two s. three d.; ed Univs of Bristol and Manchester, Univ. of California, Berkeley,

USA; eng apprentice, Bristol Aero Engines 1950–53; Lecturer in Mechanical Eng, Univ. of Manchester 1958–61; Sr Lecturer, Reader, Univ. of Sydney, Australia 1961–66, P.N. Russell Prof. of Mechanical Eng 1975–, Pro-Vice-Chancellor (Research) 1994–97; Prof., Brown Univ. Providence, RI, USA 1966–75; Fellow, Australian Acad. of Tech. Science and Eng 1979; Edgeworth David Medal 1966, Australian Soc. of Rheology Medallion 1993, A.G.M. Michell Medal 1999, British Soc. of Rheology Gold Medal 2000. *Publications include:* Engineering Rheology 1985, 2000, Rheology: An Historical Perspective 1998. *Leisure interests:* golf, opera. *Address:* Department of Aerospace, Mechanical and Mechatronic Engineering, University of Sydney, Sydney, NSW 2006 (office); 3 Sixth Mile Lane, Roseville, NSW 2069, Australia (home). *Telephone:* (2) 9351-7153 (office). *Fax:* (2) 9351-7060 (office). *E-mail:* roger.tanner@sydney.edu.au (office). *Website:* www.aeromech.usyd.edu.au (office).

TANOESOEDIBJO, Hary, BCom, MBA; Indonesian business executive; *Group President and CEO, PT Global Mediacom Tbk;* b. 26 Sept. 1965, Surabaya; m.; five c.; ed Carleton Univ., Canada, Univ. of Ottawa; co-f. PT Bhakti Investama Tbk, Surabaya 1989, Pres. Commr 1989–2009, Pres. Dir 2009–, Pres. Dir PT Global Mediacom Tbk 2002–, currently Group Pres. and CEO, CEO MNC Group 2004–; Commr PT Mobile 8 Telecom 2004–, PT MNC Sky Vision 2006–; Pres. Dir PT Rajawali Citra Televisi 2003–08; Dir MNC International Ltd 2007–; Chair. and CEO Linktone Ltd 2008–; co-f. Indonesia Recovery Co. Ltd; other holdings include Bimantara Citra, Indomilk, SCTV; mem. Partai NasDem 2011–13, Partai Hati Nurani Rakyat (Hanura) 2013–. *Address:* PT Global Mediacom Tbk, Floor 27, Kebon Sirih Tower, Kebon Sirih Street, Lot 17-19, Jakarta 10340, Indonesia (office). *Telephone:* (21) 3900885 (office). *Fax:* (21) 3909207 (office).

TANOTO, Sukanto, (Chen Jianghe); Indonesian business executive; *Founder, Chairman and CEO, RGE Pte Ltd;* b. 25 Dec. 1949; m.; four c.; ed INSEAD, France, Harvard Univ. and Wharton Business School, USA; left school aged 17 to join family business supplying parts to oil and gas cos, Medan; f. Raja Garuda Mas (RGM) (plywood mfr) 1973, later RGM Int., renamed RGE (Royal Golden Eagle) Pte Ltd 2009, (conglomerate with interests in paper, palm oil, construction, energy), associated cos include Pacific Oil & Gas Ltd, Asia Pacific Resources Int. Holdings Ltd; f. Tanoto Foundation 1984; mem. INSEAD Int. Council, World Pres Org., Wharton Bd of Overseers; named Outstanding Contributor among Asia-Pacific Chinese Entrepreneurial Leaders with the Strongest Social Responsibility 2009, Wharton School Dean's Medal Award. *Address:* RGE Pte Ltd, 80 Raffles Place, #50-01 UOB Plaza 1, Singapore 048624, Singapore (office). *Telephone:* 62169368 (office). *Fax:* 65384668 (office). *Website:* www.rgei.com (office); www.sukantotanoto.net.

TANTAWI, Field Marshal Muhammad Hussein; Egyptian army officer and government official; *Adviser to the President;* b. 31 Oct. 1935; served as infantry officer in Suez war 1956, six-days war 1967, October 1973 war; Minister of Defence and Mil. Production 1991–2012; apptd Gen. Commdr for Armed Forces 1995; Chair., Supreme Council of the Armed Forces and de facto Head of State (following resignation of Pres. Hosni Mubarak) 2011–12; Adviser to Pres. 2012–; Order of the Nile 2012, Order of Merit, Order of the Republic, Egypt, Grand Cross of the Order of Prince Henry, Portugal, Commdr of the Order of the Republic, Tunisia, Commemorative Medal of the United Arab Republic, Kt of the Order of St Michael and St George, UK, Nishan-e-Imtiaz, Pakistan; Kuwait Liberation Medal, Saudi Arabia, Egypt, Kuwait, Longevity and Exemplary Meda, 25 January Revolution Medal, Army Day Medal, Combat Injury Medal, Tenth Anniversary of the Revolution Medal, Twentieth Anniversary of the Revolution Medal.

TANTI, Tulsi R., BCom, DipEng; Indian energy industry executive; *Chairman and Managing Director, Suzlon Energy;* b. Rajkot, Gujarat; m.; three c.; ed Rajkot Coll.; began career in textile industry, Gujarat; co-f. Suzlon Energy Ltd (wind power venture) 1995, currently Chair. and Man. Dir; Pres. Gujarat Chapter, Indian Wind Turbine Manufacturers Asscn; fmr Chair. Hansen Transmissions Int., Dir 2006–; Chair. Supervisory Bd REPower Systems AG 2007–; mem. Bd of Dirs SE Forge Ltd; Solar Energy Soc. of India (SESI) Business Leadership Award 2002, World Wind Energy Award 2003, SESI Lifetime Achievement Award as Best Renewable Man of the Decade 2006, Entrepreneur of the Year, Ernst & Young 2006, Time magazine Hero of the Environment 2007, Champion of the Earth, UNEP 2009. *Address:* Suzlon Energy Ltd, One Earth, Hadapsar, Pune 411 028, Maharashtra, India (office). *Telephone:* (20) 67022000 (office). *Website:* www.suzlon.com (office).

TANTIVORAWONG, Apisak, BEng, MBA; Thai banker and government official; *Minister of Finance;* b. 28 Nov. 1953; Pres. Krung Thai Bank Public Co. Ltd 2004–12, Dir 2004–; Chair. Quality Houses Public Co. Ltd 2013–15; Dir of Investment, Thai Asset Management Corpn; Dir Siam Commercial Bank Public Co. Ltd 2014–, Adviser to Bd of Dirs 2013–14; Ind. Dir Thai Oil Public Co. Ltd 2007–15, Indorama Ventures Public Co. Ltd 2013–15, Bangkok Glass Industry Co. Ltd 2013–, Synnex (Thailand) Public Co. Ltd 2013–15, Thai-German Ceramic Industry Public Co. Ltd; Dir Siam City Bank Public Co. Ltd, Indorama Holdings Ltd, Indorama Polymers Public Co. Ltd, CP ALL Public Co. Ltd 2012–; Minister of Finance 2015–; fmr Chair. ASEAN Bankers Asscn, Thai Bankers Asscn. *Address:* Ministry of Finance, Thanon Rama VI, Samsennai, Phaya Thai, Rajatevi, Bangkok 10400, Thailand (office). *Telephone:* (2) 273-9021 (office). *Fax:* (2) 273-9408 (office). *E-mail:* webmaster-eng@mof.go.th (office). *Website:* www.mof.go.th (office).

TANTOCO, Bienvenido R., Sr; Philippine retail executive and diplomatist; b. 7 April 1921; m. Gliceria Tantoco (deceased); six c.; ed Jose Rizal Univ., Mandaluyong; opened first retail outlet with wife 1951; fmr Chair. Rustan Commercial Corpn, Rustan Supermarkets Inc., Rustan Int. Trading Corpn, Rustan Marketing Corpn, Royal Duty Free Shops, Tourist Duty Free Shops Inc., Stores Specialists Inc., Rustan Coffee Corpn, Rustan Supercenters Inc., Sta Elena Golf Club, Sta Elena Properties Inc.; Amb. of Philippines to Holy See 1983–86; Pres. Philippine–Italian Asscn 1977–86; fmr Pres. Philippine Retailers Asscn, Shopwise; Commdr, Order of Merit of the Repub. of Italy, Order of Merit of the Repub. of Portugal, Kt, Grand Cross of the Order of Pius 1X 1985; Hon. DH (Jose Rizal Univ.).

TANZI, Vito, BA, MA, MA, PhD; American/Italian economist; *Independent Scholar and Honorary President, International Institute of Public Finance;* b. 29 Nov. 1935, Italy; s. of Luigi Tanzi and Maria Tanzi; m. Maria T. Bernabé 1997; three s.; ed George Washington and Harvard Univs; Chair. of Econs Dept, American Univ., Washington, DC 1971–74, Prof. of Econs 1970–74; Head of Tax Policy Div., IMF 1974–81, Dir Fiscal Affairs Dept 1981–2000; Pres. Int. Inst. of Public Finance 1990–94, now Ind. Scholar and Hon. Pres.; Sr Assoc. Carnegie Endowment for Int. Peace 2001; Under-Sec. of State, Ministry of Economy and Finance, Italy 2001–03; Sr Consultant in Trade and Integration, IDB 2003–07; Commendatore della Repubblica Italiana; Dr hc (Córdoba, Argentina) 1998, (Liège, Belgium) 1999, (Turin, Italy) 2001, (Bari, Italy) 2003, (Lisbon, Portugal) 2007; various awards. *Publications:* 20 books, including Government versus Markets 2011, Italica 2012, Dollars, Euros and Debt 2013; more than 300 articles in professional journals. *Leisure interests:* naif art, African art, photography, music, travel, collecting old keys and old locks. *Address:* 5912 Walhonding Road, Bethesda, MD 20816, USA (home). *Fax:* (301) 229-2827 (home). *E-mail:* vitotanzi@msn.com.

TAO, Gen. Bojun; Chinese army officer; b. Dec. 1936, Yongji Co., Jilin Prov.; joined PLA 1951, CCP 1961; Chief, Wuhan Mil. Dist (Combat Div., Artillery HQ), PLA Guangzhou Mil. Region 1976–77, Dir Artillery HQ 1983; Deputy Army Commdr PLA Chengdu Mil. Region 1983–85, Chief-of-Staff 1985–92, Commdr 2000; Chief of Staff Guangzhou Mil. Region 1992, Deputy Commdr 1993–96, Commdr 2000; Commdr Guangdong Mil. Region 1996–2001; rank of Maj.-Gen. 1988, Lt-Gen. 1991, Gen. 2000; Del., 13th CCP Cen. Cttee 1987–92, 14th CCP Cen. Cttee 1992–97, mem. 15th CCP Cen. Cttee 1997–2002. *Address:* People's Liberation Army, c/o Ministry of National Defence, Jingshanqian Jie, Beijing 100009, People's Republic of China (office).

TAO, Ho, MArch; Chinese architect and artist; b. 17 July 1936, Shanghai; ed Williams Coll. and Harvard Univ., Mass, USA; worked with architect Walter Gropius; in practice as architect and Lecturer in Hong Kong 1964–; Pres. Hong Kong Inst. of Architects 1994–98; art work includes acrylic paintings, lithographs, pen-and-ink sketches and sculptures in marble, wood and rusty scrap iron; works exhibited at Hong Kong Univ. Museum; f. TAOHO Design 1968; Hon. LHD (Williams Coll., Mass) 1979; Hong Kong Inst. of Architects Prize for Outstanding Community Services to Architecture 1995, Bicentennial Medal For Career Distinction, Williams Coll., Mass 1996, World Economic Forum Crystal Award 1997, two Silver Medals and five Design Merit awards from Hong Kong Inst. of Architects. *Buildings include:* Hong Kong Arts Centre 1977, Hong Chi Pinehill Training Centre, Tai Po 2003, People's Supreme Court, Shanghai (Interior) 2004, Pu Jiang Information Technology Centre 2005. *Designs include:* Bauhinia emblem, flag of Hong Kong Special Administrative Region, Synergy of Dynamic Energy (displayed at West Hall area, Hong Kong International Airport). *Address:* Taoho Design International Limited, 4 Suffolk Road, Kowloon, Hong Kong Special Administrative Region, People's Republic of China (office). *Telephone:* 62478850 (office). *Fax:* 62478870 (office). *E-mail:* taoho_sh@taoho.com (office). *Website:* taohofoundation.org (office).

TAO, Terence, BSc, MSc, PhD, FRS; Australian mathematician and academic; *James and Carol Collins Professor of Mathematics, University of California, Los Angeles;* b. (Chi-Shen Tao), 17 July 1975, Adelaide, SA; s. of Dr Billy Tao and Grace Tao; m. Laura Tao; one s. one d.; ed Flinders Univ. of South Australia, Princeton Univ.; began learning calculus aged seven, progressed to univ.-level calculus aged 11, apptd Full Prof. aged 24; Hedrick Asst Prof. then Prof. of Math., UCLA 1996–; Visiting Prof., Univ. of New South Wales 2000; Corresponding mem. Australian Acad. of Sciences; Foreign mem. NAS; Fellow, American Acad. of Arts and Sciences 2009, American Math. Soc.; Hon. Prof., ANU 2001–03; Bronze, Silver and Gold Medals (youngest ever Gold medallist) Int. Math. Olympiads, Salem Prize 2000, Bôcher Memorial Prize 2002, Clay Research Award 2003, Australian Math. Soc. Medal 2005, Ostrowski Prize 2005, Levi L. Conant Prize, American Math. Soc. (co-recipient) 2005, Fields Medal, Int. Congress of Mathematicians 2006, SASTRA Ramanujan Prize 2006, MacArthur Fellowship Award 2006, Alan T. Waterman Award 2008, Onsager Medal 2008, King Faisal Int. Prize (co-recipient) 2010, Nemmers Prize in Math. 2010, Polya Prize 2010, Crafoord Prize (co-recipient) 2012, Simons Foundation Award 2012, Joseph I. Lieberman Award 2013, Royal Medal, Royal Soc. (co-recipient) 2014, Johns Hopkins CTY Distinguished Alumnus 2014, Breakthrough Prize in Math. (co-recipient) 2015, PROSE Award 2015. *Publications:* 17 books, including Solving Mathematical Problems: A Personal Perspective 2006, Analysis, Vols I and II 2006, Additive Combinatorics (co-author) 2006, Nonlinear Dispersive Equations: Local and Global Analysis 2006, Structure and Randomness: Pages from Year One of a Mathematical Blog 2008, Poincaré's Legacies: Pages from Year Two of a Mathematical Blog, Vols I and II 2009, An Introduction to Measure Theory 2011, An Epsilon of Room, I: Real Analysis: Pages from Year Three of a Mathematical Blog 2011, An Epsilon of Room, II: Pages from Year Three of a Mathematical Blog 2011, Topics in Random Matrix Theory 2012, Higher-order Fourier Analysis 2012, Compactness and Contradiction 2013; more than 250 articles in professional journals. *Address:* Mathematical Sciences 6183, Department of Mathematics, UCLA, Los Angeles, CA 90095-1555, USA (office). *Telephone:* (310) 206-4844 (office). *Fax:* (310) 206-6673 (office). *E-mail:* tao@math.ucla.edu (office). *Website:* www.math.ucla.edu/~tao (office); terrytao.wordpress.com.

TAO, Yiping, MBA; Chinese economist and banking executive; *President, Industrial Bank Company Ltd;* b. April 1963; ed Xiamen Univ.; worked for Bank of China for many years, including a six-year period in Bank of China Group (Hong Kong), served as Section Chief of Gen. Plan Div., Fujian Br. of Bank of China, as Sr Man. of Gen. Office, Hong Kong and Macao Admin Office, BOC Group, as Sr Man. of China Business Dept, Hong Kong Br. of Kincheng Bank, as Dir of Gen. Office and Chief of Fund Plan Div., Fujian Br. of Bank of China, as Pres. of Fuzhou Shizhong Sub-br. of Bank of China, as Asst Pres. and Vice-Pres. of Fujian Br. of Bank of China, as Pres. of Xiamen Br. of Bank of China, as Pres. of Fujian Br. of Bank of China, and as Pres. of Shandong Br. of Bank of China –2016; Pres. Industrial Bank Co. Ltd 2016–. *Address:* Industrial Bank Company Ltd, 154 Hudong Road, Fuzhou 350003, People's Republic of China (office). *Telephone:* (591) 87839338 (office). *Fax:* (591) 87841932 (office). *E-mail:* webmaster@cib.com.cn (office). *Website:* www.cib.com.cn (office).

TAPANGARARUA, Willie Jimmy; Ni-Vanuatu politician and fmr diplomatist; b. 4 March 1960; ed Malapoa Coll., Fulton Coll., Fiji; Freight and Traffic Officer, Air Melanesia 1989; Receptionist and Reservations Officer, Radisson Palms and

Casino 1992; Asst Chief Security Officer, Club Vanuatu 1993; Compliance and Freight Officer, Ifira Shipping Agencies 1994–95; Private Business (real estate) 1997–2004; MP for Port Vila constituency 1983–; Minister of Finance, Commerce, Industry and Tourism 1991–93, of Finance 1993–96, of Foreign Affairs 1996, of Trade, Commerce and Industry 2003–04, of Infrastructure and Public Utilities 2004–05, of Lands, Geology and Mines July–Nov. 2005, of Finance and Econ. Man. March–May 2013, June–Dec. 2015, of Tourism, Commerce, Industries, Trade and Ni-Vanuatu Business 2014–15; Amb. to China 2009–12; sentenced to 20 months' imprisonment (suspended) on charges of bribery and corruption Oct. 2015; Pres. Liberal Democratic Party 2012–.

TAPIA ROA, Ruth Esperanza; Nicaraguan government official and diplomatist; *Ambassador to France;* b. 21 Nov. 1960, Masaya; ed Centre d'Études Diplomatiques et Stratégiques, Paris, France, Universidad Centroamericana, Managua; First Sec., Embassy in Paris 1985–90; Spokesperson, Supreme Court of Justice 2002–07; Sec.-Gen. Ministry of Nat. Defence 2007–12; Amb. to France 2012–, also Perm. Rep. to UNESCO. *Address:* Embassy of Nicaragua, 34 avenue Bugeaud, 75116 Paris (office); Permanent Delegation of Nicaragua to UNESCO, Maison de l'UNESCO, Bureau M8.05, 1, rue Miollis, 75732 Paris Cedex 15, France (office). *Telephone:* 1-44-05-93-07 (office). *Fax:* 1-44-05-92-42 (office). *E-mail:* embanicfrancia@gmail.com (office); dl.nicaragua@unesco-delegations.org (office). *Website:* www.amb-nicaragua.fr (office).

TAPLIN, Guy Christie; British artist; b. 5 March 1939, London; s. of George Frederick Taplin and Gladys Lillian Taplin (née Peters); m. Robina Dunkery Jack 1989; one s. one d.; ed Norlington Secondary Modern School, Leyton; self-taught artist (sculptor) 1978–; fmrly worked as window cleaner; Post Office messenger 1954–58, meat porter 1960, driver 1961, ladies' hairdresser 1961–62, lifeguard 1962–68, cook 1964, birdkeeper Regent's Park 1970–76, also had own fashion business during 1960s. *Publications:* books on his work: Birds of Creation, Bird on Wire (by Ian Collins). *Leisure interests:* life, art, folk art, travel, chance.

TAPPER, Colin Frederick Herbert, MA, BCL; British lawyer and academic; b. 13 Oct. 1934, West Drayton, Hillingdon, England; s. of H. F. Tapper and F. G. Tapper (née Lambard); m. Margaret White 1961; one d.; ed Magdalen Coll., Oxford; teacher, LSE 1959–65; barrister, Grays Inn 1961; tutor, Magdalen Coll. 1965–79, Fellow 1965–2002 (Vice-Pres. 1991–92) Emer. Fellow 2002, All Souls Reader in Law 1979–92, Prof. of Law 1992–2002; mem. Bd of Dirs Butterworth Group 1979–84, Butterworth Telepublishing 1979–89; consultant to Masons (solicitors) 1990–2003. *Publications:* Computers and the Law 1973, Computer Law 1978, Cross on Evidence (ed.) 1990, Handbook of European Software Law (ed.) 1995, Cross and Tapper on Evidence (ed.) 1999. *Leisure interests:* computing, reading, writing. *Address:* Corner Cottage, Woodstock Road, Stonesfield, Witney, Oxon., OX29 8QA, England. *Telephone:* (1993) 891284. *Fax:* (1993) 891395.

TARAND, Andres; Estonian politician; b. 11 Jan. 1940, Tallinn; s. of Helmut Tarand and Leida Tarand; m. Mari Tarand (née Viiding) 1963; two s.; ed Tartu State Univ.; hydrometeorologist 1963; Research Asst, Tallinn Botanical Gardens 1965–68, Sr Engineer 1970–73, Sr Researcher 1973–76, Sector Dir 1976–79, 1981–88, Dir of Research 1979–81, Dir Tallinn Botanical Gardens 1988–90; researcher, Antarctic Expedition 1968–70; Chair. Environment Cttee Supreme Soviet Estonian SSR 1990; mem. Council of Estonia 1990–92; mem. Constitutional Ass. 1991–92; mem. Riigikogu (Parl.) 1992, 1995–2004; Minister for the Environment 1992–94, 1994–95; Prime Minister of Estonia 1994–95; mem. People's Party Moderates (Rahvaerakond Mõõdukad, renamed Sotsiaaldemokraatlik Erakond 2004) 1996–, Chair. 1996–2002, Chair. Cttee of Foreign Affairs 1999–2002; mem. European Parl. (Socialist Group) 2004–09; Regional Vice-Pres. Globe International Europe 1999–; mem. Estonian Geographical Asscn 1966–, Bd Estonian Inst. for Sustainable Devt, Stockholm Environment Inst.'s Centre, Tallinn 1988–, Bd Univ. of Tartu 1996–, Bd Estonian Nature Fund 1998–; Badge of the Order of Nat. Coat of Arms (Second Class) 2001, Commdr, Légion d'honneur 2001; Panda Award, Danish Section of WWF 1998. *Publications:* Neljakümne kiri 1991, Cassiopeia 1992, Kiri ei Põle Ära 2005; numerous articles on climatology, urban ecology, politics. *Leisure interests:* chess, ornithology, traditional style gardening. *Address:* Harju 1-1, Tallinn 10 146, Estonia.

TARANDA, Gediminas Leonovich; Russian/Lithuanian ballet dancer; b. 26 Feb. 1961, Kaliningrad; ed Moscow Acad. of Choreography, Moscow Acad. of Dance; joined Bolshoi Theatre as dancer 1980, Soloist 1982, Leading Soloist 1985–93, dismissed after conflict with admin.; Founder (with M. Plisetskaya) and Artistic Dir Imperial Russian Ballet Co. 1994–; Co-organizer European Culture Centre (under patronage of European Parl.); First Prize, USSR Championship Ballet Competition 1980. *Leading roles include:* classical and contemporary Russian repertoire including Espado (Don Quixote), Corregidor (Carmen), Forest Warden (Giselle), Kuman (Prince Igor), Severyan (Stone Flower), Yashka (Golden Age), Kurbsky (Ivan the Terrible), Abderakhman (Raimonda), Vizir (Legend of Love) and others. *Address:* Imperial Russian Ballet Company, 103001 Moscow, Trekhprudny per. 11/13, building 2B, Office 45, Russia. *Telephone:* (495) 299-13-98.

TARANTINO, Quentin Jerome; American film director, actor, screenwriter and producer; b. 27 March 1963, Knoxville, Tenn.; s. of Tony Tarantino and Connie McHugh; m. Daniella Pick 2018; fmrly worked in Video Archives, Manhattan Beach, Calif.; Officier, Ordre des Arts et des Lettres, Order of Merit (Hungary) 2010; Career Achievement Award, Casting Soc. of America 2004, Empire Film Award for Icon of the Decade 2005, Golden Eddie Filmmaker of the Year Award, American Cinema Editors 2007, Lifetime Achievement Award, Cinemanila Int. Film Festival 2007, Filmmaker on the Edge Award, Provincetown Int. Film Festival 2008, Hon. César, Acad. des Arts et Techniques du Cinéma 2011, Lifetime Achievement Award, Rome Film Festival 2013, Prix Lumière 2013. *Films include:* My Best Friend's Birthday (actor, dir, producer) 1987, Reservoir Dogs (actor, dir) 1992, Past Midnight (assoc. producer) 1992, Siunin Wong Fei-hung tsi titmalau (producer) 1993, Eddie Presley (actor) 1993, Sleep With Me (actor) 1994, Killing Zoe (exec. producer) 1994, Somebody to Love (actor) 1994, Pulp Fiction (actor, dir) (Golden Palm, Cannes Film Festival, Acad. Award for Best Screenplay 1995) 1994, Destiny Turns on the Radio (actor) 1995, Desperado (actor) 1995, Four Rooms (actor, dir, exec. producer) 1995, Red Rain (producer) 1995, Girl 6 (actor) 1996, From Dusk Till Dawn (actor, exec. producer) 1996, Curdled (actor, exec. producer) 1996, Jackie Brown (dir) 1997, God Said, 'Ha!' (exec. producer) 1998, 40 Lashes (dir) 2000, Little Nicky (actor) 2000, Kill Bill Vol. I (dir, producer) 2003, Kill Bill Vol. II (dir, producer) 2004, Daltry Calhoun (exec. producer) 2005, Hostel (exec. producer) 2005, Freedom's Fury (exec. producer) 2006, Grindhouse (actor) 2007, Death Proof (writer, producer, dir, actor) 2007, Planet Terror (actor) 2007, Sukiyaki Western Django (actor) 2007, Diary of the Dead (voice) 2007, Planet Terror (producer) 2007, Hell Ride (exec. producer) 2008, Inglourious Basterds (dir and actor) 2009, Django Unchained (dir) 2012, The Hateful Eight (dir, writer) 2015. *Film screenplays:* My Best Friend's Birthday 1992, Reservoir Dogs 1992, True Romance 1993, Natural Born Killers 1994, Pulp Fiction 1994, Four Rooms (segment: The Man from Hollywood) 1995, From Dusk Till Dawn 1996, Jackie Brown 1997, 40 Lashes (dir) 2000, Kill Bill (also novel) 2003, Inglourious Basterds 2009, Django Unchained (Golden Globe Award for Best Screenplay 2013, BAFTA Award for Best Original Screenplay 2013, Academy Award for Best Original Screenplay 2013) 2012, The Hateful Eight 2015, Once Upon a Time in Hollywood 2019. *Television includes:* ER (dir, episode 'Motherhood') 1994, Alias (actor, one episode) 2004, CSI: Crime Scene Investigation (dir, writer two episodes) 2005, Alias (actor, four episodes) 2006, From Dusk Till Dawn: The Series (series) 2014–15. *Address:* c/o WME Entertainment, 9601 Wilshire Boulevard, Beverly Hills, CA 90210-5213, USA; 6201 Sunset Boulevard, Suite 35, Los Angeles, CA 90028, USA. *Telephone:* (310) 285-9000. *Website:* wmeentertainment.com.

ŢĂRANU, Cornel, DMus; Romanian composer and conductor; b. 20 June 1934, Cluj; s. of Francisc Ţăranu and Elisabeta Ţăranu; m. Daniela Mărgineanu 1960; one d.; ed Gheorghe Dima Acad. of Music, studied with Sigismund Toduta, Paris Conservatoire, studied with Nadia Boulanger and Olivier Messiaen, also studied with György Ligeti, Bruno Maderna and Christoph Caskel; joined Faculty, Gheorghe Dima Acad. of Music, Cluj-Napoca 1957, Asst Prof. 1970–90, Prof. of Composition 1990–; Founder and Conductor of Ars Nova, contemporary music ensemble; Vice-Pres. Romanian Composers' Union 1990–; Artistic Dir Modern Festival Cluj 1995–; apptd mem. Romanian Acad. 1993, Full mem. 2012–; Chevalier, Ordre des Arts et des Lettres 2002, Great Officer, Order of Cultural Merit 2004; Prize of the Romanian Composers' Union 1972, 1978, 1981, 1982, 2001, Grand Prize 2005, Prize of the Romanian Acad. 1973, Koussevitsky Prize 1982, Nat. Prize for Music 2007. *Works include:* Sonatas for flute, oboe, clarinet and percussion, Sonata for double bass solo, viola sonata, one piano concerto, cantatas, four symphonies, Séquences, Incantations, Symmétries, Alternances, Raccords for orchestra, two Sinfoniettas for strings, Garlands for chamber orchestra, Don Giovanni's Secret for chamber opera, Chansons nomades (oratorio), Chansons sans amour (lieder), Sempre Ostinato for saxophone and ensemble, Chansons sans réponse, Hommage à Paul Célan, Memento and Dedications (cantatas), Miroirs for saxophone and orchestra, Prolégomènes for chamber orchestra, Orpheus (cantata), Tombeau de Verlaine for mixed choir, Mosaïques for saxophone and ensemble, Testament for choir 1988, Chansons interrompues for voice and ensemble 1993, Cadenze Concertante for cello and chamber orchestra 1993, Trajectoires for ensemble 1994, Crisalide for saxophone, tape and ensemble, Five Tzara Songs for voice and piano, Remembering Bartók for oboe and ensemble, Enescu's 'Caprice Roumain' for violin and orchestra (new arrangement) 1995, Responsorial for clarinet 1996, Antiphona for flute and orchestra 1996, Flaine Quintette for winds 1997, Laudatio per Clusium for voice and instruments 1997, Saturnalii for baritone and ensemble 1998, Three Labiş Poems for bass and piano 1998, Cadenze per Antiphona for flute and solo 1998, Siciliana Blues for piano and chamber orchestra 1998, Concerto for oboe and strings 1998, Oreste-Oedipe (chamber opera) 1999–2001, Concerto Breve for flute orchestra 2001, Modra Rijeka for choir 2002, Shakespeare Sonnets for voice and ensemble 2003, Baroccoco for baroque ensemble 2004, Rimembranza for orchestra 2004, Sinfonia da Requiem for choir and orchestra 2005, Sax-Sympho for saxophone and orchestra 2006, Madrigals (verse by Blaga, Vinea, Attila, Ady); also film and theatre music. *Publications include:* Enesco dans la conscience du présent 1981. *Leisure interest:* chess. *Address:* Str. Nicolae Iorga 7, 400063 Cluj-Napoca, Romania (home). *Telephone:* (264) 593879 (office); (264) 443283 (home). *Fax:* (264) 593879 (office). *E-mail:* corneltaranu@yahoo.com (office).

TARAR, Muhammad Rafiq; Pakistani politician, lawyer, judge and fmr head of state; b. 2 Nov. 1929, Pir Kot, Gujranwala Dist; m.; three s. one d.; ed Govt Islamia High School, Gujranwala, Guru Nanak Khalsa Coll., Gujranwala, Punjab Univ. Law Coll.; legal practice, Gujranwala; Additional Sessions Judge, Gujranwala, Bahawalnagar, Sargodha; mem. Lahore High Court 1974, Chief Justice of Punjab 1989; mem. Electoral Comm. of Pakistan 1980–89; mem. Supreme Court 1991–94; Senator (Pakistan Muslim League) March–Dec. 1997; Pres. of Pakistan 1998–2001. *Address:* House 457, G-3, Johar Town, Lahore, Pakistan.

TARASCON, Jean-Marie, MS, PhD, FRSC; French physicist and academic; *Professor of Chemistry, Collège de France;* b. 21 Sept. 1953; ed Univ. of Bordeaux; Post-Doctoral Fellow, Cornell Univ., USA 1980–81; Post-Doctoral Fellow, Bell Labs, Murray Hill, NJ, USA 1982–83; mem. Tech. Staff, Bellcore Solid State Chem. Div., Red Bank, NJ, USA 1983–89, Dir Energy Storage Group 1989–94, Bellcore Fellow 1994; apptd Prof. and Dir, CNRS Lab. of Reactivity and Solid State Chem., Amiens 1995; Prof. of Chem., Collège de France 2014–; Co-Ed. Journal of Solid State Ionics, Journal of Solid State Electrochemistry, Journal of Materials Chem., International Journal of Inorganic Materials; mem. Academie des Sciences 1999–; mem. ACS, Electrochemical Soc., Materials Research Soc., Institut Universitaire de France 2002–; Foreign mem. Royal Soc. 2014–; Bellcore Award of Excellence 1987, Bellcore President Award 1993, Industry Week Best Tech. of the Year Award 1994, R and D 100 Award 1994, 1995, Popular Mechanics Design and Eng Award 1995, Int. Battery Asscn Research Award 1995, Electrochemical Soc. Battery Tech. Award 1997, Thomas Alva Edison Patent Award 2001, Volta Medal Award 2002, ISI Award 2004, Prix du rayonnement français 2004, ENI Protection of the Environment Award 2011, Pierre Sue Award 2011. *Publications include:* 600 scientific papers; 75 patents. *Address:* Collège de France, 11 Place Marcelin Berthelot, 75231 Paris, Cedex 05, France (office). *Telephone:* 1-44-27-12-11 (office). *Website:* www.college-de-france.fr (office).

TARASOV, Gennady Pavlovich; Russian diplomatist and UN official; *Inspector, Joint Inspection Unit, United Nations;* b. 14 Sept. 1947, Moscow; m. Elena Tarasov; ed Moscow State Inst. of Int. Relations; on staff, Ministry of Foreign Affairs 1970–, worked in Egypt, USSR Perm. Mission to UN, New York and several other posts –1986; Deputy Head of Dept of Near E and N African Countries, USSR Ministry of Foreign Affairs 1986–90, Amb. of USSR, then of Russian Fed. to Saudi Arabia 1990–96, Dir Dept of Information and Press, Ministry of Foreign Affairs 1996–98, Amb. to Portugal 1998–2001, to Israel 2002–07; UN Sec.-Gen.'s High-Level Co-ordinator for compliance by Iraq on its obligations regarding Kuwait 2008–12, Insp., Jt Inspection Unit 2013–. *Address:* Palais des Nations, 1211 Geneva 10, Switzerland (office). *Telephone:* (22) 9173041 (office). *Fax:* (22) 9170627 (office). *E-mail:* tarasovg@un.org (office). *Website:* www.un.org (office).

TARASOVA, Elvira; Russian ballet dancer; *First Soloist, Kirov Ballet;* b. 5 Aug. 1969, St Petersburg; ed Vaganova Acad.; joined Kirov Ballet (renamed Mariinsky Theatre 1992) 1988, First Soloist 1996–, Teacher and Coach 2010–; Best Partner, Moscow Competition 1997, Honored Artist of Russia 2003. *Repertoire includes:* Cinderella (Coppelia, Krivlaka), Don Quixote (Kitri), Faust (Vakhanka), Giselle (Myrtha), La Bayadère (Gamzatti), Le Corsaire (Medora, Gulnara), Sleeping Beauty (Brilliant Fairy), Symphony in C (Allegro Vivace). *Address:* Kirov Ballet, c/o Maryinsky Theatre, One Theatre Square (Teatralnaya Ploshchad), St Petersburg 190000, Russia (office). *Telephone:* (812) 114-12-11 (office). *Fax:* (812) 314-17-44 (office). *E-mail:* elvira@kirov.com (office). *Website:* www.kirov.com (office).

TARASYUK, Borys Ivanovych; Ukrainian politician and diplomatist; b. 1 Jan. 1949, Dzerzhynsk, Zhytomyr Oblast; m.; one s. two d.; ed Kyiv State Univ.; attaché, Third, Second, then First Sec., Ukrainian Ministry of Foreign Affairs 1975–81, Second, then First Sec., Perm. Mission of Ukrainian SSR to UN, New York 1981–86, First Sec., Div. of Int. Orgs, Ukrainian Ministry of Foreign Affairs 1986–87, Instructor, Div. of Foreign Relations, Ukrainian CP Cen. Cttee 1987–90, Head, Dept of Political Analysis and Planning, Ministry of Foreign Affairs 1991–92, Deputy, First Deputy Minister of Foreign Affairs, Head, Nat. Cttee on Disarmament Problems 1992–95, Amb. to Belgium (also accred to Netherlands, Luxembourg) 1995–98, Head, Mission to NATO, Brussels 1997–98, Minister of Foreign Affairs 1998–2000, 2005–07 (resgnd); mem. Verkhovna Rada (Parl.) 2002–, Deputy Chair. Parliamentary Cttee on Foreign Affairs 2014–; fmr Vice-Pres. EURONEST Parl. Ass.; mem. Nat. Security Defence Council; Chair. Narodny Rukh Ukrainy (People's Movt of Ukraine—Rukh) 2003–12; Deputy Head, Batkivshchyna party 2013–; mem. Bd of Dirs East-West Inst. 1993–2001; Chair. Cttee on European Integration 2002–12; Dir Inst. of Social Studies and Int. Relations 2001–02; Founder and Dir Inst. of Euro-Atlantic Co-operation 2001–; Chair. Euroatlantic magazine; State Order 'For Merits', III Grade 1996, II Grade 1999, I Grade 2005; Dr hc (Rivne Int. Econ. and Humanitarian Univ.) 2000, (Ivan Franko Nat. Univ. of Lviv) 2002, (Int. Personnel Acad.) 2002; state awards from Argentina, Brazil, France, Lithuania, Portugal, Sweden, Venezuela. *Leisure interests:* table tennis, fishing, woodwork. *Address:* Batkivshchyna, 04080 Kyiv, vul. Turovska 13, 1st Floor, Ukraine (office). *Telephone:* (44) 527-70-69 (office). *E-mail:* gromprym@gmail.com (office). *Website:* ba.org.ua (office).

TARDIEU, Christophe, DESS; French government official and institute director; *Managing Director, National Film Centre and Centre of the Moving Image;* b. 20 Nov. 1964, Versailles; Insp. of Finances 2000–04; Gen. Dir Museum and Nat. Estate of Versailles 2004–07; Deputy Chief of Staff to Christine Albanel, Minister of Culture and Communication 2007–09; Deputy Head of Service, Gen. Inspectorate of Finances 2009–10; Deputy Dir Opéra nat. de Paris 2010–14; Man. Dir Centre nat. du cinéma et de l'image animée (CNC—Nat. Film Centre and Centre of the Moving Image) 2014–; mem. Bd of Dirs Cinémathèque français; Officier des Arts et des Lettres. *Address:* Centre national du cinéma et de l'image animée, 12 rue de Lubeck, 75784 Paris Cedex 16, France (office). *Telephone:* 1-44-34-34-40 (office). *Fax:* 1-47-55-04-91 (office). *E-mail:* webmaster@cnc.fr (office). *Website:* www.cnc.fr (office).

TARFUSSER, Cuno Jakob, DJur; Italian lawyer, public prosecutor and judge; *Judge, International Criminal Court;* b. 11 Sept. 1954, Merano; m. Gerda Amplatz; ed Univ. of Innsbruck, Austria, Univ. of Padua; Deputy Public Prosecutor, Bolzano, Southern Tyrol 1987–2001, Chief Prosecutor 2001–09; Judge, Pre-Trial Div., Int. Criminal Court (ICC), The Hague, Netherlands 2009–, Second Vice-Pres. ICC 2012–15. *Address:* International Criminal Court, PO Box 19519, 2500 CM The Hague, The Netherlands (office). *Telephone:* (70) 515-85-15 (office). *Fax:* (70) 515-85-55 (office). *E-mail:* pio@icc-cpi.int (office); otp.informationdesk@icc-cpi.int (office). *Website:* www.icc-cpi.int (office).

TARHOUNI, Ali Abdussalam, PhD; Libyan economist, academic and government official; b. 1951; m. Mary Li; four c.; ed Al Fateh Univ., Tripoli, Michigan State Univ., USA; in exile in USA 1973–2011; Asst Prof. of Business Econs, Michael G. Foster School of Business, Univ. of Washington, Seattle 1984–85, Sr Lecturer 1985–2011; fmr Consultant, FAO; returned to Libya Feb. 2011; Minister of Finance and Oil (apptd by Nat. Transitional Council following overthrow of Mu'ammar Gaddafi) March–Nov. 2011, also Chair. Supreme Security Cttee, interim Prime Minister of Libya Oct.–Nov. 2011; currently Pres. Libyan Constitution Drafting Ass.

TARIFA, Fatos, PhD; Albanian diplomatist and academic; *Rector, University of New York Tirana;* b. 21 Aug. 1954; ed Univ. of Tirana, Univ. of North Carolina, USA; Faculty mem., Univ. of Tirana 1979–93, Founding Chair. Sociological Research Centre, 1991–93, Dir New Sociological Research Centre 1993–98; Amb. to Netherlands 1998–2001, to USA 2001–05; has taught at Inst. of Social Studies, The Hague 1993–94, Univ. of North Carolina, Chapel Hill 1996–98, Campbell Univ. 1996–97, Webster Univ., Leiden campus 1999–2001, Eastern Michigan Univ. 2006–08, European Univ. of Tirana 2008–13; currently Rector and Prof., University of New York Tirana; mem. (fmr Pres.) Albanian Acad. of Arts and Sciences 2012–. *Publications include:* over 40 books and articles on political science and int. relations theory. *Leisure interests:* jazz, travel. *Address:* University of New York Tirana, Kodra e Diellit, Tirana, Albania (office). *Telephone:* (4) 4512345 (office). *E-mail:* info@unyt.edu.al (office). *Website:* unyt.edu.al/prof/1fatos-tarifa (office).

TARIN, Shaukat Fayaz Ahmed, MBA; Pakistani economist, banker and government official; *Advisor to Chairman, Silkbank Limited;* b. 1 Oct. 1953, Multan; s. of Jamshaid Ahmed Tarin and Mumtaz Tarin; m. Razalia Tarin; one s. two d.; ed Punjab Univ., Lahore; joined Citibank as trainee in 1975; Sr Head of Country Operations Support, Citibank NA, Dubai 1985–87, Gen. Man. Citibank Gulf 1987–90, Gen. Man. Citibank Pakistan 1991–95, Gen. Man. Citibank Thailand 1995–97; Pres. and CEO Habib Bank 1997–2000; Pres. and Group CEO Union Bank 2000–06; est. consortium, along with Sadeq Sayeed, Bank-Muscat, Nomura Holdings Inc. and International Finance Corpn to acquire 85.09% stake in bank from Saudi Pak Industrial and Agricultural Investment Co. Ltd 2008, Pres. Saudi Pak Commercial Bank –2008; Advisor to Prime Minister on Finance (with status of fed. minister) 2008–10 (resgnd), also Head of Exec. Cttee of Nat. Econ. Council and Econ. Co-ordination Cttee; elected unopposed mem. of Senate from Sindh July 2009–; fmr Chair. Karachi Stock Exchange; Advisor to Chair., Silkbank Ltd 2010–; Quaid-e-Azam Gold Medal Award 2005, Sitara-e-Imtiaz 2007. *Address:* Silkbank Ltd, 22nd Floor, Centrepoint, Shaheed-e-Millat Expressway, Near KPT Interchange, Korangi, Karachi 74900, Pakistan (office). *Telephone:* (21) 35805772 (office). *Fax:* (21) 35805774 (office). *E-mail:* shaukat.tarin@silkbank.com.pk (office). *Website:* www.silkbank.com.pk (office).

TARISA, Watanagase, BA, MA, PhD; Thai economist and fmr central banker; b. 30 Nov. 1949; m.; one d.; ed Keio Univ., Japan, Univ. of Washington and AMP program at Harvard Univ., USA; joined Bank of Thailand 1975, economist, Financial Inst. Analysis Section, Dept of Econ. Research 1975–78, Chief Analyst, Banking Analysis Section, Banking Dept 1979, study leave 1979–83, Section Chief, Policy Section, Dept of Financial Insts Supervision and Examination 1984–85, Deputy Div. Chief, Financial Insts Supervision Div. 1986–87, Asst Dir Dept of Econ. Research 1987, Deputy Dir Dept of Bank Supervision and Examination and Head of Payment System Devt Task Force 1991–93, Dir Payment System Devt Office 1993–96, Dir Payment System Dept 1996–97, Dir Financial Insts Regulations Dept 1997–98, Asst Gov., Financial Insts Regulation and Examination Group 1998–99, Asst Gov., Financial Insts Policy Group 1999–2001, Asst Gov., Financial Markets Operations Group 2001–02, Deputy Gov. Financial Insts Stability 2002–07, also mem. Bd, Financial System Policy Cttee, Monetary Policy Cttee, Gov. Bank of Thailand (first woman) 2006–10; economist, Cen. Banking Dept, IMF, Washington, DC 1988–91; mem. Bd of Dirs Insurance Comm., SCG, Ramathibodi Hospital Foundation, Heart Foundation of Thailand, Private Sector Collective Action Coalition Against Corruption; mem. Advisory Bd Promontory Financial Group, LLC; Commdr (Third Class), The Most Noble Order of The Crown of Thailand; Outstanding Leadership Award, Bank of Thailand 2001, Outstanding Individual Research Award, Nat. Defence Coll. of Thailand 2006. *Leisure interests include:* watercolour painting, yoga.

TARJAN, Robert Endre, PhD, FAAS; American computer scientist and academic; *James S. McDonnell Distinguished University Professor of Computer Science, Princeton University;* b. 30 April 1948, Pomona, Calif.; s. of George Tarjan and Helen Emma Tarjan; three d.; ed California Inst. of Tech., Stanford Univ.; Asst Prof. of Computer Science, Cornell Univ., Ithaca, NY 1972–73; Miller Research Fellow, Univ. of California, Berkeley 1973–75; Asst Prof. of Computer Science, Stanford Univ. 1974–77, Assoc. Prof. 1977–80; mem. tech. staff, AT&T Bell Labs, Murray Hill, NJ 1980–89; Adjunct Prof. of Computer Science, New York Univ. 1981–85; James S. McDonnell Distinguished Univ. Prof. of Computer Science, Princeton Univ. 1985–, Co-Dir NSF Center for Discrete Math. and Theoretical Computer Science 1989–94, 2001–; Fellow, NEC Research Inst., Princeton 1989–97; Visiting Scientist, MIT 1996; Chief Scientist, InterTrust 1997–2001, 2014–; Sr Research Fellow, STAR Labs, InterTrust Technologies Corpn, Sunnyvale, Calif. 1997–2001; Corp. Fellow, Compaq Computer Corpn, Houston, Tex. 2002; Chief Scientist, Hewlett Packard Corpn, Palo Alto, Calif. 2002–03, Sr Fellow 2003–; mem. Nat. Advisory Bd Computer Professionals for Social Responsibility 1987–, Bd of Govs Inst. for Math. and its Applications 1988–91; Ed. Princeton University Press Series in Computer Science 1985–, John Wiley Series in Discrete Mathematics 1987–97, Transactions on Mathematical Software 1978–80, Journal of the Association for Computing Machinery 1979–83, SIAM Journal on Computing 1979–83, Journal of Graph Theory 1985–88, Journal of Algorithms 1983–90, Discrete and Computational Geometry 1985–, Journal of the American Mathematical Society 1986–91, European Journal of Combinatorics 1988–91; Correspondent, Mathematical Intelligencer 1991–; mem. NAS 1987, Nat. Acad. of Eng 1988, American Philosophical Soc. 1990; Foundation Fellow, Inst. for Combinatorics and its Applications 1991; Fellow, American Acad. of Arts and Sciences 1985, Asscn for Computing Machinery (ACM) 1994, New York Acad. of Sciences 1994, Soc. of Ind. and Applied Math. 2009; Miller Research Fellowship, Univ. of California, Berkeley 1973–75, Guggenheim Fellowship 1978–79, Nevanlinna Prize in Information Science 1983, NAS Award for Initiatives in Research 1984, Lanchester Prize (Hon. Mention), Operations Research Soc. of America 1984, 1993, Distinguished mem. of Technical Staff, AT&T Bell Labs 1985, A.M. Turing Award, Asscn for Computing Machinery 1986, ACM Paris Kanellakis Award in Theory and Practice 1999, Edelman Prize, Inst. for Operations Research and Man. Sciences (INFORMS) 2009, Distinguished Alumni Award, California Inst. of Tech. 2010. *Publications:* Data Structures and Network Algorithms 1983, Notes on Introductory Combinatorics 1983; 19 patents and more than 275 articles and reports in scientific journals. *Address:* Department of Computer Science, Princeton University, 35 Olden Street, Room 324, Princeton, NJ 08544-2087 (office); 4 Constitution Hill East, Princeton, NJ 08540, USA (home). *Telephone:* (609) 258-4797 (Princeton) (office); (650) 857-2497 (Palo Alto) (office); (609) 921-0132 (home). *Fax:* (609) 258-1771 (Princeton) (office). *E-mail:* ret@cs.princeton.edu (office). *Website:* www.cs.princeton.edu/~ret (office).

TARLEV, Vasile Pavlovich, DTechSci; Moldovan business executive and politician; b. 9 Oct. 1963, Başcalia, Basarabeasca Dist; m.; three c.; ed Chişinău Polytechnical Inst.; worked as tractor driver; served in army of USSR 1981–83; Chief Mechanic, Bucuria confectionery factory, Chief Engineer Bucuria SA 1991–93, First Deputy Dir-Gen. 1993–95, Chair. Bd of Admin., Dir-Gen. 1995–2001; studied int. marketing and trade man. in USA; fmr mem. Supreme Econ. Council of Pres., Econ. Council of Govt; mem. Repub. Comm. on Collective Negotiations between Businessmen and Trade Unions 1998–99; mem. Party of Communists of the Repub. of Moldova; Prime Minister of Moldova 2001–08; fmr Chair. Nat. Asscn of Mfrs 1995–2001; mem. Council Int. Union of Mfrs, Int. Acad. of Sciences and Computing Systems 1998–; mem. Int. Acad. of Sciences and Informational Systems 1998; Order of Work Glory 1997; Businessman of the Year (six times) 1995–2000, Gold Medal for Efficient Man., Int. Acad. of Human Resources 2000, several medals for tech. inventions shown at int. exhbns 1997–. *Achievements include:* holds five patents on tech. inventions. *Publications:* more than 30 scientific publs. *Address:* Party of Communists of the Republic of Moldova, 2012 Chişinău, N. Iorga Str. 11, Moldova (office). *Telephone:* (22) 23-46-14 (office). *Fax:* (22) 23-36-73 (office). *E-mail:* info@pcrm.md (office). *Website:* www.pcrm.md (office).

TARNOPOLSKI, Vladimir Grigor'yevich; Russian composer; *Professor of Composition, Moscow Conservatory;* b. 30 April 1955, Dniepropetrovsk, Ukrainian SSR, USSR; m. Irina Ivanovna Snitkova; one s.; ed Moscow State Tchaikovsky Conservatory; freelance composer 1988–; co-f. Moscow Assen of Contemporary Music 1989; Prof. of Composition, Moscow Conservatory 1992–, Founder and Artistic Dir first Russian Centre for Contemporary Music 1993–; f. Studio for New Music Ensemble 1993–, Moscow Forum –Int. Festival of Contemporary Music 1994–; Prof., Founder and Head of Dept for Contemporary Music, Tchaikovsky Conservatory 2003–; works performed by Ensemble Modern, Intercontemporain, Klangforum Wien, Musikfabrik Ensemble, Schoenberg Ensemble, Ensemble Recherche, Bayerische Rundfunk Symphony Orchestra, Munich Philharmonic Orchestra in major European and US festivals; mem. Saxon Acad. of Arts; Dmitry Shostakovich Prize, Moscow 1991, Paul Hindemith Prize, Plon 1991, Rostrum 2001. *Compositions include:* operas: Wenn die Zeit ueber die Ufer tritt (Munich 1999), Jenseits der Schatten (Bonn 2006), Cinderella (children's opera on text by Roald Dahl); music parodies: Three Graces 1987 (St Petersburg 1988), Ah, ces russes. . . ou l'Elexir Magic (Evian 1993); ballet: Ins Theater 1998, Boxing Pushkin (a scene within a collective dance-performance); chorus and orchestral/instrumental: Psalmus poenitentialis for violin, choir and organ 1986, Wahnfried for choir, violin and ensemble 1984; orchestral: Cello Concerto 1980, The Breath of the Exhausted Time 1994, . . .Le vent des mots qu'il n'a pas dits for cello and orchestra 1996, Feux follets 2003, Foucault's Pendulum 2004, Eastanbul 2008, Red Shift 2013, Tabula Russia 2015, Be@thoven-Invocation 2017; large ensemble/chamber orchestra: Choral Prelude 'Jesus, Your Deep Wounds' 1987, Cassandra 1991, Landscape after the Battle (with bass or bass choir on the text by Reiner Maria Rilke) 1995, Foucault's Pendulum 2004; ensemble: Chevengur for voice and ensemble (text by Andrey Platonov) 2001, Last and Lost 2011, Study of a Girl Reading Pavese 2015; wind band: Welt voll Irrsinn on texts by K. Schwitters 1993; chamber music: Troïsti muziki for piano trio with singing on text by Grigory Skovoroda 1989, Echoes of the Passing Day for clarinet, cello and piano 1990, O, PÄRT – OP ART 1992, Amoretto for soprano and ensemble (text by E. Spenser) 1992, Scenes from the Real Life for soprano and three instruments on texts by E. Jandl 1995, Impression-Expression III for piano and ensemble 1996, Perpetuum Moebius 2017; solo: Impression-Expression I for piano 1989, Study of Breath for cello 2018. *Address:* Centre for Contemporary Music, Tchaikovsky Conservatoire, of. 316, Bolshaya Nikitskaya str. 13, 125009 Moscow (office); Arbat str., N 51, Apt 41-a, 119002 Moscow, Russia (home). *Telephone:* (495) 690-51-81 (office). *Fax:* (495) 690-51-81 (office). *E-mail:* vladimir.tarnopolski@gmail.com (home). *Website:* www .tarnopolski.ru.

TARR, Béla; Hungarian film director, screenwriter and producer; b. 21 July 1955, Pécs; ed Budapest Film Acad.; began making amateur films aged 16 and later worked as caretaker at nat. House for Culture and Recreation; amateur work brought him to attention of Bela Balazs Studios which helped fund his feature debut Családi tűzfészek 1979; founding mem. Tarsulas Film Studio 1981–85, TT Filmmühely Kft 2003–; Commdr, Cross of the Hungarian Repub., Kossuth Decoration of the Hungarian Repub.; Andrzej Wajda Freedom Award, France Culture Award, Lifetime Achievement Award, Jerusalem, Giraldillo Award, Seville, Lifetime Achievement Award, International Bosphorus Film Festival 2017. *Films include:* Hotel Magnezit 1978, Családi tüzfészek (Family Nest) (also screenplay) 1979, Szabadgyalog (The Outsider) (also screenplay) 1981, Panelkapcsolat (The Prefab People, USA) (also screenplay) 1982, Öszi almanach (Almanac of Fall) (also screenplay) 1985, Szörnyek évadja (Season of Monsters, USA) (actor) 1987, Kárhozat (Damnation) (also screenplay) 1987, The Last Boat (short feature, also screenwriter) 1989, City Life 1990, Sátántangó (Satan's Tango) (also screenplay) 1994, Journey on the Plain 1995, Szenvedély (Passion) (screenplay) 1998, Werckmeister harmóniák (Werckmeister Harmonies) (also assoc. producer and screenwriter) 2000, Château de sable (artistic supervisor) 2000, Visions of Europe (segment 'Prologue') 2004, A Halál kilovagolt Perzsiából (producer) 2005, The Man from London 2007, The Turin Horse 2011. *Television includes:* Macbeth (also screenplay) 1982. *Address:* c/o TTF Kft, Kolozsvár utca 6/ B. I. em. 3, Budapest 1155, Hungary. *Fax:* (1) 251-9969. *E-mail:* ttfilmmuhely@t -online.hu.

TARSCHYS, Daniel, PhD; Swedish politician and political scientist; *Professor Emeritus of Political Science and Public Administration, University of Stockholm;* b. 21 July 1943, Stockholm; s. of Bernhard Tarschys and Karin Alexanderson; m. Regina Rehbinder 1970; two d.; ed Univ. of Stockholm, Univ. of Leningrad, USSR, Princeton Univ., USA; Prof. of Political Science and Public Admin., Univ. of Stockholm 1985–2010, Prof. Emer. 2010–; City Councillor in Lidingö 1970–76; adviser with Ministry of Finance 1976–78, 1979–83; Sec. of State, Prime Minister's Office 1978–79; Prof. of Soviet and E European Studies, Uppsala Univ. 1983–85; mem. Parl. 1976–82, 1985–94; Chair. Parl. Social Affairs Cttee 1985–91, Foreign Affairs Cttee 1991–94; Vice-Pres. Liberal International 1992–94, Int. Political Science Assen 2006–09; mem. Council of Europe Parl. Ass. 1986–94, Alt. mem. 1981–83; Sec.-Gen. Liberal, Democratic and Reformers Group (LDR) 1987–91, Chair. 1991–94; Sec.-Gen. Council of Europe 1994–99; Chair. Swedish Nat. Council on Medicine and Ethics 2001–11; Chair. Edita and Ira Morris Hiroshima Foundation 2004–, Bank of Sweden Tercentenary Foundation 2006–14, European Humanities Univ. 2012–16, Swedish Research Inst., Istanbul 2013–; mem. Royal Swedish Acad. of Sciences 2008–; Sr Fellow, Zentrum für Europäische Integrationsforschung, Univ. of Bonn, 2009; mem. Bd of Trustees European Studies Inst., Moscow 2007–, Eurasia Partnership Foundation, Tbilisi 2008–; Grand Crosses of Germany, Liechtenstein, Romania, San Marino and Spain; Herbert Tingsten Award (jtly with Ingemar Hedenius) 1976, Nagrada Sloboda (Prix liberté), Centre Int. pour la Paix, Sarajevo 1995, Gold Medal, Comenius Univ. of Bratislava 1997, King's Medal (Sweden) 2004, Karl Staaff Gold Medal 2009. *Publications:* books and articles on political philosophy, budgetary policy, public admin. and comparative politics. *Address:* Department of Political Science, University of Stockholm, 106 91 Stockholm, Sweden (office). *E-mail:* daniel.tarschys@statsvet.su.se (office). *Website:* www.statsvet.su.se/forskning/vara-forskare/daniel-tarschys (office).

TARTAKOVSKY, Vladimir Aleksandrovich; Russian chemist; b. 10 Aug. 1932; m.; one d.; ed Moscow State Univ.; worked as researcher, teacher; Head of Lab., Inst. of Organic Chem., USSR (now Russian) Acad. of Sciences 1955–86, Dir N.D. Zelinsky Inst. of Organic Chem. 1988–2002, now mem. Academic and Scientific Councils, Corresp. mem., USSR (now Russian) Acad. of Sciences 1987, mem. 1992; main research in organic synthesis, chem. of nitro-compounds and polynitrogen-oxygen systems; Lenin Prize 1976, AM Butlerov Prize, Demidov Prize 1999, Lomonosov Gold Medal, Russian Acad. of Sciences 2011. *Address:* N.D. Zelinsky Institute of Organic Chemistry, 119991 Moscow, Leninsky prosp. 47, Russia (office). *Telephone:* (495) 137-29-44 (office). *Fax:* (495) 135-53-28 (office). *E-mail:* secretary@ioc.ac.ru (office). *Website:* www.ioc.ac.ru (office).

TARTT, Donna; American writer; b. 23 Dec. 1963, Greenwood, Miss.; ed Univ. of Mississippi, Bennington Coll.; published first sonnet in a Miss. literary review 1976; Best American Short Stories 2006. *Publications include:* novels: The Secret History 1992, The Little Friend (WH Smith Literary Award 2003) 2002, The Goldfinch (Pulitzer Prize for Fiction 2014, Andrew Carnegie Medal for Excellence in Fiction 2014, Malaparte Prize (Italy) 2014) 2013; short stories include: A Christmas Pageant (Harper's) 1993, A Garter Snake (GQ) 1995, True Grit (audio book narration) 2006. *Website:* www.curtisbrown.co.uk/client/donna-tartt.

TARUTA, Sergey A.; Ukrainian steel industry executive; fmr Head, Dept of Foreign Econ. Relations, AzovStal Steel Mill; Founder and mem. Bd of Dirs Industrial Union of Donbass (ISD) 1995, Chair. 2001–15; Gov. Donetsk Oblast March–Oct. 2014; mem. Verkhovna Rada 2014–; Chair. Supervisory Bd, JSC Khartsyzsk Pipe Mill; mem. Supervisory Bd OJSC AzovStal; Owner, Metallurg Donetsk football team. *Address:* Verkhovna Rada, vul. M. Hrushevskoho 5, Kyiv 01008, Ukraine. *Telephone:* (44) 255-21-15 (office). *Fax:* (44) 253-32-17 (office). *Website:* www.rada.gov.ua (office).

TARUTOKO, Shinji; Japanese politician; b. 6 Aug. 1959, Shimane Pref.; ed Osaka Univ., Matsushita Inst. of Govt and Man.; mem. House of Reps (Parl.) (Japan New Party, later DPJ) for Osaka No.12 constituency 1993–2012, Chair. Environment Cttee 2009, Fundamental Nat. Policies Cttee 2010; Minister for Internal Affairs and Communications Oct.–Dec. 2012, also of Regional Revitalization, Minister of State for Okinawa and Northern Territories' Affairs and for Promotion of Local Sovereignty Oct.–Dec. 2012; mem. Democratic Party of Japan (DPJ) 1998–, Chair. Community Interaction Cttee 2004, Diet Affairs Cttee 2010, HR Cttee on Fundamental Nat. Policies 2010, Acting Sec.-Gen. 2011. *Address:* Democratic Party of Japan, 1-11-1, Nagata-cho, Chiyoda-ku, Tokyo 100-0014, Japan (office). *Telephone:* (3) 3595-9988 (office). *Fax:* (3) 3595-9961 (office). *Website:* dpjenews@dpj.or.jp (office); www.tarutoko.jp.

TARZI, Nanguyalai, PhD; Afghan diplomatist; m.; one s. one d.; ed Kabul Univ. and Faculté de Droit et Sciences Économiques, Paris, France; Prof. of Law and Political Science, Kabul Univ. 1964–70; joined Ministry of Foreign Affairs 1970, Political Observer of OIC, Perm. Mission to UN 1979–86, Deputy Perm. Observer of OIC to UN, New York 1986–92, Perm. Observer of OIC to UN, Geneva 1992–2000, Dir UN Information Centre, Tehran 2001–02, mem. Emergency Loya Jirga 2002, Amb. to Pakistan 2002–06, Amb. to Switzerland and Perm. Rep. to UN and other Int. Orgs, Geneva 2007–10, Amb. to India (also accred to Bhutan, the Maldives, Nepal and Sri Lanka) 2010–12, Amb. to Switzerland and Perm. Rep. to UN and other Int. Orgs, Geneva 2012–15.

TASCA, Catherine, LenD; French politician and government official; b. 13 Dec. 1941, Lyon; d. of Angelo Tasca and Alice Naturel; one d.; ed Inst. d'Etudes Politiques, Paris and Ecole Nat. d'Admin; civil servant, Ministry of Culture 1967; Dir Maison de la Culture de Grenoble 1973; Gen. Man. Ensemble Intercontemporain 1978; Co-Dir Théâtre de Nanterre-Amandiers 1982; mem. Comm. Nat. de la Communication et des Libertés (CNCL) 1986; Minister Del. attached to the Minister of Culture and Communications 1988–91; Sec. of State for Francophone Countries and External Cultural Relations 1992–93; Minister of Culture and Communications 2000–02; Conseiller d'Etat en service extraordinaire 2003–04; Senator from Yvelines 2004–17; Pres. Admin. Bd Canal+Horizons 1993–97; Deputy to Nat. Ass. from Yvelines 1997–, mem. Socialist Party; Chevalier des Arts et des Lettres, Légion d'honneur. *Publication:* Un Choix de vie 2002. *Address:* Parti Socialiste (Socialist Party), 10 rue de Solférino, 75007 Paris (office); 21 rue Saint-Amand, 75015 Paris, France (home). *Telephone:* 1-45-56-77-00 (office). *E-mail:* interps@parti-socialiste.fr (office). *Website:* www.parti-socialiste.fr (office).

TASHIYEV, Kamchybek; Kyrgyzstani politician, lawyer, engineer and chemist; *Co-Chairman, Respublika-Ata Jurt Sayasiy Partiyasy;* b. 27 Sept. 1968, Barpy, Suzak Dist, Osh Oblast (now in Jalal-Abad Oblast), Kyrgyz SSR, USSR; m.; four c.; ed Chemical-Technology Faculty, Tomsk State Univ., Russian SFSR, Legal Faculty, Kyrgyz State Nat. Univ.; served in Soviet Army 1987–89; Dir Meerim-Ay Agro-productions preparation firm, Barpy 1993–95; Gen. Dir Tomas firm, Jalal-Abad 1995–2000; Chair. of Man., Elen-Kench Agricultural Co-operative, Barpy 2000–02; Asst Chief of Staff, Office of the Prime Minister 2002–03; Deputy Head of Lenin Dist Admin, Bishkek City Admin 2003–05; Deputy to Jogorku Kenesh (Parl.), Chair. Cttee on Fuel and Energy Sector and Water Resources 2005–07; Minister of Emergency Situations 2007–09; Chair. Ata-Jurt Idealisttik-Demokratiyalyk Sayasiy Partiyasy (Ata-Jurt) –2014, Co-Chair. Respublika–Ata Jurt Sayasiy Partiyasy (R-AJ—Republic-Homeland Political Party) 2014–; rank of Maj.-Gen. 2009; arrested on charges including attempting to overthrow the Govt Oct. 2012, cleared by Bishkek City Court June 2013, decision reversed by Supreme Court Aug. 2013, sentenced to 18 months' imprisonment. *Address:* Respublika-Ata Jurt Sayasiy Partiyasy, 720000 Bishkek, Gorkogo 1/2, Kyrgyzstan (office). *Telephone:* (312) 98-68-15 (office). *E-mail:* office@respublika-atajurt.kg (office). *Website:* www.respublika-atajurt.kg (office).

TASHMUHAMEDOVA, Dilorom Hafurjanovna, MD; Uzbekistani physician and politician; b. 19 Feb. 1962, Tashkent Oblast; m. P. Tashmuhamedov; four c.; ed Tashkent State Medical Inst., Faculty of Intergovernmental Relations and External Econ. Relations, Acad. of State and Social Construction; early career as teacher, Tashkent State Medical Inst.; f. Farmed (pharmaceuticals co.) 1994; Deputy, Oly Majlis (Supreme Ass.) 2001–04, Deputy to Legis. Chamber (Qonunchilik palatasi—Parl.) 2004–, mem. Cttee for Int. Affairs and Inter-parl. Communication, Deputy Speaker 2007–08, Speaker 2008–14; mem. Adolat Sotsial Demokratik Partiyasi (Justice Social Democratic Party), First Sec. Political

Council 2005–, also leader of parl. faction; unsuccessful cand. in presidential election 2007; Dustlik (Friendship) Order 2006. *Publications include:* series of academic works about medicine; numerous articles about socio-political reform, the development of a multi-party system and of democratic institutions and the increasing involvement of women in social life. *Address:* Qonunchilik palatasi (Legislative Chamber), 100035 Tashkent, Bunyedkor ko'ch. 1, Uzbekistan (office). *Telephone:* (71) 239-87-07 (office). *Fax:* (71) 239-41-51 (office). *E-mail:* info@parliament.gov.uz (office). *Website:* www.parliament.gov.uz (office).

TASMAGAMBETOV, Imangali Nurgaliuly; Kazakhstani politician and diplomatist; *Ambassador to the Russian Federation;* b. 9 Dec. 1956, Novobogat village, Maxambet dist, Guriyev (now Atiraw) Oblast, Kazakh SSR, USSR; s. of Nurgali Tasmagambetov and Mataevna Kokanova; m. Klara Bekkulova; one s. two d.; ed Pushkin Pedagogical Inst., Uralsk (now Oral); began career as geography teacher 1979; served in various govt positions including Chair. State Cttee on Youth Affairs 1991–93; Asst to Pres. 1993–94; apptd Atyrau Oblast Akim (Gov.) 1998; Deputy Prime Minister for Cultural Affairs 1991–93, in charge of Social and Ethnic Policy 2000–02; Prime Minister of Kazakhstan 2002–03; State Sec. 2003–04; Mayor of Almatı 2004–08, of Astana 2008–14; Minister of Defence 2014–16; Deputy Prime Minister 2016–17; Amb. to Russian Fed. 2017–; Order of Parasat 1998, Order of the First Pres. of Kazakhstan Nursultan Nazarbayev 2004, Astana 10-Year Medal 2008, Order of Barys, Second Class 2010, Order of Friendship (Russian Fed.), Order of Holy Prince Daniel of Moscow, Order of St Seraphim of Sarov, Second Class 2010. *Publications include:* several scientific papers and articles on socio-economic devt and political science. *Leisure interests:* history, literature. *Address:* Embassy of Kazakhstan, 101000 Moscow, Chistoprudnyi Blvd 3A, Russian Federation (office). *Telephone:* (495) 627-17-01 (office). *Fax:* (495) 608-08-32 (office). *E-mail:* pressa@kazembassy.ru (office). *Website:* www.kazembassy.ru (office).

TASSLER, Nina, BFA; American television executive; m. Jerry Levine; two c.; ed Boston Univ.; following graduation, moved to New York City and worked for Roundabout Theatre Co.; moved to Los Angeles, Calif. and worked as talent agent at Triad Artists for five years; Dir, Movies and Mini-Series, Lorimar/Warner Bros. Television from 1990, Vice-Pres., Drama Devt, Warner Bros. Television –1997; Vice-Pres., Drama, CBS Productions 1997–98, Sr Vice-Pres., Drama Devt, CBS Entertainment 1998–2003, Exec. Vice-Pres., Drama Series Devt 2003–04, Pres. CBS Entertainment 2004–16; Creative Achievement Award 2005. *Films include:* Frankie and Johnny Are Married (actress) 2003, The Optimist (producer) 2013. *Publication:* What I Told My Daughter: Lessons from Leaders on Raising the Next Generation of Empowered Women 2016.

TATA, Jamshed Rustom, DSc, FRS; British medical research scientist; *Senior Research Scientist Emeritus, Medical Research Council;* b. 13 April 1930, Bombay, India; s. of Dr Rustom J. Tata and Gool Tata (née Contractor); m. Renée S. Zanetto 1954; two s. one d.; ed Univ. of Bombay, Indian Inst. of Science, Bangalore, Coll. de France and Univ. of Paris (Sorbonne), Paris, France; Postdoctoral Fellow, Sloan-Kettering Inst., New York, USA 1954–55; Beit Memorial Fellow, Nat. Inst. for Medical Research, London 1956–60; Visiting Scientist, Wenner-Gren Inst., Univ. of Stockholm, Sweden 1960–62; mem. Scientific Staff, MRC, Nat. Inst. for Medical Research, London 1962–96, Sr Research Scientist 1996–, Head, Lab. of Developmental Biochemistry 1973–96; Visiting Prof., Univ. of California, Berkeley, USA 1969–70, Ecole Normale Superieure, Lyon, France; Fogarty Int. Scholar, NIH, Bethesda, Md, USA 1983–89, Visiting Scientist 1997; Chair. Cell and Molecular Panel, Wellcome Trust 1990–92, Int. Relations Group 1997–2004; Dir (non-exec.) Biotech Analytic 2000–04; mem. Indian Nat. Acad. of Sciences; Corresp. mem. Soc. de Biologie, France; Fellow, Third World Acad. of Sciences; Chair. and Trustee, Oxford Int. Biomedical Centre 1996–2007; several interviews and reports on BBC Radio and one documentary on BBC TV; ed. of several science journals and publs; Dr hc (Ecole Normale Superieure, Paris) 2009; various awards. *Publications include:* The Thyroid Hormones 1959, Chemistry of Thyroid Diseases 1960, Metamorphosis 1972, The Action of Growth and Developmental Hormones 1983, Metamorphosis 1986, Hormonal Signalling and Post-embryonic Development 1998; more than 250 original scientific papers and reviews. *Leisure interests:* gardening, reading, travel, tennis. *Address:* 15 Bittacy Park Avenue, Mill Hill, London, NW7 2HA, England (home). *Telephone:* (20) 8816-2108 (office); (20) 8346-6291 (home). *Fax:* (20) 8906-4477 (office). *E-mail:* jtata@nimr.mrc.ac.uk (office); jrtata134@clara.co.uk (home).

TATA, Ratan N., BSc; Indian business executive; *Chairman Emeritus, Tata Sons Ltd;* b. 28 Dec. 1937, nephew of J. R. D. Tata; ed Cornell Univ., Harvard Business School, USA; joined Tata Group 1962, apptd Dir-in-Charge Nat. Radio & Electronics Co. Ltd (NELCO) 1971, Chair. Tata Industries 1981–2012, Chair. Tata Sons Ltd (holding co. comprising 80 cos) 1991–2012, interim Chair. 2016, now Chair. Emer., also Chair. various cos in Tata Group, including Tata Steel, Tata Motors Ltd, Tata Engineering & Locomotive Co. Ltd, Tata Industries Ltd, Tata Chemicals Ltd, The Indian Hotels Co. Ltd, Tata Tea Ltd, Tata IBM Ltd, Information Technology Park Ltd, Tata Lucent Technologies Ltd, Tata Trustee Co. Ltd, Tata International AG Zug, Switzerland, Tata Ltd, London, UK, Tata Inc., New York, USA, Tata Technologies (Pte) Ltd, Singapore, Tata Communications Ltd, Tata Hydro Electric Power Supply Co. Ltd, The Andhra Valley Power Supply Co. Ltd, The Tata Power Co. Ltd, Corus (following acquisition of Corus by Tata Steel in April 2007) 2007–12, currently Chair. Sir Ratan Tata Trust, Sir Dorabji Tata Trust, Council of Man., Tata Inst. of Fundamental Research; Pres. of Court, Indian Inst. of Science; mem. Bd of Dirs The Bombay Dyeing & Mfg Co. Ltd, Haldia Petrochemicals Ltd, Antrix Corpn Ltd, Varuna Overseas Ltd, UK; Chair. Indian Investment Comm.; mem. Indian Prime Minister's Council on Trade and Industry, Nat. Hydrogen Energy Bd, Nat. Mfg Competitiveness Council, Global Business Council on HIV/AIDS, The Reserve Bank of India, Nat. Council of Applied Econ. Research; mem. International Advisory Council, Singapore Econ. Devt Bd; mem. International Investment Council, Repub. of South Africa; mem. International Advisory Bd Mitsubishi Corpn, American International Group, JP Morgan Chase, Rolls-Royce, Monetary Authority of Singapore; Trustee, Rand Corpn, Cornell Univ., Univ. of Southern California, Foundation Bd, Ohio State Univ.; Hon. Fellow, LSE, London, UK; Grand Officer, Order of Merit of the Italian Republic 2009, Hon. KBE 2009, Hon. GBE 2014; Hon. DBA (Ohio State Univ.), Hon. DTech (Asian Inst. of Tech., Bangkok), Hon. DSc (Univ. of Warwick); Padma Bhushan 2000, Medal of the Oriental Republic of Uruguay 2004, International Distinguished Achievement Award, B'nai B'rith Int. 2005, Padma Vibhushan 2008, Oslo Business for Peace Award, Business for Peace Foundation 2010. *Address:* Tata Sons Ltd, Bombay House, 24 Homi Mody Street, Mumbai 400 001, India (office). *Telephone:* (22) 66658282 (office). *Fax:* (22) 66658013 (office). *E-mail:* talktous@tatatrusts.org (office). *Website:* www.tata.com (office).

TATE, John Torrence, Jr, PhD; American mathematician and academic; *Professor Emeritus, Harvard University;* b. 13 March 1925, Minneapolis, Minn.; s. of John Torrence Tate and Lois Beatrice Fossler; m. 1st Karin Artin (divorced); three d.; m. 2nd Carol Tate; ed Harvard Coll. and Princeton Univ.; Research Asst and Instructor, Princeton Univ., NJ 1950–53; Visiting Prof., Columbia Univ., New York 1953–54; Prof., Harvard Univ. 1954–90, Prof. Emer. 2009–; fmr Visiting Prof., Institut des Hautes Études Scientifiques, Bures-sur-Yvette, France, Université Paris-Sud, Princeton Univ., École Normale Supérieure, Paris; mem. NAS 1969; Foreign mem. Acad. des sciences 1992, Norwegian Acad. of Science and Letters; Hon. mem. London Math. Soc. 1999; Cole Prize, American Math. Soc. 1956, Sloan Fellowship 1959–61, Guggenheim Fellowship 1965–66, Leroy P. Steele Prize for Lifetime Achievement 1995, Wolf Prize in Math. Wolf Foundation (co-recipient) 2003, Abel Prize, Norwegian Acad. of Science and Letters 2010. *Publications:* numerous articles in math. journals on arithmetic algebraic geometry. *Address:* Department of Mathematics, 325, Faculty of Arts & Sciences, Harvard University, 1 Oxford Street, Cambridge, MA 02138, USA (office). *Telephone:* (617) 495-2171 (office). *Fax:* (617) 495-5132 (office). *E-mail:* tate@math.harvard.edu (office). *Website:* www.math.harvard.edu/people/TateJohn.html (office).

TATLITUĞ, Kıvanç; Turkish actor and model; b. 27 Oct. 1983, Adana; s. of Erdem Tatlıtuğ and Nurten Tatlıtuğ; m. Başak Dizer Tatlıtuğ 2016; ed İstanbul Kültür Üniversitesi; began career as a model 2002, as an actor 2005; Goodwill Amb., UNICEF 2016–; Sadri Alışık Theatre and Cinema Award for Best Actor 2012, Golden Lens Award 2012, Golden Butterfly Creators of Their Own Miracles Award 2017, The Male Brand Award, Marketing Turkey 2018. *Television includes:* series: Gümüş 2005–07, Menekşe ile Halil 2007–08, Aşk-ı Memnu (Golden Butterfly Award for Best Actor in a Leading Role 2009) 2008–10, Ezel 2009–10, Kuzey Güney (Golden Butterfly Award for Best Actor in a Leading Role 2012) 2011–12, Kurt Seyit ve Şura 2014, Cesur ve Güzel 2016–17, Çarpışma 2018. *Films:* Americans at the Black Sea 2007, Kelebeğin Rüyası (SIYAD-Turkish Film Critics Asscn Best Actor Award 2014, Yeşilçam Cinema Award for Best Actor in a Leading Role) 2013, Hadi Be Oğlum 2018. *Address:* c/o Gaye Sökmen, Karanfil Cad., Yolal Sok. No: 3, 34330İç Levent, Istanbul, Turkey (office). *Telephone:* (212) 2828130 (office). *E-mail:* gaye@gayesokmen.com.tr (office). *Website:* www.gayesokmen.com (office); www.kivanctatlitug.com.

TATOLA, Col Bénaindo; Chadian army officer and government official; ed Air Command and Staff Coll., Montgomery, Ala, USA; fmr Mil. Chief of Staff to Pres.; Minister-delegate at the Presidency of the Repub., responsible for Nat. Defence and War Veterans 2011–16. *Address:* c/o Ministry of National Defence, BP 916, N'Djamena, Chad (office).

TATUM, Beverly Daniel, MA, PhD; American clinical psychologist, academic and university administrator; *President Emeritus, Spelman College;* m. Travis Tatum; two s.; ed Wesleyan Univ., Univ. of Michigan, Hartford Seminary, Conn.; clinical psychologist in ind. practice 1988–98; Dissertation Fellow, Center for Black Studies, Univ. of Calif., Santa Barbara 1980–81, Lecturer, Dept of Black Studies 1982–83; Asst Prof., Dept of Psychology, Westfield State Coll., Mass 1983–86, Assoc. Prof. 1986–89; Assoc. Prof., Dept of Psychology and Educ., Mount Holyoke Coll., Mass 1989–96, Prof. 1996–, Dept Chair 1997–98, Dean of Coll. and Vice-Pres. for Student Affairs 1998–2002, Acting Pres. 2002; Pres. Spelman Coll., Atlanta, Ga 2002–15, then Pres. Emer.; Visiting Scholar, Wellesley Coll., Mass 1991–92; mem. Bd of Dirs Smith Child Care Center at Sunnyside, Mass 1985–92, Equity Inst., Mass 1988–90; mem. Bd of Trustees, Williston Northampton School 1999–; mem. Bd of Incorporators, Hartford Seminary 2000–; Chair. Human Subjects Cttee, Psychology Dept, Mount Holyoke Coll. 1989–90; Chair. Coll. Cttee on Fellowships 1998–; mem. African-American Studies Steering Cttee, Multicultural Community and College Life Cttee, Academic Policies Cttee; Faculty Advisor, Psychology Club, Mount Holyoke Club 1990–91; Westfield State Coll. Campus Rep., Mass Teachers Asscn 1986–89; mem. American Psychological Asscn, American Educational Research Asscn, American Coll. Personnel Asscn, American Asscn of Univ. Women, Nat. Asscn of Multicultural Educ.; Elder, Martin Luther King Community Presbyterian Church 1994–97; Rackham Opportunity Fellowship, Univ. of Mich. 1975–78; Fellow, American Psychological Asscn; Ford Foundation Postdoctoral Fellow 1991–92; Nat. Achievement Award 1971–72, Distinguished Service Award, Westfield State Coll. 1986, 1987, Commonwealth Citation for Meritorious Service, Westfield State Coll. 1988, Asscn of Women in Psychology Publ. Award 1994, Nat. Asscn of Multicultural Educ. Book of the Year Award 1998. *Publications:* Assimilation Blues: Black Families in a White Community 1987, Why Are All the Black Kids Sitting Together in the Cafeteria? and Other Conversations About Race 1997, Can We Talk About Race? and Other Conversations in an Era of Resegregation 2007. *Address:* c/o Office of the President, Spelman College, 350 Spelman Lane, SW, Atlanta, GA 30314-4399, USA (office). *Telephone:* (404) 270-5001 (office). *Fax:* (404) 270-5010 (office). *E-mail:* btatum@spelman.edu (office). *Website:* www.spelman.edu/administration/office (office).

TAUB, Daniel; Israeli (b. British) diplomatist and foundation executive; *Director of Strategy and Planning, Yad Hanadiv;* ed The Haberdashers' Aske's Boys School, Elstree, Herts., University Coll., Oxford, University Coll., London, Kennedy School of Govt, Harvard Univ., USA; grad. of Bnei Akiva youth movt; served as a combat medic and as a reserve officer in Israel Defense Forces int. law div.; joined Ministry of Foreign Affairs late 1980s, served as Prin. Deputy Legal Advisor to Perm. Missions of Israel to UN in New York and Geneva; lecturer on Middle Eastern issues, int. law and negotiation theory in univs and insts world-wide, Amb. to UK 2012–15; Dir of Strategy and Planning, Yad Hanadiv (philanthropic foundation) 2016–. *Address:* Yad Hanadiv, 4 George Washington Street, 9418704 Jerusalem, Israel (office). *Telephone:* 2-5665107 (office). *E-mail:* website@yadhanadiv.org.il (office). *Website:* www.yadhanadiv.org.il (office).

TAUBES, Clifford Henry, PhD; American mathematician and academic; *William Petschek Professor of Mathematics, Harvard University;* b. 21 Feb. 1954, Rochester, NY; ed Cornell Univ., Princeton Univ., Harvard Univ.; currently William Petschek Prof. of Math., Harvard Univ.; mem. NAS 1996; Fellow, American Acad. of Arts and Sciences 1995; four-time speaker at Int. Congress of Mathematicians 1986, 1994 (plenary), 1998, 2010 (plenary; selected, but did not speak), Veblen Prize, American Math. Soc. 1991, Elie Cartan Prize, Acad. des sciences 1993, Clay Research Award 2008, NAS Award in Math. 2008, Shaw Prize in Math. (co-recipient) 2009. *Publications:* Modeling Differential Equations in Biology, The L Squared Moduli Spaces on Four Manifold with Cylindrical Ends (Monographs in Geometry and Topology), Metrics, Connections and Gluing Theorems (CBMS Regional Conf. Series in Math.); numerous papers in professional journals. *Address:* Mathematics Department, Harvard University, SC 504, Cambridge, MA 02138, USA (office). *Telephone:* (617) 495-5579 (office). *Fax:* (617) 495-5132 (office). *E-mail:* chtaubes@math.harvard.edu (office). *Website:* www.math.harvard.edu/people/TaubesCliff.html (office).

TAUBIRA-DELANNON, Christiane, DSci; French politician; b. 2 Feb. 1952, Cayenne, French Guiana; Founder and Pres. Walwari (political movt) 1993; Deputy to Nat. Ass. for French Guiana (1st constituency) 1993–2012; mem. European Parl. (Group of the European Radical Alliance, Énergie Radicale) 1994–99; mem. Parti Guyanais de Centre Gauche; mem. Cttee on Devt and Co-operation, Del. for relations with the countries of S America; joined the Socialist Party (PS) 1997; commissioned by Prime Minister Lionel Jospin for a report on gold discovery in Guiana; gave her name to the 21 May 2001 law recognizing the Atlantic slave trade and slavery as a crime against humanity; a Left Radical Party (PRG) cand. for the presidency though not belonging to the party 2002, Vice-Pres. Left Radical Party 2002–; Regional Councillor of French Guiana 2010–; Minister of Justice and Keeper of the Seals 2012–16. *Publications:* Peche en Fiches (Guyane) 1993, Mes météores: combats politiques au long cours 2012, Paroles de liberté 2014.

TAUR MATAN RUAK; Timor-Leste politician, fmr head of state and fmr army officer; *Prime Minister;* b. (José Maria Vasconcelos), 10 Oct. 1956, Baguia, Baucau region; s. of António de Vasconcelos and Albertina Amaral; m. Isabel da Costa Ferreira; one s. two d.; joined guerrilla group Falintil (resisting Indonesian occupation) 1975, rising through ranks to become Company Commdr 1979, Asst Chief of Staff 1981, mil. adviser to Deputy Chief of Staff of Falintil 1983, responsible for all mil. operations throughout Timor-Leste 1986, Deputy Chief of Staff 1986–92, Chief of Staff 1992–98, Commdr of Falintil 1998–2001, rank of Brig.-Gen. 2001, Chief of Staff of East Timor Defence Force (Falintil-ETDF) 2002–11 (following restoration of independence 2002), rank of Maj.-Gen. 2009, demobilised from Falintil 2011; Pres. of Timor-Leste 2012–17; Prime Minister 2018–; Portuguese Parl. Human Rights Prize 1999. *Address:* Office of the Prime Minister, Palácio do Governo, Av. Presidente Nicolau Lobato, Dili, Timor-Leste (office). *Telephone:* 7243559 (office). *Fax:* 3339503 (office). *E-mail:* mail@primeministerandcabinet.gov.tp (office). *Website:* timor-leste.gov.tl (office).

TAUREL, Sidney, MBA; American (b. Spanish) business executive; *Chairman, Pearson Plc;* b. 9 Feb. 1949, Casablanca, Morocco; ed École des Hautes Études Commerciales, France, Columbia Univ.; joined Eli Lilly Int. Corpn 1971, Marketing Assoc. 1971–72, Marketing Plans Man., Brazil 1971–76, marketing and sales assignments in E Europe and France 1976–81, Gen. Man., Brazil 1981–83, Vice-Pres. Lilly European Operations, London, UK 1983–86, Pres. Eli Lilly Pres. Pharmaceutical Div. 1991–93, mem. Lilly Bd Dirs 1991–, Exec. Vice-Pres. Eli Lilly & Co. and Pres. Pharmaceutical Div. 1993–96, Pres. 1996–2005, COO 1996–98, CEO 1998–99, Chair. and CEO 1999–2008, Chair. Emer. 2009–; Chair. Pearson Plc 2016–; mem. Bd of Dirs IBM Corpn, McGraw-Hill Cos Inc., RCA Tennis Championships; fmr mem. Exec. Cttee Pharmaceutical Research and Mfrs of America (PhRMA), Exec. Cttee Business Council; apptd to Pres.'s Homeland Security Advisory Council 2002–03, to Pres.'s Export Council 2003–06, Advisory Cttee for Trade Policy and Negotiations 2007–09; mem. Bd of Overseers Columbia Business School; Trustee, Indianapolis Museum of Art; became US citizen 1995; Chevalier, Légion d'honneur 2001. *Address:* Pearson Plc, 80 Strand, London, WC2R 0RL, England (office). *Telephone:* (20) 7010-2000 (office). *Website:* www.pearson.com (office).

TAUS, Josef, LLD; Austrian banker, business executive and fmr politician; b. 8 Feb. 1933, Vienna; s. of Josef Taus and G. Schinko; m. Martha Loibl 1960; ed Univ. of Vienna, Hochschule für Welthandel; early career as journalist and served in law practice; with Austrian Inst. of Econ. Research; joined Girozentrale und Bank der Österreichischen Sparkassen AG as Sec. and Head of Econ. Div. 1958, mem. Man. Bd 1967–68, Chair. and Man. Dir 1968–75; fmr Man. Sparinvest-Kapitalanlage GmbH; mem. Parl. 1975–91; State Sec., Fed. Ministry of Communications and Nationalized Enterprises 1966–67; Fed. Chair. Austrian People's Party (ÖVP) 1975–79; Man. Partner, Constantia Industrieverwaltungs GesmbH. 1979–86; mem. Supervisory Bd Management Trust Holding AG, Vienna 1989–; mem. Bd of Dirs Constantia Industrieholding AG 1986–89, ECO TRUST Holding AG 1989, Trust Invest AG 1990–; Man. Dir Fremdenverkehrsbetriebe GesmbH and Co. OHG. *Leisure interests:* skiing, music, reading, swimming. *Address:* Management Trust Holding AG, Argentinierstraße 42, 1040 Vienna (office); Zahnradbahnstrasse 17, 1190 Vienna, Austria (home). *Telephone:* (1) 535-61-03 (office). *Fax:* (1) 535-61-03 (office). *E-mail:* office@mth-gruppe.at (office). *Website:* www.mth-gruppe.at (office).

TAUTOU, Audrey; French actress; b. 9 Aug. 1978, Beaumont, Puy de Dôme, Auvergne; began acting lessons, Cours Florent, Paris; film debut in Vénus beauté (Institut) 1999. *Films include:* Vénus beauté (institut) (Venus Beauty Salon) (César Award for Most Promising Actress, Lumière Award for Most Promising Young Actress) 1999, Triste à mourir 1999, Épouse-moi 1999, Voyous Voyous (Pretty Devils) 2000, Le battement d'ailes du papillon (Happenstance) 2000, Le fabuleux destin d'Amélie Poulain (Amélie) (Chicago Film Critics Asscn Award for Most Promising Performer, Lumière Award for Best Actress, Sant Jordi Award for Best Foreign Actress) 2001, Dieu est grand, je suis toute petite (God Is Great, And I'm Not) 2001, À la folie... pas du tout (He Loves Me... He Loves Me Not) 2002, L'auberge espagnole (The Spanish Apartment) 2002, Dirty Pretty Things 2002, Pas sur la bouche 2003, Nowhere to Go But Up 2003, Les Marins perdus (Lost Seamen) 2003, Un long dimanche de fiançailles 2004, Les poupées russes 2005, The Da Vinci Code 2006, Hors de prix 2006, Ensemble, c'est tout 2007, Coco avant Chanel 2009, De vrais mensonges 2010, La Délicatesse 2011, Thérèse 2012, Mood Indigo 2013, Chinese Puzzle 2013, Microbe et Gasoil 2015 Eternity 2015, The Odyssey 2016, Open at Night 2016. *Address:* c/o Claire Blondel, Artmedia, 20 avenue Rapp, 75007 Paris, France (office). *Telephone:* 1-43-17-33-23 (office); 1-45-51-13-00. *E-mail:* info@artmedia.fr (office); bcgpresse@wanadoo.fr (office). *Website:* www.artmedia.fr (office). *Fax:* 1-45-51-18-19.

TAVARES, Carlos; French automotive industry executive; *Chairman, PSA Group;* ed Ecole Centrale de Paris; joined Renault Group 1981, Head of Ground Link Eng 1985–91, Head of Clio II platform chassis program 1991–96, Head of Architecture Dept 1996–98, Project Dir Mengame II 1998–2001, Dir Mid-Range Vehicle Program 2001–04, Exec. Vice-Pres. of Design, Corp. Planning and Product Planning, Nissan Motor Co. (strategic partner of Renault) 2004–09, Exec. Vice-Pres. and Chair. Man. Cttee, Americas Operations 2005–09, Pres. Nissan North America 2009–11, Group COO Renault SA 2011–13; mem. Man. Bd, PSA Group Jan. 2014–, Chair. March 2014–; Pres. European Automobile Manufacturers' Asscn (ACEA) 2018. *Address:* PSA Group, Steering Center, 7, Henri Ste Claire Street, Deville, 92563 Rueil-Malmaison, France (office). *Telephone:* 1-55-94-81-00 (office). *Website:* www.groupe-psa.com (office).

TAVARES, Luís Filipe Lopes, Lic.Geog; Cabo Verde university administrator and politician; *Minister of Foreign Affairs and of Defence;* b. 25 Aug. 1965, Praia; ed Univ. de Rouen, France, ILO Training Centre, Turin, Italy, Instituto Nacional de Administração de Portugal; fmr Councillor and Dir, Research and Planning Dept, Câmara Municipal da Praia; fmr Adviser to Prime Minister; fmr Gen. Dir, Office of Decentralization, Local Admin Dept, Govt of Cabo Verde; coordinated various public admin projects in Cabo Verde at central and local levels, financed by UNDP, World Bank, EU and French and Spanish devt programmes; Cabo Verde adviser for EU municipal devt programme for East Africa; Admin.-Gen., Instituto Superior de Educação, Instituto Nacional de Administração e Gestão and Universidade Jean Piaget –2016; mem. Assembleia Nacional (parl.) (MpD) for Santiago Sul; Minister of Foreign Affairs and of Defence 2016–; mem. Movimento para a Democracia (MpD), currently mem. Political Cttee and Vice-Pres.; Chevalier, Ordre Nat. du Mérite. *Address:* Ministry of Foreign Affairs and Communities, Palácio das Comunidades, Achada de Santo António, CP 60, Praia, Santiago, Cabo Verde (office). *Telephone:* 2607853 (office). *Fax:* 2619270 (office). *Website:* www.mirex.gov.cv (office).

TAVERNE, Suzanna, BA; British company director; b. 3 Feb. 1960, London; d. of Dick Taverne and Janice Taverne; m.; Marc Vlessing 1993; one s. one d.; ed Pimlico School, Westminster School, Balliol Coll., Oxford; with S.G. Warburg & Co. Ltd 1982–90; Finance Dir, Newspaper Publishing PLC 1990–94; consultant to Saatchi & Saatchi PLC 1994–95; Dir of Strategy and Devt, Pearson PLC 1995–98; Man. Dir British Museum, London 1999–2001; Dir of Operations, Imperial Coll. London 2002–05; Chair. Nat. Council for One Parent Families 2002–07, Gingerbread 2007–10, Marie Stopes Int. 2018; Dir (non-exec.) Nationwide Building Society 2005–12, FCE Bank plc 2008–; mem. Advisory Bd Manchester Business School 2010–14; Trustee, Design Museum 2006–11, StepChange Debt Charity 2009–17, Shakespeare Schools Festival 2011–15, BBC 2012–17, Age UK 2017–. *Address:* 35 Camden Square, London, NW1 9XA, England (home). *Telephone:* (20) 7482-5710 (office). *E-mail:* taverne@vlessing.com (home).

TAVERNIER, Bertrand René Maurice; French film director, producer and screenwriter; b. 25 April 1941, Lyon; s. of René Tavernier and Geneviève Dumond; m. Claudine O'Hagan 1965; one s. one d.; ed Ecole St-Martin de Pontoise, Lycées Henri-IV, Fénelon, Paris, Univ. de Paris (Sorbonne); press attaché and journalist, then film dir; mem. Société des réalisateurs de films, APR; Pres. Inst. Lumière 1982–. *Films directed include:* Le baiser de Judas 1964, Une charge explosive, La chance et l'amour 1964, L'horloger de Saint-Paul (Louis Delluc Prize 1973) 1974, Que la fête commence (César Best Screenplay, Best Direction) 1975, Le juge et l'assassin (César Best Screenplay) 1976, Des enfants gâtés 1977, La mort en direct (Foreign Press Award 1979) 1980, Une semaine de vacances 1980, Coup de torchon 1981, Mississippi Blues (documentary) 1983, La 8ème génération (short) 1983, Ciné citron (short) 1983, Un dimanche à la campagne (Best Dir Award, Cannes Film Festival, NY Critics Award) 1984, Autour de minuit 1986, La passion béatrice 1987, La vie et rien d'autre (European Film Festival Special Prize 1989) 1988, Daddy nostalgie 1990, Lest We Forget (segment Pour Aung San Suu Kyi, Myanmar) 1991, La guerre sans nom (documentary) 1991, L.627 1992, La fille de d'Artagnan 1994, L'appât 1995, Capitaine Conan (Méliès Prize for Best French Film 1996, César for Best Dir 1997) 1996, Ça commence aujourd'hui (It All Starts Today) (Prix de la Fipresci, Berlin, Prix du Public, San Sebastian and Tübingen, Prix Photogramas de Plata for Best Foreign Language Film, Spain) 1999, Histoires de vies brisées: les 'double peine' de Lyon (documentary) 2001, Laissez-passer (Safe Conduct) (Best Film, Best Dir Fort Lauderdale) 2002, Holy Lola 2004, In the Electric Mist 2009, The Princess of Montpensier 2010, The French Minister 2013. *Films produced include:* La question 1977, La trace (assoc. producer) 1983, Veillées d'Armes (documentary) 1994, Fred (exec. producer) 1997, Don't Make Trouble! (co-producer) 2001. *Television includes:* Philippe Soupault (film documentary) 1982, Lyon, Inside Out (film documentary) 1988, De l'autre côté du periph (film documentary) 1997, Les enfants de Thiès (film) 2001. *Publications:* 30 ans de cinéma américain (jtly) 1970, 50 ans de cinéma américain (jtly) 1991, Qu'est-ce qu'on attend? 1993, Amis américains 1994 and other books. *Leisure interests:* jazz, food, literature, movies. *Address:* Institut Lumière, 25 rue du Premier Film, 69008 Lyon (office); Little Bear, 7–9 rue Arthur Groussier, 75010 Paris, France. *Telephone:* 1-42-38-06-55 (office). *Fax:* 1-42-45-00-33 (office). *E-mail:* contac@institut-lumiere.org (office). *Website:* www.institut-lumiere.org (office).

TAVIANI, Paolo; Italian film director; b. 8 Nov. 1931, San Miniato; brother of Vittorio Taviani; ed Univ. of Pisa. *Films:* co-dir (with Vittorio Taviani): Un uomo da bruciare 1963, I fuorilegge del matrimonio 1963, Sovversivi 1967, Sotto il segno dello scorpione 1969, San Michele aveva un gallo 1971, Allonsanfan 1974, Padre Padrone (Cannes Film Festival Palme d'Or, FIPRESCI Prize) 1977, The Meadow 1979, La notte di San Lorenzo (The Night of the Shooting Stars) (Cannes Film Festival Grand Prix du Jury) 1981, Xaos 1984, Good Morning, Babylon 1988, Il Sole anche di Notte 1990, Fiorile 1993, The Elective Affinities 1996, 1998 Two Kidnappings 1998, The Lark Farm 2007, Caesar Must Die 2012, Wondrous Boccaccio 2015.

TAVOLA, Kaliopate, MAgrSc; Fijian government official, economist and diplomatist; b. 10 Oct. 1946, Dravuni; m. Helen Tavola; one s. two d.; ed Massey Univ., New Zealand, Australian Nat. Univ., Australia; Agric. Officer, Ministry of Primary Industries 1973–77, Sr Agric. Officer 1977–79, Prin. Economist 1979, Prin. Agric. Officer Eastern Div./Projects 1980, Chief Economist 1980–81, 1982–84, Dir of Agric. (acting) 1981–82, later Minister of Primary Industries; London Rep. Fiji Sugar Marketing Co. Ltd 1984–88, Deputy CEO 1998–2000, in Suva 2000–08; Commercial Counsellor, Fiji High Comm. 1984–88; Head of Mission to EU, Brussels 1988–98 also Amb. to Belgium (also accred to Luxembourg, Netherlands, France, Italy, Spain, Portugal, Greece), also Perm. Rep. to UNESCO, Paris, also to FAO, WTO, WCO, OPCW; responsible for IFAD, MFO, PCA, Commr-Gen. South Pacific Pavilion, EXPO '92, Seville, Spain 1992, Minister of Foreign Affairs and External Trade 2000–06; mem. Eminent Persons Group, African, Caribbean and Pacific Group of States (ACP) 2013–. *Leisure interests:* reading, gardening, music, golf. *Address:* Coordinator of the Eminent Persons Group, ACP Secretariat, Avenue Georges Henri 451, 1200 Brussels, Belgium. *E-mail:* epg@acp.int. *Website:* www.epg.acp.int.

TAWADA, Yoko, MA; Japanese novelist; b. 23 March 1960, Tokyo; ed Waseda Univ., Univ. of Hamburg, Germany; based in Germany 1982–, writes in German and Japanese; Writer-in-Residence, Villa Aurora, Pacific Palisades, USA 1997; lectured on poetry at Univ. of Tübingen 1998; Max Kade Distinguished Visitor and Writer-in-Residence, Foreign Languages and Literatures Section, MIT 1999; Writer-in-Residence, Univ. of Kentucky 2004, Washington Univ. in St. Louis 2008, Stanford Univ. 2009, Cornell Univ. 2009; City of Hamburg Prize in Literature 1990, Gunzo Prize for new writers 1991, Lessing Prize 1994, Adelbert von Chamisso Prize 1996, Izumi Kyooka Literature Prize 2000, Punkamura Prix Des Deux Magots 2002, Ito Sei Literature Prize 2003, Tanizaki Junichiro Prize 2003, Goethe Medal 2005, Erlanger Literaturpreis 2013, Kleist Prize 2016, Carl-Zuckmayer-Medaille 2018. *Publications include:* Nur da wo du bist da ist nichts (poems and stories) 1987, Das Bad (novel) 1989, Missing Heels (short story) 1991, Wo Europa anfaengt (Where Europe Begins, poems and stories) 1991, Sannin-kankei (short stories) 1991, Inumukoiri (The Bridegroom was a Dog, short stories) (Akutagawa Prize) 1993, Ein Gast (novel) 1993, Arufabetto no kizuguchi (novel) 1993, Tintenfisch auf Reisen (short stories) 1994, Gottoharutotetsudo (short stories) 1996, Talisman (essays) 1996, Seijodensetsu (novel) 1996, Aber die Mandarinen muessen heute abend noch geraubt werden (poems) 1997, Kitunet-suki (poems) 1998, Hikon (novel) 1998, Verwandlungen (essays) 1998, Katakoto no uwagoto (essays) 1999, Hikari to zerachin no raipuchihhi (short stories) 2000, Opium fuer Ovid (novel) 2000, Hinagiku no ocha no baai (short stories) 2000, Yogisha no yakoressha 2002, Kyukeijikan 2002, Exophonie (essays) 2003, Tabi wo suru hadaka no me (novel) 2004, Uni ni otoshita namae 2006, Ameika 2006, Tokeru machi sukeru toori 2007, Students of the Snow (Noma Literary Prize) 2011, Kumo o tsukamu hanashi (Yomiuri Prize 2012) 2012, Memoirs of a Polar Bear (Warwick Prize for Women in Translation – shared with translator 2017) 2016, The Emissary (trans. Margaret Mitsutani) (Nat. Book Award for Translated Literature 2018) 2018. *Address:* c/o konkursbuch Verlag Claudia Gehrke, PF 1621, 72006, Tübingen, Germany. *E-mail:* office@konkursbuch.com; tawadaoo@yahoo.co .jp. *Website:* www.konkursbuch.com/html/tawada.html; yokotawada.de.

TAX, Stergomena Lawrence, MA, PhD; Tanzanian international organisation official; *Executive-Secretary, Southern African Development Community (SADC);* b. 6 July 1960, Mwanza; m.; two c.; ed Univ. of Dar es Salaam, Univ. of Tsukuba, Japan; Finance Man. Officer, Ministry of Finance 1991–92, Officer-in-charge for World Bank Desk 1993, Officer-in-charge for Arab Funds 1994, Officer-in-charge of SADC and UNDP Desks 1995, held various other positions within Ministry of Finance –2002, also worked in Centre for Foreign Relations (under Ministry of Foreign Affairs and Int. Relations) 1993–95 and served as Researcher, World Bank Inst. for two years; CEO Business Environment Strengthening Programme for Tanzania (BESP), Office of the Pres. 2004–06, also Coordinator, Commissioned Studies, Economic and Social Research Foundation (ESRF) 2002–04; Deputy Permanent Sec., Ministry of Economic, Planning and Empowerment 2006–07; Permanent Sec., Ministry of Trade, Industry and Marketing 2006–08; Permanent Sec., Ministry of East African Cooperation 2008–13; Exec.-Sec. SADC 2013–. *Address:* Southern African Development Community (SADC) Headquarters, Plot No. 54385, Central Business District, Private Bag 0095, Gaborone, Botswana (office). *Telephone:* 3951863 (office). *Fax:* 3972848 (office). *E-mail:* registry@sadc .int (office). *Website:* www.sadc.int (office).

TAXELL, (Lars Evald) Christoffer, LLM; Finnish business executive and fmr politician; b. 14 Feb. 1948, Turku; s. of Lars Erik Taxell and Elna Hillevi Brunberg; m. Rachel Margareta Nygård 1974; two d.; ed Univ. of Turku; Chair. Youth Org., Swedish People's Party 1970–72, Party Chair. 1985–90; Political Sec. 1970–71; Asst Lecturer, School of Econ., Åbo Akademi, Turku 1973–75; mem. Parl. 1975–91; Minister of Justice 1979–87, of Educ. and Science 1987–90; mem. Bd of Dirs Partek Corpn 1984–2002, Pres. and CEO 1990–2002; Chair. Confed. of Finnish Industries EK 2005–06; Chair. Finnair Oyj 2003–11, Stockmann Oyj 2007–; mem. Bd of Dirs Sampo plc 1998–2013, Raisio plc 2003–06, Nordkalk Corpn 2003–, Luvata Group 2005–; Chair. European Services Forum, Brussels 2007–; Chancellor, Åbo Akademi Univ. 2004–; Dr hc (Åbo Akademi Univ.) 1998. *Address:* European Services Forum, Avenue de Cortenbergh 168, 1000 Brussels, Belgium. *E-mail:* esf@esf.be. *Website:* www.esf.be/new.

TAY, Simon S(eong) C(hee), LLB, LLM; Singaporean academic; *Chairman, Singapore Institute of International Affairs;* s. of Tay Seow Huah and Cheong Keong Hin; m. Siow Jin Hua; one s.; ed Nat. Univ. of Singapore, Harvard Univ., USA; served as Nominated Mem. of Parl. 1997–2001; Chair. Nat. Environment Agency 2002–08; Schwartz Fellow, Asia Soc., New York 2009; Visiting Prof., Harvard Law School 2003, has also taught at Yale Univ. and Fletcher School, Tufts Univ.; currently Assoc. Prof. of Int. Law and Public Policy, Nat. Univ. of Singapore; Visiting Prof., Yale Univ., USA; Ed.-in-Chief, Asian Journal of International Law; Sr Consultant, WongPartnership LLP (law firm); Expert and Eminent Person, ASEAN Regional Forum, representing Singapore; Vice-Chair., Asia Pacific Water Forum; Global Council Co-Chair., Asia Soc.; mem. Bd of Dirs Hyflux Ltd, Far East Organization; mem. Global Advisory Bd Toyota Motor Corpn (also Chair. for Asia), Mitsubishi UFJ Group; Fulbright Fellow, Harvard 1993–94; Laylin Prize, Harvard 1994, Singapore Young Artist of the Year 1995, Eisenhower Fellowship 2002, Nat. Day Award PBM 2006. *Publications:* Stand Alone 1993, Asian Dragons and Green Trade 1996, Reinventing ASEAN 2001, The Enemy Within: Combating Corruption in Asia 2003, Sketching Regional Futures 2005, A Mandarin and the Making of Public Policy 2006, Elections in Asia: Making Democracy Work 2006, Climate Change Negotiations 2008, City of Small Blessings (novel) (Singapore Literature Prize 2010) 2009, Asia Alone 2010. *Address:* Singapore Institute of International Affairs (SIIA), 2 Nassim Road, Singapore, 258370 (office); Faculty of Law, National University of Singapore, Eu Tong Sen Building, 469G Bukit Timah Road, Singapore, 259776 (office). *Telephone:* 67349600 (SIIA) (office). *Fax:* 67336217 (SIIA) (office). *E-mail:* lawtaysc@nus.edu.sg (office); chairman@siiaonline.org (office). *Website:* www.siiaonline.org (office); lawtaysc.wixsite.com/simonsctay.

TAYA, Col Maawiya Ould Sid'Ahmed; Mauritanian politician, fmr army officer and fmr head of state; b. 1943; served in Saharan War 1976–78, Chief of Mil. Operations, then commdr garrison at Bir Mogkrein; Minister of Defence 1978–79; Commdr nat. gendarmerie 1979–80; Minister in charge of Perm. Secr., Mil. Cttee for Nat. Recovery 1979–81; Army Chief of Staff 1980–81, March–Dec. 1984; Prime Minister and Minister of Defence 1981–84, 1984–92; Pres. of Mauritania and Chair. Mil. Cttee for Nat. Salvation 1984–92, elected Pres. of Mauritania 1992–2005 (deposed in bloodless coup).

TAYEBNIA, Ali, PhD; Iranian academic, economist and government official; b. 5 April 1960, Isfahan; ed Tehran Univ., London School of Econs, UK; fmr mem. Faculty, Dept of Econs, Tehran Univ.; Sec., Econ. Comm. 1997–2000, 2005–07; Deputy Head, Presidential Office for Planning 2001–05; Minister of Econ. Affairs and Finance 2013–17.

TAYLOR, Allan Richard, OC; Canadian banker; b. 14 Sept. 1932, Prince Albert, Sask.; s. of Norman Taylor and Anna Lydia Norbeck Taylor; m. Shirley Irene Ruston 1957; one s. one d.; joined Royal Bank of Canada 1949, Dir, Head Int. Div. 1977–83, Pres. and COO 1983–86, CEO 1986–94, Chair. 1986–95; Dir Canadian Inst. for Advanced Research, Toronto, Neuroscience Network, Montréal; Pres. Int. Monetary Conf. 1992–93; Chair. Canadian Bankers Assen 1984–86; mem. Council of Patrons, Canadian Outward Bound; mem. Advisory Council Canadian Exec. Service Overseas; mem. Advisory Bd, Canadian Journalism Foundation, Advisory Bd, Canadian Foundation for AIDS Research; Exec. Adviser, Public Policy Forum; Hon. DJur (Univ. of Regina) 1987, (Concordia Univ.) 1988, (Queen's Univ.) 1991; Hon. DBA (Laval) 1990; Dr hc (Ottawa) 1992; inducted into Canadian Business Hall of Fame 2006. *Leisure interests:* golf, tennis, fishing.

TAYLOR, Andrew Dawson, OBE, BSc, DPhil; British physicist and academic; *Executive Director, National Laboratories, Science and Technology Facilities Council, Rutherford Appleton Laboratory;* b. 1 March 1950, Falkirk, Scotland; m.; four c.; ed St John's Coll., Oxford; joined Rutherford Lab. as part of team promoting accelerator-based neutrons sources as tools to investigate microscopic structure and dynamics of condensed matter, Dir ISIS facility, Science and Tech. Facilities Council (STFC), Rutherford Appleton Lab., Didcot, Oxon. 1992–2012, Exec. Dir STFC's Nat. Labs 2012–; also worked at Los Alamos, NM, USA; Hon. Fellow, Mansfield Coll., Oxford 2011; Hon. DSc (Glasgow) 2010, (London) 2012; Glazebrook Medal, Inst. of Physics 2006. *Publications:* numerous scientific papers in professional journals on pulsed neutron source instrumentation and science. *Address:* Science and Technology Facilities Council, Rutherford Appleton Laboratory, Harwell Science and Innovation Campus, Harwell, Oxford, OX11 0QX, Oxon., England (office). *Telephone:* (1235) 446681 (office). *Fax:* (1235) 445383 (office). *E-mail:* andrew.taylor@stfc.ac.uk (office). *Website:* www.scitech.ac.uk (office).

TAYLOR, Charles Ghankay; Liberian fmr head of state; b. 28 Jan. 1948; m. 3rd Jewel Taylor (divorced); m. 4th Victoria Addison-Taylor; three d.; Leader, Nat. Patriotic Front of Liberia (NPFL), part of combined rebel force which overthrew fmr Pres. Samuel Doe; engaged in civil insurrection 1991–96; mem. Transitional Exec. Council of State 1996–97; Pres. of Liberia 1997–2003; indicted for war crimes in Sierra Leone 2003; in exile in Nigeria 2003, arrested March 2006, extradited to The Hague 2006; convicted by Special Court for Sierra Leone, based in The Hague, of 11 counts of aiding and abetting war crimes and crimes against humanity 26 April 2012, sentenced to 50 years in prison.

TAYLOR, Charles Margrave, CC, BA, MA, DPhil, FRSC; Canadian philosopher and academic; *Professor Emeritus of Philosophy, McGill University;* b. 5 Nov. 1931, Montreal, QC; s. of Walter Margrave Taylor and Simone Beaubien; m. 1st Alba Romer 1956 (died 1990); five d.; m. 2nd Aube Billard 1995; ed McGill Univ., Balliol Coll., Oxford, UK; Fellow, All Souls Coll., Oxford 1956–61; Asst Prof., Dept of Political Science, McGill Univ., Montreal 1961–62, Prof. 1962–97, Prof. Emer. of Philosophy 1998–; Prof., Univ. of Montreal 1962–71; Chichele Prof. of Social and Political Theory, Univ. of Oxford 1976–81, also Fellow, All Souls Coll.; Bd of Trustees Prof. of Law, Northwestern Univ. 2002–07; Mills Visiting Prof., Univ. of California, Berkeley 1974, 1983; mem., School of Social Science, Inst. for Advanced Studies, Princeton, NJ 1981–82; Guest Prof., J.W. Goethe Univ., Frankfurt 1984; Visiting Prof. of Political Science and Philosophy, Hebrew Univ. of Jerusalem 1985; mem. British Acad., American Acad. of Arts and Sciences; Grand Officer, Nat. Order of Quebec 2000; Alan B. Plaunt Memorial Lecturer, Carleton Univ., Ottawa 1978, Alex Corry Lecturer, Queen's Univ., Kingston, Ont. 1980, B.N. Ganguli Lecturer, Centre for the Study of Developing Socs, Delhi 1981, Suhrkamp Lecturer, Univ. of Frankfurt 1984, Massey Lecturer, CBC 1991, Tanner Lecturer, Stanford Univ. 1992, Max Horkheimer Lecturer, Univ. of Frankfurt 1996, Storrs Lecturer, Yale Univ. 1998, Gifford Lecturer, Univ. of Glasgow 1999, Templeton Prize 2007, Kyoto Prize 2008, John W. Kluge Prize for Lifetime Achievement in the Study of Humanity, Library of Congress (co-recipient) 2015, Berggruen Prize 2016. *Publications include:* The Explanation of Behaviour 1964, The Pattern of Politics 1970, Erklärung und Interpretation in den Wissenschaften vom Menschen 1975, Hegel 1975, Hegel and Modern Society 1979, Social Theory As Practice 1983, Human Agency and Language: Philosophical Papers 1 1985, Philosophy and the Human Sciences: Philosophical Papers 2 1985, Negative Freiheit? Zur Kritik des neuzeitlichen Individualismus 1988, Sources of the Self: The Making of the Modern Identity 1989, The Malaise of Modernity 1991, Multiculturalism and 'The Politics of Recognition' 1992, Rapprocher les solitudes: crits sur le fédéralisme et le nationalisme au Canada 1992, Roads to Democracy: Human Rights and Democratic Development in Thailand 1994, Philosophical Arguments 1995, A Catholic Modernity? 1999, Wieviel Gemeinschaft braucht die Demokratie? Aufsätze zur politische Philosophie 2002, Varieties of Religion Today: William James Revisited 2002, Modern Social Imaginaries 2004, A Secular Age 2007, Dilemmas and Connections: Selected Essays 2011, Retrieving Realism (co-author) 2015, The Language Animal: The Full Shape of the Human Linguistic Capacity 2016. *E-mail:* cmt1111111@aol.com (office). *Website:* www.mcgill.ca/philosophy/people/faculty/taylor (office).

TAYLOR, David Scott, BS; American business executive; *Chairman, President and CEO, Procter & Gamble Company;* b. 20 April 1958, Charlotte, North Carolina; m.; three s.; ed Duke Univ.; joined Procter & Gamble Co. (P&G) as a Production Man. 1980, worked in P&G's Product Supply org. for ten years managing production and operations at several plants, eventually managing P&G's manufacturing plant in Mehoopany, Pa, transferred to brand man. dept to work on Pampers early 1990s, Gen. Man. Greater China Hair Care 1998–2001, Vice-Pres., Western Europe Family Care 2001–03, Vice-Pres., North America Family Care 2003–05, Pres., Global Family Care 2005–07, Group Pres., Global Home Care 2007–13, Group Pres., Global Health and Grooming 2013–15, Group Pres., Global Beauty, Grooming and Health Care Feb.–Oct. 2015, Pres. and CEO Procter & Gamble Co. 2015–, Chair. 2016–; fmr Vice-Chair. Greater China Quality Brand Protection Cttee; mem. Bd of Dirs Feeding America (Chair. for two years), TRW 2010–15; mem. Bd, Cincinnati Freestore Foodbank, US–China Business Council, Business Roundtable, Bd of Visitors of Duke Univ.'s Fuqua School of Business. *Address:* The Proctor & Gamble Co., 1 Procter & Gamble Plaza, Cincinnati, OH 43202-3315, USA (office). *Telephone:* (513) 983-1100 (office). *Fax:* (513) 983-9369 (office). *E-mail:* info@pg.com (office). *Website:* www.pg.com (office).

TAYLOR, Duncan John Rushworth, CBE; British diplomatist; b. 17 Oct. 1958, New Malden, Surrey; s. of Sir Jock Taylor and Molly Rushworth; m. Marie-Beatrice (Bebe) Taylor 1981; two s. three step-d.; ed in French lycées, Highgate School, London, Trinity Coll., Cambridge; joined FCO 1982, Asst Desk Officer, West African Dept 1982–83, Head of Japan Section, Far Eastern Dept 1987–89, Personnel Operations Dept 1989–90, Head of Personnel Man. Review Implementation Task Force 1990–91, Head of Consular Div. 1997–2000; Third, later Second Sec., Chancery, British Embassy, Havana, Cuba 1983–87; Head of Commercial Section, British Embassy, Budapest, Hungary 1992–96; Dir Latin American Affairs (on loan to Rolls Royce) 1996–97; Deputy Consul-Gen., Press and Public Affairs and Deputy Head of Mission, British Consulate Gen., New York, USA 2000–05; High Commr to Barbados (also accred to Antigua and Barbuda, Dominica, Grenada, Saint Kitts and Nevis, Saint Lucia, and Saint Vincent and the Grenadines) 2005–09; Gov., Cayman Islands 2010–13; Amb. to Mexico 2013–18. *Leisure interests:* spending time with his family, travel, theatre and film, sports (especially cricket).

TAYLOR, Grace Oladunni L., PhD; Nigerian biochemist and academic; ed Univ. of London, UK and Univ. of Ibadan; Prof. of Chemical Pathology, Univ. of Ibadan (retd); has taught medicine in Nigeria and other African countries; mem. Third World Org. for Women in Science; L'Oréal-UNESCO For Women in Science Award 1998. *Publications:* numerous articles in scientific journals on lipid metabolism.

TAYLOR, John Brian, AB, DEcon; American economist and government official; *Mary and Robert Raymond Professor of Economics, Stanford University;* b. 8 Dec. 1946, Yonkers, NY; m. Allyn Taylor; two c.; ed Shady Side Acad., Princeton Univ., Stanford Univ.; taught at Columbia Univ. 1973–80, Woodrow Wilson School and Econs Dept, Princeton Univ. 1980–84; Mary and Robert Raymond Prof. of Econs, Stanford Univ., also George P. Shultz Sr Fellow in Econs, Hoover Inst., fmr Dir Stanford Inst. for Econ. Policy Research, fmr Dir Introductory Econs Center, fmr Chair. Stanford Cttee on Undergraduate Studies; Sr Staff Economist and mem. Presidential Council of Econ. Advisers under Pres Gerald Ford and George Bush, Sr; Under-Sec. of Treasury for Int. Affairs 2001–05; apptd mem. California Council of Econ. Advisers under Gov. Arnold Schwarzenegger 2005; Fellow, American Acad. of Arts and Sciences; Medal of Repub. of Uruguay 2005; Hoagland Prize 1992, Lilian and Thomas B. Rhodes Prize 1997, Alexander Hamilton Award 2005, George Shultz Award 2005, Adam Smith Award 2007. *Publications include:* The Untold Story of International Finance in the Post-9/11 World 2008, Ending Government Bailouts as We Know Them (co-ed.) 2010, The Road Ahead for the Fed (co-ed.) 2009, Getting Off Track – How Government Actions and Interventions Caused, Prolonged, and Worsened the Financial Crisis 2009, First Principles: Five Keys to Restoring America's Prosperity 2012, Bankruptcy Not Bailout: A Special Chapter 14 (co-ed.) 2012, Government Policies and the Delayed Economic Recovery (co-ed.) 2012, Principles of Economics, Macroeconomics, and Microeconomics: Seventh Edition 2012; numerous articles in professional journals. *Address:* Herbert Hoover Memorial Building, Stanford University, Stanford, CA 94305-6010, USA (office). *Telephone:* (650) 723-9677 (office). *Fax:* (650) 723-1687 (office). *E-mail:* johnbtaylor@stanford.edu (office). *Website:* web.stanford.edu/~johntayl (office); economicsone.com; www.johnbtaylor.com.

TAYLOR, John Bryan, PhD, FRS; British physicist and academic; *Consultant, Culham Centre for Fusion Energy;* b. 26 Dec. 1928, Birmingham, England; s. of Frank H. Taylor and Ada Taylor; m. Joan M. Hargest 1951; one s. one d.; ed Oldbury Co. High School and Univ. of Birmingham; served in RAF 1950–52; physicist, Atomic Weapons Research Establishment, Aldermaston 1955–59, 1961–62; Harkness Fellow, Univ. of California 1959–60; on staff of UKAEA, Culham Lab. 1962–89, Head of Theory Div. 1963–81, Chief Physicist, Culham Lab. 1981–89, Consultant 1994–; Fondren Foundation Prof. of Plasma Theory, Univ. of Texas at Austin 1989–94; Consultant, Culham Centre for Fusion Energy 1994–; mem. Inst. for Advanced Study, Princeton, NJ, USA 1969, 1980, 1981; Fellow, American Physical Soc.; Maxwell Medal, Inst. of Physics 1971, Max Born Prize and Medal, German Physical Soc. 1979, Award for Excellence in Plasma Research, American Physical Soc. 1986, James Clerk Maxwell Prize, American Physical Soc. 1999, Hannes Alfvén Prize, European Physical Soc. 2004. *Publications:* contribs to scientific learned journals. *Leisure interests:* gliding, model engineering. *Address:* Culham Centre for Fusion Energy, Culham Science Centre, Abingdon, Oxon., OX14 3DB (office); 2 The Paddock, The Street, Bishops Cannings, Devizes, Wilts., SN10 2LD, England (home). *Telephone:* (1235) 528822 (office). *E-mail:* bryan.taylor@ccfe.ac.uk (office). *Website:* www.ccfe.ac.uk (office).

TAYLOR, John Russell, (Charles Graham, William Hall, Brian Brooke), MA; British writer, broadcaster, editor and academic; b. 19 June 1935, Dover, Kent, England; s. of Arthur Russell Taylor and Kathleen Mary Taylor (née Picker); civil partner Ying Yeung Li; ed Dover Grammar School, Jesus Coll. Cambridge, Courtauld Inst. of Art; Sub-Ed., Times Educ. Supplement 1959–60; Editorial Asst, Times Literary Supplement 1960–62; Film Critic, The Times 1962–73; Dir of Film Studies, Tufts Univ. in London 1970–72; Prof., Div. of Cinema, Univ. of Southern Calif., USA 1972–78; Art Critic, The Times 1978–2005; Ed. Films and Filming 1983–90; Art Critic, Radio Two Arts Programme 1990–2000; Friend of the Festival Award, Chicago Int. Film Festival 2010. *Film:* Charles Chaplin Makes The Countess from Hong Kong 1966. *Television:* Feet Foremost 1968, The Imposter 1969, Dracula 1969, Curse of the Mummy 1970, A Letter to David 1971, A Quiet Place in the Country 1971. *Publications include:* Joseph L. Mankiewicz 1960, Anger and After 1962 (USA: The Angry Theatre 1969), Anatomy of a Television Play 1962, Cinema Eye, Cinema Ear 1964, Penguin Dictionary of the Theatre 1966, The Art Nouveau Book in Britain 1966, Art in London 1966, The Rise and Fall of the Well-Made Play 1967, The Art Dealers 1969, Harold Pinter 1969, The Hollywood Musical 1971, The Second Wave 1971, Peter Shaffer 1974, David Storey 1974, Directors and Directions 1975, The Revels History of Drama in English Vol. VII 1978, Hitch 1978, Impressionism 1981, Strangers in Paradise 1983, Ingrid Bergman 1983, Alec Guinness 1984, 2000, Vivien Leigh 1984, Hollywood 1940s 1985, Portraits of the British Cinema 1986, Orson Welles 1986, Edward Wolfe 1986, Great Movie Moments 1987, Post-War Friends 1987, Robin Tanner 1989, Bernard Meninsky 1990, John Copley 1990, Impressionist Dreams 1990, Liz Taylor 1991, Muriel Pemberton 1993, Ricardo Cinalli 1993, Igor Mitoraj 1993, Claude Monet 1995, Bill Jacklin 1997, The World of Michael Parkes 1998, Antonio Saliola 1998, The Sun is God 1999, Michael Parkes: The Stone Lithographs 2000, Peter Coker 2002, Roberto Barnardi 2002, Roboz: The Painter's Paradox 2005, One Hand, Two Fingers 2005, Philip Sutton Woodcuts 2006, The Art of Michael Parkes 2006, Adrian George 2006, The Michael Winner Collection of Donald McGill 2006, Carl Laubin 2007, The Art of Jeremy Ramsey 2007, Randy Klein: Road 2008, The Glamour of the Gods 2008, Philip Sutton 2008, Exactitude 2009, Roboz: Face to Face 2011, High Relief 2016, Robert Barnes, Man of Mysteries 2016; edited: Let the Children Write 1961, Three Plays by John Arden 1964, New English Dramatists 8 1965, Look Back in Anger: A Casebook 1968, The Pleasure Dome (USA: Graham Greene on Film) 1972, Masterworks of British Cinema 1974, The Wizard of Oz 50th Anniversary Edn 1989. *Leisure interest:* buying books, talking to strange dogs.

TAYLOR, Joseph Hooton, Jr, PhD; American radio astronomer, physicist and academic; *Emeritus James McDonnell Distinguished Professor of Physics, Princeton University;* b. 29 March 1941, Philadelphia, Pa; s. of Joseph Taylor and Sylvia Evans; m. Marietta Bisson 1976; one s. two d.; ed Haverford Coll. and Harvard Univ.; Research Fellow and Lecturer, Harvard Univ. 1968–69; Asst Prof. of Astronomy, Univ. of Mass., Amherst 1969–72, Assoc. Prof. 1973–77, Prof. 1977–81; Prof. of Physics, Princeton Univ. 1980–2006, James McDonnell Distinguished Prof. of Physics 1986–2006, Prof. Emer. 2006–, Dean of Faculty 1997–2003; Fellow, American Acad. of Arts and Sciences; mem. NAS, American Astronomy Soc., Int. Scientific Radio Union, Int. Astronomy Union; Hon. DSc (Chicago) 1985, (Mass) 1994; Wolf Prize in Physics 1992, shared Nobel Prize for Physics 1993 and other awards and distinctions. *Publication:* Pulsars 1977. *Address:* Department of Physics, Princeton University, 215 Jadwin Hall, PO Box 708, Princeton, NJ 08544 (office); 272 Hartley Avenue, Princeton, NJ 08540, USA (home). *E-mail:* jtaylor@princeton.edu (office).

TAYLOR, Lance Jerome, BS, PhD; American economist and academic; *Professor Emeritus of Economics, New School for Social Research, New School University;* b. 25 May 1940, Montpelier, Ida; s. of W. Jerome Taylor and Ruth R. Taylor; m. Yvonne S. M. Taylor 1963; one s. one d.; ed California Inst. of Tech., Harvard Univ.; Asst Prof., then Assoc. Prof., Harvard Univ. 1968–74; Prof., MIT 1974–93; Arnhold Prof. of Int. Co-operation and Devt, New School for Social Research (now New School Univ.), New York 1993–2014, Prof. Emer. 2014–, Dir Center for Econ. Policy Analysis –2008, now Faculty Research Fellow; Visiting Prof., Univ. of Brasília 1973–74, Delhi School of Econs 1987–88, Stockholm School of Econs 1990; consultant for UN agencies and numerous govts govts and agencies; Marshall Lecturer, Univ. of Cambridge 1987; V. K. Ramaswamy Lecturer, Delhi School of Econs 1988. *Publications include:* Structuralist Macroeconomics 1983, Varieties of Stabilization Experience 1988, Income Distribution, Inflation and Growth 1991, The Market Meets its Match: Restructuring the Economies of Eastern Europe 1994, Global Finance at Risk 2000, Reconstructing Macroeconomics 2004, Growth and Policy in Developing Countries: A Structuralist Approach (co-author) 2009, Maynard's Revenge: The Collapse of Free Market Macroeconomics 2010. *Leisure interest:* raising cashmere goats. *Address:* 15 Old County Road, PO Box 378, Washington, ME 04574, USA (home). *Telephone:* (207) 845-2722 (home). *Fax:* (207) 845-2589 (home). *E-mail:* lance@blacklocust.com (home).

TAYLOR, Martin; British banker and business executive; b. 8 June 1952; m. Janet Davey 1976; two d.; ed Eton Coll. and Balliol Coll., Oxford; joined Reuters news agency as journalist in Paris; subsequently ed. Lex comment column, Financial Times, London; Personal Asst to Chair. of Courtaulds, later Dir Courtaulds Clothing Div., CEO Courtaulds PLC 1990–93, Chair. 1993; CEO Barclays Bank PLC 1994–98; mem. Bd of Dirs (non-exec.) WH Smith Group PLC 1993–98, Chair. 1999–2003; adviser to Goldman Sachs Int. 1999–2005; fmr y Chair. Syngenta AG, Basel, Switzerland, also Chair. Syngenta Foundation for Sustainable Agric.; currently Vice-Chair. RTL Group SA; mem. UK Ind. Banking Comm.; fmr mem. UK Council for Science and Tech.; fmr Chair. UK Inst. of Public Policy Research Comm. on public/private partnerships. *Address:* RTL Group, 45 Board Pierre Frieden, 1543 Luxembourg, Luxembourg (office). *Website:* www.rtlgroup.com (office).

TAYLOR, Martin, MBE; British jazz musician (guitar), composer and teacher; b. 20 Oct. 1956, Harlow, Essex; s. of William 'Buck' Taylor; ed Passmore Comprehensive School, Harlow; began playing aged four, playing in local bands aged 12, professional musician 1972–; support act for Count Basie and his Orchestra, QE2; performed and recorded regularly with violinist Stéphane Grappelli 1979–90; formed Martin Taylor's Spirit of Django 1994–; played and recorded with Bill Wyman's Rhythm Kings 1998, 1999; featured on Prefab Sprout album Andromeda Heights; recordings (with Steve Howe) of guitars from Chinery Collection; Freeman of the City of London 1998; Dr hc (Paisley) 1999, (Univ. of the West of Scotland) 1999, (Royal Scottish Acad. of Music and Drama) 2010; Music Retailers

Asscn Award for Excellence 1985, British Jazz Award for Best Guitarist 1987, 1988, 1989, 1990, 1991, 1993, 1995, 1997, 1999, 2001, British Acad. of Composers & Songwriters Gold Badge of Merit 1999, Pioneer to the Life of the Nation 2003, BBC Radio 2 Jazz Award 2007, British Jazz Award 2007, Scottish Jazz Award 2012, Lifetime Achievement Award, Ards Int. Guitar Festival 2012. *Recordings include:* albums: Taylor Made 1978, Skye Boat 1981, Sarabanda (with John Patitucci and Paulinho Da Costa) 1987, Don't Fret 1990, Change Of Heart 1991, Artistry 1993, Reunion (with Stéphane Grappelli) 1993, Spirit of Django (British Jazz Awards for Best Album 1995) 1994, Portraits 1995, Years Apart 1996, Gypsy 1998, Two's Company 1999, I'm Beginning To See The Light 1999, Kiss & Tell 1999, In Concert (live) 2000, Stepping Stones 2000, Nitelife 2001, Solo (Int. Guitar Foundation Award for Best Album) 2002, Valley 2005, Gypsy Journey 2005, Freternity 2007, Double Standards 2008, Last Train to Hauteville 2010, Two for the Road 2011, One for the Road 2012, First Time Together! 2012, The Colonel and the Governor 2013, One Day 2015. *Film soundtracks include:* (with Stéphane Grappelli) Milou en Mai, Dirty Rotten Scoundrels. *Publication includes:* Martin Taylor: Autobiography of a Travelling Musician, The Martin Taylor Guitar Method. *Leisure interests:* cooking, walking, painting, cartoons, caricatures. *Address:* P3 Music Ltd (office). *E-mail:* martin@martintaylor.com; management@p3music.com (office). *Website:* www.martintaylor.com.

TAYLOR, (John) Maxwell (Percy); British insurance industry executive; *Chairman, Mitsui-Sumitomo Insurance London Companies;* b. 17 March 1948; s. of Harold Guy Percy Taylor and Anne Katherine Taylor (née Stafford); m. Dawn Susan Harling 1970; one s. one d.; joined Willis Faber & Dumas as jr aviation broker 1970; Dir Willis Faber, then Willis Corroon Group PLC, Chair. and Chief Exec. Willis, Faber & Dumas, Group Exec. Dir 1997; elected to Council of Lloyd's 1997, Chair. of Lloyd's 1998–2000; mem. Aon Corpn Group Exec. Cttee and Deputy Chair. UK Operations 2001–09 (retd), now Adviser; Chair. Mitsui-Sumitomo Insurance London Cos 2009–; mem. Bd of Dirs, Qatarlyst (fmrly Qatar Insurance Services), ANV Syndicates Ltd 2011–; Dir Financial Services Compensation Scheme 2007–13; Chair. British Insurance Brokers Asscn; Chair. Council of Univ. of Surrey; fmr Chair. Lloyd's Insurance Brokers' Cttee, London Insurance Market Network, Vice-Pres. Insurance Inst. of London. *Leisure interests:* music, skiing, golf, travelling. *Address:* Mitsui Sumitomo Insurance Group, 25 Fenchurch Avenue, London, EC3M 5AD, England (office). *Telephone:* (20) 7977-8321 (office). *Fax:* (20) 7977-8300 (office). *E-mail:* enquiries@msilm.com (office). *Website:* www.msilm.com (office).

TAYLOR, Dame Meg, DBE, LLB; Papua New Guinea lawyer, international organization official and fmr diplomatist; *Secretary-General, Pacific Islands Forum Secretariat;* b. 1951; d. of Jim Taylor and Yerima Taylor; ed Univ. of Melbourne, Australia, Harvard Univ., USA; fmr athlete (competed for Papua New Guinea in pentathlon at S Pacific Games 1971); began career as Private Sec. to Chief Minister (later Prime Minister) Michael Somare 1973–75; fmr lawyer, Office of the Public Solicitor, Port Moresby; Amb. to USA, Mexico and Canada 1989–94; Vice-Pres. and Compliance Adviser Ombudsman, Int. Finance Corpn and Multilateral Investment Guarantee Agency, World Bank Group 1999–2014; Sec.-Gen., Pacific Islands Forum Secr. (first woman) 2014–; co-f. Conservation Melanesia; fmr Dir Australian Securities Exchange; mem. Law Reform Comm. *Film:* My Father, My Country 1989. *Address:* The Secretary General, Pacific Islands Forum Secretariat, Private Mail Bag, Suva, Fiji (office). *Telephone:* (679) 331-2600 (office). *E-mail:* info@forumsec.org (office). *Website:* www.forumsec.org (office).

TAYLOR, Rev. Michael Hugh, OBE, BD, MA, DLitt, STM; British minister of religion, charity administrator and academic; *Professor Emeritus of Social Theology, University of Birmingham;* b. 8 Sept. 1936, Northampton, Northants., England; s. of Albert Taylor and Gwendolen Taylor; m. Adele May Dixon 1960; two s. one d.; ed Northampton Grammar School, Univ. of Manchester, Union Theological Seminary, New York; Baptist Minister, North Shields, Northumberland and Hall Green, Birmingham 1960–69; Prin. Northern Baptist Coll., Manchester 1970–85; Lecturer in Theology and Ethics, Univ. of Manchester 1970–85; Examining Chaplain to Bishop of Manchester 1975–85; Dir Christian Aid 1985–97; Pres. Selly Oak Colls, Birmingham 1998–99; Prof. of Social Theology, Univ. of Birmingham 1999–2004, Prof. Emer. 2004–; Dir World Faiths Devt Dialogue 2002–04; Chair. Audenshaw Foundation Trustees 1979–93; mem. Comm. on Theological Educ., WCC 1972–91, Vice-Moderator 1985–91; mem. Council, Overseas Devt Inst. 1986–2000; mem. Comm. IV: Sharing and Service WCC; Chair. Asscn of Protestant Devt Agencies in Europe 1991–94; Pres. Jubilee 2000 UK Coalition 1997–2001; Chair. Burma Campaign –2000, Health Unlimited 2002, Worcester Diocesan Bd for Social Responsibility 2009–15; Commr High Pay Comm. 2010–12; Chair. of Govs Fircroft Coll., Birmingham 2006–; Trustee, Mines Advisory Group 1998 (Chair. 2000–14), Responding to Conflict 2005–09 (Chair. 2007–09); Trustee and Vice-Chair. St Philip's Centre, Leicester 2002–19; Trustee, Mint House Oxford 2017–, Refugee Resource 2017–; Trustee and Chair., Getting Heard 2018–; Trustee and Chair., Oxford Mencap 2018–; Patron, Jubilee Debt Campaign 2001–, Student Christian Movt 2005–18; broadcast talks on radio; Hon. mem. of Foundation, Worcester Cathedral 2002–07; Fulbright Travel Award 1969. *Publications:* Variations on a Theme 1971, Learning to Care 1983, Good for the Poor 1990, Christianity and the Persistence of Poverty 1991, Not Angels but Agencies 1995, Jesus and the International Financial Institutions 1996, Past their Sell-By Date? The Role of Northern NGOs in the Future of Development 1998, Poverty and Christianity 2000, Christianity, Poverty and Wealth in the 21st Century 2003, Eat Drink and Be Merry for Tomorrow We Live 2005, Border Crossings 2006, Sorting Out Believing 2011, Christ and Capital 2015. *Leisure interests:* walking, theatre, music, cinema, cooking. *Address:* 4 Harpes Road, Oxford, OX2 7QL, England (office). *Telephone:* (1865) 511089 (home). *E-mail:* mhandamtaylor@btinternet.com (office).

TAYLOR, Philip (Phil); British professional darts player (retd); b. 13 Aug. 1960, Stoke-on-Trent; s. of Douglas Taylor and Elizabeth Taylor; m. to Yvonne Taylor; one s. three d.; ed Milfield Middle School, Stanfield Tech. High School; fmr sheet metal worker; numerous tournament victories including: Embassy World Championship 1990, 1992, World Master 1990, European Cup Singles Championship 1992, PDC World Championship 1995, 1996, 1997, 1998, 1999, 2000, 2001, 2002, 2004, 2005, 2006, PDC World Matchplay 1995, 1997, 2000, 2001, 2002, News of the World Championship 1997, PDC World Grand Prix 1998, 1999, 2000, 2002, 2003, Quebec Open 2001, North American Cup 2001, 2002, 2003, JP Sports Pro Singles 2002, Montréal Open 2002, Las Vegas Desert Classic 2002, UK Open 2003, Bobby Bourn Memorial Trophy 2003, Stan James World Matchplay 2003; first unranked player to win a major tournament (Canadian Open 1990); unbeaten for nearly two years in televised matches 1999–2001; nine-dart finish at Stan James World Matchplay 2002 (1st since 1990 in televised match); retired 2018. *Publications:* (with Sid Waddell) The Power: My Autobiography 2003. *E-mail:* philtaylor@premiumtv.co.uk. *Website:* www.philthepower.com.

TAYLOR, Richard Lawrence, BA, PhD, FRS; British/American mathematician and academic; *Robert and Luisa Fernholz Professor, Institute for Advanced Study, Princeton;* b. 19 May 1962; s. of John C. Taylor (physicist); m. Christine Taylor; one s. one d.; ed Clare Coll., Cambridge, Princeton Univ., USA; fmr research student of Andrew Wiles, returned to Princeton Univ. to help Wiles complete proof of Fermat's last theorem 1995; Savilian Chair of Geometry, Univ. of Oxford and Fellow, New Coll. Oxford 1995–96; Prof. of Math., then Herchel Smith Prof. of Math., Harvard Univ., USA 1996–2012; Distinguished Visiting Prof., Inst. for Advanced Study, Princeton, NJ, Princeton, Robert and Luisa Fernholz Prof. 2012–; Ed. Duke Mathematical Journal 2000–, Forum of Mathematics 2012–, Annals of Mathematics 2013–; mem. American Acad. of Arts and Sciences 2012; Fellow, American Math. Soc. 2013; Whitehead Prize 1990, Fermat Prize 2001, Ostrowski Prize 2001, Cole Prize, American Math. Soc. 2002, Shaw Prize in Math. Sciences (with Robert Langlands) 2007, Clay Research Award, Clay Math. Inst. (co-recipient) 2007, Invited Plenary Speaker, Amsterdam ECM 2008, Chern Lecturer, Univ. of California, Berkeley 2009, Milliman Lecturer, Univ. of Washington, Seattle 2011, UCLA Distinguished Lecture Series 2013, Breakthrough Prize in Math. (co-recipient) 2015. *Publications:* numerous math. papers in professional journals. *Address:* Institute for Advanced Study, Einstein Drive, Princeton, NJ 08540, USA (office). *Telephone:* (609) 734-8189 (office). *E-mail:* rtaylor@math.ias.edu (office). *Website:* www.ias.edu/people/faculty-and-emeriti/taylor (office).

TAYLOR, Stuart Ross, AC, MA, PhD, DSc, FAA; New Zealand geochemist and academic; b. 26 Nov. 1925, Ashburton; s. of T. S. Taylor; m. Noel White 1958; three d.; ed Ashburton High School, Canterbury Univ. Coll., Univ. of New Zealand, Indiana Univ., USA; Lecturer in Mineralogy, Univ. of Oxford, UK 1954–58; Sr Lecturer in Geochemistry, Univ. of Cape Town 1958–60; Professorial Fellow, Research School of Earth Science, ANU 1961–90, Visiting Fellow, Research School of Physical Sciences 1991, 1993–99, mem. Council, ANU 1971–76; mem. Lunar Sample Preliminary Examination Team, Houston, Tex. 1969–70, Prin. Investigator, Lunar Sample Analysis Program 1970–90; Visiting Prof., Univ. of Vienna 1992, 1996; Foreign Assoc. NAS; Fellow, Geochemical Soc., American Geophysical Union; Hon. Fellow, UK and Indian Geological Socs, Royal Soc. of New Zealand; Hon. AC 2008; Norman L. Bowen Award, American Geophysical Union 1988, Goldschmidt Medal, Geochemical Soc. 1993, Gilbert Award, Geological Soc. of America 1994, Leonard Medal, Meteoritical Soc. 1998, Bucher Medal, American Geophysical Union 2002, Shoemaker Distinguished Lunar Scientist Award 2012. *Achievements include:* Asteroid 5670 named Ross Taylor. *Publications include:* Spectrochemical Analysis (jtly) 1961, Moon Rocks and Minerals (jtly) 1971, Lunar Science: A Post-Apollo View 1975, Planetary Science: A Lunar Perspective 1982, The Continental Crust: Its Composition and Evolution (jtly) 1985, Solar System Evolution: A New Perspective 1992, Destiny or Chance: Our Solar System and Its Place in the Cosmos 1998, Planetary Crusts (with Scott McLennan) 2009; some 240 papers in scientific journals. *Leisure interests:* reading history, gardening, classical music. *Address:* 18 Sheehan Street, Pearce, ACT 2607, Australia.

TAYLOR, Wendy Ann, CBE, FZS, FRBS, FRSA; British sculptor; b. 29 July 1945, Stamford, Lincs., England; d. of Edward P. Taylor and Lilian M. Wright; m. Bruce Robertson 1982; one s.; ed St Martin's School of Art; mem. Fine Art Bd Council of Acad. Awards 1980–85, Specialist Adviser 1985–93; Specialist Adviser, Cttee for Art and Design 1988–93; mem. Cttee for Art and Design, Council of Nat. Acad. Awards; mem. Royal Fine Art Comm. 1981–99; mem. Council, Morley Coll. 1984–89; mem. Court RCA; design consultant, New Towns Comm. (Basildon) 1985–88; design consultant, London Borough of Barking and Dagenham 1989–93, 1997–2003; Advisory Bd, London Docklands Devt Corpn 1989–98; mem. Advisory Group of the Polytechnics and Colls Funding Council 1989–90; mem. Council, Royal Soc. of British Sculptors 1999–2000; Fellow, Queen Mary and Westfield Coll. (London Univ.); Trustee, Leicestershire's Appeal for Music and the Arts 1993–2010; mem. Design Panel, Thames Gateway Area 2005–07; Walter Neurath Award 1964, Pratt Award 1965, Sainsbury Award 1966, Arts Council Award 1977, Duais Na Ríochta Gold Medal, Eire 1977, Arts Council Award 1991, Civic Trust Partnership Award 2002, Building of the Year Award, Architectural Sculpture 2004. *Television:* South Bank Show (LWT) 1988. *Leisure interest:* gardening. *Address:* 73 Bow Road, London, E3 2AN, England (home). *Telephone:* (20) 8981-2037 (home). *E-mail:* wendytaylorsculptor@gmail.com (office); info.wendytaylor@gmail.com (home). *Website:* wendytaylorsculpture.co.uk (office).

TAYLOR, Sir William, Kt, CBE, BSc (Econ), PhD; British academic; *Visiting Professor, University of Winchester;* b. 31 May 1930, Crayford, Kent; s. of Herbert Taylor and Maud Taylor; m. Rita Hague 1954; one s. two d.; ed London School of Econs, Univ. of London Inst. of Educ.; fmr school teacher and deputy head teacher, Kent; later worked in two colls of educ. and Dept of Educ., Univ. of Oxford; Prof. of Educ., Univ. of Bristol 1966; Dir London Inst. of Educ. 1973–83; Prin. Univ. of London 1983–85, Chair. of Convocation 1994–97; Vice-Chancellor Univ. of Hull 1985–91; Vice-Chancellor Univ. of Huddersfield 1994–95, Thames Valley Univ. 1998–99; Visiting Prof., Univ. of Oxford 1991–97, Univ. of Southampton 1998–2010, Univ. of Winchester 2010–; Gov. Univ. of Glamorgan 1992–2002, Christ Church, Univ. Coll., Canterbury 1996–2004; Interim Head, Winchester School of Art, Univ. of Southampton 2004; Chair. Council for Accreditation of Teacher Educ. 1984–93; Chair. Bd NFER/Nelson publishing co. 1988–99; Pres. Soc. for Research in Higher Educ. 1996–2001; Specialist Adviser, House of Commons Educ. and Skills Cttee 2000–07; Chair. NI Cttee for Teacher Educ. 1994–2003; mem. Council, Hong Kong Inst. of Educ. 1998–2003; Charter Fellow, Coll. of Preceptors; Hon. Fellow, Westminster Coll. Oxford, Thames Polytechnic, Commonwealth Council for Educ. Admin., Inst. of Educ.; Dr hc (Aston, Bristol, Leeds, London, Kent, Loughborough, Open Univ., Huddersfield, Hull, Kingston, Plymouth, Oxford Brookes, Univ. of West of England, Ulster, Queen's Univ.

Belfast, Southampton, Leicester, Glamorgan, Essex, Hong Kong Inst. of Educ.). *Publications include:* The Secondary Modern School, Society and the Education of Teachers, Planning and Policy in Post-secondary Education, Heading for Change, Research and Reform in Teacher Education, The Metaphors of Education, Universities under Scrutiny. *Leisure interest:* books and music. *E-mail:* william.taylor@winchester.ac.uk (office). *Website:* www.winchester.ac.uk (office).

TAYLOR OF BOLTON, Baroness (Life Peer), cr. 2005, of Bolton in the County of Greater Manchester; **(Winifred) Ann Taylor,** PC; British politician; b. 2 July 1947, Motherwell, North Lanarkshire, Scotland; m. David Taylor 1966; one s. one d.; ed Bolton School and Univs of Bradford and Sheffield; fmr teacher and part-time tutor, Open Univ.; MP for Bolton West 1974–83, for Dewsbury 1987–2005; Parl. Pvt. Sec. to Sec. of State for Educ. and Science 1975–76, to Sec. of State for Defence 1976–77; an Asst Govt Whip 1977–79; Opposition Spokesman on Educ. 1979–81, on Housing 1981–83, on Home Affairs 1987–90, on Environment 1990–92, on Educ. 1992–94; Shadow Leader of House of Commons 1994–97; Pres. of the Council and Leader of the House of Commons 1997–98; Chief Whip 1998–2001; Chair. Select Cttee on Modernization 1997–98; Spokesperson on Citizen's Charter 1994–95; mem. Select Cttee on Standards and Privileges 1995–97; fmr Deputy Chair. Ind. Football Comm.; Vice-Chair. Forestry Group, House of Lords 2005–, Parl. Under-Sec. of State and Govt Spokesperson, Ministry of Defence 2007–; mem. Constitution Cttee, House of Lords 2014–, Leader's Group on Governance 2015–; mem. Bd of Dirs, Thales SA; mem. Labour Party; Hon. Fellow, Birkbeck Coll. London. *Address:* House of Lords, Westminster, London, SW1A 0PW, England (office). *Telephone:* (20) 7219-5353 (office). *Fax:* (20) 7219-5979 (office). *E-mail:* taylora@parliament.uk (office).

TAYLOR-JOHNSON, Sam, OBE; British artist, photographer and filmmaker; b. (Samantha Louise Taylor-Wood), 4 March 1967; m. 1st Jay Jopling (divorced 2008); two d.; m. 2nd Aaron Johnson 2012; one d.; ed Hastings Coll. of Art and Tech., Goldsmiths Coll.; uses highly choreographed photographic sequences; first solo exhbn, London 1994. *Works include:* Fuck, Suck, Spank, Wank 1993, Slut 1993, Killing Time (film) 1994, Method in Madness (film) 1994, Five Revolutionary Seconds XI 1997, Atlantic 1997, Five Revolutionary Seconds XIII 1998, Soliloquy I 1998, Soliloquy V 1998, Self Portrait in a Single Breasted Suit with Hare 2001, Hummmm 2001, Mute (film) 2001, Breach (film) 2001, Still Life (film) 2001, Self Portrait as a Tree, Strings (film) 2003, Ascension (film) 2003, David (video portrait) 2004, Crying Men 2004, Self Portrait Suspended 2004. *Films include:* Love You More (dir) 2008, Nowhere Boy (dir) 2009, Fifty Shades of Grey (dir) 2015, Gypsy (dir and exec. producer) 2017, A Million Little Pieces (dir) 2019. *Publications include:* Contact 2001, Crying Men 2004. *Address:* c/o Regen Projects, 633 North Almont Drive, Los Angeles, CA 90069, USA. *Telephone:* (310) 276-5424. *Fax:* (310) 276-7430. *Website:* samtaylorjohnson.com.

TAZAKI, Masamoto; Japanese engineer and business executive; *Advisor, Kawasaki Heavy Industries Ltd;* b. 1935, Manchuria; ed Kyushu Univ.; joined Kawasaki Aircraft Co. Ltd (now Kawasaki Heavy Industries Ltd) in 1958, has served in various exec. and man. positions including Exec. Man.-Dir and Sr Gen.-Man. Consumer Products and Machinery Group, Pres. Kawasaki Heavy Industries USA 1989–96, mem. Bd of Dirs Kawasaki Heavy Industries 1992–2009, Sr Vice-Pres. 1996–97, Sr Exec. Vice-Pres. 1997–2000, Pres. 2000–05, Chair. 2005–09, Advisor 2009–; Pres. Japan Ship Exporters Asscn 2009–. *Address:* Kawasaki Heavy Industries Ltd, Kobe Crystal Tower, 1-3 Higashikawasaki-cho 1-chome, Chuo-ku, Kobe 650-8680, Japan (office). *Telephone:* (7) 8371-9530 (office). *Fax:* (7) 8371-9568 (office). *Website:* www.khi.co.jp (office).

TCHAIKOVSKY, Aleksandr Vladimirovich; Russian composer and pianist; *Artistic Director, Moscow State Philharmonia;* b. 19 Feb. 1946, Moscow; m. 1st; one s. one d.; m. 3rd; one d.; ed Moscow State Conservatory; pianist and chamber musician 1967–; joined Faculty, Moscow P. I. Tchaikovsky Conservatory 1976, fmr Prof. and Composition Chair, Chair. of Composition Dept; Artistic Consultant, Mariinsky Theatre 1993–2002, Rector of St Petersburg State Conservatory 2004–08; Artistic Dir Moscow State Philharmonia 2003–; mem., Bd of Dirs Pervyi Kanal; winner, Hollybush Festival Prize (USA) 1987, People's Artist of Russia 1998. *Compositions include:* operas: Grandfather Is Laughing 1976, Three Sisters (after A. Chekhov) 1994; ballets: Inspector 1960, Battleship Potemkin 1988, Legend of the Ancient Town of Yelets, Tamerlane and the Virgin Mary and Violist Davydov; symphonies 1985, 1991 (Aquarius), two piano concertos, two viola concertos, Distant Dreams of Childhood for violin and viola 1990, Concerto-Buff for violin and marimba 1990, Triple Concerto for piano, violin and cello 1994, folk operas Tsar Nikita and Motya and Savely for two soloists and folk instruments, Quartet (after A. Pushkin) 1997–99; chamber music, incidental music to theatre and film productions. *Leisure interests:* collecting models of cars, table hockey. *Address:* Moscow State Philharmonia, 125047 Moscow, Triumfalnaya Place 4/31 (home); 125040 Moscow, Leningradsky prosp. 14, Apt. 4, Russia (home). *Telephone:* (495) 151-54-18 (home). *Website:* www.mariinsky.ru/en/company/orchestra/piano/alexander_tchaikovsky (office).

TCHEN, Christina (Tina) M., BA, JD; American lawyer and government official; b. 25 Jan. 1956, Columbus, Ohio; one s. one d.; ed Harvard Univ., Northwestern Univ. School of Law; Assoc., Skadden, Arps, Slate, Meagher & Flom LLP, Chicago 1984–92, Partner 1992–2009; Deputy Asst to Pres. and Dir Office of Public Engagement, The White House 2009–11, Asst to Pres. and Chief of Staff to First Lady Michelle Obama 2011–17, also Exec. Dir Council on Women and Girls; fmr Pres. Bd of Dirs Field Foundation of Illinois, Chicago Bar Foundation; fmr mem. Bd of Trustees Univ. of Chicago Medical Center, Chicago Public Library, Chinese American Service League; mem. Bd of Dirs Harvard Alumni Asscn; mem. ABA, Women's Bar Asscn of Illinois; Dr hc (Knox Coll.) 2010; Chicago Lawyer Person of the Year 1994, Women of Achievement Award, Anti-Defamation League 1996, Leadership Award, Women's Bar Asscn of Illinois 1999, Women's Professional Leadership Award, Harvard Coll. 2011, Dawn Clark Netsch Public Service Award, Northwestern Univ. School of Law 2014. *Publications include:* numerous articles in professional journals.

TCHIKAIDZE, Aleksandre; Georgian police chief and government official; b. 6 June 1985, Tbilisi; m.; two c.; ed Ivane Javakhishvili Tbilisi State Univ.; rank of Police Col; employed at various police units in Gidani-Nadzaladevi and Vake-Saburtalo Police Div. 2008–09, Asst to Detective Investigators, Gidani-Nadzaladevi Police Div. 2009, Detective Investigator, Gidani-Nadzaladevi Police Div. 2010–11, Head of Gidani-Nadzaladevi Police Div., Tbilisi Police Main Div. 2011–12, Chief of Kakheti Regional Main Div. 2012–13, Head of Tbilisi Police Main Div. May–Nov. 2013; Minister of Internal Affairs Nov. 2013–14.

TCHIMANGOA, Gen. Thomas Théophile; Central African Republic army officer and government official; served for many years in Central African Armed Forces (FACA), including as Commdr, Amphibious Bn, Head, Inst. Protection and Security Bn 2010, Project Man. and Head of Operational Command Centre 2013; Minister of Nat. Defence, in charge of Reorganization of Armed Forces, Fmr Combatants, War Victims, Disarmament, Demobilization and Reintegration Jan.–Aug. 2014. *Address:* c/o Ministry of National Defence, Bangui, Central African Republic (office).

TCHONGÓ DOMINGOS, Salvador; Guinea-Bissau politician; m.; two c.; ed Instituto Superior de Economia and Universidade Católica, Portugal; teacher of secondary education, Portugal 1981–92; Ffounding mem. Resistência da Guiné-Bissau—Movimento Bah-Fatah, Sec.-Gen. 1987–92, 1993–95, Vice-Pres. 1992–93, 1995–2002, Pres. 2002; Vice-Pres. Assembléia Nacional Popular 1994–99; unsuccessful presidential candidate 1999; Sec.-Gen. Presidência da República da Guiné-Bissau 2000–05.

TCHURUK, Serge; French engineer and business executive; *President and CEO, Joule Unlimited, Inc.;* b. 13 Nov. 1937, Marseille; s. of Georges Tchurukdichian and Mathilde Dondikian; m. Hélèna Kalfus 1960; one d.; ed Lycée Thiers à Marseille, Ecole nationale supérieure de l'armement, Ecole Polytechnique, Paris; various refining and research positions Mobil/Oil BV Rotterdam 1964–68, Dir French research centre 1968–70, Dir of Information, France 1971–73, attaché int. planning, New York and dir plans and programmes France 1973–77, Dir social and external relations 1977–79, Pres. and Dir-Gen. 1979–80; Dir-Gen. fertilizer div. Rhône-Poulenc Inc. 1981, Asst Dir-Gen. Rhône-Poulenc Group 1982, Dir-Gen. special chemicals 1983, Dir-Gen. Rhône-Poulenc Group 1983; Pres. Bd Dirs CdF Chimie 1986, Pres. Dir-Gen. 1987–90 (became Orkem 1988); mem. Bd Dirs Total 1989, 1995, Pres. 1990–95; Chair. and CEO Alcatel Alsthom (later Alcatel) 1995–2006, Chair. Alcatel-Lucent (after Alcatel acquisition of Lucent) 2006–08; Pres. and CEO Joule Unlimited, Inc., Bedford, Mass 2014–15; mem. Bd of Dirs Inst. Pasteur 2001–, Thales, Société Genérale, Vivendi; Officier, Légion d'honneur, Officier, Ordre nat. du Mérite; Manager of the Year Award, Le Nouvel Economiste 2000. *Leisure interests:* music, skiing, tennis.

TE KANAWA, Dame Kiri Jeanette Claire, CH, DBE, ONZ, AC; New Zealand singer (soprano); b. (Claire Mary Teresa Rawstron), 6 March 1944, Gisborne, North Island; adopted d. of Thomas Te Kanawa and Nell Te Kanawa; m. Desmond Park 1967 (divorced 1997); one s. one d.; ed St Mary's Coll., Auckland, London Opera Centre; first appearance at Royal Opera, Covent Garden, London 1970, Santa Fe Opera, USA 1971, Lyon Opera, France 1972, Metropolitan Opera, New York, USA 1974; appeared at Australian Opera, Royal Opera House Covent Garden, Paris Opera during 1976–77 season; appeared at Houston Opera, USA and Munich Opera 1977; debut La Scala, Milan 1978; Salzburg Festival 1979; San Francisco Opera Co. 1980; Edinburgh Festival, Helsinki Festival 1980; sang at wedding of HRH the Prince of Wales 1981; sang the premiere of Paul McCartney's Liverpool Oratorio, written by Carl Davis, at Liverpool Cathedral and in London 1991; voice of the theme of the Rugby World Cup, performing first recorded version of World in Union 1991; appeared in 2000 Today on 1 January 2000; returned to the Cologne Opera House for two final performances of the Marschallin in Rosenkavalier 2010; final opera performance before retirement was cameo role in La fille du régiment at Royal Opera House, London 2014; appeared in ITV's Downton Abbey playing Dame Nellie Melba, an Australian operatic soprano 2013; Founding Trustee and Chair. Kiri Te Kanawa Foundation 2004–; Hans Christian Andersen Amb. 2005–; Patron Ringmer Community Coll., BBC Cardiff Singer of the World 2013–; Hon. Fellow, Somerville Coll., Oxford 1983, Wolfson Coll., Cambridge 1997; Hon. Mem. RAM; Hon. LLD (Dundee) 1982; Hon. DMus (Durham) 1982, (Oxford) 1983, (Nottingham) 1992, (Waikato) 1995, (Cambridge) 1997; Hon. DLitt (Warwick) 1989, (Sunderland) 2003, (Auckland), (Chicago); Classical Brit Award for Lifetime Achievement 2010, Kiri Prize competition to find a gifted opera singer of the future est. in her honour 2010, Edison Classical Music Award 2012, World Class New Zealand Award 2012. *Operas include:* Boris Godunov, Parsifal, The Marriage of Figaro (Countess) Otello, Simon Boccanegra, Carmen, Don Giovanni, Faust, The Magic Flute, La Bohème, Eugene Onegin, Così fan tutte, Arabella, Die Fledermaus, La Traviata, Der Rosenkavalier, Manon Lescaut, Samson, Don Carlos, Capriccio, Vanessa. *Recordings include:* Don Giovanni (as Elvira), Così fan tutti (as Fiordiligi), Carmen (as Michela), Mozart Vespers, Mozart C Minor Mass, The Magic Flute (Pamina), Siegfried (Woodbird), The Marriage of Figaro, Hansel and Gretel, La Bohème, Capriccio, Otello, Die Fledermaus, French and German arias and songs, Maori songs 1999, Strauss songs with orchestra, Songs of the Auvergne, West Side Story, The Very Best of ... 2003, Kiri Sings Karl 2006, Waiata 2013. *Publications:* Land of the Long White Cloud (children's book) 1989, Opera for Lovers (with Conrad Wilson) 1997. *Leisure interests:* golf, swimming, cooking. *Address:* c/o Kiri Te Kanawa Foundation, PO Box 38387, Howick, Auckland 2045, New Zealand (office); c/o Kiri Te Kanawa Foundation (UK), 23B Prince of Wales Mansions, Prince of Wales Drive, London, SW11 4BQ, England (office). *Telephone:* (9) 5349398 (Auckland) (office); (20) 8332-9829 (London) (office). *Fax:* (9) 5340629 (Auckland) (office); (20) 8332-7049 (London) (office). *E-mail:* foundation@kiritekanawa.org (office); gillian.newson@btopenworld.com (office). *Website:* www.kiritekanawa.org (office).

TEA BANH, Gen. (retd); Cambodian politician; *Deputy Prime Minister and Minister of National Defence;* b. 5 Nov. 1945, Koh Kong Prov.; s. of Tea Toek and Nou Pheng Chenda; m. Tao Toeun 1955; three c.; platoon commdr, Koh Kong Prov. 1962–69, co. commdr 1969–70, Mil. Commdr and Dir Training 1973–79; Deputy Chief of Staff in charge of Telecommunications and Air Force 1979–80, Deputy Minister of Nat. Defence in charge of Telecommunications and Air Force 1980–82; Minister of Communications, Transport and Posts 1982–87; Vice-Chair. Council of Ministers 1984–88; mem. Parl. for Siem Reap Prov. 1988–; Minister of Nat. Defence 1987–88, 1993–94, 2006–, Deputy Minister 1988–93, Co-Minister 1994–2006; Deputy Prime Minister 2006–; Co-Deputy C-in-C Nat. Armed Forces 1994–95. *Leisure interest:* golf. *Address:* Ministry of National Defence, boulevard Confédération de la Russie, corner rue 175, Sangkat Toeuk Thla, Khan Sen Sok,

Phnom Penh, Cambodia (office). *Telephone:* (23) 883274 (office). *Fax:* (23) 883274 (office). *E-mail:* info@mond.gov.kh (office). *Website:* www.mond.gov.kh (office).

TEBBIT, Baron (Life Peer), cr. 1992, of Chingford in the London Borough of Waltham Forest; **Norman Beresford Tebbit,** PC, CH; British politician; b. 29 March 1931, Enfield, Middx, England; s. of Leonard Tebbit and Edith Tebbit; m. Margaret Elizabeth Daines 1956; two s. one d.; ed Edmonton Co. Grammar School; RAF Officer 1949–51; commercial pilot and holder of various posts, British Air Line Pilots' Asscn 1953–70; MP for Epping 1970–74, for Chingford 1974–92; Parl. Pvt. Sec. Dept of Employment 1972–73; Under-Sec. of State, Dept of Trade 1979–81; Minister of State, Dept of Industry Jan.–Sept. 1981; Sec. of State for Employment 1981–83, for Trade and Industry 1983–85; Chancellor of the Duchy of Lancaster 1985–87; Chair., Conservative Party 1985–87; mem. (Conservative), House of Lords 1992–; Dir, BET PLC 1987–96, British Telecom PLC 1987–96, Sears PLC 1987–99, Spectator Ltd; Co-Presenter, Target, Sky TV 1989–97; columnist, The Sun 1995–97, Mail on Sunday 1997–2001; blogger, Daily Telegraph 2010–. *Publications:* Upwardly Mobile 1988, Unfinished Business 1991, The Game Cook 2009, revised edn 2017, Ben's Story 2014. *Leisure interests:* peace and quiet, shooting, gardening. *Address:* House of Lords, Westminster, London, SW1A 0PW, England (office). *Telephone:* (20) 7219-3657 (office). *E-mail:* tebbitn@parliament.uk (office). *Website:* www.parliament.uk/biographies/lords/lord-tebbit/952 (office).

TEBBOUNE, Abdelmadjid; Algerian public servant and politician; b. 17 Nov. 1945, Mécheria; ed École nat. d'admin, Algiers; began career as trainee Administrator, Saoura Wilaya (admin. dist) 1969–72, Admin. 1972; Sec.-Gen. (Sub-Prefect), Djelfa Wilaya 1975–77, Adrar Wilaya 1977–79, Batna Wilaya 1979–82, M'Sila Wilaya 1982; Wali (Gov.), Adrar Wilaya 1983–84, Tiaret Wilaya 1984–89, Tizi-Ouzou Wilaya 1989–91; Minister-Del. for Local Govt 1991–92, 2000–01, Minister of Communication and Culture 1999–2000, Minister of Housing and Towns 2001–02, of Housing, Urban Planning and Towns 2012–17, also Acting Minister of Commerce Jan.–May 2017; Prime Minister May–Aug. 2017; mem. Nat. Liberation Front.

TÉCHINÉ, André Jean François; French author and filmmaker; b. 13 March 1943, Valence, Tarn-et-Garonne; René Clair Award for Lifetime Achievement 2003. *Films include:* Paulina s'en va 1969, Souvenirs d'en France 1975, Barocco 1976, Les Sœurs Brontë 1979, Hôtel des Amériques 1981, Rendez-vous 1985 (Prize for Best Director, Cannes Int. Film Festival 1985), Le Lieu du crime 1986, Les Innocents 1987, J'embrasse pas 1991, Ma Saison préférée 1993, Les Roseaux sauvages 1994 (Prix Louis-Delluc 1994, César for Best French Film, Best Dir and Best Original Screenplay or Adaptation 1995), Les Voleurs 1996, Alice et Martin 1998, Loin 2001, Les Égarés (Strayed) 2003, Les Temps qui changent 2004, Les Témoins 2007, The Girl on the Train 2009, Unforgivable 2011, In the Name of My Daughter 2014, Being 17 2016. *Television:* Hughie 1983.

TEFFT, John F., BA, MA; American diplomatist; b. 1949; m. Mariella Cellitti Tefft; two d.; ed Marquette Univ., Milwaukee and Georgetown Univ., Washington, DC; mem. Sr Foreign Service since 1973, rank of Minister-Counselor, overseas assignments in Jerusalem, Budapest and Rome, Counselor, Political-Mil. Affairs, Embassy in Rome 1986–89, Deputy Dir Office of USSR (later Russian and CIS) Affairs, Dept of State 1989–92, Dir Office of Northern European Affairs 1992–94, Chargé d'affaires a.i., Embassy in Moscow 1996–97, Deputy Chief of Mission, Moscow 1996–99, Amb. to Lithuania 2000–03, Int. Affairs Advisor, Nat. War Coll., Washington, DC 2003–04, Deputy Asst Sec. of State for European and Eurasian Affairs 2004, Amb. to Georgia 2004–09, to Ukraine 2009–13, to Russian Fed. 2014–17; Distinguished Honor Award 1992, Deputy Chief of Mission of the Year Award 1999, Presidential Meritorious Service Award 2001, 2005, Diplomacy in Human Rights Award 2012.

TEGELTIJA, Zoran, PhD; Bosnia and Herzegovina economist and politician; b. 29 Sept. 1961, Mrkonjić Grad; m.; two c.; ed Sarajevo Univ.; began career working in oil refinery, Bosanski Brod; worked with Tax and Customs Admin of Republika Srpska; Deputy, Nat. Ass. of Republika Srpska 2000–02; Mayor of Mrkonjic Grad 2004; fmr Chair. Bosnia and Herzegovina State Border Comm.; Sr Asst, Dept of Public Finance and Monetary Econs, Univ. of Business and Man. Eng, Banja Luka, later Asst Prof.; Minister of Finance of Republika Srpska 2010–18; mem. Alliance of Independent Social Democrats, head of party electoral team 2006. *Address:* c/o Ministry of Finance, 78000 Banja Luka, Trg Republike Srpske 1, Bosnia and Herzegovina (office).

TEGUEDI, Ahmed Ould; Mauritanian diplomatist and government official; b. 15 Sept. 1954, Chinguetti; m. Chekrada Mint Ahmed Ould Labeid; ed Acad. of Econ. Studies, Bucharest, Romania; joined Ministry of Foreign Affairs 1981, apptd Head, Western Europe, Eastern Europe, Americas and European Econ. Community, African-Caribbean-Pacific Divs 1981, Second Counsellor, Embassy in Washington, DC 1987–88, First Counsellor, Embassy in Cairo 1988–90, Chargé d'affaires a.i. 1990, First Counsellor and Chargé d'affaires a.i., Embassy in Sana 1991–93, in Rabat 1993–95, Head of Office responsible for Mauritanian interests in Tel-Aviv, Israel 1995–99, Amb. to Israel 1999–2009, Amb. and Perm. Rep. to UN, New York 2012–13; Minister of Foreign Affairs 2013–15. *Address:* c/o Ministry of Foreign Affairs and Co-operation, BP 230, Nouakchott, Mauritania.

TEH, Tan Sri Dato' Hong Piow, PhD; Malaysian banker; *Chairman, Public Bank Berhad;* b. 14 March 1930, Singapore; m. Puan Sri Tay Sock Noy 1956; four c.; ed Anglo-Chinese School, Singapore, Pacific Western Univ., Clayton Univ., Univ. of Malaya; began career as bank clerk in Overseas-Chinese Banking Corpn Ltd 1950, promoted to bank officer 1955–60; Man. Malayan Banking Berhad 1960–64, Gen. Man. 1964–66; est. Public Bank 1966, currently Chair. Public Bank Berhad; Fellow, Inst. of Chartered Secs and Administrators, Australia, Inst. of Bankers, Chartered Inst. of Bankers (UK), Inst. of Man. (UK), Malaysian Inst. of Man.; Hon. LLD (Univ. of Malaya) 1989; Brand Laureate Banker of the Year 2013, Asia Pacific Brands Foundation. *Address:* Public Bank Berhad, Menara Public Bank 146, Jalan Ampang, 50450 Kuala Lumpur, Malaysia (office). *Telephone:* (3) 2176-6000 (office). *Fax:* (3) 2161-9307 (office). *E-mail:* info@publicbank.com.my (office). *Website:* www.pbebank.com (office).

TEICH, Malvin Carl, PhD; American academic; *Professor Emeritus, Boston University;* b. 4 May 1939, New York; s. of Sidney R. Teich and Loretta K. Teich; ed Massachusetts Inst. of Tech., Stanford and Cornell Univs; Research Scientist, MIT Lincoln Lab., Lexington, Mass 1966–67; Prof. of Eng Science and Applied Physics, Columbia Univ., New York 1967–96, Prof. Emer. 1996–, Chair. Dept of Electrical Eng 1978–80, mem. Columbia Radiation Lab.; Prof. of Electrical and Computer Eng, Prof. of Biomedical Eng, Prof. of Physics, Boston Univ. 1995–2011, Prof. Emer. 2011–, mem. Photonics Center, Hearing Research Center, Center for Adaptive Systems, Program in Neuroscience; Deputy Ed. Journal of European Optical Society B: Quantum Optics 1988–92; mem. Bd of Editors Optics Letters 1977–79, Journal of Visual Communication and Image Representation 1989–92, Jemná Mechanika a Optika 1994–; Fellow, IEEE, AAAS, American Physical Soc., Optical Soc. of America, Acoustical Soc. of America, SPIE; IEEE Browder Thompson Memorial Prize 1969, John Simon Guggenheim Memorial Foundation Fellow 1973, Citation Classic Award, Inst. for Scientific Information 1981, Memorial Gold Medal, Palacký Univ. 1992, IEEE Morris E. Leeds Award 1997, Distinguished Scholar Award, Boston Univ. 2009. *Publications include:* Fundamentals of Photonics (with B. E. A. Saleh) 1991, 2007, Fractal-Based Point Processes (with S. B. lowen) 2005; 350 articles in tech. journals; six US patents. *Address:* Department of Electrical and Computer Engineering, Boston University, 8 Saint Mary's Street, Boston, MA 02215-2421, USA (office). *Telephone:* (617) 353-1236 (office). *Fax:* (617) 353-6440 (office). *E-mail:* teich@bu.edu. *Website:* people.bu.edu/teich (office); www.bu.edu/bme (office).

TEISSIER, Guy; French politician; b. 4 April 1945, Marseilles; ed Ecole de Notariat de Marseilles; mem. Parti Républicain (Union pour un Mouvement Populaire from 2002); Conseiller Général for Bouches de Rhône 1982–2004; elected mem. Conseil Municipal de Marseilles 1983, Mayor 9th and 10th arrondissements, Marseilles 1983–89, 1995–2014; elected Deputy to Nat. Ass. for Bouches-du-Rhône 1988 (invalidated by Conseil Constitutionel) re-elected 1993–; Sec. Nat. Ass. 1997–99, 2002; mem. Comm. of Cultural, Family and Social Affairs 1988; mem. Comm. of Nat. Defence 1993–2002, Sec. 1994–95, Pres. 2002–07. *Address:* Assemblée Nationale, 33, rue Saint-Dominique, 75007 Paris (office); Nouveau Parc Sevigne, 15 place Mignard, 13009 Marseilles, France (home). *Telephone:* 4-91-23-39-28 (home). *E-mail:* gteissier.communication@gmail.com; gteissier@assemblee-nat.fr (office). *Website:* www.guyteissier.com (office).

TEITELBAUM, Philip, PhD; American psychologist and academic; *Graduate Research Professor in Psychology, University of Florida;* b. 9 Oct. 1928, Brooklyn, New York; s. of Bernard Teitelbaum and Betty Schechter; m. 1st Anita Stawski 1955; m. 2nd Evelyn Satinoff 1963; m. 3rd Osnat Boné 1985; five s.; ed Johns Hopkins Univ.; Instructor and Asst Prof. in Psychology, Harvard Univ. 1954–59; Assoc., Full Prof., Univ. of Pa 1959–73; Prof., Univ. of Ill. 1973–85, Emer. Prof. 1985–; Fellow, Center for Advanced Studies, Univ. of Ill. 1979–85; Grad. Research Prof. in Psychology, Univ. of Fla 1984–; mem. NAS, AAAS, Soc. of Experimental Psychologists; Guggenheim Fellow; Fulbright Fellow; Distinguished Scientific Contribution Award, American Psychology Asscn. *Publications:* Fundamental Principles of Physiological Psychology 1967, Vol. on Motivation, Handbook of Behavioral Neurobiology (with Evelyn Satinoff) 1983. *Address:* Psychology Department, 337 PSY, University of Florida, Gainesville, FL 32611; 2239 NW 17th Avenue, Gainesville, FL 32605, USA (home). *Telephone:* (352) 273-2180 (office); (352) 372-5714 (home). *Fax:* (352) 392-7985 (office). *E-mail:* teitelb@ufl.edu (office); teitelb@hotmail.com (home). *Website:* www.psych.ufl.edu/~teitelb (office).

TEIXEIRA, Jose, LLB, BA; Timor-Leste lawyer and politician; ed Univ. of Queensland, Univ. of New England, Australia; left East Timor aged 11; Solicitor, Deacon and Milani Solicitors, Brisbane, Australia 1990–2000; Civil Affairs Officer/Dir, Econ. Affairs, UN, Timor–Leste 2000–02; Sec. of State for Tourism, Environment and Investment 2002–05; Minister for Natural Resources, Minerals and Energy Policy 2006–07; mem. Nat. Parl. 2007–12; mem. Nat. Exec., Frente Revolucionária do Timor Leste Independente (Fretilin) 2011–; Lawyer, Da Silva Teixeira & Associados 2013–; mem. Petroleum Fund Consultative Council 2014–; Commr, Jt Comm., JPDA Timor Sea 2003–06, Minister, Ministerial Council, JPDA Timor Sea Treaty 2006–07. *Address:* Da Silva Teixeira & Associados, Da Silva & Teixeira Building, First Floor 1A Almeida Compound, Vila Verde, Dili, Timor-Leste (office). *Telephone:* 3311010 (office). *Website:* www.dasilvateixeira.com (office).

TEIXEIRA DA CRUZ, Paula; Portuguese lawyer and politician; b. 1 June 1960, Luanda, Angola; m. Paulo Teixeira Pinto (divorced); two c.; ed Free Univ. of Lisbon; teacher of Admin. Law, Free Univ. of Lisbon 1983–87, Inst. of Financial and Fiscal Studies –1992; mem. Social Democratic Party (PSD) 1995–, mem. PSD Nat. Political Cttee 1997–98, Vice-Pres. 2005–06; worked in govt of Cavaco Silva 1990s; City Councillor, Lisbon 1998–2002, Pres. Municipal Ass. of Lisbon 2005–09; Partner, F. Castelo Branco & Associados 2006–; Minister of Justice 2011–15; mem. High Council of Public Prosecutor's Office 1999–2003, Gen. Council of Bar Asscn 2002–05, Supreme Judicial Council 2003–05; mem. Portuguese Asscn of European Law, Asscn for the Progress of Law. *Address:* F. Castelo Branco & Associados, Avenida de la Liberdade 249, 1st Floor, 1250–143 Lisbon, Portugal. *E-mail:* paulateixeiradacruz-9782@adv.oa.pt. *Website:* www.fcblegal.com (office).

TEIXEIRA DOS SANTOS, Fernando, PhD; Portuguese economist, government official and academic; *Associate Professor, Faculty of Economics, University of Porto;* b. 13 Sept. 1951; m. Maria Clementina Pereira Nunes Teixeira dos Santos; two c.; ed Univ. of Porto, Univ. of South Carolina, USA; Assoc. Prof. of Economics, Univ. of Porto 1986–95, 2011–; Sec. of State for Treasury and Finance 1995–99; Pres. Comissão do Mercado de Valores Mobiliários 2000–05; Minister of State and Finance 2005–11; Chair. Exec. Cttee, Int. Org. of Securities Comms 2000–04, Chair. European Regional Cttee 2004–05; Chair. Instituto Iberoamericano de Mercado de Valores, Cttee of European Securities Regulators Expert Group, Portuguese Securities Exchange Comm.; Grand Official of the Order Infante D. Henrique 2005. *Address:* Faculty of Economics, University of Porto, Rua Dr. Roberto Frias, 4200-464 Porto, Portugal (office). *E-mail:* geral@fep.up.pt (office). *Website:* www.fep.up.pt (office).

TEIXEIRA PINTO, Paulo Jorge; Portuguese academic and banker; *Chairman, Banco Activobank (Portugal), SA;* b. 10 Oct. 1960, Angola; m. Paula da Cruz; two c.; ed Univ. of Lisbon, Univ. of Madrid, INSEAD, Fontainebleau; Lecturer in Law, Univ. of Lisbon and Free Univ. 1983–88; Under-Sec. of State of the Presidency of the Council of Ministers 1991–92, Sec. of State of the Presidency 1992–95; Head of Legal Dept, Banco Comercial Português SA (BCP) 1995–2000, Gen. Man. 2000–05,

Co. Sec. 2000–05, Chair. 2005–07; Gen. Sec. Millennium bcp Foundation 2004–05, Chair. 2005–07, currently Chair. Banco Activobank (Portugal), SA (bank cr. by BCP and Banco Sabadell); Vice-Chair. Portuguese Banking Asscn; mem. Opus Dei 1986–; mem. Supervisory Bd Energias de Portugal; Pres. Causa Real 2008–. *Address:* Office of the Chairman, Banco Activobank (Portugal), SA Rua Augusta 84, 1149-023 Lisbon, Portugal (office). *Telephone:* (21) 4232673 (office). *Fax:* (21) 0066883 (office). *E-mail:* ab7_dop@activobank7.pt (office). *Website:* www.activobank7.pt (office).

TEJPAL, Tarun J.; Indian newspaper editor, writer and publisher; m. Geetan Batra 1984; two d.; ed Panjab Univ.; fmr reporter for The Indian Express and The Telegraph, ed. with India Today and India Express Group; has written for numerous int. publications, including The Paris Review, The Guardian, Financial Times and Prospect; co-f. India Ink publishing house; fmr Managing Ed. Outlook news magazine –2000; Founding CEO and Ed.-in-Chief, Tehelka newspaper 2000–13, initially web-only news site, relaunched as nat. weekly newspaper 2004–. *Publications:* The Alchemy of Desire (novel) (Prix Millepages) 2005, The Story of My Assassins 2009, The Valley of Masks 2011. *Website:* www.taruntejpal.com.

TEKESTE MESKEL, Abreham, PhD; Ethiopian economist and politician; ed Int. Leadership Inst., Addis Ababa; began career as jr economist, Ministry of Finance and Econ. Devt; Chief Econ. Adviser to Mayor of Addis Ababa 2004–06; Founding Dir, Policy Research and Program Devt, Ministry of Urban Devt and Construction; Minister of State, Ministry of Finance and Econ. Devt 2010–16, Minister of Finance and Econ. Co-operation 2016–18; Deputy Commr, Nat. Planning Comm.; fmr lecturer in econs and public policy at various univs in Ethiopia; mem. Tigrian Peoples Liberation Front.

TELAVI, Willy, MA; Tuvaluan politician and fmr police officer; ed Univ. of the South Pacific, Northern Territory Univ. (now Charles Darwin Univ.), Australia; long career with Tuvalu Police Force, becoming Police Commr 1993–2009; MP for constituency of Nanumea 2006–14, Minister of Home Affairs 2006–10, Prime Minister and Minister of Home Affairs 2010–13.

TELEFONI RETZLAFF, Misa, LLB, CPA; Samoan lawyer and politician; b. 21 May 1952; ed King's Coll., Auckland and Auckland Univ., NZ; with Jackson Russell Tunks and West, Auckland, NZ 1974–76; admitted to Bar as Barrister and Solicitor of the Supreme Court, NZ 1975, Western Samoa 1976; pvt. legal practice as H. T. Retzlaff, Apia, Western Samoa 1976–92 (closed office on appointment as Minister of State); apptd Attorney-Gen. 1986–88, resgnd on running as MP; elected MP for Falelatai and Samatau Dist 1988–2011, served as Opposition MP 1988–91; Minister of State with portfolios of Agric., Forests, Fisheries and Meteorology and Minister of Shipping 1992–96, of Health 1996–2001; Deputy Prime Minister and Minister of Finance 2001–06; Deputy Prime Minister and Minister of Commerce, Tourism, Industry and Labour 2006–11 (retd); Vice-Pres. WHO 1999; Chair. FAO Asia/Pacific Regional Conf. and Inaugural Meeting, FAO Ministers 1995; admitted as CPA Samoa 1977, Pres. of Samoa Chamber of Commerce 1977–79; Dir Retzlaff Group of Cos 1975–86, also of eight cos in Western Samoa, one in NZ and Suva, Fiji (resgnd from all 1992); Pro-Chancellor Nat. Univ. of Samoa 1986–98; elected to Komiti Tumau (Standing Cttee) of Methodist Church of Samoa 1996; mem. Inaugural Council of Piula Theological Coll. 1998–; Signatory Latimer House Rules on Good Governance, The Commonwealth; Order of Merit (Chile) 1994; Kelliher Econs Scholarship, NZ 1969, Sr Prize in Law, Auckland Univ., World Food Day Medal 2005. *Publications:* Love and Money 2005, To Thine Own Self be True 2006.

TELIČKA, Pavel; Czech diplomatist, lawyer and university teacher; b. 24 Aug. 1965, Washington, DC, USA; m. Eva Teličková; one s. one d.; ed Charles Univ., Prague; joined Ministry of Foreign Affairs 1986, mem. of del. for talks on Czech membership of EU 1991, with Czech Standing Mission to EU 1991–95, Deputy Amb. to Brussels 1993–95; Dir of Dept in Ministry of Foreign Affairs 1995–98, Dir-Gen. Dept for EU and NATO 1998, Deputy Chair. Comm. for Czech Integration to EU 1998, Chief Negotiator 1998–99, Deputy Minister for Foreign Affairs 1998–99, apptd State Sec. for European Affairs 1999, Amb. and Head, Perm. Mission of Czech Repub. to European Communities 2003–04, EU Commr for Health and Consumer Protection May–Nov. 2004; mem. European Parl. (Group of the Alliance of Liberals and Democrats for Europe, Vice-Chair.) 2014–, mem. Cttee on Transport and Tourism, Del. to Parl. Ass. of the Union for the Mediterranean, Del. for relations with Israel; Co-founder and Partner, BXL Consulting (business now ceased); Sr External Adviser, European Policy Centre; mem. Admin. Council, Notre Europe Foundation, Paris; mem. Europe-USA-Asia Trilateral Comm.; Hon. mem. Man. Bd Nat. Training Fund 1999–2003, Centre of Good Will 2001–; mem. Bd Govs Univ. of Tomase Bati 2001–03; mem. Tomáš Baťa Foundation 1997–, High Level Group of Ind. Stakeholders on Admin. Burdens; Pres. Czech Rugby Union 2009–; Pres. Václav Havel Commemorative Medal 2003, Commemorative Medal of King Jiří z Poděbrad 2003. *Publication:* How Were We Entering the EU? (co-author) 2003. *Leisure interests:* playing rugby and squash, fitness, cross-country skiing, biking, roller-skating, music, travel, driving. *Address:* European Parliament, Bât. Altiero Spinelli 09G358, 60 rue Wiertz, 1047 Brussels, Belgium (office). *Telephone:* (2) 284-57-87 (office). *Fax:* (2) 284-97-87 (office). *E-mail:* pavel.telicka@europarl.europa.eu (office). *Website:* www.europarl.europa.eu (office); www.telicka.eu.

TELLE, Serge; French diplomatist and politician; *Minister of State, Government of Monaco;* b. 5 May 1955, Nantes; m. Guilaine Chenu; ed Inst. d'études politiques de Paris, Inst. nat. des langues et civilisations orientales; long career with French diplomatic service, postings include Embassy in Dar es Salaam, Tanzania 1982, Perm. Mission to UN, New York 1984–88, Diplomatic Adviser to Minister Bernard Kouchner, Minister of State attached to Prime Minister with responsibility for humanitarian action 1988–92, Technical Adviser in Prime Minister's Private Office with responsibility for Africa and Middle East 1997–2002, Consul-Gen., later Amb. to Monaco 2002–07, Deputy Dir, Private Office of Dr Bernard Kouchner, Minister of Foreign and European Affairs 2007–08, Inter-ministerial Del. for Mediterranean, Ministry of Foreign Affairs –2015, Minister of State (Head of Govt), Monaco 2016–. *Address:* Ministry of State, place de la Visitation, BP 522, MC 98000 Cedex, Monaco (office). *Telephone:* 98-98-80-00 (office). *Fax:* 98-98-82-17 (office). *E-mail:* sgme@gouv.mc (office). *Website:* www.gouv.mc (office).

TELLEM, Nancy; American media executive; *Executive Chairman and Chief Media Officer, Eko;* b. 1954; m. Arn Tellem; three c.; ed Univ. of California; began career as TV industry lawyer; with Warner Bros TV (then Lorimar TV) 1987–97, Exec. Vice-Pres. of Business and Financial Affairs; Exec. Vice-Pres. of Business Affairs for CBS Entertainment and Exec. Vice-Pres. CBS Productions 1997–98, Pres. CBS Entertainment 1998–2004, Pres. CBS Paramount Network Television Entertainment Group 2004–10; Pres. Entertainment and Digital Media, Microsoft 2012–14; mem. Bd of Dirs Interlude (media and tech. co.) (now Eko) 2014–, Exec. Chair. and Chief Media Officer 2015–; Dir ThirdAge Media Inc. 2000, Artful Style Inc. 2000. *Address:* 235 Park Avenue S, New York, NY 10003, USA (office). *Website:* helloeko.com (office).

TELLEP, Daniel Michael, MS; American business executive (retd); b. 20 Nov. 1931, Forest City, Pa; m. Pat Tellep; six c.; ed Univ. of California, Berkeley, Harvard Univ.; joined Lockheed Missiles & Space Co. 1955, Chief Eng Missile Systems Div. 1969–75, Vice-Pres., Asst Gen. Man. Advanced Systems Div. 1975–83, Exec. Vice-Pres. 1983–84, Pres. 1984–86, Pres. Lockheed Missiles and Space Group 1986–89, Chair. and CEO Lockheed Corpn 1989–95 (merged with Martin Marietta to form Lockheed Martin 1994), Chair., CEO Lockheed Martin 1996–97 (retd); mem. Interstate Bancorp Bd 1991, Bd of Govs Music Center Los Angeles Co. 1991–95, Calif. Business Round Table 1992; Fellow, AIAA, American Astronautical Soc.; mem. Nat. Acad. of Eng; James V. Forrestal Award 1995, Calif. Mfrs Award 1996, Nat. Eng Award 1996, Karman Wings Award 1997 and numerous other awards.

TELLER, Juergen; German photographer; b. 28 Jan. 1964, Erlangen; pnr, Venetia Scott; one d.; ed Bayerische Staatslehranstalt für Photographie, Munich; living and working in London 1986–; Citibank Photography Prize 2003. *Publications:* Go Sees 1999, Tracht 2001, More, Stephanie Seymour 2001, Pictures and Words 2012, among numerous others. *Address:* CLM UK, Top Floor, 19 All Saints Road, London, W11 1HE, England (office). *E-mail:* thu@clmuk.com. *Website:* www.juergenteller.com.

TELLIER, Paul M., CC, LLL, LLD, PC; Canadian business executive and fmr public official; b. 1939, Joliette, Québec; ed Université Laval and Univ. of Oxford, UK; admitted to Bar, Québec 1963; Deputy Minister for Indian Affairs and Northern Devt 1979–82; Deputy Minister of Energy, Mines and Resources 1982–85; Clerk of the Privy Council and Sec. to Cabinet of Govt of Canada 1985–92; Pres. and CEO Canadian Nat. Railway Co. (CN) 1992–2003; Pres. and CEO Bombardier Inc. 2003–04; Chair. GCT Global Container Terminals Inc. 2007–15; mem. Bd of Dirs Bell Canada Enterprises Inc. 1999–2010, Bell Canada 1996–2010, Rio Tinto 2007–, GM Canada, Canadian Inst. for Advanced Research 2006–, McCain Foods Ltd 1996–2014; mem. Conf. Bd of Canada 1993–2000, Chair. 1996–98; Co-Chair. Prime Minister of Canada's Advisory Cttee on the Renewal of the Public Service 2006–14; Vice-Chair. Canadian Council of Chief Execs, Co-Chair. N America Policy Cttee; Strategic Advisor, Société Générale; mem. Int. Advisory Bd Desautels Faculty of Management, McGill Univ.; mem. Bd Dans la rue 2000–03; Trustee, Ottawa General Hospital 1984–92, International Accounting Standards Foundation 2007–12; Hon. LLD (Univ. of Alberta) 1996; Hon. PhD (Univ. of Ottawa) 2000; Hon. DComm (St Mary's Univ.) 2001; Public Policy Forum Outstanding Performance Award 1988, Gov. Gen.'s Outstanding Achievement Award 1990, Transportation Person of the Year Award, Nat. Transportation Week 1997, Grand Montréalais 1998, Canada's Outstanding CEO of the Year 1998, B'nai Brith Canada Award of Merit 2000, Les Affaires newspaper Personality of the Year 2000, McCullogh Logistics Exec. of the Year Award, Nat. Industrial Transportation League and Logistics Management & Distribution Report 2001, Industry Achievement Award, Canadian Railway Hall of Fame 2002, Fellowship Award, Inst. of Corp. Dirs 2003, Distinguished Canadian Leadership Award 2004; second St Clair tunnel named in his honour 2004, inducted into Canadian Business Hall of Fame 2010, Hon. Assoc. Award, Conf. Bd of Canada 2010.

TELMER, Frederick Harold, MA; Canadian business executive; b. 28 Dec. 1937, Edmonton, Alberta; s. of Ingar Telmer and Bernice Telmer; m. Margaret Goddard Hutchings; three s.; ed Garneau High School, Edmonton, Univ. of Alberta; joined Industrial Relations Dept, Stelco Inc. 1963, various man. positions in Marketing Div., subsequently Gen. Man. Field Sales, apptd Gen. Man. Corp. Affairs and Strategic Planning 1984, Vice-Pres. 1985, Pres. Stelco Steel 1988, Dir Stelco Inc. 1989, Chair. and CEO 1991–97, Chair. 1997–2003; Founding Dir Japan Soc.; Hon. LLD (McMaster Univ.) 1997. *Leisure interests:* golf, tennis, skiing. *Address:* 4451 Lakeshore Road, Burlington, ON L7L 1B3, Canada (home).

TELTSCHIK, Horst; German business executive and fmr politician; b. 14 June 1940, Klantendorf; s. of Richard Teltschik and Anna Teltschik; m. Gerhild Ruff 1967; one s. one d.; ed Gymnasium Tegernsee and Freie Univ. Berlin; Asst Prof., Otto-Suhr-Inst., Freie Univ. Berlin 1968–70; Head of Int. Policy and Intra-German Relations Group, CDU Fed. HQ, Bonn 1970–72; Exec. Ministerial Counsellor to Prime Minister, Rhineland-Palatinate State Chancellery 1972–76; Chief of Staff of Chair. of CDU/CSU Parl. Group, Bundestag, Bonn 1977–82; Ministerial Dir Fed. Chancellery, Head of Directorate-Gen. for Foreign and Intra-German Relations, Devt Policy, External Security 1982–90; Deputy Chief of Staff of Fed. Chancellery 1983–90; CEO Bertelsmann Foundation 1991–92; mem. Bd of Man., Econ. and Governmental Affairs, BMW AG 1993–2000, BMW Rep. of Bd of Man. for Cen. and Eastern Europe, Asia and Middle East 2000–03, Chair. BMW Foundation Herbert Quandt 1993–2003; Lecturer and Hon Prof, Pres. Boeing Germany 2003–06; Founding Pres., Korean German Inst. of Tech., Seoul 2006–09; Pres. Soc. of Munich Philharmonic Orchestra 1993–2003; Pres. German-Israeli Business Asscn 2002–11; mem. Bd of Dirs Roche Holding Ltd 2002–10; mem. German-Japanese Dialogue Forum 1991–2003, German-Indian Consultative Group 1992–2003, Univ. Council, Munich Acad. of Arts 2000–07, Senate of German Nat. Foundation 2000–, German Council on Foreign Relations (DGAP) 2000, Steering Cttee of SWP-Foundation, German Inst. for Int. Politics and Security Affairs 2000–10, German-Russian Raw Material Forum 2008–, Korea-Germany Jt Consultation Cttee on Nat. Unification 2011–; mem. Int. Advisory Bd Council on Foreign Relations, New York 2000–10; mem. Bd of Trustees Eugen Biser Foundation; organizer, Munich Conf. on Securities Policy 1999–2008; Hon. Gen. Consul of India for Bavaria and Thuringia 1992–2002; Hon. Prof. and Lecturer, Technical Univ. Munich 1996–2007; Diplompolitologe; Großen Bundesverdienstkreuz ausgezeichnet 2008, Bundesverdienstkreuz am Bande, Verdienstkreuz 1. Klasse des Verdienstordens der Bundesrepublik Deutschland, Verdienstorden des Freistaates Bayern, Das Große Verdienstkreuz des Verdienstordens der Bundesrepublik Deutschland, Commdr, Légion d'honneur, Grande Ufficiale (Italy), Commdr (Luxembourg), Bavarian Verdienstorden, Manfred Wörner Medaille 2011; also orders and distinctions from Argentina, Spain, Mexico, Cameroon, Nepal, Portugal, Finland, Tunisia, Austria, Poland, Russian Federation, Hungary, Bulgaria; Hon. DUniv (Budapest) 1991, (Sogang, Seoul) 1997; Soziale Ordnung Magazine Future-Award 1999, SCOPUS Award, Hebrew Univ. of Jerusalem 2005, British-German Community Medal, British Chamber of Commerce in Germany 2009. *Publication:* 329 Tage – Innenansichten der deutschen Einigung. *Leisure interests:* literature, tennis. *Address:* Karl-Theodor Strasse 38, 83700 Rottach-Egern, Germany. *Telephone:* (8022) 26677. *Fax:* (8022) 662849. *E-mail:* horstmt@t-online.de.

TEMARU, Oscar Manutahi; French Polynesian politician and fmr head of state; b. 1 Nov. 1944, Faa'a Dist, Tahiti; m. Marie Temaru; seven c.; in French Navy 1961–63; customs officer 1964–99; f. Front de Libération de la Polynésie—FLP (Polynesia Liberation Front) 1977 (changed party name to Tavini Huiraatira no te ao maohi—Serve the Polynesian People 1983); Mayor of Faa'a 1983–; elected mem. Territorial Ass. 1986; mem. UPD Party (Union for Democracy); Pres. of French Polynesia June–Oct. 2004, 2005–06, 2007–08, Feb.–Nov. 2009, 2011–13; cand. in presidential election 2018. *Leisure interest:* golf. *Address:* Tavini Huiraatira, rue des Remparts, Papeete, French Polynesia (office). *Telephone:* 424902. *Fax:* 434209. *E-mail:* contact@tavinihuiraatira.com. *Website:* www.tavinihuiraatira.com.

TEMATA, Tessa; New Zealand diplomatist; *High Commissioner to Cook Islands;* fmrly posted to Indonesia and Papua New Guinea, Devt Counsellor, New Zealand Agency for Int. Devt (NZAID), Ministry of Foreign Affairs (MFA), Unit Man. for Trade and Values, Pacific Regional Div., High Commr to Cook Islands 2018–. *Address:* New Zealand High Commission, 1st floor, Philatelic Bureau Building, Takuvaine Rd, Avarua, Rarotonga, PO Box 21, Cook Islands (office). *Telephone:* 22201 (office). *Fax:* 22241 (office). *E-mail:* nzhcraro@oyster.net.ck (office). *Website:* www.nzembassy.com/cook-islands (office).

TEMBO, Akihiko; Japanese oil industry executive; ed Tokyo Univ.; joined Idemitsu Kosan Co. Ltd 1964, Man. Dir, Idemitsu International Europe PLC 1988–91, Dir and Gen. Man. Treasury Dept, Idemitsu Kosan Co. Ltd 1991–98, Man. Dir Idemitsu Kosan Co. Ltd 1998–2000, Sr Managing Man. Dir 2000–02, Pres. and Rep. Dir 2002–09, Chair. and Rep. Dir 2009–13; fmr Vice-Pres. Petroleum Asscn of Japan, later Pres. *Address:* c/o Idemitsu Kosan Co. Ltd, 1-1, Marunouchi 3-chome, Chiyoda-ku, Tokyo 100-8321, Japan. *E-mail:* info@idemitsu.com.

TEMER LULIA, Michel Miguel Elias, LLB, LLD; Brazilian lawyer, politician and fmr head of state; b. 23 Sept. 1940, Tietê, São Paulo State; s. of Miguel Elias Temer Lulia and March Barbar Lulia; m. 1st Maria de Toledo (divorced), three d.; m. 2nd Marcela Tedeschi, one s.; one s. from previous relationship; ed Univ. of São Paulo, Pontifical Catholic Univ. of São Paulo; pvt. practice as labour lawyer, São Paulo from 1963; Lecturer in Law, Pontifical Catholic Univ. of São Paulo 1968; Asst Prof., FADITU (law faculty) 1969, Deputy Dir 1975–77, Dir 1977–80; Prosecutor, State of São Paulo 1970; Chief Prosecutor, Empresa Municipal de São Paulo (public co.) 1978; State Attorney-Gen. 1983–84; Sec. of Public Security 1984–86; mem. Nat. Constituent Ass. (which promulgated new constitution) 1988; mem. Chamber of Deputies (lower house of parl.) for São Paulo 1987–91, 1994–2010, Pres. (Speaker) 1997–2001, 2009–10; Vice-Pres. of Brazil 2011–16, Acting Pres. (following suspension of Dilma Rousseff) May–Aug. 2016, Pres. 2016–18; mem. Partido do Movimento Democrático Brasileiro (PMDB) 1981–, Pres. 2001–16; Grand Cross of Dannebrog, Légion d'Honneur. *Publications include:* Constitution and Policy 1994, Democracy and Citizenship 2006, Anonymous Intimacy (poems and fiction) 2013. *Address:* c/o Office of the President, Palácio do Planalto, 3° andar, Praça dos Três Poderes, 70150-900 Brasília, DF, Brazil (office).

TEMIRKANOV, Yuri Khatuyevich; Russian conductor; *Music Director and Principal Conductor, St Petersburg Philharmonic Orchestra;* b. 10 Dec. 1938, Nalchik, Repub. of Kabardino-Balkaria; s. of Khatu Sagidovich Temirkanov and Polina Petrovna Temirkanova; m. Irina Guseva (deceased); one s.; ed Leningrad Conservatoire; First Violinist with Leningrad Philharmonic Orchestra 1961–66; Conductor for Maly Theatre and Opera Studio, Leningrad 1965–68; Chief Conductor, Leningrad Philharmonic Orchestra 1968–76, Kirov Opera and Ballet Co. 1976–88; Prof., Leningrad Conservatoire 1979–88; Artistic Dir, State Philharmonia 1988–; Prin. Guest Conductor, Royal Philharmonic Orchestra and Philadelphia Orchestra; Chief Conductor, Royal Philharmonic Orchestra 1992–97; Prin. Guest Conductor, Danish Radio Orchestra 1997–2008; Music Dir, Baltimore Symphony Orchestra 1999–2007, Music Dir Emer. 2007–; Music Dir and Prin. Conductor, St Petersburg Philharmonic Orchestra 2007–; Prin. Guest Conductor, Bolshoi Theatre, Russia 2007–; Music Dir, Teatro Regio di Parma 2009–; guest conductor of major orchestras in Europe and Asia, including Berlin Philharmonic, Vienna Philharmonic, Dresden Staatskapelle, London Philharmonic, London Symphony, Royal Concertgebouw Orchestra, Santa Cecilia, Rome and La Scala and in USA the major orchestras in New York, Philadelphia, Boston, Chicago, Cleveland, San Francisco and Los Angeles; Hon. Academician, Santa Cecilia; Commdr, Order of the Star of Italy 2012; USSR People's Artist 1981, Glinka Prize, USSR State Prize 1976, 1985, 2002, Abbiati Prize for Best Conductor 2002, Pres.'s Medal 2003. *Opera productions include:* Porgy and Bess (at Maly), Peter the Great (at Kirov), Shchedrin's Dead Souls (at Bolshoi and Kirov), Tchaikovsky's Queen of Spades and Eugene Onegin (Kirov) 1979. *Address:* c/o Nicholas Mathias, IMG Artists, Capital Tower, 91 Waterloo Road, London, SE1 8RT, England (office). *Telephone:* (20) 7957-5800 (office). *Fax:* (20) 7957-5801 (office). *E-mail:* nmathias@imgartists.com (office). *Website:* imgartists.com/artist/yuri_temirkanov (office).

TEMÍSTOCLES MONTÁS, Juan, PhD; Dominican Republic politician; b. 1950; m. Carmen Artero; two s. one d.; ed Univ. Autónoma de Santo Domingo, Univ. Politécnica de Madrid, Spain; mem. Nat. Congress (Parl.) 1986–90; Admin. Corporación Dominicana de Electricidad (now Corporación Dominicana de Empresas Eléctricas Estatales) 1996–98; Tech. Sec. to the Presidency 1998–2000, 2004–06; Exec. Dir Global Foundation for Democracy and Devt

2000–04; Sec. of State for Economy, Planning and Devt 2007–16, of Industry and Trade 2016–17; mem. Partido de la Liberación Dominicana.

TEMPEST, Brian W., BSc, PhD, CSci, CChem, FRSC, FRSM; British business executive; *Editor, Journal of Generic Medicines;* b. 13 June 1947, Morecambe, Lancs., England; s. of Bill Tempest and Joan Tempest; m. Jasmin Tempest; three s.; ed Lancaster Univ.; has worked in pharmaceutical Industry since 1970; Regional Dir for Africa, Far East and Middle East, Glaxo Holdings 1985–92; Worldwide Commercial Operations Dir, Fisons plc 1993–95; Regional Dir for Europe, CIS and Africa, Ranbaxy Laboratories Ltd 1995–2000, Worldwide Pres., Pharmaceuticals 2000–04, CEO and Man. Dir 2004–05, Chief Mentor and Exec. Vice-Chair. 2006–07; Chair. Hale & Tempest Co. Ltd 2007–, Strategy Adviser 2008–15; Chair. Religare Capital Markets Europe 2009–, Religare Capital Markets UK 2009–, Religare Capital Markets (India) 2012– (Chair. Risk Cttee), Petainer-Innopac Packaging Pvt. Ltd 2015–; mem. Bd of Dirs Fortis Healthcare (India) 2011– (Chair. Audit & Risk Man. Cttee), SRL Diagnostics (India) 2011– (Chair. Audit & Risk Man. Cttee, Governance Cttee), Glenmark Pharmaceuticals (India) 2012–, Petainer Innopac Packaging Pvt. Ltd 2015–; Chair. Advisory Bd, Lancaster Univ. Man. School; Int. Advisor MAPE, India; mem. Scrip Global Awards Panel; Dir (non-exec.), Governance Bd of UN Patent Pool, also works for UNCTAD on various projects; mem. Editorial Bd, Journal of Generic Medicine 2007–, Ed. 2014–; Hon. Prof., Lancaster Univ. 2007–. *E-mail:* brian.tempest@clara.co.uk. *Website:* www.briantempest.com.

TEMPESTA, HE Cardinal Orani João, O. Cist.; Brazilian ecclesiastic and academic; *Archbishop of São Sebastião do Rio de Janeiro;* b. 23 June 1950, São José do Rio Pardo; ed Cistercian Monastery of São Bernardo, Monastery of São Bento, São Paulo, Salesian Theological Inst. of Pius IX, São Paulo; mem. of the Order of Cistercians 1969, ordained Priest of the Order of Cistercians 1974; apptd Prior of his monastery 1984, acted as Parish Priest of Parish of São Roque, as Diocesan Co-ordinator of Communications and Pastoral Care and as Prof. at Coração de Maria Inst., São João da Boa Vista; elected first Abbot when monastery of São Bernardo became an abbacy 1996; consecrated Bishop of São José do Rio Preto 1997–2004; Apostolic Admin. of Claraval, Minas Gerais 1999–2002; Archbishop of Belém do Pará 2004–09, of São Sebastião do Rio de Janeiro 2009–; cr. Cardinal (Cardinal-Priest of Santa Maria Madre della Providenza a Monte Verde) 2014–; del. to Fifth Gen. Conf. of the Bishops of Latin American and the Caribbean 2007. *Address:* Curia Metropolitana, Rua Benjamin Constant 23, 6° andar Glória, 20241-150 Rio de Janeiro RJ, Brazil (office). *Telephone:* (21) 2292-3132 (office). *Fax:* (21) 2242-9295 (office). *E-mail:* info@arqrio.org (office). *Website:* arqrio.org (office).

TEMPLETON, Richard (Rich) K., BSc; American electronics industry executive; *Chairman, President and CEO, Texas Instruments Inc.;* b. 1958; m.; three c.; ed Union Coll.; joined Texas Instruments Inc. (TI) 1980, held various positions including Exec. Vice-Pres. semiconductor business 1996–2004, COO TI 2000–04, mem. Bd of Dirs 2003–, Pres. and CEO 2004–08, Chair., Pres. and CEO 2008–; mem. Bd of Dirs Semiconductor Industry Asscn, Catalyst; mem. Business Roundtable, Dallas CEO Roundtable; Trustee, Southern Methodist Univ., Southwestern Medical Foundation. *Address:* Texas Instruments Inc., PO Box 660199, 12500 TI Blvd, Dallas, TX 75266-0199, USA (office). *Telephone:* (972) 995-2011 (office). *Website:* www.ti.com (office).

TEMU, Sir Puka, KBE, CMG; Papua New Guinea physician and politician; *Minister for Health & HIV/AIDS;* b. 7 Jan. 1954; worked for six years at Royal Melbourne and Royal Prince Alfred hosps, Australia; Sec., Papua New Guinea Health Dept 1996–2001; MP for Abau Dist 2002–; Minister of Public Service 2002, of State Enterprise and Commerce 2004; Deputy Prime Minister and Minister of Lands, Physical Planning and Mining 2007–10; led unsuccessful vote of no confidence against Prime Minister Michael Somare July 2010; Leader of the Opposition 2010–11; Minister of Agric. and Livestock 2011–12, for Transport 2012, of Public Service 2012–17, for Health & HIV/AIDS 2017–; fmr mem. Nat. Alliance Party; f. Our Development Party 2011. *Address:* Department of Health, AOPI Centre, Waigani Drive, POB 807, Waigani, NCD, Papua New Guinea (office). *Telephone:* 3013601 (office). *Fax:* 3251825 (office). *E-mail:* health_secretary@health.gov.pg (office). *Website:* www.health.gov.pg (office).

TENDULKAR, Sachin Ramesh; Indian fmr professional cricketer; b. 24 April 1973, Bombay (now Mumbai); s. of Ramesh Tendulkar and Rajni Tendulkar; m. Anjali Mehta; one s. one d.; ed Sharadashram Vidyamandir (High School); right-hand batsman, right-arm off-break, leg-break bowler (over 100 One-Day Ints (ODI) wickets); teams: Bombay 1988–96 (renamed Mumbai 1997–2013, Yorks. 1992, India 1989–2013 (Capt. 1996–98, 1999–2000), ICC (Int. Cricket Council) World ODI XI 2004, 2007, Mumbai Indians (Indian Premier League) 2008–13; First-class debut for Bombay cricket team aged 14, scored a century on debut 1988; Test debut India v Pakistan, Karachi 15–20 Nov. 1989; ODI debut: Pakistan v India, Gujranwala 18 Dec. 1989; played in 200 Tests (25 as Capt.), scored 15,921 runs (average 53.78), 51 centuries, 68 half-centuries; set new record for most runs scored by a batsman in Test cricket Oct. 2008; 463 ODIs (73 as Capt.), scored 18,426 runs (average 44.83), 49 centuries, 96 half-centuries; First-class: 310 matches, 25,396 runs (average 57.84), 81 hundreds, 116 half-centuries; highest scores: 248 not out (Test), 200 not out (ODI); balls bowled: 4,240 (Test), 8,054 (ODI); wickets taken: 46 (Test), 154 (ODI); bowling average: 54.17 (Test), 44.48 (ODI); best bowling 3/10 (Test), 5/32 (ODI); catches: 115 (Test), 140 (ODI); highest run scorer in both Test matches and ODIs and also the batsman with the most centuries in either form of the game; first player to score 50 centuries in all int. cricket combined; first player to score a double century in an ODI (v S Africa in Gwalior) 24 Feb. 2010; first batsman to score 12,000, 13,000, 14,000 and 15,000 runs in Test cricket; passed 30,000 runs in int. cricket 20 Nov. 2009; became the most-capped Test cricketer in history after taking field for his 169th match v Sri Lanka, Colombo 3 Aug. 2010; only person to hit 50 Test centuries (scored 50th v S Africa 19 Dec. 2010); first cricketer to score 2,000 ODI World Cup runs v Netherlands, Delhi 9 March 2011; first and only player to score 100 centuries in int. cricket (51 Test and 49 ODI centuries) at Mirpur against Bangladesh in the Asia Cup 16 March 2012; nominated to Rajya Sabha (Upper House of Parl.) 2012; retd 2013; UNICEF Brand Amb. for South Asia 2013–; owner of restaurants; Hon. Group Capt., Indian Air Force (first sportsperson and first personality without an aviation background) 2010; Hon. mem. Order of Australia 2012; Arjuna Award

1994, Wisden Cricketer of the Year 1997, Rajiv Gandhi Khel Ratna Award 1998, Padma Shri Award 1999, Maharashtra Bhushan Award 2001, rated by Wisden as the second greatest Test batsman after Sir Donald Bradman, and the second greatest ODI batsman behind Sir Vivian Richards 2002 (ratings revised to leave Tendulkar ranked No. 1 and Richards at No. 2 2003), Player of the Tournament, Cricket World Cup 2003, ICC World ODI XI 2004, 2007, 2010, Rajiv Gandhi Awards – Sports 2005, ICC World Test XI 2009, 2010, 2011, Sir Garfield Sobers Trophy for Cricketer of the Year, ICC Awards 2010, Wisden Leading Cricketer in the World 2010, LG People's Choice Award 2010, Outstanding Achievement in Sport and the People's Choice Award, The Asian Awards, London 2010, Castrol Indian Cricketer of the Year Award 2011, BCCI Cricketer of the Year Award 2011, Wisden India Outstanding Achievement Award 2012, Padma Vibhushan 2008, Bharat Ratna 2014, Asian Awards Fellowship 2017. *Publication:* Playing it My Way (with Boria Majumdar) 2014. *Address:* Rajya Sabha, Parliament House Annexe, New Delhi 110 001 (office); Dorab Villa, 19-A, Perry Cross Road, Opposite Joggers' Park, Bandra, Mumbai 400 050, India (home). *Telephone:* (11) 23034695 (office); (22) 26457576 (home). *Fax:* (11) 23792940 (office). *E-mail:* ast1@vsnl.net.

TENET, George J., MIA; American academic, investment industry executive and fmr government official; *Managing Director, Allen & Company LLC;* b. 5 Jan. 1953, New York; m. A. Stephanie Glakas; one s.; ed Georgetown Univ. School of Foreign Service, School of Int. Affairs, Columbia Univ.; Research Dir American Hellenic Inst. 1978–79; Legis. Asst, Legis. Dir, staff of US Senator John Heinz 1982–85; fmr head of supervision of arms control negotiations between USSR and USA, subsequently Staff Dir, US Senate Select Cttee on Intelligence 1988–93; Special Asst to Pres. and Sr Dir for Intelligence Programs, Nat. Security Council 1993–95; Deputy Dir of CIA 1995–96, Acting Dir 1996–97, Dir 1997–2004 (resgnd); Distinguished Prof. in the Practice of Diplomacy, Edmund A. Walsh School of Foreign Service and Sr Research Assoc., Inst. for the Study of Diplomacy, Georgetown Univ. 200407; Man. Dir Allen & Co. (pvt. investment bank), New York 2008–; mem. Bd of Dirs QinetiQ Group plc, UK 2006–08; Egyptian Order of Merit (First Class); Dr hc (Georgetown Univ.), (Univ. of Oklahoma), (Rochester Inst. of Technology), (Joint Military Intelligence Coll.); Canadian Security Intelligence Service Gold Medal, Presidential Medal of Freedom 2004, America's Democratic Legacy Award from Anti-Defamation League 2005. *Publications include:* The Ability of US Intelligence to Monitor the Intermediate Nuclear Force Treaty, At the Center of the Storm 2007. *Address:* Allen & Company LLC, 711 5th Avenue, 9th Floor, New York, NY 10022, USA (office). *Telephone:* (212) 832-8000 (office). *Fax:* (212) 832-8023 (office).

TENG, Teng; Chinese politician; b. 1930, Jiangyin Co., Jiangsu Prov.; ed Tsinghua Univ., Beijing and in USSR; joined CCP 1948; Deputy Dir Chemical Eng Dept, Tsinghua Univ. 1960–66, Prof., Vice-Pres. Tsinghua Univ. 1980–84; Vice-Minister in charge of State Science and Tech. Comm. 1985–86; Deputy Head, Propaganda Dept CCP Cen. Cttee 1986–87; Vice Minister in charge of State Educ. Comm. 1988–93; Vice-Chair. Exec. Bd UNESCO 1991–93; Dir Sustainable Devt Research Centre; Pres. Chinese Ecological Econs Council; Vice-Pres. Chinese Acad. of Sciences 1986–87, Chinese Acad. of Social Sciences 1993–98; mem. 8th and 9th Standing Cttee NPC 1993–2003, mem. Educ., Science, Culture and Public Health Cttee 1993–98; Pres. Chinese and Ecological Econs Council 1998–2005; Govt Prize of Science and Tech. 1978. *Publication:* Future Outlook for the Environment and Sustainable Development 2002. *Leisure interest:* classical music. *Address:* 5th Jianguomennei Dajie, Beijing 100732 (office); Cuiweisili 1-2-401, Beijing 100036, People's Republic of China (home). *Telephone:* (10) 65137697 (office); (10) 68258097 (home). *Fax:* (10) 65137815 (office); (10) 68252720 (home). *E-mail:* tengteng@cass.org.ch (office); tengcass@yahoo.com (home).

TENG, Wensheng; Chinese writer and politician; b. 1940, Changning Co., Hunan Prov.; ed Chinese People's Univ.; joined CCP 1965; Research Fellow, Research Office, Secr. of CCP Cen. Cttee; Vice-Dir, later Dir Policy Research Office of CCP Cen. Cttee; Deputy Sec.-Gen. CCP Cen. Advisory Comm. 1988–92; Dir CCP Cen. Cttee Literature Research Office 2002–; mem. 15th CCP Cen. Cttee 1997–2002, 16th CCP Cen. Cttee 2002–07; fmr chief speech writer for Pres. Jiang Zemin. *Publication:* book on evolution of Mao Zedong thought.

TENNEKES, Hendrik, DS (Eng); Dutch meteorologist; b. 13 Dec. 1936, Kampen; s. of Cornelis Tennekes and Harmpje Noordman; m. Olga Vanderpot 1964 (divorced 1998); one s. one d.; ed Delft Tech. Univ.; Asst Prof., Assoc. Prof., Prof. of Aerospace Eng, Pennsylvania State Univ. 1965–77, currently Adjunct Prof.; Dir of Research, Royal Netherlands Meteorological Inst. 1977–90, Dir of Strategic Planning 1990–95; Prof. of Meteorology, Free Univ., Amsterdam 1977–2001; Visiting Prof., Univ. of Washington, Seattle 1976–77; Visiting Sr Scientist, Nat. Center for Atmospheric Research, Boulder, Colo 1987; mem. Royal Netherlands Acad. of Arts and Sciences 1982–2010; mem. Advisory Bd Royal Palace Foundation, Amsterdam 1990–2001. *Publications:* A First Course in Turbulence (with J. L. Lumley) 1972, The Simple Science of Flight 1996; numerous publs on turbulence, predictability, chaos, boundary-layer meteorology and environmental philosophy. *Leisure interests:* poetry, landscape painting. *Address:* Velperweg 30-19, 6824 BJ Arnhem, Netherlands (home). *Telephone:* (30) 379-2247 (home). *E-mail:* henktennekes@kpnplanet.nl (home).

TENZIN, Daw; Bhutanese fmr central banker; b. 1956; ed Australian Nat. Univ.; worked in Ministry of Information and Communications; fmr Sec., Planning Comm.; Man. Dir Royal Monetary Authority (cen. bank of Bhutan) 2003–10, Gov. 2010–15; fmr Chair. Credit Information Bureau of Bhutan.

TEO, Rear-Adm. (retd) Chee Hean, BSc, MSc, MPA; Singaporean politician and fmr naval officer; *Deputy Prime Minister and Co-ordinating Minister for National Security;* b. 27 Dec. 1954; m. Chew Poh Yim; one s. one d.; ed St Michael's School, St Joseph's Inst., Singapore Armed Forces Training Inst., UMIST, Manchester, Imperial Coll., London, Kennedy School of Govt, Harvard Univ.; various command and staff appointments in Repub. of Singapore Navy and Jt Staff 1977–86, Chief of Navy 1991, rank of Rear-Adm. 1991, retd 1992; Littauer Fellow, Harvard Univ. 1986; MP for Marine Parade Group Representation Constituency 1992–97, for Pasir Ris Group Representation Constituency 1997–, becoming Minister of State in Ministries of Finance, Communications and Defence, Acting Minister for Environment and Sr Minister of State for Defence 1995–96, Minister for Environment and Second Minister for Defence 1996–97, Minister for Educ. and Second Minister for Defence 1997–2001, Minister for Defence 2003–11, Deputy Prime Minister 2009–, also Co-ordinating Minister for Nat. Security 2011–, Minister for Home Affairs 2011–15, Minister in charge of the Civil Service 2011–; Pres.'s Scholarship, Singapore Armed Forces Scholarship 1973. *Address:* Office of the Deputy Prime Minister, The Istana, Orchard Rd, Singapore 238823, Singapore (office). *Telephone:* 62358577 (office). *E-mail:* pmo_hq@pmo.gov.sg (office). *Website:* www.pmo.gov.sg (office).

TEO, Michael Eng Cheng, BBA, MA; Singaporean diplomatist and air force officer (retd); b. 19 Sept. 1947, Sarawak; s. of Teo Thian Lai and Lim Siew Kheng; m. Joyce Teo (née Ng Sinn Toh); one s. one d.; ed Auburn Univ., Fletcher School of Law and Diplomacy, Tufts Univ., USAF War Coll., USA; joined Repub. of Singapore Air Force 1968, Commdr 1985, Brig.-Gen. 1987, Chief of Air Force 1990 (retd); joined Diplomatic Service 1993, High Commr to NZ 1994–96, Amb. to Repub. of Korea 1996–2001, High Commr to UK 2002–11, to Australia 2011–14; The Most Noble Order of the Crown (Thailand) 1981, Legion of Merit, Degree of Commdr (USA) 1991, Order of Diplomatic Service Merit Gwanghwa Medal (Repub. of Korea) 2002; Public Admin Medal (Singapore) 1989, Outstanding Achievement Award (Philippines) 1989, Bintang Swa Bhuana Paksa Utama (Indonesia) 1991. *Leisure interests:* golf, hiking, reading. *Address:* Ministry of Foreign Affairs, MFA Building, Tanglin, off Napier Road, Singapore 248163, Singapore (office). *Telephone:* 63798000 (office). *Fax:* 64747885 (office). *E-mail:* mfa@mfa.gov.sg (office). *Website:* www.mfa.gov.sg (office).

TEODORO, Gilberto ('Gilbert') Cojuangco, Jr, (Gibo), BSc, LLB, LLM; Philippine lawyer, politician and air force officer; b. 14 June 1964, Manila; s. of Gilberto Teodoro, Sr and Mercedes Cojuangco; m. Monica Prieto-Teodoro; one s.; ed Xavier School, De La Salle Univ., Univ. of the Philippines (UP), Harvard Law School, USA, Air Command and Staff Coll. of the Philippine Air Force, Jt Command and Staff Coll.; Pres. Kabataang Barangay for Cen. Luzon 1980–85, for Prov. of Tarlac 1980–85; mem. Sanguniang Panlalawigan, Prov. of Tarlac 1980–86; called to the Philippines Bar 1989; lawyer, EP Mendoza Law firm 1990–97; admitted to State Bar of NY, USA 1997; Congressman of First Dist of Tarlac 1998–2007, Asst Majority Leader (11th Congress), Head of Nationalist People's Coalition House mems and mem. House contingent to Legis.-Exec. Devt Advisory Council; Sec. of Nat. Defense 2007–10; Col, Philippine Air Force, 0-133104 E (Reserve Force); Asst mem. Faculty, Command and Gen. Staff Course; Lecturer, Air Command Staff Coll.; Chair. Suricon Resources Corpn 1995; fmr Chair. Philippine Nat. Police (PNP) Foundation Inc.; mem. Bd of Dirs Philippine Geothermal Production Company, Inc., Canlubang Sugar Estate, BDO Unibank, Inc. 2014–; mem. Integrated Bar of the Philippines, UP Alumni Asscn, UP Law Alumni Asscn, Harvard Alumni Asscn, Harvard Law Alumni Asscn; Lifetime mem. Armor-Cavalry Asscn of the Philippines; Hon. Command Pilot, Philippine Air Force; Hon. mem. PMA Alumni Asscn Sponsoring Class – '76, Philippine Air Force Aviation Cadet Alumni Asscn Sponsoring Class – '80, Asscn of Chiefs of Police of the Philippines, Inc.; Mil. Merit Medal, Philippine Air Force Gen. Staff Course Badge, Presidential Flight Crew Badge, Mil. Civic Action Medal (Plain), Mil. Civic Action Medal with Bronze Service Star, Mil. Civic Action Medal with Second Service Star; Dean's Medal for Academic Excellence, Univ. of the Philippines 1989, Leadership and Seminar Academic Excellence Awardee, Air Command and Staff Coll. of the Philippine Air Force 2001, Leadership Award, Jt Command and Staff Coll. 2003; numerous mil. awards and commendations, including Basic RASS Aeronautical Badge, Caliber .45 Pistol Expert Marksmanship Badge, M-16 Rifle Marksmanship Badge.

TEODOROVICI, Eugen Orlando, BA, MA, PhD; Romanian politician; *Minister of Public Finance;* b. 12 Aug. 1971, Bucharest; ed Spiru Haret High School, Bucharest, Faculty of Commerce, Acad. of Econ. Studies, Nat. School of Political and Admin. Studies, Dept for Int. Relations and European Integration; referee, Directorate-Gen. of Man., Marketing, Prognosis and Human Resources, Ministry of Transport 1991–97, expert, Gen. Directorate for European Integration 1997–99; expert, Dept for European Integration Feb.–June 1999, Dir June–Dec. 1999; Dir Dept for European Affairs, Ministry of Foreign Affairs Jan.–Dec. 2000; Dir, Co-ordination Directorate of ISPA and SAPARD, Ministry of European Integration 2000–04; Dir-Gen. Man. Authority for Cohesion Fund, Ministry of Economy and Finance 2004–05; Dir-Gen., Infrastructure Man. Authority, Ministry of Finance 2005–07; Sec. of State, Ministry of Economy and Finance 2007–09; Dir-Gen., ISPA Man. Authority, Ministry of Public Finance Jan.–June 2009; Dir, Audit Authority, Court of Accounts of Romania 2009–12; State Adviser, Body of Advisers to Prime Minister May–Dec. 2012; Senator, Romanian Parl. Dec. 2012–; Minister of European Funds 2012–15, of Public Finance March–Nov. 2015, 2018–; Pres. Inter-Ministerial Cttee on Financing, Guaranteeing and Insuring Local Authorities (within Ministry of Public Finance), Inter-Ministerial Cttee on Financing, Guaranteeing and Insuring the Pvt. Sector (within EXIM Bank); Romanian Rep. on Bd of Dirs of EIB; Nat. Coordinator of HIPERB Programme; Rep. of Ministry of Public Finance in Export Council; expert co-ordinator in project of institutional twinning between Romania and Moldova ('Harmonization of Public Procurement Legislation in the Republic of Moldova'); mem. Bd CEC Bank SA. *Address:* Ministry of Public Finance, 050741 Bucharest 5, Str. Apolodor 17, Romania (office). *Telephone:* (21) 3199759 (office). *Fax:* (21) 3122509 (office). *E-mail:* presa.mfp@mfinante.gov.ro (office); eugenteodorovici@gmail.com. *Website:* www.mfinante.gov.ro (office).

TEPLITZ, Alaina Beth, BS; American diplomatist; *Ambassador to Sri Lanka;* d. of Jack Teplitz and Marcella Teplitz; m. 1st Joe Mellott; two s.; m. 2nd Robert D. Saul; ed Georgetown Univ. School of Foreign Service; joined State Dept 1991, first overseas assignment as First Econ. Officer, Embassy in Ulan Bator, Mongolia, also posted to Embassies in Tirana and Sydney, other positions include Man. Counsellor, Embassy in Dhaka Special Asst to State Dept, Asst Sec. for Admin, Program Analyst in Bureau of Admin, Deputy Dir, Jt Admin. Services, Brussels, Belgium, Dir, Man. Training Div., State Dept Foreign Service Inst. 2007–09, Deputy Exec. Dir, Near East and South and Central Asia Bureau Jt Exec. Office 2009–11, Minister–Counsellor for Man., Embassy in Kabul 2011–12, Dir, Office of Man. of Policy, Rightsizing, and Innovation, State Dept 2012–15, Amb. to Nepal 2015–18, to Sri Lanka (also accred to Maldives) 2018–. *Address:* US Embassy, 210 Galle Road, Colombo 3, Sri Lanka (office). *Telephone:* (11) 2498500 (office). *Fax:* (11) 2437345 (office). *Website:* lk.usembassy.gov (office).

TEPPERMAN, Jonathan D., BA, MA, LLM; Canadian journalist and editor; *Managing Editor, Foreign Affairs;* b. 10 Aug. 1971, Windsor, Ont.; s. of Bill Tepperman and Rochelle Tepperman; ed Yale Univ., Univ. of Oxford, UK, New York Univ. School of Law; fmr speechwriter for US Amb. to UN 1994–95; journalist writing for Forward 1996, Jerusalem Post 1997; Assoc. Ed. and Production Man. Foreign Affairs (journal of Council on Foreign Relations) 1998–2001, Sr Ed. 2001–04, Deputy Man. Ed. 2004–07, Man. Ed. 2011–; Deputy Ed. Newsweek International, New York 2007–09; Man. Ed. and Dir EurasiaGroup 2010. *Publications include:* numerous contribs to publs including New York Times, Newsweek, LA Times, Christian Science Monitor, Wall Street Journal, New Republic. *Address:* Foreign Affairs, Editorial Department, 58 East 68th Street, New York, NY 10065, USA (office). *Telephone:* (212) 434-9696 (office). *E-mail:* jtepperman@cfr.org (office); jt@jonathantepperman.com. *Website:* www .foreignaffairs.com (office); jonathantepperman.com (office).

TER-MINASSIAN, Teresa R., LLB, MA (Econs); Italian economist and international organization official; m.; three c.; ed Univ. of Rome, Harvard Univ., USA; Economist, Cen. Bank of Italy 1967–75, Div. Chief 1975–78, seconded to IMF as economist in Fiscal Affairs Dept (FAD) 1971–78, Sr Economist and Asst Div. Chief, Western and Southern Europe Divs, European Dept 1978–79, Div. Chief and Asst Dir, Southern Europe Div. 1980–88, Deputy Dir FAD 1988–96, Deputy Dir Western Hemisphere Dept 1996–2000, Dir FAD 2001–08, Special Advisor to the Man. Dir of IMF 2008–09 (retd); int. econ. consultant 2009–; Fulbright, Harvard and L. Einaudi Foundation scholarships. *Publication:* Fiscal Federalism in Theory and Practice 1997. *Address:* 6661 Avignon Blvd, Falls Church, VA 22043, USA (home). *Telephone:* (703) 533 8764 (home). *E-mail:* tterminassian@post.harvard .edu. *Website:* terra-space.com/teresa.

TER-PETROSYAN, Levon Hagopi, DLit; Armenian politician, philologist and fmr head of state; *President, Hay Azgayin Kongres (HAK—Armenian National Congress);* b. 9 Jan. 1945, Aleppo, Syria; m. Lyudmila Pletnitskaya; one s.; ed Yerevan State Univ., Leningrad Inst. of Orientology, Russian SFSR; family moved to Armenian SSR in 1946; jr researcher, Armenian Inst. of Literature 1972–78, sr researcher, then Scientific Sec. Matenadaran Archive 1978–90; took part in dissident movt, arrested 1966, 1988–89; mem. and Chair. Karabakh Cttee, Matenadaran Inst. of Ancient Armenian Manuscripts 1988; Deputy, Supreme Soviet of Armenian SSR 1989, Chair. 1990–91; mem. Bd, Hayots Hamazgain Sharzhum (Pan-Armenian Nat. Movt) 1989–2013 (fmr Chair.), party spearheaded formation of Hay Azgayin Kongress (HAK—Armenian Nat. Congress) 2008, coalition of 18 opposition parties in opposition to ruling govt coalition; Pres. of Armenia 1991–98; took leading role in protests as part of a wave of regional unrest 2011; led HAK during the parl. election 2012, alliance transformed into a single political party 2013. *Publications:* six books and more than 70 papers on the history of Armenia. *Leisure interests:* reading, chess. *Address:* Hay Azgayin Kongress (Armenian National Congress), 0010 Yerevan, Abovyan poghots 38 (office); 0010 Yerevan, Tsitsernakaberd mayrughi, Armenia (home). *Telephone:* (10) 52-09-74 (office); (10) 52-09-57 (office). *E-mail:* info@anc.am (office). *Website:* www.anc.am (office); www.levonpresident.am.

TERENGGANU, HM The Sultan of; Tuanku Mizan Zainal Abidin; Malaysian fmr head of state; b. 22 Jan. 1962, Kuala Terengganu; s. of Sultan Mahmud Al Muktafi Billah Shah and Bariah binti Hishamuddin Alam Shah; m. Permaisuri Nur Zahirah Cik Puan Seri Rozita Adil Bakeri 1996; two s. two d.; apptd Heir Apparent Yang di-Pertuan Muda of Terengganu 1979; 16th Sultan of Terengganu 1998–; Timbalan Yang di-Pertuan Agong (Deputy Supreme Head of State) 1999–2006; 13th Yang di-Pertuan Agong (Supreme Head of State) 2006–11; Col-in-Chief Royal Armoured Corps; Chancellor Universiti Malaysia Terengganu 2001–06. *Address:* Istana Badariah, 20500 Kuala Terengganu, Malaysia (office).

TERENIUS, Lars Yngve, PhD; Swedish medical research scientist and academic; *Professor Emeritus of Experimental Alcohol and Drug Dependence Research, Karolinska Institute;* b. 9 July 1940, Örebro; s. of Yngve Terenius and Margareta Hallenborg; m. 1st Malin Åkerblom 1962 (divorced 1986); m. 2nd Mona Hagman 1989; two s.; ed Uppsala Univ.; Asst Prof. of Pharmacology, Medical Faculty, Uppsala Univ. 1969–79, Prof. of Pharmacology, Faculty of Pharmacy 1979–89; Prof. of Experimental Alcohol and Drug Dependence Research, Karolinska Inst. 1989–2008, Prof. Emer. 2008–; Prof. of Molecular and Cellular Neuroscience, Scripps Research Inst.; Visiting Scientist Nat. Inst. for Medical Research, London 1972–73, Univ. of Aberdeen, Scotland 1975, Hebrew Univ., Jerusalem 1983, 1986; Fogarty Scholar, NIH, USA 1988–89; mem. Royal Swedish Soc. of Sciences, Royal Swedish Acad. of Sciences 1987–, Academia Europaea 1989–, Nobel Ass. on Physiology or Medicine 2003–05; Foreign Hon. mem. American Acad. of Arts and Sciences 1999–; Dr hc (Uppsala Univ.) 1981, (Norwegian Univ. of Science and Tech.) 1982, (Trondheim) 1983; Olof Rudbeck Prize 1999; Pacesetter Award 1977, Gairdner Award 1978, Jahre Award 1980, Björkén Award of Uppsala Univ. 1984, IPSEN Award 2000, Neuronal Plasticity Prize 2000. *Publications:* 500 papers on experimental endocrinology, cancer research, neurobiology. *Address:* Department of Clinical Neuroscience, K8, Tomtebodavägen 18A pl 5, 171 77 Stockholm (office); Kyrkogårdsgatan 29, 753 12 Uppsala, Sweden (home). *Telephone:* (8) 5177-48-60 (office). *Fax:* (8) 34-19-39 (office). *E-mail:* Lars.Terenius@ki.se (office). *Website:* ki.se/orgid/75 (office).

TERENZI, Gianfranco; San Marino politician and fmr head of state; b. 2 Jan. 1941; mem. Partito Democratico Cristiano Sammarinese (San Marinese Christian Democratic Party); mem. Consiglio Grande e Generale (Parl.); Co-Capt. Regent (jt head of state) of San Marino Oct. 1987–April 1988, Oct. 2000–April 2001, April–Oct. 2006, Oct. 2014–April 2015. *Address:* c/o Office of the Captains Regent, Palazzo Begni, Contrada Omerelli, 47890 San Marino (office). *Website:* www .sanmarino.sm (office).

TERESHCHENKO, Sergei, BSc; Kazakhstani politician; b. 30 March 1951, Lesozavodsk, Primorskiy Region; s. of Aleksandr Ivanovich Tereshchenko and Tamara Ivanovna Tereshchenko; m. Yevgenya Tsykunova; two d.; ed Alma-Ata Inst. of Agric., Moscow Univ. of Commerce; held offices in state power organs of Chimkent Region 1986–89, Chair. of the Exec. Cttee of Chimkent Region 1990–91; First Deputy-Chair. Council of Ministers of Kazakh Soviet Repub. 1989–90; Vice-Pres. of Kazakhstan April–May 1991; Prime Minister of Kazakhstan 1991–94; Minister of Foreign Affairs 1994–95; Chair. Bd of Dirs Integrazia Fund 1994–;

Vice-Chair. Republican (Otan) Party 1999–2002, Deputy Chair. Ass. of the Peoples of Kazakhstan Oct. 2002; Co-Chair. Int. Eco-Safety Cooperative Org. 2009–; Chair. Ordabasy Kus Ltd 2011–, JSC Rakhat 2014–; mem. Bd of Trustees First Pres. Foundation of Repub. of Kazakhstan 2007–; Order of Dostyk (First Class) 1999; State Prize for Peace and Spiritual Content 1999. *Publications include:* Kazakh Land is My Cradle 1999, Kazakhstan, Reforms, Market 2000. *Leisure interests:* hunting, swimming, fashion, travelling. *Address:* 121-18 Kounaev str., 480100 Almaty, Kazakhstan (home). *Telephone:* (727) 263-36-18 (home). *E-mail:* tyelena@ nursat.kz (home).

TERESHKOVA, Maj.-Gen. Valentina Vladimirovna, CandTechSc; Russian politician and fmr cosmonaut; b. 6 March 1937, Maslennikovo, Yaroslavl Region; d. of Vladimir Aksyonovich Tereshkov and Elena Fyodorovna Tereshkova; m. 1st Andriyan Nikolayev 1963 (divorced 1982, died 2004); one d.; m. 2nd Yuliy G. Shaposhnikov (died 1999); ed Yaroslavl Textile Coll. and Zhukovsky Air Force Engineering Acad.; fmr textile worker, Krasny Perekop textile mill, Yaroslavl; Textile Mill Sec., Young Communist League 1960; joined Yaroslavl Air Sports Club 1959 and started parachute jumping; mem. CPSU 1962–91, Cen. Cttee CPSU 1971–90; began cosmonaut training March 1962; made 48 orbits of the Earth in spaceship Vostok VI 16–19 June 1963; first woman in world to enter space; Deputy to USSR Supreme Soviet 1966–90; USSR People's Deputy 1989–91; Chair. Soviet Women's Cttee 1968–87; mem. Supreme Soviet Presidium 1970–90; Head Union of Soviet Socs. for Friendship and Cultural Relations with Foreign Countries 1987–92; apptd Chair. then Dir of Presidium, Russian Asscn of Int. Co-operation (now Russian Centre of Int. Scientific and Cultural Co-operation) 1992, Pres. Moscow House of Europe 1992; Head, Russian Centre for Int. Scientific and Cultural Co-operation 1994–2004; carrier of Olympic flag at Winter Olympics, Sochi 2014; Hon. Citizen of, Sofia, Burgas, Petrich, Stara Zagora, Pleven, Varna (Bulgaria) 1963, Bratislava (Czechoslovakia) 1963, Polizzi Generosa (Italy), Darkhan (Mongolia) 1965, Gyumri (Leninakan, Armenia) 1965, Vitebsk (Belarus) 1975, Kaluga, Yaroslavl (Russia), Karaganda, Baikonur (Leninsk, Kazakhstan) 1977, Montreux (Switzerland), Drancy (France), Montgomery (UK); Pilot-Cosmonaut of USSR; Hero of Soviet Union 1963; Honoured Master of Sports 1963; Joliot-Curie Gold Medal; Order of Lenin 1963, 1981; World Peace Council 1966; Order of the Friendship of Peoples; Order of the Nile (Egypt) 1971; Order of the October Revolution 1971; Order of the Red Banner of Labour 1987; Order of Merit for the Fatherland, Third Class 1997, Second Class 2007; Order of Honour 2003; Order of Duke Branimir, with Sash (Croatia) 2003; Order of St Euphrosyne, Grand Duchess of Moscow, Second Class 2008; Order of Friendship 2011; Order of Alexander Nevsky 2013; Russian Federation State Prize 1997, 2003, 2008, 2009; lunar crater, Tereshkova A minor and planet 1671 Chaika named in her honour.

TERFEL, Sir Bryn, Kt, CBE; Welsh singer (bass-baritone); b. (Bryn Terfel Jones), 9 Nov. 1965, Pantglas, Snowdonia, Wales; s. of Hefin Jones and Nesta Jones; m. Lesley Halliday 1987 (divorced); three s.; one d. with Hannah Stone; ed Ysgol Dyffryn Nantlle, Penygroes, Gwynedd and Guildhall School of Music and Drama; debut, Welsh Nat. Opera (WNO) as Guglielmo 1990; sang Mozart's Figaro at Santa Fe Opera and ENO 1991; Royal Nat. Opera, Covent Garden debut as Masetto in Don Giovanni 1992, repeated on tour to Japan; sang at Salzburg Festival as the Spirit Messenger in Die Frau ohne Schatten, and as Jochanaan in Salome 1992; Leporello in Don Giovanni 1994; further appearances at Vienna Staatsoper as Mozart's Figaro 1993, at Chicago as Donner in Das Rheingold, debuts at New York Metropolitan Opera 1994, Sydney Opera House 1999; frequent guest soloist with Berlin Philharmonic Orchestra; sang in the Brahms Requiem under Colin Davis and at Salzburg Easter Festival under Abbado (Herbert von Karajan In Memoriam) 1993; sang Nick Shadow in The Rake's Progress for WNO 1996, Figaro at La Scala 1997, Scarpia for Netherlands Opera 1998, Falstaff at the reopening of the Royal Opera House, Covent Garden 1999; four male roles in Les Contes d'Hoffmann and Don Giovanni, both at Metropolitan Opera, New York, and Nick Shadow in The Rake's Progress for San Francisco Opera 1999–2000; baritone roles in Les Contes d'Hoffmann at the Opéra Bastille, Sweeney Todd in Chicago, and Falstaff and Don Giovanni at Covent Garden 2002–03; Mephistopheles in Faust, Wotan in Das Rheingold and Die Walküre at Covent Garden 2004; Scarpia and the Flying Dutchman for the Royal Opera House 2009; Die Meistersinger von Nürnberg, WNO 2010; Wotan in Das Rheingold, Metropolitan Opera, New York 2010, Die Walküre 2011; Scarpia in Tosca for WNO, Staatsoper Hannover, Opera Monte Carlo, Wiener Staatsoper and Opéra Nat. de Paris 2015–16; Scarpia in Tosca, Opéra Nat. de Paris 2016, Deutsche Oper Berlin 2016–17; Wotan, Wiener Staatsoper 2017; many concert appearances in Europe, USA, Canada, Japan and Australia; Pres. Nat. Youth Choir of Wales, Festival of Wales; Vice-Pres. Llangollen Int. Eisteddfod; Founder, Faenol Festival 2000–10; Hon. Fellow, Univ. of Wales, Aberystwyth, Welsh Coll. of Music and Drama, Univ. of Wales, Bangor; Hon. DMus (Glamorgan) 1997; White Robe, Gorsedd, recipient Kathleen Ferrier Scholarship 1988, Gold Medal Award 1989, Lieder Prize Cardiff Singer of the World Competition 1989, Gramophone magazine Young Singer of the Year 1992, British Critics Circle Award 1992, Int. Classical Music Awards Newcomer of Year 1993, Classical BRIT Award for Male Artist of the Year 2004, 2005, Nordoff-Robbins Silver Clef Classical Award 2006, Queen's Medal for Music 2006. *Recordings include:* Salome, Le nozze di Figaro, An Die Musik, Wagner Arias, Britten's Gloriana, Beethoven's Ninth Symphony, Brahms' Requiem, Schwanen-gesang, Cecilia and Bryn, If Ever I Would Leave You, Handel Arias, Vagabond (Caecilia Prize 1995, Gramophone People's Award 1996) 1995, Opera Arias (Grammy Award for best classical vocal performance) 1996, Something Wonderful (Britannia Record Club Members' Award) 1997, Don Giovanni 1997, Bryn (Classical BRIT Award for Best Album 2004) 2003, Simple Gifts (Grammy Award for Best Classical Crossover Album 2007) 2005, Tutto Mozart! 2006, First Love: Songs from the British Isles 2008, Elgar's The Dream of Gerontius (Gramophone Award for Best Choral Recording) 2009, Bad Boys 2009, At His Very Best 2010, Carols & Christmas Songs 2010, Tosca (Puccini) (BBC Music Magazine DVD Performance Award 2014), Wagner: Der Ring des Nibelungen (with Met Opera, Grammy Award for Best Opera Recording 2013) 2012, Don Giovanni 2015, Der Fliegende Holländer 2015. *Leisure interests:* golf, collecting fob watches, supporting Manchester United. *Address:* c/o Matthew Todd, Harlequin Agency, Gloworks, Heol Porth Teigr, Cardiff, CF10 4GA, Wales (office). *Telephone:* (29) 2075-0821 (office). *E-mail:* matthew.todd@harlequin-agency.co.uk (office). *Website:* www .harlequin-agency.co.uk (office).

TERIUM, Peter; Dutch business executive; *CEO, RWE International SE;* b. 26 Sept. 1963, Nederweert; ed Nederlands Institut voor Registeraccountants, Amsterdam; trainee tax auditor, Tax Dept, Ministry of Finance, ind. tax auditor working for Ministry of Finance 1984–85; Audit Supervisor, KPMG, Eindhoven 1985–90; various positions at Schmalbach-Lubeca AG 1990–2002; plant controller at PET Containers Germany, Head of Controlling for White Cap Germany and Product Group Controller for White Cap Europe, Vice-Pres., Finance and Accounting, White Cap Europe and Asia, Vice-Pres., Finance and Accounting, PET Containers Europe and Asia Head of Group Controlling, RWE AG, Essen 2003–05, mem. Exec. Bd RWE Umwelt AG, Viersen 2004–05, CEO RWE Trading GmbH, Essen 2005–08, Chief Financial Officer and in dual role mem. Group Business Cttee up to its termination –2007, RWE Supply & Trading GmbH (RWEST), Essen 2008–09, Programme Man., Essen April–Oct. 2009, CEO Essent NV 2009–11, mem. Exec. Bd and CEO Bd of RWE AG, Essen 2011–12, CEO RWE AG 2012–16, CEO RWE International SE 2016–. *Address:* RWE International SE, Opernplatz 1, 45128 Essen, Germany (office). *Telephone:* (201) 1215025 (office). *Fax:* (201) 1215265 (office). *E-mail:* info@rwe.com (office). *Website:* www.rwe.com (office).

TEROKHIN, Serhiy Anatolijovych; Ukrainian economist and politician; b. 29 Sept. 1963, Kyiv; m. Svitlana Terokhina; one s. one d.; ed Nat. Taras Shevchenko Univ. of Kyiv; joined Army 1986–88; Asst Chair., Head of Marketing, Ukrainian Republican Bank, Bank for Foreign Trade of USSR 1988–91; Head of Monetary and Financial Dept, Minister of Foreign Econ. Relations 1991–92; Chief, Dept of Monetary and Financial Policy, Econ. Bd, State Duma of Ukraine June–Nov. 1992; Deputy Minister of the Economy and Head of Dept of Financial and External Econ. Activity 1992–93; Dir Ukrainian Fund on Support of Reforms 1993–94; elected mem. Parl. (Fatherland—Batkivshchyna) 1994, Head of Tax and Customs Cttee 2007–10, apptd Deputy Head of Cttee on Public Finances 2010; Scientific Researcher, Harvard Univ. 1995; Minister of the Economy 2005; Co-Chair. Open Society Inst. 1997; Head of Asscn of Tax Payers of Ukraine 1999. *Address:* Verkhovna Rada, 01008 Kyiv, vul. M. Hrushevskoho 5, Ukraine (office). *Telephone:* (44) 255-28-07 (office). *Fax:* (44) 255-25-91 (office). *E-mail:* Teriokhin .Serhii@rada.gov.ua (office). *Website:* www.rada.gov.ua (office).

TERRACCIANO, Pasquale; Italian diplomatist; *Ambassador to Russia;* b. 4 May 1956, Naples; m. Karen Lawrence; two s. one d.; ed Univ. of Naples; joined Diplomatic Service 1981, Second Sec., Human Resources Directorate, Ministry of Foreign Affairs 1982–85, Consul at Consulate-Gen., Rio de Janeiro 1985–89, First Sec., later Counsellor 1991, Perm. Representation to NATO, Brussels 1989–93, Counsellor, Econ. Affairs Directorate, Ministry of Foreign Affairs 1993–95, Counsellor, Pvt. Sec. to Sec. of State for Foreign Affairs 1995–96, Counsellor, later First Counsellor 1998, Embassy in London and Alt. Exec. Dir for Italy, EBRD 1996–2000, First Counsellor, Perm. Representation to the Atlantic Council, Brussels 2000–01, Deputy Head of Cabinet of Sec. of State for Foreign Affairs 2001–04, Head of Information and Press Office and Spokesman for Sec. of State for Foreign Affairs 2004–06, Amb. to Spain 2006–10, Chef de Cabinet, Sec. of State for Foreign Affairs 2010–11, Diplomatic Adviser to the Prime Minister and Prime Minister's G8 and G20 Sherpa Rep. 2011–13, Amb. to UK and Perm. Rep. to IMO, London 2013–18, to Russia 2018–. *Address:* Embassy of Italy, 121002 Moscow, Denezhnyi per. 5, Russia (office). *Telephone:* (495) 956-60-93 (office). *Fax:* (495) 241-03-30 (office). *E-mail:* embitaly.mosca@esteri.it (office). *Website:* www .ambmosca.esteri.it (office).

TERRAGNO, Rodolfo H., DJur; Argentine lawyer, politician and writer; *Ambassador to UNESCO;* b. 16 Nov. 1943, Buenos Aires; m. Sonía Pascual Sánchez; two s.; ed Univ. de Buenos Aires; Ed.-in-Chief Confirmed magazine, Buenos Aires 1967–68; Pres. Terragno SA de Industrias Químicas 1970–76; Ed. Magazine Survey, Buenos Aires 1973–76; Asst Prof., Univ. de Buenos Aires 1973–80; Exec. Vice-Pres. El Diario de Caracas SA 1976–80; Researcher, Inst. of Latin American Studies, London 1980–82, LSE 1980–82; Vice-Pres. ALA Enterprises Inc., Miami and New York, USA 1982–86; Minister of Works and Public Services 1987–89; mem. Parl. 1993–95, 1997–99, Vice-Pres. Budget and Finance Cttee 1997–99, mem. Group of Five who led alliance govt 1997–99; Pres. UCR 1995–97; Chief of Cabinet of Ministers of the Nat. Exec. 1999–2000; Nat. Senator for City of Buenos Aires 2001–07; Amb. to UNESCO 2016–; Dir Letters SAH, Luxembourg 1982–86, Latin American Newsletters Ltd, London and Paris 1982–86; rep. at int. conferences, including dispute with UK over Falkland Islands 1983–85; Pres. Fundación Argentina Siglo 21 1986–87, Academic Council of 21st Century Univ., Córdoba and Buenos Aires 2010–; columnist, Noticias, Debate, La Opinión, Diario Clarín; mem. American Philosophical Soc. 2010–, American Acad. of Arts and Sciences 2012–; San Martín Nat. Inst. Scholar 2010–; Academician, Argentina Acad. of History 2011–; Hon. mem. Nat. Council of the Anticorruption Civil Asscn; Ordre Nat. du Mérite 1987, Cavaliere di Gran Croce (Italy) 1987, Medalha Mérito Maua (Brazil) 1987. *Publications include:* Los dueños del poder 1972, Los 400 días de Perón 1974, Contratapas 1976, Muerte y resurrección de los políticos 1981, La Argentina del Siglo 21 1985, The Challenge of Real Development 1987, Proyecto 95 1993, El Nuevo Modelo 1994, Bases para un Modelo de Crecimiento, Empleo y Bienestar (ed.) 1996, Maitland & San Martín 1998, Falklands/Malvinas 2002, El peronismo de los 70 2005, La Simulación 2005, Historia y futuro de las Malvinas 2006, Diario íntimo de San Martín 2009, Urgente. Llamado al País 2011, Josefa 2015. *Address:* Maison de l'UNESCO, 1, rue Miollis 75015, Paris Cedex 15 France (office). *Telephone:* 1-45-68-34-38 (office). *Fax:* 1-43-06-60-35 (office). *E-mail:* dl.argentina@unesco-delegations.org (office); rodolfo@terragno.org.ar. *Website:* www.terragno.org.ar.

TERRY, (John) Quinlan, CBE, FRIBA; British architect; b. 24 July 1937, Hampstead, London, England; s. of Philip Terry and Phyllis Terry; m. Christina de Ruttié 1961; one s. four d.; ed Bryanston School, Architectural Asscn; joined the late Raymond Erith RA 1962–73; works principally in classical Palladian architectural styles; pvt. practice Quinlan Terry Architects LLP 1973–, work includes large classical pvt. houses in stone erected in England, USA and Germany, including six pvt. villas in Regent's Park for Crown Estate Commrs, offices, shops and flats at Richmond Riverside, new Lecture Theatre, Jr Common Room, Library and residential bldgs for Downing Coll. Cambridge, restoration of the three State Rooms at No. 10 Downing Street, new commercial bldg 20–32 Baker Street, new retail bldg at Merchant Square, Colonial Williamsburg, Va, USA, Queen Mother Square, Poundbury, Dorset, Kilboy, Repub. of Ireland; mem. Royal Fine Art Comm. 1996–98; Rome Scholar 1969, Philippe Rothier European Prize for the Reconstruction of the City of Archives d'Architecture Moderne 1982, Prix Int. de la Reconstruction 1983, Building of the Year Award 1994 (for Maitland Robinson Library at Downing Coll., Cambridge), Best Modern Classical House Award, British Georgian Group (for Ferne House in Wilts.) 2003, Georgian Groups' Award for Best Modern Classical House 2005, Richard H. Driehaus Prize 2005, The Georgian Group Awards 2015. *Publications include:* Architectural Monographs 1991, Architects Anonymous 1993, Radical Classicism 2006, The Practice of Classical Architecture 2015. *Leisure interest:* theology. *Address:* Quinlan Terry Architects LLP, Old Exchange, High Street, Dedham, Colchester, Essex, CO7 6HA, England (office). *Telephone:* (1206) 323186 (office); (1206) 322370 (office). *E-mail:* quinlan@qftarchitects.com (office). *Website:* www.qftarchitects.com (office).

TERZIĆ, Adnan, BA; Bosnia and Herzegovina politician; b. 5 April 1960, Zagreb; m.; one s.; ed Univ. of Sarajevo; worked in Municipality of Travnik 1987–92; served in army 1992–95; Chair. of Exec. Bd Municipality of Travnik 1995–96; Gov. Cen. Bosnia canton 1997–98, 2000–01; Prime Minister 2002–07, Head of SDA Club of Reps, House of Reps 2000–02, concurrently Minister of European Integration; mem. Party of Democratic Action (Stranka Demokratske Akcije–SDA) 1991–2009, Vice-Pres. 2001–09; Vice-Pres. Agram BiH 2008–10; mem. Bd of Dirs GP Put d.d. Sarajevo 2012–; mem. Union for a Better Future (Savez za Bolju Budućnost—SBB) 2010–, Vice-Pres. 2010–12. *Address:* Union for a Better Future, Tešanjska 24a, 71000 Sarajevo, Bosnia and Herzegovina (office). *Telephone:* (33) 942551 (office). *Fax:* (33) 261255 (office). *E-mail:* info@sbbbh.ba (office). *Website:* www.sbb.ba (office).

TESAURO, Giuseppe; Italian professor of international law and judge; b. 15 Nov. 1942, Naples; m. Paola Borrelli 1967; three c.; ed Liceo Umberto, Naples, Univ. of Naples, Max Planck Inst. Volkerrecht-Heidelberg; Asst Prof. of Int. Law, Univ. of Naples 1965–71; Prof. of Int. Law and Int. Org., Univs of Catania, Messina, Naples, Rome 1971–88; Dir EEC Law School, Univ. of Rome 1982–88; mem. Council Legal Affairs, Ministry of Foreign Affairs 1986–; Judge, First Advocate Gen. European Court of Justice 1988–98; Pres. Italian Competition Authority 1998–2004; Judge, Constitutional Court 2005–14, Pres. July–Nov. 2014; Chair. Banca Carige 2016–18. *Publications:* Financing International Institutions 1968, Pollution of the Sea and International Law 1971, Nationalizations and International Law 1976, Movements of Capital in the EEC 1984, Course of EEC Law 2012. *Leisure interests:* tennis, football, sailing.

TESCH, Peter Martin, BA (Hons); Australian diplomatist; *Ambassador to the Russian Federation;* b. 6 Dec. 1965; ed Univ. of Queensland; joined Dept of Foreign Affairs and Trade (DFAT) 1987, Third Sec., Embassy in Moscow 1989–91, Minister of Commerce Office Work, Parl. House 1993–94, Amb. to Kazakhstan 1997–99, Gen. Agents and Man. Dir World Exhbn, Hanover 2000, Deputy Perm. Rep., Perm. Mission to UN, New York 2002–05, Commr-Gen. and Exec. Dir World Expo 2010, Shanghai 2008–10, Amb. to Germany (also accred to Switzerland and Liechtenstein) 2009–15, to the Russian Fed. (also accred to Armenia, Belarus, Kazakhstan, Kyrgyzstan, Moldova, Tajikistan, Turkmenistan and Uzbekistan) 2016–, Head of Int. Security Div., DFAT. *Address:* Embassy of Australia, 109028 Moscow, Podkolokolnyi per. 10a/2, Russian Federation (office). *Telephone:* (495) 956-60-70 (office). *Fax:* (495) 956-61-70 (office). *E-mail:* austembmos@dfat.gov.au (office). *Website:* www.russia.embassy.gov.au (office).

TESFAMARIAM, Lt Gen. Yohannes Gebremeskel; Ethiopian army officer and UN official; b. 1960, Tigray; m.; three c.; ed Addis Ababa Univ.; served as Head of Peacekeeping Dept, Head of Mil. Intelligence Dept, Ministry of Nat. Defence, Commdr, Army Corps; fmr Commr, UN Mission in Ethiopia and Eritrea (UNMEE); Deputy Force Commdr, UN Interim Security Force for Abyei (UNISFA) 2012–13, Head of Mission and Force Commdr 2013–14, Force Commdr, UN Mission in South Sudan (UNMISS) 2014–16.

TESFAY, Lt-Gen. Tadesse Werede, MBA; Ethiopian army officer and UN official; b. 13 July 1958; m.; four c.; joined Nat. Defence Forces, held several posts including Head of Jt Training Dept, Commdr Army Corps, mem. Defence Commdrs Council, Head of Mission and Force Commdr, UN Interim Security Force for Abyei (UNISFA) 2011–13.

TESHABAEV, Muxammadyusuf M.; Uzbekistani politician; b. 27 Nov. 1954, Andijon; m.; three c.; ed Tashkent Nat. Econ. Inst.; Deputy Head of Trade for the Andijan region and Chair. JSC Andizhongazmol 1989–96; Head of Directorate of Strategic Planning and Internal Trade, UzDaewooAuto 1996–2002; with Noldkomeksrim Co. Ltd (food import-export co.) 2003–05; Deputy Council of People's Deputies for Andijan region 1990–94; mem. Movt of Entrepreneurs and Businessmen—Liberal Democratic Party of Uzbekistan (Tadbirkorlar va Ishbilarmonlar Harakati—O'zbekiston Liberal Demokratik Partiyasi) (O'zlidep), Vice-Chair. Exec. Cttee 2003–05, fmr Chair. Exec. Cttee; mem. Legis. Chamber (Qonunchilik palatasi) Oliy Majlis 2005–, Chair. Cttee on Agric. and Water Man. *Address:* Movement of Entrepreneurs and Businessmen—Liberal Democratic Party of Uzbekistan (O'zlidep), 100015 Tashkent, Mirobod tumani, Nukus ko'ch. 73A, Uzbekistan (office). *Telephone:* (71) 255-27-99 (office). *Fax:* (71) 255-62-11 (office). *E-mail:* uzlidep@intal.uz (office). *Website:* www.uzlidep.uz (office).

TESHOME WIRTU, Mulatu; Ethiopian politician, diplomatist and fmr head of state; b. 1956, Arjo, Welega Prov. (now Oromo Region); one s.; ed Peking Univ., People's Repub. of China; Deputy Minister of Econ. Devt and Cooperation during mid-1990s, Minister of Agric. 2001–03; Speaker, House of Fed. (upper house of parl.) 2002–05; fmr Amb. to People's Repub. of China and Japan, Amb. to Turkey 2006–13; Pres. of Ethiopia 2013–18; mem. Oromo People's Democratic Org.

TESSON, Philippe, DèsSc; French journalist and publishing executive; b. 1 March 1928, Wassigny (Aisne); s. of Albert Tesson and Jeanne Ancely; m. Dr Marie-Claude Millet 1969 (died 2014); one s. two d.; ed Coll. Stanislas, Inst. of Political Studies; Sec. of Parl. Debates 1957–60; Ed.-in-Chief, Combat 1960–74; cand. in legis. elections 1968; Diarist and Drama Critic, Canard Enchaîné 1970–83; Co-Man. and Dir Soc. d'Editions Scientifiques et Culturelles 1971, Pres. 1980; Founder, Man. Dir and Ed.-in-Chief, Quotidien de Paris 1974–94; Dir Nouvelles Littéraires 1975–83; Drama Critic, L'Express Paris 1986; Dir and Co.-

Man. Quotidien du Maire 1988; Animator (TV programme with France 3) A Quel Titre 1994–96; Ed. Valeurs actuelles 1994–; Drama Critic, Revue des deux Mondes 1990, Figaro Magazine 1995; literary and theatre corresp., Rive Droite/Rive Gauche (TV) 1997–2004; Dir Avant-scène Théâtre 2001; jury mem. Prix Interallié 2013; Chevalier, Légion d'honneur 1987, Officier, Légion d'honneur 2009. *Publications include:* De Gaulle 1er 1965, Où est passée l'autorité? 2000, La Campagne de France 2012.

TESTER, Jonathan (Jon), BS; American farmer and politician; *Senator from Montana;* b. 21 Aug. 1956, Havre, Mont.; m. Sharla Tester; one s. one d.; ed Coll. of Great Falls; took over family farm 1978, also taught music at F.E. Miley Elementary School; elected to Big Sandy School Bd, also served on Big Sandy Soil Conservation Service Cttee, Chouteau Co. Agricultural Stabilization and Conservation Service Cttee; elected to Mont. State Senate 1998, Minority Whip 2001, Minority Leader 2003, Pres. Mont. Senate 2005–06; Senator from Montana 2007–; Democrat. *Address:* 311 Hart Senate Office Building, Washington, DC 20510-2604, USA (office). *Telephone:* (202) 224-2644 (office). *Fax:* (202) 224-8594 (office). *Website:* tester.senate.gov (office).

TESTINO, Mario, OBE; Peruvian fashion photographer; b. 30 Oct. 1954, Lima; ed Universidad del Pacífico, Pontificia Universidad Católica del Perú, Univ. of San Diego, USA; portfolio includes Madonna for Versace, Princess of Wales for Vanity Fair 1997, advertising campaign for Gucci, Sir Hardy Amies, John Galliano, Jade Jagger, Naomi Campbell, Devon Aoki and Alexander McQueen for Vogue's Millennium souvenir issue 2000; work exhibited in Nat. Portrait Gallery, London 2001–02; f. MATE—Museo Mario Testino, Lima 2012; Pres. World Monuments Fund Peru 2014–; Hon. Fellow, Royal Photographic Soc. 2011; Grand Cross Order of Merit for Distinguished Service 2010, Chevalier de la Légion d'Honneur (France) 2017; Dr hc (Univ. of the Arts London) 2004; British Style Award 2003, Tiradentes Medal 2007, Hero Award, New York 2008, Walpole Award for services to the luxury industry, London 2009, Queen Sofía Spanish Inst. Gold Medal 2011, AmfAR Inspiration Award, São Paulo 2012, Best Photographer in the World Award, Spanish Vogue 2014, Int. Center of Photography Infinity Award 2015. *Publications include:* Visionaire 35: Man 2000, Mario Testino: Portraits 2003, Mario Testino: Kids 2003, Let Me In 2007. *E-mail:* info@mariotestino.com. *Website:* www.mariotestino.com.

TETANGCO, Amando M., Jr, AB (Econ), MA; Philippine fmr central banker; b. 14 Nov. 1952; m. Elvira Ma. Plana; one s. two d.; ed Ateneo de Manila Univ., Univ. of Wisconsin-Madison, USA (Central Bank scholar); worked with Man. Services Div. of SGV & Co. 1973–74; joined Bangko Sentral ng Pilipinas (BSP—Cen. Bank of the Philippines) 1974, Deputy Gov. BSP in-charge of Banking Services Sector, Econ. Research and Treasury –2005, represented BSP at Nat. Econ. and Devt Authority Bd, Nat. Food Authority Council, Industrial Guarantee and Loan Fund Review Cttee, also served as Alt. Exec. Dir IMF, Washington, DC 1992–94, closely involved with various int. and regional orgs including Exec. Meeting of East Asia and Pacific Cen. Banks, ASEAN and ASEAN +3, South East Asia Cen. Banks (SEACEN) and APEC, Gov. BSP 2005–17; named Central Banker of the Year (Asia-Pacific) by The Banker magazine 2013.

TETT, Gillian, PhD; British anthropologist, journalist and author; *US Managing Editor, Financial Times;* b. 10 July 1967; ed Clare Coll., Cambridge; joined Financial Times 1993, worked in fmr USSR and Europe and in Econs Dept, Bureau Chief, Tokyo 1997–2003, Deputy Head of Lex column 2003, fmr Asst Ed., US Managing Ed. 2010–12, 2014–; Dr hc (Baruch Coll., CUNY) 2013; Wincott Prize 2007, British Business Journalist of the Year 2008, British Press Awards Journalist of the Year 2009, British Acad. President's Medal 2011, Society of American Business Editors and Writers (SABEW) Award for best feature article 2012, Columnist of the Year, British Press Awards 2014, Royal Anthropological Institute Marsh Award 2014. *Publications include:* Saving the Sun: A Wall Street Gamble to Rescue Japan from Its Trillion Dollar Meltdown 2004, Fool's Gold: How Unrestrained Greed Corrupted a Dream, Shattered Global Markets and Unleashed a Catastrophe (Spear's Book Awards Financial Book of the Year 2009) 2009, The Silo Effect 2015. *Address:* The Financial Times Newspaper Group, 1330 Avenue of the Americas, New York, NY 10019-5436, USA (office). *E-mail:* gillian.tett@ft.com (office). *Website:* www.ft.com/comment/columnists/gillian-tett (office).

TETTEH, Hanna Serwaa, LLB; Ghanaian barrister, politician and diplomatist; *Special Representative to African Union and Head, United Nations Office at African Union;* b. 31 May 1967, Szeged, Hungary; ed Univ. of Ghana, Ghana Law School; Barrister-at-Law 1992; Legal Officer Int. Fed. of Women Lawyers (FIDA) 1992–93; Legal Practioner Ansa-Ansa & Co. 1993–94; Legal Officer Comm. on Human Rights and Admin. Justice, Accra April–Aug. 1995; Legal Adviser Ghana Agro Food Co. Ltd 1995–2000, Gen. Man. Corporate, Legal and Admin 2005–08; mem. Parl. Nat. Democratic Congress (Awutu Senya Constituency) 2001–05, for Awutu Senya West Constituency 2013–17; Communications Dir Nat. Democratic Congress May–Dec. 2008; Minister of Trade and Industry 2009–13, of Foreign Affairs and Regional Integration 2013–17; Chair. Ghana Free Zones Bd 2009–13; Chair. Council of Ministers, Econ. Community of West African States (ECOWAS) 2014–15; Sr Lawyer Oseawuo Chambers & Co. 2017–18; Dir-Gen. UN Office at Nairobi (UNON) July 2018–March 2019; Special Rep. to African Union and Head UN Office of African Union (UNOAU) 2018–; mem. Econ. Man. Team, Ghana 2009–13; mem. Bd of Dirs Millennium Devt Authority 2009–13; Richard von Weizsäcker Fellow, Robert Bosch Acad. 2018–. *Address:* United Nations Office at African Union, Menelik II Avenue, UNECA Compound, Zambezi Building, 5th and 6th floors, PO Box 1357, Addis Ababa, Ethiopia (office). *Website:* www.unoau.unmissions.org (office).

TEUFEL, Erwin; German politician; b. 4 Sept. 1939, Rottweil; m.; four c.; Dist Admin. Rottweil and Trossingen municipality 1961–64; Mayor of Spaichingen 1964–72; mem. State Parl. of Baden-Württemberg 1972–2006; Leader CDU Parl. Group 1978–91; Minister-Pres. of Baden-Württemberg 1991–2005; mem. Bundesrat 1991–2005 (Pres. 1996–97); Regional Chair. CDU-Baden-Württemberg 1991–2005, Deputy Chair. CDU 1992–98; Pres. German-French Inst., Ludwigsburg 2005–; mem. Central Cttee of German Catholics 1983–, German Ethics Council 2008–12; Foundation of Rotary Int. Paul Harris Fellow 1998; Hon. Senator, European Acad. of Sciences 2004, Univ. of Tuebingen 2005; Großes Verdienstkreuz with Star of Merit 1994, with Star and Sash of Merit 1999, Grand Cross of Merit 2004; Hon. DJur (Univ. of Massachusetts 1999); Dr hc (Univ. in Oradea, Romania) 2000, (Agricultural Univ. of Timisoara, Romania) 2000; Golden Badge of Honor 2005, Franco-German Cultural Award, European Cultural Foundation 2005. *Address:* Dreifaltigkeitsbergstrasse 44, 78549 Spaichingen, Germany (home). *Telephone:* (74) 24502259. *Fax:* (74) 24502353. *Website:* www.erwinteufel.de.

TEVDOVSKI, Dragan, MSc, PhD; Macedonian economist, academic and government official; *Minister of Finance;* b. 21 Jan. 1979, Skopje, Socialist Repub. of Macedonia, Socialist Fed. Repub. of Yugoslavia; ed Faculty of Econs, Univ. of Belgrade, Serbia, Faculty of Econs, SS Cyril and Methodius Univ., Skopje; Assoc. Prof., Faculty of Econs, SS Cyril and Methodius Univ.; Postdoctoral Research Fellow, Center for Research in Econometric Analysis of Time Series (CREATES), Aarhus Univ., Denmark 2013–14; study visit to George Washington Univ., Washington, DC, USA; has participated in numerous scientific confs, seminars and summer schools abroad; has also worked on several int. projects; has lectured at First Training of Investment Advisors, organized by Securities and Exchange Comm.; involved in training employees in largest cos in Macedonia; Minister of Finance 2017–. *Publications:* books: Business Statistics and Economics, Introduction to Time Series Analysis; five scientific articles, eight policy analyses and two scientific monographs on applied econometrics, macroeconomic policy and labour markets. *Address:* Ministry of Finance, 1000 Skopje, ul. Dame Gruev 12, North Macedonia (office). *Telephone:* (2) 3255300 (office). *Fax:* (2) 3255721 (office). *E-mail:* finance@finance.gov.mk (office). *Website:* www.finance.gov.mk (office).

TEVES, Margarito (Gary) B., BA, MSc; Philippine economist and government official; *Chairman, Think Tank Inc.;* ed Universidad Cen. de Madrid, Spain, Williams Coll., USA, London School of Econs, UK; several positions in pvt. sector with cos such as Tolong Sugar Milling Corpn, Ayala Corpn, Ayala Foundation, also taught Economics at Ateneo de Manila Univ. 1968–84; mem. Congress for 3rd district of Negros Oriental 1987–98, Chair. Cttee on Rural Devt, on Econ. Affairs; Chair. and CEO Think Tank Inc. (consultancy) 1998–2000, Chair. 2010–; Pres. and CEO Land Bank of the Philippines 2000–05; Sec. of Finance 2005–10; mem. Bd of Dirs Landbank Countryside Development Foundation, Alphaland Corpn, Atok-Big Wedge Corpn; mem. Advisory Bd Metro Bank and Trust Co.; f. Corporate Planning Soc. of the Philippines; fmr Pres. Philippine Econ. Soc.; fmr Trustee Philippine Futuristics Soc.; Dr hc (Williams Coll.) 2011; Best Finance Minister in Asia, The Banker magazine 2009. *Address:* Think Tank Inc., Great Wall Building, No. 136 Yakal Street, Makati City 1203, Philippines (office). *Website:* www.think-tank-inc.com (office).

TÉVOÉDJRÈ, Albert, LèsL; Benin politician and international civil servant; b. 10 Nov. 1929, Porto Novo; s. of Joseph Tévoédjrè and Jeanne Singbo Tévoédjrè; m. Isabelle Ekué 1953; three s.; ed Toulouse Univ., France, Fribourg Univ. and Institut Universitaire de Hautes Etudes Internationales, Switzerland, Sloan School of Management, Massachusetts Inst. of Tech., USA; teaching assignments include Lycée Delafosse, Dakar, Senegal 1952–54, Ecole Normale d'Institutrices, Cahors, France 1957–58, Lycée Victor Ballot, Porto Novo 1959–61, Geneva Africa Inst. 1963–64, Georgetown Univ., Washington, DC 1964; Sec. of State for Information 1961–62; Sec.-Gen. Union Africaine et Malgache (UAM) 1962–63; Research Assoc., Center for Int. Affairs, Harvard Univ. 1964–65; joined Int. Labour Office 1965, Regional Dir for Africa March 1966, Asst Dir-Gen. 1969–75, Deputy Dir-Gen. 1975; Dir Int. Inst. for Labour Studies 1975–84; Sec.-Gen. World Social Prospects Asscn (AMPS) 1980; fmr Chief Ed. L'Etudiant d'Afrique Noire; Minister of Planning and Employment Promotion 1997–99; Chair. Millennium for Africa Comm. –2002; Special Envoy of the UN Sec.-Gen. in Ivory Coast 2003–05; Ombudsman, Presidential Mediation Bd (OPM) 2006–13 (retd); Founding mem. Promotion Africaine (soc. to combat poverty in Africa); Founding mem. Nat. Liberation Movt and mem. Cttee 1958–60; Deputy Sec.-Gen. of Nat. Syndicate of Teachers, Dahomey 1959–60; Assoc. Prof., Sorbonne, Paris 1976–78, Univ. des Mutants, Dakar 1979, Nat. Univ. of Côte d'Ivoire 1979, Northwestern Univ. 1980; Int. Humanitarian Medal 1987. *Publications:* L'Afrique revoltée 1958, La formation des cadres africains en vue de la croissance économique 1965, Pan-Africanism in Action 1965, L'Afrique face aux problèmes du socialisme et de l'aide étrangère 1966, Une stratégie du progrès social en Afrique et la contribution de l'OIT 1969, Pour un contrat de solidarité 1976, La pauvreté—richesse des peuples 1978.

TEWARI, Manish, BA, LLB; Indian lawyer and politician; b. 8 Dec. 1965, Chandigarh; s. of Dr Vishwanath Tewari and Amrit Kaur; m. Naaznin B. Shafa 1996; one d.; ed Punjab Univ., Chandigarh, Univ. of Delhi; Coll. Unit Pres., Nat. Students' Union of India (NSUI), DAV Coll., Chandigarh 1981–82, Gen. Sec., NSUI, Chandigarh 1982–83, Jt Sec., NSUI Nat. Cttee 1984, Gen. Sec., NSUI Nat. Cttee 1985, Nat. Pres. NSUI 1988–93; mem. All India Congress Cttee 1991, Sec. 1997–98, 2004, Nat. Spokesperson 2008; Pres. Int. Union of Students 1992–93; Nat. Pres. Indian Youth Congress 1998–2000; elected to 15th Lok Sabha (lower house of Parl.) for Ludhiana (Punjab) constituency 2009–14; Union Cabinet Minister of State (Ind. Charge) for Information and Broadcasting 2012–14. *Leisure interests:* swimming, running, reading history books. *Address:* 28 - A, Sarabha Nagar, Pakhowal Road, Ludhiana 141 003, Punjab (home); C - I/3, Lodhi Garden, New Delhi 110 003, India (home). *Telephone:* (161) 2450009 (Ludhiana) (home); (11) 24644627 (Delhi) (home). *Fax:* (161) 2451009 (Ludhiana) (home); (11) 24658384 (Delhi) (office). *E-mail:* manishtewari@hotmail.com (home); manish.tewari@sansad.nic.in (office).

TEYSSEN, Johannes, DrIur; German business executive; *Chairman of the Board of Management and CEO, E.ON SE;* b. 10 Sept. 1959, Hildesheim; ed Univs of Freiburg and Göttingen; doctoral studies scholarship in Boston, Mass, USA 1984; Research Asst, Univ. of Göttingen 1984–86; law clerk, State Superior Court, Celle, Bar examination (Assessorexamen) 1986–89; Head of Energy and Corp. Law Dept, PreussenElektra AG, Hanover 1991–94, Head of Legal Affairs (Regional Utilities) 1994–98; mem. Bd of Man. HASTRA AG, Hanover 1998–99; Chair. Bd of Man. AVACON AG, Helmstedt 1999–2001; mem. Bd of Man. E.ON Energie AG, Munich 2001–03, Chair. 2003–07, mem. Bd of Man. E.ON AG, Düsseldorf 2004–08, Vice-Chair. 2008–10, Chair. (CEO) 2010– (E.ON SE from 2012). *Address:* E.ON SE, E.ON-Platz 1, 40479 Düsseldorf, Germany (office). *Telephone:* (211) 45790 (office). *Fax:* (211) 4579501 (office). *E-mail:* info@eon.com (office). *Website:* www.eon.com (office).

THABANE, Motsoahae Thomas (Tom), BA; Lesotho politician and civil servant; *Prime Minister;* b. 28 May 1939, Maseru; m. Lipolelo Thabane (died 2017); two s. two d.; ed Univ. of South Africa; worked as civil servant for 26 years, First Clerk Asst to Senate and Deputy to Clerk of the Senate, Parl. of Lesotho 1966–70, Asst Sec. (Admin), Ministries of Health and Education 1970–72, Prin. Sec. in various govt ministries including Justice 1972–76, Health 1978–83, Foreign Affairs 1983–85 and Interior 1985–86, Sec. to ruling Mil. Council and also political adviser to the Mil. 1986–88, Govt Sec. 1988–90; Minister of Foreign Affairs, Information and Broadcasting 1990–91; escaped to South Africa following mil. coup in April 1991, worked as devt consultant; following April 1993 democratic elections, re-opened an office as devt consultant and commodities broker 1994–95; joined Ind. Electoral Comm. as Prov. Office Admin. for Free State region, South Africa March–June 1994; Special Political Adviser to Prime Minister Ntsu Mokhehle 1995–98; elected mem. Parl. (Abia constituency) 1998; Minister of Foreign Affairs 2001–02, of Home Affairs and Public Safety 2002–04, of Communications, Science and Tech. 2005–07; Prime Minister and Minister of Defence, Police and Nat. Security 2012–15 (fled to South Africa accusing the military of staging a coup 30 Aug. 2014, returned four days later), Prime Minister 2017–; Pres. All Basotho Convention party 2007–. *Leisure interests:* politics, reading, physical fitness, walking, light classic and traditional music, jazz rhythm and blues. *Address:* Office of the Prime Minister, PO Box 527, Maseru 100, Lesotho (office). *Telephone:* 22326359 (office). *Fax:* 22310444 (office). *Website:* www.gov.ls/pm (office).

THAÇI, Hashim, PhD; Kosovo politician, fmr guerrilla leader and head of state; *President;* b. 24 April 1968, Burojë/Broćna, Autonomous Province of Kosovo and Metohija, Socialist Repub. of Serbia, Socialist Fed. Repub. of Yugoslavia; m. Lumnije Thaçi; one s.; ed Univ. of Prishtina, Univ. of Zurich, Switzerland; student leader and first student pres. of parallel Albanian Univ. of Prishtina 1989; joined Albanian political émigré group in Switzerland 1993, Co-founder Lëvizja Popullore e Kosovës (People's Movt of Kosovo); became mem. inner circle of Ushtria Çlirimtare e Kosovës (UÇK—Kosovo Liberation Army), later Commdr UÇK, and Dir Political Group; Chair. Partia Demokratike e Kosovës (Democratic Party of Kosovo) 2000–16, mem. Parl. Group 2006–16; mem. and Prime Minister, Interim Admin. Council, Kosovo 1999–2000, Prime Minister of Kosovo 2008–14, Deputy Prime Minister and Minister of Foreign Affairs 2014–16; Pres. of Kosovo 2016–; Key of the City of Tirana, Albania 2008; Hon. Citizen of Ulcinj, Montenegro 2015; Hon. Dr of Int. Relations (Geneva School of Diplomacy) 2012. *Address:* Office of the President, 10000 Prishtina, Rruga Nënë Terezë, Kosovo (office). *Telephone:* (38) 213222 (office). *Fax:* (38) 211651 (office). *E-mail:* protocol@president-ksgov.net (office). *Website:* www.president-ksgov.net (office).

THACKERAY, Uddhav; Indian politician; *President, Shiv Sena;* b. 27 July 1960, Mumbai; s. of Bal Keshav Thackeray; m. Rashmi Thackeray; two s.; ed J J School of Arts, Mumbai; Exec. Pres., Shiv Sena 2003–12, Party Pres. 2013–; Ed.-in-Chief, Saamna 2006–. *Publications include:* Maharashtra Desh (photo book) 2010, Pahava Vitthal (photo book) 2011. *Leisure interest:* photography. *Address:* Shiv Sena, Shiv Sena Bhavan, Ram Ganesh Gadkari Chowk, Dadar, Mumbai 400 028, India (office). *Telephone:* (22) 24328181. *E-mail:* mazamaharashtra@shivsena.org. *Website:* www.shivsena.org; uddhavthackeray.com.

THADA-THAMRONGVECH, Suchart, BA, MSc, PhD; Thai politician; b. 8 Aug. 1952; ed Thammasat Univ., London School of Econs, UK, McMaster Univ., Canada, Nat. Defence Coll.; Vice Chancellor of Int. Relations and Research Div., Ramkhamhaeng Univ. 1991–93; mem. Prov. Waterworks Authority 1992–95; mem. Audit Cttee, Bangkok Metropolitan Bank PLC 1998–2002; mem. Bd of Dirs Bank for Agric. and Agricultural Cooperatives 2001; mem. Metropolitan Waterworks Authority 2001–02; Adviser to Minister for Commerce 2003, to Minister for Energy 2003–05; Deputy Minister of Finance 2008, Minister of Finance 2008, of Educ. Jan.–Oct. 2012; Chair. Pheu Thai Party Sept.–Nov. 2008; Sr Advisor on Econs to the Prime Minister 2011; fmr mem. Securities and Exchange Comm.; fmr mem. and Chair. Examination Cttee Ratchaburi Electricity Generating PLC, PTT PLC, Siam City Bank PLC, Pan Asia Footwear PLC; Knight Grand Cordon (Special Class) of the Most Exalted Order of the White Elephant 2011.

THAHANE, Timothy T., BComm, MA; Lesotho government official and diplomatist; b. 2 Nov. 1940, Leribe; s. of Nicodemus Thahane and Beatrice Thahane; m. Dr Edith Mohapi 1972; one s. one d.; ed Lesotho High School, Univs of Newfoundland and Toronto, Canada; Asst Sec., Prin. Asst Sec., Cen. Planning Office 1968–70, Dir of Planning 1968–73; Amb. to EEC for Negotiations of Lomé Convention 1973–74; Alt. Exec. Dir (Africa Group 1) World Bank 1974–76, Exec. Dir 1976–78, representing 15 African countries and Trinidad and Tobago; Vice-Chair. and Chair., Jt Audit Cttee of World Bank Group 1976–78; Amb. to USA 1978–80; Vice-Pres. UN Affairs, IBRD 1990–96; Deputy Gov. South African Reserve Bank 1996–2002; Minister of Finance and Devt Planning 2002–12; mem. Nat. Ass. for Likhetlane Constituency No. 16 2012–; Minister of Energy, Meteorology and Water Affairs 2012–13; mem. Bd of Dirs Lesotho Bank (Vice-Chair. 1972–73), Third World Foundation, Centre for Econ. Devt and Population Activities, Global Coalition for Africa 1992; mem. Lesotho Congress for Democracy; charged by Maseru Magistrates Court with two cases of fraud relating to misrepresentations made about farming policy Nov. 2013, charges withdrawn 2016. *Publications:* articles on econ. planning and investment in Lesotho, Southern Africa and Africa in general. *Leisure interests:* reading, music.

THAIN, John A., BS, MBA; American business executive; ed Massachusetts Inst. of Tech., Harvard Univ.; Chief Financial Officer and Head of Operations, Tech. and Finance, Goldman Sachs Group LP 1994–99, also Co-CEO for European Operations 1995–97, Dir 1998–2003, Pres. and Co-COO 1999, Pres. and Co-COO Goldman Sachs Inc. 1999–2003, Pres. and COO 2003; CEO New York Stock Exchange (NYSE) 2004–07 (NYSE Euronext, Inc. following merger of NYSE Group and Euronext NV in June 2006); Chair. and CEO Merrill Lynch & Co., Inc. 2007–09 (resgnd); Chair. and CEO CIT Group Inc. 2010–16; mem. Bd of Dirs Blackrock Inc.; mem. several visiting cttees at MIT Sloan School of Management, Int. Advisory Panel of Monetary Authority of Singapore, US Nat. Advisory Bd of INSEAD (Institut Européen d'Admin des Affaires), Bd of Mans of New York Botanical Garden, Bd of Mans of New York-Presbyterian Hosp., Harvard Business School Bd of Dean's Advisors, Partnership for New York City.

THAKSIN SHINAWATRA, PhD; Thai business executive and politician; b. 26 July 1949, Chiangmai; brother of Yingluck Shinawatra; m. Pojaman Shinawatra (divorced 2008); three c.; ed Police Cadet Acad., Eastern Kentucky Univ., Sam Houston State Univ., USA; joined Royal Thai Police Dept 1973, Lt-Col 1987, resgnd 1987; Chair. Shinawatra Computer and Communications Group 1987–94; Minister of Foreign Affairs 1994–95; Leader Palang Dharma Party 1995–96; Deputy Prime Minister in charge of Traffic and Transportation in Bangkok 1995–96, Deputy Prime Minister 1997; Prime Minister of Thailand 2001–06 (re-elected 2005, briefly resigned position 4 April–23 May 2006, ousted in bloodless coup by army generals led by Gen. Sonthi Boonyaratglin for alleged "corruption and divisiveness" while abroad visiting UN Gen. Ass. in New York 19 Sept. 2006; Founder and Leader Thai Rak Thai Party 1998–2006; Founder and Vice-Chair. THAICOM Foundation for Secondary Educ. 1993; Pres. Northerners' Asscn of Thailand 1998; Chair. Manchester City Football Club 2007–08; special adviser to Cambodian govt 2009–10; convicted in absentia 2008, sentenced to two years in prison; family assets frozen by Supreme Court 2010; granted Montenegrin citizenship 2009; Hon. (External) mem. Police Cadet Acad. Council 1996–, Hon. mem. Asscn Ex-Mil. Officers 1998–; 1992 ASEAN Businessman of the Year Award, Lee Kuan Yew Exchange Fellowship 1994 and other awards.

THAKUR, Jai Ram, MA; Indian politician; *Chief Minister of Himachal Pradesh;* b. 6 Jan. 1965, Tandi Village, Himachal Pradesh; s. of Jethu Ram and Briku Devi; m. Sadhna Singh; two d.; ed Vallabh Govt Coll., Mandi, Punjab Univ.; MLA, Himachal Pradesh (HP) Legis. Ass. from Chachiot constituency (renamed Seraj 2008) 1998–, Chair. Rural Planning Cttee, Gen. Devt Cttee, Education Cttee, fmr mem. of various Cttees including Estimates, Public Undertakings, Ethics and Human Devt; HP Minister of Rural Devt and Panchayati Raj (political system) 2009–12; Chief Minister of Himachal Pradesh 2017–; Vice Chair. State Civil Supplies Corpn; mem. Bharatiya Janata Party (BJP), State Sec., Bharatiya Janta Yuva Morcha (BJP youth wing) 1993–95, State Vice-Pres., BJP 2003-05, State Pres., BJP 2006-09. *Address:* Set Nos. 109 & 110, Jawahar Vidhayak Sadan, Shimla 171004, Himachal Pradesh, India (office). *Telephone:* (177) 2622204 (office). *Fax:* (177) 2621154 (office). *E-mail:* jr.thakur@nic.in (office). *Website:* www.himachal.gov.in (office).

THAKUR, Mahantha; Nepalese politician; *President, Rastriya Janata Party—Nepal;* fmr Nepal Congress leader; Minister for Science and Tech. –2007 (resgnd); apptd Pres. Terai Madhes Loktantrik Party 2007; fmr Sr Leader, Nepali Congress Party; Pres. Rastriya Janata Party—Nepal 2017–; mem. House of Reps (Mahottari constituency) 2017–. *Address:* House of Representatives, Singerbar, Kathmandu, Nepal (office). *Telephone:* (1) 4200210 (office). *Website:* hr.parliament.gov.np.

THAKUR, Tirath Singh, BSc, LLB; Indian lawyer and judge; b. 4 Jan. 1952, Batroo, Ramban Dist; s. of Devi Das Thakur; enrolled as Pleader 1972 and joined chamber of his father Shri Devi Das Thakur; apptd Sr Advocate 1990, Additional Judge, High Court of Jammu and Kashmir Feb. 1994, then transferred to be Judge, High Court of Karnataka March 1994, apptd Permanent Judge 1995, Judge, High Court of Delhi 2004, Acting Chief Justice, High Court of Delhi April–July 2008, Chief Justice, High Court of Punjab and Haryana 2008–09, Judge, Supreme Court 2009–15, Chief Justice of India 2015–17. *Address:* c/o Office of the Chief Justice of India, Supreme Court, Tilak Marg, New Delhi 110 001, India (office).

THALER, Richard H., BA, MA, PhD; American economist, author and columnist; *Charles R. Walgreen Distinguished Service Professor of Behavioral Science and Economics, Booth School of Business, University of Chicago;* b. 12 Sept. 1945, East Orange, NJ; s. of Alan M. Thaler and Roslyn Thaler (née Melnikoff); one s. two d.; ed Newark Acad., Case Western Reserve Univ., Univ. of Rochester; Instructor, Graduate School of Man., Univ. of Rochester 1971–74, Asst Prof. 1974–78; Asst Prof. of Econs and Public Admin, Graduate School of Business and Public Admin, Cornell Univ. 1978–80, Assoc. Prof., Johnson Graduate School of Man. 1980–86, Prof. of Econs 1986–88, Henrietta Johnson Louis Prof. of Econs and Dir, Center for Behavioral Econs and Decision Research 1988–95; joined Univ. of Chicago Booth School of Business 1995, fmr Ralph and Dorothy Keller Distinguished Service Prof. of Behavioral Science and Econs, currently Charles R. Walgreen Distinguished Service Prof. of Behavioral Science and Econs; Visiting Scholar, Nat. Bureau of Econ. Research 1977–78, Russell Sage Foundation 1991–92; Visiting Prof., Univ. of British Columbia, Vancouver 1984–85; Founder, Fuller & Thaler Asset Man.; regular columnist for Journal of Economic Perspectives 1987–90, for New York Times News Service; Fellow, American Finance Asscn, Econometrics Soc.; mem. American Acad. of Arts and Sciences, American Econs Asscn (Pres. 2015); Dr hc (Case Western), (Rochester), (Erasmus); TIAA-CREF Paul Samuelson Award, Keil Global Economy Prize, Nicholas Molodovsky Prize, CFA Inst., Nobel Prize in Economic Sciences 2017. *Publications include:* numerous articles in prominent journals including the American Economics Review, the Journal of Finance and the Journal of Political Economy; books: The Winner's Curse: Paradoxes and Anomalies of Economic Life 1992, Advances in Behavioral Finance 1993, Quasi Rational Economics 1994, Advances in Behavioral Finance (Vol. II) 2005, Nudge: Improving Decisions about Health, Wealth, and Happiness (with Cass Sunstein) 2009, Misbehaving: The Making of Behavioral Economics 2015. *Leisure interests:* golf, fine wine. *Address:* University of Chicago Booth School of Business, 5807 South Woodlawn Avenue, Chicago, IL 60637, USA (office). *Telephone:* (773) 702-5208 (office). *E-mail:* richard.thaler@chicagobooth.edu (office). *Website:* www.chicagobooth.edu (office); faculty.chicagobooth.edu/Richard.Thaler.

THAM, Khai Meng, BA, MA; Singaporean advertising executive; *Worldwide Chief Creative Officer and Co-Chairman of Worldwide Board, Ogilvy & Mather Worldwide;* ed Central Saint Martins and Royal Coll. of Art, London, UK; worked in London and Chicago before returning to Asia; taught at RCA, London; worked in Singapore at McCann Erickson, Bateys; Co-Chair. and Regional Creative Dir, Ogilvy & Mather Asia Pacific 2000–08, Worldwide Chief Creative Officer and Chair. World Wide Creative Council 2009–, Co-Chair. of Worldwide Bd 2016–; mem. Bd New York's Agencies In Action (coalition of US advertising agencies to alleviate hunger in the city); Chair. Clio Jury 2005–, Cannes Lions Film and Print Jury 2012; Contributing Writer, The Guardian, Campaign, Forbes; mem. Bd of Dirs Miami Ad School, Berlin School of Creative Leadership, Future of Storytelling New York; RSA Fellow; named Creative Dir of the Year by Campaign Brief Asia,

Pres.'s Award, Pres. S. R. Nathan 2009. *Publication:* The Ugly Duckling: A Cautionary Tale of Creativity. *Address:* Ogilvy & Mather, The Chocolate Factory, 636 11th Avenue, New York, NY 10036, USA (office). *Telephone:* (212) 237-4000 (office). *E-mail:* info@ogilvy.com (office). *Website:* www.ogilvy.com (office).

THAMMAVONG, Thongsing; Laotian politician; b. 12 April 1944, Xoneneua village, Viengthong Dist; military medical student 1958, served on battlefield in Laos-Vietnam border area 1959–60; attended cultural training 1960–63; Deputy Dir Xamneua Secondary School 1963, Dir Lower Secondary School and Dir Educ. Dept, Xiengkhor Dist, Huaphan Prov., Dir Upper Secondary School and Teacher Training School, Sopbao, Viengxay Dist 1971–76, several positions with Ministry of Educ. 1976–79; mem. Phak Pasason Pativat Lao (Lao People's Revolutionary Party—LPRP) 1967–, Standby mem. Party Cen. Cttee 1981, Pres. Newspaper and Radio Cttee and Deputy Head, Party Propaganda and Training Bd 1982–83, mem. Politburo and Head, Party Cen. Cttee Office 1991–; Minister of Culture 1983–88; Vice-Pres. Nat. Ass. 1989–91, Acting Pres. 1991–92, Pres. 2006–10; Mayor of Vientiane 2002; Prime Minister of Laos 2010–16. *Address:* c/o Office of the Prime Minister, Ban Sisavat, Vientiane, Laos.

THAMRIN, Yuri Octavian, MA; Indonesian diplomatist; *Ambassador to Belgium, Luxembourg and the European Union;* b. 31 Oct. 1961, Jambi; m. Risandrani Thamrin; two s.; ed Univ. of Indonesia, Jakarta, Australian Nat. Univ.; joined Foreign Ministry 1987, Head of Section on Issues Pertaining to Law of the Sea, Outer Space and Archipelagic Concept (Wawasan Nusantara), Directorate of Int. Orgs, Dept of Foreign Affairs 1990–92, Political Officer on Disarmament and Int. Security Issues, Perm. Mission of Indonesia to the UN, Geneva 1992–95, Head of Section on UN Security Council Directorate of Int. Orgs 1996, Spokesperson, Indonesian Task Force for the Post-Popular Consultation of East Timor 1999, Head of Sub-Div. on Disarmament and Security Council, Perm. Mission of Indonesia to the UN, New York 2000–02, Head of Political Div. 1 2002–03, Head of Bureau of the Ministry 2004–05, Spokesperson 2004–06, Dir of East Asian and Pacific Affairs 2005–07, Amb. to UK 2008–11, also Perm. Rep. to IMO, London; Dir-Gen. for Asia, Pacific and African Affairs, Ministry of Foreign Affairs 2011–15, Amb. to Belgium, Brussels (also accred to the EU) 2016–; mem. UN Panel of Governmental Experts on Missiles 2001–02; Co-ordinator, Non-Aligned Movt's Working Group on Disarmament, New York 2002–03; Vice-Chair. UN ad hoc Cttee on the Indian Ocean 2002–03; Guest Lecturer, Nat. Resilience Inst., Univ. of Indonesia 2006. *Publications:* numerous articles for nat. and int. newspapers and magazines. *Address:* Embassy of Indonesia, 38 Boulevard de la Woluwe, Woluwe-Saint-Lambert, 1200 Brussels, Belgium (office). *Telephone:* (2) 779-09-15 (office). *Fax:* (2) 772-82-10 (office). *E-mail:* kbri.brussel@skynet.be (office). *Website:* brussels.kemlu.go.id (office).

THAN, Field Marshall Shwe; Myanma politician, army officer and fmr head of state; b. 2 Feb. 1933, Kyaukse; m. Daw Kyaing Kyaing; joined army aged 20, positions included time spent in dept of psychological warfare, several other positions in army after mil. coup that ousted Prime Minister U Nu in 1962, including promotion to Lt-Col 1972, to Col 1978, to Commdr of Mil. Dist of South West 1983, Asst Man. of Gen. Staff of the Army, Brig.-Gen. and Vice-Minister of Defence 1985, Maj.-Gen. 1986; mem. Cen. Exec. Cttee 1986; Prime Minister 1992–2003, Minister of Defence 1992–; Chair. State Law and Order Restoration Council (SLORC) 1992–97, Chair. State Peace and Devt Council (SDP) 1997–2011 (council dissolved).

THAN NYEIN, U; Myanma economist and fmr central banker; Gov., Central Bank of Myanmar 2007–13, demoted to Vice-Gov. 2013, later resigned; fmr Chair. Myanmar Banks Asscn.

THANAJARO, Gen. Chettha; Thai politician; *Leader, Ruam Jai Thai Chart Pattana (Thais United National Development);* fmr Deputy Army Commander, later C-in-C; fmr Minister of Science and Tech.; Minister of Defence 2004–05; currently Leader, Ruam Jai Thai Chart Pattana (Thais United Nat. Devt); Pres. Olympic Cttee of Thailand; Pres. World Muaythai Council. *Address:* Ruam Jai Thai Chart Pattana (Thais United National Development), c/o House of Representatives, Bangkok, Thailand (office).

THANHAWLA, Lal, BA; Indian politician; b. 19 May 1942, Durtlang, Aizawl, Mizoram; s. of H. P. Sailo and Lalsawmliani; m. Lal Riliani 1970; one s. two d.; ed Gauhati Univ.; joined Indian Nat. Congress 1967, mem. All India Congress Cttee 1973–, Pres. Mizoram Pradesh Congress Cttee 1973–2014; mem. Mizoram Legis. Ass. 1978, 1979, 1984, 1987, 1989, 1993, 2003–08, Chief Minister 1984–87, 1989–93, 1993–98, 2008–13, 2014–18, Leader of Opposition 1978–84, 1987–89, 2003–08; mem. Congress Working Cttee; mem. 9th Finance Comm. of India; Chair. NE Olympic Comm.; Founder-Ed. Remna Arsi & Mizo Aw (daily newspaper); Chair. Literary Cttee of Nat. Devt Council; Pres. Mizoram Olympic Asscn; mem. Nat. Interpretation Council; Life mem. YMCA, Evangelical Fellowship of India, Bible Soc. of India; 12 nat. and int. awards for contribs to peace and social work. *Leisure interests:* gardening, reading, listening to music, games and sports. *Address:* A/14 Zarkawt Main Street, Aizawl 796 001, Mizoram, India (home). *Telephone:* (389) 2343461 (home). *Fax:* (389) 2342898 (home).

THANI, Sheikh Abdul Aziz ibn Khalifa al-, BS; Qatari politician, international organization official and petroleum industry executive; b. 12 Dec. 1948, Doha; s. of Khalifa ibn Hamad al-Thani, 8th Emir of Qatar, and his first spouse, Sheikha Amna bint Hassan ibn Abdulla al-Thani; one s. three d.; ed Northern Indiana Univ., USA; Deputy Minister of Finance and Petroleum June–Dec. 1972, Minister of Finance and Petroleum, State of Qatar 1972–91; Chair. State of Qatar Investment Bd 1972–89, Qatar Nat. Bank 1972, Qatar Gen. Petroleum Corpn 1973; Gov. IMF and IBRD (World Bank) 1972; rep. at numerous int. confs including OPEC, OAPEC and Arab, Islamic and non-aligned summit confs; resident in France since 1992; Hon. GCMG 1985. *Leisure interest:* scuba diving.

THANI, Abdullah al-; Libyan politician; *Prime Minister;* b. 1954; ed Bengasi Mil. Acad.; fmr mem. Nat. Transitional Council, now Gen. Nat. Congress (Parl.); Minister of Defence 2013–14, also Acting Prime Minister March–May 2014, Prime Minister June–Aug. 2014 (resgnd), re-apptd Sept. 2014. *Address:* Office of the Prime Minister, Tripoli, Libya (office). *Website:* www.pm.gov.ly (office).

THANI, Abdullah bin Hamad al-; Qatari business executive; *Deputy Emir;* b. 9 Feb. 1988; s. of Sheikh Hamad bin Khalifa al-Thani (fmr Emir) and Sheikha Noora bint Khalid al-Thani; half-brother of Sheikh Tamim bin Hamad al-Thani (Emir of Qatar); m. Sheikha Al-Maha bint Muhammad al-Attiyah 2012; ed Qatar Acad., School of Foreign Service, Georgetown Univ., USA; Chief of Amiri Diwan (royal court) 2011–14; Deputy Emir 2014–; Vice-Pres. Qatar Investment Authority (sovereign wealth fund) 2013–14, Chair. 2014–. *Address:* Qatar Investment Authority, Q-Tel Tower, Corniche Street, West Bay Area, 23224 Doha, Qatar (office). *Telephone:* 44995900 (office). *Fax:* 44995991 (office). *E-mail:* info@qia.qa (office). *Website:* www.qia.qa (office).

THANI, Sheikh Abdullah bin Khalifa al-; Qatari politician; *Chairman, Qatar Investment and Projects Development Holding Company;* b. 25 Dec. 1959, Doha; six s.; ed Royal Mil. Acad., Sandhurst UK; various positions within Qatar Armed Forces 1976–89; Minister of the Interior 1989–96; Deputy Prime Minister 1995–96; Prime Minister of Qatar 1996–2007 (resgnd); Special Adviser to Emir of Qatar 2007–; Chair. Qatari Olympic Cttee 1979–89, Qatar Investment and Projects Devt Holding Co. 2011–; mem. Bd of Dirs Amyris Inc. 2012–. *Address:* Qatar Investment and Projects Development Holding Company, POB 8612, Doha, Qatar (office). *Telephone:* 44058800 (office). *E-mail:* enquiries@qipco.com (office).

THANI, Abdullah bin Mohamed bin Saud al-; Qatari business executive; *CEO, Qatar Investment Authority;* ed Staff and Command Coll., Egypt, Army War Coll., USA; trained as certified pilot instructor with British RAF; fmr mem. Qatar Planning Council; Chair. Ooredoo (telecommunications firm) 2000–; Chair. Qatar Telecom (Qtel) and Qtel Group 2000–; Chief of Amiri Diwan (royal court) 2000–05; CEO Qatar Investment Authority (sovereign wealth fund) 2014–; fmr Commr, ITU Broadband Comm. for Digital Devt; mem. World Bank Group Advisory Council for Gender and Devt; mem. Global Advisory Bd, World Econ. Forum Gender Parity Programme. *Address:* Qatar Investment Authority, Q-Tel Tower, Corniche Street, West Bay Area, 23224 Doha, Qatar (office). *Telephone:* 44995900 (office). *Fax:* 44995991 (office). *E-mail:* info@qia.qa (office). *Website:* www.qia.qa (office).

THANI, Sheikh Abdullah bin Nasser bin Khalifa al-; Qatari government official; *Prime Minister and Minister of the Interior;* b. 1959; s. of Nasser bin Khalifa al-Thani; m.; six c.; ed Beirut Arab Univ.; fmr Commdr, Ministry of Interior Security Force and Chair. Nat. Anti-Terrorism Cttee; Asst Dir Special Security Force Dept for Operations Affairs 2001–04; Head of Security Cttees for Doha Asian Games 2006 and Qatar World Cup 2022; Minister of State for Internal Affairs 2005–13; Prime Minister and Minister of the Interior 2013–. *Address:* Ministry of the Interior, POB 115, Doha, Qatar (office). *Telephone:* 44330000 (office). *Fax:* 44322927 (office). *E-mail:* info@moi.gov.qa (office). *Website:* www.moi.gov.qa (office).

THANI, Sheikh; Abdullah bin Saoud al-, BA (Econ), MBA (USA), MBA (UK); Qatari central banker; *Governor and Chairman, Qatar Central Bank;* b. 1 Jan. 1957, Doha; worked in Foreign Exchange Dept, Qatar Central Bank 1982–89, Deputy Gov. 1990–2001, Gov. 2006–, also currently Chair.; Chair. Qatar Devt Bank 1996–; Chair. State Audit Bureau 2001–06; Pres. Gen. Retirement and Pension Authority 2006–; mem. Bd of Dirs, Coll. of Business and Economy, Qatar Univ. 2006–; Chair. QFC Regulatory Authority 2012–, Islamic Financial Services Bd 2013–, Int. Islamic Liquidity Man. Corpn; Chair. Bd of Dirs, Gulf Monetary Council 2014; Arab Banking Personality of the Year 2011. *Address:* Qatar Central Bank, PO Box 1234, Doha, Qatar (office). *Telephone:* 44456400 (office); 44456456 (office). *Fax:* 44415587 (office). *E-mail:* g@qcb.gov.qa (office). *Website:* www.qcb.gov.qa (office).

THANI, Sheikh Ahmed bin Jasim bin Mohamed al-; Qatari oil engineer, business executive and politician; *Minister of Business and Trade;* ed Imperial Coll. of Science, Tech. and Medicine, UK, Delft Univ. of Tech., The Netherlands, Carnegie Mellon Tepper School of Business, USA; served at different levels at Qatargas and became its COO (Engineering and Ventures), mem. decision-making body and also managed around 250 capital projects for the co., both onshore and offshore; worked at Total in La Defense, Paris, for more than a year; external posting at Mobil Research Center, Meptec, Dallas, Tex., USA; Dir-Gen. Al Jazeera Network 2011–13; Minister of Business and Trade 2013–; Chair. Tech. Cttee of Gas Processing Centre, Qatar Univ. Research Centre; Vice-Chair. Qatar Investment Authority; mem. Industrial Advisory Bd Coll. of Engineering, Qatar Univ. *Address:* Ministry of Business and Trade, POB 1968, Doha, Qatar (office). *Telephone:* 4945555 (office). *Fax:* 44945000 (office). *E-mail:* mbt@mbt.gov.qa (office). *Website:* www.mbt.gov.qa (office).

THANI, Sheikh Hamad bin Jasim bin Jaber al-; Qatari politician; b. 30 Aug. 1959, Doha; s. of Jasim bin Jabr al-Thani; m. 1st Jawaher bint Fahad al-Thani; m. 2nd Noor al-Subaie 1996; 15 c.; Dir Office of the Minister of Municipal Affairs and Agric. 1982–89, Minister of Municipal Affairs and Agric. 1989–92; Deputy Minister of Electricity and Water 1990–92; Minister of Foreign Affairs 1992–2013; First Deputy Prime Minister 2003–07; Prime Minister of Qatar 2007–13; Head of Perm. Cttee for the Support of Al Quds 1998–; mem. Supreme Defence Council 1996–, Parl. Constitution Cttee 1999–, Ruling Family Council 2000–; CEO Supreme Council for the Investment of the Reserves of State (Qatar Investment Authority) 2000–; fmr Chair. Qatar Electricity and Water Co.; fmr Pres. Cen. Municipal Council, Special Emiri Projects Office; fmr Dir Special Emiri Projects Office; fmr mem. Bd of Dirs, Qatar Petroleum, Supreme Council for Planning; launched Humanitarian Appeal 2011 in Doha, together with UNO for the Co-ordination of Humanitarian Affairs (OCHA) and UNHCR 2010; Hon. DHumLitt (Lebanese American Univ.) 2010. *Address:* Qatar Investment Authority, PO Box 23224, Doha, Qatar (office). *E-mail:* info@qia.qa (office). *Website:* www.qia.qa (office).

THANI, Sheikh Hamad bin Khalifa al-; Qatari royal; b. 1 Jan. 1952, Doha; s. of Sheikh Khalifa bin Hamad al-Thani; m. 1st Sheikha Mariam bint Muhammad al-Thani; two s. six d.; m. 2nd Sheikha Mozah bint Nasser al-Missned; five s. (including Amir of Qatar Sheikh Tamim bin Hamad bin Khalifa al-Thani) two d.; m. 3rd Sheikha Noora bint Khalid al-Thani; four s. five d.; ed Royal Mil. Coll., Sandhurst, UK; apptd Heir-Apparent May 1977; Commdr First Mobile Bn (now Hamad Mobile Bn); Maj., then Maj.-Gen., C-in-C Armed Forces of Qatar; Minister of Defence 1977–2013; Amir of Qatar 1995–2013 (abdicated); Prime Minister 1995–96; fmr Supreme Pres. Higher Planning Council; Pres. Higher Youth Council 1979–91; f. Mil. Sports Fed.; mem. Int. Mil. Sports Fed.; Pres. Qatari Nat. Olympic Cttee 2000–; mem. IOC, mem. Sports for All Cttee; Chair. Organizing Cttee 15th

Asian Games 2006; Head, Upper Council of Environment and Natural Sanctuaries; Nishan-i-Pakistan 1999, Nat. Order of Merit (Malta) 2009, Grand Order of King Tomislav with Sash and Great Morning Star (Croatia) 2009, Grand Collar of the Order of the Liberator Simon Bolivar (Venezuela) 2010, Nat. Flag Order (Albania) 2015; Orders of Merit from Cote d'Ivoire, Cuba, Dominican Repub., Egypt, Finland, France, Germany, Greece, Indonesia, Italy, Lebanon, Morocco, Oman, Portugal, Romania, Saudi Arabia, Senegal, Tunis, UK, Yemen. *Leisure interest:* sports. *Address:* c/o The Royal Palace, PO Box 923, Doha, Qatar. *Website:* www.diwan.gov.qa.

THANI, Sheikh Khalid bin Khalifa bin Jasim al-; Qatari business executive; *CEO, QatarGas;* Dir of Ras Laffan Industrial City –2010; CEO QatarGas 2010–. *Address:* Qatargas Doha Head Office, Omar Al-Mukhtar Street, West Bay, Doha, Qatar (office). *Telephone:* 44736000 (office). *Fax:* 44736666 (office). *E-mail:* infos@qatargas.com.qa (office). *Website:* www.qatargas.com (office).

THANI, Sheikh Mohamed bin Abdurrahman al-; Qatari Govt official and politician; *Deputy Prime Minister and Minister of Foreign Affairs;* b. 1 Nov. 1980, Doha; ed Qatar Univ.; Econ. Researcher Supreme Council for Family Affairs 2003–05; Dir Econ. Affairs Council for Family Affairs 2005–09; Dir Dept of Public and Pvt. Sectors Partnership, Ministry of Business Trade 2009; Sec. Personal Rep. for Follow-up Affairs to His Highness the Emir Sheikh Hamad bin Khalifa al-Thani 2010; Deputy Chair. Qatar Mining Co. 2010; Chair. Aspire–Katara Investment Co. 2011; Chair. Exec. Cttee Devt of Small and Medium-sized Enterprises 2011; Asst Foreign Minister Int. Cooperation Affairs 2013; Chair. Qatar Fund for Devt 2014; Deputy Prime Minister and Minister of Foreign Affairs 2016–; currently mem. Supreme Council for Econ. and Investments Affairs. *Address:* Ministry of Foreign Affairs, PO Box 250, Doha, Qatar (office). *Telephone:* 440111111 (office). *Fax:* 44324131 (office). *E-mail:* webmaster@mofa.gov.qa (office). *Website:* www.mofa.gov.qa (office).

THANI, HH Sheikh Tamim bin Hamad bin Khalifa al-, (Amir of Qatar); Qatari; b. 3 June 1980, Doha; s. of fmr Amir of Qatar Sheikh Hamad bin Khalifa al-Thani and Sheikha Mozah bint Nasser al-Missned; m. 1st Sheikha Jawahar bint Hamad bin Sohaim al-Thani 2005; two s. two d.; m. 2nd Sheikha Anoud bint Mana al-Hajri 2009; two s. two d.; m. 3rd Sheikha Noora bint Hathal al-Dosari 2014; one s.; ed Sherborne School, Dorset, Harrow School and Royal Mil. Acad. Sandhurst, UK; commissioned as a Second Lt in Qatar Armed Forces 1998, Deputy C-in-C of the Armed Forces 2009, later C-in-C; proclaimed Heir Apparent when his elder brother Sheikh Jasim bin Hamad bin Khalifa al-Thani renounced his right to the throne 5 Aug. 2003, Amir of Qatar (following abdication of his father) 25 June 2013–; Head of Upper Council of the Environment and Natural Sanctuaries; Chair. Qatar Investment Authority –2014; fmr Chair. Supreme Council for the Environment and Natural Reserves, Supreme Educ. Council, Supreme Council of Information and Communication Tech., Public Works Authority (Ashghal), Urban Planning and Devt Authority, Bd of Regents of Qatar Univ., Ruling Family Council; fmr Deputy Chair. High Cttee for Co-ordination and Follow Up; fmr Vice-Pres. Supreme Council for Econ. Affairs and Investment; Pres. as-Sadd Sports Club 1999–2000; Chair. Qatar Nat. Olympic Cttee 2000–, Organizing Cttee Asian Games, Doha 2006; mem. IOC, Supreme Educ. Council; Chair. ictQATAR programme 2005–; headed Doha's bid for the 2020 Olympics; Necklace of Merit 2003, Issa bin Salman al-Khalifa Order of Merit-Excellence Class (Bahrain) 2004, Collar of the Order of Zayed (UAE) 2005, Grand Officier, Légion d'honneur 2010, Collar of the Order of Mubarak the Great 2013; Sheikh Essa Bin Salman Al Khalifa Medal (Bahrain) 2004, Sheikh Zayed bin Sultan al-Nahyan Medal of Honour (UAE) 2004, voted Best Sport Personality in the Arab World in popular Egyptian newspaper Al Ahram 2006, OCA Award of Merit, Olympic Council of Asia 2007. *Address:* The Royal Palace, PO Box 923, Doha, Qatar. *Website:* www.diwan.gov.qa.

THANOU-CHRISTOFILOU, Vassiliki; Greek judge; b. 1950, Chalcis, Euboea; m.; three c.; ed Nat. and Kapodistrian Univ. of Athens, Univ. of Paris II (Sorbonne), France; joined judiciary 1975, promoted to Pres., Courts of First Instance 1992, to Judge of Appellate Court 1996, to Pres. in Appellate Courts 2005, served in D Chamber, Areios Pagos (Supreme Court of Civil and Penal Law) 2008–14, Pres. D Chamber and Vice-Pres., Supreme Court 2014–15, Pres. 2015–17; Acting Prime Minister of Greece Aug.–Sept. 2015; Teacher, Nat. School of the Judiciary (Civil Law) 2009–; mem. Greek Asscn of Judges and Prosecutors (SAD), mem. Bureau 2000–, Pres. SAD 2012–.

THAPA, Arjun Bahadur; Nepalese diplomatist, government official and international organisation official; b. 12 Jan. 1956; m. Pabitra Thapa; three c.; ed Peoples' Friendship Univ., Russia, Univ. of Adelaide, Australia; Section Officer, Int. Law and Treaties Div., Ministry of Law and Justice 1983–93, Asst Sec. 1993–94, Under-Sec. 1994–99; Jt Sec., East, South East, Far East and Pacific Div., Ministry of Foreign Affairs 1999–2002, Deputy Perm. Rep. and Minister Plenipotentiary, Perm. Mission to UN, New York 2002–05, 2006–07, Charge d'Affaires, a.i 2005–06, Jt Sec., Head of SAARC and Admin. Divs and Spokesperson, Ministry of Foreign Affairs Feb.–Dec. 2007, Amb. to UAE 2007–12, Jt Sec. and Head of Europe-Americas Div., Admin. Div., SAARC and BIMSTEC and Spokesperson, Ministry of Foreign Affairs 2012–13, Jt Sec. and Head of Regional Org. Div. SAARC and BIMSTEC 2012–13, Foreign Sec., Ministry of Foreign Affairs 2013–14; Sec.-Gen. SAARC 2014–17; Prabala Gorkha Dakshin Bahu (IV class) 1995. *Publication:* The Nepalese Law of Treaties 1992.

THAPA, Kamal, MA; Nepalese politician; b. 4 Aug. 1955, Makwanpur Dist; ed Tribhuwan Univ.; Pres., Nat. Student Org. 1973–74; Asst Lecturer in Political Economy, Tribhuwan Univ. Inst. of Forestry 1977; mem. Constitution Reform Comm. 1980; Mem. Sec., Cen. Cttee of Nat. Youth Service Fund 1986–91; mem. Parl. 1986–90, 1995–98; Minister of Home Affairs 2006–07; Deputy Prime Minister and Minister of Foreign Affairs, and of Federal Affairs and Local Devt 2015–16; Pres. All-Nepal Football Asscn 1978–87; mem. Nat. Sports Council 1977–87; Exec. Mem. Asian Football Confed. 1982–90; Leader, Nepalese del. to UN Gen. Ass. 1997; to South Asian Asscn for Regional Cooperation (SAARC) Council of Ministers 1998; mem. Rastriya Prajatantra Party (RPP), party spokesman 1992–2002, Gen. Sec. 2003, Chair. 2005–06, 2008–. *Leisure interests:* football, tennis. *Address:* Rastriya Prajatantra Party, Charumati Bihar, Chabahil,

Kathmandu, Nepal (office). *Telephone:* (1) 4471071 (office). *Fax:* (1) 4474964 (office). *E-mail:* centraloff@yahoo.com (office). *Website:* rppn.org (office).

THAPA, Maj-Gen. Purna Chandra, MPhil; Nepalese army officer and fmr UN official; *Chief of Staff, Army HQ;* b. 9 Sept. 1960; m. Deepa Thapa; one s. one d.; ed Tribhuvan Univ., Univ. of Madras, India, Army Command and Staff Coll. of Nepal, Nat. Defence Coll., India; long career in Nepalese Army, roles include infantry brigade Commdr 2006–07, Mil. Sec. of Chief of Army Staff 2007–08, Dir of Army Welfare Planning 2009–12, Gen. Officer commanding Infantry Div. and Adjutant-Gen., Nepalese Army HQ 2012–13, Master Gen. of Ordnance, Nepalese Army HQ 2013–15, Chief of Staff, Army HQ 2016–; served in several UN peacekeeping operations including UNIFIL, Lebanon 1986 and 1989, UNPROFOR, fmr Yugoslavia 1994–95, led Govt of Nepal team as Vice-Pres., Jt Monitoring and Coordination Cttee (JMCC), UN Mission in Nepal (UNMIN) 2009–11, Head of Mission and Force Commdr, UN Disengagement Observer Force (UNDOF), Golan Heights 2015–16. *Address:* Nepal Army Headquarters, Bhadrakali, Kathmandu, Nepal (office). *Telephone:* (1) 4269624 (office). *E-mail:* armyhq@gmail.com (office). *Website:* www.nepalarmy.mil.np (office).

THAPA, Gen. (retd) Pyar Jung, BA; Nepalese army officer (retd); b. 15 Sept. 1946; s. of Tej Jung Thapa and Ishwori Thapa; m.; three d.; ed Tribhuvan Univ., Royal Mil. Acad., Sandhurst, UK, Staff Coll., Camberley, UK, US Army War Coll., USA; joined Royal Nepalese Army 1964, Second Lt Singh Nath Battalion, promoted to rank of Brig.-Gen. 1993, Maj.-Gen. 1998, Asst Chief of Army Staff 1998–2002, Dir Integrated Security and Devt Program, promoted to rank of Lt-Gen. 2001, Chief of Army Staff 2002–06 (retd), Battalion Commdr UN Interim Force in Lebanon 1986, Deputy Sector Commdr Sector West, UN Protection Forces in Fmr Yugoslavia 1992; Hon. Gen., Indian Army 2002; Gouravamaya Supradeepta Birendra-Prajatantra-Bhaskara (II Class), Trishakti Patt (II Class), Gorkha Dakshina-Bahu (II Class). *Leisure interests:* golf, bridge, reading classical and military related novels.

THAPA, Ram Bahadur, (Badal); Nepalese politician and fmr guerrilla commander; *Minister of Home Affairs;* b. 1955; s. of Karn Bahjadur Thapa Magar and Nanda Kumari Thapa Magar; ed gained agric. scholarship to studied in USSR; dropped out of studies and returned to Nepal to engage in revolutionary movt; self-taught communist who joined CP of Nepal (Maoist) 1981, arrested and jailed for ten months, went underground, emerged as a mem. of Maoist rebel negotiating team during peace process 2003, credited with Maoist pull-out from the peace process, mem. Cen. Cttee, co-ordinator of Cen. Advisory Council of Magar Nat. Liberation Front; co-ordinator of cand. selection cttee for Constituent Ass. election 2008; Minister of Defence 2008–09; Minister of Home Affairs 2018–. *Address:* Ministry of Home Affairs, Singha Durbar, Kathmandu, Nepal (office). *Telephone:* (1) 4211214 (office). *Fax:* (1) 4211286 (office). *E-mail:* gunaso@moha.gov.np (office). *Website:* www.moha.gov.np (office); ucpnmaoist.org.

THAPAR, Gautam; Indian chemical engineer and business executive; *Chairman, Ballapur Industries Ltd;* b. 7 Dec. 1960; nephew of Lalit Mohan Thapar; ed Doon School, St Stephen's Coll., Delhi, Pratt Inst., USA; joined family co. Ballapur Industries Ltd (BILT) 1986, held positions successively in paper mills and pulp unit, chemicals and foods businesses, Head of Finance 1997–98, CEO 1998–99, Man.-Dir Andra Pradesh Rayons (APR) Ltd 1999, Jt Man.-Dir BILT 1999–2001, Vice-Chair. and Man.-Dir BILT 2001–06, Chair. 2006–; Chair. Crompton Greaves Ltd 2004–, Confederation of Indian Industry; Vice-Chair. Governing Body and General Body, Thapar Center for Industrial Research and Development; mem. Bd of Dirs Asahi India Safety Glass Ltd 2002–, Pratham India Educ. Initiative 2003–, Compass Limited, CG Capital & Investments Ltd, Greaves Cotton Ltd, Global Green Company Ltd, KCT Papers Ltd, KCT Chemicals & Electricals Ltd, Solaris Chemtech Ltd, Osian's Connoisseurs of Art Pvt Ltd; mem. Bd of Trustees Patiala Technical Education Trust, Aspen India; mem. Bd of Govs Thapar Inst. of Engineering and Technology; mem. Man. Cttee of Associate Chambers of Commerce and Industries. *Address:* Ballapur Industries Limited, First India Place, Tower C, Mehrauli – Gurgaon Road, Gurgaon, Haryana 122 002, India (office). *Telephone:* (124) 280424243 (office). *Fax:* (124) 280426061 (office). *E-mail:* corpcom@bilt.com (office). *Website:* www.bilt.com (office).

THAROOR, Shashi, MA, MALD, PhD; Indian UN official, politician and author; b. 9 March 1956, London, England; s. of Chandran Tharoor and Lily Tharoor; m. Sunanda Pushkar Tharoor (died 2014); twin s. one step-s.; ed St Stephen's Coll., Delhi Univ., Fletcher School of Law and Diplomacy, Tufts Univ., USA; joined UN 1978, with UNHCR, served at Geneva HQ, Head of Office in Singapore; Special Asst for UN Peace-keeping operations; Exec. Asst to UN Sec.-Gen. 1997–98, Dir Communications and Special Projects, Office of the Sec.-Gen. 1998–2000; Interim Head of Dept of Public Information 2001–02, Head and Under-Sec.-Gen. for Public Information 2002–07; mem. Lok Sabha 2009–; Minister of State for External Affairs 2009–10, for Human Resource Development 2012–14; Chair., Afras Ventures (investment co.) 2008–; mem. Bd of Overseers Fletcher School of Law and Diplomacy, Bd of Trustees, Aspen Inst. India, Advisory Bd World Policy Journal, Advisory Bd Virtue Foundation, Advisory Bd Breakthrough (human rights org.); Fellow, New York Inst. of the Humanities; mem. Indian Nat. Congress; Hon. DLitt; Pravasi Bharatiya Samman 2004; Commonwealth Writers' Prize, several journalism and literary awards; named Global Leader of Tomorrow by World Econ. Forum, Davos, Switzerland 1998. *Publications include:* Reasons of State 1981, The Great Indian Novel 1989, The Five Dollar Smile and Other Stories 1990, Show Business 1992, India: From Midnight to the Millennium 1997, Riot 2001, Kerala: God's Own Country 2002, Nehru: The Invention of India 2003, Bookless in Baghdad 2005, The Elephant, the Tiger and the Cellphone: Reflections on India in the 21st Century 2007, Pax Indica: India and The World of the 21st Century 2012, India Shastra: Reflections on the Nation in our Time 2015, Inglorious Empire: What the British Did to India 2017, Why I Am a Hindu 2018. *Leisure interests:* cricket, theatre, literature, cinema. *Address:* 97, Lodhi Estate, New Delhi 110 003, India (office). *Telephone:* (11) 24644035 (office). *Fax:* (11) 24654158 (office). *E-mail:* shashi.tharoor@nic.in (office); manu@tharoor.in (office). *Website:* www.tharoor.in.

THARP, Twyla, BA; American dancer and choreographer; b. 1 July 1941, Portland, Ind.; ed Pomona Coll., Barnard Coll.; studied with Richard Thomas, Merce Cunningham, Igor Schwezoff, Louis Mattox, Paul Taylor, Margaret Craske,

Erick Hawkins; with Paul Taylor Dance Co. 1963–65; freelance choreographer with own modern dance troupe Twyla Tharp Dance and other cos, including Joffrey Ballet and American Ballet Theater 1965–87, The Paris Opera Ballet, The Martha Graham Dance Company; Artistic Assoc. Choreographer, American Ballet Theatre, New York 1988–91; re-formed Twyla Tharp Dance periodically between 1991 and present; Hon. mem. American Acad. of Arts and Letters 1997; more than 15 hon. degrees; two Emmy Awards and numerous other awards including Dance Magazine Annual Award 1981, Laurence Olivier Award 1991, Doris Duke Awards for New Work 1999, Astaire Award 2003, The Drama League Award for Sustained Achievement in Musical Theatre, the Outer Critics Circle Award for Outstanding Choreography, Kennedy Center Honor 2008. *Major works choreographed include:* Tank Dive 1965, Re-Moves 1966, Forevermore 1967, Generation 1968, Medley 1969, Fugue 1970, Eight Jelly Rolls 1971, The Raggedy Dances 1972, As Time Goes By 1974, Sue's Leg 1975, Push Comes to Shove 1976, Once More Frank 1976, Mud 1977, Baker's Dozen 1979, When We Were Very Young 1980, The Catherine Wheel (with music by David Byrne) 1981, Nine Sinatra Songs 1982, Amadeus 1984, White Nights 1985, Singin' in the Rain 1985, In the Upper Room 1986, Rules of the Game 1989; choreographed Cutting Up 1993 for US tour, Demeter and Persephone 1993, 1994, Waterbaby Bagatelles 1994, Red White and Blues 1995, How Near Heaven 1995, Mr. Worldly Wise 1996, Movin' Out (Tony Award 2003), Even the King 2003, The Times They Are A Changin' 2006, Armenia 2008, Nightspot 2008, Rabbit and Rogue 2008, Come Fly With Me (later renamed Come Fly Away) 2009; films Hair 1979, Ragtime 1980, Amadeus 1984, White Nights 1985, I'll Do Anything 1994; videotape Making Television Dance (Chicago International Film Festival Award) 1977, CBS Cable Confessions of a Corner Maker 1980, Baryshnikov by Tharp (two Emmy Awards, Director's Guild for America Award for Outstanding Director of Achievement. *Publications include:* Push Comes to Shove (autobiog.) 1992, The Creative Habit: Learn It and Use It for Life 2003, The Collaborative Habit: Life Lessons for Working Together 2009. *E-mail:* jah@twylatharp.org (office). *Website:* www.twylatharp.org (office).

THAUGSUBAN, Suthep; Thai politician; b. 7 July 1949, Surat Thani Prov.; fmr mem. Ratha Sapha (Parl.) for Surat Thani Prov. (resgnd 2009); fmr Minister of Agric., of Transport and Communications; Deputy Prime Minister and Minister for Security Affairs 2008–11; mem. Prachatipat (Democrat Party) 1979–2013 (Sec.-Gen. 2005–11), Ruamphalang Prachachartthai Party (Action Coalition for Thailand Party) 2018–.

THAWLEY, Michael, AO; Australian business executive and fmr diplomatist; b. 16 April 1950, London, England, UK; joined Foreign Affairs Dept 1972, served in Rome, Moscow, Tokyo; Int. Adviser to the Prime Minister 1996–99; fmr staff mem. Office of Nat. Assessments, Dept of Prime Minister and Cabinet; Amb. to USA 2000–05; Sr Vice-Pres. Capital Strategy Research Inc., Washington, DC 2005–14, Capital Research and Management Co. 2007–14; Sec., Dept of Prime Minister and Cabinet 2014–16; mem. Bd, Vice-Chair. and Prin. Exec. Officer World Growth and Income Fund; mem. Bd and Vice-Chair. American Funds Global Balanced Fund; mem. Bd of Dirs US Studies Centre, Univ. of Sydney, Lowy Inst. for Int. Policy, Sydney.

THEEDE, Steven M., BS; American oil industry executive; b. 1952, Hutchison, Kan.; ed Kansas State Univ.; trained as mechanical engineer; joined Conoco, Houston, Tex. 1974, worked in production, pipelines, refining, marketing, and int. relations, held positions successively as Gen. Dir Assessment and Tech. Devt, Gen. Dir Planning and Admin, Int. Refining and Marketing, Pres. Conoco Pipeline Co., CEO and Gen. Dir Conoco Ltd (UK), Gen. Dir Exploration & Production (E&P) for S and N America, Vice-Pres. Human Resources, Pres. of E&P for Europe (following merger of co. to form ConocoPhilips 2002) 2002–03, for Europe, Russia and the Caspian 2002–03; COO OAO NK Yukos (Yukos Oil Co.), Moscow, Russia 2003–04, CEO 2004–06 (resgnd); mem. Bd of Dirs Serica Energy; fmr Chair. Energy Cttee, US–Russia Business Council 2003. *Address:* 5498 Lynbrook Drive, Houston, TX 77056, USA.

THEIN SEIN, Gen. U; Myanma fmr army officer, politician and fmr head of state; b. 20 April 1945; m. Daw Khin Khin Win; three d.; ed Defence Services Acad., Command and General Staff Coll., Kalaw; served in army for 40 years, including as Commdr, Triangle Regional Mil. Command Kyaingtong, Shan State 1997–2001; mem. ruling State Peace and Devt Council junta 1997–, becoming First Sec. 2004–07; also served as Chair. govt-sponsored Nat. Convention Convening Comm.; Acting Prime Minister April–Oct. 2007, Prime Minister 2007–11; retd from army 2010; mem. Union Ass. (Parl.) for Zabuthiri 2010–11; Pres., Repub. of the Union of Myanmar 2011–16; promoted to rank of full Gen. from Lt-Gen. 2007; mem. Union Solidarity and Development Party, Chair. 2010–13. *Address:* c/o Office of the President, Yangon, Myanmar (office).

THEOCHARIS, Reghinos D., PhD; Cypriot economist and academic; *Professor Emeritus, Athens University of Economics and Business;* b. 10 Feb. 1929, Larnaca; s. of Demetrios Theocharis and Florentia Theocharis; m. Madeleine Loumbou 1954; one s. one d.; ed Athens School of Econs, Univ. of Aberdeen and London School of Econs; Insp. of Commercial Educ., Cyprus 1953–56; at LSE 1956–58; Bank of Greece, Athens 1958–59; Minister of Finance in Cyprus Provisional Govt 1959–60; Minister of Finance 1960–62; Gov. of Bank of Cyprus 1962–75; Prof., Athens Univ. of Econs and Business 1975–96, Prof. Emer. 1996–; Dir-Gen. Centre of Planning and Econ. Research (KEPE), Athens 1978–81; Hon. Fellow, LSE 1971. *Publications:* On the Stability of the Cournot Solution on the Oligopoly Problem 1960, Early Developments in Mathematical Economics 1983, The Development of Mathematical Economics: From Cournot to Jevons 1993. *Leisure interests:* chess, gardening. *Address:* 2 Raidestou Street, Kessariani, Athens, 16122, Greece (home). *Telephone:* 2107214531 (home).

THEODORAKIS, Mikis; Greek composer and politician; b. 29 July 1925, Chios; s. of Georges Michel Theodorakis and Aspasia Poulaki; m. Myrto Altinoglou 1953; one s. one d.; ed Athens Conservatoire, Paris Conservatoire, France; joined resistance against German occupation of Greece 1942; arrested and deported during civil war 1947–52; moved to Paris 1953 and studied under Olivier Messiaen; first public concert Sonatina (for pianoforte), Paris 1954; set to bouzouki music the poem Epitaphios by Iannis Ritsos 1958–59 and subsequently wrote numerous other successful songs; ballet music for Antigone (first performed in London by Dame Margot Fonteyn), Stuttgart Ballet, others; returned to Greece 1962; Leader, Lambrakis youth movt; elected mem. Parl. 1963; imprisoned for political activities 1967, released April 1970; lived in Paris 1970–74; resgnd from CP March 1972; mem. Parl. 1981–86 (resgnd), 1989–93 (resgnd), Minister of State 1990–92 (resgnd); f. Cttee for Greek-Turkish Friendship 1986; Hon. mem. Acad. of Athens 2013; Gold Medal, Moscow Shostakovich Festival 1957, Copley Prize, USA 1957, First Prize Athens Popular Song Festival 1961, Sibelius Award, London 1963, Gold Medal for Film Music, London 1970, Socrates Prize, Stockholm 1974, First Literary Prize, Athens 1987, Lenin Int. Peace Prize 1982. *Works include:* Sinfonia (oratorio) 1944, Love and Death (voice, strings) 1945–48, Assi-Gonia (orchestra) 1945–50, Sextet for Flute 1946, Oedipus Tyrannus (strings) 1946, Greek Carnival (ballet suite) 1947, First Symphony (orchestra) 1948–50, Five Cretan Songs (chorus, orchestra) 1950, Orpheus and Eurydice (ballet) 1952, Barefoot Battalion (film) 1953, Suite No. 1 (four movements, piano and orchestra) 1954, Poèmes d'Eluard (Cycle 1 and Cycle 2) 1955, Suite No. 2 (chorus, orchestra) 1956, Suite No. 3 (five movements, soprano, chorus, orchestra) 1956, Ill Met by Moonlight (film) 1957, Sonatina No. 1 (violin, piano) 1957, Les amants de Teruel (ballet) 1958, Piano Concerto 1958, Sonatina No. 2 (violin, piano) 1958, Antigone (ballet) 1958, Epitaphios (song cycle) 1959, Deserters (song cycle) 1958, Epiphania (song cycle) 1959, Honeymoon (film) 1960, Phoenician Women – Euripides (theatre music) 1960, Axion Esti (pop oratorio) 1960, Electra-Euripides (film), Phaedra (film) 1962, The Hostage (song cycle) 1962, The Ballad of the Dead Brother (musical tragedy) 1962, Zorba the Greek (film), The Ballad of Mauthausen (song cycle) 1965, Romiossini (song cycle) 1965, Lisistrata – Aristophanes (theatre music) 1966, Romancero Gitano (Lorca) (song cycle) 1967, Sun and Time (song cycle) 1967, Arcadias Nos. 1–10 (song cycles) 1968–69, Canto General (Pablo Neruda) (pop oratorio) 1972, Z (film), Etat de Siège (film) 1973, Ballads (song cycle) 1975, Symphony No. 2 (orchestra and piano) 1981, Messe Byzantine (Liturgie) 1982, Symphony No. 3 (orchestra, chorus, soprano) 1982, Sadoukeon Passion (cantata for orchestra, chorus, soloists) 1983, Liturgie No. 2 1983, Symphony No. 7 (orchestra, chorus, soloists) 1983, Requiem 1985, Kostas Kariotakis (opera in two acts) 1985, Beatrice (song cycle) 1987, Faces of the Sun (song cycle) 1987, Symphony No. 4 1987, Memory of Stone (song cycle) 1987, Like an Ancient Wind (song cycle) 1987, Canto Olympico (symphony) 1991, Medea (opera) 1990, Electra (opera) 1993. *Publications include:* La Dette, Journals of Resistance 1972, Ballad of the Dead Brother, Culture et dimensions politiques 1973, Star System, Antimanifeste, Les chemins de l'Archange (autobiog.), 4 vols 1986–92. *Address:* Epifanous 1, Akropolis, 117 42 Athens, Greece. *Telephone:* (1) 9214863. *Fax:* (1) 9236325. *Website:* en.mikis-theodorakis.net.

THEODORAKIS, Stavros; Greek journalist, television presenter and politician; *Leader, To Potami;* b. Feb. 1963, Chania, Kissamos Drapania; raised in Upper Aghia Barbara in western Athens; began career as journalist 1984; worked for numerous radio stations, magazines, TV stations and conducted political interviews for Sunday Eleftherotypia and To Vima; returned to neighbourhood where he grew up and worked in journalism and the education of the Roma for two years; began presenting TV show Protagonists on public broadcaster NET 2000–06, then on Mega TV 2006–14; created, together with other journalists, protagon.gr website 2009; columnist, Ta Nea newspaper –2014; Founder and Leader To Potami (The River) political party 2014–; mem. Vouli (Parl.) for Chania constituency 2015–. *Address:* To Potami (The River), Sevastoupoleos 22, Athens 115 26, Greece (office). *Telephone:* (210) 7470100 (office). *Fax:* (210) 7470115 (office). *E-mail:* info@topotami.gr (office). *Website:* www.topotami.gr (office).

THEOPHILOS, Theophilou V., MA; Cypriot lawyer and fmr diplomatist; b. 9 Sept. 1946, Limnia, Famagusta; ed Athens Univ., greece, Stanford Univ., USA; lawyer in Famagusta 1971–73; Attaché, Cultural Div., Ministry of Foreign Affairs 1974, Head of EEC Desk 1974–76, Sec., Political Affairs Div. (Question of Cyprus) 1977–78, Head of Cyprus Question Desk 1979–81, Deputy Dir Political Div. 1985–86, Dir Office of Minister of Foreign Affairs 1993, Dir European Div. 1993–96, Consul Gen., New York, USA 1981–84, in charge of Orgs of NAM Foreign Ministers Conf., Nicosia 1987–88, High Commr to India with concurrent accreditation to nine other countries 1989–93, Amb. to Germany (also accred to Poland and the Holy See) 1996–2000, Perm. Rep. to EU 2000–04; fmr lawyer, M&M Law Firm; mem. Bd of Dirs Laiki Group 2005; mem. Cyprus Bar Asscn, Cttee of Missing Persons in Cyprus 2013–. *Publications:* numerous articles in Cypriot newspapers and magazines.

THEOPHILUS III, His Beatitude Patriarch of the Holy City of Jerusalem and all Palestine, Syria, beyond the Jordan river, Cana of Galilee and Holy Zion (Ilija Jannopoulos); Greek ecclesiastic; b. 1952, Messinia, Greece; ed Univ. of Athens, Durham Univ.; entered Brotherhood of Holy Sepulchre 1964; attended Patriarchal school in Jerusalem 1964–70; tonsured monk withe name of Theophilus 1970; ordained deacon 1970; ordained priest 1975; attended Athens Univ. and later worked in Jerusalem at Gen. Secr. of the Holy Synod, Patriarchal School, and St Charalampy's Monastery; elevated to rank of archimandrite 1978; apptd mem. Editorial Bd Nea Zion journal 1981; sent to UK to study at Durham Univ. 1981; Sec. for Foreign Relations, Holy Synod of the Patriarchate of Jerusalem 1986–88; Rep. Patriarchate of Jerusalem in Cen. Cttee, World Council of Churches 1988–91; hegumen, Monastery of St George the Victorious, Cana Galilee 1991–96; Rep. of Patriarchate of Jerusalem with Patriarch of Moscow and All Russia and Rector, Jerusalem Representation Church, Moscow 2001–03; Patriarchal epitrop, Doha Qatar 2003–04; Senior Custodian Holy Sepulchre and mem. Holy Synod of Patriarchate of Jerusalem 2004–05; Archbishop of Mount Tabor Feb. 2005; elected Patriarch of Jerusalem Aug., enthroned Nov. 2005. *Address:* Greek Orthodox Patriarchate, PO Box 14518, 91145 Jerusalem, Israel (office). *Telephone:* 2-6271657 (office). *Fax:* 2-6261283 (office). *E-mail:* patriarch.theophilos@jerusalem-patriarchate.info (office). *Website:* www.jerusalem-patriarchate.info (office).

THERON, Charlize; South African actress; b. 7 Aug. 1975, Benoni, SA; trained as ballet dancer; went to Milan aged 16 to become a model; moved to New York to dance with Joffrey Ballet; knee injury ended dancing career; moved to Los Angeles to take up acting; appointed UN Messenger of Peace 2008–; Los Angeles Film Festival Spirit of Independence Award 2006. *Films include:* Children of the Corn III 1994, Two Days in the Valley 1996, That Thing You Do! 1996, Trial and Error 1997, Hollywood Confidential 1997, Devil's Advocate 1997, Cop Land/The Yards 1997, Mighty Joe Young 1998, Celebrity 1998, The Cider House Rules 1999, The

Astronaut's Wife 1999, The Yards 2000, Reindeer Games 2000, Men of Honor 2000, The Legend of Bagger Vance 2000, Navy Diver 2000, Sweet November 2001, The Curse of the Jade Scorpion 2001, 15 Minutes 2001, The Yards/Nightwatch 2002, Waking Up in Reno 2002, Trapped 2002, 24 Hours 2002, Sweet Home Alabama (exec. producer) 2002, The Italian Job 2003, Monster (Golden Globe Award, Best Dramatic Actress 2004, Critics' Choice Award, Best Actress 2004, Screen Actors Guild Best Actress Award 2004, Acad. Award, Best Actress 2004) 2003, The Life and Death of Peter Sellers 2004, Head in the Clouds 2004, North Country 2005, Aeonflux 2005, In the Valley of Elah 2007, Battle in Seattle 2007, Hancock 2008, The Burning Plain 2008, Young Adult 2011, Snow White and the Huntsman 2012, Prometheus 2012, A Million Ways to Die in the West 2014, Dark Places 2015, Mad Max: Fury Road 2015, The Huntsman: Winter's War 2016. *Address:* c/o Spanky Taylor, 3727 West Magnolia, Burbank, CA 91505 (office); c/o United Talent Agency, Inc., 9560 Wilshire Blvd., Suite 500, Beverly Hills, CA 90212, USA.

THEROUX, Paul Edward, BA, FRSL, FRGS; American writer; b. 10 April 1941, Medford, Mass; s. of Albert Eugene Theroux and Anne Dittami Theroux; m. 1st Anne Castle 1967 (divorced 1993), two s.; m. 2nd Sheila Donnelly 1995; ed Univ. of Massachusetts; served in Peace Corps in Malawi; Lecturer, Univ. of Urbino, Italy 1963, Soche Hill Coll., Malawi 1963–65, Makerere Univ., Kampala, Uganda 1965–68, Univ. of Singapore 1968–71; Writer-in-Residence, Univ. of Va 1972; Hon. DLitt (Tufts Univ., Trinity Univ.) 1983, (Univ. of Mass.) 1988; Playboy magazine Editorial Awards 1972, 1976, 1977, 1979, American Acad. and Inst. of Arts and Letters Award in Literature 1977. *Play:* The White Man's Burden 1987. *Screenplays:* Saint Jack 1979, Chinese Box (story) 1997. *Publications include:* fiction: Waldo 1967, Fong and the Indians 1968, Girls at Play 1969, Murder in Mount Holly 1969, Jungle Lovers 1971, Sinning with Annie 1972, Saint Jack 1973, The Black House 1974, The Family Arsenal 1976, The Consul's File 1977, Picture Palace (Whitbread Award) 1978, A Christmas Card 1978, London Snow 1980, World's End 1980, The Mosquito Coast (James Tait Black Memorial Prize 1982, Yorkshire Post Best Novel Award 1982) 1981, The London Embassy 1982, Doctor Slaughter 1984, O-Zone 1986, My Secret History 1988, Chicago Loop 1990, Dr. DeMarr 1990, Millroy the Magician 1993, My Other Life 1996, Kowloon Tong 1997, Collected Stories 1997, Collected Short Novels 1998, Hotel Honolulu 2000, The Stranger at the Palazzo d'Oro (short stories) 2002, Telling Tales (contrib. to charity anthology) 2004, Blinding Light 2005, The Elephanta Suite 2007, A Dead Hand: A Crime in Calcutta 2009, The Lower River 2012, Mother Land 2017; non-fiction: V. S. Naipaul (criticism) 1973, The Great Railway Bazaar (travel) 1975, The Old Patagonian Express (travel) 1979, The Kingdom by the Sea (travel) 1983, Sailing through China (travel) 1983, Sunrise with Sea Monsters (travel) 1985, Riding the Iron Rooster: By Train Through China (travel) (Thomas Cook Prize for Best Literary Travel Book 1989) 1988, Travelling the World (travel) 1990, The Happy Isles of Oceania: Paddling the Pacific (travel) 1992, The Pillars of Hercules (travel) 1995, Sir Vidia's Shadow: A Friendship Across Five Continents (travel) 1998, Fresh-Air Fiend (travel) 1999, The Worst Journey in the World 2000, Nurse Wolf and Dr Sacks 2000, Dark Star Safari: Overland from Cairo to Cape Town (travel) 2002, Ghost Train to the Eastern Star (travel) 2008, The Tao of Travel 2011, The Last Train to Zona Verde: My Ultimate African Safari 2013, Deep South (Four Seasons on Back Roads) 2015. *Leisure interest:* rowing. *Address:* Hamish Hamilton Ltd, 80 Strand, London, WC2, England (office); The Wylie Agency, 250 West 57th Street, New York NY 10107, USA (office).

THEWLIS, David; British actor; b. 20 March 1963; s. of Alec Raymond Wheeler and Maureen Wheeler (née Thewlis); m. Sara Jocelyn Sugarman 1992 (divorced 1993); ed Highfield High School, Blackpool, St Anne's Coll. of Further Educ., Guildhall School of Music and Drama, London; Richard Harris Award for Outstanding Contrib. to British Film 2008. *Theatre includes:* Buddy Holly at the Regal, Ice Cream, Lady and the Clarinet (winner Edin. Fringe First), The Sea. *Films include:* Road 1987, Vroom 1988, Little Dorrit 1988, Resurrected 1989, Life is Sweet 1990, Afraid of the Dark 1991, Damage 1992, The Trial 1993, Naked (Best Actor, Cannes Film Festival, Nat. Soc. of Film Critics Awards Best Actor 1994, New York Film Critics Circle Awards Best Actor 1993) 1993, Black Beauty 1994, Total Eclipse 1995, Restoration 1995, James and the Giant Peach (voice) 1996, Dragonheart 1996, The Island of Dr Moreau 1996, Seven Years in Tibet 1997, Divorcing Jack 1998, The Big Lebowski 1998, Besieged 1998, Whatever Happened to Harold Smith 1999, Gangster No. 1 2000, Timeline 2003, Harry Potter and the Prisoner of Azkaban 2004, Kingdom of Heaven 2005, All the Invisible Children 2005, The New World 2005, Basic Instinct 2 2006, The Omen 2006, The Inner Life of Martin Frost 2007, Harry Potter and the Order of the Phoenix 2007, The Boy in the Striped Pyjamas 2008, Harry Potter and the Half-Blood Prince (Best Ensemble, Scream Award 2009) 2009, Harry Potter and the Deathly Hallows: Part 1 2010, War Horse 2011, The Lady 2011, Anonymous 2011, War Horse 2011, Separate We Come, Separate We Go (short) 2012, Red 2 2013, The Fifth Estate 2013, The Theory of Everything 2013, Stonehearst Asylum 2014, Queen & Country 2014, Regression 2015, Legend 2015, Macbeth 2015, Anomalisa (voice) (Best Depiction of Nudity, Sexuality, or Seduction, Alliance of Women Film Journalists Awards) 2015, Deep Water 2016. *Television includes:* Valentine Park (series) 1985, The Singing Detective (miniseries) 1986, The Short and Curlies (film) 1987, Skulduggery (film) 1989, Bit of a Do (series) 1989, Oranges Are Not the Only Fruit (film) 1990, Journey to Knock (film) (Best Actor, Rheims Film Festival 1992) 1991, Filipina Dreamgirls (film) 1991, Prime Suspect 3 1993, Dandelion Dead (miniseries) 1994, Endgame (film) 2000, Hamilton Mattress (film) 2001, Dinotopia (miniseries) 2002, Family Guy (series) 2014, An Inspector Calls (film) 2015. *Publication:* The Late Hector Kipling (novel) 2007. *Leisure interest:* painting. *Address:* c/o Victoria Belfrage, Julian Belfrage & Associates, Adam House, 14 New Burlington Street, London, W1S 3BQ, England (office). *Telephone:* (11) 4417-1491 (office).

THIAM, Tidjane, MBA; French/Côte d'Ivoirian business executive; *CEO, Credit Suisse Group AG;* b. 29 July 1962, Côte d'Ivoire; ed École Polytechnique, Paris, École Nationale Supérieure des Mines de Paris, Institut Européen d'Admin des Affaires (INSEAD), World Bank's Young Professionals Program, USA; moved with family to Morocco aged four; brought up in France; studied engineering in France before joining McKinsey & Co. (man. consultants), Paris, London and New York 1986; Chief Exec. then Chair. Nat. Bureau for Tech. Studies and Devt in Côte d'Ivoire 1994–97; Pres. Nat. Council on Information Superhighways and Nat. Sec. for Human Resources Devt 1997–98; Minister of Planning and Devt 1998–99; arrested and held for several weeks following mil. coup 1999; returned to France to become a Pnr with McKinsey & Co. 2000–02; apptd CEO Europe, Aviva 2002, later Group Strategy and Devt Dir and Man. Dir Aviva International –2008; Exec. Dir Prudential plc 2008–15, Chief Financial Officer –2009, Group Chief Exec. 2009–15; CEO Credit Suisse Group AG 2015–; Chair. G20 High Level Panel for Infrastructure Investment Jan.–Nov. 2011; Dir (non-exec.) Arkema (France) –2009; mem. External Advisory Council of World Bank Inst. 1999–, Africa Progress Panel chaired by Kofi Annan 2007–, Council of the Overseas Devt Inst., London, Bd of Asscn of British Insurers (Chair. 2012–), Int. Business Council of World Econ. Forum, European Financial Round Table 2013–; sponsor of Opportunity International; apptd a British Business Amb. by invitation from the Prime Minister 2014; Chevalier, Légion d'honneur 2011; Grand Prix de l'Economie, Les Echos newspaper 2013. *Address:* Credit Suisse Group AG, PO Box 1, 8070 Zurich (office); Credit Suisse Group AG, Paradeplatz 8, 8001 Zurich, Switzerland (office). *Telephone:* (44) 212-16-16 (office). *Fax:* (44) 333-25-87 (office). *E-mail:* info@credit-suisse.com (office). *Website:* www.credit-suisse.com (office).

THIBAUDET, Jean-Yves; French pianist; b. 7 Sept. 1961, Lyon; ed Paris Conservatoire, Lyon Conservatory of Music; began piano studies at age five and made first public appearance at age seven; appears with major orchestras in USA and Europe including Royal Concertgebouw, London Philharmonic, Royal Philharmonic, Orchestre Nat. de France, etc.; regular visitor to major US and European music festivals; in recital has collaborated with mezzo-sopranos Brigitte Fassbaender and Cecilia Bartoli, Renee Fleming and cellist Truls Mørk; debut, BBC Promenade Concerts 1992; Chevalier, Ordre des Arts et des Lettres 2001, Officier, Ordre des Arts et des Lettres 2012; Premier Prix du Conservatoire, Paris Conservatory 1976, winner, Young Concert Artists Auditions 1981, Echo Award 1990, 1998, Schallplattenpreis 1992, Gramophone Award 1998, Edison Prize 1998, Choc de la Musique 1999, 2003, Diapason d'Or for his recordings of works by Debussy 2000, Premio Pegasus, Spoleto Festival 2002, Echo Classical Music Awards 2002, Victoire d'Honneur, Victoires de la Musique 2007. *Recordings include:* recorded more than 50 albums, including Piano Concerti Nos. 2&5 2007, Aria—Opera Without Words 2007, Gershwin 2010, Satie: The Complete Solo Piano Music, Ravel Piano Music 2011, Rachmaninov: Piano Concertos 2012, Satie: Complete Solo Piano Music 2016, Bernstein: Symphonies Nos. 1 And 2 2017; jazz albums include Reflections on Duke: Jean-Yves Thibaudet Plays the Music of Duke Ellington, Conversations With Bill Evans. *Films:* Portrait of a Lady 1997, Bride of the Wind 2001, Pride and Prejudice 2005, Atonement 2007, Extremely Loud & Incredibly Close 2012, Wakefield 2017. *Television:* Piano Grand! (PBS/Smithsonian Special) 2000. *Leisure interests:* tennis, swimming, riding, water-skiing, museums, movies, racing cars. *Address:* c/o M. L. Falcone Public Relations, 155 West 68th Street, Suite 1114, New York, NY 10023, USA (office). *E-mail:* Lydia .Connolly@harrisonparrott.co.uk (home). *Website:* www.jeanyvesthibaudet.com.

THIBAULT, Bernard; French trade union official; *Vice-President, International Labour Organisation;* b. 2 Jan. 1959, Paris; m.; two c.; apprentice, Société Nationale des Chemins de fer Français (SNCF) 1974–76; joined Confédération Générale du Travail (CGT) 1977, responsible for the Youth Cttee, Sec., local depot 1980–82, Sec. CGT, Paris-Est railway 1982–87, joined Fed. Bureau of CGT railway 1987, Deputy Sec.-Gen. 1990–93, Gen. Sec. CGT railway 1993–99, Sec.-Gen. CGT 1999–2013; joined Parti communiste français (PCF) 1987, mem. Nat. Council of PCF 1997–2001; mem. Bd Worker's Rep. ILO 2014–, Vice-Pres. ILO 2015–; mem. Organising Cttee of Olympic Games. *Publications:* Qu'est-ce que la CGT? 2002, Ma voix ouvrière: entretiens avec Pierre-Marie Thiaville et Marcel Trillat 2004. *Address:* International Labour Organisation, 4, Route des Morillons, 1211 Geneva, Switzerland (office). *Telephone:* 227996111 (office). *Fax:* 227988685 (office). *E-mail:* ilo@ilo.org (office).

THICH, Quang Do; Vietnamese Buddhist leader; b. (Dang Phuc Tue), 27 Nov. 1928, Thai Binh Prov.; in exile in India and Sri Lanka; taught Buddhist philosophy in Saigon in the 1960s and 1970s; fmr leader Unified Buddhist Church of Vietnam, then Deputy Leader, Patriarch of the Unified Buddhist Church of Vietnam 2008–; imprisoned by Communist authorities, released 1998, launched Appeal for Democracy in Vietnam plan and was placed under house arrest in Thanh Minh Temple 2001; Hon. mem. PEN Clubs in Germany, France and Sweden; Hellman-Hammet Award 2001, shared Homo Homini Award for human rights activism, People in Need (Czech Repub.) 2003, Thorolf Rafto Memorial Prize 2006, Democracy Courage Tribute, World Movement for Democracy 2006, chosen by A Different View magazine as one of the 15 Champions of World Democracy 2008. *Publications include:* Novels: Deliverance from Bondage, Under the Eaves of the Derelict Pagoda; trans. War and Non-violence: Prison Poems 2007. *Address:* Thanh Zinh Zen Monastery, Ho Chi Minh City, Viet Nam.

THIÉBA, Paul Kaba, DEA, DESS; Burkinabè economist and politician; b. 28 July 1960, Bobo Dioulasso; m.; three c.; ed Univ. de Ouagadougou, Univ. de Grenoble II, France; Portfolio Man., Financial Management Dept, Groupe Caisse des Dépôts et Consignations (CDC), Paris 1988–91, Authorized Rep., CDC Management 1992–93; long career with Banque centrale des Etats d'Afrique de l'Ouest (BCEAO), including as Authorized Rep., Monetary Markets Service 1993–98, Head of Foreign Exchange Service 1998–2000, Deputy Dir of Financial Operations 2000–06, Dir of Financial Operations 2007–08, Adviser to Dir, BCEAO Gen. Affairs Dept 2009–11, Adviser to Dir-Gen. of Operations 2012–14; Man. Dir Financial Stability Fund, W African Econ. and Monetary Union 2014–15; Prime Minister 2015–19 (resgnd). *Address:* c/o Office of the Prime Minister, 03 BP 7027, Ouagadougou 03, Burkina Faso (office).

THIEBAUD, Wayne, MA; American artist and academic; *Professor Emeritus, University of California, Davis;* b. 15 Nov. 1920, Mesa, Ariz.; m. 1st Patricia Patterson 1945 (divorced 1959); two d.; m. 2nd Betty Jean Carr 1959 (died 2015); one s. one step s.; ed Frank Wiggins Trade School, Long Beach Jr Coll., San. José State Coll. (now San José State Univ.), California State Coll. (now California State Univ.); worked as commercial artist and freelance cartoonist from 1938; served USAAF 1942–45; started career as painter 1947; Asst Prof., Dept of Art, Univ. of Calif., Davis 1960, Assoc. Prof. 1963–67, apptd Prof. 1967, Faculty Research Lecturer 1973–, currently Prof. Emer.; co-founder Artists Co-operative Gallery (now Artists Contemporary Gallery), Sacramento 1958; numerous one-man exhbns in USA since 1950; one-man exhbn Galleria Schwarz, Milan, Italy 1963; represented USA at São Paulo Bienal, Brazil 1968; commissioned to do paintings of Wimbledon tennis tournament, England 1968; selected as Nat. Juror for Nat.

Endowment for the Arts, Washington, DC 1972; commissioned by US Dept of Interior to paint Yosemite Ridge Line for Bicentennial Exhbn, America 1976; mem. American Acad., Inst. of Arts and Letters, New York City 1985, Nat. Acad. of Design, New York City; Award of Distinction, Nat. Art Schools Asscn and Special Citation Award, Nat. Asscn of Schools of Art and Design 1984, Nat. Medal of the Arts 1994. *Publication:* Wayne Thiebaud: Private Drawings—The Artist's Sketchbook 1987. *Address:* Department of Art, University of California, 1 Shields Avenue, Davis, CA 95616, USA (office). *Telephone:* (530) 752-3135 (office). *Website:* art .ucdavis.edu (office).

THIELEN, Gunter, DEng; German business executive; *Chairman, Supervisory Board, Bertelsmann SE Co. KGaA;* b. 4 Aug. 1942, Quierschied, Saarland; ed Tech. Univ. of Aachen; various man. positions with BASF, Ludwigshafen 1970; Tech. Dir Wintershall Refinery, Kassel 1976; joined Bertelsmann AG as CEO Maul Belser printing co., Nuremberg 1980, mem. Exec. Bd Bertelsmann AG 1985, Head Print and Industrial Operations Div. (renamed Bertelsmann Arvato AG) 1985–2002, Chair. and CEO 2002–07, mem. Bertelsmann SE Co. KGaA Supervisory Bd 2002–, Chair. 2007–; Chair. Bertelsmann Stiftung (Foundation), Gütersloh 2001, 2007–; Chair. Bertelsmann Verwaltungsgesellschaft mbH (BVG) 2001; Johns Hopkins Univ. Global Leadership Award 2005. *Address:* Supervisory Board, Bertelsmann SE Co. KGaA, Carl-Bertelsmann-Str. 270, 33311 Gütersloh, Germany (office). *Telephone:* (5241) 80-0 (office). *Fax:* (5241) 80-62321 (office). *Website:* www .bertelsmann.com (office).

THIEMANN, Bernd, PhD; German banker and business executive; *Chairman of the Supervisory Board, Hypo Real Estate Holding AG;* ed Univs of Münster and Freiburg; early man. positions with German Sparkasse org.; mem. Man. Bd Nord/LB 1976, Chair. 1981–91; Chair. Man. Bd and CEO DG Bank 1991–2001; Partner, Man. Dir and Sr Adviser, Leonardo & Co. GmbH & Co. KG (fmrly Drueker & Co. GmbH & Co. KG) 2005–09; Chair. Supervisory Bd Rothschild GmbH 2001–, Constantin Medien AG (fmrly EM.Sport Media AG) 2001–09, Celanese AG of Celanese Corpn 2004–, Hypo Real Estate Holding AG 2009–; Deputy Chair. Advisory Bd Wurth Group; fmr Deputy Chair. Supervisory Bd Berentzen-Gruppe AG; mem. Supervisory Bd Nordland Papier AG –2002, VEBA Oel AG –2002, Deutsche Euroshop AG 2004–14, M.M. Warburg Bank & Co. KGaA 2011–14, ThyssenKrupp Stainless AG; fmr mem. Supervisory Bd Suedzucker AG; mem. Econ. Advisory Group, Fraport AG. *Address:* Hypo Real Estate Holding AG, Gewürzmühlstra. 11, 80538 Munich, Germany (office). *Telephone:* (89) 200072800 (office). *Fax:* (89) 200072802 (office). *E-mail:* info@hreholding.de (office). *Website:* www.hyporealestate.com (office).

THIER, Samuel Osiah, MD; American physician and academic; *Professor Emeritus of Medicine and Health Care Policy, Harvard Medical School;* b. 23 June 1937, Brooklyn, NY; s. of Sidney Thier and May H. Thier; m. Paula Dell Finkelstein 1958; three d.; ed Cornell Univ., State Univ. of New York, Syracuse; Intern, Massachusetts Gen. Hosp. 1960–61, Asst Resident 1961–62, 1964–65, Postdoctoral Fellow 1965, Chief Resident in Medicine 1966, Pres. 1994–97; Clinical Assoc. Nat. Inst. of Arthritis and Metabolic Diseases 1962–64; Instructor to Asst Prof., Harvard Medical School 1967–69, Prof. of Medicine and Health Care Policy 1994–2007, Prof. Emer. 2008–; Assoc. Prof. then Prof. of Medicine, Univ. of Pennsylvania Medical School 1969–74; Prof. and Chair. Dept of Medicine, Yale Univ. School of Medicine and Chief of Medicine, Yale-New Haven Hosp. 1975–85; Pres. Inst. of Medicine, NAS 1985–91; Pres. and Prof., Brandeis Univ. 1991–94; Pres. Partners Healthcare System Inc. 1994–2002, CEO 1996–2002. *Publications:* numerous articles and chapters in medical journals and textbooks. *Address:* Massachusetts General Hospital, 55 Fruit Street, Bulfinch 370, Boston, MA 02114, USA (office). *Telephone:* (617) 726-1811 (office). *Fax:* (617) 726-1900 (office). *E-mail:* sthier@partners.org (office).

THIERSE, Wolfgang; German politician; b. 22 Oct. 1943, Breslau; ed Humboldt Univ.; fmr typesetter; teaching asst, Dept of Cultural Theory and Aesthetics, Humboldt Univ., Berlin 1964; mem. staff, Ministry of Culture, GDR 1975–76, Cen. Inst. for History of Literature, Acad. of Sciences, GDR 1977–90; Chair. Social Democratic Party, GDR (which later factioned) 1990; mem. Bundestag (Parl.) 1990–, Pres. 1998–2005, Vice-Pres. 2005–13. *Publications include:* The Right Life in a False System, The Future of the East. *Address:* Bundestag, Platz der Republik 1, 11011 Berlin (office); Hagenauer Straße 3, 10435 Berlin, Germany. *Telephone:* (30) 22777028 (office). *Fax:* (30) 22776928 (office). *E-mail:* wolfgang.thierse@ bundestag.de (office). *Website:* www.bundestag.de (office); www.thierse.de.

THIESSEN, Gordon, OC, BA, MA, PhD; Canadian economist, company director and fmr central banker; b. 14 Aug. 1938, South Porcupine, Ont.; m. Annette Hillyar 1964; two c.; ed Univ. of Saskatchewan, London School of Econs, UK; joined Bank of Canada 1963; Visiting Economist, Reserve Bank of Australia 1973–75; Adviser to Gov. Bank of Canada 1979, Deputy Gov. responsible for econ. research and financial analysis 1984, Sr Deputy Gov. 1987, Chair. Bd of Dirs, mem. Exec. Cttee 1987, Gov. 1994–2001; fmr Exec.-in-Residence, Univ. of Ottawa School of Man.; Chair. Canadian Public Accountability Bd 2003–; mem. Bd of Dirs IPSCO Inc., Inst. for Research on Public Policy, Univ. of Saskatchewan; Swedish Order of the Polar Star, Commdr, Order of the North Star; Dr hc (Univ. of Saskatchewan, Univ. of Ottawa). *Leisure interests:* skiing, sailing.

THIJS, Johan, MSc; Belgian business executive; *Group CEO, KBC Group NV;* b. 1965; ed Catholic Univ. of Louvain; various actuarial functions in life and non-life insurance, ABB Insurance 1988–95, Head of Non-life Dept, Limburg regional office, ABB Insurance 1995–98; Prov. Man., Limburg and Eastern Belgium, KBC Insurance 1998–2001, Sr Gen. Man., Non-life Insurance, KBC Insurance 2001–09, mem. Exec. Cttee KBC Group, CEO Belgium Business Unit 2009–12, Group CEO KBC Group NV 2012–. *Address:* KBC Group NV, Havenlaan 2, Brussels 1080, Belgium (office). *Telephone:* (2) 429-50-45 (office). *Fax:* (2) 429-63-40 (office). *E-mail:* johan.thijs@kbc.be (office). *Website:* www.kbc.be (office).

THIKEO, Lien; Laotian politician; several years with Ministry of Finance, including as Vice-Pres., Planning and Investment Cttee and Vice-Pres., Planning and Cooperation Cttee, fmr Deputy Minister of Industry and Handicraft, Minister of Finance 2014–16; Gov. Sayabouri Prov. and Sec., Sayabouri LPRP Party Cttee 2006–14; mem. Lao People's Revolutionary Party (LPRP), mem. Cen. Cttee. *Address:* c/o Ministry of Finance, 23 rue Singha, Ban Phonxay, BP 24, Vientiane, Laos.

THINLEY, Jigmi Yozer, MA; Bhutanese politician; b. 9 Sept. 1952, Bumthang; ed St Stephen's Coll., India, Pennsylvania State Univ., USA; mem. civil service 1954–83, Head, Royal Civil Service Comm. Secr., Dir Educ. Dept; fmr Amb. and Perm. Rep. to UN, New York, Chair. Council of Ministers 1998–99, Minister of Foreign Affairs 1998–2003; Prime Minister, Chair. and Minister of Home and Cultural Affairs 2003–04; Minister of Home and Cultural Affairs 2004–07 (resgnd); Founder-Pres. Druk Phuensum Tshogpa (DPT) party 2007–13; Prime Minister 2008–13; Red Scarf 1987, Druk Thuksey and Coronation Medals 1999, Druk Wangyal Medal 2008. *Address:* Druk Phuensum Tshogpa (DPT), Chang Lam, Thimphu, Bhutan (office). *Telephone:* (2) 336336 (office). *Fax:* (2) 335845 (office). *E-mail:* dpt@druknet.bt (office). *Website:* www.dpt.bt (office).

THINOT, Dominique Pierre; French painter, teacher and diplomatist; *Professor and Director of Programmes for Public Art, École Nationale Supérieure des Arts Décoratifs;* b. 3 Oct. 1948, Paris; s. of Pierre Thinot and Y. Hervé; m. Claire Moreau 1977; two s.; ed Diplôme d'études supérieures, Paris; Prof., École Nationale Supérieure des Arts Décoratifs, Paris 1972–, Dir of Programmes for Public Art; has taught at various univs in Asia 1980–; leader of several cultural missions to Japan, Singapore, Korea and China 1985–; Pres. Asscn of Artists of the Bateau-Lavoir, Paris; mem. Gruppe Sieben, Germany 1975–; currently Chargé de Misson pour l'Asie, Int. Relations; Prof., Xi'an Acad. of Fine Arts, China; ECPD Special Counsellor, European Centre for Peace and Devt, Univ. for Peace est. by the UN; Artistic Dir Socs de construction européennes et asiatiques; dir of public art projects; adviser to artistic projects at univs; Chevalier, Ordre des Tastevins (Clos de Vougeot); Prix de la Création Artistique, Ministry of Cultural Affairs 1971, 1974, Prix de l'Acad. des Beaux-Arts 1983, Distinction du Govt de la République Arabe d'Egypte 1996. *Television include:* numerous reports for TV networks in France, Japan, Korea, China and Taiwan. *Leisure interests:* music, oenology. *Address:* Bateau-Lavoir, 13 place Emile Goudeau, 75018 Paris (home); 13 route des Vieilles-Vignes, 17880 Les Portes, Ile-de-Ré, France (home). *Telephone:* 1-78-11-30-08 (home). *E-mail:* artpublic3000@gmail.com (office); contact@dominiquethinot .com. *Website:* www.ensad.fr (office).

THODEY, David I., BA, FAICD; Australian business executive; *Chairman, Commonwealth Scientific and Industrial Research Organisation (CSIRO);* b. Perth, WA; ed Victoria Univ., NZ, Kellogg Post-Grad. School Gen. Man. Program, Northwestern Univ., USA; began as systems engineer at IBM, held several sr exec. positions in marketing and sales across Asia Pacific, CEO IBM Australia/NZ –2001; Group Man. Dir Telstra Mobiles, Telstra Corpn Ltd 2001–02, Group Man. Dir Telstra Enterprise and Govt 2002–09, responsible for corp., govt and large business customers in Australia, TelstraClear in NZ and int. sales div., Chair. TelstraClear New Zealand 2003–09, CEO Telstra Corpn Ltd 2009–15; Chair. Basketball Australia 2008–10, Sensis Pty Ltd 2009, CSIRO 2015–, Jobs for NSW Fund; currently Special Advisor Square Peg Capital; mem. Bd GSM Asscn 2013–; Fellow, Australian Inst. of Co. Dirs. *Address:* CSIRO, GPO Box 1700, Canberra, ACT 2601, Australia.

THOHIR, Garibaldi, BBA, MBA; Indonesian coal mining executive; *President Director and CEO, PT Adaro Energy Tbk;* b. 1 May 1965, Jakarta; s. of Teddy Thohir; m. Alinda G. Thohir; one s. two d.; ed Univ. of Southern California and Northrop Univ., USA; began career by forming holding co. for family business 1991; entered coal mining industry with acquisition of minority interest in PT Allied Indo Coal (small coal jt venture), S Sumatra 1991, bought out jt venture partner 1998, currently Pres. Dir; acquired PT Padangbara Sukses Makmur 2003, currently Pres. Dir; acquired Adaro Indonesia (coal mining co.) 2005, Pres. Dir and CEO PT Adaro Energy Tbk 2008–; f. PT Wahana Ottomitra Multiartha (PT WOM Finance TbK) 1997, currently Pres. Commr; Pres. Dir PT Trinugraha Thohir, PT Alam Tri Abadi, PT Dianlia Setyamukti, PT Jasapower Indonesia; Pres. Commr PT Trinugraha Food Industri, PT Wahanaartha Harsaka, PT Wahanaartha Motorent, PT Makmur Sejahtera Wisesa, PT Karunia Barito Sejahtera; Dir PT Indonesia Bulk Terminal; mem. Supervisory Bd Adaro Bangun Negeri Foundation. *Leisure interests:* sports, travelling with family. *Address:* PT Adaro Indonesia, Menara Karya, 18th Floor, Jln. H.R. Rasuna Said, Blok X-5, Kav. 1-2, Jakarta 12950, Indonesia (office). *Telephone:* (21) 25533000 (office). *Website:* www.adaro .com (office).

THOMAS, Betty; American film director and actress; b. 27 July 1948, St Louis, Mo.; ed Ohio Univ., Chicago Art Inst., Roosevelt Univ.; fmr mem. Second City improvisation group, Chicago; performed at the Comedy Store, Los Angeles. *Films include:* as actress: Tunnelvision 1976, Chesty Anderson: US Navy 1976, Jackson County Jail 1976, Loose Shoes 1980, Used Cars 1980, Homework 1982, Troop Beverly Hills 1989; as dir: Only You 1992, The Brady Bunch Movie 1995, Private Parts 1997, Dr Dolittle 1998, 28 Days 2000, I Spy (also producer) 2002, R3 2003, John Tucker Must Die 2006, Alvin and the Chipmunks: The Squeakquel 2009; producer: Can't Hardly Wait 1998, Surviving Christmas 2004; as exec. producer: Charlie's Angels 2000. *Television includes:* as dir: Doogie Howser MD, Dream On (series) (Emmy Award 1993), Hooperman, Mancusco FBI, Arresting Behavior, Couples; My Breast (film); The Late Shift (documentary) (Directors' Guild of America Award 1997); as actress: Hill Street Blues (series) (Emmy Award 1985) 1981–87, Outside Chance (film) 1978, Nashville Grab (film) 1981, When Your Lover Leaves (film) 1983, Prison for Children (film) 1987, Kidding (series) 2018–. *Address:* c/o Creative Artists Agency, 2000 Avenue of the Stars, Los Angeles, CA 90067, USA (office).

THOMAS, Chantal; French novelist and essayist; *Director of Research, Centre National de la Recherche Scientifique (CNRS);* b. 1945, Lyon; specialist in eighteenth century history; biographical publs on Sade, Casanova, Thomas Berhard and Marie-Antoinette; debut novel Adieux à la Reine sold over 110,000 copies and translated into German, English, Korean, Greek, Italian, Japanese, Dutch and Portugese 2002; currently Dir of Research, CNRS; Prix Roger-Caillois 2014, Grand Prix de la Société des Gens de Lettres 2014, Prix Prince Pierre de Monaco 2015. *Publications include:* Marquis de Sade: L'Oeil de la letter 1978, Casanova: Un Voyage libertine 1985, The Wicked Queen: The Origins of the Myth of Marie-Antoinette 2001, Coping with Freedom: Reflections on Ephemeral Happiness 2001, Adieux à la Reine (Farewell to the Queen, Prix Femina 2002) 2002, Le Lectrice-Adjointe 2003, Lîle flottante 2004, Apolline ou L'école de la Providence 2005, Le Palias de la Reine 2005, Chemins de sable 2006, Jardinière Arlequin 2006, Cafés de la Mémoire 2008, Le Testament d'Olympe 2010, L'esprit de conversation 2011, L'Échange des princesses 2013, Un air de liberté: Variations sur l'esprit du XVIII 2014, Souvenirs de la marée basse 2017, East Village Blues 2019. *Address:* CNRS Headquarters, 3, rue Michel-Ange, 75794 Paris cedex 16, France (office). *Telephone:* 1-44-96-40-00 (office). *Fax:* 1-44-96-53-90 (office). *Website:* www.cnrs.fr (office).

THOMAS, Clarence, BA, JD; American lawyer and judge; *Associate Justice, Supreme Court;* b. 23 June 1948, Pinpoint, Savannah, Ga; m. Virginia Lamp 1987; one s.; ed Conception Seminary, Conception Junction, Mo., Holy Cross Coll. and Yale Law School; called to the Bar, Mo. 1974, served as Mo. Asst Attorney-Gen. 1974–77; pvt. legal practice as an attorney for Monsanto Co. 1977–79; Legislative Asst to Mo. Senator John Danforth, US Senate 1979–81; Asst Sec. for Civil Rights, US Dept of Educ. 1981–82; Chair. US Equal Employment Comm. 1982–90; Judge, US Court of Appeals for DC Circuit 1990–91; Assoc. Justice, US Supreme Court 1991–. *Publication:* My Grandfather's Son 2007. *Address:* United States Supreme Court, One First Street, NE, Washington, DC 20543, USA (office). *Telephone:* (202) 479-3000 (office). *Website:* www.supremecourtus.gov (office).

THOMAS, D(onald) M(ichael), MA; British novelist and poet; b. 27 Jan. 1935, Redruth, Cornwall; s. of Harold Redvers Thomas and Amy Thomas (née Moyle); m. Angela Thomas; two s. one d.; ed Redruth Grammar School, Univ. High School, Melbourne, New Coll., Oxford; English teacher, Teignmouth, Devon 1959–63; Lecturer, Hereford Coll. of Educ. 1963–78; full-time author 1978–; Gollancz/Pan Fantasy Prize, PEN Fiction Prize, Cheltenham Prize, Los Angeles Times Fiction Prize, Cholmondeley Award for Poetry, Orwell Prize for Biography. *Play:* Hell Fire Corner 2004. *Publications include:* Two Voices 1968, Logan Stone 1971, Love and Other Deaths 1975, Honeymoon Voyage 1978, The Flute-Player 1978, Birthstone 1980, The White Hotel 1981, Dreaming in Bronze 1981, Ararat 1983, Selected Poems 1983, Swallow 1984, Sphinx 1986, Summit 1987, Memories and Hallucinations 1988, Lying Together 1989, Flying in to Love 1992, The Puberty Tree (new and selected poems) 1992, Pictures at an Exhibition 1993, Eating Pavlova 1994, Lady with a Laptop 1996, Alexander Solzhenitsyn (biog.) 1998, Charlotte 2000, Dear Shadows 2003, Not Saying Everything 2006, Bleak Hotel 2008, Hunters in the Snow 2014, Flight and Smoke, Two Countries, Vintage Ghosts, Mrs English & Other Women. *Leisure interests:* travel, Russia, Cornwall, the life of the imagination. *Address:* The Coach House, Rashleigh Vale, Truro, Cornwall, TR1 1TJ, England (home). *Telephone:* (1872) 261724 (home). *E-mail:* dmthomas@btconnect.com. *Website:* www.dmthomasonline.net.

THOMAS, David; British singer (bass); b. 26 Feb. 1943, Orpington, Kent, England; m. Veronica Joan Dean 1982; three d.; ed St Paul's Cathedral Choir School, London, King's School, Canterbury, Choral Scholar, King's Coll., Cambridge; began singing as boy chorister in St Paul's Cathedral Choir, London; repertoire from Baroque and Classical, and includes works by Walton, Tippett, Britten, Stravinsky, Schoenberg and Schnittke; tours to Europe, USA and Japan; appearances at int. festivals, including Tanglewood, Salzburg, Edinburgh, Lucerne, Stuttgart, Aldeburgh and BBC Promenade Concerts; has appeared with many of the major symphony orchestras and ensembles in UK, including City of Birmingham Symphony, London Philharmonic, Royal Philharmonic, Philharmonia, Hallé, Royal Liverpool Philharmonic, Chamber Orchestra of Europe, London Classical Players, Scottish Chamber Orchestra, Manchester Camerata, Northern Sinfonia, Taverner Consort, Acad. of Ancient Music and London Baroque, and has worked regularly with conductors including Simon Rattle, John Eliot Gardiner, Nicholas McGegan and Christopher Hogwood; notable engagements in UK include TV recording of Beethoven's 9th Symphony with London Classical Players conducted by Roger Norrington, Handel's Orlando at BBC Proms conducted by Christopher Hogwood and Die Schöpfung with Chamber Orchestra of Europe and Frans Bruggen; regular concerts with soprano Emma Kirkby and lutenist Anthony Rooley; sang Sarasto in Covent Garden Festival's production of Die Zauberflöte and the Commendatore in Don Giovanni and General Spork in Cornet Cristoph Rilke's Song of Love and Death for Glyndebourne Touring Opera; other engagements have included performances of the Christmas Oratorio in Leipzig and Berlin, a series of Messiahs in Italy and concerts with the Orchestre de la Suisse Romande, Fundaçao de Sao Carlos in Lisbon, Wiener Akademie, with Kammerchor Stuttgart in concerts in Göttingen, and Handel's Serse and Resurrezione in Brighton and Göttingen; engagements in USA have included Messiah with Los Angeles Philharmonic in the Hollywood Bowl, Haydn's Creation with Boston Symphony Orchestra and Simon Rattle, Messiah at Lincoln Center with Acad. of Ancient Music, Schubert's Winterreise at Cornell University and Handel's Judas Maccabaeus, Susanna and Theodora with Philharmonia Baroque and Nicholas McGegan; currently mem. staff, Trinity Laban Conservatoire of Music and Dance, London. *Recordings include:* more than 100 records, including Handel's Serse (Hanover Band/Nicholas McGegan), Handel's Susanna, Apollo and Daphne and Judas Maccabeus (Philharmonia Baroque/Nicholas McGegan), Handel's Semele, Purcell's Fairy Queen and Bach's Magnificat (Monteverdi Choir/English Baroque Soloists/John Eliot Gardiner), Handel's Messiah, Orlando, Athalia, etc. (Acad. of Ancient Music/Christopher Hogwood), Handel's Acis, Galatea e Polifemo (London Baroque/Charles Medlam), Handel's Messiah and Israel in Egypt, Bach's B Minor Mass and St John Passion (Taverner Consort & Players/Andrew Parrot), Handel's Messiah (Bach Collegium, Japan/Masaaki Suzuki), Coffee Cantata with Emma Kirkby, Mozart's Requiem (Hanover Band/Roy Goodman), Stravinsky's Pulcinella (City of London Sinfonia/Richard Hickox) and The Creation (City of Birmingham Orchestra/Simon Rattle), Beethoven Choral Symphony (American Bach Soloists/Jeffrey Thomas); solo record Arias for Montagnana, Handel. *Leisure interests:* the island of Dominica, Koi carp. *Address:* Trinity Laban Conservatoire of Music and Dance, King Charles Court, Old Royal Naval College, London, SE10 9JF, England (office). *Telephone:* (20) 8305-4444 (office). *E-mail:* d.thomas@trinitylaban.ac.uk (office); davidthomas@london.com (home). *Website:* www.trinitylaban.ac.uk (office).

THOMAS, Sir Derek Morison David, KCMG, MA; British fmr diplomatist and business consultant; b. 31 Oct. 1929, London; s. of K.P.D. Thomas and Mali Thomas; m. Lineke Van der Mast 1956; one s. one d.; ed Radley Coll. and Trinity Hall, Cambridge; articled apprentice, Dolphin Industrial Developments Ltd 1947; entered HM Foreign Service 1953; RNVR 1953–55; appointments overseas included Moscow, Manila, Sofia, Ottawa, Paris, Washington, DC; Deputy Under-Sec. of State for Europe and Political Dir FCO 1984–87; Amb. to Italy 1987–89; European Adviser to NM Rothschild and Sons Ltd 1990–2003, Dir 1991–99; Dir Rothschild Italia 1990–97, Christow Consultants Ltd 1990–99, Rothschild Europe 1991–97; Dir, Assoc. CDP Nexus 1990–92; Dir New Court Int. Ltd, Moscow, Consilium Spa, Prague 1994–2001; mem. Export Guarantees Advisory Council 1991–97; Chair. British Invisibles Lotis Cttee 1992–96, Council S.O.S. Sahel 1991–2000, Council Royal Inst. of Int. Affairs 1994–97, Council Reading Univ. 1990–99; Chair. British Inst. of Florence 1996–2002; Hon. Fellow, Trinity Hall, Cambridge 1998; Hon. LLD (Leicester) 2003. *Leisure interests:* exploring the past and present, music, theatre, wines, reading, grandchildren, gardening. *Address:* Flat 1, 12 Lower Sloane Street, London, SW1W 8BJ, England (home). *Telephone:* (20) 7730-1473 (home). *E-mail:* derekthomas@gmail.com (home).

THOMAS, Sir Eric Jackson, Kt, MD, DCL (Hon.), FRCOG, FRCP; British physician, academic and university administrator; b. 24 March 1953, Hartlepool, Cleveland, England; s. of Eric Jackson Thomas and Margaret Mary Murray; m. Narell Marie Rennard 1976; ed Ampleforth Coll., Univ. of Newcastle upon Tyne; Lecturer in Obstetrics and Gynaecology, Univ. of Sheffield 1985–87; Sr Lecturer in Obstetrics and Gynaecology, Univ. of Newcastle upon Tyne 1987–90; Consultant, Obstetrician and Gynaecologist, Newcastle Gen. Hosp. 1987–2000; Prof. of Obstetrics and Gynaecology, Univ. of Southampton 1991–2001, Head School of Medicine 1995–98, Dean Faculty of Medicine, Health and Biological Sciences 1998–2000, Consultant, Obstetrician and Gynaecologist, Southampton Univ. Hosps Trust 1991–2001, Dir (non-exec.) Southampton Univ. Hosps Trust 1997–2000, Southampton and SW Hants. Health Authority 2000–01; Vice-Chancellor Univ. of Bristol 2001–15; Exec. Sec., Council of Heads of Medical Schools 1998–2000; mem. Council Royal Coll. of Obstetricians and Gynaecologists 1995–2001, Bd South West Regional Sports 2003–06, Bd South West Regional Devt Agency 2003–08, CASE Europe 2007–14 (Chair. 2010–14); mem. Bd, Universities UK 2006–13, Chair. Research Policy Cttee 2006–09, England and Northern Ireland Council 2009–11, Vice-Pres. Universities UK 2009–11, Pres. 2011–13; Trustee, Royal Coll. of Obstetricians and Gynaecologist 2013–, IntoUniversity 2013–, HRH Commonwealth Study Confs 2015–; Governor, Univ. of Arts London 2015–; mem. Int. Advisory Council, Ashinaga 2014–; Dir Eric Thomas Consultancy Ltd; Hon. Fellow, Univ. of Bristol 2015, Birkbeck Coll. 2015; Hon. LLD (Bristol) 2004; Hon. DSc (Southampton) 2006, (Teeside) 2008, (West of England) 2010, (South Wales) 2015; Hon. DCL (Newcastle) 2015; William Blair Bell Memorial Lecturer, Royal Coll. of Obstetricians and Gynaecologists 1987. *Publications:* Modern Approaches to Endometriosis (co-author) 1991; publs on endometriosis and reproductive medicine. *Address:* Abbey Farmhouse, Oakley Road, Mottisfont, Hants., SO51 0LQ, England (office). *E-mail:* etconsulting@btinternet.com (office).

THOMAS, Harvey, CBE, FRSA; British international public relations consultant; b. 10 April 1939, London; s. of John Humphrey Kenneth Thomas and Olga Rosina Thomas; m. Marlies Kram 1978; two d.; ed Westminster School, London, Northwestern Coll., Minn., USA, Univ. of Minnesota, Univ. of Hawaii, Honolulu; articled in law 1957–60; Billy Graham Evangelistic Asscn 1960–75, N of England Mission 1960–61, Direct Mail, Minneapolis 1961–63, Press Relations, Southern California Mission 1963, KAIM Radio, Honolulu 1963–64, London Missions 1965–67, World Congress on Evangelism, Berlin 1966, Australasian Missions 1967–69, Dir Euro 70 Crusades 1969–70, Dir European Congress on Evangelism, Amsterdam 1970–71, research in 80 countries for 1974 Int. Congress on World Evangelization Lausanne 1971–72, SPRE-E 73, London 1973, Dir Billy Graham LAUSTADE Rally, Lausanne 1974, Gen. Sec. EUROFEST Brussels 1975; int. public relations and presentation consultant 1976–; Co-ordinator Int. Exposition for Tech. Transfer 1984; Public Relations, Luis Palau Mission to London 1984; Dir of Presentation, Conservative Party 1978; Field Dir Prime Minister's Election Tour 1987; Chair. Fellowship of European Broadcasters; mem. Bd London Cremation Co. PLC; Chair. Trans World Radio UK; Fellow, Chartered Inst. of Public Relations, Chartered Inst. of Journalists; mem. Inst. of Dirs; int. political consultant; conf. speaker and moderator; broadcaster and commentator on politics, religion and media; exec. coach; Individual Achievement Int. Broadcasting Award 2000. *Publications:* In the Face of Fear 1985, Making an Impact 1989, If They Haven't Heard It – You Haven't Said It 1995. *Leisure interests:* family, travel, broadcasting, public speaking, trains. *Address:* 23 The Service Road, Potters Bar, Herts., EN6 1QA, England (home). *Telephone:* (1707) 649910 (home). *Fax:* (1707) 662653 (home). *E-mail:* harvey@hthomas.net (office). *Website:* www.hthomas.net (office).

THOMAS, Iwan, MBE, BSc; British athlete; b. 5 Jan. 1974, Farnborough, Hants., England; ed Stamford School, Brunel Univ.; fourth-ranked BMX rider, Europe 1988; Fifth, Olympic Games 400m 1996, Silver Medal 4×400m relay; Gold Medal, Amateur Athletics Asscn Championships 400m 1997 (British record, 44.36 seconds), 1998; Silver Medal, World Championships 4×400m relay 1997; Gold Medal, European Championships 400m 1998, World Cup 400m 1998, Commonwealth Games 400m 1998; Patron Norwich Union Startrack Scheme; co-presenter, MotoGp Tonight; British Athletics Writers' Male Athlete of the Year 1998. *Television:* participant in numerous reality TV programmes. *Leisure interests:* music, Playstation, socializing with friends. *Address:* c/o Nuff Respect (Agent), 107 Sherland Road, Twickenham, Middx, TW1 4HB, England (office). *Telephone:* (20) 8891-4145 (office). *Fax:* (20) 8891-4140 (office). *E-mail:* nuff_respect@msn.com (office). *Website:* www.nuff-respect.co.uk (office); www.iwanthomas.co.uk.

THOMAS, Dame Jean Olwen, CBE, DBE, SCD., FRS, CChem, FMedSci; British scientist and academic; *Emeritus Professor of Macromolecular Biochemistry, University of Cambridge;* b. 1 Oct. 1942; d. of John Robert Thomas and Lorna Prunella Thomas (née Harris); ed Llwyn-y-Bryn High School for Girls, Swansea, Univ. Coll., Swansea, Univ. of Wales; Beit Memorial Fellow 1967–69, Univ. of Cambridge 1967–69, demonstrator in Biochemistry 1969–73, Lecturer 1973–87, Reader in the Biochemisry of Macromolecules 1987–91, apptd Prof. of Macromolecular Biochemistry 1991, currently Emer. Prof., Chair. Cambridge Centre for Molecular Recognition 1993–2003, Fellow, New Hall 1969–2006, tutor 1970–76, Vice-Pres. 1983–87, Master, St Catharine's Coll. 2007–16, Fellow 2007–16, Hon. Fellow 2016–; Fellow, Royal Soc. 1986–, mem. Council 1990–02, Biological Sec. and Vice-Pres. 2008–13; Pres. Biochemical Soc. 2000–05; mem. European Molecular Biology Org. 1982–, Academia Europaea 1991–, Council and Scientific Advisory Cttee Imperial Cancer Research Fund 1994–2000, Scientific Advisory Cttee Lister

Inst. 1994–2000, Internal Merit Promotion Panel of Research Councils (Chair. 2006–), Royal Soc. of Chem.; Fellow, Acad. of Medical Sciences 2002–; Gov. Wellcome Trust Ltd 2000–; Trustee British Museum 1994–2004; Hon. Fellow, UCW Swansea 1987, Cardiff Univ. 1998, Hon. Mem. Biochemical Soc. 2008; Hon. DSc (Wales) 1992, (East Anglia) 2002; Ayling Prize 1964, Hinkel Research Prize 1967, K. M. Stott Research Prize, Newnham Coll., Cambridge 1976. *Publications:* Companion to Biochemistry: Selected Topics for Further Study Vol. 1 1974, Vol. 2 1979 (jt and contrib.); numerous papers in scientific journals. *Leisure interests:* reading, music, walking. *Address:* Department of Biochemistry, University of Cambridge, 80 Tennis Court Road, Cambridge, CB2 1QW (office); 26 Eachard Road, Cambridge, CB3 0HY, England (home). *Telephone:* (1223) 333600 (office); (1223) 362620 (home). *E-mail:* jot1@cam.ac.uk (office). *Website:* www.caths.cam.ac.uk (office).

THOMAS, Jeremy, CBE; British film producer; *Owner, Recorded Picture Company;* b. 26 July 1949, London; s. of Ralph Thomas and Joy Thomas; m. 1st Claudia Frolich 1977 (divorced 1981); one d.; m. 2nd Vivien Coughman 1982; two s.; began work in film-processing lab., later worked as asst and in cutting room; worked with Dir Philippe Mora, editing Brother Can You Spare a Dime; went to Australia where he produced first film Mad Dog Morgan 1974, then returned to England in 1976 to produce Jerzy Skolimowski's The Shout; f. Recorded Picture Co. Ltd 1975; Chair. BFI 1992–97; set up own film distribution co. Recorded Releasing 1985; f. Hanway Films 1998; Vittorio de Sica Prize 1986, Special Award, Evening Standard Film Awards 1991, Michael Balcon BAFTA Award 1991, BFI Fellowship, Screen International Prize for World Cinema Achievement, European Film Awards 2006. *Films include:* Mad Dog Morgan 1976, The Shout (Grand Prix de Jury, Cannes Film Festival) 1978, The Great Rock'n'Roll Swindle 1979, The Kids are Alright (Special Consultant) 1979, Bad Timing 1980, Eureka 1982, Merry Christmas Mr Lawrence 1982, The Hit 1983, Insignificance 1984, The Last Emperor (winner of nine Academy Awards including Best Picture) 1987, Everybody Wins 1990, The Sheltering Sky 1990, The Naked Lunch 1991, Let Him Have It (exec. producer) 1991, Little Buddha 1993, Rough Magic (exec. producer) 1994, Victory (exec. producer) 1994, Stealing Beauty 1995, The Ogre (exec. producer) 1996, The Brave (exec. producer) 1996, Crash (exec. producer) (Grand Prix de Jury, Cannes Film Festival) 1996, Blood and Wine 1996, All The Little Animals (Dir) 1998, The Cup (exec. producer) 1999, Gohatto 2000, Brother 2000, Sexy Beast 2001, Rabbit Proof Fence (exec. producer) 2002, Triumph of Love (exec. producer) 2002, Young Adam 2003, Travellers and Magicians (exec. producer) 2003, The Dreamers (producer) 2003, Dreaming Lhasa (exec. producer) 2004, Heimat 3 (exec. producer) 2004, Don't Come Knocking (exec. producer) 2004, Tideland 2004, Glastonbury (exec. producer) 2005, Fast Food Nation 2005, Mister Lonely (exec. producer) 2006, Joe Strummer: The Future is Unwritten (exec. producer) 2007, Creation 2009, 13 Assassins (exec. producer) 2010, Essential Killing (exec. producer) 2010, Pina (exec. producer) 2011, A Dangerous Method (producer) 2011, Hara-Kiri: Death of a Samurai (producer) 2011, Vara: A Blessing (exec. producer) 2012, Kon-Tiki (producer) 2012, Only Lovers Left Alive 2013, Dom Hemingway 2013, High-Rise 2015, Tale of Tales 2015, Blade Of The Immortal 2017, Dogman 2018. *Address:* Recorded Picture Co. Ltd, 24 Hanway Street, London, W1T 1UH, England (office). *Telephone:* (20) 7636-2251 (office). *Fax:* (20) 7636-2261 (office). *E-mail:* kp@recordedpicture.com (office). *Website:* www.recordedpicture.com (office).

THOMAS, Sir John Meurig, Kt, MA, DSc, LLD, FRS; British chemist and academic; *Reader in History of Science, Davy Faraday Research Laboratory, Royal Institution of Great Britain;* b. 15 Dec. 1932, Llanelli, Wales; s. of David J. Thomas and Edyth Thomas; m. Margaret Edwards 1959 (died 2002); two d.; ed Gwendraeth Grammar School, Univ. Coll., Swansea, Queen Mary Coll., London; Scientific Officer, UKAEA 1957–58; Asst Lecturer, Lecturer, Sr Lecturer then Reader, Dept of Chem., Univ. Coll. of N Wales, Bangor 1958–69; Prof. and Head Dept of Chem., Univ. Coll. of Wales, Aberystwyth 1969–78; Head of Dept of Physical Chem., Univ. of Cambridge, Professorial Fellow of King's Coll. 1978–86, Master of Peterhouse 1993–2002, Distinguished Hon. Research Fellow, Dept of Materials Science, 1993–2002, Hon. Prof. of Materials Science 2002–; Cabinet Office Advisory Cttee on Applied Research and Devt 1982–85; Dir Davy Faraday Research Labs, Royal Inst. of GB 1986–91, Resident Prof. 1986–88, Fullerian Prof. of Chem. 1988–94, Prof. of Chem. and Professorial Research Fellow 1994–2002, Reader in History of Science 2002–; Deputy Pro-Chancellor Univ. of Wales 1991–94; Chair. Chem. Research Applied to World Needs, IUPAC 1987–95; Pres. Chem. Section, BAAS 1988–89; Hon. Visiting Prof. of Physical Chem., Queen Mary Coll., London 1986, Prof. of Chem., Imperial Coll., London 1986–91, Miller Prof., Univ. of Calif., Berkeley 1998; Distinguished Visiting Prof., Ecole Nat. Supérieure de Chimie Paris 1991; Visiting Prof., Scuola Normale Superiore Pisa 2003; Advisory Prof., Shanghai Jiao Tong Univ. 2009–, Catalysis Center, Hokkaido Univ. 2010–; Trustee, British Museum (Natural History) 1986–91, Science Museum 1989–95; Commr, 1851 Royal Exhbn 1995– (Chair. Scientific Research Cttee 1996–2005); Pres. Nat. Eisteddfod of Wales 2014; Tetelman Fellow, Yale Univ. 1997; mem. Academia Europaea 1989, Chemical Heritage Foundation, Philadelphia, Nat. Inst. of Informatics, Tokyo, Lab. of Molecular Sciences, California Inst. of Tech.; Hon. Professorial Fellow, Academia Sinica (Shanghai), Imperial Coll. London, Queen Mary Coll. London; Hon. FREng; Hon. FRSE; Hon. Visiting Prof. of Nanoscience, Univ. of South Carolina 2005–10; Hon. Distinguished Prof. of Materials Chem., Cardiff Univ. 2005–13; Hon. Distinguished Prof. of Materials Chem., Univ. of Southampton 2006–10; Hon. Distinguished Prof. of Chem. and Nanoscience, Univ. of York 2008–; Hon. Fellow, Indian Acad. (Bangalore), Indian Nat. Acad. (Delhi), UMIST, Univ. Coll. Swansea, American Acad. of Arts and Science, American Philosophical Soc., Venezuelan Acad. of Sciences, Russian Acad. of Sciences, Inst. of Physics; Hon. Foreign Fellow, Eng Acad. Japan 1991, Hungarian and Polish Acad. of Sciences 1998, Royal Spanish Acad. of Sciences 1999, Göttingen Acad. of Sciences 2003, Accad. Nazionale dei Lincei 2004, Mendeleev Chemical Soc. 2005, European Acad. of Sciences 2006, Royal Swedish Acad. of Sciences 2013; Hon. Bencher, Gray's Inn 1986; Hon. LLD (Wales); Hon. DLitt (CNAA); Hon. DSc (Heriot-Watt Univ.) 1989, (Birmingham) 1991, (Claude Bernard Univ., Lyon) 1994, (Complutense Univ., Madrid) 1994, (Western Univ., Ont.) 1995, (Eindhoven Univ., Netherlands, Hull Univ.) 1996, (Aberdeen, Surrey) 1997, (American Univ. Cairo) 2002, (Sydney, Clarkson, NY) 2005, (Osaka) 2006; Hon. DUniv (Open Univ.) 1992; laureate hc (Turin Univ.) 2004; Dr hc (St Andrews) 2012, (Univ. of South Carolina) 2013; Baker Lecturer, Cornell Univ. 1983, Bakerian Prize Lectureship, Royal Soc. 1990, Rutherford Lecturer, Royal Soc. NZ 1997, Centennial Karl Ziegler Lecturer Max Planck Inst. Mülheim 1998, Linus Pauling Lectureship, California Inst. of Tech. 1999, John C. Polanyi Nobel Laureate Lecturer, Univ. of Toronto 2000, Dreichamer Lecturer, Univ. of Illinois–Urbana 2004, Ipatieff Lecturer, Northwestern Univ. 2004, Golden Jubilee Distinguished Lecturer, Hong Kong Baptist Univ. 2006, Woodward Lecturer, Yale Univ. 2006; numerous awards including Faraday and Longstaff Medals, RSC 1990, Messel Gold Medal, Soc. of Chemical Industry 1992, Davy Medal, Royal Soc. 1994, ACS Willard Gibbs Gold Medal 1995, Hon. Medal, Polish Acad. of Sciences, Warsaw 1996, Semonov Centenary Medal, Russian Acad. of Sciences 1996, Rutherford Memorial Lecturer of Royal Soc. in New Zealand 1997, ACS Award for Creative Research in Catalysis 1999, Linus Pauling Gold Medal for Advances in Science, Stanford Univ. 2003, Giulionatta Gold Medal for Contributions to Catalysis, Italian Chem. Soc. 2003; new mineral meurigite named in his honour 1995; symposium in his honour organized by Microscopy and Microanalysis Soc. of America, Philadelphia 2000 and by RSC London 2002, Sir George Gabriel Stokes Gold Medal for Analytical Science, Royal Soc. of Chem. 2005, Distinguished Achievement Award, Int. Precious Medal Inst. 2007, US Presidential Green Chem. Challenge Award 2008, Ahmed H. Zewail Gold Medal and Lectureship, Wayne State Univ. 2009, Sven Breggren Prize Lecturer, Royal Lund Acad. of Science and Tech. (Sweden) 2010, Bragg Prize Lecturer, British Crystallography Asscn 2010, Ertl Prize Lecturer, Fritz-Haber Inst. of Max Planck Gesellschaft, Berlin 2010, Kapitza Gold Medal, Russian Acad. of Natural Sciences 2011, 600th Anniversary Lecturer, Univ. of St Andrews 2012, Jayne Prize Lecturer, American Philosophical Soc. 2012, Blaise Pascal Medal for Materials Science, European Acad. of Sciences 2014, Zewail/Elsevier Gold Medal and Prize for Molecular Science 2015, Royal Medal, Royal Soc. 2016. *Radio:* BBC Annual Lecture in Welsh 1978. *Television:* Royal Inst. Christmas Lectures on Crystals 1987–88; many Welsh language broadcasts. *Publications:* Principles of Heterogeneous Catalysis 1967, Characterization of Catalysts 1980, Heterogeneous Catalysis: Principles and Practice 1997, Michael Faraday and the Royal Institution: The Genius of Man and Place 1991, Perspectives in Catalysis (with K. I. Zamaraev) 1992; Pan Edrychwyf ar y Nefoedd (Welsh Radio Lecture) 1978; Founding Co-Ed.-in-Chief Catalysis Letters 1988–, Topics in Catalysis 1992–, Current Opinion in Solid State and Materials Science; more than 1,100 research papers on catalysis solid-state and surface science and more than 100 review articles on science, education and cultural issues. *Leisure interests:* walking, Welsh literature, ancient civilizations, birdwatching, popularization of science, listening to music. *Address:* Department of Materials Science and Metallurgy, University of Cambridge, 27 Charles Babbage Road, Cambridge, CB3 0FS (office); Davy Faraday Research Laboratory, The Royal Institution, 21 Albemarle Street, London, W1S 4BS, England (office). *Telephone:* (1223) 334300 (Cambridge) (office); (20) 7670-2928 (London) (office). *Fax:* (1223) 334567 (Cambridge) (office); (20) 7670-2958 (London) (office). *E-mail:* jmt@ri.ac.uk (office). *Website:* www-hrem.msm.cam.ac.uk/people/thomas (office); www.ri.ac.uk (office).

THOMAS, Sir Keith Vivian, Kt, MA, FBA; British historian and academic; *Honorary Fellow, All Souls College, Oxford;* b. 2 Jan. 1933, Wick, Glamorgan, Wales; s. of Vivian Thomas and Hilda Thomas; m. Valerie June Little 1961; one s. one d.; ed Barry Co. Grammar School and Balliol Coll., Oxford (Brackenbury Scholar); nat. service in Royal Welch Fusiliers 1950–52; Fellow, All Souls Coll., Oxford 1955–57, 2001–, St John's Coll. Oxford 1957–86, Tutor 1957–85; Reader in Modern History, Univ. of Oxford 1978–85, Prof. 1986, Pres. Corpus Christi Coll. 1986–2000, Pro-Vice-Chancellor, Univ. of Oxford 1988–2000; Del., Oxford Univ. Press 1980–2000; mem. Econ. and Social Research Council 1985–90, Reviewing Cttee on Export of Works of Art 1990–92, Royal Comm. on Historical Manuscripts 1992–2002; Trustee, Nat. Gallery 1991–98, British Museum 1999–2008; Pres. British Acad. 1993–97; Chair. Supervisory Cttee, Oxford Dictionary of Nat. Biography 1992–2004, British Library Advisory Cttee for Arts, Humanities and Social Sciences 1997–2002, Advisory Cttee, Warburg Inst., Univ. of London 2000–08; Hon. Fellow, Balliol Coll. Oxford 1984, St John's Coll. Oxford 1986, Univ. of Cardiff 1995, Corpus Christi Coll. Oxford 2000, Warburg Inst., Univ. of London 2008, All Souls Coll. Oxford 2015; Hon. Vice-Pres. Royal Historical Soc. 2001–; Foreign Hon. mem. American Acad. of Arts and Sciences 1983, Japan Acad. 2009; Cavaliere Ufficiale, Ordine al Merito della Repubblica Italiana 1991; Hon. DLitt (Kent) 1983, (Wales) 1987, (Hull) 1995, (Leicester) 1996, (Sussex) 1996, (Warwick) 1998, (London) 2006, (Columbia) 2011; Hon. LittD (Sheffield) 1992, (Cambridge) 1995; Hon. LLD (Williams) 1988, (Oglethorpe, Atlanta, Ga) 1996; Hon. PhD (Uppsala) 2014; mem. Academia Europaea 1993; Wolfson Literary Award for History 1971, G.M. Trevelyan Lecturer, Univ. of Cambridge 1979, Ford's Lecturer, Univ. of Oxford 2000, Norton Medlicott Medal, Historical Asscn 2003, Lifetime Achievement Award, All Party Group on Archives and History 2015. *Publications:* Religion and the Decline of Magic 1971, Puritans and Revolutionaries (co-ed with Donald Pennington) 1978, Man and the Natural World 1983, The Oxford Book of Work (ed.) 1999, Roy Jenkins: A Retrospective (co-ed with Andrew Adonis) 2004, Changing Conceptions of National Biography 2005, The Ends of Life: Roads to Fulfilment in Early Modern England 2009, The Wolfson History Prize: an Informal History 2012. *Leisure interest:* looking for second-hand bookshops. *Address:* All Souls College, Oxford, OX1 4AL (office); The Broad Gate, Broad Street, Ludlow, Shropshire, SY8 1NJ, England (home). *Telephone:* (1865) 279379 (office); (1584) 877797 (home). *Fax:* (1865) 279299 (office). *E-mail:* keith.thomas@all-souls.oxford.ac.uk (home).

THOMAS, Michael Tilson (see Tilson Thomas, Michael).

THOMAS, Robert Kemeys, MA, DPhil, FRS; British chemist and academic; *Professor Emeritus, Physical and Theoretical Chemistry Laboratory, University of Oxford;* b. 25 Sept. 1941, Harpenden, Herts., England; s. of Rev. Herbert Thomas and Agnes Thomas (née McLaren); m. Pamela H. Woods 1968; one s. two d.; ed St John's Coll., Oxford; researcher, Univ. of Oxford 1968–78, Fellow, Merton Coll. 1975–78, Lecturer in Physical Chem. 1978, Fellow and Tutor, Univ. Coll. 1978, fmr Prof., Physical and Theoretical Chem. Lab., now Prof. Emer.; Hon. Prof., Inst. of Chem., Chinese Acad. of Sciences, Beijing 1999–; Tilden Lecturer, Royal Soc. of Chem. *Publications:* numerous papers in scientific journals. *Leisure interests:* music, flora, fungi, Chinese language. *Address:* Physical and Theoretical Chemistry Laboratory, South Parks Road, Oxford, OX1 3QZ, England (office). *Telephone:* (1865) 275422 (office). *Fax:* (1865) 275410 (office). *E-mail:* robert.thomas@

chem.ox.ac.uk (office). *Website:* research.chem.ox.ac.uk/robert-thomas.aspx (office).

THOMAS, (John David) Ronald, (J. D. R. Thomas), DSc, CChem, FRSC; British/Welsh chemist and academic; *Professor Emeritus of Chemistry and Applied Chemistry, University of Wales and Cardiff University;* b. 2 Jan. 1926, Carnaugwynion, Gwynfe, Wales; s. of John Thomas and Betty Thomas (née Watkins); m. Gwyneth Thomas 1950; three d.; ed Llandovery Grammar School and Univ. of Wales, Cardiff (now Cardiff Univ.); RAMC blood transfusion training, Clifton Coll. and Southmead Hosp., Bristol 1944; served in RAMC, India 1944–47; Tech. Asst British Resin Products Ltd Tonbridge 1948; analytical chemist, Spillers Ltd, Cardiff 1950–51, Glamorgan Co. Council 1951–53; Asst Lecturer, Cardiff Coll. of Tech. 1953–56; Lecturer, South East Essex Tech. Coll. 1956–58; Sr Lecturer, Newport and Monmouthshire Coll. of Tech. 1958–61; Sr Lecturer and Reader, Univ. of Wales Inst. of Science and Tech. (UWIST) and Univ. of Wales, Cardiff 1961–90; Counsellor, Open Univ. 1970–71; Prof., Univ. of Wales, Cardiff (now Cardiff Univ.) 1990–93, Prof. Emer. 1994–; mem. Court Univ. of Wales 1989–2001, 2002–08, Council 1997–2001; mem. Council UWIST, Cardiff 1976–79, Univ. of Wales Coll. of Medicine 1993–99; mem. Court Aberystwyth Univ. 1995–2015; Royal Soc. sponsored invitee to Iranian Chemical Soc. Third Int. Congress and Iranian univs 1975; British Council sponsored invitee to Asian Chemical Congress '87, Seoul and univs at Taejon and Ulsan, S Korea 1987; Foreign Expert, Academia Sinica (Nanjing), Hunan (Changsha), North West (Xian) and Shanghai Teachers Univs 1983, 1985; Visiting Prof., Japan Soc. for the Promotion of Science 1985, NEWI (now Glyndwr Univ.), Wrexham 1995–96; Assessor, Univ. Pertanian Malaysia 1992–94, 1997–99, Univ. Sains Malaysia 1996–98, Universidade Nova de Lisboa and Universidade do Porto 1998–99, Hong Kong Research Grants Council 1996–2009; RSC Schools Lecturer in Analytical Chem. 1985–86; Distinguished Visiting Fellow, La Trobe Univ., Australia 1989; mem. Govt High-Level Mission on Analytical Instrumentation to Japan 1991; Adviser to RSC on privatization of UK Lab. of Govt Chemist 1995–97; Vice-Pres. Soc. for Analytical Chem. and Analytical Div. Chem. Soc. 1974–76, mem. Council Chem. Soc. 1976–79; Hon. Sec. Analytical Div. RSC 1987–90, Pres. 1990–92, mem. Council RSC 1990–2005; Chair. Analytical Editorial Bd RSC 1985–90; Sec. Baptist Union of Wales Superannuation Appeal 1976–78; mem. Council, Baptist Union of Wales 1994–97; lectured widely in UK, Europe, Middle and Far East, Australia, USA; Hon. Ed. Newsletter, Analytical Div., RSC 1995–2007; Hon. Prof., Univ. 'Politehnica', Bucharest, Romania 1996–; Hon. Course Adviser, Hong Kong Baptist Univ. 1991–2009; Hon. Mem. Romanian Soc. of Analytical Chem. 1994–, Romanian Chem. Soc. 1999–; Commonwealth Foundation Lecturer, CSMC Research Inst., Bhavnagar, India 1978, RSC Electroanalytical Chem. Medal and Award 1981, E.A. Moelwyn-Hughes Lecturer, Univ. of Cambridge 1988, Ion-Selective Electrodes Lecturer, Third Chemical Congress of N America, Toronto, Canada 1988, J. Heyrovsky Centenary Medal, Czechoslovak Acad. of Sciences 1990, RSC symposium in his honour, Cardiff 1994, White Robe, Gorsedd of Bards 2000, RSC L.S. Theobald Lectureship, 2001, Enric Casassas Memorial Lecturer, Univ. of Barcelona 2002, Most Visited Article Award of Inst. d'Estudis Catalans 2005, Distinguished Service Award Analytical Div. RSC 2006, Medal and Award for Service to RSC 2009. *Achievements include:* famed for PVC-based ion sensors and electrochemical sensors for biomedical and technological roles. *Publications include:* ed.: Selective Electrode Reviews, Vols 1–14 1979–92; Trans. Ed.: Membrane Electrodes in Drug Substances Analysis (Cosofret) 1982; author: History of the Analytical Division, Royal Society of Chemistry 1999; co-author: Calculations in Advanced Physical Chemistry 1962–83 (Hungarian trans. 1979), Noble Gases and Their Compounds 1964, Selective Ion-Sensitive Electrodes 1971 (Chinese trans. 1975, Japanese 1977), Dipole Moments in Inorganic Chemistry 1971 (Spanish trans. 1974), Practical Electrophoresis 1976, Chromatographic Separations and Extraction with Foamed Plastics and Rubbers 1982; more than 300 articles in scientific journals on chemical and bio-sensors, reaction kinetics, separation chem. and environmental matters. *Leisure interests:* travel, reading (current affairs and history), browsing and things of Wales, genealogy. *Address:* 4 Orchard Court, Gresford, Wrexham, LL12 8EB, Wales (home). *Telephone:* (1978) 856771 (home). *E-mail:* jdrthomas@aol.com (home).

THOMAS, Hon. Tillman Joseph, (Uncle Tilly), BSc (Econ.), LLD; Grenadian lawyer and politician; *Leader, National Democratic Congress;* b. 13 June 1947, Hermitage, St Patrick; m. Sandra Thomas; ed Fordham Univ., USA, Univ. of the West Indies, Hugh Woodling Law School, Trinidad; fmr political prisoner under govt of Maurice Bishop early 1980s; mem. House of Reps for St Patrick E 1984–90, 2003–; Jr Minister, Ministry of Legal Affairs 1984–90; Founder-mem. Nat. Democratic Congress Party 1987, Asst Gen. Sec. 1987–90, Leader 2000–; Leader of Opposition 2003–08; Prime Minister 2008–13, was also Minister of Nat. Security, Foreign Affairs, Public Admin, Information, Information Communications Tech., Legal Affairs and Nat. Mobilization; currently Assoc., Franco Chambers and Co., St Andrew's. *Film:* The Island President (documentary) 2011. *Leisure interests:* yoga. *Address:* National Democratic Congress, NDC Headquarters, Lucas Street, St George's (office); Hermitage, St Patrick's, Grenada (home). *Telephone:* 440-3769 (office); 442-9340 (home). *E-mail:* ndcgrenada@ndcgrenada.org (office); tillmanjthomas@yahoo.com (home). *Website:* www.ndcgrenada.org (office).

THOMAS-GRAHAM, Pamela, BA, MBA, JD; American business executive and author; *Founder and CEO, Dandelion Chandelier Digital Media;* b. 24 June 1963, Detroit, Mich.; m. Lawrence Otis Graham; three c.; ed Detroit Lutheran West High School, Harvard-Radcliffe Coll., Harvard Business School, Harvard Law School; fmr Ed. Harvard Law Review; joined McKinsey & Co. 1989, Partner 1995–99, leader of Media and Entertainment practice –1999; Pres. and CEO CNBC.com 1999–2001, Pres. and CEO CNBC 2001–05, Chair. 2005; Group Pres. Better and Moderate Apparel, Liz Claiborne Inc. 2005–07; Man. Dir Angelo, Gordon and Co. (pvt. investment man. firm), New York 2008–10; Chief Talent, Branding and Communications Officer, Credit Suisse AG 2010–16, mem. Exec. Bds Credit Suisse Group AG and Credit Suisse AG; Founder and CEO Dandelion Chandelier Digital Media 2016–; mem. Bd of Dirs Clorox Co. 2005– (Lead Ind. Dir 2016–), Idenix Pharmaceuticals Inc. 2005–, The Bank of N.T. Butterfield & Son Ltd 2017–, Preloton Interactive 2018–, Norwegian Cruise Lines Holdings 2018–, New York Philharmonic, Parsons School of Design; mem. Council on Foreign Relations, Economic Club of New York; fmr mem. US Sec. of State Condoleezza Rice's Advisory Cttee on Transformational Diplomacy; Capt. Jonathan Fay Prize. *Publications:* A Darker Shade of Crimson 1998, Blue Blood 2000, Orange Crushed 2004. *Leisure interests:* running, skiing, books, baseball. *Address:* Dandelion Chandelier Digital Media, New York, USA (office). *E-mail:* ptg@dandelionchandelier.com (office). *Website:* dandelionchandelier.com (office).

THOMPSON, Sir Clive Malcolm, Kt, BSc; British business executive; *Deputy Chairman, Strategic Equity Capital PLC;* b. 4 April 1943, Bristol; s. of H. L. Thompson and P. D. Thompson (née Stansbury); m. Judith Howard 1968; two s.; ed Clifton Coll., Bristol and Birmingham Univ.; Marketing Exec. Royal Dutch Shell Group 1964–67; Marketing Exec. and Gen. Man. Boots Co. PLC 1967–70; Gen. Man. Jeyes Group Ltd 1970–78; Man. Dir Health and Hygiene Div., Cadbury Schweppes 1978–82; Chief Exec. Rentokil Initial PLC 1983–2003, Chair. (non-exec.) 2003–04; Pres. CBI 1998–2000; Deputy Chair. Financial Reporting Council; fmr Dir (non-exec.) Wellcome PLC, Sainsbury PLC, Seeboard PLC, Caradon PLC, BAT Industries PLC; fmr Chair. Kleeneze PLC, European Home Retail (EHR) 2002–06; Deputy Chair. Strategic Equity Capital PLC, London 2005–; mem. Hampel Cttee on Corp. Governance 1998; Hon. DSc (Birmingham) 1999. *Leisure interests:* the stock market, current affairs, walking, golf. *Address:* Strategic Equity Capital PLC, Beaufort House, 51 New North Road, Exeter, EX4 4EP, England (office). *Telephone:* (1392) 477500 (office). *Website:* www.strategicequitycapital.com (office).

THOMPSON, Daley (Francis Morgan), MBE, OBE, CBE; British fmr athlete; b. 30 July 1958, Notting Hill, London; m. Tisha Quinlan 1987; three c.; Sussex Schools 200 m title 1974; first competitive decathlon, Welsh Open Championship June 1975; European Junior Decathlon Champion 1977; European Decathlon silver medallist 1978, gold medallist 1982 and 1986; Commonwealth Decathlon gold medallist 1978, 1982 and 1986; Olympic Decathlon gold medallist 1980 (Moscow) and 1984 (Los Angeles); World Decathlon Champion 1983; est. new world record for decathlon (at Olympic Games, Los Angeles), set four world records in all and was undefeated between 1978 and 1987; retd July 1992; Amb. Summer Olympics, London 2012; invited to run leg of the Olympic Torch relay at the opening of the Sydney Olympic Games 2000, BBC Sports Personality of the Year Award. *Publications include:* Going for Gold 1987, The Greatest 1996. *Address:* c/o Jane Cowmeadow, JCCM Ltd, Matrix Studios, 91 Peterborough Road, London, SW6 3BU, England (office). *E-mail:* office@jccm-uk.com (office). *Website:* www.jccm-uk.com (office).

THOMPSON, Donald (Don), BS (ElecEng); American business executive; m. Liz Thompson; two c.; ed Purdue Univ.; began career at McDonald's as an electrical engineer 1990, has since held several leadership positions, including Div. Pres., Exec. Vice-Pres. and US COO, Pres. McDonald's USA –2011, Pres. and COO McDonald's Corpn 2011–12, Pres. and CEO 2012–15; mem. Bd of Dirs Exelon Corpn, Northwestern Memorial Hosp., Purdue Univ.; mem. Civic Cttee of the Commercial Club, The Economic Club, World Business Chicago, Brazier Foundation; Dr hc (Excelsior Coll., Albany, NY) 2008; Purdue Univ. Outstanding Electrical and Computer Eng Award, named a Purdue Univ. Old Master Fellow 2006, named by Black Enterprise as Corp. Exec. of the Year 2007, Corp. Exec. Award, Trumpet Foundation 2008, Presidential Inspiration Award, Alpha Phi Alpha fraternity 2009, Achievement Award, Exec. Leadership Council 2010, Humanitarian Award, Illinois Holocaust Museum 2012. *Address:* c/o McDonald's Corporation, 2915 Jorie Blvd, Oak Brook, IL 60523, USA.

THOMPSON, Dorothy Carrington, CBE, BSc (Hons), MSc; British energy industry executive; *CEO and Executive Director, Drax Group;* two c.; ed London School of Econs; early career in banking; Asst Group Treas. Powergen 1993–98; joined InterGen NV 1998, later Head of European Business; CEO and Exec. Dir Drax Group Ltd 2005–; Dir (non-exec.) Johnson Matthey plc. *Address:* Drax Power Ltd, Drax Power Station, Selby, N Yorks., YO8 8PH, England (office). *Telephone:* (1757) 618381 (office). *Fax:* (1757) 618504 (office). *Website:* www.draxgroup.plc.uk (office).

THOMPSON, Dame Emma, DBE; British actress and screenwriter; b. 15 April 1959; d. of Eric Thompson and Phyllida Law; m. 1st Kenneth Branagh 1989 (divorced); m. 2nd Greg Wise 2003; one d.; ed Camden Girls' School and Newnham Coll., Cambridge; appeared with Cambridge Footlights; Chair. Bd of Trustees Helen Bamber Foundation; Int. Amb., ActionAid (charity). *Stage appearances include:* The Cellar Tapes, Edin. Festival 1981–82 (Perrier Pick of the Fringe Award 1981), A Sense of Nonsense (revue tour) 1983, Short Vehicle, Edin. Festival 1984, Me and My Girl, Adelphi 1984–85, Look Back in Anger, Lyric 1989, A Midsummer Night's Dream (world tour) 1990, King Lear (world tour) 1990. *Films:* The Tall Guy 1988, Henry V 1989, Impromptu 1989, Howards End 1991 (eight awards for Best Actress, including New York Critics, LA Critics, Golden Globe, Acad. Award, BAFTA, Nat. Bd of Review; David di Donatella Award for Best Foreign Actress (Italy)), Dead Again 1991, Peter's Friends 1992, Much Ado About Nothing 1993, Remains of the Day 1993 (David di Donatella Award for Best Foreign Actress (Italy)), In the Name of the Father 1993, Junior 1994, Carrington 1995, Sense and Sensibility (nine awards for Best Screenplay, including Acad. Award, Golden Globe, LA Film Critics, New York Film Critics, Writers Guild of America, Evening Standard British Film Award; awards for Best Actress from BAFTA and Nat. Bd of Review), The Winter Guest 1996 (Panisetti Award for Best Actress, Venice Film Festival), Primary Colors 1997, Judas Kiss 1997, Imagining Argentina 2003, Love Actually 2003, Harry Potter and the Prisoner of Azkaban 2004, Nanny McPhee (also screenplay writer) 2005, Stranger Than Fiction 2006, Harry Potter and the Order of the Phoenix 2007, Last Chance Harvey 2008, Brideshead Revisited 2008, The Boat that Rocked 2009, An Education 2009, Nanny McPhee and the Big Bang 2010, Harry Potter and the Deathly Hallows Part 2 2011, Brave (voice) 2012, Men in Black III 2012, Beautiful Creatures 2013, The Love Punch 2013, Saving Mr. Banks 2013, Effie Gray 2014, A Walk in the Woods 2015, The Legend of Barney Thomson 2015, Burnt 2015, Alone in Berlin 2016, Bridget Jones's Baby 2016, Beauty & the Beast 2017. *Television appearances include:* Emma Thompson Special, Channel 4 1983, Alfresco (two series), Granada 1983–84, The Crystal Cube, BBC 1984, Tutti Frutti, BBC (BAFTA Award for Best Actress) 1986, Fortunes of War, BBC (BAFTA Award for Best Actress) 1986–87, Thompson 1988, Knuckle, BBC 1988, The Winslow Boy, BBC 1988, Look Back in Anger, Thames 1989, Cheers 1992, Blue Boy, BBC Scotland 1994, Ellen, Touchstone TV/ABC (Emmy Award for Outstanding Guest Actress in a Comedy

Series) 1998, Wit (Best Actress Award, Semana Internacional de Cine de Valladolid) 2000, Angels in America (miniseries) 2003, The Song of Lunch 2010, Walking the Dogs 2012. *Address:* c/o Hamilton Hodell Ltd, 5th Floor, 66–68 Margaret Street, London, W1W 8SR, England (office). *Telephone:* (20) 7636-1221 (office). *Fax:* (20) 7636-1226 (office). *E-mail:* info@hamiltonhodell.co.uk (office). *Website:* www.hamiltonhodell.co.uk (office).

THOMPSON, G. Kennedy (Ken), BA, MBA; American business executive; *Principal and Executive Advisor, Aquiline Capital Partners LLC;* b. 25 Nov. 1950, Rocky Mount, NC; ed Univ. of North Carolina, Wake Forest Univ.; joined First Union Corpn 1976, various man. and exec. positions including Pres. First Union Ga, Sr Vice-Pres. and Head First Union Human Resources, Pres. First Union Fla, Vice-Chair. of Corpn and Head Global Capital Markets 1998–99, Chair., Pres. and CEO First Union Corpn 1999–2001, Pres. and CEO Wachovia Corpn (after merger of First Union and Wachovia) 2001–08; Prin. and Exec. Advisor, Aquiline Capital Partners LLC 2009–; mem. Bd of Dirs Fla Rock Industries Inc., Carolinas Healthcare System; mem. Financial Services Forum, The Business Council, Bd Financial Services Roundtable; Vice-Chair. NY Clearing House; mem. Bd Teach for America, NC Blumenthal Performing Arts Center, Charlotte Latin School, YMCA Metropolitan Bd, United Way of Cen. Carolinas Inc., Charlotte Inst. for Tech. Innovation; Co-Chair. Advantage Carolina; mem. Bd Trustees Wake Forest Univ. *Address:* Aquiline Capital Partners LLC, 535 Madison Avenue, New York, NY 10022, USA (office). *Website:* www.aquiline-llc.com (office).

THOMPSON, Harold Lindsay, AM, MB, BS, FRACGP; Australian medical practitioner; b. 23 April 1929, Aberdeen, Scotland; s. of Harold Thompson and Johan D. Thompson; m. 1st Audrey J. Harpur 1957 (died 1996); three s. two d.; m. 2nd Jennifer Manton 1997; ed Aberdeen, Melbourne and Sydney Grammar Schools and postgrad. training in UK; Surgeon-Lt Royal Australian Navy 1956–60; now in gen. practice in Lakemba, NSW; Exec. Dir Canterbury Div. of Gen. Practice 1996–2002; Assoc. Prof., Faculty of Medicine, Univ. of Sydney 1996–; fmr Chair. Diagnostic Medical Cooperative Ltd; Fellow Australian Medical Asscn 1973, Pres. 1982–85; Pres. Confed. of Medical Asscns. of Asia and Oceania 1985–87, Immediate Past Pres. 1987–89; Chair. Australian Urban Divs of Gen. Practice 1995–2000; Vice-Chair. Australian Council on Healthcare Standards 1985–89; Vice-Pres. Australian Council of Professions 1985–87, Pres. 1989–91; Assoc. Prof., Faculty of Medicine, Univ. of Sadmer 1996; mem. Council, World Medical Asscn 1984–90, Pres. 1988–89; mem. Econ. Planning Advisory Cttee 1989–91, Bd Southern Sydney Area Health Service 1991–95; Chair. Council Confed. of Medical Asscns of Asia and Oceania 1989–95, GP Advisory Cttee NSW Health 1997–2002, Chair. 1998–2002; Gold Medal, Australian Medical Asscn 1986; Medal, Australian Council on Healthcare Standards 1990, Distinguished Service Award, Confed. of Medical Asscns of Asia and Oceania 1987, Award of Merit 1989, 1995, Gusi Peace Prize 2008. *Leisure interests:* croquet, fishing, bridge. *Address:* 601/2 Roseby Street, Drummoyne, NSW 2047 (office); 4/100 Milsom Road, Cremorne, NSW 2090, Australia (home). *Telephone:* (2) 9719-8391 (office); (2) 9908-2980 (home). *E-mail:* hlindsaythompson@bigpond.com.

THOMPSON, James R., JD; American lawyer and fmr politician; *Senior Chairman, Winston & Strawn LLP;* b. 8 May 1936, Chicago, Ill.; s. of Dr J. Robert Thompson and Agnes Thompson; m. Jayne Carr 1976; one d.; ed Univ. of Illinois, Washington Univ., St Louis, Northwestern Univ. Law School; admitted to Illinois Bar 1959; Prosecutor, State Attorney's Office, Cook County, Ill. 1959–64; Assoc. Prof., Northwestern Univ. Law School 1964–69; Chief, Dept of Law Enforcement and Public Protection, Office of Ill. Attorney-Gen. 1969–70; First Asst US Attorney 1970–71, US Attorney for Northern Dist of Ill. 1971–75; Counsel, Winston & Strawn (law firm), Chicago 1975–77, Partner and Chair. Exec. Cttee 1991–2006, Chair. and CEO 1993–2006, Sr Chair. 2006–; Gov. of Ill. 1977–91; mem. Exec. Cttee Nat. Govs' Asscn 1980–82, Chair. 1983–84; Co-Chair. Attorney-Gen.'s Task Force on Violent Crime 1981; Chair., Pres.s Intelligence Oversight Bd 1989–93; mem. Presidential Advisory Cttee on Federalism 1981, Advisory Bd of Fed. Emergency Man. Agency 1991–93; fmr Chair. Republican Govs' Asscn, Mid-western Govs' Conf., Nat. Govs' Asscn Task Force on Job Creation and Infrastructure 1982; Chair. Council of Great Lakes Govs 1985; Vice-Chair. Martin Luther King Jr Nat. Holiday Cttee 1985; Chair. Public Review Bd of UNITE-HEREIU Union, Ill. Math. and Science Foundation; US Chair. Midwest US-Japan Asscn; Co-Chair. Rare Isotope Accelerator Task Force, CLEAR (Illinois Criminal Code Revision), ABA Cttee on Sentencing Reform; Commr Nat. Comm. on Terrorist Attacks Upon the US (9-11 Comm.) 2003–04; mem. Bd of Dirs JBT Corpn, Navigant Consulting Group, Inc., Maximus, Inc.; Republican; Order of the Rising Sun, Gold and Silver Star (Japan) 2014; Hon. LLD (Lincoln Coll.) 1975, (Monmouth Coll.) 1981, (Marshall Law School) 1984, (Elmhurst Coll.) 1985; Hon. DHumLitt (Roosevelt Univ.) 1979; Hon. DJur (Northwestern Univ. and Illinois Coll.) 1979; Dr hc (Pratt Inst.) 1984; Justice in Legislation Award, American Jewish Congress 1984, Distinguished Public Service Award, Anti-Defamation League 1984, Swedish-American of the Year, Vasa Order of America 1985, Laureate Award of the ISBA Acad. of Illinois Lawyers 2000, Justice John Paul Stevens Award 2003. *Publications include:* co-author of four textbooks including Cases and Comments on Criminal Procedure; numerous articles in professional journals. *Address:* Winston & Strawn LLP, 35 West Wacker Drive, Suite 4200, Chicago, IL 60601-9703, USA (office). *Telephone:* (312) 558-7400 (office). *Fax:* (312) 558-5700 (office). *E-mail:* jthompson@winston.com (office). *Website:* www.winston.com (office).

THOMPSON, Jennifer (Jenny), BSc, MD; American physician and fmr swimmer; b. 26 Feb. 1973, Danvers, Mass; ed Stanford Univ., Columbia Univ.; mem. Badger Swim Club, NY 2001–; won 19 Nat. Collegiate Athletic Asscn (NCAA) titles, most in NCAA female swimming history; 26 nat. medals, 85 medals from int. competition including 14 from World Championships; competed at Olympic Games 1992, 1996, 2000, 2004 (third female swimmer to qualify for four Olympics); most decorated swimmer in Olympic history with 12 medals (eight gold medals); most Olympic gold medals among US women; holds world records 100m butterfly, 50m butterfly, 100m individual medley; intern, Memorial Sloan-Kettering Cancer Center, New York; currently resident anesthesiologist, Brigham and Women's Hosp., Boston; US All-Star swimming team 1989, 1992–95, 1997–2000, 2002–04, USA Swimming Swimmer of the Year 1993, 1998, Female Swimmer of the Meet, World Short Course Championships 1999, Female Swimmer of the Meet, Pan Pacific Championships 1999, Sports Foundation's Sportswoman of the Year 2000. *Address:* Department of Anesthesiology, Perioperative and Pain Medicine, Brigham and Women's Hospital, 75 Francis Street, Boston, MA 02115, USA (office). *Telephone:* (617) 732-8210 (office). *Website:* www.brighamandwomens.org/anesthesiology (office).

THOMPSON, John Griggs, PhD, FRS; American mathematician and academic; b. 13 Oct. 1932, Ottawa, Kan.; ed Yale Univ., Univ. of Chicago; with Inst. of Defense Analysis 1959–60; Asst Prof., Harvard Univ. 1961–62; Prof., Univ. of Chicago 1962–68; Fellow, Univ. Coll., Cambridge, UK 1968–70, Rouse Ball Prof. of Pure Math. 1970–93, Prof. Emer. 1993–; Grad. Research Prof., Univ. of Florida 1993–, now Prof. Emer.; mem. NAS 1971, Norwegian Acad. of Science and Letters; Dr hc (Illinois) 1968, (Yale) 1980, (Chicago) 1985, (Oxford) 1987, (Ohio State); Cole Prize, American Math. Soc. 1965, Fields Medal, Int. Congress of Mathematicians, Nice 1970, American Math. Soc. Colloquium Lecturer 1974, Senior Berwick Prize, London Math. Soc. 1982, Sylvester Medal, Royal Soc. 1985, Wolf Prize (Israel) 1992, Poincaré Prize, Acad. des sciences (France) 1992, Nat. Medal of Science (jtly) 2000, Abel Prize (jtly), Norwegian Acad. of Science and Letters 2008, De Morgan Medal 2013. *Publications:* numerous articles in math. journals on group theory. *Address:* Department of Mathematics, University of Florida, 365 Little Hall, corner of SW 13th Street and SW 2nd Avenue, PO Box 118105, Gainesville, FL 32611-8105, USA (office); Department of Pure Mathematics and Mathematical Statistics, University of Cambridge, E1.10, Wilberforce Road, Cambridge, CB3 0WB, UK (office). *Telephone:* (352) 392-0281 (office). *Fax:* (352) 392-8357 (office); (352) 392-8357 (Cambridge) (office). *E-mail:* J.G.Thompson@dpmms.cam.ac.uk (office). *Website:* www.dpmms.cam.ac.uk (office).

THOMPSON, John M.; Canadian banker and business executive; b. 1942, Montreal, Québec; m.; three c.; ed Univ. of Western Ontario, Richard Ivey Business School at Univ. of Western Ontario and Kellogg Grad. School, Northwestern Univ., USA; joined IBM Canada Ltd as a systems engineer 1966, later Marketing Man., Pres. and CEO 1986, Corp. Vice-Pres., Marketing and Services, IBM Corpn 1991, Head AS/400 Server business, Sr Vice-Pres. and Group Exec. IBM Software Group 1995, Vice-Chair. 2000–02; mem. Bd Dirs Toronto-Dominion Bank 1988–13, Chair. (non-exec.) TD Bank Financial Group 2003–11; Vice-Chair. Supervisory Bd Philips Electronics NV 2003–12, Hosp. for Sick Children 2003–13; Chancellor Univ. of Western Ontario 2008–15; fmr Dir Conf. Bd of Canada, Canadian Council of Chief Exec.; served on past Premier of Ontario's Councils for educ. reform, human resources reform and industrial policy; mem. Bd of Dirs, Thomson Reuters Corpn 2004–14, Atlantic Salmon Fed.; Hon. LLD (Univ. of Western Ontario) 1994. *Leisure interests:* being with his grandchildren, fly-fishing, boating, golf.

THOMPSON, John W., BBA, MBA; American computer industry executive; *Independent Chairman, Microsoft Corporation;* b. 24 April 1949, Fort Dix, NJ; ed John F. Kennedy High School, Riviera Beach, Fla (now Suncoast Community High School), Florida A&M Univ., Sloan Fellows Program of MIT Sloan School of Man.; began career with IBM Corpn 1971, held sr exec. positions in sales, marketing and software devt, latterly as Gen. Man. IBM Americas as well as membership of Worldwide Man. Council –1999; Chair. and CEO Symantec Corpn 1999–2009, Chair. 2009–11; mem. Bd of Dirs Virtual Instruments 2009–, CEO 2010–; Ind. Dir, Microsoft Corpn 2012–, Ind. Chair. 2014–; mem. Bd of Dirs, UPS, Seagate Technology, Florida A&M Univ. Cluster, Ill. Gov.'s Human Resource Advisory Council, Teach for America; mem. Nat. Infrastructure Advisory Cttee 2002–, Financial Crisis Inquiry Comm. 2009–; bought 20% share of Golden State Warriors NBA professional basketball team under the umbrella of Bay Area Basketball Partners, LLC 2005; Dr hc (Univ. of Notre Dame) 2008, (Mendoza Coll. of Business) 2008, (Florida A&M Univ.) 2014; David Packard Medal of Achievement, TechAmerica Foundation, Business Hall of Fame Laureate, Junior Achievement 2008, Pioneer Business Leader Award, Silicon Valley Educ. Foundation 2010, Spirit of Silicon Valley Lifetime Achievement Award, Silicon Valley Leadership Group 2012. *Address:* Microsoft Corporation, 1 Microsoft Way, Redmond, WA 98052-8300 (office); Virtual Instruments, 25 Metro Drive, San Jose, CA 95110, USA (office). *Telephone:* (425) 882-8080 (Redmond) (office); (408) 579-4000 (San Jose) (office). *Fax:* (425) 936-7329 (Redmond) (office); (408) 579-4001 (San Jose) (office). *E-mail:* info@microsoft.com (office); info@virtualinstruments.com (office). *Website:* www.microsoft.com (office); www.virtualinstruments.com (office).

THOMPSON, Julie Dawn, PhD; British biologist, biochemist, bioinformatician and academic; *Senior Researcher, Laboratoire des sciences de l'ingénieur, de l'informatique et de l'imagerie;* ed Univ. of Strasbourg, Alsace, France; with Vickers Shipbuilding and Eng Ltd 1984–86; with Singer Link Miles Ltd 1986–88; with Rediffusion Simulation Ltd 1988–90; European Molecular Biology Lab., Heidelberg, Germany 1991–94; Sr Researcher, Institut de Génétique et de Biologie Moléculaire et Cellulaire (CNRS/Institut Nat. de la Santé et de la Recherche Médicale—INSERM/Université Louis Pasteur), Illkirch, France 1995–2013; Sr Researcher, Laboratoire des sciences de l'ingénieur, de l'informatique et de l'imagerie, Strasbourg, France 2013–; Perm. mem. LBGI Integrative Bioinformatics and Genomics; collaborated in creation of CLUSTAL W program for nucleic acid and protein sequences; Cristal du CNRS 2005, prix Madeleine Lecoq 2007. *Publications include:* numerous articles in scientific journals on nucleic acid and protein sequence analysis programs. *E-mail:* thompson@unistra.fr (office). *Website:* www.lbgi.fr (office).

THOMPSON, Kenneth (Ken) Lane, BS, MS; American computer scientist; *Distinguished Engineer, Google Inc.;* b. 4 Feb. 1943, New Orleans, La; ed Univ. of California, Berkeley; worked with Dennis Ritchie on Multics operating system during 1960s, cr. Bon programming language; worked at Bell Labs –2000; Fellow, Entrisphere, Inc. 2000–06; Distinguished Engineer, Google Inc. 2006–, co-invented the Go programming language; mem. Nat. Acad. of Eng 1980; Fellow, Computer History Museum 1997; Turing Award (co-recipient with Dennis Ritchie) 1983, IEEE Richard W. Hamming Medal (co-recipient with Dennis Ritchie) 1990, Nat. Medal of Tech. (co-recipient with Dennis Ritchie) 1998, first IEEE Tsutomu Kanai Award 1999, Japan Prize for Information and Communications (co-recipient with Dennis Ritchie) 2011. *Achievements include:* prin. creator (with Dennis Ritchie) of Unix operating system, also invented B programming language (direct predecessor to C programming language), one of the creators and early developers of Plan 9 operating systems. *Publications:* several patents. *E-mail:* ken@google.com (office).

THOMPSON, Mark Edward, BS, PhD; American chemist and academic; *Professor of Chemistry, University of Southern California;* ed Univ. of California, Berkeley, California Inst. of Tech.; Visiting Scientist, E.I. duPont deNemours & Co., Wilmington, Del. 1983; Science and Eng Research Council (SERC) Research Fellow, Inorganic Chem. Lab., Univ. of Oxford, UK, worked with Prof. Malcolm L.H. Green studying electronic and nonlinear-optical properties of organometallic materials 1985–87; Asst Prof., Princeton Univ. 1987–95, Dir of Undergraduate Research Program 1989–91; Assoc. Prof., Dept of Chem., Univ. of Southern California 1995–99, Prof. of Chem. 1999–, Chair. Dept of Chem. 2005–08; mem. Editorial Bd Chemistry of Materials 1998–2003; mem. Sr Advisory Bd for Minority Opportunities in Research Program, California State Univ., Los Angeles 2005–; mem. External Advisory Bd, Dept of Chem., Academica Sinica, Taiwan 2005–; Distinguished Inventor of the Year, Intellectual Property Owners Asscn 1998, Thomas Alva Edison Patent Award, Research and Devt Council of New Jersey 1998, Raubenheimer Outstanding Faculty Award, Coll. of Letters, Arts and Science, Univ. of Southern California 2004, Jan Rajchman Prize for Outstanding Research in Flat Panel Displays, Soc. for Information Display 2006, MRS Medal, Materials Research Soc. 2006. *Publications include:* more than 200 scientific papers in peer-reviewed journals on organic light emitting diodes (OLEDs), organic photovoltaic devices (OPVs or solar cells), devt of nano-biotic sensors and abiotic–biotic interfaces; 71 US patents. *Address:* SGM 216, Chemistry Department, University of Southern California, 840 West 36th Place/Downey Way, Los Angeles, CA 90089-0744, USA (office). *Telephone:* (213) 740-6402 (office). *Fax:* (213) 740-0930 (office); (213) 740-8594 (office). *E-mail:* met@usc.edu (office). *Website:* chem.usc.edu; met.usc.edu (office).

THOMPSON, Mark John, MA, FRTS, FRSA; British media executive; *President and CEO, The New York Times Company;* b. 31 July 1957, London, England; s. of Duncan John Thompson and Sydney Columba Thompson (née Corduff); m. Jane Emilie Blumberg 1987; two s. one d.; ed Stonyhurst Coll., Merton Coll., Oxford; Research Asst Trainee, BBC TV 1979–80, Asst Producer Nationwide 1980–82, Producer Breakfast Time 1982–84, Output Ed. London Plus 1984–85, Newsnight 1985–87, Ed. Nine O'Clock News 1988–90, Panorama 1990–92, Head of Features 1992–94, Head of Factual Programmes 1994–96, Controller BBC2 1996–98; Dir of Nat. and Regional Broadcasting 1998–2000; Dir of TV, BBC 2000–02; CEO Channel 4 2002–04; Dir-Gen. BBC 2004–12; Pres. and CEO The New York Times Co., New York 2012–; mem. Bd of Trustees, Media Trust 2002–12; Patron Art Room (charity), Oxford. *Leisure interests:* walking, cooking. *Address:* The New York Times Company, 620 8th Avenue, New York, NY 10018, USA. *Telephone:* (212) 556-1234. *Website:* www.nytco.com.

THOMPSON, Sir Michael Warwick, Kt, DSc, FInstP; British physicist, academic and fmr university vice-chancellor; b. 1 June 1931; s. of Kelvin W. Thompson and Madeleine Walford; m. 1st Sybil N. Spooner 1956 (died 1999); two s.; m. 2nd Jenny Mitchell 2000; ed Rydal School and Univ. of Liverpool; Research Scientist, AERE, Harwell, Reactor Physics and Metallurgy 1953–65; Prof. of Experimental Physics, Univ. of Sussex 1965–80, Pro-Vice-Chancellor 1972–78; Vice-Chancellor, Univ. of E Anglia 1980–86; Vice-Chancellor and Prin., Univ. of Birmingham 1987–96, Prof. Emer. 1996–; Chair. Council John Innes Research Inst. 1980–86, British Council Cttee for Academic Research Collaboration with Germany 1988–; mem. SRC Physics Cttee (also Chair.) 1972–79, E Sussex Educ. Cttee 1973–78, E Sussex Area Health Authority 1973–80, W Midlands Regional Health Authority 1987–90 (non-exec. Dir 1990–96), Council for Nat. Academic Awards 1988–91, Council of Asscn of Commonwealth Univs 1990–95, Council for Industry and Higher Educ. 1991–96; Dir (non-exec.), Alliance Building Soc. 1979–85 (Alliance and Leicester Building Soc., now Alliance & Leicester PLC) 1985–2000, Deputy Chair. 1995–2000; mem. Bd of Dirs, COBUILD Ltd 1987–96, TPIC Ltd 1987–; mem. Council of the Cttee of Vice-Chancellors and Prins 1989–96 (Chair. Medical Cttee 1994); Trustee, Barber Inst. of Fine Art 1987–2007, St Bartholomew's Medical Coll. 1998–2000; Hon. Fellow, Univ. of Sussex 2012; Grosses Bundesverdienstkreuz (Germany) 1997; Hon. LLD (Birmingham) 1997; Hon. DSc (Sussex) 1998; C.V. Boys Prize, Inst. of Physics. *Publications:* Defects and Radiation Damage in Metals 1968; over 100 papers in scientific journals on the interaction of radiation with solids. *Leisure interests:* sailing, the arts. *Address:* Stoneacre, The Warren, Polperro, Cornwall, PL13 2RD, England.

THOMPSON, Scott, BA; American business executive; *CEO, ShopRunner;* ed Stonehill Coll., Boston, Mass; worked with Coopers and Lybrand delivering information tech. solutions to financial services clients; fmr Chief Information Officer, Barclays Global Investors; fmr Exec. Vice-Pres. of Tech. Solutions, Inovant (subsidiary of Visa formed to oversee global technology); Sr Vice-Pres. and Chief Tech. Officer, PayPal (div. of eBay Inc.) –2008, Pres. PayPal 2008–11; mem. Bd of Dirs and CEO Yahoo! Inc. 2012; CEO ShopRunner (members-only shopping service) 2012–; mem. Bd of Dirs F5 Networks Inc., Zuora Inc.; Ernst & Young Entrepreneur Of The Year Award 2011. *Address:* ShopRunner, 225 Washington Street, 3rd floor, Conshohocken, PA 19428, USA (office). *Website:* www.shoprunner.com (office).

THOMPSON, Tommy George, BS, JD; American lawyer and fmr politician; b. 19 Nov. 1941, Elroy, Wis.; s. of Allan Thompson and Julie Dutton; m. Sue Ann Mashak 1969; one s. two d.; ed Univ. of Wisconsin; legis. messenger, Wis. State Senate 1964–66; with Elroy and Mauston, Wis. 1966–87; self-employed real estate broker, Mauston 1970; mem. Wis. State Ass. for 87th Dist 1966–87, Asst Minority Leader 1972–81, Floor Leader 1981–87; Gov. of Wisconsin 1987–2001; US Sec. Health and Human Services, Washington, DC 2001–05; Partner, Akin Gump Strauss Hauer & Feld LLP, Washington, DC 2005–12; Sr Advisor, Deloitte and Touche USA LLP 2005–09, Founding Ind. Chair. Deloitte Center for Health Solutions; Pres. Logistics Health, Inc. 2005–11, Chair. 2011; CEO Thompson Family Holdings, Madison; Chair. Republican Govs Asscn 1991–92; Chair. Bd of Dirs Amtrak 1998–99; mem. Bd of Dirs Stayhealthy Inc. (Chair.), Centene Corpn, C.R. Bard, Inc., United Therapeutics Corpn, Cytori Therapeutics, Inc., TherapeuticsMD, Inc., Population Services International (foundation); mem. ABA; unsuccessful Republican cand. for Senator from Wisconsin 2012; Nature Conservancy Award 1988, Thomas Jefferson Freedom Award (American Legis. Exchange Council) 1991; Leadership in Natural Energy Conservation Award, US Energy Asscn 1994, Horatio Alger Award, and numerous other awards. *Publication includes:* Power to the People: An American State at Work 1996. *Leisure interests:* hunting, fishing, sports. *Address:* Stayhealthy, Inc., 717 South Myrtle Avenue, Monrovia, CA 91016, USA.

THOMSON, Sir Adam McClure, Kt, KCMG, CMG; British diplomatist; *Director, European Leadership Network;* m. Fariba Shirazi Thomson; three c.; joined FCO 1978, Asst Desk Officer, Defence Dept 1978–79, Desk Officer, E European and Soviet Dept 1980–81, Third, later Second Sec. (Political), Embassy in Moscow 1981–83, Second, later First Sec. Political, Econ. and CEP Cttees, UK Del. to NATO 1983–86, Head of Israel/Lebanon Team, Near East and N Africa Dept, FCO 1986–89, seconded to Cabinet Office, Assessments Staff 1989–91, First Sec., Politico-Mil., Embassy in Washington, DC 1991–95, Political Counsellor, High Comm., New Delhi 1995–98, Head of Security Policy Dept, FCO 1998–2002, Amb. and Deputy Perm. Rep., UK Mission to UN, New York 2002–06, Dir S Asia and Afghanistan Directorate, FCO 2006–09, High Commr to Pakistan 2009–13, Amb. and Perm. Rep., NATO, Brussels 2014–16; Dir European Leadership Network 2016–. *Address:* European Leadership Network, Suite 407, Southbank House, Black Prince Road, London, SE1 7SJ, England (office). *Telephone:* (20) 3176–2554 (office). *E-mail:* adamt@europeanleadershipnetwork.org (office). *Website:* www.europealeadershipnnetwork.org (office).

THOMSON, James Alan, BS, MS, PhD; American business executive, security expert, research institute director and academic; *President Emeritus and Professor, Pardee RAND Graduate School, RAND Corporation;* b. 21 Jan. 1945, Boston, Mass; m. Darlene Thomson; ed Univ. of New Hampshire and Purdue Univ.; Research Fellow, Univ. of Wisconsin 1972–74; Systems Analyst, Office of Sec. of Defense, US Dept of Defense, Washington, DC 1974–77; mem. staff, Nat. Security Council, Washington, DC 1977–81; Vice-Pres. RAND Corpn, Santa Monica, Calif. 1981–88, Pres. and CEO 1989–2011, Pres. Emer. and Prof., Pardee RAND Graduate School 2011–; Dir LA World Affairs Council, Object Reservoir Inc., AK Steel Holdings Corpn; mem. IISS (UK), Council on Foreign Relations 1985–, Los Angeles World Affairs Council; Hon. DSc (Purdue) 1992, (New Hampshire); Hon. LLD (Pepperdine) 1996. *Publications include:* Conventional Arms Control and the Security of Europe 1988; numerous articles on defence issues. *Address:* Pardee RAND Graduate School, RAND Corporation, 1776 Main Street, Santa Monica, CA 90401, USA (office). *E-mail:* thomson@rand.org (office). *Website:* www.prgs.edu (office).

THOMSON, James (Jamie) Alexander, BS, VMD, PhD; American developmental biologist and academic; *John D. MacArthur Professor, School of Medicine and Public Health, University of Wisconsin-Madison;* b. 20 Dec. 1958, Oak Park, Ill.; ed Univs of Illinois and Pennsylvania; board certified in veterinary pathology 1995; Post-doctoral Research Fellow, Primate In Vitro Fertilization and Experimental Embryology Lab., Oregon Nat. Primate Research Center 1988–90; joined Univ. of Wisconsin-Madison 1990, currently John D. MacArthur Prof., Univ. of Wisconsin-Madison School of Medicine and Public Health, Dir of Regenerative Biology, Morgridge Inst. for Research, Faculty mem. Genome Center of Wisconsin, has conducted pioneering work in isolation and culture of non-human primate and human embryonic stem cells; Adjunct Prof., Molecular, Cellular, and Developmental Biology Dept, Univ. of California, Santa Barbara; Co-founder and Chief Scientific Officer, Cellular Dynamics International, Madison; Chief Pathologist, Wisconsin Nat. Primate Research Center; mem. NAS; Hon. DSc (Univ. of Illinois, Urbana-Champaign) 2013; King Faisal Int. Prize in Medicine (co-recipient) 2011, Albany Medical Center Prize (co-recipient) 2011. *Publications:* numerous articles in professional journals; several patents. *Address:* Department of Cell and Regenerative Biology, School of Medicine and Public Health, Morgridge Institute for Research, University of Wisconsin-Madison, 330 North Orchard Street, Madison, WI 53715, USA (office). *Telephone:* (608) 316-4348 (office). *E-mail:* jthomson@morgridgeinstitute.org (office). *Website:* discovery.wisc.edu/home/morgridge/about-morgridge/leadership/james-thomson/ (office); ink.primate.wisc.edu/~thomson (office).

THOMSON, Jennifer Ann, PhD; South African microbiologist, molecular biologist and academic; *Emeritus Professor of Microbiology, Department of Molecular and Cell Biology, University of Cape Town;* b. 16 June 1947, Cape Town; ed Univ. of Cape Town, Univ. of Cambridge, UK, Rhodes Univ.; Post-doctoral Fellow, Harvard Univ., USA 1974–77; Lecturer, Dept of Genetics, Univ. of Witwatersrand 1977–78, Sr Lecturer 1979–80, Assoc. Prof. 1981–83; Visiting Scientist, MIT 1982–83; Dir Lab. for Molecular and Cell Biology, CSIRO 1984–87; Prof. and Head, Dept of Microbiology, Univ. of Cape Town 1988–2000, Prof. of Microbiology, Dept of Molecular and Cell Biology (formed by merger of Depts of Biochemistry and Microbiology) 2001–08, Emer. Prof. 2008–; Vice-Pres. Acad. of Science of South Africa 1996–98, mem. Council 2004–06; Distinguished Teacher, Univ. of Cape Town 1996; expert adviser, WHO; addressed UN Gen. Ass. on theme of genetically modified crops for developing countries 2002; Co-founder South African Women in Science and Eng; mem. African Acad. of Sciences Policy Cttee 1993–95; Fellow, Royal Soc. of South Africa 2001–; Dr hc (Sorbonne Université) 2005; Women in Science Award, South African Asscn of Women Graduates 2000, L'Oréal-UNESCO For Women in Science Award 2004. *Publications:* Genes for Africa 2002, Seeds for the Future 2006, Food for Africa: the life and work of a scientist in GM crops 2013; numerous articles in scientific journals on biological control of plant pests and diseases, genetically modified plants to improve agricultural productivity and food quality in developing countries and molecular genetics of industrially and medically important anaerobic bacteria. *Address:* Department of Molecular and Cell Biology, University of Cape Town, Private Bag Rondebosch, 7701 Cape Town, South Africa (office). *Telephone:* (21) 650-3256 (office); (21) 794-2360 (home). *E-mail:* jennifer.thomson@uct.ac.za (office). *Website:* www.mcb.uct.ac.za (office).

THOMSON, Richard Murray, OC, BASs (Eng), MBA; Canadian banker (retd); b. 14 Aug. 1933, Winnipeg, Man.; s. of H. W. Thomson and Mary Thomson; m. Heather Lorimer 1959; ed Univ. of Toronto, Harvard Business School, Queen's Univ., Kingston, Ont.; joined Toronto-Dominion Bank, Head Office 1957, Sr Asst Man., St James & McGill, Montreal 1961, Asst to Pres., Head Office 1963, Asst Gen. Man. 1965, Chief Gen. Man. 1968, Vice-Pres., Chief Gen. Man., Dir 1971, Pres. 1972–79, Pres. and CEO 1977–79, CEO 1978–97, Chair. 1978–98; mem. Bd of Dirs Nexen Inc. 1997–2009 (Chair. 1999–2005). *Leisure interests:* golf, tennis, skiing.

THOMSON, Robert James; Australian journalist, newspaper editor and business executive; *Chief Executive, News Corp;* b. 11 March 1961, Torrumbarry; m. Wang Ping; two s.; financial and gen. affairs reporter, then Sydney Corresp. The Herald, Melbourne 1979–83; sr feature writer Sydney Morning Herald 1983–85; corresp. for the Financial Times, Beijing 1985–89, Tokyo 1989–94, Foreign News Ed., London 1994–96, Asst Ed. Financial Times and Ed. Weekend FT 1996–98, US Man. Ed. Financial Times 1998–2002; Ed. The Times (UK) 2002–07, Publr, Wall Street Journal 2007–08, Man. Ed. 2008–13, Man. Ed. and Ed.-in-Chief, Dow Jones 2008–13, mem. Bd of Dirs and Chief Exec. News Corp (following restructuring of News Corporation to spin off its publishing assets into similarly named News Corp while existing News Corporation renamed 21st Century Fox and its legal successor) 2013–; mem. Knight-Bagehot Fellowship Bd, Columbia Univ.; Dr hc (RMIT) 2010; Business Journalist of the Year, The Journalist and Financial Reporting Group (TJFR) 2001. *Publications:* The Judges: A Portrait of the Australian Judiciary, The Chinese Army (co-author), True Fiction (ed.). *Leisure interests:* cinema, tennis, reading. *Address:* News Corp, 1211 Avenue of the Americas, New York, NY 10036, USA (office). *Telephone:* (212) 416-3012 (office). *Fax:* (212) 416-2790 (office). *Website:* newscorp.com (office).

THOMSON, William Reid, BSc, MSc, MPhil (Econs); British economist, geopolitical adviser, pension fund expert and writer; *Chairman, Private Capital Limited;* b. 10 Aug. 1939, London, England; s. of Wing-Commdr W. Thomson and Nellie Hendry Thomson; m. 1st Mary Cormack 1967 (divorced 1986); m. 2nd Jeannette Vinta 1987; two s. one d.; ed George Washington Univ., Univ. of Washington, USA, Univ. of Manchester; economist and operations analyst with various cos 1961–72; investment analyst, Legg Mason & Co. 1973–74; Sr Economist, US Treasury Dept 1974–85, Office of Debt Analysis and Office of Int. Devt Banks; Exec. Dir African Devt Bank 1982–83; Alt. Exec. Dir Asian Devt Bank 1985–90, Vice-Pres. 1990–94, Sr Counsellor to Pres. 1994–95; Sr Adviser Franklin Templeton Investments Asia 1995–2008; Chair. Yamamoto Int. Co (Japan) (venture capital) 1996–, Siam Recovery Fund 1997–2005, PEDCA LLC 1997–2005, Momentum Asia Ltd (hedge funds) 1998–2003, Private Capital Ltd Hong Kong 2005–; Dir, Finavestment Ltd, London 2008–14; Sr Adviser, Int. Advisory Bd Council, Global Bank, also Chair. Int. Project Preparation Facility 2014–; adviser, Axiom Alternative Fund 2004–09; Visiting Prof., Nihon Univ., Tokyo; writer on Asian political/econ. affairs, Asia Asset Management, Asia and Pacific Review, Asia Times, The Standard Hong Kong and many websites. *Publications include:* Confidential Inside Asia Report 1996–2001, Asia Asset Management 2003–. *Leisure interests:* walking, cricket, reading, writing. *Address:* 184 London Road, Guildford, GU1 1XR, England (home); Private Capital Ltd, 16/F Shun Ho Tower, 24–30 Ice House Street, Central, Hong Kong Special Administrative Region, People's Republic of China (office). *Telephone:* 2869-1996 (Hong Kong) (office); 811-8181 (Manila) (office); 7789-733467 (UK, mobile) (home); (1483) 440825 (UK) (home). *Fax:* 2110-9521 (Hong Kong) (office); 814-0130 (Manila) (office); (1483) 440825 (home). *E-mail:* wrthomson@private-capital.com.hk (office); wrthomson@btconnect.com; bill_thomson2003@yahoo.com. *Website:* www.private-capital.com.hk (office).

THOMSON OF FLEET, 3rd Baron Thomson of Fleet; **David Kenneth Roy Thomson,** MA; Canadian business executive; *Chairman, Thomson Reuters;* b. 12 June 1957; s. of Kenneth Thomson (2nd Baron Thomson of Fleet) and Nora Marilyn Lavis Thomson; m. 1st; two d.; m. 2nd (divorced); one s.; one d. with Kelly Rowan; ed Upper Canada Coll., Selwyn Coll., Cambridge, UK; has held several positions in cos controlled by his family, including Man. The Bay store at Cloverdale Mall, Etobicoke, Ont. and Pres. of Zellers (retailer); f. real estate firm Osmington Inc. (owned and operated outside of Thomson group); mem. Bd of Dirs Thomson Corpn 1988–, Chair. 2002–, now Chair. Thomson Reuters (following merger with Reuters), Chair. The Woodbridge Co. Ltd (Thomson family investment co.); Patron Art Gallery of Ontario; succeeded to title of 3rd Baron Thomson of Fleet 12 June 2006. *Address:* Thomson Reuters, 3 Times Square, New York, NY 10036, USA (office). *Telephone:* (646) 223-4000 (office). *E-mail:* info@thomsonreuters.com (office). *Website:* www.thomsonreuters.com (office).

THONDAMAN, (Savumiamoorthy) Arumugam Ramanathan; Sri Lankan politician; b. 29 May 1964; m.; ed Royal Coll., Colombo; advocate for Indian Tamils of Sri Lanka; MP for Nuwara Eliya Dist 1994–; fmr Minister of Livestock Devt and Estate Infrastructure; Minister of Housing and Plantation Infrastructure –2004; Pres. and Gen. Sec., Ceylon Workers' Congress (affiliated with United People's Freedom Alliance); Minister of Youth Empowerment and Socio-Economic Devt 2007–10, of Livestock and Rural Community Devt 2010–15. *Address:* Parliament of Sri Lanka, Parliamentary Complex, Sri Jayawardenapura (office); No. No. 45, St. Michael's Road, Colombo 3, Sri Lanka (home). *Telephone:* (11) 2777100 (office). *Fax:* (11) 2777564 (office). *E-mail:* thondaman_a@parliament.lk (office). *Website:* www.parliament.lk (office).

THONGLOUN, Sisolit; Laotian politician; *Prime Minister;* b. 10 Nov. 1945; ed Pedagogical Coll., Neo Lao Hak Sat, Houaphanh, Pedagogical Inst., St Petersburg, Russia, Acad. of Social Science, Moscow; Staff Officer, Educational Div., Neo Lao Hak Sat (Lao Nat. Patriotic Front), Houaphanh Prov. 1967–69; Staff Officer, Rep. Office, Neo Lao Hak Sat (LNPE), Hanoi 1969–73; Instructor, Vientiane Univ. 1978–79; Sec. to Ministry of Educ. and Chief, External Relations Div., Ministry of Educ. 1979–81; Dir Public Research Dept, Minister Council Bd, Office of the Prime Minister 1985–86; Vice-Minister, Ministry of Foreign Affairs 1987–92; Minister of Labour and Social Welfare 1993–97; mem. Parl. 1998–2000; Deputy Prime Minister of Laos 2001–16, Minister of Foreign Affairs 2006–16, Prime Minister 2016–; Pres. Cttee for Planning and Cooperation, Cttee for Investment and Cooperation, Lao Nat. Cttee for Energy; Hon. Pres., SOS of Lao PDR. *Address:* Office of the Prime Minister, Ban Sisavat, Vientiane, Laos (office). *Telephone:* (21) 213653 (office). *Fax:* (21) 213560 (office). *Website:* www.na.gov.la (office).

't HOOFT, Gerardus, PhD; Dutch physicist and academic; *Professor of Theoretical Physics, University of Utrecht;* b. 5 July 1946, Den Helder; s. of H. 't Hooft and M. A. van Kampen; m. Albertha A. Schik 1972; two d.; ed Dalton Lyceum Gymnasium beta, The Hague, Rijks Universiteit, Utrecht; Fellow, CERN (Theoretical Physics Div.), Geneva 1972–74; Asst Prof., Univ. of Utrecht 1974–77, Prof. of Theoretical Physics 1977–; mem. Koninklijke Acad. van Wetenschappen, Letteren en Schone Kunsten v. België, Koninklijke Nederlandse Acad. van Wetenschappen, Koninklijke Hollandsche Maatschappij der Wetenschappen 1983; Foreign Assoc. NAS; Fellow and CPhys, Inst. of Physics, London, UK 2000; Amb., Mars One Project 2012; Foreign Hon. mem. American Acad. of Arts and Sciences, Acad. des Sciences; Commdr, Nederlandse Leeuw 1999, Hon. Medal, Astana (Kazakhstan) 2000, Officier, Légion d'honneur 2001, and others; Dr hc (Chicago) 1981, (Leuven) 1996, (Bologna) 1998, (Cape Town) 2001, (Hofstra Univ.) 2001, (Marseille) 2001, (Columbus, Ohio) 2003, (Hefei) 2004, (Salamanca) 2006 and others; W. Prins Prize 1974, Akzo Prize 1977, Dannie Heineman Prize 1979, Wolf Foundation Prize in Physics, 1981, Spinoza Premium 1995, Pius XI Medal 1983, Lorentz Medal 1986, Franklin Medal 1995, G.C. Wick Medal 1997, High Energy Physics Prize, European Physical Soc. 1999, Nobel Prize for Physics (jtly) 1999, Erice Prize 2009, Asteroid 9491 Thooft named in his honour, Lomonosov Gold Medal, Russian Acad. of Sciences 2010, Niels Bohr Inst. Medal of Honour, Copenhagen 2016. *Publications include:* Under the Spell of the Gauge Principle 1994, In Search of the Ultimate Building Blocks 1996, Playing with Planets 2008, Tijd in Machten van Tien 2011; papers on Renormalization of Yang-Mills Fields, magnetic monopoles, Instantons, Gauge theories, quark confinement, quantum mechanics, quantum gravity and black holes. *Address:* Faculty of Physics and Astronomy, University of Utrecht, Prinetonplein 5, 3584 CC Utrecht, The Netherlands (office). *Telephone:* (30) 2535928 (office). *Fax:* (30) 2539282 (office); (30) 2535937 (office). *E-mail:* g.thooft@uu.nl (office). *Website:* www.staff.science.uu.nl/~hooft101 (office).

THÓRDARSON, Gudlaugur Thór, BA; Icelandic politician; *Minister of Foreign Affairs;* b. 19 Dec. 1967; s. of Thórdur Sigurdsson and Sonja Guðlaugsdóttir; m. Ágústa Johnson; two c., two step-c.; ed Univ. of Iceland; with Vátryggingafélag Íslands hf (insurance co.) 1989–93; Man. Fjárvangur (bank) 1996–97, Dir Fjárvangur/Frjálsi Investment 1998–2001; Dir Insurance Dept, Bank of Iceland 2001–03; mem. Reykjavík City Council 1998–2006; mem. Althingi (Parl.) for Reykjavík North 2003–09, 2016–, for Reykjavík South 2009–16, Deputy Chair. Independence Party Parl. Group 2005–07, 2013–16; mem. Icelandic Del. to EFTA and EEA Parl. Cttees 2013–16; Minister of Health and Social Security 2007–09, of Foreign Affairs 2017–; mem. Sjálfstæðisflokkurinn (Independence Party). *Address:* Ministry for Foreign Affairs, Rauðarárstíg 25, 105 Reykjavík, Iceland (office). *Telephone:* 5459900 (office). *Fax:* 5622373 (office). *E-mail:* postur@utn.stjr.is (office). *Website:* www.mfa.is (office).

THORENS, Justin Pierre; Swiss professor of law and attorney; b. 15 Sept. 1931, Collonge-Bellerive; s. of Paul L. Thorens and Germaine Falquet; m. Colette F. Vecchio 1963; one s. one d.; ed Univ. of Geneva, Freie Univ. Berlin, Germany, Univ. Coll. London, UK; attorney-at-law, Geneva Bar 1956–2011; Alt. Pres. Jurisdictional Court, Geneva 1971–78; Lecturer, Faculty of Law, Univ. of Geneva 1967, Assoc. Prof. 1970, Prof. 1973–96, Dean 1974–77, Rector, Univ. of Geneva 1977–83, Hon. Prof. 1996–; Visiting Scholar, Stanford Univ. 1983–84, Univ. of Calif., Berkeley 1983–84; Guest Prof., Univ. of Munich, Germany 1984; mem. Cttee European Centre for Higher Educ. (CEPES), Bucharest 1981–95, Pres. 1986–88; mem. Admin. Council Asscn des Universités Partiellement ou Entièrement de Langue Française (AUPELF), Montreal 1978–87, Vice-Pres. 1981–87, Hon. Vice-Pres. 1987–, mem. Gov. Council 1987–; Pres. Bd Int. Asscn of Univs (AIU), Paris 1985–90, Hon. Pres. 1990–; Vice-Pres. UNDL Foundation, Geneva 2001–; Pres. Int. Latsis Foundation 1989–2013; Bd mem. Fondation des Archives historiques de l'Abbaye de Saint-Maurice 2007–; mem. Council UN Univ. Tokyo 1986–92, Pres. 1988–89; mem. UNESCO Swiss Nat. Comm. 1989–2001, mem. Int. Acad. of Estate and Trust Law; mem. Soc. of Trust and Estate Practitioners, also mem. of many other nat. and int. asscns in the legal and cultural fields; various prizes, awards and distinctions. *Publications:* publs on pvt. law, civil procedure, arbitration, Anglo-American property law, univ. politics, cultural questions. *Leisure interests:* history and all its aspects, both European and the rest of the world; interaction of cultures of various times and regions. *Address:* 18 chemin du Nant d'Aisy, 1246 Corsier, Switzerland (home). *Telephone:* (22) 751-80-81 (office); (22) 751-12-62 (home). *Fax:* (22) 751-80-82 (office); (22) 751-80-82 (home). *E-mail:* justin.thorens@bluewin.ch.

THORNBURGH, Richard (Dick) Lewis, BEng, LLB; American lawyer and fmr politician; *Of Counsel, K&L Gates LLP;* b. 16 July 1932, Pittsburgh, Pa; s. of Charles G. Thornburgh and Alice Sanborn; m. Virginia W. Judson 1963; four s.; ed Yale Univ. and Univ. of Pittsburgh; admitted to Pa Bar 1958, US Supreme Court Bar 1965; attorney, Kirkpatrick & Lockhart LLP (now K&L Gates LLP), Pittsburgh 1959–79, 1977–79, 1987–88, 1994–; US attorney for Western Pa, Pittsburgh 1969–75; Asst Attorney-Gen. Criminal Div. US Justice Dept 1975–77; Gov. of Pennsylvania 1979–87; Dir Inst. of Politics, J.F. Kennedy School of Govt, Harvard Univ. 1987–88; Attorney-Gen. of USA 1988–91; Under-Sec.-Gen. for Admin. and Man., UN 1992–93; Founding Chair. State Science and Tech. Inst.; Chair. Legal Policy Advisory Bd, Washington Legal Foundation; Vice-Chair. World Cttee on Disability; mem. American Law Inst.; Trustee, Urban Inst.; mem. Nat. Acad. of Public Admin.; Lifetime Nat. Assoc., Nat. Acads of Science and Eng 2001–; Fellow, American Bar Foundation; Republican; 32 hon. degrees; Special Medallion Award, Fed. Drug Enforcement Admin. 1973, Distinguished Service Medal, American Legion 1992, Wiley E. Branton Award, Washington Lawyers Cttee 2002, American Lawyer Magazine Lifetime Achievement Award 2006. *Publications include:* Where the Evidence Leads (autobiography) 2003, Report of the Independent Review Panel on the September 8, 2004 '60 Minutes Wednesday' Segment "For the Record" Concerning President Bush's Texas Air National Guard Service (with Louis D. Boccardi) 2005, Puerto Rico's Future: A Time to Decide 2007. *Address:* K&L Gates LLP, 210 Sixth Avenue, Pittsburgh, PA 15222-2613, USA (office). *Telephone:* (412) 355-8917 (office). *E-mail:* dick.thornburgh@klgates.com (office). *Website:* www.klgates.com (office).

THORNE, David, BA, MA; American business executive and fmr diplomatist; b. 16 Sept. 1944; s. of Landon Thorne, Jr; twin brother of Julia Thorne; m. Rose Thorne; two c.; ed Yale and Columbia Univs; moved with family to Rome when his father was apptd by Pres. Eisenhower to administer Marshall Plan for Italy 1953; served in USN 1966–70; Co-founder Adviser Investments (specializes in Vanguard and Fidelity mutual funds and exchange-traded funds); has been an investor in several business ventures, including marketing consulting, real estate, publishing and financial services; sold publishing business to Martha Stewart Omnimedia; Amb. to Italy 2009–13; fmr Pres. and current Bd mem. Inst. of Contemporary Art, Boston; Public Service Award, Columbia Univ.; Cavaliere di Gran Croce dell'ordine al Merito. *Publication:* The New Soldier 1971. *Leisure interest:* plays league soccer in New England. *Address:* Adviser Investments, 85 Wells Avenue, Suite 109, Newton, MA 02459, USA (office). *E-mail:* dthorne@adviserinvestments .com (office). *Website:* www.adviserinvestments.com (office).

THORNE, Kip Stephen, BS, PhD; American research physicist, academic and writer; *Feynman Professor of Theoretical Physics Emeritus, California Institute of Technology;* b. 1 June 1940, Logan, Utah; s. of David Wynne Thorne and Alison Comish; m. 1st Linda Jeanne Peterson 1960 (divorced 1977); one s. one d.; m. 2nd Carolee Joyce Winstein 1984; ed California Inst. of Tech. and Princeton Univ.; Postdoctoral Fellow, Princeton Univ. 1965–66; Research Fellow in Physics, Calif. Inst. of Tech. 1966–67, Assoc. Prof. of Theoretical Physics 1967–70, Prof. 1970–, William R. Kenan Jr Prof. 1981–91, Richard P. Feynman Prof. of Theoretical Physics 1991–2009, Emer. 2009–; Prof. of Physics, Univ. of Utah 1971–98; Fulbright Lecturer, France 1966; Visiting Prof., Moscow Univ. 1969, 1975, 1978, 1981, 1982, 1986, 1988, 1990, 1998; Andrew D. White Prof.-at-Large, Cornell Univ. 1986–92; Chair. Topical Group on Gravity of American Physical Soc. 1997–98; Alfred P. Sloan Research Fellow 1966–68; Guggenheim Fellow 1967; mem. Int. Cttee on Gen. Relativity and Gravitation 1971–80, 1992–, Cttee on US-USSR Co-operation in Physics 1978–79, Space Science Bd, NASA 1980–83; Foreign mem. Russian Acad. of Sciences 1999; mem. American Philosophical Soc. 1999; mem. NAS 1973; Fellow, American Acad. of Arts and Sciences, American Physical Soc., AAAS; Hon. Prof., Univ. of Chinese Acad. of Sciences 2017; Hon. DSc (Illinois Coll.) 1979, (Utah State Univ.) 2000, (Glasgow) 2001, (Univ. of Chicago) 2008, (ETH, Zurich) 2017; Dr hc (Moscow State Univ.) 1981, (Univ. Politecnica de Catalunya) 2017; Hon. DHumLitt (Claremont Grad. Univ.) 2002; Science Writing Award in Physics and Astronomy, American Inst. of Physics 1969, 1994, Priroda (USSR) Readers' Choice Award 1989, 1990, Julius Edgar Lilienfeld Prize, American Physical Soc. 1996, Karl Schwarzschild Medal, German Astronomical Soc. 1996, 24th Annual Award for Excellence in Teaching, Associated Students of the California Inst. of Tech. (undergraduates) 1999–2000, Robinson Prize in Cosmology, Univ. of Newcastle 2002, California Scientist of the Year 2004, Student Council Mentoring Award 2004, Commonwealth Award in Science 2005, Albert Einstein Medal, Albert Einstein Soc. 2009, UNESCO Niels Bohr Gold Medal 2010, J.D. Jackson Award for Excellence in Grad. Educ., American Asscn of Physics Teachers 2012, Howard Vollum Award for Science and Tech., Reed Coll. 2013, Space Pioneer Award for Mass Media, Nat. Space Soc. 2015; (co-recipient): Cosmology Prize, Peter Gruber Foundation 2016, Kavli Prize in Astrophysics 2016, Special Breakthrough Prize in Fundamental Physics 2016, Shaw Prize in Astronomy 2016, Harvey Prize for Breakthroughs in Science and Tech., Israel 2016, Nobel Prize in Physics (co-recipient) 2017, Giuseppe and Vanna Cocconi Prize for an outstanding contribution to Particle Astrophysics and Cosmology (co-recipient) 2017, Princess of Asturias Award for Technical & Scientific Research (co-recipient) 2017, Fudan-Zhongzhi Science Award (co-recipient) 2017. *Achievements include:* co-founded and provided the scientific vision for Laser Interferometer Gravitational-Wave Observatory (LIGO) for the direct detection of gravitational waves 2015. *Publications include:* co-author: Gravitation Theory and Gravitational Collapse 1965, High Energy Astrophysics, Vol. 3 1967, Gravitation 1973, Black Holes: The Membrane Paradigm 1986; sole author: Black Holes and Time Warps: Einstein's Outrageous Legacy 1994, The Science of Interstellar 2014. *Address:* California Institute of Technology, TAPIR 350-17, 1200 East California Boulevard, Pasadena, CA 91125-0001, USA (office). *Telephone:* (626) 395-4598 (office). *E-mail:* kip@caltech.edu (office). *Website:* www.its.caltech.edu/~kip (office).

THORNE VETTER, Alfredo Eduardo, MEcon, PhD; Peruvian economist and government official; b. 29 Oct. 1955, Lima; s. of Jorge Thorne Larrabure and Lissy Alicia Vetter Tudela; one s. one d.; ed Pontificia Universidad Católica del Perú, Univ. of Oxford and Univ. of Cambridge, UK; Sr Economist with World Bank 1988–95, becoming Sr Country Economist for Mexico; Exec. Dir and Analysis Area Man. for Latin America, JP Morgan Chase & Co. 1995–2009; Dir-Gen. of Investment Banking and Analysis, Banorte, Mexico 2009–11; Consultant, Mexican Securities Industry Asscn 2010–11; Dir Mexican Stock Exchange 2010–11; Prin., Thorne & Assocs (economic, financial and mergers and acquisitions advisory firm) 2011–; Dir Prima AFP (investment co.) 2012–13; Minister of Economy and Finance 2016–17; fmr columnist, Poder (bi-weekly magazine), Mexico City. *Address:* c/o Ministry of Economy and Finance, Jirón Junín 319, 4°, Circado de Lima, Lima 1, Peru (office).

THORNING-SCHMIDT, Helle, MA, MSc; Danish politician and international organization official; *Chief Executive, Save the Children International;* b. 14 Dec. 1966, Rødovre; d. of Holger Thorning-Schmidt and Grete Thorning-Schmidt; m. Stephen Kinnock 1996; two d.; ed Univ. of Copenhagen, Coll. of Europe, Belgium; Int. Consultant, Danish Trades Union Congress (LO) 1997–99; Head, Socialdemokraterne (Social Democrats) Secr., European Parl. 1994–97, MEP 1999–2004; mem. Folketing (Parl.) (Social Democratic Party) for Eastern Copenhagen 2005–07, for Greater Copenhagen 2007–16; Leader, Socialdemokraterne (Social Democrats) 2005–15; Prime Minister of Denmark 2011–15; mem. Bd of Dirs Danmarks Nationalbank 2005–; UN Global Education Champion 2012–; CEO Save the Children International 2016–. *Publications include:* En dollar om dagen (A Dollar a Day) (co-author) 2001, Forsvar for Fællesskabet (In Defence of Fellowship) (co-author) 2002. *Address:* Save the Children International, St Vincent House, 30 Orange Street, London, WC2H 7HH, England (office). *Telephone:* (20) 3272-0300 (office). *Website:* www.savethechildren.net (office); www.thorning-schmidt.dk.

THORNTON, Billy Bob; American actor, director and writer; b. 4 Aug. 1955, Hot Springs, Ark.; m. 1st Melissa Lee Gatlin (divorced 1980); one d.; 2nd Toni Lawrence (divorced 1988); 3rd Cynda Williams (divorced 1992); 4th Pietra Dawn Chernak (divorced 1997); two s.; 5th Angelina Jolie 2000 (divorced 2003); one adopted s.; one d. with Connie Angland. *Films include:* Sling Blade (also dir, screenplay; Acad. Award for Best Adapted Screenplay 1996, Chicago Film Critics Award for Best Actor, Independent Spirit Awards), U-Turn 1997, A Thousand Miles 1997, The Apostle 1997, A Gun A Car A Blonde, Primary Colors 1997, Homegrown 1998, Armageddon 1998, A Simple Plan 1998, Pushing Tin 1998, All the Pretty Horses (dir), The Man Who Wasn't There 2001, Bandits 2001, Monster's Ball 2001, Daddy and Them (dir) 2001, Love Actually 2003, Intolerable Cruelty 2003, Bad Santa 2003, The Alamo 2004, Friday Night Lights 2004, Bad News

Bears 2005, The Ice Harvest 2005, School for Scoundrels 2006, The Astronaut Farmer 2007, Mr Woodcock 2007, Eagle Eye 2008, The Informers 2008, The Smell of Success 2009, Faster 2010, Puss in Boots (voice) 2011, Jayne Mansfield's Car (also dir) 2012, The Baytown Outlaws 2012, Parkland 2013, Grizzly 2014, Cut Bank 2014, The Judge 2014, Into the Grizzly Maze 2015, Entourage 2015, Our Brand Is Crisis 2015, Whiskey Tango Foxtrot 2016, Bad Santa 2 2016. *Television:* The Outsiders (series) 1990, Hearts Afire 1992–95, Fargo (Golden Globe Award for Best Actor in a TV Mini-series or Movie 2015) 2014, Trailer Park Boys: Drunk, High and Unemployed (film) 2015, Goliath (Golden Globe Award for Best Actor in TV Series 2017) 2016. *Address:* c/o Creative Artists Agency, 2000 Avenue of the Stars, Los Angeles, CA 90067, USA.

THORNTON, Dame Janet Maureen, DBE, CBE, PhD, FRS; British molecular biologist and academic; *Director Emeritus and Senior Scientist, European Bioinformatics Institute;* b. 23 May 1949; d. of Stanley James McLoughlin and Kathleen Barlow; m. Alan Thornton 1970; one s. one d.; ed Univ. of Nottingham, King's Coll. London, Nat. Inst. of Medical Research; tutor, Open Univ. 1976–83; molecular pharmacologist, Nat. Inst. of Medical Research 1978; Science and Eng Research Council Advanced Fellow 1979–83, Lecturer 1983–89, Sr Lecturer 1989–90, Bernal Chair. of Crystallography 1996–; Dir Biomolecular Structure and Modelling Unit, Univ. Coll. London 1990–, Prof. of Biomolecular Structure 1990–; consultant, European Molecular Biology Lab., European Bioinformatics Inst. (EMBL-EBI) 1994–2000, Dir EMBL-EBI 2000–15, now Dir Emer. and Sr Scientist; Head Jt Research School in Molecular Sciences, Univ. Coll. London and Birkbeck Coll. 1996–2000; Fellow, Churchill Coll. Cambridge; Foreign Assoc., NAS; Hon. Prof., Dept of Chem., Univ. of Cambridge; Hans Neurath Award, Protein Soc., USA 2000, Dorothy Hodgkin Award, Protein Soc., Zurich 2009. *Publications:* numerous articles in scientific journals. *Leisure interests:* reading, music, gardening, walking. *Address:* EMBL-EBI, Wellcome Trust Genome Campus, Hinxton, Cambridge, CB10 1SD, England (office). *Telephone:* (1223) 494648 (office); (1223) 494444 (office). *Fax:* (1223) 494468 (office). *E-mail:* thornton@ebi.ac.uk (office). *Website:* www.ebi.ac.uk (office).

THORNTON, John Lawson, BA, MA; American business executive and academic; *Chairman, Barrick Gold Corporation;* b. 2 Jan. 1954, New York; m. Margaret Thornton; ed Hotchkiss School, Harvard Coll., Univ. of Oxford, UK, Yale School of Org. and Man.; joined Goldman Sachs 1980, f. and built merger and acquisition business for co. in Europe 1983–91, apptd Partner 1988 with exec. responsibility for operations in Europe, Middle East and Africa, mem. Bd of Dirs 1996, Pres., Co-COO 1999–2003; Prof. and Dir of Global Leadership, Tsinghua Univ., China 2003–; Chair. Barrick Gold Corpn 2014–; PineBridge Investments LLC 2014–; mem. Bd of Dirs Ford Motor Co. 1996–; fmr mem. Bd Dirs Goldman Sachs Group, Inc., Intel, Inc., China Unicom Ltd, HSBC Holdings PLC, HSBC North America Holdings Inc. (Chair. 2008–13), News Corpn, British Sky Broadcasting, Laura Ashley Holdings PLC, IMG Worldwide, Inc., Hughes Electronics Corpn, Pacific Century Group Inc.; Chair. Brookings Inst. Bd of Trustees; Pres. The Hotchkiss School; mem. Council on Foreign Relations; mem. Advisory Bd Asia Society, Morehouse Coll., Tsinghua Univ. School of Econs and Man., Yale Univ. Investment Cttee, Yale School of Man. *Address:* Barrick Gold Corporation, Brookfield Place, TD Canada Trust Tower, 161 Bay Street, Suite 3700, Toronto, ON M5J 2S1, Canada (office). *Telephone:* (416) 861-9911 (office). *Website:* www .barrick.com (office).

THORP, Holden, BSc, PhD; American chemist, academic and university administrator; *Provost and Executive Vice-Chancellor for Academic Affairs, Washington University in St Louis;* b. 16 Aug. 1964, Fayetteville, NC; m. Patti Worden Thorp; one s. one d.; ed Univ. of North Carolina, California Inst. of Tech.; Postdoctoral Asst, Yale Univ. 1989–90; Asst Prof. of Chem., North Carolina State Univ. 1990–92; Asst Prof. of Chem., Univ. of North Carolina 1992–99, Prof. 1999–, Kenan Prof. and Chair. Dept of Chem. 2005, Dean Coll. of Arts and Sciences 2007–08, Chancellor Univ. of North Carolina 2008–13, Dir Morehead Planetarium and Science Center 2001–05; Provost and Exec. Vice-Chancellor for Academic Affairs, Washington Univ. in St Louis 2013–, Rita Levi-Montalcini Distinguished Univ. Prof. 2014–, holds an endowed professorship with appointments in chemistry and medicine; co-f. Viamet Pharmaceuticals Inc. 2005; Inc.; mem. Nat. Advisory Council for Innovation and Entrepreneurship, Nat. Security Higher Educ. Advisory Bd; Chair. Cttee for the NAS charged with establishing and promoting a culture of safety in academic laboratory research; mem. Bd Artizan Biosciences, Coll. Advising Corps, St Louis Symphony Orchestra, Barnes-Jewish Hospital; mem. UNC Lineberger Comprehensive Cancer Center; mem. Scientific Advisory Bd, Ohmx Corpn; fmr mem. of Tech. Advisory Bd, Plextronics, Inc.; Fellow Nat. Acad. of Inventors 2012; NSF Predoctoral Fellow with Prof. Harry B. Gray, Calif. Inst. of Tech.; numerous awards, including Nat. Science Foundation's Presidential Young Investigator Award 1991, Ruth and Philip Hettleman Prize for Artistic and Scholarly Achievement 1996, Tanner Award for Excellence in Undergraduate Teaching, David and Lucile Packard Fellowship for Science and Engineering. *Publications:* Engines of Innovation (co-author) 2010, Our Higher Calling: Rebuilding the Partnership Between America and its Colleges and Universities (co-author) 2018, more than 130 scholarly publications on the electronic properties of DNA and RNA. *Leisure interests:* playing jazz bass and keyboard. *Address:* Office of the Provost, 229 North Brookings Hall, One Brookings Drive, Campus Box 1072, St Louis, MO 63130-4899, USA (office). *Telephone:* (314) 935-3000 (office). *E-mail:* thorp@wustl.edu (office). *Website:* provost.wustl.edu (office).

THORPE, Ian James; Australian swimmer; b. 13 Oct. 1982, Sydney; s. of Kenneth William Thorpe and Margaret Grace Thorpe; ed East Hills Boys Technical High School; winner three gold medals, two silver medals, Olympic Games, Sydney 2000; set new world record in 400m freestyle and 4×200m relay; winner 11 World Championship gold medals 1998–2003; won 10 gold medals and broke own 400m freestyle world record, Commonwealth Games; won nine titles including five gold medals, Pan-Pacific Games, Yokohama 2002; winner two gold medals, one silver medal, one bronze medal, Olympic Games, Athens 2004; world-record holder for 200m and 400m freestyle; retd from competitive swimming 2006; Medal of the Order of Australia 2001; Hon. DLit (Macquarie Univ.) 2013, 2014; numerous awards including NSW Athlete of the Year 1998, three times Australian Swimmer of the Year, four times World Swimmer of the Year, Swimming World

Magazine 1998, 1999, Male Athlete of the Year, Australian Sports Awards 2000, Young Australian of the Year 2000, The Sport Australia Hall of Fame's 'Don Award' 2000, Jesse Owens American Int. Athlete Trophy Award 2001, China Sports Daily's Most Popular World Athlete 2002, Human Rights Medal 2012. *Achievements include:* launched Ian Thorpe's Fountain for Youth 2000. *Publications:* The Journey, Live Your Dreams, This is Me (autobiog.) 2012. *Leisure interests:* surfing, cooking, exercising, reading. *Address:* c/o Andrew Gibbs, SEL, Level 3, 243 Liverpool Street, East Sydney, NSW 2010, Australia (office). *Telephone:* (2) 8353 7777 (office); (4) 1734 2323 (office). *Fax:* (2) 8353 7788 (office). *E-mail:* ag@sel.com.au (office). *Website:* sel.com.au (office).

THORPE, Nigel James, CVO, BA; British diplomatist (retd); b. 3 Oct. 1945; m. 1st Felicity Thompson 1969 (divorced); two s.; m. 2nd Susan Diane Bamforth; two d.; ed East Grinstead Co. Grammar School, Cardiff Univ.; joined Diplomatic Service 1969, served in various positions including at Embassy in Warsaw 1970–72, High Comm., Dhaka 1973–74, at FCO 1975–79, High Comm., Ottawa 1979–81; seconded to Dept of Energy, London 1981–82; Deputy Head Southern Africa Dept, FCO 1982–85, Deputy Head of Mission, Embassy in Warsaw 1985–88, Deputy High Commr, Harare 1989–92, Head of Cen. European Dept, FCO 1992–96, Sr Directing Staff, Royal Coll. of Defence Studies, London 1996–98, Amb. to Hungary 1998–2003 (retd); Pres. Vodafone Hungary Foundation 2003–08. *Publications include:* Harmincad Utca 6: A Twentieth Century History of Budapest. *Leisure interests:* family, his dog, music.

THOTTUNKAL, HE Cardinal Moran Mor Baselios Cleemis, BPhil, BTh, MTh, PhD; Indian ecclesiastic; *Major Archbishop of Trivandrum (Syro-Malankarese) and Catholicos of the Syro-Malankara Catholic Church;* b. (Isaac Thottunkal), 15 June 1959, Mukkoor, nr Mallappally Town, Pathanamthitta dist, Kerala; s. of Mathew Thottunkal and Annamma Thottunkal; ed Minor Seminary Formation, Tiruvalla, St Joseph's Pontifical Inst., Mangalapuzha, Aluva, Papal Seminary, Pune, Dharmaram Coll., Bangalore, Pontifical Univ. of St Thomas Aquinas (Angelicum), Rome; ordained priest, Archdiocese of Battery (Bathery) (Syro-Malankarese) 1986; Vicar Gen. (Proto Syncellus) of the Eparchy of Bathery 1997–2001; apptd Titular Bishop of Chaialum 2001; Auxiliary Bishop of Trivandrum (Syro-Malankarese) 2001–03; founded Mar Ivanois, Malankara Catholic Center, New York 2001; Bishop of Tiruvalla (Syro-Malankarese) 2003–06; Archbishop of Tiruvalla (Syro-Malankarese) 2006–07; Major Archbishop of Trivandrum (Syro-Malankarese) 2007–; cr. Cardinal (Cardinal-Priest of San Gregorio VII) 2012; Pres. Kerala Catholic Bishops' Council 2013–, Catholic Bishops' Conf. of India 2014–; mem. Congregation for Oriental Churches 2013–, Pontifical Council for Interreligious Dialogue 2013–, Fed. of Bishops' Confs of Asia. *Address:* Major Archbishop's House, Pattom, Thiruvananthapuram 695 004, Kerala, India (office). *Telephone:* (471) 2541642 (office). *Fax:* (471) 2541635 (office). *E-mail:* catholicostvm@gmail.com (office). *Website:* www .majorarchdioceseoftrivandrum.com (office).

THRIFT, Sir Nigel John, Kt, PhD, FBA, FAcSS; British geographer, academic and university administrator; *Vice-Chancellor and President, University of Warwick;* b. 12 Oct. 1949, Bath, England; ed Nailsea School, Univ. of Wales, Aberystwyth, Univ. of Wales, Lampeter, Univs of Bristol and Oxford; fmr Head of Life and Environmental Sciences Div., Univ. of Oxford, later Pro-Vice-Chancellor for Research; Vice-Chancellor and Pres., Univ. of Warwick 2006–; Chair. Centre for Research on Socio-Cultural Change (CRESC) Advisory Bd; Commr, Marshall Aid Comm.; mem. Bd Higher Educ. Statistics Agency, Coventry and Warwickshire Local Enterprise Partnership Bd, European Inst. of Innovation and Tech. Governing Bd; mem. Nat. Curriculum Review Advisory Cttee; Trustee, Council for Industry and Higher Educ.; Fellow, Acad. of Social Sciences; Hon. LLD (Bristol) 2010; Victoria Medal, Royal Geographical Soc. 2003, Distinguished Scholarship Honors, Asscn of American Geographers 2007, Gold Medal, Royal Scottish Geographical Soc. 2008. *Publications include:* Spatial Formations 1996, Knowing Capitalism (Theory, Culture and Society) 2005, Non-Representational Theory 2007, Shaping The Day: A History of Timekeeping in England and Wales 1300–1800 (co-author) 2009; co-editor of more than 20 books, including The International Encyclopedia of Human Geography; numerous papers in professional journals on int. finance, cities and political life, non-representational theory, affective politics and the history of time; contribs to Times Higher Education, Chronicle of Higher Education. *Address:* Office of the Vice-Chancellor and President, University of Warwick, Coventry, Warwicks., CV4 8UW, England (office). *Telephone:* (24) 7652-3630 (office). *E-mail:* vcpa@warwick.ac.uk (office). *Website:* www2.warwick.ac.uk/services/vco (office).

THRUN, Sebastian Burkhard, BSc, MSc, PhD; German computer scientist and academic; b. 14 May 1967, Solingen; m. Petra Dierkes-Thrun 1995; ed Univ. of Hildesheim, Univ. of Bonn; Research Asst, German Nat. Research Centre for Information Tech., Sankt Augustin 1989–91; Research Computer Scientist, Carnegie Mellon Univ. 1995–98, Asst Prof. of Computer Science, Robotics and Automated Learning and Discovery 1998–2001; Assoc. Prof. 2001–03; Assoc. Prof. of Computer Science, Stanford Univ. 2003–07, also of Electrical Eng 2006–07; Prof. of Computer Science and Electrical Eng 2007–11, Research Prof. of Computer Science 2011–16, also apptd Dir Stanford Artificial Intelligence Lab. (SAIL) 2004; Co-founder Udacity (online private educ. org.) 2012, CEO 2012–16, now Pres.; apptd Prin. Engineer, Google, Inc. 2007, Vice-Pres. and Fellow 2011–14, lead at various projects at Google X; Sr Adviser, Charles River Ventures 2009–12; mem. Deutsche Akademie der Naturforscher Leopoldina (German Acad. of Sciences) 2007, Nat. Acad. of Eng 2007; Dr hc (National Politechnic Institute, Mexico) 2016, (Technical University of Delft) 2016; Braunschweig Research Prize 2007, AAAI Ed Feigenbaum Prize 2011, Max Planck Research Award 2011, Asscn for the Advancement of Artificial Intelligence Ed Feigenbaum Prize 2011, Smithsonian Ingenuity Award 2012, ALVA Award 2013, GABA Award of Excellence 2014, Global Impact Award, World Affairs Council 2015, James Smithson Bicentennial Medal, Smithsonian Inst. 2015. *Achievements include:* led devt of robotic vehicle Stanley, winner of Defense Advanced Research Projects Agency (DARPA) Grand Challenge 2005; involved in devt of Google's self-driving car. *Publications include:* 370 scientific papers, 11 books. *Address:* Udacity Inc., 2465 Latham Street, 3rd Floor, Mountain View, CA 94040, USA (office). *Website:* robots.stanford.edu (office).

THRUSH, Brian Arthur, MA, ScD, FRS; British scientist and academic; *Professor Emeritus of Physical Chemistry, University of Cambridge;* b. 23 July 1928, London; s. of Arthur Thrush and Dorothy Thrush; m. Rosemary C. Terry 1958; one s. one d.; ed Haberdashers' Aske's Hampstead School and Emmanuel Coll., Cambridge; Univ. Demonstrator, Asst Dir of Research, Lecturer, Reader in Physical Chem. Univ. of Cambridge 1953–78, Prof. of Physical Chem. 1978–95, now Prof. Emer.; Head Dept of Chem., Univ. of Cambridge 1988–93; Fellow, Emmanuel Coll., Cambridge 1960–, Vice-Master 1986–90; mem. Natural Environment Research Council 1985–90; Visiting Prof. Chinese Acad. of Sciences 1980–; mem. Council, Royal Soc. 1989–91, Academia Europaea 1992–98; Tilden Lecturer (Royal Soc. of Chem.) 1965; M. Polanyi Medal (Royal Soc. of Chem.) 1980, Rank Prize for Opto-Electronics 1992. *Publications:* papers on spectroscopy, gas reactions and atmospheric chemistry in learned journals. *Leisure interests:* wine, gardens. *Address:* Department of Chemistry, University of Cambridge, Lensfield Road, Cambridge, CB2 1EW (office); Brook Cottage, Pemberton Terrace, Cambridge, CB2 1JA, England (home). *Telephone:* (1223) 763137 (office); (1223) 357637 (home). *Fax:* (1223) 336362.

THUBRON, Colin Gerald Dryden, CBE, FRSL; British writer; *President, Royal Society of Literature;* b. 14 June 1939, London; s. of Brig. Gerald Ernest Thubron and Evelyn Kate Dryden; m. Margreta de Grazia 2011; ed Eton Coll.; mem. editorial staff, Hutchinson & Co. Publishers Ltd 1959–62; freelance documentary film maker 1963–64; Production Ed., The Macmillan Co., USA 1964–65; freelance author 1965–; Vice-Pres., Royal Soc. of Literature 2003–10, Pres. 2010–; Fellow, Royal Asiatic Soc. 1991; Hon. DLitt (Warwick) 2002; Silver Pen Award of PEN 1985, Thomas Cook Award 1988, Hawthornden Prize 1988, Mungo Park Medal, Royal Scottish Geographical Soc. 2000, Lawrence of Arabia Medal, Royal Soc. of Asian Affairs 2001, Soc. of Authors Travel Award 2008, Prix Bouvier 2010, Ness Award, Royal Geographical Soc. 2011. *Scenario:* The Prince of the Pagodas (ballet at The Royal Opera House, Covent Garden). *Publications:* Mirror to Damascus, The Hills of Adonis, Jerusalem, Journey into Cyprus, Among the Russians, Behind the Wall, The Lost Heart of Asia, In Siberia, Shadow of the Silk Road 2006, To a Mountain in Tibet 2011; novels: The God in the Mountain 1977, Emperor 1978, A Cruel Madness 1984, Falling 1989, Turning Back the Sun 1991, Distance 1996, To the Last City 2002, Night of Fire 2016. *Address:* 28 Upper Addison Gardens, London, W14 8AJ, England (home). *Telephone:* (20) 7602-2522 (home). *E-mail:* Thubron@hotmail.com (home). *Website:* www.rslit.org.

THULASIDAS, V., MA; Indian airline industry executive; *Managing Director Kannur International Airport Ltd;* b. 25 March 1948, Allepey dist, Kerala; ed Inst. of English, Thiruvananthapuram; fmr lecturer, Kerala; various positions in Tripura including Commr of Taxes, Dir of Settlement and Land Records, of Food and Civil Supplies; fmr Under-Sec., Ministry of Civil Aviation; Jt Sec. (Air), Ministry of Defence 1988–2003; Chief Sec. of Tripura 1995–2003; Chair. and Man. Dir Air-India 2003–08; Man. Dir Kannur Int. Airport Ltd 2010–12, 2016–; mem. Bd of Dirs Hindustan Aeronautics Ltd 1991–93, Air Mauritius 2004–08, Oman Air 2012–. *Address:* Kannur International Airport Ltd, Parvathy TC 36/1 Chacka NH Bypass, Thiruvananthapuram 695 024 (office); 22B Sterling Apartments, 38 Peddar Road, Mumbai 400 026, India (home). *Telephone:* (471) 2508670 (office). *Fax:* (471) 2508669 (office). *E-mail:* managingdirector@kannurairport.in (office). *Website:* www.kannurairport.in (office).

THULIN, Inge G.; Swedish business executive; *Chairman, President and CEO, 3M Company;* b. 9 Nov. 1953, Malmö; ed Gothenburg Univ./IHM Business School, School of Econs and Commercial Law; various Sales and Marketing positions, 3M Sweden 1979–87, Group Man., Life Sciences Sector 1987–91, Business Man., Vision Care and Orthopedic Products, 3M Europe 1991–93, European Business Unit Man., Surgical Devices 1993–95, Man. Dir 3M Russia 1995–97, Skin Health Business Unit Dir, Skin Health Div. 1997–98, Marketing Operations Dir, Skin Health Div. 1998–99, Gen. Man., Skin Health Div. 1999–2000, Div. Vice-Pres., Skin Health Div. 2000–02, Vice-Pres., Europe and Middle East 2002–03, Exec. Vice-Pres., Int. Operations 2003–11, Exec. Vice-Pres. and COO 3M Company 2011–12, Chair., Pres. and CEO 2012–; mem. Int. Programs Advisory Council, Carlson School of Man., Univ. of Minnesota 2003–; mem. Bd Toro Co. 2007–12; mem. Pres. Trump's American Manufacturing Council 2017 (resgnd). *Address:* 3M Corporate Headquarters, 3M Center, St Paul, MN 55144-1000, USA (office). *Telephone:* (651) 733-1110 (office). *Fax:* (651) 733-9973 (office). *E-mail:* info@mmm .com (office). *Website:* www.mmm.com (office).

THUMMALAPALLY, Vinai Kumar, BS, MBA; American (b. Indian) business executive, diplomatist and government official; *Executive Director, SelectUSA;* b. 1954, Hyderabad, India; s. of T. Dharma Reddy and T. Padmaja; m. Barbara Thummalapally; two c.; ed Occidental Coll., California State Univ., Univ. of Tennessee; moved to USA 1974; fmr Mfg Man., Disc Manufacturing Inc., Man. Dir Clines Printing and Office Products, Plant Man. WEA Manufacturing, Pres. MAM-A Inc. (fmrly Mitsui Advanced Media), Colo –2009, Amb. to Belize 2009–13; Exec. Dir SelectUSA (govt-sponsored initiative to promote int. investment) 2013–. *Achievements include:* holds two patents for design of optical disc mfg. *E-mail:* info@selectusa.gov (office). *Website:* www.selectusa.gov (office).

THUN, Matteo; Italian architect and designer; b. 1952, Bolzano; ed Salzburg Acad. under Oskar Kokoschka, Univ. of Florence; moved to Milan 1978; Co-founder and fmr Partner, Sottsass Associati, Milan; co-f. Memphis Group 1981; Chair of Product Design and Ceramics, Vienna Acad. for Applied Arts 1982; f. Matteo Thun studio 1984; Creative Dir Swatch 1990–93; Applied Art Chair, Vienna; mem. RIBA; numerous awards, including ADI Compasso d'Oro Award (three times), Design of the Year Award for Via col Vento 1987, Forum Design Award 1989, Design Award, North Rhine-Westphalia 1994, Baden Württemberg Int. Design Award for 'O Sole Mio' 1997, IF Contract world Award for Missoni Shop System 2000, Industrial Design Forma Forum for 'Heidis' 2000, IF Contract world Award for Fila Shop 2000, Side Hotel in Hamburg chosen as Hotel of the Year 2001, Architecture and Tech. Innovation Prize and Good Design Award for 'Thun' 2003, ADI Design System: Architecture and Tech. Int. Prize for 'Girly' 2004, ADI Design System: Architecture and Tech. Int. Prize for 'Isy' 2004, Vigilius Mountain Resort won the Wallpaper Design Award 2004, inducted into Interior Hall of Fame, New York 2004, Red Dot Award for Product Design for Porsche Design Store 2005, Radisson SAS, Frankfurt chosen as the best hotel opened in the year, Worldwide Hospitality Awards 2005, Panda d'oro Award for Vigilius Mountain Resort 2005,

Design Plus Award for 'Archetun' 2006, IF Product Design Award for 'Roma' 2006, Legambiente/Regione Lombardi Award for Vigilius Mountain Resort 2006, Good Design Award for 'Roma' 2007, Prix Acier Construction for Strategic Unit by Hugo Boss 2007, Bronze Medal for 'Valverde' 2008, Water Innovation Award 2008, IF Product Design Award for 'Muse' 2008, Good Design Award for Rapsel 'Il bagno che non c'è' 2009, Editors Awards, ICFF, New York for Rapsel 'Il bagno che non c'è' 2009, Wallpaper* Design Award for Rapsel 'Ofurò' 2010, Wallpaper* Design Award for TVS 'Terra' 2010, iF Product Design Award for Zumtobel 'Ciria' Lighting 2010, Green Good Design Award for Belux 'Arba' Lighting 2010, Green Good Design Award for Rapsel 'Ofurò' 2010, Best Bath & Material Design 2010, Best of Year Interior Design USA for Rapsel 'Ofurò' 2010, Green Good Design Award for Zucchetti 'Isy' 2011, Hon. Mention, Compasso d'Oro for TVS 'Terra' 2011, Simon Taylor Award for Lifetime Achievement 2011, Good Design award for Antrax Serie Theater 2013, Red Dot Award for Product Design 2015, Iconic Award, German Design Council 2016, ADI Design Index for Fantini Lamé, Hospitality Design Awards 2016. *Architecture projects include:* Vigilius Mountain Resort, S. Tyrol, Hugo Boss Concept Store, New York, shop interiors for Missoni 1998–2002, Fila 2001, Porsche Design 2005–06, Radisson Blu Harbour Hotel, Dusseldorf (room design), Side Hotel, Hamburg (room design), Heidis Low-Energy Prefab House System, German Pavilion for Expo 2015 in Milan, Supsi University Campus, Lugano 2016, Fontenay luxury hotel, Hamburg 2016, JW Marriott Venice Resort (European Hotel Design Award, Categories: Adaptive Reuse/Interior Design/ Suites, Best Resort, MIPIM Awards, Best Hotel & Tourism Resort, Italian Pool Award for Rooftop Pool, World Luxury Spa Award for GOCO Spa) 2016. *Design projects include:* Rapsel Ofurò (bathroom accessories), CIRIA by Zumtobel Lighting, Savoy Zucchetti (bathroom fittings), Girly (bathroom fittings), Roma (bathroom fittings), Axent One Shower Toilet (iF Product Design Award 2016). *Address:* Via Appiani 9, 20121 Milan, Italy (office). *Telephone:* (02) 6556911 (office). *Fax:* (02) 6570646 (office). *E-mail:* press@matteothun.com (office). *Website:* www .matteothun.com (office).

THUNE, John, BA, MBA; American politician; *Senator from South Dakota;* b. Murdo, SDak; m. Kimberley Weems; two d.; ed Biola Univ., Univ. of South Dakota; started career in Washington, DC working for US Senator Jim Abdnor; served in US Small Business Admin; returned to SDak as Exec. Dir of local Republican Party 1989; State Railroad Dir 1991–93; Exec. Dir SDak Municipal League 1993–96; mem. House of Reps, Washington, DC 1996–2004, served on House Transportation and Agric. Cttees; Senator from South Dakota 2005–, mem. Agric., Nutrition and Forestry Cttee, Budget Cttee, Commerce, Science and Transportation Cttee, Finance Cttee, Chair. Senate Republican Policy Cttee 2009–11, Chair. Senate Republican Conf. *Leisure interests:* spending time with his family, pheasant hunting, running. *Address:* 511 Dirksen Senate Office Building, Washington, DC 20510, USA (office). *Telephone:* (202) 224-2321 (office). *Fax:* (202) 228-5429 (office). *Website:* thune.senate.gov (office); www.johnthune.com.

THUNELL, Lars H., PhD; Swedish business executive and international organization executive; *Chairman, Global Water Development Partners;* b. 1948; m.; three c.; ed Univ. of Stockholm; Pres. and CEO Securum (asset man. co.), Stockholm 1992–94; CEO Trygg-Hansa insurance co. 1992–97; CEO Skandinaviska Enskilda Banken AB 1997–2005; CEO and Exec. Vice-Pres. IFC (mem. World Bank Group) 2006–12; Chair. Global Water Development Partners (part of Blackstone Group) 2014–; Vice-Chair. (non-exec.) and mem. Bd of Dirs Sithe Global Power LLP 2012–; mem. Bd of Dirs Standard Chartered PLC 2012–, Kosmos Energy 2012–, Middle East Investment Initiative; Sr Adviser, Centre for Strategic and International Studies (US foreign policy think-tank); fmr Chair. IBX Integrated Business Exchange AB; fmr Deputy CEO Nordbanken. *Publications include:* author of books and articles on risk and risk man. in int. business. *Address:* Global Water Development Partners, Blackstone Group, 345 Park Avenue, New York, NY 10154, USA. *Website:* www.blackstone.com.

THURLEY, Simon John, CBE, MA, PhD, FSA, FRHistS; British foundation executive, museum administrator, author and consultant; b. 29 Aug. 1962, Huntingdon, Cambs.; s. of Thomas Manley Thurley and Rachel Thurley (née House); m. 2nd Anna Keay 2008; one s. one d.; ed Kimbolton School, Cambs., Bedford Coll. and Courtauld Inst. of Art; Insp. of Ancient Monuments, Crown Buildings and Monuments Group, English Heritage 1988–90; Curator, Historic Royal Palaces 1990–97; Dir Museum of London 1997–2002; CEO English Heritage 2002–15; Chair. Cttee Soc. for Court Studies 1996–2014; Pres. City of London Archaeological Soc. 1997–; Visiting Prof. of Built Environment, Gresham Coll. 2013–; Sr Research Fellow, Inst. of Historical Research 2014–; Trustee, British Library 2014–, Andrew Lloyd-Webber Foundation 2014–; Hon. mem. Royal Inst. of Chartered Surveyors; Hon. RIBA; Hon. Fellow, Royal Holloway Coll., Univ. of London. *Television:* Lost Buildings of Britain (Channel 4) 2004, The Buildings that Made Britain (Channel 5) 2006. *Publications include:* Henry VIII: Images of a Tudor King (co-author) 1989, The Royal Palaces of Tudor England: A Social and Architectural History 1993, Whitehall Palace: An Architectural History of the Royal Apartments, 1240–1698 1999, Lost Buildings of Britain 2004, Hampton Court Palace: A Social and Architectural History 2004, Somerset House: The Palace of England's Queens 1551–1692 (co-author) 2009, Men from the Ministry: How Britain Saved its Heritage 2013, The Building of England: How the History of England has Shaped our Buildings 2013, Houses of Power: The Places that Shaped the Tudor World 2017; frequent contribs to historical publs. *Leisure interest:* ancient buildings. *E-mail:* simon@kingstaithe.com (office). *Website:* www .simonthurley.com.

THURMAN, Uma; American actress; b. 29 April 1970, Boston, Mass; d. of Robert Thurman and Nena Schlebrugge; m. 1st Gary Oldman (q.v.) 1991 (divorced 1992); m. 2nd Ethan Hawke (q.v.) 1997 (divorced 2004); two d. one s.; worked as model; mem. Main Competition jury, Cannes Film Festival 2011; Pres. Un Certain Regard jury 2017; Chevalier, Ordre des Arts et des Lettres 2006; Chicago Int. Film Festival Career Achievement Award 2009, Bambi Award for Best Int. Actress 2014, Stockholm Int. Film Festival Achievement Award 2014, David di Donatello Speciale Award 2019. *Films:* The Adventures of Baron Munchhausen 1988, Dangerous Liaisons 1988, Where the Heart Is 1990, Henry and June 1990, Even Cowgirls Get the Blues 1993, Final Analysis 1992, Mad Dog and Glory 1993, Pulp Fiction 1994, Robin Hood, Dylan, A Month by the Lake 1995, The Truth About Cats and Dogs 1996, Batman and Robin 1997, Gattaca 1997, The Avengers 1998, Les Misérables 1998, Vatel 2000, The Golden Bowl 2001, Chelsea Walls 2002, Kill Bill Vol. I 2003, Kill Bill Vol. II 2004, Be Cool 2005, The Producers: The Movie Musical 2005, Prime 2005, My Super Ex-Girlfriend 2006, The Life Before Her Eyes 2008, The Accidental Husband (also prod.) 2008, Motherhood 2009, Percy Jackson & the Olympians: The Lightning Thief 2010, Bel Ami 2012, Playing for Keeps 2012, Nymphomaniac 2013, Burnt 2015, The Con Is On 2018, The House That Jack Built 2018, Down a Dark Hall 2018. *Stage:* The Parisian Woman 2017. *Television includes:* Hysterical Blindness (Golden Globe for Best Actress in a mini-series or TV movie 2003) 2002, Smash 2012, The Slap 2015, Imposters 2017, Chambers 2019. *Address:* c/o Untitled Entertainment, 350 South Beverly Drive, Beverly Hills, CA 90212, USA (office). *Telephone:* (310) 601-2100 (office). *E-mail:* contact@ untitledent.net (office). *Website:* untitledent.com (office).

THURNHERR, Walter; Swiss politician and fmr diplomatist; *Chancellor of the Swiss Confederation;* b. 11 July 1963, Muri, Aargau; m.; two c.; ed ETH Zurich; joined Fed. Dept of Foreign Affairs (FDA) 1989, Attaché, Embassy in Moscow 1989–90, with Political Secr., FDA 1991–95, Asst to UN Sec.-Gen.'s Personal Envoy for Georgia, Bern and New York 1993–97, Minister, Embassy in Moscow 1995–97, Personal Asst to Head of FDA 1997–99, Deputy Head, FDA Political Dept VI 1999–2000, Head 2000–02, Sec.-Gen., FDA 2002–03; Sec.-Gen., Fed. Dept of Econ. Affairs 2003–10; Sec.-Gen., Fed. Dept of the Environment, Transport, Energy and Communications 2011–15; Chancellor of the Swiss Confed. 2016–; mem. Steering Cttee Swiss Econ. Forum 2008–; mem. Advisory Council WIRE (thinktank) 2013–; mem. Christian Democratic People's Party (CVP/PDC). *Address:* Federal Chancellery, Bundeshaus West, 3003 Bern, Switzerland (office). *Telephone:* 584622111 (office). *Fax:* 584631916 (office). *E-mail:* info@bk.admin.ch (office). *Website:* www.bk.admin.ch (office).

THWAITE, Anthony Simon, OBE, MA, DLitt, FRSL, FSA; British writer and poet; b. 23 June 1930, Chester, Cheshire; s. of Hartley Thwaite and Alice Thwaite (née Mallinson); m. Ann Barbara Thwaite (née Harrop) 1955; four d.; ed Kingswood School, Bath, Christ Church, Oxford; Visiting Lecturer in English Literature, Univ. of Tokyo 1955–57; radio producer, BBC 1957–62; Literary Ed., The Listener 1962–65; Asst Prof. of English, Univ. of Libya, Benghazi 1965–67; Literary Ed., New Statesman 1968–72; Co-Ed., Encounter 1973–85; Editorial Dir, Editorial Consultant, André Deutsch 1986–95; Hon. Lay Canon, Norwich Cathedral 2005; Hon. DLitt (Hull) 1989, (East Anglia) 2007; Richard Hillary Memorial Prize 1968, Cholmondeley Award 1983. *Publications include:* poetry: Home Truths 1957, The Owl in the Tree 1963, The Stones of Emptiness 1967, Inscriptions 1973, New Confessions 1974, A Portion for Foxes 1977, Victorian Voices 1980, Poems 1953–1983 1984, revised edn as Poems 1953–1988 1989, Letter from Tokyo 1987, The Dust of the World 1994, Selected Poems 1956–1996 1997, A Different Country: New Poems 2000, A Move in the Weather 2003, The Ruins of Time (ed.) 2006, Collected Poems 2007, Late Poems 2010, Going Out 2014; other: Contemporary English Poetry 1959, The Penguin Book of Japanese Verse (co-ed. with Geoffrey Bownas) 1964, Japan (with Roloff Beny) 1968, The Deserts of Hesperides 1969, Poetry Today 1973, The English Poets (co-ed. with Peter Porter) 1974, In Italy (with Roloff Beny and Peter Porter) 1974, New Poetry 4 (co-ed. with Fleur Adcock) 1978, Twentieth Century English Poetry 1978, Odyssey: Mirror of the Mediterranean (with Roloff Beny) 1981, Larkin at Sixty (ed.) 1982, Poetry 1945 to 1980 (co-ed. with John Mole) 1983, Six Centuries of Verse 1984, Philip Larkin: Collected Poems (ed.) 1988, Selected Letters of Philip Larkin (ed.) 1992, Philip Larkin: Further Requirements (ed.) 2001, Poet to Poet: John Skelton 2008, Philip Larkin: Letters to Monica (ed.) 2010. *Leisure interests:* archaeology, antiquarian beachcombing. *Address:* The Mill House, Low Tharston, Norwich, Norfolk, NR15 2YN, England (home). *Telephone:* (1508) 489569 (home).

THYSSEN, Marianne Leonie Petrus; Belgian politician and EU official; *Commissioner for Employment, Social Affairs, Skills and Labour Mobility, European Commission;* b. 24 July 1956, Sint-Gillis-Waas; ed Catholic Univ. of Louvain; early career as Asst in Faculty of Law, Catholic Univ. of Louvain, legal asst in Office of State Sec. for Health, then legal adviser and Acting Sec.-Gen. UNIZO (org. for self-employed and small and medium-sized businesses); mem. European Parl. for Flanders with the Christen-Democratisch en Vlaams (CD&V) 1991–, currently Group Vice-Chair., Group of the European People's Party (Christian Democrats) and European Democrats (EPP-ED), mem. Cttee on Internal Market and Consumer Protection, Del. to EU-Ukraine Parl. Co-operation Cttee; First Deputy Mayor of Oud-Heverlee –2008; Chair. CD&V 2008–10; Commr for for Employment, Social Affairs, Skills and Labour Mobility, European Comm. (EC), Brussels Nov. 2014–. *Address:* European Commission, 200 Rue de la Loi/ Wetstraat 200, 1049 Brussels, Belgium (office). *Telephone:* (2) 299-11-11 (switchboard) (office). *E-mail:* marianne.thyssen@europarl.europa.eu (office). *Website:* ec .europa.eu/about/juncker-commission/commissioners-designate (office); www .mariannethyssen.be.

TIAN, Chengping; Chinese politician; b. 1940, Daming, Hebei Prov.; s. of Tian Ying; ed Tsinghua Univ., Beijing; joined CCP 1964; sent to do manual labour, Huoqiucheng (Xihu Army Farm), Anhui Prov. 1968; Sec. Publicity Section, Shengli Chemical Plant, Shandong Prov. 1970; Sec. CCP Communist Youth League of China, Beijing Gen. Petrochemical Works 1970; Deputy Sec. CCP Party Cttee, Qianjin Chemical Plant, Beijing Yanshan Petrochemical Corpn 1974, Deputy Sec. CCP Party Cttee, Beijing Yanshan Petrochemical Corpn 1983; Sec. CCP Xicheng Dist Cttee, Beijing 1984; Deputy Sec. CCP 8th Qinghai Prov. Cttee 1988–97, Sec. 1997–99; Gov. of Qinghai Prov. 1993–97; Chair. Standing Cttee Qinghai Prov. People's Congress 1998–99; mem. Standing Cttee CCP Shanxi Prov. Cttee 1999–2005, Sec. CCP Shanxi Prov. Cttee 1999–2005; Chair. Standing Cttee Shanxi Prov. People's Congress 2003–05; Minister of Labour and Social Security 2005–07; Alt. mem. 13th Cen. Cttee CCP 1987–91, 14th CCP Cen. Cttee 1992–97, mem. 15th CCP Cen. Cttee 1997–2002, 16th CCP Cen. Cttee 2002–07, 17th CCP Cen. Cttee 2007–12; Deputy, 8th NPC 1993–98, 9th NPC 1998–2003.

TIAN, Fengshan; Chinese fmr politician; b. Oct. 1940, Zhaoyuan Co., Heilongjiang Prov.; ed Second Artillery Tech. Coll., Xi'an City, Shaanxi Prov.; joined CCP 1970; teacher, Zhaoyuan Co.; Sec. CCP Party Cttee, Zhaoyuan People's Commune; Chair. CCP Revolutionary Cttee, Zhaoyuan Co.; Deputy Sec. CCP Zhaoyuan Co. Cttee; Deputy Magistrate, later Magistrate Zhaoyuan Co. (Dist) People's Court; Deputy Commr Suihua Prefectural Admin. Office, Heilongjiang Prov. 1983–85, Commr 1985–88 (Deputy Sec. CCP Party Cttee); Sec. CCP Mudanjiang Municipal

Cttee 1988–89; Vice-Gov. Heilongjiang Prov. 1989–94, Acting Gov. 1994–95, Gov. 1995–2000; Sec. CCP Leading Party Group, Ministry of Land and Resources 1999–2003, Minister of Land and Resources 2000–03 (removed from post); Deputy Sec. CCP Heilongjiang Prov. Cttee; Sec. CCP Harbin Municipal Cttee 1992; Alt. mem. 13th CCP Cen. Cttee 1987–92, 14th CCP Cen. Cttee 1992–97, mem. 15th CCP Cen. Cttee 1997–2002, 16th CCP Cen. Cttee 2002–04 (expelled from CCP 2004); Deputy to 8th NPC from Heilongjiang Prov. 1996; sentenced to life imprisonment for accepting bribes Dec. 2005.

TIAN, Guoli, BA; Chinese economist and business executive; *Chairman, Bank of China Limited;* b. Dec. 1960; ed Capital Construction Dept, Hubei Coll. of Econs (later Zhongnan Univ. of Econs and Law); held various positions at China Construction Bank (CCB), including sub-br. gen. man., deputy br. gen. man., department gen. man. of CCB Head Office, and Asst Pres. of CCB 1983–99; served successively as Vice-Pres. then Pres. China Cinda Asset Management Co., later Chair. China Cinda Asset Management Corpn 1999–2010; Vice-Chair. and Pres. CITIC Group 2010–13, also Chair. and Dir (non-exec.), China CITIC Bank; Chair. Bank of China Ltd 2013–; Chair. and Dir (non-exec.), BOCHK (Holdings) 2013–. *Address:* Bank of China Ltd, 1 Fuxingmen Nei Dajie, Beijing 100818, People's Republic of China (office). *Telephone:* (10) 6659-6688 (office). *Fax:* (10) 6659-3777 (office). *E-mail:* info@boc.cn (office). *Website:* www.boc.cn (office).

TIAN, Huiyu, MA; Chinese economist and business executive; *Executive Director and President, China Merchants Bank Company Limited;* ed Columbia Univ., USA; has served in a range of banks in various posts, including as Vice-Pres., Bank of Shanghai, Deputy Man. Dir, China Construction Bank (CCB), Shanghai, Man. Dir, CCB, Shenzhen, Retail Business Dir, CCB, Man. Dir, CCB, Beijing; Exec. Dir and Pres. China Merchants Bank Co. Ltd 2013–. *Address:* China Merchants Group Ltd, 40th Floor, China Merchants Building, 168–200 Conaught Road, Central, Hong Kong Special Administrative Region (office); China Merchants Bank Co. Ltd, 7088 Shen Nan Road, Futian District, Shenzhen 518040, Guangdong, People's Republic of China (office). *Telephone:* 25428288 (Hong Kong) (office); (755) 83198888 (Shenzhen) (office). *Fax:* 25448851 (Hong Kong) (office); (755) 83195109 (Shenzhen) (office). *E-mail:* cmhk@cmhk.com (office). *Website:* www .cmhk.com (office); www.cmbchina.com (office).

TIAN, Jiyun; Chinese politician; b. June 1929, Feicheng Co., Shandong Prov.; joined CCP 1945; teacher, Guiyang People's Revolutionary Univ., Guizhou Prov.; Admin. Cadre, Prov. Training Class for Financial Cadres, Guizhou Prov.; Section Chief, later Div. Chief, later Deputy Dir Finance Dept, Guizhou Prov.; Deputy Dir, later Dir Financial Bureau, Sichuan Prov. 1969; Deputy Sec.-Gen. State Council 1981–83, Sec.-Gen. 1983–88; Dir Nat. Afforestation Cttee; Chair. China Cttee of the Int. Decade for Natural Disaster Reduction 1983–87; Vice-Premier, State Council 1983–93; Head, Commodity Prices Group, State Council 1984–93; mem. Secr. CCP Cen. Cttee 1985–87; Dir State Flood Control and Drought Relief HQ 1988–93, Cen. Forest Fire Prevention HQ 1987–93; mem. 12th CCP Cen. Cttee 1982–87, 13th CCP Cen. Cttee 1987–92, 14th CCP Cen. Cttee 1992–97, 15th CCP Cen. Cttee 1997–2002, mem. Politburo 1985–2002, Politburo Secr. 1985–87; Vice-Chair. 8th Standing Cttee of NPC 1993–98, 9th Standing Cttee of NPC 1998–2003. *Address:* c/o Standing Committee of National People's Congress, Beijing, People's Republic of China (office).

TIAN, Zengpei; Chinese diplomatist and politician; b. 8 Oct. 1930, Raoyang Co., Hebei Prov.; ed Nankai Univ.; joined CCP 1947; joined Ministry of Foreign Affairs, becoming Section Chief and Dir, Political Dept, later Deputy Dir, Dir, and Deputy Dir-Gen. Dept of Soviet Union and Eastern Europe Affairs, Counsellor, Chinese Embassy, Moscow, USSR 1976–81; Minister-Counsellor, Embassy in Yugoslavia 1982–84, Amb. to Czechoslovakia 1984–85, to Yugoslavia 1986–88, Vice-Minister of Foreign Affairs 1988–98; mem. 14th CCP Cen. Cttee 1992–97; Del., 15th CCP Nat. Congress 1997–2002; mem. Standing Cttee 9th CPPCC Nat. Cttee 1998–2003, Chair. Foreign Affairs Sub-cttee 1998–2003. *Address:* c/o National Committee of Chinese People's Political Consultative Conference, 23, Taipingqiao Street, Beijing, People's Republic of China (office).

TIAN, Zhaowu, BS; Chinese scientist and university administrator; *Professor, College of Chemistry and Chemical Engineering, Xiamen University;* b. 28 June 1927, Fuzhou City, Fujian Prov.; ed Xiamen Univ., Fujian Prov.; Prof., Xiamen Univ., Pres. 1982–89, currently Prof. Coll. of Chemistry and Chemical Eng; Pres. China Chem. Asscn 1986; Vice-Pres. Int. Electrochemistry Asscn 1996, elected Pres. 2016; mem. Dept of Chem., Chinese Acad. of Sciences 1980–, Third World Acad. of Sciences 1996–; advanced the Feature Current idea of multi-hole electrode polarization and the Uneven Liquid Film model; also promoted electrochemical tech., including a new generation of ion chromatogram suppressers, corrosion measurement systems, and the first domestic electrochemical comprehensive testers; mem. Standing Cttee 8th CCP Nat. Cttee 1993–98; Dr hc (Univ. of Wales, UK) 1984; Hon. Nat. Prize of Sciences 1987. *Address:* Xiamen University, Xiamen 361005, Fujian Province, People's Republic of China. *Telephone:* (592) 2184975 (office). *Fax:* (592) 2183047 (office). *E-mail:* zwtian@xmu.edu.cn (office). *Website:* chem.xmu.edu.cn (office).

TIANGAYE, Nicolas; Central African Republic lawyer and politician; b. 13 Sept. 1956, Bocaranga; ed Univ. Bedél Bokassa, Bangui, Univ. of Orleans, France; mem. Bangui Bar 1983, Bar Asscn of CAR 1994–98; served as lawyer for numerous years, including as defence lawyer for Jean-Bedél Bokassa (deposed emperor of Central African Repub.) 1986–87 and for Pres. François Bozizé 1989; lawyer with Int. Criminal Tribunal for Rwanda, Arusha, Tanzania 1996–98; Chair. Nat. Transitional Council (Parl.) of CAR 2003–05; took part in drafting of new constitution 2004; Spokesman, Forces of Change Collective 2010; Prime Minister and Head of Govt 2013–14; Founder mem. Inter-African Union of Human Rights, Vice-Pres. 1992–98; mem. Int. Asscn of Young Lawyers 1986–2001; Grand Officier, Ordre du Mérite Centrafricain, Grand Officier, Ordre de la Reconnaissance Centrafricain.

TIAO, (Beyon) Luc-Adolphe, MSc; Burkinabè journalist, diplomatist and politician; b. 4 June 1954, Tenkodogo; m.; four c.; ed Univ. of Dakar, Senegal, Univ. of Ouagadougou, Univ. of Montreal, Canada, Centre for Diplomatic and Strategic Studies, Paris, France; Dir of Newspapers, Directorate-Gen. of the Press 1984–85; Dir and Chief Publr state-owned daily newspaper Sidwaya 1987–90; Sec.-Gen., Ministry of Communication and Culture 1990–92; Press Attaché,

Embassy in Paris 1992–96; Adviser, Mission of Dept of Communication at Prime Minister's Office 1996–2001; Pres. Superior Council of Communication (media regulator) 2001–08; Amb. to France 2008–11; Prime Minister 2011–14 (govt dissolved by Pres. Blaise Compaoré 30 Oct. 2014); mem. Congress for Democracy and Progress party; Founding mem. and fmr Pres. Journalists Asscn of Burkina Faso; Founding mem. and Sec.-Gen. Asscn of Devt'Earth-Schools' 1991; mem. several nat. and int. asscns, including Burkinabe Movt for Human Rights and Peoples' Rights (MBDHP); Expert and Rapporteur Gen. Conf. of Information Ministers of Mem. States of Econ. Community of West African States (ECOWAS) 1989; mem. Cttee of Experts of Panos Inst. of Paris and Union of Journalists of West Africa (WAJA) charged to reflect pluralism of the press in Africa at start of democratic processes 1990–91; Communications Adviser (Strategy-Media) to Pres. of Organizing Cttee of African Cup of Nations Jan.–April 1998; consultant to Nat. Comm. for Decentralization Sept. 1998; Sr Consultant to Supreme Council of Information for org. and conduct of seminar on Media, Democracy and Nat. Languages Oct. 1998; consultant to FAO Project TCP/BKF on project for a nat. communication policy for rural devt Feb.–March 1999. *Publications include:* The Politics of Communication in Black Africa (research report) 1987, The Committees for the Defense of the Revolution and the Process of Mobilization for Development in Burkina Faso (thesis) 1987, The Process of Democratic Transition in South Africa from the Sahara, from Burkina Faso 1994. *Leisure interests:* jogging, reading, cinema.

TIBAIJUKA, Anna Kajumulo, DSc; Tanzanian agricultural economist and United Nations official; m. Wilson Tibaijuka (died 2000); five c. (one adopted); ed Swedish Univ. of Agricultural Sciences, Uppsala; Assoc. Prof. of Econs, Dar-es-Salaam Univ. 1993–98; Founding Chair. Tanzanian Nat. Women's Council; UNCTAD Special Co-ordinator for Least Developed Countries, Landlocked and Small Island Developing Countries 1998–2000; Exec. Dir UN Centre for Human Settlements (UN-HABITAT) 2000–10, Under-Sec.-Gen. 2002–10, Dir-Gen. UN Office, Nairobi (UNON) 2006–10; Minister of Lands, Housing and Human Settlement Devt 2010–14; MP for Muleba S (Chama Cha Mapinduzi) 2010–; mem. Tanzanian Govt del. to several UN Summits, including World Summit for Social Devt, Copenhagen 1995, Fourth World Conf. on Women, Beijing 1995, UN Conf. on Human Settlements, Istanbul 1996, World Food Summit, Rome 1996 (elected Co-ordinator for Eastern Africa in Network for Food Security, Trade and Sustainable Devt—COASAD); mem. Bd Int. Scientific Advisory Bd, UNESCO 1997–; Exec. Sec. for Third UN Conf. on Least Developed Countries, Brussels, Belgium 2001; mem. Comm. for Africa 2004–05; apptd UN Special Envoy to study impact of Zimbabwean Govt's campaign (known as Operation Murambatsvina) to evict informal traders and people deemed to be squatting illegally in certain areas 2005; Prince Khalifa Bin Salman Al Khalifa Award for Sustainable Devt 2016. *Address:* PO Box 45, Muleba, Tanzania (office). *Telephone:* (68) 6838722 (office). *E-mail:* a.tibaijuka@bunge.go.tz (office). *Website:* www.annatibajuka.org (office).

TIBERI, Jean, LenD; French politician; b. 30 Jan. 1935, Paris; s. of Charles Tiberi and Hélène Pallavicini; m. Xavière Casanova; one s. one d.; ed Coll. Sainte-Barbe, Lycées Montaigne and Louis-le-Grand and Faculté de Droit, Paris; Acting Judge, Colmar 1958; Deputy Public Prosecutor, Metz 1959, Meaux 1959; Judge, Beauvais 1959, Nantes 1960; Chancellery 1960–63; apptd Dir of Studies, Faculté de Droit, Paris 1961; Conseiller de Paris 1965, First Vice-Pres. Conseil de Paris 1983–95, Deputy to Mayor of Paris 1977–83, First Deputy and Mayor of 5th arrondissement of Paris 1983–95, Mayor of Paris 1995–2000, Mayor of 5th arrondissement of Paris 2001–14; Deputy, Nat. Ass. 1976–2012; Sec. of State at Ministries of Agric., Industry and Research 1976; Sec., Paris RPR 1985–2000; convicted of electoral fraud 2015. *Publications:* Le quartier latin, Paris capitale des siècles 1988, La nouvelle Athènes, Paris capitale de l'esprit 1992. *Address:* 1 place du Panthéon, 75005 Paris, France (home).

TIBILOV, Maj.-Gen. Leonid; Georgian politician; b. 28 March 1952, Verkhnyi Dvan, Znaur dist, South Ossetian Autonomous Oblast, Georgian SSR, USSR; ed South Ossetian State Pedagogical Inst. (now South Ossetian State Univ.); served in Soviet Army 1974–75; teacher of physics and mathematics in South Ossetia, Dir Znaur Middle School, Head of Math. Dept at South Ossetian Pedagogical Inst. 1975–81; joined KGB 1981, Head of Security Services of Jt Forces for Law Enforcement and Peace in Georgian–South Ossetian conflict 1992–95; elected to Parl. of 'Republic of South Ossetia' 1994; First Deputy Prime Minister of 'Republic of South Ossetia' 1998; Co-Chair. Jt Control Comm. for Settlement of Georgian–South Ossetian Conflict 1998–2002; apptd First Deputy Prime Minister 2006; unsuccessful cand. in presidential election 2006; Chair. First Republican Bank 2007–09; consultant to the 'Pres.' on post-conflict regulation of relations with Georgia 2012; Pres. 'Republic of South Ossetia' 2012–17; Ind. *Address:* c/o Office of the President of the 'Republic of South Ossetia', 100001 Tskhinvali, Government House, ul. Stalina 18, South Ossetia, Georgia. *E-mail:* ospress@mail.ru.

TICKELL, Sir Crispin (Charles Cervantes), GCMG, KCVO; British fmr university chancellor and fmr diplomatist; b. 25 Aug. 1930, London, England; s. of Jerrard Tickell and Renée Haynes; m. 1st Chloë Gunn 1954 (divorced 1976); two s. one d.; m. 2nd Penelope Thorne Thorne 1977; ed Westminster School and Christ Church, Oxford; entered HM Diplomatic Service 1954, served at Embassy in The Hague 1955–58, Embassy in Mexico City 1958–61, Embassy in Paris 1964–70; Pvt. Sec. to Chancellor of Duchy of Lancaster 1970–72; Head of Western Orgs Dept 1972–75; Fellow, Centre for Int. Affairs, Harvard Univ. 1975–76; Chef de Cabinet to Pres. of Comm. of EC 1977–81; Visiting Fellow, All Souls Coll. Oxford 1981; Amb. to Mexico 1981–83; Deputy Under-Sec. of State 1983–84; Perm. Sec. Overseas Devt Admin. 1984–87; Perm. Rep. to UN, New York 1987–90; Warden, Green Coll., Oxford 1990–97, Dir Green Coll. Centre for Environmental Policy and Understanding 1992–2006; Chancellor, Univ. of Kent 1996–2006; Chair. Trustees, St Andrew's Prize for the Environment 1998–2014; Dir Policy Foresight Programme, The James Martin 21st Century School, Univ. of Oxford 2006–10; Adviser at Large to Pres. of Arizona State Univ. 2004–; Dir (non-exec.) IBM UK 1990–95 (mem. IBM Advisory Bd 1995–2000), Govett Mexican Horizons Investment 1991–96, Govett American Smaller Companies Trust 1996–98, Govett Enhanced Income Investment Trust 1999–; mem. Friends Provident Stewardship Cttee of Reference 1999–2002; Dir BOC Foundation 1990–2003; Pres. Royal Geographical Soc. 1990–93 (Vice-Pres. 1993–2002, Hon. Vice-Pres. 2002), Marine Biological Asscn 1990–2001 (Vice-Pres. 2001–), Earth Centre 1996–2000, Nat. Soc.

for Clean Air 1997–99, Tree Aid 2007–14; Chair. Int. Inst. for Environment and Devt 1990–94, Earthwatch Europe 1990–97, Climate Inst. of Washington, DC 1990–2002, 2012–, Advisory Cttee on Darwin Initiative for the Survival of Species 1992–99, Gaia Soc. 1998–2001, Advisory Cttee on the Environment of Int. Council for Science 1999–2004, Gaia Special Interest Group of Geological Soc. of London 2000–; Convenor Govt Panel on Sustainable Devt 1994–2000; mem. Govt Task Force towards an Urban Renaissance 1998–99, on Potential Risks from Near Earth Objects 2000, Copenhagen Climate Council 2008–09; Trustee, Nat. History Museum 1992–2001, World Wildlife Fund (UK) 1993–99, Royal Botanic Garden, Edinburgh 1997–2001, Thomson-Reuters Foundation 2000–, TERI Europe 2003–; Sr Inaugural Visiting Fellow, Harvard Univ. Center for the Environment 2002–03; Fellow, Geological Soc. of London 2000–, Linnean Soc. of London 2008–, Zoological Soc. of London 2014–; mem. ASU Council for the Global Inst. for Sustainablility; Co-founder Sir Crispin Tickell High Altitude Climate Observatory in Mexico and the associated Tickell Interaction Network in Mexico and beyond 2010–; Hon. Fellow, Anglo American School, New York 1990, Westminster School 1993, St Edmund's Coll., Cambridge 1995, Green Coll., Oxford 1997, Royal Scottish Geographical Soc. 1992, Chartered Inst. of Water and Environmental Man. 1996, Royal Inst. of GB 2002, Soc. for the Environment 2013, Hon. FRIBA 2000, Hon. Sr mem. Darwin Coll., Cambridge 1997; Officer, Order of Orange-Nassau (Netherlands) 1958, Chevalier, Nat. Order of Mali 1979, Orden Academica del Derecho, de la Cultura, y de la Paz 1989, Order of Aztec Eagle with Sash (Mexico) 1994; Dr hc (Academia Mexicana de Derecho Internacional) 1983, (Univ. of Stirling) 1990, (Sheffield Hallam Univ.) 1996, (Univ. of East London) 1998, (Open Univ.) 2006, (Univ. Juarez Autonoma de Tabasco) 2011, Hon. LLD (Univ. of Massachusetts, USA) 1990, (Univ. of Birmingham) 1991, (Univ. of Bristol) 1991, Hon. DSc (Univ. of East Anglia) 1990, (Univ. of Sussex) 1991, (Cranfield Univ.) 1992, (Loughborough Univ. of Tech.) 1995, (Univ. of Exeter) 1999, (Univ. of Hull) 2001, (Univ. of Plymouth) 2001, (Univ. of St Andrews) 2002, (Univ. of Southampton) 2002, (Oxford Brookes Univ.) 2002, (Université du Littoral Cote d'Opale) 2002, Hon. DLitt (Polytechnic of Cen. London (now Univ. of Westminster) 1990, Hon. DCL (Univ. of Kent at Canterbury) 1996, Hon. DHumLitt (American Univ. of Paris) 2003, Hon. DJur (Univ. of Nottingham) 2003, Hon. DrScs (Univ. of Brighton) 2006; mem. The Global 500: Roll of Honour for Environmental Achievement of UNEP 1991, Global Environmental Leadership Award, Climate Inst. of Washington, DC 1996, Distinguished Lecturer, British Geological Survey 1994, Centennial Lecturer, Arizona State Univ. 1995, Melchett Medallist, Inst. of Energy 1996, Kelvin Medallist, Royal Philosophical Soc. of Glasgow 1996, first Happold Medallist, Nat. Construction Industry Council 1998, Patron's Medal, Royal Geographical Soc. 2000, Distinguished Environmental Lecturer, Harvard Univ. 2001, Award for Int. Co-operation on Environment and Devt, China Council for Int. Co-operation on Environment and Devt 1996, Award for Int. Co-operation on Environmental Protection, Chinese State Environmental Protection Agency (SEPA) 2003, CAB Int. Bioscience Fellow 2004, Friendship Award, Govt of People's Repub. of China 2004, Minor Planet named No. 5971 Tickell 2006. *Publications include:* Climatic Change and World Affairs 1977, Mary Anning of Lyme Regis 1996; contribs to many books and papers. *Leisure interests:* climatology, palaeohistory, art (especially African and pre-Colombian), mountains. *Address:* Ablington Old Barn, Ablington, Cirencester, Glos., GL7 5NU, England (office). *Telephone:* (1285) 740569 (office). *E-mail:* ct@crispintickell.net (office); penelopetickell@googlemail.com (office). *Website:* www.crispintickell.com.

TICKNER, Robert, LLM, BEcons; Australian lawyer, organization official and fmr politician; *Chairman, CHS Alliance;* b. 24 Dec. 1951, Sydney; m. Jody Tickner; one c.; ed Univ. of Sydney; Lecturer, Faculty of Business Studies, NSW Inst. of Tech. 1974–78, Faculty of Law 1978–79; Prin. Solicitor, Aboriginal Legal Service, Redfern, Sydney 1979–83; Alderman, Sydney City Council 1977–84; MP for Hughes, NSW 1984–96; Minister for Aboriginal and Torres Strait Islander Affairs 1990–96; CEO Job Futures Ltd 2000–05; CEO Australian Red Cross 2005–15; Chair. CHS Alliance, Geneva 2016–; Office holder, Fed. Electorate Council and other Australian Labor Party bodies; Pres. NSW Soc. of Labor Lawyers; Cttee mem. NSW Council for Civil Liberties; Founding Cttee mem. Citizens for Democracy; Convenor Labor Parliamentarians for Nuclear Free Australia; fmr Chair. Parl. Group of Amnesty Int. *Leisure interests:* golf, tennis. *Address:* CHS Alliance, Maison Internationale de l'Environnement 2, Chemin de Balexert 7, (first floor, rooms 1-08), 1219 Châtelaine, Geneva, Switzerland (office). *E-mail:* info@chsalliance.org (office). *Website:* www.chsalliance.org (office).

TIE, Ning; Chinese writer; *Chairman, China Federation of Literary and Art Circles;* b. 1957, Beijing; d. of Tie Yang and Xu Zhi-ying; mem. Council, Chinese Writers' Asscn 1985–, Vice-Pres. 2001–06, apptd Pres. (first woman) 2006; Alt. mem. 16th CCP Cen. Cttee 2002–07, 17th CCP Cen. Cttee 2007–12, mem. 18th CCP Cen. Cttee 2012–; Chair. China Fed. of Literary and Art Circles 2016–; Zhuang Zhongwen Literary Prize 1993, Lu Xun Literary Prize 1997, Lao She Literary Award 2002, Bing Xin Prose Award 2002, 2005. *Publications include:* Path in the Night 1980, Xiangxue (Nat. Short Story Prize) 1982, Red Shirt With No Buttons (Nat. Fiction Prize) 1984, Rose Gate 1988, Cotton Stack 1988, Hay Stack (short stories) 1991, Women's White Night (non-fiction) 1991, Straw Ring (non-fiction) 1992, For Ever and Ever 1999, The Great Bather 2000, The Bathing Women 2012. *Leisure interests:* music, gourmet cooking. *Address:* China Federation of Literary and Art Circles, On Court North, Chaoyang District, Beijing 100029; Chinese Writers' Association, No.25, East Tucheng Road, Chaoyang District, Beijing 100013, People's Republic of China. *Telephone:* (10) 64221865 (office). *Fax:* (10) 64222240 (office). *Website:* www.chinawriter.com.cn (office).

TIEFENSEE, Wolfgang; German politician; *Minister for Economic Affairs, Science and Digital Society, Thüringer Landtag;* b. 4 Jan. 1955, Gera; divorced; four c.; ed Technical Univ. of Leipzig; skilled telecommunications worker 1974; mil. service 1975, as a conscientious objector served in a construction unit; graduated as an industrial electronics engineer 1979; Research and Devt Engineer, VEB Communications Works, Leipzig 1979–86; studied part-time for a postgraduate degree in computer science in the construction industry 1982; Devt Engineer, Technische Hochschule Leipzig 1986–90; studied part-time for a degree in electrical eng 1988; engaged in politics with Leipzig Round Table, Deputy Mayor without portfolio and mem. City Council 1989–90, Head of School Admin Office 1990, Deputy Mayor for Schools and Educ. 1992–94, Deputy Mayor for Youth, Schools and Sport and Vice-Mayor 1994, Mayor of Leipzig 1998–2005; Fed. Minister of Transport, Building and Urban Affairs and Fed. Govt Commr for the New Fed. States 2005–09; mem. Bundestag 2009–14; Minister for Econ. Affairs, Science and Digital Soc., Thüringer Landtag 2014–; mem. SPD 1995–, Econ. Policy Spokesman 2012–13, Econ. and Energy Policy Spokesman Jan.–Dec. 2014; Vice-Pres. Saxon Asscn of Cities and Towns 2001–05; Pres. Eurocities 2002–04; mem. Exec. Cttee German Asscn of Cities, Fed. Council (Alt. mem.) 2014–; Hon. Prof., Nanjing Univ. 1999; Chevalier, Ordre national de la Légion d'honneur 2003; Goldene Henne 2003, Golden Rathausmann, Vienna 2004. *Address:* Ministry of Economy, Science and Digital Society, Thüringer Landtag, Max Reger Strasse 4-8, 99096 Erfurt (office). *Telephone:* (36) 13797005 (office). *Fax:* (36) 13797990 (home). *E-mail:* wolfgang.tiefensee@tmwwdg.thueringen.de (office). *Website:* www.thueringen.de (office).

TIEMANN, Susanne, DJur; German lawyer, politician and academic; b. 20 April 1947, Schwandorf; d. of Hermann Bamberg and Anna-Maria Bamberg; m. Burkhard Tiemann 1969; one s. two d.; ed Ludwig-Maximilian Univ. Munich; called to the Bar, Munich 1975; served as lawyer in Cologne 1980; Prof. for Social and Admin. Law, Univ. of Bonn, Catholic Univ. of Cologne, now Prof. Emer.; Vice-Pres. European Council of the Liberal Professions 1994–97; mem. Bundestag (CDU/CSU) 1994–2002; mem. Econ. and Social Cttee of EC 1987, Chair. 1992–94; mem. Bd German Fed. of Liberal Professions 1988–; mem. Exec. Bd and Vice-Pres. European Secr. of the Liberal, Intellectual and Social Professions (SEPLIS) 1988, Pres. 1989–95; Chair. German Taxpayers' Asscn 1992–94; mem. German Bar Asscn; Hon. Prof., Katholische Fachhochschule Nordrhein-Westfalen 1998–, Hon. Prof. of Social Law, Univ. of Bonn; Frauen für Europa Prize 1993. *Address:* Stefan-Lochner-Straße 11, 50999 Cologne, Germany.

TIEN, Hung-Mao, MA, PhD; Taiwanese academic and diplomatist; *President and Chairman, Institute for National Policy Research;* b. 7 Nov. 1938, Tainan; m. Amy Tien; one s. one d.; ed Tunghai Univ. and Univ. of Wisconsin, USA; fmr Prof. of Political Science, Univ. of Wisconsin; Pres. and Chair. Inst. for Nat. Policy Research 1991–; mem. Nat. Unification Research Council, Office of Pres. of Taiwan 1994, Nat. Policy Adviser to Pres. of Taiwan 1996; Dir Foundation for Int. Co-operation and Devt 1996–, Minister of Foreign Affairs 2000–02; Rep. to UK 2002–04; adviser to Carnegie Endowment for International Peace; mem. Bd of Dirs China Bills Finance Corpn. *Publications include:* Government and Politics in Kuomintang China 1927–37, The Great Transition, Social and Political Change in the Republic of China, Taiwan's Electoral Politics and Democratic Transition: Riding the Third Wave 1995, Cross-Strait Interactions in the Past Two Decades 2008. *Leisure interests:* golf, tennis, table tennis. *Address:* Institute for National Policy Research, 7F, No.11, Zhongshan South Road, Taipei 10048 (office); #225, Tung-shih Street, Hsi-chih, Taipei County, Taiwan (home). *E-mail:* inpr@ms4.hinet.net (office). *Website:* www.inpr.org.tw (office).

TIGERMAN, Stanley, MArch, FAIA; American architect; *Partner, Tigerman McCurry Architects;* b. 20 Sept. 1930, Chicago, Ill.; s. of Samuel B. Tigerman and Emma L. Stern; m. Margaret I. McCurry 1979; one s. one d.; ed Yale Univ.; architectural draughtsman, George Fred Keck, Chicago 1949–50; Skidmore Owings & Merrill, Chicago 1957–59; Paul Rudolph, New Haven 1959–61; Harry Weese 1961–62; Pnr Tigerman & Koglin, Chicago 1962–64; Prin. Stanley Tigerman & Assoc. Chicago 1964–82; Pnr Tigerman Fugman McCurry, Chicago 1982–88, Tigerman McCurry Architects, Chicago 1988–; Co-Founder Archeworks Design Lab. Chicago 1993; Prof. of Architecture Univ. of Ill., Chicago 1967–71, 1980–93, Dir School of Architecture 1985–93; Davenport Prof. of Architecture, Yale Univ. 1979, 1993, Bishop Prof. 1984; Architect-in-Residence, American Acad. Rome 1980; Visiting Prof. Univ. of Cincinnati 1980, Univ. of Houston 1981, Tulane 1981, Univ. of Nebraska 1981, Univ. of North Carolina, Charlotte 1982, Harvard 1982, Iowa State 1985 Univ., Univ. of Rotterdam 1985; mem. Advisory Cttee Princeton Univ. 1997; Resident, American Acad. in Rome 1980; Fellow Soc. of Architectural Historians; 60 nat. and local AIA awards, 115 other awards, AIA Illinois Gold Medal in recognition of outstanding lifetime service 2008, AIA/ACSA Topaz Medallion for Excellence in Architectural Educ. 2008. *Publications:* Chicago's Architectural Heritage: A Romantic Classical Image... & Work of the Current Generation of Chicago Architects 1979, VERSUS: An American Architect's Alternatives 1982, Stanley Tigerman Architoons 1988, The Architecture of Exile 1988, Stanley Tigerman, Buildings & Projects 1966–89 1989. *Leisure interests:* drawing, reading. *Address:* Tigerman McCurry Ltd, 444 North Wells Street, Suite 206, Chicago, IL 60654, USA (office). *Telephone:* (312) 644-5880 (office). *Fax:* (312) 644-3750 (office). *E-mail:* tma@tigerman-mccurry.com (office). *Website:* www.tigerman-mccurry.com (office).

TIHIPKO, Serhiy Leonidovych; Ukrainian banker and politician; b. 13 Feb. 1960; m.; one d.; ed Dnipropetrovsk Metallurgical Inst.; Head of Dept of Agitation and Propaganda, Young Communist League during late 1980s; Chair. Bd Privatbank 1992–97; Deputy Prime Minister responsible for Privatization and Econ. Devt 1997–99, apptd Minister of Economy 1999; elected to Verkhovna Rada (Parl.) June 2000; elected Leader Working Ukraine party Nov. 2000 (party reconstituted as A Strong Ukraine 2009, merged with Party of the Regions 2011); Gov. Nat. Bank of Ukraine 2002–05 (resgnd); campaign man. for Viktor Yanukovych during presidential election 2004; cand. in presidential election 2010, 2014; Deputy Prime Minister, responsible for Econ. Affairs March–Dec. 2010, Deputy Prime Minister and Minister of Social Policy 2010–12; mem. Verkhovna Rada (Parl.) 2012–; unsuccessful cand. for Pres. of Ukraine 2014. *Address:* Verkhovna Rada (Supreme Council), 01008 Kyiv, vul. M. Hrushevskoho 5, Ukraine (office). *Telephone:* (44) 255-21-15 (office). *Fax:* (44) 253-32-17 (office). *E-mail:* umz@rada.gov.ua (office). *Website:* www.rada.gov.ua (office).

TIIK, Simmu; Estonian diplomatist; b. 19 Feb. 1959, Tartu; m.; one d.; ed Univ. of Tartu, Univ. of Copenhagen, Denmark; worked at Cen. Library, City of Tartu 1980–89; with Dept of Policy Planning, Ministry of Foreign Affairs, Tallinn 1993–96, Embassy in Copenhagen 1997–99, Adviser in Foreign Affairs, Prime Minister's Office 1999–2003, Chef de Cabinet to Minister of Foreign Affairs 2003, Amb. to Ireland 2003–06, Dir-Gen. Third Political Dept, Ministry of Foreign Affairs 2006–08, Amb. to Russia 2008–12, to Norway 2012–16.

TIILIKAINEN, Teija Helena; Finnish political scientist, academic and research institute director; *Director, Finnish Institute of International Affairs;* b. 22 April 1964, Lohja; ed Åbo Akademi Univ.; Lecturer in Social Sciences, Univ. of Turku

1989–90, Acting Departmental Asst 1990–91, Lecturer in Political Sciences and Int. Relations 1993–96; Acting Departmental Asst, Dept of Political Science, Åbo Akademi Univ. 1992–93, 1996; Research Fellow, 'Citizens Europe' Research Project, financed by Acad. of Finland 1993–95; Ed.-in-Chief, Politiikka (Politics; Finnish journal of Political Science) 1995–96; Researcher, Dept of Strategic Studies, Nat. Defence Coll. 1996–98, Lecturer in European Politics 1998–; Gen. Sec., Forum for European Security 1997–99 (Chair. 1999–2001); Researcher, Coordinator of Programme on European Policy-Making, Dept of Political Science, Univ. of Helsinki, Mar–Aug. 1998, 1999–2000, Acting Prof. in Int. Relations Sept.–Dec. 1998; Lecturer, Perm. Course in European Political Integration, European Comm., Jean Monnet Project 1998–2005, Project Dir V Frame Programme 2001–04; Project Coordinator, Nordic Research Programme in Security Policy 1999–; Dir of Research, Centre for European Studies, Univ. of Helsinki 2001–03, Dir Network for European Studies 2003–07, 2009; State Sec., Ministry for Foreign Affairs 2007–08; Vice-Chair. Finnish Inst. of Int. Affairs 2007–, currently Dir; Lecturer, Finnish Defence Courses 2004–; Chair. Finnish Int. Studies Asscn 1994–96, Organization Europpanaiset (Women in Europe) 2005–07; mem. Editorial Bd Ulkopolitiikka (Finnish Journal of Foreign Affairs) 1994–2001 (currently Dir and Ed.-in-Chief); mem. Bd of Dirs Parl. Library 1999–, Foreign and Security Policy Research, Swedish Inst. of Int. Affairs, Stockholm 2000–, British Council Awards 2001–, Foundation for Finnish Foreign Policy Research 2001; mem. Cttee for Liberal Adult Education, Univ. of Helsinki 1999–, Acad. Bd EUROPEAUM 2004–, Tanner Acad. 2005–, Nat. Bd of Econ. Defence 2000–08, Asscn Cttee, Finnish Cultural Foundation 2006–; columnist, Hufvudstadsbladet (Swedish newspaper in Finland) 1997, Turun Sanomat 1999–, Etelä-Suomen Sanomat 1999–, Suomen Kuvalehti 2000–01, MTV News 2002–; Swedish-Finnish Cultural Foundation Annual Award 2001, Univ. of Helsinki Annual J.V. Snellman Award 2002, Finnish Social Scientist Asscn Social Scientist of the Year Award 2002, Tanner Award 2005. *Publications include:* numerous articles in Finnish and int. journals. *Leisure interests:* sports, reading. *Address:* Finnish Institute of International Affairs, PO Box 400, 00161 Helsinki, Finland (office). *Telephone:* (9) 432-7701 (office). *Fax:* (9) 432-7799 (office). *E-mail:* teija.tiilikainen@fiia.fi (office). *Website:* www.fiia.fi (office).

TIJDEMAN, Robert, PhD; Dutch mathematician and academic; *Professor of Mathematics, University of Leiden;* b. 30 July 1943, Oostzaan; m. Alberdina Broertjes; two d.; ed Univ. of Amsterdam; scientific worker, Univ. of Amsterdam 1967–70; mem. Inst. for Advanced Study, Princeton, NJ 1970–71; Reader, Univ. of Leiden 1971–75, Prof. of Math. 1975–, Dir Thomas Stieltjes Inst. for Math. 1999–, Chair. Dept of Math. and Computer Science 1991–93; Visiting Prof., Univ. of Cambridge 1976, Univ. of Michigan 1976, ETH 1980, Univ. of Pisa 1975, Univ. of New South Wales 1985, Univ. of Waterloo, Canada 1987, Keio Univ. 1989, Tata Inst., Mumbai 1991, 2000, MSRI 1993, Nihon Univ. 1996, Univ. Diderot (Paris 7) 2001; Vice-Pres. Dutch Math. Soc. 1982–84, Pres. 1984–86; Chair. Akademie Raad voor Wiskunde 2003–; Ed., Acta Arithmetica 1981–; mem. Wiskundig Genootschap 1966–, American Math. Soc. 1971–, London Math. Soc. 1977–, Royal Netherlands Acad. of Arts and Sciences 1987–, Societé Mathématique de France 1988–, Deutsche Mathematiker Verein 1990–, Ostrowski Prize jury 1997–; Knight in the order of the Netherlands Lion 2008; Dr hc (Kossuth Lajos Univ., Hungary) 1999. *Publications include:* Exponential diophantine equations (with T. N. Shorey) 1986. *Address:* Mathematical Institute, University of Leiden, Niels Bohrweg 1, POB 9512, 2300 RA Leiden, Netherlands (office). *Telephone:* (71) 5277138 (office). *Fax:* (71) 5277101 (office). *E-mail:* tijdeman@math.leidenuniv.nl (office). *Website:* www.math.leidenuniv.nl (office).

TIJERINO PACHECO, José María; Costa Rican lawyer and politician; b. 11 Nov. 1947; s. of José María Tijerino Rojas and Clara Pacheco Chaverri; m. Olga Cristina Picado Gatgens 1972; one s. one d.; ed Univ. de Costa Rica, Univ. de Valencia, Spain; Public Prosecutor, Cañas, Guanacaste Prov. 1976; fmr Deputy Public Prosecutor and Trial Attorney, Alajuela Prov.; fmr Deputy Head of Public Prosecutor's Office, also Co-ordinator, Third Tribunal Superior Penal, San José; Attorney-Gen. of Costa Rica 1990–95; pvt practice as lawyer, Tribunales de la República de Costa Rica 1995–; Prof. of Law, Univ. de Costa Rica; Minister of Governance, Police and Public Security 2010–11; fmr Amb. to Uruguay; mem. Partido Liberación Nacional.

TILEY, John, CBE, LLD, FBA; British lawyer and academic; *Professor Emeritus of Law of Taxation, University of Cambridge;* b. 25 Feb. 1941, Leamington Spa, Warwicks.; s. of William Tiley OBE and Audrey Tiley; m. Jillinda Draper 1964; two s. one d.; ed Winchester Coll. and Lincoln Coll. Oxford; called to the Bar, Inner Temple 1964, Hon. Bencher 1993; Recorder 1989–97; Lecturer, Lincoln Coll. Oxford 1963–64, Univ. of Birmingham 1964–67; Fellow, Queens' Coll. Cambridge 1967–; Asst Lecturer, Univ. of Cambridge 1967–72, Lecturer 1972–87, Reader 1987–90, Prof. of Law of Taxation 1990–2008, Prof. Emer. 2008–, Leverhulme Trust Fellow Emer. 2008–10, Chair. Faculty Bd of Law 1992–95, currently Deputy Dir Centre for Tax Law; Pres. Soc. of Public Teachers of Law 1995–96; Visiting Prof., Dalhousie Univ., Canada 1972–73, Univ. of Auckland 1973, Univ. of Western Ontario 1978–79, Univ. of Melbourne 1979, Case Western Reserve Univ. 1985–86, 1996, 2002; Hon. QC; Hon. Fellow, Chartered Inst. of Taxation 2009. *Publications:* Revenue Law 1976 (sixth edn 2008); ed. of various works on taxation and contribs to legal journals. *Leisure interests:* walking, visits to art galleries, listening to music. *Address:* Queens' College, Cambridge, CB3 9ET, England (office). *Telephone:* (1223) 335511 (office). *Website:* www.queens.cam.ac.uk (office).

TILGHMAN, Shirley Marie, OC, BSc, PhD, FRS; Canadian biologist, academic and fmr university president; *President Emerita, Princeton University;* b. 17 Sept. 1946; one s. one d.; ed Queen's Univ., Temple Univ., USA; secondary school teacher, Sierra Leone 1968–70; Fogarty Int. Fellow, NIH 1975–77; Asst Prof., Fels Research Inst., Temple Univ. School of Medicine 1978–79; mem., Inst. for Cancer Research 1979–86; Adjunct Assoc. Prof. of Human Genetics and Biochemistry and Biophysics, Univ. of Pennsylvania 1980–86; Howard A. Prior Prof. of the Life Sciences, Princeton Univ. 1986–2001, Dir Lewis-Sigler Inst. for Integrative Genomics, Princeton Univ. 1998, Pres. Princeton Univ. 2001–13, Pres. Emer. and Prof. of Molecular Biology 2013–, Chair. Council on Science and Tech. 1993–2000; investigator, Howard Hughes Medical Inst. 1988; Adjunct Prof., Dept of Biochemistry, Univ. of Medicine and Dentistry of NJ (UMDNJ) – Robert Wood Johnson Medical School 1988; Foreign assoc., NAS; mem. American Acad. of Arts and Sciences, American Philosophical Soc., Inst. of Medicine; mem. Nat. Advisory Council, Nat. Center for Human Genome Research 1991–96; mem. Editorial Bd, Genes and Development (journal); mem. Bd of Dirs Rockefeller Univ., NIH, Jackson Laboratory, Whitehead Inst. for Biomedical Sciences of MIT, Google Inc. 2005–18, Alphabet, Inc. 2005–18, Harvard Corpn 2015–; Trustee, Amherst Coll. 2013–, Carnegie Endowment for Int. Peace, Leadership Enterprise for a Diverse America, King Abdullah Univ. of Science and Tech.; Hon. mem. Inst. of Electrical and Electronics Engineers; Dr hc (Harvard) 2004; Princeton Pres.'s Award for Distinguished Teaching 1996, L'Oréal-UNESCO Women in Science Award 2002, Lifetime Achievement Award, Soc. of Developmental Biology 2003, Genetics Soc. of America Medal 2007, Henry G. Friesen Int. Prize in Health Research 2010. *Address:* Carl Icahn Lab, 240, Lewis-Sigler Institute of Integrative Genomics, Washington Road, Princeton, NJ 08544-1014, USA (office). *Telephone:* (609) 258-2900 (office). *E-mail:* smt@princeton.edu (office). *Website:* molbio.princeton.edu (office).

TILL, James Edgar, OC, MA, PhD, FRS, FRSC; Canadian biophysicist; *Senior Scientist Emeritus and University Professor Emeritus, Princess Margaret Cancer Centre and University of Toronto;* b. 25 Aug. 1931, Lloydminster, Sask.; s. of William Till and Gertrude Till; m. Joyce Till; three c.; ed Univ. of Saskatchewan and Yale Univ.; post-doctoral fellowship, Connaught Medical Research Labs; mem. Faculty, Dept of Medical Biophysics, Univ. of Toronto 1958, Univ. Prof. 1984–97, Assoc. Dean (Life Sciences) School of Grad. Studies for three years, Sr Scientist Ontario Cancer Inst. 1957–96, Sr Scientist Emer. 1996–, Univ. Prof. Emer. 1997–; Editorial Bd Journal of Medical Internet Research, Editorial Bd BMC Medical Informatics and Decision Making; Pres. (Volunteer) Nat. Cancer Inst. of Canada 1998–2000, Past Pres. (Volunteer) 2000–01; Chair. Man. Cttee Cancer Information Service, Canadian Cancer Soc. 1998–99, Knowledge Man. Cttee Stem Cell Network 2001–04; Vice-Chair. Institutional Advisory Bd Inst. of Cancer Research, Canadian Insts of Health Research 2001–04; mem. Research Advisory Cttee Canadian Breast Cancer Research Alliance 2001–05, Clinical Trials Network Advisory Cttee, Ontario Cancer Research Network 2002–03, Research Action Group, Canadian Strategy for Cancer Control 2002–05, Jt Preventive Oncology and Research Bd Cttee, Cancer Care Ontario 2002–05; mem. Bd of Dirs Canadian Stem Cell Foundation 2006–10, Cancer Stem Cell Consortium 2008–17; Order of Ontario 2006; Hon. DSc (Toronto) 2004, (Lethbridge) 2007, (Saskatchewan) 2008; Gairdner Foundation Int. Award (co-recipient) 1969, RSC Thomas W. Eadie Medal (co-recipient) 1991, Robert L. Noble Prize, Nat. Cancer Inst. of Canada 1993, Ernest McCulloch & James Till Award est. by American Soc. for Blood and Marrow Transplantation for the best scientific paper by a new investigator published in its journal 1999, R.M. Taylor Medal, Canadian Cancer Soc./Nat. Cancer Inst. of Canada 2001, inducted into The Canadian Medical Hall of Fame 2004, Albert Lasker Basic Medical Research Award, Albert and Mary Lasker Foundation (co-recipient) 2005, Biomedical Science Ambassador Award, Partners in Research (co-recipient) 2005, Centenary Medal, Royal Soc. of Canada (co-recipient) 2005, Diamond Jubilee Award, National Cancer Institute of Canada 2007, Innovators Hall of Fame, University of Saskatchewan 2009. *Achievements include:* with Ernest McCulloch was first to demonstrate the existence of stem cells in bone marrow. *Publications:* numerous articles in scientific journals. *Address:* Princess Margaret Hospital, Room 9-416, 610 University Avenue, Toronto, ON M5G 2M9, Canada (office). *Telephone:* (416) 946-2948 (office). *E-mail:* Jim.Till@uhnresearch.ca (office). *Website:* medbio.utoronto.ca/faculty/till.html (office).

TILL, Jeremy, MA, DipArch, RIBA; British architect and academic; *Head of Central Saint Martins and Pro Vice-Chancellor, University of the Arts London;* b. 5 April 1957, Cambridge, England; s. of Barry Till and Shirley Philipson; partner Sarah Wigglesworth; ed Univ. of Cambridge, Polytechnic of Cen. London, Middlesex Univ.; Pnr, Peter Currie Architects 1985–92; Dir Sarah Wigglesworth Architects 1992–; Sr Lecturer, Kingston Univ. 1986–92; Sr Lecturer and Sub-Dean of Faculty, The Bartlett School of Architecture, Univ. Coll. London 1992–98; Prof. of Architecture and Head School of Architecture Univ. of Sheffield 1999–2008; Dean, School of Architecture and the Built Environment, Univ. of Westminster 2008; Curator British Pavilion, Venice Architecture Biennale 2006; Head of Central Saint Martins and Pro Vice-Chancellor, Univ. of the Arts London 2012–, also Prof. of Architecture; mem. RIBA Educ. and Research Cttees 2000; Fulbright Arts Fellowship 1990, Civic Trust Award 2002, RIBA Award 2004, RIBA Sustainability Prize 2004, RIBA Pres.'s Award for Research 2007, 2009. *Radio includes:* Shaping Our Spaces (two-part series, BBC Radio 4), contrib. to Talking Allowed (Radio 4), Front Row (Radio 4). *Television includes:* Grand Designs 2002. *Publications include:* Architecture and the Everyday 1997, 9 Stock Orchard Street: A Guidebook 2002, Architecture and Participation 2005, Flexible Housing 2007, Architecture Depends 2009, Spatial Agency 2011, The Design of Scarcity 2014. *Leisure interests:* cooking, eating, drinking. *Address:* University of the Arts London, 272 High Holborn, London, WC1V 7EY (office); 9 Stock Orchard Street, London, N7 9RW, England (home). *Telephone:* (20) 7514-6000 (office). *Website:* www.arts.ac.uk (office).

TILLERSON, Rex W., BS; American energy industry executive and fmr government official; b. 23 March 1952, Wichita Falls, Tex.; m. Renda St Clair; four c.; ed Univ. of Texas, Austin; joined Exxon Co. as Production Engineer 1975, held several eng, tech. and supervisory roles 1975–87, including Business Devt Man., Natural Gas Dept 1987–89, Gen. Man. Cen. Production Div. 1989–92, moved to Dallas, Tex. as Production Advisor to Exxon Corpn and then to Florham Park, NJ as Coordinator of Affiliate Gas Sales, Exxon Corpn Int. 1992–95; Pres. Exxon Yemen Inc. and Esso Exploration and Production Khorat Inc. 1995–98, Vice-Pres. Exxon Ventures (CIS) Inc. and Pres. Exxon Neftegas Ltd 1998–99, Exec. Vice-Pres. ExxonMobil Devt Co. 1999–2001, Sr Vice-Pres. Exxon Mobil Corpn 2001–04, Pres. and mem. Bd of Dirs 2004–06, Chair. and CEO 2006–16; US Sec. of State 2017–18; fmr mem. Bd of Dirs American Petroleum Inst. (Chair. Exec. Cttee and Policy Cttee), US-Russia Business Council; fmr Dir, United Negro Coll. Fund; mem. Exec. Bd and Nat. Pres. Boy Scouts of America 2010–12; mem. Nat. Petroleum Council, Business Roundtable (and its Energy Task Force), Emergency Cttee for American Trade; mem. Chancellor's Council and Eng Advisory Bd for Univ. of Texas, Austin, Soc. of Petroleum Engineers; Vice-Chair. Ford's Theatre Soc.; Trustee, Center for Strategic and Int. Studies; mem. Exec. Cttee The Business Council 2011–12; mem. Nat. Acad. of Eng 2013; Hon. Trustee, Business Council for Int. Understanding; Distinguished Alumnus, Univ. of Texas 2007; Order of Friendship (Russian Fed.)

2013; Hon. PhD (Eng) (Worcester Polytechnic Inst.) 2011. *Address:* c/o Department of State, 2201 C Street, NW, Washington, DC 20520, USA (office).

TILLIS, Thomas (Thom) Roland, BS; American politician; *Senator from North Carolina;* b. 30 Aug. 1960, Jacksonville, Fla; s. of Thomas Raymond Tillis and Margie Tillis; m. Susan Tillis; two c.; ed Univ. of Maryland; Sr Systems Analyst, Provident Life and Accident Insurance Co. 1981–83; Research and Devt Man., Tegra Systems 1985–87; Regional Technical Marketing Man., Wang Computers, Boston 1987–90; Partner, PricewaterhouseCoopers 1990–2002; Commr, City of Cornelius, N Carolina 2003–05; mem. N Carolina House of Reps for Dist 98 2007–15, Speaker 2011–15; Senator from N Carolina 2015–; Republican. *Address:* G55 Dirksen Senate Office Building, Washington, DC 20510, USA (office). *Telephone:* (202) 224-6342 (office). *Fax:* (202) 228-2563 (office). *Website:* www .tillis.senate.gov (office).

TILLMAN, Robert (Bob) L.; American retail executive (retd); began career as store man., Lowe's Cos 1962, various man. positions including Exec. Vice-Pres. and COO, Exec. Vice-Pres. Merchandising, Sr Vice-Pres. Merchandising and Marketing, mem. Bd of Dirs 1994–2005, Pres. and CEO 1996–98, Chair. and CEO Lowe's Cos Inc. 1998–2005 (retd), Chair. and CEO Emer. 2005–; mem. Bd of Dirs Cree, Inc. 2010–, Bank of America 2005–09.

TILLMANS, Wolfgang; German artist; b. 1968, Remscheid; s. of Karl A. Tillmans and Elisabeth Tillmans; ed Bournemouth and Poole Coll. of Art and Design, UK; Artist Trustee, Bd of Tate Gallery, London 2009–14; Turner Prize, Tate Britain, London 2000, Cultural Award, German Society for Photography 2009, The Hasselblad Foundation International Award in Photography 2015, Centenary Medal and Hon. Fellowship Award, Royal Photographic Soc. 2016. *Designer:* War Requiem (Britten), ENO 2018. *Publications:* Wolfgang Tillmans 1995, For When I'm Weak I'm Strong (exhbn catalogue) 1996, Burg 1998, Soldiers: The Nineties 1999, Portraits 2001, View from Above, If One Thing Matters, Everything Matters 2002, Freischwimmer 2004, Truth Study Center 2005, Manual 2007, Lighter 2008, Wako Book 4 2008, Wolfgang Tillmans, Serpentine Gallery 2010, Abstract Pictures 2011, Neue Welt 2012, Wolfgang Tillmans, Moderna Museet 2012, Wolfgang Tillmans 2014, The Cars: Wolfgang Tillmans 2015, Wolfgang Tillmans: What's Wrong with Redistribution 2015, Conor Donlon: Wolfgang Tillmans 2016, Wolfgang Tillmans, Fondation Beyeler 2017. *Address:* c/o Maureen Paley, 21 Herald Street, London, E2 6JT, England. *Telephone:* (20) 7729-4112. *Fax:* (20) 7729-4113. *E-mail:* info@maureenpaley.com. *Website:* www.maureenpaley.com; www.tillmans.co.uk.

TILMAN, G(eorge) David, PhD; American biologist and academic; *Munzer Professor of Developmental Biology and Biochemistry, Regents' Professor and McKnight Presidential Chair in Ecology, University of Minnesota;* b. 22 July 1949, Aurora, Ill.; ed Univ. of Michigan; during doctoral research on algae, worked on math. model to predict outcome of resource competition, continued to work on model after appointment at Univ. of Minnesota, currently Munzer Prof. of Developmental Biology and Biochemistry, Regents' Prof. and McKnight Presidential Chair in Ecology, also Dir Univ.'s Cedar Creek Ecosystem Science Reserve; Prof., Santa Barbara's Bren School of Environmental Science & Man., Univ. of California; mem. Bd NSF, Nat. Research Council; mem. NAS 2002; Foreign mem. Royal Soc. 2017; Fellow, American Acad. of Arts and Sciences 1995; W.S. Cooper Award, Ecological Soc. of America 1989, MacArthur Award, Ecological Soc. of America 1997, designated by ISI Essential Science Indicators the Most Highly Cited Environmental Scientist of the Decade (1990–2000) 2000, (1996–2006) 2006, Int. Prize for Biology, Japan Soc. for the Promotion of Science 2008, Dr A.H. Heineken Prize for Environmental Sciences 2010, Alexander von Humboldt Medal 2013, Ramon Margalef Prize in Ecology 2014, BBVA Foundation Frontiers of Knowledge Award 2014. *Publications:* numerous papers in professional journals. *Address:* Ecology/Evolution/Behavior, Room 100 Ecology, 6098A (Campus Delivery Code), 1987 Upper Buford Circle, St Paul, MN 55108, USA (office). *Telephone:* (612) 625-5740 (office); (612) 625-5743 (office). *Fax:* (612) 624-6777 (office). *E-mail:* tilman@umn.edu (office); dirccgdt@umn.edu (office). *Website:* umn.edu/home/ tilman (office); www.cbs.umn.edu/explore/field-stations/cedarcreek (office).

TILMANT, Michel; Belgian banking executive; b. 21 July 1952; ed Univ. of Louvain, Louvain School for European Affairs; with Morgan Guaranty Trust Co., New York 1977–91, held various positions including Head of European Investor Services, Paris and London, Head of Operations Services, New York, Gen. Man., Brussels br.; Vice-Chair. and COO, Banque International à Luxembourg 1991–92; mem. Exec. Cttee, Bank Brussels Lambert (BBL) 1992–2000, CEO 1997–2000; mem. Exec. Bd, ING Groep NV (after acquisition of BBL by ING) 1998–2009, Chair., ING Barings 1998–99, Vice-Chair., ING Groep 2000–04, Chair. Exec. Cttee, ING Europe 2000–04, Chair. Exec. Bd, ING Groep 2004–09; Chair., European Financial Services Round Table, Institut Int. d'Etudes Bancaires; Adviser, Verlinvest SA 2010–; Sr Advisor, Cinven Ltd 2010–; fmr mem. Bd, Belgian Governance Inst., Koninklijk Concertgebouworkest, Inst. of Int. Finance, Inc., Geneva Asscn; mem. Bd of Dirs BNP Paribas 2010–, Sofina SA 2010–, Lhoist SA 2010–, Foyer Group 2010–, Université Catholique de Louvain 2010–, Royal Automobile Club of Belgium 2010–; Deputy Dir CapitalatWork Foyer Group SA 2011–; Manager, Strafin sprl; Trustee, Univ. of Louvain.

TILSON, Joseph (Joe), ARCA, RA; British artist; b. 24 Aug. 1928, London; s. of Frederick Albert Edward Tilson and Ethel Stapley Louise Saunders; m. Joslyn Morton 1956; one s. two d.; ed St Martin's School of Art, Royal Coll. of Art, British School, Rome; Visiting Lecturer, Slade School, Univ. of London, 1962–63, King's Coll., Univ. of Durham 1962–63, exhibited at Venice Biennale 1964; Lecturer, School of Visual Arts, New York 1966, Staatliche Hochschule, Hamburg 1971–72; Rome Prize 1955, Grand Prix Fifth Biennale, Kraków 1974, Henry Moore Prize, Bradford 1984, Grand Prix, 15th Biennale, Ljubljana 1985 and 21st Biennale 1995. *Art exhibitions:* retrospective exhbn, Boymans van Beuningen Museum, Rotterdam 1973, Sackler Galleries, Royal Acad., London 2002. *Address:* c/o Alan Cristea Gallery, 31 Cork Street, London, W1X 2NU, England; c/o Waddington Galleries, 11 Cork Street, London, W1S 3LT, England. *Telephone:* (20) 7439-1866; (20) 7851-2200; (20) 7259-0024 (home). *Fax:* (20) 7734-4146; (20) 7734-1549. *E-mail:* info@ alancristea.com; mail@waddington-galleries.com. *Website:* www.alancristea.com; www.waddington-galleries.com.

TILSON THOMAS, Michael, (MTT); American conductor, pianist and composer; *Music Director, San Francisco Symphony Orchestra;* b. 21 Dec. 1944, Los Angeles, Calif.; s. of Theodor Thomas and Roberta Thomas; m. Joshua Robison 2014; ed Univ. of Southern California; conductor, Young Musicians' Foundation Orchestra, Los Angeles 1963–67; conductor and pianist, Monday Evening Concerts 1963–68; musical Asst Bayreuth 1966–67; Asst Conductor, Boston Symphony Orchestra 1969, Assoc. Conductor 1970–71, Prin. Guest Conductor 1972–74; New York debut 1969; London debut with London Symphony Orchestra (LSO) 1970; Dir Young People's Concerts, New York Philharmonic 1971–77; Music Dir Buffalo Philharmonic 1971–79; Prin. Guest Conductor, Los Angeles Philharmonic 1981–85; Music Dir Great Woods Inst. 1985, Music Dir Great Woods Festival 1987–88; Prin. Conductor, LSO 1988–95, Prin. Guest Conductor 1995–; Founder and Artistic Dir New World Symphony 1988–; Music Dir San Francisco Symphony Orchestra 1995–(2020); Artistic Dir Pacific Music Festival; Dir YouTube Symphony Orchestra 2009–; guest conductor with orchestras and opera houses in USA and Europe; Chevalier, Ordre des Arts et des Lettres; Tanglewood Koussevitzky Prize 1968, Ditson Award for contrib. to American music 1994, Musical America Conductor of the Year 1994, American Music Center Award 2001, two Gramophone Awards, seven Grammy Awards including Best Classical Album 2004, 2007, 2010, Classic FM Gramophone Award for Artist of the Year 2005, Nat. Medal of Arts 2010, Int. Classical Music Award for Opera Recording of the Year 2015. *Compositions include:* Poems of Emily Dickinson, premiered by Renée Fleming and San Francisco Symphony Orchestra. *Recordings include:* more than 120 recordings, including Mahler Symphonies 1, 3 and 6 (with San Francisco Symphony Orchestra), four-hand version of Stravinsky's Rite of Spring (with Ralph Grierson), Charles Ives' 2nd Symphony (with Concertgebouw Orchestra), complete works of Carl Ruggles (with Buffalo Philharmonic), various musicals by Weill and Gershwin, works of Bach, Beethoven, Prokofiev, Reich and Cage, Mahler's Seventh Symphony (with San Francisco Symphony Orchestra) 2007, Mahler's Eighth Symphony and Adagio from Symphony No. 10 2009, Adams' Harmonielehre & Short Ride In A Fast Machine (with San Francisco Symphony Orchestra) (Grammy Award for Best Orchestral Performance 2013) 2012, Beethoven: Piano Concerto No. 3, Mass in C Major 2015, Mason Bates: Works For Orchestra 2016. *Address:* MTT Inc., 1745 Broadway, 18th Floor, New York, NY 10019 (office); San Francisco Symphony, Davies Symphony Hall, 201 Van Ness Avenue, San Francisco, CA 94102, USA (office). *Telephone:* (212) 246-7726 (New York) (office). *Fax:* (212) 489-5217 (New York) (office). *E-mail:* skashiyama@sfsymphony.org (office). *Website:* www.sfsymphony.org (office); www.michaeltilsonthomas.com.

TILTON, Glenn F.; American airline industry executive; b. 1948; m. Jackie Tilton; two c.; joined Texaco Inc. 1970, served in various marketing, corp. planning and European downstream assignments, Pres. US Refining and Marketing –1989, Vice-Pres. Texaco Inc. 1989–91, Chair. Texaco Ltd 1991–92, Pres. Texaco Europe 1992–95, Pres. Texaco USA 1995, Sr Vice-Pres. Texaco Inc. 1995–97, apptd Pres. Texaco Global Business Unit 1997, Chair. and CEO Texaco Inc. 2001, Vice-Chair. ChevronTexaco Corpn (following merger between Texaco and Chevron) 2001–02; Chair. Dynegy Inc. 2002; Chair., Pres. and CEO United Airlines (UAL) Corpn and United Airlines 2002–10, Chair. (non-exec.) United Continental Holdings, Inc. (holding co.) of United Airlines and Continental Airlines) 2010–12; Chair. of the Midwest for JPMorgan Chase and mem. of its company-wide Exec. Cttee 2011–14; named by Pres. Obama to the Presidential Export Council 2010–, by US Transportation Sec. Ray LaHood to the Future of Aviation Advisory Cttee 2010–, by Chicago Mayor Richard Daley to the O'Hare Express Blue Ribbon Cttee 2010–; mem. Bd of Dirs Chevron Corpn 2001–, Abbott Laboratories 2007–, Corning Inc. 2010–12, Northwestern Memorial Hosp., Phillips 66 2012–, AbbVie Inc. 2013–; Chair. American Cancer Soc.'s nat. programme, CEOs against Cancer 2011–; apptd Dir The Chicago Council on Global Affairs 2011, then Exec. Vice-Chair. 2014, now Chair. Emer.; mem. Bd Field Museum, Museum of Science and Industry, World Business Chicago Exec. Cttee, Commercial Club of Chicago Civic Cttee, Econ. Club of Chicago, Executives' Club of Chicago, Big Shoulders Fund, After School Matters, British American Chamber of Commerce; owns a ranch in Santa Fe, NM; Order of Lincoln 2014; inducted as Laureate, Lincoln Acad. of Illinois 2014. *Leisure interest:* horse riding.

TIMBERLAKE, Justin Randall; American singer, songwriter and actor; b. 31 Jan. 1981, Memphis, Tenn.; m. Jessica Biel 2012; one s.; started vocal training aged eight; guest appearance at Grand Ole Opry 1991; early TV appearances include Star Search 1992, The Mickey Mouse Club 1993–94; mem. *NSYNC vocal quintet 1995–, first headline US tour 1998; also solo artist 2002–; f. Justin Timberlake Foundation, a charity to fund music and art programmes in schools; founder, Chair. and CEO Tennman Records 2007–; American Music Awards for Favorite Pop/Rock Band, Duo or group 2002, for Favorite Pop/Rock Male Artist 2007, 2013, for Favorite Soul/R&B Male Artist 2013, MOBO Award for Best R&B Act 2003, MTV Award for Best Pop Video (for Cry Me A River) 2003, BRIT Award for Best Int. Male Solo Artist 2004, 2007, Grammy Awards for Best Male Pop Vocal Performance (for Cry Me A River) 2004, (for What Goes Around...Comes Around) 2008, for Best Dance Recording (for Sexy Back) 2007, (for LoveStoned/I Think She Knows) 2008, for Best Rap/Sung Collaboration (with T.I.) 2007, (for Holy Grail, with Jay-Z) 2014, for Best R&B Song (for Pusher Love Girl) 2014, for Best Song Written for Visual Media (for Can't Stop the Feeling!) 2017, MTV Europe Music Award for Best Male Artist, for Best Pop Act 2006, Meteor Ireland Music Award for Best Int. Male Artist 2007, MTV Video Music Award for Best Male Artist 2007, for Best Video (for Mirrors) 2013, MTV Video Music Michael Jackson Video Vanguard Award 2013, Billboard Music Awards for Top Artist 2014, Top Male Artist 2014, for Top Billboard 200 Artist 2014, for Top Radio Songs Artist 2014, for Top R&B Artist 2014, People's Choice Award for Favorite Male Artist 2017. *Film appearances:* Longshot 2000, On the Line 2001, Edison 2005, Alpha Dog 2006, Southland Tales 2006, Black Snake Moan 2006, Shrek the Third (voice) 2007, The Open Road 2009, The Social Network 2010, Bad Teacher 2011, Friends with Benefits 2011, In Time 2011, Trouble with the Curve 2012, Runner, Runner 2013, Inside Llewyn Davis 2013, Trolls 2016, Wonder Wheel 2017. *Recordings include:* albums: with *NSYNC: *NSYNC 1998, Home For The Holidays 1998, The Winter Album 1998, No Strings Attached 2000, Celebrity 2001; solo: Justified (Grammy Award for Best Pop Vocal Album, BRIT Award for Best Int. Album 2004) 2002, FutureSex/ LoveSounds (American Music Award for Favorite Soul/R&B Album 2007) 2006, The 20/20 Experience (American Music Award for Favorite Soul/R&B Album 2013,

Billboard Music Awards for Top Billboard 200 Album 2014, for Top R&B Album 2014) 2013, The 20/20 Experience 2 of 2 2013, Can't Stop the Feeling! (People's Choice Award for Favorite Song 2017) 2016, Man of the Woods 2018. *Publication:* Justin Timberlake (autobiography) 2004. *Address:* Wright Entertainment Group, PO Box 590009, Orlando, FL 32859-0009, USA (office). *Website:* www .justintimberlake.com; www.nsync.com.

TIMKEN, William Robert, Jr, BA, MBA; American business executive and diplomatist; b. 21 Dec. 1938, Canton, Ohio; m. Sue Timken; six c.; ed Phillips Acad., Stanford Univ. and Harvard Business School; various exec. positions, including Pres. and CEO Timken Co. 1962–2003, Chair. 1973–2003, Chair. (non-exec.) 2004–05 (retd); mem. Bd of Dirs numerous public cos; fmr Chair. Nat. Asscn of Mfrs, The Manufacturing Inst., Ohio Business Roundtable; fmr mem. Advisory Council, Stanford Univ. School of Business; fmr mem. US-Japan Business Council; apptd by Pres. George W. Bush as Chair. Securities Investor Protection Corpn 2003; Amb. to Germany 2005–08; Hon. Citizen of Colmar, France; Chevalier, Légion d'honneur; Woodrow Wilson Award for Corp. Citizenship, Adam Smith Award, Ellis Island Medal of Honor, named Ohio Business Statesman of the Year, Ohio Gov.'s Award.

TIMMERMANS, Frans Cornelis Gerardus Maria; Dutch diplomatist, politician and EU official; *First Vice-President and Commissioner in charge of Better Regulation, Inter-Institutional Relations, the Rule of Law and the Charter of Fundamental Rights, European Commission;* b. 6 May 1961, Maastricht; m.; four c.; ed Radboud Univ., Nijmegen, Univ. of Nancy, France; began career as official with Ministry of Foreign Affairs 1987, Policy Officer, European Integration Dept 1988–90, Second Sec., Embassy in Moscow 1990; fmr Deputy Head, EC Affairs Section, Ministry for Devt Cooperation; mem. staff of European Commr Hans van de Broek 1994–95; Adviser and Private Sec. to Max van der Stoel, High Commr on Nat. Minorities, OSCE 1995–98; mem. House of Reps (lower house of Parl.) (PvdA) 1998–2007, 2010–12; Minister for European Affairs 2007–10, of Foreign Affairs 2012–14; First Vice-Pres. European Comm., in charge of Better Regulation, Inter-Institutional Relations, the Rule of Law and the Charter of Fundamental Rights Nov. 2014–; fmr Guest Lecturer, Netherlands Inst. of Int. Relations, Clingendael, Netherlands Defence Coll.; mem. Exec. Cttee European Movement; mem. Partij van de Arbeid (Labour Party) 1990–; Kt, Order of Orange-Nassau 2010; Officer, Order of Merit (Poland) 2006; Commdr, Order For Merit (Romania) 2006, Chevalier, Légion d'honneur 2007, Grand Cross, Order of the Southern Cross (Brazil) 2008, First Class of Order of the Cross of Terra Mariana (Estonia) 2008, Grand Cross, Order of the Grand Duke Gediminas (Lithuania) 2008, Commdr, Order of the Polar Star (Sweden) 2009, Grand Cross, Order of Merit (Chile) 2009. *Address:* European Commission, Rue de la Loi/Wetstraat 170, 1049 Brussels, Belgium (office). *Telephone:* (2) 299-11-11 (office). *Website:* ec.europa.eu/ commission/2014-2019/timmermans_en (office).

TIMMS, Rt Hon. Stephen C., MA, MPhil; British business consultant and politician; b. 29 July 1955, Oldham, Lancs., England; s. of Ronald James Timms and Margaret Joyce Timms (née Johnson); m. Hui-Leng 1986; ed Farnborough Grammar School, Emmanuel Coll., Cambridge; worked as consultant in computer and telecommunications industries for Logica then Ovum 1978–94; Councillor, London Borough of Newham 1984–97, Chair. Planning Cttee 1987–90, Leader Newham Council 1990–94; MP for Newham North East (by-election) 1994–97, for East Ham 1997–; Parl. Pvt. Sec. to Andrew Smith MP as Minister of State, Dept for Educ. and Skills 1997–98; joint Parl. Pvt. Sec. to Marjorie Mowlam MP as Sec. of State for NI 1998; Parl. UnderSec. of State, Dept of Social Security 1998–99, Minister of State 1999; Financial Sec., HM Treasury 1999–2001, 2004–05, 2008–10; Minister of State for School Standards, Dept for Educ. and Skills 2001–02; Minister of State for Energy, E-Commerce and Postal Services, Dept of Trade and Industry 2002–04; Minister of State (Pensions Reform), Dept for Work and Pensions 2005–06; Chief Sec. to the Treasury 2006–07; Minister for Competitiveness, Dept for Business, Enterprise and Regulatory Reform 2007–08; Minister of State for Employment, Dept for Work and Pensions 2008; Minister for Digital Britain 2009–10; Govt Adviser on Faith 2007–10; Shadow Minister for Employment 2010–15, for Work and Pensions June-Sept. 2015; mem. Commons Select Cttees for Treasury 1996–97 and Public Accounts 2004–05; Sec., Parl. Labour Party Treasury Cttee 1997–98; mem. Labour Party Departmental Cttees for Educ. and Employment 1997–2001, Environment, Transport and the Regions 1997–2001, the Treasury 1997–2001, Labour Party Faith Envoy 2007–; Chair. Christians on the left 2012–, Traidcraft Foundation Trustees 2012–; Vice-Pres. Tear Fund 2012–; mem. Bd East London Partnership (now East London Business Alliance) 1990–2006; mem. Stratford Devt Partnership 1992–94; Dr hc (Univ. of East London) 2002; Computing Magazine Award for Outstanding Contrib. to UK IT 2007. *Publication:* Broadband Communications: The Commercial Impact 1986. *Address:* House of Commons, Westminster, London, SW1A 0AA, England (office). *Telephone:* (20) 7219-4000 (office). *Fax:* (20) 7219-2949 (office). *E-mail:* stephen@stephentimms.org.uk (office); timmss@parliament.uk (office). *Website:* www.stephentimms.org.uk.

TIMOFTI, Nicolae Vasilyevich; Moldovan judge, politician and fmr head of state; b. 22 Dec. 1948, Ciutuleşti, Soroca dist, Moldovan SSR, USSR; s. of Vasile Timofti and Elenda Timofti; m. Margareta Timofti; three s.; ed Moldova State Univ.; Soviet Army service 1974–76; Judge, Frunze dist court, Chişinău 1976–80, Supreme Court of the Moldavian SSR 1980–90, Deputy Chair. Supreme Court of Justice and Chair. Judicial Bd 1990–96, Chair. Appeals Chamber of Repub. of Moldova 1996–2001, Judge, Supreme Court of Moldova 2005–, Chair. Supreme Council of Magistrates 2011; Pres. of Moldova 2012–16; Chair. Asscn of Judges and mem. Supreme Council of Magistrates 1996–2001. *Address:* c/o Office of the President, 2073 Chişinău, bd. Ştefan cel Mare şi Sfânt 154, Moldova. *E-mail:* petitii@prm.md.

TIMON, Clay S., BS; American business executive (retd); b. 20 May 1943, Chicago, Ill.; s. of Clay J. Timon and Shirley Timon; m. Barbara Timon; two c.; ed Leed School of Business Univ. of Colo; fmr Bd Dir, Man. Supervisor (Paris) McCann-Erickson, Man. Services Dir (Tokyo), Sr Vice-Pres./Man. Supervisor; fmr Sr Vice-Pres. Int. Doyle Dane Bernbach; fmr Vice-Pres./Dir Worldwide Advertising Colgate-Palmolive; fmr Regional Vice-Pres. Saatchi & Saatchi, Paris; Chair., Pres., CEO Landor Assocs 1994–2004 (retd); World Pres. Int. Advertising Asscn 1988–90; fmr Chair. Int. Cttee of American Asscn of Advertising Agencies; mem.

Business Advisory Council Leeds School of Business, Univ. of Colorado; mem. Bd of Dirs LifeMasters Supported SelfCare, Inc. 2006–, Music in the Vineyards (the Napa Valley Summer Chamber Music Festival); fmr mem. Bd of Dirs WebWare Corpn (now ClearStory Systems) 2001; Outstanding Speaker Award, Leeds School of Business, Univ. of Colo 2002. *Leisure interests:* travel, reading, tennis, vintage automobiles. *Address:* 851 North San Vicente Blvdm APT 313, West Hollywood, CA 90069, USA.

TINARI, Philip, BA, AM, DPhil; American editor, museum director and academic; *Director, Ullens Center for Contemporary Art;* b. 1979, Philadelphia, Pa; ed Duke and Harvard Univs, Peking Univ., People's Repub. of China, Univ. of Oxford, UK; ran Office for Discourse Engineering (publishing imprint, editorial office, translation studio) 2007–10; Founding Ed. Artforum.com.cn 2008–11; Contributing Ed. Artforum 2007–; Founding Ed. and Acting Publr LEAP, The International Art Magazine of Contemporary China, Modern Media Group 2009–12; Dir Ullens Center for Contemporary Art, Beijing 2011–; Adjunct Prof., Coll. of Humanities, China Cen. Acad. of Fine Arts; curated the Focus: China section of The Armory Show in New York 2014; curated Bentu, Fondation Louis Vuitton, Paris 2016; Fulbright Fellow, Peking Univ. *Address:* Ullens Center for Contemporary Art, 798 Art District, 4 Jiuxianqiao Lu, Chaoyang District, Beijing 100015, People's Republic of China (office). *Telephone:* (10) 57800200 (office). *Fax:* (10) 57800220 (office). *E-mail:* visitor@ucca.org.cn (office). *Website:* www.ucca.org .cn (office).

TINDLE, David, RA; British artist; b. 29 April 1932, Huddersfield, Yorks, England; m. 1st Jillian Evans 1953 (divorced) 1957); one s. one d.; m. 2nd Sheila Pratt 1957 (divorced 1969); three s. one d.; m. 3rd Janet Trollope 1969 (divorced 1992); one s. two d.; ed Coventry School of Art; worked as scenic artist for theatre until moving to London in 1951; numerous exhbns in London and provinces since 1952; works in many public and private collections including Tate Gallery, Nat. Portrait Gallery; designed and painted set for Iolanta (Tchaikovsky), Aldeburgh Festival 1988; Visiting Tutor, Royal Coll. of Art 1973–83, Fellow 1981, Hon. Fellow 1984; Ruskin Master of Drawing, St Edmund Hall, Oxford 1985–87; lives and works in Italy; Hon. Fellow St Edmund Hall, Oxford 1988–; Hon. mem. Royal Birmingham Soc. of Artists; Hon. MA (St Edmund Hall, Oxford) 1985; Critics Award 1962, RA Johnson Wax Award 1983. *Television:* contrib. on egg tempura to A Feeling for Paint 1980. *Leisure interests:* music, films, cats and dogs, visiting the towns and museums of Italy. *Address:* c/o The Redfern Gallery, 20 Cork Street, London, W1S 3HL, England. *Telephone:* (20) 7734-1732. *E-mail:* art@redfern -gallery.com. *Website:* www.redfern-gallery.com.

TINE, Augustin; Senegalese dental surgeon and politician; b. Fandène, Thiès region; m.; three s. three d.; ed Univ. Cheikh Anta Diop, Dakar; early training as priest, Ngazobil seminary; dental surgeon, El hadji Ibrahima Niasse Hosp., Kaolack 1980–95; pvt. dental practice, Saloum 1995–; fmr mem. local council, Fandène; Minister of the Armed Forces 2012–19; mem. Parti démocratique sénégalais 1999–2007, Alliance pour la République (APR) 2007–, later APR regional co-ordinator, Thiès region; mem. Conseil national des chirurgiens dentistes du Sénégal. *Leisure interest:* football. *Address:* c/o Ministry of the Armed Forces, Bldg Administratif, 8e étage, ave Léopold Sédar Senghor, BP 4041, Dakar, Senegal (office).

TING, Samuel Chao Chung, BSE, PhD; American physicist and academic; *Thomas Dudley Cabot Professor of Physics, Massachusetts Institute of Technology;* b. 27 Jan. 1936, Ann Arbor, Mich.; s. of Prof. Kuan Hai Ting and Prof. Tsun-Ying Wang; m. 1st Kay Kuhne 1960; two d.; m. 2nd Susan Carol Marks 1985; one s.; ed primary and secondary schools in China, Univ. of Michigan; Ford Foundation Fellow, European Org. for Nuclear Research (CERN), Geneva 1963; Instructor, Columbia Univ., New York 1964, Asst Prof. 1965–67; Group Leader, Deutsches Elektronen Synchrotron (DESY), Hamburg, FRG 1966; Assoc. Prof. of Physics, MIT 1967–68, Prof. 1969–, Thomas Dudley Cabot Inst. Prof. 1977–; Programme Consultant, Div. of Particles and Fields, American Physical Soc. 1970; Assoc. Ed. Nuclear Physics B 1970; mem. Editorial Bd Nuclear Instruments and Methods 1977, Mathematical Modelling, Chinese Physics; Fellow, American Acad. of Arts and Sciences 1975; mem. American, Italian and European Physical Socs; Foreign mem. Academia Sinica, Taiwan 1975, Pakistani Acad. of Science 1984, USSR (now Russian) Acad. of Sciences 1989, Hungarian Acad. of Sciences 1993; mem. NAS 1977–, Deutsche Akademie der Naturforscher Leopoldina 1996; Hon. Prof. Beijing Normal Coll., China 1984, Jiatong Univ., Shanghai, China 1987; Hon. ScD (Michigan) 1978, (Chinese Univ. of Hong Kong) 1987, (Bologna) 1988, (Columbia) 1990, (Univ. of Science and Tech., China) 1990, (Moscow State Univ.) 1991, (Bucharest) 1993, (Tsinghua Taiwan) 2002, (Nat. Tiaotong Univ. Taiwan) 2003; Ernest Orlando Lawrence Award 1976, Nobel Prize for Physics (jtly with the lateBurton Richter) for discovery of the heavy, long-lived 'J' (or 'psi') particle 1976, Eringen Medal, Soc. of Eng Scientists 1977, De Gasperi Gold Medal for Science, Italy 1988, Gold Medal for Science, City of Brescia, Italy 1988, Forum Engelberg Prize 1996, NASA Public Service Award 2001. *Address:* Massachusetts Institute of Technology, 77 Massachusetts Ave., Building 44-120, Cambridge, MA 02139, USA (office). *Telephone:* (617) 253-8326 (office). *E-mail:* ting@lns.mit.edu (office). *Website:* web.mit.edu/physics (office).

TIONG, Tan Sri Datuk Hiew King; Malaysian/Chinese business executive; *Executive Chairman, Rimbunan Hijau Group;* b. 1935; m.; four c.; Founder and Exec. Chair. Rimbunan Hijau Group (timber co.) 1975–, with logging operations in Papua New Guinea and Russia also Exec. Chair. RH Petrogas Ltd 2008–; Senator 1985–91; Chair. Media Chinese Int. 1995–2018, Bursa Malaysia Securities Berhad 1995–, One Media Group 2012–; Founder The National (English-language newspaper in Papua New Guinea); Dir Guang Ming Daily (Chinese nat. daily newspapers in Malaysia), Ming Pao Holdings Ltd, Hong Kong, World Asscn of Chinese Newspapers; currently Pres. Chinese Language Press Inst. Ltd; Trustee, Yayasan Sin Chew; mem. Sarawak United People's Party (major party of ruling coalition govt in Sarawak); Hon. Chair. Federation of Hokkien Asscn of Malaysia, Global Chinese Media Cooperation Union, Hon. KBE; Malaysia Business Leadership Award 2010. *Address:* Rimbunan Hijau Group, 101, Pusat Suria Permata, Jalan Upper Lanang, Sibu 96000, Sarawak, Malaysia (office). *Telephone:* (84) 216155 (office). *Fax:* (84) 215217 (office). *E-mail:* info@rhg.com.my (office). *Website:* www.rhg.com.my (office).

TIPSORD, Michael L., BA, JD, CPA; American business executive; *Chairman, President and CEO, State Farm Insurance Companies;* b. 1959, Ill.; ed Illinois Wesleyan Univ., Univ. of Illinois, Urbana-Champaign; Chartered Life Underwriter 1991, Chartered Property Casualty Underwriter 1995; practised law –1988; joined State Farm 1988, served in various leadership roles, Dir, Accounting 1995–96, Asst Controller 1996–97, Exec. Asst 1997–98, Vice-Pres. and Asst Treas. 1998–2001, Vice-Pres. and Treas. 2001–02, Sr Vice-Pres. and Chief Financial Officer 2002–04, Vice-Chair. and COO 2004–15, Pres. and CEO State Farm Insurance Cos 2015–, Chair. 2016–; mem. Bd of Dirs, Navigant Consulting, Inc.; mem. ABA, Illinois State Bar Asscn; Trustee, Brookings Inst.; mem. Dean's Advisory Bd, Univ. of Illinois Coll. of Law. *Address:* State Farm Insurance Companies, 1 State Farm Plaza, Bloomingon, IL 61710-0001, USA (office). *Telephone:* (309) 766-2311 (office). *Fax:* (309) 766-3621 (office). *E-mail:* michael.tipsord@statefarm.com (office). *Website:* www.statefarm.com (office).

TIRAVANIJA, Rirkrit; Thai artist; b. 1961, Buenos Aires, Argentina; m. Elizabeth Peyton (divorced); ed Ontario Coll. of Art and Banff Center School of Fine Arts, Canada, Art Inst. of Chicago and Whitney Ind. Studies Program, USA; Co-founder The Land Foundation, Chiang Mai, Thailand; Prof., School of the Arts, Columbia Univ.; National Endowment for the Arts Visual Artist Fellowship 1994; Gordon Matta Clark Foundation Award 1991, Louis Comfort Tiffany Foundation Biennial Competition Award 1993, Central Kunst Prize 1996, Lucelia Artist Award, Smithsonian American Art Museum 2003, Solomon R. Guggenheim Foundation Hugo Boss Prize 2004, Silpathorn Award 2007, Absolut Art Award 2010. *Works include:* Untitled (Free) 1992, Untitled (Still) 1994, Utopia Station (50th Venice Biennale) 2003, Untitled (the air between the chainlink fence and the broken bicycle wheel) 2005, Untitled (Pay Attention) 2009. *E-mail:* theland@thelandfoundation.org (office). *Website:* www.thelandfoundation.org (office).

TIRIMO, Martino, FRAM, FRSAMD, Dip RAM, ARAM; British concert pianist, conductor and academic; *Professor, Trinity Laban Conservatoire of Music and Dance;* b. 19 Dec. 1942, Larnaca, Cyprus; s. of Dimitri Tirimo and Marina Tirimo; m. Mione J. Teakle 1973; one s. one d.; ed Bedales School, England (Cyprus Govt Scholarship), Royal Acad. of Music, London, Vienna State Acad.; first public recital, Cyprus 1949; conducted seven performances of La Traviata with singers and musicians from La Scala, Milan, at Cyprus Opera Festival 1955; London debut, Wigmore Hall 1965; gave first public performance of complete Schubert sonatas (including unfinished ones with own completions), London 1975; first public performance of Beethoven piano concertos cycle directed from keyboard in two consecutive evenings, Dresden 1985, London 1986; first performance of Tippett piano concerto in several European countries 1986–2013; concerto performances with major orchestras world-wide as well as recitals, radio and TV appearances in Europe, USA, Canada, SA and the Far East 1965–; four series of performances of complete Beethoven piano sonatas 2000, two series devoted to the major piano works of Robert and Clara Schumann 2001; six-concert series devoted to the major piano works of Chopin 2002; Mozart piano concertos series, directing from keyboard 2001–; f. Rosamunde Trio with violinist Ben Sayevich and cellist Daniel Veis 2002; performed with Vienna Philharmonic during Olympics, Athens Festival 2004, Olympic Games torch bearer 2004; performed complete Mozart solo piano works in several series of eight concerts, including at Cadogan Hall, London 2006; performed Chopin entire works in ten concerts in various countries, including at King's Place, London 2010; Tchaikovsky series at King's Place, London 2012; Schubert major works in six concerts at King's Place, London 2015; Great Piano Quintet series in five concerts at St John's Smith Square, London 2016–; Prof., Trinity Coll. of Music (now Trinity Laban Conservatoire of Music and Dance) 2003–; mem. jury in various int. piano competitions 1995–; Hon. Prof., Middlesex Univ. 2004–; prizewinner, Int. Beethoven Competition, Vienna 1965, Liszt Scholarship, Boise Foundation Scholarship, Gulbenkian Foundation Fellowship 1967–69, Jt Winner, Munich Int. Piano Competition 1971, Winner, Geneva Int. Piano Competition 1972, Gold Medal, Associated Bd of Royal Schools of Music 1959, Macfarren Medal, Royal Acad. of Music 1964, Silver Disc 1988 and Gold Disc 1994 for recording of Rachmaninov 2nd Concerto and Paganini Rhapsody, Nemitsas Foundation Prize 2011, and other prizes and awards. *Film score:* The Odyssey 1998. *Recordings:* more than 50 albums, including complete piano works of Mozart, Beethoven, Debussy and Janáček; Brahms piano concertos, Chopin concertos, Tippett piano concerto, Rachmaninov concertos, complete Schubert piano sonatas, complete Mendelssohn works for piano and cello, Tchaikovsky, Shostakovich and Dvořák piano trios (Rosamunde Trio), several other recordings with mixed repertoire. *Television:* live performance of Tippett piano concerto from Coventry Cathedral for BBC TV in celebration of composer's 90th birthday and 50th birthday of UN. *Publications include:* urtext edn of complete Schubert piano sonatas in three vols 1997–99. *Leisure interests:* chess, reading, self-knowledge, theatre, badminton. *Address:* 1 Romeyn Road, London, SW16 2NU, England (home). *Telephone:* (210) 6015224 (Athens) (office); (20) 8677-4847 (home). *Fax:* (210) 6994520 (Athens) (office). *E-mail:* deskaps@otenet.gr (office); m.tirimo@trinitylaban.ac.uk (home). *Website:* www.martinotirimo.com.

TIRKEY, Dilip, BA; Indian professional field hockey player (retd) and politician; b. 25 Nov. 1977, Sawnamara, Sundergarh, Orissa; s. of Vincent Tirkey and Regina Tirkey; m. Meera Sushila Tirkey 2006; one s.; ed Bhanwani Shankar School, Mohanpali Coll.; belongs to Oraon tribe of Chota Nagpur; fmr Asst Man., Indian Airlines; trained in NIS Patiala under coach A. K. Basal; started his career as inside forward but developed into defender; int. debut in Test Series vs Australia 1994; Vice-Capt. Jr World Cup, Milton Keynes, UK 1997, selected in World XI Team; Gold Medal, SAF Games, Chennai 1995, Bangkok Asian Games 1998, Prime Minister's Gold Cup 2001; Silver Medal, Asian Games, Busan 2002; Bronze Medal, Asia Cup, Kuala Lumpur, Malaysia 1999; first Adivasi captain of ind. Indian nat. team and second in Indian history; youngest Olympian when capped at Atlanta, USA 1996; signed to play with Klein Zwitserland hockey club, Netherlands 2005; fmr Capt. with Orissa Steelers; MP (Biju Janata Dal) from Odisha 2012–; Dr hc (Sambalpur Univ.) 2010; Ekalavya Puraskar 1996, ONGC-Hockey Year Book Award 1998, Arjuna Award 2002, Padma Shri 2004. *Leisure interests:* music, dance. *Address:* 16/C, Ferozeshah Road, New Delhi; Qr No.-C-I, Unit-8, PS-Nayapalli, District Khurda, Bhubaneswar 751012, India.

TIROLE, Jean, PhD; French economist and academic; *Scientific Director, Institut d'Économie Industrielle (IDEI), Université Toulouse 1 Capitole;* b. 9 Aug. 1953; ed Université Paris IX-Dauphine, École Polytechnique, École Nationale des Ponts et Chaussées, Massachusetts Inst. of Tech., USA; Researcher, CERAS, École Nationale des Ponts et Chaussées 1981–84; Assoc. Prof. of Econs, then Prof. of Econs, MIT, USA 1984–92, Visiting Prof. 1992–; Taussig Visiting Prof. of Econs, Harvard Univ. 1989; Sr Fellow, Inst. for Policy Reform 1990–95; Scientific Dir Institut d'Économie Industrielle (IDEI), Toulouse 1992–; Prof., Ecole Polytechnique 1994–96; Dir of Accumulative Studies, École des Hautes Études en Sciences Sociales 1995–; mem. Conseil d'Analyse Économique (Prime Minister's Council of Econ. Advisors) 1999–2006, 2008–; currently Chair. of the Bd, Fondation Jean-Jacques Laffont, Toulouse School of Econs 2007–09; Visiting Prof., ENSAE, Univ. of Lausanne, Wuhan Univ.; Visiting Scholar, Stanford Univ. Spring 1983, Princeton Univ. Spring 2002; Assoc. Ed., Econometrica 1984–99; Foreign Ed., Review of Economic Studies 1986–94, Assoc. Ed. 1994–96; Founder-mem. and Inaugural Fellow, European Corp. Governance Inst. 2002–; mem. Exec. Cttee, Inst. for Advanced Study in Toulouse (IAST) 2011–, currently Chair.; Pres. European Econ. Asscn 2001; mem. Econometric Soc. (Council mem. 1991–99, mem. Exec. Cttee 1993–99, Pres. 1998), French High Council for Science and Tech. 2006–, European Research Council panel 2007–10, Comité de Suivi de la LRU (Libertés et Responsabilités des Universités) 2008–10, French Strategic Research Council 2013–; mem. Acad. des Sciences Morales et Politiques 2011; Fellow, Econometric Soc. 1986, Haut Conseil de la Sciences et de la Technologie 2006–09; Foreign Hon. mem. American Acad. of Arts and Sciences 1993, American Econ. Asscn 1993; Hon. mem. Acad. des Sciences, Inscriptions et Belles Lettres de Toulouse 2008; Hon. FRSE 2013; Chevalier, Légion d'honneur 2007; Officier, Ordre nat. du Mérite 2010; Dr hc (Université Libre de Bruxelles) 1989, (London Business School) 2007, (HEC, Univ. of Montreal) 2007, (Univ. of Mannheim) 2011, (Univ. of Rome Tor Vergata) 2012, (Athens Univ. of Econs and Business) 2012, (Université de Lausanne) 2013, (Hitotsubashi Univ.) 2013, (European Univ. Inst.) 2015; Sloan Fellow 1985–87, Pew Charitable Trust/Ford Foundation grant 1987–90, Guggenheim Fellow 1988–89, Yrjo Jahnsson Prize, European Econ. Asscn 1993, Centre for Econ. Studies Prize 1996, Public Utility Research Center Distinguished Service Award, Univ. of Florida 1997, John von Neumann Award, Budapest Univ. 1998, Distinguished Fellow Award, Industrial Org. Soc. 1999, Gold Medal, CNRS 2002, 2007, Prix Dargélos de l'École Polytechnique 2002, Thomson Prize in Econs, Inst. of Scientific Information 2004, BBVA Foundation Frontiers of Knowledge Award in the Econs, Finance and Man. category 2008, Claude Levi-Strauss Prize 2011, Math. Sciences Research Inst. Prize in Innovation Quantitative Applications, CME Group 2010, European Research Council Advanced Grant 2010–14, named amongst the most influential economists in the world according to IDEAS/RePEc 2011, ILB and EIF Award for the best paper in finance (with Emmanuel Farhi) 2011, Grand Prix, Acad. d'Occitanie 2012, Stephen A. Ross Prize in Financial Econs 2013, Erwin Plein Nemmers Prize in Econs 2014, Sveriges Riksbank Prize in Econ. Sciences in Memory of Alfred Nobel for his analysis of market power and regulation 2014; lectures include Invited Symposium, 6th World Congress, Econometric Soc. 1990, Conférencier d'honneur, Asscn Canadienne de Sciences Economiques 1990, Hicks Lecture, Univ. of Oxford 1992, Walras-Pareto Lectures, Lausanne 1992, Schumpeter Lecture, European Econ. Asscn 1993, Pazner Lecture, Tel-Aviv 1993, Walras-Bowley Lecture, Econometric Soc. 1994, Munich Lectures, Munich 1996, JMCB Lecture 1999, Wicksell Lectures 1999, Baffi Lectures, Bank of Italy 2000, Scribner Lectures and the Frank Graham Lecture, Princeton Univ. 2002, Marshall Lectures, Univ. of Cambridge 2003, Tinbergen Lecture, Amsterdam 2003, David Kinley Lectures, Univ. of Illinois 2005, inaugural JEEA Lecture 2005, inaugural Telecom Italia Lecture, Milan 2005, Snyder Lecture, Univ. of California, Santa Barbara 2005, Robert Rosenthal Memorial Lecture, Boston Univ. 2006, Invited Conf., 100th Anniversary, HEC Montreal 2007, Mundell-Fleming Lecture, IMF Annual Research Conf., Washington, DC 2008, Manchot Lecture, Univ. of Bonn 2009, Eitan Berglas Lecture, Tel-Aviv Univ. 2010, Max Weber Lecture, European Univ. Inst., Florence 2011, Judge Ralph Winter Lecture, Yale Univ. 2012, SIRE Lecture, Univ. of Edinburgh 2013, Keynote Lecture, CEPR-JIE Conf. in Applied Industrial Org., Athens 2014, Gorman Lectures, Univ. Coll. London 2015. *Publications include:* Concurrence Imparfaite (in French) 1985, The Theory of Industrial Organization, Game Theory (with Drew Fudenberg) 1988, A Theory of Incentives in Procurement and Regulation (with Jean-Jacques Laffont) 1993, Incentives in Procurement Contracting (co-ed.) 1993, The Prudential Regulation of Banks (with Mathias Dewatripont) 1994, Competition in Telecommunications (with Jean-Jacques Laffont), Financial Crises, Liquidity and the International Monetary System, The Theory of Corporate Finance (Award for Excellence, Asscn of American Publrs) 2006, Balancing the Banks: Global Lessons from the Financial Crisis (co-author) 2010, Inside and Outside Liquidity (with Bengt Holmström) 2011; several book chapters and more than 180 articles in journals. *Address:* IDEI, Université Toulouse 1 Capitole, Manufacture des Tabacs, Aile Jean-Jacques Laffont, Accueil MF 529, 21 allée de Brienne, 31015 Toulouse Cedex 6, France (office). *Telephone:* (5) 61-12-86-42 (office). *Fax:* (5) 61-12-86-37 (office). *E-mail:* jean.tirole@tse-fr.eu (office); tirole@cict.fr (office). *Website:* idei.fr/vitae.php?i=3 (office).

TISA SABUNI, Aggrey, BSc, MEconSc; South Sudanese politician; b. Kajo Keji County, Eastern Equatoria State; ed Univ. of Khartoum, Univ. of Glasgow, UK; fmr Under-Sec. of Econ. Planning; Econ. Adviser to Pres. 2011–13; Minister of Finance, Commerce and Econ. Planning 2013–15; mem. Sudan People's Liberation Movt.

TISCH, Andrew H., BS, MBA; American business executive; *Chairman of the Executive Committee, Member of the Office of the President and Co-Chairman of the Board, Loews Corporation;* b. 14 Aug. 1949, Asbury Park, NJ; s. of Laurence Tisch and Wilma Tisch; m. Ann Tisch (née Rubenstein); four c.; ed Cornell and Harvard Univs; joined Loews Corpn 1971, mem. Bd of Dirs 1985–, Chair. Exec. Cttee, mem. Office of the Pres. and Co-Chair. Bd 2006–; Pres. Bulova Corpn 1979–90, currently Chair.; CEO and Chair. Lorillard Inc. 1990–95; mem. Bd of Dirs Canary Wharf Group PLC, Zale Corpn, K12 Inc., CNA Financial Corpn 2006–. *Address:* Loews Corpn, 667 Madison Avenue, New York, NY 10021-8087, USA (office). *Telephone:* (212) 521-2000 (office). *Fax:* (212) 521-2525 (office). *E-mail:* info@loews.com (office). *Website:* www.loews.com (office).

TISCH, James S., MBA; American business executive; *President, CEO and Member of the Office of the President, Loews Corporation;* b. 2 Feb. 1953, Atlantic City, New Jersey; s. of Lawrence Tisch and Wilma Tisch; m. Merryl Tisch (neé

Hiat); two s. one d.; ed Cornell Univ., Wharton Business School, Univ. of Pennsylvania; joined Loews 1977 (hotel chain est. by Lawrence Tisch 1946), various exec. positions including Dir Loews Corpn, Pres. 1998–, COO 1998–99, CEO 1999–, also Mem. Office of the Pres.; Chair. and CEO Diamond Offshore Drilling Inc.; Dir, Educational Broadcasting Corpn 2003–, Chair. 2006–; mem. Bd of Dirs CAN Financial Corpn, Vail Resorts Inc., General Electric; mem. Bd of Overseers Univ. of Pennsylvania; mem. Council on Foreign Relations. *Address:* Loews Corpn, 667 Madison Avenue, New York, NY 10065-8087, USA (office). *Telephone:* (212) 521-2000 (office). *Fax:* (212) 521-2525 (office). *E-mail:* pr@loews.com (office). *Website:* www.loews.com (office).

TISCH, Jonathan Mark, BA; American business executive; *Co-Chairman and Member of the Office of the President, Loews Corporation;* b. 7 Dec. 1953, Atlantic City, New Jersey; s. of Preston Robert Tisch and Joan T. Tisch (née Hyman); cousin of James Tisch (q.v.) and Andrew Tisch (q.v.); m. Lizzie Rudnick 2007; ed Tufts Univ.; worked as cinematographer and producer at WBZ-TV, Boston 1976–79; Sales Man. Loews Hotels, New York 1980–81, Dir of Devt 1981–82, Vice Pres. 1982–85, Exec. Vice-Pres. 1985–86, Pres. 1986, CEO 1989–, also Chair., mem. Bd of Dirs Loews Corpn 1986–, mem. Office of the Pres. 1998–, Co-Chair. 2006–; Chair. Travel Business Roundtable 1995–; Co-Chair. NYC & Co. tourism agency; Treas. and mem. Bd of Dirs, NY Giants football team 1991–; mem. Bd of Dirs Elizabeth Glaser Paediatric AIDS Foundation, Tribeca Film Inst., Business Council for the Metropolitan Museum of Art; mem. Bd of Trustees and Patron, Jonathan M. Tisch Coll. of Citizenship and Public Service, Tufts Univ.; mem. US Dept of Commerce US Travel and Tourism Advisory Bd 2003–; fmr Chair. New York Rising, American Hotel and Lodging Asscn; fmr Vice-Chair. Welfare to Work Partnership; Travel Agent magazine Hotel Person of the Year, Business Travel Industry's Most Influential Executives, Business Travel News, 25 Most Influential People in the Meetings Industry, Meeting News magazine, Tufts Alumni Asscn Distinguished Alumni Award 1996. *Television:* host, Open Exchange: Beyond the Boardroom. *Publications include:* The Power of We: Succeeding Through Partnerships 2004, Chocolates on the Pillow Aren't Enough: Reinventing the Customer Experience 2007. *Address:* Loews Corpn, 667 Madison Avenue, New York, NY 10065-8087, USA (office). *Telephone:* (212) 521-2000 (office). *Fax:* (212) 521-2525 (office). *E-mail:* pr@loews.com (office). *Website:* www.loews.com (office).

TISCH, Thomas J., BA, LLB; American business executive and university administrator; *Managing Partner, Four Partners;* b. 1955; s. of Laurence Tisch and Wilma Tisch; ed Brown Univ., New York Univ.; Man. Partner, Four Partners (pvt. investment co.) 1992–; mem. Bd of Trustees, Brown Univ. 2002–, Chancellor 2007–; mem. Bd of Dirs General Dynamics Information Technology Inc. 2002–05, Sears Holdings Corpn 2005–, Infonxx Inc., Synageva BioPharma Corpn 2012–15; mem. Bd of Trustees New York Univ. Medical Center, KIPP Acad., Manhattan Inst. for Public Policy Research. *Address:* Four Partners, 666 5th Avenue, New York, NY 10103-0001, USA (office).

TISHKOV, Valery Aleksandrovich, DHist; Russian historian and anthropologist; *Head of History and Philology Section, Institute of Ethnology and Anthropology, Russian Academy of Sciences;* b. 6 Nov. 1941; m.; one s.; ed Moscow State Univ.; teacher, Magadan State Pedagogical Inst. 1964–66; aspirant, Moscow State Pedagogical Inst. 1966–69; Docent, Dean, Magadan State Pedagogical Inst. 1969–72; Researcher, Inst. of Gen. History, USSR (now Russian) Acad. of Sciences (RAS), Scientific Sec., Div. of History, USSR Acad. of Sciences, also Head of Dept, Inst. of Ethnography, Deputy Dir, Inst. of Ethnology and Anthropology, RAS 1972–89, Dir 1989–2015, Head of History and Philology Section 2015–; Fed. Minister for Nationalities, Russian Govt 1992; Vice-Pres. Int. Union of Ethnological and Anthropological Sciences 1993 (re-elected 1998); mem. Public Chamber of Russia, Chair. Cttee on Tolerance and Freedom of Faith 2006–10; Full mem. Russian Acad. of Sciences 2008; Order of Honour 2009; Distinguished Scholar of the Russian Fed. 1998, State Prize in Science and Art 2001, 2015. *Publications:* Ethnicity, Nationalism and Conflict in and after the Soviet Union. The Mind Aflame 1997, Peoples and Religions of the World (Russian Encyclopaedia) 1998, Chechnya: Life in a War-Torn Society 2004, Tundra and Sea: Chukotka Ivory Art 2008, Peoples of Russia: Atlas of Cultures and Religions 2008, The Russian People: History and Meaning of National Identity 2013. *Leisure interests:* fishing, collection of Arctic ivory art. *Address:* Institute of Ethnology and Anthropology, Russian Academy of Sciences, Leninsky prosp. 32A, 119334 Moscow, Russian Federation (office). *Telephone:* (495) 938-17-63 (office). *Fax:* (495) 938-06-00 (office). *E-mail:* valerytishkov@mail.ru (home); tishkov@iea.ras.ru (office). *Website:* www.valerytishkov.ru.

TITO, Teburoro, BSc; I-Kiribati politician and fmr head of state; *Permanent Representative to United NationsAmbassador to USA;* b. 25 Aug. 1953, Tabiteuea North; m. Nei Keina; one c.; ed King George V Secondary School, Univ. of South Pacific, Suva, Papua New Guinea Admin. Coll.; student co-ordinator, Univ. of South Pacific Students' Asscn 1977–79; Scholarship Officer, Ministry of Educ. 1980–82, Sr Educ. Officer 1983–87; mem. Maneaba ni Maungatabu (Parl.) and Leader of Opposition 1987–94, mem. Parl. Public Accounts Cttee 1987–90; Pres. of Kiribati 1994–2003, also Minister of Foreign Affairs; Int. Trade mem. CPA Exec. Cttee for Pacific Region 1989–90; Chair. Kiribati Football Asscn 1980–94; fmr Special Envoy of the Pres. of Kiribati to UN, Permanent Rep. to UN 2017–; Amb. to USA 2018–; Dr of World Peace (Maharishi Univ. of World Peace) 2001. *Leisure interests:* sports, especially soccer, tennis and table tennis. *Address:* Permanent Mission of Kiribati, 685 Third Avenue, Suite 1109, New York, NY 10017, USA (office); Tabuarorae, Eita Village, South Tarawa, Kiribati (home). *Telephone:* (212) 867-3310 (office). *Fax:* (212) 867-3320 (office). *E-mail:* kimission.newyork@mfa.gov.ki (office).

TITOV, Konstantin Alekseyevich, CandEconSc; Russian politician; b. 30 Oct. 1944, Moscow; m. Natalia Borisovna Titova; one s.; ed Kuybyshev (now Samara) Aviation Inst., Kuybyshev Inst. of Planning; milling-machine operator, Kuybyshev aviation factory 1962–63, flight engineer 1968–69, Deputy Sec. Komsomol Cttee 1969–70; Deputy Head Students Div., Kuybyshev City Komsomol Cttee 1970–73; Sec. Komsomol Cttee, Jr, Sr Researcher, Head of Group, Head Research Lab. Kuybyshev Inst. of Planning 1973–88; Deputy Dir Research Cen. Informatika (Samara br.) 1988–90; Chair. Samara City Council 1990–91, Head of Admin. Samara Region 1991–96, Gov. Samara Region 1996–2007; mem. Council of Fed. of Russia 1993–2001, Chair. Cttee on Budget, Taxation Policy, Finance and Customs Regulation 1996–2001; Pres. Interregional Asscn of Econ. Interaction 'Bolshaya Volga' 1994; Deputy Chair. 'Our Home Is Russia' political movt 1995; Chair. of Council, Union of Right Forces 1998–; cand. for Pres. of Russian Fed. 2000; Chair. Russian Party of Social Democracy 2000, Co-Founder Union of Social Democratic Parties 2001; Order of St Faithful Prince Daniil Moskovsky (3rd Degree), Order of St Grand Duke Vladimir (2nd Degree), Order of Friendship, Order Glory of Russia 2002; Golden Mask Prize, Russian Theatre Artists Union, Green Man of the Year, Russian Ecological Union 1996, Honoured Economist of the Russian Fed., Gov. of the Year 1998, Nat. Prize of Peter the Great 2002, Nat. Olympus Laureate 2003. *Leisure interests:* football, photography, music, painting, reading.

TITOV, Col Vladimir Georgievich, MBA; Russian business executive and fmr cosmonaut; *General Director of Russian Operations, Excalibur Almaz Limited;* b. 1 Jan. 1947, Sretensk, Chita Region; s. of Georgie Titov and Vera Titova; m. Alexandra Kozlova; one s. one d.; ed Chernigov Higher Mil. Aviation School, Yuriy Gagarin Air Force Acad., International Univ., Moscow; pilot instructor, Commdr of aviation unit 1970–76; mem. cosmonauts' team since 1976; Commdr of space flights on spacecraft Soyuz T-8 1983 and record-breaking flight on Soyuz TM-4 and space station MiR; Deputy Head Dept of Man. Centre of Cosmonauts' Training 1988–99; apptd Dir for Space and Communications, Russia and CIS, Boeing Corpn, Moscow 1999; currently Gen. Dir Russian Operations, Excalibur Almaz Ltd (pvt. int. space exploration co.); Hero of the Soviet Union, Order of Lenin 1983, 1988, Commdr de la Légion d'honneur 1988; US Harmon Prize 1990. *Address:* Excalibur Almaz Ltd, 15–19 Athol Street, Douglas, Isle of Man, IM1 1LB, British Isles (office). *E-mail:* contact@excaliburalmaz.com (office). *Website:* excaliburalmaz.com (office).

TITS, Jacques Léon, DrSc; French mathematician and academic; *Professor Emeritus of Mathematics, Collège de France;* b. 12 Aug. 1930, Uccle, Belgium; s. of Léon Tits and Louisa Tits (née André); m. Marie-Jeanne Dieuaide 1956; ed Univ. of Brussels; with Belgian Nat. Fund for Scientific Research 1948–56; Asst, Univ. of Brussels 1956–57, Assoc. Prof. 1957–62, Prof. 1962–64; Prof., Univ. of Bonn 1964–74; Assoc. Prof., Collège de France, Paris 1973–74, Prof. of Group Theory (also Chair.) 1975–2000, Prof. Emer. 2000–; de la Vallée-Poussin Chair, Univ. of Louvain 2001–02; Visiting Teacher and Prof., Eidgenössische Technische Hochschule, Zürich, Switzerland 1950, 1951, 1953, Inst. for Advanced Study, Princeton, USA 1951–52, 1963, 1969, 1971–72, Univ. of Rome, Italy 1955, 1956, Univ. of Chicago, USA 1963, Univ. of California, Berkeley, USA 1963, Univs of Tokyo and Kyoto, Japan 1971, Yale Univ., USA 1966–67, 1976, 1980, 1984, 1990, 1995, 2002; mem. editorial bds of periodicals and scientific collections; Ed.-in-Chief Math. Publs of IHES 1980–99; Guest Speaker at Int. Congresses of Mathematicians, Stockholm 1962, Nice 1970, Vancouver 1974; lecture tours in USA, UK, Israel, etc.; mem. Deutsche Akad. der Naturforscher Leopoldina 1977, Norwegian Acad. of Science and Letters; Founding mem. Academia Europaea; Corresp. mem. Acad. des Sciences, Paris 1977, mem. 1979; Foreign mem. Royal Netherlands Acad. of Arts and Sciences 1988; Foreign Assoc. Royal Belgian Acad. 1991, NAS 1992, American Acad. of Arts and Sciences 1992; Hon. mem. London Math. Soc. 1993; Foreign Hon. mem. American Acad. of Arts and Sciences 1992; Commdr des Palmes académiques 1993, Chevalier, Légion d'honneur, 1995, Officier, Ordre nat. du Mérite 2001, Prix ABEL 2007; Dr hc (Utrecht) 1970, (Ghent) 1979, (Bonn) 1987, (Louvain) 1992; Prix scientifique Interfacultataire L. Empain 1955, Prix Wettrems, Acad. de Belgique 1958, Prix décennal de mathématique du gouvernement belge 1965, Grand Prix des Sciences mathématiques et physiques, Acad. des Sciences 1976, Wolf Prize 1993, Cantor Medal, Deutsche Mathematiker-Vereinigung (German Math. Soc.) 1996, Abel Prize (co-recipient) 2008. *Publications:* more than 150 scientific papers. *Leisure interests:* languages, literature, arts. *Address:* Collège de France, 11 place Marcelin Berthelot, 75231 Paris Cedex 05, France (office). *Fax:* 1-44-27-17-04 (office). *E-mail:* jacques.tits@college-de-france.fr (office).

TIZARD, Dame Catherine (Anne), ONZ, GCMG, GCVO, DBE, OBE, QSO, BA; New Zealand public official (retd); b. 4 April 1931, Auckland; d. of Neil Maclean and Helen Montgomery Maclean; m. Robert James Tizard 1951 (divorced 1983); one s. three d.; ed Matamata Coll. and Auckland Univ.; Tutor in Zoology, Univ. of Auckland 1963–83; mem. Auckland City Council 1971–83, Auckland Regional Authority 1980–83, Mayor of Auckland (first woman) 1983–90; JP 1980–86; Gov.-Gen. of New Zealand (first woman) 1990–96; Chair. New Zealand Worldwide Fund for Nature 1996–2000, New Zealand Historic Places Trust 1996–2002, Sky City Charitable Trust 1996–2002, Cancer Control Council, Kiri te Kanawa Foundation; Dir New Zealand Symphony Orchestra Trust Bd; occasional radio, TV and newspaper commentator and columnist; public speaker and debater; numerous community activities including roles with Auckland War Memorial Inst. and Museum, Library Council of New Zealand, Auckland Univ. Council, Local Govt Asscn of New Zealand, Royal New Zealand Ballet Trust; Dir XIV Commonwealth Games Ltd, America's Cup Village Bd; Hon. Fellow, Lucy Cavendish Coll. Cambridge, UK and Winston Churchill Fellow 1981, Hon. Freeman, Worshipful Co. of Butchers 1990, Freedom, City of London 1990, Hon. Capt., Royal New Zealand Navy 1997, Hon. Col Auckland (Countess of Ranfurly's Own) and Northland Bn Group 2007; Hon. LLD (Auckland) 1992; New Zealand Medal 1990, Suffrage Centennial Medal 1995. *Publication:* Cat Amongst the Pigeons 2010. *Leisure interests:* music, reading, drama, scuba diving. *Address:* 12A Wallace Street, Herne Bay, Auckland 1011, New Zealand. *Telephone:* (9) 376-2555. *E-mail:* cath.tizard@xtra.co.nz.

TJANDRANEGARA, Eka; Indonesian business executive; *Founder, Mulia Group;* b. 1946; s. of Tjandra Kusuma; m.; f. Java Marine Lines Pte Ltd 1981, renamed Jaya Holdings Ltd, Dir, later Chair.; f. Mulia Group (real estate co.), also Pres. Dir Mulia Industrindo (glass mfr); Commr Royale Jakarta Golf Club. *Address:* Wisma Mulia, Floor 56th, Jalan Jenderal Gatot Subroto No. 42, Jakarta 12710, Indonesia (office). *Telephone:* (21) 5200888 (office). *Fax:* (21) 5200872 (office). *E-mail:* enquiry@mulialand.com (office). *Website:* www.mulialand.com (office).

TJEKNAVORIAN, Loris; Iranian composer and conductor; b. 13 Oct. 1937, Iran; s. of Haikaz Tjeknavorian and Adriné Tjeknavorian; m. 1st Linda Pierce 1964 (divorced 1979); one s.; m. 2nd Julia Cory Harley-Green 1986; m. 3rd Naira 2004; ed Tehran Conservatory of Music, Vienna Acad. of Music and Salzburg Mozarteum, Austria, Univ. of Michigan, USA; several works published in Vienna following graduation 1961; given scholarship to study with the late Carl Orff 1963–64; lived in Salzburg and worked on opera Rostam and Sohrab; began studying conducting in USA 1965; Composer-in-Residence, Concordia Coll., Moorhead, Minn. 1966–67; Head of Instrumental and Opera Departments, Moorhead Univ., Minn. 1966–70; numerous recordings with leading orchestras, including London Symphony Orchestra, Royal Philharmonic Orchestra, London Philharmonic Orchestra; works have been performed by major orchestras, including Vienna Symphony, London Philharmonic, American Symphony; Prin. Conductor and Artistic Dir Armenian Philharmonic Orchestra 1989–2000; Order of Homayoun; Austrian Presidential Gold Medal for Artistic Merit 2010, Highest Medal of Repub. of Armenia, Highest Order of Arts of Iranian Islamic Repub., Ferdowsi Medal, Ministry of Culture (for his four operas based on Shahname: Rostam and Sohrab, Rostam and Esfandyar, Siyawash and Zahak) 2015. *Compositions include:* more than 80 works (five symphonies, five operas, a requiem, chamber music, concerto for piano, violin, guitar, cello and pipa (Chinese lute), ballet music, choral works and an oratorio, and more than 40 film scores), including Requiem for the Massacred 1975, Simorgh (ballet music), Lake Van Suite, Erebouni for 12 strings 1978, Credo Symphony Life of Christ (after medieval Armenian chants) 1976, Liturgical Mass, Violin Concerto, oratorios Lucifer's Fall and Book of Revelation, Mass in Memoriam 1985, Othello (ballet), ballet suites for orchestra, five symphonies, Salam (Peace, choral-orchestral composition) 2016. *Address:* Vogelsanggasse 39–41/30, 1050 Vienna, Austria. *E-mail:* ltjeknavorian@yahoo.com. *Website:* www.loristjeknavorian.com.

TKACH, Robert, BS, MS, PhD; American physicist; *Director, Advanced Photonics Research, Bell Labs;* ed Univ. of Cincinnati, Cornell Univ.; with Bell Labs 1984–, fmr Dir of Transmission Systems and Networks Research, currently Dir of Advanced Photonics Research; with AT&T Labs 1996–2000; with Celion Networks 2000–06; Chair. Optical Fiber Communications (OFC) Conf. Steering Cttee, fmr Gen. Co-Chair. OFC; mem. Tech. Advisory Bd, Optoelectronics Industry Data Asscn; fmr Vice-Pres. Optical Internetworking Forum; fmr Assoc. Ed. Journal of Lightwave Technology; Vice Chair. and mem. Bd of Dirs Marconi Soc. 2017–; mem. Nat. Acad. of Eng 2009; fmr mem. IEEE LEOS Bd Govs; Fellow, Optical Soc. of America, IEEE, AT&T; Thomas Alva Edison Patent Award, Research and Devt Council of NJ, John Tyndall Award, Optical Soc. of America and IEEE 2008, Marconi Prize and Fellowship (co-recipient) 2009, IEEE Alexander Graham Bell Medal (co-recipient) 2013. *Publications:* numerous papers in professional journals. *Address:* Bell Labs, 791 Holmdel Road, Holmdel, NJ 07733, USA (office). *Telephone:* (732) 888-7115 (office). *E-mail:* bob.tkach@nokia-bell-labs.com (office). *Website:* www.bell-labs.com (office).

TKACHENKO, Oleksander Mikolayevich, CandTechSc; Ukrainian politician; b. 7 March 1939, Shpola, Cherkassy Region; m. Larissa Mitrofanivna Tkachenko; one d.; ed Belotsekivski Agric. Inst., Higher Party School, CPSU Cen. Cttee; worked as First Sec., Tarashansk Comsomol Cttee 1966–70, then Ukrainian CP functionary in agric. sector 1970–82; State Minister, Head of Cttee on Agric. Policy and Food Ukrainian SSR 1985–91; Minister of Rural Economy 1991–92; unsuccessful cand. for Pres. 1991; Head of Agric. Asscn Zemlya i Lyudi 1992–94; Leader, Ukrainian Farmers' Party; mem. Verkhovna Rada (Parl.) 1994–, First Vice-Chair. Verkhovna Rada 1994–98, Chair. (Speaker) 1998–2000. *Address:* Verkhovna Rada, M. Hrushevskoga str. 5, 252008 Kiev, Ukraine. *Telephone:* (381) 226-28-25 (office).

TKACHEV, Aleksandr Nikolayevich, DEcon; Russian engineer and politician; b. 23 Dec. 1960, Vyselki, Krasnodar Krai; m. Olga Tkachev; two c.; ed Krasnodar Polytechnic Inst.; trained as mechanical engineer; began career as heating engineer, inter-farm feed mill, Vyselkovsky Dist 1983, becoming chief mechanic and dir of feed mill 1990, apptd CEO, Agricultural Complex JSC (following reorganization into jt stock co.) 1993; elected First Sec., Vyselkovsky Komsomol Dist Cttee 1986; elected to Krasnodar Krai regional Legis. Ass. 1994; elected to State Duma (Parl.) for Tikhoretsky Dist 1995, Deputy Chair. Duma agroindustrial group; Gov., Krasnodar Krai Admin. Dist 2000–15; Minister of Agric. 2015–18; Order For Services to the Fatherland (IV degree) 2005, Order For Merit (III degree) 2011, Order For Service to the Motherland (II degree) 2014; numerous medals including Medal in Commemoration of 850th Anniversary of Moscow 1997, Peter the Great Nat. Pride of Russia Medal 2002, Honorary Builder of Russia 2003.

TKESHELASHVILI, David, LLM; Georgian politician and academic; *Adjunct Professor, School of Law, Emory University;* b. 16 Oct. 1969, Tbilisi; m. Nino Tkeshelashvili; one s. one d.; ed Tbilisi State Univ., Emory Univ., USA; mil. service 1987–89; Head of Regional Dept of the Citizens' Union's Youth Arm 1993–95, also Political Sec. and Deputy Chair., Press Sec. 1994–95, Chair. Youth Arm of Citizens' Union 1998–2002; elected mem. Parl. (Citizens' Union) 1995, served as Deputy Majority Leader (re-elected 1999, re-elected for Nat. Movt-Democrats 2004), Chair. Sub-cttee for Relations with Media and Non-governmental Orgs for Human Rights Cttee 1999–2003; Minister of Environmental Protection and Natural Resources 2006–07, of Labour, Health and Social Affairs 2007–08, State Minister for Regional Issues 2008–09, Minister of Regional Devt and Infrastructure 2008–10, also First Deputy Prime Minister 2009–10, Chief of Pres.'s Admin 2010–13; Adjunct Prof., Emory Univ. School of Law 2013–; Edmund S. Muskie Fellowship 2005. *Address:* Emory University School of Law, G343, 1301 Clifton Road NE, Atlanta, GA 30322-2770, USA (office). *Telephone:* (404) 727-5975 (office). *E-mail:* david.tkeshelashvili@emory.edu (office). *Website:* law.emory.edu (office).

TKESHELASHVILI, Ekaterine (Eka), LLM; Georgian lawyer and government official; *President, Georgian Institute for Strategic Studies;* b. 23 May 1977, Tbilisi; m.; four c.; ed Tbilisi State Univ., Univ. of Notre Dame, USA; Chief Specialist, Centre for Foreign Policy Research and Analysis, Ministry of Foreign Affairs 1997–99; field officer, Int. Cttee of Red Cross 1998–2000; intern, Appeals Office, Int. Tribunal of fmr Yugoslavia 2001–02; lawyer and Dir Institutional Reform and Non-governmental Sector, IRIS Georgia (Tbilisi office of Univ. of Maryland's Center for Institutional Reform and the Informal Sector) 2002–04; Deputy Minister of Justice 2004–05; Deputy Minister of Internal Affairs 2005–06; Chair. Tbilisi Court of Appeals 2006–07; Minister of Justice 2007–08; Prosecutor Gen. Feb.–May 2008; Minister of Foreign Affairs May–Dec. 2008; Sec. Nat. Security Council 2008–10; Deputy Prime Minister and State Minister, responsible for Reintegration 2010–12; Pres. Georgian Inst. for Strategic Studies 2012–. *Address:* Georgian Institute for Strategic Studies, 0179 Tbilisi, 2 Ramishvili Street, Georgia (office). *Telephone:* (32) 224-04-15 (office). *E-mail:* office@giss.org.ge (office). *Website:* giss.org.ge/eng (office).

TLUSTÝ, Vlastimil; Czech politician; b. 19 Sept. 1955; early career as Researcher, Agricultural Machinery Research Inst.; Asst Lecturer, Agricultural Univ. of Prague 1990; mem. Parl. 1991–2009, mem. Civic Democratic Party (Občanská demokratická strana—ODS), Deputy Chair., Chair. ODS Parl. Club, Vice Chair. Finance Cttee; Chair. Supervisory Bd ČKA (Czech Consolidation Agency) –2006; Minister of Finance June–Oct. 2006 (resgnd); fmr Chair. Union of Land Owners and Pvt. Farmers of Czech Repub.

TOADER, Tudorel, DrLegalSci, PhD; Romanian lawyer, judge and government official; *Minister of Justice;* b. 25 March 1960, Vulturu, Constanţa County; ed Law Faculty of Alexandru Ioan Cuza Univ., Iaşi, Nat. Coll. of Defence; prosecutor, Panciu Local Procuratorate, Vrancea Co. 1986–90; passed lawyer exam at Iaşi Bar 1991; apptd Univ. Asst, Faculty of Law, Alexandru Ioan Cuza Univ. 1990, Scientific Sec., Faculty of Law Council 1993–95, mem. Senate of Univ. 1995–, Vice-Dean 1995–2003, Dean 2004, Rector 2016–17; Judge, Constitutional Court of Romania 2006, 2007–16; Minister of Justice 2017–; mem. Int. Asscn of Penal Law, Steering Cttee of Romanian Asscn of Penal Sciences, Scientific Council of Nat. Inst. of Magistracy 2004–, Francophonie Univ. Agency, Speciality Comm. for the Confirmation of Prof.'s Degree, Univ. Lecturer, First Degree Scientific Researcher and Second Grade Scientist (CNATDCU) 2006–; expert evaluator, National Council of Scientific Research (CNCSIS), Nat. Office of Scholarships Abroad Studies; Kt, Nat. Order of the Star of Romania 2012; Order of the Holy Emperors Constantine and Helen, Romanian Orthodox Church 2012. *Publications:* Criminal Law, Offences Under Special Laws 1993, Romanian Criminal Law, Special Part (co-author) 1994, Criminal Law, Special Part 2002, Criminal Law, Special Issue, Problem of Judicial Practice for Students Use 1996, Criminal Law (co-author) 2003, Medical Legislation (co-author) 2003, Transition of Criminal Procedural Systems (co-author) 2004, Criminal Code and Special Laws – Doctrine, Jurisprudence, Decisions of the Constitutional Court, ECHR Judgments (co-author) 2007, Decennium Moztanicense (co-author) 2008, Dictionary of Romanian Legal Personality (co-author) 2008, Criminal Code and Criminal Procedure Code, ECHR Judgments, Constitutional Court Decisions, Appeals in the Interest of the Law (annotated edn) 2010, The Constitution of Romania Reflected in Constitutional Jurisprudence 2011, The Offences Stipulated in the Special Laws (fifth edn) 2012, Romanian Criminal Law, Special Part (seventh edn) 2012, The New Criminal Code 2015. *Address:* Ministry of Justice, 050741 Bucharest 5, Str. Apolodor 17, Romania (office). *Telephone:* (37) 2041999 (office). *Fax:* (37) 2041226 (office). *E-mail:* relatiipublice@just.ro (office). *Website:* www.just.ro (office).

TOAFA, Maatia; Tuvaluan politician; *Minister of Finance and Economic Development and Deputy Prime Minister;* b. 1 May 1954; began career with Pacific Islands Forum Secr., Suva, Fiji; Deputy Prime Minister of Tuvalu, Minister for Works, Communications and Transport –2004; acting Prime Minister Aug.–Oct. 2004, Prime Minister and Minister of Foreign Affairs and Labour, Oct. 2004–06, Leader of the Opposition 2006–10, Prime Minister Sept.–Dec. 2010, Minister of Finance and Econ. Devt 2013–, Deputy Prime Minister 2015–. *Address:* Ministry of Finance and Economic Development, PMB, Vaiaku, Funafuti, Tuvalu (office). *Telephone:* 20202 (office). *Fax:* 20210 (office). *E-mail:* secfin@tuvalu.tv (office).

TOAN, Barrett A., AB, MBA; American business executive; *Chairman, Sigma-Aldrich Corporation;* b. 1947, Briarcliff Manor, NY; m. Polly Toan; one d. one s.; ed Kenyon Coll., Wharton School, Univ. of Pennsylvania; began career in Bureau of the Budget, Office of the Gov. of Ill.; fmr consultant to state and local govts for Price Waterhouse & Co., Washington, DC; budgetary adviser to Ark. Attorney-Gen. Bill Clinton, 1979; Commr Ark. Div. of Social Services 1980–81; Dir Mo. Dept of Social Services 1982; Exec. Dir and COO Sanus Corp. Health Systems Inc. (renamed GenCare) 1985–91; joined Express Scripts Inc. (pharmacy benefit man. co.) 1992, mem. Bd of Dirs 1992–2011, Pres. and CEO –2000, Chair., Pres. and CEO 2000–05, Chair. 2005–06 (retd); Presiding Dir, Sigma-Aldrich Corpn 2009–, Chair. 2010–; mem. Bd of Dirs United States Cellular Corpn 2001–04, Aristotle Holding, Inc. –2011; Ind. Dir, Genworth Financial Inc. 2006–10; Mentor St Louis, Kenyon Coll.; mem. Investors Council and Leadership Circle, Regional Chamber and Growth Asscn. *Leisure interests:* history, literature. *Address:* Sigma-Aldrich Corporation, 3050 Spruce Street, St Louis, MO 63103, USA (office). *E-mail:* info@sigmaaldrich.com (office). *Website:* www.sigmaaldrich.com (office).

TOATU, Teuea, MSc, PhD; i-Kiribati government official; *Minister of Finance and Economic Development;* ed Univ. of South Pacific, Fiji, Univ. of Strathclyde, UK, Australian Nat. Univ.; Head, Project Man. and Referral Unit, Commonwealth Secr. 2004–11; Exec. Dir, Phoenix Islands Protected Area Conservation Trust 2011–16; Minister of Finance and Econ. Devt 2016–. *Address:* Ministry of Finance and Economic Development, POB 67, Bairiki, Tarawa, Kiribati (office). *Telephone:* 21806 (office). *Fax:* 21307 (office). *E-mail:* admin@mfep.gov.ki (office). *Website:* www.mfed.gov.ki (office).

TOBĂ, Petre, BA, MA, PhD; Romanian police officer and government official; b. 18 June 1964; ed Inst. of Civil Eng, Inst. for Studies of Public Order, Alexandru Ioan Cuza Police Acad., Acad. of Econ. Studies, Carol I Nat. Defence Univ., Nat. Civil Service Agency; police officer, Gen. Directorate of Police, Bucharest 1990–94, with Head Office 1994–2000, Head of Police Station 10 2000–02, Head of Dept, Gen. Directorate for Personal Data Records 2002–03, Deputy Dir-Gen. and Head of Public Safety Police Gen. Directorate of Bucharest Police 2003–04, First Deputy Dir-Gen. 2004–05, Deputy Dir-Gen. 2005–07, Deputy Insp.-Gen. of Romanian Police, Gen. Inspectorate of Romanian Police 2007–09, Insp.-Gen. of Romanian Police 2009–10, 2012–15; Deputy Sec.-Gen., Minister of Internal Affairs 2011–12, State Sec. and Head of Public Order and Safety March–May 2012, Minister of Internal Affairs 2015–16 (resgnd). *Address:* c/o Ministry of Internal Affairs, 010086 Bucharest 1, Piaţa Revoluţiei 1A, Romania. *E-mail:* petitii@mai.gov.ro.

TOBGAY, Lyonchhen Tshering, BS, MPA; Bhutanese politician; *President, People's Democratic Party;* b. 19 Sept. 1965, Haa; ed Univ. of Pittsburgh, Harvard Univ., USA; began career as programme officer, Tech. and Vocational Section, Dept of Educ. 1991, promoted Officer-in-Charge, later Head of Nat. Tech. Training Authority; Dir Dept of Human Resources –2007 (resgnd); carried out groundwork to form People's Democratic Party (PDP); trained in Cambodia, Thailand, USA, Philippines, S Korea, UK and Italy; fmr mem. Bd Royal Univ. of Bhutan, Council for Higher Educ., Bhutan Bd of Examinations and several others; mem. Parl. representing Sombaykha constituency in Haa, Leader of Opposition in Nat. Ass. –2013; Pres. People's Democratic Party 2009–; Prime Minister 2013–18. *Address:* People's Democratic Party, PO Box 835, Thimphu, Bhutan (office). *Telephone:* (2) 327137 (PDP) (office); (17) 110546 (mobile). *Fax:* (2) 335757 (PDP) (office). *E-mail:* tsheringtobgay@pdp.bt (office); tsheringtobgay.blog@gmail.com. *Website:* www.tsheringtobgay.com.

TOBGYE, Lyonpo Sonam; Bhutanese judge; b. 15 Nov. 1949, Nangkor, Pemagatshel; served as (Ziminangma) Master of the household to His Majesty the Third King and (Soelpon) Chamberlain to His Majesty the Fourth King; Chief Justice, High Court 1991–2009, Supreme Court 2010–14 (retd); Pres. South Asian Asscn for Regional Cooperation in Law (SAARCLAW) 2011–14; fmr Chair. Nat. Judicial Comm.; mem. Faculty, Royal Inst. for Governance and Strategic Studies; Honorary Bencher, Inner Temple London, UK; Order of The Druk Wangyal; Dr hc (NALSAR Univ. of India); Medaille d'Honneur, Judiciary of France, Int. Jurist Award, Int. Council of Jurists. *Address:* Royal Institute for Governance and Strategic Studies, PO Box 168, Phuentsholing, Bhutan.

TÓBIÁS, József, BSc; Hungarian fmr human resources manager and politician; b. 15 July 1970, Kisvárda; m. Raba Timea; three c.; ed Vásárhelyi Pál Grammar School, Nyíregyháza, Univ. of Pécs; Founder and Vice-Chair. Youth Org., Magyar Szocialista Párt (MSzP—Hungarian Socialist Party) 1991, Chair. Youth Org. 1995–97, Dir MSzP 1998–, Dir MSzP Parl. Group 2002–06, Deputy Leader 2006–10, Leader 2010–14, Chair. MSzP 2014–16; mem. Hungarian Parl. 1997–2002. *Address:* 19 Széchenyi rakpart, 1054 Budapest, Hungary (office). *Telephone:* (1) 441-5577 (office). *E-mail:* jozsef.tobias@parlament.hu (office). *Website:* mszp.hu (office).

TOBIAS, Randall L., BS; American business executive and government official; b. 20 March 1942, Lafayette, Ind.; m. 1st Marilyn Jane Salyer 1966 (died 1994); one s. one d.; m. 2nd Marianne Williams 1995; one step-s. one step-d.; ed Indiana Univ.; served in US Army 1964–66; numerous positions, Indiana Bell 1964–81, Illinois Bell 1977–81; Vice-Pres. (residence marketing, sales and service) AT&T 1981–82; Pres. American Bell Consumer Products 1983–84, Sr Vice-Pres. 1984–85, Chair. and CEO AT&T Communications, New York 1985–91, AT&T International, Basking Ridge, New Jersey 1991–93, Vice-Chair. AT&T, New York and Chair. 1986–93; Chair., Pres. and CEO Eli Lilly & Co., Indianapolis 1993–98, Chair. Emer. 1999–; Amb. and Coordinator US Govt Activities to Combat HIV/AIDS Globally 2003–06; Dir of Foreign Assistance and Admin., USAID 2006–07 (resgnd); fmr mem. Bd of Dirs Eli Lilly & Co., Kimberly-Clark, Knight-Ridder, Phillips Petroleum, Overseas Private Investment Corpn; Chair. Bd of Trustees Indiana Univ. 2013–; fmr Chair. Bd of Trustees Duke Univ.; fmr Vice-Chair. Colonial Williamsburg Foundation; mem. Council on Foreign Relations; Dr hc (Indiana Univ., Wabash Coll., Butler Univ., Gallaudet Univ., Ball State Univ.); Hon. DEng (Rose-Hulman Inst. of Tech.); Pharmaceutical Industry CEO of the Year 1995, named CEO of the Year by Working Mother magazine 1996, Norman Vincent Peale Humanitarian of the Year 1997, Indiana Univ.-Purdue Univ.-Indianapolis (IUPUI) Urban Univ. Medal, Positive Ally Award, Nat. Asscn of People with AIDS 2005. *Publication:* Put The Moose On The Table (with Todd Tobias) 2003. *Leisure interests:* skiing, shooting.

TOBIN, Brian V., PC, OC; Canadian businessman and fmr politician; *Senior Business Adviser, Fraser Milner Casgrain LLP;* b. 21 Oct. 1954, Stephenville, Newfoundland; s. of Patrick Tobin and Mary Frye; m. Jodean Smith 1977; two s. one d.; ed Memorial Univ., St John's, Newfoundland, Inst. of Corporate Directors, Univ. of Toronto; worked as a journalist; MP for Humber-St Barbe-Baie Verte 1980–96; MP for Bonavista-Trinity-Conception 2000–02, Parl. Sec. to Minister of Fisheries and Oceans 1980; Minister of Fisheries and Oceans 1993; Premier of Newfoundland 1996–2000; Minister of Industry and Minister responsible for the Atlantic Canada Opportunities Agency and for Western Econ. Diversification and Francophonie and for the Econ. Devt Agency of Canada for the Regions of Québec 2000–02; currently Sr Business Adviser, Fraser Milner Casgrain LLP, Toronto; Sr Fellow, Fraser Inst. 2006–10; Chair. Nat. Liberal Caucus 1989; mem. numerous House of Commons Cttees; Chair. New Flyer Industries, Market Resource Corpn; mem. Bd of Dirs Aecon Group Inc., Norvista Resources, Cline Mining Corpn; Dr hc (St Francis Xavier) 2001, (Brock) 2004. *Address:* Fraser Milner Casgrain LLP, 77 King Street West, Suite 400, Toronto, ON M5K 0A1, Canada (office). *Telephone:* (416) 863-4511 (office). *Fax:* (416) 863-4592 (office). *Website:* www.fmc-law.com (office).

TODD, Damian Roderic (Ric), BA; British diplomatist; b. 29 Aug. 1959, Crawley, West Sussex; s. of George Todd and Annette Todd; m. Alison Todd; one s. two d.; ed Worcester Coll., Oxford; with Defence Dept, FCO 1980–81, Third then Second Sec., Cape Town and Pretoria 1981–84, EC Dept 1984–87, First Sec. and Consul, Embassy in Prague 1987–89, Econ. Relations Dept 1989–91, First Sec. (Econ.), Embassy in Bonn 1991–95; seconded to HM Treasury, London 1995–97, Head, Agric. Spending Team, HM Treasury 1995–97, Agricultural Team 1996–97; EU Coordination and Strategy Team 1998–2001; Amb. to Slovakia 2001–04, FCO Finance Dir 2004–13, Amb. to Poland 2007–11, Gov. Turks and Caicos Islands 2011–13, High Commr to Cyprus 2014–16. *Address:* Foreign and Commonwealth Office, King Charles Street, London, SW1A 2AH, England.

TODD, Olivier René Louis, LèsL, MA; French writer; b. 19 June 1929, Neuilly; s. of Julius Oblatt and Helen Todd; m. 1st Anne-Marie Nizan 1948; m. 2nd France Huser 1982; two s. two d.; ed Univ. of Paris (Sorbonne), Corpus Christi Coll., Cambridge, UK; teacher, Lycée Int. du Shape 1956–62; Univ. Asst, St-Cloud 1962–64; reporter, Nouvel Observateur 1964–69; Ed. TV Programme Panorama 1969–70; Asst Ed. Nouvel Observateur 1970–77; columnist and Man. Ed. L'Express 1977–81; worked for BBC (Europa, 24 Hours) and ORTF 1964–69; Chevalier, Légion d'honneur, Commdr, Ordre des Arts et des Lettres; Hon. PhD (Stirling, Bristol), Hon. DLitt (Edinburgh) 2005; Prix Cazes 1981, Prix France Télévision 1997, Prix du Mémorial 1997. *Publications:* Une demi-campagne 1957, La traversée de la Manche 1960, Des trous dans le jardin 1969, L'année du Crabe 1972, Les canards de Ca Mao 1975, La marelle de Giscard 1977, Portraits 1979, Un fils rebelle 1981, Un cannibale très convenable 1982, Une légère gueule de bois 1983, La balade du chômeur 1986, Cruel Avril 1987, La négociation 1989, La Sanglière 1992, Albert Camus, une vie 1996, André Malraux, une vie 2001, Catre d'identités, souvenirs 2005, J'ai vécu en ces temps 2011. *Leisure interests:* walking, Luxembourg Gardens. *Address:* 8 rue du Pin, 83310 La Garde Freinet, France (home). *Telephone:* 4-94-43-63-34 (home).

TODMAN, Michael, BSBA; American business executive; *President, Whirlpool North America;* b. St Thomas, US Virgin Islands; ed Georgetown Univ.; various man. roles with Wang Laboratories Inc. and Price Waterhouse & Co. –1993; Finance Dir Whirlpool UK 1993, later Gen. Man. N Europe and Vice-Pres. Consumer Services, Whirlpool Europe, Controller N America 1995, Vice-Pres. Product Man. 1996, Vice-Pres. Sears Sales and Marketing 1997, Sr Vice-Pres. Sales and Marketing, N America 1999, Exec. Vice-Pres. N America, also mem. Exec. Cttee Whirlpool Corpn 2001, Exec. Vice-Pres. and Pres. Whirlpool Europe 2001, Pres. Whirlpool International 2006–07, 2010–, mem. Bd of Dirs Whirlpool Corpn 2006–, Pres. Whirlpool N America 2007–10; mem. Bd of Dirs Newell-Rubbermaid, Georgetown University, Economic Club of Southwestern Michigan; mem. Loyola Univ. Council of Regents. *Address:* Whirlpool Corporation, 2000 North M-63 States, Benton Harbor, MI 49022-2692, USA (office). *Telephone:* (269) 923-5000 (office). *Fax:* (269) 923-3722 (office). *Website:* www.whirlpoolcorp.com (office).

TODORIĆ, Ivica, BEcons; Croatian business executive; b. 2 Jan. 1951; m. Vesna Bašic; two s. one d.; ed Faculty of Econs, Zagreb Univ.; est. co. trading in flowers 1976, expanded in 1980s to include grains, oil, fruit and vegetables, f. Agrokor (jt stock co.) 1989, Pres. Agrokor Group (acquired numerous cos including Jaska vino d.d. 1998, Kiseljak 2000, Alastor d.o.o., Frikom 2003, also owns retail chain Konzum) –2017; Co-founder and Pres. Croatian Employers Asscn 1993; extradited on fraud charges from Britain to Croatia Nov. 2018, freed on bail settlement. *Address:* c/o Agrokor d.d., Trg D. Petrovića 3, 10000 Zagreb, Croatia (office).

TODOROVSKY, Valery Petrovich; Russian filmmaker; b. 8 May 1962, Odessa; s. of Piotr Yefimovich Todorovsky and Maiya Grigoriyevna Todorovskaya; ed All-Union Inst. of Cinematography; began career as scriptwriter; producer several TV series; Lead Producer and Artistic Dir Valery Todorovsky Producer Co., Marmot Film Studio. *Films include:* A Man of the Retinue, Cynics, Live (UNICEF Prize, Chicago Film Festival), Moscow Nights (Green Apple Prize, Golden Leaf), Katafalk (dir) 1990, Lyubov (Love) (writer, dir) 1991, Otdushina (A Vent) (writer) 1991, Hearse (dir) (Mannheim Film Festival Prize 1991), Nad tyomnoy vodoy (Above Dark Water) 1993, Katya Ismailova (dir) 1994, The Source of Snakes 1997, Strana glukhikh (Country of the Deaf) (writer, dir) 1998, Poklonnik 2001, Lyubovnik (The Lover) (dir) 2002, Moy svodnyy brat Frankensteyn (My Step Brother Frankenstein) (dir) 2004, Moscow Mission 2006, Tiski 2007, Hipster (Golden Eagle Award and Nika Award) 2008, Pikap: Sem bez pravil 2009, Detyam do 16 2010, The Geographer Drank His Globe Away 2013. *Television includes:* Kamenskaya, Morskoy volk (The Sea Wolf) (writer) 1991, Kamenskaya: Stechenie obstoyatelstv 1999, Kamenskaya: Igra na chuzhom pole 2000, Moskovskye okna 2001, Kamenskaya: Muzhskie igry 2002, Kamenskaya: Sedmaya zhertva 2003, Krasnaya kapella 2004, The Master and Margarita 2005, Komnata s vidom na ogni 2007, Ottsy i deti 2008, Zhizn vzaymy 2009, Rasplata za lyubov 2011, Lubvi ctlitelnaya sila 2012, Ottepel 2013, Ladoga 2014. *Address:* Valery Todorovsky Production Company, Marmot-film Studio, Krasina Street 7 blvd 2, 123056 Moscow; Ramenki str. 11, korp. 2, Apt. 272, 117607 Moscow, Russia. *Telephone:* (499) 254-31-23 (Valery Todorovsky Production Company); (495) 931-56-63. *E-mail:* info@todorovsky-company.ru. *Website:* www.todorovsky-company.ru.

TOELLE, Michael, BS; American business executive and farmer; ed Minnesota State Univ., Moorhead, Certificate of Dir Educ., Nat. Asscn of Corp. Dirs Dir Professionalism course; operates a family grain and hog farm near Browns Valley, Minn.; served on Bd of Country Pnrs Cooperative, Browns Valley, Minn. for 15 years, Chair. for 10 years; first elected to Bd of Dirs of CHS to represent Minnesota mems 1992, Chair. CHS 2002–11, fmr mem. Finance and Investment Cttee CHS Cooperatives Foundation; mem. Bd of Dirs Nationwide Insurance 2013–. *Address:* T & T Farms, 5085 Saint Anthony Drive, Browns Valley, MN 56219, USA. *Telephone:* (320) 695-2511 (office).

TOENNIES, Jan Peter, PhD; German physicist and academic; *Director Emeritus, Max-Planck-Institut für Dynamik und Selbstorganization;* b. 3 May 1930, Philadelphia, Pa, USA; s. of Gerrit Toennies and Dita Jebens; m. Monika Zelesnick 1966; two d.; ed Amherst Coll., Brown Univ.; Asst, Bonn Univ., FRG 1962–65, Privat Dozent 1965–67, Dozent 1967–69; Scientific mem. and Dir Max-Planck-Inst. für Strömungsforschung (now Max-Planck Inst. für Dynamik und Selbstorganisation) 1969–98, Acting Dir 1998–2001, currently Dir Emer., Emer. Scientific Mem., Max-Planck-Soc. 2002–05, Admin. Dir 2001–02; Assoc. Prof., Dept of Physics, Göttingen Univ. 1971–; Visiting Miller Prof. of Chem. and Physics, Univ. of California, Berkeley 2005; Corresp. mem. Acad. of Sciences, Göttingen; mem. German Acad. of Natural Sciences 'Leopoldina'; Hon. Prof., Bonn Univ. 1971–; Hon. DPhil (Gothenburg) 2000, Hon. DSci (Amherst Coll.) 2007; Physics Prize, Göttingen Acad. of Sciences 1964, Gold Heyrovsky Medal of the Czechoslovak Acad. of Sciences 1991, Hewlett-Packard Europhysics Prize (for outstanding achievement in condensed matter research) 1991, Max Planck Prize, Alexander von Humboldt Foundation 1992, Stern-Gerlach Medal, German Physical Soc. 2002, Kolos Medal, Univ. of Warsaw 2005, Benjamin Franklin Medal for Physics (co-recipient) 2006, Herschbach Award (co-recipient) 2013, Gold Medal of the City of Toulouse 2015. *Publications include:* Chemical Reactions in Shock Waves (with E. F. Greene) 1964, A Study of Intermolecular Potentials with Molecular Beams at Thermal Energies (with H. Pauly) in Advances in Atomic and Molecular Physics 1965, Molecular Beam Scattering Experiments, contribution in Physical Chemistry, An Advanced Treatise 1974, Rotationally and Vibrationally Inelastic Scattering of Molecules (Chem. Soc. Review) 1974, Scattering Studies of Rotational and Vibrational Excitation of Molecules (with M. Faubel) 1977, Advances in Atomic and Molecular Physics 1977, The Study of the Forces between Atoms of Single Crystal Surfaces 1988, Annual Review of Physical Chemistry, Serendipitous Meanderings and Adventures with Molecular Beams 2004, Angewandte Chemie (Int. Ed.), Superfluid Helium Droplets: A Uniquely Cold Nanomatrix for Molecules and Molecular Complexes (with A. Vilesov) 2004, Atomic Scale Dynamics at Surfaces, Theory and Experimental Studies with Helium Atom Scattering (with G Benedek) 2018; more than 720 publs in scientific journals. *Leisure interest:* sailing, hiking, physics toys. *Address:* Max-Planck-Institut für Dynamik und Selbstorganisation, Am Fassberg 17, 37077 Göttingen (office); Ewaldstrasse 7, 37085 Göttingen, Germany (home). *Telephone:* (551) 5176600 (office); (551) 57172 (home). *E-mail:* jtoenni@gwdg.de (office). *Website:* wwwuser.gwdg.de/~mpisfto (office).

TOEWS, Miriam, BA; Canadian writer and journalist; b. 1 Jan. 1964, Steinbach, Manitoba; ed Univ. of Manitoba, Univ. of King's Coll., Halifax; Hon. DLit (Brandon Univ.) 2006, Hon. DCL (Univ. of King's Coll.) 2010; John Hirsch Award for Most Promising Manitoba Writer 1996, Gold Medal for Humour, Nat. Magazine Award 1999, Writers' Trust of Canada Fellowship 2016. *Film:* as actor: Luz silenciosa 2007. *Publications include:* novels: Summer of My Amazing Luck 1996, A Boy of Good Breeding (McNally Robinson Book of the Year Award) 1998, A Complicated Kindness (Margaret Laurence Award for Fiction, McNally Robinson Book of the Year, Canadian Booksellers Asscn Fiction Book of the Year 2005, Gov. Gen.'s Award for Fiction 2005) 2004, The Flying Troutmans (Rogers Writers' Trust Fiction Prize) 2008, Travails with an Aunt 2009, Irma Voth 2011, All My Puny Sorrows (Rogers Writers' Trust Fiction Priz 2014, Sinbad Prize 2015, Canadian Authors Asscn Award 2015) 2014, Women Talking 2018; other: Swing Low: A Life (memoir) (McNally Robinson Book of the Year Award 2000, Alexander Kennedy Isbister Award for Non-Fiction 2000) 2000. *Address:* c/o Knopf Canada, 210-33 Yonge Street, Toronto, ON M5E 1G4, Canada (office).

TOHÁ MORALES, Carolina Montserrat, PhD; Chilean politician and government official; b. 12 May 1965; d. of José Tohá (fmr Vice-Pres. of Chile under Salvador Allende); m. Fulvio Rossi; ed Universidad de Chile, Univ. of Milan, Italy; played role in re-establishment of Federación de Estudiantes de la Universidad de Chile (FECH) 1984, Vice-Pres. 1987; mem. Partido por la Democracia (PPD), Vice-Pres. 1999; worked on presidential campaign of Ricardo Lagos 1999; Under-Sec. to Govt Spokesperson 2000–06; mem. Nat. Congress (PPD) for Santiago 2001–09 (re-elected 2005), Pres. 2010–; managed presidential runoff campaign of Eduardo Frei Ruiz-Tagle 2009; apptd Govt Spokesperson (first woman) 2009–10; Mayor of Santiago 2012–16.

TÓIBÍN, Colm, FRSL; Irish journalist, writer and poet; *Chancellor, University of Liverpool;* b. 30 May 1955, Enniscorthy, Co. Wexford; s. of Michéal Tóibín; ed Christian Brothers School, Enniscorthy, Univ. Coll., Dublin; in Spain 1975–78; Features Ed., In Dublin 1981–82; Ed. Magill (political and current affairs magazine) 1982–85; journalist and columnist, Dublin Sunday Independent 1985; Prof. of Creative Writing, Univ. of Manchester 2011–12; currently Irene and Sidney B. Silverman Prof. of the Humanities, Columbia Univ.; Chancellor Univ. of Liverpool 2017–; Hon. DLitt (Univ. of Ulster) 2008; American Acad. of Arts and Letters E.M. Forster Award 1995, Center for Scholars and Writers Fellowship, New York Public Library, Soc. of Authors Travelling Scholarship 2004, 38th annual AWB Vincent American Ireland Fund Literary Award 2010, Irish PEN Award 2011. *Plays:* Beauty in a Broken Place 2003. *Publications include:* fiction: Infidelity (contrib.), The South (Irish Times First Novel Award 1991) 1990, The Heather Blazing (Encore Award) 1993, The Story of the Night 1996, The Blackwater Lightship 1999, Finbar's Hotel (contrib.) 1999, The Master (Los Angeles Times Novel of the Year 2004, Stonewall Book Award 2004, Lambda Literary Award 2004, Int. IMPAC Dublin Literary Award 2006) 2004, Mothers and Sons 2006, Brooklyn (Costa Book Award for Best Novel) 2009, The Empty Family 2010, The Testament of Mary 2012, Nora Webster (Hawthornden Prize 2015) 2014, House of Names 2017; non-fiction: Seeing is Believing: Moving Statues in Ireland 1985, Walking along the Border (with T. O'Shea) 1987, Homage to Barcelona 1990, Dubliners 1990, The Trial of the Generals: Selected Journalism 1980–90 1990, Bad Blood 1994, Sign of the Cross 1994, The Kilfenora Teaboy 1997, The Irish Famine 1999, Love in a Dark Time 2001, Lady Gregory's Toothbrush 2002, New Ways to Kill Your Mother: Writers and Their Families 2012, On Elizabeth Bishop 2015; as ed.: SOHO Square VI: New Writing from Ireland 1993, Enniscorthy: History & Heritage 1998, Penguin Book of Irish Fiction 1999, The Modern Library 1999, New Writing II 2002; contrib. articles. *Address:* c/o Rogers, Coleridge and White Ltd, 20 Powis Mews, London, W11 1JN, England (office). *Telephone:* (20) 7221-3717 (office). *Fax:* (20) 7229-9084 (office). *E-mail:* info@rcwlitagency.co.uk (office). *Website:* www.rcwlitagency.co.uk (office); www.colmtoibin.com.

TOIKEUSSE, Abdallah Albert Mabri, MD; Côte d'Ivoirian politician and fmr physician; b. 8 Dec. 1962, Boueneu; m.; five c.; ed Univ. d'Abidjan, George Washington Univ., USA; mem. Nat. Ass. (Parl.) for Zouan-Hounien electoral dist 2000–, Chair. Environment Cttee –2003; Minister of State, Minister of Health and Population (govt of nat. reconciliation) 2003–05, Minister of Integration 2005–07, Minister of Transport 2007–10, Minister of State for Planning and Devt 2011–16, Minister of Foreign Affairs Jan.–Nov. 2016; Chair. Conf. of African Ministers of Finance, Planning and Econ. Devt 2013–14; Del. to World Summit on Sustainable Devt, Johannesburg 2002; Founding mem. Network of African Parliamentarians for Environment; mem. Network of Parliamentarians for Global Action; mem. American Public Health Asscn, Int. Asscn of Agricultural and Rural Health; Pres. Union pour la Démocratie et pour la Paix de la Côte d'Ivoire 2005–. *Address:* Ministry of Foreign Affairs, Bloc Ministériel, blvd Angoulvant, BP V109, Abidjan, Côte d'Ivoire (office).

TŐKÉS, Very Rev. László; Romanian ecclesiastic and politician; b. 1 April 1952, Cluj/Kolozsvár; s. of István Tőkés and Erzsébet Vass; m. Edit Joó 1985; two s. one d.; ed Protestant Theological Inst. Cluj; asst minister at Braşov/Brassó, then at Dej/Dés 1975–84; discharged for political reasons and suspended from church service 1984–86; reinstated as chaplain then pastor, Timişoara/Temesvár 1986–89; banished to small parish of Mineu/Menyő, threatened with eviction; demonstration by supporters was beginning of revolution that overthrew Communist Govt 1989; Oradea Bishop of Királyhágómellék Diocese, Nagyvárad 1990–; MEP 2007–, Vice-Pres. European Parl. 2010–12; mem. Temporary Nat. Salvation Council; Co-Chair. Hungarian Reformed Synod of Romania; Pres. Reformed Hungarian World Fed.; Hon. Pres. Hungarian Democratic Alliance of Hungarians in Romania, Hungarian World Fed.; Freeman Cities of Sárospatak amd Székelyudvarhely and of 5th and 11th dists of Budapest, Hon. Pres. World Union of Hungarians 1996; mem. European Senate of Honour 1992, Kt of Johannit Order 1993, Grand Cross of the Order of the Hungarian Repub. 1999, Star of Romania National Order 2009 (withdrawn 2013); Dr hc (Theological Acad. of Debrecen) 1990, (Regent Univ., Va Beach, USA) 1990, (Hope Coll., Holland, Mich.) 1991; Berzsenyi Prize, Hungary 1989, Roosevelt Prize of The Netherlands 1990, Bethlen Gábor Prize, Hungary 1990, Geuzenpenning Prize, Netherlands 1991, Pro Fide Prize, Finland 1993, Bocskay Prize, Hungary 1995, Hungarian Heritage Prize 1996, Minority Prize of Catalan CIEMEN Centre, Spain 1996, Leopold Kunschak Prize, Austria 1998, Fidelity Prize (Hungary) 1999. *Publications:* Where the Lord's Soul, there Freedom (selections of sermons) 1990, The Siege of Timişoara '89 1990, With God for the People 1990, There is a Time to Speak (with David Porter) 1993, A Phrase: And What is Behind 1993, In the Spirit of Timişoara: Ecumenism and Reconciliation 1996, Hope and Reality: Selected Writings 1999, Timişoara Memento: Self Confessions 1999, Timişoara Siege 1999; sermons, articles in ecclesiastical and secular publs. *Address:* European Parliament, Bât. Altiero Spinelli, 12E217, 60, rue Wiertz, 1047 Brussels, Belgium (office); Str. Craiovei 1, 3700 Oradea, Romania. *Telephone:* (2) 284-58-01 (office). *Fax:* (2) 284-98-01 (office). *E-mail:* laszlo.tokes@europarl.europa.eu (office). *Website:* www.europarl.europa.eu (office).

TOKURA, Masakazu; Japanese business executive; *President, Sumitomo Chemical Company Ltd;* b. 10 July 1950; ed Univ. of Tokyo; began career at Sumitomo Chemical Co. Ltd 1974, apptd Gen. Man. Planning & Coordination Office of Fine Chemicals Sector 1998, Electronic Materials Div. 2000, Corporate Planning & Coordination Office 2000, Alliance Promotion Office 2001, Exec. Officer in Charge of Corporate Planning & Coordination Office 2003–05, New Business Devt Office and Planning & Coordination Office of Fine Chemicals Sector 2005–06, New Business Devt Office, Planning and Coordination Office and Quality Assurance Office of IT-related Chemicals Sector April–June 2006, Man. Exec. Officer in charge of New Business Devt Office, Planning and Coordination Office and Quality Assurance Office of IT-related Chemicals Sector 2006–08, Rep. Dir and Man. Exec. Officer in charge of IT-related Chemicals Sector 2008–09, Dir and Sr Man. Exec. Officer 2009–11, Pres. Sumitomo Chemical Co. Ltd 2011–. *Address:* Sumitomo Chemical Co. Ltd, 27-1, Shinkawa 2-chome, Chuo-ku, Tokyo 104-8260, Japan (office). *Telephone:* (3) 5543-5102 (office). *Fax:* (3) 5543-5901 (office). *E-mail:* info@sumitomo-chem.co.jp (office). *Website:* www.sumitomo-chem.co.jp (office).

TOKURA, Yoshinori, BS, PhD; Japanese physicist and academic; *Professor, Department of Applied Physics, University of Tokyo;* ed Univ. of Tokyo; Assoc. Prof., Dept of Physics, Univ. of Tokyo 1986–93, Prof. 1994–95, Prof., Dept of Applied Physics 1995–, Dir Quantum-Phase Electronics Center, School of Eng 2010–13; Dir RIKEN Center for Emergent Matter Science 2013–; mem. Physical Soc. of Japan, American Physical Soc., Japan Soc. of Applied Physics; Foreign mem. Royal Swedish Acad. of Sciences 2014–; Fellow, Nat. Inst. of Advanced Industrial Science and Tech.; Dr hc (Uppsala Univ.) 2014; Nishina Memorial Prize 1990, IBM Japan Science Prize 1990, Bernd Matthias Prize 1991, Nissan Science Prize 1998, Asahi Prize 2001, Medal with Purple Ribbon 2003, James C. McGroddy Prize for New Materials, American Physical Soc. 2005, 52th Fujihara Prize 2011, IUPAP Magnetism Award and Néel Medal 2012, Imperial Prize and Japan Acad. Prize 2013, 55th Honda Memorial Award 2014. *Publications:* more than 500 articles in scientific journals. *Address:* Department of Applied Physics, School of Engineering, University of Tokyo, Hongo 7-3-1, Bunkyo-ku, Tokyo 113-8656 (office); RIKEN, 2-1 Hirosawa Wako, Saitama 351-0198, Japan (office). *Telephone:* (3) 5841-6800 (office); (4) 8462-1111 (office). *Fax:* (3) 5841-6803 (office); (4) 8462-1554 (office). *E-mail:* officeap.tu-tokyo.ac.jp (office); cems@riken.jp (office). *Website:* www.ap.t.u-tokyo.ac.jp (office); www.cems.riken.jp (office).

TOLAND, John Francis, DPhil, DSc, FRS, FRSE; British/Irish mathematician, academic and research institute director; *Honorary Professor of Mathematics, University of Bath;* b. 28 April 1949, Derry, Northern Ireland; s. of Joseph Toland and Catherine Toland (née McGarvey); m. Susan Frances Beck; ed Queen's Univ., Belfast, Univ. of Sussex; Prof. of Math., Univ. of Bath 1982–2011, now Hon. Prof. of Math.; Eng and Physical Sciences Research Council Sr Research Fellowship 1997–2002; N.M. Rothschild & Sons Prof. of Math. Sciences and Dir Issac Newton Inst. for Math. Sciences, Univ. of Cambridge 2011–16, Fellow of St John's Coll. 2011–16; Scientific Dir Int. Centre for Math. Sciences 2002–10; Pres. London Math. Soc. 2005–07; Chair. Math. Sciences panel for Research Excellence Framework by Higher Educ. Funding Council for England 2010–; mem. Exec. Cttee, Int. Math. Union 2010–18; Hon. Fellow, Univ. Coll. London 2008; Hon. DSc (Queen's Univ. Belfast) 2000, (Edinburgh) 2007, (Heriot-Watt) 2007, (Essex) 2009, (Sussex) 2017, (Bath) 2017; Senior Berwick Prize, London Math. Soc. 2000, Bath Vice-Chancellor Research Medal 2011, Sylvester Medal, Royal Soc. 2012. *Publications include:* numerous papers in professional journals. *Address:* Department of Mathematical Sciences, University of Bath, Bath, BA2 7AY (office); 15 Lansdown Park, Bath, BA1 5TG, England (home). *Telephone:* (1223) 335999 (switchboard) (office); 7799 307 433 (home). *E-mail:* jft26@cam.ac.uk (office). *Website:* www.newton.ac.uk/about/history/toland (office).

TOLEDANO, Sidney; French fashion industry executive; *Executive Chairman, LVMH Fashion Group;* b. 25 July 1951, Casablanca, Morocco; s. of Boris Toledano and Ines Benezra; m. Katia Assous 1981; one s. two d.; ed École Centrale Paris; began career as researcher and marketing consultant, AC Nielsen; moved to Kickers (French footwear brand); with Lancel (handbag mfr) 1983–93; joined Christian Dior SA 1993, Pres. 1998–2003, CEO 2003–18, also responsible for overseeing strategy at Fendi, also Pres. and CEO Christian Dior Couture, Acting Pres. Galliano 2006; Exec. Chair. and CEO, LVMH Fashion Group 2018–; mem. Exec. Cttee Chambre Syndicale de Haute Couture; Dir Comité Colbert, French Inst. of Fashion; Pres. Cercle Saint-Roch; Chevalier, Légion d'honneur 2005. *Address:* LVMH, 22 SA, 30 avenue Montaigne, 75008 Paris, France (office). *Telephone:* 1-44-13-22-22 (office). *Fax:* 1-44-13-22-23 (office). *Website:* www.lvmh.com (office).

TOLEDO, Francisco; Mexican artist; b. 17 July 1940, Minatitlan, Oaxaca; two s. three d.; ed Escuela de Bellas Artes de Oaxaca, Centro Superior de Artes Aplicadas del Instituto Nacional de Bellas Artes; first solo exhbn Mexico City 1959; travelled to Paris to work at Cite Universitaire 1960, returned to Mexico 1965; f. Instituto de Artes Graficas de Oaxaca 1988; worked at Casa de la Cultura, Juchitán and Inst. de Artes Gráficas, Oaxaca; associated with Museo de Arte Contemporaneo de Oaxaca, Jorge Luis Borges Library for the Blind, Cine El Pochote, Centro Cultural de Santo Domingo; Mexican Nat. Prize 1998, Prince Claus Award 2000, Right Livelihood Award 2005. *Website:* www.franciscotoledo.net.

TOLEDO MANRIQUE, Alejandro ('Cholo'), PhD; Peruvian economist, international organization official and fmr politician; *President, Global Center for*

Development and Democracy; b. 28 March 1946, Cabana, Ancash Prov.; m. Eliane Karp; ed Univs of Stanford and San Francisco, USA; fmr mem. staff World Bank; adviser to UN, World Bank, IDB, ILO and OECD; Research Fellow, Inst. for Int. Devt, Harvard Univ., 1991–94; Perm. Prof. of ESAN, Univ. Lima; Visiting Prof., Univ. of Waseda and Japan Foundation, Tokyo; Founder-mem. and Leader Perú Posible party (opposition alliance); presidential cand. 2000, subsequently boycotted election; Pres. of Peru 2001–06; Distinguished Scholar in Residence, Center for Advanced Study in the Behavioral Sciences, Stanford Univ. 2006–08, Payne Distinguished Visiting Lecturer, Freeman Spogli Inst. for Int. Studies 2007–08, also Visiting Scholar, Center on Democracy, Devt and the Rule of Law; Founder and Pres. Global Center for Devt and Democracy; currently Distinguished Visiting Scholar, School of Advanced Int. Studies, Johns Hopkins Univ., Washington, DC; also Non-Resident Sr Fellow in Foreign Policy and Global Economy and Devt, Brookings Inst. *Publications:* Las Cartas sobre la Mesa, Social Inversion for Growth, Economic Structural Reforms, Peru's Challenge: The Transition to Sustained Economic Growth; and several books on econs and devt. *Address:* Global Center for Development and Democracy, Calle María Parado de Bellido 245, Miraflores, Lima 18, Peru (office); Global Center for Development and Democracy, 505 9th Street, NW, Suite 1000, Washington, DC 20004, USA (office); Perú Posible, Bajada Balta 131, Miraflores, Lima, Peru. *Telephone:* (1) 4458484 (Peru) (office); (202) 776-7801 (US) (office). *E-mail:* contacto@cgdd.org (office). *Website:* www.cgdd.org (office).

TOLENTINO ARAÚJO, Jorge Homero; Cabo Verde diplomatist and government official; b. 16 Jan. 1963, Mindelo, São Vicente; ed Univ. of Coimbra, Portugal; career diplomat since 1990, Asst Sec. of State to the Prime Minister 2001–02, Minister attached to the Prime Minister and Culture 2002, Deputy Minister of the Prime Minister, Culture and Sports 2002–04; Amb. to Germany 2008–10, to Spain 2010–11; Minister of the Presidency of the Council of Ministers and of Nat. Defence 2011–14, Minister of Foreign Affairs 2014–16.

TOLGFORS, Sten, BSc; Swedish business executive and fmr politician; b. 17 July 1966, Forshaga; ed Karlberg Upper Secondary School, Oakcrest High School, USA, Örebro Univ., Åmål; mem. Örebro City Ass. 1991–94; Special Adviser, Ministry of Defence 1992–93, Ministry of Industry and Commerce 1992–94; mem. Nat. Bd Moderate Party Youth Org. 1990–95, Nat. Exec. 2002–, Spokesperson for Social Insurance 2002–03, Spokesperson for Educ. 2003–06; mem. Riksdag (Parl.) 1994–2013, Del. to OSCE Parl. Ass. 1998–2002; mem. Del. to Nordic Council 1998–2002, Cttee on Foreign Affairs 1998–2002, Cttee on Social Insurance 2002–03, Cttee on Educ. 2003–06, Advisory Council on Foreign Affairs 2006; Minister for Trade 2006–07, for Defence 2007–12 (resgnd); Partner and Sr Advisor Rud Pedersen (business consulting co.). *Address:* Rud Pedersen, Kungsgatan 42, 1tr, 111 35 Stockholm, Sweden (office). *E-mail:* sten.tolgfors@rudpedersen.com (office). *Website:* www.rudpedersen.com (office).

TOLLETT, Leland E., BSA, MSA; American business executive; b. 21 Jan. 1937, Nashville, Tenn.; s. of Vergil E. Tollett and Gladys V. Tollett; m. Betty Ruth Blew 1961; two c.; ed Univ. of Arkansas; joined Tyson Foods Inc. 1959, mem. Bd of Dirs 1984–2008, Pres. and CEO 1991–98, Chair. 1995–98, Consultant 1998–, Interim Pres. and CEO Jan.–Nov. 2009; mem. Bd of Dirs Worthen Banking Corpn 1988–, JB Hunt Transport Services Inc. (fmrly Hunt J B Transport Services Inc.) 2001–. *Leisure interests:* hunting, golf.

TOLLI, Abbas Mahamat; Chadian politician; *Governor, Banque de Développement des États de l'Afrique Centrale;* Dir Customs and Excise 2001–02; Dir Civil Cabinet of Pres. 2003–04; Sec. of State Feb.–Aug. 2005; Minister of Finance and Information Tech. 2005–08, Minister of Infrastructure and Equipment 2011–12; Sec.-Gen. Banque des Etats de l'Afrique centrale 2008–10; Sec.-Gen. La Commission Bancaire de l'Afrique Centrale 2012–15; Chair. Banque de Développement des États de l'Afrique Centrale 2015–17, Gov. 2017–. *Address:* Banque de Développement des États de l'Afrique Centrale, Boulevard Denis Sassou, N'Guesso BP 1177, Brazzaville, Republic of the Congo (office). *Telephone:* 426-83-00 (office). *E-mail:* bdeac@bdeac.org (office). *Website:* www.bdeac.org (office).

TOLNAY, Lajos, PhD; Hungarian business executive; *Chairman, MAL Company Ltd;* b. 27 Sept. 1948, Sajószentpéter; m.; four c.; ed Heavy Industries Tech. Univ., Miskolc and Budapest Univ. of Econs; various positions DIMAG Co. Ltd 1971–92, Gen. Dir 1989–92; Man. Dir Dunaferr Trading House Ltd 1992–93; Pres.-Man. Dir PTW Investment Co. Ltd 1993–95; Man. Dir Rákóczi Bank 1994, Pres. 1994–; Pres. Hungarian Chamber of Commerce 1990–93, Hungarian Chamber of Commerce and Industry 1994; Man. Dir Inota Aluminium Co. Ltd 1996–; Chair. Magyar Aluminium Ltd (now MAL Co. Ltd) 1997–; Chair. Controlling Cttee Életút First Nat. Pension Fund; Chair. NAT Hungarian Accreditation Bd; mem. Exec. Bd ICC, Hon. Chair. ICC Hungary; mem. Supervisory Bd Hungexpo Co. Ltd, Bankár Investment Co. Ltd; various awards and decorations. *Address:* MAL Co. Ltd, Termelő és Kereskedelmi Rt., 1012 Budapest, Hungary (office). *E-mail:* mal@mal.hu (office). *Website:* www.mal.hu (office).

TOMALIA, Donald A., BA, PhD; American chemist, entrepreneur and academic; *CEO, NanoSynthons LLC;* b. 5 Sept. 1938; s. of Andrew Vincent Tomalia and Mary Tomalia (neé Kondel); m. Janet E. Büchtenkirch 1986; one s.; ed Univ. of Michigan, Michigan State Univ.; worked for many years at Dow Chemical Co.; co-f. Dendritech, Inc. (first commercial producer of dendrimers) 1992, Founding Pres. and Chief Scientist 1992–2000; Vice-Pres. of Tech., MMI 1998–2000; Scientific Dir for the Biologic Nanotechnology Center, Univ. of Michigan Medical School 1998–2000; f. Dendritic Nanotechnologies, Inc. (DNT), Mount Pleasant, Mich. (jt venture with Starpharma Pooled Development, Melbourne, Australia) 2002, DNT Prin. Investigator in MIT/Inst. for Soldier Nanotechnologies (MIT/ISN) 2003; Distinguished Prof. and Research Scientist, Dept of Chem., Cen. Michigan Univ. 2001–08, Dir Nat. Dendrimer Center 2002–10, Faculty mem. 2008–10; Faculty mem. Faculty 1000 Biology, London, UK 2005–; Adjunct Prof., Dept of Chemistry, Univ. of Pennsylvania 2012–; Affiliate Prof., Dept of Physics, Coll. of Humanities and Sciences, Virginia Commonwealth Univ. 2012–; Founder and CEO NanoSynthons LLC, Mount Pleasant 2010–; Assoc. Ed. Journal of Nanoparticle Research 2012–; mem. Advisory Bd, European Foundation for Clinical Nanomedicine 2008–; mem. Editorial Advisory Bd, Current Bionanotechnology, Bentham Science 2016–; Fellow, AAAS 2017; Hon. mem. Editorial Bd, Nanomedicine 2013–; Dr hc (Cen. Michigan Univ.) 2002; IR-100 Award 1978, 1986, 1991, Leonardo da Vinci Award (France) 1996, Award for Outstanding Achievement in Polymer Science and Tech., Soc. of Polymer Science (Japan) 2002, Dow/Karabatsos and Distinguished Alumni Lectureship Award 2005, Frost & Sullivan Innovation of the Year Award (Nanomaterials for Advanced Medical Applications Tech.) 2005, Chevron Lectureship, Texas A&M, College Station, Tex. 2009. *Achievements include:* discovered dendrimers (dentritic architecture) 1979, jtly invented and developed dendritic polymers. *Publications:* Dendrimers and Other Dendritic Polymers; more than 200 peer-reviewed publs and more than 110 US patents. *Address:* NanoSynthons LLC, 1200 N Fancher Avenue, Mount Pleasant, MI 48858, USA (office). *Telephone:* (989) 317-3737 (office). *E-mail:* donald.tomalia@nanosynthons.com (office); donald.tomalia@gmail.com (office).

TOMALIN, Claire, MA, FRSL; British writer; b. 20 June 1933, London; d. of Emile Delavenay and Muriel Emily Herbert; m. 1st Nicholas Osborne Tomalin 1955 (died 1973); two s. three d. (one d. and one s. deceased); m. 2nd Michael Frayn (q.v.) 1993; ed Hitchin Girls' Grammar School, Dartington Hall School, Newnham Coll., Cambridge; publr's reader and Ed. 1955–67; Asst Literary Ed. New Statesman 1968–70, Literary Ed. 1974–77; Literary Ed. Sunday Times 1979–86; Vice-Pres. English PEN 1997, Royal Literary Fund 2000; mem. London Library Cttee 1997–2000, Advisory Cttee for the Arts, Humanities and Social Sciences, British Library 1997–2000, Council RSL 1997–2000; Trustee, Nat. Portrait Gallery 1992–2002, Wordsworth Trust 2004; Hon. mem. Magdalene Coll. Cambridge 2003, Hon. Fellow, Lucy Cavendish Coll. Cambridge 2003, Newnham Coll. Cambridge 2003; Hon. DLitt (East Anglia) 2005, (Birmingham) 2005, (Greenwich) 2006, (Cambridge) 2007, (Open Univ.) 2008, (Goldsmiths Coll.) 2009, (Roehampton) 2010, (Portsmouth) 2012; Whitbread Prize 1974, James Tait Black Prize 1990, NCR Book Award 1991, Hawthornden Prize 1991, Samuel Pepys Award 2003, Rose Mary Crawshay Prize 2003. *Plays include:* The Winter Wife 1991. *Publications include:* The Life and Death of Mary Wollstonecraft 1974, Shelley and his World 1980, Katherine Mansfield: A Secret Life 1987, The Invisible Woman 1990, The Winter Wife 1991, Mrs Jordan's Profession 1994, Jane Austen: A Life 1997, Maurice by Mary Shelley (ed.) 1998, Several Strangers: Writing from Three Decades 1999, Samuel Pepys: The Unequalled Self (Whitbread Awards for Book of the Year and Best Biog.) 2002, Thomas Hardy: The Time-Torn Man 2006, Selected Poems of Thomas Hardy 2006, Charles Dickens (Galaxy Nat. Book Award for Biography of the Year) 2011, A Life of My Own 2017. *Leisure interests:* music, gardening, walking. *Address:* c/o David Godwin, David Godwin Associates, 55 Monmouth Street, London, WC2H 9DG, England (office). *Telephone:* (20) 7240-9992 (office). *Fax:* (20) 7395-6110 (office). *E-mail:* david@davidgodwinassociates.co.uk (office). *Website:* www.davidgodwinassociates.co.uk (office); www.clairetomalin.co.uk.

TÓMASDÓTTIR, Halla, BBA, MBA; Icelandic business executive; *Co-Founder and Executive Chairman, Auður Capital;* early career in USA working with M&M/Mars, later Human Resources Dept, Pepsi Cola; spent six years at Reykjavík Univ. as Asst Prof., also Dir for Exec. Educ. and Female Entrepreneurship; Man. Dir Iceland Chamber of Commerce –2007; Co-founder Auður Capital (financial services co.) 2007, currently Exec. Chair.; Co-founder Sisters Capital (sustainable investment co.) 2012; Chair. Veritas Capital (sales and marketing co. in pharmaceutical and medical device sector), TAL (mobile communication co.); Vice-Chair. Olgerdin; fmr mem. Bd of Dirs of several orgs including Icelandic Stock Exchange, Sjóvá, Vistor, Calidris; cand. in presidential election 2016; Cartier Women's Initiative Award 2009. *Leisure interest:* fly fishing. *Address:* Auður Capital, Borgartún 29, 105 Reykjavík, Iceland (office). *Telephone:* 585-6500 (office). *Fax:* 585-6515 (office). *E-mail:* audur@audur.is (office). *Website:* www.audurcapital.is (office).

TOMBINI, Alexandre Antonio, PhD; Brazilian economist and fmr central banker; b. 9 Dec. 1963, Porto Alegre; ed Univ. de Brasília, Univ. of Illinois, USA; Gen. Coordinator for Int. Affairs, Econ. Policy Secretariat, Ministry of Finance 1991–92, Gen. Coordinator for External Affairs 1992–95; Sr Adviser, Foreign Trade Bd, Office of Chief of Staff of Pres. of Brazil 1995–98; Adviser to Bd, Banco Central do Brasil 1998–99, Head, Dept of Studies and Research 1999–2001, Deputy Gov. for Financial System Regulation and Org. 2006–10, Pres. Banco Central do Brasil 2011–16, also mem. Bd of Dirs BIS and Chair. Financial Stability Bd's Standing Cttee on Budget and Resources; Sr Adviser to Exec. Dir and mem. Exec. Bd, Brazilian Office, IMF, Washington, DC 2001–05; Visiting Prof., Univ. de Brasília 1993–94.

TOMBLIN, Earl Ray, BS, MBA; American politician; b. 15 March 1952, Logan Co., W Va; s. of Earl Tomblin and Freda M. Tomblin (née Jarrell); m. Joanne Jaeger 1979; one s.; ed Univ. of West Virginia, Marshall Univ., Univ. of Charleston; self-employed business exec. and fmr school teacher; mem. W Va House of Dels 1974–80, W Va Senate 1980–2011, Senate Pres. 1995–2011; Lt-Gov. of W Va 2000–10, Acting Gov. of West Virginia 2010–11, Gov. of West Virginia 2011–17; Vice-Chair. Nat. Council of State Govts 2004, Chair. 2005; Democrat; Dr hc (South West Virginia Community and Tech. Coll.); Nat. Bulger Award for Legislative Leadership 2009.

TOMBS, Baron (Life Peer), cr. 1990, of Brailes in the County of Warwickshire; **Francis Leonard Tombs,** Kt, BSc, LLD, DSc, FREng; British engineer; b. 17 May 1924, Walsall, West Midlands, England; s. of Joseph Tombs and Jane Tombs; m. Marjorie Evans 1949 (died 2008); three d.; ed Elmore Green School, Walsall, Birmingham Coll. of Tech.; with British Electricity Authority 1948–57; Gen. Man., Gen. Electric Co. Ltd 1958–67; Dir and Gen. Man. James Howden and Co. 1967–68; Dir of Eng, South of Scotland Electricity Bd 1969–73, Deputy Chair. 1973–74, Chair. 1974–77; Chair. Electricity Council for England and Wales 1977–80; Dir N.M. Rothschild & Sons Ltd 1981–94; Chair. The Weir Group Ltd 1981–83; Chair. T&N PLC 1982–89; Dir Rolls-Royce Ltd 1982–92, Chair. 1985–92; Chair. Old Mutual SA Fund 1994–99; Dir Shell (UK) Ltd 1983–94; Chancellor Univ. of Strathclyde 1991–97; Chair. Eng Council 1985–88; mem. House of Lords 1990–2015, Leave of Absence 2008–10; Hon. FICE; Hon. FIMechE; Hon. FIChemE; Hon. FIEE (and fmr Pres.); Hon. FRSE 1996; Papal Knighthood of the Order of St Gregory 2002; Hon. DSc (Aston) 1979, (Lodz, Poland) 1980, (Cranfield Inst. of Tech.) 1985, (City Univ., London) 1986, (Bradford) 1986, (Queen's Univ., Belfast) 1988, (Surrey) 1988, (Nottingham) 1989, (Cambridge) 1990, (Warwick) 1990; Hon. DUniv (Strathclyde) 1991; Hon. DTech (Loughborough) 1979; Dr hc (CNAA) 1988. *Publications:* Nuclear Energy Past, Present and

Future—Electronics and Power 1981, Reversing the Decline in Manufacturing Industry (Mountbatten Lecture 1993), Power Politics: Political Encounters in Industry and Engineering 2010. *Leisure interest:* music. *Address:* Honington Lodge, Honington, Shipston on Stour, Warwicks., CV36 5AA, England.

TOMÉ, Carol B., BA, MBA; American business executive; *Executive Vice-President, Corporate Services and Chief Financial Officer, Home Depot, Inc.;* b. Wyo.; ed Univ. of Wyoming, Univ. of Denver; began career as commercial lender with United Bank of Denver (now Wells Fargo); spent several years as Dir of Banking for Johns-Manville Corpn; Vice-Pres. and Treas. Riverwood Int. Corpn –1995; joined Home Depot, Inc., Atlanta, Ga 1995, Chief Financial Officer 2001–, Exec. Vice-Pres. of Corp. Services 2007–; mem. Bd of Dirs, United Parcel Service 2003–, Fed. Reserve Bank of Atlanta 2008–13, (Chair. 2012–13), US Home Systems Inc. 2012–, High Museum of Art, Atlanta Botanical Garden; Chair. Advisory Bd Metropolitan Atlanta Arts Fund, Metropolitan Atlanta Chamber of Commerce 2012–; mem. The Committee of 200; Lettie Pate Whitehead Evans Award, BDN Network 2009, CFO of the Year Award, CFO Roundtable 2009, Distinguished Alumna Award, Univ. of Wyoming 2011. *Address:* The Home Depot Inc., 2455 Paces Ferry Road NW, Atlanta, GA 30339, USA (office). *Telephone:* (770) 433-8211 (office). *Fax:* (770) 384-2805 (office). *E-mail:* info@homedepot.com (office). *Website:* www.homedepot.com (office).

TOMEING, Litokwa; Marshall Islands politician and fmr head of state; b. 14 Oct. 1939, Ratak Chain; m.; seven c.; traditional tribal chief; Mayor, Wotje Atoll 1965–69; apptd Minister for Ratak 1997; mem. Nitijela (Parl.) for Wotje Atoll 1969–, Vice-Speaker 1992–95, Speaker 2000–07; fmr mem. United Democratic Party, mem. United People's Party 2007–; Pres. Marshall Islands 2008–09.

TOMESCU, Constantina; Romanian athlete; b. (Constantina Diță), 23 Jan. 1970, Turburea, Gorj Co.; m. Valeriu Tomescu (divorced 2008); one s.; ed Bucharest Sports Acad.; long-distance runner, specializes mainly in half marathon and marathon; competed at World Half Marathon Championships, Palermo 1999; finished 10th in marathon at World Championships, Edmonton 2001; finished seventh in 10,000m at European Championships Munich 2002; finished fifth at World Half Marathon Championships, Vilamoura, Portugal 2003, third at World Half Marathon Championships, New Delhi 2004; won Chicago Marathon 2004 (personal best time of 2:21:30); Bronze Medal, marathon, World Championships, Helsinki 2005; won women's half marathon at World Half Marathon Championships, Edmonton 2005; finished second in 20km at World Road Running Championships, Debrecen, Hungary 2006; finished third in London Marathon 2007; Gold Medal, women's marathon, Olympic Games, Beijing 2008 (time of 2:26:44, oldest Olympic marathon champion in history). *Address:* Sport Expert Management, str. Grigore Balan Nr.2, Sfântu Gheorghe, Romania. *E-mail:* office@sportexpertmg.com. *Website:* www.constantinadita.com.

TOMIĆ, Dragan; Serbian engineer, business executive and politician; b. 9 Dec. 1935, G. Bukovica; s. of Boško Tomić and Mitra Tomić; m. Milica Tomić 1964; two d.; ed Univ. of Belgrade; held various positions at Rekord Rubber Works, Rakovica 1962–86, Gen. Dir 1986; Pres. Simpo 1967–2015; Pres. Gradske konferencije Socijalističkog saveza radnog naroda Beograda –1989; Pres. Eng Soc. of Yugoslavia; Gen. Dir NIS–Jugopetrol Co. 1990–; Chair. Man. Bd RTV Politika Co. 1993–; mem. Nat. Parl. (Skupština) of Serbia 1994–97, Speaker 1997–2001, Acting Pres. of Serbia July–Dec. 1997; Chair. Union of Yugoslav Engineers and Technicians 1993–. *Leisure interests:* chess, walking with his dog.

TOMITA, Tetsuro; Japanese business executive; *President and CEO, East Japan Railway Company;* has held numerous exec. positions at East Japan Railway Co., including, Head of Corp. Planning HQ and Head of Health and Welfare Dept, Chief Financial Officer and Man. Dir, Head of Personnel Dept and Head of Finance Dept, Exec. Vice-Pres. Corp. Planning HQ 2008–12, Exec. Dir, Pres. and CEO 2012–. *Address:* East Japan Railway Company, 2-2-2 Yoyogi, Shibuya-ku, Tokyo 151-8578, Japan (office). *Telephone:* (3) 5334-1150 (office). *Fax:* (3) 5334-1110 (office). *E-mail:* info@jreast.co.jp (office). *Website:* www.jreast.co.jp (office).

TOMIZAWA, Ryuichi, LLB; Japanese chemical industry executive; *Senior Corporate Advisor, Mitsubishi Chemical Holdings Corporation;* b. Tokyo; m.; two s.; ed Tokyo Univ. Faculty of Law; began career with Mitsubishi Chemical Corpn (MCC), assignments in Malaysia 1990–92, Germany 1992–95, involved in cr. of Mitsubishi Tokyo Pharmaceuticals, various positions including Gen. Man., Dir, Exec. Vice-Pres. Mitsubishi Pharma Corpn –2002, Pres. and CEO Mitsubishi Chemical Holdings Corpn 2002–07, mem. Bd of Dirs and Chair. 2007–12, Sr Corp. Advisor 2012–; Exec. Dir, Taiyo Nippon Sanso Corpn; Outside Dir, Tokyo Gas Co. Ltd 2011–; Dir, Chi Mei Corpn. *Leisure interest:* golf. *Address:* Mitsubishi Chemical Holdings Corporation, 1-1 Marunouchi 1-chome, Chiyoda-ku, Tokyo 100-8251, Japan (office). *Telephone:* (3) 6748-7115 (office). *Fax:* (3) 6414-3745 (office). *E-mail:* info@mitsubishichem-hd.co.jp (office). *Website:* www.mitsubishichem-hd.co.jp (office).

TOMKA, Peter, LLM, PhD; Slovak diplomatist, lawyer, arbitrator and judge; *Judge, International Court of Justice;* b. 1 June 1956, Banska Bystrica; s. of Ján Tomka and Kornélia Tomková; m. Zuzana Halgasová 1990; one s. one d.; ed Faculty of Law, Charles Univ., Prague, Faculty of Int. Law and Int. Relations, Ukraine, Law Inst. of Peace and Devt, France, Inst. of Int. Public Law and Int. Relations, Greece, Hague Acad. of Int. Law; Asst, Faculty of Law, Charles Univ., Prague 1980–84, Lecturer 1985–86, Adjunct Lecturer 1986–91; Asst Legal Adviser, Ministry of Foreign Affairs, Czechoslovakia 1986–90, Head of Public Int. Law Div. 1990–91; Counsellor and Legal Adviser, Czechoslovakian Mission to the UN 1991–92; Deputy Perm. Rep. of Slovakia to the UN 1993–97, Perm. Rep. 1999–2003; Agent of Slovakia before the Int. Court of Justice (ICJ) 1993–2003, Judge, ICJ 2003–, Vice-Pres. 2009–12, Pres. 2012–15; Legal Adviser to Slovak Ministry of Foreign Affairs 1997–99; Chair. UN Legal Cttee 1997, Cttee of Advisers on Public Int. Law, Council of Europe 2001–02; mem. Perm. Court of Arbitration, The Hague 1994–, UN Int. Law Comm. 1999–2003, American Soc. of Int. Law 2000–, European Soc. of Int. Law 2004–; Arbitrator in the Iron Rhine case (Belgium/Netherlands) 2003–05, in Kishenganga Court of Arbitration (Pakistan versus India) 2010–, in Annex VII to the UN Convention on the Law of the Sea 2004–, and in Int. Centre for Settlement of Investment Disputes 2005–; mem. Bd of Eds Právník (The Lawyer) 1990–91; Assoc. mem. Inst. of Int. Law 2011; mem. Curatorium of the Hague Acad. of Int. Law 2013–; Hon. Pres. Slovak Soc. of Int. Law 2003–; Hon. Bencher of the Middle Temple 2013. *Publications:* numerous articles in professional journals. *Address:* International Court of Justice, Peace Palace, Carnegieplein 2, 2517 KJ The Hague, Netherlands (office). *Telephone:* (70) 302-23-23 (office). *Fax:* (70) 302-24-20 (office). *E-mail:* p.tomka@icj-cij.org (office). *Website:* www.icj-cij.org (office).

TOMKO, HE Cardinal Jozef, DTheol, DrIur, DScS; Slovak ecclesiastic; *President Emeritus of the Pontifical Committee, International Eucharistic Congresses;* b. 11 March 1924, Udavské, Humenné; s. of Andrej Tomko and Anna Tomko; ordained priest 1949; consecrated Bishop (Titular See of Doclea) 1979; cr. Cardinal (Cardinal-Deacon of Gesù Buon Pastore alla Montagnola) 1985, (Cardinal-Priest of S. Sabina) 1996; Sec.-Gen. of Synod of Bishops 1979–85; mem. Comm. for Admin. of State of Vatican 1985–2004; Prefect of the Congregation for the Evangelization of Peoples 1985–2001; Adviser, Sec. of Vatican State 1996–2004; Pres. Pontifical Cttee for Int. Eucharistic Congresses (retd) 2001–07, now Emer.; numerous missions world-wide; Gran Cruz de la Orden del Libertador San Martín (Argentina) 1989, Order of the White Double Cross, First Class (Slovak Repub.) 1995; Prize of Grand Duchy of Luxembourg 1988. *Publications include:* Light of Nations 1972, Christianity and the World 1974, Christ Yesterday and Today 1976, Ecumenism 1977, Sinodo dei Vescori 1985, La Missione verso il terzo millennio 1998, On Missionary Roads (trans. as Sulle strade della Missione 2008) 2006. *Address:* 00120 Città del Vaticano (office); Via della Conciliazione 44, 00193 Rome, Italy (home). *Telephone:* (06) 698-824-24 (home). *E-mail:* jozef.tomko@tin.it (home).

TOMKYS, Sir (William) Roger, Kt, KCMG, DL, MA; British diplomatist and academic (retd); b. 15 March 1937, Bradford, W Yorks.; s. of Arthur Tomkys and Edith Tomkys; m. Margaret Abbey 1963; one s. one d.; ed Bradford Grammar School and Balliol Coll., Oxford; entered HM Diplomatic Service 1960, served in Amman, Benghazi, Athens, Rome, Amb. to Bahrain 1981–84, to Syria 1984–86, Asst Under-Sec., later Deputy Under-Sec. of State, FCO 1986–90, High Commr in Kenya 1990–92; Master of Pembroke Coll., Cambridge 1992–2004, Chair. Arab-British Chamber of Commerce 2004–10; Commendatore dell'Ordine al Merito 1980, Order of Bahrain First Class 1984. *Leisure interests:* travel, books, golf, shooting. *Address:* 41 New Road, Barton, Cambridge, CB23 7AY, England (home). *Telephone:* (1223) 264245 (home). *E-mail:* r.tomkys@btinternet.com (home).

TOMLINSON, Lindsay Peter, OBE, MA, FIA; British financial services industry executive; b. 7 Oct. 1951, Derby; s. of P. Tomlinson and J. M. Tomlinson; m. Sarah Caroline Anne Martin 1973; four s. one d.; ed Clifton Coll., St John's Coll., Cambridge; actuarial student, Commercial Union Assurance Co. 1973–77; sr pensions consultant, Metropolitan Pensions Asscn 1977–81; Sr Investment Man. Provident Mutual Managed Pension Funds 1981–87; CEO (Europe) Barclays Global Investors (fmrly BZW Investment Man.) 1987–2003, then Vice-Chair. –2009; Chair. Code Cttee, Panel on Takeovers and Mergers –2013; mem. Bd of Dirs Legal & General Group PLC 2013–.

TOMNITZ, Donald J., BA, MBA; American construction industry executive; *Vice-Chairman, President and CEO, Western Pacific Housing, Inc.;* b. 1948, St Louis, Mo.; m. Sharon Tomnitz; two c.; ed Westminster Coll., Western Illinois Univ.; served as capt. in US Army; fmr Vice-Pres. Republic Bank of Dallas, Crow Development Co.; joined D. R. Horton Inc. as Vice-Pres. 1983, Pres. Homebuilding Div. 1996–98, CEO and Vice-Chair. 1998–2014, Pres. 2000–14; currently Vice-Chair., Pres. and CEO Western Pacific Housing, Inc. *Address:* Western Pacific Housing, Inc., 300 Continental Blvd, Suite 390, El Segundo, CA 90245, USA (office). *Telephone:* (310) 563-5335 (office). *Fax:* (310) 648-7200 (office).

TOMONO, Hiroshi; Japanese business executive; *Representative Director and Vice-Chairman, Nippon Steel & Sumitomo Metal Corporation;* fmr Vice-Pres. and Pres. in Sumitomo Metal Industries Ltd (merged with Sumitomo Metal Industries, Ltd to become Nippon Steel & Sumitomo Metal Corpn 2012), Rep. Dir, Pres. and COO Nippon Steel & Sumitomo Metal Corpn 2012–14, Rep. Dir and Vice-Chair. 2014–. *Address:* Nippon Steel & Sumitomo Metal Corpn, Marunouchi Park Building, 6-1, Marunouchi 2-chome, Chiyoda-ku, Tokyo 100-8071, Japan (office). *Telephone:* (3) 6867-4111 (office). *Fax:* (3) 6867-5607 (office). *E-mail:* info@nssmc.com (office). *Website:* www.nssmc.com (office).

TOMOS; Chinese artist; b. 26 Nov. 1932, Tumed Banner, Inner Mongolia (Nei Monggol); s. of Yun Yao and Xing Yu; m. Xiahe-xiou 1967; two s.; ed Cen. Inst. of Fine Arts, Beijing; Assoc. Prof. of Fine Arts, Inner Mongolia Normal Coll.; Dean of Fine Arts, Inner Mongolia Teachers' Training Coll. 1984–; Adviser on Fine Arts to Children's Palace, Huhehot, Inner Mongolia; Vice-Chair. Inner Mongolian Branch of Chinese Artists' Asscn 1980–; Dir Standing Cttee, Chinese Artists' Asscn 1985–, mem. Oil Art Cttee 1985–; mem. Selection Cttee for Sixth Nat. Art Exhbn of oil paintings; mem. Art Educ. Cttee of Nat. Educ. 1986–; Dir Inner Mongolia branch of China External Culture Exchange Asscn; Dir Cheng's Style Tai-Chi Chuan Asscn 1993–; Chair. Judges' Cttee for 8th Annual Chinese Art Exhbn, Inner Mongolia 1994, 8th Annual Best Chinese Artwork Exhbn 1994; Consultant, The Watercolour Asscn, Inner Mongolia 1994; Dir China Oil Painting Asscn 1995–; Chair. Inner Mongolian Artists' Asscn 1996–; Head of Del. of Inner Mongolian painters to Hong Kong 1993; First Prize for Art, Inner Mongolia, Merit of Art Educ. Award, Wu Zuo Ren Int. Art Foundation 1990, Expert and Scholar award of Govt 1991 and medals awarded for individual paintings. *Works include:* Mine, Wind on the Grasslands, Having a Break, Dawn, Milkmaid, A Woman Hay-making, At Dusk, Polo, Spring Wind, White Horse and Wind, At Dark and many others. *Publications:* Selection of oil-paintings, Tomos's Album of Paintings (sketches and oil paintings) 1993, The Techniques of Oil Painting 1999. *Leisure interests:* Chinese Gongfu, Peking opera, Chinese medicine. *Address:* Art Department, Normal College, Nei Monggol Autonomous Region, People's Republic of China (office).

TOMOWA-SINTOW, Anna; Bulgarian singer (soprano); b. 22 Sept. 1943, Stara Zagora; m. Albert Sintow; one d.; ed Nat. Conservatory of Sofia with Zlatew Tscherkin and Katja Spiridonowa; debut at Leipzig Opera 1967; joined Deutsche Staatsoper, Berlin 1973; guest engagements at all leading European and US opera houses, with conductors including Karajan, Böhm, Haitink, Kleiber, Solti, Abbado, Muti, Maazel, Mehta, Levine, Chailly, Davis, Barenboim, Thielemann; N America debut in San Francisco 1974, at Met, New York 1978, Chicago 1981; numerous tours in Japan, also with La Scala and Berlin Philharmonic under von Karajan; regular guest at Salzburg Festival 1973–91; Kammersängerin, Vienna and Berlin, two Grammy Awards (for Ariadne and Don Giovanni/Donna Anna), three Orphée d'Or awards. *Recordings include:* Lohengrin, Le Nozze di Figaro, Don Giovanni, Die Zauberflöte, Der Rosenkavalier, Ariadne auf Naxos, Madame Butterfly, La Traviata, Tosca, Eugene Onegin, Aida, Otello, Capriccio, Andrea Chénier, Simon Boccanegra, Prince Igor, Mozart Coronation Mass, Mozart Requiem, Bach Magnificat, Brahms German Requiem, Verdi Requiem, Strauss Four Last Songs (Orphée d'Or) and Capriccio monologue, Beethoven Missa Solemnis and 9th Symphony, recitals of Verdi arias and of Italian and German arias. *Roles include:* Arabella, Ariadne, Marschallin, Salome, Madelaine in Capriccio, Ägyptische Helena, Countess Almaviva, Fiordiligi, Donna Anna, Elsa in Lohengrin, Elisabeth in Tannhäuser, Sieglinde, Aida, Traviata, Leonora in La Forza del Destino, Amelia in Ballo, Simone Boccanegra, Elisabetta in Don Carlo, Yaroslavna in Prince Igor, Tatjana in Onegin, Tosca, Madama Butterfly, Turandot, Manon Lescaut, Norma, Santuzza, Das Wunder der Heliane, etc. *Leisure interests:* nature, reading books, singing. *E-mail:* contact@tomowa-sintow.com. *Website:* www.tomowa-sintow.com.

TONEGAWA, Susumu, PhD; Japanese immunologist, neuroscientist and academic; *Picower Professor of Biology and Neuroscience and HHMI Investigator, Massachusetts Institute of Technology;* b. 5 Sept. 1939, Nagoya; s. of Tsutomu Tonegawa and Miyuko Tonegawa; m. Mayumi Yoshinari 1985; three c.; ed Kyoto Univ. and Univ. of Calif., San Diego; postgraduate work at Dept of Biology, Univ. of Calif., San Diego 1968–69, The Salk Inst., San Diego 1969–70; mem. Basle Inst. for Immunology, Basle, Switzerland 1971–81; Prof. of Biology, Center for Cancer Research and Dept of Biology, MIT 1981–, now Picower Prof. of Biology and Neuroscience, Depts of Brain and Cognitive Sciences and Biology, Biology Alumni Investigator, Howard Hughes Medical Inst. 1988–, Dir Picower Inst. for Learning and Memory, MIT 1994–, also Alumni Investigator and Dir RIKEN–MIT Center for Neural Cicuit Genetics; mem. American Acad. of Arts and Sciences; Foreign Assoc. mem. NAS; Hon. mem. American Asscn of Immunologists, Scandinavian Soc. for Immunology; Bunkakunsho Order of Culture 1984; numerous awards and prizes including Avery Landsteiner Prize 1981, Gairdner Foundation Int. Award 1983, Robert Koch Prize 1986, Lasker Prize 1987, Nobel Prize for Physiology or Medicine 1987. *Address:* Picower Institute for Learning and Memory, Massachusetts Institute of Technology, 77 Massachusetts Avenue, Building 46, Room 4235, Cambridge, MA 02139-4307, USA (office). *Telephone:* (617) 324-1660 (office). *Website:* mit.edu/picower (office).

TONG, Anote, MSc; I-Kiribati politician (retd) and fmr head of state; b. 11 June 1952; m. Meme Bernadette Tong; eight c.; ed Univ. of Canterbury, NZ, London School of Econs, UK; Sr Asst Sec., Ministry of Educ. 1976–77; Sec. Ministry of Communication and Works 1980–82; Minister for Natural Resources Devt 1994–96; mem. Parl. for Maiana Island 1996–2003; Sr mem. Boutokaan Te Koaua Party 1996–2003; Beretitenti (Pres.) of Kiribati and Minister for Foreign Affairs and Immigration 2003–16; fmr Chair. National Fishing Co., Development Bank of Kiribati, Otintai Hotel Ltd, Air Tungaru Co-operative. *Address:* c/o Office of the President (Beretitenti), POB 68, Bairiki, Tarawa, Kiribati (office).

TONG, Zhiguang; Chinese economist, academic and international organization official; b. 21 Jan. 1933, Hebei Prov.; ed Beijing Inst. of Foreign Trade and Univ. of Int. Business and Econs, Bombay Univ., India; joined CCP 1973, Deputy Head, State Council Leading Group for Right to Intellectual Property 1991; Vice-Minister of Foreign Trade and Econ. Co-operation 1991–93; Chair. Export-Import Bank of China 1994–99; apptd Chair. WTO Research Soc. of China 2001; Vice-Chair. China-UK Friendship Group; mem. China-US Inter-parliamentarian Exchange Group of NPC; fmr Chief Negotiator and Del. Leader for China's accession to GATT/WTO and Sino-US Trade Negotiations; fmr sr diplomatist to India, Myanmar, USA and UN; fmr Adviser to Chinese Del. of UN Gen. Ass.; fmr Pres. and CEO China Resources (Holdings) Co. Ltd, Hong Kong; mem. 8th Standing Cttee NPC 1993–98, mem. NPC Foreign Affairs Cttee, del. of Hebei Prov. to 8th NPC 1993–98, 9th Standing Cttee NPC 1998–2003; Del., 15th CCP Nat. Congress 1997–2002; Lifelong Hon. Adviser, China Soc. for WTO Studies. *Publications:* several articles on foreign trade, int. econs and the WTO. *Leisure interests:* golf, classical music, Chinese calligraphy. *Address:* 7202 Yin Zha Hu Tong, Xicheng Qu, Beijing, People's Republic of China (home). *Telephone:* (10) 64259703 (home).

TONG HON, HE Cardinal John, MA, PhD; Hong Kong ecclesiastic; *Bishop of Hong Kong [Xianggang];* b. 31 July 1939, Hong Kong; ed Chinese Univ. of Hong Kong, Pontifical Urbaniana Univ., Rome; spent ten years living in Huadu, Guangzhou before returning to Hong Kong; ordained priest, Diocese of Hong Kong [Xianggang] 1966; served with Holy Spirit Study Center, Congregation for the Evangelization of Peoples, Hong Kong for 24 years; apptd Auxiliary Bishop of Hong Kong [Xianggang] and Titular Bishop of Bossa 1996; Coadjutor Bishop of Hong Kong [Xianggang] 2008–09, Bishop of Hong Kong [Xianggang] 2009–; cr. Cardinal (Cardinal-Priest of Regina Apostolorum) 2012; participated in Papal Conclave 2013; mem. Congregation for the Evangelization of Peoples 2003–, Secr. for the Economy 2014–; travelled to Guangzhou as Rep. of the Pope, along with other Hong Kong religious leaders 2005. *Address:* Catholic Diocese Centre 12/F, 16 Caine Road, Hong Kong Special Administrative Region, People's Republic of China (office). *Telephone:* 2522-3677 (office); 3589-2428 (office); 2843-4679 (office). *Fax:* 2522-3749 (office); 2525-4707 (office). *E-mail:* hkcsco@catholic.org.hk (office). *Website:* www.catholic.org.hk (office).

TONG SANG, Gaston, DipEng; French Polynesian engineer, politician and fmr head of state; b. 7 Aug. 1949, Bora Bora; two c.; ed Collège La Mennais, Papeete, Lycée Montaigne, Bordeaux, Ecole des Hautes études industrielles (HEI), Centre des Hautes Etudes de la Construction, Paris; engineer, Road Infrastructure Dept, Polynesian Dept of Works 1976–80, Head, Maritime Works Dept 1980–82; Cabinet Dir for Govt Counsellors 1982–84; Cabinet Dir for Minister of Works 1984–86; Minister of Works, Supplies, Energy and Mines 1986–89; Mayor of Bora Bora 1989–91; Regional Councillor for Iles sous le Vent and Minister of Supplies, Urban Areas, Works and Energy 1991–95; Minister of Works, Energy and Ports 1995–96, of Housing, Territories, Urban Areas and Real Estate 1996–98, of Property Affairs, Land Man. and Urban Areas 1998–2000, of Land Man. and Land Redistribution 2001–04, of Energy, Commerce, Industry and Small Businesses 2004–07; Pres. of French Polynesia 2007, 2008–09 (resgnd), also Minister for External Relations, Int. Transport and Communication, 2009–11; Founding mem. and Pres. O Porinetia To Tatou Ai'a (Polynesia, Our Homeland) party 2007–; Chevalier, Ordre Nat. du Mérite 1996, Chevalier des Palmes académiques 2000, Chevalier, Légion d'honneur 2004, Grand Cross of the Order of Tahiti Nui 2007. *Address:* O Porinetia To Tatou Ai'a, BP 4061, 98713 Papeete, French Polynesia (office). *Telephone:* 584848 (office). *E-mail:* contact@oporinetia.pf (office).

TÕNISTE, Toomas; Estonian politician; b. 26 April 1967, Tallinn; ed Tallinn Univ.; competed as a sailor in four Olympic Games 1988–2000 for USSR and then Estonia; fmr Chair. Viimsi Rural Municipality Council; Chair. Pro Patria group on Tallinn City Council 2006–07; mem. Riigikogu (Parl.) 2007–15, Chair. Econ. Affairs Cttee; Minister of Finance 2017–19; mem. Bd OÜ Breting 1996–, Chair. of Bd OÜ Laste Maailm 2005–; Chair. Bd EVR Cargo 2016–17; mem. Bd AS LTT 1993–, Supervisory Bd State Forest Man. Centre 2008–11; mem. Isamaa Erakond (Pro Patria Party). *Address:* c/o Ministry of Finance, Endla 13, Tallin 10122, Estonia (office).

TONKIN, Peter Frederick, BSc (Arch) (Hons), BArch (Hons), LFAIA, PhD; Australian architect; *Director, Tonkin Zulaikha Greer Architects;* b. 10 Jan. 1953, Blayney, NSW; s. of John Ebenezer Tonkin and Veronica Mariea Tonkin (née Perry); m. Ellen Claire Woolley; one s. one d.; ed Univ. of Sydney, RMIT Univ.; in practice with Lawrence Nield and Partners 1979–81; ind. practice 1981–, Co-founder Tonkin Zulaikha 1987, Tonkin Zulaikha Greer 1988–; Visiting Design Tutor, Sydney Univ., Univ. of New South Wales, Univ. of Tech., Sydney; Adjunct Prof. of Architecture, Univ. of Queensland 2003–13, Univ. of Canberra; Fellow, Royal Australian Inst. of Architects (fmr Vice-Pres. and Chair. of Practice and Design Bds), Historic Houses Trust Exhbns Cttee; Trustee, Historic Houses Trust NSW 2003–13; Life Fellow, AIA; numerous awards and prizes, including Royal Australian Inst. of Architects Merit Awards 1988, 1991, 1993, 1996, 2000, 2001, 2003 and every year 2007–13, Winner, Vietnam Memorial Competition 1990, Tomb of the Unknown Soldier Competition 1993, Master Builders Asscn Merit Award 1993, ACEA Engineering Excellence Award 1999, Property Council of NSW Devt of the Year 1999, Int. Royal Inst. of Chartered Surveyors Award for Conservation 2000, Winner, Nat. Gallery of Australia Competition 2000, Winner, Australian War Memorial London Competition 2003, Winner, Canberra Int. Arboretum Competition 2005, Winner, Australian Memorial NZ Competition 2012. *Achievements include:* design projects include refurbishment of Sydney Customs House, Fed. Museum and Library, Tenterfield, Royal Blind Soc. Library, Nat. Memorial to Australian Vietnam Forces, Tomb of the Unknown Australian Soldier, Canberra, Australian War Memorial, London, Craigieburn Bypass, Hume Freeway, Melbourne, Carriageworks Performing Arts Centre, Sydney, Paddington Reservoir Gardens Sydney, Glebe Town Hall refurbishment, Nat. Arboretum, Canberra, Walsh Bay Arts Precinct, Sydney. *Publications:* numerous books, articles, papers and essays. *Leisure interests:* mountain sports, motorcycling. *Address:* Tonkin Zulaikha Greer Architects, 117 Reservoir Street, Surry Hills, NSW 2010, Australia (office). *Telephone:* (2) 9215-4900 (office). *Fax:* (2) 9215-4901 (office). *E-mail:* peter@tzg.com.au (office). *Website:* www.tzg.com.au (office).

TØNNESSON, Stein, CandPhil, DPhil; Norwegian peace researcher; *Research Professor, Peace Research Institute Oslo (PRIO);* b. 2 Dec. 1953, Copenhagen, Denmark; s. of Kåre Tønnesson and Birgit Tønnesson; m. Eva Helene Østbye; one s.; ed Univ. of Århus, Denmark, Univ. of Oslo; taught Norwegian and History at Univ. of Oslo 1983; historian for Norwegian Asscn of Sports 1983–85; wrote doctoral thesis on Vietnam Revolution of 1945 1986–92; Research Fellow, Peace Research Inst. Oslo (PRIO) 1990–92, Dir 2001–09, Research Prof. 2009–; Research Prof. Nordic Inst. of Asian Studies 1992–95, Sr Research Fellow 1995–98; consultant to Statoil 1996–2000; Prof. of Human Devt Studies, Univ. of Oslo 1998–2001; Randolph Jennings Sr Fellow, US Inst. of Peace 2010–11; Adjunct Prof. and Leader, East Asian Peace Programme, Uppsala Univ. 2011–17; mem. Bd NORFUND 2007–15, Bd Inst. for Security and Devt Policy 2011–15, Bd Inst. of Social Research 2011–15; mem. Cttee on Devt Research, Swedish Research Council 2015–19; ICAS Book Prize for best study in the humanities 2011. *Film:* East Asia's Surprising Peace (short) 2016. *Publications include:* The Vietnamese Revolution of 1945 1991, Imperial Policy and Southeast Asian Nationalism 1930–1957 (co-ed.) 1995, Asian Forms of the Nation (co-ed.) 1996, Vietnam 1946: How the War Began 2010, Explaining the East Asian Peace 2017. *Leisure interest:* running. *Address:* PRIO, PO Box 9229, Grønland, 0134 Oslo (office); Sollisvingen 13, 1366 Lysaker, Norway (home). *Telephone:* 22-54-77-31 (office). *Fax:* 22-54-77-01 (office). *E-mail:* stein@prio.no (office). *Website:* www.prio.no (office); www.pcr.uu.se (office); www.cliostein.com (home).

TONOYAN, Col (retd) Davit; Armenian politician and fmr army officer; *Minister of Defence;* b. 27 Dec. 1967, Ust-Kamenogorsk (now Öskemen), Eastern Kazakhstan Oblast, Kazakh SSR, USSR; m.; two c.; ed Yerevan State Univ., Russian Mil. Acad.; served with USSR Armed Forces 1986–88; joined Armed Forces of the Repub. of Armenia 1992; worked at Main Dept for Combating Organized Crime, Ministry of Internal Affairs 1992–94; Div. Head, Mil. Police Dept, Ministry of Defence 1994–97; various posts at NATO Allied Command HQ 1998–2007, including as Rep. of Armenian Armed Forces to NATO 2004–07; Head, Dept of Int. Mil. Cooperation and Defence Programs, Ministry of Defence 2007–08, Head, Defence Policy Dept 2008–10, First Deputy Minister of Defence 2010–17, Minister of Emergency Situations 2017–18, Minister of Defence 2018–; Order For Services to Fatherland; Vazgen Sargsyan Medal 2005, Andranik Ozanyan Medal 2008, Medal For Meritorious Service. *Address:* Ministry of Defence, 0044 Yerevan, Bagrevand poghots 5, Armenia (office). *Telephone:* (10) 29-46-99 (office). *Fax:* (10) 29-45-31 (office). *E-mail:* modpress@mil.am (office). *Website:* www.mil.am (office).

TOOLEY, Sir John, Kt, MA; British arts administrator and arts consultant; b. 1 June 1924, Rochester, Kent; s. of H. R. Tooley; m. 1st Judith Craig Morris 1951 (divorced 1965); three d.; m. 2nd Patricia J. N. Bagshawe 1968 (divorced 1990); one s.; m. 3rd Jennifer Anne Shannon 1995 (divorced 2003); ed Repton School, Magdalene Coll., Cambridge; Sec., Guildhall School of Music and Drama 1952–55; Asst to Gen. Admin., Royal Opera House, Covent Garden 1955–60, Asst Gen. Admin. 1960–70, Gen. Admin. 1970–80, Gen. Dir 1980–88; Dir London Philharmonic Orchestra 1998–2010, Britten Estate 1989–96, South Bank Bd 1991–97, Compton Verney Opera Project 1991–97, Welsh Nat. Opera 1992–2000, David Gyngell Holdings Ltd 1996–97; Pres. Salisbury Festival 1988–2005; Chair. Rudolf Nureyev Foundation 1995–2008, Almeida Theatre 1990–97, Salisbury Cathedral Girl Choristers Trust 1995–2006, Monument Insurance Brokers Ltd 1997–2002; Gov. Royal Ballet 1994–97; consultant, Int. Man. Group 1988–97, Ballet Opera

House, Toronto 1989–90, Istanbul Foundation for Culture and Arts 1993–2008, Antelope Films 1993–; adviser, Borusan Philharmonic Orchestra, Istanbul 2005–08; Trustee Britten Pears Foundation 1988–99, Walton Trust 1988–2000, Wigmore Hall 1989–2001, Almeida Theatre 1990–2002, Performing Arts Labs 1992–97, Cardiff Bay Opera House 1995–96, Sidney Nolan Trust 1995–, Mozartfest, Bath 2001–; Hon. FRAM; Hon. FGSM; Hon. FRNCM; Hon. mem. Incorporated Soc. of Musicians; Hon. Fellow, Magdalene Coll., Cambridge 2005; Commendatore of Italian Repub. 1976; Hon. DUniv (Univ. of Central England) 1996; Queen Elizabeth II Coronation Award 2005. *Publication:* In House 1999. *Leisure interests:* walking, theatre. *Address:* 18 Grange Court, Cambridge, CB3 9BD, England (home). *Telephone:* (1223) 358737 (office); (1223) 351995 (home). *Fax:* (1223) 358737 (office). *E-mail:* tooley@btinternet.com (home).

TOOMEY, Patrick Joseph (Pat), AB; American business executive and politician; *Senator from Pennsylvania;* b. 17 Nov. 1961, Providence, RI; m. Kris Ann Duncan 1997; two s. one d.; ed La Salle Acad., Harvard Univ.; investment banker, Chemical Bank, New York 1984–86; Vice-Pres. and Dir, US subsidiary, Morgan, Grenfell & Co. 1986–91; financial consultant, Hong Kong, 1990–91; Co-founder Toomey Enterprises, Inc., Allentown, Pa 1991–, opened, with two younger brothers, Rookie's Restaurant, Allentown 1991; elected to Allentown's newly est. Govt Study Comm. 1994; mem. US House of Reps for 15th Congressional Dist of Pa 1999–2005; unsuccessful cand. for US Senate 2006; Pres. and CEO Club for Growth, Washington, DC 2004–09; Senator from Pennsylvania 2011–, mem. Banking, Housing and Urban Affairs Cttee, Budget Cttee, Commerce, Science and Transportation Cttee, Jt Econ. Cttee; mem. Bd of Dirs Commonwealth Foundation for Public Policy Alternatives 2007–; Republican; named Man of the Year, US Marine Corps 1999, Honor Roll Award, Concord Coalition 2000. *Address:* 248 Russell Senate Office Building, Washington, DC 20510, USA (office). *Telephone:* (202) 224-4254 (office). *Fax:* (202) 228-0284 (office). *Website:* www.toomey.senate.gov (office).

TOOPE, Stephen J., OC, LLB, BCL, PhD; Canadian university administrator; *Vice-Chancellor, University of Cambridge;* m. Paula Rosen; three c.; ed Trinity Coll., Cambridge, UK, McGill Univ., Harvard Univ., USA; served as Law Clerk to Chief Justice of Canada 1986–87; Research Dir, Office of the Special Rep., Royal Comm. on Aboriginal Peoples 1991; Asst Prof. of Law, McGill Univ. 1987–93, Assoc. Prof. 1993–99, Prof. 1999–2006, Assoc. Dean (Grad. Studies and Research), Faculty of Law 1991–94, Dean 1994–99; Pres. and Vice-Chancellor Univ. of British Columbia 2006–14; Dir Monk School of Global Affairs, Univ. of Toronto 2015–17; Vice-Chancellor, Univ. of Cambridge 2017–; consultant on int. law, int. human rights and legal reform to Depts of Foreign Affairs and Justice, Int. Devt Agency 1988–; Dir World Univ. Service of Canada 2004–; Chair. Research Univs Council of BC 2009–11; mem. Bd of Dirs Canadian Human Rights Foundation (now Equitas) 2001–06; mem. UN Working Group on Enforced or Involuntary Disappearances (Chair. and Rapporteur 2004–06) 2003–07; mem. Int. Advisory Bd, Faculty of Law, Nat. Univ. of Singapore 2001–, Journal of Int. Law and Int. Relations 2004–; mem. Academic Council, Inst. for Transnational Arbitration, USA 2001–, Research Council, Canadian Inst. for Advanced Research 2004–, Advisory Council, Minister of Justice 2005–06, Social Sciences and Humanities Research Council 2005–, Order of Canada Advisory Council 2011–13; mem. Exec. Cttee Asscn of Univs and Colls of Canada 2006–, Vice-Chair. 2010–11, Chair. 2011–13; Lead negotiator for the Govt of Canada, Manuge v. The Queen 2012; mem. Bd Conf. Bd of Canada 2009–, Public Policy Forum of Canada 2012—, BC Business Council 2006–; Council mem., Social Sciences and Humanities Research Council of Canada 2005–08; Fern Gertrude Kennedy Prize in Jurisprudence (jtly) 1982, F.R. Scott Prize in Constitutional Law 1983, Casimar Bielski QC Prize in Int. Law 1983, Ballon Medal 1983, Douglas J. Sherbaniuk Distinguished Writing Award, Canadian Tax Foundation (jtly) 1995, Francis Deák Publication Award, American Soc. of Int. Law (jtly) 1998, David L. Johnston Award for Distinguished Service, McGill Alumni Asscn 1997, John W. Durnford Teaching Excellence Award, McGill Univ. 2001, McGill Univ. Scarlet Key Award, Queen Elizabeth II Diamond Jubilee Medal 2012. *Publications:* Mixed International Arbitration 1990; articles in American Journal of International Law, Columbia Journal of Transnational Law, Harvard Journal of International Law, McGill Law Journal and many other int. journals in N America and Europe. *Address:* University of Cambridge, The Old Schools, Trinity Lane, Cambridge, CB2 1TN, England (office). *Telephone:* (1223) 332291 (office). *E-mail:* co.enquiries@admin.cam.ac.uk (office). *Website:* www.cam.ac.uk (office).

TOOTOO, Hunter, PC; Canadian business executive and politician; b. 18 Aug. 1963, Rankin Inlet, Nunavut; s. of Batiste Tootoo and Sally Luttmer (née Banks); Regional Coordinator for Arviat, Nunavut 1993; Admin. Officer for NWT Dept of Recreation and Tourism 1995; Co-founder, Iqaluit br. of Arctic Insurance Brokers Ltd; fmr Recreation Coordinator for Arviat, Admin. Officer for Dept of Econ. Devt and Transportation, and Asst Dir, NWT Housing Corpn, Iqaluit 1997; mem. Nunavut Legis. Ass. for Iqaluit Centre 1999–2013, Speaker 2011–13; fmr Nunavut Minister Responsible for Nunavut Housing Corpn, Homelessness, Qulliq Energy Corpn, and Minister of Educ.; mem. House of Commons (Parl.) for Nunavut 2015–; Minister of Fisheries and Oceans, and Canadian Coast Guard 2015–16 (resgnd); fmr mem. NWT Co-op Business Devt Bd, Sport North Bd of Dirs, Arctic Co-operatives Ltd; mem. Liberal Party of Canada. *Leisure interests:* watching ice hockey, hunting, competitive curling. *Address:* c/o Fisheries and Oceans Canada, Centennial Towers, 13th Floor, 200 Kent Street, Station 13E228, Ottawa, ON K1A 0E6, Canada.

TOPALLI, Jozefina Çoba, MPA; Albanian politician; b. 26 Nov. 1963, Shkodër; m.; two c.; ed Luigj Gurakuqi Univ., Shkodra, Univ. of Padua, Italy and Tirana Univ.; civil servant, Chamber of Commerce, Shkodra 1992–95; Lecturer and Chancellor, Luigi Gurakuqi Univ., Shkodra 1995–98; mem. Democratic Party of Albania—Partia Demokratike e Shqipërisë, Vice-Chair. 1997–; mem. Kuvendi Popullor (People's Ass.) 1996–, Deputy Speaker 1997–2005, Speaker 2005–13, fmr Deputy Pres. Parl. Children's Cttee, fmr mem. Social Work, Health and Family Cttee; mem. Council of Europe 2002–; mem. monitoring missions during gen. elections held in Ukraine and Palestinian Autonomous Areas 2004–05; active participant in campaigns for the Objectives of the Millennium Devt; Honorary Citizen of Cair Municipality, Macedonia 2012; Mediterranean Award, Int. Mediterranean Forum for Peace, consigned by Senator Gergio De Gregori, Pres. of Italian Parl. Del. to Ass. of NATO 2010, declared First Amb. of UNICEF for the protection of children's rights in Albania, Medal of Honour from Chair. of Legis. Ass. of St Petersburg, Millennium Peace Award: Cavaliere per la Pace, Int. Peace Union, Sacro Cuore Univ., Italy. *Address:* Kuvendi Popullor, Bulevardi Dëshmorët e Kombit 4, Tirana, Albania (office). *E-mail:* info@parlament.al (office). *Website:* www.parlament.al (office); www.jozefinatopalli.al.

TOPALOV, Veselin; Bulgarian chess master; b. 15 March 1975, Rousse; winner, World Under-14 Chess Championship, Puerto Rico 1989, silver medal, World Under-16 Championship, Singapore 1990; named Grandmaster 1992; reached last 16 in FIDE World Chess Championship 1999, quarter-finals 2000, last 16 2001, semi-finals 2004, World Champion 2005–06; losing finalist, Cands Tournament, Dortmund 2002; jt first place with Gary Kasparov, Linares 2005, 2010; winner, M-tel Masters 2005, 2006; lost title reunification match against Vladimir Kramnik 2006; unsuccessful challenger versus world champion Viswanathan Anand in World Chess Championship 2010. *Achievements include:* in Oct. 2006 had the second-highest Elo rating of all time (2813).

TOPAN, Sanné Mohamed, MLitt; Burkinabè academic and diplomatist; b. 1 Jan. 1955, Kiembara, Sourou Prov.; m.; three c.; fmr teacher; fmr mem. Parl.; Deputy Sec.-Gen. Nat. Comm. for UNESCO 1987–95; Nat. Corresp., Islamic Org. for Educ., Science and Culture 1989–91; Dir Office of the Pres. of Burkina Faso 1996–99; Minister of Employment, Labour and Social Security 1999–2000, of Parl. Relations 2000–02; Amb. to Mali 2002–13; Chief of Staff, Office of the Pres. Jan.–Nov. 2014; Officier, Ordre Nat. du Burkina Faso; Dr hc. *Publications:* numerous publs. *Address:* ACI-2000, Commune III, BP 9022, Bamako, Burkina Faso (office). *Telephone:* 20293171 (office). *Fax:* 20299266 (office). *E-mail:* ambafaso@sotelma.net.ml (office).

TOPBAŞ, Kadir, PhD; Turkish architect and politician; b. 8 Jan. 1945, Artvin; m.; two s. one d.; ed Marmara Univ., Mimar Sinan Univ., Univ. of Istanbul; worked as architect, Istanbul Metropolitan Municipality; adviser to Recep Tayyip Erdogan, Mayor of Istanbul Metropolitan Municipality 1994–98, also served as Deputy Dir Istanbul 1st Cultural Heritage Protection and Monuments Cttee of Ministry of Culture; Mayor of Beyoğlu 1999–2004; Mayor of Istanbul 2004–17; mem. Supervisory Bd TAC Foundation; mem. Adalet ve Kalkınma Partisi—AKP (Justice and Development Party); Vice-Pres. United Cities and Local Governments (UCLG) 2004–07, Co-Pres. 2007–10, Pres. 2010–; Pres. Union of Municipalities of Turkey 2009–, UN Advisory Cttee of Local Authorities 2011–; mem. Proposal Group for Local Govts Reform Project, Bd of Trustees and Bd of Dirs TAÇ (History and Environment Foundation); Order of Cultural Merit (South Korea) 2014; Istanbul Tourism Award 2010. *Publications include:* Beyoglu: Kültürleri Buluşturan Kent, Geçmişten Günümüze Beyoglu I-II, Anılarda Beyoglu. *Address:* Istanbul Büyükşehir Belediye Başkanlığı, Şehzadebaşı Cad. No. 25, Saraçhane, Istanbul, Turkey (office). *Telephone:* (212) 4551400 (office). *Fax:* (212) 4552700 (office). *E-mail:* baskan@ibb.gov.tr (office); irelations@ibb.gov.tr (office). *Website:* www.ibb.gov.tr (office); www.kadirtopbas.com.tr.

TOPCHEYEV, Yuriy Ivanovich, DTech Sc; Russian cyberneticist and academic; *Emeritus Professor, International G. Soros Science Education Programme;* b. 26 Sept. 1920, Yaroslavl; s. of Ivan Yakovlevich Topcheyev and Vera Aleksandrovna Topcheyeva; m. Inna Ivanovna Smirnova 1965; one s.; ed Moscow Aviation Inst.; mem. CPSU 1948–91; Chief Dept of Scientific Research Inst. of Automatic Systems 1943–72; mem. staff and Prof., Inst. of Physical Eng, Moscow 1968–89, Chief of Faculty 1972–88; Prof. Int. G. Soros Science Educ. Programme 1996–97, Emer. Prof. 1997–; mem. Comm. of Co-ordination Cttee on Computers of USSR (now Russian) Acad. of Sciences 1978–85, Co-ordination Cttee on Robotics 1980–87; Chair. Council on Systems of Automated Design, Ministry of Higher Educ. 1977–87; mem. Council Specialized Scientific and Technological Activities of USSR (now Russian) Acad. of Sciences 1989–, Russian Cosmonautics 1992–, World Innovation Foundation 2001–, Prof. and Grand Doctor of Philosophy, Acad. Européenne d'Informatisation (Belgium) 2003–; Order of Labour Banner 1950, State Prize 1972, Korolev Medal 1977, Gagarin Medal 1981, Gold Medal, Russian Exhbn Centre 2005. *Publications include:* Encyclopaedia for Automatic Regulation Systems Design 1989; (co-author) Basics of Automatic Regulation 1954, Modern Methods of Automatic Control System Design (ed. and co-author) 1967, Technical Cybernetics (4 Vols) 1967–89, Philosophy of Nonlinear Control Systems 1990, Nonlinear Systems of Automatic Control (Vols 1–9) 1970–92, People and Robotics (Vol. 1) 1995, (Vol. 2) 1998, Development of Robotics 2000, Robotics: A Historical Overview 2001, Robotics: History and Perspectives 2002, Robotic Assisted Human's Activity (A History of Development) 2004, Biography of Mstislav Vsevolodovich Keldysh 2002, biographies of Vladimir Mikhailovich Myasischev and Pavel Osypovich Sukhoi 2003, Robotics: Assisted Human's Activity (A History of Development) (co-author) 2005, Biography of Vladimir Mikhailovich Petlyakov 2005, History of Domestic Aviation Arms 2005; over 310 articles, including 12 on great contemporary Russian scientists in A History of Science Engineering 2002, and 2 pieces on contemporary biosphere ecology. *Leisure interests:* nonlinear systems design, the history of the development of automatic systems and robotics. *Address:* 125212 Moscow, Leningradskoye sch. 31, Apt. 147, Russia. *Telephone:* (495) 156-63-06. *E-mail:* fsg100@yandex.ru (home).

TÖPFER, Klaus, PhD; German politician and international organization official; b. 29 July 1938, Waldenburg, Silesia; m.; three c.; ed Univs of Mainz, Frankfurt am Main and Munster; family expelled from Silesia, settled in Höxter/Weser 1945; Head, Political Economy Dept, Inst. of Devt Planning, Munster 1970–71; Head, Planning and Information Section, Saarland State Chancellery, Saarbrücken; Lecturer, Coll. of Admin., Speyer 1971–78; Prof. Ordinarius, Hanover Univ., Dir Inst. of Environmental Research and Regional Planning 1978–79; Hon. Prof. Mainz Univ. 1985–86; joined CDU 1972, CDU Dist Chair., Saarbrücken, mem. CDU State Exec., Saar 1977–79; State Sec., Rhineland Palatinate Ministry of Social Affairs, Health and Environment, Mainz 1978–85; Deputy Chair. CDU Fed. Cttee of Experts on the Environment 1983; Minister of Environment and Health, Rhineland Palatinate 1985–87; CDU Dist Chair., Rhein-Hunsrück 1987–89; Fed. Minister for the Environment, Nature Conservation and Nuclear Safety 1987–94, of Regional Planning, Housing and Urban Devt 1994–98; mem. Bundestag 1990–98; Exec. Dir UNEP, Nairobi 1998–2006; Acting Dir UN Centre for Human Settlements (Habitat) 1998–2000; Chair. of the Energy Efficiency in Buildings (EEB) Assurance Group, an initiative of the World Business Council for

Sustainable Development (WBCSD); Founding Exec. Dir Inst. for Advanced Sustainability Studies e.V, Potsdam 2009–15, now Hon. Sr Fellow; mem. Advisory Bd German Foundation for World Population, Holcim Foundation for Sustainable Construction 2004–; Strategic Advisor to Desertec Industrial Initiative (Dii); Hon. Prof. (Tongji Univ. Shanghai) 1997, (Univ. of Tübingen) 2005; Order of Merit of the Federal Republic of Germany 1986, Grand Cross of the Order of Merit of the Federal Republic of Germany; Dr hc (Technical Univ. of Freiberg) 2007; TÜV Environment Prize 2000, German Environment Prize 2002, Bruno H Schubert Environment Prize 2002, German Award for Culture 2010, Wilhelmine von Bayreuth Award 2012, inducted into Kyoto Earth Hall of Fame 2012.

TOPI, Bamir Myrteza, PhD, DrSc; Albanian biologist, politician and fmr head of state; *Leader, New Democratic Spirit;* b. 24 April 1957, Tirana; m. Teuta Mema; two d.; ed Veterinary Medicine Faculty, Agricultural Univ. of Tirana; Scientific Researcher, Inst. for Veterinary Studies, Tirana 1984–87, Dir 1990–96; elected to Nat. Ass. 1996, re-elected twice; Minister of Agric. and Food 1996–97; Pres. of Albania 2007–12; fmr Deputy Chair. Democratic Party, resgnd on taking office 2007; Founder and Leader, New Democratic Spirit 2012–; Hon. Pres. KF Tirana football club 2005–07, Hon. Citizen of Prishtina, Kosovo 2008, of Rrëshen, of Burrel, of Gjakova, Kosovo; Kt Grand Cross, Grand Order of King Tomislav (Croatia) 2009; Dr hc (Univ. of Prishtina) 2008; Goddess on the Throne Gold Medal, Prishtina 2009. *Address:* New Democratic Spirit (Fryma e Re Demokratike), Rruga George W. Bush, Pallati i Kasmeve 15/1, Tirana, Albania (office). *Telephone:* (4) 2242444 (office). *Fax:* (4) 2242444 (office). *Website:* www.frd.al (office).

TOPOL, Chaim; Israeli actor, producer and director; b. 9 Sept. 1935, Tel-Aviv; s. of Yaakov Topol and Rela Goldman; m. Galia Finkelstein 1956; one s. two d.; joined entertainment unit during army service 1953, becoming its first commdr; f. The Green Onion satirical theatre 1956, Municipal Theatre of Haifa 1960; Founding Pres. Variety Israel 1967; starred in stage productions of Fiddler on the Roof in London 1967, 1983, 1994, on Broadway, New York 1990, in Melbourne 1998, in Sydney 2005, in Wellington, NZ 2007, USA tour 2009, in Ziegfield 1988; further roles include The Caucasian Chalk Circle, Romanov and Juliet, Othello, A View From The Bridge, Chichester Festival Theatre, Gigi, London 2008; actor, producer, dir for the Genesis Project, filming the Bible, New York 2003; Chair. Jordan River Village, Galilee 2011– (holiday facility for children with life-threatening or chronic illnesses); Golden Globe Award 1972, San Francisco Film Festival Winner 1972, David Donatello Award 1972. *Films include:* Cast A Giant Shadow 1965, Sallah 1966, Before Winter Comes 1969, A Talent for Loving, Fiddler on the Roof 1971, The Public Eye 1972, Galileo 1974, Flash Gordon 1972, For Your Eyes Only 1980, The Winds of War 1981, A Dime Novel, Ervinka, Left Luggage 1997, Time Elevator 1998, War and Remembrance 1989, Mr Know All 1988, War and Remembrance 1988–89; several TV films. *Albums include:* Fiddler on the Roof (cast album), It's Topol, War Songs, Topol 68, Fiddler on the Roof (film album), Topol's Israel. *Publication:* Topol by Topol (autobiography) 1981, To Life! (A Treasury of Jewish Wisdom, Wit and Humour) 1995. *Leisure interests:* book illustrations and portrait drawings. *Address:* c/o Diamond Management, 31 Percy Street, London, W1T 2DD, England (office); 22 Vale Court, Maida Vale, London, W9 1RT, England (home). *Telephone:* (20) 7631-0400 (office). *E-mail:* agents@diman.co.uk (office); fbvandoren@aol.com (office). *Fax:* (20) 7266-2155 (home).

TOPOL, Eric J., MD; American cardiologist and academic; *Director, Scripps Translational Science Institute;* b. 26 June 1954, Queens, New York; m. Susan Leah Merriman 1979; one s. one d.; ed Univ. of Virginia, Univ. of Rochester School of Medicine and Dentistry; at Univ. of Rochester School of Medicine and Dentistry 1975–79; Intern in Medicine, Moffitt Hosp., Univ. of California, San Francisco 1979–80, Asst and Sr Resident in Medicine 1980–82; Fellow in Cardiovascular Medicine, Johns Hopkins Hosp., Baltimore, Md 1982–85; Sr Fellow, Coronary Angioplasty, San Francisco Heart Inst. 1984; Asst Prof. of Internal Medicine, Univ. of Michigan School of Medicine, Ann Arbor 1985–87, Assoc. Prof., 1987–90, Prof. 1990–91; Consulting Prof. of Medicine, Duke Univ. School of Medicine, Durham, NC 1991–2002; Prof. of Medicine, Cleveland Clinic Health Sciences Center, Ohio State Univ. School of Medicine 1991–2002; Provost and Prof. of Medicine, Cleveland Clinic Lerner Coll. of Medicine, Case Western Reserve Univ. 2002–06; Co-Dir Cleveland Clinic Heart Center 1991–2006, Chair. Dept of Cardiovascular Medicine, Cleveland Clinic Foundation 1991–2006, Provost, Chief Academic Officer and mem. Bd of Govs Cleveland Clinic Foundation 2001–06, Vice-Chair. Dept of Molecular Cardiology, Cleveland Clinic Research Institute 1991–2006, Dir Joseph J. Jacobs Center for Thrombosis and Vascular Biology 1991–2006; Dir Scripps Translational Science Inst., Scripps Research Inst. 2007–, also Gary and Mary West Endowed Chair of Innovative Medicine and Prof. of Genomics, Dept of Molecular and Experimental Medicine, Chief Academic Officer, Scripps Health 2007–, Sr Consultant, Div. of Cardiology, Scripps Clinic 2007–, Founding Dean, Scripps School Medicine 2008–; Co-founder and Vice-Chair. West Wireless Health Inst.; Amon G. Carter Professorship, Univ. of Texas Health Science Center 1988; Donald and Lois Roon Visiting Professorship, Scripps Clinic and Research Foundation 1992; Barnet Berris Visiting Professorship, Univ. of Toronto 1992; Goldberg Visiting Professorship, Cedars-Sinai Medical Center 1994; Edward Massie Visiting Professorship, Washington Univ. School of Medicine 1995; Simon Dack Visiting Professorship, Mount Sinai Cardiovascular Inst. 1995; Marjorie and Gaye Grollman Visiting Professorship, Univ. of Virginia 1995; Isadore Rosenfeld Visiting Professorship, Cornell Univ. Medical School 1995; John J. Sampson Visiting Professor, Univ. of California, San Francisco Medical Center 1998; mem. Bd of Dirs Rhone-Poulenc-Rorer, Inc. 1997, Quintiles Transnational, Inc. 1997–; Ed. Current Opinion in Cardiology 1994–96, Scientific American Medicine 1995–98, Cardiology Website: TheHeart.Org 2000–; mem. Editorial Bd American Journal of Cardiology 1988–, Journal of the American College of Cardiology 1989–93, 1995–99, 2001–03, Coronary Artery Disease 1989–, International Journal of Cardiac Imaging 1990–, Cardiology 1990–, Trends in Cardiovascular Medicine 1990–, Choices in Cardiology 1990–, Clinical Cardiology 1990–, Circulation 1991– (Consulting Ed. 2001–), Cardiology in the Elderly 1991–, British Heart Journal 1992–, Journal of Myocardial Ischemia 1992–, Current Literature 1993–, Cardiovascular Drug Therapy 1993–, Primary Cardiology 1994–, Clinics in Interventional Cardiology 1995–, Journal of Women's Health 1995–, European Heart Journal 1996–, Seminars in Interventional Cardiology 1996–, Revista Espanola de Cardiologia 1996–, American Heart Journal 1996–, Journal of Clinical and Experimental Cardiology 1997–, Acute Coronary Syndromes 1997–, American Journal of Medicine 1998–, Journal of Clinical and Basic Cardiology 1998–, Current Treatment Options in Cardiovascular Diseases 1998–, Heart Disease: A Journal of Cardiovascular Medicine 1998–, Current Opinion in Cardiovascular, Renal and Pulmonary Investigational Drugs 1998–, International Journal of Cardiology 1999–, Heart Drug Journal 1999–, Cardiovascular Therapeutics 2000–, ASEAN Heart Journal 2001–; editorial consultant/manuscript reviewer for numerous journals; mem. NAS, AAAS, American Soc. of Clinical Investigation 1990, Best Doctors in America 1992–2003, American Asscn of Physicians 1995, Johns Hopkins Soc. of Scholars 1999, Int. Soc. for Fibrinolysis and Thrombolysis, American Fed. for Clinical Research, Asscn of Univ. of Cardiologists, Asscn of Profs in Cardiology, Inst. of Medicine 2004; Fellow, American Heart Asscn 1983–85, American Coll. of Chest Physicians, Soc. of Cardiac Angiography and Interventions (also Trustee), European Soc. of Cardiology, American Coll. of Cardiology, American Coll. of Physicians; Hon. mem. Columbian Soc. of Cardiology, Polish Cardiac Soc.; Outstanding Medical Specialist in the US, Town and Country 1989, Sir William Osler Award, Univ. of Miami School of Medicine 1989, 4th Annual Virginia Heart Center Award, Virginia Heart Center 1992, Distinguished Teacher Award, Cleveland Civic Foundation 1992, Best Doctors in America, American Health Magazine 1996, Distinguished Teacher Award, Cleveland Civic Foundation 1997, Most Cited Researchers in Cardiology, Science Watch 1999, Top Docs-Medicine's Most Cited, Science Watch 1999, Scientific Achievement in Clinical Research, Cleveland Clinic Foundation 2000, Innovator of the Year, American Coll. of Cardiovascular Administrators and Alliance of Cardiovascular Professionals 2001, Top 0.5% Cited Researcher, Inst. for Scientific Information 2001, America's Top Doctors, Castle Connolly Medical Publishers 2001, American Heart Asscn's Top Ten Research Advances 2001, Gill Heart Inst. Award for Outstanding Contribs to Cardiovascular Medicine 2002, Dr William Beaumont Award in Medicine, American Medical Asscn 2002, Andreas R. Gruntzig Award, Swiss Soc. of Cardiology 2002, Silver Medal for Outstanding Physician/Scientist, European Soc. of Cardiology 2004, Most Influential Physician Executive in Healthcare by Modern Healthcare journal 2012. *Publications include:* The Creative Destruction of Medicine 2012, The Patient Will See You Now: The Future of Medicine is in Your Hands 2015; ed. of 30 medical books and author of more than 1,600 articles in medical and scientific journals. *Leisure interests:* family, golf, travel, reading. *Address:* Scripps Translational Science Institute, 3344 North Torrey Pines Court, Suite 300, La Jolla, CA 92037, USA (office). *Telephone:* (858) 554-5708 (office). *E-mail:* etopol@scripps.edu (office). *Website:* www.stsiweb.org (office); www.scripps.edu/research (office).

TOPOLÁNEK, Mirek; Czech politician; b. 15 May 1956, Vsetín; m.; three c.; ed mil. high school in Opava, Brno Univ. of Tech.; Project Designer, later Ind. Designer, OKD Ostrava 1980–87; Head Designer Specialist, Energoproject Praha, Ostrava Works 1987–91; Exec. Dir then Man. Dir VAE Ltd (later VAE Inc.) 1991–96, Chair. 1996; active in citizens forum 1989; mem. Municipal Corpn of Ostrava-Poruba 1990–94; Senator 1995–2004; mem. Civic Democratic Party (ODS) 1994–, Vice-Chair. 1996–98, Chair. 2002–10; mem. Cttee for Economy, Agric. and Transport, Org. Cttee and Chair. Sub-cttee for Power Eng, Vice-Pres. of Senate 2002–04; Chair. ODS Senate Club 1990–2002; Prime Minister June–Oct. 2006 (resgnd), reinstated Jan. 2007–09 (resgnd); cand. in presidential election 2018; mem. Bd Asscn for Restoration and Devt of Northern Moravian Region and Silesia, Mining Coll., Univ. of Tech., Ostrava, Jagello Asscn.

TOPPO, HE Cardinal Telesphore Placidus, DD; Indian ecclesiastic; b. 15 Oct. 1939, Jhargaon, Gumla Dist, Jharkhand; s. of Ambrose Toppo and Sofia Xalxo; ed Lievens Barway Boys' Secondary School, Chainpur, St Xavier's Coll., Ranchi, Pontifical Urban Univ., Rome, Italy, Univ. of Ranchi; ordained priest 1969; f. apostolic school for cands to priesthood from Munda Tribe; Prof. and Asst to Dir of St Joseph's High School, Torpa; Bishop of Dumka 1978; Coadjutor Archbishop of Ranchi 1984, Archbishop of Ranchi 1985–2018; attended Eighth Ordinary Ass. of World Synod of Bishops, Vatican City 1990, Special Ass. for Asia of World Synod of Bishops, Vatican City 1998, Second Special Ass. for Europe of World Synod of Bishops, Vatican City 1999, Tenth Ordinary Ass. of World Synod of Bishops, Vatican City 2001; cr. Cardinal (Cardinal Priest of Sacro Cuore di Gesù agonizzante a Vitinia) (first tribal cardinal of India—Oraon of Kurukh tribe) 2003; participated in Papal Conclave 2005, 2013; Pres.-Del. 11th Gen. Ordinary Ass. of World Synod of Bishops 2005; Pres. Catholic Bishops' Conf. of India 2004–08; fmr Vice-Pres. Conf. of Catholic Bishops of India, Pres. 2004–06, 2011–13, mem. Special Comm. for Evangelization, Comm. for Inter-religious Dialogue; mem. Pontifical Council for Inter-Religious Dialogue, Bishops' Friends of the Focalare Movt, Cen. Cttee Fed. of Asian Bishops' Confs, Advisory Council Margareta Weisser Foundation for Indigenous Tribal Peoples in Asia, Governing Body Indo-German Social Service Soc., New Delhi, Nat. Educ. Group, Congregation for the Evangelization of Peoples; Chair. Regional Bishops' Council, Jharkhand Bishops and Major Superiors Forum; fmr Chair. Office of Peace and Harmony of the FABC; Chancellor Faculty of Theology, Ranchi; mem. Governing Body Vikas Maitri, Ranchi, St Xavier's Coll., Ranchi, Nirmala Coll., Hinoo, Ursuline BEd Coll., Lohardaga; Pres. Chotanagpur Catholic Mission Co-operative Credit Soc., Catholic Charities, Ranchi; Patron Sarva Dharma Milan Parishad, Ranchi, Citizens' Forum, Ranchi; Managing Trustee Jharkhand Antyodaya Public Charitable Trust; Jharkhand Ratan, Lok Sewa Samity, Ranchi 2002. *Address:* c/o Archbishop's House, PO Box 5, Purulia Road, Ranchi 834 001, Jharkhand, India (office). *E-mail:* telestoppo@rediffmail.com.

TOPTAN, Köksal; Turkish politician; b. 2 Sept. 1943, Rize; m.; three c.; ed Law Faculty, Istanbul Univ.; mem. Büyük Millet Meclisi (Grand Nat. Ass., Parl.) from Zonguldak 1977–91, 2007–, from Bartin 1991–2002, fmr Chair. Parl. Justice Cttee, Parl. Speaker 2007–09; Minister of State 2007–09; Minister of Educ. 1991–93; Minister of Culture Oct. 1995; Head, Türkiyem (charity); mem. Dogru Yol Party 1986–99; mem. Justice and Development Party (AKP) 2002–. *Address:* Büyük Millet Meclisi (Grand National Assembly), 06543 Bakanlýklar, Ankara, Turkey. *Telephone:* (312) 4205290. *Fax:* (312) 4205296. *E-mail:* koksal.toptan@tbmm.gov.tr (home); info@koksaltoptan.net. *Website:* www.tbmm.gov.tr; www.koksaltoptan.com.

TOQAEV, Qasım-Jomart Kemelulı, DPolSci; Kazakhstani diplomatist, politician and fmr UN official; *Acting President;* b. 17 May 1953, Almatı, Kazakh SSR,

USSR; s. of Kemel Tokayev and Turar Shabarbayeva; m. Nadezhda Tokayeva 1983; one s.; ed Moscow State Inst. of Int. Relations, Beijing Language Inst., People's Repub. of China, Diplomatic Acad., Ministry of Foreign Affairs of USSR, Moscow; joined Ministry of Foreign Affairs of USSR 1975, posted to Soviet Embassy in Singapore 1975–79, Attaché, Third Sec., Ministry of Foreign Affairs 1979–83, Second Sec. of Dept 1984–85, Second, then First Sec., then Counsellor, Soviet Embassy in Beijing 1985–91, Deputy Foreign Minister of Kazakhstan 1992–93, First Deputy Foreign Minister 1993–94, Minister of Foreign Affairs 1994–99, Deputy Prime Minister March–Oct. 1999, Prime Minister of Kazakhstan Oct. 1999–2002 (resgnd), Sec. of State – Minister of Foreign Affairs 2002–07; Chair. (Speaker) of the Senate 2007–11, 2013–19; Acting Pres. of Kazakhstan (following resignation of Nursultan Nazarbayev) 2019–; Dir-Gen., UN Office at Geneva (UNOG) 2011–13, also Under-Sec.-Gen. and Personal Rep. of UN Sec.-Gen. to Conf. on Disarmament, also Sec.-Gen., Conf. on Disarmament; signed Comprehensive Nuclear-Test-Ban Treaty (CTBT), New York 1996, Treaty on a Nuclear-Weapons-Free Zone in Cen. Asia (CANWFZ), Semipalatinsk (now Semey) 2005; Hon. Prof., Dr of the Diplomatic Acad. and mem. Bd of Trustees, Ministry of Foreign Affairs of Russian Fed.; Hon. Dean of Geneva School of Diplomacy; Parasat (Nat. Award) 1996, Astana Medal, Independence Medal, First Pres. (Nat. Award) 2004, Friendship (Russia) 2004, Yaroslav Mudry (Ukraine) 2007. *Publications include:* How it Was… Disturbance in Beijing 1993, United Nations: Half a Century of Serving for Peace 1995, Under the Banner of Independence 1997, Kazakhstani Foreign Policy in the Context of Globalisation 2000, Diplomacy of the Republic of Kazakhstan 2001, Meeting up the Challenge 2003, Light and Shadow – Essays of the Diplomat 2007. *Leisure interests:* reading, playing tennis, listening to modern music. *Address:* Office of the President of the Senate (Senat), 010000 Nur-Sultan, Abay d-h 33, Parliament House, Kazakhstan (office). *Telephone:* (7172) 74-72-39 (office). *Fax:* (7172) 24-26-19 (office). *E-mail:* smimazh@parlam.kz (office). *Website:* www.parlam.kz (office).

TORFS, Henri Maria Dymphna André Laurent (Rik), PhD; Belgian canon law scholar, academic and university administrator; *Rector, Katholieke Universiteit Leuven;* b. 16 Oct. 1956, Turnhout; ed Sint-Gummaruscollege (Lier), Katholieke Universiteit Leuven (Catholic Univ. of Louvain), Univ. of Strasbourg, France; fmr Senator for Christian Democratic and Flemish party in Belgian Fed. Parl.; Asst Prof., Faculty of Canon Law, Katholieke Universiteit Leuven 1988–96, Prof. 1996–, Dean of the Faculty 1994–2003, 2009–13, Rector Katholieke Universiteit Leuven 2013–; Guest Prof., Univ. of Stellenbosch, Univ. of Paris, Univ. of Nijmegen, Univ. of Strasbourg; mem. Academic Bd Int. Center for Law and Religion Studies, Brigham Young Univ., USA; mem. Bd of Experts, Int. Religious Liberty Asscn; fmr Pres. and Bd mem. European Consortium for Church and State Research; Founder and Bd mem. Working Group Nederlandstalige Canonisten (Dutch-speaking Canonists); mem. Comm. for Intercultural Dialogue 2005–, Commissie ter invulling van de cursus maatschappelijke oriëntatie 2006–, Les Assises de l'Interculturalité 2009–; adviser to Govt of Romania regarding the protection of religious minorities. *Publications include:* Het huwelijk als levensgemeenschap. Een kerkrechtelijke benadering 1990, Mensen en rechten in de Kerk 1993, De kardinaal heeft verdriet 2002, Voor het zinken de kerk uit 2004, Religie, vrede en onvrede 2005, Lof der lankmoedigheid 2006, Het hellend vla 2008, Wie gaat er dan de wereld redden? (Liberales Prize) 2009. *Address:* Rectorial Offices, Naamsestraat 22, Box 5000, 3000 Leuven, Belgium (office). *Telephone:* (16) 324067 (office); (16) 324066 (office). *Fax:* (16) 324196 (office). *E-mail:* rik.torfs@kuleuven.be (office). *Website:* www.kuleuven.be (office); www.riktorfs.be (office).

TORIBIONG, Johnson, LLM, DIur; Palauan lawyer, diplomatist, politician and fmr head of state; b. 22 July 1946; m. Valeria Toribiong; ed Univ. of Colorado and Univ. of Washington Law School, USA; fmr mem. Senate; Amb. to Taiwan 2001–08; Pres. of Palau 2009–13.

TORIHARA, Mitsunori; Japanese business executive; *Senior Corporate Advisor, Tokyo Gas;* b. 12 March 1943; ed Univ. of Tokyo; joined Tokyo Gas 1967, Rep. Dir, Exec. Vice-Pres., Chief Exec. of Strategic Planning Div. and in charge of Internal Audit Dept and Compliance Dept 2003–04, Rep. Dir, Exec. Vice-Pres., Chief Exec. of Corp. Communication Div. and in charge of Compliance Dept 2004–06, Rep. Dir, Pres. and CEO 2006–10, mem. Bd of Dirs and Chair. 2010–14, Sr Corp. Advisor 2014–; est. Tokyo Football Club Co. Ltd 1998; Chair. Japanese Paralympic Cttee 2011. *Leisure interests:* football. *Address:* Tokyo Gas, 1-5-20 Kaigan, Minato-ku, Tokyo 105-8527, Japan (office). *Telephone:* (3) 5400-3888 (office). *E-mail:* tgir@tokyo-gas.co.jp (office). *Website:* www.tokyo-gas.co.jp (office).

TORKUNOV, Anatoly Vasilyevich, Cand Hist, DrPolSci; Russian academic and diplomatist; *Rector, Moscow State Institute of International Relations;* b. 26 Aug. 1950, Moscow; m.; one d.; ed Moscow State Inst. of Int. Relations (MGIMO Univ.); teacher Moscow State Inst. of Int. Relations 1974–, Pro-Rector 1977–, Dean Chair. of Int. Relations, then First Pro-Rector 1986–; diplomatic service in People's Democratic Repub. of Korea 1971–72, in USA 1983–86; Rector, Moscow State Inst. of Int. Relations 1992–; Pres. Russian UN Asscn; mem. Expert Analytical Council, Attestation Bd Ministry of Russian Asscn of Int. Studies, Scientific Council of Security Council of Russian Fed., Russian Acad. of Nat. Sciences, Acad. of Sciences of Higher Schooling, Nat. Russian Cttee on problems of UNESCO; Co-Pres. Trianon Dialogue civil society forum; mem. Editorial Bd journals Global Gov. (USA), Mezhdunarodnaya Zhizn, Moscovsky Zhurnal Mezhdunarodnogo Prava, Bisnes i Politika; mem. Russian Acad. of Sciences; Order of Friendship between Peoples, Order of Merit, Order of Honour, Order of Diplomatic Merit (Repub. of Korea); Medals for Labour Merit, 850th Anniversary of Moscow, 300 Years of Russian Navy. *Publications:* seven monographs and over 170 scientific publs on int. relations, problems of Russian foreign policy, Asian-Pacific Region, Korea including: The War in Korea 1950–1953 Tokyo 2000, History of Korea, Moscow 2003, Contemporary International Relations and Russian Foreign Policy, Moscow 2004. *Leisure interests:* theatre, music. *Address:* Office of the Rector, Moscow State Institute of International Relations, 117454 Moscow, Vernadskogo prosp. 76, Russia (office). *Telephone:* (495) 434-91-63 (office). *Fax:* (495) 434-90-61 (office). *E-mail:* tork@mgimo.ru (office). *Website:* www.mgimo.ru (office).

TÖRMÄLÄ, Pertti, DPhil; Finnish scientist and academic; b. 26 Nov. 1945, Tampere; s. of Matti Törmälä and Elma Virtanen; m. 1st Kirsti Miettinen 1967 (dissolved); two d.; m. 2nd Mirja Talasoja 1995; Assoc. Prof. of Non-Metallic Materials, Tampere Univ. of Tech. 1975, Prof. of Fibre Raw Materials, Prof. of Plastics Tech. and Head Inst. of Plastics Tech. 1985–95; fmr Research Prof., Acad. of Finland, Acad. Prof. and Head of Inst. of Biomaterial Tech. 1995–2005; Chair. and Chief Scientific Officer Bioretec Ltd 2005–11; mem. Bd of Dirs Bioretec Ltd 2011–; Hon. DMed; Nat. Inventor Prize 1986, Nordic Tech. Prize 1988. *Publications include:* eight textbooks, 150 patents and more than 800 scientific papers. *Leisure interests:* exercise, music. *Address:* Lapintie 5 C 83, 33100 Tampere, Finland (home). *Telephone:* (40) 5146944 (home). *E-mail:* pertti.tormala@bioretec.com (home). *Website:* www.bioretec.com.

TORNATORE, Giuseppe; Italian filmmaker; b. 27 May 1956, Bagheria, Palermo, Sicily; debut as dir at age 16, with short film Il Carretto. *Television films include:* Ritratto di un Rapinatore, Incontro con Francesco Rosi, Scrittori Siciliani e Cinema: Verga, Pirandello, Brancati and Sciascia and Il Diario di Guttuso, Il grande Fausto 1995. *Feature films include:* writer and dir: Il Camorrista (The Professor) 1987, Cinema Paradiso (Special Jury Prize, Cannes Festival 1989) 1988, Stanno Tutti Bene (Everybody's Fine) 1991, Una Pura formalità (A Pure Formality) 1994, Uomo delle Stelle (Starmaker) 1995, La Leggenda del pianista sull'oceano (The Legend of the Pianist on the Ocean) 1998, Malèna 2000, The Unknown Woman 2006, Baarìa 2009, Deception 2013, La corrispondenza 2016. *Documentaries include:* Ethnic Minorities in Sicily (Best Documentary, Salerno Film Festival 1982), L'ultimo gattopardo: Ritratto di Goffredo Lombardo 2010.

TÖRNUDD, Klaus, PhD; Finnish diplomatist (retd) and academic; b. 26 Dec. 1931, Helsinki; s. of Allan Törnudd and Margit Niininen; m. Mirja Siirala 1960; one s. one d.; ed Univ. of Helsinki, Univ. of Paris and School of Advanced Int. Studies, Johns Hopkins Univ., Washington, DC; joined Foreign Service 1958, served at Perm. Mission to UN, New York 1961–64, Embassy in Cairo 1964–66, Embassy in Moscow 1971–73, CSCE 1973–74; Prof. of Int. Politics, Univ. of Tampere 1967–71; Deputy Dir of Political Affairs, Ministry for Foreign Affairs 1974–77, Dir 1977–81, Under-Sec. of State for Political Affairs 1983–88; Perm. Rep. to the UN, New York 1988–91; Fellow, Harvard Univ., USA 1991–92; Sr Adviser, Ministry for Foreign Affairs 1992–93; Amb. to France and to UNESCO 1993–96; mem. Sr Faculty, Geneva Centre for Security Policy 1997–98; Visiting Prof., Nat. Defence Coll. of Finland 1998–2003; Ed. Co-operation and Conflict (Nordic Journal of Int. Politics) 1968–70, mem. Editorial Bd 1976–79; mem. Editorial Bd of Ulkopolitiikka-Utrikespolitik 1983–87; Chair. of Bd Tampere Peace Research Inst. 1978–82; Chair. UN Study Group on Nuclear Weapon-Free Zones 1983–85; mem. Bd of Trustees UNITAR 1984–88; mem. of Bd of Govs IAEA 1985–87; mem. UN Sec.-Gen.'s Advisory Bd on Disarmament Matters 1991–96; Dr hc (Åbo Akademi Univ.) 2002. *Publications include:* several books on Finnish politics and int. affairs. *Address:* Tempelgatan 8 A, 00100 Helsinki, Finland (home). *Telephone:* (9) 490159 (home). *E-mail:* klaus.toernudd@kolumbus.fi (home).

TÖRÖK, László, DTech, DSc; Hungarian archaeologist and academic; *Research Professor Emeritus, Archaeological Institute, Research Centre for Humanities, Hungarian Academy of Sciences;* b. 13 May 1941, Budapest; s. of László Török and Mária Giesz; m. Erzsébet Sződy 1984 (died 2012); ed Budapest Univ. of Tech. Sciences, Eötvös Loránd Univ.; Research Fellow, Archaeological Inst., Hungarian Acad. of Sciences 1964, Sr Research Fellow 1985, Adviser 1991, Research Prof. 2004–12, Research Prof. Emer. 2012–; Lecturer, Eötvös Loránd Univ. of Arts and Sciences, Dept of Egyptology 1972, Hon. Prof. 1992–; Visiting Prof., Dept of Classics, Univ. of Bergen, Norway 1980, 1989–92, 1994–99; Overseas Visiting Scholar, St John's Coll. Cambridge 1998; Vice-Pres. of the Int. Soc. for Nubian Studies 1990–2002; Gen. Ed. of Antaeus (periodical) 1984–99; mem., Norwegian Acad. of Science and Letters 1994; mem., Hungarian Acad. of Science 2004; Albert Reckitt Archaeological Lecture, British Acad. 1995; research into ancient history and archaeology of Middle Nile Region and Hellenistic and late antique art of Egypt; Dr hc (Univ. of Bergen, Norway) 2000. *Publications:* Economic Offices and Officials in Meroitic Nubia 1978, Der meroitische Staat 1986, The Royal Crowns of Kush 1987, Late Antique Nubia 1988, Coptic Antiquities I–II 1993, Fontes Historiae Nubiorum I 1994, II 1996, III 1998, IV 2000 (with co-authors), Hellenistic and Roman Terracottas from Egypt 1995, The Birth of an Ancient African State 1995, Meroe City: An Ancient African Capital 1997, The Kingdom of Kush: Handbook of the Napatan-Meroitic Civilization 1997, The Hunting Centaur 1998, The Image of the Ordered World in Ancient Nubian Art 2002, Transfigurations of Hellenism: Aspects of Late Antique Art in Egypt AD 250–700 2005, Between Two Worlds: The Frontier Region Between Ancient Nubia and Egypt 3700 BC – 500 AD 2009, Hellenizing Art in Ancient Nubia 300 BC – AD 250 and its Egyptian Models: A Study in Acculturation 2011, Adoption and Adaptation: The Sense of Culture Transfer between Ancient Nubia and Egypt 2011, Herodotus in Nubia 2014; over 100 articles. *Leisure interest:* reading (belles-lettres). *Address:* MTA Bölcsészettudományi Kutatóközpont Régészeti Intézet, 1014 Budapest, Úri utca 49, Hungary (office). *Telephone:* 70-322-1140 (mobile). *Fax:* (1) 224-6719 (office). *E-mail:* tl.napata@freemail.hu (office).

TOROSSIAN, Tigran, PhD, DPolSci; Armenian engineer and politician; b. 14 April 1956, Yerevan; m.; one d.; ed Yerevan Polytechnic Inst.; Engineer, then Leading Engineer, Yerevan Scientific Research Inst. of Math. Machines 1978–88, Subdivision Head, then Scientific Assoc. 1988–95; mem., Cen. Electoral Comm. 1996–98; Ed.-in-Chief, Republican Party newspaper 1997–98; Deputy, Nat. Ass. (Republican Party of Armenia) 1999–, Vice-Chair. Azgayin Zhoghov (Nat. Ass.) 1999–2006, Chair. 2006–08, Chair. ad hoc Cttee on Constitutional Amendments 2001–03, ad hoc Cttee on Matters of Integration in European Structures 2003–08; Head of Armenian Del., Parl. Ass. of Council of Europe, Vice-Chair. Parl. Ass. of the Council of Europe European Democrat Group 2004–07; Vice-Chair. Cttee on the Honouring of Obligations and Commitments by Mem. States of Council of Europe 2006–07; mem. Party Bd Republican Party of Armenia 1993–2008, Deputy Chair. 1998–2005, Deputy Chair. Republican Party of Armenia 2005–08; Medal for Exceptional Services to Motherland 2006, Oder of St M. Mashtots of NKR 2007; Hon. DSc (Univ. of Artsakh); First Prize for The Best Scientific Work (Social Sciences), Competition of Nat. Science Acad. 2009. *Achievements include:* holder of ten eng patents. *Publications:* more than 30 scientific studies in math., four monographs and more than 40 scientific studies in political science and about 200 articles. *Telephone:* (10) 51-34-47 (office). *E-mail:* toros@parliament.am (office); t.tigran@yahoo.com (office).

TORP, Niels A., DipArch; Norwegian architect; *Principal, Niels Torp Arkitekter MNAL;* b. 8 March 1940, Oslo; s. of Ernst Torp and Nini Torp (née Butenschøn); m. Bente Poulsson; one s. three d.; ed Norges Tekniske Høgskole, Trondheim, The Norwegian Inst. Rome; joined Torp & Torp Arkitekter MNAL 1965, Partner 1970, Man. 1974, Man., Prin. Niels Torp Arkitekter MNAL 1984–; visiting lecturer at architectural schools in Norway and other European countries; major works: Giskehagen residential homes 1986, Scandinavian Airlines System (SAS) HQ, Stockholm 1987, Aker Brygge (dockland devt Oslo) 1988, HQ Den Norske Bank 1988, Hamar Olympiahall 1991, Alna Shopping Centre, Oslo 1996, railway station/bus terminal, Gothenburg 1996, Christiania Qvartalet 1996, BA HQ, London 1997, Colosseum Park, Oslo 1997, Oslo Airport Gardermoen (with Aviaplan) 1998, airport control tower and airport hotel, Oslo 1998, Papendrop – Utrecht, The Netherlands, five office bldgs 1999, NSB (Norwegian Railway) HQ, Oslo 1999, devt plans for towns Larvik, Sandefjord, Drammen, Ås, Elverum, Hamar and Bodø, Masterplan Tjuvholmen, Oslo 2002, Nydalen Campus BI business school, Oslo 2005, Culture Centre Larvik 2007, AkerHus office bldg, Oslo 2008, The Soloist office bldg, Belfast 2009, Værnes Hotel, Trondheim 2009, Hotel Park Inn, Oslo Airport 2010, Vulkan Hotel, Oslo 2011, Tjuvholmen F1 South, Oslo 2011, NMD Oslo 2011, Jordan Airlines HQ, Amman 2012, The Edge Hotel, Tromsø 2014, The Eagle Hotel, Bergen 2014, Statoil HQ, Bergen 2014; A.C. Houens Legacy, Sundts Prize for Architectural Merits, Awards from the Stone Asscn, Fine Art Award (Oslo City Council), Carl M. Egers Legacy, Europa Nostra Awards, Prize for Built Environment (Norwegian Dept of Environment), Kasper Salin Prize (Sweden), European Award for Steel Structures, Swedish Stone Asscn Award, Concrete Award (Norway), British Construction Industry Award 1998, Brunel Award 1998, Aesthetic Counsel Diploma, Bærum, Norway 1998, Parelius Scholarship 1998, Glulam Award 1999 (with Aviaplan), RIBA Award for Architecture 1999, Jacob Award for Design 1999, Civic Trust Award 2000, Oslo Council Jubilee Prize 2006, Int. Property Prize, Int. Real Estate Fed. (FIABCI) 2008, Houen Fonds Diploma 2008, European Commercial Property Awards 2010, City Prize 2012, Concrete Award 2012. *Leisure interests:* music, playing piano, sailing. *Address:* Industrigaten 59, PO Box 5387, 0304 Oslo, Norway (office). *Telephone:* 23-36-68-00 (office). *Fax:* 23-36-68-01 (office). *E-mail:* firmapost@nielstorp.no (office). *Website:* www.nielstorp.no (office).

TORRA, Quim; Spanish (Catalan) lawyer, writer and politician; *President of the Government of Catalonia;* b. (Joaquim Torra i Pla), 28 Dec. 1962, Blanes, Catalonia; m. Carola Miró; one s. two d.; ed Autonomous Univ. of Barcelona; worked as lawyer and exec. for 20 years in Winterthur Group; f. A Contra Vent Editors 2008; Pres. Sobirania i Justícia 2010–11; Dir, Foment de Ciutat Vella, SA 2011–15, Born Centre de Cultura i Memòria 2012–15, Revista de Catalunya 2015–, Center for Contemporary Subject Studies, Generalitat 2016–17; mem. Assemblea Nacional Catalana 2012; Vice-Pres. Catalan independence Òmnium Cultural 2013–15, Pres. July–Dec. 2015, currently mem.; Chair. Memorial Museum of Exile (MUME) 2016–; Pres. of the Govt of Catalonia 2018–; mem. Bd of Museums 2015–17; mem. Bar Asscn of Barcelona; Premi Carles Rahola d'Assaig 2009. *Publications include:* Ganivetades Suïsses 2007, Periodisme? Permetin! La vida i els Articles d'Eugeni Xammar 2008, El Bibliobús de la Llibertat 2008, Viatge Involuntari a la Catalunya Impossible 2010, Honorables: Cartes a la Pàtria Perduda 2011, Un Bohemi al Cabaret del Món: Vida de Manuel Fontdevila, un Senyor de Granollers 2013, Els Últims 100 Metres: el Full de Ruta per Guanyar la República Catalana 2016, Muriel Casals i la Revolució dels Somriures 2016, El quadern suís 2018. *Website:* www.president.cat/pres_gov/president/ca/president/biografia.html.

TORRANCE, Sam, MBE, OBE; British professional golfer and sports commentator; b. 24 Aug. 1953, Largs, Scotland; s. of Bob Torrance and June Torrance; m. Suzanne Danielle 1988; one s. two d.; professional golfer 1970–; has played in eight Ryder Cups (European Capt. 2002) and represented Scotland on numerous occasions; winner Scottish PGA Championship 1978, 1980, 1985, 1991, 1993; mem. Dunhill Cup team (eight times), World Cup team (11 times), Hennessy Cognac Cup team (five times), Double Diamond team (three times); winner of 28 tournaments world-wide since 1972, including 1976, Piccadilly MedalMartini International 1976, Carroll's Irish Open 1981, Benson & Hedges Spanish Open 1982, Portuguese Open 1982, 1983, Scandinavian Enterprise Open 1983, Tunisian Open 1984, Benson & Hedges International Open 1984, Sanyo Open 1984, Johnnie Walker Monte Carlo Open 1985, Lancia Italian Open 1987, Mercedes German Masters 1990, Jersey European Airways Open 1991, Kronenbourg Open 1993, Heineken Open 1993, Catalan Open 1993, Honda Open 1993, Hamburg Open 1993, Italian Open 1995, Murphy's Irish Open 1995, Collingtree British Masters 1995, Peugeot Open de France 1998; played US Sr Tour 2003–04, returned to European Sr Tour 2004–, winner Travis Perkins Senior Masters 2004, Irvine Whitlock Seniors Classic 2005, De Vere PGA Seniors Championship 2005, Bendinat London Seniors Masters 2005, 2007, Sharp Italian Seniors Open 2006, AIB Irish Seniors Open 2006, PGA Seniors Championship 2006, Scottish Seniors Open 2006, OKI Castellón Open España – Senior Tour Championship 2008, DGM Barbados Open 2009; Capt. winning European team in Asahi Glass Four Tours Championship, Adelaide 1991; Capt. winning British Ryder Cup Team 2002, Vice-Capt. 2014 (winners); works as a commentator for BBC Sport golf coverage; provided commentary, with Kelly Tilghman, for Tiger Woods PGA Tour 09; Sir Henry Cotton Rookie of the Year 1972, winner European Seniors Tour's Order of Merit 2005, 2006. *Television:* A Question of Sport five times since 2005. *Publications:* Sam: The Autobiography of Sam Torrance 2003. *Leisure interests:* snooker, tennis. *Address:* c/o CSA, 90 High Street, Burnham, Bucks., SL1 7JT, England. *Website:* www.europeantour.com/europeantour/players/playerid=193.

TORRES, Ralph, BA; American politician and head of government; *Governor, Commonwealth of the Northern Mariana Islands;* b. 6 Aug. 1979, Saipan; s. of Vicente Villagomez Torres and Primitiva Concepcion Deleon Guerrero; m. Diann Mendiola Tudela; six c.; ed Boise State Univ.; Admin. Torres Brothers, LLC 2004–08; Rep. Northern Marianas Commonwealth Legislature 2008–10, Senator 2010–15, Senate Pres. 2013–15, Chair. House Standing Cttee on Health, Education and Welfare 2008–10, Senate Standing Cttee on Resources and Economics 2010–13, on Health and Welfare 2010–15, on Rules and Procedures 2013–15; Lt-Gov. Commonwealth of the Northern Mariana Islands Jan.–Dec. 2015, Gov. Dec. 2015–; Chair. Pacific Islands Development Devt Bank 2019–; Republican. *Address:* Office of the Governor, Juan A. Sablan Memorial Building, Caller Box 10007, Capital Hill, Saipan MP 96950, Mariana Islands (office). *Telephone:* (670) 664-2200 (office). *Fax:* (670) 664-2211 (office). *E-mail:* scogumoro@gov.mp (office). *Website:* www.gov.mp (office).

TORRES-PEIMBERT, Silvia, PhD; Mexican astronomer and academic; *Professor Emerita, Instituto de Astronomía, Universidad Nacional Autónoma de México (UNAM);* b. (Silvia Torres Castilleja), 26 June 1940, Mexico City; d. of Antonio Torres and Virginia Castilleja; m. Manuel Peimbert; one s. one d.; ed Univ. of California, Berkeley, USA; Prof., Faculty of Sciences and Instituto de Astronomía, Universidad Nacional Autónoma de México (UNAM), Head of Grad. Programme of Astronomy, now Prof. Emer., also Coordinator of Physical, Math. and Eng Sciences 2009; Ed. Revista Mexicana de Astronomia y Astrofisica for over 20 years; mem. American Astronomical Soc., Int. Astronomical Union (fmr Vice-Pres.); mem. UNESCO Global Scientific Cttee; Fellow, Acad. of Sciences for the Developing World; Dr hc (Instituto Nacional de Astrofísica, Óptica y Electrónica) 2015; Premio Nacional de Ciencias 2007, Premio Heberto Castillo 2007, Premio Universidad Nacional en Ciencias Exactas Hans A. Bethe Award, American Physical Soc., L'Oréal-UNESCO Women in Science Award (Latin America) 2011. *Radio:* producer of radio programme PERFILES on the academic activity of UNAM. *Address:* Universidad Nacional Autonoma de Mexico, Inst de Astronomía, Circuito exterior s/n Ciudad Universitaria, México, DF 04510, Mexico (office). *Telephone:* (55) 5622-3945 (office). *E-mail:* silvia@astro.unam.mx (office). *Website:* www.astroscu.unam.mx (office).

TORRES VILLA, Carlos, BS, MS; Spanish business executive; *Group Executive Chairman and CEO, Banco Bilbao Vizcaya Argentaria SA;* b. 24 Feb. 1966, Salamanca; ed Massachusetts Inst. of Tech. and its Sloan School of Man., USA, Universidad Nacional de Educación a Distancia; with McKinsey & Co. 1990–2002, elected Partner 1997; Corp. Dir of Strategy and mem. Exec. Cttee, Endesa 2002–07, Chief Financial Officer 2007–08; Chair. and CEO Isofotón 2008; mem. Exec. Cttee and Head of Strategy and Corp. Devt, BBVA 2008–14, mem. Exec. Cttee and Head of Digital Banking 2014–15, CEO BBVA 2015–, Group Exec. Chair. 2018–. *Address:* Banco Bilbao Vizcaya Argentaria SA, Paseo de la Castellana 81, 28046 Madrid (office); Banco Bilbao Vizcaya Argentaria SA, Plaza San Nicolás 4, Bilbao 48005, Vizcaya, Spain (office). *Telephone:* (915) 5377690 (Madrid) (office); (944) 875555 (Vizcaya) (office). *Fax:* (91) 3747610 (Madrid) (office); (944) 876161 (Vizcaya) (office). *Website:* www.bbva.com (office); www.bbva.es (office).

TORRICELLI, Robert G., JD, MPA; American business executive and fmr politician; *Partner, Panepinto Properties;* b. 26 Aug. 1951, Paterson, NJ; ed Rutgers and Harvard Univs; called to the Bar, NJ 1978; Deputy Legis. Counsel, Office of Gov. of NJ 1975–77; counsel to Vice-Pres. Mondale, Washington, DC 1978–81; pvt. legal practice, Washington, DC 1981–82; mem. US House of Reps 1983–97; Senator from New Jersey 1997–2003; f. Rosemont Asscn 2003; currently Partner, Panepinto Properties; Democrat. *Address:* Panepinto Properties, Harborside Plaza 10, 3 Second Street, Suite 1203, Jersey City, NJ 07311, USA (office). *Telephone:* (201) 521-9000 (office). *Fax:* (201) 434-3218 (office). *E-mail:* info@panprop.com (office). *Website:* www.panepintoproperties.com (office).

TORRIJOS ESPINO, Martín; Panamanian business executive, politician and fmr head of state; b. 18 July 1963, Panama City; s. of Gen. Omar Torrijos; m. Vivian de Torrijos; one s.; ed Texas A&M Univ., USA; fmr man., McDonald's, Chicago, USA; Sec.-Gen. Democratic Revolutionary Party (PRD) 1999–; cand. for presidential elections 1999; Pres. of Panama 2004–09; Vice-Pres. Conference of Political Parties of Latin America and the Caribbean (COPPAL) 2002–. *Address:* c/o Partido Revolucionario Democrático (PRD), Edif. Policentro, Avda México, entre Calle 26 y 27, Panamá 3, Panama (office).

TORRY, Sir Peter James, GCVO, KCMG; British consultant and fmr diplomatist; b. 2 Aug. 1948, Berlin, Germany; m. Angela Torry; three d.; ed Dover Coll., New Coll., Oxford; joined FCO 1970, Third Sec., Embassy in Havana 1971–73, Second Sec. (Econ.), Embassy in Jakarta 1974–77, First Sec., FCO 1977–81, 1985–89 (later also Counsellor), First Sec. (Political), Embassy in Bonn 1981–85, Counsellor, Embassy in Washington, DC 1989–93, Dir for Personnel and Security, FCO 1993–98, Amb. to Spain 1998–2003, to Germany 2003–07; Sr Adviser, Centrica PLC, Betfair PLC, Celesion AG, White Owl Capital; f. Peter Torry Consultancy Ltd; mem. Advisory Bd Lloyds Pharmacy, Global Econ. Symposium, Kiel Inst.; Policy Fellow, Bonn Inst. for Employment. *Leisure interests:* golf, walking, skiing, books, antique furniture. *Address:* Peter Torry Consultancy Ltd, Flat 17, 192 Emery Hill Street, London, SW1P 1PN, England (office). *E-mail:* info@petertorry.co.uk (office). *Website:* www.petertorry.co.uk (office).

TORSHIN, Aleksander Porfiryevich; Russian politician; b. 27 Nov. 1953, Mitoga, Kamchatsk region; m. Nina Valer'yevna Torshina; two d.; ed All Union Inst. of Law, Moscow State Univ.; teacher, Docent, Acad. of Public Sciences, then functionary, Cen. CPSU Cttee; Deputy Head Div. on Public Relations with Chambers, Factions and Public Orgs, Fed. Ass. of Russian Fed. 1993–95; Statistics Sec., Deputy Chair. Cen. Bank 1995–98; Deputy Chair. Admin of Russian Fed. Govt, Rep. of Russian Fed. Gov. to State Duma (Parl.) 1998–99; Deputy Dir-Gen. Statistics-Sec., State Corp. Agency on Restructuring of Credit Orgs (ARKO) 1999–2001; mem. Yedinaya Rossiya (YeR) (United Russia); mem. Sovet Federatsii (Fed. Council) representing Mari-El Repub. 2001–15, Deputy Chair. 2002, Acting Chair. 2011; Deputy Chair. Parl. Union of Russia and Byelorussia Union 2004; mem. Cttee on Agrarian-Food Policy, Comm. on Regulation and Organization of Parl. Activities, Comm. on Controlling Council of Fed. Activities; Rep. of Govt of Mari-El Repub. to Fed. Ass.

TORSTENDAHL, Rolf, PhD; Swedish historian and academic; *Professor Emeritus of History, Uppsala University;* b. 9 Jan. 1936, Jönköping; s. of Torsten Torstendahl and Ragnhild Torstendahl (née Abrahamsson); m. 1st Anna-Maria Ljung 1960 (died 1987); two s.; m. 2nd Tamara A. Salycheva 1996; ed Uppsala Univ.; Lecturer, Dept of History, Uppsala Univ. 1964–67, Assoc. Prof. 1968–78, Sven Warburg Prof. of History 1978–80, Stockholm Univ.; Prof., Uppsala Univ. 1981–2000, Prof. Emer. 2001–; Prof., Mälardalen Univ. 2002–03; Dir Swedish Collegium for Advanced Study in the Social Sciences 1985–90, Dean of Faculty 1994–99; mem. Royal Swedish Acad. of Letters, History and Antiquities 1982, Norwegian Acad. of Science and Letters 1989, Academia Europaea 1989, Russian Acad. of Sciences, Urals Div. 1995; Dr hc (Russian State Univ. for the Humanities)

2006; Björnstiernas Prize, Royal Swedish Acad. of Letters, History and Antiquities 1976. *Publications include:* Teknologins nytta 1975, Dispersion of Engineers in a Transitional Society 1975, Professions in Theory and History (ed.) 1990, The Formation of Professions (ed.) 1990, Bureaucratization in Northwestern Europe 1880–1985 1991, State Theory and State History (ed.) 1992, History-making (ed.) 1996, State Policy and Gender System (ed.) 1999, An Assessment of Twentieth-Century Historiography (ed.) 2000, Zarozhdenie demokraticheskoi kultury 2005 (English edn 2012), Gjort, tänkt, känt (memoirs) 2011, Professionalizm istorika i istoricheskoe znanie 2015, Rise and Propagation of Historical Professionalism 2015, Den historiografiska revolutionen 1960–1990 2017. *Address:* Department of History, Uppsala University, PO Box 628, 751 26 Uppsala (office); St Olofsgatan 4, 75 312 Uppsala, Sweden (home). *Telephone:* (18) 471-7125 (office); 700-980452 (mobile) (home). *E-mail:* rolftorstendahl@gmail.com (home); rolf.torstendahl@hist.uu.se (office). *Website:* www.hist.uu.se (office).

TORTELIER, Yan Pascal; French conductor and violinist; *Chief Conductor, Iceland Symphony Orchestra;* b. 19 April 1947, Paris; s. of Paul Tortelier and Maud Tortelier; m. Sylvie Brunet-Moret 1970; two s.; ed Paris Conservatoire and Berkshire Music Centre, UK, music studies with Nadia Boulanger, studies in conducting with Franco Ferrara; debut as concert violinist, Royal Albert Hall 1962; has since toured extensively world-wide; Konzertmeister, Assoc. Conductor of Orchestre du Capitole de Toulouse 1974–83; Prin. Conductor and Artistic Dir, Ulster Orchestra 1989–92; Prin. Conductor, BBC Philharmonic 1992–2003, Conductor Laureate 2003–10, Conductor Emer. 2010–; Prin. Guest Conductor, RAM, Pittsburgh Symphony Orchestra 2005–08; Prin. Conductor, Orquestra Sinfónica de São Paulo 2009–11, Hon. Guest Conductor 2012–; Chief Conductor, Iceland Symphony Orchestra 2016–; guest conducting with San Francisco Symphony, Dresden Philharmonic, London Philharmonic, Minnesota Orchestra, Baltimore Symphony, St Petersburg Philharmonic, Sydney Symphony, Melbourne Symphony, others; Hon. DLitt (Ulster) 1992; Dr hc (Lancaster) 1999; First Prize for Violin, Paris Conservatoire 1961. *Recordings include:* Ravel/Debussy/Massenet (BBC Music Magazine Orchestral Award 2012). *Publication:* première orchestration of Ravel's Piano Trio (world première concert 1992). *Leisure interests:* skiing, windsurfing, scuba diving, nature. *Address:* c/o Nicholas Mathias, IMG Artists, Capital Tower, 91 Waterloo Road, London, SE1 8RT, England (office); Iceland Symphony Orchestra, Harpa, Austurbakki 2, 101 Reykjavík, Iceland (office). *Telephone:* (20) 7957-5800 (office). *Fax:* (20) 7957-5801 (office). *E-mail:* nmathias@imgartists.com (office). *Website:* imgartists.com/artist/yan_pascal_tortelier (office); en.sinfonia.is (office).

TORVALDS, Linus Benedict, MSc; Finnish/American computer software developer; *Fellow, Linux Foundation;* b. 28 Dec. 1969, Helsinki; s. of Nils Torvalds and Anna Torvalds; m. Tove Monni; three d.; ed Univ. of Helsinki; fmr teacher and research asst; cr. the Linux kernel and oversaw open source devt of the widely used Linux operating system; with Transmeta 1997, later Transmeta Fellow –2003; Fellow, Open Source Devt Labs Inc. (OSDL) (consortium formed by high-tech cos including IBM, Hewlett-Packard, Intel, AMD, RedHat, Novell and many others, OSDL merged with The Free Standards Group to become Linux Foundation 2007) 2003–; remains the ultimate authority on what new code is incorporated into the standard Linux kernel; Dr hc (Stockholm) 1999, (Helsinki) 2000; asteroid 9793 Torvalds named in his honour 1996, EFF Pioneer Award 1998, Lovelace Medal, British Computer Soc. 2000, InfoWorld Award for Industry Achievement 2000, Takeda Award for Social/Econ. Well-Being (co-recipient) 2001, Vollum Award, Reed Coll. 2005, inducted into Hall of Fellows of the Computer History Museum, Mountain View, Calif. 2008, C&C Prize, NEC Corpn 2010, Millennium Tech. Prize, Technology Acad. Finland (co-recipient) 2012, an inaugural inductee into the Internet Hall of Fame 2012, IEEE Computer Soc. Computer Pioneer Award 2014. *Publications include:* Just for Fun (with David Diamond) 2001; 35 patents worldwide. *Address:* Linux Foundation, 660 York Street, Suite 102, San Francisco, CA 94110, USA (office). *Telephone:* (415) 723-9709 (office). *Fax:* (415) 723-9709 (office). *E-mail:* info@linuxfoundation.org (office). *Website:* www.linuxfoundation.org (office).

TORVILL, Jayne, OBE; British ice skater; b. 7 Oct. 1957; d. of George Torvill and Betty Torvill (née Smart); m. Philip Christensen 1990; ed Clifton Hall Grammar School for Girls; insurance clerk 1974–80; British Pair Skating Champion (with Michael Hutchinson) 1971; British Ice Dance Champion (with Christopher Dean q.v.) 1978–83, 1994; European Ice Dance Champion (with Christopher Dean) 1981–82, 1984, 1994; World Ice Dance Champion (with Christopher Dean) 1981–84; World Professional Ice Dance Champion (with Christopher Dean) 1984, 1985, 1990, 1995, 1996; Olympic Ice Dance Champion (with Christopher Dean) 1984; Olympic Ice Dance Bronze Medal (with Christopher Dean) 1994; Tours include: Australia and NZ 1984, Royal Variety Performance London 1984, world tour with own co. of int. skaters 1985, guest artists with IceCapades 1987, world tour with co. of skaters from Soviet Union 1988, Australia as guests of S Australian Govt 1991, GB with co. of skaters from Ukraine 1992, Torvill & Dean, Face the Music, World Tour, UK, Australia and N America 1994, Stars on Ice tour in USA and Canada 1997, Torvill & Dean Ice Adventures in UK 1997–98, Stars on Ice Tour in USA and Canada 1997–98; choreography includes Stars on Ice in USA 1998–99, 1999–2000, O'Connor and O'Dougherty 1999–2000, GB Nat. Champion Synchronized Skating Team 1999–2000; Hon. MA (Nottingham Trent) 1994; BBC Sportsview Personality of the Year (with Christopher Dean) 1983–84; Figure Skating Hall of Fame (with Christopher Dean) 1989. *Television:* Path of Perfection (Thames Television video) 1984, Fire & Ice (also video) 1986, World Tour (video) 1988, Bladerunners (BBC documentary) 1991, Great Britain Tour (TV special and video) 1992, The Artistry of Torvill and Dean (ABC) 1994, Face the Music (video) 1995, Torvill & Dean: The Story So Far (video) 1996, Bach Cello Suite (with Yo-Yo Ma) 1996, Dancing on Ice. *Publications:* (with Christopher Dean) Torvill and Dean: An Autobiography 1984, Torvill and Dean: Fire on Ice (with Christopher Dean) 1984, Torvill and Dean: Face the Music and Dance 1995, Facing the Music (with Christopher Dean) 1995. *Leisure interests:* theatre, ballet, dogs. *Address:* POB 32, Heathfield, East Sussex, TN21 0BW, England. *Website:* www.torvillanddean.com/jayne.html.

TORY, John Howard, BA, LLB; Canadian lawyer, politician and fmr broadcaster; *Mayor of Toronto;* b. 28 May 1954, Toronto; s. of John Arnold Tory and Elizabeth Tory (née Bacon); m. Barbara Hackett; three s. one d.; ed Univ. of Trinity Coll., Univ. of Toronto, Osgoode Hall Law School, York Univ.; reporter and newscaster, CFTR and CHFI (radio stations), Toronto 1972–79; called to the Bar, Ontario 1980; various positions including Partner at Tory, Tory, DesLauriers & Binnington (law firm, now Torys LLP) 1980–81, 1986–95; Prin. Sec. to Premier and Assoc. Sec. of Cabinet, Office of the Premier of Ont. 1981–85; managed federal election campaign of Kim Campbell 1993; Pres. and CEO Rogers Media (publishing and broadcasting co.) 1995–99, Pres. and CEO Rogers Cable (subsidiary co.) 1999; Chair. Canadian Football League 1991–96; unsuccessful cand. for Mayor of Toronto 2003; mem. Ont. Legis. Ass. for Don Valley West 2005–07, Leader of the Opposition in Ont. 2005–07; Leader Progressive Conservative Party of Ontario 2004–09; hosted radio talkshow, CFRB 2009–14; Chair. Greater Toronto CivicAction Alliance 2010–14; Mayor of Toronto 2014–; fmr mem. Progressive Conservative Party of Ontario, Leader 2004–09; Order of Ont. 2012. *Address:* Office of the Mayor, Toronto City Hall, 2nd Floor, 100 Queen Street West, Toronto, ON M5H 2N2, Canada (office). *Telephone:* (416) 397-3673 (office). *Website:* johntory.ca (office).

TOSATTI, Erio, PhD; Italian physicist and academic; *Professor and Head of Condensed Matter Theory Group, International School For Advanced Studies (SISSA);* ed Univ. of Modena, CERN, Geneva, Scuola Normale Superiore, Pisa; served as Second Lt, Weather Forecast Service, Italian Air Forces 1970–71; staff mem. Italian Research Council, Univ. of Rome 1971–77; Royal Soc./NATO Fellow, Cavendish Lab., Univ. of Cambridge, UK 1972–73; Deutsche Forschungsgemeinschaft Visitor, Univ. of Stuttgart, Germany 1974; Sr NATO Fellow, Stanford Univ., USA 1977; sr staff mem. Italian Research Council and Lecturer, Univ. of Trieste 1977–80; Co-founder and consultant Condensed Matter Programme, Int. Centre for Theoretical Physics, Trieste 1977–, Deputy Head 1990–, Acting Dir 2002–03, Permanent Bd Mem., Trieste and Adriatico Research Confs; Prof. and Head, Condensed Matter Theory Group, Int. School For Advanced Studies (SISSA), Trieste 1980–; Visiting Scientist, RCA Zürich and IBM Zürich Research Labs 1984–85; Visiting Prof., Université Pierre et Marie Curie, Paris 1994, 1996, 2002, 2003, Univ. of NSW, Australia 1999, Donostia Int. Physics Centre, San Sebastian, Spain 2001, Université Pierre et Marie Curie, Paris, France 2002, 2003, Chinese Acad. of Sciences, Beijing and Fudan Univ., Shanghai, China 2004, Raman Research Inst., Bangalore, India 2006, Fudan Univ., Shanghai 2006, Renmin Univ., Beijing and Univ. of Hong Kong 2007, Université Paris-Sud, Orsay, France 2008; mem. Scientific Advisory Cttee, Elettra Synchrotron, Trieste 2002–; mem. Italian Physical Soc., American Physical Soc., European Physical Soc., Accademia Istituto Lombardo (Accademia di Brera) Milan, 2012; Corresp. mem. Accademia Nazionale del Lincei, Rome 2006; Foreign Assoc. mem. NAS; Eli Burstein Lecture Award, Univ. of Pa 1994, Francesco Somaini Triennial Physics Prize 1997, Lamina Aurea di Redù 1999, US Physics Medal for Int. Leadership 2006, Enrico Fermi Prize of the Italian Physical Soc. 2018. *Publications:* co-ed.: Physics of Intercalation Compounds 1981, Fractals in Physics 1986, High-Temperature Superconductors 1987, Towards the Theoretical Understanding of High-Temperature Superconductors 1988, Strongly Correlated Electron Systems I 1990, Strongly Correlated Electron Systems II 1991, Strongly Correlated Electron Systems III 1993, Clusters and Fullerenes 1993, The Physics of Sliding Friction 1996; contrib.: over 460 articles and reviews in int. journals. *Address:* International School For Advanced Studies (SISSA), via Bonomea 265, Room 308, 34136 Trieste, Italy (office). *Telephone:* (40) 3787438 (office). *Fax:* (40) 3787528 (office). *E-mail:* tosatti@sissa.it (office). *Website:* www.sissa.it/~tosatti (office); sites.google.com/site/tosattierio/home.

TOŠOVSKÝ, Josef, BCom; Czech banker; *Chairman, BIS Financial Stability Institute;* b. 28 Sept. 1950, Náchod; m. Bohdana Světlíková; two d.; ed Univ. of Econs, Prague; Assoc. Prof., Univ. of Econs, Prague; banker with Czechoslovak State Bank 1973–, Deputy Dir 1978–, consultant to Bank Chair. 1982; Chief Economist, Živnostenská banka, London 1984–85, Deputy Dir June–Dec. 1989; Consultant to Bank Chair., Prague 1986–89; Chair. Czechoslovak State Bank 1989–92, Gov. 1992, for Czech Nat. Bank 1993–97, 1998–2000; Prime Minister of Czech Repub. 1997–98; Chair. Financial Stability Inst., BIS, Basel, Switzerland 2000–; Dr hc (Mendelova Univ. Brno) 2002; Central Banker of the Year, IMF 1993, European Man. of the Year, European Business Press Fed. 1994, Karel Engliš Prize 1994, European Banker of the Year, Group 20+1 1996, East-West Inst. Award for Leadership in Transition (USA) 2001. *Publications include:* numerous articles in professional press. *Leisure interest:* tennis. *Address:* Financial Stability Institute, Bank for International Settlements, Centralbahnplatz 2, 4002 Basel, Switzerland (office). *Telephone:* (61) 2808074 (office). *Fax:* (61) 2809100 (office). *E-mail:* josef.tosovsky@bis.org (office). *Website:* www.bis.org (office).

TOSUNYAN, Garegin A., CandPhys, Math, Sciences, DrJur; Russian banker; *President, Association of Russian Banks;* b. 14 May 1955, Yerevan; m.; two d. one s.; ed Moscow State Univ., All-Union Jurist Inst. (by correspondence), Acad. of Nat. Economy, Govt of Russian Fed.; worked in United Inst. of Nuclear Studies in Dubna Moscow region; Researcher, All-Union Electrotechnology Inst., Moscow 1977–88, later Sr Researcher, Head of Div.; Chief Expert, Head of Div., Head of Dept, Chief of Dept on Sciences and Tech., Moscow City Council of Deputies 1988–90; Founder and Pres. Technobank 1990–98; first Vice-Pres. Asscn of Russian Banks 1990, Pres. 2002–; Chair. Bd of Dirs Interbanking Finance Corpn 1992–; Head of Dept, Acad. of Nat. Economy 1997–; Head, Banking Law Centre, Inst. of State and Law, Russian Acad. of Sciences 1999–; mem. Council of Banking Reps, Office of Mayor of Moscow 1994–; mem. Consultative Council on Banking Activities, Govt of Russian Fed. 1996–; mem. Bd of Dirs Ardshinbank 2009–; Adviser to Mayor of Moscow on financial and banking problems 1997–, to Chair. of Fed. Council of Fed. Ass. of Russian Fed. 2004–; Adviser to Chair. Govt of Russian Fed. 1998–2000; Foreign mem. Armenian Nat. Acad. of Sciences 2008–; Corresp. mem. Russian Acad. of Sciences 2011–; Honoured Scientist of the Russian Federation 2010. *Publications include:* more than 170 scientific works and articles on problems of the banking system and banking law, and 37 studies, including Banking Business and Banking Law in Russia: Experience, Problems, Perspectives 1995, State Management in the Field of Finance and Credits in Russia (textbook) 1997, Money and Power 2000, Banking Law of the Russian Federation 1999–2002, Market of Self Regulation 2004. *Address:* Association of Russian Banks, Skatertny per. 20 bldg 1, PO Box 41, Moscow 121069, Russia (office). *Telephone:* (495) 291-66-30 (office). *Fax:* (495) 291-66-66 (office). *E-mail:* arb@arb.ru (office). *Website:* www.arb.ru (office).

TOTSKY, Gen. Konstantin Vasilyevich; Russian army officer, diplomatist and government official; b. 23 Feb. 1950, Kagan, Uzbekistan; m.; two d.; ed Higher Frontier Mil. School, Frunze Mil. Acad., Gen. Staff Mil. Acad.; army service in Pacific, Cen. Asian, Transcaucasian, NW Border Dist 1977–89; participated in mil. operations in Afghanistan; Head, Acad. of Fed. Border Service of Russian Fed. 1996–; Dir Fed. Border Service 1998; Chair. Council of Border Forces of CIS Countries 1998–2003; rank of Amb.; Head of Mission of Russian Fed. to NATO 2003–08; apptd Deputy Head of Service, Fed. Service on Supervision in Nature Man. 2009; more than 30 orders and medals.

TÖTTERMAN, Richard Evert Björnson, DPhil, JurLic; Finnish diplomatist; b. 10 Oct. 1926, Helsinki; s. of B. Björn Tötterman and Katharine Clare Wimpenny; m. Camilla S. Veronica Huber 1953; one s. one d.; ed Univ. of Helsinki, Brasenose Coll., Oxford, UK; joined Ministry for Foreign Affairs 1952, diplomatic posts in Stockholm 1954–56, Moscow 1956–58, at Ministry of Foreign Affairs 1958–62, Berne 1962–63, Paris 1963–66; Deputy Dir, Ministry of Foreign Affairs 1966; Sec.-Gen., Office of Pres. of Finland 1966–70; Sec. of State, Ministry of Foreign Affairs 1970–75, Amb. to UK 1975–83, to Switzerland 1983–90, also accred to the Holy See 1988–90; Chair., Multilateral Consultations preparing CSCE 1972–73; Hon. Fellow, Brasenose Coll., Oxford 1982; Hon. GCVO, Hon. OBE; Kt Commdr, Order of the White Rose of Finland; Grand Cross, Order of the Dannebrog (Denmark), Order of Merit (Austria), Order of Orange-Nassau (Netherlands), Order of the Pole Star (Sweden), Order of the Falcon (Iceland), Order of St Olav (Norway), Order of Merit (Poland), Order of the Lion (Senegal), Order of the Banner (Hungary); Grand Officier, Ordre de la Couronne (Belgium); Commdr, Ordre nat. du Mérite; Kt, Order of Vasa (Sweden). *Leisure interests:* music, int. relations. *Address:* Parkgatan 9A, 00140 Helsinki, Finland (home). *Telephone:* (9) 627721 (home).

TOTTI, Francesco; Italian professional footballer (retd); *Director, A S Roma;* b. 27 Sept. 1976, Porta Metronia, Rome; s. of Enzo Totti and Fiorella Totti; m. Ilary Blasi 2005; one s. one d.; striker/attacking midfielder; youth player for Fortitudo 1984, Smit Trastevere 1984–86, Lodigiani 1986–89, Roma 1989–92; sr player for AS Roma 1993–2017 (retd), apptd Capt. 1998, won Serie A 2001, Supercoppa Italiana 2001, 2007, Coppa Italia 2007, 2008; mem. Italy U-16-15 team 1991–92, Italy U-18 team 1993–95, Italy U-19 team 1995–97, Italy U-21 team 1997 (won UEFA European Under-21 Football Championship 1996, Mediterranean Games 1997), Italy 1998–2006 (58 caps, nine goals, won World Cup, Germany 2006); Good-Will Amb., UNICEF 2003–, FIFA/SOS Children's Villages 2006–; runs football school, Number Ten, and owns motorcycle racing team Totti Top Sport; Dir AS Roma 2017–; Cavaliere Ordine al Merito della Repubblica Italiana (Fifth Class) 2000, (Fourth Class) 2006; Serie A Young Footballer of the Year 1999, Euro 2000 Team of the Tournament 2000, Serie A Footballer of the Year 2000, 2003, Italian Footballer of the Year 2000, 2001, 2003, 2004, 2007, ESM Team of the Year 2000/01, 2003/04, 2006/07, named in FIFA 100 2004, FIFA World Cup All-Star Team 2006, Serie A Top Scorer 2006/07, European Golden Shoe 2006/07, USSI Silver Ball (Serie A Fair Play Award) 2007/08, Roma all-time leading scorer, Roma all-time highest number of appearances. *Publications:* Tutto Totti: Mo je faccio er cucchiaio (autobiography), published two best-selling joke books (some of the jokes were filmed in short sketches featuring himself with friends and nat. team-mates in a short show called La sai l'ultima di Totti). *Leisure interest:* collects jerseys from sports teams around the world. *Address:* AS Roma, Via di Trigoria Km 3,600, 00128 Rome, Italy. *Telephone:* (06) 501911. *Fax:* (06) 5061736. *E-mail:* info@asromastore.it. *Website:* www.asroma.it; www.francescototti.com.

TOTTIE, Thomas, FilLic; Swedish fmr librarian; b. 3 July 1930, Waxholm; s. of John Tottie and Gerda Tottie (née Willers); m. 1st; two d.; m. 2nd Marianne Sandels 1972; two s.; ed Stockholm Univ.; Asst Librarian, Royal Library, Stockholm 1961; Sec. Swedish Council of Research Libraries 1966–73; Deputy Dir Stockholm Univ. Library 1975–76; Dir Library of Royal Carolingian Medico-Chirurgical Inst., Stockholm 1977; Chief Librarian, Uppsala Univ. 1978–96; mem. and official of various professional orgs; Dr hc (Uppsala) 1994. *Publications:* two books and numerous articles and reports on librarianship. *Leisure interests:* biography, sailing. *Address:* University Publications from Uppsala, Uppsala University Library, PO Box 510, 751 20 Uppsala (office); Kyrkogardsgatan 5A, 753 10 Uppsala, Sweden (home). *Telephone:* (18) 471-20-39 (office); (18) 12-32-00 (home). *E-mail:* thomas.tottie@ub.uu.se (office). *Website:* www.ub.uu.se/upu (office).

TOUADÉRA, Faustin-Archange, BSc, MSc, PhD; Central African Republic mathematician, university vice-chancellor, politician and head of state; *President;* b. 21 April 1957, Bangui; ed Barthelemy Boganda Coll., Bangui, Univ. of Bangui, Univ. of Abidjan, Côte d'Ivoire, Lille Univ. of Science and Tech. (Lille I), France, Univ. of Yaoundé I, Cameroon; Asst Lecturer in Math., Faculty of Science, Univ. of Bangui 1987, Vice-Dean Faculty of Science 1989–92, apptd Dir Coll. for Training of Teachers (ENS) 1992, Vice-Chancellor Univ. of Bangui 2004–08; mem. Inter-state Cttee for Standardization of Math. Programmes in French-speaking countries and Indian Ocean (CIEHPM) 1992–2002, Pres. CIEHPM 2001–03; mem. African Network of Math. and Applications for Devt (RAMAD) 2001–; Vice-Pres. Math. Union of Cen. African Repub. (UMAC) 2003–; Prime Minister 2008–12; Pres. of Cen. African Repub. Feb. 2016–; Chevalier of the Order, Officer of the Order, Kt of the Order (all for services to educ.). *Address:* Office of the President, Palais de la Renaissance, Bangui, Central African Republic (office). *Telephone:* 21-61-46-63 (office). *Website:* presidencerca.com (office).

TOUBERT, Pierre Marcel Paul, PhD; French academic; *Professor of Medieval History, Collège de France;* b. 29 Nov. 1932, Algiers; s. of André Toubert and Paola Garcia y Planes; m. Hélène Poggioli 1954; one s.; ed Ecole Normale Supérieure, Paris, Ecole des Hautes-Etudes, Paris, Univ. of Paris and Ecole Française d'Archéologie, Rome; mem. Ecole Française, Rome 1958–61; Dir of Studies, École des Hautes-Etudes 1964–92; Prof., Dept of History, Univ. of Paris (Sorbonne) 1969–92; Prof., Coll. de France 1991–; mem. Nat. Council for Scientific Research, CNRS 1992–; mem. Acad. des Inscriptions et Belles-Lettres, Inst. de France, Academia Europaea 1989–, Nat. Cttee of Evaluation of Univs 1996–, High Council of Technological Research 1999–, Accademia Nazionale dei Lincei, Rome 2000–, Instituto Lombardo, Milan 2003–; Officier, Légion d'honneur, Commdr, Ordre nat. du Mérite 2010, Ordre des Arts et Lettres; Commdr des Palmes académiques; Dr hc (Siena) 1999, (Liège) 2002. *Publications include:* Les structures du Latium médiéval, 2 vols 1973, Etudes sur l'Italie médiévale 1976, Histoire du haut Moyen Age et de l'Italie médiévale 1987, Castillos señores y campesinos en la Italia medieval 1990, Dalla terra ai castelli nell'Italia medioevale 1994, L'Europe dans sa première croissance 2004, Moyen Age et Renaissance au Collège de France 2009, Remploi, citation et plagiat: conduites et pratiques médiévales 2009; many other books and publs on medieval Italy, econ. and social history of the Middle Ages. *Address:* Collège de France, 11 place Marcelin Berthelot, 75231 Paris Cedex 05 (office); 34 rue Guynemer, 75006 Paris, France (home). *Telephone:* 1-44-27-10-32 (office). *Fax:* 1-44-27-10-89 (office). *E-mail:* pierre.toubert@college-de-france.fr (office).

TOUBIANA, Serge; French editor, organization executive and university administrator; *Chairman, École nationale supérieure d'architecture de Paris-Malaquais;* b. 15 Aug. 1949, Sousse, Tunisia; ed high school in Grenoble, Univ. of Paris (Sorbonne); family moved to Grenoble 1962; Co-Ed. Les Cahiers du Cinema magazine 1973–81, Ed. of relaunched edn 1981–92; Dir Cinémathèque française 2003–15; Chair. École nationale supérieure d'architecture de Paris-Malaquais 2009–; fmr Lecturer in Cinema (part-time), Univs of Paris III and Paris VII; mem. Jury, Prix Louis Delluc 1986–2001, Cannes Int. Film Festival 1992; mem. Advances sur recette 1985, Vice-Pres. 1989, 1990; Pres. Comm. d'aide à la distribution 1992; Editorial Dir, Dept DVD at MK2 2000–01; Commdr, Ordre des Arts et des Lettres 2012, Officier, Légion d'honneur 2015. *Publications:* Persévérance (with Serge Daney) 1994, L'arrière-mémoire: conversation avec Serge Toubiana (with Micheline Presle) 1994, Le cinéma vers son deuxième siècle 1995, François Truffaut (with Antoine De Baecque) 1996, Simenon 2003, Le cinéma d'Amos Gitai, Exils et territoires 2003. *Address:* École nationale supérieure d'architecture de Paris-Malaquais, 14, rue Bonaparte, 75272 Paris Cedex 06 (office). *Telephone:* 1-55-04-56-50 (office). *E-mail:* info@paris-malaquais.archi.fr (office). *Website:* www.paris-malaquais.archi.fr (office).

TOUBLANC, Yves; French business executive; began career in Saint-Gobain group 1972, held positions of responsibility in IT, management control and in Finance Dept; joined Poliet Group 1982, Chair. Bollon Point P Co., Chambéry 1994; took over and managed cos active in the transformation of cardboard 1994–2001, sold co.; Founder and Chair. Châtel Participations 2002–; mem. Steering and Supervisory Bd, Caisse d'Epargne des Alpes 1993–, Chair. 2003–07, Chair. Steering and Supervisory Bd Caisse d'Epargne Rhône-Alpes (savings bank created from merger of Caisse d'Epargne Rhône-Alpes Lyon and Caisse d'Epargne des Alpes) and Vice-Chair. Supervisory Bd Groupe BPCE 2007–12, Chair. Supervisory Bd Groupe BPCE 2012–13, Vice-Chair. 2014–15. *Address:* c/o Groupe BPCE, 50 avenue Pierre Mendès France, 75201 Paris Cedex 13, France. *E-mail:* info@bpce.fr.

TOUBON, Jacques, LenD; French politician; *Défenseur des droits;* b. 29 June 1941, Nice; s. of Pierre-Constant Toubon and Yolande (Molinas) Toubon; m. 1st Béatrice Bernascon; m. 2nd Lise Weiler 1982; ed Lycée Masséna, Nice, Lycée Jean Perrin, Lyon, Faculté de Droit, Lyon, Inst. d'Etudes Politiques, Lyon and Ecole Nat. d'Admin; civil servant 1965–76, Chef de Cabinet, to Minister of Agric. 1972–74, to Minister of Interior 1974, Tech. Adviser, Office of Prime Minister 1974–76; Asst Sec.-Gen. Rassemblement pour la République (RPR) 1977–81, Sec.-Gen. 1984–88; Deputy to Nat. Ass. 1981–93; Mayor 13th Arrondissement, Paris 1983–2001, Deputy Mayor of Paris 1983–2001; Minister of Culture and the French Language 1993–95, of Justice 1995–97; Adviser to Pres. Jacques Chirac 1997–98; mem. European Parl. 2004–09; Dir Fondation Claude Pompidou 1970–77, Pres. Eurimages, Council of Europe 2002–09; Sec.-Gen. for Anniversary of African Independence 2010; Défenseur des droits (Ombudsman) 2014–; Pres. Advisory Cttee, Centre for History of Immigration, Club 89 1993; mem. HADOPI; Chevalier du Mérite Agricole, Chevalier, Légion d'Honneur, Commdr des Arts et letters, Officier de la Légion d'honneur 2015. *Publication:* Pour en finir avec la peur 1984. *Leisure interests:* collecting modern art, opera. *Address:* Défenseur des droits, 7 rue Saint-Florentin, 75409, Paris Cedex 08 (office); 86, rue Notre Dame des Champs, 75006, Paris, France (home). *Telephone:* 1-46-33-58-30 (home); 9-69-39-00-00 (office). *Website:* www.defenseurdesdroits.fr (office).

TOULOUSE, Gérard, DSc; French scientist; *Research Scientist, Laboratoire de Physique de l'Ecole Normale Supérieure, Le Centre national de la recherche scientifique (CNRS);* b. 4 Sept. 1939, Vattetot-sur-mer; s. of Robert Toulouse and Thérèse Toulouse (née Tiret); m. Nicole Schnitzer 1970; one s. one d.; ed Ecole Normale Supérieure, Ulm, Orsay; Research Scientist, CNRS 1965–, Laboratoire de Physique de l'Ecole Normale Supérieure 1976–; Post-doctoral Fellow, Univ. of California, San Diego 1969–71; Vice-Pres. Cttee of Exact and Natural Sciences (French nat. comm. for UNESCO) 1997 (Pres. 1999); Sec.-Gen. Foundation La Ferthé 1996; Vice-Pres. Pugwash France 1998; Visitor, Ecole Supérieure de Physique et Chimie, Paris 1985–86; Fellow, Inst. for Advanced Studies, Jerusalem 1987–88; mem. Standing Cttee on Science and Ethics, ALLEA—All European Academies 1999–, Chair. 2001–06; mem. European Acad. of Sciences, Arts and Letters 2003–, Vice-Pres. 2004–10; mem. Acad. of Sciences, Paris 1990; Founding mem. French Nat. Acad. of Tech., Paris 2000–; Foreign Hon. Mem., American Acad. of Arts and Sciences 1996–, Hon. Mem. Palestine Acad. of Science and Tech. 2005–; Chevalier, Ordre nat. du Mérite; Langevin Prize 1976, Triossi Prize 1979, Holweck Prize 1983, CEA Prize 1989; Cecil Powell Medal, European Physical Soc. 1999. *Publications include:* Introduction au groupe de renormalisation 1975, Biology and Computation: a Physicist's Choice 1994, Regards sur l'éthique des sciences 1998, Les scientifiques et les droits de l'homme 2003, Quelle éthique pour les sciences? 2005. *Address:* Laboratoire de physique de l'Ecole Normale Supérieure, 24 rue Lhomond, 75231 Paris Cedex 05, France (office). *Telephone:* 1-44-32-34-87 (office). *Fax:* 1-43-36-76-66 (office). *E-mail:* toulouse@physique.ens.fr (office). *Website:* www.lpt.ens.fr/~toulouse (office).

TOUMAH, Ahmad Saleh; Syrian dentist and political activist; b. 1965, Deir ez-Zor Prov.; long-time political opponent of Assad regime; detained numerous times by Syrian Govt, sentenced to two-and-half years in prison; spent time in exile in Turkey; mem. Syrian Nat. Council (SNC), elected Prime Minister by SNC Sept. 2013–July 2014, re-elected Oct. 2014–16.

TOUMAZOU, Christofer (Chris), BSc, PhD, DEng, FRS, FREng, FIET, FIEEE, FRSM, CEng; British computer scientist and academic; *Chief Scientist of the Institute of Biomedical Engineering, Director of the Centre for Bio-Inspired Technology and Professor of Biomedical Circuit Design, Imperial College London;*

b. 5 July 1961; ed Oxford Brookes Univ., also in collaboration with UMIST (now Univ. of Manchester); Research Fellow, Dept of Electrical and Electronic Eng, Imperial Coll. London 1986, Prof. of Circuit Design 1995–, Head of Circuits and Systems Group, then Head of Dept of Bioengineering 2001, cr. Inst. of Biomedical Eng 2003, first Dir and Chief Scientist, also Dir Centre for Bio-Inspired Tech., Regius Professorship 2013, Winston Wong Chair, Biomedical Circuits; Chair. Royal Soc. Panel for Theo Murphy Blue Skies Award, UK EPSRC Healthcare Panel, UK EPSRC Electronics and Photonics Panel; mem. Wellcome Trust Tech. Transfer Challenge Cttee; fmr mem. of several govt cttees, including the Foresight Cttee on Infectious Diseases, Ministry of Defence Strategic Advisory Cttee on Critical Technologies; Ed.-in-Chief Electronics Letters; Sr Adviser, Bd of Grace Semiconductor, Taiwan; Int. Adviser on medical devices to Govt of Singapore; Chair. and CEO DNA Electronics Ltd, Toumaz Holdings Ltd, GeneOynx; f. Applied Bionics PTE, Future Waves; mem. Academia Europaea 2007; Fellow, Academia Europaea 2007, Inst. of Eng and Tech., City and Guilds Inst. 2010; Hon. Fellow, Cardiff Univ. 2014; Hon. DEng (Oxford Brookes Univ.) 2010; IEE Rayleigh Best Book Award 1991, IEEE CAS Outstanding Young Author Award 1992, IEE Electronics Letters Premium Award 1993, Clifford Paterson Lecturer, Royal Soc. 2003, IEEE CAS Educ. Award 2005, Silver Medal, Royal Acad. of Eng 2007, World Technology Network Award for Health and Medicine 2009, J.J. Thompson Medal for Electronics, Inst. of Eng and Tech. 2011, Gabor Medal, Royal Soc. 2013, European Inventor Award 2014, Faraday Medal, Inst. of Eng and Tech. (IET) 2014, IEEE Biomedical Engineering Award 2014, Lifetime Achievement Award, Elektra European Electronics Industry Awards 2016. *Publications:* more than 320 research papers in professional journals in the field of radio frequency and low power electronics; 23 int. patents. *Address:* 405 Bessemer Building, Department of Electrical and Electronic Engineering, Imperial College London, South Kensington Campus, London, SW7 2AZ, England (office). *Telephone:* (20) 7594-6255 (office). *Fax:* (20) 7581-4419 (office). *E-mail:* c.toumazou@imperial.ac.uk (office). *Website:* www3.imperial.ac.uk/people/c.toumazou (office); www3.imperial.ac.uk/circuitssystems (office).

TOUMI, Khalida, (Khalida Messaoudi); Algerian politician; b. 1958; ed Univ. of Algiers; Co-founder Algerian League of Human Rights 1985, Asscn for Equality of Men and Women Before the Law 1985, Ind. Asscn for the Triumph of Women's Rights (also Pres.) 1990, SOS Women in Distress 1991, Asscn of Solidarity and Support to Families of Victims of Terrorism 1992; mem. Nat. Consultative Comm. 1992–93; Co-founder Mouvement pour la République 1992, Vice-Pres. 1992–97; mem. Rassemblement pour la Culture et la Démocratie (RCD) 1997–2001, Vice-Pres. 1998–2000; Deputy for Algiers 1997–2001, Head of RCD Parl. Group 2000; Vice-Pres. Nat. Comm. for Educ. Reform 2000; Minister of Communication and Govt Spokesperson 2002–14, of Culture 2004–14; Hon. Citizen Commune de Caltabellotta, Italy 1997; Dr hc (Catholic Univ. of Louvain, Belgium) 1998; Alexander Langer Int. Prize 1997, Freedom Prize 1998, Pisa Donna Prize 1998, Telamone Peace Prize 1998, City of Ferrarra Prize 1999, Liberty Prize (Sociéta Libera, Milan) 2004, Gamayung Award 2004. *Address:* c/o Ministry of Culture, BP 100, Palais de la Culture 'Moufdi Zakaria', Plateau des Annassers, Kouba, Algiers, Algeria.

TOUNGUI, Paul; Gabonese politician; s.-in-law of Omar Bongo (fmr Pres.); m. Pascaline Bongo; fmr Univ. Prof. of Math.; Minister of Mines, Energy Resources, Oil and Hydro Resources 2001, Minister of State for Econ. Affairs, Finance, the Budget and Privatization 2002–08, Minister of Foreign Affairs, Int. Co-operation and Francophone Affairs 2008–12; fmr First Vice-Chair. IMF Intergovernmental Group of 24 on Int. Monetary Affairs and Devt; fmr mem. Bd of Govs African Devt Bank, Islamic Devt Bank.

TOUQAN, Umayya Salah, MBA, PhD; Jordanian fmr central banker, economist and diplomatist; b. 26 Feb. 1946, Amman; m. Lina Izziddine Mufti; ed American Univ., Beirut, Univ. of Oxford, UK, Columbia Univ., USA; joined Cen. Bank of Jordan 1967, fmr Head Econ. Research Dept, Gov. and Chair. 2001–10; Perm. Rep. to UN, New York 1973–78; Sr Economist, Arab Monetary Fund, Abu Dhabi 1989–91; Amb. to The Netherlands, Belgium, Luxembourg and the EU 1996–2000; Senator, Upper House of Parl. 2010–; Minister of Finance 2011–12, 2013–15; fmr Econ. Adviser to the Prime Minister; fmr Dir-Gen. Jordan Stock Exchange; Grand Order of Al-Istiklal (Independence) 1995, Grand Order of Al-Kawkab (Jordan) 2001, Grand Cross, Order of the Crown (Belgium) 2001; Central Banker of the Year, The Banker, London. *Address:* c/o Ministry of Finance, PO Box 85, Amman 11118, Jordan (office).

TOURAINE, Agnès, MBA; French business executive; *Founder and President, Act III Consultants, Act III Gaming;* b. 18 Feb. 1955, Neuilly-sur-Seine; d. of René Touraine and Eliane Touraine (née Bertolus); m. Joël Cordier 1987; one s. one d.; ed Institut d'Études Politiques (Diplome Sc Po), Paris, Columbia Business School, New York, USA; consultant, then Project Man., McKinsey & Co. 1981–85; Sr Vice-Pres. for Strategy then Head of Consumer Publishing Div., Hachette 1985–95; Founding Pres. and CEO Liris Interactive 1995–97, renamed Havas Interactive 1997, Exec. Vice-Pres. Consumer Products 1998–2000, Vice-Chair. and CEO Havas 2000–01, renamed Vivendi Universal Publishing 2001, Chair. and CEO Vivendi Universal Publishing 2001–03; f. Act III Consultants (man. consultancy), Paris 2003, Act III Gaming, Paris 2009; Venture Partner, JVP Israel-Paris 2009, ITV, London, Néopost Fondation de France; Chair. Supervisory Bd, SAIP/Libération; Dir (non-exec.) lastminute.com plc 2003–05, Cable & Wireless Communication PLC (fmrly Cable & Wireless plc) 2005–09, ITV PLC 2007–09, Neopost SA 2007–; Ind. Dir (non-exec.), Darty plc 2012–; Pres. Institut Français des Administrateurs (French Inst. of Dirs) 2014–; Chevalier, Ordre nat. du Mérite, Chevalier de la Légion d'honneur. *Leisure interests:* contemporary art, reading, skiing, tennis. *Address:* Act III Consultants, 44 avenue des Champs Elysées, 75008 Paris (office); Institut Français des Administrateurs, 11bis rue Portalis, 75008 Paris, France. *Telephone:* 1-58-56-19-04 (office); 1-80-05-62-20 (IFA); 1-46-33-38-66 (home). *Fax:* 1-58-56-18-78 (office). *E-mail:* atouraine@act3consultants.com (office); president@ifa-asso.com. *Website:* www.act3consultants.com (office); www.act3gaming.com (office); www.ifa-asso.com.

TOURAINE, Alain Louis Jules François, DèsSc; French sociologist; *Director of Studies, Ecole des Hautes Etudes en Sciences Sociales;* b. 3 Aug. 1925, Hermanville; s. of Albert Touraine and Odette Cleret; m. Adriana Arenas 1957 (deceased); one s. one d.; ed Lycées Montaigne and Louis-le-Grand, Paris and Ecole Normale Supérieure; Dir of Studies, Ecole Pratique des Hautes Etudes (now Ecole des Hautes Etudes en Sciences Sociales) 1960–, Founder and Dir of Studies, Centre d'Analyse et d'Intervention Sociologiques (CADIS) 1980–; Prof., Faculté des Lettres de Paris-Nanterre 1966–69; f. Lab. de Sociologie Industrielle (now Centre d'Etude des Mouvements Sociaux) 1958–80; mem. Haut Conseil à l'Intégration 1994–96; mem. Academia Europaea, American Acad. of Arts and Sciences, Polish Acad. of Sciences 1991, Mexican Acad. of Sciences 1998, Brazilian Acad. of Letters 1998, Fundación Academia Europea de Yuste 2004; Officier Légion d'honneur, Officier des Arts et des Lettres, Officier, Ordre O'Higgins (Chile), several Ordres d'honneur; 25 hon. doctorates. *Publications:* Sociologie de l'Action 1965, La Société post-industrielle 1969, Production de la société 1973, Pour la sociologie 1974, La voix et le regard 1978, Mort d'une gauche 1979, L'après-socialisme 1980, Solidarité 1982, Le mouvement ouvrier (with Dubet and Wieviorka) 1984, Le retour de l'acteur 1984, La parole et le sang. Politique et société en Amérique Latine 1988, Critique de la modernité 1992, Qu'est-ce que la démocratie? 1994, Lettre à Lionel, Michel, Jacques, Martine, Bernard, Dominique . . . et vous 1995, Le Grand refus, réflexion sur la grève de décembre 1995 (with Dubet, Khosrokhavar, Lapeyronnie and Wieviorka), Pourrons-nous vivre ensemble? Egaux et différents 1997, Comment sortir du libéralisme? 1999, La recherche de soi. Dialogue sur le sujet (with F. Khosrokhavar) 2000, Un nouveau paradigme, pour comprendre le monde d'aujourd'hui 2005, Le monde des femmes 2006, Penser autrement 2007, Si la gauche veut des idées, Ségolène Royal et Alain Touraine 2008, Après la crise 2010, Carnets de campagne 2012, La Fin des sociétés 2013. *Leisure interest:* Latin America. *Address:* CADIS, UMR 8039 CNRS-EHESS, 190-198, avenue de France, 75244 Paris cedex 13 (office); 32 blvd de Vaugirard, 75015 Paris, France (home). *Telephone:* 1-49-54-24-57 (office); 1-43-20-04-11 (home). *Fax:* 1-42-84-05-91 (office); 1-45-38-54-05 (home). *E-mail:* touraine@ehess.fr (office). *Website:* cadis.ehess.fr (office); alaintouraine.blogspot.co.uk.

TOURAY, Omar Alieu, MA, PhD; Gambian banking executive and fmr diplomatist; *Senior Officer, Islamic Development Bank;* b. 5 Nov. 1965, Farafenni; m.; three c.; ed Grad. Inst. of Int. Studies, Univ. of Geneva; joined diplomatic corps as Sr Asst Sec., Ministry of External Affairs 1995, served at Embassy in Brussels and at Mission to EU 1995–2002, Amb. to Ethiopia, Perm. Rep. to African Union and High Commr to South Africa and Kenya 2002–07, Amb. and Perm. Rep. to UN, New York 2007–08, Minister of Foreign Affairs and Int. Cooperation 2008–09, Consultant, UN Econ. Comm. for Africa, African Union, UNDP 2009–11; Sr Regional Policy Advisor, WFP 2011–2012; Sr Officer, Islamic Development Bank, Jeddah, Saudi Arabia 2012–; mem. Panel of Eminent Persons, African Center of Int. Law Practice (ACILP). *Publications:* The Gambia and the World: A History of the Foreign Policy of Africa's Smallest State, 1965–1995 2000, The African Union: The First Ten Years 2016; numerous papers on int. econ. relations. *Address:* Islamic Development Bank, PO Box 5925, Jeddah 21432, Saudi Arabia (office). *E-mail:* info@isdb.org (office). *Website:* www.isdb-pilot.org (office).

TOURÉ, Lt-Col Amadou Toumani; Malian army officer and fmr head of state; b. 4 Nov. 1948, Mopti; m.; two d.; ed Ecole Normale Secondaire de Badalabougou, Bamako; Lt, Armed Forces of Mali 1974–78, Capt. 33rd Parachute Bn 1978–84, Commdr 1984–88, rank of Lt-Col 1988, Brigade Gen. 1992–96, Army Gen. 1996–; Commdr Presidential Guard 1981–84; led coup which overthrew Gen. Moussa Traoré March 1991; Leader Nat. Reconciliation Council 1991–92; Chair. Transition Cttee for the Salvation of the People (acting Head of State) 1991–92; participated in diplomatic initiatives in Rwanda, Burundi, Togo 1996, Cen. African Repub. 1997; Head Inter-African Mission to Monitor the Implementation of the Bangui Agreements 1997–; Pres. of Mali 2002–12 (ousted in military coup then resgnd and fled to Senegal); Rotary Int. Paul Harris Fellow; Chevalier, Nat. Order of Mali 1981, Grand Cross 1993, Gold Medal of Independence, Mali 1992, Commander, Légion d'Honneur 1994, Grand Officier 1998, Grand Officier, Central African Order of Merit 1996, Grand Officer, Order of Merit of Chad 1997, Grand Medal, Int. Order of Lawyers 2005; Laureate Prize for the Promotion of Democracy in Africa, Observatoire Panafricain de la Démocratie (OPAD) 1996, Prix du Ciwara d'Exception 1997, Prix Chaba Sangare 2001.

TOURÉ, Aminata; Senegalese human rights activist and politician; b. 12 Oct. 1962, Dakar; m. Oumar Sarr (divorced); ed Univs of Dijon and Aix-en-Provence, France; began career in Marketing Dept, SOTRAC (public transport co.), Dakar 1988; fmr Programme Dir, Asscn sénégalaise pour le bien-être familial (Senegalese family planning asscn); five years with UN Population Fund (UNFPA) 1995–2000, including positions as Sr Tech. Adviser to Ministry of Family and Social Action, Burkina Faso, later UNFPA Regional Adviser for Francophone African Countries, Program Co-ordinator on Gender and HIV in West Africa for UN Fund for Women Regional Office, becoming Dir UNFPA Human Rights Dept, New York 2003–10; head of electoral campaign for Landing Savané in presidential election 1993; Chief of Staff to presidential cand. Macky Sall 2010; Minister of Justice 2012–13; Prime Minister of Senegal 2013–14; mem. Alliance pour la République (APR—Yaakaar).

TOURÉ, Hamadoun, PhD; Malian electrical engineer, fmr international organization official and politician; b. 3 Sept. 1953; m.; four c.; ed Tech. Inst. of Electronics and Telecommunications of Leningrad, Univ. of Electronics, Telecommunications and Informatics, Moscow, Russia; worked at PANAFTEL microwave terminal 1979; worked at International Switching Centre, Bamako 1980, Engineer in charge of operation and maintenance of the International Satellite earth station, Bamako 1981–84; Group Dir and Regional Dir Int. Telecommunications Satellite Org. (INTELSAT), Washington, DC 1985–96; Dir-Gen. Africa Region, ICO Global Communications 1996–98; Dir Telecommunications Devt Bureau (BDT), Int. Telecommunication Union (ITU), UN 1998–2006, Sec.-Gen. 2007–14; apptd Minister of Communication, Posts and New Technologies 2012, also Govt Spokesman; Dir Inmarsat 2015–; mem. IEEE 1986–, Asscn of Satellite Professionals 1990–, Int. Telecommunications Acad. 1999–, Royal Swedish Acad. of Eng Sciences 2010–; Kt of Nat. Order of Mali, Officer, Nat. Order of Côte d'Ivoire, Grand Officer, Nat. Order of the Dominican Republic, 2009; Dr hc (tate Odessa Nat. Acad. of Telecommunications, Ukraine), (Univ. of Belarus) 2009, (Nat. Univ. of Moldova) 2010, (Russian–Armenian (Slavonic) Univ., Armenia) 2010, (Kigali Inst. of Science and Tech.) 2010, (Wroclaw Univ. of Tech., Poland) 2010. *Address:* Inmarsat, 99 City Road, London EC1Y 1AX, England (office). *Telephone:* (20) 7728-1646 (office). *Website:* www.inmarsat.com (office).

TOURÉ, Modibo, BSc, MBA; Malian UN official; m.; three c.; ed Ecole Nationale d'Admin, Bamako, Vanderbilt Univ., USA; consultant with Shell Oil, Mali 1982–84; Inspecteur des Finances, Bamako 1984–87; Man. United Parcel Service, Nashville, Tenn., USA 1989–90; UNDP Program Officer and later Asst Resident Rep., Burkina Faso 1991–94, Deputy Resident Rep., Djibouti 1994–97, Program Man., New York 1997–98, Sr Deputy Resident Rep., Rwanda 1998–99, Sr Country Program Man., New York 1999–2001, Special Adviser to Dir, Regional Bureau for Africa, New York 2000–01, UN Resident Coordinator, Humanitarian Coordinator and UN Resident Rep., Chad 2001–04, UNDP Resident and Humanitarian Coordinator, Ethiopia 2004–05, mem. UNDP Transition Team 2005–06; Dir UN Mine Action Service 2005–06; Sec.-Gen. African Devt Bank (ADB) 2006–10; Special Adviser to the Special Envoy of the Sec.-Gen. to the Great Lakes Region, UN 2013–15; Special Rep. for Guinea-Bissau, Head UN Integrated Peacebuilding Office in Guinea-Bissau (UNIOGBIS) 2016–18.

TOURÉ, Sanoussi, PhD; Malian politician; ed Univ. of Paris X, France; Dir-Gen. of Finance Control, Ministry of Economy and Finance 1978–87, Dir-Gen. of Budget 1987–91, tech. adviser to Minister of the Economy and Finance 1991–94; consultant to the World Bank, Canadian Co-operation, US-Aid 1995–2000; Dir of Public Finances, West African Econ. and Monetary Union 2001–05, consultant 2005–; Minister and Dir of Cabinet Office 2008–09; Minister of Economy and Finance 2009–11; Lecturer in Finance and Fiscal Studies, Univ. of Mali 1980–2000; currently ind. financial services consultant.

TOURÉ, Sidia; Guinean politician; *President, Union des forces républicaines;* fmr Dir Office of the Prime Minister of Côte d'Ivoire; Prime Minister of Guinea 1996–99, Minister of Economy, Finance and Planning 1996–97; Pres. Union des forces républicaines; cand. in presidential elections 2010. *Address:* Union des forces républicaines (UFR), Immeuble 'Le Golfe', 4e étage, BP 6080, Conakry, Guinea (office). *Telephone:* 45-42-38 (office). *Fax:* 45-42-31 (office). *E-mail:* ufrguinee@yahoo.fr (office).

TOURÉ, Younoussi; Malian politician; b. 1 Jan. 1941, Niodougou, Timbuktu Region; s. of Singoro Touré and Santadji Tamoura; m. Alimata Traore 1970; two s. three d.; ed Univ. of Dakar; studied in Dakar, Senegal and Abidjan, Côte d'Ivoire; joined Cen. Bank of Mali 1969, Dir-Gen. 1983; rep. at Banque Centrale des états de l'Afrique de l'ouest (BCEAO); Prime Minister 1992–93; Special Adviser to Gov. of BCEAO 1993–94; Commr, West African Econ. and Monetary Union (UEMOA) 1994; mem. Nat. Ass. (URD) for Niafunké Dist 2007–, First Vice-Pres. Nat. Ass. 2007–13; Founding mem. Alliance pour la Démocratie au Mali (ADEMA); Founding mem. Union pour la République et la démocratie (URD), fmr Pres. *Leisure interests:* reading, sport. *Address:* Union pour la République et la démocratie, Badalabougou, rue 105, porte 483, Bamako, Mali. *Telephone:* 2021-8642. *E-mail:* contact@urd-mali.net. *Website:* www.urd-mali.net.

TOURET, Jacques Léon Robert; French geologist and academic; *Guest Scientist, Mineralogy, Université Pierre et Marie Curie;* b. 2 Jan. 1936, Fumay; s. of Martial Touret and Suzanne Gouilly; m. 1st Christiane Poinsignon 1960 (divorced 1972); one s. two d.; m. 2nd Lydie Mohammed 1974; one d.; ed Lycée Chanzy, Charleville, Ecole Nat. Supérieure de Géologie Appliquée, Nancy and Univ. of Nancy; Asst, Ecole Nat. Supérieure de Géologie, Nancy 1958–64, Asst Lecturer in Geology 1964–69; Lecturer in Geology, Univ. of Nancy 1969–74; Prof., Univ. of Paris 7 1974–80; Prof., Earth Science Inst., Free Univ., Amsterdam, Netherlands 1980–2001, Prof. Emer. 2001–; Guest Scientist, Ecoles des Mines, Paris, currently Guest Scientist, Mineralogy, Univ. Pierre et Marie Curie (Jussieu), Paris; Invited Prof., Ecole Normale Supérieure, Paris 1994–97; Chargé de mission, CNRS, Paris 1978–80; mem. Royal Netherlands Acad. of Sciences, Norwegian Acad. of Science and Letters, Academia Europaea; Hon. Fellow, European Union of Geologists; Chevalier, Ordre nat. du Mérite; Dr hc (Liège Univ., Belgium) 2001; Prix Carrière, Acad. des Sciences, Paris 1970, Dumont Medal (Belgian Geological Soc.) 1992, Van Waterschoot van der Gracht Medal (Netherlands) 1996. *Publications include:* Le Socle précambrien de Norvège méridionale 1969, The deep Proterozoic Crust in the North Atlantic province (with A. C. Tobi) 1985. *Leisure interests:* classical music, French literature. *Address:* Université Pierre et Marie Curie, 4 place Jussieu, 75005 Paris, France (office). *Website:* www.impmc.upmc.fr (office).

TOUSIGNANT, Claude, OC; Canadian artist; b. 23 Dec. 1932, Montreal, PQ; s. of Alberic Tousignant and Gilberte Hardy-Lacasse; m. Judith Terry 1968; two d.; ed School of Art and Design, Montreal Museum of Fine Arts; numerous solo and group nat. and int. exhbns 1956–; works included in major N American public and pvt. collections; fmr mem. Association des artistes non-figuratifs de Montréal; First Prize, Salon de la jeune peinture 1962, First Prize, Painting, Art Gallery of Ont. 1967, Canadian Inst. in Rome Award 1973, Victor Martyn Lynch-Staunton Award 1974, Prix Paul-Emile Borduas 1989, Gov.-Gen.'s Award in Visual and Media Arts 2010. *Address:* 181 rue Bourget, Montreal, PQ H4C 2M1(Studio); 460 avenue Bloomfield, Outremont, PQ H2V 3R8, Canada (home). *Telephone:* (514) 934-3012 (Studio); (514) 948-1463 (home).

TOVAR FAJA, Roberto; Costa Rican politician; b. 12 Nov. 1945; ed Univ. of Barcelona, Spain; Deputy, Legis. Ass. 1978–82, 1990–94, Pres. Legis. Ass. 1992–93; Head of Faction, Unidad Social Cristiana (USC—Christian Social Unit) 1991–92, fmr Sec.-Gen.; Pres. Comm. of Econ. Subjects 1978–79; fmr mem. Bd of Dirs and Consultant, Inter-American Inst. of Human Rights; fmr Minister of the Presidency and Planning; Minister of Foreign Relations 2002–06.

TOWNE, Robert; American screenwriter; b. (Robert Bertram Schwartz), 23 Nov. 1934, Los Angeles, Calif.; m. 1st Julie Payne (divorced); m. 2nd Luisa Towne; two c.; ed Pomona Coll.; Laurel Award for Screenwriting Achievement, Writers Guild of America Award 1997. *Screenplays include:* The Tomb of Ligeia 1964, Villa Rides 1967, The Last Detail (BAFTA Award for Best Screenplay 1975) 1967, Chinatown (Academy Award for Best Original Screenplay 1975, BAFTA Award for Best Screenplay 1975, Golden Globe Award for Best Screenplay - Motion Picture 1975, Edgar Award for Best Motion Picture 1975) 1974, Shampoo (with Warren Beatty) 1974, The Yazuka (jointly) 1975, Personal Best (also producer-dir 1984), Greystoke 1984, Tequila Sunrise 1988, Days of Thunder, The Two Jakes, The Firm (co-screenwriter) 1993, Love Affair (co-screenwriter), Mission Impossible (co-screenwriter), Without Limits (also dir) 1998, Mission Impossible 2 2000, Ask the Dust (also dir) 2006, Roads of Asgard 2009. *Address:* c/o Paradigm Talent Agency, 360 North Crescent Drive, North Building, Beverly Hills, CA 90210-2500, USA (office). *Telephone:* (310) 288-8000 (office). *Fax:* (310) 288-2000 (office). *Website:* www.paradigmagency.com (office).

TOWNSHEND, Peter (Pete) Dennis Blandford; British composer, musician (guitar), publisher and author; b. 19 May 1945, Isleworth, London, England; s. of Clifford Townshend and Betty Townshend; m. Karen Astley 1968; one s. two d.; ed Acton Co. Grammar School and Ealing Art Coll.; mem. rock group, The Detours, renamed The Who 1964– (various reunion tours and recordings); solo artist 1979–; appearances include: Nat. Jazz and Blues Festival 1965, 1966, 1969, Monterey Pop Festival 1967, Woodstock 1969, Rock at the Oval 1971, Farewell tour 1982–83, Live Aid, Wembley 1985, Reunion tour 1989, Quadrophenia 1996/1997, Concert for NYC 2001, Live8 2005; owner Eel Pie Recording Productions Ltd and Eel Pie Publishing Ltd 1972–; est. Eel Pie (bookshops and publishing co.) 1976–83; est. Meher Baba Oceanic (UK archival library) 1976–; Ed., Faber & Faber (publrs) 1983–; Gold Ticket Madison Square Garden 1979, Ivor Novello Award for Contribution to British Music 1982, British Phonographic Industry Award 1983, BRIT Lifetime Achievement Award 1983, BRIT Award for Contribution to British Music 1988, International Rock Living Legend Award 1991, Q Lifetime Achievement Award 1997, Ivor Novello Lifetime Achievement Award 2001, BMI Pres.'s Award 2002, BMI TV Music Awards 2004, 2005, 2006, 2007, Silver Clef Award 2005, The Who were inducted into the UK Music Hall of Fame in 2005, Q Legend Award 2006, South Bank Show Outstanding Achievement Award 2007, Kennedy Center Honor 2008, Les Paul Award 2013, Stevie Ray Vaughan, MusiCares 2015. *Compositions include:* Tommy (rock opera) (Tony Award for score 1993, Grammy Award for original cast recording 1993, Dora Mavor Moore Award 1994, Olivier Award 1997) 1969, Quadrophenia (rock opera) 1973, The Boy Who Heard Music (rock opera) 2007. *Recordings include:* albums: with The Who: My Generation 1965, A Quick One 1966, Happy Jack 1967, The Who Sell Out 1967, Magic Bus 1968, Tommy 1969, Live At Leeds 1970, Who's Next 1971, Meaty Beefy Big And Bouncy 1971, Quadrophenia 1973, The Who By Numbers 1975, The Story Of The Who 1976, Who Are You 1978, The Kids Are Alright (live) 1979, Face Dances 1981, Hooligans 1982, It's Hard 1982, Rarities Vols. 1 and 2 1983, Who's Last (live) 1984, Two's Missing 1987, Join Together (live) 1990, Live At The Isle Of Wight Festival 1970 1996, The BBC Sessions 2000, Moonlighting 2005, Endless Wire 2006, Classic Quadrophenia 2015; solo: Who Came First 1972, Rough Mix 1977, Empty Glass 1980, All The Best Cowboys Have Chinese Eyes 1982, Scoop 1983, White City: A Novel 1985, Another Scoop 1987, The Iron Man: A Musical 1989, Psychoderelict 1993, Pete Townshend Live 1999, Lifehouse Chronicles 2000, The Oceanic Concerts 2001, Live: La Jolla 2001, Live: Sadler's Wells 2001, Truancy: The Very Best of Pete Townshend 2015. *Films:* music for: Tommy 1975, Quadrophenia 1979, The Kids Are Alright 1979. *Television:* music for CSI: Miami and CSI: Crime Scene Investigation. *Publications:* The Story of Tommy (with Richard Barnes), Horse's Neck 1985, Tommy: The Musical 1995, London 1996, Who I Am (autobiography) 2012. *Leisure interest:* sailing. *Address:* c/o Trinifold Management, 12 Oval Road, Camden, London, NW1 7DH, England (office). *Telephone:* (20) 7419-4300 (office). *Fax:* (20) 7419-4325 (office). *E-mail:* info@trinifold.co.uk (office). *Website:* www.trinifold.co.uk (office); petetownshend.net; www.thewho.com.

TOYBERG-FRANDZEN, Jens Anders; Danish UN official; b. 1950; m.; ed Aarhus Univ.; fmr Acting UN Resident Coordinator, UNDP Resident Rep. in Yemen, Resident Coordinator and Resident Rep. in Bosnia and Herzegovina, Exec. Rep. of UN Sec.-Gen. and Head of the UN Integrated Peacebuilding Office in Sierra Leone (UNIPSIL) 2012–14, Resident Coordinator and Acting Resident Rep. for Ukraine 2014, Asst Sec.-Gen. ad interim for Political Affairs 2014–15; also served with UN in Bhutan, Iraq, Nepal and Turkey. *Address:* c/o Office of the Secretary-General, United Nations, New York, NY 10017, USA (office). *Telephone:* (212) 963-1234 (office). *Fax:* (212) 963-4879 (office). *Website:* www.un.org/sg (office).

TOYE, John Francis Joseph, BA, MA, MSc, PhD; British development economist and academic; *Chair of the Advisory Panel, Department of International Development, Queen Elizabeth House, University of Oxford;* b. 7 Oct. 1942, Wisbech, Cambs., England; s. of John Redmond Toye and Adele Toye (née Francis); m. Janet Toye (née Reason); one s. one d.; ed Univ. of Cambridge, School of Oriental and African Studies, Univ. of London; Asst Prin., UK Home Civil Service, HM's Treasury 1965–68; Research Fellow in Econs, School of Oriental and African Studies, Univ. of London 1970–72, currently Professorial Research Assoc.; Fellow and Tutor, Wolfson Coll., Cambridge 1972–80, Grad. Asst, Centre of South Asian Studies, Univ. of Cambridge 1972–74, Research Officer, Overseas Studies Cttee 1975–77, Asst Dir of Devt Studies 1977–80; Consultant on Third World Studies, Open Univ. 1981–83; Dir of Research Co-ordination, Commodities Research Unit Ltd, London and New York 1980–82, Dir (non-exec.) 1982–85; Prof. of Development Policy and Planning, Univ. of Wales 1982–87, also Dir; Dir Inst. of Devt Studies, Univ. of Sussex, Brighton 1987–97, Professorial Fellow 1987–97; Dir Globalization and Devt Strategies Div., UNCTAD, Geneva 1998–2000; Dir Centre for the Study of African Economies, Dept of Economics, Univ. of Oxford 2000–03, Sr Research Assoc. and Visiting Prof., Dept of Int. Devt, Queen Elizabeth House 2003–09, currently Chair. Advisory Panel; Visiting Fellow, St Antony's Coll., Oxford 2000–03; Chair. Journal of Development Studies 1976–2006; Man. Ed. Journal Oxford Development Studies 2005–09; mem. Editorial Bd, Journal of Development Studies 1976–, Oxford Development Studies 2003–; mem. Bd, Contemporary South Asia 1989–99, Journal of International Development 1989–2007, World Development 1994–97, European Journal of Development Research 1995–2007; Fellow, Human Devt and Capability Asscn 2010–; Hon. Fellow, School of Public Policy, Univ. of Birmingham 1989–92; Hon. Pres. Devt Studies Asscn of GB and Ireland 1994–96; Hon. Trustee, Inst. of Devt Studies, Univ. of Sussex 2005–; Hon. Professorial Assoc., School of Oriental and African Studies 2010–12. *Publications include:* Taxation and Economic Development (ed.) 1978, Trade and Poor Economies (co-ed.) 1979, Public Expenditure and Indian Development Policy 1960–70 1981, Dilemmas of Development: Reflections on the Counter-Revolution in Development Theory and Policy 1987, 1993, Indo-European Cooperation in an Interdependent World (ed.) 1989, Does Aid Work in India? A Country Study of Official Development Assistance (co-author) 1990, Aid and Power: The World Bank and Policy-Based Lending in the 1980s (two vols, co-author) 1991, 1995, Structural Adjustment and Employment Policy: Issues and Experience 1995, Challenging the Orthodoxies (co-ed.) 1996, A World Without Famine? (co-ed.) 1997, Keynes on Population 2000, Trade and Development:

Directions for the Twenty-first Century (ed.) 2003, The UN and Global Political Economy: Trade, Finance and Development (co-author) 2004; numerous book chapters, book reviews, commissioned reports, and articles in professional journals. *Address:* Department of International Development, Queen Elizabeth House, University of Oxford, 3 Mansfield Road, Oxford, OX1 3TB, England (office). *Telephone:* (1865) 281835 (office). *Fax:* (1865) 281801 (office). *E-mail:* john.toye@economics.ox.ac.uk (office). *Website:* www.qeh.ox.ac.uk (office); www.johntoye.net.

TOYODA, Akio, MBA; Japanese automotive industry executive; *President and Representative Director, Toyota Motor Corporation;* b. 3 May 1956, Nagoya; grandson of Kiichiro Toyoda; m. Hiroko Toyoda; two c.; ed Keio Univ., Tokyo, Babson Coll., Mass, USA; joined Toyota Motor Corpn 1984, Vice-Pres. New United Motor Manufacturing Inc., Calif., USA, mem. Bd of Dirs Toyota Motor Corpn 2000–, Man. Dir 2002–03, Sr Man. Dir and Chief Asia and China Operations Officer 2003–05, Exec. Vice-Pres. 2005–09, Pres. and Rep. Dir 2009–, Head of team that developed Gazoo.com (Toyota web site) 1996. *Address:* Toyota Motor Corpn, 1 Toyota-Cho, Toyota City, Aichi Prefecture 471-8571, Japan (office). *Telephone:* (5) 6528-2121 (office). *Fax:* (5) 6523-5800 (office). *Website:* www.toyota-global.com (office); www.toyota.co.jp (office).

TOYODA, Kanshiro; Japanese automotive industry executive; *Chairman, Aisin Seiki Company Ltd;* s. of Eiji Toyoda and Kazuko Toyoda; m. Akiko Toyoda; fmr Man. Shinkawa Seiki Co. Ltd; Pres. Aisin Seiki Co. Ltd (automotive component mfr) –2005, Chair. 2005–, Dir Aisin AW Co. Ltd, Aisin Chemical Co. Ltd, ADVICS Co. Ltd. *Address:* Aisin Seiki Co. Ltd, 2-1 Asahi-machi, Karlya, Aichi 448-8650, Japan (office). *Telephone:* (5) 6624-8239 (office). *Fax:* (5) 6624-8003 (office). *E-mail:* info@aisin.com (office). *Website:* www.aisin.com (home).

TOYODA, Shoichiro, DEng; Japanese automotive industry executive; b. 27 Feb. 1925, Nagoya; s. of Kiichiro Toyoda and Hatako Toyoda; m. Hiroko Mitsui 1952; one s. one d.; ed Nagoya and Tohoku Univs; joined Toyota Motor Corpn 1952, Man. Dir 1961, Sr Man. Dir 1967, Exec. Vice-Pres. 1972, Pres. Marketing Org. 1981, Pres., Toyota Motor Corpn 1982, Chair. 1992–99, Hon. Chair. 1999–2013, Sr Adviser and mem. Bd 1996–; Chair., Japanese Automobile Mfrs Asscn 1986–90; Vice-Chair., Keidanren (Fed. of Econ. Orgs) 1990–94, Chair. 1994–2002, Hon. Chair. 2002–; Chair., Japan Asscn for 2005 World Exposition 1997–2006, Pres., Kaiyo Acad. 2006–; Medal of Honour (Dark Blue Ribbon) 1972, (Blue Ribbon) 1984, (Dark Blue Ribbon) 1984, 1985; Grand Cordon, Order of the Sacred Treasure 1995, Hon. KBE 1995; Commdr, Légion d'honneur 1998, Grand Officier 2005; Order of Merit (Turkey) 1998, Commdr's Cross, Order of Merit (Germany) 2001, Grand Cordon, Order of the Rising Sun 2002, Kt Grand Cordon (First Class), Most Admirable Order of the Direkgunabhorn (Thailand) 2004, Grand Cross, Order of Merit (Portugal) 2005, Grand Cross, Order of Juan Mora Fernandez, Placa de Plata (Costa Rica) 2005, Commdr, Order of the Equatorial Star (Gabon) 2005, Grand Cordon, Order of the Paulownia Flowers 2007, Cavaliere di Gran Croce decorato di Gran Cordone (Italy) 2007, Grand Collar, Order of Lakandula of the Philippines 2010, numerous other hons; Deming Prize (Japan) 1980, Medal with Blue Ribbon for Outstanding Public Service (Japan) 1984, FISITA Medal (France) 2000, Manufacturing Leadership Award, Soc. of Automotive Engineers Foundation (USA) 2005, inducted into Automotive Hall of Fame, Detroit, Mich., USA 2007. *Leisure interests:* traditional Japanese music, gardening, golf. *Address:* c/o Toyota Motor Corporation, 1 Toyota-cho, Toyota, Aichi 471-8571, Japan.

TOZAKA, Milner, OBE; Solomon Islands politician and diplomatist; b. 21 Oct. 1951; m. Jane Tozaka; ed Univ. of South Pacific, Suva, Fiji; Chair. Nat. Disaster Council 1984–85; UNEP Consultant, Ministry of Prov. Govt 1995; Chair. Prov. Govt Review Cttee 1999; High Commr to Australia 2000–05; mem. Parl. for North Vella Lavella Constituency 2006–, Chair. Constitution Review Cttee 2006–07, Foreign Relations Cttee 2010–14; Minister for Public Service April–May 2006, 2007–10, for Foreign Affairs and External Trade 2014–19. *Address:* National Parliament of Solomon Islands, PO Box G19, Honiara, Solomon Islands (office). *Website:* www.parliament.gov.sb (office).

TRABER, Peter G., BS, MD; American gastroenterologist and college administrator; *Partner, Alacrita Consulting Inc.;* b. 6 April 1955; m. 1st Bobbi Traber; m. 2nd Melanie Damrell; one s. one d.; ed Univ. of Michigan, Wayne State Univ. Medical School, Northwestern Univ. School of Medicine; Asst Prof. of Medicine, Univ. of Michigan School of Medicine 1987–92; Assoc. Prof. of Medicine and Genetics, Univ. of Pennsylvania School of Medicine 1992–96, Chief of Gastroenterology 1992–97, T. Gier Prof. of Medicine and Genetics 1996–2000, Chair., Dept of Internal Medicine 1997–2000, CEO and Interim Dean Univ. of Pennsylvania Health System March–Sept. 2000, Adjunct Prof. of Medicine 2018–; Sr Vice-Pres. for Clinical Devt and Medical Affairs and Chief Medical Officer, GlaxoSmithKline 2000–03; Pres. and CEO Baylor Coll. of Medicine 2003–09, Pres. Emer. 2008–; Pres., CEO and Chief Marketing Officer, Galectin Therapeutics Inc. 2011–18; Pnr Alacrita Consulting Inc. 2018–; Sr Ed. Handbook of Gastroenterology; Assoc. Ed. Kelly Textbook of Internal Medicine; mem. Bd of Dirs Alkek Foundation, BCM Technologies, BioHouston, Federal Reserve Bank of Dallas (Houston Br.), Greater Houston Partnership, Houston Tech. Center, Nat. Space Biomedical Research Inst., Caladrius Biosciences; mem. American Soc. of Clinical Investigation; Fellow, AAAS 2003–; Wayne State Univ. School of Medicine Distinguished Alumnus Award 1999, American Gastroenterological Asscn Outstanding Service Award 2006. *Address:* Alacrita Consulting Inc., 303 Wyman Street, Waltham, MA 02451, USA (office). *E-mail:* ptraber@alacrita.com (office). *Website:* www.alacrita.com (office); petertraber.com.

TRABUCO CAPPI, Luiz Carlos; Brazilian business executive; *Chairman, Banco Bradesco SA;* b. 6 Oct. 1951, Marília, São Paulo; ed São Paulo Univ. of Philosophy, Science and Languages, Fundação Escola de Sociologia e Política de São Paulo; joined Banco Bradesco SA 1969, Departmental Dir 1984–92, Pres. Bradesco Vida e Previdência SA 1992–98, elected Man. Dir Banco Bradesco 1998, apptd Vice-Pres. 1999, later Exec. Vice-Pres., Dir and Pres. Grupo Bradesco Seguros 2003–, Vice-Chair. and CEO Banco Bradesco SA 2009–2017, Chair. and CEO Oct. 2017–March 2018, Chair. 2018–, mem. Bd of Dirs Banco Bradesco SA and several cos of Bank Bradesco SA Group; Chair. Odontoprev SA; Pres. Nat. Asscn for Pvt. Pension Plans (ANAPP) 1994–2000; mem. Deliberative Council of Federação Brasileira de Bancos (FEBRABAN); Pres. Associação Nacional da Previdência Privada (ANAPP) 1994–2000; fmr CEO Bradesco Vida e Previdência, Grupo Segurador, Marketing and Capitation Cttee of Associação Brasileira das Entidades de Crédito Imobiliário e Poupança (ABECIP), Federação Nacional de Saúde Suplementar (FENASAÚDE); fmr Vice-Chair. Bd of Reps of Confederação Nacional das Instituições Financeiras (CNF); mem. Deliberative Council of Associação Brasileira das Companhias Abertas (ABRASCA) 2000–03; fmr mem. Bd of Dirs Banco Espírito Santo, SA, Lisbon, Portugal, ArcelorMittal Brasil (ex: Companhia Siderúrgica Belgo-Mineira); fmr mem. Superior Bd and Vice-Pres. Confederação Nacional das Empresas de Seguros Gerais, Previdência Privada e Vida, Saúde Suplementar e Capitalização (CNSeg); fmr Sitting mem. Asscn Internationale pour l'Etude de l'Economie de l'Assurance—Asscn de Genève, Geneva, Switzerland; fmr mem. Hon. Council of Academia Nacional de Seguros e Previdência. *Address:* Banco Bradesco SA, 1450 Avenida Paulista, 9th floor 01310-917 São Paulo, Brazil (office). *Telephone:* (11) 3684-3311 (office). *E-mail:* info@bradesco.com.br (office). *Website:* www.bradesco.com.br (office).

TRACHTENBERG, Stephen Joel, JD, MPA; American lawyer, academic and university administrator; *President Emeritus and University Professor of Public Service, George Washington University;* b. 14 Dec. 1937, Brooklyn, New York; s. of Oscar Trachtenberg and Shoshana Weinstock; m. Francine Zorn 1971; two s.; ed Columbia, Yale and Harvard Univs; admitted New York Bar 1964, US Supreme Court Bar 1967; attorney, Atomic Energy Comm. 1962–65; Special Asst to US Educ. Comm., Health, Educ. and Welfare, Washington, DC 1966–68; Assoc. Prof. of Political Science, Boston Univ. 1969–77, Assoc. Dean 1969–70, Dean 1970–74, Assoc. Vice-Pres., Co-Counsel 1974–76, Vice-Pres. Academic Services 1976–77; Pres., Prof. of Law, Univ. of Hartford, Conn. 1977–88; Pres. George Washington Univ., Washington, DC 1988–2007, Pres. Emer. 2007–, also Univ. Prof. of Public Service; Consultant, Korn/Ferry International 2007–; Partner, Rimon Law, PC 2014–; numerous hon. degrees; numerous awards, including Sabin Vaccine Inst. Prize 2005. *Publications:* The Art of Hiring in America's Colleges and Universities (co-ed.) 1993, Speaking His Mind: Five Years of Commentary on Higher Education 1994, Thinking Out Loud: A Decade of Thoughts on Higher Education 1998, Reflections on Higher Education 2002, Write Me a Letter!: The Wit and Wisdom of Stephen Joel Trachtenberg 2006, BMOC: A University President Speaks Out On Higher Education 2008, Letters to the Next President: Strengthening America's Foundation in Higher Education (co-ed.) 2008, Presidencies Derailed (co-author) 2013. *Address:* The Trachtenberg School, George Washington University, MPA Building, 805 21st Street, NW, Suite 600, Washington, DC 20052 (office); Korn/Ferry International, 1700 K Street, NW, Suite 700, Washington, DC 20006, USA (office). *Telephone:* (202) 994-6504 (office). *E-mail:* trachtenberg@rimonlaw.com (office); trachtenberg@gwu.edu (office). *Website:* www.gwu.edu (office); www.kornferry.com (office); rimonlaw.com (office).

TRAHAR, Anthony (Tony) John, BComm, CA (SA); South African business executive; *Chairman, Bartlett Resources LLP;* b. 1 June 1949, Johannesburg; m. Patricia Trahar; one s. one d.; ed St. John's Coll., Univ. of the Witwatersrand; qualified CA 1973; man. trainee, Anglo American Corpn 1974–76, Personal Asst to Chair. of Exec. Cttee 1976–77, Exec. Dir 1991–2000, CEO 2000–07 (retd), Chair. Anglo Forest Products, Anglo Industrial Minerals Div., Financial Dir Anglo American Industrial Corpn 1982–92, Deputy Chair. 1992–2007, Chair. Anglo American Corpn of SA; Man. Dir Mondi 1986–89, Exec. Chair. 1989, Chair. Mondi Europe 1993–2003; Chair. Bartlett Resources LLP 2007–, Paleo Anthropological Scientific Trust; Dir Anglo Platinum, Anglo Gold, DB Investments; Kt Grand Commdr, Gold Cross with Star (First Class) (Austria) 2004; Hon. LLD. *Leisure interests:* shooting, fishing, gym, classic cars and music. *Address:* Bartlett Resources LLP, 22 Mallord Street, Chelsea, London, SW3 6DU, England. *Telephone:* (20) 7351-6383 (office). *E-mail:* ajtrahar@bartlettresources.co.uk.

TRAILL, Sir Alan, KStJ, GBE, QSO, MA, DMus; British arbitrator and insurance consultant; b. 7 May 1935, London; s. of George Traill and Margaret (Matthews) Traill; m. Sarah Jane Hutt 1964; one s.; ed Charterhouse and Jesus Coll., Cambridge; Dir Morice Tozer Beck (insurance brokers) 1958–73; Underwriting mem. Lloyd's 1963–89; Founder Dir Traill Attenborough (Lloyd's brokers) 1973, Chair. 1980; Man. Dir Colburn Traill Ltd 1989–96; Div. Dir First City Insurance Brokers Ltd 1996–2000; Dir City Arts Trust Ltd 1978–, Grandactual Ltd 1993–97, Int. Disputes Resolution Centre (IDRC) 2002–, Cayman Islands Monetary Authority 2003–06; Bd mem. ARIAS (Insurance Arbitration Soc.) 1997–2015, Hon. mem. 2015–; mem. Pathfinder Team Consulting 1992–; mem. Advisory Council and Educ. Cttee, London Symphony Orchestra 1997–; Chair. UK/NZ 1990 Cttee 1989–90; Chair. Trustees, Waitangi (Link) Foundation 1991–99; Trustee, St Paul's Cathedral Choir School Foundation 1985–2010, Morden Coll. 1995–; Hon. Gov. Christ's Hosp. 1980–, Chair. Gov. Menuhin School; Patron Lord Mayor Treloar Trust 1985–; mem. Court of Common Council (of City of London) 1970–2005, Alderman 1975–2005, Sheriff 1982–83, Lord Mayor of London 1984–85; Master Worshipful Co. of Musicians 2000; Vice-Pres. Bridewell Royal Hosp. 2003–06; Commemorative Medal NZ 1990. *Leisure interests:* DIY, travel, opera, music, assisting with education. *Address:* Wheelers Farm, Thursley, Godalming, Surrey, GU8 6QE, England (home). *Telephone:* (7714) 328204 (mobile); (1252) 703271 (home). *Fax:* (1252) 703271 (home). *E-mail:* atraill.granary@btinternet.com (office).

TRAINOR, Sir Richard Hughes (Rick), KBE, BA, MA, DPhil, FRHistS, AcSS, FKC; American/British historian, academic and university administrator; *Rector, Exeter College, Oxford;* b. 31 Dec. 1948, Camden, NJ, USA; s. of William Richard Trainor and Sarah Hughes Trainor; m. Marguerite Dupree 1980; one s. one d.; ed Brown Univ. and Princeton Univ., USA, Merton and Nuffield Colls Univ. of Oxford, UK; Jr Research Fellow, Wolfson Coll., Univ. of Oxford 1977–79; joined Dept of Econ. History, Univ. of Glasgow 1979, later becoming Prof., Dean of Social Sciences and Vice-Prin.; Vice-Chancellor and Prof. of Social History, Univ. of Greenwich 2000–04; Pres., Prin. and Prof. of Social History, King's Coll. London 2004–14; Rector, Exeter Coll., Oxford Oct. 2014–; Chair. Advisory Council, Inst. of Historical Research 2004–09; Pres. Universities UK 2007–09; mem. UK-US Fulbright Comm. 2003–09 (Patron 2010–), Arts and Humanities Research Council 2006–11, Inst. of Public Policy Research Comm. on the Future of Higher Educ. 2012–13, Review Bd of the Higher Educ. Funding Council for England's Review of Philanthropic Support for Higher Educ. throughout the UK 2012–13; Hon. Sec. Econ. History Soc. 1998–2004, Pres. 2013–; Gov. St Paul's School 2012–; Gov. RAM 2013–; Hon. Fellow, Merton Coll. Oxford, Trinity Coll. of Music, Inst. of Historical

Research; Hon. DCL (Kent) 2009, Hon. DHL (Rosalind Franklin Univ. of Medicine and Science) 2012. *Publications:* History and Computing III: Historians, Computers and Data: Applications in Research and Teaching (co-ed.) 1991, Towards an International Curriculum for History and Computing (co-ed.) 1992, Black Country Elites: The Exercise of Authority in an Industrialized Area 1830–1900 1993, The Teaching of Historical Computing: An International Framework (co-ed.) 1993, University, City and State: The University of Glasgow on Gilmorehill since 1870 (with J. F. Munro and M. S. Moss) 2000, Urban Governance: Britain and Beyond since 1750 (co-ed.) 2000; book chapters and articles in peer-reviewed journals. *Address:* James Clerk Maxwell Building, King's College London, 57 Waterloo Road, London, SE1 8WA, England (office). *Telephone:* (20) 7848-3434 (office). *Fax:* (20) 7848-3430 (office). *E-mail:* principal@kcl.ac.uk (office). *Website:* www.kcl.ac.uk/aboutkings/principal/ricktrainor.aspx (office).

TRAIRATVORAKUL, Prasarn, BEng, MEng, MBA, DBA; Thai economist and fmr central banker; b. 20 Aug. 1952, Bangkok; m. Nisarat Trairatvorakul; ed Chulalongkorn Univ., Asian Inst. of Tech., Thai Nat. Defence Coll., Harvard Univ., USA; Research Fellow, Int. Food Policy Research Inst., Washington, DC 1981–83; joined Bank of Thailand (cen. bank) as Economist, Dept of Econ. Research 1983, becoming Section Chief, Dept of Bank Supervision and Examination, later Deputy Dir, Dept of Financial Insts Supervision and Examination –1992, Gov. Bank of Thailand 2010–15; Deputy Sec.-Gen., Securities and Exchange Comm. of Thailand 1992–99, Sec.-Gen. 1999–2003; Pres. KASIKORNBANK Public Co. Ltd 2004–10; Chair. KFactoring Co. Ltd 2005–09, KLeasing Co. Ltd 2005–10; Vice-Chair. Muangthai Life Assurance Co. Ltd 2010, Muangthai Group Holding Co. Ltd 2010; Exec. Dir Thai Red Cross Soc. 1998–; mem. Council Chulalongkorn Univ. 2008; Dir Financial Reform Advisory Cttee, Ministry of Finance 1998–2000; Dir State Enterprises Capital Policy Cttee 2000–03; Chair. Thai Bankers Asscn 2010; mem. Bd of Investment 2014; mem. State Enterprises Supervisory Bd 2014; Commdr (Third Class), Most Noble Order of the Crown of Thailand, Commdr (Third Class), Most Exalted Order of the White Elephant; Hon. DBA (Rajamongkol Suvarnabhumi Univ.) 2013, Hon. DEcon (Khonkaen Univ.) 2015; Central Bank Governor of the Year for Asia, Emerging Markets Magazine 2011, Financier of the Year, Money and Banking Magazine 2012.

TRAN, Duc Luong; Vietnamese fmr mining engineer, politician and fmr head of state; b. 5 May 1937, Quang Ngai Prov.; m. Nguyen Thi Vinh; moved to Hanoi after leaving school 1955; studied geology and was employed as a cartographer; joined Dang Cong san Viet Nam (CP of Viet Nam) 1959, held several party roles in 1970s, mem. Politburo 1996–97; apptd Deputy Prime Minister 1987; Pres. of Viet Nam 1997–2006; Ho Chi Minh Award for Science and Tech. 2005, Gold Star Medal 2007.

TRAN, Rev. Tam Tinh, (Hoang Tam), PhD, FRSC; Vietnamese/Canadian archaeologist and academic; *Professor Emeritus of Classical Archaeology, Université Laval;* b. 16 April 1929, Nam Dinh; ed Séminaire Pontifical, Università Laterano, Université de Fribourg, Ecole Pratique des Hautes Etudes, Paris, CNRS; ordained priest 1956; excavations at Soli, Cyprus 1965–74, Pompeii and Herculaneum 1969–76; Co-founder Fraternité Vietnam 1976; Prof. of Classical Archaeology, Université Laval 1964–71, Sr Prof. 1971–94, Prof. Emer. 1994–; Tatiana Warscher Award for Archaeology, American Acad. at Rome 1973, Prix G. Mendel, Acad. des Inscriptions et Belles-Lettres, France 1978. *Publications include:* Le culte d'Isis à Pompéi 1964, Le culte des divinités orientales à Herculaneum 1971, Le culte des divinités orientales en Campanie 1972, Isis lactans 1973, Catalogue des peintures romaines au musée du Louvre 1974, Tôi vê Hanoi 1974, Tro vê nguôn 1974, I cattolici nella storia del Vietnam 1975, Dieu et César 1978, Sérapis debout 1983, Soloi I, La Basilique 1985, La casa dei Cervi à Herculaneum 1988, Corpus des lampes antiques conservées au Québec I 1991, Corpus des lampes à sujets asiatiques du musée gréco-romain d'Alexandrie 1993, Xin thay day con cau nguyen 2004, Loan bao tin mung 2004, Lay Cha 2004, Ong la ai? 2004; and numerous articles on classical iconography and religion. *Address:* Université Laval, Cité Universitaire, Québec City, PQ G1K 7P4 (office); 2995 Maricourt, Suite 300, Québec City, PQ G1W 4T8, Canada (home). *Telephone:* (418) 653-3513 (office). *E-mail:* vinhsont2005@yahoo.ca. *Website:* www.ulaval.ca (office).

TRAN, Thanh Man, PhD; Vietnamese politician; b. 12 Aug. 1962, Châu Thành A Dist, Hau Giang Prov.; ed Ho Chi Minh Nat. Political Acad.; entered into politics 1975; joined Communist Party of Vietnam 1982; mem. People's Council of Chau Thanh Dist 1986; mem. People's Council of Can Tho Prov. 1990–94, Standing mem. Party Council 2004–11, Sec. Party Cttee 2011–15; mem. Cen. Cttee of 11th Nat. Congress 2011; mem. Nat. Ass. (Parl.) 2011–; apptd Vice-Pres. Cen. Cttee of Vietnamese Fatherland Front 2014, Pres. 2017–; mem. Cen. Cttee of 12th Nat. Congress 2018–. *Address:* Vietnamese Fatherland Front and Member Organizations, 46 Trang Thi, Hanoi (office); 81 Nguyen Trãi, Ninh Kieu, Can Tho 92000, Vietnam (home). *Telephone:* (4) 3928-7401 (office). *Fax:* (4) 3825-6331 (office). *Website:* mattran.org.vn (office).

TRAN, Trong Toan, MA; Vietnamese diplomatist and international organization official; b. 12 Oct. 1952, Ha Tay Prov. (now Ha Noi); s. of Tran Trong An and Pham Thi Lan; m. Le Thi Lai; two d.; ed Faculty of Orientalistics, Tashkent State Univ., Uzbekistan; official, S Asia Dept, Ministry of Foreign Affairs 1975–80, Embassy of Viet Nam, New Delhi 1980–83, Foreign Minister's Secr. and Asst Dir-Gen. Foreign Ministry's Secr. 1984–89, Acting Dir-Gen. S Asia Dept 1990–92, Minister Counsellor, Embassy in New Delhi 1992–95, Dir-Gen. Dept of Econ. Affairs 1996–2000, Vice-Chair. Viet Nam Nat. Cttee for the Pacific Econ. Co-operation Council 1996–2000, 2004–05, Viet Nam Sr Official to APEC 1999, Amb. to Malaysia 2000–03, Dir-Gen. Foreign Minister's Advisory Bd, then Dir-Gen. Dept of Multilateral Econ. Co-operation, Ministry of Foreign Affairs 2003–04, mem. Govt Negotiation Team for Int. Econ. Integration, Amb. and Deputy Exec. Dir APEC Secr. 2005, Amb. and Exec. Dir 2006, Standing Vice-Chair. Cttee for Overseas Vietnamese, Ministry of Foreign Affairs 2007–09, Amb. to South Korea 2010–13, Amb. of Viet Nam, Ministry of Foreign Affairs 2013–; Pres. Inst. of Business Culture 2014–18; Vice-Pres. Vietnam Asscn of Business Culture Devt 2014–18; Sr Advisor, Nat. Cttee of APEC Vietnam Year 2017; currently Lecturer, Foreign Service Training Center, Vietnam Diplomatic Acad.; State Order of Labour (Third Class) 2007, (First Class) 2014; awards from Minister of Foreign Affairs and other ministers, Ambassador for Life bestowed by Vietnam Pres. of State 2013, Prime Minister's Award of Merit for Contributions to APEC Vietnam 2017. *Publications:* several books and articles, including The Asia-Pacific Economic Cooperation Forum (APEC) (author and Chief Ed.) 1998, Globalization and Vietnam's International Economic Integration (author and Chief Ed.) 1999, APEC Glossaries 2006, Collection of My Speeches as APEC Secretariat Executive Director 2006, Stories on President Ho Chi Minh and Vietnamese Diplomacy (Chief Ed.) 2010, Selective Poems of Vietnamese Diplomats (Chief Ed.) 2010, Guidebook for Chiefs of Vietnam Diplomatic Missions (author and Chief Ed.) 2014, Blue Book on Vietnam Foreign Affairs (author & Chief Ed.) 2014, Handbook on APEC and APEC Vietnam Year 2017, History of Vietnam Ministry of Foreign Affiars 1945–2015. *Leisure interests:* volleyball, badminton, table tennis, golf. *Address:* Ministry of Foreign Affairs, 1 Ton That Dam, Ba Dinh District, Hanoi (office); Vietnam Association of Business Culture Development, 8 Huynh Thuc Khang, Ba Dinh District, Ha Noi, Viet Nam (office). *Telephone:* 0833-980752 (mobile) (office). *E-mail:* tttoantt@yahoo.com (office). *Website:* www.mofa.gov.vn (office).

TRANHOLM-MIKKELSEN, Jeppe, MSc, Cand. Scient. Pol.; Danish diplomatist; *Secretary-General, Council of the European Union;* b. 30 Oct. 1962, Aden, Yemen; m. Birgitte Karnøe Frederiksen; two c.; ed London School of Econs, UK, Univ. of Aarhus; Head of Section, Ministry of Foreign Affairs 1992–95, Sec. of Embassy, Perm. Representation to EU, Brussels 1995–98, Sr Adviser (EU Policy), Prime Minister's Office 1998–2001, Head of Dept (Gen. EU Policy), Ministry of Foreign Affairs 2001, Chief Adviser (EU Policy), Prime Minister's Office 2001–03, Amb. and Deputy Perm. Rep. to EU 2003–07, Amb. to China 2007–10, Amb. and Perm. Rep. to EU, Brussels 2010–15; Sec.-Gen. Council of the EU 2015–; Gold Medal, Univ. of Aarhus 1992. *Address:* General Secretariat of the Council of the European Union, DGF, Public Information Service, 175 Rue de la Loi, 1048 Brussels, Belgium (office). *Telephone:* (2) 281-56-50 (office). *Fax:* (2) 281-49-77 (office). *E-mail:* jerome.unterhuber@consilium.europa.eu (office). *Website:* www.consilium.europa.eu (office).

TRAORÉ, Gen. Moussa; Malian politician, army officer and fmr head of state; b. 25 Sept. 1936, Kayes; ed Training Coll., Fréjus, Cadets Coll., Kati; NCO in French Army, returned to Mali 1960, promoted Lt 1964, Col 1971, Brig.-Gen. 1978; at Armed Forces Coll., Kati until 1968; led coup to depose Pres. Modibo Keita Nov. 1968; Pres. Mil. Cttee for Nat. Liberation (Head of State) and C-in-C of the Armed Forces 1968–91, also Prime Minister 1969–80; Pres. of Mali 1979–91; Minister of Defence and Security 1978–86, of the Interior 1978–79, of Nat. Defence 1988–90 (overthrown in coup, under arrest); Chair. OAU 1988–89; Sec.-Gen. Nat. Council Union Démocratique du Peuple Malien 1979–80, fmr mem. Cen. Exec. Bureau; Pres. Conf. of Heads of State, Union Douanière des Etats de l'Afrique de l'Ouest 1970; overthrown March 1991, stood trial Nov. 1992, sentenced to death for mass murder Feb. 1993, sentence commuted to life imprisonment 1997, charged with embezzlement Oct. 1998, sentenced to death Jan. 1999, sentence commuted to life imprisonment Sept. 1999, officially pardoned 2002.

TRAORÉ, Col Salif; Malian politician and military commander; *Minister of Security and Civil Protection;* ed Ecole mil. française de Saint Cyr; served in Malian army, roles include Commdr, 11th Mixed Regt, Head, Sector No 1 (Tessalit Dist), Commdr, 12th Mixed Regt and Head, Sector No 2 (Kidal Dist), Commdr, 13th Mixed Regt and Head, Sector No 3, Co-ordinator, Special Programme for peace, security and devt in northern Mali; took part in UN missions in Sudan and Liberia; Gov. Kayes Region 2012–15; Minister of Security and Civil Protection 2015–; attained rank of Gen. de Brigade 2006; Officier, ordre nat. du Mali 2014. *Address:* Ministry of Security and Civil Protection, BP E 4771, Bamako, Mali (office). *Telephone:* 2022-0082 (office).

TRAPATTONI, Giovanni; Italian professional football manager and fmr footballer; b. 17 March 1939, Cusano Milanino, Milan; defender/midfielder; sr player, AC Milan 1959–71 (274 appearances, three goals, won Serie A 1961/62, 1967/68, Italian Cup 1966/67, European Cup 1963, 1969, UEFA Cup Winners' Cup 1967/68, Intercontinental Cup 1969), Varese 1971–72, Italy 1960–64 (17 caps, one goal); Man. AC Milan 1974, 1976, Juventus 1976–86, 1991–94 (won Serie A 1976/77, 1977/78, 1980/81, 1981/82, 1983/84, 1985/86, Italian Cup 1978/79, 1982/83, European Cup 1984/85, UEFA Cup Winners' Cup 1984, UEFA Cup 1977, 1993, European Super Cup 1984, Intercontinental Cup 1985, UEFA Cup 1992/93), Inter 1986–91 (won Serie A 1988/89, UEFA Cup 1991), Bayern Munich 1994–95, 1996–98 (won German League 1996/97, German Cup 1998), Cagliari 1995–96, Fiorentina 1998–2000, Italy nat. team 2000–04; Head Coach, Benfica, Portugal 2004–05 (won Portuguese League 2004/05), VfB Stuttgart 2005–06, Red Bull Salzburg, Austria 2006–08 (won Austrian League 2006/07); Man. Repub. of Ireland nat. team 2008–13; one of only two coaches, alongside Ernst Happel, to have won the league title (ten times) in four different countries (Italy, Germany, Portugal and Austria); fourth coach with most int. competitions for clubs won in the world (second in Europe) with seven titles in eight finals, including Intercontinental Cup final (mainly with Juventus); only coach, alongside Udo Lattek, to have won all three major European club titles; only coach to have won all UEFA club competitions and World Club title; also has record of three UEFA Cup wins; UEFA Cup Winning Coach 1976–77, 1990–91, 1992–93, UEFA Cup Winners' Cup Winning Coach 1983–84, European Cup Winning Coach 1984–85, Philips Man. of the Year Award 2012, Italian Football Hall of Fame 2012. *Publication:* Fischia il Trap (biog.). *Website:* www.trapattoni.de.

TRAUTMAN, Andrzej; Polish theoretical physicist and academic; *Professor Emeritus, Warsaw University;* b. 4 Jan. 1933, Warsaw; s. of Mieczysław Trautman and Eliza Trautman (née André); m. Róża Michalska 1962; two s.; ed Warsaw Univ. of Tech., Warsaw Univ.; asst, Inst. of Radiolocation, Warsaw Univ. of Tech. 1952–53, Inst. of Applied Math. 1953–55; postgraduate studies, Inst. of Physics, Polish Acad. of Sciences (PAN) 1955–58, doctorate 1959; lecturer 1959; scientific training, Imperial Coll., King's Coll., London, Univ. of Syracuse, USA 1959–61; scientist, Inst. of Theoretical Physics, Warsaw Univ. 1961–, Asst Prof. and Head of Dept Electrodynamics and Theory of Relativity 1962–68, Extraordinary Prof. 1964–71, Ordinary Prof. 1971–2004, Prof. Emer. 2004–; Deputy Dir Inst. of Theoretical Physics 1968–74, Dir 1975–85; Corresp. mem. Polish Acad. of Sciences 1969–76, mem. 1977–, mem. Presidium 1972–83, Vice-Pres. 1978–80, Chair. Cttee of Physics; Corresp. mem. Polish Acad. of Arts and Science, Kraków; Deputy Chair. Gen. Bd of Polish Physics Asscn 1970–73, Foreign mem. Czechoslovak Acad. of Sciences 1980–90; mem. Int. Cttee of Theory of Relativity and Gravitation 1965–80, Int. Journal of Theoretical Physics, Journal of Geometry and Physics; Visiting Prof., American Math. Soc., Santa Barbara 1962, Coll. de France, Paris

1963 and 1981, Brandeis Univ., USA 1964, Univ. of Chicago 1971, Univ. of Pisa, Italy 1972, The Schrödinger Professorship, Univ. of Vienna 1972, State Univ. of NY at Stony Brook 1976–77, Univ. of Montreal 1982, 1990, Univ. of Texas at Dallas 1985, 1986; Gold Cross of Merit, Officer's Cross of Order of Polonia Restituta; Dr hc (Silesian Univ., Czech Repub.) 2001; State Prize 1st Class 1976, Alfred Jurzykowski Foundation Award in Physics 1984. *Publications:* Differential Geometry for Physicists 1984, The Spinorial Chessboard (with P. Budinich) 1988, Space Time and Gravitation (with W. Kopczyński) 1992; and numerous works on theory of gravitational waves, energy of gravitation field, modern methods of differential geometry and their application in physics, Einstein-Cartan's Theory, Dirac operator and spin structures on manifolds. *Leisure interest:* chess. *Address:* Instytut Fizyki Teoretycznej UW, ul. Pasteura 5, 02-093 Warsaw, Poland (office). *Telephone:* (22) 5532295 (office). *Fax:* (22) 6219475 (office). *E-mail:* andrzej.trautman@fuw.edu.pl (office). *Website:* www.fuw.edu.pl (office).

TRAUTZ, Volker, PhD; German business executive; b. 14 Feb. 1945, Bretten; ed Univ. of Stuttgart; worked as asst at Univ. of Stuttgart –1974; joined BASF AG 1974, served several man. positions, including 14 years in S America, Pres. BASF's Consumer Products Div. 1991–95, mem. Bd Exec. Dirs BASF 1995–2000, responsible for all polymers, including eng resins, PVC and polyurethanes, and for BASF's activities in Asia; CEO Basell (renamed LyondellBasell Industries following acquisition by Basell of Lyondell Chemical Co. Dec. 2007) 2000–09 (retd); mem. Supervisory Bd Evonik Industries AG 2007–; mem. Bd of Dirs La Seda de Barcelona SA 2011–. *Address:* Evonik Industries AG, Rellinghauser Str. 1–11, 45128 Essen, Germany (office). *Telephone:* (201) 17701 (office). *Fax:* (201) 1773475 (office). *E-mail:* info@evonik.com (office). *Website:* www.evonik.com (office).

TRAVIS, Randy; American country singer, songwriter and musician (guitar); b. (Randy Bruce Traywick), 4 May 1959, Marshville, North Carolina; m. Lib Hatcher (Mary Elizabeth Robertson) 1991 (divorced 2010); played local clubs with brothers; resident at Charlotte nightclub (owned by Lib Hatcher) 1977; early recordings as Randy Traywick; resident singer, as Randy Ray, Nashville Palace 1992; solo artist as Randy Travis 1985–; Acad. of Country Music Top Male Vocalist 1985, 1986, 1987, 1988, Grammy Award for Best Country Newcomer 1986, CMA Horizon Award 1986, Acad. of Country Music Song of the Year (for On the Other Hand) 1986, (for Forever and Ever Amen) 1987, (for Three Wooden Crosses) 2004, CMA Single of the Year (for Forever and Ever Amen) 1987, Music City News Male Artist of the Year, Star of Tomorrow and Single of the Year (for On the Other Hand) 1987, CMA Male Vocalist of the Year 1987, 1988, Music City News Entertainer of the Year, Male Artist of the Year, Single of the Year (for Forever and Ever Amen) and Entertainer of the Year 1989, Grammy Award for Best Album Collaboration (for Same Old Train 1998, CMA Song of the Year (for Three Wooden Crosses) 2003, inducted into CMA Country Music Hall of Fame 2016, Grammy Award for Best Country Collaboration with Vocals (for I Told You So with Carrie Underwood) 2010, Artist Career Achievement Award, Country Radio Broadcasters 2016, also awards from Performance magazine, AMOA Jukebox, Country Music Round Up, NECMA, TNN Viewers Choice Awards, Rolling Stone magazine, Playboy magazine, Billboard Music Awards, BBC Radio Two, Dove Awards, Christian Country Music Awards. *Recordings include:* albums: Storms Of Life (Acad. of Country Music Album of the Year 1986, Music City News Album of the Year 1986) 1986, Always And Forever (Grammy Award 1987, CMA Album of the Year 1987, Music City News Album of the Year 1988) 1987, Old 8x10 (Grammy Award 1988) 1988, An Old Time Christmas 1989, No Holdin' Back 1989, Heroes And Friends 1990, High Lonesome 1991, Wind In The Wire 1993, This Is Me 1994, Full Circle 1996, You And You Alone 1998, A Man Ain't Made Of Stone 1999, Inspirational Journey 2000, Randy Travis Live 2001, Anthology 2002, Rise And Shine (Grammy Award 2004) 2002, Worship & Faith (Grammy Award 2005) 2003, Passing Through 2004, Glory Train (Grammy Award for Best Southern, Country, Or Bluegrass Gospel Album 2007) 2005, Songs of the Season 2007, Around the Bend 2008, Blessed Assurance 2011, Influence, Vol. 1: The Man I Am 2013, Influence Vol. 2: The Man I Am 2014, On The Other Hand – All The Number Ones 2015. *E-mail:* webmaster@randytravis.com. *Website:* www.randytravis.com.

TRAVKIN, Nikolai Ilyich; Russian politician; b. 19 March 1946, Novo-Nikolskoe, Moscow region; m.; two s.; ed Kolomna Pedagogical Inst., Higher Party School; mem. CPSU 1970–90; worker, brigade-leader, Head of the Dept of Glavmosstroi; initiator self-financing and self-man. into construction industry 1969–; Deputy Head of construction union 1967–89; mem. of the movt Democratic Russia 1988–; People's Deputy of the USSR 1989–91; People's Deputy of Russia 1990–93; Co-founder and Chair. Democratic Party of Russia 1990–94; Chair. of the Sub cttee, (Supreme Soviet of the USSR (supervising local soviets and devt of self-man.) 1989–90; Chair. Cttee Supreme Soviet of Russia; supervising local soviets and devt of self-man. May–Dec. 1990; head of local admin. Shakhovskoy Dist 1991–96; Co-leader Civic Union coalition 1992–93; mem. State Duma (Parl.) Yabloko group (now Union of Right Forces faction) 1993–2003; Minister without Portfolio 1994–96; apptd mem. Cttee on Problems of Fed. and Regional Politics 1996; Pres. Fund in Support of Farmers; Order of Red Banner of Labour, Order of Merit for the Fatherland 1996; Hero of Socialist Labour 1986. *Leisure interests:* theatre, literature.

TRAVOLTA, John; American actor; b. 18 Feb. 1954, Englewood, NJ; s. of Salvatore Travolta and Helen (née Burke) Travolta; m. Kelly Preston 1991; one s. (one s. deceased) one d.; Billboard Magazine Best New Male Vocalist Award 1976, Male Star of the Year, Nat. Asscn of Theatre Owners 1983, Alan J. Pakula Prize 1998, Lifetime Achievement Award, Palm Springs Int. Film Festival 1999. *Television includes:* Welcome Back Kotter (series) 1975–77, American Crime Story (series) 2016. *Films:* Carrie 1976, The Boy in the Plastic Bubble (for TV) 1976, Saturday Night Fever (Nat. Bd of Review Award for Best Actor) 1977, Grease 1978, Moment by Moment 1978, Urban Cowboy 1980, Blow-Out 1981, Staying Alive 1983, Two of a Kind 1983, Perfect 1985, The Experts 1988, Chains of Gold 1989, Look Who's Talking 1989, Look Who's Talking Now 1990, The Tender 1991, All Shook Up 1991, Look Who's Talking 3 1994, Pulp Fiction 1994, White Man's Burden 1995, Get Shorty (American Comedy Award, Golden Globe Award for Best Actor) 1995, Broken Arrow 1996, Phenomenon 1996, Michael 1997, Face Off 1997, She's So Lovely 1997, Primary Colors 1998, A Civil Action 1998, The General's Daughter 1999, Battlefield Earth 2000, Lucky Numbers 2000, Swordfish 2001, Domestic Disturbance 2001, Basic 2003, The Punisher 2004, A Love Song for Bobby Long 2004, Ladder 49 2004, Be Cool 2005, Lonely Hearts 2006, Wild Hogs 2007, Hairspray 2007, The Taking of Pelham 123 2009, Old Dogs 2009, From Paris with Love 2010, Savages 2012, Killing Season 2013, The Forger 2014, Life on the Line 2015, Criminal Activities 2015, In a Valley of Violence 2016, I Am Wrath 2016. *Recordings include:* John Travolta 1976, Travolta Fever 1978, Grease 1978, Let Her In: The Best of John Travolta 1996, Hairspray 2007. *Publications:* Staying Fit 1984, Propeller One-Way Night Coach (juvenile) 1998. *Leisure interest:* flying. *Address:* William Morris Agency, One William Morris Place, Beverly Hills, CA 90212, USA (office); William Morris Endeavor, 9601 Wilshire Blvd, Beverly Hills, CA 90212, USA. *Telephone:* (310) 859-4000 (office). *Fax:* (310) 859-4462 (office). *Website:* www.wma.com (office).

TREACY, Philip, MA, RCA; Irish milliner; b. 26 May 1967, Ballinsoe, Co. Galway; s. of James Vincent Treacy and Katie Agnes Treacy; ed Nat. Coll. of Art and Design, Dublin, Royal Coll. of Art, London; while a student worked for designers including Rifat Ozbek, John Galliano and Victor Edelstein; f. Philip Treacy Millinery, London 1991; house milliner for Marc Bohan at Hartnell and for Victor Edelstein; has collaborated with Karl Lagerfeld, Chanel's couture and ready-to-wear shows 1991–; his own ready-to-wear range sold in New York and London 1991–; designed headdresses for Pola John's production of My Fair Lady 1992; presented own show, London 1993; launched accessory range 1997; first show in New York 1997; Interior Design Dir The G (hotel) 2005; Hon. OBE 2007; British Accessory Designer of the Year award 1991, 1992, 1993, 1996, 1997, Irish Fashion Oscar 1992, Haute Couture Paris 2000, Moet & Chandon Award 2002, Int. Designer of the Year, China Fashion Awards 2004. *Address:* Philip Treacy London Head Office, 1 Havelock Terrace, London, SW8 4AS, England (office). *Telephone:* (20) 7738-8080 (office). *Fax:* (20) 7738-8545 (office). *E-mail:* admin@philiptreacy.co.uk (office). *Website:* www.philiptreacy.co.uk (office).

TRECHSEL, Stefan, DIur, PD; Swiss lawyer and judge (retd) and academic; b. 25 June 1937, Berne; s. of Manfred F. Trechsel and Steffi Friedlaender; m. Franca Julia Kinsbergen 1967 (died 2017); two d.; ed Univ. of Berne and Georgetown Univ., Washington, DC; Asst and Main Asst for Criminal Law, Univ. of Berne 1964–71; Swiss Fed. Dept for Tech. Cooperation 1966–67; Public Prosecutor, Dist of Bern-Mittelland 1971–75; Guest Prof. of Criminal Law and Procedure, Univ. of Fribourg 1975–77; Prof., Hochschule St Gallen 1979–99; Prof. of Criminal Law and Legal Criminal Procedure, Univ. of Zurich 1999–2004, Prof. Emer. 2004–; Judge ad litem, Int. Criminal Tribunal for the Fmr Yugoslavia, The Hague, Netherlands 2006–13; mem. European Comm. of Human Rights 1975–99 (2nd Vice-Pres. 1987, Chamber Pres. 1993–94, Pres. 1995–99), AIDP 2013–, FIPP 2013–; Council of Europe Medal pro merito 2004; Dr hc (New York Univ. Law School) 1975; ASIL award for Human Rights in Criminal Proceedings. *Publications include:* Der Strafgrund der Teilnahme 1967, Die Europäische Menschenrechtskonvention, ihr Schutz der persönlichen Freiheit und die Schweizerischen Strafprozessrechte 1974, Strafrecht Allgemeiner Teil I (6th edn of textbook by Peter Noll) 1994, Schweizerisches Strafgesetzbuch, Kurzkommentar 1997, Human Rights in Criminal Proceedings 2005, Strafrecht Allgemeiner Teil Idn with Mark Pieth 2017, Praxiskommentar (third edn with Mark Pieth) 2018. *Leisure interests:* music, literature, art. *Address:* Rabbentalstr. 63, 3013 Berne, Switzerland (home). *Telephone:* 313328449 (home). *Fax:* (4179) 3650874. *E-mail:* trechsel@gmx.net (office).

TREDE, Michael, BA, MD, BChir; German surgeon; b. 10 Oct. 1928, Hamburg; s. of Hilmar Trede and Gertrud Trede (née Daus); m. Ursula Boettcher 1956; one s. four d.; ed The Leys School, Cambridge and Univ. of Cambridge; Surgeon-in-Training, Freie Universität, Berlin 1957–62, Heidelberg Univ. 1962–72; Prof. and Chair. Dept of Surgery, Klinikum Mannheim, Univ. of Heidelberg, now Prof. Emer. and Chair.; Pres. Deutsche Gesellschaft für Chirurgie, Int. Surgical Soc. 1993–95; Hon. mem. Austrian, American, Swiss, Italian and Portuguese Surgical Asscns; Hon. FRCS (England, Ireland, Glasgow, Edin.); Hon. FACS; Verdienstorden der Bundesrepublik Deutschland 1998; Dr hc (Edinburgh) 1995. *Publications:* Surgery of the Pancreas (with D. C. Carter), The Art of Surgery 1999, Der Rückkehrer. Skizzenbuch eines Chirurgen 3rd edn 2003; 500 articles on surgery in scientific journals. *Leisure interests:* painting, violin-playing, mountaineering, skiing. *Address:* Nadlerstrasse 1A, 68259 Mannheim, Germany. *Telephone:* (621) 383-2728 (office); (621) 796301.

TREGLOWN, Jeremy Dickinson, BLitt, MA, PhD, FRSL; British author, journalist and academic; *Professor Emeritus of English, University of Warwick;* b. 24 May 1946, Anglesey, N Wales; s. of Rev. G. L. Treglown and Beryl Treglown; m. 1st Rona Bower 1970 (divorced 1982); one s. two d.; m. 2nd Holly Eley (née Urquhart) 1984 (died 2010); one d. with Jennifer Lewis; m. 3rd Maria Alvarez 2013; ed Bristol Grammar School, St Peter's Coll. and Hertford Coll., Oxford; Lecturer in English Literature, Lincoln Coll. Oxford 1973–76, Univ. Coll., London 1976–79; Asst Ed. The Times Literary Supplement 1979–81, Ed. 1982–90; Prof. of English, Univ. of Warwick 1993, now Prof. Emer. (Chair. Dept of English and Comparative Literary Studies 1995–98); Chair. of Judges, Booker Prize 1991, Whitbread Book of the Year Award 1998; mem. Council, RSL 2010–; Co-Ed. Liber: A European Review of Books 1989; Contributing Ed., Grand Street magazine, New York 1991–98; Visiting Fellow, All Souls Coll., Oxford 1986; Fellow, Huntington Library 1988; Mellon Visiting Assoc., California Inst. of Tech. 1988; Ferris Visiting Prof., Princeton Univ. 1992; Jackson Brothers Fellow, Beinecke Library, Yale Univ. 1999; Leverhulme Research Fellow 2001–03; Margaret and Herman Sokol Fellow, Cullman Center for Scholars and Writers, New York Public Library 2002–03; Fellow in History, Bogliasco Foundation 2011, 2017; Fellow, Rockefeller Foundation, Bellagio 2011; Sr Research Fellow, Inst. of English Studies, School of Advanced Study, Univ. of London 2012–; Chair. of Trustees, Arvon Foundation; Hon. Research Fellow, Univ. Coll. London 1991–. *Publications include:* The Letters of John Wilmot, Earl of Rochester (ed.) 1980, Spirit of Wit: Reconsiderations of Rochester (ed.) 1982, Roald Dahl: A Biography 1994, Grub Street and the Ivory Tower: Literary Journalism, and Literary Scholarship from Fielding to the Internet (co-ed. with Bridget Bennett) 1998, Romancing: The Life and Work of Henry Green 2000, VS Pritchett: A Working Life 2004, Essential Stories/V.S. Pritchett (ed.) 2005, Roald Dahl: Collected Stories (ed.) 2006, Franco's Crypt: Spanish Culture and Memory Since 1936 2013; contrib. of introductions to recent edns of R. L. Stevenson's In the South Seas, Robert Louis Stevenson's The Lantern Bearers, the complete novels of Henry Green; various articles on poetry, drama and literary history. *Address:* Humanities Building, University Road, University of Warwick, Coventry, CV4 7AL, England (office). *E-mail:* jeremy.treglown@warwick.ac.uk (office). *Website:* www2.warwick.ac.uk/fac/arts/english (office).

TREHAN, Naresh Kumar, MD; Indian cardiovascular surgeon; *Chairman and Managing Director, Medanta-The Medicity; b.* 12 Aug. 1946; m. Madhu Trehan; ed King George's Medical Coll., Lucknow, American Bd of Surgery and American Bd of Cardiothoracic Surgery, USA; Teaching Asst and Clinical Instructor, New York Univ. Medical Center, USA 1971–74, Attending Cardiothoracic Surgeon 1979–88, Asst Prof. of Surgery 1981–88; Attending Cardiothoracic Surgeon, New York Infirmary-Beekman Downtown Hosp., St Vincent's Hospital and Medical Center, Bellevue Hospital, New York 1979–88; Chief Thoracic and Cardiovascular Surgery, Veterans Administration Hosp., New York; Personal Surgeon to Pres. of India 1991–; est. Escorts Heart Inst. and Research Centre 1988, Exec. Dir and Chief Cardiovascular Surgeon, Escorts Heart Inst. and Research Centre 1988–2007; Sr Cardiovascular and Thoracic Surgeon, Apollo Hospitals 2007–09; currently Chair. and Man. Dir Medanta-The Medicity, Haryana; Pres. Indian Health Care Fed., Int. Soc. for Minimally Invasive Cardiac Surgery 2004–05; Chair. Healthcare Industry Cttee, Confed. of Indian Industries; Fellow, Royal Soc. of Medicine, London, American Coll. of Surgeons, Int. Medical Sciences Acad.; mem. Soc. of Thoracic Surgeons of America, Asscn of Thoracic and Cardiovascular Surgeons of Asia, Scientific Council, American Coll. of Angiology, European Asscn for Cardio-thoracic Surgery, Key Advisory Group, Ministry of Health and Family Welfare, Inst. Body of Sanjay Gandhi Post Grad. Inst. of Medical Sciences, Lucknow 1996–2001, Governing Council, Sri Jayadeva Inst. of Cardiology, Bangalore; mem. Bd of Dirs Int. Soc. for Minimally Invasive Cardiac Surgery; mem. Editorial Bd Heart Surgery Forum (journal); Hon. Consultant to Cromwell Hospital, London, UK 1994, Cardiothoracic Surgery to Armed Forces Medical Services 1997, Hon. Visiting Prof., Cardiovascular Surgery, LPS Inst. of Cardiology, Kanpur 1996, Bangladesh Medical Coll., Dhaka 2000, Hon. Fellow, Royal Australasian Coll. of Surgeons 2002; Hon. DSc (Banaras Hindu Univ.) 1996, (Chhatrapati Shahu Ji Maharaj Univ., Kanpur) 2004, (King George's Medical Univ., Lucknow) 2007; Nagrik Club Jaipur Award 1991, Joshi Award, Delhi Medical Asscn 1989, Alumni Award, KG Medical Coll., Lucknow 1989, Nat. Integration Council Award 1988, Padma Shri 1991, Nat. Inst. of Punjab Studies Bhai Vir Singh Int. Award, Yuva Shakti Org. Jaipur Award 1992, Shiromani Award 1992, T.P. Jhunjhunwala Foundation Award 1992–93, Mother India Int. Award, NRI Inst. 1992, Distinguished Service Award, Indian Medical Asscn Acad. of Medical Specialities 1993, Distinguished Service Award, Acad. of Medical Specialities 1994, Sushruta Award 1994, Samajshree Award, Indian Council of Man. Exec., Bombay 1995, Rajiv Gandhi Nat. Unity Award 1995, Lok Seva Award 1995, India Int. Gold Award, NRI Inst. 1995, Rotary Ratna Award, Rotary Int. 1996, Life Time Achievement Award, Int. Medical Integration Council 1999, Dr K. Sharan Cardiology Excellence Award, Indian Medical Asscn 2000, Indira Gandhi Millennium Award, All India Feroze Gandhi Memorial Soc. 2000 AMA Physician's Recognition Award, CME Alliance at ISMICS, Germany 2001, Padma Bhushan Award 2001, Rashtriya Ratan Award 2001, Ernst & Young Entrepreneur Award, Jewel of India in the Millennium, Int. Award Cttee, Wisitex Foundation 2002, Life Time Achievement Award, Int. Soc. of Cardiovascular Ultrasound 2002, Dr B.C. Roy Nat. Award 2005, Lal Bahadur Shastri Nat. Award 2005. *Address:* Medanta-The Medicity, Sector 38, Gurgaon, Haryana 122 001, India (office). *Telephone:* (124) 4141414 (office). *Fax:* (124) 4834111 (office). *E-mail:* naresh.trehan@medanta .org (office); ntrehan@vsnl.com (office). *Website:* www.medanta.org; www .drnareshtrehan.com.

TREICHL, Andreas; Austrian banking executive; *Chairman of the Management Board, Erste Group Bank AG; b.* 1952; ed Univ. of Vienna; began career with Chase Manhattan Bank, New York 1977; joined Erste Bank in 1983 for three years, rejoined bank and apptd to Man. Bd 1994, Chair. 1997–, responsible for Group Communication, Group HR, Strategic Group Devt, Group Secr., Group Audit, Group Marketing, Group Investor Relations, Group Identity, good.bee – banking for the unbanked; Vice-Chair. Supervisory Bd Ceska Sporitelna AS 2013–; Great Silver Decoration of Honour 2001, WU Manager of the Year 2007, Great Golden Decoration of Honour 2007. *Address:* Erste Bank der oesterreichischen Sparkassen AG, Am Belvedere 1, 1100 Vienna, Austria (office). *Telephone:* (50) 100-10100 (office). *Fax:* (50) 100-910-100 (office). *E-mail:* investor.relations@erstebank.at (office). *Website:* www.erstebank.com (office).

TREITEL, Sir Guenter Heinz, Kt, QC, MA, DCL, FBA; British academic; *Professor Emeritus of English Law, University of Oxford; b.* 26 Oct. 1928, Berlin, Germany; s. of Dr Theodor Treitel and Hanna Treitel (née Levy); m. Phyllis M. Cook 1957; two s.; ed Kilburn Grammar School and Magdalen Coll., Oxford; came to UK 1939; Asst Lecturer, LSE 1951–53; Lecturer, Univ. Coll., Oxford 1953–54; Fellow of Magdalen Coll., Oxford 1954–79, Fellow Emer. 1979–; All Souls Reader in English Law 1964–79; Vinerian Prof. of English Law, Univ. of Oxford and Fellow of All Souls Coll. 1979–96, Prof. Emer. and Fellow Emer. 1996–; Visiting Lecturer, Univ. of Chicago 1963–64, Visiting Prof. 1968–69, 1971–72; Visiting Prof., Univ. of Western Australia 1976, Univ. of Houston 1977, Southern Methodist Univ. 1978, 1988–89, 1994, Distinguished Visiting Prof. 2000, 2003; Visiting Prof., Univ. of Va 1978–79, 1983–84, Univ. of Santa Clara 1981; Visiting Scholar, Ernst von Caemmerer Gedächtnisstiftung 1990; Clarendon Lecturer in Law, Univ. of Oxford 2001; consultant to Law Comm. on law of contract 1972–84; Trustee, British Museum 1983–98; mem. Council Nat. Trust 1984–93; Hon. Bencher, Gray's Inn. *Publications:* The Law of Contract (11 edns) 1962–2003, Chitty on Contracts (10 edns as jt ed.) 1968–2015, An Outline of the Law of Contract (six edns) 1975–2004, Remedies for Breach of Contract: A Comparative Account 1988, Unmöglichkeit, "Impracticability" und "Frustration" im anglo-amerikanischen Recht 1991, Frustration and Force Majeure (three edns) 1994–2014, Benjamin's Sale of Goods (nine edns as co-author) 1974–2014, English Private Law (two edns as co-author) 2000–07, Carver on Bills of Lading (three edns as co-author) 2001–11, Some Landmarks of Twentieth Century Contract Law 2002 (Chinese trans. 2010); ed. of other law books. *Leisure interests:* reading, music. *Address:* All Souls College, Oxford, OX1 4AL, England. *Telephone:* (1865) 279379. *Fax:* (1865) 279299.

TRELFORD, Donald Gilchrist, MA, FRSA; British journalist and editor (retd) and academic; *b.* 9 Nov. 1937, Coventry, West Midlands, England; s. of T. S. Trelford and Doris Gilchrist; m. 1st Janice Ingram 1963 (divorced 1978); two s. one d.; m. 2nd Katherine Louise Mark 1978 (divorced 1999); one d.; m. 3rd Claire Elizabeth Bishop 2001; one s. one d.; ed Bablake School, Coventry, Selwyn Coll., Cambridge; pilot officer, RAF 1956–58; worked on newspapers in Coventry and Sheffield 1961–63; Ed. Times of Malawi and corresp. in Africa, The Times, Observer, BBC 1963–66; joined Observer as Deputy News Ed. 1966, Asst Man. Ed. 1968, Deputy Ed. 1969–75, Dir and Ed. 1975–93, CEO 1992–93; Dir Optomen Television 1988–97, Observer Films 1989–93, Cen. Observer TV 1990–93; Dir, Prof., Dept of Journalism Studies, Univ. of Sheffield 1994–2000, Visiting Prof. 2001–04, Prof. Emer. 2004–; Chair. Soc. of Gentlemen, Lovers of Musick 1996–2002, London Press Club 2002–07 (Pres. 2007–13); mem. British Exec. Cttee, Int. Press Inst. 1976–90, Asscn of British Eds 1984–90, Guild of British Newspaper Eds 1985–93 (mem. Parl. and Legal Cttee 1987–91); Vice-Pres. British Sports Trust 1988–2002; Ind. Assessor BBC TV Regional News 1997; mem. Council, Media Soc. 1981–2003 (Pres. 1999–2002), Judging Panel, British Press Awards 1981–2005 (Chair. 2003–05), Scottish Press Awards 1985, Olivier Awards Cttee, SWET 1984–93, Defence, Press and Broadcasting Cttee 1986–93, Cttee, MCC 1988–91, Competition Comm.'s Newspaper Panel 1999–2007, Council of Advertising Standards Authority 2002–08; Vice-Pres. Newspaper Press Fund 1992– (Chair. Appeals Cttee 1991); Acting Ed. The Oldie 1994; Judge, Whitbread Literary Awards 1992, George Orwell Prize 1998; sports columnist, Daily Telegraph 1993–2008; Dir St Cecilia Int. Festival of Music 1995–2002; columnist, Majorca Daily Bulletin 2010–; Freeman of the City of London 1988; Hon. DLitt (Sheffield); Granada Newspaper of the Year Award 1983, 1993, commended, Int. Ed. of the Year (World Press Review) 1984. *Radio:* presenter, LBC Breakfast News 1994; regular panellist, BBC Radio Five Live. *Television:* presenter of sports and current affairs series, Channel 4 and BBC 2. *Publications include:* Siege 1980, Snookered 1986, Child of Change (with Garry Kasparov) 1987, Saturday's Boys 1990, Fine Glances 1990; (contrib.) County Champions 1982, The Queen Observed 1986, Len Hutton Remembered 1992, World Chess Championships (with Daniel King) 1993, W. G. Grace 1998; Ed.: Sunday Best 1981, 1982, 1983, The Observer at 200 1992; contrib. to Animal Passions 1994: Shouting in the Street, Adventures and Misadventures of a Fleet Street Survivor 2017. *Leisure interests:* reading, walking, watching rugby. *Address:* Apartado 146, 07460 Pollenca, Majorca, Spain (home). *Telephone:* 6-63453506 (mobile) (home). *E-mail:* donaldtrelford@yahoo.co .uk (home).

TREMAIN, (Edwin) Garrick; New Zealand landscape artist and cartoonist; *b.* 4 Feb. 1941, Wellington; s. of Edwin Rex Tremain and Linda Joyce Tremain; m. Jillian Mary Butland; two d.; ed Palmerston North Boys' High School; worked as shepherd; then as artist and art director for advertising agencies in NZ, UK and Malaysia; full-time artist 1973–; syndicated cartoonist 1988–; NZ Commemorative Medal 1990, Cartoonist of the Year 1996, 1999. *Publications:* Nursery Rhymes Mother Never Read You 2005, Twenty Years of Tremain 2007, The Trouble with Golf 2011, The Arrowtown Collection 2011. *Leisure interests:* golf, piano, jazz music. *Address:* Stonebridge, 103 Cotter Avenue, Arrowtown, Otago 9302, New Zealand. *Telephone:* (3) 409-8244. *E-mail:* tremain@queenstown.co.nz. *Website:* garrick-tremain.squarespace.com.

TREMAIN, Rose, CBE, BA, FRSL; British writer; *b.* (Rosemary Jane Thomson), 2 Aug. 1943, London; d. of Keith Thomson and Viola Mabel Thomson; m. 1st Jon Tremain 1971; one d.; m. 2nd Jonathan Dudley 1982 (dissolved 1990); partner Richard Holmes; ed Univ. of Paris (Sorbonne), France, Univ. of East Anglia; novelist and playwright 1971–; part-time tutor Univ. of East Anglia 1988–95; mem. judging panel, Booker Prize 1988, 2000; Chancellor, Univ. of East Anglia 2013–; Hon. DLitt (East Anglia) 2001, (Essex) 2005, (Open Univ.) 2010, Hon. Fellowship (Goldsmiths Coll., London) 2012; Univ. of Essex Fellowship 1979–80, one of Granta's Best Young British Novelists 1983, Giles Cooper Award 1985, Angel Literary Award 1986, Sony Award 1996. *Plays for radio include:* Temporary Shelter 1985, Who Was Emily Davison? 1996, The End of Love 1999, One Night in Winter 2001. *Television includes:* A Room for the Winter 1979, Daylight Robbery 1982. *Publications include:* fiction: Sadler's Birthday 1976, Letter to Sister Benedicta 1978, The Cupboard 1981, The Swimming Pool Season 1984, Restoration (Sunday Express Book of the Year Award) 1989, Sacred Country (James Tait Black Memorial Prize 1993, Prix Fémina Etranger 1994) 1992, The Way I Found Her 1997, Music and Silence (Whitbread Novel of the Year) 1999, The Colour 2003, The Road Home (Orange Broadband Prize for Fiction 2008) 2007, Trespass 2010, Merivel: A Man of His Time 2012, The Gustav Sonata 2016; for children: Journey to the Volcano 1985; short story collections: The Colonel's Daughter (Dylan Thomas Short Story Prize 1984) 1982, The Garden of the Villa Mollini 1988, Evangelista's Fan 1994, Collected Short Stories 1996, The Darkness of Wallis Simpson and Other Stories 2005, The American Lover and Other Stories 2014; non-fiction: The Fight for Freedom for Women 1971, Stalin: An Illustrated Biography 1974, Rosie: Scenes from a Vanished Life (memoir) 2018. *Leisure interests:* yoga, gardening. *Address:* 2 High House, South Avenue, Thorpe St Andrew, Norwich, NR7 0EZ, England (home). *Telephone:* (1603) 439682 (home).

TREMAINE, Scott Duncan, BSc, MA, PhD, FRS, FRSC; Canadian astrophysicist and academic; *Professor, Institute for Advanced Study; b.* 25 May 1950, Toronto, Ont.; s. of Vincent Tremaine and Beatrice Tremaine (née Sharp); m. Marilyn Tremaine; ed McMaster Univ., Hamilton, Ont., Princeton Univ., USA; mem. Inst. for Advanced Study, Princeton, NJ 1978–81, Prof. 2007–; Assoc. Prof., MIT 1981–85; Prof., Univ. of Toronto 1985–97; Dir Canadian Inst. for Theoretical Astrophysics 1985–96; Prof. and Chair. Dept of Astrophysical Sciences, Princeton Univ. 1998–2006; mem. NAS 2002; Foreign Hon. mem. American Acad. of Arts and Sciences 1992; Hon. DSc (McMaster Univ., St Mary's Univ., Univ. of Toronto); Warner Prize, American Astronomical Soc. 1983, Steacie Prize 1989, Rutherford Medal in Physics 1990, Carlyle S. Beals Award 1990, Heinemann Prize for Astrophysics 1997, Dirk Brouwer Award 1997, Tomalla Prize 2013. *Publication:* Galactic Dynamics (with J. Binney) 1987 (second edn 2008). *Address:* School of Natural Sciences, Institute for Advanced Study, Einstein Drive, Princeton, NJ 08540, USA (office). *Telephone:* (609) 734-8191 (office). *Fax:* (609) 924-7592 (office). *E-mail:* tremaine@ias.edu (office). *Website:* www.sns.ias.edu (office).

TREMBLAY, Michel; Canadian writer; *b.* 25 June 1942, Montréal; ed Graphic Arts Inst. of Québec; worked as linotypist 1963–66; Chevalier, Légion d'Honneur 2008, Grand Officier, Ordre national du Québec 2015; Dr hc (Concordia, McGill,

Stirling, Windsor, Université du Québec à Montréal); first prize for young writers sponsored by CBC (for play Le Train, written 1959) 1964, Gov.-Gen.'s Performing Arts Award 1999. *Film scripts include:* Françoise Durocher, Waitress 1972, Il était une fois dans l'Est 1973, Parlez-nous d'amour 1976, Le Soleil se lève en retard 1977. *Plays include:* Les Belles-Sœurs 1968, En pièces détachées 1969, La Duchesse de Langeais 1969, Demain matin, Montréal m'attend (musical) 1970, À toi, pour toujours, ta Marie-Lou 1971, Hosanna 1973, Bonjour là, bonjour 1974, Surprise! Surprise! 1975, Les Héros de mon enfance (musical) 1976, Sainte Carmen de la Main 1976, Damnée Manon, sacrée Sandra 1977, L'Impromptu d'Outremont 1980, Les Anciennes Odeurs 1981, Albertine en cinq temps 1984, Le Vrai Monde? 1987, La Maison suspendue 1990, Nelligan (opera libretto) 1990, Marcel poursuivi par les chiens 1992, En circuit fermé 1994, Messe solennelle pour une pleine lune d'été 1996, Encore une fois, si vous permettez 1998, L'État des lieux 2002, Le Passé antérieur 2003, Impératif présent 2003, Bonbons assortis 2006, Le Paradis à la fin de vos jours 2008, Fragments de mensonges inutiles 2009, Lettres de madame Roy à sa fille Gabrielle (songs cycle) 2012, L'Oratorio de Noël 2012. *Television:* Le Cœur découvert 2000. *Publications:* Contes pour buveurs attardés 1966, La Cité dans l'œuf 1969, C't'à ton tour, Laura Cadieux 1973, La Grosse Femme d'à côté est enceinte 1973, Thérèse et Pierrette à l'école des Saints-Anges 1980, La Duchesse et le Roturier 1982, Des nouvelles d'Edouard 1984, Le Cœur découvert 1986, Le Premier Quartier de la lune 1989, Les Vues animées 1991, Douze Coups de théâtre 1992, Le Cœur éclaté 1993, Un ange cornu avec des ailes de tôle 1994, La Nuit des princes charmants 1995, Quarante-quatre minutes, quarante-quatre secondes 1997, Un objet de beauté 1998, Hôtel Bristol, New York 1999, L'Homme qui entendait siffler une bouilloire 2001, Bonbons assortis 2002, Le Cahier noir 2003, Le Cahier rouge 2004, Le Cahier bleu 2005, Le Trou dans le mur 2006, La Traversée du continent 2007, La Traversée de la ville 2008, La Traversée des sentiments 2009, Le passage obligé 2010, La Grande Mêlée 2011, Au hasard la chance 2012, Les Cles du Paradise 2013, Survivre!, Survivre! 2014, La Traversée du malheur 2015. *Leisure interest:* painting water colours. *Address:* Agence Goodwin, 839 Sherbrooke Street East, Suite 200, Montréal, PQ H2L 1K6, Canada (office). *Telephone:* (514) 598-5252 (office). *Fax:* (514) 598-1878 (office). *E-mail:* artistes@goodwin.agent.ca (office). *Website:* www.agencegoodwin.com (office).

TREMLETT, David Rex; British artist; b. 13 Feb. 1945, Cornwall, England; s. of Rex Tremlett and Dinah Tremlett; m. Laure Florence 1987; one s. two d.; ed St Austell Grammar School, Falmouth Art Coll., Birmingham Coll. of Art and Royal Coll. of Art; exhibited widely in UK, USA, Europe, Africa, Australia, Mexico, Japan etc.; recent projects include: walls of Law Courts, Amsterdam, two rooms at Benesse Guesthouse, Naoshima Island, Japan, façade of St Denis Univ., Paris, main hall of BBL Bank Kortrijk, Belgium, walls and ceiling at Eaton Hall, Chester, UK, walls of castle of Marchese di Barolo, Barolo, Italy, lobby of Cen. Landesbank, Dresden, Germany, Chapel of Barolo, Italy, interior wall at ABN AMRO HQ, Amsterdam, Netherlands, walls of British Embassy Berlin, walls at Obayashi HQ, Tokyo, Japan, walls and floor of Palazzo Fantuzzi, Bologna, Italy, wall for the Grosvenor Estates, London, walls of Rione Alto metro station, Naples, Italy, walls, ceiling and floor of Chapel of Santa Maria dei Carcerati Bologna, wall drawings for British Council Centre, Nairobi, Kenya, walls of Esserheem Penitentiary, N Holland, all 25 stained glass windows of St Peter and St Paul Church, Villenauxe-la-Grande, France, Villa Caldogno (Palladio) Vicenza, Italy (one room of wall drawings), Zamosc Synagogue wall drawings, Zamosc, Poland, Villa Amista (Byblos Hotel) ceilings, Verona, Italy, The Qube (Atrium), Tottenham Court Road, London, two entrance rooms, Castello di Formigine, Formigine, Italy, walls of Chapelle Notre-Dame des Fleurs, Moric, Brittany, France, entrance wall of Palazzo Mantegazza, Lugano, Switzerland, portico ceiling of Beata Vergine Assunta Church, Mortorone, Italy, ceiling of Forte di Bard, Aosta, Italy, wall for the Paladian Villa Pisani, Vicenza, Italy, walls of A La Cruz restaurant, London, stained glass windows for Chapelle Notre-Dame des Fleurs, Moric, Brittany, hallway and staircase of Manton Hall, Tate Britain, London, walls for three rooms of Fernandez and Wells Bar, Somerset House, London, 3 Fernandez and Wells Bars in Soho, London, Reception Area of 26 Finsbury Square London, 'Artists House' at Roche Court Sculpture Park, Salisbury, Walls and Ceilings for Casa Giulia, Turin, Italy, Walls of QE2 hospital entrance, Welwyn Garden City, UK, The Exterior of the Chiesetta (Small Church) di Coazzolo, Italy; South Lobby Walls of BLOOMBERG LP, London; Hon. Citizen of La Morra, Italy, Citizen of Coazzolo, Italy. *Films:* Non-Improvisation (b/w) 1971, No Title 1995. *Music:* Hand Up/Too Bad (CD), A Journey with David Tremlett (soundtrack). *Television:* A Journey with David Tremlett (satellite) 2003. *Publications include:* selected artist books: Some Places to Visit 1974, On the Waterfront 1978, Scrub 1978, On the Border 1979, Restless 1983, Rough Ride 1985, Ruin 1987, Sometimes We All Do 1988, Tremlett-West Bengal 1990, Internal 1991, From Wall to Wall 1991, Mjimwema Drawings 1991, Abandoned Drawings 1993, Casa de Dibujos 1993, Nouveaux Plans 1994, Columns 1995, How Far in that Direction 1996, Walls and their Drawings 1997, Pages (Eritrea) 1998, Clear and Fuzzy 1999, If Things Could Talk 2002, Black as Midnight with the Eyes Shut 2002, Between You and Me (co-author) 2006, Texas 2007, D.T. 2008, Tools of the Trade (Outils du Metier) 2017; selected catalogues: Wall Drawings 1969–1995, Dates/Differents 1987, Written Form 1990, A Quiet Madness 1992, PAC Catalogue 1993, Rooms in Vienne 1994, Walls at the Palais Jacques Coeur, Bourges 1994, Passa Dentro 2000, If Walls Could Talk 2001, A New Light 2003, 37 Wall Drawings in Issoire 2003, David Tremlett: British Council Nairobi 2005, David Tremlett-Retrospectve Musée des Beaux Arts, Grenoble France/Pecci Museum, Prato, Italy 2006, Lumière: The Stained Glass Windows of St Peter and St Paul Church, Villenauxe-la-Grande, France 2006, Between You and Me 2006, David Tremlett: A Dialogue Between Past and Present 2008, D.T. 2008, David Tremlett: Drawn, Rubbed, Smeared 2009, Walls (Forte di Bard) 2010, Place and Material, MAMAC, Nice 2010, David Tremlett: Drawing Rooms, Hamburg Kunsthalle 2010, David Tremlett at Villa Pisani 2010, David Tremlett: The Thinking in Space 2011, David Tremlett: Architecte de Lumière 2011, 3 Drawing Rooms: Ikon Gallery, Birmingham 2013, Works on Paper: Galleria Comunale D'Arte Contemporanea Di Monfalcone 2014, Textile Projects by David Tremlett, Galleria Antonio Verolino, Modena 2016, Tools of the Trade Voix Editions, France 2017. *Leisure interests:* Davidson glass, African music, Saharan architecture, cross-country strolling. *Address:* Broadlawns, Chipperfield Road, Bovingdon, Hemel Hempstead, Herts., HP3 0JR, England (home). *E-mail:* tremlett@tremlett.demon.co.uk (home). *Website:* www.davidtremlett.com.

TREMONTI, Giulio; Italian lawyer, academic and politician; b. 18 Aug. 1947, Sondrio, Lombardy; ed Univ. of Pavia; Prof., Univ. of Pavia Law School 1974–; fmr Sr Teaching Fellow, Inst. of European and Comparative Law, Univ. of Oxford, UK; mem. Camera dei Deputati (Parl.) 1994–2013, Senator 2013–, mem. Parl. Special Cttee for Reform of Italian Constitution; Minister of Finance 1994–95, 2008–11, of Economy and Finance 2001–04 (resgnd), Sept. 2005–06, Deputy Prime Minister 2005–06; Pres. Comm. for Monetary Reform 1994–95; Chair. Aspen Inst. Italia; mem. Italy/Vatican Cttee for Treaty on Financing of Ecclesiastical Insts, Comm. on Deregulation, Lombard Acad. of Sciences and Letters; Ed. Rivista di Diritto Finanziario e Scienza delle Finanze; regular contrib., Corriere della Sera. *Publications:* La paura e la speranza 2008 and several books on tax and public policy. *Address:* Senate (Senato), Piazza Madama, 00186 Rome, Italy (office). *Telephone:* (06) 67061 (office). *Website:* www.senato.it (office); www.giuliotremonti.it.

TRENDAFILOVA, Ekaterina Panayotova, PhD; Bulgarian barrister and judge; b. 20 June 1953, Sofia; d. of Panayot Trendafilova and Tatiana Trendafilova; m. Emil Roussev Bachvarov; one d.; ed Sofia Univ. 'St Kliment Ohridski'; legal internship, Sofia City Court 1977–78; Deputy Dist Attorney, Sofia Dist Court 1985–89; specialization at Inst. of State and Law, Moscow, USSR 1983, 1985; Prof., Faculty of Law, Sofia Univ. 'St Kliment Ohridski' 1984–, Assoc. Prof. (Docent) 1996–2001, Full Prof. 2001–; Prof., Faculty of Law, Veliko Turnovo Univ. 'Sts Cyril and Methodius' 1995; Visiting Prof., Tokai Univ., Japan 1993; called to the Bar of Bulgaria 1995, barrister 1995–2005; advised the Ministry of Foreign Affairs on the establishment of the Int. Criminal Court (ICC) and served as an expert to the Ministry of Justice, Ministry of Interior, Supreme Court of Cassation and Parl. of Bulgaria where she chaired the Criminal Div. of the Legis. Consultative Council; Judge, Pre-Trial Div., ICC 2006–15; mem. Intergovernmental Comm. entrusted with the preparation of the ratification of the European Convention on Human Rights and Fundamental Freedoms 1991; Bulgarian Rep. to UN Comm. for Crime Prevention and Criminal Justice, Vienna 1992–94; Chair. Program and Analytical Center for European Law 1999–, Modern Criminal Procedure Foundation 1999–; Vice-Pres. Specialized Scientific Council on Legal Science 2003–04; mem. Comm. for Social Sciences at the Higher Accreditation Agency with the Council of Ministers of Bulgaria 2000–03, Legal Comm. Nat. Higher Attestation Comm. with the Council of Ministers of Bulgaria 2004–05; scientific advisor, Students' Internship Program between the American Govt and Bulgarian Parl. 2000–05; Head, Criminal Div. Legis. Consultative Council with Chair. (Speaker) of the Bulgarian Parl. 2001–05; Middle-term expert under the PHARE Twinning project (Bulgaria–Austria) 2002–03; mem. Consultative Council Open Soc. Inst. Project 'Access to Justice' 2002–05, Advisory Bd Open Soc. Inst. Int. Project 'Independence and Accountability of Prosecution' 2003–05; European expert within EC CARDS Regional Project 2004–05; Head of Working Group on Judicial Reform, Open Soc. Inst. Project Strategy for the Socio-econ. and Political Devt of Bulgaria 2005–2010 2004–05; mem. Editorial Bd Human Rights Review 2003–; mem. Union of Bulgarian Lawyers 1980–, Union of Bulgarian Scholars 1984– (Chair. legal section 2001–03), Bulgarian Humboldt Soc. 1994–, Bulgarian Fulbright Soc. 1997–, Women with Int. Societal Expertise (WISE), Paris 2004–; Alexander von Humboldt Scholarship, Augsburg Univ., Germany 1993–94; Fulbright Scholarship, Univ. of California, USA 1997; Hon. mem. European Correspondents Scientific Cttee, Centre Int. Constats et Prospective, Paris 1991; Best Young Lecturer of the Year Award, Nat. Soc. for Dissemination of Legal Knowledge 1984, Alexander von Humboldt Scholarship, Augsburg Univ., Germany 1993–94, Author of the Year Award for contrib. to the legal literature 2000, Legal Initiative for Training and Devt Award 2004. *Publications:* more than 70 publs in Bulgaria, USA, France, Italy and the Netherlands in the field of human rights law, criminal procedural law, int. criminal procedural law, comparative law and constitutional law. *Address:* c/o International Criminal Court, PO Box 19519, 2500 CM The Hague, Netherlands (office).

TRENTA, Elisabetta; Italian politician; *Minister of Defence;* b. 4 June 1967, Velleteri; ed La Sapienza University of Rome; Capt., Army Reserve 2008; Nat. Councillor, UN Interim Force In Lebanon 2009; Project Man., Task Force Archaeological Sites 2013–14; Researcher, Military Center for Strategic Defense Studies 2016–17; currently Deputy Dir Master in Intelligence and Security Programme, Link Campus Univ.; Vice-Pres. Children of Nassiriya Onlus, Flauto Magico; Minister of Defence 2018–; mem. Movimento 5 Stelle. *Address:* Ministry of Defence, Palazzo Baracchini, Via XX Settembre 8, 00187 Roma, Italy (office). *Telephone:* (06) 4882126 (office). *E-mail:* sgd@sgd.difesa.it (office). *Website:* www.difesa.it (office).

TRENTHAM, David Rostron, BA, PhD, FRS; British medical research scientist and academic; *Visiting Professor, Randall Division of Cell and Molecular Biophysics, King's College London;* b. 22 Sept. 1938, Solihull, West Midlands, England; s. of John A. Trentham and Julia A. M. Trentham; m. Kamalini Bhargava 1966; two s.; ed Uppingham School and Univ. of Cambridge; MRC Jr Research Fellow, Lecturer and Reader, Dept of Biochemistry, Univ. of Bristol 1966–77; Chair. and Edwin M. Chance Prof., Dept of Biochemistry and Biophysics, School of Medicine, Univ. of Pennsylvania, Phila, USA 1977–84; Head, Div. of Physical Biochemistry, MRC Nat. Inst. for Medical Research, London (now Crick Mill Hill) 1984–2003, Visiting Worker 2003–; Visiting Prof., Randall Div. of Cell and Molecular Biophysics, King's Coll. London 2003–; Hon. Prof., Randall Div., King's Coll. London 2001; Colworth Medal, Biochemical Soc. 1974, Wilhelm Feldberg Prize 1990. *Publications include:* numerous articles in biochemical and academic journals. *Address:* Randall Division of Cell and Molecular Biophysics, King's College London, School of Biomedical Sciences, New Hunt's House, Guy's Campus, London, SE1 1UL, England (office). *E-mail:* drtrentham@aol.com (home). *Website:* www.kcl.ac.uk/biohealth/research/divisions/randall (office).

TRESCHOW, Michael, MEng; Swedish business executive; b. 22 April 1943, Helsingborg; ed Inst. of Tech., Lund; divisional man. roles in Scandinavia and France with Bahco Ventilation 1970–76; joined Atlas Copco AB 1976, Pres. and CEO 1991–97; Pres. and CEO AB Electrolux 1997–2002, Chair. 2004–07; Chair. Ericsson (Telefonaktiebolaget L.M. Ericsson) 2002–11; Chair. (non-exec.), Unilever NV and Unilever PLC 2007–16 (retd); mem. Bd of Dirs, B-Business Partners 2001–, ABB Ltd 2003–, Knut and Alice Wallenberg Foundation; Dir (non-exec.), SKF 1992, Saab 1992, Parker-Hannifin Corp. 1996; mem. European Advisory Bd,

Eli Lilly & Co. 2008–; Chair. Swedish Trade Council 1996, Confed. of Swedish Enterprise 2004–07; mem. Royal Acad. of Eng Sciences; King's Medal of 12th Dimension and Ribbon of Order of Seraphims (Sweden) 2000, Gran Cruz de la Orden del Mérito Civil (Spain) 2000, Chevalier, Légion d'honneur 2002, Commr Order of the Crown (Belgium) 2004. *Leisure interests:* golf, hunting. *Address:* c/o Unilever PLC, Unilever House, 100 Victoria Embankment, London, EC4Y 0DY, England. *E-mail:* press-office.london@unilever.com.

TRETHEWEY, Natasha, AB, MA, MFA; American poet and academic; b. 26 April 1966, Gulfport, Miss.; d. of Eric Trethewey and Gwendolyn Ann Turnbough; m. Brett Gadsden; ed Univ. of Georgia, Hollins Univ., Univ. of Massachusetts, Amherst; Lehman Brady Jt Chair Prof. of Documentary and American Studies, Duke Univ. and Univ. of North Carolina 2005–06; Charles Howard Candler Prof. of English and Creative Writing, also Robert W. Woodruff Prof. of English and Creative Writing, Emory Univ.; Louis D. Rubin Writer-in-Residence, Hollins Univ. 2012; Poet Laureate of Miss. 2012; US Poet Laureate 2012–14; Prof. of English Northwestern Univ. 2017–18; James Weldon Johnson Fellow in African American Studies, Beinecke Library, Yale Univ. 2009; Dr hc (Delta State Univ.) 2007, (Hollins Univ.) 2010; Nat. Endowment for the Arts Literature Fellowship 1999, Bunting Fellowship for Radcliffe Inst. for Advanced Study, Harvard Univ. 2000, Lillian Smith Book Award 2001, 2007, Miss. Inst. of Arts and Letters Book Prizes 2001, 2003, 2007, John Simon Guggenheim Memorial Foundation Fellowship 2003, Rockefeller Foundation Fellowship 2004, Acad. of American Poets Fellowship 2016, Heinz Award, Heinz Family Foundation 2017, Sidney Lanier Prize for Southern Literature 2018. *Publications include:* Domestic Work (Cave Canem Foundation Poetry Prize 1999) 2000, Bellocq's Ophelia 2002, Native Guard (Pulitzer Prize for Poetry 2007) 2006, Beyond Katrina: A Meditation on the Mississippi Gulf Coast 2010, Thrall 2012. *Address:* c/o Alison Granucci, Blue Flower Arts, PO Box 1361, Millbrook, NY 12545, USA (office). *Telephone:* (845) 677-8559 (office). *Fax:* (845) 677-6446 (office). *E-mail:* Alison@blueflowerarts.com (office). *Website:* www.blueflowersarts.com (office).

TRETIKOV, Lila; American (b. Russian) business executive; *CEO, Terrawatt Initiative;* b. 25 Jan. 1978, Moscow, Russia; ed Lomonosov Moscow State Univ., Univ. of California, Berkeley; moved to USA at age 16; started professional career at Sun Microsystems as engineer with Sun-Netscape Alliance, working on the Java server 1999; f. GrokDigital (tech. marketing co.); Chief Information Officer and Vice-Pres. of Eng, SugarCRM, Inc. 2006–14; Exec. Dir WikiMedia Foundation 2014–16; CEO Terrawatt Initiative 2017–; Young Global Leader, World Economic Forum LLC 2017–; mem. Bd of Dirs Rackspace, OpenEd.io; Advisor to Bd, Zamurai Corpn. *Address:* Terrawatt Initiative, 6 rue de Solférino, 75007 Paris, France (office). *E-mail:* secretariat@twi.team (office). *Website:* terrawatt.org (office).

TRETYAK, Vladislav A.; Russian ice hockey player (retd) and politician; b. 25 April 1952, Orudyevo, Moscow region; s. of Alexander D. Tretyak and Vera P. Tretyak; one s. one d.; m. Tatyana Ye Tretyak; ed Moscow State Inst. of Physical Culture, Lenin Mil. Political Acad.; ice hockey player 1967–84; (13 times USSR champion); hockey goalkeeper Central Army Sports Club and USSR nat. team (10 times world champion, nine times European champion); as a nat. team player played in 117 games in world, European championships and Olympic games; fmr Pres. Int. Sports Acad.; served as goalkeeper consultant to Chicago Black Hawks professional ice hockey team in 1990s; Asst Coach, Russian national team for Olympic Winter Games 1998, 2002; mem. State Duma (faction United Russia) 2003–; Pres. Ice Hockey Fed. of Russia 2006–; Gen. Man. of Russian 2010 Winter Olympic ice hockey team; mem. Int. Ice Hockey Fed. 2016–; Order of Red Banner of Labour 1984, Order of Friendship of the People; inducted into Hockey Hall of Fame 1989, named Best Russian Hockey Player of the 20th Century 2000. *Publications include:* four books. *Address:* State Duma, 103265 Moscow, Okhotnyi ryad 1, Russia (office). *Website:* www.duma.gov.ru (office).

TRETYAKOV, Viktor Viktorovich; Russian violinist; b. 17 Oct. 1946, Krasnoyarsk; m. Natalia Likhopoi; one d.; ed Moscow Conservatory with Yury Yankelevich; concert career since mid-1960s, soloist of Moscow Philharmonic 1969; tours of Europe, USA, Japan; participant in numerous European music festivals; Artistic Dir and Conductor, Moscow (now Russian) Chamber Orchestra 1983–90; apptd Prof. and Head of Chair of Violin, Tchaikovsky Moscow State Conservatory 1979; apptd Prof., Hochschule für Musik, Cologne 1996; Jury Pres. International Tchaikovsky Competition 1986–94; First Prize, All-Union Competition of Violinists 1965, First Prize, Int. Tchaikovsky Competition 1966, Lenin Komsomol Award 1967, People's Artist of the RSFSR 1979, Glinka State Award of the RSFSR 1981, USSR People's Artist 1987, Shostakovich Premium 1997, Triumph Prize 2003.

TRETYAKOV, Vitaly Toviyevich; Russian journalist and academic; b. 2 Jan. 1953, Moscow; m.; one s.; ed Moscow State Univ.; jr ed. to Ed. Press Agency Novosti (APN) 1976–88; reviewer, political reviewer, Deputy Ed.-in-Chief Moskovskiye Novosti (weekly) 1988–90; f. Nesavisimaya Gazeta (newspaper) 1990, Ed.-in-Chief 1990–2000; Dir-Gen. Independent Publishing Group 2001–04; Ed.-in-Chief, Moskovskiye Novosti 2004–07; Ed.-in-Chief, Politicheskii Klass; currently Dean, Higher School of Television, Lomonosov Moscow State Univ.; mem. Exec. Bd Council on Foreign and Defence Policy. *Publications include:* Philanthropy in Soviet Society 1989, Gorbachev, Ligachev, Yeltsin: Political Portraits on the Perestroika Background 1990, Titus of Sovietologists: Their Struggle for Power: Essays on Idiotism of Russian Policy 1996. *Leisure interests:* theatre, collecting of art albums. *Address:* Lomonosov Moscow State University, School of Television, 119991 Moscow, GSP-1, Leninskiye Gory, 1-51, 1 Humanities Building, Russia. *Telephone:* (495) 939-44-61 (office). *E-mail:* ftv-study@mail.ru (office). *Website:* www.ftv.msu.ru (office); v-tretyakov.livejournal.com.

TREVES, Vanni E., CBE, MA, LLM; British/Italian business executive; *Chairman, Korn/Ferry International;* b. 3 Nov. 1940, Florence, Italy; s. of Giuliano Treves and Marianna Treves; m. Angela Treves; two s. one d.; ed St Paul's, London, Univ. Coll. Oxford, Univ. of Illinois; joined Macfarlanes (law firm) as articled clerk 1963, qualified 1965, Asst Solicitor 1965–68, Visiting Attorney, White & Case, New York 1968–69, Partner, Macfarlanes 1970–2002, Sr Partner 1987–99; Chair. Equitable Life Assurance Soc. 2001–09; Chair. Intertek Group plc 2002–11; Chair. Channel Four Television Corpn 1998–2004, BBA Group PLC 1989–2000, McKechnie PLC 1991–2000, Korn/Ferry Int. UK 2004–; Sr Advisor, Oliver Wyman 2007–09; mem. Bd of Dirs Amplifin, Homerton Univ. Hosp. Trust 2012–; Chair. NSPCC Justice for Children Appeal 1997–2000; Gov. Coll. of Law 1999–, Sadler's Wells Foundation 1999–; Trustee, J. Paul Getty Charitable Trust, Prisoners Education Trust; mem. Devt Bd Nat. Art Collections Fund; mem. Law Soc.; Hon. Fellow, London Business School; Kt of the Star of Italy 2014. *Television:* Chairman,Channel 4 Television 1998–2004. *Leisure interests:* art, walking, food. *Address:* Korn/Ferry International, Ryder Court, 14 Ryder Street, London, SW1Y 6QB, England (office). *Telephone:* (20) 7024-9000 (office). *E-mail:* vanni.treves@kornferry.com (office). *Website:* www.kornferry.com (office).

TREVINO, Lee Buck; American professional golfer (retd); b. 1 Dec. 1939, Dallas, Tex.; s. of Joe Trevino and Juanita Barrett; m. Claudia Bove 1983; three s. three d.; turned professional 1960; US Open Champion 1968, 1971, The Open Champion 1971, 1972, Canadian Open Champion 1971, PGA Champion 1974, 1984 and numerous other championships 1965–80; won US Sr Open 1990, PGA Sr Championship 1994, Australian PGA Sr Championship 1996; f. Lee Trevino Enterprises, Inc. 1967; US PGA Player of the Year 1971, Sr Tour Player of the Year 1990, 1992, 1994. *Publication includes:* Super Mex (autobiography) 1983. *Leisure interest:* fishing.

TRÉYÉ, Mahamat Allamine Bourma; Chadian politician; s. of Bourma Tréyé; ed Ecole Nat. d'Admin de N'Djaména, Univ. Paris II (Panthéon Assas), France; Econ. Adviser to Pres. 2004; Minister of Stockbreeding and Water Supply 2006; Nat. Dir for Chad, Banque des Etats de l'Afrique Centrale (Bank of Central African States) 2013; Minister of Finance and the Budget 2012, Feb.–Aug. 2016.

TRIA, Giovanni; Italian academic, economist and politician; *Minister of Economy and Finance;* b. 28 Sept. 1948, Rome; ed Sapienza Univ. of Rome; Consultant, Ministry of Treasury 1995; Consultant, World Bank 1998–2000; Consultant, Ministry of Foreign Affairs 1999–2000, 2002; Expert High Committee for Fiscal Federalism 2004–05; Consultant World Bank 2004–05; Delegate to Bd of Dirs ILO 2002–06, 2009–12; Dir-Gen. Antiquities and Museum 2007; Pres. Nat. School of Public Admin 2010–16; Dir CEIS Univ. of Rome Tor Vergata 2002–09, currently Prof. of Political Economics, Dean 2017–; Minister of Economy and Finance 2018–; mem. Bd of Govs EIB 2018–. *Publications include:* Reforming the Public Sector: How to Achieve Better Transparency, Service, and Leadership (with Giovanni Valotti). *Address:* Ministry of Economy and Finance, Via XX Settembre 97, 00187 Roma, Italy (office). *Telephone:* (06) 476111 (office). *E-mail:* ufficio.stampa@mef.gov.it (office). *Website:* www.mef.gov.it (office).

TRICHET, Jean-Claude, LèsSc; French fmr central banker; *Chairman, Trilateral Commission (European Region);* b. 20 Dec. 1942, Lyon; s. of Jean Trichet and Georgette Vincent-Carrefour; m. Aline Rybalka 1965; two s.; ed Ecole des Mines, Nancy, Univ. of Paris, Inst. d'Etudes Politiques, Paris, Faculté Sciences Economiques, Paris and Ecole Nat. d'Admin; Engineer, competitive sector 1966–68, Insp. of Finances 1971–76; assigned to Gen. Inspectorate of Finance 1974, assigned to Treasury Dept 1975, Sec.-Gen. Business Restructuring Interministerial Cttee 1976–78; Adviser, Minister of Economic Affairs 1978; Adviser to Pres. of Repub. 1978–81; Head of Devt Aid Office and Deputy Dir of Bilateral Affairs, Treasury Dept 1981, Head of Int. Affairs, Treasury Dept 1985; Chief of Staff to Minister of Finance 1986–87; Dir Treasury Dept 1987; Alternate Gov. IMF and World Bank 1987, Under-Sec. of Treas. and Censor Bank of France 1987–93; Gov. Bank of France 1993–2003; Chair. Paris Club 1985–93; Gov. IBRD 1993–95; Vice-Gov. IMF 1995–2003; Chair. Monetary Cttee of EC 1992–93; Dir European Cen. Bank 1998–2003, Pres. 2003–11 (retd); Chair. Group of Ten Cen. Bank Govs 2003–11; Chair. Group of Thirty, Washington DC 2012–17, Trilateral Comm. (European Region) 2012–; Pres. SOGEPA (Société de Gestion des Participations aéronautiques), Paris 2012–13; Chair. Bd of Dirs, Bruegel (think-tank) 2012–; mem. Bd of Dirs BIS 1993–2003, 2005–11, EMI 1994–98, Airbus group 2012–18; mem. Institut de France (Académie des Sciences Morales et Politiques); Hon. Gov., Banque de France; Commdr, Légion d'honneur, Ordre nat. du Mérite, also Commdr Nat. Orders of Merit in Austria, Belgium and Portugal; Commdr's Cross with star of the Order of Merit (Poland), Knight Grand Cross of the Order of Orange-Nassau (Netherlands), Grand Cross 1st class of the Order of Merit (Germany); also decorations from Argentina, Brazil, Côte d'Ivoire, Ecuador; Dr hc (Stirling, Bologna, Liege, Tel Aviv, Montreal, Sofia); Policy Maker of the Year, Int. Economy Magazine 1991, 2007, Prize Zerilli Marimo, Acad. des Sciences Morales et Politiques 1999, Int. Prize Pico della Mirandola 2002, Prix franco-allemand de la Culture/Deutsch-Französischer Kulturpreis 2006, Person of the Year, Financial Time 2007, Int. Charlemagne Prize of Aachen 2011, Global Economy Prize, Kiel Inst. for the World Economy 2011, Lifetime Achievement Award for Econ. Policy, NABC 2014. *Publications include:* numerous articles on finance and economy. *Leisure interest:* poetry. *Address:* 7, Rue Rembrandt, 75008 Paris, France (home). *Telephone:* 1-42-92-48-48 (office). *E-mail:* jean-claude.trichet0263@orange.fr (home).

TRICOIRE, Jean-Pascal, MBA; French business executive; *President and CEO, Schneider Electric SA;* b. 11 May 1963; m.; three c.; ed Ecole Supérieure d'Electronique de l'Ouest Grad. School of Eng, Angers, CESMA Business School, Lyon; began career with Alcatel, Schlumberger and St Gobain 1985–86; joined Merlin Gerin 1986; various exec. roles with Schneider Electric SA 1988–99 including posts in Italy, China and S Africa, becoming Head of Global Strategic Accounts 1999–2001, Exec. Vice-Pres. Int. Div. 2002–03, COO 2003–06, Chair. Man. Bd (Pres.) and CEO 2006–; Chair. France-China Cttee of Mouvement des Entreprises de France (MEDEF) 2009–. *Leisure interests:* multi-cultural teams, commitment, humour, curiosity, travelling off the beaten path, whitewater sports, new technologies. *Address:* Schneider Electric SA, 43–45 boulevard Franklin Roosevelt, 92500 Rueil-Malmaison, France (office). *Telephone:* 1-41-29-70-00 (office). *Fax:* 1-41-29-71-00 (office). *E-mail:* info@schneider-electric.com (office). *Website:* www.schneider-electric.com (office).

TRIESMAN, Baron (Life Peer), cr. 2004, of Tottenham in the London Borough of Haringey; **David Maxim Triesman,** BA, MA, FRSA, FRSS; British economist, politician, trade union official and company director; b. 30 Oct. 1943, Herts., England; s. of Michael Triesman and Rita Triesman (née Lubran); m. Lucy Hooberman 2004; one d.; ed Stationers' Co. School, London, Univ. of Essex and King's Coll., Cambridge; Sr Research Officer in Addiction, Inst. of Psychiatry 1970–74; secondment to Asscn of Scientific, Tech. and Managerial Staff 1974–75;

Sr Lecturer and Co-ordinator Post grad. Research, Polytechnic of the South Bank 1975–84; Deputy Sec.-Gen. (Nat. Negotiating Sec.) Nat. Asscn of Teachers in Further and Higher Educ. 1984–93; Gen. Sec. Asscn of Univ. Teachers 1993–2001; Gen. Sec. Labour Party 2001–03, Govt Whip and Lord-in-Waiting 2004–05; Parl. Under-Sec. of State for Foreign and Commonwealth Affairs 2005–07; Govt Spokesman on Higher Educ., Trade and Industry, Foreign Affairs and Aid 2004–; Prime Minister's Special Envoy on Returns 2007–08; Under-Sec. of State for Innovation, Univs and Skills, Minister for Intellectual Property and Higher Educ. 2007–08; Chair. The Football Asscn and England 2018 FIFA World Cup Bid 2008–10 (resgnd); Shadow Spokesperson (Business, Innovation and Skills), House of Lords 2010–11, Foreign and Commonwealth Affairs 2010–; Chair. (non-exec.) Mortgage Credit Corpn 1978–2001, Victoria Management Ltd 2000–01; Chair. Usecolor Foundation 2001, Triesman Assocs 2010–, Templewood Merchant Bank 2010–13; Dir, Salamanca Group 2013–; Dir (non-exec.) The Social Homes Corpn 2013–, Havin Bank 2013–; Visiting Prof. in Social Econs, St Lawrence Univ. 1977; Visiting Fellow in Econs, Wolfson Coll., Cambridge 2000–; Sr Visiting Fellow, Univ. of Warwick 2003–; Visiting Fellow, LSE 2004–; mem. Greater London Manpower Bd 1981–86, Home Office Consultative Cttee on Prison Educ. 1980–83, Burnham Further and Higher Educ. Cttee 1980–84, Univ. Entrance and Schools Exams Bd for Social Science 1980–84, Standing Cttee on Business and the Community, Higher Educ. Funding Council for England 1999–; mem. Kensington, Chelsea and Westminster Area Health Authority 1976–82; mem. Industrial Relations Public Appointments Panel, Dept of Trade and Industry 1996–2001, Ind. Review of Higher Educ. Pay and Conditions 1998–99, Cabinet Office Better Regulation Task Force 2000–03, Treasury Public Services Productivity Panel 2000–03, British N American Cttee 1999–2013; mem. Fabian Soc. 1974–, Charles Rennie Mackintosh Soc., Glasgow 1986–, Highgate Literary and Scientific Inst. 1990–; mem. Council, Ruskin Coll., Oxford 2000–03, Univ. of Northamptonshire; Trustee, The Football Foundation 2008–10; Hon. LLD (London South Bank Univ.); Hon. DUniv (Essex); Hon. Fellow, Univ. of Northampton 1995. *Publications include:* The Medical and Non-Medical Use of Drugs 1969, Football Mania (with G. Viani) 1972, Football in London 1985, College Administration (co-author) 1988, Managing Change 1991, Can Unions Survive (Staniewski Memorial Lecture) 1999, Higher Education for the New Century 2000; 18 academic papers on epidemiology, drug addiction and related statistical method. *Leisure interests:* football, art, reading, blues guitar, hill walking. *Address:* House of Lords, Westminster, London, SW1A 0PW, England (office). *Telephone:* (20) 7219-5353 (office). *Fax:* (20) 7219-5979 (office). *E-mail:* triesmand@parliament.uk (office).

TRIGUBOFF, Harry Oscar, AO, BA, AM; Australian property developer; *Chairman and Managing Director, Meriton Apartments Pty Ltd;* b. 3 March 1933, Dalian, China; s. of Moishe Triguboff and Freda Triguboff; m. 1st Hana Postel 1959 (divorced 1976); two d.; m. 2nd Rhonda Eileen 1980; ed Scots Coll., Sydney, Univ. of Leeds, UK; immigrated to Australia 1947; Founder, Chair. and Man. Dir Meriton Apartments Pty Ltd 1963–; Life mem. Housing Industry Asscn 2013; Dr hc (Hebrew Univ.) 2008, (Griffith Univ.) 2012; Sir Phillip Lynch Award, Housing Ind. Asscn 1995, Property Person of the Year, Urban Taskforce Australia 2003, 2009, Ernst & Young Entrepreneur of the Year 2008, Gold Harold Award 2011, UDIA Allen Vogan Distinguished Service Award 2015, inducted into Australian Property Hall of Fame, Property Council of Australia 2015. *Address:* Meriton Apartments Pty Ltd, Level 11, 528 Kent Street, Sydney, NSW 2000, Australia (office). *Website:* www.meriton.com.au (office).

TRILLO-FIGUEROA MARTÍNEZ-CONDE, Federico, DIur, PhD; Spanish politician, jurist and diplomatist; b. 23 May 1952, Cartagena, Murcia; s. of Federico Trillo-Figueroa and Eloísa Martínez-Conde; m. María José Molinuevo; five c.; ed Univ. of Salamanca, Univ. Complutense of Madrid; Sec.-Gen. Partido Popular (PP) Parl. Group (Conservative Party) 1982–89; mem. Nat. Exec. Cttee, PP 1987–; Chief of Staff to Manuel Fraga Iribarne, Leader of the PP and Adjunct Gen. Sec. of the Party 1989–90; mem. Parl. (PP) for Alicante 1989–2012, Deputy Speaker of the Congress 1989–96, Speaker of the Congress and Nat. Ass. 1996–2000, Speaker of the Constitutional Comm. of the Spanish Parl. 2004–08; Sec. of State for Defence 2000–04; Amb. to UK 2012–17; Grand Cross, Carlos Tercero, Grand Cross, Isabel La Católica, Grand Cross of Civil Merit, Grand Cross, San Raimundo de Peñafort Judicial Merit, Grand Cross of Naval Merit, Chevalier, Légion d'honneur, Grand Cross, Order of the Italian Repub., Grand Cross Enrique el Navegante (Portugal), Golden Grand Cross (Austria). *Publications include:* Pregones y Semblanzas 1997, El poder político en los dramas de Shakespeare (Political Power in Shakespeare's Dramas) 1999, Memoria de Entreguerras 2005. *Leisure interests:* reading, music, cycling.

TRIMBLE, Baron (Life Peer), cr. 2006, of Lisnagarvey in the County of Antrim; **(William) David Trimble,** PC, LLB; British politician, barrister and university lecturer; b. 15 Oct. 1944, Belfast, Northern Ireland; s. of William Trimble and Ivy Jack; m. 1st Heather McComb (divorced); m. 2nd Daphne Orr 1978; two s. two d.; ed Bangor Grammar School and Queen's Univ. Belfast; Lecturer in Law, Queen's Univ. Belfast 1968–77, Sr Lecturer 1977–90; mem. N Ireland Constitutional Convention 1975–76; mem. Parl. for Upper Bann 1990–2005; Leader Ulster Unionist Party (UUP) 1995–2005; First Minister, Northern Ireland 1998–2000 (Ass. suspended Feb. 2000), 2001–02 (Ass. suspended Oct. 2002); mem. N Ireland Ass. for Upper Bann 1998–; Chair. Lagan Valley Unionist Asscn 1985–90, Ulster Soc. 1985–90; left UUP and joined Conservative Party 2007; Hon. LLD (Queen's) 1999, (New Brunswick) 2000, (Wales) 2002, amonst others; shared Nobel Peace Prize 1998. *Publications:* To Raise up a New Northern Ireland 2001, Misunderstanding Ulster 2007. *Leisure interests:* music, reading, opera. *Address:* House of Lords, Westminster, London, SW1A 0PW England (office). *Telephone:* (20) 7219-5353 (office). *Fax:* (20) 7219-5979 (office). *E-mail:* trimbled@parliament.uk (office). *Website:* www.davidtrimble.org (office).

TRINH, Xuân Thuân, BSc, PhD; American (b. Vietnamese) astrophysicist and author; *Professor of Astronomy, University of Virginia;* b. 20 Aug. 1948, Hanoi, Vietnam; ed California Inst. of Technology, Princeton Univ.; Research Fellow in Astrophysics, California Inst. of Tech. and Hale Observatories 1975–76; Asst Prof. of Astronomy, Univ. of Virginia 1976–82, Assoc. Prof. of Astronomy 1982–90, Prof. of Astronomy 1990–; CNRS Visiting Prof., Observatoire de Paris-Meudon June–Aug. 1998, July–Sept. 1999, Institut d'Astrophysique de Paris Oct.–Dec. 1999; Visiting Prof. Centre d'Etudes de Saclay, France, Univ. of Paris VII, Institut d'Astrophysique de Paris; Vice-Pres. Advisory Bd, Université Interdisciplinaire de Paris 1995–; mem. UNESCO Council on Future 1999–; mem. Bd of Advisors, John Templeton Foundation 2002–04, 2008–10; mem. Exec. Cttee Int. Soc. for Science and Religion 2003–07; Order of the French Legion of Honor 2014; Glory of Vietnam Award 2004, Kalinga Award, UNESCO 2009, Prix mondial Cino del Duca, Fondation Simone et Cino del Duca, Institut de France 2012. *Publications:* La mélodie secrète: et l'homme créa l'univers (The Secret Melody: And man created the universe) 1988, Un astrophysicien 1992, Le destin de l'Univers: le Big Bang et après (The Changing Universe: Big Bang and After) 1992, Le Chaos et l'Harmonie: la fabrication du Réel (Chaos and Harmony: Perspectives on Scientific Revolutions of the 20th Century) 1998, L'Infini dans la paume de la main: Du Big Bang à l'Éveil (with Matthieu Ricard) (The Quantum and the Lotus: A Journey to the Frontiers Where Science and Buddhism Meet) (Henri Chŕetien Award, American Astronomical Soc. 2000, Asia Literary Prize, French Language Writers Asscn 2000) 2000, Origines: La nostalgie des commencements 2003, Les Voies de la lumière: Physique et Metaphysique du Clair-Obscur (Grand Prix Moron, Acad. Française 2007) 2007, Dictionnaire amoureux du Ciel et des Étoiles 2009, Désir d'infini 2013, Face à l'univers 2015, La plénitude du Vide 2016; numerous articles, proceeding and contribs to journals. *Address:* Astronomy Department, Room 253, Astronomy Building, University of Virginia, POB 400325, Charlottesville, VA 22904-4325, USA (office). *Telephone:* (804) 924-4894 (office). *Fax:* (804) 924-3104 (office). *E-mail:* txt@virginia.edu (office). *Website:* astronomy.as.virginia.edu (office).

TRINTIGNANT, Jean-Louis Xavier; French actor; b. 11 Dec. 1930, Piolenc (Vaucluse); s. of Raoul Trintignant and Claire Tourtin; m. 1st Stéphane Audran 1954 (divorced 1956); m. 2nd Nadine Marquand 1961 (divorced 1976); one s. two d. (both deceased); m. 3rd Marianne Hoepfner 2000; ed Faculté de Droit, Aix-en-Provence; Officier des Arts et des Lettres; Prix d'interprétation de l'Acad. du Cinéma (for Mata Hari, Agent H21) 1965; Prize, Cannes Festival (for Z) 1969; Prix David de Donatello, Taormina Festival 1972. *Plays include:* Macbeth, Jacques ou la Soumission (Ionesco), Hamlet, Bonheur, impaire et passe (Sagan), Deux sur la balançoire, Art 1998, Poèmes à Lou 1999, Comédie sur un quai de gare 2001, Moins deux 2005. *Films include:* Et Dieu créa la femme 1956, Club de femmes 1956, Les liaisons dangereuses 1959, L'été violent 1959, Austerlitz 1959, La millième fenêtre 1959, Pleins feux sur l'assassin 1960, Coeur battant 1960, Le jeu de la vérité 1961, Horace 62 1961, Les sept péchés capitaux 1961, Il sorpasso 1962, Il successo 1962, Chateau en Suède 1963, La bonne occase 1964, Mata Hari, Agent H21 1964, Angélique marquise des anges 1964, Meurtre à l'italienne 1965, La longue marche 1965, Le 17e ciel 1965, Paris brûle-t-il? 1965, Un homme et une femme 1966, Safari diamants 1966, Trans-Europ-Express 1966, Mon amour, mon amour 1967, L'homme qui ment 1967, Les biches 1968, Le voleur de crimes 1968, Z 1969, Ma nuit chez Maud 1969, Disons un soir à diner 1969, L'Américain 1969, La mort a pondu un oeuf 1969, Le conformiste 1970, Si douces, si perverses 1970, Le grand silence 1971, Une journée bien remplie (author and dir) 1973, Le train 1973, Les violins du bal 1973, Le mouton enragé 1974, Le secret 1974, Le jeu avec le feu 1975, Shattering 1977, Le désert des Tartares 1977, The French Way 1978, L'argent des autres 1978, Le maitre nageur 1979 (also dir), La terrasse 1980, Je vous aime 1980, La femme d'à côté 1981, Un assassin qui passe 1981, Malevil 1981, Passion d'amour 1981, Une affaire d'hommes 1981, Eaux profondes 1981, Le grand-pardon 1982, Boulevard des assassins 1982, Le bon plaisir 1983, Vivement dimanche! 1983, La crime 1983, Le bon plaisir, Femmes de personne 1984, Under Fire, Viva la vie 1984, L'été prochain, Partir, revenir 1985, Rendez-vous, David, Thomas et les autres 1985, L'homme aux yeux d'argent 1985, Un homme et une femme: vingt ans déja 1986, La femme de ma vie 1986, La vallée fantôme 1987, Le Moustachu 1987, Bunker Palace Hotel 1989, 'Merci la vie' 1991, Le Grand Pardon II (narrator) 1992, L'Instinct de l'ange 1993, L'oeil écarlate 1993, Three Colours: Red 1994, Regarde les hommes tomber 1994, The City of Lost Children (voice) 1995, Fiesta 1995, Un homme est tombé dans la rue 1996, C'est jamais loin 1996, Un héros très discret 1996, Tykho Moon 1996, Ceux qui m'aiment prendront le train 1998, Janis et John 2003, Immortel (ad vitam) (voice, uncredited) 2004, Amour 2012. *Television:* Pour un oui ou pour un non (film) 1990, Julie de Carneilhan (film) 1990, La controverse de Valladolid (film) 1992, L'interdiction (film) 1993, Rêveuse jeunesse (film) (voice) 1994, L'insoumise (film) 1996, Galilée ou L'amour de Dieu (film) 2005. *Address:* 30 rue des Francs-Bourgeois, 75003 Paris, France (office).

TRINTIGNANT, Nadine; French film director, screenwriter and writer; b. 11 Nov. 1934, Nice, Alpes-Maritimes; d. of Jean Marquand and Lucienne Marquand (née Cornillad); m. 1st Jean-Louis Trintignant 1961 (divorced 1997); two d. (both deceased) one s.; m. 2nd Alain Corneau 1998 (died 2010); ed Lycée Molière, Inst. Fénelon and Cours Lamartine, Paris; trainee, LTC Lab. 1952, trainee film ed. 1953–54, Asst Film Ed. 1954–58, Chief Ed. and Continuity Person 1958–64; Dir TV programmes in the Le Cinéma and Les Femmes Aussi series 1965–66; writer and dir of films and TV programmes; Officier Ordre des Arts et Lettres, Chevalier Ordre nat. du Mérite. *Films include:* Dir: Fragilité, ton nom est femme (Festival de Hyères Prize, Salonika Festival Prize, Greece) 1965, L'île bleue 2000; Writer and Dir: Mon amour, mon amour 1967, Le voleur de crimes 1969, Ça n'arrive qu'aux autres 1971, La semaine des quatre jeudis 1972, Défense de savoir 1973, Le voyage de noces 1976, Madame le Juge, L'innocent 1977, Premier voyage 1980, Portrait de Mikis Theodorakis, L'été prochain 1984, La maison de jade 1988, Fugueuses 1994, L'insoumise 1996. *Television includes:* film: Le tiroir secret 1985, Lucas 1988, Rêveuse jeunesse 1992, Les inséparables; Dir: Qui c'est ce garçon? (series) 1986, Victoire 1998 (Sept d'or de la mise en scène), L'île bleue 2000, Colette 2003. *Publications:* Ton chapeau au vestiaire 1998, Combien d'enfant 2000, Le jeune-homme de la rue de France 2002, Ma fille Marie 2003, Marie Trintignant 2004, J'ai été jeune un jour 2006, Une étrange peine 2007. *Leisure interests:* music, travelling. *Address:* 30 rue des Francs-Bourgeois, 75003 Paris, France. *Telephone:* (1) 42-74-47-01. *Fax:* (1) 42-74-55-03. *E-mail:* nadine.trintignant@wanadoo.fr.

TRIPATHI, Keshari Nath, BA, LLB; Indian lawyer, politician and poet; *Governor of West Bengal;* b. 10 Nov. 1934, Allahabad, Uttar Pradesh; s. of Harish Chandra Tripathi and Shiva Devi; m. Sudha Tripathi; three c.; ed Allahabad Univ.; Sr Advocate, Allahabad High Court 1956–2014; mem. Uttar Pradesh Legis. Ass. 1977–80, 1989–2007, Speaker 1991–93, 1997–2004; Uttar Pradesh State Minister of Institutional Finance 1977–79; Gov. of W Bengal July 2014–, also of Bihar 2014–15, June–Sept. 2017, of Meghalaya Jan.–May 2015, of Mizoram April–May 2015, of Tripura June–Aug. 2018; Pres., Allahabad High Court Bar Asscn 1987–89, Commonwealth Parl. Asscn (Uttar Pradesh Br.) 1991–93, 1997. *Publications* *include:* poetry anthologies: Manonukriti, Aayu Pankh. *Address:* Office of the Governor, Raj Bhavan, Kolkata 700 001, India (office). *Telephone:* (33) 22001641 (office). *Fax:* (33) 22002444 (office). *Website:* rajbhavankolkata.nic.in (office).

TRIPPE, Thomas G., PhD; American particle physicist; b. 1939; ed Univ. of California, Los Angeles; mem. Particle Data Group, Lawrence Berkeley Nat. Lab., Berkeley, Calif. 1970–2008; research work at Bevatron, CERN, SLAC and Fermilab (retd); NSF Fellowship 1969–70. *Publications:* Particle Physics: One Hundred Years of Discoveries: An Annotated Chronological Bibliography 1996, Review of Particle Physics, biennial 2010. *Leisure interests:* windsurfing, gardening, photography. *Address:* 1551 La Vereda Road, Berkeley, CA 94708, USA (home). *Telephone:* (510) 548-8435 (home). *E-mail:* trippe321@gmail.com (home).

TRITTIN, Jürgen, MA; German politician; b. 25 July 1954, Bremen; m.; one d.; ed Univ. of Göttingen; worked as journalist 1973; business man. Alternative-Greens-Initiative List (AGIL) group Göttingen City Council 1982–84; press spokesman for Green Party group Lower Saxony Landtag 1984–85, Chair. 1985–86, 1988–90, Deputy Chair. Alliance '90/Greens group 1994–95, spokesman Fed. Exec. 1994–98; mem. Lower Saxony Landtag 1985–90, 1994–95, Lower Saxony Minister for Fed. and European Affairs 1990–94, also head of state mission to fed. insts in Bonn; mem. Bundestag 1998–, mem. Cttee on Foreign Affairs 2014, Co-Chair. comm. on financing of nuclear phase-out in Germany 2015–16; Fed. Minister for the Environment, Nature Conservation and Nuclear Safety 1998–2005; Vice-Chair. Alliance '90/Greens group 2005–09, Chair. 2009–13; mem. NATO Parl. Ass. *Address:* Bundestag, Platz der Republik 1, 11011 Berlin (office); Room 2.533, Dorotheenstr.101, 10117 Berlin, Germany (office). *Telephone:* (30) 22772247 (office). *Fax:* (30) 22776203 (office). *E-mail:* juergen.trittin@bundestag.de (office). *Website:* www.trittin.de.

TROCKEL, Rosemarie; German artist and academic; b. 13 Nov. 1952, Schwerte; ed Kölner Werkschulen under Prof. Werner Schriefers; numerous solo exhbns in USA, especially at Museum of Modern Art (MoMA), New York 1980s and all over Europe; 'knitting pictures', produced in 1980s and 1990s; cr. Memorial Frankfurter Engel, Frankfurt am Main 1995; Prof., Staatliche Kunstakademie, Düsseldorf 1998–; lives and works in Cologne; Arbeitsstipendium der Stiftung Kunstfonds zur Förderung der zeitgenössischen bildenden Kunst, Bonn 1984, Stipendium, Kulturkreis der deutschen Wirtschaft, Cologne 1985, Karl Ströher Prize, Frankfurt am Main 1989, Günter Fruhtrunk Prize, Akad. der Bildenden Künste, Munich 1991, Konrad von Soest Prize, Münster 1992, Preisträgerstipendium, Günther-Peill-Stiftung, Düren 1996, Nordrhein-Westphalia State Prize 1998, Int. Arts Prize, Kulturstiftung Stadtsparkasse, Munich 1999, German Pavilion, Venice Biennale 1999, Kulturpreis, Cologne 2001, Wolfgang Hahn Prize, Gesellschaft für Moderne Kunst am Kölner Museum Ludwig 2004, Westfälische Ehrengalerie 2006, Arts Prize, Landeshauptstadt Düsseldorf 2008, Peter Weiss Prize, City of Bochum 2010, Kaiserring der Stadt Goslar 2011, Roswitha-Haftmann Prize, Zurich 2014. *Publications:* Jedes Tier ist eine Künstlerin 1993, Pro Test, mit einem Text von Rosemarie Trockel 2002, Löffel + Mirabelle 1995, Rosemarie Trockel präsentiert: Pierre Klossowski, Pierre Zucca – Lebendiges Geld (Edn Exlibris Nr 4, Gerhard Teewen (ed.)) 2005, Mutter (with Marcus Steinweg) 2006, Duras (with Marcus Steinweg) 2008. *Address:* c/o Sprüth Magers Berlin, Oranienburger Straße 18, 10178 Berlin (office); c/o Friederike Schuler, Sprüth Magers, Hebbelstraße 93, 50968 Cologne, Germany (office); c/o Sprüth Magers London, 7A Grafton Street, London, W1S 4EJ, England (office). *Telephone:* (30) 28884030 (Berlin) (office); (221) 937297513 (Cologne) (office); (20) 7408-1613 (London) (office). *Fax:* (30) 288840352 (Berlin) (office); (221) 937297517 (Cologne) (office); (20) 7499-4531 (London) (office). *E-mail:* fs@spruethmagers.com (office); info@spruethmagers.com (office). *Website:* www.spruethmagers.com (office).

TROE, Jürgen, Dr rer. nat; German chemist and academic; *Niedersachsenprofessor for Research, Georg-August-Universität Göttingen;* b. 4 Aug. 1940, Göttingen; ed Univ. of Göttingen; Prof. of Physical Chem., Ecole Polytechnique Fédérale de Lausanne, Switzerland 1971–75, Hon. Prof. 1976–; Prof. of Physical Chem., Inst. for Physical Chem., Univ. of Göttingen 1975–2008, Prof. Emer. 2008–, Niedersachsenprofessor for Research 2008–, Chair. Lab. for Laser Tech. 1987, Dir and Scientific mem. Max-Planck-Inst. for Biophysical Chem., Göttingen 1990–2008, Dir Emer. 2008–; Pres. Deutsche Bunsen-Gesellschaft für Physikalische Chemie 1999–2002; Editorial Chair. Physical Chem./Chemical Physics 2000–03; mem. Deutsche Akademie der Naturforscher Leopoldina 1980–, Akademie der Wissenschaften zu Göttingen 1982–, Academia Europaea, London 1989–, Berlin-Brandenburgische Akademie der Wissenschaften 2000–; mem. Senate, Deutsche Forschungsgemeinschaft 2002– (Chair. Physical Chem. and Chem. Sections 1984–92); mem. Nat. Science Bd of Germany 1993–98; Fellow, American Physical Soc. 2010; Foreign hon. mem. American Acad. of Arts and Science 1989–, Finnish Acad. of Sciences 2012–; Hon. Prof., Ecole Polytechnique Fédérale de Lausanne 1976, Hon. mem. Bunsen-Gesellschaft 2009; Hon. DSc (Bordeaux) 1995, (Karlsruhe) 1995; Deutsche Bunsen-Gesellschaft für Physikalische Chemie Bodenstein Award 1971, Royal Soc. of Chem. Centenary Medal 1980, Polanyi Medal 1992, Alexander von Humboldt Foundation Max-Planck Research Award 1993, Deutsche Akademie der Naturforscher Leopoldina Carus Medal 1995, Int. Combustion Inst. Bernard Lewis Gold Medal 1996, Walther Nernst Denkmünze, Bunsen-Gesellschaft 1998, Otto-Hahn Prize 2015. *Address:* Institut für Physikalische Chemie, Georg-August-Universität Göttingen, Tammannstrasse 6, D- 37077 Göttingen, Germany (office). *Telephone:* (551) 393122 (office). *Fax:* (551) 393150 (office). *E-mail:* shoff@gwdg.de (office). *Website:* www.uni-pc.gwdg.de/troe (office); www.mpibpc.mpg.de.

TROISGROS, Pierre Emile René; French hotelier and restaurateur; b. 3 Sept. 1928, Châlon-sur-Saône; s. of Jean-Baptiste Troisgros and Marie Badaut; m. Olympe Forte 1955; two s. one d.; ed Lycée Bourgneuf, Roanne; worked Roanne-Etretat 1944–45, Armenonville, Paris 1946, St Jean de Luz 1947; mil. service, Tunisia 1948; at Lucas Carton, Paris 1950–52, Point, Vienne 1954, then Maxim's and Retour à Roanne; now Pres. Supervising Cttee Restaurant Troisgros SA, Roanne; Ordre Nat. du Mérite 1969, Officier des Arts et des Lettres 1985, Chevalier, Légion d'honneur 1987. *Publications:* Cuisiniers à Roanne (with Jean Troisgros) 1977, Toc et Toque 1983, Les Petits Plats des Troisgros (with Michel Troisgros) 1985, Cuisine de famille chez les Troisgros (jtly) 1998. *Leisure interests:* tennis, basketball. *Address:* Place Jean Troisgros, 42300 Roanne; 20 route de Commelle, 42120 Le Coteau, France (office). *Telephone:* 4-77-71-66-97. *Fax:* 4-77-70-39-77 (office). *E-mail:* info@troisgros.com (office). *Website:* www.troisgros.fr (office).

TROJANOWSKI, John Quinn, BA, MD, PhD; American neuroscientist and academic; *William Maul Measey-Truman G. Schnabel, Jr, MD Professor of Geriatric Medicine and Gerontology, University of Pennsylvania;* b. 1946, Bridgeport, Conn.; m. Prof. Virginia M.-Y. Lee; ed Tufts Univ. School of Medicine and Grad. School of Arts and Sciences; Resident, Massachusetts Gen. Hosp. and Harvard Medical School 1977–79; Resident, Univ. of Pennsylvania Hospital, Philadelphia 1979–80, Asst Prof. of Pathology and Laboratory Medicine, Univ. of Pennsylvania School of Medicine 1981–90, Prof. 1990, Dir of Medical Pathology, Pennsylvania Inst. on Aging 1988–2002, Dir Pennsylvania Inst. on Aging 2002–, Co-Dir Pennsylvania Center for Neurodegenerative Disease Research 1992–, Prin. Investigator, NIA Program Project Grant on Alzheimer's (AD) and Parkinson's (PD) disease 1990–, William Maul Measey-Truman G. Schnabel, Jr, MD Prof. of Geriatric Medicine and Gerontology 2003–, Co-Dir Marian S. Ware Alzheimer Drug Discovery Program; mem. NIA Neuroscience, Behavior and Sociology of Aging Study Section 1987–91, Nat. Advisory Council on Aging (NACA) of the NIA 1994–98, NACA Working Group Chair 1996–98, Medical and Scientific Advisory Bd of Nat. Alzheimer's Asscn 1994–97, Southeastern Pennsylvania Chapter of the Alzheimer's Asscn 1992–, NIA Bd of Scientific Counselors 1998–, Scientific Advisory Bds of the Paul Beeson Physician Faculty Scholars In Aging Award 1998–, Alliance for Aging Research 2002–, Asscn of Frontotemporal Dementia 2003–, Program Cttee of the World Alzheimer Congress 2000 1998–2000; mem. editorial bds of several neuroscience and pathology journals; Pres. American Asscn of Neuropathologists 1997–98; mem. American Soc. of Clinical Investigation 1991, Asscn of American Physicians 2000; NIH MERIT Award 1986–94, Metropolitan Life Foundation Promising Investigator Award for Alzheimer's Disease Research 1991, 1996, Established Investigator Award, Nat. Alliance for Research on Schizophrenia and Depression 1994, Potamkin Prize for Research in Pick's, Alzheimer's and Related Diseases 1998, first Pioneer Award, Alzheimer's Asscn 1998, Stanley Cohen Biomedical Research Award, Univ. of Pennsylvania 2000, Irving Wright Award of Distinction, American Federation for Aging Research 2004, Rous-Whipple Award, American Soc. for Investigative Pathology 2005, J. Allyn Taylor Int. Prize in Medicine (co-recipient) 2014. *Publications:* numerous papers in professional journals. *Address:* Institute on Aging, University of Pennsylvania, 3615 Chestnut Street, Philadelphia, PA 19104-2676 (office); Pathology and Laboratory Medicine, Hospital of the University of Pennsylvania, 3rd Floor, Maloney Building, 3600 Spruce Street, Philadelphia, PA 19104, USA (office). *Telephone:* (215) 898-7801 (office); (215) 662-6399 (office). *Fax:* (215) 349-5909 (office). *E-mail:* trojanow@mail.med.upenn.edu (office). *Website:* www.med.upenn.edu/aging (office).

TROLLOPE, Joanna, (Caroline Harvey), OBE, MA, DL; British writer; b. 9 Dec. 1943, Minchinhampton, Glos., England; d. of Arthur Trollope and Rosemary Hodson; m. 1st David Potter 1966; two d.; m. 2nd Ian Curteis 1985 (divorced 2001); two step-s.; ed Reigate Co. School and St Hugh's Coll., Oxford; Information and Research Dept Foreign Office 1965–67; various teaching posts, including Farnham Girl's Grammar School, Daneshill School 1967–79; Chair. Betty Trask Prize for Soc. of Authors 1993, Advisory Cttee on Nat. Reading Initiative, Dept of Nat. Heritage 1996–97; mem. Advisory Cttee on Nat. Year of Reading, Dept of Educ. 1998, Council of Soc. of Authors 1997–, Campaign Bd St Hugh's Coll. Oxford, Council of West Country Writer's Asscn; Vice-Pres. Trollope Soc.; Judge, Costa Book Awards 2002, Chair. Advisory Bd 2007; mem. International PEN, Romantic Novelists' Asscn; Trustee, Joanna Trollope Charitable Trust 1995–; Patron County of Glos. Community Foundation 1994–2004, March Foundation, Mulberry Bush, For Dementia; Chair. Nat. Portrait Gallery Fund Raising Gala 2009; DL for Co. of Glos. 2002–08; Judge, The Melissa Nathan Awards 2005–11, The Sunday Times EFG Private Bank Short Story Award 2011–12; Chair. Orange Prize for Fiction 2012, Review Panel for UK Dept for Culture, Media & Sport (DCMS) into e-lending in libraries, Report Panel for UK DCMS, Role of Public Libraries 2013–; Trustee, Nat. Literacy Trust 2013–; Patron, Chawton House Library; Lifetime Achievement Award, Romantic Novelists Asscn 2010. *Publications include:* as Caroline Harvey: Eliza Stanhope 1978, Parson Harding's Daughter (aka Mistaken Virtues) (Historical Novel of the Year Award, Romantic Novelists' Asscn 1979, Elizabeth Goudge Historical Award 1980) 1979, Leaves from the Valley 1980, The City of Gems 1981, The Steps of the Sun 1983, The Taverners' Place 1986, Legacy of Love 1992, A Second Legacy 1993, A Castle in Italy 1993, The Brass Dolphin 1997; as Joanna Trollope: Britannia's Daughters: A Study of Women in the British Empire 1983, The Choir 1988, A Village Affair 1989, A Passionate Man 1990, The Rector's Wife 1991, The Men and the Girls 1992, A Spanish Lover 1992, The Best of Friends 1992, The Country Habit: An Anthology (ed.) 1993, Next of Kin 1996, Faith 1996, Other People's Children 1998, Marrying the Mistress 2000, Girl from the South 2002, Brother and Sister 2004, Second Honeymoon 2006, The Book Boy 2006, Britannia's Daughters 2007, Friday Nights 2008, The Other Family 2010, Daughters in Law 2011, The Soldier's Wife 2012, Sense & Sensibility 2013, Balancing Act 2014, City of Friends 2017, An Unsuitable Match 2018; contribs to newspapers and magazines. *Leisure interests:* reading, conversation, very long baths. *Address:* c/o United Agents, 12–26 Lexington Street, London, W1F 0LE, England (office). *Telephone:* (20) 3214-0800 (office). *Fax:* (20) 3214-0801 (office). *E-mail:* info@unitedagents.co.uk (office); joanna@joannatrollope.com (office). *Website:* unitedagents.co.uk (office); www.joannatrollope.com.

TRONCHETTI PROVERA, Marco, OBE; Italian business executive; *CEO and Executive Vice-Chairman, Pirelli & C. SpA;* b. 18 Feb. 1948, Milan; three c.; ed Bocconi Univ., Milan; worked in family maritime transport business 1973–86; joined Pirelli Group as Partner, Pirelli & C. 1986, Man. Dir and Gen. Man. Soc. Int. Pirelli SA, Basle 1988–92, Man. Dir and Gen. Man. (Finance and Admin. and Gen. Affairs) Pirelli SpA 1991–92, Exec. Deputy Chair. and Man. Dir Pirelli SpA 1992–96, CEO Pirelli & C. 1992–, Deputy Chair. Pirelli & C. 1995–99, Chair. and CEO Pirelli SpA 1996–, Exec. Vice-Chair. Pirelli & C. 2015–; Chair. Olivetti 2001–; Chair. Bd and Exec. Cttee CAMFIN SpA, Milan; Chair. Telecom Italia SpA 2001–06 (resgnd); Chair. Bd Il Sole 24 Ore; Deputy Chair. Confindustria (nat. employers' org.), Chair. 2000–; Chair. Prelios SpA –2013; currently Co-Chair. Italy-China Business Forum; mem. Bd Mediobanca, Banca Commerciale Italiana, Banca Intesa, GIM, RAS, Università Commerciale Luigi Bocconi, FC Internazionale Milano; mem. European Round Table of Industrialists, Int. Advisory Bd of

Allianz, Int. Council of J. P. Morgan, New York Stock Exchange Advisory Cttee, Italian Group of Trilateral Comm.; Cavaliere del Lavoro 1996, Chevalier, Légion d'Honneur 1998. *Address:* Office of the Chairman, Pirelli SpA, Viale Piero e Alberto Pirelli n. 25, 20126, Milan (office); CONFINDUSTRIA, Viale dell'Astronomia 30, EVR, 00144 Rome, Italy. *Telephone:* (02) 64421 (office); (06) 59031. *Fax:* (02) 64422670 (office). *Website:* www.confindustria.it (office); www.pirelli.com.

TROŠKA, Zdeněk, MA; Czech film and theatre director and scriptwriter; b. 18 May 1953, Strakonice; s. of Václav Troška and Růžena Troška; ed Lycée Carnot, Dijon, France, Acad. of Film and Musical Arts; Prin./Head Prize for Luck From Hell II, St Petersburg, Russia 2002. *Films:* Jak rodí chlap (How a Man Gives Birth) 1980, Bota jménem Melichar (Boot) 1983, Slunce, seno, jahody (The Sun, Hay and Strawberries) 1984, Poklad hrabete Chamaré (The Treasure of Count Chamaré) 1984, O princezne Jasněnce a létajicim sevci (About Princess Jasněnka) 1987, Flying Shoemaker 1987, Slunce, seno a pár facek (The Sun, Hay and Some Slaps) 1989, Zkouskové období (The Time of Examinations) 1990, Slunce, seno, erotika (The Sun, Hay and Erotics) 1991, Princezna ze mlejna (The Princess from the Mill) 1994, Z pekla stestí (Helluva Good Luck) 1999, Princezna ze mlejna 2 2000, Z pekla stestí 2 (Goblins and Good Luck 2) 2001, Andelská tvár 2002, Kamenák 2003, Kamenák 2 2004, Kamenák 3 2005, Nejkrasnejsi hadanka 2008, Doktor od jezera hrochu 2010, The Devil's Bride 2011, Babovresky 2013, Babovresky 2 2014, Babovresky 3 2015. *Plays:* Don Carlos (Nat. Theatre, Prague) 1989, Rusalka, Hamlet (musical version) 2000, Luck From Hell 2000, Luck From Hell II 2001. *Leisure interests:* literature, music: piano and organ, cooking, mushrooming, hiking. *Address:* Hoštice u Volyně 77, 387 01 Volyně, Czech Republic (office). *E-mail:* info@zdenektroska.cz. *Website:* www.zdenektroska.cz.

TROST, Barry Martin, PhD; American scientist and academic; *Tamaki Professor of Humanities and Science, Department of Chemistry, Stanford University;* b. 13 June 1941, Philadelphia, Pa; s. of Joseph Trost and Esther Trost; m. Susan Paula Shapiro 1967; two s.; ed Univ. of Pennsylvania and Massachusetts Inst. of Tech.; Asst Prof. of Chem., Dept of Chem., Univ. of Wis. 1965–68, Assoc. Prof. 1968–69, Prof. 1969–76, Helfaer Prof. 1976–82, Vilas Prof. 1982–87; Prof. of Chem., Stanford Univ. 1987–, Tamaki Prof. of Humanities and Sciences 1990–; consultant, E.I. du Pont de Nemours and Merck, Sharp & Dohme; mem. ARCO Science Bd; mem. Cttee on Chemical Sciences, NAS 1980–83; mem. and Chair. NIH Medicinal Chem. Study Section 1982–; Commr, Nat. Research Council Comm. on Eng and Tech. Systems; Ed.-in-Chief Comprehensive Organic Synthesis (Vols 1–9) 1991, Chair. 1996–; Ed. Chemical Tracts/Organic Chem.; mem. NAS, American Chemical Soc., AAAS; Dr hc (Univ. Claude Bernard, Lyon, Technion, Israel); ACS Award in Pure Chem. 1977, for Creative Work in Synthetic Organic Chem. 1981, Backland Award 1981, AIC Chemical Pioneer Award 1983, Alexander von Humboldt Award (Fed. Repub. of Germany) 1984, Cope Scholar Award of ACS 1989, ACS Guenther Award 1990, Dr Paul Janssen Prize for Creativity in Organic Synthesis 1990, Merit Award, NIH 1988, Roger Adams Award 1995, Herbert C. Brown Award 1999, Nichols Medal 2000, Elsevier Boss Award 2000, Yamada Prize 2001, Signature Award for Grad. Educ. in Chem. 2002, ACS Arthur C. Cope Award 2004, John Scott Award 2004, Nagoya Medal 2008. *Publications:* Problems in Spectroscopy 1967, Sulfur Ylides 1974, Organic Synthesis Today and Tomorrow (ed.) 1981, Selectivity: a Goal for Synthetic Efficiency (ed.) 1984; more than 850 scientific articles in leading chemical journals. *Address:* Department of Chemistry, Stanford University, Stanford, CA 94305-5080, USA (office). *Telephone:* (650) 723-3385 (office). *Fax:* (650) 725-0002 (office). *E-mail:* bmtrost@stanford.edu (office). *Website:* chemistry.stanford.edu/faculty/barry-trost (office); www.stanford.edu/group/bmtrost (office).

TROVOADA, Miguel dos Anjos da Cunha Lisboa; São Tomé and Príncipe UN official and fmr head of state; fmrly in charge of foreign relations for the São Tomé e Príncipe Liberation Movt (MLSTP), fmr mem. Political Bureau; Prime Minister of São Tomé e Príncipe 1975–78, also Minister of Defence and Foreign Affairs July–Dec. 1975, of Econ. Co-ordination, Co-operation and Tourism 1975–78, of Trade, Industry and Fisheries 1978–79; arrested and imprisoned 1979, released 1981, then in exile in Lisbon; Pres. and C-in-C of the Armed Forces of São Tomé e Príncipe 1991–95 (deposed in coup 15 Aug. 1995), reinstalled 1995–2001; Exec. Sec. Gulf of Guinea Comm. 2009–13; Special Rep. of Sec.-Gen. and Head, UN Integrated Peace Building Office in Guinea-Bissau (UNIOGBIS) 2014–16.

TROVOADA, Patrice Emery; São Tomé and Príncipe politician; b. 18 March 1962, Libreville, Gabon; s. of Miguel Trovoada, Pres. of São Tomé and Príncipe 1991–2001; Minister of Foreign Affairs 2001–02; oil adviser to Pres. Fradique de Menezes –2005 (sacked by Pres.); Sec.-Gen. Independent Democratic Action (ADI) Party; unsuccessful cand. in presidential election 2006; Prime Minister Feb.–June 2008, 2010–12, 2014–18. *Address:* c/o Office of the Prime Minister, Rua do Município, CP 302, São Tomé, São Tomé and Príncipe (office).

TRPEVSKI, Ljube, MSc, PhD; Macedonian politician, banker and academic; b. 3 Aug. 1947, Velmej, Ohrid; m.; one s. one d.; ed Univ. of St Cyril and St Methodius, Skopje, Univ. of Tallahassee, Fla; teaching Asst, Faculty of Econs, Univ. of St Cyril and St Methodius, Skopje 1970–77, lecturer 1977–80, Docent 1980–85, Assoc. Prof. 1985–91, Prof. 1991; Deputy Gov. Nat. Bank of Macedonia 1987–91, Gov. 1997–2004; Minister, Pres. Securities and Exchange Comm. 1992–95; Vice-Pres. of Macedonia 1996; indicted for breach of duty and embezzlement 2007, sentenced to four years in jail 2008; released from prison after Supreme Court overturned judgment Jan. 2010; currently Prof., Faculty of Econs, Sts Cyril and Methodius Univ., Skopje. *Publications:* Lexicon of Contemporary Market Economy (co-author, ed.) 1993, Money and Banking 1995, The Republic of Macedonia (co-author) 1996 and numerous articles. *Address:* University Sts Cyril and Methodius, Faculty of Economics, Blvd Goce Delchev 9V, 1000 Skopje (office); Mile Pop Jordanov 52, 91000 Skopje, North Macedonia (home). *E-mail:* ljubet@eccf.ukim.edu.mk (office).

TRUBETSKOI, Kliment Nikolayevich; Russian geochemist; *Adviser, Research Institute of Comprehensive Exploitation of Mineral Resources, Russian Academy of Sciences;* b. 3 July 1933; m.; two c.; ed Moscow Inst. of Nonferrous Metals and Gold; Jr, then Sr Researcher, Research Inst. of Comprehensive Exploitation of Mineral Resources, USSR (now Russian) Acad. of Sciences 1961–81, Head of Lab. 1981–87, Deputy Dir 1987, Dir 1987–2003, Prof. of Geotechnology 2003, now Adviser; Chair. Russian State Geological Exploration Univ. 2003; Corresp. mem. USSR (now Russian) Acad. of Sciences 1987–91, mem. 1991–; Vice-Pres. Acad. of Mining Sciences; mem. Int. Organizational Cttee, World Mining Congress 1992; Order of Merit for Country of VI Degree 1998, Order of Merit for Country of III Degree 2008; USSR State Prize 1990, N. Melnikov Gold Medal and Prize 1989, 2004, B. Krupinski Medal 1997, Russian State Prize 1999, 2000, Prize of the Pres. of Russia 2001. *Achievements include:* took part in devt of tech. to save resources in quarries, developed theoretical fundamentals of projecting, prognosis and tech. of complex utilization of mineral deposits. *Publications:* author of 30 books and 700 scientific articles in periodicals. *Leisure interests:* chess, swimming, photography, travelling. *Address:* Research Institute of Comprehensive Exploitation of Mineral Resources, 111020 Moscow, Krukovsky tupik 4, Russia. *Telephone:* (495) 360-89-60 (office); (495) 331-52-55 (home). *Fax:* (495) 360-89-60 (office). *E-mail:* trubetsk@ipkonran.ru (office). *Website:* www.ipkonran.ru (office).

TRUBETSKOV, Dmitry Ivanovich, DPhys-MathSc; Russian physicist and academic; *Head Chair of Electronics, Oscillations and Waves, Saratov State University;* b. 14 June 1938, Saratov; s. of Ivan Trubetskov and Varvara Trubetskova; m. Sofya Vasilyeva 1962; one s.; ed Saratov State Univ.; aspirant 1960–64; teacher 1961–68; docent 1968; Prof., Saratov State Univ. 1981–, Head, Chair of Electronics and Wave Processes 1981–, Rector 1994–2003; mem. IEEE Electron Devices Soc. 1995; Corresp. mem. USSR (now Russian) Acad. of Sciences 1991; Educ. Award of the Pres. of Russian Fed. 2001. *Publications include:* Analytical Methods of Calculation in Microwave Electronics (with V. N. Shevchik) 1970, Electronics of Backward-Wave Tubes 1975, Introduction into the Theory of Oscillations and Waves 1984, Oscillations and Waves in Linear and Non-linear Systems (with M. I. Rabinovich) 1989, Nonlinear Dynamics in Action (with A. A. Koronovsky) 1995, Lectures on Microwave Vacuum Microelectronics (with A. G. Rozjenev and D. V. Sokolov) 1996, Nonlinear Waves (with N. M. Ryskyn) 2000, Linear Oscillators and Waves (with A. G. Rozjenev) 2001, The Trace of Inspiration and Patient Labour 2001, Linear Oscillations and Waves, Problems (with A. P. Kuznetsov and A.G. Rozjenev) 2001, Introduction into the Theory of Self-Organization Open Systems (with E. S. Mchedlova and L. V. Krasichkov) 2002, Lectures on Microwave Electronics for Physicists, Vol. 1 (with A. Hramov) 2003, Introduction to Synergetics, Oscillations and Waves 2003, Lectures on Microwave Electronics for Physicists Vol. 2 (with A. Hramov) 2004, Introduction to Synergetics, Chaos and Patterns 2004, The Way to Synergetics (with B. Bezruchko, A. Koronovsky and A. Hramov) 2005, Synchronization: Scientist and Time 2006, Higher Education in Russia from the Point of Vew of Nonlinear Dynamics (with M. Strikhanov, A. Koronovsky, U. Sharaevsky and A. Hramov) 2007. *Leisure interest:* reading. *Address:* Saratov State University, Astrakhanskaya str. 83, 410071 Saratov, Russia (office). *Telephone:* (8452) 512-107 (office); (8452) 231-993 (home). *Fax:* (8452) 512-107 (office). *E-mail:* trubetskovdi@nonlin.sgu.ru (office).

TRUBNIKOV, Gen. (retd) Vyacheslav Ivanovich; Russian security officer, politician and diplomatist (retd); b. 25 April 1944, Irkutsk; m.; one d.; ed Moscow State Inst. of Int. Relations; served in USSR KGB (First Main Directorate, intelligence) 1967–91; staff mem. HQ of First Main Dept (intelligence) 1977–84; KGB station officer in India (as corresp. Press Agency Novosti) 1971–77; mem. Union of Journalists 1973; resident in Bangladesh and India 1984–90; Head Div. of America KGB 1990–92; First Deputy Dir Russian Intelligence Service 1992–96, Dir 1996–2000; mem. Security Council, Defence Council and Foreign Policy Council of Russia 1996; First Deputy Minister of Foreign Affairs 2000–04; Amb. to India 2004–09 (retd); mem. IISS, UK, Russian Union of Journalists, Trialogue Club Int. 2012–; mem. Exec. Bd European Leadership Network; mem. Advisory Bd PIR Center 2010–, Russian Center for Policy Studies.

TRUDEAU, Garry B., BA, MFA; American cartoonist; b. 21 July 1948, New York; m. Jane Pauley 1980; three c.; ed Yale Univ. School of Art and Architecture; cr. comic strip Doonesbury at Yale 1969, now syndicated nationwide; Creator and Exec.-Producer Alpha House Series; Fellow, American Acad. of Arts and Sciences; hon. degrees from Yale Univ., Colgate Univ., Williams Univ., Duke Univ. and 18 other univs; Pulitzer Prize for Editorial Cartooning 1975, Newspaper Comic Strip Award 1994, Reuben Award 1995, John S. Knight Lecturer 2000. *Plays include:* Doonesbury 1983, Rapmaster Ronnie, A Partisan Review (with Elizabeth Swados) 1984. *Films:* A Doonesbury Special for NBC-TV 1977 (Special Jury Prize at Cannes Film Festival). *Television:* conceived (with Robert Altman) Tanner '88 1988. *Publications include:* Any Grooming Hints for Your Fans, Rollie, But the Pension Fund was Just Sitting There, The Doonesbury Chronicles, Guilty, Guilty, Guilty, We Who are about to Fry, Salute You: selected cartoons in In Search of Reagan's Brain, Vol. 2, Is This Your First Purge, Miss?, Vol. 2, It's Supposed to be Yellow, Pinhead: selected cartoons from You Ask for Many, Seetle for June, Vol. 1, The Wreck of the Rusty Nail, Dressed for Failure 1983, Confirmed Bachelors are Just So Fascinating 1984, Sir I'm Worried About Your Mood Swings 1984, Doonesbury Dossier: The Reagan Years 1984, Check Your Egos at the Door 1986, Talking 'Bout My G-G-Generation 1988, We're Eating More Beets 1988, Read My Lips, Make My Day, Eat Quiche and Die 1989, Recycled Doonesbury 1990, You're Smoking Now Mr Butt! 1990, In Search of a Cigarette Holder Man: A Doonesbury Book 1994, Doonesbury Nation 1995, Flashbacks 1995; The Portable Doonesbury 1993; contribs. to The People's Doonesbury and many others. *Website:* doonesbury.slate.com.

TRUDEAU, Justin Pierre James, BA, BEd; Canadian politician; *Prime Minister;* b. 25 Dec. 1971, Ottawa; s. of Pierre Elliott Trudeau (fmr Prime Minister) and Margaret Sinclair Trudeau Kemper; m. Sophie Grégoire; two s. one d.; ed McGill Univ., Univ. of British Columbia; began career as teacher, West Point Grey Acad. and Sir Winston Churchill Secondary School, Vancouver; mem. House of Commons (Liberal) for Papineau constituency 2008–, mem. Parl. Cttees on Environment and Sustainable Devt and Citizenship and Immigration; Leader, Liberal Party of Canada 2013–; Prime Minister of Canada 2015–; Minister of Intergovernmental Affairs and Youth 2015–18; Dr hc (Univ. of Edinburgh) 2017, (NYU) 2018; Queen Elizabeth II Diamond Jubilee Medal 2012. *Radio:* panellist on Canada Reads (CBC Radio) 2003–04. *Address:* Office of the Prime Minister, Langevin Block, 80 Wellington Street, Ottawa, ON K1A 0A2 (office); Liberal Party of Canada, 81 Metcalfe Street, Suite 600, Ottawa, ON K1P 6M8, Canada (office). *Telephone:* (613) 941-6888 (PM) (office); (613) 237-0740 (Liberal Party) (office). *Fax:* (613) 941-6900 (PM) (office); (613) 235-7208 (Liberal Party) (office). *E-mail:*

pm@pm.gc.ca (office); info@liberal.ca (office). *Website:* www.pm.gc.ca (office); www .liberal.ca (office); justin.ca.

TRUE, Baron (Life Peer), cr. 2010, of East Sheen in the County of Surrey; **Nicholas Edward True,** BA, MA, CBE; British politician and fmr civil servant; *Leader of the Council, London Borough of Richmond-upon-Thames;* b. 31 July 1951; s. of Edward Thomas True and Kathleen Louise True; m. Anne-Marie Elena Kathleen Blanco Hood 1979; two s. one d.; ed Peterhouse, Cambridge; mem. Conservative Research Dept 1976–82; Personal Asst to Lord Whitelaw 1978–82; Special Adviser to Sec. of State, Dept of Health and Social Security 1982–86; Dir Public Policy Unit Ltd 1986–90; Deputy Head of Prime Minister (PM)'s Policy Unit 1990–95; Ministerial nominee to English Sports Council 1996–97; Special Adviser to PM's Office 1997; Pvt. Sec. to Leader of the Opposition, House of Lords 1997–2010; Councillor, Richmond upon Thames 1986–90, 1998–, Deputy Leader 2002–06, Leader of the Opposition 2006–10, Leader of the Council 2010–; mem. Leaders' Cttee, London Councils (fmrly ALG); mem. (Conservative) House of Lords 2010–; Trustee, Sir Harold Hood's Charitable Trust 1996–, Richmond Civic Endowment Trust 2006–10, Royal Parks Bd 2012. *Leisure interests:* books, cricket, Italy, Byzantium. *Address:* London Borough of Richmond upon Thames, Civic Centre, 44 York Street, Twickenham, TW1 3BZ (office); House of Lords, Westminster, London, SW1A 0PW (office); 114 Palewell Park, East Sheen, SW14 8JH, England (home). *Telephone:* (20) 8487-5001 (Richmond upon Thames) (office); (20) 7219-2562 (House of Lords) (office); (20) 8876-9628 (home). *E-mail:* Cllr .LordTrue@richmond.gov.uk (office). *Website:* www.richmond.gov.uk (office).

TRUJILLO, Solomon Dennis (Sol), BS, MBA; American telecommunications industry executive; b. 17 Nov. 1951, Cheyenne, Wyo.; ed Univ. of Wyoming; began career with Mountain Bar Telephone 1974; Pres. and CEO USWest Dex Inc. 1992–95, Pres. and CEO US est Communications 1995–98, CEO and Chair. USWest Inc. 1999–2000; Chair., Pres. and CEO Graviton Inc., La Jolla, Calif. 2000; mem. Exec. Bd Orange SA 2001–04, CEO 2003–04; mem. Bd of Dirs and CEO Telstra Corpn Ltd, Australia 2005–09 (resgnd); mem. Chair.'s Council, Alcatel 2000–03; mem. Bd of Dirs Target, Promerica Bank of Los Angeles, Silk Road Technologies, Weather Investments; fmr mem. Bd of Dirs Pepsi Co., Gannet, Bank of America, Electronic Data Systems Corpn (EDS), Tomas Rivera Policy Inst.; mem. Advisory Bd UCLA School of Public Affairs; fmr Gov. World Econ. Forum, mem. World Econ. Forum's Steering Cttee on Climate Change 2008; fmr Trustee, Boston Coll., UCLA's School of Public Policy; fmr trade policy adviser in Clinton and Bush admins; Dr hc (Univ. of Wyoming, Univ. of Colorado); Ronald H. Brown Corporate Bridge Builder Award 1999. *Website:* www.soltrujillo.com.

TRUMAN, Edwin Malcolm, BA, MA, PhD; American economist and academic; *Senior Fellow, Peterson Institute for International Economics;* b. 6 June 1941, Albany, NY; s. of David B. Truman and Elinor G. Truman; m. Tracy P. Truman; one s. one d.; ed Amherst Coll., Yale Univ.; trained as economist; Prof., Yale Univ. 1967–74; joined Div. of Int. Finance, Bd of Govs of Fed. Reserve System 1972, Dir (later Staff Dir) 1977–98; Asst Sec., US Treasury for Int. Affairs 1998–2001; Sr Fellow, Peterson Inst. for Int. Econs, Washington, DC 2001– (non-resident 2013–); Asst Sec. US Treasury (Int. Affairs) and Counsellor to Sec. of the Treasury 2009; taught at Amherst Coll. 2006, 2008, 2010, Williams Coll. 2008, 2010, 2012, 2014; mem. G-7 Working Group on Exchange Market Intervention 1982–83, G-10 Working Group on the Resolution of Sovereign Liquidity Crises 1995–96, G-10-sponsored Working Party on Financial Stability in Emerging Market Econs 1996–97, G-22 Working Party on Transparency and Accountability 1998, Financial Stability Forum's Working Group on Highly Leveraged Insts 1999–2000; Hon. LLD (Amherst Coll.) 1988. *Publications include:* Inflation Targeting in the World Economy 2003, Chasing Dirty Money: The Fight Against Money Laundering (co-author) 2004, A Strategy for IMF Reform 2006, Sovereign Wealth Funds: Threat or Salvation? 2010; numerous articles on int. monetary econs, int. debt problems, econ. devt and European econ. integration. *Address:* Peterson Institute for International Economics, 1750 Massachusetts Avenue, NW, Washington, DC 20036-1903, USA (office). *Telephone:* (202) 237-1730 (home). *Fax:* (202) 659-3225 (office). *E-mail:* ttruman@piie.com (office); tnttruman@yahoo.com (home). *Website:* www.piie.com (office).

TRUMKA, Richard Louis, JD; American lawyer and trade union official; *President, American Federation of Labor and Congress of Industrial Organizations (AFL-CIO);* b. 24 July 1949, Nemacolin, Pa; s. of Frank Richard Trumka and Eola Elizabeth Bertugli; m. Barbara Vidovich 1982; one s.; ed Philadelphia State Univ., Villanova Univ.; served at bar US Dist Court 1974, US Court of Appeals 1975, US Supreme Court 1979; Attorney United Mine Workers of America, Washington 1974–77, 1978–79; Miner-Operator Jones and Loughlin Steel, Nemacolin, Pa 1977–78, 1979–81, mem. Int. Exec. Bd Dist 4, Masontown, Pa 1981–83, Int. Pres., Washington, DC 1982–95, Pres. Emer. 1995–; Sec. Treas., AFL-CIO, Washington, DC 1995–2009, Pres. 2009–; Chair. Econ. Policy Inst., Solidarity Center, Union Sportsmens Alliance; mem. Pres. Trump's American Manufacturing Council 2017 (resgnd); mem. Bd of Dirs Union Labor Life Insurance Co.; Trustee Philadelphia State Univ.; Labor Responsibility Award, Martin Luther King Center for Non-Violent Social Change 1990, Jewish National Fund Tree of Life Award 1996, Sons of Italy Foundation's Humanitarian Award 2003. *Address:* AFL-CIO, 815 16th Street, NW, Washington, DC 20006, USA (office). *Telephone:* (202) 637-5000 (office). *Fax:* (202) 637-5058 (office). *Website:* www.aflcio.org (office).

TRUMP, Donald John, Sr, BS; American business executive, property developer, politician and head of state; *President;* b. 14 June 1946, Queens, New York; s. of Fred C. Trump and Mary Anne Trump (née MacLeod); m. 1st Ivana Zelnicek 1977 (divorced 1991); two s. one d.; m. 2nd Marla Maples 1993 (divorced 1999); one d.; m. 3rd Melania Knauss 2005; one s.; ed New York Mil. Acad., Fordham Univ., Wharton School of Finance, Univ. of Pennsylvania; worked for father's real-estate firm, Elizabeth Trump & Son, while attending univ., joined firm in 1968, given control 1971, renamed The Trump Organization, Chair. and Pres. 1971–2017; Founder Trump Entertainment Resorts; fmr Chair. Trump Plaza Assocs, LLC, Trump Atlantic City Assocs; holdings include: Trump Tower on Fifth Avenue, New York, Mar-A-Lago at Palm Beach, Fla, Trump Plaza, New Jersey, several int. holdings; acquired 50 percent stake in Empire State Bldg 1994 (sold 2002); mem. Bd of Dirs Police Athletic League; mem. Advisory Bd Lenox Hill Hosp. and United Cerebral Palsy; Dir Fred C. Trump Foundation; fmr Co-Chair. New York Vietnam Veterans Memorial Fund; Republican party nominee for US Pres. 2016; Pres. of USA Jan. 2017–; Hotel and Real Estate Visionary of the Century, UJA Fed. 2000, Time Person of the Year 2016, Financial Times Person of the Year 2016, King Abdulaziz al-Saud Collar 2017. *Radio:* Clear Channel Radio broadcasts 2004. *Television:* host and co-exec. producer, The Apprentice 2004–15. *Publications include:* Trump: The Art of the Deal 1989, Trump: Surviving at the Top 1990, Trump 1997, The Art of the Comeback 1997, The America We Deserve 2000, How to Get Rich 2004, Think Like a Billionaire 2004, Trump: Think Like a Billionaire: Everything You Need to Know about Success, Real Estate, and Life 2005, Why We Want You to Be Rich: Two Men – One Message 2006, Trump University Real Estate 101: Building Wealth with Real Estate Investments 2006, Trump 101: The Way to Success 2006, Trump: How to Get Rich 2008, Trump – Never Give Up: How I Turned My Biggest Challenges into Success 2008, Trump University Commercial Real Estate 101: How Small Investors Can Get Started and Make it Big 2008, Think Like a Champion: An Informal Education in Business and Life 2010, Think BIG: Make It Happen in Business and Life 2012, Time to Get Tough 2012, Crippled America: How to Make America Great Again 2015, Great Again: How to Fix Our Crippled America 2016. *Address:* The White House, 1600 Pennsylvania Avenue, NW, Washington, DC 20500, USA (office). *Telephone:* (202) 456-1414 (office). *Fax:* (202) 456-2461 (office). *E-mail:* president@whitehouse.gov (office). *Website:* www .whitehouse.gov (office); www.trump.com (office); www.trumpgolf.com (office).

TRUMP, Melania; American (b. Slovenian) fmr model; *First Lady;* b. (Melanija Knavs (Melania Knauss)), 26 April 1970, Novo Mesto, fmr Yugoslavia (now Slovenia); d. of Victor Knavs and Amalija Knavs (née Ulčnik); m. Donald J. Trump 2005; one s.; began modelling aged 16; signed by ID Model Management (model agency), Milan 1988; perm. resident of USA 2001, US citizen 2006; launched Melania jewellery collection on shopping channel QVC 2010; launched Melania Marks Skincare 2013; First Lady of USA Jan. 2017–. *Address:* Office of the First Lady, The White House, 1600 Pennsylvania Avenue, NW, Washington, DC 20500, USA (office). *Telephone:* (202) 456-1414 (office). *Fax:* (202) 456-2461 (office). *Website:* www.whitehouse.gov (office).

TRUONG, My Hoa; Vietnamese politician; b. 8 May 1945, Tien Giang Prov.; sister of Truong Tan Sang, Pres. of Viet Nam; m. 1975; two d.; joined People's Army aged 15; mem. CP of Vietnam 1963–; captured aged 19 and imprisoned for 11 years; Party Sec. and Chair. People's Cttee, Tan Binh dist of Ho Chi Minh City 1986–91; Pres. Nat. Cttee for Advancement of Women 1995; Pres. The Women's Union 1995; Vice-Chair. Nat. Ass. 1994–2002; Vice-Pres. Socialist Repub. of Viet Nam 2002–07; fmr Vice-Chair. Nat. Cttee for Population and Family Planning; fmr mem. Exec. Bd Cen. Party Cttee, Congress Party del.

TRUONG, Tan Sang, LLB; Vietnamese politician and fmr head of state; b. 21 Jan. 1949, My Hanh, Duc Hoa, Long An, French Indochina (now Viet Nam); m. Mai Thi Hanh; joined CP 1969; taken prisoner by S Vietnamese Govt 1971, held in Bien Hoa Prison, Phu Quoc island dist, released under Paris Peace Treaty 1973; headed Ho Chi Minh City's Forestry Dept as well as city's New Econ. Zone Devt Dept 1983–86; promoted to Standing Bd of city's Party Cttee 1986; Party Chair. for Ho Chi Minh City 1992; mem. Politburo 1996–; Party Sec. for Ho Chi Minh City 1996–2000; promoted to 10th position in nat. party at a congress April 2001; also apptd Head of party's Econ. Comm.; promoted to fifth position in party at a congress April 2006, also appointed Head of party's Secr.; promoted to party's number two slot between congresses Oct. 2009; ranked as the party's number one leader following 11th Nat. Congress, Hanoi Jan. 2011; Chair. Council for Nat. Defence and Security 2011–16; Pres. of Viet Nam 2011–16. *Address:* Dang Cong San Viet Nam (Communist Party of Viet Nam), 1 Hoang Van Thu, Hanoi, Viet Nam. *E-mail:* cpv@hn.vnn.vn. *Website:* www.cpv.org.vn.

TRUSS, Rt Hon. Elizabeth (Liz) Mary, PC, BA; British management accountant and politician; *Chief Secretary to the Treasury;* b. 26 July 1975, Oxford; m. Hugh O'Leary; two d.; ed Roundhay School, Leeds, Merton Coll., Oxford; Pres. Oxford Univ. Liberal Democrats 1994; worked for Shell as a commercial man. and for Cable & Wireless as Econs Dir for ten years; joined Conservative Party 1996; Chair. Lewisham Deptford Conservative Asscn 1998–2000; Councillor, London Borough of Greenwich 2006–10; Deputy Dir of Reform (think-tank) 2008–10; contested Hemsworth Constituency in Gen. Election 2001, Calder Valley constituency 2005; MP (Conservative) for SW Norfolk 2010–, mem. Justice Cttee 2010–12; Parl. Under-Sec. for Educ. and Childcare 2012–14; Sec. of State for Environment, Food and Rural Affairs 2014–16, Sec. of State for Justice and Lord Chancellor 2016–17, Chief Sec. to the Treasury 2017–; f. Free Enterprise Group of Conservative MPs. *Publications include:* author or co-author of several papers and reports, including The Value of Mathematics 2008, A New Level 2009, Academic Rigour and Social Mobility: How Low Income Students Are Being Kept Out of Top Jobs 2011, A Decade of Gains: Learning Lessons from Germany 2012, Affordable Quality: New Approaches to Childcare 2012, and several books, including After the Coalition 2011, Britannia Unchained 2012. *Address:* HM Treasury, 1 Horse Guards Road, London, SW1A 2HQ (office); House of Commons, London, SW1A 0AA, England (office). *Telephone:* (20) 7270-5000 (office). *E-mail:* public.enquiries@ hmtreasury.gsi.gov.uk (office). *Website:* www.hm-treasury.gov.uk (office); www .elizabethtruss.com.

TRUSS, Warren Errol; Australian farmer and politician; b. 8 Oct. 1948, Kingaroy, Queensland; m. Lyn Truss; mem. Kingaroy Shire Council 1976–90, fmr Chair.; mem. House of Reps (Parl.) (Nat. Party of Australia) for Wide Bay constituency 1990–, Nat. Party Parl. Leader 2007–; Minister for Customs and Consumer Affairs 1997–98, for Community Services 1998–99, for Agric., Fisheries and Forestry 1999–2005, for Transport and Regional Services 2005–06, for Trade 2006–07; Shadow Minister for Infrastructure and Transport 2010–13; Deputy Prime Minister 2013–16, also Minister for Infrastructure and Regional Devt 2013–16; Chair. Fraser Coast-South Burnett Regional Tourism Bd 1985–89; Deputy Chair. Bulk Grains Queensland 1985–90; fmr Deputy Chair. Queensland Grain Handling Authority; Pres. Australian Council of Rural Youth 1973–74; fmr Pres. Burnett District Local Govt Asscn, Lutheran Youth of Queensland; mem. State Council, Queensland Graingrowers Asscn 1979–90; mem. Nat. Party of Australia, Leader 2007–16; Centenary Medal 2001.

TRUSZCZYŃSKI, Jan, MA; Polish politician, diplomatist and international organization official; b. 30 July 1949, Warsaw; m.; two c.; ed Warsaw School of

Commerce, Institut für Internationale Beziehungen, Potsdam, Germany, Polish Inst. of Int. Affairs, Warsaw; trainee, then desk officer in Human Resources and Training Dept, Ministry of Foreign Affairs 1972–78; Second Sec., Embassy in The Hague 1978–82; European Integration Desk Officer, Western Europe Dept, Ministry of Foreign Affairs 1982–88; Counsellor, Embassy in Brussels (in charge of bilateral and EC matters) 1988–89; Deputy Head of Polish Mission to the European Communities, Brussels 1989–93; corresp. banking officer, then Head of Investor Relations, Bank Inicjatyw Gospodarczych (BIG) SA, Warsaw 1993–94; Head of Rep. Office of Kredietbank NV in Poland 1995–96; Amb. and Perm. Rep. to EU, Brussels 1996–2001 (mem. of Poland's EU accession negotiation team 1998–2001); Undersecretary of State, Chancellery of the Pres. of Poland (acting as Chief Adviser to the Pres. on European integration) Feb.–Oct. 2001; Undersecretary of State, Ministry of Foreign Affairs 2001–05, Govt's Plenipotentiary for Negotiations on Accession of Poland to the EU 2001–03; Sec. of State, Ministry of Foreign Affairs Jan.–Oct. 2005; Man. Dir Foundation for Polish-German Co-operation in Warsaw 2005–07; Deputy Dir-Gen. for Enlargement, EC 2007–09, Deputy Dir-Gen. for Educ. and Culture 2009–10, Dir-Gen. for Educ. and Culture 2010–14.

TRUTNEV, Yurii Petrovich; Russian politician; *Deputy Prime Minister and Presidential Representative to Far Eastern Federal Okrug;* b. 1 March 1956, Perm, Russian SFSR, USSR; m.; five c.; ed Perm Polytechnic Inst.; engineer, Perm Scientific Research Inst. of Oil 1978–81; instructor Perm City Komsomol Cttee and Sport Cttee 1981–88; Pres. EKS Int. (food business) 1996, Dir 2000–; Deputy, Perm City Duma (parl.) 1994–96, Chair. Cttee on Econ. Policy and Taxation; Mayor of Perm 1996–2000; Gov. of Perm Oblast 2000–04; Minister of Natural Resources and Ecology 2004–12; Asst to the Pres. of Russia 2012–13; Deputy Prime Minister and Presidential Rep. to the Far Eastern Fed. Okrug 2013–. *Leisure interests:* karate (3rd Dan), wrestling, rally racing. *Address:* Office of the Presidential Representative to the Far Eastern Federal Okrug, 680030 Khabarovsk, ul. Sheronova 22, Russia (office). *Telephone:* (4212) 31-39-78 (office). *Fax:* (4212) 31-38-04 (office). *Website:* www.dfo.gov.ru (office); government.ru/en/gov/persons/21/events (office).

TSACHEVA DANGOVSKA, Tsetska, LLB; Bulgarian jurist and politician; b. 24 May 1958, Dragana, Ugarchin Municipality, Lovech Prov.; m. Rumen Dangovski; one s.; ed Pleven High School of Math., Sofia Univ.; mem. Bulgarian CP –1989 (resgnd); practised as lawyer and was subsequently a head legal adviser to Pleven Municipality 1999–2007; mem. Grazhdani za Evropeysko Razvitie na Balgariya (GERB—Citizens for European Devt of Bulgaria) 2007–, Deputy Chair. GERB 2013–14; joined Pleven Municipal Council as GERB mem. 2007; GERB cand. for Mayor of Pleven 2007; headed GERB's voting list in Pleven Prov. in parl. elections and was also party's proportional cand. for that constituency 2009; mem. Narodno Sobraniye (Nat. Ass.) for 15-Pleven 2009–, Chair. 2009–13, 2014–17; second-placed cand. in presidential election 2016; Minister of Justice 2017–19 (resgnd); mem. Pleven Bar Asscn. *Address:* Narodno Sobranie (National Assembly), 1169 Sofia, pl. Narodno Sobranie 2, Bulgaria (office). *Telephone:* (2) 939-39 (office). *Fax:* (2) 981-31-31 (office). *E-mail:* predsedatel@parliament.bg (office); infocenter@parliament .bg (office). *Website:* www.parliament.bg/en/MP/946 (office).

TSAI, Eng-Meng; Taiwanese business executive; *Chairman and CEO Want Want China Holdings Ltd;* b. 1957; m.; one s.; joined Want Want China Holdings Ltd 1976, Gen. Man. I Lan Foods Industrial Co. Ltd (subsidiary), Taiwan –1987, Chair., Exec. Dir and CEO Want Want China Holdings Ltd, Shanghai 1987–, Chair. and CEO Want Want Holdings Ltd 1987–; Chair. and controlling shareholder of San Want; fmr mem. Council Standing Cttee of Taiwan Confectionery, Biscuit and Floury Food Industry Asscn, Food Devt Asscn of Taiwan; mem. Bd of Dirs Hot-Kid Holdings Ltd, Norwares Overseas Inc.; Hon. Prof., Nanjing Normal Univ. 1995; Dr hc (Chinese Culture Univ.) 2013. *Address:* Want Want China Holdings Ltd, 1088 East Hong Song Road, Shanghai 201103, People's Republic of China (office). *Telephone:* (21) 61151111 (office). *Fax:* (21) 61151777 (office). *E-mail:* info@www.want-want.com (office). *Website:* www.want-want.com (office).

TSAI, Hong-tu, BA, JD; Taiwanese insurance industry executive; *Chairman, Cathay Life Insurance Company Ltd;* s. of Tsai Wan-lin and Tsai Chou Pao-chin; ed Nat. Taiwan Univ., Southern Methodist Univ., USA; Man. Dir and Vice-Chair. Cathay Life Insurance Company Ltd –1980, Chair. 1980–, also Chair. Cathay Financial Holding Co. Ltd (parent co. Lin-Yuan Group est. by father Tsai Wan-lin); mem. Life Insurance Asscn of Repub. of China; Chair. Life Insurance Asscn of Repub. of China. *Address:* Cathay Life Insurance Co. Ltd, 296 Jen Ai Road, Section 4, Taipei 10639, Taiwan (office). *Telephone:* (22) 755-1399 (office). *Fax:* (22) 704-1485 (office). *E-mail:* info@cathlife.com.tw (office); service@cathayholdings.com.tw (office). *Website:* www.cathlife.com.tw (office).

TSAI, Ing-wen, LLB, LLM, PhD; Taiwanese politician, professor of law and head of state; *President;* b. 31 Aug. 1956; ed Nat. Taiwan Univ., Cornell Univ., USA, London School of Econs, UK; Assoc. Prof., Law Dept, Nat. Chengchi Univ. 1984–90, Prof., Grad. School of Law 1990–91, Prof. of Law, Grad. Inst. of Int. Trade 1993–2000 (mem. Int. Trade Comm.); Prof., Grad. School of Law, Soochow Univ. 1991–93; Adviser on Int. Econ. Orgs, Ministry of Econ. Affairs 1992–2000; Convener, Drafting/Research Group on 'Statute Governing Relations with Hong Kong and Macao' 1994–95; mem. Advisory Cttee Mainland Affairs Council, Exec. Yuan 1994–98, Chair. 2000–04; Nat. Policy Adviser to Pres. 2004–06; Vice-Pres. of Exec. Yuan 2006–07 (resgnd); Chair. TaiMedBiologics (biotechnology firm) 2007–08; Chair. Democratic Progressive Party 2008–12, 2014–18; mem. Fair Trade Comm., Exec. Yuan 1995–98, Advisory Cttee of Copyright Comm., Ministry of Interior 1997–99; Sr Adviser Nat. Security Council 1999–2000; unsuccessful cand. (DPP) in presidential election 2012; Pres. of Taiwan (first woman) 2016–. *Address:* Office of the President, 122 Chungking South Road, Zhongzheng District, Taipei 10048, Taiwan (office). *Telephone:* (2) 23113731 (office). *Fax:* (2) 23311604 (office). *E-mail:* public@mail.oop.gov.tw (office). *Website:* www.president.gov.tw (office).

TSAI, Michael Ming-hsien, PhD; Taiwanese politician and diplomatist; ed California Western School of Law, USA; mem. Parl. (Progressive Democratic Party), served as a legislator for two terms and as Deputy Rep. to USA; fmr Vice-Minister of Nat. Defense, adviser to Ministry of Nat. Defense –2008, Minister of Nat. Defense 2008; mem. Democratic Progressive Party. *Publications include:*

Defending Taiwan: The Future Vision of Taiwan's Defence Policy and Military Strategy (co-ed.) 2002, Submarines and Taiwan's Defense (co-author) 2004, Taiwan's Security and Air Power (co-author) 2004, (co-author of book on Taiwanese defence reform) 2006. *Address:* Democratic Progressive Party, 10/F, 30 Beiping East Road, Taipei 10051, Taiwan (office). *Telephone:* (2) 23929989 (office). *Fax:* (2) 23930342 (office). *E-mail:* dppforeign@gmail.com (office). *Website:* www.dpp.org.tw (office).

TSAI, Ming-liang; Taiwanese film dir ; b. 27 Oct. 1957; ed Chinese Culture Univ. *Films include:* Rebels of the Neon God 1992, Vive l'Amour (Venice Golden Lion Award 1994) 1994, The River (Berlin Silver Bear Award 1996) 1996, The Hole 1998, Tian bian yi duo yun 2005, Last Dance, Dong, The Wayward Cloud (Alfred Bauer Prize, Silver Bear for Outstanding Artistic Achievement) 2005, I Don't Want to Sleep Alone 2006, Face 2009, Stray Dogs 2013, Journey to the West 2014.

TSAKALOTOS, Euclid, PhD; Greek economist and politician; *Minister of Finance;* b. 1960, Rotterdam, The Netherlands; s. of Stefanos Tsakalotos; m. Heather D. Gibson; three c.; ed Univs of Oxford and Sussex, UK; Researcher, Univ. of Kent, UK 1989–90, Lecturer 1990–93; Lecturer, Athens Univ. of Econs and Business 1994–2010; Prof. of Econs, Nat. and Kapodistrian Univ. of Athens 2010–; mem. Vouli (Parl.) (Synaspismos Rizospastikis Aristeras—SYRIZA—Coalition of the Radical Left) for Athens B constituency 2012–; Deputy Minister for Int. Econ. Relations Jan.–July 2015, Minister of Finance July 2015–; mem. Cen. Political Cttee and Political Secr., Coalition of Left of Movements and Ecology; mem. Exec. Cttee, Hellenic Fed. of Univ. Teachers Asscns; mem. SYRIZA Cen. Cttee. *Publications include:* Alternative Economic Strategies: The Case of Greece 1991, Corporatism and Economic Performance: A Comparative Analysis of Market Economies (with Andrew Henley) 1993, No Return (co-author) 2011, 22 Things They Tell You about the Greek Crisis Which are Not So (co-author) 2012, Crucible of Resistance: Greece, The Eurozone and the World Economic Crisis (co-author) 2013; numerous articles in economic and political journals. *Address:* Ministry of Finance, Karageorgi Servias 10, 105 62 Athens, Greece (office). *Telephone:* (210) 3375000 (office). *Fax:* (210) 3332608 (office). *E-mail:* minister@minfin.gr (office). *Website:* www.minfin.gr (office).

TSAKHNA, Margus; Estonian politician; b. 13 April 1977, Tartu; m.; two c.; ed Univ. of Tartu, Univ. of Toronto, Canada; mem. Isamaa ja Res Publica Liit (IRL—Union of Pro Patria and Res Publica) 2001–, Chair. Noor-Isamaa (party's youth org.) 2001–04, Political Sec., IRL 2003–06, Sec.-Gen. 2007–10, Political Sec. 2010–13, Chair. Social Cttee 2011–, Asst Chair. IRL 2013–15, Chair. 2015–; mem. Tartu City Council 2001–03; mem. Riigikogu (Parl.) 2007–; Minister of Social Protection 2015–16, of Defence 2016–17; f. Christian Adolescent Home, Tartu 2000; mem. Gen. Johan Laidoner Soc., Korp! Sakala student soc. *Achievements include:* runner-up in Estonian TV singing competition Laulud tähtedega (Singing with Stars), singing with Birgit Õigemeel 2009. *Address:* c/o Ministry of Defence, Sakala 1, Tallinn 15094, Estonia (office). *Telephone:* 717-0022 (office). *Fax:* 717-0001 (office). *E-mail:* info@kaitseministeerium.ee (office). *Website:* www .kaitseministeerium.ee (office).

TSANG, Sir Donald Yam-kuen, Kt, KBE, JP, MPA; Chinese government official; b. (Tsang Yam-kuen), 7 Oct. 1944, Hong Kong; m.; two s.; ed in Hong Kong and Harvard Univ., USA; joined Govt of Hong Kong 1967, served in various govt depts and brs of Govt Secr.; attached to Asian Devt Bank, Manila 1977; Dist Officer, Shatin; Deputy Dir of Trade responsible for trade relations with N America; Deputy Sec. of Gen. Duties Br. responsible for Sino-British Jt Declaration 1985–89; Dir of Admin. Office of Chief Sec. 1989–91; Dir-Gen. of Trade 1991–93; Sec. for the Treasury 1993–95; Financial Sec. 1995–2001; Chief Sec. for Admin. 2001–05, Acting Chief Exec. March–May 2005, Chief Exec. 2005–12; charged and put on trial for bribery and misconduct 2016; Grand Bauhinia Medal 2002; Dr hc (Chinese Univ. of Hong Kong, Hong Kong Polytechnic Univ., Univ. of Hong Kong). *Leisure interests:* hiking, swimming, bird-watching, music.

TSANG, John Chun-wah, JP, MPA; Chinese government official; b. 21 April 1951; m.; two c.; ed La Salle Coll., Hong Kong, Boston State Coll., Massachusetts Inst. of Tech., Kennedy School of Govt, Harvard Univ., USA; began career working in Boston Public Schools, USA; joined Hong Kong civil service 1982, Admin. Asst to the Financial Sec. 1987–91, Asst Dir-Gen. of Trade 1991–95, Pvt. Sec. to Gov. Chris Patten 1995–97, Dir-Gen. Econ. and Trade Office, London 1997–99, Commr of Customs and Excise 1999–2002, Perm. Sec. for Housing, Planning and Lands 2002–03, Sec. for Commerce, Industry and Tech. 2003–06; Dir Office of the Chief Exec. of Hong Kong 2006–07, Financial Sec. 2007–16, mem. Exec. Council, Hong Kong Special Admin. Region; Chair. Sixth Ministerial Conference (MC6), WTO 2005. *Address:* c/o Executive Council, Central Government Offices, Lower Albert Road, Central, Hong Kong Special Administrative Region, People's Republic of China.

TSANG, Yok-Sing, BA; Hong Kong politician; b. 17 May 1947, Guangzhou, Guangdong; m. 1st Young Sun-yee (divorced); m. 2nd Ng Kar-man 2009; ed Univ. of Hong Kong; Founding Chair. Democratic Alliance for the Betterment of Hong Kong 1992–2003 (resgnd); Legis. Councillor, Special Admin. Region of Hong Kong, People's Repub. of China 1996–2016 (Pres. 2008–16), mem. Exec. Council (Cabinet) 2002–08, Chair. Cttee on Rules of Procedure, Panel on Educ.; mem. political section, Preparatory Cttee for Hong Kong Special Admin. Region (SAR); mem. Bd of Dirs Airport Authority; mem. Comm. on Strategic Devt, ICAC Complaints Cttee, Disaster Relief Fund Advisory Cttee. *E-mail:* info@ tsangyoksing.hk. *Website:* tsangyoksing.hk.

TSAO, Robert H.C., MS; Taiwanese electronics industry executive; *Chairman Emeritus, United Microelectronics Corporation;* b. 24 Feb. 1947, Shantung; ed Nat. Univ. of Taiwan, Nat. Chiao Tung Univ.; Deputy Dir Electrical Research Service Org. 1979–81; Vice-Pres. United Microelectronics Corpn 1980, Pres. 1981–91, Chair. 1991–2006 (resgnd), now Chair. Emer.; indicted for allegedly making illegal investments in a Chinese foundry 2006, found not guilty of charges by Hsinchu Dist. Court 2007; Chair. Unipac Microelectronics Corpn 1989; Vice-Chair. TECO Information System Co. Ltd 1995; mem. Standing Bd Chinese Nat. Fed. of Industry, Chair. Intellectual Property Protection Cttee 1991–94; Chair. Asscn of Allied Industries in Science-Based Industry Park 1987–93. *Address:* c/o United Microelectronics Corporation Ltd, No. 3, Li-Hsin 2nd Road, Hsinchu Science Park, Hsinchu, Taiwan.

TSAPOGAS, Makis Joakim, MD, DSc, MCh, PhD, MRCS, LRCP, FACS; Greek medical scientist and academic; *Professor of Vascular Diseases, New York University and University of London;* m. Lily Philossopoulou; ed Univs of Athens, London and New York; Lecturer, King's Coll. Hosp. Medical School, London 1961–63, Sr Lecturer 1963–67; Hunterian Prof., Royal Coll. of Surgeons, UK 1964; Assoc. Prof., Albany Medical Coll. Union Univ. New York 1967–70, Prof. 1970–75; Adjunct Prof. Rensselear Polytechnic Inst. New York 1970–75; Prof., Rutgers Medical School, NJ 1976; Prof. of Vascular Diseases, State Univ. of New York, Stony Brook 1977–; Adviser, WHO 1986–; Consultant, UN, New York 1993–; Prof. of Vascular Diseases, Univs of NY and London; Visiting Prof. in many univs in Europe and N America; Physician in charge of the Pres. of Greece and the Ecumenical Orthodox Patriarchate, Constantinople; corresp. mem. Acad. of Athens; Fellow, Archaeological Soc. of Athens; adviser to several medical schools 2009–; Hon. mem. Parnassos Literary Soc. and over 30 medical, research and biomedical scientific socs, Hon. citizen of Nea Smyrni and Kos; Hon. MD (Nice Univ.), (Athens Univ.), (Patras Univ.); Hon. PhD; Red Cross Gold Medal, Gold Medal and Cross of the Ecumenical Patriarchate, Medal of the towns of Heraklion and Alexandroupoulis. *Publications include:* Atherosclerosis in the Lower Limb 1959, Treatment of Thrombosis 1965, Management of Vascular Diseases 1985, Medical Education 1992, Venous Thrombosis and Pulmonary Embolism 2001, Biomedical Progress and Society 2004, Hypertension 2006, Lipids and Cardiovascular Disease 2007, Post-Graduate Medical Education 2008, Athersclerosis in Women 2009, Recent Advances in Medicine 2009, Molecular Biology in Medicine (contrib.) 2009, Prevention of Vascular Diseases 2009, Cardiovascular Diseases in Children 2010, Hypertension in Young People 2010, The Role of Lipids in Health and Disease 2010; over 200 articles in scientific medical journals. *Leisure interests:* classical music, reading, travelling. *Address:* 8 Merlin Street, Kolonaki, 106 71 Athens, Greece (home). *Telephone:* (21) 03390988 (home). *Fax:* (21) 03390989 (home).

TSARUKYAN, Gagik; Armenian business executive, sportsman and politician; b. 25 Nov. 1956, Arinj, Armenian SSR, USSR; s. of Nikolay Tsarukyan and Roza Tsarukyan; m. Javahir Tsarukyan; six c.; ed Armenian State Inst. of Physical Culture, Yerevan; began business activities 1980s; Exec. Dir 'Armenia' co. 1990–92; Founder and Pres. Multi Group group of cos (more than 30 enterprises, including Kotayk beer factory, Abovyan, Yerevan Chemical Pharmaceutical Co., Mek network of furniture stores, Yerevan Ararat Brandy-Wine-Vodka Factory, and others) 1995–; practised boxing, wrestling and arm wrestling, becoming world champion in arm-wrestling 1996, won European Championship 1998; Founder and fmr Leader, Bargavach Hayastani Kusaktsutyun (BHK—Prosperous Armenia Party); mem. Azgayin Zhoghov (Nat. Ass.) for Dist 42 2003–08, as BHK Rep. for Dist 28 2008–, mem. Standing Cttee on Defence, Nat. Security and Internal Affairs; announced departure from politics 2015, announced return 2017, formed the Tsarukyan dashinq (Tsarukyan Alliance), led by the BHL, before Parl. elections in Apr. 2017; Pres. Nat. Olympic Cttee; St Grigor Lousavorich Order from Supreme Patriarch of All Armenians Garegin II 2002; Movses Khorenatsi Medal 2003, 'Services Provided to the Motherland' First Rank Medal 2008, European of the Year, Int. European Movt 2009, Gold Medal, European Judo Fed. 2009. *Address:* Bargavach Hayastani Kusaktsutyun, 0010 Yerevan, Hanrapetutyan poghota 47, Armenia (office). *Telephone:* (10) 52-02-81 (office). *E-mail:* info@bhk .am (office). *Website:* www.bhk.am (office); gagiktsarukyan.am.

TSCHÜTSCHER, Klaus, LLM, DrIur; Liechtenstein politician and academic; b. 8 July 1967; m. Jeanette Tschütscher; two c.; ed Univs of St Gallen and Zurich, Switzerland; Leader, Liechtenstein Fiscal Admin Sept. 1995; mem. Exec. Cttee Liechtenstein Steuerwaltung 1996–; Dozent, Univ. of Liechtenstein 1998–; mem. Vaterländische Union (Patriotic Union); mem. Liechtenstein Del. to OECD (Harmful Tax Practices) 1999, to EU (EU tax topics, in particular EU interest taxation) 1999, for legal aid negotiations with USA 2001; Chair. Standing Working Group 'International Developments of the Tax Law' 2001–; mem. MWS Mixed Comm. 2001–; mem. Future Finance Plan Liechtenstein 2002; Deputy Prime Minister and Minister of Econ. Affairs, of Justice and of Sports 2005–09, Prime Minister of Liechtenstein 2009–13, also Minister of Gen. Govt Affairs, Finance, Family Affairs and Gender Equality 2009–13.

TSEKOA, Mohlabi Kenneth, BEd, MA; Lesotho politician, educator and diplomatist; b. 13 Aug. 1945; m.; two s. one d.; ed Nat. Univ. of Lesotho, Univ. of Botswana, Lesotho and Swaziland, Univ. of Newcastle-upon-Tyne, Univ. of London, UK, Univ. of Mass, USA; teacher, Hlotse High School 1970–74; Deputy Headmaster, St Agnes High School 1974–76; Sr Educ. Officer, Lesotho Distance Teaching Centre 1976–78, Dir 1978–84; Deputy Prin. Sec., Ministry of Educ. 1984–86, Prin. Sec. 1986–89; High Commr to UK and Amb. to Ireland, Spain and Portugal 1989–96; Govt Sec. and Head of the Public Service 1996–2001; Minister of Finance and Devt Planning 2001–02, of Foreign Affairs 2002–04, of Educ. and Training 2004–07, of Foreign Affairs and Int. Relations 2007–15. *Address:* c/o Ministry of Foreign Affairs and International Relations, POB 1387, Maseru 100, Lesotho.

TSEPKALO, Valery V.; Belarusian academic, government official and fmr diplomatist; *Director, High-Tech Park Administration;* b. 22 Feb. 1965, Grodno; m. Veronika Tsepkalo; ed Belarus Technological Inst., Moscow State Inst. of Int. Relations, Russia; mil. service 1984–86; with Embassy of USSR in Finland 1991; joined Ministry of Foreign Affairs, Repub. of Belarus 1992–93, First Deputy Minister for Foreign Affairs 1994–97; Adviser to Exec. Sec. of CIS 1993–94; lecturer on int. relations, geopolitics and neo-conservatism; Amb. to USA 1997–2002; Sr Adviser to Pres. of Belarus 2002–05, Rep. of Pres. to Nat. Ass. 2005–; Dir High-Tech Park Admin 2005–. *Publications include:* By The Road of the Dragon 1994, numerous articles on int. security, foreign policy and world economy. *Address:* Office of the President, vul. K. Marksa 38, Dom Urada, 220016 Minsk, Belarus (office). *Telephone:* (17) 268-69-11 (office). *E-mail:* info@park.by (office). *Website:* www.president.gov.by (office).

TSERETELI, Zurab Konstantinovich; Georgian sculptor and artist; *President, Russian Academy of Arts;* b. 4 Jan. 1934, Tbilisi; m. Inessa Andronikashvili (deceased); one d.; ed Dept of Painting, Tbilisi Acad. of Arts; Chief Designer, Ministry of Foreign Affairs 1970–80; Prof. Brockport Univ. New York USA 1979; Chief Designer, Summer Olympic Games, Moscow 1980; Prof. Acad. of Arts, Tbilisi 1981; Deputy, Supreme Council of Georgia 1985–89; Chair. Union of Designers of Georgia 1987–91; Sec. USSR Union of Designers; USSR People's Deputy 1989–91;

Pres. Moscow Int. Foundation for Support to UNESCO Russia 1992–; Chief Designer, War Memorial, Moscow 1995; Chief Designer, interior and exterior decoration of Cathedral of Christ the Saviour, Moscow 1995–2000; UNESCO Goodwill Amb. 1996–; Chief Designer, Manezh Square and the underground shopping mall, Moscow 1997; Vice-Pres. Russian Acad. of Informatics 1998; Dir Moscow Museum of Modern Art 1999; Dir Tsereteli Art Gallery, Moscow 2000–; mem. Russian Acad. of Arts 1989–, Pres. 1997–, Head Dept of Design; mem. Georgian Acad. of Arts 1996, Acad. of World Elite 1997, Acad. of Art of Kyrgyzstan 1998; corresp. mem. Spanish Royal Acad. of Fine Arts, Madrid, Spain 1998, French Acad. of Fine Arts, Paris, France; Vice-Pres. Russian Acad. of Creativity; author of numerous sculptures, mosaics, monumental murals, stained-glass windows, revived old technique of traditional Georgian enamel; creator of numerous monuments including Friendship in Moscow (with poet A. Voznesensky), Kindness Wins over Evil (New York, UN Bldg), Happiness for Children of the World (Univ. of Fine Arts, Brockport), Columbus (Miami), Birth of a New Man (London), Moment of Victory (Moscow), Peter the Great (Moscow), Tear of Grief (To the Struggle Against World Terrorism), Bayonne, New Jersey, and others in Tbilisi, Tokyo, Seville, Osaka, Brasília; Hero of Socialist Labour USSR 1991, Order, Friendship of Peoples, Russia 1994, Order for Services to the Fatherland (3rd Class, Russia) 1996, Hon. Cross Combattant Volontaire, Asscn of Veterans, French Resistance, France 2000, Order, Glory of Russia 2003, Int. Peace Prize, Jt Convent of Figures of Culture, USA 2003, Order for Services to the Fatherland (2nd Class) 2006, (1st Class) 2010, Chevalier, Légion d'honneur 2012; numerous awards including Lenin Prize 1976, State Prize of USSR 1978, 1983, People's Artist of Georgia 1978, of USSR 1979, of Russia 1994, Picasso Prize 1994, State Prize of Russia 1996, Vermeil Medal, Paris, France 1998, Prize of Modern Art 2000, Int. Recognition, Golden Hand (France) 2000, Medal for Services and Homeland, Russia 2003, Jewish Nat. Fund Tree of Life 2005. *Leisure interests:* collecting works of art. *Address:* Office of the President, Russian Academy of Arts, 21 Prechistenka str., 119034, Moscow (office); Bolshaya Gruzinskaya str. 17, 123557, Moscow, Russia (office). *Telephone:* (495) 201-36-65 (office), (495) 254-77-67 (home). *E-mail:* info@ tsereteli.ru. *Website:* en.rah.ru (office); www.mmoma.ru (office); www.tsereteli.ru (home).

TSHERING, Lyonpo Dago; Bhutanese diplomatist and politician; *Special Envoy of the Prime Minister and Foreign Policy Adviser to the Prime Minister;* b. 17 July 1941, Paro; ed Univ. of Bombay, Indian Admin. Service Training, Mussoorie and Indian Audit and Accounts Service Training, Simla, India, Univ. of Manchester, UK, Nat. Admin, Tokyo; Asst, Ministry of Devt 1961–62; Asst, Office of the Chief Sec. 1962–63; returned to Ministry of Devt 1963, Sec. 1965–71; mem. Nat. Ass. 1968–90; mem. Royal Advisory Council 1968–70; First Sec., Bhutan Embassy in India 1971–73; Deputy Perm. Rep. to UN 1973–74, Perm. Rep. 1974–80, 1984–85; Amb. to Bangladesh 1980–84; Minister of Home Affairs 1985–98; Amb. to India 1998–2009; currently Special Envoy of the Prime Minister and Foreign Policy Adviser to the Prime Minister; Orange Scarf, Excellence in Diplomacy Award, India-Bhutan Friendship Asscn 2004. *Address:* Cabinet Secretariat, Tashichhodzong, Thimphu, Bhutan. *Telephone:* (2) 321437. *Fax:* (2) 321438. *Website:* www .cabinet.gov.bt.

TSHERING, Goonglon Wogma (Maj.-Gen.) Dozin Batoo; Bhutanese army officer; *Chief Operations Officer, Royal Bhutan Army;* b. Nov. 1951, Toebesa, Thimphu; ed Indian Mil. Acad., Dehradun, Defence Services Staff Coll., Wellington, India; completed Young Officer's Course, Commando Course, Intelligence Staff Officer's Course, Jr Command Course and Sr Command Course; commissioned into Royal Bhutan Army 1971, has held various command posts, apptd Operations and Training Officer 1976, commanded Wing 4 and Wing 7, apptd Commdt of mil. training centre 1988, Deputy Chief Operations Officer 1991, Commdr Command Centre 1997, promoted to rank of Dozin (Brig.) 1997; Deputy Chief Operations Officer Royal Bhutan Army Feb.–Nov. 2005, Chief Operations Officer Nov. 2005–; Druk Yurgyal Medal, Drakpoi Wangyal Medal, Drakpoi Thugsey Medal, Drakpoi Khorlo Medal, Drakpoi Rinchen Tsugtor Medal 2013. *Address:* Royal Bhutan Army Headquarters, Thimphu, Bhutan (office).

TSHERING, Kinzang, BSc, MBA; Bhutanese banking executive and politician; b. 29 May 1991; ed Univ. of Kansas and School of Business, Pepperdine Univ., USA; Asst Engineer, Transmission Unit, Dept of Power 1994–96, Exec. Engineer 1996–99; Nat. Project Man. Water Resource Man. and Power Systems Master Plan Update Project Feb.–Oct. 2002; Gen. Man. Bhutan Power Corpn 2002–05; Head of Div., Renewable Energy Div., Dept of Energy, Ministry of Trade and Industry 2005–06; CEO Bhutan Electricity Authority, Ministry of Trade and Industry 2006–07; CEO Bank of Bhutan Ltd 2007–10; mem. Bd of Dirs Druk Holding and Investments Ltd 2007–08, CEO 2007–10, Project Dir Druk Holding and Investments Educ. City Project 2010, CEO DHI Infra Ltd 2011–13; mem. Nat. Ass. of Bhutan (Druk Phuensum Tshogpa) 2013–; apptd mem. Bd of Dirs Bhutan Ferro Alloys Ltd 2007; Dispute Resolution Fellow, School of Law, Pepperdine Univ., USA 1999–2001. *Address:* National Assembly, Gyelyong Tshokhang, POB 139, Thimphu, Bhutan (office). *Telephone:* (2) 336907 (office). *E-mail:* ktshering@nab .gov.bt (office). *Website:* www.nab.gov.bt (office).

TSHERING, Lotay, MBBS, MBA; Bhutanese physician and politician; *Prime Minister;* b. 1968, Dalukha village, Mewang gewog, Thimpu; m.; three c. (two adopted); ed Mymensingh Medical Coll., Medical Coll. of Wisconsin, Okayama Univ., Univ. of Dhaka, Univ. of Canberra; more than 20 years as consultant surgeon at Mongar Regional Referral Hosp., and 11 years as urologist at Jigme Dorji Wangchuk Nat. Referral Hosp.; resigned as doctor to enter politics 2013; Pres. Druk Nyamrup Tshogpa (DNT, Solidarity, Justice and Freedom) 2018–; mem. Nat. Ass. (lower house of parl.) from South Thimphu constituency (DNT) 2018–; Prime Minister 2018–; Order of Beloved of the Thunder Dragon Medal (Druk Thuksey) 2017, Royal Orange Scarf 2018; Unsung Hero of Compassion Award 2005. *Address:* Cabinet Secretariat, Gyalyong Tshokhang, POB 1011, Thimphu, Bhutan (office). *Telephone:* (2) 336842 (office). *Fax:* (2) 321438 (home). *E-mail:* cabinet@druknet.bt (office). *Website:* www.cabinet.gov.bt (office).

TSHERING, Tashi, BSc, MSc; Bhutanese mining engineer, business executive and politician; ed univs in USA; fmr Jt Dir of Geology and Mines, Ministry of Trade and Industry; fmr Deputy Man. Dir, later Officiating Man. Dir Dungsam Cement Project Authority (DCPA), fmr consultant to DCPA and other proposed cement plants; CEO Penden Cement Authority Ltd 2010; fmr Resource Person for the

Study on Strategic Partnership between PCAL and DCPA; campaigned for Nat. Council seat from Trashigang Dzongkag 2007.

TSHIBALA NZENZE, Bruno; Democratic Republic of Congo politician; b. 20 Feb. 1956, Tshilenge, Eastern Kasai Prov.; ed Marien Ngouabi Univ., Brazzaville, univ. in Belgium; began political career whilst student at age 25, in opposition to regime of Mobutu Sese Seko 1980; founder mem. Union for Democracy and Social Progress (UDPS) 1982, fmr Deputy Gen. Sec. and Spokesman; expelled from UDPS March 2017; fmr leading mem. of main opposition coalition; arrested at Kinshasa Int. Airport for his role in anti-govt demonstrations Oct. 2016, released Nov. 2016; apptd Prime Minister (in power-sharing govt) 2017–19. *Address:* c/o Office of the Prime Minister, 5 ave du Roi Baudouin, BP 8931, Kinshasa-Gombe, Democratic Republic of Congo (office).

TSHISEKEDI, Félix Antoine; Democratic Republic of the Congo politician and head of state; *President;* b. 13 June 1963, Léopoldville (now Kinshasa); s. of Étienne Tshisekedi (fmr Prime Minister of Zaire) and Marthe Tshisekedi; m. Denise Tshilombo Nyakéru; five c.; spent several years in exile in Belgium; elected mem. Nat. Ass. (parl.) for Mbuji Mayi constituency 2011 (did not take up seat); selected as UDPS presidential candidate 2017; Pres., Democratic Repub. of the Congo 2019–; mem. Union pour la Démocratie et le Progrès Social (UDPS), Pres. 2018–. *Address:* Office of the President, Hôtel du Conseil Exécutif, ave de Lemera, Kinshasa-Gombe, Democratic Republic of the Congo (office). *Telephone:* (12) 30892 (office). *Website:* www.presidentrdc.cd (office).

TSHULTIM, Dasho Jigme, BA; Bhutanese diplomatist and politician; ed St Joseph's Coll., Darjeeling, India, Univ. of Manchester, UK; served in Govt as Head of Tourism, Dzongda and Zhung Dronyer (Chief of Protocol); Amb. to Bangladesh 2004–07; mem. Bhutan People's Unity Party; mem. Parl. for Radhi-Sakteng constituency, Trashigang 2008–13 (resgnd), Speaker of Nat Ass. 2008–13.

TSIPRAS, Alexis; Greek politician; *Prime Minister;* b. 28 July 1974, Athens; partner Peristera Baziana; two s.; ed Ampelokipoi Br. High School, Nat. Tech. Univ. of Athens (NTUA); worked as civil engineer in construction industry; joined Kommunistiki Neolaia Elladas (Communist Youth of Greece) late 1980s, active in student uprising in early 1990s; mem. Exec. Bd Students' Union, Civil Eng School, NTUA, student rep. at Univ. Senate; elected rep. on Cen. Council of Nat. Ethniki Foititikí Enosi Elládos (Students Union of Greece) 1995–97; left party to remain in coalition following departure of Kommunistiko Komma Elladas (Communist Party of Greece) from Synaspismos tis Aristeras ton Kinimátõo kai tis Oikologías (Synaspismos—Coalition of the Left, of Movements and Ecology) coalition of radical parties; first person to hold position of Political Sec. of Synaspismos Neolaia Syn (Synaspismos Youth Wing) 1999–2003; elected mem. Synaspismos party's Cen. Political Cttee and to its Political Secr. 2004, Chair. Synaspismos 2008–; mem. Parl. (Vouli) for the Athens 'A' constituency 2009–; elected unanimously by Secr. of Synaspismos Rizospastikis Aristeras (SYRIZA) as Head of SYRIZA parl. group; Leader of the Opposition 2012–15; Party of the European Left nominee for Pres. of EC in European Parl. election 2014; Prime Minister of Greece Jan.–Aug. 2015, Sept. 2015–, also Minister of Foreign Affairs 2018–19; Ewald von Kleist Prize 2019. *Leisure interest:* supports Panathinaikos Football Club. *Address:* Office of the Prime Minister, Maximos Mansion, Herodou Atticou 19, 106 74 Athens (office); Synaspismos Rizospastikis Aristerás (SYRIZA—Coalition of the Radical Left), Pl. Eleftherias 1, 105 53 Athens, Greece (office). *Telephone:* (210) 3385491 (Office of the Prime Minister) (office); (210) 3378400 (Party) (office). *Fax:* (210) 3238129 (Office of the Prime Minister) (office); (210) 3217003 (Party) (office). *E-mail:* primeminister@primeminister.gr (office); international@syriza.gr (office). *Website:* www.primeminister.gr (office); www.syriza.gr (office).

TSISKARIDZE, Nikolai; Georgian ballet dancer; *Principal, Vaganova Academy of Ballet, Saint Petersburg;* b. 31 Dec. 1973, Tbilisi; s. of Maxim Tsiskaridze and Lamara Tsiskaridze; ed Tbilisi Ballet School, Bolshoi Ballet Acad., Moscow Choreographic Inst.; joined the Bolshoi Ballet 1992, prin. dancer –2013; Prin. Vaganova Acad. of Russian Ballet, St Petersburg 2014–; Prof. Emer. Tokyo Ballet Acad. 2015; mem. Pres.'s Council for Culture and Arts 2011; Order of Honour of the Republic of Georgia 2003, Chevalier de l'Ordre des Arts et des Lettres de la République Française 2006; numerous prizes including Silver Medal, 7th Japan World Ballet Competition, Osaka 1995, Soul of Dance Rising Star Nat. Prize 1995, First Prize and Gold Medal, 8th Moscow Int. Ballet Competition 1997, Merited Artist of Russia 1997, La Sylphide Russian Nat. Dance Org. Diploma Dancer of the Year 1997, Gold Mask, Russian Nat. Award for Best Male Role 1999, 2000, 2003, Benois de la Danse Int. Award, Dancer of the Year 1999, Mayor of Moscow Prize in Literature and Art 2000, State Prize of the Russian Federation 2001, 2003, People's Artist of North Ossetia-Alania Republic 2013. *Dance:* roles in numerous ballets including Sleeping Beauty, Gisèle, Raymonda, La Sylphide, La Bayadère, The Nutcracker, Swan Lake, Romeo and Juliet, Legend of Love, Narcissus, Pharaoh's Daughter, etc. *Leisure interest:* reading. *Address:* Komsomolsky Prospekt 35, Apt. 106, Moscow 119146, Russia (home). *Telephone:* (495) 242-29-79 (home). *Website:* www.vaganovaacademy.com/A/Structure/Principal.

TSKITISHVILI, Maya; Georgian politician; *Vice-Prime Minister, Minister of Regional Development and Infrastructure;* b. 2 June 1974, Tbilisi, Georgian SSR, USSR; ed Ivane Javakhishvili Tbilisi State Univ., Univ. of Econs, Prague, Caucasus School of Business; early career in aviation industry, including as Sr Man., Georgian Air and Asst to Commercial Dir and Head of Contracts Dept, Georgian Airways; fmr Project Man., JSC Bagebi City Group; fmr Deputy Head and later Head, Logistics Dept, Burji Ltd; various man. positions with Kartu Management Ltd and JSC Parcount; Head of Admin, Govt of Georgia 2012–18; Vice-Prime Minister, Minister of Regional Devt and Infrastructure 2018–. *Address:* Ministry of Regional Development and Infrastructure, 0177 Tbilisi, Al. Qazbegi 12, Georgia (office). *Telephone:* (32) 251-05-91 (office). *E-mail:* press@mrdi.gov.ge (office). *Website:* www.mrdi.gov.ge (office).

TSOGTBAATAR, Damdin, LLM; Mongolian diplomatist and politician; *Minister of Foreign Affairs;* b. 14 Jan. 1970, Ulaanbaatar; m.; two c.; ed Moscow State Inst. of Int. Relations, Australian Nat. Univ.; Desk Officer in charge of Australia, New Zealand and ASEAN countries, Asia and Africa Div., Ministry of Foreign Affairs (MFA) 1994–96, Desk Officer, Dept of Foreign Trade and Econ. Cooperation 1996–98, Deputy Dir, Dept of Multilateral Cooperation 1998–2000, Foreign Policy Advisor to Pres. of Mongolia 2002–08, State Sec., MFA 2008–09; Minister for Nature, Environment and Tourism 2012–13, Minister of Construction and Urban Devt 2015–16, Minister of Foreign Affairs 2017–; mem. State Great Khural (parl.) 2016–; part-time lecturer in int. trade law, School of Foreign Service, Nat. Univ. of Mongolia; CEO, Xillion LLC (investment consulting firm for oil and gas cos) 2012–15; Chair. Lynx Power Core LLC 2012–15. *Leisure interest:* judo. *Address:* Ministry of Foreign Affairs, Enkhtaivny Örgön Chölöö 7a, Ulaanbaatar, 14210, Mongolia (office). *Telephone:* 62262222 (office). *Fax:* (11) 322127 (office). *E-mail:* info@mfa.gov.mn (office). *Website:* www.mfa.gov.mn (office).

TSVOLAKYAN, Feliks; Armenian politician; *Minister of Emergency Situations;* b. 27 Jan. 1952, Nerkin Dzhrapi; ed Yerevan State Univ.; joined Ararat Industrial and Technological Coll. 1974; joined State Security Cttee 1980; Control Service of the Pres. 1999; Head of State Tax Service 2003–07; Deputy Dir, Nat. Security Service 2007–13; Gov. of Shirak Marz 2013–16; mem. of Parl. 2017–, Minister of Emergency Situations 2018–; Anania Shirakatsi Medal 2005, For Services Contributed to the Motherland Medal 2016. *Address:* Ministry of Emergency Situations, 0054 Yerevan, Mikoyan poghots 109/8, Armenia (office). *Telephone:* (10) 31-77-20 (office). *Fax:* (10) 31-78-43 (office). *E-mail:* mes@mes.am (office). *Website:* www.mes.am (office).

TSOLMON, Tserendash, PhD; Mongolian engineer, diplomatist and politician; b. 1953, Tsetserleg; ed Irkutsk Polytechnic Inst., Diplomatic Acad. of Moscow, USSR; electrical engineer, meat canning factory 1976–77; Engineer, Ministry of Food and Light Industry 1977–80; Dept Chief, MRYCC 1982–84; Deputy Head of Dept, Ministry of Foreign Affairs 1987–90; Minister of Labour 1990–92; Gen. Sec., Mongolian Nat. Comm. for UNESCO 1992–94; Amb. to Bulgaria 1995–96, to Russia 1996–2000; Dir Delpati Co. 2000–06; Minister of Construction and Infrastructure 2006–08; Chair. Nat. New Party 2008–12, currently mem. Justice Coalition; mem. Mongolian Great Khural (Parl.) 2012–, Chair. Standing Cttee on Security and Foreign Policy 2012–; Minister of Defence 2014–16. *Address:* c/o Ministry of Defence, Government Bldg 7, Enkhtaivny Örgön Chölöö 51, Bayanzürkh District, Ulan Bator, Mongolia (office). *E-mail:* tsolmon@parliament.mn (office). *Website:* tsolmon.parliament.mn (office).

TSONEV, Nikolai Georgiev, PhD; Bulgarian economist, academic, politician and fmr army officer; b. 9 June 1956, Pernik; ed Nat. Artillery Mil. School, Shumen, Vassilyevski Air Defence School, Kyiv, Ukrainian SSR, Univ. for Nat. and World Economy, Sofia, Sofia Univ. St Kliment of Ohrid; officer in Bulgarian Army 1978–92; man. of several limited liability firms 1992–99; Dir Public Procurement Directorate, Ministry of Defence 1999–2000, adviser to Minister of Defence 2001–02, Dir of Social Activities Directorate 2002–08, Minister of Defence 2008–09; arrested on charges of bribery 2010, acquitted and released 2012; Prof. of Strategic Planning, Civic Admin and European Integration Inst. 2002; Prof., Univ. for Nat. and World Economy, Sofia 2004.

TSONGA, Jo-Wilfried; French professional tennis player; b. 17 April 1985, Le Mans; s. of Didier Tsonga and Évelyne Tsonga; ed Univ. of Maine, USA; won US Open Juniors title against Marcos Baghdatis in the final 2003; also reached semifinals of other three Grand Slam events; turned professional 2004; suffered several injuries that kept him from playing 2004–06; won first ATP Masters Series championship at Paris Masters 2008; qualified for Tennis Masters Cup, Shanghai 2008; winner, Bangkok, Thailand 2008, Johannesburg 2009, Marseille 2009, 2013, Tokyo 2009, Metz, France 2011, 2015, Vienna 2011, Coupe Rogers, Montreal 2014; semifinalist, French Open 2013; finalist, ATP World Tour Finals 2011; mem. Tennis Club de Paris; lives in La Rippe, Switzerland. *E-mail:* agence@interactive-one.fr (office). *Website:* www.interactive-one.fr (office); www.jowiltsonga.fr.

TSUGA, Kazuhiro, BS, MS; Japanese business executive; *President and Representative Director, Panasonic Corporation;* ed Osaka Univ., Univ. of California, Santa Barbara, USA; joined Panasonic (then known as Matsushita Electric Industrial Co. Ltd) 1979, held positions of increasing responsibility, including Head of Advanced Appliances Devt Centre for Audiovisual Technologies 2001–04, Exec. Officer 2004–08, Pres. Automotive Systems Co. and Man. Exec. Officer, Panasonic Corpn 2008–11, Head of Overseas R&D Centres and Digital Network Strategic Planning Office, Pres. AVC Networks Co. 2011–12, also Sr Man. Dir and mem. Bd, Pres. and Rep. Dir Panasonic Corpn 2012–. *Address:* Panasonic Corporation, Corporate Headquarters, 1006 Oaza Kadoma, Kadoma-shi, Osaka 571-8501, Japan (office). *Telephone:* (6) 6908-1121 (office). *Fax:* (6) 6908-2351 (office). *E-mail:* info@panasonic.net (office). *Website:* www.panasonic.net (office).

TSUI, Daniel C., PhD; American (b. Chinese) physicist and academic; *Research Professor, Boston University;* b. 28 Feb. 1939, Henan, China; ed Univ. of Chicago; Arthur LeGrand Doty Prof. of Electrical Eng, Princeton Univ. 1982, now Prof. Emer.; currently Research Prof., Boston Univ.; Fellow, American Physical Soc., AAAS; mem. NAS, Acad. Sinica, American Acad. of Arts and Sciences, Chinese Acad. of Sciences; Fellow, American Physics Soc.; Dr hc (Univ. of Chicago) 1999; Buckley Prize for Condensed Matter Physics 1984, Nobel Prize in Physics for discovery of fractional quantum Hall effect (jtly with Robert B. Laughlin and Horst L. Störmer) 1998, Benjamin Franklin Medal 1998. *Publications include:* numerous articles in scientific journals. *Address:* Boston University, Department of Electrical and Computer Engineering, PHO 830, 8 Saint Mary's Street, Boston, MA 02215, USA. *Telephone:* (617) 353-1334 (office). *Fax:* (617) 353-7337 (office). *E-mail:* tsui@bu.edu (office). *Website:* www.bu.edu/ece (office).

TSUI, Lap-Chee, OC, OOnt, BSc, MPhil, PhD, FRS, FRSC; Canadian geneticist, academic and university administrator; b. 21 Dec. 1950, Shanghai, China; s. of Jing Lue Hsue and Hui Ching Wang; m. (Ellen) Lan Fong 1977; two s.; ed The Chinese Univ. of Hong Kong, Univ. of Pittsburgh, USA; staff geneticist, Dept of Genetics and scientist, The Research Inst., Hosp. for Sick Children, Toronto, Canada 1983–88, Sr Research Scientist 1988–89, Sellers Chair in Cystic Fibrosis Research 1989–, Geneticist-in-Chief 1996–2002; Asst Prof. Depts of Medical Genetics and Medical Biophysics, Univ. of Toronto 1983–88, Assoc. Prof. 1988–90, Prof., Dept of Molecular and Medical Genetics 1990–2006, Univ. Prof. 1994–2006, H.E. Sellers Chair in Cystic Fibrosis 1998–2006; Vice-Chancellor and Pres., The Univ. of Hong Kong 2002–13; Howard Hughes Int. Scholar 1991–96; Assoc. Ed. Clinical Genetics 1991–; Ed. Int. Journal of Genome Research 1990, Assoc. Ed. Genomics 1994–; mem. Editorial Bd several scientific journals; Adviser, European Journal of Human Genetics 1992–; Dir American Soc. of Human Genetics, Mon Sheong Foundation, Educ. Foundation, Fed. of Chinese Canadian Professionals;

Foreign Assoc., NAS 2004; Foreign mem., Chinese Acad. of Science 2009–; Pres. The Human Genome Org.; Lee Kuan Yew Distinguished Visitor, Singapore 2000; Foreign Mem. Chinese Academy of Science 2009; Hon. Pres., Prix Galien 1998, Hon. mem. World Innovation Foundation 2001, Hon. FRCP (UK) 2005, Hon. Fellow, Hong Kong Coll. of Physicians 2005, Hong Kong Coll. of Pathologists 2005, Hong Kong Coll. of Pathologists 2006, Univ. of Cambridge 2012; Chevalier, Légion d'honneur 2007, Gold Bauhinia Star of the Hong Kong SAR 2011; Dr hc (St Francis Xavier Univ., Antigonish, NS) 1994, (York Univ., Toronto) 2001, (Tel-Aviv Univ.) 2005, (King's Coll. London) 2009, (Univ. of Edinburgh) 2010, (Fudan Univ.) 2013; Hon. DSc (Univ. of New Brunswick) 1991, (Chinese Univ. of Hong Kong) 1992, (Univ. of Toronto) 2007, (Univ. of Aberdeen) 2007, (Western Univ.) 2013; Hon. DCL (Univ. King's Coll.) 1991; numerous prizes and awards, including Scientist Award, Medical Research Council (Canada) 1989–93, Gold Medal of Honour, Pharmaceutical Mfrs Asscn of Canada 1989, RSC Centennial Award 1989, Award of Excellence, Genetic Soc. of Canada 1990, Gairdner Int. Award 1990, Canadian Achiever Award 1991, Sarstedt Research Prize 1993, XII San Remo Int. Award for Genetic Research 1993, J.P. Lecocq Prize 1994, Henry Friesen Award, Canadian Soc. of Clinical Investigation and Royal Coll. of Physicians and Surgeons of Canada 1995, Medal of Honour, Canadian Medical Asscn 1996, Distinguished Scientist Award, MRC 2000, Zellers Senior Scientist Award, Canadian Cystic Fibrosis Foundation 2001, Killam Prize, Canada Council 2002, Queen's Golden Jubilee Medal 2002, Distinguished Achievement Award, Chinese American Physicians Soc. 2004, European Cystic Fibrosis Soc. Award 2009, Laureate, Canadian Medical Hall of Fame 2012. *Achievements include:* identified the defective gene (viz. Cystic Fibrosis Transmembrane Regulator (CFTR)) that causes cystic fibrosis. *Publications include:* numerous scientific papers and reviews. *Leisure interests:* travel, good food. *Address:* c/o Vice-Chancellor's Office, The University of Hong Kong, 10/F Knowles Building, Pokfulam Road, Hong Kong Special Administrative Region, People's Republic of China. *E-mail:* tsuilc@hku.hk.

TSUJII, Akio; Japanese transport industry executive; *Chairman, Kinki Nippon Railway Company;* Pres. Kinki Nippon Railway Co. Ltd –2003, apptd CEO 2003, Chair. 2003–; mem. Bd of Dirs Kansai Electric Power Co. 2006–; mem. Bd of Auditors Hino Motors Ltd 2002–. *Address:* Kinki Nippon Railway Company Ltd, 6-1-55 Uehommachi Tennoji-ku, Osaka 543-8585, Japan (office). *Telephone:* (6) 6775-3465 (office). *Fax:* (6) 6775-3467 (office). *Website:* www.kintetsu.co.jp (office).

TSUKAMOTO, Hiroshi; Japanese national organization official and fmr government official; b. 10 March 1946; ed Kyoto Univ.; joined Ministry of Int. Trade and Industry—MITI (now Ministry of Economy, Trade and Industry) 1968, First Sec., Embassy in Jakarta 1979–82, Dir for Int. Petroleum Affairs, Petroluem Dept, Natural Resources and Energy Agency April–Dec. 1982, Dir Middle East Office, West Europe-Africa-Middle East Div., Int. Trade Policy Bureau, Nat. Land Agency 1982–84, Office Dir Regional Devt Bureau 1984–86; Visiting Research Fellow, Royal Inst. of Int. Affairs (now Chatham House), London 1986; Dir-Gen. for Gen. Coordination Dept, MITI Osaka Bureau 1987–89, Dir Fiber and Spinning Div., Consumer Goods Industry Bureau 1989–91, Dir Policy Planning Office, Minister's Secr. 1991–92, now Special Adviser; Pres. Japan External Trade Org. (JETRO), New York 1992–94, Pres. JETRO, Tokyo 2002–07; apptd Pres. Inst. for Int. Studies and Training 2007; Commr Gen. of Japan Pavilion, Expo 2010, Shanghai 2010; mem. Bd of Dirs NHK International, Inc.; Deputy Dir-Gen. for Global Environment Affairs (MITI) 1994–95; Exec. Dir People's Finance Corpn 1995–97; Pres. Electronic Industries Asscn of Japan (later Japan Electronics and Information Tech. Industries Asscn) 1997–2002.

TSUKAMOTO, Takashi; Japanese business executive; *Honorary Advisor, Mizuho Financial Group, Inc.;* b. 2 Aug. 1950; joined Dai-Ichi Kangyo Bank Ltd 1974; Exec. Officer/Gen. Man. Human Resources Div., Mizuho Corp. Bank Ltd 2002–03, Man. Exec. Officer/Head of Risk Man. Group, Head of Human Resources Group and Gen. Man. Post-retirement Counselling, Mizuho Financial Group, Inc. 2003–04, Man. Exec. Officer/Head of Risk Man. Group and Head of Human Resources Group Feb.–April 2004, Man. Exec. Officer/Head of Europe, Middle East and Africa, Mizuho Corp. Bank Ltd 2004–06, Man. Dir/Chief Strategy Officer and Chief Financial Officer 2006–07, Deputy Pres. 2007–08, Dir 2013–, Deputy Pres.-Exec. Officer/Head of Financial Control and Accounting Group, Mizuho Financial Group, Inc. April 2008, Pres. and CEO Mizuho Financial Strategy Co. Ltd 2008–09, Deputy Pres./Head of Financial Control and Accounting Group, Mizuho Financial Group, Inc. 2008–09, Pres. and CEO/Head of Human Resources Group 2009–10, Pres. and CEO 2010–11, Chair. 2011–14, Sr Advisor 2014–17, Hon. Advisor 2017–, Pres. and CEO Mizuho Bank Ltd 2011–13; Dir Internet Initiative Japan Inc. 2017–; Outside Dir Asahi Mutual Life Insurance Co. 2016–, Aeon Co. Ltd 2017–. *Address:* Mizuho Financial Group, Inc., Marunouchi 2-chome Building, 2-5-1, Marunouchi, Chiyoda-ku, Tokyo 100-8333, Japan (office). *Telephone:* (3) 5224-1111 (office). *Fax:* (3) 3215-4616 (office). *E-mail:* info@mizuho-fg.co.jp (office). *Website:* www.mizuho-fg.co.jp (office).

TSUKANOV, Nikolay; Russian politician; *Plenipotentiary of the President, Urals Federal District;* b. 22 March 1965, Lipovo; m. Svetlana Tsukanov; one s.; ed Moscow Higher School of Privatization and Entrepreneurship, Kazan Tupolev State Technical Univ.; served in army 1983–85; Mayor of Gusev 2005–09, Head of Gusev municipal area 2009–10; mem. United Russia (Yedinaya Rossiya), Head of Kaliningrad Br. 2010–; Gov. of Kaliningrad 2010–16; Plenipotentiary of the Pres., Severo-Zapadny Fed. Dist 2016–17, Urals Fed. Dist 2018–; Asst to Pres. 2018–. *Leisure interests:* hunting, fishing. *Address:* Office of the Plenipotentiary of the President, Severo-Zapadny Federal District, 125362 Moscow, ul. Svoboda 13/2, Russia.

TSUKIOKA, Takashi; Japanese business executive; *Representative Director and CEO, Idemitsu Kosan Company Limited;* joined Idemitsu Kosan Co. Ltd in 1975, Man. of Kobe Br. 2002–05, Man. of Chubu Br. 2005–07, Exec. Officer of Man. Supply and Demand Dept 2007–08, Man. Exec. Officer and Man. Supply and Demand Dept 2008–09, Rep. Dir 2009–, Man. Dir, later Exec. Vice-Pres., Pres. Idemitsu Kosan Co. Ltd –2013, CEO 2013–. *Address:* Idemitsu Kosan Co. Ltd, 1-1, Marunouchi 3-chome, Chiyoda-ku, Tokyo 100-8321, Japan (office). *Telephone:* (3) 3213-3115 (office). *Fax:* (3) 3213-9354 (office). *E-mail:* info@idemitsu.com (office). *Website:* www.idemitsu.com (office).

TSUKUDA, Kazuo, BS, MS; Japanese engineering industry executive; *Senior Corporate Advisor, Mitsubishi Heavy Industries;* b. 1 Sept. 1943; m. Yoshiko Kazuo; ed Univ. of Tokyo; joined Mitsubishi Heavy Industries 1968, engineer 1968–79, liaison to Westinghouse 1979–81, steam-turbine engineer 1982–95, Deputy Gen. Man., Takasago Machinery Works 1995–99, Gen. Man., Nagoya Machinery Works 1999–2000, Dir 1999–2013, Gen. Man., Industrial Machinery Div. 2000–02, Man. Dir and Gen. Man., Global Strategic Planning and Operations HQ 2002–03, Pres. and CEO Mitsubishi Heavy Industries 2003–08, Chair. 2008–13, Outside Dir Mitsubishi Corpn 2008–16, Sr Corp. Advisor 2013–, Dir Mitsubishi Research Inst., Inc. 2010–; Outside Dir Fanuc Corpn 2015–. *Address:* Mitsubishi Heavy Industries, 16-5, Konan 2-chome, Minato-ku, Tokyo 108-8215, Japan (office). *Telephone:* (3) 6716-3111 (office). *Fax:* (3) 6716-5800 (office). *E-mail:* info@mhi.co.jp (office). *Website:* www.mhi.co.jp (office).

TSUMBA, Leonard Ladislas, MA, PhD; Zimbabwean economist, academic and banker; *Chairman, Dairibord Holdings Zimbabwe Limited (DHZL);* b. 27 June 1943, Harare; s. of Ladislus Million Tsumba and Regina Tsumba; m. Nola Arne Yasinski 1969; two d.; ed Georgetown Univ., Howard Univ., Virginia Polytechnic Inst. and State Univ. (Virginia Tech), Blacksburg, Va, USA; Instructor in Econs, Hampton Inst., USA 1970–72; Asst Prof. of Econs, Trinity Coll., USA 1975–77, 2007; consultant, Money and Finance Div. UNCTAD 1979; with CitiBank NA, USA 1977–81; Exec. Asst to Gov. Reserve Bank of Zimbabwe 1981–82, Gen. Man. 1982–86, Deputy Gov. 1986–87, Group Chief Exec. 1987–83, Gov. 1993–2003; Chief Exec. and Man. Dir Finhold/Zimbabwe Banking Corpn 1987–93; Chair. Central African Bldg Soc. 2004–; Chair. Dairibord Holdings Zimbabwe Ltd (DHZL) 2012–; mem. Bd of Dirs Edgars Stores Ltd 2006–; Fellow, Inst. of Dirs UK. *Leisure interest:* golf. *Address:* Dairibord Holdings Limited, 9th Floor, ZB Life Towers, 77 Jason Moyo Avenue/Sam Nujoma Streets, PO Box 587, Harare (office); 23 Shawasha Hills, PO Box Ch 147, Chisipite, Harare, Zimbabwe (home). *Telephone:* (4) 790801-8 (office); (91) 282791 (home). *Fax:* (4) 582791 (home). *E-mail:* zwtsumba@zol.co.zw. *Website:* www.dairibord.com (office).

TSUNKAWA, Satoshi; Japanese business executive; *Representative Executive Officer, President and CEO, Toshiba Corporation;* b. 21 Sept. 1955; joined Toshiba Corpn 1979, Corp. Sr Vice-Pres., Toshiba Medical Systems Corpn 2009–10 Pres. and CEO 2010–14, Gen. Man., Healthcare Business Devt Div., Toshiba Corpn 2013–14, Exec. Officer, Corp. Sr Vice-Pres. 2014–15, Dir, Rep. Exec. Officer, Corp. Sr Exec. Vice-Pres. 2015–16, Dir, Rep. Exec. Officer, Pres. and CEO 2016–. *Address:* Toshiba Corporation, 1-1, Shibaura 1-chome, Minato-ku, Tokyo 105-8001, Japan (office). *Telephone:* (3) 3457-4511 (office). *Fax:* (3) 3455-1631 (office). *E-mail:* info@toshiba.co.jp (office). *Website:* www.toshiba.co.jp (office).

TSURUOKA, Koji, LLM; Japanese diplomatist; *Ambassador to UK;* m.; ed Univ. of Tokyo, Harvard Law School; Prof. of Int. Relations, Grad. Inst. of Policy Studies 2002; Deputy Dir-Gen., Ministry of Foreign Affairs 2003–06 (later, Sr Coordinator); Amb. to UK 2016; fmr Deputy Vice-Minister for Foreign Policy, Dir-Gen. Legal Affairs Bureau, Dir-Gen. for Global Issues, also, served at Embassies of Japan, Moscow, Washington, Jakarta. *Address:* Embassy of Japan, 101–104 Piccadilly, London W1J 7JT, UK (office). *Telephone:* (20) 7465-6500 (office). *Fax:* (20) 7491-9348 (office). *E-mail:* info@ld.mofa.go.jp (office). *Website:* www.uk.emb-japan.go.jp (office).

TSUSHKO, Vasyl Petrovych; Ukrainian economist and politician; b. 1 Feb. 1963, Nadrichne, Tarutynsky Dist, Odesa Oblast; m.; one s. one d.; ed Izmayil Tech. School of Agric., Odesa Agric. Inst. and Nat. Univ. of Internal Affairs; served in Soviet Army 1983–85; Deputy Dir and Dir of various state farms 1988–97; Gov. Odesa Regional State Admin 2005–06; Minister of Internal Affairs 2006–07, of the Economy March–Dec. 2010; mem. Parl. and Leader Parl. faction Socialist Party of Ukraine (Sotsialistychna Partiya Ukrainy—SPU) –2006, Chair. SPU 2010–11; Head, Antimonopoly Cttee of Ukraine 2010–14. *Address:* c/o Socialist Party of Ukraine (Sotsialistychna Partiya Ukrainy), 02100 Kyiv, vul. Bazhova 12, Ukraine.

TSUTSUI, Yoshinobu, BA; Japanese business executive; *President and Representative Director, Nippon Life Insurance Company;* b. 30 Jan. 1954, Hyogo Pref.; ed Kyoto Univ.; joined Nippon Life Insurance Co. 1977, Gen. Man. Nagaoka Br. 1999–2001, Gen. Man. Public Affairs Dept 2001–03, Gen. Man. Corp. Planning Dept 2003–04, Dir and Gen. Man. 2004–07, Dir, Exec. Officer and Gen. Man. Corp. Planning Dept and Risk Man. Dept Jan.–March 2007, Dir, Man. Exec. Officer and Gen. Man. Legal Office, Head of Corp. Admin Sector (Corp. Planning, Public & Investors Relations, Planning and Research, Actuarial, and Legal related) 2007–09, Dir and Sr Man. Exec. Officer 2009–10, Dir and Sr Man. Exec., Head of Investment Man. Sector (Credit, and Securities Operation related) and Corp. Admin Sector 2010–11, Pres. and Rep. Dir Nippon Life Insurance Co. 2011–; Ind. Dir, Imperial Hotel Ltd 2011–. *Address:* Nippon Life Insurance Co., 3-5-12 Imabashi, Chuo-ku, Osaka 541-8501, Japan (office). *Telephone:* (6) 6209-5525 (office). *Fax:* (3) 5510-7340 (office). *E-mail:* info@nissay.co.jp (office). *Website:* www .nissay.co.jp (office).

TSUYA, Masaaki, BA (Econ), MBA; Japanese business executive; *Chairman, CEO and Representative Director, Bridgestone Corporation;* ed Hitotsubashi Univ., Univ. of Chicago, USA; Dir Div. of Int. Relations and Licenses, Bridgestone Corpn Co. Ltd 2004, served as Dir of Internal Auditing Office, Office of Group CEO and Vice-Pres. Bridgestone Corpn, served as Chief Compliance Officer, Chief Human Rights Officer, Chief Risk-Management Officer, Vice-Pres. and Sr Officer, Bridgestone Corpn, Chair. Bridgestone Americas, Inc. Jan.–March 2011, CEO Bridgestone Corpn 2012–, Chair. 2013–; Dir, Inoue Rubber Vietnam Co. Ltd; Ind. Dir, Inoue Rubber Thailand Public Co. Ltd 2001–09. *Address:* Bridgestone Corporation, 10-1, Kyobashi 1-chome, Chuo-ku, Tokyo 104-8340, Japan (office). *Telephone:* (3) 3567-0111 (office). *Fax:* (3) 3535-2553 (office). *E-mail:* info@ bridgestone.co.jp (office). *Website:* www.bridgestone.co.jp (office).

TSVETANOV, Tsvetan Genchev; Bulgarian politician; *Chairman, Citizens for European Development Parliamentary Group;* b. 8 April 1965, Sofia; m. Desislava Tsvetanova; three d.; ed Nat. Sports Acad., Sofia, Inst. of Postgraduate Studies with Univ. of Nat. and World Economy, Sofia; Specialist, Inspector, Sr Inspector, Chief Inspector, Team Leader, Ministry of the Interior (MoI) Cen. Information, Analysis and Org. Service and at MoI Information Tech. and Automation of Man. Service 1987–2001; Sr Expert, sector Nat. Services, Specialized and Gen. Admin, Schools, Research Insts, R&D Insts and Specialized Anti-Terrorism Unit, Human

Resource Man. Div., MoI, 7th Sr Rank 1997–2001; Head of Dept/Operational Asst to MoI Sec.-Gen./MoI Cen. Admin 2001–05; Deputy Mayor for Public Order and Security, Sofia Municipality Nov. 2005; mem. Nat. Ass. (Citizens for European Devt of Bulgaria—GERB) for Veliko Turnovo Constituency 2009–, Chair. GERB Parliamentary Group 2014–; Deputy Prime Minister and Minister of the Interior 2009–13; govt cand. for presidential election 2011; Silver Cross of the Order of Merit of the Spanish Civil Guard 2014; numerous awards from man. of Ministry of the Interior 1987–2005, White Cross of Law Enforcement Merit Medal, Spanish Nat. Police, Ministry of the Interior of Spain 2005, Certificate for outstanding int. operational police cooperation, Dir of Europol 2009, Insignia of Honour for outstanding performance of official duties, Minister of the Interior of Lithuania 2009. *Address:* Citizens for European Development of Bulgaria (GERB), NPC Office Building, floor 17, Pl. 1, 1000 Sofia, Bulgaria (office). *Telephone:* (2) 490-13-13 (office). *Fax:* (2) 490-09-51 (office). *E-mail:* pr@gerb.bg (office). *Website:* www.gerb.bg (office).

TSZYU, Kostya; Australian (b. Russian) professional boxer (retd); b. 19 Sept. 1969, Serov, Russia; youngest person to win Russian National Championships (aged 16); six times Russian champion, three times European champion; won gold medal World Amateur Championships, Sydney 1991; emigrated to Australia 1991; won International Boxing Federation (IBF) World Super-Lightweight Championship Jan. 1995, lost title to Vince Phillips May 1997; won World Boxing Asscn (WBA) and World Boxing Council (WBC) World Super-Lightweight Championships Feb. 2001 v. Sharmba Mitchell; won Undisputed World Super–Lightweight Championship Nov. 2001 v. Zab Judah, became first in 40 years to unify the division, one of only three undisputed champions, two defences; stripped of WBA title for failing to make mandatory defence June 2004; beat Sharmba Mitchell again to retain WBC and IBF titles; won 30 fights, including 24 knock-outs, one defeat; rated 4th best pound-for-pound boxer by USA Today Oct. 2003; trainer Johnny Lewis; inducted into Int. Boxing Hall of Fame 2011.

TU, Youyou, BSc, PhD; Chinese medical scientist, pharmaceutical chemist and academic; *Chief Scientist, China Academy of Chinese Medical Sciences;* b. 30 Dec. 1930, Ningbo, Zhejiang Prov.; m.; ed Peking Univ. School of Medicine (Medical School became ind. Beijing Medical Coll., renamed Beijing Medical Univ. 1985, latter merged with Peking Univ. to become Peking Univ. Health Science Centre); studied at Dept of Pharmaceutical Sciences, graduated 1955; trained for two and a half years in traditional Chinese medicine; worked at Acad. of Chinese Medicine (now China Acad. of Chinese Medical Sciences), Beijing following graduation, promoted to tenured researcher (as grad. tutor) 1980, promoted to academic adviser for doctorate cands 2001, currently Chief Scientist; Nat. Science Congress Prize 1978, Albert Einstein World Science Prize, World Culture Council 1987, (one of the) Ten Science and Technology Achievements in China, State Science Comm. 1992, (one of the) Ten Great Public Health Achievements in New China 1997, GlaxoSmithKline Outstanding Achievement Award in Life Science 2011, Lasker~DeBakey Clinical Medical Research Award 2011, Outstanding Contrib. Award, China Acad. of Chinese Medical Research 2011, (one of the Ten) Nat. Outstanding Females 2012, Warren Alpert Foundation Prize 2015, Nobel Prize in Physiology or Medicine (co-recipient with William C. Campbell and Satoshi Ōmura) 2015. *Achievements include:* discovered artemisinin (also known as Qinghaosu) and dihydroartemisinin, used for treating malaria. *Publications:* numerous papers in professional journals. *Address:* China Academy of Chinese Medical Sciences, Beijing 100700, People's Republic of China (office). *Telephone:* (10) 6401-4356 (office). *E-mail:* info@catcm.ac.cn (office). *Website:* www.catcm.ac.cn (office).

TUBAYYEB, Samir A. al-, BEng, PhD, MBA; Saudi Arabian petroleum industry executive; *Vice-President of Engineering Services, Saudi Aramco;* ed King Fahad Univ. of Petroleum and Minerals, Univ. of Calif., Berkeley, Harvard Business School; started working with Saudi Aramco 1981, in various positions over 25 years, including Project Man., Jt Venture and Planning; Rep. Dir and CEO S-Oil Corpn 2005–08; Exec. Dir Employee Relations and Training, Saudi Aramco 2008–12, Vice-Pres. Eng Services 2012–, Chair. Saudi Aramco Total Oil Refining Project; mem. Bd of Dirs Gen. Org. for Social Insurance, Technical and Vocational Training Corpn; Maeil Business Economy CEO of the Year 2007. *Address:* Saudi Aramco, PO Box 5000, Dhahran 31311, Saudi Arabia (office). *Telephone:* (13) 872-0115 (office). *Fax:* (13) 873-8190 (office). *Website:* www.saudiaramco.com (office).

TUBMAN, Winston; Liberian lawyer, diplomatist and politician; ed London School of Econs and Univ. of Cambridge, UK, Harvard Law School, USA; taught law at Univ. of Liberia and at univs in USA 1968–72; est. Tubman Law Firm, Monrovia 1968, Man. and Sr Partner until late 1980s; Prin. Legal Officer, Office of Legal Affairs 1973–75, 1991–96, UNEP 1975–77; served in Ministry of Foreign Affairs and Ministry of Planning and Economic Affairs 1977–79; Amb. to UN, New York (also accred to Cuba and Mexico) 1979–81; Justice Minister 1982–83; Chair. Legal and Constitutional Cttee of the group of Liberian political leaders meeting in Banjul, Gambia that established an interim govt in Liberia (later Foreign Minister and Minister of State) 1990; Exec. Sec. Comm. of Inquiry into ambushing and killing of Pakistani peace-keepers in Mogadishu 1993; assigned to UN Peace Office in Zagreb, Croatia and UN Peace-keeping Mission in Eastern Slavonia (UNTAES) –1998; Sr Adviser to Commdr UN Iraq–Kuwait Observation Mission (UNIKOM) 1998–; Rep. of UN Sec.-Gen. and Head of UN Political Office for Somalia (UNPOS) 2002–05; Leader and unsuccessful presidential cand. (Nat. Democratic Party of Liberia) 2005; unsuccessful presidential cand. (Congress for Democratic Change) 2011; mem. Bar of Supreme Court of Liberia. *Address:* Congress for Democratic Change, Bernard's Compound, Congo Town, Monrovia, Liberia (office). *Telephone:* 886524899 (mobile) (office). *E-mail:* info@cdcliberia.org (office). *Website:* www.cdcliberia.org (office).

TUCCI, Stanley, BFA; American actor; b. 11 Nov. 1960, Peekskill, New York; s. of Stanley Tucci, Sr and Joan Tucci (née Tropiano); m. Kate Tucci 1995 (died 2009); three c.; ed Purchase Coll., State Univ. of New York; Gotham Award 2009. *Films include:* Prizzi's Honor 1985, Monkey Shines 1988, Slaves of New York 1989, Billy Bathgate 1991, Beethoven 1992, The Public Eye 1992, It Could Happen to You 1994, Mrs Parker and the Vicious Circle 1994, Kiss of Death 1995, Big Night (also writer, dir and co-producer) (Boston Soc. of Film Critics Awards for Best New Dir and Best Screenplay, Independent Spirit Award for Best First Screenplay, New York Film Critics Circle Awards for Best New Dir, Sundance Film Festival Waldo Salt Screenwriting Award) 1996, A Life Less Ordinary 1997, The Impostors (also writer, dir and producer) 1998, In Too Deep 1999, America's Sweethearts 2001, Road to Perdition 2002, The Life and Death of Peter Sellers 2004, The Terminal 2004, The Devil Wears Prada 2006, The Hoax 2007, Julie & Julia 2009, The Lovely Bones 2009, Easy A 2010, Burlesque 2010, Margin Call 2011, Captain America: The First Avenger 2011, The Hunger Games 2012, Jack the Giant Slayer 2013, The Wind Rises 2014, A Little Chaos 2014, The Hunger Games: Mockingjay – Part 1 2014, Spotlight 2015, The Hunger Games: Mockingjay – Part 2 2015, Wild Card 2015. *Television:* Miami Vice 1986–88, Lifestories 1990, Conspiracy (Golden Globe Award) 2001, Frasier 2004, ER 2007–08, BoJack Horseman (series) 2014–15, Fortitude (series) 2015.

TUCKER, Mark, ACA; British business executive; *Group Chairman, HSBC;* b. 29 Dec. 1957; one s. one d.; fmr tax consultant, Price Waterhouse UK; joined Prudential 1986, sr positions in UK and USA, Chief Exec. Prudential Corpn Asia 1993–2003, Exec. Dir Prudential 1999–2003, Exec. Dir and Group Chief Exec. Prudential plc 2005–09; Group Finance Dir HBOS plc and Dir Halifax plc 2004–05; Group Exec. Chair. and Group CEO AIA Group Ltd Oct.–Dec. 2010, Group Chief Exec. and Pres. 2010–17, also Chair. and CEO AIA Co. and AIA International; Group Chair. HSBC 2017–; mem. Bd of Dirs, The Goldman Sachs Group, Inc. 2012–. *Address:* HSBC Holdings, 8 Canada Square, London, E14 5HQ, England (office). *Telephone:* (20) 7991–8888 (office). *Fax:* (20) 7992–4880 (office). *E-mail:* pressoffice@hsbc.com (office). *Website:* www.hsbc.com (office).

TUCKER, Sir Paul, Kt; British fmr central banker; ed Trinity Coll., Cambridge; several pvt. banking positions 1980–89, including working as banking supervisor, corp. financier at merchant bank and on projects to reform Hong Kong securities markets and regulatory system following the 1987 crash; Prin. Pvt. Sec. to Bank of England Gov. Leigh-Pemberton 1989–93, Head, Gilt-Edged and Money Markets Div. 1994–97, Head, Monetary Assessment and Strategy Div. 1997–98, Deputy Dir Financial Stability 1999–2002, Exec. Dir Markets and mem. Monetary Policy Cttee 2002–09, Deputy Gov. 2009–13, mem. Secr. of Monetary Policy Cttee 1997–2002; currently Fellow, Mossavar-Rahmani Center for Business and Govt, Harvard Kennedy School, and Sr Fellow, Center for European Studies, Harvard Univ. *Publication:* Unelected Power: The Quest for Legitimacy in Central Banking and the Regulatory State 2018. *E-mail:* paul_tucker@hks.harvard.edu (office). *Website:* paultucker.me.

TUDOSE, Mihai; Romanian lawyer and politician; b. 6 March 1968, Brăila; ed Faculty of Legal and Admin. Sciences, Bucharest, Higher Coll. of Nat. Security, Romanian Intelligence Service, Nat. Defence Coll. and Marshall European Centre for Security Studies, Garmisch, Germany, Nat. School of Political Science and Public Admin, Georgetown Univ., USA in collaboration with Nat. Defense Coll., Faculty of Econs, Univ. Dunărea de jos of Galaţi, Romanian Diplomatic Inst., under Ministry of Foreign Affairs, Nat. Acad. of Information; began career as Head of Senatorial Office 1992–99; Co. Councillor while working as lawyer 1999–2000; mem. Partidul Social Democrat (PSD—Social Democratic Party); Pres. PSD, Brăila 2004–08; mem. Chamber of Deputies (Camera Deputaţilor) for Constituency No. 9 Braila 2000–, Pres. Comm. for Econ. Policy, Reform and Privatization 2004; Minister of the Economy, Trade and Tourism 2014–15; Prime Minister June 2017–Jan. 2018; mem. Romanian Del. to Parl. Ass. of Council of Europe.

TUESTA CÁRDENAS, David, BA, MA, PhD; Peruvian economist and politician; b. 29 Nov. 1967; ed Pontifical Catholic Univ. of Peru, Univ. of Minnesota; Chief Economist, Tax Agency, Ministry of Treasury 1992–2000; taught econs at San Ignacio de Loyola Univ., Pontifical Catholic Univ. of Peru and Univ. of Lima 1997–2009; Chief Economist (Peru), BBVA 2000, later Chief Economist (Global Trends), Chief Economist (Pensions), BBVA Research 2007, Chief Economist (Financial Inclusion) 2013; mem. Bd of Dirs, OSINERGMIN (Peruvian Regulator of Energy and Mining) 2007–09; Corp. Dir of Strategic Affairs, Devt Bank of Latin America (CAF) 2017–18; Commr, Social Protection Comm. 2017; Minister of Economy and Finance April–June 2018 (resgnd). *Address:* c/o Ministry of Economy and Finance, Jirón Junín 319, 4°, Circado de Lima, Lima 1, Peru (office).

TUGENDHAT, Baron (Life Peer), cr. 1993, of Widdington in the County of Essex; **Christopher Samuel Tugendhat,** MA; British business executive, politician and fmr international organization official; b. 23 Feb. 1937, London; s. of Dr Georg Tugendhat; m. Julia Lissant Dobson 1967; two s.; ed Ampleforth Coll., Gonville and Caius Coll., Cambridge; Pres. Cambridge Union; Mil. Service, commissioned in The Essex Regt 1955–57; leader and feature writer, The Financial Times 1960–70; Consultant to Wood Mackenzie & Co. Ltd, stockbrokers 1968–77; Conservative MP for Cities of London and Westminster 1970–74, for City of London and Westminster South 1974–76; Dir Sunningdale Oils 1971–77, Phillips Petroleum Int. (UK) Ltd 1972–77, Nat. Westminster Bank PLC 1985–91 (Deputy Chair. 1990–91), BOC Group PLC 1985–96, Commercial Union PLC 1988–91, LWT (Holdings) PLC 1991–94; Dir (non-exec.), Eurotunnel PLC 1991–2003, Rio Tinto PLC 1997–2004; Chair. Civil Aviation Authority 1986–91, Abbey Nat. PLC 1991–2002, Blue Circle Industries PLC 1996–2001; Chair. (non-exec.) Lehman Brothers Europe 2002–07; Chair. Imperial Coll. Healthcare NHS Trust 2007–12; mem. Comm. of EEC with responsibility for Budget and Financial Control, Financial Institutions, Personnel and Admin. 1977–81, Vice-Pres. with responsibility for Budget and Financial Control, Financial Institutions and Taxation 1981–85; Chancellor Univ. of Bath 1998–; Chair. Royal Inst. of Int. Affairs (now Chatham House) 1986–95; Gov. and mem. Council of Man., Ditchley Foundation; Chair. Gonville & Caius Devt Campaign Cttee, Cambridge Univ.; Patron and Vice-Pres. British Lung Foundation; Freeman of the City of London; Hon. Fellow, Gonville and Caius Coll., Cambridge; Hon. LLD (Bath) 1998; Hon. DLitt (UMIST) 2002; McKinsey Foundation Book Award 1971. *Publications:* Oil: the Biggest Business 1968, The Multinationals 1971, Making Sense of Europe 1986, Options for British Foreign Policy in the 1990s (with William Wallace) 1988; numerous articles. *Leisure interests:* reading, family, conversation. *Address:* House of Lords, Westminster, London, SW1A 0PW (office); 35 Westbourne Park Road, London, W2 5QD, England (home). *Telephone:* (20) 7219-5353 (Westminster) (office). *E-mail:* tugendhatc@parliament.uk (office).

TUGWELL, Very Rev. Simon Charles ffoster, OP, STM, DD, STD; British ecclesiastic and historian; *Emeritus Fellow, Istituto Storico Domenicano;* b. 4 May

1943, Brighton, Sussex; s. of Maj. Herbert Tugwell and Mary Brigit Tugwell (née Hutchinson); ed Lancing Coll. and Corpus Christi Coll., Oxford; received into Roman Catholic Church 1964; joined Dominican Order 1965; ordained priest 1971; Lecturer and Tutor, Blackfriars, Oxford 1972–92, Regent of Studies 1976–90; mem. Faculty of Theology, Univ. of Oxford 1982–92; Fellow, Istituto Storico Domenicano 1987 (Pres. 1992–97), currently Emer. Fellow; Ed., Monumenta Ordinis Praedicatorum Historica 1992–2016; Visiting Lecturer, Pontifical Univ. of St Thomas, Rome 1977–93; Flannery Prof. of Theology, Gonzaga Univ., Spokane, Wash., USA 1982–83; Read-Tuckwell Lecturer on Human Immortality, Univ. of Bristol 1988; Consultor to Congregation for Causes of Saints 1994–97; has lectured in many countries around the world. *Publications include:* The Way of the Preacher 1979, Early Dominicans 1982, Ways of Imperfection 1984, Albert and Thomas 1988, The Apostolic Fathers 1989, Letters of Bede Jarrett (ed.) 1989, Human Immortality and the Redemption of Death 1990, Saint Dominic 1995, Miracula S. Dominici… Petri Calo legendae S. Dominici (ed.) 1997, Bernardi Guidonis: Scripta de Sancto Dominico (ed.) 1998, Humberti de Romanis, Legendae Sancti Dominici (ed) 2008, Pelagius Parvus and his 'Summa' 2012, Petri Ferrandi Legenda Sancti Dominici (ed) 2015; articles on aspects of theology and Dominican history, especially sources for the life of St Dominic. *Leisure interests:* music, science fiction. *Address:* c/o The Very Revd Fr Provincial OP, St Dominic's Priory, Southampton Road, London NW5 4LB, England (office).

TUHEITIA, Te Arikinui; New Zealand Maori king; b. 21 April 1955; s. of Whatumoana Paki and Te Arikinui Dame Te Atairangikaahu (previous monarch); m. Atawhai; three c.; ed Rakaumanga School, Huntly, St Stephen's Coll., Bombay (now Mumbai), India; fmr univ. man. and Tainui cultural adviser to Te Wananga o Aotearoa, Huntly; chosen as king at secret meeting and crowned following his mother's funeral 21 Aug. 2006; Officer, Venerable Order of St John 2007, Kt Commdr, Order of St Lazarus 2010. *Address:* Tūrongo House, Tūrangawaewae marae, Ngaruawahia, Waikato, New Zealand. *Website:* www.kiingitanga.com.

TUI'ONETOA, Pohiva, M.Bus; Tongan accountant and politician; *Minister of Finance and National Planning;* b. 30 June 1961; m.; ed Univ. of the S Pacific, Monash Univ., Inst. of Chartered Accountants of New Zealand; Auditor, Nat. Audit Office 1979, becoming Auditor Gen. 1983–2014; Official Liquidator, Dept of Justice, Commercial Div., Hamilton, New Zealand 1981; Private Sec. to HM King Tupou V and Clerk to Privy Council 1987–88; mem. Legis. Ass. (parl.) for Tongatapu No. 10 constituency 2014–; Minister of Police, Fire & Emergency and Prisons 2014–17, Minister of Finance and Nat. Planning, of Commerce, Consumer Affairs, Trade, Innovation and Labour, and of Revenue and Customs 2017–; mem. Bd of Govs., Asian Devt Bank 2017–. *Address:* Ministry of Finance and National Planning, St George Government Building, Nuku'alofa, Tonga (office). *Telephone:* 23066 (office). *Fax:* 26011 (office). *E-mail:* admin@finance.gov.to (office). *Website:* www.finance.gov.to (office).

TUIOTI, Sili Epa, BA; Samoan economist and politician; *Minister of Finance;* b. 1953, Sapulu Salelologa; m. Pearl Tuioti; six c.; ed Univ. of the South Pacific, Fiji; several years with Asian Devt Bank, Manila, including Deputy Dir, Dept of Econ. Planning and Devt 1978–84, Deputy Financial Sec., Treasury Dept 1984–88, Asst to Exec. Dir 1988–91; Financial Sec., Treasury Dept, Govt of Samoa 1991–99; apptd Co-Man. Dir and Prin. Consultant, KVAConsult Ltd 1999, econ. consultant to numerous int. orgs including UNDP 1999, S Pacific Regional Environment Programme 2000, AusAID 2000, World Bank/Govt of Samoa 2001, Japan Int. Cooperation Agency 2004; mem., Bd of Dirs Nat. Bank of Samoa 2004–07, Chair. 2007; mem. Legis. Ass. (Parl.) for Faasaleleaga No. 1 2016–; Minister of Finance 2016–; Dir, Samoa Breweries Ltd 2005–; mem. Exec. Council, Samoa Chamber of Commerce and Industry 2004–; Deacon, Apia Protestant Church 2004–12; Exec. Bd mem. and fmr Deputy Chair., Pacific Islands Private Sector Org. 2006–; Hon. Adviser, Samoa Women in Business Inc. 2003–08; mem. Human Rights Protection Party. *Address:* Ministry of Finance, Central Bank Building, Level 2–7, Private Bag, Apia, Samoa (office). *Telephone:* 34333 (office). *Fax:* 21312 (office). *E-mail:* helpdesk@mof.gov.ws (office). *Website:* www.mof.gov.ws (office).

TUITT, Roland S., BSc, MBA, CPA; St Maarten accountant and politician; b. Aruba; m. Italia Tuitt-Soon; ed Andrews Univ., USA; began career as Asst Accountant, Advent Hosp., Curaçao; worked as accountant for numerous orgs including Eilands Accountant Dienst, Aruba, Price Waterhouse, Curaçao, GEBE NV, St Maarten, Coopers & Lybrand, Amsterdam and St Maarten; Owner Tuitt CPA (financial services consultancy) 2010–; Chair. Audit Chamber of St Maarten 2010–12; fmr Commr of Finance, Island Territory of St Maarten (whilst still part of Netherlands Antilles); fmr Senator, Parl. of Netherlands Antilles; Minister of Finance 2012–13.

TU'IVAKANO, Lord, BA; Tongan politician; b. (Siale 'Ataongo Kaho), 15 Jan. 1952, Niutoua, Hahake; s. of Siaosi Kiu Ngalumoetutulu Kaho (16th Tu'ivakano) and Fatafehi-'o-Lapaha Liku; m. Joyce Robyn Kaho (née Sanft); six c.; ed Wesley Coll., Ardmore Teacher's Coll., NZ, Flinders Univ., Australia; Asst Teacher, Tonga High School 1975–80; Head, Physical Educ. Div., Ministry of Educ. 1974, Sr Educ. Officer for Youth, Sport and Culture 1992–96; mem. Legis. Ass. as Rep. of Nobles of Tonga 1996–, Speaker 2002–04, 2014–17; Minister of Works 2005, of Training, Employment, Youth and Sport 2006–10, Prime Minister Dec. 2010–14 (first prime minister to be elected by parl. rather than being installed by king), also Minister of Foreign Affairs, Defence, Information and Communication; succeeded to hereditary title of Tu'ivakano after death of father Jan. 1986. *Address:* Legislative Assembly of Tonga, POB 901, Nuku'alofa, Tonga (office). *Telephone:* 27911 (office). *Website:* www.parliament.gov.to (office).

TUJU, Hon. Raphael, MA; Kenyan politician, film producer, film director, broadcaster and business executive; *Secretary-General, Jubilee Party;* b. 30 March 1959, Ndori, Bondo district; s. of Henry Odiyo Tuju; m.; three c.; ed Starehe Boys' Centre and School, Univ. of Leicester; producer-dir of numerous films, and radio and TV programmes principally concerned with promotion of health awareness 1992–97; chief public relations consultant Population Services Int. Social Marketing of Condoms Project 1994–95; writer of newspaper column and leader of project to promote AIDS awareness 1995–96; chief communications consultant, STI electronic media intervention in Kenya, The World Bank 1998; communications consultant UNICEF and Ministry of Health 1998; lead public relations consultant, Kenya Re-Insurance Corporation 1998–2000 (resgnd); lead consultant and communications advisor, Int. AIDS Vaccine Initiative (IAVI) 1999–2002; lead consultant, IEC component of DFID funded HIV/AIDS Prevention and Care Project (HAPAC) in Nyanza province 1999–2003; lead consultant, Poverty Reduction Strategy Paper (PRSP) 2000–01; MP for Rarieda; Minister for Tourism and Information 2003–04; Minister for Information and Communications 2004–05; Minister of Foreign Affairs 2005–08; Advisor, Office of the Pres. 2008–11; Sec.-Gen. Jubilee Party 2017–; team leader of first African winner of Int. Emmy Awards; Dir Ace Communications Md, USA and Nairobi, Kenya; Chair. Kenya AIDS NGOs Consortium (KANCO); Chair. Devt Communications Inst.; Dir BITC; mem. Public Relations Soc. of Kenya (PRSK), Int. Mass Communication Soc. (IMCS), African Council for Communication Educ. (ACCE); Elder of the Golden Heart. *Publications:* AIDS: Understanding the Challenge. *Address:* Jubilee House, Pangani Interchange, Exit 3, Thika Road, POB 38601-00623, Nairobi, Kenya (office). *Telephone:* 771399841 (mobile) (office). *Website:* www.jubileepamoja.co.ke (office).

TUKI, Nabam; Indian politician; b. 7 July 1964, Sagalee; s. of Nabam Takeh; m.; two s. five d.; Pres., Nat. Students' Union of India (NSUI), Arunachal Pradesh 1983–86, Chair. North East NSUI Coordination Cttee 1984–86, Gen. Sec. All India NSUI 1986–88; Pres. Youth Congress, Arunachal Pradesh 1988–95; Vice-Chair. North Eastern Youth Congress Coordination Cttee 1988–93, Working Pres. 1993–95; apptd Vice-Chair. A P Cooperative Apex Bank Ltd 1992; elected to State Legis. Ass. 1995; apptd Deputy Minister of Agriculture 1995, of Transport and Civil Aviation 1998, of Environment and Forest 1999, of Public Works Dept and Urban Devt; Gen. Sec. Arunachal Pradesh Congress Cttee (APCC) 1995–96, Vice-Pres. 1999–2004, Working Pres. 2004–08, Pres. 2008–12; Chief Minister of Arunachal Pradesh 2011–16; Sitting Pres. Arunachal Cricket Asscn 2008–. *Leisure interest:* sports.

TUKUITONGA, Colin, MD; Niuean physician and international organisation official; *Director-General, Pacific Community;* ed Niue High School, Univ. of the South Pacific, Fiji, Fiji School of Medicine; Dir of Public Health, Ministry of Health, New Zealand 2001–03; apptd Dir Global Research on Obesity, WHO 2003, Head of Surveillance and Prevention of Chronic Diseases, WHO, Geneva 2003–06; Assoc. Prof. of Public Health and and Head of Pacific and International Health, Univ. of Auckland 2006–07; CEO Ministry of Pacific Island Affairs, New Zealand 2007–12; Dir of Public Health Div., Pacific Community (SPC) 2012–14, Dir-Gen. Pacific Community 2014–; Harkness Fellowship in Health Care Policy and Practice, Univ. of California 2000–01; Fellow, Royal NZ Coll. of General Practitioners, Australasian Faculty of Public Health Medicine. *Address:* Secretariat of the Pacific Community Headquarters, BP D5, 98848 Nouméa Cédex, New Caledonia (office). *Telephone:* 262000 (office). *Fax:* 263818 (office). *E-mail:* colint@spc.int (office); c.tukuitonga@gmail.com (home). *Website:* www.spc.int (office).

TULAFONO, Togiola Talalelei A.; American Samoa lawyer and government official; b. 28 Feb. 1947, Aunu'u Island; m. Mary Ann Taufa'asau Mauga; six c.; ed Samoana High School, Chadron State Coll., Neb., Washburn Univ. School of Law, Topeka, Kan., National Judicial Coll., Reno, Nev., USA; lawyer in pvt. practice for 20 years; fmr policeman; fmr Admin. Asst to Sec. of Samoan Affairs; fmr Samoan Asst to Attorney Gen.; fmr Dist Court Judge; fmr Senator for Saole Co. for four years, for Sua Co. for eight years; mem. Democratic Party; Lt Gov. of American Samoa 1997–2003, Gov. 2003–13; fmr Chair. Bd of Dirs American Samoa Power Authority; fmr first Chair. Bd of High Educ.; Chair. South Pacific Mini-Games Cttee 1997, American Samoa Centennial Cttee 2000; Deacon of Congregational Christian Church of American Samoa (CCCAS), Sailele for more than 25 years, Vice-Chair. CCCAS during its Ass. 2003, 2006–08, Chair. CCCAS 2004–06, 2008–10; Pres. American Samoa Rugby Union; Dist Pres. for American Samoa Dist, Boy Scouts of America; mem. Lions Club of Pago Pago. *Address:* American Samoa Rugby Union, PO Box 5830, Pago Pago AS 96799, American Samoa (office). *Telephone:* 684.699.8855 (office). *Fax:* 684.699.8866 (office). *Website:* www.foxsportspulse.com (office).

TULEYEV, Aman-Geldy Moldagazyevich, (Aman Gumirovich), DPolSc; Kazakhstani politician; *Chairman, Legislative Assembly of Kemerovo Region;* b. 13 May 1944, Krasnovodsk, Turkmenistan; s. of Moldagazy Kaldybayevich Tuleyev and Munira Fayzovna Vlasova (née Nasyrova); m. Elvira Fedorovna; two s. (one deceased); ed Tikhoretsk Railway Tech. School, Novosibirsk Inst. of Railway Eng, Acad. of Social Sciences at Cen. Cttee CPSU; worked on Krasnodar railway station 1961, Head Mundybash railway station 1969, Mezhdurechensk railway station 1973, Head Novokuznetsk Dept Kemerovo Railway 1978–85; Head Div. of Transport and Communications Regional Cttee CPSU 1985–88; Head Kemerovo Railway 1988; Peoples' Deputy of Russian Fed. for Kemerovo region 1990–93; Chair. Kemerovo Regional Soviet 1991; presidential cand. 1991, 1996, 2000; mem. CP of Russian Fed. 1993–2003, Yedinaya Rossiya party 2003– (mem. Supreme Council); Deputy, Fed. Council of Russia 1993–95, 1997–2001; Chair. Legis. Ass. Kemerovo Region 1994–96, 2018–; Minister of Co-operation with CIS 1996–97; Gov. Kemerovo Region 1997–2015, Acting Gov. 2015–18; Order of Honour 1999, Order of Mongolia 'Polar Star' 2000, Order of Russian Orthodox Church, Rev. Sergey Radonezhsky II degree 2001, Order for Outstanding Country Service (Fourth Degree) 2003, (Third Degree) 2008, (Second Degree) 2012, Dostyk Order (Kazakhstan) 2003, Order of Jaroslav the Wise (Ukraine) 2004; Peter the Great Int. Award 2002, Int. Millennium Award for Service to Humanity 2003, Andrey Pervozvanny Int. Award for Faith and Loyalty 2003 and more then 20 others. *Publications:* more than 20 books and several hundred publs in Russian and foreign mass media. *Leisure:* mushroom gathering, langlaufing, snow-tractor driving, taking Russian baths.

TULIN, Dmitri Vladislavovich, MBA, PhD; Russian economist, banker and academic; b. 26 March 1956, Moscow; s. of Vladislav Tulin and Emma S. Tulin; m. Vera Nerod 1977; two s.; ed Moscow Financial Inst. and USSR Inst. of Econs and Finance; economist, Int. Monetary and Econ. Dept USSR State Bank (Gosbank) 1978, Sr Economist 1980, Chief Economist 1985, Man. 1989, Man. Dir, mem. Bd Securities Dept 1990; Deputy Chair. Cen. Bank of Russian Fed. 1991–94, now mem. consultancy group to Chair.; Exec. Dir for Russian Fed. IMF 1994–96; Chair. Bd Vneshtorgbank (Bank for Foreign Trade) 1996–98; Sr Adviser to EBRD 1999–2004; Deputy Chair. Cen. Bank of Russian Fed. 2004–06; Partner, Deloitte CIS 2006–12; currently Prof., Russian Acad. of Entrepreneurship; mem. Supervisory Bd Sberbank of Russia; mem. Bd of Dirs Jsc Kazkommertsbank 2012–,

National Clearing Centre Cjsc 2013–; mem. Financiers Guild. *Publications:* numerous articles in professional journals on monetary econs and banking in Russia. *Leisure interests:* gardening, chess. *Address:* Russian Academy of Entrepreneurship, Moscow, 105005, Radio st., 14, Russia (office). *E-mail:* office@rusacad.ru (office). *Website:* www.rusacad.ru (office).

TULLY, James Hamilton, BA, PhD, FRSC; Canadian political scientist and academic; *Emeritus Distinguished Professor, University of Victoria;* b. 17 April 1946, Nanaimo, BC; s. of John Patrick Tully and Ethel Lorraine Hamilton; m. Debra Higgins Tully; ed Univ. of British Columbia, Univ. of Cambridge, UK; Prof. and Chair., Depts of Philosophy and Political Science, McGill Univ. 1977–96; Prof. and Chair. Dept of Political Science, Univ. of Victoria, BC 1996–2001, Distinguished Prof. of Political Science, Law, Indigenous Governance and Philosophy 2003–14, Emer. Distinguished Professor 2014–; Inaugural Henry N.R. Jackman Distinguished Prof. in Philosophical Studies, Univ. of Toronto in Depts of Philosophy and Political Science and Faculty of Law 2001–03; Fellow, Trudeau Foundation; Killam Prize in the Humanities, Canada Council for the Arts 2010, C.B. MacPherson Prize 2012. *Publications:* A Discourse on Property: John Locke and his Adversaries 1980, John Locke, A Letter Concerning Toleration (ed. and Introduction) 1982, Meaning and Context: Quentin Skinner and His Critics, (ed., Introduction, and contrib.) 1988, Samuel Pufendorf, On the Duty of Man and Citizen According to Natural Law, trans. Michael Silverthorne (ed. and Introduction) 1991, An Approach to Political Philosophy: Locke in Contexts 1993, Philosophy in an Age of Pluralism: The Philosophy of Charles Taylor in Question (ed., with assistance of Daniel M. Weinstock) 1994, Strange Multiplicity: Constitutionalism in an Age of Diversity 1995, Multinational Democracies (co-ed. with Alain-G. Gagnon) 2001, Rethinking the Foundations of Modern Political Thought (co-ed. with Annabel Brett) 2006, Democracy and Civic Freedom, Vol. I of Public Philosophy in a New Key 2008, Imperialism and Civic Freedom, Vol. II of Public Philosophy in a New Key 2008, On Global Citizenship 2014, Freedom and Democracy in an Imperial Context 2014, Resurgence and Reconciliation: Indigenous-Settler Relations and Earth Teachings (co-ed.) 2018; numerous papers in professional journals on contemporary political and legal philosophy (or theory) and its history, and on Canadian political and legal philosophy. *Address:* SSM A350, Department of Political Science, University of Victoria, PO Box 3060 STN CSC, Victoria, BC V8W 3R4, Canada (office). *Telephone:* (250) 721-7494 (office). *Fax:* (250) 721-7485 (office). *E-mail:* jtully@uvic.ca (office). *Website:* web.uvic.ca/~polisci (office).

TULLY, Sir (William) Mark, Kt, KBE, MA; British journalist; b. 24 Oct. 1935, Calcutta, India; s. of William S. C. Tully and Patience T. Tully; m. Frances M. Butler 1960; two s. two d.; ed Marlborough Coll., Trinity Hall, Cambridge; Regional Dir Abbeyfield Soc. 1960–64; Personnel Officer BBC 1964–65, Asst Rep. then Rep. (a.i.), BBC, Delhi 1965–69, Hindi Programme Organizer BBC External Services, London 1969–70, Chief Talks Writer 1970–71, Chief of Bureau BBC, Delhi 1971–93, BBC South Asia Corresp. 1993–94; freelance writer, broadcaster, journalist 1994–; Hon. Fellow, Trinity Hall, Cambridge 1994; Hon. DLitt (Strathclyde) 1997, Dr hc (Bradford Univ.) 2001, (York Univ.) 2008, (Open Univ.) 2009, (Queen's Univ., Belfast) 2011; Dimbleby Award (BAFTA) 1984, Padma Shri (India) 1992, Padma Bhushan (India) 2005. *Radio:* series: Raj to Rajiv BBC 1987, Something Understood BBC 1995–, Indian Army in World War II 2007. *Television:* series: Lives of Jesus BBC 1996. *Publications:* Amritsar: Mrs Gandhi's Last Battle (jtly) 1985, Raj to Rajiv (jtly) 1988, No Full Stops in India 1991, The Heart of India 1995, The Lives of Jesus 1996, India in Slow Motion (with Gillian Wright) 2002, India's Unending Journey 2007, India: The Road Ahead 2011. *Leisure interests:* bird watching, reading, railways, theology. *Address:* B.26 Nizamuddin West, New Delhi 110 013, India (office). *Telephone:* (11) 41033839 (office). *E-mail:* markandgilly@gmail.com (office).

TULLY, R(ichard) Brent, BSc, PhD; Canadian astronomer, astrophysicist and academic; *Astronomer, Institute for Astronomy, University of Hawaii;* b. 9 March 1943, Toronto; s. of William Munro Tully and Margaret Jean Tully; m. Janine Tully 1972; one s. two d.; ed Univ. of British Columbia, Univ. of Maryland, USA; postdoctoral researcher, Observatoire de Marseille, France 1972–75; Astronomer, Inst. for Astronomy, Univ. of Hawaii 1975–; Visiting Scientist, Cerro Tololo Inter-American Observatory Chile 1982–83, Observatoire de Meudon, Paris 1983, Istituto di Radioastronomia in Bologna 1989–90, Observatoire de la Côte d'Azur, Nice; mem. American Astronomical Soc., Int. Astronomical Union; Hon. mem. Royal Astronomical Soc. of Canada; Distinguished Alumnus Award, Univ. of Maryland, Regents Medal for Outstanding Research, Univ. of Hawaii, Cosmology Prize, Peter Gruber Foundation (co-recipient) 2014. *Achievements include:* pioneer of a branch of astronomy now called Near Field Cosmology. *Publications:* The Nearby Galaxies Catalog 1988, The Nearby Galaxies Atlas 1988; numerous papers in professional journals. *Address:* Institute for Astronomy, University of Hawaii, 2680 Woodlawn Drive, Honolulu, HI 96822-1839, USA (office). *Telephone:* (808) 956-8606 (office). *Fax:* (808) 988-2790 (office). *E-mail:* tully@ifa.hawaii.edu (office). *Website:* www.ifa.hawaii.edu/~tully (office).

TŮMA, Zdeněk, CSc, MCom; Czech economist and fmr central banker; *Partner, KPMG Czech Republic;* b. 19 Oct. 1960, České Budějovice; m.; two s. one d.; ed Univ. of Econs, Prague, London School of Econs, UK, studies in the Netherlands and USA; Researcher, Inst. for Forecasting, Prague 1986–90; Lecturer, School of Econs, Prague, Faculty of Social Sciences Charles Univ., Prague 1990–98, mem. Scientific Council 2003–06, mem. Graduation Council, Centre for Econ. Research and Grad. Educ.; Adviser to Minister of Trade and Industry 1993–95; Chief Economist, Patria Finance 1995–98; Exec. Dir EBRD 1998–99; Vice-Gov. Czech Nat. Bank 1999–2000, Gov. 2000–10; mem. TOP 09 party 2010–14, party nominee for office of Mayor of Prague in local elections Oct. 2010; Pres. Czech Econs Soc. 1999–2001; Chair. Finance Cttee, Prague City Council 2011–12; Partner, KPMG Czech Republic, Prague 2011–; mem. Bd of Eds Finance a úvěr (Czech Journal of Economics and Finance); mem. Bd of Trustees, Jan and Meda Mládek Foundation, Univ. of Econs, Prague; mem. Bd of Govs English Coll., Prague; mem. Scientific Council, Czech Tech. Univ. 2006–10; mem. Supervisory Bd, Econs Inst., Acad. of Sciences of the Czech Repub. 2007–12; Hon. mem. Bd of Trustees, US Business School, Prague. *Publications:* articles and chapters on econ. transition. *Leisure interests:* skiing, squash, tennis, cycling. *Address:* KPMG, Pobřežní 1a, 186 00 Prague 8, Czech Republic (office). *Telephone:* 222123390 (office). *Fax:* 222123100 (office). *Website:* home.kpmg.com/cz/en/home.html (office).

TUMEWU, Paulus; Indonesian retail executive; *President Commissioner, PT Ramayana Lestari Sentosa;* b. 1952, Ujung Pandang (now Makassar), Sulawesi; m.; three c.; began career helping out in parents' shop, Ujung Pandang; f. Ramayana 1978, opened first store on Jl Sabang, Central Jakarta 1978, inc. into PT Ramayana Lestari Sentosa Tbk 1983, currently Pres. Commr. *Address:* PT Ramayana Lestari Sentosa, Jl. K.H. Wahid Hasyim No. 220, A-B Jakarta Pusat, Jakarta 10250, Indonesia (office). *Telephone:* (21) 3914566 (office). *Fax:* (21) 3920484 (office). *Website:* www.ramayana.co.id (office).

TUMI, HE Cardinal Christian Wiyghan; Cameroonian ecclesiastic; b. 15 Oct. 1930, Kikaikelaki; ordained priest 1966, Bishop of Yagoua 1979–82, consecrated Bishop 1980, Coadjutor Bishop of Garoua 1982–84, Archbishop of Garoua 1984–91; cr. Cardinal-Priest of Ss. Martiri dell'Uganda a Poggio Ameno 1988; Archbishop of Douala 1991–2009 (retd); Cardinal Von Galen Award, Human Life International 2008, Integrity Award, Transparency International 2011. *Address:* Archdiocese of Douala, Archevêché, BP 179, Douala, Cameroon. *E-mail:* christiantumi@camnet.com (office).

TUMLINSON, James H., BS, MS, PhD; American entomologist and academic; *Ralph O. Mumma Professor of Entomology and Co-Director, Center for Chemical Ecology, Pennsylvania State University;* b. 28 Feb. 1938; ed Virginia Mil. Inst., Mississippi State Univ.; Chemist, Boll Weevil Research Lab., US Dept of Agric. (USDA)/Agric. Research Service (ARS) 1964–69, Research Chemist, Insect Attractants, Behavior, and Basic Biology Research Lab. 1970–72, Research Leader, Center for Medical, Agricultural, and Veterinary Entomology 1972–2003; Postdoctoral Researcher, New York State Coll. of Forestry 1969–70; Adjunct Asst Prof., Univ. of Florida Inst. of Food and Agric. 1970–75, Adjunct Assoc. Prof. 1975–82, Adjunct Prof. 1982–; Ralph O. Mumma Prof. of Entomology and Co-Dir Center for Chemical Ecology, Pennsylvania State Univ. 2003–; mem. NAS, Int. Soc. of Chemical Ecology (Vice-Pres. 1997, Pres. 1998); Fellow, Entomological Soc. of America 1996; numerous awards, including USDA Superior Service Awards 1968, 1975, 1983, 2003, ARS Distinguished Research Scientist of the Year 1984, Jean-Marie Delwart Foundation Prize 2003, Wolf Prize in Agric. (co-recipient) 2008. *Address:* Department of Entomology, 111 Chemical Ecology Lab, Pennsylvania State University, University Park, PA 16802, USA (office). *Telephone:* (814) 863-1770 (office). *E-mail:* jht2@psu.edu (office). *Website:* ento.psu.edu/directory/jht2 (office).

TUMLINSON, Rick; American space industry executive; *Chairman, Deep Space Industries;* b. 1956, San Angelo, Tex.; ed boarding school in Lakenheath, UK, Athens High School, Tex., Stephen F. Austin Univ.; lived in Dallas before moving to New York City; produced a series of animated videos to gain funding for various space projects; worked for scientist Gerard K. O'Neill at Space Studies Inst.; Founding Trustee, X-Prize; Co-founder and Exec. Dir Foundation for the Int. Non-Governmental Devt of Space; Co-founder and Chair. Deep Space Industries 2005; Co-founder XTreme Space 2006, Orbital Outfitters 2006, New Worlds Inst., Space Frontier Foundation; consultant, Robert A. Heinlein and Virginia Heinlein Prize Trust; World Tech. Award (Space) 2015. *Publications:* Return to the Moon (ed.); regular contrib. to Huffington Post, Space News. *Address:* Deep Space Industries, NASA Ames Research Park, Moffett Field, CA 94035, USA (office). *E-mail:* info@deepspaceindustries.com (office). *Website:* deepspaceindustries.com (office); www.ricktumlinson.com.

TUMUSIIME-MUTEBILE, Emmanuel, BA; Ugandan economist, government official and central banker; *Governor, Bank of Uganda;* b. 27 Jan. 1949; ed Balliol Coll., Oxford and Durham Univ., UK; Visiting Lecturer, Centre for Int. Briefing, Farnham, UK 1977; Lecturer in Industrial Econs, Univ. of Dar es Salaam, Tanzania 1977–79; Deputy Prin. Pvt. Sec. to the Pres. of Uganda 1979–80; Acting Under-Sec., Ministry of Planning and Econ. Devt 1981, Chief Govt Planning Economist 1982, Perm. Sec. and Chair. Agricultural Policy Cttee 1986–92; Perm. Sec. in charge of Econ. Affairs, Prime Minister's Office 1985; Sec. to the Treasury, Ministry of Finance 1992–98; Perm. Sec. to the Treasury and Chair. Agricultural Policy Cttee and Steering Cttee for Agricultural Modernization Plan, Ministry of Finance, Planning and Econ. Devt 1998–2000; mem. Bd of Dirs Bank of Uganda 1992–, Gov. 2001–; has served as consultant to IMF, OECD, World Bank, Macroeconomic and Financial Man. Inst. of Eastern and Cen. Africa, North-South Inst., Canada and the govts of Rwanda, Tanzania, Eritrea, Kenya, Nepal; Fellow, Econ. Devt Inst. of the World Bank; Hon. Prof., Makerere Univ. 2006; Dr hc (Nkumba Univ.) 2009. *Publications:* numerous articles in professional journals. *Address:* Bank of Uganda, 37–43 Kampala Road, POB 7120, Kampala, Uganda (office). *Telephone:* (41) 4258441 (office). *Fax:* (41) 4230878 (office). *E-mail:* info@bou.or.ug (office). *Website:* www.bou.or.ug (office).

TUNE, Thomas (Tommy) James, BFA; American theatrical performer, director and choreographer; b. 28 Feb. 1939, Witchita Falls, Tex.; s. of Jim Tune and Eva Tune; ed Lamar High School, Houston, Lon Morris Junior Coll., Univ. of Tex. at Austin and Univ. of Houston; began professional career as chorus dancer on Broadway 1963; appeared in films Hello, Dolly! and The Boyfriend; appeared on Broadway in Seesaw (Tony Award, Best Supporting Actor); Off-Broadway Dir The Club, Cloud 9 (Obie and Drama Desk Awards), Stepping Out 1987; Choreographer, A Day in Hollywood/A Night in the Ukraine (Tony Award); Dir The Best Little Whorehouse in Texas, Nine (Tony Award 1982); actor and choreographer, My One and Only (Tony Award 1983), Grand Hotel 1989 (London 1992), The Will Rogers Follies, Bye, Bye Birdie 1991–92; performed musical revue Steps in Time: A Broadway Biography in Song and Dance 2008–; nine Tony Awards, Nat. Medal of Arts, Helen Hayes Tribute Award 2011, Special Tony Award 2015. *Publication:* Footnotes: A Memoir 1997. *Leisure interests:* cooking, yoga, painting. *Address:* c/o Wayne J. Gmitter, Think Iconic Artists Agency, 1403 Madison Avenue, Bethlehem, PA 18018, USA (office); Tommy Tune Inc., 50 East 89th Street, New York, NY 10128, USA (office). *E-mail:* wayne@thinkiconic.com (office); tommytuneinc@aol.com. *Telephone:* (212) 695-7400. *Website:* www.tommytune.com.

TUNG, Chee-hwa, BSc; Hong Kong business executive and politician; *Chairman, China-United States Exchange Foundation;* b. 29 May 1937, Shanghai, China; m. Betty Chiu Hung Ping 1961; two s. one d.; ed Univ. of Liverpool, UK; with Gen.

Electric, USA –1969; Chair. Island Navigation Corpn Ltd, fmr Chair. Orient Overseas (Holdings) Ltd; Dir Sing Tao Newspapers Ltd, Sun Hung Kai Bank Ltd, Hsin Chong Properties Ltd, Mass Transit Railway Corpn; Vice-Chair. Preparatory Cttee for Hong Kong Special Admin. Region; mem. Exec. Council, Hong Kong Govt 1992–96; Chief Exec. of Hong Kong Special Admin. Region 1997–2005 (resgnd); mem. 8th CPPCC Nat. Cttee 1993, Vice-Chair. 10th CPPCC Nat. Cttee 2005–08, 11th CPPCC Nat. Cttee 2008–13, 12th CPPCC Nat. Cttee 2013–; Chair. China-United States Exchange Foundation 2008–; Hon. Consul of Monaco in Hong Kong 1982–96; Int. Councillor, Centre for Strategic and Int. Studies, Washington, DC 1983–97; mem. Advisory Council Inst. for Int. Studies, Stanford Univ. 1995–97, Int. Advisory Bd, Council on Foreign Relations, New York 1995–97. *Leisure interests:* reading, hiking, watching sport, Tai Chi, swimming. *Address:* China-United States Exchange Foundation, 15/F, Shun Ho Tower, 24–30 Ice House Street Central, Hong Kong Special Administrative Region, People's Republic of China (office). *Telephone:* 25232083 (office). *E-mail:* info@cusef.org.hk (office). *Website:* www.cusef.org.hk (office).

TUNG, T. H., MA; Taiwanese business executive; *Chairman, Pegatron Corporation;* ed Nat. Taipei Univ. of Tech.; joined computer maker Acer Inc. after graduation; Co-founder ASUSTeK Computer Inc. 1989, Vice-Chair. –2008; Chair. Pegatron Corpn 2008–; Chair. Unihan, Kinsus, Lumens. *Address:* Pegatron Corporation, 96 Ligong Street, Beitou, Taipei 112, Taiwan (office). *Telephone:* (2) 8143-9001 (office). *Fax:* (2) 8143-7984 (office). *E-mail:* pegatronhr@pegatroncorp.com (office). *Website:* www.pegatroncorp.com (office).

TUNON DE LARA, (José) Manuel, MD, PhD; French physician, university administrator and academic; *President, University of Bordeaux;* b. 13 Feb. 1958, Paris; s. of Spanish historian Manuel Tuñón de Lara; ed Lycée Louis-Barthou de Pau, medical studies in Bordeaux, Pasteur Inst., Paris, Univ. of Southampton, UK; intern in several hosps while specializing in treatment of respiratory diseases 1983; Asst Chef de Clinique, Centre Hospitalier Universitaire (CHU) de Bordeaux 1989–94, Univ. Hosp. Practitioner, Respiratory Diseases 1994–96; Prof. of Pneumology, Univ. Victor Segalen Bordeaux 2 1996–2003; conducted research on asthma and respiratory allergies; Vice-Pres. in charge of Int. Relations, Univ. of Bordeaux 2003–08, Pres. Univ. of Bordeaux II 2008–, Pres. Univ. of Bordeaux 2014–; Chevalier, Ordre des Palmes Académiques, Chevalier, Ordre National du Mérite, Chevalier, Légion d'Honneur. *Publications:* numerous scientific works and articles in professional journals. *Address:* Office of the President, Université de Bordeaux, 166 Cours de l'Argonne, 33000 Bordeaux, France (office). *Telephone:* (5) 56-33-80-80 (office). *Fax:* (5) 56-33-80-89 (office). *E-mail:* affaires.generales@univ-bordeaux.fr (office); secretaire.general@univ-bordeaux.fr (office). *Website:* www.u-bordeaux.fr (office).

TUOMIOJA, Erkki Sakari, MA, MBA, PhD; Finnish journalist, historian and politician; b. 1 July 1946, Helsinki; s. of Sakari Tuomioja and Vappu Wuolijoki; m. Marja-Helena Rajala 1978; ed Univ. of Helsinki; reporter 1967–69; mem. Suomen Eduskunta (Parl.) (SDP) 1970–79, 1991–, Vice-Chair. SDP Parl. Group 1991–96, Chair. 1996–99, Chair. Parl. Grand Cttee (EU Affairs) 1995–99, 2007–11; mem. Helsinki City Council 1969–79, Deputy Mayor of Helsinki 1979–91; Minister of Trade and Industry 1999–2000, of Foreign Affairs 2000–07, 2011–15; Pres. European Council July–Dec. 2006; Chief Ed. Ydin magazine 1977–91; Lecturer, Helsinki Univ. 1997–; Pres. Nordic Council 2008; Chair. Historians Without Borders 2015–; Non-Fiction Finlandia Prize 2006. *Publications:* 23 books on history, politics and int. affairs. *Leisure interests:* history, literature, running. *Address:* Suomen Eduskunta, Mannerheimintie 30, 00102, Helsinki, Finland (office). *E-mail:* erkkituomioja@hotmail.com (home). *Website:* www.eduskunta.fi (office); www.tuomioja.org.

TUPOU VI, HM The King of Tonga, MA; Tongan politician, army officer and fmr diplomatist; b. 12 July 1959, Nuku'alofa; s. of HM King Taufa'ahau Tupou IV and HM Queen Halaevalu Mata'aho; brother of HM King George Tupou V; m. HM Nanasipau'u Vaea 1982; three c.; ed in New Zealand, Britannia Royal Naval Coll., Dartmouth and Univ. of New South Wales, UK, Australian Jt Services Staff Coll., US Naval War Coll., Bond Univ., Australia; fmrly known as Aho'eitu' Unuaki'otonga Tuku'aho, then HRH Prince 'Ulukalala-Lavaka-Ata; joined Tonga Defence Services as Cadet Officer 1981, apptd Lt-Commdr 1987, Second-in-Command 1995; CO, Navy 1993; Minister of Foreign Affairs and Defence 1998–2006; Prime Minister of Tonga 2000–06, also Minister of Civil Aviation and Telecommunications, of Works and Disaster Relief Activities 2004–06 (resgnd); proclaimed Crown Prince 11 Sept. 2006; High Commr to Australia 2008–12; succeeded to the throne 18 March 2012 on death of elder brother, officially crowned 24th King of Tonga 4 July 2015; Chancellor, Univ. of South Pacific 2013–.

TURAJONZODA, Haji Akbar; Tajikistani ecclesiastic and politician; b. 16 Feb. 1954, Kofarnihon; s. of Ishan-e Tourajon; two s. four d.; ed Tashkent Islam Inst., Uzbek SSR, Amman Univ., Jordan, Mir-e Arab School, Buxora; teacher, Tashkent Islam Inst. 1987–88; Head of Office of Qaziate of Tajikistan 1988–90; apptd Chief Qazi of Tajikistan 1990, Qaziate position abolished 1993; elected mem. Supreme Soviet Tajik SSR 1990; participant in democratic movt against Islamic fundamentalists, forced to emigrate to Iran, in hiding 1993; First Deputy Chair. Hizbi Nahzati Islomii Tojikiston (HNIT—Islamic Rebirth Movt of Tajikistan) 1993–99; headed United Tajik Opposition in negotiations with the Govt leading to peace settlement 1995–97; fmr First Deputy Chair. of Tajikistan; currently Senator in Nat. Ass. (Majlisi Milliy); Ismael Somoni Medal of Honour, World Islamic Centre Prize for Peace 1999. *Publication:* Between Water and Fire: The Peace Plan. *Leisure interests:* reading, sports. *Address:* Majlisi Milliy (National Assembly), 734051 Dushanbe, Xiyoboni Rudaki 42, Tajikistan (office). *Telephone:* (372) 23-19-33 (office). *Fax:* (372) 21-51-10 (office). *E-mail:* mejparl@parliament.tojikiston.com (office). *Website:* www.parliament.tj (office).

TURANSKAYA, Tatyana Mikhailovna; Moldovan (Ukrainian) fmr civil servant and politician; b. 20 Nov. 1972, Bilhorod-Dnistrovskyi, Odesa Oblast, Ukrainian SSR, USSR; m.; ed Odesa State Econs Univ.; worked at tax inspectorate, Rîbniţa (Rybnitsa) 1999–2012; Deputy Head of Rîbniţa dist admin on econ. issues 2012, then First Deputy Head, Acting Head June–Aug. 2012, Head Aug. 2012–13; Deputy Prime Minister for Regional Devt, 'Transnistrian Moldovan Repub.' June–July 2013; Chair. of Govt of 'Transnistrian Moldovan Repub.' July 2013–Oct. 2015, Nov.–Dec. 2015 (dismissed). *Address:* c/o Office of the Chairman of the Government, 3300 Tiraspol, ul. 25 Oktyabrya 45, Moldova.

TURCAN, Raluca; Romanian politician; b. (Raluca Tatarcan), 2 April 1976, Botoşani; d. of Dumitru Tatarcan and Maria-Margareta Tatarcan; m. Valeriu Turcan 2004; one s.; ed Bucharest Acad. of Econ. Studies, Pushkin Inst., Moscow, Russian Fed., Nat. Univ. of Political Studies and Public Admin, Transilvania Univ. of Braşov, studies in Austria and USA; public relations consultant for Tofan Group 1999–2000; parl. expert at Romanian Senate 2000–04; Assoc. Prof., Transilvania Univ. of Braşov 2000–06, Romanian-German Univ. of Sibiu 2000–06; began political career as adviser to the Pres. of Nat. Council of Partidul Naţional Liberal (PNL—Nat. Liberal Party) 2000–02, adviser to PNL Pres. Theodor Stolojan 2002–04, mem. Nat. Leadership Council of PNL 2004–06, mem. PNL 2014–, Interim Pres. Dec. 2016–June 2017; mem. Chamber of Deputies (Parl.) for Sibiu Co. 2004–; mem. Partidul Liberal Democrat (PLD—Liberal Democratic Party) 2006–08, Vice-Pres. March–Dec. 2007, party merged with Democratic Party to form Partidul Democrat Liberal (PD-L—Democratic Liberal Party) Dec. 2007, Vice-Pres. PD-L 2008–14. *Publications:* Integrare şi politică fiscală europeană (Integration and European Fiscal Policy); English-Russian-Romanian dictionary of econ. terms; studies on European integration and public relations. *Address:* Partidul Naţional Liberal, 011866, Bucharest, Bd. Aviatorilor 86, Romania (office). *Telephone:* (21) 2310795 (office). *Fax:* (21) 2310796 (office). *E-mail:* dre@pnl.ro (office). *Website:* www.pnl.ro (office).

TURCHYNOV, Oleksandr Valentynovych, PhD; Ukrainian politician, economist and screenwriter; *Secretary, National Security and Defence Council of Ukraine;* b. 31 March 1964, Dnipropetrovsk (now Dnipro), Ukrainian SSR, USSR; m. Hanna Volodymyrivna Turchynova; one s.; ed Dnipropetrovsk Metallurgic Inst., Dept of Technology; began career working at Kryvorizhstal complex then moved into Komsomol and CP apparatus; worked in Dnipropetrovsk Oblast Admin; Co-founder and mem. All-Ukrainian Hromada Asscn 1993–99; apptd Adviser on Econ. Affairs to Prime Minister Leonid Kuchma 1993, then apptd Vice-Pres. Ukrainski Soyuz Promyslovtsiv i Pidpriyemtsiv (Ukrainian Union of Industrialists and Entrepreneurs); Dir Econ. Reforms Inst., Kyiv 1994–98, also Head of Ukrainian Nat. Acad. of Science Lab. of Shadow Econ. Research; mem. Verkhovna Rada (Parl.) 1998–, Chair. (Speaker) Feb.–Nov. 2014; joined Batkivshchyna (Fatherland) party 1999, First Deputy Leader –2014; Chief of Security Service of Ukraine (SBU) 2004–05; Vice-Chair. Blok Yuliya Tymoshenko (BYuT—Yuliya Tymoshenko Bloc) in charge of election campaign HQ 2006–07; First Deputy Prime Minister 2007–10, Acting Prime Minister 3–11 March 2010; Acting Pres. of Ukraine 23 Feb. 2014 (following impeachment of Viktor Yanukovych) –7 June 2014; Founding mem. Narodny Front (People's Front) political party Sept. 2014; Sec. Nat. Security and Defence Council of Ukraine Dec. 2014–; pastor/lay preacher, Baptist church, Kyiv. *Publications include:* Illusion of Fear 2004, script for the same-name film based on the book 2005 (film released in Ukraine 2008). *Address:* National Security and Defence Council of Ukraine, 01601 Kyiv, vul. Komandarma Kamenyeva 8 (office); Narodny Front (People's Front), 02068 Kyiv, vul. Akademika Kurchatova 3, Ukraine (office). *Telephone:* (44) 255-05-15 (NSDCU) (office); (44) 359-07-65 (People's Front) (office). *Fax:* (44) 255-05-85 (NSDCU) (office). *E-mail:* info@rnbo.gov.ua (office); press@nfront.com.ua (office). *Website:* www.rnbo.gov.ua (office); nfront.org.ua (office); turchynov.com.

TURGANBAYEV, Maj.-Gen. Melis; Kyrgyzstani police officer and government official; b. 19 Feb. 1962, Frunze (now Bishkek), Kyrgyz SSR, USSR; ed Kyrgyz State Univ., Higher Coll. of Interior Ministry of the USSR, Leningrad; detective with Criminal Investigation Dept (CID), Ministry of Internal Affairs, Kyrgyz SSR 1986–87, Operations Officer, Div. of Criminal Investigation, Police Sverdlovsk Dist, Bishkek 1987–93, Head of CID 1993–96, Deputy Police Chief 1996–98, Deputy Head of CID, Kyrgyz Repub. 1998–2000, Deputy Chief of CID and Head of Serious Crimes, Ministry of Internal Affairs 2000–01; Head of ATS Pervomaisky rayon, Bishkek and Deputy Chief of Police in Bishkek 2001–05; Head of Ministry of Internal Affairs and Deputy Police Chief in Bishkek 2005–06; Head of Interior Ministry 2006–08; First Deputy Minister of Internal Affairs and Dir Drug Control Agency 2008–10, First Deputy Minister of Internal Affairs 2010–12, Minister of Internal Affairs 2014–16 (resgnd); Chief of Police Dept, Bishkek 2012–14; 'Dank' Medal, 'Kyzhyrmon kyzmat otogondygy uchyun' Medal (Second Degree), Diploma of the Parl. of the Repub. *Address:* c/o Ministry of Internal Affairs, 720040 Bishkek, Frunze 469, Kyrgyzstan. *E-mail:* pressa@mvd.gov.kg.

TÜRK, Danilo, PhD; Slovenian academic, diplomatist, lawyer, politician and fmr head of state; *Chairman, Global Fairness Initiative;* b. 19 Feb. 1952, Maribor; m. Barbara Miklič; one d.; ed Univ. of Ljubljana, Univ. of Belgrade; Lecturer in Public Int. Law, Univ. of Ljubljana 1978–88, apptd Prof. of Int. Law 1988, Head Inst. of Int. Law and Int. Relations 1983–95; mem. UN Sub-comm. on Prevention of Discrimination and Protection of Minorities 1984–92; Special Rapporteur 1989–92, Chair. 1990; Perm. Rep. of Slovenia to the UN 1992–2000; mem. UN Security Council 1998–99, Pres. Aug. 1998, Nov. 1999; mem. Security Council Mission to Jakarta and East Timor, Indonesia Sept. 1999, Asst Sec.-Gen. of UN for Political Affairs 2000–05; apptd Chair. Int. Law Asscn, Slovenia 1990; Pres. of Slovenia 2007–12; currently Chair. Global Fairness Initiative; Hon. Prof., Acad. of Public Admin, Astana, Kazakhstan 2009; Grand Cross with Diamonds, Order of the Sun (Peru) 2008; Hon. GCB 2008; Commdr, First Class, Order of the White Rose of Finland 2010; Kt Grand Cross, Order of Saint-Charles (Monaco) 2011; Kt Grand Cross with Cordon, Order of the Italian Repub. 2011; Grand Star, Decoration on Honour for Services to the Repub. of Austria 2011; Grand Cross, Royal Norwegian Order of St Olav 2011; Kt Grand Cross, Order of the Falcon (Iceland) 2011; Dr hc (Univ. of Szeged, Hungary) 2010, (V.N. Karazin Kharkiv Nat. Univ., Ukraine) 2011; Gold medal, Széchenyi Scientific Soc. Hungary 2008, Arthur J. Goldberg Award, Touro Law Coll., USA 2008, Ilyas Afandiyev Int. Prize 2010. *Publications:* book on the principle of non-intervention in int. relations and int. law and over 100 articles in legal journals and other publs. *Leisure interests:* hiking, cross-country skiing, reading books, classical music. *Address:* Global Fairness Initiative, 2122 P Street, NW, Suite 302, Washington, DC 20037, USA (office). *Telephone:* (202) 898-9022 (office). *Fax:* (202) 787-1833 (office). *E-mail:* info@globalfairness.org (office). *Website:* www.globalfairness.org (office); www2.gov.si/up-rs/bp-dt.nsf (office).

TURK, Žiga, BSc, MSc, PhD; Slovenian academic and politician; *Professor and Vice Dean, Faculty of Civil and Geodetic Engineering, University of Ljubljana;* b. 4 Feb. 1962, Ljubljana; ed Univ. of Ljubljana; Founding Ed. Moj mikro (magazine on microcomputers) 1984–87; Asst Research Engineer, Inst. of Structural Eng and Earthquake and Building Informatics, Univ. of Ljubljana 1986–89, Asst in Computer Science, Dept of Architecture 1989–93, Asst Prof. 1993–98, Assoc. Prof. of Information Tech. and Documentation, Faculty of Civil and Geodetic Eng 1998–2004, Prof. 2004–, Vice-Dean 2015–; Visiting Lecturer, Royal Inst. of Tech., Stockholm, Sweden 1997–99; Visiting Prof., Istanbul Tech. Univ. 2001–07; Minister without Portfolio, responsible for Growth 2007–08, Minister of Educ., Science, Culture and Sport 2012–13; fmr mem. Scientific Council, Slovenia Research Agency; fmr Vice-Pres. Strategic Council for Culture, Educ. and Science; Co-founder and Co-ed. ITcon (int. science magazine); fmr Chair. Supervisory Bd Telecom Slovenia, Mobitel. *Address:* Faculty of Civil and Geodetic Engineering, University of Ljubljana, 1000 Ljubljana, Jamova cesta 2, Slovenia (office). *Telephone:* (1) 4768622 (office). *Fax:* (1) 4250681 (office). *E-mail:* tajnistvo@fgg.uni-lj.si (office); ziga.turk@gmail.com. *Website:* www3.fgg.uni-lj./en (office); www.zturk.com.

TURKI, Abdul Aziz al-Abdullah al-, BA; Saudi Arabian international organization official; b. 12 Aug. 1936, Jeddah; m.; two d.; ed Univ. of Cairo; with US Embassy, Jeddah 1953–54, ARAMCO 1954–66; Dir Office of Minister of Petroleum and Mineral Resources 1966–68; Dir of Gen. Affairs, Directorate of Mineral Resources 1968–70; Asst Sec.-Gen. OAPEC 1970–75, Sec.-Gen. 1990–2008; Sec.-Gen. Supreme Advisory Council for Petroleum and Mineral Affairs, Saudi Arabia 1975–90; Saudi Gov. for OPEC 1975–90; Deputy Minister, Ministry of Petroleum and Mineral Resources 1975; Chair. Arab Maritime Petroleum Transport Co., Kuwait 1981–87, Pemref 1982–89; mem. Bd of Dirs Petromin 1975–89, ARAMCO 1980–89. *Leisure interests:* tennis, swimming.

TURKSON, HE Cardinal Peter Kodwo Appiah, MTh, MDiv; Ghanaian ecclesiastic; *Prefect, Dicastery for Promoting Integral Human Development;* b. 11 Oct. 1948, Wassaw Nsuta; ed St Teresa's Minor Seminary, Amisano, St Peter's Regional Seminary, Pedu, Seminary of St Anthony-on-Hudson, Rensaleer, New York, USA, Pontifical Biblical Inst., Rome, Italy; ordained priest of Cape Coast 1975; staff mem., St Teresa's Minor Seminary 1975–76, 1980–81; staff mem. and lecturer of Sacred Scripture, St Peter's Major Seminary; visiting lecturer, Major Seminary, Anyama, Cote d'Ivoire 1983–86; part time lecturer and Chaplain, Univ. of Cape Coast 1984–86; promoted to episcopate while studying in Rome; Archbishop of Cape Coast 1992–2009; attended Special Ass. for Africa of World Synod of Bishops, Vatican City 1994, Ninth Ordinary Ass. of World Synod of Bishops, Vatican City 1994; cr. Cardinal (Cardinal Priest of San Liborio) 2003; participated in Papal Conclave 2005, 2013; Pres. Ghana Catholic Bishop's Conf. 1997–2004; Chancellor Catholic Univ. College of Ghana, Legon 2002–; Vice-Pres. Asscn of Episcopal Confs of Anglophone West Africa 2004–07 (merged with Conférence Épiscopale de l'Afrique de l'Ouest), Pres. 2007–; Chair. Ghana Chapter of The Conf. of Religions for Peace 2003–07, Ghana Nat. Peace Council 2006–, Int. Sec. of the Pontifical Mission Socs 2006–; Treas. Symposium of Episcopal Confs of Africa and Madagascar 2007–; mem. Governing Council of Univ. of Ghana 2001–06, Bd of Dirs, Pontifical Council for Christian Unity 2002–, Pontifical Comm. for the Cultural Patrimony of the Church 2002–, Pontifical Congregation for Divine Worship 2005–, Supreme Cttee of the Pontifical Missions Soc. 2006–, Pontifical Council for Justice and Peace 2007– (Pres. 2009–13, 2013–16); Prefect, Dicastery for Promoting Integral Human Devt 2016–; mem. Bd of Dirs, CEDECOM 2002–, Cen. Regional Devt Cttee, Asscn of Ghana Biblical Exegetes; Trustee, Komenda-Edina-Eguafo-Abrem Educational Fund; Hon. Pres. World Conf. of Religions for Peace; Order of the Star, Order of the Rock, Ghana; Dr hc (Univ. of Ghana, Legon), (Univ. of Educ., Winneba, Ghana), (Holy Cross Coll., Notre Dame, USA). *Publications:* several articles. *Address:* Dicastery for Promoting Integral Human Development, Piazza San Calisto 16, 00120 Città del Vaticano, Rome, Italy (office). *Telephone:* (06) 69879911 (office). *Fax:* (06) 69887205 (office). *E-mail:* pcjustpax@justpeace.va (office). *Website:* www.iustitiaetpax.va (office).

TURLINGTON, Christy, BA; American fashion model; b. 2 Jan. 1969, Walnut Creek, Calif.; d. of Dwain Turlington and María Elizabeth Turlington (née Parker); m. Edward Burns 2003; one s. one d.; ed Monte Vista High School, Fla, Gallatin School of Individualized Study, New York Univ.; discovered aged 14; moved to New York City to model full-time 1987; with Ford Models Inc. 1985; model for Calvin Klein 1987–2007; mem. Harvard Medical School Global Health Council, Advisor, Harvard School of Public Health Board of Dean's Advisors; mem. Advisory Bd New York Univ. Nursing School; f. Every Mother Counts campaign 2010. *Films include:* Catwalk 1996, appeared in George Michael's video Freedom, No Woman, No Cry (documentary, dir, as Christy Turlington Burns) 2010. *Publication:* Living Yoga: Creating A Life Practice 2003. *Address:* Every Mother Counts, 805 15th Street, NW, Suite 700, Washington, DC 20005, USA. *Telephone:* (202) 617-3899. *E-mail:* info@everymothercounts.org. *Website:* www.everymothercounts.org.

TURNAGE, Mark-Anthony, CBE; British composer; b. 10 June 1960, Corringham, Essex; s. of Roy Turnage and Patricia Knowles; m. 1st Susan Shaw 1989 (divorced 1990); m. 2nd Helen Reed 1992; two s.; ed Hassenbrook Comprehensive School, Palmers Sixth Form, Grays, Royal Coll. of Music with Oliver Knussen and John Lambert and Tanglewood, USA with Hans Werner Henze and Gunther Schuller; first opera, Greek, premiered at first Munich Biennale 1988; Composer-in-Asscn with City of Birmingham Symphony Orchestra, composing three major works 1989–93; Composer-in-Asscn with ENO 1995–99; Assoc. Composer in Asscn with BBC Symphony Orchestra 2000–03; Momentum, BBC Radio 3 composer weekend dedicated to his music, Barbican Hall, London 2003; Composer-in-Residence, London Philharmonic Orchestra 2005–, Chicago Symphony Orchestra 2006–08; one of 20 composers commissioned to write a piece of music for the 2012 Cultural Olympiad; Guinness Prize for Composition 1982, Benjamin Britten Young Composers Prize 1983, BMW Music Theatre Prize 1988, Laurence Olivier Award 2001. *Compositions include:* Night Dances for orchestra 1980, Lament for a Hanging Man for soprano and ensemble 1983, Sarabande for soprano saxophone and piano 1985, On All Fours for chamber ensemble 1985, Greek (opera) 1987, Three Screaming Popes for orchestra 1988, Greek Suite for mezzo soprano, baritone and ensemble 1989, Kai for solo cello and ensemble 1989, Some Days 1989, Killing Time (television scena) 1991, Drowned Out 1992, Your Rockaby saxophone concerto 1992, Blood on the Floor for large ensemble 1994, Dispelling the Fears 1994, Twice Through the Heart for mezzo and 16 players 1997, Country of the Blind 1997, The Silver Tassie (opera) 1997, Silent Cities for orchestra 1998, About Time for two orchestras 1999, Evening Songs for orchestra 2000, Another Set To for trombone and orchestra 2000, Scorched for jazz trio and orchestra (with John Scofield) 2000, On Opened Ground concerto for viola and orchestra 2000, Bass Inventions for double bass and ensemble 2001, The Torn Fields for orchestra 2001, Dark Crossing 2001, A Quick Blast 2001, The Game is Over for orchestra 2002, Scherzoid for orchestra 2003–04, From the Wreckage for trumpet and orchestra 2004, Riffs and Refrains 2005, Ceres for orchestra 2005, Lullaby for Hans for orchestra 2005, From all Sides for orchestra 2005–06, Chicago Remains for orchestra 2007, Milo 2009, Texan Tenebrae for orchestra 2010, Hammered Out 2010, Anna Nicole (opera) 2011, Beyond This 2012, Frieze (commissioned for bicentenary of Royal Philharmonic Soc.) 2013, Duetti d'Amore for violin and cello 2015, Remembering for orchestra 2016, Coraline (opera) 2018. *Leisure interests:* football, films, theatre. *Address:* c/o Boosey and Hawkes Music Publishers, Aldwych House, 71–91 Aldwych, London, WC2B 4HN, England. *Telephone:* (20) 7054-7200. *E-mail:* composers@boosey.com. *Website:* www.boosey.com.

TURNBERG, Baron (Life Peer), cr. 2000, of Cheadle in the County of Cheshire; **Leslie Arnold Turnberg,** Kt, MB, ChB, MD, FRCP, FMedSci; British professor of medicine; b. 22 March 1934, Manchester; s. of Hyman Turnberg and Dora Bloomfield; m. Edna Barme 1968; one s. one d.; ed Stand Grammar School, Whitefield and Univ. of Manchester; Lecturer, then Sr Lecturer in Gastroenterology, Univ. of Manchester, Manchester Royal Infirmary 1968–73; Prof. of Medicine Univ. of Manchester 1973–97, Dean Faculty of Medicine 1986–89; Hon. Consultant Physician, Hope Hosp. 1973–97; Pres. Royal Coll. of Physicians 1992–97, Asscn of Physicians of GB and Ireland 1996–97; Chair. Conf. of Medical Royal Colls 1993–95, Strategic Review of London's Health Services 1997; Pres. Medical Protection Soc. 1997–2004, Medical Council on Alcoholism 1997–2002; Chair. Bd of Public Health Lab. Service 1997–2002; Scientific Adviser Asscn of Medical Research Charities 1997–; Pres. British Soc. of Gastroenterology 1999–2000; Chair. Bd of Health Quality Service 2000–04; Chair. UK Forum on Genetics and Insurance 2000–02; Vice-Pres. Acad. of Medical Sciences 1998–2004; Hon. FRCP (Edin.), FRCP (Glasgow), FRCPI, FRCOG; Hon. Fellow, Royal Colls of Ophthalmologists, Psychiatrists, Surgeons of England, Royal Australian Coll. of Physicians, S African Coll. of Medicine, Pakistan Coll. of Physicians, Acad. of Medicine of Hong Kong and of Singapore and several others; Hon. DSc (Salford) 1996, (Manchester) 1998, (Imperial Coll. London) 2000. *Publications include:* Intestinal Secretion 1982, Mechanisms of Mucosal Protection in the Upper Gastro-Intestinal Tract 1983, Clinical Gastroenterology 1989. *Leisure interests:* reading, antiquarian books, walking, talking, Chinese ceramics. *Address:* House of Lords, Westminster, London, SW1A 0PW, England. *Telephone:* (20) 7435-8223. *Fax:* (20) 7435-9262 (office).

TURNBULL, Baron (Life Peer), cr. 2005, of Enfield in the London Borough of Enfield; **Andrew Turnbull,** KCB, CVO; British fmr civil servant; b. 21 Jan. 1945, Enfield, Middx, England; s. of Anthony Turnbull and Mary Turnbull; m. Diane Clarke 1967; two s.; ed Enfield Grammar School, Christ's Coll., Cambridge; Overseas Devt Inst. Fellow working as economist to Govt of Zambia 1968–70; joined HM Treasury 1970; Pvt. Sec. to Prime Minister 1983–85, Prin. Pvt. Sec. to Prime Minister 1988–92; Perm. Sec. Dept of Environment 1994–97, Dept of Environment, Transport and the Regions 1997–98, Perm. Sec. HM Treasury 1998–2002; Cabinet Sec. and Head of Home Civil Service 2002–05 (retd); mem. (Crossbench) House of Lords 2005–; Dir (non-exec.) Prudential plc 2006–15, British Land plc 2006–17; Chair. Bd Zambia Orphans of Aids-UK; Trustee, Global Warming Policy Foundation; Hon. Fellow, Christ's Coll., Cambridge; hon. degrees (Middlesex, Cranfield). *Leisure interests:* walking, opera, golf, sailing. *Address:* House of Lords, Westminster, London, SW1A 0PW, England (office). *Telephone:* (20) 7219-5353 (office).

TURNBULL, Lucinda (Lucy) Mary, AO, LLB, MBA; Australian lawyer and politician; b. 30 March 1958, Sydney; d. of Thomas Eyre Forrest Hughes and Joanna Fitzgerald; m. Malcolm Bligh Turnbull 1980; one s. one d.; ed Univ. of Sydney, Univ. of New South Wales; Partner, Turnbull McWilliam (solicitors) 1988–99, Turnbull & Partners Ltd 1988–92, Turnbull & Co. 1992–95, Dir Turnbull & Partners Pty Ltd 1990–; Deputy Lord Mayor of Sydney 1999–2003, Lord Mayor (first woman) 2003–04; Chair. Prima Biomed Ltd 2011–; Chair. FTR Holdings Ltd 1997–2001, NSW Ministerial Advisory Council on Biotechnology 2001–02; Deputy Chair. Committee for Sydney, Sydney Cancer Centre Foundation 2002–06; mem. Bd of Dirs Urban Renewal Organization, Waterloo Redfern Authority, Sydney Metropolitan Development Authority, US Studies Centre at Univ. of Sydney, Centre for Independent Studies, Biennale of Sydney, Redfern Foundation; mem. Australian Museum Trust 1995–99, Deputy Pres. 1995–99; Pres. Sydney Children's Hosp. Appeal, Sydney Children's Hosp. Foundation Ltd 1996–2000; Commr Australian Pavilion at Venice Architecture Biennale 2006, 2008; mem. Bd of Govs Woolcock Inst. of Medical Research; mem. Commonwealth of Nations Comm. on Respect and Understanding, NSW Cancer Council 1997–99. *Publications include:* Sydney: Biography of a City 1999. *Leisure interests:* history, politics, contemporary culture, visual arts, urban design, architecture. *Address:* Turnbull & Partners Pty Ltd, Level 38/264 George Street, Sydney, NSW 2000, Australia (office). *Telephone:* (2) 8248-3900 (office).

TURNBULL, Malcolm Bligh, BA, LLB, BCL; Australian banker, lawyer and politician; b. 24 Oct. 1954, Sydney, NSW; s. of Bruce B. Turnbull and Coral Lansbury; m. Lucinda M. F. Hughes 1980; one s. one d.; ed Sydney Grammar School, Univ. of Sydney and Univ. of Oxford (Rhodes Scholar); State Parl. Corresp. for Nation Review 1976; journalist, The Bulletin 1977–78; Exec. Asst to Chair. Consolidated Press Holdings Ltd 1978; journalist, The Sunday Times, London 1978–79; barrister, Sydney 1980–82; Gen. Counsel and Sec. Consolidated Press Holdings Ltd 1983–85; solicitor in pvt. practice, Turnbull McWilliam, Sydney 1986–87; Prin. Turnbull and Co. (solicitors) 1987; Man. Dir Turnbull & Partners Pty Ltd (investment bankers), Sydney 1987–97; Chair. Axiom Forest Resources Ltd (HK) 1991–92; Dir Perseverance Corpn Ltd 1993–94, Star Mining Corpn NL 1993–95, FTR Holdings Ltd 1995–2004; Chair. Oz Email Ltd 1994–99; Dir Australian Republican Movt 1991–93, Chair. 1993–2000; Chair. cttee to advise on changing Australia to Repub.; Chair. and Man. Dir Goldman Sachs Australia 1997–2001, Partner, Goldman Sachs (US) 1998–2001; Chair. Menzies Research Centre 2001–04; Hon. Fed. Treas., Liberal Party 2002–03, Treasury Spokesman 2007–08, Leader 2008–09, 2015–18; mem. NSW State Exec. 2002–03, mem. Fed. Finance Cttee 2002–03, mem. Fed. Exec. 2002–03; MP for Wentworth, NSW 2004–, Parl. Sec. to Prime Minister 2006–07; Minister for the Environment and Heritage 2007; Shadow Treas. 2007–08, Leader of the Opposition 2008–09, Shadow Minister for Communications and Broadband 2010–13; Minister for Communications 2013–15; Prime Minister of Australia 2015–18; Henry Lawson Prize for Poetry 1975, Centenary Medal 2003, Disraeli Prize 2017. *Publications:* The Spycatcher Trial 1988, The Reluctant Republic 1993, Fighting for the Republic 1999. *Leisure interests:* reading, walking, riding, gardening. *Address:* PO Box 545, Edgecliff, NSW 2027, Australia (office). *Website:* www.malcolmturnbull.com.au.

TURNBULL, Rt Rev. Michael, CBE, DL, MA, DipTheol, DLitt, DD; British ecclesiastic; *Honorary Assistant Bishop in the Diocese of Canterbury, Rochester and Europe;* b. 27 Dec. 1935, Yorks., England; s. of George Turnbull and Adeline Awty; m. Brenda Merchant 1963; one s. two d.; ed Ilkley Grammar School, Keble Coll. Oxford and St John's Coll. Durham; ordained deacon 1960, priest 1961; curate, Middleton 1960–61, Luton 1961–65; Domestic Chaplain to Archbishop of York 1965–69; Rector of Heslington and Chaplain, York Univ. 1969–76; Chief Sec. Church Army 1976–84; Archdeacon of Rochester 1984–88; Bishop of Rochester 1988–94, of Durham 1994–2003; Hon. Asst Bishop, Diocese of Canterbury, Rochester and Europe 2003–; mem. Gen. Synod of Church of England 1970–75, 1987–2003; mem. Archbishops' Council 1999–2001, Chair. Ministry Div. 1999–2001; Chair. Archbishops' Comm. on Org. of Church of England; mem. House of Lords 1994–2003; Chair. Foundation for Church Leadership 2002–05; DL, Co. of Kent; Hon. DLitt 1994; Hon. DD 2003. *Publications:* Unity: The Next Step? (contrib.) 1972, God's Front Line 1979, Parish Evangelism 1980, Learning to Pray 1981, 100 Minute Bible Reflections (ed) 2007, The State of the Church and the Church of the State 2012; numerous articles in journals. *Leisure interests:* cricket, family life, lecturer with Swan Hellenic Cruises, leader Holy Land Pilgrimages. *Address:* 67 Strand Street, Sandwich, Kent, CT13 9HN, England. *Telephone:* (1304) 611389. *E-mail:* bstmt@btopenworld.com. *Website:* www .bishopmichaelturnbull.com.

TURNER, David J.; British banking executive and company director; Finance Dir GKN plc –2001; Chief Financial Officer Brambles 2001–03, CEO 2003–07 (retd); Chair. Cobham plc 2008–10; mem. Bd of Dirs Commonwealth Bank of Australia 2006–17, Chair. 2010–17, Chair. Bd Performance and Renewal Cttee, mem. People & Remuneration Cttee; mem. Risk Cttee; fmr mem. Bd of Dirs Whitbread plc, Chair. Audit Cttee 2000–06; Fellow, Inst. of Chartered Accountants in England and Wales, Australian Inst. of Company Dirs.

TURNER, Grenville, MA, DPhil, FRS; British geochemist and academic; *Professor Emeritus, University of Manchester;* b. 1 Nov. 1936, Todmorden, Yorks., England; s. of Arnold Turner and Florence Turner; m. Kathleen Morris 1961; one s. one d.; ed St John's Coll., Cambridge, Balliol Coll., Oxford; Asst Prof., Univ. of California, Berkeley 1962–64; Lecturer, Univ. of Sheffield 1964–74, Sr Lecturer 1974–79, Reader 1979–80, Prof. of Physics 1980–88; Prof. of Isotope Geochemistry, Univ. of Manchester 1988–2002, Research Prof. 2002–12, Prof. Emer. 2012–; Visiting Assoc. in Nuclear Geophysics, Calif. Inst. of Tech. 1970–71; Fellow, Royal Soc. 1980, Council mem. 1990–92; Fellow, Meteoritical Soc. 1980, European Asscn of Geochemistry 1996, American Geophysical Union 1998; Rumford Medal, Royal Soc. 1996, Leonard Medal, Meteoritical Soc. 1999, Urey Medal European Asscn of Geochemistry 2002, Gold Medal Royal Astronomical Soc. 2004. *Achievements:* developed Ar-Ar method for rock dating, used it to determine first ages of Apollo lunar samples and a chronology of lunar evolution; discovered early isotopic evidence leading to discovery of pre-solar material in primitive meteorites; developed ultra-sensitive isotopic analysis by resonance ionisation mass spectrometry, used it to discover extinct plutonium-244 in ancient terrestrial zircons. *Publications:* scientific papers on the application of naturally occurring isotopes to earth science and the evolution of the solar system. *Leisure interests:* photography, walking, theatre. *Address:* School of Earth and Environmental Sciences, University of Manchester, Manchester, M13 9PL, England (office). *Telephone:* (161) 275-0401 (office). *Fax:* (161) 275-3947 (office). *E-mail:* grenville.turner@manchester.ac .uk (office). *Website:* www.sees.manchester.ac.uk (office).

TURNER, Kathleen, BFA; American actress; b. 19 June 1954, Springfield, Mo.; m. Jay Weiss 1984 (divorced); one d.; ed Cen. School of Speech and Drama, UK, Southwest Missouri State Univ., Univ. of Maryland. *Plays include:* various theatre roles including Broadway debut, Gemini 1978, The Graduate, London 2000, Who's Afraid of Virginia Woolf? (London Evening Standard Award for Best Actress 2006, London Critics' Circle Best Actress 2006) 2006, Crimes of the Heart, New York (Dir) 2007–08, The Third Story, New York 2009. *Television series include:* The Doctors 1977, Leslie's Folly (also dir) 1994, Friends at Last (also producer) 1995, Style and Substance 1996, Legalese 1998, Love and Action in Chicago 1999, Friends (series) 2001, Californication (series) 2009. *Films include:* Body Heat 1981, The Man With Two Brains 1983, Crimes of Passion 1984, Romancing the Stone 1984, Prizzi's Honour 1985, The Jewel of the Nile 1985, Peggy Sue Got Married 1986, Julia and Julia 1988, Switching Channels 1988, The Accidental Tourist 1989, The War of the Roses 1990, V.I. Warzhawski 1991, House of Cards, Undercover Blues 1993, Serial Mom 1994, Naked in New York 1994, Moonlight and Valentino 1995, A Simple Wish 1997, The Real Blonde 1997, The Virgin Suicides 1999, Baby Geniuses 1999, Prince of Central Park 2000, Beautiful 2000, Without Love 2004, Monster House 2006, The Perfect Family 2011, Nurse 3D 2013, Dumb and Dumber To 2014; producer Hard Boiled 1990. *Publication:* Send Yourself Roses (auto-biog.) 2008.

TURNER, Michael John, CBE, BA, ACIS, FRAeS; British business executive; *Chairman, Babcock International Group PLC;* b. 5 Aug. 1948, Manchester; m.; four c.; ed Didsbury Tech. High School, Manchester and Manchester Polytechnic; joined Hawker Siddeley Aviation as undergraduate commercial apprentice 1966, later Contracts Officer; Contracts Man. (Mil.) British Aerospace (BAe) Aircraft Group, Manchester Div. 1978, Admin. Man. 1980, Exec. Dir of Admin. 1981, Divisional Admin. Dir 1982 (led Advanced Turboprop Project Team 1982–84), Divisional Dir and Gen. Man., Kingston 1984, Dir Divisional Man. Cttee and Gen. Man. Mil. Aircraft Div. 1986, Dir Marketing and Product Support, Mil. Aircraft

Div. 1987, Exec. Vice-Pres. Defence Marketing, BAe PLC 1988; Chair. and Man. Dir BAe Regional Aircraft Ltd and Chair. Jetstream Aircraft 1992; Chair. Commercial Aerospace 1994 (mem. Main Bd BAe PLC), assumed responsibility for all BAe's defence export business 1996, mem. Airbus Supervisory Bd (renamed AIC) 1998, mem. Shareholders' Cttee AIC, COO BAE Systems (following merger of BAe PLC and Marconi Electronic Systems) 1999, CEO 2002–08; Chair. Defence Industries Council 2007–10; Jt Chair. Nat. Defence Industries Council 2007–10; Vice-Pres. Soc. of British Aerospace Cos 1995, Pres. 1996–97; Dir (non-exec.), Babcock International Group PLC 1996–2005 (Chair. 2008–), Lazard Ltd 2006–; Sr Ind. Dir (non-exec.), GKN plc 2009–; Hon. Doctor of Admin (Manchester Metropolitan Univ.); Dr hc (Cranfield), (Loughborough); NED FTSE 100 Chair. of the Year 2014. *Leisure interests:* Manchester United Football Club, golf, cricket, rugby. *Address:* Babcock International Group PLC, 33 Wigmore Street, London, W1U 1QX, England (office). *Telephone:* (20) 7355-5300 (office). *Fax:* (20) 7355-5360 (office). *E-mail:* mike.turner@babcock.co.uk (office). *Website:* www.babcock.co.uk (office).

TURNER, Robert (Ted) Edward, III; American broadcasting executive and yachtsman; b. 19 Nov. 1938; s. of Robert Turner and Frances Rooney; m. 1st Judy Nye (divorced); one s. one d.; m. 2nd Jane S. Smith 1965 (divorced 1988); one s. two d.; m. 3rd Jane Fonda 1991 (divorced 2001); ed McCallie School, Brown Univ.; Gen. Man. Turner Advertising, Macon, Ga 1960–63; Pres. and CEO various Turner cos., Atlanta 1963–70; Chair. Bd and Pres. Turner Broadcasting System (TBS) Inc. 1970–96, est. Cable News Network (CNN) 1980, Headline News Network 1992, CNN Int. 1985, acquired MGM library of film and TV properties 1986, launched Cartoon Network 1992; TBS merged with New Line Cinema 1994; Vice-Chair. Time Warner Inc. (after TBS merger with Time Warner Inc.) 1996–2001, Vice-Chair. AOL Time Warner (after Time Warner Inc. merger with AOL) 2001–03, mem. Bd of Dirs –2006; f. Ted Turner Pictures and Ted Turner Documentaries (film production cos) 2001; f. Ted's Montana Grill restuarant chain 2002; fmr owner and Pres. Atlanta Braves professional baseball team, fmr owner and Chair. Bd Atlanta Hawks professional basketball team; Chair. Better World Soc., Wash., DC 1985–90; f. Turner Foundation, Inc. 1991, UN Foundation 1997, Nuclear Threat Initiative 2001; Dir Martin Luther King Center, Atlanta; sponsor, creator, The Goodwill Games 1985; Man of the Year, Time Magazine 1991, Cable and Broadcasting's Man of the Century 1999, Cable TV Hall of Fame 1999, U Thant Peace Award 1999, World Ecology Award (Univ. of Missouri) 2000, named Yachtsman of Year four times, Fastnet Trophy 1979, Delta Air Lines Prize for Global Understanding (administered by Univ. of Georgia) 2006, Bower Award for Business Leadership, Franklin Inst. 2006. *Yachting achievements include:* successful defence of 1977 America's Cup in yacht Courageous. *Publication:* The Racing Edge 1979. *Leisure interests:* fishing, sailing. *Website:* www.tedturner.com (office).

TURNER, Tina; American singer and songwriter; b. (Annie Mae Bullock), 26 Nov. 1939, Brownsville, Tenn.; m. 1st Ike Turner 1956 (divorced 1978); four s. (one deceased); m. 2nd Erwin Bach 2013; singer with Ike Turner Kings of Rhythm, Ike and Tina Turner Revue 1958–78; numerous concert tours worldwide; solo artist 1978–; Chevalier, Ordre des Arts et des Lettres; Grammy Awards include for Record of the Year, Song of the Year, Best Female Vocal Performance, Best Female Rock Vocal, MTV Music Video Award 1985, American Music Awards for Favorite Soul/R&B Female Artist, for Best Video Artist 1985, for Best Female Pop/Rock Artist 1986, World Music Award for Outstanding Contribution to the Music Industry 1993, Kennedy Center Honor 2005. *Films include:* Gimme Shelter 1970, Soul to Soul 1971, Tommy 1975, Mad Max: Beyond Thunderdome 1985, What's Love Got to Do with It (vocals) 1993, Last Action Hero 1993. *Recordings include:* albums: with Ike Turner: River Deep, Mountain High 1966, Outa Season 1969, The Hunter 1969, Proud Mary 1970, Come Together 1970, Workin' Together 1971, 'Nuff Said 1971, Blues Roots 1972, Feel Good 1972, Nutbush City Limits 1974, The Gospel According to Ike and Tina 1974; solo: Let Me Touch Your Mind 1972, Tina Turns the Country On 1974, Acid Queen 1975, Rough 1978, Private Dancer 1984, Break Every Rule 1986, Foreign Affair 1989, Wildest Dreams 1996, Dues Paid 1999, Twenty Four Seven 1999, Simply the Best 2002, All the Best 2005, The Platinum Collection 2009, Love Songs 2014. *Publication:* I, Tina (autobiography) 1985. *Address:* c/o Roger Davies, RD Worldwide Management, 1158 26th Street, Suite 564, Santa Monica, CA 90403, USA (office). *Website:* www.tinaturnerofficial .com.

TURNER OF ECCHINSWELL, Baron (Life Peer), cr. 2005, of Ecchinswell in the County of Hampshire; **(Jonathan) Adair Turner,** MA; British business executive, financial administrator and academic; *Senior Research Fellow, Institute for New Economic Thinking;* b. 5 Oct. 1955, Ipswich, Suffolk; s. of Geoffrey Vincent Turner and Kathleen Margaret Turner; m. Orna Ní Chionna 1985; two d.; ed Hutcheson's Grammar School, Glasgow, Glenalmond School, Gonville & Caius Coll., Cambridge; grew up in Crawley and East Kilbride; Pres. Cambridge Union 1977, also Chair. Univ.'s Conservative Asscn; Coll. Supervisor in Econs, Gonville & Caius Coll. 1979–82, taught part time in parallel with business career; began career with BP (British Petroleum) PLC 1979; with Chase Manhattan Bank 1979–82; joined Social Democratic Party 1981; McKinsey & Co. 1982–95, Dir 1994–95; Dir-Gen. CBI 1995–99; Vice-Chair. Merrill Lynch Europe 2000–06; Strategic Adviser to British Prime Minister 2001–02; Chair. Policy Cttee, Centre for Econ. Performance 1999–2008, Low Pay Comm. 2002–06, Pensions Comm. 2003–06, Overseas Devt Inst.'s Council 2007, Cttee on Climate Change 2008–13, Financial Services Authority 2008–13 (FSA abolished and role split between Financial Conduct Authority and Prudential Regulation Authority); Sr Research Fellow, Inst. for New Econ. Thinking (think tank co-f. by George Soros), London 2013–; Dir (non-exec.) United News and Media 2000–, Netscalibur Ltd 2000–01, Standard Chartered Bank –2008; mem. British Overseas Trade Bd 1995–99, Econ. and Social Research Council (Chair. 2007), Group of Thirty Consultative Group on Int. Econ. and Monetary Affairs, Inc. (G-30), Washington, DC; Visiting Prof., LSE 1999–, City Univ. 2004–; Trustee, Save the Children UK –2008, Worldwide Fund for Nature UK 2002–08; mem. House of Lords 2005–. *Publication:* Just Capital: The Liberal Economy 2001. *Leisure interests:* skiing, opera, theatre, gardening. *Address:* c/o Institute for New Economic Thinking, 570 Lexington Avenue, 39th Floor, New York, NY 10022, USA. *Telephone:* (212) 444-9612. *E-mail:* info@ ineteconomics.org. *Website:* ineteconomics.org.

TURNQUEST, (Kevin) Peter, BBA, MBA; Bahamian accountant, business executive and politician; *Deputy Prime Minister and Minister of Finance;* b. 22 Aug. 1964, Pinefield, Acklins; s. of Geron Turnquest and Sylvia Turnquest; m. Sonia Turnquest; one s. one d.; ed Prairie View A&M Univ., Texas, Nova Southeastern Univ., Florida; Exec. Vice-Pres. Telecom Trading and Consulting Inc.; Chair. and Partner SkyBahamas Airlines Ltd; mem. House of Ass. (lower house of parl.) for East Grand Bahama 2012–; Deputy Prime Minister and Minister of Finance 2017–; fmr Pres. Grand Bahama Chamber of Commerce; mem. Bahamas Inst. of Chartered Accountants; fmr mem. Bahamas Trade Comm., Bahamas Customs Consultative Cttee, Grand Bahama Port Licensing Authority; mem. Free Nat. Movt, currently Deputy Leader. *Address:* Ministry of Finance, Cecil Wallace-Whitfield Centre, West Bay Street, POB N 3017, Nassau, Bahamas (office). *Telephone:* 327-1530 (office). *Fax:* 327-1618 (office). *E-mail:* financemail@bahamas.gov.bs (office); mofgeneral@bahamas.gov.bs (office). *Website:* www.bahamas.gov.bs/finance (office).

TURNQUEST, Orville A. T. (Tommy); Bahamian politician; b. 16 Nov. 1959, Nassau; s. of Sir Orville Turnquist (fmr Gov.-Gen.) and Lady Edith Turnquist; m. Shawn Carey; two s. one d.; ed St Anne's School, Nassau, Malvern Coll., UK and Univ. of Western Ontario, Canada; began career with Canadian Imperial Bank of Commerce; mem. Free Nat. Movt (FNM) 1985–, fmr Vice-Pres., Leader 2002–05; mem. Parl. 1992–2002, 2007–12; Parl. Sec., Office of the Prime Minister 1992–95; Minister of State for Public Service and Labour 1995–96, for Public Works 1996–97; Minister of Works 1997–98, of Public Service, Immigration and Nat. Insurance 1998–2000, of Tourism 2000–02, of Nat. Security and Immigration 2007–12. *E-mail:* tommyt@tommyturnquest.org. *Website:* www.tommyturnquest.org.

TURNQUEST, Sir Orville (Alton), GCMG, QC, LLB, JP; Bahamian lawyer, politician and judge; b. 19 July 1929, Grants Town, New Providence; s. of Robert Turnquest and Gwendolyn Turnquest; m. Edith Louise Thompson 1955; one s. two d.; ed Govt High School, Univ. of London, Lincoln's Inn, London; articled in chambers of Hon. A. F. Adderley 1947–53; called to The Bahamas Bar 1953, to English Bar (Lincoln's Inn) 1960; in pvt. practice 1953–92; stipendiary and circuit magistrate and coroner 1959; law tutor and mem. Examining Bd, The Bahamas Bar 1965–92; Sec.-Gen. Progressive Liberal Party 1960–62; MP for S Cen. Nassau 1962–67, for Montagu 1982–94; Opposition Leader in Senate 1972–79; Deputy Leader Free Nat. Movt 1987–94; Attorney-Gen. 1992–94, Minister of Justice 1992–93, of Foreign Affairs 1992–94, Deputy Prime Minister 1993–94, currently Leader; Gov.-Gen. The Bahamas 1995–2001; mem. Del. to first Bahamas Constitutional Conf., London 1963, Bahamas Independence Conf., London 1972; fmr Pres. Bahamas Bar Asscn; Chair. Bahamas Bar Council 1970–72; Pres. Commonwealth Parl. Asscn 1992–93; Patron The Bahamas Games; Chancellor of Diocese of Nassau and The Bahamas 1965–2002; mem. Anglican Cen. Educational Authority, Nat. Cttee of United World Colls, Bd of Govs St John's Coll., St Anne's High School; Chair. Bd of Trustees Gov.-Gen.'s Youth Award 2007–17; fmr mem. Prov. Synod, Anglican Church of West Indies; Life mem. Rotary Int., Salvation Army Advisory Bd; Hon. LLD (Elmira Coll. NY, USA) 1998, (Univ. of West Indies) 2000; Hon. LHD (Sojourner-Douglass Coll., USA) 2002; Hon. Bencher, Lincoln's Inn; President's Assocs (Nova Southeastern Univ. Fla USA). *Leisure interests:* tennis, swimming, music, reading. *Address:* Kalamalka, Skyline Drive, POB N-682, Nassau, Bahamas (home). *Telephone:* (242) 3277951 (home). *Fax:* (242) 3274994 (home).

TUROK, Neil Geoffrey, OC, PhD; South African/ British physicist and academic; *Director, Perimeter Institute for Theoretical Physics;* b. 16 Nov. 1958, Johannesburg, S Africa; s. of Ben Turock and Mary Turok; ed Churchill Coll., Univ. of Cambridge, Imperial Coll., London; fmr Assoc. Scientist, Fermilab, Chicago; Prof. of Physics, Princeton Univ. 1994–97; Chair. of Math. Physics, Univ. of Cambridge 1997–2008; f. African Inst. for Math. Sciences, Muizenberg 2003; Dir Perimeter Inst. for Theoretical Physics (ind. research inst.), Canada 2008–, also Mike and Ophelia Lazaridis Niels Bohr Chair in Theoretical Physics 2013–; Dr hc (Univ. of Ottawa) 2011, (Nelson Mandela Univ.) 2014, (St Mary's Univ.) 2014, (Stellenbosch Univ.) 2015; Maxwell Medal, Inst. of Physics 1992, Most Innovative People Award for Social Innovation, World Summit on Innovation and Entrepreneurship 2008, TED (Tech., Entertainment, Design Conf.) Prize 2008, John Torrence Tate Award for Int. Leadership in Physics 2016. *Publications:* Global Texture 1999, Structure Formation in the Universe (co-author) 2001, Endless Universe: Beyond the Big Bang (co-author) 2007. *Address:* Perimeter Institute for Theoretical Physics, 31 Caroline Street, North Waterloo, ON N2L 2Y5, Canada (office). *Telephone:* (519) 569-7600 (office). *Fax:* (519) 569-7611 (office). *Website:* www.perimeterinstitute.ca (office).

TUROW, Scott F., JD; American writer and lawyer; *Partner, Dentons;* b. 12 April 1949; s. of David Turow and Rita Pastron; ed Amherst Coll. and Stanford and Harvard Univs; mem. Bar, Ill. 1978, US Dist Court. Ill. 1978, US Court of Appeals (7th Circuit) 1979; Assoc., Suffolk Co. Dist Attorney, Boston 1977–78; Asst US Attorney, US Dist Court, Ill., Chicago 1978–86; Partner, Sonnenschein, Nath & Rosenthal (now Dentons), Chicago 1986–; mem. Chicago Council of Lawyers; mem. Bd of Trustees, Poetry Foundation 2016–; Order of Lincoln 2000; inducted as Laureate, Lincoln Acad. of Illinois. *Publications include:* One L.: An Inside Account of Life in the First Year at Harvard Law School 1977, Presumed Innocent 1987, The Burden of Proof 1990, Pleading Guilty 1993, The Laws of Our Fathers 1996, Personal Injuries 1999, Reversible Errors 2002, Ultimate Punishment: A Lawyer's Reflections on Dealing with the Death Penalty 2003, Ordinary Heroes 2006, The Best American Mystery Stories (ed.) 2006, Limitations 2007, Innocent 2010, Identical 2013, Testimony 2017; contribs to professional journals. *Address:* Dentons, 233 South Wacker Drive, Suite 7800, Chicago, IL 60606-6404, USA (office). *Telephone:* (312) 876-8163 (office). *E-mail:* scott.turow@dentons.com (office). *Website:* www.dentons.com (office); www.scottturow.com.

TURSUNBEKOV, Chynybay; Kyrgyzstani politician; b. 15 Oct. 1960, Jan-Bulak, Naryn Dist, Naryn Oblast, Kyrgyz SSR, USSR; m.; three c.; ed Kyrgyz State Univ., Acad. of Sciences of Kyrgyz SSR, Diplomatic Acad. of Ministry of Foreign Affairs of Kyrgyz Repub.; Ed., then Sr Ed., Kyrgyzstan politics publishing house 1983–; Lecturer, Ed. Lecturer, Vice-Dean, Faculty of Kyrgyz Philology and Journalism, Kyrgyz State Univ. 1989–92; rep. of Kyrgyz Ministry of Education in Turkey 1993–94; specialist on Kyrgyzstan, Turkish Int. Co-operation and Devt Agency 1995–97; Dir 'Manas Epics', Manas-1000 State Cttee; corresp., Radio Liberty in Turkey; Gen. Dir Akun Closed JSC 1997–2010; Dir-Gen. Bishkek Flour Mill; Chair. Kerege JSC; Pres. Union of Entrepreneurs of Kyrgyz Repub.; Co-Chair. Kyrgyz-Turkish Business Council of Turkish Bd for Foreign Econ. Relations (DEIK), Turkish Ministry of the Economy; mem. Kyrgyzstandyn Sotsial-Demokratiyalyk Partiyasy (KSDP—Social Democratic Party of Kyrgyzstan), Leader 2015–16; mem. (KSDP), Supreme Council (Jogorku Kenesh—Parl.) 2010–, Leader of Parl. Faction 2015–, Leader of Parl. Majority 2015–, Chair. 2016–17; Businessman of the Year 1999, Diploma of Kyrgyz Repub. 2000, 'Dank' Medal for services to econ. devt 2003. *Address:* Kyrgyzstandyn Sotsial-Demokratiyalyk Partiyasy (Social Democratic Party of Kyrgyzstan), 720000 Bishkek, Shabdan Batyr 46D, Kyrgyzstan (office). *Telephone:* (312) 53-33-23 (office). *Fax:* (312) 53-00-01 (office). *E-mail:* press@sdpk.kg (office). *Website:* www.sdpk.kg (office).

TURSUNKULOV, Nurlan Janyshevich; Kyrgyzstani lawyer and politician; b. 11 Aug. 1968, Bishkek; ed Kyrgyz State Univ.; served in Soviet Army 1986–88; Legal Consultant, Chui Oblast 1992–93; legal practise in Bishkek 1993–94; Asst Public Prosecutor, Bishkek 1994, Procurator Gen. 1994–96, Deputy Public Prosecutor, Naryn Oblast 1996–98, Chui Oblast 1999–2000, Public Prosecutor, Kara Suu Dist 2000–05, Talas Oblast 2005–06, Asst Mil. Prosecutor, Repub. of Kyrgyzstan 2006–08, Minister of Justice 2008–10; Prosecutor-Gen. 2009–10.

TURTELBOOM, Annemie, Licenciée en économie; Belgian politician; b. 22 Nov. 1967, Ninove; m.; two c.; ed Catholic Univ. of Leuven, Katholieke Hogeschool, Leuven; fmr Chair. Christian Democratic Students; mem. Town Council, Puurs 2001–07, Leader of Council 2007; Lector and Head of Dept, KHLeuven –2003; began political career with Christian People's Party (CVP) which later formed alliance with NCD (New Christian Democrats), NCD later joined Vlaamse Liberalen en Demokraten (Open VLD—Flemish Liberals and Democrats-Flemish-speaking wing); Fed. mem. Parl. (VLD) for Antwerp 2003–07, specializing in Social Affairs, Work and Pensions; Minister for Immigration and Asylum Policy 2008–09, Minister of Home Affairs (first woman) 2009–11, of Justice 2011–14; Minister of Finance and Energy, Flemish Govt 2014–16; mem. European Court of Auditors (ECA) 2018–. *Address:* European Court of Auditors, 12 rue Alcide De Gasperi, 1615, Luxembourg (office). *Telephone:* 524-39-81 (office). *Website:* www.eca.europa.eu (office); www.annemieturtelboom.be.

TURTURRO, John; American/Italian actor and film director; b. 28 Feb. 1957, Brooklyn, New York; s. of Nicholas Turturro and Katherine Turturro; m. Katherine Borowitz; one s.; ed State Univ. of New York at New Paltz and Yale Drama School; Obie Award for stage appearance in Danny and the Deep Blue Sea. *Films include:* Raging Bull, Desperately Seeking Susan, Exterminator III, The Flamingo Kid, To Live and Die in LA, Hannah and Her Sisters, Gung Ho, Offbeat, The Color of Money, The Italian Five Corners, Do the Right Thing, Miller's Crossing, Men of Respect, Mo' Better Blues, Jungle Fever, Barton Fink (Best Actor Award, Cannes Film Festival 1991), Brain Doctors, Mac (co-author, dir and actor), Being Human, Quiz Show, Fearless, Clockers, Search and Destroy, Unstrung Heroes, Sugartime (dir), Grace of My Heart (dir), Box of Moonlight (dir), The Truce (dir), The Big Lebowski 1997, Animals 1997, Lesser Prophets 1998, Rounders 1998, Illuminata (dir) 1998, The Source 1999, The Cradle Will Rock 1999, Company Man 1999, Two Thousand and None 1999, Oh Brother, Where Art Thou? 1999, The Man Who Cried 1999, The Luzhin Defense 1999, Thirteen Conversations About One Thing (dir) 2000, Collateral Damage (dir) 2001, Mr Deeds 2002, Fear X 2003, Anger Management 2003, 2BPerfectlyHonest 2004, Secret Passage 2004, Secret Window 2004, She Hate Me 2004, Romance and Cigarettes (dir) 2005, Quelques jours en septembre 2006, The Good Shepherd 2006, Slipstream 2007, Transformers 2007, Margot at the Wedding 2007, You Don't Mess with the Zohan 2008, What Just Happened? 2008, Miracle at St. Anna 2008, The Taking of Pelham 1 2 3 2009, Transformers: Revenge of the Fallen 2009, Transformers: Dark of the Moon 2011, Fading Gigolo 2013, Gods Behaving Badly 2013, God's Pocket 2014, Exodus: Gods and Kings 2014, Rio, I Love You 2014, Mia Madre 2015, The Ridiculous 6 2015. *Television includes:* The Bronx Is Burning 2007. *Address:* c/o Bart Walker, Creative Artists Agency LLC, 405 Lexington Avenue, 19th Floor, New York, NY 10174, USA (office).

TURUNEN, Antti; Finnish diplomatist and UN official; *Representative of the Secretary-General for Georgia, United Nations;* joined Foreign Service 1985, served in Washington, DC and Moscow, and as Adviser to EU High Rep. Javier Solana, Head of Unit for Eastern Europe and Cen. Asia, Ministry of Foreign Affairs 2004–07, led EU fact-finding mission to Tashkent, Uzbekistan Aug. 2006, Head of Perm. Mission to OSCE, Vienna 2007–10, chaired Perm. Council of OSCE during the Finnish Chairmanship 2008, was involved, among others, in settlement of Georgian-Ossetian conflict; Rep. of UN Sec.-Gen. for Georgia (Jt Incident Prevention and Response Mechanism) 2010–. *Address:* United Nations Observer Mission in Georgia (UNOMIG), 38 Krtsanisi Street, 380060 Tbilisi, Georgia (office); Office of the Secretary-General, United Nations, New York, NY 10017, USA (office). *Telephone:* (32) 926700 (Tbilisi) (office); (212) 963-1234 (New York) (office). *Fax:* (212) 963-4879 (New York) (office). *E-mail:* info@unomig.org (office). *Website:* www.unomig.org (office).

TUSA, Sir John, Kt, MA; British broadcaster and administrator; b. 2 March 1936, Zlín, Czechoslovakia (now Czech Repub.); s. of Jan Tusa and Lydie Sklenarova; m. Ann Hilary Dowson 1960; two s.; ed Gresham's School, Holt, Trinity Coll., Cambridge; joined BBC as general trainee 1960; Producer, Talks and Features, BBC World Service 1964–66; Ed., Forum World Features 1966–67; Presenter, The World Tonight, Radio 4 1970–78, 24 Hours, BBC World Service 1972–78, Newsweek, BBC2 1978–79, Newsnight, BBC2 1979–86, Timewatch, BBC2 1982–84, One O'Clock News BBC 1993–95; Chair. London News Radio 1993–94; Pres. Wolfson Coll., Cambridge Feb.–Oct. 1993; Man. Dir BBC World Service 1986–92; Man. Dir Barbican Centre 1995–2007; Chair. Advisory Cttee, Govt Art Collection 1993–2003, BBC Marshall Plan of the Mind Trust 1992–99; Chair. Clore Leadership Programme 2009–14; mem. Bd ENO 1994–2005; Freeman, City of London 1997; Chair. Wigmore Hall Trust 1999–2011, Univ. of the Arts, London 2007–13, Architecture Club 2007–13; Vice-Chair. British Museum 2000–08; Visiting Prof., Dept of Arts Policy and Man., City Univ.; Trustee, Trustee of The Turquoise Mountain Trust Foundation, Nat. Portrait Gallery 1988–2000, Design Museum 1998–2000, Journalism Foundation 2012; Hon. Chair. theartsdesk.com

2010; Hon. mem. RAM 1999, Guildhall School of Music and Drama 1999; Order of the White Rose (Finland) 1998; Dr hc (Heriot-Watt) 1993, (Kingston) 2007, Hon. LLD (London) 1993, Hon. DLitt (City Univ.) 1997, (Essex) 2006, (Kent) 2007; Royal TV Soc. (RTS) TV Journalist of the Year 1984, BAFTA Richard Dimbleby Award 1984, Broadcasting Press Guild Award 1991, RTS Presenter of the Year 1995, Broadcasting Press Guild Radio Programme of the Year (for 20/20 – A View of the Century) 1995. *Publications include:* The Nuremberg Trial (with Ann Tusa) 1983, The Berlin Blockade (with Ann Tusa) 1988, Conversations with the World 1990, A World in Your Ear 1992, Art Matters 1999, On Creativity 2003, The Janus Aspect: Artists in the 21st Century 2005, Engaged with the Arts: Writings from the Frontline 2007, Pain in the Arts 2014. *Leisure interests:* tennis, string quartets, listening. *Address:* 16 Canonbury Place, London, N1 2NN, England (home). *Telephone:* (20) 7704-2451 (home). *E-mail:* john.tusa@hotmail.co.uk (home).

TUSCHL, Thomas, PhD; German biochemist, molecular biologist and academic; *Professor, The Rockefeller University;* b. 1 June 1966, Altdorf bei Nürnberg; ed Univ. of Regensburg, Max Planck Inst. for Experimental Medicine, Göttingen; Jr Investigator, Max Planck Inst. for Biophysical Chem. 1999–2003; fmr Researcher, Biology Dept, Whitehead Inst. for Biomedical Research, MIT 1995–99; Assoc. Prof. and Head of Lab., The Rockefeller Univ. 2003–09, Prof. 2009–; Investigator, Howard Hughes Medical Inst. 2005–18; mem. German Nat. Acad. of Sciences Leopoldina; Fellow, New York Acad. of Sciences 2005; Biofuture Award, German Govt 1999, Young Investigator Award, European Molecular Biology Org. 2001, Otto Klung Weberbank Prize for Chem. and Physics, Berlin 2002, Eppendorf Young Investigator Award, Hamburg 2002, Wiley Prize in Biomedical Sciences 2003, Mayor's Award for Excellence in Science and Tech. 2003, AAAS Newcomb Cleveland Prize 2003, Ernst Schering Prize (for basic scientific research) 2005, Meyenburg Prize 2005, Irma T. Hirschl Career Scientist Award 2005, Dr Albert Wander Gedenk Prize, Bern 2005, Molecular Bioanalytics Prize 2006, Max Delbrück Medal, Berlin 2007, Ernst Jung Prize 2008, NIH Director's Transformative Research Project Award 2012. *Publications:* numerous scientific papers in professional journals on studies of RNA interference. *Address:* Howard Hughes Medical Institute Laboratory of RNA, Molecular Biology, The Rockefeller University, 1230 York Avenue, Box 186, New York, NY 10065, USA (office). *Telephone:* (212) 327-7651 (ext. 7651) (office). *E-mail:* thomas.tuschl@rockefeller.edu (office). *Website:* www.rockefeller.edu/research/faculty/labheads/ThomasTuschl (office).

TUSK, Donald Franciszek; Polish politician; *President, European Council;* b. 22 April 1957, Gdańsk; s. of Donald Tusk and Ewa Tusk; m. Małgorzata Tusk; one s. one d.; ed Gdańsk Univ.; journalist Maritime Publishing House, with magazines Pomerania and Samorządność; with Gdańsk Height Services Work Co-operative; Deputy ed. Gazeta Gdańska 1989; mem. Liquidation Cttee RSW Press-Books-Ruch; assoc. Free Trade Unions by the Coast; co.-f. Niezależne Zrzeszenie Studentów (Ind. Students Union); mem. Solidarność (Solidarity) Trade Union 1980–89; Founder and Ed. underground Publ Przegląd Polityczny; Leader Programme Council for Liberals Foundation; Leader Congress of Liberals 1989, later the Kongres Liberalno-Demokratyczny (Liberal-Democratic Congress), Chair. 1991–94; Vice-Chair. Unia Wolności (Freedom Union) 1994 following merger with Unia Demokratyczna (Democratic Union); Deputy to Sejm (Parl.) (Gdynia/Słupsk constituency) 1991–93, 2001–, Deputy Marshal of Sejm 2001–05, mem. Civic Platform Parl. Caucus 2001–; Chair. Parl. Liberal-Democratic Caucus and Special Cttee for Consideration of Constitutional Acts 1991–93; Senator (Gdańsk Voivodship) and Vice-Marshal of Senate 1997–2001; Co-founder Platforma Obywatelska (Civic Platform) 2001, Leader 2005–; unsuccessful cand. in presidential elections 2006; Prime Minister of Poland 2007–14; Pres. European Council Dec. 2014–; Grand Cross, Order of the Sun (Peru) 2008, Grand Cross, Royal Norwegian Order of Merit 2012, Order of the Cross of Terra Mariana (Estonia) 2014; Silver Mouth Award, Radio Three (Sweden) 2004, Karlspreis of the City of Aachen, Germany 2010. *Publications:* Kashubian Lake District 1985, Once There Was Gdańsk 1996, Gdańsk 1945, 1998, Old Sopot 1998, Ideas of Gdańsk's Liberalism 1998. *Leisure interests:* football, old photography. *Address:* Office of the President of the European Council, Justus Lipsius Building, 175 rue de la Loi, 1048 Brussels, Belgium (office). *Telephone:* (2) 281-61-11 (Brussels) (office). *Fax:* (2) 281-69-34 (Brussels) (office). *E-mail:* ec.president@european-council.europa.eu (office); poczta@platforma.org (office). *Website:* www.consilium.europa.eu/en/european-council/president (office).

TUSQUETS BLANCA, Oscar; Spanish architect and designer; b. 14 June 1941, Barcelona; m. Eva Blanch; one s. one d.; ed Arts & Crafts School, Barcelona, School of Architecture, Barcelona; with Luis Clotet, Studio Per 1964–84; Co-Founder BD Ediciones de Diseño 1972; Prof., School of Architecture, Barcelona 1975–76, 1979–80; f. Tusquets, Diaz & Assoc. Architects' Office, with Carlos Diaz 1987; Chevalier des Arts et des Lettres; FAD Architecture Prize (five times), FAD Design prize (six times), Sant Jordi Cross 1987, Ciutat de Barcelona Prize 1988, 1989, Nat. Prize for Design 1988, Fukuoka Beautification Award 1994, Medalla de Oro 1998. *Work includes:* Casa Fullá, Barcelona, Belvedere Regas, Girona, Casa Vittoria, Sala Mae West, Dali Museum, Figueras, remodelling of Music Palace, Barcelona, Pavilion, Parc de la Villette, Paris, Chandon Vinery, Barcelona, dwellings in Kashii, Fukuoka and in Olympic Village, Barcelona, La Coupole, Montpellier, music auditorium, Canary Islands, public square, shopping mall and dwellings, Den Bosch, Netherlands; design of furniture and objects for various producers, bus stop for Hanover, Germany. *Publications include:* Más que discutible 1994, Todo es comparable 1998, Dios lo ve 2000, Dalí y otros amigos 2003, Contra la desnudez 2007, Tiempos que fueron 2012, Amables Personajes 2014. *Leisure interest:* painting. *Address:* Arquitecturas Oscar Tusquets Blanca, Abadessa Olzet 7, 08034 Barcelona, Spain (office). *Telephone:* (93) 2520488 (office). *E-mail:* info@tusquets.com (office). *Website:* www.tusquets.com (office).

TUTKUS, Lt-Gen. (retd) Valdas; Lithuanian military officer; b. 27 Dec. 1960, Vilnius; m.; one s.; ed Frunze Mil. Acad., NATO Defence Coll., Italy; Second Lt Motorised Infantry Battalion 1982; served in Afghanistan 1983–85; promoted to First Lt 1984; Founding mem. Lithuanian Armed Forces 1991; Chief of Jt Staff, Ministry of Defence 1992–94; First Deputy Commdr, Armed Forces 1994–96, Deputy Commdr 1996–99; Mil. Rep. to NATO, Brussels, to EU, to WEU 1999–2001; Commdr Land Forces 2001–04; Chief of Defence 2004–09; Gen. Man. Hoptrans (transport and logistics co.) 2010–; Officer Order of Vytautas the Great; Commemorative Badge to mark Russian Troops Withdrawal from Lithuania, Honour Award for Merits to Nat. Defence System, Honour Award Iron Wolf, Nat. Defence System Level Medal of Merit, Nat. Defence Minister's Letters of Merit. *Address:* Hoptrans, Olimpiečių Str. 1A, Vilnius 09235, Lithuania (office). *Telephone:* (5) 200-0511 (office). *E-mail:* valdas@htpr.lt (office). *Website:* www.htpr.lt (office).

TUTTLE, Robert Holmes, MBA; American business executive and fmr diplomatist; *Co-Chairman, Pacific Council on International Policy;* b. 4 Aug. 1943, Calif.; m. Maria Denise Hummer; two d. from previous m.; ed Stanford Univ., Univ. of Southern California; Asst to US Pres. Ronald Reagan 1982–85, Dir of Presidential Personnel 1985–89; Co-Man. Partner, Tuttle-Click Automotive Group; Amb. to UK 2005–09; Co-Chair. Pacific Council on Int. Policy; fmr mem. Bd Woodrow Wilson Int. Center for Scholars, Ronald Reagan Presidential Library Foundation, Annenberg School of Communication, Univ. of Southern Calif., Los Angeles Museum of Contemporary Art (Chair. 2001–04); mem. Advisory Bd Center on Communication Leadership and Policy, Univ. of Southern Calif. Annenberg School for Communication and Journalism. *Address:* Pacific Council on International Policy, 801 South Figueroa Street, Suite 1130, Los Angeles, CA 90017, USA (office). *Telephone:* (213) 221-2000 (office). *Fax:* (213) 221-2050 (office). *E-mail:* info@pacificcouncil.org (office). *Website:* www.pacificcouncil.org (office); www.tuttleclick.com (office).

TUTU, Most Rev. Desmond Mpilo, MTh; South African ecclesiastic (retd) and academic; b. 7 Oct. 1931, Klerksdorp; s. of Zachariah Tutu and Aletta Tutu; m. Leah Nomalizo Tutu 1955; one s. three d.; ed Bantu High School, Bantu Normal Coll., Univ. of South Africa, St Peter's Theological Coll., Rosettenville, King's Coll., Univ. of London; schoolmaster 1954–57; parish priest 1960; Theological Seminary Lecturer 1967–69; Univ. Lecturer 1970–71; Assoc. Dir Theological Educ. Fund, World Council of Churches 1972–75; Dean of Johannesburg 1975–76; Bishop of Lesotho 1977–78, of Johannesburg 1984–86; Archbishop of Cape Town, Metropolitan of the Church of the Prov. of Southern Africa 1986–95, Archbishop Emer. 1995–; Chancellor Univ. of Western Cape 1988–; Chair. Truth and Reconciliation Comm. 1995–99; Pres. All Africa Conf. of Churches 1987–97; Sec.-Gen. South African Council of Churches 1979–84; Visiting Prof. of Anglican Studies, New York Gen. Theological Seminary 1984; elected to Harvard Univ. Bd of Overseers 1989; Dir Coca-Cola 1986–; Visiting Prof., Emory Univ., Atlanta 1998–2000; Visiting Prof. in Post-Conflict Studies, King's Coll., London 2004–; f. Desmond Tutu Peace Centre, Cape Town, supported by Desmond Tutu Peace Trust; Chair., The Elders (independent group of eminent global leaders) 2007–; mem. Third Order of the Soc. of St Francis; Freedom of Borough of Merthyr Tydfil (Wales), Durham, Hull, Borough of Lewisham (UK), Florence, Lecco (Italy), Kinshasa (Democratic Repub. of Congo), Krugersdorp, Cape Town (SA); Order of Jamaica; Hon. DD, DCL, LLD, ThD (Gen. Theol. Sem. New York, Kent Univ., Harvard Univ., Ruhr Bochum Univ.); Hon. DDiv (Aberdeen) 1981; Hon. STD (Columbia) 1982; Dr hc (Mount Allison Univ., Sackville, NB, Strasbourg) 1988, (Oxford) 1990; Hon. LLD (South Bank Univ.) 1994; Hon. DD (Exeter) 1997; FKC (Fellow of King's Coll. London); numerous awards including Onassis Award, Family of Man Gold Medal 1983, Nobel Peace Prize 1984, Carter-Menil Human Rights Prize 1986, Martin Luther King Jr Humanitarian Award 1986, Third World Prize (jt recipient) 1989, Grand Cross of Merit, Germany 1996, Bill of Rights Award, American Civil Liberation Union Fund 1997, Henry W. Edgerton Civil Liberties Award, American Civil Liberties Union 1997, One Hundred Black Men Award, USA 1997, Peace Prize, Int. Community of UNESCO, Athens 1997, Gandhi Peace Prize 2007, Presidential Medal of Freedom 2009, Templeton Prize 2013. *Publications include:* Crying in the Wilderness 1982, Hope and Suffering 1983 (both collections of sermons and addresses), The Rainbow People of God 1994, An African Prayer Book 1996, No Future Without Forgiveness 1999, Made for Goodness: And Why this Makes all the Difference (with Mpho Tutu) 2010, The Book of Forgiving (with Mpho Tutu) 2014. *Leisure interests* reading, music, jogging. *Address:* c/o Desmond Tutu Peace Trust, PO Box 8428, Roggebaai, 8012 Cape Town, South Africa (office). *Telephone:* (21) 4257002 (office). *Fax:* (21) 4189468 (office). *E-mail:* info@tutu.org (office). *Website:* www.tutu.org (office).

ŢUŢUIANU, Adrian; Romanian lawyer and politician; b. 1 Aug. 1965; m. Carmen Elena Ţuţuianu; ed Bucharest Univ., Nat. Defence Coll.; worked as lawyer, Târgovişte 1999–2012; Assoc. Prof., Faculty of Law and Admin. Sciences, Valahia Univ., Târgovişte 2000–; County Councillor, Dâmbovita 2004–08, Pres., Dâmbovita County Council 2012–16; mem. Senatul (upper house of Parl.) (PSD) 2008–12, 2016–; Minister of Nat. Defence June–Sept. 2017; mem. Partidul Social Democrat (PSD) 1998–, mem. PSD Nat. Council 2010–12; mem. Bd of Dirs and Vice-Chair. SC Eurofinances SA 1996–97; mem. Bd of Dirs and Chair. EUROintermed SA 1997–98; Dir SC Leader Lease SA, Bucharest 1995; mem. Romanian Bar Asscn, Romanian Soc. of European Law, Centre for Academic Excellence, Centre for Research in Social Sciences. *Address:* c/o Ministry of National Defence, 050561 Bucharest 5, Str. Izvor 110, Romania (office).

TUWAIJRI, Abdulrahman al-, PhD; Saudi Arabian economist; b. 23 Feb. 1955, Almajmaah; s. of Abdulaziz al-Tuwaijri and Hussah al-Tuwaijri; m. Norah Alabdulatif 1982; three s. two d.; ed King Saud Univ. and Iowa State Univ., USA; grad. asst, Dept of Econs, King Saud Univ. 1978–84, Asst Prof. 1985–88; Econ. Adviser, Gen. Secr. of Cooperation Council for the Arab States of the Gulf 1988–90; Alt. Exec. Dir IMF 1991–95, Exec. Dir 1995–2001; Sec.-Gen., Supreme Econ. Council 2002–08; Chair. and CEO Capital Market Authority of the Kingdom of Saudi Arabia 2008–13; Founding mem. Saudi Econ. Asscn. *Leisure interests:* reading, swimming.

TUYAKBAY, Col-Gen. Jarmakhan Aitbaiuly, CandJur; Kazakhstani politician and jurist; *Leader, Freedom National Social-Democratic Party;* b. 22 Nov. 1947, South Kazakhstan Prov., Kazakh SSR, USSR; m. Bagilya Aptayeva; two s. one d.; ed Kirov Kazakh State Univ.; worked in prosecutors' bureau in S Kazakhstan –1978; Deputy Prosecutor-Gen. Kazakh SSR 1981; Prosecutor, Mangyshlak region, then Guryev region 1987–90; mem. Supreme Soviet, Repub. of Kazakhstan 1990; Prosecutor-Gen. Repub. of Kazakhstan 1990–95, Deputy Prosecutor-Gen., Chief Mil. Prosecutor 1997–99; Chair. State Investigation Comm. 1995–97; elected mem. Majlis (Parl.) 1999, Chair. 1999–2004; Leader, For a Just Kazakhstan Movt (Social Democrats) 2005–; Leader, Nat. Social Democratic Party, announced intention to merge with Real Bright Road—Democratic Party of Kazakhstan (Naghyz Ak Jol—Kazakstanyn Demokratiyalyk

Partiyasy) 2007, merged with Freedom party to form Freedom Nat. Social Democratic Party ('Azat' Jalpyulttyk Sotsial Demokratiyalyk Partiyasy—Azat JSDP) 2009–; unsuccessful presidential cand. 2005; Order of Barys 2001, Council of the Inter-Parliamentary Ass. of the CIS Order of Sodruzhestvo 2002. *Publications:* Development Prosecution in Kazakhstan in the Period of Reforms 1997; numerous articles. *Leisure Interests:* golf, reading. *Address:* Freedom National Social-Democratic Party, 050000 Almaty, Kabanbai batyr kosh. 58, Kazakhstan (office). *Telephone:* (727) 266-36-40 (office). *Fax:* (727) 266-36-43 (office). *E-mail:* ocdp@mail.ru (office).

TUYMANS, Luc; Belgian artist; b. 14 July 1958, Mortsel; m. Carla Arocha. *Address:* c/o Zeno X Gallery, Godtsstraat 15, 2140 Antwerp, Belgium. *Telephone:* (3) 216-16-26 (office). *E-mail:* info@zeno-x.com. *Website:* www.zeno-x.com.

TVEIT, Rev. Olav Fykse, DTheol; Norwegian theologian, ecclesiastic and international organization official; *General Secretary, World Council of Churches;* b. 24 Nov. 1960; ed Norwegian School of Theology/Menighetsfakultetet, Oslo; ordained as pastor in Church of Norway, served as parish priest in Haram, Møre Diocese 1988–91 and as army chaplain during compulsory year of nat. service 1987–88; Sec. Church of Norway Doctrinal Comm. 1999–2000, Church–State Relations 2001–02; Gen. Sec. Church of Norway Council on Ecumenical and Int. Relations 2002–09; mem. Faith and Order Plenary Comm. and Co-Chair. Palestine Israel Ecumenical Forum core group, WCC, Gen. Sec. WCC 2010–; mem. Bd of Dirs and Exec. Cttee Christian Council of Norway; Moderator of Church of Norway-Islamic Council of Norway contact group, Jewish Congregation contact group; mem. Bd of Dirs Global Partnership to End Violence Against Children; fmr mem. Inter-Faith Council of Norway, Bd of Trustees, Norwegian Church Aid; Dr hc (Hanshin Univ. Seoul) 2015, (Serampore Coll., India) 2018. *Publications include:* Evangeliet i vår kultur (The Gospel in our Culture; co-ed.) 1995, Mutual Accountability as Ecumenical Attitude. A Study in Ecumenical Ecclesiology Based on Faith and Order Texts 1948–1998 (thesis) 2001, Ei vedkjennande kyrkje. Hovudforedrag på Kyrkjemøtet 2004 2004, Christian Solidarity in the Cross of Christ 2012, The Truth We Owe Each Other: Mutual Accountability in the Ecumenical Movement 2016; several articles on ecumenism. *Address:* World Council of Churches, 150 route de Ferney, PO Box 2100, 1211 Geneva 2, Switzerland (office). *Telephone:* 227916111 (office). *Fax:* 227910361 (office). *E-mail:* dcb@wcc-coe.org (office). *Website:* www.oikoumene.org (office).

TVIRCUN, Victor, PhD; Moldovan diplomatist and international organization executive; b. 18 Oct. 1955, Chisinau; m.; two c.; ed State Univ. of Moldova; Lab. Asst, Pedagogical State Univ. 1980–93, Prof. 2010–12; Counsellor, Embassy in Ankara 1995–98, Deputy Dir, Main Div. of Europe and North America, Ministry of Foreign Affairs 1993–95, Dir 1998–99, Chargé d'affaires, Embassy in Budapest Hungary 1999–2001, Amb. to Turkey (also accred to Org. of the Black Sea Econ. Cooperation) 2001–05; Minister of Educ. and Youth 2005–08; Dir Inst. of European Integration and Political Science, Chisinau 2009–10; Sec.-Gen. Black Sea Econ. Cooperation 2012–15; mem. Acad. of Pedagogical and Sociological Science, Moscow, International Acad. of the Hi Educational School, Scientific Asscn of Genealogists, Moldova, Scientific Asscn of Genealogists (Russia); Honourable Citizen, Kars, Turkey, Honourable Citizen, Gagauz Yeri, Honourable Pres. Nat. Fed. of Karate-Do; Order of Honour, Order of Gloria Muncii, First Degree, Order of Orthodox Church of Chisinau and Moldova 'Cuviosul Paisii Velicicovschi', Order of the Moldavian Orthodox Church 'Stefan cel Marc', Second Degree, Order of the Russian Orthodox Patriarchate 'St. Vladimir', Third Degree, Order of 'United Europe', Gold Medal 'Suleyman Demirel', Turkey; Dr hc (State Univ., South Korea); Man of the Year Award, Europe Liberty, Czech Republic 2007.

TVRDÍK, Lt-Col Jaroslav, MSc(Econ); Czech politician and army officer; b. 11 Sept. 1968, Prague; m. Blanka Tvrdíková; one d.; ed Mil. School, Vyškov; Head of Financial Services, Schooling and Training Centre, Ministry of Defence 1990–91, Commanding Sr Officer, Foreign Relations Section 1991–92, Head of Dept 1993–95, Dir Interior Admin. 1996, Deputy Minister of Defence 2000–01, Minister of Defence 2001–03; Dir Mil. Spa and recreations facilities 1996–2000; Chief, Financial Services, Czechoslovak contingent, UNPROFOR 1993–95; mem. Parl. 2002–03; Chair. Bd of Dirs and Pres. CSA (Ceske Aerolinie a.s.) 2003–06; ČSSD election Campaign Manager and Chief Advisor 2006–10; Chair. Jt Czech Chinese Mixed Chamber of Mutual Cooperation 2012–14, Pres. 2014–; Vice-Chair. Supervisory Bd, SK Slavia Praha 2015–; UN Medal for Activity in UNPROFOR 1992–93, Anniversary Medal of Honour, NATO 2002. *Publication:* Transformation of the Army 2001. *Leisure interests:* squash, swimming, historical literature. *Address:* Czech Chinese Mixed Chamber of Mutual Cooperation, Na příkopě 857/18, 110 00 Prague 1, Czech Republic (office). *Telephone:* (2) 28927788 (office). *E-mail:* jaroslav.tvrdik@czechchina.com (office). *Website:* www.czechchina.com (office).

TWAIN, Shania; Canadian country singer and songwriter; b. (Eileen Regina Edwards), 28 Aug. 1965, Windsor, Ont.; d. of Gerry Twain and Sharon Twain; m. 1st Robert John Lange 1993 (divorced); one s.; m. 2nd Frederic Thiebaud 2011; Country Music Television Europe Rising Video Star of the Year 1993, Female Artist of the Year 1996, Canadian Country Music Award for Female Vocalist 1995, American Music Awards for Favorite New Country Artist 1995, Favorite Female Pop/Rock Artist 2000, Favorite Female Country Artist 2000, Grammy Awards for Best Female Country Vocal Performance, Best Country Song 2000, Juno Award for Songwriter of the Year 2000, Best Country Female Artist 2000, Billboard Award for Top Country Artist 2003, inducted into Canadian Music Hall of Fame 2011. *Recordings include:* albums: Shania Twain 1993, The Woman in Me (Grammy Award for Best Country Album 1996) 1995, Come On Over 1997, On The Way 1999, Beginnings 1989–1990 1999, Wild and Wicked 2000, Complete Limelight Sessions 2001, Up! (Billboard Award for Top Country Album 2003) 2002, Greatest Hits 2004, The Will of a Woman 2008, Still The One: Live From Vegas 2015, Now 2017. *Publications:* From This Moment On 2011. *Website:* www.shaniatwain.com.

TWEAH, Samuel D., Jr; Liberian economist and politician; *Minister of Finance and Development Planning;* b. 6 May 1971; ed Univ. of Liberia; mem. Congress for Democratic Change (CDC) 2005–; Consultant, Ministry of Finance and Devt Planning, seconded as Sr Economist on Millennium Challenge Corpn (MCC, econ. growth programme) Liberia Compact Team –2016; Sr Adviser to Bd of Dirs, African Devt Bank (ADB) 2016; Minister of Finance and Devt Planning 2018–; currently Chair. Liberia Inst. of Statistics & Geo-Information Services (LISGIS). *Address:* Ministry of Finance and Development Planning, Broad St, POB 10-9013, 1000 Monrovia 10, Liberia (office). *Website:* www.mfdp.gov.lr (office).

TWEEDIE, Sir David Philip, Kt, BCom, PhD, CA, FRSE; British chartered accountant; b. 7 July 1944; s. of Aidrian Ian Tweedie and Marie Patricia Tweedie (née Phillips); m. Janice Christine Brown 1970; two s.; ed Grangemouth High School, Univ. of Edin.; accountancy training Mann, Judd, Gordon (Glasgow) 1969–72; Lecturer in Accounting, Univ. of Edin. 1973–78; Tech. Dir Inst. of Chartered Accountants, Scotland 1978–81; Pnr, KMG Thomson McLintock 1982–87, KPMG Peat Marwick McLintock 1987–90; Chair. Accounting Standards Bd 1990–2000, Int. Accounting Standards Bd 2001–11; Pres. Inst. of Chartered Accountants of Scotland 2012–13; Chair. Royal Household Audit Cttee for Sovereign Grant; Chair. of Trustees, Int. Valuation Standards Council 2012–, Leuchie House, Scotland; Fellow, Judge Business School, Univ. of Cambridge; Hon. FIA 1999; Hon. FSIP 2004; Hon. FCCA 2005; Hon. DSc (Econ.) (Hull) 1993, Hon. LLD (Lancaster) 1993, (Exeter) 1997, (Dundee) 1998), Hon. DLitt (Heriot-Watt) 1996, Hon. DBA (Napier) 1999, (Oxford Brookes) 2004, Hon. DSc (SocSci) (Edinburgh) 2001; Founding Socs Award, Inst. of Chartered Accountants in England and Wales 1997, Chartered Inst. of Man. Accounting Award 1998, inducted into The Accounting Hall of Fame 2013. *Publications:* Financial Reporting, Inflation & The Capital Maintenance Concept 1979; co-author of three other books and contribs. to professional and academic journals. *Leisure interests:* athletics, watching rugby, walking, gardening. *Address:* International Valuation Standards Council, 1 King Street, London EC2V 8AU, England (office). *Telephone:* (20) 3178-7807 (office). *Fax:* (20) 7643-4099 (office). *E-mail:* contact@ivsc.org (office). *Website:* www.ivsc.org (office).

TWIGGY (see LAWSON, Lesley).

TWIN, Peter John, BSc, OBE, PhD, FRS, FInstP, CPhys; British physicist and academic; *Professor Emeritus of Experimental Physics, University of Liverpool;* b. 26 July 1939, London; s. of Arthur James Twin and Hilda Ethel Twin; m. Jean Leatherland 1963; one s. one d.; ed Sir George Monoux Grammar School, Walthamstow, London and Univ. of Liverpool; Lecturer, Univ. of Liverpool 1964, Sr Lecturer 1973, Sir James Chadwick Prof. of Experimental Physics 1987–96, Lyon Jones Prof. of Physics 1997–2001, Sr Fellow and Prof. Emer. 2001–; Head, Nuclear Structure Facility, Daresbury Lab. Cheshire 1983–87; Weatherill Medal, Franklin Inst. USA 1991, Bonner Prize, American Physical Soc. 1991, Lisa Meitner Prize, European Physical Soc. 2004. *Publications:* articles in professional journals. *Address:* Room 213C, Oliver Lodge Laboratory, Department of Physics, University of Liverpool, Liverpool, L69 7ZE, England (office). *Telephone:* (151) 794-3378 (office). *Fax:* (151) 794-3348 (office). *E-mail:* twin@ns.ph.liv.ac.uk (office). *Website:* ns.ph.liv.ac.uk (office).

TWOMEY, Paul, MA, PhD; Australian international organization executive; b. 18 July 1961; ed Univ. of Queensland, Pennsylvania State Univ., USA, Univ. of Cambridge, UK; consultant, McKinsey & Co. –1994; Exec. Gen. Man. for Europe, Austrade-the Australian Trade Comm. 1994–97; Founding CEO Nat. Office for Information Economy 1997; Australian Fed. Govt's Special Adviser for Information Economy and Tech. 1997; Australia's Rep. at int. forums, including WTO, OECD, APEC and Internet Corpn for Assigned Names and Numbers (ICANN); Founder Argo P@cific (int. advisory and investment firm); Chair. Govt Advisory Cttee, ICANN 1999–2002, Pres. and CEO ICANN 2003–09, Sr Pres.–Jan. 2010; Co-founder Stash (Data-centric Privacy and Security) 2013–; mem. Green Source Energy LLC Strategic Advisory Group 2010–; mem. Bd of Dir Atlantic Council of the US; Founding Chair. World Econ. Forum's Global Agenda Council on the Future of the Internet; mem. Advisory Bd UN Digital He@lth Initiative.

TYABJI, Hatim A., BS, MS, MBA; American (b. Indian) business executive; b. 1945, Bombay, India; ed Coll. of Eng, Poona, India, State Univ. of NY, Buffalo and Syracuse Univ., USA; Unisys Pres., Information Systems Products and Technologies Group, Sperry Rand 1973–86; Pres. and CEO VeriFone 1986–98, Chair. 1992–98; CEO Saraide, Inc. 1998–2000; Exec. Chair. Bytemobile, Inc. 2001–; chairman of Jasper Wireless; mem. Bd of Dirs Best Buy Co. Inc. 1998–, Chair. 2012–15 (retd); mem. Bd of Dirs Merchant eSolutions, Inc., Sierra Atlantic, Inc., Touch Networks (Australia), Missile Defense Advocacy Alliance; fmr mem. Bd of Dirs Ariba Inc., Bank of America Merchant Services, Deluxe Corpn, eFunds Corpn, Novatel Wireless, Inc., PubliCard Inc., SmartDisk Corpn, Datacard Group, Depotpoint, Inc., Impresse Corpn, Norand Corpn; Amb. at Large for Benchmark Capital; mem. Bd Carnegie Inst., Dean's Council of the Leavey School of Business at Santa Clara Univ., Dean's Council of School of Eng at State Univ. of NY, Buffalo. *Publication:* Husband, Wife & Company: An Honest Perspective on Success in Life and Work 2007.

TYAGACHEV, Leonid Vassilyevich; Russian sports administrator and ski coach; b. 10 Oct. 1946, Dedenevo, Moscow region; m.; two d.; ed Moscow Pedagogical Inst., Mountain Ski School Kirschberg, Austria; participated in All-Union and int. ski competitions –1971; fmr USSR Ski Champion; Sr Ski Coach, Moscow region 1971–76; Chief Coach USSR Ski team, has coached numerous skiers, including Zhirov, Zelenskaya, Tsyganov, Makeyev, Gladyshev 1976–81; took part in organizing World Cup competitions in Saalbach, Schladming, Saint Anton 1981–95; Minister of Sport and Tourism 1995–99; First Vice-Pres. Russian Olympic Cttee 1991–2001, Pres. 2001–10, also Pres. Russian Alpine Ski and Snowboard Fed.; mem. Supervisory Bd Sochi Winter Games 2014 Organising Cttee; numerous medals.

TYAHNYBOK, Oleh Yaroslavovych; Ukrainian surgeon and politician; *Leader, Svoboda (Freedom);* b. 7 Nov. 1968, Lviv, Ukrainian SSR, USSR; s. of Yaroslav Tyahnibok; m. Olha Demchyschyn; one s. two d.; ed Lviv Medical Inst., Lviv Franko Univ.; part-time medical jobs at Lviv Medical Inst. as an orderly and nurse, later drafted into the army; returned to the Inst. and initiated creation of Med Inst. Student Brotherhood; qualified as surgeon, majoring in urology 1993; mem. Sotsial-Natsionalna Partiya Ukrainy (Social-Nat. Party of Ukraine) 1991; mem. Lviv Oblast Council 1994–98; mem. Verkhovna Rada (Parl.) 1998–2014, became mem. of Narodny Rukh Ukrainy (People's Movt of Ukraine) faction, re-elected as mem. of Victor Yushchenko's Nasha Ukraina (Our Ukraine) bloc 2002–04 (expelled from bloc); Leader Svoboda (Freedom) 2004–; cand. for election of Mayor of Kyiv 2008; unsuccessful cand. in presidential election 2010, 2014; criminal case launched by Russian Govt against him for "organizing an armed gang" that had allegedly fought against the Russian 76th Guards Air Assault Div. in the 1994–96 Chechen War March 2014; voted Person of the Year by readers of Korrespondent magazine 2012. *Address:* Svoboda (Freedom), 02140 Kyiv, vul. Vyshnyakivska 6A/70, Ukraine (office). *E-mail:* vo@svoboda.org.ua (office). *Website:* svoboda.org.ua (office); tiahnybok.info.

TYGART, Travis Thompson, BA, JD; American lawyer; *CEO, US Anti-Doping Agency;* b. 1971; ed Univ. of North Carolina, Southern Methodist Univ.; Assoc., Holme Roberts & Owen LLP 2000–02; Dir of Legal Affairs, US Anti-Doping Agency (USADA) 2002–04; Sr Man. Dir and Gen. Counsel 2004–07, CEO 2007–. *Address:* US Anti-Doping Agency, 5555 Technical Center Suite 200, Colorado Springs, CO 80919, USA (office). *Telephone:* (719) 785-2000 (office). *E-mail:* usada@usada.org (office). *Website:* www.usada.org (office).

TYLDUM, Morten; Norwegian film director; b. 19 May 1967, Bergen; m. Janne Tyldum; one c.; ed Univ. of Bergen, School of Visual Arts, USA; worked in TV for NRK Drama, also directed music videos, commercials and short films. *Films include:* Fast Forward (short) 2000, Buddy (Mannheim-Heidelberg Int. Filmfestival Special Prize and FIPRESCI Prize 2002, Norwegian Int. Film Festival Audience Award 2003, Sofia Int. Film Festival Grand Prix 2004) 2003, Fallen Angels 2008, Headhunters 2011, The Imitation Game (Hollywood Film Awards Best Dir 2014) 2014. *Television includes:* U rett og slett (series) 1991, U Åtte & 1/2 (mini-series) 1994, En mann må gjøre det han må (film) 1996. *Address:* Anonymous Content, 3532 Hayden Avenue, Culver City, Los Angeles, CA 90232, USA (office). *Telephone:* (310) 558-3667 (office). *Fax:* (310) 558-2724 (office). *Website:* www.anonymouscontent.com (office).

TYLER, Anne, BA; American writer; b. 25 Oct. 1941, Minneapolis, Minn.; d. of Lloyd Parry Tyler and Phyllis Tyler (née Mahon); m. Taghi M. Modarressi 1963 (died 1997); two c.; ed Duke Univ., Columbia Univ.; mem. American Acad. of Arts and Letters, American Acad. of Arts and Sciences. *Publications include:* If Morning Ever Comes 1964, The Tin Can Tree 1965, A Slipping-Down Life 1970, The Clock Winder 1972, Celestial Navigation 1974, Searching for Caleb 1976, Earthly Possessions 1977, Morgan's Passing (Janet Heidinger Kafka Prize 1980) 1980, Dinner at the Homesick Restaurant 1982, The Best American Short Stories (ed. with Shannon Ravenel) 1983, The Accidental Tourist (Nat. Book Critics Circle Award for Fiction 1985, Ambassador Book Award 1986) 1985, Breathing Lessons (Pulitzer Prize for Fiction 1989) 1988, Saint Maybe 1991, Tumble Tower (juvenile) 1993, Ladder of Years 1995, A Patchwork Planet 1998, Back When We Were Grown-ups 2001, The Amateur Marriage 2004, Digging to America 2006, Noah's Compass 2010, The Beginner's Goodbye 2012, A Spool of Blue Thread 2015, Vinegar Girl 2016, Clock Dance 2018; short stories in magazines. *Address:* Hannigan Salky Getzler Agency, 37 West 28th Street, 8th floor, New York, NY 10001, USA (office); 222 Tunbridge Road, Baltimore, MD 21212, USA (home). *E-mail:* atmBaltimore@aol.com (home). *Website:* www.annetyler.com.

TYLER, David, MA; British business executive; *Chairman, J Sainsbury plc;* ed Univ. of Cambridge; held sr financial and gen. man. positions with Unilever PLC 1974–86, County NatWest Ltd 1986–89, Christie's International plc 1989–96, Group Finance Dir GUS plc 1997–2006; Chair. 3i Quoted Private Equity plc 2007–09; Chair. Logica plc 2007–12; Chair. J Sainsbury plc Oct. 2009–; Chair. Hammerson plc 2013–, Domestic & Gen. Group 2015–; Dir (non-exec.) Burberry Group plc 2002–15 (Chair. Remuneration Cttee), Experian plc 2006–12, Reckitt Benckiser Group plc 2007–09; Chair. Hampstead Theatre 2012–. *Address:* J Sainsbury plc, 33 Holborn, London, EC1N 2HT, England (office). *Telephone:* (20) 7695-6000 (office). *E-mail:* info@j-sainsbury.co.uk (office). *Website:* www.j-sainsbury.co.uk (office).

TYLER, Liv; American actress; b. 1 July 1977, Portland, Me; d. of Steve Tyler and Bebe Buell; m. Royston Langdon 2003 (divorced); two s. one d.; fmr model, Eileen Ford Agency; UNICEF Goodwill Amb. 2003–. *Film appearances include:* Silent Fall 1994, Empire Records 1995, Heavy 1995, Stealing Beauty 1996, That Thing You Do! 1996, Inventing the Abbotts 1997, Plunkett and Macleane 1999, Armageddon 1998, Cookie's Fortune 1999, Onegin 1999, The Little Black Book 1999, Dr T and the Women 2000, The Lord of the Rings: The Fellowship of the Ring 2001, One Night at McCool's 2001, The Lord of the Rings: The Two Towers 2002, The Lord of the Rings: The Return of the King 2003, Jersey Girl 2004, Lonesome Jim 2005, Reign Over Me 2007, The Strangers 2008, The Incredible Hulk 2008, Super 2010, The Ledge 2011, Robot & Frank 2012, Space Station 76 2014, Jamie Marks is Dead 2014. *Television:* The Leftovers 2014–17. *Address:* c/o United Talent Agency, 9560 Wilshire Blvd, Suite 500, Beverly Hills, CA 90212-2401, USA (office).

TYLER OF ENFIELD, Baroness (Life Peer), cr. 2011, of Enfield in the London Borough of Enfield; **Claire Tyler;** British organization executive; Deputy Chief Exec., Nat. Connexions Unit 2000–02; Bd mem., Office of Deputy Prime Minister 2002–06, also Head of Govt's Social Exclusion Unit; Dir Vulnerable Children's Group, Dept for Educ. and Skills 2006–08; Chief Exec. Relate (relationship support charity) 2007–12, Vice-Pres. 2012–; Chair. CAFCASS 2012–, Making Every Adult Matter (Coalition of Charities) 2013–; Pres. National Children's Bureau 2012–; Vice-Chair. Think Ahead Development Board 2014–; mem. Advisory Group, Step Up to Serve 2014–. *Address:* House of Lords, Westminster, London, SW1A 0PW, England. *Telephone:* (20) 7219-3606. *E-mail:* tylerc@parliament.uk.

TYMOSHENKO, Yuliya Volodymyrivna, CandEcon; Ukrainian business executive and politician; *Leader, Batkivshchyna (Fatherland);* b. (Yulia Grigyan) 27 Nov. 1960, Dnipropetrovsk (now Dnipro), Ukrainian SSR, USSR; d. of Vladimir Abramovich Grigyan and Ludmila Nikolaevna Telegina (née Nelepova); m. Oleksandr Hennadyovych Tymoshenko; one d.; ed Dnipropetrovsk State Univ.; planning engineer, Dnipropetrovsk Machine-Construction Plant 1984–89; Commercial Dir Dnipropetrovsk Youth Centre Terminal 1989–91; Dir-Gen. Ukraine Benzine Corpn 1991–95; Pres. Union Unified Energy Systems of Ukraine, First Deputy Chair. and Head, Cttee on Budgetary Issues 1995–97; elected to Verkhovna Rada (Parl.) 1996, joined political union Hromada (Community) with Pavlo Lazarenko, left Hromada to form and lead Vseukrayinske Obyednannya Batkivshchyna (All-Ukrainian Fatherland Union) faction 1999–, merged with Ukrainska Konservatyvna Respublikanska Partiya (Ukrainian Conservative Republican Party) 2002, with Yabluko party 2004, absorbed the Fronta Zmin (Front for Change) and the Partiya 'Reformy i Poryadok' (Reforms and Order

Party) to become Batkivshchyna Obyednana Opozytsiya (Fatherland United Opposition) 2013, designation subsequently reverted to Batkivshchyna (Fatherland); Deputy Prime Minister responsible for energy issues 1999–2001 (resgnd); joined opposition Nat. Salvation Forum 2001; arrested on charge of corruption March 2001, released due to pressure of opposition; Leader, Blok Yulii Tymoshenko (Yuliya Tymoshenko Bloc) 2001–, led bloc in 2002 and 2006 elections; Prime Minister Jan.–Sept. 2005, 2007–10; unsuccessful cand. in presidential elections 2010, 2014, 2019; arrested for repeated violations of court rules during her trial (charged in May 2011) for abuse of office over a natural gas imports contract signed in 2009 with Russia Aug. 2011; charged with misusing $425m received by her govt in 2009 for the sale of carbon credits Dec. 2010; held at Lukyanivska Prison; sentenced to seven years' imprisonment Oct. 2011, appealed unsuccessfully Dec. 2011; verdict against her upheld by Supreme Court of Ukraine 29 Aug. 2012; went on hunger strike to protest against vote rigging in Oct. parl. election 29 Oct.–16 Nov. 2012; released from prison following removal of Pres. Viktor Yanukovych Feb 2014, Kyiv Dist court of Kharkiv closed the criminal case on financial malpractice; Higher Order of Orthodox Church St Barbara Great Martyr 1997. *Publications include:* about 50 papers on econs. *Address:* Batkivshchyna (Fatherland), 04080 Kyiv, vul. Turovska 13, First Floor, Ukraine (office). *Telephone:* (44) 527-70-69 (office). *E-mail:* gromprym@gmail.com (office). *Website:* ba.org.ua (office); www.tymoshenko.ua.

TYNDALE-BISCOE, Cecil Hugh, MSc, PhD, FAA, AM, FRSNZ; Australian research scientist and university teacher (retd); b. 16 Oct. 1929, Kashmir, India; s. of Eric Dallas Tyndale-Biscoe and Phyllis Mary Tyndale-Biscoe (née Long); m. Marina Szokoloczi 1960; two s. one d.; ed Wycliffe Coll., UK, Canterbury Univ., NZ, Univ. of Western Australia and Washington Univ., St Louis, USA; Animal Ecology, Dept of Scientific and Industrial Research, NZ 1951–55; Lecturer, Edwardes Coll., Peshawar, Pakistan 1955–58, Univ. of Western Australia, Perth 1961; Deputy Leader, Biologist, NZ Alpine Club Antarctic Expedition 1959–60; Lecturer, Sr Lecturer, Reader in Zoology, ANU, Canberra 1962–75, Adjunct Prof. 1996–2002; Sr Prin. Research Scientist, Div. of Wildlife Research, CSIRO, Canberra 1976–78, Chief Research Scientist, Div. of Wildlife and Ecology 1978–91; Dir Co-operative Research Centre for Biological Control of Vertebrate Pest Populations 1992–95; Hayward Fellow, Manaaki Whenua Landcare Research, NZ 1996–97; Fellow, Australian Acad. of Science; Fellow and Life Mem., Australian Mammal Soc.; Hon. Fellow, Sustainable Ecosystems, CSIRO 2000–05, Royal Soc. of NZ; Clarke Medal, Royal Soc. of NSW 1974, Troughton Medal, Australian Mammal Soc. 1982, Aitken Medal, Museum of S Australia 1986, CSIRO Medal 1987, Whitely Medal, Royal Zoological Soc. of NSW 2005. *Achievements include;* mountaineering in NZ, including first north-south traverse of Mt Cook, first ascent of Torres from the Balfour; in the Karakorum, including first ascents of Falak Sar, Barteen and Buni Zom, deputy leader and biologist, New Zealand Alpine Club Antarctic Expedition 1959–60, discovered most southerly insects at 84S named Biscoia sudpolaris. *Publications include:* Life of Marsupials 1973 (second edn 2005), Reproduction and Evolution (ed.) 1977, Reproductive Physiology of Marsupials (with M. B. Renfree) 1987, Developing Marsupials (co-ed.) 1988, The Missionary and the Maharajas: Cecil Tyndale-Biscoe and the Making of Modern Kashmir 2019; about 120 papers in scientific journals of reproduction, ecology and endocrinology. *Leisure interests:* mountaineering, agroforestry, earth houses, woodwork, history of Kashmir and North India. *Address:* 114 Grayson Street, Hackett, ACT 2602, Australia (home). *Telephone:* (2) 6249-8612 (home); (4) 0005-4471 (home). *E-mail:* hughtb@bigpond.com (home).

TYSON, John H., BBA; American food industry executive; *Chairman, Tyson Foods, Inc.;* b. 5 Sept. 1953, Springdale, Ark.; s. of Donald John Tyson and Twilla Jean Womochil; grandson of John Tyson; m. Kimberly McCoy; one s. one d.; ed Springdale High School, Southern Methodist Univ., Dallas, Tex.; began career with Tyson Foods Inc. (family-owned business est. by grandfather John Tyson), various positions including Retail Sales Man. for NE states, Purchasing Man., Complex Man. NC Region, Pres. Beef and Pork Div., Vice-Chair. –1998, Chair. Tyson Foods 1998–2000, Chair., Pres. and CEO 2000–01, Chair. and CEO 2001–06, Chair. 2006–; fmr Pres. Ark. Poultry Fed.; mem. Bd of Dirs Nat. Council on Alcoholism and Drug Dependence, Steering Cttee Campaign for 21st Century, Univ. of Ark.; Chair. Corpn and Foundation Relations Cttee, Univ. of Ark.; mem. Walden Woods (non-profit org.), Bridge School Project; Man of the Year, Arkansas Poultry Fed. 1994, Citizen of the Year, March of Dimes, Little Rock, Ark. 2000. *Leisure interests:* golf, deep sea fishing, music, travel, culture, philanthropy. *Address:* Tyson Foods Inc., 2200 Don Tyson Parkway, Springdale, AR 72762, USA (office). *Telephone:* (479) 290-4000 (office). *Fax:* (479) 290-4061 (office). *E-mail:* info@tysonfoods.com (office). *Website:* www.tysonfoods.com (office).

TYSON, Keith, MA; British artist; b. Ulverston, Cumbria, England; s. of David Tyson and Audrey Rigby; ed Dowdales School, Dalton-in-Furness, Barrow-in-Furness Coll. of Eng, Carlisle Coll. of Art and Univ. of Brighton; studied mechanical eng before taking up art studies; worked as metal turner and draftsman at Vickers shipyard; has exhibited across Europe and N America; fmr Artist-in-Residence, Astrophysics and Cosmology Dept, Univ. of Oxford; Dr hc (Brighton) 2005; ICA Arts and Innovation Award 1996, Turner Prize 2002. *Solo exhibitions include:* Anthony Reynolds Gallery 1995, Galerie Georges-Philippe && Nathalie Vallois, Paris 1997, Anthony Reynolds Gallery, London 2000, Arndt and Partner, Berlin 2003, The Bates Coll. Museum of Art, Maine 2005, Haunch of Venison, London 2007, Parasol Unit, London 2009, The Pace Gallery, New York 2010, Pace, London 2013, David Risley Gallery, Copenhagen 2014. *Group exhibitions include:* Inst. of Contemporary Arts 1996, Venice Biennale 2001, São Paulo Bienal 2002, Wolverhampton Art Gallery, Wolverhampton 2002, South London Gallery, London 2003, Galerie Georges-Philippe & Nathalie Vallois, Paris 2004, The Fine Art Soc., London 2007, Tate Britain, London 2008, Hayward Gallery, London 2009, MdM Museum, Porto Cervo, Italy 2011, Magasin 3, Stockholm Konsthall 2014, Project B, Milan, Italy 2015. *Publications include:* Moving Targets 2, A User's Guide To British Art Now 2000, Art Crazy Nation: The Post Blimey Art World 2001, Cream 3 2003, The Turner Prize: Twenty Years 2003, Artnow 4 2013; contrib. to numerous articles. *E-mail:* info@ktprojects.co.uk. *Website:* www.keithtyson.com.

TYSON, Laura D'Andrea, BA, PhD; American economist, academic, fmr government official and fmr university administrator; *Professor of Business*

Administration and Economics, Haas School of Business, University of California, Berkeley; b. 28 June 1947, New Jersey; m. Erik Tarloff; one s.; ed Smith Coll., Massachusetts Inst. of Tech.; Asst Prof., Princeton Univ. 1974–77; Prof., Dept of Econs, Univ. of California, Berkeley 1997–2001, Dean, Haas School of Business 1998–2001, Prof., Haas School of Business 2007–08, S. K. and Angela Chan Chair in Global Management 2008–13, Professor of Business Admin. and Econs 2013–, Dir Inst. of Int. Studies, 1978–98, Dir Inst. for Business and Social Impact 2013–; Dean, London Business School, UK 2001–06; Visiting Prof., Harvard Business School 1989–90; Chair. Council of Econ. Advisers to US Pres. Bill Clinton 1993–95, Nat. Econ. Advisor to the Pres. US Nat. Econ. Council 1995–97; Visiting Scholar, Inst. of Int. Econs 1990–92; mem. Bd of Economists, Los Angeles Times 1989–92; mem. Bd of Dirs AT&T, Inc.; Morgan Stanley 1997–, CBRE Group Inc., Silver Spring Networks 2009–, Science, Technology and Economic Policy of The National Academies 2009–; Chair. Advisory Bd KPMG International 2004–06; mem. Econ. Recovery Advisory Bd (PERAB); Sr Advisor, McKinsey Global Inst. 2007–, Center for American Progress 2007–, Rock Creek Group 2009–, Credit Suisse Research Inst. 2010–; Special Advisor, Berkeley Research Group, LLC 2010–; Econ. Advisor, Alliance for Competitive Taxation 2013–; Advisor, Samsung SDS 2012–; mem. Advisory Bd Newman's Own Foundation 2009–; Chair. Global Agenda Council on Women's Empowerment, World Econ. Forum 2008–; mem. Econ. and Business Advisory Bd, Warburg Pincus LLC 1997–2005; Nat. Fellows Program Fellowship, Hoover Inst. 1978–79; consultant to IBRD 1980–86, Pres.'s Comm. on Industrial Competitiveness 1983–84, Hambrecht & Quist 1984–86, Plan-Econ 1984–86, Western Govs Asscn 1986, Council on Competitiveness 1986–89, Electronics Industry Asscn 1989, Motorola 1989–90; mem. Council on Foreign Relations 1987–, NAS (mem. Innovation Policy Forum 2013–16), Innovation Policy Forum, American Acad. of Arts and Sciences 2002–; mem. Pres.'s Econ. Recovery Advisory Bd 2009–11, Pres. Obama's Council on Jobs and Competitiveness 2011–13; Chair. Bd Trustees, Blum Center for Developing Economies 2006–, Bay Area Council Economic Inst. 2009–; Trustee Jacobs Foundation 2012–, Hamilton Project Advisory Council of The Brookings Inst. 2005–; columnist, Business Week magazine 1998–2005; Dr hc (American Univ.) 1995, (Smith Coll.) 1994, (Univ. of Lausanne) 2011. *Publications:* The Yugoslav Economic System and its Performance in the 1970s 1980, Economic Adjustment in Eastern Europe 1984, Who's Bashing Whom?, Trade Conflict in High Technology Industries 1992; articles in professional journals. *Address:* Haas School of Business, S545, Haas, #1900, 2220 Piedmont Avenue, University of California, Berkeley, CA 94720-1900, USA (office). *Telephone:* (510) 642-1230 (office). *E-mail:* tyson@haas.berkeley.edu (office). *Website:* www.haas.berkeley.edu (office).

TYSON, Michael (Mike) Gerard; American professional boxer; b. 30 June 1966, New York City; s. of John Kilpatrick Tyson and Lorna Tyson; m. 1st Robin Givens 1988 (divorced 1989); 2nd Monica Turner 1997 (divorced 2003); two c.; m. 3rd Lakiha Spicer 2009; career record of 50 wins, five losses, two no contest; defeated Trevor Berbick to win WBC heavyweight title 1986; winner WBA heavyweight title March 1987, IBF heavyweight title Aug. 1987; fmr undefeated world champion, lost to James Buster Douglas 1990, defeated Donovan Ruddock 1991; Hon. Chair. Cystic Fibrosis Asscn 1987; sentenced to six years' imprisonment for rape and two counts of deviant sexual practice March 1992, appealed against March sentence, appeal rejected by US Supreme Court March 1994, released March 1995; regained title of heavyweight world champion after defeating Frank Bruno (q.v.) March 1996; lost to Evander Holyfield Dec. 1996; licence revoked by Nevada State Athletics Comm. after disqualification from rematch against Holyfield 1996, reinstated on appeal Oct. 1998; sentenced to a year's imprisonment for assault Feb. 1999; released on probation May 1999; fought Lennox Lewis (q.v.) June 2002 for WBC and IBF titles, knocked out in eighth round; defeated Clifford Etienne Feb. 2003; lost to Danny Williams 2004; f. Mike Tyson Collection (clothing co.), Tyrannic Productions (film production co.); BBC Sports Overseas Personality of the Year 1989, 2011 inducted into Boxing Hall of Fame 2011. *Film appearances include:* Rocky Balboa 2006, The Hangover 2009, The Hangover 2 2011. *Website:* miketyson.com.

TZABAN, Yair, BA; Israeli journalist and politician; *Chairman, Association for Modern Jewish Culture;* b. 23 Aug. 1930, Jerusalem; one s. one d.; ed Bar-Ilan and Te-Aviv Univs; Chair. political bureau of Maki (Israeli CP) 1972–75; Co-Founder of Moked 1972–77, Co-Founder of Sheli Coalition 1977; Political Sec. Mapam (United Workers' Party) 1981–, Chair. Mapam's faction in the Histadrut; Minister of Immigrant Absorption 1992–96; mem. Knesset 1981– (Meretz), served on numerous cttees 1981–92, Lecturer, School for Political Studies, Univ. of Tel-Aviv 1996–2002; fmr Chair. The College of Judaism as Culture (Meitar), mem. Exec. Bd; Founder and Chair. Asscn for Modern Jewish Culture; Dir-Gen. New Encyclopedia on Jewish Culture in the Era of Modernisation and Secularisation project 2000–07; Dr hc (Hebrew Union Coll.) 1996; Itamar Ben-Avi Shield 1984. *Publications:* New Jewish Time 2007; various articles on political, social and econ. topics and on Judaism and Zionism. *Address:* 1A Tarad Street, Ramat-Gan 52503, Israel (home). *Telephone:* 3-6735160 (office); 3-6121495 (home). *Fax:* 3-6727364 (office); 3-6121497 (home). *E-mail:* zabany@ netvision.net.il (home).

U

UBACH FONT, Maria; Andorran diplomatist and government official; *Minister of Foreign Affairs;* b. 14 June 1973, La Massana; m.; ed Univ. of Paris 1, La Sorbonne, Université de Toulouse, Université Grenoble Alpe; Desk Officer, Ministry of Foreign Affairs 1998, Dir of Multilateral Affairs and Cooperation 2006–11; Deputy Perm. Rep. of Andorra to Council of Europe, France 1998–2001; First Sec., Embassy in France 2001–06, Amb. to France (also Personal Rep. of Head of State to Perm. Council of Francophonie) 2011–15; Deputy Perm. Del. to UNESCO 2001–06, Perm. Del. 2011–15; apptd Perm. Rep. to OPCW 2015; Amb. to Belgium (also Head, Mission of Andorra to EU) 2015–17; Minister of Foreign Affairs 2017–. *Address:* Ministry of Foreign Affairs, Edif. Administratiu, Carrer Prat de la Creu 62–64, Andorra la Vella AD500, Andorra (office). *Telephone:* 875704 (office). *Fax:* 869559 (office). *E-mail:* exteriors@govern.ad (office). *Website:* www.mae.ad.

UBAIDULLOYEV, Mahmadsaid; Tajikistani politician and electrical engineer; *President, National Assembly (Majlisi Milliy);* b. 1 Feb. 1952, Farhor Dist, Kulob yat (now Khatlon Viloyat), Tajik SSR, USSR; s. of Ubaidullo Mahmudov and Sabagul Nazirova; m. R. Karimova; two s. one d.; ed Tajik Polytechnical Inst., Kharkiv Polytechnical Inst., Ukrainian SSR, Tashkent Higher CPSU School, Uzbek SSR; Sr Engineer, Kulob Viloyat Dept of Statistics 1974–75, Main Engineer 1975–76, Dir Computation Centre 1976–79; Instructor, Organizing Dept, CP Cttee of Kulob 1979–81, Head of Organizing Dept 1981–83; Deputy Head of Cen. Dept of Statistics, Dushanbe 1985–86; Head of Dept of Industry, Transport and People's Food Products, CP Cttee of Kulob 1986–88; Head of Khatlon Viloyat Dept of Statistics, Qurghonteppa (now Bokhtar) 1988–90; Deputy Chair. Exec. Cttee, Kulob Viloyat People's Deputy Council 1990–92; Deputy Chair. Council of Ministers 1992–94; First Deputy Prime Minister 1994–96; Mayor of Dushanbe 1996–2017; mem. Hizbi Khalki-demokratii Tojikiston (People's Democratic Party of Tajikistan); Pres. Nat. Ass. (Majlisi Milliy) 2000–, Interparliamentary Ass. of Eurasian Econ. Community (EURASEC) 2007–09, 2010–; Order of Dustlik (Friendship) 1998, Order of Ismoili Somoni 1999, Order of Ismoili Somoni, First Degree 2006; 21st Century Achievement Award 2001, Int. Honour Diploma and Prize, Medal in respect of IBC Leading Engineers of the World 2006, Diploma of UN-HABITAT and World Org. of United Cities and Local Govts 2006. *Publications:* The Foundation of Newest Statehood (ed.) 2002, History of Dushanbe City (from ancient times till our days) (ed.) 2004, Dushanbe: City of Peace (co-author) 2004. *Leisure interests:* politics, logic, dialectics and philosophy. *Address:* Office of the President, Majlisi Milliy (National Assembly), 734051 Dushanbe, Xiyoboni Rudaki 42 (office). *Telephone:* (372) 23-19-33 (office). *Fax:* (372) 21-51-10 (office). *E-mail:* mejparl@parliament.tojikiston.com (office). *Website:* parlament.tj (office).

UCHIDA, Dame Mitsuko; Japanese/British pianist; *Co-Artistic Director, Marlboro Music Festival;* b. 20 Dec. 1948, Tokyo; d. of Fujio Uchida and Yasuko Uchida; partner Sir Robert Cooper; ed Vienna Acad. of Music, Austria with Prof. R. Hauser; debut Vienna 1963; recitals and concerto performances with major London orchestras, Chicago Symphony, Boston Symphony, Cleveland Orchestra, Berlin Philharmonic, Vienna Philharmonic, New York Philharmonic, Los Angeles Philharmonic and others; played and directed the cycle of 21 Mozart piano concertos with the English Chamber Orchestra, London 1985–86; gave US premiere of piano concerto Antiphonies by Harrison Birtwistle 1996; Co-Artistic Dir (with Richard Goode) Marlboro Music Festival 1999–2013, Co-Artistic Dir (with Jonathan Biss) 2013–; Perspectives recital series at Carnegie Hall 2003; Artist-in-Residence, Cleveland Orchestra 2002–07, Berlin Philharmonic Orchestra 2008–09, Vienna Konzerthaus 2008–09; apptd Artistic Partner, Mahler Chamber Orchestra 2016; Trustee, Borletti-Buitoni Trust; Hon. CBE 2001; Hon. DBE 2009; First Prize, Beethoven Competition Vienna 1969, Second Prize, Chopin Competition Warsaw 1970, Second Prize, Leeds Competition 1975, Gramophone Award (Mozart Piano Sonatas) 1989, Gramophone Award (Schoenberg Piano Concerto) 2001, Royal Philharmonic Soc.'s Instrumentalist Award 2004, Royal Philharmonic Soc. Gold Medal 2012, Golden Mozart Medal, Salzburg Mozartwoche 2015, Premium Imperiale Award, Japan Arts Asscn 2015. *Recordings include:* Mozart Complete Piano Sonatas and 24 Piano Concertos (English Chamber Orchestra and Jeffrey Tate), Mozart Piano Concertos (Cleveland Orchestra), Chopin Piano Sonatas, Debussy 12 Etudes, Schubert Piano Sonatas, Beethoven Piano Concertos, Schoenberg Piano Concerto, Beethoven Piano Sonatas Op. 109, 110 and 111, Beethoven: Sonatas Op. 101 and 106, Schumann: Kreisleriana Carnaval Davidsbündlertänze Fantasie, Berg: Chamber Concerto, Mozart Piano Concertos Nos 23 & 24 (Grammy Award for Best Instrumental Soloist Performance) 2011, Schumann and Berg (with Dorothea Röschmann) (Grammy Award for Best Classical Solo Vocal Album 2017) 2016. *Address:* c/o Victoria Rowsell Artist Management Ltd, 34 Addington Square, London, SE5 7LB, England (office). *Telephone:* (20) 7701-3219 (office). *Fax:* (20) 7701-3219 (office). *E-mail:* management@victoriarowsell.co.uk (office). *Website:* www.victoriarowsell.co.uk (office); www.marlboromusic.org; mahlerchamber.com; www.mitsukouchida.com.

UCHIDA, Tsuneji; Japanese electronics industry executive; held numerous positions with Canon Inc., including Group Exec. Lens Products Group 1995–2001, Deputy Chief Exec. Camera Operations HQ 1995–97, Group Exec. Photo Products Group 1997–99, Chief Exec. Camera Operations HQ April–July 1999, in charge of promotion of digital photo, Man. Dir 2001–03, Sr Man. Dir 2003–06, Vice-Pres. 2006, mem. Bd of Dirs, Pres. and COO 2006–12.

UCHIDA, Yukio; Japanese business executive; *President and Representative Director, JX Holdings, Inc.;* fmr Exec. Corp. Officer, Japan Energy Corpn, in charge of Corp. Planning and Control Dept, Accounting Dept, Supply Coordination Dept, Logistics Dept and Crude Oil and Products Acquisition Dept; fmr Exec. Man. Dir, Japan Foods Co. Ltd; fmr Sr Officer and Dir (non-exec.), Nippon Mining Holdings Inc.; fmr Sr Vice-Pres. and Exec. Vice-Pres., JX Nippon Oil & Energy Corpn, Dir, JX Holdings, Inc. 2012–, Exec. Vice-Pres., Asst To Pres. and Exec. Officer 2014–15, Pres. and Rep. Dir 2015–. *Address:* JX Holdings Inc., 2-6-3, Ote-machi, Chiyoda-ku, Tokyo 100-0004, Japan (office). *Telephone:* (3) 3502-1131 (office). *Fax:* (3) 3502-9352 (office). *Website:* www.hd.jx-group.co.jp (office).

UCHINAGA, Yukako; Japanese business executive; ed Univ. of Tokyo; joined IBM Japan in 1971, several man. positions in devt and marketing, Dir Asia Pacific Products 1989, Gen. Man. AP Cross Industry 1995, mem. Bd of Dirs 1995–, Gen. Man. Services Offerings 1998, Vice-Pres. Multi-industry Solutions, IBM Asia Pacific –1999, Vice-Pres. Software Devt Lab., Yamato 1999–2007, Tech. Advisor 2007; Vice-Chair. Benesse Holdings Corpn and Chair. and CEO Berlitz International, Inc. 2008–13, Hon. Chair. 2013–; apptd Visiting Prof., Coll. of Business, Rikkyo Univ. 2008; Founder and Chair. Japan Women's Creative Network (J-WIN) 2007–; Pres. and CEO Globalization Research Inst. Co. Ltd 2013–; Pres. Global Workforce Diversity Council; mem. Council for Gender Equality, Prime Minister's Office; mem. Council for Education, Ministry of Educ. and Science 2001; Chair. Japan Diversity Network Association 2014–; fmr Adviser Japanese Ministry of Health and Welfare, Prime Minister's Council for Gender Equality; mem. Bd of Dirs Sony Corpn 2008–14, Hoya Corpn; inducted into Women in Tech. Int. Hall of Fame (first woman inducted from outside the USA) 1999, Upward Mobility Award, Soc. of Women Engineers 2006.

UCHITEL, Aleksei Yefimovich; Russian film director; *Founder and Director-General, Rock Studio;* b. 31 Aug. 1951, Leningrad; s. of Yefim Uchitel; ed All Union State Inst. of Cinematography; with Leningrad Studio of Documentary Films, St Petersburg 1975–90; Founder and Dir-Gen. Rock Studio 1989–; Merited Worker of Arts. *Documentaries:* Its Name is Novgorod 1974, Leningrad: Years of Achievement 1975, Leningrad – Hero City 1975, Ten Thousand I's (Molodost-78 Int. Festival Prize) 1976, Irina Kolpakova, Snow Fantasy 1977, October and Youth 1977, Starting Up: Portrait of An Event (Leipzig Film Festival Prize) 1978, How many faces does the disco have? (Leningrad Komsomol Prize) 1980, Who is for? (Krasnoyarsk All-Union Film Festival Prize) 1982, The Earth is Entrusted to You (Almaty All-Union Film Festival Prize) 1983, Aktsiya (Krakow Int. Film Festival Prize) 1983, Planet Natasha 1986, Rock 1988, Obvodny Kanal (First Prize, Int. Cinema Festival, Bornholm, Denmark) 1990, Butterfly (First Prize, Best Dir, Open Russian Festival of Documentary Cinema, Ekaterinburg) 1993, Elite 1997. *Feature films include:* Mania Giseli (Mania of Giselle) (Honfleur Film Festival Prize) 1996, Elite 1997, His Wife's Diary (Grand Prix, Kinotavr Open Russian Cinema Festival) 2000, The Stroll (First Prize, Cleveland Int. Film Festival, Syracuse Int. Film Festival, Special Jury Prize for Outstanding Artistic Concept, FIPRESSI prize and Boulder Prize, 13th Int. Festival of Eastern European Cinema, Kottbus, Best Direction Prize, Window onto Europe Film Festival, Vyborg) 2003, Dreaming of Space 2005, Captive 2008, The Edge 2010, Durak 2014, Matilda 2016. *Address:* Rock Studio, 12 Krukov Canal, 190068 St Petersburg (office); 4th Krasnokararmennaya str. 6–5, Apt 4, 198052 St Petersburg, Russia (home). *Telephone:* (812) 114-2056 (office); (812) 292-59-45 (home). *E-mail:* rockfilmstudio@mail.ru (office). *Website:* www.rockfilm.ru (office); eng.uchitel.info.

UCHIYAMADA, Takeshi, BSc; Japanese automotive industry executive; *Chairman and Representative Director, Toyota Motor Corporation;* b. 17 Aug. 1946; ed Nagoya Univ.; joined Toyota 1969, Project Gen. Man. Vehicle Devt Centre 2 1994–96, Chief Engineer 1996–98, mem. Bd of Dirs Toyota Motor Corpn 1998–, oversaw Vehicle Devt Centre 3 1998–2000, Chief Officer, Vehicle Devt Centre 2 2000–01, Man. Dir and Chief Officer, Overseas Customer Service Operations Centre 2001–03, Sr Man. Dir and Chief Officer, Vehicle Eng Group 2003–04, Chief Production Control and Logistics Officer 2004–05, Exec. Vice-Pres., Toyota Motor Corpn 2005–12, Vice-Chair. and Rep. Dir 2012–13, Chair. and Rep. Dir 2013–, fmr Corp. Auditor, Toyota Industries Corpn; Dir, Toyota Boshoku Corpn, JTEKT Corpn (fmrly Koyo Seiko Co. Ltd), Aisin AW Co. Ltd; Vice-Chair. Japan Automobile Mfrs Asscn Inc. 2012–, also Vice-Pres.; Vice-Chair. Nippon Keidanren (Japan Business Fed.) 2013–; Medal with Blue Ribbon (Govt of Japan) 2015. *Address:* Toyota Motor Corpn, 1 Toyota-Cho, Toyota City, Aichi Prefecture, 471-8571, Japan (office). *Telephone:* (5) 6528-2121 (office). *Fax:* (5) 6523-5800 (office). *Website:* www.toyota-global.com (office); www.toyota.co.jp (office).

UCISIK, Ahmet Hikmet, PhD; Turkish engineer and academic; b. 14 Feb. 1945, Istanbul; ed Istanbul Univ.; mem. staff, Mass Inst. of Tech., USA 1972–76; Visiting Prof., McGill Univ., Canada 1978–79, Univ. of Pennsylvania 1980, 1981, 1982, 1985, UCLA 1982, Universitaet des Saarlandes, Germany 1982, 1983, Osaka Univ., Japan 1986; apptd Assoc. Prof., Istanbul Tech. Univ.; Dir Marmara Scientific and Industrial Research Inst., Turkish Scientific and Tech. Research Council; instructor, Metallurgical Eng Dept, Istanbul Tech. Univ.; Prof. of Materials Science, Bogazici Univ.; currently Researcher and mem. Bd of Trustees, Atilim Univ.; mem. Gesellschaft für Metall, American Soc. for Metals, Japanese Soc. for Dental Materials, Japanese Soc. for Medical Electronics and Biological Engineers, Orthopaedic Research Soc., Materials Research Soc., American Ceramic Soc., AAAS, New York Acad. of Sciences; mem. NATO Advisory Group for Aerospace Research 1984–94; Founding Member TSA 1993–99, Fellow, Islamic Acad. of Sciences. *Address:* Atılım Üniversitesi, Kızılcaşar Mah., 06836İncek Gölbası, Ankara, Turkey (office). *Telephone:* (312) 586-80-00 (office). *E-mail:* info@atilim.edu.tr (office). *Website:* www.atilim.edu.tr (office).

UDALL, Mark Emery, BA; American politician; b. 18 July 1950, Tucson, Ariz.; s. of Morris 'Mo' Udall and Patricia Emery Udall; nephew of Stewart Udall; m. Maggie Fox; one s. one d.; ed Williams Coll.; Field Organizer, Morris K. Udall for Pres. 1974–75; Course Dir and Educator, Colo Outward Bound School 1975–85, Exec. Dir 1985–95; mem. Colo State House of Reps 1997–98; mem. US House of Reps from 2nd Colo Dist 1999–2009; Senator from Colorado 2009–Jan. 2015, mem. Cttee on Armed Services, Cttee on Energy and Natural Resources, Select Cttee on Intelligence, Special Cttee on Aging; Visiting Fellow, Univ. of Chicago Inst. of Politics 2015; mem. American Alpine Club, Parkinson's Action Network; mem. Bd of Dirs Berger Foundation; Democrat; Award for Achievement in Environmental Law, Policy, and Management, Environmental Law Inst. (co-recipient) 2009, Marks Lecturer, James E. Rogers Coll. of Law, Univ. of Arizona 2015, Civil Rights Award, ACLU of Colorado 2015. *Leisure interest:* mountaineering.

UDALL, Thomas (Tom) S., BA, LLB, JD; American lawyer and politician; *Senator from New Mexico;* b. 18 May 1948, Tucson, Ariz.; s. of Stewart Udall and Lee Udall; m. Jill Cooper; one d.; ed Prescott Coll., Univ. of Cambridge, UK, Univ.

of New Mexico School of Law; Legis. Asst, staff of US Senator Joe Biden 1973; clerk to Chief Justice Oliver Seth, US Tenth Circuit Court of Appeals, Santa Fe, New Mexico 1977–78; Asst US Attorney 1978–81; attorney in pvt. practice, Santa Fe 1981–83; Chief Counsel, New Mexico Health and Environment Dept 1983–84; attorney, Miller, Stratvert, Torgerson and Schlenker, Albuquerque 1985–90; State Attorney, New Mexico 1991–99; mem. US House of Reps from 3rd New Mexico Dist 1999–2009, mem. Cttees on Appropriations, Educ. and Related Agencies, Subcttees on Interior, Environment and Related Agencies, on Labor, Health and Human Services, on Legis. Branch; Senator from New Mexico 2009–, mem. Cttee on Foreign Relations, Cttee on Commerce, Science, and Transportation, Cttee on Environment and Public Works, Cttee on Indian Affairs, Cttee on Rules and Admin, Comm. on Security and Cooperation in Europe, Int. Narcotics Control Caucus; Pres. Nat. Asscn of Attorney Gens 1996; mem. New Mexico Environmental Improvement Bd 1986–87; mem. Kiwanis Club of Albuquerque Inc., Santa Fe Chamber Music Festival, LAW FUND, Regional Environmental Public Interest Law Firm; Democrat. *Leisure interests:* tennis, fly-fishing, mountain climbing, staying involved in his community. *Address:* 531 Hart Senate Office Building, Washington, DC 20510, USA (office). *Telephone:* (202) 224-6621 (office). *Website:* tomudall.senate.gov (office).

UDALTSOV, Sergei Stanislavovich; Russian lawyer and political activist; *Chairman, Left Front;* b. 16 Feb. 1977, Moscow, Russian SFSR, USSR; m. Anastasiya Udaltsova; two s.; Chair. Vanguard of Red Youth 1999–; Chair. Left Front 2008–; Chair. Russian United Labour Front 2010–; one of the leaders of protests against Vladimir Putin 2011–12; arrested along with Aleksei Navalnyi following anti-Putin rallies and given jail sentences Dec. 2011 and May 2012; arrested and charged with plotting riots Oct. 2012, arrested again Dec. 2012, convicted and sentenced to four and a half years 2014; campaign manager for CP of the Russian Fed. cand. Gennady Zyuganov during presidential election 2012. *E-mail:* leftfront77@gmail.com (office). *Website:* www.leftfront.ru (office); www.akm1917.org (office).

UDEN, Martin, LLB; British diplomatist (retd) and banking executive; *Government Liaison, HSBC;* m. Fiona Uden; two s.; ed Queen Mary Coll., Univ. of London; called to the Bar 1977; joined FCO 1977, held numerous positions in areas such as nuclear non-proliferation, Japan, Yugoslavia and Albania, CSCE; fmr Dir of Inward Investment, UK Trade and Investment HQ; Second Sec., Embassy in Seoul 1978–81, Political Counsellor 1994–97, served in Embassy in Bonn 1986–90, High Comm. in Ottawa 1997–2001, Consul-Gen. in San Francisco 2003–07, Amb. to South Korea 2008–11, with FCO 2011–12; Man. Dir British Business Embassy, UK Trade & Investment March–Oct. 2012, with FCO 2014–15, Deputy High Comm. in Lagos March–June 2015; Govt Liaison, HSBC, Hong Kong 2015–. *Publication:* Times Past in Korea 2003. *Address:* Hongkong and Shanghai Banking Corporation Ltd, GPO Box 64, Hong Kong Special Administrative Region, People's Republic of China (office). *Telephone:* 22333322 (office). *Website:* www.hsbc.com.hk (office).

UDUGOV, Brig.-Gen. Movladi; Russian/Chechen economist and politician; b. 9 Feb. 1962, Grozny; m. 1st; m. 2nd; four c.; ed Chechen-Ingush State Univ.; Co-founder Soc. Kavkaz, Co-founder political org. Bart and newspaper Bart 1987; Founder and Ed. Orientir (newspaper banned by Soviet regime) 1988; organizer Mil. Patriotic Union Mansur 1990; participant in Congress of Chechen People 1990; Sec. all sessions of Chechen Nat. Congress; Leader, Formation Cttee of Nat. Congress of Chechen People, anti-Russian resistance group Nov. 1991; participant in overthrow of Communist leadership of Chechen-Ingushetia 1991; Minister of Information and Press, Dudayev Govt 1991; head of propaganda service of Chechen separatists 1994–; took part in negotiations resulting in resolution of that conflict; First Vice-Minister Coalition Govt Chechen Repub. Ichkeria 1996–97, First Deputy Prime Minister 1997–98, Foreign Minister 1998–99; fmr Pres. Kavkaz-Center News Agency; fmr Chief, External Sub-Cttee of Informational Council, State Defence Council; currently Dir Information-Analytical Service of Caucasus Emirate.

UEBBER, Bodo; German business executive; b. 18 Aug. 1959, Solingen; ed Tech. Univ. of Karlsruhe; joined Messerschmitt-Bölkow-Blohm GmbH 1985, held various financial positions within DASA AG, Dornier Luftfahrt and MTU Aero Engines GmbH, mem. Bd of Man. and Chief Financial Officer, DaimlerChrysler Services AG 2001–03, apptd Deputy mem. Bd of Man. DaimlerChrysler AG (now Daimler AG) and Chair. Bd of Man. DaimlerChrysler Services AG 2003, Chair. European Aeronautic Defence and Space Co. (EADS) NV 2007–13; mem. Supervisory Bd Mercedes-Benz Bank AG, Stiftung Deutsche Sporthilfe, Talanx AG; mem. Advisory Bd Deutsche Bank AG, Munich, Landesbank Baden-Württemberg; mem. Bd of Dirs Freightliner LLC, BAIC Motor Corpn Ltd 2013–; mem. Investment Council of Stifterverband der Deutschen Wissenschaft; mem. Donor's Circle of the Jewish Museum, Berlin; mem. Bd of Trustees Museumsinsel, Berlin, Stuttgarter Galerieverein. *Address:* Daimler AG, 70546 Stuttgart, Germany (office). *Telephone:* 711-170 (office). *E-mail:* dialog@daimler.com (office). *Website:* www.daimler.com (office).

UEBERROTH, Peter Victor; American sports administrator and business executive; *Chairman and Managing Director, Contrarian Group Inc.;* b. 2 Sept. 1937, Evanston, Ill.; s. of Victor Ueberroth and Laura Larson; m. Ginny Nicolaus 1959; one s. three d.; ed Freemont High School, San Jose State Univ.; Operations Man., Trans Int. Airlines 1959, later part owner; f. Transportation Consultants, later First Travel Corpn 1962, sold in 1980; Head, Los Angeles Olympic Games Organizing Cttee 1980–84; Maj. League Baseball Commr 1984–89; Head, Rebuild Los Angeles 1992–93; Co-Chair. Doubletree Hotels Corpn 1993–97; Chair. and Man. Dir Contrarian Group Inc. (investment co.) 1989–, Pres. Contrarian Center; Chair. Aircastle Ltd 2012– (mem. Bd of Dirs since 2006); Owner and Co-Chair. Pebble Beach Co. 1999–; Chair. US Olympic Cttee –2008; mem. Bd of Dirs Coca-Cola Co. 1986–2015, Bell Riddell Giro (fmrly Easton Bell Sports); Chair. Bd Ambassadors International 1995; mem. Young Pres.'s Org.; Légion d'Honneur; 12 honorary degrees; Time magazine's Man of the Year 1984, Scopus Award 1985, Olympic Order-Gold, Int. Olympic Cttee, Youthlinks Indiana's Nat. Pathfinder Award 2005, John Wooden Global Leadership Award, Andersen School of Man., UCLA 2011. *Publications include:* Made in America (autobiography) 1985. *Leisure interests:* reading (especially historical non-fiction), golf. *Address:* Contrarian Group, Inc., 23 Corporate Plaza Drive, Suite 240, Newport Beach, CA 92660, USA.

UEHARA, Haruya; Japanese banking executive; b. 25 July 1946; ed Sophia Univ.; joined Mitsubishi Trust Bank 1969, Dir 1996–98, Man.-Dir 1998–2001, Sr Man.-Dir 2001–02, Deputy Pres. 2002–04, Pres. 2004–; Dir Mitsubishi Tokyo Financial Group Inc. 2003–, Chair. and Co-CEO 2004–05, Deputy Chair. and Pres. Mitsubishi UFJ Trust and Banking Corpn 2005–08, Chair. 2008–12, Sr Advisor 2012–; apptd mem. Bd Dirs Japanese Bankers Asscn 2004; Pres. Sophia Alumni Asscn. *Address:* Mitsubishi UFJ Trust and Banking Corpn, 4-1 Marunouchi 2-chome, Chiyoda-ku, Tokyo 100-6326, Japan.

UEMURA, Hiroyuki; Japanese insurance industry executive; b. 23 Jan. 1942; Pres. Sumitomo Marine & Fire Insurance Co. Ltd 1999–2001, Pres. Mitsui Sumitomo Insurance Co. Ltd (cr. from merger between Mitsui Marine & Fire Insurance and Sumitomo Marine & Fire Insurance Cos 2001) 2001–03, Pres. and Co-CEO 2003–06, led negotiations with CitiInsurance Int. Holdings Inc. to establish jt venture Mitsui Sumitomo CitiInsurance Co. (variable annuities life insurance business) 2002; mem. Bd of Dirs Japan Telework Asscn, Yamaha Music Foundation, Japan Earthquake Reinsurance Co. Ltd; apptd Chair. Marine and Fire Insurance Asscn of Japan 2001.

UENO, Chizuko, MA; Japanese sociologist and academic; *Professor, Ritsumeikan University;* b. 12 July 1948, Toyama; ed Kyoto Univ.; Assoc. Prof., Heian Women's Coll. 1980–89; Prof., Kyoto Seika Univ. 1989–93; Prof., Grad. School of Humanities and Sociology, Tokyo Univ. 1993–2011; Prof., Ritsumeikan Univ. 2011–; Visiting Prof., El Collegio de Mexico 1996, Barnard Coll., Columbia Univ. 1996–97, Univ. of Bonn; Mori Hamada and Matsumoto Visiting Fellow, Cornell Univ. Law School, USA 2003–04; Suntory Prize for Social Sciences and Humanities 1994, Asahi Prize for lifetime contrib. to feminism and gender studies 2012. *Publications:* Sekushi Gyaru no Daikenkyu (A Study of Sexy Girls) 1982, Explorations in Structuralism 1986, Pleasure of Womanhood 1986, Patriarchy and Capitalism 1990, The Rise and Fall of the Modern Japanese Family 1994, Nationalism and Gender 2003, Tojishashuken 2003, Miwa Yanagi (co-author) 2004, Sociology of Care 2011. *Address:* 1-11-16-2701, Nakamachi, Musashinoshi, Tokyo, Japan (office). *Telephone:* (422) 38-9770 (office). *Fax:* (422) 38-9862 (office). *E-mail:* ueno@l.u-tokyo.ac.jp (office). *Website:* wan.or.jp (office).

UGEUX, Georges, BA (Econ), DrIur; Belgian/American investment banker, lawyer, economist and financier; *Chairman and CEO, Galileo Global Advisors LLC;* b. 20 April 1945, Brussels; m. Francine Godet 1970; two s. two d.; ed Catholic Univ. of Louvain; Lecturer in Econs, Faculty of Law, Univ. of Louvain 1970–72; fmr Gen. Man. Investment Banking & Trust Div., Générale Bank; Man. Dir Morgan Stanley 1985–88; Group Finance Dir Société Générale de Belgique 1988–92; Pres. Kidder Peabody-Europe 1992–95; Chair. Belgian Privatization Comm. 1995–96; Pres. European Investment Fund 1995–96; Group Exec. Vice-Pres., Int., New York Stock Exchange 1996–2003; Chair. and CEO Galileo Global Advisors LLC 2003–; Adjunct Prof., European Banking and Finance, Columbia Law School; mem. Bd of Dirs Amoeba Capital, British American Business, Inc., French-American Chamber of Commerce; mem. Int. Advisory Bd Vlerick Leuven Gent Man. School, Oxford Analytica; Hon. Chair., Belgian American Chamber of Commerce, Catholic Univ. of Louvain Foundation; Officer of the Order of Leopold; Scientific Prize, Jean Bastien Foundation. *Publications:* Floating Rate Notes 1985, The Betrayal of Finance 2011; blog at Huffington Post and Le Monde.fr. *Leisure interests:* music, arts, philosophy, int. politics. *Address:* Galileo Global Advisors LLC, Ten Rockefeller Plaza, Suite 1001, New York, NY 10020, USA (office). *Telephone:* (212) 332-6055 (office). *Fax:* (212) 332-6033 (office). *E-mail:* gugeux@galileoadvisors.com (office). *Website:* www.galileoadvisors.com (office).

UGGLAS, Baroness Margaretha af, BA; Swedish foundation executive and fmr politician; b. 5 Jan. 1939, Stockholm; d. of Hugo Stenbeck; m. Bertil af Ugglas 1966 (died 1977); ed Harvard-Radcliffe Program in Business Admin., USA, Stockholm School of Econs; editorial writer, Svenska Dagbladet 1968–74; mem. Stockholm Co. Council 1971–73; mem. Parl. 1974–95, mem. Parl. Standing Cttee on Foreign Affairs 1982, Advisory Council on Foreign Affairs, Swedish Del. to Council of Europe; fmr Moderate Party Spokesman on Foreign Affairs; Chair. Swedish Section, European Union of Women 1981; Observer, European Parl.; Minister for Foreign Affairs 1991–94; mem. European Parl. 1995; Vice-Pres. European People's Party (EPP) 1996; Chair. Jarl Hjalmarson Foundation (Swedish Moderate Party) 1968–73, Save the Children Fed., Stockholm 1970–76, OSCE 1993; mem. Bd of Dirs Karolinska Inst., Becton, Dickinson and Co. 1997–2007; Robert Schuman Medal 1995, Alison Tennant Lecturer, European Union of Women (British Section) 1998. *Leisure interests:* art, walking, sailing, mountains, countryside.

UGOLINI, Giovanni Francesco; San Marino politician; b. 28 Feb. 1953, Borgo Maggiore; m. Loredana Mularoni; one d.; industrial chemical expert, technician in state hosp. 1974–81; with family hotel business 1981–; joined Partito Democratico Cristiano Sammarinese (PDCS) 1973–, mem. Cen. Council 1993–, Sec. Borgo Maggiore Br. 1989–93; mem. Consiglio Grande e Generale (parl.) 1998–2001; elected Mem. of Govt 2001; Co-Capt.-Regent (jt head of state) April–Oct. 2002, Oct. 2010–April 2011, April–Oct. 2016; Pres., San Marino Union of Tourist Hospitality (USOT) 1990–; mem. Foreign Policy Advisory Comm., Council of the XXII. *Address:* Partito Democratico Cristiano Sammarinese (PDCS), Via delle Scalette 6, 47890 San Marino (office). *Telephone:* (549) 991193 (office). *Fax:* (549) 992694 (office). *E-mail:* pdcs@omniway.sm (office). *Website:* www.pdcs.sm (office).

UHDE, Milan, PhDr; Czech politician, journalist and playwright; b. 28 July 1936, Brno; m. Jitka Uhdeová; two c.; ed Masaryk Univ.; Ed. of literary monthly A Guest Is Coming 1958–70; signed Charter 77; published essays in unofficial periodicals and abroad; Reader, Faculty of Philosophy, Masaryk Univ., Brno 1989–; Ed.-in-Chief, Atlantis Publishing House, Brno March–June 1990; Minister of Culture, Czech Repub. 1990–92; Pres. of Foundation for Preservation of Cultural Monuments 1991–; mem. Civic Democratic Party (ODS) 1991–98, Unie Svobody 1998; Deputy to Czech Nat. Council June 1990–92; mem. Presidium; Pres. of Parl., Czech Repub. 1993–96; Chair. Civic Democratic Party in Parl. 1996–97; Deputy Chair. State Radio Council 2002–06; Chair. Council of Czech Television 2011–14; Medal for Merit 2000; Czechoslovak Radio Prize 1966. *Plays include:* in trans.: King Vávra 1964, The Tax-Collector 1965, Witnesses 1966, The Tart from the Town of Thebes 1967, The Gang 1969, Ballad for a Bandit 1975, Professional Woman 1975, A May Fairy Tale 1976, A Dentist's Temptation 1976, Lord of the Flames 1977, The Hour of Defence 1978, The Blue Angel 1979, Ave Maria played Softly 1981, The

Annunciation 1986, The Bartered and the Bought 1987, Miracle in the Dark House (Alfred Radok Prize 2008) 2004, Depart in Peace 2004, Nana 2005. *Publications:* novels: Like Water off a Duck's Back 1961, A Mysterious Tower in B. 1967, Rozpomínky: Co na sebe vím 2013. *Address:* Barvičova 59, 60200, Brno, Czech Republic (home). *Telephone:* 602366040 (home). *E-mail:* milan.uhde@seznam.cz (home).

UHL, Petr; Czech human rights activist and journalist; b. 8 Oct. 1941, Prague; s. of Bedřich Uhl and Marie Kohoutová; m. Anna Šabatová 1974; three s. one d.; ed Czech. Univ. of Tech., Prague; designer and patent clerk 1964–66; teacher, Coll. of Tech. Prague 1966–69; imprisoned for political activities 1969–73; designer 1974–78; Co-Founder Charter 77; Co-Founder Cttee for Protection of the Unjustly Prosecuted 1978; imprisoned for political activities 1979–84; stoker 1984–89; ed. of East European Information Agency 1988–90; leading rep. of Civic Forum, Prague 1989–90; Dir-Gen., Czechoslovak News Agency 1990–92, Ed. 1992–94; Ed.-in-Chief Listy (magazine) 1994–96; Ed. Právo (daily) 1996–98, 2001–06; Commr of Govt of Czech Repub. for Human Rights 1998–2001; Deputy to House of the Nations, Fed. Ass. 1990–92; Chair., Control and Auditing Comm. of Prison Staff Corps, Czech Repub. 1990; mem. Working Group on Arbitrary Detention of UN Comm. on Human Rights 1991–2001, Chair., Cttee for Prevention of Torture of Human Rights Council of Czech Govt 2002–07, mem. Council of Czech TV 2003–09, mem. EU Monitoring Centre for Racism and Xenophobia 2004–07; State Honours of Czech Repub. 1998, of Poland 2000, of Germany 2001; Chevalier, Ordre nat. du Mérite 2002, Légion d'honneur 2006; Press Freedom Award, Reporter without Borders, Austria 2002. *Publications:* The Programme of Social Self-government 1982, On Czechoslovak Prison System (co-author) 1998, Justice and Injustice in the Eyes of Petr Uhl 1999, Dělal jsem, co jsem považoval za správné (co-author) 2013, and numerous articles in Czech and foreign press. *Address:* Londýnská 7, 120 00 Prague 2, Czech Republic (home). *Telephone:* 72-5103775 (mobile) (home). *E-mail:* uhl@seznam.cz (home).

UHLENBECK, Karen Keskulla, PhD; American mathematician and academic; *Professor Emerita, University of Texas at Austin;* b. 24 Aug. 1942, Cleveland, Ohio; m. 1st Olke C. Uhlenbeck; m. 2nd Robert F. Williams; ed Univ. of Michigan, Courant Inst., Brandeis Univ.; held temporary post in Massachusetts Inst. of Tech. 1968–69; Lecturer, Univ. of California, Berkeley 1969–71; Univ. of Illinois Urbana-Champaign 1971–76; Prof., Univ. of Chicago 1983; Sid W. Richardson Foundation Regents Chair in Mathematics, Univ. of Texas at Austin 1987–2014, Prof. Emer. 2014–; currently Visiting Assoc., Inst. for Advanced Study and Visiting Sr Research Scholar, Princeton Univ.; mem. American Acad. of Arts and Science 1985, NAS 1986; Hon. mem., London Mathematical Society 2008; Dr hc (Univ. of Illinois, Champaign) 2000, (Univ. of Ohio) 2001, (Univ. of Michigan) 2004, (Harvard Univ.) 2007, (Princeton Univ.) 2012; MacArthur Prize Fellowship 1983, President's Nat. Medal of Science 2000, Guggenheim Fellowship 2001, Leroy P. Steele Prize, American Mathematical Soc. 2007, Abel Prize, Norwegian Acad. of Science and Letters (first woman recipient) 2019. *Publications include:* Instantons and 4-Manifolds (with Dan Freed) 1984, numerous scholarly research articles. *Address:* Department of Mathematics, University of Texas, Austin TX 78712, USA (office). *Telephone:* (512) 471-7711 (office). *E-mail:* uhlen@math.utexas.edu (office). *Website:* web.ma.utexas.edu/users/uhlen (office).

UHLIG, Harald Friedrich Hans Volker Sigmar, PhD; German economist and academic; *Professor of Economics, University of Chicago;* b. 26 April 1961, Bonn; s. of Dr Sigmar Uhlig and Elfriede Uhlig; ed Technische Univ., Berlin, Univ. of Minnesota; Teaching Asst, Technical Univ., Berlin 1982–85; Research Asst, Fed. Reserve Bank of Minneapolis and Inst. for Empirical Macroeconomics 1986–89; Teaching Asst, Univ. of Minn. 1987; Asst Prof., Dept of Econs, Princeton Univ. 1990–94; Research Prof. for Macroeconomics, Centre for Econ. Research, Tilburg Univ., Netherlands 1994–2000; Visiting Prof., Dept of Econs, Stanford Univ. 1999–2000; Prof. of Macroeconomics and Econ. Policy, Humboldt Univ. 2000–07; Prof. of Econs, Univ. of Chicago 2007–, Chair. of Dept 2009–12; Guest Researcher, German Inst. for Econ. Research, Berlin 2002; Visiting Asst Prof., Univ. of Chicago 1992–93; Guest Lecturer, Univ. of Bonn 1993, 1994; Jt Ed. European Economic Review 1997–2001, Econometrica 2006–10, Journal of Political Economy 2012–; Fellow, Econometric Soc. 2003; Research Fellow, Centre for Econ. Policy Research (CEPR); Fulbright Scholarship 1985–86; consultant to Bundesbank 2004, Fed. Reserve Bank of Chicago; mem. German Scholarship Foundation 1981–85, CEPR European Business Cycle Dating Cttee (currently Chair.) 2003–12, Econometric Soc., American Econ. Asscn, European Econ. Asscn; Dissertation Support Award, Nat. Bureau of Econ. Research 1989–90, Gossenpreis, Verein für Socialpolitik 2003, Frank P. Ramsey Prize 2005. *Publications:* numerous articles in econ. journals. *Address:* Department of Economics, University of Chicago, 1126 East 59th Street, Chicago, IL 60637 (office); 5454 South Hyde Park Boulevard, Chicago, IL 60615, USA (home). *Telephone:* (773) 702-3702 (office). *Fax:* (773) 702-8490 (office). *E-mail:* huhlig@uchicago.edu (office). *Website:* economics.uchicago.edu (office).

UHOMOIBHI, Martin Ihoeghian, BA, DPhil; Nigerian diplomatist and UN official; *Joint Special Representative for Darfur and Head, African Union–UN Hybrid Operation in Darfur (UNAMID), United Nations;* b. 3 Nov. 1954; m.; four c.; ed Univ. of Ibadan, Univ. of Oxford, UK; Lecturer in diplomatic and African history, Univ. of Ibadan 1977–84; more than 30 years of service in Ministry of Foreign Affairs, including as Sr First Sec. 1984, Coordinator and Alt. Rep. of Nigeria to UN Security Council, New York 1993–95, Special Asst to Minister for Foreign Affairs 1995–99, Consul-Gen. of Nigeria in Atlanta, USA 1999, Minister and Deputy Head of Mission, Embassy in Addis Ababa 2000–03, also Rep. to African Union and Econ. Comm. for Africa 2000–03, Deputy Dir and Head of Div. for Inter-African Affairs 2003–04, Dir Office of the Perm. Sec. 2004–07, Amb. to Switzerland and Perm. Rep. to UN Office in Geneva 2007; Pres., Gen. Ass., WIPO 2008–09; Pres., UN Human Rights Council 2008–09; Jt Special Rep. for Darfur and Head, African Union–UN Hybrid Operation in Darfur (UNAMID) 2015–; Founder and Pres. Pan African Inst. for Global Affairs and Strategy. *Address:* African Union–UN Hybrid Operation in Darfur (UNAMID), El Fasher, Sudan (office). *Website:* unamid.unmissions.org (office).

UHRIG, John Allan, AC; Australian business executive (retd); b. 24 Oct. 1928, Newcastle, NSW; s. of L. J. Uhrig; m. Shirley Attwood 1956; two s. two d.; ed Newcastle Tech. High School, Univ. of New South Wales; Man. Dir Simpson Ltd 1975–85; Dir CRA Ltd (now Rio Tinto Australia Ltd) 1983–98, Chair. (non-exec.) 1987–98; Chair. Codan Pty Ltd 1986–2007 (retd); Chair. Australian Mineral Devt Laboratories Ltd (Amdel) 1989, Australian Minerals and Energy Environment Foundation 1991; fmr Chair. Australian Mfg Council; Dir Westpac Banking Corpn 1989, Chair. 1992–2000; Deputy Chair. Santos Ltd 1992–94, apptd Chair. 1994 (Dir 1991); apptd Deputy Chair. RTZ 1995; mem. Remuneration Tribunal of South Australia 1985–89; Dr hc (Univ. of Queensland) 1997. *Achievements include:* commissioned by Prime Minister John Howard to review the corp. governance of statutory authorities 2002 (called Uhrig Review), report released 2004.

UJIIE, Junichi, BA, MA, PhD; Japanese business executive; *Senior Advisor to the Board, Nomura Holdings Inc.;* b. 1945; ed Univ. of Tokyo, Univ. of Chicago and Univ. of Illinois, USA; joined Nomura Securities as an analyst 1975, Pres. Nomura Bank, Switzerland 1984–87, Gen. Man. Int. Planning Dept 1987–90, Pres. Nomura Securities Int., USA 1990–92, mem. Bd of Dirs Nomura Holdings 1990–2011, Head US Div. 1992–95, Co-Chair. Nomura Securities Int., USA 1995–97, CEO and Pres. Nomura Securities Co. 1997–2003, Chair. Nomura Holdings Inc. 2003–11, Sr Advisor to the Bd 2011–; Vice-Chair. Japan Asscn of Corp. Execs (Keizai Doyukai); Chair. Bd of Govs Tokyo Stock Exchange 2000–01; fmr Co-Chair. World Econ. Forum on East Asia, Int. Advisory Panel, Monetary Authority of Singapore; mem. Singapore Forum Advisory Bd, S Rajaratnam Endowment CLG Ltd. *Leisure interests:* skiing, sailing, fishing, tennis, classical music. *Address:* Nomura Holdings Inc., 1-9-1, Nihonbashi, Chuo-ku, Tokyo 103-8645, Japan (office). *Telephone:* (3) 5255-1000 (office). *Fax:* (3) 3278-0420 (office). *E-mail:* info@nomuraholdings.com (office). *Website:* www.nomuraholdings.com (office).

ULAAN, Chültemiin, MSc; Mongolian economist and politician; *Minister of Food, Agriculture and Light Industry;* b. 22 April 1954, Baruun, Sukhbaatar Prov.; m. Baldan-Osor Bud; three c.; ed Irkhutsk Inst. of Nat. Economy, Irkhutsk, Acad. of Social Sciences, Russia, Acad. of Social Sciences, Bulgaria; Officer, State Planning Dept 1977–82, Head of Div. 1982–85; Instructor, Cen. Cttee, Mongolian People's Revolutionary Party (MPRP) 1985–89, Deputy Dir 1989–90, Adviser to Sec.-Gen. 1990; mem. Cabinet and Minister, Nat. Devt Bd 1992–96; mem. Parl. 1996–; Minister of Finance and Economy 2000–04; Deputy Prime Minister 2004–06; Minister of Finance 2007–08, 2012–15; Minister of Food, Agriculture and Light Industry 2019–. *Address:* Ministry of Food, Agriculture and Light Industry, Government Building 9, Enkhtaivny Örgön Chölöö 16A, Bayanzürkh District, Ulaanbaatar, Mongolia (office). *Telephone:* (51) 262271 (office). *Fax:* (11) 263237 (office). *E-mail:* mofa@mofa.gov.mn (office). *Website:* www.mofa.gov.mn (office).

ULDUM, Andreas René; Greenlandic social worker, musician and politician; b. 21 April 1979, Qeqertarsuaq; s. of Nils Uldum and Anne Sofie Uldum; m. Charlotte Marie Uldum; two c.; early career as social worker; fmr Chair., Cttee for Children, Family and School, Municipality of Sermersooq; musician with pop group DDR, also solo career; mem. Inatsisartut (Greenland Parl.) 2009–16; Municipal Commr and first Deputy Mayor, Municipality of Sermersooq 2012–13; First Deputy Prime Minister and Minister for Finance and Mineral Resources 2014–16; mem. Demokraatit (Democrats), Leader 2014–16. *Address:* Grønlands Selvstyre, Imaneq 4, POB 1015, 3900 Nuuk Greenland.

ULIANOVSCHI, Tudor, LLM, PhD; Moldovan diplomatist and politician; *Minister of Foreign Affairs and European Integration;* b. 26 May 1983, Florești, Moldovan SSR, USSR; m.; one c.; ed Univ. Liberă Internațională din Moldova, Univ. de Stat din Moldova, Diplomatic Acad. of Vienna; Sec., America, Asia, Middle East and Africa Directorate, Ministry of Foreign Affairs and European Integration (MFA) 2005–07, Counsellor (Sec. I) responsible for political relations, Embassy in Washington DC 2007–10, Counsellor, Directorate of America, Asia, Middle East and Africa, MFA 2010–11, Dir for America, Asia, Middle East and Africa, MFA 2012–13, Chargé d'affaires, Embassy in Doha, Qatar 2013–14, Deputy Minister of Foreign Affairs and European Integration 2014–16, Amb. to Switzerland 2016–18, also Perm. Rep. to UN in Geneva 2016–18, Minister of Foreign Affairs and European Integration 2018–. *Publications:* numerous publications in the field of int. law, commercial law and int. humanitarian law. *Address:* Ministry of Foreign Affairs and European Integration, 2012 Chișinău, str. 31 August 1989 80, Moldova (office). *Telephone:* (22) 57-82-05 (office). *Fax:* (22) 23-23-02 (office). *E-mail:* secdep@mfa.md (office). *Website:* www.mfa.gov.md (office).

ULLMAN, Myron (Mike) Edward, III, BS; American retail executive; *Chairman, Mercy Ships International;* b. 26 Nov. 1946, Youngstown, OH; s. of Myron Edward Ullman Jr and June Cunningham; m. Cathy Emmons 1969; six c.; ed Univ. of Cincinnati, Harvard Univ.; Int. Account Man. IBM Corpn 1969–76; Vice-Pres. for Business Affairs Univ. of Cincinnati 1976–81; White House Fellow, The White House 1981–82; Exec. Vice-Pres. Sanger Harris Div., Federated Stores 1982–86; Man. Dir and COO Wharf Holdings Ltd, Hong Kong 1986–88; Man. Dir Lane Crawford Ltd, Hong Kong 1986–88; Chair. and CEO R. H. Macy & Co. 1988–95; Deputy Chair. and Dir Federated Dept Stores Inc.; Chair. and CEO DFS Group Ltd 1995–98, Group Chair. 1999–2000; Dir-Gen. and Group Man. Dir Louis Vuitton Möet Hennessy, Paris 1999–2002; Chair. De Beers LV 2000–02; Co-Chair. Global Crossing Ltd 2002–04; Chair. and CEO J. C. Penney Co. Inc. 2004–11, 2013–15; Chair. Mercy Ships Int. 1992–; mem. Bd of Dirs Starbucks Coffee, Segway LLC, Polo Ralph Lauren, Nat. Multiple Sclerosis Soc., Brunswick School, Univ. of Cincinnati Foundation, Fed. Reserve Bank of Dallas, Retail Industry Leaders Asscn, FIRST (charity); Chair. Exec. Council Univ. of California Medical Center Foundation 2002–, Nat. Retail Fed., Mercy Ships International; Int. Vice-Pres. Univ. of Cincinnati Alumni Asscn. *Address:* Mercy Ships, PO Box 2020, Garden Valley, Lindale, TX 75771, USA (office). *Telephone:* (903) 939-7000 (office). *E-mail:* info@mercyships.org (office). *Website:* www.mercyships.org (office).

ULLMAN, Tracey; British actress and singer; b. 30 Dec. 1959, Slough; d. of Anthony John Ullman and Dorin Cleaver; m. Allan McKeown 1984 (died 2013); one s. one d.; ed Italia Conti Stage School; British Acad. Award 1983, Rudolph Valentino Cinema Lifetime Achievement Award 1992, Charlie Chaplin Lifetime Achievement Award, BAFTA 2009. *Films include:* The Rocky Horror Picture Show, Give My Regards to Broad Street, Plenty 1985, Jumpin' Jack Flash 1986, I Love You To Death 1990, Robin Hood: Men in Tights 1993, Household Saints, Bullets over Broadway 1994, Pret-a-Porter 1995, Everybody Says I Love You 1996, C-Scam 2000, Panic 2000, Small Town Crooks 2000, A Dirty Shame 2004, The Cat

That Looked at a King (voice) 2004, Corpse Bride (voice) 2005, Kronk's New Groove (voice) 2005, I Could Never Be Your Woman 2007, The Tale of Despereaux (voice) 2008, Into the Woods 2014, Zog 2018. *Stage appearances include:* Gigi, Elvis, Grease, Four in a Million (London Theatre Critics' Award 1981). *Recordings:* album: You Broke My Heart in Seventeen Places 1983. *Television appearances include:* The Tracey Ullman Show 1987–90, The Best of the Tracey Ullman Show 1990, Tracey Takes On 1996, Ally McBeal 1998–99, Visible Panty Lines (series) 2001, Tracey Ullman in the Trailer Tales 2003, Once Upon a Mattress 2005, State of the Union (series) 2008–09, How I Met Your Mother (series) 2014, Good Session (film) 2015, Tracey Ullman's Show (series) 2016, Tracey Breaks the News (series) 2017–18, Howards End (mini-series) 2017, Girls (series) 2017. *Leisure interests:* hiking, riding. *Address:* Hamilton Hodell, Warwick House, 20 Golden Square, Soho, London, W1F 9JL, England (office). *Telephone:* (20) 7636-1221 (office). *E-mail:* info@hamiltonhodell.co.uk (office). *Website:* www.hamiltonhodell.co.uk (office).

ULLMANN, Liv Johanne; Norwegian actress; b. 16 Dec. 1938, Tokyo, Japan; d. of Viggo Ullmann and Janna Ullmann (née Lund); m. 1st Dr Gappe Stang 1960 (divorced 1965); one d.; m. 2nd Donald Saunders 1985 (divorced 1995); worked in Stavanger repertory co. 1956–59; has appeared at Nat. Theatre and Norwegian State Theatre, Oslo; work for UNICEF as Goodwill Amb.; Vice-Chair. Int. Rescue Cttee; Pres. Fed. of European Film Dirs; Commdr of Olav 1994, Commdr with Star of the Order of St Olav 2005; 12 hon. doctorates; Best Actress of the Year, Nat. Soc. of Critics in America 1969, 1970, 1974, NY Film Critics Award 1973, 1974, Hollywood Foreign Press Asscn's Golden Globe 1973, Best Actress of the Year, Swedish TV 1973, 1974, Donatello Award (Italy) 1975, Bambi Award (Fed. Repub. of Germany) 1975, nominated for Tony Award as Best Stage Actress, debut on Broadway in A Doll's House 1975, LA Film Critics' Award (Face to Face) 1976, New York Film Critics' Award (Face to Face) 1977, Nat. Bd of Review of Motion Pictures Award (Face to Face) 1977, Peer Gynt Award (Norway), Eleanor Roosevelt Award 1982, Roosevelt Freedom Medal 1984, Dag Hammarskjöld Award 1986, Outstanding Contribution to Int. Cinema, Int. Indian Film Acad. 2012. *Films include:* Pan 1965, Persona 1966, The Hour of the Wolf 1968, Shame 1968, The Passion of Anna 1969, The Night Visitor 1971, The Emigrants 1972, Cries and Whispers 1972, Pope Joan 1972, Lost Horizon 1973, 40 Carats 1973, The New Land 1973, Zandy's Bride 1973, Scenes from a Marriage 1974, The Abdication 1974, Face to Face 1975, The Serpent's Egg 1978, Sonate d'automne 1978, Richard's Things 1980, The Wild Duck 1983, Love Streams 1983, Let's Hope It's a Girl 1985, Baby Boy 1984, Dangerous Moves 1985, Gaby Brimmer 1986, Moscow Adieu 1986, Time of Indifference 1987, La Amiga 1987, Mindwalk, The Ox, The Long Shadow; Dir: Sophie 1993, Kristin Lavrandsdatter (wrote screenplay also), Faithless (dir) 2000, Saraband (TV) 2003, The Danish Poet (voice) 2006, I et speil, i en gåte 2008, Zwei Leben 2012, Miss Julie (dir) 2014. *Plays include:* Brand 1973, A Doll's House 1975, Anna Christie 1977, I Remember Mama 1979, Ghosts 1982, Old Times 1985, The Six Faces of Women (TV), Mother Courage. *Publications include:* Changing (autobiography) 1976, Choices (autobiography) 1984. *Leisure interest:* reading. *Address:* c/o Jean Diamond, Diamond Management, 31 Percy Street, London, W1T 2DD, England (office). *Telephone:* (20) 7631-0400 (office). *Fax:* (20) 7631-0500 (office). *E-mail:* agents@diman.co.uk (office). *Website:* www.diamondmanagement.co.uk (office).

ULLRICH, Axel, PhD; German biochemist and academic; *Director, Department of Molecular Biology, Max Planck Institute of Biochemistry;* b. 19 Oct. 1943, Lauban; ed Univs of Tübingen, Münster and Heidelberg; Asst Biochemist, Institute of Biochemistry, Univ. of Münster 1971–72; Postdoctoral Fellow, Dept of Biochemistry and Biophysics, Univ. of California, San Francisco, USA 1975–77, Asst Research Biochemist 1977–78; Sr Scientist, Genentech, Inc., South San Francisco 1979–84, Staff Scientist 1984–88; Dir Dept of Molecular Biology, Max Planck Inst. of Biochemistry, Martinsried 1988–, Man. Dir Max Planck Inst. of Biochemistry 1999, 2007; Visiting Prof., Acad. de Paris, Sorbonne, Paris, France 1996–98; Visiting Scientist and Research Dir of Singapore Oncogenome (SOG) Project, Centre for Molecular Medicine (CMM), Agency for Science, Tech. and Research (A*STAR), Singapore 2004–, Scientific Advisor and Program Dir 2007–11, mem. Int. Advisory Council 2000–04; Co-founder SUGEN, Inc., South San Francisco 1991, mem. Bd of Dirs and Science Advisory Bd 1991–99, Co-Chair. Clinical Science Advisory Bd 1999, mem. Science Advisory Bd SUGEN/Pharmacia 1999–2003; Co-founder Virgene/Axxima Pharmaceuticals AG, Martinsried 1998, mem. Bd of Dirs Axxima Pharmaceuticals AG 1998–2004; Co-founder Kinaxo Biotechnologies GmbH, Martinsried 2005; Founder U3 Pharma AG, Martinsried 2001, Chair. 2001–08; Founder and Vice-Chair. Academic Bd Cooperation Lab. for Biological Signal Transduction Research, Second Mil. Medical Univ., Shanghai, People's Repub. of China 1996–2002; mem. Science Advisory Bd, Hagedorn Research Inst., Denmark 1991–95, Receptor BioLogix, Inc., San Francisco 2006–, Centenary Inst., Newtown, Australia 2007–, The Wistar Inst., Philadelphia, USA 1995–2002, RZPD (German Resource Centre for Genome Research), Berlin 2001–03, Biomedicum, Helsinki, Finland 2001–, Univ. of Montreal, Groupe de Recherche Universitaire sur le Médicament (GRUM), Canada 2005–; mem. Advisory Bd, Max Planck Innovation GmbH, Munich 1992–, Chair. Advisory Bd 1996–2004; Vice-Chair. Advisory Bd, Hans Knöll Institut, Jena 1992–2000, Boehringer-Ingelheim, Ingelheim 2003–06, Fondazione Piemontese per la Ricerca sul Cancro, Candiolo, Italy 2008–, Nat. Center for Tumor Diseases (NCT), Heidelberg 2008–; mem. Supervisory Bd BioM AG, Martinsried 1997–2007; mem. One-North Resource Advisory Panel, JTC Corpn and Ministry for Environment, Singapore 2003–, Int. Panel for the Planning of a Research-Intensive Univ., Ministry of Educ., Singapore 2003–04; mem. Bd of Trustees, Max Delbrück Centre for Molecular Medicine, Berlin 2003–06; mem. Scientific Cttee Genoma España, Madrid, Spain 2003, Academic Research Council of Nat. Research Foundation, Singapore 2006–; Co-Ed.-in-Chief Current Signal Transduction Therapy; mem. Editorial Bd, Cancer Research, Growth Factors, Molecular Brain Research, Receptors and Channels, Journal of Cellular Physiology, Cancer Genomics & Proteomics, Molecules and Cells, Molecular Cancer Research, EMBO Molecular Medicine; mem. Academia Europaea, American Soc. for Cell Biology, European Molecular Biology Org. (EMBO) 1990, Gesellschaft für Biochemie und Molekularbiologie e.V., American Asscn for Cancer Research, Int. Union Against Cancer (UICC), Deutsche Krebsgesellschaft, Int. Life Science Forum, AAAS, Deutsche Akad. der Naturforscher Leopoldina 2000, American Acad. of Arts and Sciences 2005, Hungarian Acad. of Sciences 2013; Fellow, American Asscn for Cancer Research 2014; Hon. Prof., Second Mil. Medical Univ., Shanghai 1996, Univ. of Tübingen 2000; Hon. mem. The World Innovation Foundation 2003; Bundesverdienstkreuz 1. Klasse 2009; Laurea hc in Medicine and Surgery, Univ. of Chieti, Italy 2009, Dr hc (Univ. of Athens) 2012, (Semmelweis Univ., Budapest) 2012; numerous awards including Paul Langerhans Medal, German Diabetes Soc. 1987, John W. Cline Memorial Lecturer (sponsored by the American Cancer Soc.), UCLA 1987, first Annual Ray A. and Robert L. Kroc Lecture, Univ. of Massachusetts 1987, Berthold Medal, German Soc. for Endocrinology 1988, Prix Antoine Lacassagne, La Ligue Nationale Française Contre le Cancer, Paris, France 1991, German Cancer Prize, German Cancer Soc., Frankfurt 1998, Bruce F. Cain Memorial Award, American Asscn for Cancer Research 2000, Robert Koch Prize, Robert Koch Foundation 2001, Int. Fellow, Garvan Inst. of Cancer Research, Sydney, Australia 2001, King Faisal Int. Prize for Medicine, Saudi Arabia 2003, Meyer-Schwickerath Lecture, Soc. of Medical Science, Essen 2003, Warburg Medal, Soc. of Biochemistry and Molecular Biology (GBM) 2005, European BioBusiness Leadership Award, Univ. of Southern California Marshall School of Business 2005, Clifford Prize for Cancer Research (Shiraz Prize), Inst. of Medical and Veterinary Science, Adelaide, Australia 2005, Deutsche Krebshilfe Preis 2005, Deutsche Krebshilfe (German Cancer Aid) e.V. 2006, ASMR Medal, Australian Soc. for Medical Research 2007, Warren Alpert Prize, Harvard Medical School, Cambridge, USA (jtly) 2007, Karl Heinz Beckurts-Preis, Karl Heinz Beckurts-Stiftung, Garching 2007, Prince Mahidol Award of Medicine, Prince Mahidol Foundation, Bangkok, Thailand 2007, Hamdan Award for Medical Research Excellence, Dubai, UAE 2008, Sergio Lombroso Award in Cancer Research, Weizmann Inst. of Science, Israel 2009, Debrecen Award for Molecular Medicine, Univ. of Debrecen, Hungary 2009, Wolf Foundation Prize in Medicine 2010, Lennox K Black Int. Prize for Excellence in Biomedical Research 2012, CRRT Int. Cancer Research Award 2014, Johann-Georg-Zimmermann Medal 2017. *Publications:* numerous papers in professional journals. *Address:* Department of Molecular Biology, Max Planck Institute of Biochemistry, Am Klopferspitz 18, 82152 Martinsried, Germany (office). *Telephone:* (89) 8578-2512 (office). *Fax:* (89) 8578-2454 (office). *E-mail:* ullrich@biochem.mpg.de (office). *Website:* www.biochem.mpg.de/en/rd/ullrich (office).

ULLRICH, Jan; German professional cyclist; b. 2 Dec. 1973, Rostock; s. of Werner Ullrich and Marianne Kaatz; m. Sara Ullrich; one s. one d.; ed S.C. Dynamo sports school, Berlin; wins as an amateur include: World Championships (Road) 1993, South Africa Tour (three stage wins) 1994, Lower Saxony Tour (two stage wins); turned professional 1995; wins as a professional include: German Time Trial Champion (50km) 1995, Regio Tour (one stage win) 1996, Tour de France 1997, German Road Championships 1997, silver and gold Olympic medals, Sydney 2000; runner-up Tour de France 1996, 1998, 2000, 2001, 2003, fourth 2004, third 2005; seven stage wins, Tour de France; in 2002 tested positive in dope test and given six-month suspension by German Cycling Fed.; German Sportsman of the Year 1997, 2003, World Cyclist of the Year 1997. *Leisure interests:* skiing, motor sports, cinema. *Address:* Livewelt GmbH & Co. KG, Berliner Straße 133, 33330 Gütersloh, Germany (office). *Telephone:* (52) 412109024 (office). *Fax:* (52) 412109023 (office). *E-mail:* alina.otten@livewelt.de (office); jan@janullrich.de. *Website:* www.janullrich.de.

ULMANIS, Guntis, BEcon; Latvian fmr head of state; b. 13 Sept. 1939, Rīga; m. Aina Ulmane (née Stelce); one s. one d.; ed Univ. of Latvia; as a child was exiled to Russia together with his parents, returned to Latvia in 1946; mil. service 1963–65; Economist, bldg industry and Riga Public Transport Bd; Man. Riga Municipal Community Services 1965–92; fmr Lecturer in Construction Econs, Rīga Polytechnic Inst. and Econ. Planning, Latvian State Univ.; mem. CPSU 1965–89; mem. Bd of Cen. Bank of Latvia 1992–93, Deputy to Parl. (Saeima) June–July 1993, 2010–11; Pres. of Latvia 1993–99; f. Guntis Ulmanis Fund; Hon. Chair. Union of Farmers Party 1993–; numerous decorations, including Order of St Michael and St George (UK) 1996, Légion d'honneur 1997, Order of Merit (Germany) 1999; Dr hc (Charleston Univ., USA) 1996; Award of US Inst. for East-West Studies 1996, Cen. and E European Law Initiative Award, American Bar Asscn 1997, Distinguished Statesman Award, Anti-Defamation League 1998. *Publications:* Autobiography 1995, My Time as President 1999. *Leisure interests:* hunting, reading, playing with grandchildren. *Address:* Brīvības iela 38, Apt 5, 1050 Rīga, Latvia (home). *Telephone:* 927-8758. *Fax:* 732-5800.

ULRICH, Jing, BA, MA; Chinese investment manager and business executive; *Managing Director and Vice-Chairman, Asia Pacific, JPMorgan Chase;* b. (Li Jing), 28 June 1967, Beijing; m. Paul Ulrich; ed Harvard and Stanford Univs, USA; worked as fund man. for Greater China at Emerging Markets, Washington, DC, USA 1990–96; led team covering China market, Credit Lyonnais Securities Asia 1996–2003; Man. Dir Greater China Equities, Deutsche Bank 2003–05; Man. Dir and Chair. of Global Markets, JPMorgan Chase 2005, now Man. Dir and Vice-Chair., Asia Pacific; mem. Multinational Advisory Cttee, APEC China Business Council 2014–; mem. Bd of Dirs GlaxoSmithKline plc 2012–, Ermenegildo Zegna 2012–; mem. Int. Advisory Council, Università Bocconi; chosen by Asiamoney magazine as Best China Strategist, ranked by Institutional Investor magazine as head of the top China team world-wide 2003, 2004, 2005, 2006, 2007, chosen by The South China Morning Post and the American Chamber of Commerce in Hong Kong as Hong Kong's Young Achiever of the Year 2006. *Address:* JF Investment Centre, Walkway Level, Jardine House, 1 Connaught Place, Central, Hong Kong Special Administrative Region, People's Republic of China (office). *Telephone:* 22651133 (office). *Fax:* 28685013 (office). *E-mail:* investor.services@jpmorgan.com (office). *Website:* www.jpmorganam.com.hk/wps/portal (office).

ULRICH, Robert (Bob) J., BA; American retail executive; *Chairman Emeritus, Target Corporation;* b. 1943, Minneapolis, Minn.; ed Univ. of Minnesota; began career as merchandising trainee, Dayton Hudson 1967, Pres. and CEO Diamond Dept Stores 1981–82, Pres. Dayton Hudson Dept Store Co. 1982–84, Pres. Target Div. 1984–87, Chair. and CEO Target 1987–94, Chair. and CEO Dayton Hudson Corpn (renamed Target Corpn 2000) 1994–2008, Chair. Target Corpn 2008–09, Chair. Emer. 2009–; Founder and Chair. Musical Instrument Museum; mem. Bd of Dirs 3M, Univ. of St Thomas; Life Trustee, Minneapolis Inst. of Arts; Discounter of the Year, Discount Store News SPARC (Supplier Performance Award by Retail

Category) Award 1992. *Address:* c/o Musical Instrument Museum, 4725 East Mayo Boulevard, Phoenix, AZ 85050, USA.

ULUDONG, Ngedikes Olai, BSc, MSc; Palauan diplomatist; *Permanent Representative to United Nations;* b. 1979; ed Univ. of Guam, Univ. of South Pacific; Military Policewoman US Army Reserve, Guam 1999–2003; Lead Negotiator Alliance of Small Island States on UN Framework Convention on Climate Change 2012–14; Amb. to EU and Belgium 2015–17, concurrently Amb. on Climate Change, Perm. Rep. to UN FAO; Perm. Rep. to UN 2017–. *Address:* Permanent Mission of Palau, 866 United Nations Plaza, Suite 575, New York, NY 10017, USA (office). *Telephone:* (212) 813-0310 (office). *Fax:* (212) 813-0317 (office). *E-mail:* mission@palauun.org (office). *Website:* www.palauun.org (office).

ULVÆUS, Björn Kristian; Swedish songwriter, musician (guitar), singer and producer; b. 25 April 1945, Gothenburg; m. Agnetha Fältskog 1971 (divorced 1979); songwriter with Benny Andersson 1966–; duo with Andersson as The Hootennanny Singers; partner in production with Andersson at Polar Music 1971; mem. pop group ABBA 1973–82; winner Eurovision Song Contest 1974; concerts include Royal Performance, Stockholm 1976, Royal Albert Hall, London 1977, UNICEF concert, New York 1979, Wembley Arena 1979; reunion with ABBA, Swedish TV This Is Your Life 1986; continued writing and producing with Andersson 1982–; produced musical Mamma Mia! with Andersson, West End, London 1999; World Music Award for Best Selling Swedish Artist 1993, Ivor Novello Special International Award (with Benny Andersson) 2002. *Film:* ABBA: The Movie 1977. *Compositions include:* ABBA songs (with Benny Andersson); musicals: Chess (with lyrics by Tim Rice) 1983, The Immigrants 1994, Mamma Mia! (with Andersson) 1999. *Recordings include:* albums: with Andersson: Happiness 1971; with ABBA: Waterloo 1974, ABBA 1976, Greatest Hits 1976, Arrival 1977, The Album 1978, Voulez-Vous 1979, Greatest Hits Vol. 2 1979, Super Trouper 1980, The Visitors 1981, The Singles: The First Ten Years 1982, Thank You For The Music 1983, Absolute ABBA 1988, ABBA Gold 1992, More ABBA Gold 1993, Forever Gold 1998, The Definitive Collection 2001; singles include: with ABBA: Ring Ring 1973, Waterloo 1974, Mamma Mia 1975, Dancing Queen 1976, Fernando 1976, Money Money Money 1976, Knowing Me Knowing You 1977, The Name Of The Game 1977, Take A Chance On Me 1978, Summer Night City 1978, Chiquitita 1979, Does Your Mother Know? 1979, Angel Eyes/Voulez-Vous 1979, Gimme Gimme Gimme (A Man After Midnight) 1979, I Have A Dream 1979, The Winner Takes It All 1980, Super Trouper 1980, On And On And On 1981, Lay All Your Love On Me 1981, One Of Us 1981, When All Is Said And Done 1982, Head Over Heels 1982, The Day Before You Came 1982, Under Attack 1982, Thank You For The Music 1983. *Publication:* Mamma Mia! How Can I Resist You? (with Benny Andersson and Judy Craymer) 2006. *Address:* Södra Brobänken 41A, 111 49 Stockholm, Sweden. *Website:* www.abbasite.com.

ULYUKAYEV, Alexey Valentinovich, Dr Econ; Russian politician, economist and banker; b. 23 March 1956, Russia; m.; two s. one d.; ed Moscow State Univ.; Asst, then Assoc. Prof., Moscow Inst. of Construction Eng 1982–88; Consultant, Head of Div., Communist (journal) 1988–91; political analyst, Moskovskiye Novosti (weekly) 1991; econ. adviser to Russian Govt 1991–92; Head f Group of Advisers to Chair. of Govt, Russian Fed. 1992–93; Asst to First Deputy Chair. of Govt, Russian Fed. 1993–94; Deputy Dir Inst. of Econ. Problems of the Transition Period 1994–96, 1998–2000; Deputy, Moscow City Duma 1996–98; First Deputy Minister of Finance 2000–04; First Deputy Chair. Central Bank of the Russian Fed. 2004–13, Minister of Econ. Devt 2013–16; Dir Moscow Interbank Currency Exchange 2008–11; charged with bribery 2016; sentenced to eight years in prison Dec. 2017. *Leisure interests:* tourism, swimming, literature.

UMAR, Asad, MBA; Pakistani business executive and politician; b. 8 Sept. 1961; s. of Ghulam Umar; m.; two s.; ed Inst. of Business Admin, Pakistan; joined Exxon Chemical Pakistan (later renamed Engro Pakistan Ltd) 1985, worked in Karachi, Daharki and Edmonton, Canada in Finance, Manufacturing, Marketing and New Ventures Div., later Sr Vice-Pres. Engro Chemical Pakistan Ltd, Chair. and CEO 2004–12, Dir Engro Chemical Pakistan Ltd, Engro Vopak Terminal Ltd, Engro Asahi Polymer & Chemicals Ltd (fmr first Pres.), Port Qasim Authority 2000–01; mem. Pakistan Tehreek-e-Insaf (PTI) 2012–; mem. Nat. Ass. of Pakistan (PTI) for constituency NA-48 (Islamabad-I) 2013–18, for NA-54 (Islamabad-III) 2018–; Minister of Finance, Revenue and Econ. Affairs 2018–19; mem. Bd of Man. Pakistan State Oil; mem. Bd of Dirs Pakistan Business Council, Karachi Educ. Initiative, Pakistan Inst. of Corp. Governance, State Bank of Pakistan; mem. Overseas Investors' Chamber of Commerce and Industry's Standing Sub-cttee for Commercial and Industrial Matters 1998–2000, Man. Asscn Pakistan's Corp. Excellence Award Sub-cttee 1998–2000; fmr Chapter Chair. Young Presidents Org. (Pakistan Chapter); Trustee, Lahore Univ. of Man. Sciences, Pakistan Centre for Philanthropy; Sitara-i-Imtiaz 2010. *Address:* c/o Ministry of Finance, Revenue and Economic Affairs, Blk C, Pakistan Secretariat, Islamabad, Pakistan (office).

UMBELINA NETO, Natália Pedro da Costa, PhD; São Tomé and Príncipe politician; b. 3 Nov. 1951, Príncipe; ed Univ. Nova de Lisboa, Portugal, Univ. Aix-Marseille I, France; served two years as Sec.-Gen., São Tomé and Príncipe Comm. for UNESCO; fmr Inspector of Educ.; Sec. for Social Affairs, Regional Govt of Príncipe –2012; Minister of Foreign Affairs, Co-operation and Communities 2012–14.

UMEDA, Sadao, PhD; Japanese business executive; *Chairman and Representative Director, Kajima Corporation;* ed Kyoto Univ.; Pres. Kajima Corpn (building construction co. providing design, eng, building and real estate devt services) 1996–2005, Chair. and Rep. Dir 2005–; mem. Keidanren Japan-Hong Kong Business Cooperation Cttee 2000–, Chair. 2002; Chair. Japan Federation of Construction Contractors, Japan Civil Engineering Contractors Asscn; mem. Bd of Dirs Japan Telework Asscn 2003, Japan Fashion Asscn, Japan Water Forum Advisory Council; Pres. Ethiopian Asscn of Japan, Japanese-Turkish Econ. Council; mem. Japan Cttee, Pacific Basic Econ. Council; Councilor, Aspen Inst. Japan; Distinguished Service Award, Japan Soc. of Civil Engineers 2008. *Address:* Office of the Chairman, Kajima Corporation, 3-1 Motoakasaka 1-chome, Minatu-ku, Tokyo 107-8388, Japan (office). *Telephone:* (3) 3403-3311 (office). *Fax:* (3) 3470-1444 (office). *E-mail:* info@kajima.co.jp (office). *Website:* www.kajima.co.jp (office).

UMPLEBY, Jim, BSc; American business executive; *Chairman and CEO, Caterpillar, Inc.;* b. 1958; s. of Donald James Umpleby, Jr and Marcella Levakis Umpleby; m. Katherine Umpleby; two c.; ed Rose-Hulman Inst. of Tech., Int. Inst. for Management Devt, Lausanne; joined Solar Turbines, Inc. (wholly-owned subsidiary of Caterpillar, Inc.) as Assoc. Engineer 1980, various engineering and sales positions, becoming Dir of Power Systems Operations and Plant Man., Kearny Mesa gas turbine packaging facility 1994, Vice Pres., Oil and Gas, Solar Turbines, Inc. 2007–10, Pres. Solar Turbines, Inc. 2010–13, also Gen. Man. for Global Services, Product Support Div., Caterpillar, Inc. 2005, Vice Pres., Caterpillar, Inc. 2010–13, Pres. 2013–17, CEO, Caterpillar, Inc. 2017–18, Chair. and CEO 2018–; mem. Bd of Trustees, Rose-Hulman Inst. of Tech.; mem. Bd of Dirs US–India Business Council; mem. Business Roundtable. *Address:* Caterpillar, Inc., 501 Southwest Jefferson Avenue, Peoria, IL 61630, USA (office). *Telephone:* (309) 675-0545 (office). *Website:* www.caterpillar.com (office).

UNANUE, Emil Raphael, MD; Cuban immunologist and academic; *Paul and Ellen Lacy Professor, Pathology and Immunology, Department of Pathology and Immunology, School of Medicine, Washington University in St Louis;* b. 13 Sept. 1934, Havana; ed Inst. of Secondary Educ., Havana, Univ. of Havana School of Medicine; Intern in Pathology, Presbyterian Univ. Hosp., Pittsburgh, Pa 1961–62; Research Fellow, Dept of Experimental Pathology, Scripps Clinic and Research Foundation, La Jolla, Calif. 1962–66, Assoc. 1968–70; Research Fellow, Immunology Div., Nat. Inst. for Medical Research, London, UK 1966–68; Asst Prof. of Pathology, Harvard Medical School, Boston, Mass 1970–71, Assoc. Prof. 1972–74, Mallinckrodt Prof. of Immunopathology 1974–84; Consultant in Pathology, Dept of Pathology, Brigham and Women's Hosp. 1977–84; Visiting Prof., Kuwait Univ. School of Medicine, Kuwait 1982, Royal Postgraduate Medical School, London 1983; Pathologist-in-Chief, Barnes-Jewish Hosp., St Louis, Mo. 1985–; Mallinckrodt Prof. and Chair. Dept of Pathology and Immunology, Washington Univ. School of Medicine, St Louis 1985–2006, now Paul and Ellen Lacy Professor; Burroughs Wellcome Visiting Prof. in the Basic Medical Sciences, Tulane Univ., New Orleans, La 2000; Pres. American Asscn of Pathologists 1988–89; Assoc. Ed. Journal of Immunology 1972–77, Clinical Immunology and Immunopathology 1972–89, International Archives of Allergy and Applied Immunology 1973–91, Journal of the Reticuloendothelial Society 1974–77, Laboratory Investigation 1975–90, Immunity 1994–96 (Ed. 1996–2000); Contributing Ed. Sanguinis 1976–77; Transmitting Ed. International Immunology 1992–; mem. Editorial Bd Modern Pathology 1988–97, Molecular Medicine 1994–, Immunological Reviews 1996–; mem. American Soc. of Investigative Pathology 1966, American Asscn of Immunologists 1966, Reticuloendothelial Soc. 1977, American Soc. for Cell Biology 1984, Asscn of Pathology Chairmen 1986, US and Canadian Acad. of Pathology 1986, NAS 1987 (Chair. Section 43—Microbiology and Immunology 1998–), Alpha Omgea Alpha Hon. Medical Soc. 1988, Pew Nat. Advisory Council 1994–98, Inst. of Medicine 1995; Sr Fellow, American Cancer Soc. (Calif. Div.) 1969–70, American Acad. of Arts and Sciences 1989; Hon. mem. Venezuelan Soc. of Allergy and Immunology 1981; Hon. MA (Harvard) 1974; Dr hc (Barcelona) 1999; Helen Hay Whitney Fellowship and T. Ducket Jones Award 1966–69, NIH Research Career Development Award 1971, Parke Davis Award, American Soc. for Experimental Pathology 1973, Guggenheim Fellowship 1980–81, Marie T. Bonzainga Annual Research Award, Reticuloendothelial Soc. 1986, William B. Coley Award, Cancer Research Inst. 1989, Albert Lasker Award for Basic Medical Research 1995, Rous-Whipple Award, American Soc. for Investigative Pathology 1998, Kenneth W. Sell Memorial Lecturer, Emory Univ. 1999, Gairdner Foundation Int. Award 2000, Robert Koch Gold Medal 2005, Lifetime Achievement Award, American Asscn of Immunologists 2014. *Publications:* more than 210 articles in scientific journals. *Address:* Room 1751, 1st Floor, West Building, Department of Pathology and Immunology, School of Medicine, Washington University in St, 660 S Euclid Avenue, St Louis, MO 63110, USA (office). *Telephone:* (314) 362-7440 (office); (314) 362-8752 (Lab). *Fax:* (314) 362-4096 (office). *E-mail:* unanue@wustl.edu (office). *Website:* www.unanuelab.org; pathology.wustl.edu (office).

UNGARO, Emanuel Mattéotti; French fashion designer (retd); b. 13 Feb. 1933, Aix-en-Provence; s. of Cosimo Ungaro and Concetta Casalino; m. Laura Bernabei; one d.; ed Lycée d'Aix-en-Provence; worked as tailor at Aix-en-Provence, then with Camps, Paris, Balenciaga, Paris and Madrid 1958–64, Courrèges, Paris 1964; Couturier, Paris 1965–2004; sold Ungaro label to Asim Abdullah 2005; Chevalier, Légion d'honneur. *Leisure interests:* music, reading, skiing. *Address:* 2 avenue Montaigne, 75008 Paris, France. *Telephone:* 1-53-57-00-00 (office). *Fax:* 1-53-57-00-08 (office). *E-mail:* info@ungaro.fr. *Website:* www.ungaro.com.

UNGER, Felix, DrMed; Austrian surgeon; *President, European Academy of Sciences and Arts;* b. 2 March 1946, Klagenfurt; s. of Carl Unger and Maria Unger; m. Monika von Fioreschy 1971; two s.; Lecturer, Univ. of Vienna 1978–83; apptd Prof., Univ. of Innsbruck 1983; Head of Heart Surgery, Univ. Clinic for Cardiac Surgery, Salzburg 1984–2011; Pres., Guggenheim Asscn Salzburg 1988–90; Founder and Pres. European Acad. of Sciences and Arts 1990–; Amb., Austrian Red Cross, Club of Rome, 1993–2000; Dir European Heart Inst. 1990–, European Inst. of Health 2001–; Hon. Prof., Marburg 2006, St Petersburg 2012; Kt, Sovereign Order of Malta, Bundesverdienstkreuz 1992; Dr hc (Timisoara, Budapest, Tokyo, Maribor, Riga, Belgrade, Athens, Tbilisi, St Petersburg, Arad, Cluj-Napoca); Dr Karl Renner Prize 1975, Sandoz Prize 1980, Plannsee Prize 1982, Österreichischer Ehrenkreuz für Wissenschaft und Kunst I. Klasse 2006, Paul-Stradins-Preis, Riga 2009, Medal of the Pres. of Slovak Republic 2011, Great Silver Decoration of Honour 2012. *Publications:* 15 books and more than 500 articles in specialist journals. *Leisure interest:* arts. *Address:* European Academy of Sciences and Arts, St-Peter-Bezirk 10, 5020 Salzburg (office); Schwimmschulstrasse 31, 5020 Salzburg, Austria (home). *Telephone:* (662) 841345 (office); (662) 824741 (home). *Fax:* (662) 841343 (office); (662) 8247414 (home). *E-mail:* felix.unger@euro-acad.eu (office); f.unger@salk.at (office). *Website:* www.euro-acad.eu (office); www.euinhe.eu (office); www.salk.at.

UNGER, Pierre-François, MD; Swiss physician and politician; b. 21 Aug. 1951; m.; two c.; following medical training spent several years abroad, including a long period in Paris; Head of Emergency Dept, Hôpitaux universitaires de Genève 1986–, Prof. of Medicine 1999–; mem. Grand Conseil, Geneva 1993–99; mem. Council of State of Geneva 2001–13, State Councillor in charge of Dept of Social Welfare and Health 2001–05, of Economy and Health 2005–09, Pres. Council of State 2005–06, 2011–12 mem. Parti démocrate-chrétien. *Address:* c/o Council of

State of Geneva, 14, rue de l'Hôtel-de-Ville, CP 3984, 1211 Geneva 3, Switzerland (office).

UNGUREANU, Mihai-Răzvan, MA, PhD; Romanian academic, politician and government official; b. 22 Sept. 1968, Iaşi; m.; one s.; ed C. Negruzzi High School of Math.-Physics, Iaşi, Al.I. Cuza Univ., Iaşi, St Cross Coll., Oxford, UK; Jr Fellow, New Europe Coll. for Advanced Studies, Bucharest, mem. Admin. Bd 2002; teacher, Mihai Eminescu Philology-History High School, Iaşi 1992; Univ. Tutor, Faculty of History, Al.I. Cuza Univ., Iaşi 1992–96, Univ. Asst 1996–98, Univ. Lecturer 1998, Dir Centre for Jewish Studies 2004, mem. Senate Al.I. Cuza Univ. 1990–92; Guest Scientist, Dept for European History, Albert Ludwig Univ., Freiburg im Breisgau, Germany 1993–97; Dir Centre for Romanian Studies, Romanian Cultural Foundation, Iaşi 1996–99; Assoc. Prof., School of Slavonic and East European Studies, Univ. of London, UK 1996–98; Sr Fellow, Oxford Centre for Jewish and Hebrew Studies, St Cross Coll. Oxford 1998; Sec. of State, Ministry of Foreign Affairs 1998–2001, Regional Emissary, Stability Pact for South-Eastern Europe 2001–03, Deputy Coordinator SE European Cooperation Initiative (SECI), Vienna 2003, Minister-Counsellor 2003, Minister of Foreign Affairs 2004–07 (resgnd); Dir Serviciului de Informaţii Externe—SIE (Foreign Intelligence Service) 2007–12; Prime Minister Feb.–May 2012; Acting Minister of Environment and Forests 5–10 April 2012; mem. Senate (Right Romania Alliance party list) Dec. 2012–; Sr Reader, NATO School (SHAPE), Oberammergau, Germany 2001; Assoc. Univ. Prof., SNSPA, Bucharest 2002; Sr Reader, George C. Marshall Centre for Security Studies, Garmisch-Partenkirchen, Germany 2003; Ed.-in-Chief Revista de Istorie Sociala 1996; Ed. Dialog Magazine 1988–92, Arhiva Genealogica 1993, Revue des Etudes Roumains 1994, Scientific Council, Sever Zotta Inst. for Genealogical and Heraldic Studies, Iaşi 1998; mem. Scientific Bd Soros Foundation for an Open Society, Iaşi 1996–98; Pres. Romanian Inst. for Strategic Studies, Bucharest 2001; mem. Romanian Soc. for Heraldry, Sigillography and Genealogy of the Romanian Acad. (Iaşi Br.) 1993, European Asscn for Jewish Studies, Oxford 1997, Scientific Bd Centre for Security Policies, Szeged, Hungary 2003; Commdr (First Rank), Royal Order of the Dannebrog (Denmark) 2000, Grand Officer of Nat. Order for Merits (Romania) 2000, Kt of Star of Romania Nat. Order 2008; Republican Praiseworthy Scholarship, Al.I. Cuza Univ. 1991, Royal Soc. Mark Rich Scholarship, St Cross Coll., Oxford 1992, Studies and Research Scholarship, Albert Ludwig Univ., Freiburg im Breisgau, Germany 1994–98, NEC Fellowship, New Europe Coll., Bucharest 1996, Chevening-FCO Fellowship SEEES, Univ. of London 1997, Nat. Prize of 22 Magazine, Bucharest 1992, Felix Posen Prize, Hebrew Univ. 1996–97, 1997–98, Vasile Pogor Prize, Iaşi City Hall 1998, Corneliu Coposu Prize, Youth Org. of PNT-cd 1999, Dimitrie Onciul Prize, Magazin Istoric Cultural Foundation for the publication of the work Relatiile Romano-sovietice, Documente, 1917–1934, I, Bucharest, 1999 (in collaboration with the Ministry of Foreign Affairs of the Russian Federation). *Publications include:* Statistical Documents Regarding the City of Iaşi (1755–1828), Vols I–II (co-author) 1996–97, The Comprehensive Catalogue of Moldavian Boyars 1829–1856 1997, Marea Arhondologie a boierilor Moldovei 1998, Convertire şi integrare în societatea românească la începutul epocii moderne 2004; more than 50 scientific articles and more than 60 publs in magazines and learned reviews including Dialog, Cronica, Timpul, Convorbiri literare, Astra, România Literară, 22, Dilema, Tinerama, Contrapunct, Polis, Revue des Etudes Roumaines, The Genealogic Archives, The Romanian Review of Social History, Népszabadság 1991–2004. *Address:* Senate of Romania, 050711 Bucharest, Calea 13 Septembrie nr 1–3, sector 5, Romania (office). *Telephone:* (21) 4141111 (office). *Fax:* (21) 3160300 (office). *E-mail:* infopub@senat.ro (office). *Website:* www.senat.ro (office).

UNO, Ikuo, LLB; Japanese insurance executive; *Executive Advisor to the Board, Nippon Life Insurance Company;* b. 4 Jan. 1935; ed Univ. of Tokyo; joined Nippon Life Insurance Co. 1959, Dir 1986–89, Man. Dir 1989–92, Sr Man. Dir 1992–94, Vice-Pres. 1994–97, Pres. 1997–2005, Chair. 2005–11, Exec. Advisor to the Bd 2011–; Vice-Chair. Kansai Econ. Fed. (Kankeiren); mem. Bd of Auditors Odakyu Electric Railway Co. Ltd 2002; Corp. Auditor, Tanabe Seiyaku Co. Ltd; Chair. Life Insurance Asscn of Japan 2001–05; Outside Corp. Auditor, Sumitomo Mitsui Financial Group 2005–; Outside Dir Hotel Okura Co., Ltd 2015–; mem. Bd of Dirs Int. Insurance Soc. Inc., New York 2003–, Japan Investor Relations Asscn 2003–, Obayashi Foundation 2006–, Toyota Motor Corp. 2013–, Int. Insurance Soc. 2016. *Address:* Nippon Life Insurance Co., 3-5-12 Imabashi, Chuo-ku, Osaka 541-8501, Japan (office). *Telephone:* (6) 6209-5525 (office). *Website:* www.nissay.co.jp (office).

UNO, Sandiaga (Sandi) S., BBA, MBA; Indonesian business executive; *Managing Director, Saratoga Capital;* b. 28 June 1969; m.; two c.; ed Wichita State Univ., George Washington Univ., USA; fmr analyst; co-f. Saratoga Capital (pvt. equity firm) 1998, currently Man. Dir; Finance and Accounting Officer, Summa Group Companies, Indonesia 1990–93; Chief Financial Officer, NTI Resources Ltd, Calgary, Canada 1995–98; co-f. PT Recapital Advisors (investment bank), currently Pres. Commr; mem. Bd of Dirs PT Adaro Indonesia, PT Indonesia Bulk Terminal, PT Mitra Global Telekomunikasi Indonesia, Interra Resources Ltd; Chair. Indonesian Young Entrepreneurs Asscn 2005–08. *Address:* Saratoga Capital, 3 Phillip Street, #15-01 Commerce Point, Singapore 048693, Singapore (office). *Telephone:* 65368661 (office). *Fax:* 65368161 (office). *E-mail:* info@saratoga-asia.com (office). *Website:* www.saratoga-asia.com (office).

UNOURA, Hiroo; Japanese business executive; *President and CEO, Nippon Telegraph and Telephone Corporation (NTT);* b. 13 Jan. 1949; joined Nippon Telegraph and Telephone Public Corpn (NTT) 1973, Sr Vice-Pres. and Dir of Dept I 2002–05, Sr Vice-Pres. and Dir of Dept V 2005–07, Exec. Vice-Pres., Dir of Corp. Strategy Planning Dept and Exec. Man. Corp. Business Strategy Div. 2007–08, Exec. Vice-Pres. and Dir of Strategic Business Devt Div. 2008–11, Pres. and CEO NTT 2011–. *Address:* Nippon Telegraph and Telephone Corporation, Otemachi First Square, East Tower, 5-1, Otemachi 1-Chome, Chiyoda-ku, Tokyo 100-8116 Japan (office). *Telephone:* (3) 6838-5111 (office). *Fax:* (3) 5205-5589 (office). *E-mail:* info@ntt.co.jp (office). *Website:* www.ntt.co.jp (office).

UNTERMEYER, Charles Graves (Chase); American international business consultant and fmr diplomatist; *Founding Chairman, Qatar-America Institute;* b. 7 March 1946, Long Branch, NJ; s. of Dewitt Edward Untermeyer and Marguerite Alonza Graves Untermeyer; m. Diana Cumming Kendrick; one d.; ed Harvard Coll.; served in USN during Vietnam War as destroyer officer in Pacific and as aide to Commdr of US naval forces in the Philippines; early career as political reporter for Houston Chronicle newspaper; mem. Tex. House of Reps for Dist in Houston 1977–81; Exec. Asst to Vice-Pres. George Bush 1981–83; Asst Sec. of the Navy for Manpower and Reserve Affairs 1984–88; Dir Presidential Personnel, The White House 1988–91; Dir Voice of America 1991–93; Dir of Public Affairs, Compaq Computer Corp. 1993–2002; fmr mem. and Chair. Bd of Visitors, US Naval Acad.; fmr mem. Bd Nat. Public Radio; fmr mem. Houston Port Comm.; mem. Tex. State Bd of Educ. 1999–2003, Chair. 1999–2001; Prof. of Public Policy and Vice-Pres. for Govt Affairs, Univ. of Texas Health Science Center, Houston 2002–04; Amb. to Qatar 2004–07; US Vice-Chair. Strategic Real Estate Advisors Ltd 2007–09; ind. business consultant 2007–; Founding Chair. Qatar-America Inst.; Chair. St Luke's Episcopal Health Charities 2013–; Founding Dir Episcopal Health Foundation 2013–; Pres. Houston READ Comm. 1998–2001; mem. Defense Health Bd 2008–09, Texas Ethics Comm. 2010–17 (Chair. 2016–17), Council on Foreign Relations; fmr mem. Bd Conservation Trust of Puerto Rico. *Publications:* When Things Went Right 2013, How Important People Act 2014, Inside Reagan's Navy 2015, Zenith 2016. *Address:* 10000 Memorial Drive, Suite 920, Houston, TX 77024, USA (office). *Telephone:* (713) 683-9888 (office); (713) 542-8904 (mobile) (home). *Fax:* (713) 683-9896 (office). *E-mail:* chase@untermeyer.com. *Website:* www.untermeyer.com.

UNWIN, Eric Geoffrey (Geoff), BSc; British business executive; *Chairman, Xchanging;* b. 9 Aug. 1942, Radcliffe-on-Trent, Notts.; s. of Maurice Doughty Unwin and Olive Milburn (née Watson); m. Margaret Bronia Element 1967; one s. one d.; ed Heaton Grammar School, Newcastle upon Tyne, King's Coll., Durham Univ.; with Cadbury Bros 1963–68; joined John Hoskyns & Co. 1968, Man. Dir Hoskyns Systems Devt 1978, Dir Hoskyns Group 1982, Man. Dir 1984, Exec. Chair. 1988; COO Cap Gemini 1993–2000, CEO and Vice-Chair. Exec. Bd 1996–2000, Chair. Cap Programmator AB 1993–2000, CEO, mem. Bd Cap Gemini Ernst & Young (fmrly Cap Gemini) 2000–02; Chair. Cloud Networks Ltd 2005–06, Omnibus Systems Ltd 2005–10, 3G Lab 2002–05, Taptu 2007–12, Alliance Medical 2008–10, OpenCloud 2011–, Xchanging 2011–, RD Card Holdings 2011–; Deputy Chair., later Chair. Halma plc 2002–13; Chair. Liberata PLC 2003–11; Dir (non-exec.) Volmac Software Group NV 1990, Gemini Consulting Holding SA 1994–2000, NED United News & Media (now United Business Media) PLC 1995–2007 (Chair. 2002–07); Dir (non-voting) CGEY 2002–12; Pres. Computing Services Asscn 1987–88; mem. Information Tech. Advisory Bd 1988–91, Palamon Capital Pnrs and its Advisory Bd 2002–; Freeman of the City of London 1987. *Leisure interests:* golf, riding, skiing, gardening. *Address:* 17 Park Village West, London, NW1 4AE, England (home). *Telephone:* (1494) 789179 (High Wycombe) (office). *E-mail:* geoff.unwin@gunwin.co.uk (office).

UNWIN, Sir (James) Brian, Kt, KCB, MA (Oxon), MA (Yale); British banker and fmr government official; b. 21 Sept. 1935, Chesterfield, Derbyshire, England; s. of Reginald Unwin and Winifred Walthall; m. Diana Scott 1964; three s.; ed Chesterfield School, New Coll. Oxford and Yale Univ., USA; Asst Prin., Commonwealth Relations Office 1960; Pvt. Sec. to Minister of State 1960–61; Pvt. Sec. to British High Commr, Salisbury, Rhodesia 1961–64; First Sec., British High Comm. Accra 1964–65; with FCO 1965–68, transferred to HM Treasury 1968; Pvt. Sec. to Chief Sec. Treasury 1970–72, Asst Sec. 1972, Under-Sec. 1976, Deputy Sec. 1983–85; seconded to Cabinet Office 1981–83; Dir EIB 1983–85, Pres. 1993–2000, Hon. Pres. 2000–; Deputy Sec., Cabinet Office 1985–87; Chair. Bd HM Customs & Excise 1987–93; Gov. EBRD 1993–2000; Chair. Supervisory Bd European Investment Fund 1994–2000; mem. Advisory Bd IMPACT 1990–93; mem. Bd of Dirs ENO 1993–94, 2000–08, Fondation Pierre Werner, Centre d'Etudes Prospectives (CEPROS) 1996–2000, Dexia Bank 2000–10, European Centre for Nature Conservation 2000–13 (Pres. 2001–13, Hon. Pres. 2013–), 'Britain in Europe' Council 2002–05; Chair. Assettrust Housing 2003–12, Assettrust Housing Asscn Ltd 2012–14; Dir Fed. Trust for Educ. and Research 2003–; Pres. New Coll. (Oxford) Soc. 2004–08; Hon. Pres. Euronem (Athens) 2000–08, European Investment Bank, European Centre for Nature Conservation, Hon. Fellow, New Coll., Oxford 1996, Inst. of Indirect Taxation 2002; Commdr du Wissam Alloui (Morocco) 1999, Grand Officier, Ordre de la Couronne (Belgium) 2000, Grand Croix Ordre Grand Ducal de la Couronne de Chêne (Luxembourg) 2001; Gold Medal, Fondation du Mérite Européen. *Publications:* Corporate Social Responsibility and Socially Responsible Investing (co-author) 2002, Britain's Future and the Euro (co-author) 2004, Terrible Exile: The Last Days of Napoleon on St Helena 2010, Financial Regulation: Britain's Next European Challenge (co-author) 2010, A Tale in Two Cities: Fanny Burney and Adele, Comtesse de Boigne 2014, With Respect, Minister: A View from Inside Whitehall 2017. *Leisure interests:* opera, bird-watching, Wellingtoniana and Napoleonic history, cricket. *Address:* c/o Reform Club, 104 Pall Mall, London, SW1Y 5EW, England (home).

UOSUKAINEN, Riitta Maria, MA, PhD, LicPhil; Finnish teacher and fmr politician; b. 18 June 1942, Jääski; d. of Reino Vainikka and Aune Vainikka; m. Toivo Uosukainen 1968; one s.; ed Univ. of Helsinki; teacher, Imatrankoski Upper Second School 1969–; Prov. Instructor in Finnish Language, Kymi Prov. 1976–83; mem. Imatra Town Council 1977–92, Vice-Chair. 1980–86; mem. Eduskunta (Parl.) 1983–2003, Minister of Educ. 1991–94, Speaker of Parl. 1994–2003; presidential cand. 2000; Commdr Order of White Rose 1992, Commdr Italian Repub. 1993, Order of First Class of White Star (Estonia) 1995, Grand Cross First Class, Order of Merit (Germany) 1996, Grand Cross, Order of the Crown (Belgium) 1996, Commdr Grand Cross, Royal Order of Polar Star (Sweden) 1996, Grand Cross, Order of Honour (Greece) 1996, Commdr Cross, Order of Falcon (Iceland) 1997, Valtioneuvos (Councillor of State) 2004; Dr hc (Finlandia Univ., USA) 1997, (Lappeenranta Inst. of Tech.) 1999; Speaker of the Year Award 1985. *Publications include:* (as co-author): Clues for Mother Tongue Teaching 1979, Link Exercises in Mother Tongue 1981, Mother Tongue Fountain 1984, Liehuva Liekinvarsi (speeches and letters) 1996, Nuijanisku pöytään (writings about politics, power and passion) 2004. *Leisure interest:* literature. *Address:* Olkinuorankatu 11, 55910 Imatra, Finland (home). *Telephone:* (5) 4337766 (home). *Fax:* (5) 4337700 (home). *E-mail:* riitta@uosukainen.com (home).

UPADHAYA, Kedar Nath; Nepalese judge (retd); b. Feb. 1939, Jaleshwor, Mahottari Dist; ed Tribhuwan Univ., Inst. of World Affairs, London, UK; served in numerous positions in the state judiciary including Judge in various regional courts and zonal courts, Sr Govt Advocate in Office of Attorney-Gen., Under-Sec. in Ministry of Law and Justice; Justice, Supreme Court of Nepal 2000–04, Chief

Justice 2003–04 (retd); Chair. Nat. Human Rights Comm. 2007–13; fmr Chair. Administrative Court; fmr mem. Royal Comm. on Judicial Reform; fmr mem. Bd of Dirs Rastriya Banijya Bank.

UPRETY, Neel Kantha, MS; Nepalese government official; Project Man. and Sr Electoral Adviser to Election Comm. of Nepal 1999–2004; Sr Election Coordinator, Afghanistan 2004–05; Chief Election Commr 2009–15 (retd); fmr Chair. Forum of Election Man. Bodies of South Asia.

URA, Dasho Karma, BA, MPhil; Bhutanese economist and writer; *President, Centre for Bhutan Studies;* b. 7 April 1961, Ura, Bumthang Dist; ed St Stephen's Coll., Delhi, Magdalen Coll., Oxford, Edinburgh Univ.; spent 12 years as economist with Ministry of Planning; Founding Dir, Centre for Bhutan Studies 1999–2008, Pres. 2008–; mem. Bhutanese Nat. Comm. on UNESCO 1998–99, Nat. Bd of Sustainable Devt 1998–2007, Nat. Planning Comm. 1999–2001; Vice Chair. Nat. Council 2008–09; mem. Drafting Cttee of Bhutan's first Constitution 2001–06; mem. Exec. Cttee, School of Well-being, Chulalongkorn Univ. and San Nagarprada Foundation, Thailand 2010–; Assoc. Ed. International Journal of Asian Business and Information Management 2009–; mem. Reflection Group on Global Devt Perspectives, Global Policy Forum, Bonn 2010–; mem. Chief Economist's Advisory Panel, South Asia Region, World Bank; mem. Bd of Dirs Royal Monetary Authority (Central Bank) of Bhutan; mem. Tarayana Foundation (humanitarian project NGO); mem. UNESCO Mahatma Gandhi Inst. of Educ. for Peace and Sustainable Devt, Delhi; visiting prof. at several int. univs including Nagoya Univ., Japan, Xi'an Univ. of Architecture and Tech., People's Repub. of China; keynote speaker at numerous int. confs; also a painter (works on display at Dochula Temple near Thimphu); Druk Khorlo (Wheel of Dragon Kingdom) 2010. *Publications include:* Ballad of Pemi Tshewang Tashi 1994, The Hero with a Thousand Eyes (novel) 1995, Faith and Festival of Nimalung 2002, Deities and Archers, Leadership of the Wise: Kings of Bhutan 2009, 30 Years of Change in Bhutan 1981–2016: A Personal Perspective 2018. *Address:* Centre for Bhutan Studies, Langjuphakha, POB 1111, Thimphu 11001, Bhutan (office). *Telephone:* (2) 321003 (office). *Fax:* (2) 321001 (office). *E-mail:* dasho.k.ura@gmail.com (office). *Website:* www.bhutanstudies.org.bt (office).

URBAN, Jerzy; Polish journalist and publisher; *Editor-in-Chief, Nie;* b. 3 Aug. 1933, Łódź; s. of Jan Urban and Maria Urban; m. 1st 1957; one d.; m. 3rd Małgorzata Daniszewska 1986; ed Univ. of Warsaw; staff writer, weekly Po Prostu, Warsaw 1955–57; head of home section, weekly Polityka, Warsaw 1960–63, 1968–81; columnist of satirical weekly Szpilki, articles written under pen-names including Jan Rem and Jerzy Kibic; Govt Press Spokesman 1981–89; Minister without Portfolio, Head Cttee for Radio and Television April–Sept. 1989; Dir and Ed.-in-Chief, Nat. Workers' Agency Nov. 1989–90; Dir and Ed.-in-Chief Unia-Press Feb.–May 1990; Pres. Kier Co. Ltd 1990–; Pres. URMA Co. Ltd, Warsaw 1991–; Founder and Ed.-in-Chief, political weekly Nie 1990–; participant, Round Table debates, mem. group for mass media Feb.–April 1990; mem. Journalists' Asscn of Polish People's Repub. 1982–, Polish Writers' Union; Złoty KrzyżZast-Tugi, KrzyżKomandorski Polonia Restituta; Victor Prize (TV) 1987. *Screenplays include:* Sekret, Otello. *Publications include:* Kolekcja Jerzego Kibica 1972, Impertynencje: Felietony z lat 1969–72 1974, Wszystkie nasze ciemne sprawy 1974, Grzechy chodzą po ludziach 1975, Gorączka 1981, Romanse 1981, Robak w jabłku 1982, Na odlew 1983, Samosądy 1 1984, Felietony dla cudzych zon 1984, Samosądy 2 1984, Z pieprzem i solą 1986, Jakim prawem 1988, Rozkosze podglądania 1988, Cały Urban 1989, Alfabet Urbana 1990, Jajakobyły 1991, Prima aprilis towarzysze 1992, Klątwa Urbana 1995, Druga Klątwa Urbana 2000. *Leisure interest:* social life. *Address:* Nie, 00-789 Warsaw, ul. Słoneczna 25, Poland (office). *Telephone:* (22) 8488448 (office). *Fax:* (22) 8497258 (office). *E-mail:* nie@redakcja.nie.com.pl (office). *Website:* www.nie.com.pl (office).

URBAN, Knut W., PhD; German physicist and fmr research institute director; *Senior Distinguished Professor of Physics, RWTH Aachen University;* b. 25 June 1941, Stuttgart; m.; three d.; ed Technical Univ. of Stuttgart; Research Assoc., Max Planck Inst. of Metals Research, Stuttgart 1972–86; Prof., Dept of Materials Science and Eng, Univ. of Erlangen-Nuremberg 1986; Chair of Experimental Physics, RWTH Aachen Univ. 1987–, Prof. Emer. 2009–, Sr Distinguished Prof. of Physics 2010–; Dir Inst. of Microstructure Research, Forschungszentrum Jülich 1987–2010; Visiting Prof., Inst. for Advanced Materials Processing, Tohoku Univ., Sendai, Japan 1996–97; Dir Ernst Ruska Centre for Microscopy and Spectroscopy with Electrons 2004–11, Dir Emer. 2011–; Scientific Co-ordinator, EC Network of Excellence 'Complex Metallic Alloys' 2005–09; Scientific Co-ordinator of a nat. programme of the German Science Foundation (DFG) on 'Physical Properties of Complex Metallic Alloys' 2006–12; Lecturer, Xi'an Jiaotong Univ., mem. Bd Int. Dielectrics Centre, Advisor on the construction of High-Resolution Electron Microscopy Lab. 2009–11, currently Adjunct Prof., Faculty for Materials Science and Engineering; Chair. Scientific Council, Inst. for Solid-State and Materials Research (IFW), Dresden 2004–08; Vice-Chair. Asscn of German Scientific and Tech. Socs (DVT) 2006–08; Prin. Auditor, DFG 2007–; Senator of Leibniz Soc. 2007–14; Chief Advisor and Head of Materials, Science Advisory Bd, Thermo Fisher Scientific Co., Boston 2016–; mem. Bd of Trustees, Research Asscn Berlin 2004–08; mem. Scientific Council, Physics Dept, Univ. of Vienna 2007–; mem. German Physical Soc. (Pres. 2004–06, Vice-Pres. 2006–08, Hon. mem. 2014–), Acad. of Arts and Sciences of North-Rhine Westphalia 2009, Strategic Policy Council, Leibniz-Asscn of German Research Institutes 2014–; Hon. mem. Materials Research Soc. of India 2000, US Materials Research Soc. 2006, German Electron Microscopy Soc. 2012, German Physical Soc. 2015, Japanese Inst. of Metals and Materials; Hon. (Guest) Prof., Wuhan Univ., China 2001, Tsinghua Univ., Beijing 2009; Hon. Prof., Jiaotong Univ., Xi'an, China 2009; Dr hc (Tel Aviv Univ.) 2018; scholarship, Max Planck Soc. 1969–72, Acta Metallurgica Award 1986, Carl Wagner Award, Univ. of Göttingen 1986, Research Award, Japanese Soc. for the Promotion of Science 1996, Heyn Medal, Deutsche Gesellschaft für Materialkunde 1999, Medal for Scientific Publishing, German Physical Soc. 2000, Philip Morris Distinguished Lecturer in Materials Science and Eng, Rensselaer Polytechnic Inst., New York 2004, Von-Hippel Award, US Materials Research Soc. 2006, Karl Heinz Beckurts Award for Scientific and Tech. Innovation (jtly) 2006, Honda Award for Ecotechnology (jtly) 2008, 25th Global Vision Lecture, Tsinghua Univ., Beijing 2008, Wolf Prize in Physics (jtly) 2011, Nat. Inst. of Materials Science (NIMS) Award 2015, Lee Hsun Lecture Award 2017. *Publications:* Co-

ordinator and author of the series of the Frankfurter Allgemeine Zeitung on modern topics in physics 1999 and of the book Physik im Wandel (Changing Physics) 2000; about 400 original papers in peer-reviewed journals; ed. of proceedings and special vols of journals. *Address:* RWTH Aachen University, Room 3079, Building: 05.2, 52425 Jülich; Forschungszentrum Jülich GmbH, Wilhelm-Johnen-Strasse, 52428 Jülich, Germany (office). *Telephone:* (2461) 613153 (Forschungszentrum Jülich) (office); (2461) 613255 (RWTH Aachen University) (office). *Fax:* (2461) 616444 (Forschungszentrum Jülich) (office); (2461) 613153 (RWTH Aachen University) (office). *E-mail:* k.urban@fz-juelich.de (office). *Website:* www.fz-juelich.de (office); www.physik.rwth-aachen.de (office).

URBAN, Wolfgang; German business executive; b. 26 Aug. 1945, Oberbaumgarten, Schleisen; partner Isabelle Werth; one s.; Commercial Exec., Kaufhof AG, Cologne 1973–83, Dir Accounts Dept and Finance Dept 1983–85, Gen. Man. 1985–87, mem. Finance, Accounts and Tax Cttees 1987–95; Speaker, Exec. Bd, Kaufhof Holding AG, Cologne 1995–96; mem. Exec. Bd Schickedanz Holding-Stiftung & Co. KG, Fürth 1998–99; mem. Exec. Bd Karstadt Quelle AG, Essen 1999, Chair. Karstadt Warenhaus AG Jan.–Oct. 2000, Chair. Karstadt Quelle AG 2000–04 (resgnd).

URE, Sir John Burns, Kt, KCMG, LVO, MA, FRGS; British diplomatist, author and company director; b. 5 July 1931, London; s. of Tam Ure; m. Caroline Allan 1972; one s. one d.; ed Uppingham School, Magdalene Coll., Cambridge, Harvard Business School, USA; active service as 2nd Lt, Cameronians (Scottish Rifles), Malaya 1950–51; appointments in British Embassies in Moscow, Léopoldville, Santiago and Lisbon and at Foreign Office, London 1956–79, Asst Under-Sec. of State (Americas), FCO 1981–83; Amb. to Cuba 1979–81, to Brazil 1984–87, to Sweden 1987–91; UK Commr-Gen. for Expo '92, Seville; Dir Thomas Cook Group 1991–99, CSE Aviation Ltd 1992–94; consultant, Sotheby's Scandinavia Advisory Bd, Robert Fleming (merchant bankers) 1995–98, Ecosse Films 1996–99; Chair., Anglo-Swedish Soc. 1992–96, Brazilian Chamber of Commerce 1994–96, Panel of judges for Travel Book of the Year Award 1991–99; Trustee, Leeds Castle Foundation 1995–2006; Pres., Weald of Kent Protection Soc. 2005–11; Commdr, Mil. Order of Christ (Portugal) 1973. *Publications:* Cucumber Sandwiches in the Andes 1973, Prince Henry the Navigator 1977, The Trail of Tamerlane 1980, The Quest for Captain Morgan 1983, Trespassers on the Amazon 1986, Royal Geographical Soc. History of World Exploration (contrib. section on Cen. and S. America) 1991, A Bird on the Wing 1992, Diplomatic Bag 1994, The Cossacks 1999, In Search of Nomads 2003, Pilgrimage: The Great Adventure of the Middle Ages 2006, The Seventy Great Journeys in History (contrib.) 2006, Shooting Leave 2009, The Great Explorers (contrib.) 2010, Sabres on the Steppes 2012, Beware the Rugged Russian Bear 2015; regular book reviews in Times Literary Supplement, Country Life; travel articles for Daily Telegraph and Sunday Telegraph; numerous entries in The New Dictionary of National Biography. *Leisure interests:* travel, writing. *Address:* Netters Hall, Hawkhurst, Kent, TN18 5AS, England (home). *Telephone:* (1580) 752191 (home).

URECHEAN, Serafim, DEcon; Moldovan politician; b. 2 Feb. 1950, Larga, Briceni dist; m. Tatiana Marcenco; two c.; ed Chişinău Polytechnic Inst., Inst. of Political Studies, Leningrad (now St Petersburg), Russia; Engineer, Briceni Construction Enterprise 1976–78, later Head of Dept for Industrial Devt; Second Sec., Briceni CP Cttee 1978–83; Chair. Anenii Noi CP Exec. Cttee 1985–87; Deputy Chair., First Deputy Chair., then Chair. Fed. of Ind. Trade Unions 1987–94; mem. Parl. 1990–94, 2005–10, mem. Standing Bureau of Parl., Cttee for Social Policy, Healthcare and Family, Democratic Moldova electoral bloc; Acting Prime Minister of Moldova 5–17 Feb. 1999; Mayor of Chişinău 1994–2005; Chair. Alianţă Moldova Noastră (Our Moldova Alliance) 2003–11 (merged into Liberal Democratic Party of Moldova); Chair. Court of Auditors 2011–16; fmr Chair. Fed. of Local and Regional Authorities; Corresp. mem. Inst. for Int. Affairs, Int. Informatization Acad., Int. Acad. of Man.; Hon. mem. Int. Acad. of Eng; Order of the Repub. (USSR), Medal for Public Order Protection (Moldova), St Dumitru Order (Second Class), Sergii Radonejsky Order (Second Class), St Stanislav Order.

URIBE ESCOBAR, José Darío, PhD; Colombian economist and central banker; *Governor, Banco de la República;* b. 22 Dec. 1958, Medellín, Antioquia; m. Soraya Montoya; ed Universidad EAFIT, Medellín, Universidad de los Andes, Bogotá, Univ. of Illinois at Urbana-Champaign, USA; fmr Prof., Univ. Pontificia Universidad Javeriana and Universidad de Los Andes; Head of Global Programming Unit, Nat. Planning Dept, Bogotá 1986–87; Econ. Adviser, Federación Nacional de Cafeteros (Nat. Fed. of Coffee Growers) 1992–93; Deputy Dir of Econ. Studies, Banco de la República (central bank) 1993–98, Technical Man. 1998–2004, Gov. 2005–. *Address:* Office of the Governor, Banco de la República, Carrera 7a, No 14-78, 5°, Apdo Aéreo 3551, Bogotá DC, Colombia (office). *Telephone:* (1) 343-1111 (office). *Fax:* (1) 286-1686 (office). *E-mail:* wbanco@banrep.gov.co (office). *Website:* www.banrep.gov.co (office).

URIBE VÉLEZ, Alvaro, LLB; Colombian politician and fmr head of state; b. 4 July 1952, Medellín; m. Lina Moreno; two s.; ed Univ. of Antioquia, Harvard Univ., USA, Univ. of Oxford, UK; Sec.-Gen. Ministry of Labour 1977–78; Dir of Civil Aviation 1980–82; Mayor of Medellín 1982, Councillor 1984–86, Senator 1986–94, 2014–18; Gov. of Antioquia 1995–97; Presidential cand. for Movimiento Primero Colombia 2002, Pres. of Colombia 2002–10; Distinguished Scholar in the Practice of Global Leadership, Walsh School of Foreign Service, Georgetown Univ. 2010–11; Co-founder and Pres. Centro Democrático party 2012–; mem. Int. Advisory Council, JPMorgan Chase & Co. 2011–14 (resgnd); mem. Bd of Dirs News Corpn 2012–14 (resgnd); Light Unto The Nations Award 2007, US Presidential Medal of Freedom 2009. *Website:* www.alvarouribevelez.com.

URIN, Vladimir; Russian theatre director; *General Director, Bolshoi Theatre;* ed Russian Acad. of Theatre; began career as Dir Theatre for Youth, Kirov (now Vyatka) 1973–81; moved to Moscow 1981; apptd Head of Youth and Puppet Theatres Dept, All-Union Theatre Soc. (now Theatre Union of Russia) 1981; took active part in org. and promotion of World Congress ASSITEJ, Moscow, mem. Organizing Cttee and Dir Children's Theatre Festival; twice elected Sec. of the Bd, Theatre Union of Russia 1987–96, Deputy Pres. Theatre Union 1987–96, First Deputy Pres. Theatre Union 1991–96; produced Int. Festival of Theatre schools 'Podium' 1989, 1991, 1993, 1995, Russian-American Theatre Festival 'Baikal – Michigan' (first ever Russian-American festival held in Russia), Annual Drama

Workshop 'Shelykovo – The Author's Stage'; conceived idea of The Golden Mask Nat. Theatre Award est. 1994; Gen. Dir Stanislavsky and Nemirovich-Danchenko Moscow Academic Music Theatre 1995–2013; Gen. Dir Bolshoi Theatre 2013–; Gen. Dir Int. Contemporary Dance Festivals, held by Stanislavsky and Nemirovich-Danchenko Music Theatre and Cultural Centres and Embassies of Europe, Canada and USA 1997–. *Address:* The State Academic Bolshoi Theatre of Russia, 125009, Moscow, Teatralnaya Square 1, Russia (office). *Telephone:* (495) 692-32-00 (office). *E-mail:* pr@bolshoi.ru (office). *Website:* www.bolshoi.ru (office).

URINSON, Yakov Moiseyevich, DEcon; Russian economist, academic, business executive and fmr government official; b. 12 Sept. 1944; m.; one s. one d.; ed Moscow Plekhanov Inst. of Nat. Econs; Researcher, Centre Inst. of Econ. and Math., USSR Acad. of Sciences 1968–72; Deputy Head of Div., Deputy Dir Computation Centre, USSR State Planning Cttee 1972–91; Dir Centre of Econ. Conjuncture and Prognosis, Russian Govt 1992–94; First Deputy Minister of Econs 1993–97; Deputy Chair. Russian Govt, Minister of Econs 1997–98; mem. Defence Council 1997–98; Chief Expert on econ. and financial problems United Power Grids of Russia Jan.–Sept. 1999, Deputy Chair. Sept. 1999; Deputy Chair. Man. Bd Unified Energy System (UES) of Russia, also Head Corp. Center, UES of Russia, Chair. Bd of Dirs Russian Communal Systems (RCS) 2005–; Chair. Bd of Pvt. Pensions Fund of Energy Industry 2001; Prof., Faculty of Business Informatics, Dept of Business Analytics, Higher School of Economics, Moscow. *Publications:* over 50 papers and articles in specialized periodicals. *Leisure interest:* football. *Address:* Department of Business Analytics, Faculty of Business Informatics, Higher School of Economics, 101000 Moscow, 33 Kirpichnaya Str.; RAO UES of Russia, 119526 Moscow, 101-3 Vernadskogo Prosp., Russia (office). *Telephone:* (495) 771-32-38 (Higher School of Economics); (495) 710-40-01 (office). *Fax:* (495) 927-30-07 (office). *E-mail:* uym@rao.elektra.ru (office). *Website:* www.rao-ees.ru (office); bi.hse.ru.

URIONA GAMARRA, Katia Verónica; Bolivian lawyer and activist; *President, Supreme Electoral Tribunal;* b. 19 March 1965, Cochabamba; ed Centro Boliviano de Estudios Multidisciplinarios, Universidad Católica Boliviana; has worked for several women's groups, including as Exec. Dir, Instituto de Formación Femenina Integral (Women's Training Inst.), Cochabamba 1998–2003, mem. Asociación para los Derechos de la Mujer y el Desarrollo (Asscn for Women's Rights and Devt) 1999–2013, Dir of Human Devt, Cochabamba Dist Admin 2003–04, Co-ordinator of Women's Projects, Constituent Ass. 2005–07, Exec. Sec., Coordinadora de la Mujer (network of private non-profit insts) 2007–13; Dir Instituto para la Democracia y la Asistencia Electoral (IDEA Internacional) 2014–; Pres., Supreme Electoral Tribunal 2015–; Prof. of Communication in Native Languages, Universidad Católica Boliviana 1990–92. *Address:* Tribunal Supremo Electoral, Av. Sánchez Lima, esq. Pedro Salazar (Sopocachi), La Paz 8748, Bolivia (office). *Telephone:* 242–2338 (office). *Website:* tse.oep.org.bo (office).

URNOV, Mark Yuryevich, PhD, DSc; Russian academic and politician; *Academic Supervisor, Faculty of Politics, Higher School of Economics;* b. 12 May 1947, Moscow; m.; one s. two d.; ed Moscow State Inst. of Int. Relations; on staff Inst. of Conjuncture USSR Ministry of Foreign Trade 1970–76; researcher Inst. of World Econs and Int. Relations USSR Acad. of Sciences 1976–79; sr researcher Inst. of Culture, Ministry of Culture RSFSR 1979–82; sr researcher Leningrad Inst. of Information and Automatization 1982–86; sr researcher Inst. of Int. Workers' Movt USSR Acad. of Sciences 1986–89; leading researcher USSR Acad. of Nat. Econ. 1989–90; Dir of programmes Foundation of Social Econ. and Political Studies Gorbachev Foundation 1990–94; Head of Div., Deputy Head, Dir Analytical Centre, Russian Presidency 1994–96; mem. Political Council, Russian Presidency 1994–98; Dir Research Centre Ekspertiza 1996–98, 2000–04; First Deputy Head, Centre for Econ. Reforms 1998–2000; Dean, Faculty of Politics, Nat. Research Univ., Higher School of Econs, Moscow 2004–10, Academic Supervisor, Dept of Politics 2010–. *Leisure interest:* cycling. *Address:* Higher School of Economics, National Research University, 3 Kochnovsky Pereulok, Moscow 101000, Russia (office). *Telephone:* (495) 772-95-90 (office). *E-mail:* murnov@hse.ru (office). *Website:* www.hse.ru/eng (office).

UROSA SAVINO, HE Cardinal Jorge Liberato, PhD; Venezuelan ecclesiastic and academic; *Archbishop Emeritus of Caracas;* b. 28 Aug. 1942, Caracas; s. of Luis Manuel Urosa Joud and Ligia Savino del Castillo de Urosa; ed Colegio De La Salle Tienda Honda, Interdiocesan Seminary of Caracas, St Augustine's Seminary, Toronto, Canada, Pontifical Gregorian Univ., Rome, Pius Latin American Pontifical Coll.; ordained priest, Archdiocese of Caracas, Santiago de Venezuela 1967; served as Prof. and Rector, Seminary San José, Caracas; later served as Rector of Interdiocesan Seminary, Caracas; later Vicar Gen. Archdiocese of Caracas; apptd Titular Bishop of Vegesela in Byzacena 1982; Auxiliary Bishop of Caracas 1982–90; Archbishop of Valencia en Venezuela 1990–2005; Archbishop of Caracas 2005–18, now Emer.; cr. Cardinal (Cardinal-Priest of Santa Maria ai Monti) 2006; fmr Pres. Org. of Latin American Seminaries; f. a parochial vicariate in a slum neighbourhood of Caracas; second Vice-Pres. Venezuelan Episcopal Conf. 2006–11, Pres. 'Ad Honorem' 2011–. *Address:* Arzobispado, Apartado 954, Monjas a Gradillas, Plaza Bolivar, Caracas 1010, Venezuela (office). *Telephone:* (212) 5421611 (office); (212) 5421715 (office). *Fax:* (212) 5420297 (office). *E-mail:* infoiglesiaccs@gmail.com (office). *Website:* www.arquidiocesisdecaracas.com (office).

URPILAINEN, Jutta, MEd; Finnish politician; b. 4 Aug. 1975, Lapua; d. of Kari Urpilainen and Pirjo Urpilainen; m. Juha Mustonen 2006; ed Univ. of Jyväskylä, Helsinki Univ.; began career as schoolteacher in Helsinki 2001–02, Kokkola 2002–03; mem. Kokkola City Council 2001–; Asst to MP Säde Tahvanainen 2001–03; mem. Suomen Eduskunta (Parl.) for Vaasa constituency 2003–; Deputy Prime Minister and Minister of Finance 2011–14; mem. Social Democratic Party (SDP), Chair. 2008–14; Vice-Chair. UN Youth and Students' Asscn of Finland 1996–97; Vice-Chair. Finnish UN Asscn 2003–05, Chair. 2008–09; Chair. Regional Council of Central Ostrobothnia Ass. 2007–08; Vice-Chair. Central Ostrobothnia Hosp. Dist Bd of Dirs 2005–10; mem. Finnish Nat. Comm. for UNESCO 1999–2011. *Leisure interests:* music, sports. *Address:* c/o Ministry of Finance, Snellmaninkatu 1A, Helsinki, Finland (office). *Website:* www.juttaurpilainen.fi.

URQUHART, Sir Brian, KCMG, MBE; British international official (retd); b. 28 Feb. 1919, Bridport, Dorset; s. of Murray Urquhart and Bertha Urquhart (née Rendall); m. 1st Alfreda Huntington 1944 (dissolved 1963); two s. one d.; m. 2nd Sidney Howard 1963; one s. one d.; ed Westminster School and Christ Church, Oxford; Army service 1939–45; Personal Asst to Gladwyn Jebb, Exec. Sec. of Preparatory Comm. of UN London 1945–46; Personal Asst to Trygve Lie, First Sec.-Gen. of UN 1946–49; served in various capacities relating to peace-keeping operations in Office of UN Under-Sec.-Gen for Special Political Affairs 1954–71; Exec. Sec. 1st and 2nd UN Int. Confs on Peaceful Uses of Atomic Energy 1955, 1958; Deputy Exec. Sec. Preparatory Comm. of IAEA 1957; Asst to Sec.-Gen.'s Special Rep. in the Congo July–Oct. 1960; UN Rep. in Katanga, Congo, 1961–62; Asst Sec.-Gen. UN 1972–74; Under-Sec.-Gen. for Special Political Affairs UN 1974–86; Scholar-in-residence, Ford Foundation 1986–95; Hon. LLD (Yale Univ.) 1981, (Tufts Univ.) 1985; Dr hc (Essex Univ.) 1981, (Westminster) 1993; Hon. DCL (Oxford Univ.) 1986, (Cambridge) 2005; hon. degrees (City Univ. of New York, Grinnell Coll., State Univ. of New York at Binghamton) 1986, (Univ. of Colorado, Keele) 1987, (Hobart Coll., William Smith Coll.) 1988, (Warwick Univ.) 1989, (Williams Coll.) 1992, (Lafayette Coll.) 1993, (Ohio State Univ.) 2000, (Hamilton Coll.) 2000, (Brown Univ.) 2003, (Amherst Coll.) 2008; Roosevelt Freedom Medal 1984, Int. Peace Acad. Prize 1985. *Publications:* Hammarskjöld 1973, A Life in Peace and War 1987, Decolonization and World Peace 1989, A World in Need of Leadership: Tomorrow's United Nations (with Erskine Childers) 1990, Ralph Bunche: An American Life 1993, Renewing the United Nations System (with Erskine Childers) 1994, A World in Need of Leadership: A Fresh Appraisal (with Erskine Childers) 1996. *Address:* 50 West 29th Street, New York, NY 10001 (home); Jerusalem Road, Tyringham, MA 01264, USA (home). *Telephone:* (212) 679-6358 (New York) (home); (413) 243-0542 (Tyringham) (home). *E-mail:* brianurquhart1@yahoo.com (home).

URQUIZO MAGGIA, José Antonio; Peruvian academic and politician; b. 13 Feb. 1967, Ayacucho; ed Universidad Nacional Federico Villarreal, Lima, Universidad Nacional de Educación a Distancia de España; Lecturer, Universidad Nacional Federico Villarreal 1991–; Dir Monsignor Victor Alvarez Huapaya Higher Technological Inst. 1995–98; Regional Vice Pres. of Ayacucho 2003–06; mem. Congreso (Parl.) for Ayacucho 2006–; Minister of Production 2011–12, of Defence May–July 2012. *Address:* Congreso de la República, Plaza Bolívar, Av. Abancay s/n, Lima, Peru (office). *E-mail:* jurquizo@congreso.gob.pe (office). *Website:* www4.congreso.gob.pe (office).

URRUTIA FERNÁNDEZ, Paulina; Chilean actress and politician; b. 15 Jan. 1969, Santiago; ed Pontificia Univ. Católica; Pres. Sindicato de Actores de Chile (Sidarte) 2001–04; mem. Nat. Council of Culture 2004–08; Minister of the Nat. Comm. for Culture and the Arts 2006–10. *Films:* Johnny cien pesos 1993 (APES Prize for Best Actress), El Encierro 1996, No tan lejos de Andrómeda 1999, Piel canela 2001, Carga vital 2003, Cachimba 2004, Tendida, mirando las estrellas 2004, Fuga 2006, Chameleon 2016, Prueba de Actitud 2016. *Television includes:* Sor Teresa de los Andes 1989, El Milagro de vivir 1990, Volver a empezar 1991, Trampas y caretas 1992, Jaque mate 1993, Champaña 1994, El Amor esta de moda 1995, Marrón Glacé, el regreso 1996, Eclipse de luna 1997, Amandote 1998, Fuera de control 1999, Sabor a ti 2000, Puertas adentro 2003, Cuentos de mujeres 2003, Tentación 2004, Casados 2005, Gatas & tuercas 2005–06, Fugitives 2011, Ecos del Desierto 2013, The Red Band Society 2014, Sudamerican Rockers 2014, Juana Brava 2015.

URRUTIA MONTOYA, Miguel, PhD; Colombian economist, academic and banking executive; *Professor of Economics, Universidad de los Andes;* b. 20 April 1939, Bogotá; s. of Francisco Urrutia and Genoveva Montoya; m. Elsa Pombo 1963; three c.; ed Univ. de los Andes, Bogotá, Harvard Univ. and Univ. of California, Berkeley, USA; Gen. Sec., Ministry of Finance 1967–68, Adviser to Monetary Bd 1969; Deputy Tech. Man. Banco de la República 1970–74; Dir Nat. Planning Dept 1974–76; Minister of Mines and Energy 1977; Vice-Rector Univ. of the UN, Tokyo 1981–85; Man., Econ. and Social Devt Dept, IDB 1985–89; Exec. Dir Fedesarrollo 1978–81, 1989–91; mem. Bd of Dirs Banco de la República (cen. bank) 1991–93, Gov. Banco de la República 1993–2005; has taught various courses at Univ. de los Andes at various times, currently Prof. of Econs; fmr weekly columnist, El Tiempo newspaper; decoration from the Ministry of Culture; Dr hc (Universidad de los Andes). *Publications include:* Empleo y Desempleo en Colombia 1968, The Development of the Colombia Labor Movement 1969, Income Distribution in Colombia 1975, Winners and Losers in Colombia's Economic Growth of the 1970s 1985, Development Planning in Mixed Economies (with Setsuko Yukawa) 1988, Financial Liberalization and the Internal Structure of Capital Markets in Asia and Latin America 1988, Economic Development Policies in Resource Rich Countries (with Setsuko Yukawa) 1988, The Political Economy of Fiscal Policy (with Shinichi Ichimura and Setsuko Yukawa) 1989. *Leisure interests:* golf, reading. *Address:* Facultad de Economia, Universidad de los Andes, Carrera 1 N° 18A-70, Bloque W, Bogotá, Colombia (office). *Telephone:* (1) 349-4949 (ext. 2056) (office). *Fax:* (1) 332-4492 (office). *E-mail:* murrutia@uniandes.edu.co (office). *Website:* economia.uniandes.edu.co (office).

URUSEMAL, Joseph J., BA; Micronesian politician and fmr head of state; b. 19 March 1952, Woleai, Yap State; m. Olania Latileilam; three s. one d.; ed Xavier High School, Chuuk State, Rockhurst Coll., Kansas City, MO, USA; worked for Jackson Co., Mo., Dept of Correction, USA 1976–82; returned to Micronesia 1982; worked with State Dept of Educ., Yap as teacher and counsellor to Outer Islands High School and mem. Educ. Steering Cttee; elected Yap State's Rep. to Fifth Congress of Federated States of Micronesia (FSM) and mem. Standing Cttees on Health Educ. and Social Affairs, Resources and Devt and External Affairs; mem. Congress, Federated States of Micronesia 1987–2003, Floor Leader 1991–2003, mem. Standing Cttees on Health Educ. and Social Affairs, Resources and Devt, Transportation and Communication, and Judiciary and Governmental Operations 1991–2003; Pres. of Micronesia 2003–07; Senator (At-Large) for Yap 2015–; fmr Sec.-Gen. FSM Nat. Group to Asia-Pacific Parliamentarians' Union; Chair. Congressional Standing Cttee on Educ. 2015–, also Yap Congressional Del.

UŠACKA, Anita, DrIur; Latvian professor of law and judge; *Judge, International Criminal Court;* b. 26 April 1952, Rīga; m. Peter Wilkitzki; ed Moscow State Univ., Univ. of Latvia; Asst, Dept for Fundamental Legal Studies, Univ. of Latvia 1975–76, Prin. Lecturer 1980–82, Docent 1982–99, Head of Dept 1989–96, Assoc. Prof. 1999–, Prof., Dept for State Law 2002–; Assoc. Prof., Rīga Grad. School of Law 1999–2001; Exec. Dir Latvian Br., UNICEF 1994–96; Judge, Constitutional Court of Repub. of Latvia 1996–2004; Judge, Int. Criminal Court, The Hague 2003–, Pres. Appeals Div. 2011–12; mem. Editorial Bd Law and the Rights journal; mem. Bd Lawyers Training Centre of Latvia, Sub-comm. on Constitutional Legal Procedure, Council of Europe, Int. Women Lawyers Asscn 1997–; Hon. LLD (Lewis and Clark Law School, Portland, Oregon). *Publications:* numerous articles in professional journals, reports to int. scientific confs. *Address:* International Criminal Court, PO Box 19519, 2500 CM The Hague, The Netherlands (office). *Telephone:* (70) 5158212 (office). *Fax:* (70) 5158789 (office). *E-mail:* pio@icc-cpi.int (office). *Website:* www.icc-cpi.int (office).

UŠACKAS, Vygaudas, LLB; Lithuanian diplomatist and politician; *European Union Ambassador to the Russian Federation;* b. 16 Dec. 1964, Skuodas; m. Loreta Ušackienė-Bilkstytė; one s. one d.; ed Vilnius Univ., Univ. of Oslo, Norway, Arhus Univ., Denmark; Counsellor, Lithuanian Mission to EU, Brussels 1992–94, Rep. for Relations with NATO 1994–96, mem. Del. to WEU 1995–96; Political Dir, Ministry of Foreign Affairs 1996–99, Deputy Minister of Foreign Affairs 1999–2000, also served as Chief Negotiator for Lithuania's accession to EU; Amb. to USA (also accred to Mexico) 2001–06, to UK 2006–08; Minister of Foreign Affairs 2008–10; EU Special Rep. and Head of EU Mission for Afghanistan 2010–13, EU Amb. to the Russia Fed. 2013–. *Address:* Delegation of the European Union to Russia, 119017 Moscow, 14/1 Kadashevskaya embankment, Russian Federation (office). *Telephone:* (495) 721-20-00 (office). *Fax:* (495) 721-20-20 (office). *E-mail:* vygaudas.usackas@eeas.europa.eu (office); delegation-russia@eeas.europa .eu (office). *Website:* eeas.europa.eu/delegations/russia/index_en.htm (office).

UŠAKOVS, Nils, BEcons, MSc; Latvian editor, television producer and politician; *Chairman, Rīga City Council;* b. 8 June 1976, Rīga, Latvian SSR, USSR; ed Univ. of Latvia, Univ. of Southern Denmark, Odense; producer, Baltic Div., Russian NTV 1998–99; News Service Corresp., Latvian Public TV 1999–2000; News and Politics Section Ed., Respublika newspaper 2000–01; News and Policy Ed. Teļegraf newspaper 2001–02; Ed. 'Theme of the Week' weekly programme, TV5 channel 2001–04, also 'The Russian Question', later Ed. and Head of TV5; First Baltic Channel News Service Ed. 2004–05, Evening News Ed. for Lithuania and Estonia 2005–06; mem. Saskaņas Centrs/Tsentr Soglasiya (Harmony Centre) party, Chair. 2005–14; Leader, Saskaņa Sociāldemokrātiskā Partija (Harmony Social Democratic Party) 2014–; Deputy for Rīga Constituency, 9th Saeima (Parl.) 2006–, mem. Foreign Affairs Cttee, European Affairs Cttee, Substitute mem. Latvian del. to NATO Parl. Ass.; mem. Bd of Dirs Baltic Forum 2002–; Chair. Rīga City Council (Mayor) 2009–; Cicerona Award, Latvian Journalists' Union and Univ. of Latvia 2004. *Leisure interests:* sports, especially running and cycling. *Address:* Rīga City Council, Rātslaukums, Room 220, Rīga 1539 (office); Saskaņa Sociāldemokrātiskā Partija (Harmony Social Democratic Party), 'Spīķeru kvartāls', Maskavas iela 4, Rīga 1050, Latvia. *Telephone:* 6702-6100 (office); 6733-3515. *Fax:* 6702-6389 (office). *E-mail:* nils.usakovs@riga.lv (office); sekretariats@riga.lv (office). *Website:* www.riga.lv (office); www.ushakov.lv; www.saskana.info.

USATÎI, Renato George; Moldovan engineer, business executive and politician; *Leader, Partidul Nostru (Our Party);* b. 4 Nov. 1978, Fălești, Moldovan SSR, USSR; ed Alecu Russo State Univ. of Bălți; Supervisor, Int. Airport, Chișinău 2000–01; Sr Engineer, Moldovan Railways 2002–04; Pres. VPT-NN LLC (mfr and supplier of cutting tools), Nizhnii Novgorod, Russian Fed. 2005–; Sr Vice-Pres. Builders Union of Railways, Moscow 2013–; Leader, Partidul Politic 'Patria' (PATRIA—Fatherland Political Party, now known as Partidul Nostru (Our Party)) 2014–. *Address:* Partidul Nostru (Our Party), 2004 Chișinău, str. București 117, Moldova (office). *Telephone:* (22) 02-72-00 (office). *Fax:* (22) 02-72-01 (office). *E-mail:* secretariat.pnru@gmail.com (office). *Website:* ru1.md (office).

USHAKOV, Yuri Viktorovich, PhD; Russian diplomatist and government official; *Assistant to President of the Russian Federation;* b. 13 March 1947, Moscow; m.; one d.; ed Moscow State Inst. of Int. Relations, Diplomatic Acad.; joined diplomatic service 1970; trans., expert, attaché USSR Embassy in Denmark 1970–75, Second then First Sec. 1978–82, Minister-Counsellor 1986–92; adviser Gen. Secr. USSR Ministry of Foreign Affairs (MFA) 1982–86; Head Dept of All-Europe Co-operation, MFA 1992–96; Perm. Rep. of Russia to Org. for Security and Co-operation in Europe (OSCE) 1996–98; Deputy Minister of Foreign Affairs 1998; Amb. to USA 1999–2008; Deputy Chief of the Govt Office and Foreign Policy Asst to the Prime Minister 2008–12; Asst to Pres. of the Russian Fed. 2012–; Hon. Meritorious Diplomat of Russia; several medals and decorations. *Leisure interests:* tennis, alpine skiing. *Address:* Office of the Government of the Russian Federation, 103274 Moscow, Krasnopresnenskaya nab. 2, Russia (office). *Telephone:* (495) 605-51-45 (office). *Fax:* (495) 605-54-21 (office). *E-mail:* ushakov_yv@aprf.gov.ru (office). *Website:* www.government.ru (office).

USHER, Thomas J., PhD; American business executive; b. 11 Sept. 1942, Reading, Pa; s. of Paul T. Usher and Mary Leonard; m. Sandra L. Mort 1965; three c.; ed Univ. of Pittsburgh; with Industrial Eng Dept, US Steel Corpn 1965–75, Asst to Gen. Superintendent, Superintendent of Transportation and Gen. Services, South Works 1975, Asst Div. Superintendent, Gary Works 1978–79, Dir Corp. Strategic Planning, Pittsburgh 1979–81, Asst to Pres. 1981, Man. Dir for Facility Planning, Eng, Research and Industrial Eng 1981–82, Vice-Pres. Eng and Research US Steel Mining Co. 1982–83, Pres. 1983–84, Vice-Pres. Eng, Steel 1984, Sr Vice-Pres. Operations, Steel 1984–86, Exec. Vice-Pres. Heavy Products 1986–90, Pres. Steel Div. 1990, mem. Corp. Policy Cttee, USX Corpn 1990, Bd of Dirs 1991, Pres. US Steel Corpn 1991, Pres. and COO USX Corpn 1994, Chair. and CEO 1995–2001, Chair. US Steel Corpn 2001–06 (retd), CEO 2001–04, Pres. 2001–03; mem. Bd of Dirs Marathon Oil Corpn 1991–2011, Chair. (non-exec.) 1995–2011, mem. Bd of Dirs and Chair. (non-exec.), Marathon Petroleum Corpn 2011–16; mem. Bd of Dirs H.J. Heinz Co., PPG Industries, PNC Financial Services Group, Boy Scouts of America, Extra Mile Educ. Foundation; mem. The Business Council; mem. Bd of Trustees, Univ. of Pittsburgh; Iron and Steel Soc. Steelmaker of the Year 2002. *Leisure interests:* golf, tennis, racquetball, scuba diving, swimming. *Address:* c/o Marathon Petroleum Corporation, Corporate Headquarters, 539 South Main Street, Findlay, OH 45840, USA. *E-mail:* info@ marathonpetroleum.com.

USHERWOOD, Nicholas John, BA; British curator and art critic; *Features Editor, Galleries Magazine;* b. 4 June 1943, Bucks., England; s. of Stephen Usherwood and Hazel Usherwood (née Weston); m. 1st Henrietta Mahaffy

(dissolved 1990); one s. one d.; m. 2nd Jilly Szaybo 1991; ed Westminster School, Courtauld Inst. of Art, Univ. of London; lecturer in art history, Portsmouth Coll. of Art, Wimbledon Coll. of Art 1965–68; researcher, Pelican History of Art 1966–68; Admin., Press Officer RA 1969–74, Exhbns Sec. 1974–77; Deputy Keeper in charge of exhbns and public relations, British Museum 1977–78; freelance exhbn curator and organizer, art-critic, lecturer, writer 1978–; Features Ed., Galleries Magazine 1998–; Curator, Topolski C Sections 2001–02; Pres. UK Chapter, Int. Asscn of Art Critics (AICA) 2000–03; mem., Critics' Circle 2004–; mem. Bd of Govs, Fed. of British Artists, also Exhbns' Cttee; Trustee, Evelyn Williams Trust 1994; columnist, The Guardian, The Times, The Daily Telegraph, The Sunday Times, Arts Review and Resurgence; Chevalier, Order of Léopold II (Belgium). *Publications include:* exhbn catalogues for Algernon Newton 1980, Tristram Hillier 1983, Alfred Munnings 1986, Richard Eurich 1991, 1994, Nolan's Nolans 1997, Julian Trevelyan 1998, Joash Woodrow 2003, Norman Adams 2007, Evelyn Williams 2008. *Leisure interests:* new maps, reading poetry, talking to artists, contemporary music. *Address:* Barrington Publications, Riverside Studios, 65 Aspenlea Road, London, W6 8LH, England (office). *Telephone:* (20) 8237-1180 (office). *E-mail:* art@ galleries.co.uk (office); features@galleries.co.uk (office). *Website:* www.galleries.co .uk (office).

USMAN, Nenadi E., BSc; Nigerian politician; b. 12 Nov. 1966, Jere, Kaduna State; ed Ahmadu Bello Univ., Univ. of Jos; served as Commr of Health, for Environment and Natural Resources, for Women's Affairs, Youth and Social Devt; fmr Exec. Adviser for Youth, for Information, Home Affairs and Culture; Minister of State for Finance 2003–06, Minister of Finance 2006–07; Chair. Fed. Accounts Allocation Cttee 2003–06; mem. Govt Econ. Man. Team 2003–06; mem. House of Reps for Kachia/Kagarko Fed. Constituency; mem. Kaduna State Caucus, Defunct Nat. Republican Convention; f. Educ. and Empowerment for Women in Kaduna State; Peoples Democratic Party Senator for Kaduna South 2011–. *Address:* Peoples Democratic Party, Plot 1970, Michael Okpara Street, Wadata Plaza, Abuja 23409, Nigeria (office). *Telephone:* (9) 7822781 (office). *E-mail:* info@ nigeriansenate.org (office). *Website:* www.peoplesdemocraticparty.net (office).

USMAN, Shamsudeen, BSc, MSc, PhD; Nigerian economist and government official; m. Nenadi Usman; ed Ahmadu Bello Univ., London School of Econs, UK; Planning Officer, Kano State Ministry of Econ. Planning 1974–76; Lecturer, Ahmadu Bello Univ., Zaria 1976–81; Controller, Nigerian Industrial Devt Bank 1981–85; Gen. Man. Corp. Banking, NAL Merchant Bank 1985–98; Dir-Gen. Tech. Cttee on Privatization and Commercialization (TCPC) 1989–91; Exec. Dir United Bank of Africa Plc and later Union Bank of Nigeria 1992–94; Deputy Gov. Cen. Bank of Nigeria 1999–2007; Minister of Finance 2007–08; Minister, Chair. of the Nat. Planning Comm. 2009–13; Pres. Nigerian Econ. Soc. 1986–87, Fellow 1995; Officer of the Order of the Fed. Repub. *Address:* c/o National Planning Commission, Old Central Bank Building, 4th Floor, Garki, PMB 234, Abuja, Nigeria (office).

USMANOV, Alisher Burkhanovich; Russian steel industry executive; *Co-founder and Majority Shareholder, Metalloinvest Management Company LLC;* b. 9 Sept. 1953, Chust, Namangan Viloyat, Uzbek SSR, USSR; m. Irina Viner; two c.; ed Moscow State Inst. of Int. Relations; Owner Gallagher Holdings, Ural steel industrial complex, Ormeto-YUMZ mechanical eng corpn; Co-owner Oskol steel plant, Lebedinsky iron-ore mine, Mikhalovsky GOK iron ore mining and processing plant; has major stakes in Nosta steel co., Moldavia Metal, Olenegorsk iron-ore co., Australian Medusa mining, Tulachermet stock co.; Co-founder (with Vasiliy Anisimov) and majority shareholder Metalloinvest Man. Co. LLC; Co-owner Gazmetall steel and mining empire; Owner Kommersant newspaper, Muz TV; acquired large share-holding in Arsenal Football Club, UK through Red and White Holdings 2007; mem. Bd of Dirs Gazprominvestholding; mem. Bd Russian Union of Industrialists and Entrepreneurs, Chair. Cttee on Regulatory Activity Improvement and Removal of Admin. Barriers; Co-founder Arts and Sports Charity Foundation; Guarantor of Charity project 'One Thousand Russian Cities'; Pres. Int. Fencing Fed. (FIE) 2008–; mem. Councils of the 2014 Sochi XXII Olympic Winter Games and XI Paralympic Winter Games, Bd of Trustees of the Russian Olympian Sportsmen Support Fund; fmr Pres. Russian and European fencing asscns; Medal of Honour 2004, Order of Friendship (Kazakhstan) 2011, Order for Service to the Fatherland (Fourth Class) 2013, Order of Alexander Nevsky 2014; Medal 'For contribution to international cooperation', Russian Ministry of Foreign Affairs 2013. *Address:* Metalloinvest MC LLC, 121609 Moscow, Rublevskoye shosse 28, Russia (office). *Telephone:* (495) 981-55-55 (office). *Fax:* (495) 981-99-92 (office). *E-mail:* info@metalloinvest.com (office). *Website:* www.metalloinvest.com (office).

USPASKICH, Viktor; Lithuanian (b. Russian) business executive and politician; b. 24 July 1959, Urdoma, Russia; one s. one d. from 1st m.; m. 2nd Jolanta Blazyte; two d.; mil. service 1977; welder, Northern Lights Co., worked on projects across USSR including Lithuania 1979–90; attained Lithuanian citizenship 1991; f. Efektas Co. 1990 (became part of Vikonda Co. 1993), Pres. Vikonda Co. 1996; non-party mem. New Union 2000–03; Founder and Chair. Labour Party 2003–06 (resgnd), 2007–13, Hon. Chair. Labour Party 2013–; mem. Seimas (Parl.) 2000–05, 2008–09, 2012–14, mem. Cttee on Econs 2004–05, Labour Party Parl. Group 2004–05; Minister of the Economy 2004–05 (resgnd following allegations of violating law on combining public and private interests); mem. European Parl. 2009–12, mem. Cttee on Regional Devt, Alliance of Liberals and Democrats of Europe 2014–; Chair. Asscn of Lithuanian Employers 1997–2003; Order of Daniil Moskovsky 1999, Order of St Vladimir; Santarvés Fund Award, St Michael Statue. *Address:* European Parliament, Building Alterio Spinelli 08H153, 60 Rue Wiertz, 1047 Brussels, Belgium (office). *Telephone:* (2) 284-53-39 (office). *Fax:* (2) 284-93-39 (office). *E-mail:* viktor.uspaskich@europarl.europa.eu (office); info@uspaskich.eu. *Website:* www.europarl.europa.eu/meps/en/96698/viktor_uspaskich.html (office); www.uspaskich.eu.

USPENSKIJ, Boris, PhD, DLitt; Russian/Italian linguist, philologist, critic, semiotician and historian and academic; *Professor, Higher School of Economics, National Research University;* b. 1 March 1937, Moscow; s. of Andrej Uspenskij and Gustava Mekler; m. 1st Galina Korshunova 1963 (died 1978); two s.; m. 2nd Tatiana Vladyshevskaya 1985; ed Moscow Univ.; studied under Hjelmslev at Univ. of Copenhagen 1961; expedition to Siberia to study Ket language 1962; research at USSR Acad. of Sciences Inst. of African Languages 1963–65; research mem. Lab. of

Language Typology and Computational Linguistics, Moscow Univ. 1965–77, Prof., Moscow Univ. 1977–92; Fellow, Inst. for Advanced Studies, Russian State Univ. for the Humanities 1992–93, Prof. 2006–; Visiting Prof. Vienna Univ. 1988, Harvard Univ. 1990–91, Graz Univ. 1992, Cornell Univ. 1993, Univ. of Italian Switzerland 1997–2009; Fellow, Wissenschaftskolleg (Berlin) 1992–93; Prof., Oriental Univ. of Naples 1993–2009, Prof. Emer. 2009–; currently Prof., Higher School of Econs, Nat. Research Univ., also Dir Lab. of Linguistics and Semiotics; major publs 1962–; Foreign Corresp. mem. Austrian Acad. of Science 1987; Foreign mem. Norwegian Acad. of Science and Letters 1999, Polish Acad. of Arts and Sciences 2011; mem. Academia Europaea 1990, Russian PEN Centre 1994, Soc. Royale des Lettres de Lund 1996, Società Filologica Romana 2001; Hon. mem. Slavonic and E European Medieval Studies Group 1987, Asscn Int. de sémiologie de l'image 1990, Hon. Cttee, American Friends of the Warburg Inst. 1993; Dr hc (Russian State Univ. for the Humanities) 2001, (Konstantin Preslavsky Univ., Bulgaria) 2003, (Belgrade Univ.) 2010, (Tallinn Univ.) 2016; Annual Distinguished Scholarship Award, Early Slavic Studies Asscn 2007. *Publications include:* Principles of Structural Typology 1962, Structural Typology of Languages 1965, The Archaic System of Church Slavonic Pronunciation 1968, The History of Church-Slavonic Proper Names in Russia 1969, A Poetics of Composition 1970, The Semiotics of the Russian Icon 1976, Tipologia della cultura (with Yu. M. Lotman) 1975, The Semiotics of Russian Culture (with Yu. M. Lotman) 1984, The Semiotics of Russian Cultural History (with Yu. M. Lotman and L. Ja. Ginsburg) 1985, Storia e Semiotica 1988, Sémiotique de la culture russe (with Yu. M. Lotman) 1990, Storia della lingua letteraria russa: Dall'antica Rus' a Puškin 1993, Semiotics of Art 1995, Linguistica, semiotica, storia della cultura 1996, Tsar and Patriarch 1998, Boris and Gleb: The Perception of History in the Old Rus' 2000, "In regem unxit..." 2001, Studies in the Russian History 2002, Essays in History and Philology 2004, Il segno della croce e lo spazio sacro 2005, Cross and Circle: From the History of Christian Symbolism 2006, Ego Loquens: Language and Communicational Space 2007, Works on Trediakovskij 2008, Prospettiva divina e prospettiva umana: La pala di van Eyck a Gand 2010, "Tsar and God" and Other Essays in Russian Cultural Semiotics (co-author) 2012; numerous articles. *Leisure interest:* travelling. *Address:* Higher School of Economics, National Research University, Moscow 101000, Myasnitskaya ul., 20, Russia (office); Via Principe Eugenio 15, Rome 00185, Italy (home); Moscow 109028, Serebrianicheskij per. 9 Apartment 21, Russia (home). *Telephone:* (06) 4468157 (Rome) (home); (495) 917-40-67 (Moscow) (home). *E-mail:* borisusp@gmail.com. *Website:* www.hse.ru/en (office).

USTINOV, Vladimir Vassilyevich; Russian lawyer and government official; *Presidential Representative to the Southern Federal Okrug (District);* b. 25 Feb. 1953, Nikolayevsk-on-Amur, Khabarovsk Krai; m.; one s. one d.; ed Kharkiv Inst. of Law, Ukrainian SSR; prosecutor, Krasnodar Krai 1978–92, Sochi 1992–97; concurrently First Deputy Prosecutor Krasnodar Krai and Deputy Prosecutor-Gen. Russian Fed. 1997–2000; also Head, Dept Office of Prosecutor-Gen., N Caucasus 1998–99; Acting Prosecutor-Gen. Russian Fed. 1999–2000, Prosecutor-Gen. 2000–06; Minister of Justice 2006–08; Presidential Rep. to Southern Fed. Okrug (Dist) 2008–; Merited Jurist of Russian Fed. *Publication:* Indictment of Terror 2003. *Address:* Office of the Presidential Representative, 344052 Rostov-on-Don, ul. B. Sadovaya 73, Russia (office). *Telephone:* (863) 244-16-16 (office). *Fax:* (863) 249-99-47 (office). *E-mail:* apparat@ufo.gov.ru (office). *Website:* www.ufo.gov.ru (office).

USUBOV, Col-Gen. Ramil Idris oğlu; Azerbaijani politician and government official; *Minister of Internal Affairs;* b. 22 Dec. 1948, Xocalı, Nagornyi Karabakh; m.; three c.; ed N. Rzayev Police School, Acad. of the Ministry of Internal Affairs of the USSR; joined Ministry of Internal Affairs 1970; Head, Criminal Investigation Div., Şuşa dist Police Dept 1975–80; Deputy Head, Internal Affairs Dept, Nagornyi Karabakh Autonomous Oblast 1980–84; Head, Ali-Bayramlı Region Police Dept 1984–87; Minister of Internal Affairs, Autonomous Repub. of Naxçıvan 1987–89, 1993–94; Head, Criminal Investigation Dept, then Passport, Visa and Registration Dept, then Human Resources Div., Ministry of Internal Affairs 1989–93; Minister of Internal Affairs 1994–; promoted to Maj.-Gen. 1994, Lt-Gen. 1995, Col-Gen. 2002; Azerbaijani Banner Order. *Address:* Ministry of Internal Affairs, 1005 Baku, 7 Azerbaijan Avenue, Azerbaijan (office). *Telephone:* (12) 590-91-03 (office). *Fax:* (12) 492-45-90 (office). *E-mail:* info@mia.gov.az (office). *Website:* mia.gov.az (office).

USUPASHVILI, Davit, LLB, MA; Georgian lawyer and politician; b. 5 March 1968, Magharo, Signagi region (now in Kakheti Mkhare), Georgian SSR, USSR; m. Tinatin Khidasheli (q.v.); two c.; ed Tbilisi State Univ., Duke Univ., USA; legal adviser with State Council of Georgia, involved in drafting Constitution of Georgia 1993–95; Founding mem. Georgian Young Lawyers' Asscn 1994, Chair. 1994–97, active in its organized protests during 'Rose Revolution' that brought Mikheil Saakashvili to become Pres. of Georgia 2003; later distanced himself from alliance and withdrew into opposition; Chair. Sakartvelos Respublikuri Partia (SRP—Republican Party of Georgia) 2005–13; allied with Bidzina Ivanishvili to become a leader of Ivanishvili's Qartuli Ocneba (Georgian Dream) coalition, of which the SRP was part 2011; Chair. Sakartvelos Parlamenti (Georgian Parl.) 2012–16.

UTEEM, Cassam, LèsL; Mauritian politician and fmr UN official and fmr head of state; b. 22 March 1941, Plaine Verte; m. 1967; two c.; ed Univs of Mauritius and Paris VII; fmr supervisor, Cable & Wireless Ltd; Personnel Man. Currimjee Jeewanjee & Co., Ltd; Sec.-Gen. Mauritius Nat. Youth Council 1971–72; Treas. Mauritius Council of Social Service 1971–73; Rep. of World Ass. of Youth to UNESCO 1974–76; municipal councillor, Port Louis 1969, 1977–79, 1986–88; Lord Mayor of City of Port Louis 1986; mem. Legis. Ass. 1976–92, Chair. Public Accounts Cttee 1988–90; Minister of Employment, Social Security and Nat. Solidarity 1982–83; Opposition Whip 1983–87; Deputy Leader, Mouvement Militant Mauricien 1988; Deputy Prime Minister and Minister of Industry and Industrial Tech. 1990–92; Pres. Repub. of Mauritius 1992–2002; Special Envoy and Head of UN Electoral Observation Mission in Burundi (MENUB) 2014–15; mem. Bd Int. Inst. for Democracy and Electoral Assistance; mem. Club of Madrid, Africa Forum, Global Leadership Foundation; mem. Advisory Bd Global Peace and Unity Foundation; Hon. mem. Acad. Nationale Malgache 1995; Grand Commdr of the Order of the Star and Key of the Indian Ocean; Hon. DCL (Univ. of Mauritius) 1994; Dr hc (Univ. of Marseille III) 1994, (Academie Nationale Malgache, Madagascar), (Univ. of Buckingham, UK), (Univ. of Jamia Millia Islamia, New Delhi, India). *Address:* c/o United Nations Office in Burundi, BP 6899, Gatumba Road, Bujumbura, Burundi (office).

'UTOIKAMANU, Fekitamoeloa Tupoupai, MCom; Tongan diplomatist, economist and business executive; *High Representative of the Secretary-General for the Least Developed Countries, Landlocked Developing Countries and Small Island Developing States, United Nations;* b. Dec. 1959; m.; one d.; ed Univ. of Auckland, NZ; Macroeconomist, Cen. Planning Dept, Foreign Ministry 1983–86, Acting Planning Officer 1988–91; Acting Deputy Sec., Ministry of Finance 1987; Deputy Sec. of Foreign Affairs and Deputy European Comm. Nat. Authorizing Officer 1991–2002, Sec. of Foreign Affairs and European Comm. Nat. Authorizing Officer 2002–05; Perm. Rep. to UN, New York 2005–09, concurrently Amb. to USA; Deputy Dir-Gen. Secr. of the Pacific Community 2009–15; Deputy Pro-Chancellor and Deputy Chair. Council of Univ. of South Pacific 2009–16, apptd Acting Pro-Chancellor and Chair. 2015; CEO Ministry of Tourism 2017; High Rep. for Least Developed Countries, Landlocked Developing Countries and Small Island Developing States, UN 2017–. *Address:* Office of the High Representative for the Least Developed Countries, Landlocked Developing Countries and the Small Island Developing States (UN-OHRLLS), United Nations, Room S-770, New York, NY 10017, USA (office). *Telephone:* (212) 963-7778 (office). *Fax:* (212) 963-5051 (office). *E-mail:* ohrlls-unhq@un.org (office). *Website:* unohrlls.org (office).

UTOIKAMANU, Siosiua Tu'italukua Tupou, MCA, MScS; Tongan politician and economist; b. 1 July 1956; ed Wellington Univ. of Victoria, New Zealand, Univ. of Birmingham, UK; trainee economist, Ministry of Finance 1981, Economist 1981, Deputy Sec. 1984, Acting Dir of Planning, Cen. Planning Dept 1987, Minister of Finance 2001–08 (resgnd); Acting Finance Man. Tonga Commodities Bd 1989; Deputy Gov. Nat. Reserve Bank of Tonga 1989–91, Gov. 1991–2001; Financial Man. Adviser, Pacific Islands Centre for Public Admin 2012–.

UTSUDA, Shoei, BS; Japanese business executive; *Chairman, Mitsui & Company Limited;* b. 12 Feb. 1943; ed Univ. of Tokyo; joined Mitsui & Co. Ltd (general trading co.) 1967, mem. Bd Dirs (Dir, Gen. Man. Machinery, Information Industries Admin. Div.) 1997–, Rep. Dir, Exec. Man. Dir, Gen. Man. Corp. Planning Div. 2000–02, Rep. Dir, Sr Exec. Man. Officer, Chief Strategic Officer (responsible for Admin. Div.), COO Business Process Re-Eng Project April–Oct. 2002, Rep. Dir, Pres. and Oct. CEO 2002–09, Chair. 2009–; Chair. Keizai Doyukai Cttee on Asia-Japan Relations 2004–. *Address:* Mitsui & Co. Ltd, 2-1 Ohtemachi 1-chome, Chiyoda-ku, Tokyo 100-0004, Japan (office). *Telephone:* (3) 3285-1111 (office). *Fax:* (3) 3285-9819 (office). *E-mail:* info@mitsui.com (office). *Website:* www.mitsui.com (office).

UTSUMI, Akio; Japanese financial services industry executive; *Senior Adviser, Mitsubishi Tokyo Financial Group;* b. 7 Sept. 1942; Man. Dir Mitsubishi Trust Bank 1993–95, Sr Man.-Dir 1995–98, Deputy Pres. 1998–99, Pres. 1999–2004; Dir, Chair. and Co-CEO Mitsubishi Tokyo Financial Group Inc. (cr. following merger between Bank of Tokyo-Mitsubishi and Mitsubishi Trust & Banking Corpn 2001) 2001–04, now Sr Adviser; Corp. Auditor, Mitsubishi Materials Corpn. *Address:* Mitsubishi Tokyo Financial Group Inc., 10-1 Yurakucho 1-chome, Chiyoda-ku, Tokyo 100-0006, Japan (office). *Telephone:* (3) 3240-8111 (office). *Fax:* (3) 3240-8203 (office). *Website:* www.mtfg.co.jp (office).

UTSUMI, Yoshio, LLB, MA; Japanese civil servant and international organization official (retd); *President, Japan Telecommunications Engineering and Consulting Service;* b. 14 Aug. 1942; m. Masako Utsumi 1970; one s. one d.; ed Univ. of Tokyo, Univ. of Chicago, USA; joined Ministry of Posts and Telecommunications 1966, Head of Investment Postal Life Insurance Bureau 1986–88, Head Gen. Affairs Div., Broadcasting Bureau 1988, with Communications Policy Bureau, Deputy Minister, Asst Vice-Minister, Dir-Gen. MPT 1988–98; First Sec. Perm. Mission of Japan, Int. Telecommunications Union (ITU), Geneva 1978–81, Chair. ITU Plenipotentiary Conf. 1994, Sec.-Gen. ITU 1998–2006; Prof. of Public Admin., MPT Postal Coll. 1972; Pres. Japan Telecommunications Eng and Consulting Service 2008–; External Corp. Auditor, Kyushu Electric Power Co., Inc. 2012–; Hon. Advisor, Toyota Info Tech. Center Co., Ltd 2007–13, IEEE Hon. Member 2015; Grand Cordon of the Order of the Sacred Treasure 2013. *Address:* Japan Telecommunications Engineering and Consulting Service, Saisho Building, 8-1-14 Nishi Gotanda, Shinagawa-ku, Tokyo 141-0031, Japan (office). *Telephone:* (3) 3495-5211 (office). *Fax:* (3) 3495-5219 (office). *E-mail:* jtec@jtec.or.jp (office). *Website:* www.jtec.or.jp (office).

UTTLEY-MOORE, William James, CBE, BSc, FREng, FRAeS, FIEE, CEng; British electrical engineer; *Chairman and Managing Director, Conqueror Broadcasting Ltd;* b. 19 July 1944, Crayford, Kent, England; s. of William Uttley-Moore and Louisa Clara Dixon; m. Jennifer Benger 1966; one s.; ed Erith Tech. School, Univ. of London; student apprentice and devt engineer, Cintel Ltd 1960–68; project leader, Molins Machine Co. Ltd 1968–69; Chief Engineer, Computing Devices Co. Ltd 1969–75, Tech. Dir 1979–85, Chair. and Man. Dir 1985; Founder Chair. and Man.-Dir Southern FM 1989–92, Conqueror Broadcasting Ltd 1996–; Chair. E Sussex Econ. Partnership 1998–; mem. Bd, Defence Scientific Advisory Council 1994–; Fellow, Royal Acad. of Eng 1993–. *Publications:* numerous tech. papers on reconnaissance, avionics, digital battlefield and information warfare. *Leisure interests:* practical eng, farming, running, classical music. *E-mail:* bill.uttleymoore@btinternet.com (office).

UTZERATH, Hansjörg; German theatre director and author; b. 20 March 1926, Tübingen; m. Renate Ziegfeld 1957; one s. two d.; ed Kepler Oberschule, Tübingen; began as actor, later in theatre man. in Düsseldorf and then in production; Chief Stage Man., Düsseldorfer Kammerspiele 1955–59; Dir 1959–66; Intendant, Freie Volksbühne, Berlin 1967–73; Dir Städtische Bühnen, Nuremberg 1977–92; freelance dir 1993–; guest producer at Staatstheater Stuttgart, Municher Kammerspiele, Schauspielhaus Düsseldorf and Schiller-Theater, Berlin 1959; Visiting Prof. Universität Mozarteum, Salzburg. *Productions include:* Tango 1971, Der Vater 1972, Viele heissen Kain (TV), Waiting for Godot 1980, Mother Courage 1981, King Lear 1982, Der Hauptmann von Köpenick 1986, Liebeskonzil 1988, Richard III 1990, Lila 1990, Check-Point-Charly 1996, Besuch der Alten Dame 1998, Nathan der Weise 2002, Der Kaufmann von Venedig 2003, Purpurstaub 2005. *Publications:* Die Grossväter (novel) 2005, Fluchtlinien (novel) 2010. *Address:* Knesebeckstr. 98A, 10623 Berlin, Germany (home).

UVAROV, Andrei Ivanovich; Russian ballet dancer; *Principal Dancer, Bolshoi Ballet;* b. 28 Sept. 1971, Moscow; m. Filippova Svetlana; one d.; ed Moscow School of Choreography; apptd soloist, Bolshoi Ballet 1989, now Prin. Dancer; Benoit de la Danse Int. Prize 1993, 1st Prize Int. Ballet Competition, Japan 1995, Merited Artist of Russia 1996, People's Artist of Russia 2001, Spirit of Dance Prize, Ballet magazine 2003. *Ballets:* has danced leading roles with Bolshoi Theatre including Swan Lake, Chopiniana, Ivan the Terrible, Romeo and Juliet, Giselle, La Bayadère, Sleeping Beauty. *Address:* State Academic Bolshoi Theatre, Ballet, Teatralnaya pl. 1, 103009 Moscow, Russia (office). *Telephone:* (495) 292-99-86 (office). *Website:* www.bolshoi.ru (office).

UYEDA, Seiya, DSc; Japanese geophysicist and academic; b. 28 Nov. 1929, Tokyo; s. of Seiichi Uyeda and Hatsuo Uyeda; m. Mutsuko Kosaka 1952; one s. two d.; ed Univ. of Tokyo; Research Fellow, Earthquake Research Inst., Univ. of Tokyo 1955–63, Assoc. Prof., Geophysical Inst. 1963–69, Prof., Earthquake Research Inst. 1969–89, now Prof. Emer.; Prof., School of Marine Science and Tech., Tokai Univ. 1990–95; Harris Prof. of Geophysics, Texas A&M Univ. 1990–2008; Dir RIKEN Int. Frontier Program on Earthquake Research 1996–2002; mem. Japan Acad. 1996; Foreign Assoc., NAS 1976; Foreign mem. Russian Acad. of Sciences 1994; Fellow, Int. Union of Geodesy and Geophysics, American Geophysical Union; Hon. Foreign mem. American Acad. of Arts and Sciences 1981; Tanakadate Prize, Soc. of Terrestrial Electricity and Magnetism 1955, Okada Prize, Oceanographical Soc. of Japan 1968, Alexander Agassiz Medal, Nat. Acad. of Sciences 1972, Japan Acad. Prize 1987, George P. Woollard Award, Geological Soc. of America 1989, Walter H. Bucher Medal, American Geophysical Union 1991. *Publications include:* Debate About the Earth 1967, Island Arcs 1973, The New View of the Earth 1977, 350 scientific papers. *Leisure interest:* playing violin. *Address:* 2-39-6 Daizawa, Setagaya-ku, Tokyo 155-0032, Japan (home). *Telephone:* (3) 3412-0237 (home). *Fax:* (3) 3412-0237 (home). *E-mail:* suyeda@st.rim.or.jp (office). *Website:* www.u-tokai.ac.jp (office).

UYS, Pieter-Dirk, BA; South African playwright, performer and producer; b. 28 Sept. 1945, Cape Town; s. of Helga Bassel and Hannes Uys; ed Univ. of Cape Town, London Film School, UK; joined Space Theatre, Cape Town 1973; f. Syrkel Theatre Co.; Dir P. D. Uys Productions, Bapetikosweti Marketing Enterprises; produced and performed more than 30 plays in revues throughout SA and in UK, USA, Australia, Canada, Netherlands; several videos and TV films and documentaries; Hon. DLitt (Rhodes Univ.) 1997, (Univ. of Cape Town) 2003, (Univ. of the Witwatersrand) 2004; Hon. DEdu (Univ. of the Western Cape) 2003; Truth and Reconciliation Award 2001, Lifetime Achiever Award, Naledi Theatre Awards 2004, German Africa Foundation Prize (jtly) 2012. *Theatre:* cr. Mrs Evita Bezuidenhout – the most famous white woman in South Africa. *Television:* Evita Live and Dangerous, weekly talk/satire show 1999. *Publications:* Die van Aardes van Grootoor 1979, Paradise is Closing Down 1980, God's Forgotten 1981, Karnaval 1982, Selle ou storie 1983, Farce about Uys 1984, Appassionata 1985, Skote! 1986, Paradise is Closing Down and Other Plays 1989, No One's Died Laughing 1986, P.W. Botha: In His Own Words 1987, A Part Hate, A Part Love 1990, Funigalore 1995, Elections and Erections 2002, Between the Devil and the Deep 2005. *Leisure interests:* films, music, people, South African politics. *Address:* Evita SE Perron Theatre/Cafe/Bar Darling Station, Darling 7345 (office); 17 Station Road, Darling 7345, South Africa (home). *Telephone:* (22) 4922831 (office); (22) 4923208 (home). *Fax:* (22) 4923208 (home). *E-mail:* evita@evita.co.za (office). *Website:* www.evita.co.za; www.pdu.co.za.

UYTENGSU, Wilfred Steven, Jr, BS; Philippine business executive; b. 18 Oct. 1962; s. of Wilfred Uytengsu, Sr; m.; ed Univ. of Southern California, USA; fmr Dir General Milling Corpn, later Chief Finance Officer; Exec. Vice-Pres. and Chief Financial Officer, Alaska Milk Corpn 1994–98, Dir 1994–, COO 1998–2007, Pres. 1998–2018, CEO 2007–18; Pres. GenOSI Inc.; fmr Chair. Young Pres.' Org.; mem. Bd of Govs Philippine Basketball Asscn; Ernst & Young Philippines Entrepreneur of the Year 2007. *Address:* c/o Alaska Milk Corporation, 6th Floor, Corinthian Plaza Building, 121 Paseo De Roxas, Legaspi Village, Makati 1229, Philippines (office).

ÜZÜMCÜ, Ahmet, BA; Turkish diplomatist; b. 30 Aug. 1951, Armutlu; m.; one d.; ed Ankara Univ.; Attaché, Protocol Dept, Ministry of Foreign Affairs 1976; mil. service 1976–78; Attaché, then Second Sec., Bilateral Cultural Relations Dept 1978–79; Second, then First Sec., Embassy in Vienna, Austria 1979–82; Consul, Consulate-Gen. in Aleppo, Syria 1982–84; Chief of Section, Personnel Dept, Ministry of Foreign Affairs 1984–86; Counsellor, Del. to NATO, Brussels 1986–89, mem. Int. Staff 1989–94; Head of NATO Dept, Ministry of Foreign Affairs 1994–96; Minister, Head of Personnel Dept 1996–99; Amb. to Israel 1999–2002; Perm. Rep. to NATO 2002–04; Deputy Under-Sec., Ministry of Foreign Affairs for Bilateral Political Affairs 2004–06; Perm. Rep. to UN, Geneva 2006–09; Pres. UN Disarmament Conf. 2008; Dir-Gen. OPCW, The Hague 2010–18; Dr hc (Geneva School of Diplomacy) 2010. *Address:* c/o Organisation for the Prohibition of Chemical Weapons (OPCW) Headquarters, Johan de Wittlaan 32, 2517 JR The Hague, The Netherlands (office).

UZUNOV, Plamen, BA, LLM; Bulgarian government official and lecturer; *Secretary to the President on Legal Affairs and Anti-Corruption;* b. 1972, Plovdiv; ed Acad. of Ministry of the Interior, Paisiy Hilendarski Univ. of Plovdiv, postgraduate specialization courses at Int. Law Enforcement Acad., Budapest and in Acad. of Ministry of the Interior; worked for Plovdiv Regional Directorate, Ministry of the Interior 1993–2015, including as Dir with rank of Sr Commr; Lecturer in Forensics and Operational and Search Activities, Plovdiv Univ. of Security and Economy 2015–17; Minister of the Interior in Caretaker Govt Jan.–May 2017; Sec. to the Pres. on Legal Affairs and Anti-Corruption May 2017–; mem. Int. Police Asscn. *Address:* Office of the President, 1123 Sofia, bul. Dondukov 2, Bulgaria (office). *Telephone:* (2) 923-93-33 (office). *E-mail:* priemna@president.bg (office). *Website:* www.president.bg (office).

V

VACANTI, Joseph Philip, BS, MS, MD; American physician, medical scientist and academic; *John Homans Professor of Surgery, Harvard Medical School; Surgeon-in-Chief and Chief of Pediatric Surgery, Massachusetts General Hospital;* b. 1948; ed Creighton Univ., Univ. of Nebraska Coll. of Medicine, Harvard Medical School; trained in Gen. Surgery at Massachusetts Gen. Hosp., Boston, in Pediatric Surgery at Children's Hosp., Boston, in Transplantation at Univ. of Pittsburgh; has held academic appointments at Harvard; Surgeon-in-Chief and Chief of Pediatric Surgery at Mass Gen. Hosp. for Children, also Dir Laboratory for Tissue Engineering and Organ Fabrication and Co-Dir Center for Regenerative Medicine; Founding Co-Pres. Tissue Engineering Soc. (now Tissue Engineering Regenerative Medicine International Soc., also Founding Sr Ed. Tissue Engineering journal; mem. Inst. of Medicine of NAS 2001–; Co-Chair. Scientific Advisory Bd, Biostage, Inc. 2015–; Thomas G. Sheen Award, New Jersey Chapter of American Coll. of Surgeons, recognized by American Acad. of Anti-Aging Medicine for contribs in the area of tissue replacement, James Bartlett Brown Award, Soc. of Plastic and Reconstructive Surgery, Clemson Award, Soc. for Biomaterials, John Scott Medal, City of Philadelphia 2007, Flance-Karl Award, American Surgical Asscn, William E. Ladd Medal 2013, Jacobson Innovation Award, American Coll. of Surgeons 2015. *Achievements include:* created artificial organs using a biodegradable polymer scaffold to develop and shape tissue. *Publications:* more than 270 reports and papers in professional journals and more than 65 book chapters; more than 80 patents or patents-pending in USA, Canada, Europe and Japan. *Address:* Pediatric Surgery, Massachusetts General Hospital, 55 Fruit Street, WRN 1151, Boston, MA 02114-2696 (office); Harvard Stem Cell Institute, Holyoke Center, Suite 727W, 1350 Massachusetts Avenue, Cambridge, MA 02138, USA (office). *Telephone:* (617) 724-1725 (Boston) (office); (617) 496-4050 (Cambridge) (office). *Fax:* (617) 726-7593 (Boston) (office). *E-mail:* jvacanti@partners.org (office). *Website:* www.massgeneral.org (office); www.hsci.harvard.edu (office).

VĂCĂROIU, Nicolae; Romanian politician and economist; b. 5 Dec. 1943, Bolgrad, Bessarabia; m. Marilena Văcăroiu; one s.; ed Bucharest Acad. of Econ. Studies; Economist, Ilfov Co. Inst. of Design and Systemization; then with State Planning Cttee, promoted to Dir Econ.-Financial Synthesis Dept; apptd Deputy Minister of Nat. Economy 1990; subsequently Head of Price Dept, Ministry of Finance, Sec. of State and Head of Tax Dept, Chair. Interministerial Cttee of Foreign Trade Guarantees and Credits; Prime Minister 1992–96; Senator 1996–, Vice-Pres. of Senate 1999–2000, Pres. 2000–08, Chair. Privatization Cttee 1997–99, Vice-Pres. Parl. Group of Social Democratic Party (Partidul Social Democrat—PSD) 1996–2000; Pres. Court of Accounts 2008–; Chair. Romania–Brazil Friendship Asscn 1997–; Kt, Nat. Order Star of Romania, Nat. Order of Merit (Paraguay, Order of the Colombian Congress, Grand Cross with Gold Plaque, Decoration for Merit, Senate of Chile, First Order of the Hashemite Kingdom of Jordan. *Publications:* numerous articles on econ. and financial matters. *Leisure interests:* literature, tennis. *Address:* Senatul (The Senate), 050711 Bucharest 5, Calea 13 Septembrie 1–3 (office); B-dul Gh. Prezan, nr. 4, 2nd Floor, Apt 3, Sector 1, Bucharest, Romania (home). *Telephone:* (21) 4021111 (office). *Fax:* (21) 3121184 (office). *E-mail:* csava@senat.ro (office). *Website:* www.senat.ro (office).

VACHON, Louis, CM, MA; Canadian banker; *President and CEO, National Bank of Canada;* b. 1962, Québec; m.; two c.; ed Bates College, Fletcher School of Law and Diplomacy, Tufts Univ., USA; Vice-Pres. Capital Markets Levesque Beaubien Geoffrion (later National Bank Financial) 1986–90; with Bankers Trust 1990–96; joined National Bank of Canada 1996, Pres. and CEO Innocap Investment Management and Sr Vice-Pres. Treasury and Financial Markets, National Bank of Canada 1997, Chair. National Bank Financial Group and Natcan Investment Management 2004–05, Chair. and CEO National Bank Financial Group 2005–06, COO National Bank of Canada 2006–07, mem. Bd of Dirs 2006–, Pres. and CEO 2007–; fmr Pres. and CEO BT Bank Canada, Innocap; apptd mem. Bd of Dirs Fiera Capital Corpn 2012, Molson Coors Brewing Co. 2012–; Hon. Lt-Col, Les Fusiliers Mont-Royal, Montréal 2011; Dr hc (Bishop Univ.) 2015, (Univ. of Ottawa) 2016; Financial Personality of the Year, Finance et Investissement 2012, CEO of the Year, Canadian Business magazine 2014, Global Citizens Award, UNA in Canada. *Address:* National Bank of Canada, 600 rue de la Gauchetière ouest, Montréal, PQ H3B 4L2, Canada (office). *Telephone:* (514) 394-5000 (office). *Fax:* (514) 394-8434 (office). *Website:* www.nbc.ca (office).

VADERA, Baroness (Life Peer), cr. 2007, of Holland Park in the Royal Borough of Kensington and Chelsea; **Shriti Vadera,** PC; British investment banker, international organization official and fmr government official; *Chair, Santander UK plc;* b. 1962, Uganda; ed Northwood Coll., Somerville Coll., Oxford; investment banker, UBS Warburg 1984–99; mem. Council of Econ. Advisers, HM Treasury 1999–2007; Parl. Under-Sec. of State, Dept for Int. Devt 2007–08, Parl. Under-Sec. of State for Business and Competitiveness Jan.–Oct. 2008, Minister for Econ. Competitiveness, Small Business and Enterprise 2008–09; Sr Adviser to Chair. of Group of Twenty (G-20) Finance Ministers and Cen. Bank Govs 2009–10, Adviser to Temasek Holdings 2010–13, to govt of Dubai, UAE 2010; Chair. Santander UK plc 2015–; mem. Bd of Dirs BHP Billiton 2011–, AstraZeneca 2011–; Trustee, Oxfam 2000–05. *Address:* Santander UK plc, 2 Triton Square, Regent's Place, London, NW1 3AN (office); House of Lords, London, SW1A 0PW, England (office). *Website:* www.santander.co.uk (office).

VAGELOS, Pindaros Roy, MD; American biochemist, academic and pharmaceutical industry executive; *Chairman, Regeneron Pharmaceuticals Inc.;* b. 8 Oct. 1929, Westfield, New Jersey; s. of Roy John Vagelos and Marianthi Lambrinides; m. Diana Touliatos 1955; two s. two d.; ed Univ. of Pennsylvania and Columbia Univ. Coll. of Physicians and Surgeons; Intern in Medicine, Mass. Gen. Hosp. 1954–55, Asst Resident in Medicine 1955–56; Surgeon, Lab. of Cellular Physiology, NIH 1956–59, Surgeon, Lab. of Biochemistry 1959–64, Head of Section on Comparative Biochemistry 1964–66; Prof. of Biochemistry and Chair. Dept of Biological Chem., Washington Univ. School of Medicine, St Louis 1966–75, Dir Div. of Biology and Biomedical Sciences 1973–75; Sr Vice-Pres. Research, Merck Sharp & Dohme Research Labs, Rahway, NJ 1975–76, Pres. 1976–84, Corporate Sr Vice-Pres. Merck & Co., Inc. 1982–84, Exec. Vice-Pres. 1984–85, CEO 1985–86, Chair. and CEO 1986–95; Chair. Regeneron Pharmaceuticals Inc. 1995–, also mem. Scientific Advisory Bd; Trustee Rockefeller Univ. 1976–94, Univ. of Pa 1988– (Chair. Bd 1994–), Danforth Foundation 1978–; mem. Bd of Dirs Prudential Insurance Co. of America 1989–, Theravance, Inc 1996–2010 (Chair. –2010); fmr mem. Bd of Dirs TRW Inc., PepsiCo Inc.; mem. NAS, American Acad. of Arts and Sciences; ACS Enzyme Chem. Award 1967, New Jersey Science/Tech. Medal 1983, Pupin Medal 1995, NAS Award for Chem. in Service to Soc. 1995, Bower Award 1999. *Achievements include:* discoverer of acyl-carrier protein. *Leisure interests:* jogging, tennis. *Address:* Regeneron Pharmaceuticals Inc., 777 Old Saw Mill River Road, Tarrytown, NY 10591 (office); 82 Mosle Road, Far Hills, NJ 07931, USA (home). *Telephone:* (914) 347-7000 (office). *Fax:* (914) 347-2113 (office). *Website:* www.regeneron.com (office).

VAGHUL, Narayanan, BCom; Indian banker; b. 1936, South India; ed Ramakrishna School, Chennai, Loyola Coll., Madras Univ.; mem. of staff, State Bank of India 1957–74; fmr Dir Nat. Inst. of Bank Man.; Exec. Dir Cen. Bank of India 1978–81; Chair. Man. Dir Bank of India 1981–84; Chair. (non-exec.) Industrial Credit and Investment Corpn of India Ltd (now known as ICICI Bank) 1985–2009, fmrly also Man. Dir; Dir Wipro 1997–, Mahindra & Mahindra, Apollo Hospitals, Mittal Steel; Chair. Give India; fmr Visiting Prof. of Econs and Int. Business, Stern Business School, New York Univ.; Business Man of the Year, Business India 1991, Padma Bhushan (Trade and Industry category) 2010, Lifetime Achievement Award by the Times publs 2012. *Address:* Wipro Limited, Doddakannelli, Sarjapur Road, Bangalore 560 035, Karnataka, India (office). *Telephone:* (80) 28440011 (office). *Fax:* (80) 28440256 (office). *Website:* www.wipro.com (office).

VAGNORIUS, Gediminas, DEconSc; Lithuanian politician; b. 10 June 1957, Plunge Dist; m. Nijole Vagnorenė; one s. one d.; ed Inst. of Eng and Construction, Vilnius; engineer-economist, jr researcher, then researcher, Inst. of Econs, Lithuanian Acad. of Sciences 1980–90; Deputy to Lithuanian Supreme Soviet, mem. Presidium 1990–91; Chair. Council of Ministers (Prime Minister) of Lithuania 1991–92, 1996–99; mem. Seimas (Parl.) 1992–2004; Chair. Bd Homeland Union/Lithuanian Conservative Party 1993–2000; Chair. Krikščionių Konservatorių Socialinė Sąjunga (Christian-Conservative Social Union) 2000–10 (after merger into Krikščionių partija). *Leisure interest:* jogging.

VAHER, Ken-Marti; Estonian politician; b. 5 Sept. 1974, Tallinn; m.; one s.; ed Tallinn Secondary School No. 7, Univ. of Tartu; Adviser, Riigikogu (Parl.) Constitutional Cttee 1995–98; Adviser to Auditor Gen. on personnel and training issues 1998–99, Dir State Audit Office 1999–2001; Sec.-Gen. Res Publica party 2001–02, now mem. Union of Pro Patria and Res Publica party (following merger of two parties 2006); mem. Tallinn City Council 2002–03; mem. Riigikogu (Parl.) 2003, 2005–, Chair. Constitutional Cttee 2016–; Minister of Justice 2003–05, of the Interior 2011–14; Chair. Tallinn House Owners Asscn, Estonian Foundation for Helping the Repressed; mem. Academic Unit of Estonian Defence League. *Publications:* articles in the nat. press. *Leisure interests:* philosophy, physical education, music. *Address:* Riigikogu Lossi plats 1a, 15165 Tallinn, Estonia. *E-mail:* ken-marti.vaher@riigikogu.ee; press@riigikogu.ee. *Website:* www.vaher.ee/.

VÄHI, Tiit; Estonian engineer, business executive and fmr politician; *Commercial Director, Silmet AS;* b. 10 Jan. 1947, Valgamaa; m.; two c.; ed Tallinn Polytechnic Inst.; fmr Production Man., Valga Motor Depot, later Deputy Dir, Chief Engineer, Dir, Chair. Transport Cttee; helped organize Estonian Popular Front, led its regional committee in Valga Co.; Minister of Transport and Communications 1989–92; Govt's Special Rep. to NE Estonia 1991; Acting Prime Minister of Estonia Jan.–Oct. 1992, Prime Minister 1995–97; mem. Bd Coalition Party, Chair. 1993–99; Chair. Tallinn City Council 1993–95; Head, Estonian Asscn of Large Enterprises Bd 2008; fmr Owner and CEO Silmet AS, Commercial Dir 2010–. *Address:* Silmet AS, Kesk 2, Sillamäe 40231, Estonia (office). *Telephone:* 392-9100 (office). *Fax:* 392-9111 (office). *E-mail:* sekretar@silmet.ee (office). *Website:* www.silmet.ee (office).

VAHIDI, Brig. Gen. Ahmad, MEng, PhD; Iranian army officer and government official; *Head of the Strategic Centre of the General Staff, Iran Armed Forces;* b. Shiraz; ed Shiraz Univ., Imam Sadegh Univ.; joined Revolutionary Cttees and Islamic Revolutionary Guard Corps (IRGC) 1979, becoming Commdr, Qods Force, IRGC; responsible for security affairs, Armed Forces Gen. Command HQ during Iran–Iraq war 1980–88; fmr Deputy Head of Ministry of Defence Armed Forces Logistics; fmr Head of Political, Defence and Security Cttee of State Expediency Council; Deputy Minister of Defence 2005–09, Minister of Defence and Armed Forces Logistics 2009–13, currently Head of the Strategic Centre of Gen. Staff, Iran Armed Forces. *Address:* Office of the General Staff, Iran Armed Forces, Ministry of Defence, Shahid Yousuf Kaboli Street, Sayed Khandan Area, Tehran, Iran (office). *Telephone:* (21) 26126988 (office). *E-mail:* info@mod.ir (office). *Website:* www.mod.ir (office).

VAIL, Peter R., PhD; American oceanographer and academic; *Professor Emeritus, Earth Science Department, Rice University;* b. 13 Jan. 1930, New York; m. Carolyn Vail; three c.; ed Dartmouth Coll. and Northwestern Univ.; Research Geologist, Exxon Corpn 1956; Research Geologist, Esso Production Research Co. 1965, Sr Research Scientist 1980–86; W. Maurice Ewing Prof. of Oceanography, Rice Univ. 1986–2001, Prof. Emer. 2001–; Founder and Pres. Peter R. Vail Oil and Gas Consulting and Investing Co. 2001–; FGS (US) 1993–, FGS (UK) 1995–; Fellow, AAAS; mem. Sigma Xi (American Geophysical Union), American Geophysical Inst.; Hon. mem. Gulf Coast Section of Soc. for Sedimentary Geology, Soc. of Exploration Geologists, Houston Geophysical Soc.; Penrose Medal Award, Geological Soc. of America 2003, Legendary Geoscientist Award, American Geological Inst. 2004, Hollis D. Hedbers Award in Energy, Inst. for the Study of Earth and Man 2005, Benjamin Franklin Medal in Earth Science, The Franklin Inst. 2005. *Publications include:* numerous articles in scientific publs. *Address:* Department of Earth Science, 6100 Main Street, Houston, TX 77005, USA (office).

Telephone: (713) 348-4888 (office). *E-mail:* vail@rice.edu (office). *Website:* earthscience.rice.edu (office).

VAILE, Hon. Mark Anthony James, AO; Australian consultant and fmr politician; *Chairman, SmartTrans Holdings Ltd;* b. 18 April 1956, Sydney; s. of George Strafford Vaile and Suzanne Elizabeth Vaile; m. Wendy Jean Vaile 1976; three d.; worked as jackaroo 1973–76; farm machinery retailer 1976–79; Real Estate and Stock and Station Agent 1979–92; Chair. Wingham Chamber of Commerce 1980–85; mem. House of Reps for Lyne (Nat. Party), NSW 1993–, fmr Deputy Speaker, then Chair. House of Reps Standing Cttee on Communications, Transport and Micro-Econ. Reform, Nat. Party Whip 1994; Minister for Transport and Regional Devt 1997–98, for Agric., Fisheries and Forestry 1998–99, for Trade 1999–2006, for Transport and Regional Services 2006–07; Deputy Leader Nat. Party of Australia 1999–2005, Fed. Parl. Leader 2005–07 (resgnd); Deputy Prime Minister 2005–07; Dir Vaile and Assocs (business consultancy); Chair. Whitehaven Coal Ltd 2012–, SmartTrans Holdings Ltd 2016–; mem. Bd of Dirs Virgin Blue Holdings Ltd 2008–, Stamford Land Corpn Ltd 2009–, Aston Resources Ltd 2009–, ServCorp Ltd 2011–; Centenary Medal 2001. *Leisure interests:* squash, tennis, water skiing, golf. *Address:* SmartTrans Holdings Ltd, 1/614 Newcastle Street, Leederville, WA 6007, Australia (office). *Telephone:* (8) 9228-1199 (office). *Website:* www.smarttransholdings.com (office).

VAILLANT, Daniel; French politician; b. 19 July 1949, Lormes (Nièvre); s. of Raymond Vaillant and Germaine Andre; three c.; ed Ecole supérieure de biologie et biochimie; joined Convention des Institutions Républicaines 1966; Parti Socialiste (PS) official, 18th arrondissement Paris 1971–95; Special Asst to François Mitterrand, presidential election campaign 1981; Asst Nat. Sec. for PS Feds 1986, Nat. Sec. for PS Feds 1988–94, Nat. Sec. without specific assignment 1994–95; Campaign Dir, Lionel Jospin's parl. and regional election campaigns 1986, Organizer and Co-ordinator of Lionel Jospin's gen. election campaign 1997; City Councillor 18th arrondissement Paris 1977–95, Mayor of 18th arrondissement 1995–2001, 2003–14 (First Deputy Mayor 2001–03); Ile-de-France Regional Councillor 1986–89; Nat. Ass. Deputy for 19th Paris constituency 1988–93, 1994–97, 2002–; Minister for Relations with Parl. 1997–2000, of the Interior 2000–02. *Publications:* C'est ça ma gauche 2000, Sécurité, priorité à gauche 2003, PS: 40 ans d'histoire(s) 2011. *Address:* Assemblée Nationale, 126 rue de l'Université, 75355 Paris cedex 07, France.

VAILLAUD, Pierre; French fmr oil industry executive; b. 15 Feb. 1935, Paris; s. of Marcel Vaillaud and Rose Larrat; m. Geneviève Dreyfus 1960; two s.; ed Lycée Janson-de-Sailly, Paris, Ecole Polytechnique, Ecole des Mines, Ecole Nat. Supérieure du Pétrole et des Moteurs; engineer, Ministry of Industry 1959–63; project man. Technip 1964–68, Dir, Vice-Pres. Eng and Construction Atochem (affiliate of Total) 1968–72, Vice-Pres. Natural Gas Div., Total 1972–74, Vice-Pres. Devt and Construction Div., Vice-Pres. Exploration and Production Operations then Pres., Total Exploration Production 1974–89, Exec. Vice-Pres. Total, Pres. and COO Total Chimie 1989–92, Chair. and CEO Technip 1992–99, Elf Aquitaine SA 1999–2000, Dir Total SA 2000–09; Pres. Asscn des techniciens du pétrole 1985–87; Commdr, Ordre nat. du Mérite, Officier, Légion d'honneur. *Leisure interests:* tennis, sailing, golf. *Address:* 5 villa Madrid, 92200 Neuilly-sur-Seine, France (home). *Telephone:* (6) 03-03-00-70 (mobile) (home). *E-mail:* pierrevaillaud@gmail .com.

VAINIO, Vesa Veikko, LLM; Finnish business executive; b. 2 Dec. 1942, Helsinki; s. of Veikko Vainio and Aune Vainio; m. Marja-Liisa Harjunen 1968; two s.; ed Univ. of Helsinki; Circuit Court Notary, Rovaniemi Circuit Court 1966–67; Counsellor, Union of Finnish Lawyers 1968; Sec. Finnish Employers' Confed. 1969, Counsellor and Asst Head of Dept 1969–72; Admin. Dir Aaltonen Footwear Factory 1972, Deputy Man. Dir 1974–76; Man. Dir Aaltonen Factories Oy 1976–77; Dir Confed. of Finnish Industries 1977–83, Deputy Man. Dir 1983–85; Exec. Vice-Pres. Kymmene Corpn 1985–91, Pres. 1991–92, mem. Bd of Dirs 1996, Chair. UPM-Kymmene Corpn 2001–08; Pres. and CEO Unitas Ltd 1992–94; Chair. and CEO Union Bank of Finland 1992–94 (after merger with Kansallis-Osake-Pankki into Merita Bank Ltd) Merita Bank Ltd 1995–97, Pres. and CEO Merita Ltd 1995–97, Pres. Merita PLC 1998–2000, Chair. MeritaNordbanken PLC 1998, Vice-Chair. Nordbanken Holding PLC 1998–2000, Vice-Chair. MeritaNordbanken PLC 1999, Chair. Nordea AB (publrs) 2000–02; mem. Bd of Dirs Nokia Corpn ADS 1993–2008; fmr Vice-Chair. Wärtsilä NSD Oy Ab; Chair. Finnish Cen. Chamber of Commerce 1996–2003; Kt, Order of Finnish Lion; Commdr of Finnish White Rose. *Leisure interests:* hunting, fishing.

VAINO, Anton Eduardovich; Russian (b. Estonian) diplomatist and politician; *Chief of Staff of the Presidential Administration;* b. 17 Feb. 1972, Tallinn, Estonian SSR, USSR; m.; one s.; ed Moscow State Inst. of Int. Relations of Ministry of Foreign Affairs; worked at Embassy in Tokyo, then at Second Asian Dept of Ministry of Foreign Affairs 1996–2001; held different posts at Presidential Protocol Directorate 2002–04, Deputy Head of Presidential Protocol Scheduling Directorate 2004–07, First Deputy Head 2007; Deputy Chief of Govt Staff 2007–08, Chief of Prime Minister's Protocol and Deputy Chief of Govt Staff 2008–11, Chief of Govt Staff and Minister of Russian Fed. 2011–12; Deputy Chief of Presidential Admin 2012–16, Chief of Staff of Presidential Admin Office 2016–; Russian Fed. Presidential Certificate of Gratitude 2005, Russian Fed. Presidential Certificate of Honour 2012. *Address:* Office of the Presidential Administration, 103132 Moscow, Staraya pl. 4, Russia (office). *Telephone:* (495) 625-35-81 (office). *Fax:* (495) 606-07-66 (office). *E-mail:* president@gov.ru (office). *Website:* en.kremlin.ru/ catalog/persons/307 (office).

VAINSHTOK, Semyon Mikhailovich; Russian business executive; b. 5 Oct. 1947, Klimatsy, Moldova; m.; one d.; ed Kiev Inst. of Construction and Eng, Acad. of KGB; engineer in Chernovtsy, Ukraine 1969–74; Head, Chernovtsy regional Dept of Provision and Trade 1974–82; Deputy Head, Povkhneft 1982–86; Deputy Dir-Gen. Bashneft, W Siberia 1986–88; Deputy Head, Kolymneftgas 1988–93; Dir-Gen. LukOil–Kolymneftgas 1993–95, LukOil, W Siberia 1995, Vice-Pres., mem. Bd of Dirs LukOil co. 1995; Pres. Transneft 1999–2007 (retd); head of Olympstroi (state corpn overseeing preparations for 2014 Winter Olympics in Sochi) 2007–08 (resgnd); mem. Acad. of Mining Sciences; Order for Service to Motherland.

VAISEY, David George, CBE, MA, FSA, FRHistS; British librarian and archivist; *Fellow Emeritus, Exeter College, Oxford;* b. 15 March 1935; s. of William Thomas Vaisey and Minnie Vaisey (née Payne); m. Maureen Anne Mansell 1965; two d.; ed Rendcomb Coll., Glos., Exeter Coll., Oxford; archivist, Staffordshire Co. Council 1960–63; Asst, then Sr Librarian, Bodleian Library 1963–75, Keeper of Western Manuscripts 1975–86, Bodley's Librarian 1986–96, Bodley's Librarian Emer. 1997–; Deputy Keeper, Oxford Univ. Archives 1966–75, Keeper 1995–2000; Professorial Fellow, Exeter Coll., Oxford 1975–96, Fellow by Special Election 1997–2000, Fellow Emer. 2000–; Visiting Prof. of Library Studies, Grad. School of Library and Information Science, UCLA 1985; Commr, Royal Comm. on Historical Manuscripts 1986–98; Chair. Manuscript Cttee, The Soc. of Coll., Nat. and Univ. Libraries (SCONUL) 1981–88, Nat. Council on Archives 1988–91; Vice-Pres. British Records Asscn 1999–; Cecil and Ida Green Visiting, Prof. Texas Christian Univ. 1991; Pres. Bristol and Gloucestershire Archaeological Soc. 1992–93, Soc. of Archivists 1999–2002, Expert Panel on Museums, Libraries and Archives, Heritage Lottery Fund 1999–2005; Curtis Lecturer, Vassar Coll. 1997; mem. Advisory Council on Public Records 1989–94, London Services Advisory Cttee of British Library 1990–96, Expert Advisory Panel for Museums, Libraries and Archives 1999–2005; Fellow, Soc. of Antiquaries of London, Royal Historical Soc.; Mayer Fellow, Huntington Library, San Marino, Calif. 1994; Hon. Fellow, Kellogg Coll. Oxford 1996–; Hon. Research Fellow, Dept of Library, Archive and Information Studies, Univ. Coll. London 1987–; Encomienda, Order of Isabel La Catolica (Spain) 1989. *Publications:* Staffordshire and the Great Rebellion (co-author) 1964, Probate Inventories of Lichfield and District 1568–1680 1969, Victorian and Edwardian Oxford from Old Photographs (co-author) 1971, Oxford Shops and Shopping 1972, Art for Commerce (co-author) 1973, Oxfordshire: A Handbook for Students of Local History 1973, The Diary of Thomas Turner 1754–65 1984; numerous articles in learned journals. *Address:* Bodleian Library, Oxford, OX1 3BG, England (office). *E-mail:* david.vaisey@bodleian.ox.ac.uk (office).

VAITHILINGAM, Thiru V.; Indian politician; *Speaker, Puducherry Legislative Assembly;* b. 5 Oct. 1950, Cuddalore, Tamil Nadu; s. of V. Venkatasubba Reddiar; m. Sasikala Sambasivam 1969; ed Loyola Coll., Chennai; raised in rural Maducarai, Pondicherry, later went to Maducarai to take care of family farms; fmr Chair. Land Devt Bank of Pondicherry State; cand. for Legis. Ass. 1980; Minister of Public Works and Power 1985; MLA Nettapakkam Constituency 1980–2006, Kamaraj Nagar Constituency 2011–; Speaker, Puducherry Legis. Ass. 2016–; Leader Congress Legis. Party 1991–2000, 2008–16; Chief Minister of Puducherry 1991–96, 2008–11, Leader of Opposition 1996–2000, 2011–16. *Address:* Legislative Assembly Building, 79, Kandappa Mudaliar Street, Puducherry 605 001 (office); 27 Kamatham Street, Maducarai, Puducherry 605 105, India (home). *Telephone:* (413) 2333399 (office); (413) 2227622 (home). *E-mail:* secretary@satyam.net.in.

VAJDA, György, DSc, FIEEE; Hungarian engineer; b. 18 June 1927, Budapest; s. of László Vajda and Mária Daróczi; m. 1st Magdolna Krasznai 1969 (died 1987); one s. one d.; m. 2nd Dr Klára Berei 1988; ed Tech. Univ., Budapest; Asst Lecturer 1949–50; on staff of Hungarian Acad. of Sciences 1950–52; Deputy Dir Inst. of Measurements 1952–57, Research Inst. of Electric Energetics 1957–63; Deputy Section Leader, Ministry of Heavy Industry 1963–70; Dir Inst. for Electrical Power Research 1970–93, Prof. 1993–97; Dir-Gen. Hungarian Atomic Energy Authority 1994–99 (Vice-Pres. 1979–97), then Pres. Science Cttee; Pres. European Atomic Energy Soc.; mem. Hungarian Nat. Comm. for Tech. Devt, Hungarian Acad. of Eng; mem. Admin. Comm. Conf. Int. des Grands Reseaux Électriques, Paris; Chair. ECE Electric Power Comm. 1972–76; Corresp. mem. Hungarian Acad. of Sciences 1976–81, mem. 1982, Section Pres. 1985–92; mem. New York Acad. of Sciences, Hungarian Acad. of Engineers; Fellow, Wireless Interconnection Forum; Hon. Pres. Hungarian Electrotechnical Soc., Hon. mem. Sigma Kszi, Distinguished Mem. CIGRE (Int. Council on Large Electric Systems); Hungarian Order; State Prize 1975, Szilárd Prize 1999, Széchenyi Award 2000, Renovanda Kult. Hung Grand Award 2002, Helios Award 2004, Prize of Labour (five times), Hazám Award 2008. *Publications:* A szigetelések romlása (Deterioration of Insulations) 1964, Szigetelések villamos erőterei (Electric Power Fields of Insulation) 1970, Energia és Társadalom (Energy and Society) 1975, Energetika (Energetics), Vols I–II 1984, Risk and Safety 1998, Energy Policy 2001, Energy Today and Tomorrow 2003, Utilization of Energy 2005; more than 150 papers in int. journals. *Leisure interest:* gardening. *Address:* Bem rkp. 32, 1027 Budapest, Hungary (home).

VAKHROMEYEV, Kyril Varfolomeyevich (see Philaret).

VALA, Vajubhai Rudabhai, BSc, LLB; Indian politician and state official; *Governor of Karnataka;* b. 23 Jan. 1938; m.; two s. two d.; joined Rashtriya Swayamsevak Sangh, subsequently joined Jan Sangh 1971; Dir, Rajkot Nagarik Sahakari Bank 1971–90, Chair. 1975–76, 1981–82, 1987–90; Municipal Councillor, Rajkot 1975–93, Mayor of Rajkot 1983–88, 1991–93; mem. Bharatiya Janata Party, Pres. 1996–98, 2005–06; MLA for Rajkot-2 Constituency 1985–2001, 2002–, Speaker of Legis. Ass. 2012–14; Minister of Urban Devt, Gujarat Govt 1990, Minister of Energy, Petrochemicals and Co-operation 1995, of Finance and Energy 1995–96, of Finance and Revenue 1998–2001, of Finance 2002–05, 2006–07, of Finance, Labour and Employment, and Transport 2008–12; Gov. of Karnataka 2014–; The Best Citizens of India Award, International Publishing House, New Delhi 2006, Bharat Gaurav Award, India Int. Friendship Soc. 2007. *Address:* Raj Bhavan, Raj Bhavan Road, Bangalore 560 001, India (office). *Telephone:* (80) 22254102 (office). *Fax:* (80) 22258150 (office). *E-mail:* rajbhavan.karnataka@gmail .com (office). *Website:* www.rajbhavan.kar.nic.in (office).

VALAKIVI ÁLVAREZ, Jakke Raimo Milagro, PhD, MBA; Peruvian economist and politician; b. 1963; ed Univ. of Lima, Universidad Politécnica de Catalunya, Spain, INCAE Business School, Costa Rica; has held various posts in Peruvian public finance sector including as Vice-Pres., Globokas Peru SAC, Sr Man. Adviser, Peruvian Banking and Insurance Regulatory Body, Div. Man., Banco Internacional del Perú SA (Interbank Perú), Asst Man., Interfip Bolsa (stock exchange), fmr Head, Dept of Econ. Devt Studies, Corporación Financiera de Desarrollo SA (COFIDE, nat. devt bank); Dir Banco de Comercio 2012–; Deputy Minister of Defence 2012–15, Minister of Defence 2015–16; Peruvian del. to Mercosur Basel Accord negotiations, Montevideo; del. to numerous meetings with IMF and World Bank, Washington, DC; fmr Prof. of Int. Finance and Banking and Monetary Econs, Univ. of Lima Graduate School and Peruvian Univ. of Applied Sciences Business School; fmr mem. high-level Comm. on Reorganizing DINI (nat.

intelligence service); Merit Medal, Mil. Order Armando Revoredo Iglesias, Commdr, Mil. Order of Ayacucho 2008.

VALCOURT, (Joseph) Bernard, PC, DHC, BA, LLB, QC; Canadian politician and lawyer; b. 18 Feb. 1952, St Quentin de Restigouche, NB; s. of Bertin Valcourt and Geraldine Allain; m. (divorced); two d.; ed Académie St Joseph, Collège St Louis—Maillet, Univ. of New Brunswick; practised law, mem. Canadian Bar Asscn and New Brunswick Lawyers Asscn; mem. House of Commons for Madawaska–Victoria constituency 1984–93, for Madawaska–Restigouche constituency 2011–15, Parl. Sec. to Minister of State for Science and Tech., Parl. Sec. to Minister of Revenue 1985–86; Minister of State for Small Business and Tourism 1986–89, Minister of State for Indian Affairs (renamed Aboriginal Affairs May 2011) and Northern Devt 1987–89; Minister for Consumer and Corp. Affairs Jan.–Aug. 1989, of Fisheries and Oceans 1990–91, of Employment and Immigration 1991–93; Leader Progressive Conservative Party of New Brunswick 1995–97 (resgnd); Minister of Aboriginal Affairs and Northern Devt 2013–15; mem. New Brunswick Legis. Ass. 1995–99, Leader of Opposition 1995–97; mem. Conservative Party 2011–. *Address:* Conservative Party of Canada, 130 Albert St, Suite 1204, Ottawa, ON K1P 5G4, Canada (office). *Telephone:* (613) 755-2000 (office). *Fax:* (613) 755-2001 (office). *Website:* www.conservative.ca (office).

VÂLCOV, Darius Bogdan, DEcon; Romanian economist and politician; b. 25 March 1977, Slatina; m. Lavinia Șandru; one d.; ed Bucharest Acad. of Econ. Studies, Inst. of Public Admin and Business, Spiru Haret Univ.; Dir-Gen., Romanian People's Bank for Devt, Slatina 2000–04; Econ. Dir, SC Octagon LLC Slatina 2004; Mayor, Municipality of Slatina 2004–12; mem. Senatul (upper house of Parl.) for Olt constituency 2012–; Minister-Del. for Budget Aug.–Dec. 2014, Minister of Public Finance 2014–15; mem. Partidul Democrat 2000–07, Partidul Social Democrat (PSD—Social Democratic Party) 2012–.

VALDÉS, Juan Gabriel, PhD; Chilean politician and diplomatist; b. 2 June 1947; m. Antonia Echenique Celis; four c.; ed Catholic Univ. of Chile, Santiago, Univ. of Essex, UK, Princeton Univ., USA; Researcher, Political Science Inst. of Catholic Univ. of Chile, Inst. for Policy Studies, Washington, DC 1972–76; Officer, Latin American Inst. for Transnational Studies, Prof. of Int. Relations, Econ. Research and Devt Centre, Mexico City, Mexico 1976–84; Research Fellow, Kellogg Inst. of Int. Studies, Notre Dame Univ., USA, Center for Latin American Studies, Princeton Univ. 1984, 1987; Consultant, Econ. Comm. for Latin America 1985; Amb. to Spain 1990–94; Dir Int. Div. and Co-ordinator NAFTA Negotiating Team, Ministry of Finance 1994–96, Lead Negotiator Chile–Canada Free Trade Agreement 1996; Consultant, UN Programme for Devt, Santiago 1994; mem. Nat. TV Council 1995; Vice-Minister of Int. Econ. Affairs, Ministry of Foreign Affairs 1996–99, Minister 1999–2000, Perm. Rep. to UN, New York 2000–03, concurrently Amb. to Iran 2001, Amb. to Argentina 2003–04, Sec.-Gen.'s Special Rep., UN Stabilization Mission in Haiti (MINUSTAH) 2004–06; Dir Public Diplomacy Program, Ministry of Foreign Affairs 2007–10, apptd Rep. of Presidency of UNASUR (asscn of South American countries) 2010; apptd Prof., Inst. of Latin American Studies, Univ. of Paris (Sorbonne) 2011; Amb. to USA 2014. *Publications include:* Movimiento Sindical Y Empresas Transnacionales 1979, Chile 2000: Encuentro En Caceres De Politicos E Intelectuales Chilenos 1994, Pinochet's Economists: The Chicago School of Economics in Chile 1995; numerous articles on int. relations.

VALDES DANCUART, Gen. Oscar Eduardo; Peruvian politician and fmr army officer; b. 3 April 1949, Lima; ed Chorrillos Mil. School, US Army Command and Gen. Staff Coll., Fort Leavenworth; army service 1972–91, roles included Instructor, Chorrillos Mil. School, Army Technical School, School of Artillery, Chief of Artillery Group Armoured Unit No 211, Lima, Head of Artillery Group No 1, Tumbes, Head, Bureau of Foreign Acquisitions, Army Logistics Command, Chief, Office of Man. of Army Officers; Dir Chamber of Commerce, Industry and Production, Tacna 1992; Minister of the Interior July–Dec. 2011, Pres., Council of Ministers (Prime Minister) 2011–12; fmr Man. Dir SAC ADC Corpn; Pres. Regional Council, SENATI Tacna-Moquegua.

VALDÉS MENÉNDEZ, Ramiro (Ramirito); Cuban government official; *Vice-President;* b. 28 April 1932, Artemisa, Havana Prov.; father of Cuban composer Ramiro Valdés Puentes; fmr revolutionary and one of only four so-called 'Revolutionary Commanders'; joined Fidel Castro in failed assault on Moncada Barracks 1953, jailed for two years on Isla de los Pinos; granted political asylum by Govt of Fulgencio Batista May 1955, left prison and travelled to Mexico to join in preparations, led by Fidel Castro, for Granma expedition which sailed from Mexico for Cuba Dec. 1956; took part in Sierra Maestra uprising alongside Castro, second in command of second column, led by Che Guevara, invaded cen. Prov. of Las Villas 1958; Minister of the Interior 1960–61; apptd Founder and Chief of Departamento de Investigaciones del Ejercito Rebelde; removed from Interior Ministry by Politburo 1969, reinstalled as Interior Minister 1978, removed again as Interior Minister at Third Communist Party Congress and as mem. of Politburo 1986; Dir Nat. Electronics Group (Copextel) late 1980s; Head of newly established Industrial Group for Electronics attached to Ministry of Iron and Steel and Mechanical Industry (SIME) 1990s, subsequently absorbed by Ministry of Information Tech. and Communications; Minister of Information Tech. and Communications 2006–11; re-admitted to Politburo 2008; apptd one of seven Vice-Pres. in Council of Ministers and Council of State 2009–; Coordinator of the 'Battle of Ideas' 2009–; CEO of the Electronics Group 2009–.

VALDÉS PULIDO, Rodrigo, PhD; Chilean economist, academic and politician; b. 22 Nov. 1966, Santiago; m. Ilana Meller Rosenblut; two s. one d.; ed Univ. of Chile, Massachusetts Inst. of Tech., USA; Sr Economist, Banco Central de Chile 1996–2000, Chief Economist and Man., Research Div. 2002–07; Econ. Policy Coordinator, Ministry of Finance 2000–01; Chief Economist for Latin America, Barclays Capital Inc., New York 2008–09; Deputy Dir, European Dept and Americas Dept, IMF, Washington, DC 2009–12, also Head of Mission to USA 2009–12; Chief Economist for Andean Region and Argentina, BTG Pactual (investment bank) 2013–14; Chair. Bd and Exec. Cttee, Banco del Estado de Chile (BancoEstado) 2014–15; Minister of Finance 2015–17 (resgnd); fmr consultant to IMF and IDB; fmr Prof., Dept of Industrial Eng and Dept of Econs, Univ. of Chile; fmr Prof., Dept of Econs, Univ. of Santiago; mem. Partido por la Democracia (PPD).

VÁLDEZ ALBIZÚ, Héctor, BEconSc; Dominican Republic economist and central banker; *Governor, Banco Central de la República Dominicana;* b. 10 Nov. 1947; s. of Hector Manuel Valdez Albizu and Ana Rita Valdez Albizu; m. Fior d'Aliza Martinez 1971; one s.; ed Autonomous Univ. of Santo Domingo, Inst. of Social Studies, Catholic Univ. of Chile; Tech. Asst (Publs), Cen. Bank of Dominican Repub. (Banco Central de la República Dominicana) 1970–75, Head of Banking and Monetary Div., Tech. Co-ordinator of Econ. Studies 1975–82, Econ. Asst to Gov. 1982–84, Dir Econ. Studies Dept 1984–86, Asst Man., Monetary and Exchange Policy 1986–90, Adviser to Monetary Bd 1987–89, Rep. of Cen. Bank at Banco de Reservas (state commercial bank) 1991–92, Asst Gen. Man. and Gen. Admin. Banco de Reservas 1992–94, Gov. Cen. Bank and Pres. Monetary Bd 1994–2000, 2004–; Pres. Cen. American Monetary Council 2011; Prof., Universidad Cen. del Este and Instituto de Estudios Superiores 1975–89; mem. Bd of Dirs Consejo Estatal del Azucar (State Sugar Council) 1993–94, Dominican Coll. of Economists, Governing Bd, Center for Latin American Monetary Studies 2013–15; Medal of the Order of Merit Duarte, Sanchez and Mella 2012; Medal of Merit for Public Servants 1996, Economist of the Year 1997, Governor of the Year (Americas), The Banker magazine 2006. *Publications:* Financial Programs for the Dominican Republic 1976–1990, Dimensions of the National Banking System and its Enhancement 1976, Exchange Emergency Regime 1985. *Address:* Banco Central de la República Dominicana, Calle Pedro Henriquez Ureña, Esq. Leopoldo Navarro, Apdo 1347, Santo Domingo, DN, Dominican Republic (office). *Telephone:* 221-9111 (office). *Fax:* 687-7488 (office). *E-mail:* info@bancentral.gov.do (office). *Website:* www.bancentral.gov.do (office).

VALDIVIESO MONTANO, Luis Miguel, BA, MA, PhD; Peruvian economist, politician and diplomatist; *President, Asociación de AFP Perú;* s. of Juan 'El Mago' Valdivieso; ed Pontificia Univ. Católica del Perú, Boston Univ., USA; fmr Sr Researcher, Centre for Latin American Monetary Studies; fmr adviser to Bank and Securities Market Directorate, Ministry of Finance and Public Credit in Mexico and adviser to the Superintendence of Banks of Ecuador; also taught Introductory Econs and Advanced Macroeconomics at Boston Univ. and was an Econometrics Instructor at the Catholic Univ. of Peru; joined IMF 1980, held several exec. positions over 28-year period, including Sr Economist positions in Western Hemisphere Dept 1980–87 and Policy Devt and Review Dept 1997–99, Chief of Mission to Cambodia and Laos and Dir Asia-Pacific Region, Advisor and Div. Chief positions in European Dept 1991–99, in Asia and Pacific Dept 1999–2008; Adviser to Pres. Alberto Fujimori 1990–2000; Special Tech. Adviser to Ministry of Economy and Finance 1991; Minister of Economy and Finance July 2008–Jan. 2009 (resgnd), also Gov. for Peru in Bd Govs of World Bank and IDB, Chair. Andean Finance Corpn (CAF), Nat. Fund for the Financing of the Public Sector Entrepreneurial Activity (FONAFE), mem. Bd Peruvian Nat. Retirement Investment Fund (ONP), Pvt. Investment Promotion Agency (PROINVERSION), Interministerial Cttee of Social Affairs (CIAS); Amb. to USA 2009–11; Pres. Asociación de AFP Perú (asscn of pension fund admins) 2012–. *Address:* Asociación de AFP Perú, Estamos ubicados en Antequera N° 580, San Isidro, Lima 27, Peru (office). *Website:* www.asociacionafp.com.pe (office).

VALDIVIESO SARMIENTO, Alfonso, LLD; Colombian politician and diplomatist; b. Oct. 1949, Bucaramanga; m.; two s.; ed Javerian Univ., Bogotá, Boston Univ., USA, Univ. of Toronto, Canada, Stanford Univ., USA; Admin. Vice-Rector and Dir of Planning, Autonomous Univ. of Bucaramanga 1978–86; mem. House of Reps 1982–86; mem. Council, Bucaramanga 1988–89, Pres. 1989; Senator 1986–90, 1990–94, 2008–; Minister for Nat. Educ. 1990–91; Amb. to Israel 1992–93; Attorney-Gen. in charge of criminal investigations 1994–97; unsuccessful presidential cand. 1998; Perm. Rep. to UN 1998–2002; mem. Cambio Radical.

VALE, Ronald David, BA, PhD; American biologist and academic; *Professor Department of Cellular and Molecular Pharmacology, University of California, San Francisco;* b. 11 Jan. 1959, Los Angeles, Calif.; ed Univ. of California, Santa Barbara, Stanford Univ., NIH Marine Biological Lab.; joined Faculty, Univ. of California, San Francisco 1986, currently Prof., Dept of Cellular and Molecular Pharmacology, fmr Vice-Chair., Investigator, Howard Hughes Medical Inst. 1995–, W.K. Hamilton Distinguished Prof., Dept of Anesthesia; Pres. American Soc. for Cell Biology 2012; mem. NAS 2001; Fellow, American Acad. of Arts and Sciences 2002–; Foreign Fellow, Indian Nat. Science Acad. 2015–; Biophysical Soc. Award for Young Investigators 1993, Keith R. Porter Lecturer 2009, Wiley Prize 2012, Albert Lasker Basic Medical Research Award (co-recipient) 2012, Massry Prize 2013, Shaw Prize (with Ian R. Gibbons) 2017. *Publications:* numerous papers in professional journals. *Address:* Department of Cellular and Molecular Pharmacology, MC 2200, Room N312E, Genentech Hall, University of California, 600 16th Street, MC 2200, Room N312A, San Francisco, CA 94158-2280, USA (office). *Telephone:* (415) 476-6380 (office). *E-mail:* ron.vale@ucsf.edu (office); vale@cmp.ucsf.edu (office). *Website:* valelab.ucsf.edu (office).

VALE DE ALMEIDA, João; Portuguese diplomatist and European Union official; *Ambassador and Head of the European Union Delegation, United Nations;* b. 29 Jan. 1957, Lisbon; m.; two c.; ed Univ. of Lisbon, journalism training in France, USA and Japan, attended man. schools in UK and France; EC official since 1982, began career at representation in Lisbon, becoming mem. Spokesperson's Service in Brussels 1989, under Pres. Jacques Delors, Spokesman for Energy Policy and for External Relations with the Middle East, the Mediterranean, Latin America and Asia, Head of Unit at Econ. and Social Cttee of the European Communities 1992–94, Deputy Chief Spokesman of EC under Pres. Jacques Santer 1995–97, in charge of coordinating official positions on EU's external relations, among other issues, Dir in Directorate Gen. for Information, Communication, Culture and Audiovisual 1998–2000, Dir in Directorate Gen. for Educ. and Culture 2000–04, Head of Cabinet to EC Pres. José Manuel Barroso 2004–09, Personal Rep. ('Sherpa') for G8 and G20 Summits 2004–10, Dir-Gen. for External Relations of the EU 2009–10, Amb. and Head of EU Del. to USA 2010–14, to UN 2015–. *Leisure interests:* travelling and global affairs, supports Benfica football club, playing tennis and golf. *Address:* Delegation of the European Union to the United Nations, 666 Third Avenue, 31st Floor, New York, NY 10017, USA (office). *Telephone:* (212) 292-8600 (office). *Fax:* (212) 292-8680 (office). *E-mail:* delegation-new-york@eeas.europa.eu (office). *Website:* eu-un.europa.eu (office).

VALENÇA PINTO, Gen. (retd) Luís Vasco, BEng; Portuguese military officer (retd); b. 1949, Lisbon; m. Maria de Lourdes; two s. one d.; ed Tech. Univ. of Lisbon,

NATO Defence Coll., Italy; Engineer Platoon Leader during combat tour in Angola 1971–72, Engineer Co. Commdr 1973–75; Mil. Rep. to NATO, Brussels 1978–84, Mil. Counsellor, Del. to NATO, Brussels 1990–93, Mil. Rep. to SHAPE 1997–2000, Dir Nat. Defence Inst. 2000, Army Logistics Commdr 2001–03, Chief of Staff 2003–06, Gen. Chief of Staff of the Armed Forces 2006–11 (retd); Chair. Advisory Bd Middle Tagus Hospital (CHMT) EPE 2015–; seven Distinguished Service Medals (five Gold and two Silver), Mil. Merit Medal (three classes). *Publications:* articles on security and defence issues in mil. and academic journals.

VALENCIA AMORES, José Samuel, MPA, MPolSci, PhD; Ecuadorean politician and diplomatist; *Minister of Foreign Affairs and Migration;* ed Diplomatic School of the Ministry of Foreign Affairs of Spain, Pontifical Catholic Univ., Quito, Columbia Univ., John F. Kennedy School of Govt, Harvard Univ.; Official, Directorates of Econ. Promotion, Nat. Sovereignty and Protocol, Ministry of Foreign Affairs 1982–87, Head, Office of Admin. Asst Sec. 1987–88, Office of the Sec.-Gen. March–June 1988, Office of the Undersecretary of Political Affairs July–Aug. 1993, Dir UN Dept Feb.–Nov. 1995, Head, Cabinet of the Minister of Foreign Affairs 1997–98, Gen. Dir of Human Rights Sept–Oct. 2003, of Multilateral Policy 2003–04, Vice Minister of Foreign Affairs 2007–08, Coordinator for the Presidency and Pro Tempore Secr. of the Andean Community 2010–15, Adviser, Cabinet of the Minister of Foreign Affairs 2016, Minister of Foreign Affairs and Migration 2018– (also Perm. Rep. of Ecuador to the OAS); Prof. of Latin America-US Relations, Faculty of Human Sciences, Pontificia Universidad Católica 1995–97, Assoc. Prof. of Int. Orgs. and Political Thought, Faculty of Jurisprudence 2004–06, Lawyer, Human Rights Clinic, Faculty of Jurisprudence 2004–05; Deputy Del., ILO, Geneva 1998–2001, Del., Int. Conf. on Disarmament 2001–03, Human Rights Comm. 2002; Assoc. Prof. of Public Int. Law, Coll. of Jurisprudence, Universidad San Francisco 2006–07; Assoc. Prof. of Int. Relations Dept, Latin American Faculty of Social Sciences (FLACSO) 2005–07; Amb. to South Africa 2010–15; Exec. Dir Corporación Participación Ciudadana 2005–07; mem. Ass. of the Citizen Participation Corporation 2007–, Consultative Council, Agora Democrática 2006–. *Address:* Ministry of Foreign Affairs and Migration, Avda 10 de Agosto y Carrión E1-76, 170526 Quito, Ecuador (office). *Telephone:* (2) 299-3200 (office). *Fax:* (2) 299-3273 (office). *Website:* www.cancilleria.gob.ec (office).

VALENCIA COSSIO, Fabio, LLB; Colombian politician and diplomatist; b. 23 March 1948, Medellín; ed Univ. de Antioquia; worked at Land Credit Inst., Bogotá 1974–81; Sec.-Gen. Conservative Party 1981–84, Vice-Pres. 1984–96, Pres. Nat. Bd 1996–; mem. House of Reps 1982–91; Senator 1991–99, Pres. of Congress 1998–99; apptd negotiator in peace discussions with FARC guerilla movt 1999–2001; Amb. to Italy 2001–05; High Commr for Competitiveness 2005–08; Minister of Interior and Justice 2008–10.

VALENCIA RODRÍGUEZ, Luis, LLD; Ecuadorean diplomatist, lawyer and academic; b. 5 March 1926, Quito; s. of Pedro Valencia and María Rodríguez; m. Cleopatra Moreno 1952; two s. three d.; ed Central Univ., Quito; entered Ecuadorean Foreign Service 1944; Counsellor, Buenos Aires 1957–59; Minister-Counsellor, UN, New York 1959–64; Minister of Foreign Affairs 1965-66, 1981–84; legal adviser on foreign affairs 1964–65, 1966–69, 1980–81, 1990–94, 2001–03; Amb. to Bolivia 1969–71, to Brazil 1971–74, to Peru 1974–78, to Venezuela 1978–79, to Argentina 1988–91, to Peru 2005–06; Perm. Rep. to UN 1994–99; Prof. Cen. Univ., Quito 1984–86, Universidad Internacional del Ecuador 2001; mem. UN Cttee on the Elimination of Racial Discrimination 1974–86, 1992–96; special citation of Ecuadorean Nat. Ass. 1966 and decorations from Ecuador, Italy, Nicaragua, Bolivia, Brazil, Peru, Venezuela, Colombia, Argentina, El Salvador, Dominican Republic and Korea. *Publications:* books on legal matters, foreign affairs etc. *Leisure interests:* swimming, reading. *Address:* Calle Agustin Mentoso 273, N47–153, Quito, Ecuador (home). *Telephone:* (2) 245-8765 (home). *Fax:* (2) 292-2668 (home).

VALENSISE, Michele; Italian diplomatist; b. 3 April 1952, Polistena (Reggio Calabria); m. Elena Di Giovanni; two d.; ed Univ. La Sapienza, Rome; completed Italian State Exam in Law; joined Diplomatic Service 1975, foreign postings in Brasilia 1978, Bonn 1981–84, Beirut 1984–87, First Counsellor, Perm. Rep. to EU, Brussels 1991–97, Amb. to Bosnia and Herzegovina 1997–99, Head, Press and Information Section and Spokesman for Minister of Foreign Affairs (MFA) 2001–04, Amb. to Brazil 2004–09, to Germany 2009–12, Sec.-Gen. MFA 2012–16 (resgnd). *Address:* c/o Ministry of Foreign Affairs, Piazzale della Farnesina 1, 00194 Rome, Italy.

VALENTIĆ, Nikica; Croatian lawyer, business executive and fmr politician; *President, Niva Ltd;* b. 24 Nov. 1950, Gospić; m. Antoneta Valentić; one s. one d.; ed Law School, Zagreb Univ.; journalist for Radio Zagreb 1969–71; Ed. Pravnik (magazine) 1972–74; legal adviser in Zeljko Jurkovič office; Founder and Gen. Man. S2 Stanograd and Stanogradinvest (consultancy) 1978–83; f. law firm 1984–90; Gen. Man. INA Industria Nafte 1990–93; Prime Minister of Croatia 1993–95; mem. Parl. 1995–2003; Founder and Pres. Niva Ltd (eng and design firm), Zagreb 1995–; Econ. Adviser to the Pres. 2015–. *Leisure interests:* painting, music. *Address:* Jordanovac 71, 10000, Zagreb (home); Niva Ltd, Vlaška 83/1, 10000, Zagreb, Croatia (office). *Telephone:* (1) 4664751 (office); (1) 4664752 (office). *Fax:* (1) 4664753 (office). *E-mail:* niva-holding@niva.htnet.hr (office).

VALENTIN, Pierre; French business executive; *Chairman of the Supervisory Board, Groupe BPCE;* ed Institut des Assurances d'Aix-Marseille; began career at Mutuelle d'Assurances du Bâtiment et des Travaux Publics, Lyon 1978; served as Del. Man. Dir Crédit Coopératif SA, Chief Financial Officer and Deputy CEO, Finance Div., Crédit Coopératif SA; Consultant Adviser, Caisse d'Epargne Languedoc-Roussillon 1984–, Pres. Advisory and Supervisory Council and Chair. Steering and Supervisory Bd, mem. Supervisory Bd, Groupe BPCE SA, 2009–, Chair. 2015–; Pres. Vallée des Gardons local savings co. 2000; CEO BTP Banque; Vice-Chair. Supervisory Bd, Banque Palatine SA; Dir, Fédération Nationale des Caisses d'Epargne, Natixis 2013–; mem. Supervisory Bd, CNCE (now CE Participations) 2009–, Esfin Gestion, Groupe Banques Populaire 2009–. *Address:* Groupe BPCE, 50 avenue Pierre Mendès France, 75201 Paris Cedex 13, France (office). *Telephone:* 1-58-40-41-42 (office). *E-mail:* info@bpce.fr (office). *Website:* www.bpce.fr (office).

VALENTINE, Jean, BA; American poet and teacher; b. 27 April 1934, Chicago, Ill.; m. James Chace 1957 (divorced 1968); two d.; ed Radcliffe Coll.; teacher, Swarthmore Coll. 1968–70, Barnard Coll. 1968, 1970, Yale Univ. 1970, 1973–74, Hunter Coll., CUNY 1970–75, Sarah Lawrence Coll. 1974–, 92nd Street Y, Manhattan; taught at Graduate Writing Program, New York Univ. –2004; currently mem. faculty, Vermont Coll. of Fine Arts; Guggenheim Fellowship 1976; Fellow, Rockefeller Foundation, Nat. Endowment for the Arts, New York State Council on the Arts, Bunting Inst.; State Poet of New York 2008–10; Nat. Endowment for the Arts grant 1972, Maurice English Prize, Teasdale Poetry Prize, Poetry Soc. of America Shelley Memorial Prize 2000, Morton Dauwen Zabel Award, American Acad. of Arts and Letters 2006, Wallace Stevens Award 2009, American Acad. of Arts and Letters Award in Literature 2014, Bollingen Prize for Poetry, Yale Univ. 2017. *Publications:* Dream Barker and Other Poems (Yale Series of Younger Poets Award) 1965, Pilgrims 1969, Ordinary Things 1974, The Messenger 1979, Home Deep Blue: New and Selected Poems 1989, The River at Wolf 1992, Night Lake 1992, The Under Voice: Selected Poems 1995, Growing Darkness, Growing Light 1997, The Cradle of the Real Life 2000, The Lighthouse Keeper: Essays on the Poetry of Eleanor Ross Taylor (ed.) 2001, Door in the Mountain: New and Collected Poems 1965–2003 (Nat. Book Award for Poetry) 2004, Little Boat 2007, Break the Glass 2010, Shirt In Heaven 2015. *Address:* c/o Copper Canyon Press, POB 271, Port Townsend, WA 98368, USA (office); 527 West 110th Street, Suite 81, New York, NY 10025, USA (office). *Telephone:* (360) 385-4925 (office). *Fax:* (360) 385-4985 (office). *E-mail:* poetry@coppercanyonpress.org (office); jeanvalentine@mygait.com (office). *Website:* www.coppercanyonpress.org (office); www.jeanvalentine.com.

VALENTINI, Pasquale; San Marino politician; b. 19 July 1953, San Marino; m.; three c.; ed Università degli Studi di Bologna; various trade union posts with Democratic Confed. of San Marino Workers mid-1970s to mid-1980s; taught math., chemistry, physics and natural science 1977–93, Chair of Math., Upper Secondary School 1993; Dir, first and third Insts, Junior High School 2004–07; mem. Consiglio Grande e Generale (Parl.) 1988–, Pres. Parl. Perm. Cttee for Justice, Educ., Culture, Univ. and Scientific Research, Sport and Tourism, Pres. Cttee for Criminal Procedure Code; Sec. of State for Educ., Univ. and Cultural Insts 2001–02, 2002–03, for Finance and Budget and Relations with the Philatelic and Numismatic Autonomous State Corpn 2010–12, for Foreign and Political Affairs 2012–16; mem. Council of Twelve (judicial body); mem. Partito Democratico Cristiano Sammarinese, Political Sec. 2007–10. *Address:* c/o Secretariat of State for Foreign and Political Affairs, Palazzo Begni, Contrada Omerelli, 47890, San Marino (office).

VALENTINO (see Garavani, Valentino).

VALENZUELA, Luisa; Argentine writer and journalist; *President, PEN Center Argentina;* b. 26 Nov. 1938, Buenos Aires; d. of Luisa Mercedes Levinson and Pablo F. Valenzuela; m. Théodore Marjak 1958 (divorced); one d.; ed Belgrano Girls' School, Colegio Nacional Vicente Lopez, Buenos Aires; lived in Paris, writing for Argentinian newspapers and for the RTF 1958–61; Asst Ed. La Nación Sunday Supplement, Buenos Aires 1964–69; writer, lecturer, freelance journalist in USA, Mexico, France, Spain 1970–73, Buenos Aires 1973–79; taught in Writing Div., Columbia Univ., New York 1980–83; conducted writers' workshops, English Dept, New York Univ. and seminars, Writing Div. 1984–89; returned to Buenos Aires 1989; currently Pres. PEN Center Argentina; mem. and Fellow, Acad. of Arts and Sciences, Puerto Rico; Fellow, New York Inst. for the Humanities; Foreign Hon. mem. American Acad. of Arts and Sciences 2011; Illustrious Citizen of Buenos Aires 2014; Dr hc (Knox Coll., Ill.) 1991, (Universidad de San Martín) 2017; Fulbright Grant 1969–70, Guggenheim Fellow 1983, Machado de Assis Medal, Brazilian Acad. of Letters 1997, Instituto Literario Hispanoamericano 2004, Premio Astralba, Univ. of Puerto Rico 2004, Premio Esteban Echeverría Gente de Letras 2008, Premio Cultura 400 años, Universidad de Córdoba 2012, Gran Premio de Honor de la Sociedad Argentina de Escritores 2016, Premio León de Greiff, Medellín, Colombia 2017. *Publications include:* novels: Hay que sonreír 1966, El gato eficaz 1972, Como en la guerra 1977, Cola de lagartija 1983, Realidad nacional desde la cama 1990, Novela negra con argentinos 1990, La travesía 2001, El Mañana 2010, Cuidado con el tigre 2011, La máscara sarda, el profundo secreto de Perón 2012; short story collections: Los heréticos 1967, Aquí pasan cosas raras 1975, Libro que no muerde 1980, Cambio de armas 1982, Donde viven las águilas 1983, Simetrías 1993, Cuentos completos y uno más 1999, Brevs. Microrrelatos completos hasta hoy 2004, Generosos inconvenientes 2008, Juego de villanos 2008, Tres por cinco 2008, ABC de las microfábulas 2009, 2019, Zoorpresas Zoológicas 2013, El chiste de Dios 2017, 2019, Cuentos de Nuestra América 2018; essays and non-fiction: Peligrosas palabras (Reflexiones de una escritora) 2002, Escritura y secreto 2002, Los deseos oscuros y los otros (Cuadernos de New York) 2002, Cortázar/Fuentes Entrecruzamientos 2014, Lección de Arte (Consejos de Mentes Billantes) 2014, Diario de Máscaras 2014, Conversación con las máscaras 2016. *Leisure interests:* masks, anthropology, ceremonies. *E-mail:* monipano@yahoo.com (office). *Website:* www.luisavalenzuela.com (home).

VALEUR, Charlotte; Danish corporate governance expert and fmr merchant banker; *Chair, Institute of Directors;* b. 1964, Copenhagen; m. Giles Adu 1999 (divorced); two s.; ed Copenhagen Business School, Inst. of Danish Bankers; Trader, Capital Markets and Fixed Income, Nordea Markets 1982–91; Vice-Pres., Capital Markets Fixed Income, SG Warburg 1991–92; Dir, Capital Markets Fixed Income, BNP Paribas 1992–97; Dir, Capital Markets Fixed Income, Société Générale SA 1998–99; Founder Brook Street Partners 2003–11; Founder Global Governance Group/GGG Ltd 2009–; Chair. DW Catalyst Fund Ltd 2010–17; Chair. FSN Capital GP (private equity fund) 2013–; Founder and Chair. Board Apprentice (not for profit social enterprise) 2013–; Chair. Kennedy Wilson European Real Estate PLC 2014–17; Chair. Blackstone/GSO Loan Financing Ltd 2014–; Gov. and Dir Univ. of Westminster 2017–18; Chair. Inst. of Directors 2018–; mem. Advisory Panel, Hampton-Alexander Review 2018–; mem. Primary Markets Group, London Stock Exchange 2018–; Dir (non-exec.) 3i Infrastructure Fund 2009–13, Renewable Energy Generation Ltd 2010–16, JP Morgan Global Convertibles Income Fund Ltd 2013–, NTR PLC 2014–, Laing O'Rourke 2018–, Phoenix Spree Deutschland 2018–; Hon. Teaching Fellow, Lancaster Univ. Man. School 2017–. *Address:* Institute of Directors, 6 Pall Mall, London, SW1Y 5ED, England (office). *Telephone:* (200 7766-8888 (office). *Website:* www.iod.com (office).

VALIANT, Leslie Gabriel, DIC, PhD, FRS; British computer scientist and academic; *T. Jefferson Coolidge Professor of Computer Science and Applied*

Mathematics, School of Engineering and Applied Sciences, Harvard University; b. 28 March 1949; ed King's Coll., Cambridge, Imperial Coll., London, Univ. of Warwick; taught at Univ. of Leeds, Univ. of Edinburgh and Carnegie-Mellon Univ., Pittsburgh, Pa, USA; fmr Gordon McKay Prof. of Computer Science and Applied Math., School of Eng and Applied Sciences, Harvard Univ. 1982–2002, T. Jefferson Coolidge Prof. of Computer Science and Applied Math. 2002–; has served on numerous editorial bds and program cttees, including Soc. for Industrial and Applied Math. Journal on Computing, Machine Learning Computational Complexity, Neural Computation, Neural Networks, International Journal of Foundations of Computer Science, Symposium on Theory of Computing, Conf. on Computational Learning Theory, EuroColt, Symposium on Parallel Algorithms and Architectures, and others; Fellow, American Asscn for Artificial Intelligence; mem. NAS; Nevanlinna Prize, Int. Congress of Mathematicians 1986, Knuth Prize 1997, European Asscn for Theoretical Computer Science (EATCS) Award 2008, A.M. Turing Award, Asscn for Computing Machinery 2010. *Achievements include:* together with Vijay Vazirani, proved the Valiant-Vazirani Theorem 1986. *Publications:* Circuits of the Mind 1994, 2000, Probably Approximately Correct: Natures Algorithms for Learning and Prospering in a Complex World 2013; more than 80 articles in scientific journals on parallel computing, computational complexity theory (and physics), computational learning and cognitive computation, neural computation, large computer systems and data centres. *Address:* School of Engineering and Applied Sciences, Harvard University, 351 Maxwell Dworkin, 33 Oxford Street, Cambridge, MA 02138, USA (office). *Telephone:* (617) 495-5817 (office). *Fax:* (617) 496-6404 (office). *E-mail:* valiant@seas.harvard.edu (office). *Website:* people.seas.harvard.edu/~valiant (office).

VALINSKAS, Arūnas, MA; Lithuanian television producer and politician; b. 28 Nov. 1966, Lazdijai; m. Ingrida Valinskas; two s.; ed Vilnius Secondary School No. 12, Faculty of Law, Vilnius Univ.; 22-year career on stage and TV, host and moderator of radio and TV programmes, shows and concerts; writer and producer of popular TV shows, including TV games and quizzes: Taip ir Ne, Šeši nuliai – milijonas, and Žodžių mūšis, as well as TV entertainment show Vakarėlis jums, and music reality show Kelias į žvaigždes; co-writer TV series daily show Dviračio šou; Organizer Lithuanian Music Festival Nida; initiator and organizer of first ever beauty contest Miss Captivity at women's prison; gave more than 1,000 concerts as mem. of comic show team Dviratis; Founder Tautos prisikėlimo partija (Nat. Revival Party) 2008–11; mem. Seimas (Parl.) 2008–12, Speaker and Chair. Bd of the Seimas 2008–09, mem. Ass. of Elders, Group for Inter-parl. Relations with Iraq, Group for Inter-parl. Relations with USA, Del. of Seimas to Ass. of Seimas of Repub. of Lithuania, of Sejm and Senate of Repub. of Poland and of Supreme Rada of Ukraine; Kt, Order of Isabella the Catholic (Spain); first Golden Medal Award, Vilnius Secondary School No. 12. *Leisure interests:* fishing, sailing.

VALIONIS, Antanas, PhD; Lithuanian engineer, politician and diplomatist; b. 21 Sept. 1950, Kedainiai Dist; s. of Antanas Valionis and Stanislova Valioniene; m. Romualda Valionis; two s.; ed Kaunas Polytechnic Inst., Univ. of Warsaw, Poland; foreman, Kaunas Meat Processing Plant 1974–76, Man. Compressor House, Taurage Meat Processing Plant 1976–80; Chief Instructor, Taurage Regional Cttee, Industry and Transport Dept of Cen. Cttee, Lituanian CP 1980–85, Instructor, Agric. and Food Industry Dept 1985–90; Head of Div. of Perspective Planning and Foreign Relations, Food Industry Dept, Ministry of Agric. 1990–94; Amb. to Poland 1994–2000, also to Romania (also accred to Bulgaria) 1996–2000; mem. Seimas (New Union party) 2004–08, mem. Cttee on State Admin and Local Authorities 2004–08, Cttee on European Affairs 2006–08; Minister of Foreign Affairs 2000–06; Amb. to Latvia 2008–11; Hon. Chair. North Atlantic Council 2005–06; Commdr's Cross of Order of Lithuanian Grand Duke Gedimmas, Three-star Order of Repub. of Latvia, Chevalier de la Légion d'honeur, Grand Cross of Infante Dom Henriques (Portugal), Commdr's Cross with Star of Order of Merit (Poland); Commemorative Badge for Personal Input in the Development of Trans-Atlantic Relations and on the Occasion of Invitation of Lithuania to join NATO. *Publications:* numerous articles in nat and int press. *Leisure interests:* literature, traditional jazz, swing, rock 'n' roll 1950s–70s, classical music.

VALLANCE OF TUMMEL, Baron (Life Peer), cr. 2004, of Tummel in Perth and Kinross; **Iain David Thomas Vallance,** Kt, BA, MSc; British business executive; *Chairman, Edinburgh Business School;* b. 20 May 1943, London, England; s. of Edmund Thomas Vallance and Janet Wright Bell Ross Davidson; m. Elizabeth Mary McGonnigill 1967; one s. one d.; ed Edinburgh Acad., Dulwich Coll., Glasgow Acad., Brasenose Coll. Oxford, London Grad. School of Business Studies; Asst Postal Controller, Post Office 1966, Personal Asst to Chair. 1973–75, Head of Finance Planning Div. 1975–76, Dir Cen. Finance 1976–78, Telecommunications Finance 1978–79, Materials Dept 1979–81; mem. Bd for Org. and Business Systems, British Telecommunications (BT) 1981–83, Man. Dir, Local Communications Services Div. 1983–85, Chief of Operations 1985–86, Chief Exec. 1986–95, Chair. 1987–2001, Pres. Emer. 2001–02; Vice-Chair. Royal Bank of Scotland 1994–2005; mem. (Liberal Democrat), House of Lords 2004–, Liberal Democrat Spokesperson for Trade and Industry/Business, Enterprise and Regulatory Reform 2005–, mem. Select Cttee on Econ. Affairs 2005–08 (Chair. 2008–10), Select Cttee on European Union (Sub-cttee A) 2010–15, Science and Tech. Cttee 2015–; Chair. Royal Conservatoire of Scotland (fmrly Royal Scottish Acad. of Music and Drama) 2006–16; Chair. Edinburgh Business School 2017–; Founding mem. Pres.'s Cttee of European Foundation for Quality Man. 1988; mem. CBI Pres.'s Cttee, Pres. CBI 2000–02; mem. Advisory Council of Business in the Community, Allianz Int. Advisory Bd, Advisory Council of Prince's Youth Business Trust 1988–2001, Advisory Bd British-American Chamber of Commerce 1991–2001, Supervisory Bd Siemens AG 2002–12; Chair. European Services Forum 2002–08; Vice-Chair. European Advisory Cttee to New York Stock Exchange, Chair. 2000–02; Vice-Pres. The Princess Royal Trust for Carers; fmr mem. Bd Scottish Enterprise, Mobil Corpn; Trustee Monteverdi Trust; Fellow, London Business School 1989, Chartered Inst. of Bankers in Scotland; Liveryman, Worshipful Co. of Wheelwrights; Freeman of the City of London; Hon. Fellow, Brasenose Coll.; Hon. Gov. Glasgow Acad. 1993–; Hon. DSc (Ulster) 1992, (Napier) 1994; Hon. DTech (Loughborough) 1992, (Robert Gordon) 1994; Hon. DBA (Kingston) 1993; Hon. DEng (Heriot-Watt) 1995; Hon. DSc (City Univ.) 1996. *Leisure interests:* walking, playing the piano, listening to music. *Address:* House of Lords, Westminster, London, SW1A 0PW, England (office). *Telephone:* (20) 7219-2715 (office). *E-mail:* vallancei@parliament.uk (office). *Website:* www.parliament.uk/biographies/lords/lord-vallance-of-tummel/3697 (office); www.rcs.ac.uk (office).

VALLARINO BARTUANO, Arturo Ulises, BSc, DJurSc; Panamanian lawyer and politician; *Ambassador to Organization of American States;* b. 15 Dec. 1943, Capiro Dist, Panamá; s. of Ismael Vallarino and María Concepción Bartuano; m. Elka Aparicio de Vallarino; five c.; ed Univ. of Panama, Universidad Nacional Autónoma de México, Univ. of Costa Rica; Legal Adviser, Ministry of Foreign Affairs 1966; elected Councillor for Panamá Dist 1968; lawyer, Carillo, Villalaz & Muñoz (law firm); Sr Partner, Bufete, Vallarino y Asociados –1999; fmr Prof. of Political Science and Commercial Law Univ. of Panama; fmr Chargé d'affaires for Business, Argentina; fmr Legal Adviser Ministry of Planning and Econ. Politics, Nat. Banking Comm.; fmr Pres. Legis. Ass.; mem. Partido Movimiento Liberal Republicano Nacionalista (MOLIRENA), Sec.-Gen. –2003; First Vice-Pres. of Panama 1999–2003 (retd); joined Cambio Democrático 2009; Amb. to OAS 2013–, Chair Cttee on Juridical and Political Affairs. *Address:* Organization of American States, 17th Street and Constitution Avenue, NW, Washington, DC 20006-4499, USA (office). *Telephone:* (202) 370-5000 (office). *Fax:* (202) 458-3967 (office). *Website:* www.oas.org (office).

VALLARINO CLEMENT, Alberto, BS, MBA; Panamanian business executive and fmr politician; *President, Grupo Verdeazul SA;* b. 2 April 1951, Panamá City; s. of Alberto Vallarino Céspedes and Marta Estela Clement Linares; m. Adriana Lewis Morgan 1981; one s. two d.; ed Colegio La Salle, Cornell Univ., USA; began career at Citibank NA 1974; Man. Dir Industria Nacional de Plásticos SA 1975–88; Exec. Vice-Pres. Metalforma SA 1979–88; Exec. Vice-Pres. Banco del Istmo 1988, later becoming CEO; fmr mem. Partido Arnulfista; unsuccessful cand. in presidential election 1999; Minister of Economy and Finance 2009–11 (resgnd); Chair. Grupo Verdeazul, SA 2011–; Pres. Fundación por un Mejor Panamá; Founder Vitalicio del Instituto de Competitividad Juvenil de COSPAE; mem. Bd of Dirs Panama Canal Authority 2013–, Asociación Nacional de la Naturaleza; mem. Sindicato de Industriales de Panamá (Pres. 1981–82), Asociación de Industriales Latinoamericanos, Venezuela (Pres. 1981), Asociación Panameña de Exportadores (Pres. 1983). *Address:* Grupo Verdeazul S.A., BMW Plaza, Piso 10, Calle 50, San Francisco, Panamá, Panama (office). *Telephone:* (507) 307-5077 (office). *Fax:* (507) 307-5107 (office). *Website:* www.grupoverdeazul.com (office).

VALLAUD-BELKACEM, Najat; French politician; b. (Najat Belkacem), 4 Oct. 1977, Bni Chiker village, nr Nador, Morocco; m. Boris Vallaud 2005; two c.; ed Institut d'études politiques de Paris; moved with family to Amiens 1982; mem. Socialist Party (Parti socialiste—PS) 2002–, joined team of Gérard Collomb, Senator/Mayor of Lyons 2003; mem. Regional Council of Rhône-Alpes 2004–08, Pres. Culture Cttee 2007–08; columnist for cultural programme C'est tout vu on Télé Lyon Municipale 2005, 2006; joined Ségolène Royal's campaign team as spokesperson during the 2007 Gen. Election 2007; Conseillère Générale for Rhône 2008–15; Deputy Mayor of Lyons, responsible for major events, youth and community life 2008–12; Minister of Women's Rights and Spokesperson for the Govt 2012–14, Minister of Women's Rights, Youth and Sports April–Aug. 2014, Minister of Educ., Higher Educ. and Research 2014–17. *Publications include:* Raison de plus 2012, La vie a plus d'imagination que toi 2017. *Address:* Parti Socialiste, 10 rue de Solférino, 75333 Paris Cedex 07, France (office). *Telephone:* 1-45-56-77-00 (office). *Fax:* 1-47-05-15-78 (office). *E-mail:* interps@parti-socialiste.fr (office). *Website:* www.parti-socialiste.fr (office).

VALLEE, Rodolphe M. (Skip), BS, MBA; American business executive, politician and fmr diplomatist; *Chairman and CEO, R. L. Vallee, Inc.;* b. 1960, St Albans, Vt; s. of Rod Vallee and Betty Vallee; m. Denise Vallee; two s.; ed Williams Coll., Wharton School, Univ. of Pennsylvania; worked in exec. positions for several cos involved in devt and operation of refuse, biomass, hydro and other renewable energy facilities; Devt Prin., Catalyst Energy Corpn 1986–87, Vice-Pres. Catalyst Waste-to-Energy Corpn 1987–88; f. R. L. Vallee Inc. 1989, Chair. and CEO 1992–2005, 2007–; Lead Dir MSCI Inc. 2008–; mem. Bd Dirs MSCI, Inc. 2008–; began his political career in 1982 as regional campaign man. for US Senator Robert T. Stafford and later served as staff asst of Senate Sub-cttee on Educ.; apptd to Advisory Cttee for Trade Policy and Negotiation 2001; mem. Republican Nat. Cttee 1999–2004; Chair. Vt Del. to Republican Nat. Convention 2004; Amb. to Slovakia 2005–07; fmr Dir Mater Christi School; fmr Trustee, Nature Conservancy of Vt. *Leisure interests:* skiing, hunting, fishing, soccer. *Address:* R. L. Vallee, Inc., 280 South Main Street, Saint Albans, VT 05478-1866, USA (office). *Telephone:* (802) 524-8710 (office). *Fax:* (802) 524-8714 (office). *E-mail:* SkipV@rlvallee.com (office); contactus@rlvallee.com (office). *Website:* www.rlvallee.com (office).

VALLEE, Roy A.; American business executive; *Chairman, Teradyne, Inc.;* b. 1953, Southbridge, MA; joined Avnet 1977, Pres. Hamilton/Avnet Computer 1989–90, Sr Vice-Pres. and Dir Worldwide Electronics Operations for Avnet 1990, mem. Bd of Dirs 1991–2012, Pres. and COO 1992–98, Chair. and CEO 1998–2011, Exec. Chair. 2011–12; Founding mem. Gov. of Arizona's Council on Innovation and Tech. 2008–; mem. Bd Arizona Econ. Resource Org.; mem. Exec. Cttee Arizona Commerce Authority 2009–11; named to Twelfth Dist Econ. Advisory Council for Federal Reserve Bank of San Francisco 2010–12, Deputy Chair. Federal Reserve Bank of San Francisco 2013–14, Chair. 2014–17; mem. Bd of Dirs Teradyne, Inc. 2000–, (Chair. 2014–), Synopsys, Inc., Tallwave, LLC; mem. Greater Phoenix Leadership; inducted into CRN Industry Hall of Fame, Gail S. Carter Award, Nat. Electronic Distributors Asscn 2008, Lifetime Achievement Award, Phoenix Business Journal 2011, OneNeck IT Services People's Choice Lifetime Achievement Award 2011. *Leisure interests:* spending time with family, golf, tennis, hiking. *Address:* Teradyne Inc., 600 Riverpark Drive, North Reading, MA 01864, USA (office). *Telephone:* (978) 370-2425 (office). *Fax:* (978) 370-2910 (office). *E-mail:* investorrelations@teradyne.com (office). *Website:* www.teradyne.com (office).

VALLINI, HE Cardinal Agostino, LTh, DCL, DCL; Italian ecclesiastic and academic; *Vicar General of Rome;* b. 17 April 1940, Poli; ed Major Archiepiscopal Seminary of Naples, Theological Faculty of Southern Italy (San Tommaso d'Aquino campus), Pontifical Lateran Univ., Rome; moved with family to Barra, nr Naples, as a child; ordained priest, Archdiocese of Naples 1964; taught canon law at Theological Faculty of Southern Italy; taught ecclesiastical law at Pontifical Lateran Univ. 1971–78; also served as adviser for Italian Catholic Univ. Fed., the movement Seguimi and Union of Major Religious Superiors of Italy; later became Rector of Major Archiepiscopal Seminary of Naples and Regional Counsellor of Catholic Action; Rector Major Archiepiscopal Seminary of Naples 1978–87; Dean of San Tommaso d'Aquino campus, Theological Faculty of Southern Italy 1987–89; apptd Titular Bishop of Tortibulum 1989; Auxiliary Bishop of Naples 1989–99; Bishop of Albano 1999–2004; Prefect of the Apostolic Signatura 2004–05, 2005–08; cr. Cardinal (Cardinal-Deacon of San Pier Damiani ai Monti di San Paolo) 2006, (Cardinal-Priest of San Pier Damiani ai Monti di San Paolo) 2009; Vicar Gen. of His Holiness for Diocese of Rome 2008–; Archpriest of Arcibasilica di San Giovanni in Laterano (St John Lateran Basilica) 2008–; Grand Chancellor, Pontifical Lateran Univ. 2008–; mem. Congregation for Causes of Saints, Congregation for Bishops, Congregation for Insts of Consecrated Life and Socs of Apostolic Life, Congregation for Evangelization of Peoples, Pontifical Council for Legis. Texts, Admin of the Patrimony of Apostolic See, Council of Cardinals for Study of Organizational and Econ. Affairs of the Holy See, Secr. for the Economy 2014–; named as a Synod Father of 13th Ordinary Gen. Ass. of the Synod of Bishops on New Evangelization 2012; Cavaliere di Gran Croce, Ordine al Merito della Repubblica Italiana 2008. *Address:* Diocese di Roma, Piazza San Giovanni in Laterano 6/A, 00184 Rome, Italy (office). *Telephone:* (06) 69886207 (office); (06) 69886330 (office). *Fax:* (06) 69886528 (office). *E-mail:* SegreteriaGenerale@VicariatusUrbis.org (office). *Website:* www.vicariatusurbis.org (office).

VALLS, Manuel; French politician and author; b. (Manuel Carlos Valls Galfetti), 13 Aug. 1962, Barcelona, Spain; s. of Xavier Valls and Luisangela Galfetti; m. 1st Nathalie Soulié 1987 (divorced); four c.; m. 2nd Anne Gravoin 2010; ed Univ. of Paris I; joined Parti Socialiste (Socialist Party) 1980; fmr Moderator, Unef-ID (French student union); naturalized French citizen 1982; Parl. Attaché to Deputy Robert Chapuis 1983–86; Regional Councillor, Ile-de-France 1986–2002, Vice-Chair. Ile-de-France Regional Council 1998–2002; Special Adviser to the Prime Minister Michel Rocard 1988–91; Deputy Mayor of Argenteuil (Val d'Oise) 1989–98; Deputy Interdepartmental Asst, Winter Olympics, Albertville 1991–93; Nat. Sec., Socialist Party and Head of Communications and Media Relations in cabinet of Lionel Jospin 1995–97; Head of Communications and Media Relations in the Prime Minister's Office 1997–2001; Mayor of Évry, Essonne 2001–12; Deputy (PS) to Nat. Ass. from 1st Dist of Essonne 2002–12, mem. Comm. des affaires culturelles; Pres. Community of Agglomeration of Évry-Centre-Essonne 2008–12; Minister of the Interior 2012–14; Prime Minister 2014–16 (resgnd); announced run to be Parti Socialiste cand. for Pres. of France Dec. 2016. *Publications include:* La laïcité en face 2005, Les habits neufs de la gauche 2006, Pour en finir avec le vieux socialisme… et être enfin de gauche 2008, Pouvoir 2010. *Leisure interest:* supporter of FC Barcelona. *Address:* c/o Parti Socialiste, 10 rue de Solférino, 75333 Paris Cedex 07, France.

VALTINOS, Thanassis; Greek writer; b. 16 Dec. 1932, Karatoula Kynourias; m.; one d.; ed Univ. of Athens; Visiting Prof., War Research Inst., Frankfurt 1993; Pres. Hellenic Authors Soc. 1990–94, 2005–09; mem. European Acad. of Sciences and Arts, Int. Inst. of Theatre, Greek Soc. of Playwrights; mem. Greek Acad. 2008–; Scenario Award Cannes Festival 1984, Cavafy Prize 2001, Acad. of Athens Petros Haris Prize for lifetime achievement 2002, Gold Cross of Honour of the Pres. of the Greek Democracy 2003. *Publications include:* The Descent of the Nine 1963, The Book of Andreas Kordopatis 1964, Voyage to Kythira (film script) 1984, Data from the Decade of the Sixties (Nat. Book Award for Best Novel 1990) 2000, Accoutumance à la nicotine 2008. *Address:* 66 Astidamantos Street, 116 34 Athens, Greece (home). *Telephone:* (210) 7218793 (home).

VALZANIA, Sergio; Italian television journalist, author and broadcasting executive; b. 2 April 1951, Florence; ed Univ. of Florence; Dir Radio 2, Radiotelevisione Italiana SpA (RAI) 1999–2002, Dir RAI 2 and RAI 3 2002–09, Deputy Dir, Radio Rai 2009–13. *Television productions include:* Dadaumpa 1984–86, La clessidra, filosofi a confronto 1985, La macchina del tempo 1985–86, La TV delle ragazze 1988–89, Bambini 1989–90 (all for RAI 3), Viva Radio 2 2001–08, Alle 8 della Sera 2004–13, radio pilgrimages (La Via Lattea 2004, La Via Francigena 2005, La Via di Paolo e Giovanni 2006, La Via di Sigerico 2007, Il Cammino 2008, La Serenissima 2009, La Via di Olaf 2010, La via della Plata 2011, Da Roma a Gerusalemme 2012. *Publications:* Brodo nero. Sparta pacifica, il suo esercito, le sue guerre 1999, Napoleone 2001, Retorica della guerra. Quando la violenza sostituisce la parola 2002, Una radio strutturalista. Consigli per ascoltare e trasmettere 2002, Tre tartarughe greche 2002, Jutland. 31 maggio 1916: la più grande battaglia navale della storia 2006, Sparta e Atene. Il racconto di una guerra 2006, Austerlitz. La più grande vittoria di Napoleone 2006, Wallenstein. La tragedia di un generale nella guerra dei Trent'anni 2007, La morte dei dinosauri 2007, Le La città degli uomini. Cinque riflessioni in un mondo che cambia (with Fausto Bertinotti) 2007, Le radici perdute dell'Europa. Da Carlo V ai conflitti mondiali (with Franco Cardini) 2007, Amare il vino. Arte natura tecnica estetica (with Luca Maroni) 2007, La Via Lattea (with Piergiorgio Odifreddi) 2008, La Via Maestra (with Lorenzo Sganzini) 2009, Dal profondo. Posso scrivere di Cristo solo narrando la mia esperienza) 2010, U-Boot. Storie di uomini e di sommergibili nella seconda guerra mondiale) 2011 Napoleone 2011, Fare la pace. Vincitori e vinti in Europa 2011, La bolla d'oro 2012, I dieci errori di Napoleone. Sconfitte, cadute e illusioni dell'uomo che voleva cambiare la storia 2012, Invano veglia la sentinella 2013, U-Boot. Storie di uomini e di sommergibili nella seconda guerra mondiale 2013. *Address:* Direction Radio Rai, Radiotelevisione Italiana SpA, Via Asiago 10, 00195 Rome, Italy (office). *Telephone:* (06) 37352741 (office). *Fax:* (06) 3219215 (office). *E-mail:* valzania@rai.it (office). *Website:* www.rai.it (office).

VÁMOS, Éva, PhD Habil.; Hungarian museologist; *Senior Researcher, Hungarian Museum for Science, Technology and Transport (Magyar Műszaki és Közlekedési Múzeum);* b. 22 May 1950, Budapest; d. of Endre Vámos and Lilly Vámos (née Vigyázó); ed Eötvös Loránd Univ. of Budapest, Tech. Univ. of Budapest; affiliated to Hungarian Museum for Science, Tech. and Transport (Magyar Műszaki és Közlekedési Múzeum) 1973–, Curator 1973–78, Scientific Co-worker 1978–86, Head, Ind. Group of History of Science, Scientific Sec. in charge of Public Relations 1986–87, Sr Scientific Co-worker 1987–89, Head of Dept 1989–91, Scientific Deputy Dir-Gen. 1991–93, Dir-Gen. 1994–2004, Sr Researcher 2004–; Memorial Medal, Fed. of Scientific and Tech. Asscns 1997, Justus von Liebig Memorial Medal 2000. *Publications:* Chapters from the History of Communication 1979, History of Writing and Writing Utensils 1980–82, Creative Hungarians 1988, German-Hungarian Relations in the Fields of Science with Special Regard to Chemistry, Chemical Industry and Food Industry 1876–1914 1995, László József Bíró 1996, Women's Opportunities of Studying and Practising Engineering in Hungary 1998, Justus von Liebigs Hungarian Connections by Correspondence 2003, Memorial Sights of Chemistry at Budapest Universities 2007. *Leisure interests:* univ. women's movt, gardening, classical music. *Address:* Hungarian Museum for Science, Technology and Transport, 1114 Budapest, Városligeti Krt 14 (office); 1015 Budapest, Batthyány u. 3. VI. 32, Hungary (home). *Telephone:* (1) 338-06-22 (office); (1) 204-40-95 (office); (20) 541-26-74 (office); (1) 201-73-17 (home). *Fax:* (1) 204-40-88 (office). *E-mail:* vamos.endrene@chello.hu (office); evamos@mmkm.hu (office); vamos.eva@chello.hu (home). *Website:* www.omm.hu (office); mtesz.hu.

VÁMOS, Tibor, PhD, DSc; Hungarian research professor emeritus; *Chairman, Computer and Automation Research Institute, Hungarian Academy of Sciences;* b. 1 June 1926, Budapest; s. of Miklós Vámos and Ilona Rausnitz; m. Noémi Stenczer; one s.; ed Tech. Univ. Budapest; started in process control automation of power plants and systems, worked later in computer control of processes, robot vision, artificial intelligence; Chief Engineer, Research Inst. of Power System Eng Co. 1950–54, Automation Dept Head 1954–64; Dir Computer and Automation Research Inst., Hungarian Acad. of Sciences 1964–85, Chair. 1986–; Prof. Budapest Tech. Univ. 1969–; Distinguished Visiting Prof., George Mason Univ. 1992–93, Distinguished Affiliate Prof. 1993–94; Corresp. mem. Hungarian Acad. of Sciences 1973, mem. 1979, mem. Governing Bd 1980–; Pres. Int. Fed. of Automatic Control (IFAC) 1981–84, IFAC Lifetime Advisor 1987–; mem. Editorial Bd four int. scientific journals; mem. European Coordinating Cttee for Artificial Intelligence 2004–, Fellow 2006–; chair. and bd mem. of philanthropic foundations; Fellow, IEEE Inc. 1986–, IFAC 2006–; Hon. mem. Austrian Computer Soc. 1992, Austrian Soc. for Cybernetic Studies 1994; Hon. Pres. John v. Neumann Soc. of Computer Science 1986–; Order of Hungarian Repub. 1996; Dr hc (Tallinn Univ.); State Prize 1983, Chorafas Prize, Swiss Acads 1994, World Automation Congress Dedication 2006, Széchenyi Prize, Govt of Hungary 2008. *Publications:* Nagy ipari folyamatok irányitása (Control of Large-Scale Processes) 1970, Computer Epistemology 1991; co-author: Applications of Syntactic Pattern Recognition 1977, Progress in Pattern Recognition 1981, Hand Book of Applied Expert Systems 1997, Handbook of Automation 2009, Knowledge and Computing: A Course on Computer Epistemology 2010; co-ed.: The Neumann Compendium 1995; 130 contribs to scientific journals and 170 to other publs. *Leisure interests:* fine arts, mountaineering. *Address:* Lágymányosi u. 11, 1111 Budapest, Hungary (office). *Telephone:* (1) 209-5274 (office); (1) 320-3657 (home). *Fax:* (1) 209-5275 (office). *E-mail:* vamos@sztaki.hu (office). *Website:* www.sztaki.hu (office).

VAN AARTSEN, Jozias Johannes, LLB; Dutch politician; *Mayor of The Hague;* b. 25 Dec. 1947, The Hague; m. Henriëtte Warsen; three s.; ed Amsterdam Free Univ.; Supervisory Dir Govt Computer Centre and Printing Office; Ed. Liberal Reveille; worked for Parl. People's Party for Freedom and Democracy (VVD) 1970–74, Dir VVD Research Org. 1974–79; staff mem. Sec.-Gen.'s Office, Minister of the Interior 1979–83, Deputy Sec.-Gen. 1983–85, Sec.-Gen. 1985–94, Chair. Council of Bd of Sec.-Gens 1994; Minister of Agric., Nature Man. and Fisheries 1994–98, of Foreign Affairs 1998–2002; Leader VVD Parl. Group 2003–06; worked with EC as coordinator of EU project to lay gas pipeline from Turkey to Austria 2006; Mayor, The Hague 2008–; fmr mem. Bd Expertise Centre for Employment among Minorities; fmr Chair. Bd Nat. Inst. for Arts Educ.; Kt, Order of the Dutch Lion 1994, Officer, Order of Orange-Nassau 2002, Grand Cross, Order of Isabella the Catholic (Spain). *Address:* City Hall (Atrium), Spui 70, 2500 DP, The Hague, Netherlands (office). *Telephone:* (70) 3535043 (office). *Website:* www.denhaag.com (office).

VAN AGT, Andries (Dries) A. M.; Dutch international organization official and fmr politician; *President, The Rights Forum;* b. 2 Feb. 1931, Geldrop; s. of Frans van Agt and Anna Frencken; m. Eugenie Krekelberg 1958; one s. two d.; ed Catholic Univ., Nijmegen; worked at Ministry of Agric. and Fisheries, then Ministry of Justice 1958–68; Prof. of Penal Law, Univ. of Nijmegen 1968–; Minister of Justice 1971–77; Deputy Prime Minister 1973–77; Prime Minister and Minister of Gen. Affairs 1977–82; Minister of Foreign Affairs 1982; mem. Parl. 1982–83; Gov. Prov. of Noord-Brabant 1983–87; Amb., Head Del. of European Communities, Tokyo 1987–89, then Washington, DC 1989–95; Prime Counselor, Int. Forum for Justice and Peace; Founder and Pres. The Rights Forum 2009–. *E-mail:* info@driesvanagt.nl. *Website:* www.driesvanagt.nl; www.rightsforum.org/english.

VAN ASSCHE, Kris; Belgian fashion designer; b. 1976; ed Royal Acad. of Fine Arts, Antwerp; moved to Paris in 1998; worked with Hedi Slimane at Yves Saint Laurent and then for Dior Homme; began to show original creations in 2005; f. own label, Kris Van Assche; Artistic Dir Dior Homme 2007–18. *E-mail:* info@krisvanassche.com (office).

VAN BASTEN, Marcel (Marco); Dutch professional football manager and fmr professional footballer; b. 31 Oct. 1964, Utrecht; m. Elizabeth Van Basten 1992; one s. two d.; striker; youth player, Ajax 1981–82; sr player, Ajax 1982–97 (133 appearances, 128 goals, won UEFA Cup Winners' Cup 1987, Dutch Championship 1981/82, 1982/83, 1984/85, Dutch Cup 1983, 1986, 1987), AC Milan 1987–93 (147 appearances, 90 goals, won European Cup 1989, 1990, Intercontinental Cup 1989, 1990, European Supercup 1989, 1990, Serie A 1987/88, 1991/92, 1992/93, Italian Super Cup 1988, 1992, 1993); mem. Netherlands U-21 team 1981, Netherlands nat. team 1983–92 (58 caps, 24 goals, won UEFA European Championship 1988, Nasazzi's Baton 1985); Man. Jong Ajax 2003–04, AFC Ajax 2008–09, Heerenveen 2012–14, AZ Alkmaar 2014 (Asst Man. 2014–15); Head Coach of Dutch nat. team 2004–08, Asst Man. 2015–; European Silver Boot 1983–84, Dutch League Top Scorer 1983–84, 1984–85, 1985–86, 1986–87, Dutch Footballer of the Year 1984–85, European Golden Boot 1985–86, World Golden Boot 1985–86, Bravo Award 1987, Onze d'Argent 1987, 1992, Serie A Silver Top Scorer 1988–89, Ballon d'Or (European Footballer of the Year) 1988, 1989, 1992, UEFA European Championship Top Scorer and Best Player with 5 goals 1988, World Soccer Player of the Year 1988, 1992, Onze d'Or 1988, 1989, IFFHS Best Player of the Year 1988, 1989, 1990, Serie A Top Scorer 1989–90, 1991–92, UEFA Best Player of the Year 1989, 1990, 1992, European Cup Top Scorer 1989, FIFA World Player of the Year 1992, European Cup Silver Top Scorer 1993, named in FIFA 100 (list of greatest living footballers picked by Pelé) 2004. *Leisure interest:* golf. *Address:* KNVB

Sportcentrum, Woudenbergseweg 56–58, 3707 HX Zeist, Netherlands. *Website:* www.knvb.nl.

VAN BENTHEM, Johannes F. A. K., MA, PhD; Dutch logician and academic; b. (Johan van Benthem), 12 June 1949, Rijswijk; s. of A. K. van Benthem and J. M. G. Eggermont; ed Gravenhaags Christelijk Gymnasium and Univ. of Amsterdam; Asst Prof. of Philosophical Logic, Univ. of Amsterdam 1972–77, Chair. Dept of Philosophy 1974–75; Assoc. Prof. of Philosophical Logic, Univ. of Groningen 1977–86, Chair. Dept of Philosophy 1979–81; Prof. of Mathematical Logic, Univ. of Amsterdam 1986–2003, Univ. Prof. of Logic 2003–14, Chair. Dept of Math. and Computer Science 1987–89, Scientific Dir Research Inst. for Logic, Language and Computation 1991–98; Chair. European Asscn of Logic, Language and Information 1991–96; Sr Researcher, Center for Study of Language and Information, Stanford Univ., USA 1991–, Bonsall Visiting Chair in the Humanities 1991–2003, Henry Waldgrave Stuart Prof. of Philosophy 2003–; Distinguished Foreign Expert, Chinese Ministry of Educ. 2010–12; Changjiang Nat. Prof., Tsinghua Univ., Beijing 2013–17, Jin Yuelin Distinguished Prof. 2017–; Vice-Pres. Int. Fed. of Computational Logic 1999–; Chair. Netherlands Nat. Cognitive Science Programme 2001–03, Vienna Circle Foundation 1997–2014; fmr Man. Ed. Journal of Symbolic Logic, Logic and Computation, and other journals; Advisory Bd Journal of Philosophical Logic, Studies in Logic; mem. Academia Europaea, Royal Dutch Acad. of Sciences, Institut Int. de Philosophie, Hollandse Maatschappij van Wetenschappen, American Acad. of Arts and Sciences; First Hon. Mem. European Asscn of Logic, Language and Information, Dutch Asscn of Logic; Kt, Order of the Dutch Lion 2014; Dr hc (Liège Univ.) 1998; Spinoza Prize, Netherlands Org. for Scientific Research 1996. *Publications:* The Logic of Time 1983, Modal Logic and Classical Logic 1985, Essays in Logical Semantics 1986, A Manual of Intensional Logic 1988, Language in Action, Categories, Lambdas and Dynamic Logic 1991, Exploring Logical Dynamics 1996, Modal Logic for Open Minds 2010, Logical Dynamics of Information and Interaction 2011, Logic in Games 2014; co-author of various textbooks in logic; (ed.) Handbook of Logic and Language 1997, Handbook of Modal Logic 2006, Handbook of Spatial Logics 2007, Handbook of the Philosophy of Information 2007; more than 350 articles in scientific journals. *Address:* Institute for Logic, Language and Computation, University of Amsterdam, PO Box 94242, 1090 GE Amsterdam, Netherlands (office). *Telephone:* (20) 5256051 (office). *Fax:* (20) 5255206 (office). *E-mail:* johan.vanbenthem@uva.nl (office); johan@ stanford.edu (office). *Website:* staff.fnwi.uva.nl/j.vanbenthem (office).

VAN BERKEL, Ben (Bernard Franciscus), FRIBA; Dutch architect; *Principal Architect, UNStudio;* b. 25 Jan. 1957, Utrecht; s. of Magchiel van Berkel and Maria Therese Mattaar; m. Caroline Bos; one d.; ed Rietved Acad., Amsterdam, Architectural Asscn, London; graphic designer 1977–82; Co-founder and Prin. Architect, Van Berkel & Bos 1988–99, UNStudio 1999–; fmr Visiting Prof., Columbia Univ., Princeton Univ.; Prof., Conceptual Design, Städelschule, Frankfurt am Main 2001–; Kenzo Tange Visiting Prof. Chair, Graduate School of Design, Harvard Univ. 2011–; mem. Advisory Bd, Thnk (School of Creative Leadership); projects include: switching substation, Amersfoort 1989–93, Erasmus Bridge, Rotterdam 1990–96, Villa Wilbrink, Amersfoort 1992–94, Möbius House, 't Gooi 1993–98, Museum Het Valkhof, Nijmegen 1995–99, Masterplan station area, Arnhem 1996–, City Hall and Theatre, Ijsselstein 1996–2000, switching station, Innsbruck 1998–2001, Music Faculty, Graz 1998–, WTC 2001, Mercedes Benz Museum, Stuttgart, interior renovation, Galleria Department Store, Seoul; Hon. Fellow, AIA 2013; Eileen Gray Award 1983, British Council Fellowship 1986, Charlotte Köhler Prize 1991, winning entry for Police HQ, Berlin 1995, Museum Het Valkhof 1995, music theatre, Graz, Austria 1998, Kunstpreis, Frankfurt, Red Dot Award, Charles Jencks Award 2007, German Design Prize 2008, Red Dot Best of The Best, MYchair 2009, Hugo Haring Award 2009. *Address:* UNStudio, Stadhouderskade 113, 1073 AX Amsterdam, The Netherlands (office). *Telephone:* (20) 570-20-40 (office). *Fax:* (20) 570-20-41 (office). *E-mail:* info@unstudio.com (office). *Website:* www.unstudio.com (office).

VAN BEURDEN, Ben; Dutch oil industry executive; *CEO, Royal Dutch Shell plc;* b. 23 April 1958, Roosendaal; m. Stacey van Beurden; one s. three d.; ed Delft Univ. of Tech.; joined Shell 1983, held several operational and commercial roles in both Upstream and Downstream, including Vice-Pres. (Manufacturing Excellence) 2005–06, Exec. Vice-Pres. (Chemicals) 2006–13, Downstream Dir Jan.–Sept. 2013, CEO Royal Dutch Shell plc 2014–; mem. Bd Int. Council of Chemicals Asscns, European Chemical Industry Council. *Leisure interests:* reading, running, travelling with his family. *Address:* Royal Dutch Shell plc, PO Box 162, 2501 AN The Hague (office); Royal Dutch Shell plc, Carel van Bylandtlaan 30, 2596 HR The Hague, The Netherlands (office). *Telephone:* (70) 3779111 (office). *Fax:* (70) 3773115 (office). *Website:* www.shell.com (office).

VAN BOXMEER, Jean-François, MEcons; Belgian business executive; *Chairman of the Executive Board and CEO, Heineken NV;* b. 12 Sept. 1961, Elsene; ed Facultés Universitaires Notre Dame de la Paix S.J., Namur, Belgium; traineeship in production, sales and admin areas, Heineken Nederland, assignment in Cameroon 1984–87, Sales and Marketing Man., Heineken Bralima, Rwanda 1987–90, Democratic Repub. of Congo 1990–93, Gen. Man. 1993–96, Pres. and Gen. Man. Zywiec SA, Poland 1996–99, Vice-Pres. and Gen. Man. Grupa Zywiec SA, Poland 1999–2000, Gen. Man. Heineken Italia 2000–01, mem. Exec. Bd Heineken NV, The Netherlands 2001–, Chair. Exec. Bd and CEO 2005–; mem. Bd of Dirs Kraft Foods (re-named Mondelēz Int., Inc.) 2010–, Consumer Goods Forum; mem. Advisory Bd Louvain School of Man., Louvain-la-Neuve; mem. Bd of Govs De Nederlandse Opera (The Dutch Opera). *Address:* Heineken NV Global Corporate Affairs, PO Box 28, 1000 AA Amsterdam (office); Heineken NV, Tweede Weteringplantsoen 21, 1017 ZD Amsterdam, The Netherlands (office). *Telephone:* (20) 523-92-39 (office). *Fax:* (20) 626-35-03 (office). *E-mail:* info@ heinekeninternational.com (office). *Website:* www.heinekeninternational.com (office).

VAN BROECKHOVEN, Christine, BSc, MSc, PhD, DSc; Belgian research scientist and academic; *Professor, Director of the Department of Molecular Genetics and Group Leader of the Neurodegenerative Brain Diseases Group, University of Antwerp;* b. 9 April 1953, Antwerp; ed Univ. of Antwerp; competitive PhD Fellowship, IWT 1975–78; Post-doctoral Researcher, Prov. Inst. of Hygiene, Antwerp 1978–81; Research Assoc., Univ. of Antwerp 1983–89; Research Fellow, Nat. Research Foundation (NFWO) 1989–90; Research Dir, Lab. of Neurogenetics,

Inst. Born-Bunge 1990–96; Assoc. Prof., Univ. of Antwerp 1995–96, Scientific Dir, Dept of Molecular Genetics, VIB 1996–2007, Group Leader, Neurogenetics, VIB 1996–97, Prof., Univ. of Antwerp 1997–99, Full Prof. 1999–, Sr Group Leader, Neurodegenerative Brain Diseases, VIB 2005–07, Dept Dir, Dept of Molecular Genetics, VIB 2007–; Distinguished Alzheimer Prof., Univ. of Leiden, The Netherlands 1996; Guest Scientist, Scripps Research Inst., USA 2001; Royal Grand Officer, Order of Léopold 2006; Chevalier, Légion d'honneur 2009; Divry Prize, Belgian Soc. of Neurology 1991, Potamkin Prize, American Acad. of Neurology (co-recipient) 1993, Joseph Maisin Scientific Prize, Nat. Fund for Scientific Research 1995, Marie-Thérèse De Lava Prize, King Boudewijn Foundation 1995, Upjohn Inc. Scientific Prize, NFSR (co-recipient) 1995, Belgian Coll. of Neuropsychopharmacology and Biological Psychiatry Lundbeck Prize (co-recipient) 1997, L'Oréal/UNESCO Special Honour Award for Women in Science 2002, 55th Ark Prize, Belgian Ark Cttee of the Free Word 2005, Zenith Award, Alzheimer Asscn (USA) 2005, L'Oréal-UNESCO Int. Award for Women in Science (Europe) 2006, Award Lecture in the Frontiers in Clinical Neuroscience, Plenary Session of American Acad. of Neurology Annual Meeting, Boston 2007. *Publications:* more than 560 articles in peer-reviewed int. scientific journals. *Address:* VIB Department of Molecular Genetics, University of Antwerp – CDE, Universiteitsplein 1, Building V, Antwerp 2610, Belgium (office). *Telephone:* (3) 265-11-02 (office); (476) 29-88-27 (office). *Fax:* (3) 265-11-12 (office). *E-mail:* christine.vanbroeckhoven@ molgen.vib-ua.be (office). *Website:* www.molgen.ua.ac.be (office).

VAN CREVELD, Martin L.; Israeli academic; *Professor, Tel-Aviv University;* b. 5 March 1946, Rotterdam, The Netherlands; s. of L. van Creveld and M. van Creveld (née Wyler); two step-c.; ed Hebrew Univ., London School of Econs, UK; Lecturer, later Prof. in History, Hebrew Univ. of Jerusalem 1971–2007; Fellow, War Studies Dept, King's Coll. London 1975–76, von Humboldt Foundation, Freiburg 1980–81; mem. Faculty, Nat. Defense Univ., Washington DC 1986–87; Prof., Marine Corps Univ., Quantico, Va 1991–92; apptd Adjunct Lecturer, Security Studies Program, Tel-Aviv Univ. 2007, currently Prof.; Sr Fellow, Humboldt Foundation, Postdam 1999–2000; Fellow, Inst. for Contemporary Historical Research, Potsdam 2005–06; Best Book Award, Mil. History Inst. USA 1990. *Publications include:* Supplying War 1977, Fighting Power 1987, Command in War 1985, Technology and War 1988, The Transformation of War 1991, The Rise and Decline of the State 1999, The Changing Face of War 2007, The Culture of War 2008, The Land of Blood and Honey: The Rise of Modern Israel 2010, The Age of Airpower 2011, Wargames: From Gladiators to Gigabytes 2013, The Privileged Sex 2013, Equality: The Impossible Quest 2015, Conscience: A Biography 2015, A History of Strategy: From Sun Tzu to William S. Lind 2015, Pussycats: Why the Rest Keeps Beating the West—and What Can Be Done about It 2016. *Leisure interests:* reading, walking. *Address:* International Master's Program in Security and Diplomacy, Tel-Aviv University, Naftali Building Room 515, Ramat Aviv, Tel-Aviv 6997801, Israel (office). *Telephone:* 3-6409545 (office); 2-5344923 (home). *E-mail:* mvc.dvc@gmail .com. *Website:* secdip.tau.ac.il (office); www.martin-van-creveld.com.

VAN-CULIN, Rev. Canon Samuel, OBE, AB, DD; American ecclesiastic; *Canon Ecumenist, Washington National Cathedral;* b. 20 Sept. 1930, Honolulu, Hawaii; s. of Samuel Van-Culin and Susie Mossman; ed Princeton Univ. and Virginia Theological Seminary; Curate, St Andrew's Cathedral, Honolulu 1955–56; Canon Precentor and Rector Hawaiian Congregation, Honolulu 1956–58; Asst Rector St John's, Washington DC 1958–60; Gen. Sec. Lyman Int., Washington, DC 1960–61; Asst Sec., Overseas Dept, Exec. Council of the Episcopal Church USA 1962–68, Sec. for Africa and Middle East 1968–76, Exec. for World Mission 1976–83; Sec.-Gen. Anglican Consultative Council 1983–94, Sec. to Lambeth Conf. 1988; Asst Priest, All Hallows Church, London 1995–; Canon Ecumenist, Washington Nat. Cathedral 2004–; Trustee Friends of Canterbury Cathedral in the Unites States; Hon. Canon, Canterbury, Jerusalem, Honolulu, Ibadan and Cape Town; Hon. DD (Virginia Theological Seminary). *Leisure interests:* music and travel. *Address:* 3900 Watson Place, NW, 5D-B, Washington, DC 20016, USA (home). *E-mail:* sam .vanculin@aol.com (home).

VAN DAELE, Gen. (retd) August; Belgian army officer (retd); b. 25 Feb. 1944, Sint-Niklaas; ed Royal Cadet Training School, Royal Mil. Acad., Defence Coll.; tech. officer, Proficiency Training Centre, Brustem 1967–69; with Mobile Training Unit 1969–71; assigned as line man. Inspection and Tech. Acceptance Testing Service 1971; CO Air Maintenance Squadron, 10th Fighter-Bomber Wing, Kleine-Brogel 1980–83, CO Maintenance Group 1985–87; Deputy CO of Inspection and Tech. Acceptance Testing Service 1983–84, Head of Service 1987–88; Head of Equipment Inspection Service 1988–89, Inspection Service 1989–92, Aviation Equipment Section 1992–94; apptd Deputy Chief of Staff, Logistics, Air Force HQ 1994; Dir-Gen. for Material Resources, Defence Staff 2000–02; Chief of Defence Staff 2003–09; mem. NATO Mil. Cttee; currently Aide to the King of Belgium.

VAN DAELE, Baron Franciskus, MA; Belgian diplomatist (retd); *Head of Cabinet to His Majesty King Philippe of Belgium;* m. Baroness Christiana van Daele; one s. two d.; ed Catholic Univ. of Leuven; joined Belgian Foreign Service in 1971, served in Athens 1977–81, Rome 1986–89; Deputy Perm. Rep. to UN, New York 1989–93; Dir-Gen. for Political Affairs, Ministry of Foreign Affairs 1993–97; Amb. and Perm. Rep. to EU, Brussels 1997–2002; Amb. to USA 2002–06; Perm. Rep. to NATO, Brussels 2006–09; Dir of Cabinet, Minister of Foreign Affairs of Belgium July–Nov. 2009; Head of Cabinet of Pres. of European Council 2010–12 (retd); Head of Cabinet to His Majesty King Philippe of Belgium, Royal Palace 2013–; mem. Bd of Dirs Univ. of Leuven, Chapelle musicale Reine Elisabeth, American European Community Asscn, Fonds Baillet-Latour, Arenberg Foundation; mem. Advisory Bd Friends of Europe; mem. Fondation Jean Monnet (Lausanne); Vice-Pres. Royal Asscn of Belgian Nobility. *Address:* Royal Palace, Rue Brederode, 16, 1000 Brussels, Belgium (office). *Telephone:* (2) 551-20-20 (office). *Website:* www.monarchie.be/en/heritage/royal-palace-of-brussels (office).

VAN DAMME, Jean-Claude; Belgian actor; b. (Jean-Claude Camille François Van Varenberg), 18 Oct. 1961, Brussels; m. 1st Gladys Portugues; m. 2nd Darcy LaPier 1994; one s. one d.; fmr European Professional Karate Asscn Middleweight Champion. *Films include:* Monaco Forever 1984, Rue barbare 1984, Breakin' 1984, No Retreat, No Surrender 1986, Bloodsport 1988, Black Eagle 1988, Cyborg 1989, Kickboxer 1989, Lionheart 1990, Death Warrant 1990, Double Impact 1991, Universal Soldier 1992, Nowhere to Run 1993, Hard Target 1993, Timecop 1994, Street Fighter 1994, Sudden Death 1995, The Quest 1996, Maximum Risk 1996,

Double Team 1997, Knock Off 1998, Legionnaire 1998, Universal Soldier: The Return 1999, Coyote Moon 1999, The Order 2001, Replicant 2001, Derailed 2002, The Savage 2003, Narco 2004, Wake of Death 2004, Second in Command 2006, Sinav 2006, Until Death 2007, JCVD 2008, Universal Soldier: Regeneration 2009, The Eagle Path (also producer, dir and writer) 2010, Assassination Games 2012, The Expendables 2 2012, Univeral Soldier: Day of Reckoning 2012, 6 Bullets 2012, Alien Uprising 2012, Welcome to the Jungle 2013, Enemies Closer 2013, Swelter 2014, Full Love 2014, Pound of Flesh 2015, Jian Bing Man 2015, Kung Fu Panda 3 (voice) 2016, Kickboxer: Vengeance 2016. *Address:* Gersh Agency, 9465 Wilshire Blvd, #600, Beverly Hills, CA 90212, USA.

VAN DE KAA, Dirk Jan, PhD; Dutch demographer and academic; *Professor Emeritus, University of Amsterdam;* b. 5 Jan. 1933, Scherpenzeel; m. Anna Jacomina van Teunenbroek 1961; one s. one d.; ed Univ. of Utrecht, Australian Nat. Univ.; Dept Dir, Demographic Research Project, Western New Guinea 1961–66; Research Fellow, Dept of Demography, Research School of Social Sciences, Inst. for Advanced Studies, ANU, Canberra 1966–71; Dir Netherlands Interdisciplinary Demographic Inst., The Hague 1971–87, Hon. Fellow 2003–; Project Dir World Fertility Survey, London 1981–82; Dir Int. Statistical Research Centre, The Hague 1982–84; Prof. of Demography, Univ. of Amsterdam 1977–98, currently Prof. Emer.; Dir Netherlands Inst. for Advanced Study, Wassenaar 1987–95; Vice-Pres. Netherlands Org. for Scientific Research, The Hague 1988–98; mem. Royal Netherlands Acad. of Arts and Sciences (Vice-Pres. 1984–87); Pres. European Asscn for Population Studies 1983–87, Hon. Pres. 1987–; Kt, Order of the Netherlands Lion 1991; Dr hc (Instytut Statystyki i Demografii, Warsaw School of Econs) 2003; Laureate, Int. Union for Scientific Study of Population 2001. *Publications include:* (author, co-author or ed.) Results of the Demographic Research Project Western New Guinea 1964–67, The Demography of Papua and New Guinea's Indigenous Population 1971, Science for Better and for Worse 1984, Population: Growth and Decline 1986, Europe's Second Demographic Transition 1987. *Address:* University of Amsterdam, PO Box 19268, 1000 GG Amsterdam (office); Netherlands Interdisciplinary Demographic Institute, PO Box 11650, 2502 AR The Hague; Van Hogenhoucklaan 63, 2596 TB The Hague, The Netherlands (home). *Telephone:* (70) 356-52-00 (The Hague) (office). *Fax:* (70) 364-71-87 (The Hague) (office). *E-mail:* vandekaa@nidi.nl (office). *Website:* www.uva.nl (office); www.nidi.nl (office).

VAN DE WALLE, Leslie; French business executive; *Chairman, Robert Walters;* b. 27 March 1956, Paris; s. of Philippe Van de Walle and Marie Lucette Van de Walle; m. Domitille Noel 1982; two d.; ed Hautes Etudes Commerciales; started career with Danone Group; Man. Dir Schweppes Benelux 1990–92, France and Benelux 1992–93, Spain and Portugal 1993–94; Snacks Div., United Biscuits Continental Europe 1994–95 (CEO 1996–97), CEO McVities Group 1998, United Biscuits Group 1999–2000; Pres. Shell Latin America and Africa 2000–03, Shell Europe Oil Products 2003–04, Exec. Vice-Pres. of Global Retail, Royal Dutch Shell Group 2004–06; CEO Rexam plc 2007–10 (retd); Chair. Robert Walters (recruitment consultancy) 2012–; mem. Bd of Dirs DCC plc 2010–, SIG plc 2010– (Chair. 2011–), Cape plc 2012–. *Leisure interests:* golf, travel. *Address:* Robert Walters, 11 Slingsby Place, St Martin's Courtyard, London, WC2E 9AB (office); 34 Rose Square, Fulham Road, London, SW3 6RS, England (home). *Telephone:* (20) 7584-1218 (home). *Fax:* (20) 7584-9339 (home). *Website:* www.robertwalters.com (office).

VAN DEN BERG, Dirk Jan; Dutch economist, diplomatist and university administrator; *Chairman, Sanquin Bloedvoorziening;* b. 1953; m. Frederike Mijnlieff; two c.; ed Univ. of Groningen, École Nat. d'Admin, Paris, France; Policy Planner, Ministry of Econ. Affairs 1980–84; Head of Industrial Policy and Budget Div., Directorate-Gen. for Industry and Regional Policy 1987–88; Deputy Dir-Gen. for Foreign Econ. Relations, Head of Trade Policy Div., Directorate-Gen. for Foreign Econ. Relations 1989–92; Deputy Dir-Gen., Directorate-Gen. for Industry and Regional Policy 1992; Dir Public Finance Programme, Erasmus Univ., Rotterdam 1986–88; Sec.-Gen. Ministry of Foreign Affairs 1992–2001; Perm. Rep. to UN, New York 2001–05; Amb. to People's Repub. of China 2005–07; Pres. Exec. Bd Delft Univ. of Tech. 2008–15; Pres. IDEA League 2008–09, Vice-Pres. for European Affairs 2010–; Govt Rep., Zuidas Amsterdam 2009–10, Chair. Consultative Cttee of Commissioning Parties 2010–12; Chair. Sanquin Bloedvoorziening 2015–; mem. Advisory Bd Int. Visitors' Programme, Ministry of Foreign Affairs; Commr of Ziggo; mem. Peace and Justice Cttee, The Hague 2009, Int. Academic Advisory Panel, Ministry of Educ. in Singapore, Advisory Cttee, Wuhan (China), PolyU Int. Advisory Bd; mem. Governing Bd European Inst. of Innovation and Tech. 2016–; mem. Supervisory Bd, Dutch Devt Bank—FMO 2016–. *Leisure interests:* photography, computers, history, sailing, horse riding. *Address:* Sanquin Bloedvoorziening, Postbus 9190, 1006 AD, Amsterdam, Netherlands (office). *Website:* www.sanquin.nl (office).

VAN DEN BERGH, Maarten Albert; Dutch business executive; b. 19 April 1942, New York, NY, USA; s. of Sidney James van den Bergh and Maria Mijers; m. Marjan Désirée; two d.; ed Univ. of Groningen; joined the Shell Group 1968, held various man. positions in the Far East and UK, Group Man. Dir Royal Dutch/Shell Group 1992, Dir of Finance 1994–98, Vice-Chair. Cttee of Man. Dirs and Pres. Royal Dutch Petroleum Co. 1998–2000, Dir Royal Dutch Shell 2000–09; Dir BT Group plc 2001–09, Deputy Chair. 2006–09; Deputy Chair. Lloyds TSB Group plc 2000–01, Chair. 2001–06; Chair. Akzo Nobel NV 2006–09; Dir British Airways PLC 2002–11; mem. Steering Bd and Dutch Co-Chair. Apeldoorn Conf. 2003–09; Adviser to Chief Exec. of Hong Kong Special Admin. Region 1998–2002; mem. Int. Bd of Advisers to Pres. of Philippines 2001–05, Advisory Council Amsterdam Inst. of Finance 2001–05; Fellow and Vice-Pres. Inst. of Financial Services 2001–06; mem. Guild of Int. Bankers 2001–06; Companion Chartered Man. Inst. 2001. *Leisure interests:* European history.

VAN DEN BERGH, Robert (Rob) F., LLM; Dutch business executive; ed Univ. of Leiden; fmr Man. Dir Admedia BV; joined Nielsen 1990, later Head of Marketing Information, CEO Nielsen –2005; Adviser, CVC Capital Partners Ltd 2005–; Legal Counsel, General Affairs, Nederlandse Dagblad Unie 1975–80; mem. Bd of Dirs VNU Marketing Information, Inc. 1992–, Chair. 2000–, CEO 2003–, mem. Exec. Bd VNU NV (now Nielsen Holdings NV) 1992–, Vice-Chair. 1998–2000, Chair. 2000–; mem. Supervisory Bd Royal Ahold NV 2011–, Chair. ad interim 2014–15; Chair. Supervisory Bd NV Deli Maatschappij, Stichting holding Isala Klinieken; mem. Supervisory Bd Tomtom International BV –2014, Getronics NV 2001–, RBS Holdings NV 2005–09, ABN Amro Bank (subsidiary) 2005–, Corporate Express NV 2006–, Holding Nationale Goede Doelen Loterijen NV (Postcode Loterij), Wagenborg and Pon Holdings BV, Philips Nederland BV, Pon Holdings BV, P3 Technology and Partners BV; mem. Advisory Council ABN AMRO Holding NV; mem. Advisory Bd TomTom NV 2007–. *Address:* Royal Ahold NV, Piet Heinkade 167–173, 1019 GM Amsterdam, Netherlands (office). *Telephone:* (20) 509-51-00 (office). *Fax:* (20) 509-51-10 (office). *E-mail:* info@ahold.com (office). *Website:* www.ahold.com (office).

VAN DEN BERGH, Sidney, OC, MSc, Dr rer. nat, FRS; Canadian (b. Dutch) astronomer; b. 20 May 1929, Wassenaar, The Netherlands; s. of Sidney J. van den Bergh and S. M. van den Bergh; m. 1st Roswitha Koropp; one s. two d.; m. 2nd Gretchen Krause (died 1987); m. 3rd Paulette Gelinau; ed Leiden Univ., The Netherlands, Princeton Univ. and Ohio State Univ., USA, Univ. of Göttingen, FRG; Asst Prof., Ohio State Univ. 1956–58; Prof., Univ. of Toronto, Canada 1958–77; Dir Dominion Astrophysical Observatory, Victoria 1977–86, Astronomer 1986–98, Researcher Emer. 1998–2011; Adjunct Prof., Univ. of Victoria 1978–2011; Pres. Canadian Astronomy Soc. 1990–92; Assoc. Royal Astronomical Soc.; Hon. DSc 1998, 2001; Killam Laureate 1990, NRC Pres.'s Medal, Henry Norris Russell Lecturer 1990, Bruce Gold Medal 2009, inducted into Canadian Science and Tech. Hall of Fame 2011, Gruber Cosmology Prize (co-recipient) 2014, Bruce Gold Medal of ASP. *Publications include:* about 820 scientific publs, including Galaxy Morphology and Classification 1998, The Galaxies of the Local Group 2000. *Leisure interests:* archaeology, history. *Address:* 418 Lands End Road, Sidney, BC V8L 5L9, Canada (home). *Telephone:* (250) 656-6020 (home). *E-mail:* sidney.vandenbergh@nrc-cnrc.gc.ca (office); sidney.vandenbergh@nrc.ca (office).

VAN DEN BROEK, Hans; Dutch institution administrator and fmr politician; b. 11 Dec. 1936, Paris, France; m.; two d.; ed Alberdingk Thym Grammar School, Hilversum, Univ. of Utrecht; attended Sr Man. training, De Baak, Noordwijk; solicitor in Rotterdam 1965–68; Sec. Man. Bd ENKA BV, Arnhem 1969–73, Commercial Man., 1973–76; City Councillor, Rheden 1970–74; mem. Second Chamber, States-Gen. (Parl.) 1976–81; served on Standing Cttees on Foreign Affairs, Devt Co-operation and Justice; Sec. of State for Foreign Affairs 1981–82, Minister 1982–93; Commr for External Relations, Foreign and Security Policy Enlargement Negotiations, Comm. of EC (now European Comm.) 1993–95, for External Relations with Cen. and Eastern Europe, fmr Soviet Union and others for Common Foreign and Security Policy and External Service 1995–99; fmr Pres. Netherlands Inst. of Int. Relations; Chair. Bd of Govs Radio Netherlands (Radio Nederland Wereldomroep); mem. Global Leadership Foundation; mem. Advisory Bd Global Panel Foundation; Hon. Minister of State 2005; Kt Grand Cross, Order of Orange-Nassau 1993, Commander's Cross, Order of Merit (Poland) 2014.

VAN DEN HOUT, Tjaco T., LLM (Hons); Dutch lawyer, fmr diplomatist and international organization official; b. 23 Jan. 1949, The Hague; s. of Frederick Oscar van den Hout and Helene Elizabeth Walrave; m. Baiba Braze; three c.; ed Leiden Univ.; joined Foreign Service 1975; various postings abroad, including as Consul-Gen., Perm. Mission to UN, New York, Deputy Sec.-Gen., Ministry of Foreign Affairs 1996–99; Sec.-Gen. Perm. Court of Arbitration, The Hague 1999–2008; Amb. to Thailand (also accred to Myanmar, Cambodia and Laos) 2008–10; Visiting Prof., Riga Grad. School of Law; Kt Grand Cross (First Class), Order of the White Elephant (Thailand). *Address:* Strelnieku 4 k-2, Rīga 1010, Latvia (office); 45 Nottingham Place, London, W1U 5LY, England (home). *Telephone:* 7585-088513 (mobile) (home). *E-mail:* tjaco.vandenhout@rgsl.edu.lv (office); tvandenhout@gmail.com (office). *Website:* www.rgsl.edu.lv (office); www.tjacovandenhout.com.

VAN DEN WYNGAERT, Baroness Christine, PhD; Belgian judge and fmr singer; *Judge, Trial Division, International Criminal Court;* b. 2 April 1952, Antwerp; ed Free Univ., Brussels; Prof. of Criminal Law, Univ. of Antwerp 1985–2005; Visiting Fellow, Centre for European Legal Studies 1994–96, Research Centre for Int. Law, Univ. of Cambridge, UK 1996–97; Visiting Prof., Univ. of Stellenbosch, S Africa 2001; Judge, Int. Court of Justice in the Yerodia case 2000–02; Judge, Int. Criminal Tribunal for the Fmr Yugoslavia 2003–05, Perm. Judge 2005–09; Judge, Trial Div., ICC, The Hague 2009–; mem. Int. Asscn of Penal Law (Vice-Pres. 2014–); Dr hc (Uppsala) 2001, (Brussels) 2010, (Case Western Reserve) 2013, (Maastricht) 2013; Henri Rolin Prize for PhD thesis 1980, Human Rights Prize, Liga voor Mensenrechten 2006. *Achievements include:* alternative career as singer-songwriter, performing with (among others) Ferre Grignard and Wannes Van de Velde, and resulting in Long Play recording 1970s. *Publications include:* Political Offence Exception to Extradition: The Delicate Problem of Balancing the Rights of the Individual and the International Public Order 1980, Strafrecht en strafprocesrecht in hoofdlijnen 1991 (revised sixth edn: Strafrecht, strafprocesrecht en internationaal strafrecht in hoofdlijnen 2006); co-ed.: Criminal Procedure Systems in the European Community 1993, International Criminal Law and Procedure 1996, International Criminal Law: A Collection of International and European Instruments, and other titles. *Address:* International Criminal Court, PO Box 19519, 2500 CM The Hague, The Netherlands (office); Faculty of Law, University of Antwerp, Universiteitsplein 1, 2610 Antwerp, Belgium. *Telephone:* (70) 515-85-15 (office); (3) 820-29-23. *Fax:* (70) 515-85-55 (office); (3) 820-29-40. *E-mail:* chris.vandenwyngaert@ua.ac.be (office); otp.informationdesk@icc-cpi.int (office). *Website:* www.icc-cpi.int (office); www.ua.ac.be.

VAN DER AVOIRD, Ad, PhD; Dutch scientist and academic; *Professor Emeritus, Institute of Theoretical Chemistry, University of Nijmegen;* b. 19 April 1943, Eindhoven; s. of H. J. van der Avoird and M. A. van der Avoird (née Kerkhofs); m. T. G. M. Lange 1964; two s.; ed Tech. Univ., Eindhoven; Research Fellow, Inst. Battelle, Geneva, Switzerland 1965–67; Section Man. Unilever Research Lab., Vlaardingen 1967–71; Assoc. Prof., Univ. of Nijmegen 1968–71, Prof. Inst. of Theoretical Chemistry 1971–2008, Prof. Emer. 2008–; Visiting Miller Research Prof., Univ. of California, Berkeley 1992; mem. Royal Netherlands Acad. of Arts and Sciences 1979–, Int. Acad. of Quantum Molecular Sciences 1997–; Knight, Order of Netherlands Lion 2014. *Publications:* Interacties tussen moleculen 1989; articles in scientific journals. *Address:* Institute for Molecules and Materials, Theoretical Chemistry, Radboud University Nymegen, Heyendaalseweg 135, 6525 AJ Nymegen, Netherlands (office). *Telephone:* (24) 365-30-37 (office). *E-mail:* a.vanderavoird@theochem.ru.nl (office). *Website:* www.theochem.ru.nl (office).

VAN DER BELLEN, Alexander, DEcon; Austrian economist, academic, politician and head of state; *President;* b. 18 Jan. 1944, Vienna; s. of Alexander Konstantin van der Bellen and Alma Siebold; m. 1st Brigitte van der Bellen (divorced), two s.; m. 2nd Doris Schmidauer 2015; ed Univ. of Innsbruck; Asst Prof., Inst. für Finanzwissenschaft, Univ. of Innsbruck 1968–70, apptd Assoc. Prof. 1976; Asst Prof., Internationales Inst. für Management und Verwaltung, Berlin 1972–74; Prof. of Econs, Univ. of Vienna 1980–2009, Dean, Faculty for Social Sciences and Econs 1990–94; mem. Nationalrat (Nat. Council, lower house of parl.) 1994–2012, Chair. Green Party Parl. Group 1997–2008; City of Vienna Commr for Univs and Research 2010–15; mem. Vienna City Council 2012–15; ind. cand. (supported by Green Party) in presidential election 2016; Pres.-elect April–July 2016, election results overturned by Constitutional Court 1 July 2016, elected in second election Dec. 2016, sworn in 26 Jan. 2017; mem. Social Democratic Party –1992; mem. Austrian Green Party 1992–2016, Fed. Spokesperson 1997–2008, Leader 1997–2008; Großes Goldenes Ehrenzeichen mit Stern für Verdienste um die Republik Österreich 2004. *Address:* Office of the Federal President, Hofburg, Ballhausplatz, 1010 Vienna, Austria (office). *Telephone:* (1) 534-22 (office). *Fax:* (1) 535-65-12 (office). *Website:* www.hofburg.at (office); www.vanderbellen.at.

VAN DER EB, Alex Jan, PhD; Dutch fmr prof. of molecular carcinogenesis; *Senior Adviser, Janssen Pharmaceutical Companies;* b. 16 Jan. 1934, Bandung, Java; s. of Wijnand Jan van der Eb and Gertrude Leonie van der Eb-Blekkink; m. Titia Brongersma 1961; two s. one d.; ed Univ. of Leiden; mil. service 1962–63; Assoc. Prof. of Tumor Virology, Univ. of Leiden 1974–80, Prof. of Molecular Carcinogenesis 1980–99, Prof. Emer., Dept of Toxicogenetics 1999–; Postdoctoral Fellow, Calif. Inst. of Tech., USA 1968–69; Visiting Prof., Nagasaki Univ., Japan 2002–06; Sr Adviser, Janssen Pharmaceutical Cos (fmrly Crucell), Leiden 2002–; mem. Royal Acad. of Sciences and Letters 1987–, European Molecular Biology Org. 1981–, Academia Europaea, Royal Holland Science Asscn (Koninklijke Hollandsche Maatschappij van Wetenschappen) 1987–; Kt, Orde van de Nederlandse Leeuw 1998; AKZO Prize 1975, Korteweg Overwater Fund Award 1977, Beijerinck Virology Medal 1978, Robert Koch Prize 1989, Japan Org. for Promotion Cander Research Award 1989, Hyclone Award 1993, Fedora Award 1996, Inst. of Radiation Pathology IRS Prize 1997. *Publications:* more than 250 publs on molecular carcinogenesis and radiation biology. *Leisure interests:* bird watching, photography, travelling, camping. *Address:* Prinses Beatrixlaan 53, 2341 TW Oegstgeest, Netherlands. *Telephone:* (71) 5172178 (home). *E-mail:* lvandereb@kpnplanet.nl (home); tvandereb@hotmail.com (home).

VAN DER HEIJDEN, Paul F., LLM, PhD; Dutch lawyer, academic and fmr university administrator; *Professor Emeritus, International Labour Law, Leiden University;* b. 18 Sept. 1949, Utrecht; m.; three c.; ed Univs of Amsterdam and Leiden; Lecturer, Dept of Law, Univ. of Leiden 1978–85, Univ. of Groningen 1987–90; lawyer, Court of Law, Amsterdam 1985–89; Prof. of Employment Law, Univ. of Amsterdam 1990–2007, Rector Magnificus 2002–07; Rector Magnificus and Pres. Univ. of Leiden 2007–13, Prof. Emer., Int. Labour Law 2007–, Founding Ed.-in-Chief, Int. Labor Rights Case Law Journal 2015–; Ed.-in-Chief Jurisprudentie Arbeidsrecht; chaired Dutch Del. at Int. Labour Conf. of ILO 1995–2001, Geneva, Chair. ILO Governing Body Cttee on Freedom of Asscn 2002–17; Crown-apptd mem. Social and Econ. Council (SER); Chair. Social Justice Expertise Center; Chair. Supervisory Bd Amsterdam Univ. Press, The Clingendael Inst. 2015–; mem. Supervisory Bd NUON NV, Buhrmann Nederland NV, ING Group NV, Dutch Cancer Inst./Antoni van Leeuwenhoek Hosp., AMC-UvA; Chair. De Volkskrant Foundation; mem. Royal Netherlands Acad. of Arts and Sciences; Officer in the Order of Orange-Nassau 2019. *Publications:* Beyond Employment: Changes in Work and the Future of Labour Law in Europe 2001; numerous articles in professional journals. *Address:* Instituut voor Publiekrecht, Leiden University, Room B1.07, Kamerlingh Onnes Building, Steenschuur 25 PO Box 9500, 2311 ES Leiden, Netherlands (office). *Telephone:* (71) 5276128 (office). *E-mail:* p.f.van.der .heijden@law.leidenuniv.nl (office). *Website:* www.universiteitleiden.nl (office).

VAN DER HOEVEN, Maria Josephina Arnoldina; Dutch politician and international organization official; b. 13 Sept. 1949, Meerssen; m. Lou Buytendijk (died 2012); teacher 1969, school counsellor 1971; Head Adult Commercial Vocational Training Centre, Maastricht –1987; Head Limburg Tech. Centre 1987–91; mem. (Christian Democratic Alliance) House of Reps, States Gen. 1991–2002; Minister of Educ., Culture and Science 2002–07, of Economic Affairs 2007–10; Exec. Dir IEA 2011–15; Chair. Supervisory Bd, Alzheimer Netherlands; fmr Chair. St Nicholas Catholic Asscn of Bargees; fmr mem. Bd of Govs, Maastricht Coll. of Higher Professional Educ., Southern Dutch Opera Asscn; Officer, Order of Orange-Nassau 2010. *Address:* c/o International Energy Agency, 9 rue de la Fédération, 75739 Paris Cedex 15, France (office).

VAN DER MEER, Jan, MD; Dutch physician; b. 30 Aug. 1935, Leeuwarden; s. of L. van der Meer and G. Bakker; m. Joan Alkema 1962; one d.; ed Univ. of Amsterdam; intern 1968; Sr Registrar in Internal Medicine, Binnengasthuis, Amsterdam 1970–76; Head of Coagulation Lab., Cen. Lab. of Bloodtransfusion Service of Dutch Red Cross 1969–76; Prof. of Internal Medicine, Chair. of Dept, Acad. Hosp. of Free Univ. Amsterdam 1976–2000; Chair. Govs, Cen. Lab. of Blood Transfusion Service, Netherlands Red Cross 1994–98; Chair. Landsteiner Foundation for Blood Transfusion Research 1998–2009. *Publication:* Meting van de plasma renine-activiteit met behulp van een radioimmunologische bepaling van angiotensine I 1969. *Address:* De Wijde Blik 19, 1189 WJ Amstelveen, The Netherlands.

VAN DER MEER MOHR, Pauline F. M., LLM; Dutch lawyer and university administrator; *President, Erasmus University Rotterdam;* b. 1960; m.; four c.; ed Erasmus Univ. Rotterdam, European Univ. Inst., Italy, Univ. of Amsterdam; held several legal and man. positions with Royal Dutch Shell Group, including serving as a man. mem. Nederlandse Aardolie Maatschappij; Group Human Resources Dir TNT 2004–06; Sr Exec. Vice-Pres. and Head of Human Resources, ABN AMRO Bank 2006–08; f. Amstelbridge Human Capital Strategies (consultancy) 2008; Chair. Exec. Bd and Pres. Erasmus Univ. Rotterdam 2010–; mem. Supervisory Bd ASML Holding; mem. Programme Council, Ministries of Foreign Affairs and Econ. Affairs. *Address:* Office of the President, PO Box 1738, 3000 DR Rotterdam (office); Office of the President, Campus Woudestein, Burgemeester Oudlaan 50, 3062 PA Rotterdam, The Netherlands (office). *Telephone:* (10) 4081751 (office). *Fax:* (10) 4089073 (office). *E-mail:* ender@abd.eur.nl (office); vallejoandres@abd.eur.nl (office). *Website:* www.eur.nl (office).

VAN DER MEULEN, Robert Paul, LLM, MSc; Dutch fmr diplomatist; b. 25 May 1950; m. Majida Mouasher; two d.; ed Univ. of Leyden; Asst, European Inst., Univ. of Leyden 1974–76; with Directorate for European Integration, Foreign Econ. Relations Dept, Ministry of Econ. Affairs 1976, Head of Bureau, Accession of Greece, Spain and Portugal, Co-operation with Mediterranean Countries and EFTA 1979; with Perm. Representation of The Netherlands to EC, Brussels 1981–82; First Sec., Embassy in Washington, DC 1982–84, Counsellor 1984–85; Deputy Head, Office of Vice-Pres. of EC 1985–88; Amb. of European Comm. to Brunei, Indonesia and Singapore 1989–94, to Tunisia 1994–98; Head of Maghreb Div. (DG RELEX-F3), European Comm. 1998–2001, Dir, North Africa and the Middle East 2001–02; Amb. to Jordan (also accred to Yemen) 2002–06, to Nigeria and Perm. Rep. to Econ. Community of West African States (ECOWAS) 2006–09; bd mem. of foundations in the field of oriëntalisme; Grand Officier, Ordre de la République Tunisienne. *Leisure interest:* 19th century paintings, especially works by the orientalist Marius A. J. Bauer. *Address:* Manoir de Fourneux, 49400 Saumur, France (home). *Telephone:* 78-9300749 (mobile) (home). *E-mail:* robertvandermeulen@hotmail.com (home). *Website:* www.mariusbauer.nl (office).

VAN DER VEER, Jeroen; Dutch business executive; *Chairman of the Supervisory Board, ING Groep NV;* b. 27 Oct. 1947, Utrecht; m. Mariette van der Veer; three d.; ed Delft and Rotterdam Univs; joined Royal Dutch Petroleum Co. 1971, Area Co-ordinator Sub-Saharan Africa 1990–92, Man. Dir Shell Nederland 1992–95, Pres. and CEO Shell Chemical Co. USA 1995–97, Group Man. Dir Royal Dutch 1997–2000, Pres. 2000–04, Chair. Cttee of Man. Dirs Royal Dutch/Shell Group 2004–09, CEO Royal Dutch Shell plc 2004–09, Dir (non-exec.) 2009–14; mem. Supervisory Bd ING Groep NV 2009–, Vice-Chair. 2009–11, Chair. 2011–; mem. Supervisory Bd Koninklijke Philips Electronics NV 2009–, Chair. 2011–; Vice-Chair. and Sr Ind. Dir Unilever NV 2009–11; mem. Supervisory Bd Het Concertgebouw NV; Chair. Supervisory Council Nederlands Openluchtmuseum; Chair. Platform Bètatechniek; World Pres. Soc. of Chemical Industry 2002–04; mem. Bd Nationale Toneel (theatre); Hon. Citizen of Singapore 2010; Commdr, Order of Orange-Nassau 2009; Dr hc (Univ. of Port Harcourt, Nigeria) 2005. *Leisure interests:* visiting museums, playing golf (16 handicap), has twice skated the 200 kilometres 'Elfstedentocht' – 11 cities marathon – in the Netherlands. *Address:* ING Groep NV, PO Box 1800, 1000 BV Amsterdam, The Netherlands (office). *Telephone:* (20) 563-91-11 (office). *E-mail:* info@ing.com (office). *Website:* www.ing.com (office).

VAN DER WEE, Baron Herman Frans Anna, LLD, PhD; Belgian historian (retd) and academic; *Professor Emeritus of Economic History, Katholieke Universiteit Leuven;* b. 10 July 1928, Lier; s. of Jos Van der Wee and Martha Planckaert; m. Monique Verbreyt 1954; one s. one d.; ed Leuven Univ., Sorbonne, Paris, London School of Econs, UK; Fellow Nat. Foundation for Scientific Research of Belgium 1953–55; lecturer, Katholieke Universiteit Leuven 1955, Assoc. Prof. 1966, Prof. of Econ. History 1969–93, Prof. Emer. 1993–, Sec., Dept of Econs 1970–72, Chair. 1972–74, Chair. Bd of Trustees, Leuven Univ. Press 1971–93; Visiting Prof., St Aloysius Univ., Brussels 1972–76, Dean, Faculty of Econ., Political and Social Sciences 1972–75; Visiting Prof., Université Catholique de Louvain, Louvain-la-Neuve 1972–80, 1991–92; Research Fellow, Woodrow Wilson Int. Center for Scholars, Washington, DC 1975–76; Francqui Chair, Univ. of Brussels 1980–81; Visiting Fellow, Inst. for Advanced Study, School of Historical Studies, Princeton, NJ, USA 1981–82, 1991, All Souls Coll., Oxford 1985, Inst. for Advanced Study, Indiana Univ. 1986; J. Tinbergen Chair, Erasmus Univ. 1987; Chair of Econ. History, Univ. of Paris IV-Sorbonne 1987–88; Ellen MacArthur Chair. Univ. of Cambridge, UK 1989; P.P. Rubens Chair. Univ. of Calif., Berkeley 1994; Visiting Fellow, Inst. for Advanced Study (RSSC), Canberra, Australia 1994; Erasmus Chair, Harvard Univ. 1997; Chair. of Banking History, Univ. of St.-Gallen 1999; Guest of the Rector, Netherlands Inst. for Advanced Study, Wassenaar 2000; Guest of the Rector Wissenschaftskolleg Berlin, Germany 2004; Visiting Fellow, Wissenschaftszentrum fur Sozialforschung, Germany 2004; Anthony van Dyck Chair, UCLA 2010; Pres. Int. Econ. History Asscn 1986–90 (Hon. Pres. 1990–); Chair. Leuven Univ. Press 1972–85, Royal Acad. of Belgium (Class of Letters) 1987, Leuven Inst. of Cen. and E European Studies (LICOS) 1990–93, Advisory Council of W European Program at Wilson Int. Center for Scholars, Washington, DC 1986–91, Academic Advisory Council of European Asscn for Banking History 1991–99; mem. Research Council, European Univ. Inst., Florence 1985–94, 1999–2006, Bd of Trustees Cité Int. Universitaire, Paris 1993–2008; mem. Royal Acad. of Belgium 1977–2003, Hon. mem. 2003–; Corresp. Foreign mem. Royal Acad. of Netherlands 1983–; Foundation mem. Academia Europaea 1987–; Corresp. Fellow, British Acad. 1987, Royal Historical Soc. 1995; Foreign Hon. mem. American Acad. of Arts and Sciences 1993–; Fellow, European Econ. Asscn 2004; Dr hc (Brussels) 1994, (Leicester) 1995; Order of Leopold Belgium, Order of the Crown Belgium, knighted by King Albert II of Belgium (title of Baron) 1994; De Stassart Prize for Nat. History, Royal Acad. of Belgium 1961–67, 1968, Eugène Baie Prize 1966, Fulbright-Hayes Award 1975, 1981, Quinquennial Solvay Prize for the Social Sciences, Nat. Foundation of Scientific Research of Belgium 1976–80, 1981, Amsterdam Biannual Prize for Historical Sciences 1992, Golden Medal for Special Merits, Flemish Parl. 1995. *Publications include:* Prix et salaires: Manuel Méthodologique 1956, The Growth of the Antwerp Market and the European Economy (14th–16th centuries), 3 vols 1963, The Great Depression Revisited (ed) 1972, Monetary, Credit and Banking Systems in Western Europe, 1400–1750, in The Cambridge Economic History of Europe (Part V) 1977, Mint Statistics of Flanders and Brabant 1300–1506 (two vols) 1980, 1985, Prosperity and Upheaval, the World Economy, 1945–1980 1983 (trans. in several languages), Histoire économique mondiale (trans. in several languages) 1945–1990 1990, History of European Banking (trans. in several languages) 1991, The Economic Development of Europe, 950–1950 (13 edns) 1982–97, Constructing the World Economy 1750–1990 1992, The Low Countries in the Early Modern World 1993, The General Bank 1822–1997: A Continuing Challenge 1997, Urban Achievement in Early Modern Europe: Golden Ages in Antwerp, Amsterdam and London (ed.) 2001, A Century of Banking Consolidation in Europe: The History and Archives of Mergers and Acquisitions (ed.) 2001, The Woollen Industries (Cambridge History of Western Textiles) 2003, A Small Nation in the Turmoil of the Second World War – Money, Finance and Occupation (Belgium, its Enemies, its Friends, 1939–1945) 2009. *Leisure interests:* literature, music, tennis, skiing. *Address:* Katholieke Universiteit Leuven, Centrum voor Economische Studiën, Naamsestraat 69, 3000 Leuven (office); Ettingestraat 10, 9170 Sint-Pauwels, Belgium (home). *Telephone:* (3) 776-03-33 (home). *Fax:* (3) 765-90-28 (home). *E-mail:* ces@econ.kuleuven.ac.be (office); Herman.VanDerWee@econ.kuleuven.be (home). *Website:* www.econ.kuleuven.ac.be/ew/academic/econhist/default.htm.

VAN DIJK, Petrus, LLM, SJD; Dutch state councillor and fmr professor of international law; b. 21 Feb. 1943, De Lier; s. of A. A. M. van Dijk and J. H. van Straelen; m. Francisca G. M. Lammerts 1969; one s. one d.; ed Utrecht and Leyden Univs; Lecturer in Int. Law, Utrecht Univ. 1967–76, Prof. 1976–90; State Councillor 1990–2013, Pres. Admin. Jurisdiction Div., Council of State 2000–03, 2006–; Judge, European Court of Human Rights 1996–98, Deputy Pres. Admin. Tribunal of Council of Europe 2001–06; Vice-President, Administrative Tribunal of the Council of Europe 2001–06; Chair. Netherlands Inst. of Human Rights 1982–97, Netherlands Inst. of Social and Econ. Law 1986–90; Deputy Judge, Court of Appeal of The Hague 1986–2000, Cen. Appeal Bd Social Affairs 2001–13; mem. Perm. Court of Arbitration 2000–; Fullbright-Hays Scholar, Univ. of Mich. Law School 1970–71; Visiting Prof., Wayne State Univ. Law School 1978; mem. Bd Trustees Inst. of Social Sciences 1992–98; mem. Advisory Bd Anne Frank Foundation 1994–, Humanity in Action 1998–; mem. Royal Netherlands Acad. of Arts and Sciences; mem. Netherlands Del. to UN Gen. Ass. 1981, 1983, 1986; Kt, Order of the Netherlands Lion. *Publications include:* Theory and Practice of the European Convention on Human Rights (with G. J. H. van Hoof) 1979, The Final Act of Helsinki: Basis for a Pan-European System? 1980, Contents and Function of the Principle of Equity in International Economic Law 1987, Normative Force and Effectiveness of International Economic Law 1988, Access to Court 1993, Universality of Human Rights 1994; book chapters and ed. of numerous legal publs. *Address:* Gregoriuslaan 16, 3723 KR Bilthoven, The Netherlands. *E-mail:* pvandijk13@gmail.com (office).

VAN DÚNEM, Fernando José França, PhD; Angolan politician; b. 1952; ed Univ. Aix-en-Provence, France, Universidade de Coimbra, Portugal; Amb. to Belgium and Netherlands 1979–82; Minister of Justice 1986–90, of Planning 1990–91; fmr Minister of External Affairs; Prime Minister of Angola 1991–98; mem. Assembléia Nacional (parl.) 1999, 2008–; First Vice-Pres. Pan-African Parl. 2004–09; mem. Marxist-Leninist Popular Movt for the Liberation of Angola Workers' Party (MPLA). *Address:* Assembléia Nacional, CP 1204, Luanda, Angola (office). *Website:* www.parlamento.ao (office).

VAN FRAASSEN, Bastiaan (Bas) Cornelis, PhD; American/Canadian academic; *McCosh Professor Emeritus of Philosophy, Princeton University;* b. 5 April 1941, Goes, The Netherlands; s. of Jan Bastiaan van Fraassen and Dina Landman; m. Isabelle Peschard 2005; two s.; ed Univ. of Alberta, Canada, Univ. of Pittsburgh, USA; Asst Prof., Yale Univ. 1966–68, Assoc. Prof. 1969; Assoc. Prof., Univ. of Toronto 1969–73, Prof. 1973–82; Prof., Univ. of Southern Calif. 1976–81; McCosh Prof. of Philosophy, Princeton Univ. 1982–2008, Prof. Emer. 2008–; Distinguished Prof. of Philosophy, San Francisco State Univ. 2008–15; John Simon Guggenheim Fellowship 1970–71; Fellow, American Acad. of Arts and Sciences; Corresp. Fellow, British Acad.; Foreign mem. Royal Netherlands Acad. of Arts and Sciences; Titular mem. Acad. Int. de Philosophie des Sciences; Hon. DLett (Univ. of Lethbridge), Hon. LLD (Univ. of Notre Dame), Hon. PhD (Catholic Univ. of Leuven); Franklin Matchette Award (co-recipient) 1982, Imre Lakatos Award (co-recipient) 1986, Int. Giulio Preti Prize 2009, Inaugural Hempel Award 2012. *Publications include:* Introduction to the Philosophy of Time and Space 1970, Formal Semantics and Logic 1971, The Scientific Image 1980, Laws and Symmetry 1989, Quantum Mechanics: An Empiricist View 1991, The Empirical Stance 2002, Scientific Representation: Paradoxes of Perspective 2008. *Leisure interests:* rock climbing, flying trapeze, hiking. *Address:* 3148 Avis Way, Pinole, CA 94564, USA (home). *E-mail:* fraassen@princeton.edu (office). *Website:* www.princeton.edu/~fraassen (office); philosophy.princeton.edu (office).

VAN GAAL, (Aloysius Paulus Maria) Louis; Dutch football manager and fmr professional football player; b. 8 Aug. 1951, Amsterdam; m. 1st Fernanda van Gaal (died 1994); two d.; m. 2nd Truus van Gaal 2008; midfielder as player, youth career with RKSV de Meer; sr career with Ajax 1972–73, Royal Antwerp 1973–77, Telstar 1977–78, Sparta Rotterdam 1978–86, AZ Alkmaar 1986–87; Man. of Ajax 1991–97 (Eredivisie 1993–94, 1994–95, 1995–96, KNVB Cup 1992–93, Johan Cruijff Shield 1993, 1994, 1995, UEFA Champions League 1994–95, runner-up 1995–96, UEFA Cup 1991–92, UEFA Super Cup 1995, Intercontinental Cup 1995), Barcelona 1997–2000, 2002–03 (La Liga 1997–98, 1998–99, Copa del Rey 1997–98, UEFA Super Cup 1997), Netherlands 2000–02, 2012–14 (FIFA World Cup Third Place 2014), AZ Alkmaar 2005–09 (Eredivisie 2008–09), Bayern Munich 2009–11 (Bundesliga 2009–10, DFB-Pokal 2009–10, DFB-Supercup 2010, UEFA Champions League runner-up 2009–10), Manchester United 2014–16; Kt, Order of Orange-Nassau 1997; World Soccer Man. of the Year 1995, Onze d'Or Coach of the Year 1995, Rinus Michels Award 2007, 2009, Dutch Sports Coach of the Year 2009, Third Place, Die Sprachwahrer des Jahres 2009, German Football Man. of the Year 2010.

VAN GINKEL, Hans J. A., MSc, PhD; Dutch university administrator and academic; *Professor Emeritus, United Nations University;* b. 22 June 1940, Kota-Radjah, Indonesia; m. Bep Teepen; one s. one d.; ed Utrecht Univ.; Teacher of Geography and History, Thomas à Kempis Coll., Arnhem 1965–68; joined Faculty of Geographical Sciences, Utrecht Univ. 1968, apptd Prof. of Human Geography and Planning 1980, Dean of Faculty 1981–85, mem. Exec. Bd 1985, Rector Magnificus 1986; Treas. Netherlands Foundation for Int. Co-operation in Educ. 1986–97; mem., then Chair. Bd Netherlands Interdisciplinary Demographic Inst. 1986–2000; Ind. Chair. Regional Council of Utrecht 1988–93; Pres. Governing Bd Int. Training Centre for Aerial Survey and Earth Sciences, Enschedé 1990–98; mem. Governing Bd UN Univ. 1992–97, Vice-Pres. 1995–97, Rector 1997–2007 (retd), now Prof. Emer.; Vice-Pres. Bd European Asscn of Univs 1994–98; mem. European Science and Tech. Ass., Brussels, Belgium 1994–98; Vice-Pres. Bd Int. Asscn of Univs 1995–2000, Pres. 2000–04; mem. Nat. Council, Chair. Organizing Cttee, 28th Int. Geographical Congress, The Hague 1996; Vice-Chair. Bd of Trustees, Asian Inst. of Tech., Bangkok, Thailand 1997–; mem. Steering Cttee, UNESCO World Conf. on Higher Educ. 1998; mem. Academia Europaea 2001, Bibliotheca Alexandrina 2009–; mem. Comm. on Educ. and Communication, World Conservation Union; fmr mem. UNESCO Advisory Group for Higher Educ.; fmr Chair. Co-ordinating Cttee of Advisory Councils on Science Policy; Chair. Inst. for Social Studies 2007–, Kofi Annan Business Schools Foundation 2009–; fmr Bd mem. Utrecht Network for Innovation and Economy; fmr mem. Nat. Foresight Cttee on Science Policy; Hon. Fellow, Inst. for Aerospace Survey and Earth Sciences; Hon. mem. Comm. on the History of Geographical Thought, Int. Geographical Union; Kt Netherlands Order of the Lion 1994, Order of the Rising Sun, Grand Cordon (Japan) 2007; Dr hc (Universitatea Babes-Bolyai, Romania) 1997, (Calif. State Univ.–Sacramento) 2003, (Univ. of Ghana) 2005, (Tech. Univ. of Zvolen, Slovakia) 2006, (McMaster Univ., Canada) 2007; Medal of Utrecht Chamber of Commerce 1993, Golden Medal of City of Utrecht 1997, Plancius Medal, Royal Netherlands Geographic Soc. 2000. *Publications:* more than 100 publs in academic journals.

VAN HAMEL, Martine; Dutch/American ballerina, choreographer and teacher; *Co-founder, Kaatsbaan International Dance Center;* b. (Maria Christina van Hamel), 16 Nov. 1945, Brussels, Belgium; d. of D. A. van Hamel and Manette van Hamel-Cramer; partner Kevin Mckenzie; ed Nat. Ballet School of Canada; began ballet training aged four; debut with Nat. Ballet of Venezuela aged 11; following graduation, joined Nat. Ballet of Canada as soloist 1963; moved to New York and danced with Joffrey Ballet 1969–70; joined American Ballet Theatre 1970, Prin. Ballerina 1973–91, danced classic roles, including Swan Lake, Sleeping Beauty, Raimonda, as well as contemporary works choreographed by Balanchine, Glen Tetley, Anthony Tudor, Kenneth MacMillan, Jiri Kylian, Mark Morris, Twyla Tharp, Alvin Ailey; danced with Nederlands Dans Theater III 1993–98; Artistic Dir New Amsterdam Ballet (f. 1986); Co-founder Kaatsbaan Int. Dance Center; Teacher, The Jacqueline Kennedy Onassis School at American Ballet Theatre; Gold Medal, Varna Competition 1966, Prix de Varna 1966, Dance Magazine Award, Cue Magazine Award, Award for Excellence, Washington Coll., Dance Educators of America Award. *Films include:* Turning Point, Little Nikita. *Choreography includes:* Amnon V'Tamar for American Ballet Theatre 1984 and creator of works for Milwaukee Ballet, Washington Ballet, Royal Winnipeg Ballet and New Amsterdam Ballet. *Leisure interests:* singing, gardening, Qi Gong practice. *Address:* Kaatsbaan International Dance Center, PO Box 482, Tivoli, NY 12583, USA (office). *Telephone:* (845) 757-5106 (office); (845) 679-8584. *Fax:* (845) 757-4050 (office). *E-mail:* martinevh@rcn.com (home). *Website:* www.kaatsbaan.org (office).

VAN HEERDEN, Neil Peter, BA; South African diplomatist; b. 30 July 1939, East London; s. of J. van Heerden and C. Nel; m. Evelin Nowack 1961; one s. one d.; ed Wonderbom High School, Pretoria and Univ. of S Africa, Pretoria; joined Dept of Foreign Affairs 1959, Vice-Consul, Tokyo 1963, opened S Africa's first mission in Taipei 1967–68, opened first S African mission in Tehran 1970–71, First Sec., Embassy in Washington, DC 1971–75, Amb. to FRG 1980, Deputy Dir-Gen. Dept of Foreign Affairs 1985–87, Dir-Gen. of Foreign Affairs 1987–92, Amb. to EC (now EU) 1992–96; Exec. Dir S Africa Foundation (now Business Leadership South Africa) 1996; mem. Bd of Dirs Naspers 1996–13, BMW (SA); Trustee, Univ. of the Western Cape; Councillor, Business Unity South Africa; Hon. DLitt et Phil (Rand Afrikaans Univ.) 2000; Paul Harris Award. *Publications include:* articles in journals dealing with foreign affairs. *Leisure interests:* music, hiking, sailing, golf. *Address:* 19 Raed-na-Gael Street, Hermanus 7200 (office); PO Box 7006, Johannesburg 2000, South Africa (home). *Telephone:* (28) 3131792 (office). *E-mail:* neileve@iafrica.com (office).

VAN HOLLEN, Chris, Jr, BA, MPP, JD; American lawyer and politician; *Senator from Maryland;* b. 10 Jan. 1959, Karachi, Pakistan; s. of Christopher Van Hollen and Eliza Van Hollen (née Farnsworth); m. Katherine A. Wilkens; two s. one d.; ed Swarthmore Coll., Harvard Univ., Georgetown Univ.; Legis. Asst for Defense and Foreign Policy to US Senator from Maryland Charles Mathias 1985–87; Professional staff mem., Senate Foreign Relations Cttee 1987–89; Sr Legis. Adviser to Gov. of Maryland William Schaefer 1989–91; called to the Bar, Maryland 1990; Assoc., Arent, Fox, Kintner, Plotkin & Kahn, Washington, DC 1991–2002; mem. Maryland House of Dels 1991–95; mem. Maryland State Senate for Dist 18 1995–2002; mem. US House of Reps from 7th Maryland Dist, Washington, DC 2003–17, mem. House Ways and Means Cttee 2007–17, Govt Reform and Oversight Cttee, Budget Cttee 2011–17, Jt Select Cttee on Deficit Reduction 2011; Senator from Maryland 2017–, also Chair. Democratic Senatorial Campaign Cttee 2017–; mem. ABA; Democrat. *Address:* B40C, Dirksen Senate Office Building, Washington, DC 20510, USA (office). *Telephone:* (202) 224-4654 (office). *Website:* www.senate.gov (office).

VAN HOOFF, Jan A. R. A. M.; Dutch fmr professor of comparative physiology and ethology; b. 15 May 1936, Arnhem; s. of R. A. Th. van Hooff and L. E. Burgers; m. Anna C. M. Bluemink 1964; two s. one d.; ed Canisius Coll., Nijmegen, Univ. of Utrecht; Scientific Collaborator, Faculty of Biology, Univ. of Utrecht 1963–73, Lecturer in Comparative Physiology 1973–80, Prof. of Comparative Physiology and Ethology 1980–2001, Dean, Faculty of Biology 1993–96; apptd Dir Science Bd, Burgers Zoo, Arnhem 1969; Pres. Research Council of Ethology, Netherlands Foundation for Biological Research 1972–78, Dir 1978–83; Pres. Soc. pour l'Etude et la Protection des Mammifères 1985–89, Royal Netherlands Zoological Soc. 1996–2001, Jane Goodall Inst. 1997–2001; Sec.-Gen. Int. Primatological Soc. 2000–04; Sec. Lucie Burgers Foundation for Comparative Behaviour Research 1980–; Bd mem. Foundation Prince Bernhard Chair for Int. Nature Conservation 1995–2013, mem Curatorium Prince Bernhard Chair; mem. numerous scientific foundations and socs; Fellow, Royal Netherlands Acad. of Arts and Sciences; Hon. Prof., Universitas Nasional, Jakarta, Indonesia; Hon. mem. Assoziazione Primatologica Italiana; Officer, Royal Order of Orange-Nassau 2000; Socio Onorario, La Società di Medicina e Scienze Naturali dell'Università di Parma, Primates Social Impact Award 2016. *Publications include:* Facial Expressions in Higher Primates 1962, The Comparison of Facial Expressions in Man and Higher Primates 1976, Categories and Sequences of Behavior: Methods of Description and Analysis 1982, Oorlog 1990, Relationships Among Nonhuman Primate Males 2000, Economics in Nature 2001, Laughter and Smiling: the intertwining of nature and culture 2003. *Address:* Vermeerlaan 24, 3723 EN Bilthoven, The Netherlands. *Telephone:* (30) 228-76-39; 62-1287739 (mobile). *E-mail:* jaramvanhooff@gmail.com.

VAN HOUTEN, Frans, MA; Dutch business executive; *Chairman of the Board of Management and CEO, Royal Philips Electronics NV;* b. 26 April 1960, Eindhoven; ed Erasmus Univ., Rotterdam; began career in marketing and sales at Philips Data Systems 1986, held several leadership positions, CEO Airvision (in-flight entertainment co. in USA) 1992–93, Vice-Pres. Int. Sales and Operations, Philips Kommunikations Industrie, Germany 1993–96, joined Consumer Electronics Div. 1996, led region Asia Pacific, Middle East and Africa, based in Singapore, Co-CEO Consumer Electronics Div. 2002–03, mem. Group Man. Cttee 2003–06, CEO Philips Semiconductors 2004, mem. Bd of Man. 2006 until creation of NXP Semiconductors Sept. 2006 (CEO NXP Semiconductors 2006–10), rejoined Philips Bd of Man. 2010, CEO-designate Royal Philips Electronics NV 2010–11, COO Jan.–April 2011, Chair. Bd of Man. and CEO April 2011–, Chair. Exec. Cttee July 2011–, Acting CEO Philips Lighting; led project to separate ING Group's banking and insurance operations as an ind. adviser to Man. Bd 2006–10; Exec. Advisor and Interim Man., FVH Interventions BV 2009–10; mem. European Round Table of Industrialists 2010–; mem. Bd of Dirs Novartis 2018–. *Address:* Royal Philips Electronics NV, Breitner Center, HBT 14.12, Amstelplein 2, 1096 BC Amsterdam, Netherlands (office). *Telephone:* (20) 597-77-77 (office). *E-mail:* info@philips.com (office). *Website:* www.philips.com (office).

VAN INWAGEN, Peter Jan, PhD; American philosopher and academic; *John Cardinal O'Hara Professor of Philosophy, University of Notre Dame;* b. 21 Sept. 1942, Rochester, New York; s. of George Butler van Inwagen and Mildred Gloria Knudsen; m. 1st Margery Naylor 1967 (divorced 1988); one d.; m. 2nd Elisabeth Bolduc 1989; ed Rensselaer Polytechnic Inst., Univ. of Rochester; served in US Army 1969–70; Visiting Asst Prof. of Philosophy, Univ. of Rochester 1970–71; Asst Prof., Assoc. Prof., then Prof. of Philosophy, Syracuse Univ. 1971–95; John Cardinal O'Hara Prof. of Philosophy, Univ. of Notre Dame, South Bend, Ind. 1995–; Visiting Prof., Univ. of Ariz. 1981, Rutgers Univ. 1987; research grants from Nat. Endowment for the Humanities 1983–84, 1990–91; delivered Maurice Lectures, Kings Coll., London 1999, Wilde Lectures, Oxford 2000, Stewart Lectures, Princeton 2002, Gifford Lectures, St Andrews 2003; Pres. Soc. of Christian Philosophers 2010–13; currently Pres. Central Div., American Philosophical Asscn; mem. American Acad. of Arts and Sciences 2005–; Dr hc (Univ. of St Andrews, Scotland) 2011. *Publications include:* An Essay on Free Will 1983, Material Beings 1990, Metaphysics 1993, God, Knowledge and Mystery (essays) 1995, The Possibility of Resurrection and Other Essays in Christian Apologetics 1997, Ontology, Identity and Modality: Essays in Metaphysics 2001, The Problem of Evil 2006, Existence: Essays in Ontology 2014. *Address:* Department of Philosophy, 100 Malloy Hall, University of Notre Dame, Notre Dame, IN 46556-4619, USA (office). *Telephone:* (574) 631-5910 (office). *Fax:* (219) 631-0588 (office). *E-mail:* vaninwagen.1@nd.edu (office). *Website:* www.nd.edu/~ndphilo (office).

VAN KRALINGEN, Bridget; American business executive; *Senior Vice-President, IBM Global Business Services, International Business Machines (IBM) Corporation;* Man. Partner, Deloitte Consulting 1989–2004, led GBS Financial Services Sector, later served in Financial Services practice in USA and Strategy and Organizational Devt practice in SA; Gen. Man., Global Business Services, Northeast Europe, Middle East and Africa, London, UK, International Business Machines (IBM) Corpn 2007–10, Gen. Man. IBM North America 2010–12, Sr Vice-Pres., IBM Global Business Services 2012–; mem. Bd of Advisors, Catalyst, Inc.; mem. Bd of Dirs Royal Bank of Canada 2011–. *Address:* International Business Machines Corporation, 1 New Orchard Road, Armonk, NY 10504-1722, USA (office). *Telephone:* (914) 499-1900 (office). *Fax:* (914) 765-7382 (office). *E-mail:* info@ibm.com (office). *Website:* www.ibm.com (office).

VAN LEDE, Cornelis Josephus Antonius (Kees), MBA; Dutch business executive; b. 1942; ed Univ. of Leiden, Institut Européen d'Admin des Affaires (INSEAD), Fontainebleau, France; joined Akzo Nobel NV as mem. Bd of Man. 1991–2003, Vice-Chair. Bd of Man. 1992–94, Chair. and CEO 1994–2003, mem. Supervisory Bd 2003–09; mem. Supervisory Bd Heineken NV 2002–13, Chair. 2002–13; Chair. Supervisory Bd Dutch Cen. Bank; Chair. Supervisory Bd, Royal Imtech NV 2013–15; Chair. INSEAD (also Unit Bd mem. and mem. Supervisory Bd); Exec. Officer, mem. Supervisory Bd and mem. Remuneration Cttee Koninklijke Philips Electronics NV 2003–; mem. Bd of Dirs Air France KLM 2004–, (its subsidiary) Air France 2004–16, Sara Lee Corpn 2002–, Air Liquide Tunisie 2003–, L'Air Liquide SA (also mem. Supervisory Bd) 2005–; Dir (non-exec.) Reed Elsevier plc 2003–07, Reed Elsevier Group plc 2003–07, Reed Elsevier NV 2001– (also mem. Supervisory Bd 2003–); mem. Supervisory Bd Philips Lighting Co. 2003–, Stork NV 2007–, Philips Electronics N America Corpn 2003–, Philips Electronics Singapore Pte Ltd 2003–, Sara Lee (USA)/DE NV, Scania AB (Sweden); fmr mem. Bd of Man. Dirs HBG; served as Proposed mem. Supervisory Bd KLM Royal Dutch Airlines; mem. European Advisory Council JPMorgan Chase & Co. 2005–, Int. Council of JPMorgan Chase; Chair. Confed. of Netherlands Industry and Employers (VNO) 1984–91; Vice-Pres. Union of Industrial and Employers' Confeds of Europe (UNICE) 1991–94; mem. European Round Table of Industrialists, Bd of Trustees of The Conference Bd, Netherlands Pensions and Insurance Supervisory Authority. *Address:* c/o Royal Imtech NV, Quinterium Offices I, Kampenringweg 45A, 2803 PE Gouda, The Netherlands (office).

VAN LOAN, Peter, MA, MSc, JD; Canadian lawyer and politician; b. 18 April 1963, Niagara Falls; ed Univ. of Toronto, Osgoode Hall Law School; fmr Pnr and Chair Planning and Devt Law Group, Fraser Milner Casgrain LLP (law firm), Toronto; fmr Adjunct Prof. of Planning, Univ. of Toronto; Pres. Progressive Conservative Party of Ont. then Progressive Conservative Party of Canada –2000 (resgnd); MP (Conservative) for York–Simcoe 2004–, Critic for Human Resources and Skills Devt 2004–06, Parl. Sec. to Minister of Foreign Affairs –Nov. 2006, Pres. of the Queen's Privy Council for Canada, Minister of Intergovernmental Affairs and Minister for Sport Nov. 2006–Jan. 2007, Leader of the Govt in the House of Commons and Minister for Democratic Reform Jan. 2007–08, Minister of Public Safety 2008–10, of Int. Trade 2010–11, Leader of the Govt in the House of Commons 2011–15. *Address:* Parliament of Canada, Ottawa, ON K1A 0A9, Canada (office). *E-mail:* vanloan.p@parl.gc.ca (office). *Website:* www.parl.gc.ca (office); www.petervanloan.com.

VAN MIDDELKOOP, Eimert; Dutch politician; b. 14 Feb. 1949, Berkel en Rodenrijs; m.; three s. one d.; ed Netherlands School of Econs, Rotterdam; Lecturer, Reformed School of Social Work, Zwolle 1971–72; Asst, Calvinist Political Union (GPV) 1973–89; mem. House of Reps (GPV) 1989–2001, for Christian Union 2001–02; mem. Senate 2003–07; Minister of Defence 2007–10, also Acting Minister of Housing, Communities and Integration 2010; fmr mem. Supervisory Cttee, Social and Cultural Planning Office; fmr Chair. Policy Review Cttee European Defence; fmr Sec. Centre for Parl. History, Nijmegen; fmr mem. Advisory Board, East-West Parl. Practice Project, Royal Netherlands Air Force, Netherlands Inst. of Int. Relations, Inst. for Multiparty Democracy.

VAN MONTAGU, Baron; Marc Charles Ernest, MSc, PhD; Belgian plant geneticist; *Professor Emeritus, Ghent University;* b. 10 Nov. 1933, Ghent; s. of Jean Van Montagu and Irene Van Beveren; m. Nora Podgaetchi 1957; ed Ghent Univ.; Dir Bureau d'Étude, Tech. School for the Nuclear Industry 1956–60; Prof. (part-time), Free Univ. of Brussels –1989; Full Prof. of Molecular Genetics, Ghent Univ. –1999, Founder and Chair. Inst. for Plant Biotechnology Outreach, Prof. Emer. 1999–; Dir Dept of Genetics, Flanders Inst. for Biotechnology –1999; Scientific Dir and mem. Bd of Dirs Plant Genetic Systems NV 1982–96; Founder and mem. Bd of Dirs CropDesign (Belgium) 1998–2004; Chair. Scientific Advisory Cttee, Danforth Center, St Louis, Mo., USA 1999–; Scientific Advisor, Tibotech (Belgium), Extracta (Brazil); mem. Science Bd of Alellyx, São Paulo, Brazil 2003–09; Biotechnology Advisor, Int. Centre for Agric. Research in Dry and Arid Areas, Aleppo, Syria; Scientific Advisor, CIB-CSIC (Centro de Investigaciones Biologicas), Madrid, Spain; mem. Bd of Govs and Scientific Advisory Bd, Weizmann Inst. of Science, Rehovot, Israel; mem. Int. Advisory Bd, King Abdulaziz Univ., Jeddah, Saudi Arabia; mem. Bd of Dirs Avesthagen, Bangalore, India 1999–2010; Chair. Cobiotech/ACOGEB, ICSU Bodies for Biotech Research 1996–2003; mem. Bd of Trustees, IITA, Ibadan, Nigeria 1991–96; Advisor to Flemish Inst. for Biotechnology, Ghent; mem. Council of Scientific Advisors, Int. Centre for Genetic Eng and Biotechnology, Trieste, Italy; Pres. European Fed. of Biotechnology (Central Office), Barcelona, Spain, Black Sea Biotechnology Asscn, Public Research and Regulation Initiative, Delft, the Netherlands and Brussels, Belgium; Belgian Rep. in the Biosciences Steering Panel of European Academies Scientific Advisory Council, Leopoldina Acad., Halle, Germany; mem. Belgian Royal Acad. of Sciences 1987, Academia Europea 1989, Agricultural Acad. of Russia 1991, Acad. of Eng of Sweden 1992, Agricultural Acad. of France 1992, Royal Acad. of Overseas Sciences (Belgium) 1997, Italian Acad. of Sciences dei XL 1998, American Acad. of Microbiology 1999, TWAS, The World Acad. of Sciences 2001; Foreign Assoc. NAS 1986; title of Baron granted by King Baudoin I 1990; Francqui Chair, Faculty of Medicine, Catholic Univ. of Louvain 1971–72, Faculty of Medicine, Free Univ. of Brussels 1986–87, Faculty of Sciences, Catholic Univ. of Louvain 1994–95; Hon. DPhil (Helsinki) 1990; Dr hc (Helsinki) 1990, (Compiègne, France) 1995, (Rio de Janeiro) 1997, (Liège) 1997, (Free Univ. of Brussels) 1997, (Havana) 1999, (Sofia) 2004; Rank Prize for Nutrition (UK) 1987, IBM-Europe Prize (France) 1988, Charles Leopold Mayer Prize, Acad. of Sciences, Paris 1990, Dr A. De Leeuw-Damry-Bourlart Prize 1990, Japan Prize 1998, Theodor Bücher Medal, Fed. of European Biochemical Socs 1999, ranked as the most cited scientist in the field of Plant and Animal Science until 2004, Genome Valley Excellence Award, BioAsia (India) 2009, World Food Prize (co-recipient) 2013. *Achievements:* several pioneering contribs on plant gene discovery and regulation, herbicides, major contribs in the study of plant molecular mechanisms and genes involved in growth, development and flowering. *Publications:* more than 250 book chapters and reviewed conf. proceedings, over 600 papers in peer-reviewed journals, 250 other journal articles. *Leisure interest:* travel. *Address:* VIB/IPBO/Ghent University Institute of Plant Biotechnology Outreach (IPBO), IIC/UGent Technologiepark 3, 9052 Zwijnaarde, Belgium (office). *Telephone:* (9) 264-87-27 (office); (2) 511-25-57 (home). *Fax:* (9) 264-87-95 (office). *E-mail:* marc.vanmontagu@vib-ugent.be (office); mamon@psb.ugent.be (office). *Website:* www.ipbo.vib-ugent.be (office).

VAN OVERTVELDT, Johan, MA, MBA, PhD; Belgian editor, economist, academic, business executive and politician; b. 24 Aug. 1955, Mortsel; ed Univs of Antwerp and Leuven; journalist, Trends magazine 1978–82, Ed. 1992–99, Chief Economist 1999–2004, Chief Ed. 2010–13; Chief Ed. Knack 2011–12; Credit Officer, Bank Brussels Lambert 1982–87; Gen. Man., Shoekonfex 1987–91; adviser, BTR 1991–92; consultant, VCR Group 1993–2008; Dir, VKW Metena 2004–07, Gen. Man. VKW 2007–10; Prof. of Econs, Hasselt Univ. 2012–; Minister of Finance 2014–18; mem. Nieuw-Vlaamse Alliantie (N-VA—New Flemish Alliance) 2013–, European Parl. 2014. *Publications:* De Euroscheppers. Macht en Manipulatie achter de Euro 2003, The Chicago School. How the University of Chicago Assembled the Thinkers Who Revolutionized Economics and Business 2007, Bernanke's Test. Bert Bernanke, Alan Greenspan, and the Drama of the Central Banker 2009, Het Einde van de Euro 2011, Red de Vrije Markt, De Terugkeer van Milton Friedman 2012. *Address:* c/o Federal Public Service of Finance, 33 Boulevard du Roi Albert II, BP 70, 1030 Brussels, Belgium (office).

VAN PEEBLES, Mario, BEcons; American actor and film director; b. 15 Jan. 1957, Mexico City, Mexico; s. of Melvin Van Peebles and Maria Marx; m. Chitra Sukhu Van Peebles; three s. two d.; ed Columbia Univ.; film debut aged 11; worked as budget analyst in New York Mayor's office; studied acting and script interpretation with Stella Adler. *Theatre:* Champion, Jungle Fever, Midnight, Friday The 13th, Deadwood Dick, Bodybags (also co-dir). *Films include:* Sweet Sweetback's Baadasssss Song 1971, Exterminator 2 1984, Cotton Club 1984, Rappin 1985, Delivery Boys 1985, South Bronx Heroes 1985, 3:15 1986, Last Resort 1986, Heartbreak Ridge 1986, Hotshot 1987, Jaws: The Revenge 1987, Identity Crisis 1989, New Jack City (also dir) 1991, Posse (also dir) 1993, Letter to Dad 1994, Gunmen (also dir) 1994, Highlander III: The Sorcerer 1994, Panther (also dir, producer) 1995, Gang in Blue 1996, Solo 1996, Los Locos (also dir and screenplay) 1997, Stag 1997, Love Kills (also dir, producer) 1998, Crazy Six 1998, Judgment Day 1999, Raw Nerve 1999, Blowback 2000, Guardian 2000, Ali 2001, The Hebrew Hammer 2003, How to Get the Man's Foot Outta Your Ass 2003 (also dir, producer and screenplay), Gang of Roses 2003, Hard Luck 2006 (also dir), Confessionsofa Ex-Doofus-Itchy Footed Mutha 2008, A Letter to Dad 2009, Tied to a Chair 2009, Multiple Sarcasms 2010, All Things Fall Apart 2011, We the Party 2012, Red Sky 2014, Mantervention 2014. *Television includes:* Children of the Night 1985, D.C. Cops 1986, LA Law 1986, The Facts of Life Down Under 1987, The Child Saver 1988, Blue Bayou 1990, Malcolm Takes a Shot 1990, A Triumph of the Heart: The Ricky Bell Story 1991, Stompin' at the Savoy 1992, In the Line of Duty: Street War 1992, Full Eclipse 1993, Mama Flora's Family 1998, Killers in the House 1998, Sally Hemings: An American Scandal 2000, Rude Awakening (series) 2000–01, 10,000 Black Men Named George 2002, The Street Lawyer 2003, 44 Minutes: The North Hollywood Shoot-Out 2003, Crown Heights 2004, Sharpshooter 2007, All My Children (series) 2008, Damages (series) 2009, Mario's Green House (series) 2009, Way Black When 2010, Hellcats (series) 2011, The Game (series) 2011, Drumline: A New Beat (film) 2014, For Justice (film) 2015. *Address:* c/o Steven Small, United Talent Agency, 9336 Civic Center Drive, Beverly Hills, CA 90212, USA (office).

VAN ROMPUY, Herman, BA, MA; Belgian politician and fmr European Union official; b. 31 Oct. 1947, Etterbeek, Brussels; s. of Prof. Vic Van Rompuy and Germaine Geens; m. Geertrui Windels; two s. two d.; ed Sint-Jan Berchmans Coll., Brussels, Catholic Univ. of Leuven; attaché study service, Nat. Bank of Belgium 1972–75; Nat. Vice-Pres. CVP (Christian Democrat Party, now CD&V—Christen-Democratisch en Vlaams) Youth 1973–75, mem. Nat. CVP 1978, Nat. Pres. CVP 1988–93; adviser to Cabinet of Prime Minister Leo Tindemans 1975–78, to Minister of Finance 1978–80; Lecturer, Handelshogeschool Antwerpen 1980–87, Vlaamse Economische Hogeschool Brussel (VLEKHO) 1982–; Dir Centre for Political, Econ. and Social Studies 1980–88; Senator 1988–95; Sec. of State for Finance and Small and Medium-Sized Enterprises 1988–93; Deputy Prime Minister and Minister of Budget 1993–99; mem. Chamber of Reps 1995–2009, Pres. 2007–08; Minister of State 2004; Prime Minister of Belgium 2008–09; Pres. European Council 2009–14; Guest Lecturer Catholic Univ. of Leuven 2014; several decorations including Grand Officier, Légion d'honneur (France), Order of the Rising Sun, 1st class (Japan), Knight, Order of the Dannebrog (Denmark), Grand Ribbon, Order of Leopold 2009, Knight Grand Cross, Order of Orange-Nassau (Netherlands) 2014; Collier du Mérite européen, European Merit Foundation (Luxembourg) 2010, Hon. Citizen of De Haan 2012, of Olen 2013, Int. Charlemagne Prize 2014, Gold Medal of the Jean Monnet Foundation for Europe 2014. *Publications:* De kentering der tijden 1979, Hopen na 1984, Het christendom. Een moderne gedachte 1990, Vernieuwing in hoofd en hart. Een tegendraadse visie 1998, De binnenkant op een kier. Avonden zonder politiek 2000, Dagboek van een vijftiger 2004, Op zoek naar wijsheid 2007, Haiku 2010, In de wereld van Herman Van Rompuy (with Kathleen Cools) 2010, Europa in de storm 2014.

VAN ROOY, Yvonne Catharina Maria Theresia; Dutch politician and fmr university administrator; *President, Nederlandse Vereniging van Ziekenhuizen (NVZ) (Netherlands Organisation of Hospitals);* b. 4 June 1951, Eindhoven; ed Jeanne d'Arc Lyceum, Maastricht, Utrecht Univ.; trainee at EC, Brussels 1977; staff mem. Dutch Christian Employers' Union 1978–84; mem. European Parl. (Christian Democrats) 1984–86, 1989–90, 1994–97; Minister for Foreign Trade 1986–89, 1990–94; Pres. Exec. Bd Catholic University Brabant (renamed Tilburg Univ. 2002) 1997–2004; Pres. Exec. Bd Utrecht Univ. 2004–13; currently Pres. Nederlandse Vereniging van Ziekenhuizen (NVZ) (Netherlands Organisation of Hospitals); Chair. Bd of Foundation for Promotion of Exports; Crown mem. Social and Econ. Council of the Netherlands; mem. Advisory Bd Deloitte, Selection Cttee for the Judiciary; mem. Supervisory Bd Bank Nederlandse Gemeenten; mem. Bd of Dirs Radboud Foundation; mem. Royal Concertgebouw Orchestra; Kt, Order of the Netherlands Lion, Commdr, Order of Orange-Nassau. *Address:* Nederlandse Vereniging van Ziekenhuizen (NVZ), Oudlaan 4, 3515 GA Utrecht, Netherlands (office). *E-mail:* redactie@nvz-ziekenhuizen.nl (office). *Website:* www.nvz-ziekenhuizen.nl (office).

VAN ROSSUM, Anton, MBA; Belgian business executive; b. 1945; m.; three c.; ed Erasmus Univ. Rotterdam; various consultancy positions in banking and insurance sectors; with McKinsey & Co. 1972–2000, co-f. McKinsey & Co. Brussels Office; CEO Fortis 2000–04; mem. Supervisory Bd, Royal Vopak NV, Rotterdam 2007–17, Chair. 2008–17; Chair. Supervisory Bd Erasmus Univ. Rotterdam 2005–14; Chair. Bd of Trustees, Netherlands Econ. Inst. 2006–16; Chair. of Bd Presidents Inst. 2016–17; Int. Pres. European League for Econ. Co-operation; mem. Bd of Dirs Francqui Foundation 2004–, Credit Suisse Group AG 2005–14, Solvay SA, Brussels 2007–15, Rodamco Europe NV 2007–, Munich Re 2008–16; mem. Bd of Trustees, Conference Bd, Inc. 2005–13, Supervisory Bd Münchener Rückversicherungs-Gesellschaft 2009–16; mem. Int. Advisory Council, American EC Asscn; mem. Consultative Council, Solvay Business School, Brussels. *Address:* c/o Royal Vopak NV, PO Box 863, 3000 AW Rotterdam, Netherlands.

VAN SANT, Gus, Jr, BA; American film director and screenwriter; b. 24 July 1952, Louisville, Ky; ed Rhode Island School of Design; fmr production asst to Ken Shapiro; Nat. Soc. of Film Critics Awards for Best Dir and Screenplay 1990, New York Film Critics and LA Film Critics Award for Best Screenplay 1989, PEN Literary Award for Best Screenplay Adaptation (jtly) 1989; American Civil Liberties Union (ACLU) of Ore. Freedom of Expression Award 1992, Visionary Award, Stockholm Film Festival 2010. *Albums:* Gus Van Sant 1997, 18 Songs About Golf 1997. *Films include:* Mala Noche (dir, writer), Drugstore Cowboy 1989 (dir, writer, with Daniel Yost), My Own Private Idaho (dir, writer) 1991, Even Cowgirls Get the Blues (dir, writer) 1993, To Die For (dir) 1995, Kids (producer) 1995, Ballad of the Skeletons (dir) 1996, Good Will Hunting (dir) 1997, Psycho (dir) 1998, Finding Forrester 2000, Gerry 2002, Elephant (documentary dir, Palme d'Or and Best Dir, Cannes Film Festival) 2003, Last Days 2005, Paris, je t'aime (segment) 2006, Paranoid Park (60th Anniversary Award, Cannes Film Festival 2007) 2007, Milk 2008, Promised Land 2012. *Publications:* 108 Portraits (collection of photgraphs) 1995, Pink 1997. *Address:* William Morris Endeavor Entertainment, 9601 Wilshire Blvd, Beverly Hills, CA 90210, USA (office). *Website:* www.wmeentertainment.com (office).

VAN SCHAIK, Gerard, MA, FCIS; Dutch business executive (retd); b. 29 March 1930, Haarlem; s. of Gerard Van Schaik and Maria Mulder; m. Moyra Colijn 1963 (deceased); two s. one d.; ed Free Univ. of Amsterdam, IMEDE, Switzerland; officer Royal Netherlands Air Force 1956–58; joined Heineken's Bierbrouwerij Maatschappij N.V. 1959, mem. Exec. Bd Heineken NV 1974, Deputy Chair. 1983, Chair. 1989–93; Pres. Supervisory Bd Aegon NV 1993–2000; Dir of numerous cos; Vice Chair. CEIBS China European Business School, Shanghai; Hon. Pres. European Foundation of Man. Devt, Brussels; Hon. Fellow, London Business School; Kt, Order of the Dutch Lion; Dr hc (State Acad. for Man., Moscow) 1997. *Leisure interests:* golf, music. *Address:* Duinvoetlaan 7, 2243 GK Wassenaar, The Netherlands. *Telephone:* (70) 5110167; (31) 654387724 (mobile). *Fax:* (70) 5179008. *E-mail:* gvschaik@ziggo.nl (home).

VAN SCHALKWYK, Marthinus Christoffel Johannes, MA; South African politician; b. 10 Nov. 1959, Pietersburg; m. Suzette van Schalkwyk; one s. one d.; ed Pietersburg High School, Rand Afrikaans Univ.; fmr Nat. Pres. Afrikaanse Studentbond, Chair. Youth for S Africa, Fed. Youth Leader, Nat. Party; mil. service 1978–79; Lecturer in Political Science, Rand Afrikaans Univ., Univ. of Stellenbosch; MP for Randburg 1990–94; mem. Nat. Ass. 1994–, mem. Parl. Portfolio Cttee on Communications, Nat. Party Rep. at Int. Democratic Union and African Dialogue Group; apptd Exec. Dir Nat. Party 1997, Leader New Nat. Party 1997–2005 (party disbanded); Premier of the Western Cape 2002–04; Minister of Environmental Affairs and Tourism 2004–09, of Tourism 2009–14; mem. African Nat. Congress (ANC) 2005–; Pres. African Ministerial Conf. on the Environment 2008–; Abe Bailey Bursary to GB and Europe, Award for Academic Achievement, Transvaal Lawyers' Asscn. *Address:* Private Bag X9154, Cape Town 8000 (office); Private Bag X447, Pretoria 0001, South Africa (office). *Telephone:* (21) 4657240 (Cape Town) (office); (12) 3103611 (Pretoria) (office). *Fax:* (21) 4653216 (Cape Town) (office); (12) 3220082 (Pretoria) (office).

VAN SLINGELANDT, Diederik (Rik) Johannes Maximilianus Govert Baron, BBA; Dutch banking executive (retd); b. 17 July 1946, Delft; m.; two c.; ed Dutch High School A, Rotterdam, Univ. of Groningen; staff mem. Nationale Investeringsbank NV 1972–80; Head of Finance Dept, Rijn Schelde Verolme 1980–82; Dir of Finance, Treasury, Admin and Information Tech., Verolme Estaleiros Reunidos do Brasil ste, Rio de Janeiro 1982–85; Financial Dir Rodamco Groep 1985–89, also mem. Investment Cttee; Dir of Int. Operations, Rabobank Nederland 1989–96, mem. Bd Dirs 1996–2006, Chair. Rabobank Int. 1996–2006, Acting CEO of Exec. Bd Rabobank Group 2004, fmr Chair. Supervisory Bd Rabo Australia Ltd, Rabobank Int. Advisory Services (RIAS) BV, Interpolis NV, fmr Chair. Bd Dirs Rabobank Pension Fund; Chair. Exec. Cttee Centrale Bank Bedrijf 1989–96, Vice-Chair. Supervisory Bd Bank Sarasin & Cie; mem. Bd of Dirs Stichting Neyenburgh 2009–15; mem. Supervisory Bd ABN AMRO Group NV 2010–, Vice-Chair. 2011–14, Chair. 2014–16; mem. Supervisory Bd KAS Bank NV 2006–10, Vice-Chair. then Chair. 2006–10 (retd); mem. Supervisory Bd IHC Merwede Holland B.V., Redevco Europe Services B.V 2005–11, Robeco Groep NV, SNP Groep NV, Save the Children Nederland 2006–14; mem. Advisory Cttee Issuing Insts (Euronext), Unico Steering Cttee, Bd Dirs Ubbo Emmius Fund, Univ. of Groningen; Officer, Order of Orange-Nassau 2006.

VAN SWAAIJ, Willibrordus Petrus Maria, PhD; Dutch chemical engineer and academic; *Professor, University of Twente;* b. 18 Jan. 1942, Nijmegen; s. of Christian van Swaaij and C. Bosman; m. J. J. T. van den Berk 1966; one s. four d.; ed Tech. Univ. of Eindhoven, Univ. of Nancy, France; joined Shell Research 1965, worked in lab. Shell Research BV (KSLA), Amsterdam 1966–72, Section Chief, Gasification 1971–72; Prof. of Chemical Eng Science, Twente Univ. 1972–, mem. staff, Thermo-Chemical Conversion of Biomass Group 1999–; Scientific Dir Dutch Nat. Postgraduate School on Process Tech. 1992–2002; consultant to DSM, AKZO, Unilever, Netherlands Govt, EEC; mem. Royal Netherlands Acad. of Sciences 1986; Chair. Advisory Bd Green Energy Initiative 2012–; Hon. mem. Nat. Soc. of Dutch Engineers 2007; Kt Order of the Lion (Netherlands) 1997; Dr hc (Inst. Nat. Polytechnique de Lorraine, France) 1996; Australian European Fellowship Award 1984, Dow Energy Prize 1985, Grand Prix du Génie des Procédés, Inst. de France 1996, Golden Tesla Medal 1999, Golden Hoogewerff Medal for Lifetime Achievement 2000, Royal Dutch Shell Prize 2004. *Publications:* Chemical Reactor Design and Operation (with Westerterp and Beenackers); about 340 scientific papers, contribs to books, etc. *Leisure interests:* sailing, surfing, photography, gardening, history. *Address:* University of Twente, TNW/SPT Meander 224, PO 217, 7500 AE Enschede (office); Sportlaan 60, 7581 BZ Losser, Netherlands (home). *Telephone:* (53) 4892880 (office); (53) 5382677 (home). *Fax:* (53) 4894738 (office); (53) 5384368 (home). *E-mail:* w.p.m.vanswaaij@utwente.nl (office).

VAN VLISSINGEN, Annemiek M. Fentener, MSc, AM, MBA; Dutch business executive; *Chairman of the Supervisory Board, SHV Holdings NV;* b. 14 April 1961; d. of Frits Fentener; ed Univ. of Groningen and postgraduate studies in USA; Man. of Strategy and Business Devt, SHV Holdings NV, mem. Supervisory Bd 2003–, currently Chair.; Deputy Chair. Supervisory Bd, Draka Holding NV 2001–06; mem. Supervisory Bd, Univ. Medical Centre, Utrecht, Heineken International BV, Heineken NV 2006–18, Heineken Holding NV 2018–, Flint Holding NV, De Nederlandsche Bank; mem. NPM Capital NV; mem. Bd of Dirs Lhoist SA, Exor NV; Commr for Heineken, Draka Holding NV, NV Buco. *Address:* SHV Holdings NV, Rijnkade 1, 3511 LC Utrecht, Netherlands (office). *Telephone:* (30) 233-88-33 (office). *Fax:* (30) 233-83-04 (office). *E-mail:* info@shv.nl (office). *Website:* www.shv.nl (office).

VAN WACHEM, Lodewijk Christiaan, KBE; Dutch business executive and mechanical engineer; *General Manager, Asset Development and Improvement Limited (ADIL);* b. 31 July 1931, Pangkalan Brandan, now Indonesia; m. Elisabeth G. Cristofoli 1958; two s. one d.; ed Delft Univ. of Technology; joined Bataafsche Petroleum Maatschappij, The Hague 1953; Mechanical Engineer, Cía Shell de Venezuela 1954–63; Chief Engineer, Shell-BP Petroleum Devt Co. of Nigeria 1963–66, Eng Man. 1966–67, Chair. and Man. Dir 1972–76; Head Tech. Admin. Brunei Shell Petroleum Co. Ltd 1967–69, Tech. Dir 1969–71; Head of Production Div. Shell Int. Petroleum Maatschappij, The Hague 1971–72, Co-ordinator Exploration and Production 1976–79; Man. Dir Royal Dutch Petroleum Co. 1976–82, Pres. 1982–92; mem. Presidium of Bd of Dirs, Shell Petroleum NV 1976–92; Man. Dir Shell Petroleum Co. Ltd 1976–92, Chair. Jt Cttee of Man. Dirs of the Royal Dutch/Shell Group 1985–92, Chair. Supervisory Bd Royal Dutch Petroleum Co. 1992–2002; mem. Bd of Dirs Crédit Suisse Holding 1992–96, Zurich Insurance Group (now Zurich Financial Services) 1993–2005 (Vice-Chair. 2001–02, Chair. 2002–05); mem. Supervisory Bd Akzo-Nobel NV 1992–2002, Royal Philips Electronics NV 1993 (Chair. 1999), BMW (Munich) 1994–2002, Bayer AG 1997–2002, RAND Europe (mem. Exec. Bd 2005–); Chair. Global Crossing 2003–07; Dir (non-exec.) IBM Corpn 1992–2002, ATCO Ltd 1993–2009, AAB Brown Boveri Ltd 1996–99; Gen. Man. Asset Devt and Improvement Ltd (ADIL) 2017–; Hon. Citizen of Singapore 2004; Hon. Commdr and KBE 1989, Kt Order of Netherlands Lion 1981, Commdr, Order of Oranje Nassau 1990, Public Service Star, Singapore 1998. *Address:* Asset Development and Improvement Limited, Innovation House, Prime Four Business Park, Kingswells Causeway,

Kingswells, Aberdeen, AB15 8PU, UK (office). *Telephone:* (12) 2465-7146 (office). *E-mail:* lwachem@slb.com (office). *Website:* www.assetdev.com (office).

VAN WALSUM, (Arnold) Peter, LLB; Dutch diplomatist (retd); b. 25 June 1934, Rotterdam; m.; four c.; ed Univ. of Utrecht; served in Dutch mil. 1960–62; with Civil Emergency Planning Section, Ministry of Gen. Affairs 1962–63; First Sec., Perm. Mission to UN, New York 1970–74, First Sec., Embassy in New Delhi 1974–79, Counsellor, Embassy in London 1975–79, Counsellor, Perm. Mission to EC, Brussels 1979–81, Head of Western Hemisphere Dept, Ministry of Foreign Affairs 1981–85, Amb. to Thailand 1985–89, Dir-Gen. Political Affairs, Ministry of Foreign Affairs 1989–93, Amb. to Germany 1993–98, Perm. Rep. to UN, New York 1998–2001, Chair. Iran Sanctions Cttee 1999–2000; UN Sec.-Gen.'s Personal Envoy for Western Sahara 2005–08. *Address:* c/o Ministry of Foreign Affairs, Bezuidenhoutseweg 67, POB 20061, 2500 EB The Hague, Netherlands.

VAN WIJNGAARDEN, Leendert, PhD; Dutch scientist and academic; *Professor Emeritus of Fluid Mechanics, University of Twente;* b. 16 March 1932, Delft; s. of Cornelis M. van Wijngaarden and Jeanne Severijn; m. Willy F. de Goede 1962; two s.; ed Gymnasium B, Delft and Technological Univ. of Delft; Netherlands Ship Model Basin, Wageningen 1962–66, latterly Head of Hydrodynamics Dept; Prof. of Fluid Mechanics, Twente Univ. 1966–97, Prof. Emer. 1997–; mem. of Bureau and Treasurer Int. Union of Theoretical and Applied Mechanics 1984–88, Pres. 1992–96, Vice-Pres. 1996–2000; mem. Royal Netherlands Acad. of Arts and Sciences 1988–, Hollandsche Maatschappij der Wetenschappen, Academia Europaea; Mmem.-at-Large, Gen. Ass. of Int. Union of Theoretical and Applied Mechanics; Hon. mem. European Mechanics Soc.; Kt in the Order of the Dutch Lion 1995. *Publications:* about 70 publs in professional journals. *Leisure interests:* tennis, chess, literature, music. *Address:* University of Twente, Faculty of Science and Technology, Building Meander 264, PO Box 217, 7500 AE Enschede (office); Von Weberlaan 7, 7522 KB Enschede, Netherlands (home). *Telephone:* (53) 4893086 (office); (53) 352078 (home). *Fax:* (53) 44898068 (office). *E-mail:* l.vanwijngaarden@utwente.nl (office). *Website:* www.tnw.utwente.nl/pof (office).

VAN WYK, Andreas Herculas, BA, BPhil, LLB, LLD; South African professor of law and university rector (retd); b. 17 Sept. 1941, Pretoria; s. of Andries Hercules du Preez van Wyk and Hendrina Louise van Wyk (née Kruger); m. Magdalena Krüger 1967; two d.; ed Helpmekaar Boys' High School, Johannesburg, Univ. of Stellenbosch, Germany, Univ. of Leiden, Netherlands; admitted as advocate of Supreme Court, South Africa 1965; Lecturer, then Prof., then Dean, Faculty of Law, Univ. of Stellenbosch 1966–84, Prof. Faculty of Law 1987–91, Vice-Rector (Operations) 1991–93, Rector and Vice-Chancellor 1993–2000; Dir-Gen. Nat. Dept of Constitutional Devt and Planning 1984–87; Chair. South African Univs Vice-Chancellors Asscn 2001; mem. Bd of Dirs Volkskas Industrial Bank 1983–84, Boland Bank Ltd 1987–95, Distillers Corpn Ltd 1982–88, 1990–2000, Victoria & Alfred Waterfront Co. 1992–93; Chair. Old Mutual Life Assurance Co. (South Africa) Ltd 2008–09; Guest, USA/SA Leadership Exchange Programme 1978; Alexander von Humboldt Foundation Fellowship 1981; mem. SA Akad. vir wetenskap en kuns; Hon. LLD (Leuven Univ. 1997); William of Orange Medal (Univ. of Leiden) 1995. *Publications:* The Power to Dispose of the Assets of the Universal Matrimonial Community of Property 1976, Die Suid-Afrikaanse Kontraktereg en Handelsreg (co-author) 1992, Family, Property and Succession 1983 and numerous articles in academic journals; has drafted various pieces of legislation.

VAN ZWEDEN, Jaap; Dutch conductor and violinist; *Music Director, Hong Kong Philharmonic Orchestra and New York Philharmonic;* b. 12 Dec. 1960, Amsterdam; ed Amsterdam Conservatory and with Dorothy DeLay at Juilliard, New York; as violinist, Leader Royal Concertgebouw Orchestra 1979–; solo performances under conductors Haitink, Giulini, Solti and Bernstein; Conductor from 1995 including tours with Berlin Symphony Orchestra, Salzburg Mozarteum, Israel Concert Orchestra and Japanese Concert Orchestra; Music Dir Netherlands Symphony Orchestra 1997–2003; Buenos Aires Philharmonic Orchestra in Argentina and on tour to Europe; US debut with St Louis Symphony Orchestra 1997; Prin. Guest Conductor, Brabants Orchestra 1997; season 1999–2000 with Netherlands Symphony Orchestra on tour to USA and debut with London Philharmonic; Prin. Conductor, Residentie Orchestra, The Hague 2000–05, Hon. Guest Conductor 2005–09; Chief Conductor and Artistic Dir, Netherlands Radio Philharmonic Orchestra and Radio Kamer Filharmonie 2005–11, now Hon. Chief Conductor; Music Dir Dallas Symphony Orchestra 2008–18, Conductor Laureate 2018–; Prin. Conductor Royal Flemish Philharmonic Orchestra 2008–12; Chief Conductor Hong Kong Philharmonic Orchestra 2012–; Music Dir-Desig., New York Philharmonic 2017–18, Music Dir 2018–; Guest Conductor, Chicago Symphony, Philadelphia Orchestra, Gothenburg Symphony, WDR Symphony Orchestra Cologne, Orchestre National de France, Munich Philharmonic, Oslo Philharmonic, Cleveland Orchestra, Philadelphia Orchestra, London Philharmonic, Royal Concertgebouw Orchestra, New York Philharmonic, Boston Symphony; has appeared at BBC Proms, Carnegie Hall and Tanglewood and Aspen Festival; First Prize, Dutch Nat. Violin Competition 1977, Musical America's Conductor of the Year 2012. *Recordings include:* Beethoven, Brahms and Bruckner complete symphonies, Shostakovich's Symphony No. 5, Mahler's Symphony No. 5, Stravinsky Ballets, Haydn Symphonies, Tchaikovsky Symphonies Nos 4 and 5. *Address:* c/o IMG Artists, Capital Tower, 91 Waterloo Road, London, SE1 8RT, England (office). *Telephone:* (20) 7957-5800 (office). *Fax:* (20) 7957-5801 (office). *E-mail:* nmathias@imgartists.com (office). *Website:* www.imgartists.com (office).

VANACKERE, Steven, LenD; Belgian politician; b. 4 Feb. 1964, Wevelgem, W Flanders; s. of Leo Vanackere; m.; ed Catholic Univ. of Leuven; started career with Kredietbank SA 1987–88; adviser to Herman Van Rompuy (Chair. Christian Democratic Party) 1990–91; chief aide to Jos Chabert (Minister of Brussels-Capital Region) 1991–93; Dir-Gen. Port of Brussels 1993–95, Deputy Dir-Gen. STIB/MIVB (Brussels Public Transport Co.) 2000–05; mem. Flemish regional parl. 2004–07, Flemish Minister for Welfare, Public Health and Family Affairs 2007–08; mem. House of Reps for Brussels-Halle-Vilvoorde constituency 2010–14; Deputy Prime Minister and Minister for Institutional Reforms 2008–11, also Minister of Foreign Affairs 2009–11, Deputy Prime Minister and Minister for Finance and Sustainable Devt, in charge of Public Affairs 2011–13; Senator 2014–; mem. Christen-Democratisch en Vlaams. *Address:* Christen-Democratisch en Vlaams, Wetstraat

89, 1040 Brussels, Belgium (office). *Telephone:* (2) 238-38-11 (office). *Fax:* (2) 230-43-60. *Website:* www.cdenv.be (office); www.stevenvanackere.be.

VANDENBROUCKE, Frank, DPhil; Belgian politician and academic; b. 21 Oct. 1955, Louvain; ed Catholic Univ. of Louvain, Univs of Cambridge and Oxford, UK; Research Asst, Centrum voor Economische Studiën, Catholic Univ. of Louvain 1978–80; staff mem. SEVI (Research Dept of Socialist Party of Flemish Region) 1982–85; MP 1985–96; Leader Socialist Party 1989–94; Leader Parl. Group of Socialist Party 1995–96; Deputy Prime Minister and Minister of Foreign Affairs 1994–95; Minister of Social Affairs and Pensions July 1999–2003; Minister of Employment and Pensions 2003–04; Vice-Minister-Pres. Flemish Govt and Flemish Minister for Work, Educ. and Training 2004–09; retd from politics 2011; currently Prof., KU Leuven; also currently holds Herman Deleeck Chair, Univ. of Antwerp and Joop den Uyl Chair, Univ. of Amsterdam. *Address:* Herman Deleeck Centre for Social Policy, Faculteit Sociale Wetenschappen, Universiteit Antwerpen, Sint-Jacobstraat 2, 2000 Antwerp, Belgium (office). *Telephone:* (3) 265-53-81 (office). *E-mail:* frank.vandenbroucke@kuleuven.be (office). *Website:* www.centrumvoorsociaalbeleid.be (office).

VANDEPUT, Steven; Belgian politician; *Mayor of Hasselt;* b. 30 March 1967, Hasselt; m. Saskia Vandeput; one s. one d.; ed School of Econs, Limburg; mem. Nieuw-Vlaamse Alliantie (N-VA—New Flemish Alliance), Chair. N-VA Limburg –2010; mem. Chamber of Reps 2010–; Minister of Defence 2014–18; Mayor of Hasselt 2019–. *Address:* Office of the Mayor, Limburgplein 1, 3500 Hasselt (office); Ambachtsschool Str. 27, 3500 Hasselt, Belgium (home). *Telephone:* 475-286529 (mobile). *E-mail:* steven.vandeput@n-va.be. *Website:* www.hasselt.be/nl (office); www.stevenvandeput.be; www.n-va.be/cv/steven-vandeput.

VANDER ZALM, William N.; Canadian (b. Dutch) politician and business executive; *President, Van's International Projects Inc.;* b. (Wilhelmus Theodorus Nicholaas Maria Vander Zalm), 29 May 1934, Noordwykerhout, The Netherlands; s. of Wilhelmus Nicholaas van der Zalm and Agatha C. Warmerdam; m. Lillian B. Mihalick 1956; two s. two d.; ed Phillip Sheffield High School, Abbotsford, BC, Canada; emigrated to Canada 1947, became Canadian citizen; purchased Art Knapp Nurseries Ltd, became Co. Pres. 1956; elected to Surrey Municipal Council as Alderman 1965, as Mayor 1969–75; elected to Prov. Legis. for Social Credit Party, Minister of Human Resources 1975; Minister of Municipal Affairs and Minister responsible for Urban Transit Authority (now BC Transit) 1978; Minister of Educ. and Minister responsible for BC Transit 1982; est. Fantasy Garden World, major tourist attraction in Richmond 1983; Leader BC Social Credit Party 1986–; Premier of BC 1986–91; Pres. Van's International Projects Inc. 1991–, Mitsch Nursery Inc., Oregon, USA 1994–; Leader Reform BC Party 1996–2001; Dir EnvirEau; Leader of 'Fight HST' (first successful tax referendum in Canada) 2009; Hon. LLD (Univ. of N. British Columbia) 2004. *Publications:* Northwest's Gardener's Almanac, Vander Zalm For the People. *Leisure interests:* fishing, swimming. *Address:* 3553 Arthur Drive, Ladner, BC V4K 3N2, Canada. *Telephone:* (604) 946-1774. *Fax:* (604) 946-1981. *E-mail:* billvanderzalm@dccnet.com. *Website:* www.billvanderzalm.com; www.fighthst.com.

VANDERHAEGHE, Guy Clarence, OC, BA, BEd, MA, FRSC; Canadian writer, playwright and academic; *Assistant Professor, Department of English, St Thomas More College, University of Saskatchewan;* b. 5 April 1951, Esterhazy, Sask.; s. of Clarence Earl Vanderhaeghe and Alma Beth Allen; m. Margaret Nagel 1972 (died 2012); ed Univ. of Saskatchewan, Univ. of Regina; St Thomas More Scholar, St Thomas More Coll., Univ. of Saskatchewan 1993–, currently also Asst Prof., Dept of English; Fellow, Pierre Eliott Trudeau Foundation 2007; Saskatchewan Order of Merit 2004; Hon. DLitt (Saskatchewan) 1997; Canadian Authors' Asscn Award for Drama 1996, Saskatchewan Book Award 1996. *Publications include:* Man Descending (short stories) (Gov. Gen. Literary Award for Fiction 1982, Geoffrey Faber Memorial Prize 1987) 1982, The Trouble With Heroes (short stories) 1983, My Present Age (novel) 1984, Homesick (novel) (City of Toronto Book Award 1990) 1989, Things As They Are? (short stories) 1992, The Englishman's Boy (novel) (Gov. Gen. Literary Award for Fiction) 1996, The Last Crossing (novel) 2004, A Good Man (novel) 2011, Daddy Lenin and Other Stories (short stories) (Gov.-Gen.'s Literary Award 2015) 2015; plays: I Had a Job I Liked, Once (Canadian Authors Asscn Award for Drama 1993) 1991, Dancock's Dance 1995. *Address:* The Cooke Agency, 75 Sherbourne Street, Suite 501, Toronto, ON M5A 2P9, Canada (office); Department of English, St Thomas More College, 1437 College Drive, Saskatoon, SK S7N 0W6, Canada (office). *E-mail:* agents@cookeagency.ca (office); gvanderhaeghe@stmcollege.ca (office). *Telephone:* (306) 966-8900 (office). *Fax:* (306) 966-8904 (office). *Website:* stmcollege.ca (office).

VANDEVELDE, Luc; Belgian business executive; *Founder and Chairman, Change Capital Partners;* b. 1951; joined Kraft Gen. Foods Ltd 1971, later apptd CEO Kraft Jacobs Suchard France and Italy –1995, Pres., COO 1995–99, Chair., CEO 1999–2000; participated in merger of Promodès and Carrefour 1999 (apptd Exec. Vice-Chair. new group); Exec. Chair. Marks & Spencer PLC 2000–04, CEO 2000–02; Founder and Chair. Change Capital Pnrs (pvt. equity firm) 2003–; mem. Bd of Dirs Carrefour SA 2004–07, Chair. 2005–07; mem. Bd of Dirs Société Générale 2006–12, Vodafone Group plc 2003–, Sr Ind. Dir 2012–; Chair. of Bd, Majid Al Futtaim Ventures 2013–. *Address:* Change Capital Partners, 2nd Floor, College House, 272 Kings Road, London, SW3 5AW, England (office). *Telephone:* (20) 7808-9114 (office). *Fax:* (20) 7808-9111 (office). *E-mail:* lvandevelde@changecapitalpartners.com (office). *Website:* www.changecapitalpartners.com (office).

VANGELIS; Greek composer, musician (keyboards) and conductor; b. (Evangelos Papathanassiou), 29 March 1943, Volos; ed Acad. of Fine Arts, Athens and private tuition with Aristotelis Coudourof; began performing own compositions aged six; moved to Paris in late 1960s; composed and recorded symphonic poem Faire que ton rêve soit plus long que la nuit; returned to Greece, after period in London 1989; formed band Formynx in Greece 1960s; mem. Aphrodite's Child (with Demis Roussos) 1966–71; composer 1972–, in Paris, France, then established Nemo recording studio, London 1974; partnership with Jon Anderson as Jon & Vangelis 1980–84. *Composition for film:* O Adelfos mou o trohonomos 1963, To prosopo tis medusas 1966, 5000 psemata 1966, Sex Power 1970, scores for French wildlife films 1972, Salut, Jerusalem 1972, L'Apocalypse des animaux 1972, Amore 1973, Le Cantique des créatures: Georges Mathieu ou La fureur d'être 1974, Le Cantique des créatures: Georges Braque ou Le temps différent 1975, Ignacio 1975, Ace Up My Sleeve 1976, La Fête sauvage 1976, Prkosna delta 1980, Die Todesgöttin des Liebescamps 1981, Chariots of Fire (Acad. Award for Best Original Score 1982) 1981, Missing 1982, Le Cantique des créature: Pablo Picasso pintor 1982, Blade Runner 1982, Nankyoku monogatari 1983, Wonders of Life 1983, The Bounty 1984, Sauvage et beau 1984, Nosferatu a Venezia 1988, Le Dîner des bustes 1988, Russicum - I giorni del diavolo 1989, Francesco 1989, Terminator II 1990, La Peste 1992, Bitter Moon 1992, 1492: Conquest of Paradise 1992, De Nuremberg à Nuremberg 1994, Rangeela 1995, Kavafis 1996, I Hope 2001, Alexander 2004, El Greco 2007, Trashed 2012. *Composition for television:* L'Opera sauvage (series) 1977, Cosmos (series, BBC 1) 1980. *Recordings include:* albums: with Aphrodite's Child: Aphrodite's Child 1968, Rain & Tears 1968, End Of The World 1969, It's Five O'Clock 1970, 666 1972; solo: Terra, Dragon 1971, L'Apocalypse des animaux 1972, Earth 1973, Heaven and Hell 1975, Albedo 0.39 1976, The Vangelis Radio Special 1976, Spiral 1977, Beauborg 1978, Hypothesis 1978, China 1979, Odes 1979, See You Later 1980, To The Unknown Man 1981, Soil Festivities 1984, Invisible Connections 1985, Magic Moments 1985, Mask 1985, Direct 1988, The City 1990, Themes 1989, Voices 1995, El Greco 1995, Oceanic 1996, Reprise 1990–1999 2000, Mythodea: Music for the NASA Mission – 2001 Mars Odyssey 2001, Rosetta 2016; as Jon & Vangelis: Short Stories 1980, The Friends of Mr Cairo 1981, Private Collection 1983, Page of Life 1991.

VANHANEN, Matti Taneli, MScS; Finnish politician; b. 4 Nov. 1955, Jyväskylä; s. of Tatu Vanhanen and Anni Tiihonen; two c.; ed Univ. of Helsinki; journalist, Kehäsanomat (local newspaper) 1985–88, Ed.-in-Chief 1988–91; mem. Centre Party 1976–, mem. Bd and Chair. Youth League 1980–83, Vice-Chair. Party 2000–2003, Chair. 2003–10 (resgnd); mem. Espoo City Council 1981–84; mem. Bd Helsinki Metropolitan Area Council YTV 1983–84; mem. Nurmijärvi Municipal Council 1989–; mem. Bd Uusimaa Regional Council 1997–2000; mem. Parl. 1991–2010, 2015–, Vice-Chair. Centre Party Parl. Group 1994–2001, Parl. Environment Cttee 1991–95, Chair. Parl. Grand Cttee 2000–01; Minister of Defence April–June 2003; Prime Minister 2003–10 (resgnd); Rep. of Parl. to European Convention on the Future of the EU 2002–03; Vice-Chair. Housing Foundation for the Young 1981–97, Chair. 1998–2003; Chair. State Youth Council 1987–90; Vice-Chair. Housing Council 1991–2003; Chair. Union for Rural Educ. 1998–2003; Vice-Chair. Pro Medi-Heli Asscn 1995–2003; mem. Supervisory Bd Neste/Fortum 1991–2003, Helsingin Osuuskauppa (Cooperative) 2002–03; unsuccessful cand. in presidential election 2018; Dr hc (Budapest Univ.). *Address:* Eduskunta, Parliament of Finland, 00102 Helsinki, Finland (office). *E-mail:* matti.vanhanen@eduskunta.fi (office). *Website:* www.eduskunta.fi (office).

VANHEVEL, Jan; Belgian banking executive; *Secretary-General, Institut International d'Études Bancaires;* ed Univ. of Leuven; joined Legal Dept, Kredietbank 1971, Head of Litigation Dept 1974–81, Head of Credit Dept 1981–84, Br. Man., Kredietbank, Antwerp 1984–86, Deputy Commercial Man., Antwerp Regional Office 1986–90, Man. Antwerp Corp. Office, Kredietbank 1990–94, Gen. Man., Processing and Automation Directorate 1994–96, Man. Dir and mem. Exec. Cttee Kredietbank 1996–98; Man. Dir KBC Bank and mem. Exec. Cttee KBC Group 1998–2006, CEO Cen. and Eastern Europe and Russia Business Unit, KBC Group 2006–09, CEO KBC Group and CEO Corp. Banking Activities of Merchant Banking Business Unit 2009–12; Pres. Belgian Bankers' Asscn Febelfin 2005–08; Pres. Fédération Belge du Secteur Financier (Belgian Financial Sector Fed.) 2008–11; Sec.-Gen. Institut International d'Études Bancaires 2013–; mem. Bd of Dirs Alpha Bank 2016–, Ensur NV 2016–, Soudal 2016–; mem. Bd of Dirs Alpha Bank 2016–, Ensur NV 2016–, Soudal 2016–.

VANNI D'ARCHIRAFI, Raniero; Italian business executive and fmr diplomatist; b. 7 June 1931; entered diplomatic service 1956; attached to office of Italy's Perm. Rep. to EC, Brussels 1961–66; with Ministry of Foreign Affairs 1966–73; First Counsellor, Madrid 1973; Minister Plenipotentiary 1980; Prin. Pvt. Sec. to Minister of Foreign Affairs 1980; Amb. to Spain 1984–87, 1995–99, to Germany 1987–90; Dir-Gen. for Econ. Affairs 1990, for Political Affairs 1991; mem. Comm. for Institutional Questions, The Internal Market, Financial Services, Enterprise Policy, Small and Medium-sized Enterprises, Trade Services, Crafts and Tourism, EC 1993–95; Pres. RCS Iberica 2002; Dir Telepizza, Finmeccanica; Robert Schuman Medal, Group of the European People's Party 1994.

VANRIET, Jan; Belgian painter and poet; b. 21 Feb. 1948, Antwerp; m. Simone Lenaerts 1971; two s. one d.; ed Royal Acad. of Fine Arts, Antwerp; Dir Antwerp Acad. of Fine Arts, Hoboken 1980–2000; works in several museums in Europe, USA and Asia; Special Prize, Art Festival, Seoul 1990, Prize, Van Acker Foundation 2001. *Achievements include:* works for KCB-Bank, Brussels, Metro, Brussels, Roularta, Brussels, Bourla-Theatre Antwerp, Univ. of Antwerp. *Publications:* poetry: Staat van Beleg 1982, Geen Hond die Brood Lust 1984, Stormwoiud 2009, Many Catalogs, among Café Aurora 2000, De Reiziger is Blind 2001, Transport 2002, Stormlicht 2008, Closing Time 2010, Oud Zeer 2012, Leegstand 2012, Moederland 2016. *Address:* Louizastraat 22, 2000 Antwerp 1, Belgium. *Telephone:* (3) 232-47-76. *E-mail:* jan@janvanriet.com. *Website:* www.janvanriet.com.

VAQUINA, Alberto Clementino António, MD; Mozambican doctor and politician; ed Inst. of Biomedical Sciences at Universidade do Porto and Inst. of Hygiene and Tropical Medicine, Universidade Nova de Lisboa, Portugal, Université Bordeaux II, France; worked as intern and then as doctor in Hosp. Geral de Santo António, Porto; later worked at Hosp. de S. José, Lisbon and Clínica de Socorros Médicos 'The Vigilante', Amadora; studies in Lisbon 1994–95; returned to Mozambique 1996; medical practice in Dist of Monapo, prov. of Nampula; successively Dir of local hosp., then Dist Dir of Health; Dir of Health, prov. of Cabo Delgado 1998–2000; Dir of Health, prov. of Nampula 2001–05; Gov. prov. of Sofala 2005–10, prov. of Tete 2010–12; obtained Diplôme d'études supérieures spécialisées in France for work on health projects in developing countries 2011; Prime Minister of Mozambique 2012–15; mem. FRELIMO (Frente de Libertação de Moçambique). *Address:* c/o Office of the Prime Minister, Praça da Marinha Popular, Maputo, Mozambique.

VARADARAJAN, Srinivasan, BSc, ACA, DISA; Indian accountant and business executive; *Chairman and Managing Director, Bharat Petroleum Corporation Limited;* fmr Man. of Accounts and Admin, Malabar Spinning & Weaving Mills Ltd; Chair. Petronet India Ltd, Petronet CCK Chair.; fmr Gen. Man. Corp. Treasury and Gen. Man. Retail South, Bharat Petroleum Corpn Ltd, Exec. Dir of Finance 2011–13, Chair. and Man. Dir 2013–; mem. Bd of Dirs Bharat Oman Refineries Ltd (jt venture co. promoted by BPCL and Oman Oil Co.), Bharat PetroResources Ltd, Bharat Star Services Pvt. Ltd, Bharat Star Services (Delhi) Pvt. Ltd. *Address:* Bharat Petroleum Corpn Ltd, Bharat Bhavan 1, Mumbai 400 001, India (office). *Telephone:* (22) 2271-3170 (office). *Fax:* (22) 2271-3759 (office). *E-mail:* info@bharatpetroleum.com (office). *Website:* www.bharatpetroleum.com (office).

VARADHAN, Srinivasa S. R., MA, PhD, FRS, FAAS; American (b. Indian) mathematician and academic; *Professor, Department of Mathematics, Courant Institute of Mathematical Sciences, New York University;* b. 2 Jan. 1940, Chennai, India; s. of S. V. Rangaiyengar and S. R. Janaki; m. Vasundara Narayanan; two s.; ed Madras Univ., Indian Statistical Inst.; Visiting Mem., Courant Inst., New York Univ. 1963–66, Asst Prof. 1966–68, Assoc. Prof. 1968–72, Dir 1980–84, 1992–94, Prof. of Math. 1972–; Assoc. Fellow, Third World Acad. of Sciences 1988; mem. NAS; hon. degrees from Univ. of Paris, Indian Statistical Inst. and Chennai Inst. of Math.; Birkhoff Prize 1994, Steele Prize 1996, Abel Prize 2007. *Publications:* Multi-dimensional Diffusion Processes 1979, On Diffusion Problems and Partial Differentiation Equations 1980, Large Deviations and Applications 1984. *Leisure interests:* squash, bridge, travel. *Address:* Courant Institute, New York University, 251 Mercer Street, New York, NY 10012, USA (office). *Telephone:* (212) 998-3334 (office). *Fax:* (212) 995-4121 (home). *E-mail:* varadhan@cims.nyu.edu (office). *Website:* www.math.nyu.edu (office).

VARADKAR, Leo, MD; Irish physician and politician; *Taoiseach (Prime Minister) and Minister of Defence;* b. 18 Jan. 1979, Castleknock, Dublin; s. of Ashol Varadkar and Miriam Varadkar (née Howell); ed Trinity Coll., Dublin; joined Young Fine Gael at age 18; early career as jr doctor, Connolly Hosp., Blanchardstown and St James's Hosp., Dublin; qualified as Gen. Practitioner 2010; mem. Fingal County Council 2003–07; mem. Dáil Éireann (parl.) for Dublin West (Fine Gael) 2007–, Fine Gael Spokesperson for Enterprise, Trade and Employment 2007–10; Minister for Transport, Tourism and Sport 2011–14, for Health 2014–16, Minister for Social Protection 2016–17, Taoiseach (Prime Minister) and Minister of Defence 2017–; mem. Fine Gael, Leader 2017–. *Address:* Department of the Taoiseach, Government Bldgs, Upper Merrion St, Dublin 2, D02 R583, Ireland (office). *Telephone:* (1) 6194000 (office). *Fax:* (1) 6763302 (office). *E-mail:* webmaster@taoiseach.gov.ie (office). *Website:* www.taoiseach.gov.ie (office).

VARDANIAN, Ruben, MA; Russian business executive; b. Armenia; ed Faculty of Econs, Moscow State Univ.; intern, Merrill Lynch, New York 1992; Co-founder Troika Dialog (investment bank) 1991, COO 1992–96, Pres. 1996–2012, CEO 1997–, also Chair. Bd of Dirs Troika Dialog Group 2001–2012, CEO Rosgosstrakh (insurance co. acquired by Troika) 2002–04, Chair. 2004–05, Troika Dialog acquired by Sberbank CIB 2012, Advisor to Pres. of Sberbank of Russia and Man. Dir ZAO Sberbank CIB 2012–; mem. Russian Union of Industrialists and Entrepreneurs, Head Cttee on Corp. Governance, Arbitrator, Corp. Ethics Cttee; Pres. Skolkovo School of Management 2006–11; mem. Bd of Dirs OAO NOVATEK 2005–, AK Bars Bank 2006–, Joule Unlimited 2010–, OAO AvtoVAZ, OAO KAMAZ, Sibur Holding 2011; mem. mem. Nat. Council for Corp. Governance; Trustee Moscow State Univ.; Businessman of the Year, US Chamber of Commerce 1999, Russian National Entrepreneur of the Year 2004. *Website:* www.sberbank-cib.ru.

VAREBERG, Terje, MSc; Norwegian business executive; b. 15 Oct. 1948; m.; two d.; ed Norwegian School of Econs and Business Admin (NHH); worked for Ministry of Trade and Industry and Ministry of Petroleum –1979; joined Statoil 1979, with Refining and Marketing Div. 1979–83, Exec. Vice-Pres. and mem. Corp. Man. 1989–99, Chair. Norsk Hydro ASA (acquired by Statoil 2007) 2007–14; Man. Dir Agro Fellesslakteri 1983–89; mem. Bd of Dirs Solstad Offshore ASA 2011–18, Chair. 2014–18; mem. Bd of Dirs and Man. Dir Sparebank 1 SR-Bank 1999–2010; Chair. Norwegian Savings Bank Asscn, Nordan AS, Malthus AS 2011. *Address:* c/o Solstad Offshore ASA, POB 13, 4297 Skudeneshavn, Norway (office).

VARELA RODRÍGUEZ, Juan Carlos; Panamanian politician and head of state; *President;* b. 12 Dec. 1963, Panamá City; m. Lorena I. Castillo; three s.; ed Georgia Inst. of Tech., USA; Dir Varela Hermanos Group 1985–, Exec. Vice-Pres. –2008; mem. Partido Panameñista (PP), Pres. 2006–, selected as PP presidential cand. 2008, formed Alliance for Change coalition with Cambio Democrático party 2008; Vice-Pres. and Minister of Foreign Affairs 2009–11; Vice-Pres. of Panama 2011–14, Pres. of Panama 2014–. *Address:* Office of the President, Palacio de Las Garzas, Corregimiento de San Felipe, Panamá 1, Panama (office). *Telephone:* 527-9600 (office). *Fax:* 527-9034 (office). *E-mail:* prensa@presidencia.gob.pa (office). *Website:* www.presidencia.gob.pa (office).

VARGA, Imre; Hungarian sculptor; b. 1 Nov. 1923, Budapest; s. of Mátyás Varga and Margit Csepeli; m. Ildikó Szabó 1944; two s.; ed Budapest Coll. of Visual Arts; Pres. FÉSZEK Artists Club; mem. American Acad. of Arts and Sciences, Acad. Européenne des Arts et des Sciences, Paris; Hon. Citizen of Budapest 2004; Order of the Flag 1983, Commdr, Ordre des Arts et Lettres (France), Cavaliere dell'Ordine al Merito (Italy), Verdienstkreuz, First Class (Germany) 2004, Officer de l'Ordre Leopold (Belgium) 2004; Munkácsy Prize 1969, Kossuth Prize 1973, Merited Artist 1975, Eminent Artist 1980, Herder Prize 1981. *Works:* Prometheus 1965 and The Professor 1969 in Middelheim, Belgium, Madách Memorial 1968, Radnóti Memorial 1970, Partisans Memorial 1971, Lenin Memorial, Heroes Monument, Oslo 1974, plurifigural St Stephen composition, St Peter's Basilica, Vatican 1980, Bartók Memorial, Paris 1983, Béla Kun Memorial, Budapest 1986, Raoul Wallenberg Memorial 1987; perm. collection of work in Budapest; smaller sculptures: Erőlltetett menet (Forced March), A la Recherche, Baudelaire kedvese (Baudelaire's Sweetheart), Páholy (Theatre box), statue of St Stephen in Aachen Cathedral, Germany 1993, Bartók Memorial, Carrefour de l'Europe Square, Brussels 1995, Ferenc Rákóczi II, commemorative statue, Bad Kissingen, Germany 1992, Memorial to Konrad Adenauer and Charles de Gaulle, Rhöndorf 2004, Memorial to Béla Bartók, London 2004. *Address:* 1126 Budapest XII, Barthautca 1, Hungary. *Telephone:* (1) 2500-274 (Museum) (office); (1) 3951-983 (home). *Fax:* (1) 3951-983 (home).

VARGA, Mihály; Hungarian economist and politician; *Deputy Prime Minister and Minister of Finance;* b. 26 Jan. 1965, Karcag; m.; four c.; ed Karl Marx Univ. of Econ. Sciences; econ. adviser, Water Man. Inst. of East Hungary, Szolnok 1989–90; mem. Fiatal Demokraták Szövetsége (Fidesz—Alliance of Young Democrats) 1988, Vice-Pres. 1994, Deputy Head of Parl. Faction 1995–98; mem. Parl. 1990, mem. Parl. Cttee of State Budget and Finances 1990–98, of State Audit; Political State Sec., Ministry of Finance 1998–2001, Minister of Finance 2001–02, Head of Prime Minister's Office 2010–12, Minister without portfolio for liaising with int. financial orgs 2012–13, Minister for Nat. Economy 2013–18, Deputy Prime Minister and Minister of Finance 2018–; mem. IPU 1995, Chair. Parl. Advisory Cttee for Debtors and Banking Consolidation 1995–97; Visiting Prof., Szolnok Business School 1995–97; elder presbyter, Reformed Church Community of Karcag and Kt of St John. *Address:* Ministry of Finance, 1051 Budapest, József Nádor tér 4, Hungary (office). *Telephone:* (1) 795-1400 (office). *Fax:* (1) 318-2570 (office). *E-mail:* ugyfelszolgalat@ngm.gov.hu (office). *Website:* www.kormany.hu (office).

VARGAS LLOSA, (Jorge) Mario Pedro, PhD; Peruvian/Spanish writer and journalist; b. 28 March 1936, Arequipa, Peru; s. of Ernesto Vargas Maldonado and Dora Llosa de Vargas; m. 1st Julia Urquidi 1955 (divorced 1964); m. 2nd Patricia Llosa Urquidi 1965; two s. one d.; partner Isabel Preysler 2015; ed Colegio La Salle, Lima, Peru, Leoncio Prado Military Acad., Lima, Colegio Nacional San Miguel, Piura, Universidad Nacional Mayor de San Marcos, Lima and Universidad Complutense de Madrid, Spain; journalist on local newspapers, Piura, Peru 1951, for magazines Turismo and Cultura Peruana and for Sunday supplement of El Comercio 1955; News Ed. Radio Panamericana, Lima 1955; Spanish teacher, Berlitz School 1959; journalist, Agence-France Presse 1959; broadcaster, Latin American services of Radiodiffusion Télévision Française 1959; Lecturer in Latin American Literature, Queen Mary Coll., Univ. of London, UK 1967, Prof. King's Coll. 1969; Visiting Prof., Washington State Univ., USA 1968, Univ. de Puerto Rico 1969, Columbia Univ., USA 1975; Prof., Univ. of Cambridge, UK 1977, Harvard Univ., USA 1992, Princeton Univ., USA 1993, Georgetown Univ., USA 1994, 1999; Writer-in-Residence, Woodrow Wilson Int. Center for Scholars, Smithsonian Inst., Washington, DC, USA 1980; Prof. and Chair. Dept of Ibero-American Literature and Culture, Georgetown Univ., Washington, DC 2001–06, Distinguished Writer-in-Residence 2003–06; Weidenfeld Visiting Prof. of European Comparative Literature, St Anne's Coll., Oxford, UK 2004; Distinguished Visitor, Program in Latin American Studies, Princeton Univ. 2010; f. Movimiento Libertad political party and co-f. Frente Democrático (FREDEMO) coalition 1988; cand. for Pres. of Peru 1990; Pres. Jury, Iberoamerican Film Festival, Huelva, Spain 1995, San Sebastian Int. Film Festival 2004; mem. Jury, ECHO Television and Radio Awards 1998, Miguel de Cervantes Prize 1998; Pres. PEN Club Int. 1976–79 (Pres. Emer. 1997–2019); mem. Acad. Peruana de la Lengua 1975, Real Acad. Española 1994 (incorporation 1996), Int. Acad. of Humanism 1996, Cervantes Inst. Foundation 1998; Neil Gunn Int. Fellow, Scottish Arts Council 1986; Fellow, Wissenschaftskolleg, Berlin 1991–92, Deutscher Akademischer Austauschdienst, Berlin 1997–98; Hon. Fellow, Hebrew Univ., Israel 1976, Modern Language Asscn of America 1986, American Acad. and Inst. of Arts and Letters 1986; Hon. Prof., Universidad de Ciencias Aplicadas, Lima 2001; Chevalier, Légion d'honneur, Commdr Ordre des Arts et des Lettres 1993, Medal Orden El Sol del Perú (Great Cross of Diamonds) 2001, Medalla de Honor en el Grado de Gran Cruz (Peru) 2003; Diploma de Honor, Universidad Nacional Mayor de San Marcos 2000; numerous prizes including Crítica Española Prize 1966, Premio de la Crítica, Argentina 1981, Ritz Paris Hemingway Prize 1985, Príncipe de Asturias Prize, Spain 1986, Castiglione de Sicilia Prize, Italy 1990, Jerusalem Prize, Israel 1995, Congressional Medal of Honour, Peru 1982, T.S. Eliot Prize, Ingersoll Foundation of The Rockford Institute, USA 1991, Golden Palm Award, INTAR Hispanic American Arts Center, New York 1992, Miguel de Cervantes Prize, Ministry of Culture (Spain) 1994, Jerusalem Prize 1995, Peace Prize, German Publishers, Frankfurt Book Fair 1996, Pluma de Oro Award, Spain 1997, Jorge Isaacs Award, Int. Festival of Art, Cali, Colombia 1999, Crystal Award, World Econ. Forum, Davos, Switzerland 2001, Americas Award, Americas Foundation 2001, Caonabo de Oro Prize, Dominican Asscn of Journalists and Writers, 2002, PEN Nabokov Award 2002, Int. Prize of Letters, Cristobal Gabarron Foundation 2002, Premio Ateneo Americano, on Xth Anniversary of Casa de America 2002, Roger-Caillois PEN Club Prize 2003, Budapest Prize 2003, Presidential Medal of Hofstra Univ., New York 2003, Grinzane Cavour Prize: "A Life for Literature International Prize", Turin 2004, Konex Foundation Prize 2004, Medal of the Centenary of Pablo Neruda, Govt of Chile 2004, Medal of Honor of Peruvian Culture, Nat. Inst. of Culture 2004, Nobel Prize in Literature 2010, Pedro Henríquez Ureña 2016. *Films:* co-dir of film version of his novel Pantaleón y las visitadoras. *Television:* dir La torre de Babel 1981. *Publications include:* novels: La cuidad y los perros (Biblioteca Breve Prize) 1963, La casa verde (Premio Nacional de Novela, Peru 1967) 1966, Conversación en la catedral 1969, Pantaleón y las visitadoras 1973, La tía Julia y el escribidor (ILLA Prize, Italy 1982) 1977, La guerra del fin del mundo (Pablo Iglesias Literature Prize 1982) 1981, Historia de Mayta 1984, ¿Quién mató a Palomino Molero? 1986, Elogio de la madrastra 1988, Lituma en los Andes (Planeta Prize, Spain 1993, Archbishop Juan de San Clemente de Santiago de Compostella Literary Prize, Spain 1994, Int. Literary Prize, Chianti Ruffino Antico Fattore, Italy 1995) 1993, Los cuadernos de Don Rigoberto 1997, La fiesta del Chivo (first Book of the Year Prize, Union of Booksellers of Spain 2001, Readers of Crisol Libraries Prize, Spain 2001) 2000, El paraíso en la otra esquina (chosen for inclusion in "Books to Remember 2003" by cttee of librarians from The New York Public Library 2004) 2003, Travesuras de la niña mala 2006, El Sueño del Celta (The Dream of the Celt) 2010, El héroe discreto 2013, Cinco esquinas 2016; short stories: El desafío (Revue Française Prize) 1957, Los jefes (Leopoldo Alas Prize) 1959, Los cachorros 1967; anthologies: Contra viento y marea Vol. I (1962–72) 1986, Vol. II (1972–83) 1986, Vol. III (1983–90) 1990, Desafíos a la libertad 1994, Making Waves (Nat. Book Critics' Circle Award, New York 1998) 1996; plays: La huída del Inca 1952, La señorita de Tacna 1981, Kathie y el hipopótamo 1983, La Chunga 1986, El loco de los balcones 1993, Ojos bonitos, cuadros feos 1994, La verdad de las mentiras (II Bartolome March Prize for revised edn 2002) 1990, El loco de los balcones 1993, Ojos bonitos, cuadros feos 1996, Odiseo y Penélope 2007, Al pie del Támesis 2008, Las mil y una noches 2010; non-fiction: El pez en el agua (autobiog.) 1993, La orgía perpetua (criticism) 1975, La utopía arcaica 1978, Cartas a un joven novelista (literary essay) 1997, El lenguaje de la pasión (selection of articles) 2001, L'Herne. Mario Vargas Llosa (essays etc.) 2003, Diario de Irak (essays) 2003, La tentación de lo imposible (essay on Les Misérables de Victor Hugo) 2004, Mario Vargas Llosa. Obras Completas, Vol. I Narraciones y novelas (1959–1967) and Vol. II, Novelas (1969–1977) 2004, Un demi-siècle avec Borges (interview and essays on Borges written between 1964 and 1999, in French) 2004, Obras Completas, Vol. III 2005, Obras Completas, Vol. IV 2007, Obras Completas, Vol. V 2010, Touchstones: Essays on Literature, Art, and Politics 2011, La civilización del espectáculo 2012, In Praise of Reading and Fiction: The Nobel Lecture 2012, Mi trayectora intelectual 2014, Notes on the Death of Culture 2015, Sabers and Utopias 2018; contrib. to El País (series Piedra de Toque), Letras Libres, Mexico (series Extemporaneos). *Address:* Las Magnolias 295, 6° Piso, Barranco, Lima 4, Peru. *Telephone:* (1) 477-3868. *Fax:* (1) 477-3518. *Website:* www.mvargasllosa.com.

VARGAS MALDONADO, Miguel Octavio, BSc, MSc; Dominican Republic civil engineer, business executive and politician; *Minister of Foreign Affairs;* b. 26 Sept. 1950, Santo Domingo; s. of Pedro A. Rivera and Altagracia Maldonado; m. Maria Angeles Garcia de Vargas; three s.; ed Univ. of Puerto Rico, Pontificia Univ. Católica Madre y Maestra; joined Dominican Telephone Co. (CODETEL) as supervising engineer 1974, becoming Gen. Man. of Eng and Construction; f. Planificadora de Ingeniería y Construcciones, SA (building construction and devt co.) 1979; Dir-Gen., Santo Domingo Water Supply and Sewerage Corpn 1982–84; f. VARMA business group (comprising Inversiones Inmobiliaria HARNA, PLANINCO and Almacén Fiscal y Almacén General de Depósito—ALMADECA) early 1990s; Sec. of State for Public Works and Communications 2000–04, Minister of Foreign Affairs 2016–; cand. in presidential election 2008; Vice-Pres. Socialist International 2013–; Chair. VARMA Business Group; mem. Partido Revolucionario Dominicano (PRD) 1976–, mem. Presidium, mem. Nat. Exec. Cttee and Political Cttee, fmr Vice-Pres. and Nat. Financial Sec., Pres. 2009–; Grand Cross, Order of Duarte, Sánchez y Mella with Silver Star (Dominican Repub.), Order of Leonidas Monasterio, State of Miranda (Venezuela). *Address:* Ministry of Foreign Affairs, Avenida Independencia No. 752, Estancia San Gerónimo, Santo Domingo DN, Dominican Republic (office). *Telephone:* 987-7001 (office). *Fax:* 987-7027 (office). *E-mail:* relexteriores@mirex.gob.do (office). *Website:* www.mirex.gob.do (office).

VARIN, Philippe; French business executive; *President, France Industrie;* b. 8 Aug. 1952; m.; four c.; ed Ecole Polytechnique and Ecole des Mines, Paris; joined Pechiney Group 1978, various positions including researcher, Head of Strategic Studies, Aluminium Br., Vice-Pres. Eng and Research, Project Dir for construction of Dunkirk aluminium smelter 1989–90, Man.-Dir Aluminium Dunkirk 1990–92, Group Financial Controller, Paris and Chicago, 1993–94, Vice-Pres. Rhenlau Div. 1995–99, apptd Sr Exec. Vice-Pres. Aluminium Sector and mem. Exec. Cttee Pechiney Group 1999; CEO Corus Group PLC, London, UK 2003–09, Chair. Man. Bd 2009–10; Chair. Man. Bd PSA Peugeot Citröen SA 2009–14, Group Temporary Advisor 2014–; Dir, Compagnie de Saint-Gobain 2013–, Gefco, PCMA Holding BV (Netherlands), Institut pour la ville en mouvement, Banque PSA Finance 2009–, Faurecia SA 2009–14; Dir (non-exec.) Tata Steel Ltd 2007–09, BG Group PLC 2006–13; Pres. European Automobile Mfrs Asscn (ACEA) –2014; Chair. Areva 2015– (renamed Orano 2017); Pres. France Industrie 2018–. *Leisure interests include:* tennis, sailing, clarinet. *Address:* France Industrie, 55 avenue Bosquet, 75007 Paris, France. *Website:* www.franceindustrie.org.

VARKULEVICIUS, Rimas; Lithuanian engineer and business executive; *CEO, Marijampoles Pieno Konservai Group;* b. 10 March 1956, Vilnius; m. Auksuole Varkulevicienė; one s. one d.; ed Kaunas Tech. Univ., Moscow Food Industry Tech. Univ., Georgetown Univ., USA; Chief Engineer, Tauras State Brewery 1979–83; Adviser and Chief Engineer, Food Processing Co., Erdenet, Mongolia 1983–85; Exec. Officer, Food Industry Bd of Lithuania 1986; Head of Food Industry Devt Div., Ministry of Agric. 1989–91, Dir Dept of Int. Relations 1991–95, Dir Dept of Int. Integration 1995–97; Chief Consultant, Inst. for Nat. and Int. Meat and Food Industry IFW Heidelberg GmbH 1997–98; fmr Dir-Gen. Asscn of Lithuanian Chambers of Commerce, Industry and Crafts; Marketing Dir, Achemos Group, Vilnius 2008–12; Council Chair. Mykolas Romeris Univ. 2009–13; Adviser to Minister of Energy 2013–15; mem. Man. Bd Marijampoles Pieno Konservai Group 2014–16, CEO 2016–; fmr Dir Northtown Technology Park; has represented the Lithuanian Ministry of Agric. at numerous int. orgs and confs; adviser to Econ. Cttee of Seimas (Parl.). *Leisure interest:* yachting. *Address:* Marjimpoles Pieno Konservai Group, Kauno g 114, Marijampole 68108, Lithuania (office). *Telephone:* (3) 439-8450 (office). *Fax:* (3) 439-8431 (office). *E-mail:* mpk@milk.lt (office). *Website:* www.milk.lt (office).

VARLEY, John Silvester, BA, MA; British fmr banking executive; *Chairman, Marie Curie Cancer Care;* b. 1 April 1956; m. Carolyn Thorn Pease 1981; two c.; ed Coll. of Law, London; fmr Deputy CEO BZW Equity Div., fmr Head of BZW SE Asia; Chair. Barclays Asset Man. Div. 1995–98, mem. Group Exec. Cttee 1996, Exec. Dir 1998–2010, Chief Exec. Retail Financial Services 1998–2000, Finance Dir 2000–03, Group Deputy Chief Exec. Barclays PLC and Barclays Bank PLC Jan.–Sept. 2004, Group Chief Exec. 2004–11, Sr Advisor 2011–; Chair. Employment for Excluded Groups Leadership Team, Business in the Community 2006–, mem. Business Emergency Resilience Group Leadership Team; Chair. and Trustee, Marie Curie Cancer Care 2011–; fmr Pres. Employers' Forum on Disability, UK Drug Policy Comm. (now Hon. Pres.); mem. Int. Advisory Panel, Monetary Authority of Singapore 2006–; mem. Bd of Dirs BlackRock, Inc. 2009–, Rio Tinto Ltd & Rio Tinto PLC (Sr Ind. Dir (non-exec.) 2012–) 2011–, Astra Zeneca 2006–15; Trustee, Thornton Smith Plevins Young People's Trust, St Dunstan's; Prince of Wales' Ambassador Award 2010. *Leisure interests:* walking and fishing. *Address:* Marie Curie Cancer Care, 89 Albert Embankment, London, SE1 7TP (office); Business in the Community, 137 Shepherdess Walk, London, N1 7RQ, England (office). *Telephone:* (20) 7599-7777 (Marie Curie) (office); (20) 7566-8650 (office). *E-mail:* info@bitc.org.uk (office). *Website:* www.mariecurie.org.uk (office); www.bitc.org.uk (office).

VARLOOT, Denis; French engineer and museum administrator; b. 25 Oct. 1937, Lille; s. of Jean Varloot and Madeleine Varloot (née Boutron); m. Marie J. Kennel 1963; two s.; ed Lycées in Paris, Ecole Polytechnique and Ecole Nat. Supérieure des Télécommunications; Centre Nat. d'Etudes des Télécommunications 1962–68; with Direction Général des Télécommunications, Service des Programmes et des Etudes Economiques 1968–73, deputized for head of service 1973–75; Dir of

Telecommunications, Orléans 1975–76; Head of Telecommunications Personnel 1976–81; Dir of Scientific and Tech. Information, Ministry of Educ. 1981–82; Dir Libraries, Museums and Scientific and Tech. Information, Ministry of Educ. 1982–87; Special Adviser to Pres. of France-Télécom 1987, Adviser 1992–98; Chair. and CEO Télésystemes 1988–92; Chair. Admin. Bd Palais de la découverte 1996–2003; apptd Chair. Musée des télécommunications de Pleumeur Bodou 1994; Chair. Asscn des musées et centres pour le développement de la culture scientifique, technique et industrielle 2001–; mem. Haut Conseil des musées de France 2003–; Chevalier des Arts et Lettres, Officier, Légion d'honneur, Ordre nat. du Mérite, Ordre des Palmes Académiques. *Leisure interest:* sailing. *Address:* 14 rue Campagne Première, 75014 Paris, France (home). *Telephone:* 1-43-22-31-31 (home). *E-mail:* varloot.denis@wanadoo.fr (home).

VARMA, Shri Pavan Kumar, BA; Indian diplomatist (retd), writer and politician; b. 5 Nov. 1953, Nagpur, Maharashtra; s. of Badri Nath Varma and Shakuntala Varma; m. Renuka Varma; ed St Stephen's Coll., Univ. of Delhi; joined Foreign Service 1976, fmr Press Sec. to Pres. of India, Spokesman, Ministry of External Affairs, Jt Sec. for Africa, High Commr to Cyprus, Dir, Nehru Centre, London, Dir-Gen. Indian Council for Cultural Relations, New Delhi; Amb. to Bhutan 2009–12 (retd); apptd Cultural Adviser to Shri Nitish Kumar, Chief Minister of Bihar 2013; mem. Rajya Sabha (Janta Dal—United) 2014–16; Dr hc (Univ. of Indianapolis); Druk Thuksey Award (Bhutan). *Publications include:* Ghalib: The Man, The Times 1989, The Havelis of Old Delhi 1992, Krishna: The Playful Divine 1993, Yudhishtar and Draupadi 1993, The Great Indian Middle Class 1998, Widows of Vrindavan 2002, Being Indian: The Truth About Why the 21st Century will be India's 2004, Kama Sutra: The Art of Making Love to a Woman 2007, Becoming Indian: The Unfinished Revolution of Culture and Identity 2010, When Loss is Gain 2012, Chanakya's New Manifesto: To Resolve the Crisis within India 2013; trans: Selected Poems: Kaifi Azmi (in English) 2001, 21 Poems 2001, Selected Poems: Gulzar 2008, Neglected Poems 2012. *Address:* B-61, Paschimi Marg, Vasant Vihar, New Delhi 110 057, India (home). *E-mail:* pavankvarma@hotmail.com. *Website:* pavankvarma.com.

VARMUS, Harold Eliot, MA, MD; American microbiologist, physician and academic; *Lewis Thomas University Professor of Medicine, Weill Cornell Medical College;* b. 18 Dec. 1939, Oceanside, NY; s. of Frank Varmus and Beatrice Varmus (née Barasch); m. Constance Louise Casey 1969; two s.; ed Amherst Coll., Harvard Univ., Columbia Univ.; physician, Presbyterian Hosp., New York 1966–68; Clinical Assoc., NIH, Bethesda, Md 1968–70; Llecturer, Dept of Microbiology, Univ. of Calif. at San Francisco 1970–72, Asst Prof. 1972–74, Assoc. Prof. 1974–79, Prof. 1979–83, American Cancer Soc. Research Prof. 1984–93; Dir NIH 1993–99; Pres. and CEO Memorial Sloan-Kettering Cancer Center 2000–10; Dir National Cancer Inst., NIH 2010–15; Lewis Thomas Univ. Prof. of Medicine, Weill Cornell Medical Coll., New York 2015–; Sr Assoc. Core Mem., New York Genome Center 2015–; fmr Co-Chair. Council of Advisors on Science and Technology, The White House; Co-founder and Chair. Public Library of Science (publisher of open-access journals in the biomedical sciences); Chair. Scientific Bd of Grand Challenges in Global Health, Bill and Melinda Gates Foundation 2003–08, now Chair. Global Health Advisory Cttee; Consultant, Chiron Corp., Emoryville, Calif.; Assoc. Ed. Cell Journal; mem. Editorial Bd Cancer Surveys; mem. American Soc. of Virology, American Soc. of Microbiology, AAAS, Council on Foreign Relations; Calif. Acad. of Sciences Scientist of the Year 1982, Lasker Foundation Award 1982 (co-recipient), Passano Foundation Award 1983, Armand Hammer Cancer Prize 1984, Gen. Motors Alfred Sloan Award, Shubitz Cancer Prize, NAS 1984, Nobel Prize in Physiology or Medicine (co-recipient) 1989, Nat. Medal of Science 2001, Rave Award, Wired Magazine 2004, Double Helix Medal 2011, Vannevar Bush Award. *Publications:* Molecular Biology of Tumor Viruses (ed.) 1982, 1985, Readings in Tumor Virology (ed.) 1983, The Art and Politics of Science (memoir) 2009. *Address:* Weill Cornell Medical College, 1300 York Avenue, New York, NY 10065 (office); New York Genome Center, 101 Avenue of the Americas, New York, NY 10013, USA (office). *Telephone:* (212) 746-5454 (Weill) (office). *Website:* weill.cornell.edu (office); www.nygenome.org (office).

VARNEY, Sir David Robert, Kt, BSc, MBA; British telecommunications industry executive and government official; b. 11 May 1946, London; s. of Robert Varney and Winifred Varney; m. Patricia Ann Varney; one s. one d.; ed Univs of Surrey and Manchester; fmrly with Shell, Man. Dir AB Svenska Shell, Sweden, Dir Shell Int.; CEO BG Group (fmrly British Gas) 1996–2000; Chair. mmO2 2001–04; Exec. Chair. HM Revenue and Customs from 2004–06 (resgnd), Perm. Sec., HM Treasury; Sr Adviser to Gordon Brown on Transformational Govt Strategy (initiative to use information tech. to overhaul UK public services) 2006–09, conducted govt review of tax policy in NI 2007, conducted Varney Review of the Competitiveness of NI 2007–08; Chair. Business in the Community 2002–04; Chair. Packt Publishing 2012–17; Chair. Stroke Asscn 2014–17, Nat. Asscn of Citizens Advice Bureau 2015–18; Council mem., Univ. of Surrey 1994–2002, Vice-Chair. 2001–02, Pro-Chancellor 2016–; Hon. DTech (London Metropolitan Univ.) 2005, Hon. LLD (Univ. of Bath) 2006, Hon. DUniv (Univ. of Surrey) 2007; Outstanding Alumnus Award, Univ. of Manchester 2005. *Address:* 5 College Road, Dulwich, London, SE21 7BQ, England (home). *Telephone:* (208) 693-0377 (home). *E-mail:* david@varney.uk.com (home).

VAROUFAKIS, Yanis Georgiou, PhD; Greek/Australian political economist, academic, author and politician; b. 24 March 1961, Athens; m. 1st Margarite Anagnostopoulou (Poulos); one d.; m. 2nd Danae Stratou; ed Moraitis School, Athens, Univs of Essex and Birmingham, UK; taught econs and econometrics at Univs of Essex and East Anglia –1987; Fellow, Univ. of Cambridge, UK 1988; Sr Lecturer in Econs, Univ. of Sydney, Australia 1989–2000; Prof. of Econ. Theory, Univ. of Athens 2000–, Founder and Dir Univ. of Athens Doctoral Program in Econs (UADPhilEcon) 2002–08; taught at Lyndon B. Johnson School of Public Affairs, Univ. of Texas, USA 2013; Economist-in-Residence, Valve Corpn 2012–; econ. adviser to George Papandreou 2004–06; mem. Synaspismos Rizospastikis Aristeras (SYRIZA—Coalition of the Radical Left); mem. (SYRIZA) Vouli (Parl.) for Athens B Jan.–Sept. 2015; Minister of Finance Jan.–July 2015 (resgnd); co-f. Vital Space project 2010; co-f. Democracy in Europe Movement 2025 2016–, mem. Coordinating Council; Hon. Prof. of Comparative Law, Econs and Finance, Int. Univ. Coll. of Turin 2015. *Publications include:* Conflict in Economics (co-ed.) 1990, Rational Conflict 1991, Game Theory: A Critical Introduction (co-author) 1995, Foundations of Economics: A Beginner's Companion 1998, Game Theory: Critical Perspectives. Vols 1–5 2001, Game Theory: A Critical Text (co-author) 2004, The Globalizing Wall 2007, Modest Proposal (with Stuart Holland) 2010 (fourth edn with James K. Galbraith as third co-author 2013), Modern Political Economics: Making Sense of the Post-2008 World (co-author) 2011, The Global Minotaur: America, the True Origins of the Financial Crisis and the Future of the World Economy 2011 (second edn 2013), Economic Indeterminacy: A Personal Encounter with the Economists' Most Peculiar Nemesis 2013, And the Weak Suffer What They Must? Europe's Crisis, America's Economic Future 2015, Adults in the Room: My Battle With Europe's Deep Establishment 2017, Talking to My Daughter About the Economy: A Brief History of Capitalism 2017; articles in English and Spanish in Truman Factor. *Leisure interest:* motorcycling. *E-mail:* info@diem25.org. *Website:* diem25.org; yanisvaroufakis.eu.

VARRICCHIO, Armando, MA; Italian diplomatist; *Ambassador to USA;* b. 13 June 1961, Venice; m. Mrs Micaela Barbagallo; two s.; ed Univ. of Padua; Asst to Chief Financial Officer of Marzotto Group SpA 1985; joined diplomatic service 1986, Second Sec. and Head of Econ. Office, Embassy in Budapest 1986–92, First Sec., Perm. Mission to EC (co-ordination of Foreign Affairs, Ecofin and Justice/Home Affairs Councils, mem. Italian dels to European Summits of Heads of State and Govt) 1992–96, Counsellor, Prime Minister's Office (Head of Europe and Asia Desk) 1996–98, Chief of Staff to Minister for European Affairs 1998–99, Diplomatic Adviser to President of EC and Personal Rep. (Sherpa) at G7/G8 Summits in Okinawa, Genoa and Kananaskis 1999, First Counsellor, Embassy in Washington, DC (Head of Econ., Trade and Scientific Affairs Section) 2002–06, Minister Plenipotentiary and Deputy Diplomatic Adviser to the Pres. 2006–09, Amb. to Serbia 2009–12, Deputy Sec.-Gen., Ministry of Foreign Affairs 2012–13, Diplomatic Adviser and G7/G20 Sherpa of the Prime Minister 2013–14, rank of Amb. of Italy 2014, Amb. to USA 2016–; Grand Officer, Order of Merit of the Italian Repub.; numerous honours from other countries. *Address:* Embassy of Italy, 3000 Whitehaven Street, NW, Washington, DC 20008, USA (office). *Telephone:* (202) 612-4404 (office). *Fax:* (202) 518-2151 (office). *E-mail:* stampa.washington@esteri.it (office). *Website:* www.ambwashingtondc.esteri.it (office).

VARSHALOMIDZE, Levan, LLM, LLD; Georgian lawyer, business executive and fmr government official; *Managing Partner, LV & Partners;* b. 17 Jan. 1972, Batumi; ed Kiev Univ., Ukraine; Head, Bilateral Relations Office, Ministry of Foreign Affairs 1998–2000; Chair. Exec. Dept, Ministry of Justice 2000–02; Scientific-researcher, Int. Private Law Dept State and Law Inst. of Georgia 2002; Dir Law Dept, Ministry of Finance 2002; partner, Damenia, Varshalomidze, Nogaideli and Kavtaradze (law firm) 2002–04; Dir-Gen. Georgian Railways Ltd Jan.–May 2004; Presidential Envoy to the Autonomous Republic of Ajara May–June 2004; Chair. Govt of Autonomous Repub. of Ajara 2004–12; Man. Partner, LV & Partners 2012–; Presidential Order of Excellence 2012. *Publications:* numerous articles on int. law. *Address:* 6010 Batumi, 60 Gogebashvili Street, Mersin Business Center, Office 5, Georgia. *Telephone:* (422) 21-24-24 (office). *E-mail:* lvarshalomidze@lv.ge (office). *Website:* www.lv.ge (office).

VARSHAVSKY, Alexander Jacob, BS, PhD; American (b. Russian) biologist and academic; *Thomas Hunt Morgan Professor of Biology, California Institute of Technology;* b. 8 Nov. 1946, Moscow, USSR; s. of Jacob Varshavsky and Mary Zeitlin; m. Vera Bingham; one s. two d.; ed Dept of Chem., Moscow Univ., Inst. of Molecular Biology, Moscow; Research Fellow, Inst. of Molecular Biology, Moscow 1973–76; Asst Prof. of Biology, Dept of Biology, MIT, Cambridge, Mass. 1977–80, Assoc. Prof. 1980–86, Prof. 1986–92; Howard and Gwen Laurie Smits Prof. of Cell Biology, Div. of Biology, Calif. Inst. of Tech., Pasadena 1992–2017, Thomas Hunt Morgan Prof. of Biology 2017–; Visiting Fellow, Int. Inst. for Advanced Studies, Japan 2001; Foreign Assoc. European Molecular Biology Org. 2001; Bd mem. Encyclopedia of Molecular Cell Biology and Molecular Medicine 2002–05; mem. Molecular Cytology Study Section, NIH 1983–87, NAS 1995, American Philosophical Soc. 2001, Academia Europaea 2005, Medical Advisory Bd, Gairdner Foundation, Canada 2002–06, O'Connor Advisory Cttee, March of Dimes Foundation 2007–12; mem. NAS 1995, American Philosophical Soc. 2001; Foreign Assoc., European Molecular Biology Org. 2001; Foreign mem. Academia Europaea 2005; Fellow, American Acad. of Arts and Sciences 1987, American Acad. of Microbiology 2000, AAAS 2002; NIH Merit Award 1998, Novartis-Drew Award 1998, Gairdner Int. Award (Canada) 1999, Shubitz Prize in Cancer Research, Univ. of Chicago 2000, Hoppe-Seyler Award, Soc. for Biochemistry and Molecular Biology (Germany) 2000, Sloan Prize 2000, Merck Award, American Soc. for Biochemistry and Molecular Biology 2001, Wolf Prize in Medicine (Israel) 2001, Pasarow Award in Cancer Research 2001, Massry Prize 2001, Horwitz Prize 2001, Max Planck Research Prize (Germany) 2001, Wilson Medal, American Soc. for Cell Biology 2002, Stein and Moore Award, Protein Soc. 2005, March of Dimes Prize in Developmental Biology, March of Dimes Foundation 2006, Griffuel Prize in Cancer Research, Asscn pour la Recherche sur le Cancer, France 2006, Gagna and Van Heck Prize, Fonds Nat. de la Recherche Scientifique (Belgium) 2006, Schleiden Medal, Deutsche Akad. der Naturforscher Leopoldina 2007, Gotham Prize for Cancer Research, Gotham Foundation 2008, Vilcek Prize in Biomedical Sciences 2010, BBVA Foundation Award in Biomedicine (Spain) 2011, Otto Warburg Prize, Soc. for Biochemistry & Molecular Biology (Germany) 2012, King Faisal Int. Prize for Science 2012, Breakthrough Prize in Life Sciences (co-recipient) 2014, Albany Prize in Medicine and Biomedical Research 2014 La Grande médaille, Académie des sciences, France 2016, Heinrich Wieland Prize, Germany 2017. *Achievements include:* discoveries in fields of DNA replication, chromosome structure and segregation, ubiquitin system and regulated protein degradation; inventions of several widely used methods including the chromatin immunoprecipitation (CHIP) assay, the ubiquitin fusion technique, and the split-ubiquitin sensor of protein–protein interactions; more than 15 patents. *Publications:* more than 200 articles in professional journals in the fields of genetics and biochemistry; 16 US patents. *Address:* Division of Biology, MC 145–75, 208B Braun Laboratory, California Institute of Technology, 1200 East California Boulevard, Pasadena, CA 91125, USA (office). *Telephone:* (626) 395-3785 (office); (818) 606-1908 (mobile). *Fax:* (626) 449-0756 (office); (818) 248-5245 (home). *E-mail:* avarsh@caltech.edu (office). *Website:* www.bbe.caltech.edu/content/alexander-j-varshavsky (office); www.its.caltech.edu/~biochem/faculty/varshavsky.html (office).

VASELLA, Daniel Lucius, MD; Swiss physician and pharmaceutical industry executive; *Honorary Chairman, Novartis AG;* b. 15 Aug. 1953, Fribourg; m. Anne-Laurence Moret 1978; two s. one d.; ed Univ. of Berne; began career as hosp. physician; Head of Corp. Marketing, Sandoz Group 1993, Sr Vice-Pres. and Head of Worldwide Devt, Sandoz Pharma Ltd, COO –1995, mem. Exec. Cttee, then CEO 1995–96, CEO and Exec. mem. Bd of Dirs Novartis AG (following merger of Sandoz and Ciba-Geigy) 1996–2010, Chair. 1999–2013, Hon. Chair. 2013–; mem. Bd of Dirs Crédit Suisse 2000–, PepsiCo Inc., Alcon; mem. Chair.'s Council Daimler-Chrysler; mem. Supervisory Bd, Siemens AG, Munich; Pres. Int. Fed. of Pharmaceutical Mfrs and Asscns (IFPMA) 2004–06; mem. Int. Business Leaders Advisory Council for the Mayor of Shanghai, Global Health Program Advisory Panel of the Bill & Melinda Gates Foundation, Bd Inst. Européen d'Admin. des Affaires (INSEAD), Int. Inst. of Man. Devt, Bd of Dean's Advisors at Harvard Business School, Global Leaders for Tomorrow Group, World Econ. Forum, Davos, Switzerland, Int. Bd of Govs Peres Center for Peace, Tel-Aviv, Israel; fmr mem. Steering Cttee of the Bilderberg Group; Foreign Hon. mem. American Acad. of Arts and Sciences 2008; Ordem Nacional do Cruzeiro do Sul (Brazil), Chevalier de la Légion d'honneur; Dr hc (Univ. of Basel Faculty of Medicine) 2002; Harvard Business School's Alumni Achievement Award 2003, Appeal of Conscience Award, AJ Congress Humanitarian Award, chosen as the Most Influential European Business Leader of the Last 25 Years by the readers of the Financial Times 2004, Oliver R. Grace Award, Cancer Research Inst. 2004, Karl Winnacker Prize, Univ. of Marburg 2007, GILD Award for Leadership: Warren Bennis Award for Excellence in Leadership 2010. *Publication:* Magic Cancer Bullet: How a Tiny Orange Pill May Rewrite Medical History (with Robert Slater) 2003. *Leisure interests:* skiing, motorcycles, collecting rare books. *Address:* Novartis AG, Lichtstrasse 35, 4056 Basel, Switzerland (office). *Telephone:* (61) 324-11-11 (office). *Fax:* (61) 324-80-01 (office). *E-mail:* info@novartis.com (office). *Website:* www.novartis.com (office).

VASHADZE, Grigol; Georgian business executive and politician; b. 19 July 1958, Tbilisi; s. of Nodar Vashadze and Elene Bakradze; m. Nina Ananiashvili; two c.; ed Moscow State Inst. of Int. Relations; worked in Dept of Int. Orgs, USSR Ministry of Foreign Affairs 1981–88, also worked in Dept of Cosmos and Nuclear Weapons; postgraduate student, Diplomatic Acad. 1988–90; Founder and Dir Georgia Arts Man. and Gregory Vashadze and BR 1990–2008; Deputy Minister of Foreign Affairs Feb.–Nov. 2008; Minister for Culture, Heritage Preservation and Sport Nov. 2008, of Foreign Affairs 2008–12; cand. in presidential election 2018.

VASHCHANKA, Uladzimir Aliaksandravich; Belarusian government official; *Minister of Emergency Situations;* b. 3 Aug. 1958, Troitsko-Pechersk, Komi ASSR (now Repub. of Komi), Russian SFSR, USSR; ed Mogilev (Mahiloŭ) Eng Inst., Command and Eng Inst. of Ministry of Emergency Situations; served in Armed Forces 1976–78; tool sharpener, Strommashyna co. 1978–80; Jr Firefighter Insp., Chief of Guard, and headed several fire depts 1980–2000; Head of Mogilev Oblast Dept of Ministry of Emergency Situations 2000–10, Minister of Emergency Situations 2010–; mem. Mogilev Oblast Council of Deputies. *Address:* Ministry of Emergency Situations, 220050 Minsk, vul. Revolutsionnaya 5, Belarus (office). *Telephone:* (17) 229-35-90 (office). *Fax:* (17) 203-77-81 (office). *E-mail:* mail@mchs.gov.by (office). *Website:* www.mchs.gov.by (office).

VASILEV, Iliyan D.; Bulgarian business executive and fmr diplomatist; *Managing Partner, Innovative Energy Solutions Ltd;* Vice-Pres. BIBA (now CEIBG—Confederation of Employers and Industrialists in Bulgaria) 1993–97; Chair. Foreign Investment Agency 1977–2000; Amb. to Russia 2000–06; Chair. Deloitte Bulgaria 2007–11; Man. Partner, Innovative Energy Solutions Ltd 2011–; Co-founder and Hon. Chair. Bulgarian Econ. Forum and Southeast Europe Econ. Forum; fmr Pres. Bulgarian Int. Business Asscn; Deputy Chair. Bulgarian Reform Union Club; mem. Bd of Dirs Centre for Balkan and Black Sea Studies, Bulgarian Foreign Policy Asscn; Int. Cyril and Methodius Award 2005. *Address:* Innovative Energy Solutions Ltd, 1113 Sofia, 9B, Latinka Str., Bulgaria (office). *Telephone:* (2) 443-84-60 (office). *E-mail:* info@innoenergy.biz (office); idvassilev@gmail.com. *Website:* innoenergy.biz (office); innoenergy.biz/blog.html (office).

VASILIAUSKAS, Vitas, PhD; Lithuanian lawyer and central banker; *Chairman, Bank of Lithuania;* b. 15 Oct. 1973, Kaunas; m. Rasa Vasiliauskienė; three c.; ed Vilnius Univ.; Sr Tax Inspector, Lithuanian State Tax Inspectorate 1995–97; Dir Dept of Taxation, Treasury 1998–2001; Deputy Minister of Finance 2001–04; lawyer with Lideika, Petrauskas, Valiūnas and Pnrs (law firm) 2004–11; Chief of Staff, campaign office of Dalia Grybauskaitė during presidential election 2009; Chair. Bank of Lithuania 2011–. *Address:* Office of the Chairman, Bank of Lithuania, Gedimino pr. 6, Vilnius 01103, Lithuania (office). *Telephone:* (5) 268-0029 (office). *Fax:* (5) 262-8124 (office). *E-mail:* info@lb.lt (office). *Website:* www.lb.lt/vitas_vasiliauskas_1 (office).

VASILIEV, Vladimir Viktorovich; Russian ballet dancer, choreographer, theatre director, film director and teacher and artist; *President, Galina Ulanova Foundation;* b. 18 April 1940, Moscow; s. of Viktor Vasiliev and Tatiana Kuzmicheva; m. Ekaterina Maximova (died 2009); ed Bolshoi Theatre Ballet School, State Inst. of Theatrical Arts; with Bolshoi Theatre Ballet Co. 1958–88; toured widely 1988–94, including guest appearances with Ballet of Maurice Béjart, Ballet de Marseille of Roland Petit, Teatro di San Carlo di Napoli, La Scala, Milan, Arena di Verona, Opera di Roma, Polish Nat. Ballet, Kirov (Mariinsky) Ballet, American Ballet Theatre, Tokyo Ballet, Cuban Ballet, Co. of Teatro Colón (Argentina), Kremlin, ind. tours of 'Ekaterina Maximova & Vladimir Vasiliev – Superstars of the Bolshoi and Co.'; Head of Choreographic Dept, State Inst. of Theatrical Arts 1986–95; Artistic and Gen. Dir Bolshoi Theatre 1995–2000; Artistic Dir Open Ballet Competition 'Arabesque' 1998–; Pres. Galina Ulanova Foundation 2000–; freelance choreographer and dir 2000–; Founder and Trustee, Bolshoi School in Brazil; Prof. and Hon. Prof., Moscow State Univ.; Hon. Citizen, Buenos Aires, Argentina 1983, Tusona, USA 1989; People's Artist of USSR 1973, People's Artist of Russian Fed. 1993, Order of Lenin 1976, Order of People's Friendship 1981, Order of Red Banner of Labour 1986, Chevalier, Ordre nat. du Mérit 1999, State Order of Merit of Russian Fed. 2000, 2008, State Order of Lithuania 2002, State Order of Brazil 'Rio Branco' 2004, State Order of Merit for Altai Region 2015, State Decoration 'Coat of Arms of Perm Region' 2016; Hon. DHumLitt (Centre Coll., Danville, Ky, USA); numerous prizes including First Prize and Gold Medal, Vienna Int. Youth Festival 1959, Nijinsky Prize, Paris Dance Acad. 1964, Grand Prix,Varna Int. Competition 1964, USSR State Lenin Komsomol Prize 1968, USSR State Lenin Prize 1970, Jino Tagni Int. Prize, Rome 1989, Together for Peace Prize, Rome 1989, UNESCO Pablo Picasso Medal 1990, 2000, Diagilev Prize 1990, State Prize of Russian Fed. 1991, Moscow Mayor's Office Prize 1997, Crystal Turandot Prize – For Honor and Dignity (Russia) 2001, A Life for Dance Prize (USA) 2003, 2004, Ludwig Nobel Prize (Russia) 2006, 2008, Stanislavsky Prize (Russia) 2010, Gran Teatro La Havana Prize (fCuba) 2010, Liberty Prize (USA) 2010, Amber Faun Prize for outstanding contribution to choreographic art (Poland) 2012, Prize 'God of Dance, Master and Icarus' (Russia) 2015. *Principal ballet roles include:* Pan (Valpurgis Night), The Poet (Chopiniana), Danila (Stone Flower), Prince Charming/Step Mother (Cinderella), Batyr (Shurale), Andrei (A Page of Life), Basil (Don Quixote), Albert (Giselle), Frondoso (Laurencia), Nutcracker/Prince (Nutcracker), Ivanushka (The Little Humpbacked Horse), Spartacus (Spartacus), Petrushka (Petrushka) and Icarus (Icarus), Macbeth (Macbeth), Narcissus (Narcissus), Lukash (Song of the Woods), Paganini (Paganini), Romeo (Romeo and Juliet), Prince Desire (Sleeping Beauty), Ivan the Terrible (Ivan the Terrible), Sergey (Angara), Baron (Gaîté Parisienne), Zorba (Greek Zorba) Nijinsky (Nijinsky), Pyotr Leontyevich (Anyuta), Professor Unrat (The Blue Angel), Tchaikovsky (Lungo Viaggio Nella Notte de Natale), Diaghilev-Nizhinsky (Diaghilev Musaget); ballet miniatures: Narcissus, Fantasie, Melody, Football Player, Match, Mugam, Elegia, Ouverture on Jewish Themes, Diaghilev-Nizhinsky (Diaghilev-Musaget), Old Lonely Man (The Ballade). *Ballets choreographed include:* cr. Anyuta, Macbeth, Icarus, These Charming Sounds, Swan Lake, Cinderella, Paganini, new version of Giselle, Balda, Nostalgie, Bolshoi Theatre, Takhir and Zukhra, Uzbek Opera; Macbeth, Novosibisk Opera, Staats Oper Berlin, Budapest Opera, Kremlin Ballet; Romeo and Juliet, Moscow Musical Theatre of K. Stanislavsky and V. Nemirovich-Danchenko, Lithuanian Opera, Latvian Opera, Teatro Municipal of Rio de Janeiro; Don Quixote, Teatro di San Carlo, Naples, American Ballet Theatre, Kremlin Ballet, Lithuanian Ballet, Tokyo Ballet, Belgrade Ballet; Giselle, Opera di Roma, Bolshoi Ballet School in Brazil; Paganini, Teatro Argentino, Dresden Opera Theatre, Maggio Fiorentino: Cinderella, Kremlin Ballet, Cheliabinsk Opera, Voronezh Opera; Red Poppy, Krasnoyarsk Opera; Nutcracker Suite and Don Quixote Suite, Giselle, Bolshoi Ballet School in Brazil; Ballade, New York City Centre, Pushkin Fine Arts Museum, Perm Opera; House at Roadside, Altai State Dance Ensemble, Russia 2012, Triptych 'Ballet Chez d'Oeuvres in Opera Classics', Voronezh Opera 2012. *Plays:* choreographer: The Princess and Woodcutter, Sovremennik Drama Theatre, Moscow; Yunona and Avosj (rock opera), Lenkom Drama Theatre, Moscow; F. Zeffirelli's productions of Aida, Opera di Roma 1990, Arena di Verona 2002, La Scala 2006, Teatro Massimo 2008, La Traviata, Bolshoi Theatre, Khovanschina, Bolshoi Theatre, Aida (dir F.Zeffirelli). *Operas staged:* La Traviata, Bolshoi Theatre 1996, Oh, Mozart, Mozart…, Novaya Opera of Moscow 1999. *Films:* directed, choreographed and starred in Trapezium, Anyuta, House by the Roadside, Adam and Eva, Icarus, Gospel for the Sly, Gigolo and Gigolette, These Charming Sounds, Fouete, Fragments of One's Biography, I Want to Dance; choreographed Andersen: Life Without Love (Russia); appeared in Franco Zeffirelli's La Traviata. *Radio:* I. Turgenev Spring Waters (radio play). *Television:* starred in USSR with Open Heart, Road to the Bolshoi Ballet, Parade of Numbers, Moscow in Musical Notes, Recollecting Ninjinsky, Glory of the Bolshoi Ballet, Randez-vous with the Bolshoi, Creation of Dance, Choreographic Novellas, Choreographic Symphony, World of Dance, Pages of Modern Dance, The Bolshoi Ballet in Japan, Classical Duets, Grand Pas in the White Night, The World of Ulanova, Ulanova Forever, Commemorating Ulanova, Asaf Messerer, Anna Pavlova, Choreographic Images of Kasyan Goleizovsky, Magic of Giselle, Golden Age of Asaf Messerer, Katya, Ekaterina Maximova, When Dance becomes Life; Olga Lepeshinskaya, Dialogue with a Legend, Vladimir Vasiliev: Dance and Time, The Bolshoi Ballet, E. Maximova and V. Vasiliev: Dance of Fate. *Publications:* poems: The Chain of Days 2000; catalogues of paintings of V. Vasiliev 2004, 2005, 2007, Declaration d'Amour à Vladimir Vasiliev 2010, Pictures from My Memory 2010. *Leisure interests:* painting, writing poetry. *Address:* c/o Vorotnikovsky per., 7-4-26, 127006 Moscow, Russia (office); Smolenskaya naberezhnaya 5/13 62, 121099 Moscow, Russia (home). *Telephone:* (495) 699-21-51 (home). *Fax:* (495) 699-21-51 (home). *E-mail:* info@vasiliev.com (office). *Website:* www.vasiliev.com.

VASILYEV, Anatoli Aleksandrovich; Russian theatre director; b. 4 May 1942, Danilovka, Penza Region; m. Nadezhda Kalinina; one d.; ed Rostov State Univ., State Inst. of Dramatic Art, Moscow; Founder and Dir Theatre Co. School of Dramatic Art, Moscow 1988–2006; staged all works by Pirandello; numerous tours in Europe 1985–2002; Chevalier, Ordre des Arts et des Lettres 1989, Honoured Art Worker of Russia 1993; Nuova Realtà Europea Prize, Taormina, Italy 1990, Pirandello Prize, Agrigento, Italy 1992, Stanislavsky Fund Prize 1995, Stanislavsky Prize of Russian Fed. 1998, Golden Mask Prize of Russian Fed. for The Lamentation of Jeremiah (Martynov) 1997, Nat. State Prize of Russian Fed. for creation of School of Dramatic Art 1999, Triumph Prize 2001. *Productions include:* Vassa Zheleznova 1978, Grown-up Daughter of a Young Man (V. Slavkin) 1979, Cerceau (V. Slavkin) 1985, Six Characters in Search of an Author (Pirandello) 1987, Masquerade (Lermontov) at Comédie Française 1992, Uncle's Dream (Dostoyevsky), Budapest 1994, The Lamentation of Jeremiah (Martynov) 1996, The Queen of Spades (Tchaikovsky), German Nat. Theatre, Weimar 1996, Don Juan (Pushkin) 1998, Mozart and Salieri (Pushkin) 2000, Requiem (Martynov) 2000, Medee Materiaux (Heiner Muller) 2001. *Publications:* A propos de bal masqué de Mikhail Lermontov 1997, Szinházi Fuga 1998, Sept ou huit leçons de théâtre 1999, Ione e Menone di Platone 1999, A un unico lettore 2000.

VASILYEV, Sergei Aleksandrovich, PhD; Russian banking executive and politician; *Deputy Chairman of the Executive Board, State Corporation Bank for Development and Foreign Economic Affairs (Vnesheconombank);* b. 8 June 1957, Leningrad; m.; two d.; ed Inst. of Economy and Finance, Leningrad; Head, Research Lab., Inst. of Finance and Economy, Leningrad 1985–90, now Prof.; took part in activities of Moscow-Leningrad group of young economists; mem. Leningrad Political Club Perestroika 1986; Chair. Cttee for Econ. Reform, Leningrad City Soviet 1990–91; Head, Working Centre for Econ. Reform under Russian Govt 1991–94; Deputy Minister of the Economy, Russian Fed. 1994–97; Deputy Head, Office of Russian Govt 1997–98; Chair. Bd Int. Investment Bank, Moscow 1998–99; Pres. Int. Centre for Social and Econ. Research (Leontief Centre), St Petersburg 1999–2001, now Academic Adviser; Rep. of Leningrad

Regional Govt to Council of Fed. 2001–07, Deputy Chair. of Exec. Bd, State Corporation Bank for Development and Foreign Economic Affairs (Vnesheconombank) 2007–; Chair. Supervisory Bd, Belvneshekonombank OJSC, 2012–, Svyaz-Bank OJSC 2012–; mem. Bd of Dirs Alfa-Bank SC 2012–, Expert Media Holding Zao 2012–, Far East Development Fund 2015–; Chair. Lensoviet Standing Comm. for Econ. Reform; Chair. Russian Nat. Asscn of Securities Market Participants; mem. Collegium of the Russian Federation Ministry of Finance; Chair. Guardian Council, St Petersburg State Univ. of Economics and Finance; mem. Academic Bd Higher School of Economics; mem. Guardian Council, New Economic School. *Publications include:* Economics and Power 1998, Ten Years of Russian Economic Reform 1999, Comparative Analysis of Stabilization Programs of the '90s 2003, Economic Development of the Leningrad Region 2005. *Leisure interest:* travel. *Address:* Vnesheconombank, Moscow 107996, 9 Academika Sakharova Prospekt, Russia (office). *Telephone:* (495) 721-18-63 (office). *Fax:* (495) 721-92-91 (office). *Website:* www.veb.ru (office).

VASILYEV, Gen.-Col Vladimir A., Cand.Jur; Russian politician; b. 11 Aug. 1949, Klin, Moscow region; one d.; m.; ed School of Militia, Acad. of USSR Ministry of Internal Affairs; held several positions in Bauman dist Div. of Internal Affairs 1972–83, including Investigator, Inspector, Sr Inspector, Deputy Head, Head of Div. then Deputy Head of Dept of Property Security, Moscow Dept of Internal Affairs 1983–87, held several positions at Ministry of Internal Affairs, Moscow 1992–98, including Chief Inspector, Head of Operations Dept, Deputy Head, Head of Gen. Staff, First Deputy Minister of Internal Affairs; Deputy Sec., Security Council of Russian Fed. 1999–2001; apptd Deputy Minister of Internal Affairs 2001; mem. State Duma (United Russia) for Tversk Dist 173 –2017, Chair. Cttee for Security 2004–11, head of United Russia faction 2012–16; Acting Head Repub. of Dagestan 2017–; Order of Courage, Order of Honor. *Website:* www.vavasiliev.ru.

VASILYEVA, Tatyana Grigoryevna; Russian actress; b. 28 Feb. 1947, Leningrad; two s. one d.; ed Studio-School of Moscow Art Theatre; with Moscow Satire Theatre –1984; actress, Moscow Mayakovsky Theatre 1984–93; Order of Honour 2013; People's Artist of Russia, Nika Prize 1992. *Theatre roles include:* Ordinary Miracle, Pippi Longstocking, Run, Inspector, The Threepenny Opera, A Place Like the Heavens. *Films include:* Poedinok v tayge (The Fight in the Taiga) 1977, Prezhde chem rasstatsya (Before We Part) 1984, Salon krasoty (Beauty Salon) 1985, Bluzhdayushchiye zvyozdy (Wandering Stars) 1991, Hello, I'm Your Auntie, Uvidet Parizh i umeret (To See Paris and Die) 1992, Zhenikh iz Mayami (The Fiancé from Miami) 1994, Chyornaya vual (The Black Veil) 1995, Tsirk sgorel i klouny razbezhalis 1998, Popsa 2005, Tarif novogodniy 2008, Neporoshchennye 2009, Privet, kinder! 2009, S Novym godom, mamy! 2012. *Television includes:* Ivan Podushkin. Dzhentlmen syska (mini-series) 2006, Zakrytaya shkola (series) 2011–12, Ded Moroz vsegda zvonit... trizhdy! (film) 2012.

VASPÁL, Vilmos, BEng; Hungarian business executive; *Chairman, FreeSoft Nyrt.;* m.; two c.; software developer, Videoton 1980s; fmr Chief Information Officer, SZÜV; Founding mem. FreeSoft Nyrt., Chair. 2004–; mem. Bd Asscn of IT Cos 2003–. *Address:* FreeSoft Nyrt., Neumann Janos u. 1/C, Infopark, Budapest 1117, Hungary (office). *Telephone:* (1) 371-2910 (office). *Fax:* (1) 371-2911 (office). *E-mail:* fs.inf@freesoft.hu (office). *Website:* www.freesoft.hu (office).

VASQUEZ, Gaddi Holguin, BA; American business executive and diplomatist; *Senior Vice-President, Government Affairs, Southern California Edison;* b. 22 Jan. 1955, Carrizo Springs, Tex.; ed Univ. of Redlands; fmr Trustee Prof., Chapman Univ.; early career as police officer in Orange, California; served as appointee of three fmr California Govs; Div. Vice-Pres. of Public Affairs, Southern California Edison (SCE) 1995–2002, Vice-Pres. of Public Affairs 2009–13, Sr Vice-Pres., Government Affairs, SCE and Edison International (parent co.) 2013–; apptd by fmr Pres. George H. W. Bush to several fed. comms; Dir US Peace Corps 2002–06; Amb. and Perm. Rep. to UN, Rome 2006–09; Chair. Project Concern International 2014–; three hon. doctorates; numerous awards for leadership and community service, including Outstanding Alumni Award, American Asscn of Community Colls, Coro Foundation Crystal Eagle Award, Marine Corps Scholarship Fund Globe and Anchor Award, Jewish Nat. Fund Tree of Life Award, Salvation Army's William H. Booth Award for Service, Orange County Black Chamber of Commerce Award for Community Leadership, B'nai Brith Award for Leadership and Community Service. *Address:* Southern California Edison, PO Box 600, Rosemead, CA 91770-0001, USA (office). *E-mail:* info@sce.com (office); ambassadorvasquez@gmail.com. *Website:* www.edison.com (office); www.sce.com (office).

VÁSQUEZ MORALES, Ricaurte, PhD; Panamanian government official, economist and business executive; *Vice-President, Government Affairs & Public Policy, GE Latin America;* ed Villanova Univ., North Carolina State Univ., Rensselaer Polytechnic Inst., USA; Minister of Planning and Econ. Policy 1984–88; Pres. Sigma Man. Corpn 1988–96; Vice-Pres. Asesores y Gestores Bursátiles 1992–94; Dir Panama Holdings Inc. 1994–96; fmr econ. analyst Chase Manhattan Bank, econ. consultant Cámara Panameña de la Construcción, economist Corporación de Cobre de Cerro Colorado; Dir Office of Financial Admin, Panama Canal Comm. 1996; Vice-Admin. Panama Canal Authority –2004; Minister of Finance and the Treasury and Chair. Panama Canal Authority 2004–07; Pres. & CEO, GE Central America & Caribbean 2008–11, Vice-Pres. Govt Affairs & Public Policy, GE Latin America 2011–; has taught econs, econometrics and finance at Universidad Santa María La Antigua, Florida State Univ. Panamá, Universidad del Istmo. *Website:* www.ge.com/news/company-information/latam (office).

VASSALLI, Jean-Dominique, PhD, MD; Swiss physician, academic and university administrator; *Rector Emeritus, University of Geneva;* b. 12 Aug. 1946, Genève et Meride (Tessin); m.; two c.; ed Univ. of Geneva, The Rockefeller Univ., USA; Asst Prof., The Rockefeller Univ. 1977–81; Researcher, Dept of Morphology, Univ. of Geneva 1981–86, Assoc. Prof. 1986–90, Prof., Dept of Morphology 2004–, Prof., Dept of Genetic Medicine and Devt 1990, Vice-Dean, Faculty of Medicine 1991–99, Vice-Rector Univ. of Geneva 1999–2003 Pres., Section of Fundamental Medicine, Faculty of Medicine 2004, Rector Univ. of Geneva 2004–15, Rector Emer. 2015–; Chair. Bd of Trustees, Fondation Brocher 2009–17, Pres. 2017–; mem. Exec. Cttee Union suisse des socs de biologie expérimentale 1990–93, Devt and Planning Comm., Univ. of Geneva 1991–95, Scientific Comm., ISREC 1992–2002 (Pres. 1994–2002), Audit of Insts of Anatomy, Histology, Embryology, Univ. of Lausanne 1993–94, Review Cttee Int. Human Frontier Science Program 1995–97, Friedrich Miescher Prize Cttee, Soc. suisse de biochimie 1996, Scientific Council, Fed. Research Inst., Montpellier 1997–98, Patronage Cttee Gen Suisse 1998, Prize Comm. Dr Josef Steiner Krebsstiftung 1999, Fondation Ernest et Lucie Schmidheiny 2004, Scientific Cttee Fondation Eagle 2005; Consulting Ed., The Journal of Clinical Investigation 1998–2002; Pres. Organizing Cttee VIIth Int. Workshop on Molecular and Cellular Biology of Plasminogen Activation (Les Diablerets) 1999; Jt Organizer EMBO Conf. on Extracellular Proteases and Their Inhibitors in Development, Plasticity and Pathology of the Nervous System (Ascona) 2003; mem. Swiss Acad. of Natural Sciences, Genetic Research Forum 2004; mem. ad personam Swiss Acad. of Medical Sciences 2001; Prix de la Fondation Prof. Dr Max Cloëtta 1988, Prize of Int. Soc. for Fibrinolysis and Thrombolysis 1994. *Publications:* numerous papers in professional journals. *Address:* Université de Genève, Uni Dufour, 24 rue du Général-Dufour, 1211 Geneva 4 Switzerland (office). *Telephone:* (22) 3797111 (office). *Fax:* (22) 3791134 (office). *E-mail:* webmaster@unige.ch (office). *Website:* www.unige.ch (office).

VASSANJI, M. G., CM, BS, PhD; Canadian writer; b. 30 May 1950, Nairobi, Kenya; m. Nurjehan Vassanji (née Aziz) 1979; two s.; ed Massachusetts Inst. of Tech. and Univ. of Pennsylvania, USA; grew up in Nairobi, Kenya, and Dar es Salaam, Tanzania; Post-doctoral Fellow, Atomic Energy of Canada Ltd 1978–80; Research Assoc., Univ. of Toronto 1980–89; first novel published 1989, full-time writer 1989–; Writer-in-Residence, Int. Writing Program, Univ. of Iowa 1989; Fellow, Indian Inst. of Advanced Study 1996; Hon. DLitt (York) 2005, (McMaster) 2006, (Old Dominion) 2007, (Toronto) 2009, (Carleton, Ottawa) 2013; Harbourfront Festival Prize 1994, Giller Prize 1994, 2003, Gov. Gen.'s Prize 2009. *Publications include:* The Gunny Sack (novel) (Commonwealth First Novel Award, Africa Region 1990) 1989, No New Land (novel) 1991, Uhuru Street (short stories) 1991, The Book of Secrets (novel) (Giller Prize for Best Novel 1994, F.G. Bressani Literary Prize) 1994, Amriika (novel) 1999, The In-Between World of Vikram Lall (novel) (Giller Prize for Best Novel) 2003, When She Was Queen (short stories) 2005, The Assassin's Song (novel) 2007, A Place Within: Rediscovering India (travel memoir) (Gov. Gen.'s Literary Award for Best Non-fiction 2009) 2008, Mordecai Richler (biog.) 2009, The Magic of Saida (novel) 2012, And Home Was Kariakoo: A Memoir of East Africa 2014, Nostalgia (novel) 2016. *Leisure interests:* squash, tennis, films, music. *Address:* c/o Doubleday Canada Ltd, 5900 Finch Avenue East, Scarborough, ON M1B 0A2 (office); c/o Westwood Creative Artists, 386 Huron Street, Toronto, ON M5S 2G6, Canada (office). *Telephone:* (416) 364-4449 (Random House) (office); (20) 7908-5900 (Westwood) (office). *E-mail:* tbohan@wylieagency.co.uk (office). *Website:* bruce@wcaltd.com (office); meg@wcaltd.com (office); www.wcaltd.com (office); adunn@penguinrandomhouse.com (office); www.mgvassanji.com.

VASSILIKOS, Vassilis; Greek writer and fmr diplomatist; b. 18 Nov. 1934, Kavala; s. of Nikolaos Aikaterini; m. Vasso Papantoniou; one d.; ed Anatolia High School of Thessaloniki, Thessaloniki Law School, Yale Drama School, USA, School of Radio and Television, USA; Dir-Gen. of Greek TV (public) 1981–85; Amb. to UNESCO 1996–2004; Pres. Hellenic Authors' Soc. 1999–2005; presenter of weekly TV show on books; mem. Int. Parl. of Writers, Athens Union of Daily Newspaper Journalists; Dr hc (Univ. of Patra, Univ. of Thessaly); Commdr des Arts et des Lettres 1999; Prize of 'The Twelve' 1961, Mediterraneo Prize 1971. *Publications include:* (in English trans.): The Plant, The Well, The Angel 1963, Z 1968, The Harpoon Gun 1972, Outside the Walls 1973, The Photographs 1974, The Monarch 1976, The Coroner's Assistant 1986, ...And Dreams Are Dreams 1996, The Few Things I Know About Glafkos Thrassakis 2003. *Address:* 5 Ambrosiou Moshonision, 17123 Athens, Greece (office). *Telephone:* (210) 363-4868 (office). *Fax:* (210) 362-0844 (office). *E-mail:* newopera@otenet.gr (office).

VASSILIOU, Androulla, MIA; Cypriot lawyer, organization executive, politician and EU official; b. 30 Nov. 1943, Paphos; d. of Mr Georgiades; m. George Vassiliou 1966 (Pres. of Cyprus 1988–93); one s. two d.; ed Pancyprian Gymnasium, Nicosia, Middle Temple Inn of Court, London, Inst. of World Affairs, London; called to the Bar, Middle Temple Inn of Court, London 1964; practised law, specializing in corpn and banking law 1968–88; Legal Adviser, Standard Chartered Bank, Bank of Cyprus and others 1969–88; mem. Cypriot House of Reps 1996–, mem. Cttee of European Affairs, of Educ. and Culture, Environment Cttee; Commr for Educ., Culture, Multilingualism and Youth, EC, Brussels 2010–14; Vice-Pres. European Liberal Democrat and Reform Party, Pres. European Liberal Women Network; mem. Bd of Dirs of numerous cos; Hon. Pres. Bureau of Women's Affairs, Ministry of Justice 1988; Gen. Sec., then Hon. Pres. UN Asscn of Cyprus; mem. Exec. Cttee World Fed. of UN Asscns (WFUNA), later Pres. (first woman) 1991–95, now Hon. Pres.; Co-founder and Pres. Cyprus Asscn of Univ. Women, Cttee for Restoration of Human Rights Throughout Cyprus; Hon. Pres. Perm. Agency on Womens' Rights in Cyprus 1988; Founder and Pres. Cyprus Fund for Music and Other Fine Arts; Pres. Pancyprian Welfare Council 1988–93, Cyprus Fed. of Business and Professional Women 1996–2001; Alternate Mem. Convention for Future of Europe 2001–03; mem. Bd of Trustees, Pharos Trust 2001–; Pres. Bd of Trustees Oncology Centre of Bank of Cyprus 2003–; Hon. Pres. Cttee for Restoration of Human Rights; Patron, Muscular Dystrophy Research Trust, Cyprus Family Planning Asscn, Anti-rheumatism Soc., Asscn of Friends of Cancer Patients, Asscn of Friends of Children with Speech Problems; Grand Cross of Order of Beneficence from Pres. of Greece 1989. *Leisure interests:* walking, swimming, music. *Address:* Orpheus str. 9A, 1583 Nicosia, Cyprus (home). *Telephone:* 22765456 (home). *Fax:* 22377896 (home).

VASSILIOU, Georghios Vassos, DEcon; Cypriot politician and economist; b. 20 May 1931, Famagusta; s. of Vasos Vassiliou and Sophia Othonos Vassiliou (née Yiavopoulou); m. Androulla Georgiadou 1966; one s. two d.; ed Univ. of Budapest, Hungary; Market Researcher, Reed Paper Group, London 1960–62; Founder Middle East Marketing Research Bureau (now MEMRB Int.) and Ledra Advertising Co. 1962; f. Inst. of Dirs (Cyprus Br.); mem. Exec. Cttee Cyprus Chamber of Commerce 1970–86; mem. Bd and Exec. Cttee Bank of Cyprus 1981–88; mem. Econ. Advisory Council, Church of Cyprus 1982–88, Educational Advisory Council 1983–88; Pres. of Cyprus 1988–93; Founder United Democrats Movt, Pres. 1995–2005; Chair. World Inst. for Devt Econ. Research, UN Univ., Helsinki 1995–2000; mem. Parl. 1996–99; Chief Negotiator for the Accession of Cyprus to the EU 1998–2003; Visiting Prof., Cranfield School of Man., UK; mem. InterAction

Council 1998–, Trilateral Comm. 2000–; Hon. Prof., Cyprus Int. Inst. of Man.; Dr hc (Univs of Cyprus, Athens, Salonica, Budapest, Belgrade); Grand Cross, Order of Merit (Cyprus), Grand Cross, Légion d'honneur, Grand Cross of the Saviour (Greece), Grand Cross of the Order of the Repub. of Italy, Grand Star (Austria), Grand Collar, Order of Infante D. Henrique (Portugal), Grand Collar of the Nile (Egypt), Standard (Flag) Order decorated with diamonds (Hungary), and other distinctions, awards and decorations. *Publications:* Marketing in the Middle East 1976, The Middle East Markets Up to 1980 1977, Moyen Orient: Le Consommateur des années '80 1980, Towards the Solution of the Cyprus Problem 1992, Modernisation of the Civil Service 1992, Overcoming Indifference 1994, Tourism and Sustainable Development 1995, Towards a Larger, Yet More Effective European Union 1999, Cyprus-European Union: From the First Steps to Accession 2004; numerous articles in various int. publs. *Leisure interests:* listening to music, reading, swimming, body exercise. *Address:* PO Box 22098, 1583 Nicosia (office); 9A Orpheos Street, 1070 Cyprus (home). *Telephone:* (2) 2336142 (office); (2) 2374888 (home). *Fax:* (2) 2336301 (office). *E-mail:* gvassiliou@memrb.com.cy (office).

VASSILYEV, Alexey Mikhailovich, DrHist; Russian scientist; *Honorary President, Russian Academy of Sciences;* b. 26 April 1939, Leningrad; m.; two d.; ed Moscow State Inst. of Int. Relations; with Pravda, political columnist, corresp. in Viet Nam, Turkey, Egypt 1962–83; Deputy Dir Inst. of Africa (now Inst. for African Studies), USSR (now Russian) Acad. of Sciences 1983–92, Dir 1992–15, Hon. Pres. 2015–, Chair. Scientific Council for the Problems of Africa, also mem. Russian Pugwash Cttee; Head of the Chair for African and Arab Studies, Peoples' Friendship Univ. of Russia 2013–; Ed.-in-Chief Asia and Africa Today (magazine) 1998–; Pres. Asscn of Cultural and Business Co-operation with African Cos; Pres. Centre of Regional and Civilisation Studies; Special Rep. of Pres. of Russian Fed. for Relations with African Leaders 2006–11; mem. Council on Foreign Policy, Ministry of Foreign Affairs, Russian Fed., Editorial Council, Social Evolution & History Journal; Visiting Prof. at univs in USA, UK, France, Egypt, Saudi Arabia; Medals for Labour Merit, for Labour Heroism, Merited Scholar of the Russian Fed. 1999; Russian Acad. of Sciences E. V. Tarle Prize for Best Studies in History and Int. Relations 2003. *Publications:* 36 monographs, numerous scientific works and more than 900 articles published in Russia and abroad on Middle East, Central Asia, Africa, Arab-Israeli conflict, Islam including History of Saudi Arabia, Russian Policy in the Middle East, Egypt and the Egyptians, Post-Soviet Central Asia, King Faisal of Saudi Arabia: Personality, Faith and Times 2012. *Leisure interests:* Russian literature, skiing. *Address:* Institute for African Studies, Russian Academy of Sciences, Spiridonovka str. 30/1, 123001 Moscow (office); 11/13-103 Pravda str., 125040 Moscow, Russia (home). *Telephone:* (495) 690-63-85 (office); (495) 614-47-28 (home). *Fax:* (495) 697-19-54 (office). *E-mail:* dir@inafr.ru (office). *Website:* www.inafran.ru (office).

VASTAGH, Pál, PhD; Hungarian politician, jurist and diplomatist; b. 23 Sept. 1946; m. Erzsébet Fenyvesi; one s. two d.; ed József Attila Univ. of Arts and Sciences, Szeged; Asst Lecturer, later Lecturer, then Sr Lecturer, Dept of Theory of State and Law, József Attila Univ. of Arts and Sciences 1988–89, Dean 1989; mem. of Presidium HSP 1989; mem. Parl. 1990–2006, Parl.'s Cttee on Constitutional Affairs, Chair. 2002; mem. Codification and Justice Cttee on European Integration Affairs; Minister of Justice 1994–98; Deputy Leader of Socialist faction 1998–2002; Prof., Budapest School of Man. 1999–; mem. Convention on the Future of Europe 2002; Observer and mem. European Parl. 2003–04; Chief Adviser to Prime Minister 2004; Dir-Gen. Coll. of Man., Budapest 2004–07; Amb. to Canada 2007–11; Order of Merit of the Republic of Hungary 2010. *Publications:* articles in nat. newspapers and professional periodicals. *Leisure interests:* reading, hiking, travelling, soccer. *Address:* Ministry of Foreign Affairs, 1027 Budapest, Bem rakpart 47, Hungary (office).

VASUDEV, C(hander) M(ohan); Indian business executive; ed Univ. Coll. of Swansea, UK, Punjab Univ., Chandigarh; with Administrative Services 1966–2003; fmr Sec., Ministry of Finance, Jt Sec., Ministry of Commerce; Ind. Dir Housing Devt Financial Corpn (HDFC) 2006–10, Chair. (non-exec.) 2010–14; fmr Exec. Dir World Bank, chaired Cttee on Devt Effectiveness; currently Head, Centennial Group India. *E-mail:* cmvasudev@gmail.com. *Website:* www.centennial-group.com.

VASUDEVA, Sudhir, BE, MBA; Indian engineer and business executive; *Chairman, National Institute of Technology, Raipur;* m.; two d.; ed Nat. Inst. of Technology, Raipur, Indira Gandhi Nat. Open Univ.; joined Oil and Natural Gas Corpn as Exec. Trainee 1976, Exec. Dir 2004–09, Dir (Offshore) 2009–11, Chair. and Man. Dir 2011–14; Chair. and Man. Dir Mangalore Refinery and Petrochemicals 2011–14; Chair. Bd of Dirs Nat. Inst. of Tech., Raipur 2012–; apptd Chair. Soc. Petroleum Engineers (SPE) Mumbai Section 2012, Chair. SPE India Council; mem. Bd UN Global Compact 2012–; Hon. Fellow, Centre for Excellence in Project Man.-Project Man. Assocs 2012; Distinguished Service Award, Soc. Petroleum Engineers, Middle East, Outstanding Achievement in Exploration and Production Award. *Leisure interests:* reading, listening to music. *Address:* National Institute of Technology Raipur, G.E. Road, Raipur 492 010, India (office). *Telephone:* (771) 2254200 (office). *Fax:* (771) 2254600 (office). *Website:* www.nitrr.ac.in (office).

VATOLIN, Nikolay Anatolyevich; Russian metallurgist and academic; *Professor, Institute of Metallurgy, Urals Branch, Russian Academy of Sciences;* b. 13 Nov. 1926, Yekaterinburg; m.; one s.; ed Urals Polytechnical Inst., Sverdlovsk; scientific researcher, scientific sec., Head of Lab., Dir Inst. of Metallurgy, USSR (now Russian) Acad. of Sciences (Urals Br.) 1950–98, Prof. 1973–, Adviser, Russian Acad. of Sciences 1998–; mem. CPSU 1952–91; Corresp. mem. of USSR (now Russian) Acad. of Sciences 1970–81, mem. 1981; USSR State Prize 1982, 1991, Kurnakow Gold Medal, Russian Acad. of Sciences 1995, Govt Prize, Russian Fed. 1997, Demidov's Prize 1997, Russian Fed. State Prize 2000, Bardin's Prize, Russian Acad. of Sciences 2007. *Publications:* co-author: Physico-chemical Foundations of Steel Hot Leading 1977, Oxidation of Vanadium Slags 1978, Interparticle Interaction in Molten Metals 1979, Diffraction Studies of High Temperature Melts 1980, Computerization of Thermodynamic Calculations of Metallurgical Processes 1982, Electrical Properties of Oxide Melts 1984, Hydrometallurgy of Ferropowders 1984, Computer Simulation of Amorphous Metals 1985, Vanadium Slags 1988, Thermodynamic Modelling in High Temperature Inorganic Systems 1994, Temperature Dependences of Gibbs Reduced Energy of

Some Inorganic Substances 1997, Fire Processing of Integrated Ores 1997, Some Regularities of Changes of Thermochemical Properties of Inorganic Compounds and Computational Methods for these Properties 2001, Lead Wastes Recycling in Ionic Salt Melts 2002, Diffraction Studies of a Structure of High-Temperature Melts 2003, Nonferrous Metals Recycling in Ionic Melts 2005, Modelling of Disordered and Nano-structured Phases 2011, Thermodynamic Perturbation Theory in Studies of Metal Melts 2014, Stability and Thermal Evolution of Transition Metal and Silicon Clusters 2015. *Address:* Institute of Metallurgy, Ural Branch, Russian Academy of Sciences, 101 Amundsen Street, 620016 Yekaterinburg (office); 17 Polyanka Street, 620016 Yekaterinburg, Russia (home). *Telephone:* (343) 267-94-21 (office); (343) 267-89-01 (home). *Fax:* (343) 267-91-86 (office). *E-mail:* vatolin@imet.mplik.ru (home).

VAUGHAN, David Arthur John, CBE, QC, FRSA; British barrister and academic; *Visiting Professor of Law, Durham University;* b. 24 Aug. 1938; s. of Capt. F. H. M. Vaughan and J. M. Vaughan; m. 1st 1967 (divorced); m. 2nd Leslie A. F. Irwin 1985; one s. one d.; ed Eton Coll. and Trinity Coll. Cambridge; called to Bar, Inner Temple 1962, Bencher 1988; mem. Bar Council 1968–72, 1984–86, Bar Cttee 1987–88; mem. Int. Relations Cttee of Bar Council 1968–86, Bar/Law Soc. Working Party on EEC (now EU) Competition Law 1977– (Chair. 1978–88), UK Del. to Consultative Cttee of Bars and Law Socs of the EC 1978–81 and other cttees etc.; Chair. EC Section, Union Int. des Advocats 1987–91; a Recorder 1994–2001; Chair. Editorial Bd European Law Reports 1997–; a Deputy High Court Judge 1997–2002; Judge of the Courts of Appeal of Jersey and Guernsey 2000–09; Visiting Prof. of Law, Univ. of Durham 1989–; mem. Advisory Bd, Centre for European Legal Studies, Cambridge Univ. 1991–; mem. Council of Man., British Inst. of Int. and Comparative Law 1992–2005; mem. Editorial Advisory Bd European Business Law Review 1998–; Fellow, Soc. for Advanced Legal Studies 1998; Bronze Medal, Bar of Bordeaux 1985. *Publications:* Gen. Ed. Encyclopaedia of EU Law, Vaughan and Robertson; Co-ordinating Ed. Halsbury's Laws of England 1986; Vaughan on the Law of the European Communities (ed.) 1986–97; Consultant Ed., European Court Practice 1993, Current EC Legal Development series. *Leisure interests:* fishing, tennis. *Address:* Brick Court Chambers, 7–8 Essex Street, London, WC2R 3LD, England (office). *Telephone:* (20) 7379-3550 (office). *Fax:* (20) 7379-3558 (office). *E-mail:* vaughan@brickcourt.co.uk (office).

VAUGHAN, Michael Paul, OBE; British professional cricketer (retd); b. 29 Oct. 1974, Eccles, Greater Manchester; s. of Graham Vaughan and Deirdre Vaughan (née Greenhaugh); m. Nichola Shannon; ed St Marks, Worsley, Dore Junior School, Sheffield, Silverdale Comprehensive School, Sheffield; right-hand opening batsmen, occasional right-arm off-break bowler; teams: Yorks. 1993–2009, England Under-19, England A (Capt. 1998–99), England 1999–2008 (Capt. 2003–08, retd from One-Day Int. (ODI) team 2007), MCC; First-class debut: 1993; Test debut: South Africa v England, Johannesburg 25–28 Nov. 1999; ODI debut: Sri Lanka v England, Dambulla 23 March 2001; T20I debut: England v Australia, Southampton 13 June 2005; played in 82 Tests (23 as Capt.), scored 5,719 runs (average 41.44, highest score 197 against India 2002) with 18 hundreds and took six wickets; ODIs: 86 matches, scored 1,982 runs (average 27.15, highest score 90 not out); First-class matches: scored 16,295 runs (average 36.95, highest score 197) with 42 hundreds and took 114 wickets; first batsman for 32 years to score 600 runs in a test series in Australia 2002/03; ranked World No. 1 Batsman 2003; announced retirement from first-class cricket 30 June 2009; joined Test Match Special (BBC) as an expert summarizer during England v Australia ODI series 2009; Freeman of the City of Sheffield 2005; Professional Cricketer's Asscn Player of the Year 2002, Player of the Series Australia vs England 2002/03, Wisden Cricketer of the Year 2003, BBC Sports Personality of the Year Team Award (mem.) 2005, named in Test Team of the Year, ICC (Int. Cricket Council) Awards 2007. *Radio:* appeared on BBC Radio 5 Live's Fighting Talk. *Publications:* Michael Vaughan: A Year in the Sun 2003, Calling the Shots: The Captain's Story 2005. *Leisure interests:* golf, football (Sheffield Wednesday). *Address:* c/o International Sports Management Ltd, Cherry Tree Farm, Cherry Tree Lane, Rostherne, Cheshire, WA14 3RZ, England (office). *Telephone:* (1565) 832100 (office). *Fax:* (1565) 832200 (office). *Website:* www.michaelvaughan.net.

VAUGHN, Vincent (Vince) Anthony; American actor; b. 28 March 1970, Minneapolis, Minn.; s. of Vernon Lindsay Vaughn and Sharon Eileen DePalmo; m. Kyla Weber 2010; ed Lake Forest High School; began acting career 1989; ShoWest Convention Comedy Star of the Year 2006. *Films include:* Swingers 1996, The Locusts 1997, The Lost World: Jurassic Park 1997, Psycho 1998, Clay Pigeons 1998, Return to Paradise 1998, A Cool, Dry Place 1998, The Cell 2000, The Prime Gig 2000, Made (also producer) 2001, Domestic Disturbance 2001, Starsky & Hutch 2004, Dodgeball: A True Underdog Story 2004, Be Cool 2005, Mr & Mrs Smith 2005, Thumbsucker 2005, Wedding Crashers 2005, The Break-Up 2006, Into the Wild 2007, Wild West Comedy Show 2008, Couples Retreat 2009, The Dilemma 2011, The Watch 2012, A Case of You 2013, The Internship 2013, Delivery Man 2013, Unfinished Business 2015. *Television:* True Detective (series) 2015. *Address:* United Talent Agency, 9560 Wilshire Blvd, Suite 500, Beverly Hills, CA 90212-2401, USA (office). *Telephone:* (310) 273-6700 (office). *Fax:* (310) 247-1111 (office). *Website:* www.unitedtalent.com (office); www.vince-vaughn.com (office).

VAUZELLE, Michel Marie; French lawyer and politician; b. 15 Aug. 1944, Montelimar, Drome; s. of Fernand Vauzelle and Marine Faure; m. Sylvie Fauvet 1980; two s. one d.; ed Collège St-Joseph, Lyon, Faculty of Law, Paris, Inst. of Political Studies, Paris; barrister 1968; Chargé de mission Prime Minister's Office 1969–72; mem. Finance Section Econ. and Social Council 1972–73; joined Parti Socialiste (SP) 1976, Nat. Del. of SP Council of Civil Liberties 1978–81; Deputy Mayor of Arles 1977–83, town councillor 1983–95, Mayor of Arles 1995–98, Deputy Mayor 1998–2001; Spokesman for the President of the Republic 1981–86; Préfet hors cadre 1985; mem. Assemblée Nationale (Parl.) (Socialist) for Bouches-du-Rhône 1986–92, 1997–2002, 2007–, Chair. Comm. for Foreign Affairs 1989–92; Minister of Justice and Keeper of the Seals 1992–93; Vice-Pres. Gen. Council Bouches du Rhône 1992–97; Pres. Regional Council Provence-Alpes-Côte d'Azur 1998–2015; Vice-Pres. ARF (Association des régions de France) 2004–; Pres. Commission Interméditerranéenne, Conférence des Régions Périphériques Maritimes 2007–; Pres. Nat. School of Photography 1982–86. *Publications:* Éloge de Daniel Manin, avocat venitien 1978, La France déroutée. *Leisure interest:* riding.

Address: Assemblée nationale, 126 rue de l'Université, 75355 Paris Cedex 07, 75355 Paris Cedex 07 (office); 15 rue de la Calade, 13200 Arles, France (office). *Telephone:* 1-40-63-68-55 (office); 4-90-18-44-86 (Arles) (office). *E-mail:* mvauzelle@assemblee-nationale.fr (office). *Website:* www2.assemblee-nationale.fr (office); www.michel-vauzelle.fr.

VAVAKIN, Leonid Vassilyevich; Russian architect; b. 6 April 1932, Moscow; ed Moscow State Inst. of Architecture; Chief Architect and Chair. Moscow Cttee on Architecture and City Construction 1987–96; Prof., Moscow Inst. of Architecture; Corresp. mem. Russian Acad. of Arts, Full mem. 1995–; mem. Int. Acad. of Architecture; Academician-Sec. Russian Acad. of Architecture; USSR Council of Ministers Prize, RSFSR Merited Architect. *Address:* c/o Russian Academy of Architecture, 103874 Moscow, Dmitrova str. 24, Russia. *Telephone:* (495) 229-65-26.

VAVILOV, Andrei Petrovich, PhD; Russian economist, business executive and politician; *Chairman, SuperOx;* b. 10 Jan. 1961, Perm; m. Marina Tsaregradskaya; one d.; ed Moscow Inst. of Man., Cen. Econs and Math. Inst., Russian Acad. of Sciences; Eng Programmer, Computation Centre, USSR Ministry of Public Health 1982–85; Jr Researcher, Cen. Inst. of Econs and Math., USSR Acad. of Sciences 1985–88, Head of Lab., Inst. of Marketing Problems 1991–92; Sr Researcher, Inst. of Econ. Prognosis of Tech. Progress 1988–91; Head of Dept of Macroeconomic Policy, Ministry of Econs and Finance 1992; First Deputy Minister of Finance 1992–97; Pres. Int. Financial Initiative Bank 1997; mem. Bd of Dirs RAO Gazprom (Counsellor to Chair.) 1998–99; Co-founder and CEO Inst. of Financial Studies 1998–2002, apptd Research Council Chair 2002, currently Academic Dir; Owner and Chair. Severnaya Neft (oil co.), 2000–02 (sold co. 2002); mem. Fed. Council of Russia representing Penza Region Legis. Ass. 2002–10 (resgnd); f. IFS Hedge Fund 2007; Visiting Sr Scholar, Pennsylvania State Univ., USA 2007–10, Co-Dir Center for the Study of Auctions, Procurements and Competition Policy and Scientific Advisor, Center for Research on Int. Financial and Energy Security 2008–10; Chair. SuperOx (research and production co.), Moscow 2010–; mem. Intergovernmental Cttee for Public Debt and Property of the Russian Fed. 1992–97, Comm. for Modernisation and Technological Devt of Russia's Economy 2010–. *Publications:* The Russian Public Debt and Financial Meltdowns 2010, Gazprom: An Energy Giant and its Challenges in Europe 2014; numerous papers. *Leisure interests:* hunting, skiing, tennis. *Address:* SuperOx, 117246 Moscow, Nauchnyy pr-d, 20, Russia. *Telephone:* (495) 669-79-95 (office). *E-mail:* info@superox.ru (office). *Website:* www.superox.ru/en (office); www.ifs.ru/en; www.avavilov.ru/en.

VÄYRYNEN, Paavo Matti, MPolSci, DPolSc; Finnish politician; b. 2 Sept. 1946, Keminmaa; s. of Juho Eemeli Väyrynen and Anna Liisa (née Kaijankoski) Väyrynen; m. Vuokko Kaarina Tervonen 1968; one s. two d.; mem. Parl. 1970–2003, 2007–11; Political Sec. to Prime Minister 1970–71; Minister of Educ. 1975–76, of Labour 1976–77; Minister for Foreign Affairs 1977–82, 1991–93, Deputy Prime Minister and Minister for Foreign Affairs 1983–87, of Foreign Trade and Devt 2007–11; mem. European Parl. 1995–2007, 2014–; Vice-Chair. Suomen Keskusta (Finnish Centre Party) 1972–80, Chair. 1980–90, Hon. Chair. 2006–; mem. Nordic Council 1972–75; mem. Keminmaa Municipal Council 1973–80, 2005–; Helsinki City Councillor 1989; Assoc. Prof. of Int. Relations, Univ. of Lapland 1996–; unsuccessful cand. (Suomen Keskusta) in presidential election 1988, 1994, 2012, 2018. *Publications include:* Köyhän asialla (Speaking for the Poor) 1971, On muutoksen aika (This is a Time of Change) 1974, Kansallisia kysymyksiä 1981, Kansakunta – ihmiskunta 1987, Finlands utrikes politik 1988, Suomen ulkopolitiikka 1989, Yhteinen tehtävämme 1989, Igenom brytningstid 1993, On muutoksen aika II 1993, On totuuden aika I 1993, On totuuden aika II 1993, Suomen puolueettomuus uudessa Euroopassa 1996, Paneurooppa ja uusidealismi 1997, Itsenäisen Suomen puolesta 1999, Samankeskisten kehien Eurooppa 2000, Etiäisiä vai kaukoviisautta 2004, Pohjanranta 2005, Eameli Väyrysen Vuosisata 2009, Huonomminkin olisi voinut käydä. Esseitä elämästä, politiikasta ja yrittämisestä 2011, Suomen linja 2014, Eihän tässä näin pitänyt käydä 2016. *Address:* European Parliament, Rue Wiertz, ASP 08 H 349, 1047 Brussels, Belgium (office). *Telephone:* (2) 284-51-33 (office). *Fax:* (2) 284-91-33 (office). *E-mail:* paavo.vayrynen@europarl.europa.eu (office); pmvayrynen@gmail.com. *Website:* www.europarl.europa.eu (office); www.vayrynen.com.

VAZ, José Mário; Guinea-Bissau economist, politician and head of state; *President;* b. 10 Dec. 1957; s. of Mário Vaz and Amelia Gomes; m.; three c.; ed Office of Econ. Studies, Banco de Portugal; Mayor of Bissau 2004–09; fmr Pres. Assembléia Nacional Popular (Parl.); Minister of Finance 2009–12; Pres. of Guinea-Bissau 2014–; mem. Partido Africano da Independência da Guiné e Cabo Verde (PAIGC). *Address:* Office of the President, Bissau, Guinea-Bissau (office). *Website:* www.presidencia-gw.org (office).

VAZ, Osvaldo dos Santos; São Tomé and Príncipe economist and politician; *Minister of Planning, Finance and the Blue Economy;* b. 15 Oct. 1969, Guadalupe; ed University Agostinho Neto, Angola; teacher of Math. and Chemistry in Guadalupe 1987–92; served as Prof. of Econs at numerous higher education insts. in São Tomé 1996–2009; Head of Finance, Empresa Nacional de Combustíveis e Óleo (Nat. Oil and Gas Co.) (ENCO) 2001–03, Dir-Gen. 2003–18; mem. of Parl. 2014–; Minister of Planning, Finance and the Blue Economy 2018–; currently mem. Groupe Mouvement pour la libération de Sao Tomé-et-Principe–Parti social-démocrate (MLSTP-PSD) (political party) (Vice-Pres. 2012–17); mem. Bd of Dirs Sonangol EP (São Tomé and Príncipe) –2018. *Address:* Ministry of Planning, Finance and the Blue Economy, Largo Alfândega, CP 168, São Tomé, São Tomé and Príncipe (office). *Telephone:* 2221083 (office). *Fax:* 2222683 (office). *E-mail:* mpfc@cstome.net (office).

VAZ, Richard F., BS, MS, PhD; American engineer and academic; *Director, Center for Project-Based Learning, Worcester Polytechnic Institute;* b. 1958, Taunton, Mass; ed Worcester Polytechnic Inst.; Dean of Interdisciplinary and Global Studies, Worcester Polytechnic Inst. 2006–15, Dir Center for Project-Based Learning 2016–, Dir Bangkok Project Center 2016–; Gordon Prize, Nat. Acad. of Eng (co-recipient) 2016. *Address:* Project Center, 2nd Floor, Worcester Polytechnic Institute, 100 Institute Road, Worcester, MA 01609-2280, USA (office). *Telephone:* (508) 831-5344 (office). *E-mail:* vaz@wpi.edu (office). *Website:* wp.wpi.edu/projectbasedlearning (office).

VAZ DE ALMEIDA, Hélio Silva, BEcons, PhD; São Tomé and Príncipe economist and politician; ed Universidade de Lisboa; Inspector, Banking Supervision and Insurance, Banco Central de São Tomé e Príncipe 2006–08, Deputy Dir of Banking and Insurance Supervision 2008–10, Dir of Banking and Insurance Supervision 2010–12, Sr Adviser, Gov.'s Office 2015–16, Gov. 2016–19 (also mem. bd 2005); Minister of Planning and Finance 2012–14; mem. Movimento de Libertação de São Tomé e Príncipe—Partido Social Democrata.

VÁŽNY, Ľubomír; Slovak politician and business executive; b. 15 July 1957, Žilina; ed Faculty of Civil Eng, Slovak Tech. Univ., Bratislava; worked as construction foreman, construction man., tech. devt worker, State Enterprise, Trnava 1981–85; Head of Prices and Types, Head of Unit Typing and Design, Tech. Asst and Dir Stavoinveste, Banská Bystrica 1985–94, Dir and Man. Dir Stavoinvesta sro 1994–2002; mem. Smer (Direction), later Smer-Sociálna Demokracia (Smer-SD—Direction-Social Democracy), served as Shadow Minister for Transport and Construction, mem. Nat. Council 2002–; mem. Parl., Vice-Chair. Cttee for Economy, Privatization and Entrepreneurship, mem. Mandate and Immunity Cttee; Minister of Transport, Posts and Telecommunications 2006–10; unsuccessful cand. for Mayor of Banská Bystrica in electoral coalition of Smer-SD, Slovenská Národná Strana (Slovak Nat. Party) and Ľudová Strana-Hnutie za Demokratické Slovensko (People's Party –Movt for a Democratic Slovakia) 2010; Deputy Prime Minister, responsible for Investment 2012–16. *Address:* Smer-Sociálna Demokracia (Direction-Social Democracy), Súmračná 25, 821 02 Bratislava, Slovakia (office). *Telephone:* (2) 4342-6297 (office). *Fax:* (2) 4342-6300 (office). *E-mail:* sekretariat.fico@strana-smer.sk (office). *Website:* www.strana-smer.sk (office).

VÁZQUEZ MOTA, Josefina Eugenia; Mexican politician; b. 1961, Mexico City; m. Sergio Ocampo Muñoz; three d.; ed Universidad Iberoamerican, Panamerican Inst. for Exec. Business Admin (IPADE); fmr Head of Women's Secr., Asociación Política Nacional; adviser to Confed. of Nat. Chambers of Commerce and Tourism (Concanaco); fmr adviser to Mexican Patronal Confed. (Coparmex); mem. Congress (Nat. Action Party, PAN) 2000–11; Minister of Social Devt 2000–05 (resgnd), of Public Educ. 2006–09; man. of successful presidential campaign of Filipe Calderon Hinojosa 2006, then head of transition team; unsuccessful cand. (PAN) in 2012 presidential election; Diploma on Ideas and Insts, Autonomous Technological Inst. of Mexico (ITAM). *Publications:* Dios Mio, Hazme Viuda Por Favor 2001, Nuestra oportunidad. Un México para todos; numerous articles in newspapers including Novedades and El Economista. *Address:* Partido Acción Nacional, Avda Coyoacán 1546, Col. del Valle, Del. Benito Juárez, 03100 México, DF, Mexico (office). *Telephone:* (55) 5200-4000 (office). *E-mail:* correo@cen.pan.org.mx (office). *Website:* www.pan.org.mx (office).

VÁZQUEZ ROMERO, Antonio, BSc; Spanish business executive; *Chairman, International Airlines Group;* b. 23 Nov. 1951, Cordoba; ed Univ. of Malaga; Dir of Subsidiaries and Man. Dir, Osborne Group, Mexico 1978–83; Dir of Subsidiaries, Domecq Mexico and Man. Dir Domecq International 1983–93; Deputy Dir Int. Dept, Tabacalera 1993–96, Dir Cigar Div. 1996–2000, COO Cigar Div., Altadis (tobacco co. cr. out of merger of Seita and Tabacalera) 2000–05, CEO and Chair. Exec. Cttee 2005–08; Chair. and CEO Iberia Lineas Aereas de Espana SA 2009–13, Chair. International Airlines Group (holding co. which owns Iberia) 2013–; mem. Bd of Dirs Telefónica Internacional 2008–. *Address:* International Airlines Group, Calle Velazquez 130, Madrid 28006, Spain (office). *Website:* www.iairgroup.com (office).

VÁZQUEZ ROMERO, Antonio, BSc; Spanish business executive; *Chairman, International Airlines Group;* b. 23 Nov. 1951, Córdoba; ed Málaga Univ.; worked for Arthur Andersen & Co. 1974–78; Dir of Subsidiaries, Domecq Mexico and Man. Dir Domecq Int. 1983–93; Head of Devt of Int. Business, Tabacalera 1993–96, Gen. Man. Cigar Div. 1996–2005; Chair. Bd and Chair. Exec. Cttee and CEO Altadis Group (tobacco co. cr. out of merger of Seita and Tabacalera) 2005–08; Chair. and CEO Iberia Lineas Aereas de Espana SA 2009–13, Chair. International Airlines Group (holding co. which owns Iberia) 2013–; mem. Bd of Dirs Telefónica Internacional 2008–; Dir (non-exec.) Transtlantic Business Dialogue Bd; Manager of the Year, AED 2010. *Address:* Iberia, Líneas Aéreas de España SA, Velázquez 130, 28006 Madrid, Spain (office). *Telephone:* (91) 587-87-87 (office). *Fax:* (91) 587-74-69 (office). *E-mail:* media@iberia.es (office). *Website:* grupo.iberia.es (office); www.iairgroup.com (office).

VÁZQUEZ ROSAS, Tabaré Ramón, PhD; Uruguayan politician, physician and head of state; *President;* b. 17 Jan. 1940, Montevideo; m. Maria Auxiliadora Delgado; three c.; ed Universidad de la Republica, Gustave Roussy Inst., Paris; Prof. Faculty of Medicine, Universidad de la Republica 1987–; Mayor of Montevideo 1990–95; Leader, Encuentro Progresista-Frente Amplio (Broad Front) coalition 2001–; unsuccessful presidential cand. 2000; Pres. of Uruguay 2005–10, March 2015–; Order of Merit of Qatar 2007, Grand Collar, Nat. Order of San Lorenzo (Ecuador) 2010; WHO Dir-Gen.'s Award for coordinating tobacco control in Uruguay 2006. *Address:* Office of the President, Casa de Gobierno, Plaza Independencia 710, Torre Ejecutiva, 1° y 2°, 11000 Montevideo (office); Encuentro Progresista-Frente Amplio, Colonia 1367, 2° Montevideo, Uruguay (office). *Telephone:* 2150 2647 (office). *Fax:* 2917 1121 (office). *E-mail:* sci@presidencia.gub.uy (office). *Website:* www.presidencia.gub.uy (office).

VEBER, Francis Paul; French screenwriter and director; b. 28 July 1937, Neuilly; s. of Pierre Gilles Veber and Catherine Veber (née Agadjaniantz); m. Françoise Marie Ehrenpreis 1964; two s.; ed Paris Univ. of Science, Paris Medical School; began career as journalist, also wrote short stories, stand-up comedy material and theatre plays; wrote first film screenplay 1969; Pres. EFVE Films 1976, Escape Film Production Co. 1988; Chevalier, Légion d'honneur, Commdr des Arts et Lettres, Officier, Ordre Nat. du Mérite. *Films directed include:* first film, Le Jouet, 1976; first American film, Three Fugitives 1989, Le Dîner de Cons (also screenwriter, based on his stage play) (César Award for Best Writing 1999) 1997, Le Placard 2001, Tais-Toi 2003, La Doublure 2006, A Pain in the Ass 2008. *Films as writer include:* Le jaguar 1996, Shut Up! 2003, The Valet 2006, Cher trésor (TV) 2014, Le placard (TV) 2015. *Publications:* Le Grand Blond avec une Chaussure Noire 1972, L'Emmerdeur 1973, Le Magnifique 1973, Le Jouet 1976, La Cage aux Folles (adaptation) 1978, La Chèvre 1981, Les Compères 1983, Les Fugitifs 1986, Le Jaguar 1996, Le Dîner de Cons 1998, Le Placard 2001, Tais-Toi 2003. *Leisure* *interests:* tennis, swimming. *Address:* c/o Artmédia, 20 avenue Rapp, 75007 Paris, France.

VEBER, Janko; Slovenian politician; b. 30 July 1960, Ljubljana; ed Secondary School of Civil Eng and Tech., Ljubljana, Univ. of Ljubljana; moved to Kočevje, worked in spatial planning and inspection services at Municipality of Kočevje 1989–90; Dir Hydrovod Kočevje-Ribnica (water supply co.) 1990–96; Mayor of Municipality of Kočevje 1994–2010; Deputy (Social Democrats) of Državni zbor (Nat. Ass.) for IV Kočevje 1 1996–; Pres. 2013–14; Minister of Defence 2014–15; Pres. Women's Handball Club, Kočevje 1997–2011, Asscn of Professional Drivers and Mechanics of Slovenia 2011–.

VEDERNIKOV, Alexander Aleksandrovich; Russian conductor; *Chief Conductor, Royal Danish Opera;* b. 11 Jan. 1964, Moscow; s. of Aleksander F. Vedernikov and Natalya Guryeva; m. Olga Aleksandrovna Vedernikova; ed Moscow P. I. Tchaikovsky State Conservatory; Music Dir Stanislavsky Music Theatre, Moscow 1988–90; Asst Conductor, then Prin. Conductor, Symphony Orchestra of Russian TV and Radio 1989–95; Founder and Chief Conductor, Russian Philharmonia Symphony Orchestra 1995–98, 2000–04; Musical Dir and Chief Conductor, Bolshoi Theatre of Russia 2001–09; mem. conductor's collegium, Russian Nat. Orchestra 2003–; Chief Conductor and Artistic Adviser, Odense Symphony Orchestra 2009–; Chief Conductor, Royal Danish Opera 2017–; works as guest conductor with Orchestre de Paris, NHK Symphony, Netherlands Radio Philharmonic, City of Birmingham Symphony, Orchestra della Svizzera Italiana, Netherlands Philharmonic, Orchestra Verdi Milan, London Philharmonic, Orchestre Philharmonique de Radio France, Gothenburg Symphony, Danish National Symphony, Bergen Philharmonic, Czech Philharmonic; opera at Komische Oper, Berlin, La Scala in Milan, La Fenice in Venice, Teatro Comunale in Bologna, Teatro Regio in Turin, Opera di Roma; conducted opera and ballet productions in European theatres including Covent Garden, London, La Scala, Milan and symphony orchestras in Russia; debuts at Carnegie Hall and Kennedy Center, Washington, DC 2004. *Address:* Royal Danish Opera, August Bournonvilles Passage 2–8, PO Box 2185, 1017 Copenhagen K, Denmark (office); Pyryeva str. 4, korp. 1, apt. 24, 119285 Moscow, Russia (home). *Telephone:* 33-69-69-33 (office); (495) 147-52-17 (home). *E-mail:* admin@kglteater.dk (office). *Website:* kglteater.dk.

VÉDRINE, Hubert; French politician and civil servant; *Managing Director, Hubert Védrine Conseil;* b. 31 July 1947, Saint-Silvain-Bellegarde; s. of Jean Védrine and Suzanne Védrine; m. Michèle Froment; two s.; ed Lycée Albert Camus, Univ. of Nanterre, Institut d'Etudes Politiques, Paris, Ecole Nat. d'Admin.; Sr Civil Servant, Ministry of Culture 1974–78, Ministry for Capital Works 1978–79; Co-ordinator for Cultural Relations, Near and Middle East, Ministry of Foreign Affairs 1979–81; Technical Adviser External Affairs, Office of the Sec.-Gen. of the Pres. 1981–86, Legal Adviser, Conseil d'Etat 1986, 1995–96; Spokesman for Presidency of Repub. 1988–91, Chief of Staff 1991–95; Partner, Jeantet et Associés (law firm) 1996–97; Minister of Foreign Affairs 1997–2002; Founding Partner and Man. Dir Hubert Védrine Conseil (consultancy) 2003–; Chair. Institut François-Mitterrand 2004–; Chair. cttee to draw up report to Ministry of Economy on NATO 2012, on relations between Africa and France 2013–14; mem. Bd of Dirs LVMH 2004–, Ipsos SA 2009–; mem. Global Advisory Bd Moelis & Company (investment bank) 2011–; fmr mem. Advisory Bd Booz Allen Hamilton France. *Publications include:* Mieux aménager sa ville 1979, Les Mondes de François Mitterrand, A l'Elysée 1981–95 1996, Dialogue avec Dominique Moïsi: Les Cartes de la France à l'heure de la mondialisation 2000, Face à l'Hyperpuissance 2003, Multilateralisme: une reforme possible 2004, François Mitterand: un dessein, un destin 2006, Continuer l'Histoire, avec Adrien Abecassis et Mohamed Bouabdallah 2007, Atlas du monde global 2008, Atlas des crises et des conflits 2009, Atlas de la France 2011, Dans la mêlée mondiale 2009–2012 2012, La France au défi 2014, Le monde au défi 2016. *Address:* 6 rue de Luynes, 75007 Paris, France (home). *Website:* www.hubertvedrine.net.

VEERATHAI, Santiprabhob, BA, AM, PhD; Thai economist and central banker; *Governor, Bank of Thailand;* b. 25 Dec. 1969; ed Thammasat Univ., Harvard Univ., USA; Economist, IMF, Washington, DC 1994–98; Co-Dir Policy Research Inst., Fiscal Policy Office, Ministry of Finance 1998–2000; Exec. Vice-Pres. and Head of Business Bank, Strategic Planning Div., Siam Commercial Bank PCL 2000–08; Exec. Vice-Pres. and Chief Strategy Officer, Stock Exchange of Thailand 2009–13; Advisor, Thailand Devt Research Inst., Bangkok 2013–15; Gov. Bank of Thailand 2015–, also Commr Securities and Exchange Comm.; Chair. Asian Consultative Council, BIS 2017–; mem. Bd of Dirs SCB Life Assurance Public Co. Ltd, Siam Commercial New York Life Insurance Public Co. Ltd, Palm Oil Public Co. Ltd, Thai Airways Int. Public Co. Ltd 2014–15, Buddhadasa Indapanno Archives, Thailand Sustainable Devt Foundation, Mae Fah Luang Foundation, Royal Initiative Discovery Foundation; mem. State Enterprise Policy and Supervisory Cttee; fmr mem. Ind. Expert Oversight Advisory Cttee, WHO; fmr Ind. Dir Bangkok Dusit Medical Services PCL; Eisenhower Fellowship 2013; cttee mem., Thammasat Section, Anandhamahidol Foundation; H.M. King Bhumibol Adulyadej Award for Highest Academic Achievement in Econs, Thammasat Univ. 1989, Anandamahidol Foundation Scholarship 1989–94, Distinguished Alumnus Award, Thammasat Econs Asscn 2015. *Address:* Bank of Thailand, 273 Thanon Samsen, Wat Sam Phraya, Phra Nakhon, Bangkok 10200, Thailand (office). *Telephone:* (2) 283-5353 (office). *Fax:* (2) 280 0626 (office). *E-mail:* IRTeam@bot.or .th (office). *Website:* www.bot.or.th (office).

VEGA DE SEOANE AZPILICUETA, Javier; Spanish mining engineer and business executive; *President, Círculo de Empresarios;* b. 13 Sept. 1947, San Sebastián; s. of Joaquín Vega de Seoane and Rosa Azpilicueta; m. Mercedes Pérez de Villaamil Lapiedra 1970; two s. one d.; ed Escuela Técnica Superior de Ingenieros de Minas, Madrid and Glasgow Business School, UK; Asst Production Dir, Fundiciones del Estanda SA 1972–75; Asst to CEO, Leyland Ibérica SA 1975–77; Gen. Man. SKF Española SA 1977–83, Pres. and CEO 1983–84; Gen. Man. Instituto Nacional de Industria 1984–86; Partner TASA AG 1986; Co-Founder Gestlink (consultancy) 1987, Pres. 1991–; Sr Adviser in Spain, Wasserstein Perella & Co. 1992; Pres. Explosivos Río Tinto 1987, S.A. Cros 1987, Chair. Bd Ercros (following merger) –1991; Pres. Fujitsu España; currently Pres. DKV Seguros; mem. Bd of Dirs Ydilo Voice Solutions, Tavex Algodonera SA, Sonae Industria; Algodonera SA; mem. Exec. Bd Circulo de Empresarios, Pres.

2015–; Chair. Advisory Bd Fundación DKV Integralia; mem. Advisory Bd AON Gil y Carvajal. *Leisure interests:* golf, squash, scuba diving. *Address:* Círculo de Empresarios, Marqués de Villamagna, 3 11ª planta, 28001 Madrid, Spain (office). *Telephone:* (915) 78-14-72 (office). *Website:* circulodeempresarios.org (office).

VEGA GARCÍA, Gen. Gerardo Clemente Ricardo; Mexican politician and army officer; b. 28 March 1940, Puebla City; ed War Coll., Nat. Defence Coll.; joined army 1957; nat. security studies in USA and Panama and fmr Dir of Mil. Educ.; fmr Rector Army and Air Force Univ.; fmr Deputy Chief of Mil. Doctrine, Estado Mayor of SEDENA; fmr Mil. Attaché, embassies in USSR, Poland, and Germany; fmr Deputy Dir and Dir Nat. Defence Coll.; promoted to Div. Gen. with command of Mil. Zone One 2000; Sec. of Nat. Defence 2000–06; Legion of Honour and Merit and numerous other decorations.

VEGLIÒ, HE Cardinal Antonio Maria; Italian ecclesiastic and diplomatist; *President, Pontifical Council for Pastoral Care of Migrants and Itinerant People;* b. 3 Feb. 1938, Macerata Feltria; ordained priest, Archdiocese of Pesaro 1962; apptd Titular Archbishop of Aeclanum 1985; Apostolic Pro-Nuncio to Papua New Guinea (also accred to the Solomon Islands) 1985–89, to Senegal (also accred to Guinea-Bissau, Cabo Verde and Mali) 1989–94, Apostolic Nuncio to Senegal (also accred to Guinea-Bissau, Cabo Verde and Mali) 1994–97, to Lebanon (also accred to Kuwait) 1997–99; Sec. Congregation for the Oriental Churches 2001–09; Pres. Pontifical Council for Pastoral Care of Migrants and Itinerant People 2009–13, 2013–; cr. Cardinal (Cardinal-Deacon of San Cesareo in Palatio) 2012; participated in Papal Conclave 2013. *Address:* Pontifical Council for Pastoral Care of Migrants and Itinerant People, Piazza San Calisto 16, 00120 Città del Vaticano, Rome, Italy (office). *Telephone:* (06) 69887131 (office); (06) 69887193 (office); (06) 69887242 (office). *Fax:* (06) 69887295 (office); (06) 69887111 (office). *E-mail:* office@migrants .va (office). *Website:* www.vatican.va/roman_curia/pontifical_councils/migrants/ index.htm (office); www.pcmigrants.org (office).

VEIGA, Carlos Alberto Wahnon de Carvalho, PhD; Cabo Verde politician, lawyer and diplomatist; *Ambassador to USA;* b. 21 Oct. 1949, Mindelo; m. Maria Epifânia Cruz Almeida; apptd Attorney-Gen. 1978; Prime Minister of Interim Govt Jan. 1991, Prime Minister of Cabo Verde 1991–2000, also with responsibility for Defence; presidential cand. 2001; Amb. to USA 2017–; fmr Chair. Movimento para a Democracia (MPD). *Address:* Embassy of Cabo Verde, 3415 Massachusetts Avenue, NW, Washington, DC 20007, USA (office). *Telephone:* (202) 965-6820 (office). *Fax:* (202) 965-1207 (office). *E-mail:* admin@caboverdeus.net (office). *Website:* www.embcv-usa.gov.cv (office).

VEITIA, Diego, BS; American business executive; b. Havana, Cuba; ed Iowa State Univ.; launched Americas All Season Fund (global flexible fund) 1988, later Chief Investment Officer; f. International Assets Holding Corpn (now INTL FCStone) 1987, Exec. Chair. 1987–2006, CEO 1987–2002; currently Chair. Veitia and Associates, Inc. (pvt. investment co.); Founder Agribiotecnologia SA; Co-founder Costa Rica Stock Exchange; Chair. then Chair. Emer. Hamilton Holt School, Rollins Coll.; fmr Prof. of Int. Finance, Univ. of Central Florida; mem. Global Council, Grad. School of Int. Man. *Publications include:* Global Trends, The Best 50 Investments for the 21st Century 1997. *Address:* Veitia and Associates, Inc., 220 East Central Parkway, #2060, Altamonte Springs, FL 32701, USA (office). *Telephone:* (407) 645-1010 (office).

VĒJONIS, Raimonds, MA; Latvian politician; *President;* b. 15 June 1966, Pskov, Russian SFSR, USSR; m. Iveta Vējone; ed Univ. of Latvia, Tampere Univ. of Tech., Finland, Tallinn Univ. of Tech., Estonia; began career as teacher, Madona 1st High School 1987–89; mem. Madona City Council 1990–93; Deputy Dir Madona Regional Environmental Bd 1989–96; mem. Bd Skulte port 1997–98, 2000–02; Dir Lielrigas Regional Environmental Bd 1996–2002; State Rep. Getlini EKO (public authority) 1997–2002; Nat. Co-ordinator, EU Associated States Environmental Legislation Control 1998–2002; Minister of Environment 2002–11; mem. 11th Saeima (Parl.) 2011–14, Chair. Baltic Affairs Sub-cttee 2011–14, mem. Public Admin and Local Govt Cttee 2011–14, Nat. Security Cttee 2011–14; Head, Latvian Del. to Baltic Ass. 2011–; mem. Strategic Devt Comm. (under the auspices of Pres. of Latvia) 2012–14; Minister of Defence 2014–15; Pres. of Latvia July 2015–; mem. Zaļo un Zemnieku Savienība (ZZS—Greens' and Farmers' Union), currently Leader. *Address:* Chancery of the President, Pils laukums 3, Rīga 1900, Latvia (office). *Telephone:* 6709-2106 (office). *Fax:* 6709-2157 (office). *E-mail:* prese@ president.lv (office). *Website:* www.president.lv (office).

VEKARIC, Vatroslav, MA, PhD; Croatian research institute director; b. 4 March 1944, Dubrovnik; ed Univ. of Belgrade; began career as journalist with Radio Zagreb 1967–68; Research Fellow, Inst. for Int. Politics and Econs (IIPE) 1968–77, Dir Centre for Regional Studies 1977–80, Deputy Dir IIPE (Dir of Research) 1980–85, Dir IIPE 2000; Dir Centre for Strategic Studies, Belgrade 1985–2000; conducted UN research projects 1981–83; Lecturer, Univ. of Belgrade 1982–84, Centre for Post-Grad. Studies, Dubrovnik 1985–, Univ. of Bari, Italy 1997, 1999, Univ. of Sant Angelo, Rome 1998, Univ. of Florence 1998; Ed.-in-Chief Review of International Affairs 2001–; mem. Bd of Dirs Diplomatic Acad., Serbia and Montenegro 2001–; mem. Int. Advisory Bd Journal of International Relations; mem Int. Studies Asscn, USA 1986–, Cttee for Mediterranean Studies, Sassari, Italy 1983– (Deputy Sec.-Gen. 1984–87), Contemplating Group for Scenarios of Devt of the Mediterranean (UN-UNEP), Cannes, France 1983–87, Governing Bd AIRI, Rome 1989–, Int. Law Asscn 1993–, Editorial Bd Nuova Fase review, Edizioni Democrazia Domani, Rome 1994–, Scientific Council Inst. for the Study of the Greek Economy, Athens 1994–, Programme Cttee Centre for Euro-Mediterranean Studies, Rome 1997–99. *Publications:* seven books and more than 130 essays and articles. *Address:* c/o Institute for International Politics and Economics, Makedonska 25, 11000 Belgrade, Serbia (office).

VEKSELBERG, Viktor Felixovich, MA, PhD; Russian (b. Ukrainian) business executive; *Chairman, Renova Group;* b. 14 April 1957, Drogobych, Ukrainian SSR, USSR; m. Marina Vekselberg; one s. one d.; ed Moscow Inst. of Railroad Eng, Computing Center of USSR Acad. of Sciences; co-f. Renova (now Renova Group) 1990, Gen. Dir 1990–, currently Chair. Supervising Cttee for Renova group of cos; acquired Vlaimir Tractor Factory 1994; merged Siberian Irkutsk Aluminium with Ural Aluminium to form Siberial-Urals Aluminium (SUAL) Co. 1996, Pres. SUAL Group 1996–2003, Chair. 2003–12 (resgnd); Deputy Chair. TNK (Tyumen Oil Co.) Man. Bd 1998–2000, Chair. 2000–02, Chair. Man. Bd (merged with BP Russia to form TNK-BP 2003) 2002–03, Exec. Dir 2003–13; Head of Russian section of coordination council of Innovation Center Project in Skolkovo 2010–; apptd mem. Exec. Bd of Dirs Russian Union of Industrialists and Entrepreneurs 2003; mem. Bd of Dirs Jt Stock Commercial Bank Int. Financial Club 2012–18, Russian Industrialists Asscn (mining and metallurgy), Rusnano Man. Co.; Co-Chair. Coordinating Council on Social Partnership; mem. Bd of Trustees Bolshoi Theatre, Moscow, State Univ. Higher School of Econs; Order of Alexander Nevsky Decoration For Beneficence 2017, Order For Merit to the Fatherland. *Address:* Office of the Chairman, Renova Group, 115184 Moscow, Malaya Ordynka 40, Russia (office). *Telephone:* (495) 777-77-07 (office). *Fax:* (495) 787-96-68 (office). *Website:* www.renova.ru (office).

VELA CHIRIBOGA, HE Cardinal Raúl Eduardo; Ecuadorean ecclesiastic; *Archbishop Emeritus of Quito;* b. 1 Jan. 1934, Riobamba; ordained priest, Diocese of Riobamba 1957; Auxiliary Bishop of Guayaquil 1972–75; Titular Bishop of Ausafa 1972–89; Bishop of Azogues 1975–89; Bishop of Ecuador, Mil. 1989–2003; Titular Bishop of Pauzera 1989–98; Archbishop of Quito 2003–10, Archbishop Emer. 2010–; cr. Cardinal (Cardinal-Priest of Santa Maria in Via) 2010; participated in Papal Conclave 2013. *Address:* Archdiocese of Quito, Apartado 17-01-00106, Calle Chile 1440, Quito, Ecuador (office). *Telephone:* (2) 524002 (office). *Fax:* (2) 580973 (office). *Website:* www.arquidiocesisdequito.org (office).

VELARDE FLORES, Julio Emilio, BEcons, MA (Econs), PhD; Peruvian economist, academic and central banker; *Governor, Banco Central de Reserva del Perú;* b. 1 July 1952, Lima; ed Univ. del Pacífico, Lima, Inst. for World Econs, Kiel, Germany, Brown Univ., USA; Sr Researcher and Prof., Dept of Econs, Univ. del Pacífico 1986–2003, Dean, Faculty of Econs 2003; Dir, Banco Central de Reserva del Perú (central bank) 1990–92, 2001–03, Gov. 2006–; CEO Latin American Reserve Fund 2004–06; fmr consultant to numerous int. orgs including IDB, World Bank, USAID, ILO, Int. Devt Research Centre, Canada; Order El Sol del Perú 2011; Manuel J. Bustamante de la Fuente Award 2011. *Address:* Office of the Governor, Banco Central de Reserva del Perú, Jirón Antonio Miró Quesada 441-445, Lima 1, Peru (office). *Telephone:* (1) 4267041 (office). *Fax:* (1) 4273091 (office). *E-mail:* webmaster@bcrp.gob.pe (office). *Website:* www.bcrp.gob.pe (office).

VELASCO BRANES, Andrés, PhD; Chilean government official, economist and academic; *Professor of Professional Practice in International Development, School of International and Public Affairs, Columbia University;* b. (Andrés Velasco), 30 Aug. 1960, Santiago; s. of Eugenio Velasco Letelier and Marta Brañes Ballesteros; m. Consuelo Saavedra; one s. two d.; ed Yale and Columbia Univs, USA; Chief of Staff to Minister of Finance 1990–92, later Dir of Int. Finance; Postdoctoral Fellow in Political Economy, Harvard Univ. and MIT 1994–95; Chief Economist and Deputy Lead Negotiator, NAFTA accession team, Chile 1995; Research Assoc., NBER 1998–; fmr consultant World Bank, IMF, Inter-American Devt Bank, UN Econ. Comm. for Latin America, Fed. Reserve Bank of Atlanta; fmr Dir Center for Latin American and Caribbean Studies, New York Univ.; Sumitomo-FASID Prof. of Int. Finance and Devt, Harvard Univ. 2000–11; Minister of Finance 2006–10; Prof. of Professional Practice in Int. Devt, School of Int. and Public Affairs, Columbia Univ. 2013–; NSF Research Award 2001–04. *Publications:* Trade, Development and the World Economy: Selected Essays of Carlos Díaz-Alejandro (ed.) 1988, Vox Populi (novel) 1995, Lugares Comunes (novel) 2003, Free Trade and Beyond: Prospects for Integration in the Americas (co-ed.) 2004, Money, Crises, and Transition: Essays in Honor of Guillermo A. Calvo (with C. Reinhart and C. A. Végh) 2008, Banks and Cross-Border Capital Flows: Policy Challenges and Regulatory Responses: Report of the Committee on International Economic Policy Reform, Santiago: Editorial Debate, Random House Mondadori 2011, Contra la Desigualdad: El Empleo es la Clave. (with C. Huneeus), Rethinking Central Banking: Report of the Committee on International Economic Policy Reform. *Leisure interests:* running, scuba diving. *Address:* School of International and Public Affairs, Columbia University, 420 West 118th Street, New York, NY 10027, USA (office). *Telephone:* (212) 851-0189 (office). *E-mail:* av278@columbia .edu (office). *Website:* sipa.columbia.edu (office); andresvelasco.cl (office).

VELÁSQUEZ DE AVILÉS, Victoria Marina, LLD; Salvadorean judge, politician and international organization official; b. 1943; m.; ed Univ. of El Salvador; Sec. of Labour 1979–80; lawyer with Social Housing Fund 1983–93; Nat. Human Rights Procurator 1995–2011; Farabundo Marti Nat. Liberation Front cand. for presidency 1998; Nat. Councillor, Radda Barnen (Save the Children Sweden) 1998–99, UN Fund for Children (UNICEF) 1999; Judge, Civil Chamber of Supreme Court 2000–03, Constitutional Chamber 2003–09; Minister of Labour and Social Security 2009–11; Amb. to Switzerland and Perm. Rep. to UN in Geneva 2012–13; Chair. ILO 2013–14; Sec.-Gen., Cen. American Integration System (Sistema de la Integración Centroamericana –SICA) 2014–17.

VELASQUEZ QUESQUÉN, Angel Javier, LLM; Peruvian lawyer and politician; b. 12 March 1960; m. Maritza Suclupe; two s.; partner Jenny Obando Popuche; one s. one d.; ed Univ. Nacional Pedro Ruiz Gallo de Lambayeque, Pontificia Univ. Católica del Perú; fmr Prof. of Law, Univ. San Martín de Porres; mem. Congress representing Lambayeque 1995–, mem. Congress Exec. Council 2002–03, mem. Budget and Control Comm. 2002–03 (Pres. 2003–05), Pres. of Congress 2008–09; Pres. Council of Ministers (Prime Minister) 2009–10 (resgnd); mem. Partido Aprista Peruano (PAP), Vice-Pres. Exec. Cttee 1999, mem. PAP Nat. Strategic Comm. 2002–04, mem. PAP Nat. Exec. 2004–08. *Address:* Congress of the Republic of Peru, Plaza Bolívar, Av. Abancay s/n, Lima, Peru (office). *E-mail:* jvelasquezq@congreso.gob.pe (office). *Website:* www.congreso.gob.pe (office).

VELAYATI, Ali Akbar, MD; Iranian politician, medical scientist and academic; *Professor, Shahid Beheshti University of Medical Sciences and Health Services;* b. 1945, Tehran; s. of Ali Asghar and Zobeideh Asgah; m. Skina Khoshnevisan; four c.; ed Tehran Univ., Johns Hopkins Univ., USA; joined Nat. Front (of Mossadegh) 1961; f. Islamic Asscn of Faculty of Medicine, Tehran Univ. 1963; took part in underground political activities in support of Ayatollah Khomeini 1979; Vice-Minister, Ministry of Health 1979–80; proposed for Prime Minister by Ayatollah Khomeini Oct. 1981 (candidature rejected by the Majlis); Minister of Foreign Affairs 1981–97; Adviser to Supreme Leader in int. affairs; unsuccessful cand. in presidential election 2013; Pres. Expediency Discernment Council, Center for Strategic Research 2013–; Chair. Bd of Trustees, Islamic Azad Univ. 2017–; currently Prof., Shahid Beheshti Univ. of Medical Sciences and Health Services; Head, Islamic and Traditional Medicine Dept, Iranian Acad. of Medical Sciences; Pres. Iranian Journal of Infectious Diseases and Tropical Medicine, Iranian Soc. for Support of Patients with Infectious Diseases; mem. Int. Soc. for History of Medicine; Zmaj Od Bosne Gold Medal for Services to Peace in the Balkans 1995; Dr hc (Al-Farabi, Kazakhstan) 1992, (Teflis, Georgia) 1993, (Avecina, Tajikistan) 1995. *Publications:* several books including Infectious Diseases (3 vols) 1979; numerous articles in professional journals. *Address:* Shahid Beheshti University of Medical Sciences and Health Services, Shahid Chamran Highway, Evin, POB 4139-19395, Tehran (office); Iranian Academy of Medical Sciences, PO Box 19395/4655, Pasdaran Avenue, Tehran, Iran. *Telephone:* (21) 220109555 (office). *Fax:* (21) 220109484 (office). *E-mail:* icrd@sbmu.ac.ir (office); vlayati@ams.ac.ir (office); aavelayati@nritld.ac.ir (office). *Website:* www.sbmu.ac.ir (office); www.velayati.ir.

VELDHUIS, Johannes (Jan) G. F.; Dutch university president (retd); b. 4 Oct. 1938, Hengelo; m. Monica M. H. Thier 1969; three s.; ed Univs of Utrecht and Minnesota; Ministry of Foreign Affairs 1968–70; Sec. Univ. Bd Univ. of Leiden 1970–74; Deputy Sec.-Gen. Ministry of Educ. and Science 1974–79, Dir-Gen. and Insp.-Gen. of Educ. and Science 1979–86; Pres. Utrecht Univ. 1986–2003; Chair. Netherlands del. OECD Educ. Cttee 1984–86; Chair. Bd Netherlands-America Comm. for Educational Exchange (Fulbright Comm.) 1984–2001, Netherlands Inst. for Art History, Florence, Fondation Descartes Amsterdam, Museum Catharyneconvent Utrecht, Stichting Carmelcollege Hengelo; mem. Bd Netherlands History Inst., Rome, Netherlands Archaeological Inst., Cairo, Japan-Netherlands Inst., Tokyo; mem. bds of several hosps in The Hague area; Chevalier, Légion d'Honneur 1997, Officer, Order Orange Nassau 1998, Commdr, Order Isabel la Católica (Spain) 2001; Dr hc (Univ. of Florida) 1995; Univ. of Minn. Distinguished Leadership Award for Ints 2005. *Publications:* various publs in the field of educ. and public admin. *Leisure interests:* comparative educ., literature, botany, tennis, skiing, bridge. *Address:* Roucooppark 12, 2251 AV Voorschoten, Netherlands (home). *Telephone:* (71) 5617696 (home). *Fax:* (71) 5620029 (home). *E-mail:* monica.jan.veldhuis@planet.nl (home).

VELIAJ, Erion, BA, MA; Albanian politician; *Mayor of Tirana;* b. 17 Dec. 1979, Tirana; m. Ajola Xoxën 2014; ed Gymnasium 'Sami Frashëri', Grand Valley State Univ., Mich., USA, Univ. of Sussex, UK; worked in North and South America, East Africa and Kosovo before returning to Albania 2003; f. MJAFT movt (activist org. for Albanian youth) 2003 (renamed Kombeve të Bashkuara për shoqërinë civile 2004); mem. European Stability Initiative 2007–09; civil list G99 cand. in parl. elections 2009; mem. Partia Socialiste e Shqipërisë (PSSh—Socialist Party of Albania) 2011–, Sec. for Youth and Emigration; mem. Parl. for Gjirokastra 2013–; Minister of Social Welfare and Youth 2013–15; Mayor of Tirana 2015–. *Achievements include:* initiated process of opening files of fmr State Security and reformed compensation system for those who had suffered political persecution in Albania. *Address:* Office of the Mayor, Municipality of Tirana, Blvd Dëshmorët e Kombit, Tirana, Albania (office). *Telephone:* (4) 2253053 (office); (4) 2229100 (office). *Fax:* (4) 2228430 (office). *E-mail:* e-mayor@tirana.gov.al (office); info@tirana.gov.al (office). *Website:* www.tirana.gov.al (office); erionveliaj.al; www.ps.al/author/erion -veliaj.

VELIKHOV, Evgeny Pavlovich; Russian physicist; *President Emeritus, Kurchatov Institute;* b. 2 Feb. 1935, Moscow; s. of Pavel Pavlovich Velikhov and Natalia Vsevolodoma Velikhova; m. Natalia Alekseevna Arseniyeva 1959; two s. one d.; joined Kurchatov Inst. of Atomic Energy (later renamed Kurchatov Inst. Nat. Research Centre) as Jr Researcher 1958, becoming Head of Lab. 1962–70, Dir, Magnetic Lab. (sub-division of Kurchatov Inst.) 1971–78, Dir Russian Scientific Centre, Kurchatov Inst. 1989–92, Pres. Kurchatov Inst. 1992–2015, Pres. Emer. 2016–; Founder and Dir Inst. for Security Problems of Nuclear Energy Devt 1988–91; Prof., Moscow Univ. 1973–; Sec., Civic Chamber of Russian Fed. 2005–14, now Hon. Sec.; mem. CPSU Cen. Cttee 1989–90; mem. USSR (now Russian) Acad. of Sciences 1974–, Vice-Pres. 1978–96, Academician-Sec., Dept of Information Tech., Cybernetics and Automatic Systems 1983–; mem. Supreme Soviet of USSR 1984–89; People's Deputy of the USSR 1989–91; Chair. Cttee of Soviet Scientists for Peace against Nuclear Threat 1983–88; Co-founder Int. Foundation for Survival and Devt of Humanity 1987–; Chair. Soviet Nuclear Soc. 1989–90; Chair. Council, Int. Thermonuclear Experimental Reactor (ITER) 2010–12; mem. Presidential Council of Science and Tech. 1995–; Pres. Rosshelf (Offshore Devt Co.) 1992–2001; mem. American Geophysical Soc. 1981–; Foreign mem. Swedish Royal Acad. of Eng Sciences 1989–, Bulgarian Acad. of Sciences 1989; Order of Lenin (three times), Order of Courage 1997, Order of Merit for the Fatherland, First Class 2015, Order of the Rising Sun (Japan) 2016; Dr hc (Notre Dame), (Susquehanna), (Tufts), (London); USSR State Prize 1977, Lenin Prize 1984, Hero of Socialist Labour 1985, Karpinsky Prize 1986, Science for Peace Prize (Italy), Szillard Award, American Physical Soc., Russian Fed. State Prize 2003. *Publications:* over 1,500 publications on science and the problems of prevention of nuclear war. *Leisure interests:* skiing, underwater swimming, windsurfing. *Address:* Kurchatov Institute, 123182 Moscow, 1, Kurchatov Square (office); 123060 Moscow, 24, Pckhotnaya Street, Russia (home). *Telephone:* (499) 196-92-41 (office). *Fax:* (499) 196-17-04 (office). *E-mail:* nrcki@nrcki.ru (office); kuznetsov_vp@nrcki.ru. *Website:* www.nrcki.ru.

VELJANOSKI, Trajko; Macedonian lawyer and politician; b. 2 Nov. 1962, Skopje; m.; two c.; ed Law Faculty, SS Cyril and Methodius Univ.; passed Bar examination 1988, est. ind. law office and worked as lawyer 1988–99; began political career by joining Vnatrešno-Makedonska Revolucionerna Organizacija-Demokratska Partija za Makedonsko Nacionalno Edinstvo (VMRO-DPMNE—Internal Macedonian Revolutionary Org.-Democratic Party for Macedonian Nat. Unity) 1993, Head of Legal Affairs Cttee for several years, mem. Political System Cttee, also headed VMRO-DPMNE Forum on Legal and Political Affairs and Judicial System; elected Under-Sec., Ministry of Justice 1999, later Deputy Minister; fmr mem. Pres.'s Cttee of Appeals, Man. Bd Centre for European Integration, State Election Comm.; mem. Sobranie (Ass.) 2006–, Chair. Cttee on Election and Appointment Issues 2006–08, Pres. of Sobranie 2008–17, Chair. Cttee on Constitutional Issues, Chair. Del. of Ass. to Inter-Parl. Union. *Address:* Sobranie (Assembly), 1000 Skopje, 11 Oktomvri bb, North Macedonia (office). *Telephone:* (2) 3113268 (office); (2) 3112255 (ext. 353) (office). *Fax:* (2) 3237947 (office). *E-mail:* s.ugrinovska@sobranie.mk (office); pretsedatel@sobranie.mk (office). *Website:* www.sobranie.mk (office).

VELLA, Hon. George William, MD; Maltese physician, politician and head of state; b. 24 April 1942, Zejtun; m. Miriam Grima; one s. two d.; ed De La Salle Coll., Univ. of Malta; Medical Officer, Malta Drydocks 1966–73; Demonstrator in Physiology and Biochemistry, Univ. of Malta 1966–73; Aviation Medicine Consultant with Air Malta and Dept of Civil Aviation 1976–90; mem. House of Reps (Parl.) 1978–87, 1992–2019; Deputy Prime Minister and Minister for Foreign Affairs and Environment 1996–98, Minister for Foreign Affairs 2013–17; Pres. of Malta 2019–; mem. Partit Laburista, Deputy Leader 1992–2003; Grand Commdr, Order of Merit 2015; Grand Cross Pro Ordine Melitensi, Sovereign Mil. Order of Malta 2015. *Address:* Office of the President, The Palace, Valletta VLT 1190, Malta (office). *Telephone:* 21221221 (office). *Fax:* 21241241 (office). *E-mail:* president@gov.mt. *Website:* www.president.gov.mt (office).

VELLA, Karmenu, BA, MSc; Maltese architect, civil engineer, politician and EU official; *Commissioner for Environment, Maritime Affairs and Fisheries, European Commission;* b. 19 June 1950, Żurrieq; m. Marianne Buhagiar; two s.; ed Lyceum Secondary School, Univ. of Malta Junior Coll., Royal Univ. of Malta, Sheffield Hallam Univ., UK; mem. Labour Party (Malta) 1968–, mem. Nat. Exec. Cttee of Labour Youth Movt, later mem. Int. Union of Socialist Youth, mem. Nat. Exec. of Labour Party, mem. and Group Co-ordinator for Labour Party Parl. Group, in charge of electoral programme for Maltese Labour Party for 2013 general elections 2011–13; mem. Zurrieq Civic Council 1968–70; MP 1976–2014; Minister for Public Works 1981–84, for Industry 1984–87, for Tourism 1996–98, 2013–14; served as Shadow Minister for Tourism as well as Shadow Minister for Finance; Commr for Environment, Maritime Affairs and Fisheries, European Comm. (EC), Brussels Nov. 2014–; pvt. practice as architect and civil engineer 1973; Dir, Mid Med Bank – Malta 1973–76; Man. Dir Libyan Arab Maltese Holding Co. 1974–81, Dir of co.'s subsidiaries including Mediterranean Aviation Co. Ltd, Medelec Switchgear Co. Ltd, Mediterranean Power Electric Co. Ltd, Rotos Zirayia Pumps Co. Ltd, Plastic Processing Co. Ltd; Exec. Chair. Corinthia Hotels International 2001–07, Corinthia's Mediterranean Constuction Co. Ltd 2007–10; Chair. SMS-Mondial Travel Group –2013; Dir, Betfair Group Ltd 2010–; Founding Chair. Maltese Turkish Business Council 2007; mem. Vodafone Malta Foundation 2007–13; Hon. Pres. Birzebbugia Aquatic Sports Club, Żurrieq Bocci Club, Queen Victoria Band Club, Żurrieq. *Address:* European Commission, 200 Rue de la Loi/Wetstraat 200, 1049 Brussels, Belgium (office). *Telephone:* (2) 299-11-11 (office). *Website:* ec.europa.eu (office); www.karmenuvella.com.

VELLA, Mario, BA, MSc, DrSc; Maltese philosopher, economist, academic and central banker; *Governor and Chairman, Central Bank of Malta;* b. 1953, Tripoli, Libya; ed Univ. of Malta, London School of Econs, UK, Humboldt Universitaet zu Berlin, Germany; Visiting Sr Lecturer, Univ. of Malta 2000; Visiting Lecturer, Graduate School of Econs and Int. Relations, Università Cattolica in Milan and Università di Urbino 2005; Visiting Prof., Edinburgh Napier Univ. 2007–12; Exec. Chair. Malta Enterprise 2013–16; Gov. and Chair. Cen. Bank of Malta 2016–, also currently mem. Bd of Dirs IMF; fmr Pres. Labour Party 1990s; fmr Dir Foreign Direct Investment, Grant Thorton Malta; fmr CEO Malta Devt Corpn; fmr Advisor to Vice-Chair., Cttee for Econ. and Monetary Affairs, European Parl., later to Prime Minister of Malta, then to Leader of the Opposition; fmr Sr Associated Consultant, Direct Investment Advisory Services; Ordine al Merito (Italy). *Publications include:* Reflections in a Canvas Bag 1989, numerous articles, poetry and short stories. *Address:* Central Bank of Malta, Pjazza Kastilja, Valletta VLT 1060, Malta (office). *Telephone:* 25500000 (office). *Fax:* 25502500 (office). *E-mail:* info@centralbankmalta.org (office). *Website:* www.centralbankmalta.org (office).

VELTCHEV, Milen, MA, MBA; Bulgarian politician and business executive; *CEO, VTB Capital AD;* b. 24 April 1966; ed Univ. of Nat. and World Economy, Sofia, Univ. of Rochester and Massachusetts Inst. of Tech., USA; attaché, Int. Orgs Dept, Ministry of Foreign Affairs, Bulgaria 1990–92; Summer Assoc. in Corp. Finance, Chemical Bank, New York 1994; Assoc., Merrill Lynch & Co., London 1995–99, Vice-Pres. Emerging Markets 1999–2001; elected mem. Parl. 2001; Minister of Finance 2001–05, also Gov. for Bulgaria, World Bank, EBRD; Man. Partner, Delta Capital International 2010–12; CEO VTB Capital AD, Sofia 2012–; fmr Vice-Chair. Nat. Movt for Stability and Progress (Natsionalno dvizhenie za stabilnost i vazhod); fmr Chair. Monetary Council, Council for Internal Financial Control, Tax Policy Advisory Council; Dr hc (Univ. of Nat. and World Economy) 2004; Euromoney Finance Minister of the Year 2002. *Address:* VTB Capital AD, 1000 Sofia, 4 Kniaz Alexander I Street., Bulgaria (office). *Telephone:* (2) 805-28-85 (office). *Fax:* (2) 805-28-81 (office). *Website:* www.vtbcapital.com (office).

VELTMAN, Joris Andre, BSc, PhD; Dutch geneticist and academic; *Professor of Translational Genomics, Department of Medical Genetics, Radboud University;* b. 1971, Heerlen; ed Wageningen Univ. and Maastricht Univ.; Post-doctoral Fellowship, Dept of Cancer Genetics, Comprehensive Cancer Center, Univ. of California, San Francisco 1999–2005; Post-doctoral Fellowship, Dept of Human Genetics, Nijmegen Medical Centre, Radboud Univ. 2005–08, Asst Prof., Dept of Medical Genetics 2005–08, Assoc. Prof. 2008–13, Prof. of Translational Genomics, Dept of Medical Genetics 2013–, Head of Genome Research Div., Dept of Human Genetics; Prof., Dept of Clinical Genetics, Maastricht Univ. 2013–; mem. Scientific Program Cttee for the annual meeting of European Soc. of Human Genetics (ESHG), Chair. 2015–(20), Dir Next Generation Sequencing course of ESHG in partnership with European School of Genetic Medicine, Bologna, Italy; fmr Chair. Research Oversight Cttee of Genome Canada Project on Personalized Medicine and Genomics Project on Epilepsy; mem. Annual Review Cttee of Simons Foundation Autism Research Initiative, New York, Review Cttee, Health Research Council, Acad. of Finland; Assoc. Ed., American Journal of Human Genetics; research grants and awards from Netherlands Acad. of Arts and Sciences and EU, King Faisal Int. Prize for Medicine (co-recipient) 2016. *Publications:* numerous papers in professional journals. *Address:* Translational Genomics, Faculteit der Medische Wetenschappen, Radboud University Medical Centre, Postbus 9010, Nijmegen 6500 GL, The Netherlands (office). *Telephone:* (24) 3614941 (office). *Fax:* (24) 3668752 (office). *E-mail:* joris.veltman@radboudumc.nl (office). *Website:* www.radboudumc.nl/research (office); www.genomicdisorders.nl (office).

VELTMAN, Martinus J. G., PhD; Dutch physicist and academic; *John D. MacArthur Professor Emeritus of Physics, University of Michigan;* b. 1931; ed Univ. of Utrecht; Prof. of Physics, Univ. of Utrecht 1966–81; John D. MacArthur Prof. of Physics, Univ. of Mich. 1981, now Prof. Emer.; mem. Dutch Acad. of Sciences; High Energy and Particle Physics Prize, European Physical Soc. 1993, Nobel Prize for Physics (jtly) 1999. *Achievements include:* one of the developers of gauge theories. *Publications include:* Facts and Mysteries in Particle Physics. *Address:* Physics Department, University of Michigan, 450 Church Street, Ann Arbor, MI 48109-1040, USA (office). *E-mail:* veltman@umich.edu (office). *Website:* www.lsa.umich.edu/physics (office).

VELTRONI, Walter; Italian politician and writer; b. 3 July 1955, Rome; m.; two c.; ed Film Inst., Rome; fmr journalist and TV Asst Dir; Sec., Rome Br., Fed. of Young Italian Communists 1975, also mem. Nat. Exec.; mem. Rome City Council 1976–81; elected Deputy in Nat. Ass. 1987; mem. Nat. Secr. PCI–PDS 1988–92; Founder-mem. Democratici di Sinistra (PDS—Democratic Left) 1991, apptd to Political Co-ordination Bureau 1991, Political Sec. 1998; Ed. L'Unità daily newspaper 1992–96, now Dir; Deputy Prime Minister, Minister for Cultural Heritage, Performing Arts and Sport 1996–98; mem. European Parl. (Party of European Socialists Group) 1999–2004; Mayor of Rome 2001–08; Exec. Vice-Pres. Council of European Municipalities and Regions 2003; Vice-Pres. Socialist Int. 1999; Leader Partito Democratico (formed following the merger of the left wing Socialist Democrats and Margherita parties) 2007–09 (resgnd); mem. Exec. Bd UNICEF Italy 2014–; Hon. Chair. Lega Società di Pallacanestro Serie A; Chevalier, Légion d'Honneur 2000; Dr hc (John Cabot Univ.) 2003. *Publications include:* numerous books including Il sogno spezzato (on Robert Kennedy), La sfida interrotta (on the ideas of Enrico Berlinguer), Forse Dio è malato (travel book on Africa), Il disco del mondo – Vita breve di Luca Flores, musicista 2007, Noi 2011, L'inizio del buio 2012, L'isola e le rose 2013, Ciao 2015.

VENABLES, Terence Frederick (Terry); British professional football manager, fmr footballer and commentator; b. 6 Jan. 1943, Dagenham, London, England; m. Yvette Venables; two d.; ed Dagenham High School; youth player, Chelsea 1958–60; sr player, Chelsea 1960–66 (Capt. 1962, 202 appearances, 26 goals, won Football League Cup 1964/65), England nat. team 1964, Tottenham Hotspur 1966–69 (115 appearances, 19 goals, won FA Cup 1967), Queens Park Rangers 1969–73 (179 appearances, 19 goals), Crystal Palace 1974–76 (14 appearances), St Patrick's Athletic 1976 (two appearances); Man. Crystal Palace 1976–80, Queens Park Rangers 1980–84, Barcelona 1984–87 (won La Liga 1985); Man. Tottenham Hotspur 1987–91 (won FA Cup 1991), Chief Exec. Tottenham Hotspur PLC 1991–93; Coach, England nat. team 1994–96, Asst Coach 2006–07; Dir of Football, Portsmouth FC 1996–98; Coach, Australian nat. team 1997–98; Head Coach, Crystal Palace 1998–99; Coach, Middlesbrough (jt role with Bryan Robson) 2000–01; Man. Leeds United 2002–03; Tech. Advisor, Wembley FC 2012; football analyst, BBC mid-1980s–1994, ITV 1994–; only player to have represented England at all levels (schoolboy, youth, amateur, U-23 and for full int. team); co-devised board game, Terry Venables invites you to be... The Manager 1990; guided England Legends and Celebrities squad to victory in charity Soccer Aid programme 2006; Hon. Fellow, Univ. of Wolverhampton; Don Balón Award for Coach of the Year in La Liga 1985. *Recording:* recorded England Crazy single for World Cup together with band Rider (reached No. 46 in UK charts) 2002, recorded Elvis Presley song 'If I Can Dream' 2010 (reached No. 23 in UK charts). *Television:* co-creator Hazell (ITV detective series). *Publications:* They Used to Play on Grass (co-author) 1973; co-authored (as P. B. Yuill) four novels with Gordon Williams: The Bornless Keeper 1974, Hazell Plays Solomon 1974, Hazell and the Three Card Trick 1975, Hazell and the Menacing Jester 1976; Terry Venables: The Autobiography (with N. Hanson) 1994, Venables' England – The Making of the Team 1996, The Best Game in the World 1997. *Address:* Terance Venables Holdings Ltd, Palladium House, 1–4 Argyll Street, London, W1F 7LD, England.

VENDLER, Helen Hennessy, AB, PhD; American literary critic and academic; *A. Kingsley Porter University Professor, Department of English, Harvard University;* b. (Helen Marie Hennessy), 30 April 1933, Boston, Mass; d. of George Hennessy and Helen Conway; m. Zeno Vendler (deceased); one s.; ed Emmanuel Coll. and Harvard Univ.; Instructor, Cornell Univ. 1960–63; Lecturer, Swarthmore Coll. and Haverford Coll. 1963–64; Asst Prof., Smith Coll. 1964–66; Assoc. Prof., Boston Univ. 1966–68, Prof. 1968–85; Visiting Prof., Harvard Univ. 1981–85, Kenan Prof. 1985–, Assoc. Acad. Dean 1987–92, A. Kingsley Porter Univ. Prof. 1990–; Sr Fellow, Harvard Soc. of Fellows 1981–92; poetry critic, New Yorker 1978–90; mem. Educ. Advisory Bd, Guggenheim Foundation, Pulitzer Prize Bd 1990–99; Fulbright Lecturer, Univ. of Bordeaux 1968–69; Overseas Fellow, Churchill Coll. Cambridge 1980; Parnell Fellow, Magdalene Coll., Cambridge 1986, Hon. Fellow 1996–; mem. American Acad. of Arts and Sciences (fmr Vice-Pres.), Norwegian Acad., American Philosophical Soc., American Acad. of Arts and Letters (Bd mem. 2006–09), Modern Language Assn (Pres. 1980); Fulbright Fellow 1954, A.A.U.W. Fellow 1959, Lowell Prize 1969, Guggenheim Fellow 1971–72, American Council of Learned Socs Fellow 1971–72, Nat. Endowment for the Humanities (NEH) Fellow 1980, 1985, 1994, 2006, Wilson Fellow 1994, Siemens Fellow 2009; 26 hon. degrees; Explicator Prize 1969, Nat. Inst. of Arts and Letters Award 1975, Nat. Book Critics Award 1980, Newton Arvin Award, Jefferson Medal, Jefferson Lecturer, NEH, A.W. Mellon Lecturer in Fine Arts, Nat. Gallery of Art 2007. *Publications include:* Yeats's Vision and the Later Plays 1963, On Extended Wings: Wallace Stevens' Longer Poems 1969, The Poetry of George Herbert 1975, Part of Nature, Part of Us 1980, The Odes of John Keats 1983, Wallace Stevens: Words Chosen Out of Desire 1985, Harvard Book of Contemporary American Poetry 1985, The Music of What Happens 1988, The Given and the Made 1995, The Breaking of Style 1995, Soul Says 1995, Poems, Poets, Poetry 1996, The Art of Shakespeare's Sonnets 1997, Seamus Heaney 1998, Coming of Age as a Poet: Milton, Keats, Eliot, Plath 2003, Poets Thinking: Pope, Whitman, Dickinson, Yeats 2005, Invisible Listeners: Lyric Intimacy in Herbert, Whitman, and Ashbery 2005, Our Secret Discipline 2007, Dickinson, Selected Poems with Commentaries 2010, The Ocean, the Bird, and the Scholar: Essays on Poets and Poetry 2015. *Leisure interests:* travel, music, grandchildren. *Address:* Department of English, Harvard University, Barker Center 205, 12 Quincey Street, Cambridge, MA 02138, USA (office). *Telephone:* (617) 496-6028 (office). *Fax:* (617) 496-8737 (office). *E-mail:* vendler@fas.harvard.edu (office). *Website:* www.fas.harvard.edu/~english (office).

VENEMAN, Ann Margaret, MA, JD; American lawyer, government official and international organization official; b. 29 June 1949, Modesto, Calif.; d. of John Veneman (fmr US Under-Sec. of Health, Educ. and Welfare and mem. Calif. State

Ass.); ed Univ. of California, Davis, Univ. of California, Berkeley and Hastings Coll. of Law; staff attorney; Gen. Counsel's Office, Bay Area Rapid Transit Dist, Oakland, Calif. 1976–78; Deputy Public Defender, Modesto 1978–80; Assoc., later Pnr, Damrell, Damrell & Nelson (law firm), Modesto 1980; Assoc. Admin., Foreign Agric. Service, US Dept of Agric. 1986–89, Deputy Under-Sec. of Agric. for Int. Affairs and Commodity Programs 1989–91, Deputy Sec. of Dept 1991–93; with Patton, Boggs & Blow (law firm), Washington, DC 1993–95; Sec., Calif. Dept of Food and Agric. 1995–99; Partner, Nossaman, Guthner, Knox & Elliott (law firm) 1999–2001; US Sec. of Agric. 2001–05 (resgnd); Exec. Dir UNICEF 2005–10; currently Co-Chair. Nutrition and Physical Activity Initiative, Bipartisan Policy Center; mem. Bd of Dirs Alexion; fmr mem. Bd of Dirs Calgene (first co. to market genetically engineered food); mem. Council on Foreign Relations, Trilateral Comm.; Hon. mem. US Afghan Women's Council, US State Dept 2004, Modesto Rotary Club 2008; Dr hc (California Polytechnic State Univ., San Luis Obispo) 2001, (Lincoln Univ. of Mo.) 2003, (Delaware State Univ.) 2004, (Middlebury Coll.) 2006; Outstanding Woman in Int. Trade Award 2001, Outstanding Alumna of the Year Award, Univ. of California, Davis 2001, Food Research and Action Center Award 2001, Nat. 4-H Alumni Recognition Award 2002, Dutch American Heritage Award 2002, Statesman of the Year Award, Jr Statesman Foundation 2002, Alumnus of the Year Award, Goldman School of Public Policy 2003, American PVO Partners Award for Service to People in Need 2004, Richard E. Lyng Award for Public Service 2005, Sesame Workshop's Leadership Award for Children 2006. *Address:* Bipartisan Policy Center, 1225 Eye Street, NW, Suite 1000, Washington, DC 20005, USA (office). *Website:* bipartisanpolicy.org/projects/nutrition-and-physical-activity-initiative (office).

VENESS, Sir David, CBE, MA, LLM; British police officer and fmr UN official; *Senior Advisor, Pilgrims Group Limited;* m.; three c.; ed Raynes Park Co. Grammar School, London, Trinity Coll. Cambridge, Royal Coll. of Defence Studies; joined London Metropolitan Police Cadet Corps 1964, Metropolitan Police 1966; apptd Officer, Criminal Investigation Dept (CID) 1969, served as detective in N, E and Cen. London, various specialist depts in Scotland Yard; served as Detective Chief Superintendent in Fraud Squad (5O6) and Crime Operations Group (5O15); trained as hostage negotiator 1979, mem. negotiating team, London Iranian Embassy siege 1980; led negotiations at Libyan Peoples Bureau incident 1984; Instructor, then Dir Scotland Yard Negotiators Course 1980–87; apptd Commdr 1987; served with Royalty and Diplomatic Protection 1987–90; Commdr Public Order, Territorial Security and Operational Support 1990–91; Deputy Asst Commr, Specialist Operations, Crime 1991–94, Asst Commr 1994–2005; Under-Sec.-Gen. for Safety and Security, UN 2005–08 (resgnd); Sr Advisor, Pilgrims Group Ltd 2014–; Chair. Advisory Bd on Security & Resilience; Co-Chair. Exec. Bd of Cross Sector Safety & Security Communications; fmr mem. Service Authorities, Nat. Criminal Intelligence Service, Nat. Crime Squad; Hon. Prof. of Terrorism Studies, Univ. of St Andrews; HM Queen's Police Medal 2000. *Leisure interests:* rugby, reading. *Address:* Pilgrims Group, Pilgrims House, PO Box 769, Woking, Surrey, GU21 5EU, England (office). *Telephone:* (844) 788-0180 (office). *Fax:* (844) 788-0181 (office). *E-mail:* enquiries@pilgrimsgroup.com (office). *Website:* www.pilgrimsgroup.com (office).

VENETIAAN, Runaldo Ronald; Suriname mathematician, politician and fmr head of state; b. 1936, Paramaribo; ed Leiden Univ.; moved to Netherlands, early career as math. lecturer; fmr Minister of Educ.; fmr mem. Exec. Bd UNESCO; Leader, Suriname Nat. Party; Pres. of Suriname 1991–96, 2000–10; retd from politics 2013.

VENGEROV, Maxim; Israeli (b. Russian) violinist and conductor; *Polonsky Visiting Professor of Violin, Royal College of Music;* b. 1974, Novosibirsk, Western Siberia, USSR; s. of Alexander Vengerov and Larissa Vengerov; m. Olga Gringolts 2011; two d.; ed studied with Vag Papian in St Petersburg and with Yuri Simonov, Moscow Inst. of Ippolitov-Ivanov; began career as a solo violinist aged five; made first recording aged ten; turned his attention to conducting 2007, Carnegie Hall conducting debut during Verbier Festival Orchestra's tour 2007; has since conducted major orchestras, including the Toronto and Montreal Symphony orchestras, Enescu, Israel, London and Russian Nat. Philharmonic orchestras, as well as the English and Paris Chamber orchestras; first Chief Conductor, Gstaad Festival Orchestra 2010; returned to the violin in 2011, now divides his time equally between violin performance, conducting and teaching; Prof. of Violin, RAM, London 2005–16, Menuhin Prof. 2012–16; Amb. and Visiting Prof. of Menuhin Acad., Switzerland; Artist-in-Residence, Oxford Philharmonic 2013–; regularly serves on competition juries, including the Yehudi Menuhin Int. Violin Competition, Donatella Flick Conducting Competition, appeared at Montreal Int. Violin Competition as conductor of the competition finals 2013; Chair. Wieniawski Violin Competition 2011, 2016; Polonsky Visiting Prof. of Violin, Royal Coll. of Music, London 2016–; UNICEF Goodwill Amb. (first classical musician) 1997–; fellowships and honours from several insts; won Wieniawski and Carl Flesch int. competitions aged ten 10 and 15, respectively; First Prize, Jr Wieniawski Competition, Poland 1984, Winner Carl Flesch Int. Violin Competition 1990, Gramophone Young Artist of the Year 1994, Ritmo Artist of the Year 1994, Gramophone Record of the Year 1995, Edison Classical Music Awards 1995, 1996, 1998, 2003, ECHO Awards 1997, 2003,Gramophone Artist of the Year 2002, Grammy Award for Best Instrumental Soloist Performance (with Orchestra) 2003, World Economic Forum Crystal Award 2007. *Recordings include:* Sonatas by Beethoven and Brahms and Paganini 1st Concerto 1992, Sonatas by Mozart, Beethoven and Mendelssohn 1992, Virtuoso Violin Pieces, Bruch and Mendelssohn Violin Concertos, Britten Violin Concerto and Walton Viola Concerto with Mstislav Rostropovich and London Symphony Orchestra (Grammy Award 2004, Classical BRIT Critics' Award 2004) 2002, Best of Maxim Vengerov 2006, Phenomenal Vengerov 2011, Khrennikov Violin & Piano Concertos 2013, The Complete Recordings 1991–2007 2014. *Address:* c/o Nicola-Fee Bahl, NFBM Ltd, 3 Fergus Road, London, N5 1JS, England (office). *Telephone:* (20) 7359-4771 (office). *E-mail:* nicola-fee@nfbm.com (office). *Website:* www.nfbm.com (office).

VENIZELOS, Evangelos, PhD; Greek lawyer and politician; b. 1 Jan. 1957, Thessaloníki; m. Lila A. Bakatselou; one d.; ed Aristotle Univ. of Thessaloníki, Univ. of Paris II; Asst Prof., then Prof. of Constitutional Law, Aristotle Univ. of Thessaloniki 1984–87; Attorney at Law for Council of State and Supreme Court 1984–87; apptd mem. Bd Nat. Centre of Public Admin 1987; apptd mem. Bd Nat. Bank of Greece 1988; mem. Local Radio Cttee; elected to Cen. Cttee of the Panellinio Socialistiko Kinima (PASOK—Panhellenic Socialist Movt) 1990, unsuccessful cand. for leadership of the party 2007, Deputy Leader of PASOK 2004–12, Chair. 2012–15; mem. Vouli (Parl.) for Thessaloníki A 1993–; Deputy Minister to the Prime Minister's Office, responsible for Press Affairs 1993–94; Minister for Press and Media Affairs 1994–95, of Transportation and Communications 1995–96, of Justice Jan.–Aug. 1996, of Culture and Sport 1996–99, 2000–04, of Devt 1999–2000, of Nat. Defence 2009–11, Deputy Chair. of the Govt and Minister of Finance 2011–12; Deputy Prime Minister and Minister of Foreign Affairs 2013–15. *Address:* Panellinio Socialistiko Kinima (PASOK—Panhellenic Socialist Movement), Odos Hippocrates 22, 106 80 Athens (office); Odos Danaidon 4, 546 26 Thessaloníki, Greece (home). *Telephone:* (210) 3665000 (office); (2310) 548600 (home). *Fax:* (210) 3665209 (office). *E-mail:* pasok@pasok.gr (office). *Website:* www.pasok.gr (office); www.evenizelos.gr.

VENKATESH, Akshay, BSc, PhD; Australian (b. Indian) mathematician; *Faculty Member, Institute for Advanced Study;* b. 21 Nov. 1981, Delhi; m. Sarah Paden; two d.; ed Univ. of Western Australia, Princeton Univ.; emigrated with family to Perth, Western Australia at age two; C. L. E. Moore Instructor, Massachusetts Inst. of Tech. 2002–04; Visiting mem., Courant Inst. of Mathematical Sciences, New York Univ. 2004–05, Assoc. Prof. 2005–08; Prof. of Math., Stanford Univ. 2008–18; Distinguished Visiting Prof. of Math., Inst. for Advanced Study, Princeton 2017–18, mem. Faculty 2018–; Aisenstadt Chair, Univ. de Montréal 2010; Ed. Math Annalen 2011–16; Ed. Journal de l'institut mathematique de Jussieu; mem. Editorial Bd Cttee of American Math. Soc.; Salem Prize 2007, SASTRA Ramanujan Prize 2008, Infosys Prize 2016, Ostrowski Prize 2017, Int. Math. Union Fields Medal 2018. *Address:* Institute for Advanced Study, 1 Einstein Drive, Princeton, NJ 08540, USA (office). *Telephone:* (609) 734-8000 (office). *Website:* www.ias.edu/scholars/venkatesh.

VENNER, Sir K. Dwight, Kt, CBE, BSc, MSc; Saint Vincent and the Grenadines economist and central banker; m. Lynda Arnolde Winville Venner (née St Rose); seven c.; ed Univ. of the West Indies, Mona; fmr Research Asst, Univ. of the W Indies, Jr Research Fellow, Inst. of Social and Econ. Reseach, Lecturer, Dept of Econs; Dir Finance and Planning, Govt of St Lucia 1981–89; Chair. Air and Seaports Authority, St Lucia 1981–89, Nat. Insurance Investment Cttee 1981–89, Caricom Cen. Bank Govs, Eastern Caribbean Home Mortgage Bank; Gov. and Chair. Eastern Caribbean Cen. Bank 1989–2015; Chair. Tech. Restructuring Cttee, Org. of Eastern Caribbean States; Dir St Lucia Devt Bank, Nat. Commercial Bank, St Lucia; mem. Chancellor's Governance Cttee, Univ. of the W Indies; mem. Univ. Strategy Cttee; Dr hc (Univ. of the West Indies) 2003. *Address:* c/o East Caribbean Central Bank, Headquarters Bldg, Bird Rock, PO Box 89, Basseterre, St Kitts.

VENSON-MOITOI, Pelonomi, LLB; Botswana lawyer and politician; b. 5 Jan. 1945, Mapoka; ed Univ. of Botswana, Lesotho and Swaziland; State Counsel 1973–75, Sr State Counsel 1975–78, Prin. State Counsel 1978–80; Deputy Attorney-Gen. 1980–91, Attorney-Gen. 1992–2003; mem. Nat. Ass. (parl.) for Serowe South 2003–; Minister of Foreign Affairs and Int. Co-operation 2014–18, Minister of Local Government and Rural Development April–Dec. 2018; mem. Botswana Democratic Party.

VENTER, J(ohn) Craig, PhD; American biochemist, geneticist and entrepreneur; *President, J. Craig Venter Institute;* b. 14 Oct. 1946, Salt Lake City, UT; m. Claire Fraser; ed Univ. of California, San Diego; served in USN, served in Viet Nam 1967; Prof., State Univ. of NY, Buffalo –1984; Section and Lab. Chief, NIH, Bethesda, Md 1984–92; Founder, Chair. and Chief Scientist, The Inst. for Genomic Research 1992–; Founder, Pres. and Chief Scientific Officer, Celera Genomics Corpn, Rockville, Md 1998–2002, Chair. Scientific Advisory Bd 2002–; Pres. J. Craig Venter Inst. 2004–; Founder, Chair., CEO and Co-Chief Scientific Officer, Synthetic Genomics, Inc. 2005–; Co-founder, Chair. and CEO Human Longevity, Inc. 2014–; mem. Advisory Bd, USA Science and Engineering Festival; mem. NAS, American Acad. of Arts and Sciences, American Soc. for Microbiology; numerous hon. degrees, including Hon. DSc (Clarkson Univ.) 2010; Beckman Award 1999, Chiron Corpn Biotechnology Research Award 1999, King Faisal Int. Prize for Science 2000, Taylor Prize 2001, Paul Ehrlich and Ludwig Darmstaedter Prize 2001, Gairdner Foundation Int. Award 2002, Benjamin Rush Medal, William & Mary School of Law 2011, Dickson Prize in Medicine 2011, Leeuwenhoek Medal, Royal Netherlands Acad. of Arts and Sciences 2015. *Achievements include:* one of the first scientists to sequence the human genome; led team of scientists who were first to successfully create a cell with a synthetic genome May 2010. *Publications:* A Life Decoded (autobiog.) 2007, Life at the Speed of Light: From the Double Helix to the Dawn of Digital Life 2013; more than 200 articles in scientific journals. *Leisure interest:* sailing. *Address:* J. Craig Venter Institute, 9704 Medical Center Drive, Rockville, MD 20850 (office); Synthetic Genomics, Inc., 11149 North Torrey Pines Road, La Jolla, CA 92037 (office); Human Longevity, Inc., 4570 Executive Drive, San Diego, CA 92121, USA (office). *Telephone:* (301) 795-7000 (Venter Inst.) (office); (858) 754-2900 (Synthetic Genomics) (office); (858) 249-7500 (Human Longevity) (office). *Fax:* (858) 754-2988 (office). *E-mail:* info@jcvi.org (office); info@syntheticgenomics.com (office). *Website:* www.jcvi.org/cms/home (office); www.syntheticgenomics.com (office); www.humanlongevity.com (office).

VENTO, Sergio, MA; Italian business executive, academic and diplomatist (retd); *Chairman, Vento & Associati Srl;* b. 30 May 1938; m.; two c.; ed Univ. of Rome; joined Ministry of Foreign Affairs 1963, Second, then First Sec. Embassy in The Hague, Netherlands 1967–70, Consul in Buenos Aires, Argentina 1970–72, Counsellor in Ankara, Turkey 1972–75, Officer, Near East and N African Political Affairs Office 1975–79, Minister Plenipotentiary (Second Class) Office of Econ. Affairs 1985–87, Diplomatic Counsel to Deputy Prime Minister and Minister of Finance 1987–89, apptd Minister Plenipotentiary (First Class) 1988, Amb. to Yugoslavia 1989–92, Diplomatic Counsellor to Prime Minister 1992–95, Amb. to France 1995–99, Amb. and Perm. Rep. to UN, New York 1999–2003, Amb. to USA 2003–05; Sr Adviser, McDermott Will & Emery Studio Legale Associato (law firm), Rome 2005–07; Chair. Autostrade del Molise SpA 2008–10; Vice-Pres. Northeast Merchant Two (asset man. firm) 2011–, National Agency for Microcredit 2011–; Prof. of Int. Relations, Faculty of Econs, LUISS Guido Carli Univ., Rome 2006–; Chair. Vento & Associati Srl 2011–; Officer, Grand Cross of Order of Merit 1988, Kt, Grand Cross of Order of Merit 1994, Commdr, Légion d'honneur 1999; Dr hc (St

John's Univ., New York) 2003. *Address:* Vento & Associati Srl, Torre Velasca, Piazza Velasca 5, 20122 Milan, Italy (office). *Telephone:* (02) 36-74-44-05 (office). *E-mail:* info@ventoeassociati.it (office). *Website:* www.ventoeassociati.it (office).

VENTURA, Jesse; American radio presenter, actor, fmr professional wrestler and fmr politician; b. (James George Janos), 15 July 1951, Minneapolis, Minn.; s. of George Janos and Bernice Janos; m. Terry Ventura; two c.; ed North Hennepin Community Coll.; served in USN 1969–73, USNR 1973–75; fmr bodyguard for The Rolling Stones; professional wrestler 1973–84; TV commentator, actor 1984–97; Mayor of Brooklyn Park, Minn. 1991–95; radio talk show host 1995–98; Gov. of Minn. 1998–2002; fmr mem. Reform Party; mem. Advisory Bd Operation Truth (addresses issues of US Nat. Guard in Iraq) 2004; Spokesman for BetUS.com 2005. *Films include:* Predator 1987, Running Man 1987, Abraxas, Guardian of the Universe 1991, Demolition Man 1993, Batman & Robin 1997. *Television:* Jesse Ventura's America 2003, Conspiracy Theory with Jesse Ventura 2009–13, Off the Grid 2014–. *Publications:* I Ain't Got Time to Bleed 2000, Do I Stand Alone? Going to the Mat Against Political Pawns and Media Jackals 2000, Jesse Ventura Tells it Like it Is: America's Most Outspoken Governor Speaks Out About Government 2002, Don't Start the Revolution Without Me 2008, American Conspiracies (co-author) 2010, 63 Documents the Government Doesn't Want You to Read 2011, DemoCRIPS and ReBLOODlicans: No More Gangs in Government 2012, They Killed Our President: 63 Reasons to Believe There Was a Conspiracy to Assassinate JFK 2013, Sh*t Politicians Say: The Funniest, Dumbest, Most Outrageous Things Ever Uttered By Our "Leaders" 2016, Jesse Ventura's Marijuana Manifesto 2016. *Website:* www.ora.tv/offthegrid.

VENTURINI, Roberto, MD; San Marino physician and politician; b. 30 Dec. 1960; one s. one d.; ed Univ. of Bologna, Italy; Emergency Doctor, San Marino Hosp. 1992–; mem. Perm. Antidoping Cttee 2006–; mem. Consiglio Grande e Generale (Parl.) 2012–, mem. Consiglio dei XII, mem. Health, Land and Environment Cttees; Co-Captain Regent (jt head of state) April–Oct. 2015; mem. Federazione Medico Sportiva Sammarinese, Croce Rossa Sammarinese, Associazione Cuore e Vita; mem. Partito Democratico Cristiano Sammarinese.

VENTURONI, Adm. (retd) Guido; Italian naval officer (retd) and international organization official; b. 10 April 1934, Teramo; m. Giuliana Marinozzi; two s. one d.; ed Naval Acad. 1952–56; Navigator, Communications Officer, maritime patrol pilot and tactical instructor; Head of Naval Helicopter Studies and Projects Office; Exec. Asst to Chief of Navy Staff, to Chief of Defence at Naval Personnel Directorate; Head of Plans and Operation Dept at Navy Gen. Staff, at Defence Gen. Staff 1982–86; Commdr, First Naval Div. 1986–87; Head Financial Planning Bureau, Naval Gen. Staff 1987–89; Deputy Chief of Staff of Navy 1989–90; Vice-Adm. 1990–91; C-in-C of Fleet and NATO Commdr of Cen. Mediterranean 1991–92; Chief of Staff of Navy 1992–93, Chief of Defence Gen. Staff 1994–99; Over Commdr, Int. Security Mission to Albania 1997; Chair. Mil. Cttee, NATO 1999–2002; Pres. Selenia Communications SpA (fmrly Marconi Selenia Communications SpA) 2002–05; mem. Bd of Dirs Finmeccanica 2005–14 (also served as Vice-Pres. and interim Pres.); Kt of Grand Cross of Order of Merit, Officer, Légion d'honneur, Grand Cross of Orden de Mayo al Mérito Naval (Argentina), First Class Cross of Order of Mérito Naval (Spain), Second Class Decoration of Order of Mérito Naval (Venezuela); Silver Medal for sea duty service, Gold Medal for air service, Medal for Merit (Mauritius).

VENUGOPAL, Kottayan Katankot (K.K.); Indian lawyer and government official; *Attorney-General;* b. 1931, Kanhangad, Kerala; s. of M.K. Nambiar; ed Raja Lakhamgouda Law Coll., Karnataka, St Aloysius Coll., Mangalore; enrolled as an advocate in 1954, designated Sr Advocate, Supreme Court 1972; apptd Additional Solicitor-Gen., Morarji Desai's Govt 1979; fmr constitutional adviser, Govt of Bhutan; appeared in many high-profile cases including Demolition of the Babri Masjid; Pres. Union Internationale des Avocats 1996–97; Attorney-Gen. 2017–; Padma Bhushan, Padma Vibhushan 2015. *Address:* Office of Attorney-Gen., Supreme Court of India, Tilak Marg, New Delhi 110201 (office); Chamber No.26, Law Officers' Chambers, 2nd Floor, Supreme Court of India, Tilak Marg, New Delhi 110201 (office); A-144, Neeti Bagh, New Delhi 110049, India (office). *Telephone:* (11) 23388942 (office); (11) 23782101 (office). *Fax:* (11) 23381508 (office). *E-mail:* kkvenu@vsnl.com (office).

VERA BEJARANO, Cándido, Lic.; Paraguayan politician; b. 16 July 1957, San Pedro de Yeuamandyzú; s. of Candido Vera and Florencia Bezarano; m.; two s. two d.; ed Escuela Agricola Carlos Pfannl, Universidad del Norte, Asunción, Degree in Farm Man.; elected mem. Nat. Congress (Liberal Party) 1993, re-elected 1998; apptd Pres. Nat. Congress 2000; Senator 2003–08; Minister of Agric. and Livestock 2008–11; mem. Mercosur Parl. 2008–13. *Publications include:* Proyecto de Modificacion del Estatuto Agraiio 2002, Proyecto de ley que creo el Instituto de Desarollo Rural y de la Tierra 2003. *Telephone:* (21) 21-4612 (home). *Fax:* (21) 21-4612 (home).

VERA CRUZ, Tomé; São Tomé and Príncipe politician; ed in Romania; fmr Head, Water and Electricity Co.; Minister of Natural Resources 2003–04; Prime Minister and Minister of Information and Regional Integration 2006–08 (resgnd); fmr Sec.-Gen. Movimento Democrático Força da Mudança (MDFM).

VERANNEMAN DE WATERVLIET, Ecuyer Jean-Michel, Licencié ULB, Licentiaat VUB; Belgian diplomatist and historian; b. 11 July 1947, Bruges; s. of Jonkheer Raymond Veranneman de Watervliet and Baroness Manuela van Bogaerde de Terbrugge; m. Maria do Carmo Neves da Silveira; three s.; ed Institut d'Etudes Politiques, Paris, Université Libre de Bruxelles, Vrije Universiteit Brussel; six months as trainee European Comm., Brussels; mil. service with Chasseurs Ardennais Regt (Reserve Officer); joined Diplomatic Corps 1976, postings include Bonn, Brasilia, La Paz, UN, New York, EU, Brussels, Amb. to Mozambique 1983–86, Consul Gen., São Paulo 1991–94, Minister Plenipotentiary, London 1994–97, Amb. to Brazil 2000–03, to Israel 2004–06, to UK 2006–10, to Portugal 2010–12; Visiting Prof. Universidade Nova and Universidade Catolica, Lisbon 2014–15; Chair. Consultative Council, Estoril Confs (Portugal); Freeman of the City of London; Grand Officier, Ordre de Léopold II; Commdr, Ordre de Léopold, Ordre de la Couronne; Médaille Civique de Ière Classe (Belgium); Grand Cross, Order of the Southern Cross (Brazil); Grand Cross, Order of Merit (Portugal). *Publications:* The Portuguese Immigrant Workers, History of Africa, Is the Sovereign Nation State Obsolete?, Belgium in the Second World War. *Leisure interests:* model ships, archery, hiking, boating, reading history books. *Address:* Rua Joseph Bleck 48, 2° P, 1494-724 Dafundo, Portugal (office); Chateau de Wodémont 1B, 4608 Dalhem, Belgium (office). *Telephone:* (21) 4080725 (office); (4) 376-65-57 (office). *E-mail:* jmveranneman@hotmail.com (office). *Website:* www.unl.pt (office).

VERBERG, George H. B., PhD; Dutch business executive; *Chairman of the Supervisory Board, Berenschot Groep B.V.;* b. 2 Sept. 1942, Batavia, Dutch E Indies; ed Netherlands School of Econs, Erasmus Univ., Rotterdam, MIT and Univ. of Calif. at Berkeley; joined Ministry of Educ. and Science 1971, Ministry of Econ. Affairs 1974, positions include Gen. Econ. Policy Dir, Dir-Gen. for Trade, Industry and Services, Dir-Gen. for Energy –1988; joined NV Nederlandse Gasunie 1988, Commercial Man.-Dir 1989–92, CEO 1992–2004; Chair. Supervisory Bd UCN NV 2003–, Berenschot Groep B.V. 2006–; Chair. CultuurPakt Noord 2014–; fmr Vice-Pres. Int. Gas Union; fmr Vice-Chair. Eurogas Asscn; Vice-Chair. Supervisory Bd Univ. of Groningen; mem. Bd Advisory Council ING-Group; mem. Supervisory Bd IKN (Integrated Cancer Centre for N Netherlands); Chair. Advisory Bd Sogeo Co.; fmr Chair. Advisory Bd UN-Gas Centre. *Address:* Berenschot Groep B.V., Europalaan 40, 3526 KS Utrecht, Netherlands (office). *Telephone:* (30) 2916916 (office). *Fax:* (30) 2947090 (office). *E-mail:* contact@berenschot.com (office). *Website:* www.berenschot.com (office).

VERBITSKAYA, Ludmila Alekseyevna, PhD; Russian philologist and university administrator; *President, St Petersburg State University;* b. 17 June 1936, Leningrad (now St Petersburg); m. (deceased); two d.; ed Leningrad State Univ.; lab. asst, then jr researcher, Docent, Chair. of Philology, Leningrad (now St Petersburg) State Univ. –1979, Prof. Chair. of Phonetics 1979–85, Head Chair. of Gen. Linguistics 1985–, Pro-Rector on scientific work, First Pro-Rector 1989, Acting Rector 1993–94, Rector 1994–2008, Pres. 2008–; Vice-Pres. UNESCO Comm. on Problems of Women's Educ.; Rep. to Exec. Council of Int. Asscn of Univs; elected Pres. Int. Asscn of Teachers of Russian Language and Literature (MAPRYAL) 2003; Pres. Russian Soc. of Teachers of Russian Language and Literature (ROPRYAL) 2003–; Chair. Presidium of the Council of Univ. Rectors of the Northwest Fed. Dist; Deputy Chair. Advisory Comm. on Science, Tech. and Educ. of Pres. of the Russian Federation Fed.; Vice-Pres. Coordinating Cttee of the Russian-German St Petersburg Dialogue forum; Deputy Head, Russian Union of Rectors; Advisor to Gov. of St Petersburg on educ., science and mass media; mem. Russian Acad. of Education (RAE) 1995, Russian Acad. of Humanitarian Sciences, Acad. of Sciences of Higher School, Presidium Int. Asscn of Russian Language and Literature Teachers, Presidium Conf. of Rectors of European Univs; mem. of Council Our Home Russia Movt 1996–99; Verbitskaya planet named after her 2000; Hon. Employee of Higher Educ. in Russia, Hon. Citizen of St Petersburg 2006; Order of Friendship, Order for Nat. Service Third Degree and Fourth Degree, Commdr Academic Palm (France), Knight's Cross for Service (Poland), Chevalier, Légion d'Honneur 2005; Dr hc (Bologna Univ., New York Univ., St Petersburg State Tech. Univ., St Petersburg State Medical Univ., Novgorod State Univ. Yaroslav Mudry); Medal of Honour of Saint Grand Duchess Olga III of the Russian Orthodox Church, Medal of Honour of Grand Duchess Olga III (Ukraine), Medal of Merit in Nat. Healthcare, Queen's Anniversary Prize for Higher and Further Educ. (UK) 1997, Woodrow Wilson Award for Public Service 2008. *Publications:* over 300 publs. *Address:* St Petersburg State University, Universitetskaya nab. 7/9, 199034 St Petersburg, Russia (office). *Telephone:* (812) 3200717 (office). *Fax:* (812) 3241250 (office). *E-mail:* president@pu.ru (office). *Website:* www.spbu.ru (office).

VERDONCK, Ferdinand, BEcons, MA, LLD; business executive; b. 1942; ed Catholic Univ. of Leuven, Univ. of Chicago; began financial services career at Continental Ill. Bank of Chicago; with Lazard Frères and Co., New York –1984; Head of Operational and Admin Affairs, Bekaert 1984–92; Man. Dir and mem. Exec. Cttee Almanij NV 1992–2003 (retd); fmr Chair. Banco Urquijo, Nasdaq Europe; Pres. Dellacorte Acquisition Corpn 2007–; Chair. Supervisory Bd Amsterdam Molecular Therapeutics BV 2007–12, uniQure NV 2012; mem. Bd of Dirs Galapagos NV 2005–, Movetis NV 2008–10, JP Morgan European Investment Trust 1998–, Phoenix Funds, Groupe SNEF, Laco Information Services, Virtus Funds 2002–; mem. Supervisory Bd and Chair. Audit Cttee, Affimed Therapeutics 2014–.

VERE-JONES, David, MSc, DPhil, FRSNZ; British mathematician, academic and statistical seismologist; *Professor Emeritus, Victoria University of Wellington;* b. 17 April 1936, London; s. of Noel W. Vere-Jones and Isabel M. I. Wyllie; m. Mary To Kei Chung 1965 (died 2000); two s. one d.; ed Cheadle Hulme School, Cheshire, Hutt Valley High School, New Zealand, Victoria Univ. of Wellington and Univ. of Oxford; emigrated to New Zealand 1949; Rhodes Scholar 1958–61; Scientific Officer, Applied Math. Div. Dept of Scientific and Industrial Research, New Zealand 1962–63, Sr Scientific Officer 1963–64; Fellow, Dept of Statistics, ANU 1965–67, Sr Fellow 1967–69; Prof. of Math. with special responsibility for statistics, Victoria Univ. of Wellington 1970–2000, Prof. Emer. 2000–; Dir Statistical Research Asscn (New Zealand) Ltd 1999–2009, Assoc. 2009–; Distinguished Assoc. Statistics Research Associates Ltd 2009–; Founding Pres. New Zealand Math Soc. 1975; Pres. New Zealand Statistical Asscn 1981–83; Chair. International Statistical Inst. (ISI) Educ. Comm. 1987–91; Pres. of Interim Exec., International Asscn for Statistical Educ. 1991–92; Sr Researcher and Bd mem. New Zealand Inst. of Math. and its Applications 2002; Visiting Prof., Inst. Statistical Mathematics, Tokyo 1976, Imperial Coll., London, Univ. of Oxford 1986, Tokyo Inst. of Tech. 1995; Hon. mem. ISI, New Zealand Math. Soc. 2000, Life mem. New Zealand Statistical Asscn; Henri Willem Methorst Medal 1995, Royal Soc. of New Zealand Rutherford Medal 1999, New Zealand Science and Tech. Medal 2000, NZSA Campbell Award 2009. *Publications include:* An Introduction to the Theory of Point Processes (with D. J. Daley) 1988; about 150 papers on probability theory, seismology, mathematical educ. *Leisure interests:* table tennis, walking, languages. *Address:* Statistics Research Associates Ltd, PO Box 12-649, Thorndon, Wellington (office); 4 Forest Walk, Waikanae, New Zealand (home). *Telephone:* (4) 293-3342 (office). *E-mail:* dvj@statsresearch.co.nz (office); dvj@paradise.com.nz (office). *Website:* www.statsresearch.co.nz (office).

VEREKER, Sir John (Michael Medlicott), KCB, KStJ, BA, CIMgt, FRSA; British business executive and fmr public servant; b. 9 Aug. 1944; s. of Charles W. M. Vereker and Marjorie Vereker (née Whatley); m. Judith Diane Rowen 1971; one

s. one d.; ed Marlborough Coll., Keele Univ.; Asst Prin., Overseas Devt Ministry 1967–69, Adviser, World Bank, Washington, DC 1970–72, Prin., Overseas Devt Ministry 1972, Pvt. Sec. to Minister of Overseas Devt 1977–78, Asst Sec. 1978; Asst Sec., Prime Minister's Office 1980–83, Under-Sec. 1983–88; Prin. Finance Officer Overseas Devt Admin., FCO 1986–88; Deputy Sec. Dept of Educ. and Science, then Dept for Educ. 1988–93; Perm. Sec. Dept for Int. Devt 1994–2002; Gov. and C-in-C of Bermuda 2002–07; Ind. Dir, XL Group plc (now AXA XL) 2007–, XL Catlin Insurance Co. UK Ltd 2017–, MWH Global 2009–16; mem. Bd of Dirs XL Insurance Co. Ltd 2010–15; Chair. Students Loans Co. Ltd 1989–91; Vice-Pres. Raleigh Int. 2002–16; mem. Council, Inst. of Manpower Studies 1989–92, Bd British Council 1994–2002, IDS 1994–2001, VSO 1994–2002, Advisory Bd for British Consultants Bureau 1998–2002; Gov., Ditchley Foundation 2007–; Hon. DLitt (Keele) 1997.

VERES, János, PhD; Hungarian politician; b. 5 Feb. 1957, Nyírbátor; m. Éva Szabó; two c.; ed Univ. of Agriculture, Debrecen and Karl Marx Univ. of Econs; began career in business sector 1981–2002; mem. Nyírbátor local govt 1990–94; mem. Parl. 1994–; Chair., Chamber of Commerce and Trade, Szabolcs-Szatmár-Bereg County 1997–2002; Mayor of Nyírbátor 2002–03; mem. Exec. Cttee, Socialist Party of Hungary (Magyar Szocialista Párt—MSzP) 2004–; Sec. of State for Political Affairs, Ministry of Finance 2003–04; Chief of Staff, Office of the Prime Minister 2004–05; Minister of Finance 2005–09.

VERESHCHETIN, Vladlen Stepanovich, LLD, PhD; Russian international lawyer and judge; b. 8 Jan. 1932, Briansk; m.; one d.; ed Moscow State Inst. of Int. Relations; mem. staff, Presidium of USSR Acad. of Sciences 1958–67; First Vice-Chair. and Legal Counsel, Intercosmos, USSR Acad. of Sciences 1967–81; Prof. of Int. Law, Univ. of Friendship of Peoples 1979–82; Deputy Dir and Head, Dept of Int. Law, Inst. of State and Law, Russian Acad. of Sciences 1981–95; mem. Perm. Court of Arbitration, The Hague 1984–95; judge, Int. Court of Justice, The Hague 1995–2006; Vice-Pres. Russian (fmrly Soviet) UN Asscn 1984–97; Vice-Pres. Russian (fmrly Soviet) Asscn of Int. Law 1985–97; mem. UN Int. Law Comm. 1992–95; Foreign mem. Bulgarian Acad. of Sciences 2006; Hon. Dir Int. Inst. of Space Law 1995–; Order of Friendship of Peoples 1975, October Revolution Order 1981; Hon. Master of Sciences, Russian Fed. 1995; Hon. Awards from German Acad. of Sciences 1978, Bulgarian Acad. of Sciences 1979, Int. Acad. of Astronautics 1987, 1994, Hugo Grotius Award 2001, Int. Inst. of Space Law Lifetime Achievement Award 2009. *Publications include:* books and more than 200 articles on int. law, law of the sea, space law, int. jurisprudence. *Address:* 117420 Moscow, Profsouyaznaya str. 43, Building 1, Apt 255, Russia. *E-mail:* vsvereshchetin@ziggo.nl.

VERGARA, Sofía; Colombian actress, comedienne, television hostess and model; b. (Sofía Margarita Vergara Vergara), 10 July 1972, Barranquilla, Atlántico; d. of Julio Enrique Vergara Robayo and Margarita Vergara Dávila de Vergara; m. Joe Gonzalez 1991 (divorced 1993); one s.; ed Marymount School, Barranquilla, studied pre-dentistry at a univ. in Colombia for three years; moved to Miami, USA with members of her family 1990s; pursued modelling career; co-hosted two TV shows for Univisión late 1990s; designed clothing line for K-Mart 2011. *Films include:* Big Trouble 2002, Chasing Papi 2003, The 24th Day 2004, Soul Plane 2004, Lords of Dogtown 2005, Four Brothers 2005, Grilled 2006, Meet the Browns 2008, Madea Goes to Jail 2009, The Smurfs 2011, Happy Feet Two (voice) 2011, New Year's Eve 2011, The Three Stooges 2012, Machete Kills 2013, The Smurfs 2 2013. *Television includes:* Acapulco, cuerpo y alma (series) 1995, My Wife and Kids (series) 2002, Eve (series) 2004, El escándalo del mediodía (series) 2004, Rodney (series) 2004, Hot Properties (series) 2005, Entourage (series) 2007, Amas de casa desesperadas (series) 2007, The Knights of Prosperity (series) 2007, Dirty Sexy Money (series) 2007, Fuego en la sangre (series) 2008, Men in Trees (series) 2008, Dancing with the Stars 2009, Modern Family (series) 2009–, The Cleveland Show (series) (voice) 2011, Plaza Sésamo 2011. *Address:* c/o Latin World Entertainment Agency, 4770 Biscayne Boulevard, Suite 1100, Miami, FL 33137, USA (office). *Telephone:* (305) 572-1515 (office). *Website:* www.sofiavergara.com.

VERGARA MONTES, Rodrigo, PhD; Chilean economist, academic and central banker; *Governor, Central Bank of Chile;* b. 5 June 1962; m.; four c.; ed Universidad Católica de Chile, Harvard Univ., USA; Researcher, Central Bank of Chile 1985–87, Chief, Financial Macroeconomics Dept 1991–92, Chief Economist 1992–95, mem. of Bd 2009–, Gov. 2011–; Coordinator, Macroeconomics Dept, Center for Public Studies (think-tank) 1995–2003; Prof., Economics Dept, Universidad Católica 2003–09; has served as consultant to World Bank, IMF, Inter-American Devt Bank and UN; mem. Editorial Bd, Estudios Públicos, Economía Chilena; fmr mem. Presidential Advisory Council on Work and Equity, Advisory Council on Chile–US Free Trade Agreement, Nat. Savings Comm., Conicyt Econs Group; Economist of the Year, El Mercurio newspaper 2012, Commercial Engineer Award, Universidad Católica de Chile, 2013. *Publications include:* numerous articles published in professional journals; edited five books. *Address:* Central Bank of Chile, Agustinas 1180, Santiago, Chile (office). *Telephone:* (2) 2670-2300 (office). *Fax:* (2) 2697-2271 (office). *E-mail:* rvergara@bcentral.cl (office). *Website:* www.bcentral.cl (office).

VERHAEGEN, Georges, PhD; Belgian scientist and academic (retd); *Honorary Rector, Université Libre de Bruxelles;* b. 26 March 1937, Brussels; s. of Col J. Verhaegen and L. Neufcoeur; m. M. Van de Keere 1965; two s.; ed Ashbury Coll., Ottawa, Canada, Univ. Libre, Brussels, CNRS, France; Pres. Dept of Chem., Univ. Libre de Bruxelles 1973–75, Dean Faculty of Sciences 1978–81, Full Prof. 1979–2002, Univ. Prof. 2002–07, mem. Governing Body 1975–84, 1986–, Rector 1986–90, Pro-Rector 1990, now Hon. Rector; Pres. Belgian Conf. of Rectors (French speaking) 1986–90, Belgian NSF 1990, Network of Univs of Capital Cities of Europe (UNICA) 1989–97; Expert for Univ. Man. (European Univ. Asscn, IBRD, European Comm.) 1993–; winner of three Belgian scientific prizes. *Publications:* more than 60 scientific publs. *Leisure interests:* reading, tennis, handicrafts, travelling. *Address:* C.P. 160/09, Université Libre de Bruxelles, 50 avenue F.D. Roosevelt, 1050 Brussels (office); 2 rue du Bois des Aulnes, 7090 Braine le Comte, Belgium (home). *Telephone:* (2) 650-24-24 (office); (67) 63-82-86 (home). *E-mail:* gverhaeg@ulb.ac.be (office). *Website:* www.ulb.ac.be (office).

VERHAGEN, Maxime Jacques Marcel; Dutch historian, politician and entrepreneur; *President, Bouwend Nederland;* b. 14 Sept. 1956, Maastricht; m.; two s. one d.; ed Leiden Univ.; began career as Asst at Christian Democratic Alliance (CDA) 1984–87, Head of European Affairs, Devt Co-operation and Trade Policy 1987–89; mem. Oegstgeest Municipal Council 1986–89; MEP 1989–94; mem. House of Reps 1994–2012, Chair. Christian Democratic Appeal (CDA) 2002–12; Minister of Foreign Affairs 2007–10; Deputy Prime Minister, Minister of Econ. Affairs, Agric. and Innovation 2010–12; Advisor, VOPAK 2012–16, VDL 2012–, Chemelot 2012–, Prov. of Limburg 2012–; mem. Bd, VNO-NCW (gen. employers' org.) 2013–; Pres. Bouwend Nederland (employers' org. of building and construction cos) 2013–; Special Envoy for the Dutch participation in the F-35 programme 2014–; Vice-Pres. FIEC (European Fed. of Construction and Building Industry) 2015–; mem. Bd of Supervisors, Foundation DON, Diabetes Research Netherlands 2016–, Philips Lighting 2017–; fmr Vice-Chair. ACP-EU Joint Ass., Parl. Cttee on Foreign Affairs; fmr mem. Bd, Eduardo Frei Foundation, Netherlands Atlantic Asscn, European Movt, Univ. of Nijmegen Parl. History Foundation, Free Voice; mem. Bd of Trustees, Shellfoundation 2014–. *Leisure interests:* skiing, motorcycling, travelling, sailing. *Address:* Bouwend Nederland, Zilverstraat 69, 2718 RP Zoetermeer, The Netherlands (office). *Telephone:* (79) 3252252 (office). *E-mail:* m.verhagen@bouwendnederland.nl (office). *Website:* www.bouwendnederland.nl (office).

VERHEUGEN, Günter; German politician and academic; b. 28 April 1944, Bad Kreuznach; s. of Leo Verheugen and Leni Verheugen (née Holzhaüser); ed in Cologne and Bonn; trainee, Neue Rhein-Neue Ruhr-Zeitung 1963–65; Head of Public Relations Div., Fed. Ministry of the Interior 1969–74; Head of Analysis and Information Task Force, Fed. Foreign Office 1974–76; Fed. Party Man., Free Democratic Party (FDP) 1977–78; Gen. Sec. FDP 1978–82; joined Sozialdemokratische Partei Deutschlands (SPD) 1982; mem. Bundestag 1983–99, Chair. EU Special Cttee 1992, mem. Foreign Affairs Cttee 1983–98; Spokesman, SPD Nat. Exec. 1986–87; Ed.-in-Chief Vorwärts (SPD newspaper) 1987–89; Chair. Radio Broadcasting Council, Deutsche Welle 1990–99; Fed. Party Man. SPD 1993–95; Deputy Chair. SPD Parl. Group for Foreign, Security and Devt Policy 1994–97; Chair. Socialist Int. Peace, Security and Disarmament Council 1997–; mem. SPD Nat. Exec.; Minister of State, Fed. Foreign Office 1998–99; EU Commr for Enlargement 1999–2004, for Enterprise and Industry 2004–10, Vice-Pres EU Comm. 2004–10; currently Hon. Prof. for European Studies, Viadrina European University, Frankfurt (Oder); Commdr Distinguished Service Cross (Italy). *Publications include:* Eine Zukunft für Deutschland 1980, Das Programm der Liberalen Baden-Baden 1980, Der Ausverkauf-Macht und Verfall der FDP 1984, Apartheid-Südafrika und der Deutschen Interessen am Kap 1986. *Address:* Europa-Universität Viadrina, Professur für Europa-Studien, Logenhaus, Logenstraße 11-12, 15230 Frankfurt Oder, Germany (office). *E-mail:* verheugen@europa-uni.de (office). *Website:* www.kuwi.europa-uni.de/de/studium/master/es/index.html (office).

VERHOEVEN, Michael; German screenwriter, director and producer; *Head, Sentana Filmproduktion GmbH;* b. 13 July 1938, Berlin; s. of Paul Verhoeven and Doris Kiesow; m. Senta Berger 1966; two s.; actor stage, TV and cinema 1953–; Co-founder (with wife) and Head of Sentana Filmproduktion GmbH, Munich 1965–; medical studies Munich, Berlin and Worcester, Mass., LA, Calif., USA; worked as doctor Munich –1973; taught at Film Acad. Baden-Württemberg; Cross of Merit 1999; New York Critics Circle Award, BAFTA Award, Joseph Neuberger-Medaille 1996, Award, Festival Int. de Programmes Audiovisuels, Biarritz 2001, Visionary Award, Washington Jewish Film Festival 2009; several other awards for writing, directing and producing. *Films:* Dance of Death 1967, O.K. 1970, Great Escape 1973, Sunday Children 1979, The White Rose 1981, Killing Cars 1985, The Nasty Girl 1989, My Mother's Courage 1995, The Legend of Mrs. Goldman and the Almighty God 1996, Der unbekannte Soldat 2006, Menschliches Versagen 2008. *Plays (director and producer):* The Guns of Mrs Carrar, Believe Love Hope, The Tribades Night, Volpone. *Television (director and producer):* The Challenge 1974, The Reason 1978, Dear Melanie 1983, Gunda's Father 1986, Semmelweis MD 1987, The Fast Gerdi 1989, Land of Milk and Honey 1991, Unholy Love 1993, Tabori – Theatre is Life (documentary) 1998, Room to Let 1999, Metamorphosis 2000, The Fast Gerdi in Berlin 2002, Pictures of an Exhibition (docu-essay) 2004, The Unknown Soldier 2006, Menschliches Versagen 2008, The Second Execution of Romell Broom 2012, Let's Go! 2014. *Publications:* Liebe Melanie 1974, Sonntagskinder 1979, Die Weisse Rose 1980. *Address:* Sentana Filmproduktion GmbH, Gebsattelstr. 30, 81541 Munich (office); Robert-Koch-Str. 10, 82031 Grünwald, Germany (home). *Telephone:* (89) 4485266 (office). *Fax:* (89) 4801968 (office). *E-mail:* sentana@sentana.de (office). *Website:* www.sentana.de (office).

VERHOEVEN, Paul, PhD; Dutch film director; b. 18 July 1938, Amsterdam; ed Leiden Univ.; worked as a documentary filmmaker for Dutch navy and then for TV. *Films include:* directed: (shorts) A Lizard Too Much 1960, Let's Have a Party 1963, The Wrestler 1971; (feature length) Wat zien ik (Business is Business/Any Special Way) 1971, Turks fruit (Turkish Delight) 1973, Keetje Tippel 1975, Soldaat van Oranje 1940–45 (Soldier of Orange/Survival Run) 1978, Spetters 1980, De vierde man (The Fourth Man) 1984, Flesh and Blood 1985, RoboCop 1987, Total Recall 1989, Basic Instinct 1992, Showgirls 1995, Starship Troopers 1997, Hollow Man 2000, Black Book 2006, The Winter Queen (producer) 2010, Elle 2016. *Television includes:* Floris 1969, Starship Troopers: The Series (producer) 1999–2000.

VERHOFSTADT, Guy, LLB; Belgian politician; b. 11 April 1953, Dendermonde; s. of Marcel Verhofstadt and Gaby Stockmans; m. Dominique Verkinderen 1981; one s. one d.; ed Koninklijk Atheneum, Univ. of Ghent; began career as attorney-at-law, Ghent Bar; Councillor, Ghent 1976–82; Political Sec. to Willy De Clerq, Nat. Pres. Party for Freedom and Progress (PVV) 1977–81; mem. House of Reps Ghent-Eeklo Dist 1978–84; Nat. Pres. PVV Youth Div. 1979–81, Nat. Pres. PVV 1982–85; Deputy Prime Minister and Minister for the Budget, Scientific Research and the Nat. Plan 1985–88; Pres. of Shadow Cabinet 1988–91; Nat. Pres. of PVV 1989–92, of Flemish Liberals and Democrats (VLD) 1992–95, 1997–99; Minister of State 1995–99; Senator (VLD) 1995–99, Vice-Pres. of Senate 1995–99; Prime Minister of Belgium 1999–2007 (resgnd), reappointed Dec. 2007, resgnd March 2008; MEP 2009–, Chair. Group of the Alliance of Liberals and Democrats for Europe. *Publications include:* Het Radicaal Manifest: Handvest voor een nieuwe liberaale omwenteling 1979, Burgermanifest 1991, De Weg naar politieke vernieuwing: Het tweede burgermanifest 1992, Angst, afgunst en het algemeen belang 1994, De Belgische Ziekte: Diagnose en remedies 1997, In goede banen: VLD-plan voor meer tewerks telling 1999; De vierde golf – een liberaal project voor de nieuwe eeuw 2002, De verenigde staten van Europa, 2007 (Awarded Best European Book of the Year 2007), Een new age of empires 2009; contribs to books and articles in periodicals. *Leisure interests:* cycling, literature, Italy. *Address:* European Parliament, Altiero Spinelli, 60 rue Wiertz, 1047 Brussels, Belgium (office). *Website:* www.europarl.europa.eu (office); www.guyverhofstadt.be.

VERMA, Adm. (retd) Nirmal Kumar, ADC; Indian fmr naval officer and diplomatist; b. 14 Nov. 1950; m. Madhulika Verma; two s.; ed Royal Naval Staff Coll., UK, Naval War Coll., USA; joined Indian Navy 1970; crew mem. for first Kashin Class Destroyer inducted into Indian Navy 1980 (trained in fmr Soviet Union); specialist in communication and electronic warfare; sea tenures have included commands of INS Udaygiri (Leander Class Frigate), INS Ranvir (Kashin Class Destroyer), INS Viraat (Aircraft Carrier); commanded Indian Naval Acad. at Goa, fmr Head of Naval Training Team at Defence Services Staff Coll., Wellington and Sr Directing Staff (Navy), Nat. Defence Coll., New Delhi; promoted to Flag Rank as Rear Adm., Chief of Staff of Eastern Naval Command, later Flag Officer Commdg Maharashtra Naval Area, later Flag Officer Commdg-in-Chief (FOC-in-C) Eastern Naval Command; rank of Vice-Adm. and Chief of Personnel 2005; Asst Chief of Naval Staff (Policy & Plans) –2009, apptd Chair. Chiefs of Staff Cttee 2011; Chief of Naval Staff 2009–12; High Commr to Canada 2012–14; Hon. ADC to Pres. of India; Param Vishist Seva Medal, Ati Vishist Seva Medal. *Address:* Ministry of External Affairs, South Block, New Delhi 110 011, India (office). *Telephone:* (11) 23011127 (office). *Fax:* (11) 23013254 (office). *E-mail:* eam@mea.gov.in (office). *Website:* meaindia.nic.in (office).

VERMA, Rajani Kant, MA; Indian government official (retd); *Chairman, Infinity Advisory Services Private Limited;* b. 23 April 1959; m. Ritu Verma; ed Delhi School of Economics, Harvard Univ., USA; Research Fellow, Harvard Univ., USA 1996–98; joined Indian Admin. Service; Chair. and Man. Dir, Lakshwadweep Tourism, Infrastructure and Shipping Devt Corpn 1998–2002, Delhi State Industrial Devt Corpn 2002–03; Sec. of Finance and Planning July–Dec. 2003; Commr of Sales Tax and VAT, Govt of India, New Delhi 2003–06; Admin. Union Territories of Dadra and Nagar Haveli, and of Daman and Diu 2006–08; Prin. Sec. of Public Transport, Transport, Tourism, Forest and Mines 2008–11, of Power and Chair. Indraprastha Power Generation Co. Ltd (IPGCL) Aug. 2013–Jan. 2014; Prin. Sec. Dept of Technical and Higher Educ. and Information Tech. Jan.–Nov. 2014; Chair. Infinity Advisory Services Pvt. Limited 2015–. *Address:* Infinity Advisory Services Private Limited, 1003, Mercantile Building, 15 Kasturba Gandhi Marg, New Delhi 110001, India (office). *Telephone:* (11) 43015415 (office). *E-mail:* info@infinityadvisoryservices.com (office). *Website:* www.infinityadvisory.co (office).

VERMA, Richard Rahul, BS, JD, LLM; American lawyer, government official and diplomatist; b. 27 Nov. 1968; m. Melineh (Pinky) Verma; one s. two d.; ed Lehigh Univ., American Univ., Georgetown Univ.; Judge Advocate, USAF 1994–98; Assoc., Steptoe & Johnson LLP, Washington, DC 1998–2002, Partner 2007–09, 2011–; Sr Nat. Security Advisor to US Senator Harry Reid 2002–07; Asst Sec. for Legis. Affairs, US Dept of State 2009–11; Outside Counselor, Albright Stonebridge Group, Washington, DC 2011–15; Sr Nat. Security Fellow, Center for American Progress 2011–15; Amb. to India 2014–17; mem. Sec. of State's Foreign Affairs Policy Bd 2011–14; mem. Pennsylvania Bar Asscn 1993, DC Bar Asscn 1996; mem. Council on Foreign Relations (Int. Affairs Fellow 2002), S Asian Bar Asscn (Pres. and Bd mem. 1999–2001); Nat. Defense Service Medal, Air Force Commendation Medal, Meritorious Service Medal; S Asian Bar Asscn Pioneer Award 2011, US Dept of State Distinguished Service Award 2013.

VERMA, Seema, BS, MPH; American health policy consultant; *Administrator, Centers for Medicare and Medicaid Services;* ed Univ. of Maryland, Coll. Park, Johns Hopkins Univ.; fmr Vice Pres. of Planning, Health & Hospital Corpn, Marion County, Fla; fmr Dir, Asscn of State and Territorial Health Officials, Washington, DC; Founder and Pres. SVC, Inc. (health policy consulting firm) 2001–17; worked with Gov. of Indiana Mitch Daniels on health care policy; Admin. Centers for Medicare and Medicaid Services 2017–; mem. American Enterprise Inst. Leadership Network. *Address:* Hubert H. Humphrey Building, 200 Independence Avenue SW, Washington, DC 20201, USA (office). *Fax:* (202) 619-0630 (office). *E-mail:* Seema.Verma@cms.hhs.gov (office). *Website:* www.cms.gov (office).

VERNIER, Jacques; French politician and environmentalist; b. 3 July 1944, Paris; s. of Charles Vernier and Georgette Mangin; m. Bertille Janssen 1968; two s. two d.; ed Ecole Polytechnique and Ecole des Mines; engineer, Service des Mines, Strasbourg 1968–72; Sec.-Gen. Agence de l'eau Seine-Normandie 1972–74; Dir Agence de l'Eau Artois-Picardie 1974–83, Pres. Comité de Bassin Artois-Picardie (Agence de l'Eau) 1992–2004; Founder and Pres. Asscn Douai-Consommateurs 1976–83; Pres. PACT de Douai 1976–83; Mayor of Douai 1983–2014; Councillor, Régional du Nord-Pas-de-Calais 1983–90, 1998–2015, Pres. Communauté d'agglomération du Douaisis 2002–04, Vice-Pres. 2005–14; Vice-Pres. Syndicat mixte des transports du Douaisis 2011–14; mem. European Parl. 1984–93; Deputy (RPR) to Nat. Ass. 1993–97; Pres. Agence de l'Environnement 1994–97, Syndicat Mixte pour l'Aménagement et l'Equipement des Zones Industrielles du Douaisis 1995–2001, Comm. interministérielle du transport des matières dangereuses 1998–, Council of Admin Institut nat. de l'environnement industriel et des risques (INERIS) 2003–10, Comité départemental de l'UMP du Nord 2003–10, Conseil supérieur des installations classées 2004–, Comm. d'Harmonisation et de Médiation des Filières de collecte sélective et de traitement de déchets 2010–; Nat. Sec. then Gen. Del., Environnement au sein du RPR 1989–95, mem. Departmental Sec. RPR du Nord 1992–94, Political Bureau RPR 1993–98, l'autorité environnementale 2009–12; Chef de la mission du transport des matières dangereuses 1997–2008; Bénévole à la Croix rouge 2014–; Officier des Palmes académiques 2001, Chevalier, Légion d'honneur 2002, Commdr, Ordre nat. du Mérite 2005, Officier, Légion d'Honneur 2011. *Publications:* La bataille de l'environnement 1971, Guide Pratique pour les habitants de Douai 1981–2014, L'environnement (eighth edn) 2007, Les énergies renouvelables (fourth edn) 2007; several publs on environmental matters. *Leisure interests:* tennis, flying aircraft. *Address:* 162 quai du Petit Bail, 59500 Douai, France (home). *Website:* www.jacques-vernier.fr.

VERPLAETSE, Baron Alphonse Remi Emiel; Belgian fmr central banker; *Honorary Governor, National Bank of Belgium;* b. 19 Feb. 1930, Zulte; m. Odette Vanhee 1954; three s. two d.; ed Katholieke Universiteit Leuven; Nat. Bank of Belgium 1953–81, Dir 1988–, Deputy Gov. 1988–89, Gov. 1989–99, Hon. Gov. 1999–; Office of the Prime Minister 1981–88; Hon. Gov. and Vice-Pres. Higher Finance Council, Admin. BIS, Basle; Gov. IMF 1989–99; Deputy Gov. IBRD 1989–99, IFC 1989–99; Grand Officier, Ordre de la Couronne 1991; Grande Ufficiale, Ordine al Merito (Italy) 1986; Officier, Légion d'honneur 1994. *Address:* Schaveyslaan 25, 1650 Beersel, Belgium (home).

VERSACE, Donatella; Italian designer; b. 2 May 1955, Reggio di Calabria; d. of Antonio Versace and Francesca Versace; sister of Gianni Versace; m. Paul Beck (divorced); one s. one d.; ed Univ. of Florence; joined Versace 1978, fmrly overseer of advertising and public relations, accessories designer, children's collection designer (Versace Young) 1993, Head Designer for Versus and Isante lines; Style and Image Dir and Vice-Chair. Gianni Versace Group 1997–; solo debut for mainline collection 1998; first couture show for Versace Atelier in Paris Ritz 1998; launched her own fragrance Versace Woman 2001. *Address:* c/o Keeble Cavaco and Duka Inc., 450 West 15th Street, Suite 604, New York, NY 10011, USA (office); Versace SpA Headquarters, Via Manzoni 38, 20121 Milan, Italy (office). *Telephone:* (02) 760931 (Milan) (office). *Fax:* (02) 76004122 (Milan) (office). *Website:* www.versace.com (office).

VERSALDI, HE Cardinal Giuseppe, DCL; Italian ecclesiastic; b. 30 July 1943, Villarboit (Vercelli); ed Pontifical Gregorian Univ., Rome, Sacred Roman Rota; ordained priest, Archdiocese of Vercelli 1967; est. diocesan Family Counselling centre, Vercelli 1976; entrusted with care of parish of Larizza in diocese 1977; taught canon law and psychology at Pontifical Gregorian Univ. 1980–85; apptd to Supreme Tribunal of the Apostolic Signatura 1985–94; Vicar Gen. of Vercelli 1994–2007; Bishop of Alessandria (della Paglia) 2007–11; apptd Archbishop ad personam 2011; Pres. Pref. for Econ. Affairs of Holy See 2011–13, 2013–15; cr. Cardinal (Cardinal-Deacon of Sacro Cuore di Gesù a Castro Pretorio) 2012; participated in Papal Conclave 2013; mem., Congregation for the Evangelization of Peoples 2017–, Congregation for the Causes of Saints 2018–. *Address:* The Congregation for the Evangelization of Peoples, Piazza di Spagna 48, 00187 Rome, Italy (office). *E-mail:* segreteria@propagandafide.va (office). *Website:* www.vatican.va/roman_curia/congregations/cevang/index.htm (office).

VERSHBOW, Alexander R., BA, MA; American diplomatist; b. 3 July 1952, Boston, Mass; s. of Arthur E. Vershbow and Charlotte Z. Vershbow; m. Lisa K. Vershbow 1976; two s.; ed Yale Coll. and School of Int. Affairs, Columbia Univ.; joined Foreign Service 1977, Bureau of Politico-Military Affairs 1977–79, US Embassy, Moscow 1979–81, Office of Soviet Union Affairs 1981–85, US Embassy, London 1985–88; adviser US Del. to SALT II and START negotiations; Dir State Dept's Office of Soviet Union Affairs 1988–91; US Deputy Perm Rep. to NATO and Chargé d'affaires US Mission 1991–93; Prin. Deputy Asst Sec. of State for European and Canadian Affairs (responsibilities covered the Balkan conflict) 1993–94; Special Asst to the Pres. and Sr Dir for European Affairs at Nat. Security Council 1994–97 (worked on US policy which laid foundations of the Dayton Peace Agreement, adaptation and enlargement of NATO and its new relationship with Russia); Perm. Rep. to NATO 1998–2001; Amb. to Russian Fed. 2001–05, to S Korea 2005–08; Asst Sec. of Defense for Int. Security Affairs 2009–12, Deputy Sec.-Gen. NATO 2012–16; Anatoly Sharansky Freedom Award, Union of Councils of Soviet Jews 1990, first Joseph J. Kruzel Award for contribs to the cause of peace, US Dept of Defense 1997, Distinguished Service Award for Work at NATO, US State Dept 2001, ABA Amb.'s Award 2004, Cordell Hull Award for Economic Achievement, US State Dept 2007. *Publications:* articles on arms control, speeches on Russia and NATO issues. *Leisure interests:* music, theatre.

VERWAAYEN, Bernardus (Ben) J., LLM; Dutch telecommunications industry executive; b. Feb. 1952, Utrecht; m.; two c.; ed State Univ. of Utrecht; various man. posts with ITT Nederland BV 1975–88, rising to Gen. Man.; joined Koninklijke PTT Nederland (KPN) 1996, Chair. Unisource European Venture 1996–97, Pres. and Man. Dir PTT Telecom 1997–98; Exec. Vice-Pres. of Int. Div., Lucent Technologies Inc. Sept.–Oct. 1997, Exec. Vice-Pres. and COO 1997–99, Vice-Chair. Man. Bd 1999–2002, CEO Alcatel-Lucent (following acquisition of Lucent by Alcatel) 2008–13; CEO British Telecommunications PLC (now BT Group plc) 2002–08 (Chair. Operating Cttee); Chair. CBI Climate Change Bd; mem. Bd of Dirs Akamai Technologies 2013–, AkzoNobel 2012–, Bharti Airtel 2013–; Founding Partner, Keen Venture Partners; mem. World Econ. Forum's Foundation Bd 2010–; mem. Advisory Council ING; mem. Bd Astro All Asia Networks (ASTRO), Health Center Internet Services Inc.; Hon. KBE 2007; Officer, Order of Orange-Nassau, Chevalier, Légion d'honneur 2006. *Leisure interest:* Arsenal football club. *Address:* Keen Venture Partners, 9th Floor, No 1 Minster Court, Mincing Lane, London, EC3R 7AA, England (office). *E-mail:* ben@keenventurepartners.com (office). *Website:* www.keenventurepartners.com (office).

VERWILGHEN, Marc, BL; Belgian politician and lawyer; b. 21 Sept. 1952, Dendermonde; ed Free Univ. of Brussels; practising lawyer 1975–; Deputy 1991–99; Senator 1999–2010; Chair. Comms of Inquiry on Dutroux-Nihoul and on Missing and Murdered Children 1996–98; Chair. Chamber Comm. on Justice; mem. Vlaamse Liberalen en Demokraten-Partij van de Burger (PVV-VLD); Minister of Justice 1999–2003, of Devt Co-operation 2003–04, of Economy 2004–07; Dr hc (Univ. of Ghent) 1999, (Universidad Autonoma de Santo Domingo) 2001; Grand Officier, Ordre de Léopold 2001. *Publications:* Het V-Plan 1999, Over bruggen bouwen 1999. *Address:* Open Vld, Melsensstraat 34, 1000 Brussels, Belgium (office). *Telephone:* (2) 549-00-20 (office). *E-mail:* contact@openvld.be (office). *Website:* www.openvld.be (office).

VESELI, Kadri Fazli, BA, EMBA; Kosovo politician and fmr guerrilla leader; *President (Speaker), Kuvendi i Kosovës/Skupština Kosova (Kosovo Assembly);* b. 31 May 1967, Broboniq/Brabonjić, Mitrovicë/Mitrovica, Autonomous Province of Kosovo and Metohija, Socialist Repub. of Serbia, Socialist Fed. Repub. of Yugoslavia; m. Violeta Veseli; four c.; ed Univ. of Kamëz, Albania, Univ. of Sheffield –Int. Faculty, Greece, Univ. of Ljubljana, Slovenia; a leader of student movt 1988–90; joined Ushtria Çlirimtare e Kosovës (UÇK—Kosovo Liberation Army) late 1980s, completed mil. training with Albanian Army 1991, later took part in several operations with guerrilla groups nr Drenica, fled to Switzerland to gain political asylum and met Hashim Thaçi and Xhavit Haliti, apptd UÇK Chief of Intelligence Unit (G-2), foreign adviser to Kosovo del. and supporter of Peace Agreement signed in Rambouillet 1999; became supporter of Partia Demokratike e Kosovës (PDK—Democratic Party of Kosovo) 1999, mem. 2012–, Vice-Pres. 2013–16, Pres. 2016–; Head of Kosovo Intelligence Service –2013; Deputy, Kuvendi i Kosovës/Skupština Kosova (Kosovo Ass.) 2013–, Pres. (Speaker) 2014–. *Address:* Office of the Speaker, Kuvendi i Kosovës/Skupština Kosova (Kosovo Assembly), 10000 Prishtina, Rruga Nënë Terezë, Kosovo (office). *Telephone:* (38) 211169 (office). *Fax:* (38) 211188 (office). *E-mail:* info@assembly-kosova .org (office). *Website:* www.assembly-kosova.org (office).

VESHNYAKOV, Aleksander Albertovich, CandJurSc; Russian lawyer, government official and diplomatist; *Ambassador to Latvia;* b. 24 Nov. 1952, Baikalovo, Arkhangelsk Region; m.; two c.; ed Arkhangelsk Navigational School, Leningrad Higher School of Marine Eng, Leningrad Higher CP School, Diplomatic Acad., Russian Ministry of Foreign Affairs; worked for Arkhangelsk (Northern Sea steamship line) 1973–87; Sec., Arkhangelsk City CP Cttee 1987–90; Deputy Chair. Council of Repub. Supreme Soviet Russian Fed. 1990–91; Chair. Sub-comm. of Comm. for Transportation, Communications, Information Science and Space, Council of Repub. 1991–93; Econs Adviser, Marine Transport Dept, Ministry of Transportation 1993–94; Consultant, Information and Analysis Dept, Cen. Election Comm. 1994, Sec. 1995–99, Chair. 1999–2007; Amb. to Latvia 2008–; Defender of Free Russia Medal 1997, Medal in Commemoration of 850th Anniversary of Moscow 1997, Class IV Order for Service to the Fatherland 2000, Class II 2007. *Address:* Embassy of the Russian Federation, Antonijas iela 2, Rīga 1010, Latvia (office). *Telephone:* 6733-2151 (home). *Fax:* 6783-0209 (office). *E-mail:* rusembas@ml.lv (office). *Website:* www.latvia.mid.ru (office).

VESKIMÄGI, Taavi, BEng; Estonian business executive and fmr politician; *Managing Director, Elering OÜ;* b. 28 Nov. 1974, Rapla; m.; one d.; ed Tallinn Tech. Univ., Tallinn Pedagogical Univ.; Head of State Admin Dept and Adviser, Ministry of Finance 1996–2001; mem. Parl. 2003, 2005–06, Vice-Speaker of Parl. 2005–06; Minister of Finance 2003–05; mem. Res Publica Party, Treas. 2001–02, Chair. Parl. Group 2003, Vice-Chair. Res Publica (later Isamaa ja Res Publica Liit–Union of Pro Patria and Res Publica, after merger with Pro Patria Union in 2006) 2003–05, Co-Chair. 2006–07; Lecturer and Consultant in Public Admin and Financial Man. 1998–2003; mem. Rapla City Council and Head of Econ. Cttee 1999–2002; Man. Dir Elering OÜ (transmission grid operator) 2009–; fmr Dir Eesti Post, Tallinn Olympic Sport Centre, Tallinn Harbour, Narva Electricity, Estonian Air Navigation Services. *Leisure interests:* football, restoration of motorbikes. *Address:* Elering OÜ, Kadaka tee 42, Tallinn 12915, Estonia (office). *Telephone:* 715-1222 (office). *Fax:* 715-1200 (office). *E-mail:* info@elering.ee (office). *Website:* www.elering.ee (office).

VESTBERG, Hans, BBA; Swedish business executive; *CEO, Verizon;* b. 23 June 1965, Hudiksvall; m.; two c.; ed Univ. of Uppsala; joined Telefonaktiebolaget L. M. Ericsson 1991, held various managerial positions in China, Sweden, Chile and Brazil 1991–98, Chief Financial Officer (CFO), Brazil 1998–2000, CFO, N America, and Controller for the Americas 2000–02, Vice-Pres. and Head of Market Unit Mexico 2002–03, Sr Vice-Pres. and Head of Business Unit Global Services 2003–07, Exec. Vice-Pres. 2005–07, CFO and Head of Group Function Finance 2007–09, First Exec. Vice-Pres. –2009, mem. Bd of Dirs, Pres. and CEO 2010–16; Pres. Swedish Olympic Cttee 2016–18; Exec. Vice-Pres. and Pres. of Global Networks and Chief Tech. Officer, Verizon 2017–18, CEO 2018–; mem. Bd of Dirs UN Foundation 2015–; mem. Bd of Dirs Sony Ericsson Mobile Communications AB, Svenska Handbollsförbundet (Chair.). *Address:* Verizon, 1095 Avenue of the Americas, New York, NY 10001, USA (office). *Telephone:* (212) 395-1000 (office). *Website:* www.verizon.com (office).

VESTERDORF, Bo, LLM; Danish legal consultant and fmr judge; b. 11 Oct. 1945; ed Univ. of Copenhagen; fmr Jurist-Linguist, Court of Justice; fmr Admin. Ministry of Justice, later Head Constitutional and Admin. Law Dept, then apptd Dir Ministry of Justice; fmr Legal Attaché with Perm. Rep. to EC; fmr temporary judge, Eastern Regional Court; fmr mem. Human Rights Steering Cttee, then Bureau, Council of Europe; Judge, Court of First Instance of the European Communities 1989–2007, Pres. 1998–2007 (retd); Sr Legal Consultant, Plesner (law firm), Copenhagen 2007–; Consultant, Herbert Smith Freehills LLP 2008–. *Address:* Herbert Smith Freehills LLP, Central Plaza, Rue de Loxum 25, 1000 Brussels, Belgium (office); Plesner, Amerika Plads 37, 2100 Copenhagen, Denmark. *Telephone:* (2) 511-7450 (Brussels) (office). *E-mail:* bve@plesner.com (office); bo.vesterdorf@hsf.com (office). *Website:* www.herbertsmithfreehills.com (office); www.plesner.com (office).

VETTEL, Sebastian; German professional racing driver; b. 3 July 1987, Heppenheim, Bergstraße dist, Hesse; began racing karts in 1995, won various titles, including Jr Monaco Kart Cup 2001; upgraded to open-wheel cars 2003; won German Formula BMW Championship with 18 victories from 20 races 2004; drove for ASL Mucke Motorsport in Formula Three Euroseries 2005; was brought into Formula One by BMW Sauber; finished as runner-up in the F3 Euroseries 2006; took part in Friday practice for the 2006 Turkish Grand Prix and became youngest Formula One driver to drive at a Grand Prix meeting, aged 19 years and 53 days; went on to become sixth youngest driver to start a Grand Prix at US Grand Prix 2007, also the youngest point scorer on debut (aged 19 years and 349 days); moved to Toro Rosso 2007, youngest driver to lead a race at Japanese Grand Prix 2007; youngest Formula One driver to secure pole position, Italian Grand Prix 2008, went on to win; joined Red Bull Racing 2009, finished season as youngest ever runner-up (behind Jenson Button); winner Formula One Driver's Championship 2010 (youngest driver ever to win the championship), 2011 (youngest double champion in history), 2012 (third driver to win three consecutive championships and youngest triple champion in history), 2013 (youngest quadruple champion in history), helped Red Bull win World Constructors' Championship, along with team-mate Mark Webber 2010, 2011, 2012, 2013; joined Ferrari 2015; 52 Grand Prix victories (to Dec. 2018); DMV Jr Driver of the Award Year 2001, ADAC Jr Driver of the Year Award 2004, 2009, DMSB-Jr Award 2006, Autosport Rookie Of The Year Award 2008, DMV Driver of the Year Award 2008, Lorenzo Bandini Trophy 2009, BRDC Johnny Wakefield Trophy 2009, DHL Fastest Lap Award 2009, Motorsport Total Fahrer des Jahres Award 2010, German Athlete of the Year Award 2010, Autosport Int. Driver of the Year Award 2010, SPEED

Performance Award 2011, Silver Bay Laurel Leaf Award 2012, Sports Acad. Grand Prix Prize 2012, Milennium Bambi Award 2014. *Leisure interests:* snowboarding, mountain biking, swimming, fitness, Eintracht Frankfurt football team. *Address:* Ferrari S.p.a, Via Abertone Infiorne 4, I-41053 Maranello Italy (office); Postfach 1479, 64632 Heppenheim, Germany. *Telephone:* 0536 949111. *Website:* formula1 .ferrari.com (office); www.sebastianvettel.de.

VETTER, Hans-Jörg; German business executive; *Chairman of the Board of Managing Directors, Landesbank Berlin Holding AG;* b. 22 Aug. 1952, Göppingen; m.; three c.; with Deutsche Bank AG, Göppingen Br. 1969–76, Head of Commercial Property Financing, Export—Special Financing, Municipal Loan Business, Frankfurter Hypothekenbank (Group Deutsche Bank AG) 1976–84, Dir Cen. Construction Financing and Real Estate, Deutsche Bank AG, Frankfurt 1987–90; Dir, Head of Leasing Div. Man. of Deutsche Anlagen-Leasing (DAL), Westdeutsche Landesbank, Düsseldorf, Mainz 1985–87; mem. Bd of Man. Dirs, responsible for the Real Estate Business, Bank für Gemeinwirtschaft AG (BfG Bank), Frankfurt 1990–95, Co-mem. Bd of Man. Dirs, Corp. Customers and Pvt. Customers 1995, also mem. responsible for Treasury/Sales and Security Trading; Personally liable Pnr, M.M. Warburg & Co. KG a. A., Hamburg, responsible for Corp. Customers, Foreign Operations, Corp. Finance 1995–97; Vice-Chair. Bd of Man. Dirs, Landesbank Hessen-Thüringen (Helaba), Frankfurt 1997–2000; Vice-Chair. Bd of Man. Dirs, Bankgesellschaft Berlin AG (renamed Landesbank Berlin Holding AG 2006), Berlin Nov.–Dec. 2001, Chair. Dec. 2001–, Chair. Bd of Man. Dirs, Landesbank Berlin (renamed Landesbank Berlin AG 2006) 2002–; Chair. Bd of Man. Dirs, Landesbank Baden-Württemberg (LBBW), Stuttgart 2009–16. *Address:* Landesbank Berlin Holding AG, Alexanderplatz 2, D- 10178 Berlin, Germany (office). *Telephone:* (30) 245 500 (office). *Fax:* (30) 56950200 (office). *E-mail:* information@lbb.de (office). *Website:* www.lbb.de (office).

VETTIER, Jean-Paul; French business executive; *Chairman of the Supervisory Board, Novacap SA;* b. 1945; m.; two c.; ed Univ. of Paris; various staff and line positions with Rhône-Poulenc 1970–86, including Exec. Vice-Pres. Chemical Br.; Gen. Man. Petrochemical Div. and mem. Exec. Cttee, Orkem 1987–89; Exec. Vice-Pres., Refining and Marketing, Total 1990–93, Chair. (non-exec.) Total Petroleum N America 1992–96, Chair. and CEO Total Refining and Marketing and mem. Exec. Cttee 1993–2000, Chair. and CEO TotalFinaElf Refining and Marketing and mem. Exec. Cttee 2000–06; CEO Petroplus Holdings 2009–12; Pres. Europia (European oil industry asscn) for two terms; Sr Advisor, First Reserve Corpn (pvt. equity firm), Roland Berger Strategy Consultants 2006–09; currently Chair. Supervisory Bd Novacap SA; mem. Bd of Dirs SNC-Lavalin Group, Inc., Overseas Shipholding Group, Inc., DOMO Chemicals NV, Dresser-Rand Group, Inc. 2006–09, Eiffage SA; mem. Bd Institut Francais du Petrole; Chevalier, Légion d'honneur, Ordre nat. du Mérite. *Address:* Novacap SA, Le Carré Joannès 29, avenue Joannès Masset, CS 10619, 69258 Lyon Cedex 09, France (office). *Telephone:* 4-26-99-18-00 (office). *Fax:* 4-26-99-18-38 (office). *Website:* www .novacap.eu (office).

VETTORI, Daniel Luca; New Zealand fmr professional cricketer; b. 27 Jan. 1979, Auckland; m. Mary O'Connel; two c.; ed Marian School, St Paul's Collegiate School; all-rounder; slow left-arm orthodox spin bowler; left-handed batsman; plays for Northern Districts 1996–, New Zealand (youngest player to represent NZ in Tests and One-Day Ints (ODIs) aged 18, occasional Capt. ODI side 2005–06, overall Capt. 2007–11), Notts. 2003, Warwicks. 2006, Delhi Daredevils 2008–10, Queensland 2010, Royal Challengers Bangalore (Capt.) 2011–, Brisbane Heat 2011–, has also played for Hamilton in Hawke Cup; First-class debut: 1996/97; Test debut: NZ v England, Wellington 6–10 Feb. 19979; One-Day Int. (ODI) debut: NZ v Sri Lanka, Christchurch 25 March 1997; T20I debut: Kenya v NZ, Durban 12 Sept. 2007; youngest player to have represented NZ in Test cricket; currently NZ's leading ODI wicket-taker; stood down from captaincy and retd from ODIs and T20Is after the ICC World Cup 2011, retd from int. cricket after ICC World Cup 2015; Officer, NZ Order of Merit. *Address:* c/o Northern District Cricket, PO Box 1347, Hamilton, New Zealand. *Telephone:* (7) 839-3783. *Fax:* (7) 839-5542. *E-mail:* info@ndcricket.co.nz. *Website:* www.ndcricket.co.nz.

VETTRIANO, Jack, OBE; British artist; b. (Jack Hoggan), 17 Nov. 1951, Methil, Fife, Scotland; s. of William Hoggan; m. Gail Cormack 1981 (divorced); one adopted d.; fmr mining engineer; self-taught, full-time painter 1989–, adopting pseudonym from his mother's maiden name, Vetriano; founder Jack Vettriano Publishing Ltd 2015–; Dr hc (Univ. of St Andrews) 2003, (Open Univ.) 2004. *Publications include:* Fallen Angels 1999, Lovers and Other Strangers 2000, Vettriano: A Life 2004, Studio Life 2008, Women in Love 2009, Man's World 2009. *Address:* c/o Heartbreak Publishing Ltd, 17 Bulstrode Street, London, W1U 2JH, England (office); Jack Vettriano Publishing Ltd, 7 Hopetoun Crescent, Edinburgh, EH7 4AY, Scotland (office). *Telephone:* (20) 3219-5710 (office); (13) 1215-1025. *E-mail:* info@ heartbreakpublishing.com (office); info@jackvettriano.com. *Website:* www .heartbreakpublishing.com (office); www.jackvettriano.com.

VEVERS, Stuart; British fashion designer; *Executive Creative Director, Coach, Inc.;* b. 17 Nov. 1973; ed Univ. of Westminster, London; has worked as an accessories designer for Louis Vuitton, Calvin Klein, Givenchy and Bottega Veneta; also collaborates with Luella Bartley and Giles Deacon; Creative Dir, Mulberry, London 2005–08; Creative Dir, Loewe, Madrid 2007–13; Exec. Creative Dir, Coach Inc. 2013–; Accessory Designer of the Year Award, British Fashion Awards 2006. *Address:* Coach, Inc., 516 West 34th Street, New York, NY 10001, USA (office). *Telephone:* (904) 741-3090 (office). *Website:* world.coach.com (office).

VEYRAT, Marc; French chef and restaurant owner; *Owner and Chef, L'Auberge de l'Eridan;* b. 1950; worked as shepherd before opening first restaurant aged 29; Owner and Chef, restaurants L'Auberge de l'Eridan, Annecy 1987–, La Ferme de Mon Père Megève 1999–2006 (both received three stars from Michelin and Gault Millau magazine 2003), Le Roland Garros 2005–. *Publications include:* Fou de saveurs 1994, Herbier gourmand 1997, La cuisine paysanne 1998, Quatre saisons (à la carte) 2000, L'herbier des montagnes: Tout savoir sur les plantes et les fleurs d'altitude 2000, Déguster les plantes sauvages 2003, L'encyclopédie culinaire du XXIe siècle 2003, L'herbier à croquer 2004, Le gibier en 80 recettes 2004, Herbier gourmand 2004, Cuisine paysanne 2005. *Address:* La Maison de Marc Veyrat, Col de la Croix-Fry, 74230 Manigod, France (office). *Telephone:* 4-50-60-00-00 (office). *E-mail:* contact@marcveyrat.fr (office). *Website:* www.marcveyrat.fr (office).

VIAL, Martin Marie-Charles François; French civil servant, economist and business executive; b. 8 Feb. 1954, Lyon; s. of René Vial and Thérèse Giuliani; m. Nelly Waldmann 1978; two s. two d.; ed Lycée Ampère, Inst. of Political Studies Paris; Prof. of Econ. and Reform Inst. of Tech. of Commerce Algiers 1977–78, Prof. of Finance Higher School of Applied Commercial Sciences 1978–82; with Office of Gen. Compatibility and Budget for External Services 1982–84, also Head; Head of Office of the Treasury and Financial Man. 1984–86; with Office of Banks and Nat. Financial Cos. 1986–88, tech. adviser Postal Sector 1988–89, charged with reform of Post, Telecommunications and Broadcasting (PTT) 1989–91, Jt Dir office of Minister for Post, Telecommunications and Space 1991, Dir Ministry of Post and Telecommunications 1992–93, Jt Dir for Space Equipment, Accommodation and Transport 1991, Dir 1991–92; Pres. Aéropostale 1993–97; Dir La Poste 1997–2000, Pres. 2000–02; mem. Cen. Cttee Union of Air Transport and Nat. Fed. of Aviation Trade 1994–96, Pres. 1996–; mem. Supervisory Bd Caisse Nat. de Prévoyance (CNP) from 1998, Vice-Pres. from 2002; Conseiller-Maître, Cour des Comptes 2002–; Dir-Gen. Europ Assistance 2003–14; Chevalier, Légion d'honneur, Ordre nat. du Mérite. *Publications:* La Lettre et la Toile, Le Web, c'est la fin du papier? . . . et autres idées reçues sur internet 2000, La Care Révolution, l'Homme au cœur de la révolution mondiale 2008, Empreintes Sociales, pour en finir avec le court terme (co-author) 2011. *Leisure interests:* tennis, skiing. *Address:* c/o Europ Assistance Holding, 7 boulevard Haussmann, 75309 Paris Cedex 09, France. *E-mail:* webmaster@europ-assistance.com.

VIAN, Dominique, Maitrise de Droit; French government official; b. 25 Dec. 1944, Valence; m., three s.; ed Institut d'Etudes Politiques; Prefect of French Guyana 1997–99, Ardeche 1999–2002, Guadeloupe 2002–04, Alpes-Maritimes 2006–08; Deputy Special Rep. to UN Gen. Sec. in Kosovo 1999; Special Advisor to Pres. of Senat 2008–11; Chargé de mission, Ministry of Overseas Territories 2011–12; currently represents Minister of the Interior on Bd of L'Institut océanographique, Fondation Prince Albert 1 de Monaco; Officier de la Légion d'honneur, Officier de l'Ordre National du Mérite, Officier du Mérite Maritime, Chevalier de l'Ordre des Palmes académiques, Chevalier du Mérite Agricole, Médaille d'honneur pour Actes de Courage et de Dévouement, Commdr de la Croise du Sud (Brazil), Chevalier de l'Ordre de Saint Charles (Monaco). *Address:* Chemin du Sourcier, 83600 Fréjus, France (home).

VIAN, Giovanni Maria; Italian professor of patristic philology, journalist and editor; *Editor-in-Chief, L'Osservatore Romano;* b. 10 March 1952, Rome; s. of Nello Vian; m. Margarita Vian 1984 (died 2000); ed Virgilio Classical High School, Rome, Univ. of Rome 'La Sapienza', Inst. for Religious Sciences of Bologna; began to write for Catholic daily newspaper 1973; ed. and scientific adviser with Inst. of the Italian Encyclopedia 1976; currently Univ. Prof. of Patristic Philology, Univ. of Rome 'La Sapienza'; part-time Prof., Vita-Salute San Raffaele Univ. of Milan, teaches History of Christian Tradition and Identity; mem. Papal Cttee of Historical Sciences 1999–; editorial writer for Avvenire and Giornale di Brescia; has written for various daily papers and periodicals, including L'Osservatore Romano 1977–87 and the fortnightly of the Catholic Univ. of the Sacred Heart Vita e Pensiero; Ed.-in-Chief L'Osservatore Romano 2007–; scholarship from Nat. Research Council 1976. *Publications:* more than 90 specialist studies, including Bibliotheca divina. Filologia e storia dei testi cristiani 2001, La donazione di Costantino 2004; ed. of anthology of writings by Montini with the title Carità intellettuale 2005. *Address:* L'Osservatore Romano, Tipografica Vaticana, Via del Pellegrino, 00120 Città del Vaticano, Rome, Italy (office). *Telephone:* (06) 69883461 (office). *Fax:* (06) 69883675 (office). *E-mail:* ornet@ossrom.va (office). *Website:* www.vatican.va/news_services/or/home_ita.html (office).

VIANA, Marcelo, BSc, PhD; Brazilian mathematician and academic; *Professor of Mathematics and Director, Instituto de Matemática Pura e Aplicada (IMPA);* b. 4 March 1962, Rio de Janeiro; ed Univ. of Porto, Inst. of Pure and Applied Math.; Research Asst, Univ. of Porto 1984–91, Asst Prof. 1991–93; Research Asst, Instituto de Matemática Pura e Aplicada 1987–91, Asst Prof. 1991–92, Assoc. Prof. 1992–97, Prof. of Math. 1997–, Deputy Dir Instituto de Matemática Pura e Aplicada 2004–07, Chair. for Scientific Activities 1996–2004, Dir Instituto de Matemática Pura e Aplicada 2016–; Chair. Cttee for Math. and Statistics, CAPES 2005–07, Forum for Research and Grad. Studies in Brazil 2008–09, Regional Office for Latin America and the Caribbean, Acad. of Sciences for the Developing World (TWAS) 2009–10; Scientific Coordinator, Math. Union of Latin America and the Caribbean 2001–08; mem. Brazilian Math. Soc. 1987– (Vice-Pres. 2009–11, Pres. 2013–15), American Math. Soc. 1994–, Brazilian Acad. of Sciences 1997–, Third World Acad. of Sciences 2000– (Chair. Regional Office for Latin America and Caribbean 2009–10), Portuguese Acad. of Sciences and Letters 2006–; Elected Mem. Exec. Cttee Int. Math. Union 2007–10, Vice-Pres. 2011–14; mem. Organizing Cttee Math. Congress of Americas 2011–; Dir Math. Council of Americas 2013–; Corresp. mem. Portuguese Acad. of Sciences 2006–, Chilean Acad. of Sciences 2009–; mem. Editorial Bd Dynamics and Stability of Systems 1995–99, Nonlinearity 1996–2003, Ergodic Theory & Dynamical Systems 1998–, Dynamical Systems: An International Journal 1999–, Portugaliae Mathematica 1999–, Discrete and Continuous Dynamical Systems 1999–, Journal of Stochastics and Dynamics 2000–, Nonlinear Differential Equations and Applications 2001–08, Dynamics of Partial Differential Equations 2004–; mem. Advisory Bd Universidade do Minho 2009–11; Calouste Gulbenkian Foundation Fellowship 1988–90, Guggenheim Foundation Fellowship 1993–94; Invited Prof. Coll. de France, Paris 2002; Santaló Distinguished Lecturer, Univ. Complutense, Madrid 2005; Grand Cross of the Order of Scientific Merit 2000; Best Undergraduate in Science, António José de Almeida Foundation, Porto 1984, Third World Acad. of Sciences Award 1998, Math. Union of Latin America and the Caribbean Award 2000, Ramanujan Prize, Int. Centre for Theoretical Physics 2005, Prize Univ. of Coimbra 2007, Grande Cientista Brasileiro, Universidade Federal Fluminense 2009. *Publications include:* Dynamics beyond uniform hyperbolicity (co-author) 2004; numerous articles in professional journals. *Address:* Instituto de Matemática Pura e Aplicada, Estrada Dona Castorina, 110, Jardim Botânico, 22460-320 Rio de Janeiro, Brazil (office). *Telephone:* (21) 3958-5114 (office). *Fax:* (21) 2529-5019 (office). *E-mail:* viana@impa.br (office). *Website:* w3.impa.br/~viana (office).

VIAR OLLOQUI, Javier, BPharm; Spanish arts administrator; b. 1946, Bilbao; poet, novelist, art critic and historian; mem. Bd Bilbao Fine Arts Museum late 1980s, Dir 2002–17 (retd); tenured academic at Bilbao, Royal Acad. of Fine Arts of St Isabel of Hungary, Seville 2010–; fmr mem. Acquisitions Advisory Bd, Guggenheim Bilbao; fmr mem. Dept of Culture, Basque Govt; organizer of numerous int. and nat. exhbns; Chevalier des Arts et des Lettres 2008; Euskadi Literature Award, City of Irun Short Story Prize 1992. *Address:* c/o Museo de Bellas Artes de Bilbao, Museo Plaza 2, 48009 Bilbao, Spain.

VIARDO, Vladimir Vladimirovich, DJur; Russian/American concert pianist and academic; *Professor and Artist-in-Residence, College of Music, University of North Texas;* b. 14 Nov. 1949; ed Moscow State Conservatory; Asst Prof., later Prof., Moscow State Conservatory 1975–; resident in USA 1988–; Prof. and Artist-in-Residence, Coll. of Music, Univ. of N Texas 1988–; Visiting Prof., Moscow State Conservatory 1998–2000; Grand Prix, Marguerite Long Int. Competition, Gold Medal and 1st Prize, Van Clibern Int. Competition, USA 1973. *Performances:* played with conductors Mehta, Kitayenko, Maazel, Spivakov, Comissiona, Penderecki; toured in major European, N American and Canadian cities, Asia and S Africa, Israel, Cen. and S America. *Address:* UNT College of Music, PO Box 311367, Denton, TX 76203-1367, USA (office); c/o Concerts de Valmalete, 7 rue Hoche, 92300 Levallois Perret, France (office). *Telephone:* (940) 565-4653 (office); 1-47-59-87-59 (office). *Fax:* (940) 565-2002 (office); 1-47-59-87-50 (office). *E-mail:* vladimir.viardo@unt.edu (office). *Website:* www.music.unt.edu/bio/viardo.shtml (office); www.valmalete.com (office).

VIB-SANZIRI, Maj.-Gen. Francis, BA; Ghanaian army officer and UN official; *Head of Mission and Force Commander, United Nations Disengagement Observer Force (UNDOF);* b. 1957; m.; two d.; ed Univ. of Ghana, Ghana Inst. of Man. and Public Admin, Nigerian Armed Forces Command and Gen. Staff Coll., Ghana Armed Forces Command and Staff Coll., US Army Command and Gen. Staff Coll.; joined Ghanaian Armed Forces 1985, Asst Dir Ghana Army Operations 1996–98, Deputy Head Ghana Military Acad. 2002–04, CO Infantry Battalion 2004–09, Army Sec. Army HQ 2010–11, Dir-Gen. for Jt Operations, Gen. HQ 2014; deployed to UN Interim Force in Lebanon (UNIFIL) 1988–91, UN Assistance Mission in Rwanda (UNAMIR) 1993–94, UN Mission in Liberia (UNMIL) 2007, Strategic Military Planner, Dept of Peacekeeping Operations, UN 2011–14, Head of Mission and Force Commdr UN Disengagement Observer Force (UNDOF) 2017–; served with Econ. Community of West Africa States Monitoring Group, Liberia 1990, in Sierra Leone 1999, 2000; Dir Int. Peacekeeping Support Operations 2009; Dir-Gen. Nat. Disaster Man. Org. 2015–17. *Address:* UNDOF, Department of Peacekeeping Operations, United Nations, 405 E 42nd Street, New York, NY 10017, USA (office). *Telephone:* (212) 963-1234 (office). *Fax:* (212) 963-4879 (office). *Website:* www.un.org (office); www.peacekeeping.un.org/en/mission/undof (office).

VICKERS, Sir John Stuart, Kt, FBA, MA, DPhil; British economist and academic; *Warden, All Souls College, Oxford;* b. 7 July 1958, Eastbourne, Sussex, England; s. of Aubrey Vickers and Kay Vickers; m. Maureen Freed 1991; one s. two d.; ed Eastbourne Grammar School and Oriel Coll., Oxford; Fellow, All Souls Coll., Oxford 1979–84, 1991–2008, Warden 2008–; Shell UK Oil 1979–81; Roy Harrod Fellow, Nuffield Coll., Oxford 1984–90; Drummond Prof. of Political Economy, Univ. of Oxford 1991–2008; Chief Economist, Bank of England 1998–2000; Dir-Gen./Chair. Office of Fair Trading 2000–05; Pres. Royal Econ. Soc. 2007–10; Chair. Ind. Comm. on Banking 2010–11; Visiting Lecturer, Princeton Univ., USA 1988, Harvard Univ., USA 1989, 1990; Visiting Prof., London Business School 1996; Fellow, Econometric Soc. 1998–; Hon. DLitt (Univ. of East Anglia) 2001; Pres.'s Medal, British Acad. 2012. *Publications include:* Privatization: An Economic Analysis (co-author) 1988, Regulatory Reform (co-author) 1994; articles on competition, regulation etc. *Address:* Office of the Warden, All Souls College, Oxford, OX1 4AL, England (office). *Website:* www.all-souls.ox.ac.uk (office).

VICTORIA INGRID ALICE DÉSIRÉE, HRH Crown Princess (Duchess of Västergötland); Swedish; b. 14 July 1977, Stockholm; d. of HM King Carl XVI Gustaf and HM Queen Silvia of Sweden; m. Olof Daniel Westling Bernadotte (HRH Prince Daniel, Duke of Västergötland) 2010; one d., Princess Estelle Silvia Ewa Mary, Duchess of Östergötland, b. 23 Feb. 2012; one s., Prince Oscar, Duke of Skåne, b. 2 March 2016; ed Enskilda Gymnasiet, Stockholm, Université Catholique de l'Ouest, Angers, France, Yale Univ., USA and Nat. Defence Coll., Stockholm; internships at Embassy in Washington, DC 1999, UN, New York 2002, Swedish Trade Council, Berlin and Paris 2002; has completed study programmes at Offices of the Swedish Govt and the Swedish Int. Devt Co-operation Agency; participated in state visits to study int. aid efforts; Mem. with Collar, Royal Order of the Seraphim 1995, Royal Family Order of King Carl XVI Gustaf of Sweden, HM King Carl XVI Gustaf 50th Anniversary Medal 1996, Commemorative Ruby Jubilee Medal of HM The King 2013; more than 20 foreign decorations. *Leisure interests:* nature and outdoor pursuits. *Address:* c/o Information and Press Department, Kungliga Slottet, Stockholm 111 30, Sweden. *E-mail:* info@royalcourt.se. *Website:* www.royalcourt.se.

VIDAL SALINAS, Francisco; Chilean politician; b. 20 Sept. 1953; ed Univ. of Chile; Prof. of History and Geography, Univ. of Chile; Sec., Faculty of Econ. Sciences, Univ. Central de Chile 1993–99, Dean, Faculty of Econ. and Admin. Sciences 1998–99; Exec. Dir Fundación Chile 21 1994–2000; mem. Partido por la Democracia 1987–; consultant to Higher Educ. Council and Higher Educ. Div., Ministry of Educ. 1993; Councillor Metropolitan Regional Govt 1993–2000; Under-Sec. for Regional and Admin. Devt, Ministry of the Interior 2000–03; Minister, Sec.-Gen. of the Govt 2003–05, 2007–09; Minister of the Interior 2005–06, of Nat. Defence 2009–10; Pres. Directorate, Televisión Nacional de Chile 2006–07; Dir School of Govt, Univ. Alberto Hurtado 2006–.

VIDEANU, Adriean; Romanian business executive and politician; b. 1 June 1962, Crevenicu, Teleorman Co.; m. Mioriţa Videanu; one s. one d.; ed Faculty of Transport, Bucharest Polytechnic Inst.; business exec. in marble and granite industry; Head of Section, SUT Ploieşti 1987–90; Chair. CA Titan Mar SA 2003–04; Deputy (Democratic Liberal Party (Partidul Democrat-Liberal—PD-L)) for Teleorman Co. 1990–2003, Vice-Pres. Budget Cttee (Finance-Banks) 2000; Chair. Nat. Youth, PD-L 1992–96, Exec. Sec. PD-L 1996–2000, Vice-Pres. and Spokesman for PD-L, responsible for matters of image and media relations 2001–03, later Vice-Pres., party merged with Partidul Naţional Liberal (PNL) 2014; Minister of State and Deputy Prime Minister 2004–05; Mayor of Bucharest 2005–08; Minister of the Economy, Trade and the Business Environment 2008–10. *E-mail:* contact@videanu.ro. *Website:* www.videanu.ro.

VIDEGARAY CASO, Luis, BA, PhD; Mexican economist and politician; b. 10 Aug. 1968, México City; ed Instituto Tecnológico Autónomo de México (ITAM), Massachusetts Inst. of Tech., USA; fmr Lecturer, ITAM and Ibero-American Univ., Mexico City; mem. Partido Revolucionario Institucional (PRI) 1987–; Adviser to Sec. of Finance 1992–94, to Sec. of Energy 1996; Dir of Public Finance, Protego Asesores (bank) 1998–2005; Regional Sec. of Finance, Planning and Admin, State of Mexico 2005–09; Nat. Co-ordinator, Secr. of State for Finance 2008–09; mem. Cámara Federal de Diputados (Parl.) 2009–11, Pres. Budget and Public Accounts Debt Comm. 2009–11; PRI Pres., State of Mexico 2011–12; Gen. Co-ordinator of political campaign of Eruviel Ávila Villegas (Gov., State of Mexico) 2011, of presidential campaign of Enrique Peña Nieto (Pres. of Mexico) 2012; Co-ordinator of Public Policy and Gen. Co-ordinator of Govt Transition Team 2012; Sec. (Minister) of Finance and Public Credit 2012–16, of Foreign Affairs 2017–18; Hon. Mention from ITAM, Nat. Econs Award, Banco Nacional de México 1995. *Address:* c/o Secretariat of State for Foreign Affairs, Plaza Juárez 20, Col. Centro, Del. Cuauhtémoc, 06010 México, DF, Mexico (office).

VIDOKLE, Anton; Russian artist and editor; *Founding Director, e-flux;* b. 1965, Moscow; arrived in USA with parents 1981; Founding Dir e-flux (int. network reaching more than 50,000 visual art professionals daily through website, e-mail list and special projects), Organizer, with Julieta Aranda, e-flux video rental (travelled to numerous insts, including Portikus, Frankfurt, KunstWerk, Berlin, Extra City, Antwerp, Carpenter Center, Harvard Univ., Cambridge, Mass, and others); has produced projects such as Next Documenta Should Be Curated By An Artist, Do it, Utopia Station poster project, and organized An Image Bank for Everyday Revolutionary Life and Martha Rosler Library; set up ind. project in Berlin called Unitednationsplaza (12-month project involving more than 100 artists, writers, philosophers and diverse audiences); co-f., with Julieta Aranda, a time bank for artists, curators, writers and others in the arts to exchange their time and skills 2008, has nearly 4,000 members and operates branches in The Hague, Moscow, Berlin, Frankfurt and other cities; co-f. imprint, with the Sternberg Press, Berlin, that publishes a series of paperback readers consisting of monographic publs and thematic compilations of essays 2008; Resident Prof., Ashkal Alwan Home Workspace Program (with Jalal Toufic) in Beirut, Lebanon 2013–14. *Films and videos on contemporary art:* A Crime Against Art (directed by Hila Peleg) 2008, A Guiding Light (with Liam Gillick) 2010, New York Conversations 2011, Two Suns (with Hu Fang) 2012, 2084: A science fiction show (directed by Anton Vidokle and Pelin Tan) (TV show) (3 episodes) 2012–14, This is Cosmos 2014, The Communist Revolution Was Caused By The Sun 2015, Immortality and Resurrection For All! 2017. *Publications:* essays and texts in various publications including October, Frieze and Aprior, as well as numerous books and catalogues. *Address:* e-flux, 311 East Broadway, New York, NY 10002, USA (office). *E-mail:* newsletter@e-flux.com (office). *Website:* www.e-flux.com (office); www .unitednationsplaza.org.

VIDOVIĆ, Zora; Bosnia and Herzegovina economist and politician; *Minister of Finance of the Republic of Srpska;* b. 17 Nov. 1954, Srbac; ed Univ. of Belgrade, Serbia; began career as Financial Man., Stirokart A.D., Srbac; sr exec. positions at Banjalucka Banka A.d. (Srbac Branch), Mikrokredit Co. and Živinoprodukt d.o.o; fmr Dir of Public Revenue and Dir of Tax Admin, Govt of Repub. of Srpska; mem. Nat. Ass. of Republika Srpska (Parl.) 2002–10; Minister of Finance of the Repub. of Srpska 2018–. *Address:* Ministry of Finance of the Republic of Srpska, 78000 Banja Luka, Trg Republike Srpske 1, Bosnia and Herzegovina (office). *Telephone:* (51) 339728 (office). *Fax:* (51) 339645 (office). *E-mail:* mf@mf.vladars.net (office). *Website:* www.vladars.net (office).

VIEGAS FILHO, José; Brazilian diplomatist and politician; *Special Representative for Guinea-Bissau and Head of Office, United Nations Integrated Peacebuilding Office in Guinea-Bissau (UNIOGBIS);* b. 14 Oct. 1942, Campo Grande; s. of José Viegas and Dirce Bastos Viegas; m. Erika Stockholm de Viegas; one s. two d.; ed Diplomatic Acad. Instituto Rio Branco; joined Instituto Rio Branco 1964; Deputy Consul, New York 1969–73; Embassy Sec., Santiago 1973–78; mem. Policy Planning Unit, Ministry of External Relations 1979–84; Chargé d'affaires a.i. in Rome 1984–85, Minister-Counsellor and Chargé d'affaires a.i. in Paris 1985–86, in Havana 1986–91; Head of Multilateral Dept 1992, of Policy Planning Unit 1992–93, Undersecretary-Gen. for Policy Planning 1993–94; Amb. to Denmark 1995–98, to Peru 1998–2001, to Russia 2001–02, to Spain 2005–09, to Italy 2009–12; Minister of Defence 2003–04 (resgnd); Prof. of Brazilian Foreign Policy, Instituto Rio Branco 1982–83, mem. Examination Bd, High Studies for Diplomats 1992–94, Pres. Examination Bd, Master's Degree for Diplomats 2005–07, mem. Comm. for Examination of the Course of High Studies, Instituto Rio Branco 1992–94, Pres. Comm. for Examination of Masters' Theses 2005–07; Special Rep. for Guinea-Bissau and Head of Office, UN Integrated Peacebuilding Office in Guinea-Bissau (UNIOGBIS) 2018–; Grand Cross of Rio Branco, Grand Cross for Merit in Defence, Grand Cross for Mil. Merit, Grand Cross for Naval Merit, Grand Cross for Aeronautical Merit, Grand Cross for Mil. Judicial Merit, Grand Cross of the Order of the Sun (Peru), Grand Cross, Order of the Dannebrog (Denmark). *Leisure interests:* cosmology, translation. *Address:* UN Building, CP 179, Rua Rui Djassi, Bissau, Guinea-Bissau (office). *Telephone:* 20-36-18 (office). *Fax:* 20-36-13 (office). *Website:* uniogbis.unmissions.org (office).

VIEHBACHER, Christopher A.; Canadian/German business executive; *Managing Partner, Gurnet Point Capital;* b. 26 March 1960, Ottawa, Ont.; m.; three c.; ed Queens Univ., Ottawa; began career at PriceWaterhouseCoopers; Chief Financial Accountant, Wellcome GmbH, Germany 1988, Finance Dir 1989–93, Pres. and CEO Burroughs Wellcome Inc., Canada 1993–95, Vice-Pres. Glaxo Wellcome France 1995–96, Gen. Man. 1996–97, Chair. and Man. Dir 1997–2003, Pres. US Pharmaceuticals, GlaxoSmithKline 2003–08, Pres. North American Pharmaceuticals May–Dec. 2008, mem. Bd of Dirs GlaxoSmithKline Jan.–Sept. 2008; CEO Sanofi SA (now Sanofi) 2008–14, also Chair. Genzyme (after acquisition by Sanofi); Man. Partner, Gurnet Point Capital, Cambridge, Mass 2015–; mem. Bd of Dirs The Pharmaceutical Research and Mfrs of America (PhRMA), Chair. 2010–12; apptd Chair. CEO Roundtable on Cancer 2011; Pres. European Fed. of Pharmaceutical Industries and Asscns 2013–15; mem. Int. Business Council (WEF); mem. Bd of Visitors, Fuqua School of Business, Duke Univ.; Chevalier, Légion d'honneur 2003; Pasteur Foundation Award 2012. *Address:* Gurnet Point Capital, 55 Cambridge Parkway, Suite 401, Cambridge, MA 02142, USA (office).

Telephone: (617) 588-4900 (office). *E-mail:* info@gurnetpointcapital.com (office). *Website:* www.gurnetpointcapital.com (office).

VIEIRA, Mauro Luiz Iecker, JD; Brazilian diplomatist and politician; *Permanent Representative, United Nations;* b. 15 Feb. 1952, Niterói, state of Rio de Janeiro; s. of Mauro Vieira and Noêmia Vieira; ed Fluminense Fed. Univ., Instituto Rio Branca, Univ. of Cambridge, UK, Univ. of Michigan, USA, Univ. of Nancy, France; joined Foreign Service 1974, Asst to Chief of Political Finance Div. 1975–77, Third Sec., Embassy in Washington, DC 1978, Second Sec. 1978–80, First Sec. 1980–82, First Sec., ALADI (Associação Latino-Americana de Integração), Uruguay 1982–85, consultant, Sec.-Gen. of Foreign Affairs 1985, Adjunct Sec.-Gen., Ministry of Science and Tech. 1986–87, Nat. Sec. of Admin, Nat. Inst. of Social Pensions, Ministry of Pensions and Social Welfare 1987–88, consultant, Chief Dept of Culture 1989, Adviser, Embassy in Mexico City 1990–92, Diplomatic Adviser to Minister of State for Foreign Affairs 1993–94, Minister Counsellor, Embassy in Paris 1995–99, Chief of Cabinet of Sec.-Gen. of Foreign Affairs 1999–2002, Amb. to Switzerland 2002, Special Envoy of Pres. of Brazil to Syria and Palestine 2003, Rep. of Ministry of Foreign Affairs to Bd of Dirs of Itaipu Binacional hydroelectric power plant 2003–06, Amb. to Argentina 2004–09, to USA 2010–14, Minister of Foreign Affairs 2014–16, Perm. Rep. to UN, New York 2016–; Grand Cross, Order of Rio Branca, Order of Merit of Brazil, Commdr, Naval Order of Merit, Mil. Order of Merit, Medalla del Pacificador (Brazil); Grand Cross, Order of Bernardo O'Higgins (Chile), Nat. Order of Merit (Romania), Order of Merit (Poland), Order of Infante D. Henrique (Portugal), Order of Civil Merit (Spain), Order of Águila Azteca (Mexico), Grand Official of the Order of Danneborg (Denmark), Chevalier, Legión d'honneur; decorations from Govts of Argentina, Chile, Peru, Norway and the Netherlands. *Address:* Permanent Mission of Brazil in United Nations, 747 Third Avenue, 9th Floor, New York, NY 10017, USA (office). *Telephone:* (212) 372-2600 (office). *Fax:* (212) 371-5716 (office). *E-mail:* distri.delbrasonu@itamaraty.gov.br (office). *Website:* www.un.int/brazil (office).

VIEIRA, Meredith Louise; American television broadcaster and journalist; b. 30 Dec. 1953, East Providence, RI; d. of Edwin Vieira and Mary Elsie Vieira; m. Prof. Richard M. Cohen 1986; two s. one d.; ed Tufts Univ.; began career as news announcer for WORC Radio, Worcester, Mass 1975; started in TV working as local reporter and anchor at WJAR-TV Providence; later worked in newsroom at WCBS-TV, New York City; first came to nat. recognition as CBS reporter based in Chicago Bureau, later became a corresp. for CBS news-magazine shows including West 57th and 60 Minutes, then Co-anchor of CBS Morning News; corresp. for ABC news-magazine show Turning Point; Moderator and Co-host, The View 1997–2006; Host Lifetime's Intimate Portrait 1999–; Host, Who Wants to Be a Millionaire? 2002–13; Co-anchor, The Today Show (NBC) 2006–11, now host, nationally syndicated daytime show The Meredith Vieira Show; Founder and CEO Meredith Vieira Productions; seven Emmy Awards for her work on West 57th, 60 Minutes, Turning Point and Daytime Emmy for Outstanding Game Show Host 2005, P.T. Barnum Award, Tufts Univ. 2006. *Website:* meredithvieirashow.com.

VIEIRA VARGAS, Everton, PhD; Brazilian sociologist, academic and diplomatist; *Ambassador to European Union;* b. 23 Jan. 1955, Santo Ângelo, Rio Grande do Sul; s. of João Domingos da Luz Vargas and Iná Vieira Vargas; ed Univ. of Brasilia; served in Embassy in Bonn 1981–85, Head of Div. of Science and Tech., Ministry of Foreign Affairs 1987–88, posted to Perm. Mission to UN, New York 1988–92, to Embassy in Tokyo 1992–95, Co-ordinator of Summit of the Americas, Ministry of Foreign Affairs 1995–98, Head of Div. of Environment 1998–2001, Sec.-Gen. and Political Dir Dept of Environment and Special Issues 2001–08, Exec. Sec. Preparatory Ministry of World Summit on Sustainable Devt and Brazilian negotiator in Preparatory Cttee and Summit itself, Johannesburg, S Africa 2002, Amb. to Germany 2009–13, to Argentina 2013–16; Amb. and Head of Mission to EU 2016–; Prof. of Diplomatic Language, Instituto Rio Branco 2002–; Grã-Cruz da Ordem de Rio Branco, Grande Oficial da Ordem de Rio Branco, Medalha do Pacificador, Medalha Mérito de Tamandaré. *Publications:* several articles on environment and sustainable devt. *Address:* Brazilian Mission to the European Union, Avenue Franklin Roosevelt 30, 1050 Brussels, Belgium (office). *Telephone:* (2) 640-20-40 (office). *Website:* www.itamaraty.gov.br/en/ficha-pais/6698-european -union (office).

VIERA GALLO QUESNEY, José Antonio; Chilean politician and diplomatist; *Ambassador to Argentina;* b. 2 Dec. 1943, Santiago; s. of José Viera-Gallo Barahona and Josefina Quesney; m. María Teresa Chadwick; three d.; ed Univ. Católica de Chile, Instituto Latinoamericano de Doctrina y Estudios Sociales; fmr Prof. of Political Theory, Univ. Católica de Chile; Under-Sec. for Justice during Presidency of Salvador Allende 1970–72; exiled in Italy following mil. coup 1973; f. Chileamerica magazine (published in Rome during exile); fmr adviser to UNESCO, FAO and World Council of Churches; fmr Deputy Sec.-Gen. Institutional Documentation Service, Rome; Dir Centro de Estudios Sociales 1983–2001; returned to Chile 1985; mem. Chamber of Deputies 1990–98, Pres. 1990–93, mem. Internal Order, Constitutional, Legislation and Justice Perm. Comms, Defence Comm; Senator for Octava 1998–2005, fmr Pres. Senate Human Rights, Nationality and Citizenship Comm; Sec.-Gen. of the Presidency 2007–10, mem. Constitutional Court 2010–13; Prof. of Parliamentary Law, Faculty of Law, Univ. of Chile 2011–; Amb. to Argentina 2015–; mem. Cen. Cttee Partido Socialista; Scopus Award, Hebrew Univ. of Jerusalem 2012. *Address:* Embassy of Chile, Tagle 2762, C1425EEF, Buenos Aires, Argentina (office). *Telephone:* (11) 4808-8600 (office). *Fax:* (11) 4804-5927 (office). *E-mail:* echile.argentina@minrel.gov.cl (office). *Website:* chile.gob.cl/argentina (office).

VIERMETZ, Kurt F.; German banker and stock exchange official; b. 27 April 1939, Augsburg; m. Felicity Viermetz; began career as foreign exchange trader with Deutsche Bank AG, Frankfurt 1960–65; Asst Treasurer, JP Morgan & Co. Inc., Frankfurt 1965–70, Vice-Pres. Paris Br. 1970–75, involved in est. of Saudi Int. Bank Ltd, London 1975–77, Vice-Pres. JP Morgan, New York, responsible for foreign exchange and Euro treasury world-wide 1977–80, Sr Vice-Pres. JP Morgan, Frankfurt, responsible for German and Continental European business 1980–85, Treas. JP Morgan & Co. Inc., New York 1985–90, Vice-Chair. Man. Bd and Supervisory Bd, New York 1990–2000, mem. Bd Dirs 1998–2000; Chair. Supervisory Bd Bayerische Hypo- und Vereinsbank AG, Munich 1999–2002, Vice-Chair. Jan.–Dec. 2003; Chair. Supervisory Bd Hypo Real Estate Holding AG, Munich 2003–09 (resgnd); Chair. Supervisory Bd, Deutsche Börse AG 2005–08 (resgnd); mem. Supervisory Bd Hoechst AG, Frankfurt 1990–98 (also Chair. Bd Finance Cttee), Advisory Bd Metro Co., Zug, Switzerland 1990–98, Supervisory Bd Veba AG, Düsseldorf 1993–2003, Supervisory Bd E.ON AG, Düsseldorf 1993–2003, Supervisory Bd ERGO Versicherungs AG, Düsseldorf 2003–, Supervisory Bd E.ON-Ruhrgas AG, Essen 2003–05, KfW IPEX-Bank GmbH 2008–; Dir (non-exec.) Grosvenor Estate Holdings Ltd, London, UK 1996–2004; Chair. Int. Capital Markets Advisory Bd Cttee, New York Stock Exchange 1995–2004; Chair. Bd of Overseers, Univ. of Augsburg 2002–; Founder and mem. Man. Bd, Förderkreis Schaezlerpalais e.V.; mem. Bd Int. Advisory Cttee Fed. Reserve Bank of New York 1995–, American Council of Germany, New York 1987–; Trustee, New York Philharmonic Soc. 1988–2002, Haniel Foundation, Duisberg 1998–, Vereins Atlantik-Brücke, American Acad. in Berlin, Berlin and New York; Hon. Citizen of City of Augsburg; Order of Merit, Fed. Repub. of Germany 2006, Bavarian Order of Merit 2007. *Address:* c/o Deutsche Börse AG, Neue Börsenstrasse 1, 60485 Frankfurt, Germany.

VIGANÒ, Carlo Maria; Italian ecclesiastic and diplomatist; *Apostolic Nuncio Emeritus to USA;* b. 16 Jan. 1941, Varese; ordained priest of Pavia 1968; Titular Archbishop of Ulpiana 1992–; Apostolic Nuncio to Nigeria 1992–98; Official of the Secr. of State 1998–2009; Sec. of the Governatorate of Vatican City State 2009–11; Apostolic Nuncio to USA 2011–16, Apostolic Nuncio Emer. 2016–.

VIGENIN, Kristian Ivanov; Bulgarian politician; b. 12 June 1975, Sofia; m.; two c.; ed Univ. of Nat. and World Economy, Sofia, courses in Belgium, Sweden and USA; worked at Ministry of Finance 1999–2001; elected to Nat. Council of Bulgarian Socialist Party (BSP) 2000–, began at Foreign Policy and Int. Relations Dept of Supreme Council of Bulgarian Socialist Party (BSP) 2001, Head 2003–10, mem. Exec. Bureau responsible for Int. Relations from 2001, later mem. Exec. Bureau and Sec. Supreme Council for Foreign Affairs and Int. Relations, Chair. Foreign Affairs and Int. Relations Cttee, Nat. Council of BSP 2005–08, took part in PES Presidium and coordinated work of PES network for Southeastern Europe from 2006, Chair. Council on Foreign Affairs, Nat. Council of BSP 2010–; mem. Parl. 2005–07, mem. leadership of Parl. Group of Coalition for Bulgaria as Sec. for Int. Affairs; observer in European Parl. 2005–07, leader of six-mem. del. of Coalition for Bulgaria, mem. European Parl. 2007–13, Vice-Pres. Party of European Socialists Group 2007–13, Co-Chair. Parl. Ass. Euronest platform for inter-parl. co-operation with Eastern Partnership countries 2009–13, mem. numerous dels and cttees, Coordinator Group of Progressive Alliance of Socialists & Democrats Foreign Affairs Cttee 2009–12; Minister of Foreign Affairs 2013–14. *Address:* c/o Ministry of Foreign Affairs, 1113 Sofia, ul. Aleksandar Zhendov 2, Bulgaria. *Website:* www.vigenin.eu/en.

VIGNERON, Luc; French business executive; *CEO, Emirates Defence Industries Company;* b. 11 Oct. 1954, Senegal; m. Annie Hainneville 1976; three c.; ed Ecole Polytechnique, Ecole Nationale des Ponts et Chaussées; began career with Harbour and Shore Authority for Boulogne-sur-Mer and Calais, Ministry of Infrastructure and Territorial Devt 1978–82; Adviser, Budget Dept, Ministry of Economy, Finance and Budget 1982–84; Special Adviser, Finance Dept, Compagnie Générale d'Electricité (now Alcatel-Lucent) 1984–86, Head of Operations, Alcatel Telspace 1986, Dir, Alcatel CIT Distribution Product Lines, Dir of Strategy and New Businesses, Alcatel RSD 1990–91, Man. Dir, Alcatel Radiotéléphone 1991–94, Exec. Vice Pres., Alcatel Mobile Communication Group 1994–95, Dir of Strategy, Alcatel Alsthom 1995–98; CEO Giat Industries (renamed Nexter 2006) 1998–2001, Chair. and CEO 2001–09; Chair. and CEO Thales SA 2009–12; CEO Emirates Defence Industries Co. 2014–; Chair. Groupement des industries françaises de défense terrestre (GICCAT) 2002–06, Conseil des industries de défense françaises 2004–06. *Website:* www.edic.ae (office).

VIJAYAN, Pinarayi; Indian politician; *Chief Minister of Kerala;* b. 21 March 1944, Pinarayi, Kannur Dist; s. of Koran Vijayan and Kalyani Vijayan; m. Kamala Vijayan; two c.; ed Govt Brennen Coll., Thalassery; worked as handloom weaver for one year after leaving school; entered politics through student union activities at Govt Brennen Coll. and eventually joined Communist Party 1964; arrested during emergency period 1975–77; elected to Kerala Legis. Ass. from Koothuparamba constituency 1970, 1977, 1991, from Payyannur constituency 1996, from Dharmadom constituency 2016; Minister for Power and Co-operation, Kerala State Govt 1996–98; Chief Minister of Kerala 2016–; mem. Communist Party (Marxist) (CPI—M) 1964–, Sec. 1967–, Sec., Kerala State Cttee 1998–2015. *Address:* Cliff House, Nanthencode, Office of the Chief Minister, Government of Kerala, Secretariat, Thiruvananthapuram 695 003, Kerala, India (office). *Telephone:* (471) 2333812 (office). *Fax:* (471) 2333489 (office). *E-mail:* chiefminister@kerala.gov.in (office). *Website:* www.keralacm.gov.in (office).

VĪĶE-FREIBERGA, Vaira, MA, PhD; Latvian psychologist and fmr head of state; *President, Club de Madrid;* b. (Vaira Vīķe), 1 Dec. 1937, Rīga; m. Imants Freibergs 1960; one s. one d.; ed Univ. of Toronto and McGill Univ., Canada; Prof. of Psychology, Univ. of Montreal, Canada 1965–98, Prof. Emer. 1998–; Vice-Chair. Science Council of Canada 1984–89; Dir Latvian Inst., Rīga 1998–99; Pres. of Latvia 1999–2007; Pres. Club de Madrid 2014–; fmr Pres. Canadian Psychological Asscn, Social Science Fed. of Canada, Asscn for Advancement of Baltic Studies; Pres. Acad. des Lettres et des Sciences Humaines, RSC; mem. Latvian Acad. of Sciences, Royal Belgian Acad., Council of Women Leaders 1999–; mem. Bd of Dirs Bibliotheca Alexandrina 2010–; Vice-Chair. Reflection Group on the Future of Europe 2020–30, European Council, Chair. High Level Group on Media Freedom and Pluralism, EC 2011–; Chair. Review Panel, European Research Council 2009; thirty-four Orders of Merit, including Three Star Order of Latvia 1995, Legion of Honour 2001, Dame of GCB 2006, Officer, Nat. Order of Québec, Canada 2006; Hon. LLD (Queen's Univ., Canada) 1991, Hon. DLitt (Victoria Univ., Toronto) 2000, Hon. DSci (McGill Univ.) 2002, Dr hc (Latvia) 2000, (Vytautas Magnus Univ., Lithuania) 2002, (Astana, Kazakhstan) 2004, (Baku, Azerbaijan) 2005, (Tbilisi) 2005, (Yerevan) 2005, (Ottawa) 2006, (Liège, Belgium) 2006, (Odense, Denmark) 2007, (Dalhousie, Halifax) 2007, (Dublin) 2007, (Toronto) 2008, (York, Toronto) 2008, (Georgia) 2011; numerous awards, including Marcel-Vincent Prize 1992, Pierre Chauveau Medal 1995, American Acad. of Achievement Gold Plate 2000, awards from Georgetown Univ., USA 2002, Free Univ. of Berlin 2003, Grand Prize of Folklore, Ministry of Culture, Latvia 2003, Forbes Executive Women's Forum Trailblazer Award 2005, Medal of the American Jewish Cttee 2005, Baltic Freedom Award 2005, Hannah Arendt Prize for Political Thought 2005, Coudenhove-Kalergi Foundation Europa Prize, Pan-Europa Union 2006, Baltic Statesmanship Award of the US-Baltic Foundation 2006, J.W. Goethe Univ. Medal and Walter Hallstein Prize 2006, UN FAO Ceres Medal 2007, Von Hayek Medal 2009, Konrad Adenauer Prize 2010, Ladies First Int. Prize 2011. *Publications include:* La Frequence Lexicale des Mots au Québec 1974, Latvian Sun-Songs (co-author) 1988, Linguistic and Poetics of Latvian Folk Songs 1989, On the Amber Mountain 1993, Against the Current 1993, The Cosmological Sun 1997, The Chronological Sun 1999, The Warm Sun 2002, The Luminous Sun 2011, Latvian Sun Song Melodies 2005, Logique de la Poésie 2007, Latvian Culture and Identity 2010, The Meteorological Sun 2011, Mythological Sun 2016; contrib. of more than 400 articles and papers. *Leisure interests:* reading, crosswords, nature walks, gardening, swimming, and needlework. *Address:* Club de Madrid, Palacio del Marqués de Cañete. Calle Mayor, 69, Planta 1, 28013 Madrid, Spain (office). *Telephone:* (91) 1548230 (office). *Fax:* (91) 1548240 (office). *E-mail:* clubmadrid@clubmadrid.org (office). *Website:* www.clubmadrid.org (office).

VIKTYUK, Roman Grigoryevich; Russian/Ukrainian theatre director, actor and screenwriter; b. 28 Oct. 1936, Lvov; ed A. Lunacharcky State Inst. of Theatre Art; Chief Dir Kalinin Theatre of Lenin Komsomol 1968–71; Dir Russian Drama Theatre in Vilnius 1971–77; Artistic Dir Students Theatre of Moscow Univ. 1977–91; Founder and Artistic Dir Roman Viktyuk Theatre 1991–; US tour 1998; several TV productions; Prof., Acad. of the Performing Arts (GITIS); Honoured Artist of Russia 2003, People's Artist of Ukraine 2006, People's Artist of Russia 2009. *Films include:* Dolgaya pamyat (dir) 1985, The Turn of the Century (actor) 2001 Sex, kofe, sigarety (actor) 2014. *Television includes:* Manon Lesko (film) 1979, Rostov-papa (series) 2001, Rozygrysh (series) 2003. *Theatre includes:* The Royal Hunt 1977, The Music Lessons 1979, The Rose Tattoo 1982, The Maids 1988, M. Butterfly 1991, Salome 1998, Rudolf Nureyev 2004, The Last Love of Don Juan 2005, R&J (Romeo and Juliette) 2009, King Harlequin 2010, Masquerade of Marquis de Sade 2012, Glorious! 2013, At the Beginning and at the End of Times 2014, Phaedra 2015. *Address:* Roman Viktyuk Theatre, Leningradsky Prospect, Dom 30, Str. 2, Mosconcert building, 5th Floor, Office 100, Moscow (office); Tverskaya 4, Apt 87, 103009 Moscow, Russia (office). *Telephone:* (495) 614-01-70 (office); (495) 292-68-95 (home). *Website:* teatrviktuka.ru (office).

VILA-MATAS, Enrique; Spanish writer; b. 1948, Barcelona; fmr journalist for Fotogramas magazine, Paris; Chevalier, Légion d'honneur 2006; Premio Ciudad de Barcelona 2000, Prix au meilleur livre étranger 2000, Premio de la Crítica 2002, Premio Herralde 2002, Prix Médicis 2003, Premio Formentor de las Letras 2014, Premio Fil de Literatura 2015, Premi Nacional de Cultura de la Generalitat 2016, Premio Feronia-Città di Fiano 2017, Prix Ulysse 2017. *Publications include:* nonfiction; Al sur de los párpados 1980, Nunca voy al cine 1982, El viajero más lento 1992, Veneno en la boca, conversaciones con 18 escritores: Antón Castro 1994, Recuerdos inventados: primera antología personal 1994, El traje de los domingos 1995, Para acabar con los números redondos 1997, Desde la ciudad nerviosa 2000; fiction: La asesina ilustrada 1977, Impostura 1984, Historia abreviada de la literatura portátil 1985, Una casa para siempre 1988, Suicidios ejemplares 1991, Hijos sin hijos 1993, Lejos de Veracruz 1995, Extraña forma de vida 1997, El viaje vertical (Premio Rómulo Gallegos 2001) 1999, Bartleby y compañía 2000, El mal de Montano (trans. as Montano's Malady) 2002, París no se acaba nunca 2003, Doctor Pasavento (Premio de la Real Academia Española 2006, Internazionale Mondello Prize 2009) 2005, Exploradores del abismo 2007, Dietario voluble 2008, Dublinesca (trans. as Dublinesque) (Bottari Lattes Grinzane Prize, Prix Jean Carriere, Leteo Award) 2010, Chet Baker pense à son art 2011, Aire de Dylan 2012, The Illogic of Kassel 2015, Marienbad electrique 2015, Vampire in Love 2016, Mac y su contratiempo 2017, Esta bruma insensata 2019. *Address:* c/o Editorial Anagrama SA, Pedró de la Creu 58, 08034 Barcelona, Spain (office). *Telephone:* (93) 2037652 (office). *Fax:* (93) 2037738 (office). *E-mail:* anagrama@anagrama-ed.es (office). *Website:* www.anagrama-ed.es (office); www.enriquevilamatas.com.

VILADECANS, Joan-Pere; Spanish artist; b. 1948, Barcelona; s. of Joan-Pere Viladecans and Carme Viladecans; Chevalier, Ordre des Arts et Lettres 1996, Award of Excellence, Soc. for New Design 1997. *Solo exhibitions include:* Sala Gaspar, Barcelona 1967, Galerie Dresdnere, Toronto 1967, Galerie Dreiseitel, Cologne 1971, 1990, Galeria Pecanins, Mexico 1974, Galleri Uddenberg, Gothenburg 1975, M.L. Museum Gallery, New York 1977, Aaron Gallery, Washington, DC 1978, Guild Gallery, New York 1981, Museo Español Arte Contemporáneo, Madrid 1983, Duszka Patÿn-Karolczak Galerie d'Art, Brussels 1983, Galeria Art-Inter, Luxembourg 1985, Brompton Gallery, London 1985, Baukunst Galerie, Cologne 1988, Galerie Dreiseitel, Cologne 1990, Museo Rufino Tamayo, Mexico 1991, Casa de Goya, Bordeaux 1991, Espace Sphonisbe, Tunis 1991, Expo '92, Seville 1992, Sala Gaspar, Barcelona 1992, Galeria Quadrado Azul, Oporto 1993, Galerie Joan Gaspar, Barcelona 1994, Galeria Benedet, Oviedo 1995, Galerie Dreiseitel, Cologne 2001, 2003, Palau Solterra Museum, Fundació Vila Casas, Girona 2007–15. *Group exhibitions include:* Gallery Quadrado Azul, Porto 1995, Galerie Dreiseitel, Cologne 2001, Sala García Castañón, Caja Navarra Foundation, Pamplona 2005, Art Center Berlin Friedrichstrasse, Berlin 2007, Galería Joan Gaspar, Madrid 2008, 2011, 2012, 2014. *Address:* c/o Galería Joan Gaspar, Plaza Dr. Letamendi 1, 08007 Barcelona (office); Córcega 589, 08025 Barcelona, Spain (office). *Telephone:* (91) 33230748 (office); (60) 7833 889. *E-mail:* galeria@galeriajoangaspar.net (office); info@joanpereviladecans.com. *Website:* www.galeriajoangaspar.com (office); www.joanpereviladecans.com.

VILÁGOSI, Gábor, DJur; Hungarian lawyer and politician; b. 12 Jan. 1956, Devecser; m.; four c.; ed Univ. of Pécs; legal affairs official, Cen. Transdanubia Water Man. Directorate 1980–83; legal adviser to Alkotmány Agricultural Co-operative, then to Fehérvár Dept Store 1983–89; among first members of Alliance of Free Democrats (SZDSZ) 1989, mem. SZDSZ governing cttee for Székesfehérvár 1989–90, Chair. SZDSZ Fejér County 1999–, mem. Nat. Exec. 2007–; practised law in Székesfehérvár 1990–94; mem. Hungarian Olympic Cttee 1994–98; co-Chair. Lake Velence Regional Council 1995–98; mem. Országgyülés (Nat. Ass., parl.) 1990–2010, Keeper of the Minutes of the Országgyülés 1998–2004, Deputy Speaker 2004–10; State Sec. for Policy, Ministry of Interior 1994–98; mem. Fejér County Ass. 1998–2002, Székesfehérvár Municipal Ass. 2002–06; Founding mem. Szabadelvű Polgári Egyesület 2010.

VILARDELL, Francisco, MD, DSc (Med); Spanish physician and gastroenterologist; b. 1 April 1926, Barcelona; s. of Jacinto Vilardell and Mercedes Viñas; m.

Leonor Vilardell 1958; one s. two d.; ed Univs of Barcelona and Pennsylvania; Dir Gastroenterology Service, Hosp. Santa Cruz y San Pablo, Barcelona 1963–; Dir Postgraduate School of Gastroenterology, Autonomous Univ. of Barcelona 1969–; Pres. European Soc. for Digestive Endoscopy 1970–74, European Asscn for Study of the Liver 1975–76; Pres. World Org. of Gastroenterology 1982–90 (Sec.-Gen. 1974–82), now Hon. Pres.; Pres. Council of Int. Orgs in Medical Science 1987–93, Perm. Adviser 1994–; Dir-Gen. Health Planning, Ministry of Health 1981–82, mem. Advisory Council 1997–; f. Fundación Privada de Gastroenterología Dr. Francisco Vilardell 1992; Hon. Pres. World Gastroenterology Org.; Chevalier, Légion d'honneur; Hon. PhD (Univ. Toulouse, France 1974, (Univ. Zaragoza, Spain) 1990; Gold Medal, Barcelona Acad. of Medicine, Gold Medal, Spanish Soc. of Gastroenterology. *Publications:* ed. of six books; 170 papers in medical journals. *Leisure interests:* music, philology. *Address:* Fundación Privada de Gastroenterología Dr. Francisco Vilardell, C./ Virgen de la Salud, 78, Planta 5 Puerta F, 08024 Barcelona; Juan Sebastian Bach 11, 08021 Barcelona, Spain (home). *Telephone:* (93) 2197343; (93) 2014511 (home). *Fax:* (93) 2010191 (home). *Website:* www .fvilardell.org.

VILARIÑO PINTOS, Daría; Spanish librarian (retd); b. 26 Jan. 1928, Santiago de Compostela; d. of José Vilariño de Andrés and Daría Pintos Castro; mem. staff, state library, museum and archives depts 1957–70; Deputy Dir, Library of Univ. of Santiago 1970–73, Dir 1973–93; Insignia de Oro de la Univ. de Santiago 1993; Medalla de Bronce de Galicia 1993. *Publications:* O Libro Galego onte e hoxe (with Virtudes Pardo) 1981, Hechos de D. Berenguel de Landoria (co-author) 1983, Vasco de Aponte: Recuento de las Casas Antiguas del Reino de Galicia. Edición crítica (co-author) 1986, Ordoño de Celanova: Vida y Milagros de San Rosendo. Edición crítica (co-author) 1990, Guía do Fondo Antigo de Monografías da Biblioteca Xeral da USC: Literaturas Hispánicas Séculos XV–XVIII (co-author) 2000; articles in professional journals, bibliographical catalogues. *Leisure interest:* reading. *Address:* Calle San Miguel No. 5, 2°, 15704 Santiago de Compostela, La Coruña, Spain. *Telephone:* (981) 583658.

VILINBAKHOV, Georgy Vadimovich, D.Hist.SC; Russian historian and museum administrator; *Deputy Director, State Hermitage Museum;* b. 13 April 1949; m. Tatyana Borisovna; two c.; ed Leningrad (now St Petersburg) State Univ.; joined State Hermitage Museum 1969–, Treas., collection of mil. banners and graphic works 1970–92, Deputy, then First Deputy Dir 1991–; Head, State Heraldic Council 1992–, Head of State Heraldry 1994, then Chair. Herald Council, State Herald Master 1999–; Chair St Petersburg English Ass. 2016–; Prof. and mem. Exec. Cttee, Int. Asscn of Mil. Museums and Museum of Arms; Head, Dept of Heraldic Art, Stieglitz State Art and Industry Acad.; Order Sign of Honour 1997, Order for Service to Motherland 1999, Grand Officer, Order of Merit (Italy) 2001, Knight, First Class, Order of White Rose (Finland) 2005, Chevalier, Ordre National du Mérite 2005, Officier, Ordre National du Mérite 2011, Mil. Cross, Order of Merit (Poland) 2014. *Publications:* over 150 articles and publs on Russian mil. history and heraldry. *Leisure interests:* collecting tin soldiers, mil. music. *Address:* State Hermitage Museum, 190000 St Petersburg, Dvortsovaya nab. 34, Russia (office). *Telephone:* (812) 710-96-02 (office). *Fax:* (812) 571-90-09 (office). *E-mail:* vilinbakhov@hermitage.ru (office). *Website:* www.hermitagemuseum.org (office).

VILJOEN, Hendrik Christo, BSc, BEng, MEng, PhD (Eng); South African academic and electronics engineer; b. 31 Aug. 1937, Graaff-Reinet; s. of Hendrik Christoffel Viljoen and Anna Pienaar; m. Hana Stehlik 1965; one s. two d.; ed Univ. of Stellenbosch; engineer, Dept of Posts and Telecommunications, Pretoria 1961–65; Sr Lecturer, Stellenbosch Univ. 1966–70, apptd Prof. 1970, Dean of Eng 1979–93, Vice-Rector of Operations 1993–98, Dir Office for Intellectual Property 1998–2002; Man. Dir Unistel Group Holdings (Pty) Ltd 1999–2005; Chair. SABC 1989–93; Visiting Prof., Georgia Inst. of Tech., Atlanta, USA 1975–76, Nat. Chiao Tung Univ., Hsinchu, Taiwan 1981–82; est. Office for Intellectual Property, Dir –2002; ind. consultant 2002–; Consultant, science parks and technology transfer, Oman 2011–; Chair. Task Group on Broadcasting in SA 1987–91; mem. Council, Univ. Stellenbosch of 2006–09; Sr mem. IEEE, USA 1978; Fellow, S African Acad. for Arts & Science, Engineering Acad. of S Africa; mem. Huguenot Soc. of SA 1998–, Genealogical Inst. of SA 1998–2013; established Technopark (science park) in Stellenbosch, South Africa 1980–85); Hon. Fellow, Southern African Inst. for Industrial Eng; Order for Meritorious Service 1993; Sir Ernest Oppenheimer Memorial Trust Fellowship 1975, Computer Personality of the Year, Western Cape Chapter of Computer Asscn of S Africa 1988, Engineer of the Year, S African Asscn for Professional Engineers 1992, Merit Medal, S African Acad. for Arts and Science 2000, Genealogist of the Year, Genealogical Soc. of S Africa 2014, Award for contrib. to cultural Devt, Western Cape Minister for Culture and Sport 2012, Genealogist of the Year, Genealogical Soc. of SA 2014, DF du Toit-Malherbe Prize for Genealogical Publs, SA Acad. for Arts & Science 2014, HB Thom Award of excellence for the promotion of Afrikaans as an academic and scientific language 2016. *Publications include:* Viljoen Family Register 1978 (2nd edn 2012), Viljoen Family Memorial Book 1968, Elektronika 1971, Cyber Dictionary 2007, Pienaar Family Register 2016; 18 articles in scientific journals. *Leisure interests:* genealogy, writing, scuba diving. *Address:* 6 Hof Avenue, Stellenbosch 7600, South Africa (home). *Telephone:* (21) 8833754 (home). *Fax:* (21) 866162234 (home). *E-mail:* hcv@sun.ac.za (home); viljoen@mail.com (home). *Website:* www.hugenoot.org.za/Viljoen/index2.htm (office).

VILKS, Andris; Latvian economist and politician; b. 15 June 1963, Jaunpiebalga; m. Diāna Vilka; ed Univ. of Latvia, Nordisk Landboskole, Odense, Denmark; worked with various state-owned cos and public orgs 1986–94; Analyst, Credit Dept, Latvijas Unibanka 1995–97, Strategy and Analysis Dept 1997–99, Head of Equity Market Analysis Div. 2000–02; Analyst, SEB Merchant Banking, Stockholm 2002, Head of Market and Sector Analysis Dept, SEB Unibanka 2002–07, Chief Economist, SEB Banka 2007–09; mem. Saeima (Parl.) 2010–; Minister of Finance 2010–14; mem. Vienotība (Unity) party 2010–; Best Minister of Finance in the European Region, The Banker 2012. *Address:* Zvērinātu advokātu birojs, A. Caka iela 83/85-11/3, Rīga, Latvia (office). *Telephone:* 6729-2163 (office); 2-9485842 (mobile) (office). *E-mail:* avilks@btv.lv (office); info@andrisvilks.lv. *Website:* www .andrisvilks.lv.

VILKUL, Oleksander Yuriyovych; Ukrainian mining engineer and politician; b. 24 May 1974, Kryvyi Rih, Dnipropetrovsk Region; m.; one d.; ed Kryvyi Rih Technical Univ., Dnipropetrovsk Regional Inst. of Public Admin; started career as asst excavator driver, ore enrichment works, later becoming Head of Commercial Financial Dept, Deputy Dir-Gen. and Deputy Chair. JSC Southern Ore Enrichment Works, Kryvyi Rih 1997–2003, Chair. 2003–04, also Dir of Mining Div. JSC Metinvest Holding 2004–06; mem. Verkhovna Rada (Supreme Council, Parl.) 2006–10, Deputy Chair. Regulatory Policy and Entrepreneurship Cttee 2006–10; Gov. Dnipropetrovsk Oblast (Regional State Admin) 2010–12; Deputy Prime Minister 2012–14; Companion of the Order of Merit, Third Class 2008, Second Class 2011, Honoured Worker of Industry of Ukraine 2005, State Prize of Ukraine in Science and Tech. 2013. *Leisure interests:* history and books. *Address:* c/o Office of the Cabinet of Ministers, 01008 Kyiv, vul. M. Hrushevskoho 12/2, Ukraine.

VILLA-VICENCIO, Rev. Charles, BA, STM, PhD; South African theologian and academic; *Professor Emeritus, Department of Religious Studies, University of Cape Town;* b. 7 Nov. 1942, Johannesburg; s. of Charles Villa-Vicencio and Paula Villa-Vicencio; m. Eileen van Sittert 1968; two d.; ed Rhodes Univ., Natal Univ. and Yale Univ. and Drew Univ., USA; with Standard Bank of SA 1961–64; Probationer Minister, Methodist Church of Southern Africa 1965–70; ordained Minister 1970; Minister of various congregations in S Africa and USA; Teaching Fellow, Drew Univ. 1974–75; part-time lecturer, Univ. of Cape Town 1976–77; Sr Lecturer, Univ. of S Africa 1978–81, Assoc. Prof. 1981–82; Sr Lecturer, Univ. of Cape Town 1982, Assoc. Prof. 1984–88, Head of Dept of Religious Studies 1986–97, Prof. of Religion and Society 1988–97, now Prof. Emer.; mem. S African Theological Soc., Nat. Research Dir Truth and Reconciliation Comm., Exec. Dir Inst. for Justice and Reconciliation 2000–07, currently Sr Research Fellow; Fellow, Univ. of Cape Town 1996; Claude Ake Visiting Chair, Dept of Peace and Conflict Research, Uppsala Univ. and Nordic Africa Inst., Sweden 2007; Visiting Research Fellow, Berkley Center for Religion, Peace, and World Affairs, Georgetown Univ., USA 2008, also Visiting Research Scholar, Conflict Resolution Program; mem. Council, Stellenbosch Univ.; Hon. DHumLitt (Elmhurst Coll., Chicago) 1998; Abraham Kuyper Prize, Princeton Theological Seminary 2005. *Publications include:* Between Christ and Caesar: Classical and Contemporary Texts 1986, Trapped in Apartheid 1988, Civil Disobedience and Beyond 1990, A Theology of Reconstruction 1992, A Spirit of Hope: Conversations on Politics, Religion and Values 1993, Walk with Us and Listen: Political Reconciliation in Africa 2009, Conversations in Transition: The South African Story 2012; ed. or co-ed. of and contrib. to several vols of essays; numerous articles including many on the church and politics in S Africa. *Address:* University of Cape Town, Department of Religious Studies, Room 5.40, Leslie Social Science Building, Upper Campus, Cape Town; 14 Annerley Road, Rosebank, Cape Town 7700, South Africa (home). *Telephone:* (21) 6868643 (home); (21) 6503452 (office). *Fax:* (21) 6592721; (21) 6897575 (office). *E-mail:* ijr@grove.uct.ac .za (office). *Website:* www.religion.uct.ac.za (office).

VILLAIN, Claude Edouard Louis Etienne, LenD; French civil servant and business executive; b. 4 Jan. 1935, Paris; s. of Etienne Villain and Marie Louise (née Caudron) Villain; m. Bernadette Olivier 1962 (deceased); two s.; ed Lycée Voltaire, Lycée Louis-le-Grand, Univ. of Paris, Ecole Nat. de la FOM; trainee in French Overseas Admin 1956–59, Officer in Dept of Algerian Affairs 1959–61; Officer for Econ. Studies in Agricultural Devt Bureau 1962–64; Officer in Ministry of Econ. and Finance 1964, Head of Dept 1969, Deputy Dir of Ministry 1973; Tech. Adviser in Office of Valéry Giscard d'Estaing (then Minister of Econ. and Finance) 1973–74; Dir-Gen. of Competition and Prices in Ministry of Econ. and Finance 1974–78; Admin. Soc. Nat. des Chemins de fer Français (SNCF) 1974–78; Admin. Soc. Nat. Elf Aquitaine 1974–79; Dir-Gen. of Agric., Comm. of EEC 1979–85; Dir-Gen. Socopa Int., Vice-Pres. Socopa France 1985–86; Special Adviser to Minister of Econ. and Finance 1986–88; Inspector-Gen. of Finances 1987–2003; Del. Interministerial Mission for Cen. and Eastern Europe (MICECO) 1992–93, for Euro-Disneyland 1993–2003; Chair. Admin. Bd Comilog SA 1996–; mem. Intergovernmental Comm. of the Channel Tunnel 1990–2000, of the Lyon-Turin rail project 1996–2001; Admin., Soc. Nat. RATP 1998–2004; Officier, Légion d'honneur, Commdr, Ordre nat. du Mérite, du Mérite Agricole, Croix de Valeur Mil. *Leisure interests:* tennis, skiing. *Address:* 103 avenue Félix Faure, 75015 Paris, France (home). *Telephone:* 1-44-26-01-67 (home).

VILLALBA, HE Cardinal Luis Héctor; Argentine ecclesiastic; *Archbishop Emeritus of Tucumán;* b. 11 Oct. 1934, Buenos Aires; ordained priest, Archdiocese of Buenos Aires 1960; apptd Auxiliary Bishop of Buenos Aires and consecrated Titular Bishop of Aufinium 1984–91; Bishop of San Martín 1991–99; Archbishop of Tucumán 1999–2011, Archbishop Emer. 2011–; cr. Cardinal (Cardinal-Priest of San Girolamo a Corviale) 2015. *Address:* Arzobispado, Avenida Sarmiento 895, San Miguel de Tucumán, Argentina (office). *Telephone:* (381) 4310617 (office). *Fax:* (381) 4226345 (office). *E-mail:* info@arztucuman.org.ar (office). *Website:* www .arztucuman.org.ar (office).

VILLANI, Cédric, PhD; French mathematician, academic and research institute director; *Director, Institut Henri Poincaré;* b. 5 Oct. 1973, Brive-la-Gaillarde (Corrèze); two c.; ed Lycée Louis-le-Grand, École Normale Supérieure, Paris Dauphine Univ.; agrégé-préparateur (tutor), École Normale Supérieure –2000; Prof., École Normale Supérieure de Lyon 2000–10; Dir Univ. Pierre et Marie Curie Institut Henri Poincaré, Paris 2009–; Prof., Univ. of Lyon 2010–; Visiting Asst Prof., Georgia Tech Inst., USA 1999; Visiting Research Miller Prof., Univ. of California, Berkeley, USA 2004; Invited mem. Inst. for Advanced Study, Princeton, USA 2009; mem. Nat. Ass. (La République en Marche) for Essonne 5th constituency 2017–; Admin. for several asscns, including EuropaNova (pro-European think-tank); Pres. Scientific Bd AIMS-Senegal; mem. Editorial Bd, Inventiones Mathematicae, Journal of Functional Analysis, Journal of Mathematical Physics, Journal of Statistical Physics; mem. Strategic Research Council 2014; mem. Institut Universitaire de France 2006, Académie des sciences 2013, Académie pontificale des sciences 2016; Chevalier, Ordre nat. du Mérite 2009, Légion d'honneur 2011; Louis Armand Prize, Acad. des sciences 2001, Peccot-Vimont Prize and Cours Peccot, Collège de France 2003, Plenary Lecturer, Int. Congress of Math. Physics, Lisbon 2003, Harold Grad Lecturer 2004, Invited Lecturer, Int. Congress of Mathematicians, Madrid 2006, Jacques Herbrand Prize, Acad. des sciences 2007, Prize of European Math. Soc. 2008, Fermat Prize 2009, Henri Poincaré Prize, Int. Asscn of Math. Physics 2009, Fields Medal (co-recipient) 2010. *Publications include:* A Review of Mathematical Topics in Collisional Kinetic Theory 2002, Topics in Optimal Transportation 2003, Optimal Transport, Old and

New (Joseph L. Doob Award 2014) 2005, Théorème vivant (François-Mauriac Award 2013) 2012, Les Coulisses de la création (with Karol Beffa) 2015; more than 50 papers in professional journals on kinetic theory (Boltzmann and Vlasov equations and their variants) and optimal transport and its applications. *Leisure interests:* walking, music (piano). *Address:* Institut Henri Poincaré (UPMC/CNRS), 11 rue Pierre et Marie Curie, 75230 Paris Cedex 05, France (office). *Telephone:* 1-44-27-67-92 (office); 1-44-27-64-18 (office). *Fax:* 1-46-34-04-56 (office). *E-mail:* villani@ihp.fr (office); villani@math.univ-lyon1.fr (office). *Website:* math.univ-lyon1.fr/~villani (office); cedricvillani.org.

VILLANUEVA ARÉVALO, César; Peruvian politician; b. 5 Aug. 1946, Tarapoto, San Martín; ed Univ. Nacional Federico Villarreal; Pres., Regional Govt of San Martin 2007–13; Pres., Council of Ministers (Prime Minister) 2013–14; mem. Congreso (Parl.) from San Martin 2016–; Pres., Council of Ministers (Prime Minister) 2018–19 (resgnd); fmr mem. High Level Corruption Comm.; Chair. Agency for the Promotion of Private Investment in the Amazon; Chair. Interregional Amazon; mem. Movimiento Independiente Regional Nueva Amazonía. *Address:* c/o Office of the President of the Council of Ministers, Jirón Carabaya, cuadra 1 s/n, Anexo 1105-1107, Lima, Peru (office).

VILLAPALOS-SALAS, Gustavo, LLD; Spanish academic and university administrator; *Professor, Department of History of Law and Institutions, Universidad Complutense de Madrid;* b. 15 Oct. 1949, Madrid; s. of Gustavo Villapalos-Salas and Juana Villapalos-Salas; ed Universidad Complutense de Madrid; Prof., Faculty of Law, Universidad Complutense de Madrid 1970–75, apptd Prof. of Law 1976, Dir Dept of History of Law 1980–84, Dean, Faculty of Law 1984–87, Rector, Universidad Complutense de Madrid 1987–95, currently Prof., Dept of History of Law and Insts; Head, Ministry of Educ., Culture and Sports, Community of Madrid 1995–2001; Research Fellow, Instituto de Estudios Juridícos 1972–74, Centro de Investigaciones Juridícas, Económicas y Sociales 1975; Visiting Prof., Univ. of Calif., Berkeley 1976, Univ. of Freiburg 1976–77; Pres. Education Foundation of the Phoenix Mutual; Advisor, Fund de Ahorros de Ronda; mem. Real Academia de Jurisprudencia y Legislación; mem. Editorial Bd Yearbook of History of Spanish Law 1975–; Corresp. mem. Portuguese Acad. of History; Gran Cruz de la Orden de Alfonso X el Sabio, Gran Cruz del Mérito Civil, Hon. CBE; Dr hc (Univ. of Lisbon), (Universidad Paris XIII), (Universidad de Bratislava), (St Louis Univ., USA), (La Plata, Argentina), (Moscow State Inst. of Int. Relations—MGIMO Univ.) 2008, (Universidad Carolina de Praga), (Universidad Nacional Autónoma de México), (Universidad Rey Juan Carlos) 2014. *Publications include:* Colección Diplomática del Archivo Municipal de Santander: Documentos Reales II (1525–1599) 1982, Los Regímenes Económicos Matrimoniales en la Historia del Derecho Español: Prelección 1983, El Fuero de León: Comentarios 1984, Cortes de Castilla en el siglo XV 1986, La Baja Edad Media, Vol. IV, Historia General de Cantabria 1986, La Alta Edad Media, Vol. III 1987. *Leisure interests:* astronomy, cinema, classical music, reading. *Address:* Department of History of Law and Institutions, Universidad Complutense de Madrid, Ciudad Universitaria, 28040 Madrid, Spain (office). *Telephone:* (91) 3945666 (office). *E-mail:* salas@der.ucm.es (office). *Website:* www.ucm.es/dep-historia-del-derecho (office).

VILLAR, Manuel Bamba; Philippine politician and business executive; *President, Nacionalista Party;* b. 13 Dec. 1949, Tondo; s. of Manuel Montalban Villar and Curita Bamba; m. Cynthia Aguilar; two s. one d.; ed Univ. of the Philippines; began professional career as accountant with Sycip, Gorres, Velayo & Co.; fmr financial analyst, Private Devt Corpn of the Philippines; f. a construction business 1975, eventually becoming biggest housebuilder in SE Asia with firms Vista Land & Lifescapes and Polar Property Holdings; elected mem. House of Reps for Las Piñas-Muntinlupa constituency 1992, Speaker 1998–2000; Senator 2001–13, Pres. of Senate 2006–08; mem. Nacionalista Party (NP) 2003–, Pres. 2004–; unsuccessful NP cand. in 2010 presidential election; numerous hon. degrees. *Address:* Nacionalista Party, 2nd Floor, Starmall EDSA, cnr Shaw Blvd, Mandaluyong City, 1552 Metro Manila, Philippines (office). *Telephone:* (2) 7224727 (office). *Fax:* (2) 7274223 (office). *Website:* www.nacionalistaparty.com (office); www.mannyvillar.com.ph.

VILLARAIGOSA, Antonio R., BA; American politician and academic; *Professor of the Practice of Policy, Price School of Public Policy, University of Southern California;* b. (Antonio Villar), 23 Jan. 1953, Los Angeles, Calif.; m. Corina Raigosa (divorced); one s. one d. (and two c. from previous relationship); ed Univ. of California, Los Angeles; mem. Calif. State Ass. 1994, Speaker 1999; unsuccessful cand. for Mayor of Los Angeles 2001; Distinguished Fellow, UCLA, Univ. of Southern Calif. 2001–03; mem. LA City Council 2003; Chair. Transportation Cttee, mem. Bd Metropolitan Transportation Authority 2003; Mayor of LA 2005–13; currently Prof. of the Practice of Policy, Price School of Public Policy, Univ. of Southern California; also Sr Fellow, Bipartisan Policy Center, Washington, DC; Chair. Democratic Nat. Convention 2012. *Address:* USC Sol Price School of Public Policy, University of Southern California, Lewis Hall 312, Los Angeles, CA 90089-0626, USA (office). *E-mail:* uscprice@usc.edu (office). *Website:* priceschool.usc.edu (office).

VILLARROEL LANDER, Mario Enrique; Venezuelan lawyer, academic and international organization official; *President, Venezuelan Red Cross;* b. 20 Sept. 1947, Caracas; m. Norka Sierraalta 1969; three s. one d.; ed Cen. Univ. of Venezuela, Santa María Univ.; joined Venezuelan Red Cross as a volunteer 1967, Nat. Pres. 1978–, Pres. Int. Fed. of Red Cross and Red Crescent Socs 1987–98; Pres. Mirandino Historical Studies Inst., Henry Dunant Inst. 1992–93; Prof. of Penal Law, Chair. of Criminal Law Santa María Univ.; lawyer in pvt. legal practice, Caracas; fmr Dir La Voz del Derecho (legal review); numerous distinctions from Red Cross orgs. *Publications include:* El Cuerpo Técnico de Policía Judicial en el Proceso Penal Venezolano, Habeas Corpus y antejuicio de Mérito; legal articles in Venezuelan and foreign periodicals. *Leisure interest:* journalism. *Address:* Venezuelan Red Cross, Apartado 3185, 1010 Caracas, Venezuela (office). *Telephone:* (212) 571-4380 (office). *Fax:* (212) 576-1042 (office). *E-mail:* mariovillarroel@cantv.net (office). *Website:* www.cruzroja.org.ve (office); www.ifrc.org (office); www.mariovillarroel.com.

VILLASECA MARCO, Rafael, MBA; Spanish business executive; *President, Naturgy Foundation;* b. 30 April 1951, Barcelona; ed Tech. Univ. of Barcelona (UPC), Univ. of Navarra's IESE Business School; fmr Gen. Man. Dir Grupo Panrico; fmr Man. Dir Nueva Montaña Quijano, SA; CEO and Exec. Advisor, Unión Fenosa, SA; CEO Gas Natural SDG SA (renamed Gas Natural Fenosa following acquisition of Unión Fenosa 2008) 2005–18, Man. Dir and CEO Gas Natural SA ESP (subsidiary) 2005–18, fmr Deputy Chair. Gas Natural Fenosa Foundation, currently Pres. Naturgy Foundation (renamed); Chair. Gas Natural Aprovisio; fmr Chair. Túneles y Accesos de Barcelona SA (TABASA), Túnel de Cádiz SAC (affiliate of la Caixa), Gestión de Infraestructuras, SA, Grupo INISEL (now Grupo INDRA); Vice-Chair. Repsol-Gas Natural LNG, S.L.; fmr mem. Bd of Dirs Unión Fenosa, SA, Indra Sistemas, SA, Amper SA, Enagas SA 2002–09; fmr Chair. IESE's Alumni Asscn, Club Espanol de la Energia. *Address:* Naturgy Foundation, Av. San Luis, 77, 28033 Madrid, Spain (office). *E-mail:* fundacionnaturgy@naturgy.com (office). *Website:* www.fundacionnaturgy.org (office).

VILLEGAS ECHEVERRI, Luis Carlos, BA, DA; Colombian diplomatist, politician, government official and organization official; b. Pereira; m. Carmela Restrepo; one s. one d.; ed Universidad Javeriana, Bogotá, Univ. of Paris, France; served in various capacities, including as Deputy Minister of Foreign Affairs, Gen. Sec. Nat. Fed. of Coffee Growers, Sec. Comm. of Foreign Affairs, Sec.-Gen. and Under-Sec. for Econ. and Social Affairs, Ministry of Foreign Affairs, Econ. Counselor, Embassy in Paris 1979–89; Gov. Risaralda dept (state) of Colombia 1985–86; Int. Sec. Colombian Liberal Party 1989–94; Senator representing Risaralda dept 1990–92; Pres. Corfioccidente 1992–95, Nat. Business Asscn of Colombia (ANDI) for 17 years; mem. Colombian Govt's negotiating team in ongoing peace talks with Revolutionary Armed Forces of Colombia—People's Army (Fuerzas Armadas Revolucionarias de Colombia—Ejército del Pueblo, FARC–EP); Pres. Nat. Business Council 1998–99, 2002–12, Asscn for CEE/Latin American Business Co-operation (ACE) 1998–99, Andean Business Advisory Council 1998–99, Bd of Dirs Fund for the Reconstruction and Social Devt for the Coffee Belt (FOREC) 1999–2000; Amb. to USA 2013–15; Minister of Nat. Defence 2015–18; mem. Bd of Dirs Ecopetrol, Int. Org. of Employers, Geneva, Colombian Family Welfare Inst. (ICBF), Colombian Foundation for Educ. and Opportunities (FundaColombia-CocaCola); Pres. Colombian Chapter, Australian-Colombian Business Group 2005–13; mem. Colombian-France Business Group 2007–13; highest decorations of Colombian Govt and from Govts of Spain, Italy, France, Argentina, Ecuador, Brazil and Peru.

VILLEGAS QUIROGA, Carlos; Bolivian economist and government official; *President, Yacimientos Petrolíferos Fiscales Bolivianos;* fmr Dir of Postgraduate Devt Studies, Univ. of San Andres, La Paz; Econ. Adviser to presidential cand. Evo Morales 2005; Minister of Sustainable Devt and Planning –2006, also Gov. IDB and Inter-American Investment Corpn; Minister of Hydrocarbons and Energy 2006–09; Pres. Yacimientos Petrolíferos Fiscales Bolivianos (state-owned petrol co.) 2009–. *Address:* Yacimientos Petrolíferos Fiscales Bolivianos Calle Bueno 185, 6°, Casilla 401, La Paz, Bolivia (office). *Telephone:* (2) 237-0210 (office). *E-mail:* webmaster@ypfb.gov.bo (home). *Website:* www.ypfb.gob.bo (office).

VILLELA FILHO, Alfredo Egydio Arruda, MBA; Brazilian engineer and business executive; *Vice-Chairman, Itaú Unibanco Holding SA;* ed Escola de Engenharia Mauá, Instituto Mauá de Tecnologia, Fundação Getúlio Vargas; mem. Bd of Dirs Itaúsa – Investimentos Itaú SA 1995–, CEO and Dir-Gen. 2008–, Vice-Chair. 2011–, Chair. Ethics, Disclosure and Trading Cttee 2005–, Investment Policies Cttee and mem. Accounting Policies Cttee 2008–11, Vice-Chair. (non-exec.) Itaú Unibanco Holding SA 2003–, mem. Disclosure and Trading Cttee 2005–, Accounting Policies Cttee 2008–09, Appointment and Corp. Governance Cttee 2009–, Compensation Cttee 2011–, Vice-Chair. Itaú Unibanco SA 2001–03, Vice-Chair. Itautec SA 1997–2009, 2010–, Chair. 2009–10; mem. Bd of Dirs Elekeiroz SA 1996– (Vice-Chair. 2008–, mem. Personnel, Governance and Appointment Cttees 2009–), Duratex SA 1996– (Vice-Chair. 2008–, mem. Personnel, Governance and Appointment Cttees 2009–). *Address:* Itaú Unibanco Holding SA, Praça Alfredo Egydio de Souza Aranha 100, Torre Olavo Setubal, Parque Jabaquara, São Paulo 04344-902, Brazil (office). *Telephone:* (11) 5019-1677 (office). *Fax:* (11) 5019-1114 (office). *E-mail:* info@itau.com (office). *Website:* www.itau.com (office).

VILLELLA, Edward, BS; American ballet dancer; *Artistic Advisor, New Jersey Ballet;* b. 1 Oct. 1936, New York; s. of Joseph Villella and Mildred Villella (née De Giovanni); m. 1st Janet Greschler 1962 (divorced 1980); one s.; m. 2nd Linda Carbonetta 1981; two d.; ed New York State Maritime Coll.; joined New York City Ballet 1957, becoming soloist within a year, now Premier Dancer; originated leading roles in George Balanchine's Bugaku, Tarantella, Stars and Stripes, Harlequinade, Jewels, Glinkaiana, A Midsummer Night's Dream; first danced his famous role of Prodigal Son 1960; has also danced leading roles in Allegro Brillante, Jeux, Pas de Deux, Raymonda Variations, Scotch Symphony, Swan Lake; choreographed Narkissos; has appeared at Bolshoi Theatre, with Royal Danish Ballet and in London and made numerous guest appearances; choreographed and starred in revivals of Brigadoon, Carousel; Artistic Advisor, New Jersey Ballet 1972–, also Special Artist, New Jersey School of Ballet; Chair. New York City Comm. of Cultural Affairs 1978; Artistic Co-ordinator Eglersky Ballet Co. (now André Eglersky State Ballet of New York) 1979–84, Choreographer 1980–84; Choreographer NJ Ballet 1980; Artistic Dir Ballet Okla 1983–86, Miami City Ballet 1985–12; Heritage Chair in Arts and Cultural Criticism, George Mason Univ. 1992–93, 1993–94; mem. Nat. Council on the Arts 1968–74; Artist-in-Residence, Dorothy F. Schmidt Coll. of Arts and Letters 2000–01; Robert Kiphuth Fellow, Yale Univ. 2001; Fellow, American Acad. of Arts and Sciences 2009–; Hon. DFA (State Univ. of New York Maritime Coll.) 1998; Dance Magazine Award 1965, Golden Plate Award, American Acad. of Achievement 1971, Emmy Award 1975, Gold Medal Award, Nat. Soc. of Arts and Letters 1990, Nat. Medal of Arts Award 1997, other awards. *Publication:* Prodigal Son (co-author) 1992. *Address:* New Jersey BalletBallet, 15–17 Microlab Road, Suite 102, Livingston, NJ 07039, USA (office). *Telephone:* (973) 597-9600 (office). *Fax:* (973) 597-9442 (office). *E-mail:* info@njballet.org (office). *Website:* www.njballet.org (office).

VILLENEUVE, Denis; Canadian film director and writer; b. 3 Oct. 1967, Trois-Rivières, Quebec; m. 1st Macha Grenon; three c.; m. 2nd Tanya Lapointe; ed Université du Québec à Montréal; La Course Europe-Asie in 1990–91. *Films include:* Cosmos 1996, August 32nd on Earth 1998, Maelström (FIPRESCI Prize)

2000, Polytechnique 2009, Incendies (Acad. Award for Best Foreign Language Film 2011, Jutra Awards for Best Direction and Screenplay 2011, Genie Award for Best Direction and Best Adapted Screenplay 2011, Best Canadian Feature Film, Toronto Int. Film Festival 2011), 2010, Prisoners 2013, Enemy (Canadian Screen Awards for Best Dir 2014, Directors Guild of Canada Award for Best Feature Film 2014) 2013, Sicario 2015, Arrival (Future Film Festival Digital Award, Venice Film Festival 2016, Hugo Award For Best Dramatic Presentation, Long Form 2016) 2016, Blade Runner 2049 2017.

VILLENEUVE, Jacques, OQ; Canadian racing driver; b. 9 April 1971, Saint-Jean-sur-Richelieu, Québec; s. of Gilles Villeneuve and Joanne Barthe; m. Johanna Martinez 2006; ed Beau-Soleil School, Villars, Switzerland, Jim Russell Formula Ford School, Mont-Tremblant, Formula 2000 Racing School, Shannonville; first raced in three Alfa Italian touring car races; raced Italian Formula 3 series 1989–91; second place in Japanese F3 series for Team Tom's Toyota with three wins 1992; third place in Macao F3 Grand Prix 1992; Formula Atlantic debut and third place in Player's Grand Prix de Trois-Rivières; Forsythe-Green racing team Formula Atlantic: five wins and three second places in 15 races and third in championship 1993; named Formula Atlantic Rookie-of-the-Year 1993; IndyCar debut with team Players Forsythe-Green, three podiums, finished sixth in championship 1994; finished second in Indianapolis 500 race behind Al Unser Jt 1994; won his first IndyCar race at Elkhart Lake 1994; named IndyCar Rookie-of-the-Year 1994; sole driver for team Players Forsythe-Green 1995; named IndyCar Champion 1995 with seven podium finishes, four wins, one second place, two third places and six poles; first Canadian and youngest driver (aged 24) to win the Indianapolis 500 race 1995; moved to Williams/Renault Formula One (F1) team 1996; pole position in his first Formula One (F1) race at Australian Grand Prix; second in Formula One (F1) World Championship 1996 with 78 points, three pole positions, four wins (Europe, GB, Hungary and Portugal), five second places and two third places; named F l Rookie-of-the-Year 1996; driver for Williams/Renault Formula One (F1) team 1997; Formula One (F1) World Champion 1997 with 81 points, seven wins (Brazil, Argentina, Spain, GB, Hungary, Austria and Luxembourg) and 10 pole positions; driver for Williams/Mecachrome Formula One (F1) team 1998; fifth in Formula One (F1) World Championship with two third places (Germany and Hungary) 1998; driver for B.A.R. Formula One (F1) team 1999–2003; two third places (Spain and Germany) 2001; moved to Renault Formula One (F1) team for last three races of 2004; moved to Sauber Petronas Formula One (F1) team in 2005; driver with BMW-Sauber 2006; 150 Formula One (F1) Grand Prix races (as at Belgium Grand Prix 2005); Team Peugeot Le Mans 24h 2007; Bill Davis Racing NASCAR Team (Truck Series) 2007, (Sprint Cup) 2008; Owner, Newtown restaurant/club, Montreal; Founder and Patron Formula Charity; inductee into Canada's Walk of Fame 1998. *Recording:* first album as singer/songwriter: Private Paradise 2007. *Leisure interests:* reading, music, skiing, ice hockey, computers/gaming. *Address:* c/o Claymore SA, CP 195, 1884 Villars-sur-Ollon, Switzerland (office). *Telephone:* (24) 496-30-40 (office). *Fax:* (24) 496-30-41 (office). *E-mail:* jvmgt@claymore.ch (office). *Website:* www.jv-world.com; www .myspace.com/jvofficial.

VILLEPIN, Dominique Marie François René Galouzeau de, LenD; French diplomatist, civil servant and lawyer; b. 14 Nov. 1953, Rabat, Morocco; s. of Xavier Galouzeau de Villepin and Yvonne Hétier; m. Marie-Laure Le Guay 1985; one s. two d.; ed Paris Inst. of Political Sciences, Ecole Nationale d'Administration; responsible for Horn of Africa, Office of African Affairs 1980–81, Head of Mission attached to Dir's Office 1981–84, Asst Dir 1992–93; with Centre d'Analyse et de Prévision 1981–84; First Sec. Washington 1984–87, Embassy Press and Information Dir, Washington 1987–89, Ministerial Councillor, India 1989–92; Deputy Head of African Affairs, Ministry of Foreign Affairs 1992–93, Dir de Cabinet to Alain Juppé, Minister of Foreign Affairs 1993–95; Sec.-Gen. to Presidency 1995–2002; Minister of Foreign Affairs, Cooperation and Francophony 2002–04, Minister of the Interior, Internal Security and Local Rights 2004–05, Prime Minister 2005–07; Chair. Admin. Council Nat. Forests Office (ONF) 1996–99; Rep. Convention on the Future of Europe 2002; Founder and Chair. Villepin International, Paris 2008–; f République solidaire (political party) 2010, Pres. 2010–11; Chair. Advisory Bd, Universal Credit Rating Group (Sino-US-Russian rating agency); mem. Int. Cttee, China Minsheng (Chinese investment fund) 2015–; Hon. mem., Int. Raoul Wallenberg Foundation; Chevalier, Légion d'honneur, Grand Cross with Star, Order of Merit (Poland) 2000. *Publications include:* Parole d'Exil 1986 (poetry), Le Droit d'Aînesse 1988 (poetry), Elégies barbares (poetry) 1996, Secession (poetry) 1996, Les Cent-Jours ou l'Esprit de sacrifice (Amb.'s Prize) 2001, Le Cri de la Gargouille 2002, In Praise of Those Who Stole the Fire (poetry) 2003, Un Autre Monde – Cahiers de l'Herne 2003, Le Requin et la Mouette 2004, Toward a New World: Speeches, Essays and Interviews on the War in Iraq, the UN and the Changing Face of Europe 2004, L'Homme Européen 2005, Le Soleil Noir de la Puissance 2007, Mémoires des esclavages 2007, Hôtel de L'Insomnie 2008, La Chute ou L'Empire de la Solitude 2008, La Cite des Hommes 2009, Le Dernier Temoin 2009, De L'Esprit de Cour une Malediction Française 2010, Notre Vieux Pays 2011, Seul le Devoir Nous Rendra Libres 2012, Zao Wou-Ki et les poètes 2015, La chute de Napoléon 2015. *Leisure interest:* marathon running. *Address:* Villepin International, 35 rue Fortuny, 75017 Paris, France (office).

VILLIERS, Rt Hon. Theresa Anne, PC, LLB (Hons), BCL; British politician, barrister and lecturer; b. 5 March 1968, London, England; d. of George Edward Villiers and Anne Virginia Villiers (née Threlfall); m. Sean Wilken 1997 (divorced); ed Francis Holland School, Univ. of Bristol, Jesus Coll., Oxford; worked as Barrister and lecturer at King's Coll. London; MEP for London constituency 1999–2005; Deputy Leader, Conservatives in Europe 2001–02; MP for Chipping Barnet 2005–10, for Chipping Barnet (revised boundary) 2010–, mem. Environmental Audit Select Cttee 2005–06; Shadow Chief Sec. to the Treasury 2005–07, Shadow Sec. of State for Transport 2007–10, Minister of State, Dept for Transport 2010–12, Sec. of State for Northern Ireland 2012–16; Vice-Pres. Conservative Future, Asscn of Conservative Cands. *Publication:* Law of Estoppel, Variation and Waiver (with Sean Wilken) 1998. *Address:* Constituency Office, 163 High Street, Barnet, Herts., EN5 5SU, England (office). *Telephone:* (20) 8449-7345 (office). *Fax:* (20) 8449-7346 (office). *E-mail:* theresa@theresavilliers.co.uk (office). *Website:* www.parliament.uk (office); www.theresavilliers.com.

VILLIERS de SAINTIGNON, Philippe Le Jolis de; French politician; b. 25 March 1949, Boulogne; s. of Jacques Le Jolis de Villiers de Saintignon and Hedwige d'Arexy; brother of Pierre Le Jolis de Villiers de Saintignon; m. Dominique de Buor de Villeneuve 1973; four s. three d.; ed Saint-Joseph Inst., Ecole Nat. d'Admin.; civil servant Ministry of Interior 1978; Prin. Pvt. Sec. to Prefect of La Rochelle 1978; Deputy Prefect Vendôme 1979; f. Alouette FM (regional radio station) 1981, Fondation pour les Arts et les Sciences de la Communication, Nantes 1984; Jr Minister of Culture and Communications 1986–87; mem. Conseil Gen. de la Vendée 1987–, Pres. 1988–; Deputy to Nat. Ass. from Vendée 1988–94 (UDF), 1997– (Ind.); MEP 1994–97, 1999, 2004–; Nat. Del. of UDF in charge of youth and liaising with cultural groups 1988; Founder and Pres. Mouvement pour la France 1994–; Co-Founder Rassemblement pour la France 1999, Vice-Pres. 1999–2000. *Publications:* Lettre Ouverte aux Coupeurs de Têtes et aux Menteurs du Bicentenaire 1989, La Chienne qui Miaule 1990, Notre Europe sans Maastricht 1992, Avant qu'il ne soit trop tard 1993, La Société de connivence 1994, Dictionnaire du politiquement correct à la française 1996, La machination d'Amsterdam 1998. *Address:* Conseil Général de la Vendée, 40 rue Foch, 85923 La Roche-sur-Yon cedex 9, France (office); European Parliament, Bât. Altiero Spinelli 07H154, 60, rue Wiertz, 1047 Brussels, Belgium (office). *Telephone:* 1-40-63-82-05 (Paris) (office); (2) 284-58-95 (Brussels) (office). *Fax:* 1-40-63-82-80 (Paris) (office). *E-mail:* philippe.devilliers@europarl.europa.eu (office).

VILLIERS de SAINTIGNON, Gen. Pierre Le Jolis de; French army officer; b. 26 July 1956, Boulogne (Vendée); s. of Jacques Le Jolis de Villiers and Hedwige d'Arexy; brother of Philip Le Jolis de Villiers de Saintignon; m.; six c.; ed Saint-Cyr Mil. Acad.; joined French Army 1975, several appointments in armoured regts 1978–2003 including as Leader, AMX 30 tank troop, 2nd Dragoons Regt Haguenau (Bas-Rhin), Capt. commanding reconnaissance squadron, 7th Armoured Div., Valdahon (Doubs), Col Commanding Officer, 501st-503rd Combat Tank Regt, Mourmelonle-Grand (Marne), Commdr, Mechanised Infantry Bn, Leclerc Brigade, Kosovo (within KFOR) June–Oct. 1999; served three times as instructor, Saumur Mil. Acad.; 12 years at Army Staff HQ, Army Inspectorate and Finance Directorate of Ministry of Defence; Deputy to Head of Prime Minister's mil. staff 2004–06; Commdr, 2nd Armoured Brigade and Mil. Gov. of Orléans 2006; Commdr, one of five NATO regional commands in Afghanistan (within ISAF) 2006–07; Head of Prime Minister's mil. staff 2008–10; Vice-Chief of Defence Staff 2010–14, Chief of Defence Staff 2014–17 (resgnd); attained rank of Second Lt 1977, Lt 1978, Capt. 1982, Maj. 1988, Lt-Col 1992, Col 1997, Brig.-Gen. 2005, Maj.-Gen. 2008, Lt-Gen. 2009, Gen. 2010; Grand officier, légion d'honneur, Officier, ordre nat. du Mérite; several medals including Croix de la Valeur Militaire with citation. *Leisure interest:* football.

VILLIGER, Kaspar; Swiss business executive and fmr head of state; *Chairman, UBS International Center of Economics in Society;* b. 5 Feb. 1941, Pfeffikon, Lucerne; m.; two d.; ed Swiss Fed. Inst. of Tech. (ETH), Zurich; Co-owner, Villiger Group, Man. of cigar manufacturer Villiger Söhne AG, Pfeffikon 1966–89; fmr Vice-Pres. Chamber of Commerce of Cen. Switzerland and mem. Cttee Swiss Employers' Cen. Asscn; fmr Vice-Pres. Chamber of Industry and Commerce of the Canton of Aargau; mem. Lucerne Cantonal Parl. 1972–82; mem. Nat. Council, Liberal Party of Switzerland (FDP) 1982; mem. Council of States 1987; Swiss Fed. Councillor 1989–2003; Head, Fed. Mil. (Defence) Dept 1989–95, Dept of Finance 1996–2001, 2003; Vice-Pres. of Swiss Confed. 1994, 2001, Pres. 1995, 2002; Chair. UBS AG 2009–12, currently Chair. UBS Int. Center of Econs in Soc.; mem. Bd of Dirs Nestlé 2004–09, Swiss Re 2004–09, Neue Zürcher Zeitung 2004–09; mem. Global Leadership Foundation. *Address:* UBS International Center of Economics in Society, Universität Zürich, Institut für Volkswirtschaftslehre, Schönberggasse 1, 8001 Zürich, Switzerland (office). *Telephone:* 446345722 (office). *Fax:* 446343590 (office). *E-mail:* contact@ubscenter.uzh.ch (office). *Website:* www.ubscenter.uzh.ch (office).

VILLIS, Hans-Peter; German business executive; b. 1958, Castrop-Rauxel; m.; two c.; ed Ruhr Univ., Bochum; Commercial Dir, Bergbau AG 1987–89; Man. Planning and Control, VEBA Kraftwerke Ruhr AG 1989–92, Project Man. E Germany VEBA AG 1992–93; Man. Dir Städtische Werke Magdeburg GmbH 1993–99; mem. Bd Gelsenwasser AG 2000–02; Man. Dir Elektrizitätswerk Wesertal GmbH, Hameln Jan.–Sept. 2003, Chair. Bd of Man. E.ON Westfalen Weser AG 2003–06, Chief Financial Officer and Deputy Chair. Bd of Man. E.ON Nordic AB 2006–07, Chair. Bd of Man. and CEO Energie Baden-Württemberg AG 2007–12; Chair. Supervisory Bd, VfL-Bochum 1848 (football club) 2012–. *Leisure interests:* hiking, golf, football. *Address:* VfL Bochum 1848, Castroper Str. 145, 44791 Bochum, Germany (office). *Telephone:* (234) 951848 (office). *Fax:* (234) 951895 (office). *E-mail:* info@vfl-bochum.de (office). *Website:* www.vfl-bochum.de.

VILSACK, Thomas (Tom), BA, JD; American lawyer, government official and fmr politician; b. 13 Dec. 1950, Pittsburgh, Pa; s. of Bud Vilsack and Dolly Vilsack; m. Christine Bell 1973; two s.; ed Hamilton Coll., Albany Law School; in pvt. law practice, Mt Pleasant, Iowa 1975–98; Mayor of Mt Pleasant 1987–92; mem. Iowa State Senate 1993–98; Gov. of Iowa 1998–2007; Chair. Democratic Leadership Council 2005-07; Of Counsel, Dorsey & Whitney LLP, Des Moines 2007–08; US Sec. of Agric. 2009–17; Distinguished Visiting Prof. of Law, Drake Univ. Law School; mem. Democratic Govs Asscn 1999–2007; Distinguished Fellow, Biosafety Inst. for Genetically Modified Agricultural Products, Iowa State Univ.; mem. Bd of Dirs United Way, Mt Pleasant; unsuccessful cand. for Democratic party nomination for US Pres. 2008; Nat. Co-Chair. for Senator Hillary Clinton's presidential nomination campaign 2007–08; Fellow, Iowa Acad. of Trial Lawyers; mem. ABA, Iowa State Bar Asscn, Iowa Trial Lawyers Asscn (Pres. 1985), Council on Foreign Relations; Democrat.

VIMONT, Pierre, LenD; French diplomatist; b. 15 June 1949; ed Institut d'Etudes Politiques and Ecole Nationale d'Admin, Paris; Sec., Ministry of Foreign Affairs 1977, Second Sec., Embassy in London 1977–78, First Sec. 1978–81, with Press and Information Office, Ministry of Foreign Affairs 1981–85, seconded to Inst. for East-West Security Studies, New York 1985–86, Second Counsellor, Perm. Representation to European Communities, Brussels 1986–90, Head of Pvt. Office, Minister of European Affairs 1990–93, Dir for Devt and Scientific, Tech. and Educational Co-operation 1993–97, Dir for European Co-operation, Ministry of Foreign Affairs 1997–99, Amb. and Perm. Rep. to EU, Brussels 1999–2002, Prin. Pvt. Sec. to Minister of Foreign Affairs 2002–07, Amb. to USA 2007–10; Exec. Sec.-

Gen. European External Action Service 2010–15; fmr Pres. Group of Personal Reps to Intergovernmental Conf.; Chevalier, Ordre nat. du Mérite 1993. *Address:* c/o Ministry of Foreign Affairs and International Development, 37 quai d'Orsay, 75351 Paris Cedex 07, France.

VINCENT, Jean-Pierre, LèsL; French theatre director; b. 26 Aug. 1942, Juvisy-sur-Orge, Essonne; s. of André Vincent and Paulette Loyot; m. Hélène Vincent; one s.; ed Lycées Montaigne, Louis-le-Grand, Paris, Univ. de Paris (Sorbonne); amateur actor, Univ. Theatre, Lycée Louis-le-Grand 1958–64; mem. Patrice Chéreau theatre co. 1965–68, Dir 1968–72; Dir, Admin. Dir Espérance Theatre 1972–74; Dir at Théâtre Nat. and École Supérieure d'art dramatique, Strasbourg 1975–83; Gen. Admin. Comédie-Française 1983–86; Dir Théâtre de Nanterre-Amandiers 1990–2001; Co-Founder Studio Libre 2002; Lecturer, Inst. d'études théâtrales de Paris 1969–70; Studio Dir Conservatoire Nat. Supérieur d'art dramatique 1969–70, Prof. 1986–89; Pres. Syndicat nat. de directeurs d'entreprises artistiques et culturelles (Syndeac) 1978–82, Vice-Pres. 1992; mem. Bd of Dirs Festival d'Avignon, Théâtre de l'Odéon, Jeune Théâtre National; numerous awards, including Molière Prize for Best Dir 1987, Prix de la Critique 1988, prix Plaisir du Théâtre 2011. *Plays include:* La noce chez les petits-bourgeois 1968, Tambours et Trompettes 1969, Les acteurs de bonne foi 1970, Le marquis de Montefosco 1970, La Cagnotte 1971, Capitaine Eçço 1971, Dans la jungle des villes 1972, Le suicide 1984, Six personnages en quête de l'auteur 1986, Le Mariage de Figaro 1987, Fantasio, Les caprices de Mariane 1991, Woyzeck 1973, 1993, Violences à Vichy 1995, Tartuffe 1998, Pièces de guerre 1999, Homme pour homme, Lorenzaccio 2000, Les Prétendants 2003, Derniers remords avant l'oubli 2003–04, Onze Débardeurs 2004–05, La mort de Danton 2005, Les Antilopes 2006, Le silence des communistes 2007. *Opera includes:* Les Noces de Figaro 1994, Mitridate 2000, Le drame et la vie 2001.

VINCENT, Rev. John James, DTheol; British theologian, broadcaster and writer; b. 29 Dec. 1929, Sunderland; s. of David Vincent and Beatrice Ethel Vincent (née Gadd); m. Grace Johnston Stafford 1958; two s. one d.; ed Manchester Grammar School, Richmond Coll., London Univ., Drew Univ., USA, Basel Univ., Switzerland; ordained in Methodist Church 1956; Minister, Manchester and Salford Mission 1956–62; Supt Minister, Rochdale Mission 1962–69, Sheffield Inner City Ecumenical Mission 1970–77; Dir, Urban Theology Unit, Sheffield 1969–97, Dir Emer. and Doctoral Supervisor 1997–; Pres. Methodist Conf. 1989–90; Visiting Prof. of Theology, Boston School of Theology, USA 1969, New York Theological Seminary 1970, Theological School, Drew Univ. 1977; elected mem., Studiorum Novi Testamenti Societas 1961; Sec. Regional Working Party, WCC Faith and Order 1958–63; mem., British Council of Churches Comm. on Defence and Disarmament 1963–65, 1969–72; NW Vice-Pres., Campaign for Nuclear Disarmament 1957–69; Founding mem., Methodist Renewal Group 1961–70; Founding mem. and Leader, Ashram Community 1967–; Chair. Alliance of Radical Methodists 1971–74, Urban Mission Training Asscn of GB 1976–77, 1985–90; Co-ordinator, British Liberation Theology Project 1990–; mem. Bd, Int. Urban Ministry Network 1991–; presented Petition of Distress from the Cities to HM the Queen 1993; mem., Ind. Human Rights Del. to Colombia 1994, Partnership Bd Burngreave New Deal for Communities 2001–11; Chaplain to the Lord Mayor of Sheffield 2006–07; Chair. Methodist Report on The Cities 1997; Hon. Lecturer, Biblical Studies Dept, Univ. of Sheffield 1990–2011, Theology Dept, Univ. of Birmingham 2003–; Fellow, St Deiniol's Library 2003; Centenary Achievement Award, Univ. of Sheffield 2005. *Publications:* Christ in a Nuclear World 1962, Christ and Methodism 1964, Here I Stand 1967, Secular Christ 1968, The Race Race 1970, The Jesus Thing 1973, Stirrings, Essays Christian and Radical 1975, Alternative Church 1976, Disciple and Lord 1976, Starting All Over Again 1981, Into the City 1982, O.K. Let's Be Methodists 1984, Radical Jesus 1986, Mark at Work 1986, Britain in the 90s 1989, Discipleship in the 90s 1991, Liberation Theology from the Inner City 1992, A Petition of Distress from the Cities 1993, Liberation Theology UK (ed.) 1995, The Cities: A Methodist Report 1997, Gospel from the City (ed.) 1997, Hope from the City 2000, Journey: Explorations in Discipleship 2001, Bible and Practice (ed.) 2001, Faithfulness in the City (ed.) 2003, Methodist and Radical (ed.) 2003, Outworkings: Gospel Practice and Interpretation 2005, Mark: Gospel of Action (ed.) 2006, A Lifestyle of Sharing 2009, The City in Biblical Perspective (jtly) 2009, The Drama of Mark (jtly) 2010, Christian Communities (ed.) 2011, Stilling the Storm (ed.) 2011, Acts in Practice (ed.) 2012, British Liberation Theology – For Church and Nation (ed.) 2013, Christ in the City 2013, Radical Christianity 2014, Methodist Unbound: Christ and Methodism for the 21st Century 2015, Inner City Testament (with Grace Vincent) 2017. *Leisure interests:* jogging, writing. *Address:* 178 Abbeyfield Road, Sheffield, S4 7AY, England (home). *Telephone:* (114) 270-9907 (office); (114) 243-6688 (home). *Fax:* (114) 243-5356 (office). *E-mail:* john@utusheffield.org.uk (home).

VINCENT, John Russell, PhD; British historian and academic; *Professor Emeritus, University of Bristol;* b. 20 Dec. 1937, Cheshire; s. of J. J. Vincent; m. Nicolette Kenworthy 1972; two s. (one deceased); ed Bedales School, Christ's Coll., Cambridge; Fellow of Peterhouse, Cambridge 1962–70, Lecturer in History, Univ. of Cambridge 1967–70; Prof. of Modern History, Univ. of Bristol 1970–84, Prof. of History 1984–2002, now Prof. Emer.; Visiting Prof., Univ. of East Anglia, Norwich 2003–08. *Publications:* The Formation of the Liberal Party 1966, Pollbooks: How Victorians Voted 1967, The Governing Passion 1974, Disraeli, Derby and the Conservative Party: The Political Journals of Lord Stanley 1849–1869 1978, Gladstone and Ireland (British Acad. Raleigh Lecture) 1979, The Crawford Papers 1984, Disraeli 1990, An Intelligent Person's Guide to History 1995, Derby Diaries, 1869–1878 1995, Derby Diaries 1878–93 2003; various works on political history.

VINCHON, Lt-Gen. (retd) Pascal; French military officer (retd) and business executive; *General Manager Europe, AiRPX TECHOPS;* b. 14 Dec. 1953, Nîmes; s. of Philippe Vinchon and Claude Gaborieau; m. Carine Boissonnet; four c.; ed Air Force Acad., US Air War Coll., Montgomery Centre for Advanced Mil. Studies, Paris; promoted to Second Lt 1974, First Lt 1976, Captain 1979, participated in various operational missions over Mauritania and Chad 1980–81; Flight Commdr, Tactical Fighter Squadron 1/11 1982–84, Deputy Commdr, Fighter Squadron 2/12 1984–85, Commdr, Fighter Squadron 1/12 1985–87, Commdr, Air Force Acad. cadet class 1987–89, Deputy Commdr, 3rd Tactical Fighter Wing 1989–91, Commdr, 3rd Tactical Fighter Wing 1991–92; Mil. Adviser to Rep., Balkan Contact Group 1994, mem. French negotiating team, Dayton Peace Agreement 1995; Mil. Adviser to Perm. Rep. to UN, New York 1995–98; mem. French negotiating team for Kosovo, Rambouillet 1999; served in staff positions including Head of Balkan crisis action team, French Jt Command Centre, Asst Dir European and NATO Affairs, Ministry of Defence Policy Directorate, Chief of Personal Staff to Chief of Staff of French Air Force 2001–03; Defence attaché, Embassy in Washington, DC 2003–06, Mil. Rep., NATO, Brussels 2006–10; promoted to Maj. 1984, Lt-Col 1988, Col 1992, Brig.-Gen. 2001, Maj.-Gen. 2003, Lt-Gen. 2006; Gen. Man. Europe, AiRPX TECHOPS 2010–; Exec. Man. and Consultant, ATU SARL 2010–; Commdr, Légion d'honneur, Ordre nat. du Mérite; Medal of the Combatant, Overseas Operations Medal, Nat. Defence Medal. *Address:* AiRPX TECHOPS, 10 rue de Penthièvres, 75008 Paris, France (office); ATU SARL, 24 rue Gabriel Péri, 78210 Saint Cyr l'Ecole, France (office). *Telephone:* 6-58-56-28-84 (office). *E-mail:* pascal.vinchon@airpx.com (office); pascal.vinchon@a-tu.fr (office). *Website:* www.airpx.com (office).

VINE, Jeremy, BA; British broadcaster; b. 17 May 1965, Epsom, Surrey; s. of Guy Vine and Diana Vine; m. Rachel Vine; ed Epsom Coll. and Durham Univ.; journalist, Coventry Evening Telegraph 1986–87; joined BBC 1987, News Trainee 1987–89, Programme Reporter, Today 1989–93, Political Corresp. 1993–97, Africa Corresp. 1997–99, Presenter, Newsnight 1996–2002 (full-time 1999–2002), The Politics Show 2003–05, Panorama 2007–10, Eggheads 2008–, Points of View 2008–; Presenter, The Jeremy Vine Show, BBC Radio 2 2003–; Sony Radio Acad. Awards Speech Broadcaster of the Year 2005, 2011. *Publications:* It's All News to Me (autobiography) 2012. *Leisure interests:* Chelsea Football Club, films of Alfred Hitchcock, poems of W. H. Auden. *Address:* c/o Noel Gay, 19 Denmark Street, London, WC2H 8NA, England. *E-mail:* info@noelgay.com; vine@bbc.co.uk (office). *Website:* www.bbc.co.uk/radio2/shows/vine (office).

VINEN, William Frank, PhD, FRS; British physicist and academic; *Professor Emeritus of Physics, University of Birmingham;* b. 15 Feb. 1930, England; s. of Gilbert Vinen and Olive Maud Vinen; ed Clare Coll., Cambridge; fmr Prof. of Physics, Univ. of Birmingham, now Prof. Emer.; mem. Academia Europaea (Physics, Astrophysics and Eng Section); Fellow, Pembroke Coll., Cambridge; The Simon Memorial Prize, Inst. of Physics (co-recipient) 1963, Holweck Medal and Prize, Inst. of Physics and the French Physical Soc. 1978, Rumford Medal, Royal Soc. 1980, Guthrie Medal and Prize, Inst. of Physics 2005. *Achievements include:* the observation and measurement of quantized vortices in superfluid helium, the first direct confirmation of the application of quantum mechanics to a macroscopic body. *Publications include:* numerous scientific papers in professional journals on superfluids and superconductors. *Address:* School of Physics and Astronomy, University of Birmingham, Birmingham, B15 2TT, England (office). *Telephone:* (121) 414-4667 (office). *E-mail:* w.f.vinen@bham.ac.uk (office). *Website:* www.ph.bham.ac.uk (office).

VINES, David Anthony, PhD; British/Australian economist and academic; *Fellow and Professor of Economics, University of Oxford;* b. 8 May 1949, Oxford, England; s. of Robert Vines and Vera Vines; m. 1st Susannah Lucy Robinson 1979 (divorced 1992); three s.; m. 2nd Jane E. Bingham 1995; two step-s.; ed Scotch Coll., Melbourne, Australia and Univs of Melbourne and Cambridge; Fellow, Pembroke Coll. Cambridge 1976–85; Research Officer, Sr Research Officer, Dept of Applied Econs, Univ. of Cambridge 1979–85; Adam Smith Prof. of Political Econ. Univ of Glasgow 1985–92; Fellow and Tutor in Econs Balliol Coll. Oxford 1992–, Prof. of Econs, Univ. of Oxford 2000–, also Dir Ethics and Econs, Inst. for New Econ. Thinking, Oxford Martin School, Acting Dir Political Economy of Financial Markets Programme, St Antony's Coll.; Adjunct Prof. of Econs, Inst. of Advanced Studies, ANU 1991–; Dir ESRC Research Programme on Global Econ. Insts 1993–2000; Research Dir Framework Seven PEGGED Research Programme on European Dimension of Political Economy of Global Governance 2008–12; mem. Bd Channel 4 TV 1986–92, Glasgow Devt Agency 1990–92, Analysis, Scottish Early Music Asscn 1988–95; econ. consultant to Sec. of State for Scotland 1988–92; consultant to IMF 1988, 1989; mem. Acad. Panel, HM Treasury 1986–; mem. Research Programmes Bd, ESRC 1990–92; mem. Int. Policy Forum, HM Treasury 1999–; Houblon Norman Fellow, Bank of England 2001–02; Academic Visitor, Reserve Bank of Australia 2006. *Publications include:* Stagflation, Vol. II: Demand Management (with J. E. Meade and J. M. Maciejowski) 1983, Macroeconomic Interactions Between North and South (with D. A. Currie) 1988, Macroeconomic Policy: inflation, wealth and the exchange rate (jtly) 1989, Deregulation and the Future of Commercial Television (with G. Hughes) 1989, Information, Strategy and Public Policy (with A. Stevenson) 1991, North South Macroeconomic Interactions and Global Macroeconomic Policy (co-ed. with D. A. Currie) 1995, Europe, East Asia and APEC: a Shared Global Agenda (with P. Drysdale) 1998, The Asian Financial Crisis: Causes Contagion and Consequences (co-ed. with P. Agenor, M. Miller and A. Weber) 1999, Integrity in the Public and Private Domains (ed. with A. Montefiore) 1999, The World Bank: Structure and Policies (co-ed. with C. L. Gilbert) 2000, The IMF and its Critics: Reform of Global Financial Architecture (co-ed. with C. L. Gilbert) 2004; numerous papers in professional journals. *Leisure interests:* hillwalking, music. *Address:* Balliol College, Oxford, OX1 3BJ, England (office). *Telephone:* (1865) 277719 (office). *E-mail:* david.vines@economics.ox.ac.uk (office). *Website:* www.economics.ox.ac.uk (office).

VINGT-TROIS, HE Cardinal André Armand; French ecclesiastic; *Archbishop Emeritus of Paris;* b. 7 Nov. 1942, Paris; ed Catholic Inst., Paris; ordained priest in Paris 1969; after five years in a parish, began teaching at Issy-les-Moulineaux seminary; Vicar Gen. of Paris Archdiocese and Dir of Vocations 1981–88; Auxiliary Bishop of Paris and Titular Bishop of Thibilis 1988–99; Archbishop of Tours 1999–2005, of Paris 2005–17, Archbishop Emer. of Paris 2017–; Ordinary of France and Faithful of Eastern Rites 2005–; cr. Cardinal (Cardinal-Priest of S. Luigi dei Francesi) 2007; mem. Congregation for Bishops and the Pontifical Council for the Family 2008–, Congregation for the Clergy 2010–, Congregation for the Oriental Churches 2012–; apptd by Pope Benedict XVI to serve as a Synod Father for the Ordinary Gen. Ass. of the Synod of Bishops on the New Evangelization 2012; participated in Papal Conclave 2013; apptd by Pope Francis as Pres. of the 3rd Extraordinary Gen. Ass. of the Synod of Bishops 2014; Ordre nat. du Mérite 2007, Grand Croix de l'Ordre nat. du Bénin 2010, Officier, Légion d'honneur 2012, Chevalier Grand Croix de l'Ordre Equestre du St Sépulcre 2012. *Publications include:* Évêques, prêtres et diacres (Bishops, Priests and Deacons)

2009, Médiaspaul, Une mission de liberté (A Mission for Liberty) 2010, Prier. Pourquoi? Comment? (Prayer. Why? How?) 2010, La Famille: un bonheur à construire (Family Life: Building Happiness) 2011, Parole et Silence, Quelle société voulons-nous? (What Kind of Society Do We Want?) 2012, Découvrir Jésus en lisant saint Marc (Discover Jesus by Reading St Mark) 2017. *Address:* Archdiocese of Paris, 10 rue du Cloître Notre-Dame, 75004 Paris, France (office). *Telephone:* 1-78-91-91-91 (office). *Fax:* 1-78-91-92-73 (office). *E-mail:* communication@diocese-paris.net (office). *Website:* paris.catholique.fr (office).

VINNICHENKO, Nikolai Alexandrovich; Russian lawyer and politician; b. 10 April 1965, Oktyabrskoye Village, Shemonaikha Dist, Kazakhstan SSR; Chief Prosecutor, St Petersburg 2003–04; Chief Bailiff and Dir Russian Federal Bailiffs Service 2004–08; Plenipotentiary Rep. of Russian Pres. to Urals Fed. Okrug (Dist) 2008–11, to North-Western Federal Okrug 2011–13; First Class Councillor in Justice.

VINOGRADOV, Oleg Mikhailovich; Russian/American ballet master; *Principal Guest Choreographer, Mikhailovsky Theatre;* b. 1 Aug. 1937, Leningrad; m. Yelena Vinogradova; ed Vaganov Choreographic School, Leningrad, Institut Gosudarstvenny Teatralnovo; danced with Novosibirsk Acad. Theatre, Ballet Master 1961–, also Dir Cinderella 1964, Romeo and Juliet 1965; ballet master, Kirov Ballet, Leningrad 1968–72; Artistic Dir and Chief Choreographer, Maly (now Mikhailovsky) Ballet Theatre Co. 1973–77, Prin. Guest Choreographer 2008–; Artistic Dir and Chief Ballet Master, Kirov (now Mariinsky) Ballet 1977–2003, now Artistic Dir Emer.; Artistic Dir Universal Ballet Acad., Washington, DC 1990, later Artistic Dir Universal Ballet Acad., Seoul 1998–2008, now Artistic Dir Emer.; currently Dean of Musical Theater Direction and Artistic Dir, St Petersburg Conservatory Ballet; also currently Artistic Dir, Dept of Choreography, St Petersburg Univ. of Humanities and Social Sciences; f. Oleg Vinogradov Foundation for Preservation and Devt of Classical Ballet 2013; apptd Artistic Dir, Int. Center for Choreography and Ballet Pedagogy, Classical Dance Alliance, New York; Hon. mem. Russian Fed. Acad. of Liberal Arts Aesthetics 2011; People's Artist of USSR 1983, 1987, Ordre de Chevalerie 1986; Distinguished Artist of Dagestan Repub. 1968, RSFSR State Prize for Kazhlaev's Goryanka 1970, Honored Artist of USSR 1976, 1983, Marius Petipa Prize, Paris 1978, Paris Acad. of Dance Prize for Best Modern Choreography 1981, American Express Canada Prize 1985, Parl. of Greece Award 1985, Pablo Picasso Prize 1986, Laurence Olivier Prize 1988, Prix Lumière 1989, Nijinsky Prize 1991. *Productions include:* Useless Precaution (Hérold) 1971, Coppélia 1973, Yaroslavna (B. Tishchenko) 1974, The Hussar's Ballad (Khrennikov), The Government Inspector, The Battleship Potemkin (A. Chaikovsky), Behests of the Past 1983 and numerous others. *Publication:* The Confessions of A Choreographer 2007. *Address:* Mikhailovsky Theatre, 191186 St Petersburg, Arts Square, 1, Russia (office). *Website:* www.mikhailovsky.ru (office).

VINOKOUROV, Alexandr; Kazakhstani cyclist (retd); b. 16 Sept. 1973, Pavlodar; s. of Nikolay Vinokourov and Raisa Vinokourova; m. 1997; three c.; started cycling at the age of 11, initially competed within fmr Soviet Union, undertook initial training at a sports school in Almaty 1986–91, also trained as part of Soviet Union nat. team, participated in Tour of Ecuador 1995, Tour of Slovenia 1996, Olympic Games, Atlanta 1996, moved to France 1997; silver medal, road race, Olympic Games, Sydney 2000; found guilty of blood-doping during Tour de France 2007, banned for one year, returned to cycling 2009; gold medal, time trial, silver medal, road race, Asian Cycling Championships 2009; gold medal, road race, Olympic Games, London 2012; winner Four Days of Dunkirk 1998, Tour de l'Oise, Tour de Picardie 1998, Circuit de Lorraine 1998, Critérium du Dauphiné 1999, Volta a la Comunitat Valenciana 1999, Deutschland Tour 2001, Paris-Nice 2002, 2003, Amstel Gold Race 2003, Tour de Suisse 2003, Regio-Tour 2004, Liège-Bastogne-Liège 2005, 2010, Nat. Road Race Championship 2005, Vuelta a Castilla y León 2006, Chrono des Nations 2009, Giro del Trentino 2010; teams: Casino-Ag2r 1998–99, Team Telekom 2000–05, Liberty Seguros-Würth 2006, Astana 2007; Gen. Man. UCI ProTeam Astana 2013–; unsuccessful cand. during parl. elections 2011; Hon. Col, Kazakh Army 2000; People's Hero First Class Medal. *Address:* Astana Pro Team, Abacanto SA, 48bd Grande Duchesse Charlotte, 1330, Luxembourg. *E-mail:* info@astana.lu. *Website:* astanaproteam.kz.

VIOT, Pierre, LèsL, LenD; French barrister; b. 9 April 1925, Bordeaux; s. of Edmund Viot and Irma Viot; m. Monique Fruchier 1952 (deceased); two s. two d.; ed Faculté de droit de Bordeaux, Inst. d'études politiques de Paris, Ecole Nat. d'Admin.; Jr Official, Cour des Comptes 1953, Chief Counsel; Asst, Bureau des Commissaires aux Comptes, NATO 1957–61; Regional and Urban Dept Head, Gen. Planning Office 1961; Spokesman, Nat. and Regional Devt Cttee 1961; Sec.-Gen., Conseil des Impôts 1971; Dir-Gen., Centre nat. de la Cinématographie 1973–84; Pres., Cannes Film Festival 1984–2000, Cinefondation Cannes Film Festival 2000–; Pres. Bd of Dirs, Etablissement public de l'Opéra de la Bastille 1985–89; Commdr, Légion d'honneur, Croix de guerre, Grand Croix, Ordre nat. du Mérite, Commdr Arts et Lettres, Commdr, Ordine al Merito della Repubblica Italiana, Officier, Verdienstorden der Bundesrepublik Deutschland. *Leisure interests:* tennis, gardening. *Address:* 38 avenue Emile Zola, 75015 Paris, France (home).

VIPHAVANH, Phankham, DPhil; Laotian university administrator, party official and politician; *Vice-President;* b. 1951; ed State Univ. of Ukraine, Moscow Univ., Russia; Math. Lecturer, Teacher Training School 1970–75; mem. Youth Cttee, Ministry of Educ. 1976–77, Dir of Political School, Ministry of Educ. 1983–85; Vice-Pres., Univ. of Pedagogy, Vientiane 1988, Pres. 1989–96; mem. Lao People's Revolutionary Party, Standing mem., Nat. Leading Cttee for Human Resource Devt 1997–98, 1998–2003, Vice-Chair. Party Central Cttee Org. Bd 1998–2003, Standing mem., Admin Reform Cttee 1998–2003, mem. Politburo 2011–; Vice-Minister of Prime Minister's Office, responsible for Admin and Civil Service 1998–2003, Chief of Cabinet, Prime Minister's Office 2003–05; Gov., Houaphan Prov. 2005–10; Minister of Educ. 2010–11, of Educ. and Sports 2011–16; Vice-Pres. of Laos 2016–. *Address:* Office of the Vice-President, ave Lane Xang, Vientiane, Laos (office). *Telephone:* (21) 214200 (office). *Fax:* (21) 214208 (office).

VIRANT, Gregor; Slovenian lawyer, politician and public servant; b. 4 Dec. 1969, Ljubljana; m.; two s.; ed Univ. of Ljubljana, Glasgow Caledonian Univ., UK; worked as legal adviser to Constitutional Court of Slovenia 1995–99; Sec.-Gen., Ministry of the Interior 2000–04, one of the authors of the reform of public admin; cand. for Državni zbor (Nat. Ass.) on list of Slovenian Democratic Party (though never joined) 2004; Head of newly created Ministry of Public Admin 2004–08; Chair. Rally for the Republic (Zbor za republiko) 2008–11; mem. Council of Experts, Slovenian Democratic Party 2009–11; Leader of Gregor Virant's Civic List (renamed Civic List April 2012) 2011–14; elected to Nat. Ass. as an ind. 2011, Chair. 2011–13; Deputy Prime Minister and Minister of the Interior 2013–14. *Address:* Državljanska lista (Civic List), 1000 Ljubljana, Ukinarjeva 2, Slovenia (office). *Telephone:* (5) 1352467 (office). *E-mail:* info@d-l.si (office). *Website:* www.d-l.si (office).

VIRATA, Cesar Enrique, BS (MechEng), MBA; Philippine politician and banker; *Chairman and President, C. Virata & Associates Inc.;* b. 12 Dec. 1930, Manila; s. of Enrique Virata and Leonor Aguinaldo; m. Joy Gamboa 1956; two s. one d.; ed Univ. of Pennsylvania, USA and Univ. of the Philippines; Dean, Coll. of Business Admin., Univ. of the Philippines 1961–69; Chair. and Dir Philippine Nat. Bank 1967–69; Deputy Dir-Gen. Presidential Econ. Staff 1967–68; Under-Sec. of Industry 1967–69; Chair. Bd of Investments 1968–70; Minister of Finance 1970–86, Chair. IMF and IBRD Devt Cttee 1976–80; mem. Nat. Ass. 1978–86, Prime Minister of the Philippines 1981–86; Chair. Land Bank of the Philippines 1973–86; mem. Monetary Bd, Nat. Econ. and Devt Authority 1972–86, Comm. on the Future of the Bretton Woods Insts 1992; Adviser to Co-ordinating Council for the Philippines Aid Plan 1989–90; Chair. and Pres. C. Virata & Assocs Inc. (Man. Consultants) 1986–; Dir Philippine Stock Exchange, Inc. 1992; Consultant, Advisory Bd, Rizal Commercial Banking Corpn 1986–95, apptd Corp. Vice-Chair. 1999–, Sr Adviser, RCBC Savings Bank, Inc. 2007–; mem. Bd of Dirs Pacific Fund 1999–, YGC Corp. Services, Inc. 2001–, Malayan Insurance Co., Inc. 2005–; Trustee, Malayan Colleges, Inc.; Hon. LHD, Hon. DPA, Dr hc (Philippines). *Leisure interests:* tennis, reading. *Address:* C. Virata & Associates Inc., Development Academy of the Philippines Building, San Miguel Avenue, Pasig City, Metro Manila 1600 (office); Rizal Commercial Banking Corporation, Yuchengco Tower, RCBC Plaza, 6819 Ayala Avenue, Makati City 0727 (office); 63 East Maya Drive, Quezon City, Philippines (home). *Telephone:* (2) 631-2161 (office); (2) 844-8889 (office). *Fax:* (2) 631-2161 (office); (2) 878-3400 (office). *E-mail:* cvirata@pacific.net.ph (office); ceavirata@rcbc.com (office). *Website:* www.rcbc.com (office).

VIREN, Lasse; Finnish politician and fmr athlete; b. 22 July 1949, Myrskylä; m. Päivi Kajander 1976; three s.; competed in Olympic Games, Munich 1972, won gold medal at 5,000m and 10,000m; Montréal 1976, won gold medal at 5,000m and 10,000m, 5th in marathon; Moscow 1980, 5th in 10,000m; only athlete to retain 5,000m and 10,000m titles at successive Olympics; held world records at two miles, 5,000m and 10,000m; sports promoter in schools at the Union Bank of Finland; elected pres. of his local town council while running own transport business; mem. of Parl. (Conservative Party) 1999–2007, 2010–11; Track & Field Athlete of the Year 1972, inducted into Int. Assn of Athletics Fed. Hall of Fame 2014. *Publication:* The Golden Seconds. *Address:* Suomen Urheilulitto ry, Box 25202, 00250, Helsinki 25, Finland.

VIRSALADZE, Elisso Konstantinovna; Georgian pianist; b. 14 Sept. 1942, Tbilisi; ed studied under grandmother, Prof. Anastasia Virsaladze, then at Tbilisi Conservatory; began piano lessons aged eight; teacher, Moscow Conservatory 1962, apptd Full Prof. 1994; Prof., Musikhochschule, Munich; regular tours as piano soloist across Europe, USA, South America, Japan and Australia; f. Telavi Music Festival, Georgia; regularly serves as juror at int. piano competitions including Telekom Competition, Bonn 2015, Queen Elisabeth Competition, Brussels 2016, Sendai Int. Music Competition 2016, BNDS Int. Piano Competition, Rio de Janeiro 2016; First Prize, All-Union Competition of Performing Musicians, Moscow 1961, Bronze Medal, Tchaikovsky Competition 1962, Prize at Schumann Competition, Georgian State Prize 1983, People's Artist of the USSR 1989, Order of Merit 2007, Order of Honour 2013. *Recordings include:* Schumann Second Sonata 1973, Schumann First Sonata 1980, Brahms: String Quartet No. 2; Piano Quintet 1995, Elisso plays Mozart & Prokoviev 1996, Schubert: Wanderer-Fantasie/Impromptus 1997, Chopin: Etudes 1998, Schumann: Piano Sonata 1 & 2; Waldszenen 2000, Mozart: Chamber Music, Vol. 1 2003, Mozart: Concertos for 2 & 3 Pianos 2005, Elisso Virsaladze Live 2011. *Telephone:* (89) 26024335 (office). *Fax:* (89) 26024344 (office). *E-mail:* hahn@augstein.info (office). *Website:* www.augstein.info (office).

VIRZÌ, Paolo; Italian screenwriter, director and producer; b. 4 March 1964, Livorno, Tuscany; m. Micaela Ramazzotti; ed Univ. of Pisa, studied at Centro sperimentale di cinematografia, Rome under Gianni Amelio and Furio Scarpelli; formed artistic asscn with fmr fellow student Francesco Bruni that became important in later years; later, Furio Scarpelli became his teacher and mentor; f. Motorino Amaranto s.r.l. production house 2007. *Films:* Turnè (writer) 1990, Condominio (Condominium) (story; writer) 1991, Tempo di uccidere (Time to Kill; aka The Short Cut) (writer) 1991, Donne sottotetto (aka Centro storico) (writer) 1992, La bella vita (Living It Up) (writer and dir) (Ciak d'Oro, Nastro d'Argento and David di Donatello Award for Best New Dir 1995, Silver Ribbon for Best New Dir, Italian Nat. Syndicate of Film Journalists 1995) 1994, Ferie d'agosto (story, screenplay) (David di Donatello for Best Film of the Year 1996) 1995, Intolerance (dir segment Roma Ovest 143) 1996, Ferie d'agosto (dir) 1996, Cuba libre – velocipedi ai tropici (writer) 1997, Ovosodo (Hardboiled Egg) (story, screenplay and dir) (Grand Special Jury Prize and Little Golden Lion, Venice Film Festival 1997, Youth Audience Award, Montpellier Mediterranean Film Festival 1997) 1997, Baci e abbracci (Kisses and Hugs) (dir) 1999, Provino d'ammissione (writer and dir) 1999, My Name is Tanino (writer and dir) 2002, Caterina va in città (Caterina in the Big City) (writer, dir and co-producer) (Future Film Festival Digital Award – Special Mention, Venice Film Festival 2002) 2002, 4-4-2 – Il gioco più bello del mondo (all segments) 2006, L'estate del mio primo bacio (writer) 2006, N (Io e Napoleone) (Napoleon and Me) (screenplay and dir) 2006, Il caimano (The Caiman) (actor) 2006, Tutta la vita davanti (writer, dir and producer) (Golden Globe Award for Best Picture 2008) 2008, The First Beautiful Thing (story, screenplay, producer and dir) (David di Donatello for Best Picture and Best Screenplay 2010, Silver Ribbon for Best Film and Best Screenplay 2010) 2010, Every Blessed Day (screenplay, dir) 2012, Human Capital (screenplay, dir) (David di Donatello for Best Screenplay 2014, Silver Ribbon for Best Film and Best Screenplay 2014) 2013, La pazza gioia (dir) 2016. *Television:* Une questione privata (A Private Affair) (writer) 1991. *Address:* Motorino Amaranto s.r.l., Via della Moletta 35, 00154 Rome, Italy (office). *Telephone:* (06) 5747488 (office). *E-mail:* info@motorinoamaranto.it (office). *Website:* motorinoamaranto.proret.biz (office).

VISCHER, Ulrich, lic. iur., Dr. iur., PhD; Swiss lawyer and university administrator; *President of the University Council, University of Basel;* b. 1951; m.; two s.; ed Univ. of Basel; began career with Basler Volkswirtschaftsbund (Basel Econ. Fed.); with Schweizerischer Bankverein (Swiss Bank Corpn) 1977–78; worked with Baloise Insurance Co. 1979–92; mem. Basel City Parl. 1980–92 (Pres. 1989); Councillor, Canton Basel-Stadt and Minister of Finance 1992–2005; Partner, Vischer & Assocs (law firm), Basel 2005–; Pres. Univ. Council, Univ. of Basel 2005–; Chair. MCH Messe Schweiz Holding AG 2009–; mem. Bd of Dirs BioMedPartners AG, Warteck Invest AG 2007–; mem. Soc. of Trust and Estate Practitioners, Basel, Int. Bar Asscn. *Address:* Office of the President, University of Basel, Leimenstrasse 1, 4001 Basel (office); Vischer, Aeschenvorstadt 4, Postfach 526, 4010 Basel, Switzerland (office). *Telephone:* (61) 267-84-05 (office); (58) 211-33-34 (Vischer) (office). *Fax:* (61) 267-84-34 (office); (58) 211-33-10 (Vischer) (office). *E-mail:* uvischer@vischer.com (office). *Website:* www.vischer.com (office).

VISCO, Ignazio, MA, PhD; Italian economist and central banker; *Governor, Banca d'Italia;* b. 21 Nov. 1949, Naples; m.; three d.; ed La Sapienza Univ., Rome, Univ. of Pennsylvania, USA; Lecturer in Econometrics, La Sapienza Univ., Rome 1983–85, in Econ. Policy 1989; joined Research Dept, Banca d'Italia 1974, Head of Dept 1990, Deputy Dir-Gen. 2007–11, Gov. 2011–; Chief Economist and Dir Dept of Econs, OECD 1997–2002; Pres. European System of Central Banks Int. Relations Cttee 2009–10; Chair. Inst. for the Supervision of Insurance (IVASS) 2013–; Assoc. Ed. European Economic Review 1986–91; mem. Società Italiana degli Economisti, Società Italiana di Statistica, American Econ. Asscn; Cavaliere, Ordine al merito della Repubblica italiana 1991, Ufficiale 1993, Commendatore 2002, Grande Ufficiale 2007, Cavaliere di Gran Croce al merito 2011. *Publications include:* Le aspettative nell'analisi economica 1985, Inflazione, concorrenza e sviluppo (with S. Micossi) 1993, Saving and the Accumulation of Wealth (with A. Ando and L. Guiso) 1994, L'economia italiana (with L. F. Signorini) 2002, Investire in conoscenza 2014, Perche' i tempi stanno cambiando 2015. *Address:* Banca d'Italia, Via Nazionale 91, 00184 Rome, Italy (office). *Telephone:* (06) 47921 (office). *E-mail:* email@bancaditalia.it (office). *Website:* www.bancaditalia.it/bancaditalia/direttorio/visco (office).

VISHNEVA, Diana Viktorovna; Russian ballerina; *Principal Dancer, Mariinsky Theatre;* b. 13 July 1976, Leningrad; d. of Victor Vishnev and Guzel Vishneva; m. Konstantin Selinevich 2013; one s.; ed Vaganova Acad. of Russian Ballet; with Mariinsky Theatre 1995–, Prin. Dancer 1996–; Guest Artist, Teatro alla Scala, Milan 2001, Staatsoper Unter den Linden, Berlin 2002–, Grand d'Opera 2002; Dancer, American Ballet Theatre 2003–05, Prin. Dancer 2005–17; became the face of Discipline by Kérastase 2008; f. Diana Vishneva Foundation for the Development of Ballet 2010; f. Context (dance festival) 2013; guest appearances with various ballet companies including American Ballet Theatre, Bolshoi Ballet, Paris Opera Ballet, Teatro alla Scala; Hon. mem. Bd of Dirs Russian Children Welfare Society 2008; Prix de Lausanne 1994, Divine Isadora Prize, Benois de la danse prize 1995, Golden Sophit St Petersburg Theatre Prize 1996, State Prize of Russia, Baltika Prize 1998, Golden Mask 2001, Dance of Europe Prize 2002, Ballet Magazine Prize 2003, People's Artist of Russia 2007, Golden Mask Prize for Best Female Role 2009, 2013, Modern Dance/Female Role 2009, Critics Prize for Diana Vishneva:Beauty in Motion 2009, Best Ballet for Diana Vishneva: Dialogues 2013. *Main roles include:* Masha (Nutcracker), Kitri (Don Quixote), Aurore (Sleeping Beauty), Henriette and Raymonda (Raymonda), Gulnary (Corsare), Giselle (Giselle), Nikia (La Bayadere), Odette/Odile (Swan Lake), Juliet (Romeo and Juliet), Manon (Manon), Carmen (Carmen), Rubies (Jewels), Titania, Sylvia (Thais pas de Deux), Peri (Le Peri), Marguerite (Lady of the Camellias), Frikke, Brungilda (The Ring), Olga (On the Dnieper). *Address:* c/o Diana Vishneva Foundation, 190068 St Petersburg, POB 155; Mariinsky Theatre, 190000 St Petersburg, Teatralnaya pl. 1, Russia (office). *Telephone:* (812) 326-4141 (office); (812) 303-0607 (home). *Fax:* (812) 314-1744 (office); (812) 570-2331 (office). *E-mail:* info@dianavishneva.com (office). *Website:* www.dianavishneva.com.

VIŠKOVIĆ, Radovan, PhD; Bosnia and Herzegovina engineer and politician; *Prime Minister of Republika Srpska;* b. 1 Feb. 1964, Milici; m.; two c.; ed Univ. of Sarajevo; Asst Lecturer, Faculty of Traffic Eng, Univ. of Sarajevo 1990; Exec. Dir of Traffic Unit, Boksit a.d. (industrial co.), Milici 1966; Asst Prof., Faculty of Traffic Eng, Univ. of East Sarajevo, Doboj 2015; began political career as councillor, Municipal Ass. of Milici 2004; mem. People's Ass. of Republika Srpska 2006–18, Head of SNSD Caucus 2014–18; Prime Minister of Republika Srpska 2018–; mem. Savez Nezavisnih Socijaldemokratska (SNSD—Alliance of Ind. Social Democrats), currently Vice-Pres. *Address:* Office of the Prime Minister, 78000 Banja Luka, trg Republike Srpske 1, Bosnia and Herzegovina (office). *Telephone:* (51) 339103 (office). *Fax:* (51) 339119 (home). *E-mail:* kabinet@vladars.net (office). *Website:* www.vladars.net (office).

VISHWANATHAN, Anand, BComm; Indian chess player; b. 11 Dec. 1969, Chennai, Tamil Nadu; s. of K. Viswanathan and Susila Viswanathan; m. Aruna Anand; ed Loyola Coll., Chennai; winner of 72 int. chess tournaments; Nat. Sub-Jr Chess Champion 1983; Int. Master (aged 15) 1984; Indian Nat. Champion 1985; first Indian Int. Grandmaster 1987; World Jr Champion 1987; beat fmr world champions Mikhail Tal and Boris Spassky at Fourth Int. Games Festival 1989; Asian Champion 1990; captained Indian team at Chess Olympiad, Manila 1992; placed second in PCA ranking 1995; World Chess Champion 2000; FIDE World Cup Champion 2002, 2007, 2008; Jameo de Oro, Govt of Spain 2001, Russian Order of Friendship 2014; Dr hc (Jawaharlal Nehru Technological Univ., Hyderabad) 1988; Arjuna Award 1985, Padma Shri 1987, Soviet Land Nehru Award 1987, Nat. Citizens' Award 1987, Shri Rajiv Gandhi Award 1988, Rajiv Gandhi Khel Ratna Award 1991–92, K Birla Award 1995, Sportstar Millenium Award 1998, Oscar Best Chess Player 1997, 1998, 2003, 2004, 2007, Padma Bhushan 2000, CNN IBN Sportsperson of the Year 2007, Padma Vibhushan 2007, NDTV Indian Sportsperson of the Year 2008, 2012, Hridaynath Award 2016. *Publication:* My Best Games of Chess (Book of the Year Award, British Chess Fed. 1998). *Leisure interests:* reading, swimming, listening to music. *Address:* 7 (old No. 4) II Cross Street, Customs Colony, Besant Nagar, Chennai 600 090, India (home).

VITA, Giuseppe, DrMed; Italian business executive; *Chairman, UniCredit Group;* b. 28 April 1935, Favara, Agrigento, Sicily; m.; two c.; ed in Catania and at Univ. La Sapienza, Rome and Univ. of Rome; qualified as specialist in radiology; Asst Röntgeninstitut, Univ. of Mainz 1962; joined Schering AG as asst in clinical research 1964, Gen. Dir Schering SpA Milan 1965, Deputy mem. Man. Bd Schering AG 1987, mem. 1988, Chair. 1989–2001, Chair. Supervisory Bd 2001–06; Chair. Deutsche Bank SpA 1998–2002, Hon. Chair. 2002–; Chair. Supervisory Bd Hugo Boss AG 2000–08, Axel Springer AG 2002–, Deutz (Germany) 2006–09; Chair. RAS (Italy) 2001–06; Chair. UniCredit Group 2012–; Chair. Allianz SpA 2007–09, 2011–12, Vice-Pres. 2009–11; Chair. Gruppo Banca Leonardo 2007–12; mem. Supervisory Cttee Vattenfall Europe 1990–2008, Continental 1991–2002, Allianz Versicherung 1996–2003, Allianz Lebensvericherung (Assicurazione Vita) 1997–2004, Degussa 2000–04, Medical Park AG 2001–12, Dussmann Stiftung (Germany) 2006–12; mem. Bd of Dirs Marzotto di Agenzia Nazionale per Attrazione Investimenti e Sviluppo d'Impresa 1995–98, Marzotto (Italy) 2003–05, Barilla SpA 2005–12, Humanitas Istituto Clinico 2003–12, Istituto Europeo di Oncologia 2007–12, Fondazione IEO (Italy) 2007–12, Fondazione Cerba (Italy) 2007–12, Fondazione Feltrinelli (Italy) 2007–12, Consiglio per le relazioni fra Italia e Stati Uniti (Italy) 2007–12, Pirelli & C. (Italy) March–May 2012, RCS MediaGroup SpA 2012–13, ABI (Italian Banking Asscn) 2012–, Associazione Italiana per la Ricerca sul Cancro 2012–14; mem. Advisory Bd Lazard (Italy) 2002–06; Advisor to Bd Dirs Ikonisys 2004–; mem. Gen. Council Institue Italia 2012–, Trilateral Comm. (Italian Group) 2012–; mem. Exec. Cttee Istituto per gli Studi di Politica Internazionale 2013–; Cavaliere del Lavoro, Verdienstorden des Landes Berlin, Verdienstkreuz am Bande des Verdienstordens der Bundesrepublik Deutschland. *Address:* UniCredit Group, Piazza Cordusia, 20123 Milan, Italy (office). *Telephone:* (02) 88621 (office). *Fax:* (02) 88628503 (office). *E-mail:* info@unicreditgroup.eu (office). *Website:* www.unicreditgroup.eu (office).

VITAL, Brig. Gen. Albert Camille; Malagasy civil engineer, army officer and politician; b. 18 July 1952, Toliara; m.; five c.; ed École Spéciale Militaire de Saint-Cyr, France, Ecole Supérieure Militaire, Paris; Chief of Tech. Office, State Forces Staff Devt 1987–91, Instructor, Army Staff Coll. 1993–96, Corps Commdr, 1st Regt, Mil. Region No. 5, Toliara 1998–2001; Prime Minister of Madagascar 2009–11 (resgnd), also Minister of the Armed Forces 2010; apptd Perm. Rep. to UN Office at Geneva 2012; unsuccessful cand. for Mayor of Toliara; f. Toliara (security firm); fmr Pres. Toliara Chamber of Commerce and Industry.

VITERBI, Andrew J., BS, MS, PhD, FIEEE; American (b. Italian) telecommunications engineer, business executive and academic; *Presidential Chair and Professor of Electrical Engineering, University of Southern California;* b. 9 March 1935, Bergamo, Italy; m. Erna Viterbi; two s. one d.; ed Massachusetts Inst. of Tech., Univ. of Southern California; family moved to USA in 1939; began career at Jet Propulsion Lab., Calif. Inst. of Tech. 1968; Prof., School of Eng and Applied Science, UCLA 1963–73; Adjunct Prof. of Electrical Eng and Computer Science, Univ. of California, San Diego 1975, now Prof. Emer.; currently Presidential Chair. and Prof. of Electrical Eng, Andrew and Erna Viterbi School of Eng, Univ. of Southern California, Los Angeles; Co-founder Linkabit Corpn, Exec. Vice-Pres. 1974–82, Pres. M/A-COM Linkabit, Inc. 1982–; Co-founder Qualcomm, Inc. 1985, Vice-Chair. and Chief Tech. Officer –2000; currently Pres. The Viterbi Group, LLC (advises and invests in startup cos in communication, network and imaging technologies); fmr Chair. US Commission C, Int. Radio Scientific Union (URSI), Visiting Cttee, Electrical Eng Dept, Technion, Israel Inst. of Tech.; apptd mem. Presidential Advisory Cttee on Information Tech. 1997–2001; mem. MIT Corpn Visiting Cttee for Electrical Eng and Computer Science; fmr mem. Army Science Bd; fmr mem. or Chair. Bd Govs IEEE Information Theory Group (Transactions Assoc. Ed. for Coding); mem. Nat. Acad. of Eng 1978, NAS 1996, American Acad. of Arts and Sciences 2001; fmr Chair. NAS Computer and Information Sciences Section; developed Viterbi Algorithm, used in wide-ranging applications including mobile phones, DNA analysis and speech recognition; Grande Ufficiale della Repubblica (Italy) 2001; Dr hc (Waterloo, Rome, Technion, Notre Dame); IEEE Information Theory Group Outstanding Paper Award 1968, Christopher Columbus Int. Award, Italian Nat. Research Council 1975, AIAA Aerospace Communications Award (co-recipient) 1980, IEEE Alexander Graham Bell Medal 1984, Marconi Int. Fellowship Award 1990, Claude Shannon Award 1990, Benjamin Franklin Medal in Electrical Eng 2005, James Clerk Maxwell Medal, IEEE and Royal Soc. of Edinburgh (co-recipient) 2007, Robert Noyes Award, Semiconductor Industry Asscn (co-recipient) 2007, Nat. Medal of Science 2007, IEEE Medal of Honor 2010, John Fritz Medal, American Asscn of Engineering Socs 2011, Charles Stark Draper Prize for Eng 2016. *Publications include:* Principles of Coherent Communication 1966, Principles of Digital Communication and Coding (co-author) 1979, CDMA: Principles of Spread Spectrum Communication 1995; numerous scientific papers in professional journals. *Address:* Andrew and Erna Viterbi School of Engineering, University of Southern California, 3650 McClintock Avenue, Los Angeles, CA 90089, USA (office). *Telephone:* (213) 740-4750 (office). *E-mail:* viterbi.communications@usc.edu (office). *Website:* viterbi.usc.edu (office).

VITORGAN, Emmanuil; Russian actor and director; b. 27 Dec. 1939, Baku, Azerbaijan; m. 1st Tamara Rumyantseva; one d.; m. 2nd Alla Balter (deceased); one s.; m. 3rd Irina Mlodek-Vitorgan; ed Leningrad State Inst. of Theatre Arts; with Leningrad Theatre of Drama and Comedy 1961–63, Leningrad Theatre of Leninsky Komsomol 1964–71, Moscow Stanislavsky Drama Theatre 1971–82, Moscow Taganka Theatre 1982–84, Moscow Academic Mayakovsky Theatre 1984–; f. Vitorgan Foundation 2003–; Merited Artist of Russia 1990, People's Artist of Russia 1998. *Films include:* King Lear 1972, And This is All About Him 1974, Fortress 1978, Two People in a New House 1979, Profession – Investigator 1982, Devout Marta 1983, The Grown-up Daughter of a Young Man 1990, When Saints are Marching 1990, The Scam 2001, Lady in Spectacles with a Gun in a Car 2002, Tyazhyolyy pesok 2008, Black Rose 2014, Startap 2014, Yolki 1914 2014, Pyatnitsa 2016. *Plays include:* Westside Story, Humiliated and Insulted, Rain Seller, Shadows, Grown-Up Daughter of a Young Man, Sirano de Berjerac, Circle, The Doll's House. *Address:* Moscow Academic Mayakovsky Theatre, Bolshaya Nikitskaya str. 19/13, 103009 Moscow (office); Maly Kislovsky per.7, apt 26, 103009 Moscow, Russia (home). *Telephone:* (495) 290-30-31 (office); (495) 291-89-89 (office). *Website:* www.mayakovsky.ru (office); www.vitorgan.ru.

VITORINO, António, LLM; Portuguese lawyer and politician; *Associate, Cuatrecasas, Gonçalves Pereira & Associados;* b. 12 Jan. 1957, Lisbon; m.; two c.; ed Univ. of Lisbon; Prof., Univ. of Lisbon 1982–2008; mem. Parl. (Partido Socialista) 1980–2006; Sec. of State for Parl. Affairs 1984–85, for Admin and Justice of Macao Govt 1986–87; Judge, Portuguese Constitutional Court 1989–94; elected MEP 1994; Minister for Defence and the Presidency 1995–97; Vice-Pres. Portugal Telecom Internacional 1998–99; EU Commr for Freedom, Security and Justice 1999–2004; Assoc., Cuatrecasas, Gonçalves Pereira & Associados (law firm) 2005–; Pres., Gen. Ass., Banco Santander Totta 2005–; Pres. Notre Europe - Institut Jacques Delors (think-tank), Paris 2011–16; Chair. Res Publica Foundation; Co-Chair. Foreign Policy Scorecard, European Council on Foreign Relations; Chair. Governing Bd European Policy Centre 2005–09; Visiting Prof., Law Faculty, Universidade Nova de Lisboa 2008–10; mem. Transatlantic Council on Migrations, European Group of Trilateral Comm.; Hon. Co-Chair. World Justice Project. *Address:* Cuatrecasas, Gonçalves Pereira & Associados, Praça Marquês de Pombal, 2, 1250-160 Lisbon, Portugal (office). *E-mail:* cuatrecasasportugal@cuatrecasas.com (office). *Website:* www.cuatrecasas.com (office).

VITRENKO, Natalia Mikhailovna, DEcon; Ukrainian politician; b. 28 Dec. 1951, Kiev; m.; one s. two d.; ed Kiev State Inst. of Nat. Econs; Sr Economist Cen. Dept of Statistics 1973–76; Sr Researcher Research Inst. of Information, State Planning Comm. 1979–89; Docent Kiev Inst. of Nat. Econs 1979–89; Sr Researcher Council on Production Forces, Ukrainian Acad. of Sciences 1989–94; presidential cand. 1994, 2004; People's Deputy 1994–2002; Counsellor on Socio-econ. Problems, Verkhovna Rada; mem. Socialist Party of Ukraine 1991; mem. Progressive Socialist Party of Ukraine (Prohresyvna Sotsialistychna Partiya Ukrainy) 1996–, fmr Chair.; mem. Presidium of Political Council 1993–, Acad. of Construction, Acad. of Econ. Cybernetics 1997, Int. Acad. of Social Technologies (Russian Fed.); Corresp. mem. Peter's Acad. of Arts and Sciences (Russian Fed.); Chair. 'Gift of Life' (public women's org.) 2000–, Cathedral Orthodox Women in Ukraine 2010–, Eurasian People's Union 2011–. *Leisure interests:* fishing, camping. *Address:* Progressive Socialist Party of Ukraine (Prohresyvna Sotsialistychna Partiya Ukrainy), 01011 Kyiv, vul. P. Miroho 27/51 (office); Podgornaya/Tatarskaya str., 3/7, 98 office, 04107 Kyiv, Ukraine (office). *Telephone:* (44) 483-32-57 (office). *Fax:* (44) 483-32-57 (office). *E-mail:* n-vitrenko@yandex.ru (office). *Website:* www.vitrenko.org (office).

VITRYANSKY, Vassily Vladimirovich, DJur; Russian lawyer, academic and judge; *Deputy Chairman, Supreme Arbitration Court of the Russian Federation;* b. 8 May 1956, Gomel, Belarus; m.; one s. two d.; ed Moscow State Univ.; mem. staff, RSFSR State Court of Arbitration 1978–86; Sr Asst Admin. RSFSR Council of Ministers 1986–89, consultant, Dept of Law 1989–90; Deputy Chief State Arbiter of RSFSR 1990–92; Deputy Chair. Supreme Arbitration Court of Russian Fed. 1992–; teacher, Moscow State Univ., participated in devt of civil law in Russian Fed. *Publications include:* Protection of Property Rights of Businessmen, Protection of Property Rights of Stock Companies and Shareholders, Law and Bankruptcy; numerous publications on protection of civil rights, civil and legal responsibility, bankruptcy. *Address:* Supreme Arbitration Court, 111001 Moscow, M. Kharitonevskii per. 12, Russia (office). *Telephone:* (495) 608-11-97 (office). *Fax:* (495) 208-11-62 (office). *E-mail:* vasrf@arbitr.ru (office). *Website:* www.arbitr.ru (office).

VITTER, David, BA, LLB; American lawyer and politician; m. Wendy Vitter; four c.; ed Tulane Univ, Univ of Oxford, UK, Harvard Univ; mem. Louisiana State House of Reps 1992–99, concurrently Adjunct Law Prof., Tulane and Loyola Univs and pvt. business attorney; mem. US House of Reps, Washington, DC 1999–2004, served on House Appropriations Cttee, House Republican Policy Cttee; Senator from Louisiana 2005–17, mem. Cttee on Environment and Public Works, Cttee on Banking, Housing and Urban Affairs, Cttee on Armed Services, Cttee on Small Business and Entrepreneurship; Republican; Alliance for Good Govt Legislator of the Year, Victims and Citizens Against Crime Outstanding Legislator Award and Lifetime Achievement Award. *Website:* www.davidvitter.com.

VIVANCO CASAMADRID, Antonio, BA (Econs), MBA, MPP; Mexican government official and business executive; m. Rojas Jiménez; ed Instituto Tecnológico Autónomo de México, Harvard Univ., USA; worked in Finance and Public Credit Ministry (Hacienda) and Fed. Mortgage Soc. (SHF); Tech. Sec., Social Cabinet 2006–07, Tech. Sec., Office of Infrastructure 2007–08, Chief of Staff, Office of Pres. Felipe Calderón 2008–11; Asst Dir-Gen. Comisión Fed. de Electricidad Feb.–March 2011, Dir-Gen. 2011–12.

VIVAS LARA, Juan Jesús, BEcons; Spanish politician; *Mayor-President of Ceuta;* b. 27 Feb. 1953, Ceuta; s. of Juan Vivas and Isabel Lara; m. Lola Puya 1978; two c.; ed Univ. of Málaga; elected deputy in Ass. (Popular Party of Ceuta) 1999; Tech. Head Govt Delegate in Ceuta 1999; Sec.-Gen. Ministry of Economy, Industry and Competitiveness 1999; Mayor-Pres. of Ceuta 2001–; Prof. Universidad Nacional de Educación a Distancia. *Leisure interests:* listening to Serrat and Spanish music, soccer. *Telephone:* (956) 528222 (office). *E-mail:* consejeriapresidencia@ceuta.es (office). *Website:* www.ceuta.es (office).

VIVES, Xavier, MA, PhD; Spanish economist and academic; *Professor of Economics and Finance, IESE Business School;* b. 23 Jan. 1955, Barcelona; m. Aurora Bastida; two s.; ed Autonomous Univ. of Barcelona, Univ. of California, Berkeley, USA; Sr Researcher, Fundación de Estudios de Economía Aplicada (FEDEA); Programme Dir Applied Microeconomics and Industrial Org. Programmes, Centre for Econ. Policy Research, London; Prof. and Vice-Dir Institut d'Analisi Económica, Barcelona 1990–91, Dir 1991–2001; Prof. of Econs and Finance, Institut Européen d'Admin des Affaires (INSEAD) 2001–05; Research Prof., ICREA-UPF 2004–05; currently Prof. of Econs and Finance, IESE Business School, also Abertis Chair of Regulation, Competition and Public Policy and Academic Dir Public-Private Research Center; also Adjunct Prof., Universitat Pompeu Fabra; Special Advisor to Vice-Pres. EC and Commr for Competition Joaquín Almunia 2011–14; Visiting Prof., Harvard Univ. 1997–98, Univ. of Pa 1994, Univ. of Calif., Berkeley 1984; King Juan Carlos I of Spain Chair of Spanish Culture and Civilization, New York Univ. 1999; Co-Ed. Journal of Economics and Management Strategy 1992–; Ed. Journal of Economic Theory 2013–; Fellow, Econometric Soc. 1992, mem. Council 2006–08; Pres. Spanish Economic Asscn 2008, Hon. Mem. 2010; Pres.-Elect, European Asscn for Research in Industrial Econs 2015; mem. Advisory Bd for Economic Recovery, Govt of Catalonia 2011–15; mem. European Acad. of Sciences and Arts 2002–; columnist, La Vanguardia; Premio Extraordinario de Licenciatura, Autonomous Univ. of Barcelona 1978, King Juan Carlos I Prize for Research in Social Science 1988, Societat Catalana d'Economía Prize 1996, Premi Catalunya d'Economia 2005, Premio Rey Jaime I de Economía 2013, ECB Wim Duisenberg Fellowship 2015. *Publications include:* Monitoring European Integration: The Future of European Banking (co-author) 1999, Oligopoly Pricing: Old Ideas and New Tools 2000, Corporate Governance: Theoretical and Empirical Perspectives (ed.) 2000, Politicas Publicas y Equilibrio Territorial en el Stado Autonomico. *Address:* IESE Business School, Barcelona Campus, Avenida Pearson, 21, 08034 Barcelona, Spain (office). *Telephone:* (93) 2534200 (office). *Website:* www.iese.edu (office).

VIVES SICÍLIA, Mgr Joan-Enric, PhD; Spanish/Andorran ecclesiastic; *Archbishop of Urgell and Episcopal Co-Prince of Andorra;* b. 24 July 1949, Barcelona, Spain; s. of Francesc Vives Pons and Cornèlia Sicília Ibáñez; ed Escola 'Pere Vila', Institut 'Jaume Balmes', Barcelona, Conciliary Seminary of Barcelona, Faculty of Theology of Barcelona, Univ. of Barcelona; ordained priest 1974; apptd Prof. of Catalan, Univ. of Barcelona; apptd Prof. of Theology and Philosophy, Univ. 'Ramon Llull' and Faculty of Theology of Catalonia 1979; Auxiliary Bishop of Barcelona and Titular Bishop of Nona 1993–2001; Co-Adjutor Bishop of Urgell 2001–03; Bishop of Urgell and Episcopal Co-Prince of Andorra 2003–, Archbishop *ad personam* 2010–; Order of Cross of Christ (Portugal) 2010; Medal of Honour of the City of Barcelona 1999. *Address:* Pati Palau 1–5, 25700 La Seu d'Urgell, Lleida, Spain (home). *Telephone:* (973) 350054 (office). *Fax:* (973) 352230 (home). *E-mail:* jevs@bisbaturgell.org; secretaricoprincep@bisbaturgell.org (office). *Website:* www.bisbaturgell.org (office).

VIVIAN, Young; Niuean politician; b. 1935; Leader, Niue People's Party (disbanded 2003); Premier Dec. 1992–March 1993, 2002–08, also Minister responsible for Legis. Ass., Premier's Dept and Cabinet, Civil Aviation, Crown Law Office, Econ. Devt Planning and Statistics, External Affairs and Niueans Abroad, Niue Public Service Comm., Niue Broadcasting Corpn, Finance, Customs and Revenue, Police, Prison and Nat. Security, Environment, Niue Tourism, Public Works (Civil and Quarry, Outside Services and Heavy Plant) and Recovery Task Force.

VIZCARRA CORNEJO, Martín Alberto; Peruvian engineer, politician and head of state; *President;* b. 22 March 1963, Lima; s. of César Vizcarra Vargas and Doris Cornejo; m. Maribel Díaz Cabello; four c.; ed Nat. Univ. of Eng, School of Business Admin (ESAN); Exec. Dir, Pasto Grande Regional Special Project (water man. project) 1988–91; Operations Man., C & M Vizcarra SAC (civil eng firm) 1992–2010; Dean, Moquegua Eng Coll. 2008–09; Gov., Moquegua Region 2011–14; Minister of Transport and Communications 2016–17; Amb. to Canada 2017–18; First Vice Pres. of Peru 2016–18, Pres. 2018–; Order of the Sun of Peru. *Address:* Office of the President, Jirón de la Unión s/n, Cuadra 1, Lima 1, Peru (office). *Telephone:* (1) 3113900 (office). *Fax:* (1) 3114300 (office). *Website:* www.presidencia.gob.pe (office).

VIZJAK, Andrej, MEng; Slovenian engineer and politician; b. 6 Aug. 1964, Brežice; ed Brežice Gymnasium, Faculty of Electrical Eng and Computing, Univ. of Ljubljana; began career as electrical engineer, Litostroj, Ljubljana; researcher in computer automatisation of industrial processes, Jožef Stefan Inst. –1994; Labour Insp., Krško Unit, Nat. Labour Inspectorate 1994–2000; State Sec., Ministry of Labour, Family and Social Affairs 2000; elected mem. Nat. Ass. 2000, Leader of Slovenska demokratska stranka (SDS) Parl. Group 2000–04; Minister of Economy 2004–08, of Labour, Family and Social Affairs 2012–13; elected Mayor of Brežice 2002. *Address:* Slovenska demokratska stranka (SDS), 1000 Ljubljana, Trstenjakova 8, Slovenia (office). *Telephone:* (1) 4345450 (office). *Fax:* (1) 4345452 (office). *E-mail:* tajnistvo@sds.si (office). *Website:* www.sds.si (office).

VIZZINI, Carlo, LLB; Italian politician and academic; b. 28 April 1947, Palermo, Sicily; s. of Casimiro Vizzini; elected mem. Parl. (Social Democrat) for Palermo-Trapani-Agrigento-Caltanisetta 1976; Nat. Deputy Sec., Italian Social Democrat Party and Head of Econ. Dept 1980–88; Under-Sec. of State in Ministry of Budget and Econ. Planning; Minister for Regional Affairs 1986–87, of Cultural Heritage 1987–88, of the Merchant Navy 1989–91, of Posts and Telecommunications 1991–92; Sec. Partido Socialista Democratica Italiano (PSDI) 1992–93; Pres. Bicameral Comm. for Regional Questions; mem. of Senate from Palermo 2001–13, Pres. 1st Standing Cttee of Constitutional Affairs 2008–13, mem. Parl. Comm. of Inquiry into Organized Crime and the Mafia 2008–09, Parl. Comm. for implementation of Fiscal Federalism 2010–11; mem. delegation to Parl. Ass. of OSCE 2008–11; mem. Partito Socialista Democratico Italiano—PSDI 1976–98, Forza Italy (Forza Italia—FI) 1998–2009, People of Freedom (Il Popolo della Libertà—PDL) 2009–11, Italian Socialist Party (Partito Socialista Italiano—PSI) 2011–; Prof. of History of Econs, Univ. of Palermo.

VLĂDESCU, Sebastian; Romanian politician and business executive; b. 3 April 1958; ed Inst. Acad. of Econ. Studies, Bucharest, Merrill Lynch Inst., USA; economist, COS 1983, IRVMR Co. 1983–90; Shareholder and Dir Gas Prod Com LLC 1990–92, Banc Comp LLC 1992–94, Medist SA 1994–97 (Shareholder and Financial Dir 1998–99, Financial Dir 2001–05); Sec. of State, Ministry of Industry and Commerce Jan.–June 1997 (Adviser to the Minister July–Dec. 1997), Ministry of Finance Jan.–Dec. 2000 (Advisor to the Minister Jan.–April 1998, Oct.–Dec. 1999); mem. Guarantees for External Credits Inter-ministerial Comm., Eximbank Feb.–Aug. 1997, 2000; Chair. Trust Bd Company Bank Assets Recovery Agency 2000, Co. Chamber of Auditors 2000, Supervisory Bd Romanian Commercial Bank 2005– (mem. Privatization Comm. 2000–01); mem. Bd of Dirs CEC Savings House 2000–01, Petrom Service 2002–03, Upetrom 2002–05, Romanian Centre for Econ. Policies (CEROPE) 2003–05, Petrom SA 2005; Minister of Public Finance 2005–07, 2009–10; Sec. of State on Treasury Issues, Ministry of the Economy and Finance 2007.

VLAH, Irina; Moldovan lawyer and politician; *Başkan (Governor) of the Autonomous Territory of Gagauzia;* b. 26 Feb. 1974, Comrat, Moldovan SSR, USSR; one d.; ed State Univ. of Comrat; fmr lawyer in tax inspectorate, Ceadîr-Lunga, Head of Legal Dept of Gagauzia; mem. Partidul Comuniştilor din Republica Moldova (PCRM—Party of Communists of Repub. of Moldova); mem. Parl. (PCRM) 2005–09, 2009–10, 2010–14, 2014–15; Başkan (Gov.), Autonomous

Territory of Gagauzia April 2015–. *Address:* Office of the Başkan (Governor), Autonomous Territory of Gagauzia, 3800 Comrat, str. Lenin 196, Moldova (office). *Telephone:* (298) 2-46-36 (office). *Fax:* (298) 2-20-34 (office). *E-mail:* gagauzia.news@gmail.com (office). *Website:* www.gagauzia.md (office); vlah.md.

VLAHOVIĆ, Miodrag; Montenegrin politician and diplomatist; *President, Montenegrin Democratic Union (Crnogorska demokratska unija);* b. 1961, Djakovica; m.; three d.; ed Univ. of Montenegro, Podgorica, Univ. of Belgrade, Luxembourg Int. Univ.; f. STUDEKS Cultural Centre, Podgorica 1985; mem. Fed. Presidency and Int. Sec., Socialist Youth Union of Yugoslavia 1986–88; Sec. for Montenegro Asscn for Yugoslav Democratic Unity 1989; co-f. Citizens Cttee for Peace 1991–92, organized first peace rally in Montenegro 1991; mem. Parl., Repub. of Montenegro, mem. Parl. Cttee for Int. Relations, Cttee for Political System, Cttee for Legal and Admin. Matters 1992–94 (resgnd); Dir Centre for Regional and Security Studies (CeRS) 1999–; Minister of Foreign Affairs, Repub. of Montenegro 2004–06; Amb. to USA 2006–10 (also accred to Canada and Iceland 2007–10); Owner and CEO MConsult LLC 2010–13; served in Ministry of Foreign Affairs 2013–14; Pres. Montenegrin Democratic Union (Crnogorska demokratska unija) 2014–; Int. Sec., Liberal Party of Montenegro 1992–93; columnist for ind. weekly Monitor 1991–93, 1999–2000; Founder-mem. Montenegrin Centre for Democracy and Human Rights (CEDEM) 1998; mem. Socialiat Democratic Party of Montenegro; mem. Bd Open Society Inst. Montenegro 2002–04. *Address:* Montenegrin Democratic Union (Crnogorska demokratska unija), 81000 Podgorica, Park Side, Tološka šuma, Lamela C, Montenegro (office). *Website:* cdu.org.me (office).

VLOK, Adriaan; South African politician; b. 11 Dec. 1937, Sutherland; m. 1st Cornelia Burger (died 1994); two s. one d.; m. 2nd Antoinette du Plessis 1996; joined Dept of Justice 1957, became Prosecutor and Sr Magistrate; Asst Pvt. Sec. to Prime Minister John Vorster 1967; subsequently entered pvt. business; later Deputy Sheriff, E Pretoria; MP 1974–94; fmr Deputy Speaker of House of Ass., Leader House of Ass. 1992–94; Deputy Minister of Defence and Deputy Minister of Law and Order 1985–86, Minister of Law and Order 1986–91, of Correctional Services and the Budget 1991–92, of Correctional Services and of Housing and Works 1992, of Correctional Services 1992–94; received amnesty from Truth and Reconciliation Comm. (for involvement in attacks on Cosatu House 1987 and Khotso House 1988) 1999; received suspended ten-year sentence for involvement in plot to kill anti-apartheid activist Frank Chikane 2007; f. Feed a Child 2015. *Leisure interests:* rugby (referee in Northern Transvaal), military history, chewing biltong.

VO, Trong Nghia, PhD; Vietnamese architect; b. 1976, Quang Binh Prov.; ed Hanoi Architectural Univ., Ishikawa Coll. of Tech., Japan, Nagoya Inst. of Tech., Univ. of Tokyo; Founding Partner, Vo Trong Nghia Architects 2006; mem. Faculty, Nagoya Inst. of Tech. 2011; mem. Vietnam Asscn of Architects, Japan Inst. of Architects; World Architecture Festival Award, Int. Architecture Awards 2008, 2009, 2011, Green Good Design Award 2010, 2011, Architect of the Year 2012, Vietnam Green Architecture Award, Vietnam Asscn of Architects 2012, 21 for 21 Award, World Architecture News (UK) 2012, Building of the Year 2012, Archdaily 2013, World Architecture Festival Award 2014, ARCASIA Award 2014, FuturArc Green Leadership Award 2015. *Projects include:* Wind and Water (wNw) Café, Binh Duong (Asian Architects' Asscn Gold Arcasia Award 2007–08, Int. Acad. of Architecture—IAA Special Award 2009), Trung Nguyen Coffee Culture Centre, Hanoi (IAA Special Award 2009), Can Tho Univ. Campus, Mekong Delta (co-designer) (Silver Global Holcim Award 2009), Bamboo Wings (culture centre), Vinh Phuc Prov. *Address:* Vo Trong Nghia Architects, 8F, 70 Pham Ngoc Thach Street, Ward 6, District 3, Ho Chi Minh City, Viet Nam (office). *Telephone:* (8) 38206699 (office). *Fax:* (8) 38208439 (office). *E-mail:* hcmc@vtnaa.com (office). *Website:* votrongnghia.com (office).

VODIČKA, Jindřich; Czech politician; b. 22 July 1952, Prague; m.; two s.; ed Univ. of Maritime Studies, Odessa; sailed as deck engineer, later First Officer in merchant navy 1977–90; First Deputy Dir Office for Protection of Constitutional Officials –1990; Dir Job Centre, Prague-West Dist 1990–92; mem. Civic Democratic Party (Občanská Demokratická Strana—ODS) 1991–97, 1998–, Unie Svobody Jan.–March 1998; Deputy, House of Nations (Fed. Ass. of ČSFR) June–Dec. 1992; Minister of Labour and Social Affairs of Czech Repub. 1992–97; mem. Chamber of Deputies 1996–98; Minister of Interior 1997–98; Dir-Gen. České přístavy (Czech Ports Ltd).

VOGEL, Bernhard, DPhil; German politician; b. 19 Dec. 1932, Göttingen; s. of Prof. Dr Hermann Vogel and Caroline Vogel (née Brinz); ed Univs of Heidelberg and Munich; Lecturer, Inst. for Political Sciences, Heidelberg 1961–67; mem. Bundestag (Parl.) 1965–67, Speaker of Bundesrat (Upper House) 1976–77, 1987–88; Minister of Educ. and Culture, Rhineland-Palatinate 1967–76; Chairman/Deputy Chairman of the Joint Commission of the Federal and State Governments for Education Planning and Research Development 1970–76; mem. Rhineland-Palatinate State Parl. 1971–88, Thuringia State Parl. 1994–2004; Chair. CDU, Rhineland-Palatinate 1974–88, mem. Fed. Exec. Cttee of CDU 1975–, Chair. CDU, Thuringia 1993–2000; Minister-Pres., Rhineland-Palatinate 1976–88, Thuringia 1992–2003, Chair. Conf. of State Prime Ministers 1981–82, 1996–97; Rep. for Cultural Affairs of FRG within framework of Agreement on German-French Co-operation 1979–82; Chair. Advisory Bd of German TV Broadcasting/Second Channel (ZDF) 1979–92, Deputy Chair. 1992–2007; Chair. Konrad Adenauer Foundation 1989–95, 2001–09; Pres. Cen. Cttee of German Catholics 1972–76; Visiting Prof., NRW School of Governance, Universität Duisburg-Essen 2012; Hon. Prof., award from State of Baden-Wurttemberg; Hon. Chair. Konrad Adenauer Foundation 2010–; Grosses Bundesverdienstkreuz; decorations from France, Luxembourg, Poland, UK, and the Vatican; Grosskreuz St Gregorius; Gold Medal of Strasbourg; Dr hc (Catholic Univ. of America, Catholic Univ. of Lublin, German Coll. for Admin. Sciences, Speyer, Ben-Gurion Univ. of the Negev). *Publications:* Die Unabhangigen in den Kommunalwahlen westdeutscher Lander 1960, Wahlen und Wahlsysteme 1961, Kontrolliert der Bundestag die Regierung? 1964, Wahlkampf und Wählertradition. Eine Studie zur Bundestagswahl von 1961 1965, Wahlen in Deutschland 1848–1970 (co-author), Schule am Scheideweg 1974, Die Wahl der Parlamente und anderer Staatsorgane 1969–1978 (co-ed.), Neue Bildungspolitik (ed.) 1975, Federalismus in der Bewahrung (ed.) 1992, Sorge tragen fur die Zukunft 2002, Religion und Politik (ed.) 2003, Im Zentrum: Menschenwürde. Politisches Handeln aus christlicher Verantwortung, christliche Ethik als Orientierungshilfe (ed.) 2006, Deutschland aus der Vogel Perspektive. Eine kleine Geschichte der Bundesrepublik Deutschland (zusammen mit Hans-Jochen Vogel) 2007, Mutige Bürger braucht das Land. Chancen der Politik in unübersichtlichen Zeiten (co-ed.) 2012; Ed. Politische Meinung; numerous essays and speeches. *Leisure interests:* mountaineering, literature, swimming. *Website:* www.bernhard-vogel.at.

VOGEL, Dieter H., DrIng; German business executive; *Chairman, Lindsay Goldberg Vogel GmbH;* b. 14 Nov. 1941; m. Ursula Gross 1970; two c.; ed Tech. Univ. of Darmstadt, Tech. Univ. of Munich; Asst Prof., Thermic Turbo Engines, Tech. Univ. of Munich 1967–69; Vice-Pres. Printing Div., Bertelsmann AG 1970–74, Pegulan AG 1975–85 (Chair. 1978), apptd Chair. Supervisory Bd Bertelsmann AG 2003, Chair. Bd of Trustees Bertelsmann Stiftung 2007; Vice-Chair. Man. Bd Batig (BAT Industries) 1978–85; joined Thyssen Group 1986, Chair. Thyssen Handelsunion AG 1986–96, mem. Exec. Bd 1986–91, Deputy Chair. Thyssen AG 1991–96, Chair. 1996–98; f. Bessemer Vogel & Treichl (consultancy), Dusseldorf 1998; Founder and Chair. Lindsay Goldberg Vogel GmbH, Düsseldorf 2004–; Chair. Supervisory Bd Deutsche Bahn AG 1999–2001, Klöckner & Co. AG 2006–; Deputy Chair. Supervisory Bd VDM Metals GmbH; Chair. Ursula und Dieter Vogel Foundation; Deputy Chair. Karl-Schiller Foundation; Deputy Chair. Advisory Bd Falcon GmbH; mem. Admin. Bd HSBC Trinkaus & Burkhardt AG, Denkwerk GmbH; Hon. Prof., Tech. Univ. of Munich 2004. *Leisure interest:* skiing. *Address:* Lindsay Goldberg Vogel GmbH, Königsallee 60 A, 40212 Düsseldorf, Germany (office). *E-mail:* vogel@lindsaygoldbergvogel.com (office). *Website:* www.lindsaygoldbergvogel.com (office).

VOGEL, Hans-Jochen, DJur; German politician; b. 3 Feb. 1926, Göttingen; m. 1st Ilse Leisnering 1951 (divorced 1972); one s. two d.; m. 2nd Liselotte Sonnenholzer (née Biersack) 1972; ed Univs of Munich and Marburg; asst, Bavarian Justice Ministry 1952–54; judge, Traunstein Dist Court 1954–55; Bavarian State Chancellery 1955–58; mem. Munich City Council 1958–60, Mayor of Munich 1960–72; mem. Bundestag for Munich North constituency 1972–81, 1983–94; Minister for Regional Planning, Building and Urban Devt 1972–74, of Justice 1974–81; Mayor, West Berlin Jan.–June 1981; Chair. SPD Parl. Party 1984–91; Deputy Chair. SPD 1984–87, Chair. 1987–91; Vice-Pres. Org. Cttee for Munich Olympic Games 1972; apptd Chair. Gegen Vergessen (Against Forgetting) Project 1993; mem. Nationalen Ethikrat 2001–05; Deputy Chairman NS-Dokumentationszentrums München 2005–; Trustee Eugen-Biser-Stiftung 2002–; numerous decorations including Grosses Bundesverdienstkreuz, Bayerischer Verdienstorden, Hon. CBE and honours from France, Italy, etc.; numerous awards, including Wenzel Jaksch Prize 1996, Heinz Galinski Prize 1998, Leo Baeck Prize 2001, Albert Schulz Prize 2003, MaxFriedlaender Prize 2005, Regine Hildebrandt Prize 2007, Wilhelm Leuschner Medal 2009, Simon Snopkowski Prize 2012, Ohel Jakob Medal 2014. *Publications include:* Die Amtskette: Meine zwölf Münchner Jahre 1972, Nachsichten: Meine Bonner und Berliner Jahre 1996, Politik und Anstand: Warum wir ohne Werte nicht leben können 2005, Deutschland aus der Vogel Perspektive (with Bernhard Vogel) 2007, Es gilt das gesprochene Wort. Reden, Grundwerte, Würdigungen 2016. *Leisure interests:* mountain walking, history. *Address:* Stiftsbogen 74, 81375 Munich, Germany (home). *Fax:* (89) 70962211 (home).

VOGEL, Viola, PhD; German scientist and academic; *Professor, Department of Materials, Swiss Federal Institute of Technology, Zürich (ETH);* b. 1959, Tübingen; ed Max-Planck Inst. for Biophysical Chemistry, Göttingen, Frankfurt am Main Univ.; Postdoctoral Fellow, Univ. of California, Berkeley 1988–90; joined faculty Dept of Bioengineering, Univ. of Washington, Seattle 1990, also adjunct appointment in Physics, Founding Dir Center for Nanotechnology 1997–2003; Prof., Dept of Materials, ETH 2004–, also serves as Head, Lab. of Applied Mechanobiology and Dept of Health Sciences and Tech.; Fellow, American Inst. for Medical and Biological Eng, mem. Gordon Research Conf. Selection and Scheduling Cttee; mem. Selection Cttee British Marshall Fund Fellowships 1993–95, German Ministry of Science and Educ. (BMBF) 1998; mem. numerous advisor bds including Wyss Inst. at Harvard Univ., Max-Planck Inst. for Colloids and Interfaces (Golm), Inst. of Bioengineering and Nanotechnology (Biopolis Singapore); mem. Bd of Regents, Ludwig-Maximilians-Universität München; Fellow, Acad. of Sciences Leopoldina 2018–; Dr hc (Univ. of Tampere, Finland) 2012; Max-Planck Soc. Otto-Hahn Medal 1988, NIH First Award 1993, Philip Morris Foundation Research Award 2005, Julius Springer Award for Applied Physics 2006. *Address:* Biologisch-Orientierte Materialwissens, HCI F 443.2, Vladimir-Prelog-Weg 1-5/10, ETH-Hönggerberg, 8093 Zürich, Switzerland (office). *Telephone:* (44) 6320887 (office). *Fax:* (44) 6321073 (office). *E-mail:* viola.vogel@hest.ethz.ch (office). *Website:* www.hest.ethz.ch (office); www.appliedmechanobio.ethz.ch (office).

VOGELSTEIN, Bert E., BA, MD; American oncologist, pathologist and academic; *Clayton Professor of Oncology and Pathology, School of Medicine and Director of the Ludwig Center for Cancer Genetics and Therapeutics, Johns Hopkins University;* b. 2 June 1949, Baltimore, Md; m. Ilene Vogelstein; ed Univ. of Pennsylvania, Johns Hopkins Univ. School of Medicine, Baltimore, Md; Pediatric Intern, Johns Hopkins Hosp., Baltimore 1974–75, Pediatric Resident 1975–76; Postdoctoral research at Nat. Cancer Inst. 1976–78; Asst Prof. of Oncology, Johns Hopkins Univ. School of Medicine 1978–83, Assoc. Prof. 1983–89, Clayton Prof. of Oncology 1989–, of Pathology 1998–, Jt Appointment in Molecular Biology and Genetics 1992–, currently Dir Ludwig Center for Cancer Genetics and Therapeutics; Investigator, Howard Hughes Medical Inst., Chevy Chase, Md 1995–; Assoc. Ed. Cancer Research 1988–90, Genes, Chromosomes, and Cancer 1988–; mem. Bd of Reviewing Eds Science 1988–; mem. Editorial Bd Cancer and Metastasis 1993–, New England Journal of Medicine 1994–; mem. American Acad. of Arts and Sciences 1992, NAS 1992, American Philosophical Soc. 1995, Inst. of Medicine 2001, European Molecular Biology Org. 2005; Bristol Myers Squibb Award for Distinguished Achievement in Cancer Research 1990, Young Investigator Award, American Fed. for Clinical Research 1992, Gairdner Foundation Int. Award in Science 1992, Medal of Honor, American Cancer Soc. 1992, Shacknai Memorial Prize, Hebrew Univ. of Jerusalem 1993, Dickson Prize, Univ. of Pittsburgh 1994, Pezcoller Foundation Award 1993, NAS Richard Lounsbery Award 1993, Baxter Award, Asscn of American Medical Colls 1993, Ernst Schering

Prize 1994, Passano Award 1994, David A. Karnofsky Memorial Award, American Soc. for Clinical Oncology 1995, William Beaumont Prize in Gastroenterology, American Gastroenterological Asscn 1997, Louisa Gross Horwitz Prize 1998, Paul Ehrlich and Ludwig Darmstaedter Prize, Paul Ehrlich Foundation 1998, William Allan Award, American Soc. of Human Genetics 1998, Charles S. Mott Prize, General Motors Cancer Research Foundation 2000, John Scott Award, John Scott Trust 2003, Prince of Asturias Awards in Science 2004, Charles Rodolphe Brupbacher Prize for Cancer Research 2011, Howard Taylor Ricketts Award, Univ. of Chicago, Clowes Memorial Award, American Asscn for Cancer Research, Karnofsky Memorial Award, American Soc. for Clinical Oncology, Harvey Prize in Human Health, Technion, Israel, New York Acad. of Medicine Medal for Distinguished Contribs to Biomedical Science, Pasarow Award for Medical Research, Pioneer in Science Award, American Research Forum, Breakthrough Prize in Life Sciences (co-recipient) 2013, Warren Triennial Prize 2014. *Publications:* more than 450 articles in medical and scientific journals on molecular genetics of human cancer. *Address:* Johns Hopkins School of Medicine, Room 589, 1650 Orleans Street, Baltimore, MD 21231-1001, USA (office). *Telephone:* (410) 955-8878 (office). *Fax:* (410) 955-0548 (office). *E-mail:* vogelbe@jhmi.edu (office); bertvog@gmail.com. *Website:* www.hopkinsmedicine.org (office).

VOGT, Peter K., BS PhD; American (b. Czech) professor of molecular and experimental medicine; *Professor, Department of Molecular and Experimental Medicine, Scripps Research Institute;* b. 3 Oct. 1932, Broumov, Czechoslovakia; s. of Josef Vogt and Else Vogt; m. Hiroko Ishino 1993; ed Univ. of Würzburg, Germany, Univ. of Tübingen, Germany; worked at Max-Planck-Institut, Tübingen, Germany 1955–59; postdoctoral work at Virus Laboratory, Univ. of California, Berkeley 1959–62; Asst Prof. of Pathology, Univ. of Colorado 1962–66, Assoc. Prof. 1966–67; Assoc. Prof. of Microbiology, Univ. of Washington School of Medicine, Seattle 1967–69, Prof. 1969–71; Hastings Prof. of Microbiology, Univ. of Southern California School of Medicine 1971–78, Hastings Distinguished Prof. of Microbiology 1978–80, Chair. Dept of Microbiology 1980–; Chair. Div. of Oncovirology and Prof., Dept of Molecular and Experimental Medicine, Scripps Research Inst. 1993–, Exec. Vice-Pres. for Scientific Affairs 2012–15; mem. Bd of Dirs Foundation for Advanced Cancer Studies 1995–; Chair. Scientific Advisory Bd, Oncology Research Inst., Nat. Univ. of Singapore 2003–; mem. Scientific Advisory Bd Robert Koch Foundation 1999–, Sidney Kimmel Foundation for Cancer Research 2005–, Hormel Inst. 2014–, National Foundation for Cancer Research 2015–; mem. External Advisory Bd, Moores Cancer Center, Univ. of California, San Diego 2014–; mem. NAS 1980–, American Philosophical Soc. 1991–, American Acad. of Microbiology 1992–, Deutsche Akademie der Naturforscher Leopoldina (now German Acad. of Sciences) 1998–, Inst. of Medicine 2003–, American Acad. of Arts and Sciences 2004–, AACR Academy (elected Fellow) 2013–; Hon. mem. Japanese Cancer Asscn, Soc. of Chinese Bioscientists in America, Gesellschaft für Virologie; Dr hc (Univ. of Würzburg) 1995; numerous awards, including Calif. Scientist of the Year 1975, NAS Award 1980, Alexander von Humboldt Prize 1984, Ernst Jung Prize for Medicine 1985, Howard Taylor Ricketts Award 1991, Charles S. Mott Prize 1991, Gregor Johann Mendel Medal, Nat. Acad. of Sciences of the Czech Republic 2008, Loeffler-Frosch Medal, German Soc. of Virology 2010, Albert Szent-Györgyi Prize for Progress in Cancer Research 2010, Pezcoller Foundation-AACR Int. Award for Cancer Research 2013. *Publications include:* Genetics of RNA Tumor Viruses 1977, The Genetic Structure of RNA Tumor Viruses 1977 and numerous articles in scientific journals. *Leisure interest:* painting. *Address:* The Vogt Laboratory, Division of Oncovirology, Department of Molecular and Experimental Medicine, The Scripps Research Institute, 10550 North Torrey Pines Road, BCC-239, La Jolla, CA 92037, USA (office). *Telephone:* (858) 784-9728 (office). *Fax:* (858) 784-2070 (office). *E-mail:* pkvogt@scripps.edu (office). *Website:* www.scripps.edu/vogt/Vogt_Lab/Home.html (office).

VOHOR, Serge Rialuth; Ni-Vanuatu politician; b. 23 April 1955; began career as medical dresser/nurse/technician 1980–83; mem. Parl. (UMP) for Santo rural 1983–2015; Minister for Foreign Affairs 1991–93, Minister for Econ. Affairs 1993–95, Prime Minister 1995–96, July–Dec. 2004, April–May 2011; Minister for Trade 2001, for Foreign Affairs and External Trade 2002, Deputy Prime Minister 2001–02; Leader of Opposition 2003, 2004–07; Minister for Infrastructure and Public Utilities June 2007, Minister of Health 2013–15, Minister of Foreign Affairs and External Trade June–Oct. 2015; convicted of bribery by Vanuatu Supreme Court and sentenced to three years' imprisonment Oct. 2015; Pres. Union of Moderate Parties.

VOHRA, Narinder Nath; Indian politician (retd); b. 5 May 1936; ed Punjab Univ., Univ. of Oxford; Lecturer, Punjab Univ. 1957–59; served in Indian Admin. Service 1959–94, positions included Home Sec., Punjab, Additional Sec., Defence, Sec., Defence Production 1989–90, Defence Sec. 1990–93, Home Sec. 1993–94, Prin. Sec. to Prime Minister 1997–98, Special Services Bureau in Western Tibet border areas 1962–64; with WHO, Geneva 1982–84; mem. Nat. Security Advisory Bd 1998–2001; Co-Chair. India-European Union Round Table 2001–08; Special Rep. of Govt of India, Jammu and Kashmir Dialogue 2003–08; Gov. of Jammu and Kashmir 2008–18; Dir India Int. Centre 1995–97; Chair. Review Cttee, Inst. of Defence Studies and Analysis 1999–2001 (also life mem.), Cttee on Review of Mil. Histories 2001–02; Chair. Sarvodaya Int. Trust 2000–08; Founder and Co-Chair. India-European Union Round Table 2001–08; apptd Chair. Nat. Task Force on Internal Security 2000; Chair. Task Force to draw up Programme of Jt Civil-Mil. Training for Nat. Security Man. 2002–03; mem. Indian Inst. of Public Admin; Life Trustee, India Int. Centre, New Delhi, The Tribune Trust, Chandigarh; Visiting Fellow, Queen Elizabeth House, Oxford Univ. 1969–70; Hon. life mem. Int. House of Japan; Padma Vibhushan 2007. *Address:* c/o Raj Bhawan, Guwahati, India (office).

VOIGHT, Jon; American actor; b. 29 Dec. 1938, Yonkers, New York; s. of Elmer Voight and Barbara Voight (née Kamp); m. 1st Lauri Peters 1962 (divorced 1967); m. 2nd Marcheline Bertrand 1971 (divorced); one s. one d.; ed Catholic Univ.; f. Jon Voight Entertainment (production co.). *Theatre includes:* A View From the Bridge (New York); That Summer That Fall (New York) 1966; played Romeo at the San Diego Shakespeare Festival; Stanley Kowalski in A Streetcar Named Desire, Los Angeles 1973, Hamlet 1975. *Films include:* Hour of the Gun 1967, Fearless Frank 1968, Out of It 1969, Midnight Cowboy 1969, The Revolutionary 1970, The All-American Boy 1970, Catch 22 1970, Deliverance 1972, Conrack 1974, The Odessa File 1974, Coming Home (Acad. Award for Best Actor 1979, Golden Globe Award for Best Actor) 1978, The Champ 1979, Lookin' to Get Out (also wrote screenplay) 1982, Table for Five 1983, Runaway Train 1985, Desert Bloom 1986, Eternity, Heat, Rosewood, Mission Impossible 1996, U-Turn 1997, The Rainmaker 1997, Varsity Blues 1998, The General 1998, Enemy of the State 1998, Dog of Flanders 1999, Lara Croft: Tomb Raider 2001, Pearl Harbor 2001, Ali 2001, Zoolander 2002, Holes 2003, Superbabies 2003, Karate Dog 2003, The Manchurian Candidate 2004, National Treasure 2004, Superbabies: Baby Geniuses 2 2004, Glory Road 2006, The Legend of Simon Conjurer 2006, Transformers 2007, Bratz 2007, National Treasure Book of Secrets 2007, Pride and Glory 2008, An American Carol 2008, Four Christmases 2008, Dracula: The Dark Prince 2013. *Television includes:* End of the Game 1976, Gunsmoke and Cimarron Strip, Chernobyl: The Final Warning 1991, The Last of His Tribe 1992, The Tin Soldier (also dir), Convict Cowboy 1995, The Fixer 1998, Noah's Ark 1999, Second String 2000, Jasper Texas 2003, The Five People You Meet in Heaven 2004, Pope John Paul II 2005, 24 2009, Lonestar 2010, Ray Donovan (Golden Globe Award for Best Supporting Actor in a Series, Mini-Series, or TV Movie 2014) 2013. *Address:* c/o Martin Baum and Patrick Whitesell, CAA, 9830 Wilshire Boulevard, Beverly Hills, CA 90212; Jon Voight Entertainment, 10203 Santa Monica Blvd, Los Angeles, CA 90067, USA. *Telephone:* (310) 288-4545; (310) 843-0223 (Jon Voight Entertainment). *Fax:* (310) 553-9895 (Jon Voight Entertainment).

VOITOVICH, Aleksander Pavlavich, DrPhys-MathSci; Belarusian physicist and politician; b. 5 Jan. 1938, Rachkevich, Minsk region; s. of Pavel Voitovich and Nadezhda Voitovich; m.; one s.; ed Belarus State Univ.; mem. research staff, Inst. of Physics, Belarus Acad. of Sciences (BAS) 1962–84, Deputy Research Dir 1984–92, Deputy Research Dir then Dir Inst. of Molecular and Atomic Physics, BAS 1992–97; Chair. Nat. Ass. of Repub. of Belarus Council of Repub. 2000–03; Head of Lab., B.I.Stepanov Inst. of Physics, Nat. Acad. of Sciences of Belarus 2003–; Academician, Nat. Acad. of Sciences of Belarus 1996–, Pres. 1997–2000; Academician, European Acad. of Sciences, Arts and Humanities; Order of Francisk Skaryna 1998; Badge of Honour 1981, State Prize 1996. *Achievements include:* creator of 24 scientific inventions. *Publications include:* Magneto-Optics of Gas Lasers 1984, Lasers with Anisotropic Resonators (with V. Severikov) 1990; some 200 research papers. *Leisure interests:* fishing, carpentry. *Address:* Storojevskaia Str. 8–436, 220002, Minsk (home); Nezavisimosti Pr. 70, 220072 Minsk, Belarus. *Telephone:* (17) 2841732 (office); (17) 2840879. *E-mail:* avoitovich@gmail.com (home). *Website:* www.voitovich.org.

VOLCHEK, Galina Borisovna; Russian stage director and actress; b. 19 Dec. 1933, Moscow; d. of Boris Volchek and Vera Maimyna; m. 1st Yevgeniy Yevstigneyev 1957 (divorced 1964), one s.; m. 2nd Mark Abelev 1966 (divorced 1976); ed Moscow Art Theatre School; Co-founder, actress and Stage Dir Theatre Sovremennik 1956–72, Artistic Dir 1972–; Deputy to State Duma (Parl.) 1995–99; stage productions in numerous countries including USA (first Soviet stage dir to work in USA, Alley Theatre, Houston, Echelone by M. Roshchin), Ireland (Abbey Theatre), Hungary, Finland, Bulgaria, Germany, Czechoslovakia; masterclasses in Tisch School, New York Univ.; State Orders of USSR, Hungary, Bulgaria and Russia, Order of Labour Red Banner 1976, Order For Services to the Fatherland (3rd Degree) 1996, (2nd Degree) 2003, (1st Degree) 2008; USSR People's Artist 1988, Prize of Pres. of the Russian Fed. for Literature and Art 2002, G. A. Tovstonogov Prize 2006. *Dramatic roles include:* Martha (Who's Afraid of Virginia Woolf?), Miss Amelia (The Ballad of the Sad Café by Albee), Wife of Governor (Inspector by Gogol). *Films:* roles in films by directors Kozintsev (King Lear), Yutkevich, Danelia and others. *Leisure interest:* designing clothes. *Address:* Theatre Sovremennik, Chistoprudny blvd 19A, 101000 Moscow, Russia. *Telephone:* (495) 921-25-43. *Fax:* (495) 921-66-29 (office). *E-mail:* teatr@sovremennik.ru (office). *Website:* www.sovremennik.ru (office).

VOLCKER, Paul A., MA; American economist, banker, academic and government official; *Founder and Chairman, Volcker Alliance;* b. 5 Sept. 1927, Cape May, NJ; s. of Paul A. Volcker and Alma Klippel Volcker; m. Barbara Marie Bahnson 1954 (died 1998); one s. one d.; m. Anke Dening 2010; ed Princeton Univ., Harvard Univ. Grad. School of Public Admin. and London School of Econs, UK; Economist and Special Asst, Securities Dept, Fed. Reserve Bank of New York 1953–57; Financial Economist, Chase Manhattan Bank, New York 1957–62, Dir of Forward Planning 1965–69; Dir Office of Financial Analysis, US Treasury Dept 1962–63, Deputy Under-Sec. for Monetary Affairs 1963–65, Under-Sec. Monetary Affairs 1969–74; Sr Fellow, Woodrow Wilson School of Public and Int. Affairs, Princeton Univ. 1974–75; Pres. NY Fed. Reserve Bank 1975–79; Chair. Bd of Govs, Fed. Reserve System 1979–87; Frederick H. Schultz Prof. of Int. Econ. Policy, Princeton Univ. 1988–95, Prof. Emer. 1995–; Chair. James D. Wolfensohn Inc. 1988–96, CEO 1995–96; Henry Kaufman Visiting Prof., Stern School of Business, New York Univ. 1998; Chair. Int. Accounting Standards Cttee Foundation 2000–05; Chair. UN comm. investigating Iraq Oil for Food Program 2004–05; Chair. Bd of Trustees, Group of Thirty Consultative Group on Int. Econ. and Monetary Affairs, Inc., Washington, DC 2006; first Chair. Pres.'s Econ. Recovery Advisory Bd, The White House, Washington, DC 2009–11; Founder and Chair. Volcker Alliance 2013–; apptd by World Bank to lead ind. investigation of its Dept of Institutional Integrity 2007; mem. Bd of Dirs (non-exec.) ICI 1988–93, Nestlé 1988–2000, Prudential Insurance 1988–2002; consultant, Arthur Anderson 2002; Dr hc (Harvard, Yale, Princeton, and other univs); Admin. Fellowship, Harvard, Rotary Foundation Fellow, LSE, Arthur S. Fleming Award, Fed. Govt, US Treasury Dept Exceptional Service Award, Alexander Hamilton Award, Fred Hirsch Memorial Lecture 1978, Public Service Award, Tax Foundation 1981, Courage Award 1989. *Publications:* Changing Fortunes (with Toyoo Gyohten) 1992, Forbes Great Minds Of Business (co-author) 1997, Good Intentions Corrupted: The Oil for Food Scandal And the Threat to the U.N. (co-author) 2006. *Leisure interest:* avid fly-fisherman. *Address:* Volcker Alliance, 560 Lexington Avenue, Suite 16B, New York, NY 10022, USA (office). *Telephone:* (646) 343-0155 (office). *Fax:* (646) 343-0140 (office). *E-mail:* info@volckeralliance.org (office). *Website:* www.volckeralliance.org (office).

VOLLEBAEK, Knut, MSc; Norwegian diplomatist; *Commissioner, International Commission on Missing Persons;* b. 11 Feb. 1946, Oslo; m. Ellen Sofie Aadland Vollebaek; one s.; ed Inst. Catholique de Paris, Univ of Oslo, Univ of California, Santa Barbara, USA, Universidad Complutense, Madrid, Norwegian School of

Econs and Business Admin, Bergen; joined Foreign Service 1973; Second Sec. Embassy in Delhi 1975–78, First Sec. Embassy in Madrid 1978–81; Exec. Officer, then Sr Exec. Officer, Ministry of Foreign Affairs 1981–84; Counsellor, Embassy in Harare, Zimbabwe 1984–86; Head of First Political Affairs Div., Ministry of Foreign Affairs 1986–89, State Sec. and Deputy Minister of Foreign Affairs 1989–90; Amb. to Costa Rica 1991–93; Dir-Gen. Dept of Bilateral Devt Cooperation, Ministry of Foreign Affairs 1993–94; Gov. IDB, Asian Devt Bank and African Devt Bank 1994–97; Deputy Co-Chair. Int. Conf. on the Fmr Yugoslavia, Geneva 1993; Asst Sec.-Gen. for Devt Cooperation 1994–97; Minister of Foreign Affairs 1997–2000; Chair. Barents Euro-Arctic Council 1997–98, Council of Baltic Sea States 1999–2000; Chair.-in-Office OSCE 1999; Amb. to USA 2001–07; High Commr on Nat. Minorities, OSCE 2007–13; Commr, Int. Commission on Missing Persons (ICMP) 2013–; Commdr, Royal Norwegian Order of St Olav 2001; Hon. DJur (St Olaf Coll., Minn., USA) 2003; Hon. DHumLitt (Concordia Coll., Minn., USA) 2003. *Address:* International Commission on Missing Persons, Alipašina 45a, 71000 Sarajevo, Bosnia and Herzegovina (office). *Telephone:* (33) 280-800 (office). *E-mail:* icmp@ic-mp.org (office). *Website:* www.ic-mp.org (office).

VOLLHARDT, Dieter, Dr rer. nat, Dr rer. nat habil.; German theoretical physicist and academic; b. 8 Sept. 1951, Bad Godesberg, Germany; ed Univ. of Hamburg, Univ. of Southern California, USA; Postdoctoral Research Assoc., Max Planck Inst. for Physics and Astrophysics, Werner Heisenberg Inst., Munich 1979–84, Heisenberg Fellow, Deutsche Forschungs Gemeinschaft 1984–87; Prof. of Physics, Dir Inst. for Theoretical Physics, Rheinisch-Westfälische Technische Hochschule, Aachen 1987–96; Prof. of Theoretical Physics, Chair in Theoretical Physics, Centre for Electronic Correlations and Magnetism, Inst. for Physics, Univ. of Augsburg 1996–2018, mem. Exec. Bd, Augsburg Centre for Innovative Technologies 2007–, Man. Dir Inst. of Physics 2010–11, Vice-Dean, Faculty of Math. and Natural Sciences 2011–13, Dean 2013–15; Visiting Scientist, Inst. for Theoretical Physics, Santa Barbara, Calif., USA 1983, Bell Laboratories, Murray Hill, NJ, USA 1983; Chair. Prize Cttee for Max Planck Medal of Deutsche Physikalische Gesellschaft 2013–17; mem. Bavarian Acad. of Sciences and Humanities 2011 (Chair. Comm. for Low Temperature Research 2012–15, Scientific Advisory Bd, Walther Meissner Inst. for Low Temperature Research 2016–, mem. Scientific Advisory Bd of Center for Correlated Matter, Hangzhou, China 2016–), mem. College of Expert Reviewers of European Science Foundation 2018–; scholarships from Studienstiftung des Deutschen Volkes 1969–79, Ehrenfest Colloquium, Univ. of Leiden 2001, Europhysics Prize, European Physical Soc. 2006, Max Planck Medal, Deutsche Physikalische Gesellschaft 2010, Ernst Mach Hon. Medal, Acad. of Sciences of Czech Repub. 2011, Dvorak Lecturer, Acad. of Sciences of Czech Repub. 2011, Einstein Lecturer, Annalen der Physik 2012. *Publications include:* numerous papers in professional journals, The Superfluid Phases of Helium 3 2013.

VOLLMER, Dana; American swimmer; b. 13 Nov. 1987, Syracuse, New York; m. Andy Grant 2011; two s.; ed Univ. of Florida, Univ. of California, Berkeley; raised in Granbury, Tex.; swam for coach Ron Forrest at Fort Worth Area Swim Team (FAST) as a child; initially swam for Univ. of Florida before transferring to Univ. of California, Berkeley; youngest swimmer competing at US Olympic Trials 2000 aged 12; Goodwill Games: Brisbane 2001: bronze medal, 4×100m medley; Pan American Games: Santo Domingo 2003: gold medal, 200m freestyle, 4×200m freestyle, 4×100m medley; Olympic Games: Athens 2004: gold medal, 4×200m freestyle; World Championships (short course), Indianapolis 2004: gold medal, 4×100m freestyle, 4×200m freestyle, bronze medal, 200m freestyle, Dubai 2010: silver medal, 4×100m freestyle, 4×100m medley, bronze medal, 100m butterfly; Summer Universiade, Izmir 2005: gold medal, 4×100m freestyle, silver medal, 50m butterfly; Pan Pacific Championships, Victoria 2006: gold medal, 4×200m freestyle, Irvine 2010: gold medal, 100m butterfly, 4×100m freestyle, 4×200m freestyle, 4×100m medley, silver medal, 100m freestyle; World Championships (long course), Melbourne 2007: gold medal, 4×200m freestyle, silver medal, 4×100m freestyle, 4×100m medley, Rome 2009: silver medal, 4×200m freestyle, bronze medal, 200m freestyle, Shanghai 2011: gold medal, 100m butterfly, 4×100m medley, silver medal, 4×100m freestyle, Barcelona 2013: gold medal, 4×100m medley, bronze medal, 100m butterfly; Olympic Games, London 2012: gold medal, 100m. butterfly, 4×100m medley relay, 4×200m freestyle relay; Rio de Janeiro 2016: gold medal 4×100m medley relay, silver medal 4×100m freestyle relay, bronze medal 100m. butterfly; swims for California Aquatics and Univ. of California, Berkeley; first American mother to win an Olympic swimming gold medal; Amb. Go Red for Women programme by American Heart Asscn. *Address:* c/o Christine Reppa, United States Olympic Committee, One Olympic Plaza, Colorado Springs, CO 80909, USA (office). *E-mail:* info@danavollmer.com (office). *Website:* www.danavollmer.com.

VOLOCHKOVA, Anastasia, MBA; Russian ballet dancer; b. 20 Jan. 1976, St Petersburg; one d.; ed Russian Vaganova Acad. of Ballet; solo career 1990–; soloist, Mariinsky Theatre, St Petersburg 1994–98; with Bolshoi Theatre 1998–2003; danced with New Nat. Theatre Ballet, Tokyo, Bordeaux Ballet, English Nat. Ballet; danced as prima ballerina with Grigorovich Ballet and Hermitage Ballet; numerous gala performances and recitals in Moscow, Paris, Athens, Lausanne, Tel Aviv, Abu Dhabi, New York; performed in London at Royal Albert Hall, Royal Opera House, Coliseum, Palladium, Sadler's Wells Theatre; toured and performed in Chile 2010; worked as an actress and model; mem. Edinaya Rossiya 2003–11; Gold Medal, Serge Lifar International Ballet Competition 1996, Golden Lion 2000, Prix Benois de la Danse 2002, People's Artist of Russian Federation. *Films:* Chernyy Prints 2004. *Television:* Dancing with the Stars 2012. *Roles include:* Odyllia and Swan Princess in Swan Lake, Gisele in Gisele, Raimonda in Raimonda, Niknya in Bayder, Aurora and Lilac Fairy in Sleeping Beauty, Zarema in Fountain of Bakhchisarai, Girl in Spirit of Rose, Medora in Corsair, Carmen in Carmen-Suite, Catherine the Second in The Russian Hamlet. *Leisure interests:* walking, reading, classical and modern music. *Telephone:* (495) 126-17-53 (home).

VOLODIN, Vyacheslav Viktorovich, DJur; Russian politician; *Chairman, State Duma;* b. 4 Feb. 1964, Alekseyevka, Saratov Oblast, Russian SFSR, USSR; m.; one d.; ed Saratov Inst. of Agric. Mechanisation, Acad. of Civil Service; teacher, docent, Saratov Inst. of Agric. Mechanisation 1987–92; Deputy Head Admin. of Saratov City 1992–93; Chair., Pro-Rector Volga Region Management Personnel

Centre (now Volga Region Acad. of Govt Service) 1993–94; mem., Deputy Chair. Saratov Oblast Duma 1994–, Vice-Gov., First Deputy Chair. Saratov Oblast Govt 1996–99; Prof. Volga Region Acad. of Govt Service –1999; mem. Gosudarstvennaya Duma (State Duma, Parl.) 1999–2011, 2016–, mem. Otechestvo-Vsya Rossiya (Fatherland-All Russia) faction 1999–2001, Deputy Sec. Political Council 1999, mem. Yedinstvo i Otecestvo (Unity and Fatherland) faction 2001–03, re-elected to State Duma as mem. of Yedinaya Rossiya (YeR—United Russia) faction 2003, 2007, Deputy Chair. State Duma 2004–10, Chair. State Duma 2016–, First Sec., YeR 2005–10; Deputy Prime Minister and Chief of Staff of the Prime Minister 2010–11, First Deputy Chief of Staff of the Presidential Admin 2010–16; Order of Friendship 1997, Order of Honour 2003, Order 'For Merit to the Fatherland', Fourth Class 2006, Second Class 2012. *Leisure interests:* painting, sports. *Address:* State Duma, 103265 Moscow, Okhotnyi ryad 1, Russia (office). *Telephone:* (495) 692-62-66 (office). *Fax:* (495) 697-42-58 (office). *E-mail:* stateduma@duma.gov.ru (office). *Website:* www.duma.gov.ru (office).

VOLOSHIN, Alexander Stalyevich; Russian government official and business executive; *Chairman, JSC Freight One (PGK);* b. 3 March 1956, Moscow; m.; three s.; ed Moscow Inst. of Transport Eng, All-Union Acad. of Foreign Trade; Head of Lab. of Scientific Org. of Labour; Sec. Comsomol Org.; Moskva-Sortirovochnaya railway station 1973–83; Researcher, then Sr Researcher, Head of Sector, Deputy Head of Section Ail-Union Research Inst. of Conjuncture 1986–92; Exec. Dir Analysis, Consultations and Marketing 1992; Pres. ESTA Corpn 1993–96; Pres. Fed. Funds Corpn 1996–97; apptd Asst to Head of Admin. of Presidency (for Econ. Problems) 1997, Deputy Head 1998–99, Head 1999–2003 (resgnd); Chair. RAO UES (Unified Energy Systems) of Russia 1999–2008; Chair. Norilsk Nickel 2008–10, Uralkali OJSC 2010–14, JSC Freight One (PGK) 2012–; Head, Working Group for establishing Int. Financial Centre 2010–; mem. Presidential Council for Financial Market Devt of Russian Fed. 2008–; mem. Bd of Dirs Yandex NV 2010–, Cleome Holdings Ltd. *Address:* JSC Freight One (PGK), Moscow, 105064, Staraya Basmannaya st., 12 bld. 1, Russia (office). *Telephone:* (495) 663-01-01 (office). *E-mail:* office@pgkweb.ru (office). *Website:* eng.pgkweb.ru (office).

VON AHN, Luis, BS, PhD; Guatemalan entrepreneur, computer scientist and academic; *A. Nico Habermann Associate Professor, Computer Science Department, Carnegie Mellon University;* b. 1979, Guatemala City; ed American School of Guatemala, Duke Univ. and Carnegie Mellon Univ., USA; early research in the field of cryptography; Founder reCAPTCHA co. 2008–09 (acquired by Google, Inc.); Co-founder and CEO Duolingo (language-learning platform); Post-Doctoral Fellow, Computer Science Dept, Carnegie Mellon Univ. 2005–06, Asst Prof. 2006–11, Staff Research Scientist 2009–11, A. Nico Habermann Assoc. Prof. 2011–; MacArthur Fellowship 2006–11, Alan J. Perlis Teaching Award, Carnegie Mellon Univ. School of Computer Science 2006, Herbert A. Simon Award for Teaching Excellence in Computer Science 2008, David and Lucile Packard Foundation Fellowship 2009–14, Sloan Fellowship 2009, Presidential Early Career Award for Scientists and Engineers 2012, Grace Murray Hopper Award, Asscn for Computer Machinery 2012, World Technology Award (Communications Tech.) 2013, Lemelson-MIT Prize 2018. *Achievements include:* did early pioneering work with Manuel Blum on CAPTCHAs (computer-generated tests that humans are routinely able to pass but that computers have not yet mastered) 2000; known as a pioneer of 'crowdsourcing' (building systems that combine humans and computers to solve large-scale problems that neither can solve alone). *Publications:* numerous papers in professional journals. *Address:* GHC 7113, Computer Science Department, Carnegie Mellon University, Pittsburgh, PA 15213-3891, USA (office). *Telephone:* (412) 567-6602 (office). *E-mail:* biglou@cs.cmu.edu (office). *Website:* www.cs.cmu.edu/~biglou (office); vonahn.blogspot.com.

VON BOMHARD, Nikolaus, DrJur; German insurance industry executive; *Chairman of the Board of Management, Münchener Rückversicherungs-Gesellschaft AG (Munich Re);* b. 28 July 1956, Gunzenhausen; m. Charlotte von Bomhard; two c.; ed Univs of Munich and Regensburg; joined grad. trainee programme, Münchener Rückversicherungs-Gesellschaft AG (Munich Reinsurance Co., Munich Re) 1985–87, later worked as underwriter in Operational Div.: Fire/Treat, Deputy Head of Operational Div.: Germany 1992–97, Head, Brazil Office, São Paulo 1997–2000, mem. Bd of Man. 2000–, responsible for Europe 2/Latin America Div. 2001–04, Chair. Bd of Man. Munich Re 2004–; Chair. Supervisory Bd ERGO Versicherungsgruppe AG, Düsseldorf; Chair. Munich Health Holding AG, ERGO Versicherungsgruppe AG; mem. Bd of Dirs AIEEA of Geneva ('Geneva Asscn'), Fed. Financial Supervisory Authority (BaFin), Berlin, Freunde des Münchener Bach-Chores e.V., Freundeskreis der Münchener Assekuranz (Juniorenkreis); mem. Presiding Cttee and Gen. Cttee Gesamtverband der Deutschen Versicherungswirtschaft e.V; mem. Supervisory Bd Commerzbank AG 2009–; Dir UniCredit SpA (Unicredito Italiano) 2005–; mem. Bd of Trustees Gesellschaft Freunde der Hochschule für Musik und Theater München e.V., Munich, Pinakotheks-Verein Verein zur Förderung der Alten und Neuen Pinakothek München e.V., Munich, Verein der Freunde und Förderer der Glyptothek und der Antikensammlungen München e.V., Munich; mem. Univ. Council Ludwig-Maximilian Univ., Munich; mem. Foundation Bd Munich Re Foundation. *Address:* Münchener Rückversicherungs-Gesellschaft AG, Königinstrasse 107, 80802 Munich, Germany (office). *Telephone:* (89) 38910 (office). *Fax:* (89) 399056 (office). *E-mail:* info@munichre.com (office). *Website:* www.munichre.com (office).

VON BRAUN, Joachim, PhD; German agricultural economist, research institute director and academic; *Director, Centre for Development Research, University of Bonn;* b. 10 July 1950, Brakel; m. Dr Barbara von Braun; three d.; ed Univ. of Göttingen; Dir Food Consumption and Nutrition Div., Int. Food Policy Research Inst. (IFPRI), Washington, DC 1990–93, Dir-Gen. IFPRI 2002–09; Prof. and Dir Inst. for Food Econs and Consumer Analyses, Univ. of Kiel 1993–97; Dir Centre for Devt Research, Univ. of Bonn, Chair. of Dept and Prof. of Econ. and Tech. Change 1997–2002, 2009–; Pres. Int. Asscn of Agricultural Economists 2000–03, Lifetime Fellow 2009–; mem. Hunger Task Force, UN Millennium Devt Project 2003–05; Fellow, German Econs Asscn 1996, AAAS 2006; mem. Acad. of Science, State of North Rhine-Westphalia 1999–, German Acad. of Science and Eng 2011–, Pontifical Acad. of Sciences 2012– (Pres. 2017–); mem. Bd of Trustees, Robert Bosch Foundation 2017–; Hon. Prof., Int. Research Center for Food and Agric. Econs, Nanjing Agricultural Univ., China 2004–; Dr hc (Stuttgart-Hohenheim)

2005; Josef G. Knoll Science Prize 1988, Bertebos Prize, Royal Swedish Acad. of Agric. and Forestry 2009, Justus von Liebig Prize for World Nutrition 2011, Marsilius Medal, Univ. of Heidelberg, Germany 2016. *Publications include:* Famine in Africa: Causes, Responses and Prevention (co-author) 1999, Russia's Agro-Food Sector: Towards Truly Functioning Markets (co-ed.) 2000, Agricultural Biotechnology in Developing Countries: Towards Optimizing the Benefits for the Poor (co-author) 2000, Villages in the Future: Crops, Jobs and Livelihood (co-ed.) 2001, Information and Communication Technologies for Development and Poverty Reduction – The Potential of Telecommunications (co-ed.) 2005, Globalization of Food and Agriculture and the Poor (co-ed.) 2008. *Address:* Centre for Development Research, University of Bonn, Walter-Flex-Str. 3, 53113 Bonn, Germany (office). *Telephone:* (228) 731800 (office). *Fax:* (228) 731869 (office). *E-mail:* jvonbraun@uni-bonn.de (office). *Website:* www.zef.de (office).

VON BÜLOW, Andreas, DJur; German politician, lawyer and writer; b. 17 July 1937, Dresden; s. of Georg-Ulrich Bülow and Susanne von Bülow (née Haym); m. Anna Barbara Duden 1961; two s. two d.; law studies in Heidelberg, Berlin and Munich, studied in France and USA; entered higher admin. service of State of Baden-Württemberg 1966, on staff of Rural Dist Offices of Heidelberg and Balingen, Pres. Admin. Dist of Süd-Württemberg Hohenzollern at Tübingen; mem. Bundestag (Parl.) 1969–94; Parl. State Sec. Fed. Ministry of Defence 1976–80; Fed. Minister for Research and Tech. 1980–82; mem. Social Democratic Party 1960–, Public Services and Transport Workers' Union; Great Cross of Merit 1983. *Publications:* Die Überwachung der Erdgasindustrie durch die Federal Power Commission als Beispiel der Funktionen der unabhängigen Wirtschaftsüberwachungskommissionen der amerikanischen Bundesverwaltung 1967 (dissertation), Gedanken zur Weiterentwicklung der Verteidigungsstrategien in West und Ost 1984, Alpträume West gegen Alpträume Ost—ein Beitrag zur Bedrohungsanalyse 1984, Skizzen einer Bundeswehrstruktur der 90er Jahre 1985, Die eingebildete Unterlegenheit—das Kräfteverhältnis West-Ost, wie es wirklich ist 1985, The Conventional Defense of Europe, New Technologies and New Strategies 1986, Im Namen des Staates, CIA, BND und die Kriminellen Machenschaften der Geheimdienste 1998, Die CIA und der 11 September 2003. *Leisure interests:* music, geology, history, swimming, hiking, skiing.

VON DASSANOWSKY, Robert, (Robert Dassanowsky), BA, MA, PhD, FRHistS, FRSA; American/Austrian writer, academic, film producer and foundation director; *Professor of German and Film and Director of Film Studies, University of Colorado, Colorado Springs;* b. 28 Jan. 1960, New York, NY; s. of Elfi von Dassanowsky; ed American Acad. of Dramatic Arts, American Film Inst. Conservatory Program, Univ. of California, Los Angeles; Founding Ed. Rohwedder: International Magazine of Literature and Art 1986–93; writer/researcher, Stone-Stanley TV Productions/Disney Channnel 1990–92; Corresp. Ed. Rampike 1991–; consultant/trans., J. Paul Getty Conservation Inst., Los Angeles 1991–92; Visiting Asst Prof. of German, UCLA 1992–93, Visiting Prof. of German 2007–08; Asst Prof. of German, Univ. of Colorado, Colorado Springs 1993–99, Dir of Film Studies 1997–, Assoc. Prof. of German and Film Studies 1999–2006, Prof. of German and Film Studies 2006–, Chair. Dept of Languages and Cultures 2001–07, Chair. Dept of Visual and Performing Arts 2001–02, 2010–11; Adjunct Faculty, Media Communication and Film, Webster Univ. Vienna 2013–15; Professor of Cinema and Central/European Studies, Affiliate Core Faculty, Global Center for Advanced Studies, NY/Dublin 2017–; Owner and Producer, Belvedere Film, LLC 1999–; mem. Editorial Bd Osiris 1991–, Rampike Canada 1991–2014, Modern Austrian Literature/Journal of Austrian Studies 1997–2000, 2011–, Ariadne Press 1999–, Poetry Salzburg Review 2002–, Colloquia Germanica 2012–18, Studia Germanica Posnaniensia 2017–; Dir, Elfi von Dassanowsky Foundation 2009–; mem. Bd Los Angeles Flickapalooza Film Festival 2001–03, TIE The Int. Experimental Cinema Exposition 2002–10; Co-founder and mem. Bd Int. Alexander Lernet-Holenia Soc. 1997–; Co-founder and Vice-Pres. Austrian American Film Asscn 1998–2009, Exec. Council, Modern Austrian Literature and Culture Asscn (MALCA) 2006–09, 2010–11 (Vice-Pres. Austrian Studies Asscn (fmrly MALCA) 2011–13, Pres. 2012–14, Pres. Emer., Fundraising 2014–); mem. Modern Language Asscn, PEN/USA, Austrian PEN, Poets and Writers, Asscn of Austrian Film Producers, Film Independent Los Angeles, Soc. for Cinema and Media Studies, Screen Actors Guild, German Studies Asscn, PEN Colorado, Acad. of Austrian Film, European Film Acad.; Jury mem. and Prize Patron, Vienna Ind. Shorts Festival; Constantinian Order of St George, Order of Vitez (Hungary), Decoration of Honour in Silver (Austria); Pres.'s Fund for the Humanities grants, Univ. of Colorado 1996, 2001, Carnegie Foundation/CASE 2004, Chancellor's Award, Univ. of Colorado at Colorado Springs 2006, Taft Center Lecturer, Univ. of Cincinnati 2011, Grant Award, Botstiber Foundation Inst. for Austrian-American Studies 2014–15, Thomas Jefferson Award, Univ. of Colorado 2015. *Films include:* as producer, assoc. producer or exec. producer: Semmelweis 2001, Epicure 2001, The Nightmare Stumbles Past 2002, Believe 2002, Wilson Chance 2005, The Last Bogatyr 2009, The Retreat 2010, Vidas ambulante/The Troubadours 2011, Waking Eyes 2011, Deadline 2012, Menschen 2012, Felix Austria! (aka The Archduke and Herbert Hinkel) 2013, Styria 2013, Chariot 2013, Future Present Past 2013, The Creep Behind the Camera 2014, Noble Claim 2016, Before Anything You Say 2017, Jealous Gods 2017, Der Bauer zu Nathal 2017, Refuge 2018; audio commentary: Leni Riefenstahl's Tag der Freiheit 2000, Self: Felix Austria! 2013, Be Natural: The Untold Story of Alice Guy-Blache 2017. *Television:* writer and script supervisor, Teen Win, Lose or Draw (Disney Channel) 1989–90, Self, Porträt von Elfi von Dassanowsky, Wilkommen Österreich (ORF) 1998, Co-producer, De Expressione Humanitatis Von Schauspiel und Musik (ORF) 2014. *Publications include:* Phantom Empires: The Novels of Alexander Lernet-Holenia and the Question of Postimperial Austrian Identity 1996, Telegrams from the Metropole: Selected Poetry 1999, Alexander Lernet-Holenia: Mars in Aries (trans.) 2003, Austrian Cinema: A History 2005, Soft Mayhem: Poetry 2010, New Austrian Cinema (co-ed. and contrib.) 2011, World Film Locations: Vienna (ed. and contrib.) 2012, Screening Transcendence: Film under Austrofascism and the Hollywood Hope 1933–38 2018; other: several plays, film and TV scripts; contribs: numerous additional book chapters, poetry and articles in periodicals and anthologies. *Leisure interests:* art collecting, travel, fencing. *Address:* Department of Languages and Cultures, University of Colorado, 1420 Austin Bluffs Parkway, Colorado Springs, CO 80918, USA (office). *E-mail:* rvondass@uccs.edu (office). *Website:* www.belvederefilm.com (office); www.elfivondassanowsky.org (office).

VON DER LEYEN, Ursula, BSc, MPH; German gynaecologist and politician; *Federal Minister of Defence;* b. 8 Oct. 1958, Brussels, Belgium; m. Heiko E. von der Leyen; seven c.; ed European School, Brussels, Lehrte Gymnasium, Medizinische Hochschule Hannover (MHH), London School of Econs, UK; Asst Physician, Women's Clinic, MHH 1988–92; Residence at Stanford Univ., USA 1992–96, Auditing Guest, Grad. School of Business 1993, Market Analyst, Stanford Health Services Hosp. Admin 1995; Scientific Researcher, Epidemiology Dept, MHH 1998–2002; joined CDU 1990, mem. Physicians Team, Lower Saxony CDU 1999, mem. Parl. Group in Lower Saxony State Parl. (Landtag) 2003–, mem. Exec. German CDU 2004–, Chair. Parents, Child and Profession Cttee, Family Comm., German CDU 2005–; Lower Saxony Minister for Social Affairs, Women, the Family and Health 2003; Fed. Minister of Family Affairs, Sr Citizens, Women and Youth 2005–09, of Labour and Social Affairs 2009–13, of Defence 2013–. *Address:* Federal Ministry of Defence, Stauffenbergstr, 18, 10785 Berlin, Germany (office). *Telephone:* (30) 182400 (office). *Fax:* (30) 18245357 (office). *E-mail:* poststelle@bmvg.bund.de (office). *Website:* www.bmvg.de (office); www.ursula-von-der-leyen.de.

VON DOHNÁNYI, Christoph; German conductor; b. 8 Sept. 1929, Berlin; s. of Hans von Dohnányi and Christine von Dohnányi (née Bonhoeffer); brother of Klaus von Dohnányi; m. 1st Renate Zillessen; one s. one d.; m. 2nd Anja Silja 1979; one s. two d.; m. 3rd Barbara Koller; ed Munich Musikhochschule; abandoned legal training to study music 1948; studied in USA under grandfather, Ernst von Dohnányi 1951; répétiteur and conductor under Georg Solti, Frankfurt Oper 1952–56; Gen. Music Dir Lübeck 1957–63, Kassel 1963–66; London debut with London Philharmonic Orchestra 1965; Chief Conductor of Cologne Radio Symphony Orchestra 1964–69; Gen. Music Dir and Opera Dir, Frankfurt 1968–77; Chief Conductor and Intendant, Hamburg State Opera 1977–84; Music Dir (desig.) Cleveland Orchestra 1982–84, Music Dir 1984–2002, Music Dir Laureate 2002–; Prin. Guest Conductor Philharmonia Orchestra 1994, Prin. Conductor 1997–2008, Hon. Conductor for Life 2008–; Chief Conductor, NDR Sinfonieorchester Hamburg 2004–11; numerous guest appearances; numerous recordings of symphonies with Cleveland Orchestra and opera recordings; Commdr des Arts et des Lettres, Commdr's Cross, Order of Merit, Commdr's Cross (Austria); Dr hc (Kent State Univ.), (Case Western Univ.), (Oberlin Coll.), (Eastman School of Music), (Cleveland Inst. of Music), (RAM) 2013; Richard Strauss Prize, Bartok Prize, Goethe Medal, Frankfurt, Arts and Science Prize, City of Hamburg, Abraham Lincoln Award. *Address:* Harrison Parrott, The Ark, 201 Talgarth Road, London, W6 8BJ, England (office). *Telephone:* (20) 7229-9166 (office). *Fax:* (20) 7221-5042 (office). *E-mail:* info@harrisonparrott.co.uk (office). *Website:* www.harrisonparrott.com/artist/profile/christoph-von-dohnanyi (office); christophvondohnanyi.com/en.

VON DOHNÁNYI, Klaus, DJur, LLB; German politician and political publicist; b. 23 June 1928, Hamburg; s. of Johann-Georg von Dohnányi and Christine (née Bonhoeffer) von Dohnányi; brother of Christoph von Dohnányi; m. Ulla Hahn 1997; two s. one d.; ed Munich, Columbia, Stanford and Yale Univs; fmrly with Ford Motor Co., Detroit, Mich. and Cologne; Dir Planning Div. Ford-Werke, Cologne 1956-60; Dir Inst. für Marktforschung und Unternehmensberatung, Munich 1960–68; Sec. of State, Fed. Ministry of Economy 1968–69; mem. Bundestag 1969–81; Parl. Sec. of State, Ministry of Educ. and Science 1969–72; Minister of Educ. and Science 1972–74; Minister of State and Parl. Sec. of State, Fed. Foreign Office 1976–81, First Burgomaster and Pres. Senate, Hamburg 1981–88; Chair. Bd, TAKRAF AG, Leipzig 1990–94; fmr Co-Chair. Comm. 'Restructuring East Germany'; Chair. Bd Kirow AG Leipzig; mem. Club of Rome 1996–, Konvent für Deutschland; mem. SPD; Heuss Medal Theodor Heuss Foundation 1988; Gold Medal for Distinguished Leadership and Service to Humanity, B'nai B'rith 1988, Stolten Medal, Hamburg. *Publications:* Japanese Strategies 1969, Brief an den Deutschen Demokratischen Revolutionäre 1990, Das Deutsche Wagnis 1990, Im Joch des Profits? (The German Model) 1996, Dichter, Denker, Schulversager: Gute Schulen sind machbar – Wege aus der Bildungskrise (with Jorg Dräger) 2011. *Leisure interests:* writing, reading. *Address:* Heilwigstrasse 5, 20249 Hamburg, Germany. *Telephone:* (40) 4505789 (office). *Fax:* (40) 4505790 (office).

VON FIGURA, Kurt, DrMed; German microbiologist, academic and university administrator; b. 16 May 1944, Heiningen, Baden-Württemberg; m.; four c.; ed Tübingen Univ., Univ. of Vienna; Medical Asst, Bad Wildungen, Tübingen und Munich 1969–70; Scientific Asst, Univ. of Münster Physiologisch-Chemisches Institut 1972–76, Sr Asst 1976–77, Prof. 1977–86; Prof. of Biochemistry, Faculty of Medicine, Georg-August-Universität Göttingen 1986–2004, Pres. 2005–10; mem. Specialist Cttee, Max-Planck-Institute for Biochemistry 1994–2001, mem. Research Field Cttee of Neurobiology, Max-Planck-Society 1999–2000; mem. German-Israeli Project Cooperation (DIP) 1997–, Acad. of Sciences Göttingen 1998–, Deutsche Akademie der Naturforscher Leopoldina 2004–, Max-Planck-Gesellschaft; mem. Bd of Trustees, Max-Delbrück-Centre for Molecular Medicine 'Berlin-Buch' 2003–, Max-Planck-Institute for Biophysical Chem., Göttingen 2004–, Max-Planck-Institute for Experimental Medicine 2004–; Dr hc (Univ. of Namur, Belgium) 2002; Hoechst AG Prize 1978, Otto-Warburg-Medaille 2002.

VON FRITSCH, Rüdiger; German diplomatist; *Ambassador to Russia;* b. 1953, Siegen, Westphalia; m.; two c.; ed Univs of Erlangen and Bonn; joined Fed. Foreign Service 1984, Political Speaker, Embassy in Warsaw 1986–89, Press and Cultural Affairs, Embassy in Nairobi 1989–92, Press Office, Fed. Foreign Office 1992–95, Political Speaker, Perm. Representation to EU, Brussels 1995–99, Chief of Planning Staff, Office of the Fed. Pres. 1999–2004, Vice-Pres. Fed. Intelligence Service 2004–07, Head of Dept of Economy and Sustainable Devt, Foreign Affairs and G8-Sous Sherpa 2007–10, Amb. to Poland 2010–14, to Russia 2014–. *Address:* Embassy of Germany, 119285 Moscow, ul. Mosfilmovskaya 56, Russia (office). *Telephone:* (495) 937-95-00 (office). *Fax:* (495) 783-08-75 (office). *E-mail:* germanmo@aha.ru (office). *Website:* www.germania.diplo.de (office).

VON GERKAN, Meinhard, PhD, Dipl-Ing; German architect; *CEO, gmp – von Gerkan, Marg and Partners Architects;* b. 3 Jan. 1935, Riga, USSR (now Latvia); m. Sabine von Gerkan; six c.; freelance architect in collaboration with Volkwin Marg 1965– (four partners, one partner for China); with Freie Akad. der Künste Hamburg 1972–; Prof., Inst. für Baugestaltung A, Technische Univ. Brunswick 1974–2002; with Kuratorium Jürgen-Ponto-Stiftung Frankfurt 1982; Guest Prof., Nihon Univ., Tokyo 1988, Univ. of Pretoria 1993; Visiting Prof., Dalian Univ. of

Tech., Architecture and Art Coll., People's Repub. of China 2007; Founder and CEO gmp Foundation to enhance architectural educ. 2007–; work includes airport bldgs, cultural insts, railway stations, hotels, offices, public bldgs, housing, master plans and interior design and housing throughout Germany and in Italy, Latvia, Turkey, China, Viet Nam, Algeria, Saudi Arabia, South Africa, UAE, Poland, Ukraine, Romania, Brazil; mem. Convent Chairmanship of Bundesstiftung Baukultur, Berlin 2003; Pres. Acad. for Architectural Culture 2007–; Hon. FAIA 1995, Inst. of Mexican Architects 1995; Hon. mem. Berlin-Brandenburg Acad. of Sciences 2000; Bundesverdienstkreuz 2009; Dr hc (Philipps-Univ., Marburg) 2002; Hon Dr in Design (Christian Univ., Chung li, Taiwan) 2005; Dr hc (East China Normal Univ. Coll. of Design, Shanghai) 2007; more than 270 first prizes at nat. and int. architecture competitions, including Fritz Schumacher Award 2000, Romanian Nat. Award 2002, Plakette of Freie Akad. der Künste, Hamburg 2005, Grand Award, Asscn of German Architects (BDA) 2005; more than 150 awards for outstanding architecture. *Publications:* Architektur 1966–78 1978, Die Verantwortung des Architekten 1982, Architektur 1978–83 1983, Alltagsarchitektur, Gestalt und Ungestalt 1987, Architektur 1983–88 1988, Architektur 1988–91 1992, von Gerkan, Marg and Partners 1993, Idea and Model: 30 years of architectural models 1994, Architektur im Dialog 1994, Culture Bridge 1995, Architecture 1991–95 1995, Architecture for Transportation 1997, Architecture 1995–97 1998, Möbel Furniture 1998, Architecture 1997–99: Vol. 1 Selected Projects 2000, Modell Virtuell 2000, Architecture 1999–2000 2002, Vol. 2 Erlebnisräume – Spaces Design Construction 2002, Geometrie der Stille 2002, Luchao – Born from a Drop: Architecture for China 2003, Architecture 2000–01 2003, Vol. 3 Berliner Bauten und Projekte, 1965–2005 2005, Ideal City – Real Projects in China 2005, Architecture 2001–03 2005, Vol. 4 Private Houses 2006, Vol. 5 Möbel Furniture 2007, Bauten Buildings 2007, Architecture 2003–07 2009, From Cape Town to Brasília New Stadiums by gmp 2010. *Address:* Elbchaussee 139, 22763 Hamburg, Germany (office). *Telephone:* (40) 881510 (office). *Fax:* (40) 88151177 (office). *E-mail:* hamburg-e@gmp-architekten.de (office). *Website:* www.gmp-architekten.de (office).

VON GRÜNBERG, Hubertus, DSc; German business executive; *Chairman, ABB Ltd;* b. 20 July 1942; ed Univ. of Cologne; began his career with Alfred Teves GmbH (ITT), Frankfurt am Main, various posts in Germany, Brazil and USA 1971–82, Head of Devt and Tech., Frankfurt am Main 1982–84, Chair. Man. Bd 1984–89, Vice-Pres. ITT Corpn, New York, USA 1987–89, Pres. and CEO ITT Automotive Inc., Auburn Hills, Mich., USA 1989–91, Sr Vice-Pres. ITT Corpn; CEO Continental AG 1991–99, Chair. Supervisory Bd of Dirs 1999–2009; Chair. ABB Ltd, Zurich 2007–; Chair. Advisory Bd Sapinda Holding BV (Netherlands); mem. Bd of Dirs, Schindler Holding AG (Switzerland); mem. Supervisory Bd Deutsche Telekom AG from 2000, Allianz Versicherungs AG. *Address:* ABB Ltd, Affolternstrasse 44, 8050 Zurich, Switzerland (office). *Telephone:* (43) 317-71-11 (office). *Fax:* (43) 317-44-20 (office). *E-mail:* info@abb.com (office). *Website:* www.abb.com (office).

VON HEBEL, Herman, LLM; Dutch lawyer and international organization official; b. 22 Nov. 1961, Coevorden; m.; two c.; ed Univ. of Groningen; Legal Researcher, Univ. of Utrecht 1987–89; Legislation Expert, Ministry of Justice 1990–91; Asst Legal Adviser, Sr Legal Counsel, Ministry of Foreign Affairs 1991–2000; Sr Legal Officer of Trial Chamber II, Int. Criminal Tribunal for the fmr Yugoslavia 2001–06; Deputy Registrar, then Acting Registrar and Registrar, Special Court for Sierra Leone 2006–09; Deputy Registrar, then Acting Registrar and Registrar, Special Tribunal for Lebanon 2009–13; Registrar, Int. Criminal Court 2013–18; Chair. Int. Comm. of Jurists (Dutch section) 1988–90.

VON HIPPEL, Karin, BA, MA, PhD; American security expert and fmr UN official; *Director-General, Royal United Services Institute;* ed Yale Univ., St Peter's Coll., Oxford and London School of Econs, UK; Project Man., The Somalia Project, LSE March–Sept. 1995; Consultant on Governance, European Comm. Somalia Unit May–Nov. 1997; Political Adviser to Rep. of Sec.-Gen., UN Political Office for Somalia (UNPOS) 1998–99; Civil Affairs Officer, UN Interim Admin Mission in Kosovo (UNMIK) Jan.–Dec. 2000; Sr Research Fellow, Centre for Defence Studies, King's Coll. London 2001–05; Dir and Co-Dir, Post-Conflict Reconstruction Project, Center for Strategic and Int. Studies 2005–10; Sr Adviser, Bureau for Counterterrorism, US Dept of State 2010–11, Deputy Asst Sec. for Overseas Operations 2011–14, Chief of Staff, Special Presidential Envoy for Global Coalition to Counter ISIL 2014–; Dir-Gen. Royal United Services Inst. 2015–; mem. World Econ. Forum's Global Agenda Council on Fragile States. *Publications include:* Democracy by Force: US Military Intervention in the Post-Cold War World 2000; contribs to European Approaches to Crisis Management 1997, A Perilous Course: US Strategy and Assistance to Pakistan 2007, Debating Terrorism and Counterterrorism: Conflicting Perspectives on Causes, Contexts and Responses 2014; contribs to several journals including The Washington Quarterly, The World Today, Journal of Modern African Studies. *Address:* Royal United Services Institute, 61 Whitehall, London, SW1A 2ET, England (office). *Telephone:* (20) 7747-2600 (office). *E-mail:* information@rusi.org (office). *Website:* rusi.org (office).

VON KLITZING, Klaus; German physicist; *Director, Max Planck Institute for Solid State Research;* b. 28 June 1943, Schroda; s. of Bogislav von Klitzing and Anny von Klitzing (née Ulbrich); m. Renate Falkenberg 1971; two s. one d.; ed Tech. Univ. Brunswick, Univ. Würzburg; Prof., Tech. Univ., Munich 1980–84; Dir Max-Planck Inst. for Solid State Research, Stuttgart 1985–; Foreign mem. NAS, Russian Acad. of Sciences, Royal Soc. of London, Chinese Acad. of Science, Pontifical Acad. of Sciences, Österreichische Akad. der Wissenschaften, Deutsche Akad. der Naturforscher Leopoldina; Hon. mem. German Physical Soc.; numerous hon. doctorates; Nobel Prize in Physics 1985. *Achievements include:* discovered quantum Hall effect. *Address:* Max-Planck Institut für Festkörperforschung, Heisenbergstr. 1, Postfach 800665, 70569 Stuttgart, Germany (office). *Telephone:* (711) 6891570 (office). *Fax:* (711) 6891572 (office). *E-mail:* k.klitzing@fkf.mpg.de (office). *Website:* www.fkf.mpg.de/klitzing (office).

VON LUCIUS, Wulf D., Dr rer. pol; German scientific publisher; *Publisher and President, Lucius & Lucius Verlag;* b. 29 Nov. 1938, Jena; s. of Tankred R. von Lucius and Annelise Fischer; m. Akka Achelis 1967; three s.; ed Heidelberg, Berlin and Freiburg, Univ. of Hohenheim, Stuttgart; mil. service 1958–60; Asst Inst. of Econometrics, Freiburg 1965–66; worked in several publishing houses and as public accountant 1966–69; Partner and Man. Dir Gustav Fischer Verlag 1969–95; mem. Bd of Exec. Officers, German Publrs Asscn (Börsenverein) 1976–86; mem. Bd C. Hanser Verlag 1984–2013; Publr and Pres. Lucius & Lucius Verlag, Stuttgart 1996–; Chair. Int. Publishers Copyright Council 1995–98, Asscn of Scientific Publrs in Germany 1994–2001, Wüstenrot Stiftung 2009–; mem. Exec. Cttee Int. Publrs Asscn Geneva 1996–2004; Bd German Nat. Library 1981–; Hon. Prof., Univ. of Hohenheim, Stuttgart; Friedrich-Perthes-Medaille 1999, Antiquaria Preis 2001, Ludwig Erhard Preis 2004. *Publications:* Bücherlust–Vom Sammeln 2000, Verlagswirtschaft 2005 (third edn 2014), Das Glück der Bücher 2012; numerous articles on publishing, copyright and book history. *Leisure interests:* collecting fine prints and artists' books. *Address:* Gerokstrasse 51, 70184 Stuttgart, Germany (office). *Telephone:* (711) 242060 (office). *Fax:* (711) 242088 (office). *E-mail:* lucius@luciusverlag.com (office). *Website:* luciusverlag.com (office).

VON MOLTKE, Gebhardt, LLB; German diplomatist; b. 28 June 1938, Wernersdorf, Silesia; m. Dorothea von Moltke 1965; one s. one d.; ed Univs of Heidelberg, Grenoble, Berlin, Freiburg im Breisgau; practical legal training 1963–67; with Fed. Foreign Office, Bonn 1968–71, Personnel Admin. 1977–82, Head of US Dept 1986–91; served in Embassy in Moscow 1971–75, in Yaoundé 1975–77, in Washington, DC 1982–86; Asst Sec.-Gen. for Political Affairs NATO 1991–97; Amb. to UK 1997–99; Perm. Rep. to NATO, Brussels 1999–2003; Chair. German-British Soc. 2003–14; Hon. GCVO, Great Cross (Hungary), Grand Cross (Germany), Commdr Cross (Poland), Grand Decoration in Gold with Star (Austria); Hon. DrJur (Birmingham) 2000; US Army Commdr's Award. *Leisure interests:* tennis, music, drawings (old masters).

VON OTTER, Anne-Sofie; Swedish singer (mezzo-soprano); b. 9 May 1955, Stockholm; m. Benny Fredriksson 1989 (died 2018); ed Stockholm Conservatory, Guildhall School of Music and Drama, UK, studied interpretation with Erik Werba in Vienna and Geoffrey Parsons in London, vocal studies with Vera Rozsa; mem. Basel Opera, Switzerland 1982–85; French debut at Opéra de Marseille (Nozze di Figaro—Cherubino) and Aix-en-Provence Festival (La Finta Giardiniera) 1984, Rome, Accad. di Santa Cecilia 1984, Geneva (Così fan tutte—Dorabella) 1985, Berlin (Così fan tutte) 1985, USA in Chicago (Mozart's C minor Mass) and Philadelphia (Bach's B minor Mass) 1985, London at Royal Opera, Covent Garden (Le Nozze di Figaro) 1985, Lyon (La Finta Giardiniera) 1986, La Scala, Milan (Alceste) 1987, Munich (Le Nozze di Figaro) 1987, Stockholm (Der Rosenkavalier) 1988, The Metropolitan Opera, New York (Le Nozze di Figaro) 1988, The Royal Albert Hall, London (Faust) 1989, Handel's Ariodante 1997; Glyndebourne (Carmen) 2002, Théâtre des Champs Elysées (Handel's Serse) 2003, Metropolitan Opera, New York (Mélisande) 2005, Santa Fe (Carmen) 2006; Waltraute in Götterdammerung for Aix-en-Provence Festival 2009 and Salzburg Easter Festival 2010; appeared in Lulu at the Met 2010; Irene in Tamerlano, Liceu Barcelona 2011; Marcellina in Le Nozze di Figaro, Baden Baden 2015; Leonora in The Exterminating Angel, Salzburger Festspiele 2016, Royal Opera House, Covent Garden 2017; repertoire extends from baroque music, German lieder through opera to 20th century music; has given recitals in New York, Paris, Brussels, Geneva, Stockholm, Vienna, London, Verbier, Toulouse and numerous other cities; Hon. DSc (Bath) 1992; Frankfurter Musikpreis 2011. *Recordings include:* Speak Low (Songs by Kurt Weill) & The Seven Deadly Sins (Die Sieben Todsunden) 1995, Home for Christmas 1999, For the Stars (with Elvis Costello) 2001, Terezín/Theresienstadt 2008, Love Songs (with jazz pianist Brad Mehldau) 2010, Mahler: Des Knaben Wunderhorn 2010, Berlioz: Les Nuits d'été; Harold en Italie 2011, Sogno Barocco 2012, Swedish Romantic Songs (with Bengt Forsberg) 2012, Douce France 2013, So Many Things 2016, Sibelius: Tapiola, En Saga 2017. *Address:* c/o Shirley Thomson, Harrison Parrott Ltd, The Ark, 201 Talgarth Road, London, W6 8BJ, England (office). *E-mail:* shirley.thomson@harrisonparrott.co.uk (office). *Website:* www.harrisonparrott.com/artists/anne-sofie-von-otter (office); www.annesofievonotter.com.

VON PIERER, Heinrich, DrIur, DipEng; German business executive; b. (Heinrich Karl Friedrich Eduard Pierer von Esch), 26 Jan. 1941, Erlangen; m. Annette von Pierer; three c.; ed Univ. of Erlangen-Nuremberg; Asst Lecturer, Faculty of Law, Univ. of Erlangen-Nuremberg 1965–69; joined legal dept, Corp. Finance Div., Siemens AG 1969, various commercial assignments in sales and marketing at Kraftwerk Union AG div. and in various corp. depts 1977–87, apptd Commercial Head of Kraftwerk Union AG 1988, Group Pres. Kraftwerk Union AG, mem. Man. Bd Siemens AG 1989, mem. Corp. Exec. Cttee 1990, Deputy Chair. Man. Bd 1991, Chair. Man. Bd, Pres. and CEO 1992–2005, Chair. Supervisory Bd 2005–07; mem. Supervisory Bd Bayer AG 1993–2005, Münchener Rückversicherungs-Gesellschaft AG (Munich Re) from 1999, Hochtief AG 2000–11, Volkswagen AG from 2000, Deutsche Bank AG 2005–08, ThyssenKrupp AG 2005–08; mem. Econ. Cttee RWE AG; Chair. Asien-Pazifik-Ausschuss der Deutschen Wirtschaft (Asia-Pacific Cttee of the German Economy) 1993–2006; mem. Bd Bundesverbandes der Deutschen Industrie (Fed. Asscn of German Industry); Chair. Int. Advisory Bd Allianz AG Holding; mem. Senate Max Planck Soc.; Founding mem. UNESCO-Children in Need; Hon. Prof., Friedrich-Alexander Univ. of Erlangen-Nuremberg 2006; Hon. Citizen Award (Singapore) 2007; Großes Bundesverdienstkreuz des Verdienstordens 2001, Bayerischer Verdienstorden 2005; Dr hc (Technischen Universität München) 1997, (Katholieke Universiteit Leuven) 1998, (Tongji Univ., Shanghai) 2004, (Technischen Universität Berlin) 2004, (Technischen Universität Graz) 2005; Eduard Rhein Ring of Honour, Eduard Rhein Foundation 2000, Global Leadership Award, American Inst. for Contemporary German Studies 2002, Scopus Award, Hebrew Univ. of Jerusalem 2002, World Business Award 2003. *Address:* c/o Siemens AG, Wittelsbacherplatz 2, 80333, Munich, Germany.

VON PLOETZ, Hans-Friedrich, DrIur; German diplomatist (retd) and business executive; *Chairman, Investment Advisory Council, Wermuth Asset Management;* b. 12 July 1940, Nimptsch; m. Päivi Leinonen; two s.; ed Univs of Marburg, Berlin and Vienna, Austria; Asst Lecturer Univ. of Marburg 1965–66; joined Fed. Foreign Office, Bonn 1966; postings abroad: Trade Mission, German Embassy, Helsinki 1968–73; German Embassy, Washington, DC 1978–80; Perm. Rep. NATO Council 1989–93; Dir-Gen. for European Affairs, Bonn 1993–94; State Sec., Ministry for Foreign Affairs, Bonn and Berlin 1994–99; Amb. to UK 1999–2002, to Russian Fed. 2002–05; Chair. Foundation for German–Russian Youth Exchanges 2006–10; Chair. Investment Advisory Council, Wermuth Asset Management 2011–; Vice-Chair. Vitrulan International GmbH 2005–13; mem. Int. Advisory Council, Bosch

GmbH 2005–13; mem. Council, Baltic International Bank. *Leisure interests:* music, golf, gardening. *Address:* Wermuth Asset Management, Johannisstraße 3, 10117 Berlin (office); Schlossstr. 5, 14059 Berlin, Germany (home). *Telephone:* (30) 27890920 (office); (30) 30109170 (home). *Fax:* (30) 278909211 (office). *E-mail:* info@wermutham.com (office); vploetz@web.de (home). *Website:* www.wermutham.com (office).

VON ROHR, Hans Christoph (see ROHR, Hans Christoph von).

VON SCHIMMELMANN, Wulf, DBA; German business executive; b. 19 Feb. 1947, Steinhöring; ed Univ. of Hamburg, Univ. of Zurich, Switzerland; Partner, McKinsey & Co. 1972–78, worked in offices in Zurich, Cleveland, OH, USA, Kuwait and Dusseldorf; mem. Bd of Dirs Landesgirokasse-Bank, Stuttgart 1978–84; mem. Man. Bd DG Bank, Frankfurt am Main 1984–91; CEO and Head of Financial Services, Deutsche Postbank AG (also Head of Financial Services, Deutsche Post AG) 1999–2007, Interim Chief Financial Officer 2004–06, Deputy Chair. Deutsche Postbank Financial Services GmbH, also served as its Head of Corp. Devt, Investor Relations and Research Corp. Communications; mem. Deutsche Post AG 2007–18, Chair. 2009–18; Chair. PB (USA) Holdings Inc., Wilmington, Del., USA, PB Capital Corpn; Chair. Supervisory Bd PB Versicherung AG, PB Lebensversicherung AG, Hilden, Postbank Filialvertrieb AG, Bonn, Postbank Finanzberatung AG, Hameln, Bawag P.S.K., BHW Bausparkasse AG; Man. Partner, Regius investment co. 1991–, responsible for investment banking, payment transactions, int. business co-operation and corp. customers, Regius GmbH & Co. KG 1997–; mem. Bd of Dirs, Accenture Corpn (Ireland), Thomson Reuters Corpn (Canada); mem. Supervisory Bd, Deutsche Telekom AG 2006–09, Maxingvest AG, Allianz Deutschland AG; Ind. Dir Altadis SA 2004–; Hon. Prof., Univ. of Constance 2006; Dr hc (Univ. of Constance) 2006.

VON SCHLABRENDORFF, Fabian Gotthard Herbert, MA, DrIur; German lawyer; *Of Counsel, Clifford Chance LLP;* b. 23 Dec. 1944, Berlin; s. of Fabian von Schlabrendorff and Luitgarde von Schlabrendorff (née von Bismarck); m. Maria de la Cruz Caballero Palomero 1977; one s. one d.; ed Univ. of Geneva, Switzerland, Univ. of Frankfurt, Univ. of Chicago, USA; service in Bundeswehr 1964–68; Research Co-ordinator, Inst. of Int. and Foreign Trade and Business Law, Frankfurt 1975–82; joined Clifford Chance LLP Frankfurt 1983, Partner 1986–2009, Of Counsel 2010–; mem. Editorial Bd SchiedsVZ (German Arbitration Journal); mem. Advisory Bd Die Deutsche Institution für Schiedsgerichtsbarkeit; CEPES Award 1987. *Publications include:* Mining Ventures in Developing Countries (Parts 1 and 2) (co-author) 1979/81, The Legal Structure of Transnational Forest-Based Investments in Developing Countries (co-author) 1987, Substantive Law in International Long-term Infrastructure Contracts, ADRLJ 3-18 2000, Article 6 of the European Convention on Human Rights and its Bearing upon International Arbitratio, in Liber Amicorum Karl-Heinz Böckstiegel (co-author) 2001, Mehrparteiensituationen und Inter-Omnes-Wirkung, in DIS-Materialien VIII 2001, El Régimen Jurídico del Arbitraje en Alemania, in Anuario de Justicia Alternativa 2003, Geldwäsche in internationalen Schiedsverfahren, in Festschrift Peter Schlosser 2005, Conflict of Legal Privileges in International Arbitration (co-author) in Liber Amicorum Robert Briner 2005, SchiedsVZ (German Arbitration Journal), Parallele Verfahren, Aufnahme von Dritten, Verbindung von Verfahren: Erfahrungen aus der Praxis in der ICC, in Schriftreihe der Deutschen Institution für Schiedsgerichtsbarkeit, Band 16, Die Beteiligung Dritter an Schiedsverfahren (co-ed.) 2005, Legal Privilege and Confidentiality in Arbitration (co-author) in Privilege and Confidentiality: An International Handbook 2006. *Leisure interest:* classical music. *Address:* Clifford Chance LLP, Mainzer Landstrasse 46, 60325 Frankfurt, Germany (office). *Telephone:* (69) 7199-1441 (office). *Fax:* (69) 7199-4000 (office). *E-mail:* fabian.schlabrendorff@cliffordchance.com (office); fabian.schlabrendorff@t-online.de. *Website:* www.cliffordchance.com (office).

VON STADE, Frederica; American singer (mezzo-soprano); b. 1 June 1945, Somerville, NJ; m. 1st Peter Elkus 1973 (divorced); two d.; m. 2nd Michael G. Gorman 1991; ed Mannes Coll. of Music; opera début with Metropolitan Opera, New York (in Le Nozze di Figaro) 1970; has also sung with Paris Opera, San Francisco Opera, Lyric Opera of Chicago, LA Opera, Salzburg Festival, Covent Garden, London, Spoleto Festival, Boston Opera Co., Santa Fe Opera, Houston Grand Opera, La Scala, Milan, Vienna State Opera; appearances with Lyric Opera of Chicago in 2010 included Madeline in Three Decembers and Despina in Cose fan tutte; sang role of Myrtle Bledsoe (created for her by the composer Ricky Ian Gordon) in A Coffin in Egypt, Chicago Opera Theater 2015; Winnie Flato in Great Scott, Dallas Opera 2015, San Diego Opera 2016; Madeline in Three Decembers, Hawaii Opera 2017; mem. American Acad. of Arts and Sciences 2012; Officier, Ordre des Arts et des Lettres 1998; Dr hc (Yale Univ.), (Boston Univ.), (Georgetown Univ. School of Medicine), (Mannes School of Music), (San Francisco Conservatory of Music), (Cleveland Inst. of Music); two Grand Prix du Disc awards, Deutsche Schallplattenpreis, Premio della Critica Discografica and numerous other awards and prizes. *Recordings include:* over 70 recordings, including Frederica von Stade Sings Mozart and Rossini Opera Arias, French Opera Arias 1998, Songs of the Cat (with Garrison Keillor) 2010, Fauré: Mélodies 2011, A Portrait On Record 2014, Complete RCA and Columbia Recital Albums (box set) 2016. *Address:* c/o Matthew A. Horner, IMG Artists, Pleiades House, 7 West 54th Street, New York, NY 10019, USA (office). *E-mail:* mhorner@imgartists.com (office). *Website:* www.fredericavonstade.com.

VON SYDOW, Björn, MS, PhD; Swedish politician, political scientist and academic; b. 26 Nov. 1945, Stockholm; s. of Bengt Sköldenberg and Tullia von Sydow; m. Madeleine von Sydow; three s. one d.; ed Stockholm and Linköping Univs; worked as librarian for fmr Prime Minister Tage Erlander 1970–74; Lecturer in Political Science, Linköping Univ. 1974–78; Assoc. Prof. of Political Science, Stockholm Univ. 1978–83, 1992–2012; Prin. School of Social Work and Public Admin 1983–88; work on study of gen. election of Bd Dirs Nat. Pension Insurance Fund 1984–86; Visiting Research Scientist, Case Western Reserve Univ., Ohio 1986, Pomona and Scripps Colls Clairmont, Calif. 1992; active in municipal politics in Solna 1979–96, Chair. Swedish Social Democratic Party (SAP), Solna 1983–2000, in Sigtuna 2013–15; mem. Editorial Cttee Tiden (political journal) 1983–89; mem. SAP programme comm. 1987–2001; mem. Riksdag (Parl.) (Social Democrat) 1994–, Speaker 2002–06, mem. Parl. Cttee on Constitutional Affairs 1994–96, 2012– (Deputy Chair. 2014–), SI Cttee on Econ. Policy, Devt and Environment 1995–96, Alt. Parl. Cttee on Educ. 2010–12, Chair. SAP Cttee on EU Affairs, mem. IGC and EU Enlargement Cttee of Party of European Socialists, Chair. EU Cttee of Nordic Labour Movt (SAMAK) 1996–98; Head of Political Planning responsible for Research and Devt, Econ. Growth and Environment, Office of Prime Minister 1988–91; mem. Cttee on Civil Rights, Ministry of Justice 1993–94; Chair. Cttee on Environmental Protection, Ministry of Environment 1994–96, Parl. Cttee preparing EU Treaty revision, Ministry for Foreign Affairs 1995–96; Minister of Trade at Ministry for Industry and Commerce 1996–97; Minister of Defence 1997–2002; Chair. Univ. Centre for Physics and Astronomy, Stockholm 1992–95, Swedish Research Council 2007–09, Swedish Secr. for Environmental Earth System Sciences 2011–15; mem. Swedish Del. to Parl. Ass. of Council of Europe 2007–14, Rapporteur on Kosovo and Council of Europe 2010–14, Chair. Political Affairs Cttee 2010–12, 2013, Head, Swedish Del. to NATO Parl. Ass. 2014–; Commr, Research and Devt in Defence 2016; mem., Royal Swedish Acad. of Sciences 2007, Royal Swedish Acad. of War Sciences 2009. *Publications include:* Can We Rely on Politicians? – Public and Private Politics in the Leadership of the Swedish Social Democratic Party 1955–1960 1978, Parliamentarism in Sweden: Development and Forms up to 1945 1997, Sweden's Security in the 21st Century 1999, The Constitutional Developments of Sweden Since 1809 2009, The Swedish Social Democratic Party – Programmes 2009, Therefore a Defence – Philosophy, Defence and Constitution 2012, The Significance of Freedom of Speech for a Free People 2016. *Leisure interests:* horse riding, railway enthusiast. *Address:* Riddarhustorget 7–9, Sveriges Riksdag, 100 12 Stockholm (office); Stora Malmgatan 27, 193 35 Sigtuna, Sweden (home). *Telephone:* (8) 786-42-10 (office); (8) 27-66-80 (home); 70-576-17-29 (mobile) (home); (8) 592-500-71 (home). *E-mail:* bjorn.von.sydow@riksdagen.se (office). *Website:* www.riksdagen.se (office).

VON TRIER, Lars; Danish film director; b. 30 April 1956; s. of Ulf Trier and Inger Trier; m. 1st Cæcilia Holbek Trier (divorced); two c.; m. 2nd Bente Frøge 1997; ed Danish Film School; Co-founder and Head, Dogme School of Film 1995–. *Films include:* Orchidégartneren (The Orchid Gardener) 1977, Menthe - la bienheureuse 1979, Nocturne 1980, Den Sidste Detalje (The Last Detail) 1981, Befrielsesbilleder 1982, Forbrydelsens element (The Element of Crime; Cannes Film Festival Technical Grand Prize) 1984, Europa (aka Zentropa) 1991, Epidemic 1988, The Kingdom 1994, Breaking the Waves (Cannes Film Festival Grand Prize) 1996, The Idiots 1998, Dancer in the Dark (Cannes Film Festival Palme d'Or) 2000, Dogville 2003, Dear Wendy (script) 2005, Manderlay 2005, Direktøren for det hele (The Boss Of It All) 2006, De unge år: Erik Nietzsche sagaen del 1 2007, Antichrist 2009, Melancholia 2011, Nymphomaniac: Volume I 2013, Nymphomaniac: Volume II 2013. *Publication:* Trier on Von Trier 2004. *Address:* Zentropa, Filmbyen 22, 2650 Hvidovre, Denmark (home). *Telephone:* 36868788 (office). *Fax:* 36868789 (office). *E-mail:* zentropa@filmbyen.com (office). *Website:* www.dogme95.dk.

VON TROTTA, Margarethe; German film director and actress; b. 21 Feb. 1942, Berlin; m. 1st Jürgen Moeller (divorced 1968); m. 2nd Volker Schlöndorff 1971 (divorced 1991); one s.; has written scripts for The Sudden Wealth of the Poor People of Kombach 1971, Summer Lightning 1972, Fangschuss 1974, Unerreichbare Nahe 1984; Leo Baeck Medal 2012, Herbert Strate Prize for Cinematic Action 2013, Theodor-W. Adorno Prize 2018. *Films include:* Die Verlorene Ehre der Katharina Blum (The Lost Honour of Katharina Blum) 1975, Das zweite Erwachen der Christa Klages (The Second Awakening of Christa Klages) 1978, Schwestern, oder die Balance des Glücks (Sisters, or the Balance of Happiness) (Créteil Int. Women's Film Festival Grand Prix Award 1981) 1979, Die Bleierne Zeit (The German Sisters) 1981, Heller Wahn (Friends and Husbands) 1983, Rosa Luxemburg 1985, Felix 1987, Paura e amore (Love and Fear) 1988, L'Africana 1990, Il lungo silenzio 1992, Das Versprechen (The Promise) 1994, Rosenstrasse (Best European Film, Globo d'oro 2004) 2003, Ich bin die Andere 2006, Vision 2009, Hannah Arendt 2012 Searching for Ingmar Bergman 2018. *Television includes:* Winterkind (film) 1996, Dunkle Tage (film) 1999, Jahrestage (mini-series) 2000, Die Andere Frau (The Other Woman) (film) 2004, Tatort (TV series) 2007, Die Schwester (film) 2010, Mai per amore (mini-series) 2012. *Address:* c/o Above The Line GmbH, Theresienstr. 31, D-80333, Munich, Germany (office). *Telephone:* (89) 5990840 (office). *Fax:* (89) 5503855 (office). *E-mail:* mail@abovetheline.de (office). *Website:* www.abovetheline.de (office).

VON WERTHERN, Hans Carl, PhD; German diplomatist; *Ambassador to Japan;* b. 4 Aug. 1953; m.; three d.; ed St Albans School, Washington, DC, USA, Univ. of Mainz; mil. service 1973–75; Researcher, Univ. of Mainz 1979–84; Attaché (Educ.), Fed. Foreign Office, Bonn 1984–86, Inst. for Peace Research and Security Policy, Hamburg 1986–87, Embassy in Hanoi, Viet Nam 1987–90, Perm. Mission to NATO, Brussels 1990–92, Deputy Head of Training for the Professional Staff, Fed. Foreign Office 1992–94, Embassy in Asunción, Paraguay 1994–97, Deputy Dir, Western Europe Unit, Fed. Foreign Office, Bonn/Berlin 1997–2000, Sec. for European Policy, FDP Parl. Group, Berlin 2000–02, Royal Coll. of Defence Studies, London 2003, Head of 'Germany in Japan 2005/2006' task force, Fed. Foreign Office, Berlin 2004–05, Dir, East Asia Unit 2005–07, Envoy, Embassy in Beijing 2007–10, Lecturer of Staff, Fed. Foreign Office 2010–11, Head of Cen. Div. 2011–14, Amb. to Japan 2014–. *Address:* Embassy of Germany, 4-5-10, Minami Azabu, Minato-ku, Tokyo, 106-0047, Japan (office). *Telephone:* (3) 5791-7700 (office). *Fax:* (3) 5791-7773 (office). *E-mail:* info@japan.diplo.de (office). *Website:* www.japan.diplo.de (office).

VONA, Gábor; Hungarian politician; b. (Gábor Zázrivecz), 20 Aug. 1978, Gyöngyös; m. Krisztina Vona-Szabó; one s.; ed Eötvös Loránd Univ., Budapest; worked briefly as teacher; Co-founder Jobbik Youth Movt 1999, Founding mem. and Deputy Chair. Jobbik Magyarországért Mozgalom (Jobbik—Movt for a Better Hungary) 2003–06, Chair. 2006–18; Chair. Magyar Gárda (Hungarian Guard, uniformed paramilitary group) 2007–08 (org. banned Dec. 2008); mem. Országgyűlés (Parl.) 2010–18; Jobbik cand. for Prime Minister in parl. elections 2010, 2014, 2018. *Address:* c/o Jobbik Magyarországért Mozgalom (Movement for a Better Hungary), 1113 Budapest, Villányi u. 20A, Hungary (office). *Telephone:* (1) 3651488 (office). *Fax:* (1) 3651488 (office). *E-mail:* vona.gabor@parlament.hu (office); jobbik@jobbik.hu (office). *Website:* www.jobbik.hu (office); www.vonagabor.hu.

VONDRA, Alexandr; Czech diplomatist, politician, academic and consultant; b. 17 Aug. 1961, Prague; m. Martina Vondrova; three c.; ed Charles Univ.; worked at

Náprstek Museum of Asian, African and American Cultures, Prague 1985–87; also active in Czechoslovakia's democratic opposition mid-1980s; fmr man. rock band Národni třída; Spokesperson for Charter 77 1989; Co-founder Civic Forum Movt 1989; Foreign Policy Adviser to Pres. Václav Havel 1990–92; First Deputy Minister of International Affairs 1992, First Deputy Minister of Foreign Affairs 1993–97, Chief negotiator in process of preparing Czech-German Declaration 1995–96; Amb. to USA 1997–2001; Czech Govt Commr to Prague NATO Summit (coordinated Prague NATO Summit 2002) 2001–02; Deputy Minister of Foreign Affairs 2003; Asst Lecturer, German Marshall Fund 2003–04; Man. Dir Dutko Worldwide (consulting firm), Prague 2004–06; Minister of Foreign Affairs 2006–07; mem. Civic Democratic Party (ODS) 2006–, currently a Deputy Chair.; elected Senator (ODS) for Litoměřice, Roudnice and Slaný regions 2006–; Deputy Prime Minister, responsible for European Affairs 2007–09; Minister of Defence 2010–12 (resgnd); Adjunct Prof., New York Univ. in Prague; Pres. Czech Euro-Atlantic Council; mem. Bd of Dirs Program of Atlantic Security Studies, Prague; Hon. Chair. Czech Euro-Atlantic Council 2004–06; Gold Plaque (Slovakia) 2001, Cross of Merit (Czech Repub.) 2002, Cross of Order of Merit (Poland) 2004, Commdr of the Three Stars (Latvia) 2005; US Nat. Endowment for Democracy Medal 1999, NATO Meritorious Service Medal 2005, Award for Human Understanding, Tolerance and Peace 2006. *Address:* Civic Democratic Party, Polygon House, Doudlebská 1699/5, 140 00 Prague 4, Czech Republic (office). *Telephone:* 234707111 (office). *Fax:* 234707103 (office). *E-mail:* hk@ods.cz (office). *Website:* www.ods.cz (office); www.alexandrvondra.cz.

VONDRÁČEK, Radek; Czech lawyer and politician; *Chairman, Chamber of Deputies;* b. 30 Dec. 1973, Kroměříž, Czech Socialist Repub., Czechoslovak Socialist Repub.; m.; two c.; ed Masaryk Univ., Brno; legal practice, JUDr Jan Halas, Kroměříž 2000–03; Pnr, Access Devt s.r.o. 2009–13; Partner, IWWAL Consulting s.r.o. 2010–15; Deputy Mayor of Kroměříž 2014–17; mem. Poslanecká Sněmovna (Chamber of Deputies, parl.) 2013–, First Deputy Chair. Jan.–Oct. 2017, Chair. (speaker) Oct. 2017–; mem. Ano (Yes) 2011–. *Address:* Poslanecká Sněmovna, Sněmovní 4, 118 26 Prague 1, Czech Republic (office). *Telephone:* 257171111 (office). *Fax:* 257534469 (office). *E-mail:* posta@psp.cz (office). *Website:* www.psp.cz (office); radekvondracek.cz.

VONDRAN, Ruprecht, DrIur; German business executive and politician (retd); *Honorary Chairman, German-Japanese Industrial Co-operation Committee, and President, Association of German-Japanese Societies;* b. 31 Dec. 1935, Göttingen; s. of Rudolf Vondran and Anneliese Unterberg; m. Jutta Paul 1970; two s. two d.; ed Univs. of Göttingen, Bonn and Würzburg; mem. Bundestag 1987–94; Pres., Wirtschaftsvereinigung Stahl (Steel Industry Asscn) 1988–2000, Verband Deutsch–Japanischer Gesellschaften (Asscn of German-Japanese Socs); Hon. Chair. Deutsch-Japanischer Wirtschaftskreis (German-Japanese Industrial Co-operation Cttee); Chair. Poensgen-Stiftung; Order of the Rising Sun (Gold and Silver stars), Japan; Hon. DEng. *Publications:* Der politische Auftrag der Nato und seine Verwirklichung 1966, Wie bewältigt die japanische Wirtschaft ihre Anpassungsprobleme? 1996, Stahl ist Zukunft 1999, Warum Japan? 2005, Ewiger Friede und Bestandige Freundschaft 2005, Deutschland in Japan 2005/2006: was hat es gebracht? 2006, Für ein weltoffenes Deutschland, Japan und China: Auf der Suche nad einer neuen Ordnung, Chancen und Grenzen der Electromobilität 2010, Und Alle Fluten Leben 2010, Tobi Ishi Springsteine 2010, Ferne Gefährten 2011, Schwerkraft der Wissenschaft 2012, Gelebte Partnerschaft 2014, Mikado 2015. *Leisure interests:* modern graphics, Japanese porcelain. *Address:* Urdenbacher Allee 63, 40593 Düsseldorf, Germany (home). *Telephone:* (211) 7182231 (office). *Fax:* (211) 7118734 (office).

VONGKUSOLKIT, Isara, BA; Thai business executive; *Chairman, Mitr Phol Sugar Corporation Ltd;* b. 1946, Ratchaburi; m.; four c.; ed Univ. of North Carolina, USA; Pres. Mitr Phol Sugar Corpn Ltd –2008, Chair. 2008–; Dir and Chair. Exec. Cttee, United Standard Terminal (UST) Public Co. Ltd; Chair. Thai Chamber of Commerce 2013–; Chair. Board of Trade of Thailand 2013–; Dir Fed. of Thai Industries; Trustee, Kenan Inst. Asia 2009. *Address:* 88 Moo 2 Tiwanont Road, Muang, Pathumtani 12000; Mitr Phol Sugar Corpn, Ltd, 3rd Floor, Ploenchit Center, Building 2, Sukhumvit Road, Klongtoey, Bangkok 10110, Thailand (office). *Telephone:* (2) 656-8488 (office). *Fax:* (2) 656-8494 (office). *E-mail:* info@mitrphol.com (office). *Website:* www.mitrphol.com (office).

VONGVANICH, Tevin, BEng, MS (Chem. Eng), MS (Petrol. Eng); Thai business executive; *President and CEO, PTT Public Company Ltd;* b. 31 Aug. 1958; ed Chulalongkorn Univ., Rice Univ. and Univ. of Houston, USA, Program for Global Leadership, Harvard Business School, USA, Democratic Politics and Governance for High-Level Admins Program, King Prajadhipok's Inst., Thailand, Sr Exec. Program, Sasin Grad. Inst. of Business Admin, Chulalongkorn Univ., Top Execs Program, Capital Market Acad., The Joint State Private Sector Course, Nat. Defence Coll., The Programme for Sr Execs on Justice Admin, Thai Inst. of Dirs Asscn; Sr Vice-Pres., Operations, PTT Exploration and Production Public Co. Ltd 2002–03, Sr Vice-Pres., Regional Assets Div. 2003–04, Exec. Vice-Pres., Corp. Business Devt 2004–07, Sr Exec. Vice-Pres., Corp. Strategy and Devt 2008–09, Dir, PTT International Co. Ltd 2008–11, Chief Financial Officer and Acting Sr Exec. Vice-Pres., Corp. Strategy and Devt, PTT PLC, PTT Exploration and Production Public Co. Ltd 2009–10, Chief Financial Officer, PTT Co. Ltd 2010–12, Pres. and CEO PTT Exploration and Production Public 2012–15, Pres. and CEO PTT Public Co. Ltd 2015–; Chair. PTT ICT Solutions Co. Ltd 2009–11; Dir, Bangchak Petroleum PLC 2007–10, PTT Chemical PLC, Bangkok Aviation Fuel Services PLC 2009–10, PTT Aromatics and Refining PLC, PTT Exploration and Production Public Co. Ltd 2009–11, PTT Exploration and Production Public Co. Ltd 2009–; Chair. Thailand Man. Asscn 2009–. *Address:* PTT Public Company Ltd, 555 Vibhavadi Rangsit Road, Chatuchak, Bangkok 10900, Thailand (office). *Telephone:* (2) 537-2000 (office). *Fax:* (2) 537-3499 (office). *E-mail:* info@pttplc.com (office). *Website:* www.pttplc.com (office).

VONN, Lindsey Caroline; American skier; b. (Lindsey Caroline Kildow), 18 Oct. 1984, St Paul, Minn.; d. of Alan Kildow; m. Thomas Vonn 2007 (divorced); ed Univ. of Missouri High School; won three consecutive overall World Cup championships 2008–11 and six downhill championships 2008–13; Gold Medal, Downhill, World Championships, Val d'Isère 2009, Super-G 2009; Silver Medal, Downhill, World Championships, Åre 2007, Super-G 2007; Gold Medal, Downhill, Winter Olympics, Vancouver 2010, Bronze Medal, Super-G 2010; also won consecutive World Cup season titles in Super G and a title in the combined; won her 23rd Women's World Cup Super G, Garmisch-Partenkirchen, Germany 2015; 65 world cup victories in four disciplines (downhill, Super G, slalom, and super combined); most successful female in ski racing history; correspondent for NBC News during 2014 Winter Olympics; IOC Youth Olympic Games Amb.; US Olympic Cttee Sportswoman of the Year for 2010, Laureus World Sports Award for Sportswoman of the Year for 2010, Laureus Spirit of Sport Award 2019. *Leisure interests:* cycling, tennis, reading, listening to hip hop music. *Address:* c/o Sue Dorf, IMG, 12400 Wilshire Boulevard, Suite 800, Los Angeles, CA 90025, USA (office). *Telephone:* (970) 470-4053 (office). *Fax:* (310) 909-5901 (office). *E-mail:* sue.dorf@img.com (office). *Website:* www.imgworld.com (office); www.lindseyvonn.com.

VORA, Motilal; Indian politician; b. 29 Dec. 1928, Nagor, Rajasthan; s. of Mohanlal Vora; m. Shanti Vora; two s. four d.; fmr journalist; elected Councillor, Durg Municipality 1968, Congress Party mem. Madhya Pradesh Vidhan Sabha 1972–90; Minister of State for Educ. and Minister for Local Govt 1981–82; Minister of Transport, Science and Tech. 1982–83, of Higher Educ. 1983–84, of Health and Family Welfare and Civil Aviation 1988–89; Pres. Madhya Pradesh Congress (I) Cttee 1984–85; elected Leader, Congress (I) Legis. Party 1985; Chief Minister Madhya Pradesh 1985–88, Jan.–Dec. 1989; Gov. of UP 1993–96; mem. Lok Sabha 1998–99, mem. Cttee on Home Affairs; mem. Rajya Sabha 2002–; Treas., Indian Nat. Congress party 2000–18; currently Chair. and Man. Dir Associated Journals Ltd. *Address:* 33 Lodhi Estate, New Delhi 110 011 (office); 33, Mohan Nagar, Durg, Chhattisgarh, India. *Telephone:* (11) 23792375 (office); (11) 24651313 (home). *E-mail:* vora@sansad.nic.in (office). *Website:* rajyasabha.nic.in (office).

VOROBYEV, Andrei Ivanovich, DrMed; Russian haematologist; *Director, Haematological Scientific Centre, Russian Academy of Medical Sciences;* b. 1 Oct. 1928; m.; two s.; ed First Inst. of Medicine; worked as house painter 1941–44; practitioner, Head of Polyclinics Volokolamsk Moscow Region 1953–54; Prof., Cen. Inst. of Advanced Medical Studies 1956–66; Head of Div., Inst. of Biophysics 1966–84; mem. Acad. of Medical Sciences 1986–, Dir All-Union (now All-Russian) Scientific Cen. of Haematology 1987–; Minister of Health 1991–92; Ed.-in-Chief Gematologiya i Transfuziologiya; USSR State Prize. *Leisure interest:* history of Russian Acad. of Science. *Address:* Haematological Scientific Centre, 125167 Moscow, Novy Zhukovsky pr. 4A, Russia (office). *Telephone:* (495) 212-21-23 (office). *Fax:* (495) 438-18-00 (office). *E-mail:* tt@blood.ru (office). *Website:* www .russmed.ru/eng (office).

VOROBYEV, Yuri Leonidovich, PhD; Russian engineer and politician; *Deputy Speaker, Sovet Federatsii (Federation Council);* b. 2 Feb. 1948, Krasnoyarsk; m.: two s.; ed Krasnoyarsk Inst. of Non-Ferrous Metals, Russian Acad. of Public Admin; machine operator, Krasmash plant, Krasnoyarsk 1964–66; researcher, M. I. Kalinin Krasnoyarsk Inst. of Nonferrous Metals 1971–72; with CPSU 1972–90, Sec., Sosnovoborsk dist CPSU Cttee, Krasnoyarsk 1972–88, instructor, Krasnoyarsk regional CPSU Cttee 1988–90; Dir-Gen. Krasnoyarsk Foundation for Protection of Small Business and Devt of Econ. Reforms 1990–91; Deputy Chair. Russian Rescue Corps 1991–92; First Deputy Chair. Russian Fed. State Cttee on Problems of Civil Defence and Emergency Situations 1992–94; First Deputy Minister of Civil Defence and Emergency Situations 1994; mem. Fed. Ass. of Parl. representing Vologda Region 2007, Vice-Speaker, Fed. Council with responsibility for anti-corruption legislation 2008–, apptd Chair. Fed. Council Comm. for Interaction with Regional Legislators to Improve Anti-Corruption Legislation 2009, apptd Deputy to Speaker, Fed. Council 2011; Trustee and Chair. of the Governing Council, Russian Geographical Soc.; Merited Rescuer of the Russian Fed. 2000, Hero of the Russian Fed. 2003; Order for Personal Courage 1992, Order of Merit for the Fatherland (4th Class) 1995, Order of Merit for the Fatherland (3rd Class) 2000, Order of Honour (Belarus) 2016; Medal Veteran of Labour 1989, Medal Defender of a Free Russia 1993, Medal In Memory of the 850th Anniversary of Moscow 1997, Golden Star Medal 2003, Medal In Memory of the 100th Anniversary of Kazan 1997, Government Prize in the Field of Science and Technology 2000. *Leisure interests:* sports, tourism. *Address:* Federation Council (Sovet Federatsii), 103426 Moscow, ul. B. Dmitrovka 26, Russia (office). *Telephone:* (495) 629-70-09 (office). *Fax:* (495) 629-67-43 (office). *E-mail:* post_sf@gov.ru (office). *Website:* www.council.gov.ru (office).

VORONIN, Vladimir Nikolayevich; Moldovan economist, engineer and politician; *First Secretary, Partidul Comuniştilor din Republica Moldova (Party of Communists of the Republic of Moldova);* b. 25 May 1941, Corjova, Chişinău Dist, Moldovan SSR, USSR; m. Taisia Mihailovna 1962; one s. one d.; ed Tech. Coll., Chişinău, Union Inst. of the Alimentary Industry, Acad. of Social Sciences, Cen. CPSU Cttee, Acad. of Ministry of Internal Affairs; bakery man., Criuleni 1961–66, Dubăsari 1966–71; fmr Deputy to Supreme Council, Moldovan SSR, First Sec., Party Cttee, Bender (Tighina) 1985–89, Minister of Internal Affairs, Moldovan SSR 1989–90; mem. Police Reserve, Russian Fed. 1989–93; Co-Pres. Organizational Cttee for Consolidation of CP 1993; revived CP Party of Moldova as Partidul Comuniştilor din Republica Moldova (Party of Communists of the Republic of Moldova) 1994, First Sec. 1994–; presidential cand. (placed third) 1996; Deputy in Parl. Repub. of Moldova 1998; Pres. of Moldova 2001–09; rank of Maj.-Gen. from fmr Ministry of Internal Affairs, USSR; Kt Grand Cross, Grand Order of King Tomislav (Croatia) 2007. *Address:* Partidul Comuniştilor din Republica Moldova (Party of Communists of the Republic of Moldova), 2012 Chişinău, str. N. Iorga 11, Moldova (office). *Telephone:* (22) 23-46-14 (office). *Fax:* (22) 23-36-73 (office). *E-mail:* pressapcrm@gmail.com (office). *Website:* www.pcrm.md (office).

VORONKOV, Vladimir Ivanovich, PhD; Russian diplomatist and UN official; *Under-Secretary-General, United Nations Counter-Terrorism Office;* b. 21 June 1953, Moscow; s. of Ivan Alexandrovich Voronkov; m. Irina Pavlovna Voronkova; one d.; ed Moscow State Univ.; joined Soviet Ministry of Foreign Affairs 1989, worked as Press Attaché, Russian Embassy in Poland –1994, Deputy Chief of Mission, Russian Embassy in Poland 2000–02, Deputy Dir Personnel Dept 2002–05, Deputy Perm. Rep. to Org. for Security and Co-operation in Europe (OSCE) 2005–08, Dir Dept of European Cooperation 2008–11, Head of Russian Del., Russia–EU negotiations on visa-free travel 2010–11, Perm. Rep. to UN and other Int. Orgs in Vienna 2011–17; Under-Sec.-Gen. UN Counter-Terrorism Office 2017–; Kt Order of Merit of Poland 2002, Order of Friendship 2013. *Address:* United Nations Department of Political Affairs, 405 E 42 Street, New York, NY

10017, USA (office). *Telephone:* (212) 963-1234 (office). *Fax:* (212) 963-4879 (office). *Website:* www.un.org (office).

VOS, Marianne; Dutch cyclist; b. 13 May 1987, 's-Hertogenbosch; took up cycling aged six, initially trained with brother's cycling team, also participated in speed skating, inline speed skating, later also took to mountain biking; won (at junior level) Nat. Mountain Biking Championships 2002, Nat. Road Race Championships 2002, Nat. Mountain Biking Championships 2003; started participating in senior level events 2006; competes in cyclo-cross, road bicycle racing, track racing; bronze medal, Union Cycliste Internationale (UCI) Cyclo-cross European Championships 2006; gold medal, points race, Olympic Games, Beijing 2008; gold medal, road race, Olympic Games, London 2012; winner: Nat. Road Race Championships 2006, 2008, 2009, 2011, World Road Race Championship 2006, 2012, 2013, UCI Cyclo-cross World Championships 2006, 2009, 2010, 2011, 2012, Rund um die Nürnberger Altstadt 2007, La Fléche Wallonne Féminine 2007, 2008, 2009, 2011, 2013, UCI Women's Road World Cup 2007, 2009, 2010, 2012, 2013, Emakumeen Bira 2008, 2011, Tour de l'Aude Cycliste Féminin 2009, Holland Ladies Tour 2009, 2010, 2011, 2012, Trofeo Alfredo Binda-Comune di Cittiglio 2009, 2010, 2012, Open de Suède Vårgårda 2009, 2013, 2018, Nat. Time Trial Championship 2010, 2011, UCI Track Cycling World Championships (scratch race) 2011, GP Ciudad de Valladolid 2011, Giro d'Italia Femminile 2011, 2012, 2014, Ronde van Drenthe 2011, 2012, 2013, Nat. Cyclo-cross Championships 2011, 2012, GP de Plouay 2012, Tour of Flanders for Women 2013, La Course by Tour de France 2014, Sparkassen Giro Bochum 2014, BeNe Ladies Tour 2017, 2018, Trofee Maarten Wynants 2017, Ladies Tour of Norway 2017, 2018, European Road Race Championship 2017; rides for Rabobank Women Cycling Team (fmrly DSB-Ballast Nedam) 2006–16; leader CCC-Liv team 2019–; Amb. for Youth United for Sri Lanka; Sport FM Sportswoman of the Year 2004, 2005, Dutch Sports Talent of the Year 2006, Dutch Athlete of the Year 2008, 2009, AIOCC Trophy 2017. *Leisure interests:* sports, internet. *Address:* c/o Zeloo, PO Box 223, 5100 AE Dongen, Netherlands (office). *Telephone:* (162) 387387 (office). *Fax:* (162) 370264 (office). *E-mail:* mail@zeloo.nl (office). *Website:* mariannevosofficial.com.

VOSCHERAU, Eggert; German business executive; b. 11 May 1943, Hamburg; s. of Carl Voscherau; m. Sarah Voscherau; began career as man. trainee in business admin at Unilever; joined BASF 1969, man. position, BASF Brasileira SA 1981–84, Exec. Pres. BASF Brasileira SA 1984–87, Pres. Crop Protection Div., BASF, Ludwigshafen, Germany 1987–91, Exec. Vice-Pres. BASF Corpn, USA and Pres. North American Consumer Products Div. (Pharmaceuticals, Crop Protection and Fine Chemicals) 1991–98, Pres. Latin America North Div. 1994–98, mem. Bd of Exec. Dirs BASF AG 1996–2008, Chair. and CEO BASF Corpn, USA, responsible on Bd of Exec. Dirs for company's regional activities in the Americas (N and S America) as well as Fibre Products Div. 1997–98, responsible for the units Crop Protection, Pharmaceuticals, Fine Chemicals, Main Lab. and Europe region 1998–2001, Industrial Relations Dir, BASF, Head of Ludwigshafen Site and Verbund Site Man. Europe 2001–08, Vice-Chair. Bd of Exec. Dirs 2003–08 (retd), Chair. Supervisory Bd BASF SE 2009–14; mem. Supervisory Bd, ZEW, Mannheim 2007–, Zentrum für Europäische Wirtschaftsforschung (Centre for European Econ. Research) (Vice-Chair.) 2007–, Carl Zeiss AG 2008–10 (Chair.), Schott AG 2008–10 (Chair.), Hochtief AG 2011–12; Pres. BAVC (German Fed. of Chemical Employers' Asscns) 2005–13; Vice-Pres. BDA (Fed. of German Employers' Asscns) 2005–; mem. Bd of Trustees Foundation Wittenberg Centre for Global Ethics 2009–; Bundesverdienstkreuz 2008; Hon. DBA (Univ. of Mannheim) 2006; MRN Award 2008.

VOSER, Peter Robert, BBA; Swiss business executive; *Chairman of the Board of Trustees, St Gallen Foundation for International Studies;* b. 29 Aug. 1958; m. Daniela Voser; three c.; ed Univ. of Applied Sciences, Zurich; employed by Royal Dutch/Shell Group of Cos in a variety of finance and business roles 1982–2002, worked in Switzerland for five years, in UK for eight years, in Argentina for five years and in Chile for two years, Group Chief Internal Auditor, London 1997–99, Chief Financial Officer (CFO), Shell Europe Oil Products 1999–2001, CFO Global Oil Products Business and mem. Oil Products Exec. Cttee 2001–02, CFO Royal Dutch/Shell Group of Cos 2004–05, CFO and Exec. Dir Royal Dutch Shell plc 2004–09, CEO 2009–14; CFO and mem. Group Exec. Cttee Asea Brown Boveri (ABB) Group of Cos, Switzerland 2002–04, also responsible in Exec. Cttee for Group IT and the Oil, Gas and Petrochemicals business (upstream and downstream); mem. Supervisory Bd Aegon NV 2004–06; mem. Bd of Dirs UBS AG 2005–10, Catalyst (non-profit org.) 2010–, Roche 2011–; Chair. Bd of Trustees, St Gallen Foundation for Int. Studies 2013–; mem. Swiss Fed. Auditor Oversight Authority 2006–10, European Round Table of Industrialists, The Business Council; awarded title of Dato Seri Laila Jasa by the Sultan of Brunei 2011. *Address:* St Gallen Foundation for International Studies, St Gallen Symposium, Dufourstrasse 83, PO Box 1045, 9001 St Gallen, Switzerland (office). *Telephone:* (71) 2272020 (office). *Fax:* (71) 2272030 (office). *E-mail:* info@symposium.org (office). *Website:* www.symposium.org (office).

VOSGANIAN, Varujan, PhD; Romanian politician and writer; b. 25 July 1958, Craiova; m. Mihaela Vosganian; one d.; ed Acad. of Econ. Sciences, Bucharest and Bucharest Univ.; Assoc. Prof., Acad. of Econ. Sciences, Bucharest; Sr Researcher, Nat. Inst. of Economy; Deputy, Romanian Parl. 1990–96, 2016–, Senator 1996–2000, 2004–16, Chair. Cttee on Budget, Finances, Banking Activity and Capital Markets 1996–98, 2004–06, Pres. Econ. Comm., Industry and Services 2008–12; mem. Romanian Del. to Parl. Ass. of the Council of Europe (APCE) 2004–06, 2012, mem. Political and Econ. Comms 2004–; Minister of the Economy and Commerce 2006–07, of the Economy and Finance 2007–08, of the Economy, Trade and Business Environment 2012–14; mem. Nat. Liberal Party (PNL) 2003–15, Vice-Pres. 2007–14; mem. Alliance of Liberals and Democrats 2015–; Founding mem. Romanian Soc. of the Economy (SOREC); Vice-Pres. Romanian Writers Union 2005–; Hon. mem. Scientific Council, Nat. Inst. of Prognosis, Romania; St Andrew's Cross, Romanian Patriarchate, Order Italiana della solidarità (Italy) 2008; Dr hc (Vasile Goldis Univ.) 2006, (Leibniz Univ., Milan) 2006; Special Prize for Poetry, Nichita Stanescu Int. Poem Festival 2006, Prize for Excellency for Contrib. to the Devt of Capital Markets in Romania, Bucharest Stock Exchange 2006, Prize for Contrib. to Devt of Romanian Science and Culture, Romanian Acad. 2006, Gold Medal for Culture, Govt of Armenia, Academy Award for Literature 2009, Angelus Great Prize for Literature of the Central Europe 2016. *Publications include:* The Book of Whispers (novel) (Sadoveanu Prize for fiction) 2010, The Book of my Unwritten Poems 2015, The Children of War (novel) 2016; more then 500 econ., political and literary articles, studies, essays and poems. *Address:* c/o Ministry of the Economy, 010096 Bucharest 1, Calea Victoriei 152, Romania. *E-mail:* birou_presa@minind.ro. *Website:* vosganian.ro.

VOTRON, Jean-Paul, MA; Belgian banking executive; b. 1951; m.; two c.; ed Institut Catholique des Hautes Etudes Commerciale, Brussels; began career at Unilever 1975, various man. positions in sales, marketing and gen. man. 1975–91; joined Citibank 1991, served as Pres. Citibank Belgium, Marketing Dir for Europe, Dir for Marketing and Tech. US and European Consumer Bank, Dir of Insurance for USA, Head of US Investment Business, Chair. and CEO Citibank FSB (br. network in USA) –1997; Sr Exec. Vice-Pres., Int. Consumer Banking and E-Commerce, ABN-AMRO 1997–2001; apptd mem. Man. Cttee Citigroup 2002, CEO Citigroup Retail Bank for Western Europe, Cen. Europe, Russia, Middle E and Africa 2002–04; CEO Fortis NV and Chair. Fortis Bank and Fortis Insurance 2004–08 (resgnd), charged, found guilty and fined in 2012 for misleading investors with inaccurate information about Fortis, fines reduced 2015; Business Leader of the Year, European Business Awards Conf. 2007.

VOURLOUMIS, Panagis; Greek business executive and banker; b. 30 April 1937, Athens; s. of Andreas Vourloumis and Hypatia Pappa; m.; three c.; ed London School of Econs, UK; Head, SE Asia Div., International Finance Corpn 1966–73; Head, Commercial Bank of Greece Group 1979–81; fmr Dir Panagis Vourloumis & Assocs, Financial Advisors; fmr Chair. Askbali.com travel group; Chair. and CEO Alpha Finance, Alpha Mutual Funds and Alpha Bank Romania 1988–2000, Exec. Dir Alpha Bank 1988–2000; Chair. Frigoglass Group 2000–04, Aegean Baltic Bank SA 2000–04; Chair. and CEO Hellenic Telecommunications Org. SA 2004–10, Cosmote Mobile Telecommunications SA 2004–10, Romtelecom SA 2004–10; Pres. Athens Food Bank; currently Sr Adviser, N.M. Rothschild; mem. Exec. Cttee, Foundation for Econ. and Industrial Research (IOBE) (think-tank); mem. Bd of Dirs Hellenic Foundation for European and Foreign Policy (ELIAMEP), Spastics Soc.; mem. Trilateral Comm. 1998–2017; Bintang Jasa Dratama (Indonesia). *Publications include:* To Asfalistiko me apla logia 2006, The Importance of Good Governance 2018. *E-mail:* vourpan@yahoo.com (home).

VOUTILAINEN, Pertti Juhani, MSc, MEng; Finnish banker and business executive; b. 22 June 1940, Kuusjärvi; s. of Otto Voutilainen and Martta Voutilainen; m. Raili Juvonen 1963; two s.; ed Helsinki Univ. of Tech., Helsinki Univ. of Business Admin, Pennsylvania State Univ., USA; joined Outokumpu Oy as mining engineer 1964, Production Man. 1971–73, Corp. Planning Dir 1973–77, Corp. Planning 1976–78, mem. Exec. Bd 1977–91, Pres. 1980–91, Chair. Exec. Bd 1983–91; Chair. and CEO Kansallis-Osake-Pankki (merged with Unitas Ltd) 1992–95; Chair. and CEO Merita Bank plc 1995–2000; Pres. Merita Nordbanken 2000–02; Chair. Viola Systems Ltd 2002, Chair. Riddarhyttan Resources Ltd 2004–05; Vice-Chair. Technopolis plc 2003–05, Chair. 2006–07; Chair. Centre for Finnish Business and Policy Studies, Finnish Section of Int. Chamber of Commerce; mem. Bd of Dirs Fingrid Oyj, Lizar Oy, Riddarhyttan Resources AB, Agnico-Eagle Mines 2005–, HIM Specialty Furniture Ltd 2005–; Penn State Alumni Fellow 1994; Hon. Mining Counselor (Bergsrad) 2003; Commdr, Order of Lion of Finland. *Leisure interests:* hunting, fishing.

VOUTSIS, Nikos; Greek civil engineer and politician; *President (Speaker), Hellenic Parliament;* b. 4 March 1951, Athens; m. Angeliki Papazoglou; three c.; ed Nat. Tech. Univ. of Athens; participated in anti-dictatorship student movt as mem. of student struggle cttees (FEA); Vice-Pres. first Cen. Council of the Student Union (EFEE) 1975; Sec. of Cen. Council, EKON Rigas Feraios party 1980–85; mem. Kommunistiko Komma Elladas—Esoterikou (KKE—E—Communist Party of Greece—Interior) and nine-mem. Secr. –1986; participated in KKE—E-Ananeotikí Aristerá (KKE—E-Innovative Left) 1987–91; mem. Synaspismos tis Aristeras ton Kinimátoo kai tis Oikologías (Synaspismos—Coalition of the Left, of Movements and Ecology) 1993–2013, mem. Political Secr. 1993–2013; mem. Synaspismós Rizospastikís Aristerás (SYRIZA—Coalition of the Radical Left) 2013–, mem. Regional Council of Attica –2012, mem. Cen. Cttee 2013–; mem. Hellenic Parl. for Athens Region A 2012–, Pres. (Speaker) 2015–, Sec. SYRIZA Parl. Group; Minister of the Interior and Admin. Reconstruction Jan.–Aug. 2015. *Address:* Hellenic Parliament, Leoforos Vassilissis Sofias 2–4, 100 21 Athens (office). *Telephone:* (210) 3708011 (office); (210) 370838. *Fax:* (210) 3708010 (office); (210) 3707790. *E-mail:* nvoutsis@gmail.com (home); president@parliament.gr (office); presidentsoffice@parliament.gr (office). *Website:* www.hellenicparliament.gr/en/Organosi-kai-Leitourgia/Proedreio/Proedros (office); nikosvoutsis.wordpress.com.

VOYNET, Dominique; French physician and politician; *Inspector General of Social Affairs (IGAS);* b. 4 Nov. 1958, Montbéliard (Doubs); d. of Jean Voynet and Monique Richard; two d.; ed Faculty of Medicine, Besançon; anaesthetist and intensive care specialist, Dole (Jura) public hosp. 1985–89; activist in several ecological and other orgs, Belfort and Besançon 1976–; Co-founder Les Verts ('Green' Movt) 1984, Gen. Sec. Green Group in European Parl. 1989–91, Nat. Spokesperson 1991–2002, Nat. Sec. 2001–03; Municipal Councillor, Dole 1989–2004; mem. Regional Council of Franche-Comté 1992–94 (resgnd); cand. in presidential election 1995, 2007; elected Deputy (Les Verts and Parti Socialiste) for Dole-Arbois, Nat. Ass. 1997, Minister for Town and Country Planning and the Environment 1997–2001; Councillor-Gen., Jura 1998–2004; Senator for Seine-Saint Denis 2004–11; Mayor of Montreuil 2008–14; Insp. Gen. of Social Affairs (IGAS) 2014–. *Address:* Inspection Générale des Affaires Sociales, 39–43 quai André Citroën, 75739 Paris Cedex 15, France (office). *E-mail:* info@igas.gouv.fr (office). *Website:* www.igas.gouv.fr (office).

VRAALSEN, Tom Eric, MEcon; Norwegian diplomatist; b. 26 Jan. 1936, Oslo; m. Viebecke Vraalsen; five c.; ed Århus School of Econs and Business Admin., Denmark; joined Foreign Service 1960, various diplomatic positions in Embassies in Beijing 1962–64, 1969–70, Cairo 1964–67, Manila 1970–71, Jakarta 1971, in charge of Norwegian relations with Africa, Asia and Latin America, Political Dept, Ministry of Foreign Affairs 1971–73, in charge of UN and int. org. affairs 1973–75, Deputy Perm. Rep. to UN, New York 1975–79, Perm. Rep. 1982–89, Dir-Gen. Political Dept, Ministry of Foreign Affairs 1981–82, Minister for Devt Co-operation, for Nordic Co-operation 1989–90; Sr Vice-Pres. Saga Petroleum 1991–92; Asst Sec.-Gen. Ministry of Foreign Affairs 1992–94, Amb. to UK

1994–96, to USA 1996–2001, to Finland 2001–03; UN Special Envoy for Humanitarian Affairs for the Sudan 1998–2006; Special Adviser, Ministry of Foreign Affairs 2008–; Chair. Task Force for Int. Co-operation on Holocaust Educ., Remembrance and Research 2009–10; Dr hc (Augustana Coll.) 2000, (Luther Coll., USA) 2001; Commdr, Order of St Olav 1987. *Publications:* UN in Focus (co-author) 1975, The UN: Dream and Reality 1984. *Address:* Ministry of Foreign Affairs, 7 juni pl., POB 8114 Dep., 0032 Oslo, Norway (office). *Telephone:* 22-24-36-00 (office). *Fax:* 22-24-95-80 (office). *E-mail:* post@mfa.no (office). *Website:* www.regjeringen .no/ud (office).

VRABIE, Vitalie; Moldovan politician; *Secretary General, Democratic Party of Moldova (Partidul Democrat din Moldova);* b. 2 Oct. 1964, Costuleni Village, Ungheni Dist; m.; two c.; ed Agricultural Inst., Chişinău, Acad. of Public Admin, Russia; began career as Sr Agronomist, Prut Farm; Dir JSV Garant-impex, Ungheni 1994–99; mem. Ungheni City Council 1995–99, fmr Dir Office of Chamber of Commerce and Industry; elected Mayor of Ungheni 1999, re-elected 2003; Chair. Asscn of Mayors and Local Communities 2003–06; fmr mem. Council of Europe Congress of Local and Regional Authorities, fmr Head Nat. Del.; Minister of Local Public Admin 2006–07; Minister of Defence 2007–09; joined Democratic Party of Moldova 2010, Sec.-Gen. 2011–. *Address:* Democratic Party of Moldova (Partidul Democrat din Moldova), 2001 Chişinău, str. Tighina 32, Moldova (office). *Telephone:* (22) 27-82-29 (office). *Fax:* (22) 27-82-30 (office). *E-mail:* pdm@mtc.md (office). *Website:* www.pdm.md (office).

VRANITZKY, Franz, Dipl.-Kfm., DComm; Austrian banker, business executive and fmr politician; *Honorary President, Bruno Kreisky Forum for International Dialogue;* b. 4 Oct. 1937, Vienna; s. of Franz Vranitsky and Rosa Vernitsky; m. Christine Kristen 1962; one s. one d.; ed Coll. (now Univ.) of Commerce, Vienna; joined Siemens-Schuckert GmbH, Vienna 1961; Dept of Nat. Econs, Austrian Nat. Bank 1961–69, seconded to the Office of the First Vice-Pres. 1969–70; Adviser on Econ. and Financial Policy to Minister of Finance 1970–76; Deputy-Chair. Bd of Dirs Creditanstalt-Bankverein 1976–81, Österreichische Länderbank 1981, Chair. Bd of Dirs 1981–84; Fed. Minister of Finance 1984–86; Fed. Chancellor 1986–97; MP 1987–96; Chair. Austrian Socialist Party (now Social Democratic Party of Austria—SPÖ) 1988–97; OSCE Special Rep. to Albania March–Nov. 1997; Special Adviser, WestLB 1997–2004; apptd Co-Chair. InterAction Council 2010, now Hon. Co-Chair.; Pres. Vienna Inst. for Devt and Co-operation 1990; Founding Pres. Bruno Kreisky Forum for Int. Dialogue 1993–2004, Hon. Pres. 2005–; fmr mem. Bd of Dirs Magna International Inc., Touristik Union International (TUI), Magic Life der Club International Hotelbetriebs GmbH; Hon. Senator, Vienna Univ. of Economics 1991, Hon. Citizen, Vienna 2017; Hon. KCMG 1995, Grand Gold Decoration with Ribbon for Services to the Republic of Austria 1987, Grand Cross of Merit (Italy) 1993, Order of White Lion (Czech Republic) 2014, Commdr Legion of Honour 2017; Dr hc (Hebrew Univ. of Jerusalem) 1993, (Univ. of Santiago, Chile 1993), (Univ. of Economics, Bratislava) 1996; J. William Fulbright Prize For International Understanding 1995, Charlemagne Prize of Aachen 1995, Gold Medal of B'nai B'rith 2005. *Address:* Bruno Kreisky Forum for International Dialogue, Armbrustergasse 15, 1190 Vienna, Austria. *Website:* www.kreisky -forum.org.

VRANKIĆ, Dragan; Bosnia and Herzegovina politician; b. 23 Jan. 1955, Čapljina; m.; three c.; ed Faculty of Tourism and Foreign Trade, Univ. of Dubrovnik; began career in Energoinvest; later Head of Dept of Econs and Deputy Mayor for Financial and Econ. Affairs in Municipality of Čapljina; fmr Gov. of Herzegovina-Neretva canton; currently mem. Parl., Fed. of Bosnia and Herzegovina; Deputy Prime Minister and Minister of Finance, Fed. of Bosnia and Herzegovina 2003–07; Minister of Finance and the Treasury, Bosnia and Herzegovina 2007–12; participated in establishment of Indirect Taxation Authority, now mem. Governing Bd; mem. of the Presidency Hravstke Democratic Union of Bosnia and Herzegovina. *Address:* Federation House of Representatives, 71000 Sarajevo, Hamdije Kreševljakovića 3, Bosnia and Herzegovina (office). *Telephone:* (33) 263585 (office). *Fax:* (33) 223623 (office). *E-mail:* dragan.vrankic@parlament .ba (office). *Website:* www.parlament.ba (office).

VRDOLJAK, Ivan; Croatian electrical engineer and politician; b. 22 June 1972, Osijek; m. Ivana Vrdoljak; one c.; ed Braća Ribar Secondary School and Faculty of Electrical Eng, Osijek; AutoCad designer, RPM Engeharia, Porto Alerge, Brazil 1996; automation eng intern commissioning the Plomin 2 thermoelectric power plant, NOVA LIVANA d.o.o, Osijek 1999; Project Man. in automation and control systems of Puris Pazin, Moste Ljubljana, thermoelectric power plant of Šoštanj Velenje – Simatic S7, WinCC SCADA, PCS7 WinCC OS, FIX Intelution; Co-founder and mem. Bd of Dirs ATO Inženjering d.o.o., Osijek; with Dept for Electrical and IT Eng, transferred to Neo Inženjering d.o.o., Osijek 2000–08; mem. Croatian People's Party-Liberal Democrats 2000–, Chair. Cen. Bd 2008–; Deputy Mayor of Osijek, responsible for social services and the economy 2008–11; Minister of Construction and Physical Planning 2011–12, of the Economy 2012–16. *Leisure interests:* soccer, tennis, squash, mem. Croatian Hunting Asscn, Mursa Hunting Soc., Osijek. *Address:* c/o Ministry of the Economy, 10000 Zagreb, ul. grada Vukovara 78, Croatia.

VU, Duc Dam, PhD; Vietnamese politician; *Deputy Prime Minister;* b. 3 Feb. 1963, Thanh Mien Dist, Hai Duong Prov.; ed Université Libre de Bruxelles; Engineer, Import-Export Technical Services Co., Gen. Dept of Post and Telecommunications 1988–90, Deputy Dir-Gen., Dept of Science, Technology and Int. Cooperation 1993–94; Expert, Technical Devt and External Relations Dept, Vietnam Post and Telecommunications Corpn 1990–92, Office of the Gen. Post Office 1992–93; Deputy Dir-Gen., Int. Relations Dept, Office of the Govt 1994–95, Head of ASEAN Dept 1995–96; Sec. then Asst to Prime Minister Vo Van Kiet 1996–2003; Vice-Chair. People's Cttee, Bac Ninh Prov. 2003–05, People's Council Rep. 2004–05; Deputy Minister of Posts and Telematics 2005–07, Minister and Chair. Office of Govt 2011–13, Deputy Prime Minister 2013–; Standing Deputy Sec., Provincial Party Cttee, Quang Ninh Prov. 2007–08, Deputy Sec., Provincial Party Cttee and Chair. People's Cttee 2008–10, Sec. Provincial Party Cttee 2010–11; Standing mem. Cen. Cttee, Communist Party of Viet Nam (CPV) 2007–10, Alt. mem. 10th Party Cen. Cttee 2010–11, mem. 11th Party Cen. Cttee 2010–11, Party Cen. Cttee 2011–. *Address:* Office of the Deputy Prime Minister, 16 Le Hong Phong, Ba Dinh, Hanoi, Viet Nam (office). *Website:* www.chinhphu.vn.

VU, Van Ninh, MBA; Vietnamese government official; b. 23 Feb. 1955, Nam Dinh Prov.; ed Hanoi Univ. of Finance and Accountancy; mem. staff, Ministry of Finance 1977–82, Head of Economy Div. 1982–90, Deputy Dir of State Budget Dept 1990–93, Dir 1993–99; Vice-Minister of Finance 1999–2003; Vice-Chair. Hanoi People's Cttee 2003–06; Minister of Finance 2006–11; Deputy Prime Minister 2011–16; apptd Head of Cen. Steering Cttee for sustainable poverty reduction 2012; mem. CP of Viet Nam Cen. Cttee. *Website:* vuvanninh.chinhphu.vn (office).

VUCHKOV, Veselin Borislavov, LLM, JUDr; Bulgarian jurist and politician; *Minister of the Interior;* b. 26 Dec. 1968, Stob, nr Rila, Kyustendil Prov.; ed Sofia Univ. 'St Kliment Ohridski'; trainee judge, Sofia Dist Court 1994; Investigating Magistrate, Sofia Metropolitan Investigation Service (Fourth Regional Investigation Service) 1994–96; Teaching Asst, Criminal Law Dept, Acad. of Ministry of the Interior 1996–98, Sr Asst 1998–2001, Chief Asst 2001–09; has taught at Univ. of Plovdiv, South-West Univ. 'Neofit Rilski', Blagoevgrad, D.A. Tsenov Acad. of Econs, Svishtov, Varna Tech. Univ.; Deputy Minister of the Interior in first Borisov Cabinet 2009–13, Minister of the Interior 2014–; Deputy (GERB) for 24 MIR Sofia, Nat. Ass. (Narodno Sobraniye) 2013–14, mem. Internal Security and Public Order Cttee, Cttee on Control of Security Services, Use and Employment of Special Intelligence Means and Access to Data under Electronic Communications Act; Assoc. Prof. of Criminal Process Habilitation, Sofia Univ. 'St Kliment Ohridski' 2010–. *Publications include:* Pre-trial Police Investigation 1999, Evidence in the Criminal Procedure – Characteristics and Types 2006, Criminal Procedure Law in Schemes and Tables (co-author) 2007, Tests in Criminal Procedure Law (co-author) 2007, Comments on the Law on the State Agency for National Security (co-author) 2008, Subject and Significance of Evidence in the Criminal Procedure 2008; numerous professional papers. *Address:* Ministry of the Interior, 1000 Sofia, ul. 6-ti Septemvri 29, Bulgaria (office). *Telephone:* (2) 982-25-74 (office). *Fax:* (2) 982-20-47 (office). *E-mail:* info@mvr.bg (office). *Website:* www.mvr.bg (office).

VUČIĆ, Aleksandar; Serbian politician and head of state; *President;* b. 5 March 1970, Belgrade, Socialist Repub. of Serbia, Socialist Fed. Repub. of Yugoslavia; s. of Andjelko Vučić and Angelina Milovanov; m. 1st Ksenija Janković 2007 (divorced 2011); one s. one d.; m. 2nd Tamara Đukanović 2013; one s.; ed Belgrade Univ.; reporter, Channel S (TV channel), Pale, Bosnia and Herzegovina 1992–93; mem. Srpska Radikalna Stranka (Serbian Radical Party) 1993–2008, Gen. Sec. 1995–2008; Dir Pinki Sports and Business Centre, Zemun, Belgrade 1996; mem. Nat. Ass. (Parl. of Repub. of Serbia) 1993, 2004–08, May–July 2012, fmr Deputy Chair. SRS parl. group, mem. Admin. Cttee, Cttee on Constitutional Affairs, Deputy Chair. Cttee on Kosovo-Metohija and Cttee on Culture and Information; Minister of Information (Govt of Nat. Unity) 1998–2000; First Deputy Prime Minister, responsible for Defence, Security, the Fight against Corruption and Crime 2012–14, Minister of Defence 2012–13; Prime Minister 2014–17; Pres. of Serbia 2017–; unsuccessful cand. for Mayor of Belgrade 2004, 2008; mem. Srpska Napredna Stranka (Serbian Progressive Party) 2008–, Vice-Pres. 2008–12, Acting Pres. May–Sept. 2012, Pres. Sept. 2012–; Order of Friendship (Kazakhstan) 2018, Order of Alexander Nevsky (Russia) 2019; Dr hc (Moscow State Inst. of Int. Relations) 2017, (Azerbaijan Univ. of Languages) 2018; Vidovdan Award, City of Kruševac 2013. *Leisure interests:* chess, basketball, soccer, wine. *Address:* Office of the President, 11000 Belgrade, Andrićev venac 1, Serbia (office). *Telephone:* (11) 3111473 (office). *Fax:* (11) 3043280 (office). *E-mail:* predstavkegradjana@ predsednik.rs (office). *Website:* www.predsednik.rs (office).

VUČINIĆ, Boro, PhD; Montenegrin politician; b. 1 Sept. 1954, Podgorica; m.; four c.; ed Faculty of Law, Montenegrin State Univ.; started career at Titograd Civil Eng Org.; Dir Social Fund for Building Land, Business Premises and Roads; Deputy Municipal Ass. of Podgorica; mem. Parl. (Democratic Socialist Party), mem. Constitutional Affairs Cttee, Cttee for Drafting of Constitutional Charter of State Union of Serbia and Montenegro; Minister of Environmental Protection and Urban Planning 2004–06, of Defence 2006–12, Pres. Mandate and Immunity Comm.; Dir Nat. Security Agency 2012–14 (also mem.); fmr Chair. Nat. Rifle Ass. of Yugoslavia; fmr Vice-Chair. Yugoslav Olympic Cttee; Head, Yugoslav Sports Del., Mediterranean Games 1997; Chair. Montenegrin Olympic Cttee; mem. Advisory Council NATO; mem. Nat. Comm. for Implementation of Strategy for Prevention and Suppression of Terrorism, Money Laundering and Terrorist Financing, Coordination Team for Emergency Situations, Rule of Law Council, Bureau for Operational Coordination of Security Services Operations.

VUILLARD, Éric; French writer and film director; b. 4 May 1968, Lyon. *Films:* as dir: L'homme qui marche, Mateo Falcone. *Publications include:* Conquistadors 2009, La bataille d'Occident (Franz-Hessel-Preis 2012, Prix Littéraire Valery Larbaud 2013), Congo (Franz-Hessel-Preis 2012, Valery-Larbaud Prize 2013), Tristesse de la terre (Joseph-Kessel Prize 2015), L'Ordre du jour (Prix Goncourt 2017).

VUJANOVIĆ, Filip; Montenegrin politician, lawyer and fmr head of state; b. 1 Sept. 1954, Belgrade, Socialist Repub. of Serbia, Socialist Fed. Repub. of Yugoslavia; m. Svetlana Vujanović 1985; one s. two d.; ed Univ. of Belgrade; began career with First Municipal Court; Official Assoc., Dist Attorney's Office, Belgrade 1978–80; Sec. to Dist Court, Titograd (now Podgorica) 1980–81, mem. Attorney's Chamber, Chair. Chamber 1989; lawyer, pvt. legal practice 1982–93; Minister of Justice, Repub. of Montenegro 1992–95, of the Interior 1995–98; Prime Minister of Montenegro 1998–2002, with responsibility for Religious Affairs 2001–02; Pres. Parl. Ass. (Acting Pres. of Montenegro) 2002–03; Pres. of Montenegro 2003–18; mem. Demokratska Partija Socijalista Crne Gore (Democratic Party of Socialists of Montenegro), currently Deputy Chair. *Address:* Demokratska Partija Socijalista Crne Gore, 81000 Podgorica, ul. Jovana Tomaševića bb, Montenegro (office). *Telephone:* (20) 245292 (office). *Fax:* (20) 245282 (office). *E-mail:* portparol@dps.me (office). *Website:* www.dps.me (office).

VUJČIĆ, Boris, BSc, MSc, PhD; Croatian academic, economist and central banker; *Governor, Croatian National Bank;* b. 2 June 1964, Zagreb; ed Univ. of Zagreb; Asst Lecturer, Faculty of Econs, Univ. of Zagreb 1989–97, Asst Prof. 1997–2003, Assoc. Prof. 2003–, Visiting Prof., Faculty of Science, Dept of Mathematics 2004–; Dir Research Dept, Croatian Nat. Bank 1996–2000, Deputy Gov. 2000–12, Gov. 2012–; Deputy Chief Negotiator during Croatia's negotiations with EU 2005–12; mem. Bd Global Devt Network 2005–12; Visiting Fellow, Inst. of Devt Studies, Univ. of Sussex 1992–94; Fulbright Fellow 1994–95. *Address:*

Croatian National Bank, 10000 Zagreb, trg Hrvatskih velikana 3, Croatia (office). *Telephone:* (1) 4564553 (office); (1) 4564781 (office). *Fax:* (1) 4550598 (office). *E-mail:* info@hnb.hr (office). *Website:* www.hnb.hr (office).

VUJOVIĆ, Dušan, BA, MA, PhD; Serbian economist, academic and government official; b. 1951, Pozarevac; m.; two c.; ed Univ. of Belgrade, Univ. of California, Berkeley, USA; worked as an asst at Inst. for Int. Politics and Econs, Belgrade and at Faculty of Econs, Univ. of Belgrade, then as Asst Prof. and Assoc. Prof. there; Dir of Macro-modelling project at Inst. for Statistics, Yugoslavia 1984–92; Dir of JVI programme for govt officials from transition economies, World Bank Inst. 1992–98, Leader of econ. team, World Bank, Ukraine 1998–2001, Sr Adviser to Swiss EDs, Serbia and Montenegro 2001–03, Country Man. for Ukraine 2003–06, Lead Economist, Ind. Evaluation Group, Sierra Leone, Tajikistan, Timor-Leste, India 2007–11, consultant to World Bank 2011–12; consultant, IBI International 2011–12; Minister of Economy April–Sept. 2014, of Finance 2014–18 (resgnd), also acting Minister of Defence Feb.–March 2016; Fellow, Centre for Social and Econ. Research, Warsaw 2011–; teaches at several univs world-wide, including as Prof., Faculty of Econs, Finance and Admin, Belgrade, Prof., Univ. of Singidunum; Affiliate MOC Prof., Inst. for Strategy and Competitiveness, Harvard Business School, USA; Ed.-in-Chief Finansije journal; Ind. *Publications:* several papers in int. journals.

VUKAJ, Helga Hasanlliu, LLM, PhD; Albanian lawyer and public servant; b. 14 July 1978; ed Univ. of Tirana, Training Inst. of Public Admin, Tirana; fmr Dir Gen., State Supreme Audit Inst.; Lawyer, Office of the Pres. 2003; Dir Legal Services Dept, Ministry of Internal Affairs 2005–06; Deputy Dir-Gen., Agency for Property Restitution and Compensation 2006–12; Dir-Gen., High State Control Office (state supervisory body) 2012–16; Minister of Finance May–Aug. 2017; Assoc. Prof., Faculty of Law, Univ. of Tirana 2004–; lecturer at several insts including Univ. Luigi Bocconi, Milan 2003, Albanian School of Magistrates, Tirana 2009–, Luarasi Univ. *Address:* University of Tirana, Sheshi Nënë Tereza, POB 183, Tirana, Albania (office). *E-mail:* info@unitir.edu.al (office). *Website:* www .unitir.edu.al (office).

VULIN, Aleksandar; Serbian politician and fmr journalist; *Minister of Defence;* b. 1972, Novi Sad, Socialist Autonomous Province of Vojvodina, Socialist Repub. of Serbia, Socialist Fed. Repub. of Yugoslavia; m. Nataša Vulin; two s.; ed Univ. of Kragujevac, Asst Marketing Dir, Super Press 2000–02; Marketing Dir, Colour Press 2003–07; Deputy CEO, Colour Media International 2007–12; fmr Chief Ed. 'Pečat' (weekly magazine); columnist for several daily and weekly journals; fmr mem. City of Belgrade Legis. Ass.; fmr mem. Rakovica Municipality Legis. Ass.; fmr mem. Nat. Ass. (Parl.); Dir, Govt of Serbia Office for Kosovo and Metohija 2012–13; Minister without portfolio in charge of Kosovo and Metohija 2013–14; Minister of Labour, Employment, Veterans and Social Affairs 2014–17; Minister of Defence 2017–; Pres., Working Group for the Resolution of the Issue of Mixed Migratory Flow 2015; Pres. Serbian Group, Joint Serbian-Greek Cttee 2017; mem. Socijalistička Partija Srbije (Socialist Party of Serbia); Pres. Pokret Socijalista (Movement of Socialists). *Address:* Ministry of Defence, 11000 Belgrade, Birčaninova 5, Serbia (office). *Telephone:* (11) 3006311 (office). *Fax:* (11) 3006062 (office). *E-mail:* info@mod.gov.rs (office). *Website:* www.mod.gov.rs (office).

VUONG, Dinh Hue, PhD; Vietnamese economist, academic and politician; b. 15 March 1957, Nghi Xuan, Nghi Loc, Nghe An Prov.; s. of Vuong Dinh Sam and Vo Thi Cam; ed Univ. of Econs, Bratislava, Slovakia; Lecturer in Econs, Hanoi Univ. of Finance and Accounting 1979–85, 1991–92, Assoc. Dir Dept of Accounting 1992–93, Univ. Vice-Chancellor 1999–2001; Auditor-Gen. (Chair.), State Audit Office of Viet Nam 2006–10; Minister of Finance 2011–13; mem. Dang Cong San Viet Nam (Communist Party of Viet Nam), mem. Cen. Cttee; Hon. mem. ACCA

2011. *Address:* Dang Cong San Viet Nam, 1A Hung Vuong, Hanoi, Viet Nam (office). *E-mail:* dangcongsan@cpv.org.vn. *Website:* www.cpv.org.vn.

VURAL, Volkan, MA; Turkish journalist, business executive and fmr diplomatist; *Counselor to the Chairman, Doğan Şirketler Grubu Holding A.Ş.;* b. 29 Dec. 1941, Istanbul; m.; ed Ankara Coll. and Univ.; early career as journalist; joined Foreign Ministry 1964, Third Sec., Econ. Affairs Dept 1964–65; mil. service 1965–67; Third Sec., Dept of Bilateral and Regional Econ. Affairs 1967–68, Second then First Sec., Embassy in Seoul 1968–71, Consul, then Deputy Consul Gen. Consulate in Munich 1971–73, Acting Head of Dept of Int. Econ. Insts, Foreign Ministry 1973–76, Int. Officer, Political Dept, NATO HQ 1976–82, Deputy Dir-Gen. for Bilateral Econ. Affairs, Foreign Ministry 1982–87, Amb. to Iran 1987–88, to USSR 1988–93, Spokesman Foreign Ministry 1993, Chief Adviser to the Prime Minister 1993–95, Amb. to Germany 1995–98, Perm. Rep. to UN, New York 1998–2000, Amb. to Spain 2003–06; Counselor to Chair., Doğan Şirketler Grubu Holding A.Ş. 2006–, mem. Bd of Dirs Aydın Doğan Holding A.Ş.; fmr mem. Bd of Dirs TÜSİAD (Turkish Industry and Business Asscn); University Presidential Medal, La Salle Univ., Philadelphia 1999. *Address:* Doğan Şirketler Grubu Holding A.Ş., Burhaniye Mahallesi Kısıklı Caddesi No: 65 34676, Üsküdar İstanbul, Turkey (office). *Telephone:* (216) 5569000 (office). *Fax:* (216) 5569200 (office). *Website:* www.doganholding.com.tr (office).

VYACHORKA, Vintsuk; Belarusian linguist and politician; b. 7 July 1961, Bieraście; s. of Ryhor Viačorka and Alaucina Viačorka; m. 1980; two s. one d.; ed Belarus State Univ., Acad. of Sciences; Lecturer, Minsk Pedagogical Univ. 1986–; Co-founder and fmr Chair. Belarusian Popular Front (now Revival—Belarusian National Front), now Deputy Chair.; Deputy Ed.-in-Chief, bi-monthly Spadčyna. *Publication:* Orthography: An Attempt at Comprehensive Standardization 1994. *Leisure interest:* ethno-music. *Address:* Belaruski Narodny Front 'Adradzhennye' (Revival—Belarusian Popular Front), 220012 Minsk vul. Charnyshevskaga 3/39, Belarus (office).

VYAPOORY, Paramasivum Pillay, (Barlen Vyapoory), BSc, M.Ed; Mauritian politician and fmr diplomatist; *Acting President;* b. 1956; m. Sarojini Vyapoory; one d.; ed Univ. of Mauritius, Sam Houston State Univ., USA, Univ. of Nairobi, Kenya; Sr Lecturer, Mauritius Inst. of Educ. 1976–95; Advisor to Minister of Educ. and Science 2002–05; High Commr to South Africa 2015–16; Vice Pres. of Mauritius 2016–, Acting Pres. March 2018–; mem. Tamil League 1969–; mem. Militant Socialist Movt. *Address:* Office of the Vice-President, 30 Farquhar Ave, Quatre Bornes, Port Louis, Mauritius (office). *Telephone:* 427-1024 (office). *Fax:* 427-1487 (office). *E-mail:* ovp@govmu.org (office). *Website:* vice-president.govmu.org (office).

VYUGIN, Oleg Vyacheslavovich, CandPhys-MathSc, PhD; Russian economist, banker and fmr government official; *Chairman, Moscow Exchange;* b. 29 July 1952, Ufa, Bashkortostan; m. Irina; one d.; ed Moscow State Univ.; Researcher, then Sr Researcher and Head of Lab., Inst. of Prognosis of Nat. Econ., Russian Acad. of Sciences 1989–92; Head of Dept of Macroeconomic Policy, Ministry of Finance 1993–96, Deputy Minister of Finance 1996–99, First Deputy 1999–2000; mem. Bd, Exec. Vice-Pres. and Chief Economist Troyka-Dialog (investment co.) 2000–02; First Deputy Chair. Bank Rossii—Central Bank of the Russian Fed. 2002–04; Chair. Fed. Financial Markets Service 2004–07; Chair. MDM-Bank 2007–17; Chair. Nat. Asscn of Securities Market Participants (NAUFOR) 2010; Sr Adviser, Morgan Stanley, Moscow 2013–; Chair. Moscow Exchange 2018–, also mem. Bd of Dirs; mem. Bd of Dirs Transneft JSC. *Address:* Moscow Exchange, 125009 Moscow, Bolshoy Kislovsky per, 13, Russia (office). *Telephone:* (495) 363-32-32 (office). *Fax:* (495) 705-96-22 (office). *E-mail:* globalexchange@moex.com (office). *Website:* www.moex.com (office).

W

WA THIONG'O, Ngugi, BA; Kenyan writer, dramatist, critic and academic; *Distinguished Professor of English and Comparative Literature, University of California, Irvine;* b. (James Thiong'o Ngugi), 5 Jan. 1938, Limuru; m. 1st Nyambura 1961 (divorced 1982); m. 2nd Njeeri 1992; four s. two d.; ed Makerere Univ. Coll., Uganda and Univ. of Leeds, UK; Lecturer in Literature, Univ. Nairobi 1967–69, Sr Lecturer, Assoc. Prof. and Chair Dept of Literature 1972–77; Fellow in Creative Writing, Makerere Univ. 1969–70; Visiting Assoc. Prof., Northwestern Univ., USA 1970–71; arrested and detained in Kenya 1977, released 1978; in exile in London 1982; Visiting Prof. of English and Comparative Literature, Yale Univ. 1989–92; Prof. of Comparative Literature and Performance Studies, New York Univ. 1992–2002; currently Distinguished Prof. of English and Comparative Literature, Univ. of California, Irvine, fmr Dir Int. Center for Writing and Trans.; Ed. Penpoint 1963–64, Zuka 1965–70, Mutiiri 1992–; mem. American Acad. of Arts and Sciences 2014–; Hon. Foreign mem. American Acad. of Arts and Letters 2003; Hon. Life Mem. Council for the Devt of Social Sciences Research in Africa 2003; Dr hc (Albright Coll.), (Roskilde, Denmark), (Univ. of Leeds) 2004, (Walter Sisulu Univ.) 2004, (CSU Dominguez Hills) 2005, (Dillard Univ.) 2005, (Univ. of Auckland) 2005, (New York Univ.) 2008, (Univ. of Transkei), (Univ. of Dar es Salaam) 2013, (Univ. of Bayreuth) 2014; Hon. DLitt (Yale Univ.) 2017; Fonlon-Nicholas Award 1996, Nonino Int. Prize for Literature 2001, Medal of Presidency of Italian Cabinet, Fourth Memorial Steve Biko Lecture 2003, Grinzane for Africa Heritage Prize 2008, Nicolás Guillén Lifetime Achievement Award for Philosophical Literature 2014, Park Kyong-ni Prize 2016. *Publications include:* The Black Hermit (play) 1962, Weep Not, Child (novel) 1964, The River Between (novel) 1965, A Grain of Wheat (novel) 1967, This Time Tomorrow: Three Plays 1970, Homecoming: Essays on African and Caribbean Literature, Culture and Politics 1972, Secret Lives and Other Stories 1973, The Trial of Dedan Kimathi (with Micere Githae-Mugo) 1976, Petals of Blood (novel) 1977, Mtawa Mweusi 1978, Caitaani mutharaba-ini (trans. as Devil on the Cross) 1980, Writers in Politics: Essays 1981, Detained: A Writer's Prison Diary 1981, Njamba Nene na mbaathi i mathagu (trans. as Njamba Nene and the Flying Bus) 1982, Ngaahika Ndeena: Ithaako ria Ngerekano (play, with Ngugi wa Mirii), (trans. as I Will Marry When I Want) 1982, Barrel of a Pen: Resistance to Repression in Neo-Colonial Kenya 1983, Bathitoora va Njamba Nene, 1984, English trans. as Njamba Nene's Pistol 1986, Decolonising the Mind: The Politics of Language in African Literature 1986, Writing Against Neo-colonialism 1986, Matigari ma Ngirũũngi (trans. as Matigari) 1986, Njambas Nene no Chiubu King'ang'i 1986, Moving the Centre: The Struggle for Cultural Freedoms 1992, Wizard of the Crow 2006, Something Torn and New: An African Renaissance 2009, Dreams in a Time of War: A Childhood Memoir 2010, In the House of the Interpreter: A Memoir 2012, Globalectics: Theory and the Politics of Knowing 2012, In the Name of the Mother: Reflections on Writers and Empire 2013, Birth of a Dream Weaver: A Memoir of a Writer's Awakening (memoir) 2016, Secure the Base, 2016, Wrestling with the Devil: A Prison Memoir 2018, Minutes of Glory: And Other Stories 2019. *Address:* 279 Humanities Instruction Building, University of California, Irvine, CA 92697-2651, USA (office). *Telephone:* (949) 824-6722 (office). *Fax:* (949) 824-6723 (office). *E-mail:* ngugi@uci.edu (office). *Website:* www.humanities.uci.edu/complit (office); www.ngugiwathiongo.com.

WAAGSTEIN, Finn, MD, PhD; Danish cardiologist and academic; *Professor Emeritus in Cardiology, Institute of Internal Medicine, Sahlgrenska Academy, Gothenberg University;* b. 27 Feb. 1938, Copenhagen; s. of Peter Hans Dahl Waagstein and Elisabeth Waagstein (née Kongstad Rasmussen); m. Lisbeth Marika Ekstrand; three s. one d.; ed Sorö Academi Boarding School, Aarhus Univ.; Surgery resident, Torsby Hosp., Sweden 1964–65; Internal Medicine resident, Gävle Hosp. 1965–70; Cardiology resident, Sahlgrenska Univ. Hosp. 1970–76; Prof. of Cardiology, Inst. of Heart and Lung Diseases, Gothenberg Univ., Prof. Emer. in Cardiology, Inst. of Internal Medicine, Sahlgrenska Acad.; Hon. mem. Japanese Circulation Soc. 2012, Swedish Soc. of Cardiology 2012; Werköpriset Award, Swedish Heart & Lung Foundation 2001, King Faisal Int. Prize for Medicine 2002 (jt recipient), Silver Medal, European Soc. of Cardiology 2002. *Achievements include:* pioneered treatment of heart failure with beta-blockers 1973, first publ. 1975, mandatory treatment in patients with systolic heart failure not finally approved in Europe and USA until 2001. *Publications:* 250 peer-reviewed publs mainly on cardiovascular topics 1970–2012. *Leisure interests:* music (playing guitar and piano), sailing, hiking, gardening, reading (mainly science and history). *Address:* Wallenberg Laboratory, Bruna stråket 16, SU/Sahlgrenska, 413 45 Gothenberg, Sweden (office); Stallviksvägen 11, 428 43 Saro, Sweden (office). *Telephone:* (31) 342-30-14 (Gothenberg) (office); (31) 93-64-96 (Saro) (office); 76-1387477 (mobile). *E-mail:* finn.waagstein@wlab.gu.se (office).

WACHS, Joel, BA, MA, JD; American lawyer and arts administrator; *President, Andy Warhol Foundation for the Visual Arts;* b. 1 March 1939, Scranton, Pa; ed Univ. of California, Los Angeles, Harvard Law School, New York Univ.; began career as corp. tax lawyer, Los Angeles; mem. Los Angeles City Council 1971–2001, Pres. 1981; Lecturer, Univ. of Southern California Law Center 1999; Pres. Andy Warhol Foundation for the Visual Arts, New York 2001–; mem. Calif. Bar Assn. *Address:* Andy Warhol Foundation for the Visual Arts, 65 Bleecker Street, Seventh Floor, New York, NY 10012, USA (office). *Telephone:* (212) 387-7555 (office). *Fax:* (212) 387-7560 (office). *E-mail:* info@warholfoundation.org (office). *Website:* www.warholfoundation.org (office).

WACKERNAGEL, Mathis, BEng, PhD; Swiss engineer and environmental organization administrator; *President, Global Footprint Network;* b. 10 Nov. 1962, Basel; ed Swiss Fed. Inst. of Tech., Univ. of British Columbia, Canada; Dir Centro de Estudios para la Sustentabilidad, Anáhuac Univ., Mexico 1995–2001; Dir Sustainability Program at Redefining Progress, Oakland, Calif. 1999–2003; Co-creator Ecological Footprint and Pres. Global Footprint Network (think-tank) 2003–; mem. Adjunct Faculty, SAGE of Univ. of Wisconsin 2004; Frank H.T. Rhodes Class of 1956 Visiting Prof., Cornell Univ. 2011–13; Dr hc (Berne) 2007; Herman Daly Award, US Soc. for Ecological Econs 2005, WWF Award for Conservation Merit 2006, Skoll Award for Social Entrepreneurship (co-recipient) 2007, Int. Prize Calouste Gulbenkian (shared with Global Footprint Network) 2008, Zayed Int. Prize for Environment (co-recipient) 2011, Kenneth E. Boulding Memorial Award, Int. Soc. for Ecological Econs (co-recipient) 2012, Binding Prize for Environmental Conservation 2012, Blue Planet Prize, Asahi Foundation (co-recipient) 2012, Prix Nature Swisscanto 2013, Global Environment Award, Int. Assn for Impact Assessment (IAIA) 2015. *Publications:* Our Ecological Footprint: Reducing Human Impact on the Earth (co-author) 1995, Sharing Nature's Interest (co-author) 2001, The Winners and Losers in Global Competition: Why Eco-Efficiency Reinforces Competitiveness: A Study of 44 Nations (co-author) 2003, Der Ecological Footprint. Die Welt neu vermessen (co-author) 2010, WWF International's Living Planet Report; more then 50 peer-reviewed papers in professional journals, numerous articles and reports and various books on sustainability. *Address:* Global Footprint Network Headquarters, 312 Clay Street, Suite 300, Oakland, CA 94607-3510, USA (office). *Telephone:* (510) 839-8879 (office). *Fax:* (510) 251-2410 (office). *E-mail:* info@footprintnetwork.org (office). *Website:* www.footprintnetwork.org (office).

WADA, Akiyoshi, PhD; Japanese research director and academic; b. 28 June 1929, Tokyo; s. of Koroku Wada and Haruko Kikkawa; m. Sachiko Naito 1958; two s.; ed Gakushūin High School and Univ. of Tokyo; Prof. of Physics, Univ. of Tokyo 1971–90, Prof. Emer. 1990–, Dean Faculty of Science 1989–90; Dir Sagami Chemical Research Center 1991–2001; apptd Vice-Pres. Advanced Tech. Inst. 1988; Dir Kazusa DNA Research Inst. 1991–; mem. Science Council of Japan 1991–2000; Pres. Nestlé Science Foundation (Japan) 1992–2004; Dir Genomic Sciences Centre (RIKEN) 1998–2004, Adviser 2004–; Dir Yokohama Science Centre 2004–12; Dir Ohanomizu Univ. 2005–09; Second Order of the Sacred Treasure 2002; Matsunaga Prize 1971, Shimadu Prize 1983, Polymer Soc. Prize 1995, Purple Ribbon Medal 1995, 10th Anniversary Award, Human Frontier Science Program 1998, Yokohama Prize of Cultural Merit 2003. *Publications:* Macrodipole of α-helix 1976, Molten Globule State of Proteins 1980, Automated DNA Sequencing 1987, Stability Distribution of DNA Double Helix 1987. *Leisure interests:* orchid cultivation, stamp collection. *Address:* 11-1-311, Akasaka 8, Minato-ku, Tokyo 107, Japan. *Telephone:* (3) 3408-2932.

WADA, Isami, LLB; Japanese real estate industry executive; *Chairman, CEO and Representative Director, Sekisui House Group;* ed Kwansei Gakuin Univ.; joined Sekisui House Ltd (property devt firm) 1965, has held several exec. positions, Chair., CEO and Rep. Dir Sekisui House Group 2008–18; Pres. Japan Fed. of Housing Orgs; mem. Bd of Dirs Almetax Manufacturing Co., Ltd 1999–.

WADA, Norio, BEcons; Japanese telecommunications industry executive; b. 16 Aug. 1940; ed Kyoto Univ.; joined Nippon Telegraph and Telephone (NTT) Public Corpn 1964, Sr Vice-Pres. and Gen. Man. Tohoku Regional Communications Sector 1992–96, Exec. Vice-Pres. and Sr Exec. Man. of Affiliated Business HQ 1997–98, In June 1998, he became an Exec. Vice-Pres. and Sr Exec. Man. of Affiliated Business HQ and Exec. Man. of NTT-Holding Organizational Office 1998–99, Exec. Vice-Pres. and Sr Exec. Man. of NTT-Holding Provisional HQ 1999–2002, Sr Exec. Vice-Pres. NTT 1999–2002, Pres. NTT 2002–07, Chair. NTT 2007–12.

WADAGNI, Romuald; Benin chartered accountant and politician; *Minister of Economy and Finance;* b. 20 June 1976, Lokassa; ed École supérieure des Affaires de Grenoble, France, Harvard Business School, USA; Audit Supervisor, Deloitte & Touche, Lyons 1999–2003, Audit Man., Deloitte & Touche, Boston 2003–06, Sr Man., Global Int. Financial Reporting Standards (IFRS) and Offerings Services, Deloitte 2006–11, Dir Global IFRS and Offerings Services 2011–12, CEO Deloitte Democratic Repub. of Congo 2012–16 (est. Deloitte offices in Kinshasa and Lubumbashi 2012), Partner, Deloitte France 2012–16, Professional Practice Leader for Africa, Deloitte Audit leader for francophone Africa 2015–16; Minister of Economy and Finance 2016–. *Address:* Ministry of the Economy and Finance, BP 302, Cotonou, Benin (office). *Telephone:* 21-30-02-81 (office). *Fax:* 21-31-18-51 (office). *E-mail:* sgm@finance.gouv.bj (office). *Website:* www.finances.bj (office).

WADDELL, (John) Rankin; British photographer; *Director, Rankin Photography;* b. 1966, Glasgow, Scotland; m. Kate Hardie (divorced); one s.; ed Brighton Polytechnic, London Coll. of Printing; co-f. Dazed and Confused magazine; co-f. Vision On Publishing; photographed Golden Queen's Jubilee 2002; Dir Rankin Photography; f. Rankin Film Productions 2011. *Films:* Perfect (short), The Lives of the Saints 2006. *Television:* Germany's Next Top Model 2009, 2010, BBC 4's Seven Photographs that Changed Fashion 2009, BBC 2 Culture Show Review of Irving Penn Exhbn 2010, interview with Rankin (GMTV) 2010, CBS feature televised in USA 2010, America in Pictures – The Story of Life Magazine (BBC 4) 2011. *Publications:* Hello Sexy 1998, Rankin Photographs 1998, Female Nudes 1999, Rankin Works 2000, Snog 2000, Celebritation 2000, Male Nudes 2001, Sofasosexy 2002, Breeding 2002, Rankin Bailey 2003, This is the Work of Rankin 2003, Rankin Portraits 2004, Fashion Stories 2004, Surface Seduction 2005, Hard Sell 2005, The Lives of the Saints (production hardback) 2005–06, Breast Friends 2006, Tuulitastic 2006, Beautyfull 2007, Visually Hungry 2007, Sold Out 2009, Surface Attraction 2009, Rankin's Cheeky 2009, Heidilicious 2009, Destroy 2009, Macallan 2009, We Are Congo 2010, Portraits 2010, Painting Pretty Pictures 2010, RANKINJOZI 2010, Ten Times Rosie 2010, Blood, Sweat and Bond 2014, Andrew Gallimore 2014, Blood, Sweat & Bond 2015, For Queen and Country 2016, Heidi Klum By Rankin 2017. *Address:* Rankin Photography, Annroy, 110–114 Grafton Road, London, NW5 4BA, England (office). *Telephone:* (20) 7284-7320 (office). *Fax:* (20) 7284-7330 (office). *E-mail:* info@rankin.co.uk (office). *Website:* www.rankin.co.uk (office).

WADE, Abdoulaye; Senegalese lawyer, politician and fmr head of state; *Secretary-General, Parti Démocratique Sénégalais;* b. 29 May 1926, Kebemer; m. Viviane Wade; two c.; ed Univs of Besançon and Dijon, France, Univ. of Dakar; fmr univ. teacher of law in Senegal and abroad; barrister, Court of Appeal, Senegal; Founder and Pres. Parti Démocratique Sénégalais (Senegalese Democratic Party) 1974, now Sec.-Gen.; mem. Parl. 1974–2012; Minister of State 1991–92, 1995–97; Pres. of Senegal 2000–12; mem. Int. Acad. of Trial Lawyers; Commdr, Order of Merit, Grand Officer, Légion d'honneur; UNESCO Félix Houphouët-Boigny Peace

Prize 2005. *Publications:* author of several books and essays on law, economics and political science. *Address:* Parti Démocratique Sénégalais, blvd Dial Diop, Immeuble Serigne Mourtada Mbacké, Dakar, Senegal (office). *Telephone:* 33-823-5027 (office). *Fax:* 33-823-1702 (office). *E-mail:* cedobe@aol.com (office).

WADE, (Sarah) Virginia, OBE, BSc; British broadcaster and fmr tennis player; b. 10 July 1945, Bournemouth, Hants. (now Dorset); d. of Canon Eustace Wade (fmr Archdeacon of Durban, SA) and Joan Barbara Wade; ed Univ. of Sussex; amateur tennis player 1962–68, professional 1968–87; British Hard Court Champion 1967, 1968, 1973, 1974; USA Champion 1968 (singles), 1973, 1975 (doubles); Italian Champion 1971; Australian Champion 1972; Wimbledon Ladies Champion 1977; played Wightman Cup for GB 1965–85, Capt. 1973–80; played Fed. Cup for GB 1967–83 (a record), Capt. 1973–81; won 55 singles titles; commentator BBC 1980–; mem. Cttee All England Lawn Tennis Club 1983–91 (first woman to be elected); Hon. LLD (Sussex) 1985; Int. Tennis Hall of Fame 1989; Fed. Cup Award of Excellence 2002. *Publications:* Courting Triumph (with Mary Lou Mellace) 1978, Ladies of the Court 1984. *Leisure interest:* reading. *Address:* c/o Duncan March, Once Upon A Time, Golden House, 30 Great Pulteney Street, London, W1F 9NN, England (office). *Telephone:* (20) 7534-8804 (office); 7956-447-811 (mobile) (office). *E-mail:* duncan.march@onceuponlondon.com (office). *Website:* www.onceuponlondon.com (office); www.virginia-wade.com.

WADHWA, Anil, MA; Indian diplomatist; b. 26 May 1957; m. Deepa Gopalan Wadhwa; two s.; joined Foreign Service 1979, Third Sec., Comm. of India, Hong Kong 1981–83, Second, then First Sec., Embassy in Beijing 1983–87, Under-Sec./Deputy Sec., Ministry of External Affairs, New Delhi 1987–89, UN Disarmament Fellow, Geneva July–Nov. 1989, First Sec. (Disarmament), Perm. Mission in Geneva 1989–92, Counsellor, Embassy in Beijing Jan.–July 1993, Dir/Jt Sec. on deputation to Provisional Tech. Secr. and later to Tech. Secr. for the OPCW, The Hague 1993–2000, Chief Adviser, Earthquake Relief in Gujarat State, Ministry of External Affairs 2000–01, Jt Sec., Cen. and Eastern Europe 2001–04, Amb. to Poland 2004–07, to Oman 2007–11, to Thailand 2011–14, Sec. (East), Ministry of External Affairs responsible for SE Asia, Australasia and the Pacific, Gulf and West Asian regions, among other responsibilities 2014–16, also led sr officials to all meetings of ASEAN, Asia-Europe Meeting, Asia Co-operation Dialogue, Arab League, Mekong-Ganga Co-operation, ASEAN Regional Forum and East Asia Summit, oversaw evacuation of Indian nationals from Iraq, Libya and Yemen, Amb. to Italy 2016–17; currently Sr Fellow and Cluster Leader Vivekananda Int. Foundation. *Publications:* several articles on disarmament and int. security. *Address:* Vivekananda International Foundation, 3, San Martin Marg, Chanakyapuri, New Delhi 110021, India (office). *Telephone:* (11) 24121764 (office). *Fax:* (11) 43115450 (office). *E-mail:* info@vifindia.org (office). *Website:* www.vifindia.org (office).

WADHWANI, Sushil Baldev, CBE, BSc, MSc, PhD; British economist and investment manager; *CEO, Wadhwani Asset Management;* b. 7 Dec. 1959, Kenya; s. of Baldev Wadhwani and Meena Wadhwani; m. Renu Wadhwani; one s. one d.; ed London School of Econs; Reader in Econs, LSE 1984–91, Visiting Prof. 2000–; Visiting Prof., Sir John Cass Business School, City of London 2000–; Dir of Equity Strategy, Goldman Sachs Int. 1991–95; Dir of Research, Tudor Proprietary Trading LLC 1995–99; mem. Bank of England Monetary Policy Cttee 1999–2002; CEO Wadhwani Asset Man./Wadhwani Capital 2002–; Partner, Caxton Assocs 2011–; Gov., LSE 2004–16, Gov. Emer. 2016–; mem. Bd, Scott Trust Ltd 2015–16; Allyn Young Prize, C.S. McTaggart Scholarship, Clothworkers' Co. Exhbn, Gonner Prize, Raynes Undergraduate Prize, Sir Edward Stern Scholarship, Ely Devons Prize, Sayers Prize. *Publications include:* numerous articles in academic journals. *Leisure interest:* cricket. *Address:* Wadhwani Asset Management LLP, Ninth Floor, Orion House, 5 Upper St Martin's Lane, London, WC2H 9EA, England (office). *Telephone:* (20) 7663-3420 (office). *Fax:* (20) 7663-3410 (office). *E-mail:* sushilw@waniasset.com.

WADIA, Jamshed (Jim), FCA, FRSA; British chartered accountant; b. 12 April 1948, Mumbai, India; m. Joelle Garnier 1972; one s. one d.; ed Le Rosey, Rolle, Switzerland, Inns of Court School of Law; called to Bar, Inner Temple 1969; Pnr, Arthur Andersen 1982–2000, Man. Pnr UK 1993–97, Worldwide Man. Partner and CEO 1997–2000 (resgnd); COO Linklaters & Alliance (law firm) 2001–04; apptd Dir (non-exec.), Wragge & Co LLP (law firm) 2005; mem. RSA, Prince's Youth Business Trust Advisory Council. *Leisure interests:* tennis, theatre.

WADIA, Nusli; Indian business executive; *Chairman, Wadia Group;* b. 15 Feb. 1944, Mumbai; grandson of Muhammad Ali Jinnah; m. Maureen Wadia; two s.; Chair. Wadia Group, Bombay Dyeing & Manufacturing Co. Ltd, Gherzi Eastern Ltd, Bombay Burmah Trading Corpn Ltd, BRT Ltd, NW Exports Ltd, Britannia Industries Ltd, Nat. Peroxide Ltd, Citurgia Biochemicals Ltd, Wadia BSN India Ltd; Chair. and Man. Dir Nowrosjee Wadia & Sons Ltd; mem. Bd of Dirs Anil Starch Products Ltd, Tata Chemicals Ltd –2016, Atul Products Ltd, Naira Holdings Ltd, Radley Cotton Mills Ltd, ABI Holdings Ltd, Associated Biscuits Int. Ltd, Oberoi Group. *Address:* Wadia Group, C1- Wadia International Centre (Bombay Dyeing), Pandurang Budhkar Marg, Mumbai 400 025 (office); Bombay Dyeing, Neville House, J. N. Heredia Marg, Ballard Estate, Mumbai 400 038, India (office). *Telephone:* (22) 22618071 (office). *Fax:* (22) 22614520 (office). *E-mail:* Info@wadiagroup.com (office). *Website:* www.wadiagroup.com (office); www.bombaydyeing.com (office).

WAENA, Sir Nathaniel Rahumaea, GCMG, KStJ; Solomon Islands politician and government official; b. 1 Nov. 1945, Su'utaluhia, Ulawa Island; m. Alice Ole Unusu; six adopted c.; worked for Mobile Oil Co. 1966–71, then joined public service, eventually serving as Perm. Sec. in numerous ministries, including Provincial Govt and Rural Devt, Natural Resources, Transport, Works and Utilities, and Agric., Lands and Surveys; mem. Parl. 1984–2004; Exec. Cttee Rep. of Pacific Region, Commonwealth Parl. Asscn 1999–2002; Minister of Prov. Govt and Rural Devt 2000, Minister for Nat. Unity, Reconciliation and Peace 2001–04; Gov.-Gen. Solomon Islands 2004–09; apptd mem. Eminent Persons Advisory Council of Constitutional Congress 2010; Chair. Coll. of Higher Educ. 2011; currently Pres. People's Alliance Party; Patron, St Martins, Tenar 2004, Stuyvenberg Rural Training Centre, Nana 2006, Pawa Prov. Secondary School Fund Raising Drive 2007; Solomon Island Cross (CSI). *Address:* People's Alliance Party, Honiara, Solomon Islands.

WAFY, Abdallah; Niger civil servant and diplomatist; *Permanent Representative to United Nations;* b. 1955; m.; five c.; ed Université du Bénin, Togo, Ecole nationale supérieure de police, France; worked as Sr Security Adviser to Minister for Interior, Public Safety and Decentralization; fmr Inspector-Gen. of Police; Special Security Adviser to Pres.; Amb. to Libya; Perm. Rep. of Community of Sahel-Saharan States, Tripoli; served with Civilian Police UN Operation in Côte d'Ivoire (UNOCI) 2006–07, Deputy Head of Police Component UN Mission in Democratic Repub. of Congo (MONUC) 2009, Police Commr UN Stabilization Mission in Democratic Repub. of Congo (MONUSCO) 2010–12, Deputy Special Rep. of Sec.-Gen. Rule of Law and Operations, MONUSCO 2012–15; Perm. Rep. to UN 2015–. *Address:* Permanent Mission of Niger, 417 E 50th Street, New York, NY 10022, USA (office). *Telephone:* (212) 421-3260 (office). *Fax:* (212) 753-6931 (office). *E-mail:* nigermissionymail@ymail.com (office). *Website:* www.un.int/niger (office).

WAGENER, Hans; German business executive and accountant; b. 6 Feb. 1950, Rosdorf; ed Univ. of Göttingen; began career as bank clerk at Commerzbank; later accounting asst with Treuarbeit AG (predecessor of PricewaterhousCoopers (PwC) Germany) 1977, passed exams for both tax adviser and Certified Public Accountant in early 1980s, left co. 1985; moved to Auditing Asscn of German Banks 1985; returned to Germany 1987; mem. PwC Financial Services Bd 1992, assumed responsibility for various int. activities, CEO PwC Germany 2003–10; Chair. Supervisory Bd Landesbank Baden-Wuerttemberg 2010–15; fmr Lecturer, Dept of Accounting, Johann Wolfgang Goethe Univ., Frankfurt; mem. Bd Inst. of Chartered Accountants.

WAGGONER, Paul Edward, PhD, FAAS; American horticultural scientist; *Distinguished Scientist, Department of Forestry and Horticulture, Connecticut Agricultural Experiment Station;* b. 29 March 1923, Appanoose Co., Ia; s. of Walter Loyal Waggoner and Kathryn Maring Waggoner; m. Barbara Ann Lockerbie 1945; two s.; ed Univ. of Chicago, Iowa State Univ.; Asst, then Assoc. Plant Pathologist, Connecticut Agricultural Experiment Station, Dept of Forestry and Horticulture, New Haven, 1951–56, Chief Scientist, Soils, Climatology, Ecology 1951–71, Vice-Dir 1969–71, Dir 1972–87, Distinguished Scientist 1987–; Lecturer, Yale Forestry School, New Haven 1962–; Guggenheim Fellow 1963; mem. NAS; Fellow, American Soc. of Agronomy, American Phytopathological Soc.; Anton-de Bary Medal 1996. *Publications include:* Agricultural Meteorology (ed.) 1965, Climate Change and US Water Resources 1990, How Much Land Can 10 Billion People Spare for Nature? 1994 and articles on phytopathology. *Leisure interests:* gardening, bicycling. *Address:* Connecticut Agricultural Experiment Station, Box 1106, New Haven, CT 06504-1106 (office); 314 Vineyard Point Road, Guilford, CT 06437, USA (home). *Telephone:* (203) 974-8494 (office); (203) 453-2816 (home). *E-mail:* agwagg@comcast.net; paul.waggoner@po.state.ct.us. *Website:* www.caes.state.ct.us/Departments/forestry.htm (office).

WAGNER, Heinz Georg, Dr rer. nat; German scientist and academic; *Professor Emeritus, Institut für Physikalische Chemie, University of Göttingen;* b. 20 Sept. 1928, Hof, Bavaria; s. of Georg Wagner and Frieda Spiess; m. Renate C. Heuer 1974; ed Tech. Hochschule, Darmstadt and Univ. of Göttingen; Lecturer, Univ. of Göttingen 1960–65, Prof. of Physical Chem. 1971–97, now Prof. Emer.; Prof. Ruhr Univ. Bochum 1965–70; Dir Max-Planck-Inst. für Strömungsforschung, Göttingen 1971–97; Vice-Pres. Deutsche Forschungsgemeinschaft 1983–89; mem. Exec. Council ESF; Scientific mem. Max-Planck-Gesellschaft; mem. Göttingen Acad., Acad. Leopoldina, Int. Acad. of Astronautics, Heidelberg Acad., Acad. of Natural Sciences of Russia, Academia Europaea, American Physical Soc., Royal Soc. of Chem. etc.; Hon. mem. Bunsen-Gesellschaft; Grosses Bundesverdienstkreuz; several hon. doctorates; Fritz-Haber Prize, Bernard Lewis Gold Medal, Achema Medal, Numa Manson Medal, Dionizy Smoleński Medal, Walther-Nernst-Denkmünze, Dechema Medal. *Publications include:* articles on combustion, reaction kinetics, thermodynamics of liquid mixtures. *Address:* Institut für Physikalische Chemie, Universität Göttingen, Tammannstr. 6, 37077 Göttingen, Germany (office). *Telephone:* (551) 3933100 (office). *Fax:* (551) 3933117 (office). *E-mail:* jkupfer@gwdg.de (office). *Website:* www.uni-goettingen.de/de/sh/28451.html (office).

WAGNER, Herbert, Dr rer. nat; German theoretical physicist and academic; *Professor Emeritus, Ludwig Maximilian University of Munich;* b. 6 April 1935; fmr Postdoctoral Fellow, Cornell Univ., USA; apptd Prof. of Theoretical Solid State Physics, Ludwig Maximilian Univ. of Munich, now Prof. Emer.; Dr hc (Univ. of Essen) 1992; Max Planck Medal, Deutsche Physikalische Gesellschaft 2016. *Achievements include:* collaborated with David Mermin to prove the Mermin–Wagner theorem. *Publications:* numerous papers in professional journals. *Address:* Room A423, Faculty of Physics, Ludwig Maximilian University, Theresienstr. 37, 80333 Munich, Germany (office). *Telephone:* (89) 21804371 (office). *Fax:* (89) 21804155 (office). *E-mail:* herbert.wagner@physik.lmu.de (office). *Website:* www.theorie.physik.uni-muenchen.de (office).

WAGNER, Jaques; Brazilian politician; *Head of the Cabinet Office;* b. 15 March 1951, Rio de Janeiro; s. of Joseph Wagner and Cypa Perla Wagner; m. Maria de Fátima Carneiro de Mendonça; three s.; ed Pontifical Catholic Univ.; Chair., Student Union, Civil Eng Coll., Pontifical Catholic Univ., Rio de Janeiro in late 1960s; forced to leave univ. during mil. dictatorship 1973; left Rio de Janeiro, worked as labourer in petrochemical unit, Camaçari Industrial Complex, Bahia; Pres. Union of Petrochemical Industry Workers (Sindiquímica-BA) 1987–89; mem. Câmara dos Deputados (Parl.) for Bahia 1990–98; Minister of Labour Employment and Institutional Relations 2003–04, Chief Minister of Institutional Relations, Secr. of Brazil 2005–06, Minister of Defence Jan.–Oct. 2015; Head Cabinet Office Oct. 2015–; Gov. of Bahia 2007–15; co-f. Partido dos Trabalhadores. *Address:* Palácio do Planalto, 4° andar, Praça dos Três Poderes, 70150-900 Brasília DF, Brazil (office). *Telephone:* (61) 3411-1221 (office). *Fax:* (61) 3411-2222 (office). *E-mail:* sicplanalto@planalto.gov.br (office). *Website:* www.casacivil.planalto.gov.br (office).

WAGNER, Robert; American actor; b. 10 Feb. 1930, Detroit, MI; m. 1st Natalie Wood 1957 (divorced 1962, re-married 1972, died 1981); one d. one step-d.; m. 2nd Marion Marshall Donen 1963 (divorced 1971); one d.; m. 4th Jill St John 1990. *Films include:* Halls of Montezuma 1951, The Frogmen 1951, Let's Make It Legal 1951, With a Song in My Heart 1952, What Price Glory? 1952, Stars and Stripes Forever 1952, The Silver Whip 1953, Titanic 1953, Star of Tomorrow, Beneath the

12-Mile Reef 1953, Prince Valiant 1954, Broken Lance 1954, White Feather 1955, A Kiss Before Dying 1956, The Mountain 1956, The True Story of Jesse James 1957, Stopover Tokyo 1957, The Hunters 1958, In Love and War 1958, Mardi Gras 1958, Say One For Me 1959, Between Heaven and Hell, All the Fine Young Cannibals 1960, Sail a Crooked Ship 1961, The Longest Day 1962, The War Lover 1962, The Condemned of Altona 1962, The Pink Panther 1963, Harper 1966, Banning 1967, The Biggest Bundle of Them All 1968, Don't Just Stand There! 1968, Winning 1969, Madame Sin 1972, Journey Through Rosebud 1972, The Towering Inferno 1974, Midway 1976, The Concorde: Airport '79 1979, Curse of the Pink Panther 1983, I Am the Cheese 1983, Delirious (uncredited) 1991, Dragon: The Bruce Lee Story 1993, Overdrive 1997, Austin Powers: International Man of Mystery 1997, Wild Things 1998, Something to Believe In 1998, The Kidnapping of Chris Burden 1999, Dill Scallion 1999, Crazy in Alabama 1999, No Vacancy 1999, Love and Fear, Austin Powers: The Spy Who Shagged Me 1999, Play It to the Bone 1999, Forever Fabulous 2000, The Mercury Project 2000, The Retrievers 2001, Sol Goode 2001, Jungle Juice 2001, Nancy and Frank–A Manhattan Love Story 2002, Austin Powers in Goldmember 2002, The Calling 2002, El Padrino 2004, The Fallen Ones 2005, The Wild Stallion 2006, Hoot 2006, Man in the Chair 2007, Netherbeast Incorporated 2007, Man in the Chair 2007, A Dennis the Menace Christmas 2007, The Wild Stallion 2009, The Hungover Games 2014, Thirty Nine 2016. *Television series include:* How I Spent My Summer Vacation 1967, Hart to Hart 1979–84, It Takes a Thief (series) 1967–70, City Beneath the Sea 1971, Crosscurrent 1971, Killer by Night 1972, The Streets of San Francisco 1972, Colditz (series) 1972, The Affair 1973, The Abduction of Saint Anne 1975, Switch (series) 1975, Death at Love House 1976, Cat on a Hot Tin Roof 1976, The Critical List 1978, Pearl (mini-series) 1978, Hart to Hart (series) 1979, To Catch a King 1984, Lime Street (series) 1985, There Must Be a Pony 1986, Love Among Thieves 1987, Windmills of the Gods 1988, Indiscreet 1988, Around the World in 80 Days (mini-series) 1989, This Gun for Hire 1991, False Arrest 1991, Jewels (mini-series) 1992, The Trials of Rosie O'Neill (series) 1992, Les audacieux 1993, Hart to Hart: Hart to Hart Returns 1993, Hart to Hart: Home Is Where the Hart Is 1994, Heaven & Hell: North & South, Book III (mini-series) 1994, Hart to Hart: Crimes of the Hart 1994, Hart to Hart: Old Friends Never Die 1994, Parallel Lives 1994, Hart to Hart: Secrets of the Hart 1995, Dancing in the Dark 1995, Hart to Hart: Two Harts in Three-Quarters Time 1995, Hart to Hart: Harts in High Season 1996, Hart to Hart: Till Death Do Us Hart 1996, Camino de Santiago (mini-series) 1999, Fatal Error 1999, Die Abzocker–Eine eiskalte Affäre (aka A Sordid Affair, and The Hustle) 2000, Rocket's Red Glare 2000, Becoming Dick 2000, The Retrievers 2001, Mystery Woman 2003, Hope & Faith 2003–06, Boston Legal 2006, Two and a Half Men 2007, NCIS 2010–19; numerous other TV appearances. *Publications:* Pieces of My Heart: A Life 2008, You Must Remember This: The Life and Style of Hollywood's Golden Age 2014, I Loved Her in the Movies: Memories of Hollywood's Legendary Actresses 2016. *Website:* www.robert-wagner.com.

WAGNER, Susan L., BA, MBA; American business executive; b. 1961; ed Wellesley Coll., Univ. of Chicago; Vice-Pres., Mortgage and Savings Insts Group, Lehman Brothers –1988; Co-founder BlackRock, Inc. 1988, Man. Dir and Head of Strategy and Product Devt –2005, COO 2005–10, Co-Chair. Corp. Council and mem. Office of Chair., Operating Cttee, Corp. Risk Cttee and Leadership Cttee, Vice-Chair. BlackRock, Inc. 2006–12, mem. Bd of Dirs BlackRock, DSP BlackRock (India); mem. Bd of Dirs Swiss Re 2014–, Apple Inc. 2014–; mem. Business Leadership Council of Wellesley Coll., Bd of Trustees of Hackley School. *Publications:* assisted in writing and editing Conversations with Economists (named one of the ten best business and economics books published in 1984) 1984; author of several articles for Lehman Brothers. *Address:* Corporate Communications Department, BlackRock, Inc., 55 East 52nd Street, New York, NY 10055, USA (office).

WAGNER TIZÓN, Allan; Peruvian politician and diplomatist; b. 7 Feb. 1942, Lima; s. of Carlos Wagner Vizcarra and Antonieta Tizón Ponce; m. Julia de la Guerra Urquiaga; five d.; ed Nat. Univs of Trujillo and of Engineering, Lima, Universidad Católica and Universidad de San Marcos; joined Ministry of Foreign Affairs 1963; joined Diplomatic Service 1968; Chief of Econ. Dept, Embassy in Washington, DC 1972–74, Deputy Chief of Mission and Chargé d'affaires 1983–85; Chief of Political Dept, Embassy in Chile 1978–79; Minister of Foreign Affairs 1985–88, 2002–03; Amb. to Spain 1988–90, to Venezuela 1991–92 (resgnd); Prof. Diplomatic Acad. 1991; Dir of Devt and Adviser to Latin American Econ. System (SELA) 1992–98; Founder-mem. Peruvian Centre of Int. Studies (CEPEI), Pres. 1999–; Founder-mem. Inst. of European–Latin American Relations (IRELA); Amb. to USA 2001–02; Adviser to Sec.-Gen. of Andean Community of Nations –2002, Sec.-Gen. 2004–06; Minister of Defence 2006–07; Del. of Peru, Int. Court of Justice trying land and maritime boundary dispute with Chile 2007–; Amb. to the Netherlands 2008–14; Gran Cruz de la Orden El Sol del Perú, Orden al Mérito por Servicios Distinguidos, seven more decorations from Peru and 26 decorations from foreign countries. *Address:* c/o Embassy of Peru, Nassauplein 4, 2585 The Hague, Netherlands.

WAGONER, (Robert D.) Dan, BS; American dancer, choreographer, dance company director and academic; *Professor Emeritus, School of Dance, Florida State University;* b. 1932, West Virginia; ed Univ. of West Virginia; studied pharmacy; danced with Martha Graham co. 1956–57, with Merce Cunningham co. 1959–60, with Paul Taylor Dance Studio 1960–68; Artistic Dir/Choreographer and Prin. Dancer, Dan Wagoner and Dancers, New York 1969–2005; Artistic Dir London Contemporary Dance Theatre 1989–90; Distinguished Guest Artist and Prof., Dept of Dance, Connecticut Coll. 1995–2005; Visiting Prof., School of Dance, Coll. of Visual Arts, Theatre and Dance, Florida State Univ. 2004–05, Prof. 2005, now Prof. Emer.; Henry-Bascom Visiting Prof., Dept of Dance, Univ. of Wisconsin 2004; Visiting Prof., Dance Program, Office of the Arts, Harvard Univ. 2004–06; numerous grants, Medal of Honor in the Arts, Winthrop Univ. 2007, Undergraduate Teaching Award, Florida State Univ. 2010. *Address:* Florida State University, School of Dance, College of Visual Arts, Theatre and Dance, 201 Montgomery Hall, Tallahassee, FL 32306-2120, USA (office). *Telephone:* (850) 644-1024 (office). *Fax:* (850) 644-1277 (office). *E-mail:* rdwagoner@fsu.edu (office). *Website:* dance.fsu.edu (office).

WAGONER, David Russell, MA; American writer and academic; *Professor Emeritus of English, University of Washington;* b. 5 June 1926, Massillon, Ohio; m. 1st Patricia Parrott 1961 (divorced 1982); m. 2nd Robin H. Seyfried 1982; two d.; ed Pennsylvania State Univ., Indiana Univ.; served in USN 1944–46; Instructor, DePauw Univ. 1949–50, Pennsylvania State Univ. 1950–54; Assoc. Prof., Univ. of Washington, Seattle 1954–66, Prof. of English 1966–2000, Prof. Emer. 2000–; Ed. Poetry Northwest, Seattle 1966–2002, Ed. Princeton Univ. Press Contemporary Poetry Series 1977–81; Chancellor Acad. of American Poets 1978–99; Poetry Ed. Missouri Press 1983–2000; Guggenheim Fellowship 1956, Ford Fellowship 1964, American Acad. Grant 1967, Nat. Endowment for the Arts Grant 1969; Morton Dauwen Zabel Prize (Poetry, Chicago) 1967, Elliston Lecturer, Univ. of Cincinnati 1968, Ruth Lilly Prize 1991, Levinson Prize (Poetry, Chicago) 1994, Union League Prize (Poetry, Chicago) 1997, Pacific NW Booksellers Award 2000, Arthur Rense Prize 2011. *Play:* An Eye for an Eye for an Eye 1973. *Publications include:* novels: The Man in the Middle 1955, Money, Money, Money 1955, Rock 1958, The Escape Artist 1965, Baby, Come On Inside 1968, Where is My Wandering Boy Tonight? 1970, The Road to Many a Wonder 1974, Tracker 1975, Whole Hog 1976, The Hanging Garden 1980; poetry: Dry Sun, Dry Wind 1953, A Place to Stand 1958, Poems 1959, The Nesting Ground 1963, Five Poets of the Pacific Northwest (with others) 1964, Staying Alive 1966, New and Selected Poems 1969, Working Against Time 1970, Riverbed 1972, Sleeping in the Woods 1974, A Guide to Dungeness Spit 1975, Travelling Light 1976, Who Shall Be the Sun? Poems Based on the Lore, Legends and Myths of Northwest Coast and Plateau Indians 1978, In Broken Country 1979, Landfall 1981, First Light 1983, Through the Forest 1987, Walt Whitman Bathing 1996, Traveling Light: Collected and New Poems 1999, The House of Song 2002, Good Morning and Good Night 2005, A Map of the Night 2008, After the Point of No Return 2012; short stories: Afternoon on the Ground 1978, Wild Goose Chase 1978, Mr. Wallender's Romance 1979, Cornet Solo 1979, The Water Strider 1979, Fly Boy 1980, The Bird Watcher 1980, Snake Hunt 1980. *Address:* 5416 154th Place, SW, Edmonds, WA 98026-4348, USA (home). *Telephone:* (425) 745-6964 (home). *E-mail:* renogawd@aol.com (home).

WAGONER, G. Richard, Jr, BEcons, MBA; American automobile industry executive (retd); b. 9 Feb. 1953, Wilmington, Del.; s. of George Wagoner and Martha Wagoner; m. Kathy Wagoner (neé Kaylor) 1979; three s.; ed Duke and Harvard Univs; joined General Motors (GM) 1977, analyst, Office of the Treas., New York 1977, Treas. of GM do Brasil (GMB), São Paulo 1981–84, Exec. Dir of Finance, GMB 1984–87, Vice-Pres. and Finance Man. GM Canada Ltd 1987–88, Group Dir (Strategic Business Planning) Chevrolet-Pontiac-GM, Canada 1988–89, Vice-Pres. Finance, GM Europe, Zürich, Switzerland 1989–90, Pres. and Man. GMB 1991–92, Exec. Vice-Pres. and Chief Financial Officer 1992–94, Head of Worldwide Purchasing 1993–94, Exec. Vice-Pres. and Pres. N American Operations 1994–98, Pres. and COO 1998–2000, Chair. Automotive Strategy Bd, Pres. and CEO 2000–03, Chair. and CEO May 2003–09 (resgnd); mem. Bd of Dirs WP Co. LLC 2010–, Graham Holdings Co. 2010–, Aleris Corpn 2010–, Invesco Ltd 2013–; mem. Advisory Bd AEA Investors, Jefferies Investment Banking, Capital Markets Group; mem. Global Sr Advisory Bd Jefferies Group LLC.

WAHEED HASSAN MANIK, Mohamed, MA, PhD; Maldivian politician and fmr UN official and fmr head of state; b. 3 Jan. 1953; s. of Hassan Ibrahim Maniku and Aishath Moosa; m. Ilham Hussain; three c.; ed American Univ. of Beirut, Stanford Univ., USA; fmr Lecturer, Michigan State Univ., USA; fmr Programme Man. HSQ Technology Inc., San Francisco, USA; began political career by running first Western-style election campaign in Maldives in 1998, elected mem. Parl. for Malé 1998; served as Sec. of Educ., in Office of the Pres. and as mem. Atolls Devt Advisory Bd, Maldives Youth Council and Council for Dhivehi Language and Literature; worked with UNDP and UNESCO in Swaziland, Lesotho, Mozambique, Bangladesh, Fiji and Western Samoa 1991–92; joined UNICEF as Chief of Educ. for UNICEF in Tanzania 1992, served UNICEF as its Rep. and Head of Mission in several countries, including Acting Regional Dir UNICEF Regional Office for S Asia, Interim Rep. of Afghanistan, Yemen and Montenegro, and Acting Rep. in FYR Macedonia, Special Rep. in Afghanistan 2002–05, advised Govt of Pres. Hamid Karzai and assisted in co-ordination and rehabilitation of educ. sector on behalf of UN Assistance Mission for Afghanistan, apptd Assoc. Dir UN Devt Group (UNDG) Office, New York 2005, served as Sec. UNDG Man. Group, exercised oversight responsibilities for setting up of first UN Jt Office pilot and led HQ support to UN Resident Co-ordinator system for Europe and Middle East, UNICEF Country Rep. in Turkmenistan –2008; fmr mem. Maldivian Democratic Party (MDP), cand. for presidency at second party congress; est. Nat. Alliance party; Leader Gaumee Itthihaad Party, formed alliance with MDP Sept. 2008; Vice-Pres. of Maldives (first elected vice-pres.) 2008–12, Pres. 2012–13.

WAHL, Jacques Henri, LLB; French fmr civil servant; b. 18 Jan. 1932, Lille; s. of Abraham Wahl and Simone Kornbluth; m. Inna Cytrin 1969; two s. one d.; ed Inst. d'Etudes Politiques, Paris, Univs of Lille and Paris, Ecole Nat. d'Admin; Insp. des Finances 1961; Treasury Dept 1965–68; Special Asst to Ministers of Econ. and Finance, François Ortoli 1968–69, Valéry Giscard d'Estaing 1969–71; Asst Dir of the Treasury for Int. Affairs 1971–73; Chair. Invisible Transactions Cttee, OECD 1971–73; Lecturer Inst. d'Etudes Politiques and Ecole Nat. d'Admin., Paris 1969–73; Financial Minister, French Embassies, USA and Canada 1973–78; Exec. Dir IMF, IBRD 1973–78; Sec.-Gen. to the Presidency of the French Repub. 1978–81; Insp.-Gen. des Finances 1981; Dir-Gen. Banque Nat. de Paris 1982 (known as BNP Paribas 2000–11), Vice-Chair. 1993–97, Adviser to Chair. 1994–2001, Chair. Bd of Dirs BNP Paribas Canada 2010, mem. Bd of Dirs BancWest (subsidiary of BNP Paribas) 1998–2012, Banque Wormser Frères (current); Chair. Banque Nat. de Paris Intercontinentale 1993–97, mem. Bd 1994; Dir BICICI SA, Olympia Capital Management SA; Officier, Légion d'honneur, Officier Ordre nat. du Mérite, Commdr Ordre Nat. de Côte d'Ivoire, Officier Ordre du Mérite de la République Centrafricaine, Chevalier Ordre du Mérite de Haute Volta, also honours from Portugal, Brazil, Venezuela, Greece, Sweden and Germany. *Address:* BNP Paribas, 19 boulevard des Italiens, 75009 Paris (office); 15 avenue de la Bourdonnais, 75007 Paris, France (home).

WAHL, Philippe, MA; French business executive; *Chairman, President and CEO, La Poste;* b. 11 March 1956, Sarralbe; ed Sciences-Po Paris, École Nationale d'Admin; began career as auditor and maître des requêtes at Council of State, Special Adviser to Chair. of Bd 1986; Tech. Adviser for Econ., Financial and Tax Affairs, Office of Prime Minister Michel Rocard 1989; CEO Caisse Nationale des Caisses d'Epargne (CNCE) and mem. Man. Bd CNCE at CE Participations;

Adviser to Chair. of Compagnie Bancaire 1991–94, Sr Vice-Pres. 1994–97, apptd CEO Groupe Caisse d'Epargne, SA 1999, Adviser to Global Banking and Markets Board in London and Man. Dir for France, Belgium and Luxembourg 2008–11; Specialist Financial Services, BNP Paribas 1997–2002; Chair. Ecureuil Assurances Iard –2002, Ecureuil Gestion –2002, Ecureuil Vie –2002; Vice-Chair. Supervisory Bd Crédit Foncier de France; Vice-Chair. Bolloré group 2006–; Man. Dir Royal Bank of Scotland, France at Royal Bank of Scotland Group plc 2007–08; Group Sr Vice-Pres. La Poste SA –2013, Chair. Man. Bd, La Banque Postale SA and Sr Vice-Pres. La Poste Group 2011–13, Chair., Pres. and CEO La Poste 2013–; Chair. and CEO Holassure, Sopassure; CEO Havas Group 2005–06; Dir, Cie Financière Eulia, Caisse d'Epargne Financement; mem. Supervisory Bd CNP Assurances SA 2001–, CDC IXIS (Perm. Rep. of CNCEP on Supervisory Bd of CDC IXIS Capital Markets, CDC IXIS Asset Man., CDC IXIS Private Capital Man.); Perm. Rep. of Ecureuil Participations on Bd of Dirs of Alliance Entreprendre, of CNCEP on Bd of Dirs of Mutuelle du Mans Assurances IARD (MMA IARD) and Mutuelle du Mans Assurances Vie; Dir, CNP Assurances SA 2011–. *Address:* La Poste, 44 boulevard de Vaugirard, 75757 Paris Cedex 15, France (office). *Telephone:* 1-55-44-01-01 (office). *Fax:* 1-55-44-01-25 (office). *E-mail:* jean-paul.bailly@laposte.fr (office). *Website:* www.laposte.fr (office).

WAHLBERG, Mark Robert; American actor and musician; b. 5 June 1971, Dorchester, Boston, Mass; s. of Donal E. Wahlberg and Alma Wahlberg; m. Rhea Durham; three c. *Films:* Renaissance Man 1994, The Basketball Diaries 1995, Fear 1996, Traveller 1997, Boogie Nights 1997, The Big Hit 1998, The Corruptor 1999, Three Kings 1999, The Yards 2000, The Perfect Storm 2000, Metal God 2000, Planet of the Apes 2001, Rock Star 2001, The Truth About Charlie 2003, The Italian Job 2003, I Heart Huckabees 2004, Four Brothers 2005, Invincible 2006, The Departed (Best Supporting Actor Nat. Soc. of Film Critics 2007) 2006, Shooter 2007, We Own the Night 2007, The Happening 2008, Max Payne 2008, The Lovely Bones 2009, Date Night 2010, The Other Guys 2010, The Fighter 2010, Contraband 2012, Ted 2012, Pain & Gain 2013, 2 Guns 2013, Lone Survivor 2013, Transformers: Age of Extinction 2014, The Gambler 2014, Mojave 2015, Entourage 2015, Ted 2 2015, Daddy's Home 2015, Daddy's Home Two 2017, Mile 22 2018. *Television:* Teen Vid II (Video) 1991, The Substitute 1993; exec. producer Entourage (series). *Recordings include:* albums: Music For the People 1991, You Gotta Believe 1992 (as Marky Mark and the Funky Bunch). *Address:* c/o William Morris Endeavor Entertainment, 9601 Wilshire Blvd., Beverly Hills, CA 90210, USA. *Website:* www.markwahlberg.com (office).

WAHLROOS, Björn Arne Christer, BSc, MSc, DSc; Finnish economist, academic and banking executive; *Chairman, Nordea Bank AB;* b. 10 Oct. 1952, Helsinki; s. of Bror Wahlroos and Marita Wahlroos; m. Saara Wahlroos; one s. one d.; ed Hanken School of Econs; Acting Lecturer and Asst Prof. of Finance, Swedish School of Econs 1974–79, Prof. and Acting Prof. of Econs 1979–85; Visiting Asst Prof. of Econs, Brown Univ., USA 1980–81; Visiting Assoc. Prof. of Managerial Econs and Decision Sciences, Kellogg Grad. School of Man., Northwestern Univ., USA 1983–84; various positions with Union Bank of Finland, including Exec. Vice-Pres. and mem. Exec. Cttee 1985–92; Pres. Mandatum & Co. Ltd 1992–97; Chair. Mandatum Bank Plc 1998–2000; Pres. and Group CEO Sampo Plc 2001–09, Chair. 2009–, Chair. Sampo Bank Plc 2005–07; mem. of Bd of Dirs Nordea Bank AB 2008–, Vice-Chair. 2009–11, Chair. 2011–; Chair. UPM-Kymmene 2008–, Hanken School of Econs 2009–; rank of Capt. in Reserves, Finnish Defence Forces; mem. Finnish Business and Policy Forum 2005–, Research Inst. of Finnish Economy 2005–, Mannerheim Foundation 2007–; Founder and Chair. Bd of Trustees Saara and Björn Wahlroos Foundation 2002–. *Address:* Nordea Bank AB, Smålandsgatan 17, 105 71 Stockholm, Sweden (office). *Telephone:* (8) 614-7000 (office). *Fax:* (8) 105-069 (office). *E-mail:* info@nordea.com (office). *Website:* www.nordea.com (office); www.wahlroosfoundation.com.

WAHLSTRÖM, Margareta, BA; Swedish international organization official and fmr UN official; b. 30 March 1950; ed Univ. of Stockholm; has held numerous positions with non-governmental orgs and pvt. cos in SE Asia, Latin America and Africa; several sr positions with Int. Fed. of the Red Cross and Red Crescent Socs, Geneva 1989–2000, including Under-Sec.-Gen. for the Response and Operations Coordination Div.; ind. consultant 2000–02; fmr Chief of Staff of the Special Rep. of the Sec.-Gen., UN Assistance Mission in Afghanistan (UNAMA), Deputy Special Rep. responsible for relief, reconstruction and devt –2004, Asst Sec.-Gen. for Humanitarian Affairs and Deputy Emergency Relief Coordinator, UN 2004–08, concurrently Special Coordinator of the Sec.-Gen. for Humanitarian Assistance to Tsunami-Affected Countries, Asst Sec.-Gen. for Disaster Risk Reduction and Special Rep. of the Sec.-Gen. for Implementation of Hyogo Framework for Action in Secr. for Int. Strategy for Disaster Reduction, Geneva 2008–15; mem. Comm. on Climate Change and Devt.

WAIGEL, Theodor, DJur; German lawyer and politician; b. 22 April 1939, Oberrohr; s. of August Waigel and Genoveva Konrad; m. 1st Karin Hönig 1966 (divorced 1994); m. 2nd Irene Epple 1994; two s. one d.; ed Univs of Munich and Würzburg; Personal Asst to State Sec., Bavarian State Ministry of Finance 1969–70, Personal Asst to Bavarian State Minister for Economy and Transport 1970–72; mem. Bundestag 1972–2002, Chair. Working Group on economic and economic policy spokesman of the CDU/CSU group in the Bundestag 1980–82, CSU Land (Bavarian) Group 1982–89; Minister of Finance 1989–98; Chair. of CSU 1988–98, Hon. Chair. 2009–; joined GSK Stockmann & Kollegen (law firm), Munich 1999; apptd Chair. Supervisory Bd Löwen Entertainment 2004; Vice-Chair. Supervisory Bd Bayerische Gewerbebau AG 2007–; Compliance Monitor, Siemens AG 2008–12; Of Counsel, Waigel Lawyers, Munich 2016–; mem. Bd of Trustees Eugen Biser Foundation; Patron, Institut der Regionen Europas (IRE); Bayerischer Verdienstorden; Dr hc (Univ. of S Carolina) 1997. *Leisure interests:* climbing, theatre, football.

WAIHEE, John David, III, BA, JD; American lawyer and fmr politician; *Partner, Waihee & Nip LLC;* b. 19 May 1946, Honokaa, Hawaii; m. Lynne Kobashigawa; one s. one d.; ed Andrews Univ., Cen. Michigan Univ. and Univ. of Hawaii; admitted to Hawaii Bar 1976; Community Educ. Co-ordinator, Benton Harbor, Mich. area schools 1968–70; Asst Dir Community Educ. 1970–71; Program Evaluator, Admin. Asst to Dirs, Planner, Honolulu Model Cities Program 1971–73; Sr Planner, Office of Human Resources, City and Co. of Honolulu 1973–74, Program Man. 1974–75; Assoc. Shim, Sigal, Tam & Naito (law firm), Honolulu 1975–79; Partner, Waihee, Manuia, Yap, Pablo & Hoe (law firm), Honolulu 1979–82; mem. Hawaiian State House of Reps 1980–82; Lt Gov. of Hawaii 1982–86, Gov. of Hawaii 1986–95; Head of Hawaii office of Verner, Liipfert, Bernhard, McPherson and Handwith (law firm), Honolulu 1995–2001; Partner, Waihee & Nip LLC (law firm), Honolulu 2002–; Sr Advisor, Dubin Financial LLC (finance co.), also Of Counsel, Dubin Law LLC; mem. Advisory Bd World Wide Real Estate and Development Corpn; Democrat. *Address:* Waihee & Nip LLC, 333 Queen Street, Suite 608, Honolulu, HI 96613-4716, USA (office). *Fax:* (808) 566-0999 (office).

WAINWRIGHT, Geoffrey, MA, DD (Cantab.), DrThéol; British ecclesiastic and academic; *Robert Earl Cushman Professor Emeritus of Christian Theology, Divinity School, Duke University;* b. 16 July 1939, Yorks., England; s. of Willie Wainwright and Martha Burgess; m. Margaret H. Wiles 1965; one s. two d.; ed Gonville & Caius Coll. Cambridge, Univ. of Geneva, Switzerland; Prof. of Dogmatics, Protestant Faculty of Theology, Yaoundé, Cameroon 1967–73; Lecturer in Bible and Systematic Theology, Queen's Coll. Birmingham 1973–79; Roosevelt Prof. of Systematic Theology, Union Theological Seminary, New York 1979–83; Robert Earl Cushman Prof. of Christian Theology, Duke Univ. 1983–2012, now Prof. Emer.; mem. Faith and Order Comm. WCC 1977–91; Pres. Soc. Liturgica 1985–87; Co-Chair. Jt Comm. between World Methodist Council and Roman Catholic Church 1986–2011; Sec. American Theological Soc. 1988–95, Pres. 1996–97; Leverhulme European Fellow 1966–67; Pew Evangelical Fellow 1996–97; Hon. DD (North Park Univ.) 2001; Berakah Award, N American Acad. of Liturgy 1999, Festschrift: 'Ecumenical Theology in Worship, Doctrine and Life: Essays Presented to Geoffrey Wainwright on his Sixtieth Birthday' (ed. David Cunningham and others), Oxford Univ. Press 1999, Outstanding Ecumenist Award, Washington Theological Consortium 2003, Johannes Quasten Medal for excellence in theological scholarship, The Catholic Univ. of America 2006. *Publications include:* Christian Initiation 1969, Eucharist and Eschatology 1971, Doxology 1980, The Ecumenical Moment 1983, On Wesley and Calvin 1987, Methodists in Dialogue 1995, Worship With One Accord 1997, For Our Salvation: Two Approaches to the Work of Christ 1997, Is the Reformation Over? Protestants and Catholics at the Turn of the Millennia 2000, Lesslie Newbigin: A Theological Life 2000, Oxford History of Christian Worship 2006, Embracing Purpose: Essays on God, the World and the Church 2007, Faith, Hope and Love: The Ecumenical Trio of Virtues 2014. *Leisure interests:* music, art, cricket, tennis, travel. *Address:* 2 Carolina Meadows, Apartment 107, Chapel Hill, NC 27517, USA (home). *Telephone:* (919) 914-6059 (home). *Website:* gwainwright@div.duke.edu (office).

WAINWRIGHT, Rufus; American singer, musician (piano) and songwriter; b. 22 July 1973, Rhinebeck, NY; s. of Loudon Wainwright III and Kate McGarrigle; sister of Martha Wainwright; sang backing vocals on tour with mother and aunt (folk duo Kate and Anna McGarrigle) 1980s; left univ. to perform own songs in and around Montréal; Co-founder Kate McGarrigle Foundation; Int. Classical Music Award for DVD Documentaries 2015. *Contributions to film soundtracks:* The Myth of Fingerprints 1997, Big Daddy 1999, Shrek 2001, Moulin Rouge! 2001, Zoolander 2001, I Am Sam 2001. *Operas:* Prima Donna (premiere with Opera North, Manchester) 2009, Hadrian (premiere with Canadian Opera Co. at Toronto Four Seasons Centre) 2018. *Recordings include:* albums: Rufus Wainwright 1998, Poses 2001, Want One 2003, Want Two 2004, Release the Stars 2007, Rufus Does Judy at Carnegie Hall 2007, Milwaukee at Last! 2009, All Days are Nights: Songs for Lulu 2010, House of Rufus 2011, Out of the Game 2012, Live from the Artists Den 2014, Prima Donna 2015, Take All My Loves: 9 Shakespeare Sonnets 2016. *Address:* c/o Mark Adelman, Career Artist Management, 9350 North Civic Center Drive, Los Angeles, CA 90210, USA (office). *E-mail:* mark.adelman@camanagement.com (office). *Website:* www.rufuswainwright.com.

WAISMAN RJAVINSTHI, David; Peruvian politician and business executive; b. 4 May 1937, Chiclayo (Lambayeque); fmr Chair. Cttee for Small Industries and mem. Bd of Dirs Nat. Soc. of Industries in Peru; Nat. Spokesman, Bd of Co-ordination, Corpn of Small and Micro Enterprises; Man. Dir Industrial Gameda; Founder-mem. and Chair. COPEI 1997–2000; mem. and Congressman Perú Posible (PP) party; mem. Congreso (Parl.) 2000–11; Second Vice-Pres. of Peru and Minister of Defence 2000–06; Hon. Prof., Univ. of San Martin de Porras Lima.

WAITE, Terence Hardy (Terry), CBE; British fmr religious adviser, author and broadcaster; b. 31 May 1939, Bollington, Cheshire, England; s. of Thomas William Waite and Lena Waite (née Hardy); m. Helen Frances Watters 1964; one s. three d.; ed Wilmslow School, Stockton Heath, Cheshire, Church Army Coll., London; Lay Training Adviser to Bishop and Diocese of Bristol 1964–69; Prov. Training Adviser to Archbishop of Uganda, Rwanda and Burundi 1969–71; int. consultant working with RC Church 1972–79; Adviser to Archbishop of Canterbury on Anglican Communion Affairs 1980–92, Iranian hostages mission 1981, Libyan hostages mission 1985; kidnapped in Beirut Jan. 1987, held for four years in solitary confinement, released 19 Nov. 1991 after 1,763 days; mem. Church of England Nat. Asscn 1966–68; Founder and Co-ordinator Southern Sudan Project 1969–71; fmr mem. Royal Inst. of Int. Affairs; Founder-Pres. Y-Care Int. (YMCA Int. Devt Cttee) 1998–; Pres. Emmaus UK 1998–, Suffolk Br. of Far East Prisoners of War Asscn; Founder-Chair. Hostage UK 2005–; Chair. Prisons' Video Trust 1998–; Amb. for WWF-UK; Vice-Pres. Suffolk Asscn of Local Councils 1999, East Cheshire Hospice 2001; mem. Advisory Bd, Gorton Monastery 2003; Fellow Commoner, Trinity Hall, Cambridge 1992–93, now Fellow Emer.; Visiting Fellow, Magdalen Coll., Oxford 2006; Trustee, Butler Trust (Prison Officers Award Project) 1986–2010, now Patron; Patron, The Abbeyfield (Ipswich) Soc. 1996–, COFEPOW (Children (and families) of the Far East Prisoners of War) 1999–, Friends of the Samaritans (Bury St Edmunds Br.), One World Broadcasting Trust 1987, Strode Park Foundation for the Disabled, Hearne, Kent 1988–, Bury St Edmunds Volunteer Centre 1994–, Warrington Male Voice Choir 1996–, The Romany Soc. 1997, West Suffolk Voluntary Asscn for the Blind 1998–, The Bridge Project Sudbury Appeal 1999–, Save Our Parsonages 1999–, The British Friends of Neve Shalom, Wahat al-Salam 2003–, Underprivileged Children's Charity, Bristol 2003–, Children with Aids Charity 2004–, Habitat for Humanity 2004–, Rapid UK 2004–, Sunderland Counselling Services 2004–, and many other orgs; Freeman, City of Canterbury 1992, Borough of Lewisham 1992; Hon. DCL (Kent) 1986, (City of London) 1992, (Sussex) 1992, (Robert Gordon Univ.) 2007; Hon. LLD (Durham) 1992, (Liverpool) 1992; Hon. LHD (Wittenberg) 1992; Hon. DHumLitt (Southern

Florida) 1992, (Virginia Commonwealth) 1996; Hon. DPhil (Anglia Polytechnic) 2001, (Anglia Ruskin) 2005; Hon. DLitt (Nottingham Trent) 2001, (De Montfort) 2005, (Chester) 2008; Dr hc (Yale Univ. Divinity School) 1992, (Open Univ.) 2009; Templeton UK Award 1985, Roosevelt Four Freedoms Medal 1992. *Publications:* Taken on Trust 1993, Footfalls in Memory 1995, Travels with a Primate 2000, The Voyage of the Golden Handshake 2015; numerous contribs to journals and periodicals. *Leisure interests:* music, walking, travel, Jungian studies, int. affairs and politics. *Address:* Trinity Hall, Cambridge, CB2 1TJ, England.

WAITS, Tom; American singer, songwriter, musician (piano, guitar, percussion) and actor; b. 7 Dec. 1949, Pomona, Calif.; m. Kathleen Brennan 1980; two s. one d.; Grammy Award for Best Alternative Album 1992, for Best Contemporary Folk Album 2000, inducted into Rock N Roll Hall of Fame 2011, PEN Lyric Award Prize (co-winner) 2016. *Theatre:* Frank's Wild Years (co-writer, play and music) 1986, The Black Rider 1989, Alice 1992, Woyzeck 2002. *Films include:* Paradise Alley 1978, Wolfen 1981, One From the Heart 1982, The Outsiders 1983, Rumblefish 1983, The Cotton Club 1984, Down By Law 1986, Ironweed 1987, Candy Mountain 1988, Cold Feet 1989, Mystery Train 1989, Bearskin: An Urban Fairytale 1989, The Two Jakes 1990, Queen's Logic 1991, The Fisher King 1991, At Play in the Fields of the Lord 1991, Bram Stoker's Dracula 1992, Short Cuts 1993, Mystery Men 1999, Coffee and Cigarettes 2003, Domino 2005, Wristcutters: A Love Story 2006, Seven Psychopaths 2012, The Ballad of Buster Scruggs 2018, The Dead Don't Die 2019. *Compositions include:* Ol' 55, The Eagles 1974, Angel Wings, Rickie Lee Jones 1983, Downtown Train, Rod Stewart 1990, The Long Way Home, Norah Jones 2004, Temptation, Diana Krall 2004, Jersey Girl, Bruce Springsteen, Domino 2005. *Recordings include:* albums: Closing Time 1973, The Heart of Saturday Night 1974, Nighthawks at the Diner 1975, Small Change 1976, Foreign Affairs 1977, Blue Valentine 1978, Heartattack and Vine 1980, Bounced Checks 1981, One from the Heart 1982, Swordfishtrombones 1983, Anthology 1983, Asylum Years 1984, Rain Dogs 1985, Frank's Wild Years 1987, Big Time 1988, The Early Years 1991, The Early Years Vol. 2 1992, Night on Earth (with Kathleen Brennan) 1992, Bone Machine (Grammy Award for Best Alternative Music 1993) 1992, The Black Rider 1993, Beautiful Maladies 1998, Mule Variations 2000, Used Songs 1973–80 2001, Alice 2002, Blood Money 2002, Real Gone 2004, Orphans: Brawlers, Bawlers & Bastards 2006, Glitter and Doom Live 2009, Bad As Me 2011, Warm Beer and Cold Women (Live) 2012, My Father's Place 2013, Nighthawks on the Radio 2014, A Small Affair in Ohio (Live) 2014, Transmission Impossible 2015, Fumblin' on the Radio (Live) 2015, Minneapolis Drive Time (Live) 2016. *Address:* c/o Anti-Inc, 2798 Sunset Blvd, Los Angeles, CA 90026, USA (office). *E-mail:* info@anti.com (office). *Website:* www.anti.com (office); www.tomwaits.com (office).

WAITT, Theodore (Ted) W.; American computer industry executive; *Founder and Chairman, Waitt Foundation;* b. 18 Jan. 1963, Sioux City, Iowa; m. Joan Waitt; four c.; ed Univ. of Iowa; f. Gateway (with Mike Hammond) 1985, Pres. 1985–96, CEO 1993–99, Chair. 1993–2005, Pres. and CEO 2001–04; Founder and Chair. Waitt Foundation 1993, Waitt Inst. for Violence Prevention 2005, Waitt Inst. for Discovery 2005; Founder Avalon Capital Group (pvt. investment co.); Vice-Chair. Jonas Salk Inst. for Biological Studies; mem. Advisory Council Nat. Geographic Soc.; fmr Chair. Founding Fathers campaign of Family Violence Prevention Fund; Hon. DSc (Univ. of S Dakota); US Small Business Asscn Young Entrepreneur of the Year, US Jr Chamber of Commerce Ten Outstanding Young Americans Award, Nat. Alliance of Business Henry Ford II Award. *Address:* Waitt Foundation, PO Box 1948, La Jolla, CA 92038-1948, USA (office). *Telephone:* (858) 551-4437 (office). *Fax:* (858) 551-6871 (office). *Website:* waittfoundation.org (office); avalon.com (office).

WAJED, Sheikh Hasina, BA; Bangladeshi politician; *Prime Minister;* b. 28 Sept. 1947, Tungipara, Gopalganj dist; d. of Bangabandhu Sheikh Mujibur Rahman and Begum Fazilatunnesa; m. Dr M. A. Wazed Miah 1968 (died 2009); one s. one d.; ed Dhaka Univ.; Gen. Sec., Student League, Bodrunnessa Girl's Coll., Dhaka, 1965, Pres. 1966; Sec., Student League, Rokeya Hall br., Dhaka Univ. 1968–69, Founding mem. Abahani Krira Chakra (sports club) 1969; Pres. Bangladesh Awami League 1981–, Leader of Opposition, Bangladesh Jatiya Sangsad (Parl.) 1986–87, 1991–95, 2001–09, Prime Minister 1996–2001, 2009–, also Minister of the Armed Forces Div., the Cabinet Div., Defence, Power, Energy and Mineral Resources, Establishment, Housing and Public Works, Religious Affairs, and Women and Children's Affairs 2009–, also of Home Affairs 2013–, of Foreign Affairs 2014–; Chair. Bangabandhu Memorial Trust 1994–; mem. Council of Women World Leaders; Dr hc (Boston Univ.) 1997, (Waseda Univ., Japan) 1997, (Univ. of Abertay, Dundee, UK) 1997, (Visva-Bharati Univ., Shantiniketan, India) 1999, (ANU) 1999, (Bridgeport Univ., Conn.) 2000, (Catholic Univ. of Brussels) 2000, (Barry Univ., Fla) 2004; Head of State Medal, Int. Asscn of Lions Clubs 1996, 1998, Medal of Distinction, Int. Asscn of Lions Clubs 1997, Netaji Subhas Chandra Bosh Memorial Medal, West Bengal Cttee of All India Congress 1997, Mother Teresa Award, All India Peace Council 1998, UNESCO Houphouet-Boigny Peace Prize 1998, CERES Medal, FAO 1999, Asia Personality of 2000, Afro-Asian Lawyers Fed. for Human Rights 2000, Pearl S. Buck Award, Randolph-Macon Women's Coll. 2000. *Publications include:* Ora ṭokai kêno? (Why Are They Street Children?) 1987, Bangladeshe shoirotôntrer jônmo (Birth of Autocracy in Bangladesh) 1993, Daridro bimochon, kichhu bhabna (Thoughts on Eradication of Poverty) 1993, Amar shôpno, amar shônggram (My Dream, My Struggle) 1996, People and Democracy 1997, Amra jônogoner kôtha bolte eshechhi (We Want to Speak for the People) 1998, Brihot jônogoshṭhir jonno unnôeon (Development for the Large Masses) 1999, Development of the Masses 1999, Shamorik tôntro bônam gônotôntro (Military Rule versus Democracy) 1999, Antorjatik shômporko unnôeon (Improvement of International Relations) 2001, Bipônno gônotôntro, lanchhito manobota 2002, Democracy in Distress, Demeaned Humanity 2003, (Against Degradation of Humanity) 2003, Living with Tears 2004. *Address:* Office of the Prime Minister, Old Sangsad Bhaban, Tejgaon, Dhaka 1215 (office); Sudha Sudan, Road #5, House #54, Dhanmondi, Dhaka, Bangladesh. *Telephone:* (2) 8151159 (office). *Fax:* (2) 8113244 (office). *E-mail:* info@pmo.gov.bd (office). *Website:* www.pmo.gov.bd (office); www.albd.org.

WAJIH, Sakhr Ahmad al-; Yemeni politician; Minister of Finance 2011–14; mem. Gen. People's Congress –2011, now ind. MP; mem. Yemen Parliamentarians Against Corruption.

WAKABAYASHI, Masatoshi; Japanese politician; b. 4 July 1934; ed Univ. of Tokyo; joined Ministry of Agric. and Forestry 1957, Dir Agricultural Policy Planning Div., Agricultural Structure Improvement Bureau 1978–81; Dir-Gen. Affairs Div., Agricultural Structure Improvement Bureau, Ministry of Agric., Forestry and Fisheries 1981–83; Dir-Gen. Affairs Div., Dir-Gen.'s Secr., Nat. Land Agency 1981; elected to House of Reps 1983, re-elected 1986, 1993, served as Parl. Vice-Minister, Man. and Coordination Agency 1989–90, Dir Cttee on Transport, LDP 1994; elected to House of Councillors 1998, re-elected 2004, Chair. Cttee on Agric., Forestry and Fisheries 1999; Parl. Vice-Minister, Ministry of Finance 1999–2001, Sr Vice-Minister of Finance 2001, Dir Cttee on Financial Affairs 2001, Research Comm. on the Constitution 2002, Special Cttee on Financial Issues and Revitalization of the Economy 2002, Special Cttee on Protection of Personal Information 2003, Chair. Special Cttee on Prevention of Int. Terrorism 2003, Cttee on Discipline 2004, Dir Cttee on the Budget 2004, Chair. Special Cttee on Mountain Villages 2004; Chair. LDP Policy Bd 2005, Acting Chair. LDP Research Comms on the Constitution and Election System 2005; Minister of the Environment 2006–07, Minister in Charge of Global Environmental Problems 2006–07, Minister of Agric., Forestry and Fisheries 2007–08.

WAKEFIELD, Mary Katherine, BSN, MSN, PhD; American nurse, academic and government official; *Administrator, Health Resources and Services Administration, Department of Health and Human Services;* b. 12 Aug. 1954, Devils Lake, ND; m. Charles Christianson; ed Univ. of Mary, Bismarck, Univ. of Texas; practising nurse and nursing instructor 1975–87; Admin. and Legislative Asst to US Senator Quentin Burdick, Washington, DC 1987–92; Chief of Staff to Senator Kent Conrad 1993–96; Dir Center for Health Policy, Research and Ethics, George Mason Univ., Fairfax, Va 1996–2001; Assoc. Dean for Rural Health, School of Medicine and Health Sciences, Univ. of North Dakota 2001–09, also tenured Prof. and Dir; Admin. Health Resources and Services Admin (HRSA), US Dept of Health and Human Services, Rockville, Md 2009–; fmr Consultant to WHO's Global Programme on AIDS, Geneva; Chair. Nat. Advisory Council for Agency for Healthcare Research and Quality; mem. Pres. Clinton's Advisory Comm. on Consumer Protection and Quality in the Health Care Industry; fmr mem. Medicare Payment Advisory Comm., Nat. Advisory Cttee to HRSA Office of Rural Health Policy; mem. Inst. of Medicine Cttee; Fellow, American Acad. of Nursing. *Address:* Office of the Administrator, Health Resources and Services Administration, Department of Health and Human Services, 5600 Fishers Lane, Rockville, MD 20857, USA (office). *Telephone:* (888) 275-4772 (office). *E-mail:* ask@hrsa.gov (office). *Website:* www.hrsa.gov (office).

WAKEHAM, Baron (Life Peer), cr. 1992, of Maldon in the County of Essex; **John Wakeham,** JP, FCA, PC, DL; British politician and chartered accountant; b. 22 June 1932, Godalming, Surrey, England; s. of Maj. W. J. Wakeham and E. R. Wakeham; m. 1st Anne Roberta Bailey 1965 (died 1984); two s.; m. 2nd Alison Bridget Ward 1985; one s.; ed Charterhouse; JP Inner London 1972–; MP for Maldon 1974–83, for Colchester S and Maldon 1983–92; Asst Govt Whip 1979–81, Govt Chief Whip 1983–87; Lord Commr of HM Treasury 1981, Minister of State 1982–83; Parl. Under-Sec. of State, Dept of Industry 1981–82; Lord Privy Seal 1987–88; Leader of House of Commons 1987–89, Sec. of State for Energy 1989–92; Lord Privy Seal and Leader of the House of Lords 1992–94; Chair. House of Lords Econ. Affairs Cttee 2005–08; Lord Pres. of Council 1988–89; Chair. Carlton Club 1992–98, Press Complaints Comm. 1995–2002, British Horseracing Bd 1996–98 (mem. 1995–98); Chair. Genner Holdings Ltd 1994–, Alexandra Rose Day 1998–2010; Chair. Royal Comm. on Lords Reform 1999–2000; Chancellor Brunel Univ. 1998–2012; Trustee, HMS Warrior 1860 1997–. *Leisure interests:* sailing, reading. *Address:* House of Lords, Westminster, London, SW1A 0PW, England (office). *Telephone:* (20) 7219-3162 (office). *Fax:* (20) 7219-6807 (office); (20) 8672-8839 (office). *E-mail:* wakehamj@parliament.uk (office).

WAKEHAM, Sir William Arnot, Kt, PhD, CEng, CPhys, FREng, FIChemE, FIEE, FInstP; British chemical engineer, academic and fmr university vice-chancellor; *Chairman, Exeter Science Park Ltd;* b. 25 Sept. 1944, Bristol, England; s. of Stanley William Wakeham and Winifred Wakeham; m. Sylvia Frances Wakeham; two s.; ed Univ. of Exeter; fmr Research Assoc., Brown Univ., USA; Lecturer, Dept of Chemical Eng and Chemical Tech., Imperial Coll. London 1971–79, Reader 1979–85, Prof. of Chemical Physics 1985–96, Head of Dept of Chemical Eng 1988, Pro-Rector (Research) and subsequently also Deputy Rector and Pro-Rector (Resources), Imperial Coll. 1997–2001; Vice-Chancellor Univ. of Southampton 2001–09; Visiting Prof., Imperial Coll. London, Univ. of Exeter, Instituto Superior Tecnico, Lisbon; UK Chair. British-Italian Partnership Programme; Chair. SEPnet (South East Physics Network) 2009–; Sr Vice-Pres. Royal Acad. of Eng 2011–15; currently Chair. Exeter Science Park Ltd; mem. Eng and Physical Science Research Council 2005–11, Chair. Resource Audit Cttee; mem. SE England Devt Agency 2004–09, Bd EU Expert Panel on Philanthropy and Univs; Treas. European Council of Academies of Eng and Technological Sciences, Inc. 2009–; Dir (non-exec.) Ilika plc 2009–; Fellow, Imperial Coll. London, Portuguese Acad. of Eng 2012; hon. degrees from Univs of Lisbon, Exeter, Loughborough, Portsmouth, Southampton, Southampton Solent and Nova de Lisboa; Touloukian Medal, ASME 1997, Rossini Lecturer, Int. Conf. on Chemical Thermodynamics, Halifax, NS 2000, Ared Cezairliyan Lecturer, Int. Thermal Conductivity Conf. 2001, Lifetime Achievement Award, European Thermophysics Conference 2011. *Publications:* author, co-author or ed. of nine books; more than 4000 scientific and eng papers on thermophysical properties of fluids, intermolecular forces and thermodynamics. *Address:* Beacon Down, Rewe, Exeter, EX5 4DX, England (office). *Telephone:* (1392) 861390 (Exeter) (office). *Fax:* (1392) 861390 (office). *E-mail:* w.a.wakeham@soton.ac.uk (office).

WAKELEY, Amanda, OBE; British fashion designer; *Creative Director, Amanda Wakeley;* b. 15 Sept. 1962, Chester, England; d. of Sir John Wakeley; m. Hugh Morrison; ed Cheltenham Ladies' Coll.; launched Lifestyle Luxury Womenswear Collection label 1990; Co-Chair. Fashion Targets Breast Cancer Campaign 1996–; Hon. DArts (Univ. of Chester); Glamour Award, British Fashion Awards 1992, 1993, 1996. *Leisure interests:* travel, sailing, waterskiing, snowskiing, ski touring, fitness. *Address:* Amanda Wakeley, 3 Logan Place, London, W8 6QN, England (office). *Telephone:* (20) 3384-6671 (office). *E-mail:* reception@amandawakeley.com (office). *Website:* www.amandawakeley.com (office).

WAKUI, Yoji; Japanese business executive and fmr politician; *Special Counsel, Japan Tobacco Inc.;* b. 5 Feb. 1942; began career at Ministry of Finance 1964, Dir-Gen., Secretariat, Economic Planning Agency 1993–95, Dir-Gen., Secretariat, Ministry of Finance 1995–97, Dir-Gen., Budget Bureau, Ministry of Finance 1997–99; Vice-Chair. General Insurance Asscn of Japan 1999–2004, Corporate Auditor Feb.–June 2004; Chair. and Rep. Dir Japan Tobacco Inc. 2004–06, Chair. and Dir 2006–12, Special Counsel 2012–; Auditor, Nipponkoa Insurance Co. 2006, now Outside Dir; Auditor, Hakuho Foundation; mem. Ind. Cttee, Kewpie Corpn. *Address:* Japan Tobacco Inc., 2-1, Toranomon 2-chome, Minato-ku, Tokyo, 105-8422, Japan. *Telephone:* (3) 3582-3111. *Fax:* (3) 5572-1441. *E-mail:* info@jti.com.

WALA, Adolf; Austrian banking executive; b. 18 May 1937, Dürnholz; m.; three c.; ed Commercial School of Vienna Merchants' Asscn; Deputy Supervisor, later Supervisor, Foreign Exchange Dept, Creditanstalt-Bankverein 1957–65; joined Credit and Loans Dept, Austrian Nat. Bank (OeNB) 1965, Head of Office of First Deputy Gov. 1973–80, Deputy Exec. Dir Credit and Loans Dept 1980–88, Gen. Man. 1988–98, Pres. of OeNB 1998–2003; Deputy Chair. Supervisory Bd KA Finanz AG 2009–, Kommunalkredit Austria AG 2009–; Co-Chair. Finanzmarktbeteiligung AG des Bundes (FIMBAG) 2008–16; fmr mem. Supervisory Bd Casinos Austria AG, Burgtheater GmbH, Hypo Alpe-Adria-Bank; currently Pres. Vereins der Freunde der Wiener Polizei (Asscn of Friends of the Vienna Police); Order of Merit, Order of Kts of Malta 1998, Grand Decoration of Honour in Gold with Star for Services to Repub. of Austria 1999; Gold Medal for Outstanding Services to State of Vienna 1994, Arthur von Rosthon Medal 2000, Ehrenmedaille der Bundeshauptstadt Wien 2009. *Address:* Vereins der Freunde der Wiener Polizei (Asscn of Friends of the Vienna Police), PO Box 50, 1013, Vienna, Austria. *Website:* www.polizeifreunde-wien.at.

WALCH, Ernest Joseph, MCJ, DrIUR; Liechtenstein lawyer and politician; *Partner, Walch & Schurti;* b. 1956; ed Univ. of Innsbruck, Austria, New York Univ. School of Law., USA; admitted to Bar, USA 1983, Liechtenstein 1984; Rep. of Progressive Citizens' Party (FBP) to Steering Cttee of European Democratic Union 1983–93, Pres. FBP 2000–01; mem. Parl. 1989–96, FPB Parl. Spokesman 1992–93, Pres. of Parl. 1993; Minister of Foreign Affairs 2001–05; Co-founder and Partner, Walch & Schurti (law firm) 1991–; mem. New York State Bar Asscn, Liechtenstein Bar Asscn Europäische Anwaltsvereinigung e.V., Int. Acad. of Estate and Trust Law, Liechtenstein Asscn of Professional Trustees. *Publications include:* numerous works on int. legal issues. *Address:* Walch & Schurti, Zollstrasse 2, 9490 Vaduz, Liechtenstein (office). *Telephone:* 2372000 (office). *Fax:* 2372100 (office). *E-mail:* mail@walchschurti.net (office). *Website:* www.walchschurti.net (office).

WALCOTT, Jerome Xavier, FRCS, JP; Barbadian politician and surgeon; *Minister of Foreign Affairs and Foreign Trade;* b. 2 April 1957, Barbados; ed Univ. of West Indies; Asst Sec., Barbados Labour Party 1995–97, currently mem. and Chair. Nat. Exec. Council; Leader, Govt Business in Senate 2001–03, mem. of Parl. (Christ Church South constituency) 2003–08; fmr Minister of Health; apptd Opposition Senator 2013, Leader of Government Business in Senate 2018–; Minister of Foreign Affairs and Foreign Trade 2018–; Chair. Transport Bd; Deputy Chair. Sanitation Service Authority; Pres. Barbados Asscn of Medical Practitioners; Consultant Surgeon, Queen Elizabeth's Hospital; Assoc. Lecturer and Examiner for Final Surgery Exams, Univ. of West Indies; mem. Barbados Agricultural Soc., Barbados Cricket Asscn, Barbados Cancer Soc. *Address:* Ministry of Foreign Affairs and Foreign Trade, 1 Culloden Road, St Michael, Barbados (office). *Telephone:* 431-2200 (office). *Fax:* 429-6652 (office). *E-mail:* barbados@foreign.gov.bb (office). *Website:* www.foreign.gov.bb (office).

WALD, Sir Nicholas John, Kt, MBBS, DSc (Med), FRS, FRCP, FFPH, FRCOG, FMedSci, CBiol. FIBiol; British medical scientist and academic; *Head, Centre of Environmental and Preventive Medicine, Wolfson Institute of Preventive Medicine;* b. 31 May 1944; s. of Adolf Max Wald and Frieda Shatsow; m. Nancy Evelyn Miller 1966; three s. one d.; ed Univ. Coll. London, Univ. Coll. Hosp. Medical School; mem. science staff MRC 1971–; mem. science staff Imperial Cancer Research Fund (ICRF) Cancer Epidemiology and Clinical Trials Unit, Oxford 1972–82, Deputy Dir 1982–83, Prof. and Head, Centre for Environmental and Preventive Medicine, Barts and The London, Queen Mary's School of Medicine and Dentistry 1983–, Hon. Consultant 1983–, Dir Wolfson Inst. of Preventive Medicine 1991–95, 1997–2013, currently Head, Centre of Environmental and Preventive Medicine; Hon. Dir Cancer Research Campaign Screening Group 1986–2000; Chair. Study Monitoring Cttee of MRC Randomised Clinical Trial of Colo-Rectal Cancer Screening 1986–, Steering Cttee for Multicentre Aneurysm Screening Study 1997–; mem. Scientific Cttee on Tobacco and Health, Dept of Health 1993–2002, Medicines Control Agency Expert Advisory Panel 1996–; mem. Cttee on Ethical Issues in Medicine, Royal Coll. of Physicians 1988–, HPV/LBC Pilots Screening Group 2000–, Nat. Radiological Protection Bd Advisory Group on Nuclear Test Veterans 2000–; mem. Wellcome Trust Physiology and Pharmaceutical Panel 1995–2000; mem. Information Sub-Cttee, Faculty of Public Health 2001–; mem. Council of Trustees, Foundation for Study of Infant Deaths 2001; mem. Council, Action on Smoking and Health 2002–; Founding Ed.-in-Chief Journal of Medical Screening 1994–; Hon. DSc (Med) (London) 2005; Kennedy Foundation Int. Award in Scientific Research 2000, Foundation for Blood Research Award 2000, Obstetrical Soc. of Philadelphia Int. Speakers' Award 2001, BMA Medical Book Competition Award 2001, US Public Health Service and Centers for Disease Control Award 2002, Harvard School of Public Health Award 2004, Hamdan Award for Medical Research Excellence—Fetal Medicine 2011–12. *Publications:* Alpha-Fetoprotein Screening – The Current Issues (co-ed.) 1981, Antenatal and Neonatal Screening 1984 (2nd edn co-ed. 2000), (First Prize, BMA Medical Book Competition 2001), Nicotine Smoking and the Low Tar Programme (co-ed.) 1989, Passive Smoking: A Health Hazard (co-ed.) 1991, International Smoking Statistics (co-author) 1993 (2nd edn, co-ed.) 2004, Epidemiological Approach 2004. *Leisure interests:* economics, boating. *Address:* Barts and The London, Queen Mary's School of Medicine and Dentistry, Charterhouse Square, London, EC1M 6BQ (office); Centre for Environmental and Preventive Medicine, Wolfson Institute of Preventive Medicine, Barts and The London, Queen Mary's School of Medicine and Dentistry, Charterhouse Square, London, EC1M 6BQ; 9 Park Crescent Mews East, London, W1W 5AF, England (home). *Telephone:* (20) 7882-6269 (office); (20) 7636-2721 (home). *Fax:* (20) 7882-6270 (office). *E-mail:* n.j.wald@qmul.ac.uk (office). *Website:* www.smd.Qmul.ac.uk/wolfson (office).

WALD, Richard C., BA, MA, AB; American journalist, news executive and academic; *Fred W. Friendly Professor Emeritus of Professional Practice in Media Society, Graduate School of Journalism, Columbia University;* b. New York City; s. of Joseph S. Wald and Lily Wald (née Forstate); m. Edith May Leslie; two s. one d.; ed Columbia Univ. and Clare Coll., Cambridge, UK; reporter, later Man. Ed. New York Herald Tribune 1955–66; Asst Man. Ed. Washington Post 1967; Exec. Vice-Pres. Whitney Communications Corpn New York 1968; Pres. NBC News, 1968–77; asst to Chair. Bd Times-Mirror Co., Los Angeles 1977; Sr Vice-Pres. ABC News 1978–2000; Fred W. Friendly Prof. of Media and Society, Grad. School of Journalism, Columbia Univ. 2000, now Prof. Emer.; Chair. of Bd Columbia Spectator (Columbia Coll. daily newspaper); Chair. Worldwide TV News; mem. Advisory Bd Knight Fellowships Stanford Univ.; mem. Bd of Dirs Correspondents Fund, Center for Communication; mem. Bd of Visitors, School of Communication, Univ. of Colo. *Leisure interests:* reading, running. *Address:* Columbia University Graduate School of Journalism, Pulitzer Hall, MC 3801, 2950 Broadway, New York, NY 10027, USA (office). *Telephone:* (212) 854-0116 (office). *Fax:* (212) 854-7837 (office). *E-mail:* rcw25@columbia.edu (office). *Website:* www.journalism.columbia.edu (office).

WALD, Robert M., AB, PhD; American physicist and academic; *Charles H. Swift Distinguished Service Professor, Department of Physics, Enrico Fermi Institute, University of Chicago;* b. 29 June 1947, New York City; ed Columbia Univ., Princeton Univ.; Research Assoc., Univ. of Maryland 1972–74, Asst Prof. 1976–80, Assoc. Prof. 1980–85, Prof. 1985–2003; Charles H. Swift Distinguished Service Prof., Dept of Physics, Enrico Fermi Inst. 2002–, Chair. Dept of Physics, Univ. of Chicago 2003–; mem. NAS, American Acad. of Arts and Sciences. *Publications include:* Space, Time, and Gravity: The Theory of the Big Bang and Black Holes 1977, 1992, General Relativity 1984, Quantum Field Theory in Curved Spacetime and Black Hole Thermodynamics 1994, Black Holes and Relativistic Stars (ed.) 1999, The Thermodynamics of Black Holes 2001, A Rigorous Derivation of Gravitational Self-force 2008, Axiomatic Quantum Field Theory in Curved Spacetime 2010; more than 100 papers in professional journals. *Address:* Department of Physics, Enrico Fermi Institute, ACC 217, University of Chicago, 5720 South Ellis Avenue, Chicago, IL 60637, USA (office). *Telephone:* (773) 702-7765 (office). *Fax:* (773) 702-2045 (office). *E-mail:* rmwa@midway.uchicago.edu (office). *Website:* physics.uchicago.edu (office).

WALDEGRAVE OF NORTH HILL, Baron (Life Peer), cr. 1999, of Chewton Mendip in the County of Somerset; **William Waldegrave,** PC, JP; British banker and fmr politician; *Provost, Eton College;* b. 15 Aug. 1946; s. of Earl Waldegrave, KG, GCVO and Mary Hermione Waldegrave (née Grenfell); m. Caroline Burrows 1977; one s. three d.; ed Eton Coll., Corpus Christi Coll., Oxford, Harvard Univ., USA; fmr Pres. Oxford Union; Fellow, All Souls Coll., Oxford 1971–86, 1999–; attached to Cabinet Office as mem. Cen. Policy Review Staff 1971–73; mem. staff political office of Rt Hon. Sir Edward Heath 1973–76; worked for GEC PLC 1975–81; MP for Bristol W 1979–97; Parl. Under-Sec. of State, Dept of Educ. and Science 1981–83, Dept of Environment and Spokesman for the Arts 1983–85; Minister of State, Dept of the Environment (Minister for the Environment, Countryside and Local Govt, subsequently Minister for Housing and Planning) 1985–88; Minister of State, FCO 1988–90; Sec. of State for Health 1990–92, Chancellor of the Duchy of Lancaster 1992–94; Sec. of State for Agric., Fisheries and Food 1994–95; Chief Sec. to Treasury 1995–97; Man. Dir Dresdner Kleinwort Wasserstein 1998–2003; Man. Dir and Vice-Chair. UBS 2003–08, Consultant 2008–; Provost, Eton Coll. 2008–; Dir Waldegrave Farms Ltd 1975–, Bristol and West PLC 1997–2006, Henry Sotheran Ltd 1998– (Chair 2007–), Biotech Growth Trust PLC 1998– (Chair. 2012–), Corp. Finance, Dresdner Kleinwort Benson 1998–; Bank of Ireland Financial Services (UK) PLC 2002–06, Fleming Family and Partners Ltd 2008–; Chair. Rhodes Trust 2002–, Nat. Museum of Science and Industry 2002–10, Royal Mint Advisory Cttee 2011–; Pres. Royal Bath and West Soc. 2006; mem. IBA Advisory Council 1980–81, Int. Advisory Bd, Teijin Ltd 2006–08, Remuneration and Nomination Cttee, Bergesen Worldwide Gas ASA 2006–08; Founder Trustee and Chair., Bristol Cathedral Trust 1989–2002; Trustee, Rhodes Trust 1992–2002 (Chair. 2002–11), Beit Meml Fellowships for Medical Research 1998–2006, Mandela Rhodes Foundation 2003–11, Dyson School of Design Innovation 2007–08, Strawberry Hill Trust 2008–, Cumberland Lodge, Windsor 2009, Bd of Lewis Walpole Library, Yale Univ., USA 2008–; Hon. Fellow, Corpus Christi Coll., Oxford 1991. *Publications:* The Binding of Leviathan – Conservatism and the Future 1977, A Different Kind of Weather - A Memoir 2015. *Address:* House of Lords, London, SW1A 0PW; Provost's Lodge, Eton College, Windsor, Berkshire, SL4 6DH (office); 62 Hornton Street, London, W8 4NU, England (home). *Telephone:* (1753) 671234. *Fax:* (1753) 671283. *E-mail:* provostsecretary@etoncollege.org.uk.

WALDEN, (Alastair) Brian; British broadcaster, journalist and university lecturer; b. 8 July 1932; s. of W. F. Walden; m. Hazel Downes; one s. (and three s. from fmr marriages); ed West Bromwich Grammar School, Queen's Coll. and Nuffield Coll., Oxford; MP (Labour) for Birmingham All Saints 1964–74, Birmingham Ladywood 1974–77; TV presenter, Weekend World (London Weekend TV) 1977–86; mem. W Midland Bd, Cen. Ind. TV 1982–84; columnist, London Standard 1983–86, Thomson Regional Newspapers 1983–86, The Sunday Times; presenter, The Walden Interview (London Weekend TV for ITV network) 1988, 1989, 1990–94, Walden on Labour Leaders (BBC) 1997, Walden on Heroes (BBC) 1998, Walden on Villains 1999, A Point of View (BBC Radio 4) 2005; Chair. Paragon 1994, Ten Alps 2002–11 (mem. Bd of Dirs 2015–), Capital 2006; Shell Int. Award 1982, BAFTA Richard Dimbleby Award 1985, Aims of Industry Special Free Enterprise Award 1990, ITV Personality of the Year 1991. *Publication:* The Walden Interviews 1990. *Leisure interests:* chess, reading. *Address:* Landfall, Fort Road, St Peter Port, Guernsey, GY1 1ZU, United Kingdom. *Telephone:* (1481) 722860. *E-mail:* walden@guernsey.net.

WALES, HRH The Prince of; (Prince Charles Philip Arthur George), (Earl of Chester (cr.1958), Duke of Cornwall, Duke of Rothesay, Earl of Carrick, Baron Renfrew, Lord of the Isles and Great Steward of Scotland (cr.1952), KG, KT, GCB, OM, PC, MA; b. 14 Nov. 1948, London, England; eldest s. of HM Queen Elizabeth II q.v.) and Prince Philip, Duke of Edinburgh (q.v.); m. 1st Lady Diana Spencer (subsequently Diana, Princess of Wales) 29 July 1981 (divorced 28 Aug. 1996, died 31 Aug. 1997); two s., HRH Prince William Arthur Philip Louis, b. 21 June 1982,

HRH Prince Henry Charles Albert David, b. 15 Sept. 1984; m. 2nd Camilla Parker Bowles (subsequently The Duchess of Cornwall) 9 April 2005; ed Cheam School, Gordonstoun School, Geelong Grammar School, Trinity Coll. Cambridge and Univ. Coll. of Wales, Aberystwyth; mem. Gray's Inn 1974, Hon. Bencher 1975; Personal ADC to HM the Queen 1973–; Capt. RN 1988, Rear Adm. 1998–, Vice-Adm. 2002–; Maj.-Gen. Army 1998–, Lt-Gen. 2002–; Group Capt. RAF 1988–, Air Vice-Marshal 1998–, Air Marshal 2002–; Col-in-Chief The Royal Regt of Wales (24th/41st Foot) 1969–; Col Welsh Guards 1975–; Col-in-Chief The Cheshire Regt 1977–, Lord Strathcona's Horse (Royal Canadian) Regt 1977–, The Parachute Regt 1977–, The Royal Australian Armoured Corps 1977–, The Royal Regt of Canada 1977–, The Royal Winnipeg Rifles 1977–, Royal Pacific Islands Regt, Papua New Guinea 1984–, Royal Canadian Dragoons 1985–, Army Air Corps 1992–, Royal Dragoon Guards 1992–, Royal Gurkha Rifles 1994–; Deputy Col-in-Chief The Highlanders (Seaforth, Gordons, Camerons) 1994–; Air Cdre-in-Chief RNZAF 1977–; Col-in-Chief Air Reserve 1977–; Pres. Soc. of St George's and Descendants of Knights of the Garter 1975–; Adm. Royal Thames Yacht Club 1974–; High Steward, Royal Borough of Windsor and Maidenhead 1974–; Chair. The Mountbatten Memorial Trust 1979–, The King's Fund 1986; Pres. The Prince's Trust 1976–, The Prince's Scottish Youth Business Trust, Business in the Community 1985, Prince of Wales's Foundation for Architecture and the Urban Enviroment 1992–, Prince of Wales's Business Leaders Forum 1990–; Chancellor Univ. of Wales 1976–; mem. Bd Commonwealth Devt Corpn 1979–89; Hon. Pres. Royal Acad. Trust 1993–; Trustee, Gurkha Welfare Trust 1989; Patron, Royal Opera, Oxford Centre for Islamic Studies 1993–, British Orthopaedic Asscn 1993–, Royal Coll. of Music 1993–, Nat. Gallery 1993–, ActionAid 1995–, Help the Aged 1997–, Welsh Nat. Opera 1997–, Guinness Trust 1997–; represented HM the Queen at Independence Celebrations in Fiji 1970, at Requiem Mass for Gen. Charles de Gaulle 1970, at Bahamas Independence Celebrations 1973, at Papua New Guinea Independence Celebrations 1975, at Coronation of King of Nepal 1975, at funeral of Sir Robert Menzies 1978, at funeral of Jomo Kenyatta 1978, at funeral of Rajiv Gandhi 1990, at funeral of King Olav of Norway 1991; Pres. Royal Ballet, Birmingham Royal Ballet 2003–; Hon. FRCS 1978; Hon. FRAeS 1978; Hon. FIMechE 1978; Royal Fellowship of the Australian Acad. of Science 1977; Hon. Fellow, Trinity Coll. Cambridge 1989; Hon. mem. Hon. Co. of Master Mariners 1977 (Master 1988), Co. of Merchants of City of Edinburgh 1979; Hon. Life mem. Incorporation of Gardeners of Glasgow 1987; Hon. Air Cdre RAF Valley 1993–; received Freedom of City of Cardiff 1969, of Royal Borough of New Windsor 1970, of City of London 1971, of Chester 1973, of City of Canterbury 1978, of City of Portsmouth 1979, of City of Lancaster 1993, of City of Swansea 1994; Liveryman of Fishmongers' Co. 1971; Freeman of Drapers' Co. 1971; Freeman of Shipwrights' Co. 1978; Hon. Freeman and Liveryman of Goldsmiths Co. 1979, Liveryman of Farmers' Co. 1980, of Pewterers' Co. 1982, of Fruiterers' Co. 1989; Hon. Liveryman of Worshipful Co. of Carpenters 1992; Grand Cross of The Southern Cross of Brazil 1978, Grand Cross of The White Rose of Finland 1969, Grand Cordon of the Supreme Order of the Chrysanthemum of Japan 1971, Grand Cross of The House of Orange of the Netherlands 1972, Grand Cross Order of Oak Crown of Luxembourg 1972, Kt of The Order of Elephant of Denmark 1974, Grand Cross of The Order of Ojasvi Rajanya of Nepal 1975, Order of the Repub. of Egypt (First Class) 1981; Grande Croix, Légion d'honneur 1984; Order of Mubarak the Great of Kuwait 1993; cr. Prince of Wales and Earl of Chester (invested July 1969); KG 1958 (invested and installed 1968), KT 1977, PC 1977, GCB and Great Master of Order of the Bath 1975; Dr hc (Royal Coll. of Music) 1981; Hon. DCL (Durham) 1998; Spoleto Prize 1989, Author of the Year 1989, Premio Fregene 1990, Coronation Medal 1953, The Queen's Silver Jubilee Medal 1977, Global Environmental Citizen Prize 2007. *Publications include:* The Old Man of Lochnagar 1980, A Vision of Britain 1989, HRH The Prince of Wales Watercolours 1990, Urban Villages 1992, Highgrove: Portrait of an Estate 1993, Prince's Choice: A Selection from Shakespeare by the Prince of Wales 1995, Travels with the Prince 1998, The Garden at Highgrove (with Candida Lycett Green) 2000, The Elements of Organic Gardening (with Stephanie Donaldson) 2007, Harmony: A New Way of Looking at the World (with Tony Juniper and Ian Skelly) 2010. *Address:* Clarence House, London, SW1A 1BA; Highgrove House, Doughton, Nr Tetbury, Gloucestershire, GL8 8TN, England. *Website:* www.princeofwales.gov.uk (office).

WAŁĘSA, Lech; Polish trade union official, fmr politician and fmr head of state; b. 29 Sept. 1943, Popowo; s. of Bolesław Wałęsa and Feliksa Wałęsa; m. Danuta Wałęsa 1969; four s. four d.; ed primary and tech. schools; electrician, Lenin Shipyard, Gdańsk 1966–76, 1983; Chair. Strike Cttee in Lenin Shipyard 1970; employed Zremb and Elektromontaż 1976–80; Chair. Inter-institutional Strike Cttee, Gdańsk Aug.–Sept. 1980; Co-Founder and Chair. Solidarity Ind. Trade Union 1980–90, Chair. Nat. Exec. Comm. of Solidarity 1987–90; interned 1981–82; Founder of Civic Cttee attached to Chair. of Solidarity 1988–90; participant and Co-Chair. Round Table debates 1989; Pres. of Polish Republic 1990–95, Chair. Country Defence Cttee 1990–95, Supreme Commdr of Armed Forces of Polish Republic for Wartime 1990–95; Founder of Lech Wałęsa Inst. Foundation 1995; Founder Christian Democratic Party of the Third Republic (ChDTRP) 1997, apptd Pres. 1998, Chair. –2000, Hon. Chair. 2000–; retd from politics; resgnd from Solidarity 2006; Order of the Bath 1991, Grand Cross of Légion d'honneur 1991, Grand Order of Merit (Italy) 1991, Order of Merit (FRG) 1991, Great Order of the White Lion 1999, Orden Heraldica do Cristobal Colon 2001; numerous hon. doctorates including Harvard Univ. and Univ. of Paris; Man of the Year, Financial Times 1980, The Observer 1980, Die Welt 1980, Die Zeit 1981, L'Express 1981, Le Soir 1981, Time 1981, Le Point 1981; awarded Let Us Live Peace Prize of Swedish journal Arbetet 1981, Love Int. Award (Athens) 1981, Freedom Medal (Philadelphia) 1981, Medal of Merit (Polish American Congress) 1981, Free World Prize (Norway) 1982, Int. Democracy Award 1982, Social Justice Award 1983, Nobel Peace Prize 1983, Humanitarian Public Service Medal 1984, Int. Integrity Award 1986, Phila Liberty Medal 1989, Human Rights Prize, Council of Europe 1989, White Eagle Order (Poland) 1989, US Medal of Freedom 1989, Meeting-90 Award (Rimini) 1990, Path for Peace Award, Apostolic Nuncio to the UN 1996, Freedom Medal of Nat. Endowment for Democracy (Washington, USA) 1999, Int. Freedom Award (Memphis USA), and other awards, orders and prizes. *Publications:* autobiogs: Droga nadziei (A Path of Hope) 1987, Droga do wolności (The Road to Freedom) 1991, The Struggle and the Triumph 1992, Wszystko co robię, robię dla Polski (Everything I Do, I Do for Poland) 1995. *Leisure interests:* crossword puzzles, fishing. *Address:* Lech Wałęsa Institute Foundation, Al. Jerozolimskie 11/19, 00 508 Warsaw, Poland. *Telephone:* (22) 622 22 20 (office). *Fax:* (22) 625 14 14 (office). *E-mail:* sekretariat@ilw.org.pl (office). *Website:* www.ilw.org.pl (office).

WALEWSKA, Malgorzata; Polish singer (mezzo-soprano); b. 5 July 1965, Warsaw; one d.; ed Acad. of Music, Warsaw, Nat. Opera, Warsaw; has sung at Bremer Theater 1994, Staatsoper, Vienna 1996–98, Semperoper, Dresden 1999 and Rome (Teatro della Opera), Berlin (Deutsche Open), Düsseldorf (Deutsche Open am Rhein), Florida (Palm Bech Opera) and others; has participated in numerous festivals in Brussels, Seville, London, Bregenz, Nantes and Athens; numerous honours or prizes including 1st Prize Alfredo Kraus Int. Competition 1992, Prize for Best Mezzo-Soprano, Stanislaw Moniuszko Int. Competition, Warsaw 1992, Laureate Luciano Pavarotti Vocal Competition, Phila 1992, Best Grad., Chopin Acad. of Music, Warsaw, 1994. *Roles include:* Carmen (Carmen), Delilah (Samson and Delilah), Charlotte (Werther), Emilia (Otello), Olga (Eugene Onegin), Jocaste (Oedipus Rex). *Recordings include:* Voce di Donna (a compilation of famous mezzo-soprano arias) 2000, Mezzo (songs and arias in contemporary arrangements) 2000. *Address:* c/o Isabel Wolf, Wolf Artists International LLC, PO Box 492, Gracie Station, New York, NY 10028, USA (office). *E-mail:* bogdanwaskiewicz@wp.pl (office); info@walewska.net (office). *Website:* www.walewska.net (office).

WALI, Aminu Bashir; Nigerian diplomatist and business executive; b. 3 Aug. 1941, Kano; m.; two s.; ed School of Arabic Studies, Kano, Fed. Training Centre, Lagos, North-Western Polytechnic, North London Univ., Nat. Inst. for Policy and Strategic Studies, Kuru; Co. Sec. to Sayen Nagari Co. Ltd 1962–69; Gen. Man., Nigerian Match and Chemical Industries, Kano 1969–72; Man. Dir, Intersales W Africa Ltd, Kano 1972–86; Founding mem. Democratic Party of Nigeria (PDP), Deputy Nat. Chair. 1998, mem. Bd of Trustees 1998; Special Adviser to Pres. on Nat. Ass. Matters 1999–2003; Amb. and Perm. Rep. to UN, New York 2004–07, Amb. to People's Repub. of China 2007–12; Minister of Foreign Affairs 2014–15; serves as Chair. for numerous cos including Philip Morris Nigeria Ltd, Int. Tobacco Co. Ltd, Int. Bank for West Africa Ltd, Nigerian Eng and Construction Co. Ltd; fmr Dir Barclays Bank of Nigeria Ltd, Nigeria Hotels Ltd, Nigerbras Shipping Line; mem. Nat. Inst. for Policy and Strategic Studies 1986. *Leisure interests:* golf, squash.

WALKEN, Christopher; American actor; b. 31 March 1943, Astoria, NY; s. of Paul Walken and Rosalie Walken; m. Georgianne Thon 1969; ed Hofstra Univ. *Films include:* Me and My Brother 1969, The Anderson Tapes 1971, The Happiness Cage 1972, Next Stop Greenwich Village 1976, Roseland 1977, The Sentinel 1977, Annie Hall 1977, The Deer Hunter (New York Film Critics and Acad. Awards for Best Supporting Actor) 1978, Last Embrace 1979, Heaven's Gate 1980, Shoot the Sun Down 1981, The Dogs of War 1981, Pennies from Heaven 1981, The Dead Zone 1983, Brainstorm 1983, A View to a Kill 1984, At Close Range 1986, Deadline 1987, The Milagro Beanfield War 1988, Biloxi Blues 1988, Homeboy 1988, Communion 1989, The Comfort of Strangers 1989, King of New York 1990, McBain 1991, Mistress 1992, Batman Returns 1992, Day of Atonement 1992, True Romance 1993, Wayne's World II 199, A Business Affair 1994, Scam 1994, Pulp Fiction 1994, Wild Side 1995, Search and Destroy 1995, Things To Do In Denver When You're Dead 1995, The Prophecy 1995, The Addiction 1995, Nick of Time 1995, Celluloide 1996, Basquiat 1996, The Funeral 1996, Last Man Standing 1996, Touch 1997, Excess Baggage 1997, Suicide Kings 1997, Mousehunt 1997, Illuminata 1998, New Rose Hotel (also producer) 1998, Trance 1998, Antz (voice) 1998, Blast from the Past 1999, Sleepy Hollow 1999, Kiss Toledo Goodbye 1999, The Opportunists 2000, Jungle Juice 2001, Scotland, Pa. 2001, Joe Dirt 2001, America's Sweethearts 2001, The Affairs of the Necklace 2001, Poolhall Junkies 2002, The Country Bears 2002, Plots with a View 2002, Catch Me If You Can (BAFTA Award for Best Supporting Actor) 2003, Kangaroo Jack 2003, Gigli 2003, The Rundown 2003, Man on Fire 2004, Envy 2004, The Stepford Wives 2004, Around the Bend 2004, Romance & Cigarettes 2005, Wedding Crashers 2005, Domino 2005, Man of the Year 2006, Fade to Black 2006, Hairspray 2007, Balls of Fury 2007, Five Dollars a Day 2008, The Maiden Heist 2009, The Irishman 2011, Dark Horse 2011, Seven Psychopaths 2012, Stand Up Guys 2012, Gods Behaving Badly 2013, Jersey Boys 2014, One More Time 2015, The Jungle Book 2016, Father Figures 2017, Irreplaceable You 2018, The War with Grandpa 2019; writer and dir: Popcorn Shrimp 2001. *Stage appearances include:* West Side Story, Macbeth, The Lion in Winter (Clarence Derwent Award 1966), The Night Thoreau Spent in Jail (Joseph Jefferson Award 1970–71), Cinders 1984, A Bill of Divorcement 1985, The Dead 2000, The Seagull 2001, A Behanding in Spokane 2010. *Address:* ICM New York, 825 8th Avenue, New York, NY 10019, USA. *Telephone:* (212) 556-5600.

WALKER, Alice Malsenior, BA; American writer; b. 9 Feb. 1944, Eatonton, Ga; d. of Willie L. Walker and Minnie Walker (née Grant); m. Melvyn R. Leventhal 1967 (divorced 1977); one d.; ed Sarah Lawrence Coll.; Hon. PhD (Russell Sage Univ.) 1972; Hon. DHL (Univ. of Mass.) 1983; Bread Loaf Writers Conf. Scholar 1966, Ingram Merrill Foundation Fellowship 1967, McDowell Colony Fellowships 1967, 1977–78, Nat. Endowment for the Arts Grants 1969, 1977, Richard and Hinda Rosenthal Pound Award, American Acad. and Inst. of Arts and Letters 1974, Lillian Smith Award 1974, Rosenthal Award, Nat. Inst. of Arts and Letters 1973, Guggenheim Fellowship 1977, O. Henry Award 1986, Nora Astorga Leadership Award 1989, Freedom to Write Award, PEN Center West 1990, LennonOno Grant for Peace 2010. *Publications include:* Once 1968, The Third Life of George Copeland 1970, Five Poems 1972, In Love and Trouble 1973, Langston Hughes, American Poet 1973, Revolutionary Petunias 1974, Meridian 1976, I Love Myself When I am Laughing 1979, You Can't Keep a Good Woman Down 1981, Good Night Willi Lee, I'll See You in the Morning 1979, The Color Purple (Nat. Book Award 1983, Pulitzer Prize 1983) 1982, In Search of Our Mothers' Gardens 1983, Horses Make a Landscape Look More Beautiful 1984, To Hell with Dying 1988, Living By the Word 1988, The Temple of My Familiar 1989, Her Blue Body Everything We Know: Earthling Poems (1965–90) 1991, Finding the Green Stone 1991, Possessing the Secret of Joy 1992, Warrior Marks (with Pratibha Parmar) 1993, Double Stitch: Black Women Write About Mothers and Daughters (jtly) 1993, Everyday Use 1994, Alice Walker Banned 1996, Everything We Love Can Be Saved 1997, The Same River Twice 1997, By the Light of my Father's Smile 1998, The Way Forward is with a Broken Heart (ed.) 2000, Absolute Trust in the Goodness of the Earth: New Poems 2003, The Third Life of Grange Copeland 2003, Now is the Time to Open Your Heart 2004, We Are the Ones We Have Been

Waiting For (essays) 2007, Overcoming Speechlessness 2010, The World Has Changed: Conversations with Alice Walker 2010, Hard Times Require Furious Dancing 2010, Chicken Chronicles, A Memoir 2011, The Cushion in the Road: Meditation and Wandering as the Whole World Awakens to Being in Harm's Way 2013, The World Will Follow Joy: Turning Madness into Flowers (New Poems) 2013, Taking the Arrow Out of the Heart (New Poems) 2018. *Website:* www.alicewalkersgarden.com.

WALKER, Sir David Alan, Kt, MA; British banking executive; *Chairman, Winton Capital Group;* b. 31 Dec. 1939; m. Isobel Cooper 1963; one s. two d.; ed Chesterfield School and Queens' Coll., Cambridge; joined HM Treasury 1961, Pvt. Sec. to Jt Perm. Sec. 1964–66, Asst Sec. 1973–77; seconded to staff IMF, Washington, DC 1970–73; joined Bank of England as Chief Adviser, then Chief Econ. Intelligence Dept 1977, Dir 1981–88 (non-exec. 1988–93); Chair. Johnson Matthey Bankers Ltd (later Minories Finance Ltd) 1985–88, Financial Markets Group, LSE 1987–95, Securities and Investments Bd 1988–92, Agric. Mortgage Corpn PLC 1993–94, Morgan Stanley (Europe) (now Morgan Stanley Dean Witter (Europe) Ltd) 1994–2000, Morgan Stanley Int. 1995–2000, 2004–05 (Sr Adviser 2001–04, 2005–12), Reuters Venture Capital; Chair. Barclays PLC 2012–15; Chair. Winton Capital Group 2015–; Vice-Chair. Legal and Gen. group; Deputy Chair. Lloyds Bank Ltd 1992–94; British Co-Chair. British-Moroccan Business Council; UK Chair. Univ. of Cambridge 800th Anniversary Campaign; Chair. London Investment Bankers' Asscn 2001–04; Dir (non-exec.) British Invisibles 1993–, Nat. Power 1990–93; part-time Bd mem. Cen. Electricity Generating Bd 1987–89; mem. Council, Lloyd's of London 1988–92; Gov. Henley Man. Coll. 1993–99, LSE 1993–; Chair. Exec. Cttee of Int. Org. of Securities Comms 1990–92, Cttee of Inquiry into Lloyd's Syndicate Participations and the LMX Spiral; mem. Group of Thirty Consultative Group on Int. Econ. and Monetary Affairs, Inc. (G-30), Washington, DC 1993–; Co-Chair. Univ. of Cambridge 800 Anniversary Appeal; St Paul's Cathedral Devt Appeal, Cicely Saunders Foundation; Amb. for Community Links (East End charity); Hon. Fellow, Queens' Coll. Cambridge 1989; Hon. LLD (Exeter) 2002. *Leisure interests:* music, long-distance walking. *Address:* Winton Capital Group, Grove House, 27 Hammersmith Grove, London, W6 0NE, England (office). *Telephone:* (20) 8576-5800 (office). *Website:* www.wintoncapital.com (office).

WALKER, Donald J., BMechEng; Canadian automotive industry executive; *CEO, Magna International Inc.;* ed Univ. of Waterloo; began career with Gen. Motors Corpn, served in numerous mfg and eng positions; joined Magna Int. Inc. 1987, served as Vice-Pres. for Product Devt and Strategic Planning, COO 1991–92, Pres. 1992–94, mem. Bd of Dirs 1994–2002, 2005–, CEO 1994–2005, Co-CEO 2005–10, CEO 2010–, also Pres. and CEO Intier Automotive Inc. (subsidiary of Magna); Co-Chair. Canadian Automotive Partnership Council; Founding mem. Yves Landry Foundation. *Address:* Magna International Inc., 337 Magna Drive, Aurora, ON L4G 7K1, Canada (office). *Telephone:* (905) 726-2462 (office). *Fax:* (905) 726-7164 (office). *E-mail:* info@magnaint.com (office). *Website:* www.magnaint.com (office); www.magna.com (office).

WALKER, Sir John Ernest, Kt, MA, DPhil, ScD, FRS, FMedSci; British biochemist and academic; *Emeritus Director, Mitochondrial Biology Unit, Medical Research Council;* b. 7 Jan. 1941, Halifax, W Yorks.; s. of Thomas Ernest Walker and Elsie Walker (née Lawton); m. Christina Jane Westcott 1963; two d.; ed Rastrick Grammar School, W Yorks., St Catherine's Coll., Oxford; Visiting Research Fellow, Univ. of Wisconsin, USA 1969–71; NATO Research Fellow, CNRS, Gif-sur-Yvette, France 1971–72; European Molecular Biology Org. (EMBO) Research Fellow, Pasteur Inst., Paris 1972–74; Staff Scientist, MRC Lab. of Molecular Biology, Cambridge 1974–98; Dir MRC Mitochondrial Biology (fmrly MRC Dunn Human Nutrition Unit), Cambridge 1998–2012, Dir Emer. 2012–; Prof. of Molecular Bioenergetics, Univ. of Cambridge 2002; Visiting Prof., Dept of Life Sciences, Imperial Coll., London 2013; mem. EMBO 1983; Fellow, Sidney Sussex Coll., Cambridge 1997–; mem. Academia Europaea 1998; Foreign mem. Royal Netherlands Acad. of Arts and Science 1999, Accad. Nazionale dei Lincei, Rome 2003; Foreign Assoc. NAS 2004; Founding Fellow, Acad. of Medical Sciences, London 1998; Millennium Fellow, Royal Soc. of Chem. 2000; Fellow, Science Museum, London 2009; Lee Kong Chian Distinguished Prof., Nanyang Technological Univ. 2010; Hon. Prof., Peking Union Medical Coll., Beijing 2001, Univ. of Cambridge 2002; Hon. Fellow, St Catherine's Coll. Oxford 1998, Inst. of Biology 2002, Soc. of Biology, London 2009, FMedSci 2012; Hon. mem. Biochemical Soc. 1998, British Biophysical Soc. 2000; Hon. DSc (London) 2002, (Sussex) 2003, (Liverpool) 2004, (East Anglia) 2006, (Moscow State Univ.) 2007, (Tokyo Univ., Japan) 2007; Dr hc (Bradford, Leeds, Oxford, Gröningen, Manchester, Huddersfield, Buenos Aires), (Univ. Paul Sabatier, Toulouse) 2007, (KIIT, India) 2015; A. T. Clay Gold Medal for academic distinction 1959, Johnson Foundation Prize, Univ. of Pennsylvania 1994, CIBA Medal and Prize, Biochemical Soc. 1995, Peter Mitchell Medal, European Bioenergetics Congress 1996, Nobel Prize in Chem. (co-recipient with Paul Boyer) 1997, Gaetano Quagliariello Prize for Mitochondrial Research, Univ. of Bari, Italy 1997, Soc. of Chemical Industry Messel Medal 2000, Royal Soc. of Chem. Award of Biomembrane Chem. 2003, JSPS Award for Eminent Scientists, Japanese Soc. for the Promotion of Science 2004, Lifetime Achievement Award for the topic Molecular mechanisms in mitochondrion and associated human diseases, GeneExpression Systems Inc., Waltham, Mass, USA 2008, Ahmed Zewail Medal, Wayne State Univ. 2010, The Skou Award, Århus Univ. 2011, Gold Seal, Univ. of Bari Aldo Moro 2011, Keilin Memorial Medal and Award of the Biochemical Soc. 2012, Copley Medal, Royal Soc. 2012. *Publications include:* research papers and reviews in scientific journals. *Leisure interests:* cricket, opera music, walking, European history. *Address:* MRC Mitochondrial Biology Unit, Wellcome Trust/MRC Building, Hills Road, Cambridge, CB2 2XY, England (office). *Telephone:* (1223) 252701 (office). *Fax:* (1223) 252705 (office). *E-mail:* walker@mrc-mbu.cam.ac.uk (office); john.walker@mrc-mbu.cam.ac.uk (office). *Website:* www.mrc-mbu.cam.ac.uk/people/walker (office).

WALKER, Lucy, BA (Hons), MA, MFA; British film director; b. London; ed New Coll., Oxford, New York Univ. Tisch School of the Arts (Fulbright Scholar), USA; directed and produced Querm at Oxford which won the Oxford Univ. Dramatic Soc. Cuppers Awards; fmr Artistic Dir New Company (theatre group), produced outdoor musical productions of The Jungle Book and Tintin and the Broken Ear; appeared frequently at the Soundlab and all over New York City as well as in Los Angeles, San Francisco and Europe, performing mostly solo and also as mem. of experimental ensemble Byzar. *Films include:* documentaries: Devil's Playground (Best Documentary, American Film Inst. (AFI) DV Fest 2001, Grand Prize Best Film, AFI DV Fest 2001, Audience Award for Best Film, Sarasota Int. Film Festival 2002, Special Jury Prize for Best Documentary, Karlovy-Vary Int. Film Festival 2002) 2002, Blindsight (Audience Award for Best Film (tie), AFI Film Festival 2006, Audience Award Panorama Publikumspreis for Best Film, Berlin Int. Film Festival 2007, Audience Award for Best Documentary, Palm Springs Int. Film Festival 2007, Audience Award for Best Film, Ghent Film Festival 2007) 2006, Waste Land (Audience Award for Best World Cinema Documentary, Sundance Film Festival 2010, Audience Award Panorama Publikumspreis for Best Film, Berlin Int. Film Festival 2010, Amnesty International Award, Berlin Int. Film Festival 2010, Audience Award for Best Film, Full Frame Film Festival 2010, HBO Audience Choice Award for Best Documentary Feature, Provincetown Int. Film Festival 2010, Audience Award for Best World Cinema Documentary, Maui Int. Film Festival 2010, Audience Award for Best Film, Paulinia Film Festival 2010, Best Film, Paulinia Film Festival 2010, Best Documentary Feature $25,000 Target Filmmaker Award, Dallas Int. Film Festival 2010, Best Documentary Golden Space Needle Award, Seattle Int. Film Festival 2010, Best Documentary, Durban Int. Film Festival 2010, Audience Choice Best Film, Durban Int. Film Festival 2010, Amnesty International Durban Human Rights Award, Durban Int. Film Festival 2010, Crystal Heart Best Documentary Award, Heartland Film Festival 2010, Human Spirit Award, EcoFocus Film Fest 2010, Audience Award for Best Feature Film, EcoFocus Film Fest 2010, Best Documentary, Trinidad & Tobago Film Festival 2010, Jury Award, Flagstaff Mountain Film Festival 2010, Roger's People's Choice Award, Vancouver Int. Film Festival 2010, Prêmio Itamaraty for Best Documentary Feature, São Paulo Int. Film Festival 2010, Special Jury Prize for Best Feature, Amazonas Film Festival 2010, Audience Award, Int. Documentary Film Festival, Amsterdam 2010, Audience Award, Stockholm Int. Film Festival 2010, Pare Lorentz Award, Int. Documentary Asscn Awards 2010, Best Documentary, Int. Documentary Asscn Awards 2010, Grand Prix du Festival, Int. Environmental Film Festival 2010, Jury Award, Frozen River Film Festival 2011, Best of Festival, Wild & Scenic Film Festival 2011, Best in Festival, Princeton Environmental Film Festival 2011, Best Documentary, Movies For Grownups Awards 2011, Best Documentary Feature Film Audience Choice Award, Sedona Int. Film Festival 2011, Keen Hybrid Life Filmmaker Grant, Boulder Int. Film Festival 2011) 2010, The Crash Reel 2013, The Lion's Mouth Opens 2014, A History of Cuban Dance 2016, Buena Vista Social Club: Adios 2017. *Television includes:* Blue's Clues (series) 1998–2001, Countdown to Zero (documentary) 2010, Independent Lens (series documentary: Waste Land) 2011, The New Yorker Presents 2016; acted in: Doc Talk (series) (episodes, War: Past, Present & Future 2010, Episode #2.6 2010). *Publication:* contrib., with Moby, of a chapter to 'Sound Unbound, Sampling Digital Music and Culture' (ed. Paul D. Miller aka DJ Spooky that Subliminal Kid) 2008.

WALKER, Sir Miles Rawstron, CBE; British fmr politician and business executive; *Chairman, Hospice Isle of Man;* b. 13 Nov. 1940, Isle of Man; s. of George D. Walker and Alice Rawstron; m. Mary L. Cowell 1966; one s. one d.; ed Castle Rushen High School and Shropshire Agricultural Coll.; co. dir farming and retail trade; mem. and fmr Chair. Arbory Parish Commrs 1970–76; mem. House of Keys (Ind.) 1976–; mem. Bd of Agric., Local Govt Bd, Manx Museum 1976–81; Chair. Broadcasting Comm. 1979, Local Govt Bd 1981–86; mem. Exec. Council 1981–; mem. Assessment Bd 1983–86; Vice-Chair. Post Office Authority 1984–86; Chief Minister, Isle of Man Govt 1986–96; mem. Isle of Man Treasury 1996–2000; Dir (non-Exec.) Manx Telecom 2003–16, Chair. 2010–14; Chair. Isle of Man Swimming Asscn 1997–2005, Hospice Isle of Man 2010–; apptd Chair. Sefton Group PLC 2010; Pres. Rotary Club 2000–01, Southern Amateur Swimming Club, Port St Mary Rifle Club 1988–2006; Hon. LLD (Liverpool) 1994. *Publication:* Isle of Man Government Policy Documents 1987–1996. *Leisure interest:* Rotary Club, charitable fund raising. *Address:* Hospice Isle of Man, Strang, Douglas, IM4 4RP (office); Magher Feailley, Main Road, Colby, IM9 4AD, Isle of Man (home). *Telephone:* (1624) 833728 (home). *Fax:* (1624) 833728 (office). *E-mail:* miles.walker@manx.net. *Website:* www.hospice.org.im (office).

WALKER, Neil, LLB, LLD, PhD, FRSE, FBA; British academic; b. 5 July 1960; m.; three c.; ed Univ. of Strathclyde; research work and part-time lecturing at Univ. of Strathclyde 1981–86; Lecturer, Faculty of Law, Univ. of Edinburgh 1986–92, Sr Lecturer 1992–95, Prof. of Legal and Constitutional Theory 1996–2006, Hon. Tercentenary Prof. of Law 2007–; Visiting Prof., Univ. of Puerto Rico, Univ. of Tilburg 2000; Prof. of European Law European Univ. Inst. 2000–08, Dean of Studies 2003–05; Regius Prof. of Public Law 2008–; Global Prof. of Law, New York Univ. 2001–02, Visiting Prof. of Law, Yale Law School 2004–05; Francqui Int. Chair, Univ. of Leuven 2017; mem. Ed. Bds Edinburgh Law Review, European Law Journal; Gen. Ed., Oxford Constitutional Theory; Francqui Medal (Belgium). *Publications include:* Managing the Police: Law, Organisation and Democracy (jtly) 1986, The Scottish Community Charge (jtly) 1989, Edinburgh Essays in Public Law (co-ed) 1991, Policing the European Union (jtly) 1996, Legal Aspects of the European Single currency (co-ed) 1999, Policing in a Changing Constitutional Order 2000, Convergence and Divergence in European Public Law (co-ed) 2002, Sovereignty in Transition (ed) 2003, The Area of Freedom, Security and Justice (ed) 2004, Civilizing Security 2007, The Paradox of Constitutionalism (co-ed) 2007, Relocating the Rule of Law (co-ed) 2008, Europe's Constitutional Mosaic (co-ed) 2010, MacCormick's Scotland (ed) 2012, After Public Law (co-ed) 2013, Intimations of Global Law 2014. *Address:* School of Law, Edinburgh University, Old College South Bridge, Edinburgh, EH8 9YL, England (office). *Telephone:* (131) 650-2353. *Fax:* (131) 650-2005. *E-mail:* neil.walker@ed.ac.uk. *Website:* www.law.ed.ac.uk/staff/neilwalker.

WALKER, Roger Neville, BArch, FNZIA; New Zealand architect; *Principal, Walker Architecture and Design;* b. 21 Dec. 1942, Hamilton; s. of Andrew Frank Walker and Margaret Clothier; m. 1985; three s. one d.; ed Hamilton Boys' High School, Univ. of Auckland School of Architecture; joined Calder, Fowler and Styles 1967; f. own practice 1971, currently Prin., Walker Architecture and Design; designs include Rainbow Springs, Rotorua, Waitomo Visitor Centre, Whakatane Airport, Gardens Park Royal Hotel, Queenstown, City Centre Shopping Devt, New Plymouth, Marist Provincial Bldg, Ropata Medical Centre, Thorndon New World Shopping Devt, Willis Street Village, Wellington, over 120 houses and apartment devts in New Zealand, Australia and UK; Assoc., New Zealand Inst. of Architects 1973; Lecturer, Auckland School of Architecture, Wellington School of Architecture; New Zealand Order of Merit for services to architecture 1999; New Zealand Steel Award 1984, 16 NZ Inst. of Architecture Awards, five NZ Tourism Awards. *Leisure interests:* photography, travel, motor sport, basketball. *Address:* Walker Architecture and Design, PO Box 27464, Marion Square, Wellington; Roger Walker Architects Ltd, 1920 Egmont Street, Te Aro, Wellington, New Zealand. *Telephone:* (4) 385-9307. *Fax:* (4) 385-9348. *E-mail:* office@rogerwalker.co.nz. *Website:* www.rogerwalker.co.nz.

WALKER, Sarah Elizabeth Royle, CBE, FRCM, FGS, LRAM; British singer (mezzo-soprano); *Professor, Vocal Department, Royal Academy of Music;* b. 11 March 1943, Cheltenham, Glos.; d. of Alan Royle Walker and Elizabeth Brownrigg; m. Graham Allum 1972; ed Pate's Grammar School for Girls, Cheltenham and Royal Coll. of Music, studied violin and cello and then voice with Ruth Packer and Cuthbert Smith; Martin Musical Trust Scholarship to begin vocal studies with Vera Rozsa 1967; operatic debuts: Kent Opera, Ottavia in Coronation of Poppea 1969, Glyndebourne Festival, Diana/Giove in La Calisto 1970, Scottish Opera, Didon in Les Troyens 1971, ENO, Wellgunde in The Ring 1971; Prin. Singer with ENO 1972–76; debut at Royal Opera House, Covent Garden as Charlotte in Werther 1979; debut at Metropolitan Opera, New York, as Micha in Handel's Samson 1986; also at opera houses worldwide including La Scala Milan, Théâtre du Châtelet Paris, Lyric Opera of Chicago, San Francisco, Geneva, Vienna and Brussels; concert repertoire includes, in addition to standard works, contemporary and avant-garde works by Berio, Boulez, Cage, Ligeti, Xenakis and others; sang Rule Britannia at last night of 1985 and 1989 BBC Promenade Concerts, London; recital début, Wigmore Hall, London 1979; recital tours Australia, N America, Europe; numerous recordings including Handel's Hercules and Julius Caesar and Stravinsky's Rake's Progress; video recordings of Gloriana (title role), Julius Caesar (Cornelia) and King Priam (Andromache); Prince Consort Prof. of Singing, Royal Coll. of Music 1993–; vocal performance consultant, Guildhall School of Music and Drama 1999–; Prof., Vocal Dept, RAM 2009–; Pres. Cheltenham Bach Choir 1986–; Liveryman, Worshipful Co. of Musicians. *Leisure interests:* interior design, gardening, battling against incipient laziness. *E-mail:* megamezzo@sarahwalker.com. *Website:* www.sarahwalker.com.

WALKER, Scott Kevin; American politician and fmr state governor; b. 2 Nov. 1967, Colorado Springs, Colo; s. of Llewellyn Scott Walker and Patricia Ann Walker (née Fitch); m. Tonette Marie Tarantino 1993; two s.; ed Delavan-Darien High School, Marquette Univ.; family moved to Delavan, Wis. 1977; Accountant-Admin., IBM 1988–90; Marketing and Devt position at the Red Cross 1990–93; mem. Exec. Cttee, Wisconsin State Republican Party 1991–, Chair. 5th Congressional Dist 1991–93; elected in special election to Wisconsin State Ass. for 14th Dist 1993–2002 (re-elected several times), Chair. Cttee on Elections and Constitutional Law 1995, Cttee on Corrections and the Courts 1997, mem. Cttee on Health, Cttee on Census and Redistricting, Cttee on Financial Insts, Cttee on Housing; won special election for Milwaukee Co. Exec., Wis. 2002–10; Gov. of Wisconsin (first US gov. to have successfully kept his seat in a recall election June 2012) 2011–19; Council mem. Milwaukee Co. Boy Scouts America; mem. Wauwatosa Area chamber of Commerce, Wauwatosa Historical Soc.; Republican. *Publications:* Unintimidated – A Governor's Story and A Nation's Challenge (co-author) 2013.

WALKER, William (Bill) M., BS, JD; American lawyer, politician and fmr state governor; b. 16 April 1951, Fairbanks, Alaska; s. of Ed Walker and Frances Walker; m. Donna P. Walker; four c.; ed Lewis and Clark Coll., Univ. of Puget Sound School of Law (now Seattle Univ.); began career as commercial fisherman, Prince William Sound –1969; construction worker, Trans-Alaska Pipeline and mem. Alaska Laborers, Carpenters and Teamsters Unions 1970–74; fmr Gen. Counsel, Alaska Gasline Port Authority; Owner, Bill Walker Construction Co., Valdez 1975–80; City Councilman, City of Valdez 1978–80, Mayor of Valdez 1979–80; Attorney, Chair., Municipal Law Dept and Man. Partner, Hughes, Thorsness, Gantz, Powell and Brundin 1983–95; Attorney/Owner, Walker Richards LLC (law firm) 1995; Gov. of Alaska 2015–18 (retd); Lifetime mem. Nat. Rifle Asscn; Republican –2014; Ind. 2014–.

WALKER OF ALDRINGHAM, Baron (Life Peer), cr. 2006, of Aldringham in the County of Suffolk; **Gen. Michael John Dawson Walker,** GCB, CMG, CBE, DL; British army officer (retd); b. 7 July 1944, Salisbury, Rhodesia (now Harare, Zimbabwe); s. of William Hampden Dawson Walker and Dorothy Helena Walker (née Shiach); m. Victoria Margaret Holme 1973; two s. one d.; ed Royal Mil. Acad., Sandhurst; joined Royal Anglian Regt 1966, Regimental and Staff Duties 1966–82, with Staff Coll. 1976–77, Mil. Asst to Chief of Gen. Staff 1982–85, CO 1985–87, Col 1996–; Commdr 20th Armoured Brig. 1987–89; Chief of Staff 1 (Br.) Corps 1989–91; GOC NE Dist and Commdr 2nd Infantry Div. 1991–92; Col Commdt Queen's Div. 1991–2000, Army Air Corps 1994–2004; Col Royal Anglian Regt 1997–2002; GOC Eastern Dist 1992; Asst Chief of the Gen. Staff Ministry of Defence 1992–94; Commdr Ace Rapid Reaction Corps 1994–97; Head NATO Ground Forces, Bosnia 1995–96; C-in-C Land Command 1997–2000; ADC Gen. to the Queen 1997–2006; Chief of the Gen. Staff 2000–03; Chief of the Defence Staff 2003–06; mem. NATO Mil. Cttee 2003–06; Gov. Royal Hospital Chelsea 2006–11; Hon. LLD, Hon. DSc. *Leisure interests:* skiing, sailing, golf, shooting, motorcycling. *Address:* House of Lords, Westminster, London, SW1A 0PW, England (office). *Telephone:* (20) 7219-5353 (office). *Fax:* (20) 7219-5979 (office). *E-mail:* walkermjd@parliament.uk (office).

WALKER PRIETO, Ignacio, PhD; Chilean lawyer, politician and diplomatist; b. 7 Jan. 1956, Santiago; m. Cecilia Echenique; three c.; ed Saint George's Coll., Univ. of Chile, Princeton Univ., USA; lawyer, Vicariate of Solidarity, Archbishop of Santiago 1978–82; Research Assoc., CIEPLAN (Economic Research Corporation for Latin America) 1985–90, Exec. Dir 2003–04; Dir of Policy and Institutional Relations, Gen. Secr. of the Presidency 1990–93; mem. Chamber of Deputies 1994–2002; fmr Prof. Pontifical Catholic Univ., Univ. of Chile; Head of Political Studies, Andrés Bello Univ. 2002–03; Amb. to Italy 2004; Minister of Foreign Affairs 2004–06; Visiting Prof. and Researcher, Princeton Univ. 2007–08; mem. Senate for Quinta, de Valparaíso (Cordillera) 2010–; Pres. Partido Demócrata Cristiano (Christian Democratic Party) 2010–15; Visiting Prof., Kellogg Inst. for Int. Relations, Univ. of Notre Dame 1987; mem. Advisory Council Latin America

Studies Program, Princeton Univ. 1994–97; mem. Advisory Council, Kellogg Inst. for Int. Relations, Univ. of Notre Dame 2000. *Address:* Senado de la República de Chile, Avenida Pedro Montt s/n Valparaíso, Chile (office). *Telephone:* (32) 25-4688 (office). *Fax:* (32) 25-4752 (office). *E-mail:* iwalker@senado.cl (office). *Website:* www.ignaciowalker.cl (office).

WALL, Brad, BPA; Canadian politician (retd); b. 24 Nov. 1965, Swift Current, Sask.; m. Tami Wall; one s. two d.; ed Univ. of Saskatchewan, Saskatoon, Investment Funds Inst. of Canada; fmr Ministerial Asst, Prov. Govt of Sask.; fmr owner of several businesses, including The Last Stand Adventure Co.; Dir of Business Devt, City of Swift Current 1991; MLA, Sask. Legislature (Swift Current) 1999–17; Leader Saskatchewan Party 2004–18; Premier of Sask. and Pres. Exec. Council 2007–18, Minister of Intergovernmental Affairs 2009–18; Founding mem. and Western Co-Chair. Alliance for the Future of Young Canadians late 1980s; Founding Bd mem. Southwest Centre for Entrepreneurial Devt; Co-Chair. Health Care Innovation Working Group, Council of Federation 2012–13; Econ. Developer of the Year Award for 1998, Saskatchewan Econ. Developers Asscn 1999. *Leisure interests:* spending his time with family, reading, cooking, golfing, Saskatchewan Roughriders.

WALL, Brian; American sculptor and academic (retd); *Professor Emeritus, University of California, Berkeley;* b. 5 Sept. 1931, London, England; s. of Arthur F. Wall and Dorothy Seymour; m. Sylvia Brown 1973; two s.; ed Luton Coll. of Art, UK, Univ. of California, Berkeley; Asst Prof. of Art, Univ. of Calif., Berkeley 1975–77, Assoc. Prof. 1977–81, Prof. 1981–94, Prof. Emer. 1994–. *Address:* Department of Art Practice, 347 Kroeber Hall, University of California, Berkeley, CA 94720-3750, USA (office). *Telephone:* (510) 642-2582 (office). *Fax:* (510) 643-0884 (office). *Website:* www.art.berkeley.edu (office).

WALL, Charles Terence Clegg (Terry), PhD, FRS; British mathematician and academic; *Professor Emeritus of Pure Mathematics, University of Liverpool;* b. 14 Dec. 1936, Bristol, England; s. of Charles Wall and Ruth Wall (née Clegg); m. Alexandra Joy Hearnshaw 1959; two s. two d.; ed Marlborough Coll. and Trinity Coll., Cambridge; Fellow of Trinity Coll. 1959–64; Harkness Fellow, Inst. for Advanced Study, Princeton, USA 1960–61; Lecturer, Univ. of Cambridge 1961–64; Reader in Math. and Fellow of St Catherine's Coll., Oxford 1964–65; Prof. of Pure Math., Univ. of Liverpool 1965–99, Prof. Emer. 1999–; Royal Soc. Leverhulme Visiting Prof., CIEA, Mexico 1967; Science and Eng Research Council Sr Research Fellow 1983–88; mem. Council of Royal Soc. 1974–76, Council of London Math. Soc. 1972–80, 1992–96, Pres. 1978–80; Treas. Wirral Area SDP 1985–88, Wirral West Liberal Democrat Party 1988–2013; Foreign mem. Royal Danish Acad. 1990; Hon. mem. Irish Math. Soc. 2001; Jr Berwick Prize 1965, Sr Whitehead Prize 1976, Polya Prize, London Math. Soc. 1988, Sylvester Medal, Royal Soc. 1988. *Publications include:* Surgery on Compact Manifolds 1971, A Geometric Introduction to Topology 1971, The Geometry of Topological Stability 1995, Singular Points of Plane Curves 2004, Differential Topology 2016; more than 170 research publs in math. journals. *Leisure interests:* reading, walking, gardening. *Address:* 5 Kirby Park, West Kirby, Wirral, Merseyside, CH48 2HA, England. *Telephone:* (151) 625-5063. *E-mail:* ctcw@cantab.net.

WALL, Frank A., BCL, LLB, LLM; Irish public official and solicitor; b. 10 Oct. 1949, Limerick; s. of Frank M. Wall and Eileen Pierse; m. Margot Hourigan 1977; three s. one d.; ed Mungret Coll., Limerick, Univ. Coll., Cork, Inc. Law Soc., Dublin and Free Univ. of Brussels; Adviser Group of European Progressive Democrats, European Parl. 1974–79; Adviser to Minister for Agric., Dublin 1980; Nat. Dir of Elections 1982; Senator 1982–83; mem. Exec. Cttee, European Movt 1980–91, Chair. 1987–91; Gen. Sec. Fianna Fáil 1981–91; mem. Bd, Friends of Fianna Fáil Inc., USA 1986–91; Co-founder Inst. of Int. and European Affairs 1990, Chair. Brussels Br. 1998–2001, 2011–12; Dir Inter-Institutional Affairs, Council of the EU 1991–2004; apptd Dir Fisheries Policy 2004, now retd. *Publications:* European Regional Policy (with Sean Brosnan) 1978, Changing Balance between European Institutions 1999. *Leisure interests:* politics, Gaelic football, golf, rugby (Chair. Munster Rugby Supporters Club, Brussels).

WALL, Jeffrey (Jeff) D., OC, MA, FRSC; Canadian artist and academic; b. 29 Sept. 1946, Vancouver, BC; ed Univ. of British Columbia, Courtauld Inst., Univ. of London, UK; Asst Prof., Nova Scotia Coll. of Art and Design 1974–75; Assoc. Prof., Simon Fraser Univ., Vancouver 1976–87; fmr Prof. of Fine Arts, Univ. of British Columbia; mem. Faculty, European Graduate School; Int. Photography Prize, Hasselblad Foundation 2002, Audain Prize for Lifetime Achievement (BC's annual award for the visual arts) 2008. *Works include:* The Destroyed Room 1978, Picture for Women 1979, The Children's Pavilion (with Dan Graham), Woman and Her Doctor 1980, Mimic 1982, The Storyteller 1986, The Outburst 1989, The Vampires' Picnic 1991, Dead Troops Talk 1992, A Sudden Gust of Wind (after Hokusai) 1993. *Publications include:* Jeff Wall: Transparencies 1987, De Duve, Thierry and Boris Groys 1996.

WALLACE, Sir David James, Kt, BSc, CBE, FRS, FREng, FInstP, FRSE, PhD; British theoretical physicist, fmr university vice-chancellor and fmr college master; b. 7 Oct. 1945, Hawick, Scotland; s. of Robert Elder Wallace and Jane McConnell Wallace (née Elliot); m. Elizabeth Anne Yeats 1970; one d.; ed Hawick High School and Univ. of Edinburgh; Harkness Fellow, Princeton Univ., USA 1970–72; Lecturer in Physics, Univ. of Southampton 1972–78, Reader 1978–79; Tait Prof. of Math. Physics, Univ. of Edinburgh 1979–93, Head of Physics 1984–87; Vice-Chancellor Loughborough Univ. 1994–2005; Master of Churchill Coll. Cambridge 2006–14, N. M. Rothschild & Sons Prof. of Math. Sciences, Univ. of Cambridge and Dir Isaac Newton Inst. 2006–11; Dir Edin. Concurrent Supercomputer 1987–89, Edinburgh Parallel Computing Centre 1990–93; mem. Science and Eng Research Council 1990–94, subsequently Eng and Physical Sciences Research Council 1994–98, Chair. Physics Cttee 1987–90, Chair. Science Bd 1990–94, Chair. Tech. Opportunities Panel 1994–98; mem. EC Physics Panel, Human Capital and Mobility Programme 1991–94, EC Large Scale Facilities Evaluation Panel 1995–97; mem. European Science and Tech. Ass. 1997–98; Chair. CVCP/SCOP Task Force on Sport in Higher Educ. 1995–97, Value for Money Steering Group, Higher Educ. Funding Council for England 1997–2003; mem. Royal Soc. Scientific and Industrial Award Cttees 1990–95, Scottish Higher Educ. Funding Council 1993–97, LINK Bd, Office of Science and Tech. 1995–98, LINK/Teaching Co. Scheme Bd 1999–2001; Chair. e-Science Steering Cttee, Office of Science and Tech.

2001–06, Teaching Co. Scheme Quinquennial Review 2001; Dir (non-exec.) The Scottish Life Assurance Co. 1999–2001, Taylor & Francis Group PLC 2000–04, UK e-Universities Ltd 2001–04; Pres. Physics Section Br. Asscn for the Advancement of Science 1994, Inst. of Physics 2002–04; mem. Council, Royal Soc. 2001–02, Treas. and Vice-Pres. 2002–07; Chair. Council for the Math. Sciences 2006–10; Vice-Pres. and mem. Council, Royal Soc. of Edinburgh 2013–17; Chair. Int. Centre for Mathematical Sciences 2017–; mem. Court, Univ. of St Andrews 2014–; DL for Leics. 2001–06; Trustee, Bill McLaren Foundation 2016–; Hon. Fellow, Inst. of Math. and Its Applications 2009; Hon. DEng (Heriot Watt) 2002, Hon. DSc (Edinburgh) 2003, (Leicester) 2005, (Loughborough) 2006, (Southampton) 2006, (East Anglia) 2009; Maxwell Medal, Inst. of Physics 1980. *Publications include:* numerous publs in research and review journals on a number of areas of theoretical physics and computing. *Leisure interests:* exercise, building stone walls, eating well, mycophagy. *E-mail:* djw25@st-andrews.ac.uk (office). *Website:* www.chu.cam.ac.uk/people/view/david-wallace (office).

WALLACE, Dame Helen, DBE, CMG, PhD, FBA; British fmr professor of European studies; *Chairman, Europe Liaison, British Academy;* b. (Helen Rushworth), 25 June 1946, Manchester, England; d. of Edward Rushworth and Joyce Rushworth (née Robinson); m. William Wallace (now Lord Wallace of Saltaire) 1968; one s. one d.; ed Univs of Oxford, Bruges, Belgium and Manchester; Lecturer in European Studies, UMIST 1974–78, Visiting Prof., Coll. of Europe, Bruges 1976–2001; in Public Admin., Civil Service Coll. 1978–85; mem. Planning Staff, FCO 1979–80; Head W European Programme, Royal Inst. of Int. Affairs 1985–92; Prof. of Contemporary European Studies and Dir Sussex European Inst., Univ. of Sussex 1992–2001, Professorial Fellow 2001–06; Dir Robert Schuman Centre for Advanced Studies, European Univ. Inst. 2001–06; Centennial Prof., European Inst., LSE 2006–11, Prof. Emer. 2011–13; Foreign Sec., British Acad. 2013–15, Chair. Europe Liaison 2015–; mem. Better Regulation Comm. 2006–07; Assoc. mem. Acad. Royale des Sciences, des Lettres et des Beaux-Arts, Belgium; Foreign Sec. and Int. Vice-Pres. British Acad. 2011–15; mem. Acad. for Learned Socs for the Social Sciences 2000; mem. Bd of Dirs British Library 2015–19; Chevalier, Ordre nat. du Mérite 1996; Hon. LLD (Sussex) 2002, Hon. DLitt (Loughborough) 2004, (Aston) 2009, Dr hc (Sciences Po) 2011, (Athens) 2017; Lifetime Achievement in European Studies, Univ. Asscn for Contemporary European Studies 2006, Madame de Staël Prize for Cultural Values, All European Academies 2015, Tartufari Int. Prize 2015. *Publications include:* French and British Foreign Policies in Transition (co-author) 1990, The Wider Western Europe (ed.) 1991, The European Community: The Challenge of Enlargement (co-author) 1992, Participation and Policy-Making (co-author) 1997, Interlocking Dimensions of European Integration (ed.) 2001, The Council of Ministers (co-author) 2006, Policy Making in the European Union (ed.) 2014. *Leisure interests:* gardening, walking. *Address:* British Academy, 10–11 Carlton House Terrace, London, SW1Y 5AH, England (office). *E-mail:* h.s.wallace@btopenworld.com (home). *Website:* www.britac.ac.uk (office).

WALLACE-CRABBE, Christopher (Chris) Keith, AM, MA, FAHA; Australian poet, critic and academic; b. 6 May 1934, Melbourne, Vic.; s. of Kenneth Eyre Inverell Wallace-Crabbe and Phyllis Vera May Wallace-Crabbe (née Cock); m. 1st Helen Margaret Wiltshire 1957; one s. one d.; m. 2nd Marianne Sophie Feil 1979; two s.; m. 3rd Kristin Headlam; ed Univ. of Melbourne, Yale Univ., USA; cadet metallurgist 1951–52; then journalist, clerk, schoolteacher; Lockie Fellow in Australian Literature, Univ. of Melbourne 1962; Harkness Fellow, Yale Univ., USA 1965–67; Sr Lecturer in English, Univ. of Melbourne 1967, Reader 1976, apptd Prof. 1987, Personal Chair 1987–97, Prof. Emer. Australian Centre 1997–; Visiting Chair in Australian Studies, Harvard Univ., USA 1987–88; Chair. Australian Poetry Centre 2007; Hon. DLitt (Melbourne) 2006; Masefield Prize for Poetry 1957, Farmer's Poetry Prize 1964, Grace Leven Prize 1986, Dublin Prize 1987, Christopher Brennan Award 1990, Age Book of the Year Prize 1995, Philip Hodgins Memorial Medal 2002, Centenary Medal 2003, Melbourne Prize for Literature 2015. *Publications include:* The Music of Division 1959, Selected Poems 1974, Melbourne or the Bush 1974, The Emotions are not Skilled Workers 1980, Toil and Spin: Two Directions in Modern Poetry 1980, Splinters (novel) 1981, The Amorous Cannibal 1985, I'm Deadly Serious 1988, Sangue è l'Acqua 1989, For Crying out Loud 1990, Falling into Language 1990, Poetry and Belief 1990, From the Republic of Conscience 1992, Rungs of Time 1993, Selected Poems 1956–94 1995, Whirling 1998, By and Large 2001, The Universe Looks Down 2005, Read It Again 2005, The Thing Itself 2007, Telling a Hawk from a Handsaw 2008, Puck 2010, New and Selected Poems 2012, My Feet are Hungry 2014, Afternoon in the Central Nervous System 2015. *Leisure interests:* drawing, tennis, beachwalking, making artist's books. *Address:* School of Culture and Communication, University of Melbourne, Parkville, Vic., 3052 (office); 7 De Carle Street, Brunswick, Vic. 3056, Australia (home). *Telephone:* (3) 9386-6938 (home). *E-mail:* ckwc@unimelb.edu.au (office); chriswallacecrabbe@gmail.com (home).

WALLACE OF SALTAIRE, Baron (Life Peer) cr. 1995, of Shipley in the County of West Yorkshire; **William John Lawrence Wallace,** BA, PhD; British academic; *Professor Emeritus of International Relations, London School of Economics;* b. 12 March 1941, Leicester, England; s. of William Edward Wallace and Mary Agnes Wallace (née Tricks); m. Dame Helen Wallace 1968; two c.; ed Univ. of Cambridge, Cornell Univ., USA; Dir of Studies, Royal Inst. of Int. Affairs 1978–90; Walter F. Hallstein Fellow, St Antony's Coll., Oxford 1990–95; Prof. of Int. Studies, Cen. European Univ., Budapest 1994–97; fmr Prof. of Int. Relations, LSE, Prof. Emer. 2005–; mem. (Liberal Democrat), House of Lords 1995–, mem. European Union Cttee 1996–2001, Chair. Sub-cttee on Justice and Home Affairs 1997–2000, Lord in Waiting (HM Household) (Whip) 2010–15, Lords Spokesperson, FCO 2010–15, Cabinet Office 2011–15; Privy Councillor 2012–; Chevalier, Ordre pour le Mérite 1995, Legion d'honneur 1993; hon. degree from Universite Libre de Bruxelles 1992. *Publications include:* Regional Integration: the West European Experience 1994, Integration in a Larger and More Diverse European Union (jtly) 1995, Policy-making in the European Union (co-author) 2000, Rethinking European Order: West European Responses, 1989–97 (co-author) 2001, Non-State Actors in International Relations (co-author) 2001. *Leisure interests:* singing, gardening. *Address:* House of Lords, Westminster, London, SW1A 0PW, England (office). *Website:* www.parliament.uk/biographies/lords/lord-wallace-of-saltaire/1816 (office).

WALLACE OF TANKERNESS, Baron (Life Peer), cr. 2007, of Tankerness in Orkney; **Rt Hon. James Robert (Jim) Wallace,** PC, QC, MA, LLB; British politician; *Advocate General for Scotland;* b. 25 Aug. 1954, Annan, Dumfries and Galloway, Scotland; s. of John F. T. Wallace and Grace Hannah Maxwell; m. Rosemary Janet Fraser 1983; two d.; ed Annan Acad., Downing Coll. Cambridge, Univ. of Edinburgh; Chair. Edinburgh Univ. Liberal Club 1976–77; called to Scots Bar 1979; advocate 1979–83; mem. Scottish Liberal Exec. 1976–85; Vice-Chair. (Policy) Scottish Liberal Party 1982–85; MP for Orkney and Shetland 1983–2001 (Liberal 1983–88, Liberal Democrat 1988–2001), MSP for Orkney 1999–2007; Hon. Pres. Scottish Young Liberals 1984–85; Liberal Spokesman on Defence 1985–87; Deputy Whip 1985–87; Chief Whip 1987–88; first Liberal Democrat Chief Whip 1988–92; Alliance Spokesman on Transport 1987; Liberal Democrat Spokesman on Employment and Training 1988–92, on Fisheries 1988–97, on Scottish Affairs 1992–2001, on Maritime Affairs 1994–97; Leader Scottish Liberal Democrats 1992–2005; Deputy First Minister of the Scottish Exec. 1999–2005, Minister for Justice 1999–2003, for Enterprise and Lifelong Learning 2003–05; mem. (Liberal Democrat), House of Lords 2007–, Lords Spokesperson (Wales Office) 2010–12, Lords Spokesperson (Attorney-Gen.'s Office) 2010–, Lords Spokesperson (Scotland Office) 2010–, Deputy Leader of the House of Lords 2013–; Chair. Relationships Scotland 2008–10; mem. Comm. on Scottish Devolution 2008–09; Advocate Gen. for Scotland 2010–; Hon. DLitt (Heriot Watt) 2007; Hon. DUniv (Open) 2009; Dr hc (Edinburgh) 2009. *Leisure interests:* golf, music, travel. *Address:* House of Lords, Westminster, London, SW1A 0PW, England (office); Northwood House, Tankerness, Orkney, KW17 2QS, Scotland (home). *Telephone:* (20) 7219-3526 (office); (1856) 861383 (home). *Fax:* (1856) 861383 (home); (20) 7219-5979 (office). *E-mail:* wallacej@parliament.uk (office).

WALLBERG-HENRIKSSON, Harriet, MD, PhD; Swedish university administrator, academic and physiologist; *Professor of Physiology, Karolinska Institutet;* b. 25 May 1956; two c.; ed Karolinska Institutet, Univ. Coll. of Physical Educ. and Sports; fmr Dir of Gymnastics; fmr Assoc. Prof. of Physiology, Karolinska Institutet, Prof. of Physiology 1999–2001, Pres. (first female) 2004–12, currently Prof. of Physiology and mem. Nobel Ass.; Dean and Chair., Bd of Research, Royal Swedish Acad. of Sciences 1999–2001, mem. Physiology Cttee; Asst Sec.-Gen. Scientific Council for Medicine, Swedish Research Council 1996–98, Sec.-Gen. 2001–03; Vice-Chair. European Asscn for the Study of Diabetes (EASD); has led Swedish dels to Japan and UN; rep. of Sweden on Bds of European Science Foundation, WHO Agency for Cancer Research, Heads of Int. Research Orgs (HIRO); mem. EU Expert Group, EU strategy for competitive research environments; Order of the Rising Sun (Japan); several hon. Doctorates; H. M. the King's Medal 2008. *Publications:* approx. 140 scientific articles on diabetes and clinical physiology. *Address:* Department of Physiology and Pharmacology, C3, Krook Anna group-Integrative Physiology, Solnavägen 9, Karolinska Institutet, 171 65 Solna, Sweden (office). *Telephone:* (0) 70-629-64-70 (office). *Fax:* (8) 31-11-01 (office). *E-mail:* harriet.wallberg@ki.se (office). *Website:* www.ki.se (office).

WALLENBERG, Jacob, BS (Econs), MBA; Swedish business executive; *Chairman, Investor AB;* b. 1956, Stockholm; s. of Peter Wallenberg; m. Marie Wallenberg; three c.; ed Wharton School, Univ. of Pennsylvania, Royal Swedish Naval Acad.; officer in Royal Swedish Naval Reserve; extensive training programmes at several int. banks; joined Skandinaviska Enskilda Banken (SEB) AB 1984, held various posts, primarily in Sweden but also in Singapore, Hong Kong, London and New York, rejoined SEB as Adviser to CEO 1993, CEO 1997, Chair. 1998–2005; Deputy Man. Dir Investor AB (Wallenberg family fund man. firm) 1990–92, Vice-Chair. 1999–2005, Chair. 2005–; Vice-Chair. Atlas Copco AB, SAS AB; mem. Bd of Dirs ABB Ltd, Coca-Cola Co. 2008–, Atlas Copco AB 1998–2012, Electrolux, Stockholm Chamber of Commerce, Stora, WM-data; mem. Bd Nobel Foundation, Knut and Alice Wallenberg Foundation AB, Wharton European Advisory Bd, Stockholm School of Econs, Mayor of Shanghai's Int. Business Leaders Advisory Council, Royal Swedish Acad. of Eng Science, European Round Table of Industrialists, Confed. of Swedish Enterprise. *Leisure interests:* golf, sailing. *Address:* Investor AB, Arsenalsgatan 8C, 103 32 Stockholm, Sweden (office). *Telephone:* (8) 614-20-00 (office). *Fax:* (8) 614-21-50 (office). *E-mail:* fredrik.lindgren@investorab.com (office). *Website:* www.investorab.com (office).

WALLENBERG, Marcus, BSc; Swedish business executive and international organization official; *Vice-Chairman, Investor AB;* b. 1956; s. of Marc Wallenberg; ed Edmund A. Walsh School of Foreign Service, Georgetown Univ., USA; Dir Stora Feldmühle AG 1990–93, Düsseldorf; apptd Dir Investor AB 1990, Exec. Vice-Pres. –1999, Pres. and CEO 1999–2005, Vice-Chair. 2005, 2015–; mem. Bd of Dirs Saab AB 1992–, Deputy Chair. 1993–2006, Chair. 2006–; mem. Bd of Dirs Skandinaviska Enskilda Banken (SEB) AB 2002–, Chair. 2005–; mem. Bd of Dirs Electrolux AB 2005–, Chair. 2007–14; mem. Bd of Dirs L. M. Ericsson 1996–2011, Vice-Chair. 2006–; mem. Bd of Dirs AstraZeneca 1999–, Stora Enso Oyj 1998–2014, Foundation Asset Man. Sweden AB, SAS Ass. of Rep., Hi3G Access AB, Inst. of Int. Finance, EQT Partners AB, Knut and Alice Wallenberg Foundation, Temasek Holdings Ltd 2008–, Luossavaara-Kiirunavaara AB 2011–; Chair. ICC 2006–08, Hon. Chair. 2008–; fmr mem. Advisory Council, Stanford Grad. School of Business, Founder Wallenberg Global Learning Center at Stanford Univ.; mem. Royal Swedish Acad. of Eng and Sciences; European Business Leadership Award, Stanford Business School Alumni Asscn 2003. *Address:* Investor AB, Arsenalsgatan 8C, 103 32 Stockholm, Sweden (office). *Telephone:* (8) 614-20-00 (office). *Fax:* (8) 614-21-50 (office). *Website:* www.investorab.com (office).

WALLER, Rev. Ralph, KBE PhD; British minister of religion and academic; *Director, Farmington Institute, Harris Manchester College, University of Oxford;* b. 11 Dec. 1945, Scunthorpe; m. Carol Roberts 1968; one d.; ed John Leggott Grammar School, Scunthorpe, Richmond Coll. Divinity School, Univ. of London, Univ. of Nottingham, King's Coll. London; service in India, teaching math. and physical educ., House Master Shri Shivah Mil. School, Pune 1967–68; Math. Teacher, Riddings Comprehensive School, Scunthorpe 1968–69; Methodist Minister, Melton Mowbray 1972–75; ordained 1975; Minister Elvet Methodist Church, Durham City, Methodist Chaplain, Univ. of Durham 1975–81, Chaplain St Mary's Coll. and St Aidan's Coll. 1979–81; Chaplain, Tutor in Theology and Resident Tutor, Westminster Coll., Oxford 1981–88; Prin. and Tutor in Theology, Harris Manchester (fmrly Manchester) Coll., Univ. of Oxford 1988–2018, Chair. Faculty of Theology, Univ. of Oxford 1995–97, mem. Hebdomadal Council 1997–2000,

Chair. Environmental Cttee 1997–2000, Dir Farmington Inst. 2001–; Hon. DLitt (Menlo Coll., Calif.) 1994, Hon. DHum (Ball State Univ., Ind.) 1998, Hon. DHL (St Olaf Coll., Minn.) 2001, (Christopher Newport) 2005, Hon. DTheol (Uppsala) 1999, Hon. DD (Hartwick) 2003, Hon. DD (Univ. of Wales); Templeton Prize UK 1993. *Publications:* Christian Spirituality (co-ed.) 1999, John Wesley 2003, Basic Texts in Christian Spirituality (co-ed.) 2003. *Address:* Farmington Institute, Harris Manchester College, Mansfield Road, Oxford, OX1 3TD, England (office). *Telephone:* (1865) 271985 (office). *E-mail:* ralph.waller@hmc.ox.ac.uk (office). *Website:* www.farmington.ac.uk (office).

WALLIAMS, David Edward; British comedian, actor and author; b. (David Edward Williams), 29 Aug. 1971, London; s. of Peter Williams and Kathleen Williams; m. Lara Stone (divorced); one s.; ed Univ. of Bristol; Nat. TV Awards Landmark Achievement Award 2012. *Television includes:* Little Britain (series) 2003–06, Little Britain USA (series) 2008, Come Fly with Me (series) 2010–11, Britain's Got Talent (as judge) 2012–, Mr Stink (film) 2012, Big School 2013–14, Gangsta Granny (film) 2013, Walliams & Friend (series) 2015, Partners in Crime (series) 2015, Ratburger (film) 2017, The Queen and I (film) 2018. *Films include:* A Cock and Bull Story 2005, Stardust 2007, Marmaduke 2010, Dinner for Schmucks 2010, Great Expectations 2012, The Look of Love 2013, Missing Link 2019. *Achievements include:* completed 21-mile swim across English Channel to France 2006. *Publications:* children's fiction: The Boy in the Dress (illustrated by Quentin Blake) 2008, Mr Stink (illustrated by Quentin Blake) (People's Book Prize Children's Award 2010) 2009, Billionaire Boy (illustrated by Tony Ross) 2010, Gangsta Granny (illustrated by Tony Ross) 2011, Ratburger (Nat. Book Awards Children's Book of the Year) 2012, Demon Dentist 2013, The Slightly Annoying Elephant 2013, Awful Auntie 2014, The First Hippo on the Moon 2014, The Queen's Orang-utan 2015, The Bear Who Went Boo! 2015, Grandpa's Great Escape 2015, The World's Worst Children 2016, The Midnight Gang 2016, The World's Worst Children 2 2017, Bad Dad 2017; other titles: Inside Little Britain (with Boyd Hilton and Matt Lucas) 2006, Camp David (autobiography) 2012. *Address:* Troika Talent Ltd, 10A Christina Street, London, EC2A 4PA, England (office). *Telephone:* (20) 7336-7868 (office). *E-mail:* info@troikatalent.com (office). *Website:* www.troikatalent.com (office); david-walliams.co.uk; www.worldofwalliams.com.

WALLIN, Stefan Erik; Finnish politician; *Chairman, Swedish People's Party;* b. 1 June 1967, Vaasa; m. Elina Pirjatanniemi; two d.; ed Åbo Akademi Univ., Turku; summer reporter for Vasabladet newspaper 1989–93, for Åbo Underrättelser newspaper 1993–94; Special Adviser to Minister of Transport 1994–95, to Minister for Foreign Trade 1995–98, to Minister of the Interior 1998–99, to Minister of Defence 1999–2000; Deputy Ed.-in-Chief Åbo Underrättelser 2000–05; State Sec. for Minister of the Environment 2005–07; mem. Suomen Eduskunta (Parl.) 2007–; Minister of the Environment and Minister at the Ministry for Foreign Affairs Jan.–April 2007, Minister of Culture and Sport 2007–10, 2010–11, Minister at the Ministry of Social Affairs and Health 2007–10, 2010–11, Minister of Defence 2011–12; mem. Swedish People's Party (SPP), Chair. 2006–; mem. Turku City Council 2009–; mem. Ass., Regional Council of SW Finland 2009–. *Leisure interests:* cooking, reading, gym, English Premier League football. *Address:* Svenska Folkpartiet, Simonkatu 8a, PO Box 430, 00101 Helsinki, Finland (office). *Telephone:* (9) 693070 (office). *E-mail:* info@sfp.fi (office). *Website:* www.sfp.fi (office); www.stefanwallin.fi.

WALLINGER, Mark; British artist; b. 1959, Chigwell, Essex; ed West Hatch High School, Chigwell, Loughton Coll., Chelsea School of Art, London, Goldsmiths Coll.; represented GB at the Venice Biennale 2001; video work, Via Dolorosa, permanently installed in a crypt in the Duomo in Milan; his sculpture Ecce Homo was the first project chosen for the vacant Fourth Plinth in Trafalgar Square; installation State Britain on display at Tate Britain 2007; curated Hayward touring exhbn, The Russian Linesman 2009; proposal for a 165ft high White Horse won the Ebbsfleet Landmark Comm.; work is represented in major museum collections in Europe, USA and the Far East; Hon. Fellow, London Inst. 2002; Dr hc (Univ. of Central England) 2003; Henry Moore Fellowship, British School, Rome 1998, DAAD Artists Programme, Berlin 2001–02, Turner Prize 2007. *Dance:* UNDANCE, Sadler's Wells 2011, Metamorphoses: Titian 2012, Royal Opera House 2012. *Publication:* Mark 2011. *Address:* c/o Hauser & Wirth, 23 Savile Row, Mayfair, London, W1S 2ET, England. *Telephone:* (20) 7287-2300. *E-mail:* london@hauserwirth.com. *Website:* www.hauserwirth.com.

WALLIS, Stanley (Stan) David Martin, AC, BCom, FAIM, FCPA, FCIS, FCIM; Australian financial services executive (retd); b. 23 July 1939, Melbourne; s. of S. E. Wallis; m. Judith Logan 1962; three s. two d.; ed Wesley Coll., Melbourne, Univ. of Melbourne, Stanford Univ., USA; joined AMP/Amcor 1960, Chief Accountant 1986, Financial Man. 1972, Deputy Man. Dir 1975, Man. Dir 1977–96; Chair. Amcor Ltd 1997–2000; Dir AMP Ltd 1990–2003, Chair. 2000–03; Chair. Pineapplehead Ltd 2000–02; Dir Coles Myer Ltd 1996–2002, Chair. 1997–2002; currently Chair. SANE Australia; Dir Walter & Eliza Hall Inst. of Medical Research; Chair. and Dir Santos Ltd 1989–94; Dir Australian Foundation Investment Co. 1987–2009, AMCIL Ltd 2004–13; fmr Dir Nicholas-Kiwi Australasia Ltd, NZ Forest Products Ltd, Mayne Nickless Ltd, Spicers Paper Ltd; Chair. 1997–2002; currently Chair. SANE Australia (mental health charity); Chair. Inquiry into Australian Financial System 1996–97; Pres. Business Council of Australia 1996–98; fmr Vice-Pres. Melbourne Business School, Univ. of Melbourne; Hon. LLD (Monash); Award for Outstanding Achievement in Business, Melbourne Univ. Grad. School of Man. 1990, Bulletin Deloitte Business Leader Award 1995. *Leisure interests:* tennis, skiing, sailing. *Address:* c/o SANE Australia, PO Box 226, South Melbourne, Vic. 3205, Australia.

WALLNER, Nicolai; Danish gallery owner; f. Galleri Nicolai Wallner in Copenhagen 1993, moved to Islands Brygge 1999, opening second kunsthal in Charlottenborg 2011. *Address:* Ny Carlsbergvej 68, 1760 Copenhagen V, Denmark (office). *Telephone:* 32-57-09-70 (office). *Fax:* 32-57-09-71 (office). *E-mail:* info@nicolaiwallner.com (office). *Website:* www.nicolaiwallner.com (office).

WALLSTRÖM, Margot; Swedish politician and UN official; *Minister of Foreign Affairs;* b. 28 Sept. 1954, Kåge, Västerbotten Co.; m. Håkan Wallström; two s.; ed Nordanå Upper Secondary School, Skellefteå; Organizing Sec. Värmland br., Social Democratic Youth League; Accountant, Alfa Savings Bank, Karlstad 1977–79, Sr Accountant 1986–88; mem. Parl. 1979–85; fmr mem. Värmland Co. Council, Directorate of Bd of Civil Aviation, Directorate of Nat. Environment Protection Bd; Minister with responsibility for Ecclesiastical, Consumers, Equality and Youth Affairs, Ministry of Public Admin 1988–92; Minister of Cultural Affairs 1994–96, of Health and Social Affairs 1996–98, of Foreign Affairs 2014–; Exec. Vice-Pres. Worldview Global Media, Sri Lanka 1998–99; EU Commr for the Environment 1999–2004, First Vice-Pres. and Commr for Institutional Relations and Communication Strategy 2004–10; Special Rep. of the UN Sec.-Gen. on Sexual Violence in Conflict 2010–14 (resgnd); Chair. of Ministerial Initiative, Council of World Women Leaders 2007; Adviser, Inst. for Human Rights and Business 2012–14; mem. Advisory Bd, Int. Inst. for Democracy and Electoral Assistance (IDEA) 2011–14; mem. Bd Lund Univ. 2013–14, Global Challenge Foundation 2013–14, ICA Gruppen 2013–14; mem. UN High-Level Panel on Humanitarian Financing 2015–; Royal Order of the Seraphim 2008, Commdr, Ordre nat. de la Légion d'honneur (France) 2014; Dr hc (Chalmers Univ.) 2001, (Mälardalen Univ.) 2004, (Univ. of Massachusetts, Howell) 2005; IAIA Global Environmental Award 2003, Gothenburg Award for Sustainable Devt 2008, The Agent of Change Award, UN Women 2017. *Publications include:* The People's Europe or Why is It So Hard to Love the EU? (with Göran Färm) 2004, EU Elite Project? No! The People's Europe (with Göran Färm) 2008. *Address:* Ministry for Foreign Affairs, Gustav Adolfs torg 1, 103 39 Stockholm, Sweden (office). *Telephone:* (8) 405-10-00 (office). *Fax:* (8) 723-11-76 (office). *E-mail:* margot.wallstrom@gov.se (office). *Website:* www.government.se/government-of-sweden/ministry-for-foreign-affairs/margot-wallstrom (office).

WALMSLEY, David George, PhD, DSc, FInstP, MRIA; British physicist and academic; *Professor Emeritus of Physics, Queen's University Belfast;* b. 3 Feb. 1938, Newtownstewart, Northern Ireland; s. of Robert Gwynne Walmsley and Elizabeth Johnston; m. Margaret Heather Edmonstone 1965; two s.; ed Royal School, Armagh, Queen's Univ. Belfast and McMaster Univ., Hamilton, Ont.; NRC Canada Post-doctoral Fellow, MacMaster Univ. 1965; Scientific Officer, Sr Scientific Officer, AERE Harwell 1966–70; Lecturer, Sr Lecturer, Reader in Physics, New Univ. of Ulster 1970–84; Prof. of Physics, Univ. of Ulster 1984–88; Prof. of Physics, Queen's Univ. Belfast 1988–2003, Prof. Emer. 2003–, Dir School of Math. and Physics 1993–98, Dean Faculty of Science and Agric. 1998–2002; Chair. Northern Ireland Regional Medical Physics Agency 2001–09; Fellow, American Physical Soc. 2001. *Publications:* numerous articles on superconductivity and the electron tunnel effect in scientific journals. *Address:* Department of Physics and Astronomy, Queen's University, Belfast, BT7 1NN (office); 5 Newforge Grange, Belfast, BT9 5QB (home); 25 Swilly Road, Portstewart, BT55 7DJ, Northern Ireland (home). *Telephone:* (28) 9097-1903 (office); (28) 9066-4141 (home); (28) 7083-3257 (home). *Fax:* (28) 9027-3110 (office). *E-mail:* dg.walmsley@qub.ac.uk (office). *Website:* www.qub.ac.uk/mp (office).

WALMSLEY, Emma, MA; British business executive; *CEO, GlaxoSmithKline PLC;* b. 1969, Barrow-in-Furness, Cumbria; d. of Sir Robert Walmsley and Lady Christina Walmsley; m. David Owen; four c.; ed Oxford Univ.; worked with L'Oréal for 17 years, various marketing and gen. man. roles in Paris, London and New York, becoming Gen. Man., Consumer Products, L'Oréal China, Shanghai 2007–10; Pres. of Consumer Healthcare Europe, GlaxoSmithKline (GSK) PLC 2010–11, mem. GSK Corp. Exec. Team 2011–, CEO, GSK Consumer Healthcare 2015–17, CEO, GlaxoSmithKline PLC 2017–; Dir (non-exec.) Diageo PLC Jan.–Sept. 2016. *Address:* GSK House, 980 Great West Road, Brentford, TW8 9GS, Middx, England (office). *Telephone:* (20) 8047-5000 (office). *Fax:* (20) 8047-7807 (office). *Website:* www.gsk.com (office).

WALPORT, Sir Mark Jeremy, Kt, MB, BChir, MA, PhD, FRS, FRCP, FRCPath, FMedSci; British physician, academic and trust executive; *Chief Executive, UK Research and Innovation (UKRI);* b. 25 Jan. 1953, London; s. of Samuel Walport and Doreen Walport (née Music); m. Julia Elizabeth Neild 1986; one s. three d.; ed St Paul's School, London, Clare Coll. Cambridge, Middx Hosp. Medical School; House Officer, Middx Hosp. and Queen Elizabeth II Hosp., Welwyn 1977–78, House Officer 1978–80; Hon. Registrar, Brompton Hosp. 1980; Registrar, Hammersmith Hosp. 1980–82, Hon. Consultant Physician 1985–, Dir Research and Devt 1994–98; MRC Training Fellow, MRC Mechanisms in Tumour Immunity Unit, Cambridge 1982–85; Harrison–Watson Student, Clare Coll. Cambridge 1982–85; Sr Lecturer in Rheumatology, Imperial Coll. School of Medicine 1985–90, Reader Rheumatological Medicine 1990–91, Prof. of Medicine 1991–2003, Head of Div. of Medicine 1997–2003, Fellow, Imperial Coll. 2006–, Hon. Distinguished Prof. of Medicine 2013–; Gov. Wellcome Trust 2000–03, Dir 2003–13; Chief Scientific Adviser to the Govt 2013–17; Chief Exec. UK Research and Innovation (UKRI) 2017–; mem. Scientific Advisory Bd, Cantab Pharmaceuticals, Cambridge 1989–2000, Research and Devt Advisory Bd, Smithkline Beecham 1998–2000; mem. Council, British Soc. for Rheumatology 1989–95, British Soc. for Immunology 1998–2000; Asst Ed. British Journal of Rheumatology 1990–97; Ed. Clinical and Experimental Immunology 1990–97; Series Ed. British Medical Bulletin 1998–; Hon. DSc (Univ. of Sheffield, King's Coll. London); Roche Prize for Rheumatology 1991, Graham Bull Prize in Clinical Science 1996. *Publications:* Immunobiology (co-author); Clinical Aspects of Immunology (co-ed.); numerous papers published in scientific journals on immunology and rheumatology. *Leisure interest:* natural history. *Address:* UK Research and Innovation, Polaris House, Swindon, SN2 1FL, England (office). *E-mail:* communications@ukri.org (office). *Website:* www.ukri.org (office); www.gov.uk/government/people/mark-walport (office).

WALSER, Martin, DPhil; German writer, playwright and poet; b. 24 March 1927, Wasserburg, Bodensee; s. of Martin Walser and Augusta Schmid; m. Käthe Jehle 1950; four d.; ed Theologisch-Philosophische Hochschule, Regensburg and Univ. of Tübingen; Grosses Bundesverdienstkreuz mit Stern 1997, Officier, L'Ordre des Arts et des Lettres; Group 47 Prize 1955, Hermann-Hesse Prize 1957, Gerhart-Hauptmann Prize 1962, Schiller Prize 1980, Büchner Prize 1981, Orden pour le mérite 1994, Friedenspreis des Deutschen Buchhandels 1998. *Publications include:* novels include: Ehen in Philippsburg 1957, Halbzeit 1960, Das Einhorn 1966, Fiction 1970, Die Gallistlische Krankheit 1972, Der Sturz 1973, Jenseits der Liebe 1976, Ein fliehendes Pferd 1978, Seelenarbeit 1979, Das Schwanenhaus 1980, Brief an Lord Liszt 1982, Brandung 1985, Dorle und Wolf 1987, Jagd 1988, Die Verteidigung der Kindheit 1991, Ohne einander 1993, Finks Krieg 1996, Ein springender Brunnen 1998, Der Lebenslauf der Liebe 2001, Tod eines Kritikers

2002, Der Augenblick der Liebe 2004, Die Verwaltung des Nichts 2004, Leben und Schreiben 2005, Angstblüte 2006, Der Lebensroman des Andreas Beck 2006, Das geschundene Tier 2007, Ein Liebender Mann 2008; short stories: Ein Flugzeug über dem Haus 1955, Lügengeschichten 1964; plays: Der Abstecher 1961, Eiche und Angora 1962, Überlebensgross Herr Krott 1963, Der schwarze Schwan 1964, Die Zimmerschlacht 1967, Ein Kinderspiel 1970, Das Sauspiel 1975, In Goethe's Hand 1982, Die Ohrfeige 1986, Das Sofa 1992, Kaschmir in Parching 1995; essays: Beschreibung einer Form, Versuch über Franz Kafka 1961, Erfahrungen und Leseerfahrungen 1965, Heimatkunde 1968, Wie und wovon handelt Literatur 1973, Wer ist ein Schriftsteller 1978, Selbstbewusstsein und Ironie 1981, Messmers Gedanken 1985, Über Deutschland reden 1988, Vormittag eines Schriftstellers 1994, Messmers Reisen 2003; poetry: Der Grund zur Freude 1978, Die Verwaltung des Nichts 2004. *Address:* Zum Hecht 36, 88662 Überlingen-Nussdorf, Germany (home). *Telephone:* (7551) 4131 (home). *Fax:* (7551) 68494 (home). *E-mail:* nussdorf@t-online.de (home).

WALSH, Arthur Stephen, CBE, MA, FEng, FIEE; British business executive; b. 16 Aug. 1926, Wigan, Greater Manchester, England; s. of Wilfrid Walsh and Doris Walsh; m. 1st. Gwendoline Mary Walsh (divorced 1983); m. 2nd Judith Martha Westenborg 1985; one s. one d.; ed Selwyn Coll., Cambridge; joined GEC 1952, various sr appointments, including Tech. Dir of GEC/AEL 1952–79; Man. Dir Marconi Space and Defence Systems 1979–82; Man. Dir The Marconi Co. 1982–85; Chief Exec. STC PLC (now Northern Telecom Europe Ltd) 1985–91; Chair. Telemetrix PLC 1991–97, Simoco Int. Ltd 1997–2001; Dir FKI PLC 1991–99, Deputy Chair. 1993–96; Hon. DSc (Ulster) 1988, (Southampton) 1993. *Leisure interests:* sailing, skiing, golf. *Telephone:* (1923) 770883 (office); 0034952856021 (home). *E-mail:* alvecote@aol.com.

WALSH, Christopher T., AB, PhD; American biochemist and academic; *Emeritus Professor, Harvard Medical School;* b. 16 Feb. 1944, Boston, MA; ed Harvard Univ., The Rockefeller Univ.; Postdoctoral Fellow, Brandeis Univ. 1970–72, Helen Hay Whitney Foundation Fellow, Grad. Dept of Biochemistry 1970-72; Asst, Assoc. and Full Prof. of Chemistry and Biology, MIT 1972–87, Uncas and Helen Whitaker Prof. 1980–85, Chair. Dept of Chem. 1982–87, Karl Taylor Compton Prof. 1985–87; Chair. Dept of Biological Chem. and Molecular Pharmacology, Harvard Medical School 1987–95, Hamilton Kuhn Prof. of Biological Chem. and Molecular Pharmacology 1987–13, Emer. Prof. 2014–; Pres. Dana-Farber Cancer Inst. 1992–95; Co-Chair. Gordon Research Conf. on Conference on Enzymes, Coenzymes and Molecular Biology 1978, Conf. on Methanogenesis 1984; Panel mem. NSF Research Grants Study 1977–79, NIH Study Section in Biochemistry 1978–82 (Chair. 1982); mem. NIH Gen. Medical Sciences Advisory Council 1996–99; Biology Section Ed. Annual Reports in Medicinal Chemistry 1978–80; Assoc. Ed. Protein Science 1991–92, Annual Review of Biochemistry 1990–95; mem. Editorial Bd Journal of Biological Chemistry 1978–80, Journal of the American Chemical Society 1991–94, Chemistry and Biology 1993–; currently Adjunct Prof. of Chemistry, Stanford Univ., mem. Advisory Bd Stanford ChEM-H Inst.; mem. Bd of Dirs, Whitehead Inst., Versicor, Kosan Biosciences, Transform Pharmaceuticals; mem. Structural Biology Review Group, Howard Hughes Medical Inst.; mem. Scientific Advisory Bd, Epix Medical, KOSAN Biosciences, Caliper Technologies, Dyax, Millenium Pharmaceuticals, MPM Asset Management; mem. American Acad. of Arts and Sciences 1988, Inst. of Medicine 1989, NAS 1989; Alfred P. Sloan Foundation Fellow 1975–77, Camille & Henry Dreyfus Teacher-Scholar Grant Recipient 1976–80, Eli Lilly Award in Biochemistry 1979, ACS Arthur C. Cope Scholar Award 1998, ACS Repligen Award 1999, Welch Award in Chem. (co-recipient) 2010. *Publications:* Enzymatic Reaction Mechanisms 1978, Antibiotics: Actions, Origins, Resistance 2003, Post-translation Modification of Proteins: Expanding Nature's Inventory 2006; numerous papers in professional journals. *Address:* Department of Biological Chemistry and Molecular Pharmacology, Harvard Medical School, Armenise Building, Room 616, 200 Longwood Avenue, Boston, MA 02215, USA (office). *Telephone:* (617) 432-1000 (office). *Website:* walsh.med .harvard.edu (office); bcmp.med.harvard.edu (office).

WALSH, Courtney Andrew, OJ; Jamaican fmr cricketer; b. 30 Oct. 1962, Kingston; s. of Joan Woollaston; right-hand batsman, right-arm fast bowler; player for Jamaica 1981–2001, Glos. 1984–98, West Indies 1984–2001 (Capt. 1993/94–97/98); Test debut with West Indies against Australia at Perth 9-12 Nov. 1984; played in 132 Tests, took 519 wickets (average 24.44), best bowling (innings) 7/37, (match) 13/55, scored 936 runs (average 7.54, highest score 30 not out); played in 132 One-Day Ints, took 227 wickets (average 30.47), best bowling 5/1, scored 321 runs (average 6.97, highest score 30); played in 429 First-class matches, took 1,807 wickets (average 21.71), best bowling 9/72, scored 4,530 runs (average 11.32, highest score 66); world record 519 Test wickets (average 24.44) at time of his retirement in April 2001 and 1,807 first-class wickets (average 21.71); currently a regular feature of the Lashings World XI; Owner Cuddy'z Sports Bar, Kingston; Wisden Cricketer of the Year 1987, Jamaica Sportsman of the Year 1998–2000. *Leisure interests:* cooking, dancing, music, cars.

WALSH, Capt. Don, BS, MA, MS, PhD; American business executive, fmr university administrator and fmr naval officer; *President and CEO, International Maritime, Inc.;* b. 2 Nov. 1931, Berkeley, Calif.; s. of J. Don Walsh and Marta G. Walsh; m. Joan A. Betzmer 1962; one s. one d.; ed San Diego State Coll., Texas A&M Univ., US Naval Acad.; entered USN 1950, submarine service 1956–64, became Officer-in-Charge Submersible Test Group and Bathyscaph Trieste 1959, made record dive to 35,840 ft Jan. 1960, designated USN submersible pilot No. 1 1960; at Dept of Oceanography, Texas A&M Univ. 1965–68; commanded submarine Bashaw 1968–69, Scientific Liaison Officer, Submarine Devt Group One 1969–70, Special Asst (submarines) to Asst Sec. of Navy for Research and Devt, Washington, DC 1970–73; Resident Fellow, Woodrow Wilson Int. Center for Scholars 1973–74; Deputy Dir Naval Labs. 1974–75; retd from navy with rank of Capt. 1975; Dir Inst. for Marine and Coastal Studies and Prof. of Ocean Eng, Univ. of Southern Calif. 1975–83; Pres. and CEO International Maritime, Inc. 1976–; Vice-Pres. Parker Diving Service 1985–94; mem. Marine Bd, Nat. Research Council 1990–93, Ocean Studies Bd 2010–; Exec. Dir Deep Ocean Eng 1990–2000; mem. Bd of Dirs Explorers Club 1994–2000; mem. US Naval Inst., Nat. Advisory Cttee on Oceans and Atmosphere 1979–86, Law of the Sea Advisory Cttee (US State Dept) 1979–83, Soc. of Naval Architects and Marine Engineers, American Soc. for Naval Engineers; mem. Bd of Govs, Calif. Maritime Acad. 1985–94; Ed. Marine Technical Society Journal 1976–80; mem. Nat. Acad. of Eng 2001–, Ocean Elders 2011–; Fellow, Marine Tech. Soc. 1980; Hon. Life mem. Explorers' Club (Hon. Pres. 2008–), Adventurers' Club, American Geographical Soc. 2000; Legion of Merit (two awards), Meritorious Service Medal (two awards), Antarctic Service Medal, USN Dept Distinguished Civilian Service Medal, US Coast Guard Meritorious Service Medal, Admin.'s Award (Medal), Nat. Oceanic and Atmospheric Admin; The Walsh Spur (ridge) in the Antarctic, NSF 1973, Gold Medals from City of Trieste and Chicago Geographic Socs, US Coast Guard Meritorious Public Service Medal 1980, Meritorious Service Medal (two awards), Lowell Thomas Award, Explorers' Club 1987, Compass Distinguished Achievement Award, Marine Tech. Soc. 1996, Explorers' Medal, Explorers' Club 2001, L'Etoile Polaire, Jules Verne Aventures 2001, Hubbard Medal, Nat. Geographic Soc., NOGI Award, Acad. of Underwater Arts and Sciences, Peter Benchley Award, Blue Frontier Foundation, Ralph White Memorial Award, Los Angeles Chapter of the Explorers Club, Distinguished Public Service Award, USN, NOAA Administrators Award, Lifetime Achievement Award, BLUE Underwater Film Festival, Distinguished Achievement Award, Nat. Maritime Historical Soc. *Achievements include:* made 57 expeditions to the Arctic and Antarctic from 1955, including five to the North Pole. *Publications:* author of more than 200 papers, articles, etc. on marine subjects; ed. and contrib. Law of the Sea: Issues in Ocean Resources Management; Energy and Resource Development of the Continental Margins (co-ed.) 1980, Energy from the Sea: Challenge for the Decade (ed.) 1982, Waste Disposal in the Oceans: Minimum Impact, Maximize Benefits (co-ed.) 1983, Twenty Thousand Jobs Under the Sea: A History of Diving. *Leisure interests:* writing, travel, sailing, flying his aeroplane. *Address:* International Maritime Inc., 14758 Sitkum Lane, Myrtle Point, OR 97458, USA (office). *Telephone:* (541) 572-2313. *Fax:* (541) 572-4041. *E-mail:* imiwalsh@mac.com (office).

WALSH, Edward (Ed) M., BEng, MSc, PhD, FIEE, FRSA, MRIA; Irish chartered engineer, fmr university administrator and consultant; *Founding President, University of Limerick;* b. 3 Dec. 1939, Cork; s. of Michael Walsh and Margaret Walsh (née Leonard); m. Stephanie Barrett 1965; three s. one d.; ed Nat. Univ. of Ireland, Iowa State Univ., USA; Assoc., US Atomic Energy Comm. Lab., Ames, Ia 1963–65; Assoc. Prof., Virginai Polytechic Inst. and State Univ. 1965–69; Dir Energy Research Group Programme, Va 1966–69; Founding Pres. Nat. Inst. for Higher Educ., Limerick 1970–98, Univ. of Limerick 1989–98, Pres. Emer. 1998–, mem. Bd Univ. of Limerick Foundation 2006–; Prin. of Oakhampton Consultants 1999–; Founding Chair. Nat. Self-Portrait Collection of Ireland 1979–2002, Nat. Technological Park 1983–88, Nat. Council for Curriculum and Assessment 1984–90; Chair. Advisory Bd, Barrington's Hosp., Shannon Development 1987, Cttee of Heads of Irish Univs 1991–92, Birr Historic Science Foundation 1994–99, IAUP Int. Comm. on Educational Tech. 1996–2002, Irish Council for Science, Tech. and Innovation 1997–2004, Citywest Growcorp 1998–2011, Project Biostart 2000–02, ECET Int. Group 2000–03, of the Nat. Science, Tech. and Innovation Framework 2002, Nat. Allocation Advisory Group (Carbon Trading) 2003–12, Steering Group, Adare Hosp. and Clinic 2005–10, Stokes Bio 2006–10; Deputy Chair. Irish Chamber Orchestra 2002–08; Vice-Pres. Int. Asscn of Univ. Presidents 1987–99; mem. Bd of Dirs Nat. Microelectronics Applications Centre 1981–84, Shannon Devt 1976–2002 (Chair. 1987), Wind Energy Direct 2008–; Advisory Council, Transparency International 2004–05, Legal Affairs Council, Gerson Lehrman Group, New York 2005–08, mem. Advisory Bd, Ryan Acad. for Entrepreneurship 2009–13, Pontificio Ateneo S. Anselmo, Rome 2010–14; mem. New York Acad. of Science 1988; Fellow, Inst. of Engineers of Ireland 1995, Irish Acad. of Eng 1998 (mem. Energy Standing Cttee 2008–), World Innovation Foundation 2001; Patron, Asscn for Children and Adults with Learning Disabilities 1998–2004; Registered Silversmith, Co. of Goldsmiths of Dublin; Freeman, City of Limerick 1995, Hon. mem. Royal Hibernian Acad. of Arts 1994, Nat. Coll. of Art and Design 1997; Hon. LLD (Dublin) 1992, (Queen's Univ., Belfast) 1995, (Nat. Univ. of Ireland) 1998, (Limerick) 2010, Hon. DSc (Ulster) 1997; Paul Harris Fellow, Rotary Int. 1990. *Publications include:* Energy Conversion: Electromechanical, Direct, Nuclear 1967, Fluid Dynamic Energy Conversion 1967, Vision 2020: What Future for Business? 1995, Upstart: Friends, Foes and Founding a University (memoir, with Kieran Fagan) 2011; more than 50 publs in various journals and proceedings. *Leisure interests:* sailing, skiing, walking, gardening, playing violin, piano, clarinet. *Address:* University of Limerick, Limerick (office); Oakhampton House, Newport, Co. Tipperary, Ireland (home). *Telephone:* (61) 213198 (office). *Fax:* (61) 213197 (office). *E-mail:* oakhampton@gmail.com (office). *Website:* www.edwalsh.ie.

WALSH, Katie; American government official; *White House Deputy Chief of Staff for Implementation;* b. 1986, St Louis, MO; ed George Washington Univ.; high school intern for re-election campaign of Missouri Senator John Ashcroft 2000; field rep. for Matt Blunt's campaign for Gov. of Missouri 2004; Asst to Finance Dir for presidential campaign of Tennessee Senator Fred Thomson 2007–08; Regional Finance Dir for John McCain presidential campaign April–Nov. 2008; Deputy Finance Dir, Nat. Republican Senatorial Cttee 2009–12; Deputy Finance Dir, Republican Nat. Cttee (RNC) Jan.–May 2013, Finance Dir June 2013–16, Chief of Staff to Reince Priebus (RNC Chair.) 2016; White House Deputy Chief of Staff for Implementation 2017–. *Address:* The White House Office, 1600 Pennsylvania Avenue, NW, Washington, DC 20500, USA (office). *Telephone:* (202) 456-1414 (office). *Fax:* (202) 456-2461 (office). *E-mail:* vice_president@whitehouse.gov (office). *Website:* www.whitehouse.gov (office).

WALSH, Patrick Craig, AB, MD; American urologist and academic; *University Distinguished Service Professor of Urology, Johns Hopkins University School of Medicine;* b. 13 Feb. 1938, Akron, Ohio; s. of Raymond Walsh and Catherine Walsh; m. Margaret Louise Campbell 1964; three s.; ed Case Western Reserve Univ. School of Medicine; internship, Peter Bent Brigham Hosp., Boston, Mass 1964–65, Jr Asst Resident in Surgery 1965–66; Asst Resident in Pediatric Surgery, The Children's Hosp. Medical Center, Boston 1966–67; Resident in Urology, UCLA, Calif. 1967–71, Fellow in Endocrinology, UCLA School of Medicine, Harbor Gen. Hosp. Campus 1968–70; tour of mil. service as Urologist at US Naval Hosp., San Diego 1971–73; Asst Clinical Prof. of Surgery/Urology, Univ. of California, San Diego 1971–73; Visiting Asst Prof. of Medicine, Div. of Metabolism, Univ. of Texas Southwestern Medical School, Dallas 1973–74; David Hall McConnell Prof. and Dir Dept of Urology, Johns Hopkins Univ. School of Medicine, Baltimore, Md 1974,

Urologist-in-Chief, The James Buchanan Brady Urological Inst. 1974–2004, Univ. Distinguished Service Prof. of Urology 2004–, fmr Vice-Chair. Exec. Cttee for Medical Institutional Campaign Fund for Johns Hopkins Univ., served on Professional Promotions Cttee, Research Space Planning Cttee, Finance Cttee of Advisory Bd; serves as consultant to US Naval Hosp., Walter Reed Hosp., Clinical Center of NIH, Advisory Bd of Nat. Inst. of Diabetes, Digestive and Kidney Diseases, as well as several local hosps; Trustee, American Bd of Urology; Ed.-in-Chief Campbell's Textbook of Urology 1980–2005 (renamed Cambell Walsh in his honour); mem. Editorial Bd Journal of Urology, New England Journal of Medicine; mem. 14 professional socs, including Inst. of Medicine of NAS, Soc. of Univ. Surgeons, Clinical Soc. of Genitourinary Surgeons (fmr Pres.), American Asscn of Genito-Urinary Surgeons (fmr Pres.), Endocrine Soc., Peripatetic Club; Fellow, American Coll. of Surgeons 1976–80; Paul Harris Fellow, Int. Rotary Foundation 1999; Hon. mem. Urological Soc. of Australasia, German Soc. of Urology, British Asscn of Urologic Surgeons 1998, Royal Coll. of Surgeons of Ireland 2003, Royal Coll. of Surgeons of England 2004, American Urological Asscn 2007; Hon. Dr of Medical Sciences (Masaryk Univ., Brno, Czech Repub.) 2007; prizes for lab. research, American Urological Asscn 1970, 1974, Gold Cystoscope Award, American Urological Asscn 1978, Eugene Fuller Award, American Urological Asscn 1978, Grand Prize, William R. Smart Film Award, American Urological Asscn 1985 and Golden Eagle Award, Council on Nontheatrical Events 1985 for two teaching films, Charles F. Kettering Medal, Gen. Motors Cancer Research Foundation 1996, Robert V. Day Lecturer, Bruce Stewart Lecturer, Southern Lecturer, King Faisal Int. Prize in Medicine, King Faisal Foundation (co-recipient) 2007, Nat. Physician of the Year for Clinical Excellence 2007. *Films:* The Art of Retropubic Prostatectomy 1969, Visits in Urology – Renal Revascularization for Hypertension 1984, Radical Retropubic Prostatectomy and Cystoprostatectomy: Surgical Technique for Preservation of Sexual Function 1985, Radical Cystectomy with Preservation of Sexual Function 'Neuroanatomical Considerations and Surgical Technique' 1987, Radical Retropubic Prostatectomy with Preservation of Sexual Function – An Update after 500 Cases 1987, Radical Retropubic Prostatectomy: Evolution of the Surgical Technique 1993, Radical Prostatectomy, Simultaneous Demonstration by Patrick C. Walsh, M.D. and Fritz H. Schroder, M.D 1993, Alpha Omega Alpha Leaders in American Medicine, Radical Retropubic Prostatectomy: A Detailed Description of the Surgical Technique 2004. *Publications:* Male Infertility (co-ed.) 1977, The Prostate: A Guide for Men and the Women Who Love Them (with Janet F. Worthington) 1995, Campbell's Urology, Seventh Edn (co-ed.) 1997, Dr. Patrick Walsh's Guide to Surviving Prostate Cancer (with Janet F. Worthington) 2001; more than 500 scientific papers in professional journals. *Leisure interests:* sailing, swimming, cycling. *Address:* James Buchanan Brady Urological Institute, Johns Hopkins Medical Institutions, 600 North Wolfe Street, Baltimore, MD 21287, USA (office). *Fax:* (410) 614-3695 (office). *E-mail:* webmaster@urology.jhu.edu (office). *Website:* urology.jhu.edu (office).

WALSH, Paul S.; British business executive; *Chairman, Compass Group;* joined GrandMet's brewing div., Watney Mann and Truman Brewers 1982, Finance Dir 1986, Chief Financial Officer Inter-Continental Hotels 1987, GrandMet's Food Div. 1989, CEO Pillsbury 1992, mem. Bd 1995; mem. Bd Diageo plc (f. after merger of GrandMet and Guinness) 1997, CEO 2000–14; Chair. Compass Group 2014–; Chair. Scottish Whisky Asscn 2008–11; mem. Bd of Dirs (non-exec.) Federal Express Corpn, Unilever plc, Unilever NV, Avanti Communications Group PLC 2012–. *Address:* Compass Group, Parkview, 82 Oxford Road, Uxbridge, UB8 1UX, England (office). *Website:* www.compass-group.co.uk (office).

WALSH, Sam Maurice Cossart, AO, BCom, FAIM; Australian business executive; *Chief Executive, Rio Tinto Group;* b. 27 Dec. 1949, Middle Brighton, Vic.; s. of Maurice John Walsh and Winifred Margaret Lois Cossart; m. Leanne Roki; two s. one d.; ed Brighton Grammar School, Melbourne, Univ. of Melbourne, Kettering Univ., USA (Fellowship Program); spent 20 years in sr positions in automotive industry at General Motors and Nissan Australia; joined Rio Tinto 1991, Vice-Pres. Rio Tinto Iron Ore 2000–01, Chief Exec. Aluminium Group of Rio Tinto Ltd 2001–04, Chief Exec. Rio Tinto Australia –2009, mem. Bd of Dirs Rio Tino Group 2009–, Chief Exec. Iron Ore Group 2009–13, Chief Exec. Rio Tinto Group 2013–; Man. Dir Hamersley Sales and Marketing 1994–97, Hamersley Operations 1997–2000; Dir, North Ltd 1997–2000, Australian Chamber of Commerce and Industry 2003–05, Western Australian Chamber of Commerce and Industry 2005–13; Dir (non-exec.), Seven West Media 2008–13; Chair. WA chapter of Australian Business Arts Foundation 2008; Past Pres. Western Australia Br. of Scouts Australia; Patron State Library of Western Australia, Univ. of Western Australia's Hackett Foundation; Trustee, Royal Opera House Covent Garden Foundation 2014–; Fellow, Australasian Inst. of Mining and Metallurgy, Chartered Inst. of Purchasing and Supply Man., Australian Inst. of Company Dirs; Hon. Dr of Commerce (Edith Cowan Univ.) 2010; Western Australian Citizen of the Year, Industry and Commerce and an Australian Export Hero 2007, Richard Pratt Business Arts Leadership Award, Australia Business Arts Foundation 2011, Gold Medal, Australian Inst. of Company Dirs 2012. *Address:* Rio Tinto plc, 2 Eastbourne Terrace, London, W2 6LG, England (office); Rio Tinto Ltd, 120 Collins Street, Melbourne, Vic. 3000, Australia (office). *Telephone:* (20) 7781-2000 (London) (office); (3) 9283-3333 (Melbourne) (office). *Fax:* (20) 7781-1800 (London) (office); (3) 9283-3707 (Melbourne) (office). *E-mail:* info@riotinto.com (office). *Website:* www.riotinto.com (office).

WALSH, William (Willie), MSc, FRAeS; Irish airline executive; *CEO, International Airlines Group;* b. 1961, Dublin; m.; one d.; ed Trinity Coll., Dublin; Cadet Pilot, Aer Lingus 1979, later Capt., CEO Futura (Aer Lingus Spanish charter operation) 1998–2000, COO Aer Lingus 2000–01, CEO 2001–05, mem. Bd 2001–; mem. Exec. Bd and Chief Exec.-Designate British Airways plc May–Oct. 2005, Chief Exec. Oct. 2005–11, CEO Int. Airlines Group (following merger with Iberia) 2011–; Chair. Bd of Govs, IATA 2016–; mem. Bd of Dirs, Fyffes plc 2004–; Pres. Heathrow Br. of Royal Aeronautical Soc.; mem. Chartered Inst. of Logistics and Transport (UK); Hon. Bd mem. Flight Safety Int.; Hon. mem. The Aviation Club; Aviation Week & Space Technology magazine Laureate for Commercial Aviation 2014. *Leisure interests:* all sports, especially soccer, rugby and motor sports. *Address:* International Airlines Group, Waterside (HAA2), PO Box 365, Harmondsworth, Middx, UB7 0GB, England (office); Company Secretary, IAG Registered Office, Calle Velázquez 130, Madrid 28006, Spain (office). *Telephone:*

(20) 8564-2800 (UK) (office). *E-mail:* media.relations@iairgroup.com (office). *Website:* www.iairgroup.com (office).

WALTER, Andrew, DPhil; Australian academic; ed Univ. of Western Australia, Univ. of Oxford, UK; Tutor in Int. Relations, Univ. of Oxford 1985–86, Lecturer in Int. Relations, Lady Margaret Hall, Oxford 1987–88, Univ. Lecturer in Int. Relations and Fellow, St Anthony's Coll. Oxford 1990–97, European Studies Centre Fellow, Lecturer in Int. Trade and Finance, Univ. of Oxford Foreign Service Programme 1990–97; Assoc., European Mergers and Acquisitions Group, Leveraged Finance Group, JP Morgan, London 1987–90, JP Morgan Finance Program, New York, USA 1989; Sr Lecturer in Int. Relations and Dir MSc Politics of the World Economy Programme, LSE 1997–2012, Reader in Int. Political Economy 2009–12, London Academic Dir TRIUM EMBA Programme; Sr Visiting Fellow, Inst. of Defence and Strategic Studies, Nat. Technological Univ., Singapore 2001–02; other visiting fellowships include Univ. of British Columbia 1994, Int. Univ. of Japan 1994, Pacific Council on Int. Policy and Center for Int. Studies (Univ. of Southern California, Los Angeles) 1996, Univ. of Melbourne Business School 2008; mem. Chatham House Council 2009–. *Publications include:* World Power and World Money; The Role of Hegemony and International Monetary Order (revised edn) 1993; numerous articles on political economy of int. finance and investment and history of thought. *E-mail:* c.easom@lse.ac.uk.

WALTER, Peter, BSc, MSc, PhD; German/American molecular biologist, biochemist, biophysicist and academic; *Professor, Biochemistry and Biophysics Department, University of California, San Francisco;* ed Freie Universitat Berlin, Germany, Vanderbilt Univ. and The Rockefeller Univ., USA; Direct Exchange Fellow, Vanderbilt Univ. 1976–77; Grad. Fellow, The Rockefeller Univ. 1977–81, Postdoctoral Fellow 1981–82, Asst Prof., Lab. of Cell Biology 1982–83; Asst Prof., Biochemistry and Biophysics Dept, Univ. of California, San Francisco 1983–86, Assoc. Prof. 1986–91, Prof. 1991–, Chair. Dept of Biochemistry and Biophysics 2001–09; Investigator, Howard Hughes Medical Inst. 1997–; mem. NAS 2004, Leopoldina Acad. of Scientists 2006; Assoc. mem. European Molecular Biology Org. 2004; Fellow, American Acad. of Microbiology 1998, American Acad. of Arts and Sciences 2001; Searle Scholar Award 1983, Eli Lilly Award for Fundamental Research in Biological Chem. 1988, Passano Award 1988, Alfred P. Sloan Award 1989, NIH MERIT Award 1993, Harvey Lecturer, The Rockefeller Univ. 1996, Feodor-Lynen-Lecturer, Mosbach Kolloquium, Germany 1998, Virchow Lecturer, Universität Würzburg 2004, Wiley Prize in Biomedical Sciences (co-recipient) 2005, George E. Palade Distinguished Lecturer, Wayne State Univ. School of Medicine 2005, 47th Stadtler Lecturer, Univ. of Texas 2006, Gairdner Award (co-recipient) 2009, E.B. Wilson Medal 2009, The Otto Warburg Medal 2011, Paul Ehrlich and Ludwig Darmstaedter Prize 2012, Shaw Prize (co-recipient) 2014, Albert Lasker Basic Medical Research Award (co-recipient) 2014, Breakthrough Prize in Life Sciences 2018. *Publications include:* Molecular Biology of the Cell (co-author); numerous papers in professional journals. *Address:* Walter Lab, UCSF/HHMI MC 2200, Genentech Hall N316, 600 16th Street, San Francisco, CA 94158-2517, USA (office). *Telephone:* (415) 476-5017 (office); (415) 476-4636 (Lab.) (office). *Fax:* (415) 476-5233 (office). *E-mail:* peter@walterlab.ucsf.edu (office); pwalter@biochem.ucsf.edu (office). *Website:* cancer.ucsf.edu (office); walterlab.ucsf.edu (office).

WALTER, Robert D., BA, MBA; American health care industry executive; m. Margaret (Peggy) McGreevey 1967; three s.; ed Ohio Univ., Harvard Business School; Engineer, North American Rockwell 1968; Founder Cardinal Foods Inc., Dublin, Ohio 1971–88 (acquired by Roundy's Inc. 1988); Founder and CEO Cardinal Foods 1971 (renamed Cardinal Distribution Inc. 1979, renamed Cardinal Health Inc. 1994) 1979–2006, Chair. 2006–09 (retd); mem. Bd of Dirs Bank One Corpn, Viacom Inc., Westinghouse Electric; mem. Bd of Trustees Battelle Memorial Inst., Ohio Univ.; fmr mem. Bd of Trustees Ohio Univ. Foundation. *Address:* c/o Cardinal Health Inc., 7000 Cardinal Place, Dublin, OH 43017, USA. *E-mail:* info@cardinal.com.

WALTERS, Barbara, BA; American broadcast journalist and producer; b. 25 Sept. 1929, Brookline, Mass.; d. of Lou Walters and Dena Walters (née Selett); m. 1st Robert Henry Katz (m. annulled); m. 2nd Lee Guber 1963 (divorced 1976); one adopted d.; m. 3rd Merv Adelson 1986 (divorced 1992); ed Sarah Lawrence Coll., Bronxville, NY; fmr writer and producer with WNBC-TV, then with Station WPIX and CBS TV morning broadcasts; Producer, NBC TV; joined Today programme, NBC TV 1961 as a writer, then gen. reporter, regular panel mem. 1963–74, Co-Host 1974–76; moderator, Not for Women Only (syndicated TV programme) for five years; Corresp., ABC News, Co-Anchor of evening news programme 1976–78, Co-Host 20/20 1979–2004; Host Barbara Walters Specials 1976–, Ten Most Fascinating People 1994–; Co.-Exec. Producer and Co-Host The View (ABC), NY 1997–; Hon. LHD (Ohio State Univ., Marymount Coll., New York Temple Univ., Wheaton Coll., Hofstra Univ.); Broadcaster of the Year, Int. Radio and TV Soc. 1975, Emmy Award of Nat. Acad. of TV Arts and Sciences 1975, 1983, Silver Satellite Award, American Women in Radio and TV 1985, Pres.'s Award, Overseas Press Club 1988, Lowell Thomas Award for Journalism 1990, 1994, Lifetime Achievement Award, Int. Women's Media Foundation 1992, Lifetime Achievement Award, Daytime Emmy Awards 2000, and several other awards. *Publications:* How to Talk with Practically Anybody about Practically Anything 1970, Audition: A Memoir 2008; contribs to Good Housekeeping, Family Weekly, Reader's Digest, and other periodicals. *Address:* Barwall Productions, 320 West 66th Street, New York, NY 10023 (office); c/o 20/20, 147 Columbus Avenue, 10th Floor, New York, NY 10023, USA. *Website:* abc.go.com/daytime/theview.

WALTERS, Carl John, BSc, MSc, PhD, FRSC; American marine biologist and academic; *Professor Emeritus, Institute for the Oceans and Fisheries and Department of Zoology, University of British Columbia;* b. 14 Sept. 1944, Albuquerque, New Mexico; s. of Carl H. Walters and Eleanor Jonathan; m. Sandra Buckingham; two s.; ed Humboldt State Univ., Colorado State Univ.; Prof., Fisheries Centre, Univ. of British Columbia 1969, now Prof. Emer., Inst. for the Oceans and Fisheries and Dept of Zoology; mem. several NSERC grant cttees 1970–; has done extensive fisheries advisory work for public agencies and industrial groups; has conducted numerous workshops for Int. Canadian Fisheries Service, US Fish and Wildlife Service and Int. Inst. for Applied Systems Analysis 1997–2007; Grand Canyon Sr Scientist 2008–; Ed. Open Fish Science Journal; mem. Editorial Bd Coastal and Estuarine Fisheries, Canadian Journal of Fisheries and Aquatic Sciences; keynote speaker, American Fisheries Soc. 1992, Award of Excellence, American Fisheries Soc. 2006, Volvo Environment Prize, Volvo Environment Foundation (co-recipient) 2006, Timothy Parsons Medal for Oceanography 2007, American Inst. of Fisheries Research Biologists Award for Outstanding Individual Achievement 2011. *Publications include:* numerous scientific papers in professional journals on fish population dynamics, fisheries assessment and sustainable man. *Address:* Institute for the Oceans and Fisheries, Faculty of Science, Vancouver Campus, Fisheries Centre, University of British Columbia, 2202 Main Mall, Vancouver, BC V6T 1Z4, Canada (office). *Telephone:* (604) 822-6320 (office). *Fax:* (604) 822-2416 (office). *E-mail:* c.walters@oceans.ubc.ca (office). *Website:* www.oceans.ubc.ca/quantitative-modeling-group (office).

WALTERS, John P., BA, MA; American fmr government official; *Chief Operating Officer, Hudson Institute;* ed Michigan State Univ., Univ. of Toronto, Canada; fmr Lecturer, Michigan State Univ. and Boston Coll.; Acting Asst Dir and Program Officer, Educ. Programs Div., Nat. Endowment for the Humanities 1982–85; Asst to US Sec. of Educ., Dept of Educ., Washington, DC 1985–88; Chief of Staff, White House Office of Nat. Drug Control Policy (ONDCP) 1989–91, Deputy Dir Supply Reduction 1991–93, Dir ONDCP 2001–09; Visiting Fellow, Hudson Inst. 1993, COO and Exec. Vice-Pres. 2009–; Pres. New Citizenship Project –1996; Pres. Philanthropy Round Table 1996–2001. *Publications include:* Body Count: Moral Poverty and How to Win America's War Against Crime and Drugs (with William J. Bennett and John J. Di Iulio Jr). *Address:* Hudson Institute, Washington, 1015 15th Street, NW, 6th Floor, Washington, DC 20005, USA (office). *Telephone:* (202) 974-2400 (office). *Fax:* (202) 974-2410 (office). *E-mail:* info@hudson.org (office). *Website:* www.hudson.org (office).

WALTERS, Julie, DBE, CBE; British actress; b. (Julia Mary Walters), 22 Feb. 1950, Birmingham, England; d. of Thomas Walters and Mary Bridget O'Brien; m. Grant Roffey 1998; one d.; ed St Pauls Prep. School, Edgbaston, Holly Lodge Grammar School for Girls, Smethwick, Manchester Polytechnic; Variety Club Best Newcomer Award 1980, Best Actress Award 1984, British Acad. Award for Best Actress 1984, Golden Globe Award 1984, Show Business Personality of the Year Variety Club Award 2001, Richard Harris Award for Outstanding Contrib. by an Actor 2013, BAFTA Fellowship 2014. *Stage appearances include:* Educating Rita 1980, Fool for Love 1984–85, When I was a Girl I used to Scream and Shout 1986–87, Frankie and Johnny in the Clair de Lune 1989, The Rose Tattoo 1991, All My Sons (Olivier Award 2001) 2000, Acorn Antiques 2005, The Last of the Haussmans 2012. *Films include:* Educating Rita 1983, She'll be Wearing Pink Pyjamas 1984, Personal Services 1986, Prick Up Your Ears 1986, Buster 1987, Mack the Knife 1988, Killing Dad 1989, Stepping Out (Variety Club Award for Best Actress 1991) 1991, Just Like a Woman 1992, Sister My Sister 1994, Intimate Relations 1996, Titanic Town 1997, Girls Night 1997, All Forgotten 1999, Dancer 1999, Billy Elliot (Evening Standard Award, BAFTA Award) 2000, Harry Potter and the Philosopher's Stone 2001, Before You Go 2002, Harry Potter and the Chamber of Secrets 2002, Calendar Girls 2003, Harry Potter and the Prisoner of Azkaban 2004, Mickybo and Me 2005, Wah-Wah 2005, Driving Lessons 2006, Becoming Jane 2007, Harry Potter and the Order of the Phoenix 2007, Mamma Mia! 2008, Harry Potter and the Half-Blood Prince 2009, Harry Potter and the Deathly Hallows, Part I 2010, Gnomeo and Juliet 2010, Harry Potter and the Deathly Hallows, Part II 2011, Brave (voice) 2012, One Chance 2013, Justin and the Knights of Valour (voice) 2013, The Harry Hill Movie 2013, Effie Gray 2014, Paddington 2014, Brooklyn 2015, Paddington 2 2017, Mary Poppins Returns 2018, Mary Poppins Returns (voice) 2019. *Television includes:* Talent 1980, Wood and Walters (with Victoria Wood) 1981–82, Boys from the Blackstuff 1982, Say Something Happened 1982, As Seen On TV 1984, 1986, 1987, The Birthday Party 1986, Her Big Chance 1987, GBH 1991, Stepping Out 1991, Julie Walters and Friends 1991, Clothes in the Wardrobe 1992, Wide Eyed and Legless 1993, Bambino Mio 1993, Pat and Margaret 1994, Jake's Progress 1995, Little Red Riding Hood 1995, Intimate Relations 1996, Julie Walters is an Alien 1997, Dinnerladies 1998–99, Jack and the Beanstalk 1998, Oliver Twist 1999, My Beautiful Son (BAFTA Award) 2001, Murder (BAFTA and Royal TV Soc. Awards for Best Actress 2003) 2002, The Canterbury Tales (mini-series, The Wife of Bath) 2003, The Return 2003, Ahead of the Class 2005, The Ruby in the Smoke 2006, Filth! The Mary Whitehouse Story 2007, A Short Stay in Switzerland 2009, Victoria Wood's Midlife Christmas 2009, Mo (BAFTA Award for Best Actress, Int. Emmy Award for Best Actress 2011) 2010, The Jury 2011, The Hollow Crown (mini-series) 2012, Indian Summers (mini-series) 2015–16, National Treasure 2016. *Publications include:* Baby Talk 1990, Maggie's Tree (novel) 2006, That's Another Story (autobiography) 2008. *Leisure interests:* reading, travel. *Address:* c/o Independent Talent Group, 76 Oxford Street, London, W1D 1BS, England (office). *Telephone:* (20) 7636-6565 (office).

WALTERS, Sir Peter Ingram, Kt, BCom; British business executive; b. 11 March 1931, Birmingham, England; s. of Stephen Walters and Edna F. Walters (née Redgate); m. 1st Patricia Anne Tulloch 1960 (divorced 1991); two s. one. d.; m. 2nd Meryl Marshall 1992; ed King Edward's School, Birmingham and Univ. of Birmingham; served in Royal Army Service Corps 1952–54; joined BP 1954, Vice-Pres. BP North America 1965–67, Gen. Man. Supply and Devt 1969–70, Regional Dir Western Hemisphere 1971–72; Dir BP Trading Ltd 1971–73, BP Chemicals Int. 1972, Chair. 1978–90; Deputy Chair. British Petroleum Co. Ltd 1980–81, Chair. 1981–90; Vice-Pres. Gen. Council of British Shipping 1974–76, Pres. 1977–78; Pres. Soc. of Chemical Industry 1978–79, Inst. of Manpower Studies 1980–86; Dir Post Office 1978–79, Nat. Westminster Bank 1981– (Deputy Chair. 1988–89); Dir Thorn EMI (now EMI) 1989, Deputy Chair. 1990–99; Dir SmithKline Beecham PLC 1989–2000, apptd Deputy Chair. GlaxoSmithKline PLC 2000, Deputy Chair. 1990–94, Chair. 1994–2000; Chair. Blue Circle Industries Ltd 1990–96, Midland Bank PLC 1992; Deputy Chair. HSBC Holdings 1992–2001; Adviser Union Bank of Switzerland 1990–92; Dir (non-exec.) Nomura Int. plc, Saatchi and Saatchi 1993–2000; Pres. Police Foundation; Pres. Advisory Council, Inst. of Business Ethics 2004–08; Chair. Advisory Bd TNK Int. 2002–06; mem. of Council, Industrial Soc.; Gov. London Business School 1981–91; Pres. Inst. of Dirs 1986–92; Trustee, mem. Foundation Bd, Nat. Maritime Museum 1982–89; Chair. Int. Man. Inst., Geneva 1984–86; Trustee Inst. of Econ. Affairs; Hon. DUniv (Birmingham) 1986, (Stirling) 1987; Commdr, Order of Léopold (Belgium). *Leisure interests:* golf, gardening, sailing. *Address:* 1 St James's Square, London, SW1Y 4PD, England (office). *Telephone:* (20) 7496-5821 (office). *Fax:* (20) 7496-4436 (office). *E-mail:* sjs1@bp.com.

WALTON, Jim; American broadcasting news executive; b. 1958; m.; two s.; ed Univ. of Maryland; joined Cable News Network (CNN) 1980, various positions including video journalist, tape editor, exec. producer, launched CNN/Sports Illustrated (all-sports TV channel), served as Pres. 1996–2000, Deputy Pres., Pres. CNN Domestic Networks 2001, Pres. and COO 2001–03, Pres. CNN News Group 2003–12; Emmy Award for coverage of 1996 Olympic Park bombing, Atlanta, several Cable Ace awards. *Leisure interests:* Nebraska football, Allman brothers.

WALTON, Samuel Robson (Rob), BA, JD; American retail executive; b. 1944, Tulsa, Okla; s. of Sam Moore Walton (founder of Wal-Mart); m. Carolyn F. Walton (divorced); three c.; ed The Coll. of Wooster, Ohio, Univ. of Arkansas, Columbia Univ., New York; fmrly with Conner, Winters, Ballaine, Barry & McGowen (law firm), Tulsa –1969; joined Wal-Mart Stores Inc. (now called Walmart), Bentonville, Ark. 1969–, mem. Bd of Dirs 1978–, Sr Vice-Pres., Sec. and Gen. Counsel 1978–82, Dir and Vice-Chair. 1982–92, Chair. 1992–2015; currently involved with several non-profit and educational orgs, including Conservation International (Chair. Exec. Cttee); Emer. Life Trustee, Coll. of Wooster. *Address:* Walmart, 702 SW 8th Street, Bentonville, AR 72716-8611, USA (office). *Telephone:* (479) 273-4000 (office). *Fax:* (479) 277-1830 (home). *Website:* www.walmart.com (office); corporate.walmart.com (office).

WALTZ, Christoph; Austrian/German actor; b. 4 Oct. 1956, Vienna, Austria; s. of Johannes Waltz and Elisabeth Urbancic; three adult c. from a prior m.; m. 2nd Judith Holste; one d.; ed Max Reinhardt Seminar, Vienna, Lee Strasberg Theatre and Film Inst., New York, USA; began as a stage actor, performing at venues including Schauspielhaus Zürich, Burgtheater, Vienna and the Salzburg Festival; numerous TV appearances; directorial debut with the German-language TV production, Wenn man sich traut 2000; Österreichisches Ehrenzeichen für Wissenschaft und Kunst (Austria) 2012. *Films include:* Kopfstand 1981, Fire and Sword 1982, Wahnfried 1986, Quicker Than the Eye 1990, Zycie za zycie 1991, St. Petri Schnee 1991, Ein Anfang von etwas 1995, Our God's Brother 1997, Sieben Monde 1998, Das merkwürdige Verhalten geschlechtsreifer Großstädter zur Paarungszeit 1998, Die Braut 1999, Ordinary Decent Criminal 2000, Falling Rocks 2000, She 2001, Queen's Messenger 2001, Death, Deceit & Destiny Aboard the Orient Express 2001, Angst 2003, Gun-shy 2003, Herr Lehmann 2003, Dorian 2004, Lapislazuli – Im Auge des Bären 2006, Inglourious Basterds (Best Actor Award, Cannes Film Festival, BAFTA, Golden Globe, Screen Actors Guild Award and Academy Award for Best Supporting Actor 2009) 2009, The Green Hornet 2011, Water for Elephants 2011, The Three Musketeers 2011, Carnage 2011, Django Unchained 2012, The Zero Theorem 2013, Epic (voice) 2013, Horrible Bosses 2 2014, Big Eyes 2014, Spectre 2015, The Legend of Tarzan 2016, Tulip Fever 2017, Alita: Battle Angel 2019. *Television includes:* Der Einstand (film) 1977, Feuer! (film) 1979, Parole Chicago (series) 1979, Die Weltmaschine (film) 1981, Dr. Margarete Johnsohn (film) 1982, The Mysterious Stranger (film) 1982, Der Sandmann (film) 1983, A Case for Two (series) 1985, Lenz oder die Freiheit (mini-series) 1986, Derrick (series) 1986–88, The Old Fox (series) 1986–90, Das andere Leben (film) 1987, Tatort (series) 1987–2008, The Alien Years (film) 1988, Goldeneye (film) 1989, The Gravy Train (mini-series) 1990, The Gravy Train Goes East (mini-series) 1991, Die Angst wird bleiben (film) 1992, 5 Zimmer, Küche, Bad (film) 1992, König der letzten Tage (mini-series) 1993, Die Staatsanwältin (film) 1994, Tag der Abrechnung – Der Amokläufer von Euskirchen (film) 1994, Jacob (film) 1994, Man(n) sucht Frau (film) 1995, Prinz zu entsorgen (film) 1995, Die Staatsanwältin (series) 1995, The All New Alexei Sayle Show (series) 1995, Catherine the Great (film) 1996, Du bist nicht allein – Die Roy Black Story (film) 1996, Rosa Roth (series) 1996, Rex: A Cop's Best Friend (series) 1996, Der Tourist (film) 1996, Maître Da Costa (series) 1997, Faust (series) 1997, Schimanski (series) 1997, Rache für mein totes Kind (film) 1998, Mörderisches Erbe – Tausch mit einer Toten (film) 1998, Einsteins Ende (film) 1998, Vickys Alptraum (film) 1998, Schock – Eine Frau in Angst (film) 1998, Das Finale (film) 1998, Dessine-moi un jouet (film) 1999 The Beast (film) 2000, Engel sucht Flügel (film) 2001, Riekes Liebe (film) 2001, Der Tanz mit dem Teufel – Die Entführung des Richard Oetker (film) 2001, Dienstreise – Was für eine Nacht (film) 2002, Weihnachtsmann gesucht (film) 2002, Jagd auf den Flammenmann (film) 2003, Der Fall Gehring (film) 2003, Zwei Tage Hoffnung (film) 2003, Jennerwein (film) 2003, Tigeraugen sehen besser (film) 2003, Scheidungsopfer Mann (film) 2004, Mörderische Suche (film) 2004, Schöne Witwen küssen besser (film) 2004, Die Patriarchin (mini-series) 2005, Der Elefant – Mord verjährt nie (series) 2005, Die Spezialisten: Kripo Rhein-Main (series) 2006, Polizeiruf 110 (series) 2006, Stolberg (series) 2006, Franziskas Gespür für Männer (film) 2006, Der Staatsanwalt (series) 2007, Die Verzauberung (film) 2007, Der letzte Zeuge (series) 2007, Under Suspicion (series) 2007, Die Zürcher Verlobung – Drehbuch zur Liebe (film) 2007, Die Anwälte (series) 2008, Das jüngste Gericht (film) 2008, Todsünde (film) 2008, Das Geheimnis im Wald (film) 2008. *Address:* c/o Players Agentur Management GmbH, Sophienstrasse 21, 10178 Berlin - Mitte, Germany (office); c/o ICM, 730 Fifth Avenue, New York, NY 10019-4105, USA. *E-mail:* info@players.de (office). *Website:* www.players.de (office).

WALZ, Timothy (Tim) James, BS, MS; American politician; *Governor of Minnesota;* b. 6 April 1964, West Point, Neb.; s. of James 'Jim' F. Walz and Darlene R. Walz; m. Gwen Walz 1994; two c.; ed Chadron State Coll., Minnesota State Univ., Mankato; Command Sergeant Maj., Army Nat. Guard 1981–2005; teacher, World Teach 1989–90, Alliance Public Schools 1991–96, Mankato West High School 1996–2006; founder Educational Travel Adventures, Inc.; mem. US House of Reps 2007–19; Gov. of Minn. 2019–; mem. Chamber of Commerce, Rochester Area 2006, Nat. Org. for Women, Nat. Educ. Asscn, Nat. Guard and Reserve Caucus, Congressional-Exec. Comm. on China, House Agriculture Cttee; life mem., Enlisted Asscn of the Nat. Guard; ranking mem., Veterans' Affairs Cttee; Fellow of Int. Relations, Macau Polytechnic Inst.; Nebraska Citizen Soldier of the Year 1989, Outstanding Young Nebraskan, Nebraska Jr Chamber of Commerce 1993, Minn. Ethics in Educ. Award 2002, Congressional Silver Helmet Award 2010, Charles Dick Medal of Merit 2014, Friend of Farm Bureau Award 2014, Golden Triangle Award 2017, L. Mendel Rivers Award 2017, Nat. Leadership Award, Nat. Environmental Achievement for Federal Public Service Award, Nat. Asscn of Clean Water Agencies, Bronze Star and Army Commendation Medal,

Achievement Medal, Reserve Components Achievement Medal, Global War on Terrorism Service Medal. *Address:* Office of the Governor, 130 State Capitol, 75 Rev Dr. Martin Luther King Jr. Bvd, St. Paul, MN 55155, USA (office). *Telephone:* (651) 201-3400 (office). *Fax:* (651) 797-1850 (office). *Website:* www.mn.gov/governor (office).

WALZER, Michael, BA, PhD; American writer, academic and editor; *Professor Emeritus, School of Social Science, Institute for Advanced Study;* b. 3 March 1935, New York, NY; m. Judith Borodovko 1956; two d.; ed Brandeis and Harvard Univs; Asst Prof. of Politics, Princeton Univ. 1962–66; Assoc. Prof., Harvard Univ. 1966–68, Prof. of Govt 1968–80; Ed. Dissent 1964–2014; Prof. of Social Science, School of Social Science, Inst. for Advanced Study, Princeton, NJ 1980–2005, Prof. Emer. 2005–; Fellow, Straus Inst. for the Advanced Study of Law and Justice, New York Univ. School of Law 2010–11; mem. Conf. on the Study of Political Thought, Soc. of Ethical and Legal Philosophy; mem. Editorial Bd Political Theory; mem. Bd of Govs, Hebrew Univ.; Fulbright Fellow, Univ. of Cambridge 1956–57; Dr hc (Lawrence Univ.) 1980, (Brandeis Univ.) 1981, (Georgetown Univ.) 1992, (Kalamazoo Coll.) 1994, (Tel-Aviv Univ.) 2003, (Athens) 2007, (Hebrew Univ.) 2012, Brandeis Univ. Doctorate Alumni Award 2001; Harbison Award 1971, Spinoza Lens 2008. *Publications include:* The Revolution of the Saints: A Study in the Origins of Radical Politics 1965, The Political Imagination in Literature (co-ed. with Philip Green) 1968, Obligations: Essays on Disobedience, War and Citizenship 1970, Political Action: A Practical Guide to Movement Politics 1971, Regicide and Revolution: Speeches at the Trial of Louis XVI (ed.) 1974, Just and Unjust Wars: A Moral Argument with Historical Illustrations 1977, Radical Principles: Reflections of an Unreconstructed Democrat 1977, Spheres of Justice: A Defense of Pluralism and Equality 1983, Exodus and Revolution 1985, Interpretation and Social Criticism 1987, The Company of Critics: Social Criticism and Political Commitment in the Twentieth Century 1988, Civil Society and American Democracy (selected essays in German) 1992, What it Means to be an American 1992, Thick and Thin: Moral Argument at Home and Abroad 1994, Pluralism, Justice and Equality (with David Miller) 1995, Toward a Global Civil Society (ed.) 1995, On Toleration 1997, Arguments from the Left (selected essays in Swedish) 1997, Pluralism and Democracy (selected essays in French) 1997, Reason, Politics and Passion (The Horkheimer Lectures, in German) 1999, The Jewish Political Tradition, Vol. 1 Authority (co-ed with Menachem Lorberbaum, Noam Zohar and Yair Lorberbaum) 2000, Exilic Politics in the Hebrew Bible 2001, War, Politics, and Morality (selected essays in Spanish) 2001, The Thread of Politics: Democracy, Social Criticism, and World Government (selected essays in Italian) 2002, Erklärte Kriege—Kriegserklärungen (selected essays in German) 2003, Arguing About War (selected essays and articles) 2004, Politics and Passion 2004, Law, Politics, and Morality in Judaism 2006, Thinking Politically 2007, In God's Shadow: Politics in the Hebrew Bible 2012, The Paradox of Liberation: Secular Revolutions and Religious Counterrevolutions 2015, A Foreign Policy for the Left 2018; contribs to professional journals. *Address:* School of Social Science, Institute for Advanced Study, Einstein Drive, Princeton, NJ 08540, USA (office). *Telephone:* (609) 734-8253 (office). *Fax:* (609) 951-4457 (office). *E-mail:* walzer@ias.edu (office). *Website:* www.sss.ias.edu (office).

WAMALA, HE Cardinal Emmanuel, DipEd; Ugandan ecclesiastic; *Archbishop Emeritus of Kampala;* b. 15 Dec. 1926, Kamaggwa; s. of Cosma Kyamcra and Theresa Nnamayanja; ed Minor Seminary, Bukalasa, Major Seminary, Katigondo, Pontifical Urban Univ. and Pontifical Gregorian Univ., Rome, Italy, Makerere Univ., Kampala, Univ. of Notre Dame, South Bend, Ind., USA; ordained priest 1957; worked at parish of Villa Maria, acted as Diocesan School Supervisor in Diocese of Masaka 1960–62; mem. Faculty, Minor Seminary of Bukalasa 1964–68; Chaplain, Faculty mem. and Rector Univ. of Makerere 1968–74; Vicar Gen., Diocese of Masaka 1974–81; Parish Priest of Nkoni 1975–77, of Kimaanya 1977–79; Chaplain of His Holiness Pope Paul VI 1977; Bishop of Kiyinda-Mityana 1981; attended Sixth Ordinary Ass. of World Synod of Bishops, Vatican City 1983; Coadjutor Archbishop of Kampala 1988–90, Archbishop of Kampala 1990–2006, Archbishop Emer. 2006–; Pres. Episcopal Conf. of Uganda 1990–94; First Rector Nuova Uganda Martyrs Univ. 1993–; attended Special Ass. of World Synod of Bishops for Africa, Vatican City 1994; cr. Cardinal (Cardinal Priest of Sant'Ugo) 1994; Pres. Uganda Joint Christian 1990–. *Publication:* The Family of Cardinal Wamala (co-author) 2013. *Address:* Archdiocese of Kampala, PO Box 14125, Mengo-Kampala, Uganda (office). *Telephone:* (41) 270183-4 (office), (41) 342622 (office). *Fax:* (41) 345441 (office).

WAMBACH, Abby; American fmr professional football player and coach; b. 2 June 1980, Rochester, NY; d. of Pete Wambach and Judy Wambach; m. 1st Sarah Huffman 2013 (divorced 2016); m. 2nd Glennon Doyle Melton 2017; ed Our Lady of Mercy High School, Rochester, Univ. of Florida, Gainesville; played as a forward; youth career: Our Lady of Mercy High School 1994–98, Rochester Spirit (Capt.) 1995–97, Univ. of Florida 1998–2001; senior career: Washington Freedom 2002–03, 2009–10, USA 2003–, magicJack (also Coach) 2011; began playing football aged four; at high school, scored 142 goals, including 34 in 1997; mem. Olympic Devt Team (ODP) U-16 Nat. Team 1996, Nat. U-20 Pool 1997; trained and played with US Nat. Team while competing in US Soccer Festival, Blaine, Minn. 1997; travelled to Beijing, China as a mem. of the first American youth football team to compete there 1997; played for coach Becky Burleigh's Florida Gators women's football team in Nat. Collegiate Athletic Asscn (NCAA) competition 1998–2001, won an NCAA nat. championship 1998, four consecutive Southeastern Conf. (SEC) championships 1998, 1999, 2000, 2001, set school career records for goals (96), assists (49), points (242), game-winning goals (24) and hat tricks (10); second overall draft pick for the Women's United Soccer Asscn (WUSA)'s second season; went on to play for the Washington Freedom 2002, won Founders Cup III (WUSA championship match) 2003; returned to the Washington Freedom for the 2010 WPS season (team relocated to Boca Raton, Fla and became magicJack 2011); named to US World Cup team 2003 (bronze medal), 2007 (bronze medal), 2011 (silver medal); gold medal, Olympic Games, Athens 2004, London 2012; won FIFA Women's World Cup 2015; retd 2015; co-founder Wolfpack Endeavor; mem. Bd of Advisors Oath 2018; named to Parade magazine's high school All-America team and voted Nat. Player of the Year by Umbro and the Nat. Soccer Coaches Asscn of America (NSCAA), named All-Greater Rochester Player of the Year 1995, 1997, named NSCAA Regional Player of the Year 1997, NSCAA State of New York Player of the Year 1997, Gatorade Circle of Champions New York Player of the

Year 1997, SEC Freshman of the Year 1998, a freshman All-American 1998, a first-team All-SEC selection 1998, 1999, 2000, 2001, two-time SEC Player of the Year 2000, 2001, SEC Tournament Most Valuable Player 2000, 2001, named a first-team All-American for her sophomore, junior and senior seasons 1999, 2000, 2001, WPS Rookie of the Year 2002, US Soccer Athlete of the Year Award 2003, 2004, 2007, 2010, 2011, Associated Press Female Athlete of the Year 2011, ESPN's ESPY Award for Best Play of the Year 2011, FIFA Women's World Cup Silver Ball 2011, FIFA Women's World Cup Bronze Boot 2011, inducted into Univ. of Florida Athletic Hall of Fame 2012, FIFA World Player of the Year 2012, FIFA Women's World Player of the Year 2013, Excellence in Sports Performance Yearly Award for Icon Award 2016. *Publication:* Forward: A Memoir 2016. *E-mail:* contact@abbywambach.com. *Website:* www.abbywambach.com.

WAMBAUGH, Joseph, MA; American author and screenwriter; b. 22 Jan. 1937, East Pittsburgh, Pa; s. of Joseph A. Wambaugh and Anne Malloy; m. Dee Allsup 1955; two s. (one deceased) one d.; ed California State Univ., Los Angeles; served in US Marine Corps 1954–57; police officer in Los Angeles 1960–74; Rodolfo Walsh Prize, Int. Asscn of Crime Writers 1989, Grand Master Award, Mystery Writers of America 2004, Lifetime Achievement Award, Strand Magazine 2012. *Publications include:* The New Centurions 1971, The Blue Knight 1972, The Onion Field (Mystery Writers of America Edgar Allan Poe Award 1974) 1973, The Choirboys 1975, The Black Marble 1978, The Glitter Dome 1981, The Delta Star 1983, Lines and Shadows 1984, The Secrets of Harry Bright 1985, Echoes in the Darkness 1987, The Blooding 1989, The Golden Orange 1990, Fugitive Nights 1992, Finnegan's Week 1993, Floaters 1996, Fire Lover: A True Story 2002, Hollywood Station 2007, Hollywood Crows 2008, Hollywood Moon 2009, Hollywood Hills 2010, Harbor Nocturne 2012. *E-mail:* copbooks@cox.net. *Website:* www.josephwambaugh.net.

WAMMEN, Nicolai, MSc; Danish politician; b. 7 Feb. 1971; s. of Christian Frederik Wammen and Lotte Wammen; one s.; ed Univ. of Aarhus; Pres. Frit Forum Aarhus (social democrat student org.) 1996–97; mem. Aarhus City Council 1998–2006; mem. Folketing (Parl.) (Social Democratic Party) 2001–05; Mayor of Aarhus 2006–11; Minister for European Affairs 2011–13, Minister of Defence 2013–15; mem. Bd Aarhus Festival 1997–2001 (fmr Chair.); fmr Chair. Port of Aarhus; mem. Bd Danish Ports; mem. Growth Forum Central Jutland.

WAMYTAN, Roch, MA; New Caledonian politician; b. 13 Dec. 1950, Nouméa; s. of Benjamin Wamytan and Philomène Pidjot; three s. one d.; ed Grand Séminaire St Paul, Nouméa, Univ. of Lyon II and Centre d'Etudes Financières Economiques et Bancaires, Paris; fmr Head of Office for the Devt of the Interior and Islands; Attaché to Econ. Devt Sec. 1988; mem. Union Calédonienne, Pres. 1999–2001; Minister of Govt of New Caledonia, responsible for Customary Affairs 1999–2001, 2002–04; High Chief, St Louis tribal village 1987–; mem. Mt Dore Town Council, Advisory Customary Council, Djubea-Kapone region; mem. Southern Prov. Govt; mem. Congress of New Caledonia, Deputy Speaker responsible for external relations 1989, Pres. 2011–12, 2013–14; Senator for Ajie Aro Customary Area 2005–10; Pres. Council of Ajie Aro Customary Area 2002–05, Customary Senate 2009–10; Vice-Pres. Kanak Socialist Nat. Liberation Front (FLNKS) 1990–95, Pres. 1995–2001, Pres. FLNKS group, Congress of New Caledonia 1989–95, 2009–11; Pres. New Caledonian Diocese Pastoral Council 1996; Chair. Melanesian Spearhead Group 2001–03. *Address:* BP 288, Mont-Dore, 98810 New Caledonia. *Telephone:* 26-58-83; 27-31-29. *Fax:* 26-58-88; 27-32-04.

WAN, Feng, MBA, DEcon; Chinese insurance executive; *Chairman and CEO, New China Life Insurance Company Limited;* b. 1958; ed Open Univ. of Hong Kong, Nankai Univ.; Dir and Sr Vice-Pres. Tai Ping Life Insurance Co., Hong Kong –1977; fmr Deputy Chief, Life Insurance Div., People's Insurance Co. of China, Jilin br., becoming Gen. Man. Shenzhen br., People's Insurance Co. of China Life 1997–99; fmr Asst Pres. China Life Insurance Co. Ltd Hong Kong br., Vice-Pres. and Gen. Man. Shenzhen br. 1999, Dir China Life-CMG 1999, Vice-Pres. China Life Insurance Co. Ltd 2003–07, Exec. Dir 2006–14, Acting Pres. Jan.–Oct. 2007, Pres. Oct. 2007–14, Vice-Pres. China Life Insurance (Group) Co. 2007–14, also Dir China Life Property and Casualty Insurance Co. Ltd 2006–, China Life Insurance Asset Man. Co. Ltd 2006–14, China Life Pension Insurance Co. Ltd 2007–14; Pres. and COO New China Life Insurance Co. Ltd 2014–16, Chair. and CEO 2016–. *Address:* New China Life Insurance Co. Ltd, New China Insurance Tower, Beijing, 100022, People's Republic of China (office). *Telephone:* (10) 85210000 (office). *Fax:* (10) 85210101 (office). *E-mail:* info@newchinalife.com.cn (office). *Website:* www.newchinalife.com (office).

WAN, Gang, MEng, PhD; Chinese mechanical engineer, academic and politician; *Chairman, China Zhi Gong Party;* b. 1 Aug. 1952, Shanghai; ed Northeast Forestry Univ., Tongji Univ.; Teacher, Dept of Physics, Northeast Forestry Univ. 1978–79; mem. Faculty, Dept of Mechanics, Tongji Univ. 1981–85, Dean, New Energy Automobile Eng Centre April–Aug. 2001, Asst Pres. Tongji Univ. 2001–03, Vice-Pres. 2003–04, Pres. 2004–07; Eng, Tech. Devt Dept, Audi Corpn, Germany 1991–2001; Visiting Prof., Dept of Mechanical Eng, Clausthal Univ. of Tech., Germany 1994, 1995; Vice-Chair. China Zhi Gong Party Dec. 2006–April 2007, Chair. 2007–; Minister of Science and Tech. 2007–18; mem. Nat. Cttee and Standing Cttee 10th CPPCC 2003, Vice-Chair. 11th CPPCC Nat. Cttee 2008–13, 12th CPPCC Nat. Cttee 2013–18. *Address:* China Zhi Gong Dang, 11 Dongbinghe Lu, Deshengmen, Xicheng Qu, Beijing, People's Republic of China (office). *Telephone:* (10) 51550800 (office). *Fax:* (10) 51550900 (office). *E-mail:* czgpwz@zg.org.cn (office). *Website:* www.zg.org.cn (office).

WAN, Lee, BFA; South Korean artist and sculptor; b. 1979, Seoul; ed Dongguk Univ.; Artist-in-residence, Nat. Art Studio, Changdong 2010; Solomon Artist Residence & Gallery, Seoul 2011; Space Can Residence, Seoul 2012; Joong-Ang Fine Arts Prize 2005, Art Spectrum Award, Leeum, Samsung Museum of Art 2014. *Solo exhibitions include:* Gallery Ssamzie, Seoul 2005, Miro Space, Seoul 2008, Total Museum, Seoul 2009, Artspace Hue, Seoul 2010, Artspace Pool, Seoul 2011, AR Festival, Paju 2012, Daegu Art Museum, Daegu 2013. *Group exhibitions include:* Seoul Arts Center, Seoul 2005, 2011, Seoul Foundation for Arts & Culture, Seoul 2006, Gallery M, Daegu 2006, Gallery SUN Contemporary, Seoul 2006, Shin Han Museum, Seoul 2006, Insa Art Center, Seoul 2006, Gallery Curiosity, Seoul 2007, Duplex Gallery, Seoul 2007, Clayarch Gimhae Museum, Gimhae 2008, Doosan Gallery, Seoul 2008, 2012, Nat. Museum of Contemporary Art, Gwacheon

2008, 2010, Seoul Museum of Art 2009, Samsung D'light Gallery, Seoul 2009, Sangsang Madang, Seoul 2010 Ryu Hwarang, Seoul 2010, Green and Brown, Seoul 2010, Ilmin Museum, Seoul 2012, Sungkok Art Museum, Seoul 2012, Nam June Paik Art Center, Yongin-si 2013, La Biennale di Venezia 2017. *Telephone:* 82 10 91492365 (office). *E-mail:* ewan-21@hanmail.net (office). *Website:* www.leewanstudio.com.

WAN, Zhexian; Chinese mathematician and academic; b. Nov. 1927, Shandong Prov.; s. of Wan Cheggui and Zhou Weijin; m. Wang Shixiau; two d.; ed Qinghua Univ.; Prof. of Math., Division of Pure Math. and Applied Math., Inst. of Systems Science (now Chinese Acad. of Math. and System Sciences) 1978–; Chair. Academic Cttee, Center for Combinatorics; Ed.-in-Chief Algebra Colloquium (journal); Ed. Annals of Combinatorics, Finite Fields and Their Applications, Journal of Combinatorics, Information and Systems Science; mem. Chinese Acad. of Sciences 1991; Distinguished Scientific Work Award (jtly with L.K. Hua), All China Science and Tech. Congress 1978, Nat. Science Prize of the Third Degree (jtly) 1986, Chinese Acad. Science and Tech. Progress Prize of the First Degree 1987, Hua Lookeng Award for Math. 1995, Guanghua Foundation Prize of the First Degree 1995, Chinese Acad. Natural Science Price of the First Degree 1997. *Publications:* Classical Groups 1963, Geometry of Classical Groups over Finite Fields 1993, Geometry of Matrices 1996; published more than 140 research papers, 20 popular papers, and 22 books. *Address:* Academy of Mathematics and System Science, 55 East Road, Haidian District, Beijing 100190, People's Republic of China (office). *Telephone:* (10) 82541777 (office); (10) 62559148 (home). *Fax:* (10) 82541972 (office). *E-mail:* wan@amss.ac.cn (office). *Website:* www.amss.ac.cn (office).

WANAMAKER, Zoë, CBE; British/American actress; b. New York, USA; d. of Sam Wanamaker and Charlotte Wanamaker; m. Gawn Grainger 1994; one step-s. one step-d.; ed Cen. School of Speech and Drama, London; professional debut as Hermia in A Midsummer Night's Dream, Manchester 1970; repertory at Royal Lyceum 1971–72, Oxford Playhouse 1974–75, Nottingham 1975–76; Assoc., Royal Nat. Theatre; Patron Prisoners of Conscience; Vice-Patron The Actors Centre; Hon. Pres. Shakespeare's Globe Theatre; Hon. Vice-Pres. Dignity in Dying; Hon. DLitt (South Bank Univ.) 1993; Dr hc (Richmond American Int. Univ. of London); Soc. of West End Theatres (SWET) Award (Once in a Lifetime) 1979, Gold Hugo for Narration 1998, Award for Excellence in the Arts, Theatre School, DePaul Univ., Chicago 2004. *RSC and Royal Nat. Theatre includes:* Toine in Piaf, London and New York 1980, Viola in Twelfth Night 1983, Adriana in A Comedy of Errors 1983, Kitty Duval in Time of Your Life 1983, Kattrin in Mother Courage (Drama Award 1985) 1984, Othello 1989, The Crucible 1990, The Last Yankee 1993, Battle Royal 1999, His Girl Friday 2003, The Rose Tattoo 2007, The Rose Tattoo 2007, Much Ado About Nothing 2007–08, The Cherry Orchard 2011. *Other theatre includes* Fay in Loot, Broadway 1986, Ellie in Terry Johnson's Dead Funny, London 1994, Amanda in The Glass Menagerie, London 1995/96, Sylvia 1996, Electra, Chichester and London (Olivier Award for Best Actress 1998, Variety Club Award for Best Actress 1998, Calaway Award (New York) for Best Actress 1998) 1997, Princeton and Broadway 1998, The Old Neighbourhood, Royal Court 1998, Boston Marriage, Donmar Warehouse, London 2001, New Ambassadors, London 2001–02, Awake and Sing!, Lincoln Center Production, The Belasco Theater, New York (Drama Desk Best Revival, Out of Critics Circle Best Ensemble, Tony Award for Best Revival and Joan Cullman Award for Best Revival), All My Sons, Apollo Theatre, London (Whatsonstage.com Theatre Award for Best Actress 2011) 2010, Passion Play, Duke of York's Theatre 2013, Stevie, Chichester 2014, Stevie, Hampstead Theatre 2015, Zorba the Greek, New York City Theatre 2015, All On Her Own/Harlequinade, Garrick Theatre 2015–16, Elegy, Donmar Warehouse 2016. *Films include:* The Raggedy Rawney 1987, Wilde (BAFTA Award for Best Actress) 1997, Swept by the Sea 1997, Harry Potter and The Philosopher's Stone 2001, Five Children and It 2004, It's a Wonderful Afterlife 2010, My Week with Marilyn 2011, The Man 2012, An Innocent Abroad 2013. *Video:* Fable 2, 3 & 4: Theresa (Xbox game). *Radio:* The Golden Bowl, Plenty, Bay at Nice, A February Morning, Carol, Such Rotten Luck, The Older Woman. *Television includes:* Inside the Third Reich 1982, The Tragedy of Richard the Third 1983, Edge of Darkness 1985, Paradise Postponed 1986, Poor Little Rich Girl (mini-series) 1987, Morse 1990, Prime Suspect 1990, The Blackheath Poisonings 1992, Love Hurts (series) (BAFTA Award for Best Actress) 1992–94, The Widowing of Mrs. Holroyd 1995, The English Wife 1995, Dance to the Music of Time 1997, David Copperfield 1999, Gormenghast 2000, Adrian Mole: The Cappucino Years 2000, My Family (series) (Best Sitcom Actress, Rose d'Or Awards) 2000–11, Miss Marple: Murder is Announced 2004, A Waste of Shame 2005, Dr Who 2005, 2006, Agatha Christie: Poirot (series; Cards on the Table 2005, The Third Girl 2008, Mrs McGinty's Dead 2008, The Hallowe'en Party 2010, Elephants Can Remember 2013, Dead Man's Folly 2013), Johnny and the Bomb (series) 2006, The Old Curiosity Shop (film) 2007, Who Do You Think You Are? 2009, National Theatre Live (series) – The Cherry Orchard 2011, Playhouse Presents (series) – The Man 2012, Wodehouse in Exile (film) 2013, Mr Selfridge (series) 2015, Britannia (series) 2017, Girlfriends (series) 2018. *Address:* c/o Conway van Gelder Grant Ltd, 3rd Floor, 8–12 Broadwick Street, London, W1F 8HW, England (office). *Telephone:* (20) 7287-0077 (office). *Fax:* (20) 7287-1940 (office). *Website:* www.zoewanamaker.com.

WANANDI, Jusuf; Chinese/Indonesian lawyer, politician and educator; *Senior Fellow, Center for Strategic and International Studies;* b. (Liem Bian Kie), 15 Nov. 1937, Sawahlunto, West Sumatra; brother of Sofjan Wanandi; ed junior high school study, Padang, Jesuit Kanisius High School, Jakarta, Faculty of Law, Universitas Indonesia, took part in Catholic leadership course taught by Father Joop Beek; leader in Catholic Univ. Students Asscn (PMKRI) in 1960s; taught at Kanisius High School; later Asst Lecturer, Universitas Indonesia; apptd Gov. East West Centre, Hawaii 1984; political career in Golongan Karya (Golkar Party), Vice-Gen. Sec.; currently Sr Fellow, Center for Strategic and Int. Studies (CSIS), Jakarta, Vice-Chair. Bd of Trustees, CSIS Foundation; Co-Chair. Pacific Econ. Cooperation Council, Chair. Indonesian Nat. Cttee; Chair. Council for Security Cooperation in the Asia-Pacific (CSCAP) Indonesia, Co-Chair. Steering Cttee of CSCAP; Pres. Dir Jakarta Post (national English daily); Chair. Grad. School of Man. Prasetiya Mulya, Foundation of Panca Bhakti Univ., Pontianak; mem. Int. Advisory Council of the Asia Soc., New York, Bd of Govs Pacific Forum/CSIS, HI, Council of IISS, London, Int. Advisory Bd Babson Coll., Wellesley, Mass, USA; fmr Sec. Indonesian Supreme Advisory Council; fmr Sec.-Gen. Nat. Educ. Council; fmr four-term Rep. in People's Consultative Ass. *Publications:* Strategic Issues and Linkages; has edited several books, written several book chapters and published numerous articles in professional journals on political and security developments in the Asia Pacific region; articles in nat. and int. magazines and newspapers. *Address:* Center for Strategic and International Studies, The Jakarta Post Building, Third Floor, Jl. Palmerah Barat 142–143, Jakarta 10270, Indonesia (office). *Telephone:* (21) 5365-4601 (office). *Fax:* (21) 5365-4607 (office). *E-mail:* info@csis.or.id (office). *Website:* www.csis.or.id (office); www.pecc.org (office).

WANASUNDERA, Shanthi Eva, LLM, PC; Sri Lankan lawyer, judge and fmr government official; *Judge, Supreme Court;* b. Kurunegala; d. of Hector Jayasena and Sumana Jayasena; m. Indrajith Wanasundera; one s. one d.; ed Canyon del Oro High School, Tucson, Ariz., USA, Sri Lanka Law School, Univ. of Leicester, UK, Dharmapala Vidyalaya, Pannipitiya; early career as Attorney-at-Law, Gangodawila Magistrate Court (Nugegoda), Dist Courts in Mount Lavinia and Colombo; apptd State Counsel, Attorney-Gen.'s Dept 1979, also served as Sr State Counsel, Deputy Solicitor-Gen., Additional Solicitor-Gen., Solicitor-Gen., Attorney-Gen. 2011–; Judge, Supreme Court 2012–. *Leisure interests:* meditation, speaking with strangers as and when I meet them. *Address:* Supreme Court, Superior Court Complex, POB 01200, Colombo 12 (office); 237/6 3rd Lane, Bankhill Gardens, Pahalawela Road, Pelawatta, Battaramulla, Sri Lanka (home). *Telephone:* (11) 2327852 (office); (11)2787244 (home). *Fax:* (11) 2327852 (office). *E-mail:* wshanthieva@yahoo.com (office); iwanasundera@yahoo.com (home). *Website:* www.supremecourt.lk (office).

WANCER, Józef, MA; Polish banker and economist; *Chairman of the Supervisory Board, BGZ BNP Paribas SA;* b. 26 May 1942, Komi, Russia; s. of Jakub Wancer and Edwarda Wancer; m. Krystyna Antoniak; one s. one d.; ed City Univ. of New York and Webster Univ., USA; Vice-Pres. Citibank of New York, managerial posts at Citibank units, including Japan, Austria, UK, France; Vice-Pres., then Pres. Raiffeisen Centrobank, Warsaw 1995–2000; Pres. Man. Bd Przemyslowo-Handlowy Bank (BPH) 2000–01, Pres. BPH PBK (following merger with HVB, now Bank BPH SA) 2001–10; Advisor to Man. Bd, Deloitte Poland 2010–15; mem. Supervisory Bd Alior Bank 2011–13; Pres. BGZ BNP Paribas SA 2013–15, Chair. Supervisory Bd 2015–; mem. Supervisory Bd Gothaer Insurance Co., KRUK; Chair. American Chamber of Commerce in Poland 2011–, Financial Cttee of Foundation Auschwitz-Birkenau; Gold Cross of Merit and Order of the Rebirth of Polish Polonia Restituta. *Leisure interests:* cycling, logotherapy, history. *Address:* BGZ BNP Paribas SA, ul. Kasprzaka 10/16, Warsaw, 01-211, Poland (office). *Telephone:* (22) 8604400 (office). *Fax:* (22) 8605000 (office). *Website:* www.bgzbnpparibas.pl (office).

WANDREY, Christian, MSc, PhD (Habil.); German chemist and academic; b. 12 April 1943, Plauen; m.; three c.; ed Univ. of Hanover, Univ. of Bristol, UK; mil. service 1962–64; Asst Prof., Univ. of Hanover 1976, Habilitation, venia legendi Privat-Dozent (Lecturer) in Chemical Eng 1977; Assoc. Prof. of Chemical Eng, Univ. Clausthal Zeller Yield 1977–79; Prof. of Biotechnology, Univ. of Bonn and Dir Inst. of Biotechnology at Research Centre, Jülich 1979–2008; Visiting Prof., Inst. for Physical and Chemical Research (RIKEN), Wako-Shi, Saitama, Japan 1983; mem. Editorial Bd Chemie Ingenieur Technik, Weinheim Advances in Biochemical Engineering, Journal of Molecular Catalysis B: Enzymatic, Biocatalysis and Biotransformation, The Chemical Record; consultant on biochemical eng and process econs, Degussa AG, DSM Research, Netherlands, Novartis, Basel; mem. Bd of Dirs ScheBo, Biotech AG, Dahlem Biomed AG; Co-initiator of four start-up cos, DSM Biotech GmbH, Jülich, Papaspyrou biotechnologie GmbH, Jülich, Jülich Fine Chemicals, AC Biotec GmbH Jülich; mem. Working Party on Biochemical Eng, Gesellschaft Verfahrenstechnik und Chemieingenieurwesen, Working Party on Biotechnology, DECHEMA, Germany Working Party on Catalysis, DECHEMA; Corresp. mem. Braunschweigische Wissenschaftlichen Gesellschaft (Div. of Math. and Natural Science), Sächsische Akad. der Wissenschaften zu Leipzig (Div. of Tech. Science), Schweizerische Akad. der Technischen Wissenschaften; mem. Scientific Advisory Bd PolyAn GmbH; undergraduate scholarship, Konrad-Adenauer-Stiftung, Bonn 1965–70, Karmarsch-Stipendium, City of Hannover 1967, graduate scholarship, Konrad-Adenauer-Stiftung, Bonn 1971–73, Christian-Kuhlemann-Stipendium, Univ. of Hanover for best PhD thesis in natural science 1973, Tech. Transfer Prize, Minister for Research and Tech. (FRG) 1983, Philip Morris Research Award for development of a biogas high performance process for treatment of highly polluted waste waters 1987, Enzyme Eng Award, Eng Foundation, New York 1995, Carl Friedrich Gauss Medal, Braunschweigische Wissenschaftliche Gesellschaft 1999, Friedrich Wöhler Award, German Chemical Soc. (Gesellschaft Deutscher Chemiker) 2002, Wilhelm Exner Medal, Austrian Asscn for SME (Oesterreichischer Gewerbeverein—OGV) (jtly) 2009. *Achievements include:* development of the Enzyme Membrane Reactor (in cooperation with Degussa AG, Hanau) for the production of L-amino acids 1977–. *Publications:* editor of three books, including Biotechnology 1989, Industrial Biotransformations (co-ed.) 2000; more than 330 scientific publs on enzyme and fermentation technology, cell culture technology, waste water and bioorganic chemistry; about 100 patents and patent applications. *Address:* Forschungszentrum Jülich, Wilhelm-Johnen-Strasse, 52425 Jülich, Germany (office). *Telephone:* (2461) 61-3955 (office). *Fax:* (2461) 61-3870 (office). *E-mail:* c.wandrey@fz-juelich.de (office). *Website:* www.fz-juelich.de (office).

WANG, Alexander; American fashion designer; *Chairman and Creative Director, Alexander Wang, Inc.;* b. 1983, San Francisco, Calif.; ed The New School for Design New York; moved to New York City aged 18; several internships; launched first full collection of women's wear for spring 2007; launched full accessories collection 2008; designs sold to more than 500 boutiques and retail stores worldwide; labels include Alexander Wang, T by Alexander Wang founded in 2005; Creative Dir Balenciaga 2012–15; CEO Alexander Wang, Inc. 2016–17, Chair. Bd of Dirs and Creative Dir 2017–; Vogue/CFDA Fashion Fund Award 2008, CFDA Swarowski Women's Wear Designer of the Year 2009, Swiss Textile Award 2009, CFDA Swarovski Accessories Designer of the Year 2010, GQ Menswear Designer of the Year 2011. *Address:* Alexander Wang, Inc., 386 Broadway, New York, NY 10013, USA (office). *Telephone:* (212) 532-3103 (office). *Fax:* (212) 532-3110 (office). *E-mail:* corporate@alexanderwang.com (office). *Website:* www.alexanderwang.com (office).

WANG, Anshun; Chinese government official; b. 1957, Henan Prov.; ed Nankai Univ., Tianjin; began career working in oil exploration, Jilin Prov.; held positions with North China Petroleum Geology Bureau, Ministry of Geology and Mineral Resources; joined CCP 1984; Sec. CCP Standing Cttee, Gansu Prov. 1999–2001; Sec., CCP Municipal State-Owned Assets Supervision and Admin Comm., Shanghai Municipality 2003–07; Deputy Sec., Shanghai Municipal CCP Cttee 2003–07, Beijing Municipal CCP Cttee 2007–; Alt. mem. 17th CCP Cen. Cttee 2007–; Deputy, 11th NPC 2008–; Chair. Beijing CPPCC Municipal Cttee 2011–; Acting Mayor of Beijing 2012–13, Mayor 2013–16; CCP Chief, State Council Devt Research Centre 2016–. *Address:* Development Research Center of the State Council, 225 Chaoyangmennei Avenue, Dongcheng, Beijing, People's Republic of China (office). *Telephone:* 6523-6066 (office). *Website:* en.drc.gov.cn (office).

WANG, Anyi; Chinese writer and academic; *Professor, Department of Chinese Language and Literature, Fudan University;* b. 6 March 1954, Tong'an, Fujian Prov.; d. of Ru Zhijuan; m. Li Zhang; ed Xiangming Middle School; joined as musician, Xuzhou Pref. Song and Dance Ensemble 1972; Ed. Children's Time 1978; Prof., Dept of Chinese Language and Literature, Fudan Univ., Shanghai 2004–; Vice-Chair. Shanghai Writers Asscn, Chair. 2001–; Vice-Pres. Writers' Asscn of China; Outstanding Writer Award, Chinese Language Literary Media Awards 2008. *Publications include:* Song of Eternal Hatred (Mao Dun Prize for Literature), Xiaobao Village, The Love of a Small Town, The Story of a School Principal, Self-selected Works of Wang Anyi (six vols), Lapse of Time, The Song of Everlasting Sorrow 2008. *Address:* Department of Chinese Language and Literature, Fudan University, 220 Handan Road, Shanghai 200433, People's Republic of China (office).

WANG, Bingqian; Chinese politician; b. 1925, Li Co., Hebei Prov.; Deputy Section Chief, Auditing Div., Dept of Finance 1948–49; Section Chief, later Dir, Vice-Minister, Minister of Finance, Cen. Govt; Dir Budget Dept 1963; Deputy Minister of Finance 1973–80, Minister of Finance 1980–92; mem. 12th Cen. Cttee CCP 1982, 13th Cen. Cttee 1987–92; Pres. Accounting Soc. 1980–; Hon. Chair. Bd of Dirs China Investment Bank 1981–; State Councillor 1983–93; Chair. Cen. Treasury Bond Sales Promotion Cttee 1984–; Vice-Chair. Standing Cttee of 8th NPC 1993–98; mem. State Planning Comm. 1988–92; NPC Deputy Hebei Prov.; Hon. Pres. Auditing Soc. 1984–, China Scientific Research Soc. for Policy Study. *Address:* c/o Standing Committee of National People's Congress, Beijing, People's Republic of China (office).

WANG, Bingzhang, MD; Chinese political activist; b. 30 Dec. 1947; one d.; ed Beijing Medical Univ., McGill Univ., Canada; jailed twice by Chinese authorities during Cultural Revolution; moved to USA 1979; f. China Spring magazine 1980s; Founder and Leader Chinese Alliance for Democracy, New York 1980s; attempted to return to China, but expelled 1998; entered Viet Nam to hold meetings with activists 2002; allegedly abducted by Chinese security forces and held at secret location July 2002; arrested in Fanchenggang City, S China Dec. 2002; convicted of espionage and leading terrorist group (sentenced to life imprisonment), Guangdong Prov. Court, S China Jan. 2003; imprisoned in Shaoguan Prison, Guangdong Prov.

WANG, Chaowen; Chinese politician; b. 1930, Huangping, Guizhou Prov.; joined CCP 1951; Sec. Guizhou Communist Youth League 1973; Vice-Chair. Prov. Revolutionary Cttee, Guizhou 1977–79; Sec. CCP Guizhou Prov. Cttee 1980–81, Deputy Sec. 1981; Vice-Gov. of Guizhou 1977–83, Gov. 1983–93; Chair. Guizhou Prov. 8th People's Congress 1994–98; mem. 12th CCP Cen. Cttee 1982–87, 13th CCP Cen. Cttee 1987–92, 14th CCP Cen. Cttee 1992–97; mem. 8th Standing Cttee of NPC 1993–98, 9th Standing Cttee of NPC 1998–2003, Chair. Nationalities Cttee 1998–2003; Del., 15th CCP Nat. Congress 1997–2002. *Address:* c/o Standing Committee of the National People's Congress, 19 Xi-Jiaoming Xiang Road, Xicheng District, Beijing 100805, People's Republic of China (office).

WANG, Chen, MScS; Chinese journalist, editor and government official; *Director, China Law Society;* b. 1950, Beijing; ed School of Postgraduate Studies, Chinese Acad. of Social Sciences, Beijing; joined CCP 1969; reporter, CCP Yijun Co. Cttee 1970–73, CCP Yan'an Municipal Cttee, Shaanxi Prov.; reporter, Guangming Daily 1974, then successively Ed., Dir Chief Ed.'s Office, Assoc. Chief Ed. 1982–95, Chief Ed. 1995–2000; Deputy Dir Dept of Propaganda, CCP Cen. Cttee 2000–01; Ed.-in-Chief Renmin Ribao (People's Daily) 2001–02, Pres. 2002–08; Deputy Dir CCP Cen. Cttee Publicity Dept 2008–; Dir State Council Information Office 2008–11, Dir State Internet Information Office 2011–17, China Law Soc. 2019–; mem. CPPCC Nat. Cttee 1998–2003; mem. 16th CCP Cen. Cttee 2002–07, 17th CCP Cen. Cttee 2007–12, 18th CCP Cen. Cttee 2012–; Sec.-Gen. 12th NPC Standing Cttee 2013–18, Vice-Chair. 2013–18, Chair. 2018–. *Address:* China Law Society, Beijing, People's Republic of China (office).

WANG, Cher, MA (Econs); Taiwanese computer industry executive; *Chairperson, HTC Corporation;* b. 14 Sept. 1958; d. of Wang Yung-ching and Liao Chiao; m. Wenchi Chen; two c.; ed Univ. of California, Berkeley, USA; Gen. Man. PC Div., First International Computer 1982–87; Co-founder and Chair. VIA Technologies 1987–, High Tech Computer (HTC) Corpn 1997–. *Address:* HTC Headquarters, 23 Xinghua Road, Taoyuan 330, Taiwan (office). *Telephone:* (3) 3753252 (office). *Fax:* (3) 3753251 (office). *E-mail:* info@htc.com (office). *Website:* www.htc.com (office).

WANG, Chien-shien, BA, MA; Taiwanese politician and government official; b. 7 Aug. 1938, Hefei, Anhwei; m. Fa-jau Su; ed Nat. Cheng Kung Univ., Nat. Chengchi Univ., Harvard Univ., USA; Sr Specialist, Taxation & Tariff Comm., Ministry of Finance 1971–73; Dir First Div., Dept of Taxation 1973–76, Fourth Dept, Exec. Yuan 1976–80; Dir-Gen. Dept of Customs Admin, Ministry of Finance 1980–82, Public Finance Training Inst. 1982–84; Admin. Vice-Minister of Econ. Affairs 1984–89, Political Vice-Minister 1989–90, Minister of Finance 1990–92; mem. Legis. Yuan 1993–; Founder and Sec.-Gen. New Party 1994; Chair. Chinese Man. Asscn 1990–; Pres. The Control Yuan 2008–14; Asian Finance Minister of the Year 1992. *Publications:* several works on income tax and business.

WANG, Dazhong, DSc; Chinese professor of nuclear engineering; b. 1935, Changli, Hebei Prov.; ed Nankai Middle School, Tianjin, Tsinghua Univ., Beijing; Visiting Scholar, Nuclear Research Centre, Juelich (KFA Juelich), FRG 1980–82; fmr Chief Scientist, First Expert Cttee on Energy, Nat. High Tech. Devt Programme; Assoc. Prof., Prof., Research Fellow, Dir of Nuclear Energy Research Inst., Tsinghua Univ. 1958–99, Vice-Chair. Univ. Council, Pres. Tsinghua Univ. 1999–2003; Pres. Beijing Nuclear Soc.; Vice-Pres. China Nuclear Soc.; mem. Chinese Acad. of Sciences 1993–, 4th Presidium of Depts Chinese Acad. of Sciences 2000–; Hon. Dr rer. nat (Aachen Univ. of Tech.) 1982; Hon. LLD (Univ. of Hong Kong) 1998; Nat. Advanced Scientist 1989, Nat. Award of Science & Technology Progress 1992, 2002, Ho Leung Ho Lee Foundation Science & Technology Achievement Award 1994.

WANG, Dazong, MEng, PhD; Chinese business executive; *Chairman, Ophoenix Capital Management;* ed Huazhong Univ. of Science and Tech., Cornell Univ., USA; Sr Research Engineer, Research Labs, General Motors (GM) 1985; Country Man. and Chief Engineer, Delphi Energy and Engine Man. Systems, China 1994–97; Dir of Eng, GM North America Technical Center 1997–2006; Vice-Pres., Shanghai Automotive Industry (GM's Chinese production partner) 2006–08; joined Beijing Automotive Group 2008, Pres. and CEO from 2011; currently Chair. Ophoenix Capital Man.; Founding Pres. and Adviser, Chinese Asscn of Greater Detroit 1992, Council for Asian Pacific Americans; Chair. US China Automotive Exchange, China Global Automotive Exec. Council. *Address:* Ophoenix Capital Management, 1 Guanghua Road, Chaoyang District, Beijing Kerry Centre, North Building 502, Beijing 101300, People's Republic of China (office). *E-mail:* lzhao@ophoenixcap.com (office). *Website:* www.ophoenixcap.com (office).

WANG, Demin; Chinese petroleum engineer; b. 9 Feb. 1937, Tangshan, Hebei Prov.; ed Beijing Petroleum Inst.; technician, engineer, Chief Engineer, Daqing Petroleum Admin Bureau, Vice-Pres.; Prof. Daqing Petroleum Inst.; Fellow, Chinese Acad. of Eng 1994; 10 nat. level and 26 ministerial level awards. *Address:* Daqing Petroleum Administration, Daqing 163453, Heilongjiang Province, People's Republic of China (office).

WANG, Deshun; Chinese mime artist and actor; b. 1938, Shenyang, Liaoning Province; m. Zhao Aijun; one s. one d.; fmr street performer; with army drama co. 1960–70; joined state-run Changchun Theatre Troupe, NE China 1970; since 1984 has been appearing in 'modelling pantomime' show in which he adopts series of sculpture-like poses to develop a theme; has taken his show to France, Germany and Macao and China's first int. mime festival, Shanghai 1994. *Films include:* Warriors of Heaven and Earth 2003, Legend of the Book's Tower (TV Series) 2005, The Park 2007, The Forbidden Kingdom 2008, Empire of Silver 2009, Tiger Team: The Mountain of the 1000 Dragons 2010, Reign of Assassins 2010, Detective Dee: Mystery of the Phantom Flame 2010, What Women Want 2011, Here, There 2011, Full Circle 2012, Saving General Yang 2013, Miss Granny 2015, Seven Days 2015, Chronicles of the Ghostly Tribe 2015.

WANG, Dianzuo; Chinese metallurgist and academic; *Professor and Honorary President, General Research Institute for Nonferrous Metals;* b. 23 March 1934, Linghai, Liaoning Prov.; ed Central-South Univ.; Pres. Gen. Research Inst. for Nonferrous Metals 1992–97, Prof. and Hon. Pres. 1997–; Chair. Int. Mineral Processing Congress Beijing 2008; Dir (non-exec.) Aluminum Corpn of China Ltd 2001–; Foreign Assoc. mem. Nat. Acad. of Eng, USA 1990–; Fellow, Chinese Acad. of Sciences 1991, Chinese Acad. of Eng 1994 (Vice-Pres. 1998–2006); made pioneering contribs in flotation theory for mineral processing; many nat., provincial and ministerial awards including He Liang and He Li Prizes 1994, IMPC Lifetime Achievement Award. *Publications:* eight monographs and over 300 research papers. *Address:* General Research Institute for Nonferrous Metals, 2 Xinjiekou Wai Street, Beijing 100088, People's Republic of China (office). *Telephone:* (10) 62014488 (office). *Fax:* (10) 62015019 (office). *E-mail:* webmaster@grinm.com (office). *Website:* www.grinm.com (office).

WANG, Enge, BS, MS, PhD, FInstP; Chinese physicist, academic and university administrator; *President, Peking University;* b. 1957, Shenyang; ed Liaoning Univ., Peking Univ.; post-doctoral fellow and research scientist, Chinese Acad. of Sciences (CAS), Institut d'Electronique, de Microelectronique et de Nanotechnologie, France, Univ. of Houston, USA; Prof., Inst. of Physics, CAS 1995, Dir 1999–2007; Founding Dir Int. Centre for Quantum Structures 2000; Dir Beijing Nat. Lab. for Condensed Matter Physics 2004–09; Deputy Sec.-Gen. CAS 2008–09, Exec. Pres. CAS Grad. Univ. 2008–09; Chair Prof. of Physics, Peking Univ. 2009–, Dean, School of Physics and Grad. School 2009–11, Provost and Vice-Pres. Peking Univ. 2011–12, Provost and Exec. Vice-Pres. 2012–13, Pres. 2013–; Academician, CAS, Acad. of Sciences for the Developing World (TWAS); Fellow, American Physical Soc.; JSPS Prof., Tohoku Univ., Japan; AvH Scholar, Fritz-Haber Inst. der MPG, Germany; GCEP Scholar, Stanford Univ., USA; KITP Visiting Prof., Univ. of California, Santa Barbara, USA; Visiting Prof., Univ. of California, Berkeley, USA, Int. Centre for Theoretical Physics, Italy; several nat. and int. academic awards. *Publications:* more than 280 papers in peer-reviewed journals on kinetics of formation and decay of surface-based nanostructures, development of chemical vapour deposition of light-element nanomaterials, and studies of behaviour of water in confined systems. *Address:* Office of the President, Administrative Building, Peking University, 5 Yiheyuan Road, Haidian District, Beijing 100871, People's Republic of China (office). *Telephone:* (10) 62751201 (office); (10) 62751301 (office). *Fax:* (10) 62751207 (office). *E-mail:* webmaster@pku.edu.cn (office). *Website:* www.office.pku.edu.cn (office).

WANG, Fengying, MA (Econs); Chinese automotive industry executive; *General Manager and President, Great Wall Motor Company Ltd;* ed Tianjin Inst. of Finance; joined Great Wall Group 1991, Exec. Dir 2001–, Gen. Man. Great Wall Automobile Sales Network Co. Ltd and Great Wall Bus Sales Co., currently Pres. and Gen. Man. Great Wall Motor Co. Ltd (fmrly Great Wall Automobile Holding Co. Ltd), mem. Strategic Cttee, also Gen. Man. Baoding Great Wall Automobile Sales Co. Ltd; Fifth Anniversary Hebei Outstanding Young Entrepreneur, Chinese Marketing Professional Golden Tripod Outstanding Marketing Gen. Man. Award 2000, 8th of March Red Signal Soldier of Hebei Province 2004, Model Staff of Hebei Province 2004, Luding Award for PRC Marketing Gen. Man. 2008, Top Marketing Professional of the Year 2009. *Address:* Great Wall Motor Co. Ltd, 2266 Chaoyang South Avenue, Baoding City, Hebei Province, People's Republic of China (office). *Telephone:* (312) 2197688 (office). *Fax:* (312) 2197680 (office). *E-mail:* gwmomd@gwm.cn (office). *Website:* www.gwm.com.cn (office).

WANG, Fosong; Chinese chemist; b. 23 May 1933, Xingning Co., Guangdong Prov.; ed Wuhan Univ.; Researcher and Vice-Pres. Chinese Acad. of Sciences 1988, Fellow 1999–, mem. 4th Presidium of Depts Chinese Acad. of Sciences 2000–;

Deputy Chair. China Petroleum Asscn; mem. 8th NPC 1993–98; mem. Standing Cttee of NPC 1993–2003; mem. Bd of Dirs Hong Long Holdings Ltd 2008–11; fmr mem. 7th CPPCC; second class Nat. Prize in Nature Science 1982, 1986, third class Nat. Prize in Nature Science 1991, Japanese Soc. of Polymer Science Int. Award 2002. *Publications:* more than 300 scientific papers. *Address:* Chinese Academy of Sciences, 52 San Li He Road, Beijing 100864, People's Republic of China (office).

WANG, Gang; Chinese archivist and party official; *Ambassador to Uruguay;* b. Oct. 1942, Fuyu Co., Jilin Prov.; ed Jilin Univ.; clerk, Publicity Section, No. 8 Company, 7th Bureau, Ministry of Construction 1968–69, Publicity Div., Political Dept, 7th Bureau 1969–77; joined CCP 1971; Sec.-Gen. Office of CCP Xinjiang Autonomous Region Cttee 1977–81; Sec. (rank of Div. Dir) Taiwan Affairs Office of CCP Cen. Cttee 1981–85; Deputy Dir-Gen. Petition Letters Bureau, Gen. Office of CCP Cen. Cttee and Gen. Office of the State Council 1985–87, Exec. Deputy Dir-Gen. 1987–90; Exec. Deputy Dir CCP Cen. Cttee Cen. Archives 1990–93, Sec. Head Office 1990–93, Dir Cen. Archives 1993–99, Dir State Archives Bureau 1993–94, Dir-Gen. 1994–99; Deputy Dir-Gen. Office CCP Cen. Cttee 1994–99, Dir 1999–2007; Chair. Int. Archives Council 1996–; Alt. mem. 15th CCP Cen. Cttee 1997–2002 (Sec. Work Cttee of Dept CCP Cen. Cttee 1999–), mem. 16th CCP Cen. Cttee 2002–07 (Alt. mem. Politburo, mem. Politburo Secr.), mem. 17th CCP Cen. Cttee 2007–12 (mem. Politburo 2007–12); Vice-Chair. 11th CPPCC Nat. Cttee 2008–11; Amb. to Uruguay 2018–. *Address:* Miraflores 1508, esq. Pedro Blanes Viale, Carrasco, Casilla 18966 Montevideo, Uruguay (office). *Telephone:* (2) 6062958 (office). *Fax:* (2) 6042637 (office). *E-mail:* embchina@adinet.com.uy (office). *Website:* uy.china-embassy.org (office).

WANG, Guangtao, MEng; Chinese politician; b. June 1943, Shanghai; s. of Wang Daohan; ed Tongji Univ., Shanghai; technician, Urban Construction Bureau, Xuzhou City, Jiangsu Prov. 1965; engineer, Technique Section, Urban and Rural Construction Cttee, Xuzhou City 1980–81, Chief 1981, Deputy Chief Engineer and Deputy Dir Urban and Rural Construction Cttee 1981–82; joined CCP 1983; Vice-Mayor of Xuzhou City 1988; Dir and Chief Engineer, Urban Construction Dept, Ministry of Construction 1989–95, apptd Minister of Construction 2001; Deputy Sec. Harbin Municipal Cttee 1995; Acting Mayor, then Mayor of Harbin, Helongjiang Prov. 1995–98; Vice-Mayor of Beijing 1998–2001; mem. CCP Leading Party Group, Ministry of Construction 2001–07; mem. 16th CCP Cen. Cttee 2002–07; Chair. 11th NPC Environmental and Resources Protection Cttee 2008–13; Hon. Prof., Dept of Architecture, Chinese Univ. of Hong Kong 2005.

WANG, Gungwu, CBE, PhD, FAHA; Australian historian, academic and university vice-chancellor; *University Professor, National University of Singapore;* b. 9 Oct. 1930, Indonesia; s. of Wang Fo Wen and Ting Yien; m. Margaret Lim Ping-Ting 1955; one s. two d.; ed Nat. Cen. Univ., Nanjing, Univ. of Malaya and Univ. of London; Asst Lecturer, Univ. of Malaya, Singapore 1957–59, lecturer 1959; lecturer, Univ. of Malaya, Kuala Lumpur 1959–61, Sr Lecturer 1961–63, Dean of Arts 1962–63, Prof. of History 1963–68; Rockefeller Fellow, Univ. of London 1961–62, Sr Visiting Fellow 1972; Prof. of Far Eastern History, ANU 1968–86, Prof. Emer. 1986–, Dir Research School of Pacific Studies 1975–80; Visiting Fellow, All Souls Coll. Oxford 1974–75; Vice-Chancellor, Univ. of Hong Kong 1986–95; Chair. Inst. of E Asian Political Economy, Nat. Univ. of Singapore 1996–97, Dir East Asian Inst. 1997–, Univ. Prof. 2007–; Distinguished Sr Fellow Inst. of Southeast Asian Studies, Singapore 1996–99, Distinguished Professorial Fellow 1999–2003; Univ. Fellow and Hon. Corresp. mem. for Hong Kong of Royal Soc. of Arts 1987–95; Pres. Australian Acad. of the Humanities 1980–83, Asian Studies Asscn of Australia 1978–80; Chair. Australia-China Council 1984–86, Asia-Pacific Council, Griffith Univ. 1997–2001; mem. Exec. Council, Hong Kong 1990–92; Adviser Chinese Heritage Centre, Nanyang Tech. Univ. 1995–2000 (Vice-Chair. 2000–), Southeast Asian Studies, Academia Sinica, Taipei 1994–; mem. Council Int. Inst. for Strategic Studies, London 1992–2001; mem. Nat. Arts Council, Singapore 1996–2000, Nat. Heritage Bd 1997–99 (Adviser 2000–), Nat. Library Bd 1997–2003; mem. Academia Sinica, Taipei, DD Social Science Research Council, NY 1999–; Foreign Hon. mem. American Acad. of Arts and Science; Hon. Fellow, SOAS, London; Hon. Sr Fellow, Chinese Acad. of Social Sciences, Beijing; Hon. Prof., Beijing Univ., Fudan Univ., Hong Kong Univ., Nanjing Univ., Tsinghua Univ.; Hon. DLitt (Sydney, Hull, Hong Kong); Hon. LLD (Monash, ANU, Melbourne); Hon. DUniv (Griffith, Soka). *Publications:* 21 books, including The Chineseness of China 1991, China and the Chinese Overseas 1991, Community and Nation: China, South-East Asia and Australia 1992, Zhongguo yu Haiwai Huaren 1994, The Chinese Way: China's Position in International Relations 1995, Hong Kong's Transition: A Decade after the Deal (ed.) 1995, Global History and Migrations (ed.) 1997, The Nanhai Trade 1998, The Chinese Overseas: From Earthbound China to the Quest for Autonomy 2000, Joining the Modern World: Inside and Outside China 2000, Don't Leave Home: Migration and the Chinese 2001, To Act is to Know: Chinese Dilemmas 2002, Bind Us in Time: Nation and Civilisation in Asia 2002, Anglo-Chinese Encounters since 1800: War, Trade, Science and Governance 2003, Ideas Won't Keep: the Struggle for China's Future 2003, Reform, Legitimacy and Dilemmas: China's politics and Society (ed.) 2003, Damage Control: the Chinese Communist Party in the era of Jiang Zeming (ed.) 2004, Diasporic Chinese Ventures 2004; also numerous articles on Chinese and South-East Asian history; Gen. Ed. East Asian Historical Monographs series. *Leisure interests:* music, reading, walking. *Address:* National University of Singapore, Kent Ridge, Singapore 117571. *Telephone:* 7752033. *Fax:* 7793409. *E-mail:* eaiwgw@nus.edu.sg (office). *Website:* nus.edu.sg/nusinfo/eai (office).

WANG, Gen. Hai; Chinese army officer (retd); b. 1925, Weihai City, Shandong Prov.; ed China's North-East Aviation Acad.; joined PLA 1945; Group Commdr, air force brigade and sent to Korean battlefield 1950; promoted Col PLA 1964; Commdr, Air Force of Guangzhou Mil. Region 1975–83; Deputy Commdr PLA Air Force 1983–85, Commdr 1985; mem. CCP 12th Cen. Cttee 1982–87, 13th CCP Cen. Cttee 1987–92, 14th CCP Cen. Cttee 1992–97; promoted Gen. PLA 1988.

WANG, Hanbin; Chinese party official; b. 28 Aug. 1925, Fujian Prov.; m. Peng Peiyun; two s. two d.; joined CCP in Burma 1941; Deputy Sec.-Gen. NPC Legal Comm. 1979–80; Vice-Chair. and Sec.-Gen. NPC Legal Comm. 1980–83; Deputy Sec.-Gen. Political and Legal Comm. of CCP Cen. Cttee 1980–82, Constitution Revision Cttee of People's Repub. of China 1980–82; Vice-Pres. Chinese Law Soc. 1982–91, Hon. Pres. 1991–; Chair. Legis. Affairs Comm. 1983–87; Vice-Chair. Cttee for Drafting Basic Law of Hong Kong Special Admin. Zone of People's Repub.

of China 1985–90, for Drafting Basic Law of Macau Special Admin. Region of People's Republic of China 1988–, Preparatory Cttee, Hong Kong Special Admin. Region 1995–97; mem. 12th CCP Cen. Cttee 1982–87, 13th Cen. Cttee 1987–92, 14th Cen. Cttee 1992–97; Sec.-Gen. NPC Standing Cttee 1983–87, Vice-Chair. NPC 7th Standing Cttee 1988–93; Alt. mem. Politburo CCP 1992–97; Vice-Chair. Standing Cttee 8th NPC 1993–98. *Leisure interest:* bridge.

WANG, Hongzhang, BA, MA; Chinese economist, certified accountant and business executive; *Chairman and Executive Director, China Construction Bank;* ed Liaoning Inst. of Finance and Econs (now Dongbei Univ. of Finance and Econs); worked successively in Credit Bureau, Savings Dept and Industrial and Commercial Credit Dept, People's Bank of China 1978–84, worked successively in Industrial and Commercial Credit Dept and Gen. Admin Office of Industrial & Commercial Bank of China 1984–89, Asst Pres. Qingdao City Br. 1989–91, served in various positions including Deputy Dir of Gen. Admin Office, Deputy Dir of Finance Planning Dept and Gen. Man. of Operations Office, Industrial & Commercial Bank of China 1991–96, Deputy Dir-Gen. Supervision Bureau and Dir-Gen. Internal Auditing Dept, People's Bank of China 1996–2000, Pres. Chengdu Br. and Admin. of Sichuan Br. of State Admin of Foreign Exchange 2000–03, Party Cttee mem. and Chief Disciplinary Officer, People's Bank of China 2003–12; Chair. and Exec. Dir, China Construction Bank 2012–. *Address:* China Construction Bank, 25 Finance Street, Xicheng District, Beijing 100032, People's Republic of China (office). *Telephone:* (10) 6759-7114 (office). *Fax:* (10) 6360-3194 (office). *E-mail:* info@ccb.com (office). *Website:* www.ccb.com (office).

WANG, Huning; Chinese academic and party official; *Director, CCP Central Policy Research Centre;* b. 1955, Laizhou City, Shandong Prov.; ed Shanghai Normal Univ., Fudan Univ.; began career as Cadre, Municipal Publication Admin, Shanghai 1977–78; Prof., Dept of Int. Politics, Fudan Univ., Shanghai 1981–89, Dean, Dept of Int. Politics 1989–94, Dean, Law School 1994–95; joined CCP 1984; Dir CCP Cen. Cttee Policy Research Office, Policy Div. 1995–98, Deputy Dir, Policy Research Office 1998–2002, Dir Cen. Policy Research Centre 2002–; mem. 16th CCP Cen. Cttee 2002–07, 17th CCP Cen. Cttee 2007–12, also mem. 17th CCP Cen. Cttee Politburo Secr. 2007–12; mem. 18th CCP Cen. Cttee 2012–17 and 18th CCP Cen. Cttee Politburo 2012–17; mem. 19th CCP Cen. Cttee 2017–, also mem. 19th CCP Cen. Cttee Politburo 2017– and Politburo Standing Cttee 2017–; Visiting Prof., Univ. of Iowa and Univ. of California, Berkeley, USA 1988–89. *Publications include:* Logic of Politics: The Principal of Marxist Politics, America against America 1991, General Introduction to New Politics, Analysis of Modern Western Politics, Analysis of Comparative Politics, Debate Contest in Lion City, New Authoritarianism. *Address:* Central Committee Central Policy Research Centre, Chinese Communist Party, Quanguo Renmin Diabiao Dahui, Zhongguo Gongchan Dang, 1 Zhongnanhai, Beijing, People's Republic of China (office). *Website:* www .cppcc.gov.cn (office).

WANG, J. T., BEng, MBA; Taiwanese computer industry executive; *Chairman and CEO, Acer Inc.;* m.; two d.; ed Nat. Taiwan Univ., Nat. Cheng-Chi Univ.; sales engineer, Multitech (forerunner of Acer) 1981, held increasingly sr posts until Pres. Acer Sertek 1990–2000, Pres. Acer Inc. 2000–05, Chair. Acer Inc. 2005–, CEO 2005–08, 2011–, CEO Acer Group 2008–; Pres. Taipei Computer Asscn (Taiwan) 2008–. *Address:* Acer Inc., 9F, 88 Hsin Tai Wu Road, Sec 1, Hsichih, Taipei 221, Taiwan (office). *Telephone:* (2) 696-1234 (office). *Fax:* (2) 696-3535 (office). *Website:* www.acer-group.com (office); www.acer.com (office).

WANG, Jianlin; Chinese business executive and fmr public servant; *Chairman, Dalian Wanda Group Co Ltd;* b. 1954; m.; one s.; ed Liaoning Univ.; joined People's Liberation Army as border guard 1970, eventually becoming Regt Commdr, left PLA 1986; Office Admin., Xigang Dist, city of Dalian 1986–89, Gen. Man., Xigang Residential Devt 1989; Gen. Man., Dalian Wanda Group Co. Ltd (real estate developer) 1992–93, Chair. 1993–; owns 20% of Atlético Madrid (Spanish football club); mem. CCP 1976–; Deputy, 17th Nat. Congress 2007; mem. CPPCC 2008–; Vice-Chair. All-China Fed. of Industry and Commerce, China Folk Chamber of Commerce, China Enterprise Confed., China Enterprise Dirs Asscn, China Gen. Chamber of Commerce, China Charity Confed. (Hon. Pres. 2013–); Vice-Chair. Global Advisory Council, Harvard Univ. 2015–; Hon. citizen of Changchun city; China Charity Awards from Ministry of Civil Affairs 2005, 2008, 2013, named CCTV's Chinese Economic Person of the Year 2008 and 2012, Outstanding Individual for Poverty Alleviation by State Council 2014. *Address:* Wanda Group Co Ltd, Tower B, Wanda Plaza, No. 93 Jianguo Road, Chaoyang District, Beijing 100022, People's Republic of China (office). *Telephone:* (10) 85853888 (office). *Fax:* (10) 85853222 (office). *Website:* www.wanda-group.com/chairman (office).

WANG, Jianzhou, DBA; Chinese telecommunications industry executive; *Senior Advisor, GSMA;* b. Dec. 1948, Wenzhou, Changxing Co., Zhejiang; ed Zhejiang Univ., Hong Kong Polytechnic Univ.; professor-level sr engineer with experience in telecommunications industry since 1970s; served as Dir-Gen. Posts and Telecommunications Bureau, Hangzhou; Dir-Gen. Planning and Construction Dept, Ministry of Posts and Telecommunications 1996–99; Dir-Gen. Gen. Planning Dept, Ministry of Information Industry 1996–99; Dir China Unicom 1999–2001, Exec. Vice-Pres. 2001–02, Pres. 2002–04, Exec. Dir, Chair. and CEO China Mobile Communications Corpn 2004–10, Exec. Dir and Chair. 2010–12 (retd); Sr Advisor, GSMA 2013–; World Telecommunication and Information Soc. Award, ITU 2010, Chairman's Award, GSMA 2011. *Address:* GSMA, Floor 2 The Walbrook Building, 25 Walbrook, London EC4N 8AF, England (office). *Telephone:* (20) 7356-0600 (office). *Fax:* (20) 7356-0601 (office). *E-mail:* info@gsma.com (office). *Website:* www .gsma.com (office).

WANG, Jida; Chinese sculptor; b. 27 Oct. 1935, Beijing; s. of Wang Sho Yi and Chiu Chen Shin; m. Jin Gao 1971 (died 2006); one s. one d.; ed Cen. Inst. of Fine Arts, Beijing; worked in Nei Monggol 1966, 1976–84; took part in the large-scale sculpture project of Chairman Mao Memorial Hall (Mausoleum of Mao Zedong) in 1979; moved to USA 1984; Asst Dir Standing Council, Nei Monggol Sculptors' Asscn; mem. Chinese Artist's Asscn, American Nat. Sculpture Soc. 1988–, Chinese Pottery and Porcelain Art Asscn, Inner Mongolian Sculpture Asscn, China Sculpture Institute; Honour Prize, China 1977. *Works include:* The Struggle (commissioned by Exec. Council on Foreign Diplomats) 1987, Natural Beauty (a collection of 18 pieces portraying women and animals) 1987, Statue of Liberty (commissioned by Statue of Liberty/Ellis Island Foundation), several monumental sculptures in Chairman Mao's image, in China. *Leisure interests:* athletics, music, literature. *Address:* Inner Mongolia Artist's Association, 33 West Street, Hohhot, Inner Mongolia, People's Republic of China (office); 76-12 35th Avenue, Apartment 3E, Jackson Heights, NY 11372, USA. *Telephone:* 25775 (China); (718) 651-3944 (USA).

WANG, Jin, PhD; Chinese physicist and academic; ed Jilin Univ., Univ. of Illinois, USA; Post-doctoral Research Assoc. (Chem. and Biophysics), Univ. of Illinois 1991–96; Guest Scientist, NIH 1996–97; Adjunct Prof. of Physics, Jilin Univ. 1997–; Adjunct Prof. of Chem., State Univ. of New York at Stony Brook 1999–2004, Adjunct Prof., Dept of Applied Math. and Statistics 2006–, also Adjunct Prof., Harriman School of Man. 2008–; Adjunct Prof., Changchun Inst. of Applied Chem., Chinese Acad. of Sciences 2002–; Nat. Science Foundation Career Award 2005. *Publications:* more than 40 articles in scientific journals on mechanism of biomolecular folding and recognition, especially protein folding and protein-protein/protein-DNA interactions. *Address:* Department of Chemistry, State University of New York, Stony Brook NY 11794, USA (office). *E-mail:* jin.wang .1@stonybrook.edu (office). *Website:* www.sunysb.edu/chemistry/index.html (office).

WANG, Jin-Pyng, BS; Taiwanese politician; b. 17 March 1941, Kaohsiung Co.; m. Chen Tsai-Lien; one s. two d.; ed Nat. Taiwan Normal Univ.; teacher, Chin-Teh High School, Changhwa 1965; Chair. Kaohsiung Co. Industrial 1975–81; elected mem. (Kuomintang—KMT), Legis. Yuan 1976–, Co-Chair. Finance Cttee 1981–88, Vice-Chair. KMT Cen. Policy Cttee 1990–91, Chair. Finance Cttee, Cen. Policy Cttee 1990, Vice-Pres. (Deputy Speaker) Legis. Yuan 1993–99, Pres. 1999–2016; Pres. Taiwan-Japan Interparliamentary Friendship Asscn 1992–99; Dir KMT Party and Govt Coordination Cttee in Legislature and KMT Caucus Whip in Legis. Yuan 1992–93; mem. KMT Cen. Standing Cttee 1992–2000, Vice-Chair. KMT 2000–05, Chair. KMT Cen. Advisory Cttee 2005–; Chair. Asscn of mem. of the Legis. Yuan 2001–09, Repub. of China (ROC) Legislators' Asscn 2009–; Chair. Formosa Cancer Foundation 1997–, Inst. for Biotechnology & Medical Industry 2001–09, Ten Outstanding Young Persons' Foundation 2002–, Taiwan Foundation for Democracy 2003–, ROC Volunteer Fire-Fighter Council 2004–, ROC Volunteer Police Council 2006–, Research Centre for Biotechnology and Medicine Policy 2009–; Pres. Taiwan Major League (professional baseball) 1997–2002, ROC Volunteer Fire-Fighter Asscn 1997–2006, Union Against Cancer (Taiwan) 2003–, Chinese Taipei Gateball Asscn 2008–; SKKU Distinguished Fellow, Sungkyunkwan Univ. 2012; Hon. PhD (Nat. Taiwan Normal Univ.) 2007; Highest Recognition Award, European Parl. 2009. *Address:* c/o Legislative Yuan, 1 Chuanshan South Road, Taipei 10051, Taiwan.

WANG, Jiong; Chinese business executive; *Vice-Chairman and President, CITIC Group Corporation;* fmr Chair. and Dir, CITIC Heavy Industries Co. Ltd (alternative name CITIC HIC), fmr Chair. Citic Heavy Machinery Co. Ltd, Man. Dir and Vice-Pres. Citic Group Co. –2013, Exec. Dir, Vice-Chair. and Pres. CITIC Group Corpn 2013–. *Address:* CITIC Group Corporation, Capital Mansion, 6 Xinuan Nanlu, Beijing 10004, People's Republic of China (office). *Telephone:* (10) 64660088 (office). *Fax:* (10) 64661186 (office). *Website:* www.citic.com (office); www .citic.com.cn (office).

WANG, Joseph, BSc, MSc, DSc, FRSC; American electrochemist, nanoengineer and academic; *Distinguished Professor, Department of Nanoengineering, University of California, San Diego;* b. 1948; ed Technion – Israel Inst. of Tech.; Research Assoc., Univ. of Wisconsin-Madison 1978–80; Asst Prof., later Assoc. Prof. of Chem., New Mexico State Univ. (NMSU) 1980–88, Prof. of Chem. 1988–2004, Regents Prof. and Manasse Chair 2002–04; Prof. of Chemical Eng and Chem., Arizona State Univ. and Dir Center for Bioelectronics and Biosensors, Biodesign Inst. 2004–08; Distinguished Prof. of Nanoengineering, Univ. of California, San Diego 2008–; NAS Visiting Scientist Fellowship to People's Repub. of China 1986; Founder and Chief Ed. Electroanalysis 1988–2017; Assoc. Ed. Wiley Encyclopedia of Analytical Chemistry 2007–; mem. Editorial Advisory Bd Analyst 1989–95, Talanta 1990–, Analytical Instrumentation 1991–, Encyclopedia of Analytical Sciences 1991–, Analytica Chimica Acta 1992–2007, Croatian Chemica Acta 1992–, Analytical Letters 1991–95, Analysis Europa 1994–98, Analytical Communications 1995–2000, Current Topics in Analytical Chemistry 1996–, Quimica Analitica 1997–, Electrochemistry Communications 1998–, General Physiolgy and Biophysics 1998–, Sensors 2001–, Sensors Letters 2003–, Journal of Microfluidics and Nanofluidics 2005–, International Journal of Electrochemical Science 2006–, Wiley Nanoscience and Nanotechnology Series 2007–, International Journal for Analytical Chemistry 2008–, Medical Devices 2008–, Reviews in Environmental Science and Bio/Technology 2008–, Sensors and Actuators B 2008–, Journal of Chinese Clinical Medicine International 2009–, Current Nanoscience 2010–, Nano-Bio-Analysis 2010–, Nanoscience & Nanotechnology-ASIA 2010–, Current Nanoscience 2011–, Research and Reports in Transdermal Drug Delivery 2011–, Theranostics 2011–, Advanced Carbon Materials 2012–, ChemElectroChem 2013–; served as instructor ACS Short Course 'Electrochemical Sensors'; mem. IUPAC Comm. for Electroanalytical Chem.; Fellow, Japan Soc. for Promotion of Science 2000, American Inst. for Medical and Biological Eng 2009; more than 150 plenary lectures and keynote addresses at int. meetings (among over 350 presentations) in 50 countries; Hon. Prof., Nat. Univ., Cordoba, Argentina 2003, Univ. of Science and Tech., Beijing 2011; Nanyang Prof., Nanyang Technological Univ., Singapore 2007–; Hon. mem. Nat. Inst. of Chem. (Slovenia) 2007; Dr hc (Nat. Univ., Cordoba) 2003, (Complutense Univ., Madrid) 2007, (Univ. of Alcalá, Spain) 2011, (Central Michigan Univ.) 2012, (Charles Univ.) 2017; Young Faculty Award, Soc. of Analytical Chemists, Pittsburgh 1981, Heyrovsky Memorial Medal (Czech Repub.) 1994, ACS Award for Chemical Instrumentation 1999, ISI 'Citation Laureate' Award as Most Cited Scientist in Eng in the World 1991–2001, Westhafer Award for Research, NMSU 1990, most-cited electrochemist in the world 1995, 1997, ranked the Most Cited Researcher in Eng 1997–2007, ranked the Most Cited Chemist in ISI's list of Most Cited Researchers in Chem. 1997–2007, ACS Nat. Award for Electrochemistry 2006, B. Breyer Medal, Royal Australian Chemical Inst. 2012, Kapp Lecturer, Univ. of Virginia, Richmond 2012, Best Teacher Award, UCSD Dept of Nanoengineering 2012, RSC Spiers Memorial Award 2013, listed in the World Analytical Power List (100 most influential people in the analytical sciences) 2013, Outstanding Sensor Award, ECS 2018, SEAC C. Reiley Award 2019. *Publications:* 11 books, including Stripping Analysis,

Electroanalytical Techniques in Clinical Chemistry and Laboratory Medicine, Biosensors and Chemical Sensors, Analytical Electrochemistry (third edn) 2006, Biosensors and Chemical Sensors, Biosensors for Direct Monitoring of Environmental Pollutants in Field, Electrochemistry of Nucleic Acids and Proteins, Electrochemical Techniques in Clinical Chemistry and Laboratory Medicine, Stripping Analysis: Principles, Instrumentation, and Applications, Electrochemical Sensors, Biosensors and their Biomedical Applications, NanoBiosensing, Nanomachines: Fundamentals and Applications 2013; 25 patents, 35 chapters and more than 1020 articles in scientific journals on nanobioelectronics and electroanalytical techniques. *Address:* Room 245E, SME Building, Department of Nanoengineering, University of California, San Diego, La Jolla, CA 92093-0448, USA (office). *Telephone:* (858) 246-0128 (office); (858) 822-1588 (Lab.) (office). *Fax:* (858) 534-9553 (office). *E-mail:* josephwang@ucsd.edu (office). *Website:* joewang .ucsd.edu (office).

WANG, Jun; Chinese business executive; *Chairman and Executive Director, Goldbond Group Holdings Ltd;* b. 11 April 1941, Munan, Human; s. of Wang Zhen; joined China Int. Trust and Investment Corpn (CITIC) 1979, served as Deputy Gen. Man. then Gen. Man. Business Dept, Vice-Pres., Vice-Chair. and Pres. CITIC Hong Kong (Holdings), Vice-Pres. CITIC 1986–93, Pres. 1993–95, Chair. of Bd 1995–2006; Chair. Bd of Dirs Poly Group 1991–2007; Chair. Planning Comm. Gansu Prov. People's Govt; Chief Procurator Guangdong Prov. People's Procuratorate; Chair. and Exec. Dir Goldbond Group Holdings 2007–; Chair. China Professional Golfers' Asscn; mem. 10th CPPCC Nat. Cttee. *Leisure interests:* golf. *Address:* Goldbond Group Holdings Ltd, 1901-06, Tower 1, Lippo Centre, 89 Queensway, Hong Kong Special Administrative Region, People's Republic of China (office). *Telephone:* 21115666 (office). *E-mail:* kellyli@goldbondgroup.com (office). *Website:* (office).

WANG, Gen. Ke; Chinese army officer; b. Aug. 1931, Xiaoxian Co., Jiangsu Prov.; ed Mil. Acad. of the Chinese PLA; joined CCP-led armed work team 1944; joined CCP 1947; Asst Literacy Teacher, E China Field Army, PLA Services and Arms 1947–48; Deputy Political Instructor, Field Army, Regimental Training Team, PLA Services and Arms 1949; tool part in Jiaozhou Counterattack Battle 1949, Huaihai Campaign 1949; Regimental Staff Officer, Jiangsu Mil. Dist, PLA Nanjing Mil. Region 1949–51; Bn Commdr, PLA, Korea War 1953–56; Deputy Regimental Commdr, later Chief of Staff, Artillery Force, PLA Services and Arms, Korea 1956–61; Section Chief, Training Dept, PLA Artillery School, Beijing 1961–62; Deputy Dir Training Dept, PLA Wuwei Artillery School 1962–64; Deputy Commdr Garrison Div., PLA Lanzhou Mil. Region 1970–72, Political Commissar 1972–78; Div. Commdr PLA 1980–83, Army Commdr 1983–85; Commdr Xinjiang Mil. Dist, Xinjiang Mil. Region 1986–90, Commdr Lanzhou Mil. Region 1990–92; Commdr Shenyang Mil. Region 1992–95; Dir PLA Gen. Logistics Dept 1995–2002; rank of Lt-Gen. 1988, Gen. 1994; mem. 14th CCP Cen. Cttee 1992–97, 15th CCP Cen. Cttee 1997–2002; mem. CCP Cen. Cttee Cen. Mil. Comm. 1992–97; mem. Cen. Mil. Comm. of People's Repub. of China 1995–; Commdr Chengdu Mil. Region –2017.

WANG, Kefen; Chinese dance historian; b. 1 April 1927, Yunyang, Chongqing; d. of Wang Baifan and Liao Huiqing; m. Zhang Wengang 1949; one s. one d.; choreographer and dancer Cen. Nat. Song and Dance Co. 1952–58; Research Fellow, Chinese Nat. Dance Asscn 1956–66, Inst. of Dance, China Nat. Arts Acad. (CNAA) 1977–; Academic Prize, Arts Acad. of China 1989, Award for Special Contrib., State Council of China, Award for Outstanding Contribs of Culture and Educ. Exchange, Columbus, USA. *Publications:* The History of Chinese Dance 1980, The Stories of Ancient Chinese Dancers 1983, The History of Chinese Dance: Ming Dynasty, Qing Dynasty 1984, Sui Dynasty and Tang Dynasty 1987 (CNAA Research Excellence Award 1989), The History of Chinese Dance Development (CNAA Research Excellence Award 1994, Chinese Ministry of Culture Art Research Award 1999), Dictionary of Chinese Dance (Chief Ed.) (Nat. Award for Best Dictionary 1995); Chief Ed. on subject of dance in 10-vol. History of Chinese Civilization (Nat. Award for Best Book 1994); Sui and Tang Culture (Co-Ed. and contrib.) 1990 (Social Science Book Award 1992), Chinese Dance of the 20th Century 1991 (Nat. Best Book Award 1993), Buddhism and Chinese Dance 1991, Chinese Ancient Dance History (co-author), The Chinese Contemporary History of Dance 1840–1996 (Ed.-in-Chief), The Music and Dance of the Tang Dynasty recorded in Japanese History 1999, The Culture of the Wei Dynasty, Jin Dynasty, Northern Dynasty and Southern Dynasty (jtly) 2000, The Complete Works of Dunhuang Caves – Dance Vol. 2001, Chinese Dance: An Illustrated History (First Prize, Chinese Ministry of Culture Art Research Awards 2006) 2002, On the Development and Far-reaching Significance of the Chinese Palace Dance 2004, Dance from Heaven to Earth (Dunhuang Myth series) 2007, and other works on Chinese Dance. *Leisure interests:* choreography, writing and dance.

WANG, Kui; Chinese chemist; *Professor, Department of Chemical Biology, Beijing Medical University;* b. 7 May 1928, Tianjin; ed Yenching Univ.; teaching asst, Beijing Medical Univ. 1952–56, Instructor 1956–78, Assoc. Prof. 1978–83, Prof. 1983–2000, Dean Coll. of Pharmaceutics (also, Chair.) 1983–88, Prof., Dept of Chemical Biology, School of Pharmaceutical Sciences 2000–, apptd Dir Nat. Laboratory of Natural Medicine and Bionic Medicine 1950; Chair. Chem. Dept of Nat. Natural Science Foundation 1978–91; Fellow, Chinese Acad. of Science 1991–; mem. 4th Presidium, Chinese Acad. of Sciences 1999–; Ho Leung Ho Lee Prize 2000, Cai Yuanpei Prize 2006, Chinese Acad. of Sciences Award for Advancement in Science and Tech. (2nd Class), State Educ. Comm. Award for Advancement in Science and Tech. (2nd Class). *Publications:* over 100 research papers. *Address:* Department of Chemical Biology, School of Pharmacy, Peking University, 38 Xue Yuan Ju, Haidian Qu, Beijing 100191, People's Republic of China (office). *Telephone:* (10) 82802539 (office). *E-mail:* wangkuipku@bjmu.edu .cn (office). *Website:* dcb.sps.bjmu.edu.cn (office).

WANG, Lequan; Chinese politician (retd); *President, China Law Society;* b. 1 Dec. 1944, Shouguang Co., Shandong Prov.; sent to do manual labour, Jiaonan Co., Shandong Prov. 1965–66; joined CCP 1966; Deputy Head, Houzhen Commune, Shouguang Co. 1966–75, mem. Standing Cttee CCP Revolutionary Cttee and Standing Cttee CCP Party Cttee 1966–75, Deputy Sec. CCP Shouguang Co. Cttee and Vice-Chair. CCP Revolutionary Cttee 1975–82; Deputy Sec. CCP Party Cttee, Chengguan Commune 1966–75; Deputy Sec. CCP Communist Youth League of China Shandong Prov. Cttee 1982–86; Deputy Sec. CCP Liaocheng Prefectural Cttee 1986–88, Sec. 1988–89; Vice-Gov. Shandong Prov. 1989–91; Vice-Chair.

Xinjiang Uygur Autonomous Regional People's Congress 1991–95; Deputy Sec. CCP Xinjiang Uygur Autonomous Regional Cttee 1992–94, Acting Sec. 1994–95, Sec. 1995–2010; First Political Commissar, Production and Construction Corps, Xinjiang Uygur Autonomous Region 1995–2010; Alt. mem. 14th CCP Cen. Cttee 1992–97, mem. 15th CCP Cen. Cttee 1997–2002, 16th CCP Cen. Cttee 2002–07 (mem. Politburo 2002–07), 17th CCP Cen. Cttee 2007–12 (mem. Politburo 2007–12) (retd); Pres. China Law Soc. *Address:* China Law Society, People's Republic of China (office).

WANG, Lianzheng, MTAA, PhD; Chinese agronomist and administrator; *Honorary Chair of Academy Committee, Chinese Academy of Agricultural Sciences;* b. 15 Oct. 1930, Haicheng, Liaoning Prov.; s. of Wang Dianche and Wang Youzhen; m. Li Shuzhen 1959; two d.; ed Northeast Agricultural Coll., Harbin and Moscow Timiryazeev Agricultural Acad.; Asst Prof., Heilongjiang Acad. of Agricultural Sciences (HAAS) 1964–78, Assoc. Prof. 1979–82, Prof. 1983–; Dir Soybean and Crop Breeding Inst. HAAS 1970–78; Vice-Pres. HAAS 1978–82, Pres. 1983–86, Vice-Gov. Heilongjiang Prov. (in charge of Agricultural Production, Science and Tech.) 1983–87; Vice-Minister of Agric. 1988–91; mem. Agricultural Devt Group at State Council 1988–93; mem. and Convenor Plant Genetics, Breeding, Cultivation Academic Degree Cttee at State Council 1991–96; Pres. Chinese Acad. of Agricultural Sciences (CAAS) 1987–94, Pres. and Prof. Grad. School CAAS 1988–95, Hon. Chair. Acad. Cttee of CAAS 1995–; Vice-Chair. Chinese Crop Science Soc. 1988–94, Chair. 1994–2002; Vice-Chair. Scientific Tech. Cttee (Ministry of Agric.) 1988–96, Chinese Cttee for Release of New Crop Varieties 1989–96, Vice-Pres. China Asscn for Science and Tech. 1991–2001, Heilongjiang Asscn of Science and Tech., Chinese Asscn of Agricultural Science Socs; Chair. China Int. Exchange Asscn of Agricultural Science and Tech. 1992–96; mem. Bd IFAD 1988–91, Centre for Agric. and Biosciences (CABI) 1994–97; Co-Chair. Advisory Cttee China-EC Centre for Agricultural Tech. 1992–97; Pres. China Seed Asscn 1998–2006, China Agricultural Tech. Soc. 2000–06; mem. Chinese dels to numerous int. confs; Deputy to NPC; mem. Agricultural and Rural Affairs Cttee of Congress 1998–2003; has developed 34 soya bean cultivars; Foreign mem. Russian Acad. of Agricultural Sciences 1988–; Foreign Fellow Indian Nat. Acad. of Agricultural Sciences 1994–; Second Class Chinese State Prize for Invention, for new soyabean cultivar 'Heinong 26', Second Class Chinese State Prize for Invention, for new potato cultivar 'Kexin No. 1', First Class Prize for Scientific Progress, Ministry of Agric., for collection and investigation of wild soya bean; Second Class Heilongjiang Prov. Prize for Tech. Progress, for high-yielding high-protein soyabean cultivar 'Heinong 35' 1994, Winner of Timiryazeev Award for Science and Education in Agriculture, Moscow 2009, First Class Beijing Science and Technology Award (for soyabean cultivar 'Zhonghuang 13' with high yield and broad adaptability) 2010, First Class Chinese State Science and Technology Award (for 'Zhonghuang 13') 2012, Winner of Award for Agronomy, Ho Leung Ho Lee Foundation Prize for Scientific and Technological Progress, Hong Kong, China 2012. *Publications:* Feeding a Billion (co-author) 1987, Soyabean Breeding and Genetics (Ed.-in-Chief) 1992, Agriculture in Modern China (co-ed.) 1992, Soyabean Cultivation for High Yielding (Ed.-in-Chief) 1994, Soybean in Mordesa China (co-ed.) 2007, Seed Industry of Field Crops in China 2007, Soybean Research for 50 Years (Ed.-in-Chief) 2010, and more than 164 papers. *Leisure interest:* classical music. *Address:* Chinese Academy of Agricultural Sciences, 12 Zhongguancun Nan (Southern) Street, Haidian District, Beijing 100081 (office); Cui wei xili 14-12-2, Haidian District, Beijing, 100036, People's Republic of China (home). *Telephone:* (10) 82103007 (office); (10) 68258061 (home). *Fax:* (10) 82105805 (office). *E-mail:* wanglz@mail.caas.net.cn (office).

WANG, Linxiang; Chinese business executive; *President and Chairman, Erdos Group;* b. 1951, Baotou, Nei Monggol Autonomous Region; joined CCP 1974; Dir Erdos Cashmere Sweater Mill 1983–89; Pres. and Chair. Bd Erdos Group 1989–; Standing Dir Asscn of Inner Mongolia Import and Export Firms 1997; Vice-Chair. CPPCC Yih Ju Autonomous League Cttee, Inner Mongolia Autonomous Region; Deputy to NPC; mem. All-China Youth Fed.; Hon. Chair. Asscn of Friendship Liaison of Yih Ju League 1999; numerous awards including Sr Economist, Silver Medal of Nat. Frontier Talents, State Econ. and Trade Comm., named Inner Mongolia Most Outstanding Entrepreneur, Model Worker in China's Textile Circle, Nat. Model Worker, Nat. Most Outstanding Young Entrepreneur, Most Outstanding Member of CCP. *Address:* Erdos Group, Baotou, Nei Monggol, People's Republic of China (office).

WANG, Liqin; Chinese table tennis player; b. 18 June 1978, Shanghai; began playing aged six and was picked for Chinese men's nat. squad aged 15 in 1993; numerous titles; winner men's singles: Asian Youth Championships 1994, Pro Tour Grand Finals 1998, 2000, Asian Championships 1998, World Championships, Osaka 2001, Asian Games, Busan 2002, World Championships, Shanghai 2005, World Championships, Zagreb 2007; winner men's doubles: Pro Tour Grand Finals 1996, 1998, 2000, 2007, Olympic Games, Sydney 2000 (gold medal), World Championships 2001, 2003; winner mixed doubles: Asian Championships 1998, Asian Games 1998; winner team events: Asian Championships 1998, 2000, Asian Games 1998, 2000, World Championships, Osaka 2001, World Championships 2006, Olympic Games, Beijing 2008 (gold medal); men's singles, Olympic Games, Athens 2004, Beijing 2008 (bronze medal); has won highest number of pro tours, winning more than 20; ranked No. 1 (Int. Table Tennis Fed.—ITTF) in the world 2005, No. 3 2007, No. 4 July 2008, No. 8 Oct. 2011, No. 12 Nov. 2013; played for Shanghai city team, retd from Nat. team 2013; apptd Dir Shanghai Table Tennis and Badminton Centre 2013; Head Coach Shanghai Team, Table Tennis Super League 2014. *Address:* c/o Chinese Table Tennis Federation, C3 Longtan Road, Chongwen District, Beijing 100061, People's Republic of China.

WANG, Luolin; Chinese economist; b. June 1938, Wuchang City, Hunan Prov.; ed Beijing Univ.; joined CCP 1978; fmr Asst Lecturer Xiamen Univ., Lecturer 1961–80, Assoc. Prof., Econs Dept 1980–81, Deputy Dean, Econs Dept 1981–84, Vice-Pres. 1984–93, mem. CCP Standing Cttee 1984–89; fmr Dean, Zhejiang Univ. Coll. of Econs, currently Hon. Dean; Vice-Pres. Chinese Acad. of Social Sciences 1993–2005, now Special Adviser and Prof.; Vice-Chair. State Academic Degrees Cttee 1999; Alt. mem. 13th CCP Cen. Cttee 1987–92, 14th CCP Cen. Cttee 1992–97, mem. 15th CCP Cen. Cttee 1997–2002, Alt. mem. 16th CCP Cen. Cttee 2002–07; Vice-Chair. CPPCC Econ. Sub-Cttee 2005–; Hon. PhD (Hong Kong Lingnan Univ.). *Publications:* Blue Book of China's Economy (co-ed. annually).

Address: Chinese Academy of Social Sciences, Jianguomennei Dajie 5 Hao, Beijing 100732, People's Republic of China (office). *Telephone:* (10) 65137744 (office). *Fax:* (10) 65138154 (office). *E-mail:* wangll@cass.net.cn (office). *Website:* www.cass.net.cn (office).

WANG, Maolin; Chinese party and government official; b. Dec. 1934, Qidong, Jiangsu Prov.; ed Shanghai Financial and Econ. Coll.; joined CCP 1956; Vice-Chair. Shanxi Prov. Revolutionary Cttee 1977–78; Mayor Taiyuan City, Shanxi Prov. 1979–83; Vice-Gov. Shanxi Prov. 1979–83; Vice-Chair. Shanxi Prov. People's Congress 1981–88; Deputy Sec. Shanxi Prov. Cttee 1988–91, Sec. 1991; Chair. 7th CPPCC Shanxi Prov. Cttee 1993; Sec. 7th CCP Hunan Prov. Cttee 1993–98; mem. 13th CCP Cen. Cttee 1987–92, 14th CCP Cen. Cttee 1992–97, 15th CCP Cen. Cttee 1997–2002; Vice-Chair. 10th NPC Law Cttee 2003–; Prin. Adviser China Int. Council for the Promotion of Multinational Corpns. *Address:* China International Council for the Promotion of Multinational Corporations, 11th Floor, Section A, United International Building, 19 East Third Ring Road, Chaoyang District, Beijing, People's Republic of China (office). *Website:* www.cicpmc.org (office).

WANG, Gen. Maorun; Chinese army officer; b. May 1936, Rongcheng, Shandong Prov.; ed Mil. Acad. of the Chinese PLA; joined PLA 1951, CCP 1956; staff officer, Qingdao Garrison 1962; various posts in a corps political dept 1969–73; Deputy Sec.-Gen. Political dept Jinan Mil. Region 1973–76; Dir of a corps political dept 1976–83; corps deputy political commissar 1983–85; Dir Political Dept PLA Lanzhou Mil. Region 1985–90; Deputy Political Commissar and Sec. CCP Comm. for Inspecting Discipline, Lanzhou Mil. Region 1990; apptd Political Commissar, Nat. Defence Univ. 1990; rank of Maj.-Gen. 1988, Lt-Gen. 1993, Gen. 1998; mem. 15th CCP Cen. Cttee 1997–2002; Del., 11th CCP Nat. Congress 1977–82.

WANG, Meng; Chinese politician and writer; b. 15 Oct. 1934, Beijing; s. of Wang Jindi and Tong Min; m. Cui Ruifang 1957 (died 2012); two s. one d.; joined CCP 1948; criticized 1957–76; rehabilitated 1979; Minister of Culture 1986–89; mem. Secr. Chinese Writers' Asscn 1981–86, Vice-Pres. 1986–89, Vice-Chair. 2001; Vice-Pres. China PEN Centre 1982–; Vice-Pres. Asscn for Int. Understanding 1985–; Chief Ed. People's Literature 1983–86; Alt. mem. 12th Cen. Cttee CCP 1982–85, mem. 12th Cen. Cttee CCP 1985–87, 13th Cen. Cttee 1987–92; mem. Standing Cttee 8th CPPCC Nat. Cttee 1993–98, Standing Cttee 9th CPPCC Nat. Cttee 1998–2003; Hon. Fellow, United Int. Coll. 2015; Award for Excellent Chinese Biographic Works 2013, Mao Dun Literature Prize 2015. *Publications include:* The Young Newcomer in the Organization Department 1956, Long Live the Youth 1957, Bolshevik State: A Modernist Chinese Novel 1979, The Barber's Tale 1979, A Night in the City 1979, A Spate of Visitors 1980, The Butterfly 1980, The Metamorphosis of Human Nature 1986, Selected Works (Vols I–IV) 1986, Adventures of a Soccer Star 1990, You Can Come into My Dream Again 1991, Revelation from The Dream of Red Mansion 1991, Notes on Styles (collection of literary criticisms) 1991, The Seasons for Love 1992, Hard Gruel (short stories) 1992, The Season for Losing Self-Control 1995, The Season for Hesitation 1997, The Season for Carnivals 2000. *Leisure interests:* swimming, drinking. *Address:* China PEN, Shatan Beijie 2, Beijing, People's Republic of China (office).

WANG, Mingming; Chinese artist; b. 4 May 1952, Beijing; ed Beijing Fine Art Acad.; Chair. Beijing Artists Asscn; Vice Chair., Chinese Artists Asscn, Beijing Fed. of Literary and Art Circles Cttee; Vice Pres., China Overseas Friendship Asscn, Beijing Asscn of Intellectuals, Beijing Municipal People's Asscn for Friendship; Dean, Beijing Fine Art Acad.; Deputy Dir, Beijing Municipal Bureau of Culture, CPPCC Nat. Cttee (also mem. CPPCC Standing Cttee); currently lives and works in Beijing; Hon. title, Advanced Individual Made Outstanding Contribs. to the Capital Construction, Beijing Municipal Cttee.

WANG, Nan; Chinese table tennis player; b. 23 Oct. 1978, Fushun City, Liaoning Prov.; m. Guo Bin; started playing aged seven; joined Liaoning prov. table tennis team in 1989 and nat. team in 1993; numerous titles; winner women's singles: Swedish Open 1994, Asian Youth Championships 1994, World Cup 1997, 1998, 2003, Pro Tour Grand Finals 1998, 2001, Asian Games, Bangkok 1998, World Championships 1999, 2001, 2003, Olympic Games, Sydney 2000 (gold medal); winner women's doubles: Asian Championships 1996, Pro Tour Grand Finals 1997, 1998, 1999, Asian Games 1998, World Championships 1999, 2001, 2003, 2005, 2007, Olympic Games, Sydney 2000 (gold medal), Athens 2004 (gold medal); winner mixed doubles: Asian Games 1998, Asian Championships 1998, World Championships 2003; winner women's team events: Asian Youth Championships 1994, Asian Championships 1996, 1998, World Championships 1997, 2000, 2001, 2004, 2006, 2008, Asian Games 1998, Olympic Games, Beijing 2008 (gold medal); runner-up in women's singles and women's team events, Asian Games, Busan 2002; women's singles, Olympic Games, Beijing 2008 (silver medal); ranked World No. 1 1999–2001; retd 2008; f. Pingpong Hut 2014; led Chinese women's table-tennis team following retirement of Deng Yaping. *Leisure interests:* listening to music, watching television, reading, playing tennis.

WANG, Pinxian; Chinese marine geologist; *Professor of Marine Geology, Tongji University;* b. 14 Nov. 1936, Suzhou, Jiangsu Prov.; ed Moscow State Univ., USSR; joined Geology and Geography Dept, East China Normal Univ., Shanghai 1960; moved to Tongji Univ. 1972, later Prof. of Marine Geology, Head of Marine Geology Dept 1982–90; mem. Chinese Acad. of Science 1991–, Vice-Chair. Earth Sciences Div. 1997–2002; mem. NPC (legislature) 1986–92; Co-Chief Scientist, ODP Leg 184 (first scientific deep-sea drilling operation in China Seas) 1999; Pres. Chinese Cttee on Ocean Research 1994–2002; Vice-Pres. Int. Scientific Cttee for Ocean Research 1994–98, Oceanological and Limnological Soc. of China; von Homboldt Research Fellow, Kiel Univ., Germany 1981–82; Vice-Chair. Chinese Cttee for Quaternary Research, PAGES (Past Global Changes) Scientific Steering Cttee 2004–07; Hon. Fellow, Geological Soc., London 1991; Ho Leung Ho Li Earth Sciences Prize 2006, European Geosciences Union Milutin Milankovic Medal for long-term climatic research 2007. *Achievements include:* first to study paleoceano-graphy in China early 1980s. *Publications:* book: Marine Micropaleontology of China 1985, Proceeding, Ocean Drilling Program, Initial Reports, 184 2000, The South China Sea – Paleoceanography and Sedimentology 2009; research: Distribution of Calcareous Microfossils in the China Seas and its Paleoenvironmental Significance (State Educ. Comm. first prize for Advancement of Science and Tech.), Dynamic Progression and Development Trend of the Evolution of Environment in the last 150,000 years in Drought and Semi-drought Areas (Chinese Acad. of

Science first prize for Advancement of Science and Tech.) 1998. *Address:* School of Ocean and Earth Science, Tongji University, 1239 Siping Road, Shanghai, People's Republic of China (office). *Telephone:* (21) 65983207 (office). *Fax:* (21) 65988808 (office). *E-mail:* pxwang@tongji.edu.cn (office). *Website:* tongji.edu.cn (office).

WANG, Qimin; Chinese petroleum executive; *General Manager, Qinghai Wutong (Group) Industry Co., Ltd;* b. 1937; ed Beijing Petroleum Inst.; joined CCP 1978; technician, Vice-Chief Geologist, Sr Engineer and then Vice-Pres. Daqing Research Inst. of Oilfield Exploration and Devt 1961–96, apptd Pres. 1996; took part as torch-bearer in Olympic Flame Relay, Daqing July 2008; currently Gen. Man. Qinghai Wutong (Group) Industry Co., Ltd; China Gen. Co. of Oil and Natural Gas Iron Man Achievement Prize. *Address:* Qinghai Wutong (Group) Industry Co., Ltd, 16, Chaidamu Road, Chengbei District, Xining 810003, People's Republic of China (office). *Telephone:* (97) 15131513 (office). *Fax:* (97) 15131960 (office).

WANG, Qinghai; Chinese business executive and engineer; Gen. Man. and Vice-Chair. Shougang Corpn 2001–12, concurrently Chair. Beijing Shougang Flourish Coil Coating Co. Ltd, Vice-Chair. Beijing Shougang Co. Ltd 2006–12, Shougang Gen. Co., Shougang Jingtang Iron & Steel United Co. Ltd; mem. Bd of Dirs Beijing Shougang Co. Ltd, Shougang Holding (Hong Kong) Ltd.

WANG, Qishan; Chinese economist and politician; *Vice-President;* b. July 1948, Tianzhen, Shanxi Prov.; ed Northwest China Univ.; Researcher, Modern History Inst., Chinese Acad. of Social Sciences 1982, Researcher, Secr. (Rural Policies Dept) CCP Cen. Cttee Politboro 1982; joined CCP 1983; Div. Head, Rural Devt Research Centre of State Council, Acting Dir then Dir Rural Devt Inst. 1982–87; Gen. Man. China Rural Trust and Investment Corpn 1988–89; Vice-Pres. Construction Bank of China 1989–93, Pres. 1994–97; Vice-Gov. People's Bank of China 1993–94, Gov. 1994 (Sec. CCP Party Cttee); Chair. of China Investment Bank 1994–97; Chair. China Int. Capital Corpn Ltd 1995–97; mem. CCP Standing Cttee Guangdong Prov. Cttee 1997–2000; Exec. Vice-Gov. Guangdong Prov. 1998–2000; Dir Econ. Restructuring Office of the State Council 2000–; Sec. Econ. System Reform Scheme Office, CCP Party Cttee 2000–02; Sec. CCP Hainan Prov. Cttee 2002–03; Chair. Standing Cttee Hainan Prov. People's Congress 2003; Acting Mayor of Beijing 2003–04, Mayor 2004–07; Exec. Chair. Beijing Organizing Cttee for XXIX Olympiad and Deputy Sec. Leading Party Mem.'s Group 2004–07; Vice-Premier State Council and mem. CCP Leading Party Group 2008–13; Sec. CCP Cen. Comm. for Discipline Inspection 2012–17; Vice-Pres. People's Republic of China 2018–; Alt. mem. 15th CCP Cen. Cttee 1997–2002; mem. 16th CCP Cen. Cttee 2002–07, 17th CCP Cen. Cttee 2007–12; mem. Standing Cttee CCP Beijing Municipal Cttee 2003–07, Deputy Sec. CCP Beijing Municipal Cttee 2003–07; mem. 18th CCP Cen. Cttee 2012–17, Politburo 2012–17, Politburo Standing Cttee 2012–17. *Address:* Great Hall of the People, West Edge, Tiananmen Square, Beijing, People's Republic of China (office). *Telephone:* (10) 88050813 (office). *Fax:* (10) 63070900 (office). *Website:* english.gov.cn/2008-03/16/content_921792.htm (office).

WANG, Senhao; Chinese government official; b. 1933, Cixi, Zhejiang Prov.; two s.; joined CCP 1955; Dir Mining Admin, Shanxi Prov. 1970–82; Sec. CCP Party Cttee, Shanxi Prov. 1970–82; Deputy Sec. CCP Party Cttee, Shaanxi Prov. 1983–93; Gov. of Shanxi Prov. 1983–92; Minister of Coal Industry 1993–98; mem. CCP 12th Cen. Cttee 1982–87, 13th Cen. Cttee 1987–92, 14th Cen. Cttee 1992–97; mem. Standing Cttee 9th CPPCC Nat. Cttee 1998–2003, Chair. Soc. and the Rule of Law Cttee. *Address:* National Committee of Chinese People's Political Consultative Conference, 23 Taipingqiao Street, Beijing, People's Republic of China (office).

WANG, Shenghong; Chinese fmr university administrator; b. 1942, Shanghai; ed Shanghai Univ. of Science and Tech., Purdue Univ. and Univ. of Texas, USA; fmr Dir and Party Sec., Higher Educ. Bureau, Shanghai, fmr Chair. Shanghai Educ. Asscn for Int. Exchange; fmr Pres. Shanghai Univ. of Science and Tech.; apptd Head, CCP Municipal Cttee, United Front Work Dept, Shanghai 1984, Vice-Chair., CPPCC Municipal Cttee, Shanghai 1995–; Assoc. Dir, China Electro-Mechanical Eng Asscn 1980–90; del. to 15th Nat. CCP Congress, 9th CPPCC 1998–2003, 6th and 7th CCP Congress of Shanghai, 7th and 10th People's Congress of Shanghai; Pres. Fudan Univ. 1998–2009; mem. Univ. Grants Cttee of Hong Kong, Int. Academic Advisory Panel, Ministry of Educ., Singapore; Dr hc (Univ. of Manchester, UK, Nat. Univ. of Ireland, Waseda Univ., Japan, Chonnam Nat. Univ., South Korea); Chinese Acad. of Sciences Award for Scientific and Technological Breakthroughs 1986, First Prize, Nat. Awards for Scientific and Technological Advancement 1987, First Prize, Shanghai Awards for Scientific and Technological Advancement 1990, Outstanding Worker in the Frontline of Science and Tech. of Shanghai, Outstanding Worker in the Frontline of Educ. of Shanghai, Shanghai Model Worker, Pres.'s Medal, George Washington Univ., USA. *Publications:* Structural Design of Electronic Apparatus, Finite Element Method and Its Application; over 40 papers in scientific journals.

WANG, Sheping; Chinese business executive; *Chairman and President, Jizhong Energy Group Company Ltd;* Chair. Jizhou Energy Resources Co. Ltd, currently Chair. and Pres. Jizhong Energy Group Co. Ltd, also Chair. and Gen. Man. Jizhou Energy Resources Group; Dir, HeBei Jinniu Chemical Industry Co. Ltd (Chair. 2008–), fmr Chair. Hebei Jinniu Energy Group Co. Ltd, Heibei Jinniu Energy Resources Co. Ltd; fmr Chair. Xingtai-based mining co., of a Handan-based mining co. *Address:* Jizhong Energy Group Company Ltd, 191 West Zhongxing Avenue, Xingtai 054000, People's Republic of China (office). *Telephone:* (319) 2098828 (office). *Fax:* (319) 2068666 (office). *E-mail:* info@hbjnjt.com (office). *Website:* www.jznyjt.com (office); www.hbjnjt.com (office); www.jnny.com.cn (office).

WANG, Shi; Chinese business executive; b. 23 Jan. 1951, Liuzhou, Guanxi Prov.; ed Lanzhou Railway Inst.; worker, Railway Bureau, Guangzhou City (Shenzhen Econ. Special Zone), Guangdong Prov.; f. Modern Scientific and Educational Instrument Exhbn Centre, Shenzhen City, Guangdong Prov., Gen. Man. Shenzhen Vanke Co. Ltd Exhbn Centre 1984, Corp. Rep., Shenzhen Vanke Co. Ltd 1988, Gen. Man. 1988–99, Chair. and CEO China Vanke Co. Ltd 1988–99, Chair. 1999–2017; Vice-Chair. Shenzhen Real Estate Asscn, Shenzhen Gen. Chamber of Commerce; Standing Dir China Real Estate Asscn (Vice-Dean City House Devt Cttee); initiated and organized 'New Residence Forum' Shanghai Conf. and promoted New Residence Campaign 2000; visiting scholar, Harvard Univ. 2011–13; elected one of the Top Ten Econ. Figures in China 2000. *Leisure interest:* mountaineering (succeeded in reaching the highest summits of seven continents, including two ascents of Mount Everest).

WANG, Shouguan; Chinese astronomer and academic; b. 15 Jan. 1923, Fuzhou; s. of B. L. Wang and S. Y. Gao; m. Lin Zhihuan 1955; one s. one d.; Deputy Head, Div. of Math. and Physics, Chinese Acad. of Sciences 1981–; apptd Prof., Beijing Normal Univ. 1987, Univ. of Science and Tech. of China 1991; Chief Ed. Vol. Astronomy, Chinese Encyclopaedia 1980; Chief Ed. Astrophysics Sinica; mem. Chinese Acad. of Sciences 1981; Hon. Dir Beijing Astronomical Observatory 1987–; Hon. Pres. Chinese Astronomical Soc. 1988–; Nat. Science Congress Award 1978, Nat. Science and Tech. Progress Award 1985. *Leisure interest:* poetry.

WANG, Shu, PhD; Chinese architect; *Dean, School of Architecture, China Academy of Art;* b. 4 Nov. 1963, Ürümqi, Xinjiang Uyghur Autonomous Region; m. Lu Wenyu; ed Nanjing Inst of Tech., Tongji Univ.; co-f. (with Lu Wenyu) Amateur Architecture Studio, Hangzhou 1997; Prof., China Acad. of Art 2000–, Head, Architecture Dept 2003–, Dean, School of Architecture 2007–; Kenzo Tange Visiting Prof. (first Chinese), Harvard Grad. School of Design 2011; Schelling Architecture Prize 2010, French Acad. of Architecture Gold Medal 2011, Pritzker Architecture Prize 2012. *Address:* School of Architecture, China Academy of Art, 18 Nanshan Road, Shangcheng, Hangzhou, Zhejiang Province, People's Republic of China (office). *Telephone:* (571) 8716-4630 (office). *E-mail:* caaic@163.com (office). *Website:* eng.caa.edu.cn (office).

WANG, Shucheng; Chinese politician; b. Dec. 1941, Liyang, Jiangsu Prov.; ed Tsinghua Univ., Beijing; joined CCP 1965; technician, then Deputy Sec. Eng Bureau No. 6, Ministry of Water Resources and Power Industry 1968–84; Deputy Chief, 1st Eng Section, 6th Eng Bureau, Ministry of Power Industry 1980; Deputy Gen. Man. Water Conservancy and Hydroelectric Power Construction Co. 1984–86, Deputy Dir 1986–87, Dir 1987–88; Dir Dept of Hydroelectric Devt, Ministry of Energy 1988–93; Vice-Minister of Power Industry 1993–97; Deputy Gen. Man. State Power Corpn 1997–98; Minister of Water Resources 1998–2007; mem. 16th CCP Cen. Cttee 2002–07.

WANG, Shuguo, DEng; Chinese engineer and university administrator; *President, Xi'an Jiaotong University;* b. Oct. 1958, Hebei Prov.; ed Harbin Inst. of Tech.; joined CCP 1976, Sec., CCP Prov. Cttee, Heilongjiang Prov. Science and Tech. Comm. 1993–2003; Visiting Scholar, Univ. of Paris VI, Pierre et Marie Curie, France 1987–89; Prof. of Mechanical Design, Harbin Inst. of Tech., becoming Deputy Dean, Inst. of Robotics Research 1989–93, Dean, Mechanical and Electrical Eng Coll. 1993–98, Vice-Pres., Harbin Inst. of Tech. 1998–99, Pres. 2003–14; Deputy Dir State 863 Project, Intelligent Robot Research Programme 1993–2003; Deputy, 10th NPC 2003–08, 11th NPC, 12th NPC; Pres. Xi'an Jiaotong Univ. 2014–, mem. CCP Cttee and Standing Cttee; seven consecutive awards of Advanced Prize in Science and Tech. from Heilongjiang Prov. Govt. *Publications:* over 70 academic papers. *Address:* The President's Office, Xi'an Jiaotong University, 28, Xianning West Road, Xi'an, Shaanxi 710049, People's Republic of China (office). *Telephone:* (29) 82668231 (office). *Fax:* (29) 83234781 (office). *E-mail:* dbc@mail.xjtu.edu.cn (office). *Website:* en.xjtu.edu.cn (office).

WANG, Sung; Chinese zoologist and conservationist; b. 1933, Jiangsu; ed Fudan Univ., Shanghai; researcher, Inst. of Zoology, Chinese Acad. of Science, Beijing, later Pres.; was part of first team to catalogue flora and fauna in some of remotest parts of China; work interrupted during Cultural Revolution late 1960s; scientific adviser to Cities Treaty early 1980s; mem. China Council for Int. Cooperation on Environment and Devt; reintroduced Père David deer, extinct in China since 1901, from captive stock in UK; highlighted importance of indigenous domestic stock such as yak of high Tibetan plateau; brought in outside conservation expertise from countries such as UK, Japan and USA; involved with Eco Security Task Force, set up to control 'alien invasive species' in China; Joseph Grinnell Award 1998, Edinburgh Medal 2003. *Publications:* numerous articles in scientific journals. *Address:* c/o Institute of Zoology, Chinese Academy of Sciences, 25 Beisihuanxi Road, Haidan, Beijing 100080, People's Republic of China (office). *Telephone:* (10) 6254-7675 (office). *Fax:* (10) 6256-5689 (office). *E-mail:* wangs@panda.ioz.ac.cn (office). *Website:* www.oiz.ac.cn (office).

WANG, Taihua; Chinese politician; b. Oct. 1945, Xingguo, Jiangxi Prov.; ed Jiangxi Teachers' Coll., CCP Cen. Cttee Cen. Party School; worker, No. 9 Regiment, Jiangxi Production and Construction Corps, Jiangxi Prov. 1968–70; joined CCP 1973; Vice-Principal No. 3 Secondary School, Ganzhou City, Jiangxi Prov. 1978; Vice-Pres. Ganzhou City Educ. School 1979; mem. Standing Cttee CCP Ganzhou City Cttee and Head, Publicity Dept 1980; Deputy Commr Ganzhou Prefectural Admin. Office 1983; mem. Standing Cttee CCP Jiangxi Prov. Cttee and Head, Publicity Dept 1985; Vice-Sec. CCP Anhui Prov. Cttee 1992–2000, Sec. 2000–04; Sec. CCP Hefei City Cttee 1992–98; Vice-Gov. Anhui Prov. 1998–99, Gov. 1999–2001; Chair. Standing Cttee Anhui Prov. People's Congress 2003–04; Dir State Admin for Radio, Film and TV 2004–11; Alt. mem. 14th CCP Cen. Cttee 1992–97, 15th CCP Cen. Cttee 1997–2002, mem. 16th CCP Cen. Cttee 2002–07, 17th CCP Cen. Cttee 2007–12; Deputy 8th NPC 1983–88; Del., 13th CCP Nat. Congress 1987–92, 14th CCP Nat. Congress 1992–97, 15th CCP Nat. Congress 1997–2002, 16th CCP Nat. Congress 2002–07.

WANG, Tao; Chinese geologist and business executive; *Honorary Chairman, Sino Union Petroleum & Chemical International Ltd;* b. 1931, Leting, Hebei Prov.; ed Moscow Inst. of Oil; joined CCP 1948; Chief Geologist, Dagang Oil Field; Chief Geologist, Liaohe Petroleum Prospecting Bureau; Gen. Man., South China Sea Eastern Br. of China Nat. Offshore Oil Corpn; Minister of Petroleum Industry 1985–88; Pres. China Nat. Petroleum Corpn 1988–97; Exec. Dir Sino Union Petroleum & Chemical Int. Ltd 2006–11, currently Hon. Chair.; Prof., China Univ. of Petroleum, China Nanjing Univ.; Chair. Chinese Nat. Cttee for World Petroleum Council; Vice-Chair. Chinese-Arab Friendship Asscn, Chair. Chinese-Saudi Arabia Friendship Asscn; mem. CCP 12th Cen. Cttee 1982–87, 13th Cen. Cttee 1987–92, 14th Cen. Cttee 1992–97; Hon. Chair. and Exec. Dir Yanchang Petroleum Int. Ltd 2006–11; mem. Standing Cttee 9th NPC 1998–2003, Vice-Chair. Environment and Resources Protection Cttee 1998–2003; Foreign Academician, Russian Acad. of Natural Sciences; Sr Consultant, Hoifu Energy Group Ltd; mem. Bd of Dirs CNOOC Ltd 2008–14; World Petroleum Congress Outstanding Contribution Award 2005. *Address:* Sino Union Petroleum & Chemical International Ltd, Unit 1909A–1912, China Merchants Tower, Shun

Tak Centre, 168–200 Connaught Road Central, Hong Kong Special Administrative Region, People's Republic of China.

WANG, Tianpu, MBA, PhD; Chinese oil industry executive; ed Qingdao Chemical Inst., Dalian Polytechnic Univ., Zhejiang Univ.; Vice-Pres. Qilu Petrochemical Co., China Petrochemical Corpn (Sinopec Group) 1999–2000, Vice-Pres. Qilu Co., Sinopec Group 2000, Pres. Qilu Co., Sinopec Group 2000–01, Vice-Pres. Sinopec Group 2000–03, Sr Vice-Pres. 2003–11, Pres. 2011–15, Dir 2006–15, mem. Party Cttee 2001–, placed under investigation by the CCP's anti-corruption agency April 2015.

WANG, Tianren; Chinese sculptor, artist and calligrapher; b. 26 July 1939, Henan; s. of Zheng-gang Wang and Shu-zheng Ren; m. Zhang Pei 1969; one s.; ed Xian Acad. of Fine Arts; worked as art designer and sculptor at Shaanxi Exhbn Hall 1963–79, worked on construction 1964–65; cr. sculptures for Yanan Revolution Memorial Hall 1968–71; Dir group sculptures for Shaanxi Exhbn Hall 1972–75; participated in group sculptures for Chairman Mao Memorial Hall 1976–78; calligraphy works exhibited in Chinese and Japanese cities; Pres. Shaanxi Sculpture Inst. 1996–2000; Vice-Dir of Sculpture Art Cttee, Shaanxi Br. Nat. Asscn of Artists; Art Dir, Dir of Creation Office, Shaanxi Sculpture Inst.; mem. Nat. Calligraphers Asscn, Shaanxi Folk Art Inst., Shaanxi Industrial Artists Asscn. *Works include:* Hou Ji 1980–81, Flower, The Morning Rooster, Qin Ox, Zebra, Tang Dynasty Musicians in Nishang and Yuyi (Copper Medal, Nat. City Sculptures Designing Exhbn 1983), Letter Carrier Goose (Copper Medal, Nat. City Sculptures Designing Exhbn 1983), Biaoqi General of Han Dynasty Huo Qu-bing (Excellent Prize, 6th Nat. Art Works Exhbn 1984, First Prize, Shaanxi Art Works Exhbn 1984), Rising to the Sky (for Urumuqi, Xinjing; Prize for Excellence, Nat. Ministry of Urban Construction, Nat. Asscn of Artists 1987) 1985, Qin Unification 1992, Unification of Qin Dynasty (selected for 2nd Nat. City Sculpture, Nat. Prize from Nat. Construction Ministry, Ministry of Culture and Asscn of Nat Artists) 1994, Yu Youren (selected for 8th Nat. Arts Exhbn) 1994, sign sculpture for Xijiang Chemical Fertilizer Factory 1995, civic scenery sculpture for Hejin, Shaanxi Prov. 1995, Soar Aloft (sign sculpture for Xian Yanliang city) 1996, Zhao Hongzhang (granite-sculpture) 1996, Hou Ji (stone sculpture for Shaanxi) 1996, large city sign sculpture for Shanxi 1996, Flying Phoenix 1997, Wang Ding 1997, Surpass 1998, Flying 1998, Fountain 1999, Unlimited 1999, Phoenix Sing 1999, Unrestrained and Far-Ranging 2000, Liang Sicheng 2001, Yu Hua Long 2001, Space Navigation 2001, Li Xiaolong 2002, Happy Fish 2002, Shi Qingyun 2002, Doctor Bethune 2002, A group of little girls and boys 2003, Soul of poetry 2004, Canyon of poetry 2004, A group of figures 2004, Yellow Emperor 2010. *Leisure interests:* Chinese classical literature, poetry, music. *Address:* Shaanxi Sculpture Institute, Longshoucun, Xian, Shaanxi 710016 (office); 9 Wenyibeilu, Wenhua Guangxia 14–1, Xian, Shaanxi 710054, People's Republic of China (home). *Telephone:* (29) 6261002 (office); (29) 87855551 (home). *Fax:* (29) 87855551 (home).

WANG, Vera; American fashion designer; *Chairman and CEO, Vera Wang Bridal House Ltd;* b. 27 June 1949, New York, NY; d. of Cheng Ching and Florence Wu; m. Arthur Becker; two d.; ed Chapin School, NY, Sarah Lawrence Coll. and Sorbonne Univ., France; trained as figure skater before moving into fashion; Fashion Ed., Vogue USA 1971–87; Design Dir, Ralph Lauren 1987–89; Founder, Chair. and CEO Vera Wang Bridal House Ltd 1990–, opened flagship salon at Carlyle Hotel, New York; known for bridal collections, began selling bath, bedding and house wares 2002, launched mass-market line Simply Vera By Vera Wang, for chain store Kohls 2007–; Womenswear Designer of the Year, Council of Fashion Designers of America 2005, André Leon Talley Lifetime Achievement Award, Savannah Coll. of Art and Design 2006, Geoffrey Beene Lifetime Achievement Award, Council of Fashion Designers of America 2013. *Publication:* Vera Wang on Weddings 2001. *Address:* Vera Wang Bridal House Ltd, 225 West 39th Street, 9th Floor, New York, NY 10018, USA (office). *Telephone:* (212) 575-6400 (office). *Fax:* (212) 354-2548 (office). *E-mail:* prassistant@verawang.com (office); webcustomercare@verawang.com (office). *Website:* www.verawang.com (office).

WANG, Wayne; Chinese/American film director, producer and screenwriter; b. (Wang Ying), 12 Jan. 1949, Hong Kong; m. Cora Miao (fmr Miss Hong Kong); ed California Coll. of Arts and Crafts, Oakland; raised in Hong Kong and named after his father's favourite film star, John Wayne. *Films include:* A Man, a Woman, and a Killer 1975, Chan is Missing 1982, Dim Sum Take Out (short) 1985, Slam Dance 1987, Eat a Bowl of Tea 1989, Life is Cheap... But Toilet Paper is Expensive 1989, Strangers (erotic film consisting of three shorts, co-directed by Joan Tewkesbury and Daniel Vigne) 1991, The Joy Luck Club 1993, Smoke 1995, Blue in the Face 1995, Chinese Box 1997, Anywhere But Here 1999, The Centre of the World 2001, Maid in Manhattan 2002, Because of Winn-Dixie 2005, Last Holiday 2006, A Thousand Years of Good Prayers (Golden Shell for Best Film, San Sebastian Film Festival) 2007, The Princess of Nebraska 2007, Chinatown Film Project 2009, Snow Flower and the Secret Fan 2011, Soul of a Banquet (documentary) 2014, While the Women Are Sleeping 2016. *Address:* 916 Kearny Street, San Francisco, CA 94133, USA (office).

WANG, Weicheng; Chinese party official; b. 1929, Tonglu Co., Zhejiang Prov.; joined CCP 1948; Dir Research Office of the State Council 1977–83; Deputy Head of Propaganda Dept, CCP Cen. Cttee 1987; Dir Cen. Policy Research Center 1989–; Vice-Pres. China Asscn for Int. Exchange of Personnel, Soc. for study of Workers' Political and Ideological Work; mem. 14th CCP Cen. Cttee 1992–97; mem. 9th Standing Cttee of Cttee 1998–2003, Chair. Legal Affairs Cttee 1998–2003. *Address:* c/o Standing Committee of National People's Congress, Beijing, People's Republic of China (office).

WANG, Weimin; Chinese business executive; *Chairman, China International Travel Service Ltd;* b. 1961; ed Acad. of Armoured Force Eng; fmrly with Cadre, Training Dept of Acad. of Armoured Force Eng, Armoured Force Political Section of Gen. Staff Dept of PLA, Gen. Office of Economy and Trade Office under State Council, Personnel Dept of State Econ. and Trade Comm. (SETC); fmr Deputy Dir, later Dir, later Deputy Dir-Gen. of Tech. Progress Dept and Arms and Equipment Dept of SETC 1995–2003; fmr Deputy Dir-Gen. High-tech Industry Dept of Nat. Devt and Reform Comm.; fmr Deputy Insp., Gen. Office of State-owned Assets Supervision and Admin Comm. under State Council, Sec. of Party Cttee (Directorate Grade) 2006–07; Vice-Chair. and Sec. of Party Cttee, China Metallurgical Group Corpn 2009–12; fmr Chair. MCC Paper Group Co., Ltd; Chair. China Int. Travel Service Ltd 2012–; mem. Bd of Dirs CITS Group Corpn. *Address:* China International Travel Service Limited, Building No. 1, Dongdan Beidajie, Dongcheng District, Beijing, People's Republic of China (office). *Telephone:* (10) 65222991 (office). *E-mail:* info@cits.com.cn (office). *Website:* www.cits.net (office).

WANG, Wenyin; Chinese business executive; *Chairman, Amer International Group;* b. Anqing, Anhui Prov.; Pres. Anhui Chamber of Commerce in Guangdong Prov., Shenzhen-Anhui Enterprise Asscn; Vice-Pres. China Enterprise Dirs Asscn, Anhui Enterprise Confed.; Vice-Chair. Anhui Fed. of Industry and Commerce; Econ. Adviser to Hefei City; Chair. Confed. of Top 500 Chinese Companies 2010–11, 2012; Founder and Chair. Amer International Group Co. Ltd; mem. Anhui CPPCC; Vice-Pres. China Enterprise Directors Asscn; Standing mem. CPPCC Shenzhen Municipal Cttee; Vice-Chair. Anhui Fed. of Industry and Commerce; Pres. Anhui Chamber of Commerce in Guangdong Prov., Shenzhen-Anhui Enterprise Asscn; Vice-Pres. Anhui Enterprise Confed.; Chair. Confed. of Top 500 Chinese Cos 2010, 2011, 2012, Guangdong Zhisland Inst., Shenzhen Business Fed.; honoured as The Most Creative Chinese Business Leader and Outstanding Chinese Entrepreneur Venture Influential Man of Shenzhen's new generation, named as one of the ten outstanding chairmen of the Chamber of Commerce 2012, Shenzhen Business Big Men of the Honour 2013, named as one of the Shenzhen business leaders who influence China, named by Fortune as the most influential business leader in China 2013, Nat. Outstanding Entrepreneur 2013–14, Guangdong Econ. Influential Man 2014. *Address:* East Pacific International Center, 7888th Shennan Boulevard, Shenzhen 518040, People's Republic of China (office). *Telephone:* (755) 82785868 (office). *Fax:* (755) 27118899 (office). *E-mail:* webmaster@amer.com.cn (office). *Website:* www.amer.com.cn (office).

WANG, Wilfred, BEng; Taiwanese business executive; *Managing Director, Formosa Petrochemical Corporation;* ed Univ. of London, UK; Exec. Vice-Pres. Formosa Petrochemical Corpn 1998–2003, Pres. 2003–09, Chair. 2006–11, Exec. Dir 2012–; Chair. Mailiao Harbor Admin Corpn, Formosa Plastics Marine Corpn, Nan Ya Photonics Inc.; Exec. Dir Formosa Plastics Corpn, Nan Ya Plastics Corpn, Formosa Ha Tinh Steel Corpn; Man. Dir Formosa Chemicals & Fibre Corpn. *Address:* Formosa Petrochemical Corpn, 1-1, Formosa Plastics Group Industrial Zone, Mailiao, Yunlin, Taiwan (office). *Telephone:* (5) 6812345 (office). *Website:* www.fpcc.com.tw (office); www.fpg.com.tw (office).

WANG, Xianzhang; Chinese insurance executive; b. May 1942, Hebei Prov.; ed Liaoning Finance and Econ. Inst. (now Northeastern Univ. of Finance and Econs); began career in insurance industry 1965, held positions successively as Gen. Man. People's Insurance Co. of China, Liaoning Br., Vice-Pres. People's Insurance Co. of China, Vice-Pres. People's Insurance (Group) Co. of China, Pres. and Vice-Chair. China Insurance H.K. (Holding) Co. Ltd, Chair. and Pres. China Life Insurance Co. Ltd 2000–05; Chair. Insurance Industry Asscn of China; Vice-Pres. Insurance Inst. of China; mem. China Enterprise Confed. & China Enterprise Dirs Asscn (CEC-CED); mem. Bd of Dirs Beijing Enterprises Holdings Ltd 1997–2008, Ageas Asia Holdings Ltd 2000–, Wonder Auto Tech., Inc. 2009–, Eagle Ride Investment Holdings Ltd 2013–; mem. CCP, Del. to CCP Nat. and mem. CPPCC. *Publications include:* China Insurance Dictionary, Insurance Marketing Psychology, An Insurance Specialist's Comments of Insurance.

WANG, Xiaochu, DBA; Chinese telecommunications industry executive; *Chairman, China United Network Communications Group Company Ltd;* b. 1953, Beijing; ed Beijing Inst. of Posts and Telecommunications, Hong Kong Polytechnic Univ.; fmr Deputy Dir and Dir Hangzhou Telecommunications Bureau, Zhejiang Prov.; fmr Dir-Gen. Tianjin Posts and Telecommunications Admin; Dir China Mobile (Hong Kong) Ltd 1999–, also fmr CEO and Chair.; fmr Vice-Pres. China Mobile Communications Corpn; Gen. Man. China Telecommunications Corpn 2004, Exec. Dir 2005–15, Chair. and CEO 2004–15; Hon. Chair. China Communications Services Corpn Ltd 2008–, Sec. Party Leadership Group; Chair. China United Network Communications Group Co. Ltd 2015–, Chair. and CEO China Unicom (Hong Kong) Ltd 2015–; Alt. mem. 17th CCP Cen. Cttee 2007–12, 18th CCP Cen. Cttee 2012–; Class Three Nat. Science and Tech. Advancement Award, Ministry of Posts and Telecommunications, Class One Science and Tech. Advancement Award. *Address:* China United Network Communications Group Co. Ltd, 29/F 1033 Changning Road, Changning District, Shanghai 100032, People's Republic of China (office). *Telephone:* (21) 5273-2228 (office). *E-mail:* info@chinaunicom-a.com (office). *Website:* www.chinaunicom-a.com (office).

WANG, Xiaodong, BS, PhD; American (b. Chinese) biochemist and academic; *Investigator and Co-Director, National Institute of Biological Sciences, Beijing;* b. 1963, Wuhan, China; ed Beijing Normal Univ., Univ. of Texas Southwestern Medical Center, USA; grew up in Xingxiang, Henan Prov.; Post-doctoral Researcher, Univ. of Texas Southwestern Medical Center 1991–95, Asst Prof., Dept of Biochemistry 1996–99, Assoc. Prof. 1999–2001, George L. MacGregor Distinguished Chair Prof. in Biomedical Science 2001–; Asst Prof., Dept of Biochemistry, Emory Univ. School of Medicine 1996–99; Asst Investigator, Howard Hughes Medical Inst. 1997–2002, Investigator 2002–; Investigator and Co-Dir Nat. Inst. of Biological Sciences, Beijing 2003–; Consultant, Idun Pharmaceuticals 1998–2002; mem. Editorial Bd Molecular Biology of the Cell 2002–, Journal of Biological Chemistry 2002–; mem. American Asscn of Cancer Research, American Soc. of Biochemistry and Molecular Biology, American Soc. of Cell Biology, NAS 2004–, Soc. of Chinese Biomedical Scientists in America; Damon Runyon-Walter Winchell Cancer Research Fund Postdoctoral Fellowship 1991–94, ACS Eli Lilly Award 2000, Paul Marks Prize, Memorial Sloan-Kettering Cancer Center 2001, Hackerman Award, The Welch Foundation 2002, NAS Molecular Biology Award 2004, Shaw Prize in Life Science and Medicine, The Shaw Foundation 2006, NAS Richard Lounsbery Award 2007. *Publications include:* numerous scientific papers in professional journals on biochemical mechanism of programmed cell death, or apoptosis, in human cells. *Address:* National Institute of Biological Sciences, 7 Science Park Road, ZGC Life Science Park, Beijing 102206, People's Republic of China (office). *Telephone:* (10)-80726688 (office). *Fax:* (10)-80726689 (office). *E-mail:* wangxiaodong@nibs.ac.cn (office). *Website:* www.nibs.ac.cn (office).

WANG, Xiaofeng; Chinese politician; b. Oct. 1944, Cili Co., Hunan Prov.; ed Beijing Mining Inst.; technician, later Deputy Dir, later Dir Changde July 1st Machinery Plant, Hunan Prov. 1970–83; joined CCP 1973; Deputy Sec. CCP

Changde Prefectural Cttee 1983–86, Commr Changde Prefectural Admin. Office 1983–86; Dir Hunan Provincial Planning Cttee 1986–90; Vice-Gov. Hunan Prov. 1990–93, Exec. Vice-Gov. 1993–98; Deputy Sec. CCP Hunan Prov. Cttee 1992–93; Deputy Sec. CCP Hainan Prov. Cttee 1993–98, Sec. 2004–06; Vice-Gov. Hainan Prov. 1993–98, Gov. 1998–2003; Pres. Hainan Prov. Entrepreneurs Asscn 1993; Chair. Standing Cttee Hainan Prov. People's Congress 2004–06; Alt. mem. 14th CCP Cen. Cttee 1992–97, mem. 15th CCP Cen. Cttee 1997–2002, 16th CCP Cen. Cttee 2002–07; Chief of Office, Three Gorges Dam project (Sandouping, Yiling District, Hubei) 2007–10; mem. Standing Cttee CPPCC (Vice-Chair.) 2008–13 (retd).

WANG, Xiaoshuai; Chinese film director and screenwriter; b. 22 May 1966, Shanghai; ed Beijing Film Acad.; mem. jury BigScreen Italia Film Festival 2006; Chevalier, Ordre des Arts et des Lettres (France) 2010. *Films include:* Dongchun de rizi (The Days) (Silver Charybdis, Taormina Int. Film Festival 1994, Golden Alexander, Thessaloniki Film Festival 1994) 1993, Da youxi 1994, Jidu hanleng (Frozen) (FIPRESCI Prize-Special Mention, Rotterdam Int. Film Festival 1997) 1996, Biandan, guniang (So Close to Paradise) (FIPRESCI/NETPAC Award, Singapore Int. Film Festival 2000) 1998, The House 1999, Beijing Bicycle (Silver Bear for Best Dir, Berlin Film Festival 2001, Audience Award, Jeonju Film Festival 2001) 2001, After War (segment) (Golden Leopard-Video (co–recipient), Locarno Int. Film Festival 2002) 2002, Drifters (Netpac Award, Cinefan-Festival of Asian and Arab Cinema 2003) 2003, Shanghai Dreams (Jury Prize, Cannes Film Festival 2005, Golden Orange Award for Best Film, Antalya Golden Orange Film Festival 2005, Grand Prize, Tallinn Black Nights Film Festival 2005) 2005, In Love We Trust (Silver Bear Best Script 2008) 2007, Chongqing Blues (China Film Directors' Guild Award for Best Director 2011) 2010, 11 Flowers 2011, Red Amnesia (ARRI/OSRAM Award-Special Mention, Munich Film Festival 2015) 2014; as actor: Weekend Lover 1994, The Red Violin 1998, The World 2004, Karmic Mahjong 2006.

WANG, Xiji, BEng, MS; Chinese engineer; b. 1921, Dali, Yun'nan Prov.; ed Southwest China United Univ., Virginia Polytechnic Inst., USA; returned to China 1950; fmrly Assoc. Prof. Dalian Polytechnic; Prof., Shanghai Jiaotong Univ. and Shanghai Univ. of Science and Tech.; Chief Engineer, Shanghai Mechanical and Electrical Designing Inst., Chinese Acad. of Sciences; Chief Engineer, Ministry of Aerospace Industry; Vice-Pres. Research Inst. No. 5, Ministry of Aerospace Industry; researcher and adviser, China Aerospace Science and Tech. Corpn, China Space Tech. Research Inst.; mem. Int. Acad. of Astronautics 1987, Chinese Acad. of Sciences 1993–; was in charge of the research and devt of 12 types of sounding rockets and the technical design of China's first launch vehicle Long March I in the 1960s; was first chief designer of Chinese recoverable satellites (CRSAT) and successfully conducted China's micro-gravity space experiments on CRSAT; Special Prize of Nat. Science and Tech. Advancement Award 1985, Meritorious Service Medal for the devt of China's Atomic and Hydrogen Bombs and Satellites by the CCP Cen. Cttee, the State Council and the Cen. Mil. Comm. 1999. *Address:* c/o Chinese Academy of Sciences, 52 Sanlihe Road, Beijing 100864, People's Republic of China (office).

WANG, Xudong; Chinese politician; b. Jan. 1946, Yancheng, Jiangsu Prov.; ed Tianjin Coll. for Advanced Studies in Science and Tech.; joined CCP 1972; fmrly Sec. of Chinese Communist Youth League Cttee; Vice-Sec. CCP Cttee PLA 1418 Research Inst.; Dir Research Inst. No. 18, Ministry of Electronics Industry; Dir Org. Dept, CCP Tianjin Municipal Cttee, also Deputy Sec.; Vice-Dir Org. Dept, CCP Cen. Cttee 1993–2000; mem. Standing Cttee CCP Hebei Prov. Cttee 2000–02, Sec. Prov. Cttee 2000–02; Minister of Information Industry 2003–08; Chair. State Electricity Regulatory Comm. 2008–11; apptd Vice-Chair. CPPCC Nat. Cttee, Cttee for Social and Legal Affairs 2011; Alt. mem. 15th CCP Cen. Cttee 1997–2002, mem. 16th CCP Cen. Cttee 2002–07, 17th CCP Cen. Cttee 2007–12.

WANG, Xuebing; Chinese banker; b. 1946, Beijing; ed Univ. of Int. Business and Econs, Beijing; Adviser Steering Group, Gold and Exchange Rate Man. of State Council 1987; Gen. Man. US Operations, Bank of China 1988–93; Chair. and Pres. Bank of China 1993–2000; Pres. and CEO China Construction Bank 2000–02 (dismissed following alleged financial irregularities at Bank of China); expelled from CCP 2002; sentenced to 12 years in prison for taking bribes 2003; Alt. mem. 15th CCP Cen. Cttee 1997–2002.

WANG, Yang; Chinese politician; *Chairman, Chinese People's Political Consultative Conference;* b. 1955, Suzhou City, Anhui Prov.; ed CCP Cen. Cttee Central Party School; joined CCP 1975; began career working in food processing factory, becoming supervisor 1972–76; teacher, CCP Party School, Suxian, Anhui Prov. 1980–81; Deputy Dir, later Dir Anhui Provincial Sports Bureau 1984–88; Mayor, Tongling City, Anhui Prov. 1988–98; Vice-Gov. Anhui Prov. 1993–99; Vice-Minister, Nat. Devt and Reform Comm. 1999–2003; Deputy Sec.-Gen., State Council 2003–05; Sec., Chongqing Municipality CCP Cttee 2005–07, Chair., Standing Cttee, Chongqing Municipality Municipal People's Congress 2006–08; Sec., CCP Provincial Cttee, Guangdong Prov. 2007–12, also mem. Standing Cttee, CCP Provincial Cttee, Guangdong Prov. 2007–12; Vice-Premier 2013–18; mem. State Council CCP Leading Party Group 2013–; Dir Nat. Afforestation Cttee 2013–; alt. mem. 16th CCP Cen. Cttee 2002–07; Chair., Chinese People's Political Consultative Conf. 2018–; mem. 17th CCP Cen. Cttee 2007–12, also mem. 17th CCP Cen. Cttee Politburo 2007–12; mem. 18th CCP Cen. Cttee 2012–17, also mem. 18th CCP Cen. Cttee Politburo 2012–17; mem. 19th CCP Cen. Cttee 2017–, also mem. 19th CCP Cen. Cttee Politburo 2017– and Politburo Standing Cttee 2017–. *Address:* Chinese Communist Party Politburo, Quanguo Renmin Diabiao Dahui, Zhongguo Gongchan Dang, 1 Zhongnanhai, Beijing, People's Republic of China. *Website:* cpc.people.com.cn (office).

WANG, Yi, MEconSc; Chinese diplomatist and government official; *Minister of Foreign Affairs;* b. 8 Oct. 1953, Beijing; m.; one d.; ed Beijing Second Foreign Language Inst.; with Intelligence Research Inst., Ministry of Post and Telecommunications 1977–78; Attaché, Deputy Office Dir the Office Dir, Dept of Asian Affairs, Ministry of Foreign Affairs 1982–89; Counsellor, Embassy in Japan 1989–94; returned to Asian Affairs Dept as Deputy Chief 1994–95, Chief 1995–98, Asst to Minister for Foreign Affairs 1998–2001, Vice-Minister for Foreign Affairs 2001–04, 2007, Minister 2013–, Amb. to Japan 2004–07, Dir Taiwan Affairs Office 2008–13; mem. State Council 2018–; mem. 17th CCP Cen. Cttee 2007–12, 18th

CCP Cen. Cttee 2012–17, 19th CCP Cen. Cttee 2017–. *Address:* Ministry of Foreign Affairs, 225 Chaoyangmen Nan Dajie, Chaoyang Qu, Beijing 100701, People's Republic of China (office). *Telephone:* (10) 65961114 (office). *Fax:* (10) 65962146 (office). *E-mail:* webmaster@mfa.gov.cn (office). *Website:* www.fmprc.gov.cn (office).

WANG, Yidong, BFA, MFA; Chinese artist; b. 1 May 1955, Le Shan, Sichuan; ed Shandong Univ. of Tech., Central Acad. of Fine Arts; fmr prof. of painting, Shandong Univ. of Technology and Central Acad. of Fine Arts; Vice Chair. Beijing Artists Asscn; Councillor, mem., Chinese Artists Asscn; Golden Prize of the Sixth Nat. Art Exhibition, Nat. Gallery, Beijing. *Exhibitions include:* Solo: Schoeni Art Gallery, Hong Kong; Group: Modern Art Museum, Dallas 1990, Schoeni Art Gallery, Hong Kong 1997, 2001, 2002, 2004, 2007, Museum Küppersmühle für Moderne Kunst, Duisburg 2005, Galerie Kaysser, Ruhpolding 2006, Triumph Art Space, Beijing 2010, 2011. *Address:* c/o Yang Gallery, 3rd Taoci Street, 798 Art District, No. 4 Jiuxianqiao Road, Chaoyang District, Beijing 100015, People's Republic of China. *Telephone:* (10) 57623020. *E-mail:* beijing@yanggallery.info. *Website:* www.yanggallery.com.sg.

WANG, Yifang, MSc; Chinese engineer and steel industry executive; b. 1948, Pingxiang, Hebei Prov.; ed Wuhan Steel and Iron Coll., Beijing Steel and Iron Coll.; joined CCP 1948; Dir and Deputy Gen. Man. Handan Steel and Iron Co. Ltd (Hangang Group), Hebei Prov. 2000–08, Gen. Man. 2003–08; Chair., Gen. Man. and Deputy Party Sec., Hebei Iron and Steel Group Co. Ltd (HeSteel Group Co. Ltd (HBIS), formed from merger of Tangsteel Co. Ltd and Hansteel Co. Ltd 2008) 2008–13; Hebei Prov. Award for Excellent Science and Tech. 2000, State Award for Top Worker 2000, State Award for Excellent Promoter.

WANG, Yifang, BSc, PhD; Chinese physicist and academic; *Director, Institute of High Energy Physics, Chinese Academy of Sciences;* b. Feb. 1963, Jiangsu; ed Nanjing Univ., Univ. of Florence, Italy; Temporary Researcher, Nat. Inst. of Nuclear Physics, Italy 1991–92; Researcher, MIT Lab. of Nuclear Science 1992–96; Research Assoc., Dept of Physics, Stanford Univ. 1996–2001; Researcher then apptd Prof., Inst. of High Energy Physics, Chinese Acad. of Sciences 2001, currently Dir, also fmrly Standing mem. Science Cttee, Deputy Dir Experimental Physics Centre 2001–05, later Dir; Breakthrough Prize in Fundamental Physics (co-recipient) 2016. *Publications:* numerous papers in professional journals. *Address:* Institute of High Energy Physics, Chinese Academy of Sciences, 19B Yu Quan Lu, Shijingshan District, Beijing 100049, People's Republic of China (office). *Telephone:* (10) 88233992 (office). *E-mail:* yfwang@mail.ihep.ac.cn (office). *Website:* english.ihep.cas.cn (office).

WANG, Yilin, PhD; Chinese geologist and oil industry executive; *Chairman, China National Petroleum Corporation (CNPC);* ed China Univ. of Petroleum; Deputy Dir and Chief Exploration Geologist, Xinjiang Petroleum Admin Bureau 1996–99; Gen. Man. Xinjiang Oilfield Co. 1999–2003; Asst Pres. China Nat. Petroleum Corpn (CNPC) July–Dec. 2003, Vice-Pres. Dec. 2003–11, concurrently Chief HSE Officer, CNPC 2004–11, mem. Bd of Dirs, PetroChina 2005–11, Chair. China Nat. Offshore Oil Corpn (CNOOC) 2011–15, Chair. CNPC April 2015–, Chair. PetroChina June 2015–; mem. 18th CCP Cen. Comm. for Discipline Inspection 2012–. *Address:* China National Petroleum Corporation (CNPC), 9 Dongzhimen North Street, Dongcheng District, Beijing 100007, People's Republic of China (office). *Telephone:* (10) 62094114 (office). *Fax:* (10) 62094205 (office). *E-mail:* admin_eng@cnpc.com.cn (office). *Website:* www.cnpc.com.cn (office).

WANG, Yong, MEng; Chinese government official; *State Councillor and Director, National Committee for Disaster Reduction;* b. 1955, Gaizhou City, Liaoning Prov.; ed Harbin Inst. of Tech.; began working 1969; joined CCP 1974; worked in Heilongjiang Construction Corps, Seventh Ministry of Mechanical Industry, Ministry of Aerospace, No. 230 Factory under China Aerospace Corpn, held successive posts of Asst to the Dir, Deputy Chief Economist, Deputy Dir, Exec. Deputy Dir, Dir and Deputy Party Sec. (Dir-Gen. level); transferred to China Astronautics Corpn, Deputy Dir and Head of Personnel Dept 1997–98; Deputy Gen. Man. China Aerospace Mechanic and Electronic Corpn 1999–2000; Dir Org. Dept, Enterprise Cadre Office, CCP Cen. Cttee 2000–01, Dir 5th Dept 2001–03; Deputy Dir State-owned Assets Supervision and Admin Comm. (SASAC) 2003–08, Dir 2010–13, also mem. CCP Party Cttee 2003–05, Deputy Sec. 2005–08, Sec. 2010–; State Councillor 2013–; Dir-Gen. Admin of Quality Supervision, Inspection and Quarantine 2008–10, Sec. CCP Leading Party Group 2008–10; Dir, Nat. Cttee for Disaster Reduction 2013–; mem. Cen. Comm. for Discipline Inspection, 16th CCP Cen. Cttee 2003–07, 17th CCP Cen. Cttee 2007–12, 18th CCP Cen. Cttee 2012–17, 19th CCP Cen. Cttee 2017–. *Address:* National Committee for Disaster Reduction, Department of Foreign Affairs, 147 Beiheyan Street, Beijing 100721, People's Republic of China (office). *Telephone:* (10) 65235511 (office). *Fax:* (10) 65121882 (office). *E-mail:* kp@mca.gov.cn (office). *Website:* www.mca.gov.cn (office).

WANG, Yongyan; Chinese physician; b. Sept. 1938, Tianjin; ed Beijing Chinese Medical Coll.; Assoc. Prof., then Prof., Chief Doctor, Pres., Beijing Chinese Medical Univ.; Dir Chinese Acad. of Traditional Chinese Medicine; Vice-Chair. Chinese Medical Soc. of China; Prof. and Founding Dir Inst. of Basic Research in Clinical Medicine, China Acad. of Chinese Medical Sciences; mem. Expert Group, Nat. Key Basic Research and Devt Plan, 5th Standing Cttee, China Asscn of Science and Tech., mem. Nat. Cttee for Terms in Science and Tech., Academic Degrees Cttee of the State Council, 6th and 7th Standing Cttees; Chief Ed. Clinical Chinese Internal Medicine, Series on Today Chinese Medicine Clinic and other academic works; mem. Editorial Bd Journal of Traditional Chinese Medicine; Fellow, Chinese Acad. of Sciences, Chinese Acad. of Engineering; Hon. Pres. China Acad. of Chinese Medical Sciences; Medal of Nat. Labor Day, Ho Leung Ho Lee Foundation Prize for Scientific and Technological Progress. *Publications include:* more than 120 academic papers. *Address:* Institute of Basic Research in Clinical Medicine, 16 Nanxiaojie, Dongzhimennei Street, Dongcheng District, Beijing 100700, People's Republic of China (office). *E-mail:* wangyyan@public.bta.net.cn.

WANG, Yongzhi; Chinese aerospace scientist; b. 17 Nov. 1932, Changtu, Liaoning Prov.; m.; ed Moscow Aviation Inst.; Dir Research Section, Dir Design Dept, Pres. No. 1 Research Inst. of Ministry of Aerospace Industry; Gen. Designer of Rockets 1961–91; Vice-Dir Science and Tech. Cttee, Ministry of Aerospace Industry 1991–98; designer of rocket launcher series 1991–; Sr Consulting

Engineer for manned space programme, including launch of Shenzhou VII spacecraft Sept. 2008; Academician, Int. Astronautical Acad., Foreign Academician Konstantin Eduardovich Ziolkowski Acad., Russia 1992–; Academician Chinese Acad. of Eng 1994–; mem. 11th CPPCC Nat. Cttee 2008–13; Prize of Nat. Scientific Conf., Scientific Advancement Prize, State Pre-eminent Science and Technology Award 2003, Meritorious Scientist of Manned Spaceflight 2005, HoLeung Ho Lee Foundation Technological Science Prize. *Address:* Chinese Academy of Engineering, 2 BingJiaoKou HuTong, Beijing 100088, People's Republic of China (office). *Telephone:* (10) 59300264 (office). *Fax:* (10) 59300140 (office). *E-mail:* info@cae.cn (office). *Website:* en.cae.cn (office).

WANG, You-Tsao, MSc, PhD; Taiwanese politician and agricultural adviser; b. 2 July 1925, Chinchiang Co., Fukien; s. of Wang Hsiao-kwei and Wang-Huang Pei-feng; m. Jean Eng-ling 1954; two s. one d.; ed Nat. Taiwan Univ., Iowa State Univ., USA; Asst, Instructor, Assoc. Prof., Dept of Agric. Econs, Nat. Taiwan Univ. 1954–60, Prof. 1960–73; Specialist, Rural Econs Div., Jt Comm. on Rural Reconstruction (JCRR) 1960–63, Sr Specialist 1965–66, Chief, Rural Econs Div. 1966–71, Chief, Office of Planning and Programming 1971–72, Deputy Sec.-Gen. JCRR 1972–73, Sec.-Gen. 1973–79; Sec.-Gen. Council for Agric. Planning and Devt, Exec. Yuan 1979, Vice-Chair. 1979–84, Chair. 1984, Chair. and Chief Operating Admin. 1984–88, Adviser 1990–2004; Minister without Portfolio, Exec. Yuan 1988–90; Nat. Policy Adviser to Pres. 1990–96; Dir Asian Agric. Tech. Service Center 1993–95; Pres. Rural Devt Foundation 1995–98 (Chair. 1998); Chair. Bd of Dirs Harvest (farm magazine) 1995–2002; mem. Agric. Asscn of China, Rural Econs Asscn of China. *Publications:* Statistical Analysis of Resources Productivity in Shihmen Reservoir Area of Taiwan 1963, Technological Changes and Agricultural Development of Taiwan 1946–65 1966. *Address:* 7F, No. 2, Alley 8, Lane 216, Sect. 4, Chung Hsiao East Road, Taipei, Taiwan (home).

WANG, Yuan; Chinese mathematician; b. 30 April 1930, Zhejiang Prov.; s. of Maoqing Wang; ed Zhejiang Univ.; Acting Dir Inst. of Math., Acad. Sinica March–Oct. 1946–49, apptd Dir 1985; mem. Dept of Math. and Physics, Acad. Sinica 1985–; mem. Nat. Cttee 6th CPPCC 1986; Pres. Chinese Math. Soc. 1989–92; mem. Presidium Chinese Acad. of Sciences 1996; numerous awards including Hua Loo-Keng Math. Prize. *Publications:* Applications of Number Theory to Numerical Analysis 1978, Goldbach Conjecture 1984, Popularising Mathematical Methods In The People's Republic Of China (with Hua Loo Keng) 1989, Diophantine Equations And Inequalities In Algebraic Number Fields 1991, Number Theoretic Methods In Statistics 1994, Hua Loo Keng: A Brief Outline of his Life and Works 1995, Calculus (with Fong Yuen) 1997. *Leisure interest:* calligraphy.

WANG, Yunkun; Chinese politician; b. Dec. 1942, Liyang Co., Jiangsu Prov.; ed Tianjin Univ.; joined CCP 1966; Chief, Publicity Section, Chemical Machinery Plant, Jilin Chemical Industry Co., Deputy Dir, later Dir Political Dept, engineer, Refinery, Research Inst. and Organic Synthesis Plant; Vice-Mayor Jilin City 1982–83, Mayor 1983–86; Dir Dept of Electronic Industry, Jilin Prov. 1986–88; Chair. Comm. for Restructuring the Economy, Jilin Prov. 1988; Sec.-Gen. People's Govt, Jilin Prov. 1988–89; Vice-Gov. Jilin Prov. 1989–92, Acting Gov. 1995, Gov. 1996–98; Sec. CCP Changchun City Cttee 1992–95; Deputy Sec. Jilin Prov. Cttee 1995–98, Sec. 1998–2006; fmr Chair. Standing Cttee Jilin Prov. People's Congress 1999; mem. 15th CCP Cen. Cttee 1997–2002, 16th CCP Cen. Cttee 2002–07.

WANG, Yupu, BA, MA, PhD; Chinese energy industry executive; b. 1956, Xinmin Co., Liaoning Prov.; ed China Univ. of Petroleum, Faculty of Quarry Machinery, Daqing Petroleum Inst., Cen. Party School (Cadre Training Class); Deputy Dir No. 7 Production Plant, Daqing Petroleum Admin Bureau, Heilongjiang Prov., Daqing City 1994–97, No. 4 Production Plant 1994–96, Oilfield Devt Dept 1997–98, No. 1 Oil and Gas Devt Div. 1997–98, Deputy Chief Engineer, Daqing Petroleum Admin Bureau 1998–99; Deputy Chief Engineer, PetroChina Co. Ltd, Heilongjiang Prov. 1999–2000, Dir No. 1 Production Plant 2000–01, Deputy Gen. Man. and Sec. CCP Party Cttee, PetroChina Co. Ltd 2000–01, Exec. Deputy Gen. Man. 2001–03, Vice-Chair., PetroChina Co. Ltd 2001–03, Chair. and Gen. Man., PetroChina Co. Ltd and Deputy Sec., CCP Party Cttee 2003–09; Chair. China Petrochemical Corpn (Sinopec Group) 2015–17; Vice-Gov. Heilongjiang Prov. 2009–; mem. CCP 1985–, Alt. mem. 17th CCP Cen. Cttee 2007–12, mem. 18th CCP Cen. Cttee 2012–; Academician, Chinese Acad. of Eng 2007.

WANG, Zhaoguo; Chinese party official; *Chairman, All-China Federation of Trade Unions;* b. 14 July 1941, Fengrun, Hebei Prov.; one s.; ed Harbin Technological Univ., Dalian Univ. of Tech.; joined CCP 1965; technician, later Deputy Dir Axle Plant, Second Automotive Works 1968–79 (mem. Standing Cttee, later First Sec. CCP Party Cttee 1968–79), Dir Second Automotive Works 1979–82 (Sec. CCP Party Cttee 1979–82); mem. Standing Cttee CCP Shiyan Municipal Cttee, Hubei Prov. 1968–79; First Sec. CCP Communist Youth League of China and Pres. Party School 1982–84; Deputy for Hubei to 6th NPC 1983; Dir-Gen. Office Cen. Cttee CCP 1984–86; Chief Rep. 21st Century Cttee for Chinese-Japanese Friendship 1984–89; Vice-Gov. and Acting Gov. of Fujian 1987–88, Gov. 1988–90; Dir Taiwan Affairs Office, State Council 1990–96; Chair. All-China Fed. of Trade Unions 2002–; mem. 12th CCP Cen. Cttee 1982–87, 13th CCP Cen. Cttee 1987–92, 14th CCP Cen. Cttee 1992–97, 15th CCP Cen. Cttee 1997–2002, 16th CCP Cen. Cttee 2002–07 (mem. Politburo 2002–07), 17th CCP Cen. Cttee 2007–12 (mem. Politburo 2007–12); mem. Secr., CCP Cen. Cttee 1985–87; mem. Presidium 6th NPC 1983–88, Standing Cttee 6th NPC 1983–88, Vice-Chair. Standing Cttee 10th NPC 2003–08, Standing Cttee 11th NPC 2008–; Head, United Front Work Dept 1992–2007; Vice-Chair. 8th CPPCC Nat. Cttee 1993–98, 9th CPPCC Nat. Cttee 1998–2003; Pres. China Overseas Friendship Asscn 1997–. *Address:* All-China Federation of Trade Unions, 10 Fu Xing Men Wai Jie, Beijing 100865, People's Republic of China (office). *Telephone:* (10) 68592114 (office). *Website:* www.acftu.org (office).

WANG, Zhen-Yi, DMed; Chinese haematologist; *Honorary Director, Shanghai Institute of Haematology;* b. 30 Nov. 1924, Shanghai; m. Xie Jin-xiong; three s.; ed Aurora Univ. Medical Coll.; Pres. Shanghai Second Medical Univ. 1984–88; currently Prof. Emer. of Medicine and Pathophysiology, School of Medicine, Shanghai Jiao Tong Univ.; Foreign Corresp., French Acad. of Sciences 1992–; mem. Chinese Acad. of Eng 1994–; Hon. Dir Shanghai Inst. of Haematology; Chevalier, Légion d'honneur (France) 1993; numerous awards, including Kettering Prize 1994, Charles Rodolphe Brupbacher Prize 1997, Prix mondial Cino Del Duca 1998, State Supreme Science and Tech. Award 2011. *Publications:* chief ed. of five books and author of more than 320 scientific papers. *Leisure interest:* listening to classical music. *Address:* Shanghai Institute of Haematology, Rui-jin Hospital, 197 Rui-jin Er Road, Shanghai 200025, People's Republic of China (office). *Telephone:* (21) 6437-0045 (office). *Fax:* (21) 6474-3206 (office). *E-mail:* xiejx@sh163.net (office). *Website:* www.sih.org.cn (office).

WANG, Zhengwei; Chinese government official; *Minister of State Ethnic Affairs Commission;* b. June 1957, Ningxia Hui Autonomous Region; ed Ningxia Univ., Central Univ. for Nationalities; joined CCP 1981; Sec., Gen. Office, CCP Autonomous Regional Cttee, Ningxia Hui Autonomous Region 1984–89, Deputy Dir, Policy Research Office 1989–97, Dir, Publicity Dept 1997–2001; Acting Chair., Autonomous Region People's Govt, Ningxia Hui Autonomous Region 2007–08, Chair. 2008–13; Minister of State Ethnic Affairs Comm. 2013–; Vice-Chair., 12th CPPCC Nat. Cttee 2013–; mem. 16th CCP Cen. Cttee 2002–07, 17th CCP Cen. Cttee 2007–12, 18th CCP Cen. Cttee 2012–. *Address:* State Ethnic Affairs Commission, 252 Taipingqiao Dajie, Xicheng Qu, Beijing 100800, People's Republic of China (office). *Telephone:* (10) 66080952 (office). *Fax:* (10) 66057719 (office). *E-mail:* webmaster@seac.gov.cn (office). *Website:* www.seac.gov.cn (office).

WANG, Zhibao; Chinese administrator; *Chairman, China Green Foundation;* b. July 1938, Zhaoyuan, Shandong Prov.; ed Northeast Electric Power Inst.; joined CCP 1965; Deputy Chief, Machinery and Electrical Div., Yikeshi Forestry Admin 1975; Dir Planning Dept, Ministry of Forestry 1986; Vice-Minister of Forestry 1992–98; Dir State Forestry Bureau 1998–2000; Pres. China Wildlife Conservation Asscn 1998; currently Chair. China Green Foundation; mem. 9th CPPCC Nat. Cttee 1998–2003. *Address:* China Green Foundation, 18 Hepingli Dongjie Street, Dongcheng District, Beijing 100714, People's Republic of China (office). *Telephone:* (10) 84238200 (office). *Fax:* (10) 84239264 (office). *E-mail:* cgf@cgf.org.cn (office). *Website:* www.cgf.org.cn (office).

WANG, Zhixin, PhD; Chinese biophysicist; *Professor of Biological Sciences and Biotechnology, Tsinghua University;* b. 10 Aug. 1953, Beijing; ed Tsinghua Univ., Beijing; Research Fellow and Vice-Dir, Biophysics Research Inst. of Chinese Acad. of Sciences 1993–, Dir Nat. Biomacromolecules Lab. 1997–2003, Dir Inst. of Biophysics 1999–2003; Vice-Pres. Biophysical Soc. of China 2002–06; Prof., Dept of Biological Sciences and Biotechnology, Tsinghua Univ. 2003–; Prof. Medical Coll., Soochow Univ. 2015–; Pres. Chinese Soc. of Biochemistry and Molecular Biology 2005–14; Dir SinoBiomed Inc. 2007–; mem. Chinese Acad. of Sciences 1997–; Fellow Acad. of Sciences for Developing World (TWAS) 1999; Hon. DSc (Biophysics Research Inst. of Chinese Acad. of Sciences) 1988; Natural Science Award 1990, Young Scientist Award 1993, Chinese Acad. of Sciences, Nat. Natural Science Prize 1993, Outstanding Young Scientist Award, Hong Kong Qiushi Foundation 1994. *Address:* Department of Biological Sciences and Biotechnology, Tsinghua University, 30 Shuangqing Rd, Haidan Qu, Beijing 100101, People's Republic of China (office). *Telephone:* (10) 64889890 (office). *Fax:* (10) 64871293 (office). *E-mail:* zhixinwang@mail.tsinghua.edu.cn (office). *Website:* www.biosci.tsinghua.edu.cn (office).

WANG, Zhizhong; Chinese business executive; joined Tianjin Enterprise Group (Tewoo) 1999, Chair. Tianjin Materials and Equipments Group Corpn (fmrly Bureau of Materials, f. 1993) –2014, Tewoo Metals International Trade Co. Ltd.

WANG, Zhongyu; Chinese politician; b. Feb. 1933, Changchun, Jilin Prov.; two s. one d.; ed Light Industry Sr Vocational School, Shenyang City, Liaoning Prov., CCP Cen. Cttee Party School; technician, Deputy Workshop Dir, engineer, Deputy Planning Section Chief, Jilin Paper Mill 1953–67, Deputy Head of Production Man. Group, Deputy Dir, Dir Office of CCP 1970–75, Deputy Dir and Chief Engineer 1975–80; joined CCP 1956; Deputy Dir Light Industry Bureau, Jilin Prov. 1980–81, Dir CCP Leading Party Group, 1982–83; mem. Standing Cttee, Dir Research Office and Sec.-Gen. CCP Jilin Prov. Cttee 1983–85, Deputy Sec. 1985–92; Vice-Gov. Jilin Prov. 1983–85, Acting Gov. 1985–92; Deputy, Jilin Prov., 7th NPC 1988–93; Vice-Gov. Jilin Prov. 1988–89, Gov. 1989–93; Deputy Dir Production Office of the State Council 1992–93 (also Deputy Sec. CCP Party Cttee); Minister in charge of State Econ. and Trade Comm. 1993–98; State Councillor and Sec.-Gen. State Council 1998–2003; Pres. Nat. School of Admin 1998–2003; Head, 5th Nat. Census Leading Group 1998; mem. Govt Del., Macao Hand-Over Ceremony, Macao Special Admin. Region Preparatory Cttee 1999; Alt. mem. 13th Cen. Cttee CCP 1987–92, mem. 14th Cen. Cttee 1992–97, mem. 15th CCP Cen. Cttee 1997–2002, 16th CCP Cen. Cttee 2002–07; apptd Vice-Chair. 10th CPPCC Nat. Cttee 2003. *Address:* Chinese People's Political Consultative Conference, Beijing, People's Republic of China (office).

WANG, Zikun, DSc; Chinese professor and university administrator; b. 30 April 1929, Jiangxi Prov.; s. of Wang Zhao-ji and Guo Xiang-e; m. Tian Der-Lin 1958; two s.; ed Wuhan Univ., Moscow Univ., USSR; Asst Prof., then Prof., Nankai Univ. 1952–84; Prof. and Pres. Beijing Normal Univ. 1984; Prof., Shantou Univ. 1993–; Dir China Math. Soc.; mem. Standing Bd China Probilistical-Statistics Soc., China Higher Educational Soc.; mem. Editorial Bd Soc., Scientia Sinica, Science Bulletin of China; mem. Chinese Acad. of Sciences 1991–; Hon. DSc (Macquarie Univ., Australia) 1988; China Science Conf. Award 1978, China Natural Science Prize 1982, China Excellent Popular Science Works Award 1981, Ho Leung Ho Lee Foundation Math. and Mechanics Prize, and numerous other awards. *Publications:* Theory of Stochastic Processes 1965, Foundations of Probability Theory and Their Applications 1976, Probability Theory and Statistical Prediction 1978, Talks on Scientific Discovery 1978, Brownian Motion and Potentials 1982, Birth-Death Processes and Markov Chains 1992 and many other math. articles and popular scientific publs. *Leisure interest:* literature. *Address:* Shantou University, Shantou, Guangdong Province, People's Republic of China (office). *E-mail:* web@stu.edu.cn (office). *Website:* www.stu.edu.cn (office).

WANG, Zuji, PhD; Chinese government official and banking executive; *Vice-Chairman, Executive Director and President, China Construction Bank;* ed Jilin Univ.; Deputy Dir, Loan Dept II (NE China Loan Dept), China Devt Bank 1997–2000, Pres. Changchun Br. 2000–03, Dir Business Devt Dept, China Devt Bank 2003–04, Dir Comprehensive Planning Dept 2004–05; Asst Gov., People's Govt of Jilin Prov. Feb.–May 2005, Asst Gov. and Dir-Gen. State-owned Assets Supervision and Admin Comm., People's Govt of Jilin Prov. 2005–06, Asst Gov.,

Dir-Gen. Devt and Reform Comm., People's Govt of Jilin Prov. and concurrently Dir-Gen. Leadership Team Office of Revitalizing Jilin Old Industrial Base 2006–08, Vice-Gov. People's Govt of Jilin Prov. 2008–12; Vice-Chair. China Insurance Regulatory Comm. 2012–15; Vice-Chair., Exec. Dir and Pres. China Construction Bank 2015–. *Address:* China Construction Bank, 25 Finance Street, Xicheng Dist, Beijing 100032, People's Republic of China (office). *Telephone:* (10) 6759-7114 (office). *Fax:* (10) 6360-3194 (office). *E-mail:* info@ccb.com (office). *Website:* www.ccb.com (office).

WANGCHUCK, HM Dasho Jigme Khesar Namgyel, (The Druk Gyalpo — 'Dragon King'— of Bhutan), MPhil; b. 21 Feb. 1980; s. of King Jigme Singye Wangchuck and Queen Ashi Tshering Yandon Wangchuck; m. Jetsun Pema 13 Oct. 2011; one s. HRH Crown Prince Jigme Namgyel Wangchuck, Druk Gyalsey (Dragon Prince) of Bhutan, b. 5 Feb. 2016; ed Cushing Acad. and Wheaton Coll., USA, Magdalen Coll., Oxford, UK; proclaimed Crown Prince Oct. 2004; succeeded to throne 14 Dec. 2006, on the abdication of his father; participated in official visits; officially crowned 6 Nov. 2008; Supreme C-in-C, Royal Bhutan Army; Chair. Bhutan Trust Fund for Environmental Conservation; Pres. Bhutan-India Friendship Asscn; Chancellor, Royal Univ. of Bhutan; Chief Patron, Scouts Asscn of Bhutan; Patron, Royal Soc. for the Protection of Nature, Bhutan Chamber of Commerce and Industry, India-Bhutan Foundation, European Convention of Bhutan Socs, Oxford Centre for Buddhist Studies, Bhutan Shooting Fed.; Hon. Royal Bencher, Hon. Soc. of the Inner Temple, UK; Red Scarf 2002, Grand Master, Order of the Dragon King 2008, Grand Master, Royal Order of Bhutan 2008, Grand Master, Nat. Order of Merit 2008, Grand Master, Order of Great Victory of the Thunder Dragon 2008, Medal of the Great Victory of the Thunder Dragon 2008, Kt Grand Cross, Order of Queen Sālote Tupou III (Tonga) 2010; Hon. LLD (Univ. of New Brunswick, Canada) 2005, (Univ. of Calcutta) 2010; Hon. Dr of Philosophy, Politics and Econs (Rangsit Univ., Thailand); Hon. DEcon (Keio Univ., Japan). *Address:* Royal Palace, Thimphu, Bhutan. *Website:* www.bhutan.gov.bt.

WANGCHUCK, HM Jigme Singye; Bhutanese fmr ruler; b. 11 Nov. 1955, Thimphu; s. of Druk Gyalpo Jigme Dorji Wangchuk and Queen Ashi Kesang; m.; ten c. (including HM King Dasho Jigme Khesar Namgyal Wangchuck); ed North Point, Darjeeling, Ugyuen Wangchuk Acad., Paro, also in UK; Crown Prince March 1972; succeeded to throne 24 July 1972, crowned 2 June 1974, abdicated 14 Dec. 2006; Chair. Planning Comm. of Bhutan 1972–; C-in-C of Armed Forces; Chair. Council of Ministers 1972–98. *Address:* Royal Palace, Thimphu, Bhutan (office). *Website:* www.bhutan.gov.bt.

WANGCHUCK, Lyonpo Khandu, BA; Bhutanese politician; b. 24 Nov. 1950; ed St Stephen's Coll., India; Asst Sec., Ministry of Trade, Industry and Forests 1974, Deputy Dir 1976, Man. Dir Industrial Devt Corpn 1978, Dir of Trade and Commerce 1980–84; Dir of Agric. 1986, Dir-Gen. 1987–89, Sec. 1989–1991; Sec. Royal Civil Service Comm. 1991–94; Prime Minister and Chair. 2001–02, 2006–07 (resgnd); Minister of Trade and Industry 1998–2003, of Foreign Affairs 2003–07 (resgnd), of Econ. Affairs 2008–13; mem. Nat. Ass. for Lamgong-Wangchang constituency; mem. Druk Phuensum Tshogpa party; fmr Chair. Bhutan Nat. Bank; Red Scarf 1987, Orange Scarf 1998, Coronation Medal 1999. *Address:* Jangsa, Shari Geog, Paro, Bhutan (home). *Telephone:* (2) 336907 (office). *E-mail:* kwangchuk@nab.gov.bt (office). *Website:* http://www.nab.gov.bt (office).

WANGCHUK, Dasho Lhatu; Bhutanese diplomatist, government official and airline industry executive; b. 15 Dec. 1951, Rongthung, Trashigang; Accountant, Foreign Affairs Dept 1972–74, Attaché 1974–75, Under-Sec. 1975–76; Third Sec., Perm. Mission to UN, New York 1976–79; Second Sec., Embassy in New Delhi 1979–81; Deputy Sec. 1981–83; Sec. Nat. Urban Devt Corpn 1983–88; Promotions Officer, Marketing and Promotions Div.; Chief of Protocol, Ministry of Foreign Affairs –1994, also Acting Foreign Sec.; Amb. to Bangladesh 1998–2001; apptd Admin. Officer, Admin. and Finance Section of then Ministry of Trade and Industry 1998; Dir-Gen. Dept of Tourism, Ministry of Econ. Affairs 2004–08; Chair. Druk Air (Royal Bhutan Airlines) 2007–08; Amb. and Perm. Rep. to UN, New York (also accred as Amb. to Canada) 2009–14; Bd mem. Bhutan Foundation. *Address:* Ministry of Foreign Affairs, Gyalyong Tshokhang, PO Box 103, Thimphu, Bhutan (office). *Telephone:* (2) 322459 (office). *Fax:* (2) 331465 (office). *E-mail:* ugyen@mofa.gov.bt (office). *Website:* www.mfa.gov.bt (office).

WANGCHUK, Dasho Penden; Bhutanese government official (retd); began career as Officer in Royal Bhutan Army; served 38 years in govt service in various capacities including Sec., Ministry of Home and Cultural Affairs then Cabinet Sec. –2015 (retd); fmr mem. Royal Civil Service Comm.; fmr Sec.-Gen. Bhutan Olympic Cttee; Patron, Asian Art Museum; mem. Advisory Council, Friends of Bhutan's Culture; Red Scarf 1998.

WANGCHUK, Sonam, BTech, MArch; Indian engineer, teacher and inventor; *Co-founder and Teacher, Students' Educational and Cultural Movement of Ladakh (SECMOL);* b. 1 Sept. 1966, Ladakh, Jammu and Kashmir; s. of Sonam Wangyal; ed Nat. Inst. of Tech., Srinagar, Craterre School of Architecture, Grenoble, France; co-founder and teacher, Students' Educational and Cultural Movement of Ladakh (SECMOL) 1988–, worked in training programmes and experiments in school reforms, also currently adviser to the bd and fmr dir; launched Operation New Hope movt in asscn with govt educ. dept 1994; founder and ed., Ladags Melong 1993–2005; apptd adviser for educ., Hill Council Govt 2001, mem. Drafting Cttee for Vision Document Ladakh 2025, served in formulating policy on Education and Tourism 2004, apptd to Jammu and Kashmir State Bd of School Educ. 2013, mem. of expert panel, State Educ. Policy and Vision Document 2014; co-f. Ladakh Voluntary Network (LVN) 2002, Sec. Exec. Cttee –2005; Educ. Adviser, MS (NGO) 2007–10; founder The Ice Stupa Project 2014–; co-founder Himalayan Inst. of Alternatives 2015–; founder FarmStays Ladakh initiative 2016–; apptd mem. Nat. Governing Council for Elementary Educ., Ministry of Human Resource Devt 2005; Fellow for Social Entrepreneurship, Ashoka, USA 2002–; UNESCO Chair Earthen Architecture, Craterre France 2014; Governor's Medal for educational reform 1996, State Award for outstanding environmentalist 2017, Jammu & Kashmir State Govt, Green Teacher Award, Sanctuary Asia 2004, Real Heroes Award, CNN-IBN TV 2008, Int. Terra Award for best earth building 2016, Rolex Award for Enterprise 2016, Global Award for Sustainable Architecture 2017, GQ Men of the Year Award for Social Entrepreneur 2017, Indians for Collective Action (ICA) Honor Award, San Francisco, Calif. 2017, Eminent Technologist of the Himalayan Region, Indian Inst. of Tech. Mandi 2018, Ramon Magsaysay Award (co-recipient) 2018. *Achievements:* invented a prototype of Ice Stupa which stores stream water in the form of giant artificial ice cones/stupas reserved in winters and to be potentially used by farmers during spring. *Address:* SECMOL, PO Box 4, Leh, Ladakh, 194101, Jammu & Kashmir, India (office). *Telephone:* (19) 82252421 (office). *Website:* www.secmol.org (office); www.hial.edu.in (office).

WANGCHUK, Lyonpo Tshering, (CJB), BA, LLB, LLM; Bhutanese judge; *Chief Justice, Supreme Court;* b. (Karma Tshering), 20 Oct. 1963, Lungtenphu, Bhutan; s. of Dorji Lingpa Lineage; m. Chhimi Wangmo; two d.; ed Sherubtse Coll., Kanglung, St Stephen's Coll. and Delhi Univ., India, George Washington Univ., USA; began career as Trainee Officer with High Court 1987, then served as Judicial Officer, Sr Section Officer of Crime Section 1988–90, Dist Judge 1999–2006, High Court Drangpon 2006–10; Justice, Supreme Court 2010–14, Chief Justice 2014–; apptd Chief Advisor to pre-election interim Govt Aug. 2018, Interim Chief Advisor, Ministry of Foreign Affairs and of Home and Cultural Affairs Aug.–Nov. 2018; Second Lt, Royal Bhutan Army 1990–95; Druk Yuegyal Medal, Coronation Gold Medal 2008, Bura Maap (Red Scarf) 2013, Orange Scarf 2014. *Address:* Supreme Court of Bhutan, Royal Court of Justice, Lhadrong, Hejo, Thimphu, Bhutan (office). *Telephone:* (2) 322447 (office). *Fax:* (2) 322921 (office). *E-mail:* twangchuk@judiciary.gov.bt (office); tshering.wangchuk@gmail.com (office). *Website:* www.judiciary.gov.bt (office).

WANGDI, Kesang; Bhutanese diplomatist, government official and fmr airline industry executive; *Cabinet Secretary;* m.; one s. one d.; joined Ministry of Foreign Affairs 1982, served in various positions including Head of Chancery and Head of Econ. Section, Embassy in Delhi, Head of Finance and Admin Div., Ministry of Foreign Affairs, represented Bhutan at UN, New York including at Security Council, Non-Aligned Group, Asian Group and Forum of Small States, served as Consul Gen. in USA, Chief of Protocol and Head of Protocol Dept, Ministry of Foreign Affairs, served as Dir of SAARC at SAARC in Kathmandu and Head of SAARC and Others Div. Ministry of Foreign Affairs, fmr Planning Officer, Policy and Planning Div., Ministry of Trade and Industry; Dir Dept of Bilateral Affairs, Ministry of Foreign Affairs –2008, 2016–18; Dir-Gen. Tourism Council of Bhutan 2008–12; Chair. Druk Air Corpn Ltd (nat. airline) 2008–11; Amb. to Thailand (concurrently accred to Australia and Singapore) 2013–16; Cabinet Sec. 2018–. *Address:* Cabinet Secretariat, Gyalyong Tshokhang, POB 1011, Thimphu, Bhutan (office). *Telephone:* (2) 336842 (office). *Fax:* (2) 321438 (office). *E-mail:* cabinet@druknet.bt (office). *Website:* www.cabinet.gov.bt (office).

WANGDI, Dasho Kunzang, BA, MPA; Bhutanese government official; b. 17 July 1953, Ura, Bumthang; s. of Sithar Norbhu and Choki; m. Pem Tandi; ed Delhi Univ., India, Pennsylvania State Univ., USA, London School of Econs, UK; worked in various capacities in govt ministries for more than 28 years; Auditor-Gen. 1999–2005; Chief Election Commr 2006–15, in charge of two rounds of trial parl. elections in 2007 and first-ever parl. elections in 2008; Druk Thuksey Medal from the Fifth King of Bhutan. *Publications:* drafted Royal Charters, Audit Act, Anti-Corruption Act, Election Acts. *Leisure interests:* reading, photography, cinema.

WANGDI, Dasho Phuntsho, BL; Bhutanese government official; ed Sherubtse Coll., Royal Inst. of Man., Univ. of Mumbai, India, Univ. of Adelaide, Australia; began career as Judicial Officer, High Court; Chief Prosecutor and Head, Prosecution and Litigation Div., Office of Attorney-Gen. –2010, Attorney-Gen. 2010–15.

WANIEK, Danuta, DJur; Polish politician and political scientist; b. 26 Oct. 1946, Włocławek; d. of Jerzy Waniek and Jozefina Wisniewski; m. (husband deceased); two s.; ed Univ. of Warsaw, Institut für Höhere Studien und Wissenschaft, Austria; with Inst. of Political Studies, Polish Acad. of Sciences (PAN) 1989; mem. Polish United Workers' Party (PZPR) 1967–90; mem. Social Democracy of Polish Repub. (SDRP) 1990–; Deputy to Sejm (Parl.) 1991–2001, mem. Parl. Cttee of Nat. Defence; Deputy Minister of Nat. Defence 1994–95; Minister of State and Head of Chancellery of Pres. of Poland 1995–97; Chair. Nat. Council of Radio and Television 2003–05; Prof., ALMAMER Szkoła Wyższa 2005–, also mem. Faculty, Krakowska Akademia; Chair. Women's Democratic Union 1990–; with Instytut Problemów Strategicznych 2007–; Krzyz Zaslugi (Cross of Merit). *Publications:* Compromise within the Political System of Germany: Partnership or Struggle? 1988, Constitution and Political Reality 1989, Debate over 'Little Constitution' (ed.) 1992, Creating New Constitutional Order in Poland (ed.) 1993. *Leisure interests:* opera, reading newspapers, embroidering, painting, music (listening and playing). *Address:* ul. Protazego 61, 03-606, Warsaw, Poland (home).

WANKA, Johanna, DrRerNat; German academic and politician; b. (Johanna Müller), 1 April 1951, Rosenfeld, Saxony; m. Gert Wanka; two c.; ed Univ. of Leipzig; Academic Assoc., Technical Univ. Merseburg 1974–85, Sr Academic Assoc. 1985–93, Prof. of Eng Math., Merseburg Univ. of Applied Sciences 1993–, Rector 1994–2000; Founding mem. Neues Forum (citizens' movt in former GDR), Merseburg 1989; Vice-Pres. Saxony-Anhalt Rectors Conf. 1994–98; Deputy Chair. Saxony-Anhalt Advisory Council for Science and Research 1995–98; mem. Bd of Trustees, Körber Foundation Hamburg's German Study Award 1996–2004; mem. Standing Cttee for Planning and Org. of German Rectors Conf. (HRK) 1998–2000, mem. HRK Senate 1999–; mem. Brandenburg Higher Educ. Council 1999–2000; Brandenburg Regional Minister of Science, Research and Culture 2000–09; Lower Saxony Regional Minister of Science and Culture 2012–13; Fed. Minister for Educ. and Research 2013–18; mem. CDU 2001–, CDU Party Chair. in Brandenburg Land Parl. 2009–10, mem. Brandenburg CDU Land Exec. Cttee 2003–10, Chair. Brandenburg CDU 2009–10; Deputy Chair. Konrad Adenauer Foundation 2010–11.

WAQA, Baron Divavesi; Nauruan politician and head of state; b. 31 Dec. 1959; m. Louisa Waqa; mem. Parl. for Boe constituency 2003–; held various portfolios including Health, Repub. of Nauru Telecommunications Corpn and Public Works, Minister of the Interior and of Educ. 2004–07; Pres. of Nauru 2013–, also currently Minister of Public Service, of Foreign Affairs and Trade, of Climate Change, and of Police and Emergency Services. *Address:* Office of the President, Yaren, Nauru (office). *Telephone:* 557-3133 (office). *Fax:* 444-3776 (office). *E-mail:* andromeda.amram@naurugov.nr (office).

WAQAR YOUNIS; Pakistani sports commentator, cricket coach and fmr professional cricketer; b. (Waqar Younis Maitla), 16 Nov. 1971, Vehari; m.; one s. two d.; ed Sadiq Public School, Bahawalpur, Pakistani Coll. Sharjah, Govt Coll., Vehari; right-hand lower-order batsman, right-arm fast bowler; played for Multan 1987/88–97/98, United Bank Ltd 1988–97, Pakistan 1989–2003 (Capt. 2001–03), Surrey 1990–91, 1993, Glamorgan 1997–98 (took career-best 8 for 17 against Sussex), Karachi 1998–99, Rawalpindi 1998–99, REDCO Pakistan Ltd 1999–2000, Lahore Blues 2000–01, Nat. Bank of Pakistan 2001–03, Warwickshire 2003, Allied Bank Ltd 2003–04; Test debut: Pakistan v India, Karachi 15–20 Nov. 1989; played in 87 Tests for Pakistan (17 as Capt.) taking 373 wickets (average 23.56), best bowling (innings) 7/76, (match) 13/135, scored 1,101 runs (average 10.20, highest score 45); played in 262 One-Day Ints (ODIs), 56 as Capt., took 416 wickets (average 23.84), best bowling 7/36, scored 969 runs (average 10.30, highest score 37); played in 228 First-class matches, took 956 wickets (average 22.33), best bowling 8/17, scored 2,972 runs (average 13.38, highest score 64); only bowler to have taken five-wicket hauls in three consecutive ODIs; took the fastest 50, 300, 350 and 400 wickets in ODI matches and fastest 150, 200, 250, 300 and 350 wickets in Test matches; only batsman to pass 1,000 run mark without ever scoring a 50; has best strike rate for any bowler with more than 200 Test wickets; first player to be banned for ball tampering, fined 50% of match fee July 2000; retd April 2004; bowling coach for Pakistan 2006–07 (resgnd); TV cricket commentator for Australia's Nine Network; Pakistan Head Coach 2010–11, 2014–15 (resgnd); commentator, Indian TV channel Sony coverage of Indian Premier League 2016–; Team Dir and Bowling Coach, Islamabad United 2017–; Wisden Cricketer of the Year 1992. *Leisure interests:* football, badminton, squash.

WARBURTON, Sam, OBE; Welsh rugby union player (retd); b. (Sam Kennedy-Warburton), 5 Oct. 1988, Cardiff, Wales; s. of Jeremy Warburton and Carolyn Warburton; m. Rachel Thomas 2014; ed Whitchurch High School; openside flanker; played for Glamorgan Wanderers 2007–09, Cardiff Blues 2009–18, Wales (Capt. 2011–17) 2009–17, British and Irish Lions (Capt.) 2013, 2017; retd July 2018; mem., Order of St John 2018. *Address:* c/o Welsh Rugby Union, Principality Stadium, Westgate Street, Cardiff, CF10 1NS, Wales (office). *E-mail:* info@wru.co.uk (office). *Website:* www.wru.co.uk (office).

WARCHUS, Matthew, BA; British theatre and film director; *Artistic Director, The Old Vic;* b. 24 Oct. 1966, Rochester, Kent, England; m. Lauren Ward; three c.; ed Selby High School, Univ. of Bristol; Dir Nat. Youth Theatre 1989, 1990, Bristol Old Vic 1991; Asst Dir RSC 1991–92; Assoc. Dir West Yorkshire Playhouse 1993; has directed for Donmar Warehouse, Royal Nat. Theatre, Opera North, West Yorkshire Playhouse, Welsh Nat. Opera, ENO and in the West End; Artistic Dir The Old Vic 2015–; Shakespeare's Globe Award 1994, Sydney Edwards Award 1995, Evening Standard Award 1995. *Plays directed include:* for RSC: Henry V 1995, The Devil is an Ass 1995, Hamlet 1997; (for West Yorkshire Playhouse) Life is a Dream, Who's Afraid of Virginia Woolf?, The Plough and the Stars, Death of a Salesman, Betrayal, True West; other productions The Stuff of Life (Donmar Warehouse) 1994, Volpone (Royal Nat. Theatre) 1995, Art (Wyndhams) 1996, The Unexpected Man (Duchess) 1998, Life x 3 (West End) 2001, Art, True West, Follies (all Broadway), The Lord of the Rings 2007, Boeing Boeing 2008, The Norman Conquests 2008. *Opera:* Troilus and Cressida (Opera North), The Rake's Progress, Falstaff, Cosí fan tutte (ENO). *Films include:* Simpático (also screenwriter and co-producer) 1999, Pride (Queer Palm Award, Cannes Film Festival) 2014. *Address:* c/o Hamilton Asper Management, 24 Hanway Street, London, W1T 1OH, England (office); c/o The Old Vic, The Cut, Waterloo, London, SE1 8NB, England. *Telephone:* (20) 7636-1221 (office); (20) 7928-2651. *Website:* www.oldvictheatre.com.

WARD, Jacqueline (Jackie) M., LLD; American business executive; *Chairman (Non-Executive), Sysco Corporation;* ed Georgia State Coll. for Women, Univ. of Georgia Extension Center, London School of Business, UK, Mercer Univ.; co-f. Computer Generation Inc. 1968, Pres. and CEO 1968–2000, Chair. May–Dec. 2000; Outside Man. Dir Intec Telecom Systems 2000–06; Dir, Anthem Southeast, Inc. (fmrly Trigon Healthcare Inc.) 1993–2002, Anthem Insurance (subsidiary of WellPoint Inc. 2002–03, Dir WellPoint Inc. 2002–13, Lead Ind. Dir, Chair. (non-exec.) 2012–13; Sr Dir of Human Resources, Digg Inc. 2013–; mem. Bd of Dirs Sysco Corpn 2001–, Chair. (non-exec.) 2013–; mem. Bd of Dirs Sanmina, Inc. (fmrly SCI Systems Inc.) 1992–2002, Bank of America Corpn 1994–2009, PRG-Schultz International Inc. 1999–2004, PRGX Global Inc. (fmrly Profit Recovery Group International Inc.) 1999–, Flowers Industries, Inc. (renamed Keebler Holdings Corpn) 1999–, Equifax Inc., Matria Healthcare Inc., Premier Technologies Inc., PTEK Holdings Inc.; Ind. Dir, Flowers Foods Inc. 2001–, Sanmina-SCI Corpn 2001–; mem. Bd of Govs, The Ravinia Club, Inc.; ind. licensee, Blue Cross and Blue Shield Asscn. *Address:* Sysco Corporation, 1390 Enclave Parkway, Houston, TX 77077-2099 (office); Digg Inc., 135 Mississippi Street, 3rd Floor, San Francisco, CA 94107-2536, USA (office). *Telephone:* (281) 584-1390 (Houston) (office); (415) 436-9638 (San Francisco) (office). *Fax:* (281) 584-2721 (Houston) (office); (415) 621-6461 (San Francisco) (office). *E-mail:* info@sysco.com (office); info@digg.com (office). *Website:* www.sysco.com (office); digg.com (office).

WARD, Richard, PhD, FRSA; British insurance company executive; *Chairman, Brit Insurance Ltd;* b. 1957; m.; two s.; ed Univ. of Exeter; Sr Physicist, Science and Eng Research Council, Rutherford Appleton Lab., Oxford 1982–88; Sr Man., Research, BP plc 1988–91, Head, Business Devt and Marketing, BP Oil Trading Int. 1991–94; Head, Marketing and Business Devt, Tradition Financial Services 1994–95; Dir Product Devt and Research, Int. Petroleum Exchange (ICE) 1995–96, Exec. Vice-Pres. 1996–99, CEO 1999–2005, Vice-Chair. ICE Futures 2005; CEO Lloyd's of London 2006–14; Chair. Brit Insurance and Brit Syndicates Ltd 2014–; Chair. Cunningham Lindsey 2014–; Sr Ind. Dir DLIG 2016–; Non-Ind. Dir Partnership Assurance Group 2013–. *Address:* Brit Insurance Ltd, 55 Bishopsgate, London, EC2N 3AS, England (office). *Telephone:* (20) 7984-8500 (office). *E-mail:* info@britinsurance.com (office). *Website:* www.britinsurance.com (office).

WARD, Vincent; New Zealand film director, screenwriter and artist; b. 16 Feb. 1956, Greytown; ONZM; ed St Patrick's Coll., Silverstream, Ilam School of Fine Arts at the Univ. of Canterbury, Christchurch; while still at art school, began writing and directing films; named by the Boston Globe as "one of the world's great image-makers". *Films include:* A State of Siege (Miami Film Festival Special Jury Prize, Chicago Film Festival Golden Hugo) 1978, Sons for the Return Home (art dir) 1979, In Spring one Plants Alone (documentary) (Silver Hugo at Chicago Film Festival 1980, Grand Prix Co-Winner Cinéma du Réel 1982) 1980, Vigil (also co-writer) (Grand Prix Prades and Madrid Film Festivals) 1984, The Navigator: A Medieval Odyssey (Grand Prix Film Festivals in Rome, Munich, Sitges 1988, Oporto Film Festival 1989, Best Film and Best Director Australian Film Inst. and New Zealand Listener Awards 1989) 1988, Alien^3(writer) 1991, Map of the Human Heart (also story and co-writer, producer) (Most Significant Artistic Achievement Tokyo Film Festival 1993) 1992, Leaving Las Vegas (actor) 1995, The Shot (actor) 1996, One Night Stand (actor) 1997, What Dreams May Come (Acad. Award for Best Visual Effects, Best Renting Drama Video Australian Video Ezy Prestige Awards 1999) 1998, The Last Samurai (exec. producer) 2003, Spooked (actor) 2004, River Queen (also story and co-writer) 2005, Rain of the Children (documentary) (also writer and producer) 2008. *Publications:* The Navigator, A Medieval Odyssey 1989, Edge of the Earth: Stories and Images from the Antipodes 1990, The Past Awaits, people, images, film (large format, full colour photographic book of images and stories) 2010, Inhale | Exhale (large format, full colour reproductions of his artwork from his 2011–12 exhbns) 2013. *Address:* PO Box 78-078, Grey Lynn, Auckland 1245, New Zealand. *E-mail:* info@vincentwardfilms.com. *Website:* vincentwardfilms.com.

WARDAK, Gen. Abdul Rahim; Afghan government official and military officer; b. 1945, Wardak Prov.; s. of Abdul Ghani; ed Habibia High School, Ali Naser Acad. of Cairo, Egypt; previous positions include Lecturer Cadet Univ., Asst of Protocol, Ministry of Defence, Mil. Attaché, India, Dir Mil. Officers Soc., Educ. Comm., Disarmament Program; apptd Chief of Army Staff 1992; fmr Deputy Minister of Defence, Minister of Defence 2004–12 (resgnd), Sr Adviser to Pres. Hamid Karzai in Afghan army reform, development and equipment sector 2012–13 (resgnd); unsuccessful cand. in presidential election 2014; Ghazi Amanullah Khan Medal.

WARDAK, Capt. Moin Khan; Afghan airline industry executive; *CEO, Afghan Jet International Airlines;* Chief Pilot Ariana Afghan Airlines Co. Ltd 2003–05, Captain and CEO 2003–12, Vice-Pres. (Operation and Technical) 2005–07, Pres. and CEO 2007–11; Captain A320, Safi Airways Jan.–May 2013; Captain A320, Kam Air May 2013–June 2014; Owner and CEO Interport Aviation Services 2012–; CEO Afghan Jet Int. Airlines 2014–. *Address:* Afghan Jet International Airlines, 8th floor Kalemzai plaza, Baraki Square, Kabul, Afghanistan (office). *Telephone:* (70) 1110303 (office). *E-mail:* info@flyaji.com (office). *Website:* www.flyaji.com (office).

WARDLE, Len; British business executive; following graduation, worked for PriceWaterhouse in North East England then spent five years teaching in the Midlands; entered local govt in East Sussex, spent two years with Eastbourne Borough Council before moving to East Sussex Co. Council and holding several man. positions, culminating in Head of Resources; later Fellow, Univ. of Surrey in School of Man.; first elected to Co-operative Group 1992, Chair. 2007–13 (resgnd); held appointments in Co-operative Financial Services, The Co-operative Bank, Co-operative Insurance Soc. Ltd, CIS General Insurance Ltd, ICA (ex officio), Mutuo, PACE Trustees Ltd, CIS Pension Scheme Nominee Ltd.

WARINER, Jeremy; American athlete; b. 31 Jan. 1984, Irving, Tex.; s. of Danny Wariner and Linda Wariner; ed Lamar High School, Arlington, Tex. and Baylor Univ.; coached by Clyde Hart; volunteer asst coach; mem. USA World Jr Team; three-time Jr All-American in 400m 2002; Nat. Collegiate Athletic Asscn (NCAA) Outdoor Champion, 400m 2004, 4×400m relay 2004; NCAA Indoor Champion, 400m 2004, 4×400m relay 2004; US Olympic Trials 400m Champion 2004; gold medal, 400m, Olympic Games, Athens 2004, 4×400m relay 2004; first athlete in history to win both collegiate titles, US Championship and Olympic Gold Medal in 400m; turned professional 2004; USA Outdoor Champion 2005; gold medal, 400m, World Outdoor Championships, Helsinki, Finland 2005, 4×400m relay 2005; silver medal, 400m, Olympic Games, Beijing 2008; gold medal, 4×400m relay, Olympic Games, Beijing 2008; current coach Michael Ford; Jesse Owens Award 2004, named by ESPN.com Top Rookie of 2004, named Mondo Track Athlete of the Year 2004. *Address:* c/o USA Track and Field, 1 RCA Dome, Suite 140, Indianapolis, IN 46225, USA. *E-mail:* Sariyu.Suggs@usatf.org. *Website:* www.usatf.org.

WARJIYO, Perry, MSc, PhD; Indonesian economist and central banker; *Governor, Bank Indonesia;* b. 25 Feb. 1959, Sukoharjo; ed Gadjah Mada Univ., Iowa State Univ.; Asst Lecturer, Gajah Mada Univ. and Islamic Univ. Indonesia 1980–82; Staff, Credit Rescue Desk, Inspection and Affairs Credit Control 1984–86; Head of Section of Foreign Exchange Analysis and Research, Foreign Exchange Affairs 1991–92, Deputy Head of Foreign Loan Section 1992–95, Head of Balance of Payments Section 1995–97, Head of Analysis and Formulation of Monetary Policy 1997–98, Head of Gov.'s Bureau 1998–2000, Deputy Dir of Econ. Research and Monetary Policy 2000–02; Project Leader Bank Indonesia Monetary Transformation Program 2002–03; Dir of Center for Educ. and Studies, Kebentrality 2003–05; Dir of Econ. Research and Monetary Policy, Bank Indonesia 2005–07, 2009–13, Deputy Gov. 2013–18, Gov. 2018–; Exec. Dir South East Asia Voting Group, IMF 2007–09. *Address:* Bank Indonesia, Jl. MH. Thamrin No. 2, Jakarta 10350 (office); Jl. Gandaria V No. 18 Kebayoran Baru, Jakarta 12130, Indonesia (home). *Telephone:* (21) 3818190 (office). *Fax:* (21) 3800394 (office). *Website:* www.bi.go.id (office).

WARLOW, Charles Picton, BA, MB, BChir, MD, FRCP, FRSE, FMedSci; British neurologist, epidemiologist and academic; *Professor of Medical Neurology, University of Edinburgh;* b. 29 Sept. 1943, Nottingham, England; s. of Charles Edward Picton Warlow and Nancy Mary Maclennan Hine; partner Cathie Sudlow; two s. two d.; ed Univ. of Cambridge and St George's Hosp. Medical School, London; Lecturer in Medicine, Aberdeen 1971–74; specialist training in neurology, London and Oxford 1974–77; Clinical Reader in Neurology and Hon. Consultant Neurologist, Oxford 1977–87; Prof. of Medical Neurology, Univ. of Edinburgh 1987–; Pres. Asscn of British Neurologists 2001–03; Ed. Practical Neurology; Tenovus-Scotland Margaret MacLellan Award 1989–90, Soc. of Authors and Royal Soc. of Medicine Medical Book Award, Advanced Author Book Category 1997, Osler Oration, Royal Coll. of Physicians 1998, Willis Lecturer, American Heart Asscn 2003, Asscn of British Neurologists Medal 2005. *Publications include:* Handbook of Clinical Neurology 1991, Transient Ischaemic Attacks of the Brain and Eye (with G. J. Hankey) 1994, Stroke: A Practical Guide to Management (co-author) (second edn) 2001, Lancet Handbook of Treatment in Neurology (ed.) 2006.

Leisure interests: sailing, photography, mountains. *Address:* Department of Clinical Neurosciences, University of Edinburgh, Western General Hospital, Crewe Road, Edinburgh, EH4 2XU (office); 6 South Gray Street, Edinburgh, EH9 1TE, Scotland (home). *Telephone:* (131) 537-2082 (office). *Fax:* (131) 332-5150 (office). *E-mail:* charles.warlow@ed.ac.uk (office); cpw@skull.dcn.ed.ac.uk (office). *Website:* www.dcn.ed.ac.uk/pages/profiles/profiles.asp?ProfileId=10 (office).

WARNE, Shane Keith; Australian sports commentator, cricket coach and fmr professional cricketer; b. 13 Sept. 1969, Upper Ferntree Gully, Melbourne, Vic.; s. of Keith Warne and Bridgette Warne; m. Simone Callahan 1995 (divorced 2005); one s. two d.; ed Hampton High School, Mentone Grammar School; right arm leg break bowler; right-hand lower-order batsman; played for Victoria 1990–2007 (Capt. 1996–99), Australia 1992–2007 (Capt. ODI side 1997–99), Hants. 2000–07 (Capt. 2004–07), ICC (Int. Cricket Council) World XI, Rajasthan Royals (Coach and Capt.) 2008–11 (apptd Team Mentor 2018), Melbourne Stars (Capt.) 2011–13; First-class debut: Feb. 1991; Test debut (cap 350): Australia v India, Sydney 2–6 Jan. 1992; One-Day Int. (ODI) debut: NZ v Australia, Wellington 24 Mar 1993; played in 145 Tests, took 708 wickets and scored 3,154 runs, bowling average 25.41, best bowling (innings) 8/71, (match) 12/128, economy rate 2.65, highest batting score 99, batting average 17.32, 12 fifties; took hat-trick against England, Melbourne 1994; ODIs (11 as Capt.): 194 matches, took 293 wickets and scored 1,018 runs; First-class cricket: 301 matches, took 1,319 wickets and scored 6,919 runs; toured England 1993, 1997, 2001, 2005; received 12-month ban for testing positive for a banned substance Feb. 2003; works for Shane Warne Foundation 2004–; announced retirement from limited-overs ints 2004, from int. cricket 2007, from First-class cricket 2008, from IPL (Indian Premier League) cricket 2011; Captain, Rest of the World side, Bicentenary Celebration, Lord's 2014; leading wicket-taker in test cricket; has scored the most Test runs (3,154) without making a century; Wisden Cricketer of the Year 1994, One-Day Int. Player of the Year 2000, selected as one of five Wisden Cricketers of the Century 2000, Wisden Leading Cricketer in the World 2005, Overseas Personality of the Year, BBC Sports Personality of the Year Awards 2005, Test Player of the Year 2006, inducted into ICC Hall of Fame 2013. *Publication:* Shane Warne: The Autobiography 2001, My Illustrated Career 2006, Shane Warne's Century – My Top 100 Cricketers 2008. *Leisure interest:* collecting cars. *E-mail:* gareth@shanewarne.com. *Website:* www.shanewarne.com.

WARNER, Bishop Bennie Dee, MSc, ThM, DD; Liberian ecclesiastic and politician; b. 30 April 1935, Caresburg Dist; ed Monrovia Gbargna United Methodist Mission School, Booker Washington Inst., Kakata, Cuttington Univ. Coll., Suakoto, Syracuse Univ. and Boston Univ. School of Theology, USA; ordained deacon 1961; Acting Dir Pastors' Inst. of the United Methodist Church 1961; educ. counsellor and maths and social studies teacher, W.V.S. Tubman Elementary School 1962–68; fmr Chair. Nat. Student Christian Council of Liberia; later ordained Elder; fmr Pastor, St John's United Methodist Church, Gbarnga and Reeves Memorial United Methodist Church, Crozierville; fmr Chair. Interim Cttee for the Admin of the Coll. of West Africa (later Chair. Bd of Trustees), Bd of Ministry, Liberia Annual Conf. of United Methodist Church; ordained Bishop 1973; Vice-Pres. of Liberia 1977–80; mem. Bd of Trustees, Cuttington Coll. and Divinity School, Bd of the Booker Washington Inst., Nat. Disaster Comm., Council of Bishops, World Methodist Council; in exile in USA; Interim Pastor, Wesley United Methodist Church, Oklahoma City, USA 2007; Grand Band, Order of the Star of Africa. *Address:* c/o Wesley United Methodist Church, 1401 NW 25th Street, Oklahoma City, OK 73106, USA. *E-mail:* wesleyokc@coxinet.net.

WARNER, Brian, BSc, MA, PhD, DSc; British astronomer and academic; *Distinguished Professor Emeritus of Natural Philosophy and Senior Scholar, University of Cape Town;* b. 25 May 1939, Crawley Down, Sussex, England; s. of Leslie Warner and Edith M. Warner (née Bashford); m. 1st Carole Christian 1965 (divorced 1973); one s. one d.; m. 2nd Nancy Russell 1976 (divorced 1987); ed Univs of London and Oxford; Research Asst, Univ. of London Observatory 1964–65; Radcliffe-Henry Skynner Sr Research Fellow, Balliol Coll. Oxford 1965–67; Asst Prof., Univ. of Texas at Austin 1967–69, Assoc. Prof. 1969–72; Prof. and Head, Dept of Astronomy, Univ. of Cape Town 1972–99, Distinguished Prof. of Natural Philosophy 1999–2004, Distinguished Prof. Emer. 2005–, Fellow 1978–, Sr Scholar 2011–; Alfred P. Sloan Fellow 1969–71; Visiting Fellow, Univ. of Colorado 1977; Visiting Sr Fellow, Dept of Astrophysics, Univ. of Oxford 1985; Visiting Prof., Dartmouth Coll. and Univ. of Texas 1986–87, Univ. of Sussex 1997, Univ. of Southampton 2007, 2008, 2009, 2010, 2011, 2012; Visiting Fellow, Univ. of California, Santa Cruz 1990, ANU 1989, 1993, 1996, 1998, 2000, 2003; Visiting Scientist, European Southern Observatory 1996; Sr Fellow, Copernicus Centre, Warsaw 2003; Adjunct Prof., James Cook Univ., Townsville 2006–09; Fellow, Stellenbosch Inst. of Advanced Study 2013; Pres. Royal Soc. of S Africa 1981–83, Foreign Sec. 1996–2001, Hon. Fellow 2009–; mem. Acad. of Sciences of S Africa 1994–; Pres. Comm. 41 of Int. Astronomical Union (IAU) 1978–82 (Vice-Pres. IAU 2003–09), Astronomical Soc. of Southern Africa 1977–78, The Owl Club 1985–86; mem. Bd of Trustees, S African Museum 1981–99, Deputy Chair. 1988–91, Chair. 1991–99; mem. Council S Africa Library 1991–99; Ernest Oppenheimer Travelling Fellowship 1990; Fellow, TWAS, Acad. of sciences for the developing world 2009; Hon. Fellow, Royal Astronomical Soc. 1994; Hon. mem. Royal Astronomical Soc. of NZ 1995; Hon. Fellow, Univ. Coll. London 2009; Hon. DSc (Univ. of Cape Town) 2009; Boyden Premium, Franklin Inst. 1980; McIntyre Award, Astronomical Soc. of Southern Africa 1983, John F.W. Herschel Medal, Royal Soc. of South Africa 1988, South African Medal, South African Asscn for the Advancement of Science 1989, Gill Medal, Astronomical Soc. of Southern Africa 1992, Univ. of Cape Town Book Award 1997, Science for Soc. Gold Medal, Acad. of Sciences of South Africa 2004. *Publications include:* Astronomers at the Royal Observatory, Cape of Good Hope 1979, Charles Piazzi Smyth 1983, Maclear and Herschel 1984, The Journal of Lady Jane Franklin 1985, High Speed Astronomical Photometry 1988, William Mann 1989, Lady Herschel 1991, Cataclysmic Variable Stars 1995, Dinosaurs' End 1996, Flora Herscheliana 1998, Cape Landscapes 2006, Scatological Verse 2007; more than 400 scientific research papers. *Leisure interests:* 19th-century science and exploration, baroque music. *Address:* Department of Astronomy, University of Cape Town, Rondebosch, 7700 Cape (office); 401 Blenheim, Marlborough Park, Claremont, 7700 Cape, South Africa (home). *Telephone:* (21) 650-2391 (office); (21) 671-1850 (home). *Fax:* (21) 650-4547 (office). *E-mail:* Brian.Warner@uct.ac.za (office). *Website:* www.ast.uct.ac.za/brianwarner (office).

WARNER, David; British actor; b. 29 July 1941, Manchester; s. of Herbert Simon Warner and Ada Doreen (née Hattersley); m. 1st Harriet Lindgren 1969 (divorced 1972); m. 2nd Sheilah Kent 1981 (divorced 2002); one c.; ed Feldon School, Leamington Spa and Royal Acad. of Dramatic Art; worked as bookseller; stage début as Snout in A Midsummer Night's Dream, Royal Court 1962; film début in Tom Jones 1963; joined RSC 1963 and appeared as Trinculo in The Tempest, title role in Henry VI, Edward IV in adaptation of Henry VI (Parts I, II and III) comprising first two parts of trilogy The Wars of the Roses (Stratford). *Other roles include:* Henry VI in The Wars of the Roses, Aldwych 1964; Richard II, Mouldy in Henry IV (Part II) and Henry VI in The Wars of the Roses, RSC, Stratford 1964; Valentine Brose in Eh?, Aldwych 1964, Hamlet, Stratford and Aldwych 1965; the Postmaster in The Government Inspector, Aldwych 1965; Hamlet, Sir Andrew Aguecheek in Twelfth Night, Stratford 1966; Claudius in I, Claudius, Hampstead 1972. *Films include:* Morgan – A Suitable Case for Treatment 1966, Work is a Four Letter Word 1967, The Bofors Gun, The Fixer, The Seagull 1968–69, The Ballad of Cable Hogue 1970, Straw Dogs 1971, A Doll's House 1972, The Omen 1975, Cross of Iron, Providence, Silver Bears 1976, The Disappearance 1977, The Thirty Nine Steps 1978, Nightwing, Time After Time 1979, The Island 1980, Hanna's War 1988, The Secret Life of Ian Fleming 1990, Dark at Noon, Mortal Passions, In the Mouth of Madness, Titanic 1997, Scream 2 1997, Money Talks 1997, Shergar 2000, In the Beginning 2000, Planet of the Apes 2001, The Code Conspiracy 2002, Kiss of Life 2003, Terry Pratchett's Hogfather 2007, Black Death 2010, A Thousand Kisses Deep 2011, Before I Sleep 2013, You, Me and Him 2017, Mary Poppins Returns 2018. *Television includes:* Clouds of Glory 1977, Holocaust 1978, Masada 1981 (Primetime Emmy Award for Outstanding Supporting Actor in a Miniseries or Special 1981), Charlie 1984, The Larry Sanders Show 1993–94, The Choir 1995, Toonsylvania (Voice) 1998, Hornblower 2001, In Love with Barbara 2008, Dark Shadows: Kingdom of the Dead 2010, The Secret of Crickley Hall 2012. *Address:* c/o Julian Belfrage Associates, 3rd Floor, 9 Argyll Street, London, W1F 7TG, England (office). *E-mail:* davidwarnerfilm@hotmail.co.uk. *Website:* www.davidwarnerfilm.co.uk.

WARNER, Deborah, CBE; British theatre and opera director; b. 12 May 1959, Oxford; d. of Ruth Warner and Roger Warner; ed Sidcot School, Avon, St Clare's, Oxford, Cen. School of Speech and Drama; Founder and Artistic Dir Kick Theatre Co 1980–86; Resident Dir RSC 1987–89; Assoc. Dir Royal Nat. Theatre 1989–98; Assoc. Dir Abbey Theatre, Dublin 2000; has also staged productions at ENO Glyndebourne Festival Opera, Royal Opera House, Opera North, London Proms, La Scala, and has staged productions for Fitzroy Productions, Odeon Theatre, Chaillot and Bobigny Theatre, Paris, Salzburg Festival, LIFT and Perth Int. Arts Festival, Lincoln Center Festival, New York, Venice Festival, Bavarian State Opera; Dir Fitzroy Productions; Chevalier, Ordre des Arts et des Lettres 2000; Evening Standard Award 1988, 1998, 2002, Laurence Olivier Award 1989, 1992, New York Drama Desk Award 1997, South Bank Arts Award 1998, OBIE Award 2003. *Productions include:* Titus Andronicus (RSC), King John (RSC), Electra (RSC), Hedda Gabler (Abbey Theatre, Dublin/West End), The Good Person of Sichuan (Royal Nat. Theatre), King Lear (Royal Nat. Theatre), Richard II (Royal Nat. Theatre), The Powerbook (Royal Nat. Theatre), The Waste Land (Fitzroy Productions), Medea (Abbey Theatre/West End/Broadway), The St Pancras Project (LIFT), The Tower Project (LIFT) The Angel Project (Perth Int. Arts Festival and Lincoln Center Festival), Readings (Fitzroy Productions); Tchaikovsky's Eugene Onegin, Metropolitan Opera, New York 2013–14, 2017, Fidelio, La Scala, Milan 2015, Between Worlds (ENO, Barbican) 2015; Billy Budd, Teatro Real de Madrid 2017. *Films:* The Waste Land 1996, The Last September 1999. *Television includes:* Richard II (BBC), Hedda Gabler (BBC), Don Giovanni (Channel 4). *Leisure interest:* travelling. *Website:* www.askonasholt.co.uk/artists/directors/deborah-warner (office).

WARNER, Douglas Alexander III, BA; American banker; b. 9 June 1946, Cincinnati; s. of Douglas Alexander Warner Jr and Eleanor Warner (née Wright); m. Patricia Grant 1977; two s. one d.; ed Yale Univ.; Officer's Asst, Morgan Guaranty Trust Co., New York 1968–70, Asst Treas. 1970–72, Asst Vice-Pres. 1972–75, Vice-Pres. 1975–85, Sr Vice-Pres. Morgan Guaranty Trust Co., London 1983–87, Exec. Vice-Pres. Morgan Guaranty Trust Co., New York 1987–89, Man. Dir 1989–90, Pres. 1990–95, Chair. and CEO 1995–2000; Chair. J.P. Morgan Chase & Co. 2000–01; mem. Bd of Dirs Gen. Electric Co., Anheuser-Busch Cos Inc., Motorola Inc.; Chair. Bd of Man. Overseers Memorial Sloan-Kettering Cancer Center, New York; Trustee, Pierpoint Morgan Library, Cold Spring Harbor Lab. *Leisure interests:* golf, tennis, shooting. *Address:* PO Box 914, New York, NY 10268, USA (home).

WARNER, H. Ty; American business executive and philanthropist; *Chairman and CEO, Ty Inc.;* b. 3 Sept. 1944, Chicago, Ill.; s. of Harold Warner and Georgia Warner; ed St. John's Military Acad., Wis., Kalamazoo Coll., Mich.; early career selling toys for Dakin LLC, San Francisco; f. Ty Inc. 1986, currently Chair. and CEO; creator of Beanie Babies; significant investments in hotels, property and golf courses, Ty Warner Hotels and Resorts include the Four Seasons Hotel, New York, Sandpiper golf course, Four Seasons Resort, Santa Barbara, Calif., San Ysidro Ranch, Montecito, Calif., Kona Village resort, Hawaii, Montecito Country Club and Las Ventanas al Paraiso Resort, Los Cabos, Mexico; bought the beachfront Miramar resort and Rancho San Marcos golf course 2005; sentenced to two years' probation plus community service for tax evasion 2014; Children's Champion Award, Children's Hunger Fund 2006. *Address:* Ty Inc., 280 Chestnut Avenue, Westmont, IL 60559, USA (office). *Telephone:* (630) 920-1515 (office). *Fax:* (630) 920-1980 (office). *E-mail:* info@ty.com (office). *Website:* www.ty.com (office); www.tywarnerhotelsandresorts.com (office).

WARNER, Jack Austin, BA; Trinidad and Tobago fmr football executive and politician; *Leader, Independent Liberal Party;* b. 26 Jan. 1943, Rio Claro, South Trinidad; ed Coll. of St Phillip and St James (now Presentation Coll.), Chaguanas, Mausica Teacher Training Coll., Univ. of the West Indies; teacher, Polytechnic Inst., Port of Spain 1970–93; Gen. Sec. Trinidad and Tobago Football Fed. 1973–90, Special Adviser 1990; Gen. Sec. Caribbean Football Union 1978–83, Pres. 1983; mem. FIFA Exec. Cttee 1983–2011, Vice-Pres. FIFA 1997; Pres. Confed. of North, Central American and Caribbean Asscn Football 1990–2011; mem. House of Reps (Parl.) for Chaguanas West 2007–; Minister of Works and Transport 2010, of Nat. Security 2012–13 (resgnd); Leader, Independent Liberal Party; Founding

Chair. Joe Public Football Club 1996–; mem. United Nat. Congress. *Address:* Independent Liberal Party, 113 Edward Street, Port of Spain, Trinidad and Tobago (office). *Website:* www.ilptnt.com (office).

WARNER, John William, BS, LLB; American lawyer and fmr politician; *Senior Advisor, Hogan Lovells US LLP;* b. 18 Feb. 1927, Washington, DC; s. of Dr John W. Warner and Martha Warner (née Budd); m. 1st Catherine Conover Mellon (divorced 1973); one s. two d.; m. 2nd the late Elizabeth Taylor 1976 (divorced 1982, died 2011); m. 3rd Jeanne van der Myde 2003; ed school of Naval Research Lab., Washington, DC, Washington and Lee Univ., Univ. of Virginia Law School; served in USN, attained rank of Electronic Technician 3rd Class 1944–46; subsequently enlisted in US Marine Corps Reserve, active duty as Communications Officer 1950–52, Capt. in US Marine Corps Reserve 1952–61; admitted to the Bar 1954; pvt. practice 1954–56; served in US Attorney's office as Special Asst 1956, Asst 1957; joined campaign staff of then Vice-Pres. Richard Nixon 1960; Assoc. Hogan & Hartson (now Hogan Lovells US LLP) 1960, Gen. Partner 1964–69, Sr Advisor 2009–; Dir of Ocean Affairs as rep. of US Dept of Defense 1971; Under-Sec. of US Navy 1969–72, Sec. 1972–74; Dir American Revolution Bicentennial Admin. 1974–76; Senator from Virginia 1979–2009 (retd), Chair. Armed Services Cttee; fmr Head of US Del. to Moscow on Naval Affairs; Hon. KBE 2009; Nat. Intelligence Distinguished Public Service Medal, Office of the Dir of Nat. Intelligence (first ever awarded) 2008. *Address:* Hogan Lovells US LLP, Columbia Square, 555 Thirteenth Street, NW, Washington, DC 20004, USA (office). *Telephone:* (202) 637-8875 (office). *Fax:* (202) 637-5910 (office). *E-mail:* john.warner@hoganlovells.com (office). *Website:* www.hoganlovells.com/john-warner (office).

WARNER, Dame Marina Sarah, DBE, MA, FBA, FRSL; British writer, historian and academic; *Professor of English and Creative Writing, Birkbeck College, London;* b. 9 Nov. 1946, London; d. of Esmond Warner and Emilia Terzulli; m. 1st William Shawcross 1971 (divorced); one s.; m. 2nd John Dewe Mathews 1981 (divorced); m. 3rd Graeme Segal; ed St Mary's Convent, Ascot and Lady Margaret Hall, Oxford; Getty Scholar, Getty Centre for History of Art and Humanities 1987–88; Tinbergen Prof., Erasmus Univ., Rotterdam 1990–91; Visiting Prof., Queen Mary and Westfield Coll., London 1994, Univ. of Ulster 1994, Univ. of York 1996–2000, Birkbeck Coll., London; Prof. of Literature, Film and Theatre Studies, Univ. of Essex 2004–14 (resgnd); Prof. of English and Creative Writing, Birkbeck Coll., London 2014–; Visiting Prof., RCA 2008–12; Distinguished Visiting Prof., Queen Mary, Univ. of London 2009–12, New York Univ., Abu Dhabi 2012–; Fellow, Commonership, Trinity Coll., Cambridge 1998, Italian Acad., Columbia Univ., New York, 2003, All Souls College, Oxford 2013–15; Visiting Fellow, All Souls Coll., Oxford 2001, Univ. of Paris XIII 2003; Sr Fellow, Remarque Inst., New York Univ. 2006, Italian Acad. for Advanced Studies in America, Columbia Univ. 2018; Pres. Virgil Soc. 2004; Vice-Pres. Inst. of Greece, Rome, and Classical Studies, Univ. of Bristol 2004; mem. Exec. Cttee Charter 88 –1997, Literature Panel Arts Council of England –1997, Advisory Council, British Library –1997, Man. Cttee, Nat. Council for One-Parent Families, Bd of Artangel, Cttee of London Library, Cttee of PEN, Council of the British School at Rome 2009–; Judge, Man Booker Int. Prize 2015; Trustee, Nat. Portrait Gallery; Hon. Fellow, Queen Mary and Westfield Coll., London 1994, Lady Margaret Hall, Oxford 2000, London Inst. of Pataphysics 2007, Mansfield Coll., Oxford 2013, St Cross Coll., Oxford 2013; Chevalier des Arts et des Lettres 2000, Commendatore dell'Ordine della Stella di Solidarietà (Italy) 2005; Hon. DLitt (Exeter) 1995, 1997, (York) 1997, (St Andrews) 1998, (Leicester) 2006, (Oxford) 2006; Dr hc (Sheffield Hallam) 1995, (Univ. of North London) 1997, (Tavistock Inst., Univ. of East London) 1999, (RCA) 2004, (Kent) 2005, (Leicester) 2006, (King's Coll., London) 2009, British Acad. Medal 2017; Runner Up, WH Smith Children's Poetry Prize 1964, Young Writer of the Year (Daily Telegraph Award) 1971, Daily Express Award 1972, Fawcett Prize 1986, PEN Silver Pen Award 1988, Commonwealth Writer's Prize (Eurasia) 1989, Mythopoeic Scholarship Award 1996, Harvey Darton Prize 1996, Tanner Lecturer, Yale Univ., USA 1999, Katharine Briggs Memorial Prize 1999, Rose Mary Crawshay Prize, British Acad. 2000, Clarendon Lecturer, Univ. of Oxford 2001, Aby Warburg Prize 2004, Nat. Book Critics Circle Award for Criticism 2012, Truman Capote Award for Literary Criticism 2013, Sheikh Zayed Book Award for Arab Culture in Non-Arabic Languages 2013, Holberg Prize 2015. *Radio:* short stories, criticism. *Publications include:* The Dragon Empress: Life and Times of Tz'u-hsi 1835–1908 1972, Alone of All Her Sex: The Myth and the Cult of the Virgin Mary 1976, In a Dark Wood 1977, Queen Victoria Sketch Book 1979, The Crack in the Tea-Cup: Britain in the 20th Century 1979, Joan of Arc: The Image of Female Heroism 1981, The Impossible Day 1981, The Impossible Night 1981, The Impossible Bath 1982, The Impossible Rocket 1982, The Skating Party 1982, The Wobbly Tooth 1984, Monuments and Maidens: The Allegory of the Female Form 1985, The Lost Father 1988, Into the Dangerous World 1989, Imagining a Democratic Culture 1991, Indigo 1992, L'Atalante 1993, Mermaids in the Basement (short stories) 1993, Richard Wentworth 1993, From the Beast to the Blonde: On Fairy Tales and Their Tellers 1994, Managing Monsters: Six Myths of Our Time (Reith Lectures) 1994, Wonder Tales: Six Stories of Enchantment (ed.) 1994, Six Myths Of Our Time: Little Angels, Little Monsters, Beautiful Beasts, and More 1995, Donkey Business Donkey Work: Magic and Metamorphoses in Contemporary Opera 1996, The Inner Eye: Art Beyond the Visible 1996, No Go the Bogeyman: On Scaring, Lulling and Making Mock 1998, The Leto Bundle 2001, Fantastic Metamorphoses, Other Worlds: The Clarendon Lectures 2002, Murderers I Have Known and Other Stories 2002, Signs and Wonders: Essays on Literature and Culture 2003, Phantasmagoria: Spirit Visions, Metaphors, and Media 2006, Stranger Magic: Charmed States and the Arabian Nights (Sheikh Zayed Book Award for Arab Culture in Non-Arabic Languages 2013) 2011, Scheherazade's Children: Global Encounters with the Arabian Nights (co-ed.) 2013, Once Upon a Time: A Short History of Fairy Tale 2014, Fly Away Home 2015, Fairy Tale: A Very Short Introduction 2018, Forms of Enchantment: Writings on Art and Artists 2018; contrib. to The London Review of Books, New Statesman, Sunday Times, The Telegraph, Vogue. *Address:* c/o Rogers, Coleridge & White Literary Agency, 20 Powis Mews, London, W11 1JN, England (office); Department of English and Humanities, Birkbeck College, 43–46 Gordon Square, London, WC1H 0PD, England (office). *Telephone:* (20) 7221-3717 (office). *Fax:* (20) 7229-9084 (office). *E-mail:* info@rcwlitagency.co.uk (office); englishandhumanities@bbk.ac.uk (office). *Website:* www.rcwlitagency.co.uk (office); www.bbk.ac.uk/english (office); www.marinawarner.com.

WARNER, Mark Robert, BA, JD; American lawyer and politician; *Senator from Virginia;* b. 15 Dec. 1954, Indianapolis, Ind.; m. Lisa Collis; three d.; ed Rockville High School, Conn., George Washington Univ., Harvard Law School; Founding Partner, Columbia Capital Corpn; Gov. of Virginia 2002–06; Senator from Virginia 2009–, mem. Cttee on Banking, Housing, and Urban Affairs, Cttee on the Budget, Cttee on Commerce, Science and Transportation, Cttee on Rules and Admin, Select Cttee on Intelligence, Jt Econ. Cttee; Chair. Nat. Govs' Asscn 2004–05; involved in farming and winemaking at his Rappahannock Bend farm; Democrat; fmr Hon. Chair. Forward Together Political Action Cttee; Economic Patriots Award 2011. *Address:* 703 Hart Senate Office Building, Washington, DC 20510, USA (office). *Telephone:* (202) 224-2023 (office). *Website:* warner.senate.gov (office).

WARNOCK, John Edward, MS, PhD; American computer industry executive; b. 6 Oct. 1940, Salt Lake City, Utah; m. Marva E. Warnock; three c.; ed Univ. of Utah; fmrly with Evans & Sutherland Computer Corpn, Computer Sciences Corpn, IBM and Univ. of Utah; Prin. Scientist, Xerox Palo Alto Research Centre (PARC) 1978–82; Co-founder, with Charles Geschke, Adobe Systems Inc. 1982, Pres. 1982–84, Co-Chair. and CEO 1984–2000, Co-Chair. 2000–17, Chief Tech. Officer 2000–01; Chair. Salon Media Group, Inc. 2006–17; mem. Bd of Dirs Octavo Corpn, mem. Bd, fmr Chair. Tech. Museum of Innovation; mem. Entrepreneurial Bd Advisory Cttee, American Film Inst.; mem. Nat. Acad. of Eng, Utah Information Tech. Asscn 2000, American Acad. of Arts and Sciences, American Philosophical Soc.; Fellow, Asscn for Computing Machinery (ACM) 1999, Computer History Museum 2002; Dr hc (Univ. of Utah, American Film Inst., Univ. of Nottingham); numerous awards, including Distinguished Service to Art and Design Int. Award and Corp. Outstanding Achievement Award, Rhode Island School of Design 1998, Award for Tech. Excellence, Nat. Graphics Asscn, Lifetime Achievement Award for Tech. Excellence, PC Magazine, Cary Award, Rochester Inst. of Tech., Software Systems Award, ACM 1989, Distinguished Alumnus Award, Univ. of Utah 1995, Edwin H. Land Medal, Optical Soc. of America 2000, Bodley Medal, Bodleian Library, Univ. of Oxford 2003, Lovelace Medal, British Computer Soc. 2004, Medal of Achievement, American Electronics Asscn (with Charles Geschke) 2006, Computer Entrepreneur Award, IEEE Computer Soc. (with Charles Geschke) 2008, Nat. Medal of Tech. and Innovation (with Charles Geschke) 2009, Marconi Prize (with Charles Geschke) 2010. *Publications:* numerous articles in technical journals and industry magazines. *Address:* c/o Adobe Systems Inc., 345 Park Avenue, San Jose, CA 95110-2704, USA.

WARRELL, David Alan, MA, DM, DSc, FRCP, FRCPE, FMedSci, FRGS, FZS; British specialist in tropical medicine and venoms; *Professor Emeritus of Tropical Medicine, University of Oxford;* b. 6 Oct. 1939, Singapore; s. of A. T. Warrell; m. Dr Mary J. Prentice 1975; two d.; ed Portsmouth Grammar School, Christ Church, Oxford and St Thomas's Hosp. Medical School, London; Oxford Univ. Radcliffe Travelling Fellow, Univ. of Calif. at San Diego 1969; Sr Lecturer, Ahmadu Bello Univ., Nigeria and Lecturer and Consultant Physician, Royal Postgrad. Medical School, London and Hammersmith Hosp. 1970–75; Founding Dir Wellcome-Mahidol Univ., Oxford Tropical Medicine Research Programme, Bangkok and Wellcome Reader in Tropical Medicine, Univ. of Oxford 1979–86; Prof. of Tropical Medicine and Infectious Diseases and Dir Emer. (fmrly Dir) Centre for Tropical Medicine, Univ. of Oxford 1987–2001, Head Nuffield Dept Clinical Medicine 2002–04, Deputy Head 2004–06, Prof. Emer. of Tropical Medicine 2006–; Int. Dir (Hans Sloane Fellow), Royal Coll. of Physicians 2012–; Sr Adviser to MRC on tropical medicine 2001–; Hon. Consultant in Malariology to British Army 1989–2018; Hon. Medical Adviser, Royal Geographical Soc. 1993–2018, Earthwatch Int. 2007–12, Foreign and Commonwealth Office 2002–; WHO Consultant 1979–; mem. WHO Expert Advisory Panel on Malaria 1989–2016; Fellow, St Cross Coll. 1975–2007, Hon. Fellow 2007–; Chair. AIDS Therapeutic Trials Cttee, MRC; Trustee, Tropical Health and Education Trust; Pres. British Venom Group 1992–, Int. Fed. for Tropical Medicine 1996–2000, Royal Soc. of Tropical Medicine and Hygiene 1997–99; Del., Oxford Univ. Press 1999–2006; Adjunct Prof., Univ Xi'an, People's Repub. of China 2009–; Visiting Prof., Capital Medical Univ., Beijing 2011–; Int. Advisor, Australian Myanmar Snakebite Project 2014–18; Prof. Emer. Gorgas Institute, Universidad Peruana Cayetano Heredia, Lima, Peru 2017–; Advisor, Hamish Ogston Foundation (Health) 2018–; Hon. mem. Asscn of Physicians GB and NI 2003, American Soc. of Tropical Medicine and Hygiene 2003, Instituto de Medicina Tropical 'Alexander von Humboldt', Universidad Peruana Cayetano Heredia, Lima, Peru 2010; Hon. Fellow, Ceylon Coll. of Physicians, Hon. FZS; Profesor Honorario, Universidad Nacional Mayor de San Marcos, Lima, Peru 2005; Hon. Prof., Tropical Medicine, University of Medicine-1, Yangon, Myanmar 2016–; Companion, Order of the White Elephant (Thailand) 2004; Chalmer's Medal, Royal Soc. of Tropical Medicine and Hygiene 1981, Ambuj Nath Bose Prize, Royal Coll. of Physicians 1994, Runme Shaw Lecturer, Acad. of Medicine, Singapore 1997, Queen's Award for Higher and Further Educ. 2000, Marc Daniels, Bradshaw, Croonian and Coll. Lecturer and Harveian Orator, Royal Coll. of Physicians 2001, Guthrie Medal, Royal Army Medical Corps (RAMC) 2004, Mary Kingsley Medal, Liverpool School of Tropical Medicine 2005, Lloyd-Roberts Lecturer, Royal Soc. of Medicine 2008, Osler Memorial Medal, Univ. of Oxford 2010, Redi Award, Int. Soc. on Toxinology 2012. *Publications include:* scientific papers and book chapters; Ed.: Oxford Textbook of Medicine, Essential Malariology, Oxford Handbook Expedition and Wilderness Medicine. *Leisure interests:* book-collecting, music, bird-watching, hill-walking. *Address:* Nuffield Dept of Clinical Medicine, University of Oxford, John Radcliffe Hospital, Headley Way, Oxford, OX3 9DU, England (office). *Telephone:* (1865) 234664 (office); (1865) 766865 (office). *E-mail:* david.warrell@ndm.ox.ac.uk (office). *Website:* www.ndm.ox.ac.uk (office).

WARREN, Christopher (Chris), BA (Hons), MBA; Australian fmr journalist and international organization executive; *Federal Secretary, Media, Entertainment & Arts Alliance;* ed Univ. of Sydney, Australian Grad. School of Man.; completed journalist cadetship at The Sydney Morning Herald and worked as a staff and freelance journalist for various employers 1976–86; Fed. Sec., Australian Journalists Asscn 1986–92, Media Entertainment & Arts Alliance 1992–; Pres. Int. Fed. of Journalists 1998–2007. *Address:* Media, Entertainment & Arts Alliance, PO Box 723, Strawberry Hills, NSW 2012, Australia (office). *Telephone:* (1300) 656513 (office). *Fax:* (1300) 730543 (office). *E-mail:* christopher.warren@alliance .org.au (office). *Website:* www.alliance.org.au (office).

WARREN, Sir David Alexander, Kt, KCMG, MA (Oxon.); British diplomatist (retd); b. 11 Aug. 1952, London, England; s. of Alister Warren and Celia Warren; m. Pamela Warren; ed Epsom Coll., Exeter Coll., Oxford; began FCO career at S East Asian Dept 1975–76, Second, later First Sec., Embassy in Tokyo 1977–81, Head of Recruitment Section, Personnel Policy Dept, FCO 1981–83, EC Dept (External) 1983–86, First Sec. and Head of Chancery, High Comm. in Nairobi 1987–90, Asst Head of Far East Dept 1990–91, Dir Int. Div. Office of Science and Tech., Cabinet Office 1991–93, Commercial Counsellor, Embassy in Tokyo 1993–98, Head of China Hong Kong Dept, FCO 1998–2000, Dir UK Trade and Investment 2000–04, Dir Human Resources, FCO 2004–07, Amb. to Japan 2008–12 (retd); Chair. The Japan Soc., London 2013–18; Chair. Council Univ. of Kent; Dir (non-exec.) Aberdeen Japan Investment Trust; mem. Advisory Council, London Symphony Orchestra, Advisory Bd Migration Matters Trust; Bd mem. Sainsbury Inst. for the Study of Japanese Arts and Culture; Assoc. Fellow, Royal Inst. for Int. Affairs, Chatham House; Hon. Fellow, Exeter Coll., Oxford; Hon. DLitt (Sheffield), (De Montfort). *Publications:* Contrib. to various periodicals. *Address:* The Royal Institute of International Affairs, Chatham House, 10 Street James's Square, London, SW1Y 4LE, England (office). *Telephone:* (20) 7957-5700 (office). *Fax:* (20) 7957-5710 (office). *E-mail:* contact@chathamhouse.org (office). *Website:* www.chathamhouse.org (office).

WARREN, Sir Frederick Miles, Kt, KBE, CBE, ONZ, FNZIA, ARIBA, DipArch; New Zealand architect; b. 10 May 1929, Christchurch; s. of M. B. Warren and J. Warren (née Hay); ed Christ's Coll., Auckland Univ. School of Architecture; worked for the late C. W. Wood, 1946–47, for the late R. C. Munroe,ANZIA 1948; joined partnership with the late G. T. Lucas 1956; started firm Warren & Mahoney 1958, Sr Partner 1958–95 (retd); Pres. Canterbury Soc. of Arts 1972–76; Warren & Mahoney awarded New Zealand Inst. of Architects (NZIA) Gold Medal for Dental Nurses' Training School 1959, for Christchurch Memorial Garden Crematorium 1964, for Christchurch Coll. Halls of Residence 1969, for Christchurch Town Hall and Civic Centre 1973; won Architectural Competition for design of Condominium Offices, New Hebrides 1966; gifted his house and garden to the people of NZ through the Ohinetahi Charitable Trust 2012; Dr hc (Auckland) 2001; AIA Pan Pacific Citation 1966, NZIA Gold Medal 1980, 1981, 1983, 1984, 1985, 1986, 1988–91, 2000 (individual), Icon Award, Arts Foundation of NZ 2003, commemorated as one of the Twelve Local Heroes and a bronze bust of him unveiled outside Christchurch Arts Centre 2009. *Works include:* Dorset Street Flats 1956–57, Dental Nurses Training School 1958–59, Carlton Mill Road Flats 1960, MB Warren House 1961, Architect's Office and Flat 1962–79, Harewood Memorial Gardens and Crematorium 1962–63, Christchurch Wool Exchange 1962–64, Christchurch Coll., Univ. of Canterbury 1964–70, I. Munro House 1968, Christchurch Town Hall 1966–72, NZ Chancery, Washington, DC 1975–81, Canterbury Public Library, Christchurch 1982, The Oaks Complex, Wellington 1982, Michael Fowler Centre, Wellington 1983, Rotorua Civic Offices 1985–86, Clarendon Tower 1986–87, AXA New Zealand Wellington Office 1987–89, Compudigm House, Wellington 1989, TVNZ Centre, Auckland 1990. *Television:* profiled on Artsville (TVNZ arts documentary series) 2011. *Publications:* Warren & Mahoney Architects 1990, Miles Warren: An Autobiography 2008. *Leisure interests:* yachting, water-colouring, sketching. *Address:* 65 Cambridge Terrace, Christchurch 1, New Zealand. *Telephone:* 799640. *Website:* www.warrenandmahoney.com.

WARREN, John Robin, AC, MB, BS, MD, FAA, FRCPA, FRCP; Australian pathologist; b. 11 June 1937, Adelaide, S Australia; s. of Roger Warren and Helen Warren (née Verco); m. Winifred Teresa Williams; four s. two d.; ed Univ. of Adelaide and Royal Melbourne Hosp.; Jr Resident Medical Officer, Queen Elizabeth Hosp., Woodville, S Australia 1961; Registrar in Haematology and Clinical Pathology, Inst. of Medical and Veterinary Science, Adelaide 1962; Registrar in Clinical Pathology, Royal Melbourne Hosp. 1964–66, Registrar in Pathology 1966–68; Sr Pathologist, Royal Perth Hosp., Western Australia 1968–99; demonstrated, with Barry J. Marshall, the association of *Helicobacter pylori* and peptic ulcers, particularly duodenal ulcers; Fellow, Royal Coll. of Pathologists of Australasia 1967; Hon. Fellow, Royal Australian Coll. of Physicians 2006; Hon. Mem. Polish Soc. of Gastroenterology, German Soc. of Pathology 2007; Hon. MD (Univ. of Western Australia) 1997; Dr hc (Univ. of Adelaide) 2006, (Univ. of Toyama, Japan) 2007, (Otto-von-Guericke Universität, Magdeburg) 2007; Distinguished Fellows Award, Coll. of Pathologists 1995, Inaugural Award, First Western Pacific Helicobacter Congress 1996, Medal of Univ. of Hiroshima 1996, Australian Medical Asscn (WA) Award 1995; jtly with Prof. Barry Marshall: Warren Alpert Foundation Prize, Harvard Medical School 1995, Paul Ehrlich and Ludwig Darmstaedter Award, Goethe-Universität, Frankfurt, Germany 1997, Inaugural Florey Medal Award 1998, Nobel Prize in Physiology or Medicine 2005, Australian Medical Asscn Gold Medal 2006, Western Australian of the Year 2007, Medal of the Hirosaki Univ. School of Medicine 2007, Special Recognition Award for Distinguished Service to Surgical Pathology, American Soc. for Clinical Pathology 2007, Govt of Western Australia Premier's Science Awards, Western Australian Science Hall of Fame 2007. *Publications include:* numerous articles in scientific journals. *Leisure interest:* photography.

WARREN, Kelcy L., BS; American business executive; *Chairman and CEO, Energy Transfer Equity, LP;* b. 9 Nov. 1955; m.; one c.; ed Univ. of Texas, Arlington; Pipeline Engineer, Lone Star Gas Co., Dallas, Tex. 1978–81; worked for Endevco 1981–92; Pres. and COO Cornerstone Natural Gas, Inc., Dallas 1993–96; Pres. Energy Transfer Partners, Dallas 1996–2004, co-f. entities that acquired and operated midstream assets contributed in merger of Energy Transfer Partners and Heritage Propane 2004, Co-Chair. and Co-CEO Energy Transfer Equity, LP 2004–07, Chair. and CEO 2007–; co-f. own recording studio, Music Road Records, with Jimmy LaFave and Fred Remmert 2007. *Leisure interest:* collecting music memorabilia including autographs of Jackson Browne and drumsticks signed by the Eagles. *Address:* Energy Transfer Equity, LP, Dallas Office, 3738 Oak Lawn Avenue, Dallas, TX 75219, USA (office). *Telephone:* (214) 981-0700 (office). *Fax:* (214) 981-0703 (office). *E-mail:* info@energytransfer.com (office). *Website:* www.energytransfer.com (office).

WARREN-GASH, Haydon Boyd, MA (Cantab.); British business executive, consultant and fmr diplomatist; b. 8 Aug. 1949, Nairobi, Kenya; m. Caroline Emma Bowring; one s. one d.; ed Marlborough Coll., Univ. of Cambridge; joined FCO 1971, Latin America Dept 1971–72, Third Sec., Chancery, Ankara 1973–76, Rhodesia Dept 1976–77, Second Sec., Chancery, Madrid 1977–81, Perm. Under-Sec.'s Dept 1981–82, Pvt. Sec., Minister of State's Office 1982–85, Asst Head, Southern European Dept 1989–90, Deputy High Commr, Nairobi 1991–94, Head of Southern European Dept 1994–97, Amb. to Côte d'Ivoire 1997–2001, HIV/AIDS Special Project Coordinator 2001–02, Amb. to Morocco 2002–05, to Colombia 2005–08; Chair. British and Colombian Chamber of Commerce 2013 (now mem. Bd); Dir FORO Consulting 2010–14, BTV Ltd 2014–19. *Address:* 98 Overstrand Mansions, Prince of Wales Drive, London, SW11 4EU, England (home). *Website:* www.britishandcolombianchamber.com (office).

WARRINGTON, Elizabeth Kerr, PhD, DSc, FRS; British academic; *Professor Emerita of Clinical Neuropsychology, National Hospital for Neurology and Neurosurgery;* b. Edinburgh, Scotland; d. of Prof. John A. V. Butler, FRS and Margaret L. Butler; m.; one d.; ed Univ. Coll. London; Research Fellow, Inst. of Neurology 1956; Sr Clinical Psychologist, Nat. Hosp. for Neurology and Neurosurgery 1960, Prin. Psychologist 1962, Top Grade Clinical Psychologist 1972–82, Prof. of Clinical Neuropsychology 1982–96, Hon. Consultant Neuropsychologist to Dementia Research Centre 1996–, Prof. Emer. of Clinical Neuropsychology, Univ. of London 1996–; Fellow, Univ. Coll. London; Dr hc (Bologna) 1998, (York) 1999, (Univ. Louis Pasteur) 2006; Ipsen Foundation Prize 2008. *Publications include:* Cognitive Neuropsychology (co-author) 1990; numerous papers in professional journals. *Leisure interests:* entertaining granddaughters. *Address:* Dementia Research Centre, Box 16, National Hospital for Neurology and Neurosurgery, Queen Square, London, WC1N 3BG, England (office). *Telephone:* (20) 3448-3291 (office). *E-mail:* e.warrington@ucl.ac.uk (office). *Website:* www.uclh.org/about/nhnn.shtml (office).

WARRIOR, Padmasree, BS, MS; Indian/American engineer and business executive; b. 1961, Vijayawada, AP, India; m.; ed Maris Stella Coll., Vijayawada, Indian Inst. of Tech. (IIT), New Delhi, Cornell Univ., Ithaca, NY; Vice-Pres. Motorola, Inc. 1999, Motorola's Liaison Exec. for Cornell Univ. 2001, Exec. Vice-Pres. and Chief Tech. Officer, Motorola, Inc. 2003–07; Chief Tech. Officer, Cisco Systems Inc. 2007–12, Chief Tech. and Strategy Officer 2012–15; mem. Bd of Dirs Corning Corpn 2005–08, Gap Inc. 2013–, Box 2014–; mem. Bd Joffrey Ballet, Chicago, Museum of Science and Industry, Chicago, Singapore Agency for Science, Tech. and Research (ASTAR), Chicago Mayor's Tech. Council, Cornell Univ. Eng Council, IIT Advisory Council; mem. Selection Bd for White House Fellows 2001; fmr mem. Texas Gov.'s Council for Digital Economy, Tech. Advisory Council Fed. Communications Comm., Advisory Cttee NSF Computing and Information Science and Eng; Dr hc (New York Polytechnic) 2007; Women Elevating Science and Tech. Award, Working Woman Magazine (co-recipient) 2001, achievements recognized by American Immigration Law Foundation 2003, Nat. Medal of Tech. 2004, IIT Distinguished Alumni Award 2006. *Leisure interests:* novels of P. G. Wodehouse, arts and crafts, exercising, meditation. *Address:* c/o Cisco Systems Inc., 170 West Tasman Drive, Building 10, San Jose, CA 95134-1706, USA.

WARSH, Kevin Maxwell, BA, JD; American financier and fmr government official; *Shepard Family Distinguished Visiting Fellow in Economics, Hoover Institution;* b. 13 April 1970, Albany, NY; m. Jane Lauder 2002; ed Stanford Univ., Harvard Law School, Harvard Business School, MIT Sloan School of Man.; worked for Morgan Stanley & Co., New York 1995–2002, becoming Exec. Dir, Mergers and Acquisitions Dept; Special Asst to the Pres. for Econ. Policy, also Exec. Sec., Nat. Econ. Council 2002–06; mem. Bd of Govs, Fed. Reserve System 2006–11; currently Shepard Family Distinguished Visiting Fellow in Econs, Hoover Inst., also Lecturer, Stanford Grad. School of Business; mem. Bd of Dirs United Parcel Service (UPS), Inc.; mem. Advisory Bd Rubicon Global. *Address:* Hoover Institution, 434 Galvez Mall, Stanford University, Stanford, CA 94305-6003, USA (office). *Telephone:* (650) 723-1754 (office). *Website:* www.hoover.org/profiles/kevin-warsh (office).

WARSHEL, Ariel, BS, MS, PhD; American/Israeli chemist and academic; *Distinguished Professor of Chemistry and Biochemistry, University of Southern California;* b. 20 Nov. 1940, Kibbutz Sde Nahum, Beit She'an Valley; m. Tamar Warshel; two c.; ed Israel Inst. of Tech., Weizmann Inst. of Science; served in Israel Defense Forces (attained rank of capt.); Research Fellow, Dept of Chemistry, Harvard Univ. 1970–72; Research Assoc., Weizmann Inst. of Science 1972–73, Sr Scientist 1973–77, Assoc. Prof. 1977–78; Visiting Scientist, MRC Lab. of Molecular Biology, Cambridge, UK 1974–76; Asst Prof. of Chemistry, Univ. of Southern Calif. 1976–78, Assoc. Prof. 1979–84, Prof. 1984, Prof. of Chemistry and Biochemistry 1991, Distinguished Prof. of Chemistry and Biochemistry and Dana and David Dornsife Chair in Chemistry 2011–; Fellow, Biophysical Soc.; mem. NAS 2009; Hon. FRSC 2014; several awards including Tolman Medal 2003, Royal Soc. of Chemistry Soft Matter and Biophysical Chemistry Award 2012, Nobel Prize in Chemistry (jtly with Martin Karplus and Michael Levitt) 2013, Founders Award of the Biophysical Soc. 2014, Israel Chemical Soc. Gold Medal 2014. *Address:* University of Southern California, Department of Chemistry, SGM 406, Los Angeles, CA 90089, USA (office). *Telephone:* 213) 740-4114 (office). *Fax:* (213) 740-2701 (office). *E-mail:* warshel@usc.edu (office). *Website:* chem.usc.edu (office).

WARSI, Baroness (Life Peer), cr. 2007, of Dewsbury in the County of West Yorkshire; **Rt Hon. Sayeeda Hussain Warsi,** LLB, PC; British lawyer and politician; b. 1971, Dewsbury, Yorks.; ed Birkdale High School, Dewsbury Coll., Univ. of Leeds, York Coll. of Law; completed Legal Practice Course and trained with Crown Prosecution Service and Home Office Immigration Dept; worked for John Whitfield (last Conservative MP for Dewsbury) at Whitfield Hallam Goodall Solicitors; later est. specialist practice, George Warsi Solicitors, Dewsbury; also worked overseas for Ministry of Law in Pakistan and in Kashmir as Chair. Savayra Foundation (women's empowerment charity); Conservative Party parl. cand. for Dewsbury at Gen. Election (first Muslim woman to be selected by Tories) 2005; served as special adviser to Michael Howard on Community Relations; apptd by David Cameron as Vice-Chair. Conservative Party with specific responsibility for cities 2005–07; mem. (Conservative) House of Lords 2007–; Shadow Minister for Community Cohesion and Social Action 2007–10; Minister without Portfolio (Minister of State) 2010–12; Govt Spokesperson, Cabinet Office 2011–12; Sr Minister of State and Govt Spokesperson, FCO 2012–14 (resgnd); Minister for Faith and Communities 2012–14 (resgnd); Co-Chair. Conservative and Unionist Party 2010–12; Dir, Shire Bed Co. (family business), Azam Assocs Ltd (food consultancy, owned jtly with husband); Trustee, Savayra Foundation UK; Pro Vice-Chancellor, Bolton Univ. 2016–; Visiting Prof., St Mary's Univ.; Adviser to Bridge Initiative, Georgetown Univ., Washington, DC. *Address:* House of Lords, Westminster, London, SW1A 0PW, England (office). *Telephone:* (20) 7219-6097 (office). *E-mail:* warsis@parliament.uk (office). *Website:* www.sayeedawarsi.com.

WARWICK, Dionne; American singer; b. (Marie Dionne), 12 Dec. 1941, East Orange, NJ; m. Bill Elliott (divorced 1975); two s.; pnr Bruce Garrick; ed Hartt Coll. of Music; as teenager formed Gospelaires; later sang background for recording studio 1966; début, Philharmonic Hall, Lincoln Center, New York 1966; appearances at London Palladium, Olympia, Paris, Lincoln Center; apptd US Amb. of Health by President Ronald Reagan 1987; apptd Global Amb. for Health and FAO Amb. 2002; Co-founder Carr/Todd/Warwick Production, Inc., Dionne Warwick Design Group Inc.; Dr hc (Lincoln Coll., Ill.) 2010; five Grammy Awards, Luminary Award, American Soc. of Young Musicians 1997, Chairman's Award for Sustained Creative Achievement, Nat. Asscn of Record Merchandisers 1998, History Maker, History Makers Org. of Chicago 2001, Heroes Award, New York Chapter of Recording Acad. 2002, Lifetime Achievement Award, R&B Foundation 2003, Steve Chase Humanitarian Arts & Activism Award, Desert Aids Project 2011, Ellis Island Medal of Honor 2013, inducted into New Jersey Hall of Fame 2013. *Films:* The Slaves 1969, No Night, So Long, Hot! Live and Otherwise. *Television includes:* co-host, Solid Gold; host, A Gift of Music 1981; Dionne Warwick Special; appeared in Sisters in the Name of Love 1986. *Recordings include:* albums: Presenting Dionne Warwick 1963, Anyone Who Had a Heart 1964, Make Way for Dionne Warwick 1964, The Sensitive Sound of Dionne Warwick 1965, Here I Am 1965, Here Where There Is Love 1966, Dionne Warwick in Paris 1966, On Stage and in the Movies 1967, The Windows of the World 1967, Dionne Warwick in Valley of the Dolls 1968, The Magic of Believing (with The Drinkard Singers) 1968, Promises, Promises 1968, Soulful 1969, I'll Never Fall in Love Again 1970, Very Dionne 1970, The Dionne Warwick Story: A Decade of Gold 1971, Dionne 1972, Just Being Myself 1973, Then Came You 1975, Track of the Cat 1975, Love at First Sight 1977, A Man and a Woman (with Isaac Hayes) 1977, Dionne 1979, No Night So Long 1980, Hot! Live and Otherwise 1981, Friends in Love 1982, Heartbreaker 1982, How Many Times Can We Say Goodbye 1983, Finder of Lost Loves 1985, Friends 1985, Reservations for Two 1987, Dionne Warwick Sings Cole Porter 1990, Friends Can Be Lovers 1993, Aquarela do Brazil 1994, Christmas in Vienna II (with Plácido Domingo) 1994, Dionne Sings Dionne 1998, Dionne Sings Dionne, Vol. 2 2000, My Favorite Time of the Year 2004, My Friends & Me 2006, Why We Sing 2008, Only Trust Your Heart 2011, Now 2012, Feels So Good 2014. *Publications:* My Point of View 2003, My Life, As I See It 2010. *Website:* www.dionnewarwickonline.com.

WARWICK OF UNDERCLIFFE, Baroness (Life Peer), cr. 1999, of Undercliffe in the County of West Yorkshire; **Diana Mary Warwick,** BA; British academic; b. 16 July 1945, Bradford; d. of Jack Warwick and Olive Warwick; m. Sean Young 1969; ed Bedford Coll., Univ. of London; Gen. Sec. Asscn of Univ. Teachers 1983–92; Chief Exec. Westminster Foundation for Democracy 1992–95; Chair. VSO 1994–2005; Chair. Human Tissue Authority 2009–, NED Pension Protection Fund 2011–; mem. Standing Cttee on Standards in Public Life (Nolan/Neill Cttee) 1994–99, OST Tech. Foresight Steering Group 1997–2000; Chief Exec. Universities UK (fmrly Cttee of Vice-Chancellors and Prins) 1995–2009; Chair. Modern Records Centre, Univ. of Warwick; Chair. Bd of Trustees, Int. Students House; Commr, Fulbright Comm.; mem. Bd Pensions Protection Agency, British Council 1985–95, Commonwealth Inst. 1988–95; mem. RIIA, Inter-Parl. Union, Commonwealth Parl. Asscn, British American Parl. Group, Employment Appeals Tribunal 1984–99; mem. of Council, Univ. Coll. London; Trustee, St Catharine's Foundation, Windsor 1996–2008; Hon. DLitt (Bradford) 1993, (Open Univ.) 1998, (Royal Holloway Coll., Univ. of London) 2007, (London Metropolitan) 2008, (Brunel) 2009,. *Address:* House of Lords, London, SW1A 0PW, England (office). *Telephone:* (20) 7219-5353 (office).

WARWICK-THOMPSON, Paul, BA, PhD; British museum director and university rector; *Rector, Royal College of Art;* b. 9 Aug. 1959, Oxford; s. of Sir Michael Thompson; m. Adline Finlay 1984; one s. one d.; ed Bryanston School, Univ. of Bristol, Univ. of East Anglia; Curator Design Museum, London 1989–92, Dir 1992–2000; Dir Cooper-Hewitt Nat. Design Museum, New York 2001–09; Rector RCA 2009–; Adjunct Prof., Inst. for Global Health Innovation, Imperial Coll.; Trustee, Victoria and Albert Museum, London; Hon. Fellow, RCA 2000. *Leisure interests:* theatre, cinema, gardening. *Address:* Royal College of Art, Kensington Gore, London SW7, England (office). *Telephone:* (20) 7590-4444 (office). *E-mail:* press@rca.ac.uk (office).

WĄSACZ, Emil, MEng; Polish economist, business executive and fmr government official; *Chairman and CEO, Stalexport Autostrady SA;* b. 1 Aug. 1945, Zabratówka, Rzeszów Prov.; m.; three c.; ed Łódź Tech. Univ., Main School of Commerce (SGH), Warsaw; employee, Katowice Steelworks 1976–94, Supreme Dir then Chair. Katowice Steelworks SA 1991–94; adviser to Chair. Bank Śląski SA, Bank PeKaO SA and enterprise Stalexport SA; Chair. Szczecin Steelworks SA 1995–97; Vice-Leader Supervisory Bd, later Chair. Progress Nat. Investment Fund 1995–97; Minister of the Treasury 1997–2001; CEO Stalexport Serwis-Centrum SA (steel products co.) 2001, then Chair. Man. Bd, suspended from position 2006, Chair. and CEO Stalexport Autostrady SA (fmrly Stalexport SA) 2000–; mem. Solidarity Trade Union, Leader Plant Cttee in the Katowice Steelworks 1989–90; voluntary worker, Catholic Family Clinic, Sosnowiec 1983–90. *Leisure interests:* tourism, history, astronomy, literature, romantic poetry. *Address:* Stalexport Autostrady SA, 41-404 Myslowice, ul. Sand 20, Poland (office). *Telephone:* (32) 7627545 (office). *Fax:* (32) 7627556 (office). *E-mail:* relacje .inwestorskie@stalexport-autostrady.pl (office); walne.zgromadzenie@stalexport -autostrady.pl (office). *Website:* www.stalexport-autostrady.pl (office).

WASE, Brenson S.; Marshall Islands politician; *Minister of Finance;* b. 28 May 1952; m. Antonia U. Wase; five c.; ed Univ. of Hawaii-Hil; Senator from Arno 1988–99, from Majuro Atoll 1999–; Minister of Social Service 1984–87, of Resources and Devt 1988–91, of Interior and Outer Islands Affairs 1991–95, of Internal Affairs 1995–99, of Transportation and Communications 2000–02, of Finance 2002–08, 2016–, of Justice 2009–12; Gov. of the Marshall Islands to ADB 2000–, Vice-Chair. Bd of Dirs 2004–; Acting Pres. of Repub. of Marshall Islands 2003. *Address:* Ministry of Finance, POB D, Majuro MH 96960, Marshall Islands (office). *Telephone:* (625) 8311 (office). *E-mail:* secfin@ntamar.net (office). *Website:* rmi-mof.com (office).

WASHIDA, Kiyokazu; Japanese philosopher, academic and fmr university administrator; *Professor, Otani University;* b. 2 Sept. 1949, Kyoto; ed Kyoto Univ.; fmr Prof., School of Letters and Dean, Grad. School of Letters, Kyoto Univ., later Vice-Pres. in charge of Educ. and Information; Asst Prof., Faculty of Literature, Osaka Univ. Grad. School 2005, becoming Univ. Vice-Pres., then Pres. 2007–11; Prof., Otani Univ. 2011–; mem. Kyoto Nat. Festival Planning Cttee; Assoc. mem. Science Council of Japan; Dir Japan Asscn of Nat. Univs; mem. Cabinet Office Council for Science and Tech. Policy Expert Panel on Bioethics; Medal of Honour with Purple Ribbon 2004; Suntory Prize for Social Sciences and Humanities 1989, Kuwabara Takeo Prize 2000. *Publications:* Bunsansuru risei: Genshogaku no shisen 1989, Modo no meikyu 1989, Kimochi no ii hanashi 2001, Talking to Myself (co-author) 2002. *Address:* Otani University, Koyama-Kamifusacho, Kita-ku, Kyoto 603-814, Japan (office). *Telephone:* (75) 411-8161 (office). *Fax:* (75) 411-8162 (office). *Website:* www.otani.ac.jp (office).

WASHINGTON, Denzel Hayes, Jr, BA; American actor, film director and film producer; b. 28 Dec. 1954, Mt Vernon, New York City; s. of Rev. Denzel Hayes Washington, Sr and Lennis 'Lynne' Washington; m. Pauletta Pearson 1983; two s. two d.; ed Mainland High School, Daytona Beach, Fla, Fordham Univ. and American Conservatory Theater, San Francisco; worked at New York Shakespeare Festival and American Place Theater; off-Broadway appearances include: Ceremonies in Dark Old Men, When the Chickens Come Home to Roost and A Soldier's Play (Negro Ensemble Co.), Public Theater's production of Shakespeare's Richard III 1990, as Marcus Brutus in Julius Caesar on Broadway 2005; played young doctor in TV series St Elsewhere; Harvard Foundation Award 1996, Cecil B. DeMille Award, Golden Globe Awards 2016. *Films include:* A Soldier's Story 1984, The Mighty Quinn, Cry Freedom 1987, Heart Condition 1989, Glory (Acad. Award for Best Supporting Actor) 1990, Love Supreme 1990, Mo' Better Blues 1990, Ricochet 1991, Mississippi Masala 1991, Much Ado About Nothing, Malcolm X 1992, The Pelican Brief 1993, Philadelphia 1993, Hank Aaron: Chasing the Dream (documentary) (exec. producer) 1995, Devil in a Blue Dress 1995, Courage Under Fire 1996, The Preacher's Wife 1996, Fallen 1997, He Got Game 1998, The Siege 1998, The Bone Collector 1999, The Hurricane 1999, Remember the Titans 2001, Training Day (Acad. Award for Best Actor 2002) 2001, John Q (Award for Best Actor, Nat. Asscn for the Advancement of Colored People (NAACP) Awards 2003) 2002, Antwone Fisher (also producer and dir; Awards for Best Supporting Actor and Best Dir, NAACP Awards 2003) 2002, Out of Time 2003, Man on Fire 2004, The Manchurian Candidate 2004, Inside Man 2006, Deja Vu 2006, American Gangster 2007, The Great Debaters (also dir) 2007, The Taking of Pelham 1 2 3 2009, The Book of Eli (also producer) 2010, Unstoppable 2010, Safe House (also exec. producer) 2012, Flight 2012, 2 Guns 2013, The Equalizer 2014, Fences (SAG Award for Outstanding Performance by a Male Actor in a Leading Role 2017) 2016. *Television includes:* Half Past Autumn: The Life and Works of Gordon Parks (documentary) (producer) 2000. *Leisure interests:* cooking, reading, basketball. *Address:* c/o WME Entertainment, 9601 Wilshire Blvd, Beverly Hills, CA 90210-5213, USA (office). *Website:* www.wma.com (office).

WASIM AKRAM; Pakistani sports commentator, coach and fmr professional cricketer; b. 3 June 1966, Lahore, Punjab; m. 1st Huma Akram (died 2009); two s.; m. 2nd Shaniera Thompson 2013; one d.; ed Islamia Coll., Lahore; left-hand middle-order batsman, left-arm fast bowler; played for Pakistan Automobile Corpn 1984/85–85/86, Lahore City Whites 1985–86, Pakistan 1985–2002 (Capt. 1999–2000), Lahore City 1986–87, 1997–98, Lancashire 1988–98 (Capt. 1998), Pakistan International Airlines 1992/93–2001/02, Lahore Blues 2000–01, Hampshire 2003; regarded as one of the greatest fast bowlers ever, holds world records for the most wickets taken in List A cricket (881), and is second only to Muttiah Muralitharan in terms of One-Day Int. (ODI) wickets (502); considered to be a pioneer of reverse swing bowling; only bowler to have captured more than 400 wickets both in Test and ODI cricket; Test debut: NZ v Pakistan, Auckland 25 Jan. 1985; played in 104 Tests (25 as Capt.), scoring 2,898 runs (average 22.64, highest score 257 not out) including three hundreds and taking 414 wickets (average 23.62), best bowling (innings) 7/119, (match) 11/110; achieved highest score by a No. 8 batsman in Test cricket: 257 not out from 363 balls against Zimbabwe at Sheikhupura, innings contained 12 sixes which is also a world record for Test cricket; played in 350 ODIs (109 as Capt.), scoring 3,717 runs (average 16.52, highest score 86) and taking 502 wickets (average 23.52), best bowling 5/15; played in 257 First-class matches, scoring 7,161 runs (average 22.73) and taking 1,042 wickets (average 21.64), best bowling 8/30; retd 2003; currently sportscaster for ESPN Star network and ARY Digital; commentated on Int. Cricket Council (ICC) Women's Cricket World Cup in Australia 2009, ICC World Twenty20 in England 2009, Champion's Trophy in S Africa 2009; Dir Islamabad United –2017; f. Akram Foundation; Wisden Cricketer of the Year 1993, one of five new members inducted into ICC Cricket Hall of Fame 2009. *Publication:* Wasim (autobiography). *Leisure interest:* Manchester United Football Club. *Website:* wasimakramlive.com; theakramfoundation.com.

WASMOSY, Juan Carlos, DCE; Paraguayan civil engineer, politician and fmr head of state; b. 15 Dec. 1938, Asunción; s. of Dr Juan Bautista Wasmosy and María Clotilde Monti Paoli; m. Maria Teresa Carrasco Dos Santos; five s. (one deceased) one d.; ed San José School, Asunción and Nat. Univ. of Asunción; fmr Asst Prof. Univ. of Asunción; sometime Pres. ECOMIPA, CONEMPA, COCEP, GOYA (pvt. construction and industrial cos); other business affiliations; mem. construction holding which built Itaipú Hydroelectric Power Station; currently engaged in construction of Yacyretá power station; Pres. Int. Fed. of Zebu Cattle Breeders; mem. Colorado Party 1973–; Minister of Integration 1993; Pres. of Paraguay 1993–98, Senator for Life 1998–; Orden de Solidaridad de Brasil; numerous awards. *Address:* The Senate, Calle 14 de Mayo, esq. Avda de la República, 1°, Asunción, Paraguay.

WASSENER, Albert; German cultural institute director; b. 25 April 1936, Essen; s. of Albert Wassener and Gertrud Wassener (née Forstbauer); m. Renate Wassener 1962; one s. one d.; ed Univs of Bonn and Munich; Dir Goethe Inst., Tripoli, Libya 1965–66, Officer, Cultural Programmes, Goethe Inst., Rome 1966–74, Head, Teachers' Training Dept, Goethe Inst. Head Office, Munich 1974–78, Dir Goethe Inst., Tel-Aviv 1978–84, Copenhagen 1984–89, Istanbul

1989–90, Head, Talks Dept, Goethe Inst. Head Office, Munich 1990–95, Dir Goethe Inst., London and Regional Dir, GB and NI 1995–2000. *Publication:* German Foreign Cultural Politics: Principles, Perspectives and the Future (Discussion Papers in German Studies) 1998. *Address:* c/o Goethe-Institut Berlin, Neue Schönhauser Str. 20, Berlin 10178, Germany. *Telephone:* (30) 259063. *Fax:* (30) 25906400. *E-mail:* berlin@goethe.org. *Website:* www.goethe.de.

WASSERMAN, Baron (Life Peer), cr. 2011, of Pimlico in the City of Westminster; **Gordon Wasserman,** BA, MA; Canadian/British civil servant and consultant; b. 26 July 1938, Montreal, Quebec; ed McGill Univ., Univ. of Oxford, UK (Rhodes Scholar); ind. consultant specializing in public sector man.; began service to UK Govt as Econ. Adviser to the Home Office 1967–73, Head of Urban Deprivation Unit 1973–81, apptd Asst Under-Sec. of State and Dir of Social Policy in Cabinet of Margaret Thatcher 1981, Asst Under-Sec. of State for Police Science and Tech. 1983–95; spent a year working at Nat. Asscn for the Advancement of Colored People (NAACP) Legal Defense Fund, Inc., New York City while on sabbatical from UK Govt; Special Adviser on Science and Tech. to Police Commissioner, New York City 1996–98; Sr Adviser and Chief of Staff to Philadelphia Police Commr 1998–2002; CEO The Gordon Wasserman Group, LLC 2002–08; fmr Chair. (non-exec.) Ion Track Inc. (developer of trace detection tech. for explosives and narcotics), Yes Please Foods GmbH, The Public Safety Forum; Pres. Inst. of Public Safety, Crime and Justice, Univ. of Northampton; mem. Bd of Dirs BBL Foundation; Chair. Advisory Bd Center for Criminal Justice Science and Tech., Georgia Tech. Inst.; Strategic Adviser to Man. Dir, Public Sector Business, Telefonica UK and Safety and Graphics Business Group, 3M United Kingdom plc; Advisor, Policing and Criminal Justice to British Prime Minister and Home Sec. 2010–12; mem. Council of Advisors, Inst. for Int. Criminal Investigations, Ind. Reference Group to the Police Fed. of England and Wales; Trustee, Centre for Justice Innovation. *Address:* House of Lords, Westminster, London, SW1A 0PW, England. *Telephone:* (20) 7219-5353. *Fax:* (20) 7219-5979.

WASSON, Gregory (Greg) D.; American business executive; ed Purdue Univ.; joined Walgreen as pharmacy intern, Houston, Tex. 1980, managed several drugstores then promoted to dist man. 1986, Regional Vice-Pres. Walgreens store operations 1999–2001, Vice-Pres. and Exec. Vice-Pres. Walgreens Health Initiatives 2001–02, Pres. 2002–04, Sr Vice-Pres. 2004–05, Exec. Vice-Pres. 2005–07, Pres. and COO Walgreen Co. 2007–09, Pres. and CEO 2009–14, Pres. and CEO Walgreens Boots Alliance (following purchase of remaining stake in Alliance Boots GmbH) Aug.–Dec. 2014; mem. or fmr mem. Bd of Dirs, AmerisourceBergen, Verizon Communications Inc., Nat. Asscn of Chain Drug Stores, Retail Industry Leaders Asscn, Healthcare Leadership Council, Consumer Goods Forum, World Business Chicago, The Field Museum, Museum of Science and Industry, Midtown Educational Foundation; mem. British-American Business Council Int. Advisory Bd; mem. The Economic Club of Chicago, The Business Council, The Wall Street Journal CEO Council, Civic Cttee of Commercial Club of Chicago, Illinois chapter of American Cancer Soc.'s CEOs Against Cancer (Co-Chair. Discovery Ball 2014).

WÄSTBERG, Olof (Olle), BA; Swedish politician, writer and diplomatist; *President of the Board, Isaak Hirsch Foundation;* b. 6 May 1945, Stockholm; s. of Erik Wästberg and Greta Hirsch; m. Inger Claesson 1968; two s.; ed Univ. of Stockholm; Vice-Pres. Liberal Youth Sweden 1968–71; mem. Bd Liberal Party 1972–93, 1997–, Pres. Exec. Cttee 1982–83, teacher of political science, Univ. of Stockholm 1967–68; journalist, political Dept Expressen 1968–71, Ed. 1994–95; Research Fellow, Business and Social Research Centre 1971–76; Pres. Akiefram-jandet 1976–82; mem. Parl. 1976–82; Pres. Swedish Newspaper Promotion Asscn 1983–91; Under-Sec. of State, Ministry of Finance 1991–93; Ed.-in-Chief Expressen 1993–95; Consul Gen. of Sweden, New York 1999–2004; Dir-Gen. Swedish Inst., Stockholm 2005–11; Sec.-Gen. Raoul Wallenberg Centennial 2011–13; Head of Governmental Comm. on Democracy 2014–16; Pres. Nordic Investment Bank 1992–94; Chair. Swedish Broadcasting Corpn 1996–99, Stockholm City Theatre 1998–99; Dir, Stockholm Stock Exchange 1977–82, 1988–94; Pres. Isaak Hirsch Foundation 2004–; mem. Bd, Swedish American Foundation 2009–, Govt comms on S African consumer politics, stock market, globalization and media; The Royal Medal (12th Grade); Gold Medal, Swedish Marketing Group 1982, Bertil Ohlin Medal 1996, Man of the Year, Swedish-American Community of New York 2003, Karl Staaf Gold Medal 2013. *Publications:* books on African problems, immigration policies and economic topics; articles in professional journals. *Address:* Bellmangatan 6, 118 20 Stockholm, Sweden (home). *Telephone:* 73-6842050 (mobile) (office). *E-mail:* olle@wastberg.se (office). *Website:* www.wastberg.se.

WASUM-RAINER, Susanne Marianne, PhD; German lawyer and diplomatist; *Ambassador to Italy;* b. 31 July 1956; widowed; one c.; research at Stiftung Wissenschaft und Politik 1984–86, preparatory service for Higher Foreign Service 1986–87, career examination for Higher Foreign Service 1987, served at Fed. Foreign Office, Bonn 1987–89, Embassy in Rabat, Morocco 1989–91, Fed. Foreign Office 1991–93, Embassy in Tel-Aviv 1993–97, Perm. Representation to Int. Orgs, Geneva 1997–2000, Deputy Dir, Int. Law Policy Unit, Fed. Foreign Office 2000–02, Head of Int. Law Policy Unit, Dept of State 2002–06, Commr for Issues of Gen. and Special Law, Fed. Foreign Office 2006–09, Gen. Counsel and Int. Law Adviser to Fed. Govt 2009–12, Amb. to France 2012–15, to Italy (also accred to San Marino) 2015–. *Address:* Embassy of Germany, Via San Martino della Battaglia 4, 00185 Rome, Italy (office). *Telephone:* (06) 492131 (office). *Fax:* (06) 4452672 (office). *E-mail:* info@rom.diplo.de (office). *Website:* www.rom.diplo.de (office).

WASZCZYKOWKI, Witold Jan, MA (Hist), MA (Int. Studies), PhD; Polish diplomatist and politician; b. 5 May 1957, Piotrków Trybunalski; ed Univ. of Łódź, Univ. of Oregon, USA, Geneva Centre for Security Policy, Switzerland; joined Ministry of Foreign Affairs 1992, Amb. to Iran 1999–2002, Deputy Minister of Foreign Affairs 2005–08, Chief Negotiator with USA on missile defence; Deputy Head, Nat. Security Bureau 2008–10; Minister of Foreign Affairs 2015–18; mem. Sejm (Parl.) 2011–; mem. Prawo i Sprawiedliwość (PiS—Law and Justice) party.

WATANABE, Katsuaki; Japanese automotive industry executive; *Senior Advisor, Toyota Motor Corporation;* b. 14 Feb. 1942, Mie Pref.; m.; three d.; ed Keio Univ.; joined Toyota Motor Corpn 1964, Gen. Man. Secretarial Div. 1988–89, Gen. Man. Corp. Planning Div. 1989–97, mem. Bd of Dirs 1992–2011, Man. Dir 1997–99, Sr Man. Dir 1999–2001, Exec. Vice-Pres. 2002–05, Pres. and Rep. Dir 2005–09, Vice-Chair. 2009–11, Sr Advisor 2011–. *Address:* Toyota Motor Corporation, 1 Toyota-cho, Toyota, Aichi 471-8571, Japan (office). *Telephone:* (565) 28-2121 (office). *Fax:* (565) 23-5800 (office). *Website:* www.toyota.co.jp (office).

WATANABE, Kazuhide; Japanese automotive industry executive; b. 1941; Man. Dir in charge of Personnel and Human Affairs, Mazda Motor Corpn 1998, later Sr Man. Dir in charge of Secretarial, Personnel and Human Devt, Vice-Chair. Jan.–July 2000, Chair. and Rep. Dir 2000–06; mem. Council. Japan Productivity Centre for Socio-Econ. Devt (JPC-SED); mem. Bd of Dirs Energy Conservation Center Japan 2001–03, also Trustee.

WATANABE, Ken; Japanese stage, film and television actor; b. 21 Oct. 1959, Koide, Niigata; m. 1st Yumiko Watanabe 1983 (divorced 2004); two c.; m. 2nd Kaho Minami 2005; one adoped s.; ed Niigata Prefectural Koide High School; moved to Tokyo to begin acting career, got break with Tokyo-based theatre troupe En, cast as the hero in the play Shimodani Mannencho Monogatari, directed by Yukio Ninagawa, left group 2002; TV debut in Michinaru Hanran (Unknown Rebellion), first appearance on TV as a samurai in Mibu no koiuta; feature-film debut with MacArthur's Children 1984; joined the K-Dash agency 2002; mostly known in Japan for playing samurai. *Theatre includes:* Britannicus henso 1980, Shitaya mannencho monogatari 1981, Fuyu no raion (The Lion in Winter) 1981, Pajaze 1981, Platonof 1982, Kafun netsu 1982, Pizarro 1985, Hamlet 1988, Hamlet no gakuya-anten 2000, Towa part1-kanojo 2000, Towa part2-kanojo to kare 2001. *Films include:* Setouchi shonen yakyu dan 1984, Kekkon annai mystery 1985, Tampopo 1985, Umi to dokuyaku (The Sea and Poison) (Newcomer Award, Elandor Awards 1987) 1986, Bakumatsu jyunjyoden 1991, Kimitachi ga ite boku ga iru 1992, Rajio no jikan 1997, Kizuna 1998, Oboreru sakana 2000, Supêsutoraberâzu (Space Travelers) 2000, Zawa-zawa Shimokita-sawa 2000, Sennen no koi – Hikaru Genji monogatari 2001, Hi wa mata noboru 2002, T. R. Y. 2003, The Last Samurai (Special Award, Blue Ribbon Awards) 2003, Kita no zeronen 2005, Batman Begins (video game) 2005, Memoirs of a Geisha 2005, Ashita no kioku (Memories of Tomorrow) (also producer) (Best Lead Actor, Japanese Academy Awards, Best Actor, Hochi Film Awards, Nikkan Sports Film Awards, Blue Ribbon Awards, Kinema Junpo Awards 2007, Fujimoto Prize 2007) 2006, Letters from Iwo Jima 2006, The Unbroken 2009, Cirque du Freak: The Vampire's Assistant 2009, Shanghai 2010, Inception 2010, Hayabusa: The Long Voyage Home 2012, Unforgiven 2013, Godzilla 2014, Transformers: Age of Extinction 2014, Sea of Trees 2015, Silence 2015. *Television includes:* Mibu no koiuta (series) 1983, Sanga moyu (series) 1984, Dokugan-ryu Masamune (series) 1987, Takeda Shingen (mini-series) 1990, Ikebukuro West Gate Park (series) 2000, Hôjô Tokimune (series) 2001, Suna no utsuwa (Best Supporting Actor, Television Drama Academy Awards (Winter)) 2004, Hoshi hitotsu no yoru (film) 2007, Keiji ichidai: Hiratsuka Hachibei no Shôwa jiken shi (series) 2009, Clouds Over the Hill (series) 2009, Tômawari no ame (film) 2010, Hei no naka no chûgakkô (film) 2010, Ai inochi - Shinjuku Kabukicho Kakekomi Dera (film) 2011, Makete katsu – sengo wo tsukutta otoko Yoshida Shigeru (mini-series) 2012, Silver Jack (film) 2014. *Publication:* Dare? – Who Am I? (autobiog.) 2006. *Address:* c/o WME Entertainment, 9601 Wilshire Boulevard, Beverley Hills, CA 90210-5213, USA (office). *Telephone:* (310) 285-9000 (office). *Fax:* (310) 285-9010 (office). *Website:* www.wma.com (office).

WATANABE, Koichiro, BEcons; Japanese insurance industry executive; *President and Representative Director, Dai-ichi Life Insurance Company Ltd;* ed Tohoku Univ.; joined Dai-ichi Life Insurance Co. Ltd 1976, served as Sr Man. Exec. Officer, Dir of Research, Chief Dir of Planning and Research, Dir of First Planning, Man. Dir and Man. Exec. Officer –2010, Pres. and Rep. Dir 2010–. *Leisure interests:* karate, kendo. *Address:* Dai-ichi Life Insurance Co. Ltd, 13-1, Yurakucho 1-chome, Chiyoda-ku, Tokyo 100-8411, Japan (office). *Telephone:* (3) 3216-1211 (office). *E-mail:* info@dai-ichi-life.co.jp (office). *Website:* www.dai-ichi-life.co.jp (office).

WATANABE, Shigeo, BS; Japanese business executive; *Member of the Board and Adviser, Bridgestone Corporation;* b. 10 April 1942; ed Keio Univ.; joined Bridgestone Tire Co. Ltd (renamed Bridgestone Corpn) 1965, Tech. Adviser Bridgestone Tire Mfg USA Inc., Gen. Man. Truck and Bus Devt Dept 1988, Tech. Adviser Firestone Tire and Rubber Co. Int. Tech. Centre 1988–90, Gen. Man. Mfg and Tech. 1990–93, Dir Quality Assurance Div. 1993–94, Dir Tire Devt Div. 1994–97, mem. Bd 1994–, Vice-Pres. and Dir Tire Devt Div. 1997, Vice-Pres. and Dir Commercial Tire Devt and Tire Tech. Admin 1997–98, Sr Vice-Pres. Tire Devt 1998–2000, Sr Vice-Pres. Tire Devt and Quality Assurance 2000–01, Chair., Pres. and CEO 2001–06, mem. Bd and Adviser 2006–. *Address:* Bridgestone Corporation, 10-1 Kyobashi 1-chome, Chuo-ku, Tokyo 104-8340, Japan (office). *Telephone:* (3) 3567-0111 (office). *Fax:* (3) 3535-2553 (office). *E-mail:* bfspr@bfusa.com (office). *Website:* www.bridgestone.com (office).

WATANABE, Shuichi; Japanese health care industry executive; *Representative Director, President and CEO, Medipal Holdings Corporation;* apptd Dir Kuraya Sanseido Inc. 2001, Pres. and Rep. Dir Kuraya Sanseido Inc. (following separation of pharmaceutical distribution from purchasing businesses to form new Kuraya Sanseido Inc., took over prescription pharmaceutical wholesale business of Medipal Holdings Corpn, merged with Senshu Yakuhin Co. Ltd, Ushioda Kuraya Sanseido Inc., Yamahiro Kuraya Sanseido Inc., Heisei Yakuhin Co. Ltd and Izutsu Kuraya Sanseido Inc. and changed its corp. name to Mediceo Corpn) 2004–12, Rep. Dir, Pres. and CEO Medipal Holdings Corpn 2012–, Rep. Dir and Chair. Mediceo Corpn 2012–. *Address:* Medipal Holdings Corporation, 2-7-15, Yaesu, Chuo-ku, Tokyo 104-8461, Japan (office). *Telephone:* (3) 3517-5800 (office). *Fax:* (3) 3517-5011 (office). *E-mail:* info@medipal.co.jp (office). *Website:* www.medipal.co.jp (office).

WATANABE, Tsuneo; Japanese newspaper executive; *Chairman and Editor-in-Chief, Yomiuri Shimbun;* b. 30 May 1926, Tokyo; began career with Yomiuri Shimbum newspaper as reporter 1950, fmr Washington, DC corresp., chief editorial writer, Pres. 1991–, currently Chair. and Ed.-in-Chief, also Chair. Yomiuri Group; Man. Exec. Officer, Tanker Div. and Dir Mitsui OSK Lines Ltd 2008–; Owner, Yomiuri Giants Co., Ltd 2002–; mem. Bd of Dirs Nippon Television Network Corpn. *Publication:* Memoirs of Tsuneo Watanabe 2000. *Address:* Yomiuri Shimbum, 1-7-1, Otemachi, Chiyoda-ku, Tokyo 100-8055, Japan (office).

Telephone: (3) 3242-1111 (office). *E-mail:* webmaster@yomiuri.co.jp (office). *Website:* www.yomiuri.co.jp (office).

WATARI, Fumiaki, BA; Japanese energy industry executive; *President and Representative Director, Private Finance Initiative Promotion Corporation of Japan;* b. 3 Oct. 1936; ed Keio Univ.; joined Nippon Oil 1960, numerous positions in Marketing Dept 1960–95, Marketing Dir 1995–98, Vice-Pres. 1998–99, Vice-Pres. Nippon Mitsubishi Oil 1999–2000, Pres. Nippon Oil Corpn 2000–05, then Chair. and Rep. Dir; Pres. and Rep. Dir, Private Finance Initiative Promotion Corpn of Japan 2013–; Chair. Seijo Gakuen 2014–; Chair. Bd of Councilors, Japan Business Fed.; fmr Pres. Petroleum Asscn of Japan; mem. Bd of Dirs Japan Post Holdings Co., Ltd 2013–; Sr Exec. Consultant, JX Holdings, Inc., now Hon. Exec. Consultant; Vice-Chair. Japan-China Economic Asscn; mem. Bd of Councilors, Keio Univ.; mem. Advisory Council, Bai Xian Asia Inst.; mem. Advisory Bd, US Japan Research Inst.; Grand Cordon of the Order of the Rising Sun 2014.

WATERMAN, Ewen Leith, BEcons; Australian civil servant; b. 2 Dec. 1943, Adelaide, S Australia; s. of Gordon Waterman and Elsie Waterman (née Batty); m. Barbara Prideaux 1966; two s. one d.; ed Pulteney Grammar School, Adelaide, Univ. of Adelaide; Gen. Financial and Econ. Policy Div., Australian Treasury 1967–72, Overseas Econ. Relations Div., 1973–75, Asst Sec. State and Local Govt Finances Br. 1982–84, Prin. Adviser, Gen. Financial and Econ. Policy Div., 1984–85, First Asst Sec., Revenue Loans and Investment Div. 1985–87, Capital Markets Div. 1987–89, Deputy Sec. (Financial) 1989–93; Prime Minister's Dept 1972; Counsellor (Financial), Embassy in Washington, DC 1976–79; Sec., Australian Loan Council 1986–87, Australian Nat. Debt Comm. 1986–87; Exec. Dir IMF, Washington, DC 1993–97; Exec. Dir Access Economics 1997–2001; Man. Dir Export Finance and Insurance Corpn (EFIC) 2001–03. *Leisure interests:* tennis, golf.

WATERS, John; American film director, actor, producer and screenwriter; b. 22 April 1946, Baltimore, Md; formed repertory troupe Dreamland Players to produce films. *Films include:* dir, producer, actor, writer, ed. and cinematographer: Hag in a Black Leather Jacket 1964, Roman Candles 1966, Eat Your Makeup 1968, The Diane Linkletter Story 1969, Mondo Trasho 1969, Pink Flamingos 1972, Hairspray (co-producer) 1988; producer, dir and writer: Multiple Maniacs 1970, Female Trouble 1974, Desperate Living 1977, Polyester 1981; dir, actor and writer: Cry-Baby 1990, Serial Mom 1994, Pecker 1998, Cecil B. DeMented 2000; dir and writer: A Dirty Shame 2004, This Filthy World 2006; actor: Sweet and Lowdown 1999, Blood Feast 2: All U Can Eat 2002, Seed of Chucky 2004, The Junior Defenders 2007, Mangus! 2011, Excision 2012, Suburban Gothic 2014, Mugworth 2014, Alvin and the Chipmunks: The Road Chip 2015. *Television includes:* Family Album (actor) 1994. *Publications include:* Shock Value: A Tasteful Book About Bad Taste 1981, Crackpot: The Obsession of John Waters 1986, Role Models 2010; articles for National Lampoon. *Address:* c/o Creative Artists Agency, 9830 Wilshire Blvd, Beverly Hills, CA 90212-1825, USA. *Telephone:* (310) 288-4545. *Fax:* (310) 288-4800. *Website:* www.caa.com.

WATERS, Ralph Graham, MBus, CPEng; Australian engineer and business executive; ed Curtin Univ. of Technology; has eng and man. experience in London and the Middle East; fmr Man. Dir Email Ltd; fmr Chief Exec. Fletcher Building Ltd, mem. Bd of Dirs 2001–14, Chair. 2010–14; Dir, Fisher & Paykel Appliances Holdings Ltd 2001–11, Chair. 2009–11; mem. Bd of Dirs, Woolworths Ltd 2011–15, Chair. 2012–15; Chair. Fisher & Paykel Appliances Holdings Ltd 2009–11, Fletcher Building Ltd 2010–14; Dir, Fonterra Co-operative Group Ltd 2006–13, Westpac New Zealand Ltd 2006–12, Asciano Ltd 2012–; Chair. Cricket World Cup 2015 Ltd; Fellow, Inst. of Engineers Australia; Hon. FIEAust. *Address:* Asciano Ltd, 476 St Kilda Road, Melbourne, Vic. 3004, Australia (office). *Telephone:* (3) 9248-7000 (office). *Fax:* (3) 9699-2869 (office). *E-mail:* info@asciano.com.au (office). *Website:* asciano.com.au (office).

WATERS, Sarah, PhD, FRSL; British author; b. 1966, Neyland, Wales; ed Univs of Kent, Lancaster and London; fmr Assoc. Lecturer, Open Univ.; mem. Council of The Soc. of Authors; Hon. Fellowship (Univ. of London) 2012, (Cardiff Metropolitan Univ.) 2013, (Cardiff Univ.) 2016, (Goldsmiths, Univ. of London) 2016; Dr hc (Univ. of Kent) 2005, (Open Univ.) 2014, (Queen Mary); Betty Trask Award 1999, Mail on Sunday/John Llewellyn Rhys Prize 1999, CWA Ellis Peters Historical Dagger 2002, British Book Award for Author of the Year 2002, Stonewall Award for Writer of the Decade 2015. *Play:* co-author (with Christopher Green) The Frozen Scream 2014. *Publications include:* Tipping the Velvet 1998, Affinity 1999, Fingersmith 2002, The Night Watch 2006, The Little Stranger 2009, The Paying Guests 2014. *Leisure interests:* cinema, theatre. *Address:* c/o Greene & Heaton (Authors' Agents) Ltd, 37 Goldhawk Road, London, W12 8QQ, England (office). *Telephone:* (20) 8749-0315 (office). *Website:* www.greeneheaton.co.uk (office); www.sarahwaters.com.

WATERSTON, Robert Hugh, BSE, MD, PhD; American geneticist and academic; *William H. Gates III Endowed Chair in Biomedical Sciences and Chairman of the Department of Genome Sciences, University of Washington, Seattle;* b. 17 Sept. 1943, Detroit, Mich.; ed Princeton Univ., courses in biology in Germany, Univ. of Chicago; NIH Predoctoral Trainee 1968–71; American Cancer Soc. Postdoctoral Fellowship 1972–74; Muscular Dystrophy Asscn Postdoctoral Fellowship 1975–76; Postdoctoral Researcher, MRC Lab. of Molecular Biology, Cambridge, UK 1972–74, 1975–76, Sabbatical Visitor, Dir's Div. 1985–86; Postdoctoral Researcher, Children's Hosp. Medical Center, Boston, Mass 1974–75; Asst Prof., Dept of Anatomy and Neurobiology, Washington Univ., St Louis, Mo. 1976–80, Asst Prof. of Genetics, Washington Univ. School of Medicine 1980–81, Assoc. Prof. of Genetics 1981–87, Prof. of Genetics 1987–91, Prof. and Acting Head, Dept of Genetics 1991–93, James S. McDonnell Prof. and Chair. Dept of Genetics 1993–2002; William H. Gates III Endowed Chair in Biomedical Sciences and Chair. Dept of Genome Sciences, Univ. of Washington, Seattle, Wash. 2003–; American Heart Asscn Established Investigator 1980–85; John Simon Guggenheim Fellowship 1985–86; City of Medicine Award, Dan David Prize, The Dan David Foundation, Gairdner Award (co-recipient), The Gairdner Foundation, Gen. Motors Prize (co-recipient), George W. Beadle Medal, Genetics Soc. of America, Gruber Genetics Prize, The Peter and Patricia Gruber Foundation 2005. *Publications:* numerous scientific papers in professional journals. *Address:* Department of Genome Sciences, Foege S-350D, Box 355065, University of Washington School of Medicine, 1705 NE Pacific Street, Seattle, WA 98195-5065, USA (office). *Telephone:* (206) 685-7347 (office). *Fax:* (206) 685-7301 (office). *E-mail:* waterston@gs.washington.edu (office). *Website:* waterston.gs.washington.edu (office).

WATERSTONE, Sir Timothy John Stuart, Kt, MA; British business executive; b. 30 May 1939; s. of Malcolm Waterstone and Sylvia Sawday; m. 1st Patricia Harcourt-Poole (divorced); two s. one d.; m. 2nd Clare Perkins (divorced); one s. two d.; m. 3rd Mary Rose (Rosie) Alison; two d.; ed Tonbridge School and St Catharine's Coll., Cambridge; Carritt Moran, Calcutta 1962–64; Allied Breweries 1964–73; W. H. Smith 1973–81; Founder, Chair. and Chief Exec. Waterstone's Booksellers Ltd 1982–93; Chair. Priory Investments Ltd 1990–95, Golden Rose Radio (London Jazz FM) 1992–93; Founder and Chair. Chelsea Stores Ltd children's stores 1996–; Chair. HMV Media Group PLC 1998–2001; Deputy Chair. Sinclair-Stevenson Ltd 1989–92; mem. Bd Yale Univ. Press 1992–, Futurestart 1992–, Virago Press 1995–96, Hill Samuel UK Emerging Cos Investment Trust PLC 1996–2000, Downing Classic VCT 1998–; Chair. Dept of Trade and Industry Working Group on Smaller Quoted Cos and Pvt. Investors 1999, Shelter 25th Anniversary Appeal Cttee 1991–92; mem. Bd London Philharmonic Orchestra 1990–97 (Trustee 1995–98), Portman House Trust 1994–96; Chair. Acad. of Ancient Music 1990–95, London Int. Festival of Theatre 1991–92, Elgar Foundation 1992–98, King's Coll. Library Bd 2000–; Co-Founder BOOKAID 1992–93; Advisory mem. Booker Prize Man. Cttee 1986–93; Chair. of Judges Prince's Youth Business Trust Awards 1990. *Publications:* Lilley and Chase 1994, An Imperfect Marriage 1995, A Passage of Lives 1996, Swimming Against the Stream: Ten Rules for Creating Your Business and Making your Life 2006, In for a Penny, In for a Pound 2010. *Leisure interest:* being with Rosie Alison. *Address:* c/o Ed Victor Ltd, 6 Bayley Street, London, WC1B 3HB, England (office).

WATHRA, Ashraf Mahmood, MBA; Pakistani central banker; worked with BRR Capital Modaraba, Emirates Bank Int., American Express Bank Ltd, ANZ Grindlays Bank 1978–92; served as Dir Habib Finance Int., Hong Kong, Habib Finance, Australia; held several positions at Faysal Bank Ltd, including Exec. Vice-Pres., Country Risk Man., Exec. Vice-Pres., Regional Man., Sr Vice-Pres., Chief Man. 1992–99; Regional Gen. Man. (Bangladesh) Habib Bank Ltd, Exec. Vice-Pres., Regional Gen. Man. (Singapore), Exec. Vice-Pres., Group Exec., Risk Man., Sr Credit Officer, Asset Remedial Man. Group 1999–2012; Sr Exec. Vice-Pres. Nat. Bank of Pakistan (NBP), Group Chief, Credit Man. Group 2012–13; Deputy Gov. State Bank of Pakistan 2013–14, Acting Gov. Jan.–April 2014, Gov. 2014–17; mem. Bd of Dirs IMF, Asian Clearing Union, ECO Trade and Devt Bank, Monetary and Fiscal Policies Coordination Bd, Nat. Financial Inclusion Strategy Council, Nat. Exec. Cttee on Anti Monetary Laundering; Co-Chair. Financial Stability Bd, Regional Consultative Group for Asia (FSB-RCG Asia) 2015–.

WATKINS, David John, BA, FRSA; British jewellery artist, sculptor and academic; *Professor Emeritus, Royal College of Art;* b. 14 Nov. 1940, Wolverhampton; m. Wendy Ann Jopling Ramshaw 1962; one s. one d.; ed Wolverhampton Grammar School and Univ. of Reading; sculptor, musician, special effects model maker (including for film 2001: A Space Odyssey) and jewellery designer 1963–71; co-f. with Wendy Ramshaw the fashion jewellery co. Something Special 1965; Visiting Lecturer, Berkshire Coll. of Art, Guildford School of Art 1964–66; own studios for jewellery and sculpture 1971–; est. second studio/workshop for large-scale forged and fabricated steel, utilising combination of eng and hot metal processes for sculpture and public art projects 1980s; mem. Membership Cttee, Crafts Council 1976–78; Artist-in-Residence, Western Australian Inst. for Tech. 1978 Collection Cttee, Crafts Council 1983–84; Visiting Prof., Bezalel Acad., Jerusalem, Israel 1984; mem. Bd of Trustees Haystack Mountain School of Crafts, Me, USA 1999–; Head of Dept and Prof. of Goldsmithing, Silversmithing, Metalwork and Jewellery, RCA, London 1984–2009, Prof. Emer. 2009–; works in major collections, including American Craft Museum, Australian Nat. Gallery, Birmingham City Museum and Art Gallery, Crafts Council, London, Die Neue Sammlung, Munich, Kunstgewerbe Museum, Berlin, Kunstindustrimuseet, Oslo, Musée des Arts Decoratifs, Paris, Museum für Angewandte Kunst, Cologne, Museum für Kunst und Gewerbe, Hamburg, Nat. Gallery of Victoria, Nat. Museum of Modem Art, Tokyo, Nat. Museums of Scotland, Schmuckmuseum, Pforzheim, Science Museum, London, Stedelijk Museum, Amsterdam, Victoria & Albert Museum, London; Fellow, Chartered Society of Designers 1984; Freeman, Goldsmiths' Co. 1988, Liveryman 1989; De Beers Diamonds Today 1974, Crafts Advisory Cttee Bursary 1976, Japan Foundation Travel Award 1978, Art for Architecture Award, Royal Soc. of Arts 1995. *Publications include:* The Best in Contemporary Jewellery 1994, A Design Sourcebook: Jewellery 1999, The Paper Jewellery Collection 2000; subject of biog., David Watkins–Wendy Ramshaw: A Life's Partnership 2009. *Leisure interest:* listening to jazz and classical music. *Address:* Royal College of Art, Kensington Gore, London, SW7 2EU, England (office). *Telephone:* (20) 7590-4261 (office). *E-mail:* david.watkins@rca.ac.uk (office). *Website:* www.rca.ac.uk (office).

WATSON, Edward, MBE; British ballet dancer; *Principal Dancer, The Royal Ballet;* b. 21 May 1976, Bromley, Kent, England; ed Royal Ballet School, trained with Anatoly Grigoriev; began ballet lessons aged three; joined The Royal Ballet School aged 11, graduated into The Royal Ballet 1994, First Artist 1998–2000, Soloist 2000–02, First Soloist 2002–05, Prin. 2005–, roles for Resident Choreographer Wayne McGregor include: Symbiont(s), Qualia, Chroma, Infra, Limen, Carbon Life, Raven Girl, Tetractys, Woolf Works, for Artistic Assoc. Christopher Wheeldon: Lewis Carroll/The White Rabbit (Alice's Adventures in Wonderland), Leontes (The Winter's Tale); has worked with numerous other contemporary choreographers, including Alastair Marriott, Ashley Page, Siobhan Davies, Arthur Pita, Cathy Marston; other significant roles with Royal Ballet include Count Albrecht (Giselle), Des Grieux (Manon), Palemon (Ondine), Ivan Tsarevich (The Firebird); prin. roles in the works of Kenneth MacMillan include Crown Prince Rudolf (Mayerling), Romeo, The Chosen One (The Rite of Spring), Woyzeck (Different Drummer) and roles in Gloria and Song of the Earth; Season 2014–15: danced in newly created mixed programme with Wendy Whelan in Linbury Studio Theatre; Best Male Dancer, Nat. Dance Awards 2008, Olivier Award for Outstanding Achievement in Dance for role as Gregor Samsa in Pita's The Metamorphosis 2012, Prix Benois de la Danse for performance as Leontes in The Winter's Tale 2015. *Address:* Royal Ballet, Royal Opera House, Bow Street, Covent

Garden, London, WC2E 9DD, England (office). *Telephone:* (20) 7240-1200 (office). *E-mail:* info@roh.org.uk (office). *Website:* www.roh.org.uk/people/edward-watson (office).

WATSON, Emily Margaret, OBE; British actress; b. 14 Jan. 1967, London, England; m. Jack Waters; one s. one d.; ed London Drama Studio, Univ. of Bristol; began career on stage and joined RSC 1992. *Theatre includes:* School for Mothers and The Mistake (double-bill of one-act plays, White Bear Theatre, London) 1991, All's Well That Ends Well (RSC, Swan Theatre, Stratford-upon-Avon) 1992, (later Pit Theatre, London) 1993, The Taming of the Shrew (RSC, Barbican Theatre, London) 1993, The Changeling (RSC, Pit Theatre) 1993, A Jovial Crew (RSC, Pit Theatre) 1993, The Lady from the Sea (Lyric Hammersmith Theatre, London) 1994, The Children's Hour (Lyttelton Theatre, London) 1994, Three Sisters (Out of Joint) 1995, Othello 1996, Uncle Vanya/Twelfth Night (both at Donmar Warehouse, London) 2002, (at Brooklyn Acad. of Music, New York) 2003. *Films include:* Breaking the Waves (New York Soc. of Film Critics Award, Nat. Soc. of Film Critics Award, European Film Award, Evening Standard Film Award) 1996, Mill on the Floss 1997, Metroland 1997, The Boxer 1997, Hilary and Jackie (British Independent Film Award) 1998, Angela's Ashes 1999, Trixie 2000, The Luzhin Defense 2000, In Search of the Assassin 2001, Gosford Park 2001, Red Dragon 2002, Punch-Drunk Love 2002, Equilibrium 2002, Boo, Zino and the Snurks (voice) 2004, The Life and Death of Peter Sellers 2004, The Proposition 2004, Separate Lies 2005, Corpse Bride (voice) 2005, Wah Wah 2005, Crusade in Jeans 2005, Miss Potter 2006, The Waterhorse 2007, Fireflies in the Garden 2008, Synecdoche, New York 2008, Within the Whirlwind 2008, Cold Souls 2009, Oranges and Sunshine 2010, Cemetery Junction 2010, War Horse 2011, Little Boy 2012, Anna Karenina 2012, Some Girl(s) 2013, Molly Moon 2013, Belle 2013, The Book Thief 2013, The Theory of Everything 2014, Little Boy 2015, Testament of Youth 2015, Molly Moon: The Incredible Hypnotist 2015, Girls' Night Out 2015, Everest 2015, Genius 2017. *Radio includes:* The Wolves of Willoughby Chase 1994, Wuthering Heights (series) 1995. *Television includes:* A Summer Day's Dream 1994, The Memory Keeper's Daughter 2008, Appropriate Adult (BAFTA Award for Best Leading Actress 2012) 2011, The Politician's Husband 2013, Marilyn (mini-series) 2015, A Song for Jenny (film) 2015, The Dresser (film) 2015, Apple Tree Yard 2017. *Address:* c/o Independent Talent, 40 Whitfield Street, London, W1T 2RH, England (office). *Telephone:* (20) 7636-6565 (office). *Fax:* (20) 7323-0101 (office). *E-mail:* info@independenttalent.com (office). *Website:* www.independenttalent.com (office).

WATSON, Emma Charlotte Duerre; British actress; b. 15 April 1990, Paris, France; d. of Chris Watson and Jacqueline Luesby; ed Dragon School, Headington School, Oxford; learned acting, singing and dancing at Stagecoach Theatre Arts, Oxford; performed in several school plays including Arthur: The Young Years and The Happy Prince; model representing Burberry; Visiting Fellow, Lady Margaret Hall, Oxford 2016-. *Films include:* Harry Potter and the Philosopher's Stone (Young Artist Award for Best Performance in a Feature Film – Leading Young Actress 2002) 2001, Harry Potter and the Chamber of Secrets 2002, Harry Potter and the Prisoner of Azkaban 2004, Harry Potter and the Goblet of Fire 2005, Harry Potter and the Order of the Phoenix 2007, December Boys 2007, The Tale of Despereaux (voice) 2008, Harry Potter and the Half-Blood Prince 2009, Harry Potter and the Deathly Hallows: Part 1 2010, Harry Potter and the Deathly Hallows: Part 2 2011, My Week with Marilyn 2011, The Perks of Being a Wallflower 2012, The Bling Ring 2013, Noah 2014, Colonia 2015, Beauty and the Beast (Best Actor in a Movie 2017) 2017. *Television includes:* Ballet Shoes 2007. *Address:* Special Artists Agency Inc, 9465 Wilshire Blvd, Suite 470, Beverly Hills, CA 90210, USA (office). *Telephone:* (310) 859-9688 (office). *E-mail:* info@ specialartists.com (office). *Website:* www.specialartists.com (office).

WATSON, James Dewey, BS, PhD; American biologist and academic; *Chancellor Emeritus, Cold Spring Harbor Laboratory;* b. 6 April 1928, Chicago, Ill.; s. of James D. Watson and Jean Mitchell Watson; m. Elizabeth Lewis 1968; two s.; ed Univs of Chicago and Indiana; Research Fellow, US Nat. Research Council, Univ. of Copenhagen, Denmark 1950–51; Fellow, US Nat. Foundation, Cavendish Lab., Univ. of Cambridge, England 1951–53, 1955–56; Sr Research Fellow in Biology, Calif. Inst. of Tech. 1953–55; Asst Prof. of Biology, Harvard Univ. 1956–58, Assoc. Prof. 1958–61, Prof. 1961–76; Dir Cold Spring Harbor Lab. 1968–93, Pres. 1994–2003, Chancellor 2003–07, Chancellor Emer. 2007–; Assoc. Dir NIH, USA 1988–89, Dir Nat. Center for Human Genome Research, NIH 1989–92; Newton-Abraham Visiting Prof., Univ. of Oxford, UK 1994; mem. NAS, Danish Acad. of Arts and Sciences, American Acad. of Arts and Sciences, American Soc. of Biological Chemists; Sr Fellow, Soc. of Fellows, Harvard Univ. 1964–70; mem. American Philosophical Soc. 1978; Foreign mem. Royal Soc. 1981, USSR (now Russian) Acad. of Sciences 1989; Hon. Fellow, Clare Coll., Cambridge 1967; Hon. KBE 2002; Hon. DSc (Chicago, Indiana, Long Island, Adelphi, Brandeis, Hofstra, Harvard, Rockefeller, State Univ. of New York, Albert Einstein Coll. of Medicine, Clarkson Coll., Stellenbosch, Fairfield, Cambridge, Oxford, Charleston Medical Coll., Washington Coll., Univ. of Judaism, Univ. Coll. London, Wesleyan, Widener, Dartmouth, Trinity Coll. Dublin); Hon. LLD (Notre Dame) 1965; Hon. MD (Buenos Aires) 1986, (Charles Univ., Prague) 1998; Hon. DSc (Rutgers Univ.) 1988, (Bard Coll.) 1991, (Melbourne) 1997; Dr hc (Barcelona) 2005, (Royal Irish Acad.) 2002, (Int. Acad. of Humanism) 2005; Eli Lilly Award in Biochemistry 1959, Lasker Prize (American Public Health Asscn) 1960, Nobel Prize for Medicine (with F.H.C. Crick and M.F.H. Wilkins) 1962, John J. Carty Gold Medal (Nat. Acad. of Sciences) 1971, Medal of Freedom 1977, Gold Medal Award, Nat. Inst. of Social Sciences 1984, Kaul Foundation Award for Excellence 1992, Copley Medal of Royal Soc. 1993, Nat. Biotechnology Award 1993; Lomosonov Medal 1994, Nat. Medal of Science 1997, Liberty Medal Award 2000, Benjamin Franklin Medal 2001, Gairdner Award 2002, Lotos Club Medal of Merit 2004, Othmer Gold Medal, Chemical Heritage Foundation 2005. *Achievements include:* discovered structure of DNA (with Francis Crick) 1953. *Publications include:* Molecular Biology of the Gene 1965, The Double Helix 1968, The DNA Story (with John Tooze) 1981, Recombinant DNA – A Short Course 1983 (co-author), The Molecular Biology of the Cell (co-author) 1986, Recombinant DNA (2nd edn) (co-author) 1992, A Passion for DNA 2000, Genes, Girls and Gamow 2001, DNA – The Secret of Life 2003, Avoid Boring People: And Other Lessons from a Life in Science (auto-biog.) 2007, Darwin: The Indelible Stamp (Ed.) 2007; papers on structure of deoxyribonucleic acid (DNA), on protein synthesis and on the induction of cancer by viruses.

Address: c/o Cold Spring Harbor Laboratory, One Bungtown Road, Cold Spring Harbor, New York, NY 11724, USA (office).

WATSON, James Kay Graham, BSc, PhD, FRS, FRSC; British/Canadian research scientist; *Researcher Emeritus, National Research Council of Canada;* b. 20 April 1936, Denny, Scotland; s. of Thomas Watson and Mary C. Miller; m. Carolyn M. L. Kerr 1981; ed Denny High School, High School of Stirling and Univ. of Glasgow; Carnegie Sr Scholar, Dept of Chem., Univ. Coll. London 1961–63; Postdoctoral Fellow, Nat. Research Council, Ottawa, Canada 1963–65; ICI Research Fellow, Univ. of Reading 1965–66, Lecturer in Chemical Physics 1966–71; Visiting Assoc. Prof. in Physics, Ohio State Univ. 1971–75; SRC Sr Research Fellow in Chem., Univ. of Southampton 1975–79, 1980–82; Visiting Scientist, Nat. Research Council, Ottawa, Canada 1979–80, Sr Research Officer 1982–87, Prin. 1987–2007, Researcher Emer. 2008–; Fellow, American Physical Soc. 1990; Chem. Soc. Award 1974, Plyler Prize, American Physical Soc. 1986, RSC Henry Marshall Tory Medal 1999, ACS E.B.Wilson Award 2004. *Publications:* more than 160 articles on molecular physics in learned journals. *Leisure interests:* music, golf, tree-watching. *Address:* Steacie Institute for Molecular Sciences, National Research Council of Canada, Ottawa, ON K1A 0R6 (office); 183 Stanley Avenue, Ottawa, ON K1M 1P2, Canada (home). *Telephone:* (613) 990-0739 (office); (613) 745-7928 (home). *Fax:* (613) 991-2648 (office). *E-mail:* james.watson@nrc -cnrc.gc.ca (office).

WATSON, Jim, BA; Canadian politician; *Mayor of Ottawa;* b. 1961; ed Carleton Univ.; mem. Ottawa City Council for Capital Ward 1992–98; Mayor of Ottawa 1997–2000, 2010–; Pres. and CEO Canadian Tourism Comm. 2000–03; host, The New RO@Noon, CHRO-TV 2003; regular contrib. to CFRA (radio station) and Ottawa Citizen (daily newspaper); mem. Ont. Prov. Parl. for Ottawa West-Nepean 2003–10, Minister of Consumer and Business Services 2003–05, of Health Promotion 2005–07, of Municipal Affairs and Housing 2007–10; mem. bd of several community orgs, including Riverside Hosp., Nat. Arts Centre, Christmas Exchange of Ottawa, Forum for Young Canadians; Chair. United Way 2002 campaign; Carleton Univ. Honours Award, City of Ottawa Key to the City, Queen's Golden Jubilee Medal, Ontario Pharmacists' Asscn Visionary Award, Canadian Council for Tobacco Control Nat. Leadership Award. *Address:* 110 Laurier Avenue West, Ottawa, ON K1P 1J1, Canada (office). *Telephone:* (613) 580-2496 (office). *Fax:* (613) 580-2509 (office). *E-mail:* jim.watson@ottawa.ca (office). *Website:* ottawa .ca/en/city-hall/mayor-and-city-councillors/jim-watson (office); www .jimwatsonottawa.ca.

WATSON, John S., BA, MBA; American business executive; *Chairman and CEO, Chevron Corporation;* b. 1956, Calif.; ed Univ. of California, Davis, Univ. of Chicago; joined Chevron Corpn as financial analyst 1980, held financial, analytical and supervisory positions before being elected Pres. Chevron Canada Ltd 1996, named Vice-Pres. Chevron Corpn, with responsibility for strategic planning and mergers and acquisitions 1998, led co.'s integration effort following Chevron-Texaco merger, Chief Financial Officer 2001–05, Pres. Chevron Int. Exploration and Production 2005–07, Exec. Vice-Pres. for Strategy and Devt 2008–09, Vice-Chair. Chevron Corpn 2009–10, Chair. and CEO 2010–; Chair. Bd of Dirs and Exec. Cttee, American Petroleum Inst.; mem. Nat. Petroleum Council, The Business Council, Business Roundtable, J.P. Morgan Int. Council, American Soc. of Corp. Execs, Univ. of California, Davis Chancellor's Bd of Advisors. *Address:* Chevron Corporation, 6001 Bollinger Canyon Road, San Ramon, CA 94583, USA (office). *Telephone:* (925) 842-1000 (office). *Fax:* (925) 842-3530 (office). *E-mail:* corpgov@chevron.com (office). *Website:* www.chevron.com (office).

WATSON, Sir Robert Tony, Kt, CMG, PhD, FRS; British environmental scientist and academic; *Professor of Environmental Sciences and Director of Strategic Development, Tyndall Centre, University of East Anglia;* b. 21 March 1948; ed Queen Mary Coll., London; fmr Dir Science Div. and Chief Scientist for the Office of Mission to Planet Earth, NASA; fmr Assoc. Dir for Environment, Office of the President, The White House, Washington, DC, USA; joined the World Bank as Sr Scientific Adviser in Environment Dept 1996, apptd Dir of Environment Dept and Head of Environment Sector Bd 1997, later Chief Scientist and Dir for Environmentally and Socially Sustainable Devt; Prof. of Environmental Sciences and Dir of Strategic Devt, Tyndall Centre, Univ. of East Anglia 2007–; apptd Chief Scientific Adviser, Dept for Environment, Food and Rural Affairs (Defra) 2007; Chair. Global Environment Facility's Scientific and Tech. Advisory Panel 1991–94, Intergovernmental Panel on Climate Change (IPCC) 1997–2002; Co-Chair. Millennium Ecosystem Assessment 2000–05, Int. Scientific Assessment of Stratospheric Ozone; Chair. Intergovernmental Science-Policy Platform on Biodiversity and Ecosystem Services (IPBES) 2016–; Dir Int. Assessment of Agricultural Science and Tech. for Devt; fmr Chair. or Co-Chair. of other int. scientific assessments, including the IPCC Working Group II, UNEP/WMO, UNEP Global Biodiversity Assessment; NAS Award for Scientific Reviewing 1992, AAAS Award for Scientific Freedom and Responsibility 1993, UN Champions of the Earth Award 2014. *Publications:* numerous papers in professional journals. *Address:* School of Environmental Sciences, University of East Anglia, Norwich Research Park, Norwich, NR4 7TJ, England (office). *Telephone:* (1603) 593900 (office). *E-mail:* robert.watson@uea.ac.uk (office). *Website:* people.uea.ac.uk (office); tyndall.ac.uk (office).

WATSON, Shane Robert; Australian professional cricketer; b. 17 June 1981, Ipswich, Queensland; m. Lee Furlong 2010; all-rounder; right-handed batsman; right-arm fast-medium bowler; plays for Tasmania 2001–04, Australia 2002– (Vice-Capt. Test, ODI and T20I teams 2011–13), Queensland 2004–09, Hants. 2005, Rajasthan Royals 2008–, NSW 2009–, Sydney Sixers 2011–12, Brisbane Heat 2012–; First-class debut: 2000/01; Test debut: Australia v Pakistan, Sydney 2–5 Jan. 2005; One-Day Int. (ODI) debut: S Africa v Australia, at Centurion 25 March 2002; T20I debut: S Africa v Australia, Johannesburg 24 Feb. 2006; has played in 51 Tests, taken 68 wickets, average 31.83 and scored 3,343 runs (4 centuries, 22 half-centuries), highest score 176, average 36.33, best bowling (innings) 6/33, (match) 6/51; ODIs: 173 matches, scored 5,256 runs, average 41.06, highest score 185 not out, took 163 wickets, average 30.26, best bowling 4/36; First-class: 124 matches, 8,822 runs, average 43.67, highest score 203 not out, took 202 wickets, average 28.77, best bowling 7/69; mem. winning Australian ODI team, ICC (Int. Cricket Council) Cricket World Cup 2003, 2007; made 185 not out off 96 balls against Bangladesh 11 April 2011, hitting 15 sixes and breaking record held by Xavier Marshall, also highest ODI score by an Australian batsman, passing Matthew Hayden's score of 181 not out set in 2007; mem. Ashes-winning team against England 2013–14; Allan Border Medal 2010, 2011, Test Player of the Year 2011, One Day Int. Player of the Year 2011, named Player of the Tournament, ICC World Twenty20 2012. *Address:* c/o Cricket NSW, PO Box 333, Paddington, NSW 2021; c/o Cricket NSW, Driver Avenue, Moore Park, NSW 2021, Australia. *Telephone:* (2) 8302-6000. *Fax:* (2) 8302-6080. *E-mail:* info@cricketnsw.com. *Website:* www.cricketnsw.com.

WATSON, Thomas Sturges (Tom), BS; American professional golfer; b. 4 Sept. 1949, Kansas City, Mo.; s. of Raymond Etheridge Watson and Sarah Elizabeth Ridge; m. 1st Linda Tova Rubin 1972; one s. one d.; m. 2nd Hilary Watson 1999; three step-c.; ed Stanford Univ.; turned professional 1971; The Open Champion 1975, 1977, 1980, 1982, 1983; record low aggregate for The Open Championship of 268, record two single round scores of 65, lowest final 36-hole score of 130, Turnberry 1977; won US Masters title 1977, 1981; won US Open 1982; won World Series 1975, 1977, 1980; winner of numerous other open championships; top money winner on US Professional Golf Assen (PGA) circuit 1977, 1978, 1979, 1980; first player ever to win in excess of $500,000 in prize money in one season 1980; Ryder Cup Player 1977, 1981, 1983, 1989, Capt. at The Belfry 1993 (won), Capt. at Gleneagles 2014; Sr Tour victories: Bank One Championship 1999, IR Sr Tour Championship 2000, Sr PGA Championship 2001, Sr Tour Championship 2002, Sr British Open 2003, 2005, 2007; joined European Seniors Tour 2011; 71 professional wins; became involved with golf course design early 1990s, has designed courses through his co. Tom Watson Design, Kan. in USA, Ireland and Japan; visited US troops in Iraq with Corey Pavin and Tim Simpson 2007, 2009; active in Kansas City-area charitable endeavours, including Children's Mercy Hosp. and devt of golf courses for junior players; Hon. mem. Royal and Ancient Golf Club of St Andrews 1999; US PGA Player of the Year 1977, 1978, 1979, 1980, 1982, 1984, PGA Tour leading money winner 1977, 1978, 1979, 1980, 1984, Vardon Trophy 1977, 1978, 1979, Bob Jones Award 1987, PGA World Golf Hall of Fame 1988, Old Tom Morris Award 1992, ranked by Golf Digest magazine as the 10th greatest golfer of all time 2000, Payne Stewart Award 2003, Charles Schwab Cup 2003, 2005, Card Walker Award 2003. *Publications:* Getting Back into Basics (co-author) 1992, Tom Watson's Strategic Golf 1995, The Timeless Swing 2011; has written a golf instruction column in Golf Digest magazine since the mid-1970s. *Leisure interests:* current affairs, outdoor life, baseball (Kansas City Royals fan). *Address:* c/o PGA Tour, 100 PGA TOUR Boulevard, Ponte Vedra Beach, FL 32082; 1901 West 47th Place, Suite 200, Shawnee Mission, KS 66205, USA. *Website:* www.pgatour.com/players/player.02256.tom-watson.html; www.tomwatson.com.

WATTS, Charles (Charlie) Robert; British musician (drums); b. 2 June 1941, London, England; m. Shirley Anne Shepherd 1964; one d.; fmr mem. Blues Incorporated; mem. The Rolling Stones 1963–, numerous tours world-wide; toured with Charlie Watts Orchestra 1985–86; Nordoff-Robbins Silver Clef 1982, Grammy Lifetime Achievement Award 1986, Ivor Novello Award for Outstanding Contribution to British Music 1991. *Recordings include:* albums: with The Rolling Stones: The Rolling Stones 1964, The Rolling Stones No. 2 1965, Out Of Our Heads 1965, Aftermath 1966, Between The Buttons 1967, Their Satanic Majesties Request 1967, Beggar's Banquet 1968, Let It Bleed 1969, Get Yer Ya-Ya's Out 1969, Sticky Fingers 1971, Exile On Main Street 1972, Goat's Head Soup 1973, It's Only Rock And Roll 1974, Black And Blue 1976, Some Girls 1978, Emotional Rescue 1980, Tattoo You 1981, Still Life 1982, Undercover 1983, Dirty Work 1986, Steel Wheels 1989, Flashpoint 1991, Voodoo Lounge 1994, Stripped 1995, Bridges to Babylon 1997, Forty Licks 2002, Live Licks 2004, A Bigger Bang 2005, Blue & Lonesome (Grammy Award for Best Traditional Blues Album 2018) 2016; solo: Live at Fulham Town Hall 1986, From One Charlie 1992, Tribute To Charlie Parker With Strings 1991, Warm & Tender 1993, Long Ago and Far Away 1996, Charlie Watts/Jim Keltner Project 2000, Watts At Scott's 2004, The Magic of Boogie Woogie 2010, The ABC&D of Boogie Woogie Live In Paris 2012. *Films include:* Sympathy For The Devil 1969, Gimme Shelter 1970, Ladies and Gentlemen, The Rolling Stones 1977, Let's Spend the Night Together 1983, Flashpoint 1991, Shine a Light 2007. *Publications include:* Ode to a High Flying Bird 1965, According to the Rolling Stones (autobiog., jtly) 2003. *Leisure interest:* jazz music. *Address:* c/o Rosebud Agency, PO Box 170429, San Francisco, CA 94117, USA (office). *Telephone:* (415) 386-3456 (office). *E-mail:* info@rosebudus.com (office). *Website:* www.rosebudus.com (office); www.rollingstones.com.

WATTS, Donald Walter, AM, PhD, FACE; Australian business executive and academic administrator; *Senior Policy Advisor, University of Notre Dame, Australia;* b. 1 April 1934, Western Australia; s. of Horace Frederick Watts and Esme Anne White; m. Michelle Rose Yeomans 1960; two s.; ed Hale School, Perth, Univ. of Western Australia, Univ. Coll. London, UK; CSIRO Postdoctoral Fellow 1959; Dept of Scientific and Industrial Research Postdoctoral Fellow 1961; Personal Chair. in Physical and Inorganic Chem., Univ. of Western Australia 1977–79; Dir Western Australian Inst. of Technology 1980–86; Japan Foundation Visiting Fellow 1984; Vice-Chancellor Curtin Univ. of Tech. 1987; Pres. and Vice-Chancellor Bond Univ. 1987–90, Prof. Emer. 1990–; CEO Trade Devt Zone Authority, Darwin 1990–91; Chair. NT Employment & Training Authority 1991–93; Prof. of Science and Educ. and Dean Coll. of Arts and Sciences, Univ. of Notre Dame, Western Australia 1995–97, Dean of Research 1998–2004, Sr Policy Adviser (part-time) 2004–; Dir Advanced Energy Systems 1995–96 (Chair. 1997–2003); Chair. and Dir Tech. Training Inst. Pty Ltd 2001–03; Councillor Australian Acad. of Technological Sciences and Eng 2001–; mem. ACS, Chemical Educ. Sub-cttee, Australian Acad. of Science; Fellow, Royal Australian Chemical Inst., Australian Acad. of Tech. Sciences and Eng; Hon. Fellow, Marketing Inst. of Singapore; Hon. DTech (Curtin Univ. of Tech.) 1987, Hon. DUniv (Bond Univ.) 2009, Dr hc (Univ. of Western Australia) 2001; Hackett Scholar 1953, Gledden Fellow 1957, Fulbright Scholar 1967, Rennie Medal 1967, Leighton Medal, Royal Australian Chemical Inst. 1987, Australian and New Zealand Assen for the Advancement of Science (ANZAAS) Medal 1998. *Publications include:* The School Chemistry Project – A Secondary School Chemistry Syllabus for Comment (with N. S. Bayliss) 1978, Chemical Properties and Reactions (with A. R. H. Cole and R. B. Bucat) 1978, Chemistry for Australian Secondary School Students (with N. S. Bayliss) 1979, Elements of Chemistry: Earth, Air, Fire and Water 1984, Higher Education in Australia: A Way Forward, Policy Paper No. 8 1986, The Private Potential of Australian Higher Education 1987, A Private Approach to Higher Education 1987; numerous scientific publs and articles on education and policy. *Leisure interests:* golf, tennis, reading. *Address:* University of Notre Dame Australia, Mouat Street, PO Box 1225, Fremantle, WA 6959 (office); 87 Evans Street, Shenton Park, WA 6008, Australia (home). *Telephone:* (8) 9433-0862 (office); (8) 9381-1667 (home). *E-mail:* dwatts@nd.edu.au (office); don9chel@bigpond.com. *Website:* www.nd.edu.au (office).

WATTS, Sir Philip Beverley, Kt, KCMG, BA, BSc, MSc, FInstP, FEI, FRGS, FGS, FRSA; British oil company executive (retd); b. 25 June 1945, Leicester, England; s. of Samuel Watts and Philippa Watts (née Wale); m. Janet Edna Watts (née Lockwood) 1966; one s. one d.; ed Wyggeston Grammar School, Leicester and Univ. of Leeds, Open Univ., Oxford Brookes Univ.; science teacher, Methodist Boys High School, Freetown, Sierra Leone 1966–68; joined Shell Int. 1969, held various posts: seismologist, Indonesia 1970–74, geophysicist UK/Europe 1974–77, Exploration Man., Norway 1978–81, Div. Head, Malaysia, Brunei, Singapore, London 1981–83, Exploration Dir, UK 1983–85; Head EP Liaison—Europe, The Hague 1986–88, Head EP Econs and Planning, The Hague 1989–91, Man. Dir, Nigeria 1991–94, Regional Co-ordinator, Europe, The Hague 1994–95; Dir Planning, Environment and External Affairs, London 1996–97; Chair. Royal Dutch/Shell Group 2001–04 (Group Man. Dir 1997–2004); Chair. Shell Transport and Trading 2001 (Man. Dir 1997–2004); Chair. World Business Council for Sustainable Devt 2001–03 (mem. Exec. Cttee 1998–2004); Chair. ICC-UK 1998–2004 (mem. Governing Body 1997–2004), Worldwide ICC, Exec. Bd 1997–2000; Asst Curate, Binfield Parish, Oxford Diocese; Priest-in-Charge, Waltham St Lawrence Parish Church 2013–16; Sr Priest, Warfield Church 2017. *Leisure interests:* travel, gardening, reading. *Address:* Sunnyridge, Hill Farm Lane, Binfield, Berks., RG42 5NR, England (home). *E-mail:* philbwatts@googlemail.com (home).

WAU, Guma; Papua New Guinea politician; fmr mem. Nat. Parl. for Kerowagi constituency; Minister for Tourism, Arts and Culture 2010, Minister of Defence 2011–12; mem. United Resource Party.

WAUGH, Richard (Rick) E., OC, B.AV, BComm (Hons), MBA, FICB; Canadian banking executive; m. Lynne Waugh; three s.; ed Univ. of Manitoba, York Univ.; began career with The Bank of Nova Scotia (Scotiabank), Winnipeg 1970, served in investment, corp., int. and retail banking areas, Sr Exec. of US Operations, New York 1985–93, Sr Exec. Vice-Pres. of Corp. Banking, responsible for Global Corp. Banking, Toronto 1993–95, Vice-Chair. of Corp. Banking 1995–98, Vice-Chair. of Int. Banking and Wealth Man. 1998–2003, mem. Bd of Dirs, Pres. and CEO 2003–14; Co-Chair. Canada-Brazil CEO Forum 2011; mem. Bd of Dirs Catalyst Inc. (Chair. Catalyst Canada Advisory Bd), Inst. of Int. Finance (IIF), Int. Monetary Conf.; Trustee, IIF's Principles for Stable Capital Flows in Emerging Markets; mem. Council of the Americas, Chair.'s Int. Advisory Council for the Americas Soc., Advisory Council of the Schulich School of Business at York Univ., Guanghua School of Man. at Peking Univ., Canadian Museum of Human Rights, amongst others; Campaign Chair. United Way of Greater Toronto 2006; has worked extensively with the MS Soc., both as Hon. Chair. endMS Capital Campaign and as mem. Bd Scientific Research Foundation; Dir St Michael's Hosp., Co-Chair. Hosp.'s Campaign to build the Li Ka Shing Knowledge Inst.; Fellow, Inst. of Canadian Bankers; Order of Merit (Dominican Repub.) 2010; Hon. LLD (York Univ., Assumption Univ.); Merit of Honor, Council of the Americas, Award of Merit, B'nai Brith Canada 2008, Corp. Social Responsibility Award, Foreign Policy Assen, New York 2009, Int. Award, Horatio Alger Assen of Distinguished Americans 2011.

WAUGH, Scott L., BA, PhD; American historian, academic and university administrator; *Executive Vice-Chancellor and Provost, University of California, Los Angeles;* ed Univ. of California, Los Angeles, Univ. of London, UK; taught in Dept of History, UCLA from 1975, Dean of Div. of Social Sciences 1992–2006, Acting Exec. Vice-Chancellor and Provost, UCLA 2006–08, Exec. Vice-Chancellor and Provost 2008–; honours, fellowships and grants from Nat. Endowment for the Humanities, American Philosophical Soc., and others, UCLA Distinguished Teaching Award, Harvey L. Eby Award for Art of Teaching, Univ. of California Pres.'s Fellowship in Humanities, UCLA Faculty Devt Award. *Publications:* two books and co-ed. of a third; numerous articles in scholarly journals. *Address:* Office of the Chancellor, University of California, Los Angeles, 2147 Murphy Hall, 405 Hilgard Avenue, Los Angeles, CA 90095-1405, USA (office). *Telephone:* (310) 825-2052 (office). *Fax:* (310) 206-6030 (office). *E-mail:* evc@conet.ucla.edu (office). *Website:* evc.ucla.edu/biography (office).

WAUGH, Stephen Rodger (Steve), AO; Australian foundation director and fmr professional cricketer; b. 2 June 1965, Canterbury, Sydney, NSW; s. of Rodger Waugh and Beverley Waugh; elder twin of Mark Edward; m. Lynette Waugh; one s. two d.; ed East Hills High School; right-hand batsman and right-arm medium-fast bowler; teams: New South Wales 1984/85–2003/04, Australia 1985–2004 (Capt. 1999–2004), Somerset 1987–88, Ireland 1998, Kent 2002; Test debut: Australia v India, Melbourne 26–30 Dec. 1985; played in 168 Tests (most capped Test player in history), scoring 10,927 runs (average 51.06, highest score 200) including 32 hundreds, taking 92 wickets (average 37.44), best bowling (innings) 5/28, (match) 8/169; played in 325 One-Day Ints (106 as Capt.), scoring 7,569 runs (average 32.90, highest score 120 not out) including three hundreds, taking 195 wickets (average 34.67), best bowling 4/33; played in 356 First-class matches, scoring 24,052 runs (average 51.94, highest score 216 not out) including 79 hundreds, taking 249 wickets (average 32.75), best bowling 6.51; shared world record 5th wicket stand of 464 (unbroken) with brother M. E. Waugh for NSW vs Western Australia, Perth 1990–91; retd Jan. 2004; Patron Camp Quality, Cerebral Palsy Assen, Udayan Home for Girls, India; Chair. Steve Waugh Foundation; Wisden Cricketer of the Year 1989, Australian Sports Medal 2000, Australian Cricketer of the Year 2000–01, Allan Border Medal 2001, Laureus Sports Award (World's Best Team) 2001, Australian of the Year 2004, an Australian Living Treasure, one of five new members inducted into ICC (Int. Cricket Council) Cricket Hall of Fame 2009. *Publications:* South African Tour Diary 1995, Steve Waugh's West Indies Tour Diary 1996, Steve Waugh's World Cup Diary 1997, Images of Waugh, Never Satisfied, Ashes Summer (co-author), Ashes Diary 1997, 2001, Out of My Comfort Zone: Captain's Diary 2002, Never Say Die 2003. *Leisure interests:* golf, photography, reading, writing. *Address:* c/o Team-Duet, 3 Winnie Street, Cremorne, NSW 2090, Australia (office); The Steve Waugh Foundation, GPO Box 3331, Sydney, NSW 2001, Australia. *Telephone:* (2) 9909-2188 (office); (1300)

669935. *Fax:* (2) 9909-2157 (office); (2) 9964-6255. *E-mail:* admin@duetgroup.com (office); info@stevewaughfoundation.com.au. *Website:* www .stevewaughfoundation.com.au.

WAWRINKA, Stanislas (Stan); Swiss/German professional tennis player; b. 28 March 1985, Lausanne, Switzerland; s. of Wolfram Wawrinka and Isabelle Wawrinka; m. Ilham Vuilloud 2009; one d.; ed distance educ. with Centre nat. d'enseignement à distance, France; right-handed (one-handed backhand); began playing int. junior events aged 14, entered the satellite circuit 2000, turned professional 2002; won French Open Junior championships 2003; gold medal for Switzerland, Men's Doubles, Summer Olympics, Beijing partnering Roger Federer 2008; won Croatia Open Umag 2006, Grand Prix Hassan II, Casablanca, Morocco 2010, Aircel Chennai Open, India 2011, 2014, 2015, 2016, Portugal Open 2013, Monte Carlo Rolex Masters 2014; won doubles, with Benoît Paire, Chennai Open 2013, Japan Open 2015; Grand Slam Singles results: fourth round, Wimbledon 2008, 2009, fourth round, US Open 2008, quarterfinalist, French Open 2013, semifinalist, US Open 2013, winner, Australian Open 2014, French Open 2015; other tournaments: semifinalist, ATP World Tour Finals, London 2013; team competitions: won Davis Cup (with Roger Federer, Marco Chiudinelli and Michael Lammer), Lille, France 2014; ranked World No. 3 27 Jan. 2014; coached by Dimitri Zavialoff 1993–2010, Peter Lundgren 2010–11, Magnus Norman 2013–; Flag-bearer for Switzerland, Summer Olympic Games, London 2012; mem. Admin. Council Lausanne HC ice hockey club 2011–; Swiss Team of the Year Award 2008. *Address:* c/o Nicolas Lamperin, IMG, 5 bis rue Mahias, 92100 Boulogne-Billancourt, France.

WEAH, George Tawlon Manneh Oppong Ousman; Liberian politician, head of state and fmr professional footballer; *President;* b. 1 Oct. 1966, Clara Town, Monrovia; s. of William T. Weah, Sr and Anna Quayeweah; raised by his paternal grandmother, Emma Klonjlaleh Brown; m. Clar Weah; four c.; ed Wells Hairston High School, univ. in Fla, USA; worked for Liberia Telecommunications Corpn as switchboard technician; played as forward for Liberian and Cameroonian clubs, Young Survivors Clareton 1981–84, Bongrange Company 1984–85, Mighty Barolle 1985–86, Invincible Eleven 1986–87, Africa Sports 1987, Tonnerre Yaoundé 1987–88 (won LFA Championship 1987, Cameroon Championship 1988); player, AC Monaco 1988–92 (102 games, 47 goals), Paris Saint-Germain 1992–95 (96 games, 32 goals, won French Championship 1994, French Cup, 1991, 1993, 1995, French League Cup 1995), AC Milan 1995–2000 (114 games, 46 goals, won Serie A 1995, 1999), Chelsea (on loan) 2000 (11 games, four goals, won FA Cup 2000), Manchester City 2000 (seven games, one goal), Olympique Marseille 2000–01 (19 games, five goals), Al Jazira, UAE 2001–03 (eight games, 13 goals); player, Cameroon nat. team 1988–92 (93 games, 47 goals), Liberia nat. team 1988–2002 (60 games, 22 goals), also Tech. Dir until retd after African Nations Cup Jan. 2002; UNICEF Goodwill Amb. 1997–; Amb. for SOS Children's Villages; unsuccessful cand. for Pres. of Liberia 2005; returned from USA to campaign for Congress for Democratic Change cand. in Montserrado senatorial by-election 2009, then Leader, Congress for Democratic Change; Senator from Montserrado Co. 2014–18; Pres. of Liberia 2018–; Dr hc (Cuttington Univ., Suakoko) 2018; African Player of the Year 1989, 1994, 1995, European Player of the Year 1995, FIFA Football Player of the Year 1995, FIFA Fair Player 1996, African Footballer of the Century 1998. *Address:* Executive Mansion, PO Box 10-9001, Capitol Hill, 1000 Monrovia 10, Liberia (office). *E-mail:* gmoore@emansion.gov.lr (office). *Website:* www.emansion.gov.lr (office).

WEAIRE, Denis Lawrence, PhD, FRS, MRIA, MAE; British/Irish physicist and academic; *Professor Emeritus, Trinity College Dublin;* b. 17 Oct. 1942, Dalhousie, India; s. of Allen M. Weaire and Janet E. Rea; m. Colette O'Regan 1969; one s.; ed Belfast Royal Acad., Univ. of Cambridge; Harkness Fellowship 1964–66; Fellow, Clare Coll., Cambridge 1967–69; Research Fellow, Harvard Univ. 1969–70; Instructor, Assoc. Prof. Yale Univ. 1970–74; Sr Lecturer, then Prof., Heriot-Watt Univ. 1974–79; Chair. of Experimental Physics, Univ. Coll. Dublin 1980–84; apptd Erasmus Smith's Prof. of Natural and Experimental Philosophy, Trinity Coll. Dublin 1984, Head of Dept 1984–89, Fellow 1987, Dean of Science 1989–92, now Prof. Emer.; mem. Belfast Royal Acad. 1954–61, Royal Irish Acad. 1987– (Vice-Pres. 2001–02); mem. Academia Europaea 1998– (Vice-Pres. 2005–08); Hon. Sec., European Asscn of Deans of Science 1991–93; Vice-Pres. European Physical Soc. 1995–96, 1999–2000, Pres. 1997–99; Vice-Pres. Inst. of Physics 2008–; Dr hc (Tech. Univ., Lisbon) 2001; Cecil Powell Medal 2002, RIA Cunningham Medal 2005, IOP/ French Physics Soc. Holweck Medal 2008. *Publications:* Introduction to Physical Mathematics (co-author) 1985, The Physics of Foams (co-author) 2000, The Pursuit of Perfect Packing (co-author) 2000; co-ed. of several other vols. *Leisure interests:* sport, sea-fishing, theatre, humorous writing, book collecting. *Address:* School of Physics, Trinity College, Dublin 2; 26 Greenmount Road, Terenure, Dublin, Ireland (home). *Telephone:* (1) 8961675 (office); (1) 4902063 (home). *Fax:* (1) 6711759 (office). *E-mail:* Denis.Weaire@tcd.ie (office). *Website:* www.tcd.ie/ Physics (office).

WEALE, Martin Robert, CBE, MA, ScD; British economist; b. 4 Dec. 1955, Barnet, Herts.; s. of R. A. Weale and M. E. Weale; ed Clare Coll., Cambridge; Overseas Devt Inst. Fellow, Nat. Statistical Office, Malawi 1977–79; Researcher and Lecturer, Faculty of Econs and Politics, Univ. of Cambridge 1979–95, Econs Fellow, Clare Coll. 1981–95; Dir Nat. Inst. of Econ. and Social Research 1995–2010, mem. Statistics Commr 2000–07; mem. Bd for Actuarial Standards 2006–11; External mem. Monetary Policy Cttee, Bank of England 2010–; Hon. Fellow, Inst. of Actuaries 2001; Hon. DSc (City Univ.) 2007. *Publications include:* Macroeconomic Policy: Inflation, Wealth and the Exchange Rate (co-author) 1989, Reconciliation of National Income and Expenditure (co-author) 1995, Econometric Modelling: Techniques and Applications (co-ed.) 2000; numerous journal articles. *Leisure interests:* bridge, walking, art exhbns, music. *Address:* Bank of England, Threadneedle Street, London, EC2R 8AH (office); 63 Noel Road, London, N1 8HE, England (home). *Telephone:* (20) 7601-4271 (office); (20) 7359-8210 (home). *Fax:* (20) 7601-5460 (office). *E-mail:* martin.weale@bankofengland.co.uk (office). *Website:* www.bankofengland.co.uk (office).

WEARING, Gillian, OBE, BA, RA; British artist; b. 1963, Birmingham; ed Chelsea School of Art, Goldsmiths Coll., London; first solo exhbn City Racing, London 1993, numerous exhbns worldwide; concentrates on video and photog-raphy; public commissions include Trentino Family, Galleria Civica di Arte Contemporanea, Trento, Italy 2007, A Real Birmingham Family, Birmingham 2014, A Real Danish Family, Copenhagen, Denmark 2016, Millicent Fawcett Statue, Parliament Square, London 2018; Hon. Fellow, Univ. of the Arts, London 2015; Dr hc (Birmingham City Univ.) 2016; BT Young Contemporaries 1993, Turner Prize 1997, Prize of Ministry of Employment, Social Affairs and Urban Devt, Culture and Sport 1998, Oberhausen Short Film Festival Award 1998, British Television Advertising Award, Public Service: Gold 2002, Grazia o2 X Award for Art 2007. *Film:* Self Made 2010. *Publications include:* Gillian Wearing City Projects Prague 1996, Signs that say what you want them to say and not Signs that say what someone else wants you to say 1997, Gillian Wearing Secession 1997, A Woman Called Theresa 1999, Gillian Wearing 1999, 2000, 2001, 2012, 2015, Broad Street 2001, Unspoken 2001, Sous Influence 2001, Mass Observation 2002, A Trilogy 2002, Living Proof 2006, Family History 2007, Family Stories 2017. *Address:* c/o Maureen Paley, 21 Herald Street, London, E2 6JT, England (office). *Telephone:* (20) 7729-4112 (office). *Fax:* (20) 7729-4113 (office). *E-mail:* info@maureenpaley.com (office). *Website:* www.maureenpaley.com (office).

WEATHERALL, Vice-Adm. Sir James (Lamb), KCVO, KBE; British naval officer; b. 28 Feb. 1936, Newton Mearns, Renfrewshire, Scotland; s. of Lt Commdr Alwyne Weatherall and Joan Cuthbert; m. Hon. Jean Stewart Macpherson 1962; two s. three d.; ed Glasgow Acad., Gordonstoun School; commanded HM Ships Soberton 1966–67, Ulster 1970–72, Tartar 1975–76, Andromeda 1982–84 (in Falklands Conflict), Ark Royal 1985–87; on staff of Supreme Allied Commander Europe (NATO) as Rear-Adm. 1987–89; Deputy Supreme Allied Commdr Atlantic 1989–91; HM Marshal of the Diplomatic Corps 1992–2001; Extra Equerry to HM The Queen 2001; DL for Hampshire 2004; one of HM The Queen's Commrs of the Lieutenancy for the City of London 2001; Liveryman Worshipful Co. of Ship-wrights 1985, Asst to Court 1989, Prime Warden 2001–02; Younger Brother Trinity House 1986; Trustee, Marwell Zoological Preservation Trust 1992 (Chair. 1999–2007); Gov. Box Hill School 1992–2003 (Chair. 1994–2003, Warden 2003–), Gordonstoun School 1994–2003 (Chair. 1996–2003, Warden 2004–11); Pres. Int. Social Service 1996–2001; Chair. Lord Mayor of London's Appeal 1997–98; Chair. Sea Cadet Asscn 1992–98, Vice-Pres. 2009–; Trustee, World Wildlife Fund UK 2001–07; Patron, Marwell Wildlife; Sea Cadet Medal 1998. *Leisure interests:* fishing, stamp collecting. *Address:* Craig House, Street End, Bishop's Waltham, Hants., SO32 1FS, England (home). *Telephone:* (1489) 892483 (home). *E-mail:* jimweatherall@btinternet.com (home).

WEAVER, Jacqueline (Jacki) Ruth; Australian actress; b. 25 May 1947, Sydney; d. of Arthur Weaver and Edith Weaver (née Simpson). *Television includes:* Homicide 1967–77, Trial by Marriage 1980, The Challenge (mini-series) 1986, Hammer Bay (film) 2007, Satisfaction 2009, Gracepoint (mini-series) 2014, Blunt Talk 2015–16, Sister Cities (film) 2016, Secret City 2016–18. *Films include:* Stork (Australian Film Inst. Award for Best Actress in a Leading Role) 1971, Picnic at Hanging Rock 1975, The Removalists 1975, Caddie (Australian Film Inst. Award for Best Actress in a Supporting Role) 1976, The Perfectionist 1987, Animal Kingdom (Australian Film Inst. Award for Best Actress in a Leading Role, Nat. Bd of Review Award for Best Supporting Actress, Los Angeles Film Critics Asscn Award for Best Supporting Actress, San Francisco Film Critics Circle Award for Best Supporting Actress, Satellite Award for Best Supporting Actress – Motion Picture, Utah Film Critics Asscn Award for Best Supporting Actress) 2010, Summer Coda 2010, The Five-Year Engagement 2012, Silver Linings Playbook 2012, Stoker 2013, Parkland 2013, The Voices 2014, Haunt 2014, Magic in the Moonlight 2014, Reclaim 2014, Six Dance Lessons in Six Weeks 2014, Last Cab to Darwin 2015, Goldstone 2016, The Polka King 2017, The Disaster Artist 2017, Irreplaceable You 2018, Bird Box 2018, Poms 2019, Zeroville 2019, Grudge 2020. *Address:* c/o International Casting Service & Associates Pty Ltd, 2/218 Crown Street, Darlinghurst, Sydney, NSW 2010, Australia (office).

WEAVER, Sigourney, BA, MFA; American actress; b. (Susan Alexandra Weaver), 8 Oct. 1949, New York; d. of 'Pat' Laflin Weaver and Elizabeth Inglis (née Desiree Mary Lucy Hawkins); m. James Simpson 1984; one d.; ed Stanford Univ., Yale Univ.; f. Goat Cay Productions (film production co.); Hon. Chair. Dian Fossey Gorilla Fund Int. *Films include:* Annie Hall 1977, Tribute to a Madman 1977, Camp 708 1978, Alien 1979, Eyewitness 1981, The Year of Living Dangerously 1982, Deal of the Century 1983, Ghostbusters 1984, Une Femme ou Deux 1985, Half Moon Street 1986, Aliens 1986, Gorillas in the Mist (Golden Globe Best Actress Award) 1988, Working Girl (Best Supporting Actress Award Golden Globe) 1988, Ghostbusters II 1989, Aliens 3 1992, 1492: Conquest of Paradise 1993, Dave 1993, Death and the Maiden 1994, Jeffrey 1995, Copycat 1996, Snow White in the Black Forest 1996, Ice Storm 1996, Alien Resurrection 1997, A Map of the World 1999, Galaxy Quest 1999, Get Bruce 1999, Company Man 1999, Airframe 1999, Heartbreakers 2001, Tadpole 2002, The Guys 2002, Holes 2003, The Village 2004, Imaginary Heroes 2004, Snow Cake 2006, The TV Set 2006, Infamous 2006, Happily N'Ever After (voice) 2006, The Girl in the Park 2007, Be Kind Rewind 2008, Vantage Point 2008, Baby Mama 2008, Wall-E (voice) 2008, The Tale of Despereaux (narrator) 2008, Avatar 2009, Crazy on the Outside 2010, You Again 2010, Cedar Rapids 2011, The Cold Light of Day 2012, Red Lights 2012, The Cabin in the Woods 2012, Vamps 2012, Exodus: Gods and Kings 2014, Chappie 2015, Finding Dory (voice) 2016, A Monster Calls 2016, Rakka 2017, Avatar 2 2020. *Television includes:* Somerset (series) 1970, The Best of Families (mini-series) 1977, 3 by Cheever: The Sorrows of Gin 1979, 3 by Cheever: O Youth and Beauty! 1979, Snow White: A Tale of Terror 1997, Late Night with Conan O'Brien 1997, Futurama: Planet Express Ship 2002, Love and Rocket 2002, The TV Set 2006, Eli Stone: The Path 2008, Prayers for Bobby 2009, Political Animals (mini-series) 2012, Doc Martin (series) 2015, The Defenders (series) 2017, Not The White House Correspondents' Dinner 2019. *Telephone:* (212) 421-8293. *Fax:* (212) 421-8294.

WEBB, Sir Adrian Leonard, Kt, BSocSci, MSc, DLitt, FRSA, FCGI; British academic and university administrator; b. 19 July 1943, Newport, Wales; s. of Leonard Webb and Rosina Webb; m. 1st Caroline Williams 1966 (divorced 1995); two s.; m. 2nd Monjulee Dass 1996; ed St Julian's High School, Newport, Gwent, Univ. of Birmingham, London School of Econs, Loughborough Univ.; Lecturer, LSE 1966–74; Research Dir Personal Social Services Council 1974–76; Prof. of Social Policy, Loughborough Univ. 1976–93; Dir Centre for Research in Social Policy 1983–90, Dean, later Pro-Vice-Chancellor, 1986–93; Vice-Chancellor, Univ.

of Glamorgan 1993–2005; Visiting Prof., Cardiff Business School; Chair. Bd of Govs, Volunteer Centre 1978–84, Cttee on Workforce Planning and Training in Social Services 1987–88, Dept of Health Task Force on Nursing Research 1992–93, Heads of Higher Educ. in Wales 2000–03, Pontypridd and Rhondda NHS Trust 2005–08, Enquiry into Further Educ. Wales 2006–07, Wales Employment and Skills Bd 2008–11, Tenovus (cancer charity) 2008–11, Enquiry into Higher Educ. in NE Wales 2012–13, Review of Post 14 Educ. in Wales (published as Promise and Performance); Wales Commr, UK Comm. for Employment and Skills –2012; mem. DHSS Research Liaison Groups 1975–90 (science adviser, Chief Scientist's Departmental Research Cttee, DHSS 1987–90), Sociology and Social Admin Cttee, SSRC 1976–80, Council on Tribunals 1985–91, English Nat. Bd on Nursing Midwifery and Health Visiting 1988–93, CBI Council Wales 1993–98, Nat. Cttee of Inquiry into Higher Educ. (Dearing Cttee) 1996–97, BBC Broadcasting Council for Wales 1998, Public Services Productivity Panel, HM Treasury 2000–06, Admin. Justice and Tribunals Council 2008– (also Chair. Welsh Cttee), Big Lottery Fund 2012– (also Chair. Wales Cttee), Beecham Review of the Delivery of Public Services in Wales (published as Beyond Boundaries), Wales Cttee Royal Soc. for the Protection of Birds; Vice-Pres. Leics. Regional Council Guideposts Trust Ltd 1988–93; Chair. Social Admin Asscn 1977–80; Dir (non-exec.), East Glamorgan NHS Trust 1997–, Nat. Council Educ. and Learning Wales (ELWa) 2001–06, Nat. Ass. for Wales 2003–08, Bd Inst. of Welsh Affairs 2008–, Bd Wales Govt 2012–; adviser on social policy and social work, Univ. Funding Council 1989–92, Leics. DHA 1992–93, NHS Wales R&D Forum 1993–96; mem. Social Policy Asscn, British Sociological Asscn, Political Studies Asscn; Founding Trustee, Bevan Foundation. *Publications include:* Change, Choice and Conflict in Social Policy 1975, Planning Need and Scarcity 1986, The Economic Approach to Social Policy 1986, Social Work, Social Care and Social Planning 1987, Joint Approaches to Social Policy 1988. *Leisure interests:* walking, painting (water colour), ornithology. *Address:* Welsh Government, Cathays Park, Cardiff, CF10 3NQ, Wales (office). *Website:* wales.gov.uk (office).

WEBB, James (Jim) H., Jr, JD; American writer and politician; b. 9 Feb. 1946, Arlington, Va; m. Hong Le Webb; one s. three d. one step-d.; ed US Naval Acad., Georgetown Univ.; Asst Minority Counsel, House Cttee on Veterans Affairs, Washington, DC 1977–78, Chief Minority Counsel 1979–81; Visiting Writer, US Naval Acad. 1979; Asst Sec. for Reserve Affairs, Dept of Defense 1984–87; Sec. of the Navy 1987–88 (resgnd); Senator from Virginia 2007–13 (retd), mem. Cttee on Foreign Relations (Chair. East Asian and Pacific Affairs Subcommittee), Cttee on Armed Services (Chair. Key Personnel Subcommittee), Veterans' Affairs Cttee, Jt Econ. Cttee; Fellow, Harvard Inst. of Politics 1992; Democrat; Distinguished Public Service Medal, Dept of Defense, Patriot Award, Medal of Honor Soc., Public Service Award, American Legion Nat. Commdr, VFW Media Service Award, Mil. Order of the Iron Mike Award, Marine Corps League, John Russell Leadership Award, Robert L. Denig Distinguished Service Award, Emmy Award for 1983 PBS coverage of US Marines in Beirut. *Film:* Rules of Engagement (wrote story and exec. producer) 2000. *Publications:* Fields of Fire 1978, A Sense of Honor 1981, A Country Such as This 1983, Something to Die For 1991, A Sense of Honor 1995, The Emperor's General 1999, Lost Soldiers 2001, Born Fighting 2004. *Website:* www.jameswebb.com.

WEBB, Leslie Roy, AO, BCom, PhD; Australian university vice-chancellor (retd); b. 18 July 1935, Melbourne, Vic.; s. of Leslie Hugh Charles Webb and Alice Myra Webb; m. Heather Brown 1966; one s. one d.; ed Wesley Coll., Melbourne, Univ. of Melbourne, London School of Econs; Sr Lecturer in Econs, Univ. of Melbourne 1964–68, Truby Williams Prof. of Econs 1973–84, Prof. Emer. 1985–, Pro-Vice-Chancellor 1982–84, Chair. Academic Bd 1983–84; Reader in Econs, La Trobe Univ. 1969–72; Vice-Chancellor Griffith Univ. 1985–2002; Chair. Queensland Non-State Schools Accreditation Bd 2001–09; Visiting Prof. Cornell Univ., USA 1967–68; Consultant, UNCTAD 1974–75; Jt Ed. The Economic Record 1973–77; Chair. Cttee of Inquiry into S Australian Dairy Industry 1977, Library Bd of Queensland 2002–08; Assoc. mem. Prices Justification Tribunal 1978–79, 1980–81; mem. Council of Advice, Bureau of Industry Econs 1982–84; Chair. Australian-American Educational Foundation (Fulbright Program) 1986–90; mem. Bd of Govs Foundation for Devt Co-operation 1990–2007; Dir and mem. Australian Vice-Chancellors' Cttee Bd of Dirs 1991–94; Cavaliere, Ordine al Merito (Italy) 1995; Hon. DUniv (Queensland Univ. of Tech.) 2002, (Griffith Univ.) 2002, Hon. DLitt (Univ. of South Queensland) 2002; Award for Outstanding Achievement, US Information Agency 1987. *Publications include:* Industrial Economics: Australian Studies (co-ed.) 1982; articles in learned journals. *Leisure interests:* music, art, gardening. *Address:* 3 Davrod Street, Robertson, Queensland 4109, Australia (home). *Telephone:* (7) 3345-7141 (home). *E-mail:* lroywebb@optusnet.com.au.

WEBBER, Tristan, BA, MA; British fashion designer; b. 1973; ed SE Essex Coll. of Arts and Tech., Cordwainers Coll., London and St Martin's School of Art and Design; work exhibited at Colette, Paris and Powerhouse Exhbn, London 1998; third collection shown at London Fashion Week 1998 and MTV Fashionably Loud event, Miami 1998; fmr Visiting Lecturer, Royal Coll. of Art, currently Sr Tutor, Fashion Womenswear Programme, School of Material. *Address:* c/o Royal College of Art, Kensington Gore, London, SW7 2EU, England (office). *Website:* www.tristanwebber.com.

WEBER, Axel A., MA, PhD Habil.; German economist, academic and banking executive; *Chairman, UBS AG;* b. 8 March 1957, Kusel, Rhineland-Palatinate; ed Univs of Siegen and Konstanz; Prof. for Monetary Econs, Sr Research Fellow and Dir Centre for Financial Studies, Goethe Univ., Frankfurt am Main 1998–2001; Prof. for Int. Econs and Dir Centre for Financial Research, Univ. of Cologne 2001–04, on leave of absence; Visiting Prof., Booth School of Business, Univ. of Chicago 2011–12; Research Fellow, Centre for Econ. Policy Research, London, UK, Centre for Financial Research, Cologne; Pres. Bundesbank 2004–11, mem. Governing Council, European Cen. Bank 2004–11, mem. Bd of Dirs BIS 2004–11, Gov. for Germany, IMF 2004–11, mem. G7 and G20 Ministers and Govs 2004–11; Chair. UBS AG 2012–; mem. Financial Stability Bd 2010–11, Steering Cttee, European Systemic Risk Bd 2011; mem. German Council of Econ. Experts 2002–04; mem. Group of Thirty, Washington, DC, Swiss Bankers Asscn; mem. Bd Int. Inst. of Finance; mem. Monetary Econs Council and Int. Econs Council Verein für Socialpolitik, Advisory Bd German Market Economy Foundation, Advisory Council (Hochschulrat) Goethe Univ.; mem. Bd of Trustees Avenir Suisse; Dr hc (Duisburg-Essen), (Konstanz). *Address:* UBS AG, Bahnhofstrasse 45, 8021 Zurich, Switzerland (office). *Telephone:* (44) 234-11-11 (office). *Fax:* (44) 239-91-11 (office). *E-mail:* info@ubs.com (office). *Website:* www.ubs.com (office).

WEBER, Bruce; American photographer, film director and producer; b. 29 March 1946, Greensburg, Pa; ed Hun School at Princeton, Denison Univ., Ohio, New York Univ. Art and Film Schools, New School for Social Research, New York; numerous exhbns in New York, Los Angeles, Chicago, Dallas, San Francisco, Atlanta, New Orleans, St Louis, Paris, London, Dortmund, Basel, Lausanne, Tokyo, Frankfurt etc. 1973–; photographs in perm. collections of Victoria and Albert Museum, London and Photography Div., City of Paris; numerous commercials 1988–; numerous awards, including Council of Fashion Designers of America for Achievement in Photography 1984, 1985, American Soc. of Magazine Photographers Fashion Photographer of the Year 1984, Int. Film and TV Festival of New York Silver Medal 1985, Cannes Int. Advertising Film Festival Silver Lion for Beauty Brothers (commercial) 1988, Int. Center of Photography Award for use of Photography in Advertising 1994, Best Advertising in Print and TV, Fragrance Foundation 1997, First Alfred Eisenstaedt Award for Portrait Photography, Life magazine 1998. *Films produced and directed include:* Broken Noses (Int. Documentary Asscn Award 1988) 1987, Let's Get Lost (Critics' Award, Venice Film Festival 1988, Int. Documentary Asscn Award 1989) 1988, Backyard Movie 1991, Gentle Giants 1994, The Teddy Boys of the Edwardian Drape Society 1996, Chop Suey 1999; music videos: Being Boring, The Pet Shop Boys (Video of the Year Award, Music Week 1990) 1990, Blue Spanish Sky, Chris Isaak 1991, Se A Vida E, The Pet Shop Boys 1996. *Film directed:* A Letter to True 2003. *Publications:* Sam Shepard 1990, Bear Pond 1990, Hotel Room with a View (photographs) 1992, Gentle Giants: A Book of Newfoundland 1994, A House is Not a Home 1996, Branded Youth and other stories 1997, The Chop Suey Club 1999, Mother's Days: Imogen Cunningham 2002, Like a Moth to a Flame: Jim French 2003, Blood Sweat and Tears 2005, People I May Know 2006, Live Here, Rent Free 2007; All American Series: All American 2001, All-American: Short Stories 2002, All-American: Family Albums 2003, All-American IV: Otherworldly 2004, All-American V: Is Love Enough? 2005, All-American VI: Larger Than Life 2006, All-American VII: Till I Get It Right 2007, All-American VIII: Nature's Way 2008, All-American IX: A Near-Perfect World 2009, All-American X: Written in the Stars 2010, All American XI: Just Life 2011, All American XII: A Book of Lessons 2012, All American XIII: Born Ready 2013, All American XIV: Affairs of Heart 2014, All American XV: Leap of Faith 2015, All American XVI: Wild Blue Yonder 2016, All American XVII: Glory Be 2017. *Address:* c/o Little Bear Inc., 135th Watts Street, 5th Floor, New York, NY 10013, USA (office). *Telephone:* (212) 226-0814 (office). *Fax:* (212) 334-5180 (office). *Website:* www.bruceweber.com.

WEBER, Christophe, MFin, MPM, DPharm; French pharmaceutical industry executive; *President and CEO, Takeda Pharmaceutical Company Ltd;* ed Univ. of Lyon; began career in Australia, working for Rhône-Poulenc-Rorer Pharmaceuticals; joined GlaxoSmithKline 1993, positions included Gen. Man. Swiss subsidiary, Chair. and CEO GSK France 2003–08, Sr Vice-Pres. and Regional Dir of Asia Pacific 2008–11, mem. Corp. Exec. Team, Pres. and Gen. Man. GlaxoSmithKline Vaccines (GSK Biologicals SA) 2011–14; apptd COO and Corp. Officer, Takeda Pharmaceutical Co. Ltd April 2014, Pres. and Rep. Dir June 2014–15, Pres., CEO and Rep. Dir 2015–. *Address:* Takeda Pharmaceutical Co. Ltd, 1-1, Doshomachi 4-chome, Chuo-ku, Osaka 540-8645, Japan (office). *Telephone:* (6) 6204-2111 (office). *Fax:* (6) 6204-2880 (office). *E-mail:* info@www.takeda.com (office). *Website:* www.takeda.com (office).

WEBER, George Brian, MA; Canadian national organization official and fmr Red Cross official; *President and CEO, Royal Ottawa Health Care Group;* b. 18 April 1946, Montreal; s. of Harry Weber and Johanna Alexopoulos; m. Mary Morris 1976; ed McGill Univ., Harvard Univ., USA; voluntary instructor/examiner, Canadian Red Cross 1963–73, Field Del. Viet Nam, Int. Red Cross 1973–74, Disaster Relief Officer, Chief Del., League of Red Cross Socs 1974–76, Nat. Dir of Int. Affairs, Canadian Red Cross 1976–81, Nat. Dir of Programmes 1981–83, Sec.-Gen. Canadian Red Cross 1983–92, Hon. Vice-Pres. 1993–, Sec.-Gen. and CEO Int. Fed. of Red Cross and Red Crescent Socs 1992–2000, Sec.-Gen. Emer. 2000–11; Chair. Canadian Soc. Assoc. Execs; Exec. Dir/CEO Canadian Dental Asscn 2000–07; Pres. and CEO Royal Ottawa Health Care Group 2007–; CEO Continovation Services Inc.; mem., Dir numerous bodies, including Canadian Inst. of Int. Affairs, Amundsen Foundation, Earth Foundation, American Coll. of Sports Medicine; Vanier Award 1984. *Leisure interests:* diving, tennis, squash, skiing. *Address:* Royal Ottawa Mental Health Centre, 1145 Carling Avenue, Ottawa, ON K1Z 7K4, Canada (office). *Telephone:* (613) 722-6521 (office). *E-mail:* info@theroyal.ca (office). *Website:* www.theroyal.ca (office).

WEBER, Jonathan Norden, FMedSci, FRCP, FRCPath; British clinical professor; *Dean, Faculty of Medicine, Imperial College London;* Wellcome Clinical Training Fellow, St Mary's Hosp. Medical School 1982–85; Wellcome Trust Lecturer in Cell and Molecular Biology, Inst. for Cancer Research Chester Beatty Labs 1985–88; Sr Lecturer in Infectious Diseases, Royal Postgraduate Medical School, Hammersmith Hosp. 1988–91; Jefferiss Prof. of Communicable Diseases and GU Medicine, Faculty of Medicine, Imperial Coll. London 1990–, also Dean; Founding Ed. AIDS (journal) 1987–92; co-f. WHO Network for HIV Characterisation 1992; Adviser on HIV to numerous orgs including WHO, UNAIDS, EC, Elton John Foundation, Wellcome Trust, Dept for Int. Devt, Russian Fed. AIDS Centre, Ivanovsky Inst. of Virology; Collaborator, European Vaccine Effort Against HIV/AIDS, Int. AIDS Vaccine Initiative; Dir Weber Investments 1996–. *Publications:* over 200 scientific papers on HIV and other STIs. *Address:* 15, Level 2, Faculty of Medicine, Imperial College, Exhibition Road, London, SW7 2AZ, England (office). *Telephone:* (20) 7594-3905 (office). *E-mail:* j.weber@imperial.ac.uk (office). *Website:* www.imperial.ac.uk/people/j.weber (office).

WEBER, Jürgen, Dipl-Ing, FRAeS; German business executive; *Honorary Chairman of the Supervisory Board, Deutsche Lufthansa AG;* b. 17 Oct. 1941, Lahr; m. Sabine Rossberg 1965; one s. one d.; ed Stuttgart Tech. Univ., Massachusetts Inst. of Tech., USA; with Lufthansa Eng Div. 1967–74, Dir Line Maintenance Dept 1974–78, with Aircraft Eng Sub-div. 1978–87, COO (Tech.) 1987–89, deputy mem. Exec. Bd 1989–90, CEO (Tech.) 1990–91, Chair. Exec. Bd Deutsche Lufthansa AG 1991–2003, CEO 1998–2003, mem. Supervisory Bd

1998–2005, Chair. –2013, Hon. Chair. 2013–; Chair. Supervisory Bd Deutsche Post AG 2006–; Chair. Supervisory Bd Thomas Cook AG; mem. Supervisory Bd, Allianz-Lebensversicherungs AG, Bayer AG, Deutsche Bank AG, Voith AG, Loyalty Partner GmbH, Tetra Laval Group (Switzerland), Willy Bogner GmbH & Co. KGaA; Hon. DEng (Stuttgart) 1998; Bambi Award for Industry 1994, Anti-Defamation League Champion of Liberty Award, Man. Magazin Man. of the Year 1999, Wirtschaftswoche Best Man. 2002, L. Welch Pogue Award, Airline Business Award 2003. Bambi Award 2003,. *Leisure interests:* jogging, skiing. *Address:* Deutsche Lufthansa AG, Flughafen-Bereich West, 60546 Frankfurt, Germany (office). *E-mail:* impressum_de@lufthansa.com (office). *Website:* www.lufthansa.com (office).

WEBER, Manfred, Dr rer. pol; German economist and banking official; b. 18 Dec. 1950, Altenkofen, Landshut; ed Johann Wolfgang Goethe Univ., Frankfurt am Main; Research Asst, Research Dept, Deutsche Bundesbank 1976–80, with Econs Dept 1980–85, Head, Office of Deputy Gov. 1986–90; with Monetary and Econ. Dept, Bank of International Settlements, Basle 1991–92; CEO Bundesverband deutscher Banken, Berlin 1992–2010, mem. Bd of Dirs 1997–2010; mem. Exec. Cttee European Banking Fed. 1992–2010 (Chair. 2000–02); Hon. Prof., Faculty of Econs and Social Sciences, Univ. of Potsdam 2004–. *Address:* Linienstr. 56, 10119 Berlin, Germany. *Telephone:* (30) 28385344. *Fax:* (30) 28385346. *E-mail:* office@manfredweber.net. *Website:* www.manfredweber.net.

WEBSTER, Peter; Irish business executive; ed Univ. Coll., Dublin; spent early career in oil industry in West Africa; joined Jefferson Smurfit Group 1978, fmr Regional Operations Dir, Chair. and Chief Exec. Smurfit Ireland Group 1995–2000, now Dir Smurfit Ireland Group; Chair. Beaumont Hosp. 2000–03; Pres. Dublin Chamber of Commerce 2002, now mem. Council; Chair. Metro Herald, Ryco Book Protection, Image Now Group, Epilepsy Care Foundation; Dir of several Irish and US cos; Dir (non-exec.) Carra (Ireland) Ltd 2011–. *Address:* Carra (Ireland) Ltd, Carra House, 12 West Pier, Howth, County Dublin, Ireland. *Telephone:* (1) 8323955. *Fax:* (1) 8326874. *E-mail:* info@carra.ie. *Website:* www.carra.ie.

WEBSTER, Toby; British gallery owner; *Director, The Modern Institute;* ed Glasgow School of Art; held first show in flat in Glasgow entitled The World of Ponce; worked for Transmission Gallery; co-f. (with Will Bradley) the Modern Institute 1998; artists represented include Dirk Bell, Martin Boyce, Jeremy Deller, Alex Dordoy, Urs Fischer, Kim Fisher, Luke Fowler, Henrik Håkansson, Mark Handforth, Thomas Houseago, Richard Hughes, Chris Johanson, Andrew Kerr, Jim Lambie, Duncan MacQuarrie, Victoria Morton, Scott Myles, Nicolas Party, Toby Paterson, Simon Periton, Manfred Pernice, Mary Redmond, Anselm Reyle, Eva Rothschild, Monika Sosnowska, Simon Starling, Katja Strunz, Tony Swain, Spencer Sweeney, Joanne Tatham & Tom O'Sullivan, Padraig Timoney, Hayley Tompkins, Sue Tompkins, Cathy Wilkes, Michael Wilkinson, Gregor Wright and Richard Wright; curated My Head is on Fire, but My Heart is Full of Love, in Copenhagen; guest curator, Centre for Contemporary Arts, Glasgow, Inst. for Contemporary Arts, London and at numerous venues; co-opened, with New York gallerist Gavin Brown, a space in Rome called Roma Roma Roma 2009; Movers and Makers: The Most Powerful People in the Art World, The Guardian 2014. *Address:* The Modern Institute, 14–20 Osborne Street, Glasgow, G1 5QN, Scotland (office). *Telephone:* (141) 248-3711 (office). *Fax:* (141) 552-5988 (office). *E-mail:* mail@themoderninstitute.com (office). *Website:* www.themoderninstitute.com (office).

WEBSTER, William Hedgcock, LLB, JD; American lawyer, judge and fmr government official; *Chairperson, Homeland Security Advisory Council;* b. 6 March 1924, St Louis, Mo.; s. of Thomas M. Webster and Katherine Webster (née Hedgcock); m. 1st Drusilla Lane 1950 (died 1984); one s. two d.; m. 2nd Lynda Clugston 1990; ed Amherst Coll., Mass, Washington Univ. in St Louis Law School; served as Lt USNR 1943–46, 1951–52; admitted to Missouri Bar 1949; attorney with Armstrong, Teasdale, Kramer & Vaughan and predecessors, St Louis 1949–50, 1952–59, Partner 1956–59, 1961–70; US Attorney, Eastern Dist, Mo. 1960–61; Judge, US Dist Court, Eastern Mo. 1971–73, US Court of Appeals 1973–78; Dir FBI 1978–87; Dir CIA 1987–91; apptd Sr Partner, Millbank, Tweed, Hadley & McCloy LLP 1991 (now retd); Chair. Homeland Security Advisory Council 2002–; head of investigation into police response to LA Riots 1992; head of ind. investigation of the FBI's actions surrounding the Fort Hood shooting 2009; Trustee, Washington Univ. 1974–; mem. Univ. of Colorado Law School Bd of Visitors; mem. Nat. Advisory Bd of American Univ.; mem. ABA, Fed., Mo. and St Louis Bar Asscns, American Law Inst., Council 1978–, Inst. of Judicial Admin Inc.; Fellow, American Bar Foundation; Hon. Chair. The OSS Soc.; Hon. Fellow, American Coll. of Trial Lawyers; Order of the Coif; Hon. LLD (Amherst Coll.) 1975, (DePauw Univ.) 1978, (Washington Univ.) 1978, (William Woods Coll.) 1979, (Inst. of World Politics) 2008 and numerous others; Washington Univ. Distinguished Alumnus Award 1977, American Legion Distinguished Service Award 1979, St Louis Globe-Democrat Man of the Year 1980, Washington Univ. William Greenleaf Elliot Award 1981, Riot Relief Fund of New York Award 1981, Young Lawyers of the ABA Award 1982, Fordham-Stein Award 1982, William Moss Inst.-American Univ. Award 1983, Freedoms Foundation Medal 1985, Presidential Medal of Freedom 1991, Nat. Security Medal 1991, Justice Award, American Judicature Soc. 2001, ABA Medal 2002, Distinguished Public Service Medal from NASA, William J. Donovan Award, The OSS Soc. 2005. *Leisure interest:* tennis. *Address:* Homeland Security Advisory Council, Washington, DC 20528, USA (office). *Telephone:* (202) 282-8000 (office). *Website:* www.dhs.gov/homeland-security-advisory-council-members (office).

WEDER, Hans, PhD, DHabil; Swiss theologian, university rector and academic; b. 27 Dec. 1946, Diepoldsau; m. Veronika Altherr; two d.; ed Gymnasium, St Gallen, Univ. of Zürich, Univ. of St Andrews, UK; Prof. of New Testament Science, Univ. of Zürich 1980–2000, Dean Theological Faculty 1986–88, Dir Inst. of Hermeneutics 1994–98, Head of Theological Seminary 1998–2000, Rector, Univ. of Zürich 2000–08, Prof. ad personam of New Testament Studies 2008–12; Chair. Univ. Council, Ludwig Maximilian Univ. of Munich 2011–19; Co-editor Journal for Theology and Church 1993–; mem. Scientific Soc. for Theology 1981–, Int. Acad. of Sciences Religieuses 1996–; fmr Pres. Rectors' Conf. of Swiss Univs; Dr hc (Univ of Jena) 2012. *Publications:* numerous articles in professional journals on hermeneutics and philosophy. *Address:* c/o Institut für Hermeneutik und Religionsphilosophie, University of Zurich, Kirchgasse 9, 8001 Zürich, Switzerland (office). *E-mail:* weder.hans@access.uzh.ch (office). *Website:* www.hermes.uzh.ch (office).

WEDGEWORTH, Robert, AB, MS, LHD, LLD, PhD; American university librarian, academic and association executive; b. 31 July 1937, Ennis, Tex.; m. Chung-Kyun Wedgeworth; one d.; ed Wabash Coll., Univ. of Illinois, Rutgers Univ.; Exec. Dir American Library Asscn (ALA) 1972–85; Dean School of Library Service, Columbia Univ. 1985–92; Librarian, Prof. of Library Admin, Univ. of Ill. at Urbana-Champaign 1993–99; Pres. Int. Fed. of Library Asscns and Insts (IFLA) 1991–97, Hon. Pres. 1997–; fmr interim Pres. Laubach Literacy Int. (LLI), fmr Vice-Chair., Bd of Trustees, Pres. and CEO ProLiteracy Worldwide (formed by merger of Laubach Literacy Int.and Literacy Volunteers of America, Inc.) 2000–07; Chair. Advisory Cttee ALA Office of Information Tech. Policy 1995–97; mem. Cttee to Visit Harvard Coll. Library 1994–97; mem. Nat. Comm. on Adult Literacy 2006–09; Trustee, Newberry Library, Chicago; mem. Bd of Trustees Poetry Foundation; mem. Bd of US Inst. of Museum and Library Services; ALA Joseph Lippincott Award 1989, Medal of Honor, Int. Council of Archives 1996, Melvil Dewey Award 1997. *Publications include:* World Encyclopaedia of Library and Information Services (ed.) 1993, Issues Affecting the Development of Digital Libraries in Science and Technology (UNESCO) 1996, Courtship, Marriage and Librarianship: A Vision of a 21st Century Profession (IFLA) 1996, Beyond Unification 1997, Reaffirming Professional Values 1997. *Address:* 2626 North Lakeview, Suite 3603, Chicago, IL 60614, USA (home). *Telephone:* (773) 525-6609 (home). *E-mail:* rwedge@illinois.edu (home).

WEE, Cho Yaw; Singaporean banker; *Chairman Emeritus and Adviser, United Overseas Bank Group;* s. of Wee Kheng Chiang, founder of United Chinese Bank; m.; five c.; ed high school in China; joined Bd of Dirs of United Chinese Bank (now United Overseas Bank) 1958, Man. Dir 1960–74, Chair. and CEO United Overseas Bank Group 1974–2007, Chair. 2007–13, Chair. Emer. and Adviser 2013–, also Chair. Emer. and Adviser, Far Eastern Bank, United Overseas Bank (Malaysia), currently Pres. Commr PT Bank UOB Indonesia, Supervisor of United Overseas Bank (China), Chair. United Overseas Bank (Thai) Public Co. and United Overseas Insurance; Pres. Singapore Fed. of Chinese Clan Asscns; Pro-Chancellor, Nanyang Technological Univ.; Chair. Haw Par Corpn, UOL Group, Pan Pacific Hotels Group, United Industrial Corpn, Marina Centre Holdings, Wee Foundation; Hon. Pres. Singapore Chinese Chamber of Commerce and Industry, Singapore Fed. of Chinese Clan Asscns, Singapore Hokkien Huay Kuan; Hon. DLit (Nat. Univ. of Singapore) 2008, (Nanyang Technological Univ.) 2014; Public Service Star, Singapore Govt 1971, named Businessman of the Year 1990, 2001, inaugural Credit Suisse-Ernst & Young Lifetime Achievement Award 2006, Lifetime Achievement Award, Asian Banker 2009, Distinguished Service Order (Singapore) 2011. *Address:* United Overseas Bank, 80 Raffles Place, UOB Plaza, 048624 Singapore (office). *Telephone:* 6533-9898 (office). *Fax:* 6534-2334 (office). *E-mail:* info@uobgroup.com (office). *Website:* www.uobgroup.com (office); www.uob.com.sg (office).

WEEKES, Sir Everton de Courcy, KCMG, GCM, OBE; Barbadian fmr cricketer; b. 26 Feb. 1925, Pickwick Gap, Westbury, St Michael; ed St Leonard's School, Bridgetown; right-hand batsman; teams: Barbados 1944–64, West Indies 1948–58; played in 48 Tests, scoring 4,445 runs (average 58.61, highest score 207) including 15 hundreds, took one wicket for eight runs (average 77.00); played in 152 First-class matches, scoring 12,010 runs (average 55.34, highest score 304 not out) including 36 hundreds, took 17 wickets (average 43.00), best bowling 4/38; Umpire, Int. Cricket Council (ICC) (four Tests, three One-Day Ints); Wisden Cricketer of the Year 1951, inducted into ICC Cricket Hall of Fame 2009. *Leisure interest:* int. bridge player.

WEEKES, Paula-Mae, LLB; Trinidad and Tobago lawyer, judge (retd), government official and head of state; *President;* single; ed Univ. of the West Indies, Cave Hill, Hugh Wooding Law School; called to the Bar 1982; worked in Office of Dir of Public Prosecutions 1982–93; entered pvt. legal practice 1993; Puisne Judge, Supreme Court of Trinidad and Tobago (Criminal Jurisdiction) 1996–2005; Judge, Court of Appeal 2005–16 (retd); Judge, Turks and Caicos Islands Court of Appeal 2017–18; Chancellor, Anglican Diocese of Trinidad & Tobago 1998–; Course Dir in Ethics, Hugh Wooding Law School 2011–16; Pres. of Trinidad and Tobago (first woman) 2018–. *Address:* President's House, Circular Rd, St Ann's, Port of Spain, Trinidad and Tobago (office). *Telephone:* 624-1261 (office). *Fax:* 624-1264 (office). *E-mail:* info@thepresident.tt (office). *Website:* www.thepresident.tt (office).

WEEKS, Milton A.; Liberian banking executive and central banker; b. 8 March 1964; s. of Rocheforte L. Weeks and Euphemia Weeks; two c.; ed George Mason Univ. and Syracuse Univ., USA; worked with financial insts in various sr positions for 25 years in several African countries, including Liberia, Zambia, Ghana, Malawi, South Africa and Nigeria; Asst Man. Citibank Liberia 1984–87, Citibank Zambia 1987–90; Gen. Man. Meridian Bank Liberia 1992–94; Vice-Pres. and CEO, First Commercial and Investment Bank 1994; Project Consultant (Information), CIBank, Malawi 1996–97, Dir 1997–98; worked for Standard Bank, South Africa; Man. Dir, Loita Investment Bank 1998–2001; Man. Dir, Stanbic Bank, Nigeria 2001–07; returned to Liberia 2007; joined Devin Corpn (financial man. and consultancy firm) as Man. Dir and CEO 2007; mem. Bd of Govs, Cen. Bank of Liberia 2014–, Exec. Gov. 2016–18; Head of Secr., Liberia Bankers Asscn 2008–14; Chair. Bd of Dirs Nat. Social Security and Welfare Corpn 2009–12; Chair. Bd of Dirs Safeway Cargo Handling Services; Pres. Rotary Club of Monrovia 2013–14; mem. Bd of Dirs Du Investment Corpn, Du Devt Corpn, MILCHAR Inc., Business Development Services & Incubator, Auriole Enterprises; mem. Exec. Council, Liberia Chamber of Commerce; Fellow, Inst. of Credit and Risk Man., Nigeria, Inst. of Credit Admin, Nigeria; Hon. mem. Chartered Inst. of Bankers, Nigeria. *Address:* c/o Office of the Executive Governor, Central Bank of Liberia, corner Warren and Carey Streets, POB 2048, 1000 Monrovia, Liberia (office).

WEERASETHAKUL, Apichatpong (Joe), MFA; Thai artist and filmmaker; b. 1970, Bangkok; ed Khon Kaen Univ., Art Inst. of Chicago, USA; began career as architect and multi-media artist before becoming filmmaker; f. Kick the Machine (production co.) 1999; mem. jury, Cannes Film Festival 2008; commissioned by UN to make short film (Mobile Men) to mark 60th anniversary of the Universal Declaration of Human Rights 2008; Chevalier, Ordre des arts et des lettres 2008, Officier, Ordre des arts et des lettres 2011; Silpathorn Award, Thai Office of

Contemporary Culture 2005, winner, Asia Art Award Forum (South Korea) 2010, Sharjah Biennial Prize (UAE) 2013, Fukuoka Prize 2013, Yanghyun Art Prize 2014, Artes Mundi Prize 2018, numerous other awards. *Films include:* Blissfully Yours (Prix Un Certain Regard, Cannes Film Festival 2002, Silver Screen Award: Young Cinema Award, Singapore Int. Film Festival 2003, FIPRESCI Prize, Buenos Aires Film Festival 2003) 2002, Tropical Malady (Jury Prize, Cannes Film Festival 2004, Grand Prize, Tokyo FilmEx 2004, Special Jury Prize, Singapore Int. Festival 2005, Best Film and Special Jury Prize, Int. Gay & Lesbian Film Festival, Turin, 2005) 2004, Syndromes and a Century 2006, A Letter to Uncle Boonmee (Grand Prize of the City of Oberhausen, Germany, Prize of the Jury of the Minister Pres. of N Rhine-Westphalia, Best Film, Prize of the Jury of the Pernambuco Asscn of Filmmakers, Janela Internacional de Cinema do Recife, Brazil) 2009, Uncle Boonmee Who Can Recall His Past Lives (Palme d'Or, Cannes Film Festival 2010) 2010. *Address:* Kick The Machine, 44/17 Ladprao 15, Jatujak, Bangkok 10900, Thailand (office). *E-mail:* kickthemachine.info@gmail.com (office). *Website:* www .kickthemachine.com (office).

WEERASOORIYA, Gen. C. S.; Sri Lankan army officer (retd) and diplomatist; m. Dilhani Weerasooriya; ed St Thomas Coll., Pakistan Mil. Acad., Nat. Defence Coll., India; commanded Operation Jayasikurui to regain the Liberation Tigers of Tamil Eelam-held Wanni and Mullaitivu areas and subsequently to open a land route through Wanni and Kilinochchi dists to link up with Jaffna Peninsula 1997; Commdr of the Army (rank of Lt-Gen.) 1998–2000; High Commr to Pakistan (also accred as Amb. to Tajikistan and Kyrgyzstan) 2001–07; mem. Bd of Dirs Ceylinco Life PLC 2010–; Patron, Pakistan-Sri Lanka Friendship Asscn, Pakistan-Sri Lanka Business Forum; Rana Wickrama Padakkama, Rana Sura Padakkama, Vishista Seva Vibhushanaya, Uttama Seva Padakkama; Sitara-i-Pakistan 2014.

WĘGLEŃSKI, Piotr, Dr habil.; Polish molecular geneticist; b. 29 June 1939, Swidniki; m. Teresa Juszczyk; two d.; ed Univ. of Warsaw; academic, Univ. of Warsaw 1961–, Pro-Rector 1985–88, 1990–96, Ordinary Prof. 1989–, Rector 1999–2002, 2002–05; Visiting Prof., MIT, USA 1987–88, Univ. of Paris-Sud 1991; mem. Programme Bd of Polish Radio 2010–; mem. Polish Genetic Soc., Warsaw Scientific Soc., Corresp. mem. Polish Acad. of Sciences 1994; Officier des Palmes académiques 2002, Commdr's Cross, Order of Polonia Restituta Polish 2005; Dr hc (Prikarpatsky State Univ.) 2002, (Sofia Univ.) 2003, (Podgorica Univ.) 2006, (Arequipa Univ.) 2008. *Publications:* Genetic Engineering (co-author) 1980, Molecular Genetics (co-author and ed.) 1996; numerous scientific articles. *Leisure interests:* tennis, travel, volleyball, ornithology. *Address:* Uniwersytet Warszawski, 00-927 Warsaw, ul. Krakowskie Przedmieście 26/28 (office); Centrum Nowych Technologii, Uniwersytet Warszawski, 00-927 Warsaw, ul. Banacha 2C, Poland (office). *Telephone:* (22) 5922243 (office). *Fax:* (22) 5540808 (office). *E-mail:* wegle@adm.uw.edu.pl (office). *Website:* www.uw.edu.pl (office).

WEHNER, Rüdiger, BA, PhD; German zoologist, neurobiologist and academic; *Professor, Institute of Molecular Life Sciences, University of Zurich;* b. 6 Feb. 1940, Nuremberg; m. Sibylle Segesser Brunegg; ed Univs of Frankfurt and Munich; Research Asst, Univ. of Frankfurt 1966–70; Asst, Inst. of Zoology, Univ. of Zurich 1967–70, Asst Prof. of Animal Physiology 1970–72, assoc. Prof. 1972–73, Prof. 1974–2005, Research Prof. Emer. 2005–08, Dir Inst. 1986–2005; Sr Research Fellow, Dept of Biology, Yale Univ., USA 1973–74; Andrew Dixon White Prof. (at Large), Cornell Univ., USA 1988–94; Non-Resident Perm. Fellow, Wissenschaftskolleg (Inst. for Advanced Study) 1991–2008; Visiting Prof., Biozentrum, Univ. of Würzburg 2007–10; mem. Advisory Bd Inst. for Integrative Life Sciences, Humboldt Univ., Berlin 2007; Assoc., Neurosciences Research Program (USA) 2010; mem. Academic Foundation of German People 1960–67; mem. Acad. of Natural Scientists Leopoldina, Halle (Saale) 1985, Academia Europaea 1989, Berlin-Brandenburg Acad. of Sciences 1995, Royal Swedish Physiographic Soc. 2000; Corresp. mem. Acad. of Sciences and Literature, Mainz 1977, Acad. of Sciences, Göttingen 1996, Bavarian Acad. of Sciences 1987; Corresp. mem. (abroad), Austrian Acad. of Sciences 1998; Chair. Section of Organismic and Evolutionary Biology, German Nat. Acad. of Sciences Leopoldina 2004–05; Senator for Leopoldina Adjunktenkreis Switzerland 2005; Fellow, Int. Soc. for Neuroethology 2012; Hon. mem. German Zoological Soc. 2006; Foreign Hon. mem. American Acad. of Arts and Sciences 2005; Hon. Dr rer. nat (Carl von Ossietzky Univ., Oldenburg) 2002, (Humboldt Univ., Berlin) 2005; Carus Medal, Leopoldina and Carus Award, City of Schweinfurt 1993, Karl-von-Frisch Medal, German Zoological Soc. 1994, Distinguished Scientist Award, UCLA 1996, Marcel Benoist Prize 2002, Humboldt Research Award 2007, King Faisal Int. Prize for Science 2008, Univ. Medal in Silver, Univ. of Tübingen 2009. *Publications:* numerous papers in professional journals. *Address:* Institute of Molecular Life Sciences, University of Zurich, Winterthurerstrasse 190, 8057 Zurich, Switzerland (office). *Telephone:* (44) 6354831 (office). *Fax:* (44) 6355716 (office). *E-mail:* rwehner@zool .uzh.ch (office). *Website:* www.neuroscience.ethz.ch (office); www.imls.uzh.ch (office).

WEI, Gen. Fenghe; Chinese army officer and government official; *Minister of National Defence;* b. 1954, Chiping, Liaocheng, Shandong Prov.; ed Second Artillery Corps Command Coll., Wuhan; joined CCP 1972; Deputy Head, PLA Operational Dept 2010–12; several command roles with PLA Second Artillery Force including Chief of Staff, Services and Arms, 53rd Base 2001–02, Commdr 2002–05, Deputy Chief of Staff 2005–06, Chief of Staff 2006–12, Commdr in Chief 2012–18; Head of PLA Strategic Missile Force 2012–15, Commdr PLA Rocket Force 2016–18; rank of Maj.-Gen. 2004, Lt-Gen. 2008, Gen. 2012; mem. State Council 2018–; Minister of Nat. Defence 2018–; Alt. mem. 17th CCP Cen. Cttee 2007–12; mem. 18th CCP Cen. Cttee 2012–17, 19th CCP Cen. Cttee 2017–; mem. 18th CCP Cen. Mil. Comm. 2012–17, 19th Cen. Military Comm. 2017–. *Address:* Ministry of National Defence, 20 Jingshanqian Jie, Beijing 100009, People's Republic of China (office). *Telephone:* (10) 66730000 (office). *Fax:* (10) 65962146 (office). *E-mail:* chinamod@chinamil.com.cn (office). *Website:* www.mod.gov.cn (office).

WEI, Ing-chou; Taiwanese business executive; *Chairman and CEO, Tingyi (Cayman Islands) Holdings Corporation;* m.; three c.; more than 30 years' experience in factory construction, production man. and research in relation to food production; joined Tingyi (Cayman Islands) Holdings Corpn (China's largest instant noodle producer) 1991, currently Chair. and CEO, introduced Master Kong instant noodles to Chinese consumers 1990s. *Address:* Tingyi (Cayman Islands)

Holdings Corpn, No. 15 The 3rd Street, Tianjin Economic-Technological Development Area, Tianjin 300457 (office); Tingyi (Cayman Islands) Holdings Corpn, Suite 5607, 56/F, Central Plaza, 18 Harbour Road, Wanchai, Hong Kong Special Administrative Region, People's Republic of China (office). *Telephone:* 2511-1911 (Hong Kong) (office). *Fax:* 2511-7911 (Hong Kong) (office). *E-mail:* info@tingyi.com (office). *Website:* www.tingyi.com (office).

WEI, Jiafu, MEng, PhD; Chinese shipping industry executive; b. 1950, Jiangsu; ed Wuhan Marine Coll., Dalian Maritime Univ., Tianjin Univ.; with Guangzhou Ocean Shipping Co. 1967–92; Gen. Man. Chinese-Tanzanian Jt Shipping Co., Tanzania 1992–93; Pres. COSCO Holdings Pte Ltd, Singapore 1993–95; Gen. Man. and CEO Tianjin Ocean Shipping Co. 1995–97, COSCO Bulk Carriers Co. Ltd 1997–98, Exec. Pres. and CEO China Ocean Shipping (Group) Co. (COSCO) Group 1998–2011, Chair. 2011–13, Sec. CCP Party Cttee; Chair. China Shipowners' Asscn, China Shipowners Mutual Assurance Asscn, China Fed. of Industrial Econs, China Group Cos Promotion Asscn; apptd Vice-Chair. China Merchants Bank 2001; mem. Panama Canal Authority Advisory Bd, Harvard Business School Asia-Pacific Advisory Bd; mem. 17th CCP Cen. Cttee Cen. Comm. for Discipline Inspection 2007–12; mem. Hong Kong Man. Asscn 2006; Hon. Dean, Shanghai Maritime Univ. School of Econs and Man., Hon. Chief Commdr with Four Star rank of Massport Police, AAPA Security Cttee and Massachusetts Port Authority 2011; Commdr, Order of Leopold II (Belgium) 2005; Hall of the Fame, Lloyd's List and Maritime Asia 2003, Port Authority of Long Beach Port Pilot Award 2004, Int. Who's Who Professional, Int. Who's Who Historical Soc. 2004, Valuable Man. of the Year, China's leading media 2004, Economic Booster Award, Massachusetts Alliance for Econ. Devt 2004, Port Pilot Award, Port Authority of Long Beach 2004, Int. Maritime Achievement Award 2005, CCTV Annual Econ. Leaders 2005, Leader in Global Shipping and Logistics, US Journal of Commerce 2006, Outstanding Dir's Award, Hong Kong Dirs Asscn 2008, CMA Commodore Award 2009, named China Charity Amb. by China Charity Asscn 2009, Personality Award, Sea Trade 2009, CCTV Outstanding Contrib. Award of Chinese Brands 2009, commended by US House of Reps as a People's Amb. 2009, Guardian of American Workers Award, Int. Longshoremen Asscn (USA) 2011.

WEI, Jingsheng; Chinese dissident; fmr mem. Red Guards and PLA; active in pro-democracy movt, contrib. to underground magazine Exploration 1978; sentenced to 15 years' imprisonment for allegedly leaking mil. secrets to a foreign journalist and for counter-revolutionary activities Spring 1979, released Sept. 1993; held incommunicado and without charge April 1994; sentenced to 14 years' imprisonment for alleged subversive activities 1995; deported March 1998; f. Wei Jingsheng Foundation, New York City 1998; f. Overseas Chinese Democracy Coalition 1998; Olof Palme Memorial Prize 1994, Sakharov Prize for Freedom of Thought 1996, Robert F. Kennedy Human Rights Award 1996, Nat. Endowment for Democracy Award 1997. *Publication:* The Courage to Stand Alone. *Address:* Wei Jingsheng Foundation, PO Box 15449, Washington, DC 20003, USA. *Telephone:* (1) 202-270-6980. *Website:* www.weijingsheng.org.

WEI, Wei; Chinese singer; b. 28 Sept. 1963, Hohhot, Inner Mongolia; m. Michael J. Smith (divorced 2004); three s.; singer at 11th Asian Games, Beijing 1990, performed a duet with Julio Iglesias at East Asian Games, Shanghai 1993; represented Asia at the ceremony of the Olympic Games, Atlanta, USA 1996; performed at closing ceremony, Beijing 2008 Summer Olympics; winner Nat. Young Singers' contest on Chinese TV 1986, Sopot Int. Music Festival 1987. *Film appearance:* The Singer's Story. *Recordings include:* albums: The Album 1986, Bright Eyes 1987, Endless Love 1989, I Love My Motherland 1990, Famous Songs 1992, The Twilight 1994, Wei Wei 1998, Wei Wei's Devotion 1999, Dedication of Love 2001, Myths of China 2005, Yang-Chin 2006, 20x20 2008. *Address:* Wei Wei International Management, Jing Da International 4E, Chao Yang Park West Road 11, 100026 Beijing, People's Republic of China (office). *E-mail:* info@weiweiint.com (office).

WEI, Yang, BS, MS, PhD; Chinese engineer and academic; b. 16 Feb. 1954, Beijing; ed Tsinghua Univ., Brown Univ., USA; Prof. of Solid Mechanics, Tsinghua Univ. 1989, Chair. Dept of Eng Mechanics 1997–2004, Yantz Prof. of the Ministry of Educ. 1999–2004, Chair. Univ. Academic Cttee 2004–06, Dean, School of Aerospace 2004, Adjunct Prof. 2005–; Pres. Zhejiang Univ. 2006–13; Visiting Scientist, Univ. of Sheffield, UK 1987–88, Univ. of Calif., Santa Barbara, USA 1993, 1995, Taiwan Univ. 1996–97, Princeton Univ., USA 1998; Visiting Prof. Inst. of Mechanics, Grenoble, France 1988, Brown Univ., USA 1990, Tokyo Inst. of Tech., Japan 2000–01, Univ. of Illinois, Urbana-Champaign, USA 2002; Vice-Pres. 1998–2006, 2010–14, Chinese Soc. of Theoretical and Applied Mechanics, now Pres. 2014–; Ed.-in-Chief, Acta Mechanica Sinica 1999–2003; Pres. Far East and Oceanic Fracture Soc. 2004–08; Pres. Nat. Natural Sciences Foundation 2013, also Chair., Cttee for Nat. Natural Science Award; Chair. Nat. Postdoctoral Funds of China 2016–; Council Mem. China Asscn of Science and Tech. 1996–2005, 2011–15; mem. Scientific Cttee, Ministry of Educ. 1996–2005; mem. Gen. Ass. 2000–, Int. Union of Theoretical and Applied Mechanics, also Chair. Working Party 7 2000–12 and Bureau Mem. 2012–16; mem. Chinese Acad. of Sciences 2003–, also Chair. Technological Science Division 2008–12, 2016–; mem. Nat. People's Congress (NPC) 2007–; Int. Academic Advisory Panel for High Educ., Singapore 2012–; mem. Editorial Bds International Journal of Damage Mechanics, Fatigue and Fracture of Engineering Materials and Structures, International Journal of Solids and Structures, Archive in Applied Mechanics; Fellow, Third World Acad. of Sciences 2004–, also Head of Division, Eng Science 2008–12; Hon. Pres. Nat. Natural Sciences Foundation; Hon. DEng (Hong Kong Polytechnic Univ.) 2011, DS (Brown Univ.) 2012, DJur (Univ. of Bristol) 2013; three Scientific Achievement Awards, State Educ. Comm., Young Scientists Award 1994, Nat. Natural Science Award 1995, Scientific Achievement Award, Ministry of Educ. 2002, Brown Univ. Engineering Alumni Medal (BEAM) 2009. *Publications:* Mesoplasticity and its Applications (jtly) 1993, Macroscopic and Microscopic Fracture Mechanics 1995, Mechatronic Reliability 2001, Interfacial and Nanoscale Failure (co-ed.) 2003; over 240 technical papers. *Address:* National Natural Sciences Foundation, 83 Shuangqing Rd, Haidian, Beijing 100085, People's Republic of China (office). *Telephone:* (10) 62327001 (office). *Fax:* (10) 62327004 (office). *E-mail:* bic@nsfc.gov.cn (office). *Website:* www.nsfc.gov.cn (office).

WEICKER, Lowell Palmer, Jr, LLB; American fmr politician; b. 16 May 1931, Paris, France; s. of Lowell Palmer Weicker and Mary Paulsen Weicker (née

Bickford); m. 1st Camille Di Lorenzo Butler; eight c.; m. 2nd Claudia Testa Ingram 1984; ed Lawrenceville School, Yale Univ. and Univ. of Virginia; State Rep. in Conn. Gen. Ass. 1963–69; US Rep., Fourth Congressional Dist, Conn. 1969–71; Senator from Conn. 1971–89; Gov. of Conn. 1991–95; 1st Selectman of Greenwich 1964–68; mem. Select Cttee for Investigation of the Watergate Case 1973; fmr mem. Senate Appropriations Cttee, Senate Labor and Human Resources Cttee, fmr Chair. Senate Small Business Cttee, Sub-cttee on State, Justice, Commerce, the Judiciary and related agencies, Senate Energy and Natural Resources Cttee; fmr Republican, then Ind.; Pres. Bd of Dirs, Trust for America's Health 2001–11; mem. Bd of Dirs Compuware Co. 1996–, World Wrestling Entertainment 1996–2011, Medallion Financial Corpn 2003–, Phoenix, Duff & Phelps Mutual Funds; Chair. Pew Foundation Environmental Health Comm. 2000, Century Fund Comm. 2001; fmr Dir United States Tobacco. *Publication:* Maverick: My Life in Politics 1995. *Leisure interests:* tennis, scuba, history.

WEIDEL, Alice Elisabeth, Dr.rer.pol; German management consultant and politician; *Co-Chair, AfD Parliamentary Group;* b. 6 Feb. 1979, Gütersloh; pnr Sarah Bossard; two c.; ed Univ. of Bayreuth; analyst, Goldman Sachs, Frankfurt 2005–06; worked for Allianz Global Investors 2011–13; with Heristo AG, Bad Rothenfelde 2013–14; freelance business consultant 2014–; mem. Bundestag (AfD) for Lake Constance 2017–; mem. Alternative for Germany (AfD) 2012–, AfD Leader in Bundestag 2017–, co-Lead Cand. at 2017 election, co-Chair., AfD Parl. Group 2017–. *Address:* Alternative für Deutschland, Schillstr. 9, 10785 Berlin, Germany (office). *Telephone:* (30) 22056960 (office). *Fax:* (30) 220569629 (office). *E-mail:* bgs@alternativefuer.de (office). *Website:* www.afd.de (office); www.afd.de/alice-weidel/.

WEIDENFELD, Werner, DPhil; German political scientist and academic; *Professor of Political Science and Director, Center for Applied Policy Research, Geschwister Scholl Institute for Political Science, Ludwig-Maximilians-Universität München;* b. 2 July 1947, Cochem; s. of Dr Josef Weidenfeld and Maria Weidenfeld (née Walther); m. Gabriele Kokott-Weidenfeld 1976; ed Univ. of Bonn; Prof. of Political Science, Univ. of Mainz 1976–95; Assoc. Prof., Sorbonne, Paris 1986–88; Co-ordinator for German-American Co-operation 1987–99; Prof. of Political Science, Ludwig-Maximilians-Universität München 1995–, Dir Centre for Applied Policy Research; Perm. Guest Prof., Remnim Univ., Beijing, People's Repub. of China 2000–; mem. Exec. Bd Bertelsmann Foundation, Gütersloh 1992–2007; Bundesverdienstkreuz (First Class) 1998, Commdr, Ordinul serviciul Credincios of the Repub. of Romania; Dr hc; Columbus Medal, German-American Soc., Munich 1991, Europe Medal (Bavaria) 1996, Bavarian Europe-Schoolbook Award 1997, Gen. Lucius D. Clay Medal, Asscn of German-American Clubs 1998, World of Difference Award, Anti-Defamation League 1999, European Cultural Award, European Cultural Foundation 2001. *Publications:* Die Englandpolitik Gustav Stresemanns 1972, Konrad Adenauer und Europa 1976, Europa 2000 1980, Die Frage nach der Einheit der deutschen Nation 1981, Die Identität der Deutschen 1983, Die Bilanz der Europäischen Integration 1984, Nachdenken über Deutschland 1985, 30 Jahre EG 1987, Geschichtsbewusstsein der Deutschen 1987, Der deutsche Weg 1990, Jahrbuch der Europäischen Integration (ed.) 1980, Die Deutschen – Profil einer Nation 1991, Europa von A bis Z, Taschenbuch der Europäischen Integration (co-ed. with Wolfgang Wessels) 1991, Handwörterbuch zur deutschen Einheit 1992, Osteuropa: Herausforderungen-Probleme-Strategien 1992, Technopoly, Europa im globalen Wettbewerb 1993, Maastricht in der Analyse, Materialien zur Europäischen Union (ed.) 1994, Europa '96: Reformprogramm für die Europäische Union (ed.) 1994, Reform der Europäischen Union 1995, Kulturbruch mit Amerika? 1996, Handbuch zur deutschen Einheit 1996, Demokratie am Wendepunkt? (ed.) 1996, Europa öffnen–Anforderungen an die Erweiterung (ed.) 1997, Aussenpolitik für die deutsche Einheit: Die Entscheidigungsjahre 1989/90 1998, Amsterdam in der Analyse: Strategien für Europa (ed.) 1998, Handbuch zur deutschen Einheit 1949–1989–1999 (ed.) 1999, Deutschland-Trendbuch (ed.) 2001, Herausforderung Terrorismus 2004, Wie Zukunft ensteht 2002, Europa-Handbuch (ed.) 2004, Die Europäische Verfassung in der Analyse (ed.) 2005, Managing Integration (ed.) 2005, Rivalität der Partner (ed.) 2005, Die Europäische Verfassung verstehen 2006, Partners at Odds 2006, Werte 2006, Understanding the European Constitution 2007, Europa leicht gemacht 2007, Reformen kommunizieren (ed.) 2007, Europäische Identität: Voraussetzungen und Strategien (co-ed. with Nida Rümelin) 2007, Lissabon in der Analyse – Der Reformvertrag der Europäischen Union (ed.) 2008, Die Europäische Union – Politisches System und Politikbereiche (ed.) 2008, Die Staatenwelt Europas (ed.) 2009, Die Europäische Union 2010, Deutsche Kontraste (co-ed. with Manuela Glaab and Michael Weigl) 2010. *Address:* Center for Applied Policy Research, Geschwister Scholl Institute for Political Science, Ludwig-Maximilians-Universität München, Maria-Theresia-Str. 21, 81675 Munich (office); Oettingenstr. 67, 80538 Munich, Germany (home). *Telephone:* (89) 21801300 (office). *Fax:* (89) 21809042 (office). *E-mail:* cap.office@lrz.uni-muenchen.de (office). *Website:* www.cap-lmu.de/english/index.php (office).

WEIDMANN, Jens, PhD; German economist and central banker; *President, Deutsche Bundesbank;* b. 20 April 1968, Solingen; m. Anja Weidmann; one s., one d.; ed Université de Droit, d'Economie et des Sciences, Aix-Marseille III, France, Rheinische Friedrich-Wilhelms Univ., Bonn; internship at Banque de France; Research Asst, Inst. for Int. Econ. Policy, Univ. of Bonn 1994–97; Economist with IMF, Washington, DC 1997–99; Sec.-Gen. German Council of Econ. Experts 1999–2003; Head of Monetary Policy and Analysis Div. and Deputy Head of Econs Dept, Deutsche Bundesbank 2003–06; Head, Dept of Econ. and Financial Policy, Fed. Chancellor's Office 2006–11, also personal rep. of Chancellor Angela Merkel charged with preparations for world econ. summits of G8 and G20 countries; Pres. Deutsche Bundesbank 2011–; Chair. BIS, Basel, Switzerland 2015–; mem. Governing Council, European Cen. Bank 2011–. *Address:* Deutsche Bundesbank, Wilhelm-Epstein-Strasse 14, 60431 Frankfurt am Main, Germany (office). *Telephone:* (69) 95663511 (office). *Fax:* (69) 95663077 (office). *E-mail:* info@bundesbank.de (office). *Website:* www.bundesbank.de (office); www.bis.org (office).

WEILL, Sanford I., BA; American banker and philanthropist; *Chairman Emeritus, Citigroup Inc.;* b. 16 March 1933, New York City; s. of Max Weill and Etta Weill (née Kalika); m. Joan Mosher 1955; one s. one d.; ed Peekskill Mil. Acad., Cornell Univ. School Business and Public Admin.; co-f. Carter, Berlind, Potoma & Weill, New York 1960 (became Carter, Berlind & Weill 1962, then Cogan, Berlind, Weill & Levitt 1968), Chair. 1965–84 (co. became CBWL-Hayden, Stone, Inc. 1970, Hayden Stone, Inc. 1972, Shearson Hayden Stone (following merger with Shearson Hammill & Co. 1974), Shearson Loeb Rhoades (following merger with Loeb, Rhoades, Hornblower & Co. 1979), co. sold to American Express 1981, Pres. American Express Co. 1983–84, Chair. and CEO Fireman's Fund Insurance Co. (subsidiary) 1984–85 (resgnd); apptd Chair., Pres., CEO Commercial Credit Co., Baltimore 1986; Chair., CEO Primerica Corpn 1989–, Pres. 1989–92; Chair., CEO Travelers Group 1996–98, Co-Chair. Citigroup (following merger between Citicorp and Travelers Group) 1998–2000, CEO 1998–2003, Chair. 2000–06, Chair. Emer. 2006–; f. Nat. Acad. Foundation 1982; Dir Terra Nova Insurance Co. 1984–; Class A Dir, Fed. Reserve Bank of New York 2001; Chair. Carnegie Hall 1991–; mem. Midwest Stock Exchange Bd; Assoc. mem. New York Stock Exchange, Bd of Overseers Cornell Medical Coll., Business Cttee Museum of Modern Art, New York; mem. American Acad. of Arts and Sciences 2012; Baruch Medal for Business and Civic Leadership, Baruch Coll. 2003, Carnegie Medal of Philanthropy Award (with his wife) 2009. *Address:* Citigroup Inc., 399 Park Avenue, New York, NY 10013, USA (office). *Telephone:* (212) 559-1000 (office). *Fax:* (212) 793-3946 (office). *Website:* www.citigroup.com (office).

WEINBACH, Lawrence A., BS (Hons), CPA; American business executive; *Managing Director, Yankee Hill Capital Management LLC;* b. 8 Jan. 1940, Brooklyn, New York; s. of Max Weinbach and Winnefred Weinbach; m. Patricia Lieter 1961; two s. one d.; ed Wharton School, Univ. of Pennsylvania; joined Arthur Andersen 1961, Man. Pnr, Stamford, Conn. office 1974–83, Man. Pnr, New York office 1983–87, COO 1987–89, Man. Pnr and CEO 1989–97; Chair., Pres. and CEO Unisys Corpn 1997–2004, Exec. Chair. 2005–06; Man. Dir Yankee Hill Capital Man. LLC 2006–; Chair. Great Western Products Holdings LLC 2009–; mem. Bd of Dirs Avon Products 1999–2013, UBS AG 2001–08, Quadra Realty Trust Inc. 2007–, Discover Bank 2009–; Outside Ind. Dir, Discover Financial Services LLC 2007–, Lead Dir 2009–; Trustee, Univ. of Pennsylvania, Carnegie Hall, Wharton School; fmr Trustee, The Carnegie Hall Corpn; mem. Bd Nat. Security Telecommunications Advisory Cttee. *Leisure interests:* reading, golf. *Address:* Yankee Hill Capital Management LLC, 300 East 42nd Street, Suite 1400, New York, NY 10017, USA (office). *Telephone:* (646) 356-8450 (office). *Fax:* (212) 661-2601 (office). *E-mail:* lawrence.weinbach@yankeehillcapital.com (office). *Website:* www.yankeehillcapital.com (office).

WEINBERG, Adam D., BA, MFA; American museum director; *Alice Pratt Brown Director, Whitney Museum of American Art;* ed Brandeis Univ., State Univ. of NY at Buffalo; Dir of Educ. and Asst Curator, Walker Art Center, Minneapolis 1981–89; Artistic and Program Dir, American Center in Paris 1989–93; Sr Curator of Perm. Collection, Whitney Museum of American Art, NY 1993–99, Alice Pratt Brown Dir of Museum 2003–, also Trustee; Mary Stripp and R. Crosby Kemper Dir Addison Gallery of American Art at Phillips Acad., Andover 1999–2003, also Curator of Temporary Exhbns; mem. Bd of Dirs Andy Warhol Foundation for the Visual Arts, Storm King Art Center, Colby Coll. Museum of Art. *Address:* Whitney Museum of Modern Art, 945 Madison Avenue at 75th Street, New York, NY 10021, USA (office). *Telephone:* (212) 570-3633 (office). *Fax:* (212) 570-4169 (office). *E-mail:* info@whitney.org (office). *Website:* www.whitney.org (office).

WEINBERG, Robert A., PhD; American biochemist and academic; *Daniel K. Ludwig Professor for Cancer Research, Massachusetts Institute of Technology;* b. 11 Nov. 1942, Pittsburgh, Pa; s. of Dr Fritz E. Weinberg and Lore W. Weinberg (née Reichhardt); m. Amy Shulman 1976; one s. one d.; ed Massachusetts Inst. of Tech.; Instructor in Biology, Stillman Coll., Ala 1965–66; Fellow, Weizmann Inst., Israel 1969–70, Salk Inst., Calif. 1970–72; Research Assoc. Fellow, MIT 1972–73, Asst Prof., Dept of Biology and Center for Cancer Research 1973–76, Assoc. Prof. 1976–82, Founding mem. and Prof., Whitehead Inst. for Biomedical Research 1982–, currently Daniel K. Ludwig Prof. for Cancer Research; mem. NAS; Hon. ScD (Northwestern Univ.) 1984; numerous awards, including 'Scientist of the Year', Discover magazine 1982, Bristol-Myers Award for Distinguished Achievement in Cancer Research 1984, Nat. Medal of Science 1997, Wolf Prize in Medicine 2004, Landon-AACR Prize for Cancer Research 2006, Otto Warburg Medal 2007, Breakthrough Prize in Life Sciences (co-recipient) 2013. *Achievements include:* identified and characterized both the first oncogene and the first tumour suppressor gene. *Leisure interests:* house building, gardening, genealogy. *Address:* Whitehead Institute, 9 Cambridge Center, Cambridge, MA 02142 (office); Department of Biology, Massachusetts Institute of Technology, Cambridge, MA 02139, USA (office). *Telephone:* (617) 258-5159 (office). *Fax:* (617) 258-5213 (office). *E-mail:* weinberg@wi.mit.edu (office). *Website:* www.wi.mit.edu/research/faculty/weinberg.html (office); weinberglab.wi.mit.edu (office); biology.mit.edu/people/robert_weinberg (office); wi.mit.edu/people/faculty/weinberg (office).

WEINBERG, Serge, LenD; French business executive; *Chairman, Sanofi SA;* b. 10 Feb. 1951; ed Univ. of Paris, Institut d'Etudes Politiques de Paris, École Nationale d'Admin, Strasbourg; Pvt. Prin. Sec. to Budget Minister 1981–82; Deputy Dir-Gen. FR3 1982–83; Chair. Havas Tourisme 1983–87; Dir-Gen. Pallas Finances 1987–90; Chair. Rexel (affiliate of Pinault) 1991–95, mem. Man. Bd, Pinault Printemps-Redoute (PPR) 1993–2005, Chair. and CEO 1995–2005, mem. Supervisory Bd, PPR Interactive; Founder and Chair. Weinberg Capital Partners 2005–; Chair. (non-exec.), Accor 2006–09; mem. Bd of Dirs, Sanofi-Aventis 2009–, Chair. 2010– (name changed to Sanofi May 2011), Interim CEO 2014–15, Ind. Dir 2015–; Chair. Supervisory Bd, Conforama Holding, France-Printemps, Guilbert SA, Redcats; Vice-Chair. Supervisory Bd, Schneider Electric; mem. Supervisory Bd, Boucheron Holding, Gucci Group NV (Netherlands), Yves Saint Laurent Perfumes; Dir, Fnac SA, Artémis, Gucci, French Asscn of Pvt. Enterprises, Soc. des Amis du Musée d'Orsay); mem. Growth Release Cttee (Attali Cttee) 2007–08; Founding mem. and Treas., Institut du Cerveau et de la Moelle Épinière (IM—Brain and Spinal Cord Inst.); mem. Nat. Econ. Comm. *Address:* Weinberg Capital Partners, 40 rue La Boétie, 75008 Paris (office); Sanofi SA, 174 avenue de France, 75013 Paris Cedex 13, France (office). *Telephone:* 1-53-53-55-00 (Weinberg) (office); 1-53-77-42-23 (Sanofi) (office). *Fax:* 1-53-53-55-19 (Weinberg) (office); 1-53-77-42-65 (Sanofi) (office). *E-mail:* serge.weinberg@weinbergcapital.com (office); info@sanofi.com (office). *Website:* www.weinbergcapital.com (office); www.sanofi.com (office).

WEINBERG, Steven, PhD; American physicist and academic; *Jack S. Josey-Welch Foundation Chair in Science and Regental Professor and Director, Theory*

Research Group, Department of Physics, University of Texas; b. 3 May 1933, New York; s. of Fred Weinberg and Eva Weinberg; m. Louise Goldwasser 1954; one d.; ed Cornell Univ., Univ. of Copenhagen, Denmark, Princeton Univ.; mem. staff, Columbia Univ. 1957–59, Lawrence Radiation Lab. 1959–60, Univ. of Calif., Berkeley 1960–69; Prof. of Physics, MIT 1969–73; Higgins Prof. of Physics, Harvard Univ. 1973–83; Sr Scientist, Smithsonian Astrophysical Observatory 1973–83, Sr Consultant 1983–; Josey Chair and Regental Prof. of Science, Univ. of Texas, Austin 1982–, also Dir Theory Research Group; Co-Ed. Cambridge Univ. Press Monographs on Mathematical Physics 1978; Dir Jerusalem Winter School of Theoretical Physics 1983–93; mem. A.P. Sloan Foundation Science Book Cttee 1985–90, Einstein Archives Int. Advisory Bd 1988–, Scientific Policy Cttee, Supercollider Lab. 1989–93, American Acad. of Arts and Sciences 1968–, NAS 1972–, Council for Foreign Relations, President's Cttee on the Nat. Medal of Science 1979–80, Royal Soc. 1982–, American Philosophical Soc. 1983–; fmr mem. Council, American Physical Soc., Int. Astronomical Union, Philosophical Soc. of Tex. (Pres. 1994); Loeb Lecturer, Harvard Univ. and Visiting Prof. MIT 1966–69, Richtmeyer Lecturer of American Asscn of Physics Teachers 1974, Scott Lecturer, Cavendish Lab. 1975, Silliman Lecturer, Yale Univ. 1977, Lauritsen Lecturer, Calif. Inst. of Tech. 1979, Bethe Lecturer, Cornell Univ. 1979, Harris Lecturer, Northwestern Univ. 1982, Cherwell-Simon Lecturer, Oxford Univ. 1983, Bampton Lecturer, Columbia Univ. 1983, Hilldale Lecturer, Univ. of Wisconsin 1985, Brickweede Lecturer, Johns Hopkins Univ. 1986, Dirac Lecturer, Univ. of Cambridge 1986, Klein Lecturer, Univ. of Stockholm 1989, Sackler Lecturer, Univ. of Copenhagen 1994, Brittin Lecturer, Univ. of Colorado 1994, Gibbs Lecturer, American Math. Soc. 1996, Bochner Lecturer, Rice Univ. 1997, Sanchez Lecturer, Witherspoon Lecturer, Washington Univ. 2001; Hon. DSc (Knox Coll.) 1978, (Chicago, Yale, Rochester) 1979, (City Univ., New York) 1980, (Clark Univ.) 1982, (Dartmouth) 1984, (Weizmann Inst.) 1985, (Columbia) 1990, (Salamanca) 1992, (Padua) 1992, (Barcelona) 1996, (Bates Coll.) 2002, (McGill Univ.) 2003, (Univ. of Waterloo) 2004, (Renssalear Polytechnic Inst.) 2016, Hon. DLitt (Washington Coll.) 1985; J. R. Oppenheimer Prize 1973, Dannie Heinemann Mathematical Physics Prize 1977, American Inst. of Physics-U.S. Steel Foundation Science Writing Award 1977, Elliott Cresson Medal, Franklin Inst. 1979, Joint Winner, Nobel Prize for Physics 1979, James Madison Medal (Princeton) 1991, Nat. Medal of Science 1991, Andrew Gemant Award 1997, Piazzi Prize 1998, Lewis Thomas Prize Honoring the Scientist as Poet 1999, Benjamin Franklin Medal, American Philosophical Soc. 2004, James Joyce Award, Univ. Coll. Dublin) 2009, Career Research Excellence Award, Univ. of Texas Co-Op 2012, Award for Excellence in General Nonfiction, Austin Public Library Friends Foundation 2013. *Publications include:* Gravitation and Cosmology 1972, The First Three Minutes 1977, The Discovery of Subatomic Particles 1982, Elementary Particles and the Laws of Physics (with R. P. Feynman) 1987, Dreams of a Final Theory 1993, The Quantum Theory of Fields (Vol. I) 1995, (Vol. II) 1996, (Vol. III) 2000, Facing Up 2001, Lake Views: This World and the Universe 2010, Lectures on Quantum Mechanics 2012, To Explain the World: The Discovery of Modern Science 2015, Third Thoughts 2018; and over 250 articles. *Leisure interest:* medieval history. *Address:* Department of Physics, University of Texas, Theory Group, 2515 Speedway, Stop C1600, Austin, TX 78712-1192, USA (office). *Telephone:* (512) 471-4394 (office). *Fax:* (512) 471-4888 (office). *E-mail:* weinberg@physics.utexas.edu (office). *Website:* www.ph.utexas.edu/~weintech/weinberg.html (office).

WEINBERGER, Mark A., BA, MBA, JD; American business executive; *Global Chairman and CEO, EY;* b. Scranton, Pa; m. Nancy Weinberger; four c.; ed Emory Univ., Case Western Reserve Univ., Georgetown Univ. Law Center; joined Ernst & Young (now EY) Tax Dept 1987, co-f. Washington Counsel, PC 1996 (acquired by EY May 2000), Head, EY US Nat. Tax Dept 2000–01, becoming EY Global Vice-Chair. of Tax 2008–2013, Global Chair. and CEO 2013–; fmr Chief Tax and Budget Counsel to Senator John Danforth; apptd by Pres. Bill Clinton as Chief of Staff, Bipartisan Comm. on Entitlement and Tax Reform 1994; Asst Sec. of the Treasury for Tax Policy 2001–02; Co-Chair., Russia Foreign Investment Advisory Council; Chair., Int. Business Leaders Advisory Council to Mayor of Shanghai; mem. World Econ. Forum Int. Business Council; mem. Exec. Cttee US Business Roundtable; mem. Bd of Dirs American Council for Capital Formation, The Tax Council; Vice-Chair. Corp. Fund Bd, Kennedy Center for the Performing Arts; mem. Bd of Trustees US Council for Int. Business, Greater Washington Partnership, The Concord Coalition, Emory Univ., Case Western Reserve Univ.; Dr hc (American Univ. Kogod School of Business); Cornell Univ. Robert S. Hatfield Fellowship in Econ. Educ. Award 2015, Tax Council Policy Inst. Pillar of Excellence Award 2015. *Address:* EY, 1101 New York Avenue, NW, Washington, DC 20005, USA (office). *Telephone:* (202) 327-6000 (office). *Fax:* (202) 327-6200 (office). *Website:* www.ey.com (office).

WEINER, Matthew, MFA; American television producer and writer; b. 29 June 1965, Baltimore; m. Linda Brettler; four s.; ed Wesleyan Univ., Univ. of Southern California. *Television includes* The Naked Truth (writer) 1995, Becker (producer and writer) 1999–2002, Andy Richter Controls the Universe (producer) 2002–03, The Sopranos (writer and exec. producer) 2004–07 (Emmy for Outstanding Drama Series 2004, 2007, TV Producer of Year awards in Episodic, Producers' Guild of America 2005, 2008, Best Dramatic Series award, Writers' Guild of America 2007), Mad Men (creator and exec. producer) 2007–15 (Best New Series award, Writers' Guild of America 2008, Emmy for Outstanding Writing for a Drama Series 2008, 2010, Emmy for Outstanding Drama Series 2008, 2010, 2011, Best TV Series - Drama, Golden Globe award, Hollywood Foreign Press Asscn 2009, 2010, Norman Felton Producer of Year award in TV - Drama, Producers' Guild of America 2009, 2010, Best Dramatic Series, Writers' Guild of America 2009). *Address:* c/o AMC, 11 Penn Plaza, 15th Floor, New York, NY 1000, USA (office). *Website:* www.amctv.com/shows/mad-men/crew/matthew-weiner (office).

WEINGARTEN, David Michael, BA, MArch; American architect; *Principal, Ace Architects;* b. 22 Jan. 1952, Fort Ord, Calif.; s. of Saul M. Weingarten and Miriam E. Moore; one s.; ed Monterey High School, Yale Univ. and Univ. of California, Berkeley; Partner, Ace Architects 1979–, now Prin.; Lecturer, Univ. of California, Berkeley 1980–81; Founder and Partner, Piraneseum LLC 2012–; Graham Foundation for Advances Studies Award 1987, Interiors Magazine '40 under 40' Award 1990, Architectural Digest 'AD 100' Award 1994, 1996. *Publications:* Souvenir Buildings/Miniature Monuments 1996, Monumental Miniatures 1997, Bay Area Style: San Francisco Bay Region Houses 2004, Ten Houses: Ace Architects 2000, California Ranch Houses (co-author) 2009; articles for several design and other periodicals. *Address:* Ace Architects, 330 Second Street #1, Oakland, CA 94607, USA (office). *Telephone:* (510) 452-0775 (office). *Fax:* (510) 452-1175 (office). *E-mail:* ace@aceland.com (office). *Website:* www.aceland.com (office); www.piraneseum.com (office).

WEINGARTNER, Paul Andreas, DPhil; Austrian academic; *Professor Emeritus of Philosophy, Institut für Philosophie, Universität Salzburg;* b. 8 June 1931, Innsbruck; s. of Karl Weingartner and Maria Weingartner; five s. one d.; ed Univ. of Innsbruck; Research Fellow, Univ. of London 1961–62; Research Asst Inst. für Wissenschaftstheorie, Int. Research Centre, Salzburg 1962–67, Chair. Dept I (Philosophy of Natural Science) 1967–72; Assoc. Prof. of Philosophy, Univ. of Salzburg 1970, Prof. of Philosophy 1971, now Prof. Emer., Chair. Inst. für Philosophie 1971–79, 1988–90, 1994–98, Chair. Inst. für Wissenschaftstheorie 1972–; mem. Acad. Internationale de Philosophie des Sciences 1975–; New York Acad. of Sciences 1997–; Dr hc (M. Curie Univ., Poland) 1995. *Publications include:* Wissenschaftstheorie (two vols) 1976, 1978, Logisch-philosophische Untersuchungen zu Werten und Normen 1996, Zu philosophie-historischen Themen 1996, Basic Questions on Truth 2000; Evil, Different Kinds, In the Light of a Modern Theodicy 2003; Laws of Nature (with P. Mittelstaedt) 2005, Omniscience: From a Logical Point of View 2008; ed of 36 vols; about 150 research articles. *Leisure interests:* sport (climbing, skiing), photography. *Address:* Department of Philosophy, University of Salzburg, Franziskanergasse 1, 5020 Salzburg, Austria (office). *E-mail:* paul.weingartner@sbg.ac.at (office). *Website:* www.uni-salzburg.at/phs (office).

WEINRIB, Ernest J., BA, LLD, PhD, FRSC; Canadian professor of law; *Cecil A. Wright Professor of Law, University of Toronto;* b. 1943, Toronto; m. Lorraine Eistenstat; one s. two d.; ed Univ. of Toronto, Harvard Univ., USA; Asst Prof. of Classics, Univ. of Toronto 1968–72, Asst Prof. of Law 1972–75, Assoc. Prof. of Law 1975–81, Prof. of Law 1981, apptd Univ. Prof. 1999, Cecil A. Wright Prof. of Law 2000–; Visiting Prof. of Law, Univ. of Tel-Aviv, Israel 1979, Yale Law School, USA 1984; served as Book Review Ed. Univ. of Toronto Law Journal; mem. Editorial Cttee Ratio Juris, Law and Philosophy Library; mem. Advisory Bd Israel Law Review; Fellow, Royal Soc. of Canada; Killam Research Fellowship 1986–88, Connaught Senior Fellowship, Univ. of Toronto 1990–91; Foreign Hon. mem. American Acad. of Arts and Sciences 2008; Teaching Award, Ontario Confed. of Univ. Faculty Asscns 2007, Canada Council for the Arts Killam Prize 2009. *Publications:* The Idea of Private Law 1995, Tort Law: Cases and Materials 1997; numerous essays and articles. *Address:* Faculty of Law, University of Toronto, 84 Queen's Park, Toronto, ON M5S 2C5, Canada (office). *Telephone:* (416) 978-8581 (office). *E-mail:* e.weinrib@utoronto.ca (office). *Website:* www.law.utoronto.ca (office).

WEINSTEIN, Alan D., BSc, MA, PhD; American mathematician and academic; *Professor Emeritus, Department of Mathematics, University of California, Berkeley;* b. 17 June 1943, New York; m. Margo Weinstein; ed Massachusetts Inst. of Tech., Univ. of California, Berkeley; conducted postdoctoral research at Institut des Hautes Etudes Scientifiques, France and Univ. of Bonn, Germany; joined Faculty of Dept of Math., Univ. of California, Berkeley 1969, Full Prof. 1976–2009, Prof. of the Grad. School 2009, now Prof. Emer.; Visiting Prof., Univ. of Paris, France 2009; mem. American Acad. of Arts and Sciences 1992–; Fellow, American Mathematical Soc. 2012; Dr hc (Utrecht) 2003; Guggenheim Fellowship, Sloan Fellowship. *Address:* Department of Mathematics, University of California, 825 Evans Hall, Berkeley, CA 94720-3840, USA (office). *Telephone:* (510) 642-6550 (office). *Fax:* (510) 642-8204 (office). *E-mail:* alanw@math.berkeley.edu (office). *Website:* math.berkeley.edu/~alanw (office).

WEINSTEIN, Harvey; American film industry executive; b. 19 March 1952, Buffalo, New York; s. of Mira Weinstein and Max Weinstein; brother of Robert Weinstein (q.v.); m. 1st Eve Chilton (divorced); three c.; m. 2nd Georgina Chapman 2007; two c.; Co-Chair. Miramax Films Corpn, New York (with brother Robert) 1979–2005; Co-founder (with brother) The Weinstein Co. 2005, Co-Chair. 2005–17 (dismissed), mem. Bd of Dirs –2017 (resgnd). *Films produced include:* Playing for Keeps 1986, Scandal 1989, Strike it Rich 1990, Hardware 1990, A Rage in Harlem 1991, The Crying Game 1992, The Night We Never Met 1993, Benefit of the Doubt 1993, True Romance 1993, Mother's Boys 1994, Like Water for Chocolate 1994, Pulp Fiction 1994, Pret-A-Porter 1994, Smoke 1995, A Month by the Lake 1995, The Crossing Guard 1995, The Journey of August King 1995, Things To Do In Denver When You're Dead 1995, The Englishman Who Went Up A Hill But Came Down A Mountain 1995, Blue in the Face 1995, Restoration 1995, Scream 1996, The Pallbearer 1996, The Last of the High Kings 1996, Jane Eyre 1996, Flirting with Disaster 1996, The English Patient 1996, Emma 1996, The Crow: City of Angels 1996, Beautiful Girls 1996, Addicted to Love 1997, Shakespeare in Love 1998, Allied Forces, She's All That 1999, My Life So Far 1999, The Yards 1999, Bounce 2000, Scary Movie 2000, Boys and Girls 2000, Love's Labour's Lost 2000, Scream 3 2000, About Adam 2000, Highlander: Endgame 2000, Chocolat 2000, Dracula 2000, Spy Kids 2001, Texas Rangers 2001, Daddy and Them 2001, Scary Movie 2 2001, The Others 2001, Jay and Silent Bob Strike Back 2001, Lord of the Rings: Fellowship of the Ring 2001, Iris 2001, Shipping News 2001, Kate and Leopold 2001, Imposter 2002, Only the Strong Survive 2002, Heaven 2002, Halloween: Resurrection 2002, Full Frontal 2002, Spy Kids 2 2002, Below 2002, Equilibrium 2002, Waking Up in Reno 2002, Lord of the Rings; Two Towers 2002, Gangs of New York 2002, Chicago 2002, Confessions of a Dangerous Mind 2002, Spy Kids 3–D 2003, Human Stain 2003, Duplex 2003, Kill Bill (Vol. 1) 2003, Scary Movie 3 2003, Bad Santa 2003, Lord of the Rings: Return of the King 2003, Cold Mountain 2003, The I Inside 2003, Mindhunters 2004, Jersey Girl 2004, Ella Enchanted 2004, Kill Bill (Vol. 2) 2004, Paper Clips 2004, Fahrenheit 9/11 2004, Shall We Dance 2004, Cursed 2004, Aviator 2004, Derailed 2005, Nine 2009, The King's Speech 2010, My Week with Marilyn 2011, The Artist 2011, Silver Linings Playbook 2012, Django Unchained 2012, One Chance 2013, Escape from Planet Earth 2013, Sin City: A Dame to Kill For 2014, War and Peace 2015, Scream 2015, The Founder 2016, Amityville: The Awakening 2017, Leap! 2017.

WEINSTEIN, Robert (Bob); American film industry executive; b. 1954, Flushing, NY; s. of Max Weinstein and Mira Weinstein; brother of Harvey Weinstein (q.v.); m. 1st; two d.; m. 2nd Anne Clancy 2000; one s. one d.; produced rock concerts with brother Harvey as Harvey & Corky Productions, Buffalo 1970s; Co-founder and Co-Chair, Miramax Film Corpn with brother Harvey 1979–2005; Co-founder with brother The Weinstein Co. 2005, Chair. Bd 2005–18; Founder and Head of Dimension Films. *Broadway productions:* co-producer: The Real Thing (revival) (Tony Award for Best Revival of a Play, Drama Desk Award for Outstanding Revival of a Play) 2000, The Producers (musical) (Tony Award for Best Musical, Drama Desk Award for Outstanding New Musical) 2001, Sweet Smell of Success (musical) 2002, La bohème (revival) 2003, All Shook Up (musical) 2005, The Color Purple (musical) 2005. *Screenplay:* The Burning 1981. *Films produced include:* (all with Harvey Weinstein q.v.) Playing for Keeps (with Alan Brewer) (also writer and dir) 1986, Scandal (with Joe Boyd and Nik Powell) 1989, Strike it Rich 1990, Hardware (with Nik Powell, Stephen Woolley and Trix Worrell) 1990, A Rage in Harlem (with Terry Glinwood, William Horberg and Nik Powell) 1991, The Night We Never Met (with Sidney Kimmel) 1993, Benefit of the Doubt 1993, True Romance (with Gary Barber, Stanley Margolis and James G. Robinson) 1993, Clerks 1994, Mother's Boys (with Randall Poster) 1994, Pulp Fiction (with Richard N. Gladstein) 1994, Pret-A-Porter (with Ian Jessel) 1994, Smoke (with Satoru Iseki) 1995, A Month By the Lake (with Donna Gigliotti) 1995, The Crossing Guard (with Richard N. Gladstein) 1995, The Journey of August King 1995, Things To Do In Denver When You're Dead (with Marie Cantin) 1995, The Englishman Who Went Up a Hill But Came Down a Mountain (with Sally Hibbin and Robert Jones) 1995, Blue in the Face (with Harvey Keitel) 1995, Restoration (with Donna Gigliotti) 1995, Flirting with Disaster 1996, The English Patient 1996, Scream 1996, The Faculty 1998, Halloween H20: 20 Years Later 1998, Good Will Hunting 1998, Velvet Goldmine 1998, Jackie Brown 1998, Shakespeare in Love 1998, Allied Forces 1999, My Life So Far 1999, The Yards 1999, Music of the Heart 1999, The Cider House Rules 1999, She's All That 1999, Down To You 2000, Committed 2000, The Crow: Salvation 2000, The Prophecy 3: The Ascent 2000, Boys and Girls 2000, Scream 3 2000, Love's Labour's Lost 2000, Scary Movie 2000, Highlander: Endgame 2000, Backstage 2000, Malena 2000, Bounce 2000, Chocolat 2000, Dracula 2000 2000, Serendipity 2001, Spy Kids 2001, Texas Rangers 2001, Daddy and Them 2001, Scary Movie 2 2001, The Others 2001, Legend of Zu 2001, Jay and Silent Bob Strike Back 2001, Lord of the Rings: Fellowship of the Ring 2001, Shipping News 2001, Kate and Leopold 2002, Ritual 2001, Imposter 2002, Only the Strong Survive 2002, Halloween: Resurrection 2002, Full Frontal 2002, Spy Kids 2 2002, Darkness 2002, Below 2002, Waking Up in Reno 2002, Lord of the Rings: Two Towers 2002, Equilibrium 2002, Gangs of New York 2002, Chicago 2002, Confessions of a Dangerous Mind 2002, Spy Kids 3-D: Game Over 2003, My Boss's Daughter 2003, Human Stain 2003, Duplex 2003, Kill Bill: Vol. 1 2003, Scary Movie 3 2003, Bad Santa 2003, Lord of the Rings: Return of the King 2003, Cold Mountain 2003, The I Inside 2003, Mindhunters 2004, Jersey Girl 2004, Ella Enchanted 2004, Kill Bill: Vol. 2 2004, Paper Clips 2004, The Great Raid 2004, Fahrenheit 9/11 2004, Finding Neverland 2004, Shall We Dance 2004, Cursed 2004, The Aviator 2004, Derailed 2005, Sin City 2005, Breaking and Entering 2006, Clerks 2 2006, Pulse 2006, Halloween 2007, The Mist 2007, Rogue 2007, Sicko 2007, The Great Debaters 2007, Fanboys 2008, The Reader 2008, Zack and Miri Make a Porno 2008, Capitalism: A Love Story 2009, Youth in Revolt 2009, Janky Promoters 2009, Inglourious Basterds 2009, Nine 2009, Hurricane Season 2009, Shanghai 2010, Piranha 3-D 2010, The King's Speech 2010, My Week with Marilyn 2011, Scream 4 2011, Hoodwinked Too! Hood vs. Evil 2011, The Artist 2011, Spy Kids: All the Time in the World in 4D 2011, Apollo 18 2011, Butter 2011, I Don't Know How She Does It 2011, My Week with Marilyn 2011, Piranha 3DD 2012, The Sapphires 2012, Silver Linings Playbook 2012, Song for Marion 2012, Django Unchained 2012, Ain't Them Bodies Saints 2013, Escape from Planet Earth 2013, Dark Skies 2013, Scary Movie 5 2013, Beyond Memories (short) 2013, A Better Tomorrow (short) 2013, uwantme2kill-him? 2013, The Butler 2013, August: Osage County 2013, The Art of the Steal 2013, Philomena 2013, Vampire Academy 2014, Sin City: A Dame to Kill For 2014, Big Eyes 2014, The Amityville Horror: The Lost Tapes 2015. *Television includes:* Project Runway (series) 2004–13, After the Runway (series) 2011, Project Accessory (series) 2011, Supermarket Superstar (series) 2012, Mob Wives: The Sit Down (series) 2012, Mob Wives Chicago (series) 2012, Big Ang (series) 2012, Code Name: Geronimo (film) 2012, Project Runway All Stars (series) 2012–14, Under the Gunn (series) 2014. *Address:* The Weinstein Company, 345 Hudson Street, 13th Floor, New York, NY 10014, USA. *E-mail:* info@weinsteinco.com. *Website:* www.weinsteinco.com.

WEIR, Dame Gillian Constance, DBE, LRAM, LTCL, FRAM, FRCM; British concert organist, harpsichordist, broadcaster, lecturer and clinician; *Prince Consort Professor of Organ, Royal College of Music;* b. 17 Jan. 1941, Martinborough, New Zealand; d. of Cecil Alexander Weir and Clarice Mildred Foy Weir (née Bignell); m. 1st Clive Rowland Webster 1967 (divorced 1971); m. 2nd Lawrence Irving Phelps 1972 (died 1999); ed Wanganui Girls Coll., NZ and Royal Coll. of Music, with Cyril Smith (piano) and Ralph Downes (organ), pvt. studies in London and Paris with Anton Heiller, Marie-Claire Alain and Nadia Boulanger; débuts at Royal Festival Hall and Royal Albert Hall, London 1965; worldwide career since 1965 as concert organist, comprising some 2,000 appearances in major concert halls etc., including more than 50 at South Bank Centre, London; has appeared with all leading British orchestras and many abroad, including Vienna Symphony, Boston Symphony, San Francisco Symphony, ORF, under leading conductors; many radio and TV appearances; adjudicator in int. competitions and artist-in-residence at major univs including Yale; gives lectures and master classes in many countries; organ consultant, Birmingham Symphony Hall; Visiting Prof. of Organ, RAM, London 1997–98; Prince Consort Prof. of Organ, Royal Coll. of Music, London 1999–; Int. Chair. in Organ, Royal Northern Coll. of Music, Manchester 2006–07; Distinguished Visiting Artist, Peabody Conservatory of Music, Baltimore, USA 2006–12; Visiting Tutor, Curtis Inst., Philadelphia 2006–09; numerous premières including first British performance of Messiaen's *Méditations* of 1972; numerous works written for her including concertos by William Mathias and Peter Racine Fricker; numerous recordings including complete organ works of Olivier Messiaen 1995 and César Franck 1997; recognized world-wide as authority on and pre-eminent performer of Messiaen; Concerto soloist First Night of the Proms 1967 and Last Night of the Proms 1999, numerous other Proms appearances; Pres. Inc. Asscn of Organists (first woman Pres.) 1981–83, Inc. Soc. of Musicians 1992–93, Soloists' Ensemble 1998–2000; mem. Exec. Council, Royal Coll. of Organists (first woman mem.) 1981–85, Council (first woman mem.) 1977–, Pres. (first woman Pres.) 1994–96; mem. Council of Royal Philharmonic Soc. 1995–2001; mem. Royal

Soc. of Musicians of GB 1996–; Trustee, Eric Thompson Charitable Trust 1993–2013; Patron Friends of Young Artists' Platform 1991–, Oundle Int. Festival 1998–, Cirencester Early Music Festival 1999, Northern Ireland Int. Organ Competition 2011–, various organ socs in UK and abroad; Hon. FRCO 1975; Hon. Fellow, Royal Canadian Coll. of Organists 1983; Hon. RAM 1989; Hon. Bencher of the Middle Temple, London 2012; Hon. Freeman, Worshipful Co. of Musicians 2015; Hon. DMus (Victoria Univ. of Wellington, NZ) 1983, (Hull) 1999, (Exeter) 2001, (Leicester) 2003, (Aberdeen) 2004, (London) 2008, (Durham) 2012; Hon. DLitt (Huddersfield) 1997; Hon. DUniv (Univ. of Central England) 2001; Winner, St Albans Int. Organ Festival Competition 1964, Countess of Munster Award 1965, Int. Performer of the Year Award, American Guild of Organists 1981, Musician of the Year, Int. Music Guide 1982, Turnovsky Foundation Award for Outstanding Contrib. to the Arts (first musician) 1985, Silver Medal, Albert Schweitzer Asscn (Sweden) 1998, Evening Standard Award for Outstanding Solo Performance 1999, Lifetime Achievement Award, The Link Foundation 2005. *Television:* presenter and performer, The King of Instruments (six-part series, BBC) 2000, A Year in the Life of Gillian Weir (NZTV), appearances on Omnibus (BBC), South Bank Show (ITV) 2000, and numerous other programmes. *Publications include:* contrib. to Grove's Dictionary of Music and Musicians 1980, Faber's The Messiaen Companion 1995; numerous articles in professional journals. *Leisure interests:* theatre, reading. *E-mail:* gw@gillianweir.com (home). *Website:* gillianweir.com.

WEIR, Jeremy, BSc (Hons); Australian business executive; *CEO, Trafigura Beheer BV;* ed Univ. of Melbourne; with N.M. Rothschild 1992–2000; joined Trafigura Group as Head of Metals Derivatives, Structured Products and Risk Man. 2001, mem. Man. Bd, Head of Risk and CEO Galena Asset Man. and Trafigura Mining Group –2014, CEO Trafigura Beheer BV 2014–, also responsible for co.'s Metals and Minerals Trading Div. May 2015; Dir, Iberian Minerals Corpn 2006–, Cadillac Ventures Inc. 2009–14, Anvil Mining Ltd 2009–. *Address:* Trafigura Beheer BV, 20th Floor, ITO Tower, Gustav Mahlerplein 102, 1082 MA Amsterdam, The Netherlands (office). *Telephone:* (20) 504-1800 (office). *E-mail:* info@trafigura.com (office). *Website:* www.trafigura.com (office).

WEIR, Judith, CBE, MA; British composer; *Master of the Queen's Music;* b. 11 May 1954, Cambridge; ed North London Collegiate School, King's Coll., Cambridge; Composer-in-Residence, Southern Arts Asscn 1976–79; Fellow in Composition, Univ. of Glasgow 1979–82, Creative Arts Fellowship, Trinity Coll. Cambridge 1983–85, Composer-in-Residence, Royal Scottish Acad. of Music and Drama (RSAMD) 1988–91; Fairbairn Composer in Asscn with City of Birmingham Symphony Orchestra 1995–98; Artistic Dir Spitalfields Festival 1995–2000; Hambro Visiting Prof. in Opera Studies, Univ. of Oxford 1999–2000; Visiting Lecturer, Princeton Univ., USA 2001; Fromm Foundation Visiting Prof., Harvard Univ. 2004; Distinguished Visiting Research Prof. in Composition, School of Music, Cardiff Univ. 2006–13; Master of the Queen's Music 2014–; Assoc. Composer, BBC Singers 2015–; Trustee, Royal Opera House 2002–11; mem. Council, Spitalfields Music 2010–16; Hon. Fellow, St Hilda's Coll. Oxford 2000, King's Coll., Cambridge 2003; Hon. RAM 1997; Hon. FRCM 2006; Dr hc (Aberdeen) 1995, (Univ. of Central England) 1999, (RSAMD) 2001, (Queen's Univ. Belfast) 2001, (Glasgow) 2005, (King's Coll. London) 2007, (Glasgow Caledonian) 2008; Critics' Circle Award 1994, Elise L Stoeger Prize 1997, South Bank Award 2000, Queen's Medal for Music 2007, Distinguished Musician Award, Incorporated Soc. of Musicians 2010, Ivor Novello Award 2015. *Compositions include:* King Harald's Saga 1979, The Consolations of Scholarship 1985, The Black Spider 1985, A Night At The Chinese Opera 1987, Missa Del Cid 1988, Heaven Ablaze In His Breast 1989, The Vanishing Bridegroom 1990, Music Untangled 1991–92, Heroic Strokes of the Bow 1992, Blond Eckbert 1993, Musicians Wrestle Everywhere 1994, Moon and Star 1995, Forest 1995, Storm 1997, Piano Concerto 1997, Piano Trio 1998, Natural History 1999, We Are Shadows (South Bank Show Award 2001) 2000, Piano Quartet 2000, The Welcome Arrival of Rain 2001, Tiger under the Table 2002, The Voice of Desire 2004, Piano Trio No. 2 2004, Armida 2005, Blond Eckbert Pocket Version 2006, Winter Song 2007, Concrete 2008, Miss Fortune 2009–11, Blue-Green Hill 2012, I give you the end of a golden string 2011–13, Day Break Shadows Flee 2014, Good Morning, Midnight 2013–15, In the Land of Uz (British Composer Awards 2018). *Address:* c/o Promotion Department, Chester Music, 14–15 Berners Street, London, W1T 3LJ, England (office). *Telephone:* (20) 7612-7400 (office). *Fax:* (20) 7612-7549 (office). *E-mail:* promotion@musicsales.co.uk (office). *Website:* www.judithweir.com; www.royal.gov.uk/TheRoyalHousehold/OfficialRoyalposts/MasterofTheQueensMusic.aspx.

WEIR, Peter Lindsay; Australian film director; b. 21 Aug. 1944, Sydney; s. of Lindsay Weir and Peggy Barnsley; m. Wendy Stites 1966; one s. one d.; ed Scots Coll., Sydney, Univ. of Sydney; worked in real estate sector until 1965; worked as stagehand in television, Sydney 1967; dir of film sequences in variety show 1968; dir of amateur univ. reviews 1967–69; dir for Film Australia 1969–73; made own short films 1969–73, Ind. feature-film dir and screenwriter 1973–; Broadcast Film Critics Asscn Passion in Film Award 2004. *Films:* Cars that Ate Paris 1973, Picnic at Hanging Rock 1975, The Last Wave 1977, The Plumber (television) 1978, Gallipoli 1981, The Year of Living Dangerously 1982, Witness 1985, The Mosquito Coast 1986, Dead Poets Society 1989, Green Card 1991, Fearless 1994, The Truman Show (BAFTA Award for Best Dir) 1997, Master and Commander: The Far Side of the World (BAFTA Award for Best Dir) 2003, The Way Back 2010.

WEIR, Stuart Peter, BA; British journalist, political scientist and academic; *Associate Director, Democratic Audit, Human Rights Center and Visiting Professor, Government Department, University of Essex;* b. 13 Oct. 1938, Frimley, Surrey, England; s. of Robert H. Weir and Edna F. Lewis; m. 1st Doffy Burnham 1963; two s.; m. 2nd Elizabeth E. Bisset 1987; one s. two d.; ed Peter Symonds School, Winchester and Brasenose Coll. Oxford; Feature Writer, Oxford Mail 1964–67; Diarist, The Times 1967–71; Dir Citizens Rights Office 1971–75; Founding Ed. Roof Magazine (Shelter) 1975–77; Deputy Ed. New Society 1977–84; Ed. New Socialist 1984–87; Political Columnist, London Daily News 1987; Ed. New Statesman 1987–88, New Statesman and Society 1988–90; Founder Charter 88 1988; Dir Democratic Audit 1991–2009, now Assoc. Dir, Prof. and Sr Research Fellow, Human Rights Centre, Univ. of Essex 1991–; Visiting Prof. 1999–; Series Consultant, The People's Parl. (Channel 4 TV) 1994–97; Consultant, State of Democracy Project, Int. IDEA, Stockholm 1997–2003; Assoc. Consultant (Governance) British Council 1997; Consultant on Governance Dept for Int. Devt

1999–2002; Sr Int. Facilitator Namibian Govt and Democracy Project 1994–95; UK Facilitator Zimbabwe Parl. Democracy Project; Chair. Parl. Assessment Team, Zimbabwe 2002–03; Lecturer on Politics and the Media, LSE 1994. *Publications:* Manifesto 1981; contributor to: The Other Britain 1982, Consuming Secrets 1982, Defining and Measuring Democracy 1995; Ego Trip (ed.) 1995, Behind Closed Doors 1995, The Three Pillars of Liberty 1996, Making Votes Count 1997, Political Power and Democratic Control in Britain 1998, Voices of the People (jtly.) 2001, The IDEA Handbook on Democracy Assessments (jtly) 2001, The State of Democracy (jtly) 2002, Democracy Under Blair 2003. *Leisure interests:* children, cooking, walking, football. *Address:* Butts Orchard, Butts Batch, Wrington, Bristol, BS40 5LN, England. *Telephone:* (1934) 863668. *E-mail:* stuart@democraticaudit.demon.co.uk (office). *Website:* www.essex.ac.uk (office).

WEIR, Viscount; **William Kenneth James Weir,** FRSA, BA; British business executive; b. 9 Nov. 1933, Glasgow, Scotland; s. of Lord Weir and Lady Weir (née Crowdy); m. 1st Diana Lucy MacDougall 1964 (divorced 1972); one s. one d.; m. 2nd Jacqueline Mary Marr 1976 (divorced); m. 3rd Marina Sevastopoulo 1988; one s.; ed Eton Coll., Trinity Coll. Cambridge; served Royal Navy 1955–56; Chair. Weir Group PLC 1972–99, Balfour Beatty PLC (fmrly BICC PLC) 1996–2003, CP Ships Ltd 2001–04; Dir Bank of England 1972–84, British Steel Corpn 1972–76, British Bank of Middle East 1977–79, Canadian Pacific Ltd 1989–2001, St James Place Capital 1990, Canadian Pacific Railway Co. 2001; Pres. British Electrotechnical Mfrs Asscn 1988-89, 1993–95; mem. London Advisory Cttee, Hong Kong Shanghai Bank 1980–92, Export Credit Advisory Cttee 1991–98; Chair. British Water 1999–2000; Hon. FREng; Hon. DEng (Glasgow). *Publication:* The Weir Group 2008. *Leisure interests:* shooting, golf. *Address:* Rodinghead, Mauchline, Ayrshire, KA5 5TR, Scotland (home). *Telephone:* (1563) 884233 (home).

WEISBROD-WEBER, Wolfgang; German UN official; b. 1955, Hanau; m.; three c.; ed Freie Universität, Berlin; various appointments within UN Secr. and in UN field operations, including Dir Europe and Latin American Div., UN Dept of Peacekeeping Operations 2004–06, Chief of Staff, UN Integrated Mission in Timor-Leste 2006–08, Dir of Asia and Middle East Div., UN Dept of Peacekeeping Operations 2008–12, Deputy Special Rep. of Sec.-Gen. ad interim for UN Assistance Mission in Afghanistan 2009, 2010, Special Rep. of Sec.-Gen. for Western Sahara and Head of UN Mission for Referendum in Western Sahara 2012–14. *Address:* Federal Ministry of Foreign Affairs, Werderscher Markt 1, 10117 Berlin, Germany (office). *Telephone:* (30) 18170 (office). *Fax:* (30) 18173402 (office). *E-mail:* poststelle@auswaertiges-amt.de (office). *Website:* www.auswaertiges-amt.de (office).

WEISFELDT, Myron Lee, BA, MD; American cardiologist and academic; *University Distinguished Service Professor and Professor of Medicine, Johns Hopkins University;* b. 25 April 1940, Milwaukee, Wis.; m. Linda Weisfeldt 1963; three c.; ed Johns Hopkins Univ.; intern then resident, Columbia-Presbyterian Medical Center, New York 1965–67; Fellow in Cardiology, Mass Gen. Hosp., Boston 1970–72; Asst Prof. of Medicine, Johns Hopkins Univ., Baltimore 1972–78, Prof. of Medicine 1978–91, Robert L. Levy Prof. of Cardiology 1979–91, Dir, Cardiology Div., Johns Hopkins Univ. School of Medicine 1975–91, William Osler Prof. of Medicine and Physician-in-Chief, Johns Hopkins Hosp. 2001–14, also Dir, Dept of Medicine –2014, currently Univ. Distinguished Service Prof. and Prof. of Medicine; Samuel Bard Prof. of Medicine and Chair. Dept of Medicine, Columbia-Presbyterian Medical Center 1991–2001; Pres. American Heart Asscn 1989–90; Fellow, AAAS, American Coll. of Physicians, American Coll. of Cardiology; mem. NAS Inst of Medicine, American Soc. for Clinical Investigation, Asscn of American Physicians, Asscn of Profs of Medicine, Nat. Inst. on Aging Nat. Advisory Council; mem. Bd of Advisers KBL Healthcare Acquisition Corpn; numerous awards including American Heart Asscn Golden Heart Award 1998, Phillips Award in Clinical Medicine, American Coll. of Physicians 2006, Diversity Award, Asscn of Profs of Medicine 2008. *Address:* Johns Hopkins Hospital, 600 North Wolfe Street, Sheikh Zayed Tower, Baltimore, MD 21287, USA (office). *Website:* www.hopkinsmedicine.org (office).

WEISLER, Dion J.; American business executive; *President and CEO, HP, Inc.;* b. 20 Aug. 1968, Australia; m.; two c.; fmr Man. Dir Acer UK, helped build Acer's business in cen. and Eastern Europe; Head of businesses in South Korea, ASEAN and Australia and NZ, Lenovo Group Ltd –2008, Vice-Pres. and COO Product and Mobile Internet Digital Home Groups, Lenovo Group Ltd 2008–11; Sr Vice-Pres. and Man. Dir, Printing and Personal Systems, Asia Pacific and Japan, Hewlett-Packard Co. 2012–13, Exec. Vice-Pres., Printing and Personal Systems Group 2013–15, mem. Bd of Dirs, Pres. and CEO HP, Inc. (printer and personal computer business co. split from Hewlett-Packard Co.) 2015–. *Address:* HP, Inc., 3000 Hanover Street, MS 1050, Palo Alto, CA 94304-1185, USA (office). *Telephone:* (650) 857-1501 (office). *Fax:* (650) 857-5518 (office). *E-mail:* bod@hp.com (office). *Website:* www.hp.com (office).

WEISS, Rainer (Rai), SB, PhD; American (b. German) physicist and academic; *Professor Emeritus of Physics, Massachusetts Institute of Technology;* b. 29 Sept. 1932, Berlin, Germany; m. Rebecca Young 1957; two d.; ed Massachusetts Inst. of Tech.; Instructor of Physics, Tufts Univ. 1960–61, Asst Prof. of Physics 1961–62; Research Assoc. in Physics, Princeton Univ. 1962–64; Asst Prof. of Physics, MIT 1964–67, Assoc. Prof. of Physics 1967–73, Prof. of Physics 1973–2001, Prof. Emer. 2001–; Adjunct Prof. of Physics, Louisiana State Univ. 2001–; fmr Chair. COBE Science Working Group; mem. NASA Physical Sciences Cttee 1970–74, Infrared Detector Panel 1978, SSSC Cttee 1982, Panel on Jt Inst. of Lab. Astrophysics, NAS Bd on Assessment of NBS Programs 1985–; Co-ordinator NSF Panel on Interferometric Observatory for Gravitational Waves 1986; mem. NAS Space Sciences Bd 1983–86; mem. NAS 2000, American Astronomical Soc., New York Acad. of Sciences; Fellow, American Acad. of Arts and Sciences 1998, AAAS; MIT Baker Award for Excellence in Teaching 1968, NASA Achievement Award (Monolithic Bolometers) 1984, NASA/GSFC Group Achievement Award 1990, Exceptional Science Achievement Medal 1991, Group Achievement Medal 1991, Gruber Prize in Cosmology 2006, Einstein Prize, American Physical Soc. (shared with Ronald Drever) 2007; (shared with Ronald Drever and Kip Thorne): Cosmology Prize, Peter Gruber Foundation 2016, Kavli Prize in Astrophysics 2016, Special Breakthrough Prize in Fundamental Physics 2016, Shaw Prize in Astronomy 2016, Nobel Prize in Physics (shared with Barry Barish and Kip Thorne) 2017, Joseph Weber Award for Astronomical Instrumentation 2018. *Achievements include:* known for inventing the laser interferometric technique; jointly conceived and designed the Laser Interferometer Gravitational-Wave Observatory (LIGO) for the direct detection of gravitational waves. *Publications:* numerous papers in professional journals. *Address:* Room NW22-281, Department of Physics, 4-304 Massachusetts Institute of Technology, 77 Massachusetts Avenue, Cambridge, 02139-4307, USA (office). *Telephone:* (617) 253-3527 (office); (617) 253-4824 (LIGO Lab) (office). *E-mail:* weiss@ligo.mit.edu (office). *Website:* web.mit.edu/physics (office); space.mit.edu/LIGO (office).

WEISS, Ulrich, DBA; German banker; b. 3 June 1936; ed Univ. of Hamburg; fmr mem. Bd of Man. Dirs, Deutsche Bank AG, Frankfurt, Chair. Admin. Council, Deutsche Bank SAE, Barcelona/Madrid, Deutsche Bank de Investimento SA, Lisbon, Deutsche Bank Luxembourg SA, Chair. Admin. Council, Deutsche Bank SpA, Milan 1979–88; fmr Chair. O&K Orenstein & Koppel AG, Heidelberg; fmr Deputy Chair. Südzuker AG, Mannhei and Deputy Chair. Supervisory Bd; Chair. Supervisory Bd Continental AG –2005, Hanover; Dir, Ducati Motor Holding SpA from 1998, Bego Medical AG, Bremen, Edizione Holding SpA, Mittel SpA, Mittel Private Equity SpA; Ind. Dir, Benetton Group SpA 1997–2007; mem. Supervisory Bd HeidelbergCement AG (fmrly Heidelberger Zement AG) –2004, Asea Brown Boveri AG –2005, Mannheim, BASF AG, Ludwigshafen, Heidelberger Zement AG, Klein, Schanzlin & Becker AG, Frankenthal, Rheinelektra AG, Mannheim; mem. Admin. Council Fiat SpA, Turin; mem. Advisory Bd Deutsche Bahn AG, EPCI Srl, ECPI Group SpA, Bausparkasse Schwaebisch Hall AG; Co-founder and mem. Bd Stiftung Marktwirtschaft, Berlin (think tank).

WEISSER, Alberto, BBA; American business executive; b. 26 June 1955, Argentina; ed Univ. of São Paulo, Harvard Business School, Institut Européen d'Admin des Affaires (INSEAD), France; began career with BASF Group, worked in Brazil, Germany, USA and Mexico 1978–93; joined Bunge Ltd as Chief Financial Officer 1993–99, mem. Bd of Dirs 1997–2013, Chair. and CEO 1999–2013, Exec. Chair. June–Dec. 2013; Dir, Ferro Corpn 2000–07, Int. Paper Co. 2006–12; Ind. Dir, Pepsico, Inc. 2011–; mem. North American Agribusiness Advisory Bd of Rabobank; mem. Council on Foreign Relations, Council of the Americas, Latin America Conservation Council, in partnership with The Nature Conservancy. *Address:* PepsiCo Inc., 700 Anderson Hill Road, Purchase, NY 10577, USA (office). *Telephone:* (914) 253-2000 (office). *Fax:* (914) 253-2070 (office). *E-mail:* info@pepsico.com (office). *Website:* www.pepsico.com (office).

WEISSER, Hellmuth; German business executive; *Chairman of the Supervisory Board, Marquard & Balhs AG;* CEO Marquard & Bahls AG 1981–2003, Chair. Supervisory Bd 2003–; Pres. Union Pétrolière Européenne Indépendante, Paris, AFM+E (Aussenhandelsverband für Mineralöl und Energie e.V.), Hamburg; mem. EC Energy Consultative Cttee. *Address:* Marquard & Bahls AG, Admiralitaetstr. 55, 20459 Hamburg, Germany (office). *Telephone:* (40) 37004-0 (office). *Fax:* (40) 37004-225 (office). *E-mail:* office@marquard-bahls.com (office). *Website:* www.marquard-bahls.com (office).

WEISSLEDER, Ralph, MD, PhD; German radiologist and academic; *Professor of Radiology, Harvard Medical School;* ed Univ. of Heidelberg; Resident, Massachusetts Gen. Hosp., joined Harvard Medical School 1991, currently Prof. of Radiology and Dir Center for Systems Biology, mem. Prin. Faculty, Harvard Stem Cell Inst., mem. Dana Farber Harvard Cancer Center, Assoc. mem. Broad Inst. (Chemical Biology Program), also Dir Center for Molecular Imaging Research and Attending Clinician (Interventional Radiology), Massachusetts Gen. Hosp.; Researcher, Breast Cancer Research Foundation, New York; Founding-mem. Soc. for Molecular Imaging Research (Pres. 2002); mem. Inst. of Medicine 2009–, Radiological Soc. of North America, German Nat. Acad. of Sciences (Leopoldina) 2015–; J. Allyn Taylor Int. Prize in Medicine 2004, Millenium Pharmaceuticals Innovator Award, Memorial Award, Asscn of Univ. Radiologists, Pres.'s Award, American Roentgen Ray Soc., Soc. for Molecular Imaging Lifetime Achievement Award, Acad. of Molecular Imaging Distinguished Basic Scientist Award 2006, RSNA Outstanding Researcher Award 2008, European Soc. of Radiology Gold Medal 2011. *Publications:* Primer of Diagnostic Imaging (co-author) 2002; 10 US and int. patents and more than 600 articles in medical journals on molecular imaging research in living organisms; several textbooks. *Address:* Center for Systems Biology, Simches Research Bldg, 185 Cambridge Street, 5th Floor, Boston, MA 02114, USA (office). *Telephone:* (617) 726-8226 (office); (617) 726-8396 (Clinic) (office). *Fax:* (617) 726-5078 (office); (617) 726-4891 (Clinic) (office). *E-mail:* rweissleder@mgh.harvard.edu (office); rweissleder@partners.org (office). *Website:* csb.mgh.harvard.edu/weissleder (office); www.massgeneralimaging.org (office).

WEISSMAN, Irving L., BS, MD, FAAS; American biologist and academic; *Director, Institute for Stem Cell Biology and Regenerative Medicine, Stanford University School of Medicine;* b. 21 Oct. 1939, Great Falls, Mont.; ed Dartmouth Coll., Montana State Coll., Univ. of Oxford, UK, Stanford Univ.; Montana Cancer Soc. Student Research Fellow, Lab. for Experimental Medicine, Montana Deaconess Hosp., Great Falls 1961; Medical Student Research Fellow, Dept of Genetics, Stanford Univ. School of Medicine 1961, NIH Student Traineeship, Dept of Radiology 1961–64, NIH Postdoctoral Fellowship 1965–67, Research Asscn 1967–68, Asst Prof., Dept of Pathology 1969–74, Assoc. Prof. 1974–81, Prof. 1981–, Chair. Stanford Univ. Immunology Program 1986–2001, Karel and Avice Beekhuis Prof. of Cancer Biology 1987–, Prof. of Developmental Biology 1989–, Investigator, Howard Hughes Medical Inst., Stanford Univ. 1990–92, Prof. (By Courtesy) of Neurosurgery and of Biological Sciences 1990–, Dir Inst. of Stem Cell Biology and Regenerative Medicine, School of Medicine 2003–; NIH Student Traineeship, Cellular Immunology Research Unit, Sir William Dunn School of Pathology, MRC, Oxford 1964; Sr Dernham Fellow, American Cancer Soc. (Calif. Div.) 1969–73; Josiah Macy Foundation Scholar 1974–75; Co-Founder and mem. Bd of Dirs SyStemix, Palo Alto, Calif. 1988, Chair. Scientific Advisory Bd 1988–97; Founder Stem Cells, Inc., Palo Alto 1998; mem. Scientific Advisory Bd Amgen, Calif. 1981–89, DNAX, Germany 1981–92, T Cell Sciences, Inc., Mass 1988–92; Pres. American Asscn of Immunologists 1994–95; mem. Nat. Bd of Govs Project Inform; Assoc. Ed. Molecular Therapy 1999–; mem. Editorial Bd Journal of Cellular Biochemistry 1980–, Molecular Marine Biology and Biotechnology 1991–, Biology of Blood and Marrow Transplantation 1995–, Experimental Hematology 1996–, Journal of Clinical Investigation 1998–; mem. NAS 1987 (mem. Council 2011)), American Acad. of Arts and Sciences 1990, American Acad. of Microbiology 1997, American Asscn of Immunologists, American Asscn of Univ. Pathologists

(PLUTO), American Asscn of Pathologists, American Soc. for Microbiology, American Asscn of Cancer Research, American Acad. of Microbiology, Clinical Immunology Soc., American Soc. of Hematology, Int. Soc. of Experimental Hematology, American Soc. for Blood and Marrow Transplantation, Int. Cytokine Soc., Molecular Medicine Soc.; Hon. mem. Israel Immunological Soc. 1995; Hon. Dir Centre for Biotech/BioMedicine and Shenzhen Key Lab. of Gene and Antibody Therapy, Grad. School of Shenzhen, Tsinghau Univ., People's Repub. of China; Hon. Investigator, State Key Lab. of Experimental Hematology, Chinese Acad. of Medical Sciences and Peking Union Medical Coll. 2010; Hon. Prof., Peking Union Medical Coll. 2010; Hon. DSc (Montana State Univ.) 1992; Faculty Research Award, American Cancer Soc. 1974–78, NIH Outstanding Investigator Award 1986, Kaiser Award for Excellence in Pre-clinical Teaching 1987, Harvey Lecturer 1989, Pasarow Award for Outstanding Contrib. to Cancer Biology 1989, Selected Top 100, Alumni, Montana State Univ. 1993, de Villier's Int. Achievement Award, Leukemia Soc. of America 1999, E. Donnall Thomas Prize to Recognize Pioneering Research Achievements in Hematology, American Soc. of Hematology 1999, J. Allyn Taylor Prize in Medicine 2003, The Cockrell Foundation Award in Clinical or Translational Research, The Methodist Hospital Research Inst. 2009, Simon M. Shubitz Award for Excellence in the Field of Cancer Research, Univ. of Chicago 2010. *Publications:* more than 410 articles in scientific journals on hematopoietic stem cells, lymphocyte differentiation, lymphocyte homing receptors, normal and neoplastic hematolymphoid devt, phylogeny of stem cells and alloreactivity in protochordates. *Address:* Stanford University School of Medicine, Mail Code 5501-0, 265 Campus Drive, Room G3167, Stanford, CA 94305-5461, USA (office). *Telephone:* (650) 723-6520 (office). *Fax:* (650) 723-4034 (office). *E-mail:* irv@stanford.edu (office). *Website:* biology.stanford.edu (office); med.stanford.edu/profiles/faculty/Irving_Weissman (office).

WEISSMAN, Myrna M., BA, MSW, PhD; American epidemiologist and academic; *Diane Goldman Kemper Family Professor of Psychiatry and Epidemiology, College of Physicians and Surgeons and Mailman School of Public Health, Columbia University;* b. (Myrna Milgram), Boston, Mass; d. of Samuel Milgram and Jeanette Milgram; m. 1st Gerald Klerman (deceased); m. 2nd Dr Marshall Nirenberg (deceased); m. 3rd James Frauenthal; ed Brandeis Univ., Univ. of Pennsylvania, Yale Univ. Medical School; Psychiatric Social Worker, Inst. for Juvenile Research, Chicago, Ill. 1958–59; Psychiatric Social Worker, Dept of Psychological Medicine, Southern Gen. Hosp., Glasgow, Scotland 1959–60; Social Worker, NIH, Clinical Center and Bethesda, Md 1960–67; from Research Assoc. to Prof. of Psychiatry and Epidemiology, Yale Univ. School of Medicine 1967–87, also Dir Depression Research Unit; apptd Prof. of Psychiatry and Epidemiology, Coll. of Physicians and Surgeons and Mailman School of Public Health, Columbia Univ. 1987, Diane Goldman Kemper Family Prof. 2013–; Chief of Dept, Clinical-Genetic Epidemiology, New York State Psychiatric Inst. 1987–2007, Chief, Div. of Epidemiology 2007–; Visiting Sr Scholar, Inst. of Medicine, NAS, Washington, DC 1979–80 (mem. 1996–); mem. editorial bd of several journals including Early Intervention in Psychiatry 2007–, Journal of Clinical Psychiatry 2009–, Brazilian Journal of Psychiatry 2010–, Brain Disorders & Therapy, 2011–, Current Psychopharmacology 2011–, F1000 Research 2012–; mem. Nat. Advisory Mental Health Council, Inst. of Medicine, NAS 1998–, Nat. Inst. of Mental Health 1999–2000, Council, American Coll. of Neuropsychopharmacology 1999–2002; Pres. American Psychopathological Asscn, New York 1998–99; Fellow, Royal Soc. of Psychiatrists (UK) 1998–, New York Acad. of Sciences; numerous awards, including American Psychiatric Asscn Foundation's Fund Prize 1978, Rema Lapouse Mental Health Epidemiology Award, American Public Health Asscn 1985, Research Award, American Suicide Foundation 1990, Joseph Zubin Award, American Psychopathological Asscn 1996, Distinguished Scholar Award, Partnership for Gender-Specific Medicine, Columbia Univ. 2003, Perry Award, New York Hospital-Cornell Medical Center 2005. *Publications include:* author or co-author of over 500 scientific articles and book chapters and seven books including The Depressed Woman: A Study of Social Relationships 1974, Interpersonal Psychotherapy of Depression 1984, A Comprehensive Guide to Interpersonal Psychotherapy 2000, The Treatment of Major Depression: Bridging the 21st Century (ed.) 2001, Mastering Depression through Interpersonal Psychotherapy 2005, A Clinician's Quick Guide to Interpersonal Psychotherapy 2007, The Guide to Interpersonal Psychotherapy (with John C. Markowitz and Gerald L. Klerman) 2018. *Leisure interests:* running, hiking, family. *Address:* College of Physicians and Surgeons, Nyspi-Unit 24, 1051 Riverside Drive, Columbia University, New York, NY 10032, USA (office). *Telephone:* (646) 774-6427 (office). *Fax:* (212) 568-3534 (office). *E-mail:* weissman@nyspi.columbia.edu (office); mmw3@columbia.edu (office). *Website:* www.mailman.columbia.edu (office); www.columbiapsychiatry.org.

WEISSMANN, Charles, MD, PhD, FMedSci; Swiss (b. Hungarian) molecular biologist and academic; *Professor Emeritus, Department of Infectious Diseases, The Scripps Research Institute;* b. 14 Oct. 1931, Budapest, Hungary; ed Univ. of Zurich; Prof. and Dir Inst. of Molecular Biology, Zurich –1999, Prof. Emer. 1999–; fmr Sr Researcher, Neurogenetics Unit, Imperial Coll. School of Medicine, London, UK; Sr Research Scientist, Dept of Neurodegenerative Diseases, Inst. for Neurology, Univ. Coll., London 1999–2004; Prof. and Chair. Dept of Infectious Diseases, The Scripps Research Inst., Palm Beach Co., Fla 2004–12, Prof. Emer. 2012–, mem. Scripps Bd of Scientific Govs 2004–; Distinguished Research Prof., Dept of Biological Sciences, Florida Atlantic Univ. 2004; Co-founder Biogen (first European biotechnology co.); Pres. Roche Research Foundation; co-publr several journals; mem. Bd of Dirs F. Hoffman-La Roche –2001, Speedel 2003–, several startup firms in Switzerland and Germany; mem. Bd of Govs Tel-Aviv Univ. 1997–; mem. Editorial Bd Proceedings of the Royal Soc. 1999–; mem. Akad. der Naturforscher Leopoldina, American Soc. of Biological Chem.; Foreign mem. Royal Soc.; Foreign Assoc. NAS; Fellow, American Acad. of Microbiology 1999; first to genetically engineer Interferon-Alpha; Hon. Sr Fellow, Inst. of Neurology, Univ. Coll. London 2004; Orden Pour le Mérite (Germany); seven hon. doctorate degrees, including from New York Univ. 2011; many leading scientific prizes including Dr H.P. Heineken Prize for Biochemistry and Biophysics 1982, Betty and David Koetser Award, Zürich 2001, Friedrich-Bauer-Prize for Medical Research, Univ. of Munich 2001, Warren Alpert Foundation Prize, Harvard Medical School 2004, Betty and David Koetser Award, Zurich 2001, Friedrich-Bauer-Prize for Medical Research, Univ. of Munich 2001, Warren Alpert Foundation Prize, Harvard Medical School, Boston 2004, Fifth Annual Dart/NYU Biotechnology Award, New York Univ. 2006, Ernst Jung Gold Medal for Medicine 2014. *Publications:* numerous articles in scientific journals on RNA phages, terferon and prion diseases. *Leisure interest:* art collection. *Address:* Department of Infectious Diseases, The Scripps Research Institute, 5353 Parkside Drive, Jupiter, FL 33458, USA (office). *Telephone:* (561) 543-2500 (office); (561) 228-3450 (office). *Fax:* (561) 297-0329 (office). *E-mail:* charlesw@scripps.edu (office). *Website:* www.scripps.edu/florida/research/faculty/weissmann (office).

WEISSMANN, Mariana, PhD; Argentine physicist and academic; *Senior Researcher, Argentine National Research Council;* ed Univ. of Buenos Aires; Practical Work Asst, Dept of Physics, Univ. of Buenos Aires 1957–61, Chief of Practical Works, Dept of Meteorology 1963–65, Assoc. Prof., Dept of Meteorology 1965–66, Assoc. Prof., Dept of Physical Chem. 1973–74, Contracted Lecturer, Dept 1989; Visiting Prof., Univ. of Oregon, USA 1966–67; Research Assoc., Syracuse Univ. 1967; Research Officer, Univ. of Chile 1968–71; Assoc. Prof., Dept of Physics, Univ. Simon Bolivar, Venezuela 1979–81; Sr Assoc., Int. Centre for Theoretical Physics, Trieste, Italy 1985–94; Prof. on Sabbatical, Dept of Condensed Matter Physics, Univ. Autonoma de Madrid, Spain 1990–91; Career Investigator, CONICET 1972–; Sr Researcher, Dept of Physics, Nat. Comm. Atomic Energy; currently Sr Researcher, Argentine Nat. Research Council, Buenos Aires; mem. Nat. Acad. of Exact, Physical and Natural Sciences of Argentina (first woman); UNESCO-L'Oréal Award for Women in Science (Latin America) 2003. *Publications include:* numerous papers in scientific journals on condensed matter and solid-state physics. *Address:* c/o Sección de Matemática, Física y Astronomía, Academía Nacional de Ciencias Exactas, Físicas y Naturales, Avda. Alvear 1711, 4° piso, 1014 Buenos Aires, Argentina (office). *Telephone:* (11) 4811-2998 (office); (11) 4815-9451 (office). *Fax:* (11) 4811-6951 (office). *E-mail:* acad@ancefn.org.ar (office). *Website:* www.ancefn.org.ar (office).

WEISZ, Rachel; British actress; b. 7 March 1970, London; d. of George Weisz and Edith Ruth (née Teich); m. Daniel Craig 2011; one d.; one s. with Darren Aronofsky; ed Univ. of Cambridge; London Critics Circle Theatre Award for Most Promising Newcomer 1994. *Films include:* Seventeen, Chain Reaction, Stealing Beauty, Going All the Way, Amy Foster, Bent, I Want You 1998, Land Girls 1998, The Mummy 1999, Sunshine 2000, Beautiful Creatures 2001, Enemy at the Gates 2001, The Mummy Returns 2001, About a Boy 2002, Confidence 2003, Runaway Jury 2003, Envy 2004, Constantine 2005, The Constant Gardener (Golden Globe Award for Best Supporting Actress, Screen Actors Guild Award for Best Supporting Actress, Acad. Award for Best Supporting Actress 2006) 2005, The Fountain 2006, Eragon (voice) 2006, My Blueberry Nights 2007, Fred Claus 2007, Definitely, Maybe 2007, The Lovely Bones 2009, The Whistleblower 2010, The Deep Blue Sea 2011, The Bourne Legacy 2012, Oz the Great and Powerful 2013, The Lobster 2015, Youth 2015, Complete Unknown 2016, The Light Between Oceans 2016, My Cousin Rachel 2017, The Mercy 2017, The Favourite (BAFTA Award for Best Actress in a Supporting Role 2019) 2018. *Plays include:* Design for Living 1994, Suddenly Last Summer 1999, The Shape of Things 1999, 2001, A Streetcar Named Desire 2009, Betrayal 2013, Plenty 2016. *Address:* c/o Actors Department, Independent Talent Group Ltd, 40 Whitfield Street, London, W1T 2RH, England (office). *Telephone:* (20) 7636-6565 (office). *Website:* www.independenttalent.com (office).

WEITZMANN, Horst, Dipl.-Ing; German business executive; b. 1941, Riesa, Saxony; m. Marlis Weitzmann 1967; two d.; Man. Dir Vereinigten Schraubenwerke Thyssen/Otto Wolff 1972–77; Man. Dir American Airfilter Co., Düsseldorf 1978–80; Jt Owner, Badische Stahlwerke (following man. buyout 1982); Man. Partner, NDW Beteiligungsgesellschaft mbH; Chair. Supervisory Bd Südweststahl AG, BCT Technology AG; Chair. Bd of Trustees Albert-Ludwigs-Universität Freiburg, also Hon. Senator and Chair. Univ. Council; fmr Pres. European Steel Works Asscn; mem. Int. Advisory Bd, IEDC (fmrly Int. Exec. Devt Center) Bled School of Man. *Leisure interest:* collecting contemporary art. *Address:* NDW Beteiligungsgesellschaft mbH, Friedrichstr. 16, Eberbach 69412, Germany (office).

WEK, Alek; Sudanese fashion model; b. 1977, Wau, southern Sudan; fled with younger sister to UK to escape civil war between Muslim north and Christian south of Sudan 1991; discovered at an outdoor market in Crystal Palace, south London by Fiona Ellis (scout for Models 1) 1995; first appeared on catwalks 1995; later moved to USA; has modelled for fashion designers John Galliano, Donna Karan, Calvin Klein and Ermanno Scervino; also designs range of designer handbags called Wek 1933; mem. US Cttee for Refugees' Advisory Council; named Model of the Year by MTV 1997, Venus de la Mode Award. *Publication:* Alek (autobiography) 2007. *Address:* c/o Storm Models, 1st Floor, 5 Jubilee Place, Chelsea, London, SW3 3TD, England (office). *E-mail:* info@alekwek.com. *Website:* alek-wek.com.

WELBY, Most Rev. and Rt Hon. Justin Portal, PC, BA, DipMin; British ecclesiastic, writer, theologian and fmr oil industry executive; *Archbishop of Canterbury;* b. 6 Jan. 1956, London; s. of Gavin Bramhall James Welby (b. Bernard Gavin Weiler) and Jane Gillian (née Portal), later Baroness Williams of Elvel; m. Caroline Eaton; two s. four d. (one deceased); ed Eton Coll., Trinity Coll., Cambridge, St John's Coll., Durham; worked in the oil industry for 11 years, including with Société Nationale Elf Aquitaine, Paris 1978–83, Elf UK plc, London 1983–84; Treas. Enterprise Oil PLC, London 1984–89; studied theology and trained for the priesthood 1989–92; Deacon 1992, Priest 1993; Asst Curate, All Saints, Chilvers Coton and St Mary the Virgin, Astley, Nuneaton 1992–95; Rector St James, Southam, later Vicar of St Michael and All Angels, Ufton, Diocese of Coventry 1995–2002; Canon Residentiary, Coventry Cathedral and Co-Dir for Int. Ministry, Int. Centre for Reconciliation 2002–05; Canon Residentiary and Sub-Dean, Coventry Cathedral 2005–07; Priest-in-Charge, Holy Trinity, Coventry 2007; Dean of Liverpool Cathedral 2007–11; Bishop of Durham 2011–12; Archbishop of Canterbury 2013–; mem. House of Lords 2012–, mem. Parl. Comm. on Banking Standards 2012; Chair. an NHS hosp. trust in S Warwicks. 2000–02; mem. Sec.-Gen.'s High-Level Advisory Bd on Mediation, UN 2017–. *Publications:* Managing the Church?: Order and Organisation in a Secular Age, Explorations in Financial Ethics, Can Companies Sin?: 'Whether', 'How' and 'Who' in Company Accountability 1992; articles on ethics, international finance and reconciliation. *Leisure interests:* French culture, sailing, politics. *Address:* Lambeth Palace, London, SE1 7JU, England (office). *Telephone:* (20) 7898-1200 (office). *Fax:* (20) 7261-9836 (office). *E-mail:* contact@lambethpalace.org.uk (office). *Website:* www.archbishopofcanterbury.org (office).

WELCH, C. David, MA; American business executive and fmr diplomatist; *Senior Vice-President for International Relations and Government Affairs, Bechtel Group;* b. 1953, Munich, Germany; m. Gretchen Gerwe Welch; three d.; ed London School of Econs, UK, Georgetown Univ., Washington, DC, Fletcher School of Law and Diplomacy, Tufts Univ., Medford, Mass; Political Officer, Embassy in Islamabad 1979–81, Officer responsible for Syria, Bureau of Near Eastern Affairs and South Asian Affairs, Dept of State, Washington, DC 1981–82, for Lebanon 1982–83, Chief of Political Section, US Embassy, Damascus, Syria 1984–86, Political Counselor, US Embassy, Amman, Jordan 1986–88, mem. staff, Nat. Security Council, White House, Washington, DC 1989–91, Exec. Asst to Under-Sec. of State for Political Affairs 1991–92, Chargé d'Affaires, US Embassy, Riyadh, Saudi Arabia 1992–94, Deputy Chief of Mission 1994–95, Prin. Deputy Asst Sec., Bureau of Near Eastern Affairs 1995–98, Asst Sec. of State for Int. Org. Affairs 1998–2001, Amb. to Egypt 2001–05, Asst Sec., Bureau of Near Eastern Affairs 2005–08; Pres. of Europe, Africa, Middle East Region, Bechtel Ltd, London 2008–13, Dubai 2013–16, Sr Vice-Pres. for Int. Relations and Govt Affairs, Bechtel Group, Reston, Va 2016–; mem. Council on Foreign Relations, American Foreign Service Asscn, American Acad. of Diplomacy; mem. ME Advisory Group for Fletcher School, Tufts Univ.; presidential appointments under Democrat and Republican admins; several Awards for exceptional service to US Govt. *Address:* Bechtel Group, 12011 Sunset Hills Road, Suite 110, Reston, VA 20190, USA (office). *Telephone:* (571) 392 6300 (office). *Website:* www.bechtel.com (office).

WELCH, John Francis (Jack), Jr, BS, MS, PhD; American business executive; *Senior Advisor, Clayton, Dubilier & Rice, LLC;* b. 19 Nov. 1935, Peabody, Mass; s. of John Francis Welch and Grace Welch (née Andrews); m. 1st Carolyn B. Osburn 1959 (divorced 1987); two s. two d.; m. 2nd Jane Beasely 1989 (divorced 2003); m. 3rd Suzy Wetlaufer 2004; ed Univs of Massachusetts and Illinois; joined Gen. Electric Co., Fairfield, Conn. 1960, Vice-Pres. 1972, Vice-Pres. Exec. Components and Materials Group 1973–77, Sr Vice-Pres. Sector Exec., Consumer Products and Services Sector 1977–79, Vice-Chair and CEO 1979–81, Chair. and CEO 1981–2001, Pres. and CEO Nat. Broadcasting Co. 1986–2000; mem. Bd of Dirs Fiat 2002–03, Idealab 2000; Sr Advisor, Clayton, Dubilier & Rice, LLC 2001–; f. Jack Welch Man. Inst. (programme at Chancellor Univ., acquired by Strayer Univ. 2011) 2009; Chair. The Business Council 1991–92; mem. Pres.'s Strategic and Policy Forum Jan.–Aug. 2017. *Publications:* Jack Welch and the GE Way 1998, Jack: Straight from the Gut 2000, Winning (with Suzy Welch) 2005. *Address:* Clayton, Dubilier & Rice, LLC, 375 Park Avenue, 18th Floor, New York, NY 10152, USA (office). *Telephone:* (212) 407-5200 (office). *Fax:* (212) 407-5252 (office). *E-mail:* info@cdr-inc.com (office). *Website:* www.cdr-inc.com (office).

WELCH, Raquel; American actress; b. (Jo Raquel Tejada), 5 Sept. 1940, Chicago, Ill.; d. of Armand Tejada and Josepha Tejada (née Hall); m. 1st James Westley Welch 1959 (divorced); one s. one d.; m. 2nd Patrick Curtis (divorced); m. 3rd Andre Weinfeld 1980 (divorced); m. 4th Richard Palmer 1999 (divorced 2003); Lifetime Achievement Award, NALIP Latino Media Awards 2015. *Films include:* Fantastic Voyage 1966, One Million Years BC 1967, Fathom 1967, The Biggest Bundle of Them All 1968, Magic Christian 1970, Myra Breckinridge 1970, Fuzz 1972, Bluebeard 1972, Hannie Caulder 1972, Kansas City Bomber 1972, The Last of Sheila 1973, The Three Musketeers 1974, The Wild Party 1975, The Four Musketeers 1975, Mother, Jugs and Speed 1976, Crossed Swords 1978, L'Animal 1979, Right to Die 1987, Scandal in a Small Town 1988, Trouble in Paradise 1989, Naked Gun 33 1/3: The Final Insult 1994, Folle d'Elle 1998, Chairman of the Board 1998, The Complete Musketeers 1999, Tortilla Soup 2001, Legally Blonde 2001, Forget About It 2006. *Television includes:* Central Park West (series) 1996, American Family (series) 2002, Welcome to the Captain (series) 2008. *Plays include:* Woman of the Year (Broadway) 1982, Torch Song 1993. *Videos:* Raquel: Total Beauty and Fitness 1984, A Week with Raquel 1987, Raquel: Lose 10lbs in 3 Weeks 1989. *Publications:* The Raquel Welch Total Beauty and Fitness Program 1984, Raquel: Beyond the Cleavage 2010.

WELD, Tuesday Ker; American actress; b. (Susan Ker Weld), 27 Aug. 1943, New York City; d. of Lathrop M. Weld and Aileen Ker; m. 1st Claude Harz 1965 (divorced 1971); one d.; m. 2nd Dudley Moore 1975 (divorced); one s.; m. 3rd Pinchas Zukerman 1985; ed Hollywood Professional School; fashion and catalogue model aged three; regular appearances as magazine cover-girl and in child roles on TV by age twelve. *Films include:* Rock Rock (debut) 1956, Serial, Rally Round the Flag Boys, The Five Pennies, The Private Lives of Adam and Eve, Return to Peyton Place, Wild in the Country, Bachelor Flat, Lord Love a Duck, Pretty Poison, I Walk the Line, A Safe Place, Play it as it Lays, Because They're Young, High Time, Sex Kittens Go to College, The Cincinnati Kid, Soldier in the Rain, Looking for Mr Goodbar, Thief, Author!, Once Upon a Time In America 1984, Heartbreak Hotel 1988, Falling Down 1993, Feeling Minnesota 1996, Chelsea Walls 2001, Investigating Sex 2002. *Television includes:* appeared in numerous TV programmes and TV films including The Many Loves of Dobie Gillis 1959 and numerous guest roles.

WELD, William (Bill) Floyd, AB, JD; American business executive and politician; *Principal, Mintz Levin, PC;* b. 31 July 1945, Smithtown, NY; s. of David Weld and Mary Weld (née Nichols); m. 1st Susan Roosevelt 1975 (divorced 2002); two s. three d.; m. 2nd Leslie Marshall; ed Middlesex School, Mass, Harvard Coll., Univ. Coll., Oxford, UK, Harvard Univ.; admitted Mass Bar 1970; law clerk, Supreme Judicial Court, Mass 1970–71; Partner, Hill & Barlow, Boston 1971–81; Assoc. Minority Counsel, US House of Reps Judiciary Comm. Impeachment Inquiry 1973–74; US Attorney for Dist of Mass 1981–86; Asst Attorney-Gen. Criminal Div. US Justice Dept, Washington, DC 1986–88; Gov. of Massachusetts 1991–97; nominated as Amb. to Mexico but was never confirmed; Prin., Leeds Weld & Co. (pvt. equity firm) –2005, CEO Decker Coll., Louisville, Ky (after acquisition by Leeds Weld) Jan.–Oct. 2005; announced candidacy for Gov. of NY Aug. 2005; admitted to practise law in NY State 2008; Co-Chair. for Mitt Romney's presidential campaign in NY State 2007–08; currently Prin., Mintz Levin and ML Strategies, Boston; co-chaired Ind. Task Force on North America under the Council on Foreign Relations, which studied the integration of the USA, Canada and Mexico; served by appointment as mem. US Holocaust Memorial Council; Libertarian Party cand. for Vice-Pres. for US presidential election 2016; mem. ABA, American Law Inst., Boston Bar Asscn, Council on Foreign Relations; Assoc. mem. InterAction Council; Republican. *Film:* Traffic (as himself) 2000. *Publications:* novels: Mackerel By Moonlight 1988, Big Ugly 1999, Stillwater 2002. *Address:* Mintz Levin, PC, One Financial Center, Boston, MA 02111, USA (office). *Telephone:* (617) 348-4412 (office). *E-mail:* BWeld@mintz.com (office). *Website:* www.mintz.com (office).

WELDON, Fay, CBE, MA, FRSA; British author and academic; *Professor of Creative Writing, Bath Spa University;* b. 22 Sept. 1931, Alvechurch, Worcs., England; d. of Frank T. Birkinshaw and Margaret J. Birkinshaw; m. 1st Ronald Weldon 1960 (divorced 1994); four s.; m. 2nd Nicolas Fox 1995; ed Girls' High School, Christchurch, New Zealand, South Hampstead School for Girls and Univ. of St Andrews; fmr advertising copywriter; Chair. of Judges, Booker McConnell Prize 1983; Writer-in-Residence, Savoy Hotel, London Oct.-Dec. 2002; apptd Prof. of Creative Writing, Brunel Univ. 2006; Prof. of Creative Writing, Bath Spa Univ. 2012–; fmr mem. Arts Council Literary Panel; mem. Video Censorship Appeals Cttee; Fellow, City of Bath Coll. 1999; Hon. DLitt (Bath) 1989, (St Andrews) 1992, (Birmingham), (Univ. of Connecticut), (Worcester) 2011; Women in Publishing Pandora Award 1997. *Plays:* Words of Advice 1974, Friends 1975, Moving House 1976, Mr Director 1977, Action Replay 1979, I Love My Love 1981, Woodworm 1981, Jane Eyre 1986, The Hole in the Top of the World 1987, Jane Eyre (adaptation), Playhouse Theatre, London 1995, The Four Alice Bakers, Birmingham Repertory 1999, Breakfast with Emma, Lyric Hammersmith 2003; more than 30 television plays, dramatizations and radio plays. *Television:* wrote pilot episode of Upstairs, Downstairs; Big Women (series), Channel 4 1999. *Publications include:* novels: The Fat Woman's Joke (aka And the Wife Ran Away) 1967, Down Among the Women 1972, Female Friends 1975, Remember Me 1976, Little Sisters (aka Words of Advice) 1977, Praxis 1978, Puffball 1980, The President's Child 1982, The Life and Loves of a She-Devil 1984, The Shrapnel Academy 1986, The Heart of the Country 1987, The Hearts and Lives of Men 1987, The Rules of Life (novella) 1987, Leader of the Band 1988, The Cloning of Joanna May 1989, Darcy's Utopia 1990, Growing Rich 1992, Life Force 1992, Affliction (aka Trouble) 1994, Splitting 1995, Worst Fears 1996, Big Women 1997, Rhode Island Blues 2000, Bulgari Connection 2001, She May Not Leave 2005, The Spa Decameron 2007, The Stepmother's Diary 2008, Chalcot Crescent 2009, Kehua 2010, Habits of the House 2012, Long Live the King 2013, The New Countess 2013; children's books: Wolf the Mechanical Dog 1988, Party Puddle 1989, Nobody Likes Me! 1997; short story collections: Watching Me Watching You 1981, Polaris 1985, Moon Over Minneapolis 1991, Wicked Women 1995, Angel All Innocence and Other Stories 1995, A Hard Time to be a Father 1998, Nothing to Wear, Nowhere to Hide 2002; other: Letters to Alice 1984, Rebecca West 1985, Godless in Eden (essays) 2000, Auto da Fay (autobiography) 2002, Mantrapped (autobiography) 2004, What Makes Women Happy 2006, The Spa Decameron 2007, The Stepmother's Diary 2008, Chalcot Crescent 2009, Kehua! 2010, Habits of the House 2012, Long Live the King 2013, The New Countess 2013, Mischief 2015, Before the War 2016. *Address:* c/o Georgina Capel, Capel Land, 29 Wardour Street, London, W1V 6HB, England (office); Department of Creative Writing, Bath Spa University, Newton St Loe, Bath, BA2 9BN, England (office). *Telephone:* (20) 7734-2414 (office). *Website:* www.fayweldon.co.uk.

WELDON, William C., BS; American pharmaceutical industry executive; b. 26 Nov. 1948, Brooklyn, New York; m. Barbara Weldon; one s. one d.; ed Quinnipiac Univ., Hamden, Conn.; joined Johnson & Johnson 1971, served in sales and marketing positions with McNeil Pharmaceuticals affiliate 1971–82, led pharmaceutical orgs for Johnson & Johnson in SE Asia and UK 1982–89, Vice-Pres. Sales and Marketing Janssen Pharmaceutica 1989–92, Pres. Ethicon Endo-Surgery 1992–95, Group Chair. 1995–98, mem. Exec. Cttee and Worldwide Chair. Pharmaceuticals Group 1998–2001, mem. Bd of Dirs Johnson & Johnson 2001–, Vice-Chair. 2001–02, Chair. and CEO 2002–12, then Chair. 2012; mem. Bd of Dirs JPMorgan Chase & Co. 2005–; Chair. CEO Roundtable on Cancer; Vice-Chair. The Business Council; mem. The Sullivan Comm. on Diversity in the Health Professions Workforce, Liberty Science Center Chair.'s Advisory Council; fmr Chair. Pharmaceutical Research and Mfrs of America; Trustee, Quinnipiac Univ.

WELLER, Malcolm Philip Isadore, MB BS, MA, FRCPsych, FBPS, Chartered Psychologist, Int. FAPA; British medical practitioner; *Emeritus Consultant, St Ann's Hospital* and*Honorary Research Professor, Middlesex University;* b. 29 May 1935, Manchester; s. of Solomon George Weller and Esther Weller; m. Davina Reisler 1966; two s.; ed Perse School, Cambridge, Univ. of Cambridge, Newcastle Univ.; Consultant Neuropsychiatrist Emer., Barnet Enfield & Haringey Mental Health NHS Trust, Chartered Psychologist (Neuropsychology Section); Emer. Consultant, St Ann's Hosp.; Hon. Sr Lecturer, Mental Health Sciences, School of Medicine, Univ. of London –1997; Hon. Research Prof., Middlesex Univ. 1997–; Chair. N Thames Region Psychiatric Cttee 1997, London Region Psychiatric Cttee 1995–2000; Vice-Chair. NE Thames Regional Cttee for Hosp. Medical Services 1984–96; Hon. Medical Adviser, Nat. Alliance of Relatives of the Mentally Ill, Jewish Asscn of the Mentally Ill, Nat. Schizophrenia Fellowship and Founder-mem. Parl. Cttee; Chair. CONCERN 1992–99; co-opted mem. Bd of Studies in Psychology, London Univ. and Higher Degrees Sub-cttee 1976–; Royal Coll. of Psychiatry Examiner for Master in Medicine (Psychiatry) Degree, Nat. Univ. of Singapore 1988, 1989; External Examiner, Univ. of Manchester PhD degree 1990; mem. Standing Cttee, Bd of Studies in Medicine, Univ. of London 1981–84, Cen. Cttee of BMA 1994–96, Gen. Psychiatry Exec. Cttee of Royal Coll. of Psychiatry, also of Pharmacology and Social, Community and Rehabilitation; previously Royal Coll. Rep. to Asscn of the British Pharmaceutical Industry; Exec. mem. Neuropsychiatry and Academic Faculties, Royal Coll. of Psychiatrists 2011–16; Council mem. Psychiatry Section, Royal Soc. of Medicine (RSM), RSM Rep. to Nat. Inst. for Clinical Excellence, also RSM Prize Adjudicator; Visiting Fellow, Fitzwilliam Coll., Cambridge 1993–94; Concert organizer, Newcastle Festival 1970–71; co-opted mem. Laing Art Gallery Cttee 1972–73; Chair. Govs Gosforth Middle School 1971–74; Fellow, British Psychological Soc., Royal Coll. of Psychiatrists; Int. Fellow, American Psychiatric Asscn; initiated and ran courses for British Postgraduate Fed. and prepared teaching videos and a rating scale for WHO; Hon. Lifetime Achievement Fellow, Int. Coll. of Neuropsychopharmacology (CINP); Scholarship, Mental Health Research Fund, Ver Heyden de Lancey Prize, Univ. of Cambridge, Wilfred Kingdom Prize, Univ. of Newcastle, Brit Council Travel Award, Invited Fellow, Royal Soc. of Arts. *Radio:* adviser and participant in BBC radio feature: Breakdown (Italia Prize). *Publications include:* Founder and

Ed.-in-Chief, Baillière's Clinical Psychiatry series (11 vols); Progress in Clinical Psychiatry 1997, Genetics of Mental Disorder, Vols I and II, Epidemiological Psychiatry, Hypnotics and Anxiolytics, Pharmacological Management of Chronic Psychiatric Disorders, Post Traumatic Stress Disorder, Drugs of Abuse, Psychiatric Issues in Women, Sexual Dysfunction, Eating Disorders, Psychosocial Aspects of Chronic Fatigue Syndrome; editor: Scientific Basis of Psychology 1983, 1992, International Perspectives in Schizophrenia 1989, Dimensions of Community Care 1993; about 200 editorials and papers in learned journals, mainly on psychosis, depression, head injury, psychological medicine and medico-legal matters; about 100 publs on music in various music journals. *Leisure interests:* fine art, music. *Address:* 30 Arkwright Road, Hampstead, London, NW3 6BH, England (home). *Telephone:* (20) 7794-5804 (home). *E-mail:* malcolm@weller.tv (home); office@malcolmweller.com (office). *Website:* malcolmweller.com.

WELLER, Paul; British musician (guitar, piano), singer and songwriter; b. 25 May 1958, Woking, Surrey; Founder-mem. and lead singer, The Jam 1972–82, The Style Council 1983–89, The Paul Weller Movement; solo artist 1990–; est. own record label Freedom High; Ivor Novello Awards for Outstanding Contemporary Song Collection 1994, for Lifetime Achievement 2010, Brit Awards for Best Male Artist 1995, 1996, 2009, for Outstanding Contribution 2005, Mojo Award for Best Songwriter 2005, Q Award for Outstanding Contribution to Music 2005, for Best Act in the World Today 2018, Silver Clef Award 2007. *Recordings include:* albums: with The Jam: In the City 1977, This is the Modern World 1977, All Mod Cons 1978, Setting Sons 1979, Sound Affects 1980, The Gift 1982; with The Style Council: Introducing The Style Council 1983, Café Bleu 1984, Our Favourite Shop 1985, Home and Abroad 1986, The Cost of Loving 1987, Confessions of a Pop Group 1988, Singular Adventures of the Style Council 1989, Here's Some That Got Away 1993, Modernism: A New Decade 1998; solo: Paul Weller 1992, Wild Wood 1993, Live Wood 1994, Stanley Road 1995, Heavy Soul 1997, Modern Classics 1998, Heliocentric 2000, Days of Speed 2001, Illumination 2002, Fly on the Wall: B-Sides and Rarities 2003, Studio 150 2004, As Is Now 2005, Catch-Flame! 2006, Hit Parade 2006, 22 Dreams 2008, Wake Up the Nation 2010, Sonik Kicks 2012, More Modern Classics 2014, Saturns Pattern 2015, A Kind Revolution 2017, True Meanings 2018. *Film:* JerUSAlem 1987. *Website:* www.paulweller.com.

WELLINK, Arnout (Nout) H. E. M., PhD; Dutch international banking executive and fmr central banker; b. 27 Aug. 1943, Bredevoort; m. M. V. Volmer; five c.; ed Leyden Univ., Univ. of Rotterdam; teacher, Leyden Univ. 1965–70; mem. staff, Ministry of Finance 1970–75, Head of Directorate-Gen. Financial and Econ. Policy 1975–77, Treas.-Gen. 1977–82; Exec. Dir De Nederlandsche Bank NV 1982–97, Pres. 1997–2011; Extraordinary Prof., Free Univ., Amsterdam 1988–98; Chair. Banking Supervision, Basel Cttee 2006–11; mem. Bd Bank of China 2012–; Chair. of Bd and Pres. Bank for Int. Settlements (BIS) 2002–06; Chair. Public Interest Cttee, PricewaterhouseCoopers Accountants NV 2015–; Chair. Supervisory Bd, Leyden Univ. 2008–; Pres. Wim Drees Foundation for Public Finance 2011–, Foundation Bontius 2013–; mem. Governing Council, European Cen. Bank 1999–2012; mem. Bd of Trustees Museum Mauritshuis, Supervisory Bd Openlucht Museum; Kt, Order of the Netherlands Lion 1980, Commdr, Order of Orange-Nassau 2011; Dr hc (Tilburg Univ.) 2008.

WELLS, George Andre; Ni-Vanuatu politician; worked for Sofrana Line (shipping co.) 1980–85; Minister of Internal Affairs 2004, 2007, 2011–13; fmr Minister of Nat. Defence; Minister of Foreign Affairs, External Trade and Telecommunications 2007, 2010–11; mem. Parl. for Luganville (suspended 2013), Leader of Govt Business 2002–03, Speaker of Parl. 2010–13; fmr mem. Vanuaaku Pati and Nat. United Party; currently mem. Nat. Community Asscn Party (NCAP).

WELLS, Michael (Mike) Andrew, BS; American (b. Canadian) business executive; *Group Chief Executive, Prudential plc;* b. 9 April 1960, Canada; m.; two s.; ed San Diego State Univ.; spent ten years working for various financial services firms in USA, including Wood Logan, Smith Barney, McGinness & Assocs, Dean Witter; joined Prudential Group as Pres. Jackson Nat. Life Distributors, Mich. (part of Group's US arm, Jackson Nat. Life Insurance Co.—Jackson) 1995, spent 20 years in various sr positions, CEO Jackson 2011–15, mem. Bd of Dirs, Prudential plc (parent co.) 2011–, Group Chief Exec. Prudential plc 2015–. *Leisure interests:* music, collecting Gibson guitars, European Renaissance history. *Address:* Prudential plc, Laurence Pountney Hill, London, EC4R 0HH, England (office). *Telephone:* (20) 7548-3901 (office); (20) 7220-7588 (switchboard) (office). *Fax:* (20) 7548-3631 (office). *E-mail:* info@prudential.co.uk (office). *Website:* www .prudential.co.uk (office).

WELLS, Rufus Michael Grant, PhD, DSc, FRSNZ; New Zealand marine biologist and academic; *Professor, Marine Biology Group, University of Auckland;* b. 3 July 1947, Cardiff, Wales; s. of Peter F. Wells and Jean Chiles; m. Jane Nelson 1969; one s. one d.; ed Hamilton Boys' High School, Univ. of Auckland, Bedford Coll., Univ. of London, UK; researcher in molecular physiology of haemoglobin and respiration (medical, animal and fisheries science), Antarctic biology; Asst Lecturer in Statistics, Univ. of Auckland 1970–71; Research Asst and PhD student Bedford Coll., London 1971–74; Biochemist and MRC Fellow, Univ. Coll. Hosp., London 1974–75; Lecturer, then Sr Lecturer in Zoology, then Prof., Univ. of Auckland 1975–; biological and editorial consultant, specializing in Antarctic Science and Science Educ.; fmr mem. Nat. Comm. for Antarctic Research; Physiological Soc. of NZ Medal 1983, Royal Soc. of NZ Hutton Medal 1989. *Publications:* more than 220 scientific papers. *Address:* School of Biological Sciences, Marine Biology Group, Thomas Building, Level 1, Room 138, 3 Symonds Street, City Campus, University of Auckland, Auckland 1, New Zealand (office). *Telephone:* (9) 373-7999 (ext. 87206) (office). *Fax:* (9) 373-7668 (office). *E-mail:* r.wells@auckland.ac.nz (home). *Website:* www.sbs.auckland.ac.nz (office).

WELSER-MÖST, Franz; Austrian conductor; *Music Director, Cleveland Orchestra;* b. 16 Aug. 1960, Linz; m.; ed Musikgymnasium, Linz and Staatliche Musikhochschule, Munich; Chief Conductor, Jeunesse Orchestra, Linz 1982–85, Norrköping Symphony Orchestra 1985, Musikkollegium Winterthur, Switzerland 1986; Music Dir London Philharmonic Orchestra 1990–96; Music Dir Zürich Opera 1995–2002, Principal Conductor 2002–05, Music Dir 2005–08; Music Dir Cleveland Orchestra 2002–; Gen. Music Dir Vienna Staatsoper 2010–14; has appeared at Deutsche Oper Berlin, Glyndebourne Festival, Salzburg Festival;

regularly works with Berlin Philharmonic, Vienna Philharmonic, Royal Concertgebouw Orchestra, Gewandhausorchester Leipzig, Staatskapelle Dresden, Symphonieorchester des Bayerischen Rundfunks and Gustav Mahler Youth Orchestra; has conducted all major US orchestras; Academician, European Acad. of Yuste; Hon. mem. Gesellschaft der Musikfreunde Wien and Wiener Singverein; Decoration of Honour; Outstanding Achievement Award, Western Law Centre, LA, for work for people with disabilities, Musical America's Conductor of the Year 2003, Diapason d'Or, Japanese Record Acad. Award, Gold Medal of Upper Austria, Kilenyi Medal of Honour, Bruckner Soc. of America. *Recordings include:* Mendelssohn Symphonies Nos 3 and 4, Schumann Symphonies Nos 2 and 3, Bruckner Symphony No. 7, Strauss Waltzes, Carl Orff's Carmina Burana, Stravinsky's Oedipus Rex, Bartók's Miraculous Mandarin, Kodaly's Peacock Variations, Kancheli's Symphony No. 3, Pärt's Symphony No. 3, Fratres, Schmidt's Symphony No. 4 (Gramophone Award 1996) (all with LPO), world premiere recording of Johann Straus Jr's Simplicius with Zurich Opera Orchestra, Beethoven's Symphony No. 9 (with The Cleveland Orchestra), The Welser-Möst Edition, New Year's Day Concert (Vienna Musikverein) on CD and DVD 2011, 2013. *Publication:* Kadenzen: Notizen und Gespräche 2007. *Leisure interests:* literature, mountain hiking, marathons. *Address:* c/o IMG Artists, Capital Tower, 91 Waterloo Road, London, SE1 8RT, England (office); The Cleveland Orchestra, Severance Hall, 11001 Euclid Avenue, Cleveland, OH 44106-1796, USA (office). *Telephone:* (20) 7957-5800 (office); (20) 7957-5801 (office); (216) 231-7300 (office). *E-mail:* jchadwick@imgartists.com (office); jchadwick@enticottmusicmanagement .com (office); info@clevelandorchestra.com (office). *Website:* www.imgartists.com (office); www.clevelandorchestra.com (office).

WELSH, Irvine, MBA; British writer; b. 1958, Edinburgh, Scotland; m. 1st Anne Antsy 1984 (separated 2003); m. 2nd Beth Quinn 2005 (separated 2017); ed Heriot-Watt Univ.; Co-owner, 4 Way Productions film studio; Amb. for UNICEF. *Publications include:* Trainspotting (novel) 1993, The Acid House (short stories) 1994, Marabou Stork Nightmares: A Novel 1995, Ecstasy: Three Chemical Romances 1996, The Wedding (with Nick Waplington) 1996, You'll Have Had Your Hole (play) 1997, Filth: A Novel 1998, Glue (novel) 2000, Porno (novel) 2002, Soul Crew (screenplay, also dir) 2003, Meat Trade (screenplay) 2004, The Bedroom Secrets of the Master Chefs (novel) 2006, Babylon Heights (with Dean Cavanagh) 2006, If You Liked School, You'll Love Work (short stories) 2007, Crime (novel) 2008, Reheated Cabbage (short stories) 2009, Skagboys 2012, The Blade Artist 2016, Dead Men's Trousers 2018; contrib. to newspapers; contrib. to anthologies, including Children of Albion Rovers 1996, Disco Biscuits 1996, Ahead of its Time 1997, The Weekenders 2002, One City 2006; contrib. to Loaded, Guardian, Daily Telegraph. *Address:* c/o Jonathan Cape, 20 Vauxhall Bridge Road, London, SW1V 2SA, England. *Website:* www.irvinewelsh.net.

WELSH, Jennifer M., BA; Canadian academic and UN official; *Professor and Chairman, International Relations, European University Institute;* b. Regina, Sask.; m.; two c.; ed Univ. of Saskatchewan, Univ. of Oxford, UK; fmr Jean Monnet Fellow, European Univ. Inst., currently Prof. and Chair in Int. Relations; fmr Cadieux Research Fellow, Policy Planning Staff of Canadian Dept of Foreign Affairs; fmr Prof. of Int. Relations and Co-Dir, Oxford Inst. for Ethics, Law and Armed Conflict, Univ. of Oxford, UK; fmr Assoc. Dir, Peace and Conflict Studies Programme, Univ. of Toronto; Special Adviser to UN Sec.-Gen. on the Responsibility to Protect, Office of the Special Adviser on the Prevention of Genocide 2013–16; currently Prof. and Chair., Int. Relations, European Univ. Inst.; Sr Research Fellow, Somerville Coll., Univ. of Oxford; has also taught int. relations at McGill Univ. and Central European Univ.; fmr consultant to Govt of Canada on int. policy; frequent commentator in Canadian media on foreign policy and int. relations; Distinguished Visiting Fellow, Massey Coll., Univ. of Toronto 2005; mem. Bd of Trustees, Walter and Duncan Gordon Foundation 2006; mem. Editorial Bd, BISA Series in Int. Relations, Cambridge Univ. Press 2008; Leverhulme Trust Research Fellowship 2006, Trudeau Fellowship 2006. *Publications include:* Edmund Burke and International Relations 1995, Chips & Pop: Decoding the Nexus Generation (co-author) 1998, Empire and Community: Edmund Burke's Writings and Speeches on International Relations (co-author) 1999, At Home in the World: Canada's Global Vision for the 21st Century 2004. *Address:* European University Institute, Via dei Roccettini 9, 50014 Fiesole, Italy (office). *Telephone:* (55) 4685436 (office). *Fax:* (55) 4685201 (office). *E-mail:* Jennifer.Welsh@eui.eu (office). *Website:* www.eui.eu/DepartmentsAndCentres/ PoliticalAndSocialSciences/People/Professors/Welsh (office).

WELSH, Moray Meston, BA, GradDip, LRAM, ARCM; British cellist, teacher and painter; b. 1 March 1947, Haddington, East Lothian, Scotland; s. of D. A. Welsh and C. Welsh (née Meston); partner Jonathan Papp; ed York Univ. and Moscow Conservatoire, Russia; debut, Wigmore Hall 1972; cello solo appearances in UK, USA, USSR, Europe and Scandinavia; principal cellist, London Symphony Orchestra 1992–2007; appeared with major UK orchestras, including Royal Philharmonic Orchestra, BBC Symphony; festivals at Bath, Edinburgh, Aldeburgh, Bergen and Helsinki; appeared as soloist internationally under Colin Davis, André Previn, Rafael Frühbeck de Burgos, Bernard Haitink; chamber music performances with Previn, Bashmet, Midori, Galway and Chung; Prin. Cellist, London Symphony Orchestra 1992–2005; mem. Cropper-Welsh-Roscoe Trio 2005–15; recitals with Jonathan Papp, Martin Roscoe and Caroline Palmer; teaches privately and in master-classes; British Council Scholarship 1969, Gulbenkian Fellowship 1970. *Recordings include:* concertos by Boccherini, Vivaldi, Alexander Goehr, Hoddinott, Hugh Wood (Sunday Times Record of the Year); recorded with James Galway, Kyung-Wha Chung, Allegri Quartet, Alberni Quartet; cello and orchestra music by Herbert Howells with LSO; Rachmaninov Complete Works for Cello and Piano. *Film:* Barry Lyndon (soundtrack). *Radio includes:* frequent broadcasts on BBC Radio 3. *Publications:* articles in The Strad Magazine and nat. newspapers. *Leisure interests:* art, gardening, skiing, writing. *Address:* 32 Dartmouth Road, London, NW2 4EX, England (home). *Telephone:* (20) 8933-3032 (home). *E-mail:* moraywelsh@thecello.net (home). *Website:* www .moraywelsh.com.

WELTEKE, Ernst; German economist; b. 21 Aug. 1942, Korbach; ed Univ. Marburg, Univ. Frankfurt am Main; Chair. Parl. Group of Social Democratic Party in Hessen Land Parl. 1984–87, 1988–91; Minister for the Economy, Transport and Tech. in Hessen 1991–94, for Finance 1994–95; Pres. Land Cen. Bank, Hessen

1995–99; Pres. Deutsche Bundesbank Sept. 1999–2004 (resgnd); mem. Governing Council European Cen. Bank 1999–2004. *Address:* Westerbachstraße 23E, 61476 Kronberg im Taunus, Germany (office).

WELTY, John D., MA, EdD; American academic and fmr university administrator; *Associate, American Association of State Colleges and Universities–Penson Center for Professional Development;* b. 24 Aug. 1944, Amboy, Ill.; s. of John D. Welty and Doris E. Donnelly; m. Sharon Brown 1996; three d. two s.; ed Western Illinois, Michigan State and Indiana Univs; Admissions Counsellor, Michigan State Univ. 1966–67; Asst Vice-Pres. for Student Affairs, Southwest Minnesota State Univ. 1967–74; Dir of Residences and Asst Prof., State Univ. of NY, Albany 1974–77, Assoc. Dean of Students and Dir of Residences 1977–80; Vice-Pres. for Student and Univ. Affairs, Ind. Univ. of Pennsylvania 1980–84, Pres. 1984–91; Pres. California State Univ., Fresno 1991–2013 (retd), also Prof., Kremen School of Educ. and Human Devt; Assoc., American Asscn of State Colls and Univs–Penson Center for Professional Devt (AASCU–Penson Center) 2014–; Dr hc (Western Illinois Univ.); Chief Exec. Leadership Award, Council for Advancement and Support for Educ. 1999, Fresno Business Council's Excellence in Public Service Award 2003, Fresno Compact's Harold H. Haak Award for Outstanding Business Partnership Educator of the Year 2007, American Coll. Personnel Asscn Educational Leadership Foundation Diamond Honoree 2009, Sequoia Award, Great Valley Center 2010, William M. Lyles Vision Award 2012. *Publication:* Alcohol and Other Drugs: A Guide for College Presidents and Governing Boards. *Leisure interests:* golf, jogging, reading, racquetball. *Address:* AASCU-Penson Center, 1307 New York Avenue, NW, 5th Floor, Washington, DC 20005, USA (office). *Website:* www.aascupenson.org (office).

WEN, Carson, BA, BA, MA, JP (Hong Kong); Hong Kong lawyer; *Chairman, Sancus Capital Ltd;* b. 16 April 1953, Hong Kong; s. of Sir Yung Wen and Tsi Fung Chu; m. Julia Fung Yuet Shan 1983; one c.; ed Diocesan Boys' School, Hong Kong, Nat. Jr Coll. Singapore, Columbia Univ., USA and Univ. of Oxford, UK; Singapore Govt Scholar 1971–72; Partner, Siao, Wen and Leung (Solicitors and Notaries), Hong Kong 1982–, Jones Day; Dir and Sec.-Gen. Hong Kong Kwun Tong Industries and Commerce Asscn 1982–, Pres. Emer. 1989–; mem. Kwun Tong Dist Bd 1983–85; Dir Banco Delta Asia SARL, Macau 1992–; Hon. Pres. Hong Kong Industrial Dists., Industry and Commerce Asscn Ltd 1993–; Attesting Officer apptd. by Ministry of Justice of China 1992–; Special Adviser to China Sr Prosecutors Educ. Foundation under the auspices of the Supreme People's Procurate of People's Repub. of China 1993–; Hong Kong Affairs Adviser to Govt of China 1993–; mem. Selection Cttee for First Govt of Hong Kong Special Admin. Region 1996; Vice-Chair. The Hong Kong Progressive Alliance 1994–; Deputy, Nat. People's Congress, People's Repub. of China for three terms from 1998; Partner, Hong Kong Office, Heller Ehrman (pvt. law practice) as Head, China Practice Group 2003–07; Chair. Sancus Capital Ltd 2007–; Founding Exec. Cttee mem. China M&A Asscn; mem. Bd China-Africa Business Council (Hong Kong), Pacific Basin Econ. Council, California Asscn of Hong Kong and China; mem. Business Advisory Council of the UN Econ. and Social Comm. for Asia Pacific (UNESCAP); fmr Vice-Chair. Democratic Alliance for the Betterment and Progress of Hong Kong; Guest Prof., Law School of Sun Yat-Sen Univ. (Zhongshan Univ.), Guangzhou, China; Hon. Life Pres. Hong Kong Sze Yap Industry and Commerce Asscn 1983–; Bronze Bauhinia Star. *Publications:* contribs to 13 lectures on Hong Kong Law; articles in journals, magazines and newspapers. *Leisure interests:* reading, golf. *Address:* Sancus Group, Level 18, Wheelock House, 20 Pedder Street, Central, Hong Kong Special Administrative Region, People's Republic of China (office). *E-mail:* info@sancusgroup.com (office). *Website:* sancuscapital.com (office).

WEN, Gang, PhD; Chinese engineer and business executive; *General Manager and President, China North Industries Group Corporation (NORINCO Group);* b. Aug. 1966, Taiyuan, Shanxi Prov.; ed Cen. Party School, CCP Cen. Cttee, Nanjing Univ. of Science and Tech.; Deputy Gen. Man. China North Industries Group Corpn (NORINCO Group) 1997–99, Dir, Gen. Office 1999–2003, Deputy Gen. Man. 2003–14, mem. Bd of Dirs, Beijing Auxin Chemical Technology Ltd, NORINCO 2005–11, Chair. Sichuan Nitrocell Co. Ltd, NORINCO 2005–10, mem. Bd of Dirs, North Huajin Chemical Industries Group Corpn, NORINCO 2006–09, Chair. Beiben Trucks Group Corpn, NORINCO 2008–13, Gen. Man. and Pres. China North Industries Group Corpn (NORINCO Group) 2014–. *Address:* China North Industries Group Corporation (NORINCO Group), 46 Sanlihe Road, Beijing 100821, People's Republic of China (office). *Telephone:* (10) 68594210 (office). *Fax:* (10) 68594232 (office). *E-mail:* webmaster@norincogroup.com.cn (office). *Website:* www.norincogroup.com.cn (office).

WEN, Jiabao; Chinese party and state official and geologist; b. 15 Sept. 1942, Tianjin; m. Zhang Peili; one s. one d.; ed Beijing Inst. of Geology; joined CCP 1965; technician and political instructor, Geomechanics Survey Team, Gansu Prov. Geological Bureau, Ministry of Land and Resources 1968–78, Deputy Head 1978–79; Engineer and Deputy Section Head, Gansu Prov. Geological Bureau 1979–81, Deputy Dir-Gen. 1981–82; Dir Reform Research Office of the Geological and Mining Bureau of the State Council 1982–83; Deputy Minister of Geology and Mining 1983–85; Deputy Dir, Gen. Office of 12th CCP Cen. Cttee 1985–86, Dir, Gen. Office of 13th and 14th CCP Cen. Cttee 1986–93; Alt. mem. Secr. of Cen. Cttee 1987; Sec. CCP Cen. Organs Working Cttee 1988; mem. 13th CCP Cen. Cttee 1987–92, 14th CCP Cen. Cttee 1992–97, Alt. mem. CCP Politburo 1992–97, mem. 1997–2012; Sec. Secr. of Cen. Cttee 1992; mem. 15th CCP Cen. Cttee 1997–2002, 16th CCP Cen. Cttee 2002–07 (mem. Standing Cttee of the Politburo 2002–07), 17th CCP Cen. Cttee 2007–12 (mem. Standing Cttee of the Politburo 2007–12); Sec. Financial Work Cttee of Cen. Cttee 1998–2002; Vice-Premier State Council 1998–2003, Premier State Council (Prime Minister) 2003–13; Chair. State Comm. for Public Sector Reform 2003, Nat. Defence Mobilization Comm. 2003; Leader of the Leading Group for Financial and Econ. Affairs 2003.

WEN, Shizhen; Chinese party official; b. Jan. 1940, Haicheng Co., Liaoning Prov.; ed Faculty of Mechanical Eng, Dalian Inst. of Tech.; Deputy Dir, later Dir Dalian Oil Pump Nozzle Plant, Liaoning Prov. 1965–82; joined CCP 1979; Deputy Dir Dalian City Machinery Bureau 1982–83, Machine Building Industry Dept 1983–85; Asst Gov. Liaoning Prov. 1985–86, Deputy Gov. 1986–93, Vice-Gov. 1993–95, Gov. 1995; Deputy Sec. CCP Liaoning Prov. Cttee 1986–97, Sec. 1997–2004, mem. Standing Cttee 2001; Chair. Standing Cttee Liaoning Prov. People's Congress 2003–04; Alt. mem. 13th CCP Cen. Cttee 1987–91, mem. 14th

CCP Cen. Cttee 1992, 15th CCP Cen. Cttee 1997–2002, 16th CCP Cen. Cttee 2002–07; Deputy, 8th NPC 1993–98, 9th NPC 1998–2003.

WEN, Gen. Zongren; Chinese army officer; b. Nov. 1940, Chaoxian Co., Anhui Prov.; ed PLA Tank School, PLA Political Acad., PLA Mil. Acad.; joined PLA 1959, CCP 1961; platoon leader, Tank Regt, PLA Services and Arms, Beijing 1962–67 (also Sec. Political Dept); clerk, Org. Section (Political Dept), Tank Div. and Armoured Force, PLA Services and Arms, Nanjing City Jiangsu Prov. 1967–73; Political Commissar, Tank Regt, PLA Services and Arms 1973–79; Dir 2nd Tank Div. Political Dept 1980–83; Div. Political Commissar 1980–83; Dir 12th Group Army Political Dept 1983–85; 12th Group Army Political Commissar 1985–94; rank of Maj.-Gen. 1988, Lt-Gen. 1996, Gen. 2002; Dir Political Dept of Nanjing Mil. Area Command 1994–96; Political Commissar, Lanzhou Mil. Area Command 1996–2000; Political Commissar, PLA Mil. Acad. of Sciences 2000–05; Alt. mem. 14th CCP Cen. Cttee 1992–97, mem. 15th CCP Cen. Cttee 1997–2002, 16th CCP Cen. Cttee 2002–07.

WENDER, Paul Anthony, BS, PhD; American chemist and academic; *Francis W. Bergstrom Professor, Professor of Chemistry and, by courtesy, of Chemical and Systems Biology, Stanford University;* b. 1947, Wilkes-Barre, Pa; ed Wilkes Coll., Yale Univ.; Post-doctoral Fellow, Columbia Univ. 1974; Asst Prof., then Assoc. Prof., Harvard Univ. 1974-81; Prof. of Chemistry, Stanford Univ. 1981–, Francis W. Bergstrom Prof. 1994–, also, by courtesy, Prof. of Chemical and Systems Biology; Founder CellGate Inc.; Co-founder Progen Pharmaceuticals, Inc. 1998; mem. NAS 2003; Fellow, American Acad. of Arts and Sciences 1992, AAAS 2001; A.P. Sloan Fellow 1979, Eli Lilly Grantee Award 1979, Dreyfus Teacher Scholar 1980, Ernest Guenther Award 1988, Stuart Award for Excellence in Chem., ICI Pharmaceutical Group 1988, ACS Arthur C. Cope Scholar Award 1990, Alexander von Humboldt Stiftung Award 1991, Teaching Award, Associated Students of Stanford Univ. 1991, Hoagland Prize for Undergraduate Teaching, Stanford Univ. 1991, Bing Teaching Award, Stanford Univ. 1992, NIH MERIT Award 2003, 2006, Pfizer Research Award for Synthetic Organic Chem. 1995, ACS Award for Creative work in Synthetic Organic Chem. 1998, Dean's Award for Distinguished Teaching 2000, ACS H.C. Brown Award for Creative Research in Synthetic Methods 2003, The Hamilton Award, Univ. of Nebraska 2008, Wilbur Lucius Cross Medal, Yale Grad. Alumni 2010, Tetrahedron Prize for Creativity in Organic Chem. 2012, Prelog Medal, ETH (Switzerland) 2013, ACS Arthur C. Cope Award 2015. *Publications:* numerous papers in professional journals. *Address:* Wender Research Group, Stanford University, Chemistry Department, 333 Campus Drive, Stanford, CA 94305-5080, USA (office). *Telephone:* (650) 723-0208 (office). *Fax:* (650) 725-0209 (office). *E-mail:* wenderp@stanford.edu (office). *Website:* www .stanford.edu/group/pawender (office); chemsysbio.stanford.edu (office).

WENDERS, Ernst Wilhelm (Wim); German film director, writer and artist; b. 14 Aug. 1945, Düsseldorf; m. 1st Edda Köchl 1968–74; m. 2nd Lisa Kreuzer 1974–78; m. 3rd Ronee Blakley 1979–81; m. 4th Isabelle Weingarten 1981–82; m. 5th Donata Schmidt 1993; ed studied medicine and philosophy in Munich, Freiburg and Düsseldorf, Hochschule für Fernsehen und Film, Munich; film critic, Die Suddeutsche Zeitung, Filmkritik 1968–70; Chair. European Film Acad. 1991–96, Pres. 1996–; Prof., Hochschule für Bildende Künste (School of Fine Arts), Hamburg 2001; numerous solo exhbns; mem. Akad. der Künste 1989; lives and works in Berlin; Hon. Prof., HFF (Acad. of Film and Television), Munich 1993; Dr hc (Sorbonne, Paris) 1989, (Univ. of Fribourg, Switzerland) 1995, (Univ. of Louvain) 2005, (Univ. of Catania, Italy) 2010; Pour le mérite for science and the arts 2005, Großes Verdienstkreuz mit Stern 2006; Friedrich Wilhelm Murnau Award 1991, Hon. Golden Bear, Berlin Int. Film Festival 2015, Großer Kulturpreis, Sparkasse Culture-Foundation Rhineland 2016, Max-Herrmann-Prize, Asscn of Friends of the State Library of Berlin 2016. *Films include:* Summer in the City 1970, The Goalie's Anxiety at the Penalty Kick 1972, The Scarlet Letter 1973, Alice in the Cities 1974, The Wrong Move 1975, Kings of the Road 1976, The American Friend 1977, Lightning Over Water 1980, The State of Things (Golden Lion, Venice Film Festival) 1982, Hammett 1982, Paris, Texas (Palme d'Or, Cannes Film Festival) 1984, Wings of Desire (Cannes Film Festival Award) 1987, Aufzeichnungen zu Kleidern und Städten 1989, Until the End of the World 1991, Faraway, So Close! (Grand Jury Prize, Cannes Film Festival) 1993, Lisbon Story, The Million Dollar Hotel (Silver Bear Jury Prize, Berline Int. Film Festival 2000) 1999, Buena Vista Social Club 1999, Vill Passiert 2002, Soul of a Man 2003, Land of Plenty 2004, Don't Come Knockin' 2004, Palermo Shooting 2008, Pina (documentary) (Gilde Film Prize, European Film Award, Documentary Prix Arte Award, German Film Prize for Best Documentary, German Documentary Film Prize, The Dokville tradeshow Ludwigsburg) 2011, The Salt of the Earth 2014, Every Thing Will Be Fine 2015, The Beautiful Days of Aranjuez 2016, Submergence 2017. *Publications include:* Emotion Pictures 1986, Written in the West 1987, Die Logik der Bilder 1988, The Act of Seeing 1992. *Address:* c/o Paul Kohner, 9300 Wilshire Boulevard, #555, Beverly Hills, CA 90212, USA (office). Blain Southern, 4 Hanover Square, London, W1S 1BP, England (office). *E-mail:* office@neueroadmovies.com (office); info@blainsouthern.com (office). *Telephone:* (20) 7493-4492 (office). *Website:* www.blainsouthern.com/artists/wim-wenders (office); www.wim -wenders.com.

WENDT, Henry, III, AB; American business executive; *Co-Founder, Healthcare Investment Partners;* b. 19 July 1933, Neptune City, NJ; s. of Henry Wendt and Rachel Lindsey Wendt; m. Holly Ann Peterson 1956; one s. one d.; ed Hackley School, Tarrytown, NY and Princeton Univ., NJ; joined SmithKline and French Labs 1955; Pres. SmithKline Corpn 1976–89, CEO 1982–89, Chair. SmithKline Beckman Corpn Feb.–July 1989, Chair. SmithKline Beecham PLC 1989–94; Founder and Chair. Global Health Care Partners 1995–2001; Chair. DLJ Merchant Banking 1997–, Computerized Medical Systems, Inc.; Co-founder Healthcare Investment Partners 2004–; Dir West Marine Inc. 1997–2001; Chair. Computerized Medical Systems Inc., Arrail Dental (China) Ltd; Dir, Bio Partners SA 2000–, Cambridge Laboratories, PLC, Wilson Greatbatch Technologies Ltd, Focus Technologies Inc., Seven Hills Group LLC, Prometheus Laboratories Inc.; Propr Quivira Estate Vineyards and Winery 1983–; mem. Advisory Bd CTPartners Board Consultants; Chair. Community Foundation of Sonoma Co.; Dir The Pacific Basin Inst., Pomona Coll.; Trustee Emer., American Enterprise Inst.; Order of the Rising Sun with Gold and Silver Star (Japan) 1994; Hon. CBE 1995. *Publications:* Global Embrace 1993 Mapping the Pacific Coast 2004; various articles. *Leisure* *interests:* viticulture, oenology, 16th and 18th century cartography, fly fishing, sailing. *Address:* Healthcare Investment Partners, 111 Monte Vista Avenue, Suite A, Healdsburg, CA 95448, USA (office).

WENG, Yueh-Sheng, LLB, DrJur; Taiwanese judge and academic; *Professor, National Chengchi University;* b. 1 July 1932, Chia-yi; m. Chuan Shu-Chen; three d.; ed Nat. Taiwan Univ., Heidelberg Univ., Germany; Assoc. Prof., Nat. Taiwan Univ. 1966–70, Prof. 1970–72; Commr Legal Comm., Exec. Yuan 1971–72, Commr Research, Devt and Evaluation Comm. 1972, Commr and Convenor Admin. Procedure Act Research Comm., Judicial Yuan 1981–92; Grand Justice, Judicial Yuan 1972–99, Presiding Justice, Constitutional Court 1992–99, Pres. Judicial Yuan 1999–2007, Chief Justice of Constitutional Court 2003–07; currently Prof., Nat. Chengchi Univ., Nat. Taiwan Univ.; mem. Council of Academic Review Evaluation, Ministry of Educ. 1998–99; Visiting Prof., School of Law, Univ. of Washington, USA 1991; Commr Academic Consultation Comm., Sun Yat-Sen Inst. of Social Sciences and Philosophy, Academia Sinica 1991–2001, Convenor 1998–2001; mem. Bd of Dirs, Chiang Ching-kuo Foundation for Int. Scholarly Exchange 2004–; Pres. Taiwan Admin. Law Asscn 1998–2004 (Hon. Pres. 2004–07), Chinese Soc. of Constitutional Law 1999–2004 (Hon. Pres. 2004–); Chair. Nat. Taiwan Univ. Law Foundation 2010–16; Hon. Fellow, Soc. for Advanced Legal Studies (UK) 2002; Hon. Pres. Taiwan Jurist Asscn 2003–06; Order of Propitious Clouds with Special Grand Cordon by Pres. of Taiwan 2000; Judicial Medal of the First Grade, Merit and Achievement Medal of the First Grade, Judicial Yuan of Taiwan 1994, Golden Medal of the Distinguished Justice, Supreme Court of the Repub. of Guatemala 2000, Chung-Cheng Medal of Honour, Pres. of Taiwan 2007. *Publications include:* Die Stellung der Justiz im Verfassungsrecht der Republik China 1970, Administrative Law and Rule of Law 1976, Administrative Law and Judiciary in a State Under the Principle of the Rule of Law 1994, Administrative Law I and II (co-author and co-ed.) 1998, 2000, Annotation of Administrative Procedure Act (co-author and ed.) 2003. *Leisure interests:* reading, hiking. *Address:* 19 Alley 9, Lane 65, He-Ping E. Road Sector-4, Taipei 116, Taiwan (home). *Telephone:* (2) 2230-6339 (home). *Fax:* (2) 2230-6339 (home). *E-mail:* weng.ys21@msa.hinet.net (home). *Website:* www.cckf.org.tw (office).

WENNEMER, Manfred, BSc, MBA; German business executive; b. 19 Sept. 1947, Ottmarsbocholt, Münsterland; m.; three s.; ed Univ. of Münster, Institut Européen d'Admin des Affaires (INSEAD), Fountainebleau, France; Project Man. Procter & Gamble, Schwalbach 1974–77, Arthur D. Little, Wiesbaden 1978–80; Head of Planning and Controlling Non-Woven Fabrics Div. Freudenberg & Co., Weinheim 1980–82, Gen. Man. Lady Esther, Weinheim 1982–84, Man. Dir Freudenberg Nonwovens, Capetown, SA 1984–87, Pres. and CEO Nonwovens N America USA 1987–92, Head of Special Nonwoven Fabrics Business Unit for Europe, Weinheim 1992–93, Head of Spunbounded Fabrics Operations, Kaiserlautern 1993–94; Head Exec. Bd Benecke-Kaliko AG, Hannover 1994–98; joined Continental Aktiengesellschaft (Continental AG) 1998, mem. Exec. Bd ContiTech Group 1998–2001, Chair. Exec. Bd and CEO Continental AG 2001–08; Deputy Chair. Supervisory Bd Knorr-Bremse 2009–16; Chair. Supervisory Bd Kion 2009–11, Springer Science + Business Media SA 2010–, Hochtief AG 2011–12; Chair. Sulzer Ltd March–Dec. 2013; Ind. Dir Bekaert 2009–; mem. Advisory Bd Allianz Deutschland AG 2008–; Mentor, Bernotat & Cie. GmbH. *Leisure interests:* skiing, football, travelling. *Address:* Bernotat & Cie. GmbH, Brüsseler Platz 1, 45131 Essen, Germany. *E-mail:* manfred.wennemer @ bernotat-cie.com. *Website:* bernotat-cie.com/en/mentors/manfred-wennemer.

WENNER, Jann S.; American publisher; *Editor and Publisher, Rolling Stone;* b. 7 Jan. 1946, New York; m. Jane Schindelheim (divorced); six c.; ed Univ. of California, Berkeley; Founder, Ed. and Publisher, Rolling Stone magazine 1967–; TV appearances include Crime Story 1987–88; Chair. Wenner Media Inc., Rock & Roll Hall of Fame Foundation, Inc.; Owner, Us and Men's Journal magazines; inducted into American Soc. of Magazine Eds Hall of Fame 1997, Publishing Exec. of the Year, Adweek 1994, Lifetime Achievement Award (non-performer category), Rock & Roll Hall of Fame 2004, Norman Mailer Prize for Lifetime Achievement in Magazine Publishing 2010. *Film appearances:* Up Your Legs Forever 1970, Perfect 1985, Jerry Maguire 1996, Almost Famous 2000. *Publications include:* Lennon Remembers (ed.) 1972, 20 Years of Rolling Stone: What a Long Strange Trip It's Been 1987, Rolling Stone Environmental Reader 1992, Gonzo: The Life of Hunter S. Thompson (edited with Corey Seymour) 2007, Fear and Loathing at Rolling Stone: The Essential Writing of Hunter S. Thompson (ed.) 2011. *Address:* Rolling Stone, Wenner Media Inc., 1290 Avenue of the Americas, New York, NY 10104-0298, USA (office). *Telephone:* (212) 484-1616 (office). *E-mail:* editors@rollingstone .com (office). *Website:* www.rollingstone.com (office); www.jannswenner.com.

WENNING, Werner; German business executive; *Chairman of the Supervisory Board, Bayer AG;* b. 21 Oct. 1946, Leverkusen-Opladen; m.; two d.; joined Bayer AG, Leverkusen 1966, Commercial Trainee, mem. staff Corp. Auditing Dept, Man. Finance and Accounting Dept Bayer Industrial SA, Lima, Peru 1970–75, Man. Dir and Admin. Head 1978–83, Head of Staff Dept Health Care Sector, Leverkusen 1983–86, Head Marketing Thermoplastics, Plastics Business Group 1986, Head Worldwide Marketing Operations 1987–91, seconded to Treuhandanstalt privatization agency, Berlin 1991–92, Man. Dir Bayer Hispania Industrial SA, Sr Bayer Rep. Spain 1992–96, Head Corp. Planning and Controlling, Leverkusen 1996–97, mem. Bd of Man., Bayer AG 1997–2010, Chair. 2002–10, Chair. Supervisory Bd 2012–; mem. Shareholders' Cttee Henkel AG & Co. KGaA; Chair. Supervisory Bd, E.ON SE 2011–16; mem. Supervisory Bd, Deutsche Bank AG; Pres. German Chemical Industry Asscn (VCI) 2005–07, Vice-Pres. 2007–. *Address:* Bayer AG, Building W11, Kaiser-Wilhelm-Allee, 51368 Leverkusen, Germany (office). *Telephone:* (214) 301 (office). *Fax:* (214) 3066328 (office). *E-mail:* info@bayer.com (office). *Website:* www.bayer.com (office).

WENSLEY, Penelope Anne, AC, AO, BA; Australian diplomatist and government official; *Chairman, Australian Institute of Marine Science (AIMS);* b. 18 Oct. 1946, Toowoomba, Qld; d. of William Neilsen Wensley and Doris Eileen McCulloch; m. Dr Stuart McCosker 1974; two d.; ed Univ. of Queensland; diplomatic service 1968–2008, Paris 1969–73, Mexico City 1975–77, Wellington, NZ 1982–85, Consul Gen. Hong Kong 1986–88; Head Int. Orgs Div., Dept of Foreign Affairs and Trade 1991–92, Perm. Rep. to UN, Geneva 1993–95, also Amb. for Environment, UN 1992–95, Head of N Asia Div. 1996–97; Amb. and Perm. Rep. to UN, New York 1997–2002; High Commr to India 2002–04; Amb. to Bhutan 2002–04, to France (also accred to Algeria, Mauritania, Morocco, Monaco) 2005–08; Gov. of Queensland 2008–14; Sr Adviser, Australian del. to UN Conf. on Environment and Devt 1992; Vice-Pres. World Conf. on Human Rights, Vienna 1993; Vice-Chair. UN Climate Change Convention Negotiations 1993–96; Coordinator Western Group Negotiations on UN Conventions on Biodiversity and Desertification 1994–96; Chair. Preparatory Process UN Conf. for the Sustainable Devt of Small Island Developing States 1993–94; Chair. Int. Coral Reef Initiative Conf. 1995; Vice-Chair. UN Inst. for Training and Research; Chair. Australian Inst. of Marine Science (AIMS) 2015–; mem. WHO High Level Advisory Council on Health and the Environment; Chair. UN Gen. Ass. Fifth Cttee (Admin. and Budgetary) 1999; Co-Chair. Preparatory Process for UN Gen. Ass. Special Session on HIV/AIDS 2001; Adjunct Prof., Univ. of Queensland 2000; Patron UN Youth Asscn of Australia; Fellow, Women's Coll., Univ. of Queensland; Grand Officer, French Nat. Order of Merit 2009; Hon. PhD and Alumnus of the Year (Univ. of Queensland) 1994; Hon. PhD (Griffith Univ.) 2008, (Queensland Univ. of Tech.) 2011, Hon PhD (James Cook Univ.) 2012. *Leisure interests:* music, theatre, reading, bushwalking. *Address:* Australian Institute of Marine Science, 1526 Cape Cleveland Road, Cape Cleveland, 4810, Queensland, Australia (office). *Telephone:* (7) 4753-4444 (office). *Fax:* (7) 4772-5852 (office). *E-mail:* web@aims.gov.au (office). *Website:* www .aims.gov.au (office).

WENT, David, BA, LLB, BL; Irish barrister, banker and business executive; b. 25 March 1947, Dublin; s. of Arthur Went and Phyllis Went (née Howell); m. Mary Christine Milligan 1972; one s. one d.; ed Trinity Coll. Dublin; Barrister-at-Law, King's Inns, Dublin; grad. trainee, Citibank, Dublin 1970, Gen. Man. 1975, Gen. Man., Jeddah 1975–76; Dir Ulster Investment Bank 1976, Chief Exec. 1982, Deputy Chief Exec. Ulster Bank Belfast 1987, Chief Exec. 1988–94; CEO Coutts & Co. Group 1994–97; CEO Irish Life Assurance PLC 1998–; Group CEO Irish Life and Permanent PLC 1999–2007; Gov., The Irish Times Trust 2002–07, Chair. The Irish Times Ltd 2007–13; Chair. Trinity Foundation; fmr Chair. Financial Services Consultative Industry Panel; mem. Bd of Dirs Allianz (Ireland); Dir (non-exec.), Goldman Sachs Bank (Europe) Ltd; fmr Dir (non-exec.), VHI Healthcare; Paul Prize, Trinity Coll. 1969, Brook Scholar, King's Inns 1970. *Leisure interests:* tennis, reading. *Address:* c/o The Irish Times, PO Box 74, 24–28 Tara Street, Dublin 2, Ireland. *E-mail:* services@irishtimes.com.

WENTWORTH, Timothy (Tim) C., BA; American business executive; *President and CEO, Express Scripts Holding Company;* ed Cornell Univ., Monroe Community Coll.; fmrly with, PepsiCo, Inc.; Sr Vice-Pres., Account Man., Medco Health Solutions, Inc. 1998, Sr Vice-Pres., Human Resources and Pres., International, Mary Kay, Inc., Exec. Vice-Pres., Client Strategy and Service, Medco Health Solutions, Inc. 2002–03, Group Pres., Nat. Accountants 2004–06, Pres. and CEO Accredo Health Group, Inc. (co.'s speciality pharmacy subsidiary) 2006–08, Group Pres., Employer Accountants, Medco Health Solutions, Inc. 2008–12, joined Express Scripts when it merged with Medco April 2012, Sr Vice-Pres. and Pres., Sales and Account Man., Express-Scripts 2012–14, Pres. Express Scripts Holding Co. 2014–, CEO 2016–. *Address:* Express Scripts Holding Company, 1 Express Way, St Louis, MO 63121, USA (office). *Telephone:* (314) 996-0900 (office). *E-mail:* info@express-scripts.com (office). *Website:* www.express-scripts.com (office).

WERGER, Marinus Johannes Antonius, BSc, MSc, PhD; Dutch biologist and academic; *Professor Emeritus of Plant Ecology and Vegetation Science, Utrecht University;* b. 3 May 1944, Enschede; s. of Johannes G. Werger and Gezina M. Zwerink; m. Karin E. Klein 1968; one d.; ed Jacobus Coll. Enschede and Utrecht, Groningen and Nijmegen Univs; biology teacher, Erasmus Coll., Rotterdam 1968; Researcher, Botanical Research Inst. Pretoria, S Africa 1968–73 (Sr Researcher 1971–73); Assoc. Prof. of Geobotany, Nijmegen Univ. 1974–79; Reader, Plant Ecology and Vegetation Science, Utrecht Univ. 1979–80, Prof. 1980–2009, now Prof. Emer., Dir Inst. of Environmental Biology 2006–09, Chair Curator, Prins Bernhard Chair for Int. Nature Conservation, Dean Faculty of Biology 1990–93, Functional Head, Dept of Landscape Ecology 1991–2000, Functional Head, Dept of Plant Systematics 1994–99; Consultant Prof., SW China Univ., Beibei 1984–; Visiting Prof., Univ. of Tokyo 1985, Kyoto Univ. 1985, Hebrew Univ. 1994, 1997; mem. Editorial Bd Vegetatio/Plant Ecology 1975–2010, Webbia 1980–, Bothalia 1985–, Journal of Tropical Ecology 1985–, Journal of Vegetation Science 1989–91, Ecological Research 1992–97, 2007, Folia Geobotanica 1993–2007, Phytocoenologia 1998–, Acta Botanica Sinica 1999–2006; mem. Royal Netherlands Acad. of Arts and Sciences 1987–, Sec., Biology Section 1989–91, Chair. Biology Section 1991–98; Hon. Prof., Southwest Univ., China 1985–, Hon. mem. Academic Senate, Southwest Univ., China 1998–; Mid-America State Univs Asscn Award 1986, Andrew W. Mellon Award, Smithsonian Inst. 1998, Friendship Award (China0 1998. *Publications include:* Biogeography and Ecology of Southern Africa (two vols) 1978, The Study of Vegetation 1979, Man's Impact on Vegetation 1983, Plant Form and Vegetation Structure 1988, Tropical Rain Forest Ecosystems 1989; Ed.-in-Chief Geobotany book series 1980-2005, Monographiae Biologicae book series 1982–, Plant and Vegetation book series 2005–; about 180 research papers in int. scientific journals; co-authored 12 books, edited more than 35 books, published more than 80 book reviews. *Leisure interests:* history, travel, cooking. *Address:* Department of Plant Ecology and Biodiversity, Utrecht University, PO Box 80084, 3508 TB Utrecht (office); Nieuwe Gracht 145, 3512 LL Utrecht, Netherlands (home). *Telephone:* (30) 311969 (home). *Fax:* (30) 2518366 (office). *E-mail:* m.j.a .werger@uu.nl (office). *Website:* www3.bio.uu.nl/peb (office).

WERNER, Hans-Joachim, DipChem; German chemist and academic; *Professor and Director, Institute of Theoretical Chemistry, University of Stuttgart;* b. 16 April 1950, Hamburg; ed Univ. of Mainz, Univ. of Göttingen, Univ. of Frankfurt; Visiting Prof., Los Alamos Nat. Lab., Los Alamos, NM, USA 1983–84; Fellow, Churchill Coll., Cambridge, UK 1984–85; Heisenberg Fellowship, Deutsche Forschungsgemeinschaft, Univ. of Frankfurt 1985–87; Prof., Univ. of Bielefeld 1987; Prof. and Dir Inst. for Theoretical Chem., Univ. of Stuttgart 1994–, Dean (Dekan), Faculty of Chem. 2006–12, Vice-Rector for Organisation and Research 2012–; mem. Editorial Bd Zeitschrift für Physikalische Chemie, International Reviews in Physical Chemistry, Theoretical Chemistry Accounts, Physical Chemistry/Chemical Physics; Ed. Molecular Physics; mem. Int. Acad. of Quantum Molecular Science, Akad. der Wissenschaften zu Göttingen, Deutsche Bunsengesellschaft; City of Mainz Gutenbergpreis 1972, Max-Planck Research Award for Int. Collaboration 1996,

Akad. der Wissenschaften zu Göttingen Jost Medal 1999, Deutsche Forschungs-gemeinschaft Gottfried Wilhelm Leibniz Award 2000, Gay-Lussac-Humboldt Award 2008, ERC Advanced Grant 2013. *Address:* Institute of Theoretical Chemistry, University of Stuttgart, Pfaffenwaldring 55, 70569 Stuttgart, Germany (office). *Telephone:* (711) 685-64401 (office). *Fax:* (711) 685-64442 (office). *E-mail:* werner@theochem.uni-stuttgart.de (office). *Website:* www.theochem.uni -stuttgart.de/~werner (office).

WERNER, Helmut, Dr rer. nat; German chemist and academic; *Professor Emeritus of Inorganic Chemistry, University of Würzburg;* b. 19 April 1934, Mühlhausen; ed Univ. of Jena, Technische Hochschule, Munich, Calif. Inst. of Tech. (Caltech), Pasadena, Calif., USA; Lecturer in Inorganic Chem., Technische Hochschule, Munich, 1967–68; Asst Prof., Univ. of Zürich, Switzerland 1968–70, Prof. of Inorganic Chem. 1970–75; Prof. of Inorganic Chem. and Head, Inorganic Dept, Univ. of Würzburg 1975–2002, Prof. Emer. 2002–, Dean, Faculty of Chem. and Pharmacy 1987–89; Visiting Prof., Chemical Lab., Univ. of Cambridge, UK 1983, Chem. Dept, Universidad Catolica de Chile 1984, Research Unit, CNRS, Toulouse, France 1990, Univ. of Zaragoza, Spain 2003; mem. Editorial Advisory Bd Journal of Organometallic Chem. 1988–, Gazzetta Chimica Italiana 1990–97, Comments on Inorganic Chem. 1990–, Monatsheft für Chemie 1993–96, Journal of the Chemical Society 1994–96; mem. German Chemical Soc., ACS, Royal Soc. of Chem. (Fellow 1987–), Swiss Chemical Soc., Nat. Acad. of Science, Leopoldina 1988–, New York Acad. of Sciences 1997–; Dr hc (Zaragoza) 2001, (Jena) 2006; Lessing Medal 1952, German Chemical Soc. Alfred Stock Memorial Prize 1988, Max-Planck Research Award 1994, Royal Soc. of Chem. Centenary Medal 1994, Spanish Ministry of Science Mutis Award 1995, Paolo Chini Memorial Lecturer 1995, Gordon Stone Lecturer 2004. *Address:* Institut für Anorganische Chemie, Universität Würzburg, Am Hubland, 97074 Würzburg (office); Georg-Sittig-str. 1, 97074 Würzburg, Germany (home). *Telephone:* (931) 31-85270 (office). *Fax:* (931) 31-84623 (office). *E-mail:* helmut.werner@mail.uni-wuerzburg.de (office). *Website:* www-anorganik.chemie.uni-wuerzburg.de/werner/eng-index.html (office).

WERNER, Patrick; French banking executive; ed Institut d'Études Politiques de Paris, École Nat. d'Admin; began career as Chief of Service of Internal Audit, Caisse des Dépôts 1980–83; mem. Bd then Man. Dir C3D (holding co. of subsidiaries of Caisse des Dépôts) 1983–91; Man. Dir groupe d'assurances Victoire 1991–95; joined Fédération Française des Socs d'Assurances 1996, Acting Man. Dir then Acting Vice-Pres. 1997; Dir-Gen. La Poste, in charge of Financial Affairs 1999, Chair. Man. Bd La Banque Postale (subsidiary of La Poste) 2006–11; CEO Gras Savoye SAS 2011–12.

WERNER, Wendelin, PhD; French (b. German) mathematician and academic; *Professor of Mathematics, Eidgenössische Technische Hochschule Zürich;* b. 23 Sept. 1968; ed École Normale Supérieure, Université Paris VI; became a French national 1977; Research Officer, CNRS 1991–97; postdoctoral work as a Leibniz Fellow, Univ. of Cambridge, UK 1993–95; Prof. of Math., Université Paris-Sud 1997–2013, École Normale Supérieure (part time) 2005–13; Prof. of Math., ETH Zürich 2013–; mem. Acad. des sciences 2008; Rollo Davidson Prize 1998, Doisteau-Blutet Prize (Academie des Sciences) 1999, EMS Prize 2000, Fermat Prize 2001, Jacques Herbrand Prize (Academie des Sciences) 2003, Loeve Prize 2005, Soc. for Industrial and Applied Math. Polya Prize (co-winner) 2006, Fields Medal 2006. *Films:* actor in La Passante du Sans-Souci 1982, A Christmas Tale (math. demonstrations) 2008. *Publications:* numerous papers in professional journals on self-avoiding random walks, Schramm-Loewner evolution and related theories in probability theory and mathematical physics. *Address:* Room HG.G.66.3, Department of Mathematics, ETH, Rämistrasse 101, 8092 Zurich, Switzerland (office). *E-mail:* wendelin.werner@math.ethz.ch (office). *Website:* www.math.ethz.ch/ ~wewerner (office).

WERTENBAKER, Timberlake, FRSL; British playwright; *Artistic Director, Natural Perspective Theatre Company;* m. John Man; one d.; Resident Playwright, Royal Court Theatre 1984–85; Dir English Stage Co. 1991–99; mem. Exec. Cttee PEN 1999–2002; Royden B. Davis Visiting Prof. of Theatre, Georgetown Univ., Washington, DC 2005–06; Artistic Dir Natural Perspective Theatre Co. 2007–; Leverhulme Artist-in-Residence, Freud Museum, London 2011–; UNESCO City of Literature Visiting Prof. of Creative Writing, Univ. of East Anglia 2012, Chair. Playwriting 2013–; mem. Artistic Advisory Panel, Royal Acad. of Dramatic Art 2008–, Council of the Royal Soc. of Literature 2011–18; Dr hc (Open Univ.); Plays and Players Most Promising Playwright (for The Grace of Mary Traverse) 1985, Evening Standard Most Promising Playwright, Olivier Play of the Year (for Our Country's Good) 1988, Eileen Anderson Drama Award (for The Love of the Nightingale) 1989, Critics' Circle Best West End Play 1991, Writers' Guild Best West End Play, Susan Smith Blackburn Award (for Three Birds Alighting on a Field) 1992, Mrs Giles Whiting Award (for gen. body of work) 1989, Guggenheim Fellowship 2004. *Plays include:* (for the Soho-Poly): Case to Answer 1980; (for the Women's Theatre Group): New Anatomies 1982; (for the Royal Court): Abel's Sister 1984, The Grace of Mary Traverse 1985, Our Country's Good 1988, Three Birds Alighting on a Field 1991, Credible Witness 2001; (for Out of Joint): The Break of Day 1995; (for RSC): The Love of the Nightingale 1988, The Ant and the Cicada 2014, trans. Successful Strategies, False Admissions, La Dispute (Marivaux), Pelléas and Mélisande (Maeterlinck), (Mnouchkine), The Theban Plays (Sopho-cles); (for Hampstead Theatre): After Darwin 1998; (for Birmingham Rep.): The Ash Girl 2000; (for Theatre Royal, Bath): Galileo's Daughter 2004; (for Arcola Theatre, London) The Line 2009, trans. Jenufa (Preissová); (for Southwark Playhouse, London): Our Ajax 2012; (for Watford Palace Theatre): Jefferson's Garden (Writers' Guild of Great Britain Best Play 2016) 2015; (for Salisbury Playhouse): We Sell Right 2015; (for Unicorn Theatre): My Father Odysseus 2016; (for Octagon Theatre, Bolton): Winter Hill 2017; (for San Francisco ACT): trans. Euripides' Hecuba; (for Peter Hall Co.): trans. Eduardo de Filippo's Filumena (Piccadilly Theatre) 1998; (for Chichester): Wild Orchards (Anouilh) 2002; trans. Euripides' Hippolytus (Riverside Studios, London) 2009; trans. Racine's Phèdre (Stratford, Ontario) 2009, (ACT, San Francisco) 2010, Sophocles' Elektra (Getty, Los Angeles) 2010. *Libretto:* The Love of the Nightingale (music by Richard Mills, Sydney Opera House) 2011. *Films:* The Children (Channel 4), Do Not Disturb (BBC TV). *Radio includes:* Credible Witness, Dianeira, Hecuba (trans. and adaptation), The H. File (adaptation of novel by Ismail Kadaré), Scenes of Seduction 2005, Divine Intervention 2006, What is the Custom of Your Grief?

2009, adaptation of A. S. Byatt's Possession 2011, Tolstoy's War and Peace 2015, Elena Ferrante's Neapolitan novels 2017. *Television:* Belle and the Beast (BBC). *Publications:* Timberlake Wertenbaker: Plays 1 1996, The Break of Day 1996, After Darwin 1999, Filumena 1999, The Ash Girl 2000, Credible Witness 2001, Timberlake Wertenbaker: Plays 2 2002, Jenufa (Adaption) 2007, Hippolytus 2009, The Line 2009, Britannicus (trans.) 2011, Timberlake Wertenbaker: Teatro: Dopo Darwin, Testimone Credibile, Le Leggi del Moto 2011, Our Ajax 2012, Jefferson's Garden 2015, My Father Odysseus 2016, Winter Hill 2017. *Leisure interest:* mountains. *Address:* c/o The Agency, 24 Pottery Lane, Holland Park, London, W11 4LZ, England (office).

WERTMULLER, Lina; Italian film director; b. (Arcangela Felice Assunta Wertmuller von Elgg), 14 Aug. 1928, Rome; m. Enrico Job (died 2008); ed Rome Theatre Acad.; toured Europe with a puppet show after graduating; worked in theatre for ten years as actress, director and playwright; First Asst to Federico Fellini in Ottoemezzo; Commendatore Repubblica Italiana. *Plays:* Amore e magia nella cucina di mamma, Storia d'amore e d'anarchia, Lasciami andare madre, La vedova Scaltra. *Films as director and screenwriter:* I Basilischi (The Lizards) 1963, Questa Volta parliamo di Uomini (Let's Talk About Men) 1965, Rita la zanzara (Rita the Mosquito) 1966, Non stuzzicate la zanzara (Don't Sting the Mosquito) 1967, Mimi Metallurgio Ferito nell'Onore (The Seduction of Mimi) 1972, Film d'amore e d'anarchia (Love and Anarchy) 1973, Tutto a Posto e Niente in Ordine (All Screwed Up), Travolti da un Insolito Destino nell'Azzurro Mare d'Agosto (Swept Away) 1974, Pasqualino Settebellezze (Seven Beauties) 1976, The End of the World in our Usual Bed in a Night Full of Rain, Shimmy Lagano Tarantelle e Vino 1978, Revenge 1979, Summer Night, On a Moonlit Night, Saturday, Sunday, Monday, Ciao, Professore! 1993, The Nymph 1996, Ferdinando e Carolina 1999, Francesca e Nunziata 2001, Il giornalino di Gianburrasca. *Music:* La Pappa con il pomodoro. *Radio:* Sceicchi e femministe. *Television:* Peperoni ripieni e pesci in faccia (dir) 2004, Canzonissima, Studio Uno. *Address:* Via P. Clotilde 5, 00196 Rome, Italy.

WESCOT-WILLIAMS, Sarah; St Maarten politician; m. Louis E. Wescot (deceased); fmr Commr of Finance, of Educ., of Constitutional Affairs, fmr Leader of Govt; Prime Minister of St Maarten 2010–14 (first Prime Minister following dissolution of Netherlands Antilles), also Minister of Gen. Affairs and Acting Minister of Tourism, Econ. Affairs, Transport and Telecommunication; Leader, Democratic Party; Person of the Year Award, Paul Harris Fellow Award, Woman of Great Esteem Award. *Leisure interests:* music, reading, volleyball. *Address:* Democratic Party, Tamarind Tree Dr. 4, Union Rd, Cole Bay, Sint Maarten (office). *Telephone:* 543-1166 (office). *Fax:* 542-4296 (office).

WESSELS, Wolfgang, Dr rer. pol; German academic; *Director, Centre for Turkey and European Union Studies, University of Cologne;* b. 19 Jan. 1948, Cologne; s. of Theodor Wessels and Emma Wessels; m. Aysin Wessels 1973; two d.; Dir Institut für Europäische Politik, Bonn 1973–94; Dir Admin. Studies and Prof., Coll. of Europe, Bruges, Belgium 1980–96; Visiting Prof. 1996–; Jean Monnet Chair., Univ. of Cologne 1994–2016, Dir Centre for Turkey and European Union Studies (CETEUS) 2016–; Chair. Trans European Policy Studies Asscn 1995–2016; Vice-Pres. Konsortiums zur Gründung der Türkisch-Deutschen Universität, Istanbul 2010–; mem. of Editorial Bds of numerous publications including Integration magazine 1978–, European Foreign Policy Review 1990–; Jean Monnet – European Studies GOLD Lifelong Learning Award, European Comm. 2007, UACES Award for Lifetime Achievement in Contemporary European Studies 2011, Universitätspreis Forschung for excellence in research, Univ. of Cologne 2015, Vision for Europe Award, Prague European Summit 2016. *Publications include:* The European Council, Decision-Making in European Politics (with Simon Bulmer) 1987; Co-Ed.: Die Europäische Politische Zusammenarbeit in den achtziger Jahren—Eine gemeinsame Aussenpolitik für Westeuropa? 1989, Jahrbuch der Europäischen Integration 1980–2016, Europa vom A-Z. Taschen-buch der Europäischen Integration 1991–2016, Foreign Policy of the European Union. From EPC to CFSP and Beyond 1997, Die Öffnung des Staates. Modelle und Wirklichkeit grenzüberschreitender Verwaltungspraxis 2000, Das politische System der Europäischen Union. Die institutionelle Architektur des EU-Systems 2008; papers and articles on European integration. *Address:* Centre for Turkey and European Union Studies, University of Cologne, Gottfried-Keller-Strasse 1, 50931 Cologne, Germany (office). *Telephone:* (221) 4704131 (office). *Fax:* (221) 4701492 (office). *E-mail:* wessels@uni-koeln.de (office). *Website:* www.ceteus.uni -koeln.de (office).

WESSEX, HRH The Earl of; (Prince Edward Antony Richard Louis), (Viscount Severn), KCVO, ADC, KG, MA; British; b. 10 March 1964; s. of Queen Elizabeth II (q.v.) and Prince Philip, The Duke of Edinburgh; m. Sophie Rhys-Jones (now HRH The Countess of Wessex) 1999; one s. one d.; ed Heatherdown Prep. School, Gordonstoun School, Jesus Coll. Cambridge; fmrly Second Lt Royal Marines; worked in theatre production with Really Useful Group, Theatre Div.; f. Ardent Productions Ltd 1993; opened Commonwealth Games, Auckland 1990 and Malaysia 1998, Pres. Nat. Youth Music Theatre, Commonwealth Games Fed.; Co-f. (with The Countess of Wessex) The Wessex Youth Trust 1999; Chancellor, Univ. of Bath 2013–; Chair. Int. Council and Trustee, The Duke of Edinburgh's Award Int. Asscn 2015–; Pres. Sport and Recreation Alliance; UK and Int. Trustee, The Duke of Edinburgh's Award; Patron, ADC Theatre Appeal Cambridge, BADMINTON Scotland, British Paralympic Asscn, British Ski and Snowboard Fed., Cen. Caribbean Marine Inst., Chetham's School of Music, Manchester, The Church Army 121 Club, City of Birmingham Symphony Orchestra, Glassworks Theatre, Cambridge, Globe Theatre, Saskatchewan, Canada, Gordon's School Stepping Forward Appeal, Haddo Arts Trust, Aberdeen Haddo House Choral and Operatic Soc. (Royal Patron), Headway Dorset, His Majesty's Theatre Aberdeen, The Stage Man. Asscn, UNITEC, Auckland, Nat. Youth Orchestras of Scotland, Nat. Youth Theatre of Great Britain, Northern Ballet Theatre, The Orpheus Trust, Queen Victoria School, Auckland, Real Tennis Professionals Asscn, Royal Exchange Theatre Co., Royal Fleet Auxiliary Asscn, Manchester, Royal Wanganui Opera House, The London Gardens Soc., London Mozart Players, Royal Wolverhampton School, The Tennis and Rackets Asscn; Patron of Appeal, St Thomas Church Appeal, Newport; Col-in-Chief Hastings and Prince Edward Regt, Saskatchewan Dragoons; Vice Patron, Commonwealth Games Fed.; Royal Hon. Col Royal Wessex Yeomanry 2003; Hon. Deputy Commr, Royal Canadian Mounted Police 2007; hc

Liveryman, Worshipful Company of Haberdashers, of Gardeners 2008; Hon. Freeman, City of London 2011; Hon. mem., Court of Assistants, Worshipful Company of Haberdashers, of Gardeners 2011; Hon. Master, Worshipful Company of Gardeners 2013; Hon. Chair. The Duke of Edinburgh's Award, Young Canadian's Challenge Charter for Business; Hon. MA (Univ. of Cambridge) 1991, DIur (Univ. of Victoria) 1994, (Univ. of Prince Edward Island) 2007, (Univ. of Bath) 2013; Commander, RVO 1989–2003, Kt Grand Cross, RVO 2011; Queen Elizabeth II Silver Jubilee Medal 1977, Queen Elizabeth II Golden Jubilee Medal 2002, Queen Elizabeth II Diamond Jubilee Medal 2012. *Publication:* Crown and Country 1999. *Leisure interests:* the arts, horse-riding, sailing, skiing, badminton, Real Tennis. *Address:* Buckingham Palace, London, SW1A 1AA; Bagshot Park, Bagshot, Surrey, GU19 5PL, England. *Website:* www.royal.gov.uk.

WEST, Owen (see KOONTZ, Dean Ray).

WEST, Richard G., MA, ScD, FRS; British botanist and academic; b. 31 May 1926, Hendon, Middx; m. 1st Janet Abram 1958; one s.; m. 2nd Hazel Gristwood 1973 (died 1997); two d.; ed King's School, Canterbury and Univ. of Cambridge; Fellow, Clare Coll., Cambridge 1954–; Lecturer in Botany, Univ. of Cambridge 1960–68, Reader in Quaternary Research 1968–74, Prof. of Palaeoecology 1974–77, Prof. of Botany and Head, Dept of Botany 1977–91, Dir Sub-Dept of Quaternary Research 1966–87; Hon. mem. Royal Belgian Acad.; Foreign mem. Finnish Acad. of Sciences and Letters 1999; Hon. MRIA; Bigsby Medal, Geological Soc. 1968, Lyell Medal, Geological Soc. 1988, Albrecht Penck Medal, Deutsche Quartärvereinigung 1988. *Publications:* Pleistocene Geology and Biology 1968, The Ice Age in Britain (jtly) 1972, The Pre-glacial Pleistocene of the Norfolk and Suffolk Coasts 1980, Pleistocene Palaeoecology of Central Norfolk 1991, Plant Life in the Quaternary Cold Stages 2000, Brandon to Bungay 2009. *Leisure interest:* sailing. *Address:* Clare College, Cambridge (office); 3A Woollards Lane, Great Shelford, Cambridge, CB22 5LZ, England (home). *Telephone:* (1223) 842578 (home).

WEST, Stephen Craig, PhD, FRS, FMedSci; British scientist; b. 11 April 1952, Hull, England; s. of Joseph West and Louisa West; ed Univ. of Newcastle upon Tyne, Yale Univ., USA; Research Scientist, Yale Univ. 1983–85; Sr Scientist, Imperial Cancer Research Fund (now Cancer Research UK) 1985–89, Prin. Scientist, Sr Group Leader; mem. European Molecular Biology Org. 1994–; Hon. Prof., Univ. Coll. London 1997–; Swiss Bridge Prize 2001, 2009, Louis-Jeantet Prize for Medicine 2007, Novartis Prize 2008, GSK Prize 2010, Genetics Soc. Medal 2012, Genome Stability Network Medal 2015. *Publications include:* more than 240 research articles. *Leisure interests:* sport, music. *Address:* Meadowbank, Riverside Avenue, Broxbourne, Herts., EN10 6RA, England (home). *Telephone:* (1992) 470147 (home).

WEST, Timothy Lancaster, CBE, FRSA; British actor and director; b. 20 Oct. 1934, Bradford, Yorks., England; s. of H. Lockwood West and Olive Carleton-Crowe; m. 1st Jacqueline Boyer 1956 (dissolved); one d.; m. 2nd Prunella Scales (q.v.) 1963; two s.; ed John Lyon School, Harrow and Regent Street Polytechnic; repertory seasons, Wimbledon, Hull, Salisbury, Northampton 1956–60; mem. Royal Shakespeare and Prospect Theatre Cos. 1962–79; Artistic Dir, Old Vic 1980–81; Dir-in-Residence Univ. of WA 1982; Assoc. Dir Bristol Old Vic. –1991; Pres. London Acad. of Music and Dramatic Art 1986–2018; currently Pres. Soc. for Theatre Research; Patron, Nat. Piers Soc., The Associated Studios; Hon. DLitt (Easy Anglia), (West of England), (London), (Hull); Hon. DUniv (Bradford); Hon. LLD (Westminster); Hon. Dr of Drama (Royal Scottish Acad. of Music and Drama). *Theatre includes:* (in London): Caught Napping 1959, Galileo 1960, Gentle Jack 1963, The Trigon 1963, The Italian Girl 1968, Abelard and Heloise 1970, Exiles 1970, The Critic as Artist 1971, The Houseboy 1973, A Month in the Country 1974, A Room with a View 1975, Laughter 1978, The Homecoming 1978, Beecham 1980, Master Class 1984, The War at Home 1984, When We are Married 1986, The Sneeze 1988, Long Day's Journey into Night 1991, It's Ralph 1991, Twelve Angry Men 1996, Henry IV Parts 1 and 2 1996, King Lear 1997, The Birthday Party 1999, Luther 2001, King Lear 2003, HMS Pinafore 2003, National Hero 2005, Galileo 2006, The Old Country 2006, A Number 2006, Coriolanus 2007, The Collection 2007, The Lover/ The Collection 2008, Romany Wood (narrator) 2009, The Winslow Boy 2009, Uncle Vanya 2012, The Handyman 2012, The Vote 2015; numerous appearances with Prospect Theatre Co., Royal Shakespeare Co. and regional theatres. *Films include:* The Looking Glass War 1969, Nicholas and Alexandra 1971, The Day of the Jackal 1973, The Devil's Advocate 1978, The Thirty-Nine Steps 1978, Agatha 1979, Rough Cut 1980, Cry Freedom 1987, Consuming Passions 1988, The Tempest (voice) 1992, Ever After 1998, The Messenger: The Story of Joan of Arc 1999, 102 Dalmatians 2000, The Fourth Angel 2001, Iris 2001, Shrink 2002, Villa des Roses 2002, Sinbad: Legend of the Seven Seas (voice) 2003, Beyond Borders 2003, Endgame 2009. *Radio:* has appeared in more than 500 programmes since 1960. *Television includes:* Persuasion (mini-series) 1960, Witch Hunt (mini-series) 1967, Feet Foremost 1968, Big Breadwinner Hog (series) 1969, The Tragedy of King Richard II 1970, Edward II 1970, The Edwardians (mini-series) 1972, Horatio Bottomley 1972, Edward the King (mini-series) 1975, Hard Times (series) 1977, Henry VIII 1979, Churchill and the Generals 1979, Crime and Punishment (mini-series) 1979, Masada (mini-series) 1981, Murder Is Easy 1982, Oliver Twist 1982, Brass (series) 1983, The Last Bastion (mini-series) 1984, A Pocket Full of Rye 1985, Florence Nightingale 1985, Tender Is the Night (mini-series) 1985, The Good Doctor Bodkin-Adams 1986, The Monocled Mutineer (series) 1986, When We Are Married 1987, What the Butler Saw 1987, Harry's Kingdom 1987, Breakthrough at Reykjavik 1987, Strife, Beryl Markham: A Shadow on the Sun 1988, The Contractor, Blore M.P. 1989, Lenin: The Train 1990, The Tragedy of Flight 103: The Inside Story (aka Why Lockerbie?) 1990, Bye Bye Columbus 1991, Shakespeare: The Animated Tales (mini-series) (voice) 1992, Framed 1992, Survival of the Fittest, Smokescreen (mini-series) 1994, Reith to the Nation, Eleven Men Against Eleven 1995, Hiroshima 1995, The Place of the Dead 1996, Over Here 1996, Cuts 1996, Rebecca 1997, Animated Epics: Beowulf (voice) 1998, Bramwell: Our Brave Boys 1998, King Lear 1998, The Big Knights (series) (voice) 1999, Midsomer Murders 2000, Bedtime (series) 2001, Murder in Mind 2001, Station Jim 2001, Martin Luther 2002, Dickens 2002, The Alan Clark Diaries 2004, The Inspector Lynley Mysteries: In Pursuit of the Proper Sinner 2004, London 2004, Essential Poems for Christmas 2004, Waking the Dead 2004, Colditz 2005, Bleak House (mini-series) 2005, A Room With a View 2007, Terry

Pratchett's Going Postal 2010, Exile 2011, Titanic 2012, Coronation Street 2013, Last Tango in Halifax 2013, EastEnders 2014–15, Inside No. 9 2014, Canal Journeys 2014–. *Concerts:* with London Philharmonic Orchestra, Royal Philharmonic Orchestra, Britten Ensemble, Sinfonia 21 etc. *Publications:* I'm Here I Think, Where Are You? 1997, A Moment Towards the End of the Play 2001, So You Want To Be an Actor (with Prunella Scales) 2005. *Leisure interests:* music, travel, inland waterways, old railways. *Address:* c/o Gavin Barker Associates, 2D Wimpole Street, London, W1M 7AA, England (office).

WESTDAL, Christopher (Chris), BA, MBA; Canadian fmr diplomatist; ed St John's Coll., Univ. of Manitoba; previous positions beginning 1973 with Canadian Int. Devt Agency (CIDA); Amb. to Bangladesh and Burma 1982–85, to South Africa 1991–93, to Ukraine 1995–98, to UN, Geneva 1999–2003, to Russian Fed. 2003–06; mem. Bd of Dirs Silver Bear Resources Inc. 2007–, Consolidated Puma Minerals Corpn 2008–, Sage Gold, Inc. 2009–, Black Iron, Inc. 2010–, Canada-Eurasia-Russia Business Asscn; Contrib., Literary Review of Canada. *Website:* www.silverbearresources.com.

WESTERBERG, Bengt, MedKand, FilKand; Swedish politician and banker; b. 23 Aug. 1943, Solna; s. of Carl-Eric and Barbro Westerberg; m. 2nd Marie Ehrling; one s. two d. from a previous marriage; ed Karolinska Inst., Univ. of Stockholm; joined Liberal Youth League 1965, held elected office at all levels, Chair. Exec. Cttee 1970–71; joined Liberal Party 1965, Pres. 1993–95; Deputy Sec. to Commr for Greater Stockholm 1969, Sec. to Commr for Municipal Services 1970, Sec. to Stockholm County Council Traffic Commr 1971, Research Dir Traffic Cttee 1972, Adviser, Govt Comm. on Traffic Policy 1975, Ministry of Labour 1976, Liberal Party's Coordination Office 1978; State Sec., Ministry of Industry 1978, Ministry of the Budget 1979–82; f. Foundation for Market-Economy Alternative for Sweden 1983; mem. Parl. 1984–94; Minister of Social Affairs and Deputy Prime Minister 1991–94; Research and Devt Leader, Centre of Gender Studies, Univ. of Karlstad 1995–2000; Chair. Telia AB 1995–98, BTJ 1995–98, Swedish Petrol Inst., Finansinspektionen (Swedish Financial Supervisory Authority) 2003–15, Swedish Inst. of Disabilty Research, Cirkus Cirkor, Bonus-Presskopia, Swedish Author's Foundation, Inst. of Future Studies, Univ. of Linkoping –2016; Vice-Chair. Riksbank (Cen. Bank of Sweden) 1994–98, mem. Bd 2002–06; Pres. Swedish Athletics Asscn 1995–2004, Swedish Foundation of Dyslexia 1995–2005, Swedish Red Cross; Vice-Pres. Int. Fed. of Red Cross and Red Crescent Socs; mem. Bd Swedish Sports Confed. 1999–2005; Dr hc (Univ. of Karlstad) 2008.

WESTERBERG, Lars, BBA, MSc; Swedish business executive; b. 1948; ed Univ. of Stockholm, Royal Inst. of Tech.; began career with ASEA 1972, later Sales Man., ASEA Robotics –1984; joined Esab 1984, Pres. and CEO 1991–94; Pres. and CEO Gränges AB 1994–99; Pres. and CEO Autoliv AB 1999–2007, Chair. 2007–11; Ind. Chair. Vattenfall AB 2008–14; fmr Chair. Husqvarna AB, Ahlsell AB; mem. Bd of Dirs SSAB Svenskt Stål AB 2006–, Sandvik AB 2010–, Stena AB 2011–, Meda AB 2012–, AB Volvo 2007–, Plastal AB.

WESTERFIELD, Putney, BA; American business executive; b. 9 Feb. 1930, Yale Univ. campus, New Haven, Conn.; s. of Ray Bert Westerfield and Beatrice Westerfield (née Putney); m. Anne Montgomery 1954; two s. one d.; ed Choate School and Yale Univ.; Vice-Pres. and Co-founder, Careers Inc. 1950–52; Man. SE Asia Operations, Swen Publs; service with CIA in Hong Kong and SE Asia 1951–52, Seoul, Korea 1953–54, Saigon, Viet Nam 1955–57; Asst to Publr of Time Inc. 1957–59, Asst to Circulation Dir 1959–61, Circulation Dir 1961–66, Asst Publr 1966–68; Asst Publr of Life 1968–69; Publr of Fortune 1969–73; Pres. Chase World Information Corpn 1973–75; Vice-Pres. Boyden Assocs International 1976–80, Sr Vice-Pres., Western Man. 1980–84, Pres. and CEO 1984–90, Man. Dir 1990, now Chair. Emer.; Dir East Meets West Foundation 1991; Chair. Upside Media Inc.; Chair. Choate Alumni Fund, Choate Alumni Asscn 1960s, Trustee 1967–77; mem. Communication Bd Yale Univ., Founding Bd of the Asscn of Yale Alumni 1971, Reunion Chair. Yale '51, Vice-Chair. Reunion Class Gifts; mem. Bd US-South Africa Leaders Exchange Program 1971–95; Founder East Meets West Foundation (Viet Nam) 1989; Distinguished Service Award, Choate School. *Leisure interests:* travel, reading, music, tennis, swimming. *Address:* c/o Boyden International, 275 Battery Street, Suite 420, San Francisco, CA 94111 (office); 10 Green View Lane, Hillsborough, CA 94010, USA (home). *Website:* putneywesterfield.com.

WESTMACOTT, Sir Peter John, Kt, GCMG, KCMG, LVO; British diplomatist; b. 23 Dec. 1950, Edington, Somerset, England; m. Susan Nemazee; two s. two d.; ed New Coll., Oxford; joined FCO in 1972, in Middle East Dept and Persian language training 1973–74, Second Sec., Embassy in Tehran 1974–78, Perm. Mission to EU, Brussels 1978–80, First Sec. for Econs, Embassy in Paris 1980–84, with FCO 1984–87, Head of Chancery, Embassy in Ankara 1987–90, Deputy Pvt. Sec. to HRH Prince of Wales 1990–93, Counsellor for Political and Public Affairs, Embassy in Washington, DC 1993–97, Dir for Americas, later Deputy Under-Sec., FCO 1997–2002, Amb. to Turkey 2002–07, to France 2007–11, to USA 2012–16; Commdr, Légion d'honneur 2008. *Address:* Foreign and Commonwealth Office, King Charles Street, London, SW1A 2AH, England (office). *Telephone:* (20) 7008-1500 (office). *E-mail:* fcocorrespondence@fco.gov.uk (office). *Website:* www.gov.uk/government/organisations/foreign-commonwealth-office (office).

WESTON, (Willard Gordon) Galen, OC, OOnt, BA, LLD; Canadian business executive; *Executive Chairman, George Weston Ltd;* b. 29 Oct. 1940, grandson of George Weston; m. Hilary Weston; one s. one d.; ed Univ. of Western Ontario; Chair. and Pres. George Weston Ltd (family business est. by grandfather) –2011, Exec. Chair. 2011–; Chair. Holt Renfrew & Co. Ltd, Brown Thomas Group Ltd, Selfridges & Co. Ltd, De Bijenkorf BV 2011–; fmr Chair. Loblaw Cos Ltd; Pres. Garfield Weston Foundation (majority owner of Wittington Investments Ltd, owner of Associated British Foods, Fortnum & Mason, Heal's); Hon. LLD (Univ. of Western Ontario). *Leisure interest:* art collecting. *Address:* George Weston Ltd, 22 St Clair Avenue East, Suite 1901, Toronto, ON M4T 2S7, Canada (office). *Telephone:* (416) 922-2500 (office). *Fax:* (416) 922-4395 (office). *E-mail:* info@weston.ca (office). *Website:* www.weston.ca (office).

WESTON, Sir (Philip) John, Kt, KCMG; British diplomatist, company director and poet; b. 13 April 1938, nottingham; s. of Philip G. Weston and Edith Ansell; m. Sally Ehlers 1967; two s. one d.; ed Sherborne School and Worcester Coll. Oxford; served Royal Marines 1956–58; entered HM Diplomatic Service 1962; Treasury Centre for Admin. Studies 1964; Chinese language student, Hong Kong 1964–66;

Beijing 1967–68; Office of UK Perm. Rep. to EEC 1972–74; Asst Pvt. Sec. to Sec. of State for Foreign and Commonwealth Affairs 1974–76; Counsellor, Head of EEC Presidency Secr., FCO 1976–77; Visiting Fellow, All Souls Coll. Oxford 1977–78; Counsellor, Washington, DC 1978–81; Head, Defence Dept FCO 1981–84, Asst Under-Sec. of State 1984–85; Minister, Paris 1985–88; Deputy Sec. to Cabinet, Cabinet Office 1988–89; Deputy Under-Sec. of State, FCO 1989–90, Political Dir 1990–91; Amb. and Perm. Rep. to N Atlantic Council (NATO) 1992–95; Amb. and Perm. Rep. to UN 1995–98; Dir (non-exec.) British Telecommunications 1998–2002, Rolls Royce Group 1998–2005, Hakluyt & Co. 2001–07; mem. Council IISS 2001–05; Pres. Community Foundation Network (UK) 1998–2008, Worcester Coll. Soc. 2003–12; Gov. Ditchley Foundation 2000–11; Chair. Govs Sherborne School 2002–07; Chair. of Trustees The Poetry School 2004–08; mem. Council and Trustee, The Poetry Soc. 2005–08; Trustee, Nat. Portrait Gallery 1999–2008; Hon. Pres. Community Foundation Network (UK) 1998–2008, Hon. Fellow, Worcester Coll., Oxford 2003; Order of Merit (with Star) (FRG). *Publications include:* Take Five – 04 (poetry anthology) 2004, Chasing the Hoopoe (first poetry collection) 2005, Echo Soundings (second poetry collection) 2012, Poetry in the Blood (essay anthology) 2014; poems published by The Guardian, The Spectator, The London Magazine and many other literary magazines. *Leisure interests:* poetry, beekeeping, fly-fishing, running, birds, drawing, Chinese language. *Address:* 139 Queens Road, Richmond, TW10 6HF, England (home). *E-mail:* john.weston-pjweston@btinternet.com (home).

WESTON, John Pix, CBE, BA, MA, FRAeS, FRSA, FREng; British business executive; *Chairman, International Advisory Board, ASPIDE;* b. 16 Aug. 1951, Kendal, Cumbria, England; s. of John Pix Weston and Ivy Weston (née Glover); m. Susan West 1974; one s. one d.; ed Kings School, Worcester and Trinity Hall, Cambridge; under-grad. apprentice, British Aircraft Corpn 1970–75; various sales appointments, Panavia Aircraft GmbH 1975–82, seconded to Ministry of Defence as Project Officer P110 and Tornado, Defence Sales Org. 1982–84; Middle East Sales Man., British Aerospace Mil. Aircraft 1984–85, Exec. Project Dir, Al-Yamamah Programme 1985–87, Dir in Charge, Saudi Arabia 1987–90, Man. Dir Mil. Aircraft Div. 1990–92, Group Man. Dir and Chair. British Aerospace Defence Businesses 1992–98, mem. Bd 1993–2002, Chief Exec. BAe (later BAE Systems following merger with Marconi Electric Systems) 1998–2002; Chair. (non-exec.) Spirent plc 2002–06, Acra Controls Ltd 2003–, Inbis PLC 2004–05, University for Industry (Learn-Direct) 2004–, ISOFT PLC 2005–07, MB Aerospace 2006–, Insensys PLC 2007–08, AWS PLC 2008–; currently Chair. Int. Advisory Bd, ASPIDE; mem. CBI Pres.'s and Chair.'s Cttees 2000–09, Chair. CBI European Group 2000–09; Vice-Pres. Royal United Services Inst. 1992–; Dir, The German/British Forum 2002–, Assystem-Brime, Paris 2005–06; mem. Council Royal Acad. of Eng 2003–06; Patron Combined Services Winter Sports Asscn 2003–; Fellow, Royal Acad. of Eng; Freeman, City of London; Commdr, Order of the Pole Star (Sweden); Gold Medal, Royal United Services Inst. *Leisure interests:* skiing, photography, mountain walking. *Address:* ASPIDE, Pariser Platz 4A 10117 Berlin, Germany (office). *Telephone:* (30) 2067356-0 (office). *Fax:* (30) 2067356-10 (office). *E-mail:* mail@ASPIDEpartners.com (office). *Website:* www.aspidepartners.com (office).

WESTON, Sir Michael Charles Swift, Kt, KCMG, CVO, MA; British diplomatist (retd); b. 4 Aug. 1937, Crowborough, Sussex, England; s. of Edward C. S. Weston and Kathleen M. Mockett; m. 1st Veronica A. Tickner 1959 (divorced 1990); two s. one d.; m. 2nd Christine J. Ferguson 1990; one s. one d.; ed Dover Coll. and St Catharine's Coll., Cambridge (Exhibitioner); joined HM Diplomatic Service 1961; Third Sec. Kuwait 1962; First Sec. Tehran 1968; UK mission, New York 1970; Counsellor Jeddah 1977; Royal Coll. of Defence Studies 1980; Counsellor Paris 1981, Cairo 1984; Head S European Dept, FCO 1987–90; Amb. to Kuwait 1990–92; Leader UK Del. to Conf. on Disarmament, Geneva 1992–97; mem. Special Immigration Appeals Comm. 1999–2007, apptd Advisory Group of the Comprehensive Nuclear Test Ban Treaty Org. 2006 (apptd Chair. 2009–). *Leisure interests:* squash, tennis, walking. *Address:* Beech Farm House, Beech Lane, Matfield, Kent, TN12 7HG, England (home). *Telephone:* (1892) 824666 (home). *E-mail:* michael.c.s.weston@talk21.com (home).

WESTPHAL, Cheyenne, BA (Hons), MA; German art dealer; *Co-Worldwide Head, Contemporary Art, Sotheby's;* ed St Andrews Univ., Univ. of California, Berkeley, USA; joined Sotheby's, London 1990, joined Contemporary Art Dept 1992, Head of European div. 1999–2006, mem. Bd of Dirs 2002, Chair. Contemporary Art, Sotheby's Europe 2006–13, Co-Worldwide Head, Contemporary Art 2013–. *Address:* Sotheby's, 34–35 New Bond Street, London, W1A 2AA, England (office). *Telephone:* (20) 7293-5390 (office); (20) 7293-5000 (office). *Fax:* (20) 7293-5989 (office). *E-mail:* cheyenne.westphal@sothebys.com (office). *Website:* www.sothebys.com (office).

WESTPHAL, Joseph William, BA, MA, PhD; American political scientist, academic, government official and diplomatist; *Senior Adviser to Global Industrial Market Practice, Korn Ferry;* b. 26 Jan. 1948, Santiago, Chile; m.; four c.; ed Adelphi Univ., Oklahoma State Univ., Univ. of Missouri; moved to USA with his family at an early age; fmr Prof., Dept of Political Science, Oklahoma State Univ., later Head of Dept; has lectured at numerous univs world-wide and taught public policy as an Adjunct Prof. at Georgetown Univ., while working in Washington, DC; fmr Chancellor Univ. of Maine System and Prof. of Political Science, Univ. of Maine; fmr Provost, Sr Vice-Pres. for Research and Prof. of Environmental Studies, The New School, New York City; worked as policy adviser to Asst Sec. for Land and Water Resources, Dept of the Interior 1990s; Sr Policy Advisor for Water Resources, Environmental Protection Agency during Clinton Admin 1990s; also worked in US Congress in various capacities, from directing a bi-partisan congressional caucus in the House and Senate, as a budget analyst and asst to the Chair. of the House Cttee on the Budget; Asst Sec. of the Army for Civil Works 1998–2001, Acting Sec. of the Army 2001, later Under-Sec. of the Army and the Army's first Chief Man. Officer; mem. Pres. Obama's Transition Team for Defense Matters –2014; Amb. to Saudi Arabia 2014–17; Sr Adviser to Global Industrial Market Practice, Korn Ferry 2018–; Sr Global Fellow, Joseph H. Lauder Inst. of Man. and Int. Studies, Univ. of Pennsylvania, Sr Fellow, Wharton Leadership Program. *Telephone:* (310) 226-6352 (office). *Website:* www.kornferry.com (office).

WESTWOOD, Lee John, OBE; British professional golfer; b. 24 April 1973, Worksop, Notts.; s. of John Westwood and Trish Westwood; m. Laurae Coltart 1999; one s. one d.; began to play golf aged 13; England Boys, Youths and Srs amateur teams 1989–93, won Peter McEvoy Trophy 1990, Lagonda Trophy 1992, British Youths Championships 1993; turned professional 1993, won Volvo Scandinavian Masters 1996, 2000, Sumitomo VISA Taiheiyo Masters 1996, 1997, 1998, Benson and Hedges Malaysian Open 1997, Volvo Masters Andalucia 1997, Holden Australian Open 1997, McDermott-Freeport Classic 1998, Deutsche Bank SAP Open TPC of Europe 1998, 2000, Nat. Car Rental English Open 1998, The Standard Life Loch Lomond 1998, Belgacom Open 1998, 2000, Dunlop Phoenix Tournament 1998, Macau Open 1999, TNT Dutch Open 1999, Smurfit European Open 1999, 2000, Canon European Masters 1999, Dimension Data Pro Am 2000, Compaq European Grand Prix 2000, Cisco World Match Play Championship 2000, BMW Int. Open 2003, Dunhill Links Championship 2003, Nelson Mandela Invitational (with Simon Hobday) 2003, Valle Romano Open de Andalucia 2007, Quinn Direct British Masters 2007, Portugal Masters 2009, Dubai World Championship 2009, Nedbank Golf Challenge (South Africa) 2010, Indonesian Masters (Asian Tour) 2011, Ballantines Championship 2011, Thailand Golf Championship 2011, Nordea Masters 2012, Maybank Malaysian Open 2014, Thailand Golf Championship 2014, CIMB Niaga Indonesian Masters 2015; PGA Tour wins: Freeport-McDermott Classic 1998, St Jude Classic 2010; won renamed Race to Dubai 2009; best results in major championships: The Masters: tied for sixth place 1999, second 2010, tied for third place 2012, tied for eighth place 2013, seventh 2014, tied for second place 2016, US Open: tied for seventh place 1998, tied for fifth place 2000, third 2008, tied for third place 2011, tied for tenth place 2012, The Open Championship: tied for tenth place 1997, fourth 2004, tied for third place 2009, second 2010, tied for third place 2013, PGA Championship: tied for third place 2009, tied for eighth place 2011; results in World Golf Championship events: CA Championship tied for fourth place 1999, second 2000, Bridgestone Invitational: tied for ninth place 2004, tied for second place 2008, ninth 2009, HSBC Champions: tied for eighth place 2009, second 2010, Dell Match Play: round of 16 2015; Team appearances: Ryder Cup (representing Europe): 1997 (winners), 1999, 2002 (winners), 2004 (winners), 2006 (winners), 2008, 2010 (winners), 2012 (winners), 2014 (winners), Alfred Dunhill Cup (representing England): 1996, 1997, 1998, 1999, Seve Trophy (representing GB & Ireland): 2000, 2002 (winners), 2003 (winners), Royal Trophy (representing Europe): 2007 (winners); spent over 180 weeks in top 10 of Official World Golf Rankings 1998–2001, returned to top 10 at end of the 2008 season and again after 2009 PGA Championship; ranked World No. 1 31 Oct. 2010–26 Feb. 2011, 25 April–28 May 2011; announced creation of Lee Westwood Acad. (set of three-day acads across nine venues in England) 2009; opened his first golf school 2010; Hon. DSc (Nottingham Trent Univ.) 2007; named Player of the Year 1998, 2000, 2009, European Tour Order of Merit 2000, Volvo Order of Merit 2000, 'Spirit of Golf' Award, Golf Foundation 2010, Nottingham Trent Univ. named its sports hall after him 2010. *Leisure interests:* snooker, horse racing (racehorse owner), sports cars, Nottingham Forest Football Club, cinema, shows. *Address:* c/o International Sports Management Ltd, Cherry Tree Farm, Cherry Tree Lane, Rostherne, Cheshire, WA14 3RZ, England (office). *E-mail:* ism@golfism.net (office). *Website:* www.leewestwood.golf.

WESTWOOD, Dame Vivienne Isabel, OBE, DBE; British fashion designer; b. (Vivienne Isabel Swire), 8 April 1941, Tintwistle, Derbyshire; d. of Gordon Swire and Dora Swire; m. 1st Derek Westwood 1962, one s.; one s. with Malcolm McLaren; m. 2nd Andreas Kronthaler 1993; worked with Malcolm McLaren 1970–83, developing 'punk' look, and her clothes were sold at McLaren's shop on King's Road, London; designed for the Sex Pistols, Boy George and Bananarama; created first catwalk collection, Pirate (adopted by Adam Ant and Bow Wow Wow) 1981; showed in Paris 1983, in Tokyo 1984; moved to Italy with new business pnr Carlo D'Amario 1984; opened first Vivienne Westwood shop, London 1990; launch of signature fragrance, Boudoir 1998, further fragrances Libertine 2000, Boudoir Sin City 2007, Let it Rock 2007; Prof. of Fashion Acad. of Applied Arts 1989–91, Hochschule der Künste, Berlin 1993–; Trustee, Civil Liberties Trust 2007–; Hon. Sr Fellow, Royal Coll. of Art 1992; Dr hc (Heriot-Watt) 1995, (Acad. of Art Univ. School of Fashion) 2006; Designer of the Year 1990, 1991, Queen's Award for Export 1998, Moet & Chandon Red Carpet Dresser 2006, Outstanding Achievement in Fashion Award, British Fashion Awards 2007. *Television:* South Bank Show: Vivienne Westwood 1990. *Address:* Vivienne Westwood Ltd, Westwood Studios, 9–15 Elcho Street, London, SW11 4AU, England (office). *Telephone:* (20) 7924-4747 (office). *Fax:* (20) 7738-9655. *E-mail:* info@viviennewestwood.co.uk. *Website:* www.viviennewestwood.com.

WETANG'ULA, Moses Masika, LLB; Kenyan lawyer and politician; b. 13 Sept. 1956, Western Kenya; m.; c.; ed Univ. of Nairobi, Kenya School of Law; Professional Dist Magistrate, Chief Magistrate's Court, Nakuru 1982, Dist Magistrate's Court, Rongo, South Nyanza 1983; Sole Practitioner, M. M Wetang'ula Advocate Chambers, Nairobi 1983–85, currently Proprietor, Wetangula, Adan, Makokha & Co. Advocates (law firm), Nairobi; mem. Parl. (FORD–Kenya) for Sirisia constituency 1993–97, 2003–13, Senator for Bungoma County March–Oct. 2013, Senate Minority Leader April–Oct. 2013; Asst Minister for Int. Affairs –2008, Minister of Foreign Affairs 2008–12, of Trade 2012–13; Chair. Electricity Regulatory Bd 1998–2001; mem. Law Soc. of Kenya, Commonwealth Parl. Asscn, Int. Bar Asscn, Int. Comm. of Jurists, Kenya Chapter, Parliamentarians for Global Action, Inter-Parliamentary Union. *Leisure interests:* reading, swimming and other health activities, farming, traveling, intellectual debates and politics. *Address:* Wetangula, Adan, Makokha & Co. Advocates, 12th Floor, Bruce House, Standard Street, PO Box 10741, 00100 Nairobi, Kenya (office). *E-mail:* info@wetangulawam.co.ke (office). *Website:* www.wetangulawam.co.ke (office).

WETHINGTON, Charles T., Jr, PhD; American fmr university president; b. 2 Jan. 1936, Merrimac, Ky; m. Judy Woodrow 1962; two c.; ed Brescia Coll., Eastern Kentucky Univ., Syracuse Univ., Univ. of Kentucky; Instructor, Univ. of Kentucky 1965–66; Dir Maysville Community Coll. 1967–71; Asst Vice-Pres. for the Community Coll. System, Univ. of Kentucky 1971–81, Vice-Pres. 1981–82, Chancellor 1982–88, Chancellor for the Community Coll. System and Univ. Relations 1988–89, Interim Pres. Univ. of Kentucky 1989–90, Pres. 1990–2001, then Fund Raiser; Bd mem. Nat. Coll. Athletic Asscn Foundation 1999–2002. *Address:* c/o University of Kentucky, 5-52 Wm. T. Young Library, Lexington, KY 40506 (office); 2926 Four Pines Drive, Lexington, KY 40502, USA (home). *Telephone:* (606) 257-5646 (office). *Fax:* (859) 323-3777 (office).

WETTER, HE Cardinal Friedrich; German ecclesiastic; *Archbishop Emeritus of Munich and Freising;* b. 20 Feb. 1928, Landau, Rhineland-Palatinate; s. of Peter Wetter and Hedwig Böttinger; ed Sankt Georgen Grad. School of Philosophy and Theology and Univ. Gregoriana, Rome; ordained priest 1953; chaplain in Speyer 1956–58; taught in seminary in Speyer 1958–60; Asst Parish Priest in Glanmünchweiler 1960–61; Prof. of Fundamental Theology, Eichstätt 1962–67; Prof. of Dogmatic Theology, Johannes Gutenberg Univ. of Mainz 1967–68; Bishop of Speyer 1968–82; Archbishop of Munich and Freising 1982–Feb. 2007, Apostolic Admin. of Munich and Freising Feb.–Nov. 2007, Archbishop Emer. 2007–; cr. Cardinal (Cardinal-Priest of Santo Stefano al Monte Celio) 1985; participated in Papal Conclave 2005; Hon. Prof., Univ. of Mainz 1967–; Grosses Bundesverdienstkreuz mit Stern, Bayerischer Verdienstorden. *Publications:* Zeit-Worte 1993, Er allein trägt 1996, Mit Euch auf dem Weg 1998. *Address:* Archdiocese of München und Freising, Postfach 330360, Rochusstrasse 5–7, 80063 Munich, Germany. *Telephone:* (89) 21370. *Fax:* (89) 21371585. *Website:* www.erzbistum-muenchen.de.

WEVER-CROES, Evelyn Christina; Aruban lawyer and politician; *Prime Minister and Minister of General Affairs, Integrity, Innovation and Energy;* b. 5 Dec. 1966; ed Univ. of the Netherlands Antilles, Leiden Univ.; worked for Netherlands Antilles Tax Dept 1989–2003, becoming Head, Tax Inspectorate Office; Tax Adviser, Croes Wever & Tchong (law firm) 2003–10, Tax Lawyer 2008–10; mem. Staten (Parl.) 2009–17, Leader, MEP parl. group 2013–17; Prime Minister (first female) and Minister of Gen. Affairs, Integrity, Innovation and Energy 2017–; mem. Movimiento Electoral di Pueblo (MEP. *Address:* Office of the Prime Minister, Government Offices, L. G. Smith Blvd 76, Oranjestad, Aruba (office). *Telephone:* 5830001 (office). *Fax:* 5880024 (office). *E-mail:* info@kabinet.aw (office).

WEXLER, Nancy Sabin, AB, PhD, FRCP; American neurologist and academic; *Higgins Professor of Neuropsychology, Departments of Neurology and Psychiatry, College of Physicians and Surgeons, Columbia University;* b. 19 July 1945, Washington, DC; d. of Milton Wexler and Leonore Wexler; ed Radcliffe Coll., Univ. of the West Indies, Jamaica (Fulbright Scholarship), Hampstead Clinic Child Psychoanalytic Training Inst., UK, Univ. of Michigan; Psychological Intern and Teaching Fellow, Univ. of Michigan 1968–74; Licensed Psychologist, New York State 1974–; Asst Prof. of Psychology, New School of Social Research, Grad. Faculty, New York City 1974–76; pvt. practice, psychologist, New York City 1974–76; Exec. Dir Congressional Comm. for Control of Huntington's Disease and Its Consequences, based in Nat. Inst. of Neurological, Communicative Disorders and Stroke, NIH, Bethesda, Md 1976–78; Co-organizer, Public Forum on Nat. Genetic Diseases Act 1977; Health Science Admin. Demyelinating, Atrophic and Degenerative Diseases Program, Nat. Inst. of Neurological, Communicative Disorders and Stroke, NIH 1978–83; Pres. Hereditary Disease Foundation 1983; Assoc. Prof. of Clinical Neuropsychology, Depts of Neurology and Psychiatry, Coll. of Physicians and Surgeons, Columbia Univ. 1985–92, mem. Center for Brain and Behavior 1985, Prof. of Clinical Neuropsychology 1992–93, Higgins Prof. of Neuropsychology 1993–; Chair. Jt NIH/DOE Ethical, Legal and Social Issues Working Group of Nat. Center for Human Genome Research, Human Genome Org. (HUGO); Councillor, Soc. for Neuroscience 2000; mem. Inst. of Medicine, NAS 1997 (mem. Council 2007); mem. Bd Dirs AAAS, Advisory Cttee on Research on Women's Health, NIH; mem. American Psychological Asscn, American Psychological Soc., American Soc. for Human Genetics, Soc. for Neuroscience, World Fed. of Neurology, Research Group on Huntington's Disease, American Neurological Asscn, American Soc. of Law and Medicine, Inst. of Medicine, NAS, European Acad. of Sciences and Arts 2001, American Acad. of Arts and Sciences 2005; Fellow, New York Acad. of Sciences 1998, AAAS 2002, Royal Coll. of Physicians; Order of Merit in Work First Class (Venezuela) 1990; Hon. DHumLitt (New York Medical Coll.) 1991; Hon. DSc (Univ. of Michigan) 1991, (Bard Coll.) 1998; Hon. Doctor of Medical Sciences (Yale Univ.) 2006; PHS-NIMH Fellowship 1969–70, Univ. Fellowship 1973–74, PHS Certificate of Merit 1980, NIH Director's Award 1980, Hon. Declaration, Community of San Luis, Venezuela 1982, 1987, Award for Research, Nat. Huntington's Disease Soc. 1984, Landacre Day Award, Ohio State Univ. 1986, Maracaibo Rotary Club Award (Venezuela) 1986, Award for Research, Huntington's Disease Soc. of America 1986, The SOMA Distinguished Prof. Lecture Series, Univ. of California, San Diego School of Medicine 1987, First Robert J. and Claire Pasarow Foundation Award 1987, Living Legacy Award, Women's Int. Soc. 1988, Esquire Magazine Register 1988, Alumnae Athena Award, Alumnae Council, Univ. of Michigan 1989, Award from Gov.'s Office, State of Zulia, Venezuela 1989, Huntington's Disease Benefit Dinner Honoree 1989, Legislative Resolution of Commendation, New York State 1990, 21st Annual Louis B. Flexner Lecturer, Univ. of Pennsylvania 1992, Dean's Distinguished Lecture in the Clinical Sciences, Columbia Univ. 1992, Distinguished Service Award for Enhancing Educ. Through Biological Research, Nat. Asscn of Biology Teachers 1993, Foster Elting Bennett Memorial Lecturer, 118th Annual Meeting of American Neurological Asscn, Boston 1993, Nat. Health Council Nat. Medical Research Award to Huntington's Disease Collaborative Research Group 1993, Albert Lasker Public Service Award 1993, American Captains of Achievement Golden Plate Award, American Acad. of Achievement 1994, J. Allyn Taylor Int. Prize in Medicine 1994, Asscn of Neuroscience Depts and Programs' Educ. Award 1997, Venezuela Award, Casa Hogar 1999, Soc. for Neuroscience Public Advocacy Award 2003, Distinguished Investigator Award, NARSAD 2006, NARSAD Lieber Investigator 2006, Benjamin Franklin Medal in Life Science 2007. *Achievements include:* important scientific contrib. on Huntington's disease; 20-year study of world's largest family with Huntington's disease, in Venezuela, developing pedigree of more than 18,000 individuals and collecting more than 4,000 blood samples helped lead to identification of Huntington's disease gene on human chromosome 4. *Publications:* numerous scientific papers in professional journals. *Address:* Columbia University Department of Psychiatry, 1051 Riverside Drive, Unit 6, PI Annex 371, New York, NY 10032 (office); Hereditary Disease Foundation, 601 West 168th Street, Suite 54, New York, NY 10032, USA (office). *Telephone:* (646) 774-5000 (Dept of Psychiatry) (office); (212) 928-2121 (Hereditary Disease Foundation) (office). *Fax:* (212) 928-2172 (Hereditary Disease Foundation) (office). *E-mail:* wexlern@pi.cpmc.columbia.edu (office); cures@hdfoundation.org (office). *Website:* www.columbiapsychiatry.org (office); www.hdfoundation.org (office).

WEXNER, Leslie (Les) Herbert; American retail executive and philanthropist; *Chairman and CEO, L Brands, Inc.;* b. 8 Sept. 1937, New Albany, Ohio; s. of Bella Wexner; m. Abigail S. Koppel 1993; two s. two d.; ed Ohio State Univ.; Founder, Chair. and CEO Ltd Inc. fashion chain (now L Brands, Inc.), Columbus, OH 1963–; est. the Wexner Foundation 1984; Dir and mem. Exec. Comm. Banc One Corpn, Sotheby's Holdings Inc.; mem. Business Admin Advisory Council, Ohio State Univ.; Chair. Retail Industry Trade Action Coalition, Columbus Urban League 1982–84, Hebrew Immigrant Aid Soc. 1982–; Co-Chair. Int. United Jewish Appeal Cttee; Nat. Vice-Chair. and Treas. United Jewish Appeal; mem. Bd of Dirs and Exec. Cttee American Jewish Jt Distribution Cttee Inc.; Founding mem. and first Chair. The Ohio State Univ. Foundation; mem. Exec. Cttee American Israel Public Affairs Cttee; fmr mem. Governing Cttee Columbus Foundation; Trustee, Columbus Jewish Fed. 1972–, Columbus Jewish Foundation, Aspen Inst., Ohio State Univ. 1988–97, 2005–12 (Chair. 2009–12), Columbus Capital Corpn for Civic Improvement; fmr Trustee, Columbus Museum of Art, Columbus Symphony Orchestra, Whitney Museum of American Art, Capitol South Community Urban Redevelopment Corpn; mem. Young Presidents Org.; considered to have one of the 50 largest art collections in the world; Hon. Vice-Chair. Congregation Agudas Achim, Bexley; Hon. mem. 104th Class of SPHINX Sr Class Hon., Ohio State Univ. 2010; Cavaliere of Repub. of Italy; Hon. HHD 1986; Hon. LLD (Hofstra Univ.) 1987; Hon. LHD (Brandeis Univ.) 1990; Hon. PhD (Jewish Theological Seminary) 1990; American Marketing Asscn Man of the Year 1974, Woodrow Wilson Award for Corporate Citizenship 2004, The Medical Center at Ohio State Univ. officially changed its name to the Wexner Medical Center at The Ohio State Univ. 2012, Women's Wear Daily Beauty Inc. Visionary Award 2013. *Address:* L Brands, Inc., 3 Limited Way Parkway, Columbus, OH 43230, USA (office). *Telephone:* (614) 415-7000 (office). *Fax:* (614) 415-7440 (office). *E-mail:* info@lb.com (office). *Website:* www.lb.com (office).

WEYMOUTH, Katharine Bouchage, BA, JD; American lawyer and publishing executive; b. 1966; d. of Yann R. Weymouth and Lally Weymouth; grand-d. of Katharine Graham (Chair. Washington Post and publr); niece of Tina Weymouth; m. Richard Alan Scully 1998 (divorced 2004); one s. two d.; ed Harvard Coll., Univ. of Oxford, UK, Stanford Univ. Law School; mother's family has owned The Washington Post newspaper since 1933; Assoc., Williams & Connolly (law firm), Washington, DC 1993–96; Asst Counsel, The Washington Post 1996–98, Advertising Liason 2000–02, Dir Advertising Jobs Unit 2002–04, Dir Advertising Sales 2004–05, Vice-Pres. Advertising 2005–08, Publr The Washington Post and CEO Washington Post Media 2008–14; Advisor, FiscalNote Inc. 2015–; mem. Bd of Dirs Online Publrs Asscn. *Address:* FiscalNote Inc., 1155 F Street, NW, Suite 475, Washington, DC 20004, USA. *Website:* www.fiscalnote.com.

WHALLEY, Joanne; British actress; b. 25 Aug. 1964, Salford; m. Val Kilmer 1988 (divorced 1996); one s. one d.; stage career began during teens and has included season of Edward Bond plays at Royal Court Theatre, London and appearances in The Three Sisters, What the Butler Saw (NW Manhattan Theatre Club), Lulu (Almeida, London). *Films include:* Pink Floyd: The Wall 1982, Dance With a Stranger 1985, No Surrender 1985, The Good Father 1985, Will You Love Me Tomorrow 1987, Willow 1988, To Kill a Priest 1988, Scandal 1989, Kill Me Again 1989, The Big Man 1990, Navy Seals 1990, Miss Helen, Shattered 1991, Crossing the Line, Storyville 1992, The Secret Rapture 1993, Mother's Boys 1994, A Good Man in Africa 1994, Trial By Jury 1994, The Man Who Knew Too Little 1997, A Texas Funeral 1999, Run the Wild Fields 2000, The Guilty 2000, Breathtaking 2000, Virginia's Run 2001, Before You Go 2002, The Californians 2005, Played 2006, 44 Inch Chest 2009, Golf in the Kingdom 2010, Twixt 2011. *Television includes:* Coronation Street (series) 1974, Emmerdale Farm (series) 1977, A Kind of Loving (series) 1982, Reilly: Ace of Spies (mini-series) 1983, Edge of Darkness (mini-series) 1985, The Singing Detective (mini-series) 1986, A TV Dante (mini-series) 1989, Scarlett (mini-series) 1994, Jackie Bouvier Kennedy Onassis (mini-series) 2000, 40 2003, Child of Mine 2005, Life Line 2007, Flood 2007, Diverted 2009, Gossip Girl (series) 2011–12, The Challenger 2013, The Borgias (series) 2011–13, Jamaica Inn (series) 2014, Wolf Hall (mini-series) 2015, A.D. The Bible Continues (mini-series) 2015. *Address:* Creative Artists Agency, 2000 Avenue of the Stars, Los Angeles, CA 90067, USA.

WHALLEY, John, BA (Hons), MA, MA, MPhil, PhD, FRSC; British/Canadian economist and academic; *Professor of Economics, University of Warwick and University of Western Ontario;* ed grammar school, Lancs., Univ. of Essex, Yale Univ., USA; Teaching Assistant, Univ. of Essex 1968–69, Yale Univ. 1970-73; Lecturer in Econs, LSE 1973–76; Assoc. Prof. of Econs, Univ. of Western Ontario, Canada 1976–78, Prof. of Econs 1978–, Dir Centre for the Study of Int. Econ. Relations 1979–, William G. Davis Prof. of Int. Trade 1986–90, 2004–09; Research Assoc., Nat. Bureau of Econ. Research, Cambridge, Mass 1985–; Sr Advisor, Tax Policy Br., Dept of Finance, Govt of Canada 1985–86; Visiting Fellow, Inst. for Int. Econs, Washington, DC 1990–91; Sr Research Fellow, Inst. for Policy Reform, Washington, DC 1992–93; Prof. of Int. and Devt Econs, Univ. of Warwick 1994–98, 2010–, Assoc. Dir Centre for the Study of Globalisation and Regionalisation; Guest Prof., Univ. of Peking, People's Repub. of China 2003–04; Co-ordinator, Global Economy Research Group, Univ. of Munich, Germany 2003–; Distinguished Fellow, Centre for Int. Governance Innovation, Waterloo, Ont. 2006–; Co-Investigator, Centre for Competitive Advantage in the Global Economy (CAGE); has served on a Canada-US trade dispute panel; fmr Research Dir for the MacDonald Royal Comms in Canada; Co-Ed. CESifo Econ. Studies; fmr Jt Man. Ed. The World Economy; Foreign mem. Russian Acad. of Natural Sciences; Fellow, Econometric Soc.; Hellmuth Prize for Achievement in Research 2009, Killam Prize (co-recipient), Canada Council for the Arts 2012. *Publications:* The International Taxation of Multinational Enterprises in Developed Countries (with John Adams) 1977, Tax Policy Options in the 1980s (co-ed.) 1982, Federalism and the Canadian Economic Union (co-ed.) 1983, Trade Liberalization Among Major World Trading Areas 1985, A General Equilibrium Model for Tax Policy Evaluation (with John Shoven, Charles Ballard and Don Fullerton) 1985, UK Tax Policy and Applied General Equilibrium Analysis (with John Piggott) 1985, New Developments in Applied General Equilibrium Analysis (with John Piggott) 1985, Canada/United States Trade and Investment Issues (co-ed.) 1985, Canadian Trade Policies and the World Economy (with Colleen Hamilton and Rod Hill), Vol. 9 of the Research Studies for the Royal Commission on the Economic Union and Development Prospects for Canada 1985, Canada and the Multilateral Trading System, Vol. 10

of the Research Studies for the Royal Commission on the Economic Union and Development Prospects for Canada 1985, Canada-United States Free Trade (co-ed.), Vol. 11 of the Research Studies for the Royal Commission on the Economic Union and Development Prospects for Canada 1985, Domestic Policies and the International Economic Environment (co-ed. with Rod Hill), Vol. 12 of the Research Studies for the Royal Commission on the Economic Union and Development Prospects for Canada 1985, Canada's Resource Industries (ed.), Vol. 14 of the Research Studies for the Royal Commission on the Economic Union and Development Prospects for Canada 1986, Regional Aspects of Confederation (with Irene Trela), Vol. 68 of the Research Papers for the Royal Commission on the Economic Union and Development Prospects for Canada 1986, General Equilibrium Trade Policy Modeling (co-ed.) 1986, Dealing with the North: Developing Countries and the Global Trading System (ed. CSIER Research Monograph) 1987, Perspectives on a US-Canadian Free Trade Agreement (co-ed.) 1987, Developing Countries and the Global Trading System, Vol. I, Thematic Studies From a Ford Foundation Project 1989, Developing Countries and the Global Trading System, Vol. II, Country Studies From a Ford Foundation Project 1989, The Uruguay Round and Beyond, Final Report From the Ford Foundation Supported Project on Developing Countries and the Global Trading System 1989, Economic Impacts of Tax Reform (co-ed. 1989, The Economics of the Goods and Services Tax (with Deborah Fretz), Canadian Tax Paper No. 88 1990, Applied General Equilibrium, Studies in Empirical Economics (co-ed.) 1991, Applying General Equilibrium (with John Shoven) 1992, Canada-U.S. Tax Comparisons (co-ed.) 1992, Applying General Equilibrium (with John Shoven) 1993, The Trading System After the Uruguay Round (with Colleen Hamilton) 1996, Environmental Issues in the New World Trading System (with Peter Uimonen) 1997, Uruguay Round Results and the Emerging Trade Agenda: Quantitative-Based Analyses from the Developmental Perspective (co-ed.) 1998, 30, Fiscal Reform and Structural Change in the Developing Countries, Vols 1 and 2 (co-ed.) 2000, The WTO, Trade and the Environment (co-ed.) 2005, Frontiers in Applied General Equilibrium Modeling (co-ed.) 2005, Privatization Experiences in the European Union (co-ed.) 2006, Globalisation and the Labour Market: Trade, Technology and Less-Skilled Workers in Europe and the United States (co-ed.) 2006, China's Integration Into The World Economy (ed.) 2011, Puzzles over International Taxation of Cross-Border Flows of Capital Income, Chapter 17 in International Handbook on the Economics of Integration, Vol. II 2011, Global General Equilibrium Modelling (ed.) 2012; numerous papers in professional journals. *Address:* Department of Economics, University of Warwick, Coventry, CV4 7AL, England (office); Department of Economics, Faculty of Social Science, University of Western Ontario, London, ON N6A 5C2, Canada. *Telephone:* (519) 661-3509 (Western Ontario) (office). *Fax:* (24) 7652-3032 (Warwick) (office); (519) 661-3064 (Western Ontario) (office). *E-mail:* jwhalley@uwo.ca (office). *Website:* www2.warwick.ac.uk/fac/soc/csgr/people/staff/jwhalley (office); economics.uwo.ca/faculty/whalley (office).

WHARTON, Clifton R., Jr., PhD; American academic, university administrator, financial services executive and government official; *President Emeritus, Michigan State University;* b. 13 Sept. 1926, Boston, Mass.; s. of Hon. Clifton R. Wharton Sr and Harriette B. Wharton; m. Dolores Duncan 1950; one s.; ed Boston Latin School, Harvard Univ., Johns Hopkins Univ. School of Advanced Int. Studies and Univ. of Chicago; Head of Reports and Analysis Dept, American Int. Asscn for Econ. and Social Devt 1948–53; Research Assoc., Univ. of Chicago 1953–57; Assoc., Agricultural Devt Council 1957–58, stationed in SE Asia 1958–64, Dir of the Council's American Univs. Research Program 1964–66, Vice-Pres. 1967–69, mem. Bd of Dirs 1973–80; Pres. Mich. State Univ. and Prof. of Econs 1970–78, now Pres. Emer.; Chancellor, State Univ. of New York System 1978–87; Chair. and CEO TIAA-CREF 1987–93; Deputy Sec. of State, US Dept of State 1993; Visiting Prof., Univ. of Malaya 1958–64, Stanford Univ. 1964–65; fmr Chair. Bd for Int. Food and Agric. Devt (AID), US Dept of State; mem. Presidential Comm. on World Hunger, Presidential Mission to Latin America, Presidential Mission to S Viet Nam; Chair. Bd Rockefeller Foundation 1982–87; mem. Knight Foundation Comm. on Inter-collegiate Athletics 1989– (fmr Co-Vice Chair.); dir of numerous cos and orgs including Ford Motor Co. 1973–93, 1994–97, Tenneco Inc. 1994–99, New York Stock Exchange 1991–93, 1994–2000, Harcourt Gen. 1994–2001, Equitable Life 1969–82, Overseas Devt Council 1969–79, 1994–2000, Aspen Inst. 1980–93, Time Inc. 1982–89, Federated Dept Stores 1985–88, Rockefeller Foundation 1970–87; Comm. for Econ. Devt 1980–93, 1994–; Deputy Chair. Fed. Reserve Bank, New York 1985–86; mem. Knight Foundation Comm. on Inter-collegiate Athletics 1990–93, Council on Foreign Relations 1983–93, Advisory Comm. on Trade Policy and Negotiations 1990–93; numerous hon. degrees; numerous awards including President's Award on World Hunger 1983, American Council on Education Distinguished Service Award for Lifetime Achievement 1994, John Hope Franklin Award 2005. *Publications include:* Subsistence Agriculture and Economic Development (ed.) 1969, Patterns for Lifelong Learning (co-author) 1973, Privilege and Prejudice: The Life of a Black Pioneer 2015.

WHEATCROFT, Baroness (Life Peer), cr. 2010, of Blackheath in the London Borough of Greenwich; **Patience Wheatcroft,** LLB; British journalist; b. 28 Sept. 1951, Chesterfield, Derbyshire, England; m. Tony Salter; three c.; ed Univ. of Birmingham; launched, with her husband, Retail Week 1988, Ed. 1988–92; has worked on financial sections of The Daily Mail, The Sunday Times and The Daily Telegraph; Deputy City Ed. Mail on Sunday –1997; Business and City Ed. The Times 1997–2006; Ed. The Sunday Telegraph 2006–07; Ed.-in-Chief The Wall Street Journal Europe 2009–10; Dir (non-exec.) Barclays Bank 2007–09, Shaftesbury plc 2008–09, St James's Place PLC 2012–, Fiat Chrysler Automobiles N.V. 2014–; Head of Mayor of London's Forensic Audit Panel 2008; Dir Asscn of Leading Visitor Attractions; mem. Bd British Museum 2010–18, Advisory Bd, British Olympic Asscn 2011–12; Trustee, Reuters Inst. for Study of Journalism; Visiting Fellow, Centre for Corporate Reputation, Oxford Univ.; mem. (Conservative) House of Lords 2010–; Hon. Dr of Arts (City Univ.) 2011; Wincott Sr Journalist of the Year Award 2001, London Press Club Business Journalist of the Year 2003. *Leisure interests:* opera, theatre. *Address:* House of Lords, Westminster, London, SW1A 0PW, England (office). *Telephone:* (20) 7219-5353 (office); (20) 7219-5979 (office). *E-mail:* contactholmember@parliament.uk (office).

WHEATLEY, Martin; British business executive and banking regulator; worked for London Stock Exchange for 18 years, including six years on its bd, later Deputy Chief Exec. –2003; fmr Chair. FTSE Int.; mem. Listing Authority Advisory Cttee,

Financial Services Authority (FSA); Exec. Dir for Market Supervision, Securities and Futures Comm., Hong Kong 2004–05, Chair. 2005–06, CEO 2006–11; Man. Dir FSA Conduct Business Unit 2011–13, mem. Bd of Dirs and Chief Exec. Financial Conduct Authority (successor of FSA, along with Prudential Regulatory Authority) 2013–15 (resgnd); mem. Financial Stability Bd Standing Cttee on Standards Implementation, Int. Org. of Securities Comms (IOSCO) Tech. Cttee, Chair. IOSCO Tech. Cttee Task Force on Short Selling. *Address:* c/o Financial Conduct Authority, 25 The North Colonnade, Canary Wharf, London, E14 5HS, England.

WHEDON, Joss; American screenwriter, director, producer, comic book writer and composer; b. (Joseph Hill Whedon), 23 June 1964, New York City; s. of Tom Whedon and Ann Lee Stearns; m. Kai Cole (divorced 2016); two c.; ed Winchester Coll., Wesleyan Univ.; Hon. DLitt (Wesleyan Univ.) 2013. *Films:* Serenity (director & writer) 2005, The Cabin in the Woods (writer) 2012, Avengers (director & writer) (Saturn Award for Best Director 2013) 2012, Much Ado About Nothing (director & writer) 2012, In Your Eyes (writer) 2014, Avengers: Age of Ultron (director & writer) 2015, Justice League (writer) 2017. *Television:* exec. producer: Parenthood 1990, Buffy the Vampire Slayer 1996–2003, Angel 1999–2004, Firefly 2002–03, Dollhouse 2009–10, Agents of S.H.I.E.L.D. 2013–; writer: Roseanne 1989–90, Dr. Horrible's Sing-Along Blog (Emmy Award for Outstanding Short-Format Live-Action Entertainment Program 2009) 2008, The Cabin in the Woods 2012. *Publications include:* Astonishing X-Men series: Gifted 2004, Dangerous 2005, Torn 2007, Unstoppable 2008; Fray series: Big City Girl 2001, The Calling 2001, Ready, Steady...2001, Out of the Past 2001, The Worst of It 2001, Alarums 2002, The Gateway 2003, All Hell 2003; Tales of the Vampires series: Stacy 2003, Tales of the Vampires I–VI 2003–04; Buffy the Vampire Slayer Season Eight series: The Long Way Home 2007, The Chain 2007, Anywhere But Here 2008, A Beautiful Sunset 2008, Time of Your Life 2008, Turbulence 2010, Last Gleaming 2010; Buffy the Vampire Slayer Season Nine: Freefall, Part I 2011; Angel: After the Fall series: Vol. 1-5 2007–09. *Address:* c/o Creative Artists Agency, 2000 Avenue of the Stars, Los Angeles, CA 90067, USA (office). *Telephone:* (424) 288-2000 (office). *Fax:* (424) 288-2900 (office). *Website:* www.caa.com (office).

WHEELDON, Christopher Peter, OBE; British ballet dancer and choreographer; b. 22 March 1973, Yeovil, Somerset, England; m. Ross Rayburn 2013; ed Royal Ballet School, London; began training to be ballet dancer aged eight; joined Royal Ballet 1991; moved to USA to join New York City Ballet (NYCB) 1993, Soloist 1998, began choreographing for NYCB 1997, retd as dancer to focus on choreography 2000, Resident Choreographer and first Resident Artist 2001–08; dances commissioned by several other ballet cos, including San Francisco Ballet, Bolshoi Ballet, Royal Ballet, London; Co-founder and Artistic Dir Morphoses/The Wheeldon Company (transatlantic co. with a US base at City Center, New York and in UK at Sadler's Wells Theatre, London) 2007–10; has collaborated with composers James MacMillan, Bright Sheng and Michael Nyman, with artists Ian Falconer, James Buckhouse and Jean Marc Puissant, with designers Adrianne Lobel and Narciso Rodriguez, with author and actor John Lithgow, and with dir Nicholas Hytner; Gold Medal Prix de Lausanne competition 1991, Mae L. Wien Award, School of American Ballet, Martin E. Segal Award, Lincoln Center, New York City, London Critics' Circle Award for Best New Ballet for Polyphonia 2005, American Choreography Award, Dance Magazine Award for Best New Ballet for Polyphonia 2005, Olivier Award 2006, South Bank Show Award 2007. *Ballets choreographed include:* Slavonic Dances for Diamond Project, NYCB 1997, cr., in collaboration with artist Ian Falconer, Scènes de Ballet for School of American Ballets Workshop Performances 1999 and NYCB's 50th anniversary season, Mercurial Manoeuvers for NYCB's Spring Diamond Project 2000, Polyphonia, set to piano music by Györgi Ligeti 2000, Variations Sérieuses, set to a score by Felix Mendelssohn 2001, Morphoses and Carousel (A Dance) 2002, Carnival of the Animals and Liturgy 2003, After the Rain 2005, An American in Paris 2005, Klavier 2006, The Nightingale and the Rose 2007; for other cos: Continuum, for San Francisco Ballet 2002, Tryst and DGV (Danse à Grande Vitesse), for The Royal Ballet 2002, 2006 (respectively), Swan Lake, for Pennsylvania Ballet 2004, Dance of the Hours, for The Metropolitan Opera's production of Ponchielli's La Gioconda 2006, Misericors, for the Bolshoi Ballet 2007, ballet based on Lewis Carroll's Alice's Adventures in Wonderland, for The Royal Ballet 2011, Cinderella by Sergei Prokofiev, for Dutch Nat. Ballet (Prix Benois de la Danse for Best Choreography) 2013, The Winter's Tale, for the Royal Ballet, Covent Garden (Prix Benois de la Danse for Best Choreography 2015) 2014; ballet sequences for feature film Center Stage 2000, stage version of Broadway's Sweet Smell of Success 2002. *Address:* c/o Morphoses Ltd, The Wheeldon Company, 800 Fifth Avenue, Suite 18F, New York, NY 10065, USA (office).

WHEELER, Andrew R., BA, JD, MBA; American lawyer and government official; *Administrator, Environmental Protection Agency;* b. 23 Dec. 1964, Hamilton, Ohio; s. of Ron Wheeler and Pat Wheeler; ed Washington Univ., George Mason Univ., Case Western Reserve Univ.; began career as Special Asst to Dir of Information Management Div., Environmental Protection Agency (EPA) Office of Pollution Prevention and Toxics 1991–95, Deputy Admin., EPA April–July 2018, Acting Admin. July 2018–Feb. 2019, Admin. Feb. 2019–; Chief Counsel to Senator Jim Inhofe 1995–97; Majority Staff Dir, Senate Sub-Cttee on Clean Air, Climate Change, Wetlands, and Nuclear Safety 1997–2003; Chief Counsel, Senate Cttee on Environment and Public Works 2003–09; Prin. and Team Leader, Energy and Environment Practice Group, FaegreBD Consulting 2009–17; Chair. Emer. Nat. Energy Resources Org.; Vice Pres. Washington Coal Club; Environmental Protection Agency Bronze Medal 1993, 1994. *Address:* Environmental Protection Agency, William Jefferson Clinton Bldg, 1200 Pennsylvania Ave, NW, Washington, DC 20460, USA (office). *Telephone:* (202) 272-0167 (office). *Website:* www.epa .gov (office).

WHEELER, Fraser William; British diplomatist (retd) and business executive; *CEO, Sambora Communications Inc.;* b. 23 March 1957; m. Sarah Wheeler; one s. one d.; with Finance Dept, FCO 1980–81, Defence Dept 1981–82, Entry Clearance/Consular Officer, Accra 1982–84, Third Sec., UK Mission to UN, Geneva 1984–87, Soviet Dept, FCO 1987–91, Second Sec. (Trade), Moscow 1991–94, Deputy Consul Gen., Vancouver 1994–98; Vice-Pres. Nat. Communications plc (Canada) 1998–2000; Strategic Policy Adviser, Directorate for Strategy and Innovation, FCO 2000–02, Head of Partnerships and Networks Devt Unit, Directorate for

Strategy and Innovation 2002–04, Deputy Head of Mission, Basra 2004–06, High Commr to Guyana (also accred as Amb. to Suriname) 2006–10; UK Rep., Handsome Hero 2010–11; CEO Sambora Communications Inc. 2011–. *Address:* Sambora Communications Inc., 2 Avenue of the Republic, Georgetown, Guyana (office). *E-mail:* business@samboracommunications.com (office); sekoub@samboracommunications.com (office). *Website:* samboracommunications.com (office).

WHEELER, Graeme; New Zealand international organization official and central banker; ed Univ. of Auckland; Adviser, later Sr Adviser, NZ Treasury 1973–84, Dir of Macroeconomic Policy and Strategy 1990–93, Treas., NZ Debt Man. Office and Deputy Sec. NZ Treasury 1993–97; Econ. and Financial Counsellor to NZ Del. to OECD, Paris 1984–90; Dir Financial Products and Services Dept, World Bank (IBRD) 1997–2001, Vice-Pres. and Treas. 2001–05, Acting Man. Dir, then Man. Dir 2005–10; Dir (non-exec.) Thyssen-Bornemisza Group 2010–12; Gov. and Chief Exec., Reserve Bank of New Zealand (central bank) 2012–17; Chair. Asian Consultative Council, BIS 2016–17.

WHEELER, Gen. Sir Roger Neil, GCB, CBE, MA, FRGS; British army officer (retd); b. 16 Dec. 1941, Fulmer, Bucks.; s. of Maj.-Gen. T.N.S. Wheeler, C.B., CBE; m. Felicity Hares 1980; three s. one d. (from previous marriage); ed All Hallows School, Devon and Hertford Coll. Oxford; commissioned Royal Ulster Rifles 1964; early service in Borneo, Middle East and Cyprus; Chief of Staff, Falkland Islands June–Dec. 1982; Command, 11th Armoured Brig. 1985–87; Dir Army Plans 1987–89; Command, 1st Armoured Div. 1989–90; Asst Chief of Gen. Staff, Ministry of Defence 1990–92; GOC Northern Ireland 1993–96; C-in-C Land Command 1996–97; Chief of Gen. Staff 1997–2000; ADC Gen. to Queen 1996–2000; Constable HM Tower of London 2001–09; Pres. Army Rugby Football Union 1995–99, Army Rifle Assoc. 1995–2000; Col The Royal Irish Regt 1996–2001; Col Commdt Intelligence Corps 1996–2001; Pres. Combat Stress 2001–09, Forces Pension Soc. 2006–13; Dir Thales UK Plc 2001–, Aegis Specialist Risk Man. 2005–, Serious and Organised Crime Agency 2005–09; Patron Police Foundation 2001–; Hon. Fellow, Hertford Coll., Oxford. *Leisure interests:* fly fishing, ornithology, cricket, shooting.

WHELAN, Máire, BA, LLB, LLM, SC; Irish barrister and politician; *Judge, Court of Appeal;* b. 1962, Kinvara, Co. Galway; m. Bernard McCabe; one c.; ed Univ. Coll., Galway, King's Coll., London, UK; called to the Bar 1985, apptd Sr Counsel 2005; fmr Financial Sec., Labour Party; Attorney-Gen. 2011–17; Judge, Court of Appeal 2017–; fmr Rep. of Bar Council, Property Registration Authority; Vice-Chair. Inc. Council of Law Reporting for Ireland; fmr Chair. Free Legal Advice Centres; fmr Advisor to Irish Comm. for Prisoners Overseas. *Publication:* National Asset Management Agency Act 2009: A Reference Guide (co-author) 2011. *Address:* Court of Appeal, Áras Uí Dhálaigh, Ground Floor, Inns Quay, Dublin 7, Ireland (office). *Telephone:* (1) 8886120 (office). *E-mail:* courtofappealcivil@courts.ie (office).

WHELAN, Michael John, MA, PhD, FRS, FInstP; British scientist and academic; *Professor Emeritus and Fellow, Linacre College, University of Oxford;* b. 2 Nov. 1931, Leeds; s. of William Whelan and Ellen Whelan (née Pound); ed Gonville and Caius Coll., Cambridge; Royal Soc. Mr and Mrs John Jaffé Donation Research Fellow 1959–61; Demonstrator in Physics, Univ. of Cambridge 1961–65, Asst Dir of Research 1965–66, Fellow of Gonville and Caius Coll. 1958–66; Reader, Dept of Materials, Univ. of Oxford 1966–92, Prof. 1992–97, Prof. Emer. 1997–; Fellow, Linacre Coll., Univ. of Oxford 1968–; Hon. Prof., Univ. of Science and Tech., Beijing 1995; Hon. Fellow, Royal Microscopical Soc. 2001, Japanese Soc. of Microscopy 2003, Microscopy Soc. of America 2009; C.V. Boys Prize, Inst. of Physics 1965, Hughes Medal, Royal Soc. 1988, Distinguished Scientist Award, Microscopy Soc. of America 1998, Gjønnes Medal in Electron Crystallography, Int. Union of Crystallography 2011. *Publications:* Electron Microscopy of Thin Crystals (co-author) 1965, Worked Examples in Dislocations 1990, High-Energy Electron Diffraction and Microscopy (co-author) 2004, numerous papers and articles in scientific journals. *Leisure interests:* gardening, tinkering, Japanese language. *Address:* Department of Materials, Engineering and Technology Buildling, Room 50.14, Parks Road, Oxford, OX1 3PH (office); 18 Salford Road, Old Marston, Oxford, OX3 0RX, England (home). *Telephone:* (1865) 273742 (office); (1865) 244556 (home). *Fax:* (1865) 273789 (office); (1865) 244556 (home). *E-mail:* michael.whelan@materials.ox.ac.uk (office). *Website:* www.materials.ox.ac.uk/peoplepages/whelan.html (office).

WHELAN, Noel, BComm, MEconSc, PhD, DPA, FIMInst; Irish civil servant, international public servant, academic and banker; *Vice-President, Dean and Professor Emeritus, University of Limerick;* b. 28 Dec. 1940, Cork; s. of Richard Whelan and Ann Whelan (née Crowley); m. Joan Gaughan 1970; two s. two d.; ed Sacred Heart Coll., Buttevant, Univ. Coll., Dublin; Exec. Officer, Irish Civil Service 1960–62; Sr Admin. Officer and Head of Research Evaluation, an Foras Taluntais (Agricultural Research Inst. of Ireland) 1962–69; Asst Gen. Man. Córas Iompair Éireann (Irish Transport Authority) 1969–74; Deputy Sec. Dept of Public Service and Dept of Finance 1974–77; Special Consultant, OECD (part-time) 1975–80; Sec. Dept of Econ. Planning and Devt 1977–80; Sec. Dept of the Taoiseach (Prime Minister) 1979–82, 1988–; Chair. Sectoral Devt Cttee, Irish Govt 1980–82; Vice-Pres. and Vice-Chair. Bd of Dirs European Investment Bank, Luxembourg 1982–88, Hon. Vice-Pres. 1988–; Vice-Pres. External Univ. of Limerick, Dean, Coll. of Business 1989–, Prof. of Business and Man. 1989–2005; Chair. Sectoral Devt Cttee 1989–97; Special Consultant, UN and World Bank 1989–; Chair./Dir Corp. Bds 1989–; Chair. Nat. Econ. and Social Council of Ireland 1978–84; Adviser to Irish Ministry of Foreign Affairs on Ireland's Foreign Aid Programme 1999–; Chair. St Vincent's Healthcare Group 1988–2014, Telephone Users' Advisory Council 1993–98, Caritas Consultative Forum (Health Sector) 1998–2005, Nat. Adult Learning Council of Ireland 2000–05, Dublin Area Teaching Hosps' Group 1998–2009, State Claims Agency 2002–15; Pres. European Univ. Foundation 2002–07, Pres. Emer. 2008–, mem. Strategic Evaluation Panel, European Univ. Asscn; Dir (non-exec.) on various pvt. sector corp. bds; Pres. and Chair. Inst. of Public Admin. (part-time); Council mem. and mem. Exec. Cttee, Econ. and Social Research Inst.; Council mem. Statistical and Social Enquiry Soc.; Council mem. and Fellow, Irish Man. Inst. 1984; mem. Chartered Accountants Regulatory Bd of Ireland 2008–. *Publications:* miscellaneous papers and reports in various academic and research journals. *Leisure interests:* reading, photography, music. *Address:* 93 Burleigh Court, Burlington Road, Dublin 4, Ireland (home). *Telephone:* 87-2530565 (mobile) (office). *E-mail:* noel.whelan@ul.ie (office); noelwhelan2@gmail.com (home).

WHISHAW, Anthony Popham Law, RA, ARCA; British painter; b. 22 May 1930, London; s. of Robert Whishaw and Joyce Wheeler; m. Jean Gibson 1957; two d.; ed Chelsea School of Art, Royal Coll. of Art; featured in BBC Monitor arts programme 1960s; work in collections including Arts Council of GB, Royal Acad., London, Tate Gallery, London, Christchurch, Kensington, London, Nat. Gallery of Wales, Royal West of England Acad., Bristol, Bolton Art Gallery, Chantrey Bequest, City Art Galleries, Sheffield, Coventry Art Gallery, Dept of the Environment, Huddersfield Museum and Art Gallery, Leicester City Art Gallery, European Parl., Strasbourg, Museu de Arte da Bahia, Brazil, Museo de Murcia, Spain, Nat. Gallery of Victoria, Melbourne, Australia, Power Art Gallery Sydney, Australia, Museum of Contemporary Art, Helsinki, Seattle Museum of Art, USA, Western Australia Gallery, Ben Uri Gallery, Bolton Gallery, Canaccord Genuity, Wellcome Trust, Royal Astronomical Soc., Tavistock Centre, Portman Trust, Shell BP, Stanhope PLC, The Royal Collection, Ladbrokes, and several pvt. and corp. collections; Hon. mem. Royal West of England Acad.; Royal Coll. of Art Travelling Scholarship 1952, Royal Coll. of Art Drawing Prize 1953, Abbey Minor Scholarship 1954, Spanish Govt Scholarship 1954, Spanish Govt Scholarship 1955, Perth Int. Drawing Biennale Prize 1973, Byer Int. Painting Prize 1973, South East Arts Asscn Painting Prize 1975, Greater London Arts Council Award 1978, Greater London Council Painting Prize 1981, Abbey Premier Scholarship 1982, Lorne Scholarship 1982, Jt Winner, Hunting Group Nat. Art Competition 1986, Korn Ferry Carre Oban Int. Picture of the Year 1996. *E-mail:* info@anthonywhishaw.com (home). *Website:* www.anthonywhishaw.com.

WHITACRE, Edward Earl (Ed), Jr, BEng; American business executive; b. 4 Nov. 1941, Ennis, Tex.; ed Texas Tech. Univ.; joined Southwestern Bell Telephone Co., Dallas, Tex. 1963, subsequently facility engineer, Lubbock and various posts in operational depts, Tex., Ark. and Kan.; Pres. Kan. Div. 1982–85; Group Pres., subsequently Vice-Pres. (Revenues and Public Affairs), Vice-Chair. and Chief Financial Officer, Southwestern Bell Corpn 1986–88, Pres. and COO 1988–90, Chair. and CEO (subsequently called SBC Communications Inc.) 1990–2005, Chair. and CEO AT&T Inc. (after merger of SBC Communications and AT&T) 2005–07 (retd); Chair. Gen. Motors Corpn, Detroit July 2009–10, CEO Dec. 2009–Aug. 2010; mem. Bd of Dirs Anheuser-Busch Cos Inc., May Dept Stores Co., Emerson Electric Co., Burlington Northern Inc.; mem. Bd of Regents, Tex. Tech. Univ. and Tex. Tech. Univ. Health Sciences Center; mem. Bd of Govs, Southwest Foundation for Biomedical Research; Trustee, Southwest Research Inst.; actively involved with Boy Scouts of America; Dr hc (Univ. of the Incarnate Word) 2004; Int. Citizen of the Year Award, World Affairs Council, San Antonio 1997, Spirit of Achievement Award, Nat. Jewish Medical and Research Center 1998, Freeman Award, San Antonio Chamber of Commerce 1998, several awards for contribs to business and civic affairs, including Corp. Leadership Award from Nat. Minority Supplier Devt Council and Obelisk Leadership Award, Texas Tech coll. of eng renamed Edward E. Whitacre Jr Coll. of Eng in his honour 2008, inducted into Junior Achievement US Business Hall of Fame 2009, Amistad Award, San Antonio-Mexico Friendship Council Inc. 2011. *Publication:* American Turnaround: Reinventing AT&&T and GM and the Way We Do Business in the USA 2013.

WHITAKER, Forest; American actor and film director; b. 15 July 1961, Longview, Tex.; s. of Forest Steven Whitaker Jr and Laura Francis (née Smith); m. Keisha Nash 1996; four c.; ed School of Theater, Univ. of Southern California; f. Spirit Dance Entertainment (production co.) –2005; UNESCO Goodwill Amb. for Peace and Reconciliation 2011–; Co-Chair. JuntoBox Films 2012–; Founder and CEO, Whitaker Peace & Devt Initiative (WPDI); Co-founder and Chair., Int. Inst. for Peace (IIP), Rutgers Univ., New Jersey 2011–; Hon. DHumLitt (Xavier Univ. of Louisiana) 2009, (California State Univ., Dominguez Hills) 2015, DFA (Univ. of Southern California) 2018; BET Award for Best Actor 2007. *Films include:* Tag: The Assassination Game 1982, Fast Times at Ridgemont High 1982, Vision Quest 1985, The Color of Money 1986, Platoon 1986, Stakeout 1987, Good Morning, Vietnam 1987, Bloodsport 1988, Bird 1988, Johnny Handsome 1989, Downtown 1990, A Rage in Harlem 1991, Diary of a Hitman 1991, Article 99 1992, The Crying Game 1992, Consenting Adults 1992, Body Snatchers 1993, Bank Robber 1993, Blown Away 1994, Jason's Lyric 1994, Prêt-à-Porter 1994, Waiting to Exhale (dir) 1995, Smoke 1995, Species 1995, Phenomenon 1996, Body Count 1998, Hope Floats (dir) 1998, Ghost Dog: The Way of the Samurai 1999, Light It Up 1999, Battlefield Earth 2000, Four Dogs Playing Poker 2000, Green Dragon 2001, The Fourth Angel 2001, Panic Room 2002, Phone Booth 2002, First Daughter (dir, producer and voice) 2004, Mary 2005, A Little Trip to Heaven 2005, American Gun 2005, The Marsh 2006, Even Money 2006, The Last King of Scotland (Best Actor, Nat. Bd of Review 2006, Best Actor, Los Angeles Film Critics Asscn 2006, Nat. Soc. of Film Critics 2007, Golden Globe for Best Actor (drama) 2007, Screen Actors' Guild Award for Outstanding Performance by an Actor in a Leading Role 2007, Best Actor, London Film Critics' Circle Awards 2007, BAFTA Award for Best Actor 2007, Acad. Award for Best Actor 2007) 2006, Everyone's Hero (voice) 2006, The Air I Breathe 2007, Ripple Effect 2007, The Great Debaters 2007, Vantage Point 2008, Street Kings 2008, Winged Creatures 2009, Where the Wild Things Are (voice) 2009, Repo Men 2010, My Own Love Song 2010, Catch .44 2011, Crossfire 2012, A Dark Truth 2012, The Last Stand 2013, Repentance 2013, Pawn 2013, Zulu 2013, The Butler 2013, Out of the Furnace 2013, Black Nativity 2013, Two Men in Town 2014, Taken 3 2014, Southpaw 2015, Arrival 2016, Rogue One: A Star Wars Story 2016, The Forgiven 2017, Sorry to Bother You 2018, Black Panther 2018, How It Ends 2018, City of Lies 2018. *Television includes:* North and South (mini-series) 1985, Strapped (dir) 1993, North and South, Book II (mini-series) 1986, Black Jaq (dir) 1998, Witness Protection 1999, Twilight Zone (series) 2002–03, Deacons for Defense 2003, The Shield (series) 2006, Criminal Minds 2010, Criminal Minds: Suspect Behavior 2011, Roots (mini-series) 2016, Star Wars: Go Rogue (short mini-series) 2016, Star Wars Rebels (series) 2017, Empire (series) 2017–18, The Godfather of Harlem (series) 2019. *Address:* c/o Brillstein Entertainment Partners, 9150 Wilshire Blvd, Suite 350, Beverly Hills, CA 90212 (office); c/o William Morris Endeavor, 9601 Wilshire Blvd, Beverly Hills, CA 90210, USA (office). *Telephone:* (310) 275-6135 (Brillstein Entertainment) (office); (310) 285-9000 (William Morris Endeavor) (office). *Website:* www.bepmedia.com (office); www.wmeentertainment.com (office).

WHITAKER, Mark Theis, BA, LLD; American journalist, editor and media executive; b. 7 Sept. 1957, Lower Merion, Pa; m. Alexis Lynn Gelber; one s. one d.; ed Harvard Univ., Univ. of Oxford, UK, Wheaton Coll.; Marshall Scholar, Balliol Coll., Oxford 1979–81; Assoc. Ed. Newsweek 1981–83, Gen. Ed. 1983, Sr Writer 1984–86, Sr Ed., Business Ed. 1987–91, Asst Man. Ed. 1991–95, Man. Ed. 1996–98, Ed. 1998–2006; Vice-Pres. and Ed.-in-Chief of New Ventures, Digital Division, Washington Post 2006–07; Sr Vice-Pres. for News, NBC 2007–11, Washington bureau chief, NBC News 2008–11; Exec. Vice-Pres. and Man. Ed., CNN Worldwide 2011–13; mem. Nat. Asscn of Black Journalists, Bd of Dirs American Soc. of Magazine Eds 1999– (Pres. 2004–06), Council on Foreign Relations, Century Asscn. *Publications include:* My Long Trip Home (autobiography) 2011, Cosby 2014. *Website:* authors.simonandschuster.co.uk/Mark -Whitaker/79846463.

WHITBREAD, Sir Samuel Charles, Kt, KCVO; British business executive; b. 22 Feb. 1937, London; s. of Maj. Simon Whitbread and H. B. M. Trefusis; m. Jane M. Hayter 1961; three s. one d.; ed Eton Coll.; served in Beds. and Herts. Regt 1955–57; Dir Whitbread & Co. 1972, Deputy Chair. 1984, Chair. Whitbread & Co. (Whitbread PLC from 1991) 1984–92, Dir 1972–2001; Chair. Herts. Timber Supplies 2000–; Vice-Pres. East Anglia TA and VRA 1991–; Lord-Lt of Beds. 1991–2012; Hon. LLB (Bedfordshire). *Publications include:* Southill and the Whitbreads 1995, Straws in the Wind 1997, Plain Mr Whitbread 2007. *Leisure interests:* shooting, travel, painting, music. *Address:* Glebe House, Southill, Biggleswade, Beds., SG18 9LL, England (home). *Telephone:* (1462) 813272 (home).

WHITE, B. Joseph, BA, MBA, PhD; American academic and university administrator; *James F. Towey Professor of Business and Leadership and President Emeritus, University of Illinois;* b. 6 April 1947, Detroit, Mich.; m. Mary White; two c.; ed Georgetown Univ. School of Foreign Service, Washington, DC, Harvard Univ., Univ. of Michigan; Asst Prof. of Organizational Behavior and Industrial Relations, Stephen M. Ross School of Business, Univ. of Michigan 1975–78, Assoc. Prof. 1978–80, Assoc. Dean 1987–90, Interim Dean 1990–91, Dean 1991–2001, Dean Emer. 2005–; Pres. William Davidson Inst. 1993–2001, Wilbur K. Pierpont Collegiate Prof. of Leadership in Man. Educ., Prof. of Business Admin 1995–2004, Interim Pres., Univ. of Michigan 2001–02, Research Prof., Life Sciences Inst. and Head, Project for a Positive Healthcare Future 2002–05; Pres. Univ. of Illinois 2005–09, Pres. Emer. 2010–, James F. Towey Prof. of Business and Leadership, Univ. of Illinois, Urbana-Champaign 2010–, mem. Strategic Planning Cttee, Coll. of Business 2013–; Vice-Pres. for Man. Devt, later Vice-Pres. for Personnel and Public Affairs, Cummins Engine Co., Inc. 1981–87; Man. Dir Fred Alger Man., Inc. 2003; ind. dir or trustee of several cos, including Equity Residential, Chicago, Gordon Food Service, Kaydon Corpn, Kelly Services, American Council on Educ. 2006–09, Nat. Merit Scholarship Corpn 2007–09, Catholic Theological Union 2011–12; mem. Bd of Dirs W.E. Upjohn Inst. for Employment Research 2006–; mem. Bd American Council on Educ., Nat. Merit Honor Scholarship Program, Argonne Nat. Lab. 2005–09; fmr chair. several large healthcare orgs, including Univ. of Mich. Health System, St Joseph Hosp., Ann Arbor, Catherine McAuley Health System; Hon. DHumLitt (Wabash Coll.) 2003; Leadership Award, Illinois Legis. Latino Caucus Foundation 2005, Martin Luther King Jr Leadership Award, Illinois Comm. on Diversity and Human Relations 2007. *Publications:* The Nature of Leadership 2007, Boards That Excel: Candid Insights and Practical Advice for Directors 2014; numerous articles on leadership, man. and organizational matters. *Address:* 4027 Business Instructional Facility, 515 East Gregory Drive, Champaign, IL 61820, USA (office). *Telephone:* (217) 244-1947 (office). *E-mail:* bjwhite@illinois.edu (office). *Website:* www.business.illinois .edu/facultyprofile/faculty_profile.aspx?ID=10711 (office); illinois.edu.

WHITE, Sir Christopher John, CVO, PhD, FBA; British fmr arts administrator; b. 19 Sept. 1930; s. of Gabriel Ernest E. F. White; m. Rosemary Katharine Desages 1957; one s. two d.; ed Downside School, Courtauld Inst. of Art, Univ. of London; army service 1949–50; Asst Keeper, Dept of Prints and Drawings, British Museum 1954–65; Dir P. and D. Colnaghi 1965–71; Curator of Graphic Arts, Nat. Gallery of Art, Washington, DC 1971–73; Dir of Studies, Paul Mellon Centre for Studies in British Art 1973–85; Assoc. Dir Yale Centre for British Art, New Haven 1976–85; Adjunct Prof. of History of Art, Yale Univ. 1977–85; Dir Ashmolean Museum, Oxford 1985–97; Prof. of the Art of the Netherlands, Oxford 1992–97; Hermione Lecturer, Alexandra Coll., Dublin 1959; Adjunct Prof., Inst. of Fine Arts, New York Univ. 1973, 1976; Visiting Prof., Yale Univ. 1976; Conf. Dir, European-American Ass. on Art Museums 1975; Reviews Ed., Master Drawings 1967–80; Gov. British Inst. of Florence 1994–2002; mem. Exec. Cttee NACF 1998, Raad van Toezicht, Mauritshuis, The Hague 1999; Dir Burlington Magazine 1981– (Chair. 1995–2001); Fellow, Worcester Coll., Oxford 1985–97; Trustee, Victoria and Albert Museum 1997–2004; Visiting Curator, Courtauld Inst. Gallery, London 2011. *Publications include:* Rembrandt and His World 1964, The Flower Drawings of Jan van Huysum 1965, Rubens and His World 1968, Rembrandt's Etchings: a catalogue raisonné (co-author) 1970, Dürer: the Artist and His Drawings 1972, English Landscape 1630–1850 1977, The Dutch Paintings in the Collection of HM The Queen (second edn 2015) 1982, Rembrandt in Eighteenth Century England (ed.) 1983, Peter Paul Rubens: Man and Artist 1987, Drawing in England from Hilliard to Hogarth (co-author) 1987, Rubens in Oxford (co-author) 1988, One Hundred Old Master Drawings from the Ashmolean Museum (co-author) 1991, Dutch and Flemish Drawings at Windsor Castle (co-author) 1994, Anthony van Dyck: Thomas Howard, the Earl of Arundel 1995, Rembrandt by Himself (co-author) 1999, Ashmolean Museum Catalogue of the Dutch, Flemish and German Paintings 1999, Rembrandt as an Etcher (second edn) 1999, The Later Flemish Paintings in the Collection of HM The Queen 2007, Dutch and Flemish Drawings in the Victoria & Albert Museum (co-author) 2014. *Address:* 34 Kelly Street, London, NW1 8PH, England (home). *Telephone:* (20) 7485-9148 (home).

WHITE, Sir David Harry, Kt, DL; British business executive; b. 12 Oct. 1929, Nottingham, England; s. of Harry White and Kathleen White; m. Valerie White 1971; one s. four d. (one deceased); ed Nottingham High School and Master Mariner, Liverpool; Master Mariner's Certificate, HMS Conway; apprentice, Shell Co. 1946–56; Terminal Man., Texaco (UK) Ltd 1956–64; Operations Man., Gulf Oil (GB) 1964–68; Asst Man. Dir Samuel Williams, Dagenham 1968–70; Man. Dir Eastern British Road Services 1970–76; Group Man. Dir British Road Services 1976–82, Pickfords 1982–84; Deputy Chair. Nat. Freight Corpn 1984–89; Group Man. Dir Nat. Freight Consortium Property Group 1984–87; Chair. Pension Fund, Nat. Freight Co. 1985–99; Chair. Nottingham Devt Enterprise 1987–93; Dir (non-exec.) British Coal 1993–94; Chair. Nottingham Health Authority 1986–98, Bd of Govs Nottingham Trent Univ. 1988–99, Mansfield Brewery PLC 1993–99, The Coal Authority 1994–99, EPS Ltd 1997–2000; Dir Hilda Hanson 1997–2010, James Bell 1998–2010, Nottingham Forest 1999–2002, Coutts & Co. 1999–2010, Alkane Ltd 2000–02; DL 1989; Hon. DBA (Nottingham Trent) 1999; Hon. LLD (Nottingham) 2011. *Leisure interests:* football, walking. *Address:* Whitehaven, 6 Croft Road, Edwalton, NG12 4BW, England (home). *Telephone:* (115) 923-4199 (home). *E-mail:* sdw@pobox.com (home).

WHITE, Edmund Valentine, III, BA; American writer and academic; *Professor of Creative Writing, Princeton University;* b. 13 Jan. 1940, Cincinnati, OH; s. of E. V. White and Delilah Teddlie; ed Univ. of Michigan; writer, Time-Life Books, New York 1962–70; Sr Ed. Saturday Review, New York 1972–73; Asst Prof. of Writing Seminars, Johns Hopkins Univ. 1977–79; Adjunct Prof., Columbia Univ. School of the Arts 1981–83; Exec. Dir New York Inst. for the Humanities 1982–83; Prof. of English, Brown Univ. 1990–92; Prof. of Humanities, Princeton Univ. 1999, now Prof. of Creative Writing in Lewis Center for the Arts; Guggenheim Fellowship; mem. Acad. of Arts and Letters 1998; Officier, Ordre des Arts et des Lettres 1999; PEN/Saul Bellow Award for Achievement in American Fiction 2018. *Play:* Terre Haute 2006. *Publications:* fiction: Forgetting Elena 1973, Nocturnes for the King of Naples 1978, A Boy's Own Story 1982, Aphrodisiac (with others) 1984, Caracole 1985, The Darker Proof: Stories from a Crisis (with Adam Mars-Jones) 1987, The Beautiful Room is Empty 1988, Skinned Alive 1995, The Farewell Symphony 1997, The Married Man 2000, Fanny: A Fiction 2003, Chaos 2007, Hotel de Dream 2007, Jack Holmes and His Friend 2013, Our Young Man 2016; non-fiction: The Joy of Gay Sex: An Intimate Guide for Gay Men to the Pleasures of a Gay Lifestyle (with Charles Silverstein) 1977, States of Desire: Travels in Gay America 1980, The Faber Book of Gay Short Fiction (ed.) 1991, Genet: A Biography (Nat. Book Critics' Circle Award 1994) 1993, The Selected Writings of Jean Genet (ed.) 1993, The Burning Library (essays) 1994, Our Paris: Sketches from Memory 1994, Our Paris 1995, Proust 1998, The Flâneur 2001, My Lives (autobiog.) 2005, Rimbaud: The Double Life of a Rebel 2008, City Boy: My Life in New York During the 1960s and '70s 2009, Inside a Pearl: My Years in Paris 2014. *Address:* c/o Amanda Urban, ICM, 825 8th Avenue, New York, NY 10019, USA (office); New South Building, Floor 6, Lewis Center for the Arts, Princeton, NJ 08544, USA (office). *Telephone:* (212) 556-5764 (office); (609) 258-8561 (office). *E-mail:* ewhite@princeton.edu (office). *Website:* www.princeton.edu/~visarts/cwr (office); www.edmundwhite .com.

WHITE, Jack; American singer and musician (guitar, drums); b. (John Anthony Gillis), 9 July 1975, Detroit, Mich.; m. 1st Meg White 1996 (divorced 2000); m. 2nd Karen Elson 2005 (divorced 2013); one s. one d.; fmrly played in a number of Detroit-based bands; Founder-mem. The White Stripes 1997–2011; Founder-mem. The Raconteurs 2006–, The Dead Weather 2009–; f. Third Man Records 2001; MTV Europe Music Award for Best Rock Act 2003, BRIT Award for Best Int. Group 2004, Grammy Awards for Best Rock Song (for Seven Nation Army) 2004, for Best Rock Performance by a Duo or Group with Vocals (for Icky Thump) 2008, Music City Amb. Award, City of Nashville 2011. *Film appearances:* Cold Mountain 2003, Coffee and Cigarettes 2003. *Recordings include:* albums: with The White Stripes: White Stripes 1999, De Stijl 2000, White Blood Cells 2001, Elephant (Grammy Award for Best Alternative Album) 2003, Get Behind Me Satan (Grammy Award for Best Alternative Music Album 2006) 2005, Icky Thump (Grammy Award for Best Alternative Music Album 2008) 2007, Under Great White Northern Lights 2010; with The Raconteurs: Broken Boy Soldiers 2006, Consolers of the Lonely 2008; with The Dead Weather: Horehound 2009, Sea of Cowards 2010, Dodge and Burn 2015; solo: Blunderbuss 2012, Lazaretto (Grammy Award for Best Rock Performance 2015) 2014, Boarding House Reach 2018. *Address:* Third Man Records, 623 7th Avenue South, Nashville, TN 37203 (office); Monotone Management, 820 Seward Street, Hollywood, CA 90038, USA (office). *Telephone:* (615) 891-4393 (Nashville) (office); (323) 308-1818 (office). *Fax:* (323) 308-1819 (office). *Website:* jackwhiteiii.com (office); www.thirdmanrecords.com (office); www .theraconteurs.com (office); www.thedeadweather.com (office); www.whitestripes .com (office).

WHITE, Jake; South African rugby union coach; b. (Jacob Westerduin), 19 March 1963, Johannesburg; ed Jeppe High School for Boys; played as hooker in First XV for Jeppe High School for Boys and for Jeppe Old Boys Under 20, also for Johannesburg Coll. of Educ. First XV; began coaching career as high school rugby coach at Parktown Boys High School's First XV 1982–85; worked as physical educ. teacher 1986–94; coached 14a, 15a 1986–88; returned to his old school as teacher and as coach of First XV 1989–94; Dir of Coaching, Transvaal Rugby Union 1995–97; Fitness Coach and Tech. Adviser for Gauteng Lions in Super 12; Nat. Coaching Congress 1997; Asst Coach to Natal Sharks 2000, Asst Coach to South African Nat. Rugby Union Team (Springboks) 2000–01, Head Coach 2004–07; Head Coach, Brumbies Rugby Team 2012–13; Coach and Dir of Rugby, Natal Sharks 2014–; coached various Under 19 and Under 21 sides, including Under 21 Springbok side that won U-21 Rugby Union World Cup 2002; won Tri Nations trophy 2004; won Rugby World Cup, Paris 2007; mem. Int. Rugby Bd; Int. Rugby Bd (IRB) Int. Coach of the Year 2004, 2007, inducted into Int. Rugby Bd Hall of Fame 2011. *E-mail:* jakewhitetv@gmail.com. *Website:* jakewhiterugby.blogspot .com.

WHITE, James Boyd, AM, LLB; American academic; *L. Hart Wright Professor Emeritus of Law, University of Michigan;* b. 28 July 1938, Boston, Mass.; s. of Benjamin White and Charlotte Green White; m. 1st Constance Southworth 1959; m. 2nd Mary Fitch 1978; two s. two d.; ed Groton School, Amherst Coll. and Harvard Univ.; pvt. practice of law, Foley Hoag & Eliot 1964–67; Prof. of Law, Univ. of Colorado 1967–75, Univ. of Chicago 1975–82; Hart Wright Prof. Emer. of Law, Prof. Emer. of English Language and Literature and Adjunct Prof. of Classics, Univ. of Mich. 1982–. *Publications include:* The Legal Imagination 1973, When Words Lose Their Meaning 1984, Heracles' Bow: Essays on the Rhetoric and Poetics of the Law 1986, Justice as Translation: An Essay in Cultural and Legal Criticism 1990, This Book of Starres: Learning to Read George Herbert 1994, Acts of Hope: Creating Authority in Literature, Law and Politics 1994, From Expectation to Experience: Essays in Law and Legal Education 1999, The Edge of

Meaning 2001, Living Speech 2006. *Leisure interests:* reading, walking, swimming. *Address:* University of Michigan Law School, 332 Hutchins Hall, Ann Arbor, MI 48109 (office); 1606 Morton, Ann Arbor, MI 48104, USA (home). *Telephone:* (734) 936-2989 (office); (734) 662-6464 (home). *Fax:* (734) 763-9375 (office). *E-mail:* jbwhite@umich.edu (office). *Website:* www-personal.umich.edu/~jbwhite (office).

WHITE, Marco Pierre; British chef and restaurateur; b. 11 Dec. 1961, Leeds, Yorks., England; s. of Frank White and Maria Rosa Gallina; m. 1st Alexandra McArthur 1988 (divorced 1990); one d.; m. 2nd Lisa Butcher 1992 (divorced 1994); m. 3rd Matilda Conejero-Caldera 2000; two s. one d.; ed Allerton High School, Leeds; Commis Chef Hotel St George, Harrogate 1978, Box Tree, Ilkley 1979; Chef de Partie Le Gavroche 1981, Tante Claire 1983; Sous Chef Manoir aux Quat' Saisons 1984–85; Propr and Chef Harveys 1986–93, The Canteen Restaurant, Chelsea Harbour (co-owner Michael Caine) 1992–96, Restaurant Marco Pierre White 1993–, Criterion Marco Pierre White (co-owner Sir Rocco Forte) 1995–, Quo Vadis 1996–, Oak Room, Le Meridien 1997–99, MPW Canary Wharf 1997–, Café Royal Grill Room 1997–, Mirabelle Restaurant, Curzon Street 1998–, L'Escargot, Belvedere 1999, Wheelers of St James 2002, Frankie's Bar and Grill; Catey Award for Newcomer of the Year 1987, Chef of the Year, Egon Ronay 1992, youngest and first British chef to win 3 Michelin stars 1995, Restaurant of the Year, Egon Ronay (for The Restaurant) 1997. *Television includes:* Hell's Kitchen (presenter) 2007, The Chopping Block (host) 2008, Marco Pierre White's Kitchen Wars 2012. *Publications include:* White Heat 1990, White Heat II 1994, Wild Food from Land and Sea 1994, Canteen Cuisine 1995, Glorious Puddings 1998, The Mirabelle Cookbook 1999, White Slave (autobiography) 2006, The Devil in the Kitchen 2007, Frankie's: Recipes from an Italian Family (with Frankie Dettori) 2007, Marco Made Easy: A Three-Star Chef Makes It Simple 2010. *Leisure interests:* fishing, shooting, bird-watching. *Website:* www.mpwrestaurants.co.uk; www.marcopierrewhite.org.

WHITE, Mary Jo, BA, MA, JD; American lawyer and government official; b. 27 Dec. 1947, Kansas City, Mo.; d. of Carl Monk and Ruth King Monk; m. John White 1970; ed Coll. of William and Mary, New School for Social Research, New York, Columbia Univ.; called to the Bar, New York 1975; clerk to Marvin E. Frankel, US Dist Court (Southern Dist), New York 1975–76; Assoc., Debevoise & Plimpton LLP 1976–78, Litigation Partner 1983–90, Partner and Chair., Litigation Dept 2002–13; Asst US Attorney, Chief Appellate Attorney, Criminal Div., US Dept of Justice (Southern Dist), New York 1978–81, Chief Asst and Acting US Attorney (Eastern Dist), Brooklyn 1990–93, US Attorney (Southern Dist), New York 1993–2002; Chair. SEC, Washington, DC 2013–17; Dir Nasdaq Stock Exchange and mem. Exec., Audit and Policy Cttees 2002–06; Lecturer in Professional Responsibility and Ethics, Columbia Law School 1981–; mem. ABA, New York State Bar Asscn, New York City Bar Asscn; Fellow, American Coll. of Trial Lawyers; Sandra Day O'Connor Award for Distinction in Public Service 2002, FBI Jefferson Cup Award 2002, George W. Bush Award for Excellence in Counter-terrorism 2002, CIA Agency Seal Medallion 2002.

WHITE, Michael D.; American business executive; *Chairman, President and CEO, The DIRECTV Group;* joined Frito-Lay as Vice-Pres. of Planning 1990, later Exec. Vice-Pres. and Chief Financial Officer (CFO) PepsiCo Foods Int. and CFO Frito-Lay North America, later Sr Vice-Pres. and CFO PepsiCo 1998–2000, Pres. and CEO Frito-Lay's Europe/Africa/Middle East div. 2000–03, Chair. and CEO PepsiCo International 2003–09, mem. Bd of Dirs and Vice-Chair. PepsiCo 2006–09; mem. Bd of Dirs, Chair., Pres. and CEO The DIRECTV Group 2009–; mem. Bd of Dirs Whirlpool Corpn. *Address:* The DIRECTV Group, Inc. 2230 East Imperial Highway, El Segundo, CA 90245, USA (office). *E-mail:* info@directv.com (office). *Website:* www.directv.com (office).

WHITE, Miles D., BA, MBA; American pharmaceutical industry executive; *Chairman and CEO, Abbott Laboratories;* b. 1955, Minneapolis, Minn.; m.; ed Stanford Univ.; began career as Man. Consultant with McKinsey & Co.; Man. Nat. Account Sales and later other Sr Man. posts, Diagnostics Div., Abbott Laboratories 1984–93, Vice-Pres. Diagnostics Systems and Operations 1993–94, Sr Vice-Pres. 1994–98, Exec. Vice-Pres. 1998–99, mem. Bd of Dirs 1998–, CEO Jan. 1999–, Chair. April 1999–; mem. Bd of Dirs Fed. Reserve Bank of Chicago 2002–04, Chair. 2005–07; mem. Bd of Dirs Caterpillar Inc., McDonald's Corpn, Northwestern Memorial Hosp.; Chair. Civic Cttee of the Commercial Club of Chicago, Dean's Advisory Bd at Kellogg School of Man., The Culver Educational Foundation; mem. Bd of Trustees Northwestern Univ., Museum of Science and Industry, The Field Museum in Chicago (fmr Chair.); fmr Chair. Fed. Reserve Bank of Chicago, The Econ. Club of Chicago, Pharmaceutical Research and Mfrs of America (PhRMA); Distinguished Executive Award, Lake Forest Grad. School of Man. 2004. *Address:* Abbott Laboratories, 100 Abbott Park Road, Abbott Park, IL 60064-3500, USA (office). *Telephone:* (847) 937-6100 (office). *E-mail:* info@abbott.com (office). *Website:* www.abbott.com (office).

WHITE, Raymond P., DDS, PhD; American oral and maxillofacial surgeon and academic; *Dalton L. McMichael Distinguished Professor of Oral and Maxillofacial Surgery, University of North Carolina;* b. 13 Feb. 1937, New York, NY; s. of Raymond P. White and Mabel S. White; m. Betty P. White 1961; one s. one d.; ed Medical Coll. of Virginia Commonwealth Univ., Washington & Lee Univ.; Asst Prof. of Oral Surgery, Univ. of Kentucky 1967–70, Assoc. Prof. 1970–71, Chair. Oral Surgery Dept 1969–71; Prof. of Oral Surgery, Virginia Commonwealth Univ. 1971–74; Dalton L. McMichael Prof. of Oral and Maxillofacial Surgery, School of Dentistry, Univ. of North Carolina 1974–, Dean 1974–81, Assoc. Dean. Univ. of North Carolina School of Medicine 1981–93, Research Assoc., Health Services Research Center 1982–98; Co-Ed. International Journal of Adult Orthodontics and Orthognathic Surgery; Asst Ed. The Journal of Oral & Maxillofacial Surgery; mem. Inst. of Medicine, NAS; William Gies Award, American Asscn of Oral and Maxillofacial Surgeons 2000, Distinguished Service Award, American Asscn of Oral and Maxillofacial Surgeons 2003, Torch Distinguished Service Award, Oral and Maxillofacial Surgery Foundation 2006. *Publications:* co-author: Fundamentals of Oral Surgery 1971, Surgical Correction of Dentofacial Deformities 1980, Surgical Orthodontic Treatment 1990, Rigid Fixation for Maxillofacial Surgery 1991, Contemporary Treatment of Dentofacial Deformity 2002; more than 100 papers on dentistry, surgery and health policy. *Leisure interests:* tennis, sailing. *Address:* 149 Brauer Hall, School of Dentistry, University of North Carolina, CB 7450, Chapel Hill, NC 27599-7450 (office); 1506 Velma Road, Chapel Hill, NC

27514, USA (home). *Telephone:* (919) 537-3944 (office); (919) 967-4064 (home). *Fax:* (919) 966-6019 (office). *E-mail:* ray_white@dentistry.unc.edu (office). *Website:* www.dentistry.unc.edu (office).

WHITE, Simon David Manton, BA, MSc, PhD, DSc, FRS; British/German astrophysicist, academic and research institute director; *Director, Max Planck Institute for Astrophysics;* b. 30 Sept. 1951, Ashford, Kent, England; m. Guinevere Alice Mei-Ing Kauffmann; one s.; ed Jesus Coll., Cambridge, Univ. of Toronto, Canada; Lindemann Fellow, Dept of Astronomy, Univ. of California, Berkeley 1977–78; Visiting Research Astronomer, Nat. Radio Astronomy Observatory, Charlottesville, Va Sept.–Dec. 1978; Research Fellow, Churchill Coll., Cambridge 1979–80; Attaché au CNRS, Institut d'Astrophysique de Paris Jan.–June 1980; Sr Fellow, Space Sciences Lab., Univ. of California, Berkeley 1980–84, Adjunct Asst Prof., Astronomy Dept 1981–84; mem. Inst. for Advanced Study, Princeton, NJ, USA 1982, Inst. for Theoretical Physics, Santa Barbara, Calif. 1984, Inst. for Advanced Study, Jerusalem 1990; Assoc. Prof./Astronomer, Steward Observatory, Univ. of Arizona 1984–87, Prof./Astronomer 1987–91, Research Prof. 1992–; Sheepshanks Reader in Astronomy, Univ. of Cambridge 1991–94; Dir European Asscn for Research in Astronomy 1992–94; Scientific mem. Max Planck Soc. 1994–, Dir Max Planck Inst. for Astrophysics, Garching, Germany 1994–; Visiting Prof., Durham Univ. 1994–; mem. Council of the Royal Soc. 2015–18; mem. Academia Europaea 2009, European Physical Soc. 2011; Foreign Assoc., NAS 2007; Foreign mem. Chinese Acad. of Sciences 2015; Fellow, Leopoldina, Nationale Akad. der Wissenschaften 2005; Hon. Prof., Ludwig Maximilians Univ., Munich 1995–, Shanghai Astronomical Observatory 1999–, Nat. Observatory, Beijing 2001–; Hon. Citizen of City of Padua 2010; Hon. DSc (Durham) 2007; NSF Presidential Young Investigator 1984–89, Helen B. Warner Prize, American Astronomical Soc. (AAS) 1986, Grubb Parsons Lecturer, Durham Univ. 1996, George Darwin Lecturer, Royal Astronomical Soc. 1998, Lansdowne Lecturer, Univ. of Victoria, BC 1999, Max-Planck-Forschungspreis, Internationale Kooperation 2000, Sackler Lecturer, Physics Dept, Princeton Univ. 2003, Blaauw Lecturer, Groningen Univ. 2005, Dannie Heineman Prize, American Inst. of Physics/AAS 2005, Gold Medal, Royal Astronomical Soc. 2006, Dirk Brouwer Award, Dynamical Div. of AAS 2008, Oort Professorship 2008, European Latsis Prize, Leiden Univ., European Science Foundation 2008, Max Born Prize, Inst. of Physics and German Physical Soc. 2010, Cosmology Prize, Peter Gruber Foundation 2011, Marsilius-Vorlesung, Univ. of Heidelberg 2012, Shaw Prize in Astronomy 2017. *Publications:* numerous papers in professional journals on the structure, formation, evolution and clustering of galaxies; dark matter and dark energy; gravitational dynamics, simulation of cosmic structure formation; cosmology. *Address:* Max-Planck-Institut für Astrophysik, Karl-Schwarzschild-Str. 1, Postfach 1523, 85740 Garching, Germany (office). *Telephone:* (89) 30000-2211 (office). *Fax:* (89) 30000-2899 (office). *E-mail:* swhite@mpa-garching.mpg.de (office). *Website:* www.mpa-garching.mpg.de (office); www.mpg.de/379074/astrophysik_wissM2 (office).

WHITE, Terrence (Terry) Harold, PhD; Canadian academic and fmr university president; *President Emeritus, University of Calgary;* b. 31 March 1943, Ottawa; s. of William H. White and Shirley M. Ballantine; m. Susan E. Hornaday 1968; two d.; ed Univ. of Wisconsin–Oshkosh and Central Michigan Univ., USA Univ. of Toronto; Head, Dept of Sociology and Anthropology, Univ. of Windsor 1973–75; Chair. Dept of Sociology, Univ. of Alberta 1975–80, Dean, Faculty of Arts 1980–88; Pres. and Vice-Chancellor, Brock Univ. 1988–96; Pres. and Vice-Chancellor, Univ. of Calgary 1996–2001, Pres. Emer. 2001–; Vice-Chair. Whyte Museum of the Canadian Rockies, Peter and Catharine Whyte Foundation, Western Watersheds Research Collaborative; mem. Bd of Dirs Academics Without Borders, Rosebud Theatre Centre, Miller Thompson Education Foundation; Rotary Int. Paul Harris Fellow, Canada 125 Commemorative Medal 1999, Queen's Jubilee Medal 2004. *Publications:* Power or Pawns: Boards of Directors in Canadian Corporations 1978, Quality of Working Life 1984. *Leisure interests:* hockey, skiing, squash, tennis, painting.

WHITE, Tony L.; American business executive; b. 1947; ed Western Carolina Univ.; Exec. Vice-Pres. Baxter Int. Inc., Group Vice-Pres. 1986–92; Dir and Chair., Pres. and Chief Exec. PE Corpn (subsequently called Applera Corpn, then Applied Biosystems, Inc.) 1995–2008; co-f. Celera Genomics Group 1998, Pres. (acting) 2002; mem. Bd of Dirs CVS Health 2011–, Ingersoll-Rand Co., C.R. Bard, Inc.; mem. Advisory Bd Kellogg Center for Biotechnology, Northwestern Univ.; Trustee, North Carolina Univ., Centenary Coll.

WHITE, Sir Willard Wentworth, Kt, OM, CBE, BA; Jamaican/British singer (bass); *President, Royal Northern College of Music;* b. 10 Oct. 1946, Ewarton, St Catherine, Jamaica; s. of Egbert White and Gertrude White; m. Gillian Jackson 1972; three s. one d.; ed Excelsior School, Kingston and Juilliard School of Music, USA; early mem. Jamaica Amateur Operatic Soc.; Founding mem. Jamaican Folk Singers; debut with New York City Opera as Colline in La Bohème 1974–75; European debut as Osmin with Welsh Nat. Opera 1976; has performed in most int. opera houses, including Royal Opera House, La Scala, Glyndebourne; roles include Porgy, Orestes, Banquo, King Henry (Lohengrin), Pizarro, Wotan, Mephistopheles, Boris Godunov, Golau, Leporello, Prince Kovansky, Napoleon; extensive concert appearances; appeared as Othello, RSC, Stratford-upon-Avon; Falstaff at Aix Festival 2001, Klingsor in Parsifal, Covent Garden 2001, Bartok's Bluebeard 2002, Messiaen's St Francis, San Francisco 2002, Wotan in the Ring, Aix and Salzburg 2005; Méphistophélès in La Damnation de Faust, Geneva 2008; appeared in Janáček's From the House of the Dead at the Met, New York 2009, La Scala 2010 and Unter den Linden, Berlin 2011; Bottom in A Midsummer Night's Dream for ENO 2011; other appearances include: Klingsor in Parsifal, Royal Opera House, Covent Garden 2013; Wotan in Rheingold, Astana Opera 2014; roles in Mahagonny, Royal Opera and Opera Roma 2015; Arkel in Pelleas and Melisande, Los Angeles 2016; roles in Giasone, Grand Théâtre de Genève 2017; Pres. Royal Northern Coll. of Music 2008–; Patron, London Southbank Scheme for Young Singers; Order of Merit 2000; Prime Minister of Jamaica's Medal of Appreciation 1987, Gold Musgrave Medal, Inst. of Jamaica 2000, Golden Mask Award for Best Male Artist (for his role of Bottom in Midsummer Night's Dream at Mariinsky Theatre), Theatre Union of Russia 2012. *Recordings include:* Porgy and Bess 1991, Mozart Requiem, Orfeo, Die Aegyptische Helena, Acis and Galatea, Willard White Sings: Copland; American Spirituals; Folk Songs 1999, Willard White in Concert 2004, The Paul Robeson Legacy 2007, Dvořák: Rusalka 2014, Ol' Man River/I Got

Plenty O' Nuttin' 2015. *Address:* IMG Artists, Capital Tower, 91 Waterloo Road, London, SE1 8RT, England (office); Royal Northern College of Music, 124 Oxford Road, Manchester, M13 9RD, England. *Telephone:* (20) 7957-5800 (office); (161) 907-5200. *Fax:* (20) 7957-5801 (office). *E-mail:* bsegal@imgartists.com (office). *Website:* www.imgartists.com (office); www.rncm.ac.uk.

WHITE, William James, BS, MBA; American business executive (retd) and academic; *Professor, Department of Industrial Engineering and Management Sciences, Northwestern University;* b. 30 May 1938, Kenosha, Wis.; s. of William H. White and Dorothy Caroline White; m. Jane Schulte 1960; two s. two d.; ed Northwestern and Harvard Univs; Mechanical Planning Engineer, Procter & Gamble Corpn 1961–62; Corp. Vice-Pres. Hartmarx Corpn, Chicago 1963–74; Group Vice-Pres. Mead Corpn, Dayton, Ohio 1974–81; Pres., COO and Dir Masonite Corpn, Chicago 1981–85; Exec. Vice-Pres. and Dir USG Corpn 1985–88; Pres., CEO Whitestar Enterprises Inc. 1989–90; Chair., Pres., CEO Bell & Howell Co. 1990–95, Chair. CEO Bell and Howell Holdings Co. 1995; Chair. ContextMedia Company; Prof., Dept of Industrial Eng and Man. Sciences, Northwestern Univ. 1998–; Visiting Prof., Univ. of Virginia Darden School of Business 2000–01, Univ. of Chicago Business School 2000–04; fmr Dir Midwest Stock Exchange, Evanston Hosp., Ill. Math. and Science Foundation, Business Advisory Council, Univ. of Ill.; mem. The Chicago Cttee, Advisory Council Tech. Inst., Northwestern Univ.; Trustee, Northwestern Univ. *Publication:* Creative Collective Bargaining (co-author) 1965, From Day One: CEO Advice to Launch an Extraordinary Career 2005. *E-mail:* white@iems.northwestern.edu. *Website:* www.williamjwhite.com.

WHITEHOUSE, Sheldon; American lawyer and politician; *Senator from Rhode Island;* b. 20 Oct. 1955, New York; s. of Charles Whitehouse; m. Dr Sandra Thornton; one s. one d.; ed St Paul's School, Concord, New Hampshire, Yale Univ., Univ. of Virginia School of Law; worked as clerk for Judge Richard F. Neely, Supreme Court of Appeals of W Va 1982–83; Special Asst Attorney-Gen., RI Attorney-Gen.'s Office 1985–90, Chief of Regulatory Unit 1988–90, Asst Attorney-Gen. 1989–90; Exec. Counsel for Gov. Bruce Sundlun of RI 1991–94, later Dir of Policy, Dir of Business Regulation 1992–94; US Attorney for RI 1994–98; State Attorney-Gen. 1998–2006; cand. for Gov. 2002; Senator from Rhode Island 2007–, mem. Budget Cttee, Environment and Public Works Cttee, Judiciary Cttee, Health, Educ., Labor, and Pensions Cttee, Special Cttee on Aging; f. Rhode Island Quality Inst.; Democrat. *Address:* 530 Hart Senate Office Building, Washington, DC 20510, USA (office). *Telephone:* (202) 224-2921 (office). *Fax:* (202) 228-6362 (office). *Website:* whitehouse.senate.gov (office).

WHITEMAN, Bernard (Ben) Denzil, MD; Curaçao politician and fmr health administrator; b. 20 Aug. 1954; m.; ed Universidad del Norte, Barranquilla, Colombia; began career as Asst Physician, Dept of Gynaecology and Obstetrics, St Elisabeth Hospital, Willemstad 1983, held various medical positions 1983–94 including Coordinator of Primary Care, Curaçao Public Health Dept, becoming Head of Public Health Service –1994; Dir, Dept of Health and Environment, Netherlands Antilles 1994–2002, later Dir, Netherlands Antilles Public Health Directorate 2002–07, Sec. to Bd, Medical Services Office 2007–10; Inspector-Gen. for Public Health, Ministry of Health, Environment and Nature, Curaçao (following break-up of Netherlands Antilles 2010) 2010–12, Minister of Public Health, Environment and Nature 2012–16, Prime Minister 2015–16; mem. Pueblo Soberano (PS).

WHITEREAD, Rachel, CBE; British artist and sculptor; b. 20 April 1963, London, England; d. of Thomas Whiteread and Patricia Whiteread; m. Marcus Taylor; two s.; ed Brighton Polytechnic, Slade School of Art, Univ. Coll. London; some works use casts of sinks, baths, beds, mattresses, floors and mortuary slabs; work includes 'Ghost', a white plaster cast of an entire room shown at Chisenhale Gallery, London 1990, 'House', a cast of an entire London terraced house on show in Bow, East London 1993–94, 'Water Tower', Museum of Modern Art, New York, 1998, Fourth Plinth Project, Trafalgar Square 2000, Holocaust Memorial, Judenplatz, Vienna 2000, 'Embankment', Tate Modern, London 2005, 'Gran Boathouse', Røykenvik, Norway 2010, 'Cabin', Governors Island, New York 2016, 'Chicken Shed', Tate Britain, London 2017; Hon. DLitt (Brighton Polytechnic) 1998, (Univ. of East London) 1998; Turner Prize 1993, Venice Biennale Award for Best Young Artist 1997, Ada Louise Huxtable Prize, Women in Architecture 2017. *Publication:* Whiteread 2007. *Address:* c/o Gagosian Gallery, 6–24 Britannia Street, London, WC1X 9JD, England. *Telephone:* (20) 7841-9960. *Fax:* (20) 7841-9961. *E-mail:* info@gagosian.com (office). *Website:* www.gagosian.com.

WHITESIDE, Barry, BA, MA (Econs); Fijian economist and central banker; m. Margaret Whiteside; four d.; ed Univ. of South Pacific, Simon Frazer Univ., Canada; joined Reserve Bank of Fiji as Asst Research Officer, Econs Dept in 1977, Head of Dept 1991–98, Chief Man., Dept of Financial Markets 1998–2002, of Currency and Corp. Services 2002–04, of Financial Insts 2004–08, Acting Deputy Gov. 2008–09, Deputy Gov. 2009–10, Acting Gov. 2010–11, Gov. 2011–17; Pres. Fiji Badminton Asscn; USP Award for Studies in Admin. *Achievements include:* Team Man. Fijian Badminton Team, Oceania Tournament 2003 (Suva), 2005 (Auckland), South Pacific Games 2003 (Suva), 2007 (Apia), Commonwealth Games 2006 (Melbourne). *Leisure interests:* hockey, cricket, badminton.

WHITESIDES, George M., PhD, FInstP; American chemist and academic; *Mallinckrodt Professor of Chemistry, Harvard University;* b. 3 Aug. 1939, Louisville, Ky; ed Harvard Univ. and Calif. Inst. of Tech.; mem. Faculty, MIT 1963–82; mem. Faculty, Dept of Chem., Harvard Univ. 1982–86, Chair. 1986–89, Mallinckrodt Prof. of Chem. 1989–; mem. Defense Advanced Research Projects Agency, Defense Science Research Council, US Dept of Defense 1984–, Defense Science Bd 1993–, Threat Reduction Advisory Cttee to Defense Threat Reduction Agency 1998–; Chair. NSF Chem. Advisory Cttee 1986, Nat. Research Council Bd of Chemical Sciences and Tech. 1986–99, NSF Materials Research Advisory Cttee 1993; mem. Scientific Advisory Cttee, Scripps Research Inst. 1993–; mem. NSF Sr Assessment Panel: Int. Assessment of US Math. Sciences 1997; mem. Nat. Research Council Bd on Physics and Astronomy 1997–; Ed. Science Reviewing; mem. Editorial Bd Journal of Applied Biochemistry and Biotechnology, BioOrganic Chemistry, BioOrganic and Medicinal Chemistry Letters, Chemistry of Materials, Journal of Physical Chemistry, Angewandte Chemie, Chemistry and Biology, Langmuir, Nanotechnology, Colloids and Surfaces B: Biointerfaces; mem. American Acad. of Arts and Sciences, NAS, Nat. Acad. of Eng, American Philosophical Soc., World Tech. Network, Royal Netherlands Acad. of Arts and Sciences, Institut de France-Acad. des sciences 2010; Fellow, AAAS, New York Acad. of Science; Foreign Fellow, Indian Nat. Science Acad. 2000; Hon. mem. Materials Research Soc. of India; Hon. Fellow, Chemical Research Soc. of India 2000; Hon. FRSC; Wallac Oy Innovation Award in High Throughput Screening, Soc. for Biomolecular Screening, ACS (Sierra Nevada Section) Distinguished Chemist Award, Alfred P. Sloan Fellowship 1968, ACS Award in Pure Chem. 1975, ACS (Rochester Section) Harrison Howe Award 1979, Alumni Distinguished Service Award, Calif. Inst. of Tech. 1980, ACS (Maryland Section) Remsen Award 1983, ACS Arthur C. Cope Scholar Award 1989, 1995, ACS (New England Section) James Flack Norris Award 1994, ACS Madison Marshall Award 1996, Award for Significant Tech. Achievement, Defense Advanced Research Projects Agency 1996, Nat. Medal of Science, Nat. Science Bd 1998, Award for Excellence in Surface Science, Surfaces in Biomaterials Foundation 1999, Von Hippel Award, Materials Research Soc. 2000, Dan David Prize 2005, ACS Priestley Medal 2007, Scientist of the Year, R&D Magazine 2007, August Wilhelm von Hofmann Lecture, German Chemical Soc. 2007, Gold Medal, American Inst. of Chemists 2007, Wheland Medal, Univ. of Chicago 2008, Outstanding Achievement Award in Nanotechnology, Ohio State Univ. 2008, Nanoscience Prize, Int. Soc. for Nanoscale Science, Computation and Eng 2008, Prince of Asturias Award in Science and Tech. (Spain) 2008, Benjamin Franklin Medal in Chem., Franklin Foundation 2009, Popular Mechanics Breakthrough Award 2009, 100 Most Creative People, FAST Company 2009, Dreyfus Prize in the Chemical Sciences 2009, IKCOC Prize, Int. Kyoto Conf. on Organic Chem. 2009, Othmer Gold Medal, Chemical Heritage Foundation 2010, King Faisal Int. Prize for Science (co-recipient) 2011. *Publications:* more than 630 articles in scientific journals on materials science, biophysics, surface science, polyvalency, microfluidics, optics, self-assembly, microfabrication, nanotechnology and cell surface biochemistry. *Address:* Department of Chemistry and Chemical Biology, Harvard University, Mallinckrodt 232, 12 Oxford Street, Cambridge, MA 02138, USA (office). *Telephone:* (617) 495-9430 (office). *Fax:* (617) 495-9857 (office). *E-mail:* gwhitesides@gmwgroup.harvard.edu (office). *Website:* gmwgroup.harvard.edu (office).

WHITMAN, Christine Todd, BA; American consultant and fmr politician; *President, Whitman Strategy Group;* b. 26 Sept. 1946, New York, NY; d. of Webster Bray Todd and Eleanor Schley Todd; m. John R. Whitman 1974; two c.; ed Wheaton Coll.; fmr freeholder, Somerset Co., NJ; fmr Pres. State Bd of Public Utilities; Gov. of New Jersey 1994–2001; Admin. US Environmental Protection Agency, Washington, DC 2001–03; Pres. Whitman Strategy Group (consulting firm), Washington, DC 2006–; Co-Chair. Republican Leadership Council 2007–11, Clean and Safe Energy; mem. Bd of Dirs S.C. Johnson & Son, Inc., Texas Instruments Inc., United Technologies Corpn, American Security Project, Center for Sustainable Shale Devt, 2014 NY/NJ Super Bowl Host Cttee, Council on Foreign Relations; Trustee, Eisenhower Fellowships; adviser, Aspen Rodel Fellowship Program; mem. Advisory Bd, Corporate Eco Forum; Republican. *Publication:* It's My Party Too 2005. *Address:* Whitman Strategy Group, 116 Village Boulevard, Suite 200, Princeton, NJ 08540 (office); Whitman Strategy Group, 888 16th Street NW, Suite 800, Washington, DC 20006, USA (office). *Telephone:* (609) 524-4068 (Princeton) (office); (202) 355-1374 (Washington, DC) (office); (646) 330-4850 (NY) (office). *E-mail:* christie@christiewhitman.com (office). *Website:* www.whitmanstrategygroup.com (office); www.christiewhitman.com.

WHITMAN, Margaret (Meg) Cushing, AB, MBA; American business executive and fmr politician; *President and CEO, Hewlett Packard Enterprise;* b. 4 Aug. 1956, Cold Spring Harbor, Long Island, New York; d. of Hendricks Hallett Whitman and Margaret Whitman (née Goodhue); m. Griffith R. Harsh IV 1980; two s.; ed Cold Spring Harbor High School, Princeton Univ., Harvard Business School; Brand Asst, Procter & Gamble, Cincinnati, Ohio 1979–81; with Bain & Co., San Francisco, Calif. 1982–89, becoming Vice-Pres.; Sr Vice-Pres. Marketing in Consumer Products Div., Walt Disney Co. 1989–92; Pres. Stride Rite Div., Stride Rite Corpn 1993–95, Exec. Vice-Pres. Keds Div.; Pres. and CEO Florists Transworld Delivery 1995–97, leading launch of co.'s internet strategy; Gen. Man. Hasbro Inc.'s Pre-school Div., Brand Man. responsible for global marketing of Playskool and Mr Potato Head brands 1997–98; mem. Bd of Dirs, Pres. and CEO eBay Inc. 1998–2008, mem. Bd of Dirs, eBay Foundation –2009; co-f., with her husband, Griffith R. Harsh IV and Margaret C. Whitman Charitable Foundation 2006; unsuccessful Republican cand. for Gov. of Calif. 2010; mem. Bd of Dirs, Hewlett-Packard Co. Jan. 2011–15, Pres. and CEO Sept. 2011–15, Chair. 2014–15, (co. split into HP Inc. and Hewlett Packard Enterprise Nov. 2015), Chair. HP Inc. Nov. 2015–17, Pres. and CEO Hewlett Packard Enterprise Nov. 2015–; Strategic Advisor (part-time), Kleiner Perkins Caufield & Byers March–Sept. 2011; mem. Bd of Dirs Goldman Sachs 2001–02, Gap Inc. 2003–06, Procter & Gamble 2003–09, DreamWorks Animation SKG, Inc. 2005–09; Co-Trustee, Princeton Univ. *Publication:* The Power of Many: Values for Success in Business and in Life 2010. *Address:* HP Inc., 3000 Hanover Street, MS 1050, Palo Alto, CA 94304-1185, USA (office). *Telephone:* (650) 857-1501 (office). *Fax:* (650) 857-5518 (office). *E-mail:* bod@hp.com (office). *Website:* www.hpe.com (office).

WHITMAN, Marina von Neumann, BS, MA, PhD; American economist and academic; *Professor of Business Administration and Public Policy, Stephen M. Ross School of Business Administration and Professor of Public Policy, Gerald R. Ford School of Public Policy, University of Michigan;* b. (Marina von Neumann), 6 March 1935, New York; d. of John von Neumann and Mariette Kovesi (Mrs J. B. H. Kuper); m. Robert F. Whitman 1956; one s. one d.; ed Radcliffe Coll., Columbia Univ.; Lecturer in Econs, Univ. of Pittsburgh 1962–64, Asst Prof. 1964–66, Assoc. Prof. 1966–71, Prof. of Econs 1971–73, Distinguished Public Service Prof. 1973–79; Sr Staff Economist, Council of Econ. Advisors 1970–71; mem. Pres.'s Price Comm. 1971–72; mem. Pres.'s Council of Econ. Advisors (with special responsibility for int. monetary and trade problems) 1972–73; Vice-Pres. and Chief Economist, Gen. Motors Corpn, New York 1979–85, Group Exec. Vice-Pres. for Public Affairs 1985–92; Distinguished Visiting Prof. of Business Admin. and Public Policy, Univ. of Michigan 1992–94, Prof. 1994–, currently Prof. of Business Admin. and Public Policy, Stephen M. Ross School of Business Admin. and Prof. of Public Policy, Gerald R. Ford School of Public Policy; mem. Trilateral Comm. 1973, Peterson Inst.; mem. Bd of Dirs J. P. Morgan Chase Corpn 1973–2002, Procter and Gamble Co. 1976–2003, Council on Foreign Relations 1977–87, Alcoa 1993–2002, Unocal 1993–2005; mem. Bd of Overseers Harvard Univ. 1972–78, Bd of Trustees,

Princeton Univ. 1980–90, Nat. Bureau of Econ. Research 1993–; mem. Group of Thirty Consultative Group on Int. Econ. and Monetary Affairs, Inc. (G-30), Washington, DC 1979–, American Acad. of Arts and Sciences, Council on Foreign Relations; more than 20 hon. degrees. *Publications include:* New World, New Rules: The Changing Role of the American Corporation 1999, The Martian's Daughter: A Memoir 2012; numerous books and articles on econ. topics. *Address:* Gerald R. Ford School of Public Policy, University of Michigan, Weill Hall, 735 South State Street, Suite 3228, Ann Arbor, MI 48109-3091, USA (office). *Telephone:* (734) 763-4173 (office). *Fax:* (734) 763-9181 (office). *E-mail:* marinaw@umich.edu (office). *Website:* fordschool.umich.edu (office).

WHITMER, Gretchen Esther, BA, JD; American politician; *Governor of Michigan;* b. 23 Aug. 1971, Lansing, Mich.; d. of Richard Whitmer and Sharon H. Reisig; m. 1st Gary Shrewsbury (divorced); two d.; m. 2nd Marc Mallory 2011; three step-s.; ed Mich. State Univ.; Assoc. Attorney, Dickinson Wright 1998–2000, Of Counsel 2015–16; mem. State House of Reps, Mich. 2000–06, Senate 2006–14, Minority Leader 2011–14, also Policy Analyst; Gov. of Mich. 2019–; Lecturer, Gender and the Law, Mich. State Univ. 2015; Towsley Policy Maker in Residence, Gerald R. Ford School of Public Policy, Univ. of Mich. 2015–16; Prosecutor, Ingham Co. 2016, mem. Bar Asscn; Vice-Chair. Democratic Women's Leadership Caucus; mem. State Bar of Mich., Women's Economic Club. *Address:* Office of the Governor, PO Box 30013, Lansing, MI 48909, USA (office). *Telephone:* (517) 373-3400 (office). *Website:* www.michigan.gov (office).

WHITNEY, John Norton Braithwaite, CBE, FRSA; British broadcasting executive; b. 20 Dec. 1930, Gerrards Cross, Bucks., England; s. of Willis Bevan Whitney and Dorothy Anne Whitney; m. Roma Elizabeth Hodgson 1956; one s. one d.; ed Leighton Park Friends' School, Reading; radio producer 1951–64; set up Ross Radio Productions Ltd 1951, Autocue Ltd 1955; f. Radio Antilles 1963; Man. Dir Capital Radio 1973–82; Dir-Gen. Ind. Broadcasting Authority 1982–89; Man. Dir The Really Useful Group 1989–90, Chair. 1990–95, Dir 1990–97; Dir VCI PLC 1995–98; Chair. The Radio Partnership Ltd 1996–99; Chair. Caspian Publishing Ltd 1996–2002; Dir Galaxy Media Corp PLC 1997–2000, Bird and Co. International 1999–2001, Friends Provident PLC 2001–02; wrote, edited and devised numerous TV series 1956–82; mem. Bd Royal Nat. Theatre 1992–94, City of London Sinfonia 1994–2001; Founder-Dir Sagitta Productions 1968–82; Dir Duke of York's Theatre 1979–82, Consolidated Productions (UK) Ltd 1980–82, Friends' Provident Life Office 1982–2001 (Chair. Friends' Provident Stewardship Cttee of Reference 1985–2000); Chair. Theatre Investment Fund 1990–2001, Trans-World Communications PLC 1992–94, Sony Music Pace Partnership (Nat. Bowl) 1992–95, Rajar Ltd 1992–2002, Friends' Provident Ethical Investment Trust PLC 1992–2001; Trustee, Pension and Life Assurance Plan RNT 1994–2003; Chair. and co-f. Local Radio Asscn 1964; Chair. Asscn of Ind. Local Radio Contractors 1973–75, 1980; f. Recidivists Anonymous Fellowship Trust 1962; mem. Films, TV & Video Advisory Cttee, British Council 1983–89, Royal Coll. of Music Centenary Devt Fund 1982–84 (Chair. Media & Events Cttee 1982–94), Royal Jubilee Trusts Industry & Commerce Liaison Cttee 1986–88 (mem. Admin. Council of Trusts 1981–85); mem. Council Royal London Aid Soc. 1966–90, Fairbridge Drake Soc. 1981–96, Intermediate Tech. Group 1982–85, Council for Charitable Support 1989–92; Pres. TV & Radio Industries Club 1985–86, London Marriage Guidance Council 1983–90; Vice-Pres. Commonwealth Youth Exchange Council 1982–85, RNID 1988–2003; Chair. Bd of Trustees, Soundaround 1981–2000, Artsline 1983–2000; Chair. Festival Media Cttee 1991–92, British American Arts Asscn 1992–95, Sony Radio Awards 1992–98, Friends Provident Charitable Foundation 2002–06, RADA 2003–07; mem. Bd Open Coll. 1987–89; Gov. English Nat. Ballet 1989–91, Performing Arts and Tech. School; Fellow and Vice-Pres. Royal Television Soc. 1986–89; Trustee, Venture Trust 1982–86, Japan Festival Educ. Trust 1992–2003; Patron, Music Space Trust 1990–; Hon. FRCM, Hon. mem. BAFTA. *Publication:* To Serve the People 2013. *Leisure interests:* chess, photography, sculpture. *Address:* The Long Barn, 5 Church Close, Todber, Dorset, DT10 1JH, England (home). *E-mail:* john@johnwhitney.co.uk (office).

WHITNEY, Meredith Ann, BA; American business analyst; *CEO, Meredith Whitney Advisory Group LLC;* b. 20 Nov. 1969; m. John 'Bradshaw' Layfield 2005; ed Brown Univ., Providence, RI; joined Oppenheimer & Co. Inc. as a research analyst 1993, with Specialty Finance Group 1995–98, returned to Oppenheimer & Co. Inc. 2004, Man. Dir and Sr Financial Analyst 2008–09; Head of Financial Insts Research, Wachovia Securities 1998–2001; Analyst, FrontPoint Partners 2001–04; Sr Financial Insts Analyst, CIBC World Markets 2004–07; Founder and CEO Meredith Whitney Advisory Group LLC 2009–; frequent contrib. to CNBC, Fox Business and Bloomberg News programs; Power Player of the Year, CNBC 2008. *Address:* Meredith Whitney Advisory Group LLC, 50 West 57th Street, 2nd Floor, New York, NY 10019, USA (office). *Telephone:* (212) 542-4320 (office). *E-mail:* info@meredithwhitneyllc.com (office). *Website:* www.meredithwhitneyllc.com (office).

WHITTLE, Peter, PhD, FRS; New Zealand mathematician and academic; *Professor Emeritus, Statistical Laboratory, University of Cambridge;* b. 27 Feb. 1927, Wellington; s. of Percy Whittle and Elsie (née Tregurtha) Whittle; m. Käthe Hildegard Blomquist 1951; three s. three d.; ed Wellington Boys' Coll., Victoria Univ. Coll., Uppsala Univ., Sweden; NZ Sr Prin. Scientific Officer 1953–59; Lecturer in Math., Univ. of Cambridge, UK 1959–61, Churchill Prof. of the Math. of Operational Research 1967–94, Prof. Emer. Statistical Lab. 1994–, Fellow of Churchill Coll.; Prof. of Math. Statistics, Univ. of Manchester 1961–67; Sr Fellow, Science and Eng Research Council 1988–91; mem. Royal Soc. of NZ 1981; Hon. DSc (Victoria Univ. of Wellington) 1987; Guy Medal in Silver, Royal Statistical Soc. 1966, in Gold 1996; Lanchester Prize, Operational Research Soc. of America 1987, Sylvester Medal, Royal Soc. 1994, J. von Neumann Theory Medal, Inst. of Operational Research Man. Science 1997. *Publications:* Hypothesis Testing in Time Series Analysis 1951, Prediction and Regulation 1963, Probability 1970, Optimisation Under Constraints 1971, Optimisation Over Time 1982, Optimization Over Time: Dynamic Programming and Stochastic Control 1983, Systems in Stochastic Equilibrium 1986, Risk-Sensitive Optimal Control 1990, Probability via Expectation 1992, Optimal Control: Basics and Beyond 1996, Neural Nets and Chaotic Carriers 1998, Networks: Optimisation and Evolution 2007. *Leisure interests:* variable. *Address:* Statistical Laboratory, Pavilion D, Centre for Mathematical Studies, Wilberforce Road, Cambridge, CB3 0WB (office); 268 Queen Edith's Way, Cambridge, CB1 8NL, England (home). *Telephone:* (1223) 337964 (office); (1223) 245422 (home). *Fax:* (1223) 337956 (office). *E-mail:* whittle@statslab.cam.ac.uk (office). *Website:* www.statslab.cam.ac.uk (office).

WHITTLE, Stephen Charles, OBE, LLB, FRSA; British broadcasting executive; b. 26 July 1945, London, England; s. of Charles William Whittle and Vera Lillian Whittle (née Moss); m. 1st Claire Walmsley 1988 (divorced 1999); m. 2nd Eve Salomon 2004; ed St Ignatius Coll., Stamford Hill, Univ. Coll., London; Asst Ed. New Christian 1968–70; Communications Officer, World Council of Churches, Geneva 1970–73; Ed. One World 1973–77, Asst Head Communications Dept 1975–77; Sr Producer BBC Religious Programmes, Manchester 1977–82, Producer Newsnight 1982, Ed. Songs of Praise and Worship 1983–89, Head of Religious Programmes 1989–93, Chief Adviser, Editorial Policy 1993–96; Dir Broadcasting Standards Council 1996–97, Broadcasting Standards Comm. 1997–2001; Controller of Editorial Policy, BBC 2001–05; Chair. Broadcast Equality and Training Regulator 2007–11; Gov. European Inst. for the Media, Düsseldorf 1997–2002; Visiting Fellow, Reuters Inst. for the Study of Journalism, Oxford 2007–; mem. Solicitors Regulation Authority 2005–12, Gen. Medical Council 2009–12; Expert for Council of Europe; Chair. Time and Talents; Trustee, The Fifth Trust; Freeman, City of London 1990; Personal Award, Sandford St Martin Trust 1993. *Publication:* Privacy, Probity and Public Interest 2009. *Leisure interests:* cinema, theatre, music, reading, walking. *Address:* 4 Carmarthen Place, London, SE1 3TS, England (home). *Telephone:* (20) 7407-2016 (home). *E-mail:* stephen_whittle@btopenworld.com (office).

WHITWAM, David R., BS; American business executive; b. Madison, Wis.; ed Univ. of Wisconsin; joined Whirlpool Corpn 1968, various sr and marketing positions including Vice-Pres. Whirlpool brand business 1983–85, mem. Bd of Dirs 1985, Vice-Chair. and Chief Marketing Officer 1985–87, Pres. 1987–92, Chair. and CEO 1987–2004 (retd); mem. Bd of Dirs PPG Industries Inc., Business Roundtable Policy Cttee and Educ. Task Force; Chair. Mich. Business Leaders for Educational Excellence Org.; Trustee Univ. of Wis. Alumni Research Foundation.

WHITWORTH-JONES, Anthony, CA; British arts administrator; b. 1 Sept. 1945, Bucks., England; s. of Henry Whitworth-Jones and Patience Martin; m. Camilla Barlow 1974; one d.; ed Wellington Coll.; Admin. Dir London Sinfonietta 1972–81; Admin. Glyndebourne Touring Opera 1981–89, Opera Man. Glyndebourne Festival Opera 1981–89, Gen. Dir Glyndebourne 1989–98; Chair. Michael Tippett Musical Foundation 1998–; Gen. Dir The Dallas Opera 2000–02; Artistic Dir Casa da Musica, Oporto, Portugal 2004–05, Artistic Consultant 2007–08; Gen. Dir Garsington Opera 2005–12; mem. Bd Spitalfields Festival 2003–06, Young Classical Artists Trust 2006–14, ENO 2012–; Trustee, Leonard Ingrams Foundation 2006–16. *Leisure interests:* the arts, golf, mountains. *Address:* 60 Marquis Road, London, NW1 9UB, England (home). *Telephone:* (20) 7267-3154 (home). *E-mail:* antwjones@gmail.com (home).

WHYBROW, John W., BSc, MBA; British business executive; *Chairman, AZ Electronic Materials SA;* b. 11 March 1947; m.; two c.; ed Imperial Coll. London, Manchester Business School; joined Philips 1970, apptd Man.-Dir Philips Power Semiconductors and Microwave business 1987, Chair. and Man.-Dir Philips Electronics UK –1995, Pres. and CEO Philips Lighting Holding BV, The Netherlands 1995–2001, Exec. Vice-Pres. Royal Philips Electronics and mem. Bd of Man. 1998–2002; Dir (non-exec.) Wolseley PLC 1997, Chair. Remuneration Cttee 1998–2002, Deputy Chair. April–Dec. 2002, Chair. 2002–11, Chair. Nominations Cttee; Chair. CSR PLC 2004–07; Dir (non-exec.), DSG Int. PLC 2003–10; Chair. Petworth Cottage Nursing Home; Chair. AZ Electronic Materials SA, Chair. Remuneration Cttee, Disclosure Cttee, Nominations Cttee; Order of Merit for Services to Econ. Devt of Poland (Poland) 2002. *Leisure interests:* sailing, shooting. *Address:* AZ Electronic Materials SA, 32–36 Boulevard d'Avranches, 1160 Luxembourg, Luxembourg (office). *Telephone:* (26) 4979-1116 (office). *Fax:* (26) 4979-8888 (office). *E-mail:* info@azem.com (office). *Website:* www.azem.com (office).

WIATR, Jerzy Józef, MPh, PhD; Polish politician and sociologist; *Rector, European School of Law and Administration;* b. 17 Sept. 1931, Warsaw; s. of Wilhelm Wiatr and Zofia Wiatr; m. Ewa Żurowska-Wiatr; one s.; ed Warsaw Univ.; Asst Warsaw Univ. 1951–59; Mil. Political Acad. 1959–65; Polish Acad. of Sciences (PAN) 1965–69; Prof., Warsaw Univ. 1969–2001, Dean of Social Sciences 1977–80; participant Round Table debates 1989; Deputy to Sejm (Parl.) 1991–2001; mem. Cttee for Nat. Defence and Cttee for Constitutional Responsibility 1991–97; Minister of Educ. 1996–97; Dir Inst. for Social and International Studies, Keller-Krauz Foundation 1998–; Pres. Cen. European Political Science Asscn 2000–03; Vice-Pres. Int. Political Science Asscn 1979–82; Vice-Pres. Int. Studies Asscn 1980–81; mem. Polish United Workers Party (PZPR) 1949–90; mem. Social Democracy of Polish Repub. (SdRP) 1990–99; mem. Democratic Left Alliance 1999–; Rector, European School of Law and Admin, Warsaw 2007–; Hon. Senator Univ. of Ljubljana 2006, Hon. Pres. Cen. European Political Science Asscn 2009; Commdr's Cross with Star of Polonia Restituta Order 1996. *Publications include:* over 30 books including Education For and In the 21st Century 1997; numerous articles on sociology and political science. *Leisure interests:* tourism, books, chess. *Address:* European School of Law and Administration, Grudzienska 21/29, 03 750 Warsaw (office); ul. Komisji Edukacji Narodowej 98/49, 02 777 Warsaw, Poland (home). *Telephone:* (22) 619-90-11 (office); (22) 643-54-41 (home). *Fax:* (22) 643-54-41 (home). *E-mail:* jwiatr@ewspa.edu.pl (office). *Website:* www.ewspa.edu.pl (office).

WIBERG, Kenneth Berle, PhD; American academic; *Professor Emeritus of Chemistry, Yale University;* b. 22 Sept. 1927, New York; s. of Halfdan Wiberg and Solveig Berle; m. Marguerite Louise Koch 1951; two s. one d.; ed Massachusetts Inst. of Tech., Columbia Univ.; Instructor, Univ. of Washington 1950–52, Asst Prof. 1952–55, Assoc. Prof. 1955–57, Prof. 1958–62; Prof., Yale Univ. 1962–68, Chair. Dept of Chem. 1968–71, Whitehead Prof. of Chem. 1968–90, Eugene Higgins Prof. 1990–97, Prof. Emer. 1997–; Visiting Prof., Harvard Univ. 1957–58; mem. NAS, AAAS; Sloan Foundation Fellow 1958–62, Guggenheim Fellow 1961–62, ACS California Section Award 1962, ACS J.F. Norris Award 1973, ACS Arthur C. Cope Award 1988, Linus Pauling Award 1992. *Publications include:* Laboratory Technique in Organic Chemistry 1960, Interpretation of NMR Spectra 1964, Physical Organic Chemistry 1964, Oxidation in Organic Chemistry (ed.)

1965, Computer Programming for Chemists 1966, Sigma Molecular Orbital Theory (with Sinanoglu) 1970; approx. 400 articles in scientific journals. *Address:* 865 Central Avenue, Apartment A404, Needham, MA 02492, USA (home). *Telephone:* (781) 400-5039 (home). *E-mail:* kenneth.wiberg@yale.edu (home).

WICKER, Roger Frederick, BA, JD; American lawyer and politician; *Senator from Mississippi;* b. 5 July 1951, Pontotoc, Miss.; m. Gayle Long; one s. two d.; ed Univ. of Mississippi; Judge Advocate and Capt. in USAF 1976–80, Lt-Col in USAF Reserve 1980–2004; Partner, Sparks, Wicker & Colburn (law firm) 1982–94; public defender, Lee Co., Miss. 1984–87; judge pro tempore, Tupelo, Miss. 1986–87; mem. Mississippi State Senate 1987–94; mem. US House of Reps from 1st Miss. Dist 1995–2007, Deputy Majority Whip; Senator from Mississippi 2007–, mem. Armed Services Cttee, Commerce, Science, and Transportation Cttee, Veterans' Affairs Cttee; Chair. Nat. Republican Senatorial Cttee 2014; Republican, mem. Republican Policy Cttee 2001–. *Address:* 555 Dirksen Senate Office Building, Washington, DC 20510, USA (office). *Telephone:* (202) 224-6253 (office). *Fax:* (202) 228-0378 (office). *Website:* www.wicker.senate.gov (office).

WICKER-MIURIN, Fields, OBE, BA, MA, FRSA, FKC; American/British company director; *Co-founder and Partner, Leaders' Quest Ltd;* b. (Jane Fields Wicker), 30 July 1958, USA; d. of Warren Jake Wicker and Marie Peachee Wicker; m. Paolo Miurin; ed Univ. of Virginia, l'Institut d'Etudes Politiques, France, Johns Hopkins School of Advanced International Studies, Bologna, Italy and Washington, DC; Chief Financial Officer and Dir of Strategy, London Stock Exchange 1994–97; fmr Vice-Pres. A.T. Kearney (strategy consultancy), London; fmr Sr Partner, Mercer Man. Consulting London; fmr Man. Dir Vesta Capital Advisors (venture capital firm); Co-founder and Partner, Leaders' Quest Ltd 2002–; Dir (non-exec.), BNP Paribas 2011–, SCOR SE (also Chair. Social and Societal Responsibility Cttee and Sustainable Devt Cttee) 2013–, UK Dept of Digital Culture, Media and Sport (also Chair. Audit and Risk Cttee) 2016–, Prudential plc 2018–; fmr Dir (non-exec.), BILT Industries, CDC Group, Bd of UK Dept of Trade and Industry (DTI), D. Carnegie & Co. AB, Royal London Insurance, United Business Media plc, Savills plc, UK Ministry of Justice; fmr Chair. DTI Investment Cttee, mem. Ballapur Nominations, Remuneration and CSR Cttees, DTI Tech. Strategy Bd 2002–08, Royal London Investment Cttee, Savills Audit Cttee; fmr mem. Advisory Council, Univ. of Virginia Batten School of Leadership, Nasdaq Tech. Advisory Cttee, Panel of Experts to advise EU Parl. on harmonization of financial services; fmr Fellow, World Econ. Forum; fmr Gov., King's Coll. London, now Fellow; fmr Trustee, London Int. Festival of Theatre, Tate Members, London Musici, Arts and Business; Global Leader for Tomorrow, World Econ. Forum. *Publications:* numerous articles in the financial press. *Leisure interests:* horses, nature, music, ideas and the world. *Address:* Leaders' Quest Ltd, 11–13 Worple Way, Richmond-upon-Thames, Surrey, TW10 6DG, England (office). *Telephone:* (20) 8948-5200 (office). *Fax:* (20) 8332-6423 (office). *E-mail:* info@leadersquest.org (office). *Website:* www.leadersquest.org (office).

WICKRAMASINGHE, Nalin Chandra, BSc, MA, PhD, ScD (Cantab.), FIMA, FRAS, FRSA; British mathematician, astronomer, astrobiologist and academic; *Honorary Professor and Director, Buckingham Centre for Astrobiology, University of Buckingham;* b. 20 Jan. 1939, Colombo, Sri Lanka; s. of Percival H. Wickramasinghe and Theresa E. Wickramasinghe; m. Nelum Priyadarshini Pereira 1966; one s. two d.; ed Royal Coll., Colombo and Univs of Colombo and Cambridge; Research Fellow, Jesus Coll., Cambridge 1963–66, Fellow 1967–73, Tutor 1970–73; Staff mem. Inst. of Theoretical Astronomy, Univ. of Cambridge 1968–73; Prof. and Head of Dept of Applied Math. and Astronomy, Univ. Coll., Cardiff 1973–88; Prof. of Applied Math. and Astronomy, Univ. of Wales Coll. of Cardiff (now Cardiff Univ.) 1988–2006, Dir Cardiff Centre for Astrobiology 2000–10; Dir Buckingham Centre for Astrobiology, Univ. of Buckingham 2010–, Ruhuna Univ. Centre for Astrobiology; Adjunct Prof., Ruhuna Univ., Sri Lanka; Dir Inst. of Fundamental Studies, Sri Lanka 1982–83; UNDP Consultant and Scientific Adviser to Pres. of Sri Lanka 1970–81; Visiting Prof., Univs of Ceylon, Maryland, Arizona and Kyoto 1966–70, Univ. of Western Ontario 1974–76, Inst. of Space and Astronomical Science, Japan 1993, Univ. of the West Indies, Mona, Kingston, Jamaica 1994, Univ. of Peradeniya; Fellow, Inst. of Math. and Its Applications; Hon. Prof., Univ. of Buckingham, Kotelawala Defence Univ. of Sri Lanka 2017; Vidya Jyothi (Sri Lanka Nat. Honour) 1992; Hon. DLitt (Tokyo, Soka Univ.) 1996, Hon. DSc (Ruhuna Univ.), (Soka Univ. Japan); Dag Hammarskjöld Laureate in Science 1986, Scholarly Achievement Award of Inst. of Oriental Philosophy, Japan 1989, Sahabdeen Award for Science 1996. *Publications include:* Interstellar Grains 1967, Light Scattering Functions for Small Particles with Applications in Astronomy 1973, The Cosmic Laboratory 1975; with Sir Fred Hoyle: Life Cloud: The Origin of Life in the Universe 1978, Diseases from Space 1979, The Origin of Life 1980, Evolution from Space 1981, Space Travellers, The Bringers of Life, Is Life an Astronomical Phenomenon? 1982, Why Neo-Darwinism Doesn't Work 1982, Proofs That Life Is Cosmic 1982, Fundamental Studies and the Future of Science 1984, From Grains to Bacteria 1984, Living Comets 1985, Archaeopteryx, the Primordial Bird: a case of fossil forgery 1986, Cosmic Life Force 1987, The Theory of Cosmic Grains 1991, Our Place in the Cosmos: the Unfinished Revolution 1993, Life on Mars? The Case for a Cosmic Heritage 1996; with F. D. Kahn and P. G. Mezger: Interstellar Matter 1972; with D. J. Morgan: Solid State Astrophysics 1976; with Daisaku Ikeda: 2000 A.D. – Emergent Perspectives 1992, Glimpses of Life, Time and Space 1994, Space and Eternal Life 1997, Cosmic Dragons 2001, A Journey with Fred Hoyle 2004, Comets and the Origin of Life (with J. Wickramasinghe and W. M. Napier) 2010, A Destiny of Cosmic Life: Chapters in the Life of an Astrobiologist 2014, Search for Our Cosmic Ancestry 2015, Where Do We Come From 2015, Vindication of Cosmic Biology 2015, Big Bang and God 2016, Cosmic Womb (with R. Bauval) 2018. *Leisure interests:* photography, poetry. *Address:* Buckingham Centre for Astrobiology, University of Buckingham, Buckingham, Bucks., MK18 1EG England (office); 24 Llwynypia Road, Lisvane, Cardiff, CF14 0SY, Wales (home). *Telephone:* (29) 2075-2146 (home); 7778-389243 (mobile) (home). *E-mail:* chandra.wickramasinghe@buckingham.ac.uk (office); ncwick@gmail.com (home). *Website:* www.buckingham.ac.uk/directory/professor-chandra-wickramasinghe (office); profchandra.org.

WICKREMASINGHE, Nishanta; Sri Lankan business executive; *Chairman, SriLankan Airlines Ltd.;* brother-in-law of Mahinda Rajapaksa; m.; ed St Thomas Coll.; fmr Gen. Man. James Finlay Plantation Holdings Ltd; mem. Bd of Dirs SriLankan Airlines Ltd 2006–, Exec. Dir 2008–09, Acting Chair. 2008–09, Chair. 2009–; fmr mem. Volunteer Army. *Address:* SriLankan Airlines Ltd., Airline Centre, Bandaranaike International Airport, Katunayake, Sri Lanka (office). *Telephone:* (19) 7335555 (office). *Fax:* (19) 7335122 (office). *Website:* www.srilankan.lk (office).

WICKREMESINGHE, Ranil, LLB; Sri Lankan politician and lawyer; *Prime Minister and Minister of National Policy and Economic Affairs;* b. 24 March 1949, Colombo; s. of Esmond Wickremesinghe and Nalini Wickremesinghe; m. Maithree Wickremasinghe 1995; ed Royal Coll. of Colombo, Univ. of Colombo and Sri Lanka Law Coll.; enrolled as Advocate of Supreme Court of Sri Lanka 1972; mem. Parl. 1977–, Leader of House 1989–93, Leader of the Opposition 1994–2001, 2004–15, Prime Minister of Sri Lanka 1992, 2001–04, 2015–Oct. 18 (removed), Dec. 2018–, also Minister of Nat. Policy and Econ. Affairs 2015–, fmr Minister of Policy Planning, of Econ. Affairs, and of Child, Youth and Cultural Affairs, Deputy Minister of Foreign Affairs 1977–79, Minister of Youth Affairs and Employment 1978–89, of Educ. 1980–89, of Industries 1989–90, of Industries, Science and Tech. 1990–94, of Policy Devt and Implementation 2001–04, of Buddha Sasana (Buddhism) and Religious Affairs 2015; Leader, United Nat. Party 1994–, unsuccessful party cand. in presidential elections 1999, 2005; Robert E. Wilhelm Fellow, Center for Int. Studies, MIT, USA 2014; Chair. of Dhayakasabha, Kelaniya Vihara temple and Dhayakaya of Gangaramaya, Walukaramaya and Weragodalla (Sedawatte) temples. *Address:* Prime Minister's Office, 58 Sir Ernest de Silva Mawatha, Colombo 7 (office); No. 115, 5th Lane, Colombo 3, Sri Lanka. *Telephone:* (11) 2575317 (office). *Fax:* (11) 2575310 (office). *E-mail:* info@pmoffice.gov.lk; wickremesinghe_r@parliament.lk (office). *Website:* www.pmoffice.gov.lk (office); ranilwickremesinghe.com.

WICKS, Sir Nigel Leonard, Kt, GCB, CVO, CBE, MA (London), MA (Cantab.); British business executive and civil servant (retd); *Chairman, British Bankers Association;* b. 16 June 1940; s. of Leonard Charles Wicks and Beatrice Irene Wicks; m. Jennifer Mary Coveney 1969; three s.; ed Beckenham and Penge Grammar School, Portsmouth Coll. of Tech., Univ. of Cambridge, Univ. of London; British Petroleum 1958–68; served HM Treasury 1968–75, 1978–83, Second Perm Sec. (Finance) 1989–2000; Pvt. Sec. to Prime Minister 1975–78; mem. Bd BNOC 1980–82; Econ. Minister Embassy, Washington and UK; Exec. Dir IMF and IBRD 1983–85; Prin. Pvt. Sec. to Prime Minister 1985–88; Pres. Monetary Cttee of EC 1993–98; Chair. Cttee on Standards in Public Life 2001–04, panel appointing initial members of the then-new Judicial Appointments Comm. 2005; Commr Jersey Financial Services Comm. 2007–12; Chair. CRESTCo (settlement system for UK and Irish securities) 2001–02, Deputy Chair. (following merger with Euroclear plc) 2002–06, Chair. 2007–13; Chair. British Bankers Asscn 2012–; Dir (non-exec.), Morgan Stanley 2004–06, The Edinburgh Investment Trust 2005–; mem. EU Cttee of 'Wise Men' on European Securities Regulation (the Lamfalussy group) 2000–01; Gov., King's Coll. School, Wimbledon; Grand Officier, Ordre grand-ducal de la Couronne de Chêne (Luxembourg); Hon. LLD (Bath) 1999, (Portsmouth). *Address:* British Bankers Association, Pinners Hall, 105–108 Old Broad Street, London, EC2N 1EX (office); Steeple Ashton, Lime Grove, West Clandon, Guildford, Surrey, GU4 7UT, England (home). *Telephone:* (20) 7216-8800 (office). *Fax:* (20) 7216-8811 (office). *E-mail:* info@bba.org.uk (office); nigel.wicks@bigfoot.com (home). *Website:* www.bba.org.uk (office).

WIDMER-SCHLUMPF, Eveline, LLB, JD; Swiss lawyer and politician; b. 16 March 1956, Felsberg, Graubünden; d. of Leon Schlumpf and Trudi Rupp; m.; three c.; ed Univ. of Zürich; admitted to the bar, Graubünden, pvt. practice as lawyer and notary public 1987–98; elected to Dist Court, Trin 1985, Pres. 1991–97; mem. Grosser Rat (Great Council), Graubünden 1994–98; elected to Regierungsrat 1998, Head, Cantonal Dept of Finance 1999–2007, Pres. Cantonal Council 2001, 2005; mem. Fed. Council 2008–15, Head, Fed. Dept of Justice and Police 2008–10, Head, Fed. Dept of Finance 2010–15, Vice-Pres. of Switzerland Jan.–Dec. 2011, Pres. Jan.–Dec. 2012; fmr mem. Swiss People's Party; mem. Conservative Democratic Party 2008–.

WIDNALL, Sheila Evans, BSc, MS, PhD, FAAS; American astrophysicist and academic; *Institute Professor and Professor of Aeronautics and Astronautics, Massachusetts Institute of Technology;* b. 13 July 1938, Tacoma, Wash.; d. of Rolland Evans and Genevieve Krause; m. William Widnall 1960; one s. one d.; ed Massachusetts Inst. of Technology; Research Staff Engineer, MIT 1961–62, Research Asst 1962–64, Asst Prof. 1964–70, Assoc. Prof. 1970–74, Prof. 1974–86, Abby Rockefeller Mauze Prof. of Aeronautics and Astronautics 1986–93, Assoc. Provost 1992–93, Inst. Prof. 1998–, Dir Fluid Dynamics Research Lab. 1979–90, Chair. of Faculty 1979–80, Assoc. Provost 1992–93; Dir Univ. Research, US Dept of Transportation, Washington, DC 1974–75; Sec. of US Air Force 1993–98, Co-Chair. Dept of Defense Task Force on Sexual Harassment and Discrimination; fmr Dir Aerospace Corpn, Draper Laboratories, ANSER Corp., Chemical Fabrics Inc.; fmr Pres. AAAS; Dir GenCorp Inc.; Vice-Pres. Nat. Acad. of Eng 1998; Fellow, American Inst. of Aeronautics and Astronautics (AIAA), mem. Bd of Dirs 1975–77, Pres. 2000–01; mem. Nat. Research Council Governing Bd 1999; Fellow, APS, American Acad. of Arts and Sciences, Royal Aeronautical Soc.; fmr mem. Carnegie Comm. on Science, Council of Smithsonian Inst. of Washington; mem. Exec. Cttee, Nat. Research Council of the Nat. Acads; mem. Int. Acad. of Astronautics, Seattle Mountaineers, Appalachian Mountain Club, Eastern Yacht Club, Charles River Wheelman, Potomac Peddlers; fmr consultant, Macarthur Foundation; fmr Trustee, Carnegie Corpn (also Vice-Chair.), Boston Museum of Science; Trustee, Sloan Foundation, Inst. for Defense Analysis; Hon. DSc (Princeton) 1994; American Inst. of Aeronautics Lawrence Sperry Achievement Award 1972, Soc. of Women Engineers Outstanding Achievement Award 1975, Boston Museum of Science Washburn Award 1987, Nat. Acad. of Eng Distinguished Service Award 1993, Barnard Coll. Medal of Distinction 1994, Air Force Asscn W. Stuart Symington Award 1995, Air Force Asscn Maxwell A. Kriendler Memorial Award 1995, Boston USO Mil. Award 1995, ASME Applied Mechanics Award 1996, New England Council New Englander of the Year 1996, Women's Int. Center Living Legacy Award 1998, Nat. Space Club Goddard Award 1998, NDIA Hartinger Award 1999, AIAA Reed Aeronautics Award 2000, ASME Spirit of St Louis Medal 2001, Arthur M. Bueche Award, Nat. Acad. of Eng 2009. *Publications:* contrib. articles to professional journals. *Address:* Room 33-411, Department of Aeronautics and Astronautics, Massachusetts Institute of Technology, 77 Massachusetts

Avenue, Cambridge, MA 02139-4307, USA (office). *Telephone:* (617) 253-3595 (office). *E-mail:* sheila@mit.edu (office). *Website:* web.mit.edu/aeroastro/www (office).

WIDODO, Joko (Jokowi); Indonesian politician and head of state; *President;* b. 21 June 1961, Solo; s. of Noto Mihardjo and Sudjiatmi Notomihardjo; m. Iriana Widodo; three c.; ed Gadjah Mada Univ.; worked at father's furniture workshop from age 12; worked at BUMN PT Kertas Kraft, Aceh (state-owned cement co.) 1985; f. own furniture business CV Rakabu 1988; Pres. Solo Br., Furniture Mfrs' Asscn 2002; Mayor of Solo 2005–12; Gov. of Jakarta 2012–14; Pres. of Indonesia 2014–; mem. Partai Demokrasi Indonesia Perjuangan (Indonesian Democratic Struggle Party); Bintang Jasa Utama (Main Service Star) 2011. *Address:* Office of the President, Istana Merdeka, Second Floor, Jakarta 10110, Indonesia (office). *Telephone:* (21) 3840946 (office). *Website:* www.presidenri.go.id (office).

WIDOM, Benjamin, PhD; American chemist and academic; *Goldwin Smith Professor Emeritus of Chemistry, Cornell University;* b. 13 Oct. 1927, Newark, New Jersey; s. of Morris Widom and Rebecca Hertz Widom; m. Joanne McCurdy 1953; two s. one d.; ed Stuyvesant High School, New York and Columbia and Cornell Univs; Research Assoc., Univ. of North Carolina 1952–54; Instructor in Chem., Cornell Univ. 1954–55, Asst Prof. 1955–59, Assoc. Prof. 1959–63, Prof. 1963–, Goldwin Smith Prof. Emer. 1983–; van der Waals Prof., Univ. of Amsterdam 1972; Visiting Prof. of Chem., Harvard Univ. 1975; IBM Visiting Prof. of Theoretical Chem., Univ. of Oxford 1978; Lorentz Prof., Leiden Univ. 1985; Visiting Prof., Katholieke Univ., Leuven 1988, Université d'Aix Marseille III 1995; Kramers/Debye Prof., Univ. of Utrecht 1999; Fellow, American Acad. of Arts and Sciences, New York Acad. of Sciences; mem. NAS, American Philosophical Soc.; Hon. DSc (Chicago), Dr hc (Utrecht); Boris Pregel Award, New York Acad. of Sciences, ACS Langmuir Award, Dickson Prize for Science, Carnegie-Mellon Univ., ACS Hildebrand Award, Hirschfelder Prize in Theoretical Chem., Univ. of Wisconsin, Bakhuis Roozeboom Medal, Royal Netherlands Acad. of Arts and Sciences, Onsager Medal, Univ. of Trondheim, Boltzmann Medal, IUPAP Comm. on Statistical Physics, ACS Award in Theoretical Chem. *Publications include:* Molecular Theory of Capillarity (with J. S. Rowlinson) 1982, Statistical Mechanics: A Concise Introduction for Chemists 2002. *Address:* Department of Chemistry, 220 Baker Laboratory, Cornell University, Ithaca, NY 14853, USA (office). *Telephone:* (607) 255-3363 (office). *Fax:* (607) 255-4137 (office). *E-mail:* bw24@cornell.edu (office). *Website:* www.chem.cornell.edu (office).

WIEANDT, Axel, MBA, Dr rer. pol; German banker, business executive and academic; b. 19 Sept. 1966, Bochum; s. of Paul Wieandt; m.; two c.; ed Kellogg School of Man., Northwestern Univ., USA, Koblenz School of Man.—WHU, Germany; began career as Man. Consultant in Financial Services and Media Industry at McKinsey & Co., Inc., Düsseldorf, followed by one year at Morgan Stanley Ltd & Co., London, UK; Deputy Global Head of Corp. Strategy, Deutsche Bank Group, Frankfurt am Main 1998–99, Man. Dir Deutsche Asset Man. Europe GmbH/Deutsche Asset Man. Int. GmbH, Frankfurt am Main 1999–2000, Global Head of Corp. Devt (AfK), Deutsche Bank Group 2000–08, Global Head of Corp. Investments, Deutsche Bank Group 2003–08, Man. Dir responsible for Integration Man. 2010–11; Chair. Man. Bd and CEO Hypo Real Estate Holding AG 2008–10; Man. Dir Credit Suisse 2011–12; Chair. Man. Bd and CEO Valovis Bank 2012–15; Lecturer, Goethe Business School, Frankfurt Univ. 2013–; Adjunct Prof. of Finance, Kellogg School of Man., Northwestern Univ. 2016–; mem. Bd of Dirs auxmoney GmbH; mem. Supervisory Bd Atradius NV, Amsterdam 2003–; mem. Advisory Bd Aquila Capital 2011–, Alceda Fund Man., SA 2015–16; Hon. Prof., (Koblenz School of Man.—WHU) 2005–. *Address:* Kellogg School of Management, Northwestern University, 2001 Sheridan Road, Evanston, IL 60208, USA (office). *Telephone:* (847) 491-3300 (office). *E-mail:* axel.wieandt@kellogg.northwestern.edu (office). *Website:* www.kellogg.northwestern.edu (office).

WIEDEKING, Wendelin, Diplom Ingenieur; German business executive; b. 28 Aug. 1952, Ahlen; m.; ed Aachen Univ. of Tech.; studied mechanical eng and worked as scientific asst Machine Tool Lab. Rhine-Westphalian Coll. of Advanced Tech. Aachen; Dir's Asst Production and Materials Man. Porsche AG 1983–88; Div. Man. Glyco Metall-Werke KG 1988, advanced to CEO and Chair. Bd of Man. 1990; Production Dir Porsche 1991, CEO 1992–2009, Chair. of Exec. Bd 1993–2009, also Pres.; Founder Tialini AG (chain of pizza and pasta restaurants) 2012; mem. Bd of Dirs Novartis AG, Eagle Picher Inc.; mem. Advisory Bd Signa Holdings; European Man. of the Year, European Business Press 2008. *Publications:* Das Davidprinzip, Anders ist Besser. *Website:* www.tialini.com.

WIEGHARDT, Karl Ernst, DipChem, PhD; German chemist and academic; *Director Emeritus, Max-Planck-Institut für Bioanorganische Chemie;* b. 25 July 1942, Göttingen; s. of Karl Eugen Wieghardt and Elisabeth Wieghardt (née Klinkenborg); m. Gertraud Willfahrt; one c.; ed Univ. of Heidelberg; Postdoctoral Fellow, Univ. Heidelberg 1969–72, Asst Prof. of Inorganic Chem., 1974–75; Postdoctoral Fellow, Univ. of Leeds, UK 1972; Assoc. Prof. of Inorganic Chem., Univ. of Hanover 1975–81; Prof. of Inorganic Chem., Ruhr-Univ. Bochum 1981–94, Hon. Prof. 1994–; Dir Max-Planck-Institut für Bioanorganische Chemie (now MPI für Chemische Energiekonversion), Mulheim 1994–2010, Emer. 2010–; mem. Gesellschaft Deutscher Chemiker; Alexander von Humboldt Research Award 1995, John Bailar Medal, Univ. of Illinois 2000, Wilhelm Klemm Medal, German Chemical Soc. 2000, RSC Centenary Medal 2002, ACS Inorganic Chemistry Award 2006. *Address:* Max-Planck-Institut für Chemische Energiekonversion, Stiftstrasse 34–36, Postfach 10 13 65, 45470 Mülheim an der Ruhr, Germany (office). *Telephone:* (208) 3063609 (office). *Fax:* (208) 3063952 (office). *E-mail:* karl.wieghardt@cec.mpg.de (office). *Website:* www.cec.mpg.de/emeriti.

WIEKER, Gen. Volker; German army officer; *Chief of Defence, Federal Armed Forces (Bundeswehr);* b. 1 March 1954, Delmenhorst, Lower Saxony; m. Sabine Wieker; two c.; ed Fed. Armed Forces Univ., Munich, Command and Gen. Staff Coll. (Führungsakademie), Hamburg, US Army Command and Gen. Staff Coll., Fort Leavenworth, Kan., USA; grad. engineer; joined Bundeswehr (Fed. Armed Forces) 1974, trained as artillery officer, 315 Armoured Artillery Bn, Wildeshausen, posts held include platoon leader, battery officer, battery commdr, later Asst Br. Chief, Personnel Div., Fed. Ministry of Defence, Bonn 1989, becoming G3 Staff Officer, 21 Armoured Brigade, Augustdorf, Commdr, 215 Armoured Artillery Bn 1993–96, Staff Officer for Training and Operations and Chief of Operations Centre, German Army Contingent, IFOR Multinational Force, Bosnia-Herzegovina 1996, Exec. Asst, Admin. Control, Fed. Ministry of Defence, Mil. Asst to Fed. Minister of Defence 1997–99, Commdr, Armoured Infantry Brigade 40 Mecklenburg, Schwerin 1999–2001, Commdr, Multinational Brigade S and Nat. Commdr in Theatre, 3rd KFOR Contingent, Kosovo June–Dec. 2001, Chief of Staff, Army Office in Cologne 2002–04, Chief of Staff in the Army Staff 2004–07, Deputy Commanding Gen., 1 German–Netherlands Corps, Münster 2007–08, Commanding Gen. 2008–09, Chief of Staff, Int. Security Assistance Force (ISAF), Afghanistan Oct. 2009–Jan. 2010, Chief of Defence, Fed. Armed Forces (Bundeswehr) 2010–; Gold Cross of Honour of the Bundeswehr 1999, Order of Merit of Bulgaria 2001, Officer, Legion of Merit (USA) 2010, Grand Officer, Royal Order of Merit (Norway) 2012, Hon Emblem of the Romanian Gen. Staff 2012, Order of Merit (Germany) 2013, Commdr's Cross with Star, Order of Merit (Hungary) 2015, Grand Decoration of Honour in Silver with Star for Service (Austria) 2015, Commdr, Legion of Merit 2015; Bundeswehr Foreign Duty Medal (IFOR) 1996, NATO Service Medal 1996, Bundeswehr Foreign Duty Medal (KFOR) 2001, Bundeswehr Foreign Duty Medal (ISAF) 2010, Medal of Merit in Gold (Netherlands) 2011, North Star Medal (Sweden) 2013. *Address:* Office of the Chief of Defence, Bundeswehr, Federal Ministry of Defence, Stauffenbergstr. 18, 10785 Berlin, Germany (office). *Telephone:* (30) 18240 (operator) (office). *E-mail:* poststelle@bmvg.bund.de (office). *Website:* www.bmvg.de (office).

WIELGUS, Archbishop Stanisław Wojciech; Polish ecclesiastic and professor of history of philosophy; b. 23 April 1939, Wierzchowiska; ed Catholic Univ. of Lublin, Univ. of Munich; ordained priest 1962; curate and parish catechist 1962–69; Prof., Catholic Univ. of Lublin 1969–, Pro-Rector 1988–92, Rector 1989–98; Bishop of Płock 1999–2006; apptd Archbishop of Warsaw Jan. 2007 (resgnd Jan. 2007), Archbishop Emer. 2007–; Head, Dept of the History of Philosophy in Poland, Head, Interdisciplinary Centre of the History of Medieval Culture; Head, Catholic Univ. of Lublin (KUL) Catholic Encyclopaedia Editing Offices; Vice-Pres. Conf. of Polish Univ. of Rectors 1990–93; del. Extraordinary Synod of European Bishops, Rome 1991; canon Lublin Cathedral Chapter; leader Coll. of Rectors, Lublin Region 1992–93; mem. Ethical Team of Scientific Research attached to Minister of Educ. 1998–; Chair. Educ. Council of the Nat. Conf. of Bishops in Poland 2001–; Chair. Council of the Polish Rectors Foundation 2001; mem. KUL Science Soc. (Gen. Sec. 1985–88), Acad. Council of the John Paul Second Inst., mem. numerous socs; Officer's Cross, Order of Polonia Restituta 1993; Award of the Minister of Nat. Educ., Catholic Soc. Civitas Christiana Award 1998, Honour of the Societas Scientiarum Lublinensis Resolutio Pro Laude 1999. *Publications:* Quaestiones Nicolai Peripatetici 1973, Benedykta Hessego Quaestiones super octo libros Physicorum Aristotelis 1983, Bible Research in Ancient Times and in the Middle Ages 1990, Foreign Biblical Literature in Medieval Poland 1990, Mediaeval Biblical Literature in the Polish Language 1991, Mediaeval Polish Bible Studies in the Latin Language 1992, From Research into the Middle Ages 1995, The Medieval Polish Doctrine of the Law of Nations: Jus Gentium 1998, Deo et Patriae, vol. 1 1996, vol. II 1999, Dobra jest więcej 2001, Na Skale budujmy nasz świat 2002, Z obszarów średniowiecznej mysli islamskiej, żydowskiej i chrzescijańskiej 2002, Filozofie w Rzeczypospolitej 2002, Ducha nie gaście 2004, Zachodnia i polska nauka średniowieczna 2005, Mocni w wierze 2005, Moja umilowana Ojczyzna 2010, Zyc prawdziwie 2010, Chrześcijaństwo zobowiązuje 2011, Stanąć po stronie Dobra 2013, Przestańcie się lękać! 2014, Tobie, Panie, zaufałem 2014. *Leisure interests:* factual literature, memoirs, film. *Address:* ul. Jana Pawla II, 11, 20-585 Lublin, Poland (home).

WIELICKI, Krzysztof; Polish mountaineer and business executive; b. 5 Jan. 1950, Szklarka Przygodzka; m.; one s. two d.; ed Tech. Univ. of Wrocław; owner of four commercial cos (distribution of alpine and outdoor equipment and garments) and mountain agencies; began climbing 1970; joined 27 high mountain expeditions including Dolomites, Alps, Caucasus, Pamir, Hindukush, Karakoram and Himalayas; leader of 12 expeditions; the fifth man in the world to climb all 14 8,000m peaks; first person to climb in winter: Mount Everest (with partner Leszek Cichy) 1980, Kanchenjunga 1986, Lhotse (solo) 1988; led climbing expedition on K-2 (Karakoram); mem. The Explorers' Club 1997–, Group de Haute Montagne (France) 2001–; Pres. Jury, Piolet d'Or 2004; Lowell Thomas Award 2001. *Publications:* Talks about Everest (co-author) 1980, The Crown of the Himalayas 1997. *Leisure interest:* travelling. *Website:* www.wielicki.wpthemes.pl.

WIELOWIEYSKI, Andrzej Jan, (Wir, Jan Nowak), LLM; Polish fmr politician, economist and publicist; b. 16 Dec. 1927, Warsaw; s. of Zbigniew Wielowieyski and Katarzyna Wielowieyska; m. Zofia Wielowieyska 1951; one s. six d.; ed Jagiellonian Univ., Kraków; trainee, Radomsko Forest Inspectorate 1942–44; mem. Wici Rural Youth Union (ZMW Wici) 1945–48; Head, Foreign Dept Bratnia Pomoc students' org. Jagiellonian Univ., Kraków 1946–47, mem., Club of Logofags 1946–47; subsequently councillor and inspector in Ministry of Finance 1948–52; Ed., Słowo Powszechne, Warsaw 1948; inspector, Head Office of Workers' Housing Estates Enterprise Warsaw-South, subsequently Warsaw-Śródmieście 1952–55; inspector, Head Urban Devt Dept, Municipal Comm. of Econ. Planning, Warsaw 1956–62; Head of Section Więź, Warsaw 1961–80; Lecturer, Doświadczenie i Przyszłość (Experience and the Future) Conversatorium, Warsaw 1978–82; Ed. Królowa Apostołów, Warsaw 1982–84, Gość Niedzielny, Katowice 1982–90; mem. Solidarity Ind. Self-governing Trade Union 1980–, adviser to Nat. Comm. of Solidarity 1980; Head of Social and Labour Study Centre attached to Nat. Comm. of Solidarity, Warsaw 1981; adviser to Nat. Executive Comm. of Solidarity 1987–89; mem. Civic Cttee attached to Lech Wałęsa (q.v.), Chair. of Solidarity 1987–90; participant Round Table plenary debates, Co-Chair. group for economy and social policy Feb.–April 1989; Senator 1989–91, 2001–05 (Pres. Freedom Union Group), Vice-Marshal of the Senate 1989–91, Deputy Speaker 2001–05; mem. European Parl. 2008–09; Chair. Civic Parl. Caucus of Senate 1989–90; Deputy to Sejm (Parl.) 1991–2001, fmr mem. Parl. Comm. Foreign Affairs; Polish del. and Vice-Pres. Council of Europe Parl. Ass. 1993–2005; Chair., Polish Council of European Movement 1993–2005, Asscn of Commons Metropolia Warszawa 2000–11; mem. Democratic Action of Civic Movement (ROAD), Democratic Union, Freedom Union 1990–2002; mem. Pax Romana Catholic Intelligentsia Int. Fed., mem. of Council 1979–83; mem. of European Council 1987–89; co-f. Int. Fed. of Family Life Promotion 1979–; Cross of Valour 1944, Silver Cross of Merit with Swords, Partisan Cross, Cross of Home Army (AK) 1946–50, Chevalier de la Legion d'Honneur 2003, Commdr's Cross, Order of Polonia Restituta 2006, Kt, Order of the White Eagle 2011. *Publications:* Przed trzecim przyśpieszeniem 1969, Przed nami małżeństwo 1972, Tajemnice i Niespodzianki Historii 2004, Na Rozdrożach Dziejów 2011, Losowi na Przekór 2015; over 400 articles on politics, religion, educ. and history. *Leisure interests:* gardening, skiing, yachting, historical and detective stories. *Address:* ul. Kłodzka 59, 04-913 Warsaw, Poland (home). *E-mail:* awielowieyski@tlen.pl (home).

WIEMAN, Carl Edwin, BS, PhD; American physicist and academic; *Professor of Physics and of the Graduate School of Education, Stanford University;* b. 26 March 1951, Corvallis, Ore.; s. of N. Orr and Alison Wieman; ed Massachusetts Inst. of Tech., Stanford Univ.; Asst Research Scientist, Dept of Physics, Univ. of Michigan 1977–79, Asst Prof. 1979–84; Assoc. Prof. of Physics, Univ. of Colorado, Boulder 1984–87, Prof. 1987–97, Distinguished Prof. 1997–2013, Fellow, Jt Inst. for Lab. Astrophysics 1985–2007, Chair. 1993–95, Presidential Teaching Scholar 2004–13, Dir Science Educ. Initiative 2006–13, Founder and Chair. of PhET; Prof. of Physics, Univ. of British Columbia 2007–13, Dir Carl Wieman Science Educ. Initiative 2007–13; Prof. of Physics and of Grad. School of Educ., Stanford Univ. 2013–; Assoc. Dir of Science, White House Office of Science and Tech. Policy 2010–12; mem. Advisory Bd USA Science and Eng Festival; mem. Optical Soc. of America, American Asscn of Physics Teachers, Nat. Acad. of Educ. 2008; Fellow, American Physical Soc. 1990, NAS 1995, American Acad. of Arts and Sciences 1998; Hon. DS (Univ. of Chicago) 1997; numerous awards, including Sloan Research Fellowship 1984, Guggenheim Fellowship 1990–91, E.O. Lawrence Award in Physics 1993, Fritz London Award 1996, King Faisal Int. Prize for Science 1997, Lorentz Medal 1998, Schawlow Prize for Laser Science 1999, Benjamin Franklin Medal in Physics 2000, Nobel Prize in Physics (shared with Eric Allin Cornell and Wolfgang Ketterle) 2001, named US Prof. of the Year, Carnegie Foundation for the Advancement of Teaching and Council for Advancement and Support of Educ. 2004 Oersted Medal, American Asscn of Physics Teachers 2007, Vollum Award for Distinguished Accomplishment in Science and Tech., Reed Coll. 2009, Science Educ. Research Award, Council of Scientific Socs 2011, Presidential Citation for Lifetime Achievement, Nat. Science Teachers Asscn 2012. *Address:* Department of Physics, Stanford University, 382 Via Pueblo Mall, Stanford, CA 94305-4060, USA (office). *Telephone:* (650) 497-3491 (office). *E-mail:* cwieman@stanford.edu (office). *Website:* physics.stanford.edu/people/faculty/carl-wieman (office).

WIESCHAUS, Eric Francis, BS, PhD; American molecular biologist and academic; *Squibb Professor in Molecular Biology, Princeton University;* b. 8 June 1947, South Bend, Ind.; s. of Leroy Joseph Wieschaus and Marcella Carner Wieschaus; m. Gertrud (Trudi) Schüpbach 1982; three d.; ed John Carroll Catholic High School, Birmingham, Ala, Univ. of Notre Dame, Yale Univ.; Research Fellow, Zoological Inst., Univ. of Zurich 1975–78; Group Leader European Molecular Biology Lab., Germany 1978–81; Asst Prof. then Assoc. Prof., Princeton Univ. 1981–87, Prof. of Biology 1987–, Squibb Prof. in Molecular Biology 2005–; Adjunct Prof. of Biochemistry, Robert Wood Johnson Medical School, Univ. of Medicine and Dentistry of New Jersey 2005–; Prof. of Molecular Biology, Lewis-Sigler Inst. for Integrative Genomics; Visiting Researcher, Center for Pathobiology, Univ. of California, Irvine 1977; Fellow, Laboratoire de Génétique Moléculaire, France; mem. Damon Runyon-Walter Winchell Cancer Fund 1987–92; mem. NAS; Fellow, AAAS; Nobel Prize for Medicine and Physiology (shared with Edward B. Lewis and Christiane Nüsslein-Volhard) 1995. *Publications:* numerous articles. *Address:* Moffett Lab-435, Department of Molecular Biology, Princeton University, Princeton, NJ 08544, USA (office). *Telephone:* (609) 258-5383 (office); (609) 258-5401 (Lab.) (office). *E-mail:* efw@princeton.edu (office). *Website:* molbio.princeton.edu/faculty/molbio-faculty/140-wieschaus (office); www.molbio1.princeton.edu/wieschaus (office).

WIESE, Christoffel Hendrik, BA, LLB, CA; South African business executive; *Chairman, Shoprite Holdings Ltd;* b. 10 Sept. 1941; m.; three c.; ed Univs of Cape Town, Stellenbosch; Exec. Dir Pep Stores 1967–73; Dir (non-exec.) Shoprite Holdings Ltd 1979–, Chair. 1991–; Chair. and Dir (non-exec.) Pepkor Ltd 1981–; Chair., Instore plc 1994–2008, Tradehold Ltd 2000–14, African Dawn Capital Ltd 2011, Orion Selections Holdings Ltd, Industrial Devt Corpn of South Africa Ltd, Smart Centre Holdings, BoE (Pty) Ltd, Brown and Jackson plc, Pepgro Ltd; mem. Bd of Dirs Invicta Holdings Ltd 2004–, Chair. (non-exec.) 2006–; mem. Bd of Dirs KWV Holdings Ltd –2009, Brait SA Ltd 2011–, Primedia (Pty) Ltd, PSG Financial Services Ltd 2007–12, New Look Retail Group Ltd 2015–18, Metropolitan Life Ltd, Monex Group of Cos, Titan Financial Services, Co-Operative Winegrowers of South Africa, Lenco Holdings Ltd, Luna Group (Pty) Ltd; mem. Supervisory Bd Steinhoff International Holdings NV 2015–17, Chair. 2016–17; Owner, Lanzerac Manor and Winery, Stellenbosch, Lourensford Estate (wine producer); also owns pvt. game reserve in Kalahari Desert; Dr hc (Univ. of Stellenbosch); Diagonal Strategic Communicator of the Year, Marketing Man. of the Year, Inst. of Marketing Man., Business Leader of the Year, Cape Town Sakekamer, Pioneer of the 20th Century Award, South African Council of Shopping Centres, MS Louw Award for Exceptional Business Achievements. *Address:* Shoprite Holdings Ltd, PO Box 215, Brackenfell, Cape Town 7561, South Africa (office). *Telephone:* (21) 9804000 (office). *Fax:* (21) 9804050 (office). *Website:* www.shopriteholdings.co.za (office).

WIESEL, Torsten Nils, MD; Swedish neurobiologist, university administrator and academic; *President Emeritus and Vincent and Brooke Astor Professor Emeritus, The Rockefeller University;* b. 3 June 1924, Uppsala, Sweden; ed Karolinska Inst. Stockholm; Instructor, Karolinska Inst. 1954–55; Asst, Karolinska Hosp. 1954–55; Fellow in Ophthalmology, Johns Hopkins Univ. Medical School, Baltimore, Md, USA 1955–58, Asst Prof. of Ophthalmic Physiology 1958–59; Assoc. in Neurophysiology/Neuropharmacology, Harvard Medical School, Boston 1959–60, Asst Prof. 1960–64, Asst Prof. Dept of Psychiatry 1964–67, Prof. of Physiology 1967–68, Prof. of Neurobiology 1968–74, Chair. Dept of Neurobiology 1973–82, Robert Winthrop Prof. of Neurobiology 1974–83; Vincent & Brooke Astor Prof. and Head, Lab. of Neurobiology, The Rockefeller Univ. New York 1983–2001, Gen. Sec. Human Frontier Science Program 2000–09, Pres. The Rockefeller Univ. 1991–98, Pres. Emer. 1998–; Pres. Int. Brain Research Org. 1999–2005; Dir Shelby White & Leon Levy Center for Mind, Brain and Behavior 1999–; Chair. Borderline Personality Disorder Research Foundation 2001–02, New York Acad. of Sciences 2001–; Chair. Bd Govs, Okinawa Inst. of Science and

Tech. 2002–; mem. American Physiology Soc., American Acad. of Arts and Sciences, AAAS, NAS etc.; Foreign mem. Royal Soc.; Nobel Prize in Physiology or Medicine 1981, Nat. Medal of Science 2005; numerous other honours and awards. *Publications include:* more than 80 articles in medical journals. *Address:* The Rockefeller University, 1230 York Avenue, New York, NY 10065, USA (office). *Telephone:* (212) 327-7093 (office). *Fax:* (212) 327-8988 (office). *E-mail:* wiesel@rockefeller.edu (office). *Website:* www.rockefeller.edu/research/faculty/labheads/TorstenWiesel (office); www.nobelprize.org/nobel_prizes/medicine/laureates/1981/wiesel-autobio.html (office).

WIESENDANGER, Roland, PhD (Habil.); German (b. Swiss) physicist and academic; *Professor of Experimental Solid State Physics, University of Hamburg;* b. 5 Oct. 1961, Basel, Switzerland; ed Univ. of Basel; Pvt. Lecturer, Univ. of Basel 1991–92; Ordinary Prof. of Experimental Solid State Physics, Univ. of Hamburg 1992–, foundation and extension of the Microstructure Advanced Research Centre 1993–, Man. Dir Inst. of Applied Physics 2003–12, Vice-Dean, Dept of Physics 2003–04; Chair. Nanoscience and Tech. Div., German Vacuum Soc. 1996–2004, Nanoscience and Tech. Div., Int. Union for Vacuum Science, Techniques and Applications 1998–2001; Co-ordinator, German Centre of Competence in Nanotechnology 'Nanoanalytics' 1998–2003 and 'HanseNanoTec' 2003–06; Scientific Co-ordinator, Interdisciplinary Nanoscience Centre, Hamburg 2001–; Speaker and Scientific Co-ordinator, DFG Collaborative Research Centre 2006–17; Speaker and Scientific Co-ordinator, Hamburg Cluster of Excellence 'Nanospintronics' 2009–12; Chair. Int. Cttee for Nanoscience and Nanotechnology 2010–13; Co-Ed. Springer Series in Nanoscience and Technology; mem. German Acad. of Sciences Leopoldina 2000, German Acad. of Tech. Sciences acatech 2008, Polish Acad. of Sciences 2013; Founder-mem. Hamburg Acad. of Sciences 2005; Fellow, American Vacuum Soc. 2012; Int. Fellow, Surface Science Soc. of Japan 2015; Hon. Prof., Harbin Inst. of Tech., China 2012; Dr hc (Poznań Univ. of Tech., Poland) 2015; Gaede Prize, German Vacuum Soc. 1992, Max Auwärter Prize 1992, Kepler Lecturer, Univ. of Tübingen 1998, Karl Heinz Beckurts Prize 1999, Kronig Lecturer, Delft Univ. of Technology, The Netherlands 2001, Philip Morris Research Prize (co-recipient) 2003, Kavli Lecturer, California Inst. of Tech., USA 2007, Advanced Grant, European Research Council (ERC) 2008, AVS Nanotechnology Recognition Award 2010, Zernike Lecturer, Univ. of Groningen, The Netherlands 2011, ERC Advanced Grant 2013, Distinguished iNANO Lecturer, Univ. of Aarhus, Denmark 2013, Heinrich Rohrer Grand Medal and Prize 2014, Hamburg Science Prize, Hamburg Acad. of Sciences 2015, Distinguished Lecturer, Dresden Univ. of Tech. 2015, Julius Springer Prize for Applied Physics (co-recipient) 2016. *Publications:* two textbooks, ed. or co-ed. of eight books and seven conf. proceedings, 30 review papers and book chapters and 550 papers in professional journals. *Address:* Room 302, Department of Physics, University of Hamburg, Jungiusstr. 11A, 20355 Hamburg, Germany (office). *Telephone:* (40) 428385244 (office). *Fax:* (40) 428386188 (office). *E-mail:* wiesendanger@physnet.uni-hamburg.de (office). *Website:* www.nanoscience.de/HTML/group/wiesendanger.html (office).

WIGDERSON, Avi, BSc, MSE, MA, PhD; Israeli computer scientist and academic; *Herbert H. Maass Professor, School of Mathematics, Institute for Advanced Study;* b. 9 Sept. 1956; m.; three c.; ed Technion-Israel Inst. of Tech., Princeton Univ., NJ, USA; Visiting Asst Prof., Prof., Dept of Computer Science, Univ. of California, Berkeley 1983–84; Visiting Scientist, IBM Research, San José, Calif. 1984–85; Fellow, Math. Sciences Research Inst., Berkeley 1985–86; Sr Lecturer, Dept of Computer Science, Hebrew Univ. of Jerusalem 1986–87, Assoc. Prof. (with tenure) 1987–92, Prof., Computer Science Inst. 1991–2003, Chair. Computer Science Inst. 1993–95; Visiting Assoc. Prof., Dept of Computer Science, 1990–92, Prof., Computer Science Inst. 1991–2003; Visiting Prof., Inst. for Advanced Study (IAS), Princeton and Dept of Computer Science, Princeton Univ. 1995–96, Prof., School of Math., IAS 1999–2003, Herbert H. Maass Prof. 2003–; Rothschild Visiting Fellow, Isaac Newton Inst. 2011; mem. Editorial Bd Society for Industrial and Applied Mathematics (SIAM) Journal on Discrete Mathematics, Information and Computation, Complexity Theory; mem. American Acad. of Arts and Sciences 2011, NAS 2013; Pres.'s List of Excellence, The Technion 1977–80, IBM Grad. Fellowship, Princeton Univ. 1982–83, Alon Fellowship 1986–89, Bergman Fellowship 1989, Invited Speaker, Int. Congress of Mathematicians, Kyoto 1990, Zurich 1994, Nevanlinna Prize 1994, Yoram Ben-Porat Presidential Prize for Outstanding Research, ICM Plenary Lecturer, Madrid 2006, Gibbs Lecturer, San Diego 2008, Conant Prize 2008, Gödel Prize 2009, Fields Inst. Distinguished Lecture Series 2010. *Publications:* more than 150 articles in math. journals on complexity theory, parallel computation, combinatorics and graph theory, combinatorial optimization algorithms, randomness and cryptography, distributed and neural networks. *Address:* Simonyi Hall 013, School of Mathematics, Institute for Advanced Study, Einstein Drive, Princeton, NJ 08540, USA (office). *Telephone:* (609) 734-8115 (office). *E-mail:* avi@math.ias.edu (office); avi@ias.edu (office). *Website:* www.math.ias.edu/avi (office); www.ias.edu/people/faculty-and-emeriti/wigderson (office).

WIGEMARK, Lars-Gunnar, AB, MA; Swedish diplomatist; *Head of Delegation to Bosnia and Herzegovina and Special Representative, European Union;* b. 20 March 1960, Gothenburg; ed Harvard Univ. and Fletcher School of Law and Diplomacy, Tufts Univ., USA; joined Foreign Service 1988, postings to Belgrade, Washington, DC, Brussels and Kabul, Deputy Head and Minister, Embassy in Moscow 2003–07; Head of Security Policy Unit, EC, Brussels 2008–10, with External Action Service, EU, Brussels 2010–11, apptd as one of first EU Ambs under Treaty of Lisbon 2010, Head of EU Del. to Pakistan 2011–14, Head of EU Del. to Bosnia and Herzegovina and EU Special Rep. 2015–. *Address:* Delegation of the European Union to Bosnia and Herzegovina and European Union Special Representative, 71000 Sarajevo, Skenderija 3A, Bosnia and Herzegovina (office). *Telephone:* (33) 254700 (Del.) (office); (33) 560800 (EU Special Rep.) (office). *Fax:* (33) 666037 (Del.) (office); (33) 668390 (EU Special Rep.) (office). *E-mail:* delegation-bih@eeas.europa.eu (office). *Website:* europa.ba (office).

WIGGINS, Sir Bradley Marc, Kt, CBE, OBE; British fmr professional road and track racing cyclist; b. 28 April 1980, Ghent, Belgium; s. of Gary Wiggins and Linda Wiggins; m. Cath Wiggins; one s. one d.; ed St Augustine's Church of England High School; began racing at South London's Herne Hill Velodrome aged 12, represented Camden in London Youth Games; began career as track cyclist (specialized in pursuit and madison events), later took to road cycling; turned professional with Francaise des Jeux team 2002; silver medal, team pursuit, 100m, Commonwealth Games, Kuala Lumpur 1998; bronze medal, team pursuit, Olympics Games, Sydney 2000; silver medal, team pursuit, Union Cycliste Internationale (UCI) World Championships (track cycling), Manchester 2000; silver medal, team pursuit, UCI World Championships (track cycling), Antwerp 2001; silver medal, 4km individual pursuit, team pursuit, 100m, Commonwealth Games, Manchester 2002; bronze medal, team pursuit, UCI World Championships (track cycling), Copenhagen 2002; gold medal, 4km individual pursuit, silver medal, team pursuit, UCI World Championships (track cycling), Stuttgart 2003; gold medal, 4km individual pursuit, silver medal, team pursuit, bronze medal, madison, Olympics Games, Athens 2004; gold medal, 4km individual pursuit, gold medal, team pursuit, UCI World Championships (track cycling), Palma de Mallorca 2007; gold medal, 4km individual pursuit, team pursuit, Olympics Games, Beijing 2008; gold medal, 4km individual pursuit, team pursuit, Madison, UCI World Championships (track cycling), Manchester 2008; UCI World Championships (road cycling): silver medal, individual time trial; UCI Road World Championships 2011, 2013; gold medal, road time trial, Olympics Games, London 2012; gold medal, road time trial, UCI Road World Championships 2014, Track World Championship (with Mark Cavendish) 2016, Team Pursuit, Olympic Games, Rio 2016, Six Days of Ghent (with Mark Cavendish) 2016; winner: British Nat. Time Trial Championships 2009, Herald Sun Tour 2009, Nat. Time Trial Champion 2009, 2010, British Nat. Road Race Championships 2011, Critérium du Dauphiné 2011, 2012, Paris–Nice 2012, Tour de Romandie 2012, Olympic Time Trial Champion 2012, Tour de France (first British cyclist, also two individual stages) 2012, Tour of Britain 2013; set new hour record with a distance of 54.526km (33.881mi) 2015; only cyclist to have won Tour de France and an Olympic gold medal in the same year; teams: Linda McCartney Racing Team 2001, Française des Jeux 2002–03, Crédit Agricole 2004–05, Cofidis 2006–07, Team High Road 2008, Garmin-Slipstream 2009, Team Sky 2010–16; Bradley Wiggins X Fred Perry Collaboration clothing range launched 2012; f. Bradley Wiggins Foundation 2012; coached by Rod Ellingworth; retd from all forms of professional cycling Dec. 2016; inducted into London Youth Games Hall of Fame 2010, BBC Sports Personality of the Year 2012. *Publication:* In Pursuit of Glory (autobiography) 2008. *Leisure interests:* owns a collection of classic motor scooters and guitars from the 1960s and 1970s, supports Liverpool Football Club and Wigan Warriors rugby league club, spending time with family. *Address:* M&C SaatchiMerlin, 36 Golden Square, London, W1F 9EE, England (office); Bradley Wiggins Foundation, Suite 19, Hattersley House, Hattersley Court, Ormskirk, L39 2AY, England. *E-mail:* enquiries@mcsaatchimerlin.com (office). *Website:* www.bradleywigginsfoundation.org.

WIGGINS, David, MA, FBA; British academic; *Professor Emeritus, University of Oxford;* b. 8 March 1933, London; s. of Norman Wiggins and Diana Wiggins (née Priestley); m. 1st Hideko Ishiguro 1969 (separated 1973); m. 2nd Jennifer Hornsby 1980 (separated 1987); one s.; m. 3rd Phillida Gili (née Stone) 2010; ed St Paul's School and Brasenose Coll., Oxford; Asst Prin. Colonial Office 1957–58; Jane Eliza Procter Visiting Fellow, Princeton Univ. 1958–59; Lecturer, New Coll., Oxford 1959, Fellow and Lecturer 1960–67; Prof. of Philosophy, Bedford Coll., London 1967–78; Fellow and Praelector in Philosophy, Univ. Coll., Oxford 1981–89; Prof. of Philosophy, Birkbeck Coll., London 1989–94, Visiting Prof. 2008–10; Wykeham Prof. of Logic, New Coll., Oxford Univ. 1993–94, now Prof. Emer.; visiting appointments at Stanford Univ. 1964, 1965, Harvard Univ. 1968, 1972, All Souls Coll., Oxford 1973, Princeton Univ. 1980, Univ. Coll., Oxford 1989–; Findlay Visiting Prof., Boston Univ. 2001; Fellow, Center for Advanced Study in Behavioral Sciences, Stanford 1985–86; mem. Independent Comm. on Transport 1973–74, Cen. Transport Consultative Cttee; Chair. Transport Users' Consultative Cttee for South-East 1977–79; Foreign Hon. mem. American Acad. of Arts and Sciences 1992, Hon. Fellow, Brasenose Coll. 2010; Dr hc (York) 2005. *Publications:* Identity and Spatio Temporal Continuity 1967, Truth, Invention and the Meaning of Life 1978, Sameness and Substance 1980, Needs, Values, Truth 1987, Sameness and Substance Renewed 2001, Ethics: Twelve Lectures on the Philosophy of Morality 2006, Univ. of Kansas Lindley Lecture: Solidarity at the Root of the Ethical 2008; articles in learned journals. *Address:* New College, Oxford, OX1 3BN, England. *Telephone:* (20) 7584-9009.

WIGLEY, Baron (Life Peer), cr. 2011, of Caernarfon in the County of Gwynedd; **Dafydd Wigley,** PC, BSc; Welsh politician, writer and business executive; b. (David Wigley), 1 April 1943, Derby, England; s. of Elfyn Edward Wigley and Myfanwy Wigley (née Batterbee); m. Elinor Bennett Owen 1967; three s. (two deceased) one d.; ed Sir Hugh Owen School, Caernarfon, Rydal School, Colwyn Bay, Victoria Univ. of Manchester; Econ. Analyst, Ford Motor Co. 1964–67; Chief Cost Accountant, Mars Ltd 1967–71; Financial Controller, Hoover Ltd 1971–74; Pres. S Caernarfon Creamery 1987–2002; Co. Borough Councillor, Merthyr Tydfil 1972–74; Vice-Chair. Plaid Cymru 1972–74, Pres. (Party Leader) 1981–84, 1991–2000, Hon. Pres. 2001–; MP for Caernarfon 1974–2001, Ass. Mem. 1999–2003; Chair. All Party House of Commons Reform Group 1983, Vice-Chair. All-Party Disablement Group 1992–2001; Vice-Chair. Parl. Social Services Group 1985–88; mem. Nat. Ass. for Wales 1999, Leader of the Opposition 1999–2000, Chair. Audit Cttee of Nat. Ass. 2002; Chair. Ymddiriedolaeth Hybu Gwydoniaeth 2002, now retd; Pres. Spastic Soc. of Wales 1985–90, Mencap Wales 1991–; Pres. Nat. Library of Wales 2007–11; Vice-Pres. Welsh Asscn of Community Councils 1978–2001, Nat. Fed. of Industrial Devt Authorities 1981–2001; Sponsor, Disabled Persons Act 1981; Chair. Alpha Dyffryn Cyf/Ltd 1980–91; Dir (non-exec.), Gwernafalau Cyf/Ltd 2001–; Pro-Chancellor Univ. of Wales 2003–06; mem. (Plaid Cymru) House of Lords 2011–; Freeman of the Borough of Arfon 1994, Royal Town of Caernafon 2001; Hon. mem. Gorsedd of Welsh Bards; Hon. Fellow, Univ. of N Wales Bangor 1995, Hon. Pres., Plaid Cymru; Hon. LLD (Univ. of Wales) 2002; Grimshaw Memorial Award, Nat. Fed. of the Blind 1982. *Publications:* An Economic Plan for Wales 1970, O Ddifri 1992, Dal Ati 1993, A Democratic Wales in a United Europe 1995, A Real Choice for Wales 1996, Maen i'r Wal 2001, Be Nesa! (autobiog.) 2013. *Leisure interests:* football, tennis, chess, hill walking, writing. *Address:* c/o Rhian Medi Roberts (PA), Room 4/1, Norman Shaw North, House of Lords, Victoria Embankment, London, SW1A 1AA (office); House of Lords, Westminster, London, SW1A 0PW, England; Hen Efail, Bontnewydd, Caernarfon, Gwynedd, LL54 7YH, Wales (home). *Telephone:* (20) 7219-5021 (office). *Fax:* (20) 7219-5979. *E-mail:* wigleyd@parliament.uk (office); dafydd.wigley@hotmail.com (home).

WIGZELL, Hans Lennart Rudolf, MD, PhD; Swedish physician, immunologist, academic and company director; *Professor Emeritus of Immunology, Karolinska Institute;* b. 28 Oct. 1938, Stockholm; m. Kerstin Largell 1964; one s. three d.; ed Karolinska Inst., Stockholm; Prof. of Immunology, Uppsala Univ. 1972–82; Prof. of Immunology, Karolinska Inst. 1982–2003, Prof. Emer. 2003–, Pres. 1995–2003, fmr Dir Centre for Medical Innovation; Dir Nat. Bacteriological Lab., Stockholm 1988–; Chair. Nobel Cttee, Karolinska Inst. 1990–92; Chair. Nobel Cttee 1990–92, Nobel Ass. 2000, Stockholm School of Entrepreneurship; scientific adviser to Govt of Sweden 1999–; one of 11 appointed Advisors to the EU Commr for research on life science issues; Chair. Karolinska Devt AB 2006–13; fmr Chair. WHO-UNAIDS Vaccine Advisory Cttee 2002–; fmr Sec.-Gen. Swedish Inst. for Infectious Disease Control; fmr Dir-Gen. Nat. Bacteriological Lab., Stockholm; mem. Council of Trustees, TuBerculosis Vaccine Initiative; mem. Bd of Dirs Sobi AB, Biovitrum AB, uMabs (Switzerland), RaySearch Laboratories AB 2004–, Apogee Technology, Inc. 2005–, Intercell AG 2006–, Mertiva AB 2006–, Probi AB 2007–10, Sarepta Therapeutics Inc. 2010–; mem. editorial bds of several int. journals; mem. Royal Acad. of Sciences, Royal Swedish Acad. of Eng Sciences, Finnish Soc. of Sciences and Letters, Danish Acad. of Sciences and Letters, European Molecular Biology Org., Academia Europea, American Acad. of Arts and Sciences; Hon. mem. American Asscn of Immunologists; Dr hc (Univ. Tor Vergata, Rome), (Univ. of Turku, Finland); Anders Jahres Medical Prize, Oslo 1975, Erik Fernström Prize for Young Scientists, Uppsala 1979, Russel Weiser Lecturer Prize, Smith Lecture Award. *Play:* The Gene Scene 1989. *Publications:* more than 700 scientific articles, textbooks and popular science books. *Leisure interests:* music, nature, tropical plants, Japanese carp. *Address:* Karolinska Institute, Department of Microbiology, Tumor and Cell Biology, C1, Martin Rottenberg group, Box 280, Nobels Väg 16, 171 77 Stockholm, Sweden (office). *Telephone:* (8) 52486680 (office). *Fax:* (8) 31-11-01 (office). *E-mail:* hans.wigzell@ki.se (office); hans.wigzell@mtc.ki.se (office). *Website:* ki.se/mtc (office).

WIIG, Ole, BArch, MArch; Norwegian architect; *Architectural Director and Chairman, NSW Arkitektur;* b. 22 Oct. 1946, Trondheim; s. of Thorvald Wiig and Esther-Marie Wiig; m. 1st Alison Wiig 1972; two d.; m. 2nd Cathrine Lerche 2002; ed Harvard Univ., USA, Univs of Manchester and Dundee, UK; joined Kallmann, McKinnel & Wood, Boston 1973; Community Design Services, Boston 1974; City Architects Dept, Edin. 1974–80; Lecturer and Studio Critic, Dept of Architecture, Univ. of Edin. 1979–80, Visiting Lecturer and Studio Critic 1999–2000; External Examiner, Dept of Architecture, Dublin Inst. of Tech. 2000–04; Founding Partner, Narud-Stokke-Wiig AS 1979–, (restructured as NSW Arkitektur), later Sr Partner, now Architectural Dir and Chair.; Pres. Nat. Asscn of Norwegian Architects 1990–94; Pres. Council Colletta di Castelbianco, Italy; lecturer at univs and confs in Europe and USA; initiated Ligurian Int. Workshop for architecture students; mem. RIBA, Royal Incorporation of Architects, Scotland; British Tourist Authority Certificate of Distinction, Museum of the Year Award, Edin. Civic Trust Award 1981, RIBA Award, Civic Trust Award, Disabled Design Award 1983, Homansbyen Environmental Award 1991, Nordic Copper Award 1994, First Prize Int. Competition for Scottish Architecture and Design Centre 1995; several first prizes in Norwegian and int. architecture competitions. *Publications:* numerous articles on architecture and planning topics in books, newspapers and magazines. *Leisure interest:* introducing modern architecture and design into medieval Italian villages. *Address:* NSW Arkitektur, Rådhusgaten 27, 0158, Oslo (office); Bryggegaten 16, 0250 Oslo, Norway (home). *Telephone:* 93-00-41-86 (office); 22-83-41-01 (home). *Fax:* 22-83-21-86 (home). *E-mail:* ow@nsw.no (office). *Website:* www.nsw.no (office).

WIJAYATHILAKE, Yuwanjana Wanasundera, LLM; Sri Lankan lawyer and government official; s. of S.R. Wijayathilake; ed Ananda Coll., Sri Lanka Law Coll., Kings Coll., London, UK; enrolled as Attorney-at-Law of Supreme Court 1979; joined Attorney-Gen.'s Dept 1980 as State Counsel, subsequently promoted to Sr State Counsel, Deputy Solicitor Gen., Additional Solicitor Gen. and Solicitor Gen. 2012–14, Attorney-Gen. 2014–16 (retd); apptd Pres.'s Counsel 2007; admitted as Solicitor of England and Wales 1988.

WIJDENBOSCH, Jules Albert, PhD; Suriname fmr head of state; b. 2 May 1941, Paramaribo; one d.; customs officer 1962–66; civil servant, Municipality of Amsterdam 1966–81; mem. State Cttee on Remigration of Surinamese est. by Dutch Govt 1978–81; sr civil servant, Ministry of Dist Admin. and Decentralization 1981, Under-Dir in charge of Bureau for Decentralization of Admin. 1983, Dir of Dist Admin, Ministry of Dist Admin and Decentralization and Nat. Mobilization 1985; Minister of Home Affairs, Dist Admin and Nat. Mobilization and Minister of Justice and Police 1986–87; Prime Minister, Minister of Gen. Affairs and Minister of Foreign Affairs 1987–88; sr civil servant, Ministry of Regional Devt 1988–91; Vice-Pres. Repub. of Suriname and Minister of Finance Jan.–Sept. 1991, Pres. 1996–2000; first Chair. Nationale Democratische Partij (NDP) 1987–91, Deputy Chair. 1992–96, mem. Nat. Ass. and Floor Leader NDP 1991, political coordinator in Saramacca 2014; Chair. Union of Customs Officers 1962–66; Chair. Surinamese Basketball Fed., Deputy Chair. Surinamese Football Fed.; mem. Editorial Bd Lanti; Grand Master, Order of the Yellow Star, Order of the Palm. *Publications:* Schets voor de Republiek Suriname eigen stijl (A Personal View of the Republic of Suriname) 1974, Bestuurlijke organisatie in een leefgemeenschap (Administrative Organisation in Surinamese Society) 1980, Politieke orde en legitimiteit (Political Order and Legitimacy) 1981, Statuut van het Koninkrijk der Nederlanden (Charter for the Kingdom of the Netherlands) 1979, Participatie in een waarachtige democratie (Participating in a Modern Democracy) 1983.

WIJEGUNARATNE, Adm. Ravindra (Ravi) C., BSc, MPhil; Sri Lankan naval officer; *Chief of Defence Staff;* m. Yamuna de Saram; one s.; ed Royal Coll., Colombo, Karachi Univ., Pakistan, Univ. of Madras, India, Naval and Maritime Acad., Trincomalee, Britannia Royal Naval Coll., Dartmouth, UK; joined Sri Lankan Navy as officer cadet 1980, has held various command, operational and staff positions, command positions include Commdr, SLNS Sayura, helped establish then commanded Special Boat Squadron (SBS) and led numerous SBS operations, staff assignments include as Commdt Naval and Maritime Acad., Flag Officer Commdg Naval Fleet, First Sec. and Defence Adviser, High Comm. in New Delhi, Dir of Naval Operations, Special Forces and Maritime Surveillance,

Commdr, Southern Naval Area, Commdr Western Naval Area, Commdr Northern Naval Area, Commdr Eastern Naval Area, Dir-Gen., Sri Lanka Coast Guard, Chief of Staff of Navy 2014–15, Commdr of the Navy 2015–16; Chief of Defence Staff 2017–, also promoted to rank of Adm.; Pres. Naval Golf Club; fmr Pres. Nat. Rifle Asscn; Weerodara Vibhushanaya, Rana Wickrama Padakkama (twice), Rana Sura Padakkama, Vishista Seva Vibhushanaya, Uttama Seva Padakkama. *Address:* Office of Chief of Defence Staff, Block No.5, Buddhaloka Mawatha, Colombo 7, Sri Lanka (office). *Telephone:* (11) 2674503 (office). *Fax:* (11) 2674506 (office). *E-mail:* ocds@army.lk (office); ocdsmail@gmail.com (office). *Website:* www.ocds.lk (office).

WIJERS, G(erardus) J(ohannes) (Hans), MA, PhD; Dutch business executive; *Chairman of the Supervisory Board, Heineken NV;* b. 11 Jan. 1951, Oostburg; ed Univ. of Groningen, Erasmus Univ. of Rotterdam; Asst Prof. of Econs, Erasmus Univ. of Rotterdam 1976–82; participation in two think-tanks for govt ministers 1982–84; sr consultant and partner for various consulting firms 1984–86; Man.-Partner Horringa and De Koning 1986–93; Man.-Partner Amsterdam Office, Boston Consulting Group (BCG) 1993–94; Minister for Econ. Affairs 1994–98; Sr Vice-Pres. BCG and Chair. Dutch Office 1999–2002; adviser to Man. Bd AkzoNobel NV 2002, mem. Bd 2002–12, Chair. Man. Bd and CEO AkzoNobel NV 2003–12; Chair. Supervisory Bd Heineken NV 2013–, AFC Ajax NV; Chair. Oranje Fonds, Ubbo Emmius Fund Foundation at Univ. of Groningen; Dir (non-exec.), Royal Dutch Shell plc 2009–, Deputy Chair. and Sr Ind. Dir 2014–; Dir (non-exec.), GlaxoSmithKline plc 2013–; Vice-Pres. Young Pianist Foundation; mem. Bd of Dirs Concertgebouw; mem. European Roundtable of Industrialists. *Address:* Heineken NV, Global Corporate Relations, PO Box 28, 1000 AA Amsterdam (office); Heineken NV, Tweede Weteringplantsoen 21, 1017 ZD Amsterdam, The Netherlands (office). *Telephone:* (20) 523-92-39 (office). *Fax:* (20) 626-35-03 (office). *E-mail:* info@theheinekencompany.com (office). *Website:* www.theheinekencompany.com (office).

WIJN, Joannes Gerardus (Joop), MA, LLM; Dutch business executive and politician; b. 20 May 1969, Haarlem; ed Univ. of Amsterdam; worked while a student as an intern with Royal Dutch Shell in Jakarta, Indonesia; taught course for entrepreneurs Schoevers Acad., Amsterdam 1989–94, also taught course in marketing at Netherlands Marketing Inst. and course in business econs at sr secondary vocational level 1991–94; owned and operated personnel recruitment agency, Amsterdam 1992–94; trainee then Investment Man., ABN AMRO Private Equity 1994–98, joined Man. Dir Bd ABN AMRO and Fortis Bank Nederland Transition Team responsible for integration of ABN AMRO and Fortis Bank Nederland up to 1 April 2010 2009–; mem. (Christen-Democratisch Appèl—Christian Democratic Appeal) House of Reps of the States Gen. 1998–2002; Sec. of State for Econ. Affairs 2002–03, for Finance 2003–06, Cabinet Minister for Econ. Affairs 2006–07; Sr Exec. Vice-Pres., Rabobank 2007–09; Chair. Oranje Fonds; mem. Supervisory Bd, Schiphol Group, Royal Jaarbeurs Utrecht (Congress and Meeting Centre, Fairs and Events), Stadsherstel Amsterdam; mem. Bd VNO-NCW (Confed. of Netherlands Industry and Employers). *Address:* ABN AMRO Bank NV, Gustav Mahlerlaan 10, 1082 PP Amsterdam, The Netherlands (office). *Telephone:* (10) 2411720 (office). *E-mail:* info@abnamro.com (office). *Website:* www.abnamro.com (office).

WIJNHOLDS, Johannes de Beaufort (Onno), MA, PhD; Dutch banker, international civil servant and economist; b. 24 Oct. 1943, Amsterdam; s. of Heiko W. de Beaufort Wijnholds and Benudina M. de Beaufort Wijnholds; m. Jolanthe de Graaf 1968; one s. one d.; ed Univ. of Amsterdam; economist, De Nederlandsche Bank, Amsterdam 1968, various positions in bank 1974–84, Deputy Exec. Dir 1987–94; Asst to Exec. Dir IBRD and IMF, Washington, DC 1972–74, Alt. Exec. Dir IMF 1985–87, Exec. Dir 1994–2003; Perm. Rep. of European Cen. Bank, Washington, DC and its Observer at the IMF –2008; Alt. mem. Social Econ. Council of the Netherlands 1987–94; Prof. of Money and Banking, Univ. of Groningen 1992–95; Order of the Duke of Branimir (Croatia) 2003. *Publications:* The Need for International Reserves and Credit Facilities 1977, The International Banking System (in Dutch) 1985, A Framework for Monetary Stability (co-ed.) 1994, The Dollar's Last Days? 2009; numerous articles on int. financial subjects.

WIKTORIN, Gen. Owe Erik Axel; Swedish air force general; b. 7 May 1940, Motala; s. of Erik Wiktorin and Ester Wiktorin (née Johnsson); m. Cajs Gårding 1965; two s.; ed AF Flying Training School, AF Acad., Armed Forces Staff and War Coll., USAF Air Command and Staff Coll.; fighter pilot, Skaraborg Wing 1964–69, CO squadron 1969–71; staff officer, Swedish Defence Staff 1973–79, Head of Planning Section 1980–83, Dir of Plans and Policy and Deputy Chief 1986–91, Chief 1991–92; Deputy CO Jämtland (Sector) Wing 1983–84; Head of Planning Section AF Staff 1984–86; CO Southern Jt Command Swedish Armed Forces 1992–94, Supreme Commdr 1994–2000; Chair. Swedish Asscn for Hunting and Wildlife Man. 2003–07; Fellow, Royal Swedish Acad. of War Sciences 1985; Hon. mem. Lund Academic Officer Soc. 1998; Kt Commdr of White Rose of Finland, Chevalier, Légion d'honneur; Gold Medal for Merit, Southern Skåne Regt, Swedish Home Guard, Gold Medal for Merit, Nat. Fed. of AF Asscns. *Leisure interests:* sailing, skiing, cooking, sky-diving, hunting.

WILANDER, Mats Arne Olof; Swedish fmr professional tennis player and sports commentator; *Tennis Instructor, WilanderOnWheels, LLC;* b. 22 Aug. 1964, Vaxjo; s. of Einar Wilander and Karin Wilander; m. Sonya Mulholland 1987; turned professional 1981; Australian Open Champion 1983, 1984, 1988 (finalist 1985), French Open Champion 1982, 1985, 1988 (finalist 1983, 1987), US Open Champion 1988 (finalist 1987); winner Wimbledon Men's Doubles Championship (with Joakim Nystrom) 1986; mem. victorious Swedish Davis Cup Team 1984, 1987, 1988; ranked world No. 1 1988; voted official World Champion 1988; won 33 singles and six doubles titles (including seven Grand Slam titles); coach of Russian player Marat Safin 2001; Capt. Swedish Davis Cup Team 2002–; mem. Sr Tour; International Tennis Hall of Fame 2003. *Music:* released CD 1991. *Leisure interests:* art, music, skiing, golf. *E-mail:* wilanderonwheels@gmail.com (office). *Website:* www.wilanderonwheels.com (office).

WILBUR, Hon. Richard Sloan, MD, JD; American physician and association executive; *Chairman, American Medical Foundation for Peer Review and Education;* b. 8 April 1924, Boston, Mass; s. of Blake Colburn Wilbur and Mary Caldwell Sloan; m. Betty Lou Fannin 1951; three s.; ed John Marshall Law School, Stanford Univ. Medical School; Intern, San Francisco County Hosp. 1946–47; Resident, Stanford Hosp. 1949–51, Univ. of Pennsylvania Hosp. 1951–52; mem. of Staff, Palo Alto Medical Clinic, Calif. 1952–69; Deputy Exec. Vice-Pres., American Medical Asscn, Chicago 1969–71, 1973–74; Asst Sec., Health and Environment Defense Dept 1971–73; Sr Vice-Pres., Baxter Labs Inc., Deerfield, Ill. 1974–76; Exec. Vice-Pres. Council Medical Speciality Socs 1976–91, Emer. 1992–; Sec., Accreditation Council for Continuing Medical Educ. 1979–91; Assoc. Prof. of Medicine, Stanford Medical School 1952–69, Georgetown Univ. Medical School 1971–77; Vice-Pres. Nat. Resident Matching Plan 1990–91, Pres. 1991–92; Chair. Bd Calif. Medical Asscn 1968–69; Chair. Calif. Blue Shield 1966–68; Chair. American Medical Foundation 1987–, Professional Advisory Bd, Royal Soc. of Medicine Foundation 1995–; Pres. American Coll. of Physician Executives 1988–89; Pres. American Bd Medical Man. 1992–93; Pres. MedicAlert Foundation Int. 1992–94, MedicAlert Foundation, USA 1992–94, Dir MedicAlert Germany 1992–94, Iberica 1992–94, Europe (UK) 1992–95; Chair. Bd and CEO Inst. for Clinical Information 1994–; Sr Vice-Pres. Healthcare, Buckeye Corpn Pte. Ltd 1997–2000; Chair. Medical Advisory Bd, Medical City, Bangalore 1997–2000; Pres. Royal Soc. of Medicine Foundation 1998–, American Coll. of Legal Medicine 2006–07; Ed. World Association Medical Law Bulletin 2009–; mem. numerous other medical asscns; Scroll of Merit, Nat. Medical Asscn 1970, Distinguished Service Medal, US Dept of Defense 1973, Gold Medal, American Coll. of Legal Medicine 2008. *Publications include:* Medicine and Law (ed.) 2015; contribs to medical journals. *Address:* APT Management Inc., 736 North Western Road, Suite 222, Lake Forest, IL 60045 (office); 985 North Hawthorne Place, Lake Forest, IL 60045, USA (home). *Telephone:* (847) 234-6337 (office). *Fax:* (847) 234-5294 (office). *E-mail:* aptmgmnt@aol.com (office). *Website:* www.medicalfoundation.org (office).

WILBY, James; British actor; b. 20 Feb. 1958, Rangoon, Burma; s. of Geoffrey Wilby and Shirley Wilby; m. Shana Louise Magraw 1988; three s. one d.; ed Sedbergh School, Durham Univ., Royal Acad. of Dramatic Art, London; Outstanding Performance by a Cast, Screen Actors' Guild 2001. *Theatre includes:* Another Country (West End début), Who's Afraid of Virginia Woolf (Belgrade Theatre, Coventry), Chips With Everything (Leeds Playhouse), As You Like It (Royal Exchange Theatre, Manchester and tour), Jane Eyre (Chichester), A Patriot for Me (Barbican), Helping Harry (Jermyn Street), Don Juan (Lyric Hammersmith). *Films include:* Dreamchild, Maurice (Best Actor, Venice Film Festival 1988), A Handful of Dust (Best Actor, Bari Film Festival 1989), A Summer Story, Howards End 1991, Immaculate Conception 1992, Une partie d'echec, Regeneration, An Ideal Husband, Tom's Midnight Garden, Cotton Mary, Jump Tomorrow, Gosford Park, C'est Gradiva qui vous appelle 2006, The Wreck 2007, Lady Godiva 2008, Shadows in the Sun 2009, We Need to Talk About Kieran 2011, ChickLit 2016, The Sense of an Ending 2017. *Television includes:* Sherlock Holmes, The Crooked Man, Dutch Girls, A Tale of Two Cities, Mother Love, Tell Me That You Love Me, Adam Bede, You, Me And It, Lady Chatterley, Crocodile Shoes, Woman in White 1997, The Dark Room, Trial and Retribution IV, Bertie and Elizabeth, Island at War, Jericho 2005, Marple: The Sittaford Mystery 2005, Little Devil 2006, Nero 2006, Lewis 2006, The Last Days of the Raj 2007, Clapham Junction 2007, Impact Earth 2008, A Risk Worth Taking 2008, Shadows in the Sun 2009, We Need to Talk About Keiran 2011, Titanic 2012, The Best Possible Taste 2012, The Great Train Robbery 2013, Strike Back 2015, Casualty 2016, Poldark 2017. *Leisure interests:* playing piano, tennis, sailing. *Address:* c/o Sue Latimer, A.R.G., 4 Great Portland Street, London, W1W 8PA, England. *Telephone:* (20) 7436-6400. *Fax:* (20) 7436-6700.

WILBY, Peter, BA (Hons); British journalist; *Columnist, New Statesman and Guardian;* b. 7 Nov. 1944, Leicester, England; m. Sandra James; two s.; ed Univ. of Sussex; reporter, The Observer 1968–72, Educ. Corresp. 1972–75; Educ. Corresp. The New Statesman 1975–77, Ed. 1997–2005, now writes weekly column; Educ. Corresp., The Sunday Times 1977–86; Educ. Ed., The Independent 1986–89, Home Ed., Independent on Sunday 1989–91, Deputy Ed. 1991–95, Ed. 1995–96; Press Commentator, The Guardian newspaper 2007–09; Hon. LLD (Leicester); Comments Award, Media Commentator 2011, Educ. Journalism Award, Ted Wragg Award for sustained contrib. to Educ. Journalism 2013. *Publication:* Anthony Eden 2006. *Address:* 51 Queens Road, Loughton, Essex, IG10 1RR, England (home). *E-mail:* peter.wilby@gmail.com (home).

WILCZEK, Frank, BS, MA, PhD; American physicist and academic; *Herman Feshbach Professor of Physics, Massachusetts Institute of Technology;* b. 15 May 1951, New York; s. of Frank Wilczek and Mary Cona; m. Elizabeth Devine 1973; two d.; ed Univ. of Chicago, Princeton Univ.; Instructor, Princeton Univ. 1974, Asst Prof. 1974–76, 1977–78, Visiting Fellow, Inst. for Advanced Study 1976–77, Assoc. Prof. 1978–80, Prof. 1980–81, R. J. Oppenheimer Prof., Inst. for Advanced Study, School of Natural Sciences 1989–2000; mem. Inst. for Theoretical Physics, Univ. of Calif., Santa Barbara 1980–88, Robert Huttenback Prof. of Physics 1980–88; Visiting Prof., Harvard Univ. 1987–88; Herman Feshbach Prof. of Physics, MIT 2000–; Adjunct Prof., Centros Estudios Cientificos, 2002–; Schrödinger Prof., Vienna 2002; Rudolf Peiriels Visiting Prof., Univ. of Oxford 2008; mem. Editorial Bd, Zeitschrift für Physik C 1981–87, Annual Reviews of Nuclear & Particle Science 1985–89; mem. Scientific Advisory Cttee, CERN 2002–, Perimeter Inst. for Theoretical Physics 2003–; Ed.-in-Chief Annals of Physics 2001–; Editorial Adviser Daedalus 2002–; mem. American Acad. of Arts and Sciences 1993–, NAS 1990–; foreign mem. Royal Netherlands Acad. of Arts and Sciences 2000–; Fellow AAAS 2000–, American Physical Soc. 2004–, American Philosophical Soc. 2005–, Polish Acad. of Arts and Sciences 2007–; numerous hon. doctorates; Sakurai Prize, American Physical Soc. 1986, Lorentz Medal, Royal Netherlands Acad. of Arts and Sciences 2002, Michelson-Morley Prize, Case Western Reserve Univ. 2002, Lillienfeld Prize, American Physical Soc. 2003, High Energy and Particle Physics Prize, European Physical Soc. 2003, Nobel Prize in Physics (jt recipient) 2004, King Faisal Prize 2005, Julius Wess Award 2008, Casimir Funk Award 2008; hon. lecturerships at numerous int. univs. *Publications include:* Longing for the Harmonies 1989, Fantastic Realities: 49 Mind Journeys and A Trip to Stockholm 2006, The Lightness of Being: Mass, Ether and the Unification of Forces 2008, A Beautiful Question: Finding Nature's Deep Design 2015; more than 200 contribs to academic journals and books. *Leisure interests:* music, learning things, solving puzzles. *Address:* Department of Physics, Massachusetts Institute of Technology, 77 Massachusetts Avenue, 6-301, Cambridge, MA 02139 (office); 4 Wyman Road, Cambridge, MA 02138, USA (home). *Telephone:* (617) 253-0284 (office). *Fax:* (617) 253-8674 (office). *E-mail:* wilczek@mit.edu (office). *Website:* www.web.mit.edu/physics (office); www.frankwilczek.com.

WILD, Christopher, PhD; British medical scientist and academic; *Director, International Agency for Research on Cancer;* ed Univ. of Manchester; postdoctoral fellow, Int. Agency for Research on Cancer (IARC), Lyon, France 1984–85, staff scientist 1987, later Chief of Unit of Environmental Carcinogenesis, Dir IARC 2009–; Royal Soc. European Exchange Fellowship, Netherlands Cancer Inst., Amsterdam 1986–87; apptd Prof. of Molecular Epidemiology, Univ. of Leeds and Head of Centre for Epidemiology and Biostatistics 1996, later Dir Leeds Inst. of Genetics, Health and Therapeutics 2005–08, Hon. Prof. of Molecular Epidemiology 2008–; Chair. UK Molecular Epidemiology Group 2001–05; Founding mem. Ethics and Governance Council of the UK Biobank; mem. American Asscn for Cancer Research, British Asscn for Cancer Research, Int. Epidemiological Asscn, Int. Soc. of Exposure Science, Soc. of Socuak Medicine; Fellow, European Acad. of Cancer Sciences, European Cancer Org. 2010–; Science Award for Outstanding Scientific Article 2003, UK Molecular Epidemiology Group 10th Anniversary Medal 2006. *Publications:* Molecular Epidemiology of Chronic Disease 2008; more than 170 peer-reviewed scientific papers in professional journals on the interplay between environmental and genetic risk factors in the causation of human disease. *Address:* IARC, 150 Cours Albert Thomas, 69372 Lyon CEDEX 08, France (office). *Telephone:* (4) 72-73-84-85 (office). *Fax:* (4) 72-73-85-75 (office). *E-mail:* www@iarc.fr (office). *Website:* www.iarc.fr (office).

WILDENTHAL, Kern, MD, PhD; American university administrator and physician; *President Emeritus, University of Texas Southwestern Medical Center;* b. 1 July 1941, San Marcos, Tex.; m. Margaret Wildenthal (née Dehlinger) 1964; two d.; ed Sul Ross Coll., Univ. of Tex. Southwestern Medical Center, Univ. of Cambridge, UK; Intern, Bellvue Hosp., New York 1964–65; Resident, Parkland Hospital, Dallas 1965–67; Asst Prof. then Prof. of Internal Medicine and Physiology, Univ. of Tex. Southwestern Medical School, Dallas 1970–76, Prof. and Dean of Grad. School 1976–80, Prof. and Dean Southwestern Medical School 1980–86, Pres. Univ. of Tex. Southwestern Medical Center 1986–2008, also Prof. of Internal Medicine and Physiology, now Pres. Emer. and Prof. Emer.; CEO Southwestern Medical Foundation 2008–12; Pres. Children's Medical Center Foundation 2013–16, now Consultant; fmr Chair. N-American Section, Int. Soc. for Heart Research, Science Policy Cttee, Asscn of Academic Heart Centers, Basic Science Council, Science Advisory Cttee, American Heart Asscn, Program Project Research Review Cttee, Nat. Heart, Lung and Blood Inst.; mem. NAS Inst. of Medicine, American Soc. for Clinical Investigation, Asscn of American Physicians; mem. Bd of Dirs Dallas Center for the Performing Arts, Dallas Museum of Art, Dallas Symphony Asscn, Dallas Opera, Greater Dallas Chamber of Commerce, Dallas Citizens Council, Southwestern Medical Foundation, Hoblitzelle Foundation, Wendy and Emery Reves Foundation, Hamon Charitable Foundation; Hon. Fellow, Hughes Hall, Univ. of Cambridge; Hon. DrSc (Southern Methodist Univ.) 2006, (Austin Coll.) 2010; Guggenheim Fellowship 1975–76. *Publications include:* 130 scientific papers in basic research and clinical cardiology, numerous articles on health and educ. policy issues. *Address:* 3963 Maple Avenue, Suite 340, Dallas, TX 75219, USA (office). *Telephone:* (214) 532-6438 (office). *E-mail:* kern.wildenthal@utsouthwestern.edu (office). *Website:* www.kernwildenthal.com.

WILDER, C. John, BS, MBA; American energy industry executive; *Chairman, Bluescape Resources;* b. 1958, Missouri; ed SE Missouri State Univ., Univ. of Texas; joined Royal Dutch/Shell Group 1980, various man. positions including CEO Shell Capital, London, UK –1998; Exec. Vice-Pres. and Chief Financial Officer Entergy Corpn 1998–2004; Pres., CEO and Dir TXU Corpn 2004–07; currently Chair. Bluescape Resources; served as dir of more than 65 Entergy-related cos and 75 Shell-related cos; mem. Bd of Dirs Univ. of Tex. and Tulane Univ. Business Schools; mem. Financial Execs Inst., Edison Electric Inst., United Methodist Church Admin. Bd. *Address:* Bluescape Resources, 200 Crescent Court, Suite 1900, Dallas, TX 75201, USA (office). *Telephone:* (214) 855-2260 (office). *Fax:* (214) 855-2265 (office). *Website:* www.bluescaperesources.com (office).

WILDEROTTER, Maggie, BA; American business executive; *Chairman and CEO, Frontier Communications Corporation;* b. (Mary Agnes Sullivan), 9 Feb. 1955, Neptune, NJ; ed Holy Cross Coll., Worcester, Mass; with CableData for 12 years following graduation; later Sr Vice-Pres. McCaw Cellular Communications Inc., a Regional Pres. managing the co.'s Calif., Nev. and Hawaii Region, remained with AT&T following its acquisition of McCaw, later Exec. Vice-Pres. Nat. Operations for AT&T Wireless Services Inc. and CEO AT&T's Aviation Communications Div. (Claircom) –1997; fmr Pres. and CEO Wink Communications Inc. (acquired by Liberty Media) 1997–2002; Sr Vice-Pres. Worldwide Public Sector, Microsoft Corpn 2002–04; mem. Bd of Dirs, Pres. and CEO Citizens Communications (renamed Frontier Communications 2008) 2004–06, Chair. and CEO 2006–; mem. Bd of Dirs Xerox Corpn, Procter & Gamble Co.; Vice-Chair. Pres. Obama's Nat. Security Telecommunications Advisory Cttee 2010–12, Chair. 2012–; mem. Directorship 100 (list compiled by Nat. Asscn of Corp. Dirs), Bd of Advisors of BoardroomIQ, WomenCorporateDirectors Global CEO Task Force; mem. Exec. Cttee Business Roundtable 2012–; fmr mem. Bd of Trustees, Holy Cross Coll.; The Business Media Award, Women's Media Center 2011, Distinguished Achievement Award, B'nai B'rith International 2012. *Address:* Frontier Communications Corporation, 3 High Ridge Park, Stamford, CT 06905-1390, USA (office). *Telephone:* (203) 614-5600 (office). *Fax:* (203) 614-4602 (office). *E-mail:* frontier@frontiercorp.com (office). *Website:* www.frontier.com (office).

WILDERS, Geert; Dutch politician; *Leader, Partij voor de Vrijheid;* b. 6 Sept. 1963, Venlo; m. Krisztina Wilders 1992; ed Open Univ.; lived in Israel 1981–83; began career working for health insurance co., Utrecht; mem. Volkspartij voor Vrijheid en Democratie (VVD) 1998–2004, becoming speech-writer and public spokesman 2002; VVD mem. Utrecht city council 1998; Parl. Asst to VVD leader Frits Bolkestein, specializing in foreign policy 1990–98; mem. House of Reps 1998–2002, 2002–; f. Groep Wilders 2004 (renamed Partij voor de Vrijheid, Freedom Party 2006). *Films:* Fitna (short film about Islam) 2008. *Publication:* Marked for Death: Islam's War Against the West and Me 2012. *Address:* Partij voor de Vrijheid, POB 20018, 2500 EA The Hague, Netherlands (office). *E-mail:* g.wilders@tweedekamer.nl (office). *Website:* www.pvv.nl (office); www.geertwilders.nl (home).

WILDHABER, Luzius, DrIur, LLM, JSD; Swiss judge and professor of law; b. 18 Jan. 1937, Basle; m. 1st Simone Wildhaber-Creux 1963 (died 1994); m. 2nd Gill Reilly 1998 (divorced 2004); two d.; ed Univ. of Basle, Univ. of Paris, France, Univ. of Heidelberg, Germany, Univ. of London, UK, Yale Univ., USA; Int. Law Div. Fed. Dept of External Affairs 1968–71; Prof. of Int. Constitutional and Admin. Law, Univ. of Fribourg 1971–77; Prof. of Int. and Constitutional Law, Univ. of Basle 1977–98, Rector (desig.) 1990–92, Rector 1992–94, Pro-Rector 1994–96; Judge, Supreme Court of Liechtenstein 1975–88, Admin. Tribunal, IDB 1989–94, European Court of Human Rights 1991–2007; Pres. European Court of Human Rights 1998–2007; Pres. Admin Tribunal, Council of Europe 2009–11; Pres. Advisory Panel of Experts on Cands for Election as Judge to European Court of Human Rights 2011–13; Hon. Bencher, Inner Temple 2002, King's Inns Soc. Dublin 2005, Hon. mem. Int. Comm. of Jurists 2008; Star of Romania 2000, Order of Merit of Lithuania 2003, Order of St Agata (San Marino), Great Gold Badge of Honour with Sash (Austria) 2006, Commdr, Order of Orange-Nassau (Netherlands) 2007; Dr hc (Charles Univ., Prague) 1999, (Sofia Univ.) 1999, (American Univ., Bulgaria) 1999, (Bratislava) 2000, (State Univ. of Moldova) 2000, (Bucharest) 2000, (Russian Acad. of Sciences) 2000, (Law Univ. of Lithuania) 2000, (Tbilisi) 2001, (Nat. Law Acad. of Ukraine) 2001, (Neuchâtel) 2004, Hon. LLD (McGill Univ., Montreal) 2002, (Augsburg) 2009; Marcel Benoist Prize 1999, Anna Göldi Prize 2009, Award of Merit, Yale Law School Asscn 2011. *Publications:* Advisory Opinions – Rechtsgutachten höchster Gerichte 1962, Treaty-making Power and Constitution 1971, Erfahrungen mit der Europäischen Menschenrechtskonvention 1979, Wechselspiel zwischen Innen und Aussen 1996, Praxis des Völkerrechts (with J. P. Müller, 3rd edn) 2001, The European Court of Human Rights: History, Achievements, Reform 2006; more than 200 articles. *Leisure interests:* travel, skiing, hiking, mountaineering. *Address:* Auf der Wacht 21, 4104 Oberwil, Switzerland. *Telephone:* (61) 401-25-21. *Fax:* (61) 401-25-75. *E-mail:* luzius.wildhaber@unibas.ch (office).

WILES, Sir Andrew John, KBE, PhD, FRS; British mathematician and academic; *Royal Society 2010 Anniversary Research Professor, University of Oxford;* b. 11 April 1953, Cambridge, England; s. of Rev. Prof. Maurice Frank Wiles and of Patricia Wiles (née Mowll); m.; two d.; ed King's Coll. School, Cambridge, The Leys School, Cambridge, Merton Coll., Oxford and Clare Coll., Cambridge; fmr Fellow, Clare Coll., Cambridge; mem. Inst. for Advanced Study, Priceton, NJ, USA 1981; Prof. of Math., Princeton Univ. 1982–88, 1990–2011; Royal Soc. Research Prof. in Math. and Professorial Fellow, Merton Coll., Oxford 1988–90, Royal Soc. 2010 Anniversary Research Prof. in Math. and Professorial Fellow in Math., Merton Coll. 2011–; Foreign mem. NAS 1996; Hon. DSc (Oxford) 1999; Guggenheim Fellow, Institut des Hautes Études Scientifiques, Paris and École Normale Supérieure 1985–86, Jr Whitehead Prize, London Math. Soc. (co-recipient) 1988, Wolf Prize 1995–96, Wolfskehl Prize (for proving Fermat's Last Theorem), Göttingen 1997, Silver Plaque, Berlin Int. Congress of Mathematicians 1998, King Faisal Prize 1998, asteroid 9999 Wiles named for him 1999, Clay Research Award 1999, Pythagoras Award 2004, Shaw Prize 2005, Math. Inst. building at Oxford named the Andrew Wiles Building in his honour 2013, Abel Prize 2016. *Address:* Mathematical Institute, University of Oxford, Andrew Wiles Building, Radcliffe Observatory Quarter, Woodstock Road, Oxford, OX2 6GG (office); Merton College, Merton Street, Oxford, OX1 4JD, England. *Telephone:* (1865) 273525 (office); (1865) 276310. *Fax:* (1865) 276361. *E-mail:* andrew.wiles@merton.ox.ac.uk (office). *Website:* www.maths.ox.ac.uk (office).

WILEY, John Duncan, BS, MS, PhD; American physicist, academic and fmr university administrator; *Professor Emeritus of Electrical and Computer Engineering, University of Wisconsin-Madison;* b. 23 March 1942, Evansville, Ind.; ed Indiana Univ., Grad. School, Univ. of Wisconsin-Madison (NSF Fellow); mem. tech. staff, Bell Telephone Labs, Murray Hill, NJ 1968–74; at Max Planck Inst., Stuttgart, Germany (awardee of Alexander von Humboldt Sr US Service Award for Research and Training) 1974–75; mem. Faculty, Dept of Electrical and Computer Eng, Univ. of Wisconsin-Madison 1975–, Assoc. Dean for Research, Coll. of Eng 1986–89, Dean Grad. School and Sr Research Officer 1989–94, Provost and Vice-Chancellor for Academic Affairs 1994–2000, Chancellor 2001–08, Prof. Emer. 2008–, Interim Dir Wisconsin Inst. for Discovery 2008–11; Co-founder several research centres, including Center for X-ray Lithography, Eng Research Center for Plasma-Aided Manufacturing; Chair. Materials Science Program 1982–86, Big Ten Council of Pres and Chancellors, Bd for the Council on Higher Educ. Accreditation; mem. Nat. Security Higher Educ. Advisory Cttee; also serves on several local and community bds, including William T. Evjue Foundation, Greater Madison Chamber of Commerce. *Address:* 3120A Wisconsin Institute For Discovery, 333 North Randall Avenue, Madison, WI 53715, USA (office). *Telephone:* (608) 316-4339 (office); (608) 265-4927 (office). *E-mail:* jdwiley@wisc.edu (office). *Website:* www.wisc.edu (office).

WILHELM, Ivan, CSc; Czech physicist, academic and university administrator; *Government Plenipotentiary, Ministry of Education, Youth and Sports;* b. 1 May 1942, Trnava, Slovakia; m.; one d.; ed Czech Tech. Univ. (CVUT), Prague; Asst, Dept of Nuclear Physics, CVUT 1964–67; study attachment to Neutron Physics Lab., United Inst. for Nuclear Research, Dubna, USSR 1967–71; Sr Research Officer, Faculty of Math. and Physics, Charles Univ. 1971–89, Chief Research Officer 1989–91, Dir Nuclear Centre 1990–94, Vice-Rector for Devt 1994–2000, Rector of Charles Univ. 2000–06; Pres. Czech Rectors' Conf. 2000–06; mem. Exec. Council European Univ. Asscn 2000–06, Admin. Council Int. Asscn of Univs 2000–; Govt Plenipotentiary, Ministry of Educ., Youth and Sports 2006–; Ordre des Palmes académiques, St Gregory Order of the Holy Sea; Dr hc (Univ. of Lyon 1-Claude Bernard) 2003, (Comenius Univ., Bratislava) 2006. *Publications include:* more than 100 research papers on nuclear and neutron physics. *Leisure interests:* cycling, walking, skiing. *Address:* Ministry of Education, Youth and Sports, Karmelitska 8, 11812 Prague 1, Czech Republic (office). *Telephone:* (2) 34811749 (office). *E-mail:* ivan.wilhelm@msmt.cz (office); ivan.wilhelm@ruk.cuni.cz. *Website:* www.msmt.cz (office).

WILKIE, Robert Leon, BA, JD, LLM; American lawyer and government official; *Secretary of Veterans Affairs;* b. 2 Aug. 1962, Frankfurt, Germany; s. of Robert Leon Wilkie, Sr; m. Julia Wilkie; ed Coll. of Naval Command and Staff, US Army War Coll., Jt Forces Staff Coll., Wake Forest Univ., Loyola Univ. Coll. of Law, Georgetown Univ.; Counsel and Advisor on Appropriations and Senate Rules and Procedure, US Senate 1997–2000; Counsel and Advisor on Int. Security Affairs to Senate Majority Leader 2000–03; served in US Navy Reserve 2001–07; Special Asst to Pres. for Nat. Security Affairs 2003–05; Asst Sec. of Defense 2005–09; Vice-

Pres. for Strategic Programs, CH2M HILL (eng and program man. firm) 2010–15; fmr Sr Dir Nat. Security Council; Under-Sec. of Defense for Personnel and Readiness 2017–18; Sec. of Veterans Affairs 2018–; Reserve Officer, US Air Force Reserve. *Address:* Department of Veterans Affairs, 810 Vermont Ave, NW, Washington, DC 20420, USA (office). *Telephone:* (202) 461-7600 (office). *Website:* www.va.gov (office).

WILKINS, David Horton, BA, JD; American lawyer, politician and diplomatist; *Partner, Nelson Mullins Riley & Scarborough LLP;* b. 12 Oct. 1946, Greenville, South Carolina; s. of William Walter Wilkins and Evelyn Wilkins; m. Susan Clary; two s.; ed Greenville High School, Clemson Univ., Univ. of S Carolina; served in US Army as a First Lt; practised law for 30 years while serving in S Carolina House of Reps for 25 of those years; Chair. Greenville Co. Legis. Del. 1985–86, 1989–94; Chair. Judicial Comm. 1986–92; Chair. Southern Legis. Conf. 1998; Pres. Nat. Speakers Conf. 2001; Speaker Pro Tempore, S Carolina Legislature 1992–94, Speaker 1994–2005; State Chair. Bush-Cheney Re-election Campaign; Amb. to Canada 2005–09; Partner, Nelson Mullins Riley & Scarborough LLP 2009–; Chair. Clemson Univ. 2009–; Chair. Public Policy and Int. Law practice group; mem. Bd of Dirs Porter Airlines 2009–; Dr hc (Clemson Univ.) 2003; William M. Bulger Excellence in State Legis. Leadership Award 2004. *Address:* Nelson Mullins Riley & Scarborough LLP, Poinsett Plaza, Suite 900, 104 South Main Street, Greenville, SC 29601-2122, USA (office). *Telephone:* (864) 250-2231 (office). *Fax:* (864) 250-2925 (office). *E-mail:* david.wilkins@nelsonmullins.com (office). *Website:* www.nelsonmullins.com (office).

WILKINSON, Jonathan Peter (Jonny), CBE, OBE; British fmr professional rugby football player (rugby union) and sports coach; b. 25 May 1979, Frimley, Surrey, England; s. of Philip Wilkinson and Philippa Wilkinson; m. Shelley Jenkins 2013; ed Lord Wandsworth Coll., Hants., Durham Univ., fly-half; player for Farnham, Newcastle Falcons 1997–2009 (mem. winning squad, Allied Dunbar Premiership 1997/98, Powergen Cup 2001, 2004), England Under-18s, England 1998–2011 (debut vs Ireland, second youngest England int. at 18 years and 314 days, apptd Capt. Nov. 2004), Rugby Club Toulonnais (France) 2009–14 (mem. Heineken Cup winning squad 2013), mem. coaching staff 2014–; 91 Test caps for England (won 67 of them), 1,179 points, has also scored 67 Test points for British and Irish Lions, total of 1,246 points (second only to Dan Carter's 1,442); mem. Grand Slam winning squad 2003, Five Nations Championship winners 1999, Six Nations Championship winners 2000, 2001, 2011, World Cup winning squad 2003, 2nd place 2007, 4th place 1995, 1999; mem. British Lions' team Australia 2001 (three test caps), New Zealand 2005 (two Test caps); scored most points at World Cup 2003 (113), all-time highest points scorer in history of World Cup with 277; announced retirement from int. rugby union Dec. 2011, from all rugby union May 2014; Co-founder Fineside Ltd (clothing co.) 2011–; Freeman, City of Greater London, Newcastle-upon-Tyne 2004; Hon. DCL (Northumbria) 2005; Dr hc (Surrey) 2009; Int. Rugby Board Int. Player of the Year 2003, BBC Sports Personality of the Year 2003, ERC European Player of the Year 2013. *Publications:* Lions and Falcons: My Diary of a Remarkable Year 2001, Jonny Wilkinson: The Perfect 10 (DVD) 2003, Jonny Wilkinson – The Real Story (DVD) 2003, My World 2004, Jonny's Hotshots: How to Play Rugby My Way 2005, Tackling Life 2008, Jonny – My Autobiography 2011. *Leisure interests:* tennis, swimming, basketball, cricket, playing guitar and piano, travelling, speaking and reading French and Spanish. *Address:* Rugby Club Toulonnais SASP, 53 rue Melpomène, 83100 Toulon, France (office); Fineside, Unit B4, Benfield Business Park, Newcastle upon Tyne, NE6 4NQ, England (office). *Telephone:* (8) 92-68-06-80 (Toulon) (office); (191) 265-9446 (Newcastle upon Tyne) (office). *Fax:* (4) 94-41-92-16 (office). *E-mail:* info@fineside.com (office); rctoulon-sasp@rctoulon.com (office). *Website:* www.rctoulon.com (office); www.fineside.com (office); www.jonnywilkinson.com.

WILKINSON, Tom, OBE; British actor; b. (Thomas Geoffrey Wilkinson), 12 Dec. 1948, Leeds, Yorks., England; m. Diana Hardcastle; two d.; ed Univ. of Kent, Royal Acad. of Dramatic Arts; London Critics Circle Theatre Award Best Supporting Actor (for Ghosts) 1986, Best Actor (for An Enemy of the People) 1988; Dr hc (Univ. of Kent) 2001. *Plays:* plays with Royal Nat. Theatre, RSC and Oxford Playhouse include Peer Gynt, Brand, Henry V, Three Sisters, Uncle Vanya, Julius Caesar, Hamlet, The Merchant of Venice, The Crucible, As You Like It. *Films include* Sylvia 1985, Wetherby 1985, Sharma and Beyond 1986, Paper Mask 1990, In the Name of the Father 1993, All Things Bright and Beautiful 1994, Priest 1994, A Business Affair 1994, Sense and Sensibility 1995, The Ghost and the Darkness 1996, Oscar and Lucinda 1997, Smilla's Sense of Snow 1997, Wilde 1997, The Full Monty 1997, Jilting Joe 1997, The Governess 1998, Shakespeare in Love 1998, Rush Hour 1998, Father Damien 1999, Ride with the Devil 2000, Chain of Fools 2000, Black Knight 2001, The Importance of Being Earnest 2002, The Gathering Storm 2002, Girl with a Pearl Earring 2003, If Only 2004, Eternal Sunshine of the Spotless Mind 2004, Stage Beauty 2004, Piccadilly Jim 2004, Ripley Under Ground 2005, Batman Begins 2005, The Exorcism of Emily Rose 2005, A Good Woman 2005, Separate Lies 2005, The Night of the White Pants 2006, The Last Kiss 2006, Dedication 2007, Michael Clayton 2007, Cassandra's Dream 2007, RocknRolla 2008, Valkyrie 2008, Duplicity 2009, 44 Inch Chest 2009, The Ghost 2010, Jackboots on Whitehall (voice) 2010, The Debt 2010, The Conspirator 2010, Burke and Hare 2010, The Green Hornet 2010, The Best Exotic Marigold Hotel 2011, Mission: Impossible – Ghost Protocol (uncredited) 2011, The Samaritan 2012, Belle 2013, The Grand Budapest Hotel 2014. *Television includes:* Prime Suspect 1991, Martin Chuzzlewit 1994, Crossing the Floor 1996, Eskimo Day 1996, Cold Enough for Snow 1997, David Copperfield 1999, The Gathering Storm 2002, An Angel for May 2002, Normal 2003, John Adams (series, HBO) (Golden Globe Award for Best Supporting Actor in a Series 2009) 2008, Recount 2008, A Number 2008, The Gruffalo (film) (voice) 2009, The Kennedys (mini-series) 2011, The Gruffalo's Child (film) (voice) 2011. *Address:* c/o The Gersh Agency, 232 North Canon Drive, Suite 201, Beverly Hills, CA 90210, USA (office). *Telephone:* (310) 274-6611 (office). *Fax:* (310) 278-6232 (office). *Website:* www.gershcomedy.com (office).

WILLATS, Stephan; British artist; b. 17 Aug. 1943, London; m. Stephanie Craven 1983; three s.; ed Drayton School and Ealing School of Art; Ed. and Publr Control magazine 1965–; Lecturer, Ipswich School of Art 1965–67; Lecturer, Nottingham Coll. of Art 1968–72; Organiser, Centre for Behavioural Art, Gallery House, London 1972–73; numerous group exhbns in the UK, Netherlands, Italy, FRG, Switzerland, Belgium, Australia; numerous project works, including Inside an Ocean, Mile End, London 1979, Two Worlds Apart, Hayes 1981 and Blocks, Avondale Estate, London 1982, Brentford Towers, W London 1985, White Towers, Helsinki 1989, Private Network, Oxford 1990; DAAD Fellowship, Berlin 1979–81. *Publications include:* several books, including The Artist as an Instigator of Changes in Social Cognition and Behaviour 1973, Art and Social Function 1976, The Lurky Place 1978, Doppelgänger 1985, Intervention and Audience 1986, The House that Habitat Built 1989, Between Buildings and People 1996, The Art Museum in Society: Collected Writings 1997, Through Symbolic Worlds 2002, The Speculative Diagram 2008, Street Talk 2011, Artwork as Social Process 2012; numerous articles in art magazines. *Address:* c/o Victoria Miro Gallery, 16 Wharf Road, London, N1 7RW, England. *E-mail:* info@victoria-miro.com. *Website:* stephenwillats.com.

WILLCOX, Peter John, MA; Australian business executive; ed Univ. of Cambridge, UK; began career in oil industry 1975; CEO BHP Petroleum Ltd 1986–94; apptd Dir AMP Ltd 2002, Chair. 2003–05; Chair. Mayne Group Ltd 2002–05, Mayne Pharma Ltd 2005–07; Chair. Telstra Corpn Ltd 2006–09; Chair. and Dir, CSIRO 2006–07; mem. Bd of Dirs F.H. Faulding & Co. Ltd, Woodside Petroleum Ltd 1986–93, Hamilton Oil Corpn (USA) 1987–91, Tejas Gas Corpn (USA) 1987–94, BHP Ltd 1988–94, James Hardie Industries Ltd (now James Hardie Industries SE) 1992–2001, Schroders Holdings Australia Ltd 1994–99, Lend Lease Corpn Ltd 1994–2000, North Ltd 1994–2000, Energy Developments Ltd 1994–2002; fmr Dir, The Broken Hill Pty Co. Ltd, MLC Ltd; mem. Advisory Bd CVC Asia Pacific (Australia) Ltd; (non-exec.), F.H Faulding & Co. Ltd 1996–2000; Fellow, Australian Inst. of Co. Dirs. *Address:* c/o Telstra Corpn Ltd, 363 Oxford Street, Paddington, Sydney, NSW 2021, Australia. *E-mail:* info@telstraglobal.com.

WILLEM-ALEXANDER, HM King of The Netherlands Willem-Alexander Claus George Ferdinand, MA; Dutch; b. 27 April 1967, Utrecht; s. of HRH Princess Beatrix and Prince Claus; m. Máxima Zorreguieta (now Queen Maxima of The Netherlands) 2002; three d.; ed Baarns Lyceum, Eerste Vrijzinnig Christelijk Lyceum, The Hague, Atlantic Coll. Llantwit Major, Wales, Leiden Univ.; succeeded to the throne 30 April 2013, on the abdication of his mother HM Queen Beatrix (now HRH Princess Beatrix); mil. service in Royal Netherlands Navy 1985–87, gained Mil. Pilot's Licence 1993, attended Netherlands Defence Coll. 1994, currently holds ranks of Commodore Navy Reserve and Air Force Reserve, Brig.-Gen. Army Reserve and Royal Mil. Constabulary Reserve; ADC Extraordinary to HM The Queen –2013; Patron Global Water Partnership 1998; fully-qualified pvt, commercial and airline pilot, volunteer pilot African Medical Research and Educ. Foundation 1989, Kenya Wildlife Service 1991; mem. founding cttee World Water Vision 1999–2000; Chair. Second World Water Forum, The Hague 2000; mem. Panel of Eminent Persons, UN conf. on sustainable devt, Johannesburg 2002; Chair. Integrated Water Man. Comm. 2002–04; Chair. Water Advisory Cttee 2004–13; mem. IOC 1998–2013; Patron Orange Fund; ADC to HM The Queen –2013; Hon. mem. Royal Naval Yacht Club, Royal Dutch Yachting and Rowing Asscn; Sovereign of the Mil. William Order, Sovereign and Kt Grand Cross, Order of the Netherlands Lion, Sovereign of the Order of Orange-Nassau, Co-Sovereign and Kt, Order of the Gold Lion of the House of Nassau, Sovereign and Grand Cross, Order of the House of Orange, Sovereign of the Order of the Crown, Sovereign of the Order for Loyalty and Merit, Hon. Commdr, Order of St John in the Netherlands, Recipient of the Eleven Cities Cross, Recipient of the Officers' Long Service Cross 2001, Recipient of the Queen Beatrix Inauguration Medal; Kt Grand Cross, Order of the Crown (Belgium), Grand Cross, Order of the Southern Cross (Brazil), Kt Grand Cross, Order of the Most Esteemed Family Order of Brunei, First Class, Grand Cross, Order of Merit of Chile, Kt Grand Cross, Order of the Elephant (Denmark), Grand Croix, Légion d'honneur, Grand Croix, Ordre nat. du Mérite, Grand Cross, Order of Merit of the FRG, Special Class, Adipurna Grand Cross, Order of the Star of the Repub. of Indonesia, Kt Grand Cordon with Collar, Order of the Chrysanthemum (Japan), Kt Grand Cross, Order of Adolphe of Nassau (Luxembourg), Kt Grand Cross, Order of the Oak Crown (Luxembourg), Grand Cross, Order of the Aztec Eagle (Mexico), Kt Grand Cross, Order of St Olav (Norway), Kt Grand Cross with Collar, Order of Oman, Special Class, Grand Cross, Order of the White Eagle (Poland), Kt Grand Cross, Order of Isabella the Catholic (Spain), Kt Grand Cross, Order of the Seraphim (Sweden), Kt Grand Cross, Order of Chula Chom Klao (Thailand), Grand Cross, Order of Union (UAE), Grand Cross, Order of the Liberator (Venezuela); IOC Gold Olympic Order. *Address:* Noordeinde Palace, Postbus 30412, The Hague 2500 GK, The Netherlands (office). *Website:* www.koninklijkhuis.nl (office).

WILLEMS, Lodewijk, MA; Belgian diplomatist; *Adviser to the CEO, BNP Paribas Fortis;* b. 6 April 1948, Etterbeek; m. Lindsay Edwards; four c.; ed Vrije Universiteit, Brussels, Yale Univ.; began career at IAEA 1977; adviser to Deputy Prime Minister and Minister for Econ. Affairs 1977–81; Deputy Sec.-Gen. Benelux Econ. Union 1981–85; Political Counselor, Embassy in Kinshasa 1985–88; Advisor to Deputy Prime Minister and Minister for Econ. Affairs 1988–91; Deputy Perm. Rep. to EC 1991–92; Chief of Cabinet to Minister of Foreign Affairs 1992–94, Perm. Rep. to UN, Geneva 1994–97, Amb. to UK 1997–2002, to Germany 2002–06; fmr Chair. ECE; Dir of External and Governmental Affairs, BNP Paribas Fortis 2006–12, currently Adviser to the CEO; mem. Advisory Bd, LSE Alumni Asscn, Belgium. *Leisure interests:* opera. *Address:* BNP Paribas Fortis, Montagne du Parc 3, 1000 Brussels, Belgium (office). *Telephone:* (2) 565-52-16 (office). *Fax:* (2) 565-27-39 (office). *Website:* www.bnpparibasfortis.com (office).

WILLES, Mark Hinckley, PhD; American economist and media executive (retd); b. 16 July 1941, Salt Lake City, Utah; s. of Joseph Simmons Willes and Ruth Willes (née Hinckley); m. Laura Fayone 1961; three s. two d.; ed Columbia Univ.; with Banking and Currency Cttee, US House of Reps 1966–67; Asst Prof. of Finance, Univ. of Pennsylvania 1967–69; Economist, Fed. Reserve Bank 1967, Sr Economist 1969–70, Dir of Research 1970–71, Vice-Pres. 1971, First Vice-Pres. 1971–77; Pres. Fed. Reserve Bank of Minneapolis 1977–80; Exec. Vice-Pres. and Chief Finance Officer, Gen. Mills Inc. 1980–85, Pres. and COO 1985–92, Vice-Chair. 1992–95; Chair., Pres. and CEO Times Mirror Co. 1995–2000; Pres. and CEO Deseret Man. Corpn 2009–12; Publr Los Angeles Times 1997–99; Pres. Hawaii Honolulu Mission, Church of the Latter Day Saints 2001. *E-mail:* willesmh@deseretmgt.com (home). *Website:* www.deseretmanagement.com.

WILLIAMS, (Elizabeth) Betty; Irish campaigner for children's rights, peace and justice; *Founder and President, World Centers of Compassion for Children*

International; b. 22 May 1942, Belfast, Northern Ireland; ed Queen's Univ., Belfast; worked as office receptionist; jt winner of Nobel Peace Prize for launching the Northern Ireland Peace Movt (later renamed Community of the Peace People then Peace People) 1976, Jt Leader 1976–78; fmr Visiting Prof., Sam Houston State Univ.; Founder and Head, The Global Children's Studies Center 1992; Founder and Pres. World Centers of Compassion for Children Int. 1997–; Co-f. Nobel Women's Initiative 2006; Chair. Inst. for Asian Democracy, Washington DC; Distinguished Visiting Prof., Nova Southeastern Univ.; mem. Bd of Dirs Adoption Options, Inc.; Founding mem. Alliance for the New Humanity; mem. Advisory Bd Dalai Lama Center for Peace and Educ., Camfed Int., Mahatma Gandhi Center for Global Non-violence, Vermont Peace Acad., Int. Cttee of Artists for Peace Council, The Pangaea Project; mem. Council of Honour UN Univ. for Peace, Costa Rica; mem. Bd of Trustees Pax Natura; Patron, Int. Peace Foundation, Vienna; Hon. mem. Club of Budapest, World Wisdom Acad., Global Vision for Peace; Hon. DHumLitt (Coll. of Siena Heights) 1977, (Monmouth Coll.), Hon. LLD (Yale Univ., Beloit Coll., St Norbert Coll., Williams Woods Univ.), Hon. Dr of Humanities (Mount Merry Coll.), Laurea hc (Università degli Studi Della Basilicata, Potenza, Italy); Nobel Peace Prize (jtly) 1976, People's Peace Prize of Norway 1976, Carl von Ossietzky Medal for Courage (Berlin Section, Int. League of Human Rights), Schweitzer Medallion for Courage, Eleanor Roosevelt Award 1984, Frank Foundation Child Assistance Int. Oliver Award, Together for Peace Foundation Peace Building Award 1995, Gandhi, King, Ikeda Community Builders Prize 2003, Ischia Peace Award (Italy) 2003, Soka Gakkai Int. Peace and Culture Award 2004, The Martin Luther King, Jr Award, Paul Harris Fellowship, Rotary Club Int., The Raoul Wallenberg Humanitarian Award, Old Dominion Univ., The Max and Betty Walker Distinguished Speaker Series Certificate of Honor, Fed. of World Peace and Love Humanity in the Arts Founders Award, Int. Cttee of Artists for Peace, Premio Mediterraneo Award, Eleanor Roosevelt Global Women's Rights Award. *Leisure interest:* gardening. *Address:* World Centers of Compassion for Children International, Knock Inverin, Co. Galway, Ireland (office). *Telephone:* (91) 593304 (office). *E-mail:* bwccc@eircom.net (office). *Website:* www.wccco.org (office).

WILLIAMS, Brian Douglas; American television journalist; b. 5 May 1959, Elmira, NY; s. of Gordon Lewis Williams and Dorothy May Williams (née Pampel); m. Jane Gillan Stoddard 1986; one s. one d.; ed Mater Dei High School, Brookdale Community Coll., Catholic Univ of America, George Washington Univ; intern with admin of Pres. Jimmy Carter, The White House; TV reporter KOAM-TV, with WTTG-TV, WCAU-TV; joined WCBS-TV 1993; joined NBC 1993, Chief White House Corresp. 1994–96; anchor, Man. Ed. The News With Brian Williams MSNBC 1996–2004, Anchor and Man. Ed. NBC Nightly News 2004–15, suspended for six months Feb. 2015, breaking news anchor, MSNBC 2015–; host of Rock Center with Brian Williams (news magazine programme) 2011–13; mem. Council on Foreign Relations; Hon. DHumLitt (Bates Coll.) 2005; Emmy Awards for reporting 1987, 1989, 1993. *Leisure interests:* NASCAR racing, New York Giants (American football team). *Address:* MSNBC, One MSNBC Plaza, Secaucus, NJ 07094, USA (office). *Website:* www.msnbc.com (office).

WILLIAMS, Sir Daniel Charles, GCMG, QC, LLB; Grenadian lawyer, consultant and fmr government official; *Lawyer and Business and Legal Consultant, Law Office of Danny Williams & Company;* b. 4 Nov. 1935, Grenada; s. of Adolphus D. Williams and Clare Stanislaus; m. Cecilia Patricia Gloria Modeste 1970; two s. four d.; ed Holborn Coll. of Law, Languages and Commerce, Univ. of London, UK Council of Legal Educ.; called to the Bar, Lincoln's Inn, London 1968; barrister 1969–70, 1974–84, 1990–96; Magistrate, St Lucia 1970–74; mem. Parl. (New Nat. Party) 1984–89; Minister of Health, Housing and Environment 1984–89, of Legal Affairs and Attorney-Gen. 1988–89; Acting Prime Minister July 1988; Gov.-Gen. of Grenada 1996–2008; currently lawyer and business and legal consultant, Law Office of Danny Williams & Co.; fmrly several lay positions in RC Church; Chief Scout; Founder-mem. Grenada Foundation for Needy Students Inc. 1996; sole sponsor of cricket competition of the six primary schools in parish of St David's, Grenada 1985–. *Publications:* Index of Laws of Grenada 1959–79, The Office and Duties of the Governor-General of Grenada 1998, A Synoptic View of the Public Service of Grenada 1999, Prescription of a Model Grenada 2000, God Speaks 2001, The Layman's Lawbook 2002, The Love of God 2003, Government of the Global Village 2007; contrib. to Modern Legal Systems Cyclopedia: Central America and the Caribbean, Vol. 7 1985. *Leisure interests:* lawn tennis, gardening. *Address:* PO Box 346, St George's, Grenada (office).

WILLIAMS, Hon. Daniel (Danny) E., QC, JD; Canadian fmr politician; b. 4 Aug. 1949, St John's, Newfoundland; m. Maureen Williams; four c.; ed Memorial Univ. of Newfoundland, Univ. of Oxford, UK, Dalhousie Univ.; practised law in Newfoundland and Labrador 1972; led Cable Atlantic (cable TV co.) in series of acquisitions 1975; Pres. OIS Fisher (offshore oil and gas supply and services co.); apptd QC 1984; MLA for Humber West, Newfoundland 2001–; Leader Progressive Conservative Party 2001–, also Opposition Leader; Premier of Newfoundland and Labrador 2003–10 (resgnd); Founder and Pres. St John's Jr Hockey League; fmr Chair. Canadian Parl. Channel, Newfoundland and Labrador Film Devt Corpn, Provincial Govt Offshore Oil Impact Advisory Council; mem. Bd of Dirs Alderon Iron Ore Corpn 2012–14 (resgnd); fmr mem. Bd of Govs Canadian Sports Hall of Fame; fmr mem. Terry Fox Marathon of Hope, Big Brothers/Big Sisters, Iris Kirby House, Arthritis Soc. *Telephone:* (709) 753-6043 (office).

WILLIAMS, Eliud Thaddeus, BSc, MBA; Dominican accountant, politician and fmr head of state; *Management Consultant, WHITCO Inc.;* b. 21 Aug. 1948, St Joseph, Dominica; m. Cornelia Henry; two s.; ed Univ. of the West Indies, ICTC, Loughborough, UK, Manitoba Inst. of Man., Canada, Univ. of Florida, USA; Financial Controller, Dominica Banana Growers Asscn 1978–79; Licensed Public Accountant, Inland Revenue, Dominica 1985–; Commr of Cooperatives 1985–87; Perm. Sec., Ministry of Agric. and Environment 1987–92, 1996–2000, Ministry of Health and Social Security 1992–96, Ministry of Communications, Works and Housing 2000–04; Man. Dir Eastern Caribbean Telecommunications Authority (ECTEL) 2004–08; Man. Consultant, WHITCO Inc. 2008–, also mem. Bd of Dirs; Pres. of Dominica 2012–13; Chair. Ind. Regulatory Comm. 2010–12; fmr Dir Caribbean Agricultural Research & Devt Inst., Caribbean Food Corpn, Org. of Caribbean Utility Regulators; Pres. Roseau Coop Credit Union 1997–99; Dir Cooperative Socs League 1999–2002; fmr Chair. and mem. Bd of Govs Dominica State Coll.; fmr Vice-Pres. Helping Hands Inc.; mem. Inst. of Financial Account-

ants (UK) 1985, Fellow 1995, Fellow, Chartered Management Inst. (UK) 2004; mem. Manitoba Inst. of Man. 1990; Dominica Award of Honour 2012. *Leisure interests:* walking, swimming. *Address:* Whitco Inc., PO Box 2130, 37 Kennedy Avenue, Roseau, Dominica (office). *Telephone:* 4499800 (office). *Fax:* 4499777 (office). *E-mail:* info@whitco-inc.com (office). *Website:* (office).

WILLIAMS, Evan Clark; American internet industry executive; *Co-Founder, Obvious Ventures;* b. 31 March 1972, Clarks, Neb.; s. of Monte Williams and Laurie Howe; m. Sara Morishige; two c.; ed Univ. of Nebraska–Lincoln; began career as Web Application Developer with O'Reilly Media, Hewlett Packard Co. and Intel Corpn; Co-founder and CEO, Blogger (weblog-authoring software), Pyra Labs 1998–2003 (co. acquired by Google Inc. 2003), Head Blogger, Google, Inc. 2003–04; Co-founder and Prin. Owner, Odeo, Inc. 2004–07 (co. acquired by Sonic Mountain, Inc. 2007); Co-founder, Obvious Ventures 2006; Co-founder and mem. Bd of Dirs, Twitter, Inc. 2007–19, CEO 2008–10; Founder and CEO Medium (online writing platform), San Francisco 2012–. *Address:* Obvious Ventures, 220 Halleck Street, Suite 120, San Francisco, CA 94129, USA (office). *E-mail:* info@obvious.com (office); obvious.com (office). *Website:* medium.com (office).

WILLIAMS, Sir Francis Owen Garbatt, Kt, CBE; British motor racing team owner; *Team Principal, Williams F1 racing team;* b. 16 April 1942, South Shields, Tyne and Wear; ed St Joseph's Coll., Dumfries, Scotland; worked as travelling grocery salesman; brief career as driver and mechanic; f. Frank Williams Racing Cars 1966; hired drivers including Piers Courage and Tony Trimmer for several years in Formula Two and Formula Three; bought Brabham Formula One chassis for 1969 Formula One season, two second place finishes; brief partnership with Alessandro de Tomaso 1970; raced Henri Pescarolo with chassis bought from March Engineering 1971; first F1 car built by Williams works, Politoys FX3 designed by Len Bailey 1972, crashed by Pescarolo and destroyed in first race; sought sponsorship from Marlboro and Iso Rivolta (Italian car co.); partnership with oil magnate Walter Wolf 1976; left team along with fmr employee, engineer Patrick Head, and acquired empty carpet warehouse in Didcot, Oxon. 1977, announced formation of Williams Grand Prix Engineering 1977, now known as Williams F1, Team Principal 2012–; first win with Clay Regazzoni 1979, first title with Alan Jones 1980, second championship with Keke Rosberg 1982; six further drivers' championships and eight constructors' championships 1981–97; Chevalier, Légion d'honneur; Wheatcroft Trophy 2008, BBC Sports Personality of the Year Helen Rollason Award for "outstanding achievement in the face of adversity" 2010. *Address:* Williams F1, Grove, Wantage, Oxon., OX12 0DQ, England (office). *Telephone:* (1235) 777700 (office). *Fax:* (1235) 764705 (office). *E-mail:* enquiries@williamsf1.com (office). *Website:* www.williamsf1.com (office).

WILLIAMS, (John) Gwynn, CBE, MA; British historian and academic; b. 19 June 1924, Wales; s. of John Ellis Williams and Annie Maude Rowlands; m. Beryl Stafford Thomas 1954; three s.; ed Holywell Grammar School, Univ. Coll. of North Wales; with RN 1943–46; staff tutor Dept of Extra Mural Studies Univ. of Liverpool 1951–54; Asst lecturer Univ. of North Wales 1955, Prof. of Welsh History 1963–83, Dean Faculty of Arts 1972–74, Vice-Prin. 1974–79, Vice-Pres. 1993–98; Chair. Press Bd Univ. of Wales 1979–91; Dir Gregynog Press 1979–2002; Vice-Pres. Nat. Library of Wales 1984–86, Pres. 1986–96; Pres. Cambrian Archaeological Asscn 1987–88; Vice-Pres. Hon. Soc. of Cymmrodorion 1988–; mem. Royal Comm. on Ancient and Historical Monuments in Wales 1967–91; Hon. mem. Gorsedd of Bards 1983, Hon. Fellow Bangor Univ. 2007; Hon. DLitt (Univ. of Wales) 1999; Prince Llywelyn Medal 1952. *Publications include:* The Founding of the University College of North Wales, Bangor 1985, The University College of North Wales: Foundations 1985, University and Nation 1893–1939 (The Thomas Jones Pierce Memorial Lecture) 1992, The Report on the Proposed University of Wales (ed.) 1993, The University Movement in Wales 1993, The University of Wales 1893–1939 1997; numerous articles on 17th-century Wales for learned journals. *Leisure interests:* travelling, walking. *Address:* Llywenan, Siliwen, Bangor, Gwynedd, LL57 2BS, Wales (home). *Telephone:* (1248) 353065 (home).

WILLIAMS, Jody, BA, MA; American international organization official, activist, academic and writer; *Chairwoman, Nobel Women's Initiative;* b. 9 Oct. 1950, Poultney, Vt; d. of John C. Williams and Ruth C. Williams; m. Stephen D. Goose 2001; ed Univ. of Vermont, School for Int. Training, Vt, Johns Hopkins School of Advanced Int. Studies, Washington, DC; English teacher, Mexico, UK and Washington, DC 1978–81; worked to spread awareness of US policy in Cen. America 1981–92; Co-ordinator Nicaragua-Honduras Educ. Project 1984–86; Deputy Dir Medical Aid for El Salvador, Los Angeles 1986–92; Founding Co-ordinator Int. Campaign to Ban Landmines (ICBL) 1992–98, ICBL Campaign Amb. 1998–; Tech. Adviser, UN Study on Impact of Armed Conflict on Children 1996; Distinguished Visiting Prof. of Social Work, Grad. Coll. of Social Work, Univ. of Houston 2003–14, Sam and Cele Keeper Endowed Prof. in Peace and Social Justice 2007–; Founding Chair. Nobel Women's Initiative 2006–; Co-f. Campaign to Stop Killer Robots 2013–; Head, UN Human Rights Council High-Level Mission to Darfur 2007; more than 20 hon. degrees in USA, Canada and Peru, including from the Royal Mil. Coll. of Canada, Smith Coll., Wesleyan Univ., Penn State Univ.; Nobel Peace Prize (jt recipient with ICBL) 1997, Distinguished Peace Leadership Award, Nuclear Age Peace Foundation 1998, Olender Foundation Peacemaker of the Year 1999, Public Service Award, Center for Public Policy and Administration, Univ. of Massachusetts Amherst 2005, Global Women's Rights Award, Feminist Majority Foundation 2006, Global Peacemaker Award, Wayne State Univ. 2017, Eleanor Roosevelt Val-Kill Medal 2017, 31st International Joan B. Cendrós i Carbonell Prize, Òmnium Cultural, Barcelona 2017. *Publications:* After the Guns Fall Silent: The Enduring Legacy of Landmines (with Shawn Roberts) 1995, Banning Landmines: Disarmament, Citizen Diplomacy and Human Security 2008, My Name is Jody Williams: A Vermont Girl's Winding Path to the Nobel Peace Prize 2013; more than 24 chapters and articles for books and journals; numerous articles for newspapers around the world, including The Wall Street Journal, The Independent (UK), the Economist. *Address:* Nobel Women's Initiative, 1 Nicholas Street, Suite 430, Ottawa, ON K1N 7B7, Canada (office). *Telephone:* (613) 569-8400 (office). *Fax:* (613) 563-0682 (office). *E-mail:* jwilliams@nobelwomensinitiative.org (office). *Website:* www.nobelwomensinitiative.org (office).

WILLIAMS, John Peter Rhys (J.P.R.), MBE, MB, BS, LRCP, MRCS, FRCS, FRCSE; British orthopaedic surgeon (retd) and fmr rugby union player; *President,*

Bridgend Ravens Rugby Club Ltd; b. 2 March 1949, Cardiff, Wales; s. of Peter Williams and Margaret Williams; m. Priscilla Parkin 1973; one s. three d.; ed Bridgend Grammar School, Millfield, St Mary's Hosp. Medical School; British Jr Tennis Champion, Wimbledon 1966; Welsh int. rugby player 1969–79, 1980–81; 55 caps for Wales; Capt. of Welsh rugby team 1978–79; on tour with British Lions to NZ 1971, South Africa 1974; eight test matches for British Lions, winning both series; qualified as medical doctor 1973; surgical Registrar, Cardiff Hosp. 1977–80, Orthopaedic Registrar 1980–82; Orthopaedic Sr Registrar, St Mary's Hosp., London 1982–85; Consultant Orthopaedic Surgeon, Princess of Wales Hosp., Bridgend 1986–2005; Primary FRCS 1976; Pres. Bridgend Ravens Rugby Club Ltd; Amb. Portugal Rugby Festival 2012; inducted into Int. Rugby Hall of Fame 1997, Int. Rugby Bd Hall of Fame 2014. *Publications:* Irish Conference on Sporting Injuries, Dublin (ed.) 1975, JPR (autobiog.) 1979, Cervical Neck Injuries in Rugby Football, British Medical Journal 1978, Trans-Oral Fusion of the Cervical Spine, Journal of Bone and Joint Surgery 1985, Given the Breaks 2006. *Leisure interests:* sport, music. *Address:* Bridgend Ravens Rugby Club Ltd, Bridgend Ford Brewery Field, Tondu Road, Bridgend, CF31 4JE, Wales (office); Llansannor Lodge, Llansannor, nr Cowbridge, Vale of Glamorgan, CF71 7RX, Wales (home). *Telephone:* (1446) 772590 (home). *E-mail:* jprw15@aol.com (home).

WILLIAMS, John Towner; American composer, conductor and pianist; b. 8 Feb. 1932, Flushing, NY; ed Juilliard School, New York, Univ. of California, Los Angeles, studied composition with Mario Castelnuovo-Tedesco; pianist, Columbia Pictures; jazz pianist working with Henry Mancini on television scores; Conductor, Boston Pops Orchestra 1980–98; numerous hon. degrees; five Academy Awards, seven BAFTA Awards, three Emmy Awards, four Golden Globes, 21 Grammy Awards, recipient of Kennedy Center Honors 2004, Classical BRIT Award for Soundtrack Composer of the Year 2005, Grammy Awards for Best Instrumental Composition (for A Prayer for Peace, from Munich) 2007, (for The Adventures of Mutt, from Indiana Jones and the Kingdom of the Crystal Skull) 2009, Nat. Medal of Arts 2009, Ken Burns Lifetime Achievement Award 2013. *Film scores:* The Secret Ways 1961, Diamond Head 1962, None But the Brave 1965, How to Steal a Million 1966, Valley of the Dolls 1967, The Cowboys 1972, The Poseidon Adventure 1972, Tom Sawyer 1973, Earthquake 1974, The Towering Inferno 1974, Jaws (Acad. Award) 1975, The Eiger Sanction 1975, Family Plot 1976, Midway 1976, The Missouri Breaks 1976, Raggedy Ann and Andy 1977, Black Sunday 1977, Star Wars (Acad. Award) 1977, Close Encounters of the Third Kind 1977, The Fury 1978, Jaws II 1978, Superman 1978, Dracula 1979, 1941 1979, The Empire Strikes Back 1980, Raiders of the Lost Ark 1981, E.T.: The Extra Terrestrial (Acad. Award) 1982, Return of the Jedi 1983, Indiana Jones and the Temple of Doom 1984, The River 1985, Space Camp 1986, The Witches of Eastwick 1987, Empire of the Sun (BAFTA Award for Best Score) 1988, Always 1989, Born on the Fourth of July 1989, Indiana Jones and the Last Crusade 1989, Stanley and Iris 1990, Presumed Innocent 1990, Home Alone 1990, Hook 1991, JFK 1993, Far and Away 1993, Home Alone 2: Lost in New York 1993, Jurassic Park 1993, Schindler's List (Acad. Award) 1993, Sabrina 1995, The Reivers 1995, Nixon 1995, Sleepers 1996, Rosewood 1996, Land of the Giants 1997, Seven Years in Tibet 1997, The Lost World: Jurassic Park 1997, Amistad 1997, Lost in Space 1997, Time Tunnel 1997, Saving Private Ryan 1998, Star Wars: Episode I – The Phantom Menace 1999, Angela's Ashes 1999, Harry Potter and the Sorcerer's Stone 2001, Star Wars: Episode II – Attack of the Clones 2001, Minority Report 2002, Harry Potter and the Chamber of Secrets 2002, Catch Me if You Can 2002, Harry Potter and the Prisoner of Azkaban 2004, The Terminal 2004, Star Wars: Episode III – Revenge of the Sith 2005, War of the Worlds 2005, Harry Potter and the Goblet of Fire 2005, Memoirs of a Geisha (Golden Globe for Best Original Score in a Motion Picture 2006, BAFTA Anthony Asquith Award for Achievement in Film Music 2006, Grammy Award for Best Score Soundtrack Album for Motion Picture 2007) 2005, Munich 2005, Superman Returns 2006, Harry Potter and the Order of the Phoenix 2007, Indiana Jones and the Kingdom of the Crystal Skull 2008, Harry Potter and the Half-Blood Prince 2009, Lincoln (Critics Choice Award 2013) 2012, The Book Thief 2013, Star Wars: the Force Awakens (Grammy Award for Best Score Soundtrack for Visual Media 2017) 2015. *Recordings include:* John Williams Plays The Movies 1996, Music From The Star Wars Saga 1999, Jane Eyre 1999, Themes From Academy Award Winners, Over The Rainbow: Songs From The Movies 1992, John Williams Conducting The Boston Pops 1996, The Hollywood Sound 1997, From Sousa To Spielberg, Best Of John Williams 1998, Treesong 2001, Call Of The Champions (official theme of 2002 Winter Olympics, Salt Lake City) 2001, John Williams Trumpet Concerto 2002, American Journey 2002; recordings of film scores. *Address:* c/o Michael Gorfaine, Gorfaine/Schwartz Agency, 4111 West Alameda Avenue, Suite 509, Burbank, CA 91505, USA (office). *Website:* www .johnwilliams.org.

WILLIAMS, Keith, BA (Hons); British chartered accountant and business executive; *Deputy Chairman, John Lewis Partnership PLC;* ed Univ. of Liverpool; worked for Apple, Arthur Andersen and Boots plc; joined British Airways as Head of Taxation 1998, Group Treas. 2000–06, mem. Exec. Bd and Chief Financial Officer British Airways 2006–11, Chief Exec. 2011–15 (following merger with Iberia), mem. Bd of Dirs, Iberia Lineas Aéreas de España SA 2009–, Int. Airlines Group (parent co.) 2011–14; Dir (non-exec.), John Lewis Partnership PLC 2014–, Deputy Chair. 2016–; Dir (non-exec.), Transport for London; Accountancy Age Award for Blue Chip Finance Dir of the Year 2010. *Address:* John Lewis Partnership, Carlisle Place, London, SW1P 1BX, England (office). *Website:* www .johnlewispartnership.co.uk (office).

WILLIAMS, Mack Geoffrey Denis, BA; Australian diplomatist and consultant; *Senior Advisor, AFG Venture Group;* b. 16 July 1939, Sydney, NSW; s. of Bernard George Williams and Thelma A. McMillan; m. Carla Lothringer 1966; one s. three d.; ed Fort Street Boys High School, Sydney and Univ. of Sydney; joined Dept of Foreign Affairs 1961, Third Sec., Embassy in Brussels 1962–65, Second Sec., Embassy in Saigon 1965–67, First Sec., Embassy in Phnom Penh 1969–71, Counsellor, Embassy in Washington, DC 1971–74, Office of Minister of Foreign Affairs, Canberra 1975–76, Deputy High Commr in Papua New Guinea 1977–78, Royal Coll. of Defence Studies, London 1979, High Commr to Bangladesh 1980–82, Dept of the Prime Minister, Canberra 1986–87, First Asst Sec., Dept of Foreign Affairs and Trade 1987–89, Amb. to the Philippines 1989–94, to South Korea 1994–98; Bd mem. Australia-Korea Foundation 1998–; Exec. Australia-Korea Business Council from 1998, Vice-Pres. from 2000; Hon. Investment and Trade Rep., Repub. of Philippines from 1999; fmr Dir, Piedmont Triad Partnership; Sr Advisor, Asean Focus Group Pty Ltd (now AFG Venture Group); Hon. Fellow, Univ. of Sydney 1996; Korean Pres. Order of Merit 1998. *Leisure interests:* golf, travel. *Address:* AFG Venture Group, 15/9 Castlereagh Street, Sydney, NSW 2000 (office); 87 Ferry Road, Glebe, NSW 2037, Australia. *Telephone:* (2) 9241-4777 (office). *E-mail:* info@aseanfocus.com (office). *Website:* www.aseanfocus.com (office).

WILLIAMS, Mark James, MBE; British professional snooker player; b. 21 March 1975, Cwm, Ebbw Vale, Wales; s. of Dilwyn Williams; m. Joanne Dent; three s.; won first junior event aged 11; made first century break aged 13; turned professional 1992; winner of 23 titles (18 ranking, 1 minor-ranking, 4 non-ranking); ranking titles: Welsh Open 1996, 1999, Grand Prix 1996, 2000, British Open 1997, Irish Open 1998, Thailand Masters 1999, 2000, 2002, UK Championship 1999, 2002, Embassy World Snooker Championship 2000 (first left-handed player), 2003, China Open 2002, 2006, 2010, LG Cup 2003, German Masters 2011, Rotterdam Open European Tour 2013; minor-ranking event title: Players Tour Championship – Event 1 2010; non-ranking titles: Benson & Hedges Championship 1994, Masters 1998, Masters 2003, Pot Black 2006; Pro-am event title: Finnish Snooker Challenge 2010; winner Nations Cup (with team Wales) 1999; became second player to hold all four major titles at one time 2003; ranked World No. 1 2000–01, 2003, 2011; 284 competitive century breaks, including two maximum (147) breaks; Owner, Tredegar Snooker Club, Wales. *Leisure interests:* golf, badminton, poker, cars, fmr amateur boxer. *Address:* Tredegar Snooker Club, Park Place, Tredegar, NP22 4LD, Wales.

WILLIAMS, Mark R., PhD; American business executive; *Chairman (Non-Executive), Hess Corporation;* ed Stanford Univ.; joined Royal Dutch Shell plc's upstream oil business in USA 1979, held several upstream and downstream positions in Shell's upstream business, including Exec. Vice-Pres. of Supply and Distribution in Oil Products at Shell's upstream business, Downstream Dir 2009–12; Chair. (non-exec.) Hess Corpn 2013–; Dir (non-exec.), Intertek Group Plc 2013–; Chair. Exec. Cttee of Athabasca Oil Sands Project, Downstream Cttee of American Petroleum Inst. *Address:* Hess Corporation, 1185 Avenue of the Americas, New York, NY 10036, USA (office). *Telephone:* (212) 997-8500 (office). *Fax:* (212) 536-8390 (office). *E-mail:* info@hess.com (office). *Website:* www.hess.com (office).

WILLIAMS, Martin John, CVO, OBE, BA; British consultant and diplomatist (retd); b. 3 Nov. 1941; s. of John Henry Stroud Williams and Barbara Williams (née Benington); m. Susan Dent 1964; two s.; ed Manchester Grammar School, Corpus Christi Coll. Oxford; joined Commonwealth Relations Office 1963; various posts including service at Embassy in Manila 1966–69, Consulate-Gen. in Milan 1970–72, Embassy in Tehran 1977–80, High Comm. in New Delhi 1982–86, Embassy in Rome 1986–90; Head of S. Asian Dept, FCO 1990–92; seconded to NI Office, Belfast as Asst Under-Sec. (Political Affairs) 1993–95; High Commr in Zimbabwe 1995–98, in NZ (also accred to Samoa and Gov. Pitcairn Island) 1998–2001; UK Consultant to New Zealand Antarctic Heritage Trust 2002–12; Chair. Link Foundation for UK-NZ Relations 2004–09. *Leisure interests:* music, gardening, woodwork, theatre. *Address:* Russet House, Lughorse Lane, Yalding, Kent, ME18 6EG, England (home). *Telephone:* (1622) 815403 (home).

WILLIAMS, Michael (Mike) J., BS, MBA; American business executive; *Chairman, Prospect Mortgage, LLC;* ed Drexel Univ.; began career with DuPont Co.; Sr Man., Strategic Systems Practice, KPMG Peat Marwick's information tech. consulting group –1991; joined Fannie Mae (Fed. Nat. Mortgage Asscn) 1991, served in several areas of co., developed tech. tools, Sr Vice-Pres., e-Commerce 1999–2000, Pres. Fannie Mae eBusiness 2000–05, Exec. Vice-Pres., Regulatory Agreements and Restatement Feb.–Nov. 2005, Exec. Vice-Pres. and COO Fannie Mae, responsible for Tech., Enterprise Operations, Human Resources, Community and Charitable Giving, Compliance and Ethics, Corp. Facilities and Security, and Corp. Procurement 2005–09, mem. Bd of Dirs, Pres. and CEO Fannie Mae 2009–12; Operating Partner, Sterling Partners 2012–; Chair. Prospect Mortgage, LLC 2012–; mem. Bd of Dirs Realogy Holdings Corpn 2012–, Livingston Int. 2013–; Trustee Drexel Univ. 2012–. *Website:* www.myprospectmortgage.com; www .sterlingpartners.com.

WILLIAMS, Michelle Ingrid; American actress; b. 9 Sept. 1980, Kalispell, Mont.; d. of Larry Williams and Carla Williams (née Swenson); m. Phil Elverum 2018; one d. with Heath Ledger (died 2008); began career with appearances in several 1990s TV series, including Baywatch, Step by Step, Home Improvement; mem. Acad. of Motion Picture Arts and Sciences 2009. *Films include:* Lassie 1994, Species 1995, Timemaster 1995, A Thousand Acres 1997, Halloween H20: 20 Years Later 1998, Dick 1999, But I'm a Cheerleader 1999, Perfume 2001, Me Without You 2001, Prozac Nation 2001, The United States of Leland 2003, The Station Agent 2003, A Hole in One 2004, Imaginary Heroes 2004, Land of Plenty 2004, The Baxter 2005, Brokeback Mountain (Broadcast Film Critics Asscn Award for Best Supporting Actress, Phoenix Film Critics Soc. Award for Best Supporting Actress) 2005, The Hawk Is Dying 2006, The Hottest State 2006, I'm Not There 2007, Incendiary 2008, Deception 2008, Wendy and Lucy (Online Film Critics Soc. Award for Best Actress, Toronto Film Critics Asscn Award for Best Actress) 2008, Synecdoche, New York 2008, Mammoth 2009, Blue Valentine (San Francisco Film Critics Circle Award for Best Actress) 2010, Shutter Island 2010, Meek's Cutoff 2010, Take This Waltz 2011, My Week with Marilyn (Golden Globe Award for Best Performance by an Actress in a Motion Picture – Comedy or Musical 2012) 2011, Tar 2012, Oz the Great and Powerful 2013, Manchester by the Sea (Chicago Film Critics Asscn Award for Best Supporting Actress 2016, Florida Film Critics Circle Award for Best Supporting Actress 2016, NSFC Award for Best Supporting Actress 2017) 2016, Certain Women 2016, Wonderstruck 2017, The Greatest Showman 2017, All the Money in the World 2017, I Feel Pretty 2018, Venom 2018, After the Wedding 2019. *Television includes:* Baywatch (series) 1993, Step by Step (series) 1994, Raising Caines (series) 1995, Home Improvement (series) 1995, My Son is Innocent (film) 1996, Killing Mr. Griffin (film) 1997, If These Walls Could Talk 2 (film) 2000, Dawson's Creek (six seasons) 1998–2003. *Address:* c/o William Morris Agency, 9560 Wilshire Blvd, Beverly Hills, CA 90210, USA (office). *Telephone:* (310) 285-9000 (office). *Website:* wmeentertainment.com (office).

WILLIAMS, Nigel, MA; British writer and television producer; b. 20 Jan. 1948, Cheadle, Cheshire, England; s. of David Ffrancon Williams; m. Suzan Harrison 1973; three s.; ed Highgate School, Oriel Coll., Oxford; trainee, BBC 1969–73, Producer/Dir Arts Dept 1973–85, Ed. Bookmark 1985–92, Omnibus 1992–96, writer and presenter 1997–2000. *Stage plays include:* Class Enemy (Plays and Players Award for Most Promising Playwright) 1978, Trial Run 1980, Line 'Em 1980, Sugar & Spice 1980, My Brother's Keeper 1985, Country Dancing 1986, Nativity 1989, Harry & Me 1995, The Last Romantics 1997, Lord of the Flies (adapted from William Golding's novel). *Radio:* HR Series 1–5 (BBC) 2009–14. *Television includes:* Double Talk, Talking Blues, Real Live Audience 1977, Baby Love 1981, Breaking Up 1986, The Last Romantics 1992, Skallagrig (BAFTA Award) 1994, Elizabeth I (Emmy Award, Golden Globe Award) 2006, Wodehouse at War 2013. *Publications include:* novels: My Life Closed Twice (jt winner Somerset Maugham Award) 1977, Jack Be Nimble 1980, Star Turn 1985, Witchcraft 1987, The Wimbledon Poisoner 1990, They Came from SW19 1992, East of Wimbledon 1994, Scenes from a Poisoner's Life 1994, Stalking Fiona 1997, Fortysomething 1999, Hatchett and Lycett 2002; travel: Wimbledon to Waco 1995, Unfaithfully Yours 2013. *Leisure interests:* dogs, drinking, talking, family, swimming, walking. *Address:* 18 Holmbush Road, Putney, London, SW15 3LE, England. *Telephone:* (20) 8964-8811. *Fax:* (20) 8964-8966.

WILLIAMS, Sir Peter, Kt, CBE, MA, PhD, FRS; British physicist, academic and university administrator; *Chairman, Daiwa Anglo-Japanese Foundation;* m. 1970; one s.; ed Hymers Coll., Hull, Trinity Coll., Cambridge; Research Fellow, Univ. of Cambridge –1970; Lecturer, Dept of Chemical Eng and Chemical Tech., Imperial Coll., London 1970–75; joined VG Instruments 1975, later Deputy Group Man. Dir; joined Oxford Instruments (first spin-off co. of Univ. of Oxford) 1982, Chief Exec. 1985–91, Chair. 1991–99 (retd); Master, St Catherine's Coll., Oxford 2000–02; Chancellor, Univ. of Leicester 2005–10; Chair. Bd of Trustees, Nat. Museum of Science and Industry 1996–2002; Chair. Particle Physics and Astronomy Research Council 1990s, Eng and Tech. Bd 2001–06, Nat. Physical Lab. 2002–; Pres. Inst. of Physics 2000–02, BAAS 2003; Dir (non-exec.) GKN plc (Sr Ind. Dir) 2001–10, W.S. Atkins plc 2004–11; Vice-Pres. and Treas. The Royal Soc. 2006–12; Chair. Daiwa Anglo-Japanese Foundation 2012–; Fellow, Imperial Coll. London 1996; Hon. Fellow, Univ. Coll., London 1997, Selwyn Coll., Cambridge 1997, St Catherine's Coll., Oxford 2002, City & Guilds 2002; Hon. FICE 2004; Hon. FIEE 2004; Hon. Fellow, Inst. of Measurement and Control 2006; Hon. FIMechE 2008; Hon. DSc (Leicester) 1995, (Nottingham Trent) 1995, (Loughborough) 1996, (Brunel) 1997, (Univ. of Wales, Swansea) 1997, (Univ. of Wales, Cardiff) 1999, (Sheffield) 1999, (Warwick) 1999, (Staffordshire) 2004, (City) 2007, (Hull) 2010, (Bedford) 2010; Glazebrook Medal, Inst. of Physics 2005. *Leisure interests:* travelling, hiking, skiing, music, collecting wine. *Address:* Daiwa Foundation, Japan House, 13–14 Cornwall Terrace, London, NW1 4QP, England (office). *Telephone:* (20) 7486-4348 (office). *Fax:* (20) 7486-2914 (office). *E-mail:* office@dajf.org.uk (office). *Website:* www.dajf.org.uk (office).

WILLIAMS, R. Stanley (Stan), BA, PhD; American physicist, academic and industrial researcher; *HP Senior Fellow and Founding Director, HP Quantum Science Research Group, Hewlett-Packard Laboratories;* b. 1951, Kodiak, Alaska; s. of Bobby L. Williams and Shirley A. Williams; ed Rice Univ., Univ. of California, Berkeley; mem. Tech. Staff, AT&T Bell Labs 1978–80; Asst Prof., Dept of Chem., UCLA 1980–84, Assoc. Prof. 1984–86, Prof. 1986–95, now Adjunct Prof. of Chem.; Adjunct Prof. of Computer Science, Univ. of N Carolina; joined Hewlett-Packard Labs 1995, HP Sr Fellow and Founding Dir HP Quantum Science Research Group 1995–; consultant to several corpns and law firms; mem. Defense Science Study Group; Advisor, Defense Science Bd, Frontier Research Program, Inst. for Physics and Chem. Research (RIKEN), Japan, Nat. Inst. for Materials Science, Japan; Julius Springer Award for Applied Physics 2000, Feynman Prize in Nanotechnology 2000, Dreyfus Teacher-Scholar Award, Sloan Foundation Fellowship, Scientific American Top 50 Technology Leaders 2002, Peter Debye Lecturer, Cornell Univ. 2004, Herman Block Lecturer, Univ. of Chicago 2004, Joel Birnbaum Award 2005, EETimes Innovator of the Year 2009, HP CEO Innovation Award 2010. *Achievements include:* holder of 34 US patents. *Publications include:* more than 290 papers in peer-reviewed scientific journals and more than 130 patents worldwide. *Leisure interests:* cookery, long beach walks with wife and dogs. *Address:* Hewlett-Packard Company, 3000 Hanover Street, Palo Alto, CA 94304-1185, USA (office). *Telephone:* (650) 857-1501 (office). *Website:* www.labs.hpe.com.

WILLIAMS, Richard Edmund; Canadian animated film producer, director and writer; b. 19 March 1933, Toronto, Ont.; s. of Kenneth D. C. Williams and Kathleen Williams (née Bell); m. 2nd Margaret French 1976; four c. (including two from a previous m.); m. 4th Imogen Sutton; ed Northern Secondary School, Royal Ontario Coll. of Art; emigrated from Toronto to Ibiza 1953, to London 1955; famous for his animation of Who Framed Roger Rabbit 1988; f. Richard Williams Animation Ltd 1962; mem. Acad. of Motion Picture Arts and Sciences; est. Richard Williams Animation Masterclasses for professionals and students world-wide 1995–; mem. Asscn of Cinematographers and TV Technicians; more than 250 int. awards. *Films include:* produced and/or directed: The Little Island (short) (British Acad. Award, First Prize, Venice Film Festival) 1958, Love Me, Love Me, Love Me 1962, A Lecture on Man (short) 1962, The Apple 1963, Diary of a Madman 1963, The Dermis Probe (short) 1965, The Sailor and the Devil 1965, The Ever-Changing Motor Car 1965, A Christmas Carol (Academy Award for Best Animated Short Subject) 1971, The Thief and the Cobbler 1993, Circus Drawings (short) 2010; designed film sequences and titles for: What's New Pussycat 1965, The Liquidator 1965, A Funny Thing Happened on the Way to the Forum 1966, The Spy with a Cold Nose 1966, Casino Royale 1967, Sebastian 1968, Here We Go Round the Mulberry Bush 1968, The Charge of the Light Brigade 1968, 30 Is a Dangerous Age, Cynthia 1968, Prudence and the Pill 1968, Can Heironymus Merkin Ever Forget Mercy Humppe and Find True Happiness? 1969, Murder on the Orient Express (uncredited) 1974, The Return of the Pink Panther 1975, The Pink Panther Strikes Again 1976; animation for Raggedy Ann & Andy: A Musical Adventure 1977, Who Framed Roger Rabbit (two Academy Awards, including for Special Achievement) 1988, Arabian Knight (produced and directed) 1995, The Animator's Survival Kit – Animated (16-DVD boxed set) 2008; Tummy Trouble (voice of Droopy) 1989. *Television includes:* Ziggy's Gift (short) 1982. *Publication:* The Animator's Survival Kit 2002 (revised edn 2009). *Address:* Richard Williams Animation Masterclass, PO Box 3016, Bristol, BS6 9HH, England. *E-mail:* enquiries@theanimatorssurvivalkit.com. *Website:* www.theanimatorssurvivalkit.com.

WILLIAMS, Robert (Robbie) Peter; British singer; b. 13 Feb. 1974, Stoke-on-Trent, Staffs.; s. of Pete Williams and Theresa Janette Williams; m. Ayda Field 2010; one d., one s.; played the Artful Dodger in Oliver 1982; mem. group Take That 1990–95, 2010–12; solo artist 1995–; tours: The Show Off Must Go On 1997, The Ego Has Landed 1998, One More for the Rogue Tour/For a Few Dollars More… Tour 1998–99, Robbie Williams North American Tours 1999, The Sermon on the Mount Tour 2000–01, Weddings, Barmitzvahs & Stadiums Tour/Sing When You're Pacific Rimming Tour 2001, Weekends of Mass Distraction Tour/Cock of Justice/Aussie Typo Tour 2003, Close Encounters Tour 2006, Take the Crown Stadium Tour 2013; recording collaborators as soloist include: Kylie Minogue, Nicole Kidman, Maxi Jazz, Pet Shop Boys, Dean Martin, Gary Barlow, Thalia, Trevor Horn; mem. Equity, Musicians' Union, Mechanical-Copyright Protection Soc., Performing Right Soc., ADAMI, GVC, AURA; numerous including: nine Smash Hits Awards 1992–98; with Take That: Brit Awards for Best British Single (for Could It Be Magic) 1993, (for Pray) 1994, (for Back for Good) 1996, for Best British Video (for Pray) 1994, for Best British Group 2011, Q Idol Award 2006; solo: Brit Awards for Best British Single (for Angels) 1998, (for She's the One) 2000, (for Rock DJ) 2001, for Best British Video (for Millennium) 1999, (for She's the One) 2000, (for Rock DJ) 2001, for Best British Male Solo Artist 1999, 2001, 2002, 2003, for Best British Song of 25 Years (for Angels) 2005, for Outstanding Contrib. to Music 2010, for Icon 2017, Levi's Nordoff-Robbins Music Therapy Original Talent Award 1998, MTV Award for Best Male 1998, Echo Award for Best Int. Male Rock and Pop Artist, Germany 2005, 2006, MTV Europe Music Award for Best Male 2005, MTV Latin America Music Award for Best Int. Pop Artist 2006, Q Idol Award 2013, Echo Award for Best Int. Male 2010, NRJ Music Award for Best Int. Male Artist 2010, Virgin Media Award for Best Male Artist 2010. *Films:* Nobody Someday 2002, De-Lovely 2004, The Magic Roundabout (voice) 2005. *Recordings include:* albums: with Take That: Take That And Party 1992, Everything Changes 1993, Nobody Else 1995, Greatest Hits 1996, Progress 2010; solo: Life Thru' a Lens 1997, I've Been Expecting You 1998, The Ego Has Landed 1999, Sing When You're Winning 2000, Swing When You're Winning 2001, Escapology 2002, Live At Knebworth 2004, Intensive Care 2005, Rudebox 2006, Reality Killed the Video Star 2009, Take the Crown 2012, Swings Both Ways 2013, The Heavy Entertainment Show 2016. *Publications:* F for English 2000, Robbie Williams: Performance (with Mark McCrum) 2001, Robbie Williams: Somebody Someday 2001, Feel (with Chris Heath) 2004, You Know Me (with Chris Heath) 2010. *Leisure interests:* golf, rollerblading. *Address:* IE Music Ltd, 111 Frithville Gardens, London, W12 7JG, England (office). *Telephone:* (20) 8600-3400 (office). *Fax:* (20) 8600-3401 (office). *E-mail:* info@iemusic.co.uk (office). *Website:* www.iemusic.co.uk (office); www.takethat.com; www.robbiewilliams.com.

WILLIAMS, Sir Rodney; Antigua and Barbuda politician and fmr physician; *Governor-General;* s. of Ernest Emmanuel Williams; early career as medical doctor; mem. Parl. for St Paul constituency 1984–2004; several ministerial posts 1992–2004, including portfolios of culture, econ. devt, environment, educ., tech. and tourism; Gov.-Gen. 2014–; mem. Antigua Labour Party. *Address:* Office of the Governor-General, St John's, Antigua and Barbuda (office).

WILLIAMS, Roger Stanley, CBE, MD, FRCP, FRCS, FRCPE, FRACP, FRCPI, FMedSci; British consultant physician; *Director, Institute of Hepatology, Foundation for Liver Research;* b. 28 Aug. 1931; s. of Stanley George Williams and Doris Dagmar Clatworthy; m. 1st Lindsay Mary Elliott 1954 (deceased); two s. three d.; m. 2nd Stephanie Gay de Laszlo 1978; one s. two d.; ed St Mary's Coll., Southampton, London Hosp. Medical School, Univ. of London; House Doctor, London Hosp. 1953–56; Jr Medical Specialist, Queen Alexandra Hosp. 1956–58; Medical Registrar and Tutor, Royal Postgraduate Medical School 1958–59; Lecturer in Medicine Royal Free Hosp. 1959–65; Consultant Physician Royal S. Hants. and Southampton Gen. Hosp. 1965–66; Consultant Physician and Dir, Inst. of Liver Studies, King's Coll. Hosp. (now King's Coll. School of Medicine and Dentistry), London 1966–96, Prof. of Hepatology; Dir Inst. of Hepatology, London, Foundation for Liver Research 1996–, Hon. Consultant Physician, Univ. Coll. London Hosps NHS Trust 1996–2010; mem. WHO Scientific Group on Viral Hepatitis, Geneva 1972, Transplant Advisory Panel DHSS 1974–83, Advisory Group on Hepatitis DHSS 1980–, European Asscn for the Study of the Liver (Pres. 1983) 1966–, Harveian Soc. of London (Pres. 1974–75), British Asscn for the Study of the Liver (Pres. 1984), Royal Soc. of Medicine, British Soc. of Gastroenterology (Pres. 1989); Vice-Pres. Royal Coll. of Physicians 1991; Hon. Consultant in Medicine to the Army 1988–98; Rep. to Select Cttee of Experts on Organizational Aspects of Co-operation in Organ Transplantation, Congress of Europe; Sir Ernest Finch Visiting Prof., Univ. of Sheffield 1974; Hon. FACP; Hon. FRCPI. *Publications include:* Fifth Symposium on Advanced Medicine (ed.) 1969, Immunology of the Liver 1971, Artificial Liver Support 1975, Immune Reactions in Liver Disease 1978, Drug Reactions and the Liver 1981, Clinics in Critical Care Medicine – Liver Failure 1986, Liver Tumours (Baillière's Clinical Gastroenterology) 1987, The Practice of Liver Transplantation 1995, International Developments in Health Care. A review of Health Systems in the 1990s 1995, Acute Liver Failure 1997; more than 2,500 papers, reviews and book chapters. *Leisure interests:* tennis, sailing, opera. *Address:* Institute of Hepatology, 111 Coldharbour Lane, London, SE5 9NT, England (office). *Telephone:* (20) 7255-9830 (office). *E-mail:* r.williams@researchinliver.org.uk (office). *Website:* www.liver-research.org.uk (office).

WILLIAMS, Ronald Allen, MS; American business executive; b. 11 Nov. 1949, Chicago, Ill.; ed Roosevelt Univ., Sloan School of Management, Massachusetts Inst. of Tech.; Sr Vice-Pres. of Marketing Blue Cross of California 1987–95, Pres. 1995–99; Co-founder and fmr Sr Vice-Pres. Vista Health Corpn; fmr Group Marketing Exec. Control Data Corpn; Co-founder and fmr Pres. Integrative Systems; Group Pres., Large Group Div. WellPoint Health Networks Inc. 1999–2001; Exec. Vice-Pres. and Chief of Health Operations, Aetna Inc. 2001–02, Pres. 2002–07, mem. Bd of Dirs 2002–11, Chair. and CEO 2006–10, Chair. 2010–11 (retd); mem. Bd of Dirs American Express Co. 2007–, The Boeing Co., Johnson & Johnson; mem. or fmr mem. MIT Sloan Dean's Advisory Council, MIT North America Exec. Bd 2002–10, Alfred P. Sloan Man. Soc., Business Council (Vice-Chair. 2008–10), Business Roundtable, Council for Affordable Quality Healthcare (Chair. 2007–10), Int. Fed. of Health Plans, Healthcare

Leadership Council, GE Healthymagination Advisory Cttee, The Wall Street Journal CEO Council; Co-Chair. World Econ. Forum's Annual Meeting, Davos, Switzerland Jan. 2010; f. RW2 Enterprises, LLC (consultancy) 2010; mem. Pres. Obama's Man. Advisory Bd 2011–; mem. Bd of Dirs Peterson Inst. for Int. Economics, Save the Children; Trustee, Connecticut Science Center. *Publications:* author or co-author of op-ed articles in The Wall Street Journal, Washington Post, The Financial Times and the Seattle Post-Intelligencer. *Address:* RW2 Enterprises, LLC, 2255 Glades Road, Suite 324A, Boca Raton, FL 33431, USA (office). *Telephone:* (561) 235-7795 (office). *Website:* www.ronwilliams.net.

WILLIAMS, Serena Jameka; American professional tennis player; b. 26 Sept. 1981, Saginaw, Mich.; d. of Richard Williams and Oracene Williams; partner Alexis Ohanian; one d.; sister of Venus Williams (q.v.); began playing tennis aged five; turned professional 1995; coached by her father Richard Williams; singles semi-finalist, Sydney Open 1997, Chicago 1998; won mixed doubles (with Max Mirnyi) at Wimbledon 1998, US Open 1998; doubles winner (with Venus Williams), Oklahoma City 1998, French Open 1999, 2010, Hanover 1999, US Open 1999, 2009, Wimbledon 2000, 2002, 2008, 2009, 2012, 2016, Australian Open 2001, 2003, 2009, 2010, Olympic Games, London 2012; winner (singles), US Open 1999, 2002, 2008, 2012, 2013, 2014, Paris Indoors 1999, 2003, Indian Wells 1999, 2001, LA 1999, 2000, Grand Slam Cup 1999, Hanover 2000, Tokyo 2000, Canadian Open 2001, French Open 2002, 2013, 2015, Wimbledon 2002, 2003, 2009, 2010, 2012, 2015, 2016, Australian Open 2003, 2005, 2007, 2009, 2010, 2015, 2017, Miami 2002, 2003, 2004, 2007, 2008, 2013, 2014, Madrid 2012, Olympic Games, London 2012, Brisbane International 2013, Family Circle Cup, Charleston 2013, Mutua Madrid 2013 China Open 2013, Italian Open 2014, 2016; singles finalist, US Open 2001, 2011, Wimbledon 2004, 2008, Australian Open 2016, French Open 2016; US Fed. Cup Team 1999; winner WTA Tour Championships, Munich 2001, Doha 2009, Istanbul 2012, 2013, Singapore 2014; doubles gold medal with sister, Venus, Olympic Games, Sydney 2000, Beijing 2008; singles quarter-finalist, Olympic Games, Beijing 2008; 775 career singles wins, 129 defeats, 184 career doubles wins, 30 defeats; 39 Grand Slam titles: 23 in singles (record for the most Major wins in Open Era and second on all-time list behind Margaret Court with 24), 14 in women's doubles and 2 in mixed doubles; debuted The Serena Williams Collection by Nike, an apparel and footwear collection 2005; f. clothing label Aneres; numerous appearances as actress on TV programmes; f. Serena Williams Foundation (educational foundation); Sanex WTA Tour Most Impressive Newcomer Award 1998, WTA Most Improved Player 1999, Tennis Magazine Player of the Year 1999, Teen Awards Achievement Award (shared with sister, Venus) 2000, WTA Doubles Team of the Year Award (with Venus Williams) 2000, 2009, WTA Player of the Year 2002, 2008, 2009, 2012, 2013, 2014, 2015, ITF Women's Singles World Champion 2002, 2009, 2012, 2013, 2014, 2015, Associated Press Female Athlete of the Year 2002, World Sportswoman of the Year 2002, 34th NAACP Image Awards Pres.'s Award 2003, ESPY Award for Best Female Athlete 2003, ESPY Award for Best Female Tennis Player 2003, 2004, 2009, 2010, 2011, 2013, Laureus World Sportswoman of the Year 2003, 2010, 2016, 2018, Avon Foundation Celebrity Role Model Award 2003, BET Award for Sportswoman of the Year 2003, 2004, 2005, 2007, 2009, 2010, 2011, 2012, 2014, 2015, 2016, 2017, Family Circle/Prudential Financial Player Who Makes a Difference Award 2004, WTA Comeback Player of the Year 2004, Laureus World Comeback of the Year 2007, Glamour Magazine Women of the Year Award 2009, SI.com Best Female Athlete of the Decade 2009, AP Female Athlete of the Year Award 2002, 2009, 2013, 2015, ITF Women's Doubles World Champion (with Venus Williams) 2009, Doha 21st Century Leaders Awards – Outstanding Leadership 2009, Teen Choice Awards – Female Athlete Award 2010, ESPY Award for Best Female Athlete 2013, Sportsperson of the Year, Sports Illustrated magazine 2015, BET Award for Sportswoman of the Year 2018. *Publication includes:* On the Line (autobiog.) 2009. *Leisure interests:* watching movies, playing football and basketball, reading, acting, music, designing clothing. *Address:* c/o William Morris Endeavor Entertainment, 9601 Wilshire Blvd. 3rd Floor, Beverly Hills, CA 90210, USA (office). *Website:* www.serenawilliams.com.

WILLIAMS, Steven (Steve) W., BSc (ChemEng), FIChemE; British oil industry executive; *President and CEO, Suncor Energy Inc.;* ed Univ. of Exeter, Harvard Business School, Univ. of Oxford; was responsible for Octel Corpn's global operation; also managed operation of largest refinery in UK for Esso; joined Suncor 2002, Exec. Vice-Pres., Corp. Devt and Chief Financial Officer 2002–07, also served as Exec. Vice-Pres., Oil Sands, COO Suncor Energy 2007–11, mem. Bd of Dirs Suncor Energy 2011–, Pres. 2011–, CEO 2012–; Chair. Suncor United Way campaign, Fort McMurray 2003–07, Suncor United Way campaign 2011; Co-Chair. Oil Sands Leadership Initiative 2009–; mem. Alberta Govt Oil and Gas Econs Advisory Council 2010, Canadian Assn of Petroleum Producers Bd Govs 2009–10, Nat. Roundtable on the Environment and the Economy 2007–09, CEO Cttee of Syncrude Canada Ltd 2009–, Business Advisory Council, School of Business, Univ. of Alberta 2004–, Alberta Carbon Capture and Storage Devt Council 2008–10, Bd Alberta Chamber of Resources 2003–07, Bd Northern Lights Regional Hosp. Foundation 2003–07, Bd Alcoa Corpn 2016–; Founding Bd mem. Oil Sands Safety Assn 2003, Chair. 2005; Founding mem. COSIA 2012; mem. Inst. of Dirs. *Address:* Suncor Energy Inc., PO Box 2844, 150 – 6 Avenue SW, Calgary, Alberta, T2P 3E3, Canada (office). *Telephone:* (403) 296-8000 (office). *Fax:* (403) 296-3030 (office). *E-mail:* sef@suncormail.com (office). *Website:* www.suncor.com (office).

WILLIAMS, HE Cardinal Thomas Stafford, ONZ, STL, BSocSc; New Zealand ecclesiastic (retd); *Archbishop Emeritus of Wellington;* b. 20 March 1930, Wellington; s. of Thomas S. Williams and Lillian M. Williams (née Kelly); ed St Patrick's Coll., Wellington, Victoria Univ., Wellington, St Kevin's Coll., Oamaru, Holy Cross Coll., Mosgiel, Pontifical Urban Coll. de Propaganda Fide, Rome and Univ. Coll., Dublin; ordained priest, Rome 1959; Asst St Patrick's Parish, Palmerston North 1963; Dir of Studies, Catholic Enquiry Centre, Wellington 1965; parish priest, St Anne's, Leulumoega, Western Samoa 1971, Holy Family Parish, Porirua East, Wellington 1976; Archbishop of Wellington and Metropolitan of NZ 1979–2005, Archbishop Emer. 2005–; Bishop of New Zealand, Mil. 1995–2005; cr. Cardinal (Cardinal-Priest of Gesù Divin Maestro alla Pineta Sacchetti) 1983. *Address:* 40 Walton Avenue, Waikanae Park, Kapiti 5036, New Zealand. *Telephone:* (4) 293-4684. *E-mail:* t.williams@wn.catholic.org.nz.

WILLIAMS, Venus Ebone Starr; American professional tennis player; b. 17 June 1980, Lynwood, Calif.; d. of Richard Williams and Oracene Williams; sister of Serena Williams (q.v.); ed Art Inst. of Fort Lauderdale; made professional debut Bank of West Classic, Oakland, Calif. 1994; Bausch & Lomb Championships 1996; winner numerous singles titles (WTA Tour) including Oklahoma City 1998, Lipton 1998, 1999, Hamburg 1999, Italian Open 1999, Grand Slam Cup 1998; seven Grand Slam singles titles: Wimbledon 2000, 2001, 2005, 2007, 2008, US Open 2000, 2001; 14 Grand Slam doubles titles (with Serena Williams): French Open 1999, 2010, US Open 1999, 2009, Wimbledon 2000, 2002, 2008, 2009, 2012, 2016, Australian Open 2001, 2003, 2009, 2010; two Grand Slam mixed doubles titles: Australian Open 1998, French Open 1998; singles finalist, Wimbledon 2002, 2003, 2009, 2017, French Open 2002, Australian Open 2003, 2017; mixed doubles finalist, Wimbledon 2006; with Serena Williams, first sisters in tennis history to have each won a Grand Slam singles title; singles Gold Medal, Olympic Games, Sydney 2000; doubles Gold Medal (with sister Serena), Olympic Games, Sydney 2000, Beijing 2008, London 2012; only sisters in 20th century to win a Grand Slam doubles title together; US Fed. Cup Team 1995, 1999; 742 career singles wins, 208 defeats, 174 career doubles wins, 30 defeats, 28 career mixed doubles wins, seven defeats; 49 career singles titles, 22 doubles titles, two mixed doubles titles; highest ranking (singles): No. 1 25 Feb. 2002, (doubles): No. 3 14 Sept. 2009; awarded largest-ever endorsement contract for a female athlete by Reebok 2002; Founder and CEO V Starr Interiors (design firm), Jupiter, Fla 2002–; apptd Global Amb. for UNESCO to address worldwide gender issues 2006; teamed up with retailer Steve & Barry's to launch own fashion line EleVen 2007; Sports Image Foundation Award 1995, WTA Newcomer of the Year 1997, September's Olympic Cttee Female Athlete 1997, Tennis Magazine's Most Impressive Player 1998, WTA Player of the Year 2000, Sports Illustrated for Women's Sportswoman of the Year 2000, Teen Awards Achievement Award 2000, Sanex WTA Tour Player of the Year and Doubles Team of the Year (with sister, Serena) 2000, Women's Sports Foundation Athlete of the Year 2000, WTA Most Improved Player of the Year 2001, ESPY Awards for Best Female Athlete and Best Female Tennis Player of 2001, 2002, Certificate of Achievement Howard Univ. 2002, 34th NAACP Image Awards' Pres.'s Award 2003, Harris Poll Most Favorite Female Sports Star 2004, 2006, Glamour Magazine's Woman of the Year Award 2005, ESPY Award for Best Female Tennis Player 2006, BET's Best Female Athlete of the Year 2006, Whirlpool 6th Sense Player of the Year Awar 2008, 2009, Anti-Defamation League Americanism Award 2009, ITF Women's Doubles World Champion (with Serena Williams) 2009, Caesars Tennis Classic Achievement Award 2010, YWCA GLA Phenomenal Woman of the Year Award 2010, WTA Fan Favorite Doubles Team of the Year Award (with Serena Williams) 2010, World TeamTennis Finals Most Valuable Player 2012, WTA Player Service Award 2012, 2013, US Open Sportsmanship Award 2015, WTA Comeback Player of the Year 2015. *Leisure interests:* sumo wrestling, surfing, reading, languages, antique furniture, writing poetry. *Address:* c/o IMG Tennis, IMG Center, 1360 East 9th Street, Suite 100, Cleveland, OH 44114-1782, USA (office); V Starr Interiors, 1102 West Indiantown Road, Suite 11, Jupiter, FL 33458, USA (office). *Telephone:* (216) 522-1200 (office). *Fax:* (216) 436-3477 (office). *E-mail:* cleresumes@imgworld.com (office). *Website:* www.imgworld.com (office); www.vstarrinteriors.com; elevenbyvenuswilliams.com; www.venuswilliams.com.

WILLIAMS OF CROSBY, Baroness (Life Peer), cr. 1993, of Stevenage in the County of Hertfordshire; **Rt Hon. Shirley Williams,** CH, PC, MA; British politician and academic; *Public Service Professor of Electoral Politics, Emerita, John F. Kennedy School of Government, Harvard University;* b. 27 July 1930, London, England; d. of Sir George Catlin and Vera Brittain; m. 1st Bernard Williams 1955 (divorced 1974, died 2003); one d.; m. 2nd Prof. Richard Neustadt 1987 (died 2003); ed Summit School, Minn., USA, St Paul's Girls' School, Somerville Coll., Oxford and Columbia Univ., New York; Gen. Sec., Fabian Soc. 1960–64; Labour MP for Hitchin 1964–74, for Hertford and Stevenage 1974–79; SDP MP for Crosby 1981–83; Parl. Pvt. Sec., Minister of Health 1964–66; Parl. Sec. Minister of Labour 1966–67; Minister of State, Dept of Educ. and Science 1967–69; Minister of State, Home Office 1969–70; Opposition Spokesman on Health and Social Security 1970–71, on Home Affairs 1971–73, on Prices and Consumer Affairs 1973–74; Sec. of State for Prices and Consumer Protection 1974–76, for Educ. and Science 1976–79; Paymaster-Gen. 1976–79; Sr Research Fellow (part-time), Policy Research Inst. 1979–85; mem. Labour Party Nat. Exec. Cttee 1970–81; mem. Council for Social Democracy Jan.–March 1981; left Labour Party March 1981; Co-Founder SDP March 1981, Pres. 1982–88; Public Service Prof. of Elective Politics, John F. Kennedy School of Govt, Harvard Univ. 1988–2000, Prof. Emer. 2000–, Dir Inst. of Politics 1988–89; mem. Social and Liberal Democratic Party 1988–; Deputy Leader Liberal Democrat Party, House of Lords 1999–2001, Leader Nov. 2001–04; Visiting Fellow, Nuffield Coll., Oxford 1967–75; Fellow, Inst. of Politics, Harvard 1979–80 (mem. Sr Advisory Council 1986–); Regents Lecturer and Fellow, Inst. of Politics, Univ. of Calif., Berkeley; Vice-Pres. CAFOD; mem. EC Comité des Sages 1996–97, Council Int. Crisis Group 1998–, Int. Advisory Council, Council on Foreign Relations; Chair. EC Job Creation Competition 1997–98; Trustee, The Century Foundation, New York, Inst. for Public Policy Research, London, RAND Europe UK; Gov. The Ditchley Foundation; mem. Bd Moscow School of Political Studies, Nuclear Threat Initiative; Hon. Fellow, Somerville Coll., Oxford, Newnham Coll., Cambridge; Grand Cross (FRG); Hon. DEd, CNAA; Hon. DrPolEcon (Univ. of Leuven, Belgium, Radcliffe Coll., Harvard, USA); Hon. LLD (Leeds) 1979, (Southampton) 1981, (Ulster) 1997; Dr hc (Aston, Bath, Essex, Heriot-Watt, Napier, Sheffield, Washington Coll. (USA)); Janeway Lecturer, Princeton Univ.; Pick Lecturer, Univ. of Chicago; Godkin Lecturer, Harvard Univ.; Montgomery Lecturer, Dartmouth Coll.; Heath Fellow, Grinell Coll.; Rede Lecturer and Darwin Lecturer, Univ. of Cambridge; Hoover Lecturer, Strathclyde Univ.; Dainton Lecturer, British Library; Gresham Lecturer, Mansion House; RSA Silver Medal. *Radio:* Snakes and Ladders: A Political Diary (BBC Radio 4) 1996, Women in the House (BBC Radio 4) 1998. *Television:* Shirley Williams in Conversation (BBC series) 1979. *Publications:* Youth Without Work (OECD Study) 1981, Politics is for People 1981, A Job to Live 1985, 'Human Rights in Europe' for Human Rights: What Work? (ed. Power and Alison) 2000, Making Globalisation Good (Chapter 15: Global Social Justice – The Moral Responsibilities of the Rich to the Poor) (ed. John Dunning) 2003, God and Caesar 2003, Climbing the Bookshelves: The Autobiography 2009; pamphlets on EC and economics of Central Africa; articles for The Times, Guardian, Independent, Int. Herald Tribune,

Political Quarterly, Prospect etc. *Leisure interests:* riding, rough walking, music. *Address:* House of Lords, Westminster, London, SW1A 0PW, England (office). *Telephone:* (20) 7219-5850 (office); (20) 7219-3242 (office). *Fax:* (20) 7219-1174 (office). *E-mail:* williamss@parliament.uk (office); shirley_williams@ksg.harvard.edu. *Website:* www.hks.harvard.edu.

WILLIAMS OF ELVEL, Baron (Life Peer), cr. 1985, of Llansantffraed in Elvel in the County of Powys; **Charles Cuthbert Powell Williams,** PC, CBE, MA; British business executive, author and politician; b. 9 Feb. 1933, Oxford; s. of Dr Norman P. Williams and Muriel Cazenove; m. Jane G. Portal 1975; one step-s.; ed Westminster School, Christ Church, Oxford and London School of Econs; British Petroleum Co. Ltd 1958–64; Bank of London and Montreal 1964–66; Eurofinance SA, Paris 1966–70; Baring Brothers & Co. Ltd 1970–77, Man. Dir 1971–77; Chair. Price Comm. 1977–79; Man. Dir Henry Ansbacher & Co. Ltd 1980–82, Chair. 1982–85; Chief Exec. Henry Ansbacher Holdings PLC 1982–85; Chair. Acoustiguide UK Ltd 1989–95; Pres. Campaign for the Protection of Rural Wales 1989–95, Pres. Radnor Br. 1995–; Pres. Fed. of Econ. Devt Authorities 1990–96; parl. cand. (Labour) 1964; Opposition Spokesman for Trade and Industry, House of Lords 1986–92, for Defence 1990–, for Environment 1992–; Deputy Leader of Opposition in House of Lords 1989–92; Chair. Acad. of St Martin in the Fields 1989–91, Mid Wales Chamber Orchestra Ltd 2009–13; Patron Llandrindod Wells Spa Town Trust 1991–. *Publications:* The Last Great Frenchman: A Life of General de Gaulle 1993, Bradman: An Australian Hero 1996, Adenauer: The Father of the New Germany 2000, Pétain 2005, Harold Macmillan 2009, Gentlemen and Players 2012. *Leisure interests:* cricket, music. *Address:* 48 Thurloe Square, London, SW7 2SX, England.

WILLIAMS OF OYSTERMOUTH, Baron (Life Peer), cr. 2013, of Oystermouth in the City and County of Swansea; **Most Rev., Rt Hon. Rowan Douglas Williams,** PC, MA, DPhil, DD, FRSL, FBA; British ecclesiastic, academic and college principal; *Master, Magdalene College, Cambridge;* b. 14 June 1950, Ystradgynlais, Swansea, Wales; s. of Aneurin Williams and Delphine (Del, Nancy) Morris; m. Jane Paul 1981; one s. one d.; ed Dynevor School, Swansea, Christ's Coll., Cambridge, Wadham Coll., Oxford; lectured at Coll. of the Resurrection, Mirfield, W Yorks. 1975–77; deacon, Ely Cathedral 1977; priest 1978; tutor, Westcott House, Univ. of Cambridge 1977–80, Lecturer in Divinity 1980–86, Dean and Chaplain, Clare Coll. 1984–86; Canon Theologian Leicester Cathedral 1981–82; Canon Residentiary, Christ Church, Oxford 1986–92; Lady Margaret Prof. of Theology, Univ. of Oxford 1986–92; consecrated Bishop of Monmouth in the Church in Wales 1992–2002; Archbishop of Wales 2000–02; Archbishop of Canterbury, Metropolitan of the Prov. of Canterbury and Primate of All England 2002–12; Master of Magdalene Coll., Cambridge 2013–; inaugurated as first Chancellor of Canterbury Christ Church Univ. 2005; Visitor at King's Coll., London, Univ. of Kent, Keble Coll., Oxford; Chancellor Univ. of South Wales 2013–; mem. (Crossbench) House of Lords 2013–; Chair. Lambeth Palace Library Trustees, Christian Aid Bd of Trustees 2013–; Pres. John Townsend Trust, Royal School of Church Music, St Edmund's School, Canterbury, Friends of Anglican Centre, Rome, Charles Williams Soc., Council of Christians and Jews, Soc. for the Promotion of Christian Knowledge; Vice-Pres. Barnardo's, MIND—Nat. Asscn for Mental Health, Royal Nat. Coll. for the Blind, Welsh Music Guild; Trustee, Philip Usher Memorial Fund; Gov. of Charterhouse School; Patron Peace Mala Youth Project for World Peace 2002–, Canterbury Open Centre run by Catching Lives; Founding Fellow, Learned Soc. of Wales 2010; Hon. Student of Christ Church, Oxford; Hon. Curate, St George's, Chesterton, Cambridge 1980–83, Hon. Fellow, Univ. of Wales, Bangor 2003, Univ. of Wales, Swansea, Newport, Aberystwyth, Cardiff, Clare Coll., Cambridge, Christ Church, Oxford, Wadham Coll., Oxford, Christ's Coll., Cambridge; Order of Friendship (Russia) 2010; Hon. DD (Kent) 2003, (Univ. of Wales) 2003, (Cambridge) 2006, (Trinity Coll., Univ. of Toronto) 2007, (Wycliffe Coll., Univ. of Toronto) 2007, (Durham) 2007, (St Vladimir's Orthodox Theological Seminary) 2010, (Catholic Univ. of Louvain) 2011, (King's Coll., London) 2011; Hon. DrTheol (Evangelisch-Theologische Fakultät, Univ. of Bonn) 2004; Hon. DCL (Oxford) 2005; Dr hc (Erlangen, Nashoteh House, Exeter, Aberdeen, Open Univ., Roehampton). *Television:* Conversations with Rowan Williams 2003. *Publications include:* The Wound of Knowledge 1979, Resurrection 1982, The Truce of God 1983, Arius: Heresy and Tradition 1987, Teresa of Avila 1991, Open to Judgement: Sermons and Addresses 1994, Sergei Bulgakov: towards a Russian political theory 1999, Christ on Trial: How the Gospel Unsettles our Judgement 2000, Lost Icons: Reflection on Cultural Bereavement 2000, On Christian Theology 2000, Love's Redeeming Work (ed.) 2001, Ponder These Things: Praying With Icons of the Virgin 2002, Writing in the Dust: Reflections on 11th September and its Aftermath 2002, Silence and Honey Cakes 2003, The Dwelling of the Light 2003, Anglican Identities 2004, Why Study the Past? 2005, Grace and Necessity 2006, Tokens of Trust: An Introduction to Christian Belief 2007, Wrestling with Angels: Conversations in Modern Theology 2007, Dostoevsky: Language, Faith and Fiction 2008; poetry: After Silent Centuries 1994, Remembering Jerusalem 2001, The Poems of Rowan Williams 2002, Headwaters 2008, Uncommon Gratitude (with Joan Chittister) 2010, Crisis and Recovery (with Larry Elliot) 2010. *Leisure interests:* music, fiction, languages. *Address:* House of Lords, London, SW1A 0PW (office); Magdalene College, Cambridge, CB3 0AG, England (office). *Telephone:* (20) 7219-5353 (House of Lords) (office); (1223) 332144 (office). *Fax:* (20) 7219-5979 (House of Lords) (office). *E-mail:* jeh34@cam.ac.uk (office). *Website:* www.magd.cam.ac.uk (office).

WILLIAMSON, David Keith, AO, BE, MA; Australian playwright and screenwriter; b. 24 Feb. 1942, Melbourne, Vic.; s. of Edwin Keith David Williamson and Elvie May Williamson (née Armstrong); m. Kristin Ingrid Lofven 1974; five c.; ed Monash Univ., Univ. of Melbourne; Design Engineer, Gen. Motors-Holden's 1965; Lecturer, Swinbourne Tech. Coll. 1966–72; freelance writer 1972–; Hon. DLitt (Sydney), (Monash), (Swinburne), (Queensland); numerous writing, TV and cinema awards including JC Williamson Award for Lifetime Achievement, Live Performance Australia 2005. *Plays:* The Removalists (Australian Writers Guild Awgie Award) 1972, Don's Party 1973, Three Plays 1974, The Department 1975, A Handful of Friends 1976, The Club 1977, Travelling North (Australian Film Institute Award for Best Screenplay 1987) 1979, The Perfectionist 1981, Sons of Cain 1985, Emerald City 1987, Top Silk 1989, Siren 1990, Money and Friends 1992, Brilliant Lies 1993, Sanctuary 1994, Dead White Males 1995, Corporate Vibes 1999, Face to Face 1999, The Great Man 2000, Up for Grabs 2001, A Conversation 2001, Charitable Intent 2001, Soulmates 2002, Amigos 2004, Influence 2005, Scarlett O'Hara at the Crimson Parrot 2008, Let The Sunshine 2009, Rhinestone Rex & Miss Monica 2010, Don Parties On 2011, At Any Cost? 2011, Nothing Personal 2011, When Dad Married Fury 2011, Managing Carmen 2012, Happiness 2013, Rupert 2013, Cruise Control 2014, Dream Home 2015. *Screenplays:* Don's Party (Australian Film Institute Award for Best Screenplay 1977) 1971, Gallipoli (Australian Film Institute Award for Best Screenplay 1981) 1981, Phar Lap 1983, The Year of Living Dangerously 1983, Travelling North 1986, Emerald City 1988, The Four Minute Mile (two-part TV series) 1988, A Dangerous Life (six-hour TV series) 1988, Top Silk 1989, Siren 1990, Money and Friends 1992, Dead White Males 1995, Heretic 1996, Brilliant Lies 1996, Third World Blues 1997, After the Ball 1997, On the Beach 2000, Balibo (Australian Film Institute Award for Best Screenplay 2009) 2009, Face to Face 2011. *Address:* c/o, Level 7, 61 Marlborough Street, Surry Hills, NSW 2010, Australia (office). *Telephone:* (2) 9319-7199 (office). *E-mail:* info@cameronsmanagement.com.au (office). *Website:* www.cameronsmanagement.com.au (office).

WILLIAMSON, Rt Hon. Gavin Alexander, CBE, BSc; British politician; b. 25 June 1976, Scarborough; m. Joanne Eland; two d.; ed Univ. of Bradford; began career working at Aynsley China, Staffordshire; fmr Man. Dir architectural design firm; County Councillor, Seamer Division, North Yorkshire County Council 2001–05; MP (Conservative) for S Staffordshire 2010–, mem. Northern Ireland Affairs Cttee 2010–11; Parl. Private Sec. to Minister of State for N Ireland 2011–12, Parl. Pvt. Sec. to Sec. of State for Transport 2012–13, Parl. Pvt. Sec. to the Prime Minister 2013–16, Parl. Sec. to the Treasury and Chief Whip 2016–17; Sec. of State for Defence 2017–19; fmr Deputy Chair. Staffordshire Area Conservatives, Chair. Stoke-on-Trent Conservative Asscn, Vice-Chair. Derbyshire Dales Conservative Asscn. *Address:* House of Commons, London, SW1A 0AA, England (office). *Telephone:* (20) 7218-9000 (office). *E-mail:* gavin@gavinwilliamson.org. *Website:* www.gavinwilliamson.org.

WILLIAMSON, Geordie, BA (Hons), PhD; Australian mathematician and academic; *Professor of Mathematics, University of Sydney;* b. 1981, Bowral, NSW; ed Univ. of Sydney; Scientific Asst, Univ. of Sydney Feb.–July 2004, currently Assoc. Prof., Prof. of Math. 2017–; Wissenschaftlicher Mitarbeiter, Albert-Ludwigs-Universität Freiburg 2004–08; Jr Research Fellow, St Peter's Coll., Oxford 2008–11; EPSRC Postdoctoral Research Fellow, Math. Inst., Univ. of Oxford 2008–11; Advanced Researcher (W2 Research Prof.), Max Planck Inst. for Math., Bonn 2011–16; Visiting Prof., Research Inst. for Math. Sciences, Kyoto, Japan Sept.–Dec. 2017; Univ. Medal, Univ. of Sydney 2003, Eleanor Sophia-Wood Travelling Scholarship, Universität Freiburg (awarded by Univ. of Sydney) 2005–07, ING Excellence Award, Univ. of Sydney 2006, Liegrits Predoctoral Scholarship, Univ. of Aarhus, Denmark Sept.–Dec. 2006, Feit Memorial Lecturer, Yale Univ., USA 2014, Séminaire Bourbaki, Paris, France 2016, Takagi Lecturer, Univ. of Tokyo 2016, Chevalley Prize, American Math. Soc. 2016, European Math. Soc. Prize 2016, Clay Research Award, Clay Math. Inst. (co-recipient) 2016, Distinguished Lecture Series, Stanford Univ., USA 2017. *Publications:* numerous papers in professional journals. *Address:* Room F07, School of Mathematics and Statistics, Carslaw Building, University of Sydney, Sydney, NSW 2006, Australia (office). *Telephone:* (2) 9351-2222 (switchboard) (office). *E-mail:* geordie@mpim-bonn.mpg.de (office). *Website:* sydney.edu.au/science/people/g.williamson.php (office); people.mpim-bonn.mpg.de/geordie (office).

WILLIAMSON, Kevin Meade; American screenwriter, producer, director and actor; b. 14 March 1965, New Bern, NC; ed East Carolina Univ., Univ. of California, Los Angeles; fmr actor, asst dir, music videos; f. Outerbanks Entertainment 1995; Entertainer of the Year, Entertainment Weekly 1997, mem. Power 100 List, Premiere Magazine 1998. *Films include:* Scream (writer) 1996, Scream 2 1997, I Know What You Did Last Summer (writer) 1997, Halloween H20: 20 Years Later (producer) 1998, The Faculty (writer) 1998, Teaching Mrs. Tingle (writer, dir) 1999, Scream 3 2000, Cursed (writer, producer) 2005, Venom 2005, Retribution 2006, Scream 4 2011, Horror Movie: The Movie (short) 2012. *Television series include:* Dawson's Creek (creator) 1998–99, 2003, Wasteland (writer, producer) 1999, Glory Days (creator) 2002, Hidden Palms 2007, The Vampire Diaries 2009–, The Secret Circle 2011–12, The Following 2013–, Stalker 2014–. *Address:* c/o WME Entertainment, 9601 Wilshire Boulevard, Beverley Hills, CA 90210-5213, USA. *Telephone:* (310) 285-9000. *Fax:* (310) 285-9010. *Website:* www.wma.com.

WILLIAMSON, Sir (George) Malcolm, Kt, FCIB; British banker; *Chairman, Strategy and Development Board, Cass Business School;* b. 27 Feb. 1939, Oldham, Lancs., England; s. of George Williamson and Margery Williamson; m. Hang Thi Ngo; one s. one d.; one s. one d. by previous marriage; local dir, Barclays Bank PLC, N London 1978–79; Asst Gen. Man. Barclays Bank PLC 1979–82, Treas. UK 1982–83, Regional Man. 1983–85; Man. Dir Girobank PLC and mem. Bd The Post Office 1985–89; Group Exec. Dir Banking (Eastern Hemisphere), Standard Chartered Bank 1989–90, Group Exec. Dir Banking 1990–91, Group Man. Dir 1991–93, Group Chief Exec. 1993–98; Dir Nat. Grid Group 1995–99; UK Chair. Thai-British Group 1997; Pres. and Chief Exec. Visa Int. 1998–2004; Chair. Britannic Group 2004–05; Chair. CDC Group PLC 2004; Dir Group 4 Securicor plc (now G4S PLC) 2004–08; mem. Bd of Dirs, Nat. Australia Bank 2004–12, Chair. Nat. Australia Group Europe Ltd 2004–12, Clydesdale Bank 2004–12, (all mems Nat. Australia Bank Group); Deputy Chair. Resolution plc 2005–08; Dir, JP Morgan Cazenove Holdings 2005–; Chair. Signet Group plc 2006; Chair. Advisory Bd, Youth Business Int. (now Princes Youth Business Int.) 2005–08; Dir, The Prince of Wales Int. Business Leaders Forum 2006–; Chair. Friends Life Group Ltd 2012–, NewDay Group Ltd, Governing Council of the Centre for the Study of Financial Innovation; Chair. Bd of Trustees, Youth Business Int., Cass Business School Strategy and Devt Bd. *Leisure interests:* mountaineering, walking, chess, bridge. *Address:* Cass Business School, 106 Bunhill Row, London, EC1Y 8TZ, England (office). *Telephone:* (20) 7040-8600 (office). *E-mail:* execed@city.ac.uk (office). *Website:* www.cass.city.ac.uk (office).

WILLIAMSON, Matthew, BA; British fashion designer; b. 23 Oct. 1971, Chorlton, Manchester, England; ed Loreto Coll., Manchester, Saint Martin's School of Art and Design (now Central Saint Martin's); worked as a freelance designer for two years; travelled frequently to India for Marni, Georgina von Ertzdorf and Monsoon fashion retailers; Founder and Creative Dir Matthew Williamson (with Joseph Velosa) 1997–; debuted collection 'Electric Angels' at

London Fashion Week 1997; collections displayed during New York Fashion week 2002; shop at 28 Bruton Street, Mayfair, London opened 2004; launched own perfume range 2005; Creative Dir Emilio Pucci 2006–; restrospective exhbn of his work (Matthew Williamson – 10 years in Fashion) hosted by Design Museum, London 2007; returned to London full-time to focus on own label's forthcoming ventures and expansion 2008; signed new licensing deal with MBFG to begin new line – Muse by Matthew Williamson 2010; Elle Designer of the Year 2004, Moet and Chandon Fashion Tribute Award 2005, Red Carpet Designer Award, British Fashion Awards 2008. *Film:* XV (short) 2012. *Television:* guest appearance on US reality TV series Project Runway 2010. *Address:* Matthew Williamson Head Office, Unit 10–11, The Quadrant, 135 Salusbury Road, London, NW6 6RJ (office); Matthew Williamson Communications Office (Press, Marketing and Sales), 28 Bruton Street, London, W1J 6QH, England (office). *Telephone:* (20) 7491-6220 (Head Office) (office); (20) 7629-6200 (Communications Office) (office). *Fax:* (20) 7491-6252 (Head Office) (office). *E-mail:* info@matthewwilliamson.co.uk (office). *Website:* www.matthewwilliamson.com (office).

WILLIAMSON, Oliver E., SB, MBA, PhD; American economist and academic; *Professor of the Graduate School and Edgar F. Kaiser Professor Emeritus of Business, Economics, and Law, University of California, Berkeley;* b. 27 Sept. 1932, Superior, Wis.; s. of Scott Williamson and Lucille Williamson; m. Dolores Celeni 1957; three s. two d.; ed Massachusetts Inst. of Tech., Stanford Univ., Carnegie Mellon Univ.; Project Engineer with US Govt 1955–58; Asst Prof. of Econs, Univ. of California, Berkeley 1963–65, Prof. of Business, Econs and Law 1988–94, Edgar F. Kaiser Prof. of Business Admin and Prof. of Econs and Law 1994–2008, Prof. in the Grad. School and Prof. Emer. 2008–; Assoc. Prof., Pennsylvania State Univ. 1965–68, Prof. 1968–83, Charles and William L. Day Prof. of Econs and Social Science 1977–83; Gordon B. Tweedy Prof. of Econs of Law and Org., Yale Univ. 1983–88; visiting prof. at numerous int. univs; Special Econ. Asst to Asst Attorney-Gen. for Antitrust, US Dept of Justice 1966–67, consultant to US Dept of Justice 1967–69; consultant, NSF 1976–77; consultant to US Fed. Trade Comm. 1978–80; Fellow, American Acad. of Arts and Sciences 1983, Econometrics Soc. 1977, American Acad. of Political and Social Science 1997; mem. NAS 1994–, American Econ. Asscn 1960–, Western Econs Asscn 1995– (Pres. 1999–2000), American Law and Econs Asscn (Pres. 1997–98), Int. Soc. for New Institutional Econs 1997– (Pres. 1999–2001); mem. numerous advisory and editorial bds; Distinguished Fellow, Industrial Org. Soc. 2005, American Econ. Soc. 2007; several hon. degrees; Alexander Henderson Award for Excellence in Econ. Theory 1962, Irwin Award for Scholarly Contributions to Man. 1988, John von Neumann Award, Laszlo Rajk Coll. for Advanced Studies, Budapest 1999, Horst Claus Recktenwald Prize in Econs 2004, Nobel Prize in Econs (with Elinor Ostrom) 2009. *Publications include:* The Economics of Discretionary Behavior: Managerial Objectives in a Theory of the Firm 1964, Corporate Control and Business Behavior: An Inquiry into the Effects of Organization Form on Enterprise Behavior 1970, Markets and Hierarchies: Analysis and Antitrust Implications 1975, The Economic Institutions of Capitalism: Firms, Markets, Relational Contracting 1985. *Address:* Walter A. Haas School of Business, S545 Student Services Building, #1900, Berkeley, CA 94720-1900, USA (office). *Telephone:* (510) 642-8697 (office). *Fax:* (510) 642-4700 (office). *E-mail:* owilliam@haas.berkeley.edu (office). *Website:* groups.haas.berkeley.edu/bpp/oew (office).

WILLIAMSON, Sir (Robert) Brian, Kt, CBE, MA, FRSA; British business executive; b. 16 Feb. 1945; m. Diane Marie Christine de Jacquier de Rosée 1986; ed Trinity Coll., Dublin; Personal Asst to Maurice Macmillan (later Viscount Macmillan) 1967–71; Ed. Int. Currency Review 1971; Man. Dir Gerrard & Nat. Holdings (later Gerrard Group PLC) 1978–89, Chair. 1989–98; Dir London Int. Financial Futures and Options Exchange (LIFFE) 1982–89, Chair. 1985–88, 1998–2003; Chair. GNI Ltd 1985–89; Dir Fleming Int. High Income Investment Trust PLC 1990–96, Deputy Chair. Fleming Worldwide Investment Trust PLC 1996; Dir Bank of Ireland 1990–98 (mem. Bd Bank of Ireland Britain Holdings 1986–90); Chair. MT Fund Man. Ltd, Armed Forces Charities Advisory Co., Electra Partners LLP; Group Chair. Resolution Life Group Ltd –2005; Chair. London Int. Financial Futures and Options Exchange (alternative name, LIFFE (Holdings) plc) 1985–88, 1998–2003; Chair. Gerrard Group PLC 1989–98; Chair. Electra Private Equity PLC (fmrly Electra Investment Trust PLC) 2009–10, Electra Private Equity Investments PLC –2010; Chair. NASDAQ's Int. Markets Advisory Bd of Army Common Investment Fund UK 1995–98; Chair. Macmillan Trustees Fund Man. Ltd; fmr Chair. Fleming Worldwide Investment Trust plc; Dir, Politeia, Live-Ex Ltd, Barlows PLC 1986–98, Electra Partners LLP, Electra Private Equity PLC 1994–2010, Templeton Emerging Markets Investment Trust PLC 2002–03, Pearl Group Holdings (No. 1) Ltd from 2005, AMP Holdings Plc, Winston Churchill Memorial Trust, Edenberg Ltd Partnership, Liv-Ex Ltd; Ind. Dir, Climate Exchange Plc 2007–11; Dir (non-exec.), MT Fund Management Ltd 1995–, Resolution PLC 2004–08, NYSE Euronext, Inc. 2007–13, Waverton Investment Man. Ltd 2010–; Ind. Dir (non-exec.), HSBC Holdings Plc 2002–12; mem. Supervisory Bd Euronext NV 2002–07; mem. Dean and Canons Advisory Cttee on Finance of the Coll. of St George's Chapel, Windsor Castle, Finance Cttee of St George's House Trust, Windsor Castle; Pres. St Moritz Tobogganing Club; Hon. Bencher of the Inner Temple; HM Lt for the City of London. *Leisure interests:* tobogganing, hot air ballooning. *Address:* Waverton Investment Management Ltd, 21 St James's Square, London, SW1Y 4HB, England (office); MT Fund Management Ltd, Calton Square, 1 Greenside Row, Edinburgh, EH1 3AN, Scotland (office); 8 Canada Square, London, E14 5EQ, England. *Telephone:* (20) 7484-7484 (Waverton) (office). *Fax:* (20) 7484-7400 (Waverton) (office). *E-mail:* info@waverton.co.uk (office). *Website:* www.waverton.co.uk (office).

WILLIS, Bruce Walter; American actor; b. 19 March 1955, Idar-Oberstein, Germany; s. of David Willis and Marlene Willis; m. 1st Demi Moore (q.v.) 1987 (divorced 2000); three d.; m. 2nd Emma Heming 2009; one d.; ed Montclair State Coll.; moved to USA 1957; studied with Stella Adler; mem. First Amendment Comedy Theatre; Officier, Ordre des Arts et des Lettres. *Stage appearances:* (off-Broadway): Heaven and Earth 1977, Fool for Love 1984, The Bullpen, The Bayside Boys, The Ballad of Railroad William. *Films:* Blind Date 1987, Sunset 1988, Die Hard 1988, In Country 1989, Die Hard 2, Die Harder 1990, Bonfire of the Vanities 1990, Hudson Hawk 1991, The Last Boy Scout 1991, Billy Bathgate 1991, Death Becomes Her 1992, Striking Distance 1993, Color of Night 1994, North 1994, Nobody's Fool 1994, Pulp Fiction 1994, Die Hard with a Vengeance 1995, 12 Monkeys 1995, Four Rooms, Last Man Standing 1996, The Jackal 1997, The Fifth Element 1997, Mercury Rising 1998, Armageddon 1998, Breakfast of Champions 1998, The Story of US 1999, The Sixth Sense 1999, Unbreakable 2000, Disney's the Kid 2000, Bandits 2001, Hart's War 2002, Tears of the Sun 2003, The Whole Ten Yards 2004, Hostage 2005, Sin City 2005, Alpha Dog 2006, Lucky Number Slevin 2006, 16 Blocks 2006, Over the Hedge (voice) 2006, Hammy's Boomerang Adventure (voice) 2006, Fast Food Nation 2006, The Hip Hop Project 2006, The Astronaut Farmer 2007, Perfect Stranger 2007, Grindhouse 2007, Live Free or Die Hard (also producer) 2007, Planet Terror 2007, Assassination of a High School President 2008, What Just Happened? 2008, Surrogates 2009, Red 2010, Catch 44 2010, Setup 2011, Lay the Favorite 2012, Moonrise Kingdom 2012, G.I. Joe: Retaliation 2012, The Expendables 2 2012, Looper 2012, The Cold Light of Day 2012, RED 2 2013, Sin City: A Dame to Kill For 2014, The Prince 2014, Vice 2015. *Television includes:* Moonlighting 1985–89 (series; People's Choice award 1986, Emmy award 1987, Golden Globe award 1987), Friends 2000. *Recordings:* The Return of Bruno 1987, If It Don't Kill You, It Just Makes You Stronger 1989. *Address:* CAA, 2000 Avenue of the Stars, Los Angeles, CA 90067; 22470 Pacific Coast Highway, Malibu, CA 90265, USA.

WILLIS, Ralph, AO, BCom; Australian politician; b. 14 April 1938, Melbourne, Vic.; s. of Stanley Willis and Doris Willis; m. Carol Joyce Dawson 1970; one s. two d.; ed Univ. High School and Univ. of Melbourne; research officer, Australian Council of Trade Unions 1960, industrial advocate 1970; mem. (Australian Labor Party) Fed. Parl. for Gellibrand 1972–98; Minister for Employment and Industrial Relations and Minister assisting Prime Minister in Public Service Industrial Matters 1983–87, Minister for Industrial Relations and Minister assisting Prime Minister in Public Service Matters 1987–88, for Transport and Communications 1988–90, for Finance 1990–91, Treas. 1991, Minister for Finance 1991–93, Treas. 1993–96; Vice-Pres. Exec. Council 1992; Chair. Western Health Bd 2004, Construction and Building Industry Superannuation Fund (C+BUS), Melbourne City Opera, LeadWest 2008–11; Dir, Australian Super Developments; Chair. and Treas., Mietta Foundation; mem. Australian Council of Superannuation Investors, UN Sec.-Gen.'s High Level Panel on Youth Employment, Bd Westgate Community Initiatives Group, Bd Stan Willis Trust; Centenary Medal 2001; Hon. DUniv (Victoria Univ.) 2009. *Leisure interests:* tennis, reading, watching football. *Address:* 24 Gellibrand Street, Williamstown, Vic. 3016, Australia.

WILLMOTT, Peter S., BA, MBA; American business executive; *Chairman and CEO, Willmott Services Inc.;* ed Williams Coll., Harvard Univ.; began career as sr financial analyst American Airlines; fmr Man. Consultant Booz, Allen & Hamilton; fmr Vice-Pres. ITT Continental Banking Co.; fmr Chief Financial Officer, then Pres. and COO Federal Express Corpn; fmr Chair. and Pres. Carson Pirie Scott, Zenith Electronics Corpn; currently Chair. and CEO Willmott Services (consultancy), Chicago; mem. Bd Fleming Cos Inc. 2002–, interim CEO and Pres. March–Aug. 2003; apptd Man. Partner Berkshires Capital Investors (BCI) 2001; mem. Bd of Dirs Federal Express, Security Capital Group; mem. bd several civic orgs in Chicago and Berkshires; fmr Chair. Bd of Trustees Williams Coll. *Address:* Willmott Services Inc., 333 North Michigan Avenue, Suite 2200, Chicago, IL 60601, USA. *Telephone:* (312) 244-6505.

WILLOCH, Kåre Isaachsen, Cand Oecon; Norwegian politician (retd); b. 3 Oct. 1928, Oslo; s. of Haakon Willoch and Agnes Saure; m. Anne-Marie Jørgensen 1954; one s. two d.; ed Ullern Gymnasium and Univ. of Oslo; Sec. Fed. of Norwegian Shipowners 1951–53, Counsellor Fed. of Norwegian Industries 1954–63; mem. Storting 1958–89; mem. Nat. Cttee Conservative Party 1961–89, Sec.-Gen. Conservative Party 1963–65, Chair. 1970–74, Chair. Conservative Party Parl. Group 1970–81; Minister of Trade and Shipping 1963, 1965–70; Chair. World Bank Group 1967; mem. Nordic Council 1970–86, Pres. 1973; Prime Minister 1981–86; Chair. Int. Democratic Union 1987–89; Chair. Foreign Affairs Cttee of Parl. 1986–89; Co-Gov. of Oslo and Akershus 1989–98; Chair. Norwegian Defence Comm. 1990–92; Chair. Supervisory Bd, Norwegian Bank 1990–96; Chair. Bd of Norwegian Broadcasting Corpn 1998–2000; Chair. Norwegian Comm. on the Vulnerability of Soc. 1999–2000; Dir Fridtjof Nansen Inst. 1999–2001; Commdr with Star, Royal Norwegian Order of St Olav; Dr hc (St Olav's Coll. Minn., USA); Fritt Ords Pris, Norwegian Inst. for Free Speech 1997, Opinion Maker of the Year, Asscn of Norwegian Eds 1996, C.J. Hambro's Prize 2000. *Publications include:* Personal Savings 1955, Price Policy in Norway (with L. B. Bachke) 1958, Memoirs (Vol. I) 1988, (Vol. II) 1990, Krisetid 1992, A New Policy for the Environment 1996, Ideas (Tanker i Tiden) 1999, Myths and Realities ((Myter og virkelighet) (memoirs) 2002, Alvorlig talt (Seriously Speaking) (with fmr Prime Minister Odvaar Nordli) 2008, Erfaringer for fremtiden (Experience for the Future) 2010, Strid og samarbeid (Strife and cooperation) 2015. *Leisure interests:* skiing, touring. *Address:* Blokkaveien 6B, 0282 Oslo, Norway. *Telephone:* 22-50-72-89. *E-mail:* fmoa@firsurf.no.

WILLOTT, (William) Brian, CB, PhD; British public official; b. 14 May 1940, Swansea, Wales; s. of William Harford and Beryl P. M. Willott; m. Alison Leyland Pyke-Lees 1970; two s. two d.; ed Trinity Coll., Cambridge; Research Assoc., Univ. of Md 1965–67; Asst Prin. Bd of Trade 1967–69, Prin. 1969–73; HM Treasury 1973–75; Asst Sec. Dept of Industry 1975–78, Sec. Ind. Devt Unit 1978–80; Sec. Nat. Enterprise Bd 1980–81; CEO British Tech. Group (Nat. Enterprise Bd and Nat. Research and Devt Corpn) 1981–84; Head, Information Tech. Div., Dept of Trade and Industry 1984–87, Head, Financial Services Div. 1987–91; Chief Exec. Export Credit Guarantee Dept 1992–97; CEO Welsh Devt Agency 1997–2000; Chair. Gwent NHS Healthcare Trust 2003–08 (re-apptd 2008); Dir Dragon Int. Studios Ltd; mem. Council Nat. Museums and Galleries of Wales 2001–09; Visiting Prof., Univ. of Glamorgan 2000. *Leisure interests:* music, reading, ancient history, gardening. *Address:* Coed Cefn, Tregare, Monmouth, NP25 4DT, Wales.

WILLOUGHBY, Christopher R., MA; British economist; b. 24 Feb. 1938, Guildford; s. of Ronald James Edward Willoughby and Constance Louisa (née Sherbrooke) Willoughby; m. Marie-Anne Isabelle Normand 1972; ed Lambroke School, Marlborough Coll., Univ. of Grenoble, Jt Services School for Linguists, Balliol Coll., Oxford, Univ. of California, Berkeley; served in RN 1956–58, Lt, RNR 1958; New York Times Wash. Bureau 1962–63; Economist, World Bank 1963, Dir Operations Evaluation Dept 1973–76, Transport, Water and Telecommunications Dept 1976–83, Econ. Devt Inst. 1983–90, Chief, World Bank Mission in Bangladesh 1990–94, in Belarus 1994–97, Infrastructure Lead Adviser, Europe and Cen. Asia Region 1997, Lead Specialist Infrastructure Dept 1999, now retd; Assoc. Consultant, Oxford Policy Man. *Leisure interests:* running, swimming, house re-modelling. *Address:* c/o Oxford Policy Management, 6 St Aldates Courtyard, 38 St Aldates, Oxford, OX1 1BN, England.

WILLS, Dean Robert, AO; Australian business executive; b. 10 July 1933; s. of Walter W. Wills and Violet J. Dryburgh; m. Margaret F. Williams 1955; one s. two d.; ed Sacred Heart Coll., South Australian Inst. of Tech.; Dir W. D. & H. O. Wills (Australia) 1974–, Man. Dir 1977–83, Chair. 1983–86; apptd Dir AMATIL Ltd 1975, Deputy Chair. 1983–84; Man. Dir Coca-Cola AMATIL Ltd 1984–94, Chair. 1984–99; mem. Business Council of Australia 1984–94, Vice-Pres. 1987–88, Pres. 1988–90; mem. Bd Australian Grad. School of Man. (Univ. of NSW) 1985–92; Gov. Medical Foundation (Univ. of Sydney) 1990–94; mem. Corps. and Securities Panel 1991–94; Vice-Chair. Nat. Mutual Life 1992–97, Chair. 1997–2000; Deputy Chair. Nat. Mutual Holdings 1995–97, Chair. 1997–2000; Chair. Transfield Services Ltd 2001–05, Coca-Cola Australia Foundation Ltd 2002–05; Dir John Fairfax Holdings Ltd 1994–2005 (Chair. 2002–05); Gov. Australian Naval Aviation Museum; Deputy Chair. Australian Grand Prix Corpn 1994–2002; Trustee, Museum of Applied Arts and Sciences 1986–90. *Leisure interests:* tennis, performance cars. *Address:* 71 Circular Quay East, Sydney, NSW 2000, Australia. *Telephone:* (2) 9259-6420. *Fax:* (2) 9259-6628.

WILLS, Garry, BA, MA, PhD; American writer, journalist and academic; *Professor of History Emeritus, Northwestern University;* b. 22 May 1934, Atlanta, Ga; m. Natalie Cavallo 1959; two s. one d.; ed St Louis Univ., Xavier Univ., Univ. of Cincinnati and Yale Univ.; Fellow, Center for Hellenic Studies 1961–62; Assoc. Prof. of Classics 1962–67, Adjunct Prof. 1968–80, Johns Hopkins Univ.; newspaper columnist, Universal Press Syndicate 1970–; Henry R. Luce Prof. of American Culture and Public Policy, Northwestern Univ. 1980–88, Adjunct Prof., later Prof. of History Emer. 1988–; mem. American Philosophical Soc., American Acad. of Arts and Letters, American Acad. of Arts and Sciences; Dr hc (Coll. of the Holy Cross) 1982, (Bates Coll.) 1995; Nat. Humanities Medal 1998, St Louis Literary Award, St Louis Univ. Library Associates 2004. *Publications include:* Chesterton 1961, Politics and Catholic Freedom 1964, Roman Culture 1966, Jack Ruby 1967, Second Civil War 1968, Nixon Agonistes 1970, Bare Ruined Choirs 1972, Inventing America 1978, At Button's 1979, Confessions of a Conservative 1979, Explaining America 1980, The Kennedy Imprisonment 1982, Lead Time 1983, Cincinnatus 1984, Reagan's America 1987, Under God 1990, Lincoln at Gettysburg (Nat. Book Critics Circle Award 1993, Pulitzer Prize for General Non-Fiction 1993) 1992, Certain Trumpets: The Call of Leaders 1994, Witches and Jesuits: Shakespeare's Macbeth 1994, John Wayne's America 1997, Saint Augustine 1999, A Necessary Evil: A History of American Distrust of Government 1999, Papal Sin: Structures of Deceit 2000, Saint Augustine's Childhood 2001, Why I Am a Catholic 2002, President 2003, Saint Augustine's Sin 2004, Saint Augustine's Conversion 2004, Bush's Fringe Government 2006, Head and Heart: American Christianities 2007, What the Gospels Meant 2008, Martial's Epigrams (trans.) 2008, Bomb Power 2010, Outside Looking In: Adventures of an Observer 2010, Augustine's 'Confessions': A Biography 2011, Verdi's Shakespeare: Men of the Theater 2011, Rome and Rhetoric: Shakespeare's Julius Caesar 2011, Font of Life: Ambrose, Augustine, and the Mystery of Baptism 2012, Why Priests? 2013. *Address:* Department of History, Northwestern University, Harris Hall 202, 1881 Sheridan Road, Evanston, IL 60208, USA (office). *Telephone:* (847) 491-3406 (office). *Fax:* (847) 467-1393 (office). *E-mail:* g-wills@northwestern.edu (office). *Website:* www.history .northwestern.edu (office).

WILLSON, C. Grant, BS, MS, PhD; American chemist and academic; *Professor of Chemistry and Chemical Engineering Rashid Engineering Regents Chair, University of Texas;* b. 30 March 1939; ed Univ. of California, Berkeley, San Diego State Univ.; Asst Prof., California State Univ., Long Beach 1973–74; Asst Prof., Univ. of California, San Diego 1974–78; IBM Fellow and Man. of Polymer Science and Tech., IBM San Jose Research Center 1978–93; Prof. of Chem. and Chemical Eng and Rashid Eng Regent's Chair, Dept of Chem. and Biochemistry, McKetta Dept of Chemical Eng, Univ. of Texas 1993–; affiliated with Microelectronics Research Center, Center for Nano- and Molecular Science and Tech., Environmental Science Inst., Texas Materials Inst.; Fellow, Int. Soc. for Optics and Photonics (SPIE) 2007, Materials Research Soc. 2012; Inaugural Fellow, ACS 2009; SPIE Frits Zernike Award 2005, ACS Heroes of Chem. Award 2005, AIChE Arthur Dehon Little Award for Chemical Eng Innovation 2005, Teaching Excellence Award in Chemical Eng 2006, SEMI North America Award 2007, Nat. Medal of Tech. and Innovation 2007, Gordon E. Moore Medal 2009, ACS Award in Applied Polymer Science 2004, Inventor of the Year, Univ. of Texas 2012, Japan Prize (co-recipient) 2013. *Publications:* numerous papers in professional journals. *Address:* Department of Chemistry and Biochemistry, University of Texas, 1 University Station A5300, NHB 5.130, Austin, TX 78712-0165, USA (office). *Telephone:* (512) 471-4342 (office); (512) 471-3975 (office). *Fax:* (512) 471-7222 (office). *E-mail:* willson@che.utexas.edu (office). *Website:* www.cm.utexas .edu/grant_willson (office); willson.cm.utexas.edu (office).

WILLUMSTAD, Robert B.; American insurance executive; *Senior Adviser, Brysam Global Partners;* b. Brooklyn, New York; m. Carol Willumstad; two c.; ed Adelphi Univ.; worked in various positions in operations, retail banking and computer systems, Chemical Bank 1967–87; joined Commercial Credit, Baltimore (later CitiFinancial div. of Citigroup) 1987, Chair. and CEO Consumer Financial Services, Travelers Group –1998, Vice-Chair. Global Consumer Group and Chair. Global Consumer Lending, Citigroup Inc. (following merger of Citicorp and Travelers Group in 1998) 1998–2002, Chair. and CEO Citigroup Global Consumer Group 2000–03, Pres. Citigroup Inc. 2002–05, COO 2003–05, also CEO and Pres. Citibank NA 2003–05; mem. Bd of Dirs AIG 2006–08, Chair. 2006–08, CEO June–Sept. 2008; Co-founder and Sr Adviser, Brysam Global Partners 2007–; mem. Bd of Dirs S.C. Johnson & Son Inc., Habitat for Humanity, MasterCard International; mem. Adelphi Univ. Bd of Trustees 2005–; Hon. LLD (Adelphi) 2005; New York City Urban League Frederick Douglass Award 2002. *Address:* Brysam Global Partners, 515 Madison Avenue, New York NY 10022, USA (office). *Telephone:* (212) 297-2777 (office). *E-mail:* marge.magner@brysam.com (office). *Website:* www.brysam.com (office).

WILMOTT, Peter Graham, CMG, MA; British consultant and fmr civil servant; b. 6 Jan. 1947, Cuckfield, West Sussex, England; s. of John Wilmott and Violet Wilmott; m. Jennifer Plummer 1969; two d.; ed Hove Grammar School and Trinity Coll., Cambridge; Asst Prin., HM Customs & Excise 1968, Prin. 1973, Asst Sec. 1983, Commr 1988; seconded to UK Perm. Rep. to EC 1971–73, 1977–79, to EC Court of Auditors 1980–82; Dir-Gen. Customs and Indirect Taxation, EC Comm. 1990–96; partner with Prisma Consulting Group 1996–2000; Chair. Int. Value Added Tax Asscn 1998–2000; Pres. Office du Développement par l'Automatisation et la Simplification du Commerce Extérieur (ODASCE), Paris 2000–04, First Vice-Pres. 2004–08; Dir Ad Valorem Int. Ltd 2002–08, GlobalLink Border Solutions Ltd, SITPRO 2001–07.

WILMUT, Sir Ian, Kt, OBE, PhD, FRS, FRSE, FMedSci; British geneticist; *Professor Emeritus, University of Edinburgh;* b. 7 July 1944, Hampton Lucy, Warwicks., England; s. of Leonard (Jack) Wilmut and Mary Wilmut; m. Vivienne Mary Craven 1967; two d. one adopted s.; ed Univ. of Nottingham and Darwin Coll., Cambridge; Post-doctoral Fellow, Unit of Reproductive Physiology and Biochemistry, Cambridge 1971–73; various research posts, Animal Breeding Research Org. (ARC, now BBSRC Roslin Inst.) 1973–2005, Head of Div. Gene Expression and Devt, jtly responsible (with Keith Campbell) for cloning of Dolly (a sheep, first animal produced from an adult cell) 2000–05; Prof. of Reproductive Science, Univ. of Edin. 2005–06, also Chair. Scottish Centre for Regenerative Medicine 2005–, Founding Dir MRC Centre for Regenerative Medicine 2006–11, currently Prof. Emer.; Foreign Assoc. NAS 2004; Hon. DSc (Nottingham) 1998, (North Eastern Univ., Boston) 1999, (Edin.) 2002; Shaw Prize (co-recipient) 2008. *Publications:* The Second Creation (co-author) 2000, After Dolly: The Uses and Misuses of Human Cloning 2006; and contribs to numerous papers on cloning of Dolly the sheep. *Leisure interests:* curling, photography, walking in the countryside. *Address:* MRC Centre for Regenerative Medicine, SCRM Building, University of Edinburgh, Edinburgh bioQuarter, 5 Little France Drive, Edinburgh, EH16 4UU, Scotland (office). *Telephone:* (131) 651-9500 (office). *Fax:* (131) 651-9501 (office). *E-mail:* ian.wilmut@ed.ac.uk (office). *Website:* www.crm.ed.ac.uk/ research/group/redirecting-cell-fate (office).

WILSEY, Gen. Sir John Finlay Willasey, GCB, CBE, DL; British fmr army officer and business executive; b. 18 Feb. 1939, Frimley, Hants., England; s. of Maj.-Gen. J. H. O. Wilsey and B. S. F. Wilsey; m. Elizabeth P. Nottingham 1975; one s. one d.; ed Sherborne School and Royal Mil. Acad., Sandhurst; commissioned 1959; served in Cyprus, North Africa, Guyana, USA, Malta, Germany, UK (mem. Blue Nile Expedition 1968), Staff Coll. 1973; Commdg 1st Bn, The Devonshire & Dorset Regt 1979–82, Col 1990–97; Chief of Staff, HQ, NI 1982–84; Commdg 1st Infantry Brigade and UK Mobile Force 1985–86; Royal Coll. of Defence Studies 1987; Chief of Staff, HQ UK Land Forces 1988–90; GOC and Dir Mil. Operations, NI 1990–93; last C-in-C, UK Land Forces 1993–95, first C-in-C Land Command 1995–96; ADC Gen. to the Queen 1994–96; Chair. Western Provident Asscn 1996–2009; Vice-Chair. Sherborne School 1996–2001; mem. Council Royal Bath & West 1996–, Commonwealth War Graves Comm. from 1998 (Vice-Chair. from 2001); Commr, Royal Hosp., Chelsea from 1996; Gov. Suttons Hosp. in Charterhouse 1996–2001, Sherborne School for Girls 1996–2001; Hon. Col, Royal Jersey Militia, Royal Engineers 1993–. *Publications:* Service for the Nation 1987, H. Jones VC: The Life and Death of an Unusual Hero 2002. *Leisure interests:* skiing, fishing, sailing, breeding alpacas. *Address:* c/o Western Provident Association, Rivergate House, Blackbrook Park, Taunton, Somerset, TA1 2PE, England.

WILSON, Sir Alan Geoffrey, Kt, MA, FRS, FBA, FCGI, FAcSS; British geographer, mathematician, academic and fmr university vice-chancellor; *CEO, Alan Turing Institute;* b. 8 Jan. 1939, Bradford, Yorks.; s. of Harry Wilson and Gladys Naylor; m. Sarah Fildes 1987; ed Queen Elizabeth Grammar School, Darlington, Corpus Christi Coll., Cambridge; Scientific Officer, Rutherford High Energy Lab. 1961–64; Research Officer, Inst. of Econs and Statistics, Univ. of Oxford 1964–66; Math. Adviser to Ministry of Transport 1966–68; Asst Dir Centre for Environmental Studies, London 1968–70; Prof. of Urban and Regional Geography, Univ. of Leeds 1970–2004, Pro-Vice-Chancellor 1989–91, Vice-Chancellor 1991–2004; Dir-Gen. for Higher Educ., Dept for Education and Skills 2004–06; Prof. of Urban and Regional Systems, Centre for Advanced Spatial Analysis, Univ. Coll. London 2007–; Chair. Arts and Humanities Research Council 2007–13; Ed. Environment and Planning 1969–91; Dir GMAP 1991–2001; Chair. Home Office Science Advisory Council 2013–; CEO Alan Turing Inst. 2016–; mem. Academia Europaea 1991–, Acad. of Learned Socs for the Social Sciences; Hon. Fellow, Univ. Coll. London 2003, Corpus Christi Coll. Cambridge 2004; Hon. DSc (Pennsylvania State), Hon. DEd (Leeds Metropolitan) 2004, Hon. LLD (Leeds) 2004, (Teesside) 2006, Hon. DSocSci (King's Coll. London) 2010, Hon. DLitt (School of Advanced Study, Univ. of London) 2017; Gill Memorial Award, Royal Geographical Soc. 1978, Hons Award, Asscn of American Geographers 1987, Founders Medal, Royal Geographical Soc. 1992. *Publications include:* Entropy in Urban and Regional Modelling 1970, Urban and Regional Models in Geography and Planning 1974, Spatial Population Analysis (with P. H. Rees) 1977, Mathematics for Geographers and Planners (with M. J. Kirkby) 1980, Models of Cities and Regions (co-ed.) 1977, Catastrophe Theory and Bifurcation: applications to urban and regional systems 1981, Geography and the Environment: Systems Analytical Methods 1981, Mathematical Methods in Geography and Planning (with R. J. Bennett) 1985, Urban Systems (co-ed.) 1987, Urban Dynamics (co-ed.) 1990, Modelling the City: Performance, Policy and Planning (with Bertuglia, Clarke and others) 1994, Intelligent Geographical Information Systems (with Birkin, Clarke and Clarke) 1996, Complex Spatial Systems 2000. *Leisure interests:* writing, miscellaneous fads. *Address:* Alan Turing Institute, British Library, 96 Euston Road, London, NW1 2DB, England. *Telephone:* (20) 3108-3327 (Ext. 53901) (office). *Fax:* (20) 3108-3258 (office). *E-mail:* awilson@turing.ac.uk (office). *Website:* info@turing.ac.uk (office); www.casa.ucl.ac.uk (office); www.turing.ac.uk (office).

WILSON, A(ndrew) N(orman), MA, FRSL; British writer; b. 27 Oct. 1950; s. of N. Wilson and Jean Dorothy Wilson (née Crowder); m. 1st Katherine Dorothea Duncan-Jones 1971 (divorced 1989); two d.; m. 2nd Ruth Guilding 1991; one d.; ed Rugby School and New Coll., Oxford; Asst Master Merchant Taylors' School 1975–76; Lecturer, St Hugh's Coll. and New Coll., Oxford 1976–81; Literary Ed. Spectator 1981–83, Evening Standard 1990–97; columnist, The Daily Mail; Hon. mem. American Acad. of Arts and Letters 1984; Chancellor's Essay Prize 1975, Ellerton Theological Prize 1975. *Publications include:* fiction: The Sweets of Pimlico 1977, Unguarded Hours 1978, Kindly Light 1979, The Healing Art

(Somerset Maugham Award) 1980, Who Was Oswald Fish? 1981, Wise Virgin (WHSmith Award) 1982, Scandal 1983, Gentleman in England 1985, Love Unknown 1986, Stray 1987, Incline Our Hearts 1988, A Bottle in the Smoke 1990, Daughters of Albion 1991, The Vicar of Sorrows 1993, Hearing Voices 1995, A Watch in the Night 1996, Hazel the Guinea-pig (for children) 1997, Dream Children 1998, My Name is Legion 2004, A Jealous Ghost 2005, Winnie and Wolf 2007, The Potter's Hand 2012, Aftershocks 2018; non-fiction: The Laird of Abbotsford 1980, A Life of John Milton 1983, Hilaire Belloc 1984, How Can We Know? An Essay on the Christian Religion 1985, The Church in Crisis (jtly) 1986, Landscape in France 1987, The Lion and the Honeycomb 1987, Penfriends from Porlock: Essays and Reviews 1977–86 1988, Tolstoy (Whitbread Award for Biography and Autobiography) 1988, Eminent Victorians 1989, John Henry Newman: prayers, poems, meditations (ed.) 1989, C. S. Lewis: A Biography 1990, Against Religion 1991, Jesus 1992, The Faber Book of Church and Clergy (ed.) 1992, The Rise and Fall of the House of Windsor 1993, The Faber Book of London (ed.) 1993, Paul: The Mind of the Apostle 1997, God's Funeral 1999, The Victorians 2003, Beautiful Shadow: A Life of Patricia Highsmith 2003, Iris Murdoch as I Knew Her 2004, London: A Short History 2004, After the Victorians 2005, Betjeman (biog.) 2006, Harold Robbins: The Man Who Invented Sex 2007, Our Times: The Age of Elizabeth II 2008, Dante in Love 2011, The Elizabethans 2011, Hitler: A Short Biography 2011, Victoria: A Life 2014, Charles Darwin: Victorian Mythmaker 2017. *Address:* c/o Daily Mail, Northcliffe House, 2 Derry Street, London, W8 5TT; 5 Regent's Park Terrace, London, NW1 7EE, England.

WILSON, Blake Shaw, PhD, DSc, DEng; American medical scientist, electrical engineer and academic; b. 7 March 1948, Orlando, Fla; s. of Joseph Richard Hoyle Wilson and Lucy Jacqueline Jones Wilson; m. Doris Jane Rouse; two d.; worked full time at Research Triangle Inst. (now RTI International) 1974–2007; Adjunct Prof. of Surgery, of Biomedical Eng, of Electrical and Computer Eng and Co-Dir Duke Hearing Center, Duke Univ. 2007–, helped establish the Duke Cochlear Implant Program 1984, Duke Hearing Center 2008, Scholar-in-Residence, Pratt School of Eng 2013–, mem. affiliated faculties for Duke Global Health Inst. and Duke Inst. for Brain Sciences 2013–; Chief Strategy Advisor for MED EL GmbH 2007–; Adjunct Prof. of Electrical Eng, of Bioengineering and of Behavioral and Brain Sciences, Univ. of Texas, Dallas 2015–; Prin. Investigator for 27 projects, including 13 for NIH; Life Fellow, IEEE 2014; Fellow, Acoustical Soc. of America 2016; Hon. Prof., Univ. of Warwick, UK 2008–; DrMed hc (multiple), including from Uppsala Univ., Sweden and Univ. of Salamanca, Spain; Distinguished Alumnus Award, Pratt School of Eng, Duke Univ. 2007, Lasker–DeBakey Clinical Medical Research Award (co-recipient) 2013, Russ Prize, Nat. Acad. of Eng (co-recipient) 2015, Gold Medal, Paul Sabatier Univ. (co-recipient) 2015, Eduard Rhein Tech. Prize (co-recipient) 2016, Helmholtz-Rayleigh Interdisciplinary Silver Medal in Psychological and Physiological Acoustics, Speech Communication, and Signal Processing in Acoustics 2017. *Publications:* numerous papers in professional journals. *Address:* Biomedical Engineering Department, Room 136, Hudson Hall, Box 90281, Durham, NC 27708-0281, USA (office). *Telephone:* (919) 493-7231 (office). *Fax:* (919) 684-4488 (office). *E-mail:* blake.wilson@duke.edu (office). *Website:* ece .duke.edu/faculty/blake-shaw-wilson (office).

WILSON, Brian; American musician (bass, keyboards), singer, songwriter and producer; b. 20 June 1942, Inglewood, Calif.; m. 2nd Melinda Ledbetter 1995; two d.; Founder-mem., The Beach Boys 1961–; retired from live performance to concentrate on composing and recording 1964; numerous live appearances, tours; band est. Brother Records label 1967; simultaneous solo artist 1988–; Pet Sounds 50th Anniversary World Tour 2016–17; American Music Awards Special Award of Merit 1988, Grammy Lifetime Achievement Award 2001, Ivor Novello Award for Lifetime Achievement 2003, Musicares Person of the Year Award 2005, Kennedy Center Honor 2007, inducted into Rock and Roll Hall of Fame (as mem. of Beach Boys) 1988, Songwriters Hall of Fame, UK Music Hall of Fame. *Recordings include:* albums: with The Beach Boys: Surfin' Safari 1962, Surfer Girl 1963, Little Deuce Coupe 1963, Shut Down Vol. 2; All Summer Long 1964, Christmas Album 1964, The Beach Boys Today! 1965, Summer Days (and Summer Nights) 1965, Beach Boys Party 1966, Pet Sounds 1966, Smiley Smile 1967, Wild Honey 1968, Friends 1968, 20/20 1969, Sunflower 1970, Surf's Up 1971, Carl and the Passions – So Tough 1972, Holland 1973, The Beach Boys in Concert 1973, Endless Summer 1974, 15 Big Ones 1976, The Beach Boys Love You 1977, M.I.U. 1978, LA (Light Album) 1979, Keepin' The Summer Alive 1980, The Beach Boys 1985, Still Cruisin' 1989, Two Rooms 1991, Summer in Paradise 1992, The Sounds of Summer – The Very Best of The Beach Boys 2003, Smile Sessions (Grammy Award for Best Historical Album 2013) 2011, That's Why God Made the Radio 2012; solo: Brian Wilson 1988, I Just Wasn't Made For These Times 1995, Imagination 1998, Pet Projects: The Brian Wilson Productions 2003, Smile 2004, What I Really Want For Christmas 2005, That Lucky Old Sun 2008, Brian Wilson Reimagines Gershwin 2010, In The Key Of Disney 2011, No Pier Pressure 2015. *Compositions for stage:* Shine 2002, That Lucky Old Sun (a Narrative) 2007. *Publication:* I Am Brian Wilson: A Memoir 2016. *Address:* c/o Elliott Lott, Boulder Creek Entertainment, PO Box 91002, San Diego, CA 91269, USA (office). *Telephone:* (858) 793-4141 (office). *Website:* www.thebeachboys.com; www.brianwilson.com.

WILSON, Brian G., AO, BSc, PhD; Australian/British physicist and university administrator (retd); b. 9 April 1930, Belfast, NI; s. of Charles W. Wilson and Isobel C. Wilson (née Ferguson); m. 1st Barbara Wilkie 1959 (divorced 1975); two s. one d.; m. 2nd Jeanne Henry 1978 (divorced 1988); m. 3rd Joan Opdebeeck 1988; three s.; ed Methodist Coll., Belfast, Queen's Univ. Belfast and Nat. Univ. of Ireland; Postdoctoral Fellow, Nat. Research Council of Canada 1955–57; Officer-in-charge, Sulphur Mount Lab., Banff, Alberta 1957–60; Assoc. Prof. of Physics, Univ. of Calgary 1960–65, Prof. 1965–70, Dean of Arts and Science 1967–70; Vice-Pres. Simon Fraser Univ., Burnaby, BC 1970–78; Vice-Chancellor Univ. of Queensland 1979–95; Deputy Chair. Australian Vice-Chancellors' Cttee 1987–88, Chair. 1989–90; mem. Council, Northern Territory Univ. 1988–93, Univ. of the South Pacific 1991–95; Pres. Int. Devt Program of Australian Univs and Colls 1991–92; Chair. Australian Cttee for Quality Assurance in Higher Educ. 1993–95; Founder-Chair. Uniquest Pty Ltd (Australia), UQ Tech. Transfer Co. 1984–95; Fellow, Acad. of Technological Sciences and Eng (Australia); Hon. LLD (Calgary) 1984; Hon. DUniv (Queensland Univ. of Tech.) 1995; Hon. DSc (Queensland) 1995. *Publications:* one book and more than 50 scientific articles in int. journals. *Leisure*

interest: golf. *Address:* Les Grezes, 11400 Montauriol, France. *Telephone:* (4) 68-23-14-06. *E-mail:* opdebeeck.wilson2@aliceadsl.fr.

WILSON, Charles Martin; British journalist; b. 18 Aug. 1935, Glasgow, Scotland; s. of Adam Wilson and Ruth Wilson; m. 1st Anne Robinson 1968 (divorced 1973); one d.; m. 2nd Sally O'Sullivan 1980 (divorced 2001); one s. one d.; m. 3rd Rachel Pitkeathley 2001; ed Eastbank Acad., Glasgow; copy boy, The People 1951; later reporter with Bristol Evening World, News Chronicle and Daily Mail; Deputy Ed. Daily Mail (Manchester) 1971–74; Asst Ed. London Evening News 1974–76; Ed., Evening Times, Glasgow 1976; later Ed., Glasgow Herald; Ed. Sunday Standard, Glasgow 1981–82; Exec. Ed., The Times 1982, Jt Deputy Ed. 1984–85, Ed. 1985–90; Int. Devt Dir News Int. 1990–91; Ed.-in-Chief, Man. Dir The Sporting Life 1990–98; Editorial Dir Mirror Group Newspapers 1991–92, Group Man. Dir Mirror Group 1992–98; Acting Ed., The Independent 1995–96; Dir (non-exec.), Chelsea and Westminster Hosp. 1999–2011; mem. Newspaper Panel, Competition Comm. 1999–2007, Jockey Club 1993–, Youth Justice Bd 1998–2004, Bd of Ind. Press Standards Org. 2014–; Trustee, World Wildlife Fund-UK 1997–2004, Royal Naval Museum 1999–2012, Nat. Museum of the Royal Navy 2012–, Addaction 2000–16. *Leisure interests:* current affairs, National Hunt racing, hunting, reading. *Address:* 23 Campden Hill Square, London, W8 7JY, England. *Telephone:* (7831) 623522 (home). *E-mail:* wcampden@gmail.com.

WILSON, Sir David Mackenzie, Kt, LittD, FBA, FSA; British fmr museum director; b. 30 Oct. 1931, Dacre Banks, N Yorks., England; s. of Rev. J. Wilson; m. Eva Sjögren 1955; one s. one d.; ed Kingswood School, St John's Coll., Cambridge, Lund Univ., Sweden; Asst Keeper, The British Museum 1955–64; Reader in Archaeology, Univ. of London 1964–71, Prof. of Medieval Archaeology 1971–76; Dir British Museum 1977–92; Commr English Heritage 1990–97; mem. Royal Swedish Acad. of Science, Norwegian Acad. of Science and Letters; Hon. Fellow, Univ. Coll. London; numerous honours and awards. *Publications include:* The Anglo-Saxons 1960, Catalogue of Anglo-Saxon Metalwork 700–1100 in the British Museum 1964, Anglo-Saxon Art 1964, The Bayeux Tapestry 1965, Viking Art (with O. Klindt-Jensen) 1966, Three Viking Graves in the Isle of Man (with G. Bersu) 1966, The Vikings and their Origins 1970, The Viking Achievement (with P. Foote) 1970, St Ninian's Isle and its Treasure (with A. Small and A. C. Thomas) 1973, The Viking Age in the Isle of Man 1974; editor: The Archaeology of the Anglo-Saxons 1976, The Northern World 1980, The Art of the Anglo-Saxons 1984, The Bayeux Tapestry 1985, The British Museum: Purpose and Politics 1989, Awful Ends 1992, Showing the Flag 1992, Vikingetidens Konst 1995, Vikings and Gods in European Art 1997, The British Museum – A History 2002, The Vikings in the Isle of Man 2008, Aggersborg, The Viking-Age Settlement and Fortress (co-ed.) 2014; numerous articles and pamphlets. *Address:* The Lifeboat House, Castletown, IM9 1LD, Isle of Man (home). *Telephone:* (1624) 822800 (home). *E-mail:* dmw@mcb.net.

WILSON, Edward Osborne, Jr, BS, MS, PhD; American biologist, academic and writer; *University Professor Emeritus, Harvard University;* b. 10 June 1929, Birmingham, Ala; s. of Edward Osborne Wilson, Sr and Linnette Freeman Huddleston; m. Irene Kelley 1955; one d.; ed Univ. of Alabama, Harvard Univ.; Jr Fellow, Soc. of Fellows, Harvard Univ. 1953–56, Prof. of Zoology 1964–76, F.B. Baird Prof. of Science 1976–94, Pellegrino Univ. Prof. 1994–97, Univ. Research Prof. 1997–2002, Prof. Emer. 2002–; Curator of Entomology, Museum of Comparative Zoology 1974–97, Hon. Curator of Entomology 1997–; apptd Lecturer, Duke Univ. 2014; Fellow, Guggenheim Foundation 1977–78, mem. Advisory Bd 1979–90, mem. Selection Cttee 1982–90; mem. Bd of Dirs World Wildlife Fund 1983–94, Org. for Tropical Studies 1984–91, American Museum of Natural History 1992–, American Acad. of Liberal Educ. 1993–2004, Nature Conservancy 1993–98, Conservation Int. 1997–; Foreign mem. Royal Soc. 1990, Finnish Acad. of Science and Letters 1990, Russian Acad. of Natural Sciences 1994; Founding mem. Int. Centre of Insect Physiology and Ecology, Org. for Tropical Studies, Ecosystems Center of Marine Biological Lab.; mem. NAS 1969; Fellow, American Acad. of Arts and Sciences 1959, American Philosophical Soc. 1976, Animal Behavior Soc. 1976, Deutsche Akad. der Naturforscher Leopoldina 1977, Royal Soc. of Sciences of Uppsala 1989, World Econ. Forum 2000; Hon. Life mem. American Genetic Asscn 1981, British Ecological Soc. 1983, Entomological Soc. of America 1987, Darwin Soc., Univ. of Bergen 1987, American Humanist Asscn 1989, Zoological Soc. of London 1992, Linnean Soc. of London 1994, Netherlands Entomological Soc. 1995, Asscn for Tropical Biology 1999, European Sociobiological Soc. 2000, Royal Entomological Soc. 2001; mem. Hon. Bd World Knowledge Dialogue and Scientist in Residence for symposium organized in Crans-Montana, Switzerland 2008; Silver Cross of Columbus (Dominican Repub.) 2003, Commdr (First Class), Royal Order of the Polar Star (Sweden) 2009; Hon. DHC (Univ. of Madrid Complutense) 1995; Hon. DPhil (Uppsala University) 1987; Hon. Dr rer. nat (Univ. of Wurzburg) 2000; Hon. DSc (Duke Univ.) 1978, (Grinnell Coll.) 1978, (Univ. of West Florida) 1979, (Muhlenberg Coll.) 1998, (Yale Univ.) 1998, (Cedar Crest Coll.) 1999, (State Univ. of NY, Albany) 1999; Hon. LHD (Univ. of Alabama) 1980, (Hofstra Univ.) 1986, (Pennsylvania State Univ.), (Lawrence Univ.) 1979, (Fitchburg State Coll.) 1989, (Macalester Coll.) 1990, (Univ. of Massachusetts) 1993, (Univ. of Oxford) 1993, (Ripon Coll.) 1994, (Univ. of Connecticut) 1995, (Bates Coll.) 1996, (Ohio Univ.) 1996, (Coll. of Wooster) 1997, Univ. of Guelph 1997, (Univ. of Portland) 1997, (Bradford Coll.) 1997; Hon. LLD (Simon Fraser Univ.) 1982; Nat. Medal of Science 1976, Tyler Prize for Environmental Achievement 1983, Ingersoll Foundation Weaver Award for Scholarly Letters 1989, Crafoord Prize, Royal Swedish Acad. of Sciences 1990, Int. Prize for Biology, Govt of Japan 1993, Carl Sagan Award for Public Understanding of Science 1994, Audubon Soc. Medal 1995, Los Angeles Times Book Prize for Science 1995, Schubert Prize (Germany) 1996, German Ecological Foundation Book Award 1998, Franklin Prize for Science, American Philosophical Soc. 1999, Nonino Prize (Italy) 2000, Lewis Thomas Prize for Writing about Science 2000, King Faisal Int. Prize for Science (Saudi Arabia) 2000, Foundation for the Future Kistler Prize 2000, Nierenberg Prize 2001, Addison Emery Verrill Medal, Peabody Museum of Natural History 2007, TED (Tech. Entertainment Design) Prize (co-recipient) 2007, XIX Premi Internacional Catalunya 2007, EarthSky Science Communicator of the Year 2010, and others. *Achievements include:* coined the term 'sociobiology'. *Publications include:* The Theory of Island Biogeography (with R. H. MacArthur) 1967, The Insect Societies 1971, Sociobiology: The New Synthesis 1975, On Human Nature (Pulitzer Prize for Gen. Non-Fiction 1979) 1978, Caste and Ecology in the Social Insects (with G. F. Oster) 1978, Genes, Mind and Culture (with C. J.

Lumsden) 1981, Promethean Fire (with C. J. Lumsden) 1983, Biophilia 1984, Biodiversity (ed.) 1988, The Ants (with Bert Hölldobler) (Pulitzer Prize for Gen. Non-Fiction 1991) 1990, Success and Dominance in Ecosystems 1990, The Diversity of Life 1991, In Search of Nature (with Laura Simonds Southworth) 1996, Journey to the Ants (with Bert Hölldobler) 1994, Pheidole in the New World: A Dominant, Hyperdiverse Ant Genus 2002, From So Simple a Beginning: Darwin's Four Great Books 2005, The Creation: An Appeal to Save Life on Earth 2006, Nature Revealed: Selected Writings 1949–2006 2006, The Superorganism: The Beauty, Elegance, and Strangeness of Insect Societies (with Bert Hölldobler) 2009, Anthill: A Novel (Heartland Prize 2010) 2010, The Social Conquest of Earth 2012, Letters to a Young Scientist 2013, A Window on Eternity: A Biologist's Walk Through Gorongosa National Park 2014, The Meaning of Human Existence 2014, Half-Earth 2015; numerous articles on evolutionary biology, entomology and conservation. *Address:* Museum of Comparative Zoology, Harvard University, 26 Oxford Street, 418, Cambridge, MA 02138-2902 (office); 1010 Waltham Street, A-208, Lexington, MA 02421-8062, USA (home). *Telephone:* (617) 496-1034 (office). *Fax:* (617) 495-1224 (office). *E-mail:* khorton@oeb.harvard.edu (office). *Website:* www.mcz.harvard.edu/Departments/Entomology (office).

WILSON, Heather Ann, BS, MPhil, PhD; American educational administrator and fmr air force officer; *President, South Dakota School of Mines & Technology;* b. 30 Dec. 1960, Keene, NH; d. of George Douglas Wilson and Martha Lou Wilson; m. Jay Hone; three c.; ed US Air Force Acad., Jesus Coll., Oxford; served in US Air Force 1982–89; Dir European Defense Policy and Arms Control, Nat. Security Council 1989–91; f. Keystone Int., Inc., Albuquerque, New Mexico 1991; sr advisor to several large defence and scientific cos including Nevada Test Site, Battelle, Sandia, Los Alamos and Oak Ridge Nat. Laboratories as well as several major defence firms; Cabinet Sec. for Children, Youth & Families Dept, New Mexico 1995–98; mem. US House of Reps from New Mexico 1st Dist 1998–2009, mem. House Energy and Commerce Cttee, Chair. House Sub-Cttee on Technical and Tactical Intelligence, mem. Congressional Panel on the Nuclear Security Enterprise; mem. Republican Main Street Partnership; Pres. South Dakota School of Mines & Tech. 2013–; nominated as US Sec. of the Air Force Jan. 2017; mem. Bd of Dirs South Dakota Science and Technology Authority, Peabody Energy, Raven Industries; Republican. *Publications:* International Law and the Use of Force by National Liberation Movements (Paul Reuter Prize of Int. Cttee of the Red Cross 1988) 1990. *Leisure interests:* private pilot; hiking and fly fishing. *Address:* South Dakota School of Mines & Technology, 501 E. Saint Joseph Street, Rapid City, SD 57701, USA (office). *Telephone:* (605) 394–2511 (office). *Website:* www.sdsmt.edu (office).

WILSON, Dame Jacqueline, DBE, OBE, FRSL; British writer, academic and university administrator; *Pro-Chancellor, Roehampton University;* b. 17 Dec. 1945, Bath, England; d. of Harry Aitken and Margaret Aitken (née Clibbons); m. William Millar Wilson 1965 (divorced 2004); one d.; ed Coombe Girls' School; journalist, D.C. Thomsons 1963–65; teenage magazine Jackie named after her; Amb. Reading is Fundamental, UK 1998–; mem. Cttee Children's Writers and Illustrators Group, Soc. of Authors 1997–; Advisory mem. Panel Costa (fmrly Whitbread) Book Awards 1997–; Judge, Rhône-Poulenc Prizes for Jr Science Books 1999, Orange Prize for Fiction 2006, Prince Maurice Award 2006; mem. Bd Children's Film and TV Foundation 2000–; Children's Laureate 2005–07; Visiting Prof. of Children's Literature, Roehampton Univ. 2010–, Pro-Chancellor, Roehampton Univ. 2011–; Hon. DLitt (Winchester) 2005, (Bath) 2005, (Roehampton) 2007; Hon. DEd (Kingston Univ.) 2006; Hon. LLD (Dundee) 2007; Oak Tree Award 1992, Sheffield Children's Book Award, WHSmith Children's Book of the Year 2002, BT Childline Award 2004, British Book Award for Services to Bookselling 2004. *Plays:* books adapted for the stage include Lottie Project 1999, Double Act 2003, Bad Girls 2004, Midnight 2005, Tracy Beaker Gets Real 2006, Suitcase Kid 2007, Secrets 2008. *Television:* novels Girls in Love, Girls Under Pressure, Girls Out Late and Girls in Tears adapted into 13-part TV series, Granada 2003; The Story of Tracy Beaker adapted into five series on BBC children's TV; The Illustrated Mum adapted for Channel 4 children's TV (two BAFTA Awards, one Emmy Award). *Publications include:* fiction: Hide and Seek 1972, Truth or Dare 1973, Snap 1974, Let's Pretend 1975, Making Hate 1977; juvenile fiction: Nobody's Perfect 1982, Waiting for the Sky to Fall 1983, The Other Side 1984, Amber 1986, The Power of the Shade 1987, Stevie Day Series 1987, This Girl 1988, Is There Anybody There? 1990, Deep Blue 1993, Take a Good Look 1990, The Story of Tracy Beaker 1991, The Suitcase Kid (Children's Book of the Year Award 1993) 1992, Video Rose 1992, The Mum-minder 1993, The Werepuppy 1993, The Bed and the Breakfast Star (The Young Telegraph/Fully Booked Award 1995) 1994, Mark Spark in the Dark 1994, Twin Trouble 1995, Glubbslyme 1995, Jimmy Jelly 1995, The Dinosaur's Packed Lunch 1995, Cliffhanger 1995, Double Act (Children's Book of the Year Award, Smarties Prize) 1995, My Brother Bernadette 1995, Werepuppy on Holiday 1995, Bad Girls 1996, Mr Cool 1996, Monster Story-teller 1997, The Lottie Project 1997, Girls in Love 1997, Connie and the Water Babies 1997, Buried Alive! 1998, Girls Under Pressure 1998, How to Survive Summer Camp 1998, The Illustrated Mum (Guardian Children's Book of the Year Award, Children's Book of the Year Award 1999) 1999, Girls Out Late 1999, Lizzie Zipmouth 1999, The Dare Game 2000, Vicky Angel 2000, The Cat Mummy 2001, Sleepovers 2001, Dustbin Baby 2001, Secrets 2002, Girls in Tears 2002, The Worry Website 2002, Lola Rose 2003, Midnight 2004, The Diamond Girls 2004, Clean Break 2005, Love Lessons 2005, Best Friends (Red House Children's Book Award) 2005, Candyfloss 2006, Starring Tracy Beaker 2006, Kiss 2007, My Sister Jodie 2008, Cookie 2008, Hetty Feather 2009, Little Darlings 2010, The Longest Whale Song 2010, Lily Alone 2011, Sapphire Battersea: Hetty Feather 2 2011, Lily Alone 2011, Green Glass Beads 2011, The Worst Thing About My Sister 2012, Big Day Out 2012, Four Children and It 2012, Emerald Star 2012, Queenie 2013, Opal Plumstead 2014, Paws and Whiskers 2014, The Butterfly Club 2015; other: Jacky Daydream (autobiog.) 2007, My Secret Diary (autobiog.) 2009. *Leisure interests:* reading, swimming, going to art galleries and films, shopping, dancing. *Address:* c/o David Higham Associates, 7th Floor, Waverley House, 7–12 Noel Street, London, W1F 8GQ, England (office). *Telephone:* (20) 7434-5900 (office). *Website:* www.jacquelinewilson.co.uk.

WILSON, Jean Donald, MD, FRCP; American endocrinologist and academic; *Professor Emeritus of Internal Medicine, University of Texas Southwestern Medical School;* b. 26 Aug. 1932, Wellington, Tex.; s. of J. D. Wilson and Maggie

E. Wilson (née Hill); ed Hillsboro Coll., Univ. of Texas at Austin and Univ. of Texas Southwestern Medical School, Dallas; Medical Intern and Asst Resident in Internal Medicine, Parkland Memorial Hosp. Dallas 1955–58; Clinical Assoc. Nat. Heart Inst. Bethesda, Md 1958–60; Instructor, Univ. of Texas Health Science Center 1960–, apptd Prof. of Internal Medicine 1968, Charles Cameron Sprague Distinguished Chair in Biomedical Science, Southwestern Medical School, Dallas, then Prof. Emer.; Established Investigator, American Heart Asscn 1960–65; Travelling Fellow, Royal Soc. of Medicine, Strangeways Research Lab. Cambridge 1970; mem. NAS, Inst. of Medicine of NAS, American Philosophical Soc., American Acad. of Arts and Sciences, Royal Coll. of Physicians; Amory Prize, American Acad. of Arts and Sciences 1977, Henry Dale Medal, Soc. for Endocrinology 1991, Gregory Pincus Award, Worcester Foundation for Experimental Biology 1992, Fred Conrad Koch Award, The Endocrine Soc. 1993, Kober Medal, Asscn of American Physicians 1999. *Publications include:* more than 300 scientific articles in various medical journals. *Leisure interests:* birding, opera. *Address:* Division of Endocrinology and Metabolism, Department of Internal Medicine, University of Texas Southwestern Medical Center at Dallas, 5323 Harry Hines Boulevard, Dallas, TX 75390-8857, USA (office). *Telephone:* (214) 648-3469 (office). *Fax:* (214) 648-8917 (office). *E-mail:* jean.wilson@utsouthwestern.edu (office). *Website:* www.swmed.edu (office).

WILSON, Linda S., BA, PhD, FAAS; American chemist and fmr university administrator; *President Emerita, Radcliffe College;* b. (Linda Lee Smith), 10 Nov. 1936, Washington DC; d. of Fred M. Smith and Virginia T. Smith; m. 1st Malcolm C. Whatley 1957 (divorced); one d.; m. 2nd Paul A. Wilson 1970; one step-d.; ed Tulane Univ., Univ. of Wisconsin-Madison; Post-Doctoral Research Assoc., Univ. of Maryland 1962–64, Research Asst Prof. 1964–67; Visiting Fellow, Univ. of Southampton, England 1967; Visiting Asst Prof., Univ. of Missouri-St Louis 1967–68; Asst Vice-Chancellor for Research, Washington Univ., St Louis, Mo. 1968–74, Assoc. Vice-Chancellor 1974–75; Assoc. Vice-Chancellor for Research, Univ. of Illinois, Urbana 1975–85, Assoc. Dean, Grad. Coll. 1978–85; Vice-Pres. for Research, Univ. of Michigan, Ann Arbor 1985–89; Pres. Radcliffe Coll., Cambridge, Mass. 1989–99, Pres. Emer. 1999–; Chair. Advisory Cttee Office of Science and Eng Personnel, Nat. Research Council 1990–96; mem. Council on Govt Relations 1971–77, Nat. Inst. of Health Advisory Council on Research Resources 1978–82, Nat. Comm. on Research 1978–80, NSF Dirs Advisory Council 1980–89, Govt-Univ.-Industry Research Roundtable (NAS) 1984–88, Inst. of Medicine Council 1986–89, Inst. of Medicine Cttee on Govt-Industry Collaboration in Research and Educ. 1988–89, Inst. of Medicine Cttee on NIH Priority-Setting 1998–99; mem. Bd of Dirs AAAS 1984–88, Mich. Materials Processing Inst. 1986–89, Mich. Biotechnology Inst. 1986–89, Inst. of Medicine, ACS, AAAS; mem. Bd of Overseers Museum of Science, Boston 1992–2001; Trustee, Mass. Gen. Hosp. 1992–99 (Hon. Trustee 1999–2002), Cttee on Econ. Devt 1995–; mem. Bd of Dirs Citizens Financial Group 1996–99, Inacom Corpn 1997–2003, ValueLine Inc. 1998–2000, Myriad Genetics Inc. 1999–2010, Internet Corpn for Assigned Names and Numbers (ICANN) 1998–2003; Friends of DaPonte String Quartet 2002–07; mem. Bd of Admins (Trustee) Tulane Univ. 2002–14, Trustee Emer. 2014–; Trustee, Bigelow Laboratory for Ocean Sciences 2013–; elected to Inst. of Medicine 1983; Dr hc (Tulane Univ.), (Univ. of Maryland); Distinguished Contribution to Research Admin. Award, Soc. of Research Admins, Distinguished Service Award, Univ. of Illinois Coll. of Medicine, Centennial Award for Outstanding Accomplishments, Newcomb Coll., Distinguished Alumni Award, Univ. of Wisconsin 1997, Endowed Chair. for Dir of Radcliffe Public Policy Center 1999, Radcliffe Medal 1999. *Publications:* seven book chapters, 10 journal articles, six maj. reports, four commissioned studies, 12 papers on chem., science policy and research policy. *Leisure interests:* cello, reading, music. *Address:* 26 Honey Locust Drive, Topsham, ME, 04086, USA (office). *Telephone:* (207) 729-9129 (office). *E-mail:* llswilson@comcast.net (office).

WILSON, Lynton Ronald, OC, BA, MA; Canadian business executive; b. 3 April 1940, Port Colborne, Ont.; s. of Ronald Alfred Wilson and Blanche Evelyn Matthews; m. Brenda Jean Black; two d. one s.; ed Port Colborne High School, McMaster Univ., Cornell Univ., USA; Foreign Service Officer, Dept of Trade and Commerce 1962; Asst Commercial Sec., Embassy in Vienna 1963–65; Second Sec., Embassy in Tokyo 1967–68; Corp. Economist and Dir of Econ. Research, John Labatt Ltd 1969–71; Coordinator, Industrial R & D Policy, Ministry of State, Science and Tech. 1972; Strategic Planning and Devt Officer, MacMillan Bloedel Ltd 1973–74, Vice-Pres. and Dir, MacMillan Bloedel Enterprises Inc. 1974–77; Exec. Dir, Policy and Priorities, Ministry of Industry and Tourism, Govt of Ont. 1977–78, Deputy Minister 1978–81; Pres. and CEO Redpath Industries Ltd, Toronto 1981–88, Chair. Bd 1988–89; Man. Dir N America, Tate & Lyle PLC 1986–89; Vice-Chair. Bank of Nova Scotia, Toronto 1989–90; Pres. and COO BCE Inc., Montreal 1990–92, Pres. and CEO 1992–93, Chair., Pres. and CEO 1993–96, Chair. and CEO 1996–98, Chair. Bd Dirs 1998–2000; Chair. Bell Canada, CAE Inc. 1999–2013, Nortel Networks Corpn 2000–05; Chair. Govt's Competition Policy Review Panel 2007–08; Chancellor McMaster Univ. 2007–13; Founding Chair. Historica Foundation of Canada; Dir BCE Mobile Communications Inc., Bell Canada Int. Inc., Northern Telecom Ltd, Bell-Northern Research Ltd, Teleglobe Inc., Chrysler Canada Ltd, Chrysler Corpn, Tate & Lyle PLC, UK, Stelco Inc., CD Howe Inst., Canadian Inst. for Advanced Research; mem. Business Council on Nat. Issues (Policy Cttee), Trilateral Comm., Int. Council JP Morgan & Co., New York, Bd of Trustees Montreal Museum of Fine Arts Foundation; Gov. Olympic Trust of Canada, McGill Univ.; six hon. degrees including Dr hc (Montreal) 1995, Hon. LLD (McMaster) 1995, (Cape Breton) 1998, (Mount Allison) 2000. *Address:* c/o CAE Inc., 8585 Côte de Liesse, Saint-Laurent, Montreal, Quebec H4T 1G6 (office); 2038 Lakeshore Road East, Oakville, Ont. L6J 1M3, Canada (home).

WILSON, Hon. Margaret, DCNZM, LLB (Hons), M.jur; New Zealand lawyer, politician and academic; *Professor of Law and Public Policy, University of Waikato;* b. 20 May 1947, Gisborne; ed St Dominic's Coll., Northcote, Morrinsville Coll., Univ. of Auckland; sec. for Legal Employers Union 1970–71; law clerk and solicitor, Peter Jenkins, barrister and solicitor in Auckland 1970–72; taught at Univ. of Auckland; Founder-mem. Industrial Relations Soc. 1973; Acting Ed. Recent Law 1974; Founding Ed. New Zealand Journal of Industrial Relations 1976–77, mem. Editorial Bd 1994–; Exec. mem., Vice-Chair. and Chair. Auckland Br., Asscn of Univ. Teachers 1976–84; Founder-mem. and Vice-Pres. Auckland Women Lawyers' Asscn 1984, Life mem. 1985–; Convenor, Govt Working Party on

Equal Pay and Equal Opportunities 1988; Dir Reserve Bank of New Zealand 1985–89; Chief Political Adviser and Head of Prime Minister's Office 1987–89; Chair. Nat. Advisory Council on Employment of Women 1987–91; Chair. TV3 News Ltd 1988–89; Law Commr of the Law Comm. 1988–89; apptd Foundation Dean and Prof. of Law, Univ. of Waikato 1990; mem. Advisory Cttee to establish the Ministry of Women's Affairs 1985, Advisory Group on restructuring of the Ministry of Justice 1995, team to review the Crown Forestry Rental Trust 1995, Judicial Working Group on Gender Equality 1995–97; Chief Govt Law Officer; Attorney-Gen. 1999–2005; Minister of Labour 1999–2004; Minister in charge of Treaty of Waitangi Negotiations 1999–2005; Assoc. Minister of Justice 1999–2004, Assoc. Minister of State Services 2000–02; Minister responsible for the Law Comm. 2001–02; Minister for Courts 2002–03, Assoc. Minister 2003–04; Minister of Commerce 2004; Speaker of House of Reps 2005–08; Prof. of Law and Public Policy, Univ. of Waikato 2008–; Pres. NZ Labour Party 1984–87; Hon. LLD (Waikato) 2004. *Address:* School of Law, University of Waikato, Private Bag 3105, Hamilton, New Zealand (office). *Telephone:* (7) 856-2889 (office). *E-mail:* mwilson@ waikato.ac.nz (office). *Website:* www.waikato.ac.nz/law (office).

WILSON, Mark, BMS; New Zealand business executive; *Group CEO, Aviva plc;* b. Aug. 1966, Rotorua; ed Univ. of Waikato; held several sr man. positions at Nat. Mutual in New Zealand –2001; CEO AXA South East Asia (insurance) 2001–03, CEO AXA China (insurance) 2003–06, Pres. and CEO AIA Group (insurance), Hong Kong 2006–10, mem. Bd of Dirs Aviva plc (as Group CEO-designate) Dec. 2012–, Group CEO Jan. 2013–; UK New Zealander of the Year Award, The New Zealand Soc. 2016. *Address:* Aviva plc, St Helen's, 1 Undershaft, London, EC3P 3DQ, England (office). *Telephone:* (20) 7283-2000 (office). *E-mail:* aviva.info@aviva .com (office). *Website:* www.aviva.com (office).

WILSON, Nigel, PhD; British business executive; *Group Chief Executive, Legal & General Group Plc;* m.; five d.; ed Massachusetts Inst. of Tech. (Kennedy Scholar), USA; fmr consultant, McKinsey & Co.; fmr Man. Dir Stanhope Properties Plc; fmr Chief Exec., Corp., Guinness Peat Aviation; fmr Group Commercial Dir Dixons Group Plc; Sr Ind. Dir/Chair. Halfords Group Plc 2006–11; Deputy Chief Exec. and Chief Financial Officer (CFO) United Business Media plc –2009; Group CFO Legal & General 2009–12, Group Chief Exec. 2012–; Sr Ind. Dir, The Capita Group plc 2010–; apptd to Prime Minister's Business Advisory Group 2015; City AM Business Personality of the Year 2014. *Achievements include:* current 800m British Masters Athletics Champion. *Address:* Legal & General Group Plc, One Coleman Street, London, EC2R 5AA, England (office). *Telephone:* (20) 3124-2000 (office). *Fax:* (20) 7528-6222 (office). *E-mail:* info@legalandgeneralgroup.com (office). *Website:* www.legalandgeneralgroup.com (office).

WILSON, Nigel Guy, MA, FBA; British academic; b. 23 July 1935, London; s. of Noel Wilson and Joan L. Wilson; m. Hanneke Marion Wirtjes 1996; ed Univ. Coll. School and Corpus Christi Coll., Oxford; Lecturer, Merton Coll., Oxford 1957–62; Fellow and Tutor in Classics, Lincoln Coll., Oxford 1962–2002; James P. R. Lyell Reader in Bibliography 2003; Kenyon Medal 2015; Hon. LittD (Uppsala) 2001, (Cyprus) 2013; Gordon Duff Prize 1968, Premio Anassilaos 1999. *Publications:* Scribes and Scholars (with L. D. Reynolds) (fourth edn) 2013, An Anthology of Byzantine Prose 1971, Medieval Greek Bookhands 1973, St Basil on the Value of Greek Literature 1975, Scholia in Aristophanis Acharnenses 1975, Menander Rhetor (with D. A. Russell) 1981, Scholars of Byzantium 1983, Oxford Classical Text of Sophocles (with Sir Hugh Lloyd-Jones) 1990, From Byzantium to Italy 1992, Photius: the Bibliotheca 1994, Aelian: Historical Miscellany 1997, Pietro Bembo: Oratio pro litteris graecis 2003, Oxford Classical Text of Aristophanes 2007, Aristophanea 2007, A Descriptive Catalogue of the Greek Manuscripts of Corpus Christi College, Oxford 2011, The Archimedes Palimpsest (with R. Netz, W. Noel and Natalie Tchernetska) 2011, Oxford Classical Text of Herodotus 2015, Herodotea 2015, Aldus Manutius: the Greek Classics 2015. *Leisure interests:* bridge, real tennis, wine. *Address:* Lincoln College, Oxford, OX1 3DR, England (office). *Fax:* (1865) 279802 (office).

WILSON, Owen; American actor; b. 18 Nov. 1968, Dallas, Tex.; s. of Robert Andrew Wilson and Laura Cunningham Wilson; one s. with Jade Duell. *Films include:* The Cable Guy 1996, Armageddon 1998, The Haunting 1999, Meet the Parents 2000, Shanghai Noon 2000, The Royal Tenenbaums (also writer and exec. producer) 2001, Zoolander 2001, Shanghai Knights 2003, The Life Aquatic with Steve Zissou 2004, Meet the Fockers 2004, Around the World in 80 Days 2004, Starsky & Hutch 2004, Wedding Crashers 2005, You, Me and Dupree (also producer) 2006, Cars (voice) 2006, The Darjeeling Limited 2007, Marley & Me 2008, Fantastic Mr Fox (voice) 2009, How Do You Know 2010, Little Fockers 2010, Midnight in Paris 2011, The Big Year 2011, The Internship 2013, Are You Here 2013, The Grand Budapest Hotel 2014, She's Funny That Way 2014, Inherent Vice 2014, Night at the Museum: Secret of the Tomb 2014, No Escape 2015. *Address:* c/o United Talent Agency, 9560 Wilshire Blvd, Suite 500, Beverly Hills, CA 90212-2410, USA (office).

WILSON, Peter (Pete) Barton, LLB, JD; American fmr politician and lawyer; *Distinguished Visiting Fellow, Hoover Institution, Stanford University;* b. 23 Aug. 1933, Lake Forest, Ill.; s. of James Boone Wilson and Margaret (née Callahan) Wilson; m. 1st Betty Robertson (divorced); m. 2nd Gayle Edlund Graham 1983; two step-s.; ed Yale Univ., Univ. of California, Berkeley; admitted to Calif. Bar; Asst Exec. Dir Republican Asscn, San Diego Co. 1963–64; Exec. Dir San Diego Co. Republican Cen. Comm. 1964–65; legal service officer, Calif. State Republican Cen. Comm. 1965; mem. Calif. Ass. 1967–71; Mayor of San Diego 1971–83; Senator from Calif. 1983–91; Gov. of Calif. 1991–99; ran unsuccessfully for Republican nomination for Pres. 1996; Man. Dir Pacific Capital Group, Calif. 1999–2001; Dir, Irvine Company, TelePacific Communications, Inc., Nat. Information Consortium Inc.; adviser, Crossflo Systems, IDT Entertainment; mem. Bd of Advisors, Thomas Weisel Partners, San Francisco; fmr Chair. Japan Task Force of the Pacific Council on Int. Policy; Distinguished Visiting Fellow, Hoover Inst., Stanford Univ. 1999–; Co-Chair. campaign for Republican Gov. Arnold Schwarzenegger 2003; Chair. Meg Whitman for Gov. Campaign 2009; Founding Dir California Mentor Foundation; mem. Governing Bd National D-Day Museum, Ronald Reagan Presidential Foundation, Richard M. Nixon Library and Birthplace Foundation, Donald Bren Foundation; mem. Presidential Advisory Cttee on Environmental Quality, Task Force Land Use and Urban Growth Policy; Republican; hon. degree from San Diego State Univ. of Professional Studies and

Fine Arts 2009; Woodrow Wilson Inst. Award for Distinguished Public Service, Patriots Award, Congressional Medal of Honor Soc., Distinguished Alumnus Award, Boalt Hall, Univ. of California, Berkeley, Bernard E. Witkin Amicus Curiae Award given by the Judicial Council of California, statue of him erected on San Diego Walk of Fame 2007. *Address:* c/o Hoover Institution, Stanford University, 434 Galvez Mall, Stanford, CA 94305-6010, USA. *Telephone:* (650) 723-1754. *Fax:* (650) 723-1687. *Website:* www.hoover.org/fellows/pete-wilson.

WILSON, Peter L., A.A. Diploma; Australian architect; b. 27 Sept. 1950, Melbourne, Vic.; s. of Jack Wilson and Betty Wilson; m. Julia B. Bolles; one s. one d.; ed Univ. of Melbourne, Architectural Asscn School of Architecture, London; Asst Teacher, Architectural Asscn School of Architecture, London 1974–75, Intermediate Unit Master 1976–79, Diploma Unit Master 1980–88; f. Wilson Partnership, London (with Julia Bolles-Wilson) 1980, Architekturbüro Bolles + Wilson (now Bolles+Wilson GmbH & Co. KG), Münster 1988; Visiting Prof., Kunsthochschule Weisensee, Berlin 1996–98, Accad. di Architettura, Mendrisio, Switzerland 2006–07; Int. Fellow, RIBA 2014; winner of more than 20 int. architectural competitions; Brick Award 2012, Worldwide Bricke (Haarlem Raaks), Gold Medal, Australian Inst. of Architects 2013. *Buildings include:* Suzuki House, Tokyo 1993, New City Library, Münster 1993, WLV Office Bldg, Münster 1993, Quay Landscape, Rotterdam 1998, Falkenried Urban Quartier, Hamburg 1999–2004, New Luxor Theatre, Rotterdam 2001, Water purification plant, Münster 2001, Teatro Luxor, Rotterdam 2001, BEIC Library and Media Centre, Milan 2001–06, Nord LB Bank, Cathedral Square, Magdeburg, Germany 2002, Nat. Library, Luxembourg 2003–04, Kaldewei kompetenz center, Ahlen 2005, Spuimarkt Block, L'Aia 2008, Raakspoort City Hall + Bioscoop, Haarlem 2011, Masterplan Talmalaan e Snaketower, Utrecht 2012, St Sebastian Church, Münster 2013. *Publications include:* El Croquis No 105 – Bolles Wilson 1995–2001, Bolles Wilson Monograph Electra 2004, Bolles Wilson Monograph, A Handful of Productive Paradigms 2009, Bolles Wilson Monograph/Sketchbook, Inspiration and Process in Architecture, Moleskine 2012, Bolles Wilson Monograph Tacuit et fecit, arianuova 18 2014, Bolles Wilson Monograph, Reasons for Travelling to Italy 2016. *Address:* Bolles+Wilson GmbH & Co. KG, Hafenweg 16, 48155 Münster, Germany (office). *Telephone:* (251) 482720 (office). *Fax:* (251) 4827224 (office). *E-mail:* info@bolles-wilson.com (office). *Website:* www.bolles-wilson.com (office).

WILSON, Robert M.; American theatre and opera director and artist; b. 4 Oct. 1941, Waco, Tex.; s. of D. M. Wilson and Velma Loree Wilson (née Hamilton); ed Univ. of Texas, Pratt Inst.; began creating theatre in New York in the 1960s; worked mainly in Europe in 1980s and 1990s, directed original works as well as traditional opera and theatre; Guggenheim Fellow 1971, 1980; f. The Watermill Center 1992; Trustee, Nat. Inst. of Music Theatre; mem. Dramatists Guild, Soc. des Auteurs et Compositeurs Dramatiques, Soc. of Stage Dirs and Choreographers, PEN American Center, American Acad. of Arts and Letters; Hon. Dir American Repertory Theatre; Commdr des Arts et des Lettres, Officier, Légion of d'Honneur 2014, Officer's Cross, Order of Merit (Germany) 2014; Dr hc (Calif. Coll. of Arts and Letters), (Pratt Inst.); Maharam Award for Best Set Design 1975, Lumen Award 1977, First Prize, San Sebastian Film and Video Festival 1984, Picasso Award 1986, Inst. Skowhegan Medal for drawing 1987, Grand Prix Biennale, Barcelona Festival of Cinema Art 1989, Germna Theatre Critics Award 1990, Brandeis Univ. Poses Creative Arts Award 1991, Venice Biennale Golden Lion Award for Sculpture 1993, Dorothy and Lillian Gish Prize Prize for Lifetime Achievement 1996, Tadeusz Kantor Prize 1997, Harvard Excellence in Design Award 1998, Pushkin Prize 1999; Most Outstanding Theater Designer of the Seventies, US Inst. of Theater Tech. 1977, Goethe-Medaille, Goethe-Institut, Germany 2014. *Dance created and choreographed:* Snow on the Mesa (for Martha Graham Dance Co.) 1995. *Stage appearances include:* Deafman Glance 1970, The Life and Times of Joseph Stalin (Dir) 1974, A Letter for Queen Victoria 1974, Einstein on the Beach 1976, 1984, Death, Destruction and Detroit 1979, The Golden Windows 1982, 1985, The Civil Wars 1983–85, Hamletmachine 1986, Doktor Faustus 1989, The Black Rider 1990, King Lear 1990, The Magic Flute 1991, Alice 1993, Der Mond in Gras 1994, The Death of Molière 1994, Hamlet: A Monologue 1995, Prometeo 1997, Saints and Singing 1997, Monsters of Grace 1998, Dream Play 1998, Scourge of Hyacinths 1999, The Days Before 1999, Hot Waters 2000, Relative Light 2000. *Plays directed and designed include:* Deafman Glance 1970, Einstein on the Beach 1976, Death, Destruction and Detroit 1979, The Golden Windows 1982, the CIVIL warS 1983–85, Hamletmachine 1986, Doktor Faustus 1989, The Black Rider 1990, The Magic Flute 1991, Doktor Faustus Lights the Lights 1992, Alice 1992, Madame Butterfly 1993, Hanjo 1994, Hamlet: A Monologue 1995, Time Rocker 1996, Lady from the Sea 1998, Das Rheingold 2000, POEtry 2000, Woyzeck 2001, Three Penny Opera, Spoleto Festival, Italy 2008. *Films include:* Overture for a Deafman, Monsters of Grace 1998. *Videos include:* The Spaceman 1976, 1984, Video 50 1978, Stations 1982, La Femme à la Cafétière 1989, Mr. Bojangles' Memory 1991, La Mort de Molière 1994. *Publications include:* The King of Spain 1970, Einstein on the Beach: An Opera in Four Acts (with Philip Glass) 1976, A Letter for Queen Victoria 1977, Death, Destruction and Detroit 1979, the CIVIL warS 1985, Mr. Bojangles' Memory 1991, RW Notebook 1999. *Leisure interest:* collecting fine art and design. *Address:* The Watermill Center, 39 Watermill Towd Road, Water Mill, NY 11976 (office); RW Work Ltd, 155 Wooster Street, Suite 4F, New York, NY 10012, USA. *Telephone:* (212) 253-7484. *Fax:* (212) 253-7485 (office). *Website:* www.robertwilson.com (office); www.watermillcenter.org (office).

WILSON, Sir Robert Peter, KCMG, FRSA, CIMgt; British business executive; *Senior Adviser, Morgan Stanley;* b. 2 Sept. 1943, Carshalton, Surrey, England; s. of Alfred Wilson and Dorothy Wilson (née Mathews); m. Shirley Elisabeth Robson 1975; one s. one d.; ed Epsom Coll., Univ. of Sussex, Harvard Business School, USA; Asst Economist, Dunlop Ltd 1966–67; Economist, Mobil Oil Co. Ltd 1967–70; with Rio Tinto PLC (fmrly RTZ Corpn PLC) starting 1970, Man. Dir AM & S Europe 1979–82, Project Dir RTZ Devt Enterprise 1982–83, Head of Planning and Devt RTZ Corpn PLC 1984–86, Dir 1987–2003, Chief Exec. 1991–97, Chair. 1997–2003; Dir Rio Tinto Ltd (fmrly CRA Ltd) 1990–2003, Deputy Chair. 1995–98, Chair. 1999–2003; Chair. BG Group plc 2004–12; currently Sr Adviser Morgan Stanley; Dir (non-exec.), BP PLC, The Boots Co. PLC 1991–98, GlaxoSmithKline plc 2003–14; Sr Ind. Dir 2009–13); fmr Dir (non-exec.), Diageo PLC; mem. Bd of Dirs, The Economist Group Ltd 2002–09, Chair. 2003–09; Trustee, Camborne School of Mines 1993–99; Hon. DSc (Exeter) 1993, (Birmingham) 2002, (Sussex) 2004; Hon. LLD (Dundee) 2001. *Leisure interests:* theatre, opera. *Address:* Morgan

Stanley, 1585 Broadway, New York, NY 10036, USA (office). *Website:* www.morganstanley.com (office).

WILSON, Robert Woodrow, PhD; American radio astronomer; *Senior Scientist, Harvard-Smithsonian Center for Astrophysics;* b. 10 Jan. 1936, Houston, Tex.; s. of Ralph Woodrow Wilson and Fannie May Wilson (née Willis); m. Elizabeth Rhoads Sawin 1958; two s. one d.; ed Rice Univ., California Inst. of Tech.; mem. Tech. Staff, AT&T Bell Labs, Holmdel, NJ 1963–76, Head of Radio Physics Research Dept 1976–94; Sr Scientist, Harvard-Smithsonian Center for Astrophysics 1994–; mem. NAS, American Astronomical Soc., American Physical Soc., Int. Astronomical Union; Henry Draper Award 1977, Herschel Award 1977, Nobel Prize for Physics (shared with Arno Allan Penzias for their discovery of the cosmic microwave background) 1978. *Publications:* numerous articles in scientific journals. *Address:* Harvard-Smithsonian Center for Astrophysics, 60 Garden Street, #42, Cambridge, MA 02138 (office); 9 Valley Point Drive, Holmdel, NJ 07733, USA (home). *Telephone:* (617) 496-7744 (office). *Fax:* (617) 496-7554 (office). *E-mail:* rwilson@cfa.harvard.edu (office). *Website:* cfa-www.harvard.edu (office).

WILSON, Thomas Joseph (Tom), BBA, MBA; American business executive; *Chairman, President and CEO, The Allstate Corporation;* b. 1958, St Clair Shores, Mich.; m. Jill Wilson (neé Garling); three c.; ed Univ. of Michigan, J.L. Kellogg Grad. School of Man., Northwestern Univ.; held various financial positions at Amoco Corpn 1980–86; Man. Dir Mergers and Acquisitions, Dean Witter Reynolds 1986–93; Vice-Pres., Strategy and Analysis, Sears, Roebuck and Co. 1993–95; Chief Financial Officer Allstate Corpn 1995–98, Chair. and Pres. Allstate Financial 1999–2002, Pres. Allstate Protection 2002–06, Pres. and COO 2005–06, Pres. and CEO 2007–, Chair. 2008–; apptd Vice-Chair. Fed. Reserve Bank of Chicago 2008; Co-f. Get IN Chicago Foundation; mem. Bd, Rush Univ. Medical Center, Museum of Science and Industry, Financial Services Roundtable, Catalyst, World Business Chicago, State Street Corpn; mem. World Presidents' Org., Financial Services Forum, The Business Roundtable, Civic Cttee of Commercial Club of Chicago; CFO Magazine's Excellence Award 1998. *Address:* The Allstate Corporation, 2775 Sanders Road, Suite F7, Northbrook, IL 60062-6127, USA (office). *Telephone:* (847) 402-5000 (office). *Fax:* (847) 326-7519 (office). *E-mail:* directors@allstate.com (office). *Website:* www.allstate.com (office).

WILSON, Trevor Gordon, AM, MA, DPhil, FRHistS, FAHA; New Zealand military historian and academic; *Professor Emeritus and Honorary Visiting Research Fellow, School of History and Politics, University of Adelaide;* b. 24 Dec. 1928, Auckland; s. of Gordon Wilson and Winifred Wilson; m. Jane Verney 1957; two d.; ed Mount Albert Grammar School, Univs. of Auckland and Oxford; Asst Lecturer in History Canterbury Univ. 1952, Auckland Univ. 1953–55; Research Asst in Govt, Univ. of Manchester 1957–59; Lecturer then Sr Lecturer in History, Univ. of Adelaide 1960–67, Prof. 1968–, now Prof. Emer. and Hon. Visiting Research Fellow; Commonwealth Fellow, St John's Coll., Cambridge 1972; Visiting Fellow, Magdalen Coll., Oxford 1987; Drinko Distinguished Visiting Prof., Marshall Univ. 1989; Nuffield Dominion Travelling Fellowship 1964–65; Univ. of NZ Overseas Travelling Scholarship 1953; Gilbert Campion Prize (jt winner) 1960, Higby Prize 1965, Adelaide Festival of Arts Literature Award 1988. *Publications:* The Downfall of the Liberal Party (1914–35) 1966, The Political Diaries of C. P. Scott 1911–28 1970, The Myriad Faces of War: Britain and the Great War 1914–18 1986, Command on the Western Front: The Military Career of Sir Henry Rawlinson 1914–1918 (with Robin Prior) 1992, Passchendaele: the Untold Story (with Robin Prior) 1996, The First World War (Cassell History of Warfare) (with Robin Prior) 1999, The Somme (with Robin Prior) 2005. *Leisure interests:* listening to jazz, watching musical movies, ten-pin bowling. *Address:* Department of History and Politics, Room 314, Napier Building, University of Adelaide, North Terrace, South Australia 5005, Australia. *Telephone:* (8) 8303-5633 (office). *Fax:* (8) 8303-3443 (office). *E-mail:* tjwilson@senet.com.au (home). *Website:* www.arts.adelaide.edu.au/historypolitics (office).

WILSON-JOHNSON, David Robert, BA, FRAM; British baritone; b. 16 Nov. 1950, Northampton; s. of Harry K. Johnson and Sylvia C. Wilson; ed Wellingborough School, Northants., British Inst. of Florence, St Catharine's Coll., Cambridge and Royal Acad. of Music; debut at Royal Opera House, Covent Garden in We Come to the River 1976; regular appearances for over 20 years including in Billy Budd, L'Enfant et les Sortilèges, Le Rossignol, Les Noces, Boris Godunov, Die Zauberflöte, Turandot, Werther, Madame Butterfly, Così fan tutte; Wigmore Hall recital debut 1977; BBC Promenade Concert debut 1981; debut at Edin. Festival 1976, Glyndebourne Festival 1980 and at festivals in Bath, Bergen, Berlin, Geneva, Graz, Netherlands, Hong Kong, Jerusalem, Orange, Paris, Salzburg, Tanglewood and Vienna; Paris Opera debut in Die Meistersinger 1989; American debut in Paulus (title role) 1990; ENO debut (in Billy Budd) 1991; Netherlands Opera debut in Birtwistle's Punch and Judy 1993; Founder Dir Ferrandou Summer Singing School 1985–; numerous concert tours with David Owen Norris (voice and piano duo for 40 years), Pierre Boulez/ Ensemble Intercontemporain, Gennadi Rozhdestvensky /BBCSO, David Atherton/London Sinfonietta/Hong Kong Symphony, Charles Dutoit Philadelphia Orchestra/Tonhalle Orchestra/ NHK Symphony, Frans Bruggen/Orchestra of the 18th Century, Robert King/The King's Consort; Prof. of Voice, Amsterdam Conservatorium 2005–10; Gulbenkian Fellowship 1978–81; Nat. Fed. of Music Soc. Award 1977, Evening Standard Award for Opera 1989. *Films include:* Give My Regards to Broad Street (The Beatles), A Midsummer Marriage (Michael Tippett) 1988, Or Shall We Die? (Michael Berkeley/Ian McEwan). *Television includes:* BBC Handel 250th Anniversary Celebrations from Westminster Abbey 1985, BBC TV Purcell Tercentenary Celebration from Westminster Abbey 1995, Olivier Messiaen's 80 birthday Concert from Royal Festival Hall (title role in St François d'Assise) 1988. *Recordings include:* Schubert's Winterreise with David Owen Norris, Mozart Masses from King's Coll., Cambridge, Haydn's Nelson Mass (English Concert/ Trevor Pinnock), Schoenberg's Ode to Napoleon (Ensemble Intercontemporain), King Priam, Punch and Judy, The Ice Break (London Sinfonietta/ David Atherton), La Traviata, Lucrezia Borgia (Joan Sutherland, Luciano Pavarotti/ Richard Bonynge), Michael Berkeley's Or Shall We Die?, Belshazzar's Feast, The Kingdom, Caractacus (LSO/Richard Hickox), Odes (Purcell), Black Pentecost (BBCPO/Maxwell Davies), Mass in B Minor (Bavarian Radio Symphony Orchestra/Carlo Maria Giulini, Peter Grimes (ROH /Bernard Haitink), Roméo et Juliette, Damnation of Faust, Oedipus Rex (Philadelphia Orchestra/Charles Dutoit). *Leisure interests:* swimming, slimming, gardening and growing walnuts in the Dordogne. *Address:* c/o Ben Rayfield, Rayfield Artists, Southbank House, Black Prince Road, London, SE1 7SJ, England (office); Prinsengracht 455, 1016 HN Amsterdam, Netherlands (home); 28 Englefield Road, London, N1 4ET, England (home). *Telephone:* (20) 7193-1531 (office); (20) 7254-0941 (London); 5-65-10-94-11 (France); (20) 7728104 (home). *E-mail:* ben.rayfield@rayfieldallied.com (office); info@ferrandou.org (office). *Website:* www.rayfieldartists.com (office); www.ferrandou.org (office); www.davidwilsonjohnson.com.

WILSON OF DINTON, Baron (Life Peer), cr. 2003, of Dinton in the County of Buckinghamshire; **Richard Thomas James Wilson,** GCB, MA, LLM; British civil servant and college principal; b. 11 Oct. 1942, Cardiff, South Wales; s. of Richard Ridley Wilson and Frieda Bell Wilson (née Finlay); m. Caroline Margaret Lee 1972; one s. one d.; ed Radley Coll., Clare Coll., Cambridge; called to the Bar 1965; Asst Prin. Board of Trade 1966, Pvt. Sec. to Minister of State, Board of Trade 1969–71, Prin. Cabinet Office 1971–73, Dept of Energy 1974, Asst Sec. Dept of Energy 1977–82, Under-Sec. 1982, Prin. Establishment and Finance Officer 1982–86; on loan to Cabinet Office Man. and Personnel Office 1986–87, Deputy Sec. Cabinet Office 1987–90; Deputy Sec. (Industry) HM Treasury 1990–92; Perm. Sec. Dept of Environment 1992–94; Perm. Under-Sec. of State, Home Office 1994–97; Cabinet Sec. and Head of the Home Civil Service 1997–2002; Master, Emmanuel Coll., Cambridge 2002–12; mem. (Crossbench) House of Lords 2003–; Chair. C Hoare & Co. 2006–16, now Life Fellow; Dir (non-exec.) BSkyB 2003–13; Chair. Radley Coll. Council 2004–10; Trustee, Ewing Foundation 1994–2014, Cicely Saunders Int. 2004–14, Cambridge Arts Theatre 2007–11; Pres. Chartered Inst. of Personnel and Devt 2004–06. *Address:* Emmanuel College, St Andrew's Street, Cambridge, CB2 3AP, England (office). *Telephone:* (1223) 334247 (office). *Website:* www.emma.cam.ac.uk (office).

WILSON OF TILLYORN, Baron (Life Peer), cr. 1992, of Finzean in the District of Kincardine and Deeside and of Fanling in Hong Kong; **David Clive Wilson,** KT, GCMG, PhD, FRSE; British diplomatist and public servant; b. 14 Feb. 1935, Alloa, Clackmannanshire, Scotland; s. of Rev. William Skinner Wilson and Enid Wilson; m. Natasha Helen Mary Alexander 1967; two s.; ed Glenalmond and Keble Coll., Oxford; nat. service, The Black Watch 1953–55; entered Foreign Service 1958, Third Sec., Vientiane 1959–60, Second then First Sec., Peking 1963–65, FCO 1965–68 (resgnd 1968, rejoined Diplomatic Service 1972), Cabinet Office 1974–77, Political Adviser, Hong Kong 1977–81, Head S. European Dept, FCO 1981–84, Asst Under-Sec. of State 1984–87; Gov. and Commdr-in-Chief of Hong Kong 1987–92; Chancellor, Univ. of Aberdeen 1997–2013; Vice-Pres. Royal Scottish Geographical Soc. 1996–; Language Student, Hong Kong 1960–62; Ed. China Quarterly 1968–74; Visiting Scholar, Columbia Univ., New York 1972; Chair. Scottish Hydro-Electric PLC 1993–2000 (Scottish and Southern Energy PLC 1998–2000); mem. Bd of Govs. SOAS 1992–97; mem. Bd British Council 1993–2002 (Chair. Scottish Cttee 1993–2002); Chancellor's Assessor, Univ. of Aberdeen 1993–96; Chair. Council, Glenalmond Coll. 2000–05, Scottish Peers' Asscn 2000–02; Dir Martin Currie Pacific Trust 1993–2003; mem. Advisory Cttee on Business Appointments 2000–09 (Chair. 2008–09); Pres. Bhutan Soc. of the UK 1993–2008, Hong Kong Asscn 1994–, Hong Kong Soc. 1994–2013; Fellow, Royal Soc. of Edinburgh 2000–, Pres. 2008–11; Registrar of the Most Distinguished Order of St Michael and St George 2001–10; Chair. Bd of Trustees Nat. Museums of Scotland 2002–06; Chair., St Paul's Cathedral Advisory Council 2009–; Lord High Commr to Gen. Ass., Church of Scotland 2010, 2011; Hon. Fellow, Keble Coll. Oxford; Hon. Burger of Guild of City of Aberdeen 2003; Hon. LLD (Aberdeen) 1990, (Chinese Univ., Hong Kong) 1996; Hon. DLitt (Sydney) 1991, (Abertay Dundee) 1994, (Univ. of Hong Kong) 2006; Dr hc (Edinburgh) 2011. *Leisure interests:* mountaineering, reading, theatre. *Address:* House of Lords, Westminster, London, SW1A 0PW, England (office). *Telephone:* (20) 7219-3107 (office). *Fax:* (20) 7219-5979 (office). *E-mail:* wilsondc@parliament.uk (office).

WILSON-RAYBOULD, Jody, PC, BA, LLB; Canadian lawyer and politician; b. 23 March 1971, Vancouver, BC; d. of Bill Wilson and Sandra Wilson; m. Tim Raybould 2008; ed Univ. of Victoria, Univ. of British Columbia; called to the bar 2000; Provincial Crown Prosecutor, Ministry of the Attorney-Gen., Vancouver 2000–03; Commr, BC Treaty Comm. 2003–09; Commr, First Nations Summit 2004; Lawyer and CEO, KaLoNa Group (consulting firm providing advice to First Nation govts) 2004; Councillor, We Wai Kai First Nation 2009, also We Wai Kai rep. to First Nations Finance Authority, Chair. FNFA 2013–15; Regional Chief, BC Assembly of First Nations 2009–15; mem. House of Commons for Vancouver Granville 2015–; Minister of Justice and Attorney-Gen. of Canada 2015–19; Assoc. Minister of Nat. Defence Jan.–Feb. 2019; Minister of Veterans Affairs Jan.–Feb. 2019; fmr Dir Capilano Univ.; mem. Bd of Dirs Minerva Foundation for BC Women 2008–10; mem. Liberal Party of Canada; Minerva Foundation for BC Women Award 2011, Indigenous Women in Leadership Award, Canadian Council for Aboriginal Business 2017.

WILUAN, Kris Taenar, BSc; Indonesian business executive; *Chairman, Citramas Group;* b. 1948; s. of Henk Wiluan; m.; three c.; ed Univ. of London, UK; began career as computer programmer, Guest, Keen and Nettlefold, England; moved to Singapore 1973; Gen. Man. United Motor Works 1973–77; f. own business as logistics contractor for oil cos, Indonesia 1977; f. PT Citra Bonang 1979 (currently Chair.) PT Citra Bonindo 1983, PT Citra Tubindo Tbk 1983 (currently Pres. and CEO), Chair. Citramas Group (holding co. with interests in oil, tourism, real estate, logistics and transportation); Chair. and CEO KS Energy 2006–; Chair. and CEO Aqua-Terra Supply Co. Ltd; Exec. Chair. and CEO SSH Corpn Ltd; Pres. Asean Taekwondo Fed., Vice-Chair. World Taekwondo Federation; Pres. Riau Porlasi (sailing asscn); Ernst and Young Indonesian Entrepreneur of the Year Award 2009. *Address:* PT Citramasjaya Teknikmandiri, Jl Diponegoro No. 108, Tambun, Bekasi 17510, Indonesia (office). *Telephone:* (21) 8822149 (office). *Fax:* (21) 8807335 (office). *E-mail:* cti@citramas.co.id (office). *Website:* www.citramas.co.id (office).

WIN, Myint, BSc; Myanma politician; *President;* b. 8 Nov. 1951, Danubyu, Ayeyarwady Region, Burma; s. of Tun Kyin and Daw Than; m. Cho Cho; one d.; ed Rangoon Arts and Science Univ.; Sr Lawyer, High Court 1981, then Lawyer, Supreme Court; Advocate, High Court 1985; mem. Nat. League for Democracy 1988–; Political Prisoner 1988–90; elected mem. Pyithu Hluttaw (House of Rep.) 1990, mem. Pathein Township 2012–16, Tamwe Township 2016–18, Second

Speaker 2016–18; Pres. 2018–. *Address:* President's Office, Building 18, Nay Pyi Taw, Myanmar (office). *Website:* www.president-office.gov.mm.

WINBERG, (Sven) Håkan, LLB; Swedish politician and lawyer; b. 30 July 1931, Ånge; s. of Sven Winberg and Sally Angman; m. Ulla Greta Petersson 1957; Justice, Court of Appeal; mem. Parl. 1971–82; mem. Exec. Swedish Moderate Party 1972–, mem. Steering Cttee 1975–; mem. Press Assistance Bd 1971–79, Bd of Council for Prevention of Crime 1974–79, Co. Boundaries Cttee 1970–74, Cttee of Inquiry into the Press 1972–75, New Labour Laws Cttee 1976–78, Nat. Police Bd 1977–79, Nordic Council 1977–82; County Councillor 1974–79; Minister of Justice 1979–81; Pres. Court of Appeal, Sundsvall from 1982; mem. Election Review Cttee of the Riksdag from 1983; mem. Parl. Comm. for Investigation into the murder of Prime Minister Olof Palme 1987–88, new Comm. for same investigation 1994; mem. Security Police Cttee from 1989, Court of Law Cttee from 1990. *Leisure interest:* skiing.

WINBLAD, Ann L., BA, MA, PhD; American investment company executive; *Managing Director, Hummer Winblad Venture Partners;* b. 1 Nov. 1950, Red Wing, Minn.; ed Univ. of St Thomas, St Paul, Minn.; began career as systems programmer with San Francisco Fed. Reserve Bank; co-f. Open Systems Inc. 1976, sold co. 1983; Co-founder and Man. Dir Hummer Winblad Venture Partners 1989–; Co-Chair. SDForum; serves as adviser to many entrepreneurial orgs; mem. Bd of Dirs Voltage Security Inc. 2002–15, Ace Metrix 2008–, Karmasphere 2010–14, Sonatype Inc. 2010–, Optimine Software Inc. 2014–, Richard M. Schulze Family Foundation; mem. Bd of Trustees Univ. of St Thomas 2000–; Hon. LLD (Univ. of St Thomas). *Publication:* Object-Oriented Software (co-author) 1990; numerous articles in industry journals. *Address:* Hummer Winblad Venture Partners, One Lombard Street, Suite 300, San Francisco, CA 94111, USA (office). *Telephone:* (415) 979-9600 (office). *Website:* www.humwin.com (office).

WINCHESTER, Robert J., MD; American physician and academic; *Professor of Pediatrics, Pathology, and Medicine, Division of Rheumatology, Department of Medicine, Columbia University;* ed Cornell Univ.; Internship and Residency, Cornell Medical Center, New York Hosp.; currently Prof. of Pediatrics, Pathology, and Medicine, Div. of Rheumatology, Dept of Medicine, Columbia Univ.; mem. NIH Study Section: Gen. Medicine A 1980–84, AIDS-Related Research-2 1995–97; Assoc. Ed., Journal of Clinical and Experimental Immunology 1995–97; mem. American Soc. for Clinical Investigation, American Fed. for Clinical Research, Asscn of American Physicians, American Coll. of Rheumatology, American Asscn of Immunologists; Fellow, AAAS 1992; Councillor, Int. Workshop on Human Leukocyte Differentiation Antigens 1989–96, Lee C. Howley, Sr Prize for Arthritis Research, Arthritis Foundation 1990, Crafoord Prize, Royal Swedish Acad. of Sciences (co-recipient) 2013. *Publications:* numerous papers in professional journals. *Address:* New York-Presbyterian Hospital/CUMC, 630 West 168th Street, P&S Building, 10th Floor, Room 10-445, New York, NY 10032, USA (office). *Telephone:* (212) 305-8250 (office). *Fax:* (212) 305-9078 (office). *E-mail:* rjw8@columbia.edu (office). *Website:* www.rheumatologyatcolumbia.org/rwinchester.html (office); nyp.org/physician/rjwinchester (office).

WINCKLER, Georg; Austrian university rector and academic; *President, ERSTE Foundation;* b. 27 Sept. 1943, Ostrava, Czechoslovakia; m.; two d.; ed Princeton Univ., USA, Univ. of Vienna; with Austrian Inst. of Econ. Research, Vienna 1967; Univ. Asst, Dept of Econs, Univ. of Vienna 1968–75, Docent 1976–78, Prof. 1978–, Head 1980–82, Dir Centre for Int. and Interdisciplinary Studies 1994–99, mem. Senate 1997–99, Univ. Rector 1999–2011; Visiting Prof., Univ. of Graz, Université Fribourg, Switzerland 1977–78, Univ. of Linz 1985–86, Georgetown Univ., USA 1995, Comenius Univ. of Bratislava, Slovakia 1998; with Research Dept IMF 1990–91; Rector Univ. of Vienna 1999–2011; Pres. Austrian Rectors Conf. 2000–05; Vice-Pres. European Univ. Asscn 2001–05, Pres. 2005–09; Gen. Sec. Austrian Econ. Asscn 1978–85, Vice-Pres. 1985–99; apptd Lecturer, Diplomatic Acad., Vienna 1974, Bd mem. 1985–2011; mem. cadre, Pont-à-Mousson SA, France 1971–72; mem. Council of Scientists, INTAS-Int. Asscn for Promotion of Cooperation with Scientists from New Ind. States of fmr Soviet Union, EC, Brussels 1993–96, TRM Panel 1995–99; mem. Bd of Société Universitaire Européenne de Recherches Financières, Netherlands 1990–98; Speaker, Chair. Confs of IMF 1992–94, EFTA, Bulgaria 1994, OECD 1996, Euromoney, England, Centre for Econ. Policy Research 1997–99; mem. European Research Advisory Bd 2004–07, European Research Area Board, EC, Brussels 2008–12, People Advisory Group 2009–12; Pres. ERSTE Foundation 2011–; Vice-Chair. Supervisory Bd UNIQA AG 2009–, ERSTE Group AG. *Publications include:* as co-author or co-ed.: Handbook of Austrian Economic Policy 1982, Financial Liberalisation and Tax Harmonisation in Europe 1992, Central and Eastern Europe: Roads to Growth 1992, International Trade and Restructuring in Eastern Europe 1994, Output Decline in Eastern Europe: Unavoidable, External Influence or Homemade? 1995, Macroeconomic Policy Games 1995, Central Banks and Seigniorage: A Study of Three Economies in Transition (European Econ. Review) 1996, Grundzüge der Wirtschaftspolitik Österreichs (third edn) 2001. *Leisure interests:* mountaineering, skiing, reading. *Address:* ERSTE Stiftung Graben 21, 3rd floor, 1010 Vienna, Austria (office). *Telephone:* (43) 50100-11584 (office); (1) 328-12-72 (home). *E-mail:* georg.winckler@erstestiftung.org (office). *Website:* www.erstestiftung.org (office).

WINDLE, Alan Hardwick, PhD, FRS, FIM, FInstP; British scientist and academic; *Emeritus Professor of Materials Science, University of Cambridge;* b. 20 June 1942, Croydon, Surrey, England; s. of Stuart George Windle and Myrtle Lillian Windle (née Povey); m. Janet Susan Carr 1968; one s. three d.; ed Whitgift School, Imperial Coll. London, Trinity Coll., Cambridge; ICI Research Fellow, Imperial Coll., London 1966–67, Lecturer in Metallurgy 1967–75; Lecturer in Metallurgy and Materials Science, Univ. of Cambridge 1975–92, Fellow, Trinity Coll. 1978–, Lecturer and Dir of Studies in Natural Sciences, Trinity Coll. 1978–92, Tutor 1983–91, Prof. of Materials Science 1992, Head of Dept of Materials Science, Univ. of Cambridge 1996–2001, now Emer. Prof.; Visiting Prof., N Carolina State Univ., USA 1980; Exec. Dir Cambridge-MIT Inst. 2000–03; Vice-Pres. Inst. of Materials 2001–; Dir Pfizer Inst. for Pharmaceutical Materials Science 2005–; Commr Royal Comm. for Exhbn of 1851 2001–11; mem. Indian Acad. of Science; Fellow, American Physical Soc.; Bessemer Medal, Imperial Coll. 1963, RSA Silver Medal 1963, Rosenhain Medal & Prize 1987, Swinburne Medal & Prize, Plastics and Rubber Inst. 1992, Founders' Medal and Prize, Polymer Physics Group, Inst. of Physics and Royal Soc. of Chem. 2007, Royal Soc. Armourers and Braziers Medal and Prize 2007. *Publications:* A First Course in Crystallography 1978, Liquid Crystalline Polymers (with A. M. Donald) 1992 (second edn with A. M. Donald and S. Hanna 2005). *Leisure interest:* flying light aircraft. *Address:* Department of Materials Science and Metallurgy, University of Cambridge, 27 Charles Babbage Road, Cambridge, CB3 0FS, England (office). *Telephone:* (1223) 334321 (office). *E-mail:* ahw1@cam.ac.uk (office). *Website:* www.mml.msm.cam.ac.uk/directory/alanwindle (office).

WINDSOR, Colin, DPhil, FRS, FInstP; British physicist and academic; *Consultant, Tokamak Energy;* b. 28 June 1938, Beckenham, Kent, England; s. of George Thomas and Mabel Rayment; m. 1st Margaret Lee 1963; one s. two d.; m. 2nd Maureen Watkins 2005; ed Magdalen Coll., Oxford, Clarendon Lab., Oxford; Research Assoc., Yale Univ., USA 1963–64; scientist, UKAEA 1964–96, Programme Area Man. UKAEA Fusion 1996–98; Visiting Fellow, Japanese Asscn for the Advancement of Science, Sendai 1980; Consultant, UKAEA Fusion (now Culham Centre for Fusion Energy) 1998–2015; Sr Consultant, PenOp UK 1998–2000; Consultant, Tokamak Energy 2013–; Hon. Prof. of Physics, Univ. of Birmingham 1990–; Duddell Medal, Inst. of Physics 1986. *Publications include:* Pulsed Neutron Scattering 1981, Four Computer Models 1983, Solid State Science, Past, Present and Predicted (ed.) 1987. *Leisure interests:* singing, playing piano, organ and recorder, composing, cycling to work, naturism. *Address:* Tokamak Energy United Kingdom Ltd, 120A, Olympic Avenue, Milton Park, Abingdon, OX14 4SA (office); 116 New Road, East Hagbourne, Oxon., OX11 9LD, England (home). *Telephone:* (1235) 812083 (home). *E-mail:* colin.windsor@tokamakenergy.co.uk (office). *Website:* www.tokamakenergy.co.uk (office); www.colin.windsor.talktalk.net.

WINE, Bobi, (Robert Kyagulanyi Ssentamu), BA; Ugandan musician, actor and activist; b. 12 Feb. 1982, Gomba Dist; m. Barbara Itungo; four c.; ed Makerere Univ., Kampala; adopted stage name Bobi Wine 1999; well known for Afrobeat music; uses music to address Uganda's political and social issues; MP (ind.) for Kyaddondo East constituency 2017–; arrested and detained 2018, charged with treason Aug. 2018. *Recordings include:* albums: Bobi Wange, Hosanah, Kansubize, Ontabira, Sweet.

WINELAND, David Jeffery, BS, MS, PhD; American physicist; *Group Leader, Time and Frequency Division, National Institute of Standards and Technology (NIST);* b. 24 Feb. 1944, Milwaukee, Wis.; m. Sedna Helen Quimby; two s.; ed Univ. of California, Berkeley, Harvard Univ.; Group Leader, Time and Frequency Div., Nat. Inst. of Standards and Tech. (NIST), Boulder, Colo 1975–, also NIST Fellow; Prof. Adjoint, Univ. of Colorado 2000–; Davisson-Germer Prize in Atomic or Surface Physics 1990, William F. Meggers Award, Optical Soc. of America (OSA) 1990, Einstein Prize for Laser Science, Soc. of Optical and Quantum Electronics 1996, IEEE Rabi Award 1998, Arthur L. Schawlow Prize in Laser Science 2001, OSA Ives Medal 2004, Nat. Medal of Science 2007, OSA Herbert Walther Award 2009, Benjamin Franklin Medal, Franklin Inst. (with Juan Ignacio Cirac and Peter Zoller) 2010, Nobel Prize in Physics (shared with Serge Haroche) 2012, Galileo Ferraris Prize, Istituto Nazionale di Ricerca Metrologica, Turin, Italy 2014. *Address:* National Institute of Standards and Technology, 325 Broadway, Mailcode 847.10, Boulder, CO 80305-3328, USA (office). *Telephone:* (303) 497-5286 (office). *E-mail:* david.wineland@nist.gov (office). *Website:* www.nist.gov/pml/div688/index.cfm (office).

WINFREY, Oprah, BA; American broadcaster, actress and producer; *Chairman, Harpo Inc.;* b. (Orpah Gail Winfrey), 29 Jan. 1954, Kosciusko, Miss.; d. of Vernon Winfrey and Vernita Lee; ed Tennessee State Univ.; worked for WVOL radio, Nashville, Tenn. while still at school, subsequently as reporter/anchor, WTVF-TV, Nashville; joined WJZ-TV news, Baltimore, as co-anchor 1976, became co-host, People Are Talking 1978; joined WLS-TV, Chicago as host, AM Chicago, subsequently renamed The Oprah Winfrey Show 1985–2011; f. Harpo Productions Inc. 1986, Owner and Producer 1986–; Founder and Editorial Dir O, The Oprah Magazine 2000–, O at Home 2004–; f. The Oprah Winfrey Foundation; Partner, Oxygen Media 2000–; launched Oprah & Friends (XM Satellite Radio network) 2006; f. OWN: The Oprah Winfrey Network 2011; est. Leadership Acad. for Girls, S Africa 2007–; Hon. LLD (Harvard) 2013; numerous awards, including Int. Radio and TV Soc.'s Broadcaster of the Year Award 1988, 1995 Individual Achievement Award, George Foster Peabody Awards 1996, Int. Radio and TV Society's Foundation Gold Medal Award 1996, TV Guide Television Performer of the Year 1997, named by Newsweek as the Most Important Person in Books and Media 1997, Nat. Acad. of TV Arts and Sciences Lifetime Achievement Award 1998 (in 1999 Oprah removed herself from future Emmy consideration and the show followed suit in 2000), Oprah and The Oprah Winfrey Show received more than 40 Daytime Emmy Awards: seven for Outstanding Host, nine for Outstanding Talk Show, more than 20 in the Creative Arts categories, and one for Oprah's work as supervising producer of the ABC After School Special Shades of Single Protein), Nat. Book Foundation 50th Anniversary Gold Medal 1999, Broadcasting & Cable Hall of Fame 2002, Bob Hope Humanitarian Award, 54th Annual Primetime Emmy Awards 2002, named the Greatest Pop Culture Icon of All Time by VH1 2003, elected to Nat. Women's Hall of Fame, Seneca, NY, Asscn of American Publrs AAP Honors Award 2003, Nat. Asscn of Broadcasters Distinguished Service Award 2004, UNA of the USA Global Humanitarian Action Award 2004, Int. Acad. of TV Arts and Sciences Int. Emmy Founders Award 2005, Nat. Asscn for the Advancement of Colored People Hall of Fame 2005, Nat. Civil Rights Museum Nat. Freedom Award 2005, ranked by Forbes magazine amongst The World's Most Powerful People (45th) 2009, (64th) 2010, Kennedy Center Honor 2010. *Achievements include:* helped initiate US Nat. Child Protection Act 1991, signed by Pres. Clinton ('Oprah's Law') 1993. *Theatre:* Broadway debut as a producer of The Color Purple 2005. *Films include:* acting roles: Sofia in The Color Purple 1985, Mrs Thomas in Native Son 1986, Throw Momma From The Train 1988, Mattie Michael in The Women of Brewster Place (TV) 1989, Listen Up: The Lives of Quincy Jones 1990, LaJoe Rivers in There Are No Children Here (TV) 1993, Sethe in Beloved 1998, Coretta Scott King (voice) in Our Friend, Martin (video) 1999, Charlotte's Web (voice) 2006, Bee Movie (voice) 2007, The Butler 2013; producer and/or exec. producer of several TV films, including Nine 1992, Overexposed 1992, Beloved 1998, Their Eyes Were Watching God 2005, Legends Ball 2006. *Publications:* Oprah (autobiog.) 1993, In the Kitchen with Rosie 1996, Make the Connection (with Bob Greene) 1996. *Address:* Harpo Inc., 110 North Carpenter Street,

Chicago, IL 60607, USA (office). *Telephone:* (312) 633-1000 (office). *Fax:* (312) 633-1976 (office). *Website:* www.oprah.com (home).

WINGER, Debra; American actress; b. 16 May 1955, Cleveland, Ohio; d. of Robert Winger and Ruth Winger; m. 1st Timothy Hutton 1986 (divorced); one s.; m. 2nd Arliss Howard 1996; one c.; ed California State Univ., Northridge; first professional appearance in Wonder Woman TV series 1976–77. *Films include:* Thank God It's Friday 1978, French Postcards 1979, Urban Cowboy 1980, Cannery Row 1982, An Officer and a Gentleman 1982, Terms of Endearment (Nat. Soc. of Film Critics Award for Best Actress 1983) 1983, Mike's Murder 1984, Legal Eagles 1986, Black Widow 1987, Made in Heaven 1987, Betrayed 1988, The Sheltering Sky, Everybody Wins 1990, Leap of Faith 1992, Shadowlands 1993, A Dangerous Woman (Tokyo Int. Film Festival Award for Best Actress) 1993, Forget Paris 1995, Big Bad Love (also producer) 2001, Radio 2003, Eulogy 2004, Dawn Anna (TV) 2005, Sometimes in April (TV) 2005, Rachel Getting Married 2008, Lola Versus 2012, Boychoir 2014, The Lovers 2017. *Television includes:* Special Olympics (movie) 1978, Dawn Anna 2005, In Treatment (series) 2010, The Ranch 2016–. *Publication:* Undiscovered 2008. *Address:* c/o CAA, 2000 Avenue of the Stars, Los Angeles, CA 90067, USA (office).

WINGTI, Rt Hon. Paias, CMG, PC; Papua New Guinea politician; *Governor of Western Highlands Province;* b. 2 Feb. 1951, Moika Village; five s.; ed Univ. of Papua New Guinea; MP 1977–97, 2002–07, 2012–, apptd. Asst Speaker and mem. Public Accounts Cttee; elected Govt Whip; Minister for Transport and Civil Aviation 1978–80; Deputy Prime Minister and Minister for Nat. Planning and Devt 1982–84, for Educ. 1984–85; resgnd from Govt, co-f. People's Democratic Movt 1985; Leader of Opposition March–Nov. 1985, 1988–92, 1994; Prime Minister 1985–88, 1992–94; Gov. Western Highlands Prov. 1995–97, 2002–07, 2012–. *Leisure interests:* playing golf and watching Rugby League. *Address:* People's Democratic Movement, P.O. Box 635, Gordons, NCD, Papua New Guinea. *Telephone:* 72175054. *Website:* www.parliament.gov.pg.

WINIGER, Matthias; Swiss geographer, academic and fmr university administrator; b. 1943, Berne; ed Univ. of Berne; Prof. of Geography, Univ. of Berne 1978–88; Prof. of Geography, Rheinische Friedrich-Wilhelms-Universität, Bonn, Germany 1988–, Dean, Faculty of Math. and Natural Sciences 2002–04, Rector 2004–09; mem. Acad. Science and Literature, Mainz. *Address:* Department of Geography, Rheinische Friedrich-Wilhelms-Universität, Meckenheimer Allee 166, 53115 Bonn, Germany (office). *Telephone:* (228) 73-7293 (office). *Fax:* (228) 73-7506 (office). *E-mail:* winiger@uni-bonn.de (office). *Website:* www.uni-bonn.de (office).

WINKELMANN, Helen Diana, BA, LLB, ONZ; New Zealand lawyer, judge and politician; *Chief Justice, Supreme Court of New Zealand;* b. 1962; d. of Douglas Winkelmann and Kathleen Winkelmann (née Papich); m. Martin James; four c.; ed Univ. of Auckland; admitted to the bar 1985; Law Clerk, Nicholson Gribbin, Partner 1988–2001; Barrister, Shortland Chambers 2001–04; Judge, High Court 2004, Chief Judge 2010–15; Court of Appeal Bench 2015; Chief Justice Supreme Court of New Zealand 2019–; Chair. Inst. of Judicial Studies; mem. Bd of Dirs Myanmar Investments Int. Ltd, All The Answers Ltd, NZ Telemed Services Ltd; Trustee, Starship Foundation, Lynfield Coll. Devt Trust; Australasian Inst. of Judicial Admin Award for Excellence 2013. *Address:* Supreme Court of New Zealand, 85 Lambton Quay, Wellington DX SX11224, New Zealand (office). *Telephone:* (4) 918-8222 (office). *Fax:* (4) 914-3560 (office). *E-mail:* supremecourt@justice.govt.nz (office). *Website:* www.courtsofnz.govt.nz/the-courts/supreme-court (office).

WINKLER, Josef; Austrian writer; b. 3 March 1953, Kamering, Kärnten; ed Handelsakademie, Klagenfurt; administrator, Univ. of Klagenfurt 1973–82, now teacher; Publisher, literary magazine Schreibarbeiten 1979; freelance writer and novelist 1982–; Writer-in-Residence, Bergen 1994–95; Anton Wildgans Prize 1980, Theodor Körner Foundation Funds literary grant 1990, Robert Musil Scholarship 1990, German Literary Fund's Kranich mit dem Stein Prize 1990, Bettina von Arnim Prize 1994, Berlin Literature Prize 1996, Otto Stoessl Prize 2000, André-Gide Prize 2000, Alfred Döblin Prize 2001, George Saiko travel grant 2004, Franz Nabl Prize 2005, Georg Büchner Preis 2008. *Publications include:* Das wilde Kärnten (trilogy): Menschenkind 1979, Der Ackermann aus Kärnten 1980, Muttersprache 1982, Die Verschleppung 1983, Der Leibeigene (trans. as The Serf) (novel) 1987, Friedhof der bitteren Orangen (novel) 1990, Das Zöglingsheft des Jean Genet (trans. as Flowers for Jean Genet) (essay) 1992, Das Wilde Kärnten 1995, Domra 1996, Wern es soweit ist 1998, Natura morta (novella) 2001, Leichnam, seine Familie belauernd 2003, Requiem für einen Vater 2004, Roppongi 2007, Ich eiss mir eine Wimper aus und stech dich damit tot 2008, Wortschatz der Nacht 2013, Mutter und der Bleistift 2013, Winnetou, Abel und ich 2014. *Address:* c/o Suhrkamp Verlag, Pappelallee 78-79, 10437 Berlin, Germany (office). *E-mail:* geschaeftsleitung@suhrkamp.de (office). *Website:* www.suhrkamp.de (office).

WINOCK, Michel, LèsL, DèsL; French historian, academic, writer and publisher; *Professor Emeritus, Institut d'Etudes politiques;* b. 19 March 1937, Paris; s. of Gaston Winock and Jeanne Winock (née Dussaule); m. Françoise Werner 1961; two s.; ed Sorbonne; teacher, Lycée Joffre, Montpellier 1961–63, Lycée Hoche, Versailles 1963–66, Lycée Lakanal, Sceaux 1966–68; Lecturer, Sr Lecturer Univ. of Paris VIII-Vincennes à St-Denis 1968–78; Sr Lecturer, Institut d'Etudes politiques (Sciences-Po), Paris 1978–90, Prof. 1990, now Prof. Emer.; Publr Editions du Seuil, Paris 1969–; radio producer, France-Inter 1983–85; Ed.-in-Chief L'Histoire magazine 1978–81, Editorial Adviser 1981–. *Publications include:* Histoire politique de la revue esprit 1930–1950 1975, La république se meurt 1978, Les grandes crises politiques 1971–1968 1986, La Fière hexagonale 1986, Nationalisme, antisemitisme et fascisme en France 1990, Le socialisme en France et en Europe XIXe–XXe siècle 1992, Le siècle des intellectuels (essays) 1997, La guerre de 1914–1918 racontée aux enfants 1998, La France politique XIXe–XXe siècle 1999, Les Voix de la liberté 2001, Les écrivains engagés au XIXe siècle 2001, La France et les juifs (Prix Montaigne de Bordeaux 2005) 2004, Pierre Mendès France 2005, Victor Hugo dans l'arène politique 2005, La Gauche au pouvoir: L'héritage du Front populaire 2006, La France antijuive de 1936: L'agression de Léon Blum à la Chambre des députés 2006, L'Agonie de la IVe République 2006, La Gauche en France 2006, La Mêlée présidentielle 2007, Clemenceau 2007, Madame De Stael (Prix Goncourt de la Biographie 2010) 2010. *Leisure interest:* tennis. *Address:* Institut d'Etudes politiques, 25 Rue Gaston De Saporta, Aix En Provence, 13100 Paris, France (office). *Telephone:* 4-42-17-01-91 (office). *Fax:* 4-42-96-36-99 (office). *E-mail:* wimi@cybercable.fr; wimi@noos.fr.

WINSER, Kim, OBE; British business executive; *President and CEO, Aquascutum Ltd;* b. 1959, Helensburgh, Scotland; one s.; ed Purbrook Grammar School, Hampshire; man. trainee Marks & Spencer 1977, various positions including Exec. for Menswear Buying, Div. Dir for Ladies Casualwear Group, est. Corp. Marketing Group 1999, Dir Marks & Spencer (first female in position) –2000; Chief Exec. Pringle of Scotland 2000–06; Pres. and CEO Aquascutum Ltd 2006–; Chair. Charity Events and Exec. mem. Co-operation Ireland 1996–; Hon. DLitt (Heriot-Watt) 2002. *Leisure interests:* being with her family, entertaining, sports, fashion. *Address:* Aquascutum Flagship Store, 100 Regent Street, London, W1B 5SR, England. *Telephone:* (20) 7675-9113 (office). *Website:* www.aquascutum.com (office).

WINSLET, Kate Elizabeth, CBE; British actress; b. 5 Oct. 1975, Reading, Berks.; d. of Roger Winslet and Sally Winslet; m. 1st Jim Threapleton 1998 (divorced 2001), one d.; m. 2nd Sam Mendes (q.v.) 2003 (divorced 2010); one s.; m. 3rd Ned Rocknroll 2012; one s.; ed Theatre School, Maidenhead; Grammy Award for Best Spoken Word Album for Children 2000, Film Critics' Annual Achievements Award for Best Supporting Actress 2002, Honorary César Award 2012. *Stage appearances include:* Peter Pan, What the Butler Saw (Manchester Evening News Award for Best Supporting Actress), A Game of Soldiers, Adrian Mole. *Films include:* Heavenly Creatures (New Zealand Film and TV Award for Best Foreign Actress, London Film Critics Circle Award for Best British Actress, Empire Magazine Award for Best British Actress 1995) 1994, A Kid in King Arthur's Court 1995, Sense and Sensibility (BAFTA Award for Best Supporting Actress 1996, Screen Actors' Guild Award for Best Supporting Actress 1996, Evening Standard British Film Award for Best Actress 1997) 1995, Jude 1996, Hamlet 1996, Titanic (Variety Club of Great Britain Film Actress of the Year 1998, European Film Acad. Award for Best European Actress 1998, BAFTA Award, Empire Magazine Award for Best British Actress 1998) 1997, Hideous Kinky 1998, Holy Smoke 1998, Faeries (voice) 1999, Quills (Evening Standard British Film Award for Best Actress 2002) 2000, Enigma (Empire Magazine Award for Best British Actress 2002) 2001, A Christmas Carol: The Movie (voice) 2001, Iris (European Film Acad. Award for Best European Actress 2002) 2001, War Game 2001, The Life of David Gale 2003, Plunge: The Movie 2003, Pride (TV film, voice) 2004, Eternal Sunshine of the Spotless Mind (London Film Critics Circle Award, Empire Magazine Award for Best British Actress 2005) 2004, Finding Neverland 2004, Romance & Cigarettes 2005, All the King's Men 2006, Little Children (Desert Palm Achievement for Acting, Palm Springs Int. Film Festival 2007) 2006, The Holiday 2006, Flushed Away (voice) 2006, The Fox & the Child (voice) 2007, The Reader (Golden Globe Award for Best Supporting Actress 2009, BAFTA Award for Leading Actress 2009, Acad. Award for Best Actress 2009) 2008, Revolutionary Road (Golden Globe Award for Best Actress 2009) 2008, Carnage 2011, Contagion 2011, Movie 43 2012, Labor Day 2013, Divergent 2014, A Little Chaos 2014, The Divergent Series: Insurgent 2015, Daisy Chain 2015, Steve Jobs (Golden Globe Award for Best Actress in a Supporting Role in Motion Picture 2016, BAFTA Award for Best Supporting Actress 2016) 2015, The Dressmaker (Australian Acad. of Cinema and Television Arts Award for Best Actress 2015) 2015. *Television includes:* Shrinks (series) 1991, Dark Season (series) 1991, Anglo Saxon Attitudes (mini-series) 1992, Get Back (series) 1992, Casualty (series) 1993, Pride (film) 2004, Mildred Pierce (mini-series) (Emmy Award for Outstanding Lead Actress in a Miniseries or Movie 2011, Golden Globe Award for Best Actress in a Mini-series or Motion Picture Made for Television 2012) 2011. *Address:* c/o Dallas Smith, United Agents, 12–26 Lexington Street, London, W1F 0LE, England (office); c/o Hylda Queally, CAA, 2000 Avenue of the Stars, Los Angeles, CA 90067, USA (office). *E-mail:* info@unitedagents.co.uk (office). *Website:* unitedagents.co.uk (office); www.caa.com (office).

WINSTON, Baron (Life Peer) cr. 1995, of Hammersmith in the London Borough of Hammersmith and Fulham; **Robert Maurice Lipson Winston,** MB, BS, DSc, FRCP, FRCOG, FRCPE, FRCPS, FMedSci, FIBiol, FRSA; British medical researcher, academic and writer; *Professor of Science and Society and Professor Emeritus of Fertility Studies, Imperial College, London;* b. 15 July 1940, London; s. of Laurence Winston and Ruth Winston-Fox; m. Lira Feigenbaum 1973; two s. one d.; ed St Paul's School, London and London Hosp. Medical Coll., Univ. of London; Registrar and Sr Registrar, Hammersmith Hosp. 1970–74; Wellcome Research Sr Lecturer, Inst. of Obstetrics and Gynaecology 1974–78, Sr Lecturer 1978–81, Consultant Obstetrician and Gynaecologist 1978–2005; Prof. of Gynaecology, Univ. of Texas at San Antonio, USA 1980–81; Reader in Fertility Studies, Royal Postgraduate Medical School 1982–86, Prof. 1987–97; apptd Prof. of Fertility Studies, Imperial Coll., London 1997, now Prof. of Science and Soc. and Prof. Emer. of Fertility Studies, mem. Devt Cttee; Dir NHS Research and Devt, Hammersmith Hosps Trust 1998–2005; Chancellor, Sheffield Hallam Univ. 2001–; Visiting Prof., Univ. of Leuven, Belgium 1976–77, Mount Sinai Hosp., New York, USA 1985; mem. (Labour) House of Lords 1995–, Chair. Select Cttee of Science and Tech. 1999–2002; Chair. Royal Coll. of Music 2008–; Vice-Chair. Parl. Office of Science and Tech. 2005–; Founder-mem. British Fertility Soc.; mem. Eng and Physical Sciences Research Council 2008–13, Council mem. Surrey Univ. 2008–, Scottish Scientific Advisory Council, The Athenaeum; Trustee, Genesis Research Trust; numerous other professional appointments; Hon. Fellow, Queen Mary and Westfield Coll. 1996; Hon. FRCSE; Hon. Fellow, Royal Coll. of Physicians and Surgeons (Glasg); Hon. FIBiol; 20 hon. doctorates at British univs, including: Hon. DSc (Cranfield) 2001, (UMIST) 2001, (Oxford Brookes) 2001, (St Andrews) 2003, (Exeter) 2004, (Trinity Coll. Dublin) 2005, (Univ. of Auckland) 2008; Victor Bonney Prize, Royal Coll. of Surgeons 1991–93, Chief Rabbinate Award for Contribution to Soc. 1992–93, Cedric Carter Medal, Clinical Genetics Soc. 1993, Gold Medal, Royal Soc. of Health 1998, Michael Faraday Award, Royal Soc. 1999, Wellcome Award for Science in the Media 2001, Edwin Stevens Medal, Royal Soc. of Medicine 2003, Gold Medal, North of England Zoological Soc. 2004, VLV Individual Award for Best contribs to UK Broadcasting 2004, Al Hammadi Medal, Royal Coll. of Surgeons, Edin. 2005. *Director:* Each in his Own Way (Pirandello), Edinburgh Festival 1969. *Radio:* Robert Winston's Musical Analysis 2009. *Television:* Presenter, Your Life In Their Hands (BBC) 1979–87, Making Babies 1996, The Human Body 1998, The Secret Life of Twins 1999, Child of our Time (BBC) 2000, Superhuman 2000, Human Instinct 2002, 2003, Threads of Life (BBC) 2003, The Human Mind (BBC)

2004, Story of God (BBC) 2005, Child Against All Odds (BBC) 2006, Superdoctors 2008. *Publications include:* Reversibility of Sterilization 1978, Tubal Infertility (jtly) 1981, Infertility: A Sympathetic Approach 1987, Getting Pregnant 1989, Making Babies 1996, The IVF Revolution 1999, Superman 2000, Human Instinct 2002, The Human Mind 2003, What Makes Me, Me? (Aventis Jr Prize, Royal Soc. 2005) 2004, Human (BMA Award for Best Popular Medicine Book) 2005, The Story of God 2005, Body 2005, A Child Against All Odds 2006, It's Elementary 2007, Evolution Revolution 2009, What Goes On in My Head? 2010, Bad Ideas? 2010, Science Experiments (Royal Society Young People's Book Prize 2012) 2011, That's Life 2012, Science Year by Year 2013, Utterly Amazing Science 2014, Home Lab: Exciting Experiments for Budding Scientists 2016, My Amazing Body Machine 2017; more than 300 scientific articles on reproduction. *Leisure interests:* theatre, broadcasting, music, wine, festering. *Address:* Imperial College, Exhibition Road, London, SW7 2AZ (office); House of Lords, Westminster, London, SW1A 0PW, England. *Telephone:* (20) 7594-5959 (office); (20) 7219-6020 (House of Lords). *Fax:* (20) 8458-4980 (home). *E-mail:* r.winston@imperial.ac.uk (office); info@ robertwinston.org. *Website:* www.robertwinston.org.uk.

WINTER, Sir Gregory (Greg), Kt, CBE, PhD, FRS, FMedSci; British biochemist and academic; *Master, Trinity College, Cambridge;* b. 14 April 1951; ed Trinity Coll., Cambridge; fmr Postdoctoral Researcher, Lab. of Molecular Biology, Cambridge, Deputy Dir, Lab. of Molecular Biology, MRC and Head of Div. of Protein and Nucleic Acids Chem.; Fellow, Trinity Coll., Cambridge, Master of Trinity Coll. 2012–; Co-founder Cambridge Antibody Technology 1989; Founder Domantis 2000 (acquired by GlaxoSmithKline 2006), Bicycle Therapeutics Ltd; mem. Scientific Advisory Bd, Covagen; Dr hc (Nantes Univ.) 2001; Hon. DrScNat (ETH) 2002; Dr Scientiarum hc (Aarhus Univ.) 2015; Prix Louis Jeantet de Medecine 1989, King Faisal Int. Prize for Medicine (Molecular Immunology) 1995, William B. Coley Award, Cancer Research Inst. 1999, Royal Medal, Royal Soc. 2011, Prince of Asturias Award for Technical & Scientific Research 2012, Canada Gairdner Int. Award 2013, Wilhelm Exner Medal, Österreichischer Gewerbeverein 2015, Prince Mahidol Award, Thailand 2016, Nobel Prize in Chemistry (co-recipient) 2018. *Publications include:* numerous papers in professional journals. *Address:* Trinity College, Cambridge, CB2 1TQ, England (office). *Telephone:* (1223) 338595 (office). *E-mail:* masters.secretary@trin.cam.ac.uk (office). *Website:* www .trin.cam.ac.uk (office).

WINTER, William Forrest, BA, LLB; American lawyer and politician; *Senior Partner and Shareholder, Watkins Ludlam Winter & Stennis P.A.;* b. 21 Feb. 1923, Grenada, Miss.; s. of William A. Winter and Inez P. Winter; m. Elise Varner 1950; three d.; ed Univ. of Miss.; Miss. House of Reps. 1948–56; Miss. state tax collector 1956–64; State Treas. 1964–68; Lt-Gov. of Miss. 1972–76, Gov. 1980–84; Sr Pnr, Shareholder, Watkins, Ludlam Winter & Stennis P.A. (law firm), Jackson, Miss. 1985–; Eudora Welty Prof. of Southern Studies, Millsaps Coll. 1989; Jamie Whitten Prof. of Law, Univ. of Miss. 1989; Chair. Advisory Comm. on Intergovernmental Relations 1993–97, Ole Miss Alumni Asscn 1978, Southern Growth Policies Bd 1981, Southern Regional Educ. Bd 1982, Appalachian Regional Comm. 1983, Comm. on the Future of the South 1986, Foundation for the Mid South 1990–92, Kettering Foundation 1990–93, Nat. Comm. on the State and Local Public Service; Fellow, Miss. Bar Foundation; Fellow, Inst. of Politics, Harvard Univ. 1985; mem. American Bar Asscn, DC Bar, Miss. Bar, Hinds Co. Bar Asscn, Nat. Advisory Bd on Race Relations 1997–; Pres. Bd of Trustees Miss. Dept of Archives and History; Dr hc (Univ. of North Carolina, Tougaloo Coll.) 2004; Miss. Bar Lifetime Achievement Award 1998, Martin Luther King, Jr. Memorial Award, Nat. Educ. Asscn 2001. *Address:* Watkins Ludlam Winter & Stennis P.A., 633 North State Street, PO Box 427, Jackson, MS 39202, USA (office). *Telephone:* (601) 949-4800 (office). *Fax:* (601) 949-4804 (office). *E-mail:* wwinter@watkinsludlam .com (office). *Website:* www.watkinsludlam.com (office).

WINTERBOTTOM, Michael; British film director; b. 29 March 1961, Blackburn, Lancs.; ed Univ. of Oxford; fmr ed., Thames TV. *Films include:* Butterfly Kisses 1995, Go Now, Jude 1996, Welcome to Sarajevo 1997, I Want You 1998, Resurrection Man (exec. producer) 1998, Wonderland 1999, With or Without You 1999, The Claim 2000, 24 Hour Party People 2002, In This World (Golden Bear, Berlin Film Festival 2003) 2002, Code 46 2003, 9 Songs 2004, A Cock and Bull Story 2005, The Road to Guantánamo (Silver Bear Berlin Film Festival 2006) 2005, A Mighty Heart 2007, Genova 2008, The Shock Doctrine 2009, The Killer Inside Me 2010, The Trip 2010, Trishna 2011, 2012 Everyday 2012, The Look of Love 2013. *Television includes:* Cracker Mysteries – The Mad Woman in the Attic 1993, Family 1994, Cinema Europe: The Other Hollywood (mini-series) 1996, The Trip (series) 2010, The Trip to Italy 2014, The Trip to Spain 2017. *Address:* Independent Talent Group, Oxford House, 76 Oxford Street, London, W1D 1BS, England.

WINTERBOTTOM, Michael, DPhil, FBA; British classicist; b. 22 Sept. 1934, Sale, Cheshire; s. of Allan Winterbottom and Kathleen Mary Winterbottom (née Wallis); m. 1st Helen Spencer 1963 (divorced 1983); two s.; m. 2nd Nicolette Janet Streatfeild Bergel 1986; ed Dulwich Coll., London and Pembroke Coll. Oxford; Domus Sr Scholar, Merton Coll. Oxford 1958–59; Research Lecturer, Christ Church Oxford 1959–62; Lecturer in Latin and Greek, Univ. Coll. London 1962–67; Fellow and Tutor in Classics, Worcester Coll. Oxford 1967–92, Reader in Classical Languages 1990–92; Corpus Christi Prof. of Latin, Fellow, Corpus Christi Coll., Oxford 1993–2001, Fellow Emer. 2001–; Craven Scholar 1954; Derby Scholar 1956; Dr hc (Besançon) 1985. *Publications include:* Quintilian (ed.) 1970, Ancient Literary Criticism (with D. A. Russell) 1972, Three Lives of English Saints 1972, The Elder Seneca (ed. and trans.) 1974, Tacitus, Opera Minora (co-ed. with R. M. Ogilvie) 1975, Gildas (ed. and trans.) 1978, Roman Declamation 1980, The Minor Declamations Ascribed to Quintilian (ed., with commentary) 1984, Sopatros the Rhetor (with D. C. Innes) 1988, Cicero, De Officiis (ed.) 1994, William of Malmesbury, Gesta Regum Anglorum Vol. I (co-ed. and co-trans. with R. A. B. Mynors and R. M. Thomson) 1998, William of Malmesbury, Saints' Lives (co-ed. and co-trans. with R. M. Thomson) 2002, Quintilian, Institutio Oratoria Book 2 (co-ed. with T. Reinhardt) 2006, William of Malmesbury, Gesta Pontificum Anglorum Vol. I (ed. and trans.) 2007, William of Malmesbury, Liber super explanationem Lamentationum Ieremiae prophetae (co-ed. with R. M. Thomson) 2011, William of Malmesbury, On Lamentations (trans.) 2013, The Miracles of the Blessed Virgin Mary (co-ed. with R.M. Thomson) 2015. *Leisure interests:* travel, geology, walking.

Address: 53 Thorncliffe Road, Oxford, OX2 7BA, England (home). *Telephone:* (1865) 513066 (home).

WINTERKORN, Martin, Dr rer. nat; German automotive industry executive; b. 24 May 1947, Leonberg; m.; two c.; ed Univ. of Stuttgart, Max-Planck-Inst. for Metal Research and Metal Physics; Special Asst in Process Eng, Robert Bosch GmbH 1977, Head, Substances and Processes Group, Bosch-Siemens-Hausgeräte GmbH 1978–81; Asst to Mem. of Bd for Quality Assurance, AUDI AG 1981–83, Head, Measuring Tech./Sampling and Test Lab. 1983–88, Dept Head, Cen. Quality Assurance 1988–90, Head, Audi Quality Assurance 1990–93, Head, Group Quality Assurance, Volkswagen AG 1993, Gen. Man. Volkswagen AG 1994–96, Head, Volkswagen Group Product Man. 1995–96, mem. Brand Bd of Man. for Tech. Devt 1996–2002, mem. Group Bd of Man. for Tech. Devt 2000–02, Chair. Bd of Man., Audi AG 2002–06, also Chair. Bd of Dirs, SEAT, also responsible for Audi AG Tech. Devt 2003–06, mem. Bd of Man., Volkswagen AG 2002–15, mem. Bd of Man. with responsibility for Group Research and Devt and Chair. Bd of Man., Volkswagen AG 2007–15 (resgnd), Chair. Supervisory Bd, Audi AG 2007–15 (resgnd), Chair. Bd of Man., Porsche Automobil Holding SE 2009–15, investigated by German prosecutors for alleged fraud over diesel emissions tests scandal Sept. 2015; Hon. Prof., Budapest Univ. of Tech. and Econs 2003, Dresden Univ. of Tech. 2004, Tongji Univ., Shanghai 2007; Hon. Dr-Ing (Chemnitz Univ. of Tech.) 2011; Hon. Dr rer. pol (Tech. Univ. of Munich) 2012.

WINTERS, L(eonard) Alan, CB, BSc, MA, PhD; British economist and academic; *Professor of Economics, University of Sussex;* b. 8 April 1950, London, England; s. of Geoffrey Walter Horace Winters and Christine Agnes Ive; m. 1st Margaret Elizabeth Griffin 1971; m. 2nd Zhen Kun Wang 1997; one s. two d.; ed Chingford Co. High School, Univs of Bristol and Cambridge; Jr, Research Office, Dept of Applied Econs, Univ. of Cambridge 1971–80; Lecturer in Econs, Univ. of Bristol 1980–86; economist, World Bank 1983–85, Div. Chief/Research Man. 1994–99; Prof. of Econs, Univ. of Wales at Bangor 1986–90, Univ. of Birmingham 1990–94, Univ. of Sussex 1999–; Dir World Bank Devt Research Group, Washington, DC 2004–07; Chief Economist, UK Dept for Int. Devt 2008–11; fmr adviser to OECD, UK Dept for Int. Devt, Commonwealth Secr., EC, European Parl., UNCTAD, WTO, Inter-American Devt Bank; Founder-Dir and Co. Sec. Cambridge Econometrics Ltd 1978–80; Sec., Int. Econs Study Group, Univ. of Stockholm 1979–83, Visiting Research Fellow 1987–88, 1991; Visiting Prof., Swedish Nat. Univ. of Agricultural Sciences, Uppsala 1988, Univ. of Bordeaux 1 1992, Argentine Council for Int. Relations, Buenos Aires 1993; Research Fellow, Centre for Econ. Policy Research 1985–, Co-Dir Int. Trade Programme 1987–94; Vice-Pres. British Asscn for Advancement of Science, Econs Section 1989–94, Treas. 1990–94; Econs Advisory Bd, Royal Inst. for Int. Affairs 1992–94; Exec. Cttee, Royal Econ. Soc. 1992–94; Visiting Lecturer, Finnish Doctoral Programme, Helsinki 1993; mem. Advisory Bd, Vienna Inst. for Comparative Econ. Studies 1998–2006; Sr Visiting Research Fellow, Centre for Econ. Policy, LSE 1999–2004; Research Fellow, IZA Inst. for Study of Labor 2005–; mem. European Devt Network 2000–; mem. Bd Global Devt Network 2005–07, 2009–, Chair. 2011–; mem. Steering Cttee, Cttee of Heads of Univ. Depts of Econs, Royal Econs Soc. 1988–93; mem. UGC Research Assessment Panel in Econs 1989, Council of Royal Econ. Soc. 1991–94; mem. UFC Research Assessment Panel in Economics 1992. *Publications:* Econometric Model of the British Export Sector 1981, International Economics 1984, Europe's Domestic Market 1987, Eastern Europe's International Trade 1994, Sustainable Development 1995, The Uruguay Round and the Developing Countries 1996, Trade Liberalisation and Poverty 2001, Making Sense of Globalization: A Guide to the Economic Issues 2002, Regional Integration and Development 2003, Challenges to Globalization: Analyzing the Economics 2004, Poverty and the WTO: Impacts of the Doha Development Agenda 2006, Dancing with Giants: China, India, and the Global Economy 2007, Critical Perspectives on the World Trading System: The WTO and Poverty and Inequality 2007. *Leisure interests:* walking, music, cricket. *Address:* Jubilee Building 280, University of Sussex, Falmer, Brighton, BN1 8SL, England (office). *Telephone:* (1273) 678332 (office). *E-mail:* l.a.winters@sussex.ac.uk (office). *Website:* www .sussex.ac.uk/economics (office).

WINTERSON, Jeanette, CBE, OBE, BA (Hons) (Oxon.); British writer; b. 27 Aug. 1959, Manchester; m. Susie Orbach 2015; ed Accrington Girls' Grammar School, St Catherine's Coll., Oxford; Prof. of Creative Writing, Centre for New Writing, Univ. of Manchester 2010–; Hon. Fellow, Royal Acad.; Golden Gate Award, San Francisco Int. Film Festival 1990, Best of Young British Novelists Award 1992, Int. Fiction Award, Festival Letteratura Mantua 1999. *Play:* The Power Book (Royal Nat. Theatre, London, Théâtre de Chaillot, Paris). *Screenplay:* Great Moments in Aviation 1992. *Television:* Oranges Are Not The Only Fruit (BBC) (BAFTA Award for Best Drama 1990, FIPA d'Argent Award for screenplay, Cannes Film Festival 1991) 1990, Orlando – Art That Shook the World (BBC) 2002, South Bank Show 2004, Ingenious (BBC) 2009, My Monster and Me (BBC 2) 2012. *Publications include:* fiction: Oranges Are Not The Only Fruit (Whitbread Prize for Best First Novel 1985) 1985, Boating for Beginners 1985, The Passion (John Llewellyn Rhys Prize 1987) 1987, Sexing the Cherry (E. M. Forster Award 1989) 1989, Written on the Body (Lambda Literary Award – Lesbian Fiction 1994) 1992, Art and Lies 1994, Gut Symmetries 1997, The World and Other Places (short stories) 1998, The Power Book 2000, The King of Capri (juvenile) 2003, Lighthousekeeping 2004, Weight: The Myth of Atlas and Heracles 2005, Tanglewreck (juvenile novel) 2006, The Stone Gods 2007, The Battle of the Sun (juvenile novel) 2009, The Lion, The Unicorn and Me (juvenile picture book) 2009, The Daylight Gate 2012, The Gap of Time 2015, Christmas Days 2016; non-fiction: Fit for the Future 1986, Art Objects (essays) 1994, Why Be Happy When You Could Be Normal? (memoir, Lambda Literary Award – Memoir or Biography 2013) 2011; editor and contrib.: Midsummer Nights (short stories). *Leisure interests:* opera, champagne, Paris, house building. *Address:* c/o Caroline Michel, PFD, Drury House, 34–43 Russell Street, London, WC2B 5HA, England (office). *E-mail:* cmichel@pfd.co.uk (office). *Website:* www.petersfraserdunlop.com/clients/jeanette -winterson (office); www.alc.manchester.ac.uk/centrefornewwriting (home); www .jeanettewinterson.com.

WINTON, Timothy (Tim) John; Australian writer; b. 4 Aug. 1960, nr Perth, WA; m. Denise Winton; two s. one d.; ed Western Australian Inst. of Tech.; Patron Tim Winton Award for Young Writers sponsored by City of Subiaco, WA, Australian

Marine Conservation Soc., Stop the Toad Foundation; Centenary Medal for service to literature and the community 2001, Australian Soc. of Authors Medal 2003. *Publications include:* An Open Swimmer (Australian Vogel Nat. Literary Award 1981) 1981, Shallows (Miles Franklin Award) 1985, Scisson and Other Stories (Western Australian Council Literary Award 1985) 1985, That Eye, The Sky 1986, Minimum of Two 1987, In the Winter Dark 1988, Jesse 1988, Lockie Leonard, Human Torpedo (Western Australian Premier's Book Award for Children's Fiction 1990, American Library Asscn Best Book for Young Adults Award 1993) 1990, The Bugalugs Bum Thief 1991, Cloudstreet (Miles Franklin Award 1991, NBC Banjo Award for Fiction 1991, West Australian Fiction Award 1991, Deo Gloria Award 1992) 1991, Lockie Leonard, Scumbuster (Wilderness Soc. Environment Award 1993) 1993, Land's Edge (with Trish Ainslie and Roger Garwood) 1993, Local Colour: Travels in the Other Australia 1994, The Riders (Commonwealth Writers Prize (South East Asia and South Pacific Region), Best Book 1994) 1994, Lockie Leonard, Legend (Family Award for Children's Literature) 1997, Blueback (Wilderness Soc. Environment Award 1998, WAYRBA Hoffman Award for Young Readers 1999) 1997, The Deep 1998, Down to Earth 1999, Dirt Music (Western Australian Premier's Book Award Premier's Prize 2001, Australian Booksellers Asscn Book of the Year Award 2002, Miles Franklin Award 2002, New South Wales Premier's Literary Award, Christina Stead Prize for Fiction 2002) 2001, The Turning (Colin Roderick Award 2004, Queensland Premier's Literary Awards, Best Fiction Book 2005, New South Wales Premier's Literary Awards, Christina Stead Prize for Fiction 2005) 2004, Breath (Age Book of the Year, Fiction 2008, Miles Franklin Literary Award 2009) 2008, Smalltown 2010, Land's Edge 2010, Rising Water 2012, Signs of Life 2013, Eyrie 2013, Island Home 2016. *Address:* c/o Jenny Darling & Associates, PO Box 5328, South Melbourne, Vic. 3205, Australia (office). *Telephone:* (3) 9696-7750 (office). *E-mail:* jenny@jennydarling.com.au (office). *Website:* jennydarling.com.au (office).

WINTOUR, Anna, OBE; British editor; *Editor-in-Chief, Vogue (US);* b. 3 Nov. 1949, London, England; d. of Charles Wintour and Eleanor ('Nonie') Trego Baker; m. David Shaffer 1984 (divorced); one s. one d.; ed Queen's Coll. School, London, North London Collegiate School; Deputy Fashion Ed., Harpers & Queen 1970–76; moved to New York 1976; Jr Fashion Ed., Harper's Bazaar, New York 1976–77; Fashion and Beauty Ed., Viva magazine 1977–78; contributing ed. for fashion and style, Savvy Magazine 1980–81; Sr Ed. New York Magazine 1981–83; Creative Dir US Vogue 1983–86; returned to London 1986; Ed.-in-Chief, UK Vogue 1986–87; moved back to New York 1987; Ed. House & Garden 1987–88; Ed.-in-Chief Vogue (US) 1988–, Artistic Dir Condé Nast 2013–; Co-Chair. Metropolitan Museum of Art's Costume Inst. Gala 1995; host, VH1/Vogue Fashion Awards 1999; est. CFDA/Vogue Fashion Fund 2003; produced Fashion Rocks (music supplement to Vogue) 2006; instigated first Fashion's Night Out event 2009; Trustee, Metropolitan Museum of Art 2011; Chevalier, Légion d'honneur 2011. *Address:* Vogue, 4 Times Square, 12th Floor, New York, NY 10036, USA (office). *Telephone:* (212) 286-2810 (office). *Fax:* (212) 286-8593 (office). *Website:* www.vogue.com/magazine (office).

WINWOOD, Stephen (Steve) Lawrence; British musician and composer; b. 12 May 1948, Birmingham; s. of Lawrence Samuel Winwood and Lillian Mary Winwood (née Saunders); m. Eugenia Crafton 1987; one s. three d.; singer and musician, Spencer Davis Group 1964–67, Traffic 1967–74, Blind Faith 1969; British tours with The Rolling Stones 1965, The Who 1966, The Hollies 1967; solo artist 1974–; Dir F.S. Ltd/Wincraft Music Ltd; Dr hc (Berklee Coll. Of Music), (Aston Univ.), (Univ. of Gloucestershire); 14 Gold Record Awards, four Platinum Record Awards, Ivor Novello Outstanding Song Collection, Musicians Union Classic Rock Award. *Recordings include:* albums include: with Spencer Davis Group: Spencer Davis Group 1966, Spencer Davis Group: The Second Album 1966, Autumn '66 1966, Gimme Some Lovin' 1967, I'm A Man 1967; with Traffic: Mr Fantasy 1968, Traffic 1968, John Barleycorn Must Die 1970, The Low Spark of High Heeled Boys 1972, When the Eagle Flies 1974; with Blind Faith: Blind Faith 1969; solo: Steve Winwood 1977, Arc of a Diver 1980, Talking Back to the Night 1982, Back in the Highlife 1986, Roll With It 1988 (Grammy Award 1989), Chronicles, Refugees of the Heart 1991, Far from Home 1994, The Finer Things 1995, Junction 7 1997, About Time 2003, Eric Clapton and Steve Winwood Live From Madison Square Garden 2009, Nine Lives 2008, Revolutions: The Very Best Of Steve Winwood 2010; singles: with Spencer Davis Group: Keep On Running 1966, Somebody Help Me 1966, Gimme Some Lovin' 1966, I'm a Man 1967; with Traffic: Paper Sun 1967, Hole in My Shoe 1967, solo singles: While You See A Chance 1980, Freedom Overspill 1986, Higher Love (two Grammy Awards: Record of the Year and Best Pop Vocal Performance 1987) 1986, The Finer Things 1987, Valerie 1987, Roll With It 1988, Don't You Know What the Night Can Do 1988, Holding On 1989, One and Only Man 1990, I Will Be Here 1991, Reach for the Light 1995, Spy in the House of Love 1997; other session work includes: Lou Reed, Berlin 1973, John Martyn, Inside Out 1973, Viv Stanshall, Men Opening Umbrellas Ahead 1974, Marianne Faithfull, Broken English 1979, Talk Talk, The Colour of Spring 1986, Paul Weller, Stanley Road 1995, Eric Clapton, Back Home 2005, Eric Clapton, Clapton 2010, Slash, Hey Joe 2010, Miranda Lambert, Four the Record 2011, Eric Clapton, Old Sock 2013, Gov't Mule, Shout! 2013. *Address:* Wincraft Music, Ltd, PO Box 41, Cheltenham, Glos., GL54 4WA, England (office). *E-mail:* management@wincraftmusic.com (office). *Website:* www.wincraftstudios.co.uk (office); www.stevewinwood.com.

WIRAJUDA, Nur Hassan, MA, LLM, SJD; Indonesian politician and academic; b. 9 July 1948, Tangerang; m.; four c.; ed Univ. of Indonesia, Univ. of Oxford, UK, Tufts Univ., Harvard Univ. and Univ. of Virginia, USA; practising lawyer (legal aid) and univ. lecturer, Jakarta 1972–75; Legal Council Corp. Sec., Dockyard State Enterprise, Jakarta 1972–73; Head of Section, Secr. of the Foreign Affairs Cttee of the Nat. Council for Political and Security Stabilization, Secr. Gen., Dept of Foreign Affairs 1974–75, Third Sec., then Second Sec. for Political Affairs, Embassy in Cairo 1977–81, Head of Section, Politics-Legal Affairs, Directorate of Int. Orgs, Dept of Foreign Affairs 1981, Counsellor, later Minister Counsellor for Political Affairs, Perm. Mission in Geneva 1989–93, Dir for Int. Orgs 1993–97, Amb. to Egypt (also accred to Djibouti) 1997–98, Amb. and Perm. Rep. to the UN, Geneva, WTO and the Conf. on Disarmament 1998–2000, Dir Gen. for Political Affairs 2000–01, Minister of Foreign Affairs 2001–09; currently mem. Faculty, School of Govt and Public Policy–Indonesia; mem. Council of Presidential Advisors, Global Comm. on Elections, Democracy and Security; Ed.-in-Chief Strategic Review: The Indonesian Journal of Leadership, Policy and World Affairs; Patron Inst. for Peace and Democracy. *Address:* SGPP-INDONESIA, Equity Tower, 39th Floor, Jl. Jend Sudirman Kav 52–53 (SCBD), Jakarta 12190, Indonesia (office). *E-mail:* info@sgpp.ac.id (office). *Website:* sgpp.ac.id (office).

WIRANTO, Gen. (retd) H.; Indonesian politician and army officer (retd); *Minister for Political, Legal and Security Affairs;* Minister of Defence and Security and C-in-C of Armed Forces –1999; Co-ordinating Minister for Politics and Security 1999–2000, Minister for Political, Legal and Security Affairs 2016–; indicted by UN for crimes against humanity in E Timor in 1999 Feb. 2003; unsuccessful presidential cand. for Partai Golongan Karya (Golkar) party 2004 elections, unsuccessful cand. for Vice-Pres. 2009; Chair. Partai Hati Nurani Rakyat (Hanura) (People's Conscience Party) 2006–16. *Address:* Office of the Co-ordinating Minister for Political, Legal and Security Affairs, Jalan Medan Merdeka Barat 15, Jakarta 10110, Indonesia (office). *Telephone:* (21) 3521121 (office). *Fax:* (21) 3450918 (office). *E-mail:* dkpt@polkam.go.id (office). *Website:* www.polkam.go.id (office).

WIRTH, Iwan; Swiss gallery owner and art dealer; *Director, Galerie Hauser & Wirth;* b. 1970, Zurich; m. Manuela Hauser; bought first art work aged 13; opened first gallery aged 16; f. Galerie Hauser & Wirth, Zurich (with Ursula Hauser) 1992; est. London br., Piccadilly 2003, Hauser & Wirth, New York 2009, Hauser & Wirth, London, Savile Row 2010; Co-founder and Partner, with David Zwirner, Zwirner & Wirth Gallery, New York City 2000–09. *Publications:* numerous catalogues and monographs. *Address:* Galerie Hauser & Wirth, Limmatstrasse 270, 8005 Zurich, Switzerland (office). *Telephone:* (44) 4468050 (office). *Fax:* (44) 4468055 (office). *E-mail:* zurich@hauserwirth.com (office). *Website:* www.hauserwirth.com (office); www.zwirnerandwirth.com (office).

WIRTH, Timothy (Tim) Endicott, PhD; American international organization executive and fmr politician; *Vice-Chairman, United Nations Foundation;* b. 22 Sept. 1939, Santa Fe, NM; s. of Cecil Wirth and Virginia Maude Davis; m. Wren Winslow 1965; one s. one d.; ed Harvard Coll., Stanford Univ.; Special Asst to Sec., Dept of Health, Educ. and Welfare 1967, Deputy Asst Sec. for Educ. 1969; Asst to Chair., Nat. Urban Coalition 1968; Vice-Pres. Great Western United Corpn, Denver 1970; Man. Arthur D. Little Inc. 1971–73; mem. US House of Reps 1975–87; Senator from Colorado 1987–92; Counsellor, Dept of State 1993–97; Pres. UN Foundation and Better World Fund 1998–2013, Vice-Chair. 2013–; Fellow, Kennedy School of Govt, Harvard Univ. 2013; Ford Foundation Fellow 1964–66; Pres. White House Fellows Asscn 1968–69; mem. Exec. Cttee Denver Council Foreign Relations 1974–75, Harvard Bd of Overseers; mem. Bd of Visitors, USAF Acad. 1978–; Adviser, Pres. Comm. on the 80s 1979–80; Democrat; numerous awards and hon. degrees; honoured by UNEP as a Champion of the Earth 2008. *Address:* United Nations Foundation, 1800 Massachusetts Avenue, NW, Washington, DC 20036, USA (office). *Telephone:* (202) 887-9040 (office). *Fax:* (202) 887-9021 (office). *E-mail:* kmiller@unfoundation.org (office). *Website:* www.unfoundation.org (office).

WISE, Phyllis, BS, PhD; American physiologist, academic and university administrator; *Chancellor, University of Illinois at Urbana-Champaign;* ed Swarthmore Coll., Univ. of Michigan; mem. Faculty, Univ. of Maryland, Baltimore 1976–93, Full Prof. of Physiology 1987–93; Prof. and Chair. Dept of Physiology, Univ. of Kentucky 1993–2001; Dean of Div. of Biological Sciences, Univ. of California, Davis 2002–05; Vice-Pres. for Academic Affairs and Provost, Univ. of Washington 2005–07, Exec. Vice-Pres. and Provost 2007–10, 2011, Interim Pres. 2010–11; Chancellor, Univ. of Illinois at Urbana-Champaign 2011–; mem. American Acad. of Arts and Sciences, Inst. of Medicine of NAS 2008; Fellow, AAAS 2008; Dr hc (Swarthmore Coll.) 2008; Ford Foundation Postdoctoral Fellowship 1972–74, NIH Research Career Devt Award 1982–87, NIH MERIT Award 1986–96, 2001–10, Nathan W. Shock Award for outstanding research in aging 1991, Presidential Speaker, Soc. of Neuroscience 1997, Burroughs-Wellcome Professorship 1997, Solomon Berson Award, American Physiological Soc. 1998, Robert W. Kleemeier Award, Gerontological Soc. of America 1999, Albert D. and Elizabeth H. Kirwan Memorial Prize 2000, FASEB Excellence in Science Award 2002, Women in Endocrinology Mentor Award 2003, Roy O. Greep Award for Excellence in Endocrine Research 2004, Women of Influence Award, Puget Sound Business Journal 2008, Asscn of Chairs of Depts of Physiology Service Award 2009, Chang-Lin Tien Award for Educational Leadership 2011. *Publications:* numerous papers in professional journals on issues concerning women's health and gender-based biology. *Address:* Office of the Chancellor, Swanlund Administration Building, 601 East John Street, Champaign, IL 61820, USA (office). *Telephone:* (217) 333-6290 (office). *E-mail:* pmwise@illinois.edu (office). *Website:* oc.illinois.edu (office).

WISE, Robert (Bob) E., BA, JD; American politician and lawyer; *President, Alliance for Excellent Education;* b. 6 Jan. 1948, Washington, DC; m. Sandy Wise; one s. one d.; ed Duke Univ., Tulane Univ. Coll. of Law; pvt. law practice, Charleston, W Va 1975–80; attorney, legis. council for judiciary comm., W Va House of Dels 1977–78; mem. W Va State Senate 1980–82; mem. US House of Reps from W Va Second Dist) 1983–2001, Whip-at-Large 1986–2001, mem. House Transportation and Infrastructure Cttee; Gov. of W Va 2001–05; Pres. Alliance for Excellent Education, Washington, DC 2005–; Chair. National Bd for Professional Teaching Standards; mem. Bd of Trustees America's Promise Alliance and West Virginia Wesleyan Coll.; mem. ABA, W Va State Bar Asscn; Education Award, National Asscn of State Bds of Education 2011, Charles W. Eliot Award, New England Asscn of Schools and Colls 2012, Thought Leader Award, Corporation for Public Broadcasting 2013, Bammy Award for Education Policy/Researcher 2014. *Leisure interests:* keeping fit, bluegrass music. *Address:* Alliance for Excellent Education, 1201 Connecticut Avenue, NW, Suite 901, Washington, DC 20036, USA (office). *Telephone:* (202) 828-0828 (office). *Fax:* (202) 828-0821 (office). *E-mail:* wise@all4ed.org (office). *Website:* www.all4ed.org (office).

WISEMAN, Debra (Debbie), OBE, MBE, FGSM, FTCL; British composer and conductor; b. 10 May 1963, London; d. of Paul Wiseman and Barbara Wiseman; m. Tony Wharmby 1987; ed Trinity Coll. of Music, Kingsway Princeton/Morley Coll., Guildhall School of Music and Drama; composer and conductor of music for film and TV productions 1989–; Visiting Prof. of Film Composition, Royal Coll. of Music 1995–; mem. Performing Right Soc., BAFTA, Musicians' Union, British Acad. of Composers and Songwriters, Acad. of Motion Pictures, Arts & Sciences; Hon.

Fellow, Trinity Coll. of Music, London 2006, Guildhall School of Music and Drama 2007; Hon. DMus (Univ. of Sussex) 2015. *Compositions include:* Inside Looking Out 1989, Squares and Roundabouts 1989, Echoes of Istria 1989, The Guilty, Lighthouse, Female Perversions, The Dying of the Light, Shrinks (Silents to Satellite Award for Best Original TV Theme Music 1991), The Good Guys (Television and Radio Industries Club Award for TV Theme Music of the Year 1993), Tom and Viv 1994, The Project, Judge John Deed, P.O.W., Wilde Stories, The Upper Hand, The Churchills, Serious and Organised, The Second Russian Revolution, Little Napoleons, Children's Hospital, Death of Yugoslavia, Haunted 1995, Wilde 1997, The Fairy Tale of the Nightingale and the Rose 1999, The Fairy Tale of the Selfish Giant 1999, It Might be You, A Week in Politics, People's Century, What Did You Do In The War, Auntie?, The Cuban Missile Crisis, Vet's School, The Missing Postman, Tom's Midnight Garden, Absolute Truth, Warriors (Royal TV Soc. Award) 2000, My Uncle Silas 2001, Othello 2001, Oscar Wilde Fairy Stories 2002, Freeze Frame 2004, He Knew He Was Right 2004, The Andrew Marr Show, The Truth About Love 2004, Arsène Lupin 2004, Johnny and the Bomb 2005, Middletown 2005, Feather Boy: The Musical 2005, Middletown (film music) 2006, Jekyll 2007, Walter's War 2008, Stephen Fry in America 2008, The Passion 2008, Lesbian Vampire Killers 2009, The Hide 2009, Land Girls 2009, 2010, 2011, Joanna Lumley's Nile 2010, Martin Clunes: Horsepower 2010, The Promise 2011, Joanna Lumley's Greek Odyssey 2011, Fry's Planet Word 2011, Lost Christmas 2011, The Whale 2013, Father Brown 2013–18, WPC 56 2013–14, A Poet in New York 2014, Wolf Hall 2015, The Coroner 2015–16, Dickensian 2015–16, Red Rock 2016, The State 2017, Shakespeare and Hathaway—Private Investigators 2018, Edie 2018. *Recordings include:* Music for The Queen's Diamond Jubilee Pageant 2012, Music for The Queen's 90th Birthday Celebration 2016, Signature music for Viking Cruises 2017. *Leisure interests:* swimming, snooker. *Address:* c/o Roz Colls, Music Matters International, Crest House, 102–104 Church Road, Teddington, Middx, TW11 8PY, England (office). *Telephone:* (20) 8979-4580 (Teddington) (office). *E-mail:* rozcolls@music-matters.co.uk (office); wisemaninfo@aol.com (office). *Website:* www.debbiewiseman.co.uk.

WISEMAN, Frederick, BA, LLB; American documentary filmmaker and theatre director; b. 1 Jan. 1930, Boston, Mass; ed Williams Coll., Yale Univ.; Lecturer-in-Law, Boston Univ. Law School 1959–61; Research Assoc., Department of Sociology, Brandeis Univ. 1962–64; Treasurer, Org. for Social & Technical Innovation 1966–70; turned to television documentary film making 1967; Founder and Gen. Man. Zipporah Films Inc. 1971–; mem. Bd of Dirs Int. Documentary Asscn 1986–, Theater for a New Audience (also mem. Artistic Council) 1998–; mem. Advisory Bd New York Documentary Festival 1997–; mem. Advisory Cttee Learning from Performers, Harvard Univ. 1991–, Margaret Mead Film Festival, American Museum of Natural History 1992–; mem. Festival Cttee Human Rights Watch Int. Film Festival 1994–; mem. Massachusetts Bar Asscn 1955–; Russell Sage Foundation Fellowship, Harvard Univ. 1961–62; Fellow, American Acad. of Arts and Letters 1991–; mem. Hon. Advisory Cttee, American Repertory Theatre, Harvard Univ. 1986–; Hon. mem. Les Amis du Cinéma du Réel Association 1987–; mem. Boston Jewish Film Festival, Hon. Cttee 1994–; Fellow, American Acad. of Arts and Letters 1991–; Chevalier, Ordre des Arts et des Lettres 1987, Commdr, Ordre des Arts et des Lettres 2000; Hon. DHumLitt (Cincinnati) 1973, (Williams Coll.) 1976, (John Jay Coll. of Criminal Justice) 1994; Hon. DFA (Lake Forest Coll.) 1991, (Princeton) 1994, (Bowdoin Coll.) 2005, (CUNY) 2009; Dr hc (Universitat Pompeu Fabra) 2016; Peabody Award for Significant and Meritorious Achievement 1990, Rosenberger Medal, Univ. of Chicago 1999, Yale Law Asscn Award of Merit 2002, Dan David Prize Laureate 2003, American Soc. of Cinematographers Distinguished Achievement Award 2006, George Polk Career Award 2006, Lifetime Achievement Award, The Chicago Int. Documentary Festival 2007, Int. Documentary Filmfestival Amsterday Living Legend Award 2009, Dartmouth Film Award 2009, Career Achievement Award, Los Angeles Film Critics Asscn Awards 2013, Golden Lion Hon. Award, 67th Venice Film Festival 2014, New York Film Critics Circle Award for Best Non-Fiction Film (Documentary) 2015, France Culture Prix Consécration, Cannes Film Festival 2016, Hon. Oscar, Bd of Govs. Acad. of Motion Picture Arts & Sciences. *Documentary films include:* Titicut Follies 1967, High School 1968, Law and Order 1969, Hospital 1969, Basic Training 1971, Essene 1972, Juvenile Court 1973, Primate 1974, Welfare 1975, Meat 1976, Canal Zone 1977, Sinai Field Mission 1978, Manoeuvre 1979, Model 1980, Seraphita's Diary 1982, The Store 1983, Racetrack 1985, Blind 1986, Deaf 1986, Adjustment & Work 1986, Multi-Handicapped 1986, Missile 1987, Near Death 1989, Central Park 1989, Aspen 1991, Zoo 1993, High School II 1994, Ballet 1995, La Comedie Francaise 1996, Public Housing 1997, Belfast, Maine 1999, Domestic Violence 2001, La Dernière lettre 2002, Domestic Violence II 2002, The Garden 2005, State Legislature 2007, La danse 2009, Boxing Gym 2010, Crazy Horse 2011, At Berkeley 2013, National Gallery 2014, In Jackson Heights 2015, Ex Libris: The New York Public Library 2017, Monrovia, Indiana 2018. *Plays include:* as dir: The Last Letter (adaptation from the novel Life and Fate by Vasily Grossman), Hate by Joshua Goldstein, Welfare: The Opera, Oh Les Beaux Jours (Happy Days) by Samuel Beckett. *Publications:* numerous articles in journals and magazines including The Threepenny Review. *Address:* Zipporah Films, One Richdale Avenue, Unit 4, Cambridge, MA 02140, USA (office). *Telephone:* (617) 576-3603 (office). *Fax:* (617) 864-8006 (office). *E-mail:* info@zipporah.com (office). *Website:* www.zipporah.com (office).

WISNER, Frank George, BA; American business executive and fmr diplomatist; b. 2 July 1938, New York, NY; s. of Frank G. Wisner and Mary E. Knowles; m. 1st Genevieve de Virel 1969 (deceased 1974); one d.; m. 2nd Christine de Ganay 1976; one s. one d. and one step-s. one step-d.; ed Woodberry Forest School, Rugby School and Princeton Univ.; joined US Foreign Service 1961; various posts 1961–75; Special Asst to Under-Sec. for Political Affairs 1975–76; Dir Office of Southern African Affairs 1976–77; Deputy Exec. Sec. 1977–79; Amb. to Zambia 1979–82; Deputy Asst Sec. for African Affairs 1982–86; Amb. to Egypt 1986–91, to Philippines 1991–92, to India 1994–97; Under-Sec. of Defence 1993–94; fmr Vice-Chair. for External Affairs, American Int. Group (AIG); mem. Bd of Dirs, Ethan Allen Interiors, EOG Resources, Pangea3 LLC 2009–; Dir (non-exec.), Commercial Int. Bank (Egypt) SAE from 2009; mem. Advisory Bd, Global Precision Research, LLC 2013–; Romanian Order of Merit; Presidential Meritorious Service Awards, Dept of State Honor Awards, Repub. of Vietnam Mil. Medal of Honour, Dept of Defense Service Medal. *Leisure interests:* hunting, horseback riding, golf. *Address:* 164 East 72nd Street, Apt 5B, New York, NY 10021, USA (home). *Telephone:* (212) 517-2028 (home).

WISSMANN, Matthias; German lawyer and politician; b. 15 April 1949, Ludwigsburg; s. of Paul Wissmann and Margarete Kalcker; ed Univs of Tübingen and Bonn; practised as lawyer; mem. Fed. Exec. of CDU 1975–; mem. Bundestag 1976–; Pres. European Union of Young Christian Democrats 1976–82; Minister of Research and Technology Jan.–May 1993, of Transport 1993–98; Chair. Parl. Cttee of Econ. and Tech. 1998–2001, Speaker Parl. Group for Econ. and Tech. 2001–02, Chair. Cttee of European Affairs; apptd Sr Int. Counsellor, Wilmer Cutler Pickering Hale and Dorr (law firm), Berlin 1999, currently Partner; Pres. German Automotive Industry Asscn 2007–18, Organisation Internationale des Constructeurs d'Automobiles 2016–; Vice-Pres. Bundesverband der Deutschen Industrie 2017–; mem. Int. Rolls-Royce Advisory Bd; mem. Supervisory Bd ODDO BHF; Vice-Chair. Supervisory BD Seeburger AG; mem. Advisory Bd EnBW 2004–09, Landesbank Baden-Württemberg –2010, Transatlantic Trade and Investment Partnership 2014, Freitag & Co. 2016–; mem. Bd of Trustees, Stifterverband für die Deutsche Wissenschaft, Ludwigsburg Festival; Grand Order of Merit (Germany), Grand Order of Merit (Austria), Grand Cross (Chile), Chevalier de Légion d'Honneur. *Publications include:* Zukunftschancen der Jugend 1979, Einsteigen statt Aussteigen 1983, Marktwirtschaft 2000 1993, Soziale Marktwirtschaft 1998. *Leisure interests:* piano, literature, hockey, tennis, skiing, golf. *Address:* WilmerHale, Friedrichstr. 95, 10117 Berlin, Germany (office); Am Zuckerberg 79, 71640 Ludwigsburg, Germany (home). *Telephone:* (30) 20226426 (office). *Fax:* (30) 20226500 (office). *E-mail:* christine.cosentino@wilmerhale.com (office). *Website:* www.wilmerhale.com (office).

WISZNIEWSKI, Andrzej, PhD, DSc; Polish electrical engineer, politician and academic; *Professor, Institute of Electrical Power Engineering, Wrocław University of Technology;* b. 15 Feb. 1935, Warsaw; s. of Tadeusz Wiszniewski and Ewa Wiszniewski (née Ciechomska); m. Ewa Lutosławska; one d.; ed Wrocław Univ. of Tech.; researcher, Wrocław Univ. of Tech. 1957, Extraordinary Prof. 1972, Ordinary Prof., Inst. of Electrical Power Eng 1990–, Rector 1990–96; at Univ. of Garyounis Benghazi, Libya 1976–79; Head of Scientific Research Cttee and mem. Council of Ministers 1997–99; Minister of Science 1999–2001; mem. Speech Communication Asscn, USA, Solidarity Trade Union 1980–, Social Movt of Solidarity Election Action 1998–2001; Distinguished mem. Int. Conf. on Large Electric Systems 2000; Hon. mem. IEE 1999; Kt's Cross, Order of Polonia Restituta 1979, Officer's Cross 2004, Commdr's Cross 2009; Grand Cross, Order of St Stanisław with Star 1998; Commdr, Order of St Sylvester 1998; Grand Cross, Order of Merit (Peru) 2001; Dr hc (Cen. Conn. State Univ., USA) 1993, (Tech. Univ. of Lvov) 1999, (Wrocław Univ. of Tech.) 2001; City of Wrocław Award 1996, Council of Rectors Award 1998. *Publications include:* Measuring Transformers 1983, Algorithms of Numeral Measurements in Electroenergetic Automatics 1990, Schutztechnik in Elektroenergiesystemen (co-author) 1994, Protective Automatics in Electroenergetics Systems 1998, How to Speak and Make Speeches Convincingly 1994, Aphorisms and Quotations: for Orators, Disputants and Banqueters 1997, Measuring and Decision Making Algorithms (co-author), Art of Writing 2003; over 130 articles on electrotechnics and electroenergetics. *Leisure interests:* contemporary literature, dog walking, skiing, mountaineering, rhetoric. *Address:* Institute of Power Engineering, Wrocław University of Technology, Wybrzeze Wyspianskiego 27, 50-370 Wrocław (office); Krasickiego 18, 51-144 Wrocław, Poland (home). *Telephone:* (71) 3203487 (office); (71) 3726477 (home); (601) 381944 (home). *Fax:* (71) 3202656 (office). *E-mail:* andrzej.wiszniewski@pwr.wroc.pl (office); awiszniewski@wr.home.pl. *Website:* www.pwr.wroc.pl (office); www.wme.pwr.wroc.pl (office).

WIT, Antoni; Polish conductor and academic; *Artistic Director, Orquesta Sinfónica de Navarra;* b. 7 Feb. 1944, Kraków; m. Zofia Ćwikilewicz; ed State Higher School of Music, Kraków, Jagiellonian Univ., studied with Nadia Boulanger, Paris; Asst Conductor Nat. Philharmonic Orchestra of Poland, 1967–70, Man. Dir and Artistic Dir 2002–13; Conductor, Poznań Nat. Philharmonic 1970–72; Artistic Dir Pomeranian Philharmonic, Bydgoszcz 1974–77; Man. and Artistic Dir, Polish Radio Symphony Orchestra and Choir, Kraków 1977–83; Dir Polish Nat. Radio Symphony Orchestra, Katowice 1983–2000; Artistic Dir Orquesta Filarmonica de Gran Canaria, Las Palmas 1987–91; First Guest Conductor, Orquesta Sinfónica de Navarra, Pamplona 2010–, Artistic Dir 2013–; Prof., Fryderyk Chopin Acad. of Music, Warsaw 1997–; has conducted LPO, RPO, BBC Symphony Orchestra, Berliner Philharmoniker, Orchestre National de Belgique, Tokyo Symphony Orchestra, Montreal Symphony Orchestra, Orquesta Nacional de España, Staatskapelle Dresden, Accad. di Santa Cecilia, Rome, Tonhalle-Orchester, others; Hon. Conductor, Krakow Philharmonic; Chevalier, Légion d'Honneur 2015; numerous prizes include Second Prize, Herbert von Karajan Conducting Competition, Berlin 1971, Orpheus (Warsaw Autumn Festival Critics' Award) 1984, 1996, Diapason d'Or, Grand Prix de Disque de la Nouvelle Académie du Disque 1992, Diamond Baton Award of Polish Public Radio 1998, Cannes Classical Award, Midem Classique 2002, Classical Internet Award 2004, Record Acad. Award of Japanese music magazine Record Geijutsu (for Penderecki's Polish Requiem) 2005, Karol Szymanowski Foundation Award 2010, Int. Classical Music Award for Best Contemporary Music Recording 2012, four Fryderyk Awards, Polish Phonographic Acad. *Compositions include:* soundtracks: Kronika wypadków miłosnych (The Chronicle of Love Affairs) 1986, Korczak 1990, Pan Tadeusz (Last Foray in Lithuania) 1999. *Recordings include:* more than 90 recordings, albums include symphonies by Tchaikovsky, Górecki, Schumann, Penderecki, Lutosławski (all), Olivier Messiaen (Turangalila Symphony) (Cannes Classical Award—Midem Classique 2002), Penderecki: Fonogrammi; Horn Concerto; Partita; The Awakening of Jacob; Anaklasis (Grammy Award for Best Classical Compendium 2013). *Address:* International Classical Artists Ltd, 26–28 Hammersmith Grove, 6th Floor, London, W6 7BA, England (office); Orquesta Sinfónica de Navarra, Calle Sandoval, 6, 1 Izq., 31002 Pamplona, Navarra, Spain (office). *E-mail:* mwiktorowicz@icartists.co.uk (office). *Website:* www.icartists.co.uk/artists/antoni-wit (office); www.orquesta-pablo-sarasate.com (office).

WITHEROW, John Moore, BA (Hons); British journalist and editor; *Editor, The Times;* b. 20 Jan. 1952, Johannesburg, S. Africa; m. Sarah Linton 1985; two s. one d.; ed Bedford School, Univ. of York, Univ. of Cardiff; voluntary service in Namibia (then SW Africa) after school; posted to Madrid for Reuters; covered Falklands War for The Times 1982; joined The Sunday Times 1984, successively Defence and Diplomatic Corresp., Focus Ed., Foreign Ed., Man. Ed. (news), Ed., The Sunday Times 1994–2012, Acting Ed. The Times Jan.–Sept. 2013, Ed. Sept. 2013–. *Publications include:* The Winter War: The Falklands (with Patrick Bishop) 1982, The Gulf War 1993. *Leisure interests:* sailing, skiing, tennis. *Address:* Office of the Editor, The Times, 3 Thomas More Square, London, E98 1TT, England (office). *Website:* www.thetimes.co.uk (office).

WITHERSPOON, Reese; American actress and producer; b. 22 March 1976, Baton Rouge, La; d. of John Witherspoon; m. 1st Ryan Phillippe 1999 (divorced 2007); one s. one d.; m. 2nd Jim Toth 2011; ed Harpeth Hall, Nashville, Stanford Univ.; f. production co. Type A Films. *Films:* The Man in The Moon 1991, Wildflower (for TV) 1991, Solomon's Choice (for TV), Return to Lonesome Dove (TV mini-series) 1993, A Far Off Place 1993, Jack the Bear, S.F.W. 1995, Fear, Freeway 1996, (Best Actress, Catalonian Int. Film Festival, Cognac Film Festival) 1996, Twilight, Overnight Delivery, Pleasantville 1998, Cruel Intentions (Best Supporting Actress in a Drama Romance, Blockbuster Entertainment Awards) 1999, Election (Best Actress, Nat. Soc. of Film Critics) 1999, Best Laid Plans 1999, American Psycho 2000, Little Nicky 2000, The Trumpet of the Swan (voice) 2001, Legally Blonde (Best Actress, Cosmo Movie Awards, Best Comedic Performance, MTV Movie Awards) 2001, Sweet Home Alabama 2002, The Importance of Being Earnest 2002, Legally Blonde 2: Red, White & Blonde 2003, Vanity Fair 2004, Just Like Heaven 2005, Walk the Line (Best Actress Critics' Choice Awards 2006, Golden Globe Award for Best Performance by an Actress in a Musical or Comedy, Screen Actors Guild Award for Best Actress 2006, BAFTA Award for Best Actress in a Leading Role 2006, Acad. Award for Best Actress 2006) 2005, Penelope 2006, Rendition 2007, Four Christmases 2008, Monsters vs. Aliens (voice) 2009, How Do You Know 2010, This Means War 2012, Mud 2013, Gone Girl (producer) 2014, Wild (also producer) 2014, The Good Lie 2014, Inherent Vice 2014, Hot Pursuit 2015, Home Again 2017, A Wrinkle in Time 2018. *Television:* Friends 2000, King of the Hill 2000, Saturday Night Live 2001, Big Little Lies 2017–, Shine On With Reese 2018. *Publication:* Whiskey in a Teacup: What Growing Up in the South Taught Me About Life, Love and Baking Biscuits 2018. *Address:* c/o CAA, 2000 Avenue of the Stars, Los Angeles, CA 90067, USA (office).

WITKIN, Evelyn M., PhD; American geneticist and academic; *Professor Emerita, Waksman Institute of Microbiology, Rutgers University;* b. 9 March 1921, New York, NY; m. Herman A. Witkin (died 1979); two s.; ed New York Univ., Columbia Univ.; worked at Cold Spring Harbor Lab. (CSHL) 1944, 1945–47, employed by Carnegie Inst. to continue work at CSHL 1947–55; worked at Downstate Medical Center, State Univ. of New York, Brooklyn 1955–71; Prof. of Biological Sciences, Douglass Coll., Rutgers Univ. 1971–79, Barbara McClintock Prof. of Genetics 1979–83, with Waksman Inst. of Microbiology 1983, now Prof. Emer.; mem. NAS 1977; Fellow, American Acad. of Arts and Sciences 1978, AAAS 1980, American Acad. of Microbiology; Thomas Hunt Morgan Medal 2000, Nat. Medal of Science 2002, The Wylie Prize in Biomedical Sciences 2015, Albert Lasker Basic Medical Research Award, Lasker Foundation (co-recipient) 2015. *Publications:* numerous papers in professional journals. *Address:* 1 Firestone Court, Princeton, NJ 08540-5220, USA. *Telephone:* (609) 921-8780. *E-mail:* ewitkin@aol.com.

WITKIN, Joel-Peter, BFA, MA, MFA; American art photographer; b. 13 Sept. 1939, Brooklyn, New York; s. of Max Witkin and Mary Pelligrino; m. Barbara Anne Witkin 2008; one s.; ed The Cooper Union, Columbia Univ., Univ. of New Mexico; began photography at age 11; photographer, US Army 1961–64; art photographer 1970–; Chevalier des Arts et des Lettres 1990, Commdr 2000; four Nat. Endowment Awards 1982, 1984, 1986, 1992, Int. Center of Photography Award, New York City 1988, The Augustus Saint Gaudens Medal, The Cooper Union 1996, New York Times Award (for The Plague Years) 2000. *Publications:* Joel-Peter Witkin (monograph) 1984, Gods of Earth and Heaven 1994, Guggenheim Museum monograph 1995, The Bone House 1998, Joel-Peter Witkin, Disciple and Master 2000; illustrated editions of William Blake's poetry: Songs of Experience 2002, Songs of Innocence 2003, Songs of Innocence and Experience 2004–05, Bourgeoisie-in-de-Nile 2007, The Journal of Joel-Peter Witkin 2010, Maestro Witkin, Master of Photography Collection 2010, 2014, Heaven and Hell 2012, Witkin, Witkin and Witkin, Museo Cuatro Caminos, Mexico City 2016. *Address:* 1707 5 Points Road, SW, Albuquerque, NM 87105, USA (home). *Telephone:* (505) 843-6682 (office); (505) 842-6511 (home). *Fax:* (505) 842-1611 (home). *E-mail:* jwitkin1@gmail.com (home).

WITSCHEL, (Johann) Georg (Michael), PhD; German lawyer and diplomatist; *Ambassador to Brazil;* b. May 1954; m. Sabine Witschel; one c.; ed high school in Nuremberg, Univ. of Erlangen; mil. service 1972–73; legal studies in Erlangen, barrister exam, doctoral thesis, various internships, public int. law summer schools, language courses in Geneva, Lima, Salamanca, The Hague 1975–82; training with Fed. Foreign Office, Bonn 1983–85, Speaker in Dept of the Fed. Chancellery, Bonn 1985–86, in Int. Law Dept 1986–89, Political Counsellor, Embassy in Tel-Aviv 1989–92, Deputy Head of Mission and Head of Econ. Dept, Embassy in Ljubljana, Slovenia 1992–95, Deputy Head of Human Resources Unit, Higher Service, Fed. Foreign Office, Bonn 1995–98, Deputy Head of Political Div. and Legal Adviser, Perm. Mission to UN, New York 1998–2001, Head of Policy Issues, UN, Security Council, Peacekeeping Measures, Fed. Foreign Office, Berlin 2001–02, Fed. Govt Commr for Combating Int. Terrorism 2002–06, Head of Legal Dept of Fed. Foreign Office, Int. Law Adviser to the Fed. Govt 2006–09, Amb. to Canada 2009–12, to Indonesia (also accred to Timor Leste) and Perm. Rep. to ASEAN 2012–16, to Brazil 2016–; Bundesverdienstkreuz. *Publications:* several publs on int. law, disarmament issues, counter-terrorism and on econ. issues concerning Slovenia. *Address:* Embassy of Germany, SES, Av. das Nações, Quadra 807, Lote 25, 70415-900 Brasília, DF, Brazil (office). *Telephone:* (61) 3442-7000 (office). *Fax:* (61) 3443-7508 (office). *E-mail:* info@alemanja.org (office). *Website:* www.brasilia.diplo.de (office).

WITTEN, Edward, BA, MA, PhD; American physicist and academic; *Charles Simonyi Professor, School of Natural Sciences, Institute for Advanced Study;* b. 26 Aug. 1951, Baltimore, Md; s. of Louis Witten and Lorraine Wollach Witten; m. Chiara R. Nappi 1979; one s. two d.; ed Brandeis and Princeton Univs; Postdoctoral Fellow, Harvard Univ. 1976–77, Jr Fellow, Harvard Soc. of Fellows 1977–80; Prof. of Physics, Princeton Univ. 1980–87; Prof., School of Natural Sciences, Inst. for Advanced Study, Princeton, NJ 1987–, Charles Simonyi Prof. 1997–; Visiting Prof., California Inst. of Tech. 1999–2001; mem. Bd of Dirs, Americans for Peace 1992–; Foreign mem. Royal Soc. 1998; mem. Pontifical Acad. of Sciences 2006; Fellow, American Acad. of Arts and Sciences 1984, American Physical Soc. 1984, NAS 1988, American Philosophical Soc. 1994, American Math. Soc. 2013; Hon. Citizen of Padua, Italy 2009; Dr hc (Brandeis Univ.) 1988, (Hebrew Univ. of Jerusalem) 1993, (Columbia Univ.) 1996, (Univ. of Southern California) 2004, (Johns Hopkins Univ.) 2005, (Harvard Univ.) 2005, (Univ. of Cambridge, UK) 2006; Hon. PhD (UNESP, São Paulo) 2011; MacArthur Fellowship 1982, Einstein Medal, Einstein Soc. of Berne, Switzerland 1985, Award for Physical and Math. Sciences, New York Acad. of Sciences 1985, Dirac Medal, Int. Center for Theoretical Physics 1985, NSF Alan T. Waterman Award 1986, Fields Medal, Int. Union of Mathematicians 1990, Madison Medal, Princeton Univ. 1992, New Jersey Pride Award 1996, Award of the Golden Plate, American Acad. of Achievement 1997, Klein Medal, Stockholm Univ. 1998, Dannie Heineman Prize 1998, Nemmers Prize in Math., Northwestern Univ. 2000, Clay Research Award 2001, Shalom Award, Americans for Peace 2002, Nat. Medal of Science 2003, Harvey Prize, Technion 2006, Poincaré Prize, Int. Asscn of Math. Physics 2006, Crafoord Prize (co-recipient) 2008, Lorentz Medal, Royal Dutch Acad. of Sciences 2010, Isaac Newton Medal, Inst. of Physics 2010, Solomon Lefschetz Medal, Math. Soc. of Mexico 2011, Fundamental Physics Prize, The Milner Foundation 2012, Kyoto Prize, Inamori Foundation (co-recipient) 2014, Medal for Exceptional Achievement in Research, American Physical Soc. 2015. *Publications:* Superstring Theory, Vols 1 and 2 (with M. B. Green and J. H. Schwarz) 1987; more than 300 scientific papers. *Address:* Institute for Advanced Study, School of Natural Sciences, Einstein Drive, Princeton, NJ 08540, USA (office). *Telephone:* (609) 734-8021 (office). *E-mail:* witten@ias.edu (office). *Website:* www.sns.ias.edu/witten (office).

WITTIG, (Hans) Peter; German academic and diplomatist; *Ambassador to UK;* b. 11 Aug. 1954; m. Huberta von Voss-Wittig; two s. two d.; ed Univs of Bonn and Freiburg, Univs of Canterbury and Oxford, UK; Asst Prof., Univ. of Freiburg for three years; joined Foreign Service 1982, served in Madrid, New York (Perm. Mission to UN), Bonn (Pvt. Sec. to the Foreign Minister), as Amb. to Lebanon and as Amb. to Cyprus (also acted as Special Envoy of German Govt for the Cyprus Question), Deputy Head of Directorate-Gen. for the UN and Global Issues 2002–06, Dir-Gen. 2006–09, Amb. and Perm. Rep. to UN, New York 2009–14, Amb. to USA 2014–18, to UK 2018–. *Publications:* numerous articles on the history of ideas and on foreign policy. *Address:* Embassy of Germany, 23 Belgrave Square, London, SW1X 8PZ, England (office). *Telephone:* (20) 7824-1300 (office). *Fax:* (20) 7824-1449 (office). *E-mail:* info@london.diplo.de (office). *Website:* uk.diplo.de (office).

WITTY, Sir Andrew, Kt, BA (Econ); British business executive; m.; two c.; ed Univ. of Nottingham; joined Glaxo UK 1985, held various positions in UK, including Dir of Pharmacy and Distribution, Int. Product Man. and a variety of other sales and marketing positions, later served as Man. Dir Glaxo South Africa and Area Dir for South and East Africa, then Vice-Pres. and Gen. Man. Marketing for Glaxo Wellcome Inc. (US subsidiary), Sr Vice-Pres., Asia Pacific, based in Singapore –2003, Pres. Pharmaceuticals Europe, GlaxoSmithKline 2003–08, mem. Corp. Exec. Team, CEO Designate 2007–08, CEO 2008–17; served as Econ. Advisor to Gov. of Guangzhou, People's Repub. of China 2000–02; mem. Singapore Econ. Devt Bd 2000–02, Econ. Devt Bd Audit Cttee 2000–02, Singapore Land Authority Bd 2000–02; Pres. European Fed. of Pharmaceutical Industries and Asscns 2010–; Chancellor Univ. of Nottingham 2013–; mem. INSEAD UK Council, Interim Bd of Office for Strategic Coordination of Health Research, Imperial Coll. Commercialisation Advisory Bd, London Council for the Advancement of Science and Tech.; mem. Pharma Futures Working Group, Health Innovation Council (UK); Lead Non-Exec. Bd mem. Dept of Business, Innovation and Skills 2011–; Bd mem. INSEAD Business School 2011–; mem. Prime Minister's Business Advisory Group; Public Service Medal, Govt of Singapore 2003, Public Service Star 2012. *Leisure interests:* tennis, running, watching rugby and cricket.

WŁOSOWICZ, Zbigniew; Polish lawyer, diplomatist and UN official; *Deputy Chief, National Security Office;* b. 1955; ed Jagiellonian Univ.; First Sec., Perm. Del. to UN, New York 1990–91, Deputy Rep. 1991–93, Rep. to UN Security Council 1993–97; Special Adviser on Inter-Governmental Affairs, UNDP 1998–2000, Special Rep. of the UN Sec.-Gen. in Cyprus and Chief of Mission, UNFICYP 2000–05; Dean, Faculty of Int. Relations, School of Business Admin, Bielsko-Biala 2006–07, Lecturer 2009–10; Lecturer, Higher School of European Studies, Krakow 2008–10; Sec. of State for Int. Affairs, Ministry of Defence 2010–12; Deputy Chief, Nat. Security Office 2013–. *Address:* National Security Office, 00-909 Warsaw, ul. Karowa 10, Poland (office). *Telephone:* (22) 6951850 (office). *Website:* en.bbn.gov.pl (office).

WNENDT, Werner Franz, MSc; German diplomatist; m.; five c.; ed geosciences and law studies; worked for German Devt Agency in Myanmar 1976–78; joined Fed. Foreign Service 1980, held positions in missions to EU, Brussels, Washington, DC, Islamabad and Nairobi, Chef de Cabinet to Minister of State for European Integration 1995–98, Deputy Head of Mission, Embassy in Prague 1998–2000, Foreign Adviser to the Fed. Pres. 2000–03, Sr Deputy High Rep. of Int. Community to Bosnia and Herzegovina 2003–05, Head of OSCE Mission in Kosovo 2005–07, Asst Deputy Minister for Culture and Communication, Fed. Foreign Office 2007–12, Amb. to Canada 2012–18.

WOBBE, Kristin K., BA, PhD; American chemist and academic; *Associate Professor of Chemistry and Biochemistry, Associate Dean of Undergraduate Studies and Director, Great Problems Seminars, Worcester Polytechnic Institute;* ed St Olaf Coll., Harvard Univ.; spent one year as Research Assoc., Harvard Univ., then three years as Research Assoc. and NSF Fellow at Rutgers Univ., then one year as Research Assoc. and NSF Fellow, Massachusetts General Hosp.; apptd Asst Prof., Worcester Polytechnic Inst. 1995, Leonard P. Kinnicutt Asst Prof. 1999–2012, apptd John C. Metzger Prof. of Chemistry 2008, apptd Head of Chemistry and Biochemistry Dept 2008, Assoc. Prof. of Chem. and Biochemistry 2009–, Assoc. Dean for First Year Experience 2009–11, Assoc. Dean of Undergraduate Studies 2011–, Dir Great Problems Seminars; Romeo L. Moruzzi Young Faculty Award for Innovation in Undergraduate Educ., Gordon Prize, Nat. Acad. of Eng (co-recipient) 2016. *Publications:* numerous papers in professional journals. *Address:* Room 234, Rubin Campus Center, Worcester Polytechnic Institute, 100

Institute Road, Worcester, MA 01609-2280, USA (office). *Telephone:* (508) 831-5375 (office). *E-mail:* kwobbe@wpi.edu (office). *Website:* www.wpi.edu/people/faculty/kwobbe (office).

WOELKI, HE Cardinal Rainer Maria, DTheol; German ecclesiastic; *Archbishop of Cologne;* b. 18 Aug. 1956, Köln-Mühlheim; ed Theological Faculties, Univs of Bonn and Freiburg im Breisgau, Pontifical Univ. of the Holy Cross, Rome; ordained priest, Archdiocese of Cologne 1985; Asst Priest, St Mary's Parish, Neuss 1985–89; mil. chaplain in Münster 1989; Pvt. Sec. to Archbishop of Cologne 1990–97; Dir Collegium Albertinum (residence for major seminarians of the archdiocese studying at Univ. of Bonn) 1997–2011; rank of Chaplain of His Holiness, with title of Mgr 1999; apptd Auxiliary Bishop of Cologne and Titular Bishop of Scampa 2003; Archbishop of Berlin 2011–14, of Cologne 2014–; cr. Cardinal (Cardinal-Priest of San Giovanni Maria Vianney) 2012; participated in Papal Conclave 2013; mem. Congregation of the Clergy 2014–, Congregation for Divine Worship and the Discipline of the Sacraments 2016–, Comm. for Spiritual Professions and church Services (Deputy Chair. 2016–), Pontifical Council for Promoting Christian Unity, Administration of the Patrimony of the Apostolic See; Comm. for Vocations and Ministries of the Church and for Science and Culture (Chair. 2018–), German Bishops' Conf.; Consultor of the Holy See's Congregation for Catholic Educ.; Dr hc (Sophia Univ., Tokyo) 2016. *Address:* Archdiocese of Cologne, Marzellenstrβe 32, 50606 Cologne (office); Cardinal Frings Street 10, 50668 Cologne, Germany (home). *Telephone:* (21) 16421411 (office). *E-mail:* erzbischof@erzbistum-koeln.de (office). *Website:* www.erzbistum-koeln.de (office).

WOERTH, Éric; French business executive and politician; *Mayor of Chantilly;* b. 29 Jan. 1956, Creil; m.; two c.; ed HEC School of Man., Paris; legal and tax adviser, Arthur Andersen Int. 1981–82; Head of Internal Audit and Asst Head of Service Operations and Financial Negotiations, Pechiney (aluminium producing co.) 1982–90; Dir, then Pnr Bossard Consultants 1990–97; Assoc. Dir Arthur Andersen 1997–2002; mem. Regional Council, Picardy 1986–2002, Vice-Pres. 1992–98; Mayor of Chantilly 1995–2004, 2005–, Deputy Mayor 2004–05; Adviser, Cabinet of the Prime Minister 1995–97; mem. Union pour un Mouvement Populaire (UMP), Treas. 2002–10, party became Les Républicains 2015, Sec.-Gen. 2015–16; Deputy for Oise, Nat. Ass. 2002–04, 2005–07; Treas., Jacques Chirac's presidential campaign 2002; Sec. of State for Reforms 2004–05; Minister of Budget, Public Accounts and Civil Service 2007–10, of Labour, Solidarity and the Civil Service March–Nov. 2010; mem. Finance Comm., Nat. Ass. 2005–07. *Address:* Conseil Municipal, 60500 Chantilly, France (office). *Telephone:* 3-44-62-42-00 (office). *E-mail:* eric.woerth@wanadoo.fr (home). *Website:* www.blog-ewoerth.com.

WOERTZ, Patricia (Pat) A., BA, CPA; American business executive; b. 17 March 1953, Pittsburgh, Pa; m.; three c.; ed Pennsylvania State Univ. and Columbia Univ.; joined Ernst & Young, Pittsburgh as a certified public accountant 1974; positions in refining and marketing, strategic planning and finance with Gulf Oil Corpn, Pittsburgh 1977–81, head of US upstream audit group, Houston, Tex. 1981–85, worked on asset divestitures during merger of Gulf and Chevron 1985–87, Finance Man. Chevron Information Tech. Co. 1989–91, Strategic Planning Man. Chevron Corpn 1991–93, Pres. Chevron Canada Ltd, Vancouver, BC 1993–96, Pres. Chevron Int. Oil Co. and Vice-Pres. Logistics and Trading for Chevron Products Co. 1996–98, Pres. Chevron Products Co. and Vice-Pres. Chevron Corpn 1998–2001, Exec. Vice-Pres. Global Downstream, ChevronTexaco Corpn 2001–06; mem. Bd of Dirs, Archer Daniels Midland Co. (ADM) 2006–15, Pres. and CEO 2006–14, Chair. 2007–15 (retd); apptd to the Pres.'s Export Council by Pres. Obama 2010–; mem. Bd of Dirs Procter & Gamble Co., US-China Business Council, American Petroleum Inst., Bd of Visitors Pennsylvania State Univ.; Vice-Chair. Kennedy Center Corp. Fund; mem. Nat. Petroleum Council, Int. Business Council of the World Econ. Forum, US Chamber of Commerce, The Business Council, Business Roundtable; Trustee, Univ. of San Diego; mem. Bd of Visitors Pennsylvania State Univ.

WOESSNER, Mark Matthias, DrIng; German business executive; b. 14 Oct. 1938, Berlin; m.; two c.; ed Tech. Univ., Karlsruhe; Man. Asst Bertelsmann AG 1968–70; Production Man. Mohndruck Printing Co. 1970–72, Tech. Dir 1972–74, Man. Dir 1974–76; mem. Exec. Bd Bertelsmann AG, Pres. Printing and Mfg Div. 1976–83, Pres. and CEO 1983–98, Chair. Supervisory Bd 1998–2000; Deputy Chair. Exec. Bd Bertelsmann Foundation 1996–98, Chair. Exec. Bd 1998–2000; Chair. Supervisory Bd, Heidelberger Druckmaschinen AG, eCircle AG; Deputy Chair. Supervisory Bd, Loewe AG; mem. Supervisory Bd DaimlerChrysler AG, Dussmann AG & Co. KGaA, Douglas Holding AG; mem. Bd of Trustees, Univ. of Munich; Hon. Senator, Univ. of St Gallen, Univ. of Witten/Herdecke; Hon. Prof. of Business Admin, Univ. of Munich 2005–. *Leisure interest:* sport.

WOESTE, Albrecht, Dipl-Ing; German business executive; *President, Direktoriums für Vollblutzucht und Rennen—DVR;* b. 30 Oct. 1935, Düsseldorf; ed Berlin Tech. Univ.; f. Woeste GmbH & Co. KG 1963, Man. Dir and Chair. Advisory Bd; mem. Supervisory Bd Henkel KGaA 1988–2009, Chair. Supervisory Bd 1990–2009; Vice-Pres. Düsseldorfer Reiter- und Rennvereins e.V. 2003–; Pres. Direktoriums für Vollblutzucht und Rennen—DVR (bd for thoroughbred horse breeding and racing) 2009–; mem. Supervisory Bd Fortuna Dusseldorf (football club); Pres. IHK Düsseldorf (football club) 1991–99, Hon. Pres. 1999–; mem. Bd of Dirs Ecolab Inc. 1991–2001; mem. Supervisory Bd Deutsche Bank AG 1993–2006; mem. Advisory Bd IKB Deutsche Industriebank AG; mem. Int. Advisory Bd IESE Business School, Univ. of Navarra; Hon. Citizen of Düsseldorf 2015; Order of Merit (1st Class) 1992, Great Cross of Merit 2001. *Website:* www.direktorium.de.

WOGAN, Gerald Norman, BS, MS, PhD; American chemist and academic; *Professor Emeritus of Chemistry and Underwood-Prescott Professor Emeritus of Toxicology, Massachusetts Institute of Technology;* b. 11 Jan. 1930, Altoona, Pa; s. of Thomas B. Wogan and Florence E. (Corl) Wogan; m. Henrietta E. Hoenicke 1957; one s. one d.; ed Juniata Coll., Pa and Univ. of Illinois, Urbana; Teaching Asst in Mammalian Physiology, Univ. of Illinois 1953–54, Teaching Asst in Human Anatomy 1954–55, Dept Fellow in Metabolic Physiology 1955–56, Instructor in Physiology 1956–57; Asst Prof. of Physiology, Rutgers Univ., NJ 1957–61; Research Assoc. in Food Toxicology, MIT 1961–62, Asst Prof. of Food Toxicology 1962–65, Assoc. Prof. of Food Toxicology 1965–69, Prof. of Toxicology 1969–2001, Dir Environmental Health Sciences Center 1978–96, Underwood-Prescott Prof. and Head, Dept of Applied Biological Sciences 1979–88, Prof. of Chem. 1988–2001, Underwood-Prescott Prof. and Dir Div. of Toxicology, Whitaker Coll. of Health Sciences and Tech. 1988–96, Prof. of Toxicology and Prof. of Chem. 1996–2001, Prof. Emer. of Chem. 2001–, Underwood-Prescott Prof. Emer. of Toxicology 2001–; Scientific Advisor, Lab. of Human Carcinogenesis, Nat. Cancer Inst., NIH 1999–, Sr Research Fellow 2001–; Scholar-in-Residence, Fogarty Int. Center 1997–99; Visiting Prof. of Environmental Health Sciences, Johns Hopkins Univ. 1997–; Visiting Prof., Distinguished Visitor Program, Nat. Univ. of Singapore 1999; consultant to nat. and int. govt agencies and industries; Section Ed. Journal of Environmental Pathology, Toxicology and Oncology 1992–; mem. Editorial Bd Journal of the American College of Toxicology 1987–, Methods in Toxicology 1994–; mem. Editorial Acad. International Journal of Molecular Medicine 1997–; mem. NAS 1977, Inst. of Medicine 1994, American Asscn for Cancer Research, ACS, Soc. for Free Radicals in Biology and Medicine, The Nitric Oxide Soc., Environmental Mutagen Soc., American Soc. for Preventive Oncology, Soc. of Toxicology, American Coll. of Toxicology, American Soc. for Microbiology, American Soc. of Pharmacology and Experimental Therapeutics, American Soc. for Nutrition Sciences, AAAS; Fellow, American Acad. of Microbiology 1992; Lecturer, Japan Foundation for the Promotion of Cancer Research 1988, Distinguished Alumnus Award, Univ. of Illinois 1995, Distinguished Lectureship, Republic of Singapore Cancer Society 1991, Harvard School of Public Health 1996, Founders' Award, Chemical Industry Institute of Toxicology 1999, George H. Scott Memorial Award, Toxicology Forum 2003, Award of Merit, Princess Takamatsu Cancer Research Fund (Japan) 2001. *Publications:* articles and reviews in professional journals. *Address:* Room 26-009, Biological Engineering Division, Massachusetts Institute of Technology, 77 Massachusetts Avenue, Cambridge, MA 02139, USA (office). *Telephone:* (617) 253-3188 (office). *Fax:* (617) 258-9733 (office). *E-mail:* wogan@mit.edu (office). *Website:* web.mit.edu/be/people/wogan.shtml (office); web.mit.edu/gnwlab (office).

WOICKE, Peter L., MBA; German banker and international finance official; ed Univ. of Saarbruecken; with J. P. Morgan for over 30 years, in particular in Latin America and the Middle East, Head of Banking Div., Beirut, Lebanon, Man. Global Gas and Petroleum Group, fmr mem. Exec. Man. Group, Chair. J.P. Morgan Securities Asia, Singapore; Man. Dir Pvt. Sector Operations, IBRD (World Bank) 1999–2005, Exec. Vice-Pres. IFC 1999–2005; Chair. Int. Save the Children Alliance 2008–09; mem. Supervisory Bd Raiffeisen Int. Bank-Holding AG (Raiffeisen Int., subsidiary of RZB Group) 2005–07, ProCredit Holding 2005–, Anglo American 2006–13; mem. Bd of Dirs MTN Group Ltd 2006–08, Int. Youth Foundation, Chesapeake Bay Foundation, Inst. of Human Rights and Business, Saudi Aramco; mem. Bd of Trustees Ashesi Univ. Foundation, Global Communities 2014–; Diageo Africa Business Reporting Award 2005. *Address:* 7308 Drum Point Road, St. Michaels, MD 21663, USA.

WOJCICKI, Susan D., AB, MA, MBA; American business executive; *CEO, YouTube;* b. 5 July 1968, Santa Clara Co., Calif.; d. of Prof. Stanley Wojcicki and Esther Wojcicki; m. Dennis Troper; four c.; ed Harvard Univ., Univ. of California, Santa Cruz, Univ. of California, Los Angeles Anderson School of Man.; worked at Intel; man. consultant at Bain & Co. and R.B. Webber & Co.; joined Google Inc. as co.'s first marketing man. 1996–2006, worked on initial marketing programmes and branding and then the syndication of Google search to partners, also led initial Devt of Google Images, Google Books and Google Video, Vice-Pres., Product Man. 2006–10, Sr Vice-Pres., Product Man. 2010–11, Sr Vice-Pres. of Advertising and Commerce 2013–14, CEO YouTube 2014–; mem. Bd of Dirs HomeAway, Inc. 2011–12. *Address:* Google Inc., 1600 Amphitheatre Parkway, Mountain View, CA 94043, USA (office). *Telephone:* (650) 253-0000 (office). *Fax:* (650) 253-0001 (office). *Website:* www.google.com (office).

WOJTYŁA, Andrzej Franciszek; Polish politician and paediatrician; b. 1 May 1955, Kalisz; s. Franciszek Wojtyła and Stanisława Wojtyła; m. Ewa Wojtyła; one s. one d.; ed Medical Acad., Poznań, George Washington, Georgetown and La Salle Univs, USA; paediatrician, Children's Ward Municipal Hosp., Pleszew 1980–89; Head, Village Health Service Centre, Jastrzębniki 1985–92; Visiting Researcher, George Washington Univ., USA 1995, Visiting Prof., Center for Health Policy and Research 1995–96; mem. Solidarity Trade Union 1980–89, Solidarity of Individual Farmers Trade Union 1989–91; Councillor of Commune of Blizanów 1990; mem. Polish Peasant Party Solidarity (PSL Solidarność) 1990–92, Peasant Christian Party (SLCh) 1992–97; Pres. SLCh Voivodship Bd, Kalisz, mem. SLCh Nat. Political Council; mem. Conservative Peasant Party (SKL) 1997–; Deputy to Sejm (Parl.) 1991–93, 1997–2005, Vice-Chair. Parl. Health Cttee; mem. Parl. Constitutional Responsibility Cttee 1991–93; Minister of Health and Social Welfare 1992–93, Sec. of State, Ministry of Health 2005–06; Chief Sanitary Insp. 2006–10; Dir Inst. of Rural Health, Lublin from 2010; fmr Sec.-Gen. World Org. of Rural Medicine; fmr mem. Scientific Cttee, International Journal of Rural Health; Gold Cross of Merit 2010. *Publication:* Third International Conference: Health Education for Children, International Conference: Health Care Reform in Poland 1995. *Leisure interests:* fitness, walking, history, health care reforms in the world. *Address:* c/o Instytut Medycyny Wsi im. Witolda Chodzki (Institute of Rural Health), 20-090 Lublin, Jaczewsk iego 2, Poland. *E-mail:* imw@galen.imw.lublin.pl (home).

WOLDEZGU, Maj.-Gen. Gebre Adhana; Ethiopian army officer, government official and UN official; *Head of Mission and Force Commander, United Nations Interim Security Force for Abyei (UNIFSA);* b. 1963; m.; two c.; ed Ethiopian Civil Service Univ.; worked for 38 years in Ethiopian Army, deployed to Sudan, South Sudan, Kenya, Uganda, African Union Mission in Somalia, Mechanized Deputy Div. Commdr 1995–98, Div. Commdr 1999–2008; Dir Ministry of Nat. Defence 2008–18; Head of Mission and Force Commdr, UN Interim Security Force for Abyei (UNISFA) 2018–. *Address:* United Nations Interim Security Force for Abyei, Department of Peacekeeping Operations, Room S-3727B, United Nations, New York, NY 10017, USA (office). *Telephone:* (212) 963-8077 (office). *Fax:* (212) 963-9222 (office). *Website:* peacekeeping.un.org (office).

WOLF, (Richard Anthony) Dick; American television producer; b. 20 Dec. 1946, New York, NY; s. of George Wolf and Marie G. Wolf (née Gaffney); m. 1st Susan Scranton 1970 (divorced 1981); m. 2nd Christine Marburg 1983 (divorced 2005); three c.; m. 3rd Noelle Lippman 2006; ed Saint David's School, New York, Phillips Acad., The Gunnery, Univ. of Pennsylvania; worked as advertising copywriter at Benton & Bowles; moved to Los Angeles and had three screenplays produced, including Masquerade 1988; began TV career as staff writer on Hill Street Blues; moved over to Miami Vice as supervising producer; f. Wolf Films (production co.); creator and producer of Law & Order series which equalled Gunsmoke as the longest-running dramatic show in TV history 1990–2010; several awards, including an Emmy Award. *Television includes:* exec. producer: Skateboard (producer, as Richard A. Wolf) 1978, No Man's Land (producer) 1987, Masquerade 1988, Miami Vice (series) (co-producer) 1986–87, (co-exec. producer) 1987–88, (exec. producer) 1989, The Last Plane from Coramaya (video) (producer) 1989, Gideon Oliver (series) 1989, Christine Cromwell (series) 1989, H.E.L.P. (series) 1990, Law & Order (series) 1990–2010, Mann & Machine (series) 1992, The Human Factor (series) 1992, Crime & Punishment (series) 1993, South Beach (series) 1993, New York Undercover (series) 1994–99, The Wright Verdicts (series) 1995, Swift Justice (series) 1996, Feds (series) 1997, Players (series) 1997, The Invisible Man (film) 1998, Exiled (film) 1998, Law & Order: Special Victims Unit (series) 1999–2018, D.C. (series) 2000, Arrest & Trial (series documentary) 2000, Deadline (series) 2000–01, Law & Order: Criminal Intent (series) 2001–11, Crime & Punishment (series documentary) 2002, Twin Towers (short) (producer) (Academy Award for Best Short Documentary) 2003, Dragnet (series) 2003–04, Law & Order: Trial by Jury (series) 2005–06, Conviction (series) 2006, Bury My Heart at Wounded Knee (film) 2007, Lost & Found (film) 2009, American Masters (series documentary) (producer) 2009, Home Is Where You Find It (documentary short) (producer) 2009, Law & Order: Los Angeles (series) 2010–11, Law & Order: UK (series) (exec. producer, Wolf Films) 2009–11, (exec. producer) 2010, Stars Earn Stripes (series) 2012, Chicago Fire (series) 2012, Cold Justice: Sex Crimes 2013–15, 2017, Chicago P.D. 2014, Chicago Med 2015, Chicago Justice 2017, FBI 2018. *Address:* Wolf Films, 100 Universal City Plaza Bldg, 2252, Universal City, CA 91608-1085, USA (office).

WOLF, Günter, PhD; German particle physicist and academic; *Senior Researcher, Deutsches Elektronen-Synchrotron (DESY);* b. 23 Nov. 1937, Ulm/Donau; ed Univs of Tübingen and Hamburg; worked at Stanford Linear Accelerator Center (SLAC), Stanford Univ., Calif., USA 1960s; co-spokesman for DASP experiment at Electron-Positron Storage Ring DORIS, Deutsches Elektronen-Synchrotron (DESY), Hamburg; spokesman for TASSO experiment at Electron-Positron Storage Ring PETRA, (DESY); C-discoverer of the gluon with the TASSO experiment, Hamburg 1979; spokesman for ZEUS experiment at Electron-Proton Storage Ring HERA (DESY) 1986–94, mem. of ZEUS collaboration –2011; apptd Prof. of Physics 1994; European Physical Soc. High Energy and Particle Physics Prize (jtly) 1995, Stern-Gerlach Medal, German Physical Soc. 2011. *Publications:* numerous articles in scientific journals. *Address:* Deutsches Elektronen-Synchrotron DESY, ZEUS/F1, 1B/252, Notkestraße 85, 22607 Hamburg, Germany (office). *Telephone:* (40) 8998-3841 (office). *E-mail:* guenter.wolf@desy.de (office). *Website:* www.desy.de (office).

WOLF, Martin Harry, CBE, MA, MPhil; British economist and journalist; *Associate Editor and Chief Economics Commentator, Financial Times;* b. 16 Aug. 1946, London; s. of Edmund Wolf and Rebecca Wolf; m. Alison Margaret Wolf; two s. one d.; ed Univ. of Oxford; joined World Bank 1971 Sr Economist in 1974; Dir of Studies, Trade Policy Research Centre, London 1981; Chief Econs Leader Writer, Financial Times 1987–96, Assoc. Ed. 1990, Chief Econs Commentator 1996, currently Assoc. Ed. and Chief Econs Commentator; Hon. Prof., Univ. of Nottingham; mem. Council of Royal Econ. Soc. 1991–96; Forum Fellow, World Econ. Acad. 1999–, mem. Int. Media Council 2006–; Hon. Fellow, Corpus Christi Coll., Oxford, Oxford Inst. for Econ. Policy (Oxonia), European Int. Business Acad. 2012; Hon. DLitt (Nottingham) 2006, (Kingston Univ.) 2010, (Macquarie Univ.) 2012, Hon. DSc (Econ) (LSE) 2006, (Warwick Univ.) 2009; Wincott Foundation Sr Prize for excellence in financial journalism (jtly) 1989, 1997, Commemoration Medal 1990, RTZ David Watt Memorial Prize 1994, Business Journalist of the Year Decade of Excellence Award 2003, Newspaper Feature of the Year Award, Workworld Media Awards 2003, First Magazine Award for Advocacy of Responsible Capitalism 2005, sixth winner, Journalism Prize, Fundacio Catalunya Oberta (Open Catalonia Foundation) 2006, Lifetime Achievement Award, AMEC 2007, Ischia Int. Journalism Award 2012, Wincott Award for Best Radio Programme 2014. *Publications:* Why Globalization Works 2004, Fixing Global Finance 2008, The Shifts and the Shocks: What We've Learned—and Have Still to Learn—from the Financial Crisis 2014. *Address:* Financial Times Group, 1 Southwark Bridge, London, SE1 9HL, England (office). *Telephone:* (20) 7873-3673 (office). *Fax:* (20) 7873-3421 (office). *E-mail:* martin.wolf@ft.com (office). *Website:* www.ft.com (office).

WOLF, Naomi, BA; American writer and feminist; b. 15 Nov. 1962, San Francisco, Calif.; d. of Leonard Wolf and Deborah Wolf; m. David Shipley 1993 (divorced 2005); one c.; ed Yale Univ., New Coll., Oxford, UK; Rhodes Scholar 1986; Co-founder Woodhull Inst. for Ethical Leadership 1997, now Scholar-in-Residence and Woodhull Fellow; fmr columnist, George magazine; consultant, Al Gore Presidential campaign 2000. *Publications include:* The Beauty Myth: How Images of Beauty Are Used Against Women 1990, Fire With Fire: The New Female Power and How It Will Change in the 21st Century 1993, Promiscuities: The Secret Struggle for Womanhood 1997, Misconceptions: Truth, Lies and the Unexpected on the Journey to Motherhood 2001, The Treehouse: Eccentric Wisdom from my Father on How to Live, Love and See 2006, The End of America: A Letter of Warning to a Young Patriot 2007, Give Me Liberty: A Handbook for American Revolutionaries 2008, Vagina: A New Biography 2012. *Website:* www.harpercollins.com/cr-105876/naomi-wolf.

WOLF, Siegfried; Austrian business executive; *Chairman, GAZ Group;* b. 31 Oct. 1957, Feldbach; m.; two d.; trained as tool and die-maker and then as mem. of tech. staff, Quality Lab. at Philips; joined VereinigteMetallwerke Wien (VMW) as Quality Man. and Asst Dir of Quality Control; joined Hirtenberger AG, positions included Dir for Quality Control, then Gen. Man. and Vice-Pres.; joined Magna Europe 1994, Pres. 1995–2001, mem. Bd of Dirs and Vice-Chair. Magna Int. Inc. 1999–2001, Pres. and CEO Magna Steyr 2001–02, Exec. Vice-Chair. Magna Int. Inc. 2002–05, Co-CEO 2005–10; Chair. GAZ Group and Glavstroy JSC 2010–, Chair. Russian Machines Corpn, Gazprom Open JSC 2010–; Chair. Sberbank Europe AG (fmrly Volksbank Int. AG—VBI) 2012–; mem. Supervisory Bd Verbundgesellschaft (Austria Hydro Power), Österreich Industrieholding AG 2002– (Second Vice-Chair. 2006–08, First Vice-Chair. 2008–), Siemens AG

Österreich, HGI Beteiligungs AG; mem. Bd Decoma Int. Inc. –2005, Intier Automotive Inc. –2005, Tesma Int. Inc. –2005; mem. Supervisory Bd Strabag SE 2007–10, Continental AG 2010–; Hon. Senator, Technical Univ. of Vienna 2002, Hon. Prof., Technical Univ. of Graz 2009; Great Silver Decoration of Honour 2000; Golden Badge of Honour Award 2008, Order of Friendship Award, Russia 2016. *Address:* GAZ Group, 603004 Nizhny Novgorod, 88 Lenina Prospect, Russia (office). *Telephone:* (831) 299-09-90 (office). *Fax:* (831) 299-09-99 (office). *E-mail:* UKGG@gaz.ru (office). *Website:* www.gazgroup.ru (office).

WOLF, Stephen M., BA; American business executive; *Chairman, R.R. Donnelley & Sons Company;* b. 7 Aug. 1941, Oakland, Calif.; ed San Francisco State Univ., with American Airlines 1966–81, Vice-Pres. Western Div.; Sr Vice-Pres., Pan American World Airways 1981; Pres. and COO Continental Airlines 1982–83; Pres. and CEO Republic Airlines 1984–86; Chair., Pres. and CEO Tiger Int. Inc. 1986–88; Chair. and CEO UAL Corpn 1987–94, also fmr Pres.; Chair. and CEO United Airlines 1992–94; Chair. US Air Group Inc. 1996–98 (Pres. 1987–92), Chair. USAIR Inc. (later US Airways) 1998–2002; Sr Adviser, Lazard Frères 1994–2003; Man. Partner, Alpilles LLC 2003–; Dir R.R. Donnelley & Sons Co. 1995–, Chair. 2004–; Chair. Lehman Brothers Pvt. Equity Advisory Bd 2005–08, Trilantic Capital Partners (fmrly Lehman Brothers Merchant Banking) 2009–; mem. Bd of Dirs Altria Group Inc. 1993–2008, Philip Morris Int. 2008–, Chrysler Group, LLC 2009–; fmr Dir Air Transport Asscn of America; Trustee, Georgetown Univ., World Wide Fund for Nature; Hon. Trustee, The Brookings Inst. *Address:* R.R. Donnelley Global Headquarters, 111 South Wacker Drive, Chicago, IL 60606-4301, USA (office). *Telephone:* (312) 326-8000 (office). *Fax:* (312) 326-8001 (office). *E-mail:* info@rrdonnelly.com (office). *Website:* www.rrdonnelly.com (office).

WOLF, Thomas (Tom) Westerman, AB, PhD; American business executive and politician; *Governor of Pennsylvania;* b. 17 Nov. 1948, York, Pa; s. of William Wolf and Cornelia Rohlman Wolf (née Westerman); m. Frances Wolf; two d.; ed Dartmouth Coll., Univ. of London, UK, Massachusetts Inst. of Tech.; Chair. The Wolf Organization Inc. (family-owned business) –2014; Sec., Pennsylvania Dept of Revenue 2007–08; Gov. of Pennsylvania 2015–; Chair. York County United Way, York County Community Foundation, York Coll. Bd of Trustees, York County Chamber of Commerce; Democrat. *Address:* Office of the Governor, Main Capitol Bldg, Room 225, Harrisburg, PA, 17120 USA (office). *Telephone:* (717) 787-2500 (office). *Fax:* (717) 772-8284 (office). *E-mail:* governor@pa.gov (office). *Website:* www.governor.state.pa.us (office).

WOLFE, Nathan, BA, MA, DSc; American virologist and academic; *Founder, CEO and Director, Global Viral;* b. 24 Aug. 1970, Detroit, Mich.; ed Stanford Univ., Harvard Univ.; Postdoctoral Fellow, Dept of Int. Health, Johns Hopkins Univ. 1999–2003, Asst Prof., Dept of Epidemiology, Dept of Molecular Microbiology and Immunology 2003–06, Adjunct Prof., Bloomberg School of Public Health 2006–; Prof., Dept of Epidemiology, UCLA 2006–08; Lorry I. Lokey Visiting Prof. of Human Biology, Stanford Univ. 2008–; Founder, CEO and Dir, Global Viral Forecasting Initiative (now Global Viral) 2008–; Fulbright Fellowship 1997; mem. AAAS, Int. Soc. of Ecosystem Health, Int. Primatological Soc., Ecological Soc. of America, American Soc. of Virology, American Soc. of Tropical Medicine and Hygiene, American Soc. of Microbiology; NIH Dir's Pioneer Award 2005, Nat. Geographic Emerging Explorers Award 2009. *Publications include:* The Viral Storm: The Dawn of a New Pandemic Age 2011; numerous articles in scientific journals. *Address:* Global Viral, 425 California Street, Suite 200, San Francisco, CA 94104, USA (office). *Telephone:* (415) 398-4712 (office). *Fax:* (415) 398-4716 (office). *E-mail:* nwolfe@gvfi.org (office). *Website:* www.globalviral.org (office); www.nathanwolfe.net.

WOLFE-SIMON, Felisa, BM, BA, PhD; American biologist; *Astrobiology Research Fellow, NASA Astrobiology Institute;* ed Oberlin Coll., Rutgers Univ.; studied oboe performance before turning to biology; Grad. Fellow, Grad. Asst/Teaching Asst, Dept of Oceanography, Rutgers Univ. 2000–06; Postdoctoral Research Fellow in Biology, NSF 2006–09; Astrobiology Research Fellow, NASA Astrobiology Inst. 2010–; mem. Soc. of Bio-inorganic Chemistry, Soc. of Molecular Biology and Evolution, Int. Soc. for the Study of the Origin of Life, American Soc. of Plant Biologists, American Soc. of Limnology and Oceanography, American Geophysical Union, ACS; NAS Kavli Fellow 2010. *Address:* PO Box 985, Berkeley, CA 94701, USA (office). *E-mail:* felisawolfesimon@gmail.com (office). *Website:* felisawolfesimon.com (office).

WOLFENDALE, Sir Arnold (Whittaker), Kt, PhD, FRS, FRAS, FInstP; British physicist and academic; *Professor Emeritus, Department of Physics, Durham University;* b. 25 June 1927, Rugby; s. of Arnold Wolfendale and Doris Wolfendale; m. Audrey Darby 1951; twin s.; ed Univ. of Manchester; Asst Lecturer, Univ. of Manchester 1951–54, Lecturer 1954–56; Lecturer, Durham Univ. 1956–59, Sr Lecturer 1959–63, Reader in Physics 1963–65, Prof. 1965–92, Prof. Emer. 1992–, Head of Dept 1973–77, 1980–83, 1986–89; Chair., Northern Region Action Cttee, Manpower Services Comm. Job Creation Programme 1975–78; Pres. Royal Astronomical Soc. 1981–83, Durham Univ. Soc. of Fellows 1988–, Inst. of Physics 1994–96, European Physical Soc. 1999–; Prof. of Experimental Physics, Royal Inst. of GB 1996–; mem. Science and Eng Research Council 1988–94; Astronomer Royal 1991–95; Fellow, Tata Inst. Fund 1996; mem. Academia Europaea 1998; Foreign Fellow, Nat. Acad. of Sciences of India 1990, Indian Nat. Science Acad.; Foreign Assoc., Royal Soc. of SA 1996; Pres. Antiquarian Horological Soc.; Freeman Worshipful Co. of Clockmakers, Worshipful Co. of Scientific Instrument Makers; Hon. Fellow, Lancs. Polytechnic 1991; Dr hc (Potchefstroom, Łódź, Teesside, Newcastle, Open Univ., Paisley, Lancaster, Bucharest, Durham, Neofit Rilski Southwest Univ. (Bulgaria); Silver Jubilee Medal 1977, Univ. of Turku Medal 1987, Armagh Observatory Medal 1992, Marian Smoluchowski Medal (Polish Physics Soc.) 1992, Powell Memorial Medal, European Physical Soc. 1996, Royal Soc. Bakerian Lecture and Medal 2002, Il Fiorino d'Oro, City of Florence 2004. *Publications include:* Cosmic Rays 1963; Ed. Cosmic Rays at Ground Level 1973, Origin of Cosmic Rays 1974, Gamma Ray Astronomy 1981, Progress in Cosmology 1982, Gamma Ray Astronomy (with P. V. Ramana Murthy) 1986, Secular, Solar and Geomagnetic Variations in the last 1,000 years 1988; Origin of Cosmic Rays (co-ed.) 1981, Observational Tests of Cosmological Inflation (co-ed.) 1991; numerous papers on cosmic radiation. *Leisure interests:* walking, gardening, foreign travel. *Address:* Department of Physics, Durham University, Rochester Building, Science Laboratories, South Road, Durham, DH1 3LE (office); Ansford, Potters

Bank, Durham, England (home). *Telephone:* (191) 334-3580 (office); (191) 384-5642 (home). *Fax:* (191) 374-3749 (office). *E-mail:* a.w.wolfendale@durham.ac.uk (office). *Website:* www.dur.ac.uk/Physics (office).

WOLFENSOHN, James (Jim) D., KBE, AO, BA, LLB, MBA; American (b. Australian) international organization official, business executive, arts administrator and diplomatist; *Chairman, Wolfensohn and Co.;* b. 1 Dec. 1933, Sydney, Australia; s. of Hyman Wolfensohn and Dora Weinbaum; m. Elaine Botwinick 1961; one s. two d.; ed Univ. of Sydney, Harvard Business School; Pres. J. Henry Schroder Banking Corpn 1970–76; Chair. Salomon Brothers Int. 1977–81; Owner, Pres. James D. Wolfensohn Inc. 1981–95, fmr Chair., also CEO; Pres. World Bank 1995–2005; US Special Envoy for Gaza Disengagement 2005–April 2006 (resgnd); apptd Sr Advisor and Chair. Int. Advisory Bd, Citigroup Inc., New York 2006; Chair. Wolfensohn and Co. (corp. advisory and investment firm), New York 2005–; Chair. Kennedy Center for the Performing Arts 1990–95, Chair. Emer. 1995–; Chair. Advisory Group, Wolfensohn Center, Brookings Inst.; Chair. Bd Inst. for Advanced Study, Princeton, New Jersey; mem. Bd Carnegie Hall; Trustee, Rockefeller Univ. 1985–94, Howard Hughes Medical Inst. 1987–96; mem. Global Bd of Dirs Endeavor (non-profit org.), Conservation Int.; mem. Council on Foreign Relations; Montblanc de la Culture Award 1992; sponsor of The Elaine and Jim Wolfensohn Gift. *Achievements include:* Capt. Australian Olympic fencing team. *Publications include:* Voice for the World's Poor: Selected Speeches and Writings 2005, A Global Life: My Journey among Rich and Poor, from Sydney to Wall Street to the World Bank 2010. *Leisure interest:* playing the cello. *Address:* Wolfensohn and Co., 1350 Avenue of the Americas, 29th Floor, New York, NY 10019, USA (office). *Telephone:* (212) 974-0111 (office). *E-mail:* info@wolfensohn.com (office). *Website:* www.wolfensohn.com (office).

WOLFF, Hugh; American conductor and academic; *Stanford and Norma Jean Calderwood Director of Orchestras, New England Conservatory of Music;* b. 21 Oct. 1953, Paris, France; m. Judith Kogan; three s.; ed Harvard Univ.; began career as Asst Conductor, Nat. Symphony Orchestra, with the late Mstislav Rostropovich; Musical Dir New Jersey Symphony 1985–92; Prin. Conductor, Saint Paul Chamber Orchestra 1988–92, Musical Dir 1992–2000; Prin. Conductor, Frankfurt Radio Symphony Orchestra 1997–2006; Stanford and Norma Jean Calderwood Dir of Orchestras, New England Conservatory of Music 2008–; Music Dir Orchestre National de Belgique 2017–; regularly guest-conducts the major orchestras in N America and Europe; Seavor/Nat. Endowment for the Arts Conducting Prize 1985, Cannes Classical Award 2001. *Address:* International Classical Artists, 26–28 Hammersmith Grove, 6th Floor, London, W6 7BA, England (office); New England Conservatory of Music, 290 Huntingdon Avenue, Boston, MA 02115, USA (office). *E-mail:* mwiktorowicz@icartists.co.uk (office). *Website:* www.icartists.co.uk/artists/hugh-wolff (office); necmusic.edu (office); www.nob-onb.be (office); www.hughwolff.com. *Telephone:* (617) 585-1100 (office).

WOLFF, Tobias Jonathan Ansell, BA, MA; American writer; *The Ward W. and Priscilla B. Woods Professor, Stanford University;* b. 19 June 1945, Birmingham, Ala; s. of Arthur S. Wolff and Rosemary Loftus; m. Catherine Dolores Spohn 1975; two s. one d.; ed The Hill School, Univ. of Oxford, UK, Stanford Univ.; served in US Army 1964–68; reporter, Washington Post 1972; Writing Fellow, Stanford Univ. 1975–78, Prof. of English and Creative Writing 1997–, currently The Ward W. and Priscilla B. Woods Prof.; Writer-in-Residence, Ariz. State Univ. 1978–80; Peck Prof. of English, Syracuse Univ. 1980–97; Wallace Stegner Fellowship 1975–76, Nat. Endowment Fellow 1978, 1984; Arizona Council on the Arts and Humanities Fellowship 1980, Guggenheim Fellow 1983; mem. PEN; Fellow, American Acad. of Arts and Sciences 2009–; Fellow, American Acad. of Arts and Letters 2014–; Hon. Fellow, Hertford Coll., Oxford 2000; St Lawrence Award for Fiction 1982, Rea Award for Short Story 1989, Whiting Foundation Award 1989, Los Angeles Times Book Prize for Biography 1989, Amb. Book Award 1990, Lila Wallace/Reader's Digest Award 1993, Lyndhurst Foundation Award 1994, Esquire-Volvo-Waterstones Award for Non-Fiction 1994, Award of Merit, American Acad. of Arts and Letters 2001, Fairfax Award for Lifetime Achievement in Fiction 2007, The Story Prize 2009, Nat. Medal of Arts 2015. *Publications include:* Ugly Rumours 1975, Hunters in the Snow 1981, The Barracks Thief (PEN/Faulkner Award for Fiction 1985) 1984, Back in the World 1985, A Doctor's Visit: The Short Stories of Anton Chekhov (ed.) 1987, The Stories of Tobias Wolff 1988, This Boy's Life 1989, The Picador Book of Contemporary American Stories (ed.) 1993, In Pharaoh's Army: Memories of a Lost War 1994, The Vintage Book of Contemporary American Short Stories 1994, The Best American Short Stories 1994, The Night in Question (short stories) 1996, Writers Harvest 3 (ed.) 2000, Old School 2003, Our Story Begins (short stories) 2008. *Address:* English Department, Building 460, Room 218, Stanford University, Stanford, CA 94305-2087, USA (office). *Telephone:* (650) 723-0504 (office). *Fax:* (650) 725-0755 (office). *E-mail:* twolff@stanford.edu (office). *Website:* english.stanford.edu (office).

WOLFOWITZ, Paul Dundes, BA, PhD; American academic, government official and fmr international organization official; b. 22 Dec. 1943, Brooklyn, New York; s. of Jacob Wolfowitz and Lillian Dundes; m. Clare Selgin; three c.; ed Cornell Univ., Univ. of Chicago; Man. Intern Bureau of the Budget 1966–67; Prof., Dept of Political Science, Yale Univ. 1970–73; mem. staff Arms Control and Disarmament Agency 1973–77, also Special Assst Strategic Arms Limitation Talks (SALT); Deputy Asst Sec. of Defense for Regional Programs 1977–80; Dir of Policy Planning, US Dept of State 1981–82, Asst Sec. of State for E Asia and Pacific Affairs 1982–86; Amb. to Indonesia 1986–89; Under-Sec. of Defense for Policy 1989–93, Deputy Sec. of Defense 2001–05; George F. Kennan Prof. of Nat. Security Strategy, Nat. War Coll. 1993; Visiting Prof., Paul H. Nitze School of Advanced Int. Studies (SAIS), Johns Hopkins Univ. 1980–81, Dean and Prof. of Int. Relations 1994–2001; Pres. World Bank Group 2005–07 (resgnd); Visiting Scholar, American Enterprise Inst. 2007–; mem. Advisory Bd Foreign Affairs, National Interest (journals); numerous awards including Presidential Citizen's Medal, Dept of Defense Distinguished Public Service Medal, Distinguished Honor Award, Distinguished Civilian Service Medal, Arms Control and Disarmament Agency Distinguished Honor Award. *Address:* American Enterprise Institute, 1150 Seventeenth Street, NW, Washington, DC 20036, USA (office). *Telephone:* (202) 862-5948 (office). *Fax:* (202) 862-7177 (office). *Website:* www.aei.org (office).

WOLFRAM, Herwig, DPhil; Austrian historian and academic; b. 14 Feb. 1934, Vienna; s. of Dr Fritz Wolfram and Rosa Wolfram; m. Adelheid Schoerghofer 1958; three s. one d.; ed Univ. of Vienna; Lecturer, Univ. of Vienna 1959–68, Docent 1967; Assoc. Prof., Los Angeles 1968; Assoc. Prof. of Medieval History, Vienna 1969, Prof. of Medieval History and Auxiliary Sciences 1971–2002, Dean Faculty of Arts 1981–83; Dir Institut für Österreichische Geschichtsforschung, Vienna 1983–2002; Fellow, Austrian Acad. of Sciences 1985; Corresp. Fellow, Monumenta Germaniae Historica, Medieval Acad. of America 1990, Royal Historical Soc., London 1995, British Acad. 1996; Theodor-Koerner Foederungspreis 1962, 1964, Kardinal Innitzer-Foederungspreis 1964, Kardinal Innitzerpreis fuer Geisteswissenschaft 1994, Austrian Medal for Science and Art 2000, Cardinal Innitzer Prize 2011. *Television:* adviser to Sturm Ueber Europa I–IV (ZdF, ORF, Arte) 2002. *Publications include:* Splendor Imperii 1963, Intitulatio I 1967, II 1973, III 1988, History of the Goths 1988, Die Geburt Mitteleuropas 1987, Die Goten (seventh edn) 2001, Das Reich und die Germanen 1990–92, Salzburg, Bayern, Oesterreich. Die Conversio Bagoariorum et Carantanorum und die Quellen ihrer Zeit 1995, Grenzen und Räume 1995, The Roman Empire and its Germanic Peoples 1997, Konrad II (990–1039): Kaiser dreier Reiche 2000 (English trans. 2006), Die Goten und ihre Geschichte 2001, Gotische Studien 2005, Die 101 wichtigsten Fragen. Germanen 2008, Die Germanen (ninth edn) 2009, 99 Fragen an die Geschichte Österreichs 2009, Conversio Bagoariorum et Carantanorum 2012, Tassilo III. 2016. *Leisure interests:* sport, music, theatre. *Address:* Sommeregg 13, 5301, Eugendorf, Austria (home). *Telephone:* (6221) 77-43 (home). *Fax:* (6221) 77-43 (home). *E-mail:* herwig.wolfram@univie.ac.at.

WOLFSON, Dirk (Dik) Jacob, PhD; Dutch economist; *Professor Emeritus of Economics, Erasmus University;* b. 22 June 1933, Voorburg; s. of Dirk Wolfson and Gerdina Akkerhuys; m. Anna Maaike Hoekstra 1960; three c.; ed Univ. of Amsterdam; Teaching Asst Univ. of Amsterdam 1961–63; Economist, IMF, Washington, DC 1964–70; Dir (Chief Economist), Econ. Policy Div. Netherlands Treasury Dept 1970–75; Prof. of Public Finance, Erasmus Univ., Rotterdam 1975–86, Prof. of Econs 1992–99, Prof. Emer. 1999–; Rector, Inst. of Social Studies, The Hague 1986–90; mem. Social and Econ. Council 1982–96, Scientific Council for Govt Policy 1990–98; Royal Supervisor, Netherlands Cen. Bank and Chair. Banking Council 1990–99; mem. Senate (Social Democratic Party) 1999–2003; mem. Royal Netherlands Acad. of Arts and Sciences 1989–; Kt, Order of the Netherlands Lion, Commdr, Order of Orange Nassau. *Publications include:* Public Finance and Development Strategy 1979; numerous books and articles on econ. theory and policy. *Leisure interests:* theatre, hiking. *Address:* Aelbrechtskolk 41A, 3025 HB Rotterdam, Netherlands (home). *Telephone:* (10) 4779497 (home). *E-mail:* dwolfson@xs4all.nl (home).

WOLINSKY, Leo C., BA; American journalist and editor; b. 9 May 1949, Los Angeles; m. Roberta Leith (née Wardle); ed Univ. of Southern California; joined Los Angeles Times newspaper in 1977, positions included staff writer South Bay Bureau 1977–79, transportation and environment corresp. Orange Co. Edn 1979–82, City Co. Bureau 1982–85, Sacramento Bureau 1985–87, Asst Bureau Chief 1987–88, Asst City Ed. 1989–90, Calif. Political Ed. 1990–91, City Ed. 1991–93, Metropolitan Ed. 1994–97, Man. Ed. of News 1997–2000, Exec. Ed. Los Angeles Times 2000–01, Deputy Man. Ed. 2001–05, Man. Ed. 2005–08; Ed. Daily Variety 2009–10; Prin., Creative Media (consultancy), Los Angeles 2009–; mem. Bd of Dirs CALmatters 2015–. *Achievements include:* directed teams that won Pulitzer Prizes for coverage of the Los Angeles Riots in 1992 and the Northridge Earthquake in 1994.

WOLPERT, Lewis, CBE, DIC, PhD, FRS, FRSL; British biologist and academic; *Professor Emeritus of Biology as Applied to Medicine, University College, London and Middlesex School of Medicine;* b. 19 Oct. 1929, South Africa; s. of William Wolpert and Sarah Wolpert; m. Elizabeth Brownstein; two s. two d.; ed Univ. of Witwatersrand, Imperial Coll. London, King's Coll. London; civil engineer, S African Council for Scientific and Industrial Research and Israel Water Planning Dept 1951–54; Reader in Zoology, King's Coll. London 1964–66; Prof. of Biology as Applied to Medicine, Dept of Anatomy and Developmental Biology, Univ. Coll., London and Middlesex School of Medicine (fmrly at Middx Medical School) 1966–2005, Prof. Emer. 2005–; presenter, Antenna (BBC 2) 1988–89, TV documentaries and radio interviews with scientists; Chair. MRC Cell Bd 1984–88; Chair. Comm. on the Public Understanding of Science 1994–; Hon. DSc (Leicester) 1996, (Westminster) 1997, (Bath); Hon. DUniv (Open Univ.) 1998; Medanear Lecturer, Royal Soc. 1998, Michael Faraday Medal, Royal Soc. 2000. *Publications include:* A Passion for Science 1988, The Triumph of the Embryo 1991, The Unnatural Nature of Science 1992, Principles of Development 1998, Malignant Sadness: The Anatomy of Depression 1999, Six Impossible Things Before Breakfast 2006, How We Live and Why We Die 2009. *Leisure interests:* cycling, tennis. *Address:* Department of Anatomy and Developmental Biology, University College London, Gower Street, London, WC1E 6BT (office); 63A Belsize Park Gardens, London, NW3 4JN, England (home). *Telephone:* (20) 7679-1320 (office); (20) 7586-7694 (home). *E-mail:* l.wolpert@ucl.ac.uk (office); lewiswolpert@yahoo.com.

WOLSZCZAN, Aleksander, PhD; Polish astronomer; *Evan Pugh Professor of Astronomy and Astrophysics, Pennsylvania State University;* b. 29 April 1946, Szczecinek; m.; one d.; ed Nicolaus Copernicus Univ., Toruń; Dir Astronomy Centre, Nicolaus Copernicus Univ. 1997–2000; Evan Pugh Prof. of Astronomy and Astrophysics, Penn State Univ. 2000–; Kt's Cross, Order of Polonia Restituta 1997; Young Astronomer Prize, Polish Astronomical Soc. 1977, Annual Award, Foundation of Polish Science 1992, Annual Award, Alfred Jurzykowski Foundation 1993, Faculty Scholar Medal, Pa State Univ. 1994, Beatrice M. Tinsley Prize, American Astronomical Soc. 1996, Casimir Funk Natural Sciences Award, Polish Inst. of Arts and Sciences of America 1996, M. Smoluchowski Medal, Polish Physical Soc. *Publications include:* Interstellar Interferometry of the Pulsar PSR 1237+25 1987 (co-author), Experimental Constraints on Strong-Field Relativistic Gravity 1992 (co-author), A Planetary System Around the Millisecond Pulsar PSR 1257+12 1992 (co-author), Confirmation of Earth-Mass Planets Orbiting the Millisecond Pulsar PSR B1257+12 1994, Binary Pulsars and Relativistic Gravitation 1994. *Leisure interests:* climbing, hiking. *Address:* 501 Davey Laboratory, Department of Astronomy and Astrophysics, Penn State University, University Park, PA 16802, USA (office). *Telephone:* (814) 863-1756 (office). *Fax:* (814) 863-3399 (office). *E-mail:* alex@astro.psu.edu (office). *Website:* www.astro.psu.edu (office).

WOLTER, Frank; German international civil servant; b. 22 Nov. 1943, Seehausen, Bavaria; s. of Dr Hans Wolter and Ilse Wolter (née Henrici); m. Birgit Rein 1975; one s. one d.; ed Univs of Freiburg, Saarbrücken and Kiel; Research Fellow, Kiel Inst. of World Econs 1969–74, Head of Research Groups 1974–83; Dir Research Project, German Research Foundation 1977–79; Sr Economist, Econ. Research and Analysis Unit, GATT Secr., Geneva 1983–89, Dir Trade Policies Review Div. 1989–91, Dir Agric. and Commodities 1991. *Publications:* numerous studies and articles on structural change in industry, int. trade and econ. growth. *Leisure interests:* tennis, skiing, classical music, historical literature, golf. *Address:* 38 La Clé des Champs, 01280 Moens, France (home). *E-mail:* wolterfrank@aol.com (home).

WONDER, Stevie; American singer, musician and composer; b. (Steveland Judkins Morris), 13 May 1950, Saginaw, Mich.; step-s. of Paul Hardaway; m. 1st Syreeta Wright 1971 (divorced 1972, died 2004); m. 2nd Yolanda Simmons; m. 3rd Kai Millard Morris; seven c.; ed Michigan School for the Blind; first appeared as solo singer at Whitestone Baptist Church, Detroit 1959; recording artist with Motown, Detroit, initially as Stephen Judkins, 1963–70; Founder and Pres. Black Bull Music Inc. 1970–, Wondirection Records 1982–; Owner, KJLH, LA; Edison Award 1973, Nat. Asscn of Record Merchandisers Best Selling Male Soul Artist of Year 1974, and Presidential Award 1975, Golden Globe (for I Just Called To Say I Love You) 1985, numerous American Music Awards, including Special Award of Merit 1982, Acad. Award for Best Song 1984, Soul Train Heritage Award 1987, numerous Grammy Awards, including Grammy Award (for Superstition) 1974, Grammy Award (for You are the Sunshine of My Life) 1974, Grammy Award (for Living For The City) 1975, Grammy Award (for Boogie on Reggae Woman) 1975, Grammy Award (for I Wish) 1977, Grammy Lifetime Achievement Award 1990, Nelson Mandela Courage Award 1991, IAAAM Diamond Award for Excellence 1991, National Acad. of Songwriters Lifetime Achievement Award 1992, NAACP Image Award 1992, Polar Music Prize, Swedish Acad. of Music, Grammy Award for Best Male Pop Vocal Performance (for From the Bottom of my Heart) 2006, Grammy Award for Best R&B Performance by a Duo or Group with Vocals (for So Amazing, with Beyoncé) 2006, Grammy Award for Best Pop Collaboration with Vocals (with Tony Bennett) 2007, Gershwin Prize for Popular Song, US Library of Congress 2009, Presidential Medal of Freedom 2014. *Film appearances:* Bikini Beach 1964, Muscle Beach Party 1964. *Recordings include:* albums: Little Stevie Wonder: The Twelve-Year-Old Genius 1963, Tribute To Uncle Ray, Jazz Soul, With A Song In My Heart, At The Beach, Uptight 1966, Down To Earth 1966, I Was Made To Love Her 1967, Someday At Christmas 1967, For Once In My Life 1969, My Cherie Amour 1969, Signed Sealed and Delivered 1969, Music Of My Mind 1972, Talking Book 1972, Innervisions (Grammy Award 1974) 1973, Fulfillingness' First Finale (Grammy Award 1975) 1974, Songs in the Key of Life (Grammy Award 1977) 1976, Journey Through the Secret Life of Plants 1979, Hotter than July 1980, Original Musiquarium 1982, Woman in Red (soundtrack) 1984, Love Songs 1984, In Square Circle 1985, Characters 1987, Jungle Fever (film soundtrack) 1991, Conversation Peace 1995, Motown Legends 1995, Natural Wonder 1996, Song Review 1996, At The Close Of A Century 1999, A Time To Love 2005. *Address:* Steveland Morris Productions LLC, 4616 West Magnolia Boulevard, Burbank, CA 91505, USA. *Website:* www.steviewonder.net.

WONG, Andrea, BS, MBA; American television and media executive; *President, International Production, Sony Pictures Television;* ed Massachusetts Inst. of Tech., Stanford Univ. Grad. School of Business; Analyst, High Yield Investment Banking, The First Boston Corpn 1988–90; Strategic Planning Analyst, PepsiCo 1990–91; Researcher, ABC News 1993–94; Exec. Asst to the Pres. of ABC Television 1994–96, Vice-Pres. and Exec. Asst to the Pres. of ABC, Inc. 1996–98, Vice-Pres., Alternative Series, Specials & LateNight, ABC Entertainment 1998–2000, Sr Vice-Pres. 2000–04, Exec. Vice-Pres. 2004–07; Pres. and CEO Lifetime Entertainment Services 2007–10; mem. Bd Liberty Media Corpn 2010–; Pres., Int. Production, Sony Pictures Television and Pres., Int., Sony Pictures Entertainment, London, UK 2011–; Gov. BFI 2014–; mem. Visiting Cttee, MIT Media Lab Cttee of 100, Stanford Women on Bds Initiative; Henry Crown Fellow, Aspen Inst. 2010. *Address:* Sony Pictures Entertainment, 25 Golden Square, London, W1F 9LU, England (office). *Telephone:* (20) 7533-1000 (office). *E-mail:* info@sonypictures.co.uk (office). *Website:* www.sonypictures.com (office).

WONG, Anthony Chau-Sang; Hong Kong actor, screenwriter and film director; b. 2 Sept. 1961, s. of Frederick Perry and Wong Juen Yee; m. Jane Ng Wai Zing; two s.; ed Acad. of Performing Arts; began acting career at ATV; film debut in Flower Street Era 1985; writer and dir films New Tenant 1995 and Top Banana Club 1996; lead singer in punk music band; Chair. Hong Kong Acad. of Performing Arts Alumni Asscn 2010–14, now Hon. Chair.; Co-founder and Co-Artistic Dir, Dionysus Contemporary Theatre 2013–; mem. Hong Kong Arts Devt Council 2014–16;. *Films include:* No Risk, No Gain: Casino Raiders – The Sequel 1990, The Big Score 1990, Dancing Bull 1990, Angel Hunter 1991, Her Fatal Ways 1991, Lucky Encounter 1992, Lady Hunter 1992, The Untold Story (Best Actor Hong Kong Film Award, Golden Horse Award) 1992, Hard Boiled 1992, Executioners 1992, Legal Innocence 1993, The Tigers 1993, Taxi Hunter 1993, Love to Kill 1993, Full Contact 1993, Physical Weapon 1994, Rock n' Roll Cop 1994, Now You See Me, Now You Don't 1994, Highway Man 1994, Husbands and Wives 1995, Another Chinese Cop 1996, Mangkok Story 1996, Blind Romance 1996, Beyond the Cop Line 1996, Young and Dangerous 1996, Armageddon 1997, Midnight Zone 1997, Beast Cops (Best Actor, Hong Kong Film Award 1999, Hong Kong Film Critics Soc. Awards 1999) 1998, Ordinary Heroes 1998, Haunted Mansion 1998, The Deadly Camp 1999, A Man Called Hero 1999, The Mission 1999, When a Man Loves a Woman 2000, Violent Cop 2000, What is a Good Teacher 2000, Ransom Run 2000, Runaway 2001, U-Man 2002, Just One Look 2002, Infernal Affairs (Best Supporting Actor, Hong Kong Film Awards 2003, Golden Horse Awards 2003, Best Actor, Hong Kong Film Critics Soc. 2003) 2002, The Twins Effect 2002, Princess D (Best Supporting Actor, Taiwan Golden Horse Awards) 2002, Infernal Affairs 2 (Hong Kong Film Award) 2003, Infernal Affairs 3 2003, Magic Kitchen 2004, Kung Fu Soccer 2004, House of Fury 2005, Initial D (Best Supporting Actor 2005, Asia-Pacific Film Festival 2005, Hong Kong Film Awards 2006) 2005, Exiled 2006, The Painted Veil 2006, On the Edge 2006, Sweet Revenge 2007, Great Uncle 2007, Mr Cinema 2007, Simply Actors 2007, Secret 2007, The Sun Also Rises 2007, Bullet and Brain 2007, The Mummy: Tomb of the Dragon Emperor 2008, Plastic City 2008, Underdog Knight 2008, True Women for Sale 2008, I Corrupt All Cops 2009, Vengeance 2009, McDull, Kung Fu Kindergarten 2009, Turning Point 2009, Legend of the Fist: The Return of Chen Zhen 2010, Punished 2011, A Beautiful Life 2011, A Simple Life 2011, The Woman Knight of Mirror Lake 2011, White Vengeance 2011, Motorway 2012, McDull: The Pork of Music (voice) 2012, The Four (as Anthony Wong) 2012, Naked Soldier 2012, Westgate Tango 2012, Ip Man: The Final Fight 2013, The Four 2 2013, Golden Chickensss 2014, Si da ming bu 3 2014, Hot Blood Band 2015, 12 Golden Ducks 2015, The Mobfathers 2016, Heaven in the Dark 2016, Cook Up a Storm 2017, 77 Heartbreaks 2017, Still Human 2018, A Home with a View 2019. *Television includes:* The Iron Butterfly (film) 1989, Ta loi ji kong wu (series) 1989, Ng ye tai yong (series) 1990, 1:99 Shorts (film) 2003, Kung Fu Soccer (series) 2004, Jintai-Pan (series) 2009, White Dragon (series) 2018. *Leisure interests:* martial arts, kung fu, singing. *E-mail:* admin@dctheatre .com.hk (office). *Website:* www.dctheatre.com.hk (office).

WONG, Chi-Huey, BS, MS, PhD; American/Taiwanese chemist, biochemist and academic; *Ernest W. Hahn Professor of Chemistry, The Scripps Research Institute;* b. 3 Aug. 1948, Chiayi Co., Taiwan; ed Nat. Taiwan Univ., Massachusetts Inst. of Tech.; Postdoctoral Fellow, Harvard Univ. 1982–83; Asst Prof. of Chem., Texas A&M Univ. 1983–86, Assoc. Prof. 1986–87, Prof. 1987–89; Prof. and Ernest W. Hahn Chair in Chem., Scripps Research Inst. 1989–; Dir Genomics Research Center, Academia Sinica, Taipei 2003–06, now Distinguished Research Fellow; jt appointment as Distinguished Prof. of Chem. and Biochemical Sciences, Nat. Taiwan and Nat. Tsing-Hua Univ.; Scientific Adviser, Max Planck Inst.; Founding Scientist and Chair. Scientific Advisory Bd, Optimer Pharmaceuticals, Inc.; Head of Frontier Research Program on Glycotechnology, RIKEN (Inst. of Physical and Chemical Research, Japan) 1991–99; mem. Bd US Nat. Research Council on Chemical Sciences and Tech. 2000–03; Ed.-in-Chief, Bioorganic & Medicinal Chemistry; mem. Exec. Bd, Tetrahedron Publications; mem. Academia Sinica 1994 (Pres. 2006–), American Acad. of Arts and Sciences 1996, NAS 2002; Searle Scholar Award in Biomedical Sciences 1985, Presidential Young Investigator in Chemistry 1986, ACS Arthur C. Cope Scholar Award 1993, IUPAC Int. Carbohydrate Award 1994, ACS Harrison Howe Award in Chem. 1998, ACS Claude S. Hudson Award in Carbohydrate Chem. 1999, Int. Enzyme Eng Award 1999, Presidential Green Chem. Award 2000, ACS Award for Creative Work in Synthetic Organic Chem. 2006, Humboldt Research Award for Sr Scientists 2008, F.A. Cotton Medal for Excellence in Chemical Research 2008, ACS Arthur C. Cope Award 2012, Wolf Prize in Chem., Wolf Foundation 2014. *Publications:* about 700 papers in professional journals; 105 patents. *Address:* The Scripps Research Institute, 10550 North Torrey Pines Road, BCC-338, La Jolla, CA 92037, USA (office). *Telephone:* (858) 784-2487 (office). *Fax:* (858) 784-2409 (office). *E-mail:* wong@scripps.edu (office). *Website:* www.scripps.edu/research/faculty/wong (office); www.scripps.edu/wong (office).

WONG, Kan Seng, BA, MBA; Singaporean fmr politician and business executive; *Chairman, Ascendas-Singbridge;* b. 8 Sept. 1946; m. Ruth Wong; two s.; ed Univ. of Singapore, London Business School, UK; began career as trainee teacher, Teacher's Training Coll. 1964–67; joined Admin. Service, Ministry of Labour 1970; called to Nat. Service, Singapore Armed Forces 1970–71; Admin. Officer, Ministry of Defence 1971; Head of Navy Personnel, Dir of Manpower Div., then Deputy Sec., Ministry of Defence 1971–81; Personnel Man., Hewlett Packard, Singapore 1981–85; MP (People's Action Party) for Kuo Chuan Constituency 1984–88, Toa Payoh Constituency 1988–91, Thomson Constituency 1981–97, Bishan-Toa Payoh Constituency 1997–2001, 2001–15; Minister of State for Home Affairs, then for Community Devt 1985–86; Minister of State for Communications and Information 1985–87; Acting Minister for Community Devt 1986–87, Minister 1987–91; Leader of the House of Parl. 1987–2007; Second Minister for Foreign Affairs 1987–88, Minister 1988–94; Deputy Chair. of the People's Asscn 1992–2006; Minister for Home Affairs 1994–2010; Deputy Prime Minister 2005–11; mem. Cen. Exec. Cttee, People's Action Party 1987–2015, Second Asst Sec.-Gen. 1992–2004, First Asst Sec.-Gen. 2004; Adviser to Nat. Transport Worker's Union 1985–2012; Chair. Chinese Devt Assistance Council 1992–2004, Trustee 2004–12; apptd Chair. Singbridge 2011, Chair. Ascendas-Singbridge 2015–; mem. Global Advisory Bd, London Business School 1999–; Chair. Advisory Council Temasek Foundation-Connects CLG; mem. Bd of Dirs Bo'ao Forum for Asia, United Overseas Bank 2017–, Chair. 2018–; Public Admin Medal (Silver) 1976, Nat. TUC May Day Medal of Honour 1998. *Leisure interests:* working out at gym, golf. *Address:* Ascendas Pte Ltd, 1 Fusionopolis Place, Galaxis, #10-10, Singapore 138522, Singapore (office). *Telephone:* 66902998 (office). *Fax:* 67749852 (office). *E-mail:* ascendas@ascendas-singbridge.com (office). *Website:* www .ascendas-singbridge.com (office).

WONG, Kar-Wai, BA; Chinese film director and screenwriter; b. 17 July 1958, Shanghai; m. Ye-cheng Chan; one s.; ed Hong Kong Polytechnic; TV drama production training programme Hong Kong TV Broadcasts Ltd 1980–82; Pres. Cannes Film Festival 2006; Pres. of the Jury, Berlin Int. Film Festival 2013; has also directed numerous TV commercials and music videos; Foreign Hon. Fellow, American Acad. of Arts and Sciences 2009; Kt, Ordre national de la Légion d'honneur (France) 2006, Commdr d'Ordre des Arts et des Lettres (France) 2013; Douglas Sirk Award, Filmfest Hamburg 2000, Lifetime Achievement Award, Int. Film Festival of India 2014. *Films:* As Tears Go By 1988, Days of Being Wild (Best Dir Award, Asia-Pacific Film Festival 1991, Best Dir Award, Golden Horse Film Festival 1991, Hong Kong Film Award for Best Dir 1991) 1990, Ashes of Time 1994, Chungking Express (Hong Kong Film Award for Best Dir 1995) 1994, Fallen Angels 1995, Happy Together (Best Dir, Cannes Film Festival 1997) 1997, In the Mood for Love 2000, 2046 (New York Film Critics Circle Award for Best Dir 2005) 2004, My Blueberry Nights 2007, The Lady from Shanghai 2009, The Grandmaster (Asian Film Award for Best Dir 2013, Best Dir Award, Beijing Int. Film Festival 2014, Hong Kong Film Award for Best Dir 2014) 2013, Xuanzang 2016, See You Tomorrow 2016, Europe Raiders 2018. *Television:* Don't Look Now 1981. *Address:* c/o Jet Tone Films, 21/f, Park Commercial Center, 180, Tung lo Wan Road, Hong Kong Special Administrative Region, People's Republic of China (office). *Telephone:* 23361102. *Fax:* 23379849. *E-mail:* jettone@netvigator.com. *Website:* www.jettone.net.

WONG, Penny, BA, LLB; Australian politician; *Shadow Minister for Foreign Affairs;* b. 5 Nov. 1968, Kota Kinabalu, Sabah, Malaysia; ed Scotch Coll., Vic., Univ. of Adelaide; moved to Australia aged eight years; Del., Australian Labor

Party (ALP) State Conventions 1989–94, 1996–, ALP Nat. Conference 2000–; began career as industrial officer, Adelaide 1990–96, barrister and solicitor 1996–2000, legal officer 2000–02; Deputy Convener, ALP State Platform Cttee 1990–94; mem. ALP State Exec. 1996–99, Industry, Infrastructure and Regional Development, ALP Nat. Policy Cttee; fmr Adviser to Carr Govt, NSW; Labor Senator for S Australia 2001–, Deputy Leader in the Senate Feb.–June 2013, Leader 2013–16, Leader of the Opposition 2013–; Minister for Climate Change and Water 2007–10, for Finance 2010–13, Shadow Minister for Employment and Workforce Participation and for Corp. Governance and Responsibility 2004–07, also for Public Admin and Accountability 2006–07, for Trade and Investment 2013–16, for Foreign Affairs 2016–; McKinnon Prize in Political Leadership 2018. *Address:* Electorate Office, Level 4, 19 Gouger Street, Adelaide, SA 5000, Australia (office). *Telephone:* (8) 8212-8272 (office). *Fax:* (8) 8212-8273 (office). *E-mail:* info@pennywong.com.au. *Website:* www.pennywong.com.au.

WONG YICK MING, Dame Rosanna, DBE, JP, BSc, MS, MA, PhD; Hong Kong administrator and government official; b. 15 Aug. 1952, Hong Kong; m. Alfred Tam Yat-chung (divorced 1992); two c.; ed St Stephen's Girls' School, Univ. of Hong Kong, Univ. of Toronto, Canada, London School of Econs. UK, Chinese Univ. of Hong Kong, Univ. of California, Davis, USA; Exec. Dir Hong Kong Fed. of Youth Groups 1980–; Chair. Hong Kong Housing Authority 1993–2000, Complaints Cttee of Hong Kong Ind. Comm. Against Corruption, Children's Thalassaemia Foundation, Social Welfare Advisory Cttee 1988–91, Comm. on Youth 1990–91, Police Complaints Cttee 1993; mem. Legis. Council 1985–91, Exec. Council 1988–91, 1992–97, Exec. Council of Hong Kong Special Admin. Region 1997–2002; Chair. Educ. Comm. 2001, 2003–07; Hong Kong mem., CPPCC Nat. Cttee 2003–; mem. Judicial Officers Recommendation Comm. 2005–07; mem. Bd of Dirs Hongkong and Shanghai Banking Corpn Ltd 1996, Cheung Kong (Holdings) Ltd 2001–15, Hong Kong and Shanghai Hotels, Ltd 2013–; Founding Dir Dragon Foundation; Patron Mother's Choice, Children's Kidney Trust Fund; mem. Co-ordinating Cttee for Children and Youth at Risk, Exec. Cttee Hong Kong Council of Social Service; Hon. Fellow, Hong Kong Inst. of Housing 1994; Hon. mem. Chartered Inst. of Housing 1994; Dr hc (Hong Kong Univ.), (Hong Kong Polytechnic Univ.) 2002. *Address:* c/o Hong Kong and Shanghai Hotels, Limited, 8/F, Saint George's Building, 2 Ice House Street, Central, Hong Kong Special Administrative Region, People's Republic of China. *Website:* www.hshgroup.com/en/about/leadership/people-profiles/dr-rosanna-yick-ming-wong-dbe-jp.

WONGSUWAN, Gen. Prawit; Thai army officer and government official; *Deputy Prime Minister and Minister of Defence;* b. 11 Aug. 1945, Bangkok; s. of Prasert Wongsuwan and Saisunee Wongsuwan; ed Chulachomklao Royal Mil. Acad., Army Command and Gen. Staff Coll., Nat. Defence Coll.; rifle platoon leader, 2nd Bn, 3rd combat team 1969; heavy mortar platoon leader, 21st Regt 1971; Commdr infantry co., 2nd Bn 1974; Operations and Training Officer, 2nd Infantry Bn 1976; Officer Student, Command and Gen. Staff Coll. 1977; Officer, Operations Unit 1979; Deputy Commdr 1st Infantry Bn, 21st Regt 1980; Commdr 2nd Infantry Bn, 2nd Regt 1981; Commdr 3rd Infantry Bn, 12th Regt 1984; Deputy Commdr 12th Infantry Regt 1986, Commdr 1989; Deputy Commdg Gen. 2nd Infantry Div. 1993, Commdg Gen. 1996–97; Deputy Commdg Gen. 1st Army Area 1997–98, Commdg Gen. 2002–03; Commdg Gen. 1st Corps 1998–2000; Army Specialist 2000–01; Asst Chief of Staff, Operations 2001–02; Asst C-in-C Royal Thai Army 2003–04, C-in-C 2004–06; Minister of Defence 2008–11, 2014–; Deputy Prime Minister 2014–; Pres. Nat. Olympic Cttee 2017–; Kt Grand Cross, Most Exalted Order of White Elephant (1st Class) 1997, Kt Grand Cordon, Most Exalted Order of White Elephant (special) 2004, Grand Companion, Most Illustrious Order of Chulachomklao (3rd Class) 2005. *Leisure interests:* jogging, golf. *Address:* Ministry of Defence, Thanon Sanam Chai, Bangkok 10200, Thailand (office). *Telephone:* (2) 222-1121 (office). *Fax:* (2) 226-3117 (office). *E-mail:* webmaster@mod.go.th (office). *Website:* www.mod.go.th (office).

WONGTSCHOWSKI, Pedro, BEng, MEng, DEng; Brazilian chemical engineer and business executive; ed Escola Politécnica da Universidade de São Paulo; with Ultrapar (chemical fertilizer co.) 1970–72, rejoined Ultrapar 1977, officer of Ultrapar 1985–2002, mem. Bd of Dirs Ultraprev 1989–2006, CEO Ultrapar Holdings 2007–12, Dir 2013–; officer of Oxiteno and Oxiteno Nordeste 1992–2006; mem. Bd Arteris SA, Brazilian Asscn for Chemical Eng, Latin American Petrochemical and Chemical Asscn (APLA, Pres. –2012); Vice-Chair. ABIQUIM –2010; Chair. Nat. Asscn for Research, Devt and Eng of Innovative Cos (ANPEI), Nat. Centre for Research in Energy and Materials (CNPEM); mem. Council of Tech. and Competitiveness of FIESP. *Publication:* Indústria Química – Riscos e Oportunidades (Chemical Industry – Risks and Opportunities) 2002. *Address:* Ultrapar Holdings, Avenida Brigadeiro Luiz Antônio 1343, São Paulo 01317-910, Brazil (office). *Telephone:* (11) 3177-7014 (office). *Fax:* (11) 3177-6107 (office). *E-mail:* info@ultra.com.br (office). *Website:* www.ultra.com.br (office).

WONOWIDJOJO, Susilo; Indonesian business executive; *President, PT Gudang Garam Tbk;* b. (Cai Daoping), spent entire career with family business PT Gudang Garam Tbk (clove cigarette mfr), Dir 1990–, Deputy Pres. Dir 2008–09, Pres. Dir Feb.–June 2009, Pres. June 2009–; Founder and Owner PT Matahari Kahuripan Indonesia (Makin Group) (plantation). *Address:* PT Gudang Garam Tbk, Jl. Semampir II/1, Kediri 64121, Indonesia (office). *Telephone:* (354) 682091 (office). *Fax:* (354) 681555 (office). *Website:* www.gudanggaramtbk.com (office).

WOO, John; Chinese film director and producer; b. (Yu Sum Woo), 23 Sept. 1946, Guangzhou; m. Annie Woo Ngau Chun-lung 1976; three c.; ed Matteo Ricci Coll., Hong Kong; family moved to Hong Kong 1951; started making experimental 16mm films in 1967; entered film industry 1969 as production asst Cathay Film Co., asst dir 1971; later joined Shaw Bros as asst ir to Zhang Che; arrived in Hollywood 1992, debut with Hard Target 1993; Silver Bauhinia Star, Hong Kong 2010. *Films include:* The Young Dragons (debut) 1973, The Dragon Tamers, Countdown in Kung Fu, Princess Chang Ping, From Riches to Rags, Money Crazy, Follow the Star, Last Hurrah for Chivalry, To Hell with the Devil, Laughing Times, Sunset Warriors (Heroes Shed No Tears), The Time You Need a Friend, Run Tiger, Run, A Better Tomorrow 1986, A Better Tomorrow II, Just Heroes, The Killer 1989, Bullet in the Head, Once a Thief 1990, Hard Boiled 1992, Hard Target 1993, Broken Arrow 1996, Face/Off 1997, King's Ransom, M: I-2 2000, The Last Word (producer), Windtalkers 2002, The Hire: Hostage 2002, Bulletproof Monk (producer) 2003, Paycheck 2003, All the Invisible Children 2005, Red Cliff 2008, Red Cliff II 2009,

Reign of Assassins 2010, The Killer (producer) 2012, The Crossing 2014. *Television includes:* Once a Thief 1996, Blackjack 1998, The Robinsons: Lost in Space 2004.

WOO, Peter Kwong Ching, JP, MBA, DLitt, DSC; Chinese business executive; *Chairman, Wheelock & Company Ltd;* b. 1946, Shanghai; m. Bessie Pao; ed St Stephen's Coll., Hong Kong, Univ. of Cincinnati and Columbia Business School, USA; family moved to Hong Kong 1949; worked at Chase Manhattan Bank and Worldwide Shipping Group following graduation; Chair. Wheelock & Co. Ltd 1986–96, 2002–; Chair. Wharf (Holdings) Ltd 1986–94, Hon. Chair 1994–; Founding Chair. Wheelock NatWest Ltd 1995–, The Wharf (Holdings) Ltd 1992–, Chair. and Dir Wheelock Properties (Singapore) Ltd 2006–13; Hong Kong (now Hong Kong Special Admin. Region) Affairs Adviser to People's Repub. of China 1993–; non-official mem. Comm. on Strategic Devt 2007–; mem. Int. Advisory Bd Chemical Banking Corpn 1981–, Nat. Westminster Bank PLC 1992–, Gen. Electric 1994–, Elf Aquitaine 1994–; Dir Standard Chartered Bank PLC 1986–89; mem. Hong Kong (now Hong Kong Special Admin. Region)/US Econ. Co-operation Cttee 1989–95, Hong Kong Gov.'s Business Council 1993–97; Chair. Hong Kong (now Hong Kong Special Admin. Region) Environment and Conservation Fund Cttee 1994–, Hong Kong Hosp. Authority 1995–, Hong Kong Trade Devt Council 2000–08; Deputy Chair. Prince of Wales Business Leaders' Forum 1991–; mem. Court of Hong Kong Polytechnic Univ.; cand. for Chief Exec. of Hong Kong 1996; Officer, Order of Leopold (Belgium) 1993, Gold Bauhinia Star 1998, Grand Bauhinia Medal 2012. *Publication:* The Challenge of Hong Kong Plus 1991. *Leisure interests:* golf, tennis. *Address:* Penthouse, Wheelock House, 20 Pedder Street, Central, Hong Kong Special Administrative Region, People's Republic of China. *Website:* www.wheelockcompany.com.

WOO, Sir Po-shing, FCIA, FID; British solicitor; *Chairman, Kailey Enterprises Ltd;* b. 19 April 1929, Hong Kong; s. of Seaward Woo and Ng Chiu Man; m. Helen Woo Fong Shuet Fun (Lady Woo) 1956; four s. one d.; ed La Salle Coll., Hong Kong and King's Coll., London; admitted to practice as solicitor in England and Hong Kong 1960; Notary Public 1966; admitted to practice as barrister and solicitor, Supreme Court of Victoria, Australia 1983; Founder Woo Kwan Lee & Lo, Solicitors and Notaries 1973; Chair. Kailey Enterprises Ltd; Dir Sun Hung Kai Properties Ltd, Henderson Devt Co. Ltd and more than 40 other cos; mem. Inst. of Admin. Man., Inst. of Trade Mark Agents; f. Woo Po Shing Medal in Law (Hong Kong Univ.) 1982, Woo Po Shing Overseas Summer School Travelling Scholarship (Hong Kong Univ.) 1983, The Po-Shing Woo Charitable Foundation 1994, Woo Po Shing Chair of Chinese and Comparative Law (City Univ.) 1995; fmr mem. Council Univ. of Hong Kong; Hon. Voting mem. Hong Kong Jockey Club, Po Leung Kuk Advisory Bd, Tung Wah Group of Hosps; Legal Adviser Chinese Gold and Silver Exchange Soc.; Hon. Pres. and Legal Adviser, South China Athletic Asscn; Patron, Woo Po Shing Gallery of Chinese Bronze, Shanghai Museum, The Auckland Observatory (renamed Sir Po-Shing Woo Auckland Observatory Bldg); Patron, RCA, Tsinghua Univ., Beijing; Fellow, Inst. of Man., King's Coll., London Univ., Hong Kong Man. Asscn; Hon. Prof., Nankai Univ. of Tianjin, China; Chevalier, Ordre des Arts et des Lettres 2004; Hon. LLD (City Univ. Hong Kong), Hon. LLB (King's Coll. London); World Fellowship of Duke of Edinburgh's Award. *Leisure interests:* travelling, viewing and collecting antiques including Chinese paintings, bronzes and ceramics, racehorses. *Address:* Kailey Enterprises Ltd, 21-23/F Kailey Tower, 14-16 Stanley Street, Central, Hong Kong Special Administrative Region, People's Republic of China (office). *Telephone:* 2526-6373 (office). *Fax:* 2845-1514 (home). *Website:* www.kailey.com.hk (office).

WOOD, Adrian John Bickersteth, CBE, MA, MPA, PhD; British economist and academic; *Professor Emeritus of International Development, University of Oxford;* b. 25 Jan. 1946, Woking, Surrey; s. of John H. F. Wood and Mary E. B. Wood (née Ottley); m. Joyce M. Teitz 1971; two d.; ed Bryanston School, King's Coll., Cambridge, Harvard Univ., USA; Fellow, King's Coll. Cambridge 1969–77; Asst Lecturer, then Lecturer, Univ. of Cambridge 1973–77; Economist, Sr Economist, IBRD 1977–85; Professorial Fellow, Inst. of Devt Studies, Univ. of Sussex 1985–2000; Chief Economist, Dept for Int. Devt 2000–05; Prof. of Int. Devt, Univ. of Oxford 2005–11, Prof. Emer. 2011–; Harkness Fellowship 1967–69. *Publications include:* A Theory of Profits 1975, A Theory of Pay 1978, Poverty and Human Development (with others) 1981, China: Long-Term Development Issues and Options (with others) 1985, North-South Trade, Employment and Inequality 1994. *Leisure interests:* music, art, tennis. *E-mail:* adrian.wood@qeh.ox.ac.uk (office).

WOOD, Anne, CBE, FRTS; British television producer; *Chairman and Creative Director, Ragdoll Productions Ltd;* b. 18 Dec. 1937, Spennymoor, Co. Durham; m. Barrie Wood; one s. one d.; teacher of English Language and Literature 1960s; f. Books For Your Children magazine; co-creator and producer, TV programme The Book Tower 1979, Ragdolly Anna; Head of Children's Programmes TV AM (ITV) 1982–84; f. Ragdoll Ltd (TV production co.) 1984, Creative Dir 1984–, currently also Chair.; creator of Pob, Rosie and Jim, Tots TV, Brum, Open a Door, Teletubbies (shown in 120 countries worldwide), Boohbah, In The Night Garden, Dipdap, Twirlywoos; Hon. LittD; Eleanor Farjeon Award for Services to Children's Books 1969, Ronald Politzer Award 1974, BAFTA 1979, 1982, 1996, 1997, Prix Jeunesse 1980, 1996, Baird Medal Royal TV Soc. 1997; numerous awards for Teletubbies including Grand Prize, Winner Pre-School Educ. Category, Prize Int. Contest (Japan) 1997, Children's BAFTA for Best Pre-School Programme 1998, Indies Nickleodeon UK Children's Award 1999, five awards at Int. Licensing Industry Merchandisers' Asscn 1999, BBC Audiocall Children's Award 2000, Veuve Clicquot Award for Business Woman of the Year 1999, BAFTA Special Award for Outstanding Contrib. in Children's TV and Film 2000, Olswang Business Award, Women in Film and Television 2003, Harvey Lee Award, Broadcasting Press Guild 2007. *Leisure interests:* gardening, reading. *Address:* Ragdoll Productions Ltd, 9 Timothys Bridge Road, Stratford Enterprise Park, Stratford-upon-Avon, Warwicks., CV37 9NQ, England (office). *Telephone:* (1789) 404100 (office). *Fax:* (1789) 404136 (office). *E-mail:* info@ragdoll.co.uk. *Website:* www.ragdoll.co.uk (office).

WOOD, Brian Kuan; American writer and artist; was based in Cairo 2000–05, produced publs and sound projects in collaboration with artists, and began an on-line journal with artist Iman Issa featuring artists based in Cairo and Alexandria; with Anton Vidokle and Julieta Aranda, began a set of projects related to their interests, including an art collective (e-flux), a school (unitednationsplaza; Night

School), an archive (e-flux video rental; Martha Rosler Library) and an activist group (The Next Documenta Should Be Curated By an Artist) 2008; co-f., with Julieta Aranda, a time bank for artists, curators, writers and others in the arts to exchange their time and skills 2008, has nearly 4,000 members and operates branches in The Hague, Moscow, Berlin, Frankfurt and other cities; co-f. imprint, with the Sternberg Press, Berlin, that publishes a series of paperback readers consisting of monographic publs and thematic compilations of essays 2008; Visiting Prof. Ashkal Alwan 2013–14; currently faculty mem. Master of Arts degree in Curatorial Practice by School of Visual Arts: a two-year program that focuses on relevant study of history, research and theory. *Publications include:* Selected Maria Lind Writing (ed.) 2010; writing has appeared in Bidoun, CAC Interviu, Paletten, e-flux journal and various artist-initiated platforms and publs. *Address:* e-flux, 311 East Broadway, New York, NY 10002, USA (office). *E-mail:* info@e-flux.com (office). *Website:* www.e-flux.com (office); www.unitednationsplaza.org (office); www.macp.sva.edu (office).

WOOD, David M., BSc; British/American oil industry executive; ed Univ. of Nottingham; served in various positions in exploration for oil co. 1980–94; Man. of Frontier Exploration, Murphy Oil Corpn 1994–95, Gen. Man. Frontier Exploration 1995–97, Vice-Pres. of Frontier Exploration and Production 1997–99, Sr Vice-Pres. 1999–2003, Pres. Murphy Exploration & Production Co.-International 2003–06, Exec. Vice-Pres. of Worldwide Exploration and Production Operations 2007–08, Pres. Murphy Exploration & Production Co. for Murphy Oil Corpn 2007–08, mem. Bd of Dirs, Pres. and CEO Murphy Oil Corpn 2009–12 (resgnd).

WOOD, Elijah; American actor; b. 28 Jan. 1981, Cedar Rapids, Iowa. *Films include:* Back to the Future Part II 1989, Internal Affairs 1990, Avalon 1990, Paradise 1991, Radio Flyer 1992, Forever Young 1992, The Adventures of Huck Finn 1993, The Good Son 1993, North 1994, The War 1994, Flipper 1996, The Ice Storm 1997, Deep Impact 1998, The Faculty 1998, Black and White 1999, The Bumblebee Flies Anyway 1999, Chain of Fools 2000, The Lord of the Rings: The Fellowship of the Ring 2001, Ash Wednesday 2002, The Adventures of Tom Thumb and Thumbelina (voice) 2002, Try Seventeen 2002, The Lord of the Rings: The Two Towers 2002, Spy Kids 3-D: Game Over 2003, The Lord of the Rings: The Return of the King 2003, Eternal Sunshine of the Spotless Mind 2004, Christmas on Mars 2005, Sin City 2005, Hooligans 2005, Everything Is Illuminated 2005, Paris, je t'aime 2006, Bobby 2006, Legend of Spyro: A New Beginning (voice) 2006, Happy Feet (voice) 2006, Day Zero 2007, The Oxford Murders 2008, 9 (voice) 2008, The Romantics 2010, The Hobbit: An Unexpected Journey 2012. *Address:* c/o William Morris Agency, Inc., 1 William Morris Place, Beverly Hills, CA 90212, USA. *Telephone:* (310) 859-4550. *Fax:* (310) 248-5650. *E-mail:* nd@wma.com. *Website:* www.wma.com.

WOOD, L. John, QSO, MA; New Zealand diplomatist and academic; *Chancellor, University of Canterbury;* b. 31 March 1944, Kaikoura; s. of Lionel Wood and Margaret Wood; m. 1st Rosemary Taunt 1969 (died 1995); one s.; m. 2nd Rose Newell; ed Lincoln Country Dist High School, Christchurch Boys' High School, Univ. of Canterbury, Balliol Coll., Oxford; joined Ministry of Foreign Affairs 1969, seconded to Treasury 1971–72, Second Sec., later First Sec., Embassy in Tokyo 1973–76, seconded to Prime Minister's Dept 1976–78, First Sec., later Counsellor and Consul-Gen. Bonn 1978–82, at Ministry of Foreign Affairs 1982–83, Minister, Deputy Chief of Mission, Embassy in Washington, DC 1984–87, Amb. to Iran (also accred to Pakistan and Turkey) 1987–90, Dir N Asia Div., Ministry of External Relations and Trade 1990–91, Deputy Sec. Econ. and Trade Relations 1991–94, Amb. to USA 1994–98, 2001–06, Deputy Sec. External Econ. and Trade Policy, Ministry of Foreign Affairs and Trade 1991–94, 1998–2002; Adjunct Prof. of Political Science, Univ. of Canterbury 2006–, Trustee, Univ. of Canterbury Foundation 2006–, elected by Court of Convocation to Univ. of Canterbury Council 2007, 2010–, Pro-Chancellor 2008–10, Chancellor 2012–; Pres. Canterbury History Foundation 2013–; mem. Advisory Bd NZ/US Council 2006–; mem. Governing Bd Econ. Research Inst. for ASEAN and East Asia (ERIA), Jakarta 2008–; mem. Council, Lincoln Univ. 2013–; Chief Crown Treaty of Waitangi Negotiator 2007–; mem. Canterbury Museum Trust Bd 2013, Te Urewera Governing Bd 2014–; Companion, Queen's Service Order for Public Service 2006, Companion, New Zealand Order Of Merit 2015; Hon. DLitt (Canterbury) 2006; Consumers for World Trade Hall of Fame 2004, Paul Harris Fellow, Rotary Int. 2005. *Publications include:* Negotiating within Washington: Thrown in at the Deep End – A New Zealand Diplomat Looks Back, In 'American Negotiating Behaviour, Wheeler-Dealers, Legal Eagles, Bullies, And Preachers' 2010. *Leisure interests:* rare books and bindings, New Zealand literature, sport, V8 cars. *Address:* 'Blue Ridge', 215 Bay Paddock Road, R.D.I. Hapuku, Kaikoura (home); Office of the Chancellor, University of Canterbury, Private Bag 4800, Christchurch, New Zealand (office). *Telephone:* (3) 319-7074 (home). *E-mail:* blue-duck@xtra.co.nz (home). *Website:* www.posc.canterbury.ac.nz (office).

WOOD, Mark William, BA (Hons), MA; British journalist and broadcasting executive; *CEO, Ten Alps PLC;* b. 28 March 1952, Rochester, Kent; m.; one d. one s.; ed Univs of Leeds, Warwick and Oxford; joined Reuters 1976, Corresp. in Vienna, East Berlin and Moscow 1977–85, Chief Corresp., W Germany 1985–87, European Ed. 1987–89, Ed.-in-Chief 1989–2000, Exec. Dir 1990–96, Chair. Visnews Reuters TV 1992–2002, Man. Dir Reuters Contents Partners 2000–02; Dir (non-Exec.) Ind. TV News (ITN) 1993–2002, Chair. 1998–2009, CEO 2003–09; Chair. Scottish News Consortium 2010; CEO Future Publishing PLC 2011–14; CEO Ten Alps PLC (broadcasting and production co.) 2014–; Chair. Meteor GmbH 2000–02; Dir London News Radio 1999–2002; Chair. Museums, Libraries and Archives Council 2003–08. *Address:* Ten Alps PLC, Commonwealth House, 1 New Oxford Street, High Holborn, London, WC1A 1NU, England (office). *Telephone:* (20) 7878-2311 (office). *Website:* www.tenalps.com (office).

WOOD, Sir Martin (Francis), Kt, OBE, MA, FRS, DL; British engineer and business executive; b. 19 April 1927; s. of Arthur Henry Wood and Katharine Mary Altham Wood (née Cumberlege); m. Audrey Buxton Wood (née Stanfield) 1955; one s. one d. one step-s. one step-d.; ed Gresham's, Trinity Coll., Cambridge, Imperial Coll., London, Christ Church, Oxford; with Nat. Coal Bd 1953–55; Sr Research Officer, Clarendon Lab., Oxford of Oxford 1956–69; f. Oxford Instruments PLC 1959, Chair. 1959–83, Deputy Chair. 1983–, now Hon. Pres.; Chair. Nat. Comm. for Superconductivity 1987–91; mem. Advisory Bd for Research Councils 1983–89, ACOST 1990–93, Central Lab. of Research Councils 1995–98; Dir Orbit Precision

Machining Ltd 1965–, Oxford Seedcorn Capital Ltd 1986–, Oxford Ventures Group Ltd 1988–, ISIS Innovation Ltd 1989–, Oxford Innovation Ltd 1989–, Newport Tech. Group Ltd 1989–, FARM Africa Ltd 1985–; Tech. Consultant African Medical and Research Foundation; f. Northmoor Trust (for nature conservation), Oxford Trust (for encouragement of study and application of science and tech.); Trustee Oxon. Council for Voluntary Action 1994–; Fellow, Wolfson Coll., Oxford 1967–94, Hon. Fellow 1994; Hon. Fellow, UMIST 1989; Hon. DSc (Cranfield Inst. of Tech.) 1983; Hon. DTech (Loughborough Univ. of Tech.) 1985; Hon. DEng (Birmingham) 1997; Hon. DUniv (Open Univ.) 1999; Mullard Medal, Royal Soc. 1982; Sir Martin Wood Science Prize for Japan awarded annually by Millennium Science Forum; Oxford Instruments est. Sir Martin Wood China Prize for research in physical science 2013.

WOOD, Michael M.; American business executive and fmr diplomatist; *Chairman, Investment Committee, Redwood Investments;* b. 1947; m. Judy Wood; one s. one d.; Co-founder and CEO Hanley Wood, LLC 1976–2005, mem. Bd 2005; mem. Bd of Advisors, Veronis Suhler Stevenson 2005; f. Redwood Investments, LLC 2005, currently Chair. Investment Cttee; mem. US del. attending inauguration of Pres. Lucio Gutierrez Borbua of Ecuador 2003; organized Building the American Dream housing industry round table with US Pres. Ronald Reagan 1984; Amb. to Sweden 2006–09; mem. Bd of Dirs Capital Partners for Education, Washington, DC; fmr mem. Harvard Jt Center for Housing Studies; has served on Nat. Asscn of Home Builders Long-Range Planning Cttee; mem. Bd of Trustees American-Scandinavian Foundation; Commdr Grand Cross, Order of the Polar Star (Sweden) 2009; Hon. DHumLitt (Kettering Univ.) 2009; Top Executive of the Year Award, Media Business magazine 2005. *Leisure interests:* mountain biking, golf. *Address:* Redwood Investments, PO Box 25327, Washington, DC 20027, USA (office). *Telephone:* (202) 333-1395 (office). *E-mail:* mail@redwoodinvestments.net (office). *Website:* www.redwoodinvestments.net (office).

WOOD, Sir Peter John, Kt, CBE; British insurance industry executive and entrepreneur; *Chairman, Esure;* b. 1946, Surrey, England; m. (divorced); five d.; Founder and CEO Direct Line Insurance 1985–96, Chair. 1996–97; Chair. Privilege Insurance 1993–98; Vice-Chair. Plymouth Rock Co. 1994–; Founder and Chair. Esure 2000– (purchased Lloyds Banking Group's 70% stake in the co. 2010), First Alternative 2003–, also set up two insurance cos in USA, Response 1995 and Homesite 1997, involvement ended 2004; est. a women-only specialist insurance brand, Sheilas' Wheels 2005; Dir (non-exec.), The Economist Newspaper Ltd 1998–2004. *Address:* Esure at The Observatory, Reigate, Surrey, RH2 0SG, England (office). *Telephone:* (1737) 222222 (office). *Fax:* (1737) 235000 (office). *E-mail:* info@esure.com (office). *Website:* www.esure.com (office).

WOOD, Richard; British diplomatist; *Ambassador to Norway;* m. Xavier Piot; ed Leeds Polytechnic; Press Officer and Minister for Africa, FCO 1997–2001, Head of Future of Europe 2001–02, First Sec. (Human Rights) to UN 2002–07, Consul-Gen. in South Africa 2007–11, in Iraq 2011–12, Deputy Head, Int. Orgs. Dept, FCO 2012–14, Head of Sanctions and Econ. Security June–Oct. 2014, Counsellor, Embassy in Washington, DC, USA Oct. 2014–Sept. 2015, Head of EU Dept, FCO 2015–18, Amb. to Norway 2018–. *Address:* British Embassy, Thomas Heftyesgate 8, 0244 Oslo, Norway (office). *Telephone:* 23-13-27-00 (office). *Fax:* 23-13-27-41 (office). *E-mail:* UKinNorway@fco.gov.uk (office). *Website:* www.gov.uk/world/organisations/british-embassy-oslo (office).

WOOD, Ronald (Ronnie) David; British musician (guitar, bass guitar); b. 1 June 1947, Hillingdon, London, England; m. 1st; one s.; m. 2nd Jo Howard 1985 (divorced 2009); one s. one d.; guitarist with Jeff Beck Group 1968–69, The Faces 1969–75, The Rolling Stones 1976–; tours worldwide; has also played with Bo Diddley, Rod Stewart, Jerry Lee Lewis; Nordoff-Robbins Silver Clef 1982, Grammy Lifetime Achievement Award 1986, Ivor Novello Award for Outstanding Contribution to British Music 1991. *Recordings include:* albums: with Jeff Beck Group: Truth 1968, Beck-Ola 1969; with The Faces: First Step 1970, Long Player 1971, A Nod's As Good As A Wink... To A Blind Horse 1971, Ooh La La 1973, Coast To Coast Overtures and Beginners 1974; with The Rolling Stones: Black And Blue 1976, Some Girls 1978, Emotional Rescue 1980, Tattoo You 1981, Still Life 1982, Undercover 1983, Dirty Work 1986, Steel Wheels 1989, Flashpoint 1991, Voodoo Lounge 1994, Stripped 1995, Bridges to Babylon 1997, Forty Licks 2002, Live Licks 2004, A Bigger Bang 2005, Blue & Lonesome (Grammy Award for Best Traditional Blues Album 2018) 2016; solo: I've Got My Own Album To Do 1974, Now Look 1976, Mahoney's Last Stand 1976, Gimme Some Neck 1979, 1234 1981, Live At The Ritz 1988, Slide On This 1992, Slide On Live: Plugged In And Standing 1994, Live & Eclectic 2000, Not For Beginners 2002, Live At Electric Ladyland 2002, Always Wanted More 2003, Buried Alive 2006, The First Barbarians 2007, I Feel Like Playing 2010. *Film:* Shine a Light 2007. *Publications include:* According to the Rolling Stones (autobiography, jtly) 2003, Ronnie Wood: The Autobiography 2007. *Website:* www.rollingstones.com; www.ronniewood.com.

WOOD, Sir (James) Sebastian (Lamin), Kt, KCMG, CMG; British diplomatist; *Ambassador to Germany;* b. 6 April 1961; m.; four c.; EC Dept (External), FCO 1983, Thai language training, Thailand 1984–86, Second, later First Sec., Bangkok 1986–89, Security Policy Dept, FCO 1989–91, Mandarin language training, Taiwan 1991, First Sec. and Consul for Macao BTC, Hong Kong 1992–94, First Sec., UKREP Jt Liaison Group, Hong Kong 1994–96, Security Policy Dept then UN Dept, FCO 1996–98, Prin. Pvt. Sec. to Cabinet Sec. 1998–2000, Weatherhead Centre for Int. Affairs, Harvard Univ., USA 2000–01, Counsellor (Political), Washington, DC 2001–05, Dir Asia Pacific, FCO 2005–08; secondment to Rolls-Royce Group 2008–09; Amb. to China 2010–15, to Germany 2015–. *Address:* British Embassy, Wilhelmstraße 70–71, 10117 Berlin, Germany (office). *Telephone:* (30) 204570 (office). *E-mail:* ukingermany@fco.gov.uk (office). *Website:* www.gov.uk/government/world/organisations/british-embassy-berlin (office); www.gov.uk/government/world/germany (office).

WOOD, William B., III, PhD; American biologist and academic; *Distinguished Professor Emeritus, University of Colorado;* b. 19 Feb. 1938, Baltimore, Md; s. of Dr W. Barry Wood, Jr and Mary L. Hutchins; m. Renate Marie-Elisabeth Hartisch 1961; two s.; ed Harvard Coll., Stanford Univ. and Univ. of Geneva, Switzerland; NAS-Nat. Research Council Postdoctoral Fellow, Univ. of Geneva 1964; Asst Prof. of Biology, California Inst. of Tech. 1965–68, Assoc. Prof. 1968–70, Prof. 1970–77; Prof. of Molecular Biology, Univ. of Colorado, Boulder 1977–2008, Distinguished

Prof. Emer. 2008–, Chair. of Dept 1978–83; Co-Chair. NRC Cttee tasked with initiating the Nat. Acads Summer Inst. on Undergraduate Educ. 2003; Ed.-in-Chief CBE-Life Sciences Education 2005–10; mem. NAS, American Acad. of Arts and Sciences, AAAS, American Soc. of Biological Chemists, Soc. for Developmental Biology; US Steel Award in Molecular Biology, NAS 1969, Bruce Alberts Award, American Soc. for Cell Biology 2004, Viktor Hamburger Outstanding Educator Prize, Soc. for Developmental Biology 2013. *Publications include:* Biochemistry, A Problems Approach (co-author) 1974, 1981, Molecular Design in Living Systems 1974, The Molecular Basis of Metabolism 1974, Molecular Biology of Eucaryotic Cells (co-author) 1975, Immunology (co-author) 1978, 1984, The Nematode Caenorhabditis Elegans (ed.) 1988, Learning and Understanding (report) 2002; articles in professional journals. *Leisure interests:* music, tennis, camping. *Address:* Molecular, Cellular and Developmental Biology, University of Colorado, PORT B345A, Boulder, CO 80309-0347, USA (office). *Telephone:* (303) 492-6680 (office); (303) 492-2272 (Lab.) (office). *E-mail:* wood@colorado.edu (office). *Website:* mcdb.colorado.edu/directory/wood_b.html (office).

WOOD OF ANFIELD, Baron (Life Peer), cr. 2011, of Tonbridge in the County of Kent; **Lord Stewart Martin Wood,** MA, PhD; British politician, political adviser, academic, writer and commentator; *Fellow in Practice, Blavatnik School of Government, University of Oxford;* b. 25 March 1968, Kent, England; s. of Brian Wood and Gisela Wood; m. Camilla Bustani; two c.; ed Univ. of Oxford, Harvard Univ., USA, Wissenschaftszentrum Berlin, Germany; Lecturer, Univ. of Oxford 1996–2011, Fellow in Politics, Magdalen Coll. Oxford, Fellow in Pratice, Blavatnik School of Govt, Univ. of Oxford 2015–; co-f. 'Third Way' think-tank, Nexus 1996; became Special Adviser to the Treasury under Chancellor of the Exchequer, Gordon Brown 2001; Sr Foreign Policy Adviser to Prime Minister Gordon Brown 2007–10, also advised Prime Minister on NI and culture, media and sport; Communications Chief for Labour Party Leader, Ed Miliband 2010–11; mem. (Labour), House of Lords 2011–; Shadow Minister without Portfolio 2011–15; Shadow Spokesperson (Cabinet Office) 2011–15; Chair. UNA (UK) 2016–; mem. Bd of Dirs Janus Henderson Diversified Income Trust 2017–, The Good Law Project 2018–; mem. Bd, English Stage Co., Royal Court Theatre 2006–, Marshall Scholarship Comm. 2016–; Fulbright Scholar 1989–90. *Leisure interests:* movies, playing music, theatre, cricket, Liverpool Football Club. *Address:* House of Lords, Westminster, London, SW1A 0PW, England (office). *Telephone:* (20) 7219-5854 (office). *E-mail:* stewart.wood@parliament.uk (office). *Website:* www.parliament.uk/biographies/lords/lord-wood-of-anfield/4217 (office).

WOODLAND, Alan Donald, PhD, FASSA; Australian economist and academic; *Scientia Professor, School of Economics, Australian School of Business, University of New South Wales;* b. 4 Oct. 1943, Dorrigo, NSW; s. of C. J. Woodland and E. Shephard; m. Narelle Todd 1966; one s. two d.; ed Univ. of New England, Armidale, NSW; Lecturer, Univ. of New England 1967–69; Asst Prof., Univ. of British Columbia, Canada 1969–74, Assoc. Prof. 1974–78, Prof. of Econs 1978–81; Prof. of Econometrics and Australian Professorial Fellow, Faculty of Econs and Business, Univ. of Sydney 1982–2008; Scientia Prof., School of Econs, Australian School of Business, Univ. of New South Wales 2008–; Jt Ed. The Economic Record 1987–92; Fellow, Reserve Bank 1981; Fellow, Econometric Soc.; Distinguished Economist Award, Econ. Soc. of Australia 2008. *Publications include:* International Trade and Resource Allocation 1982, International Trade Policy and the Pacific Rim, Institute of Economic Affairs Conference Vol. Number 120 (co-ed.) 1999, Economic Theory and International Trade: Essays in Honour of Murray C. Kemp (ed.) 2002, The Economics of Illegal Immigration (co-author) 2005, Elsevier Handbook on the Economics of Population Aging (co-ed.) 2016. *Leisure interests:* bridge, tennis. *Address:* Room 416, School of Economics, Australian School of Business Building, University of New South Wales, Sydney, NSW 2052 (office); 5 Rosebery Road, Killara, NSW 2071, Australia (home). *Telephone:* (2) 9385-9707 (office); (2) 9416-3100 (home). *Fax:* (2) 9313-6337 (office). *E-mail:* a.woodland@unsw.edu.au (office). *Website:* www.asb.unsw.edu.au/schools/economics (office).

WOODROW, William (Bill) Robert, DipAD, RA; British artist and sculptor; b. 1 Nov. 1948, nr Henley-on-Thames, Oxon., England; s. of Geoffrey W. Woodrow and Doreen M. Fasken; m. Pauline Rowley 1970; one s. one d.; ed Barton Peveril Grammar School and Winchester, St Martin's and Chelsea Schools of Art; works in numerous public collections in UK and abroad; Trustee, Tate Gallery 1996–2001, Imperial War Museum 2003–11, Roche Court Educational Trust 2008–17; Gov. Univ. of the Arts, London 2003–08; elected to Royal Acad. of Arts 2002; finalist in Turner Prize 1986, winner, Anne Gerber Award, Seattle Museum of Art, USA 1988. *Publications include:* Bill Woodrow, Sculpture 1980–86, A Quiet Revolution – Recent British Sculpture, Bill Woodrow, Eye of the Needle, Sculptures 1987–1989, Bill Woodrow, XXI Bienal de São Paulo 1991, In Awe of the Pawnbroker 1994, Fools' Gold 1996, Lead Astray 2004, Brood 2007, The sculpture of Bill Woodrow 2013. *E-mail:* bill@billwoodrow.com (office). *Website:* www.billwoodrow.com.

WOODRUFF, Judy Carline, BA; American broadcast journalist; *Co-anchor and Managing Editor, PBS Newshour;* b. 20 Nov. 1946, Tulsa, Okla; d. of William Henry Woodruff and Anna Lee Woodruff (née Payne); m. Albert R. Hunt, Jr 1980; two s. one d.; ed Meredith Coll., Duke Univ.; News Announcer and Reporter WAGA-TV, Atlanta 1970–75; News Corresp. NBC News, Atlanta 1975–76; White House Corresp., NBC News, Washington 1977–83; Corresp., MacNeil-Lehrer News Hour, PBS, Washington 1983–93, Sr Corresp. and Political Ed. The News Hour With Jim Lehrer (now PBS Newshour) 2007–13, Co–anchor and Man. Ed. 2013–; Anchor and Sr Corresp. Cable News Network (CNN) 1993–2005, also anchored Judy Woodruff's Inside Politics; anchor for Frontline (PBS documentary series) 1983–90; Visiting Fellow, Joan Shorenstein Center on the Press, Politics and Public Policy, Harvard Univ. 2005–; Visiting Prof. of Media and Politics, Duke Univ. 2006; mem. Bd of Advisers Henry Grady School of Journalism, Univ. of Georgia 1979–82, Bd of Visitors Wake Forest Univ. 1982–88, Bd of Advisers Benton Fellowship in Broadcast Journalism, Univ. of Chicago 1984–90, Families and Work Inst. 1989–, Freedom Forum First Amendment Center 1992–, Comm. on Women's Health 1993–, Radio and TV News Dirs' Foundation 1994–; Co-Chair. Int. Women's Media Foundation 1991– (Founder, Dir 1989–); mem. Nat. Acad. of TV Arts and Sciences, White House Corresps Asscn; Trustee, Duke Univ. 1985–97, now Trustee Emer.; Knight Fellowship in Journalism, Stanford Univ. 1985–99, Edward Weintal Award 1987, Joan Shorenstein Barone Award 1987, Helen Bernstein Award for Excellence in Journalism, New York Public Library 1989, Pres.'s 21st Century Award, Nat. Women's Hall of Fame 1994, CableAce Award for Best Newscaster 1995, CableAce Best Anchor Team Award 1996, Allen H. Neuharth Award for Excellence in Journalism 1995, News and Documentary Emmy Award 1997, Int. Matrix Award, Asscn for Women in Communications 2003, Leonard Zeidenberg First Amendment Award, Radio-TV News Dir Asscn and Foundation 2003; elected to Georgia Asscn of Broadcasters Hall of Fame 2003. *Publication:* This is Judy Woodruff at the White House 1982. *Address:* The PBS Newshour, 3620 27th Street South, Arlington, VA 22206-2350, USA (office). *Telephone:* (703) 998-2481 (office). *Fax:* (703) 998-4154 (office). *E-mail:* newshour@pbs.org (office). *Website:* www.pbs.org/newshour/author/jwoodruff (office).

WOODS, Darren W., BSc, MBA; American petroleum industry executive; *Chairman and CEO, ExxonMobil Corporation;* b. 1965, Wichita, KS; ed Texas A&M Univ., Northwestern Univ. Kellogg School of Man.; joined Exxon Co. International as planning analyst 1992, becoming Vice-Pres., ExxonMobil Chemical Co. 2005–08, Dir of Refining for Europe, Africa, and the Middle East, ExxonMobil Refining and Supply Co., Brussels 2008–10, Vice-Pres. of supply and transportation, Fairfax, Virginia 2010–12, Pres., ExxonMobil Refining and Supply Co. and Vice-Pres., ExxonMobil Corpn 2012–14, Sr Vice-Pres., ExxonMobil Corpn 2014–16, mem. Bd of Dirs 2016–, Pres., ExxonMobil Corpn 2016–17, Chair. and CEO 2017–; mem. Bd US-China Business Council, Texas A&M Univ. Engineering Advisory Council 2015. *Address:* ExxonMobil Corporation, 5959 Las Colinas Boulevard, Irving, TX 75039-2298, USA (office). *Telephone:* (972) 444-1000 (office). *Website:* corporate.exxonmobil.com (office).

WOODS, Eldrick Tont (Tiger); American professional golfer; b. 30 Dec. 1975, Cypress, Calif.; s. of Lt-Col Earl Woods and Kultida Woods; m. Elin Nordegren 2004 (divorced 2010); one s. one d.; ed Stanford Univ.; winner Int. Jr World Championship 1984–91, Nat. Youth Classic 1990, US Jr Amateur Championship 1991 (youngest winner), 1992, 1993, US Amateur Championships 1994 (youngest winner), 1995, 1996; turned professional 1996; winner, Las Vegas Invitational competition 1996, Walt Disney Classic 1996, Honda Asian Classic 1997, Mercedes Championships 1997, 2000, US Masters 1997 (youngest winner, broke records for lowest score and greatest margin of victory), 2001, 2002, 2005, Bell South Classic 1998, US PGA Championship 1999, 2000, 2006, 2007, Nat. Car Rental Golf Classic 1999, WGC American Express Championship 1999, 2006, AT&T Pebble Beach Nat. Pro-Am 2000, Bay Hill Invitational 2000, 2001, 2002 US Open 2000, 2002, 2008, British Open 2000, 2005, 2006, PGA Tour's Arnold Palmer Invitational Golf Tournament 2012, 2013, Memorial Tournament 2012, AT&T National 2012, and numerous other titles; mem. US team World Amateur Team Championship 1994, US Walker Cup team 1995, US Ryder Cup team 1997, 1999, 2002 (postponed from 2001), 2004, 2006, 2010, 2012, 2018; first ranked World No. 1 following maiden victory at The Masters, Augusta 1997, held World No. 1 ranking Aug. 1999–Sept. 2004, June 2005–Oct. 2010, also for most consecutive weeks and for greatest total number of weeks; contract with Nike 1999 (biggest sponsorship deal in sporting history); co–founder TGR Foundation 1996, Tiger Woods Learning Center (now TGR Learning Lab) 2006, TGR Design; announced indefinite leave from professional golf 11 Dec. 2009, returned to competition for The Masters 8 April 2010; won Chevron World Challenge title 2011; regained World No. 1 ranking after winning Arnold Palmer Invitational 25 March 2013; won Tour Championship, Atlanta 2018; co-f. with his father The Tiger Woods Foundation 1996; numerous awards, including Sports Star of the Year Award 1997, PGA Player of the Year and PGA Tour Player of the Year 1997, 1999–2003, 2005–06, 2009, Sports Illustrated Sportsman of the Year 1996, 2000, Mark H. McCormack Award 2006, Byron Nelson Award for lowest adjusted scoring average a record nine times, inducted into the California Hall of Fame 2007, named Athlete of the Decade by the Associated Press 2009, named Associated Press Male Athlete of the Year four times, Laureus World Sports Award for Comeback of the Year 2019. *Leisure interests:* basketball, fishing, sport in general. *Address:* c/o Mark Steinberg, Excel Sports Management, 1700 Broadway, 29th Floor, New York, NY 10019, USA (office); TGR Foundation, 121 Innovation Drive, Suite 150, Irvine, CA 92617. *Fax:* (646) 366-8480 (office). *Website:* www.excelsm.com (office); tgrfoundation.org; www.tigerwoods.com. *E-mail:* help@tgrfoundation.org.

WOODS, James Howard; American actor; b. 18 April 1947, Vernal, Utah; s. of Gail Woods and Martha Woods; m. 1st Kathryn Greko 1980 (divorced 1983); m. 2nd Sarah Owen 1989 (divorced 1990); ed Univ. of California, Los Angeles and Massachusetts Inst. of Tech.; first Broadway appearance in Brendan Behan's Borstal Boy; Obie Award for appearance in Brooklyn Acad. of Music Production of Edward Bond's Saved, New York 1971; other stage appearances in 1970s include Moonchildren 1972, The Trial of the Catonsville Nine, Finishing Touches, Conduct Unbecoming; two Emmy Awards. *Films include:* The Visitors 1971, The Way We Were 1972, The Gambler 1974, Distance 1975, Alex and the Gypsy 1976, The Choirboys 1977, The Onion Field 1979, Black Marble 1980, Fast Walking 1982, Split Image 1982, Videodrome 1983, Once Upon a Time in America 1984, Against All Odds 1984, Joshua Then and Now 1985, Best Seller 1987, Cop 1987, The Boost 1989, True Believer 1989, Immediate Family 1989, Straight Talk 1992, Diggstown, Chaplin 1992, The Getaway 1994, Curse of the Starving Class 1994, Casino 1995, Nixon 1996, Killer: A Journal of Murder, Ghosts of Mississippi 1996, Hercules (voice) 1997, Contact 1997, Vampires 1998, True Crime 1999, Virgin Suicides 2000, Race to Space 2001, John Q 2001, Recess, School's Out (voice) 2001, Riding in Cars with Boys 2001, Scary Movie 2 2001, Northfork 2003, This Girl's Life 2003, Ark 2004, Pretty Persuasion 2005, Be Cool 2005, End Game 2006, Surf's Up (voice) 2007, An American Carol 2008, Jobs 2013, White House Down 2013, Jamesy Boy 2014. *Television include:* Holocaust 1978, Badge of the Assassin 1985, Promise 1986, My Name is Bill. W. 1989, Citizen Cohn 1992, Jane's House 1994, Next Door 1994, Indictment: The McMartin Trial 1995, The Summer of Ben Tyler 1996, Dirty Pictures 2000, Showtime 2000, Rudy: The Rudy Giuliani Story 2003, Shark (series) 2006–08, Too Big to Fail (film) 2011, Coma (mini-series) 2012, Mary and Martha (film) 2013, Ray Donovan (series) 2013. *Leisure interest:* poker. *Address:* c/o Guttman Associates, 118 S Beverly Drive, Suite 201, Beverly Hills, CA 90210, USA.

WOODS, Michael, PhD, DSc; Irish politician (retd); b. 8 Dec. 1935, Bray, Co. Wicklow; m. Margaret Maher; three s. two d.; ed Univ. Coll., Dublin, Harvard Business School, USA; Lecturer, Franciscan Coll. of Agric., Multyfarnham, Co.

Westmeath 1958–59; Head of Dept and Prin. Officer, Agric. Research Inst. 1960–70; Man. Dir F11 Produce Ltd 1970–73, Associated Producer Groups Ltd 1974–79; TD (mem. Dáil) 1977–2011; Minister of State, Depts of Taoiseach and Defence 1979; Minister for Health and Social Welfare 1979–81, March–Dec. 1982, for Social Welfare 1987–91, for Agric. 1991–92, for the Marine 1992, for Social Welfare 1993–94, for Health 1994, Spokesperson on Equality and Law Reform 1994–97, Minister for Marine and Natural Resources 1997–2000, for Educ. and Science 2000–02, Chair. Jt Cttee of Foreign Affairs 2002–11; Fellow, Inst. of Public Admin; mem. Fianna Fáil. *Publications:* Research in Ireland: Key to Economic and Social Development; numerous tech. and scientific papers. *Address:* 13 Kilbarrack Grove, Raheny, Dublin 5, Ireland (home). *Telephone:* (1) 8392439 (home). *E-mail:* michaelwoods.dsc@gmail.com.

WOODWARD, Dame Barbara, DCMG; British diplomatist; *Ambassador to China;* joined Official Devt Assistance (now Dept for Int. Devt), seconded to FCO Jt Assistance Unit 1990–91, joined FCO 1994, Cabinet Office, European Fast Stream, seconded to FCO EU Directorate including on 1992 EU Presidency 1991–93, Second, later First Sec. (Commercial/Political), Embassy in Moscow 1994–98, Agenda 2000 Negotiating Team, EU Dept, FCO 1998–99, Head of EU Enlargement Section 1999–2001, Deputy Head of Human Rights Policy Dept 2001–03, Political Counsellor, later Minister and Deputy Head of Mission, Embassy in Beijing 2003–09, Int. Dir, UK Border Agency 2009–11, Dir-Gen. (Econ. and Consular), FCO 2011–14, Amb. to China 2015–. *Address:* British Embassy, 11 Guang Hua Lu, Jian Guo Men Wai, Beijing 100600, People's Republic of China (office). *Telephone:* (10) 51924000 (office). *Fax:* (10) 51924239 (office). *E-mail:* consular.beijing@fco.gov .uk (office). *Website:* www.gov.uk/government/world/organisations/british -embassy-beijing (office); www.gov.uk/government/world/china (office).

WOODWARD, Robert (Bob) Upshur, BA; American journalist and writer; *Associate Editor, The Washington Post;* b. 26 March 1943, Geneva, Ill.; s. of Alfred Woodward and Jane Upshur; m. Elsa Walsh 1989; two c.; ed Yale Univ.; reporter, Montgomery Co. (Md) Sentinel 1970–71; reporter, Washington Post 1971–78, Metropolitan Ed. 1979–81, Asst Man. Ed. 1981–2008, Assoc. Ed. 2008–; Heywood Broun Award 1972, Worth Bingham Prize for Investigative Reporting 1972, 1986, Sigma Delta Chi Award 1973, George Polk Award 1972, William Allen White Medal 2000, Gerald R. Ford Prize for Reporting on the Presidency 2002. *Publications include:* All the President's Men (with Carl Bernstein, Pulitzer Prize 1972) 1973, The Final Days (with Carl Bernstein) 1976, The Brethren (with Scott Armstrong) 1979, Wired 1984, Veil: The Secret Wars of the CIA 1987, The Commanders 1991, The Man Who Would Be President (with David S. Broder) 1991, The Agenda: Inside the Clinton White House 1994, The Choice 1996, Shadow: Five Presidents and the Legacy of Watergate 1999, Maestro, Greenspan's Fed and the American Boom 2000, Bush at War... Inside the Bush White House 2002, Plan of Attack 2004, The Secret Man 2005, State of Denial: Bush at War, Part III 2006, The War Within: A Secret White House History 2006–2008 2008, Obama's Wars 2010, The Price of Politics 2012. *Address:* The Washington Post, 1150 15th Street, NW, Washington, DC 20071, USA (office). *E-mail:* woodwardb@ washpost.com (office). *Website:* bobwoodward.com.

WOODWARD, Sir Clive, Kt, OBE, BSc; British professional rugby (union) football coach, business executive and former rugby player; *Co-founder, Captured;* b. 6 Jan. 1956, Ely, Cambs., England; m. Jayne Woodward; two s. one d.; ed Loughborough Univ.; centre; player for Leicester 1979–85, Manly 1985–88, England Under-23, England 1980–84, British Lions (two tours: 1980, 1983); 21 caps for England (mem. Grand Slam winning side 1980), two caps for British Lions in 1980; coach for Henly 1993–95, London Irish 1995, Bath (Asst Coach) 1996–97, England Under-21 1996–97, England 1997–2004 (winners Grand Slam 2003, World Cup 2003); coached England to record 14 consecutive victories in 2002–03; apptd Head Coach of British Lions for tour of NZ 2005 (resgnd); Dir of Football, Southampton Football Club 2004–06; Dir of Elite Performance, British Olympic Asscn 2006–12; Co-founder Captured 2013; mem. Bd of Dirs, Leicester Tigers 2007; Hon. Pres. Wooden Spoon Soc.; Freeman, City of Greater London, Royal Borough of Windsor and Maidenhead; Dr hc (Loughborough) 2004. *Publication:* Winning 2004. *Leisure interests:* golf, skiing, football. *Address:* Captured, One Hammersmith Broadway, London, W6 9DL, England (office). *E-mail:* clive@ clivewoodward.com (office); press@capturedhq.com (office). *Website:* www .capturedhq.com (office); www.clivewoodward.com.

WOODWARD, Joanne Gignilliat; American actress; b. 27 Feb. 1930, Thomasville, Ga; d. of Wade Woodward and Elinor Trimmier; m. Paul Newman 1958 (died 2008); three d.; ed Louisiana State Univ.; Trustee, Westport (Conn.) Country Playhouse; numerous awards including Foreign Press Award for Best Actress 1957, Acad. Award 1957, Nat. Bd Review Award 1957, Best Actress Award, Soc. of Film and TV Arts 1974; Franklin D. Roosevelt Four Freedoms Medal 1991, Kennedy Center Honor 1992. *Films include:* Count Three and Pray 1955, A Kiss Before Dying 1956, The Three Faces of Eve 1957, The Long Hot Summer 1958, Rally Round the Flag Boys 1958, The Sound and the Fury 1959, The Fugitive Kind 1959, From the Terrace 1960, Paris Blues 1961, The Stripper 1963, A New Kind of Love 1963, Signpost to Murder 1964, A Big Hand for the Little Lady 1966, A Fine Madness 1966, Rachel Rachel 1968, Winning 1969, W.U.S.A. 1970, They Might Be Giants 1971, The Effects of Gamma Rays on Man-in-the-Moon Marigolds 1972, The Death of a Snow Queen 1973, Summer Wishes, Winter Dreams 1973, The Drowning Pool 1975, The End 1978, The Shadow Box 1980, Candida (Play) 1981, Harry and Son 1984, The Glass Menagerie 1987, Mr and Mrs Bridge 1990, Philadelphia 1993, My Knees Were Jumping: Remembering the Kindertransports (voice) 1998, Lucky Them 2013. *Television includes:* All the Way Home, See How She Runs 1978, Streets of LA 1979, Crisis at Central High 1981, Do You Remember Love? 1985, Blind Spot 1993, Breathing Lessons 1994, James Dean: A Portrait 1996, Empire Falls 2005. *Address:* 246 Post Road East, Westport, CT 06880, USA.

WOODWARD, Shaun Anthony; British politician; b. 26 Oct. 1958, Bristol, England; m. Camilla Davan Sainsbury 1987; one s. three d.; ed Bristol Grammar School, Jesus Coll., Cambridge; Researcher, BBC 1981–91; Dir of Communications, Conservative Party 1991–92; Lecturer on Politics, Queen Mary and Westfield Coll. 1992–94; Fellow, Inst. of Politics, Kennedy School, Harvard Univ., USA 1994; MP (Conservative) for Witney 1997–99, MP (Labour) for St Helens S 2001–10, St Helens S and Whiston 2010–15, mem. Parl. Jt Cttee on Human Rights 2001–05, fmr mem. Foreign Affairs Select Cttee, EU Scrutiny

Select Cttee, Minister for Creative Industries and Tourism and Parl. Under-Sec. of State for NI 2005–06, Parl. Under-Sec., Dept for Culture, Media and Sport 2006–07, Sec. of State for NI 2007–10; Shadow Sec. of State for NI 2010–11; Dir ENO 1994–2002; fmr Trustee, Homes for Homeless People, Marine Stewardship Council; fmr Chair. Understanding Industry; mem. Advisory Council, Royal Shakespeare Co. *Address:* c/o St Helens South and Whiston Parliamentary Office, Century House, Hardshaw Street, St Helens, WA10 1QW, England.

WOOL, Christopher; American artist and photographer; b. 1955, Chicago, Ill.; s. of Ira Wool and Glorye Wool; m. Charline von Heyl 1997; ed Sarah Lawrence Coll., New York Studio School; fmrly worked in film and music during late 1970s; part-time studio asst to Joel Shapiro 1980–84. *Publications include:* 93 Drawings of Beer on the Wall 1984, Untitled 1988, Black Book 1989, Low and Slow 1991, Cats in Bag Bags in River 1991, Absent Without Leave 1993, Shut Up Stupid I'm Working 1995, Incident on 9th Street 1996, Christopher Wool: Los Angeles: Museum of Contemporary Art, Zurich, Scalo 1998, Focus 1999, 9th Street Rundown 2001, Christopher Wool: Vienna 2001, Maybe Maybe Not 2001, Pass the Bitch Chicken 2001, Crosstown Crosstown 2003, East Broadway Breakdown 2002, Christopher Wool: New York 2004, Christopher Wool Camden Arts Centre, London 2004, Christopher Wool: London 2006, Christopher Wool: Los Angeles 2006, Christopher Wool: Valencia, Strasbourg 2006, Christopher Wool: Berlin 2007, Pattern Paintings 1987–2000 2007, Can Your Monkey Do the Dog (with Josh Smith) 2007, Christopher Wool: Cologne: Taschen 2008, Porto-Köln 2008, Psychopts 2008, Roma Termini 2010, Sound on Sound 2010, Musee d'Art Moderne de la Ville de Paris 2012, Christopher Wool: New York 2013. *Website:* wool735.com.

WOOLARD, Edgar Smith, Jr, BSc; American business executive; b. 15 April 1934, Washington, NC; s. of Edgar Smith and Mamie Woolard (née Boone); m. Peggy Harrell 1956; two d.; ed North Carolina State Univ.; fmr Lt, US Army; industrial engineer, Du Pont at Kinston, NC 1957–59, various supervisory and managerial posts 1959–75, Man. Dir textile marketing div. 1975–76, Man. corp. plans dept 1976–77, Gen. Dir products and planning div. 1977–78, Gen. Man. textile fibres, Wilmington, Del. 1978–81, Vice-Pres. textile fibres 1981–83, Exec. Vice-Pres. 1983–85, Vice-Chair. 1985–87, Pres. and COO 1987–89, Chair., CEO 1989–96, Chair. 1996–98, also mem. Bd of Dirs 1996–2000; Advisor, Acorn Energy, Inc. 2010, mem. Bd of Dirs 2014–; mem. Bd of Dirs Telex Communications Inc. 1998 (Chair. 2000–03); fmr mem. Bd of Dirs Citicorp, New York Stock Exchange, Council for Aid to Educ., IBM, Apple Computer Inc., Bell Atlantic, Jt Council on Econ. Educ., Raleigh, Seagram Co. (Canada); Chair. The Business Council 1995–96; mem. Bretton Woods Cttee, North Carolina Textile Foundation; mem. Bd of Trustees NC Textile Foundation, Christiana Care Corpn; mem. Nat. Acad. of Eng, American Philosophical Soc.; Distinguished Engineering Alumnus Award, North Carolina State Univ. 1988, Int. Palladium Medal Soc. Chimie Industrielle (American Section) 1995; Edgar S. Woolard Chair at Univ. of Delaware is named after him. *Address:* c/o Acorn Energy, Inc., 3903 Centerville Road, Wilmington, DE 19807, USA.

WOOLCOTT, Richard, AC, AO, BA; Australian consultant, company director and fmr diplomatist; *Founding Director, Asia Society AustralAsia Centre;* b. 11 June 1927, Sydney; s. of A. R. Woolcott; m. Birgit Christensen 1952 (deceased); two s. one d.; ed Frankston High School, Geelong Grammar School, Univ. of Melbourne and London Univ. School of Slavonic and East European Studies; joined Australian Foreign Service 1951; served in Australian missions in London, Moscow (twice), South Africa, Malaya, Singapore and Ghana; attended UN Gen. Ass. 1962; Acting Commr to Singapore 1963–64; High Commr to Ghana 1967–70; accompanied Prime Ministers Menzies 1965, Holt 1966, McMahon 1971, 1972, Whitlam 1973, 1974 and Hawke 1988–91 on visits to Asia, Europe, the Americas and the Pacific; Adviser at Commonwealth Heads of Govt Confs London 1965, Ottawa 1973, Kuala Lumpur 1989; Pacific Forum 1972, 1973, 1988; Australia-Japan Ministerial Cttee 1972, 1973, 1988, 1989; Head, S Asia Div., Dept of Foreign Affairs 1973; Deputy Sec. Dept of Foreign Affairs 1974; Amb. to Indonesia 1975–78, to Philippines 1978–82; Perm. Rep. to UN 1982–88; Sec. of Dept of Foreign Affairs and Trade 1988–92; Prime Minister's Special Envoy to develop Asia Pacific Econ. Co-operation 1989; Australian Rep. on UN Security Council 1985–86; rep. of Australia at Non-aligned Summit meeting, Harare 1986; ASEAN Post-Ministerial Conf. 1989, 1990, 1991; Alt. Australian Gov., inaugural EBRD meeting 1991; Chair. Australia Indonesia Inst. 1992–98, Official Establishments Trust 1992–99, Nat. Cttee on Population and Devt 1993–95, Across Asia Multimedia (Hong Kong) 2000–, Cttee to review the Australian Citizenship Test 2008; Dir Auric Pacific (Singapore) 2001–02; mem. int. council of The Asia Soc.; Vice-Pres. Multiple Sclerosis Soc. of Australia 1995–2000; Founding Dir Australasia Centre, Asia Soc. 1997–; Founding Dir or consultant several firms; mem. Bd of Commrs, Lippo Bank, Indonesia 1999–2002; apptd Special Envoy to develop idea of an Asia Pacific community 2008; Life Fellow, Trinity Coll., Melbourne Univ. 1995; Bintang Mahaputra Utama (Indonesia) 2000. *Publications include:* Australian Foreign Policy 1973, The Hot Seat: Reflections on Diplomacy From Stalin's Death to the Bali Bombings 2003, Undiplomatic Activities 2006; numerous articles, including special features for The Australian, articles for International Herald Tribune, Time. *Leisure interests:* writing, cricket, photography. *Address:* Asia Society, AustralAsia Centre, Level 1, 175 Collins Street, Melbourne, Vic. 3000 (office); PO Box 3926, Manuka, Canberra, ACT 2603 (office); 19 Talbot Street, Forrest, Canberra, ACT 2603, Australia (home). *Telephone:* (2) 6295-3206 (office). *Fax:* (2) 6295-3066 (office). *E-mail:* rwoolcot@ozemail.com.au. *Website:* www.asiasociety.org (office).

WOOLDRIDGE, Hon. Michael Richard Lewis, BSc, MB BS, MBA; Australian fmr politician; b. 7 Nov. 1956; m. Michele Marion Colman 1988; two s.; ed Scotch Coll., Melbourne, Univ. of Melbourne, Monash Univ.; Resident Medical Staff (Surgical), Alfred Hosp. 1982–85; MP (Liberal Party) for Chisholm, Vic. 1987–88, for Casey, Vic. 1998–2001; pvt. practice 1985–87; Shadow Minister for Aboriginal Affairs 1990–92, for Aboriginal and Torres Strait Islander Affairs 1992–93; Deputy Leader of the Opposition, Shadow Minister for Educ., Employment and Training 1993–94, for Community Services, Sr Citizens and Aged Care 1994–95, for Health and Human Services 1995–96; Minister for Health and Family Services 1996–98, for Health and Aged Care 1998–2001; Ind. Dir (non-exec.), Australian Pharmaceuticals Industry Ltd 2006–15; mem. or fmr mem. Bd Resonance Health Ltd, Dia-B Tech Ltd 2009 (resgnd, co. since de-listed), Prime Trust Ltd, CogState Ltd,

Vision Eye Inst. Ltd; Chair. Neurosciences Australia, Healthsource Australia (Ministerial Advisory Cttee on AIDS, Sexual Health and Hepatitis), CRC for Mental Health, Oral Health Co-operative Research Centre; mem. Bd Waubra Foundation (anti-wind energy org.); Assoc. Prof., Univ. of Melbourne; fined and banned from managing a corpn for two years and three months over collapse of retirement village co. Prime Retirement and Aged Care Property Trust 2014; Hon. Fellow, Australasian Faculty of Public Health Medicine; Hon. LLD. *Leisure interests:* tennis, skiing, reading.

WOOLF, Baron (Life Peer), cr. 1992, of Barnes in the London Borough of Richmond; **Rt Hon. Harry Kenneth Woolf,** CH, PC, LLB; British judge; b. 2 May 1933, Newcastle upon Tyne, England; s. of Alexander Woolf and Leah Woolf; m. Marguerite Sassoon 1961; three s.; ed Glasgow Acad., Fettes Coll., Univ. Coll. London; Nat. Service, 15/19th Royal Hussars 1954, Capt., Army Legal Services 1955; called to Bar, Inner Temple 1955, began practising 1956; Recorder, Crown Court 1972–79; Jr Counsel, Inland Revenue 1973–74; First Treasury Counsel (Common Law) 1974–79; Judge, High Court, Queen's Bench Div. 1979–86; Presiding Judge, S Eastern Circuit 1981–84; Lord Justice of Appeal 1986–92; Lord of Appeal in Ordinary 1992–96; Master of the Rolls 1996–2000; Lord Chief Justice of England and Wales 2000–05; mem. (Crossbench), House of Lords 1992–, fmr Chair. Parl. Standards Sub-cttee, mem. Constitution Cttee; non-perm. judge, Court of Final Appeal, Hong Kong 2003–; mediator and arbitrator, Blackstone Chambers, London 2005–; Founding Pres. Civil, Commercial and Appeal Court, Qatar Financial Centre 2006–; conducted review of working methods of the European Court of Human Rights 2005; fmr Chair. Bank of England Financial Market's Law Cttee; Visiting Prof. of Law and fmr Chair. of Council, Univ. Coll. London; mem. Bd of Man., Inst. of Advanced Legal Studies 1985–94 (Chair. 1986–94); Chair. Lord Chancellor's Advisory Cttee of Legal Educ. 1986–94, Middx Advisory Cttee on Justices of the Peace 1986–90, Magna Carta Trust 1996, Lord Chancellors' Advisory Cttee on Public Records 1996–2000, Council of Civil Justice 1997–2000, Civil Procedure Rules Cttee 1997–2000; Pro-Chancellor Univ. of London 1994–2002; Visitor, Nuffield Coll. Oxford 1996–2000, Downing Coll. Cambridge 2000–, Univ. Coll. London 1996–2000; Trustee, Butler Trust 1991–96, Chair. 1992–96, Pres. 1996–; Hon. Visiting Prof., Chinese Univ. of Hong Kong; Hon. FBA 2002; Hon. FMedSci; Hon. Fellow, Univ. Coll. London, Coll. of Trial Lawyers, USA; Hon. LLD (Buckingham) 1992, (Bristol) 1992, (London) 1993, (Anglia Poly Univ.) 1994, (Manchester Metropolitan) 1994, (Hull) 2001, (Cranfield) 2001, (Cambridge) 2002, (Exeter) 2002; Hon. DLitt (London) 2002; Hon. DSc (Cranfield) 2002; Dr hc (Oxford) 2004, (Open Univ.) 2010. *Publications:* Protection of the Public – The New Challenge 1990, Declaratory Judgement (co-ed.) 1993, Judicial Review of Administrative Action (co-ed.) (fifth edn) 1995; reports: Prisons in England and Wales 1991, Access to Justice (Interim) 1995, (Final) 1996, Principles of Judicial Review (co-author) 1999, Pursuit of Justice 2008. *Address:* House of Lords, Westminster, London, SW1A 0PW, England (office). *Telephone:* (20) 7219-1788 (office). *Fax:* (20) 7219-0785 (office).

WOOLFSON, Michael Mark, MA, PhD DSc, CPhys, FRAS, FInstP, FRS; British physicist and academic; *Professor Emeritus, University of York;* b. 9 Jan. 1927, London, England; s. of Maurice Woolfson and Rose Woolfson (née Solomons); m. Margaret Frohlich 1951; two s. one d.; ed Jesus Coll., Oxford, Univ. of Manchester Inst. of Science and Tech.; Nat. Service, Royal Engineers 1947–49; Research Asst, Cavendish Lab., Cambridge 1952–54; ICI Fellow, Univ. of Cambridge 1954–55; Lecturer, Faculty of Tech., Univ. of Manchester 1955–61, Reader 1961–65; Prof. of Theoretical Physics, Univ. of York 1965–94, Prof. Emer. 1994–; Chair. Royal Soc. Planetary Sciences Sub-cttee 1979–83, British Crystallographic Asscn 1985–90, British Nat. Cttee for Crystallography 1985–90; Pres. Yorks. Philosophical Soc. 1985–99; Hughes Medal, Royal Soc. 1986, Patterson Award, American Crystallographic Asscn 1990, Gregori Aminoff Medal and Prize, Royal Swedish Acad. of Sciences 1992, Dorothy Hodgkin Prize, British Crystallographic Asscn 1997, Ewald Prize, Int. Union of Crystallography 2002. *Publications:* Direct Methods in Crystallography 1960, The Origin of the Solar System, The Capture Theory 1989, Physical and Non-physical Methods of Solving Crystal Structures 1995, An Introduction to X-ray Crystallography 1997, An Introduction to Computer Simulation 1999, The Origins and Evolution of the Solar System 2000, Planetary Science 2002, Mathematics for Physics 2007, The Formation of the Solar System: Theories Old and New 2007, Everyday Probability and Statistics 2008, Time, Space, Stars and Man 2008, Materials, Matter and Particles 2010, On the Origin of Planets 2011, The Fundamentals of Imaging 2011, Time and Age 2014, Colour 2016, A Dialogue Concerning the Two Chief Models of Planet Formation 2017. *Leisure interest:* writing. *Address:* Department of Physics, University of York, York, YO1 5DD (office); 61 Thackrah Court, 1 Squirrel Way, Leeds, South Yorks., LS17 8FQ, England (home). *Telephone:* (1904) 432230 (office); (113) 4692343 (home). *Fax:* (1904) 432214 (office). *E-mail:* mmw1@york.ac.uk (office). *Website:* www.york.ac.uk/physics/people/emeritusprof/woolfson (office).

WOOLGAR, Stephen, BA (Hons), MA, PhD, DPhil; British sociologist and academic; b. 14 Feb. 1950; ed Emmanuel Coll., Cambridge; Visiting Lecturer, McGill Univ., Montréal, Canada 1979–81, MIT 1983–84, École Nat. Supérieure des Mines, Paris 1988–89, Univ. of California, San Diego 1995–96; Prof. of Sociology, Brunel Univ. 1996–2000, Head of Dept of Human Sciences –2000, Dir Centre for Research into Innovation, Culture and Tech. Technology 1998–2000; Dir Virtual Society Program, Econ. and Social Research Council 1997–2002; Prof. of Marketing and Head, Science and Tech. Studies Academic Area, Inst. for Science, Innovation and Society, Saïd Business School, Univ. of Oxford 2000, now Sr Research Fellow (part time); mem. Man. Bd, Oxford e-Science Centre, Oxford Internet Inst.; mem. Council Consumer's Asscn, Acad. of Social Sciences; mem. Research Assessment Exercise Sociology Panel, Higher Educ. Funding Council for England 1996, 2001; fmr mem. EC (VALUE) Think Tank, Information Tech., Electronics and Communications Foresight Panel for UK Govt, Leisure and Learning Foresight Panel; fmr Adviser to Cabinet Office Better Govt Team; fmr mem. E-Commerce and Consumer Affairs Ministerial Advisory Groups; fmr Adviser to Research Councils of Denmark, Netherlands and Norway; Fulbright Scholarship, Fulbright Sr Scholarship, ESRC Sr Research Fellowship, Econ. and Social Research Council; Bernal Prize, Soc. for Social Studies of Science 2008. *Publications:* Laboratory Life: The Social Construction of Scientific Facts (co-author) 1979, Science: The Very Idea 1988, The Cognitive Turn: Sociological and Psychological Perspectives on Science (co-author) 1989, Representation in Scientific Practice (co-author) 1990, The Machine at Work: Technology, Work and Society (co-author) 1997, Virtual Society? Technology, Cyberbole, Reality (ed.) 2002. *Leisure interest:* hot air ballooning. *Address:* Saïd Business School, University of Oxford, Park End Street, Oxford, OX1 1HP, England (office). *Telephone:* (1865) 288934 (office). *E-mail:* steve.woolgar@sbs.ox.ac.uk (office). *Website:* www.sbs.ox.ac.uk (office).

WOOLLISCROFT, James O., BSc, MD; American physician and medical educator; *Dean of the Medical School, University of Michigan;* ed Univ. of Minnesota; Chief Resident, Univ. of Michigan Medical School 1980, Faculty mem., Dept of Internal Medicine 1980, Prof. of Internal Medicine 1993, Josiah Macy Jr Prof. of Medical Educ. 1996–2001, Lyle C. Roll Prof. of Medicine 2001–, Exec. Assoc. Dean 1999–2006, Interim Dean 2006–07, Dean 2007–; Fellow, Council of Deans, Asscn of American Medical Colls (AAMC) 2003–04; mem. Inst. of Medicine 2013; Soc. of Gen. Internal Medicine Medical Educ. Award 2004, Merril Flair Award, AAMC, GEA 2008, Flexner Award, AAMC, 2014. *Address:* Office of the Dean, University of Michigan Medical School, 1301 Catherine Road, Ann Arbor, MI 48109, USA (office). *Telephone:* (734) 764-8175 (office). *Fax:* (734) 763-4936 (office). *E-mail:* woolli@umich.edu (office). *Website:* www.med.umich.edu/medschool/dean (office).

WOOLSEY, R. James, LLB, MA; American lawyer and fmr government official; *Chairman, Foundation for Defense of Democracies;* b. 21 Sept. 1941, Tulsa, Okla; m. Suzanne Haley; three s.; ed Tulsa Cen. High School, Stanford Univ., Univ. of Oxford, UK and Yale Law School; mem. staff, Nat. Security Council 1968–70; Advisor, US Del. to Strategic Arms Limitation Talks 1969–70; Gen. Counsel to US Senate Cttee on Armed Services 1970–73; Under-Sec. of the Navy 1977–79; del.-at-large to US–Soviet Strategic Arms Reduction Talks and space talks 1983–86; Amb. and US Rep. to negotiations on Conventional Armed Forces in Europe Treaty 1989–91; Chair. CIA task force on future of satellite spying 1991; Dir of CIA 1993–95; Partner, Shea & Gardner 1991–93, 1995–2002; Vice-Pres. Global Assurance, Booz Allen Hamilton 2002; Chair. Advisory Cttee, Clean Fuels Foundation; currently Chair. Foundation for Defense of Democracies; Chair. Strategic Advisory Group, Paladin Capital Group; mem. Pres.'s Comm. on Strategic Forces 1983, Pres.'s Blue Ribbon Comm. on Defense Man. 1985–86, Pres.'s Comm. on Fed. Ethics Law Reform 1989, Comm. to Assess the Ballistic Missile Threat to the US 1998, Nat. Comm. on Terrorism 1999–2000; Annenberg Distinguished Visiting Fellow, Hoover Inst., Stanford Univ. 2009; Sr Fellow, Jackson Inst. for Global Affairs, Yale Univ. 2010–11; mem. Bd of Advisors BioDefense Corpn 2004; Trustee, Center for Strategic and Int. Studies; mem. Bd of Govs Philadelphia Stock Exchange. *Address:* Foundation for Defense of Democracies, PO Box 33249, Washington, DC 20033, USA (office). *Telephone:* (202) 207-0190 (office). *E-mail:* info@defenddemocracy.org (office). *Website:* www.defenddemocracy.org (office).

WOOSNAM, Ian Harold, OBE; British (Welsh) professional golfer; b. 2 March 1958, Oswestry, Wales; s. of Harold Woosnam and Joan Woosnam; m. Glendryth Pugh 1983; one s. two d.; ed St Martin's Modern School; professional golfer 1976–; tournament victories: News of the World under-23 Matchplay 1979, Cacharel under-25 Championship 1982, Swiss Open 1982, Silk Cut Masters 1983, Scandinavian Enterprise Open 1984, Zambian Open 1985, Lawrence Batley TPC 1986, 555 Kenya Open 1986, Hong Kong Open 1987, Jersey Open 1987, Cepsa Madrid Open 1987, Bell's Scottish Open 1987, 1990, Lancome Trophy 1987, Suntory World Match-Play Championship 1987, 1990, 2001, Volvo PGA Championship 1988, 1997, Carrolls Irish Open 1988, 1989, Panasonic Euro Open 1988, Am Express Mediterranean Open 1990, Torras Monte Carlo Open 1990, Epson Grand Prix 1990, US Masters 1991, USF+G Classic 1991, Fujitsu Mediterranean Open, Torras Monte Carlo Open 1991, European Monte Carlo Open 1992, Lancôme Trophy 1993, Murphy's English Open 1993, British Masters 1994, Cannes Open 1994, Heineken Classic 1996, Scottish Open 1996, Volvo German Open 1996, Johnnie Walker Classic 1996, Parkridge Polish Seniors' Championship 2008, Russian Seniors' Open 2008, Irish Seniors' Open 2009, Professional Golfers' Asscn (PGA) Handa Cup 2009, Berenberg Bank Masters 2011, Dutch Senior Open 2014, Insperity Invitational 2015; team events: Ryder Cup 1983–97, Dunhill Cup 1985, 1986, 1988, 1989, 1990, 1991, 1993, 1995, World Cup 1980, 1982, 1983, 1984, 1985, 1987, 1990, 1991, 1992, 1993, 1994, 1996, 1997; finished top Order of Merit 1987, 1990 and Seniors' Order of Merit 2008; ranked No. 1, Sony world rankings 1991; World Cup Individual, PGA Grand Slam 1991; Pres. World Snooker Asscn 1999–2002; eighth on all-time European Tour earnings list; 29 European PGA Tour titles; Capt. European Ryder Cup Team 2006; BBC Wales Sports Personality of the Year Award 1987, 1990, 1991. *Publications:* Ian Woosnam's Golf Masterpieces (with Peter Grosvenor) 1991, Golf Made Simple: The Woosie Way 1997, Woosie: My Autobiography 2002. *Leisure interests:* snooker, water skiing, sports, fishing. *Address:* c/o Sharron Elkabas, M2NS Agency, Notcutt House, 36 Southwark Bridge Road, London, SE1 9EU, England (office). *Telephone:* (20) 7234–9455 (office). *E-mail:* www.mn2s.com (office). *Website:* www.ianwoosnam.com.

WORCESTER, Sir Robert Milton, KBE, BSc, FRSS, FMRS; British (b. American) company chairman; *Senior Adviser, Ipsos MORI;* b. 21 Dec. 1933, Kansas City, Mo., USA; s. of C. M. Worcester and Violet Ruth Worcester; m. 1st Joann Ransdell 1958 (deceased); two s.; m. 2nd Margaret Noel Smallbone 1982; ed Univ. of Kansas; Consultant, McKinsey & Co. 1962–65; Chief Financial Officer, Opinion Research Corpn 1965–68; Man. Dir Market & Opinion Research Int. Ltd (MORI) 1969–94, Chair. 1973–2005; Int. Dir, Ipsos 2005–08, Sr Adviser, Ipsos MORI 2008–; Pres. World Asscn for Public Opinion Research 1983–84; Visiting Prof., Grad. Centre of Journalism, City Univ. 1990–2002, LSE 1992– (Hon. Fellow 2005), Univ. of Strathclyde 1996–2001; Pres. Environmental Campaigns Ltd 2002–06; Chair. Magna Carta 2015 800th Anniversary Commemoration Cttee 2009–15; Vice-Pres. Int. Soc. Science Council, UNESCO 1989–94, European Atlantic Group, UNA 1999–, Royal Soc. for Wildlife Trusts 1995–; Co-Chair. Jamestown 2007 British Cttee 2004–07; mem. Pilgrims Soc. of GB (Chair. 1993–2010, Vice-Pres. 2010–); mem. Court of Govs LSE 1995–, Advisory Bd European Business Journal, Fulbright Comm. 1995–2005, Court Univ. of Middx 2001–, Council Univ. of Kent 2002–13 (also mem. Court, Chancellor 2006–13), Advisory Bd Nat. Consumer Council 2002–, Media Standards Trust 2006–, Camelot Advisory Panel for Corp. Responsibility 2006–11, GovNet 2008–, Advisory Council Inst. of Business Ethics (Pres. 2010–13, Vice-Pres. 2013–); Gov. Ditchley

Foundation, English-Speaking Union; Dir (sr non-exec.) Kent Messenger Group 2004–08; Chair. Maidstone Radio Ltd (CTR 105.4 fm) 2004–06; Founding Co-Ed. Int. Journal of Public Opinion Research; wrote monthly columns for Profile (magazine of C. Inst. of Public Relations) and Parliamentary Monitor; Trustee, WorldWide Fund for Nature (WWF-UK) 1988–94, Amb. 1995–2001; Trustee, Natural History Museum Devt Trust 1989–94, Magna Carta Trust 1993– (Deputy Chair. 2009–), Wildfowl and Wetlands Trust 2002–08 (currently Vice-Pres.); Adjunct Prof., Univ. of Kansas 2012–, Chancellor's Lecture 2012–14; Fellow, Market Research Soc. 1997–, King's Coll. 2007; Dir What on Earth Publishing? 2016– (Chair. What on Earth Publishing North America 2016–), Medway Maritime NHS Trust 2001–04; apptd Kent Amb., Environment Champion by Kent Co. Council; Freeman of the City of London 2001, Hon. Prof. of Politics (Kent) 2002, Hon. DL (Kent) 2004, Hon. Prof. (Warwick) 2005, Hon. Fellow (LSE, King's Coll. London); Hon. DSc (Buckingham) 1998, Hon. DLitt (Bradford) 2001, Hon. DUniv (Middlesex) 2001, Hon. LLD (Greenwich) 2002, Hon. DCL (Kent) 2006, (Warwick) 2012, Distinguished Grad. (Univ. of Kansas) 2006, Hon. DLaws (Richmond American Int. Univ. in London) 2009; Helen Dinerman Award, World Asscn for Public Opinion Research 1996. *Publications include:* Political Communications (with Martin Harrop) 1982, Political Opinion Polling: An International Review (ed.) 1983, Consumer Market Research Handbook (3rd edn, co-ed. with John Downham) 1986, Private Opinions, Public Polls (with Lesley Watkins) 1986, We British (with Eric Jacobs) 1990, British Public Opinion: History and Methodology of Political Opinion Polling in Great Britain 1991, Typically British (with Eric Jacobs) 1991, Dynamics of Societal Learning about Global Environmental Change (with Samuel H. Barnes) 1992, The Millennial Generation (with Madsen Pirie) 1998, The Next Leaders (with Madsen Pirie) 1999, Explaining Labour's Landslide (with Roger Mortimore) 1999, The Big Turn Off (with Madsen Pirie) 2000, How to Win the Euro Referendum: Lessons from 1975 2000, Facing the Future (with Madsen Pirie) 2000, The Wrong Package (with Madsen Pirie) 2000, Explaining Labour's Second Landslide (with Roger Mortimore) 2001, Explaining Labour's Landslip (with Roger Mortimore and Paul Baines) 2005, Explaining Cameron's Coalition: How It Came About: An Analysis of the 2010 General Election 2011, Explaining Cameron's Comeback (with Roger Mortimore, Paul Baines and Mark Gill) 2015. *Leisure interest:* castles, choral music, gardening. *Address:* Ipsos MORI, 3 Thomas More Square, London, E1W 1YW, England (office). *Telephone:* (20) 3059-5000 (office). *E-mail:* rmworcester@yahoo.com (office). *Website:* www.ipsos-mori.com (office); www.magnacarta800th.com (office).

WORMS, Gérard Etienne; French business executive and company director; *Honorary Chairman, International Chamber of Commerce (ICC);* b. 1 Aug. 1936, Paris; s. of André Worms and Thérèse Dreyfus; m. Michèle Rousseau 1960; one s. one d.; ed Lycées Carnot and Saint-Louis, Ecole Polytechnique and Ecole Nat. Supérieure des Mines, Paris; Engineer, Org. commune des régions sahariennes 1960–62; Head of Dept, Délégation à l'Aménagement du Territoire et à l'Action Régionale 1963–67; Tech. Adviser, Office of Olivier Guichard (Minister of Industry, later of Planning) 1967–69, Office of Jacques Chaban-Delmas (Prime Minister) 1969–71; Asst Man. Dir, Librairie Hachette 1972–75, Man. Dir 1975–81, Dir 1978–81; Prof., Ecole des Hautes Etudes Commerciales 1962–69, Supervisor of complementary courses, Faculty of Letters and Human Sciences, Paris 1963–69; Prof. Ecole Polytechnique 1974–85; Vice-Pres. Syndicat nat. de l'édition 1974–81; Exec. Vice-Pres. Rhône-Poulenc SA 1981–83; Exec. Vice-Pres. Compagnie de Suez 1984–90, Chair. and CEO 1990–95; Pres. Banque Indosuez 1994–95; Pres. Supervisory Bd Rothschild, Compagnie Banque Paris 1995–99, Man. Partner Rothschild et Cie and Rothschild et Cie Banque 1999–, Vice-Chair. Rothschild Europe; Chair. Int. Chamber of Commerce (ICC) France 2006–, ICC 2011–13, Hon. Chair. ICC 2013–; Pres. Centre for research into econ. expansion and business Devt 1996–, Supervisory Council for health information systems 1997–2000, History channel 1997–; Hon. Chair. Nat. Technical Research Asscn, Société d'Economie Politique; mem. bd Telecom Italia 1998–2001, Publicis, Métropole Télévision; Chevalier, Ordre nat. du Mérite, Ordre du Mérite maritime, Commdr Légion d'honneur 2007. *Publications include:* Les méthodes modernes de l'économie appliquée 1965; various articles on econ. methods in specialized journals. *Address:* International Chamber of Commerce, 38 cours Albert 1er, 75008 Paris (office); 61 bis avenue de la Motte Picquet, 75015 Paris, France (home). *Telephone:* 1-49-53-28-28 (office); 1-47-83-99-43 (home). *Fax:* 1-49-53-28-59 (office). *E-mail:* icc@iccwbo.org (office). *Website:* www.iccwbo.org (office).

WÖRNER, Johann-Dietrich; German professor of engineering and international organization official; *Director-General, European Space Agency;* b. 18 July 1954, Kassel; ed Technische Hochschule Berlin, Technische Hochschule Darmstadt; began career with König und Heunisch, Frankfurt (consulting civil engineers) –1990; Prof. of Civil Eng, Technische Hochschule (TU) Darmstadt 1990–2007, also Head of Testing and Research Inst., Dean of Civil Eng Faculty 1992–94, Pres., TU Darmstadt 1995–2007; Chair. Exec. Bd German Aerospace Centre 2007–15; Dir-Gen. European Space Agency 2015–; Vice-Pres. Helmholtz Asscn; fmr mem. Bd of Dirs École Centrale de Paris, École Centrale de Lyon, Convention for Tech. Sciences, Röhm GmbH; mem. Berlin Brandenburg Acad. of Sciences, German Acad. of Sciences Leopoldina 2002; Dr h.c (State Univ. New York) 1998, (Tech. Univ. of Moldova) 1999, (Tech. Univ. of Bucharest), (St Petersburg Univ. for Economy and Finance) 2000, (École Centrale de Lyon) 2003, (Tech. Univ. of Mongolia) 2005; Fraunhofer Medal 2007. *Address:* European Space Agency, 8–10 rue Mario Nikis, 75738 Paris Cedex 15, France (office). *Telephone:* 1-53-69-76-54 (office). *Fax:* 1-53-69-75-60 (office). *E-mail:* contactesa@esa.int (office). *Website:* www.esa.int (office).

WORRALL, Denis John, PhD; South African business executive, politician, diplomatist and lawyer; b. 29 May 1935, Benoni; s. of Cecil John Worrall and Hazel Worrall; m. Anita Denise Ianco 1965; three s.; ed Univ. of Cape Town, Univ. of South Africa, Cornell Univ., USA; taught political science, Cornell Univ., UCLA, Univ. of Natal, Univ. of South Africa and Univ. of Witwatersrand; Cornell Research Fellow, Univ. of Ibadan, Nigeria 1962–63; Founder-Ed. New Nation 1967–74; Research Prof. and Dir Inst. for Social and Econ. Research, Rhodes Univ. –1974; Senator for Cape 1974–77; Amb. to Australia 1983–84, to UK 1984–87; Advocate, Supreme Court of SA; MP for Cape Town-Gardens 1977–83; independent cand. for Helderberg in 1987 Election; mem. Pres.'s. Council 1980–83; f. Ind. Movt 1988; Leader Ind. Party 1988–89; Co-founder Democratic Party 1989; MP for Berea, Durban 1989–94; Chair. Omega Investment Research Ltd. *Publication:*

South Africa: Government and Politics. *Leisure interests:* reading, cycling. *E-mail:* denisw@omegainvest.co.za.

WORRELL, R. DeLisle, BSc (Econs), PhD; Barbadian economist and central banker; *Principal, DeLisle Worrell and Associates;* b. 12 Jan. 1945; m. Monica Drayton; ed Univ. of the West Indies, Mona, Jamaica, McGill Univ., Canada; joined Cen. Bank of Barbados 1973, held several positions at bank, including Dir of Research, Deputy Gov. –1998; Sr Economist, IMF 1998–2008; Gov. Cen. Bank of Barbados 2009–17, also Alt. mem. IMF Bd of Govs; apptd Gen. Chair. Int. Symposium on Forecasting 1997; Exec. Dir Caribbean Centre for Money and Finance –2008; Prof. of Econs, Univ. of the West Indies, St Augustine; Co-Chair. Regional Consultative Group for Americas, Financial Stability Bd; Principal, DeLisle Worrell and Associates; fmr Consultant, Inter-American Devt Bank, Foundation for Devt Cooperation, Australia, US Agency for Int. Devt, World Bank, UN Econ. and Social Council, Caribbean Community Secr.; fmr Research Fellow, Smithsonian Inst., Peterson Inst., Federal Reserve System, Washington, DC, Yale Univ., Princeton Univ., Univ. of the West Indies; mem. Bretton Woods Cttee. *Publications include:* Small Island Economies: Structure and Performance in the English Speaking Caribbean since 1970 1987, Policies for Stabilization and Growth in Small Very Open Economies 2012; numerous articles in professional and journals. *Leisure interests:* photography, swimming, Caribbean festival arts. *Address:* DeLisle Worrell and Associates, Glenisla, Fisherpond, St Joseph BB21000, Barbados (office). *Telephone:* 433-1251 (office). *E-mail:* info@ delisleworrell.com (office). *Website:* www.delisleworrell.com (office).

WORSTHORNE, Sir Peregrine Gerard, Kt, MA; British journalist, writer and broadcaster; b. 22 Dec. 1923, London; s. of Col A. Koch de Gooreynd and Baroness Norman; m. 1st Claudia Bertrand de Colasse 1950 (died 1990); one d. one step-s.; m. 2nd Lady Lucinda Lambton 1991; ed Stowe School, Peterhouse, Cambridge and Magdalen Coll., Oxford; mem. editorial staff, Glasgow Herald 1946–48; mem. editorial staff, The Times 1948–50, Washington corresp. 1950–52, leader writer 1952–55; leader writer, Daily Telegraph 1955–61; Deputy Ed. Sunday Telegraph 1961–76, Assoc. Ed. 1976–86, Ed. 1986–89, Ed. Comment Section 1989–91; columnist, The Spectator 1997–, The New Statesman; fmr columnist, The First Post (online news magazine); Granada TV Journalist of the Year 1981. *Publications include:* The Socialist Myth 1972, Peregrinations 1980, By The Right 1987, Tricks of Memory (memoirs) 1993, In Defence of Aristocracy 2004. *Leisure interests:* walking, tennis. *Address:* The Old Rectory, Hedgerley, Bucks., SL2 3UY, England (home). *Telephone:* (1753) 646167 (home). *Fax:* (1753) 646914 (home). *E-mail:* therectory.hedgerley@virgin.net.

WORTH, Richard, OBE, LLB, MJur, MBA, PhD; New Zealand fmr politician and lawyer; *Director, Aubade Global Resources Ltd;* b. 3 July 1948, Auckland; ed Univ. of Auckland, Massey Univ., Institut Européen d'Admin des Affaires (INSEAD), France, Royal Melbourne Inst. of Tech., Australia; Pnr, Simpson Grierson 1972–99, Exec. Chair. 1986–99; MP for Epsom 1999–2005, mem. Select Cttees on Regulations Review 1999–2002, on Law and Order 2001–02, on Justice 2005–06, Chair. Regulations Review Cttee 2005–08; Head of Mission, Govt of Monaco 2002–; Spokesman on Defence 2002–03, on Veterans' Affairs 2002–03, Justice 2003–06; Assoc. Spokesman on Local Govt 2005–06; Minister of Internal Affairs 2008–09 (resgnd), also Minister for Land Information, Minister Responsible for Archives New Zealand and for Nat. Library and Assoc. Minister of Justice; Fellow, NZ Inst. of Dirs, NZ Inst. of Man.; Chair. PF Olsen Ltd; fmr Chair. Korea/ NZ Business Council, Korean Parl. Group; fmr Pres. Hong Kong–NZ Business Asscn; Deputy Chair. India Trade Alliance; Trustee, Royal NZ Coastguard Foundation; fmr Dir Prada America's Cup NZ Ltd; Dir Aubade Global Resources Ltd 2017; mem. Council of Legal Educ.; fmr Chair. Willis NZ Ltd; fmr mem. and Treas. NZ Law Soc. Bd; mem. and fmr Dir Auckland Rotary Club; fmr Pres. The Northern Club, Outward Bound Trust Bd of NZ; Hon. Consul of Colombia; Hon. Consul of Monaco to NZ 2002–; Kt, Justice Order of St John, Kt Grand Officer, Portugal, Order of St Michael (Portugal), Kt of Rizal (Philippines). *Publications:* numerous articles on maritime and regulatory affairs in int. trade publs. *Leisure interests:* mountaineering, sailing. *Address:* PO Box 246, Shortland Street, Auckland 1140, New Zealand (office). *E-mail:* rwworth@gmail.com (office).

WOUK, Herman, AB; American writer and dramatist; b. 27 May 1915, New York, NY; s. of Abraham Isaac Wouk and Esther Levine; m. Betty Sarah Brown 1945 (died 2011); three s. (one deceased); ed Columbia Univ.; radio scriptwriter for leading comedians, New York 1935–41; presidential consultant to US Treasury 1941; served in USNR 1942–46; Visiting Prof. of English, Yeshiva Univ., New York 1952–57; Trustee, Coll. of the Virgin Islands 1961–69; mem. Authors' Guild, Authors League, Center for Book Nat. Advisory Bd, Library of Congress, Advisory Council, Center for US–China Arts Exchange; Hon. LHD (Yeshiva Univ.); Hon. DLitt (Clark Univ.), (George Washington Univ.) 2001; Hon. DLitt (American Int. Coll.) 1979; Hon. PhD (Bar Ilan) 1990, (Hebrew Univ.) 1997; Hon. DST (Trinity Coll.) 1998; Columbia Univ. Medal for Excellence, Alexander Hamilton Medal, Columbia Univ. 1980, Ralph Waldo Emerson Award, Int. Platform Asscn 1981, Univ. of Calif., Berkeley Medal 1984, Yad Vashem Kazetnik Award 1990, USN Memorial Foundation Lone Sailor Award 1987, American Acad. of Achievement Golden Plate Award 1986, Bar Ilan Univ. Guardian of Zion Award 1998, Univ. of California, San Diego Medal 1998, Lifetime Literary Achievement Award, Jewish Book Council 2000, Lifetime Achievement Award for Writing of Fiction, Library of Congress (first) 2008. *Publications include:* fiction: Aurora Dawn 1947, The City Boy 1948, Slattery's Hurricane (screenplay) 1949, The Caine Mutiny (Pulitzer Prize for Fiction 1952) 1951, Marjorie Morningstar 1955, Slattery's Hurricane 1956, Youngblood Hawke 1961, Don't Stop the Carnival 1965, The Lomokome Papers 1968, The Winds of War (also TV screenplay) 1971, War and Remembrance (also TV screenplay) 1978, Inside, Outside (Washingtonian Book Award 1986) 1985, The Hope 1993, The Glory 1994, A Hole in Texas 2004, The Lawgiver 2012, Sailor and Fiddler 2016; plays: The Man in the Trench Coat 1941, The Traitor 1949, Modern Primitive 1951, The Caine Mutiny Court-Martial 1953, Nature's Way 1957; non-fiction: This is My God: The Jewish Way of Life 1959, The Will to Live On: The Resurgence of Jewish Heritage 2000, The Language God Talks: On Science and Religion 2010, Sailor and Fiddler (memoir) 2015. *Leisure interests:* Hebraic studies. *Address:* BSW Literary Agency, 303 Crestview Drive, Palm Springs, CA 92264, USA (office). *Website:* www.hermanwouk.com (office).

WOWEREIT, Klaus, LLB; German politician; *Vice-Chairman, Sozialdemokratische Partei Deutschlands (SPD);* b. 1 Oct. 1953, Berlin; partner Jörn Kubicki; ed Free Univ. of Berlin; adviser to Senator for Internal Affairs, Berlin 1981–84; mem. Regional Cttee and Del. to SPD, Tempelhof Regional Council 1984–95; Chair. SPD Group, Tempelhof Dist 1981–84, Vice-Chair. 1995–99, Chair. SPD Group, Parl. of Berlin 1999–2001; Mayor of Berlin 2001–14; Vice-Chair. SPD 2009–; Partner, Tempelhof Haus-, Wohnungs- und Grundstückseigentümerverein Berlin-Lichtenrade eV, European Acad.; mem. Tempelhof Art and Cultural Union (TKK); Commdr, Légion d'honneur 2004. *Publications:* ... und das ist auch gut so 2007, Mut zur Integration: Für ein neues Miteinander 2011. *Address:* Sozialdemokratische Partei Deutschlands (SPD), Willy-Brandt-Haus, Wilhelmstr. 141, 10963 Berlin, Germany. *Telephone:* (30) 25991500. *Fax:* (30) 25991507. *E-mail:* parteivorstand@spd.de. *Website:* www.spd.de; www.klaus-wowereit.de.

WOZNIACKI, Caroline; Danish professional tennis player; b. 11 July 1990, Odense; d. of Piotr Wozniacki and Anna Wozniacki; plays right-handed (two-handed backhand); won several jr tournaments in 2005, including Orange Bowl tennis championship, Fla, Osaka Mayor's Cup, Japan; debut on WTA (Women's Tennis Asscn) Tour at Cincinnati's Western & Southern Financial Group Women's Open 2005; winner Girls' Singles Jr Championship, Wimbledon 2006; winner Pilot Pen, New Haven, USA 2008, Nordic Light Open, Stockholm, Sweden 2008, Mirage Cup, Las Vegas, USA 2008, Ortisei ITF, Italy 2008, Ponte Vedra Beach 2009, 2010, Eastbourne 2009, New Haven 2009, 2010, Copenhagen 2010, 2011, Montreal 2010, US Open Summer Series 2010, Tokyo 2010, Beijing 2010, Dubai 2011, Indian Wells 2011, Brussels 2011; Grand Slam results: fourth round, Wimbledon 2009, 2010, 2011, finalist, US Open 2009, 2014, quarter-finalist, French Open 2010, semi-finalist, Australian Open 2011; finalist, WTA Tour Championships, Doha 2010; also holds two WTA titles in doubles: China Open, Beijing, China 2008, Cellular South Cup, Memphis, Tenn. 2009; three-time mem. Danish Fed. Cup Team 2009; WTA Tour Most Impressive Newcomer of the Year 2008, Youngest Player in the WTA Top 10 2009, ITF Player of the Year 2010, Danish Sports Name of the Year 2010. *Leisure interests:* playing handball and football, swimming, playing the piano, Liverpool Football Club. *Address:* c/o Lagardère Unlimited, 5335 Wisconsin Avenue, NW, Suite 850, Washington, DC 20015, USA (office). *Website:* www.lagardere-unlimited.com (office); www.carolinewozniacki.dk. *E-mail:* contact@carolinewozniacki.dk.

WOŹNIAK, Piotr Grzegorz, MSc; Polish business executive and government official; b. 13 Feb. 1956, Warsaw; m.; five c.; ed Warsaw Univ.; Asst Prof. State Geological Inst. 1980–84, 1986–89; head field group Geopol-Polservice in Libya 1985; adviser to Minister of Agric. and Food Economy 1989–90; adviser to Minister of Industry 1990–91; Dir TUW (mutual insurance soc.) 1991; Vice-Chair., mem. of Bd RUCH SA; Rep. of Poland UNIDO Programme; Commercial Consul Polish Embassy Ottawa and Montreal Consulate 1992–96; mem. Bd PAKTO SA 1997–98; Prime Minister's adviser on infrastructure 1998–2000; mem. Supervisory Bd EkoFundusz Foundation 1998–2001, KUKE SA 1998–2002, Polish Oil and Gas Extraction Co. (PGNiG S.A) 1999–2000, Gas Trading S.A. 2000–02, EuRoPol Gaz SA 2000–01; mem. Council for Motorways 1998–2002; Vice-Pres. of Man. Bd for Trade and Restructuring PGNiG SA 2000–02; Deputy of Warsaw Council, Vice-Chair. Econ. Development and Infrastructure Cttee 2002; econ. adviser on fuel gas trading and power industry 2002–05; Chair. Bd of Dirs Ence.Eko Ltd 2004–05; expert, Sejm Investigative Comm. investigating PKN Orlen SA 2004–05; Minister of the Economy 2005–07; mem. Catholic Intelligentsia Club.

WOZNIAK, Stephen (Steve) Gary, BS; American computer scientist and business executive; *Chief Scientist, Fusion-io;* b. 11 Aug. 1950, San Jose, Calif.; m. 1st Alice Robertson 1980 (divorced); m. 2nd Candice Clark Wozniak 1987 (divorced), three c.; m. 3rd Suzanne Mulkern 1990 (divorced); m. 4th Janet Hill 2008; ed Univ. of California, Berkeley; joined Hewlett Packard Co. as designer of calculator chips 1976; Co-founder (with the late Steve Jobs) Apple Computer Inc. 1976, co-designed world's first personal computers, the Apple I and II, Vice-Pres., Research and Devt 1976–81, Designer 1979–81, Vice-Pres., Eng 1983–85, consultant 1985–; Co-founder and Pres. CL9 Remote Control Co. 1985–89; Co-Chair. Axlon Inc. 1986–; Co-founder Wheels of Zeus (wOz) 2002, CEO and Chair. 2002–04, Pres. 2004–06; Co-founder and Exec. Vice-Pres. Acquicor Tech Inc. (now Jazz Technologies, Inc.) 2005–; mem. Bd of Dirs Fusion-io, Salt Lake City 2008–, Chief Scientist 2009–; Founder, Electronic Frontier Foundation; Founding Sponsor, Tech Museum, Silicon Valley Ballet, Children's Discovery Museum of San Jose; Hon. DSc (North Carolina State Univ.) 2004, (Kettering Univ.) 2005, (ESPOL Univ., Ecuador) 2008, (Michigan State Univ.) 2011, (State Engineering Univ., Armenia) 2011, (Santa Clara Univ.) 2012, (Univ. Camilo Jose Cela, Spain) 2013, (Universidad San Juan Bautista, Peru) 2015; Grace Murray Hopper Award, Asscn of Computing Machinery 1979, Nat. Medal of Tech. 1985, Inventors Hall of Fame 2000, Heinz Award for Tech. 2000, Global Award of Pres. of Armenia for Outstanding Contrib. to Humanity Through IT 2011, Hoover Medal 2014, Lifetime Achievement Award, New York City Chapter of Young Pres Org. 2014, Alumnus of the Year Award, Cal Alumni Asscn 2015. *Publications include:* iWoz: Computer Geek to Cult Icon 2006. *Leisure interests:* children, dogs. *Address:* Fusion-io, 6350 South 3000 East, 6th Floor, Salt Lake City, UT 84121 (office); Acquicor Tech Inc., 4910 Birch Street, Suite 102, Newport Beach, CA 92660, USA (office). *Website:* www.fusionio.com (office); www.woz.org (office).

WOŹNICKI, Jerzy, PhD, DSc; Polish scientist and business executive; *President, Polish Rectors Foundation;* b. 22 May 1947, Kotuń; ed Warsaw Univ. of Tech.; Dean, Faculty of Electronics and IT, Warsaw Univ. of Tech. 1990–96, Rector 1996–2002; Deputy Chair. Supervisory Bd, Bank Pekao SA 1999–2005, 2011–12, Chair. 2005–11, 2012–17; fmr Polish Govt Scientific Expert, UNESCO; Deputy Pres. Conf. of Rectors of Academic Schools in Poland (CRASP) 1997–99, Pres. 1999–2002, Hon. Pres. 2002–05, Head, CRASP Commission for Legislative and Organisational Issues 1997–99, 2005–08, 2008–14; Chair. of team of experts for preparing a new Law on Higher Educ. 2003–05; Leader, group of experts working on Strategy for Development of Higher Educ. 2010–; Pres. Nat. Council for Science and Higher Educ., Poland 2014–17; currently Pres. Polish Rectors Foundation; Dir, Inst. of Knowledge Soc.; Chair. Poland in the United Europe Cttee, Polish Acad. of Sciences; Deputy Chair. Nat. Council of European Integration; mem. Cttee of Ethics in Science operating at Presidium of Polish Acad. of Sciences; originator and co-author of Code of Best Practices for Higher Education Institutions; Kt's Cross, Order of Polonia Restituta 1994, Chevalier, Légion d'honneur 1996, Commdr's Cross with Star of Order of Rebirth of Poland 2012, Chevalier, Légion d'honneur; Dr hc (Univ. of Warmia and Mazury, Olsztyn), (Wrocław Univ. of Environmental and Life Sciences, Poland), (Taras Shevchenko Nat. Univ. of Kyiv, Ukraine); numerous awards from Ministry of Nat. Educ., Award of Stefan Batory Foundation, Medal 'For Merit to Banking', Pres. of Nat. Bank of Poland. *Publications:* A Flexible System of Two Cycles (ed.) 1996, The Basic Techniques of Image Processing 1996, Public Management Model Academic Institution 1999, Colleges in Partnership with its Environment. Selected Speeches and Other Public Appearances 2002, Benefits and Costs Associated with the Polish Accession to the European Union in the Field of Higher Education (co-author) 2003, Academic Institutions as Institutions of Public Life 2007, The University as an Institution of Public Domain: The English Perspective 2009. *Address:* 00-432 Warsaw, Górnośląska 14, Poland (office). *Telephone:* (22) 6210972 (office). *Fax:* (22) 6210973 (office). *E-mail:* frpfund@mbox.pw.edu.pl (office). *Website:* www.pekao.com.pl (office); www.frp.org.pl.

WRAGG, John, ARCA, RA; British sculptor; b. 20 Oct. 1937, York, England; s. of Arthur Wragg and Ethel Wragg; ed York School of Art and Royal Coll. of Art, London; ARA 1983, RA 1991; taught at Chelsea School of Art 1961–90; work represented in several public collections, including Tate Gallery, London, Arts Council of GB, Arts Council of NI, Contemporary Art Soc., Nat. Gallery of Modern Art, Edin., Israel Museum, Jerusalem, Wellington Art Gallery, NZ, Sainsbury Centre for Visual Arts, Univ. of East Anglia; mem. Royal Soc. of British Sculptors 1996; Sainsbury Award 1960, winner, Sainsbury Sculpture Competition, Chelsea 1966, Arts Council of GB Major Award 1977, Chantrey Bequest 1981. *Leisure interests:* walking, listening to music, reading. *Address:* 6 Castle Lane, Devizes, Wilts., SN10 1HJ, England. *Telephone:* (1380) 727087. *E-mail:* john@johnwraggra.co.uk. *Website:* www.johnwraggra.co.uk.

WREN, John D.; American advertising executive; *Chairman and CEO, Omnicom Group Inc.;* b. 1 July 1952, New York; joined Needham Harper Worldwide as an Exec. Vice-Pres. 1984; part of team that created Omnicom 1986, CEO Omnicom's Diversified Agency Services div. 1990, grew Diversified Agency Services into Omnicom's largest operating group, comprising cos ranging from public relations to branding, Pres. Omnicom Group 1996–2013, CEO 1997– (merged with Publicis Groupe 2013), Chair. 2018–; mem. Int. Business Council, World Economic Forum; mem. Bd of Dirs, Lincoln Center for Performing Arts; Trustee, Arthus Ashe Foundation; Ellis Island Medal of Honor 1999. *Address:* Omnicom Group Inc., 437 Madison Avenue, New York, NY 10022, USA (office). *Telephone:* (212) 415-3600 (office). *Fax:* (212) 415-3530 (office). *Website:* www.omnicomgroup.com (office).

WRIGHT, Alexander (Alastair) Finlay, MBE, MD; British fmr medical practitioner; b. 19 March 1933, Blantyre, Scotland; s. of Alexander Finlay Wright and Mary Paterson; m. Barbara Lattimer 1957; three s. one d.; ed Hamilton Acad., Univ. of Glasgow; gen. medical practitioner, medical researcher, teacher 1961–92; Council of Europe Fellowship, France 1976; Chair. Clinical and Research Div. Royal Coll. of Gen. Practitioners 1990–91; mem. Scientific Cttee, Jt Royal Coll. 'Defeat Depression' Campaign 1991–98; Ed. British Journal of Gen. Practice 1991–99; Fellow, Royal Coll. of Gen. Practitioners; Hon. Fellow, Royal Coll. of Psychiatrists 1998; Sima/Jansson Prize for Research in Gen. Practice 1981, George Abercrombie Award, Royal Coll. of Gen. Practioners 2000. *Publications include:* Medicine and the New Towns of France 1976, Female Sterilisation: The View From General Practice 1981, Depression: Recognition and Management in General Practice 1993, Psychiatry and General Practice (co-author) 1994. *Leisure interests:* walking, spoken French, grandchildren. *Address:* 5 Alburne Crescent, Glenrothes, Fife, KY7 5RE, Scotland (home). *E-mail:* drafw@blueyonder.co.uk (home).

WRIGHT, Charles Penzel, BA, MFA; American poet, writer and academic; b. 25 Aug. 1935, Pickwick Dam, Tenn.; m. Holly McIntire 1969; one s.; ed Davidson Coll., Univ. of Iowa, Univ. of Rome, Iowa Writers Workshop; served in US Army in Italy; mem. Faculty, Univ. of California, Irvine 1966–83; Asst Prof., then Prof., Univ. of Virginia 1983, now Souder Family Prof. Emer. of English; Poet Laureate of US 2014–15; Fulbright Lecturer, Venice, Italy 1968–69; Distinguished Visiting Prof., Universita Degli Studi, Florence, Italy 1992; mem. Acad. of American Poets (mem. Bd of Chancellors 1999–2002), American Acad. of Arts and Letters, Fellowship of Southern Writers, American Acad. of Arts and Sciences, PEN American Centre; Brandeis Creative Arts Citation for Poetry 1987, Ruth Lilly Poetry Prize for Lifetime Achievement 1993, Critics Award 1999, Artico Fattore Poetry Prize, Italy 1999, Leoncino d'Oro, Commune di Pistoia, Italy. *Publications include:* Grave of the Right Hand 1970, Hard Freight 1973, Bloodlines (Acad. of American Poets Edgar Allan Poe Award 1976) 1975, China Trace 1977, Southern Cross 1981, Country Music (Nat. Book Award for Poetry 1983) 1982, The Other Side of the River 1984, Zone Journals 1988, The World of the 10,000 Things 1990, Chickamauga (Lenore Marshall Poetry Prize 1996) 1995, Black Zodiac (Pulitzer Prize for Poetry 1998, Nat. Book Critics Circle Award 1998, Los Angeles Times Book Prize, Ambassador Book Award) 1997, Appalachia 1998, Negative Blue: Selected Later Poems 2000, A Short History of the Shadow, Snake Eyes 2004, Buffalo Years 2004, Scar Tissue (Griffin Int. Poetry Prize) 2006, Littlefoot 2007, Sestets 2009, Outtakes (with Eric Appleby) 2010, Bye-and-Bye: Selected Late Poems (Bollingen Prize 2013) 2011, Caribou: Poems 2014; trans. of Eugenio Montale's The Storm and Other Poems (PEN Trans. Prize 1979); contrib. to numerous journals and magazines. *Address:* 940 Locust Avenue, Charlottesville, VA 22901, USA (home).

WRIGHT, Sir David John, Kt, GCMG, LVO, MA; British diplomatist and banker; *Vice-Chairman, Barclays Capital;* b. 16 June 1944; s. of J. F. Wright; m. Sally Ann Dodkin 1968; one s. one d.; ed Wolverhampton Grammar School, Peterhouse, Cambridge; Third Sec., Foreign Office 1966, Third Sec., later Second Sec., Tokyo 1966–72, FCO 1972–75, Ecole Nat. d'Admin., Paris 1975–76, First Sec., Paris 1976–80, Pvt. Sec. to Sec. of Cabinet 1980–82, Counsellor (Econ.), Tokyo 1982–85, Head Personnel Services Dept FCO 1985–88; Deputy Pvt. Sec. to HRH the Prince of Wales 1988–90 (on secondment); Amb. to Repub. of Korea 1990–94, to Japan 1996–99; Deputy Under-Sec. of State, FCO 1994–96; Group Chief Exec. (Perm. Sec.) British Trade Int. 1999–2002; Vice-Chair. Barclays Capital 2002–; Hon. Fellow, Peterhouse, Cambridge 2002; Grand Cordon, Order of the Rising Sun (Japan) 1998; Hon. LLD (Wolverhampton) 1997, (Birmingham) 2000. *Leisure interests:* golf, cooking, military history. *Address:* Barclays Capital, 5 North

Colonnade, Canary Wharf, London, E14 4BB, England (office). *Telephone:* (20) 7773-5599 (office). *Fax:* (20) 7773-1806 (office). *E-mail:* david.wright@barcap.com (office).

WRIGHT, James E., PhD; American historian, academic and university administrator; *President Emeritus and Eleazar Wheelock Professor of History, Dartmouth College;* b. 16 Aug. 1939, Madison, Wis.; m. Susan DeBevoise Wright; two s. one d.; ed Galena High School, Wisconsin State Univ. (now Univ. of Wisconsin-Platteville), Univ. of Wisconsin-Madison; served for three years in US Marine Corps, postings that included Calif., Hawaii and Japan; Asst Prof. of History, Dartmouth Coll., Hanover, NH 1969–74, Assoc. Prof. 1974–80, Prof. of History 1980, Dean, Faculty of Arts and Sciences 1989–97, Provost and Acting Pres. 1995, Acting Provost, then Provost 1997, Pres. Dartmouth Coll. 1998–2009, Pres. Emer. and Eleazar Wheelock Prof. of History 2009–; Sr Historian, Univ. of Mid-America (consortium of nine Midwestern univs) 1976–77; mem. American Acad. of Arts and Sciences, Org. of American Historians, Western History Asscn; mem. Bd of Trustees Sherman Fairchild Foundation; fellowships from Danforth Foundation and IBM Corpn, Social Science Research Council Grant, Guggenheim Fellowship, Charles Warren Fellowship, Harvard Univ., American Acad. of Arts and Sciences, Marine Corps Scholarship Foundation's Semper Fidelis Award, New Englander of the Year, New England Council 2007, Semper Fidelis Award, Marine Corps Scholarship Foundation 2008, C-in-C's Gold Medal of Merit Award and Citation, Veterans of Foreign Wars 2009, Eleanor M. McMahon Award for Lifetime Achievement, New England Bd of Higher Educ. 2010. *Television includes:* Sr Historian for award-winning six-film series on history of the Great Plains 1976–78; participated in confs on 'TV and the Historian' and 'The Historian as Film-Maker' 1978; served as Chair. American Historians' Cttee on TV, Film and Media. *Publications include:* author or ed. of six books: The Galena Lead District: Federal Policy and Practices, 1824–1847 1966, The West of the American People 1970, The Politics of Populism: Dissent in Colorado 1974, The Great Plains Experience: Readings in the History of a Region 1978, The Progressive Yankees: Republican Reformers in New Hampshire 1987, Those Who Have Borne the Battle: A History of America's Wars and Those Who Fought Them 2012. *Address:* History Department, Dartmouth College, 300 Carson Hall, 2 Dorrance Place, Suite A, 6166, Hanover, NH 03755, USA (office). *Telephone:* (603) 646-0016 (office). *E-mail:* James.E.Wright@Dartmouth.edu (office). *Website:* history.dartmouth.edu (office).

WRIGHT, James R., BA, MA; Canadian diplomatist (retd); b. Montreal; m. Donna Thomson; one s. one d.; ed McGill Univ., Montreal; joined Dept of Foreign Affairs 1976, fmr Dir of Personnel, Dir-Gen. for Cen., East and S Europe Bureau 1996–2000, Political Dir and Asst Deputy Minister, Int. Security Br. 2000–06; served at Embassy in Moscow 1978–80, Embassy in Washington, DC 1983–87, Minister Political and Public Affairs, High Comm. to UK 1992–96, High Commr 2006–11; ex officio Gov. Ditchley Foundation; mem. Bd of Dirs Commonwealth War Graves Comm., Imperial War Museum; worked with Canadian actor R. H. Thomson on an int. First World War centennial project entitled The World Remembers; Dr hc (Univ. of Ulster) 2008; Queen's Diamond Jubilee Medal 2013.

WRIGHT, Rt Hon. Jeremy Paul, QC, PC, LLB; British politician; *Secretary of State for Digital, Culture, Media and Sport;* b. 24 Oct. 1972, Taunton, Somerset; m. Yvonne Salter 1998; one s. one d.; ed Taunton School, Trinity School, New York, USA, Univ. of Exeter, Inns of Court School of Law; called to the Bar 1996, specialized in criminal law (prosecution and defence); mem. No. 5 Chambers, Birmingham; MP (Conservative) for Rugby and Kenilworth 2005–10, for Kenilworth and Southam 2010–, mem. Constitutional Affairs Cttee 2005–07, Justice Cttee, f. All-Party Parl. Group on Dementia 2007; Opposition Whip (Commons) 2007–10; Lord Commr (HM Treasury) (Whip) 2010–12; Parl. Under-Sec. for Justice 2012–14; Attorney-Gen. for England and Wales and Advocate-Gen. for NI 2014–18; Sec. of State for Digital, Culture, Media and Sport 2018–. *Address:* Department for Digital, Culture, Media and Sport, 100 Parliament St, London, SW1A 2BQ, England (office); House of Commons, Westminster, London, SW1A 0AA, England (office). *Telephone:* (20) 7211-6000 (Dept) (office); (20) 7219-8299 (Westminster) (office). *E-mail:* enquiries@culture.gov.uk (office); pickeringc@parliament.uk (office). *Website:* www.gov.uk/government/organisations/department-for-digital-culture-media-sport (office); www.jeremywrightmp.co.uk.

WRIGHT, Joe; British film and television director; b. 25 Aug. 1972, London; m. Anoushka Shankar (d. of Ravi Shankar) (divorced 2018); two s. *Films directed:* Pride & Prejudice 2005 (numerous awards including Boston Soc. of Film Critics Award for Best New Filmmaker 2005, BAFTA Carl Foreman Award 2006), Atonement 2007, The Soloist 2009, Hanna 2011, Anna Karenina 2012, Pan 2015, Darkest Hour (Hollywood Film Award for Director of the Year 2017) 2017. *Films produced:* exec. producer: Small Gifts (short) 2010, Plagium (short) 2011, Redemption 2013, Locke 2013. *Television includes:* Nature Boy (mini-series) 2000, Bob & Rose (series) 2001, Bodily Harm (mini-series) 2002, Charles II: The Power & the Passion (mini-series) (BAFTA TV Award for Best Drama Serial 2004, jtly) 2003.

WRIGHT, Rt Rev. N(icholas) T(homas), BA, MA, DPhil, DD . FRSE; British theologian, academic and fmr Anglican bishop; *Professor of New Testament and Early Christianity, School of Divinity, St Mary's College, University of St Andrews;* b. 1 Dec. 1948, Morpeth, Northumberland; s. of Nicholas Irwin Wright and Rosemary Wright (née Forman); m. Margaret Elizabeth Anne Fiske 1971; two s. two d.; ed Sedbergh School, Exeter Coll., Oxford, Wycliffe Hall, Oxford; ordained deacon 1975, priest 1976; Jr Research Fellow, Merton Coll., Oxford 1975–78, Jr Chaplain 1976–78; Fellow and Chaplain, Downing Coll., Cambridge 1978–81; Asst Prof. of New Testament Studies, McGill Univ., Montreal and Hon. Prof., Montreal Diocesan Theological Coll., Canada 1981–86; Lecturer in Theology, Univ. of Oxford and Fellow, Tutor and Chaplain, Worcester Coll., Oxford 1986–93; Dean of Lichfield 1994–99; Canon Theologian of Coventry Cathedral 1992–99; Canon Theologian of Westminster 2000–03; Bishop of Durham 2003–10 (retd); Prof. of New Testament and Early Christianity, St Mary's Coll., Univ. of St Andrews 2010–; Fellow, Inst. for Christian Studies, Toronto 1992–; mem. Doctrine Comm., Church of England 1979–81, 1989–95, Lambeth Comm. 2004; regular broadcasts on TV and radio; Hon. Fellow, Downing Coll., Cambridge 2003, Merton Coll., Oxford 2004; Burkitt Medal for Biblical Studies, British Acad. 2014; Hon. DD (Aberdeen) 2000, (Nashotah House) 2006, (Wycliffe Coll., Toronto) 2006, (Durham) 2007, (St Andrews) 2009, (Northumbria) 2010, (London) 2010, (St Mary's Baltimore) 2012, (Fribourg, Switzerland) 2014, (Sewanee) 2015, (Huron Coll., Ontario) 2015, Hon. DHumLitt (Gordon Coll., Mass) 2003; Mark O. Hatfield Leadership Award, Council for Christian Colls and Univs 2014, Dallas Willard Award 2017, Gifford Lecturer 2018. *Publications include:* Small Faith, Great God 1978, The Work of John Frith 1983, The Epistles of Paul to the Colossians and to Philemon 1987, The Glory of Christ in the New Testament (co-ed.) 1987, The Interpretation of the New Testament 1861–1986 (co-author) 1988, The Climax of the Covenant 1991, New Tasks for a Renewed Church 1992, The Crown and the Fire 1992, The New Testament and the People of God 1992, Who Was Jesus? 1992, Following Jesus 1994, Jesus and the Victory of God 1996, The Lord and His Prayer 1996, What Saint Paul Really Said 1997, For All God's Worth 1997, Reflecting the Glory 1998, The Meaning of Jesus (co-author) 1999, The Myth of the Millennium 1999, Romans and the People of God (co-ed.) 1999, Holy Communion for Amateurs 1999, The Challenge of Jesus 2000, Twelve Months of Sundays, Year C 2000, Easter Oratorio (co-author) 2000, Twelve Months of Sundays, Year A 2001, Luke for Everyone 2001, Mark for Everyone 2001, Paul for Everyone: Galatians and Thessalonians 2002, John for Everyone 2002, Twelve Months of Sundays, Year B 2002, New Interpreter's Bible, Vol. X (contrib.) 2002, The Contemporary Quest for Jesus 2002, Paul for Everyone (The Prison Letters) 2002, Matthew for Everyone 2002, Paul for Everyone (I Corinthians 2003), Paul for Everyone (II Corinthians) 2003, Quiet Moments 2003, The Resurrection of the Son of God 2003, For All the Saints? 2003, Hebrews for Everyone 2003, Paul for Everyone (The Pastoral Letters) 2003, Paul for Everyone: Romans 2004, Scripture and the Authority of God 2005, Paul: Fresh Perspectives 2005, Simply Christian 2006, Evil and the Justice of God 2006, Judas and the Gospel of Jesus 2006, The Cross and the Colliery 2007, Surprised by Hope 2007, Acts for Everyone 2008, Jesus: the Final Days 2008, Anglican Evangelical Identity 2008, Justification 2009, For Everyone Bible Study Guides 2009, Lent for Everyone 2009, Virtue Reborn 2010, Simply Jesus: A New Vision of Who He Was, What He Did, and Why He Matters 2011, How God Became King: The Forgotten Story of the Gospels 2012, Lent for Everyone: Mark 2012, The Case for the Psalms 2013, Pauline Perspectives 2013, Paul and the Faithfulness of God 2013, Creation Power and Truth 2013, Surprised by Scripture 2014, Simply Good News 2015, The Paul Debate 2015, Paul and His Recent Interpreters 2015, God in Public 2016, The Day the Revolution Began 2016, Advent for Everyone (Matthew) 2016, Spiritual and Religious: The Gospel in an Age of Paganism 2017, Paul: A Biography 2018, The Bible for Everyone (with John Goldingay) 2018. *Leisure interests:* music, hill walking, poetry, golf. *Address:* School of Divinity, St Mary's College, University of St Andrews, South Street, St Andrews, Fife, KY16 9JU, Scotland (office). *Telephone:* (1334) 462827 (office). *E-mail:* ntw2@st-andrews.ac.uk (office). *Website:* www.st-andrews.ac.uk/divinity (office); www.ntwrightpage.com; www.ntwrightonline.org.

WRIGHT, Sir Peter Robert, Kt, CBE; British ballet director and choreographer; *Director Laureate, Birmingham Royal Ballet;* b. 25 Nov. 1926, London, England; s. of Bernard Wright and Hilda Wright (née Foster); m. Sonya Hana 1954; one s. one d.; ed Bedales School and Leighton Park School, Reading; 1944 debut as professional dancer with Ballets Jooss; during 1950s worked with several dance cos. including Sadler's Wells Theatre Ballet; created first ballet, A Blue Rose, for Sadler's Wells 1957; Ballet Master, Sadler's Wells Opera and teacher, Royal Ballet School 1959–61; teacher and ballet master to ballet co. formed by John Cranko in Stuttgart 1961–65; choreographed several ballets in Stuttgart including The Mirror Walkers, Namouna, Designs for Dancers, Quintet and mounted his first production of Giselle; producer of TV ballets and choreographer of various London West End musicals and revues during 1960s; Asst Dir The Royal Ballet 1969, later Assoc. Dir; Dir Sadler's Wells Royal Ballet (Birmingham Royal Ballet since 1990) 1977–95, Dir Laureate, Birmingham Royal Ballet 1995–; Gov. Royal Ballet School 1976–2002, Sadler's Wells Theatre 1987–2000; Special Prof. of Performance Studies, Univ. of Birmingham 1990–; Fellow, Birmingham Conservatoire of Music 1991–; Pres. Council of Dance Educ. and Training 1994–99, Friends of Sadler's Wells Theatre 1995–2003, Benesh Inst. of Choreology 1994–; Vice-Pres. Royal Acad. of Dancing 1993–; Hon. DMus (London) 1990, Hon. DLitt (Birmingham) 1994; Evening Standard Award for Ballet 1981, Elizabeth II Coronation Award, Royal Acad. of Dancing 1990, Digital Premier Award 1991, Critics' Award for Services to the Arts 1995, De Valois Award for Outstanding Achievement, Critics' Circle Nat. Dance Awards 2004, Critics' Circle Centenary Award 2014. *Ballets directed include:* many new productions in various countries of the full-length classics Giselle, Coppelia, Swan Lake, The Sleeping Beauty, The Nutcracker, but particularly for The Royal Ballet and the Birmingham Royal Ballet; original works for Sadlers Wells Royal Ballet include: A Blue Rose, Arpège, El Amor Brujo, Summer's Night, Summertide; for the Stuttgart Ballet: Mirror Walkers, Designs for Dancers, Quintet; for Western Theatre Ballet: Musical Chairs. *Leisure interests:* ceramics, gardens, travel, music. *Address:* Flat 5, Wedderburn House, 95 Lower Sloane Street, London, SW1W 8BZ, England (home). *Telephone:* (20) 7823-4530 (home). *E-mail:* petsoprods@aol.com (home).

WRIGHT, Robert (Bob) Charles, LLB; American broadcasting executive (retd); b. 23 April 1943, Hempstead, NY; m. Suzanne Wright 1967; one s. two d.; ed Chaminade High School, Holy Cross Coll., Univ. of Virginia Law School; career in gen. man. marketing, broadcasting, strategic planning and law; fmr Pres. Cox Cable Communications; later Pres. Gen. Electric Financial Services, Vice-Chair. 2001; Pres. and CEO NBC 1986–2001, Chair. and CEO 2001–04, then Chair. and CEO NBC Universal Inc. (following NBC merger with Vivendi Universal) 2004–07; Co-founder (with wife) Austism Speaks (foundation); mem. Bd of Dirs Ralph Lauren Corpn, Mission Product, LLC, AMC Networks Inc.; Trustee, New York Presbyterian Hospital; Chair. and CEO Palm Beach Civic Asscn; Sr Advisor, THL Capital; Double Helix Medal Honoree, Cold Spring Harbor Lab. (co-recipient with his wife) 2006, Dean's Medal, Johns Hopkins Bloomberg School of Public Health (co-recipient with his wife) 2013. *Address:* Autism Speaks, 1 East 33rd Street, 4th Floor, New York, NY 10016, USA. *Website:* www.autismspeaks.org.

WRIGHT OF RICHMOND, Baron (Life Peer), cr. 1994, of Richmond-upon-Thames in the London Borough of Richmond-upon-Thames; **Patrick Richard Henry Wright,** KStJ, GCMG, MA, FRCM; British diplomatist (retd); b. 28 June 1931, Reading, Berks., England; s. of Herbert H. S. Wright and Rachel Wright (née Green); m. Virginia Anne Gaffney 1958; two s. one d.; ed Marlborough Coll., Merton Coll., Oxford; served with RA 1950–51; joined Diplomatic Service 1955, Middle East Centre for Arabic Studies 1956–57, Third Sec., Embassy in Beirut

1958–60, Pvt. Sec. to Amb., later First Sec., Embassy in Washington, DC 1960–65, Pvt. Sec. to Perm. Under-Sec., FCO 1965–67, First Sec. and Head of Chancery, Embassy in Cairo 1967–70, Deputy Political Resident, Bahrain 1971–72, Head of Middle East Dept, FCO 1972–74; Pvt. Sec. (Overseas Affairs) to Prime Minister 1974–77; Amb. to Luxembourg 1977–79, to Syria 1979–81, to Saudi Arabia 1984–86, Deputy Under-Sec., FCO 1982–84, Chair. Jt Intelligence Cttee 1982–84, Perm. Under-Sec. of State, FCO and Head of Diplomatic Service 1986–91; Dir Barclays Bank PLC 1991–96, BP 1991–2000, De La Rue 1991–2000, Unilever 1991–99, British Airports Authority 1992–98; mem. Council, Royal Coll. of Music 1991–2001; Chair. Royal Inst. for Int. Affairs 1995–99, Home-Start Int. 2004–07, currently Hon. Pres.; mem. (Crossbench), House of Lords 1994–, Chair. Sub-cttee F (Home Affairs) 2004–07, mem. European Select Cttee 2004–07, Sub-cttee E (Law and Insts) 2008–12, UK Del. to Parl. Ass. of the Council of Europe (PACE) 2016–; Gov. Wellington Coll. 1991–2001, Fellow 2012–; Hon. Fellow, Merton Coll., Oxford; Parliamentary Speech of the Year, House Magazine 2004. *Publication:* Behind Diplomatic Lines: Relations with Ministers 2018. *Leisure interests:* philately, piano duets. *Address:* House of Lords, Westminster, London, SW1A 0PW, England. *Telephone:* (20) 8876-4176 (home). *E-mail:* prhwright@btinternet.com.

WRIGHTON, Mark Stephen, BS, MS, PhD; American professor of chemistry and university administrator; *Chancellor, Washington University in St Louis;* b. 11 June 1949, Jacksonville, Fla; s. of Robert Wrighton and Doris Wrighton; m. Risa Zwerling Wrighton; ed Florida State Univ., California Inst. of Tech.; Asst Prof. of Chem., MIT 1972–76, Assoc. Prof. 1976–77, Prof. 1977–81, Frederick G. Keyes Chair in Chem. 1981–89, Ciba-Geigy Chair in Chem. (first holder) 1989, Head of Dept of Chem. 1987–90, Provost of MIT 1990–95; Chancellor, Washington Univ. in St Louis 1995–; mem. numerous advisory cttees including Chem. Research Evaluation Panel for Air Force Office of Scientific Research 1976–80, American Physical Soc. Study Group on Solar Photovoltaic Energy Conversion 1977–79, Advisory Cttee of Chem. Div., Oak Ridge Nat. Lab. 1983–85, Advisory Cttee for NSF Chem. Div. 1984–87 (Chair. 1986–87), Basic Energy Sciences Advisory Cttee of Dept of Energy 1986–89, Science Advisory Cttee of Electric Power Research Inst. 1990–92, NSF Materials Research Advisory Cttee 1990–91, Defense Sciences Research Council of Advanced Research Projects Agency 1981–97, Corpn of Woods Hole Oceanographic Inst. 1991–95, Corpn of Draper Lab. 1994–96; mem.-at-large Gordon Research Council 1986–89; presidential appointee to Nat. Science Bd 2000–06; fmr Chair. Cabot Corpn, Business-Higher Educ. Forum, Asscn of American Univs; mem. Bd of Dirs A.G. Edwards, Inc. 2001–07, Chemical Heritage Foundation 1998–2002, Brooks Automation, Inc., Donald Danforth Plant Science Center, Universities Research Asscn, St Louis Regional Chamber and Growth Asscn, Missouri Botanical Garden; mem. Editorial Advisory Bd numerous journals; Trustee Higher Learning Comm. of North Cen. Asscn of Colls and Schools 1998–2002, Barnes-Jewish Hosp., BJC Healthcare, Innovate St Louis, St Louis Art Museum, St Louis Science Center, St Louis Symphony Orchestra; mem. American Philosophical Soc. 2001; Fellow, AAAS 1986, Acad. Academy of Arts and Sciences 1988; Hon. Prof., Shandong Univ., Jinan, People's Repub. of China 2002; Hon. DSc (Univ. of West Florida) 1983, Dr hc (Fudan Univ.) 2010; numerous awards including Monsanto Chem. Award for outstanding research, Florida State Univ., Alfred P. Sloan Research Fellowship 1974–76, Dreyfus Teacher-Scholar Grant 1975–80, ACS Pure Chem. Award 1981, MIT Chem. Dept Grad. Teaching Award 1981, ACS Award in Inorganic Chem. 1988, MacArthur Prize Fellowship 1983, Gregory and Freda Halpern Award in Photochemistry, New York Acad. of Sciences 1983, E.O. Lawrence Award, US Dept of Energy 1983, MIT School of Science Teaching Prize 1987, first recipient of Herbert Newby McCoy Award, Calif. Inst. of Tech., Distinguished Alumni Award, Calif. Inst. of Tech. 1992, named by the Arthritis Foundation's Eastern Missouri Chapter Humanitarian of the Year 2000, Right Arm of St Louis Award, St Louis Regional Chamber and Growth Asscn 2010. *Publications:* Organometallic Photochemistry (co-author) 1979; 14 patents and 300+ articles published in professional and scholarly journals on transition metal catalysis, photochemistry, surface chemistry, molecular electronics and photoprocesses at electrodes. *Address:* Office of the Chancellor, Washington University in St Louis, Campus Box 1192, One Brookings Drive, St Louis, MO 63130, USA (office). *Telephone:* (314) 935-5100 (office). *Fax:* (314) 935-4744 (office). *E-mail:* wrighton@wustl.edu (office). *Website:* www.wustl.edu (office).

WRIGLEY, Sir Edward Anthony, Kt, MA, PhD, FBA; British academic; b. 17 Aug. 1931, Manchester, England; s. of Edward Wrigley and Jessie Wrigley; m. Maria Laura Spelberg 1960; one s. three d.; ed King's School, Macclesfield and Peterhouse, Cambridge; William Volker Research Fellow, Univ. of Chicago 1953–54; Fellow, Peterhouse 1958–79, Sr Bursar 1964–74, Hon. Fellow 1996–; Lecturer in Geography, Univ. of Cambridge 1958–74; Assoc. Dir Cambridge Group for the History of Population and Social Structure 1964–95; mem. Inst. of Advanced Study, Princeton 1970–71; Hinkley Visiting Prof., Johns Hopkins Univ. 1975; Tinbergen Visiting Prof., Erasmus Univ., Rotterdam 1979; Prof. of Population Studies, LSE 1979–88; Pres. Manchester Coll. Oxford 1987–96; Sr Research Fellow, All Souls Coll. Oxford 1988–94, Acad. Sec. 1992–94, Fellow 2002–05; Prof. of Econ. History, Univ. of Cambridge 1994–97; Master, Corpus Christi Coll., Cambridge 1994–2000; Ed. Econ. History Review 1985–92; Treas. British Acad. 1989–95, Pres. 1997–2001; Pres. British Soc. for Population Studies 1977–79; Chair. Population Investigation Cttee 1984–90; Hon. Fellow, LSE 1997; Hon. DLitt (Manchester) 1997, (Sheffield) 1997, (Bristol) 1998, (Oxford) 1999, (Leicester) 1999, (Queen Mary) 2004; Hon. DScS (Edin.) 1998; James Ford Special Lecturer, Oxford 1986, Ellen Macarthur Lecturer, Cambridge 1987, Linacre Lecturer, Oxford 1998, Laureate of the Int. Union for the Scientific Study of Population 1993, Founder's Medal, Royal Geographical Soc. 1997, Leverhulme Medal, British Acad. 2005. *Publications include:* Continuity, Chance and Change 1989, Poverty, Progress and Population 2004, several works on econ. and demographic history. *Leisure interest:* gardening. *Address:* 13 Sedley Taylor Road, Cambridge, CB2 8PW, England (home). *Telephone:* (1223) 247614 (home). *E-mail:* eaw20@cam.ac.uk (office).

WU, Aiying; Chinese politician; *Minister of Justice;* b. 1951, Changle Co., Shandong Prov.; ed Shandong Univ., Cen. Communist Party School; joined CCP 1970, began career 1973; served successively as teacher in Communist Party (CP) School of Party Cttee of Changle Co., Deputy Sec.-Gen. CP Cttee of Gaoya Communist Soc. under Changle Co., Perm. mem. CP Cttee of Changle Co., Deputy

Sec.-Gen. Chengguan Communist Soc. under Changle Co., Deputy Sec.-Gen. CP Cttee of Changle Co., Deputy Dir Revolutionary Cttee of Co. and concurrently Sec.-Gen. CP Cttee and Dir Revolutionary Cttee of Chengguan Communist Soc. 1973–78; served successively as Sec. Gen. Changwei Regional Cttee of Communist Youth League and Sec.-Gen. Regional Party Group 1978–82; worked successively as Deputy Sec.-Gen. Shandong Prov. Cttee of Communist Youth League, Vice-Pres. and Pres. Shandong Prov. Youth Union and Dir-Gen. Shandong Provincial Youth Working Cttee 1982–89; Vice-Chair. Shandong Prov. Women's Fed. 1989–90, Chair. 1990–93; Deputy Sec.-Gen. Prov. Party Group 1989–93; Sec.-Gen. Party Group and concurrently Pres. Shandong Br. of China Women Leaders' Training Coll. 1989–93; Vice-Gov. Shandong Prov. and mem. Shandong CP Prov. Cttee 1993–98; Deputy Sec.-Gen. Shandong CP Prov. Cttee 1998–2002, Pres. Prov. Cttee of CPPCC and Sec.-Gen. Party Group of Cttee 2002–04; Vice-Minister of Justice and Deputy Sec.-Gen. of Party Group, Ministry of Justice (with rank of Prin. Minister) 2003–05; Minister of Justice and Sec.-Gen. Party Group, Ministry of Justice 2005–; Alt. mem. 14th CCP Cen. Cttee 1992–97, 15th CCP Cen. Cttee 1997–2002, 16th CCP Cen. Cttee 2002–07, mem. 17th CCP Cen. Cttee 2007–12, 18th CCP Cen. Cttee 2012–; mem. 10th Nat. People's Political Consultative Conf. 2003–08. *Address:* Ministry of Justice, 10 Chaoyangmen, Nan Dajie, Chao Yang Qu, Beijing 100020, People's Republic of China (office). *Telephone:* (10) 65205114 (office). *Fax:* (10) 65205316 (office).

WU, Bai; Taiwanese rock singer, songwriter, musician and actor; b. (Wu Chun-lin), 14 Jan. 1968, Suantou, Lioujiao, Chaiyi Prov., Taiwan; m. Chen Wen-pey 2003; formed the band Wu Bai and China Blue, with Dean 'Dino' Zavolta (drums), Yu Ta-hao (keyboards), Chu Chien-hui (bass guitar) and himself on lead guitar and lead vocals 1992. *Films include:* Zheng hun qi shi (The Personals) 1998, Meili xin shijie (A Beautiful New World) 1999, Seunlau ngaklau (Time and Tide) 2000, San ging chaat goo si (New Police Story) 2004, Arthur and the Minimoys (voice) 2007. *Television includes:* Say Yes Enterprise (series) 2004, In a Good Way 2014. *Albums include:* Loving Others is a Happy Thing 1992, Wanderer's Love Song 1994, The End of Love 1996, Lonely Tree, Lonely Bird 1998, (EP) 1998, White Dove 1999, Wu Bai & China Blue Movie Song Book/Time and Tide Soundtrack 2000, Dream River 2001, Tear Bridge (CD and VCD) 2003, Two Faced Man 2005, GO PA 2005, Innocent Years (CD and DVD) 2006, 1015 (CD and DVD) 2007, Spacebomb 2008, Rock and Poetry (CD and DVD) 2009, One Way Ticket 2011, Endless Sorrow Shiny 2013. *Publications:* Moonlight Symphony 2001, Wandering Soul 2002, Scenery (book of his photography) 2007, Story 2009. *Leisure interest:* Japanese pro wrestling. *E-mail:* clubwubai@gmail.com. *Website:* wubai.com.

WU, Bangguo; Chinese party official and engineer; b. 12 July 1941, Feidong Co., Anhui Prov.; m. Zhang Ruizhen; ed Tsinghua Univ., Beijing; joined CCP 1964; worked at Shanghai No. 3 Electronic Tube Factory, progressing from freight worker to Factory Dir 1967–78; Deputy Man. Shanghai Municipal Electronics Components Industry Co., Shanghai Municipal Electrical Vacuum Device Co. 1979–81; Deputy Sec. Parl. Cttee Shanghai Municipal Instruments Bureau 1981–83; mem. Standing Cttee Shanghai Municipal CCP Cttee 1983–85, Deputy Sec. 1986–89, Sec. 1991–94; a Shanghai del. to 8th NPC 1993; mem. CCP Secr. 1994–97; Vice-Premier of State Council 1995–2007; Alt. mem. 13th CCP Cen. Cttee 1987–92, mem. 14th CCP Cen. Cttee 1992–97, 15th CCP Cen. Cttee 1997–2002, 16th CCP Cen. Cttee 2002–07, 17th CCP Cen. Cttee 2007–12; mem. CCP Politburo 1992–2012, CCP Politburo Standing Cttee 2002–12; Chair. Standing Cttee 10th NPC 2003–07, Standing Cttee 11th NPC 2008–13.

WU, Dechang; Chinese toxicologist; b. 22 Oct. 1927, Beijing; m. Lin Rhi-zhu 1951; one s. two d.; ed Peking Univ. and in USSR; Asst Lecturer, later Lecturer, Xiehe Hosp., Beijing 1949; Prof. of Toxicology, Inst. of Radiation Medicine, Beijing 1981; Commdt Mil. Medical Science Acad. of PLA 1990–94; Del. to 14th Nat. Conf. CCP 1992–97; mem. 8th Nat. Cttee CPPCC 1993–97; Deputy Rep., UN Atomic Radiation Effectiveness Science Cttee; Pres. Chinese Soc. of Toxicology 1995, now Hon. Pres.; Academician, Chinese Acad. of Eng 1994–; Nat. Science and Tech. Awards 1985, 1993, 1995, Prize for Outstanding Contributions 1991, Ho Leung Ho Lee Medical Sciences and Materia Medica Prize 2003. *Publications:* Radiation Risk and Assessment 1999, Radiation Medicine 2000. *Leisure interest:* classical music. *Address:* c/o Military Medical Science Academy of People's Liberation Army, 27 Tai-Ping Road, Beijing 100850, People's Republic of China (office).

WU, Den-Yih, BA; Taiwanese politician; *Chairman, Kuomintang (KMT);* b. 30 Jan. 1948, Tsaotun, Nantou Co.; m. Tsai Ling-yi; three s. one d.; ed Nat. Taiwan Univ.; Pres. and Ed.-in-Chief Univ. News, Nat. Taiwan Univ. 1968–69; Instructor, Military Acad. 1970–71; journalist and editorial writer, China Times newspaper 1971–73; mem. Taipei City Council 1973–83; Magistrate, Nantou Co. 1981–89; Chair. Kuomintang (KMT) Taipei Municipal Cttee 1989–90, mem. KMT Cen. Standing Cttee 1993–2000, Vice Chair. and Sec.-Gen., KMT 2007–09, First Vice Chair. 2014, Acting Chair. 2014–15, Chair. 2017–; Mayor of Kaohsiung City 1990–98; Chair. (volunteer), Nantou Co. Cttee, China Youth Corps 2000–02; mem. Legis. Yuan (Parl.) 2002–09; Premier, Repub. of China (Taiwan) 2009–12; Vice-Pres. 2012–16. *Address:* Kuomintang (KMT), 232–234 Bade Road, Sector 2, Taipei 10492, Taiwan (office). *Telephone:* (2) 87711234 (office). *Fax:* (2) 23434561 (office). *Website:* www.kmt.org.tw (office).

WU, Dingfu; Chinese government official; b. July 1946, Hubei; m.; ed Hubei Univ.; joined CCP 1972; has held numerous govt positions including Magistrate, Guangji Co. 1983–84, Deputy Commr, Huanggang Pref., Hubei Prov. 1987–90, Auditor-Gen., Prov. Auditing Office, Hubei Prov. 1991–95; joined Nat. Audit Office 1995, Head, Comm. for Discipline Inspection 1998–2000; Vice-Chair. China Insurance Regulatory Comm. 1998–2000, Chair. 2002–11; mem. Cen. Comm. for Discipline Inspection, CCP Cen. Cttee 2000–02, Sec.-Gen. 2001–02; Alt. Mem. 16th CCP Cen. Cttee 2002–07, 17th CCP Cen. Cttee 2007–12.

WU, Sir Gordon Ying Sheung, Kt, KCMG, FICE, BSc; Chinese real estate executive; *Chairman, Hopewell Holdings;* b. 3 Dec. 1935, Hong Kong; s. of Wu Chung and Wu Sum (née Kang); m. Kwok San-Ping Wu 1970; two s. two d.; ed Princeton Univ., USA; Man. Dir Hopewell Holdings, Hong Kong 1972–2001, Chair. 2001–, Chair. and Exec. Dir Hopewell Highway Infrastructure Ltd 2003–18, non-Exec. Dir April–May 2018; responsible for construction of Hong Kong's tallest bldg, Hopewell Holdings HQ; projects constructed include China Hotel, Canton, China, coal-fired power station for Prov. of Guangdong, China, motorway linking Hong

Kong to Shenzhen and Canton; responsible for design of many of his own bldgs; Vice-Pres. Hong Kong Real Estate Developer's Asscn 1970–; mem. CPPCC 1984–13, Vice-Chair. Cttee for Liaison with Hong Kong, Macao, Taiwan and Overseas Chinese (Special Cttee of CPPCC) 2003–13; Chair. Hong Kong Polytechnic Univ. Council; Adviser, Xiamen Special Econ. Zone, Guangxi Zhuang Autonomous Region, Urban Renewal Authority; mem. UNA of China, Chinese People's Political Consultative Conf.; mem. Int. Advisory Bd, Inst. for Int. Business Communication; mem. Business Advisory Council, IFC of the World Bank Group, APEC; mem. Comm. on Strategic Devt of the Hong Kong Special Admin. Region, Hong Kong Trade Devt Council, Hong Kong Logistic Devt Council; currently Trustee, Princeton Univ.; Fellow, Inst. of Civil Engineers, UK, Hong Kong Acad. of Eng Sciences; Hon. Fellow, The Hong Kong Inst. of Engineers; Hon. Citizen, New Orleans, USA, Guangzhou, People's Repub. of China, Prov. of Quezon, Repub. Philippines; Hon. Vice-Pres. Hong Kong Football Asscn Ltd; numerous honours including Gold Bauhinia Star 2004, Officer de l'Ordre de la Couronne (Belgium) 2007, Order of Danica Hvratska 2007, Lifetime Achievement Award, CNBC Asia Business Leaders Awards 2010, Lifetime Achievement Award, Hong Kong Business Awards 2013, Gold Medal, Hong Kong Inst. of Engineers 2015; several hon. degrees. *Leisure interest:* classical music. *Address:* 64/F, Hopewell Centre, 183 Queen's Road East, Wan Chai, Hong Kong Special Administrative Region, People's Republic of China (office). *Telephone:* 25284975 (office). *Fax:* 28612068 (office). *E-mail:* ir@hopewellholdings.com (office). *Website:* www.hopewellholdings.com (office).

WU, Lt-Gen. Guangyu; Chinese air force officer; b. Dec. 1940, Hongze Co., Jiangsu Prov.; ed middle school and Air Force Aviation School; joined PLA 1958, CCP 1964; air force pilot and squadron leader 1962–70; various posts in Air Force Aviation 1970–85; Commdr Air Force units, PLA Shanghai Base 1985; Commdr PLA Air Force Command Post 1985–90; Deputy Commdr Nanjing Mil. Regional Air Force 1990–93; Deputy Commdr and Air Force Commdr Jinan Mil. Region 1993; Deputy Commdr PLA Air Force 1995; Deputy to 6th NPC 1983; Alt. mem. 14th CCP Cen. Cttee 1992–97, 15th CCP Cen. Cttee 1997–2002.

WU, Guoxiong, PhD; Chinese meteorologist; *Academician, Chinese Academy of Sciences;* b. March 1943, Chaoyang, Guangdong; ed Nanjing Meteorological Inst., Beijing Univ., Imperial Coll. London, UK; Visiting Scientist, ECMWF 1983–84; Research Fellow, Inst. of Atmospheric Physics, Chinese Acad. of Sciences 1985–, currently Sr Scientist; Deputy Chair. Advisory Cttee, Nat. Key Lab. of Atmospheric Sciences and Geophysical Fluid Dynamics 1993–2000; Sr Visiting Research Prof., Geophysical Fluid Dynamics Lab., Princeton Univ., USA 1989–91; Chair. Chinese Cttee for Int. Council for Science (ICSU), mem. Exec. Bd, ICSU; Academician, Chinese Acad. of Sciences 1997–; Hon. Fellow, Royal Meteorological Soc., UK 2012; Second Nat. Natural Science Prize 2007. *Publications:* Time-Mean Statistics of Global General Circulation 1987, Dynamics of the Formation and Variation of the Subtropical Anticyclones 2002. *Address:* Institute of Atmospheric Physics, Chinese Academy of Sciences, Qijiahuozi, Beijing 100029 (office); Room 1302, Building 801-B, Huangzhuang Dwelling, Beijing 100080, People's Republic of China (home). *Telephone:* (10) 82995266 (office). *Fax:* (10) 82995172 (office). *E-mail:* gxwu@lasg.iap.ac.cn (office). *Website:* www.lasg.ac.cn (office).

WU, Hongbo; Chinese diplomatist and UN official; b. May 1952, Shandong Prov.; m.; one d.; ed Beijing Foreign Studies Univ., Victoria Univ. of Wellington, New Zealand; with Beijing Service Bureau for Diplomatic Missions 1976–78, advanced training, Victoria Univ. of Wellington, NZ 1978–80, posted to Embassy in Wellington 1980–81, Beijing Service Bureau for Diplomatic Missions 1981–83, Third Sec., Dept for Dolmetsch and Trans. Service, State Dept of People's Repub. of China 1983–87, Second Sec., Section Chief of Office for Affairs of Hong Kong and Macao 1987–88, Second Sec., Sino-British Jt Liaison Group 1988–89, First Sec., Section Chief of Office for Affairs of Hong Kong and Macao 1991–95, Rep. (with rank of Amb.), Sino-British Jt Liaison Group 1995–97, Amb., Office of the Commr of Ministry of Foreign Affairs, Hong Kong Special Admin. Region 1997–98, Chief Rep. (with rank of Amb.), Sino-British Jt Liaison Group 1998–99, Leader, Dept for Western Europe, State Dept of People's Repub. of China 1999–2000, Leader, Dept for Affairs of Hong Kong and Macao 2000–02, Amb. to Philippines 2003–05, Asst Minister of Foreign Affairs 2007–09, Amb. to Germany 2009–12; Under-Sec.-Gen., Dept of Econ. and Social Affairs, UN 2012–17.

WU, Hsing-kuo; Taiwanese theatre and film actor; *Artistic Director, Contemporary Legend Theatre;* ed Fu-Hsing Chinese Opera School, Taiwan, Theatre Dept of Chinese Culture Univ., Taipei, trained under Chou Cheng-jung (Zhou Zhengrong); became leading dancer of Lin Hwai-min's Cloud Gate Dance Theatre; co-f. Contemporary Legend Theatre, Taipei 1986, sought to revive traditional Chinese theatre by adapting Western classical plays to the style and techniques of Peking Opera; currently Artistic Dir Contemporary Legend Theatre; Chevalier, Ordre des Arts et Lettres 2011; Fulbright Scholarship to study in New York with Richard Schechner 1992, Best New Performer, Hong Kong Film Awards 1992. *Films include:* Shi ba 1993, Temptation of a Monk 1993, Green Snake 1993, The Great Conqueror's Concubine 1994, What Price Survival 1994, Rock 'n' Roll Cop 1994, Red Rose White Rose 1994, God of Gamblers Returns 1994, Shanghai Grand 1996, The Soong Sisters 1997, The Accidental Spy 2001, Master Swordsman Lu Xiaofeng 2001. *Television includes:* Metropolitan Opera: Live in HD (series) 2007. *Address:* Contemporary Legend Theatre, No. 40, 3F-1, Ting Zhou Road Section 2, Taipei 10077, Taiwan (office). *Telephone:* (2) 2369-2616 (office). *Fax:* (2) 2369-2667 (office). *E-mail:* info@cl-theatre.com (office). *Website:* clients.mingisland.com/CLT (office).

WU, Hualun; Chinese artist; b. June 1942, Tianjin; s. of Wu Bing-Zheng and Wang Yaxin; m. Zeng Wan 1985; ed Cen. Acad. of Arts and Crafts; mem. China Artists' Asscn 1982–, China Calligraphists' Asscn 1986–; Sr Art Ed., China People's Fine Art Publishing House; Prof. 1999–; First Prize, Chinese Paintings Competition 1988, Gold Medal, Japan-China Art Exchange Centre 1988. *Publication:* Chinese Paintings by Wu Hualun 1989. *Leisure interests:* travelling, playing badminton. *Address:* People's Fine Arts Publishing House, 32 Bei Zong Bu Hutong, Beijing 100735, People's Republic of China (office). *Telephone:* (10) 65244901 (office).

WU, Huatai, BA; Chinese engineer and mining industry executive; b. 1959, Shanxi; fmr capt., electromechanical section chief and deputy dir, Xishan Mining Bureau Xiqu Coal Mine, Sec. of Party Cttee, Xiqu Coal Mine, Xishan Coal Electricity Group Co., mem. Party Cttee, Shanxi Coking Coal Group Tunlan Mine, Deputy Gen. Man. and mem. Party Cttee Standing Cttee, Xishan Coal Corpn (Xishan Coal Electricity Group Co.), Sec. of Party Cttee and Chair. Huajin Coking Coal Co., mem. Bd of Dirs, Chair. Shanxi Coking Coal Group Co., mem. Party Standing Cttee, Xishan Coal and Electricity (Group) Ltd and Sec. of Party Cttee; apptd Chair. and Sec. of Party Cttee, Shanxi Jincheng Anthracite Mining Group Ltd 2010; part-time Chair. Taiyuan Coal Gasification Co. 2013; mem. 18th CCP Nat. Congress 2012–. *Address:* c/o Shanxi Jincheng Anthracite Mining Group, Beishidian Town, Jincheng 048006, Shanxi, People's Republic of China.

WU, Jianchang; Chinese engineer and business executive; *Honorary Chairman, China Nonferrous Metals Industry Association;* b. June 1939, son-in-law of Deng Xiaoping; m. Deng Lin; ed Henyang Mining Coll.; fmr Deputy Gen. Man. China Nat. Nonferrous Metals Import and Export Corpn; Vice-Pres. China Nat. Nonferrous Metals Industry Corpn 1984–94, later Pres.; Dir (non-exec.) Jianxi Copper Co. Ltd 2008–, Shanxi Tai Gang Stainless Steel Co. 2007–, Silver Grant Int. Industries (Hong Kong), Ind. Dir (non-exec.) Aluminum Corpn of China Ltd 2013–; Consultant China Iron and Steel Asscn; Hon. Chair., China Nonferrous Metals Industry Asscn, China Council for the Promotion of Int. Trade. *E-mail:* www.cmra.cn/en (office).

WU, Jichuan; Chinese fmr politician; b. 1937, Changning Co., Hunan Prov.; m. Gong Shuangjin 1960; two d.; ed Beijing Inst. of Posts and Telecommunications (BIPT), Beijing Univ.; joined CCP 1960; technician, later Div. Chief, later Bureau Dir, Ministry of Posts and Telecommunications 1960–84; taught at BIPT 1962–65; Vice-Minister of Posts and Telecommunications 1984–90, Minister 1993–98; Minister of Information Industry 1998–2003 (retd); Deputy Sec. Henan Prov. CCP Cttee 1990–93; Vice-Chair. State Radio Regulatory Cttee; Deputy Head, State Leading Group for Information 1996; Dir (non-Exec.) China Telecom Corpn Ltd 2007–14 (retd); Alt. mem. 14th CCP Cen. Cttee 1992–97, mem. 15th CCP Cen. Cttee 1997–2002, 16th CCP Cen. Cttee 2002–07.

WU, Jinglian; Chinese economist; *Senior Researcher, State Council Development Research Centre (DRC);* b. Jan. 1930, Nanjing, Jiangsu Prov.; ed Fudan Univ.; Asst Research Fellow, Econs Research Inst. of Chinese Acad. of Sciences 1954–79; Assoc. Research Fellow, Econs Inst. of Chinese Acad. of Social Sciences 1979–83, Research Fellow and Prof. 1983–; Vice-Dir Office for Econ. Reform Programmes of State Council; Sr Researcher, State Council Devt Research Centre; mem. Standing Cttee 9th CPPCC Nat. Cttee 1998–2003, Vice-Chair. Econ. Cttee of CPPCC 1998–2003; Faculty mem., China Europe Int. Business School (CEIBS) 1996–, currently Baosteel Chair Prof. of Econs; Hon. Pres. Int. Econ. Assc 2011; elected one of China's Top Ten Econ. Figures 2000. *Publications:* Explorations into Problems of Economic Reform, Planned Economy or Market Economy, Fifteen Critical Issues of the Reform of SOEs 1999, Reform: Now at a Critical Point 2001, Understanding and Interpreting Chinese Economic Reform 2005. *Address:* Development Research Center of the State Council, No. 225, Chaoyangmen Nei Dajie, Dongcheng District, Beijing 100010, People's Republic of China (office). *Website:* www.drc.gov.cn/english/ (office).

WU, Joseph, (Wu Jaushieh), BA, MA, PhD; Taiwanese politician; *Minister of Foreign Affairs;* b. 31 Oct. 1954, Dacheng; ed Nat. Chengchi Univ., Univ. of Missouri-St Louis, Ohio State Univ.; Research Fellow, Inst. of Int. Relations, Nat. Chengchi Univ. 1989–2002; Deputy Sec.-Gen., Office of the Pres. 2002–04, Sec.-Gen. 2017–18; Chair., Mainland Affairs Council 2004–07; Rep., Taipei Econ. and Cultural Rep. Office in USA 2007–08; mem. Democratic Progressive Party (DRP), DRP Rep. to USA 2012–16, Exec. Dir, DRP Policy Research and Coordination Cttee 2012–14, DRP Sec.-Gen. 2014–16; Sec.-Gen., Nat. Security Council 2016–17; Minister of Foreign Affairs 2018–. *Address:* Ministry of Foreign Affairs, 2 Kaitakeland Blvd, Zhongzheng District, Taipei 10048, Taiwan (office). *Telephone:* (2) 23482999 (office). *Fax:* (2) 23805678 (office). *E-mail:* eyes@mofa.gov.tw (office). *Website:* www.mofa.gov.tw (office).

WU, Liang-Yong; Chinese architect; b. 7 May 1922, Nanjing, Jiangsu Prov.; m. Yao Tong-zhen; two s.; ed Nat. Cen. Univ. China, Cranbrook Acad. of Art, USA; Assoc. Prof. of Architecture and Urban Planning, Tsinghua Univ. 1951–61, Prof. 1961–; Dir Inst. of Architectural and Urban Studies 1983–, Centre for Human Settlements 1995–; Visiting Prof., Centre of Urban Studies and Urban Planning, Univ. of Hong Kong 1983, Ecole de Hautes Etudes Sociales, Paris 1987, Univ. of California, Berkeley 1988, Sydney Univ. of Tech. 1993, Univ. of Cambridge, UK 1995; Vice-Pres. Chinese Soc. for Urban Studies 1984–, Int. Union of Architects 1987–90; Pres. Urban Planning Soc. of China 1993–; mem. Academia Sinica 1980; Fellow, Chinese Acad. of Science 1980–, Int. Acad. of Architecture 1989, Chinese Acad. of Eng 1995–; Hon. mem. Architectural Inst. of Japan 1994; Hon. Fellow, American Inst. of Architects 1990, Royal Inst. of British Architects 1998; Chevalier des Arts et Lettres 1999; numerous awards including Gold Medal in Architecture for the Ju'er Project 1992, Jean Tschumi Prize, Int. Union of Architects 1996, Architectural Soc. of China First Prize of Architecture Design Award for Research Institute of Confucius 2006, State Supreme Science and Tech. Award 2011, Nanjing Univ. Distinguished Alumnus Award 2012. *Publications include:* A Brief History of Ancient Chinese City Planning 1985, Selected Essays on Urban Planning and Design 1987, Rehabilitating the Old City of Beijing 1999, Reflections at the Turn of the Century: The Future of Architecture 1999, Buildings, Cities and Human Settlements 2003; more than 200 academic papers. *Leisure interests:* fine arts including painting and calligraphy. *Address:* School of Architecture, Tsinghua University, Beijing 100084 (office); No. 12, Apt 10, Tsinghua University, Beijing 100084, People's Republic of China (home). *Telephone:* (10) 62784567 (office); (10) 62784507 (home). *Fax:* (10) 6562768 (office); (10) 62781048 (home). *E-mail:* engach@mail.cae.ac.cn (office); wuly@public.bta.net.cn (home).

WU, Min, DMed; Chinese geneticist; *Academician, Chinese Academy of Sciences;* b. 16 Dec. 1925, Peping (now Beijing); ed Tongji Univ. Medical Coll., USSR Acad. of Medical Science; Research Fellow, Chinese Acad. of Medical Sciences, apptd Dir Cytobiology Section of Tumour Research Inst. 1961, Dir Dept of Cell Biology 1974, Nat. Lab. of Molecular Oncology 1988; Academician, Chinese Acad. of Sciences 1980–, fmr Dir Biology Div., mem. Standing Cttee, mem. 4th Presidium 2000–; one of the initiators of nat. Human Genome project in China; fmr Deputy Sec.-Gen. and Deputy Dir-Gen., Council of Chinese Genetics Soc.; Dir Life Science Div., Natural Science Foundation of China; Chair. Chinese Soc. of Genetic Medicine; several awards including Nat. Award of Progress in Science and Tech., Second Class 1985, Golden Bull Prize for Devt of Nat. Labs 1990, 1994, China Tech. Science Prize 1996, Ho Leung Ho Lee Medical Sciences Prize 1998. *Publications:* The Mitotic Caryotype of the Chinese; more than 300 scientific publications. *Address:* Chinese Academy of Sciences, 52 Sanlihe Rd., Xicheng District, Beijing 100864, People's Republic of China (office). *Telephone:* (10) 68597521 (office). *Fax:* (10) 68511095 (office). *E-mail:* cas_en@cas.cn (office). *Website:* english.cas.cn (office).

WU, Poh-Hsiung, BSc; Taiwanese politician; *Honorary Chairman, Kuomintang (KMT);* b. 19 June 1939, Taoyuan County; m. Dai Mei-yu; two s. one d.; ed Nat. Cheng Kung Univ., Sun Yat-sen Inst. of Policy and Research and Devt; school teacher 1963–65; mem. Taiwan Prov. Ass. 1968–72; Assoc. Prof., Nan Ya Jr Coll. of Tech. 1972–73; Magistrate, Taoyuan Co. 1973–76; Dir Inst. of Industry for Workmen and Friends of Labour Asscn, Dir-Gen. Taiwan Tobacco and Wine Monopoly Bureau 1976–80; Dir Inst. of Industrial and Vocational Training for Workmen 1976–80; Chair. Repub. of China Amateur Boxing Asscn 1981–82; Dir Secr., Cen. Cttee, Kuomintang (KMT) 1982–84, Chair. Cen. Exec. Cttee, Vice-Chair. KMT 2000–07, Chair. 2007–09, now Hon. Chair.; Minister of Interior 1984–88, 1991–94; Mayor of Taipei 1988–90; Minister of State 1990–91; apptd Sec.-Gen. Office of the Pres. 1994; Chair. Cen. Election Comm. 1991–94, Political Party Review Cttee 1991–94; Dr hc (Nanjing Univ.) 2009.

WU, Rong-i, MA, MS, PhD; Taiwanese government official and economist; *Chairman, Taiwan Brain Trust;* b. 15 Dec. 1939; m.; one d. one s.; ed Nat. Taiwan Univ., Université Catholique de Louvain, Belgium; Prof. and Dir Dept of Econs, Nat. Chung Hsing Univ. 1975–93; Visiting Scholar, Yale Univ., USA 1982–83; Vice-Pres. Taiwan Inst. of Econ. Research 1991–92, apptd Pres. 1993; Commr Fair Trade Comm., Exec. Yuan 1992–93, mem. Science and Tech. Advisory Group 2004–; Nat. Policy Adviser to Pres. 2000–, mem. Econ. Advisory Group to Pres. 2000–; Vice-Premier and Minister of the Consumer Protection Commission 2005; fmr Chair. Taiwan Stock Exchange; mem. Eminent Persons Group, Asia-Pacific Econ. Co-operation 1993–94; Prof. of Econ. Devt and Industrial Policy, Nat. Chung Hsing Univ.; Chair. Taiwan Brain Trust, Taiwan Think Tank. *Address:* Taiwan Brain Trust, 3F., No.42, Sec. 2, Minquan East Road, Zhongshan Dist, Taipei 10469, Taiwan (office). *E-mail:* info@braintrust.tw (office). *Website:* www.braintrust.tw (office).

WU, Adm. Shengli; Chinese naval officer; *Commander, People's Liberation Army Navy;* b. 1945, Wuqiao City, Hebei Prov.; ed PLA Inst. of Surveying and Mapping; joined PLA 1964, eventually becoming Deputy Commdr, East China Sea Fleet, later Commdr, South China Sea Fleet, Deputy Commdr, Guangzhou Mil. Region, Navy Deputy Chief, HQ of Gen. Staff 2004–06, Commdr, PLA Navy 2006–; rank of Rear-Adm. 1994, Vice-Adm. 2003, Adm. 2007; Del. 17th CCP Nat. Congress 2007–12; Deputy 11th NPC 2008–13; mem. State Central Mil. Comm. 2008–; mem. 17th CCP Cen. Cttee 2007–12, also 17th CCP Cen. Cttee Cen. Mil. Comm. 2007–12; mem. 18th CCP Cen. Cttee 2012–, also 18th CCP Cen. Cttee Cen. Mil. Comm. 2012–. *Address:* Office of the Commander, People's Liberation Army Navy, Ministry of National Defence, 20 Jingshanqian Jie, Beijing 10009, People's Republic of China (office). *E-mail:* chinamod@chinamil.com.cn (office). *Website:* www.mod.gov.cn (office).

WU, Lt-Gen. Shuangzhan; Chinese police officer; b. Feb. 1945, Qingfeng, Henan Prov.; ed PLA Nat. Defence Univ.; joined PLA 1963, CCP 1965; promoted to rank of Maj.-Gen. 1990, Lt-Gen. 1997; Deputy Chief of Staff of Beijing Mil. Area Command 1993; Chief of Staff of the People's Armed Police Force 1993–99, Deputy Commdr-in-Chief 1996–99, C-in-C 1999–2009; mem. 16th CCP Cen. Cttee 2002–07, 17th CCP Cen. Cttee 2007–12; Deputy Dir 11th NPC Internal and Judicial Affairs Cttee 2010–13.

WU, Shuoing; Chinese economist; b. Jiangyin, Jiangyin Prov.; ed Shanghai East-China People's Revolution Univ.; research student of political econ., Renmin Univ.; fmrly Prof., Pres. of Grad. School, Vice-Pres. Renmin Univ.; Prof., Pres. Peking Univ. 1989–96; mem. Standing Cttee 8th and 9th NPC 1993–2003. *Publications:* Shenme Shi Zhengzhi Jingyixue (What Is Political Economy?), Zhongguo Shehuizhuyi Jianshe (China's Socialist Construction), Moshi, Yunxing and Kongzhi (Model, Operation and Control).

WU, Weiran; Chinese surgeon (retd); *Honorary President, Beijing Hospital;* b. 14 Oct. 1920, Changzhou, Jiangsu Prov.; s. of Wu Jingyi and Zheng Zhixia; m. Huang Wuchiung 1951; three d.; ed West China Union Univ.; joined CCP 1956; Deputy Dir Surgery Soc., attached to the Medical Soc. 1972; Deputy Dir Surgery Dept, Beijing Union Medical Coll. Hosp., Chinese Acad. of Medical Sciences 1972; now Prof. of Surgery, Surgical Dept, Beijing Union Medical Coll. Hosp., Chinese Acad. of Medical Sciences; Hon. Pres. Beijing Hosp.; Alt. mem. 12th CCP Cen. Cttee 1982, mem. 1985, 13th Cen. Cttee 1987–92; Del., 14th CCP Nat. Congress 1992–97; mem. 9th CPPCC Nat. Cttee 1998–2003; Nat. Class 2 Award for Scientific and Technological Progress, Nat. Award for his special contribs to work related to health and care, Ministry of Health Class 2 Award for his research into the 'artificial gut' technique. *Publication:* Surgery (co-author). *Leisure interest:* gardening. *Address:* Surgery Department, Beijing Hospital, 1 Dahalu, Dondan, Beijing 100730, People's Republic of China. *Telephone:* 65132266. *Fax:* 65132969.

WU, Xiucheng, PhD; Chinese physicist; *President and Chief Technology Officer, D-Tech Optoelectronics, Incorporated;* held various sr eng positions with Perkin Elmer, Agere and Finisar; fmr Researcher, Centre for Electrophotonic Materials and Devices, McMaster Univ., Hamilton, Ont., Canada; mem. Man. Team AdTech Optics Inc., USA; Pres. and Chief Tech. Officer D-Tech Optoelectronics Inc. 2008–. *Publications:* numerous articles in scientific journals. *Address:* D-Tech Optoelectronics Inc., 18062 Rowland St., City of Industry, CA 91748, USA (office). *Telephone:* (626) 269-1102 (office). *Fax:* (626) 269-1198 (office). *E-mail:* xiucheng.wu@atoptics.com (office). *Website:* www.dtechopto.com (office).

WU, Yajun, BEng; Chinese real estate executive; *Chairman and CEO, Longfor Properties Ltd;* b. 1964, Hechuan, Chongqing; m. Cai Kui (divorced 2012); ed Northwestern Polytechnical Univ.; began career as engineer, Qianwei Meter Factory 1984–88; reporter and ed., China Shirong News Agency 1989–93; f. Jiacheng Econ. Devt Co., Chongqing 1993; f. Longhu Real Estate Devt Co. Ltd 1995; Exec. Dir Longfor Properties Ltd 2007–, also Chair. and CEO; mem. NPC; Vice-Chair. Fed. of Industry and Commerce of Chongqing Municipality; Vice-Chair. Real Estate Br., Chongqing Gen. Chamber of Commerce. *Address:* Longfor Properties Ltd, 7/F Tower 2, FuSheng Building, 4 Huixin East Street, Beijing, People's Republic of China (office). *Telephone:* (10) 8466-1857 (office). *Website:* www.longfor.com (office).

WU, Yan, PhD; Chinese insurance executive; *Executive Chairman, People's Insurance Company (Group) of China Ltd (PICC);* ed Xinjiang Coll. of Finance and Econs, China Acad. of Social Sciences; Deputy Sec. and Party Sec., Communist Youth League of Xinjiang Autonomous Region and Vice-Minister of Cen. Communist Youth League Org. Dept 1985–98; Party Sec., Cen. Finance League and Pres. Nat. Finance Youth Union 1998–2003; Pres. China Life Insurance Assets Man. Co. Ltd 2003–05; Vice-Pres. China Life Insurance (Group) Co. 2003–06, Pres. 2006–07; Pres. and Gen. Man. People's Insurance Co. (Group) of China Ltd (aka PICC Holding Co.) 2009–12, Exec. Chair. 2012–, Chair. PICC Life Insurance Co. Ltd March 2007–, PICC Asset Man. Co. Ltd April 2007–. *Address:* People's Insurance Co. (Group) of China Ltd, 28 Qinghua Xi Road, Haidian District, Beijing 100084, People's Republic of China (office). *Telephone:* (10) 62616611 (office); (10) 82653062 (office). *E-mail:* bianji@picc.com.cn (office). *Website:* www.picc.com (office); www.picc.cn (office); www.epicc.com.cn (office).

WU, Yigong; Chinese film director; b. 1 Dec. 1938, Chongqing, Sichuan Prov.; s. of Wu Tiesan and Yu Minhua; m. Zhang Wen Rong 1967; one s.; Dir Shanghai Film Bureau, Gen. Man. Shanghai Film Corpn, Vice-Pres. China Film Artists' Asscn 1985–; Vice-Chair. China Fed. of Literary and Art Circles 1996–; Alt. mem. 14th CCP Cen. Cttee 1992–97, 15th CCP Cen. Cttee 1997–2002. *Films include:* University in Exile, The Tribulations of a Chinese Gentleman, Bitter Sea, Evening Rain 1980, My Memories of Old Beijing (Golden Rooster Award for Best Dir 1984), A Man Aged 18 (Magnolia Prize 1988), A Confucius Family 1992. *Leisure interests:* music, sports. *Address:* 52 Yong Fu Road, Shanghai, People's Republic of China. *Telephone:* 4332558. *Fax:* 4370528.

WU, Yingjie; Chinese party official; *Communist Party Secretary, Tibet Autonomous Region;* b. Dec. 1956, Changyi County, Shandong Prov.; ed Tibet Minzu Univ., CCP Central Party School; began career working at insect breeding farm, Linzhi, Tibet Autonomous Region (TAR) 1974–77; Teacher, Dept of Chinese Language and Literature, Tibet Minzu Univ. 1979–83; joined TAR Dept of Educ. 1983, becoming Deputy Dir, Gen. Educ. Dept 1986–87, Deputy Dir, Primary and Secondary Educ. Dept, Science and Tech. Comm. 1987–90, Deputy Dir, Office of the Educ. Comm. 1990–93, Deputy Dir, TAR Educ. Cttee, also mem. Teaching and Research Cttee 1994–98, Deputy Dir, TAR Bd of Educ. 1998–2000, Deputy Sec.-Gen., Dept of Educ. March–May 2000; joined CCP May 1987, becoming mem. TAR CCP Standing Cttee 2005–11, Deputy Party Sec., TAR 2011–13, Exec. Deputy Party Sec. 2013–16, CCP Sec., TAR 2016–; Vice-Chair., TAR Govt 2003–11, also Minister of Propaganda Dept 2005–06. *Address:* Office of the Party Secretary, Zhongguo Gongchan Dang (Communist Party of China), Lhasa, Tibet Autonomous Region, People's Republic of China (office).

WU, Zuqiang; Chinese musician, composer and academic; *Vice-Chairman, China Federation of Literary and Art Circles;* b. 24 July 1927, Beijing; s. of Wu Jingzhou and Wu Qinqi (née Zhou); m. Li-qin Zheng 1953; one s. one d.; Vice-Pres. Cen. Conservatory of Music 1978–82, Pres. 1982–88, now Prof. and Hon. Pres.; Vice-Pres. Chinese Musicians' Asscn 1985, now Hon. Chair.; Vice-Exec. Chair. China Fed. of Literary and Art Circles 1988–92, Vice-Chair. 1992–; Adviser to China Nat. Symphony Orchestra 1996; Alt. mem. 12th CCP Cen. Cttee 1982–87; Perm. mem. Nat. Cttee 7th, 8th and 9th CPPCC 1988–2003; Artistic Adviser, Yong Siew Toh Conservatory of Music; Artistic Adviser for opening and closing ceremonies, Beijing Summer Olympic Games 2008. *Compositions include:* Sunrise at the Tu Mountains – Fighting against the Floods, Little Sisters at the Grasslands, The Moon's Reflection On ErQuan, Listening to the Pines, A Lovely Night, Revival. *Publications:* Musical Form, Analysis of Music Works 1962. *Leisure interests:* literature, fine arts, tourism. *Address:* Central Conservatory of Music, 43 Baojiajie Street, Xicheng District, Beijing 100031, People's Republic of China (office). *Telephone:* (10) 66414887 (office). *Fax:* (10) 66417211 (office). *E-mail:* fao@ccom.edu.cn (office). *Website:* en.ccom.edu.cn (office).

WUERL, HE Cardinal Donald William, STD; American ecclesiastic and academic; *Archbishop Emeritus of Washington, DC;* b. 12 Nov. 1940, Pittsburgh, Pa; s. of Francis J. Wuerl and Mary Anne Wuerl (née Schiffauer); ed Mount St Mary's Seminary, Cincinnati, Ohio, Catholic Univ. of America, Washington, DC (Basselin Scholar), Pontifical Gregorian Univ. and Pontifical Univ. of St Thomas Aquinas, Rome; ordained priest, Diocese of Pittsburgh 1966; first assignment as Asst Pastor at St Rosalia Parish, Greenfield, Pittsburgh and as Sec. to the then Bishop of Pittsburgh, John Wright; full-time Sec. to Cardinal Wright in Vatican City 1969–79; Rector St Paul Seminary, Pittsburgh 1981–85; Exec. Sec. to Bishop John Marshall for papally mandated study of US seminaries 1982; Titular Bishop of Rossmarkaeum and Auxiliary Bishop of Seattle 1985–87; Bishop of Pittsburgh 1988–2006; taught at Duquesne Univ., Pittsburgh as Distinguished Service Prof.; Chaplain for the Order of Malta, Fed. Asscn, USA (div. of Sovereign Mil. Order of Malta, commonly referred to as the Knights of Malta) 1999–; Archbishop of Washington, DC 2006–18, Archbishop Emer. 2018–; cr. Cardinal (Cardinal-Priest of San Pietro in Vincoli) 2010; participated in Papal Conclave 2013; Chair. Nat. Catholic Educational Asscn 2005–; Chancellor Catholic Univ. of America; apptd by Congregation for the Doctrine of the Faith as Del. in USA to facilitate mass receptions of Anglicans in accord with norms of Anglicanorum Coetibus issued in Nov. 2009 2010–; heads US Bishops' ad hoc cttee in implementing the apostolic constitution. *Television:* launched and hosted programme, The Teaching of Christ 1990. *Publications include:* The Forty Martyrs: New Saints of England and Wales 1971, Fathers of the Church 1975, The Catholic Priesthood Today 1976, The Teaching of Christ: A Catholic Catechism for Adults 1976, St Christopher: A Military Martyr (unpublished) 1979, A Visit to the Vatican: For Young People 1981, The Gift of Faith: A Question and Answer Version of The Teaching of Christ 2001; has written regular columns in Columbia, the major publ. of the Knights of Columbus in USA. *Address:* c/o Archdiocese of Washington, PO Box 29260, Washington, DC 20017-0260 (office); c/o Archdiocese of Washington, 5001 Eastern Avenue, Hyattsville, MD 20782-3447, USA (office).

WUFFLI, Peter A.; Swiss banking executive; *Chairman, IMD Foundation;* b. 26 Oct. 1957; s. of Heinz Wuffli; m.; three c.; ed Univ. of St Gallen; began career as econs journalist, Neue Zurcher Zeitung 1978–84; Man. Consultant, McKinsey & Co. 1984–90, Partner, McKinsey Switzerland 1990–94; joined Swiss Banking Corpn 1994, Chief Financial Officer (CFO), mem. Exec. Cttee 1994–98; CFO UBS Group (following merger with UBS) 1998–99, Chair. and CEO UBS Asset Management 1999–2001, Pres. and CEO UBS AG 2001–07; currently Chair. IMD Foundation and Supervisory Bd; Chair. Partners Group, Zug; mem. Bd of Dirs, Inst. of Int. Finance Inc., Zurich Opera House; Vice-Chair. Int. Inst. for Man. Devt, Swiss-American Chamber of Commerce; European Banker of the Year 2005. *Address:* IMD Foundation, PO Box 915, Ch. de Bellerive 23, 1001 Lausanne, Switzerland (office). *Telephone:* (21) 6180111 (office). *Fax:* (21) 61807070 (office). *E-mail:* info@imd.org (office). *Website:* www.imd.org (office).

WULF-MATHIES, Monika, PhD; German consultant, business executive, government official and fmr politician; *CEO, Wulf-Mathies Consult;* b. 17 March 1942, Wernigerode; d. of Carl-Hermann Baier and Margott Baier (née Meisser); m. Dr Carsten Wulf-Mathies 1968; ed Univs of Hamburg and Freiburg; Br. Asst Fed. Ministry of Econs 1968–71; Head of Dept for Social Policy, Fed. Chancellery 1971–76; mem. ÖTV (Public Services and Transport Workers' Union) 1971–, mem. Man. Exec. Cttee 1976–95, Chair. of ÖTV (representing around 2.3 million workers) 1982–95; Pres. Public Services Int. 1989–94; Commr for Regional Policies of EU 1995–99; Adviser to the Chancellor on European Policy 2000; mem. Supervisory Bd Deutsche Lufthansa AG 1978–95 (Deputy Chair. 1988–95), VEBA 1989–95; joined mem. SPD 1965; Exec. Vice-Pres. Corp. Public Policy and Sustainability, Deutsche Post AG 2001–08 (retd), now Adviser; Pres. Netzwerks Europäische Bewegung Deutschland 2001–06, Hon. Pres. 2006–; Founding mem. and Policy Fellow, Institut zur Zukunft der Arbeit (IZA) (Inst. for the Study of Labour), Bonn 2005; CEO Wulf-Mathies Consult 2010–; Chair. Beethoven-Foundation for Arts and Culture, Bonn 2007–; Vice-Chair. Supervisory Bd Univ. of Bonn 2008–13; mem. Senate Leibniz-Gemeinschaft 2010–18; mem. EC; patron of hospice foundation, Bonn 2007–; Grand Cross of the Order of Infante D. Henrique (Portugal). *Leisure interests:* gardening, cross-country skiing. *Address:* Wolf-Mathies Consult, Hoffmann Str. 5, 53113 Bonn, Germany (office). *Telephone:* (228) 24969137 (office). *E-mail:* buero@wulf-mathies.de (office). *Website:* www.wulf-mathies.com.

WULFF, Christian Wilhelm Walter; German lawyer, politician and fmr head of state; b. 19 June 1959, Osnabrück; s. of Rudolf Wulff and Dagmar Wulff; m. 1st Christiane Vogt 1988, one d.; m. 2nd Bettina Körner 2008, one s.; ed Osnabrück Univ.; mem. Christlich-Demokratische Union (CDU) 1975–2010, Chair. CDU in Lower Saxony 1994–2008, Deputy Fed. Chair. CDU 1998–2010; mem. Osnabrück city council 1986, leader of CDU group 1989–94; mem. Lower Saxony Landtag (regional parl.) 1994, Ministerpräsident (Prime Minister) of Lower Saxony 2003–10; Pres. of Germany 2010–12 (resgnd); cleared of corruption charges by Landgericht Hannover 2014; Asparagus Amb., Niedersächsische Spargelstraße 2016–; Dr hc (Tongji Univ., Shanghai), (Univ. of Tokyo-Tsukuba); Leo Baeck Prize 2011, St Georgs Orden 2016.

WUNSCH, Carl Isaac, PhD; American oceanographer and academic; *Cecil and Ida Green Professor Emeritus of Physical Oceanography, Massachusetts Institute of Technology;* b. 5 May 1941, Brooklyn, New York City, NY; s. of Harry Wunsch and Helen Wunsch (née Gellis); m. Marjory Markel 1980; one s. one d.; ed Massachusetts Inst. of Tech.; Lecturer in Oceanography, MIT 1966–67, Asst Prof. 1967–70, Assoc. Prof. 1970–75, Prof. of Physical Oceanography 1975–76, apptd Cecil and Ida Green Prof. of Physical Oceanography 1976, Sec. of Navy Research Prof. 1985–89, now Cecil and Ida Green Prof. Emer. of Physical Oceanography; Sr Visiting Fellow, Dept of Applied Math. and Theoretical Physics, Univ. of Cambridge, UK 1969, 1974–75, 1981–82; currently Visiting Prof., Harvard Univ.; Fulbright Scholar 1981–82; John Simon Guggenheim Foundation Fellow 1981–82; Visiting Sr Scientist, GFDL, Princeton Univ. 1993–94; Visiting Scientist, CNES/CNRS, Toulouse, France 1994; Moore Distinguished Scholar, Calif. Inst. of Tech. 2000; Visiting Prof., Univ. Coll., London 2001; Visiting Scientist, Southampton Oceanography Centre 2001; Distinguished Visiting Scientist, Jet Propulsion Lab. 1994–2011; George Eastman Visiting Prof., Balliol Coll., Oxford, 2011–12; Chair. Ocean Studies Bd, NRC; consultant to NAS, NSF; mem. NAS, Soc. for Industrial and Applied Math.; Foreign mem. Royal Soc. 2002, American Philosophical Soc. 2003; Fellow, American Acad. of Arts and Sciences, American Geophysical Union, American Meteorological Soc., AAAS; Hon. Fellow, Royal Meteorological Soc. 2012; James R. Macelwane Award 1971, Maurice Ewing Medal 1990, American Geophysical Union, Founders Prize, Texas Instrument Foundation 1975, A.G. Huntsman Prize 1988, NASA Public Service Medal 1993, Henry Stommel Prize, American Meteorological Soc. 2000, Bowie Medal, American Geophysical Union 2006, Prince Albert 1er Medal 2007, Walter Munk Medal, Oceanography Soc. and USN 2015. *Publications include:* Evolution of Physical Oceanography (co-ed.), Ocean Acoustic Tomography (co-author), The Ocean Circulation Inverse Problem, Discrete Inverse and State Estimation Problems; many tech. papers. *Leisure interests:* sailing, history, reading. *Address:* Geological Museum 451, Harvard University, Cambridge, MA 02138 (office); 78 Washington Avenue, Cambridge, MA 02140, USA (home). *Telephone:* (617) 496-0194 (office); (617) 253-5937 (office). *Fax:* (617) 253-4464 (office). *E-mail:* cwunsch@fas.harvard.edu (office). *Website:* ocean.mit.edu/~cwunsch (office).

WURTH, Hubert, LLB; Luxembourg diplomatist and painter; *Ambassador to Austria, Slovakia and Slovenia;* b. 15 April 1952; m. 1st Lydie Polfer (q.v.) (divorced 1998); one c.; m. 2nd Francisca Passchier; one c.; ed Univ. de Paris II Inst. d'Etudes Politiques, Paris; called to the Luxembourg Bar 1977; Attaché, Dept of Int. Econ. Relations, Ministry of Foreign Affairs 1978, Deputy Perm. Rep. to Council of Europe 1979, Chief Sec. to Vice-Pres. of the Govt and Minister for Foreign Affairs, Econ. Affairs and Justice 1981, Deputy Dir of Political Affairs 1986; Amb. to USSR (also accred to Poland, Finland and Mongolia) 1988–92, to the Netherlands 1992–98 (also served as rep. for the Pact on Stability in Europe 1993–95 and on special mission in Fmr Yugoslavia 1996), Perm. Rep. to UN, New York 1998–2003, to OECD 2003–, to UNESCO 2003–07, Amb. to France 2003–07, to UK 2007–11 (also accred to Ireland 2007–11 and Iceland 2008–11), to Austria, Slovakia and Slovenia 2011–; Perm. Rep. OSCE and int. orgs in Vienna. *Publication:* Monography on Hubert Wurth as a Painter 1998. *Address:* Embassy of Luxembourg, 81 Sternwartestrasse, 1180 Vienna, Austria (office). *Telephone:* (1) 478-2142 (office). *Fax:* (1) 478-2144 (office). *E-mail:* vienne.amb@mae.etat.lu (office). *Website:* vienne.mae.lu (office).

WÜRTH, Reinhold; German trading company executive; *Chairman, Supervisory Board, Würth Group's Family Trusts;* b. 20 April 1935, Öhringen; m. Carmen Würth; three c.; joined father's wholesale screw business as second employee, Künzelsau 1949, took over man. of business 1954–94, Chair. Advisory Bd Würth Group 1994–2006, Chair. Supervisory Bd Würth Group's Family Trusts; Head Interfacultative Inst. for Entrepreneurship, Univ. of Karlsrühe 1999–2003; Chair. Advisory Bd Entrepreneurs of the Soc. of Int. Cooperation Baden-Württemberg GmbH; Chair. Gesellschaft zur Förderung des württembergischen Landesmuseums e.V., Freunde der Burgfestspiele Jagsthausen e.V., Pro Region Heilbronn-Franken; mem. Supervisory Bd IKB Deutsche Industriebank AG, Düsseldorf; mem. Bd Trustees Robert-Bosch-Foundation; made his art collection of over 15,000 items by Edvard Munch, Max Beckmann, Pablo Picasso and others accessible to the public 1991–; est. Kunsthalle Würth, Schwäbisch Hall 2001–; Hon. Senator, Univ. of Tübingen; Distinguished Service Cross (First Class) of the Order of Merit (FRG); Chevalier des Arts et des Lettres 2000, Légion d'honneur 2004; Officer, Order of Orange-Nassau (Netherlands) 2005; Dr hc (Tübingen); Medal of Econ. Merits (Baden-Württemberg); Freedom of Erstein (France) 1997, Künzelsau 2003. *Leisure interests:* flying, motor bikes, art collecting. *Address:* Adolf Würth GmbH & Co. KG, Reinhold-Würth-Str. 12–17, 74653 Künzelsau, Germany (office). *Telephone:* (7940) 15-0 (office). *Fax:* (7940) 15-1000 (office). *E-mail:* info@wuerth.de (office). *Website:* www.wuerth.com (office).

WURTZ, Robert H., AB, PhD; American psychologist, neuroscientist and academic; *NIH Distinguished Investigator Emeritus, Laboratory of Sensorimotor Research, National Eye Institute, National Institutes of Health;* b. (Robert Henry Wurtz, Jr), 28 March 1936, St Louis, Mo.; m. Emily O. Wurtz; ed Oberlin Coll., Univ. of Michigan; Research Asst, Univ. of Michigan 1958–61, PHS Predoctoral Fellow 1961–62, Predoctoral Instructor 1962; Research Assoc., Cttee for Nuclear Information, St Louis, Mo. 1962–63; Postdoctoral Fellow, Dept of Physiology and Research Fellow, Dept of Neurology, Washington Univ. School of Medicine, St Louis 1962–65; Research Psychologist, Spinal Cord Section, Lab. of Neurophysiology, Nat. Inst. of Neurological Diseases and Blindness, NIH 1965–66, Physiologist, Lab. of Neurobiology, Nat. Inst. of Mental Health, NIH 1966–78, Founding Chief, Lab. of Sensorimotor Research, Nat. Eye Inst., NIH 1978–2002, Sr Investigator, Lab. of Sensorimotor Research 2002–, NIH Sr Investigator 2007, fmr NIH Distinguished Investigator (then Emer. 2016–), apptd to Sr Exec. Service, NIH 1984, apptd to Sr Biomedical Research Service, NIH 1996; Visiting Scientist, Physiological Lab., Univ. of Cambridge, UK 1975–76, Assoc., Neuroscience Research Program 1989–94; mem. Scientific Bd McGovern Inst. for Brain Research, MIT; Pres. Soc. for Neuroscience 1990–91; mem. Nat. Acad. of Medicine 1987, NAS 1988 (mem. Council 1996), Inst. of Medicine 1997; non-resident Fellow, Salk Inst.; Fellow, AAAS 1990, American Acad. of Arts and Sciences 1990; Hon. DSc (Oberlin Coll.) 2009; Grass Foundation Research Fellow, Marine Biological Lab. 1961, Gordon Holmes Lecturer, European Neuroscience Soc. 1985, James M. Sprague Lecturer, Univ. of Pennsylvania 1986, Morris B. Bender Lecturer, Mount Sinai Medical School 1986, W. Alden Spencer Award, Columbia Univ. 1987, George H. Bishop Lecturer, Washington Univ. 1988, Clinton N. Woolsey Lecturer 1991, Keynote Lecturer, Neural Control of Movement Meeting 1992, Presidential Award, Soc. for Neuroscience 1993, AAAS John P. McGovern Award 1995, Karl Spencer Lashley Award, American Philosophical Soc. 1995, NIH G. Burroughs Mider Lecturer 1995, Friedenwald Award, Asscn for Research in Vision and Ophthalmology 1996 Distinguished Scientific Contrib. Award, American Psychological Asscn 1997, Plenary Lecturer, Japanese Neuroscience Soc. 2000, Seventh Annual Lecturer, Center for Neural Basis of Cognition, Univ. of Pittsburgh 2001, Eighth Annual American Legion Lecturer, Univ. of Minnesota Brain Sciences 2002, Keynote Lecturer, Salk Inst. Annual Faculty Meeting 2003, Nat. Eye Inst. Dir's Award 2004, Dan David Prize for the Future Time Dimension: Brain Sciences (with William T. Newsome and Amiram Grinvald) 2004, Ralph W. Gerard Prize, Soc. for Neuroscience 2006, Albert and Ellen Grass Lecture Soc. for Neuroscience 2009, Gruber Neuroscience Prize 2010, NIH Director's Award 2017. *Publications include:* more than 180 scientific papers in professional journals on neurobiology of vision, eye movements and brain circuits for corollary discharge. *Address:* National Eye Institute, Building 49, Room 2A50, Bethesda, MD 20892-4436, USA (office). *Telephone:* (301) 466-7528 (office). *Fax:* (301) 402-0511 (office). *E-mail:* bob@lsr.nei.nih.gov (office). *Website:* www.nei.nih.gov (office).

WÜTHRICH, Kurt, PhD; Swiss scientist and academic; *Cecil H. and Ida M. Green Professor of Structural Biology, The Scripps Research Institute;* b. 4 Oct. 1938, Aarberg; s. of Hermann Wüthrich and Gertrud Bertha Wüthrich-Kuchen; m. Marianne Briner 1963; one s. one d.; ed Univs of Bern, Basel and Calif. at Berkeley, USA; mem. tech. staff Bell Telephone Labs 1967–69; Privatdozent, ETH, Zürich 1970–72, Asst Prof. 1972–76, Assoc. Prof. 1976–80, Prof. of Biophysics 1980– (Chair. Biology Dept 1995–2000); Visiting Miller Research Prof., Univ. of Calif., Berkeley 1988; Scholar-in-Residence, Johns Hopkins Univ., Baltimore, USA 1992; Sherman Fairchild Distinguished Scholar, Caltech, Pasadena, Calif. 1994, Visiting Assoc. in Biology and Chem. 1995; Guest Scientist, The Scripps Research Inst., Calif. 1994, Cecil H. and Ida M. Green Prof. of Structural Biology 2001–; Visiting Prof., Inst. of Physical and Chemical Research (RIKEN), Tokyo, Japan 1997–98, Univ. of Edinburgh, UK 1997–2000; Adjunct Distinguished Prof., Daegu Gyeongbunk Inst. of Science and Tech., South Korea 2013–; Distinguished Sr Prof., iHuman Inst., Shanghai Tech. Univ. 2014–; consultant, Hoechst AG, Frankfurt, Germany 1985–92, Sandoz Pharma AG, Basel 1987–96, Hoffman-La Roche AG, Basel 1987–2004, Ciba-Geigy AG, Basel 1989–96, Tripos Inc., St Louis, USA 1992–94, Novartis AG, Basel 1997–; mem. European Molecular Biology Org. (EMBO) 1984, Deutsche Akad. der Naturforscher Leopoldina 1987, Academia Europaea 1989, Schweizerische Akad. der Technischen Wissenschaften 2001, Schweizerische Akad. der Medizinischen Wissenschaften 2002; Foreign Fellow, Indian Nat. Science Acad. 1989; Foreign Assoc. NAS 1992, Acad. des Sciences, Institut de France 2000; Fellow, AAAS 1998; mem. Schweiz Kommission für Molekularbiologie 1973–76, Pres. 1977–82; mem. Council Int. Union of Pure and Applied Biophysics (IUPAB) 1975–78, 1987–90, Sec.-Gen. 1978–84, Vice-Pres. 1984–87; Pres. Züricher Chemische Gesellschaft 1990–91; mem. Exec. Cttee Schweiz Gesellschaft für Biochemie 1986–92, Pres. Biophysics Section 1985–88; mem. IUPAC, Comm. on Biophysical Chem. 1969–99, Chair. 2000–01; mem. Bds

Centro Stefano Franscini, Monte Verità and ETH Zürich 1989–98, European Molecular Biology Lab., Heidelberg, Germany 1989–95, Nat. Lab. of Biomacromolecules, Academia Sinica, Beijing, China 1989, Deutsche Forschungsgemeinschaft, Bonn, Germany: Schwerpunktsprogramm 'Protein Design' 1989–95, Inst. für Molekulare Biotechnologie, Jena, Germany 1993–96, Ciba Foundation, London, UK 1994–96, Institut de Biologie Structurale Jean-Pierre Ebel, Grenoble, France 1994–97, Inst. of Biotechnology, Univ. of Helsinki, Finland 1997–2005, Novartis Foundation, London 1997–2005, Triad Therapeutics Inc., San Diego, Calif. 1998–2004, Genomics Sciences Centre, RIKEN, Tokyo 2000–05, Syrrx Inc., San Diego 2000–04, Nat. Inst. of Chemical Physics and Biophysics, Tallinn, Estonia 2001–05, Nat. High Field NMR Center (NANUC), Univ. of Alberta, Edmonton, Canada 2001–04, Eidogen Inc., Pasadena, Calif. 2002–06; Titular mem. European Acad. of Arts, Sciences and Humanities 2003; mem. Prix Marcel Benoist, Conseil de Fondation, Berne 2001–15, Solvay Scientific Cttee for Chemistry, Int. Solvay Inst, Brussels 2005– (Chair. 2011–), Hon. Advisory Bd, Int. Union of Biochemistry and Molecular Biology 2007–, Scientific Advisory Bd, Dept of Biosciences and Bioengineering, Indian Inst. of Tech., Indore 2012–; Foreign mem. Latvian Acad. of Sciences 2004, Korean Acad. of Science and Tech. 2005, Royal Soc., UK 2010; Corresponding mem. Nordrhein-Westfälische Akademie der Wissenschaften 2005, Academia Brasileira de Ciências 2013; ISMAR Fellow, Weizmann Inst. of Science 2008; JMR Fellow, Journal of Magnetic Resonance, USA 2017; Hon. Prof., Dalian Inst. of Chemical Physics, Chinese Acad. of Sciences, Dalian Inst. of Light Industry; Hon. Fellow, Nat. Acad. of Sciences, India 1992, Royal Soc. of Chem., UK 2003, Latvian Inst. of Organic Synthesis 2008; Hon. FRSE 2003; Foreign Hon. mem., American Acad. of Arts and Sciences 1993; Hon. mem. Japanese Biochemical Soc. 1993, Nat. Magnetic Resonance Soc. of India 1998, The World Innovation Foundation 2003, Swiss Chemical Soc. 2003, Int. Soc. for Magnetic Resonance in Medicine 2003, Wallisellen Football Club 2003, Hungarian Acad. of Sciences 2004, World Acad. of Young Scientists 2004, World High Tech. Soc., Dalian, China 2004, European Acad. of Sciences and Arts 2004, Groupement Ampère 2004, The Nuclear Magnetic Resonance Soc. of Japan 2004, Indian Biophysical Soc. 2005, Korean Magnetic Resonance Soc. 2005; Hon. Fellow, The Spanish Biophysical Soc. 2012; Hon. DPhil (Zürich) 1997; Hon. DSc (Sheffield) 2004, (King George's Medical Univ., Lucknow, India) 2005; Dr hc (Siena) 1997, (Ecole Polytechnique Fédérale de Lausanne) 2001, (Valencia) 2004, (Lomonosov Moscow State Univ.) 2007, (Verona) 2007, (Pécs) 2007, (Univ. del Norte, Asunción) 2007, (Univ. René Descartes, Paris) 2007, (Napoli) 2012, (Patras) 2015, (Buenos Aires) 2015, (Córdoba) 2016; numerous awards including Friedrich-Miescher-Preis, Schweizerische Gesellschaft für Biochemie 1974, Shield of the Faculty of Medicine, Tokyo Univ. 1983, Médaille P. Bruylants, Université Catholique de Louvain, Belgium 1986, Stein and Moore Award of the Protein Soc., USA 1990, Louisa Gross Horwitz Prize, Columbia Univ., New York 1991, Gilbert Newton Lewis Medal, Univ. of Calif., Berkeley 1991, Marcel Benoist-Preis, Swiss Confed. 1992, Distinguished Service Award, The Miami Bio/Technology Winter Symposia, USA 1993, Prix Louis Jeantet de Médecine, Fondation Louis Jeantet, Geneva 1993, Kaj Linderstrom-Lang Prize, Carlsberg Foundation, Copenhagen, Denmark 1996, Eminent Scientist of RIKEN, Tokyo 1997, Kyoto Prize in Advanced Tech., Inamori Foundation, Kyoto 1998, Otto-Warburg-Medaille, Gesellschaft für Biochemie und Molekularbiologie, Germany 1999, Médaille d'Honneur en Argent, Soc. d'Encouragement au Progrès, Paris, France 2001, Nobel Prize in Chem. 2002, World Future Award, The World Awards, Vienna, Austria 2002, Johannes M. Bijvoet Medal, Utrecht Univ., The Netherlands 2008, Paul Walden Medal, Riga Tech. Univ., Latvia 2008, Jabir ibn Hyyan (Geber) Medal, Saudi Chemical Soc., Saudi Arabia 2009, Ralph and Helen Oesper Award, Univ. of Cincinnati 2010, Pres.'s Gold Medal, Govt of India 2012, Theodor Bücher Medal, Fed. of European Biochemical Socs 2013, IUBMB Medal 2015, Shanghai 1000 Talents Award 2016, Genome Valley Excellence Award, India 2017. *Publications:* NMR in Biological Research: Peptides and Proteins 1976, NMR of Proteins and Nucleic Acids 1986, NMR in Structural Biology – A Collection of Papers by Kurt Wüthrich 1995; also published 800 papers and reviews. *Leisure interests:* sports, French literature, wine. *Address:* Institut für Molekularbiologie & Biophysik, ETH Zürich, HPK, 8093 Zürich, Switzerland (office); The Scripps Research Institute, MB-44, 10550 North Torrey Pines Road, La Jolla, CA 92037, USA (office); Fliederstrasse 7, 8304 Wallisellen, Switzerland (home). *Telephone:* (44) 633-1151 (Zürich) (office); (858) 784-8011 (La Jolla) (office). *Fax:* (44) 6331151 (Zürich) (office); (858) 784-8014 (La Jolla) (office). *E-mail:* wuthrich@mol.biol.ethz.ch (office); wuthrich@scripps.edu (office). *Website:* www.mol.biol.ethz.ch (office).

WYATT, Christopher Terrel, BSc, FREng, FICE, FRSA, FIStructE, DIC, CBIM; British business executive and engineer; b. 17 July 1927, Ewell, Surrey; s. of Lional H. Wyatt and Audrey Vere Wyatt; m. 1st Doreen Mary Emmerson; three s.; m. 2nd Geertruida Willer 1970; one s.; m. 3rd Patricia Perkins 1990; ed Kingston Grammar School, Battersea Polytechnic and Imperial Coll., London; Charles Brand & Son, Ltd, 1948–54; joined Richard Costain Ltd, 1955, Dir 1970–87, Group Chief Exec. 1975–80, Deputy Chair. 1979–80, Chair. Costain Group PLC 1980–87; Chair. W. S. Atkins Ltd 1987–97; Fellow, Royal Acad. of Eng, Inst. of Structural Engineers. *Leisure interests:* sailing, music, painting. *Address:* Ryderwells Farm, Uckfield Road, Lewes, East Sussex, BN8 5RN, England (home). *Telephone:* (1273) 812219 (home).

WYATT, (Alan) Will, BA, CBE, FRTS; British executive, author and TV producer; b. 7 Jan. 1942, Oxford; s. of Basil Wyatt and Hettie Wyatt (née Hooper); m. Jane Bridgit Bagenal 1966; two d.; ed Magdalen Coll. School, Oxford, Emmanuel Coll. Cambridge; trainee reporter, Sheffield Telegraph 1964; Sub-Ed. BBC Radio News 1965; joined BBC TV 1968, Producer, Late Night Line-Up, In Vision, The Book Programme, B. Traven – a mystery solved, etc. 1970–77, Asst Head of Presentation (Programmes) 1977, Head Documentary Features 1981, Features and Documentaries Group 1987, Asst Man. Dir BBC Network TV 1988–91; Man. Dir BBC Network TV 1991–96; Chief Exec. BBC Broadcast 1996–99; Chair. Human Capital Ltd 2001–, Goodwill Assocs (Media) Ltd 2003–; Vice-Chair. Shadow Racing Trust 2003–; Chair. BBC Guidelines on Violence 1983, 1987; Dir Broadcasters' Audience Research Bd 1989–91, BBC Subscription TV 1990–93, BBC Enterprises 1991–93, UKTV 1997–99; Vice-Pres. Royal TV Soc. 1997, Pres. 2000–04; Vice-Pres. Euro Broadcasting Union 1998–99; Gov. Univ. of the Arts, London (fmrly London Inst.) 1990–2007, Chair. 1999–2007; Huw Wheldon Memorial Lecture 1996; Royal Inst. Discourse 1996; Dir Coral Eurobet 2000–02, Vitec Group plc 2002–11, Racing UK 2004–12 (Chair. 2008–12), Racecourse Media Services 2007–12 (Chair. 2008–12); Chair. Teaching Awards Trust 2008–13; mem. British Horseriding Bd Comm. into Stable and Stud Staff 2003–04, Welsh Nat. Opera Board 2013–; Gov. Magdalen Coll. School 2000–06; Trustee, Services Sound and Vision Corpn 2007–13. *Television includes:* The Fifties, Late Night Line Up, The Book Programme, Edition, All the Buildings Fit to Print, The Golden Trashery of Ogden Nashery, Robinson's Travels – The Mormon Trail, B. Traven – A Mystery Solved, Toni and Rosi (documentary film) 2012. *Publications include:* The Man Who Was B. Traven 1980, Masters of the Wired World (contrib.) 1999, The Fun Factory – A Life in the BBC 2003, Oxford Boy—A Post War Townie Childhood 2018; articles on broadcasting in Evening Standard, The Times, Daily Telegraph etc. *Leisure interests:* fell walking, horse racing, opera, theatre. *Address:* 46 Flanders Mansions, Flanders Road, London, W4 1NF, England (home). *Telephone:* (20) 8995-8557 (office). *E-mail:* will.wyatt@btinternet.com (home).

WYDEN, Ronald (Ron) Lee, BA, JD; American politician; *Senator from Oregon;* b. 3 May 1949, Wichita, Kan.; s. of Peter Wyden and Edith Wyden; m. 1st Laurie Oseran 1978; one s. one d.; m. 2nd Nancy Wyden 2005; one s. one d.; ed Univ. of Santa Barbara, Stanford Univ. and Univ. of Oregon; campaign aide, US Senator Wayne Morse 1972, 1974; Instructor in Gerontology, Univ. of Oregon 1976, Portland State Univ. 1979, Univ. of Portland 1980; Co-Founder and Co-Dir Oregon Gray Panthers 1974–80; Dir Oregon Legal Services for Elderly 1977–79; mem. US House of Reps from 3rd Oregon Dist 1981–95; Senator from Oregon 1996–, mem. Energy and Natural Resources Cttee (Chair. Subcommittee on Public Lands and Forests), Finance Cttee (Chair. Subcommittee on Int. Trade, Customs and Global Competitiveness), Budget Cttee, Select Cttee on Intelligence, Special Cttee on Aging; mem. ABA; Democrat. *Address:* 221 Dirksen Senate Office Building, Washington, DC 20510, USA (office). *Telephone:* (202) 224-5244 (office). *Fax:* (202) 228-2717 (office). *Website:* wyden.senate.gov (office).

WYLIE, Andrew, BA; American literary agent; *President, The Wylie Agency;* b. 4 Nov. 1947, New York City; s. of Craig Wylie; m. 1st Christina Meyer 1969; one s.; m. 2nd Camilla Carlini; two d.; ed St Paul's School, Harvard Coll.; Founder and Pres. The Wylie Agency, New York 1980–, London 1996–, Madrid 1999–; f. Odyssey Editions (e-book publishing co.) 2010. *Address:* The Wylie Agency, 250 West 57th Street, Suite 2114, New York, NY 10107, USA. *Telephone:* (212) 246-0069. *Fax:* (212) 586-8953. *E-mail:* mail@wylieagency.com. *Website:* www.wylieagency.com.

WYLLER, Egil A., DPhil; Norwegian professor of philosophy; *Professor Emeritus of Philosophy, University of Oslo;* b. 24 April 1925, Stavanger; s. of Trygve Wyller and Anne-Kathrine Wyller; m. Eva Middelthon 1949; three s.; ed Univs of Oslo, Tübingen and Freiburg im Breisgau; Prof. of History of the Ideas of Antiquity, Dept of Philosophy, Univ. of Oslo 1969–95, now Prof. Emer.; Commdr, Order of Phoenix (Greece), Kt First Class, Order of St Olav 2000; Gold Medal of HM King of Norway 1958, Cultural Prize of City of Oslo 1986. *Publications include:* Platons 'Parmenides' 1960, Der späte Platon 1965–1970, Enhet og Annethet I–III 1981, Johannes' Aapenbaring 1985, Prinsesse Europa 1989, Platonismus/Henologie in der Antike und im Mittelalter I–II (textbook) 1993, Henologisk Skriftserie I–XX 1994–2002, Henologische Perspektiven I–II 1995, Platon und Platonismus Tre 1996, Henrik Ibsen I–II: 1999–2002, Gestern und Morgen Heute 2005, Himmelharpen 2015. *Leisure interests:* music, poetry, natural life. *Address:* Kaptein Oppegaards v. 15, 1164 Oslo, Norway (home). *Telephone:* 22-28-36-00 (home).

WYLLIE, Peter John, BSc, PhD, FRS; American geologist, academic and polar explorer; *Professor Emeritus of Geology, Division of Geological and Planetary Sciences, California Institute of Technology;* b. 8 Feb. 1930, London, England; s. of George W. Wyllie and Beatrice G. Weaver; m. F. Rosemary Blair 1956; one s. one d. (and one s. and one d. deceased); ed Univ. of St Andrews, Scotland; glaciologist, British West Greenland Expedition 1950; geologist, British North Greenland Expedition 1952–54; Asst Lecturer in Geology, Univ. of St Andrews 1955–56; Research Asst to O. F. Tuttle, Pennsylvania State Univ. 1956–58, Asst Prof. of Geochemistry 1959–60; Research Fellow in Chem., Univ. of Leeds 1959–60, Lecturer in Experimental Petrology 1960–61; Assoc. Prof. of Petrology, Pennsylvania State Univ. 1961–65, Acting Head of Dept of Geochemistry and Mineralogy 1962–63; Prof. of Petrology and Geochemistry, Univ. of Chicago 1965–83, Master of Physical Sciences, Collegiate Div., Assoc. Dean Physical Sciences, Assoc. Dean of the Coll. 1972–73, Homer J. Livingston Prof. 1978–83, Chair. Dept of Geophysical Sciences 1979–82; Chair. Div. of Geological and Planetary Sciences, Calif. Inst. of Tech. 1983–87, Prof. of Geology 1983–99, Academic Officer 1994–99, Prof. Emer. 1999–; Chair. Comm. Experimental Petrology, Int. Union of Geological Sciences 1976–80; Vice-Pres. Mineralogical Soc. of America 1976–77, Pres. 1977–78; Vice-Pres. Int. Mineralogical Asscn 1978–86 (Pres. 1986–90), Int. Union of Geodesy and Geophysics 1991–95 (Pres. 1995–99); Foreign Assoc. NAS 1981; Fellow, American Acad. of Arts and Sciences 1982; Corresp. Fellow, Edin. Geological Soc. 1985–; Foreign Fellow (Corresp. mem.) Indian Geophysical Union 1987; Foreign mem. USSR (now Russian) Acad. of Sciences 1988, Academia Europaea 1996; Foreign Fellow, Indian Nat. Science Acad. 1991, Nat. Acad. of Science of India 1992, Chinese Acad. of Science 1996; Louis Murray Visiting Fellow, Univ. of Cape Town March 1987; Hon. Prof., China Univ. of Geosciences, Beijing 1996–, Hon. mem. Mineralogical Soc. of GB and Ireland 1986, German Geological Soc. 2001, Mineralogical Soc. of Russia 1987, Hon. mem. and Fellow, Int. Union of Geodesy and Geophysics 2015; Miller Prize (St Andrews) 1952, Hon. DSc (St Andrews) 1974; Polar Medal 1954, Mineralogical Soc. of America Award 1965, Quantrell Award 1979, Wollaston Medal, Geological Soc., London 1982, Abraham-Gottlob-Werner-Medaille, German Mineralogical Soc. 1987, Roebling Medal, Mineralogical Soc. of America 2001, Leopold von Buch Medal, German Geological Soc. 2001. *Sport:* Heavyweight Boxing Champion, RAF Scotland 1949, Pres. Athletic Union, Univ. of St Andrews 1951–52. *Publications include:* Ultramafic and Related Rocks (ed.) 1967, The Dynamic Earth 1971, The Way the Earth Works 1976, Solid-Earth Sciences and Society (Chair. NAS Cttee) 1993; numerous book chapters and articles in scientific journals. *Leisure interests:* writing science. *Address:* Division of Geological and Planetary Sciences, California Institute of Technology, Pasadena, CA 91125, USA (office). *E-mail:* wyllie@gps.caltech.edu (office). *Website:* www.gps.caltech.edu/~wyllie (office).

WYMAN, Bill; British musician (bass guitar); b. (William George Perks), 24 Oct. 1936, Lewisham, London; m. 1st Diane Cory 1959 (divorced 1968); one s.; m. 2nd

Mandy Smith 1989 (divorced 1991); m. 3rd Suzanne Accosta 1993; three d.; Founder-mem. The Rolling Stones 1962–91; numerous tours and concerts worldwide; solo artist and mem. Willie and the Poor Boys 1985, Bill Wyman's Rhythm Kings 1998–2004; Owner WGW Holdings, WGW Enterprises, Wytel Music, Ripple Records, Ripple Music, Ripple Publications, Ripple Productions, KJM Nominees, Sticky Fingers Restaurant; Lord of the Manor of Gedding and Thormwoods 1968–; Nordoff-Robbins Silver Clef 1982, Grammy Lifetime Achievement Award 1986, Ivor Novello Award for Outstanding Contribution to British Music 1991, Blues Foundation Memphis Literary Award 2002. *Films include:* Sympathy for the Devil 1970, Gimme Shelter 1970, Ladies and Gentlemen the Rolling Stones 1974, Let's Spend the Night Together 1982, Digital Dreams 1983. *Recordings include:* albums: with The Rolling Stones: The Rolling Stones 1964, The Rolling Stones No. 2 1965, Out Of Our Heads 1965, Aftermath 1966, Between The Buttons 1967, Their Satanic Majesties Request 1967, Beggar's Banquet 1968, Let It Bleed 1969, Get Yer Ya-Ya's Out 1969, Sticky Fingers 1971, Exile On Main Street 1972, Goat's Head Soup 1973, It's Only Rock And Roll 1974, Black And Blue 1976, Some Girls 1978, Emotional Rescue 1980, Tattoo You 1981, Still Life 1982, Undercover 1983, Dirty Work 1986, Steel Wheels 1989, Flashpoint 1991; solo: Monkey Grip 1974, Stone Alone 1976, Green Ice (film soundtrack) 1981, Bill Wyman 1981, Digital Dreams (film soundtrack) 1983, Stuff 1991, Struttin' Our Stuff 1998, Anyway the Wind Blows 1999, Groovin' 2000, Double Bill 2001, Blues Odyssey 2001, Rude Dudes 2003, Just For The Thrill 2004; singles: with The Rolling Stones: Come On 1963, I Wanna Be Your Man 1963, Not Fade Away 1964, It's All Over Now 1964, Little Red Rooster 1964, The Last Time 1965, (I Can't Get No) Satisfaction 1965, Get Off Of My Cloud 1965, 19th Nervous Breakdown 1966, Paint It Black 1966, Have You Seen Your Mother Baby, Standing In The Shadow 1966, Let's Spend The Night Together/Ruby Tuesday 1967, We Love You 1967, Jumping Jack Flash 1968, Honky Tonk Women 1969, Brown Sugar 1971, Tumbling Dice 1972, Angie 1973, It's Only Rock 'N' Roll 1974, Fool To Cry 1976, Miss You 1978, Emotional Rescue 1980, Start Me Up 1981, Waiting On A Friend 1981, Undercover Of The Night 1983, Harlem Shuffle 1986, Mixed Emotions 1989, Rock And A Hard Place 1989, Highwire 1991; solo: (Si Si) Je Suis Un Rock Star 1981, Come Back Suzanne 1981, A New Fashion 1981, Groovin' 2000, (Si Si) Je Suis Un Rock Star – The Best Of Bill Wyman and Bill Wyman's Rhythm Kings 2016. *Publications include:* Stone Alone – The Story of a Rock and Roll Band (with Ray Coleman) 1990, Wyman Shoots Chagall 2000, Bill Wyman's Blues Odyssey (with Richard Havers) 2001, Rolling With The Stones (with Richard Havers) 2002, Bill Wyman's Treasure Islands 2005, The Stones: A History in Cartoons 2006. *Address:* Ripple Productions Ltd, 344 Kings Road, London, SW3 5UR, England. *Website:* www.billwyman.com.

WYNAENDTS, Alexander Rijn; Dutch business executive; *CEO and Chairman of the Executive and Management Boards, AEGON NV;* b. 1960; began career with ABN Amro, working in Amsterdam and London in bank's capital markets, asset man., corp. finance and pvt. banking operations 1985; joined AEGON NV as Sr Vice-Pres. for Group Business Devt 1997, mem. Exec. Bd 2003–, COO 2007–08, CEO and Chair. Exec. and Man. Bds 2008–; Chair. Supervisory Bd, Mauritshuis, The Hague 2010–18; Chair. Supervisory Bd, Rijksmuseum, Amsterdam 2018–; mem. Supervisory Bd, Air France/KLM 2016–. *Address:* AEGON NV, PO Box 202, 2501 The Hague, The Netherlands (office). *Telephone:* (70) 344-3210 (office). *E-mail:* info@aegon.com (office). *Website:* www.aegon.com (office).

WYNDHAM, Henry Mark; British art expert and company director; *Chairman, Sotheby's Europe;* b. 19 Aug. 1953, London, England; s. of Hon. Mark Wyndham and Anne Wyndham; m. Rachel Pritchard 1978; three s.; ed Wellesley House, Broadstairs, Eton Coll., Sorbonne, Paris and Sotheby's Fine Art Course; joined Christie's 1974, Head, 19th Century European Picture Dept, Christie's, New York 1978–82, Vice-Pres. 1979, Dir Christie's, London 1983–87; set up Henry Wyndham Fine Art of St James's Art Group 1987–93; set up Portrait Commissions 1992; Chair. Sotheby's UK 1994–, Sotheby's Europe 1997–, also Sr Auctioneer; Amb. and Patron, Orbis (charity) 2014–; Trustee, Glyndebourne Opera, Prince of Wales Drawing School, Chatsworth House Trust. *Films:* Entrapment 1999, Tomb Raider 2001, And Now Ladies and Gentlemen 2002. *Television:* Antiques Roadshow 1980s, 1990s. *Leisure interests:* cricket, golf, fishing, shooting, travelling, soccer (Brighton & Hove Albion supporter), visiting museums and art, galleries, opera, landscape. *Address:* Sotheby's, 34 New Bond Street, London, W1S 2RT (office); The Old Rectory, Southease, nr Lewes, Sussex, BN7 3HX (home); 18 St Leonards Terrace, London, SW3 4QG, England (home). *Telephone:* (20) 7293-5057 (office). *Fax:* (20) 7293-5065 (office). *E-mail:* henry.wyndham@sothebys.com (office); henrymwyndham@gmail.com (home). *Website:* www.sothebys.com (office).

WYNNE, Kathleen O., BA, MA; Canadian politician; b. 21 May 1953, Richmond Hill, Ont.; divorced; three c.; pnr Jane Rounthwaite; ed Univ. of Toronto, Ontario Inst. for Studies in Educ., Harvard Univ., USA; Public School Trustee, Toronto 2000–03; MPP, Legis. Ass. of Ont. for Don Valley West (Ont. Liberal Party) 2003–, Parl. Asst to Ont. Minister of Training, Colls and Univs 2003–04, to Minister of Educ. 2004–06, Ont. Minister of Educ. 2006–10, of Transportation 2010–11, of Municipal Affairs and Housing and of Aboriginal Affairs 2011–12, Premier of Ont. (first woman) 2013–18; Leader, Ont. Liberal Party 2013–18; fmr Chair. Liberal Women's Caucus. *Address:* c/o Office of the Premier, Legislative Bldg, Room 281, Queen's Park, Toronto, ON M7A 1A1, Canada (office). *Website:* www.kathleenwynne.ca.

WYNNE-MORGAN, David; British public relations executive; *Founding Partner, Chairman and CEO, WMC Communications Ltd;* b. 22 Feb. 1931; s. of John Wynne-Morgan and of Marjorie Wynne-Morgan; m. 1st Romaine Ferguson; two s.; m. 2nd Sandra Douglas-Home (divorced); m. 3rd Karin E. Stines; two s.; ed Bryanston School; reporter, Daily Mail 1952–55; Foreign Corresp., later William Hickey, Daily Express 1955–58; contracted to Sunday Times to write biographical features including ghosting autobiog. of the late Pres. Nasser of Egypt; Founder, Chair. and Man. Dir Partnerplan 1964–80; Man. Dir Extel Public Relations 1980–83, Chair. 1983–84; Chair. and Chief Exec. Hill & Knowlton (UK) Ltd 1984–90, Pres. Hill & Knowlton Europe, Middle East and Africa 1990–94; Chair. Worldwide Exec. Cttee 1994, Marketing Group of GB 1989–90; Founding Partner, Chair. and CEO WMC Communications Ltd 1997–; Dir Horsham Corpn 1995–97; Council mem. Lord's Taverners 1992–96; mem. Inst. of Public Relations. *Publications:* biogs of Pietro Annigoni, Margot Fonteyn, Sir Malcolm Sargent. *Leisure interests:* squash (fmr Welsh int.), cricket, tennis, riding, golf. *Address:* WMC Communications Ltd, 11–12 Pall Mall, London, SW1Y 5LU (office); Lowndes Flat, 136 Brompton Road, London, SW3 1HY, England. *Telephone:* (20) 7930-9030 (office). *Fax:* (20) 7930-9038 (office). *Website:* www.wmccommunications.com (office).

WYNTER, Brian Hector, BSc; Jamaican lawyer, banking executive and central banker; *Governor and Chairman, Bank of Jamaica;* b. 1959, Kingston; s. of Hector Wynter and Jacqueline Wynter (née Antrobus); ed London School of Econs and City Univ. London, UK, Columbia Univ., USA; called to the Bar of England and Wales 1983; worked with Chase Investment Bank and Schroder Wertheim Int. Co. –1988; fmr Dir of Investment, Nat. Investment Bank of Jamaica; fmr Sr Gen. Man., Mutual Security Merchant Bank; enrolled as Attorney, Supreme Court of Judicature, Jamaica 1990; Vice-Pres. Citibank, NA 1991–95; Deputy Gov. Bank of Jamaica 1995–99, Gov. and Chair. 2009–, also mem. Bd of Govs IMF; apptd Tech. Advisor to Minister of Finance 1999; First Exec. Dir Financial Services Comm. 2001–07; Capital Markets/Financial Sector Advisor, Caribbean Regional Tech. Assistance Centre (CARTAC), Barbados 2007–09; Order of Distinction in the Rank of Commdr 2013; Cen. Bank Gov. of the Year for the Caribbean 2016. *Address:* Bank of Jamaica, Nethersole Pl., POB 621, Kingston, Jamaica (office). *Telephone:* 922-0750 (office). *Fax:* 922-0854 (office). *E-mail:* info@boj.org.jm (office). *Website:* www.boj.org.jm (office).

WYPLOSZ, Charles, PhD, DipEng; French professor of economics; *Professor of Economics, Graduate Institute, Geneva;* b. 5 Sept. 1947, Vichy; s. of Jacob Wyplosz and Félicia Zanger; m. Claire-Lise Monod 1967; one s. three d.; ed Ecole Centrale de Paris, Harvard Univ.; Asst, Assoc., then Full Prof. of Econs, Institut Européen d'Admin des Affaires (INSEAD), Fontainebleau 1978–, Assoc. Dean (Research and Devt) 1986–89; Directeur d'études, École des hautes études en sciences sociales (EHESS), Paris 1988–95; Prof. of Econs, Grad. Inst. of Int. Studies, Geneva 1995–; Dir Int. Center for Monetary and Banking Studies 1998–; Man. Ed. Econ. Policy 1984–2001; mem. Council of Econ. Advisors to Prime Minister of France 1999–2006, Comm. Economique, Ministry of Finance, France 1999–2005; mem. Panel of Econ. and Monetary Experts, Cttee for Econ. and Monetary Affairs, European Parl. 2000–15, Group of Econ. Analysis, EC 2001–10, Advisory Scientific Cttee of European Systemic Risk Bd 2010–15, Consultative Group to the Monetary and Capital Markets Dept, IMF 2010–; European Comm. Fellow 2012, 2014; Chevalier, Légion d'honneur. *Publications include:* numerous publs in professional journals; occasional contribs to press. *Leisure interests:* skiing, music, family. *Address:* Graduate Institute of International Studies, Chemoin Eugène-Rigot 2, 1202 Geneva (office); 3 rue du Valais, 1202 Geneva, Switzerland (home). *Telephone:* (22) 9085946 (office). *Fax:* (22) 7333049 (office). *E-mail:* charles.wyplosz@graduateinstitute.ch (office). *Website:* www.wyplosz.eu (office).

WYZNER, Eugeniusz, LLM; Polish diplomatist and UN official; *Member, International Civil Service Commission;* b. 1931; s. of Henryk Wyzner and Janina Wyzner; m. Elżbieta Laudańska; one s.; ed Jagiellonian Univ., Univ. of Warsaw, Acad. of Int. Law, The Hague; Deputy Perm. Rep. to UN 1961–68, Deputy Dir Dept at Ministry of Foreign Affairs 1968–71, Dir of Dept 1971–73, Amb. and Perm. Rep. to UN, Geneva 1973–78, Dir of Dept, Ministry of Foreign Affairs 1978–81; UN Under-Sec.-Gen. 1982–94; Deputy Minister for Foreign Affairs and Parl. Sec., Ministry of Foreign Affairs 1994–97, Acting Minister for Foreign Affairs Dec. 1995, Amb. and Rep. to UN, New York 1998–99, mem. Int. Civil Service Comm. 1999–; Chair. UN Steering Cttee on Status of Women 1989–91, UN Appointments and Promotion Bd 1991–94, UN Exhibits Cttee 1992–94; mem. UN Sr Bd on Services to the Public 1989–94; mem. Bd of Dirs Int. Inst. of Space Law, Int. Peace Acad., New York, Int. Congress Inst. 1987–; Vice-Pres. Jan Karski Soc. 2009–; Amb. ad personam 1999–; Gold Cross of Merit, Grand Commdr's Cross, Order of Polonia Restituta, Grand Commdr, Order of the Phoenix (Greece), Commdr, Légion d'honneur and other decorations; Testimonial from UN Sec.-Gen. for dedicated service in support of UN peacekeeping operations 2009, Citation, Int. Inst. of Space Law. *Publications include:* Wybrane zagadnienia z działalności ONZ w dziedzinie kodyfikacji i postępowego rozwoju prawa międzynarodowego, Niektóre aspekty prawne finansowania operacji ONZ w Kongo i na Bliskim Wschodzie, Poland and 50 Years of the United Nations Existence 1995. *Leisure interests:* cross-country skiing, mountain walking, theatre. *Address:* International Civil Service Commission, 2 United Nations Plaza, New York, NY 10017, USA (office). *Telephone:* (212) 963-8465 (office). *Fax:* (212) 963-1717 (office). *E-mail:* wyzner@un.org (office). *Website:* icsc.un.org (office).

X

XAYRULLOYEV, Col-Gen. Sherali; Tajikistani government official and army officer; b. 8 Nov. 1949, Danga City, Khatlon Prov.; m.; c.; ed Tajikistan State Univ.; conscripted to serve in USSR Ministry of Internal Affairs 1970, served in various positions including Platoon Commdr 1970–77, subsequently served in various Ministry depts; Deputy Internal Affairs Minister 1988–95; Minister of Defence 1995–2013.

XHAFAJ, Fatmir; Albanian lawyer and politician; b. 17 May 1959, Vlorë; m. Mimoza Berberi; two d.; ed Univ. of Tirana; Legal Advisor and Judge, Krujë Dist Court 1982–84; Dist Investigator, Krujë Prosecutor's Office 1984–85; practised as lawyer 1993–97, 1999–2000; Legal Advisor for consultancy co. 1994–97; mem. People's Ass. (Parl.) (PSSh) for Pogradec, Korçë County 2001–09, for Tirana County 2009–, Chair. Parl. Cttee for Legal Issues, Public Admin and Human Rights 2013–, Ad Hoc Parl. Cttee on Judicial System Reform 2014–; Gen. Sec., Council of Ministers 1997–99, Minister for Territorial Regulation and Tourism 2002, Minister of Justice 2003–05, Minister of Internal Affairs 2017–18; mem. Partia Socialiste e Shqipërisë (Albanian Socialist Party) 1991–. *Address:* c/o Ministry of Internal Affairs, Sheshi Skënderbej 3, 1001 Tirana, Albania (office).

XHAFERI, Musa; Macedonian politician; b. 7 July 1959, Zajaz, Kičevo; m.; one c.; ed Prishtina Univ., Univ. of Zurich and Acad. for Adult Educ., Lucerne, Switzerland; teacher in Lucerne, Switzerland 1996–2001; Deputy Prime Minister, responsible for the implementation of the Ohrid Framework Agreement 2002–06, 2011–16; Minister of Local Self-Govt 2008–11; Co-founder and mem. Bashkimi Demokratik për Integrim (BDI—Democratic Union for Integration), Sec.-Gen. 2002–03, mem. Cen. Cttee 2002–, Sec. Human Resources Secr. 2003–09, Sec. Local Self-Govt and Decentralization Secr. 2009–. *Address:* Bashkimi Demokratik për Integrim (Democratic Union for Integration), 1200 Tetovo, Rruga 170 No 2, Reçicë e Vogël, North Macedonia. *E-mail:* bdi@bdi.org.mk. *Website:* www.bdi.org.mk.

XHAFERI, Talat, MA; Macedonian fmr army officer and politician; *Chairman, Sobranie (Assembly);* b. 15 April 1962, Forino, Gostivar, Socialist Repub. of Macedonia, Socialist Fed. Repub. of Yugoslavia; m.; two c.; ed Mil. High School, Belgrade, Land Forces Mil. Acad.–Infantry, Belgrade and Sarajevo, General Mihailo Apostolski Mil. Acad., Skopje; ethnic Albanian; Officer in Yugoslav People's Army 1985–91; Macedonian army officer 1992–2001; mem. Bashkimi Demokratik për Integrim (BDI—Democratic Union for Integration); mem. Sobranie (Ass.) (BDI) 2002–04, Chair. 2017–; Deputy Minister of Defence 2004–06, 2008– Minister of Defence 2013–14. *Address:* Office of the Chairman of the Sobranie (Assembly), 1000 Skopje, 11 Oktomvri b.b., North Macedonia (office). *Telephone:* (2) 3113268 (office); (2) 3112255 (ext. 353) (office). *Fax:* (2) 3237947 (office). *E-mail:* pretsedatel@sobranie.mk (office). *Website:* www.sobranie.mk (office).

XI, Guohua, PhD; Chinese business executive; b. 1951; ed Hefei Univ. of Tech., Jiaotong Univ., Tongji Univ.; Chair. Shanghai Bell Co. Ltd, Shanghai 2000–01, Exec. Vice-Pres. 2000–01; Vice-Minister, Ministry of Industry and Information Tech. 2001–11; Gen. Man. China Network Communications Group Corpn 2002–11, Sec. CCP Leading Party Group 2002–11; Exec. Dir and Chair. China Mobile Communications Corpn 2011–15; Deputy Dir State Internet Information Office 2011–16; Alt. mem. 16th CCP Cen. Cttee 2002–07, mem. Cen. Comm. for Discipline Inspection, 17th CCP Cen. Cttee 2007–12.

XI, Jinping, LLD; Chinese politician and head of state; *President and General Secretary, CCP Central Committee;* b. 1953, Fuping, Shaanxi Prov.; s. of Xi Zhongxun (fmr Vice-Premier and a founder of Communist guerrilla movt in northern China); m. 1st Ke Lingling (divorced); m. 2nd Peng Liyuan 1987; one d.; ed Tsinghua Univ., Beijing; sent to do manual labour, Yanchuan Co., Shaanxi Prov. 1969; joined CCP 1974; Sec.-Gen. Office of the State Council 1979–82; served as Sec. to Geng Biao 1982; Vice-Sec., Sec. CCP Zhengding Co. Cttee 1982–85; First Political Commissar, Chinese People's Armed Police Force, Hebei Prov. 1983–85; Vice-Mayor of Xiamen, Fujian Prov. 1985–88; Sec. CCP Ningde Pref. Cttee 1988–90; First Sec. Fujian Mil. Dist (Ningde Mil. Sub-Area Command), PLA Nanjing Mil. Region 1988; Sec. CCP Fuzhou Municipal Cttee, Chair. Standing Cttee Fuzhou Municipal People's Congress 1990–96; Deputy Sec. CCP Fujian Prov. Cttee 1995–2002; Deputy, 9th NPC 1998–2003; Vice-Gov. of Fujian Prov. 1999–2000, Gov. 2000–02; Acting Gov. of Zhejiang Prov. 2002–07; Deputy Sec. CCP Zhejiang Prov. Cttee 2002, Sec. 2002–07; Chair. Standing Cttee of Zhejiang Prov. People's Congress 2003–07; Sec. CCP Shanghai Municipal Cttee 2007; First Sec., Cen. Secr., CCP 2007–12; Pres. CCP Central Party School 2007–13; Gen. Sec. CCP Cen. Cttee 2012–; Vice-Pres. People's Repub. of China 2008–13, Pres. 2013–; Chair. CCP Cen. Mil. Comm. 2012–, State Cen. Mil. Comm. 2013–; Chair. Nat. Security Comm. 2014–; Deputy, 13th NPC 2018–; Del., 14th CCP Nat. Congress 1992–97; Alt. mem. 15th CCP Cen. Cttee 1997–2002; mem. 16th CCP Cen. Cttee 2002–07; mem. 17th CCP Cen. Cttee 2007–12, also mem. 17th CCP Cen. Cttee Politburo 2007–12 and Politburo Standing Cttee 2007–12; mem. 18th CCP Cen. Cttee 2012–17, also mem. 18th CCP Cen. Cttee Politburo 2012–17 and Politburo Standing Cttee 2012–17; mem. 19th CCP Cen. Cttee 2017–, also mem. 19th CCP Cen. Cttee Politburo 2017– and Politburo Standing Cttee 2017–. *Publications include:* Research on Developing Chinese Rural Market-orientated Economy, Science and Patriotism (Chief Ed.). *Leisure interests:* reading, sports. *Address:* Office of the President, Great Hall of the People, West Edge, Tiananmen Square, Beijing, People's Republic of China (office). *Website:* www.gov.cn (office).

XIANG, Junbo, MEconSc, PhD; Chinese fmr financial services executive; b. Jan. 1957, Sichuan Prov.; ed Peking Univ., Nankai Univ., Renmin Univ. of China; Vice-Pres. Nanjing Audit Inst. 1993–96; Deputy Dir-Gen., Supervision Dept, Nat. Audit Office of China (CNAO) 1996, Special CNAO Attaché to Beijing, Tianjin and Hebei Prov. 1996–99, Dir-Gen. Personnel and Educ. Dept 1999–2000, Dir-Gen. Personnel Dept 2000–02, Deputy Auditor 2002–04; Deputy Gov. People's Bank of China (PBC) 2004–07, also Pres. PBC Shanghai Head Office 2005–07; Pres. Agricultural Bank of China Head Office 2007–09, Exec. Chair. Agricultural Bank of China 2009–11; Chair. China Insurance Regulatory Comm. 2011–17; Adjunct Prof., China Europe Int. Business School; Guest Prof., Fudan Econ. Forum 2007; mem. Expert Cttee for Devt of Shanghai as Int. Financial Centre 2007–; Alt. mem. 17th CCP Cen. Cttee 2007–12, mem. 18th CCP Cen. Cttee 2012–17; Research Fellow, Peking Univ.; investigated on charges of corruption and expelled from CCP April 2017.

XIAO, Gang, LLM; Chinese banker; b. 1959, Changsha, Hunan Prov.; m. Wu Touhong; ed Hunan Inst. of Finance and Econs, Renmin Univ. of China; joined People's Bank of China (PBC) 1981, various roles including Gen. Man. China Foreign Exchange Trading Center, Dir-Gen. Policy Research Dept, Asst Gov. PBC 1996–98, Deputy Gov. 1998–2003, also mem. PBC Monetary Policy Cttee 1998–2003; Chair., Pres. and Sec. Party Cttee, Bank of China Ltd 2003–04, Chair. and Sec. Party Cttee 2003–13, Chair. BOC Hong Kong (Holdings) 2003–13; Chair. China Asscn of Banks 2003–04, China Securities Regulatory Comm. (CSRC) and Sec. CSRC Party Cttee 2013–16; fmr Deputy 9th Nat. People's Congress; fmr Alt. mem. 8th Chinese CP Guangdong Prov. Cttee; Alt. mem. 17th CCP Cen. Cttee 2007–12, mem. 18th CCP Cen. Cttee 2012–17.

XIAO, Jie, PhD; Chinese engineer and politician; *Secretary-General, State Council;* b. June 1957, Kaiyuan County, Liaoning Prov.; ed CCP Central Party School, Ministry of Finance Financial Sciences Research Inst., Renmin Univ. of China; began career as engineer, Research Inst. of Mechanics and Research Inst. of Mechanics and Electronics, Beijing 1976–78; joined CCP 1985; Long-term Planning Officer, Gen. Planning Dept, Ministry of Finance 1982–87, Deputy Head of Long-term Planning 1987–91, Head of Long-term Planning and Forecasting 1991–93, Deputy Section Chief, Gen. Planning Dept 1993–94, Deputy Section Chief, Gen. Reform Dept 1994–98, Chief, Ministry of Finance Admin. Office 1998–2000, Head, Nat. Treasury Dept 2000–01, Dir, State Admin of Taxation 2007–13, Vice-Minister of Finance 2001–05, Minister of Finance 2016–18; Deputy Dir, Fuxin Econ. Planning Comm., Liaoning Prov. 1991–92; Vice-Gov. of Hunan Prov. 2005–07, also mem. Hunan Provincial CCP Standing Cttee 2005–07; Deputy Sec.-Gen., State Council 2013–16, mem. State Council and Sec. Gen. 2018–; mem. 17th CCP Cen. Cttee 2007–12, 18th CCP Cen. Cttee 2012–17, 19th CCP Cen. Cttee 2017–. *Address:* State Council, Great Hall of the People, West Edge, Tiananmen Square, Beijing, People's Republic of China (office). *Website:* english.gov.cn (office).

XIAO, Yaqing; Chinese engineer, business executive, academic and government official; *Director, State-Owned Assets Supervision and Administration Commission;* b. Sept. 1959, Beijing; ed Cen. South Univ. of Tech.; began working as engineer 1982; fmr Dept Head and Chief Engineer, Tech. Div., Northeast Light Alloy Fabrication Plant; fmr Gen. Man. Northeast High Alloy Corpn Ltd; fmr Factory Man. Southwest Aluminum Fabrication Plant (renamed Southwest Aluminum Industry Group 1999), Chair. and Gen. Man. 1999–2003; Pres. China Aluminum Corpn (CHINALCO) 2003–09; Chair. and CEO Aluminum Corpn of China (CHALCO) Ltd 2004–09; Deputy Sec.-Gen., State Council 2009–13; Deputy Dir, State Council Leading Group for Promoting Medium and Small Enterprise Devt 2013–16, Nat. Construction Leading Group for Manufacturing Powerful Country 2015–16; Dir State-Owned Assets Supervision and Admin Comm. 2016–; Vice-Chair. China Non-ferrous Metals Fabrication Asscn; part-time Prof., Cen. South Univ. of Tech., Chongqing Univ.; mem. CCP 1981–; Del., Nat. Congress, 16th CCP 2002–07; Alt. mem. 17th CCP Cen. Cttee 2007–12, mem. 18th CCP Cen. Cttee 2012–17, 19th CCP Cen. Cttee 2017. *Address:* No. 26, Xidajie, Xuanwumen, Xicheng District, Beijing 100053, People's Republic of China (office). *Telephone:* (10) 63192000 (office). *E-mail:* iecc@sasac.gov.cn (office). *Website:* en.sasac.gov.cn (office).

XIE, Heping, DEng, PhD; Chinese mining engineer, academic and university administrator; b. Jan. 1956, Shuangfeng Co., Hunan Prov.; ed China Univ. of Mining and Tech.; joined CCP 1986; Prof., China Univ. of Mining and Tech., Beijing 1990, Dean, Postgraduate Dept 1992, Pres. China Univ. of Mining and Tech. 1998, also Deputy Sec., China Univ. of Mining and Tech. CCP Cttee 1999–2000, Sec. 2000; Pres. Sichuan Univ. 2003–17; Alt. mem. 17th CCP Cen. Cttee 2007–12; mem. Chinese Acad. of Eng 2001–; Hon. DEng (Hong Kong Polytechnic Univ.) 2012; numerous awards including Award of Chinese Youth Scientists 1993, Nat. Prize of Natural Sciences 1995, Nat. Prize of Progress in Science and Tech. 1999, 2000, St Edmund Fellowship 2017, Ho Leung Ho Lee Prize. *Publications:* five books in English and Chinese and over 150 journal papers.

XIE, Qihua; Chinese steel industry executive; b. June 1943, Shanghai; ed Tsinghua Univ., Beijing Municipality; trained as engineer; began career in steel industry 1968; joined Shanghai Baoshan Iron & Steel Group 1978, held positions successively as Planning Section Chief, Asst Commdr and Vice-Commdr of Baosteel Project HQ, Dir and Deputy Man. of Group Eng HQ, Dir of Planning and Devt Dept 1993–94, Deputy Pres. and Gen. Man. 1994–98, Vice-Chair. and Pres.; Pres. Shanghai Baosteel Group Corpn (following merger of Baoshan Iron & Steel with Shanghai Metallurgical and Meishan Steel to form new co. 1998) 1998–2004, 2005, Chair. and Pres. 2004–07 (retd); Alt. mem. 16th CCP Cen. Cttee 2002–07; Chair. China Fed. of Industrial Econs Presidium; fmr Chair. China Metallurgical Council; Vice-Chair. China Iron & Steel Asscn (Chair. 2005–), China Asscn of Women Entrepreneurs, China Group Cos Promotion Asscn, China Investment Asscn, China Enterprise Confed., China Enterprise Dirs Asscn, Chinese Entrepreneur Asscn, Investment Asscn of China; Dir Standard Chartered 2007–; Hon Dir Chinese Soc. for Metals 2011–; Shanghai Excellent Entrepreneur 1995, Outstanding Entrepreneur of Shanghai Municipality, Nat. Outstanding Female Entrepreneur, Outstanding Contrib. to Chinese Enterprise Prize 2004. *Address:* Metallurgical Council of China, 46 Dongsi Xidajie, Beijing 100711, People's Republic of China (office). *Telephone:* (10) 65227956 (office). *Website:* www.mcchina.org.cn (office).

XIE, Shijie; Chinese administrator; b. Sept. 1934, Liangping Co., Sichuan Prov.; ed South-West Agricultural Coll.; joined CCP 1954; Dir Ya'an Agricultural School, Sichuan Prov. 1959–71; Deputy Sec., later Sec. CCP Ya'an Prefectural Cttee 1980–85, Sichuan Prov. Govt 1985–92; mem. Standing Cttee CCP Sichuan Prov. Cttee 1985–92, Deputy Sec. CCP Sichuan Prov. Cttee 1992–93, Sec. 1993–2000;

Vice-Gov. of Sichuan Prov. 1985–1992; Deputy, 8th NPC 1993–98, 9th NPC 1998–2003; Chair. Standing Cttee of NPC, Sichuan Prov. 1998–2003; mem. 14th CCP Cen. Cttee 1992–1997, 15th CCP Cen. Cttee 1997–2002. *Address:* c/o Standing Committee of Sichuan People's Congress, Chengdu, Sichuan Province, People's Republic of China (office).

XIE, Xuren; Chinese economist and government official; b. 1947, Ningbo City, Zhejiang Prov.; ed Zhejiang Univ.; began career as technician, Ningbo Zhenhai Machinery Factory, Ningbo City 1967, served as Section Chief and later Deputy Dir –1981; Magistrate, People's Court, Zhejiang Prov. 1984–85; Dir Investment and Planning Offices, Prov. Planning and Econ. Comm., Zhejiang Prov. 1985–88; Deputy Dir Prov. Planning and Econ. Comm. 1988–90; Deputy Dir Budget Dept, Ministry of Finance 1990–91, Deputy Dir Planning Dept 1990–93, Dir Planning Dept and Asst to Minister 1993–94, Dir Reforms Dept 1994–95, Vice-Minister 1995–98; Pres. Agricultural Devt Bank of China 1998–2000; Vice-Minister, State Econ. and Trade Comm. 2001–03; Dir State Admin of Taxation 2003–07; Minister of Finance 2007–13; joined CCP 1980, Deputy Sec., Yinxian Co. Cttee 1984–85, Deputy Sec., Work Cttee Depts, Financial Work Cttee, CCP Cen. Cttee 2000–01, Deputy Sec., Leading Party Group, CCP 2001–03, Alt. mem. 16th CCP Cen. Cttee 2002–07, mem. 17th CCP Cen. Cttee 2007–12; named by Emerging Markets Magazine as Asian Finance Minister of the Year 2009.

XIE, Yi, BSc, PhD, FRSC; Chinese chemist and academic; *Professor, University of Science and Technology of China;* b. 23 July 1967, Fuyang, Anhui Prov.; ed Xiamen Univ., Univ. of Science and Tech. of China, State Univ. of New York, Stony Brook, USA; assigned as asst engineer to a chemical plant in Hefei 1988; mem. Faculty, Univ. of Science and Tech. of China 1996–, Prof. 1998–, Doctoral Supervisor 1999–; Prin. Investigator, Dept of Nanomaterials and Nanochemistry, Hefei Nat. Lab. for Physical Sciences at Microscale; mem. Int. Editorial Advisory Bd, Dalton Transactions; mem. Editorial Bd, Chinese Journal of Inorganic Chemistry, Journal of University of Science and Technology of China, Chemistry Central Journal; mem. Chinese Acad. of Sciences 2013; Cheung Kong Scholar, Ministry of Educ. 2000, China Young Scientist Award 2002, Chinese Acad. of Sciences-Bayer Young Scientist Award 2003, China Young Female Scientist Award 2006, Laureate, L'Oréal-UNESCO Awards for Women in Science (Asia Pacific) 2015, Springer Nano Research Award, Tsinghua University Press 2017. *Publications include:* numerous papers in professional journals on nanotechnology, materials chemistry, energy science and theoretical physics. *Address:* Department of Chemistry, University of Science and Technology of China, Hefei 230026, Anhui Province, People's Republic of China (office). *Telephone:* (551) 63603987 (office). *Fax:* (551) 63606266 (office). *E-mail:* yxie@ustc.edu.cn (office). *Website:* dsxt.ustc .edu.cn (office); staff.ustc.edu.cn/~yxie (office).

XIE, Zhenhua; Chinese civil servant; b. Oct. 1949, Tianjin; ed Tsinghua Univ., Beijing, Wuhan Univ. Environmental Law Research Inst.; joined CCP 1969; Sec. Production and Construction Corps, Heilongjiang Prov. 1979–80; teaching asst, No. 2 Subsidiary School, Tsinghua Univ. 1979–80 (Sec. CCP Revolutionary Cttee); Org. Sec. CCP Party Cttee State Construction Comm. 1980–82; various man. roles, Ministry of Urban and Rural Construction and Environmental Protection 1982–88; Deputy Dir State Environment Protection Bureau 1990–93, Dir 1993–2007; apptd Vice-Chair. and Sec.-Gen. Environmental Protection Cttee of the State Council 1993, Nat. Cttee for the Patriotic Public Health Campaign 1994; apptd Chair. Chinese Comm. for Certification of Produce Conformity and Environmental Standards 1994; apptd Dir Specialists Examination Cttee of Nuclear Environment 1994; Vice-Minister, State Devt and Reform Comm. 2007–15; Del., 15th CCP Nat. Congress 1997–2002; mem. 15th CCP Cen. Cttee for Discipline Inspection 1997–2002, 16th CCP Cen. Cttee 2002–07, 17th CCP Cen. Cttee for Discipline Inspection 2007–12, mem. 18th CCP Cen. Cttee 2012–17; Global Environment Facility (GEF) Leadership Award (jt winner) 2002, UNEP Sasakawa Environment Prize (jt winner) 2003.

XIMENES BELO, Mgr Carlos Filipe, SDB; Timor-Leste ecclesiastic; b. 3 Feb. 1948, Baucau, Dili; ordained priest (mem. Salesians of St John Bosco) 1980; consecrated Titular Bishop of Lorium 1988; Papal Admin., Dili; active in campaign for human rights in Timor-Leste; fmr Apostolic Admin. to Bishopric of Dili (resgnd 2002); Nobel Peace Prize (shared with José Ramos-Horta q.v.) 1996. *Address:* c/o Camara Eclesiaastica, Av. Direitos Humanos, Bidau Lecidere, Dili 88010, Timor-Leste. *Telephone:* (390) 3322850. *Fax:* (390) 3322308.

XING, Bensi; Chinese philosopher and academic; b. 7 Oct. 1929, Sheng Co., Zhejiang Prov.; s. of Xing Tinxu and Guei Yuyin; m. Zhou Bangyuan 1953; two d.; ed Special School of Russian Language of CCP Cen. Cttee; joined CCP 1950; teacher, Beijing Inst. of Russian Language 1952–56; Asst Researcher and Academic Sec., Inst. of Philosophy, Chinese Acad. of Sciences 1957–66, Deputy Dir, Dir, Vice-Chair. Academic Cttee under Chinese Acad. of Social Sciences 1978–82, Academician 1983–85; Prof. Tsinghua Univ. 1984–, apptd Chair School of Marxism 2011; mem. Council for Int. Cultural Exchange 1984; Deputy Gen. Ed. Philosophy Vol. of Chinese Encyclopaedia 1983–; Vice-Pres. CCP Cen. Cttee Party School 1988–; Ed.-in-Chief Party journal Qiushi 1994–; NPC Deputy, Zhejiang Prov.; mem. NPC Law Cttee; Visiting Scholar Columbia Univ. 1981. *Publications:* The Dualism of Ludwig Feurbach's Anthropology 1963, The Social Theory and Historical Viewpoint of Saint-Simon 1964, Humanism in the History of European Philosophy 1978, Philosophy and Enlightenment 1979, The Anthropology of Ludwig Feurbach 1981, Philosophy and Time 1984, Philosophy (Introduction to Philosophy Vol. of Chinese Encyclopaedia) 1987, The Past, Present and Future of Philosophy (Introduction, Little Encyclopaedia of Philosophy) 1987 and many other essays. *Leisure interests:* music, literature, Peking Opera, Chinese calligraphy. *Address:* Tsinghua University, School of Marxism, Haidian District, Beijing, People's Republic of China (office). *Telephone:* (10) 62795238 (office). *Fax:* (10) 62789940 (office). *Website:* www.smarx.tsinghua.edu.cn (office).

XIONG, Shen; Chinese mechanical engineer and academic; b. 13 Sept. 1935, Jiangsu Prov.; s. of Shen Baozhang and Xu Shifeng; m. Xia Xuejian 1965; one d.; ed Tsinghua Univ., Beijing; Prof. Dept of Eng Mechanics, Tsinghua Univ. 1959; several prizes including State Prize of Science Congress 1978, Prize of Science and Tech. of State Bureau of Instrumentation Industry 1981, Prizes of Science and Tech., State Educational Comm. 1986, 1988, State Prize of Invention 1992, Prize of Zhou Peiyuan Foundation 1992, State Prize of Excellent Book in Science and Tech.

1992. *Publications include:* Modern Techniques and Measurements in Fluid Flows 1989, Fluid Velocity Measurement Techniques (in Chinese) 1987, Laser Doppler Velocimetry and Its Applications (in Chinese) 2004. *Leisure interests:* music, playing piano and accordion.

XIONG, Weiping, PhD; Chinese academic and business executive; Prof. of Mineral Eng, Cen. South Univ. of Industry; fmr Exec. Vice-Pres., Cen. South Univ. of Industry, fmr Dean of School of Man.; fmr Deputy Gen. Man. China Copper, Lead and Zinc Group Co.; fmr Deputy Gen. Man. and Vice-Pres. China Aluminum Corpn (CHINALCO), Pres. and Sec.-Gen. Exec. Cttee 2009–14, joined Aluminum Corpn of China (CHALCO) 2000, served as Sr Vice-Pres., Pres. 2004–06, Chair. and CEO 2009–14; Vice-Chair. and Pres. China Nat. Travel Service (HK) Group Corpn and China Travel Service (Holdings) Hong Kong Ltd as well as Vice-Chair. and Pres. China Travel International Investment Hong Kong Ltd 2006–09; PhD Supervisor, Guanghua School of Man., Beijing Univ.

XOLMURADOV, Suxrob R.; Uzbekistani banking executive and politician; *Deputy Prime Minister, responsible for Investment, Innovative Development, Co-ordination of Free Economic and Small Industrial Zones;* b. 1973, Samarqand Viloyat, Uzbek SSR, USSR; ed Tashkent Financial Inst.; began career in banking sector 1993; fmr Vice-Chair., Open Jt Stock Commercial Bank Hamkorbank; First Deputy Chair., Nat. Bank for Foreign Econ. Activity (NBU) 2016–17, Chair. 2017–18; Deputy Prime Minister, responsible for Investment, Innovative Devt, Co-ordination of Free Econ. and Small Industrial Zones 2017–; Head State Cttee for Investment. *Address:* Office of the Cabinet of Ministers, 100078 Tashkent, Mustaqillik maydoni 5, Uzbekistan (office). *Telephone:* (71) 239-86-76 (office). *Fax:* (71) 239-84-63 (office). *Website:* www.gov.uz (office).

XU, Bin; Chinese automotive industry executive; Pres. China South Industries Group Corpn (state-owned enterprise run by Cen. Govt and an investment inst. authorized by the State Council) –2012, owns more than 40 industrial enterprises, including Chang'an Automobile (Group) Corpn Ltd, China Jialing (Group) Corpn Ltd, Jianshe Industries (Group) Corpn Ltd, four research insts and 23 research and devt centres) 2003–, also Chair. China Chang'an Automobile Group. *Address:* c/o China South Industries Group Corpn, 10 Chedaogou, 69 Zizhuyuan Road, Haidian District, Beijing 100089, People's Republic of China. *E-mail:* info@csgc .com.cn.

XU, Bing, MFA; Chinese artist; *Professor, Department of Art History and Theory, Central Academy of Fine Arts (CAFA);* b. 8 Feb. 1955, Chongqing; s. of Hua-min Xu and Shi-ying Yang; ed Cen. Acad. of Fine Arts, Beijing; grew up in Beijing; relocated to the countryside for two years 1975–77; apptd Asst Prof. Printmaking Dept, Cen. Acad. of Fine Arts (CAFA) 1987, Assoc. Dir 1988–89, Prof., Dept of Art History and Theory 2008–, Vice-Pres. CAFA 2008–14, also Dir of Acad. Cttee; following Tiananmen Square Protests his recent work came under govt scrutiny and was heavily criticized 1989; moved to USA as an honour artist under invitation from Univ. of Wisconsin 1990–2007; Andrew D. White Prof.-at-Large, Cornell Univ. 2015–; exhbns in China, France, USA, Switzerland, UK, Italy, Japan, Germany, Turkey 1979–; one man exhbns Beijing Art Gallery 1988, Taipei 1988, Taiwan 1990; mem. Chinese Engraving Artists' Asscn 1981–, Chinese Artists' Asscn 1982–, Dir 1985–; Dir Chinese Engraving Artists' Asscn 1986–; mem. Printmaking Artists' Cttee, Chinese Fine Arts Asscn 1989–; mem. Appraisal Cttee, 7th Chinese Nat. Exhbn of Fine Arts 1989; best known for his print-making skills and installations pieces, as well as creative artistic use of language, words and text; Hon. Adviser, Dept of Art, Beijing Univ. 1989–; Hon. Fellow, Art Dept, Univ. of Wisconsin, Madison 1990; Hon. DHumLitt (Columbia Univ., New York) 2010; prizes from Art Exhbns of Chinese Young Artists' Works 1980, 1985, 8th Exhbn of China's Wooden Paintings 1983, Medal, 9th Chinese Engraving Exhbn 1986, Award for Excellent Prints, Taiwan 1988, Young Univ. Teacher First Prize, State Educ. Comm. and Huo Yingdong Educ. Fund 1988, Henry E.T. Kok Educ. Foundation Prize for Young Instructors at Insts of Higher Learning 1989, Pollack Krasner Foundation Prize 1998, MacArthur Award 1999, Fukuoka Asian Culture Prize 2003, Coca-Cola Fellowship, American Acad. in Berlin 2004, inaugural Artes Mundi Prize 2004, The Youth Friends Award, New York 2005, Int. Asscn of Art Critics Award for "Best Installation or Single Work of Art in a Museum, New England" 2006, Lifetime Achievement Award, Southern Graphics Council 2006, Lifetime Engraving Achievement Award, US Nat. Engraving Artists Soc. 2007, Medal of Arts, US Dept of State 2014. *Publications:* Wooden Painting Sketches of Xu Bing 1986, Engravings of Xu Bing; numerous articles in magazines and newspapers. *Leisure interest:* hiking. *Address:* Central Academy of Fine Arts, No. 8 Hua Jia Di Nan Street, Chao Yang District, Beijing 100102, People's Republic of China (office); Xu Bing Studio, Inc., 540 Metropolitan Avenue, Brooklyn, NY 11211, USA (office). *Telephone:* (10) 64771018 (Beijing) (office); (718) 388-4228 (Brooklyn, NY). *Fax:* (10) 64771136 (Beijing) (office). *E-mail:* xujia@cafa.edu.cn (office); xubing@xubing.com. *Website:* www.cafa.edu.cn (office); www.xubing.com.

XU, Guanhua; Chinese scientist and politician; b. 16 Dec. 1941, Shanghai; m.; ed Beijing Inst. of Forestry; research intern, teacher, Asst Research Fellow, Chinese Acad. of Forestry Sciences; Researcher, Stockholm Univ., Sweden 1979–81, Research Fellow and Dir Natural Resources Information Inst.; joined CCP 1984; Asst Research Fellow, Inst. of Remote Sensing Application, Chinese Acad. of Sciences 1964–93, Fellow, Chinese Acad. of Sciences 1991, Research Prof., Dir 1993, Vice-Pres. 1994–95, Chair. Div. of Earth Sciences 1996; Vice-Chair. State Science and Tech. Comm. 1995; Vice-Minister of Science and Tech. 1998, Minister 2001–07; Hon. Prof., Chinese Univ. of Hong Kong 2005–08; apptd Wei Lun Research Prof. of Space and Earth Sciences, Inst. of Space and Earth Information Science 2009; mem. 9th CPPCC Nat. Cttee 1998–2003; mem. 16th CCP Cen. Cttee 2002–07; mem. Third World Acad. of Sciences, Royal Swedish Acad. of Eng Sciences, Int. Acad. of Astronautics, Helmholtz-Zentrum Geesthacht; awarded title of Outstanding Scientist.

XU, Heyi; Chinese business executive; *Chairman and President, Beijing Automotive Industry Holding Company Limited (Beijing Automotive Group);* serves as a Consultant of Shunyi People's Govt; Pres. and Sec., Party Cttee, Beijing Automotive Industry Holding Co. Ltd, Vice-Chair. –2006, Chair. 2006–; Chair. Beijing Hyundai Motor Co., Beijing Benz-Daimler Chrysler Automotive Co. Ltd, Beijing Automotive Investment Co. Ltd, Beiqi Foton Motor Co. Ltd, Beijing Hyundai Mobis Automotive Parts Co. Ltd; Assoc. Pres. Beijing Asscn of Automobile Mfrs, Beijing Entrepreneurs Asscn, Beijing Consumers Asscn; Exec. Dir China Asscn of Automobile Mfrs; Deputy Dir Capital Entrepreneurs Club; mem. Standing Cttee, Beijing Asscn of Science and Tech.; China Outstanding Quality Model Award 2015. *Address:* Beijing Automotive Industry Holding Co. Ltd, 99 Shuanghe Street, Shunyi District, Beijing 101300, People's Republic of China (office). *Telephone:* (10) 87664009 (office). *Fax:* (10) 87664048 (office). *E-mail:* info@baicgroup.com.cn (office). *Website:* www.baicgroup.com.cn (office); www.baihc.com (office).

XU, Houze; Chinese geodesist and geophysicist; b. 4 May 1934, Anhui; s. of Xu Zuoren and Jiang Xinghua; m. Yang Huiji 1967; one s. one d.; ed Tongji Univ., Shanghai, Chinese Acad. of Sciences; Asst Researcher, Inst. of Geodesy and Geophysics, Chinese Acad. of Sciences 1963, Assoc. Prof. 1978, Prof. 1982–, Dir 1983–, Fellow 1991–; Dir Survey and Geophysics Inst. 1992–; mem. Chinese Geophysics Soc. 1978–; Vice-Pres. Int. Gravimetry Cttee and Pres. Perm. Cttee of Earth Tides, Int. Asscn of Geodesy 1983–; Vice-Pres. Science-Tech. Soc. of Hubei Prov. 1984–, Chinese Survey and Mapping Soc. 1985–; Prof., Tongji Univ. 1985–, Wuhan Tech. Univ. of Survey and Mapping 1986–, Shandong Univ. of Tech.; NPC Deputy, Hubei Prov.; Ho Leung Ho Lee Foundation Earth Sciences Prize. *Publications:* The Approximation of Stokes' Function and the Estimation of Trunction Error 1981, The Effect of Oceanic Tides on Gravity Tide Observations 1982, The Tidal Correction in Astrometry 1982, Accuracy Estimation of Loading Correction in Gravity Observation 1984, The Effect of Different Earth Models on Load Tide Correction 1985, Representation of Gravity Field outside the Earth using Fictitious Single Layer Density 1984, Collected Papers on Earth Tides 1988, Model of Oceanic Load Tide Correction in Chinese Continent 1988. *Address:* 54 Xu Dong Road, Wuchang 430077, Hubei Province, People's Republic of China. *Telephone:* 813405.

XU, Jian; Chinese business executive; *General Manager, China National Machinery Industry Corporation (Sinomach);* Dir and Gen. Man. China Nat. Machinery Industry Corpn (Sinomach) 2013–. *Address:* China National Machinery Industry Corporation, 3 Danling Street, Haidian District, Beijing, 100080, People's Republic of China (office). *Telephone:* (10) 82688888 (office). *Fax:* (10) 82688811 (office). *E-mail:* office@sinomach.com.cn (office). *Website:* www.sinomach.com.cn (office).

XU, Jianyi, MBA; Chinese business executive and government official; b. Dec. 1953, Fushan Dist, Yantai, Shandong Prov.; ed Jilin Univ.; Vice-Chair. FAW Car Co. Ltd –2008, Chair. 2008–15, Pres. China FAW Group Corpn 2007–10, Chair. 2010–15; mem. Jilin Prov. Standing Cttee and Sec. of Jinlin City 2006–07; Mayor of Jilin City 2006–07; expelled from CCP for alleged corruption Aug. 2015.

XU, Jiayin; Chinese real estate executive; *President, Evergrande Real Estate Group Ltd;* b. 1958, Henan; ed Wuhan Univ. of Science and Tech.; Founder, Guangzhou Hengda Group 1996, renamed Evergrande Real Estate Group Ltd, currently Pres. and Sec.; mem. CCP; Deputy Chair. China Enterprise Confed. 2003, China Entrepreneur Asscn, China Real Estate Asscn, Guangdong Fund for Justice and Courage, Guangdong Private Enterprise Chamber, Guangdong General Chamber of Commerce; Pres. Guangzhou Real Estate Asscn; f. Evergrande Football School 2013–; owner Guangzhou Evergrande Taobao Football Club; Hon. Chair. Guangdong Charity Fed.; mem. 13th CPPCC Nat. Cttee 2018–; Deputy 12th Guangzhou NPC; numerous awards including one of the People of the Year, Guangzhou Business Circles Award 2005. *Address:* Evergrande Real Estate Group, Tianlun Building, No. 45 Tianhe Road, Guangzhou, Guangdong, People's Republic of China (office). *Website:* www.gzhengda.com.cn (office).

XU, Kuangdi; Chinese engineer, academic and politician; b. 11 Dec. 1937, Tongxiang Co., Zhejiang Prov.; ed Beijing Metallurgy Inst.; asst, Beijing Metallurgy Inst. 1959–63; May 7th Cadre School (Fengyang) 1971–72; Asst, later Lecturer, Metallurgical Dept, Shanghai Inst. of Mechanical Eng 1972–79; Deputy Dean and Assoc. Prof., later Dean and Prof., Metallurgical Dept, Shanghai Polytechnical Univ. 1980–86, Exec. Vice-Pres. Shanghai Polytechnical Univ. 1986–89; joined CCP 1983; Deputy Dir Educ. and Public Health Office, Shanghai 1989–91; Dir Shanghai Higher Educ. Bureau 1989–91; Dir Shanghai Planning Comm. 1991–92; Vice-Mayor of Shanghai Municipality 1992–95, Mayor 1995–2001; mem. Standing Cttee CCP Shanghai Municipal Cttee 1992, Deputy Sec. 1994–2001; Dir Labour and Wages Cttee, Shanghai Municipality 1993; Vice-Pres. China Mayors' Asscn 1996; Sec. CCP Leading Party Group of Chinese Acad. of Eng 2001–, Pres. Chinese Acad. of Eng 2002, also Chair. China Fed. of Industrial Econs (CFIE); Alt. mem. 14th CCP Cen. Cttee 1992–97, mem. 15th CCP Cen. Cttee 1997–2002, 16th CCP Cen. Cttee 2002–07; Vice-Chair. 10th CPPCC Nat. Cttee 2003–; Fellow, Chinese Acad. of Sciences (Div. of Chemical, Metallurgical and Materials Eng) 1995–; Hon. DEng (Polytechnic Inst. of New York Univ.) 2007; Hon. Pres. Red Cross Soc. of China 1996, Hon. Chair. Governing Bd Chinese Acad. of Engineering; honoured for his achievements in some key projects in 6th Five-Year Plan 1986, Royal Acad. of Eng Int. Medal 2008. *Publication:* The Refining of Stainless Steel. *Address:* Chinese Academy of Engineering, 2 Bingjiaokou Hutong, Xicheng District, Beijing 100088, People's Republic of China (office). *Fax:* (10) 59300071 (office). *E-mail:* carees2@139.com. *Website:* www.cae.cn (office).

XU, Lejiang, MBA; Chinese steel industry executive; *Chairman, Baosteel Group Corporation;* b. Feb. 1959; ed Jiangxi Metallurgy Inst., Univ. of West Virginia, USA, Fudan Univ.; mem. CCP; joined Baosteel 1982, mem. Bd of Dirs 1998–, Vice-Pres. 1998–2004, Pres. 2004–07, Chair. Baoshan Iron and Steel Co. Ltd 2006–07, 2007–10, Standing mem. CCP Cttee 2007–10, Dir and Pres. Baosteel Group Corpn 2005–07, Chair. 2007–, also Dir, CCP Sec. and Standing mem. CCP Cttee, Baosteel Group Corpn 2014–; Deputy Chair. HKU Alumni Asscn of Chinese Mainland; Alt. mem. 17th CCP Cen. Cttee 2007–12, 18th CCP Cen. Cttee 2012–17, 19th CCP Cen. Cttee 2017–. *Address:* Baosteel Group Corporation, Baosteel Tower, 370 Pudian Road, Shanghai 200122 (office); Office of the Board of Directors, Baoshan Iron & Steel Co. Ltd, Baosteel Administrative Centre, 885 Fujin Road, Baoshan District, Shanghai 201990, People's Republic of China. *Telephone:* (21) 58350000 (office); (21 26647000. *Fax:* (21) 68404832 (office); (21) 26646999. *E-mail:* info@baosteel.com (office); ir@baosteel.com. *Website:* www.baosteel.com (office).

XU, Liuping, BA, MA; Chinese business executive; *Chairman, China FAW Group;* b. b. 1964; ed Jiangsu Polytechnic Univ., Univ. of Tech., Beijing; Sec., Gen. Office, State Admin for Science, Tech. and Industry for Nat. Defence 1999–2000; Deputy Dir Devt and Planning Dept, China South Industries Motors Co. (CSIMC) 2000–03, Dir 2003–04, mem. CCP Leading Party Group 2004–07, Asst Gen. Man. CSIMC 2004–05, Dir Automobile Dept 2004–05, Sr Vice-Pres., CSIMC 2005–07, Exec. mem. Bd of Dirs 2005–07, Deputy Gen. Man. China South Industries Group Corpn 2005–09, Sec., CCP Party Cttee, China Changan Automobile Group 2007–10, Pres. China Changan Automobile Group 2007–10, Vice-Chair. 2010, Chair. 2010–13, Gen. Man. and Pres. China South Industries Group Corpn 2013–17; Chair. China FAW Group 2017–. *Address:* China FAW Group, 3025 Dongfeng Street, Changchun 130011, People's Republic of China (office). *Fax:* (431) 87614780 (office). *E-mail:* info@faw.com (office). *Website:* www.faw.com (office).

XU, Ning; Chinese business executive; ed Party School of Chinese Communist Party Cen. Cttee; joined Shougang Corpn (holding co. of Shougang Holding) 1970, apptd Dir and Exec. Deputy Gen. Shougang General Co. 2002, Chair. and Gen. Man. Shougang Corpn, Chair. Shougang Holding (Hong Kong) Ltd 2012, Shougang Concord International Enterprises Co. Ltd 2012, Chair. and Dir (non-exec.) 2014, fmr Chair. Nomination Cttee; Vice-Chair. Beijing Zhongguancun Software Park Development Co. Ltd; Dir (non-exec.) Shougang Concord International Enterprises Co. Ltd 2012–, Beijing Shougang Co. Ltd, Shougang Jingtang Iron & Steel United Co. Ltd.

XU, Ping, BEng; Chinese automobile industry executive; *General Manager and President, China South Industries Group Corporation;* b. 1957; ed Hefei Univ. of Tech.; joined Dongfeng Motor Corpn 1982, fmr Pres. thermo-electricity factory, served as Sec. CCP and Deputy Gen. Man. Dongfeng Motor Corpn 2001–03, Vice-Pres. 2003–05, Gen. Man. and Sec. CCP 2005–, mem. Bd of Dirs 2004–, Chair. and CEO 2005–11, Chair. 2011–15, Chair. Dongfeng Peugeot Citroën Automobiles Co. Ltd 2005–15, Dongfeng Automobile Co. Ltd 2005–15; Chair. China FAW Group Corpn 2015–17; Gen. Man. and Pres., China South Industries Group Corpn 2017–; Rep. of 11th NPC, 17th CCP Cen. Cttee; Vice Pres. China Auto Talents Soc.; consultant, Global Automotive Exec. Council. *Address:* China South Industries Group Corpn, 10 Chedaogou, 69 Zizhuyuan Road, Haidian District, Beijing 100089, People's Republic of China (office). *Telephone:* (10) 68963764 (office). *Fax:* (10) 68963765 (office). *E-mail:* info@chinasouth.com.cn (office). *Website:* www.csgc.com.cn (office); www.chinasouth.com.cn (office).

XU, Gen. Qiliang; Chinese air force officer; *Vice-Chairman, State Central Military Commission;* b. 1950, Shandong Prov.; ed Air Force 1st Aviation Reserve Coll., 8th Aviation School, 5th Aviation School, Univ. of Nat. Defence; joined PLA and CCP 1967; Aviator, Air Force Div. Command 1969–83, becoming Bn Chief and Deputy Div. Commdr, later Div. Commdr 1983–84, Deputy Army Commdr (Air Force) 1984–85, Chief of Staff (Air Force), Shanghai Municipality 1985–88, Chief of Staff (Air Force) 1989–93, 1994–99, Deputy Chief of Staff 1993–94, Deputy Commdr, Shenyang Mil. Region, Liaoning Prov. 2000, Commdr (Air Force), Shenyang Mil. Region 2000–07, Commdr PLA Air Force 2007–12; Vice-Chair. State Cen. Mil. Comm. 2013–; attained rank of Maj.-Gen. 1991, Lt-Gen. 1996, Gen. 2007; Alt. mem. 14th CCP Cen. Cttee 1992–97, mem. 15th CCP Cen. Cttee 1997–2002, 16th CCP Cen. Cttee 2002–07, 17th CCP Cen. Cttee 2007–12, also mem. 17th CCP Cen. Cttee Cen. Mil. Comm. 2007–12, mem. 18th CCP Cen. Cttee 2012–17, also mem. 18th CCP Cen. Cttee Politburo 2012–17 and Vice-Chair. 18th CCP Cen. Cttee Cen. Mil. Comm. 2012–17. *Address:* Ministry of National Defence, 20 Jingshanqian Jie, Beijing 10009, People's Republic of China (office). *Website:* www.mod.gov.cn (office).

XU, Rongmao, (Hui Wing Mao), MBA; Chinese business executive and property developer; *Chairman, Shimao Corporation;* b. 1950, Shishi, Fujian Prov.; m.; two c.; ed Univ. of South Australia; moved to Hong Kong to work as stockbroker in 1970s; returned to China to export textiles 1980s; Founder and CEO Shimao Group 1985, currently Chair. Shimao Corpn; investor in high-end property market in Fujian Prov., Beijing and Shanghai; Chair. Shanghai Overseas Chinese Chamber of Commerce; Vice-Chair. Shanghai Business Asscn; mem. 10th Chinese People's Political Consultative Conf. (CPPCC), Sub-Cttee Social and Legal Affairs of CPPCC, Standing Cttee Nat. Business Asscn; mem. Standing Cttee All-China Fed. of Industry and Commerce, Vice-Pres. 2007–; Chair. Shanghai Overseas Chinese Chamber of Commerce, Shanghai Real Estate Chamber of Commerce; Vice-Chair. China Real Estate Chamber of Commerce, Hong Kong Chinese Cultural Asscn, Fujian Overseas Friendship Asscn, Beijing Univ. of Chemical Tech.; Life Hon. Chair. Hong Kong Fed. of Overseas Chinese Asscns, Friends of Hong Kong Asscn; Hon. Chair. Conf. on Non-Independence and Pro-Reunification of China; Hon. Vice-Chair. Council of Shanghai Charity Foundation; Vice-Pres. Chinese Red Cross Foundation; mem. Council of Chinese Overseas Friendship Asscns; Hon. JP; Hon. Prof., Tongji Univ.; Shanghai Magnolia Award, Lilac-Bauhinia Golden Award (govt of Heilongjiang) 2006, Gold Bauhinia Star 2011. *Address:* Shimao Group, Jin Mao Tower, 45th Floor, 88 Shi Ji Avenue, Shanghai, 200121 People's Republic of China (office). *Telephone:* (21) 50473399 (office). *Website:* www.shimaogroup.com (office).

XU, Shaoshi, MEcons; Chinese geologist and government official; b. Oct. 1951, Ningbo, Zhejiang Prov.; ed Changchun Univ. of Earth Sciences, CCP Central Party School, Nankai Univ., Tianjin; sent to countryside to do manual labour during Cultural Revolution, Jilin Prov. 1969–71; joined CCP 1974; Officer, Policy Office, Ministry of Geology and Mineral Resources (now Ministry of Land and Resources) 1980–86, Dir Minister's Office 1986–88, Deputy Dir-Gen.'s Office 1988–93, Dir 1993, Minister of Land and Resources 1987–2013, also Sec., CCP Leading Party Group 2007–13; Deputy Dir, Mining Bureau, Shenzhen City 1991–93; Dir Secr., Gen. Office of State Council 1996–2000, Deputy Sec.-Gen. 2000–07; Head, Nat. Devt and Reform Comm. 2013–17; mem. 17th CCP Cen. Cttee 2007–12, 18th CCP Cen. Cttee 2012–17. *Address:* c/o National Development and Reform Commission, 38 Yuetannan Jie, Xicheng Qu, Beijing 100824, People's Republic of China (office).

XU, Xianming, LLB; Chinese lawyer; b. 12 April 1957, Laixi, Shandong Prov.; ed Jilin Univ., Wuhan Univ.; Vice-Pres. Shandong Univ. 1985–2001, also Head of Grad. School and Dean of Law School, Pres. Shandong Univ. 2008–13; Pres. China Univ. of Political Science and Law, Beijing 2001–08; Deputy Dir, General Office, Central Governance Cttee 2013–; Deputy Procurator Gen. Supreme People's Procuratorate 2017–18; Deputy, 10th NPC 2003–08; Commr, 10th NPC Law Cttee 2003–08; Vice-Chair. China Law Soc.; First Nat. Social Science Achievement Award for Young Scholars, Ministry of Educ. Social Science Achievement Award.

Address: c/o Office of the President, Shandong University, 27 Shanda Nanlu, Jinan 250100, Shandong Province, People's Republic of China (office).

XU, Xianping, MBA; Chinese engineer and business executive; *President, China FAW Group Corporation;* b. Sept. 1964, Jilin Prov.; ed Dalian Univ. of Tech., Enterprise Reorganization Dept of MSM Holland; began career with FAW Group 1989, assumed posts of workshop head, Deputy Man. FAW Carburetor Plant, responsible for JV programme between FAW Group and Kazakhstan, Man. Parts Supplying Dept, FAW Group, Man. Procurement Dept, Gen. Man. Tianjin FAW Xiali Automobile Co. Ltd, Gen. Man. FAW Jiefang Truck Co. Ltd, Asst Pres., then and Vice-Pres., FAW Group, mem. Bd of Dirs and Pres. China FAW Group Corpn 2011–, Deputy Sec. FAW Group CCP Standing Cttee 2013–. *Address:* China FAW Group, 2259 Dongfeng Street, Changchun 130011, People's Republic of China (office). *Fax:* (431) 87614780 (office). *E-mail:* info@faw.com (office). *Website:* www .faw.com (office).

XU, Yinsheng; Chinese government official; b. 12 June 1938, Suzhou City, Jiangsu Prov.; m. Chen Liwen; one s.; World Table Tennis Champion three times; joined CCP 1961; Vice-Minister State Physical Culture and Sport Comm. 1977–98; Vice-Dir State Gen. Admin. of Physical Culture; apptd Pres. Chinese Table Tennis Asscn 1979, Chinese Boxing Asscn 1987; Exec. Vice-Chair. Preparatory Cttee for 6th Nat. Games 1985; Vice-Pres. Chinese Olympic Cttee 1986–89, 1994–99, Hon. Pres. 2010–; apptd Vice-Pres. All-China Sports Fed. 1989; apptd Exec. Vice-Pres. XIth Asian Games Organizing Cttee 1990; Pres. Int. Table Tennis Fed. 1995–99; Deputy, 4th NPC 1975–78, 5th NPC 1978–83, 6th NPC 1983–88, 7th NPC 1988–93, 8th NPC 1993–98; inducted into Int. Table Tennis Fed. Hall of Fame 2010. *Publication:* How to Play Table Tennis by Dialectics. *Leisure interests:* tennis, fishing.

XU, Yongyue; Chinese politician; b. July 1942, Zhenping Co., Henan Prov.; ed Beijing Municipal People's Public Security School; joined CCP 1972; served consecutively as Sec. Beijing Municipal People's Public Security School, Gen. Office of Chinese Acad. of Sciences, Gen. Office of Ministry of Educ., Gen. Office of Ministry of Culture 1960–83; Political Sec. to Chen Yun 1983–93; Deputy Sec.-Gen. CCP Cen. Cttee Cen. Advisory Comm. 1988; Deputy Sec. Hebei Prov. Cttee 1994–98; Minister of State Security 1998–2007; Alt. mem. 15th CCP Cen. Cttee 1997–2002, mem. 16th CCP Cen. Cttee 2002–07.

XU, Yuanhe; Chinese philosopher; b. 1942, Rugao, Jiangsu Prov.; ed Peking Univ.; Asst Research Fellow, Assoc. Research Fellow then Research Fellow Inst. of Philosophy, Chinese Acad. of Social Sciences; Dir Oriental Philosophy Research Centre, Chinese Acad. of Social Sciences; State Council Prize 1993. *Publications:* Origin and Development of Luo Studies, The School of Reason and the Yuan Society, Confucianism and Oriental Culture, Survey of Chinese Civilization. *Address:* 502 F2, 2T Bei tai pin zhuang Road, Haichian District, Beijing, People's Republic of China (home). *Telephone:* (10) 63240875 (home). *Fax:* (10) 63240815 (home).

XU, Zhenshi; Chinese photographer, artist and publisher; b. 18 Aug. 1937, Songjiang Co., Shanghai; s. of Xu Weiqing and Jiang Wanying, step-s. of Cheng Shi-fa; m. Zhang Fuhe 1967; one d.; ed No. 1 High School, Songjiang Co., Zhejiang Acad. of Fine Arts; moved to Beijing 1965; Ed. People's Fine Arts Publishing House 1965–86, apptd Dir Picture Editorial Dept 1986, Ed.-in-Chief 1992; mem. China Artists' Asscn; Deputy Sec.-Gen. Spring Festival Pictures Research Centre, Publrs' Asscn of China; Deputy Sec.-Gen. and Assoc. Dir Photography Research Centre; mem. Selection Cttee 3rd, 4th and 5th Nat. Exhbns of Spring Festival Pictures and other exhbns; Assoc. Dir Standing Cttee Spring Festival Pictures; apptd Sr Adviser, Office of East China–UN TIPS Nat. Exploit Bureau 1994; exhbns in China, Japan, Korea, Hong Kong, Thailand; Vice-Ed.-in-Chief Gouache Vol. of Anthology of Contemporary Chinese Fine Arts 1996; Vice-Pres. Chinese Fan Art Soc. 1997; organized 1st Nat. Exhbn of Calligraphy and Paintings to Help the Poor 1998; Dir Foundation for Underdeveloped Regions in China 1998–; prepared 6th Nat. Exhbn of Spring Festival Pictures 1998; union art exhib., St Petersburg, Russia 2006, Royal Acad. of Arts Hon. Academician and Visiting Prof. 2013; Lifetime Hon. Pres. Cultural Figure magazine 2012–; numerous awards including Bronze Medal for albums of photographs, Leipzig Int. Book Exhbn 1987, Nat. Award 1993, Model Ed. Nat. Press and Publs System 1997, 1998, State Prize for Spring Festival Pictures 2001, two 6th Nat. Exhbn of Spring Festival Pictures Prizes (China) 1998, Chinese Contemporary Art Achievement Prize, Hong Kong, State Prize of Spring Festival Pictures 2001, Prize of A Brilliant Contrib. 2001, Outstanding People's Artist Award, 60 Years Outstanding and Contributing Figure Award 2009, Top Ten Heroic Model Figures Honor Award 2010, World Peace Artist Honor 2012, Chinese Art Flying Awards for Outstanding Contributing Figure and Lifetime Achievement 2013. *Publications include:* China's Cultural Relics Unearthed during the Great Cultural Revolution 1973, Travel in China (four vols) 1979–80, Tibet 1981, Travel in Tibet 1981, Costumes of China's Minority Nationalities 1981, Travel in Guilin 1981, Travel Leisurely in China 1981, Travel in Yunnan 1982, China's Flowers in Four Seasons 1982, Poet Li Bai 1983, Native Places of Tang Dynasty Poems 1984, Travel along the Yangtse River 1985, Through the Moongate: A Guide to China's Famous Historical Sites 1986, Waters and Mountains in China 1986, Travel in Guangzhou 1986, China 1987, The Chinese Nation 1989, Poet Du Fu 1989, Selected Works of Xu Zhenshi 1990, 1993, Selected Paintings of Xu Zhenshi 1993, 1994, Boat on the Plateau 1998, Album of

Xu Zhenshi's Sketches 1999, Love for China 2003; collection of Xu Zhenshi published in 2003, Love for China 2003; ed Olympic Games picture book 2008, World Culture Art Masters Dictionary (Chinese section) 2013, The Classical Album of Chairman Mao 2014; as contrib.: Complete Works of Modern Art 2012. *Leisure interest:* sports. *Address:* People's Fine Arts Publishing House, No. 32 Beizongbu Hutong, Beijing, People's Republic of China (office). *Telephone:* (10) 65244901 (office); (10) 65246353 (home).

XU, Zhihong, BSc; Chinese plant physiologist and academic; *Professor of Life Sciences, Peking University;* b. 14 Oct. 1942, Wuxi, Jiangsu Prov.; ed Peking Univ.; research student, Chinese Acad. of Sciences Shanghai Plant Physiology Research Inst. 1969; Researcher, Assoc. Research Fellow, Research Fellow, Vice-Dir Chinese Acad. of Sciences Shanghai Plant Physiology Research Inst. 1969–91, Dir 1991–94; Vice-Pres. Chinese Acad. of Sciences and Dir Shanghai Life Science Research Centre 1992–2003, mem. 4th Presidium of Depts, Chinese Acad. of Sciences 2000–; Fellow, Third World of Sciences 1995–, Acad. Chinese Acad. of Sciences 1997– (also Deputy Dean); Pres. Peking Univ. 1999–2008, apptd Dean Coll. of Modern Agric. Science 2018, currently Prof. of Life Sciences; Pres. Int. Asscn of Plant Tissue Culture and Biotechnology 2002–06; Hon. Prof. Hong Kong Univ.; Hon. DrSc (De Montfort) 1994, (Nottingham) 2000, (Hong Kong City) 2001, (Waseda) 2002, (McGill) 2003, (La Trobe) 2007, (East Anglia) 2008; Hon. DIur (Melbourne) 2003; Dr hc, (Edinburgh) 2008, (Dublin) 2008; Natural Science First Prize, Third Prize (Chinese Acad. of Science) 1990, 1991. *Publications include:* more than 200 papers on plant development, plant cell culture and genetic manipulation, and plant biotechnology. *Address:* Peking University School of Life Sciences, 5 Yiheyuan Road, Haidian District, Beijing 100871, People's Republic of China (office). *Telephone:* (10) 62751051 (office). *Fax:* (10) 62761008 (office). *E-mail:* hqf@pku .edu.cn (office). *Website:* www.pku.edu.cn (office).

XU, Zhijun, (Eric Xu), PhD; Chinese business executive; *Deputy Chairman and Rotating CEO, Huawei Technologies Company Ltd;* b. 1967; ed Nanjing Univ. of Science and Tech.; joined Huawei 1993, served successively as Pres. of Wireless Product Line, Chief Strategy and Marketing Officer, Chief Products and Solutions Officer, Chair. Investment Review Bd, Corp. Exec. Vice-Pres., Chair. SDC, Deputy Chair. and Rotating CEO, Huawei Technologies Co. Ltd Oct. 2013–. *Address:* Huawei Technologies Co. Ltd, Bantian, Longgang District, Shenzhen 518129, People's Republic of China (office). *Telephone:* (755) 28780808 (office). *E-mail:* hwtech@huawei.com (office). *Website:* www.huawei.com (office).

XU, Zhizhan, MSc; Chinese optical scientist; *Professor, Shanghai Institute of Optics and Fine Mechanics;* b. Dec. 1938, Changzhou, Jiangsu Prov.; ed Fudan and Beijing Univs; research student of physics, Peking Univ.; Prof., Shanghai Inst. of Optics and Fine Mechanics, East China Normal Univ., Chinese Acad. of Sciences, Dir 1992–2001, currently Chair. Academic Council; Vice-Chair. Optical Soc. of China 1993–2012; Chair. Academic Cttee, State Key Laboratory of Optoelectronic Materials and Technologies, Sun Yat-sen Univ.; Chief Ed. Journal of Optics; Founding Ed. and Ed.-in-Chief Chinese Optics Letters; Fellow, Chinese Acad. of Sciences 1992–, Third World Acad. of Sciences (now TWAS) 2004–, Optical Soc. of America; mem. Standing Cttee 9th CPPCC Nat. Cttee 1998–2003; Nat. Natural Science Awards (II class) 1995, 2001, Ho Leung Ho Lee Foundation Award 1998, Nat. Innovation Award (II class) 1999, Nat. Science and Tech. Progress Award (I class) 2004. *Publications:* over 350 essays on laser and related studies, presented about 20 invited papers at int. conferences. *Address:* Shanghai Institute of Optics and Fine Mechanics, Chinese Academy of Sciences, Shanghai 201800, People's Republic of China (office). *Telephone:* (21) 69918020 (office). *Fax:* (21) 69918021 (office). *E-mail:* zzxu@mail.shcnc.ac.cn (office). *Website:* www.siom.cas.cn (office).

XU, Zhonglin; Chinese politician; b. Dec. 1943, Wujin Co., Jiangsu Prov.; ed PLA Survey and Cartography Inst., Zhengzhou, CCP Cen. Acad., Beijing; teaching asst, PLA Survey and Cartography Inst. 1962; joined CCP 1964; Deputy Sec., City Instrument, Meter and Electronics Bureau, Xuzhou City, Jiangsu Prov. 1975–80; Deputy Dir Planning and Science Cttees, Xuzhou City 1975–80; Deputy Dir, CCP Revolutionary Cttee, Xuzhou City 1980; Vice Mayor of Xuzhou 1980-86, Mayor 1986–89; mem. Standing Cttee CCP Xuzhou Municipal Cttee 1984–89, Dir Org. Dept 1984–86, Deputy Sec. Xuzhou Municipal Cttee 1986–89; Deputy Dir Org. Dept, CCP Jiangsu Prov. Cttee 1989–91, Dir 1991–94 (mem. Standing Cttee 1992–99), Deputy Sec. CCP Jiangsu Prov. Cttee 1994–99; mem. Standing Cttee CCP Anhui Prov. Cttee 1999–2002, Deputy Sec. CCP Anhui Prov. Cttee 1999–2002; Gov. Anhui Prov. 2001–02; mem. Standing Cttee CCP Jiansu Prov. Cttee 2002, Deputy Sec. CCP Jiangsu Prov. Cttee 2002; Chair. CPPCC Jiangsu Prov. Cttee 2003–08.

XUE, Wei; Chinese violinist; b. 21 Dec. 1963, Henan; s. of Xue-Ming and Shang Yi-qing; ed Shanghai Conservatory, Beijing Conservatory of Music and Guildhall School of Music, London; appears regularly with the major London orchestras; performs in solo recitals and as concert soloist at int. music festivals; guest soloist with Shanghai Symphony on tour in Japan; Prof., RAM, London 1989–; numerous prizes including Silver Medal, Tchaikovsky Int. Competition (violin), Moscow 1986; Gold Medal, Carl Flesch Int. Competition 1986; London Philharmonic Soloist of the Year 1986. *Recordings include:* Great Violin Concertos 2001, Dreamland: Xue Wei Plays Chinese Violin Pieces 2002, Xue Wei and the Romance of Cremona 2003, Jue Ban 2008. *Leisure interests:* reading, chess, poker.

Y

YA NDAKOLO, Penda; Namibian politician and fmr resistance fighter; *Minister of Defence;* b. 23 March 1960, Oshigambo; ed Eastern and Southern Man. Inst., South Africa; mil. training and political studies, Lubango, Angola 1979–80; anti-air defence platoon Commdr, People's Liberation Army of Namibia (PLAN) 1979–80, Political Commissar, Deputy Commdr on Political Matters and specialist in radio communications warfare 1980–89; Head of Voter Educ., Onkumbula Centre, Ondangwa 1989; teacher, Onkumbula Junior Primary School 1990; SWAPO Party of Namibia Dist Coordinator, Omutsegonime Dist 1990–92; Oshikoto Regional Councillor for Omuthiyagwiipundi Constituency 1993–2010; mem. Nat. Council (second chamber of parl.) for Oshikoto Region 1998–2004, 2015–; Gov. Oshikoto Region 2004–15; Minister of Defence 2015–; Most Distinguished Order of Namibia, First Class 2014. *Address:* Ministry of Defence, PMB 13307, Windhoek, Namibia (office). *Telephone:* (61) 2049111 (office). *Fax:* (61) 232518 (office). *E-mail:* psecretary@mod.gov.na (office). *Website:* www.mod.gov.na (office).

YAACOB, Tan Sri Nik Mohamed Bin Nik, BE; Malaysian business executive; *Chairman, Scomi Energy Services Bhd;* ed Monash Univ., Asian Inst. of Man.; with Sime Darby, fmrly Regional Dir, Dir of Operations, Malaysia, mem. Bd 1990–2004, mem. Exec. Cttee, CEO 1993–2004 (retd); mem. Bd of Dirs Scomi Group Bhd 2004–, Chair. Scomi Energy Services Bhd 2013–; mem. Bd of Dirs Perbadanan Nasional Bhd, GuocoLand (Malaysia) Bhd 2005–, Symphony Life Bhd 2005–, Bolton Bhd, Scomi Marine Bhd 2005–09, Kencana Petroleum Bhd 2008–12, SapuraKencana Petroleum Bhd 2013–, Yayasan Kepimpinan Perdana; fmr mem. Bd of Dirs DMIB, Tractors Malaysia Holdings, Consolidated Plantations, Port Dickson Power, SD Holdings, SIRIM. *Address:* Scomi Energy Services Bhd, Level 17, 1 First Avenue Bandar Utama, Selangor Darul Ehsan, 47800 Petaling Jaya, Malaysia (office). *Telephone:* (3) 77173000 (office). *Fax:* (3) 77285258 (office). *E-mail:* info@my.scomienergy.com (office). *Website:* www.scomienergy.com.my (office).

YAAKOB, Datuk Muhammad Shahrul Ikram bin, BSc; Malaysian diplomatist; *Permanent Representative to United Nations;* b. 21 May 1961, Bentong, Pahang; m. Izdina Izaidin; four s.; ed Univ. of Malaya, Kuala Lumpur, Harvard Business School; apptd to Admin. and Diplomatic Service, Ministry of Foreign Affairs 1988, also Asst Sec. East Asia Div., Asst Sec. Int. Orgs Div. 1989–91, Second Sec. Embassy of Malaysia, Beijing 1991–94, First Sec. (Econs), Embassy of Malaysia, Washington DC 1994–98, Sr Asst Sec. American Affairs Div. 1998, Prin. Asst Sec. 1999–2002, Counsellor, Embassy of Malaysia, Vienna 2002–05, also Deputy Head of Mission UN Office; Undersecretary Multilateral Political Div. 2005–07; Amb. to Qatar 2007–10, to Austria and other int. orgs in Vienna 2010–13; Deputy Sec.-Gen. Bilateral Affairs, Ministry of Foreign Affairs 2016–17, Sec.-Gen. Ministry of Foreign Affairs 2018–; Perm. Rep. to UN 2017–; Chair. Bd of Govs Int. Atomic Energy Agency 2009–10; Dir-Gen. ASEAN-Malaysia Nat. Secr. 2013–16; Ahli Ahmad Shah Pahang 2004, Setia Ahmad Shah Pahang 2006, Darjah Indera Mahkota Pahang 2007, Darjah Sultan Ahmad Shah Pahang 2014. *Address:* Permanent Missions of Malaysia, 313 E 43rd Street, New York, NY 10017, USA (office); Ministry of Foreign Affairs, Aras 3, Wisma Putra, Presint 2, Pusat Pentadbiran Kerajaan Persekutuan, 62602 Putrajaya, Malaysia (office). *Telephone:* (212) 986-6310 (office); (3) 88874000 (Ministry of Foreign Affairs) (office). *Fax:* (212) 490-8576 (office); (3) 88891717 (Ministry of Foreign Affairs) (office). *E-mail:* mwnewyorkun@kln.gov.my (office); anifah@kln.gov.my (office). *Website:* www.un.int/malaysia (office); www.kln.gov.my (office).

YA'ALON, Lt-Gen. (retd) Moshe, BA; Israeli politician and army officer (retd); b. (Moshe Smilansky), 24 June 1950, Kiryat Haim; m.; three c.; ed Command and Staff Coll., Camberley, UK, Univ. of Haifa; drafted into Israeli Defence Forces (IDF) 1968, served in Nahal Paratroop Regt; reserve paratrooper during Yom Kippur War 1973, participated in liberation of Suez Canal; held several command positions in IDF Paratroop Brigade, Commdr reconnaisance unit during Litani Operation 1978, later Deputy Commdr, apptd Commdr 1990; served in elite unit 1979–82, later Deputy Commdr; fought in Operation Peace for Galilee; retrained in IDF Armoured Corps 1989–90; apptd CO Judea and Samaria, promoted Brig.-Gen. 1992; Commdr of Ground Forces, Tze'elim 1993; apptd CO Intelligence, rank Maj.-Gen. 1995; apptd CO Cen. Command 1998, IDF Deputy Chief-of-Staff 2000, Chief-of-Staff 2002–05; mem. Knesset (Likud) 2009–; Vice-Prime Minister and Minister of Strategic Affairs 2009–13, Minister of Defence 2013–16 (resgnd); Pres. Shekel: Community Services for People with Special Needs; Chair. Center for Jewish Identity and Culture; Chair. Bd of Dirs Bishvil Hamachar. *Publications include:* The Long Short Road 2008. *Address:* Knesset, Kiryat Ben-Gurion, Jerusalem 91950, Israel (office). *Telephone:* 2-6753333 (office). *Fax:* 2-6753665 (office). *E-mail:* mshenkar@knesset.gov.il (office). *Website:* www.knesset.gov.il (office).

YABLONOVITCH, Eli, BSc, AM, PhD; American physicist and academic; *Professor and James and Katherine Lau Chair in Engineering, Department of Electrical Engineering and Computer Sciences, University of California, Berkeley;* b. 15 Dec. 1946; ed McGill Univ., Canada, Harvard Univ.; Teaching Fellow, Harvard Univ. 1971, 1972, Asst Prof. of Applied Physics 1974–76, Assoc. Prof. 1976–79, Research Assoc. and Head of Optical Sciences Group; mem. Tech. Staff, Bell Telephone Labs 1972–74; mem. Tech. Staff, Exxon Research Center 1979–84; mem. Tech. Staff Bell Communications Research 1984–90, Distinguished Mem. of Staff 1990–93, Dir Solid State Physics Research 1991–93; Northrop-Grumman Chair Prof. of Electrical Eng, UCLA 1992–2007, Adjunct Prof. of Electrical Eng 2007–; Prof. and James and Katherine Lau Chair in Eng, Dept of Electrical Eng and Computer Sciences, Univ. of California, Berkeley 2007–, Dir NSF Center for Energy Efficient Electronics Science (E^3S) 2010; apptd Visiting Prof., Inst. for Advanced Study, Princeton, NJ 2010, Hong Kong Univ. of Science and Tech. 2010–; Distinguished Visiting Prof., Technion, Haifa, Israel 2012–; f. W/PECS series of Photonic Crystal Int. Workshops 1999; mem. NAS 2003, Nat. Acad. of Eng 2003, American Acad. of Arts and Sciences 2012; Foreign mem. Royal Soc. 2013; Fellow, Optical Soc. of America 1982, American Physical Soc. 1990, IEEE 1992; Moore Distinguished Scholar, Caltech 2003–04; Dr hc (Royal Inst. of Tech., Sweden) 2004, (Hong Kong Univ. of Science and Tech.) 2011; Alfred P. Sloan Fellow 1978–79, Adolf Lomb Medal, Optical Soc. of America 1978, IEEE/LEOS W. Streifer Scientific Achievement Award 1993, R.W. Wood Prize, Optical Soc. of America 1996, Clifford Paterson Lecturer, Royal Soc. of London 2000, Julius Springer Prize in Applied Physics 2001, Edison Lecture, Notre-Dame Univ. 2004, Anson L. Clark Memorial Lecture, Univ. of Texas, Dallas 2004, Morris Loeb Lecturer, Harvard Univ. 2005, Mountbatten Medal, Inst. of Eng and Tech. (UK) 2010, IEEE Photonics Award 2012, Harvey Prize, Technion, Israel (co-recipient) 2012, Rank Prize (UK) 2014. *Publications:* more than 200 scientific papers in professional journals; 15 patents. *Address:* 267M Cory Hall, Electrical Engineering and Computer Sciences Department, University of California, Berkeley, Berkeley, CA 94720-1770, USA (office). *Telephone:* (510) 642-6821 (office). *Fax:* (510) 666-3409 (office). *E-mail:* eliy@eecs.berkeley.edu (office). *Website:* www.eecs.berkeley.edu (office); www.e3s-center.org (office).

YACHROUTU, Mohamed Caabi El; Comoran politician and diplomatist; fmr Counsellor to Pres. of Repub.; Prime Minister 1995–96; interim Pres. 1995–96; Vice-Pres., with responsibility for Finance, the Budget, the Economy, Foreign Trade, Investments and Privatization 2002–06; apptd Amb. to Seychelles 2013.

YACOB, Halimah, LLB, LLM; Singaporean politician and head of state; *President;* b. 23 Aug. 1954; m. Mohammed Abdullah Alhabshee; five c.; ed Nat. Univ. of Singapore; called to bar 1981; worked as a legal officer at Nat. Trades Union Congress, apptd Dir Legal Services Dept 1992; apptd Dir Singapore Inst. of Labour Studies 1999; served as Exec. Sec., United Workers of Electronics and Electrical Industries, Dir Women's Devt Secretariat 2008–11; Vice-Chair. Standards Cttee, Int. Labour Conference (ILC), Geneva 2000–02, 2005, Spokesperson, Cttee on Human Resources Devt and Training 2003–04; mem. Parl. for Jurong constituency 2001–15, for Marsiling-Yew Tee constituency 2015–17, Speaker 2013–17; apptd Minister of State, Ministry of Community Devt, Youth and Sports 2011, Ministry of Social and Family Devt 2012; Pres. of Singapore 2017–; Chair. Jurong Town Council, Govt Parl. Cttee on Manpower, Tripartite Workgroup on Enhancing Employment Choices for Women; Co-Chair. Employability Network, UFUK Co-operative; Pres. Malay Teachers' Union Co-operative; Patron, Young Muslim Women's Asscn, Ain Society, Club HEAL, Singapore Asscn of Mental Health, Sian Chay TCM, Casa Raudha; mem. Bd of Dirs SMRT Trains Ltd, SMRT Road Holdings Ltd; mem. Bd Temasek Cares CGL Ltd, Mendaki Holdings Pte Ltd; mem. Bd of Trustees Nat. Univ. of Singapore; mem. People's Action Party –2017; Hon. DIur (Nat. Univ. of Singapore) 2016; Berita Harian/McDonald's Achiever of the Year Award 2001, Her World Woman of the Year Award 2003, Heroine Award, AWARE 2011, inducted into Singapore Women's Hall of Fame, Singapore Council of Women's Orgs 2014. *Address:* Office of the President, The Istana, Orchard Road, Singapore 238823 (office). *E-mail:* istana_feedback@istana.gov.sg (office). *Website:* www.istana.gov.sg (office).

YACOUB, Sir Magdi Habib, Kt, FRCS, FRS; British/Egyptian cardiac surgeon and academic; *Professor of Cardiothoracic Surgery, National Heart and Lung Institute, Imperial College London;* b. 16 Nov. 1935, Cairo, Egypt; m. Marianne Yacoub; one s. two d.; ed Univ. of Cairo; Rotating Sr Surgical Registrar, Nat. Heart and Chest Hospitals, London 1964–68; Instructor and Asst Prof., Univ. of Chicago 1969; Consultant Cardiothoracic Surgeon, Harefield Hosp., Middx 1973–2001, Royal Brompton Hosp. 1986–2001, British Heart Foundation Prof. of Cardiothoracic Surgery 1986–2006; Prof. of Cardiothoracic Surgery, Nat. Heart and Lung Inst., Imperial Coll. London 1986–, also Founder and Dir of Research, Harefield Heart Science Centre (Magdi Yacoub Inst.); Founder and Pres. Chain of Hope (charity) 1995–; Founder and Dir of Research, Magdi Yacoub Research Inst. 2001–; Co-Chair and Research Dir Qatar Cardiovascular Research Center 2010–; MRCP 1986; Fellow, Acad. of Medical Sciences 1999; Hon. FRCP 1990, Hon. citizenship of the city of Bergamo, Italy 2007; Order of Pakistan, Order of Lebanon; numerous hon. degrees including Hon. MCh (Wales) 1986, Dr hc (Univ. of Lund, Sweden) 1988, Hon. DSc (Brunel Univ.) 1985, (Univ. of Cardiff) 1986, (American Univ. at Cairo) 1989, (Loughborough Univ. of Tech.) 1990, (Keele) 1995, (Univ. of Middx) 2002, (London Univ.) 2011; WHO Prize for Humanitarian Services, Int. Soc. for Heart & Lung Transplantation Lifetime Achievement Award 2004, European Soc. of Cardiology Gold Medal 2006, Pride of Britain Lifetime Achievement Award, Daily Mirror 2007, Medal of Merit, Int. Acad. of Cardiovascular Sciences 2007, Greatest Nile Collar for Science and Humanity 2011, Legend of Cardiovascular Medicine, American Coll. of Cardiology 2012. *Achievements include:* performed first live lobe lung transplant in UK 1984; pioneered techniques of repair of complex congenital heart disease, homograft valve surgery and heart, heart-lung and lung transplantation. *Publications:* numerous medical papers. *Leisure interest:* orchid growing. *Address:* National Heart and Lung Institute, Dovehouse Street, London, SW3 6LY, England (office). *Telephone:* (0)1895828 893 (office); (20) 7351-8534. *Fax:* (20) 7351-8229. *E-mail:* m.yacoub@imperial.ac.uk (office). *Website:* www1.imperial.ac.uk/medicine/about/divisions/nhli (office).

YACOUBA, Ibrahim; Niger trade unionist and politician; b. 8 Aug. 1971, Maradi; m.; four c.; ed École Nat. d'Admin, Niamey; fmr customs inspector; Sec.-Gen., Syndicat nat. des agents des douanes (trade union) 2003–12; Founding mem., Confédération démocratique des travailleurs du Niger (trade union) 2003–06; Co-ordinator, Réseau Nat. Dette et Développement (anti-debt campaign group) 2004–10; Minister of Transport 2012–13; Adviser on Communications and Chef de cabinet of Pres. Issoufou Mahamadou 2013–15; Minister of Foreign Affairs, Co-operation, African Integration and Nigeriens Abroad 2016–18; Chair. Niger Basketball Fed. 2009–12; Vice-Chair. Niger Football Fed. –2012; Owner, Dan Kassawa Football Club.

YADAV, Akhilesh, BEng, MEng; Indian politician; *President, Samajwadi Party;* b. 1 Aug. 1973, Saifai village, Etawah Dist; s. of Mulayam Singh Yadav and Malti Devi; m. Dimple Yadav 1999; three c.; ed Dholpur Mil. School, Rajasthan, Sri Jayachamarajendra Coll. of Eng, Mysore, Univ. of Sydney, Australia; mem. 13th Lok Sabha (Parl.) from Kannauj constituency 2000–04, 14th Lok Sabha 2004–09, 15th Lok Sabha 2009–12, mem. Cttee on Science and Tech., Environment & Forests, Cttee on Food, Civil Supplies and Public Distribution; Chief Minister of

Uttar Pradesh 2012–17; mem. Samajwadi Party, Pres. 2017–. *Leisure interests:* reading, music, films, football, cricket. *Address:* Samajwadi Party, 18 Copernicus Lane, New Delhi, India (office). *Telephone:* (11) 23386842 (office). *Fax:* (11) 23382430 (office). *E-mail:* www.samajwadiparty.in (office).

YADAV, Ayodhi Prasad, PhD; Nepalese academic and government official; *Chief Election Commissioner;* b. 1954, Banauli, Praswani VDC, Saptari dist; ed Babasaheb Bhimrao Ambedkar Bihar Univ., Muzaffarpur, India; spent 24 years as univ. teacher; apptd Election Commr 2007, Acting Chief Election Commr 2015–16, Chief Election Commr 2016–. *Publications include:* Election Cost in Nepal, Constituent Assembly Election 2008: At a Glance, Voter Registration System in Nepal; numerous articles and research papers. *Address:* Election Commission of Nepal, Bahadur Bhawan, Kantipath, Kathmandu, Nepal (office). *Telephone:* (1) 4228663 (office). *Fax:* (1) 4229227 (office). *E-mail:* info@election.gov.np (office). *Website:* www.election.gov.np (office).

YADAV, Lalu Prasad, BA, LLB; Indian politician; *Leader, Rashtriya Janata Dal (National People's Party);* b. 11 June 1948, Gopalganj; m. Rabri Devi; two s. seven d.; ed Patna Univ.; elected to Lok Sabha 1977, re-elected 1989, 1998, 2004, 2009; Chief Minister of Bihar 1990–97; mem. Bihar Legis. Ass. 1995–98; Founder and Leader Rashtriya Janata Dal (Nat. People's Party) 1997–; elected to Rajya Sabha 2002; Minister of Railways 2004–09. *Address:* Rashtriya Janata Dal, 13 V. P. House, Rafi Marg, New Delhi 110 001 (office); Vill. Samanpura, Bihar Veterinary College, Patna 800 014, Bihar, India (home). *Telephone:* (11) 23357182 (office). *E-mail:* info@rjd.co.in (office). *Website:* rjd.co.in (office).

YADAV, Mulayam Singh, MA; Indian politician; b. 22 Nov. 1939, Safayee, Etawah Dist; s. of Sudhar Singh; m.; two s.; elected mem. UP Legis. Ass. 1967; Minister of Co-operative and Animal Husbandry, UP 1977; Pres. Lok Dal 1980; Leader of the Opposition, UP Legis. Council 1982–85, of UP Legis. Ass. 1985–89; Leader Janata Dal Legis. Party UP 1989; Chief Minister of Uttar Pradesh 1989, 1993–95, 2003–07; elected to Lok Sabha 1996, re-elected 1998, 1999, 2004, 2005; Minister of Defence 1996–98; Founder-Pres. Samajwadi Party (Socialist Party) 1992–2017; Convenor, Rashtriya Loktantrik Morcha (Nat. Democratic Front). *Address:* Samajwadi Party, 18 Copernicus Lane, New Delhi 110 001, India (office). *Telephone:* (11) 23386842 (office). *Fax:* (11) 23382430 (office). *E-mail:* samajwadipartynewdelhi@gmail.com (office).

YADAV, Ram Baran, MBBS, DCP, MD; Nepalese physician, politician and fmr head of state; b. 4 Feb. 1948, Sapahi, Dhanusa dist; s. of Thani Yadav and Ramrati Yadav; m. Julekha Yadav (deceased); two s. one d.; ed Calcutta Medical Coll., Tropical School of Medicine, Post Graduate Inst. of Medical Educ. and Research, India; worked as physician for more than two decades in hospitals in south Nepal's Terai region; joined Nepali Congress Party 1987, Gen. Sec. –2008 (resgnd); elected to House of Reps 1991, 1994, 1999, 2008; Minister for Health 1991–94, 1999–2001; Pres. of Nepal (first elected Pres.) 2008–15.

YADAV, Sharad, BSc, BEE; Indian politician; b. 1 July 1947, Babai Dist, Hoshangabad, Madhya Pradesh; m. Rekha Yadav; one s. one d.; ed Jabalpur Eng Coll.; active youth leader, took part in several mass movements; detained 1969–70, 1972, 1975; mem. Lok Sabha (Parl.) 1974–; Pres. Yuva Janata 1977, Yuva Lok Dal 1979; mem. Rajya Sabha 1986–87, 2004 (2nd term), 2016 (3rd term); Minister of Textiles and Food Processing Industries 1989–90, of Civil Aviation 1999–2001, of Labour 2001–02, of Consumer Affairs, Food and Public Distribution 2002–04; Gen. Sec. Janata Dal 1989–97, Acting Pres. 1995–97, Pres. Janata Dal—United 1997–2016 (Janata Dal merged with Lok Shakti to form Janata Dal—United 1999); Outstanding Parliamentarian Award 2012. *Leisure interests:* reading, music, cricket. *Address:* Janata Dal (United), 7 Jantar Mantar Road, New Delhi 110 001 (office); 7 Tughlak Road, New Delhi 110 003, India (home). *Telephone:* (11) 23368833 (office); (11) 23792738 (home). *Fax:* (11) 23368138 (office); (11) 23017118 (home). *Website:* www.janatadalunited.org (office).

YADAV, Upendra, BA, BL, MSc; Nepalese politician; *Deputy Prime Minister and Minister of Health and Population;* b. 8 Jan. 1961, Sunsari Dist; s. of Dhani Lal and Phudani Devi; one s.; joined Maoists and was briefly in dist leadership; apptd Chair. Madhesi Jana Adhikar Forum Nepal (Madhesi People's Rights Forum Nepal) 2006; Minister of Foreign Affairs 2008–09, Deputy Prime Minister and Minister of Foreign Affairs May–Sept. 2011, Deputy Prime Minister and Minister of Health and Population 2018–; Chair. Federal Socialist Forum—Nepal 2015–. *Leisure interest:* reading books. *Address:* Office of Prime Minister, Singha Durbar, POB 23312, Kathmandu (office); Ministry of Health and Population, Singha Durbar Plaza, Ramshah Path, Kathmandu (office); Federal Socialist Forum—Nepal, Central Committee, Tinkune, Kathmandu, Nepal (office). *Telephone:* (1) 4262802 (Ministry of Health and Population) (office); (1) 4211000 (Office of Prime Minister) (office). *Fax:* (1) 4262896 (Ministry of Health and Population) (office); (1) 4211065 (Office of Prime Minister) (office). *E-mail:* info@mohp.gov.np (office); info@nepal.gov.np (office). *Website:* www.mohp.gov.np (office); www.opmcm.gov .np (office).

YADE, Ramatoulaye (Rama); French politician and consultant; b. 13 Dec. 1976, Dakar, Senegal; m. Joseph Zimet; one d.; ed Institut d'études politiques, Paris; immigrated to France with family 1987; Admin. Sénat Local Authorities Dept 2002–07, Deputy Dir Programmes Public Sénat (Parl. TV channel), becoming Dir of Communication 2005–07; Exec. Sec. France–W Africa Friendship Group; joined UMP (Union pour un Mouvement Populaire) 2005, UMP Nat. Sec. for Francophone Affairs 2006; Minister of State, attached to Ministry of Foreign and European Affairs, responsible for Foreign Affairs and Human Rights 2007–09; Minister-Del. for Sport 2009–10; left UMP and joined Parti Radical 2011, Vice-Pres. 2011–15; Pres. Allons Enfants! (think-tank); joined Cursus Management (consultancy), Paris 2011; Regional Adviser in Ile-de-France 2010–; Amb. of France to UNESCO 2010–11; mem. municipal council, Colombes 2008–14. *Publications include:* Noirs de France 2007, Les droits de l'homme expliqués aux enfants de 7 à 77 ans 2008, Lettre à la jeunesse 2010, Plaidoyer pour une instruction publique 2011. *Address:* Cursus Management, 242 Rue de Rivoli, 75001 Paris, France (office). *Telephone:* 1-77-35-94-45 (office). *Fax:* 1-47-03-66-45 (office). *E-mail:* contact@cursus-management.com (office). *Website:* www.cursus -management.com (office); www.allons-enfants.org; www.rama-yade.fr.

YADLIN, Aharon, BA; Israeli politician and educationalist; b. 17 April 1926, Tel-Aviv; s. of Haim Yadlin and Zipora Yadlin; m. Ada Hacohen 1950; three s.; ed Hebrew Univ.; Co-founder Kibbutz Hatzerim; fmr mem. Presidium, Israel Scouts Movement; mem. Exec. Council Histadrut (Israel Fed. of Labour) 1950–52; Prin. Beit Berl (Labour Party's Centre for Educ.) 1956–58; mem. Knesset (Parl.) 1959–79; Deputy Minister of Educ. and Culture 1964–72; Gen. Sec. Israel Labour Party 1972–74; Minister of Educ. and Culture 1974–77; Chair. Educational and Cultural Cttee, Knesset 1977–79; Chair. Beit Berl Coll. of Educ. 1977–85; Chair. Bialik Inst., Books Publishing House and Acad. for Philosophy, Jewish Studies and World Literature 1990–; Sec.-Gen. United Kibbutz Movt (TAKAM) 1985–89; Chair. Beer-Sheva Theatre, Janush Korczak Asscn in Israel, Scientific Cttee Ben Gurion Research Inst. and Archives 1979–85, Yad Tabenkin (Research Centre of Kibbutz Movt), Beith Yatziv Educational Centre, Beer-Sheva, World Labour Zionist Movt 1992; Chair. Exec. Cttee, Ben Gurion Univ. of the Negev; lecturer and researcher in EFAL (educ. centre of TAKAM); Dr hc (Ben Gurion Univ. of the Negev) 1988; Israel Prize 2010. *Publications:* Introduction to Sociology 1957, The Aim and The Movement 1969, articles on sociology, educ. and youth. *Leisure interests:* stamps, gardening.

YAFTALI, Gen. Mohammad Sharif; Afghan army officer; *Chief of General Staff National Defence and Security Forces;* b. Yaftal-e Sufla, Badakhshan; s. of Muhammad Jama Yaftali; m.; eight c.; ed Army Mil. School, Army Mil. Univ.; joined as Co. Grade and Field Grade Officer 17th Div., Chief of Staff, 40th Infantry Div., Kabul Garrison Command, Commdr, Nat. Military Acad., Ground Forces Command, 203rd Afghan Nat. Army Corps, Chief of Gen. Staff Afghan Nat. Defence and Security Forces 2017–; Afghan Medal for Bravery, Loya Jirga Service Medal, Afghan Medal for Heroism, Wazir Mohammed Akbar Khan Medal, Second Tier Achievement Medal. *Address:* Ministry of Defence, Shash Darak, Kabul, Afghanistan. *Telephone:* (20) 2100451. *Fax:* (20) 2104172. *Website:* mod.gov.af.

YAGHI, Omar Mwannes, PhD; Jordanian/American chemist and academic; *James and Neeltje Tretter Chair Professor of Chemistry, University of California, Berkeley;* b. 9 Feb. 1965, Amman, Jordan; ed Hudson Valley Community Coll., State Univ. of New York at Albany, Univ. of Illinois, Urbana-Champaign; moved to USA aged 15; NSF Postdoctoral Fellow, Harvard Univ. 1990–92; mem. Faculty, Arizona State Univ. 1992–98, Univ. of Michigan 1999–2006; Jean Stone Prof. of Chem., UCLA 2007–12; James and Neeltje Tretter Chair Prof. of Chem., Univ. of California, Berkeley 2012–, Co-Dir Kavli Energy NanoSciences Inst. of the Univ. of California, Berkeley and the Lawrence Berkeley Nat. Lab.; Solid State Chem., ACS and Exxon Co. 1998, Sacconi Medal, Italian Chemical Soc. 1999, second most cited chemist in the world 2000–10, listed by Popular Science Magazine amongst the 'Brilliant 10' scientists and engineers in USA for his work on hydrogen storage 2006, Hydrogen Program Award for outstanding contribs to hydrogen storage, US Dept of Energy 2007, Materials Research Soc. Medal, ACS Chem. of Materials Award 2009, King Faisal Int. Prize in Chem. (co-recipient) 2015, Mustafa Prize 2015, TÜBA Academy Prize 2016, RSC Spiers Memorial Award 2017, Albert Einstein World Award of Science 2017, BBVA Foundation Frontiers of Knowledge Award in Basic Sciences 2018, Wolf Prize for Chemistry (co-recipient) 2018. *Achievements include:* widely known for inventing several extensive classes of new materials termed metal-organic frameworks, zeolitic imidazolate frameworks and covalent organic frameworks. *Publications:* more than 130 scientific papers in professional journals on the synthesis, structure and properties of inorganic compounds and the design and construction of new crystalline materials. *Address:* 602 Latimer Hall, University of California, Berkeley, Berkeley, CA 94720 (office); Lawrence Berkeley National Lab, Materials Sciences Division, 1 Cyclotron Road, Berkeley, CA 94720, USA (office). *Telephone:* (510) 643-5507 (UC, Berkeley) (office); (510) 495-2168 (LBNL) (office). *Fax:* (310) 206-5891 (UC, Berkeley) (office); (510) 486-5846 (LBNL) (office). *E-mail:* yaghi@berkeley.edu (office); oyaghi@lbl .gov (office). *Website:* yaghi.berkeley.edu (office).

YAGI, Makoto; Japanese business executive; *Chairman, Kansai Electric Power Company Inc.;* b. 13 Oct. 1949; ed Kyoto Univ.; joined Kansai Electric Power Co. Inc. in 1972, has held numerous exec. positions including Deputy Chief Dir of Electric System Business and Exec. Vice-Pres., served as Man. Dir –2010, Pres. and Dir 2010–16, Chair. 2016–; Chair. Fed. of Electric Power Cos of Japan, Japan Nuclear Fuel Ltd 2011–; Gov., Tokyo Centre, World Asscn of Nuclear Operators (WANO); Chevalier, Ordre nat. de la Légion d'honneur 2015. *Address:* Kansai Electric Power Co. Inc., 6-16 Nakanoshima 3-chome, Kita-ku, Osaka 530-8270, Japan (office). *Telephone:* (6) 6441-8821 (office). *Fax:* (6) 6447-7174 (office). *E-mail:* finance@kepco.co.jp (office); info@kepco.co.jp (office). *Website:* www.kepco.co.jp (office).

YAGI, Takeshi; Japanese diplomatist; *Ambassador to Germany;* b. 12 July 1954, Niigata; m.; ed Univ. of Tokyo, Ludwig Maximilian Univ. of Munich, Germany; joined diplomatic service 1977, Head of Supporting the CIS, Dept of Europe and Oceania, Ministry of Foreign Affairs (MFA) 1994–96, Head of Cen. and Eastern Europe 1996–97, Head of Repayment Free Devt Co-operation, Dept of Econ. Co-operation 1997–99, Minister, Embassy in Washington, DC 1999–2001, Chargé d'affaires a.i., Embassy in Berlin 2001–03, Deputy Vice-Minister (Parl. Affairs), MFA 2003–05, Deputy Head of European Dept 2005–07, Envoy and Deputy Perm. Rep. to OECD, Paris 2007–10, Head of Econ. Affairs, MFA 2010–12, Amb. to India (also accred to Bhutan) 2012–16, to Germany 2016–. *Address:* Embassy of Japan, Hiroshimastr. 6, 10785 Berlin, Germany (office). *Telephone:* (30) 210940 (office). *Fax:* (30) 21094228 (office). *E-mail:* info@botschaft-japan.de (office). *Website:* www .de.emb-japan.go.jp (office).

YAGODIN, Gennadiy Alekseyevich; Russian physical chemist and academic; b. 3 June 1927, Vyass, Penza region; s. of Alexei Yagodin and Alexandra Yagodina; m. 1949; one s. one d.; ed Mendeleyev Chemical Tech. Inst., Moscow; mem. CPSU 1948–91; Deputy Dean, Mendeleyev Chemical Tech. Inst., Moscow 1956–59, Dean, Dept of Physical Chemistry 1959–63, Prof. of Chemical Tech. 1959–63, 1966–73, Rector 1973–85; Deputy Dir-Gen., IAEA, Vienna 1963–66, Head of Dept of Training and Tech. Information 1963–64, Head of Dept of Tech. Operations 1964–66; USSR Minister of Higher and Secondary Specialized Educ. 1985–89; Chair. State Cttee for Nat. Educ. 1988–91; Founder and Rector Int. Univ. in Moscow 1992–2001, First Vice-Pres. 2001–03; Head of Environmental Science Dept, Mendeleyev Chemical Tech. Univ. from 2002; Deputy, USSR Supreme Soviet 1986–89; mem. Cen. Cttee CPSU 1986–89; Corresp. mem. USSR (now

Russian) Acad. of Sciences 1976; mem. Russian Acad. of Educ.; Order of Lenin; D.Y. Mendeleyev Prize 1981, USSR State Prize 1985, Koptyug Prize 2003. *Leisure interest:* collecting butterflies.

YAHAV, Yona, LLB; Israeli lawyer and politician; b. 19 June 1944, Haifa; m. Rivka Yahav; three c.; ed Hebrew Univ., Jerusalem, London Univ., UK; served as Lt-Col in Israeli Mil. Police; mem. 14th Knesset (Parl.) 1996–1999, parl. posts included Chair. Subcommittee for Banking, mem. Constitution, Law and Justice Cttee, substitute mem., Finance Cttee; fmr Deputy and Alternating Mayor of Haifa, Mayor of Haifa 2003–18; Chair. Haifa Econ. Co.; fmr Chair. Petrol and Gas Resources, Govt Co., Municipal Theatre Exec., Haifa Int. Film Festival Org.; fmr Dir-Gen. Haifa Tourist Devt Org., David Ben-Gurion Foundation; fmr Sec.-Gen. World Jewish Student Union; mem. Israel Labour Party –2006, mem. Kadima party 2006–; Legion d'honneur 2008; Global Citizenship Award, Tufts Univ. 2009, Rambam Award, Rambam Health Care Campus 2014. *Publications:* The Anatomy of the Fall of the Labor Party (with Prof. Shevach Weiss) 1977, Libel and Slander 1987. *Address:* c/o Office of the Mayor, Municipality of Haifa, Haifa, Israel (office). *Telephone:* 4-8356767 (office). *Fax:* 4-8356020 (office). *E-mail:* haifa@haifa.muni.il (office). *Website:* www.haifa.muni.il (office).

YAKCOP, Tan Sri Nor Mohamed, MBA; Malaysian economist and politician; b. 24 Aug. 1947, Butterworth, Penang; m.; ed St Xavier's Inst., George Town, Univ. of Malaya, Kuala Lumpur, Leuven Catholic Univ., Belgium; worked at Bank Negara Malaysia 1968–2000, positions included Deputy Man. in 1985, Man. 1986; Special Econ. Adviser to Prime Minister Tun Dr Mahathir Mohamad 1997–98; Deputy Chair. Khazanah Nasional Bhd 2013–17, mem. Bd of Dirs 2002–17, Chair. Khazanah Research Inst. –2017; Minister of Finance II 2004–09, Minister in the Prime Minister's Dept 2009–13; mem. Parl. for Tasek Gelugor 2008–13; mem. Exec. Cttee Nat. Econ. Action Council; mem. Bd Khazanah Berhad; mem. Barisan Nasional.

YAKÉTÉ, Joseph, DSc; Central African Republic politician; b. 14 Nov. 1960, Sibut; ed Inst. de Sciences Politiques, France; spent several years in France, becoming mem. Parti socialiste français 1997 and Parl. Asst in Assemblée nationale (French parl.); elected to Muncipal Council, Paris Thirteenth Dist 2008; f. FORAC (Forum pour le Rassemblement Centrafricain); unsuccessful cand. (Union de la Gauche) in presidential election Oct. 2015; Minister of Defence 2016–17. *Publication:* Socialisme sans discriminations 2005.

YAKIŞ, Yaşar, BA; Turkish politician; b. 1938, Akçakoca; m.; one c.; ed Ankara Univ.; joined Ministry of Foreign Affairs 1962; Councillor, Turkish Embassy, Damascus, Syria 1980; est. OIC's Standing Cttee for Econ. and Commercial Co-operation 1985; Amb. to Saudi Arabia 1988–92; Deputy Under-Sec., Ministry of Foreign Affairs, responsible for Econ. Affairs 1992–95; Amb. to Egypt 1995–98; Perm. Rep. to UN, Vienna 1998–2002; Minister of Foreign Affairs 2002–03; Chair. EU Cttee in Turkish Parl. 2003–11, co-Chair. Turkey-EU Joint Parliamentary Commission 2003–11; Chair. French caucus in the Turkish Parliament 2007–11; Decoration of King Abdul Aziz, Saudi Arabia 1992, Ordine della Stella della Solidericà Italiana 2007, Légion d'Honneur, France 2009, Grand Cross of the Order of King Leopold II of Belgium 2012. *E-mail:* www.yasaryakis.com.tr.

YAKORO, Rémi; Central African Republic economist and government official; ed Univ. Félix Houphouët-Boigny, Abidjan, Côte d'Ivoire; several years with Direction Générale des Douanes (Directorate-Gen. of Customs) including as Inspector of Taxes 2008, Dir-Gen. of Customs and Excise 2013–14; Minister of Finance and the Budget Jan.–Aug. 2014. *Address:* c/o Ministry of Finance and the Budget, BP 696, Bangui, Central African Republic (office).

YAKOVENKO, Alexander Vladimirovich, DIur, CandJurSc; Russian diplomatist; *Ambassador to UK;* b. 1954, Homel, Byelorussian SSR, USSR; m.; one d.; ed Moscow State Inst. of Int. Relations; joined Foreign Services 1976, served with USSR Mission to UN, New York 1981–86, Head of Div., Dept on Security and Co-operation in Europe, Ministry of Foreign Affairs, Russian Fed. 1986–92, Deputy Dir Dept of Int. Scientific and Technological Cooperation 1993–95, Deputy Dir Dept on Problems of Security and Disarmament, Ministry of Foreign Affairs 1995–97, Perm. Rep. to Int. Orgs, Vienna 1997–2000, Dir Information and Press Dept, Ministry of Foreign Affairs 2000–04, Deputy Minister of Foreign Affairs 2005–11, Amb. to UK 2011–; Head of Russian del. to intergovernmental negotiations on Int. Space Station 1993–98; mem. Russian Acad. of Natural Sciences, Space Council of the Russian Acad. of Sciences, Int. Inst. of Space Law, Int. Acad. of Astronautics; Corresp. mem. Tatarstan Acad. of Sciences. *Publications:* several books and a manual on int. law; more than 150 publs on int. relations and Russian foreign policy, science, education and cultural issues. *Address:* Russian Ambassador's Residence, 13 Kensington Palace Gardens, London, W8 4QX, England (office). *Telephone:* (20) 7229-6412 (office). *Fax:* (20) 7727-8625 (office). *E-mail:* info@rusemb.org.uk (office); office@rusemblon.org (office). *Website:* www.rusemb.org.uk (office).

YAKOVLEV, Aleksandr Maksimovich, DJur; Russian lawyer; b. 30 Aug. 1927, Leningrad; s. of Maxim Yakovlev and Maria Yakovleva; m. Eugenia Yakovleva 1950; ed Moscow Inst. of Law; sr research fellow Inst. of Law, USSR Ministry of Internal Affairs, then USSR Ministry of Justice 1957–75; Head Dept of Criminal Law and Criminology USSR (now Russian) Inst. of State and Law, Prof. 1975–94, apptd Chief Researcher 1996; in democratic movt since late 1980s; USSR People's Deputy 1989–91; mem. Perm. Cttee on Legis. USSR Supreme Soviet 1989–91; Plenipotentiary Rep. of Pres. of Russia at Federal Ass. 1994–96, Expert to Council of Fed. 1997; apptd Rector New Moscow Law Inst. 1998; Visiting Prof., Univ. of Manitoba 1990, Rutgers Univ. 1991, Alberta Univ., New York and Toronto Univ. 1992, Emory Univ. Atlanta 1993, 1997; mem. Bd of Dirs Int. Soc. of Social Defence, Paris, UN Cttee Against Torture 1994, Inst. of Sociology of Law for Europe; Hon. LLD (Alberta Univ., Canada) 1991; Merited Lawyer of Russia. *Publications:* The Bear That Wouldn't Dance: Failed Attempts to Reform the Former Constitution of the Soviet Union (with Dale Gibson) 1992, Striving for Law in a Lawless Land 1995, Sociology of Crime 2000, The Social Structure of Society 2003; several other books and more than 100 articles on various aspects of constitutional law, publs in journals. *Leisure interest:* travelling. *Address:* Dolgorukovskaya str. 40, Apt. 153, 127030 Moscow, Russia (home). *E-mail:* yakovlev.27@mail.ru (home).

YAKOVLEV, Vladimir Anatolyevich, CandEconSc; Russian politician (retd); b. 25 Nov. 1944, Olekminsk, Yakutia; m. Irina Ivanovna Yakovleva; one s.; ed NW Polytech. Inst.; master on construction sites, Head Repair-Construction Trust 1965–80, Deputy Man. Housing Dept, Leningrad (St Petersburg) 1980–93; First Deputy Mayor of St Petersburg, Russia. Head Cttee on Man. of Municipal Econ. 1993–96; Mayor (Gov.) of St Petersburg 1996–2003; Deputy Chair. (Deputy Prime Minister) Govt of the Russian Fed. 2003–04; Rep. of the Pres. in the S Fed. Dist 2004–05; Minister of Regional Development 2005–07; mem. Council of Fed. of Russia 1996–2001; Pres. Ass. of Heads of Regions and Repubs of NW Russia 1997; Pres. Basketball Club Spartacus; Founder and Leader of Vsya Rossiya Movt 1999; Pres. Fed. of Bicycle Sports of St Petersburg; Order of Honour 2000; Merited Constructor of Russia. *Leisure interests:* tennis, basketball, football, Russian history, numismatics.

YAKOVLEV, Gen. Vladimir Nikolayevich, CAND.MIL.SC.; Russian army officer; b. 17 Aug. 1954, Tver; s. of Nikolai Vassilyevich Yakovlev and Erika Alexeyevna Yakovleva; m. Raisa Anatolyevna Yakovleva; two d.; ed Dzerzhinsky Mil. Acad., Mil. Acad. of Gen. Staff; served with strategic rocket forces incl. Commdr rocket regt 1985–89; Deputy Commdr rocket div. 1989–91, Commdr 1991–93; Head of Staff Rocket Army 1993–94, Commdr 1994–97; Head of Gen. Staff Rocket Troops Jan. 1999; C-in-C Rocket Strategic Forces of Russian Fed. 1997–2001; Head of Staff for Co-ordination of Mil. Co-operation within CIS 2001–04; Adviser to Gen. Dir Rosoboroneksport 2006–09; Chief, Military Acad. of the Gen. Staff 2009–12; mem. Russian Acad. of Eng; Corresp. mem. Russian Acad. of Rocket and Artillery Sciences; mem. Council on Foreign and Defense Policy; Order of Red Star, Order for Mil. Service; Prize of Russian Pres. for Achievement in Educ. 1998. *Publications include:* Military Work: Science, Art, Vocation 1998, Organizational Activities of General Staff in Rocket Strategic Forces 1999, Rocket Shield of the Motherland 1999, co-author Mil. Encyclopaedic Dictionary of Rocket Strategic Forces; over 50 journal articles and 18 scientific-technical reports. *Leisure interests:* music, reading, tennis, swimming.

YAKUNIN, Vladimir I., PhD; Russian transport industry executive; *Founding President, World Public Forum—Dialogue of Civilizations;* b. 30 June 1948, Zakharovo, Vladimir prov.; m.; two s.; ed Leningrad Mechanical Inst.; Jr Research Asst, State Inst. of Applied Chem. 1972–75; mil. service 1975–77; worked for Cttee on Foreign Econ. Relations, USSR Ministerial Council 1977–82; Chief of Foreign Dept, Inst. of Physics and Technics, USSR Acad. of Sciences 1982–85; Second then First Sec., Perm. Rep. to UN, New York 1985–91; Co-founder and Chair. Cttee of Dirs CJSC Int. Center For Business Partnership 1991–97; Head North-Western Revision, Chief Control Dept of Pres. of Russian Fed. 1997–2000; Deputy Minister of Transport 2000–02; First Deputy Minister of Transport 2002–03; First Vice-Pres. Russian Railways OAO (Rossiiskiye zheleznyye dorogi—RZhD) 2003–05, Pres. and CEO 2005–15; Founding Pres. World Public Forum—Dialogue of Civilizations, Vienna 2013–; Chair. Bd Trustees, Centre of Nat. Glory, Andrew the First-Called Foundation; Order of Saint Equal-to-the-Apostles Grand Duke Vladimir (Second Degree), Russian Orthodox Church, Order for Merit to the Fatherland of the Fourth Class, Medal for Mil. Merit and Medal for the Development of Railways, Orders of the Russian Orthodox Church: Order of St Seraphim of Sarov (Second Class), Order of Venerable Andrew Rublyov (First Class), Order of Honour of the Russian Muftis Council (First Class), Order of the Holy Sepulchre of the Jerusalem Orthodox Church, Chevalier, Légion d'honneur, Decoration of Honour for Services to the Repub. of Austria, Order of Friendship (Order Dostyk) of the Repub. of Kazakhstan, Grande Ufficiale, Ordine al Merito (Italy). *Address:* Russian Headquarters, World Public Forum—Dialogue of Civilizations, 105062 Moscow, 42/5 Pokrovka, Russia (office). *Telephone:* (495) 641-52-10 (office). *Fax:* (495) 641-52-10 (office). *E-mail:* info@wpfdc.org (office). *Website:* wpfdc.org (office); v-yakunin.livejournal.com.

YAM, Joseph C. K., CBE, BSc; Hong Kong banker and academic; *Distinguished Research Fellow, Lau Chor Tak Institute of Global Economics and Finance, Chinese University of Hong Kong;* b. 9 Sept. 1948, Canton, China; s. of Shun Yam and Hok-chun Shum; m. Grace Fong 1972; one s. one d.; ed Univ. of Hong Kong, Inst. of Social Studies, The Hague, Netherlands; Demonstrator in Econs, Econs Dept, Univ. of Hong Kong 1970–71; statistician, Census and Statistics Dept, Hong Kong Govt 1971–76, Economist, Econ. Services Br. 1976–77, Sr Economist 1977–79, Prin. Asst Sec. (Econ. Services) 1979–82, (Monetary Affairs) 1982–85, Deputy Sec. for Monetary Affairs 1985–91; Dir Office of the Exchange Fund 1991–93; Chief Exec. Hong Kong Monetary Authority 1993–2009; Exec. Vice-Pres. China Soc. for Finance and Banking (serving as adviser to People's Bank of China) 2009–; mem. Int. Advisory Council, China Investment Corpn; Distinguished Research Fellow, Lau Chor Tak Inst. of Global Econs and Finance, Chinese Univ. of Hong Kong 2010–, also Hon. Prof., Business School; mem. Bd of Dirs Johnson Electric Holdings Ltd 2010–, Swiss Bank UBS AG 2011– (UBS Group AG after restructuring), UnionPay International Co., Ltd, Community Chest of Hong Kong; Hon. Prof., Dept of Asian and Policy Studies, Hong Kong Inst. of Educ. (HKIEd) 2015–; Hon. DScS (Hong Kong Univ.) 2008, Hon. DBA (Hong Kong Univ. of Science and Tech.) 2009. *Leisure interests:* golf, horse racing, swimming, hiking. *Address:* Lau Chor Tak Institute of Global Economics and Finance, The Chinese University of Hong Kong, 13/F Cheng Yu Tung Building, 12 Chak Cheung Street, Shatin, N.T., Hong Kong Special Administrative Region, People's Republic of China (office). *Website:* www.igef.cuhk.edu.hk (office).

YAM, Vivian Wing-Wah, BSc, PhD, CChem, FRSC; Hong Kong chemist and academic; *Chair of Chemistry and Philip Wong Wilson Wong Professor in Chemistry and Energy, University of Hong Kong;* ed Univ. of Hong Kong; mem. Faculty, City Polytechnic of Hong Kong 1988–90; joined Dept of Chem., Univ. of Hong Kong 1990, Chair of Chem. and Prof. 1999–, Head of Chem. Dept 2000–05, Philp Wong Wilson Wong Prof. in Chem. and Energy 2009–; Academician, Chinese Acad. of Sciences 2001–; Croucher Foundation Sr Research Fellow 2000–01; Royal Soc. of Chem. Chartered Scientist; Fellow, TWAS, The World Acad. of Sciences; Foreign Assoc., NAS 2012–; Dr hc (Université de Rennes 1) 2013; Centenary Medal, Royal Soc. of Chem. 2005, State Natural Science Award 2005, Hong Kong Fulbright Distinguished Scholar 2007, Japanese Photochemistry Asscn Eikohsha Award 2006, L'Oréal-UNESCO Women in Science Award (Asia/Pacific) 2011, Ho Leung Ho Lee Foundation Prize for Scientific and Technological Progress 2011, Seaborg Lectureship, Univ. of California, Berkeley 2013, Chinese Chemical Soc.-

China Petroleum and Chemical Corpn (Sinopec) Chemistry Contribution Prize 2014, Ludwig Mond Award, Royal Soc. of Chem. 2015. *Address:* Room 504, Chong Yuet Ming Chemistry Building, University of Hong Kong, Pokfulam Road, Hong Kong Special Administrative Region, People's Republic of China (office). *Telephone:* (852) 2859-2153 (office). *E-mail:* wwyam@hku.hk (office). *Website:* www.chemistry.hku.hk (office); web.hku.hk/~wwyam/yam/homepage (office).

YAMADA, Akira, LLB; Japanese diplomatist; *Ambassador to Brazil;* b. 27 Jan. 1958; ed Univ. of Tokyo; joined Ministry of Foreign Affairs (MFA) 1981, Attaché, Embassy in Madrid 1982–84, Third Sec., Embassy in Buenos Aires 1984–85, Second Sec. 1985–86, Deputy Dir, First Affairs Div. of Latin America and the Caribbean, MFA 1986–88, Deputy Dir, Research and Planning Div., Dept of Econ. Co-operation 1988, Official Interpreter (Spanish–Japanese) 1988–92, First Sec., Embassy in Washington, DC 1992–95, Prin. Deputy Dir, Div. of Policy Assistance, Dept of Econ. Co-operation 1995–97, Sr Co-ordinator for Econ. Co-operation 1997–98, Dir, Div. of Trade in Services (WTO), Dept of Econ. Affairs 1998–99, Co-ordinator, Second Affairs Div. of Latin America and the Caribbean 1999–2001, Dir, Sec. of Audit Comm. Disclosure, Cabinet Office 2001–03, Dir, Div. of Grant Aid, Dept of Econ. Co-operation 2003–04, Minister (Trade), Embassy in Baghdad 2004–06, Minister (Trade), Embassy in Madrid 2006–08, Dir-Gen., Dept of Int. Co-operation and African Affairs (Amb. for Non-governmental Orgs—NGOs) 2008–10, Dir-Gen., Global Affairs (Amb. for NGOs) 2010–12, Dir-Gen. for Latin American Affairs and the Caribbean 2012–14, Amb. to Mexico 2014–17, to Brazil 2017–. *Address:* SES, Av. das Nações, Quadra 811, Lote 39, 70425-900 Brasília, DF, Brazil (office). *Telephone:* (61) 3442-4200 (office). *Fax:* (61) 3443-9685 (office). *E-mail:* comunicacaojapao@bs.mofa.go.jp (office). *Website:* www.br.emb-japan.go.jp (office).

YAMADA, Noboru; Japanese business executive; *Representative Director, Chairman and CEO, Yamada Denki Company Ltd;* with JVC –1976; f. Yamada Denki Co. Ltd 1983, currently Rep. Dir, Chair. and CEO, listed on JASDAQ 1989, started business as internet service provider 1996, promoted to first section of Tokyo Stock Exchange 2000, acquired Daikuma from Ito Yokado as subsidiary 2002, opened Tecc Land Gushikawa store in Gushikawa (now Uruma), Okinawa 2004, first city-based store, main Hiroshima store, opened 2004, invested in Kouziro Co. Ltd, Owner of Shopland PC 2004, entered business alliance (and capital alliance) with Kyūshū-based consumer electronics retailer, Shōichi Denki 2006, moved co. HQ from Maebashi to new Takasaki store 2007, cos in group include Daikuma, Minami Kyūshū Yamada Denki Co. Ltd, Okinawa Yamada Denki Co. Ltd, Kansai Yamada Denki Co. Ltd, Chūgoku/Shikoku Tecc Land, Cosmos Berry's, Pres. Techplanning Inc. 1992–, Yamada BroadBand Corpn 2002–. *Address:* Yamada Denki Co. Ltd, 4-40-11 Hiyoshi-cho, Maebashi 371-0017, Gunma, Japan (office). *Telephone:* (2) 7233-5522 (office). *Fax:* (2) 7233-3309 (office); (2) 7233-3568 (office). *E-mail:* info@yamada-denki.jp (office). *Website:* www.yamada-denki.jp (office).

YAMADA, Tadataka (Tachi), BA, MD; American (b. Japanese) physician, academic and foundation executive; *Executive Vice-President, Chief Medical and Scientific Officer, Takeda Pharmaceuticals International Inc.;* b. Tokyo, Japan; ed Phillips Acad., Stanford Univ., New York Univ. School of Medicine; emigrated to USA aged 15; began career in Dept of Gastroenterology, UCLA; Chief of Gastroenterology then Chair. Dept of Internal Medicine and Physician-in-Chief, Univ. of Michigan Medical Center 1989–99, now Adjunct Prof. of Internal Medicine, Univ. of Michigan Medical School; mem. Bd of Dirs SmithKline Beecham (now GlaxoSmithKline) 1994–2006, Pres. SmithKline Beecham Healthcare Services 1996–99, Chair. Research and Devt, Pharmaceuticals 1999–2001, Chair. Research and Devt 2001–06; Pres. Global Health Program, Bill and Melinda Gates Foundation 2006–11; Chair. Man. and Operations Cttee 3, Takeda Pharmaceuticals International Inc. Feb. 2011–, Dir, Medical and Scientific Advisor to CEO and Exec. Vice-Pres. June 2011–, Chief Medical and Scientific Officer Nov. 2011–; mem. Bd of Dirs Research!America, Agilent Technologies, Inc. 2011–; mem. Advisory Bd Quaker BioVentures, Inc.; Sr Advisor, Frazier Healthcare Ventures 2006–; mem. Pres.'s Council of Advisors on Science and Tech. 2004–; mem. Advisory Cttee to Dir NIH 2004–; fmr Pres. Asscn of American Physicians, American Gastroenterological Asscn; Master, American Coll. of Physicians; mem. Inst. of Medicine, NAS, Acad. of Medical Sciences (UK); fmr mem. American Bd of Medical Examiners; Trustee Rockefeller Brothers Fund; Hon. KBE; Dr hc (Univ. of East Anglia, Univ. of Warwick, Washington Coll., Loyola Univ. of Chicago); numerous awards, including Distinguished Achievement Award in Gastrointestinal Physiology, American Physiological Soc., Friedenwald Medal, American Gastroenterological Asscn, Distinguished Faculty Achievement Award, Univ. of Michigan, Distinguished Medical Scientist Award, Medical Coll. of Virginia. *Publications:* Textbook of Gastroenterology (ed.), Yamada Textbook of Medicine (ed.); more than 150 original manuscripts in professional journals. *Address:* Takeda Pharmaceuticals Co. Ltd, 1-1, Doshomachi 4-chome, Chuo-ku, Osaka 540-8645, Japan (office). *Telephone:* (6) 6204-2111 (office). *Fax:* (6) 6204-2880 (office). *E-mail:* info@takeda.com (office). *Website:* www.takeda.com (office).

YAMAGUCHI, Kenji, MA (Econs); Japanese government official and economist; *Representative, WELL (World Economy and Land Laboratory);* b. 19 July 1933, Yamagata; s. of Futao Yamaguchi and Yoshi Yamaguchi; m. Momoe Matsumoto 1962; one s. one d.; ed Univ. of Tokyo; entered Budget Bureau, Ministry of Finance 1956; Nat. Tax Admin. Agency 1963; Ministry of Interior 1966; Econ. Planning Agency 1968; First Sec., Okinawa Reversion Preparatory Cttee, Foreign Minister's Office and Counsellor, Okinawa Bureau, Prime Minister's Office 1969; Int. Finance Bureau, Ministry of Finance 1971; Consul for Japan, Sydney 1972; Counsellor, Personnel Bureau, Prime Minister's Office 1975; Finance Bureau, Ministry of Finance 1977; Dir-Gen. North East Japan Finance Bureau, Ministry of Finance 1981; Special Asst to Minister of Foreign Affairs 1982–87; Exec. Dir for Japan, IBRD and affiliates 1982–87, Dean IBRD Bd 1985–87; Sr Exec. Dir Water Resources Devt Public Corpn 1988–; Co-ordination Leader, Org. for Industry, Science and Cultural Advancement (OISCA) 1987–99; Exec. Adviser Mitsui Trust Bank, Tokyo 1993–97; Chair. Mitsui Trust Int. Ltd, London 1993–97, Mitsui Trust Bank Ltd, Switzerland 1993–97; Exec. Adviser Chiyoda Mutual Life Insurance Co., Tokyo 1997–99; f. WELL (World Economy and Land Lab.) a think-tank seeking a balanced relationship between the nat. econ. and land ownership 1998; Human Life Rescue Award 1954, Zuihou Chuujushou conferred by the Emperor 2004. *Publications:* The World Bank – How Can Japan Contribute to the World? 1988, Land Policy for Prosperity – Land as Public Property 1997, Land is to be Owned by the Public 2000, A Cool Observation on the Japanese Economy 2006; several books on financial matters and foreign affairs. *Leisure interests:* reading, swimming, music. *Address:* World Economy and Land Laboratory, 3-16-43 Utsukushiga-Oka, Aoba-ku, Yokohama City 225-0002, Japan (office). *Telephone:* (45) 901-7309 (office). *Fax:* (45) 901-7309 (office). *E-mail:* well@mx7.ttcn.ne.jp (office). *Website:* www2.ttcn.ne.jp/~well (office).

YAMAGUCHI, Masanori; Japanese business executive; *President and CEO, Sun Corporation;* Vice-Pres., then Pres. Kinki Nippon Railway Co. –2004, Chair. Kinki Nippon Tourist Co. Ltd (now KNT-CT Holdings Co. Ltd) 2008–, Adviser, KNT-CT Holdings Co. Ltd 2013–; Man. Dir Kintetsu Corpn 1993–97, Sr Man. Dir 1997–98, Chief of Secr. Office 1998–99, Vice-Pres. 1999–2003, CEO and Pres. 2003–07, Chair. 2007–, Chair. Kintetsu Department Store Co. Ltd 2007–; fmr Pres. Origin Electric Shoji Co. Ltd; Dir, Sr Man. Dir Sun Corpn from 2008, Dir, Pres. and CEO 2012–; Chair. CelleBrite USA Corpn, Kintetsu World Express, Inc., Wakayama Kintetsu Department Store Co. Ltd; mem. Bd of Dirs Int. Business Org. of Osaka Inc., Asahi Broadcasting Corpn 2007–, Nippon Pallet Pool Co. Ltd 2007–; External Dir, KNT-CT Holdings Co. Ltd 2002–. *Address:* Sun Corporation, 250 Asahi Konan, Aichi 483-8555, Japan (office). *Fax:* (5) 8755-3851 (office). *E-mail:* info@sun-denshi.co.jp (office). *Website:* www.sun-denshi.co.jp (office).

YAMAGUCHI, Nobuo; Japanese business executive; Chair. and Rep. Dir Asahi Kasei Corpn (changed name from Asahi Chemical Industry Co. Ltd 2000) –2010, Hon. Chair. April–Sept. 2010; apptd Chair. Japan Chamber of Commerce and Industry 2001, Tokyo Chamber of Commerce and Industry 2001; mem. Bd of Dirs Asahi Breweries Ltd, Nippon Television Network Corpn; mem. Pacific Basin Econ. Council.

YAMAGUCHI, Yutaka; Japanese business executive; ed Univ. of Tokyo; joined Bank of Japan as staff economist 1964, spent most of career in policy planning and policy-related research areas, experiences at sr man. level included being Bank of Japan's Chief Rep. in New York 1989–91, Dir of Research and Statistics 1991–92, of Policy Planning 1992–96, Exec. Dir 1996–98, Deputy Gov. 1998–2003 (retd); also chaired Cttee for Global Financial System, Basel, Switzerland 1998–2003; currently advises Japanese and int. firms on econ. and policy devts; mem. Group of Thirty Consultative Group on Int. Econ. and Monetary Affairs, Inc. (G-30), Washington, DC, Keizai Doyukai (a leading business group in Japan). *Address:* The Group of Thirty, 1701 K. Street, NW, Suite 950, Washington, DC 20006, USA. *Telephone:* (202) 331-2472. *Website:* group30.org.

YAMAMOTO, Keith R., BSc, PhD; American biochemist, academic and writer; *Vice-Chancellor for Research, University of California, San Francisco;* ed Iowa State Univ., Princeton Univ., Univ. of California, San Francisco; Asst Prof. of Biochemistry, Univ. of California, San Francisco 1976–79, Assoc. Prof. of Biochemistry 1979–83, Prof. of Biochemistry 1983–2003, Vice-Chair. Dept of Biochemistry and Biophysics 1985–94, Dir Biochemistry and Molecular Biology Program in Biological Sciences 1988–2001, Prof. of Cellular and Molecular Pharmacology 1994–, Chair. Dept of Cellular and Molecular Pharmacology 1994–2003, Vice-Dean for Research, School of Medicine 2002–03, Exec. Vice-Dean, School of Medicine 2004–, Vice-Chancellor for Research 2011–; Chair. Coalition for Life Sciences, NAS Bd on Life; Founding Ed., Molecular Biology of the Cell; mem. Nat. Advisory Group on Genome Editing 2015–; Hon. DSc (Iowa State Univ.) 2001; NIH Research Career Development Award 1977–82, Vanderbilt Medal of Merit 1999, Allan Munck Prize, Dartmouth Univ. 2004, Edwin B. Astwood Award, Endocrine Soc. 2012, Public Service Award, American Soc. for Cell Biology 2012, John V. Atanasoff Discovery Award 2013. *Publications include:* co-author: Gene Wars: Military Control over the New Genetic Technologies 1988, Transcriptional Regulation: Monograph 22 1992; contrib. to numerous academic publs. *Address:* Cellular and Molecular Pharmacology, University of California, Mission Bay, 600 16th Street, GH-S574, PO Box 2280, San Francisco, CA 94143-2280, USA (office). *Telephone:* (415) 476-3128 (office). *Fax:* (415) 514-4112 (office). *E-mail:* Yamamoto@ucsf.edu (office). *Website:* yamamotolab.ucsf.edu (office); www.cancer.ucsf.edu (office).

YAMAMOTO, Masami; Japanese business executive; *Chairman and Representative Director, Fujitsu Limited;* b. 11 Jan. 1954; ed Kyushu Univ.; joined Fujitsu 1976, Corp. Vice-Pres. Fujitsu Ltd –2007, Corp. Sr Vice-Pres. 2007–10, Corp. Sr Exec. Vice-Pres. 2007–10, Pres. and Rep. Dir Fujitsu Ltd 2010–15, also Corp. Vice-Pres. Fujitsu Microelectronics Ltd, Dir of Fujitsu Technology Solutions (Holding) BV, Dir at Fujitsu Laboratories Ltd, Chair. Fujitsu Ltd 2015–. *Address:* Fujitsu Headquarters, Shiodome City Centre, 1-5-2 Higashi-Shimbashi, Minato-ku, Tokyo 105-7123, Japan (office). *Telephone:* (3) 6252-2220 (office). *Fax:* (3) 6252-2783 (office). *E-mail:* info@fujitsu.com (office). *Website:* www.fujitsu.com (office).

YAMAMOTO, Tadamichi, BSc, BA; Japanese diplomatist and UN official; *Secretary-General's Special Representative and Head, UN Assistance Mission in Afghanistan, United Nations;* b. 1950; m.; two c.; ed Dept of Eng, Tokyo Inst. of Tech., Univ. of Oxford, UK; passed Higher Diplomatic Service Examination 1973; entered Diplomatic Service 1974, First Sec., Political Section, Embassy in Manila 1983–85, First Sec., Political Section, Embassy in Washington, DC 1985–87, Deputy Dir First Int. Econ. Orgs Div., Econ. Affairs Bureau, Ministry of Foreign Affairs 1987–91, Dir First SE Asia Div., Asian Affairs Bureau 1991–94, Dir Tech. Co-operation Div., Econ. Co-operation Bureau Feb.–April 1994, Pvt. Sec. to Minister of Foreign Affairs 1994–96, Dir Policy Planning Div., Foreign Policy Bureau, Ministry of Foreign Affairs Jan.–July 1996, Dir First N American Div., N American Affairs Bureau 1996–98, Minister of Political Affairs, Embassy in Seoul 1998–2000, Consul-Gen. in Boston 2000–02, Minister of Political Affairs, Embassy in Washington, DC 2002–06, Dir-Gen. Public Policy Dept, Ministry of Foreign Affairs 2006–09, Amb. and Perm. Del. to UNESCO, Paris 2008–10, Amb. in Charge of Afghanistan and Pakistan Assistance Co-ordination, Ministry of Foreign Affairs 2010–12, Amb. to Hungary 2012–14; Deputy Special Rep. of the Sec.-Gen., UN Assistance Mission in Afghanistan (UNAMA) 2014–16, Special Rep. and Head, UNAMA 2016–. *Address:* UNAMA, Compound B, Building 5 – Annex, Kabul, Afghanistan (office). *Website:* unama.unmissions.org (office).

YAMAMOTO, Yohji; Japanese fashion designer; b. 3 Oct. 1943, Tokyo; one d.; ed Keio Univ. and Bunkafukuso Gakuin School of Fashion, Tokyo; launched first collection Tokyo 1977, Paris 1981, New York 1982, first menswear collection, Paris 1984; costume designer for Opéra de Lyon's production of Madame Butterfly 1990, Wagner Opera's production of Tristan und Isolde, Bayreuth 1993, Kanagawa Art Festival Opera Susanoo 1994; launched first perfume Yohji 1996, second perfume Yohji Essential 1998; participant in 25th Anniversary of Pina Bausch Co., Wuppertal 1998; launched first perfume Yohji Homme 1999; designed costumes for the Ryuichi Sakamoto Opera 'Life' 1999; subject of Wim Wenders' film Notebook on Cities and Clothes 1989; designed costumes for Dir Takeshi Kitano's films, Dolls and Zatoichi; debut of Y-3 line 2003; designs costumes for Elton John's The Red Piano show in Las Vegas 2003; invited to curate second issue of A MAGAZINE curated by 2005; co. restructured following debts 2009–10; Yohji Yamamoto Fund for Peace est. to foster devt of China's fashion industry and to help heal China–Japan relations 2008; Chevalier des Arts et des Lettres 1994, Medal of Honour with Purple Ribbon, Chevalier, Ordre nat. du Mérite; So-en Award, Endo Award 1969, Fashion Eds Club Award, Tokyo 1982, 1991, 1997, Mainichi Fashion Award, Tokyo 1986, 1994, Night of Stars Award Fashion Group, New York 1997, Arte e Moda Award, Pitti Imagine, Florence 1998, Int. Award Council of Fashion Designers of America 1999, Royal Designer for Industry, Master of Design Award, Fashion Group International. *Publication:* Talking to Myself. *Address:* Yohji Yamamoto Inc., 133 2-2-43 Higashi-Shinagawa, Shinagawa-ku, Tokyo 140-0002, Japan (office). *E-mail:* info@yohjiyamamoto.co.jp (office). *Website:* www.yohjiyamamoto.co.jp (office).

YAMAMOTO, Yuji, BA; Japanese politician; b. 11 May 1952; ed Waseda Univ.; began career as lawyer; mem. Kochi Prefectural Ass. 1985–90; mem. (LDP), House of Reps for Kochi 3 constituency 1990–, State Sec. for Home Affairs 1996, State Sec. for Justice 1999, 2000, Chair. House of Reps Cttee on Economy, Trade and Industry 2001, Cttee on Judicial Affairs 2002; Sr Vice-Minister of Finance 2003, Minister of State for Financial Services 2006–07; Acting Dir Judicial Affairs Div., Policy Research Council, LDP 1995, mem. LDP Gen. Council 1997–, Dir Infrastructure Div., Policy Research Council 1998, Exec. Deputy Sec.-Gen., LDP 2000–. *Address:* Liberal Democratic Party (Jiyu-Minshuto), 1-11-23, Nagata-cho, Chiyoda-ku, Tokyo 100-8910, Japan (office). *Telephone:* (3) 3581-6211 (office). *E-mail:* koho@ldp.jimin.or.jp (office). *Website:* www.jimin.jp/english/profile/members/114799.html (office).

YAMANAKA, Shinya, MD, PhD; Japanese medical scientist and academic; *Director, Center for iPS Cell Research and Application, Kyoto University;* b. 4 Sept. 1962, Higashiōsaka; ed Kobe Univ., Osaka City Univ. Grad. School; resident in orthopedic surgery, Nat. Osaka Hosp. 1987–89; postgraduate studies 1989–93; Post-doctoral Fellow, Gladstone Inst. for Cardiovascular Disease, San Francisco, USA 1993–95, Staff Research Investigator 1995–96, currently Sr Investigator and L.K. Whittier Foundation Investigator in Stem Cell Biology; Asst Prof., Osaka City Univ. Medical School 1996–99; Assoc. Prof., Nara Inst. of Science and Tech., Nara 1999–2003, Prof. 2003–05; Prof., Inst. for Frontier Medical Sciences, Kyoto Univ. 2004–10, Inst. for Integrated Cell-Material Sciences (iCeMS) 2007–12, Dir Centre for iPS Cell Research and Application (CiRA), iCeMS 2008–10, Dir Centre for iPS Cell Research and Application (CiRA) 2010–, Prof. 2012–; Prof. of Anatomy, Univ. of California, San Francisco; Pres. Int. Soc. for Stem Cell Research 2012–13; mem. Pontifical Acad. of Sciences 2013–; Fellow, NAS 2012; Honorable Emer. Prof., Hiroshima Univ. 2016; Medal of Honour with Purple Ribbon 2008, Bunka-kunsho (Order of Culture) 2012; Hon. DSc (Mount Sinai School of Medicine) 2010; Prize of the Japan Soc. for the Promotion of Science 2007, Asahi Award 2007, Inoue Prize for Science 2007, Special Prize for Science and Tech., Minister of Educ., Culture, Sports, Science and Tech. 2008, Shaw Prize (co-recipient) 2008, Robert Koch Award 2008, Gairdner International Award 2009, Gairdner Award 2009, Albert Lasker Basic Medical Research Award 2009, Kyoto Prize for Advanced Tech. (co-recipient) 2010, March of Dimes Prize 2010, The Imperial Prize, The Japan Acad. 2010, Balzan Prize 2010, Frontiers of Knowledge Award, BBVA Foundation 2010, Wolf Prize in Medicine 2011, McEwen Award for Innovation (co-recipient) 2011, King Faisal Int. Prize in Medicine (co-recipient) 2011, Millennium Tech. Prize (co-recipient) 2012, Nobel Prize in Physiology or Medicine (with Sir John Gurdon) 2012, Breakthrough Prize in Life Sciences (co-recipient) 2013, 150th Anniversary Alumni Excellence Awards, Univ. of California, San Francisco 2014. *Achievements include:* discovered how to make induced pluripotent stem cells (iPS cells) from ordinary skin cells. *Publications:* numerous articles in professional journals. *Address:* Center for iPS Cell Research and Application (CiRA), Kyoto University, 53 Kawahara-cho, Shogoin Yoshida, Sakyo-ku, Kyoto 606-8507, Japan (office). *Telephone:* (75) 366-7000 (office). *Fax:* (75) 366-7023 (office). *E-mail:* yamanaka-g@cira.kyoto-u.ac.jp (office). *Website:* www.cira.kyoto-u.ac.jp/e/research/yamanaka_master.html (office).

YAMANI, Sheikh Ahmed Zaki; Saudi Arabian government official and oil industry executive; b. 30 June 1930, Mecca; ed Cairo Univ., New York and Harvard Univs, USA; Saudi Arabian Govt Service; pvt. law practice; Legal Adviser to Council of Ministers 1958–60; mem. Council of Ministers 1960–86; Minister of State 1960–62; Minister of Petroleum and Mineral Resources 1962–86; Dir Arabian American Oil Co. 1962–86; Chair. General Petroleum and Mineral Org. (PETROMIN) 1963–86, Coll. of Petroleum and Minerals, Dhahran 1963–86, Saudi Arabian Fertilizer Co. (SAFCO) 1966–86; f. Centre for Global Energy Studies; Sec.-Gen. OAPEC 1968–69, Chair. 1974–75; mem. several int. law asscns; state decorations from many countries; Dr hc from univs in N and S America, Europe, Asia and Africa. *Publication:* Islamic Law and Contemporary Issues. *Address:* PO Box 14850, Jeddah 21434, Saudi Arabia.

YAMANI, Hashim bin Abdullah bin Hashim al-, PhD; Saudi Arabian politician; b. 1945; ed Harvard Univ., USA; Prof. and later Chair. of Physics Dept, King Fahd Univ. of Petroleum and Minerals; Vice-Pres. King Abdul Aziz City for Science; Minister of Industry and Electricity 1995–2003, Minister of Commerce and Industry 2003–08; Chair. Sabic.

YAMANI, Khaled Hussein al-; Yemeni politician and diplomatist; *Minister of Foreign Affairs;* b. 2 May 1960, Aden; m.; three s.; ed Univ. of Havana; Ed. of Pvt. Publications, Dept of Press and Information, Ministry of Foreign Affairs 1991–94, Expert Overlooking Yemeni African Relations, Office of Foreign Minister 1995–97, Expert Overlooking Yemeni American Relations, Asst and Pvt. Sec. 2003–05, Counsellor 2004, Rep. Ministry of Foreign Affairs, Supreme Technical Cttee of Human Rights 2004–05, Deputy Dir July–Sept. 2009, Minister Plenipotentiary 2009, Deputy Dir and Acting Dir 2011–12, Dir Jan.–June 2013, Amb. 2014; Political and Press Officer, Embassy of Yemen in Malaysia 1997–2000, USA 2000–03; Ed.-in-Chief, The Diplomat 2003–05; Deputy Coordinator, San'a Conference on Democracy, Human Rights and role of the Int. Criminal Court 2005; Deputy Chief of Mission, Embassy of Yemen in UK 2005–09; Chief Negotiator, Perm. Mission to UN, New York 2009–10, Deputy Perm. Rep. 2013–14, Perm. Rep. 2014, apptd Vice-Pres. UN Gen. Ass. 2015, Vice-Chair. Bureau of Least Developed Countries 2016–17; Minister of Foreign Affairs 2018–; mem. Yemeni negotiating team, Gulf Cooperation Council Secr. 2005, Joint Political Cttee, San'a Forum for Cooperation. *Address:* Ministry of Foreign Affairs, POB 1994, San'a, Yemen (office). *Telephone:* (1) 485500 (office). *Fax:* (1) 536926 (office). *E-mail:* media@mofa.gov.ye (office). *Website:* www.mofa.gov.ye (office).

YAMANISHI, Kenichiro; Japanese business executive; *Executive Corporate Adviser, Mitsubishi Electric Corporation;* b. 1951, Osaka Pref.; ed Kyoto Univ.; joined Mitsubishi Electric Corpn 1975, first served as a researcher in Applied Equipment Lab., Exec. Officer and Group Pres. of Corp. Total Productivity Man. and Environmental Programs 2006–08, Sr Exec. Officer and Group Pres. of Semiconductor & Devices 2008–10, Rep. Exec. Officer, Pres. and CEO Mitsubishi Electric Corpn 2010–14, Chair. 2014–18, Exec. Corporate Adviser 2018–; mem. Bd of Dirs Toyota Industries Corpn 2015–; Co-Chair. Japan-Turkey Econ. Cttee, Keidanren. *Address:* Mitsubishi Electric Corpn, Tokyo Bldg, 2-7-3, Marunouchi, Chiyoda-ku, Tokyo 100-8310, Japan (office). *Telephone:* (3) 3218-2111 (office). *E-mail:* info@mitsubishi.com (office). *Website:* global.mitsubishielectric.com (office); www.mitsubishi.com (office).

YAMANOUCHI, Takashi; Japanese automotive industry executive; b. 10 Jan. 1945; ed Keio Univ.; joined Toyo Kogyo Co. Ltd (renamed Mazda Motor Corpn) 1967, Gen. Man. Corp. Planning Div. 1996, Dir 1996–97, Man. Dir 1997–99, Sr Man. Dir 1999–2002, Sr Man. Exec. Officer of Corp. Liaison, Purchasing, Human Resources, Admin, Secr. and Global Auditing 2002–07, Dir and Exec. Vice-Pres. April–June 2007, Exec. Vice-Pres. and Rep. Dir June 2007–08, Rep. Dir, Pres. and CEO 2008–13, Chair. and Rep. Dir 2010–14 (retd); Order of the Aztec Eagle (Mexico) 2013. *Address:* c/o Mazda Motor Corporation, 3-1 Shinchi, Fuchu-cho, Aki-gun, Hiroshima 730-8670, Japan.

YAMASHITA, Ryuichi; Japanese automobile industry executive; ed Tohoku Univ.; joined Yamaha 1962, Sr Gen. Man. Automotive Engine operation 1983–2001, apptd Dir 1983, Exec. Vice-Pres. 2001, then Chair. Yamaha Motor Co. Ltd –2005, Dir and Corp. Adviser from 2005; Chair. Motorcycle Cttee, Japan Automobile Manufacturers Asscn, Inc. *Address:* c/o Yamaha Motor Co. Ltd, 2500 Shingai, Iwata, Shizuoka 438-8501, Japan. *E-mail:* info@yamaha-motor.co.jp.

YAMASHITA, Yasuhiro, MA; Japanese judo coach and judo player (retd) and academic; *Professor and Dean, School of Physical Education, Tokai University;* b. 1 June 1957, Yamato, Kumamoto; m. Midori Ono 1986; two s. one d.; ed Kyushu Gakuin High School, Tokai Univ. Sagami High School and Tokai Univ.; winner nine consecutive times, All Japan Judo Tournament; four-time World Judo Champion, +95kg, Paris 1979, +95kg, Maastricht 1981, Open, Maastricht 1981, +95kg, Moscow 1983; achieved unbroken record of 203 consecutive wins from 1977 till he retd in 1985; gold medal, Summer Olympic Games, Los Angeles 1984; Prof., Dept of Sports, Tokai Univ. 1986–, now Dean, School of Physical Educ., fmr Team Man. Univ. Judo Team; Man. Japanese Nat. Judo Team 1992–; currently works as an instructor or adviser for orgs including Int. Judo Fed. (Dir of Educ. 2003–), All Japan Judo Fed.; Chair. Solidarity of Int. Judo Educ.; has trained youth Judo teams in Israel and Palestine and local children at China-Japan Friendship Judo Hall est. in Tsingtao and Nanjing; mem. Laureus World Sports Acad.; Nat. Honour Prize (Japan, first amateur sportsman to achieve award) 1984, Foreign Minister's Commendation 2011. *Film:* compiled an instructional judo video with Russian Pres. Vladimir Putin (black belt). *Publications include:* Young Days with Black Belt, Enjoyable Judo, The Moment of Fight, Osoto-Gari, Judo with Fighting Spirits. *Leisure interests:* reading, playing with my kids, karaoke (with family), dining out. *Address:* 4-1-1 Kitakaname, Hitatsuka-shi, Kanagawa 259-1292 (office); Tokai University, 661-104 Higashi Koiso, Oiso-machi, Naka-gun, Kanagawa -ken, Japan (home). *Telephone:* (463) 581211 (ext. 3532) (office). *Fax:* (463) 502405 (office). *E-mail:* info@yamashitayasuhiro.com (office). *Website:* www.u-tokai.ac.jp/international/undergraduate/physical_education.html (office); www.yamashitayasuhiro.com.

YAMASSOUM, Nagoum, Dr rer. pol; Chadian politician and diplomatist; *President, COSUMAF;* b. 1 Jan. 1954, Danamadji; s. of Jean Yamassoum and Alice Titingone; m. Brigitte Boukar Belingar; two s.; ed Univ. of Bordeaux, Univ. of Paris XI, France; Pres. Constitutional Council –1999, 2014, fmr Chair.; Prime Minister 1999–2002; Minister of State, Minister of Foreign Affairs and African Integration 2003–05; apptd Chair. Hydrocarbons Company of Chad (Societe des Hydrocarbures du Tchad, SHT) 2007; Sec.-Gen. Mouvement Patriotique du Salut –2011; Head of African Union observation mission to presidential election in Benin 2011; Pres. COSUMAF 2017–; Nat. Order of Chad, Nat. Order of Taiwan. *Leisure interests:* tennis, soccer, gardening. *Address:* COSUMAF, BP 1724 Libreville Gabon (office); POB 4321, N'Djamena, Moursal, Chad (home). *Telephone:* 01-74-75-91 (office); 65-10-10-10 (home). *Fax:* 01-74-75-88 (office); 51-70-21 (home). *E-mail:* info@cosumaf.org (office); nagoumyamassoum@gmailcom; conseilconstitutioneltchad@gmail.com. *Website:* cosumaf.org (office).

YAMATAMI, Eriko, BA; Japanese politician and fmr journalist; b. 19 Sept. 1950; widowed; two s. one d.; ed Univ. of the Sacred Heart; began career as journalist 1976; worked as US-based correspondent for various Japanese media cos, including radio, magazines and newspapers; Ed.-in-Chief Sankei Living Shimbun (daily newspaper for female readers) 1985; mem. House of Reps (lower house of Parl.) 2000–03, House of Councillors (upper house of Parl.) 2004–; Parl. Sec. in Cabinet Office 2005; Special Adviser to Prime Minister Shinzo Abe 2006–07; Chair. Nat. Public Safety Comm., also Minister in charge of the Abduction Issue, of Ocean Policy and Territorial Issues, and of Building Nat. Resilience 2014–15; mem. Liberal Democratic Party. *Address:* House of Councillors, 1-7-1 Nagatacho, Chiyoda-ku, Tokyo 100-0014, Japan (office). *Telephone:* (3) 3581-3111 (office). *E-mail:* webmaster@sangiin.go.jp (office). *Website:* www.sangiin.go.jp (office).

YAMAUCHI, Yasuhito; Japanese automotive industry executive; joined Toyota 1968, Man. Dir, also Chair. Plant Production Environmental Sub-cttee, Overseas

Production Environmental Sub-Cttee 1999–2001, Sr Man. Dir 2001–03, Chair. Production Environment Cttee 2003; Pres. Aisin Seiki Co. 2005–09, apptd Vice-Chair. 2009; mem. Bd of Dirs Sintokogio Ltd.

YAMEEN ABDUL GAYOOM, Abdulla, BBA, MA; Maldivian politician and head of state; b. 21 May 1959, Malé; s. of Abdul Qayyoom Ibrahim; half brother of fmr Pres. Maumoon Abdul Gayoom; m. Fathimath Ibrahim; two s. one d.; ed Majeediyya School, American Univ. of Beirut, Lebanon, Claremont Graduate Univ., USA; began govt career as a Surveyor, Land Registrations Div. 1978; returned from studies in Lebanon 1982, served as Sec., Dept of Finance, then Research Officer, Research and Int. Orgs Div., Maldives Monetary Authority; returned after completing postgraduate studies abroad and held several positions in Ministry of Trade and Industries, including Foreign Trade Devt Officer, Under-Sec., Asst Dir, Deputy Dir, Dir, Dir-Gen. then Minister 1993; mem. Parl. 1993–2013; apptd Chair. State Electric Company Ltd (STELCO) 1997; also served as Chair. Island Aviation Services, State Trading Organisation (STO), Vice-Chair. Addu Development Authority; apptd Chair. Machchangolhi Ward of Male' 2004; Minister of Higher Educ., Employment and Social Security 2005–07, of Tourism and Civil Aviation Sept.–Nov. 2008; left Dhivehi Raiyyithunge Party—DRP 2007, Founder and Leader People's Alliance party 2008, joined forces with DRP reformists to form Progressive Party of Maldives 2011–; Pres. of Maldives 2013–18, also C-in-C Maldives Nat. Defence Force; Dr Kalam Puraskar for Excellence in Governance Award 2016, Asia HRD Lifetime Achievement Award 2017. *Address:* c/o Office of the President, Boduthakurufaanu Magu, Malé 20113, Maldives.

YAMEY, Basil Selig, CBE, BComm, FBA; British economist and academic; *Professor Emeritus of Economics, London School of Economics;* b. 4 May 1919, Cape Town, South Africa; s. of Solomon Yamey and Leah Yamey; m. 1st Helen Bloch 1948 (died 1980); one s. one d.; m. 2nd Demetra Georgakopoulou 1991; ed Tulbagh High School and Univ. of Cape Town; Prof. of Econs LSE 1960–84, Prof. Emer. 1984–; mem. Monopolies and Mergers Comm. 1966–78; Trustee Nat. Gallery, London 1974–81, Tate Gallery, London 1977–81, Inst. of Econ. Affairs 1987–91; Hon. Fellow LSE 1988. *Publications:* Economics of Resale Price Maintenance 1951, Economics of Underdeveloped Countries (with P. T. Bauer) 1956, Economics of Futures Trading (with B. A. Goss) 1976, Essays on the History of Accounting 1978, Art and Accounting 1989. *Address:* 27B Elsworthy Road, London, NW3 3BT, England. *Telephone:* (20) 7586-9344. *Fax:* (20) 7586-9344.

YAN, Bing; Chinese business executive; fmr Vice-Pres. and Gen. Man. of Sinopharm Foreign Trade, China Nat. Pharmaceutical Group Corpn (Sinopharm), fmr Pres., currently mem. Bd of Dirs. *Address:* Sinopharm, 20 Zhichun Road, Beijing 100088, People's Republic of China (office). *Telephone:* (10) 82287727 (office). *E-mail:* webmaster@sinopharm.com (office). *Website:* www.sinopharm.com (office).

YAN, Haiwang; Chinese politician; b. Sept. 1939, Zhengzhou City, Henan Prov.; ed Harbin Architectural Eng Inst.; joined CCP 1966; Dir Urban and Rural Construction Cttee, Gansu Prov. 1983–87; Vice-Gov. Gansu Prov. 1987–93, Gov. 1993–97; Deputy Sec. CCP Gansu Provincial Cttee 1988–93; Sec. CCP Gansu Provincial Cttee 1993–98; Deputy Gov. People's Bank of China 1998–2000; Deputy Sec. Financial Work Committee, CCP Cen. Cttee Work Cttee Depts 1998–2003; Vice-Chair. China Banking Regulatory Comm. 2003–05; Alt. mem. 14th CCP Cen. Cttee 1992–97, mem. 15th CCP Cen. Cttee 1997–2002, 16th CCP Cen. Cttee 2002–07, 10th CPPCC Cen. Cttee 2003–08.

YAN, Hao; Chinese business executive; *Chairman and CEO, Pacific Construction Group Company Limited;* b. 1986, Huai'an, Jiangsu Prov.; s. of Yan Jiehe; began career as Deputy Dir Gen., office of subsidiary co. of Pacific Construction Group Co. Ltd, promoted to Asst Gen. Man., Office Dir, Deputy Gen. Man., Gen. Man. and CEO, Chair. and CEO Pacific Construction Group Co. Ltd 2011–; Vice-Chair. China Private-owned Business Asscn; Exec. Vice-Chair. China Private Economy Research Soc.; Outstanding CEO 2011, Hurun Report's Outstanding Entrepreneur Successor 2013, amongst others. *Address:* Pacific Construction Group Co. Ltd, 1 Wutaishan, Nanjing 210029, People's Republic of China (office). *Telephone:* (25) 57911111 (office). *Fax:* (25) 57908000 (office). *E-mail:* cpcg@cpcg.com.cn (office). *Website:* www.cpcg.com.cn (office).

YAN, Jiehe; Chinese business executive; b. 1960, Huai'an, Jiangsu Prov.; taught Chinese language in middle school in Huai'an 1980s; took job as clerk at local cement factory, then apptd man.; expanded into construction materials business by taking over bankrupt state-owned collective; started construction co. in Huai'an 1992; launched his first pvt. business, Jiangsu Pacific Eng Ltd in 1995; Chair. and CEO Pacific Construction Group Co. Ltd (leading pvt. co. in building nat. expressways, urban construction and hydraulic projects) –2011; purchased ST Zongheng (Shanghai-listed machinery manufacturer based in Jiangsu Prov.) 2003; Chair. Pacific Architect Group; Chair. Huatuo CEO Forum. *Address:* Pacific Construction Group Co. Ltd, 1 Wutaishan, Nanjing 210029, People's Republic of China (office). *Telephone:* (25) 57911111 (office). *Fax:* (25) 57908000 (office). *E-mail:* cpcg@cpcg.com.cn (office). *Website:* www.cpcg.com.cn (office).

YAN, Zhiyong, BSc, MSc; Chinese engineer and business executive; *Chairman, Power Construction Corporation of China (PowerChina);* ed Coll. of Water Resource and Hydropower, Sichuan Univ., China Inst. of Water Resources and Hydropower Research; Chair. Power Construction Corpn of China (PowerChina) 2016–; mem. Nat. Energy Advisory Cttee. *Address:* Power Construction Corporation of China, No. 7 & 8 Building, Beijing Xiyuan Hotel, 1 Sanlihe Road, Haidian District, Beijing 100040, People's Republic of China (office). *Telephone:* (10) 58382266 (office); (10) 88358715 (office). *Fax:* (10) 58382888 (office). *E-mail:* infocenter@powerchin.com (office). *Website:* www.powerchina.cn (office); en .powerchina.cn (office).

YANAGIMACHI, Ryuzo, PhD; American/Japanese biologist and academic; *Professor Emeritus of Anatomy and Reproductive Biology, Institute for Biogenesis Research, John A. Burns School of Medicine, University of Hawaii-Manoa;* b. 27 Aug. 1928, Ebetsu, Hokkaido, Japan; s. of Kyuzo Yanagimachi and Hiroko Yanagimachi; ed Hokkaido Univ., Sapporo; mem. staff, Worcester Foundation for Experimental Biology, Shrewsbury, Mass 1960–64; returned to Japan 1964–66; Asst Prof., John A. Burns School of Medicine, Univ. of Hawaii-Manoa 1966–74,

Prof. of Anatomy and Reproductive Biology 1974–2005, Prof. Emer. 2005–, Founding Dir Inst. for Biogenesis Research 1999–2004; mem. NAS 2001–, mem. Editorial Bd Proceedings of the National Academy of Sciences; Marshall Medal, Soc. of Study of Fertility 1994, Int. Prize of Biology 1996, Distinguished Andrologist Award, American Soc. of Andrology 1998, Carl G. Hartman Award, Soc. of Study of Reproduction 1999, inducted into Hall of Honor, Nat. Inst. of Child Health and Human Devt 2003, Pioneer Award in Reproduction Research 2012, Recognition Award, Soc. of Reproductive Biologists and Technologists 2014. *Achievements include:* pioneering work on in vitro fertilization, assisted fertilization and animal cloning. *Publications include:* numerous articles in scientific journals on assisted fertilization, freeze-dried sperm tech. and cloning. *Address:* Institute for Biogenesis Research, John A. Burns School of Medicine, University of Hawaii-Manoa, 1960 East-West Road, Honolulu, HI 96822, USA (office). *Telephone:* (808) 956-8746 (office). *Fax:* (808) 956-7316 (office). *E-mail:* yana@hawaii .edu (office). *Website:* www.ibr.hawaii.edu (office).

YANAGISAWA, Hakuo; Japanese politician; b. 18 Aug. 1935, Fukuroi, Shizuoka; ed Tokyo Univ.; joined Ministry of Finance 1961; Consul in New York 1971–75; Sec. to Chief Cabinet Sec. 1978–79; mem. House of Reps for Shizuoka Pref. 3rd Dist (LDP) from 1980, Parl. Vice-Minister, Ministry of Foreign Affairs 1994–95, Chair. House of Reps Educ. Cttee 1995–96, Health and Welfare Cttee 1998, Minister of State, Dir-Gen., Nat. Land Agency 1998, Minister of State for Financial Reconstruction 1998, Minister of State and Chair. Financial Reconstruction Comm. 1998–99, 2000–01, Minister of State for Financial Services 2001–02, Minister of Health, Labour and Welfare 2006–07; Man. Chair. LDP Admin. Reform Task Force 1995–98, Chair. LDP Research Comm. on Tax System 2005–06. *Address:* Liberal Democratic Party (Jiyu-Minshuto), 1-11-23, Nagata-cho, Chiyoda-ku, Tokyo 100-8910, Japan (office). *Telephone:* (3) 3581-6211 (office). *E-mail:* koho@ldp.jimin.or.jp (office). *Website:* www.jimin.jp (office).

YANAI, Tadashi; Japanese retail executive; *Chairman, President and CEO, Fast Retailing Co. Ltd;* b. 7 Feb. 1949; s. of Hitoshi Yanai; m.; two c.; ed Waseda Univ.; joined Fast Retailing Co. Ltd (family retail business) 1972, Dir 1972, Sr Man. Dir 1973, Pres. and CEO 1984–, currently also Chair., also Chair., Pres. and CEO Uniqlo Co. Ltd (subsidiary), Chair. Uniqlo USA Inc. 2004–, Uniqlo France SAS 2005–, Uniqlo UK Ltd 2005–; Chair. Link Theory Holdings Co. Ltd 2004–, Cabin Co. Ltd 2006–, Gov Retailing Co. Ltd 2008–; Dir Softbank Corpn 2001–, Nippon Venture Capital Co. Ltd 2009–; Retailer of Year, Nat. Retailer Fed., USA 2010. *Publications:* One Win, Nine Losses 1991, Throw Away Your Success in a Day 2009. *Address:* Office of the Chairman, Fast Retailing Co. Ltd, 717-1 Sayama, Yamaguchi City, Yamaguchi 754-0894, Japan (office). *Website:* www.fastretailing .com (office).

YÁÑEZ-BARNUEVO, Juan Antonio, LLM; Spanish foundation director and fmr diplomatist; *Director-General, Women for Africa Foundation;* b. 15 Feb. 1942, Coria del Río, Seville; s. of Luis Yáñez-Barnuevo and Angeles García; m. Isabel Sampedro 1969; one s.; ed Univs of Seville and Madrid, Univ. of Cambridge, UK, School for Int. Civil Servants, Hague Acad. of Int. Law and Spanish Diplomatic School; Sec. of Embassy, Perm. Mission to UN, New York 1970–73, Deputy Head, Office of Int. Legal Affairs, Ministry of Foreign Affairs 1975–78, Deputy Perm. Rep. to Council of Europe, Strasbourg 1978–82; Dir of Int. Dept of Presidency of Govt (Foreign Policy Adviser to Prime Minister) 1982–91; Amb. and Perm. Rep. to UN, New York 1991–96, Rep. in Security Council 1993–94, Deputy Dir Diplomatic School 1996–98, Amb.-at-Large 1998–2004, Head of Spanish Del. to UN negotiations on Int. Criminal Court 1998–2004, Head of Legal Dept, Ministry of Foreign Affairs 2002–04, Amb. and Perm. Rep. to UN, New York 2004–10, Rep. in Security Council 2004, Chair. Sixth Cttee (Legal) of UN Gen. Ass. 2005–06, Vice-Pres. UN Gen. Ass. 2008–09, Co-Chair. consultations leading to adoption by UN Gen. Ass. Counter Terrorism Strategy 2006, Co-Chair. consultations leading to adoption of UN Gen. Ass. Resolution on UN system-wide coherence, including reform of UN gender architecture; Sec. of State for Foreign Affairs, Ministry of Foreign Affairs and Co-operation 2010–11; Dir-Gen. Women for Africa Foundation (Fundacion Mujeres por Africa) 2013–; mem. Int. Humanitarian Fact-finding Comm. 2002–06; mem. Perm. Court of Arbitration 2008–; head of Socialist Int. fact-finding mission to Western Sahara 2015; Grand Cross, Order of Civil Merit, Grand Cross, Order of Merit (Germany); Francisco Tomás y Valiente Prize (Seville) 1998, Jurist of the Year (Madrid Law School) 1999. *Publication:* La Justicia Penal Internacional: Una perspectiva iberoamericana 2001. *Leisure interests:* reading, music, nature. *Address:* Fundacion Mujeres por Africa, Paseo de la Castellana, 144, 28046 Madrid (office); Carretera de Húmera, 1 (Aravaca), 28023 Madrid, Spain (home). *Telephone:* (914) 570945 (office); (913) 078017 (home). *E-mail:* juan.yanezb@ mujeresporafrica.es (office); juanyanezb@hotmail com. *Website:* www .mujeresporafrica.es (office).

YANG, Chao, MBA; Chinese insurance industry executive; b. 1950; ed Shanghai Int. Studies Univ., Univ. of Middlesex, UK; served in various man. positions with People's Insurance Co. of China 1976–96, including Deputy Gen. Man. and Asst Gen. Man. Shanghai Br., Gen. Man. Shanghai Pudong Br.; Chair. and Pres. China Insurance (Holdings) Co., Europe 1996–2000, China Insurance (Holdings) Co. 2000–05, China Insurance HK (Holding) Co. 2000–05; Pres. China Life Insurance (Group) Co. Ltd 2005–11, Chair. China Life Insurance Co. Ltd 2005–11; currently Dir (Ind. and Non-Exec.) FOSUN; mem. Bd of Dirs Pacific Century Insurance Holdings, CITIC Int. Financial Holdings; CPPCC Nat. Cttee.

YANG, Chen Ning (Frank), (Yang Zhenning), MSc, PhD; American (b. Chinese) physicist and academic; *Albert Einstein Professor Emeritus of Physics, State University of New York at Stony Brook;* b. 1 Oct. 1922, Hefei, Anhui Prov.; s. of Ke Chuan Yang and Meng Loh Yang; m. 1st Chih Li Tu 1950 (died 2003); two s. one d.; m. 2nd Weng Fan 2004; ed Nat. Southwest Associated Univ., Kunming, Tsinghua Univ., Univ. of Chicago, USA; Research Student, Univ. of Chicago, USA 1946, Instructor 1948; joined Inst. for Advanced Study, Princeton, NJ 1949, Prof. 1955–66; naturalized US citizen 1964; Albert Einstein Prof. of Physics, State Univ. of NY at Stony Brook 1966–99, Prof. Emer. 1999–; Distinguished Prof.-at-Large, Chinese Univ. of Hong Kong 1986–; Prof., Tsinghua Univ., People's Repub. of China 1998–; Pres. Nat. Asscn of Chinese Americans 1977–80, Asscn of Asia Pacific Physical Socs 1989–94, Asia Pacific Center of Theoretical Physics 1996–; mem./Foreign mem. NAS, Royal Soc. (London), Chinese Acad. of Sciences, Russian Acad. of Sciences, Brazilian Acad. of Sciences, Polish Acad. of Sciences, Royal

Spanish Acad. of Science, Korean Acad. of Science and Tech., Venezuelan Acad. of Sciences, Pontifical Acad. of Sciences; Fellow, American Physical Soc., Academia Sinica (Taiwan); now lives in China, granted permanent residency 2005; 18 hon. degrees, including Dr hc (Princeton) 1958, (Moscow State Univ.) 1992, (Chinese University of Hong Kong) 1997, (State Univ. of NY, Stony Brook) 1999, (Baptist Univ., Hong Kong) 1999, (Chung-Cheng Univ., Taiwan) 2000, (Hong Kong Univ. of Science and Tech.) 2002, (Ecole Normale Superieure, Paris) 2003; Nobel Prize in Physics (shared with Tsung-dao Lee) 1957, Albert Einstein Commemorative Award 1957, Rumford Prize 1980, Nat. Medal of Science 1986, Benjamin Franklin Medal 1993, Bower Award 1994, N. Bogoliubov Prize 1996, Lars Onsager Prize 1999, King Faisal Int. Prize 2001, Yang Coll. at Stony Brook Univ. named in his honour 2010. *Publications:* numerous articles in scientific journals. *Address:* Department of Physics and Astronomy, State University of New York at Stony Brook, Stony Brook, NY 11794, USA (office). *Telephone:* (631) 632-8100 (office). *Fax:* (631) 632-8176 (office). *E-mail:* yang@insti.physics.sunysb.edu (office). *Website:* insti.physics.sunysb.edu/~yang (office); www.castu.tsinghua.edu.cn/cnyang.

YANG, Cheng-Zhi, BSc; Chinese petroleum engineer; b. 8 Aug. 1938, Henan; s. of Yang Xian-zun and Hou Yang; m. Li Yan-qin 1969; one s. one d.; ed Beijing Univ. of Petroleum; Asst Prof., Beijing Univ. of Petroleum 1961–75; Asst Prof., Vice-Dir Dept of Petroleum Eng, Sheng-li Coll. of Petroleum 1976–78; Prof., Sr Research Engineer and Dir of Research for Interface Chem., Research Inst. of Petroleum Exploration and Devt of Beijing 1979–; apptd Dir Jr Lab. for Colloid and Interface Science, Acad. Sinica and China Nat. Petroleum Co. 1990; Visiting Sr Research Engineer, Inst. Français du Pétrole 1979–80, 1985–87, 1989–90; mem. China Petroleum Soc., Soc. of Petroleum Engineers of USA; Hon. Prof., Da-qing Univ. of Petroleum 1988; Science-Tech. Award in Petroleum Eng 1991, 1996, World Lifetime Achievement Award, ABI, USA 1992 and other awards. *Publications:* Petroleum Reservoir Physics 1975, World Fine Chemical Engineering Handbook (jtly), Enhanced Oil Recovery Theory and Practice 1995, Improved Oil Recovery 1997, Enhanced Oil Recovery by Chemical Flooding 1999; more than 60 articles in professional journals. *Leisure interests:* collecting stamps and badges. *Address:* No. 1107, West-Beido Lodging House, Zhixing Road, Beijing 100083, People's Republic of China (home). *Telephone:* (10) 62397956 (home). *Fax:* (10) 62397956 (home).

YANG, Chin-tien (Timothy), BA; Taiwanese diplomatist and politician; b. 1 July 1942; ed Nat. Chengchi Univ., Univ. of Witwatersrand, SA; Officer, Dept of African Affairs, Ministry of Foreign Affairs (MFA) 1972–74; Third, later Second and First Sec., Embassy in Lesotho 1974–83; Sr Specialist, MFA 1986–88; Rep., Taipei Rep. Office, Ireland 1988–91; Dir-Gen. Taipei Econ. and Cultural Office, Houston, Tex., USA 1991–95; Dir-Gen., Dept of African Affairs, MFA 1995–99, Sec.-Gen., MFA 1999–2000; Rep., Taipei Econ. and Cultural Office, Australia 2000–06; positions at MFA 2006–07; Rep., Taipei Econ. and Trade Office, Indonesia 2007–09; Minister of Foreign Affairs 2009–12; Sec.-Gen., Office of the Pres. 2012–15.

YANG, Chuantang; Chinese government official; b. 1954, Yucheng County, Shandong Prov.; ed Shandong Normal Univ., CCP Cen. Cttee Cen. Party School, Chinese Acad. of Social Sciences; began career as worker, Shengli Petrochemical Complex, No. 2 Fertilizer Plant, Shandong Prov. 1975–78; Deputy Group Chief, Qilu Petrochemical Corpn, Ethylene Production Headquarters, Shandong Prov. 1978–81, Deputy Chief, Admin Office 1983–84, Deputy Sec. CCP Party Cttee 1984–87; Pres., Young Cadres Management Coll., Shandong Prov. 1987–92; Administrative Vice-Chair., Autonomous Region People's Govt, Tibet Autonomous Region 1993–96, 1998–2003, Chair. 2004–06; Acting Gov., Qinghai Prov. 2003–04, Gov. 2004; Vice-Chair., State Ethnic Affairs Comm. 2004–06; Minister of Transport 2013–16; alt. mem. 16th CCP Cen. Cttee 2002–07, mem. 17th CCP Cen. Cttee 2007–12, 18th CCP Cen. Cttee 2012–.

YANG, Deqing; Chinese army officer and politician; b. Sept. 1942, Yingcheng, Hubei Prov.; joined PLA 1963, CCP 1964; mem. Secr., Wuhan Mil. Dist, PLA Guangzhou Mil. Region 1973–77, Political Commissar PLA Armoured Force Regt 1977–80, Dir Political Dept, Armoured Force Regt 1982–85; Dir Political Dept, 54th Group Army of Ground Force 1985–89; Dir Political Dept and Political Commissar, Acad. of Mil. Economy 1989–91; Dir PLA Gen. Logistics Dept 1991–94, Sec., later Deputy Sec. CCP Party Cttee Comm. for Discipline Inspection 1994–99; Political Commissar, PLA Chengdu Mil. Region 1999–2005; Sec. CCP Party Cttee, Chengdu City, PLA Guangzhou Mil. Region 1999–2007; mem. Cen. Comm. for Discipline Inspection; Mayor Zhangjiakou City, Hebei Prov.; mem. 15th CCP Cen. Cttee 1997–2002, 16th CCP Cen. Cttee 2002–07.

YANG, Fudong; Chinese artist; b. 1971, Beijing; ed China Acad. of Fine Arts, Hangzhou; Shanghai-based multimedia artist, works include paintings, photography and film. *Films include:* An Estranged Paradise 2003, Seven Intellectuals in Bamboo Forest, Part 4 2008, Seven Intellectuals in Bamboo Forest, Part 5 2008. *Address:* c/o Marian Goodman Gallery, 24 West 57th Street, New York, NY 10019, USA.

YANG, Fujia, BSc; Chinese nuclear physicist and fmr university administrator; *Chancellor Emeritus, University of Nottingham;* b. June 1936, Shanghai; ed Fudan Univ.; Lecturer, Dept of Physics, Fudan Univ., later Prof. and Pres. Fudan Univ. 1993–99; Dir Shanghai Inst. of Nuclear Research 1987–2001; Chancellor, Univ. of Nottingham, UK 2001–12 (first Chinese academic to become Chancellor of a UK univ.), Chancellor Emer. 2013–; fmr Visiting Prof., Niels Bohr Inst., Copenhagen, Rutgers Univ., State Univ. of NY, Univ. of Tokyo; Chair. Shanghai Science and Tech. Union 1992–96, currently Hon. mem.; apptd Vice-Chair. Chinese Asscn for Science and Tech. 2001; Pres. Asscn of Univ. Presidents of China 1997–99; mem. Int. Asscn of Univ. Presidents, Asscn of Univ. Presidents of the Pacific Rim; Fellow, Chinese Acad. of Sciences; Dr hc (Soka Univ., Tokyo), (State Univ. of NY), (Univ. of Hong Kong), (Univ. of Nottingham), (Univ. of Connecticut). *Address:* Office of the Vice-Chancellor, University of Nottingham, University Park, Nottingham, NG7 2RD, England (office). *Telephone:* (115) 951-3001 (office). *Fax:* (115) 951-3005 (office).

YANG, Fuqing; Chinese computer scientist and academic; *Professor, Faculty of Information and Engineering Sciences, Peking University;* b. 6 Nov. 1932, Wuxi, Jiangsu Prov.; ed Tsinghua and Peking Univs; Prof., Dept of Computer Science and Tech., Peking Univ. 1983–, Dean 1983–99, apptd Dean Faculty of Information and Eng Sciences 1999 and Dir Nat. Eng Research Center for Software Eng Research 1997, Dir Computer Science and Tech. Dept 1983–99, currently Prof.; mem. Chinese Acad. of Sciences 1991–, Academic Degree Cttee of the State Council; Fellow, IEEE 2003–; mem. Communist Party of China (CPC); numerous awards and prizes including Special Prize for Advancement of Science and Tech., Electronics Industry Admin. 1996, First Class Prize of the Guang Hua Tech. Fund from the Nat. Defence Tech. Ministry 1996, Science and Tech. Progress Awards of He Liang and He Li Fund 1997, Pioneer of Software Engineering in China. *Publications:* Operating System, Compiler, The Fundamental Theory of Software Engineering, Software Engineering Environment, Software Production Industrialization Technology; more than 150 papers. *Address:* Department of Computer Science and Technology, Peking University, Beijing 100871, People's Republic of China (office). *Telephone:* (10) 62756233 (office). *E-mail:* yang@sei.pku.edu.cn. *Website:* www.sei.pku.edu.cn/en/yangfuqing.html (office).

YANG, Henry T. Y., BS, MS, PhD; American (b. Chinese) engineer and university administrator; *Chancellor, University of California, Santa Barbara;* b. 29 Nov. 1940, Chungking, China; m. Dilling Yang 1966; two d.; ed Nat. Taiwan Univ., West Virginia Univ., Cornell Univ.; Asst Prof., School Aeronautics and Astronautics, Purdue Univ. 1969, Assoc. Prof. 1972–76, Prof. 1976–88, Neil A. Armstrong Distinguished Prof. of Aeronautics and Astronautics 1988–94, Head, School of Aeronautics and Astronautics 1979–84, Dean of Eng and Dir, Computer Integrated Design, Mfg and Automation Center 1984–94; Chancellor and Prof., Dept of Mechanical Eng, Univ. of Calif., Santa Barbara 1994–; mem. Nat. Acad. of Eng 1991, Academia Sinica 1992; Fellow, American Inst. of Aeronautics and Astronautics 1985, American Soc. for Eng Educ. 1993, ASME 2008; has served on numerous bds and cttees including Defense Science Board, USAF Scientific Advisory Bd, Naval Research Advisory Cttee, NASA's Aeronautical Advisory Cttee, NSF Eng Advisory Cttee; Dr hc (Purdue Univ.) 1996, (Hong Kong Univ. of Science and Tech.) 2002, (Nat. Taiwan Univ.) 2004, (City Univ. Hong Kong) 2005, (Chinese Univ. of Hong Kong) 2008, (West Virginia Univ.) 2011, (Hong Kong Polytechnic Univ.) 2011; numerous awards, including USAF Meritorious Civilian Service Award 1989, Centennial Medal, American Soc. of Eng Educ. 1993, Benjamin Garver Lamme Award, American Soc. of Eng Educ. 1998, Structures, Structural Dynamics and Materials Award, AIAA 2008, Arthur M. Bueche Award, NAE 2016, 12 outstanding teaching awards, Purdue Univ. 1971–94, Hon. Distinguished Teaching Award, Univ. of Calif., Santa Barbara 2007. *Publications include:* Finite Element Structural Analysis (textbook); author or co-author of more than 180 articles for scientific journals. *Address:* Office of the Chancellor, 5221 Cheadle Hall, University of California, Santa Barbara, CA 93106-2030, USA (office). *Telephone:* (805) 893-2231 (office). *Fax:* (805) 893-8717 (office). *E-mail:* henry.yang@ucsb.edu (office). *Website:* www.chancellor.ucsb.edu (office).

YANG, Hua, BSc, MBA; Chinese oil industry executive; *Chairman, China National Offshore Oil Corporation (CNOOC);* b. 1961; ed China Univ. of Petroleum, Sloan School of Man., Massachusetts Inst. of Tech. (Sloan Fellow), USA; joined China Nat. Offshore Oil Corpn (CNOOC) Ltd 1982, served in several positions in CNOOC Research Centre, including Man. of Reservoir Eng Dept and Dir of Field Devt Dept 1982–92, Deputy Chief Geologist and Deputy Dir for the Overseas Devt Dept of CNOOC and Vice-Pres. CNOOC Overseas Oil and Natural Gas Ltd 1993–99, Sr Vice-Pres. CNOOC Ltd 1999–2005, Exec. Vice-Pres. 2005–06, Pres. CNOOC Southeast Asia Ltd (subsidiary of CNOOC) 2002–03, Pres. CNOOC International Ltd 2004–05, Chief Financial Officer CNOOC Ltd 2005–06, Asst Pres. 2006–10, Pres. 2009–10, Vice-Pres. and Party Leadership Group mem. May–Sept. 2010, Vice-Chair. and CEO CNOOC Ltd 2010–11, Pres. and Party Leadership Group mem. CNOOC 2011–15, Chair. and Party Leadership Group Sec. CNOOC April 2015–, Chair. CNOOC Ltd May 2015–, CEO June 2016–April 2017. *Address:* China National Offshore Oil Corpn, Box 4705, 25 Chao Yangmen North Street, Dongcheng District, Beijing 100010, People's Republic of China (office). *Telephone:* (10) 84521010 (office). *Fax:* (10) 64602600 (office). *E-mail:* info@cnooc.com.cn (office). *Website:* www.cnooc.com.cn (office).

YANG, Hyong-sop; North Korean politician; *Vice-President, Presidium of the Supreme People's Assembly;* b. 1 Oct. 1925, Hamhung; ed Kim Il Sung Univ.; Speaker, Supreme People's Ass. 1983, Chair. 1983–98, Assoc. mem. Politburo 1993–, Vice-Pres. Presidium of the Supreme People's Ass. 1998–; Vice-Chair. Peaceful Reunification of Fatherland Cttee 1984–; Chair. Korean Asscn of Social Sciences 1997–; Alt. mem. Political Bureau of Cen. Cttee of the Workers' Party; Head of Del. to China 2004, to S Africa 2005, to Venezuela 2005. *Address:* Presidium of the Supreme People's Assembly, Pyongyang, Democratic People's Republic of Korea (office).

YANG, Jerry, BS, MS; American computer industry executive; *Founding Partner, AME Cloud Ventures;* b. (Yan Chih-Yuan), 6 Nov. 1968, Taipei, Taiwan; m. Akiko Yamazaki; one c.; ed Stanford Univ.; moved to San Jose, Calif. at age 10 years; Co-Creator Yahoo! (internet navigational guide) 1994, Co-Founder, Yahoo! Inc. 1995, mem. Bd of Dirs 1995–2012, Chief Yahoo! 1995–2007, 2009–12, CEO 2007–09, mem. Bd of Dirs 1995–2012; Founding Partner, AME Cloud Ventures, Palo Alto, Calif. 2012–; mem. Bd of Dirs (non-exec.) Cisco Systems Inc. 2000–, Alibaba 2005–12, 2014–, Asian Pacific Fund; mem. Bd of Trustees, Stanford Univ. (Vice-Chair.); Board Observer, Lenovo; Co-Chair. (with wife) $1B Campaign for Undergraduate Educ., Stanford Univ. *Website:* www.amecloudventures.com.

YANG, Jian; Chinese automotive industry executive; *Vice-Chairman, Zhejiang Geely Holding (Group) Company Limited;* ed Zhejiang Radio and Television Univ.; joined Zhejiang Geely Holding (Group) Co. Ltd 1995, involved in several different job functions within the group, including Production Man., Quality Control, Gen. Admin, Research and Devt, and Project Man., later First Vice-Pres. Zhejiang Geely Holding Group Co. Ltd and Head of Zhejiang Geely Automobile Research Inst. Ltd, responsible for overall admin of Zhejiang Geely JV, Exec. Dir 2005–, Vice-Chair. Geely Automobile Holdings Ltd 2008–, fmr Pres. Zhejiang Geely Holding (Group) Co. Ltd, currently Vice-Chair. *Address:* Zhejiang Geely Holding Group, 1760 Jiangling Road, Hangzhou 310051, People's Republic of China (office). *Telephone:* (571) 28001111 (office). *Website:* www.zgh.com (home).

YANG, Jie, BEng, DBA; Chinese engineer and business executive; *Executive Director, Chairman and CEO, China Telecommunications Corporation;* b. July 1962, Shanxi Prov.; ed Beijing Univ. of Posts and Telecommunications, Norwegian School of Man., ESC Rennes School of Business, France; Gen. Man., Business

Dept, Northern Telecom 1991–95; Vice-Pres. Beijing Research Inst., China Telecom 1996–99; Deputy Dir Gen. Shanxi Posts and Telecommunications Admin 1999–2000, Gen. Man. Shanxi Telecommunications Corpn 2000–04, Exec. Vice-Pres., Pres. and COO China Telecommunications Corpn from 2004, Vice-Pres. and Pres. –2015, Exec. Dir, Chair. and CEO 2015–. *Address:* China Telecommunications Corporation, 31 Jinrong Street, Xicheng District, Beijing 100032, People's Republic of China (office). *Telephone:* (10) 6602-7217 (office). *Fax:* (10) 6602-1147 (office). *E-mail:* info@chinatelecom.com.cn (office). *Website:* www.chinatelecom .com.cn (office); www.chinatelecom-h.com/en/global/home.php (office).

YANG, Jiechi, PhD; Chinese diplomatist and government official; *Member, State Council;* b. May 1950, Shanghai; m.; one d.; ed Univ. of Bath, London School of Econs, UK, Nanjing Univ.; staff mem., then Second Sec. Trans. and Interpretation Dept, Ministry of Foreign Affairs 1975–84, Counsellor, then Div. Dir 1987–93, Counsellor, later Div. Dir, later Dir-Gen. North American and Oceania Affairs Dept 1990–93, Asst Minister, Ministry of Foreign Affairs 1995–98, Vice-Minister 1998–2000; Second Sec., later First Sec., later Counsellor, Chinese Embassy, Washington, DC, USA 1983–87, Minister and Deputy Chief of Mission 1993–95, Amb. to USA 2001–05; Vice-Minister of Foreign Affairs in charge of region of N America and Oceania and Latin America, foreign-related affairs involving Hong Kong, Macao and Taiwan, work of translation and interpretation 2005–07, Minister of Foreign Affairs 2007–13; State Councillor 2013–; Alt. mem. 16th CCP Cen. Cttee 2002–07, mem. 17th CCP Cen. Cttee 2007–12, 18th CCP Cen. Cttee 2012–17, 19th CCP Cen. Cttee 2017–, Leading Small Group (LSG) for Finance and Economy, CCP 2017–, LSG for Taiwan Affairs, CCP 2017–, Deputy Dir LSG for Foreign Affairs Work, CCP 2017–, mem. LSG for Hong Kong and Macao Work, CCP 2017–; Hilal-i-Pakistan (Crescent of Pakistan) 2013; Dr hc (Geneva School of Diplomacy) 2009. *Leisure interests:* playing table tennis, listening to choral music, writing poems. *Address:* State Council, Beijing, People's Republic of China (office).

YANG, Jing; Chinese politician; b. Dec. 1953, Jungar Banner, Inner Mongolia; ed Inner Mongolia Univ.; began career as worker at agricultural equipment factory, Jungar Banner, Inner Mongolia Autonomous Region 1970–74; joined CCP 1976; Sec., Communist Youth League of China Regional Cttee, Ih Ju League 1982–97; Magistrate, County (Dist) People's Court, Inner Mongolia Autonomous Region 1985–88; Deputy Dir, Statistics Bureau, Inner Mongolia Autonomous Region 1991–92; Dir, Tourism Bureau, Inner Mongolia Autonomous Region 1992–93; Deputy Sec., Inner Mongolia Autonomous Region CCP Cttee 2003–08, Acting Chair. Inner Mongolia Regional Govt 2003–04, Chair. 2004–08; Minister of State Ethnic Affairs Comm. 2008–13; Sec.-Gen., State Council (first from ethnic minority background) 2013–18; Pres. Chinese Acad. of Governance 2013–; alt. mem. 16th CCP Cen. Cttee 2002–07, mem. 17th CCP Cen. Cttee 2007–12, 18th CCP Cen. Cttee 2012–17, also mem. 18th CCP Cen. Cttee Politburo Secr. 2012–17; investigated for severe disciplinary violations and dismissed from posts Feb. 2018.

YANG, Jingyu; Chinese politician; b. Sept. 1936, Xingyang, He'nan Prov.; ed Beijing Foreign Trade Inst.; joined CCP 1954, Deputy Dir Econ. Law Office, Dir Research Office, Deputy Sec.-Gen., Deputy Dir Comm. of Legis. Affairs, Standing Cttee of 5–7th NPC 1981–91; Dir Bureau of Legis. Affairs, State Council 1991–98, Deputy Sec.-Gen. 1995–98, Minister, Office of Legis. Affairs 1998–2002; Del. to 14–16th CCP Nat. Congress 1992–2007; Chair. Law Cttee, 10th NPC 2003–08, Hon. Expert, Standing Cttee of 11th NPC 2008; Visiting Prof., Renmin Univ. of China, China Univ. of Int. Business and Econs, Nat. Admin School. *Publications:* Rational Explorations in the Process of Rule of Law 2002, My Meditations 2006, Reflections on the Practice of Rule of Law 2008. *Address:* National People's Congress, 23, Xijiaominxiang, Xicheng Qu, Beijing 100805, People's Republic of China (office).

YANG, Kaisheng, DEcon; Chinese banking executive; *Deputy Chairman, ICBC Credit Suisse Asset Management Limited;* b. Nov. 1949, Beijing; ed Beijing Coll. of Chemical Tech., Wuhan Univ.; joined Industrial & Commercial Bank of China (ICBC) 1985, Head of Planning and Information Dept 1985–90, Gen. Man. Shenzhen City Br. 1990–95, Vice-Gov. ICBC 1995–99, Pres. 2005–13, also Vice-Chair. and Exec. Dir and Deputy ICBC Party Sec. and Chair. ICBC Credit Suisse Asset Man. Co. Ltd 2005–2013, Deputy Chair. and Dir (non-Exec.) 2014–; Pres. China Huarong Asset Man. Corpn 1999; Dir (non-exec.) and Deputy Chair. Standard Bank Group (South Africa) 2008–14; Adjunct Prof., Wuhan Univ.; Deputy Dir 16th Cttee, China Int. Econ. and Trade Arbitration Comm., consultant to 17th Cttee. *Address:* ICBC Credit Suisse Asset Management Ltd, 8/F Bank of Beijing Building, 17th Floor, Financial Street, Xicheng Qu, Beijing 100140, People's Republic of China.

YANG, Lan, BA, MA; Chinese journalist, broadcaster and media executive; *Chairperson, Sun Media Group;* b. 31 March 1968, Beijing; m. 1st Yibin Zhang (divorced); 2nd m. Bruno Wu Zheng 1995; two c.; ed Beijing Foreign Studies Univ., Columbia Univ., USA; Presenter, Zheng Da variety show, China Cen. TV Station 1990–94; Producer and Presenter, Chinese Channel Phoenix Satellite TV, Hong Kong 1997–99; Co-founder and Chair. Sun Media Investment Holdings Ltd (Sun Media Group) 1998–; Founder and Chair. Sun Cultural Foundation, Hong Kong 2005; creator Her Village website; apptd image Amb. for Beijing 2008 Olympics bid; Global Amb. for Special Olympics Movt; first UNICEF Ambassador in Amb.; Co-Chair. Lincoln Center China Advisory Council; mem. 10th CPPCC Nat. Cttee 2003–; mem. Columbia Univ. Int. Advisory Council 2005–; Golden Microphone Winner 1994, Chinese Women of the Year Award, Top Ten Women Entrepreneurs Award, 'She Made It' Award, The Paley Center for Media, Global Leadership Award, SIPA of Columbia Univ., Nat. Philanthropy Award, Women's Achievement Award in China. *Address:* Sun Media Investment Holdings, No. 387 Yong Jia Road, Shanghai 200031, People's Republic of China (office). *Telephone:* (21) 68419980 (office). *Website:* www.chinasunmedia.com (office).

YANG, Le, (Lo Yang); Chinese mathematician; b. Nov. 1939, Nantong, Jiangsu Prov.; m. Qieyuan Huang; two d.; ed Peking Univ. and Inst. of Math., Chinese Acad. of Sciences; Pres. Acad. of Math. and System Sciences, Chinese Acad. of Sciences 1998–; mem. 4th Presidium of Depts, Chinese Acad. of Sciences 2000–; Research Fellow and Dir Inst. of Math., Chinese Acad. of Sciences; Fellow, Chinese Acad. of Sciences; invited to deliver lectures in 60 univs abroad and to speak at over 20 int. confs; Nat. Natural Science Prize, Hua Luogeng Math. Prize, Tan Kah Kee Prize, Ho Leung Ho Lee Math. Prize. *Publication:* Value Distribution Theory 1993.

Address: Institute of Mathematics, Chinese Academy of Sciences, 55 Zhongguan-cun, Haidian District, Beijing, People's Republic of China (office). *Telephone:* (10) 62541848 (office). *Fax:* (10) 62568356 (home). *Website:* www.mcm.ac.cn (office).

YANG, Maj.-Gen. Liwei; Chinese astronaut; b. 21 June 1965, Suizhong Co., Liaoning Prov.; m.; one s.; joined PLA 1983, entered No. 8 Aviation Coll. of PLA, became fighter pilot 1987; selected to fly Project 921 (later Shenzhou) spacecraft 1988, in training Astronaut Training Base, Beijing 1988–93; became first Chinese citizen launched aboard a Chinese spacecraft (Shenzhou-5) Oct. 2003; Deputy Dir China Manned Space Eng Office 2010–18; rank of Col 2003, Maj.-Gen. 2008; Alt. mem. 17th CCP Cen. Cttee 2007–12; Space Hero 2003; Dr hc (Chinese Univ. of Hong Kong) 2004; Arthur Chen's Aviation Achievement Honor 2005, UNESCO Medal on Space Science 2017.

YANG, Marjorie Mun-tak, BS, MBA; Hong Kong business executive; *Chairman and CEO, Esquel Group;* b. 1952, d. of Yang Yuan-loong; m. Dickson Poon (divorced); one d.; ed Baldwin School, Bryn Mawr, Pa, Massachusetts Inst. of Tech., Harvard Business School, USA; Assoc. in Corp. Finance, Mergers and Acquisitions, First Boston Corpn, New York 1976–77; Chair. YTT Tourism Advisor Ltd, Hong Kong 1978–87; helped her father to found Esquel Group in 1978, Chair. and CEO 1995–; mem. Bd of Dirs of Assocs, Harvard Business School 1997–; mem. Bd of Dirs Wuxi Int. Man. Services Pte Ltd 1997–, Gillette Co. 1998–, RandD Corpn Ltd, Hong Kong Univ. of Science and Tech. 2000–, Pacific Century Regional Devts 2000–, BlueDot Capital Pte Ltd 2000–, Clarke Quay Ltd 2001–, China Exploration and Research Soc. 2000–; business adviser to Chair. Sembcorp Industries Ltd; Council Chair. Hong Kong Polytechnic Univ.; Chair. HK-US Business Council, Quality Migrant Program; Yang Yuan-Loong Educ. Fund, Suzhou, People's Repub. of China 1995–; mem. MIT Corpn; Vice-Pres. and Exec. Dir Women Entrepreneur Asscn 1995–; mem. Govt's Strategic Devt Comm.; mem. Standing Cttee CPPCC, Xinjian Prov. 1998, Foshan, Guangdong Prov. 1998, mem. Cttee CPPCC, Gaoming, Guangdong Prov. 1998; mem. Hong Kong Exec. Council 2009–; apptd by Gov. of Hong Kong as Immigration Tribunal Adjudicator 1982–88; mem. Asia Advisory Bd of MIT/China Int. Man. Educ. Project, Dean's Council of Advisors, Sloan School of Man., MIT; Hon. Pres. Hong Kong Fed. of Women 1994–; Hon. Citizen of Foshan, Guangdong Prov. 1995, of Turpan, Xinjiang Prov. 1996; Hon. Darjah Setia Pangkuan Negeri, Penang State, Malaysia 1996; Hon. Chargé d'affaires, China Nat. Table Tennis Team 1997–; Commdr of the Star and Key of the Indian Ocean (Mauritius) 1997; Alumnae Award, Baldwin School, Bryn Mawr, Pennsylvania, USA 1996, Gold Bauhinia Star 2013. *Address:* Esquel Enterprises Limited, 12/F, Harbour Centre, 25 Harbour Road, Wanchai, Hong Kong Special Administrative Region, People's Republic of China (office). *Telephone:* 28118077 (office). *Fax:* 29606988 (office). *E-mail:* questions@esquel.com (office). *Website:* www.esquel.com (office).

YANG, Mianmian; Chinese business executive; b. 1945; ed Shandong Industrial Inst.; joined Qingdao Refrigerator General Factory 1984, co-f. Haier Electronics Group Co., Ltd (Haier Group), Exec. Pres. –2000, Pres. 2000–05, Exec. Dir and Chair. 2005–06, Pres. 2006–13 (resgnd), Sr Adviser 2013–, Deputy Dir Techno-logical Centre, also Chair. Qingdao Haier Co., Ltd 2001–13; Vice-Pres. China Asscn of Women Entrepreneurs. *Address:* Haier Group Company, No. 1 Haier Road, Hi-tech Zone, Qingdao 266101, People's Republic of China (office). *Website:* www.haier.com (office).

YANG, Mingsheng, MA; Chinese economist and banking executive; *Chairman and Executive Director, China Life Insurance (Group) Company;* b. 1955; ed Nankai Univ.; joined Agricultural Bank of China 1980, Deputy Gen. Man., Shenyang Br. 1987–90, Gen. Man., Tianjin Br. 1990–97, Exec. Vice-Pres. 1997–2003, Pres. and CEO 2003–07; Vice-Chair. China Insurance Regulatory Comm. 2007–12; Chair. and Exec. Dir China Life Insurance (Group) Co. 2012–. *Address:* China Life Insurance Co. Ltd, China Life Centre (22–28 Floor), 17 Financial Street, Xicheng District, Beijing, 100140, People's Republic of China (office). *Telephone:* (10) 85659999 (office). *Fax:* (10) 85252232 (office). *E-mail:* info@ chinalife.com.cn (office). *Website:* www.chinalife.com.cn/publish/yw/index.html (office).

YANG, Mu, BA, DipMus, PhD; Chinese ethnomusicologist; *Senior Lecturer, School of Humanities and Languages, University of New South Wales;* b. 16 Aug. 1949, Fuzhou; ed Central Conservatory of Music, Beijing, Univ. of Queensland, Australia; violinist, composer, conductor 1971–78; Music Editor and Programme Producer, Nat. Broadcasting Service, Beijing 1983–85; Sessional Lecturer, Project Dir, Research Fellow in Ethnomusicology, Monash Univ., Melbourne 1990–95; Visiting Fellow, ANU 1995–98; Research Fellow, Northern Territory Univ. 1999–2002; currently Sr Lecturer, Univ. of New South Wales; mem. Society for Ethnomusicology; Int. Council of Traditional Music; Musicological Society of Australia; Asscn for Chinese Music Research, USA; Jaap Kunst Prize, Society for Ethnomusicology, USA 1998. *Publications include:* Chinese Musical Instruments: An Introduction, 1993; Articles in Music Research (Beijing), Musicology Australia, Ethnomusicology, International Journal of Music Education, Yearbook for Trad-itional Music, Asian Music, Journal of the Central Conservatory of Music (Beijing). *Address:* School of Humanities and Languages, UNSW, Sydney, NSW 2052, Australia (office). *Telephone:* (4) 3440-3479 (office). *E-mail:* yang.mu@unsw.edu.au (office). *Website:* www.hal.arts.unsw.edu.au (office).

YANG, Pan-chyr, MD, PhD; Taiwanese physician, academic and university administrator; *Distinguished Professor and Chair professor, National Taiwan University;* ed Nat. Taiwan Univ.; Attending Physician, King Fahad Hosp., Hofuf, Saudi Arabia 1984–86; Attending Physician, Dept of Internal Medicine, Nat. Taiwan Univ. Hosp. (NTUH) 1986–, Prof., Dept of Internal Medicine, Coll. of Medicine, Nat. Taiwan Univ. 1993–, Chair. Dept of Internal Medicine, NTUH 1998–2004, Jt Appointment, Inst. of Biomedical Sciences, Academia Sinica 1999–, Assoc. Dean for Academic Affairs, Coll. of Medicine, Nat. Taiwan Univ. 2001–07, Vice-Supt, NTUH 2004–07, Dir NTUH Nat. Clinical Trial and Research Centre 2005–07, Distinguished Prof. and Chair Prof., Nat. Taiwan Univ. 2006–, Dean, Coll. of Medicine 2007–13, Supt, Nat. Taiwan Univ. Cancer Centre 2011–, Pres. Nat. Taiwan Univ. 2013–17, currently Distinguished Prof. and Chair Prof.; Dir Advisory Office, Ministry of Educ. 2002–05, mem. Cttee on Medical Science Educ. 2008–09, Chair. and mem. Perm. Cttee, Cttee on Medical Science Educ. 2012–; Adjunct Investigator, Nat. Health Research Inst. 2006–; Dir and Co-Prin.

Investigator, Nat. Research Program for Biopharmaceuticals 2011–; Ed.-in-Chief MicroRNA 2011–, Lung Cancer: Targets and Therapy 2012–; Academic Ed. PLoS One 2010–; mem. Editorial Bd Journal of the Formosan Medical Association 2005–10, Carcinogenesis 2007–, American Journal of Respiratory Cell Molecular Biology 2007–, The International Journal of Tuberculosis and Lung Disease 2007–, Journal of Clinical Oncology 2008–, European Respiratory Journal 2012–, Journal of Thoracic Oncology 2012–; Academician, Academia Sinica 2006, Acad. of Sciences for the Developing World 2008; Ten Outstanding Youth Award 1993, Distinguished Clinical Teacher Award, NTUCMAF 1993, 1997, Outstanding Research Award, Nat. Science Council 1994–95, 1996–97, 1998–99, The 7th Annual Wang Ming-Ning Award 1997, Distinguished Teacher Award, Nat. Taiwan Univ. 1999, 2012, Outstanding Scholar Award, Foundation for the Advancement of Outstanding Scholarship 2001–06, Academic Award, Ministry of Educ. 2002, 10th TECH Tech. Award 2003, Nat. Chair Prof., Ministry of Educ. 2007–09. *Publications:* numerous papers in professional journals. *Address:* National Taiwan University, 1 Roosevelt Road, Section 4, Taipei 106, Taiwan (office). *Telephone:* (2) 3366-2000 (office). *E-mail:* pcyang@ntu.edu.tw (office). *Website:* www.ntu.edu.tw (office).

YANG, Peidong, BA, PhD; American (b. Chinese) chemist and academic; *Professor of Chemistry, University of California, Berkeley;* b. 1971, Suzhou; m. Mei Wang; one d.; ed Univ. of Science and Tech. of China (USTC), Hefei, Harvard Univ., USA; Postdoctoral Fellow, Univ. of Calif., Santa Barbara 1997–99; joined Chem. Dept, Univ. of Calif., Berkeley 1999, Chevron Texaco Asst Prof. 2003–04, Assoc. Prof. 2004, now Prof. of Chemistry and S.K. and Angela Chan Distinguished Prof. of Energy; Co-Founder Nanosys Inc.; Assoc. Ed. Journal of the American Chemical Soc.; mem. ACS (Chair., Nanoscience Div. 2003–), American Physical Soc., Materials Research Soc., American Acad. of Arts and Sciences 2012; known for work in nanotechnology; USTC Guo Moruo Prize 1993, Camille and Henry Dreyfus New Faculty Award 1999, 3M Untenured Faculty Award 2000, Research Innovation Award 2001, NSF Career Award 2001, Hellman Family Faculty Award 2001, ACS ExxonMobil Solid State Chem. Award 2001, Beckman Young Investigator Award 2002, Camille Dreyfus Teacher-Scholar Award 2004, Materials Research Soc. Outstanding Young Investigator Award 2004, ACS Pure Chem. Award 2005, NSF Waterman Award 2007, Scientific American 50 Award 2008. *Address:* Department of Chemistry, University of California, Berkeley, CA 94720-1460, USA (office). *Telephone:* (510) 643-1545 (office). *Fax:* (510) 642-7301 (office). *E-mail:* p_yang@berkeley.edu (office). *Website:* www.cchem.berkeley.edu (office).

YANG, Philémon Yunji; Cameroonian lawyer, politician and fmr diplomatist; b. 14 June 1947, Jiketum-Oku, NW Prov.; ed Univ. of Yaoundé; began career as Prosecutor, Court of Appeal, Buea 1975; Vice-Minister of Territorial Admin 1975–78, Minister of Mines and Power, Livestock and Animal Industries 1978–80, Minister of Mines and Power 1980–84; Amb. to Canada 1984–95, High Commr to Canada 1995–2004; Asst Sec.-Gen. at the Presidency 2004–09; Prime Minister 2009–19; mem. Rassemblement démocratique du peuple camerounais. *Address:* c/o Office of the Prime Minister, Yaoundé, Cameroon (office).

YANG, Sung-chul, BA, MA, PhD; South Korean academic, politician and diplomatist; *Distinguished Professor, Korea University;* b. 20 Nov. 1939; m. Daisy Lee Yang; one s. one d.; ed Seoul Nat. Univ., Univ. of Hawaii and Univ. of Kentucky, USA; served in Korean Army 1960–62; taught at Eastern Kentucky Univ. and Univ. of Kentucky Fort Knox Center, USA 1970–75, Prof. of Political Science, Lexington 1978; Visiting Prof., Northwestern Univ., Pembroke State Univ., Indiana Univ., USA and Seoul Nat. Univ.; taught at Grad. Inst. of Peace Studies (GIP), Kyung Hee Univ., Seoul 1986, Dean of Academic Affairs at GIP 1987–94; mem. Korean Nat. Ass. 1996–2000, Vice-Chair. Unification and Foreign Affairs Cttee; Amb. to USA 2000–03; currently Distinguished Prof., Korea Univ.; Sec.-Gen. Asscn of Korean Political Scientists in N America; Pres. Korean Asscn of International Studies; mem. Advisory Cttee, Ministry of Foreign Affairs, Ministry of Nat. Defence, Nat. Unification Bd; fmr Chair. Advisory Cttee Kim Dae-jung Peace Foundation; Presidential Award 1964, Distinguished Service to Korean Community in Kentucky Award 2001, inducted into Hall of Distinguished Alumni, Univ. of Kentucky 2010. *Publications include:* North and South Korean Political Systems: A Comparative Analysis, Polemics and Foibles: Fragments on Korean Politics, Society and Beyond, numerous articles and essays. *Address:* Korea University, Anam-dong Seongbuk-gu, Seoul 136-70, Republic of Korea (office). *Telephone:* (2) 3290-1152 (office). *Website:* www.korea.edu (office).

YANG, Tae-jin, BA; South Korean business executive; *Co-CEO and Representative Director, Trade Division, Hanwha Corporation;* ed Seoul Nat. Univ., Grad. School of Business Admin, Yonsei Univ.; joined Korea Explosives 1971, Dir in charge of Business, Golden Bell Trading Inc. 1994–97, Man. Dir Hanwha Japan 1997–2002, Officer in charge of Hanwha Corpn/Trade Div. 2002–04, Rep. Dir Hanwha Corpn/Trade Div. 2004–10, Co-CEO and Rep. Dir Trade Div., Hanwha Corpn 2010–. *Address:* Hanwha Corporation, Hanwha Building, 1 Changgyo-dong, Chung-ku, Seoul 100-797, Republic of Korea (office). *Telephone:* (2) 729-2700 (office); (2) 729-1114 (office). *Fax:* (2) 729-1762 (office). *E-mail:* hanwhacorp@hanwha.co.kr (office). *Website:* english.hanwhacorp.co.kr (office).

YANG, Hon. Sir Ti Liang, Kt, LLB, FCIA; Chinese judge (retd); b. 30 June 1929, Shanghai; s. of Shao-nan Yang and Elsie Chun; m. Eileen Barbara Tam 1954 (died 2006); two s.; ed The Comparative Law School of China, Soochow Univ., Shanghai, Univ. Coll. London, UK; called to Bar (with Hons), Gray's Inn 1954; Magistrate, Hong Kong 1956, Sr Magistrate 1963, Dist Judge, Dist Court 1968, Judge of High Court 1975, Justice of Appeal 1980, Vice-Pres. Court of Appeal 1987, Chief Justice of Hong Kong 1988–96; mem. Exec. Council, Hong Kong Special Admin. Region 1997–2002; Pres. of Court of Appeal of Negara Brunei Darussalam 1988–92; Rockefeller Fellow, London Univ. 1963–64; Chair. Kowloon Disturbances Claims Assessment Bd 1966, Compensation Bd 1967, Comm. of Inquiry into the Rainstorm Disasters 1972, into Lelung Wing-sang Case 1976, into McLennan Case 1980; mem. Law Reform Comm. (Chair. Sub-Cttee on law relating to homosexuality 1980) 1980–96; Chair. Chief Justice Working Party on Voir Dire Procedures and Judges' Rules 1979, Univ. and Polytechnic Grants Cttee 1981–84, Hong Kong Univ. Council 1987–2001; Chair. ICAC Complaints Cttee 1999–2002; apptd Chair. Hong Kong Red Cross 1998, now Patron; Pro-Chancellor, Hong Kong Univ. 1994–2001, Life Mem. of the Court 2001–; mem. Advisory Cttee, Chinese Univ. of Hong Kong Law School 2009–; Patron The Soc. for the Rehabilitation of Offenders, Hong Kong; Vice-Patron Hong Kong Scouts Asscn; Hon. Prof., Open Univ. of Hong Kong 2006, Chinese Univ. of Hong Kong; Order of Chivalry (First Class), SPMB, Negara Brunei Darus-salam 1990; Hon. LLD (Chinese Univ. of Hong Kong) 1984, (Hong Kong Polytechnic) 1992; Hon. DLitt (Hong Kong Univ.) 1991; Grand Bauhinia Medal 1999. *Publications:* (trans.) General Yue Fei (by Qian Cai) 1995, (trans.) Peach Blossom Fan (novel by Gu Shifân 1948) 1998, (trans.) Officialdom Unmasked (novel by Li Boyuan) 2001. *Leisure interests:* philately, reading, walking, oriental ceramics, travelling, music. *Address:* GPO Box 1123, Central, Hong Kong Special Administrative Region, People's Republic of China (office). *Telephone:* (852) 91373067 (office). *Fax:* (852) 28498099 (home).

YANG, Xiaowei, BEng, MEng; Chinese engineer and business executive; *Executive Director, President and Chief Operating Officer, China Telecommunications Corporation;* b. 1963; ed Chongqing Univ.; served as Asst to Dir Gen. and Deputy Dir Gen. Chongqing Telecommunications Bureau, as Deputy Dir Gen. Chongqing Telecommunications Admin Bureau and as Dir Gen. of Chongqing Municipal Communication Admin Bureau; served as Gen. Man. Chongqing br. and Guangdong br. of Unicom Group, as Vice-Pres. of Unicom Group, as Dir of Unicom Group, as Exec. Dir and Vice-Pres. China Unicom Ltd, as Dir and Vice-Pres. China Unicom Corpn Ltd, as Chair. Unicom Huasheng Telecommunications Tech. Co. Ltd; Vice-Pres. and Exec. Vice-Pres. China Telecommunications Corpn –2015, Exec. Dir, Pres. and COO 2015–. *Address:* China Telecommunications Corporation, 31 Jinrong Street, Xicheng District, Beijing 100032, People's Republic of China (office). *Telephone:* (10) 6602-7217 (office). *Fax:* (10) 6602-1147 (office). *E-mail:* info@chinatelecom.com.cn (office). *Website:* www.chinatelecom.com.cn (office); www.chinatelecom-h.com (office).

YANG, Yanyi; Chinese diplomatist; b. June 1955; m. Wang Weiguo; one s.; began career in Head Office of China Int. Travel Service 1975–81; began diplomatic career in Embassy in Dar es Salaam, Tanzania 1981–83, Deputy Dir, Dept of African Affairs, Ministry of Foreign Affairs (MFA) 1983–89, Deputy Director and First Sec., Dept of Int. Orgs and Confs 1989–92, Counsellor, Perm. Mission to UN, New York 1992–96, Counsellor and Deputy Dir Gen., Asian Affairs Dept, MFA 1996–2001, Deputy Dir-Gen., Policy Planning Dept 2001–04, Amb. to Brunei 2004–07, Dir-Gen. Asian Affairs Dept, MFA 2007–10, Asst Minister, Int. Dept, CCP Cen. Cttee 2010–13, Amb. and Head of Perm. Mission to EU, Brussels 2014–17. *Leisure interests:* reading, yoga, tai chi, calligraphy, photography, travelling.

YANG, Yong-eun; South Korean professional golfer; b. 15 Jan. 1972, Jeju-do; m. Ju Pak Young 1999; three c.; served with S Korean Army; professional golfer, Korean Professional Golfers' Asscn (PGA) Tour, Japan Golf Tour, European Tour 2006–, PGA Tour 2008–; mem. Asian team Royal Trophy 2007; won Korean Tour event, SBS Championship 2002, Japan Golf Tour events, Sun Chlorella Classic 2004, Asahi Ryokuken Yomiuri Asolizuka 2004, Coca-Cola Tokai Classic 2005, Suntory Open 2006, Asian Tour event, Kolon Hana Bank Korea Open 2006, European Tour event, HSBC Champions 2006, PGA Tour events, The Honda Classic 2009, PGA Championship 2009; Rookie of Year, Korean PGA Tour 1997. *Address:* c/o IMG Korea, 5th Floor, Namdo Building 823–24, Yeoksam-Dong, Kangnam-Gu, Seoul 135-080, South Korea. *Telephone:* (2) 558-8544. *Fax:* (2) 558-8540.

YANG, Yu-liang, BSc, PhD; Chinese chemist, academic and university administrator; b. Zhejiang; ed Fudan Univ.; post-doctoral researcher, Max Planck Inst. for Polymer Research 1986–88; mem. Faculty, Fudan Univ., Vice-Pres. for Research 1999–2006, Pres. Fudan Univ. 2009–14; Dir Gen. Dept of Degree and Postgraduate Educ., State Council of People's Repub. of China 2006–09; Sr Adviser, Shanghai Municipal Govt; serves on the boards of several academic journals including Chinese Journal of Chemistry and Science in China; leads Nat. 973 Project and Nat. 863 Project; mem. Chinese Acad. of Sciences 2003; Cheung Kong Scholar, Nat. Scientific and Technological Progress Award, First Prize, Science and Tech. Progress Awards, China Petroleum and Chemical Corpn 2003, Second Prize 2004, Science and Tech. Progress Award, Ho Leung Ho Lee Foundation 2007, Outstanding Scientist Award, Qiushi Foundation 2008, amongst others. *Publications:* about 260 papers in professional journals on condensed matter physics and polymer science; several domestic and int. patents.

YANG, Yuanqing, MSc; Chinese computer industry executive; *Chairman and CEO, Lenovo Group;* b. 12 Nov. 1964; ed Univ. of Science and Tech. of China; joined Lenovo Group 1989, CEO 2001, later Pres. and CEO Lenovo Group Ltd, Exec. Chair. 2004–09, CEO 2009–, Chair. 2011–; mem. New York Stock Exchange (now NYSE Euronext) Int. Advisory Cttee, Nat. Youth Asscn Cttee; mem. Bd of Dirs China's Entrepreneurs' Asscn; Guest Prof., Univ. of Science and Tech. of China; Edison Achievement Award 2014. *Address:* Lenovo Group, No. 6 Chuang Ye Road, Shangdi Information Industry Base, Haidian District, Beijing 100085, People's Republic of China (office). *Telephone:* (10) 58868888 (office). *E-mail:* info@lenovo.com (office). *Website:* www.lenovo.com (office).

YANG, Zhengwu; Chinese politician; b. Jan. 1941, Longshan Co., Hunan Prov.; ed Jishou Univ.; joined CCP 1969; Deputy Sec. CCP Longshan Co. Cttee 1970, Sec. 1970–77; Sec. CCP Tujia-Miao Autonomous Prefectural Cttee, Hunan Prov., Xiangxi 1985–90, Deputy Magistrate, Intermediate People's Court 1985–90; mem. Standing Cttee CCP Hunan Prov. Cttee 1985–90, Deputy Sec. CCP Hunan Prov. Cttee 1990–98, Sec. 1998; Chair. Standing Cttee of People's Congress 1999–2006; Chair. Comm. for Comprehensive Man. of Social Security 1993; Gov. of Hunan Prov. 1995–98; Alt. mem. 12th CCP Cen. Cttee 1982–87, mem. 13th CCP Cen. Cttee 1987–92, 14th CCP Cen. Cttee, 15th CCP Cen. Cttee 1997–2002, 16th CCP Cen. Cttee 2002–07.

YANGIBAEV, Baxadir; Uzbekistani politician; b. 25 Aug. 1960, Beruni dist, Kara-Kalpak ASSR (now Repub. of Qoraqalpog'iston), Uzbek SSR, USSR; ed Tashkent Highways Inst., Tashkent State Econs Univ., specializing as Engineer-Constructor; economist responsible for highways repairs and construction in Beruni dist 1982, worked in various Komsomol and CP cttees 1982–93, Man. Insp., Head of Econ.-Analytical Dept of Qoraqalpog'iston br. of Tadbirkorbank 1993–95, Aide to the Chair. of Council of Ministers of Sovereign Repub. of Qoraqalpog'iston 1995–96; First Deputy Chair., Chief Dept of Cen. Bank of Uzbekistan for Qoraqalpog'iston 1996–99, Head of regional br. in Qoraqalpog'iston of Gallabanka; Minister of Finance, Sovereign Repub. of Qoraqalpog'iston 2002–06, Chair.

Council of Ministers 2006–16; mem. Council of Ministers of Uzbekistan; fmr Gov. To'rtku'l dist.

YANIN, Valentin Lavrentyevich, DHist; Russian archaeologist and academic; *Professor Emeritus, Archaeology Department, Moscow State University 'M. V. Lomonosov';* b. 6 Feb. 1929, Vyatka (now Kirov); m.; ed Moscow State Univ.; Jr then Sr Researcher, Moscow State Univ. 'M. V. Lomonosov' 1954, apptd Prof. 1963, now Distinguished Prof., now Prof. Emer., also Chair. of Archaeology Dept; Chair. of Bd Russian Humanitarian Scientific Fund (RGNF) 1996; Corresp. mem. USSR (now Russian) Acad. of Sciences 1966, mem. 1990, mem. Presidium 1991–2002; Hon. Citizen of Novgorod, Hon. mem. Novgorod Society of Antiquity Lovers; USSR State Prize 1970, Lenin Prize 1984, Demidov Prize 1993, State Prize of Russian Fed. 1996, Triumph Prize 2002, Alexander Solzhenitsyn Prize 2010. *Publications include:* Money and Weight Systems of Medieval Russia 1956, Novgorod Posadniki 1962, I Have Sent You a Birch Bark 1965, Act Stamps of Old Russia X–XV Centuries 1970, Novgorod Feudal Ancestral Lands 1982, Novgorod Acts XII–XV Centuries 1991; more than 700 scientific and popular science books and articles. *Leisure interest:* collecting old vocal recordings. *Address:* Department of Archaeology, Moscow State University 'M. V. Lomonosov', Moscow 119991, GSP-1, Leninskie Gory, Russia (office). *Telephone:* (495) 939-56-47 (office); (495) 335-54-28 (home). *Website:* www.hist.msu.ru/Departments/Arch (office).

YANNARAS, Christos, PhD, DrTheol; Greek philosopher and academic; *Professor Emeritus of Philosophy, Panteion University of Political and Social Studies;* b. 10 April 1935, Athens; ed Univ. of Athens, Univ. of Bonn, Germany, Univ. of Paris (Sorbonne), France, Faculty of Theology, Aristotle Univ. of Thessaloniki, Faculté des Lettres et Sciences Humaines, Sorbonne; Visiting Prof., Catholic Univ. of Paris 1971–73, Univ. of Geneva, Switzerland 1977–79, Univ. of Lausanne, Switzerland 1978–79, Univ. of Crete (Rethymnon) 1979–82; Prof. of Philosophy, Panteion Univ. of Political and Social Studies, Athens 1982–2005, Prof. Emer. 2005–; mem. Hellenic Authors' Soc., Acad. Int. des Sciences Humaines, Brussels, Belgium, St. Vladimir's Seminary, New York, Holy Cross School, Boston, Dept. of Theology, National and Kapodistrian Univ. of Athens; Hon. DPhil (Belgrade), Hon. DD (St Vladimir's Orthodox Theological Seminary, New York), (Holy Cross Coll., Boston) 2011, (Dept of Theology, National and Kapodistrian Univ. of Athens). *Publications include:* more than 60 books, including Critical Ontology (3rd edn) 1995, The Real and the Imaginary in the Political Economy (2nd edn) 1996, Heidegger and the Areopagite (4th edn) 1998, The Linguistic Boundaries of Realism in Metaphysics 1999, The Inhuman Character of Human Rights (3rd edn) 2000, The Freedom of Morality (3rd edn) 2002, Discontinuity in Philosophy (5th edn) 2002, Cultural Diplomacy (2nd edn) 2003, Postmodern Metaphysics (2nd edn) 2004, The Relational Ontology 2004, Variations on the Song of Songs (6th edn) 2005, Culture as the Central Problem in Politics (2nd edn) 2005, Orthodoxy and the West (5th edn) 2006, The Religionization of the Ecclesial Event (2nd edn) 2007, Person and Eros (8th edn) 2018; translated into many European languages. *Address:* 84 Plastira Street, 171 21 Nea Smyrni, Athens, Greece (home). *Telephone:* (210) 935-3697 (home). *Fax:* (210) 935-3697 (home). *E-mail:* anpa@uom.gr (home).

YANO, Akiko; Japanese singer and musician (piano, keyboards); b. 1955, Tokyo; m. Ryuichi Sakamoto (divorced 2006); ed classical training; child piano prodigy; familiar with jazz, pop and R&B at early age; working musician in Tokyo club scene during high school and began singing at this time; played on many albums as session musician in Japan; appeared in concert with Tin Pan Alley; recorded track album by Little Feat, Los Angeles; first solo album Japanese Girl 1976; participated in Yellow Magic Orchestra world tour 1979–80; double solo album co-produced by herself and her husband titled Gohan Ga Dekitayo (Dinner's Ready!) 1980; f. Akiko Yano Trio 2009. *Albums include:* Nagatsuki Kan Nazuki 1976, I Rohani Konpeitou 1977, To Ki Me Ki 1978, Gohan Ga Dekitayo 1980, Tadaima 1981, Ai Ga Nakuchane 1982, O.S.O.S. 1984, Brooch 1986, Granola 1987, Welcome Back Akiko Yano 1989, Love Life 1991, Super Folk Song 1992, Love Is Here 1993, Elephant Hotel 1994, Piano Nightly 1996, Oui Oui 1997, Ego Girl 1999, Home Journey Girl 2000, Reverb 2002, Honto No Kimochi 2004, Hajimete No Yano Akiko 2006, Akiko 2008, Ongakudo 2010, Yano Akiko, Imawano Kiyoshirō o Utau 2013, Tobashite Ikuyo 2014, Welcome to Jupiter 2015, Soft Landing 2017. *Website:* www.akikoyano.com.

YANO, Kaoru, MSc; Japanese electronics industry executive; *Chairman, NEC Corporation;* b. 23 Feb. 1944; ed Univ. of Tokyo, Stanford Univ., USA; joined NEC Corpn 1966, based in USA 1985–90, Gen. Man. Transmission Div. 1990–94, Exec. Gen. Man. Transmission Operations Unit 1994–95, Assoc. Sr Vice-Pres. 1995–99, Pres. NEC USA Inc. 1998–2000, Sr Vice-Pres. 1999–2002, mem. Bd of Dirs 2000–, served as Assoc. Sr Vice-Pres., Sr Vice-Pres., Exec. Vice-Pres. NEC Networks Co., Deputy Pres. NEC Networks Co. 2000–02, Pres. NEC Networks Co. 2002–03, Dir NEC Corpn 1995–2016, Exec. Vice-Pres. 2002–04, Sr Exec. Vice-Pres. and Rep. Dir 2004–06, Pres. and Rep. Dir 2006–10, Chair. and Rep. Dir 2010–12, Chair. 2012–. *Address:* NEC Corporation, 7-1, Shiba 5-chome, Minato-ku, Tokyo 108-8001, Japan (office). *Telephone:* (3) 3454-1111 (office). *Fax:* (3) 3798-1510 (office). *E-mail:* info@nec.com (office). *Website:* www.nec.com (office).

YANSANÉ, Kerfalla; Guinean economist and politician; *Ambassador to USA ;* fmr Gov. Banque Centrale de la République de Guinée; many roles as int. econ. consultant, including assignments with World Bank, African Devt Bank, UN Econ. Comm. for Africa, UNDP, Int. Lawyers and Economists against Poverty, Toronto, Canada; fmr Vice-Chair. African Econ. Research Consortium, Nairobi, Kenya; fmr Chair. Operations Cttee, African Capacity Building Foundation, Harare, Zimbabwe; fmr Lead Consultant, New Partnership for Africa's Devt African Peer Review Mechanism; Minister of the Economy and Finance 2010–14, of Mines and Geology 2014–17, Amb. to USA 2017–. *Address:* 2112 Leroy Pl., NW, Washington DC 20008, USA (office). *Telephone:* (202) 986-4300 (office). *Fax:* (202) 986-3800 (office). *E-mail:* info@guineaembassyusa.com (office). *Website:* www .guineaembassyusa.com (office).

YANUKOVYCH, Viktor Fedorovych, DEcon; Ukrainian politician and fmr head of state; b. 9 July 1950, Yenakiyevo, Donetsk Oblast, Ukrainian SSR, USSR; m. Lyudmyla Oleksandrivna Yanukovych 1971 (divorced 2016); two s. (one deceased); ed Donetsk Polytechnic Inst., Ukrainian Acad. of Foreign Trade; worked in a variety of early jobs including welder, Yenakiyevo metal works 1969–70, fitter and mechanic in automobile factory 1972–76, dir of transport depot

1976–84; mem. CP of Soviet Union 1980–91; moved to Donetsk 1984, held exec. positions at transport cos; fmr Dir-Gen. of major production firms including Donbastransremont, Ukrvuhlepromtrans, Donetsk Oblast Motor Transport Territorial Production Asscn 1994–96; Deputy Gov., then First Deputy Gov. of Donetsk Oblast State Admin 1996–97, Gov. 1997–2002; Chair. Donetsk Oblast Council 1999–2001 (resgnd); Prime Minister of Ukraine 2002–7 Dec. 2004, 28 Dec. 2004–5 Jan. 2005, 2006–07; unsuccessful presidential cand. 2004; Pres. of Ukraine 2010–14 (fled the capital following popular protests, then travelled to southern Russia, impeached by Parl. Feb. 2014, warrant for arrest issued, placed on US sanction list March 2014, listed by Interpol as "wanted by the judicial authorities of Ukraine for prosecution/to serve a sentence" on charges of "misappropriation, embezzlement or conversion of property by malversation, if committed in respect of an especially gross amount, or by an organized group" Jan. 2015); officially deprived of title of Pres. of Ukraine June 2015; removed from Interpol's 'most wanted' list pending further investigations July 2015; received temporary asylum certificate in Russia for one year Nov. 2015 (later extended until Nov. 2017); announced interest in returning to Ukrainian politics Dec. 2015; Gen. Persecutor's Office submitted documents to court relating to case on state treason March 2017; Chair. Partiya Rehioniv (Party of Regions) 2003–10; Prof., mem. Acad. of Econ. Sciences of Ukraine; Pres. Nat. Olympic Cttee of Ukraine 2002–05; mem. Presidium Nat. Acad. of Sciences of Ukraine; Merited Worker of Ukrainian Transport; Order of Merit (Third Class) 1998, (Second Class) 2000, (First Class) 2002; Order 'Miner's Award' (3, 2, 1 Class); Order 'Miner's Glory' (3, 2, 1 Class); Certificate from the Cabinet of Ministers of Ukraine 2000; Order of Saint Nestor 1998; Order of St Prince Volodmyr (Third Class) 1998, (Second Class) 2004, (First Class) 2010; Order of St Daniyel of Moscow 2004; Order of St Sergius (First Class) 2004; Grand Croix, Légion d'honneur 2010; Order of the Precious Wand (Mongolia) 2011; Order of St Mashtots (Armenia) 2011; Order of José Martí (Cuba) 2011; Order Ismoili Samoni (Tajikistan) 2011. *Leisure interests:* sport (especially tennis), hunting, pigeon raising.

YAO, Ming; Chinese professional basketball player (retd); b. 12 Sept. 1980, Shanghai; s. of Yao Zhiyuan and Fang Fengdi; m. Ye Li; ed Shanghai Sports Coll.; center; played for Chinese Basketball Asscn Shanghai Sharks 1997–2002; drafted first overall by Nat. Basketball Asscn (NBA) Houston Rockets 2002; retd 2011; Owner Shanghai Sharks, Chinese Basketball Asscn 2009–; mem. Chinese Olympic team 2000 Sydney, 2004 Athens; carried Olympic Flame into Tiananmen Square during Olympic torch relay August 2008; led Chinese delegation during Olympic opening ceremony; mem. Chinese nat. team, Beijing Summer Olympics 2008; Chinese Basketball Asscn (CBA) Most Valuable Player 2001, 2002; CBA Sportsmanship Award 2002; selected for NBA All-Rookie Team 2002; selected for NBA All-Star Game 2003, 2004, 2005, 2006, 2007; Laureus World Newcomer of the Year 2003, Laureus China Prominent Achievement of the Year 2011, Laureus World Sports Award for Best Sportsmanship 2015, also elected to Laureus World Sports Acad. 2015. *Publications:* Yao: A Life in Two Worlds (with Ric Bucher) 2004. *E-mail:* shanghaisharks@shanghaisharks.CN. *Website:* www.shanghaisharks.cn.

YAO, Yan; Chinese engineer and business executive; *Vice-Chairwoman, China National Building Materials Group;* b. Shanghai; successively held posts of Supt of Building Architecture Station, China Building Materials Acad., Pres. Asst, Supt of Cement and New Material Research Inst., Pres. and Deputy Gen. Man. China Nat. Building Materials Group, later Dir, Gen. Man., Pres. and Vice-Sec. Party Cttee, currently Vice-Chair.; Pres. China Building Materials Acad. *Address:* China National Building Materials Group, 17 Fuxing Road, Beijing 100036, People's Republic of China (office). *Telephone:* (10) 68138199 (office). *Fax:* (10) 68138088 (office). *E-mail:* cnbmadmin@cnbm.com.cn (office). *Website:* www.cnbm.com.cn (office).

YAO, Zhonghua; Chinese artist; b. 17 July 1939, Kunming, Yunnan; s. of Yao Penxien and Wang Huiyuan; m. Ma Huixian 1969; two s.; ed Cen. Acad. of Fine Arts; one-man show, Beijing 1980, Cité Int. Arts, Paris 1985 and exhbns in Paris and Eastern Europe; numerous group exhbns in China, also China Oil Paintings of Present Age Exhbn, New York, USA 1987, Melbourne, Sydney, Australia 1987, Wan Yu Tang Art Gallery, Hong Kong 1989; group exhbn Beijing Art Gallery 1992; one-man exhbn Taiwan 1992, Calif., USA 1995; mural for Parl. Hall, Yunnan People's Congress; mem. Council China Artists' Asscn; Vice-Pres. Yunnan Painting Inst. *Works include:* Oh, the Land!, Sani Minority's Festival, The Yellow River, Zhenghe's Voyage, The Jinsha River Flowing beside the Jade Dragon Mountain, Chinese Ink and Water. *Publications:* paper on painter Dong Xi Wen, in Chinese Oil Painting and Art Research 1990, Selected Works of Yao Zhonghua 1993. *Leisure interests:* music, literature. *Address:* c/o China Art Networks, 7/F, Xinzhong Mansion, Gongti Beilu, Beijing, People's Republic of China.

YAQUB, Muhammad, BA, MA PhD; Pakistani banker and economist; b. 1937, Jalandar, India; s. of Haji Muhammad Shah and Bibi Karim; m. Nasreen Yaqub; two s. one d.; ed Punjab Univ., Yale Univ. and Princeton Univ., USA; mem. Pakistan Taxation Comm. 1966–72; Asst Dir, Research Dept State Bank of Pakistan 1966–68, Deputy Dir 1968–69, Sr Deputy Dir 1969–72, Sr Prin. Officer, Dir Research Dept 1975, Gov. 1993–99; Sr Economist and Resident Rep., IMF, Saudi Arabia 1975, Fund Resident Adviser to Saudi Arabian Govt, IMF 1977, Div. Chief, Middle Eastern Dept IMF 1977–80, Asst Dir 1981–82, IMF Rep. to Paris Club, London Club, OECD and co. aid consortia; Consultant IMF, Washington; Prin. Econ. Adviser, Special Section, Ministry of Finance 1992–93; Gov. State Bank of Pakistan 1993–99; has headed IMF missions to numerous Middle Eastern countries; mem. Bd of Dirs MCB Bank; columnist, The News International. *Publications include:* Major-Macro Economic Policy Issues in Pakistan.

YARDIM, Ümit; Turkish diplomatist; *Deputy Under-Secretary, Ministry of Foreign Affairs of Culture for Eastern Europe and Asia Affairs;* b. 1961, Balıkesir, Denizli-Acıpayam; m. Nurtop Yardım; two c.; ed Eskişehir Anatolian High School, Bosphorus Univ., Gazi Univ., Ankara; intern, Div. of Eastern Europe and Asia, Ministry of Foreign Affairs (MFA) 1985, mil. service 1985–86, trainee, then Third Sec., Third Div., Econ. Affairs Div., MFA 1986–88, Third Sec., Embassy in Islamabad 1988–90, Third, then Second Sec., Embassy in Moscow 1990–93, Second, then First Sec., First Dept of the Slavic Countries, MFA 1993–95, First Sec., Embassy in Athens 1995–97, First Sec., Embassy in Baku 1997–2000, Head of First Div. of Eastern Europe, MFA 2000–02, Counsellor, then First Counsellor, Embassy in Lisbon 2002–04, Consul-Gen. in Komotini, Greece 2004–06, Head of

Second Dept of Cen. Asia and the Caucasus, MFA 2006–07, Acting Deputy Dir, then Deputy Dir-Envoy of Dept of Cen. Asia and the Caucasus 2007–08, Consul-Gen., First Class, Consulate-Gen. in Stuttgart 2008–10, Amb. to Iran 2010–14, to Russian Fed. 2014–16; currently Deputy Under-Sec., Ministry of Foreign Affairs of Culture for Eastern Europe and Asia Affairs; Dr hc (Inst. of Fine Arts). *Address:* Ministry of Foreign Affairs, Dr Sadık Ahmet Cad. 8, 06100 Balgat, Ankara, Turkey (office). *Telephone:* (312) 2921000 (office). *Fax:* (495) 246-49-89 (office). *E-mail:* info@mfa.gov.tr (office). *Website:* www.mfa.gov.tr (office).

YARK, Col Damehane; Togolese police officer and government official; *Minister of Security and Civil Protection;* b. 31 Dec. 1963, Worgou, Tône Dist; Dir-Gen. Gendarmerie nationale (police force) 2008–12; Minister of Security and Civil Protection 2012–. *Address:* Ministry of Security and Civil Protection, rue Albert Sarraut, Lomé, Togo (office). *Telephone:* 22-22-57-12 (office). *Fax:* 22-22-61-50 (office). *E-mail:* info@republicoftogo.com (office).

YARMOSHYN, Uladzimir Vasilyevich; Belarusian politician and engineer; b. 26 Oct. 1942, Pronsk, Ryazan Region, Russia; m.; two c.; ed Novocherkassk Polytech. Inst., Leningrad Civil Aviation Acad.; turner, Electric Locomotive plant, Novocherkassk; Sr Engineer, Chief Mechanical Engineer, Deputy Dir Minsk Civil Aviation plant 1965–90; Chair. Exec. Cttee Dist Soviet of People's Deputies, Minsk 1990; Deputy Chair. Minsk City Exec. Cttee, also Head Cttee on Housing and Power Eng 1990–92; First Deputy Chair. then Chair. Minsk City Exec. Cttee 1995–2000; mem. Council in Nat. Ass.; Chair. Council of Ministers 2000–01; Head of Belorussian Reps, Mobil Telesystems 2002–03; lived in Moscow for a short period; with Vnesheconombank from 2003; supervised building of Minsk-Arena sporting complex c. 2009; Hon. Citizen of Minsk.

YARON, Hadas; Israeli actress; b. 21 Sept. 1990; ed Tichon Eroni Alef Art School, Aleph High School of the Performing Arts; began acting aged eight; served in Israel Defense Forces for two years. *Films include:* Out of Sight 2006, On Air (short) 2008, Girls' Night (short) 2009, Alone in the Dark (short) 2012, Fill the Void (Volpi Cup for Best Actress, Venice Film Festival, Ophir Award for Best Actress) 2012, Has Anyone Seen Eyal Nurich? (short) 2013, Felix and Meira (Best Actress, Amiens Int. Film Festival, Torino Film Festival, Whistler Film Festival) 2014, La felicità e un sistema complesso (Happiness is a Complex System) 2014. *Address:* c/o Allison Band, Gersh, 9465 Wilshire Boulevard, Sixth Floor, Beverly Hills, CA 90212, USA (office). *E-mail:* hadas@add-ca.com. *Website:* www.hadasyaron.com.

YAROSH, Dmytro; Ukrainian politician; *Leader, Derzhavnytska Initsiatyva Yarosha (DIYa—Governmental Initiative of Yarosh);* b. 30 Sept. 1971, Dniprod-zerzhynsk, Ukrainian SSR, USSR; m. Olha Yarosh; one s. two d.; ed High School No. 24, Dniprodzerzhynsk, State Univ. of Educ., Drohobych; drafted and served two years in Soviet Army as a private 1989–91; as student, mem. Young Pioneers, later of Komsomol (youth-based org. of CPSU); mem. Narodny Rukh Ukrainy (People's Movt of Ukraine) 1989–94, Tryzub (Trident) 1994– (Leader 2005–); Head, Pravy Sektor (Right Sector) (formed with Tryzub as its core) 2013–15; arrest ordered by Basmanny Court, Moscow on charges of publicly inciting terrorism, placed on int. wanted list by Interpol at request of Russian Fed. Govt Feb. 2014, listing removed from Interpol website Jan. 2016; mem. Verkhovna Rada (Supreme Council) 2014–; adviser to Ukrainian Armed Forces April 2015–; Founder and Leader Derzhavnytska Initsiatyva Yarosha (DIYa—Governmental Initiative of Yarosh) 2016–. *Address:* Derzhavnytska Initsiatyva Yarosha (Governmental Initiative of Yarosh), Kyiv, Ukraine (office). *Telephone:* 97-4168468 (mobile) (office).

YAROSHENKO, Fedir O.; Ukrainian politician; various positions within Ministry of Finance, including First Deputy Minister of Finance 2002–04, Chair. State Tax Admin of Ukraine 2004, Deputy Chair. –2010, Minister of Finance 2010–12 (resgnd).

YAROU ROBERT, Théophile, DESS; Benin politician; ed Ecole Nat. d'Admin du Bénin, Univ. d'Abomey-Calavi; worked as expert on Projet d'Appui au Développe-ment des Communes (funded by UNDP) 2006–08; Dir of Financial Resources, Ministry of Decentralisation 2009–12; Dir-Gen. Centre de Formation pour l'Administration Locale (CeFAL) 2012–14; mem. Ass. Nat.; Minister of Nat. Defence 2014–16. *Address:* c/o Ministry of National Defence, BP 2493, Cotonou, Benin (office).

YAROV, Yuri Fedorovich; Russian politician; b. 2 April 1942, Mariinsk, Kemerovo Oblast; m.; one s. one d.; ed Leningrad Tech. Inst., Leningrad Eng Econ. Inst.; worked in factories in Latvia 1964–68, Leningrad Oblast 1968–76; Dir factory Burevestnik 1978–85; First Sec. Gatchina City CPSU Cttee (Leningrad Oblast) 1985–87; Deputy Chair. Exec. Cttee Leningrad Oblast Soviet of Deputies 1987–89, Chair. 1989–90; Chair. Leningrad Oblast Soviet of People's Deputies 1990–91; People's Deputy of Russian Fed. 1990–92; Deputy Chair. Supreme Soviet of Russia 1991–92; Deputy Prime Minister 1992–96; Presidential Rep. to Fed. Council; Deputy Head of Presidential Admin 1996–97, First Deputy 1997–98; Plenipotentiary Rep. of Pres. of the Russian Fed. in Federation Council 1998–99; Chair. Exec. Cttee of CIS 1999–2004.

YASAY, Perfecto 'Jun' Rivas, Jr, BA, LLB, MBA; Philippine lawyer and politician; b. 27 Jan. 1947; s. of Perfecto Yasay, Sr and Deborah Rivas; m. Cecile Joaquin; three c.; ed Central Philippine Univ., Univ. of the Philippines, Ateneo de Manila Univ.; fmr mem. Bar, US Supreme Court and US Circuit Court of Appeals; Sr Partner, Maceda, Yasay & Tolentino (law firm), New York 1979–85, Yasay & De Castro (law firm), New York 1985–90; Man. Dir, Maceda Philippine News, New York 1983–87; Sr Partner, San Jose, Yasay & Santos Law Office, Manila 1987–93; Assoc. Commr, Philippine Securities and Exchange Comm. 1993–95, Chair. 1995–2000; Sec. of Foreign Affairs 2016–17 (cabinet appointment rejected by Comm. on Appointments March 2017); fmr Visiting Prof. of Law, Richardson School of Law, Univ. of Hawaii; Chair. and Pres. Central Philippine Univ.; mem. Bangon Pilipinas (Rise Philippines). *Publications include:* Out of the Lion's Den: The Travails and Triumphs of a Public Servant, Terminal Four: Corruption in America's Only Colony in Asia. *Website:* perfectoyasay.com.

YASIN, Yevgeny Grigoryevich, DEconSc; Russian economist, academic and fmr government official; *Professor, National Research University Higher School of Economics;* b. 7 May 1934, Odessa; s. of Grigory Yasin and Yevgenia Yasina; m. Lydia Yasina (née Fedoulova); one d.; ed Odessa Inst. of Construction Eng, Moscow

State Univ.; worked at USSR Cen. Dept of Statistics 1963–73, Researcher, Cen. Inst. of Econs and Math., USSR (now Russian) Acad. of Sciences 1973–89; Head of Div. State Comm. on Econ. Reform, USSR Council of Ministers (Abalkin Comm.) 1990–91; apptd Prof., Nat. Research Univ. Higher School of Econs (HSE), Moscow 1992, Scientific Head 1998, now Prof., Faculty of Econ. Sciences, Dept of Applied Econs and Academic Supervisor, Expert Inst., mem. HSE Academic Council; mem. Council of Enterprise of Pres. of Russia 1992; Plenipotentiary Rep. of Govt in Parl. 1992–93; Head of Analytical Centre of Pres. 1994; Minister of Economy of Russia 1994–97, Minister without Portfolio 1997–98; mem. Russian Council of Defence 1996; head of govt legislation drafting teams 1992–97, one of authors of econ. programme 500 Days; Dir-Gen. Direction on Econ. Policy of Russian Union of Industrialists and Entrepreneurs 1991, Founder and Dir Expert Inst. of Russian Union of Industrialists and Entrepreneurs 1992–93; Pres. Liberalnaya Missiya Foundation 2000–; apptd mem. Civic Chamber of Russian Fed. 2009; mem. European Acad. of Sciences, Russian Fed. Public Chamber Comm. on Educ. and Science; Hon. Prof., Jilin Univ.; Hon. DUniv (Univ. of Birmingham) 2005. *Address:* National Research University Higher School of Economics, Moscow 101000, Room 212 K, 20, Myasnitskaya ul., Russia (office). *Telephone:* (495) 621-33-13 (office). *Fax:* (495) 623-28-58 (office). *E-mail:* yassin@hse.ru (office). *Website:* www.hse.ru (office); www.hse.ru/en/org/hse/expert (office).

YASINZAI, Aman Ullah Khan; Pakistani politician and justice (retd); *Governor of Balochistan;* b. 7 Aug. 1954, Quetta, Balochistan; ed Forman Christian Coll.; Justice, High Court of Balochistan 1997–2009, Chief Justice 2005–09; Gov. of Balochistan 2018–. *Address:* Governor House, Zarghoon Road, Quetta, Balochi-stan, Pakistan (office). *Telephone:* (81) 9202973 (office). *Fax:* (81) 9202178 (office). *E-mail:* psgb@balochistan.gov.pk (office). *Website:* www.balochistan.gov.pk (office).

YASSIN, Magdi Hassan; Sudanese politician; *Minister of Finance and Economic Planning;* Minister of State for Finance and Deputy Minister of Finance and Nat. Economy –2019, Minister of Finance and Econ. Planning 2019–. *Address:* Ministry of Finance and Economic Planning, POB 735, Khartoum, Sudan (office). *Telephone:* (183) 777672 (office). *Fax:* (183) 775630 (office). *E-mail:* info@mof.gov .sd (office). *Website:* www.mof.gov.sd (office).

YASSUKOVICH, Stanislas Michael, CBE; British/American banker and busi-ness executive; b. 5 Feb. 1935, Paris, France; s. of Dimitri Yassukovich and Denise Yassukovich; m. Diana Townsend 1961; two s. one d.; ed Deerfield Acad., Mass. and Harvard Univ., USA; served in US Marine Corps 1957–61; joined White, Weld and Co. 1961, London Office 1962, Branch Man. 1967–69, Gen. Partner, New York 1969–73, Man. Dir, London 1969–73; Man. Dir European Banking Co. SA Brussels 1983–85, Chief Exec. European Banking Group 1983–85; Chair. Merrill Lynch Europe Ltd 1985–89, Hemingway Properties 1993–; Vice-Chair. Jt Deputy Chair. London Stock Exchange 1986–89, Bristol and West Bldg Soc. (now Bristol & West PLC) 1991–2000, ABC Int. Bank 1993–; fmr Chair. S.M. Yassukovich & Co. Ltd; Chair. Securities Asscn 1988–91; Chair. Cragnotti & Partners Capital Investment (UK) 1991–96, Park Place Capital 1994, Henderson EuroTrust PLC 1995, Easdaq SA 1997–99, Manek Investment Man. Ltd 1997–2018; Deputy Chair. Flextech PLC 1989–97, South West Water (now Pennon Group PLC) 1993–2000; Dir Royal Nat. Theatre 1991–96, Chair. City Disputes Panel 1993–99; Dir (non-exec.) Henderson Group PLC 1990–98, Telewest PLC 1998–, Atlas Capital Ltd 1999–. *Leisure interests:* hunting, shooting and polo.

YASTRZHEMBSKY, Sergey Vladimirovich, CandHistSc; Russian journalist, government official, diplomatist and documentary filmmaker; b. 4 Dec. 1953, Moscow; m. Anastassia Yastrzhembskaya; three c.; ed Moscow State Inst. of Int. Relations, Inst. of Int. Workers' Movt; Jr Researcher, Acad. of Social Sciences, Cen. Cttee CPSU 1979–81; on staff journal Problems of the World and Socialism (Prague) 1981–89; sr staff mem., Int. Div., Cen. Cttee CPSU 1989–90; Deputy Ed.-in-Chief Megapolis (journal) 1990–91, Ed.-in-Chief VIP journal 1991–92; Dir Dept of Information and Press, Russian Ministry of Foreign Affairs 1992–93; Amb. to Slovakia 1993–96; Press Sec. to Pres. Boris Yeltsin 1996; Deputy Head, Pres. Yeltsin's Admin. 1997–98; Vice-Chair. Moscow Govt 1998–99; Asst to Pres. Vladimir Putin (q.v.) 2000–08; Special Envoy to EU 2004; f. Film Co. Yastreb-Film 2009, now directing and producing documentary films about Africa; Order of Courage, Order of Merit for the Fatherland, Order of Merit (Luxembourg), Order of Isabella of Castile (Spain), Légion d'honneur, Order of Merit (Italy), Rank II Order of the White Cross (Slovakia), Order of St Daniil, Russian Orthodox Church; 850th Anniversary of Moscow Commemorative Medal. *Films directed include:* Africa, Blood & Beauty 2012, The Death Charmers 2012, Possessed by Voodoo 2012, Wolfhound 2014, Ivory: A Crime Story 2016. *Publications:* Social Democracy in the Contemporary World 1991, Patriarchal Africa: The Last Sunrise Photo-Chronicle of the Vanishing Life 2015; essays and articles on current events, contemporary devt of Portugal and European social democracy, and relations between Russia and EU. *Leisure interests:* tennis, stamp collecting, reading, hunting, downhill skiing, photography. *E-mail:* www.yastrebfilm.com.

YASUNAGA, Tatsuo; Japanese business executive; *Representative Director, President and CEO, Mitsui & Company Limited;* Gen. Man., Planning and Admin. Div., Infrastructure Projects Business Unit, Mitsui & Co. Ltd 2008–10, Deputy Gen. Man., Corp. Planning and Strategy Div. March–July 2010, Gen. Man. 2010–13, Man. Officer, COO Integrated Transportation Systems Business Unit 2013–15, Pres. and CEO Mitsui & Co. Ltd April 2015–, Rep. Dir June 2015–. *Address:* Mitsui & Co. Ltd, 2-1 Ohtemachi 1-chome, Chiyoda-ku, Tokyo 100-0004, Japan (office). *Telephone:* (3) 3285-1111 (office). *Fax:* (3) 3285-9819 (office). *E-mail:* info@mitsui.com (office). *Website:* www.mitsui.com (office).

YATHOTOU, Pany; Laotian politician and fmr central banker; *President of the National Assembly;* b. 18 Feb. 1951, Xiangkhouang Prov.; m.; Cabinet mem. 1987–98; Chair. Cen. Bank 1988–90, Gov. 1990–92, Gov. Bank of the Lao People's Democratic Repub. 1995–97; mem. Nat. Ass. 2001–, Chair. Cttee of Ethnic Affairs and Deputy Pres. Nat. Ass. 2001–10, Pres. Nat. Ass. 2010–; mem. Politbureau Cen. People's Democratic Repub. 1995–97; Pres. Asean Inter-Parliamentary Ass. 2014–15; Chair. Cttee of Lao People's Revolutionary Party. *Address:* Office of the President, National Assembly of the Lao People's Democratic Republic, Vientiane, Laos (office). *Telephone:* 45188990 (office). *Fax:* (21) 451890 (office). *E-mail:* info_na@na.gov.la (office). *Website:* www.na.gov.la (office).

YATIM, Dato' Rais bin, MA, LLB, PhD; Malaysian politician; b. 15 April 1942, Jelebu, Negeri Sembilan; m. Datin Masnah Mohamat; three s. one d.; ed Univs of Northern Illinois, Singapore and London; lecturer at ITM, School of Law and also managed own law firm in Kuala Lumpur 1973; mem. Bar Council 1973; mem. Parl. 1974; Parl. Sec. Ministry of Youth, Sport and Culture 1974; Deputy Minister of Law 1976, of Home Affairs 1978; elected to State Ass., Negeri Sembilan 1978; Menteri Besar, Negeri Sembilan 1978; Minister of Land and Regional Devt 1982, of Information 1984–86, of Foreign Affairs 1986–87; Advocate and Solicitor, High Court of Malaysia 1988–; returned to law practice, Kuala Lumpur 1988–; mem. United Malays' Nat. Org. (UMNO) Supreme Council of Malaysia 1982–; Deputy Pres. Semangat 1989–; Minister in Prime Minister's Dept 1999; Minister of Foreign Affairs 2008–09, of Information, Communications and Culture 2009–13; mem. Civil Liberty Cttee Bar Council, Kuala Lumpur 1996–98. *Publications:* Faces in the Corridors of Power 1987, Freedom under Executive Power in Malaysia 1995, Zaman Beredar Pesaka Bergilir 1999. *Leisure interests:* photography, writing, travel. *Address:* 41 Road 12, Taman Grandview, Ampang Jaya, 68000 Ampang, Selangor, Malaysia (home).

YATSENYUK, Arseniy Petrovych, PhD; Ukrainian lawyer and politician; *Head of Political Council, Narodny Front (People's Front);* b. 22 May 1974, Chernivtsi, Ukrainian SSR, USSR; m. Tereziya Victorivna Hur 2000; two d.; ed Chernivtsi State Univ. and Kyiv Univ. of Trade and Econs; Pres. Yurek Ltd (law firm), Chernivtsi 1992–97; consultant to credit dept, Aval Jt Stock Postal Pensions Bank, Kyiv 1998, Adviser to Chair. of Bd 1998–2001, Deputy Chair. of Bd Aug.–Sept. 2001; Minister of Economy, Autonomous Repub. of Crimea, Simferopol 2001–03; First Deputy Chair. Nat. Bank of Ukraine 2003–05; First Deputy Gov. Odesa Oblast March–Sept. 2005; Minister of Economy 2005–06, of Foreign Affairs March–Dec. 2007; Deputy Head, Presidential Secr. 2006–07; Chair. Verkhovna Rada 2007–08; mem. Nat. Security and Defence Council 2007; Founder Front Zmin (Front for Change) political party 2007 (merged into Batkivshchyna—Fatherland 2013), Open Ukraine Benevolent Foundation; Head of the Political Council, Batkivshchyna (Fatherland) 2013–14; Prime Minister of Ukraine 2014–16 (resgnd); Head of Political Council, Narodny Front (People's Front) 2014–. *Address:* Narodny Front (People's Front), 02068 Kyiv, vul. Akademika Kurchatova 3, Ukraine (office). *Telephone:* (44) 59-07-65 (office). *E-mail:* press@nfront.com.ua (office). *Website:* nfront.org.ua; www.yatsenyuk.org.ua.

YATSKEVICH, Boris Alexandrovich, CandGeol; Russian geologist and government official; b. 7 Jan. 1948, Lignice, Poland; ed Voronezh State Univ.; Sr Technician, Sr Geologist, Chief Geologist, Ukhta geological expedition, Komi Autonomous Repub. 1972–86; Chief Geologist, Polar-Urals production geological co., Vorkuta 1986–90; Head of Div., State Cttee on Geology, RSFSR 1990–92; Deputy Chair. State Cttee on Geology and Use of Mineral Wealth 1992–96; First Deputy Minister of Natural Resources, Russian Fed. 1996–99, Minister 1999–2001; mem. Observation Council, ALROSA (Diamonds of Russia and Sakha). *Address:* c/o Ministry of Natural Resources and Environmental Protection, 123995 Moscow, ul. B. Gruzinskaya 4/6, Russia. *E-mail:* admin@mnr.gov.ru.

YAU, Shing-tung, PhD, FAAS; Chinese mathematician and academic; *William Casper Graustein Professor of Mathematics, Harvard University;* b. 4 April 1949, Shantou, Guangdong Prov.; s. of Chen ying Chiu and Yeuk Lam leung; Yu-yun Kuo, Isaac Chiu Yau and Michael Chiu; ed Univ. of California, Berkeley; Asst Prof. of Math., State Univ. of New York, Stony Brook 1972–73, Distinguished Visiting Prof. 1990; Prof. of Math., Stanford Univ. 1974–79; Prof. of Math., Inst. for Advanced Study, Princeton NJ 1979–84; Chair and Prof. of Math., Univ. of California, San Diego 1984–87; Visiting Prof. and Sid Richardson Centennial Chair in Math., Univ. of Texas, Austin 1986; Prof. of Math., Harvard Univ. 1987–, Higgins Prof. (Chair Prof.) 1997–2000, William Casper Graustein Prof. 2000–, Chair. Math. Dept 2008–; Fairchild Distinguished Scholar, Calif. Inst. of Tech. 1990; Wilson T. S.Wang Distinguished Visiting Prof., The Chinese Univ. of Hong Kong 1991–92, Adjunct Prof. of Math. 1994–2003, Dir Inst. of Math. Sciences 1994–, Distinguished Prof.-at-Large 2003–; Special Chair, Nat. Tsinghua Univ., Hsinchu, Taiwan 1991–92; Eilenberg Visiting Prof., Columbia Univ., New York 1999; mem. Bd of Math. Sciences, National Acad. of Science –1989); Mem.-at-Large Council of the American Math. Soc. 1990–92; mem. Scientific Advisory Council Math. Sciences Research Inst. –1989; Ed.-in-Chief Journal of Differential Geometry 1980–, Methods and Application of Analysis 1994–, Asian Journal of Mathematics 1997–; Ed. Communications in Mathematical Physics 1982–99, Mathematical Research Letters, 1993–, Advances in Mathematics 1994–, Journal of Mathematical Physics 1997–; mem. Editorial Advisory Bd Methods and Applications of Analysis, 1993–, Communications in Analysis and Geometry 1993–; mem. American Acad. of Arts and Sciences 1982; Academic Sinica 1984, NAS 1993, New York Acad. of Science, American Physical Soc., Soc. for Industrial and Applied Math.; Foreign mem. Chinese Acad. of Sciences 1995, Russian Acad. of Sciences 2003, Accad. Nazionale dei Lincei; Fellow, American Math. Soc. 2012; Hon. Prof., Fudan Univ. 1983–, Chinese Acad. of Sciences 1983, Hangzhou Univ. 1987–, Tsinghua Univ. 1987–, Nankai Univ. 1993–, Beijing Univ. 1998–, Univ. of Science and Tech. of China 1999–, Zhejiang Univ. 2002–; Hon. mem. Academic Cttee Inst. of Math., Chinese Acad. of Sciences 1980–; Hon. Ed. Communications in Information and Systems 2001–; Hon. Fellow, Shaw Coll. of The Chinese Univ. of Hong Kong 2007; Hon. DSc (Chinese Univ. of Hong Kong) 1981, (Chao Tung Univ.) 1997, (Nat. Tsinghua Univ., Beijing) 2000, (Macao Univ.) 2002, (Zhejing Univ.) 2003, (Hong Kong Science and Tech. Univ.) 2004, (Cen. Univ. of Taiwan) 2005, (Polytechnic Univ., Brooklyn) 2005, (Nat. Taiwan Univ.) 2006, (Lehigh Univ.) 2009, (Nat. Cheng Kung Univ.) 2010; Hon. Dr of Math. (Univ. of Waterloo) 2011; Hon. MA (Harvard) 1987; Sloan Fellow 1975–76, California Scientist of the Year 1979, Veblen Prize 1981, Carty Prize, Nat. Acad. 1981, Guggenheim Fellowship 1982, Fields Medal, Int. Math. Union, Warsaw 1982 (presented 1983), America's 100 Brightest Scientists Under 40, Science Digest 1984, MacArthur Fellow 1985, American Math. Soc. Lecturer 1986, Crafoord Prize, Royal Swedish Acad. 1994, John Harvard Fellow, Univ. of Cambridge 1996, US Nat. Medal of Science 1997, Bowen Lecturer, Univ. of California, Berkeley 1997, Run Run Shaw Distinguished Lecturer, The Chinese Univ. of Hong Kong 1998, Bergman Lecturer, Stanford Univ. 1999, Radamacher Lecture, Univ. of Pennyslvania 1999, Int. Scientific and Technological Co-operation Award 2003, Wolf Prize in Math. (co-recipient) 2010. *Publications:* The Shape of Inner Space: String Theory and the Geometry of the Universe's Hidden Dimension (co-author) 2010; numerous articles in math. journals on partial differential equations, the Calabi conjecture in algebraic geometry, the positive mass conjecture of general relativity theory, and real and complex Monge-Ampère equations. *Address:* Department of Mathematics, Harvard University, One Oxford Street, Cambridge, MA 02138, USA (office); The Institute of Mathematical Sciences, Unit 601, 6/F, Academic Building No. 1, The Chinese University of Hong Kong, Shatin, Hong Kong Special Administrative Region, People's Republic of China. *Telephone:* (617) 495-0836 (Harvard) (office); 2609-8038 (Hong Kong) (office). *Fax:* 2603-7636 (Hong Kong) (office). *E-mail:* yau@math.harvard.edu (office); yau@ims.cuhk.edu.hk (office). *Website:* math.harvard.edu (office); www.math.cuhk.edu.hk (office); www.doctoryau.com.

YAV MULANG, Henri; Democratic Republic of Congo politician; *Minister of Finance;* b. 1955, Lubumbashi; began career with Asscn nat. des entreprises du Zaïre (industry confed.) 1979; Dir of Studies, Fédération des chambres de commerce des États d'Afrique centrale 1984–89; fmr Prin. Tech. Adviser, GATT (later WTO), Libreville and Geneva; Deputy Chief of Staff to Minister of Industry and Small and Medium-sized Enterprises 2005–06; Deputy Admin., Fédération des entreprises du Congo 2006–09; Deputy Chief of Staff to the Presidency 2009–14; Minister of Finance 2014– (also Acting Minister of Mines); Gov. Eastern and Southern African Trade and Devt Bank; mem. Bd of Govs., ADB. *Address:* Ministry of Finance, Blvd du 30 juin, BP 12998 KIN I, Kinshasa-Gombet, Democratic Republic of Congo (office). *Telephone:* (12) 33232 (office). *Website:* www.minfinrdc.cd (office).

YAVLINSKII, Grigorii Alekseevich, PhD, CEconSc; Russian politician, economist and academic; *Professor, Department of Applied Economics, National Research University Higher School of Economics;* b. 10 April 1952, Lviv, Ukrainian SSR; m. Elena Yavlinskaya; two s.; ed Plekhanov Inst. of Econ., Cen. Inst. of Econs and Math., Russian Acad. of Sciences; electrician, Lviv Co., Raduga 1968–69; Sr Researcher, Research Inst. of Man., Ministry of Coal Industry, Moscow 1976–80; Head of Div. Research Inst. of Labour 1980–84; Deputy Chief, Chief of Div., Chief of Dept of Man. USSR State Labour Cttee 1984–89; Chief of Div. State Cttee on Econ. Reform USSR Council of Ministers 1988–90; mem. Pres.'s Political Advisory Council 1990–; Deputy Chair. Council of Ministers of Russian Fed., Chair. State Cttee on Econ. Reform 1990, author of econ. programme 500 days July–Nov. 1990; Econ. Counsellor of Prime Minister of Russia 1991; Chair. of Council of Scientific Soc. EPI-CENTRE (Cen. for Political and Econ. Studies) 1991; mem. Econ. Council of Pres. of Kazakhstan 1991; Deputy Chair. USSR Cttee on Operational Man. of Nat. Econ. Aug.–Dec. 1991; mem. Political Advisory Council of Pres. Gorbachev Oct.–Dec. 1991; elected mem. State Duma (Parl.) 1993; Co-leader (with Y.U. Boldyrev and V. Lukin) of pre-election bloc (later political movt then political party) Yabloko Russian Democratic Party (Rossiisskaya demokraticheskaya partiya 'Yabloko') 1993, Leader 1995–2008, also party Chair. in Duma; cand. in presidential elections 1996, 2000; Prof., Dept of Applied Econs, Nat. Research Univ. Higher School of Econs 2009–; mem. Trilateral Comm.; Int. Prize for Freedom 2004. *Achievements include:* Ukraine Jr Boxing Champion 1967, 1968. *Publications include:* Russia–The Search for Landmarks 1993, Incentives and Institutions: The Transition to a Market Economy in Russia 2000, Realeconomik: The Hidden Cause of the Great Recession (And How to Avert the Next One) 2011; over 60 books on economy of USSR, numerous articles. *Address:* Department of Applied Economics, National Research University, Higher School of Economics, 101000 Moscow, Myasnitskaya Ulitsa 20, Russia (office). *Telephone:* (495) 625-02-11 (office). *E-mail:* mmitkina@hse.ru (office); mmitkina@gmail.com. *Website:* www.hse.ru/en (office).

YAWER, Ghazi Mashal Ajil al-, BSc, MSc; Iraqi engineer, business executive and fmr head of state; b. 11 March 1958, Mosul; m. 1984; four c.; ed King Fahd Univ. for Petroleum and Minerals, Saudi Arabia, studies in UK, American University and Georgetown Univ., Washington, DC, USA; prominent mem. of Shammar tribe; left Iraq mid-1980s; Vice-Pres. Hicap Technology Co., Riyadh –2003; apptd to Iraqi Governing Council 2003, Pres. of Iraq under Iraqi Interim Govt 2004–05, Vice-Pres. under Iraqi Transitional Govt 2005–06. *Address:* c/o Office of the Vice-President, Baghdad, Iraq.

YAYA BRAHIM, Gen. Daoud; Chadian military commander, politician and fmr diplomatist; *Minister-delegate at the Presidency, responsible for National Defence, War Veterans and War Victims;* fmr Commdr, Chadian army regt deployed in Bosso, Niger (wounded in combat); fmr Dir Gendarmerie Nat. (nat. police force); Amb. to Central African Repub. 2016–18; Minister-del. at the Presidency, responsible for Nat. Defence, War Veterans and War Victims 2018–; rank of army gen. 2018. *Address:* Ministry of National Defence, War Veterans and War Victims, BP 916m N'Djamena, Chad (office). *Telephone:* 2-52-35-13 (office). *Fax:* 22-52-65-44 (office).

YAYI, Boni, PhD; Benin economist, banker and fmr head of state; b. 1952, Tchaourou; m. Chantal Yayi; five c.; ed Nat. Univ. of Benin, Univ. of Dakar, Senegal, Univ. of Orleans and Paris Univ., France; worked for Cen. Bank of the States of West Africa (BCEAO) becoming Deputy Dir 1980–88; Deputy Dir for Professional Devt, West African Centre for Banking Studies, Dakar 1988; worked in office of Pres. of Benin in charge of monetary and banking policies 1992–94; Pres. West African Devt Bank 1994–2006; Pres. of Benin 2006–16, also Minister of Defence 2012–13; Chair. African Union 2012–13; Chevalier, Ordre Nat. de Mérite (France), Officier, Ordre Nat. de Burkina Faso, Grand Officier, Ordre Nat. de Benin, Commdr, Ordre Nat. de Mali, de Niger, de Senegal.

YAZAMI, Rachid, MSc, PhD; Moroccan/French chemist, chemical engineer and academic; *Professor, School of Materials Science and Engineering and Director, Battery Programs, Energy Research Institute, Nanyang Technological University;* b. 16 April 1953, Fez, Morocco; s. of Abdelkader Yazami and Fatma Attar Yazami; m. Michele Dauriat; one d.; ed Grenoble Inst. of Tech., France; Research Assoc., CNRS, Grenoble 1985–88, Research Dir (Prof.) 1988–; Visiting Prof., Kyoto Univ. and Shinshu Univ., Japan 1988–90; Visiting Assoc. in Materials Science and in Chem., California Inst. of Tech. (Caltech), Jet Propulsion Lab., under a co-operative exchange programme with CNRS and co-f. a jt CNRS-Caltech int. lab. on Materials for Electrochemical Energetic (LIA-ME2) with Dept of Material Science 2000–10; Prof., School of Materials Science and Eng, Nanyang Technological Univ., Singapore 2009–, Dir Battery Programs, Energy Research Inst. (ERIAN) 2010–; Prin. Investigator, TUM-Create Center of Electromobility, Singapore; Co-founder CFx Battery, Inc. (now Contour Energy Systems, Inc.) (Caltech-CNRS start-up co. in Azusa, Calif.); Founder KVI PTE Ltd, Singapore 2011; fmr Pres. Int. Battery Asscn (IBA); fmr mem. Int. Scientific Advisory Bd of several int. meetings, including Int. Meetings on Lithium Batteries; mem. Hassan II Acad. of Science and Tech., Morocco; Wissam al-Kafaâ al-Fikria (Order for Intellectual Competence), Morocco 2014, Chevalier, Legion d'Honneur 2016; NATO Science for Peace Award, two Tech. Innovation Awards, NASA, IBA Research Award, Hawaii Battery Conf., IEEE Medal for Environmental and Safety Technologies 2012, Charles Stark Draper Prize, Nat. Acad. of Eng (co-recipient) 2014. *Achievements include:* best known for research on lithium ion batteries and fluoride ion batteries; inventor of the graphite anode (negative pole) of lithium ion batteries. *Publications include:* co-author of more than 200 papers in professional journals; more than 125 patents. *Leisure interests:* soccer, travelling, culinary arts, jazz, classical music. *Address:* KVI PTE Ltd, 18 Nanyang Drive #219-220, Singapore 637723, Singapore (home). *Telephone:* 6592-3545 (office); 8189-6674 (home). *Fax:* 6694-2617 (office). *E-mail:* rachid@ntu.edu.sg (office). *Website:* erian.ntu.edu.sg/aboutus/organisation/PD/Pages/Rachid-Yazami.aspx (office).

YAZGHI, Muhammad al-, LenD; Moroccan politician, lawyer and newspaper executive; b. 28 Sept. 1935, Fez; m. Balafrej Souada 1972; two s.; ed Moulay Youssef Coll., Lycée Gouraud, Univ. of Rabat and Ecole Nat. d'Admin., Paris, France; Dir of Budget, Ministry of Finance 1957–60; Dir Al-Moharir (daily paper) 1975–81, Liberation (daily paper) 1989; First Sec., Moroccan Press Union 1977–93; elected Deputy in Parl. 1977; mem. Political Bureau, Union Socialiste des Forces Populaires (USFP) 1975–91, Joint Vice-Sec. 1992, First Sec. –2007 (resgnd); Minister of Territorial Admin, the Environment, Urban Planning and Housing, then Minister of Territorial Administration, Water Resources and the Environment –2007; Minister of State 2007. *Publications:* articles in magazines and journals. *Leisure interests:* reading, travel.

YAZICI, Hayati, BS; Turkish politician and lawyer; *Minister of Customs and Trade;* b. 1952, Rize; m.; two c.; ed Istanbul Univ.; served as judge and freelance lawyer 1976–2002; elected mem. Grand Nat. Ass. representing Istanbul 2002; Deputy Prime Minister 2007–09, Minister of Customs and Trade 2011–; Co-founder, Bd Mem. and Deputy Chair. (Organizational Affairs), AKP (Adalet ve Kalkinma Partisi/Justice and Devt Party). *Address:* Ministry of Customs and Trade, Dumlupinar Boulevard 151, Eskisehir Yolu 9 Km.06530, Çankaya, Ankara, Turkey (office). *Telephone:* 449-10-00 (office). *E-mail:* bilgi@gtb.gov.tr (office). *Website:* www.gtb.gov.tr (office); www.hayatiyazici.com.tr.

YAZOV, Marshal Dmitri Timofeevich; Russian military official (retd); b. 1923; ed Frunze Mil. Acad. and Mil. Acad. of Gen. Staff; entered Soviet army 1941; active service 1941–45; command posts 1945–76; Deputy Commdr of Far Eastern Mil. Dist 1976–79; Commdr of Cen. Group Forces in Czechoslovakia 1979–80; Deputy to USSR Supreme Soviet 1979–89; Commdr of Cen. Asian Mil. Dist 1980; Deputy Minister of Defence Feb.–June 1987, Minister of Defence and Head of Armed Forces 1987–91; mem. of Cen. Cttee of Kazakh CP 1981–87; mem. Presidential Council 1990–91; Cand. mem. of Cen. Cttee of CPSU 1981–91; fmr mem. Politburo; rank of Marshal 1990; arrested 1991, for participation in attempted coup d'état, charged with conspiracy 1992; on trial 1993; released 1994; Chief Mil. Adviser, Ministry of Defence 1998; Chair. Marshal G. Zhukov Memorial Cttee; numerous Russian and int. decorations and awards. *Leisure interests:* theatre, poetry.

YE, Gongqi; Chinese administrator; b. 1930; ed Shanghai High School; joined CCP 1948; Deputy Dir of Shanghai Light Industry Bureau 1976; Vice-Mayor Shanghai 1985; Chair. Shanghai Municipal 9th and 10th People's Congress 1988–98; apptd Chair. Shanghai Consumers Asscn 2004; Sr Consultant China Shipping (Group) Co.; Pres. Shanghai Asscn for Int. Friendly Contact. *Address:* c/o Shanghai Consumers Association, 14th Floor, No. 301 Zhaojiabang Road Shanghai 200032, People's Republic of China.

YE, Jianming, BA; Chinese business executive; *Chairman, CEFC China Energy Company Ltd;* b. 5 June 1977, Hong Kong; Exec. Dir and Chair. CEFC China Energy Co. Ltd, Chair. China Energy Fund Cttee; Chair. China Inst. of Culture Ltd; Chair. CEFC Shanghai Charity Fund; Dir Shanghai Energy Security Research Centre. *Publication:* Building an Economic Community. *Address:* Head Office, CEFC China Energy Company Ltd, 111 Xingguo Road, Xuhui District, Shanghai, People's Republic of China (office). *Telephone:* (21) 33633178 (office). *E-mail:* enquiry@cefc.co (office). *Website:* en.cefc.co (office).

YE, Liansong; Chinese politician and engineer; b. 1935, Shanghai; ed Jiaotong Univ., Shanghai; engineer, Shijiazhuang Municipal Diesel Plant 1960–80; Vice-Mayor Shijiazhuang 1982–85; mem. Standing Cttee Hebei Prov. CCP Cttee 1983–2000, Deputy Sec. 1998–2000; Vice-Gov. Hebei Prov. 1985–93, Gov. 1993–98; Alt. mem. 13th Cen. Cttee CCP 1987–92, mem. 14th Cen. Cttee 1992–97, 15th CCP Cen. Cttee 1997–2002; Deputy to 8th NPC 1993–98; mem. 10th Nat. Cttee, CPPCC 2003, also Vice-Chair. Subcommittee of Economy.

YE, Weilin; Chinese writer; b. 1935, Huiyang Co., Guangdong Prov.; s. of Ye Wei; m. Chen Jieni; two c.; joined PLA 1950; apptd Chair. Hainan Writers' Asscn 1990; has written film screenplays. *Publications:* The Blue Mulan Rivulet, On the River without Navigation Marks, The First Farewell, Passing the Night at Meiziguo.

YE, Xiaogang; Chinese composer; *Vice-President, Central Conservatory of Music;* b. 23 Sept. 1955, Shanghai; s. of Ye Chunzi and Ho Ying; m. Xu Jing 1987; ed Eastman School of Music, USA (postgraduate); Vice-Pres. Cen. Conservatory of Music, Beijing 2009–, Chair. Composition Division; piano concerto Starry Sky was premiered during opening ceremony of Beijing Olympic Games by pianist Lang Lang, August 2008; mem. China Fed. of Literature and Art; Vice Chair. Chinese Musicians Asscn; mem. Council, China Film Workers Asscn; Fellow Metropolitan Life Foundation, Pennsylvania Council of the Arts 1996; mem. judging penal, numerous nat. and int. competitions including Himalayas Cup Int. Piano Composition Competition, Luxembourg Int. Composition Competition; Alexander Tcherepnin Prize 1982, Japan Dance Star Ballet Prize 1986, Ministry of Culture Ou Yongxi Excellent Music Education Award. *Compositions:* Xi Jiang Yue Symphony 1984, Horizon Symphony 1985, Piano Ballade 1987, Dance Drama: The Love Story of Da Lai VI 1988, Last Paradise, Song of the Earth, Twilight in Tibet, My Far Away Nanjing, Nine Horses. *Address:* Central Conservatory of Music, 43 Baojiajie, Beijing 100031, People's Republic of China (office). *E-mail:* ao@ccom.edu.cn (office). *Website:* en.ccom.edu.cn (office).

YEANG, Dato' (Darjah Mulia Panguan Negeri) Kenneth (Ken) King Mun, AADipl, PhD, RIBA; Malaysian architect, ecologist, academic and author; *Principal, T. R. Hamzah & Yeang Sdn Bhd;* b. 6 Oct. 1948, Penang; m. Priscilla Pit-Ling Yeang; ed Architectural Asscn (AA), London, UK, Univ. of Pennsylvania, USA, Wolfson Coll., Cambridge, UK; internship with S.T.S. Leong, Singapore 1969; Louis de Soisson Partnership 1970; freelance graphic design work for AD and AAQ magazines and for the AA; architect at Akitek Bersekutu 1975; Prin., T. R. Hamzah & Yeang Sdn Bhd 1976–, Llewely Davies Yeang 2005–11, Ken Yeang Design International, UK, North Hamzah Yeang Architectural and Eng Co., China; Willis Visiting Prof., Univ. of Sheffield, UK 1994–2004; Provost's Distinguished Visitor, Univ. of Southern California, USA 1999; Distinguished Plym Prof., Univ. of Illinois, USA 2006–; Hon. Fellow, Singapore Inst. of Architects 1998; Hon. FAIA 1999; Hon. Academician, Int. Acad. of Architecture, Sofia 2000; Hon. LittD (Sheffield) 2004; Hon. PhD (Univ. of Malaya) 2013; Aga Khan Award for Architecture 1992, Norway Award 1992, Far Eastern Econ. Review Innovation Award 1998, Auguste Perret Prize 1999, Asia Pacific Distinguished Scholar Award 1999, Enterprise 50 Award, Govt of Malaysia 1999, Prinz Claus Fonds Award, Netherlands 1999, CAA Sir Robert Mathew Award 2000, Lynn S. Beedle Lifetime Achievement Award, Council on Tall Buildings and Urban Habitat (USA), Merdeka Award, Govt of Malaysia 2011, Malaysian Inst. of Architects Gold Medal 2014, Green Building Council Lifetime Achievement Award, Singapore 2015. *Works include:* has completed more than 200 built projects since 1975, known for his signature ecoarchitecture and ecomasterplans; The Roof Roof House, Selangor 1985, Menara Mesiniaga Tower, Selangor (Aga Khan Award for Architecture, Royal Australian Inst. of Architects Int. Award, Malaysian Inst. of Architects Design Award) 1992, Kowloon Waterfront Masterplan, Hong Kong 1998, Nat. Library, Singapore (BCA Green Mark Platinum Award, Singapore Inst. of Architects Award) 2005, SOMA Masterplan, Bangalore, India 2006, DiGi Technical Office, Shah Alam (Malaysian Inst. of Architects Design Award (Commendation) and Green Building Index Gold rating) 2010, Solaris Tower, 1-north, Singapore (with CPG Consult) (Singapore Inst. of Architects Award 2011, Malaysian Inst. of Architects Gold Award 2011, World Asscn of Chinese Architects Gold Medal 2011, BCA Green Mark Platinum rating) 2010, Spire Edge Tower, Gurgaon, Haryana, India 2013, Ganendra Art House, Petaling Jaya (Malaysian Inst. of Architects Design Award (Commendation) 2010, Green Building Index certification rating) 2011, Great Ormond Street Children's Hospital Extension Phase 1 (with Llewelyn Davies Yeang), London, UK 2011, Calvary Convention Centre, Kuala Lumpur 2012, Fu Gong Shan Monastery, Johore Baru 2013, Fu Gong Shan, Johore 2016, Putrajaya Phase 2C5 Towers (offices and retail) 2016, LGT Hijauan Towers, Kuala Lumpur (completion 2018). *Publications:* The Tropical Verandah City 1989, Designing with Nature 1995, The Skyscraper Bioclimatically Considered: A Design Primer 1997, The Green Skyscraper: The Basis for Designing Sustainable Intensive Buildings 1999, Reinventing the Skyscraper: A Vertical Theory of Urban Design 2002, Eco Skyscrapers 2007, Ecodesign: A Manual for Ecological Design 2008, EcoMasterplanning 2009, Ecoarchitecture: The Work of Ken Yeang 2011, Ginza Pocket Park (Japan), Tokyo Designer's Space (Japan), Washington Building Museum, ADES Gallery (Germany), Bulding Centre, London, Netherlands Inst. of Architecture, Rotterdam, IFA Gallery, Stuttgart, Berlin. *Publications:* more than 12 books on ecological design. *Leisure interests:* reading, writing. *Address:* T. R. Hamzah & Yeang Sdn Bhd, 8 Jalan 1, Taman Sri Ukay, Ampang, Selangor, 68000 Kuala Lumpur, Malaysia (office); Ken Yeang Design International, 13 Grosvenor Gardens, London, SW1W 0BD, England (office). *Telephone:* (3) 4257-1948 (Kuala Lumpur) (office); (20) 7592-7264 (London) (office). *Fax:* (3) 4256-1005 (Kuala Lumpur) (office). *E-mail:* janet@trhamzahyeang.com (office); kynnet@kyeang.com (office); kynnet@kyeang.com. *Website:* www.hamzahyeang.com (office).

YECHURY, Sitaram, PhD; Indian politician; *General Secretary, Communist Party of India—Marxist;* b. 12 Aug. 1952, Chennai; s. of Sarveswara Somayajula Yechury and Kalpakam Yechury; m. 1st; one s. one d.; m. 2nd Seema Chisti; ed St Stephen's Coll., Delhi Univ., Jawaharlal Nehru Univ.; joined Students Fed. of India (SFI) 1974, elected All India Jt Sec. 1978, then All India Pres., left SFI in 1986; joined Communist Party of India—Marxist (CPI—M) 1975, elected mem. Cen. Cttee 1984, Cen. Secr. 1988, Politibureau 1992, fmr Head Int. Dept, Parl. Group Leader, Gen. Sec. 2015–; mem. Rajya Sabha (Parl.) 2005–17. *Publications:* What is This Hindu Rashtra?: On Golwalkar's Fascistic Ideology and the Saffron Brigade's Practice 1993, Pseudo Hinduism Exposed: Saffron Brigade's Myths and Reality 1993, Caste and Class in Indian Politics Today 1997, Oil Pool Deficit or Cesspool of Deceit 1997, Ghrina Ki Rajniti 2006, Socialism in a Changing World 2008, Communalism vs. Secularism 2008; as ed.: People's Diary of Freedom Struggle 2008, The Great Revolt: A Left Appraisal, Global Economic Crisis. *Address:* Communist Party of India—Marxist, A. K. Gopalan Bhavan, 27–29 Bhai Vir Singh Marg, New Delhi 110 001, India (office). *Telephone:* (11) 23344918 (office). *Fax:* (11) 23747483 (office). *E-mail:* cc@cpim.org (office). *Website:* www.cpim.org.

YEDDYURAPPA, B(okanakere) S(iddalingappa), BA; Indian politician and government official; b. 27 Feb. 1943, Bookanakere village, Mandya Dist, Karnataka; s. of Siddalingappa Yediyurappa and Puttathayamma Yediyurappa; m. Maithra Devi Yediyurappa 1967 (died 2004); two s. three d.; first-div. clerk in social welfare dept 1965; clerk, Veerabhadra Shastri's Shankar rice mill, Shikaripur 1965–67; set up hardware shop in Shimoga; Sec. Shikaripur unit, Rashtriya Swayamsevak Sangh 1970–72; Pres. Taluk unit, Jan Sangh 1972–75; Pres. Town Municipality of Shikaripur 1975; imprisoned during Emergency in India 1975–77, lodged in Bellary and Shimoga jails; Pres. Shikaripur Taluk unit of BJP 1980–85, Shimoga Dist unit of BJP 1985–88, BJP unit, Karnataka 1988; mem. Lower House, Karnataka Legis. Ass. for Shikaripura constituency 1983–99, 2004, 2008–12, nominated by BJP to become mem. Legis. Council (Upper House) of Karnataka 1999–2004; mem. Lok Sabha (Lower House of Parl.) for Shimoga 2006–07, 2014–; Deputy Chief Minister and Minister of Finance, Karnataka Govt 2006–07; Chief Minister of Karnataka (prior to collapse of coalition govt) 12–19 Nov. 2007 (first BJP mem. to become Chief Minister of a South Indian state), 2008–11 (resgnd), 17–19 May 2018; arrested and charged with illegally selling govt land 2011 (case overturned; mem. Bharatiya Janata Party (BJP). *Address:* No.

381, "Dhavalagiri" 6th Cross, 80 ft. Road, RMV II Stage, Dollars Colony, Bengaluru Karnataka 560094 India (home); 3, South Avenue Lane, New Delhi 110004 India.

YEGOROV, Vladimir Konstantinovich; Russian politician, philosopher and journalist; *Professor, Russian Academy of State Service;* b. 30 Oct. 1947, Kanash, Chuvash ASSR, USSR; m.; one s.; ed Kazan State Univ.; Deputy Ed. Molodoi Komsomolets, also Head, Dept of Propaganda, Cen. Comsomol Cttee 1974–85; Rector, Gorky. Inst. of Literature in Moscow 1985–87; Deputy Head, Div. of Culture, Ideological Dept, CPSU Cen. Cttee 1987–90; Asst to Pres. Mikhail Gorbachev (q.v.) on Problems of Culture and Religion 1990–91; Chief Scientific Researcher, Analytical Centre at Ministry of Science 1992–96; Prof., Russian Acad. of State Service 1993–, Rector from 2000; mem. Co-ordination Council, My Motherland; Dir Russian State Library 1996–98; Minister of Culture Russian Fed. 1998–2000. *Publications:* books including History in our Lives, Intelligentsia and Power, The Star Turns Pale: Reflections on Russian History, Out of a Dead End into the Unknown: Notes on Gorbachev's Perestroika 1993, Many Faces of Russia; numerous articles. *Address:* Academy of State Service, Vernadskogo prosp. 84, 119571 Moscow, Russian Federation (office). *Telephone:* (495) 436-90-12 (office).

YEHOSHUA, Abraham B., MA; Israeli writer and academic; *Professor Emeritus of Comparative and Hebrew Literature, University of Haifa;* b. 9 Dec. 1936, Jerusalem; s. of Yaakov Yehoshua and Malka Rosilio; m. Rivka Kirsninski; two s. one d.; ed Hebrew Univ., Jerusalem; served in paratroopers unit 1954–57; Dir Israeli School in Paris 1964; Gen. Sec. World Union of Jewish Studies, Paris 1963–67; Dean of Students, Haifa Univ. 1967–72, apptd Prof. of Comparative and Hebrew Literature 1972–, now Prof. Emer.; Visiting Prof., Harvard Univ., USA 1977, Univ. of Chicago 1988, 1997, 2000, Princeton Univ. 1992–, Rome Univ. 2003; Co-Ed. Keshet 1965–72, Siman Kria 1973–, Tel Aviv Review 1987–; mem. Israeli Peace Movt; Dr hc (Hebrew Union Coll.) 1990, (Tel-Aviv Univ.) 1998, (Univ. of Turin) 1999, (Bar Ilan Univ.) 2000, (Weizman Inst.) 2009, (Ben Gurion Univ.) 2011, (Scuola Normale Superiore di Pisa) 2012; Brener Prize 1983, Alterman Prize 1986, Bialik Prize 1989, Booker Prize 1992, B'nai B'rith of Europe Prize 1993, Jewish Quartely Prize 1993, Grinzanne Cavour Prize (Italy) 1994, Boccaccio Prize 2005, Viarrego Prize 2006, Rome Prize 2008, Prix Médicis étranger 2012, Emet Prize 2016, Dan David Prize 2017, Feltrinelli Prize, Accademia Nazionale dei Lincei 2017. *Opera:* A Journey to the End of the Millennium, music by Josef Bardanashvili and libretto by A. B Yehoshua, Israel Opera 2005. *Plays include:* A Night in May 1969, Last Treatments 1973, Possessions 1992, Night's Babies 1993, Can Two Walk Together 2012. *Film adaptations include:* The Lover, Facing the Forests, Continuing Silence, Mr Mani, Open Heart, A Voyage to the End of the Millennium, Early in the Summer of 1970, A Late Divorce. *Publications:* short fiction: The Death of the Old Man (short stories) 1962, Facing The forests (short stories) 1968, Early in the Summer of 1970 (novella) 1971, The Continuing Silence of a Poet: The Collected Stories of A.B. Yehoshua 1999; novels: The Lover 1977, A Late Divorce (Flaiano Int. Poetry Prize, Italy 1996) 1982, Five Seasons (Nat. Jewish Book Award 1990, Cavour Prize, Italy 1994) 1987, Mr. Mani (Israeli Booker Prize 1992, Nat. Jewish Book Award 1993, Wingate Prize, UK 1994) 1990, Open Heart 1994, A Journey to the End of the Millennium (Koret Prize) 1997, The Liberated Bride (Napoli Prize, Lampedusa Prize) 2001, A Woman in Jerusalem (The Mission of the Human Resource Man) (Los Angeles Times Book Prize for Fiction) 2004, Friendly Fire 2007, The Retrospective (Spanish Grace) 2010, The Extra 2014; collected essays: Between Right and Right 1980, The Wall and the Mountain 1988, The Terrible Power of a Minor Guilt 1998, Homeland Grasp 2008; children's books: Tamar and Gaya's Mouse (picture book) 2005, Ofri's Beloved Pet (picture book) 2007. *Address:* 258 Ben Gurion Road, Givatayim, 53326, Israel (home). *Telephone:* 3-7524539 (home). *Fax:* 3-5274412 (home). *E-mail:* bulli@research.haifa.ac.il (home).

YEKHANUROV, Yuriy Ivanovych; Ukrainian economist and politician; b. 23 Aug. 1948, Belkachi, Yakut ASSR (now the Repub. of Sakha—Yakutiya), Russian Fed.; s. of Ivan Mikhailovich Yekhanurov and Galina Mikhailovna Yekhanurova; m. Olena Lvivna Yekhanurova; one s.; ed Kyiv Construction Tech. Coll.; Higher School of Econ. State Planning, Kyiv Inst. of Nat. Econs, Academic Research Econ. Inst. of State Planning; master, then head of workshop, Chief Engineer, Dir, Kyivmiskbur Co. 1967–77, Head of Kyivmiskbudkomplekt Co. 1977–88; Head, Buddetal Co. 1977–88; Deputy Chief, Golovkyivmiskbud Co. 1988–91; elected to Kyiv City Rada (Council) 1990; Head of State Econ. Council, Cabinet of Ministers 1991–92; Deputy Head of Bd of Verkhovna Rada (Parl.) 1992; Deputy Head of Kyiv City Admin. 1992–93; Deputy Minister of the Economy 1993–94; Head of State Property Fund 1994–97; Minister of Economy Feb.–July 1997; Head of State Cttee on Entrepreneurship Devt 1997–98; mem. Verkhovna Rada 1998–, Deputy Head, Cttee on Econ. Policy, Man. Economy, Property and Investment 1998–99; First Deputy Prime Minister 1999–2001; Deputy Head of Presidential Admin 2001, 2004, re-elected mem. Verkhovna Rada for Our Ukraine bloc 2002, Head of Parl. Cttee on Industrial Policy and Entrepreneurship 2002; Deputy Head of Viktor Yushchenko's presidential campaign team 2004; Head of Cen. Exec. Cttee, Our Ukraine People's Union party March 2005; Gov. Dnipropetrovsk Oblast April–Sept. 2005; apptd Acting Prime Minister Sept. 2005, Prime Minister Sept. 2005–06; Minister of Defence 2007–09; First Deputy Head of the Presidential Secr. 2009–10; unsuccessful cand. of Revival party for Mayor of Kiev 2015. *Publications:* more than 60 publs on econs.

YELCHENKO, Volodymyr, MA; Ukrainian diplomatist; *Permanent Representative to United Nations;* b. 27 June 1959, Kiev; s. Yuriy Nykyforovych Yelchenko; m. Iryna Yelchenko; one d.; ed Kyiv State Univ.; Third Sec./Second Sec., Dept of State Protocol, Ministry of Foreign Affairs (MFA) 1981–84, Second Sec. Dept of Int. Orgs 1984–86, First Sec. to Chief of Section 1992–93, Deputy Dir 1993–95, Dir 1995–97, Second Sec. Perm. Mission to UN 1986–92; Perm. Rep. to UN 1997–2000, Rep. to UN Security Council 2000–01 (Pres. March 2001), 2016–17; Deputy Minister of Foreign Affairs 2000–01, Deputy Sec. of State for Foreign Affairs 2001–03, Sec. of State March–May 2003, First Deputy Minister of Foreign Affairs 2003–05; Chair. Nat. Comm., UNESCO 2004–05, also mem. Exec. Bd; Amb. to Austria 2005–08, to Russia 2010–15, Perm. Rep. to int. orgs in Vienna 2005–10; Perm. Rep. to UN 2016–; Order of Merit, III and II Grades. *Address:* Permanent Mission of Ukraine, 220 E 51st Street, New York, NY 10022, USA (office). *Telephone:* (212) 759-7003 (office). *Fax:* (212) 355-9455 (office). *E-mail:* uno_us@mfa.gov.ua (office). *Website:* ukraineun.org (office).

YELLAND, David, BA, AMP; British business executive and fmr journalist; *Partner, Brunswick Group LLP;* b. 14 May 1963, Harrogate, N Yorks., England; s. of John Michael Yelland and Patricia Ann McIntosh; m. 1st Tania Farrell 1996 (died 2006); one s.; m. 2nd Charlotte Marjorie Elston 2010; one d.; ed Brigg Grammar School, Lincs., Univ. of Coventry, Harvard Business School, USA; grad. trainee, Westminster Press 1985; trainee reporter, Buckinghamshire Advertiser 1985–87; industrial reporter, Northern Echo 1987–88; gen. news and business reporter, North West Times and Sunday Times 1988–89; city reporter, Thomson Regional Newspapers 1989–90; joined News Corpn 1990; city reporter, then City Ed. The Sun 1990–92, New York Corresp. 1992–93, Ed. 1998–2003; Deputy Business Ed. Business Ed., then Deputy Ed. New York Post 1993–98; Sr Vice-Pres. News Corpn, New York 2003–04; Vice-Pres. Weber Shandwick Worldwide (public relations consultancy) 2004–06; Partner, Brunswick Group LLP 2006–; Trustee, Action on Addiction 2012–; Campaign UK Media Achiever of the Year 2002. *Publication:* The Truth About Leo (novel) 2010. *Leisure interests:* writing, reading, recovering, swimming, Manchester City Football Club. *Address:* Brunswick Group LLP, 16 Lincoln's Inn Fields, London, WC2A 3ED, England (office). *Telephone:* (20) 7404-5959 (office). *Fax:* (20) 7936-7730 (office). *E-mail:* dyelland@brunswickgroup.com (office). *Website:* www.brunswickgroup.com (office).

YELLEN, Janet Louise, PhD; American economist, academic and fmr central banker; b. 13 Aug. 1946, Brooklyn, New York; d. of Julius Yellen and Anna Ruth Yellen (née Blumenthal); m. George Arthur Akerlof (Nobel Laureate 2001) 1978; one s.; ed Brown Univ., Yale Univ.; Grad. Fellow, NSF 1967–71; Asst Prof. of Econs, Harvard Univ. 1971–76; consultant, Div. of Int. Finance, Bd of Govs of US Fed. Reserve System 1974–75, economist, Trade and Financial Studies section 1977–78; consultant, US Congressional Budget Office, Washington, DC 1975–76; Research Affiliate, Yale Univ. 1976; Lecturer, LSE 1978–80; Asst Prof. of Econs, School of Business Admin., Univ. of California, Berkeley 1980–82, Assoc. Prof. 1982–85, Prof., Haas School of Business 1985, Bernard T. Rocca Jr Prof. of Int. Business and Trade 1992, Eugene E. and Catherine M. Trefethen Prof. of Business Admin, now Prof. Emer., fmr mem. Haas Econ. Analysis and Policy Group; mem. Bd of Govs US Fed. Reserve System 1994–97; Chair. Council of Econ. Advisers 1997–99, also Chair. Econ. Policy Cttee of OECD; Pres. and CEO Fed. Reserve Bank of San Francisco 2004–10, Vice-Chair. Bd of Govs, Fed. Reserve System 2010–14, Chair. 2014–18; Research Fellow, MIT 1974; mem. Panel of Econ. Advisers, US Congressional Budget Office 1993; mem. Advisory Panel on Econs NSF 1977–78, 1991–92; mem. Brookings Panel on Econ. Activity 1987–88, 1990–91, Sr Adviser 1989–; Lecturer on Macroeconomic Theory, Yrjö Jahnsson Foundation, Helsinki 1977–78; mem. Council on Foreign Relations 1976–81, American Econ. Asscn; Guggenheim Fellow 1986–87; Fellow, American Acad. of Arts and Sciences 2001–, Yale Corpn 2000–; Assoc., Journal of Econ. Perspectives 1987–91; Hon. Woodrow Wilson Fellow 1967; Dr hc (London School of Econs) 2014, (Yale) 2015; Maria and Sidney Rolfe Award for Nat. Econ. Service, Women's Econ. Roundtable 1997, Wilbur Lucius Cross Medal, Yale Univ. 1997, Adam Smith Award, Nat. Asscn for Business Economics 2010. *Publications include:* The Limits of the Market in Resource Allocation (co-author) 1977, contrib. articles to professional journals.

YEMENIDJIAN, Alex, MA; American business executive; *Chairman and CEO, Armenco Holdings LLC;* ed California State Univ., Northridge, Univ. of Southern California; Man. Partner, Parks, Palmer & Yemenidjian; joined Metro-Goldwyn-Mayer (MGM) Grand Inc., Las Vegas 1989, Chief Financial Officer 1994–98, Pres. and COO 1995–99, mem. Bd of Dirs 1999–2005, Dir MGM Grand Inc. (now MGM MIRAGE), Santa Monica 1989–, Chair. and CEO 1999–2005; Chair. and CEO Armenco Holdings LLC 2005–; Exec. Tracinda 1990–97, 1999; Chair., Pres. and CEO Tropicana Las Vegas Hotel & Casino, Inc. 2009–, Pres. and CEO Tropicana Las Vegas, Inc. 2013–; Chair. and CEO Hotel Ramada of Nevada; Chair. United Armenian Fund; Ind. Dir Kirk Kerkorian's Lincy Foundation 1989–, Guess Inc. 2005–; Trustee, Baron Investment Funds Trust 2006–, Baron Select Funds, Mutual Funds; Co-Chair. Imagine the Arts Campaign at California State Univ., Northridge 2005–. *Address:* Armenco Holdings LLC, 1925 Century Park East, Los Angeles, CA 90067-2701, USA (office). *Telephone:* (310) 788-3000 (office).

YEN, Ching-Chang, LLB, MA; Taiwanese government official; b. 7 April 1948, Tainan; m.; one s. one d.; ed Nat. Taiwan Univ., Univ. of Michigan, USA; joined Ministry of Finance 1972, Sr Customs Officer, Taipei Customs Bureau 1972–73, Specialist, Dept of Customs Admin. 1973–77, Sr Specialist in Secr. 1977–78, 1980–84, Exec. Sec. Legal Comm. 1984–85, Taxation and Tariff Comm. 1985–92, Deputy Minister of Finance 1996–2000, Minister of Finance 2000–02; Deputy Dir-Gen. First Bureau, Office of the Pres. 1992–93, Dir-Gen. 1993–96; Prof., Nat. Taiwan Univ., Nat. Chengchi Univ. and Soochoe Univ. 1981–86; Rep. to WTO 2002–05; Chair. and CEO Yuanta Financial Holding Co., Ltd (fmrly Fuhwa Financial Holding Co.) 2005–13; fmr Chair. Yuanta Commercial Bank Co., Ltd, Dir 2007–; fmr Visiting Chair, Law School, Univ. of Wisconsin-Madison; Eisenhower Fellowship, USA 1995; Chevalier, Ordre nat. du Mérite 1998, Order of Brilliant Star with Grand Cordon in 2005; Class One Merit Medal, Exec. Yuan 2000. *Publications:* Anti-dumping Act and Customs Policy 1981, Legal Problems of Sino-American Trade Negotiations 1987, Unveiling GATT: Order and Trend of Global Trade 1989, International Economic Law 1991, Laws and Regulations of International Economic Relations 1995, Taxation Law 1998, Understanding and Appreciating French Wines 1997; (in English) Taiwan Trade and Investment Law 1994.

YEN, De-fa; Taiwanese politician and fmr military commander; *Minister of National Defense;* b. 1952; m. Zhu Taiying; ed Repub. of China Mil. Acad., Nat. Defense Univ. War Coll.; long career in army, roles include Commdr and Prin., Army Armored Forces Training Command and Armored Forces School 2006, Commdr, Eighth Army Corps 2008–10, Deputy Chief of Staff 2011–13, 5th Commdr, Repub. of China (RoC) Army 2014–15, Chief of Gen. Staff, RoC Armed Forces 2015–16; Vice Minister of Nat. Defense for armaments 2013–14, Minister of Nat. Defense 2018–; Sec.-Gen., Nat. Security Council 2017–18. *Address:* Ministry of National Defense, 409 Bei An Rd, Zhongshan District, Taipei 10462, Taiwan (office). *Telephone:* (2) 23116117 (office). *Fax:* (2) 23144221 (office). *Website:* www.mnd.gov.tw (office).

YEN, Gen. Ming; Taiwanese army officer and politician; b. 14 Nov. 1949; ed Repub. of China Air Force Acad., Nat. Defense Univ.; spent long career in Repub. of China Air Force (ROCAF) including as Wing Chief, later Superintendent, ROCAF, Chief of Staff of Combined Logistics Command, Commdr, ROCAF Logistics Command, Deputy Commdr, later Commdr, Deputy Chief of Staff and Chief of Staff ROCAF Command HQ, Commanding Gen. of ROCAF 2011–13, Chief of Gen. Staff Jan.–Aug. 2013; Minister of Nat. Defense 2013–15; attained rank of Gen. 2008.

YENEL, Selim; Turkish diplomatist; *Under-Secretary, Ministry of European Union Affairs;* b. 9 June 1956, Istanbul; m.; ed Univ. of Ankara; Attaché and Third Sec., Dept of Nuclear Energy, Ministry of Foreign Affairs (MFA) 1979–80, mil. service, Third Sec., Cabinet of the Minister of Foreign Affairs 1980–81, Third Sec., then Second Sec., Perm. Representation of Turkey to OECD, Paris 1981–84, First Sec., Embassy in Kabul 1984–86, First Sec., Dept of the Middle East and Africa, MFA 1986–88, First Sec., Special Advisory Office of the Minister of Foreign Affairs Feb.–Aug. 1988, First Sec. and Counsellor, Perm. Representation to the UN, New York 1988–93, Head of Section, Special Advisory Office of the Undersecretary, MFA 1993–94, Chief of Cabinet of the Undersecretary, MFA Feb.–Sept. 1994, Counsellor and First Counsellor, Perm. Del. of Turkey to the EEC, Brussels 1994–99, Head of Dept for EU Econ. Affairs, MFA 1999–2001, Deputy Dir Gen. and Minister Plenipotentiary, Deputy Directorate Gen. for EU Econ. Affairs 2001–05, Amb. to Austria 2005–09, Amb. and Deputy Undersecretary for European Affairs, MFA 2009–10, Amb. and Deputy Undersecretary for Bilateral Political Affairs 2010–11, Amb. and Perm. Rep. to the EU, Brussels 2011–16; Under-Sec., Ministry of EU Affairs 2017–. *Address:* Mustafa Kemal Mah. 2082 Cad. 4, 06510 Bilkent, Ankara, Turkey (office). *Telephone:* (312) 2181300 (office). *Fax:* (312) 2181464 (office). *E-mail:* bilgiedinme@ab.gov.tr (office). *Website:* www.abgs.gov.tr (office).

YENNIMATAS, George, LLB; Greek diplomatist; *Secretary-General, Presidency of the Hellenic Republic;* m. Athena Yennimata-Kritikou; ed Univ. of Athens; joined Foreign Service 1972, has served as Minister Counsellor and Chargé d'affaires, Embassy in Paris, Minister Counsellor, Embassy in Moscow, Amb. to Syria 1992–96, to Portugal 1996–2000, Gen. Sec. (Political), Ministry of Foreign Affairs 2003–05, also Dir Int. Orgs Dept, Amb. to Turkey 2005–07; currently Sec.-Gen., Presidency of the Hellenic Republic. *Address:* Office of the President, Odos Vassileos Georgiu 2, 100 28 Athens, Greece (office). *Telephone:* (210) 7283111 (office). *Fax:* (210) 7248938 (office). *Website:* www.presidency.gr (office).

YENTOB, Alan, LLB; British media executive; *Chairman, BBC Films;* b. 11 March 1947, London, England; s. of Isaac Yentob and Flora Yentob (née Khazam); partner Philippa Walker; one s. one d.; ed King's School, Ely, Univ. of Grenoble, France, Univ. of Leeds; BBC gen. trainee 1968, apptd Producer/Dir 1970, including Omnibus 1973–75, Ed. Arena 1978–85, Head of Music and Arts, BBC-TV 1985–88, Controller, BBC 2 1988–93, BBC 1 1993–97, BBC Dir of Programmes 1997–98, BBC Dir of TV 1998–2000, of Drama, Entertainment and Children's Programmes 2000–04, Creative Dir, BBC 2004–15 (resgnd), presenter of arts series Imagine (BBC 1) 2003–, Chair. BBC Films; mem. British Film Inst. Production Bd 1985–93, British Screen Advisory Council, Advisory Cttee, Council Royal Court Theatre; Chair. Inst. of Contemporary Arts –2010; Gov. Nat. Film School 1998–; mem. South Bank Bd 1999–2008, Int. Acad. of Television Arts and Sciences; Trustee, Kids Co. (charity) 1997–2015 (Chair. 2003–15), Architecture Foundation 1992–2000, Timebank 2001–04; Hon. Fellow, RCA, RIBA, Royal Television Soc. *Leisure interests:* swimming, books. *Address:* BBC Films, Zone A, 7th Floor, BBC Broadcasting House, Portland Place, London, W1A 1AA, England (office). *Telephone:* (20) 3614-4445 (office). *Website:* www.bbc.co.uk/bbcfilms (office).

YEO, Cheow Tong, BEng; Singaporean politician; b. 1947; m. Helen Yeo; three d.; ed Anglo-Chinese School, Univ. of Western Australia; worked in Econ. Devt Bd 1972–75; joined LeBlond Makino Asia Pte. Ltd (LMA) as Staff Engineer 1975, subsequently promoted to Eng Man., then Operations Dir; Man. Dir LMA and subsidiary co., Pacific Precision Castings Pte. Ltd 1981–85; MP for Hong Kah 1984–2011; Minister of State for Health and for Foreign Affairs 1985–87; Acting Minister for Health, Sr Minister of State for Foreign Affairs 1987–90, of Health 1990–94, for Community Devt 1991–94, for Trade and Industry 1994–97, of Health and for the Environment 1997–99; Minister for Communications and Information Tech. 1999–2001; Minister of Transport 2001–06 (resgnd); mem. Bd of Dirs KillyInvest Pte Ltd; mem. Investment Cttee, Tembusu Partners Pte Ltd; mem. Global Advisory Bd, Univ. of Chicago Grad. School of Business 2006–; Adviser, Raffles Education Corpn 2006–, Neftech Pte Ltd. *Address:* Neftech Pte Ltd, 17 Jurong Port Road, 619092, Singapore (office). *Website:* www.neftech.com.sg (office).

YEO, George Yong-Boon, BA, MBA; Singaporean business executive and fmr politician; *Chairman, Kerry Logistics Network;* b. 13 Sept. 1954; m. Jennifer Leong Lai Peng 1984; three s. one d.; ed Univ. of Cambridge, UK, Harvard Business School, USA; fmr Signals Officer, Singapore Armed Forces, later Head of Air Plans Dept, Chief of Air Staff 1985; Dir Jt Operations and Planning, Ministry of Defence 1986–88, attained rank of Brig.-Gen. 1988; mem. Parl. 1988–2011; Minister of State for Finance and Minister of State for Foreign Affairs 1988–90, Acting Minister for Information and the Arts and Second Minister of State for Foreign Affairs 1990–91, Minister for Information and the Arts 1991–99, Second Minister for Foreign Affairs 1991–94; Minister for Health 1994–97, Second Minister for Trade and Industry 1997–99, Minister for Trade and Industry 1999–2004, Minister of Foreign Affairs 2004–11; Chair. Kerry Logistics Network 2012–, Exec. Dir 2013–, Dir Kerry Holdings Ltd; Strategic non-business Adviser, Sea Ltd; Sr Adviser, Brunswick Corpn; mem. Bd of Dirs, AIA Group Ltd 2012–, Pinduoduo Inc., New Yangon Devt Co. Ltd 2017–; mem. Foundation Bd, World Economic Forum; mem. Berggruen Inst. on Governance, Asia-Pacific Advisory Bd of Harvard Business School, Int. Advisory Bd of IESE Business School, Hong Kong Econ. Devt Comm., Int. Advisory Cttee of Nat. Grad. Inst. for Policy Studies, Int. Advisory Cttee of Mitsubishi Corpn, Int. Advisory Council of China Eco Forum, Int. Advisory Panel of Peking Univ.; mem. Pontifical Comm. for Reference on Econ.-Admin. Structure of the Holy See 2013–14, also mem. Vatican Council for the Economy 2014–; Hon. AO; Order of Sikatuna (Philippines); Padma Bhushan (India). *Publication:* George Yeo on Bonsai, Banyan and the Tao 2015. *Leisure interests:* reading, swimming, jogging. *Address:* Kerry Logistics Network, 16/F Kerry Cargo Centre, 55 Wing Kei Road, Kwai Chung, Hong Kong Special Administrative Region, People's Republic of China (office). *Telephone:* 24103600 (office). *Fax:* 24805958 (office). *E-mail:* corpcom@kerrylogistics.com (office). *Website:* www.kerrylogistics.com (office).

YEOH, Tan Sri Michelle, BA; Malaysian actress; b. (Nee Yeoh Choo-Keng), 6 Aug. 1962, Ipoh, Perak; m. Dickson Poon 1988 (divorced 1992); ed Royal Acad. of Dance, London; fmr Bond girl in Tomorrow Never Dies 1997; deported and barred from entering Myanmar after playing role of freed democracy leader Aung San Suu Kyi in film, The Lady, about her life June 2011; Chevalier, Légion d'honneur 2007, Officier, Légion d'honneur 2012; Darjah Datuk Paduka Mahkota Perak 2001, Darjah Seri Paduka Mahkota Perak 2012, Panglima Setia Mahkota 2013, Excellence in Asian Cinema Award, Hong Kong Int. Film Festival Soc. 2013. *Films include:* Owls vs. Dumbo 1984, In the Line of Duty 2 1985, The Target 1985, Magnificent Warriors 1987, Easy Money 1987, The Heroic Trio 1993, Police Story 3 1992 (Part 2 1993), Butterfly Sword 1993, Heroic Trio 2: Executioners 1993, Seven Maidens 1993, Tai-Chi 1993, Wonder Seven 1994, The Stunt Woman 1996, The Soong Sisters 1997, Tomorrow Never Dies 1997, Moonlight Express 1999, Crouching Tiger, Hidden Dragon 2000, The Touch 2002, Fei ying 2004, Memoirs of a Geisha 2005, Fearless 2006, Sunshine 2007, Far North 2007, Purple Mountain 2008, The Children of Huang Shi 2008, The Mummy: Tomb of the Dragon Emperor 2008, Babylon A.D. 2008, True Legend 2010, Reign of Assassins 2010, Kung Fu Panda 2 (voice) 2011, The Lady 2011, Final Recipe 2013, Crouching Tiger, Hidden Dragon: Sword of Destiny 2016, Guardians of the Galaxy Vol. 2 2017, Master Z: Ip Man Legacy 2018. *Television includes:* Jackie Chan Adventures (series) 2002, Strike Back (series) 2015, Marco Polo 2016, Star Trek: Discovery 2017–19.

YEOM, HE Cardinal Andrew Soo-jung, MEduc; South Korean ecclesiastic; *Archbishop of Seoul;* b. 5 Dec. 1943, Ansong, Gyeonggi Prov.; ed Catholic Univ. of Korea, Korea Univ., East Asian Pastoral Inst., the Philippines; ordained priest, Archdiocese of Seoul 1973; Pastoral Vicar 1971–73; Pres. Minor Seminary, Songshin High School 1973–77; Pastor 1977–78; Rector of the Major Seminary 1987–92; Chancellor of the diocesan curia 1992–98; apptd as one of the Seoul Archdiocese's Vicar Foranes, a Pastor and mem. Presbyteral Council 1998–2001; consecrated Titular Bishop of Thibiuca 2001; Auxiliary Bishop of Seoul 2001–12, Archbishop of Seoul 2012–; cr. Cardinal (Cardinal-Priest of San Crisogono) 2014–; also Apostolic Admin. Diocese of Pyongyang, North Korea; fmr Chair. Peace Broadcasting Corpn. *Address:* Archbishop's House, Chung-gu, Myong-dong 2-ga, Seoul 100-809, Republic of Korea (office). *Telephone:* (2) 727-2021 (office). *Fax:* (2) 773-1947 (office). *E-mail:* info@catholic.or.kr (office). *Website:* www.catholic.or.kr (office).

YEOMANS, Donald Keith, BA, MS, PhD; American astronomer; b. 3 May 1942, Rochester, New York; s. of George E. Yeomans and Jessie Yeomans; m. Laurie Robyn Ernst; one s. one d.; ed Middlebury Coll., Univ. of Maryland; Supervisor, Computer Sciences Corpn 1973–76; Sr Research Scientist, NASA Jet Propulsion Lab. 1976–, Supervisor 1992–2014 (retd); Discipline Specialist, Int. Halley Watch 1982–89; Chief Investigator, NASA Comet Mission 1987–91, Near-Earth Asteroid Rendezvous Mission 1994–2001, Multi-Comet Flyby Mission 1997–2002, Comet Impact Mission 1999–2006, NASA Project Scientist for Japanese Asteroid Sample Return Mission 1998–2010; Man. NASA Near-Earth Object Program Office 1998–2015; mem. American Astronomical Soc.; JPL Fellow 2010; American Inst. of Aeronautics and Astronautics Space Achievement Award 1985, NASA Exceptional Service Medal 1986, Distinguished Service Medal 2009, named NASA/JPL Senior Research Scientist 1993, Sagan Medal 2013. *Publications include:* Comet Halley: Once in a Lifetime 1985, The Distant Planets 1989, Comets: A Chronological History of Observation, Science, Myth and Folklore 1991, Near-Earth Objects: Finding Them Before They Find Us 2013; over 200 publications. *Leisure interests:* golf, ancient Roman coins. *Telephone:* (818) 395-9271 (office). *E-mail:* dkyeomans@gmail.com. *Website:* www.jpl.nasa.gov (office).

YEREMIN, Yuri Ivanovich; Russian theatre director and drama instructor; *Acting and Directing Instructor, Institute for Advanced Theatre Training;* b. 9 March 1944, Kolomna, Moscow Region; s. of Evdokiya Fillippovna Yeremina; m. Nina Petrovna Yeremina 1974; one s. one d.; with Youth Theatre, Rostov-on-Don 1973–77; Gorky Drama Theatre, Rostov-on-Don 1978–80; Cen. Army Theatre, Moscow 1981–87; Dir Pushkin Theatre, Moscow 1987–2000; Acting and Directing Instructor, American Repertory Theater/Moscow Art Theatre (ART/MXAT) Inst. for Advanced Theatre Training, Harvard Univ., USA 1997–; mem. Faculty, Moscow Art Theatre School USA; US debut with production of The Paper Gramophone, Hartford Stage Co. 1989; Ward No. 6, dramatic adaptation of Chekhov story, performed at int. drama festivals in USA, France, Italy, Switzerland, Belgium, UK and Canada 1989–91; Vice-Pres. Int. Assen of Theatre Producers 1991–; People's Artist of Russia 1986, Chevalier des Arts et des Lettres 1989. *Productions include:* The Possessed (Dostoevsky adaptation) 1989, Black Monk (Chekhov adaptation) 1990, At Kingdom Gate (Hamsun) 1991, Erick XIV (Strindberg) 1992, The Ghosts (De Filippo) 1992, The History of one Staircase (Buero Valejo) 1993, To Moscow! To Moscow! (adaptation of Chekhov's Three Sisters) 1994, Madame Bovary (Flaubert adaptation) 1994, The Inspector (Gogol) 1994, King Oedipus (Sophocles) 1995, The Old Man (Gorky), Ward No. 6 (Chekhov) (toured extensively throughout Europe, USA and Canada, was part of New York Int. Theatre Festival), Paper Nickelodeon (Chervinsky), Shelter (based on The Lower Depths by Maxim Gorky). *Productions at American Repertory Theater (Cambridge, Mass):* The Idiot (Dostoevsky) 1998, Ivanov (Chekhov) 1999, Three Farces and a Funeral (based on Chekhov's comedies) 2000, Othello (Shakespeare) 2001, Silver Age (Roshchin) 2001. *Leisure interests:* painting, writing. *Address:* ART/MXAT Institute, Loeb Drama Center, 64 Brattle Street, Cambridge, MA 02138, USA (office); 7 Soviet Army Street, Apt 213, 01827 Moscow, Russia. *Telephone:* (617) 495-2668 (Cambridge) (office); (495) 281-83-20 (Moscow) (home); (495) 299-41-36 (Moscow). *Fax:* (617) 495-1705 (Cambridge) (office). *E-mail:* yuryer@mail.ru (home); institute@amrep.org (office). *Website:* americanrepertorytheater.org/person/yuri-yeremin (office).

YERGIN, Daniel, BA, PhD; American writer and business executive; b. 6 Feb. 1947; ed Yale Univ., Univ. of Cambridge (Marshall Scholar), UK; taught at Harvard Business School and John F. Kennedy School of Govt, Harvard Univ.; Co-founder and Vice-Chair. Cambridge Energy Research Assocs, acquired by IHS Inc. 2004, now Vice-Chair. IHS Inc.; Dir US-Russian Business Council, Atlantic Partnership, New America Foundation; Global Energy Analyst, NBC; Adjunct

Prof., China Univ. of Petroleum, Beijing 2012–; mem. Bd of Dirs Council on Foreign Relations, New America Foundation, US Energy Asscn; mem. Advisory Bd US Sec. of Energy; mem. Advisory Bd MIT Energy Initiative, Yale Univ. Climate and Energy Inst.; mem. Nat. Petroleum Council, Russia Acad. of Oil and Gas; Trustee Brookings Inst.; fmr Chair. US Dept of Energy Task Force on Strategic Energy Research and Devt; mem. Pres.'s Strategic and Policy Forum Jan.–Aug. 2017; Pres.'s Medal (Italy) 2005; Dr hc (Univs of Houston and Missouri); US Energy Asscn Award, James Schlesinger Medal for Energy Security, US Department of Energy 2014, Lifetime Achievement Award from the Prime Minister of India 2014, Carnot Prize, Kleinman Center for Energy Policy, Univ. of Pennsylvania 2015. *Publications include:* Shattered Peace: Origins of the Cold War and the National Security State 1978, Energy Future: Report of the Energy Project at the Harvard Business School (with Robert Stobaugh) 1981, Dependence Dilemma 1984, The Prize: The Epic Quest for Oil, Money and Power (Pulitzer Prize for Gen. Nonfiction 1992) 1993 (also PBS/BBC documentary series), Russia 2010 and What It Means for the World (with Thane Gustafson) 1995, Commanding Heights: Battle for the World Economy (with Joseph Stanislaw) (also PBS/BBC documentary series—CINE Golden Eagle Award, New York Festivals Gold World Medal), The Quest: Energy, Security, and the Remaking of the Modern World 2011. *Website:* www.danielyergin.com.

YÉRIMA, Denis Ali; Benin politician; Préfet, Borgou and Alibori Départements 2008–13; Minister of Nat. Defence 2013–14. *Address:* c/o Ministry of National Defence, BP 2493, Cotonou, Benin (office).

YERMOLOVICH, Maksim L.; Belarusian government official; *Minister of Finance;* b. 26 June 1977, Lepel; ed Polotsk State Univ., Acad. of Public Admin, Minsk; began career as State Tax Inspector, Frunzensky Dist, Minsk 1999; various positions with State Tax Cttee of Belarus (now Ministry of Taxes and Duties) 1999–2002; Adviser, Budget Revenue Planning and Analysis Dept, Ministry of Finance 2002, later Deputy Head of Dept, Head of Budget Revenue Planning Office, Head of Main Dept for Budget Policy, Deputy Minister of Finance 2011–14, First Deputy Minister of Finance 2014–18, Minister of Finance 2018–. *Address:* Ministry of Finance, 220010 Minsk, vul. Savetskaya 7, Belarus (office). *Telephone:* (17) 222-61-37 (office). *Fax:* (17) 222-45-93 (office). *E-mail:* minfin@minfin.gov.by (office). *Website:* minfin.gov.by (office).

YEROFEYEV, Victor Vladimirovich; Russian writer and critic; b. 19 Sept. 1947, Moscow; s. of Vladimir Yerofeyev; m. Veslava Yerofeyeva (née Skura); one s.; ed Moscow State Univ.; did postgraduate work at Inst. for World Literature, Moscow 1970–73; expelled from USSR Writers' Union for participation in almanac Metropol, membership restored 1986; Lecturer, Maxim Gorky Literature Inst.; seminars on Modern Russian Literature at Univ. of Southern California, USA; contribs to Moscow News, Moscow Magazine, New York Review of Books, Times Literary Supplement, The New Yorker, International Herald Tribune; mem. Bd Russian PEN Centre; lives in Moscow and frequently appears on Russian TV where he has his own programme on Kultura channel, also has a programme on Radio Liberty, Moscow; Chevalier, Légion d'honneur 2013; named Man of the Year by Moscow Magazine 1990. *Publications:* Anna's Body and End of the Russian Avant-garde (collection of short stories) 1980, Life with an Idiot (novel) 1980, Russian Beauty (novel) 1981, In the Maze of Cursed Questions (collection of essays) 1990, The Pocket Apocalypse 1993, Collected Works (three vols) 1994–95, The Doomsday 1996, Men 1997, Five Rivers of Life 1998, Encyclopedia of the Russian Soul 2000, Men 2001, God X 2001, The Good Stalin 2004. *Leisure interest:* travelling. *Address:* 1st Smolensky per. 9, Apt 1, 119121 Moscow, Russia. *Telephone:* (495) 241-02-08.

YERSHOV, Yuri Leonidovich, DMathSci; Russian scientist and mathematician; b. 1 May 1940, Novosibirsk; m.; three c.; ed Tomsk State Univ., Novosibirsk State Univ.; worked at Novoasibirsk State Univ. 1964–2002, Prof. 1968–2002, Dean, Dept of Math. 1973–76, Rector 1985–93; Jr, Sr Researcher, then Head of Div., Sobolev Inst. of Math., Siberian br., USSR (now Russian) Acad. of Sciences 1963–85, Dir 2003–11; Ed.-in-Chief Siberian Mathematical Journal, Algebra i Logika; Corresp. mem. Russian Acad. of Sciences 1970, Academician 1990; fmr mem. CP; several Russian State Orders; Malcev Award, Russian Acad. of Sciences 1992, Russian State Award in the area of Science and Technics 2002, 2003, Lavrentjev Foundation Award 2007. *Achievements include:* proved decidability of the elementary theory of the field of p-adic numbers (independently proven by J. Ax and S. Kochen), undecidability of the elementary theory of finite symmetric groups, decidability of the elementary theory of relatively complemented distributive lattices. *Publications:* numerous scientific publs on algebra, field theory, mathematical logic, algorithm theory, model theory, constructive models, computer science and philosophical aspects of mathematics. *Address:* Sobolev Institute of Mathematics, Siberian Branch of the Russian Academy of Sciences, 4 Acad. Koptyug Avenue, 630090 Novosibirsk, Russian Federation. *Telephone:* (383) 333-28-92. *Fax:* (383) 333-25-98. *E-mail:* ershov@math.nsc.ru; im@math.nsc.ru. *Website:* www.math.nsc.ru/english.html.

YESENBAYEV, Mazhit Tuleubekovich, CandEcon, Docent; Kazakhstani politician, engineer and economist; *Chairman, Agency for Competition Protection (Antimonopoly Agency);* b. 28 April 1949, Pavlodar; m.; three c.; ed Kazakh Polytechnic Inst., Almaty; fmr Gov. Cen. Karaganda Region; Minister of Finance 1999–2001, of Economy and Trade 2002–03, of Industry and Trade 2003; Presidential Aide on Econ. Affairs 2003; Akim of Akmolinskaya Oblast 2004–08; Chair. Agency for Competition Protection (Antimonopoly Agency) 2008–; First Pres. Order 1997, Parasat Order 1999. *Publications:* more than 50 publs on issues of territorial production arrangements, education process optimization, current competition policy and its prospects. *Leisure interests:* judo, alpine skiing, tennis, reading. *Address:* #4 Entrance, House of Ministries Building, 010000 Nur-Sultan, Kazakhstan (office). *Telephone:* (7172) 749068 (office). *Fax:* (7172) 749637 (office). *E-mail:* m.yessenbayev@azkrk.kz (office).

YESIMOV, Akhmetzhan S., PhD; Kazakhstani politician; *Chairman, Management Board Samruk-Kasyna;* b. 15 Dec. 1950, Almaty; ed Kazakh Inst. of Agric., Acad. of Social Sciences, Moscow, Russia; mechanical engineer 1979–80; worked for econ. orgs in Almaty Region 1979–90; First Vice-Chair., State Agricultural and Industrial Cttee 1990–91; First Deputy Minister of Agric. of Kazakh SSR 1991–92; Head of Almaty Regional Admin 1992–94; Deputy Prime Minister of Kazakhstan 1994–96, State Sec. of Kazakhstan 1996, First Deputy Prime Minister and Chair. of State Cttee on Investments 1996–98; Head, Admin of Pres. 1998; Minister of Agric. 2001–06; Amb. and Head of Perm. Del. of Kazakhstan to NATO, Brussels, Belgium, then Rep. to EU 1998–2001; Chair. Almaty Affiliate, Nur Otan Khalyktyk Demokratiyalyk Partiyasy (Light of the Fatherland People's Democratic Party) 2008–; Mayor of Almaty 2008–15; Chair. NC EXPO-2017 Astana JSC 2015–17; Chair. Man. Bd Samruk-Kazyna JSC 2017–, also mem. Bd; Order of Badge of Honor 1982; Parasat Medal 2002, Otan Medal 2007. *Address:* Samruk-Kasyna, 010000, Nur-Sultan, E10 Street, 17/10, Kazakhstan (office). *Telephone:* (7172) 55-40-77 (office). *Website:* sk.kz (office).

YEVTUSHENKOV, Vladimir Petrovich, DEcon; Russian economist and business executive; *Chairman, AFK Sistema;* b. 25 Sept. 1948, Kamenshchina, Smolensk region; m.; one s. one d.; ed D. Mendeleev Moscow Chemical Eng Inst., Moscow State Univ.; Deputy Dir and Chief Engineer Karacharovo Factory of Plastics, Moscow 1975–82; Chief Engineer, First Deputy CEO Polymerbyt Research and Manufacturing Asscn 1982–87; Head Tech. Dept, then Chief Dept of Science and Tech., Moscow City Exec. Cttee 1987–90, Head Cttee on Science and Tech. 1990–93; Founder and Pres. AFK Sistema (jt stock financial holding corpn) 1993–95, Chair. 1994–2005, 2006–, Pres. 2005–06; mem. Bureau of Bd of Dirs Russian Union of Industrialists and Entrepreneurs 2000–, Head of Cttee on Industrial Policy 2001–; mem. Presidium of Bd of Dirs, Russian Chamber of Commerce and Industry 2002–, Head of Russian-Arab Business Council 2003–; Chair. Bd of Trustees, Russian Museum Devt Fund 2004. *Leisure interests:* hunting, tennis. *Address:* AFK Sistema, 125009 Moscow, 13 Mokhovaya Street, Russia (office). *Telephone:* (495) 228-15-01 (office). *Fax:* (495) 629-12-52 (office). *E-mail:* chairman@sistema.ru (office). *Website:* www.sistema.ru (office); www.sistema.com (office).

YEZHEL, Adm. (retd) Mykhailo Bronislavovych; Ukrainian politician and fmr naval officer; b. 19 Oct. 1952, Sloboda-Yaltushkivska, Barskyi Dist, Vinnytsia Oblast; m. Natalya Klimentivna; one s. one d.; fmrly served in Soviet Pacific Fleet 1975–93; joined Ukrainian Navy 1993, becoming Deputy C-in-C 1996–2000, C-in-C 2001–03; Adviser to Viktor Yanukovych June–Dec. 2007; Insp., Main Inspectorate of Ministry of Defence 2008; Minister of Defence 2010–12; apptd adviser to Pres. Viktor Yanukovych 2012; Amb. to Belarus 2013–15.

YHAP, Laetitia, DFA; British artist; b. 1 May 1941, St Albans, Herts., England; d. of Leslie Neville Yhap and Elizabeth Yhap (née Kogler); one s.; ed Camberwell School of Arts and Crafts, Slade School of Fine Art, Univ. Coll. London; Artist-in-Residence, Chatham House Grammar School, Ramsgate 1981; works in public collections in UK; mem. of London Group 1971–; exhibited in many nat. and museum-curated shows, British Council, Arts Council, Contemporary Art Soc. etc.; Leverhume Research Award 1962–63, John Moores Prize 1973. *Leisure interests:* music, attending concerts, playing badminton, choral singing. *Address:* c/o Tate Britain, Millbank, London, SW1P 4RG, England (office). *Telephone:* (20) 7887-8888 (office). *E-mail:* information@tate.org.uk (office). *Website:* www.tate.org.uk (office).

YHOMBI-OPANGO, Brig.-Gen. Jacques-Joachim; Republic of the Congo army officer and fmr head of state; b. 1939; trained in French army; fmr military attaché at Congolese Embassy, Moscow; Chief of Staff, People's National Army 1968–73, Insp.-Gen. 1973–74; Sec.-Gen. of Council of State with rank of Minister 1974–75, Council of State Delegate responsible for Defence and Security 1974–75; Pres. of Republic, Pres. Council of Ministers, Pres. Mil. Council of Congolese Labour Party 1977–79; arrested 1979, detained 1979–84, released from detention Nov. 1984, rearrested Sept. 1987; Prime Minister of Congo 1993–96; fmr Leader, Rassemblement pour la défense et le développement (RDP); fmr Leader Rassemblement pour la démocratie et le développement (RDD); went into exile 1997, returned 2007, currently Pres. RDD; Order of Nat. Flag (N Korea) 1978.

YI, Gang, BA, DEcon, PhD; Chinese economist and central banker; *Governor, People's Bank of China;* b. 5 March 1958, Beijing; ed Peking Univ., Hamline Univ., USA, Univ. of Illinois at Urbana-Champaign; Asst Prof., later Assoc. Prof., Dept of Econs, Univ. of Illinois at Urbana-Champaign 1986–94; co-f., Prof. and Deputy Dir, Peking Univ. China Econ. Research Centre 1994–; joined People's Bank of China (PBC) 1997, becoming Deputy Sec.-Gen., Monetary Policy Dept 1997–2002, Sec.-Gen. 2002–08, Pres., Operations Office 2006–07, Deputy Gov., People's Bank of China 2008–18, Gov. 2018–; Dir State Admin of Foreign Exchange (SAFE) 2009–16; consultant for Scandinavian Journal of Statistics, the Journal of Econometrics, Comparative Economic Studies, Economic Theory, Contemporary Policy Issues; mem. Editorial Bd China Economic Review, Journal of Asian Economics; alt. mem. 19th CCP Cen. Cttee 2017–. *Publications include:* 10 books, more than 40 articles in Chinese and 20 academic papers in English. *Address:* People's Bank of China, 32 Chengfang Jie, Xicheng Qu, Beijing 100800, People's Republic of China (office). *Telephone:* (10) 66194114 (office). *Fax:* (10) 66195370 (office). *E-mail:* webbox@pbc.gov.cn (office). *Website:* www.pbc.gov.cn (office).

YI, Huiman, MA; Chinese business executive; *Chairman, President and Executive Director, Industrial & Commercial Bank of China Limited;* ed Guanghua School of Man., Peking Univ.; joined Industrial & Commercial Bank of China Ltd (ICBC) 1985, apptd mem. of Sr Man. 2005, served in several positions at ICBC, including Deputy Head of Zhejiang Br., Deputy Head and Head of Jiangsu Br., and Head of Beijing Br., Sr Exec. Vice-Pres. Industrial & Commercial Bank of China Ltd 2008–13, Pres. May 2013–, Vice-Chair. and Exec. Dir July 2013–16, Chair. and Exec. Dir 2016–, concurrently Chair. Industrial and Commercial Bank of China (Malaysia) Berhad. *Address:* Industrial & Commercial Bank of China Ltd, 55 Fuxingmennan Dajie, Xicheng Qu, Beijing 100140, People's Republic of China (office). *Telephone:* (10) 66106070 (office). *Fax:* (10) 66106053 (office). *E-mail:* ir@icbc.com.cn (office). *Website:* www.icbc.com.cn (office); www.icbc-ltd.com (office).

YI, Jun, MSc; Chinese engineer and business executive; *Chairman, China State Construction Engineering Corporation;* ed studied Construction Project Man. at Cardiff Univ. and at Taylor Woodrow Ltd, UK, Chongqing Inst. of Construction and Eng; Dir and Gen. Man. China State Construction Contracting Co. 1993–2001, Vice-Pres. and mem. Party Cttee of China State Construction Engineering Corpn (CSCEC) 2001–02, Chair. and Pres. China State Construction International Co. Ltd 2002–, Chief Engineer, CSCEC 2005–, Pres. CSCEC and mem. Party Cttee of CSCEC 2005–10, Chair. and Sec. Party Leadership Group 2010–, Chair. China Overseas Holdings Ltd (Hong Kong) 2010–; Exec. Dir Fourth Council of China Int.

Econ. Co-operation Soc.; Pres. Chartered Inst. of Building in China; Vice Chair. China Construction Industry Asscn, China Asscn of Construction Enterprise Man., China Civil Eng Soc., China Int. Contractors Asscn, China Asscn of Trade Services; Nat. Model Worker, Nat. Excellent Project Man., Excellent Party Mem. of Cen. and State Organs. *Address:* China State Construction Engineering Corporation, CSCEC Mansion, 15 Sanlihe Road, Haidian District, Beijing 100037, People's Republic of China (office). *Telephone:* (10) 88082888 (office). *Fax:* (10) 88082888 (office). *E-mail:* info@cscec.com (office); ir@cscec.com.cn (office). *Website:* www.cscec.com (office); english.cscec.com (office).

YIIN, Chii-ming, BS, MBA, PhD; Taiwanese economist and politician; b. 2 June 1952; m.; one s. one d.; ed Nat. Chiao Tung Univ., Nat. Chengchi Univ.; Sr Specialist, Council for Econ. Planning and Devt, Exec. Yuan 1978–85; Dir Industrial Devt Bureau, Ministry of Econ. Affairs 1985–90, Deputy Dir-Gen. 1990–94, Dir-Gen. 1994–97, Deputy Minister of Econ. Affairs 1997–2005, Minister 2008–09, adviser to Exec. Yuan 2005–06, Minister without Portfolio 2009–11, Minister of the Council for Econ. Planning and Devt 2012–; Chair Prof., Chung Hua Univ. 2007–08.

YILDIRIM, Binali; Turkish politician; b. 20 Dec. 1955, Refahiye; m. Semiha Yıldırım 1976; three c.; ed İstanbul Tech. Univ., World Maritime Univ.; served in various positions in Gen. Directorate of Turkish Shipping Industry and Camialtı Shipyard; Chair. Bd of Dirs, İstanbul Fast Ferries Co. 1994–2000; mem. Grand Nat. Ass. (Parl.) (AKP) for İstanbul I electoral dist 2002–07, for Erzincan 2007–11, for Izmir II 2011–15, Speaker July 2018–Feb. 2019; Minister of Transport 2002–07, 2007–11, July–Nov. 2011, of Transport, Maritime Affairs and Communication 2015–16; Prime Minister 2016–18 (post abolished); special adviser to Pres. Recep Tayyip Erdoğan 2014–15; mem. Justice and Devt Party (AKP), Leader 2016–17; Dr hc (Girne American Univ., Cyprus) 2006, (Ondokuz Mayıs Univ.) 2009, (Cumhuriyet Univ., Bozok Univ.) 2010, (Anadolu Univ., Erzincan Univ., Kırklareli Univ., Tech. Univ. of Berlin) 2011, (Pamukkale Univ., World Maritime Univ., Sweden) 2012, (Okan Univ.) 2013.

YILMAZ, A(hmet) Mesut; Turkish politician; b. 6 Nov. 1947, Istanbul; s. of Hasan Yilmaz and Güzide Yilmaz; m. Berna Müren; two s.; ed Istanbul High School for Boys, Faculty of Political Studies, Ankara Univ., Univ. of Cologne, Germany; worked in various exec. positions in cos in chemical, textile and transportation sectors 1975–83; mem. Grand Nat. Ass. (Parl.) for Rize 1983–2002; Minister of Culture and Tourism 1986–87, of Foreign Affairs 1987–90, Prime Minister of Turkey June–Nov. 1991, 1996, 1997–98, Deputy Prime Minister and Minister of State –2002; Founding mem. and Chair. Anavatan Partisi–ANAP (Motherland Party) 1991–2002; Vice-Chair. EDU.

YILMAZ, Durmuş, MA; Turkish politician and fmr central banker; b. 1947, Uşak; ed City Univ., London and Univ. Coll., London, UK; joined Cen. Bank of Turkey 1980, worked in Foreign Debt Rescheduling, Exchange Rates and Foreign Exchange Reserve Man. 1993, Deputy Dir Foreign Exchange Transactions Div. 1995, Dir Interbank Money Market Div. 1996; Dir Balance of Payments Div. 1996, Deputy Exec. Dir Markets Dept to supervise Foreign Exchange Risk Man., Credits, Foreign Exchange and FX Banknotes Markets and Open Market Operations 2002, Exec. Dir Workers' Remittances (Non-Resident FX Deposits) Dept 2003, mem. Bd 2003–06, Gov. 2006–11; Chief Econ. Adviser to the Pres. 2011–15; mem. Grand Nat. Ass. (Parl.) from Uşak 2015–. *Address:* Grand National Assembly, TBMM 06543, Bakanlıklar, 06100 Ankara, Turkey (office). *Telephone:* (312) 4205000 (office). *Fax:* (312) 4206756 (office). *E-mail:* assembly@tbmm.gov.tr (office). *Website:* www.tbmm.gov.tr (office).

YILMAZ, İsmet, MA, PhD; Turkish engineer, lawyer and politician; b. 10 Dec. 1961, Sivas; m.; three c.; ed Faculty of Maritime Studies, Istanbul Tech. Univ., Faculty of Law, İstanbul Univ., World Maritime Univ., Malmö, Sweden, Inst. of Social Sciences, Marmara Univ., Inst. of Social Sciences, Ankara Univ.; worked for 20 years as engineer and accountant in the public and private sectors; Under-Sec. of Maritime Affairs 2002; Under-Sec., Ministry of Culture and Tourism 2007; Minister of Transport and Communications May–Aug. 2007, Minister of Nat. Defence 2011–15, 2015–16, Minister of Nat. Educ. 2016–18; mem. Büyük Millet Meclisi (Grand Nat. Ass., Parl.) 2011–, Speaker July–Nov. 2015; fmr Vice-Chair. Turk Telekom; mem. Justice and Development Party (AKP). *Address:* c/o Grand National Assembly, TBMM 06543, Bakanlıklar, Ankara, Turkey.

YIM, Jong-yong, BEcons, MEcons; South Korean economist and politician; b. 1959; ed Yonsei Univ., Univ. of Oregon, USA; started govt career with Ministry of Finance and Economy 1981, held several positions including Minister, Embassy in London 2006–07, Deputy Dir Gen., Financial Policy Bureau, Dir Gen., Econ. Policy Bureau and Planning and Coordination Bureau, Ministry of Strategy and Finance, Presidential Econ. and Financial Sec. 2009–10, First Vice-Minister of Strategy and Finance 2010, Minister for Govt Policy Coordination at Prime Minister's Office 2011, Chair. Financial Services Comm. 2015–17; Chair. and CEO NongHyup Financial Group 2013–15.

YIN, Jiaxu, MA, MBA; Chinese engineer and business executive; *Chairman, China North Industries Group Corporation (NORINCO Group);* ed Univ. of Chongqing; fmr Gen. Man. CSG Automobile Co. Ltd; Pres. and Sec., Changan Automobile Group Co. (CAC) from 1998, Man. Yuzhou Gear Factory, Chair. and Pres. Changan Minsheng APLL Logistics Co. Ltd 2004–10; fmr Vice-Gen. Man. and Vice-Pres. China South Industries Group Corpn and China North Industries Group Corpn (NORINCO Group), Chair. 2013–; Dir Admin. Office and Deputy Gen. Dir Southwest Industries Bureau of China Industries Co.; Chair. Nanjing CMSC Logistics Co. Ltd; Exec. Dir Chongqing Changan Automobile Co. Ltd 1998–, South Automobile Corpn Ltd; Dir, Jiangling Motors Corpn Ltd. *Address:* China North Industries Group Corporation (NORINCO Group), 46 Sanlihe Road, Beijing 100821, People's Republic of China (office). *Telephone:* (10) 68594210 (office); (10) 68787608 (office). *Fax:* (10) 68594232 (office); (10) 68594555 (office). *E-mail:* webmaster@norincogroup.com.cn (office). *Website:* www.norincogroup.com.cn (office).

YIN, Jun; Chinese politician; b. Sept. 1932, Eryuan, Yunnan Prov.; joined CCP 1949; Sec. CCP Xiaguan City Cttee, Yunnan Prov.; fmr Mayor of Xiaguan City; Sec. CCP Yunlong Co. Cttee, Yunnan Prov.; Chair. and Gov., Dali Bai Autonomous Pref., Yunnan Prov. 1982–84; Sec. Discipline Inspection Cttee, Yunnan CCP Prov. Cttee 1985; Deputy Sec. Yunnan Prov. Cttee 1990; Alt. mem. 12th CCP Cen. Cttee 1982–87, 13th CCP Cen. Cttee 1987–92; apptd Chair. Standing Cttee Yunnan Prov. People's Congress 1993; Deputy, 8th NPC 1993–98, 9th NPC 1998–2003; Del., 15th CCP Nat. Congress 1997–2002.

YIN, Weimin; Chinese government official; b. 1953, Lingshou County, Hebei Prov.; ed Jilin Univ.; joined CCP 1973; Vice-Minister of Human Resources and Social Security 2000–07, Minister of Human Resources and Social Security 2007–18; Deputy Dir CCP Cen. Cttee Org. Dept 2007–12; Dir State Admin of Civil Service 2008–14; mem. 17th CCP Cen. Cttee 2007–12, 18th CCP Cen. Cttee 2012–17.

YIN, Wenying; Chinese entomologist and academic; *Professor, Institute of Plant Physiology and Ecology, Chinese Academy of Sciences;* b. Oct. 1922, Pingxiang Co., Hebei Prov.; ed Nat. Cen. Univ., Nanking, Cen. Univ. for Nationalities, Beijing and Zhongyang Univ.; worked at Inst. of Zoology, Shanghai 1947–49; joined Chinese Acad. of Sciences 1950, worked at Inst. of Hydrobiology, Wuhan 1950–62, Shanghai Inst. of Entomology 1963, 1981, 1987–2000, apptd Academician, Chinese Acad. of Sciences 1991, Prof., Inst. of Plant Physiology and Ecology 2001–; conducted research on fish parasites and fish disease prevention and treatment in the early stages of contamination; est. a new classification system according to her research; Two Nat. Natural Sciences Prizes, two Chinese Acad. of Sciences Prizes of Natural Sciences, four prizes both of the Nat. and Chinese Acad. of Sciences Prizes of Progress on Sciences and Tech., Ho Leung Ho Lee Life Sciences Award. *Publications:* China Animal Records: Original Tail Item 1999, Chinese Sub-tropical Soil Animals, Chinese Soil Animal Search Illustrated Handbook, Chinese Soil Animals; more than 130 research articles and four monographs. *Address:* Institute of Plant Physiology and Ecology, Chinese Academy of Sciences, 300 Feng Lin Road, Shanghai 200032, People's Republic of China (office). *Telephone:* (21) 54924181 (office). *Fax:* (21) 54924015 (office). *E-mail:* wyyin@sibs.ac.cn (office). *Website:* www.sippe.ac.cn (office).

YINGLUCK SHINAWATRA, BA, MA; Thai business executive and politician; b. 21 June 1967, San Kamphaeng; d. of Lert Shinawatra and Yindee Shinawatra; sister of fmr Prime Minister Thaksin Shinawatra; m. Anusorn Amornchat; one s.; ed Chiang Mai Univ., Kentucky State Univ., USA; worked at Shinawatra Directories Co. Ltd; mem. Cttee and Sec. Thaicom Foundation; fmr Pres. Advanced Info Service Public Co. Ltd (AIS) (mobile phone operator) before its sale to Singapore's Temasek Holdings; mem. Bd of Dirs SC Asset Corpn Public Co. Ltd (family business) 2004–11, Chair. Exec. Cttee 2006–11, Acting Pres. Dec. 2006–09, Acting CEO 2009–11; also managed finances for opposition Pheu Thai Party; nominated by Pheu Thai Party as cand. for Prime Minister in 2011 elections (first woman to run for country's highest political office), Prime Minister 2011–14 (ordered to step down by Constitutional Court); Minister of Defence 2013–14, impeached and banned from politics for five years for involvement in rice subsidy scheme while Prime Minister Jan. 2015.

YISHAI, Eliyahu; Israeli politician; b. 26 Dec. 1962, Jerusalem; m.; five c.; served in Israel Defence Forces 1980–83; mem. Jerusalem Municipal Council 1987–88; Asst, Minister of Interior, Aryeh Deri 1988–90; fmr Head of Interior Minister's bureau; acting Sec.-Gen., then Chair. Shas (Sephardic Torah Guardians) 1991, Head 2000–14; Dir-Gen. Shas-affiliated El ha-Ma'ayan Movt 1994–96; mem. Knesset (Parl.) 1996–2015; Minister of Labour and Social Affairs 1996–2001, of Internal Affairs 2001–02, also Deputy Prime Minister 2001–02; Deputy Prime Minister 2002–13, Minister of Industry, Trade and Labour 2006–09, of the Interior 2009–13; f. Yachad 2015. *Website:* www.elieyshay.com.

YMERI, Visar; Kosovo sociologist, activist and politician; b. 11 Oct. 1973; ed City and Islington Coll., London, UK, Univ. of Prishtina; worked in Kosovo Pension Trust –2008; activist and leading mem. and Spokesman of Vetëvendosje! (Self-Determination!) 2005–, Chair. 2015–18; mem. (Vetëvendosje!), Kuvendi i Kosovës (Parl.) 2010–, mem. Parl. Cttee for Econ. Devt, Infrastructure, Trade and Industry. *Address:* Vetëvendosje! (Self-Determination!), 10000 Prishtina, Qyteza Pejton, Rruga Bajram Kelmendi 10, Kosovo (office). *Telephone:* (44) 411174 (office). *E-mail:* info@vetevendosje.org (office). *Website:* www.vetevendosje.org (office).

YOAKAM, Dwight; American country singer, musician (guitar), songwriter and actor; b. 23 Oct. 1956, Pikeville, Ky; ed Ohio Univ.; solo artist 1978–; numerous tours; Acad. of Country Music Award for Best New Male Artist 1986, Music City News Country Award for Best Vocal Collaboration (for Streets of Bakersfield, with Buck Owens) 1988, Grammy Awards for Best Country Male Vocal Performance 1994, for Best Country Collaboration with Vocals 1999, Cliffie Stone Pioneer Award 2011, Americana Music Award for Artist of the Year 2013. *Films include:* Red Rock West 1992, The Little Death 1995, Sling Blade 1996, Painted Hero 1996, The Newton Boys 1998, The Minus Man 1999, South of Heaven, West of Hell (also dir) 2000, Panic Room 2002, Hollywood Homicide 2003, 3-Way 2004, The Three Burials of Melquiades Estrada 2005, Wedding Crashers 2005, Bandidas 2006, Crank 2006, Four Christmases 2008, Crank: High Voltage 2009, The Last Rites of Ransom Pride 2010, Bloodworth 2010, Dirty Girl 2010, 90 Minutes in Heaven 2015, Boomtown 2016. *Television includes:* Roswell (film) 1994, Don't Look Back (film) 1996, When Trumpets Fade (film) 1998, Wilfred (series) 2011–13, Under the Dome (series) 2014, To Appomattox (mini-series) 2015, Goliath (series) 2016. *Recordings include:* albums: Guitars, Cadillacs, Etc., Etc. 1986, Hillbilly Deluxe 1987, Buenas Noches From A Lonely Room 1988, Just Looking For A Hit 1989, If There Was A Way 1990, La Croix D'Amour 1992, This Time 1993, Dwight Live 1995, Gone 1996, Under The Covers 1997, Come On Christmas 1997, A Long Way Home 1998, dwightyoakamacoustic.net 2000, Tomorrow's Sounds Today 2000, South Of Heaven, West Of Hell 2001, Population Me 2003, In Others' Words 2003, Blame The Vain 2005, Dwight Sings Buck 2007, 3 Pears 2012, Second Hand Heart 2015, Swimmin' Pools, Movie Stars... 2016. *Address:* Paradigm Talent Agency, 360 North Crescent Drive, North Building, Beverly Hills, CA 90210, USA (office). *Website:* www.dwightyoakam.com.

YOCCOZ, Jean-Christophe, PhD; French mathematician and academic; *Professor, Collège de France;* b. 29 May 1957, Paris; ed Ecole Normale Supérieure, Paris and Ecole Polytechnique, Paris; mil. service in Brazil 1981–83; Attaché, then Head of Research, CNRS, l'Ecole Polytechnique 1979–88; Prof., Univ. of Paris-Sud 1988–96; Prof., Collège de France 1996–; mem. Institut Universitaire de France 1990, Unité Recherche Associé 'Topology and Dynamics', CNRS, Acad. des sciences

1994, Brazilian Acad. of Sciences 1994; Assoc. mem. Third World Acad. of Sciences 2004–; Chevalier, Légion d'honneur 1995; Order of Scientific Merit (Brazil) 1998; Officier, l'Ordre nat. du Mérite 2000; Bronze Medal, CNRS 1984, IBM Math. Prize 1985, Cours de la Fondation Claude-Antoine PECCOT, Collège de France 1987, Salem Prize 1988, Invited Speaker, Kyoto Int. Congress 1990, Jaffe Prize, Acad. des sciences 1991, Fields Medal, Int. Congress of Mathematicians, Zürich 1994. *Publications:* numerous articles in math. journals on dynamical systems. *Address:* Collège de France, 11 Place Marcelin Berthelot, 75231 Paris Cedex 05, France (office). *Telephone:* 1-44-27-12-11 (office). *Website:* www.college-de-france.fr (office).

YODA, Alain Bédoum, LLB, DEcon; Burkinabè politician; b. 31 Dec. 1951, Komtoèga; m.; two c.; ed Univ. of Youndé, Cameroon, Univ. of Clermont Ferrand, France; with Ministry of Trade, Industry and Mines Jan.–March 1978, Ministry of Trade 1978–85, Tech. Adviser to Minister of Trade 1985; Econ. and Financial Adviser to Pres. of Burkina Faso 1985–87; Dir-Gen. Nagansgani Air Freight Co. 1986–92; assigned to Gen. Secr., Ministry of Transport and Communications 1992; Deputy, Nat. Ass. 1992–, Chair. Working Group on Mid-Term Review of Lomé IV Convention 1994, Finance and Nat. Ass. Planning Comm. 1996–97, Pres. Parl. Group of Congrès pour la Démocratie et le Progrès 2013–; Minister for Transport and Tourism 1997–2000, for Trade and the Promotion of Business and Crafts 2000–02, of Health 2002–08, of Foreign Affairs and Regional Co-operation 2008–11. *Leisure interests:* swimming, board games, cinema, music, reading. *Address:* National Assembly, 01 BP 6482, Ouagadougou 01, Burkina Faso (office). *Telephone:* 50-31-46-84 (office). *Fax:* 50-31-45-90 (office).

YOH-HAMURA, Shoei, BA (Econs); Japanese architect; *Design and Architectural Principal, Shoei Yoh + Architects;* b. 7 March 1940, Kumamoto City; ed Univ. of Keio, Tokyo, Wittenberg Univ., USA; interior designer at Int. Design Assocs, Tokyo 1964–67; project designer with Nic, Fukuoka 1967–70; Design and Architectural Prin., Shoei Yoh + Architects 1970–; Visiting Prof., Grad. School of Architecture, Urban Design and Preservation, Columbia Univ., New York 1992; Prof., Grad. School of Architecture and Urban Design, Keio Univ. 1996–2005; Mainichi Design Award 1983, Japan Inst. of Architects Award 1983, 1989, Architectural Inst. of Japan Award, IAKS Award 1993, City of Fukuoka Award 1994, Benedictus Award 1994, Fukuoka Pref. Award 1998, Wittenberg Fellow 2003. *Works include:* Ingot, Coffee Shop, Fukuoka 1977, Kinoshita Clinic, Fukuoka 1979, Stainless Steel House with Light Lattice, Nagasaki 1981, Egami Clinic, Nagasaki 1982, Aspecta, Out Door Theatre in Volcano Aso, Kumamoto 1987, Oguni Dome, Wooden Structure Gymnasium, Kumamoto 1988, Saibu Gas Museum for Natural Phenomenart, Fukuoka 1989, Matsushita Clinic, Nagasaki 1990, Wakita Hitecs, Office, Fukuoka 1990, Pyramid of Sea, Ferry Terminal, Kumamoto 1990, Another Glass House Between Sea and Sky, Fukuoka 1991, Galaxy Toyama, Gymnasium 1992, Toyama 1992, Prospecta Toyama '92, Observatory Tower for Natural Phenomena, Toyama 1992, Glass Station, Kumamoto 1993, Harada Bldg, Kumamoto 1993, 6 Cubes in Light, Kumamoto 1994, Naiju Community Centre and Nursery School, Fukuoka 1994, Kanada Children Training House, Fukuoka 1994, Uchino Community Centre for Seniors and Children, Fukuoka 1995, Oguni Community Centre, Parasol Centre, Kumamoto 1995, Sundial, Welfare Facility for Seniors, Fukuoka 1996, Ms. REIKO TOKYO, Tokyo 1997, Health and Welfare Facilities in Chikuho-machi, Fukuoka 1998, SFC Digital Labo, Kanagawa 2000, BOLIZIA, Tokyo 2002, Kyushu Gakuin Lutheran Junior High School, Kumamoto 2003, Muse Kitano, Kobe 2004, Tohno Clinic Dining Cafe Lounge, Fukuoka 2004, Tenjin Minami Subway Station, Fukuoka 2005, dental office Ryu, Fukuoka 2007. *Publications:* Ambient V Matrix 1970–1987 1987, Shoei Yoh – In Response to Natural Phenomena 1997, Calisthenics for Architecture 1997. *Leisure interest:* travel. *Address:* Shoei Yoh + Architects, 1-12-30 Heiwa, Minami-ku, Fukuoka-shi, Fukuoka 815-007, Japan (office). *Telephone:* (92) 521-4782 (office); (92) 521-4110 (home). *Fax:* (92) 521-6718 (office). *E-mail:* shoeiyoh.plus.architects@galaxy.dti.ne.jp (office); yohshoei@jade.dti.ne.jp (office). *Website:* www.jade.dti.ne.jp/shoeiyoh (office).

YOKOI, Yutaka; Japanese diplomatist; *Ambassador to China;* joined diplomatic service 1979, language training in China, has held several China-related posts, including Dir China and Mongolia Div., Consul-Gen. in Shanghai and Chief Minister, Embassy in Beijing 2010–11, Amb. to Turkey 2013–16, to China 2016–. *Address:* Embassy of Japan, 7 Ri Tan Lu, Jian Guo Men Wai, Beijing 100600, People's Republic of China (office). *Telephone:* (10) 65322361 (office). *Fax:* (10) 65324625 (office). *E-mail:* info@eoj.cn (office); info@pk.mofa.go.jp (office). *Website:* www.cn.emb-japan.go.jp (office).

YOKOMICHI, Takahiro, LLB; Japanese lawyer and politician; b. 3 Jan. 1941, Sapporo; ed Tokyo Univ.; worked as lawyer in pvt.; elected to House of Reps as mem. for Japan Socialist Party 1969, served five terms 1969–83; Gov. of Hokkaido 1983–95; joined Democratic Party of Japan 1995, fmr Vice-Pres.; mem. House of Reps for Hokkaido No. 1 constituency 1996–, Deputy Speaker 2005–09, Speaker 2009–12. *Address:* House of Representatives, 7-1, Nagata-cho, Chiyoda-ku, Tokyo 100-0014, Japan (office). *Telephone:* (3) 3581-5111 (office). *E-mail:* webmaster@shugiin.go.jp (office). *Website:* www.shugiin.go.jp (office); www.yokomichi.com (office).

YOKOO, Hiroshi; Japanese business executive; *Chairman, AEON Company Limited;* joined AEON Co. Ltd (fmrly Jusco Co. Ltd) 1974, Man. and Store Adviser, Ministop Co. Ltd 1985–89, Devt Div. Man. 1989–93, Regional Devt Section Man. 1993–99, Sr Man. Dir and Sales Div. Man. 1999–2000, Pres. 2000–08, Chair. Ministop Co. Ltd 2008–11, Sr Exec. Officer and Sr Man. Dir 2011–12, Sr Exec. Vice-Pres. and Asst to Pres. of AEON Co. Ltd 2012–13, CEO Strategic Small Store Business and Chief in charge of Group Merchandise 2012–13, Vice-Pres., Exec. Officer of Retail Store Business Strategy and CEO Aeon Co. Ltd 2008–14, Chair. 2014–; mem. Bd of Dirs, Aeon Retail Co. Ltd 2010–, Origin Toshu Co. Ltd 2012–, Yamaya Corpn 2013–. *Address:* AEON Co. Ltd, 1-5-1 Nakase, Mihama-ku, Chiba-shi, Chiba 261-8515, Japan (office). *Telephone:* (4) 3212-6042 (office). *Fax:* (4) 3212-6849 (office). *E-mail:* info@aeon.info (office). *Website:* www.aeon.info (office).

YOKOYAMA, Shinichi; Japanese insurance industry executive; *Corporate Advisor, Sumitomo Life Insurance Company;* b. 10 Sept. 1942; joined Sumitomo Life Insurance Co. 1966, Dir 1992–95, Man. Dir 1995–98, Sr Man. Dir 1998–2000, Dir and Vice-Pres. 2000–01, Dir and Pres. 2001–03, Pres. and CEO 2003–07,

Chair. and Rep. Dir 2007–10, now Corporate Advisor; Outside Corp. Auditor, Sumitomo Chemical Co. Ltd 2010–, Rengo Co. Ltd 2014–; Standing Corp. Auditor, Shionogi & Co. Ltd 2008–; apptd Chair. Life Insurance Asscn of Japan 2002; mem. Bd Corp. Auditors, NEC Corpn 2003–. *Address:* Sumitomo Life Insurance Co., 1-4-35 Shiromi, Chuo-ku, Osaka 540-8512, Japan (office). *Telephone:* (6) 6937-1435 (office). *E-mail:* info@sumitomolife.co.jp (office). *Website:* www.sumitomolife.co.jp (office).

YO'LDOSHEV, Nig'matilla To'lqinovich; Uzbekistani lawyer and politician; *Speaker of the Senate;* b. 5 Nov. 1962, Tashkent; ed Tashkent State Univ.; Prosecutor, Almalyk, Tashkent region 1986–91; Investigator, Abad Dist of Tashkent city prosecutor's office, becoming Sr Investigator, Tashkent city prosecutor's office, later head of Investigation Dept, Ministry of Internal Affairs and Office of Prosecutor-Gen., also head of Investigation Dept of Gen. Govt Admin 1991–2000; Head of Internal Security Inspection, Office of the Prosecutor-Gen. 2000–03; Head of coordination, law enforcement and regulatory agencies under Gen. Prosecutor 2003–06; Investigator, Tax, Currency Crimes and Criminal Income Dept, Office of the Prosecutor Gen. 2006–08; Deputy, Oliy Majlis (Supreme Ass., Parl.) 2008–11; Minister of Justice 2011–15; Speaker of the Senate 2015–; Acting Pres. for a week in Sept. 2016. *Address:* Office of the Speaker, Senate, 100078 Tashkent, Mustaqillik maydoni 6, Uzbekistan (office). *Telephone:* (71) 238-26-38 (office). *Fax:* (71) 238-29-01 (office). *E-mail:* senat@tps.uz (office). *Website:* www.senat.uz (office).

YONATH, Ada E., BSc, MSc, PhD, FRSC; Israeli chemist and academic; *Martin S. and Helen Kimmel Professor of Structural Biology and Director, Helen and Milton A. Kimmelman Center for Biomolecular Structure and Assembly, Weizmann Institute of Science;* b. 22 June 1939, Jerusalem; ed Hebrew Univ. of Jerusalem, Weizmann Inst. of Science; post-doctoral work at Carnegie Mellon Univ. 1969 and MIT 1970; Scientist, Dept of Chem., Weizmann Inst. of Science 1970–74, Sr Scientist 1974–83, Assoc. Prof. 1984–88, Prof. 1988–, Dir Mazar Center for Structural Biology 1988–, Martin S. and Helen Kimmel Prof. of Structural Biology 1988–, Dir Helen and Milton A. Kimmelman Center for Biomolecular Structure and Assembly 1989–, Chair. Dept of Structural Chem. 1989–92, of Dept of Structural Biology 1992–94; Visiting Scientist, Univ. of Chicago 1977–78; Visiting Prof., Southern Univ. of Valdivia, Chile 1978; Head, Max Planck Research Units for Ribosomal Structure, Hamburg, Germany 1986–2004; Jt Ed. of numerous journals, including European Molecular Biology Organization (EMBO) Journal; mem. Israeli Acad. for Science and Humanities, NAS, European Acad. of Sciences, EMBO, German Nat. Acad. of Sciences Leopoldina, American Acad. of Art and Sciences, Korean Acad. of Sciences and Tech., Int. Acad. of Astronautics, Int. Acad. for Microbiology; mem. Council for Higher Education, Nat. Advisory Cttee for Science Vision, Israel, Advisory Cttee on Biological Functions, Finnish Acad., Int. Cttee for Synchrotron Radiation; Hon. mem. Israeli Crystallographic Soc. 2001, Hon. Supreme Prof. of KEK, Photon Factory, Tsukuba, Japan 2010, Hon. Guest, Medical Univ., Baku, Azerbaijan 2012; Dr hc (Ben-Gurion Univ.) 2002, (Tel-Aviv Univ.) 2003, (Oxford) 2008, (Bar-Ilan Univ.) 2010, (Open Univ., Israel) 2011, (Fujou Univ., China) 2011, (Hebrew Univ.) 2011, (New York Univ.) 2011, (Oslo) 2011, (Toulouse) 2012, (Hamburg) 2012 (Mount Sinai Medical Univ., NYC) 2012, (Patras Univ., Greece) 2013, (Cambridge) 2013, (Xiamen Univ., China) 2014, (Baptist Univ., Hong Kong) 2014, (Moscow State Univ.) 2015, (Univ. of Strasbourg) 2016, (Mendel Univ., Czech Repub.) 2017; Somach Sachs Award 1974, Kolthof Award 1990, European Crystallography Prize (first winner) 2000, Kilby Int. Award 2000, Israel Prize 2002, Harvey Prize 2002, Louisa Gross Horwitz Prize for Biology or Biochemistry 2005, Paul Ehrlich and Ludwig Darmstaedter Prize (with Harry Noller) 2007, Wolf Prize in Chem. (with George Feher) 2006–07, 2008, Albert Einstein World Award of Science, Princeton Univ. 2008, UNESCO-L'Oréal Award for European Woman in Life Science 2008, George E. Palade Gold Medal 2008, Linus Pauling Gold Medal, Stanford 2008, Nobel Prize in Chem. (with Venkatraman Ramakrishnan and Thomas A. Steitz) 2009, Eminent Scientists Award, Japan Soc. for the Promotion of Science 2010, Wilhelm Exner Medal, Austrian Asscn for SME (Oesterreichischer Gewerbeverein—OGV) (jtly) 2010, Erna Hamburger Prize, EFEL-WISH Foundation, Lausanne 2011, Gold Medal of Distinction, Prime Minister of India 2011, Maria Sklodowska-Curie Medal, Polish Chemical Soc. 2011, Pres. of Panama Award 2011, Cite of Florence Award 2011, Academia Sinica Award (Taiwan) 2012, Prakash S. Datta Medal, FEBS, Seville 2012, The Roentgen Medal, Germany 2015, Indian Prime Minister's Gold Medal for Outstanding Scientific Contributions 2017. *Address:* Department of Structural Biology, Weizmann Institute of Science, Rehovot 76100, Israel (office). *Telephone:* (8) 934-6440 (office). *Fax:* (8) 934-3361 (office). *E-mail:* ada.yonath@weizmann.ac.il (office). *Website:* www.weizmann.ac.il/sb/faculty_pages/Yonath/home.html (office).

YONGYUTH, Wichaidit; Thai politician and political scientist; b. 15 July 1942, Surat Thani; ed Chulalongkorn Univ., Nat. Inst. of Devt Admin; fmr Permanent Sec., Ministry of Interior; fmr Deputy Minister of Interior; fmr Dir-Gen. Dept of Lands; fmr Chair. of Metropolitan Electricity Authority; fmr Chair. Audit Cttee of Govt Lottery Office; Deputy Minister to Sudarat Keyuraphan, Health Minister 2003–05; Adviser to Minister of Interior 2008; Leader Pheu Thai Party 2008–12; Deputy Prime Minister and Minister of Interior 2011–12 (resgnd); Knight Grand Cordon of the Most Exalted Order of the White Elephant, Knight Grand Cordon of the Most Noble Order of the Crown of Thailand.

YONLI, Paramanga Ernest, PhD; Burkinabè politician, agricultural economist and diplomatist; b. 31 Dec. 1956, Tansarga, Tapoa Prov.; m.; ed Univ. of Benin, Univ. of Paris I (Panthéon-Sorbonne), France, Nat. Inst. of Agric., Paris-Grignon, Ouagadougou Univ., Univ. of Groningen, Netherlands; mem. Congress for Democracy and Progress (CDP) party; Dir of Prime Minister's Office Feb.–Sept. 1996, then Minister of the Civil Service and Institutional Devt; Prime Minister of Burkina Faso 2000–07 (resgnd); elected to Nat. Ass. from Tapoa Prov. as CDP cand. May 2007 (resgnd); Amb. to USA 2008–11; Pres. Econ. and Social Council (ECOSOC) 2012–15. *Publication:* Stratégies paysannes en matière de sécurité alimentaire et commercialisation céréalière: le rôle des banques de céréales dans le Nord du Plateau Central du Burkina Faso.

YOO, Chong-ha; South Korean politician and diplomatist; b. 28 July 1936; m.; three s.; ed Seoul Nat. Univ., Bonn Univ.; joined Ministry of Foreign Affairs 1959, Third Sec., Embassy in Bonn 1963–68, Consul, Chicago May–Oct. 1968, Islamabad

1968–71, Dir SE Asia Div. Ministry of Foreign Affairs 1971–74, Counsellor, Embassy in Washington, DC 1974–77, Deputy Dir-Gen. American Affairs Bureau, Ministry of Foreign Affairs 1977–78, Dir-Gen. 1978–80, Minister, Embassy in London 1980–83, Amb. to Sudan 1983–85, Asst Minister for Econ. Affairs, Ministry of Foreign Affairs 1985–87, Amb. to Belgium 1987–89, to EC Feb.–Dec. 1989, Vice-Minister of Foreign Affairs 1989–92, Perm. Rep. to UN, New York 1992–94; Sr Adviser to Pres. for Foreign Policy and Nat. Security 1994–96; Minister of Foreign Affairs 1996–98; Pres. Korean Red Cross –2010; Order of Service Merit (Red Stripes).

YOO, Heung-soo; South Korean fmr police official, politician and diplomatist; b. 1937; spent early childhood in Japan, including elementary school in Kyoto; fmr Chief of nat. police agency; fmr Gov. of South Chungcheong Prov.; elected to Parl. 1985, sr official in South Korea–Japan Parliamentarians' League under Prime Minister Kim Dae-jung 2000–04 (retd); Amb. to Japan 2014–16.

YOO, Il-ho, BEcons, PhD; South Korean economist and politician; b. 30 March 1955; ed Seoul Nat. Univ., Univ. of Pennsylvania, USA; Research Fellow, Korea Devt Inst. (KDI) 1989–96, Prof., KDI School of Public Policy and Man. 2002–12; Pres., Korea Inst. of Public Finance 1998–2001; mem. Nat. Ass. (Parl.) 2008–, mem. Nat. Policy Cttee 2012–15; Chief Sec. to Pres.-elect Park Geun-hye 2012–13; Minister of Land, Infrastructure and Transport March–Nov. 2015, Deputy Prime Minister and Minister of Finance 2016–17; Acting Prime Minister May 2017; mem. Saenuri Party, Party Spokesperson 2013–14, Chair., Saenuri Party Policy Cttee March–May 2014. *Address:* National Assembly (Kuk Hoe), 1 Uisadang-daero, Yeongdeungpo-gu, Seoul 07233, Republic of Korea (office). *Telephone:* (2) 788-2001 (office). *Fax:* (2) 788-3375 (office). *E-mail:* webmaster@assembly.go.k (office). *Website:* www.assembly.go.kr (office).

YOOBAMRUNG, Capt. Chalerm, PhD; Thai police officer and politician; b. 10 June 1947, Bangkok; m. Lamnao Yubamrung; three s.; ed Royal Thai Police Acad., Ramkhamhaeng Univ.; Minister of Justice 1995–96; mem. House of Reps. (Parl.) (Pheu Thai Party), Leader of Opposition 2009–11; fmr police capt.; arraigned for murder of a police officer 2001, acquitted due to insufficient evidence; cand. in election for Gov. of Bangkok Metropolitan Admin 2004; Minister of the Interior 2008; Deputy Prime Minister 2011–13; Minister of Labour 2013–14; arrested after Thai coup d'état 2014.

YOON, Boo-keun (BK), BS; South Korean electronics engineer and business executive; *President and CEO, Samsung Electronics;* b. 6 Feb. 1953; ed Hanyang Univ.; Head, R&D Team, Visual Display Business, Samsung Electronics 2003–07, Head, Visual Display Business 2007–11, Head, Consumer Electronics Div. 2011–12, Pres. and Head, Consumer Electronics 2012–17, Pres., CEO and Rep. Dir, Samsung Electronics 2013–. *Address:* Samsung Electronics Building, 1320-10 Seocho-2-dong, Seocho-gu, Seoul 137-857, Republic of Korea (office). *Telephone:* (2) 2255-0114 (office). *Fax:* (2) 2255-2133 (office). *Website:* www.samsung.com (office).

YOON, Jeung-hyun, BA, MA; South Korean banking executive and politician; b. 19 Oct. 1946, Masan; ed Seoul Nat. Univ., Univ. of Wisconsin, USA; Dir Int. Finance Div., Ministry of Finance 1983–86, Banking Div. 1986–87, Financial Policy Div. 1987–89, Dir-Gen. Tax and Customs Office 1992, Securities Bureau 1992–94, Finance Bureau 1994, Dir-Gen. Financial Policy Bureau, Ministry of Finance and Economy 1994–96, Deputy Minister, Tax and Customs Office 1996–97, Financial Policy Bureau 1997–98; Dean, Nat. Tax Coll. 1998–99; Exec. Dir Asian Devt Bank 1999–2004; Chair. Financial Supervisory Comm. 2004–07; Minister of Strategy and Finance 2009–11, also Acting Prime Minister Aug.–Oct. 2010; Sr Adviser to Kim & Chang (law firm) 2008; mem. Nat. Econ. Advisory Council 2008–; mem. Bd of Dirs Doosan Infracore Co. Ltd 2015–, Hyundai Oilbank Co. 2015–; Service Merit Medal 1978, Asian Banker Achievement Award 2006, Daesan Insurance Prize 2008. *Address:* c/o Hyundai Oilbank Co., 182, Pyeongsin 2-ro, Daesan-eup, Seosan City 31902, Chungcheongnam-do, Republic of Korea (office). *Telephone:* (1) 660-5114 (office). *E-mail:* wchun@oilbank.co.kr (office). *Website:* www.oilbank.co.kr (office).

YOON, Adm. Kwang-ung; South Korean politician; b. 13 Oct. 1942, Busan; ed Busan Commercial High School, Repub. of Korea Naval Acad., US Naval Command and Staff Coll., Repub. of Korea Nat. Defence Univ.; CO, ROKS Chungnam, Repub. of Korea Navy 1985–86, Dir Org. Div., Repub. of Korea Navy HQ 1987–89, Commdr Flotilla Five 1991–92, Naval Forces Devt Command 1996–97, C-in-C ROKFLT 1997–98, Vice-Chief of Naval Operations 1998–99; Dir Acquisition and Devt Bureau, Ministry of Nat. Defence 1995–96; Adviser, Hyundai Heavy Industries Co. Ltd 2000–03; Chair. Emergency Planning Comm., Office of the Prime Minister 2003–04; Adviser to the Pres. on Nat. Defence Jan.–July 2004; Minister of Nat. Defence July 2004–06 (resgnd); US Legion of Merit, Korean Order of Nat. Security Merit.

YORDANOV, Svetoslav, BEcons; Bulgarian business executive; b. 28 May 1960, Bourgas; ed Varna Univ. of Econs; fmr Deputy Chief Accountant, Neftochim, later becoming Financial Dir and Commercial Dir; fmr Exec. Dir, Multigroup AD; mem. Man. Bd, Chair. and CEO Petrol AD 1999–2014. *Address:* c/o Petrol AD, 43 Cherni Vrah, 1407 Sofia, Bulgaria. *E-mail:* office@petrol.bg.

YORK, HRH The Duke of; (Prince Andrew Albert Christian Edward), (Earl of Inverness, Baron Killyleagh), KG, GCVO, CD, ADC, FRS; British; b. 19 Feb. 1960, London, England; s. of HM Queen Elizabeth II (q.v.) and Prince Philip, Duke of Edinburgh (q.v.); m. Sarah Ferguson 1986 (divorced 1996); two d., Beatrice Elizabeth Mary, b. 8 Aug. 1988, Eugenie Victoria Helena, b. 23 March 1990; ed Heatherdown Preparatory School, Ascot, Gordonstoun School, Scotland, Lakefield Coll. School, Ont., Canada, Britannia Royal Naval Coll., Dartmouth; joined Royal Navy as Seaman Officer, specializing as a pilot 1979, before entering Royal Naval Coll.; flying training with RAF Leeming, Yorks. and helicopter training at Royal Naval Air Station (RNAS) Culdrose, Cornwall; received Wings 1981; joined front-line unit 820 Naval Air Squadron and embarked in Anti-Submarine Warfare Carrier HMS Invincible; participated in Falklands conflict; rank of Lt 1984; Personal ADC to HM The Queen 1984; served as Flight Pilot in NAS, Type 22 Frigate HMS Brazen 1984–86; returned to 702 NAS as Helicopter Warfare Instructor 1987; joined Type 42 Destroyer HMS Edinburgh as Officer of the Watch 1988–89; returned to RNAS Portland to form HMS Campbeltown Flight; served as Flight Commdr, 829 NAS 1989–91; Army Command and Staff Course, Staff Coll., Camberley 1992; rank of Lt Commdr 1992; commanded Hunt Class Minehunter HMS Cottesmore 1993–94; Sr Pilot, 815 NAS, RNAS Portland 1995–96; joined Ministry of Defence, London as a staff officer, Directorate of Naval Operations 1997–99; rank of Commdr, with Diplomacy Section of Naval Staff, London 1999–2001; Special Rep. for Int. Trade and Investment 2001–11; rank of Hon. Capt. 2005, Hon. Rear Adm. 2010, Hon. Vice Adm. 2014; Adm. of the Sea Cadet Corps 1992–; Col-in-Chief Staffordshire Regt 1989–, Royal Irish Regt 1992–, Royal NZ Army Logistic Regt, Small Arms School Corps, Royal Highland Fusiliers (Princess Margaret's Own and Ayrshire Regt), 9th/12th Royal Lancers (Prince of Wales's), Queen's York Rangers (1st American Regt), Royal Highland Fusiliers of Canada, Princess Louise Fusiliers, Canadian Airborne Regt (disbanded), Yorkshire Regt (14th/15th, 19th and 33rd/76th Foot); Royal Col of the Royal Highland Fusiliers, 2nd Bn Royal Regt of Scotland; Hon. Air Cdre, RAF Lossiemouth, Morayshire; Cdre-in-Chief of the Fleet Air Arml Adm. of the Sea Cadet Corps; Patron of more than 90 orgs, including Greenwich Hosp., Fight for Sight, Defeating Deafness, Jubilee Sailing Trust, Royal Aero Club; Trustee Nat. Maritime Museum, Greenwich; Chair. Trustees Outward Bound Trust; Capt. Royal and Ancient Golf Club of St Andrews; mem. Advisory Bd of Govs, Lakefield Coll. School; Cdre, Royal Thames Yacht Club; Elder Brother, Trinity House; Queen Elizabeth II Silver Jubilee Medal 1977, South Atlantic Medal, with Rosette 1982, NZ 1990 Commemoration Medal 1990, Queen Elizabeth II Golden Jubilee Medal 2002, Commemorative Medal for the Centennial of Saskatchewan 2005, Queen Elizabeth II Diamond Jubilee Medal 2012; Grand Cross of the Royal Norwegian Order of St Olav 1988, Order of the Fed. (UAE) 2010. *Address:* Buckingham Palace, London, SW1A 1AA, England. *Website:* www.royal.gov.uk; www.thedukeofyork.org.

YORK, Michael, OBE, BA; British actor; b. (Michael Hugh York-Johnson), 27 March 1942, Fulmer, Bucks., England; s. of Joseph Gwynne Johnson and Florence Edith May Johnson (neé Chown); m. Patricia McCallum 1968; ed Hurstpierpoint Coll., Sussex, Univ. Coll., Oxford; began career in production of The Yellow Jacket 1956; West End debut with a small part in a production of Hamlet 1959; with Dundee Repertory Co. 1964, Nat. Theatre Co. 1965, guest lecturer; Chair. Calif. Youth Theatre; Chevalier des Arts et des Lettres 1995; named to Int. Best Dressed List Hall of Fame 1977, star on the Hollywood Walk of Fame. *Stage appearances include:* Any Just Cause 1967, Hamlet 1970, Outcry (Broadway) 1973, Ring Round the Moon 1975, Bent, Cyrano de Bergerac, Whisper in the Mind 1990, The Crucible 1991, Someone to Watch Over Me 1993. *Films include:* Accident 1967, Confessions of Loving Couples 1967, The Taming of the Shrew 1967, Smashing Time 1967, Red and Blue (short) 1967, Romeo and Juliet 1968, The Strange Affair 1968, The Guru 1969, Alfred the Great 1969, Justine 1969, Something for Everyone 1970, Zeppelin 1971, Touch and Go 1971, Cabaret 1972, Lost Horizon 1973, England Made Me 1973, The Three Musketeers 1973, The Four Musketeers: Milady's Revenge 1974, Murder on the Orient Express 1974, Conduct Unbecoming 1975, Logan's Run 1976, Seven Nights in Japan 1976, The Island of Dr. Moreau 1977, The Last Remake of Beau Geste 1977, The Riddle of the Sands 1979, Final Assignment 1980, Beauty and the Beast (short, voice) 1981, The White Lions 1981, For Those I Loved 1983, Success Is the Best Revenge 1984, L'aube 1986, Spaceballs (uncredited) 1987, Der Joker 1987, Phantom of Death 1988, Killing Blue 1988, The Return of the Musketeers 1989, Come See the Paradise 1990, Eline Vere 1991, The Wanderer 1991, The Long Shadow 1992, Wide Sargasso Sea 1993, Discretion Assured 1994, Gospa 1995, Not of This Earth 1995, A Young Connecticut Yankee in King Arthur's Court 1996, Austin Powers: International Man of Mystery 1997, Goodbye America 1997, Dark Planet 1997, A Christmas Carol (video, voice) 1997, Merchants of Venus 1998, Wrongfully Accused 1998, 54 1998, The Treat 1998, Tex Murphy: Overseer (video game) 1998, Lovers and Liars 1998, Die by the Sword (video game) 1998, A Monkey's Tale (English version, voice) 1999, Austin Powers: The Spy Who Shagged Me 1999, Puss in Boots 1999, The Omega Code 1999, The Haunting of Hell House 1999, Borstal Boy 2000, One Hell of a Guy 2000, The Land Before Time VII: The Stone of Cold Fire (video, voice) 2000, Megiddo: The Omega Code 2 2001, Austin Powers in Goldmember 2002, Superman: Shadow of Apokolips (video game) 2002, Winnie the Pooh: A Very Merry Pooh Year (voice) 2002, Moscow Heat (as Maykl York) 2004, William Powell: A True Gentleman (video short, narrator) 2005, Scarface: The World Is Yours (video game) 2006, Flatland: The Movie (short, voice) 2007, Transformers: Revenge of the Fallen (voice) 2009, Tom and Jerry Meet Sherlock Holmes (video, voice) 2010, The Justice of Wolves 2010, The Mill and the Cross 2011, Flatland 2: Sphereland (video) 2012, Sleeping Beauty (voice) 2014. *Radio:* Jane Eyre 2002, Alice in Wonderland 2002, The Trial of Walter Raleigh 2003. *Television includes:* Arrest and Trial (series) 1964, The Forsyte Saga (mini-series) 1967, The Wednesday Play (series) – Rebel in the Grave 1968, Great Expectations (film) 1974, Jesus of Nazareth (mini-series) 1977, BBC 2 Play of the Week (series) 1977, Much Ado About Nothing (film) 1978, A Man Called Intrepid (mini-series) 1979, CBS Library (series) 1981, Vendredi ou la vie sauvage (film) 1981, Twilight Theater (film) 1982, The Phantom of the Opera (film) 1983, Parade of Stars (film) 1983, The Weather in the Streets (film) 1983, The Master of Ballantrae (film) 1984, Au nom de tous les miens (mini-series) 1985, Space (mini-series) 1985, ABC Afterschool Specials (series) 1986, Dark Mansions (film) 1986, Tall Tales & Legends (series) 1986, Sword of Gideon (film) 1986, Knots Landing (series) 1987–88, The Secret of the Sahara (mini-series) 1988, The Far Country (film) 1988, The Four Minute Mile (film) 1988, The Lady and the Highwayman (film) 1989, Hunt for Stolen War Treasures (film) 1989, Till We Meet Again (mini-series) 1989, The Heat of the Day (film) 1989, Night of the Fox (film) 1990, Avonlea (series) 1991, Duel of Hearts (film) 1991, The Legend of Prince Valiant (series, voice) 1992, Batman: The Animated Series (series, voice) 1992–93, The Magic Paintbrush (film, voice) 1993, Tracey Takes on New York (film) 1993, David Copperfield (film, voice) 1993, TekWar: TekLab (film) 1994, ABC Weekend Specials (series) – The Magic Flute (voice) 1994, Fall from Grace (film) 1994, Rochade (film) 1994, Shadow of a Kiss (film) 1995, The Naked Truth (series) 1995, The Magic School Bus (series, voice) 1995, SeaQuest 2032 (series) 1995–96, 1914–1918 (mini-series, voice) 1996, La nouvelle tribu (mini-series) 1996, September (film) 1996, Babylon 5 (series) 1996, Adventures from the Book of Virtues (series) – Compassion (voice) 1996, The Ring (film) 1996, Superman (series, voice) 1997, Austin Powers' Electric Pussycat Swingers Club (film) 1997, Sliders (series) 1997, True Women (film) 1997, Un coup de baguette magique (film) 1997, The Ripper (film) 1997, Dead Man's Gun (series) 1998, Perfect Little Angels (film) 1998, A Knight in Camelot (film) 1998, Glory, Glory (film) 1998, The Lot (series) 2001, Orson Welles Tales from the Black Museum (series) 2002, Liberty's Kids: Est. 1776 (series, voice) 2002, Presidio Med (series) 2002, Curb Your Enthusiasm (series) 2002, Gilmore Girls (series) 2003–04, The Lady Musketeer (film) 2004, Justice League (series, voice) 2004, Super Robot Monkey Team Hyperforce Go! (series) 2005, Icon (film) 2005, Crusader (film) 2005, The Simpsons (series, voice) 2006, Law & Order: Criminal Intent (series) 2006, The Replacements (series, voice) 2007, Ben 10: Alien Force (series, voice) 2008, Four Seasons (mini-series) 2008–09, Star Wars: The Clone Wars (series) 2009, How I Met Your Mother (series) 2010, Family Guy (series, voice) 2010. *Music:* Christopher Columbus: A Musical Journey 2002, Enoch Arden (Tennyson/Strauss) 2003. *Publications:* The Courage of Conviction (contrib.) 1986, Voices of Survival (contrib.) 1987, Travelling Player (autobiog.) 1991, Accidentally on Purpose (autobiog.) 1992, A Shakespearean Actor Prepares 2000, Dispatches From Armageddon 2002. *Address:* c/o Roger Carey, Roger Carey Associates, Suite 909, The Old House, Shepperton Studios, Studios Road, Shepperton, Middx, TW17 0QD, England (office); c/o Bradford Bricken, Bricken Entertainment, PO Box 46190, Los Angeles, CA 90046, USA (office). *Telephone:* (1932) 582890 (office). *Fax:* (1932) 569602 (office). *Website:* www.michaelyork.net.

YORKE, James A., AB, PhD; American mathematician, physicist and academic; *Distinguished University Professor Emeritus of Mathematics and Physics, Institute for Physical Sciences and Technology, University of Maryland;* b. 3 Aug. 1941, Plainfield, NJ; ed Columbia Coll., Columbia Univ., Univ. of Md; Research Assoc., Inst. for Physical Sciences and Tech. (IPST), Univ. of Maryland, College Park 1966–67, Research Asst Prof. 1967–69, Research Assoc. Prof. 1969–73, Prof. 1973–, has held jt appointments with Math. 1976– and Physics 2000–, Acting Dir IPST 1985–88, Dir 1988–2001, Distinguished Univ. Prof. of Math. and Physics 1995–2013, Emer. 2013–; Expert (part-time), Nat. Cancer Inst. 1978–79; mem. Editorial Bd, International Journal of Bifurcation and Chaos, Journal of Complex Systems Chaos, Solitons and Fractals, SIAM Journal of Applied Dynamical Systems (SIADS), Journal of Difference Equations and Applications; mem. Math Asscn of America, Soc. for Industrial and Applied Math. (SIAM); Fellow, AAAS 1998, American Physical Soc. 2003, American Math Soc. 2012; Guggenheim Fellow 1980, 38th Annual Chaim Weizmann Memorial Lecturer, Weizmann Inst., Rehovot, Israel 1997, First recipient, Univ. of Md Regents Faculty Award for Excellence in Research/Scholarship 1998, American Physical Soc. Centennial Speaker 1998–99, Distinguished Alumnus Award, Univ. of Md Coll. of Computer, Math, and Physical Sciences 2002, Japan Prize (with Benoit Mandelbrot) 2003. *Achievement:* best known to gen. public for jtly coining the math. term 'chaos' with T.Y. Li in a paper entitled Period Three Implies Chaos 1975. *Publications:* Gonorrhea Transmission: Dynamics and Control 1984, Dynamics: Numerical Explorations (co-author) 1994, Coping with Chaos (co-author) 1994, Chaos: An Introduction to Dynamical Systems (co-author) 1997; more than 300 articles in scientific journals. *Leisure interest:* photography. *Address:* Institute for Physical Sciences and Technology, University of Maryland, College Park, MD 20742-2431, USA (office). *Telephone:* (301) 405-4875 (office). *Fax:* (301) 314-9363 (office). *E-mail:* yorke2@ipst.umd.edu (office); yorke@umd.edu (office). *Website:* www.umd.edu (office); yorke.umd.edu (office); www.chaos.umd.edu/~yorke (office).

YORKE, Thomas (Thom) Edward; British singer, songwriter and musician (guitar, keyboards); b. 7 Oct. 1968, Wellingborough, Northamptonshire, England; one s.; ed Univ. of Exeter; mem. and lead singer, On A Friday 1985, renamed Radiohead 1991–; also designer of record sleeves; numerous tours, festivals and television appearances; guest vocalist with Drugstore on White Magic for Lovers and El President 1998; guest vocalist with Velvet Goldmine 1998, MTV's 120 Minutes Live 1998; other collaborations include UNKLE, P. J. Harvey; Founder-mem. Atoms for Peace 2009–; Q Award for Best Act in the World Today 2001, 2002, 2003. *Recordings include:* albums: with Radiohead: Pablo Honey 1993, The Bends 1995, OK Computer (Grammy Award for Best Alternative Music Performance) 1997, Kid A (Grammy Award for Best Alternative Music Album) 2000, Amnesiac 2001, I Might Be Wrong (live recordings) 2001, Hail To The Thief 2003, In Rainbows (Ivor Novello Album Award 2008, Grammy Award for Best Alternative Music Album 2009) 2007, The King of Limbs 2011, A Moon Shaped Pool 2016; solo: The Eraser 2006, Tomorrow's Modern Boxes 2014; with Atoms for Peace: Amok 2013. *Address:* Courtyard Management, 21 The Nursery, Sutton Courtenay, Abingdon, Oxfordshire OX14 4UA, England (office). *Website:* www.radiohead.com.

YORONGAR, Ngarledjy; Chadian politician and editorial director; m.; five c.; ed schools and univs in Chad, Canada and France; civil servant and govt official; also worked for int. orgs including OECD, Science and Educ. Admin. and Financial Office in Zaire, Int. Insurance Inst. (IIA) in Cameroon; Cand. in Presidential Elections 1996, 2001; campaigner against human rights violations and corruption, arrested numerous occasions including 1996 and on winning 2001 elections, imprisoned 1998–99; Leader, Fédération Action pour le République–Parti fédération; Fed. Exec. Co-ordinator of Federalist Party; Pres. of Foundation for the Respect of Law and Liberties (FORELLI); Editorial Dir of newspapers La Roue and Le Phare Républicain. *Publication:* Tchad: le Proces d'Idriss Deby. *Address:* Fédération Action pour la République–Parti fédération, BP 4197, N'Djamena, Chad (office). *Fax:* 22-51-78-60 (office). *E-mail:* yorongar@gmail.com (office).

YOSANO, Kaoru, LLB; Japanese politician; b. 22 Aug. 1938, Tokyo; ed Faculty of Law, Tokyo Univ.; joined Japan Atomic Power Co. 1963; mem. House of Reps (Tokyo 1st Dist) 1976–2009; Parl. Vice-Minister of Int. Trade and Industry 1985–89; Chair. Parl. Cttee on Commerce and Industry 1989–90, Cttee on Science and Tech. 1990–94; Minister of Educ. 1994; Deputy Chief Cabinet Sec. 1996–98; Minister of Int. Trade and Industry 1998–2005; Minister of State for Econ. and Fiscal Policy and Financial Services 2005–06; Deputy Chair., Policy Research Council, Liberal Democratic Party 1995–2004, Chair. 2004–06; Chief Cabinet Sec. Aug.–Sept. 2007; State Minister in charge of Econ. and Fiscal Policy and for Regulatory Reform 2008–09; Minister of Finance and Minister of State for Financial Affairs and for Econ. and Fiscal Policy 2009.

YOSELIANI, Otar Davidovich; Georgian film director; b. 2 Feb. 1934, Tbilisi; s. of David Yoseliani and Maria Yoseliani (née Mikaberidze); m. Rita Semenova 1956; one d.; ed Moscow Univ., Moscow Cinema Inst.; worked as sailor and miner; Tbilisi film studio 1959–76; teacher of cinema, Tbilisi Acad. of Fine Arts; working in France 1982–. *Films include:* Avril 1962, La Chute des Feuilles (Fipresci Prize, Cannes) 1966, Il était une fois un merle chanteur (Best Foreign Film of the Year, Italy) 1970, Pastorale (Fipresci Prize, Berlin) 1976, Sept pièces pour le cinéma noir et blanc 1982, Euskadi 1983, Les favoris de la lune (Grand Prix, Venice Festival) 1984, Le petit monastère en Toscane 1988, Et la lumière fut (Grand Prix, Venice Festival) 1989, Hunting Butterflies (Tarkovsky Prize 1993) 1992, Georgia Alone (TV documentary) 1994, Les Brigandeurs 1996, In Vino Veritas 1999, Lundi matin (Monday Morning) 2002, Jardins en automne 2006, Chantrapas 2010, Winter Song 2015. *Leisure interest:* speleology. *Address:* Mitskewitch 1 korp., 1 Apt 38, 380060 Tbilisi, Georgia; 14 rue de Rivoli, 75004 Paris, France. *Telephone:* (32) 38-50-58 (Tbilisi); 1-40-26-07-18 (Paris).

YOSHIDA, Saori; Japanese wrestler; b. 5 Oct. 1982, Tsu Mie; d. of Eikatsu Yoshida; ed Chukyo Univ.; gold medal, World Championships Chalkida 2002, New York 2003, Budapest 2005, Guangzhou 2006, Baku 2007, Tokyo 2008, Herning 2009, Moscow 2010, Istanbul 2011, Alberta, Canada 2012, Budapest 2013, Tashkent 2014; gold medal, World Univ. Championships 2002; gold medal, Women's 55kg Freestyle, Asian Games, Busan 2002, Doha 2006, Guangzhou 2010; gold medal, Women's 55kg Freestyle, Olympic Games, Athens 2004, Beijing 2008, London 2012; won 100th consecutive contest Sept. 2006, defeated after 119th consecutive victory by Marcie Van Dusen during Team World Cup series, Beijing 2008; coached by Kazuhito Sakae; Female Wrestler of the Year 2002, Japanese Athlete of the Year, Japan Sports Awards 2007, People's Honour Award 2012. *Leisure interests:* singing karaoke songs.

YOSHIMOTO, Takashi; Japanese medical research scientist and university administrator; ed Tohoku Univ.; began teaching career at School of Medicine, Tohoku Univ. 1981, Assoc. Prof. 1982–88, Prof., Dept of Neurosurgery 1988–, Dir Univ. Hosp. 1999, Dean Grad. School of Medicine 2001–02, Pres., Tohoku Univ. 2002–08; Chair. Japan Neurosurgical Soc. 2003–; mem. Liaison Cttee for Cerebral Neurology, Science Council of Japan 1994–, Cttee of Nat. Inst. for Academic Degrees 1996–, Devt and Promotion for Medical Care in the 21st Century Cttee, Ministry of Health, Labour and Welfare 2002–; Int. mem. American Asscn of Neurological Surgeons 1998–; Active mem. Academia Eurasiana Neurochirurgica 2000–; Award of the Japanese Stroke Soc. 1979, Gold Medical Award, School of Medicine, Tohoku Univ. 1984, Nikkei BP Tech. Award, Medical and Bio Section 2000.

YOSHIMURA, Yukio, BA (Econs); Japanese business executive and fmr international organization official; *Executive Officer and Head of Government Affairs, Citigroup Japan Holdings Corporation;* b. 9 June 1947, Nishinomiya; s. of Kazuo Yoshimura and Itoko Iijima; m. Tomoko Shibazaki 1977; three s.; ed Tokyo Univ.; Dir Int. Orgs Div., Ministry of Finance 1991–92, Int. Banking Div. 1992–95; Counsellor, Minister's Secr., in charge of Int. Public Relations 1995–96, Deputy Dir-Gen. Int. Finance Bureau 1996–97; Exec. Dir for Japan, IMF 1997–2001; Sr Adviser to Pres. World Bank Group 2001–02, Vice Pres. and Special Rep. for Japan 2002–07; Man. Dir, Govt Affairs, Citibank Japan Ltd 2007–08, mem. Bd of Dirs 2008–12; Head of Govt Affairs, Nikko Citi Holdings Inc. 2008–, renamed Citigroup Japan Holdings Corpn, also Exec. Officer; mem. Basle Cttee on Banking Supervision 1984–85; Alt. Exec. Dir World Bank 1988–91; Exec. Dir Inter-American Investment Corpn 1990–91; mem. Group of Ten Working Party on Electronic Money 1996–97. *Address:* Shin Marunouchi Building, 1-5-1 Marunouchi, Chiyoda-ku, Tokyo 100-6524, Japan (office). *E-mail:* yuyoshi@mc.rosenet.ne.jp (home). *Website:* www.citigroup.jp (office).

YOSHINO, Akira, BSc, MSc, DrEng; Japanese electrochemist and industrial researcher; *General Manager, Yoshino Laboratory;* b. 30 Jan. 1948, Suita, Osaka; ed Kyoto Univ., Osaka Univ.; joined Asahi Kasei Corpn 1972, with Kawasaki Lab. 1982–92, Man. of Product Devt Group, Ion Battery Business Promotion Dept 1992–94, Man. of Tech. Devt, A&T Battery Corpn (LIB mfr, jt venture co. between Asahi Kasei and Toshiba) 1994–97, Man. of Rechargeable Ion Battery Dept, Asahi Kasei Corpn 1997–2001, Man. of Battery Materials Business Devt Dept 2001–05, Fellow, Asahi Kasei Corpn 2003–, Gen. Man., Yoshino Lab. 2005–, Gen. Man., Battery Materials Business Devt Dept, Asahi Kasei E-materials Corpn 2009–; Pres. Lithium Ion Battery Tech. and Evaluation Centre (LIBTEC) 2010–; Medal with Purple Ribbon, Govt of Japan 2004; Chemical Tech. Prize, Chemical Soc. of Japan 1998, Battery Div. Tech. Award, The Electrochemical Soc. 1999, Ichimura Prizes in Industry—Meritorious Achievement Prize 2001, Commendation for Science and Tech., Minister of Educ., Culture, Sports, Science and Tech.—Prize for Science and Tech., Devt Category 2003, Yamazaki-Teiichi Prize, Foundation for Promotion of Material Science and Tech. of Japan 2011, C&C Prize, NEC C&C Foundation 2011, IEEE Medal for Environmental and Safety Technologies 2012, Global Energy Prize (Russia) 2013, Kato Memorial Prize, Kato Foundation for Promotion of Science 2013, Charles Stark Draper Prize, Nat. Acad. of Eng (co-recipient) 2014. *Publications:* numerous papers in professional journals on the lithium-ion battery; several patents. *Address:* Asahi Kasei Corporation, 1-105 Kanda Jinbocho, Chiyoda-ku, Tokyo 101-8101, Japan (office). *E-mail:* info@asahi-kasei.co.jp (office). *Website:* www.asahi-kasei.co.jp (office).

YOST, R. David, MBA; American business executive; ed US Air Force Acad., Univ. of California, Los Angeles; joined Kauffman-Lattimer, Columbus, Ohio 1974, served in a variety of operational, sales and exec. positions, including Pres., Exec. Vice-Pres. Operations 1995–97, Co-COO; CEO AmeriSource Health Corpn 1997–2001, Chair. 2000–01, CEO AmerisourceBergen Corpn (cr. through merger of Bergen Brunswick Corpn and AmeriSource Health Corpn) 2001–11, Pres. 2001–02, 2007–11; mem. Bd of Dirs Tyco International 2009–, ITT Exelis Inc., Marsh & McLennan Companies 2012–; Trustee, Penn Medicine, US Air Force Academy Endowment Bd.

YOULA, Mamady, DEA; Guinean economist, business executive and politician; b. 1951, Conakry; ed Univ. Félix-Houphouët-Boigny, Abidjan, Centre d'Etudes Financières Economiques et Bancaires, Paris, IMF Inst., Washington; joined Banque Centrale de la République de Guinée 1989, becoming Economist and Man. Dir, Head of Econ. Research Service, Asst Dir of Research Studies, Dir, Dept of Research and Publications 1994–97; Dir Société Guinéo-Norvégienne de Transport Maritime (GUINOMAR) 1997–2003; Chair. Technical Cttee, Société minière de Dinguiraye 1997–2003; Adviser on Econ. and Financial Affairs, Ministry of Natural Resources and Energy, later Ministry of Mining, Geology and Environment 1997–2003; Admin., Port Autonome de Conakry 1999–2003; Adviser on Econ. and Mining Affairs to Prime Minister 2003–04; Dir-Gen., Guinea Alumina Corpn

SA 2004–15; First Vice-Pres., Chambre des Mines de Guinée 2009–11, Pres. 2012–15; Founder-mem. and First Pres., Plateforme de Concertation du Secteur Privé Guinéen (private sector consultation body) 2015–; Prime Minister 2015–18.

YOUN, Kong-hi (Victorinus), STD, DD; South Korean ecclesiastic; *Archbishop Emeritus of Kwangju;* b. 8 Nov. 1924, Nampo City (now North Korea); s. of (Peter) Sang Youn and (Victoria) Sang Sook Choi; ed St Willibrord's Major Seminary, Dok-Won, Urban Coll., Rome, Gregorian Univ., Rome; ordained priest 1950; Asst Priest, Cathedral of Seoul (Myong-Dong) 1950; Chaplain, Pusan UN POW Camp 1951, Vice-Pres. Catholic Library, Pusan 1953; teacher, Song-Shin (Holy Ghost) Middle and High School 1954; Sec. Catholic Conf. of Korea 1960; consecrated Bishop of Suwon 1963–73; Ordinary of Su-Won Diocese 1963–73; Admin. Seoul Archdiocese 1967; Archbishop and Ordinary of Kwangju Archdiocese 1973–2000, Archbishop Emer. 2000–; Rep., Kwangju Catholic Coll. Foundation 1974; Chair. Episcopal Conf. of Korea 1975; Rep. of Episcopal Cttee of Bicentennial of Catholic Church in Korea 1980; Episcopal Moderator, Justice and Peace Cttee 1979. *Publication:* Radio Message 1963. *Leisure interest:* mountain climbing. *Address:* Kwangju Catholic University, PO Box 101, Jung-Nam-Kil 12–25, Nampyeong-eup, Naju-si, Jeonnam 58230, Republic of Korea. *Telephone:* (61) 337-2181. *Fax:* (61) 337-2185. *E-mail:* vkyoun@mail.kjc.ac.kr (office).

YOUNG, Sir Colville Norbert, Kt, GCMG, MBE, JP, DPhil; Belizean government official and academic; *Governor-General;* b. 20 Nov. 1932, Belize City; s. of Henry Oswald Young and Adney Wilhelmina Young (née Waite); m. Norma Eleanor Trapp 1956; three s. one d.; ed Univ. of West Indies, Univ. of York; Prin. St Michael's Coll., Belize 1974–76; Lecturer in English and Gen. Studies Belize Tech. Coll. 1976–86; Pres. Univ. Coll. of Belize 1986–90, Lecturer 1990–93; Gov.-Gen. of Belize 1993–; Hon. PhD (York) 2003; Arts Faculty Prize, Univ. Coll. of the West Indies 1959, Student of the Year, Univ. Coll. of the West Indies 1960, Outstanding Teacher's Award 1987. *Compositions include:* Misa Caribeña, Tiger Dead (folk opera), Ode to Independence (secular cantata for mixed voices and orchestra). *Publications:* Creole Proverbs of Belize 1980, Caribbean Corner Calling 1988, Language and Education in Belize 1989, Pataki Full 1990, From One Caribbean Corner (poetry) 1983, contrib. drama and poetry in various anthologies, articles in various publs. *Leisure interests:* creative writing, playing and arranging steel band music, musical composition. *Address:* Belize House, Belmopan, Belize. *Telephone:* (822) 2521 (office); (822) 3081 (office). *Fax:* (822) 2050 (office). *E-mail:* govgenbz@btl.net (office).

YOUNG, Rev. Frances Margaret, OBE, PhD, FBA; British academic; *Professor Emerita, Department of Theology, University of Birmingham;* b. (Frances Margaret Worrall), 25 Nov. 1939, Frome, Somerset; d. of A. Stanley Worrall and Mary Frances Worrall (née Marshall); m. Robert Charles Young 1964; three s.; ed Bedford Coll., Univ. of London, Girton Coll., Cambridge and Chicago Divinity School; Research Fellow, Clare Hall, Cambridge 1967–68; temporary lecturer, Univ. of Birmingham 1971–73, Lecturer 1973–84, Sr Lecturer 1984–86, Edward Cadbury Prof. 1986–2005, Prof. Emer. 2005–, Head, Dept of Theology 1986–95, Head of School of Philosophy and Theology 1989–93, Dean Faculty of Arts 1995–97, Pro-Vice-Chancellor 1997–2002; ordained Methodist Minister 1984; Hon. DD (Univ. of Aberdeen) 1994, (Liverpool Hope Univ.) 2013, Hon. DTheol (MF Norwegian School of Theology) 2008, Hon. DUniv (Oxford Brookes Univ.) 2010. *Publications:* Sacrifice and the Death of Christ 1975, Can These Dry Bones Live? 1982, From Nicaea to Chalcedon 1983 (second edn 2010), Face to Face: A Narrative Essay in the Theology of Suffering 1985, The Art of Performance 1990, The Theology of the Pastoral Letters 1994, Biblical Exegesis and the Formation of Christian Culture 1997, Cambridge History of Early Christian Literature (co-ed.) 2004, Cambridge History of Christianity: Origins to Constantine (co-ed.) 2006, Brokenness and Blessing 2007, Holiness and Mission (with Morna Hooker) 2010, Exegesis and Theology in Early Christianity 2012, Arthur's Call 2014, Construing the Cross 2015. *Leisure interests:* walking, cycling, camping, travel, music, poetry, literature. *Address:* 142 Selly Park Road, Birmingham, B29 7LH, England (home). *Telephone:* (121) 472-4841 (home). *E-mail:* francesmyoung@gmail.com (home).

YOUNG, Ian, AO, BE (Hons), MEngSc, PhD, FTSE; Australian civil engineer, academic and university administrator; *Kernot Professor of Engineering, University of Melbourne;* b. 17 Jan. 1957, Cunnamulla; s. of Richard Young and Mary Stella Young; m. Heather Young; one d.; ed James Cook Univ., North Queensland; began academic career at Max Planck Institut für Meteorologie, Hamburg Germany; later Prof. of Civil Eng, Univ. of New South Wales; consultant to USN and offshore oil and gas industry in Australia, Asia and N America; Exec. Dean of Faculty of Eng, Computer and Math. Sciences, Univ. of Adelaide 1999–2003, also held position of Pro Vice-Chancellor (Int.) for part of this time; Vice-Chancellor, Swinburne Univ. of Tech. 2003–11; Vice-Chancellor and Pres. ANU 2011–16; Kernot Prof. of Eng, Univ. of Melbourne 2016–; Chief Exec., Conviro Pty Ltd 2016–; fmr Chair. Education Australia Ltd; fmr Dir IDP Education Pty Ltd; mem. Australian Qualifications Framework Council 2009–11; Chair. Group of Eight 2014–15, VERNet Pty Ltd 2015–; Fellow, Acad. of Technological Sciences and Eng; Hon. Fellow, Inst. of Engineers Australia; numerous awards, including C.N. Barton Medal, Lorenz G. Straub Medal, Centenary Medal for services to Australian Soc. 2003. *Publications include:* three books and more than 100 papers in peer-reviewed journals on coastal and ocean engineering and physical oceanography. *Address:* 34 Freemantle Drive, Wantirna South, Vic. 3152, Australia (home). *Telephone:* (4) 0813-3185 (home). *E-mail:* ian.young@conviro.com.au (office).

YOUNG, Michael K., BA, JD; American lawyer, university administrator and fmr government official; *President, Texas A&M University;* m. Suzan Young; three c.; ed Brigham Young Univ., Harvard Law School; Law Clerk, US Supreme Court, Washington, DC 1977–78; Assoc. Prof., then Prof., then Fuyo Prof. of Japanese Law, Columbia Univ. 1978–98, also Dir Center for Japanese Legal Studies, Center for Korean Legal Studies; Deputy Legal Adviser to US Dept of State 1989–91, Deputy Under-Sec. for Econ. and Agricultural Affairs 1991–93, Amb. for Trade and Environmental Affairs 1992–93; Dean and Lobingier Prof. of Comparative Law and Jurisprudence, George Washington Univ. Law School 1998–2004; Pres. and Distinguished Prof. of Law, Univ. of Utah 2004–11, Pres. Emer. and Distinguished Prof. of Law 2011–; Pres. and Prof. of Law, Univ. of Washington 2011–15; Pres. Texas A&M Univ. 2015–; Visiting Scholar, Faculty of Law, Univ. of Tokyo, Japan 1978–80, 1983; Visiting Prof., Nihon Univ., Tokyo 1985, Waseda Univ., Tokyo 1989; mem. US Comm. on Int. Religious Freedom 1998–2005, Brown v. Bd of Educ. 50th Anniversary Comm.; fmr mem. US Judicial Conf. Cttee on Int. Judicial Relations; fmr mem. Bd of Visitors, USAF Acad.; mem. Council on Foreign Relations, Worldwide Univs Network 2011, Asscn of American Univs 2011, Asscn of Pacific Rim Univs 2011, Asscn of Public and Land-grant Univs 2011, Asscn of Governing Bds of Colls and Univs 2011, Pac-12 Conf. of Chief Exec. Officers 2011; Fellow, POSCO Research Inst. 1996, American Bar Foundation; Order of St Michael of the Wing (Portugal) 2007; Honored Alumni of the Year, Coll. of Humanities, Brigham Young Univ. 1995, Award for Excellence in Ethics, Utah Valley State Univ. 2004, Award of Excellence in Educ., Utah Hispanic Chamber of Commerce 2005, Communicator of the Year Award, Utah Chapters of the Public Relations Soc. of America and Int. Asscn of Business Communicators 2005, Award for Distinguished Service in Promoting Religious Freedom, Int. Center for Law Religious Studies, Brigham Young Univ. 2005, Distinguished Service Award, J. Reuben Clark Soc., Los Angeles Chapter 2006, Award in Recognition of Excellence in the Promotion of Int. Religious Freedom, Church of Jesus Christ of Latter-Day Saints 2006, Helping Hands Award, Utah Youth Village 2006, US-China Educational Collaboration Leadership Award, Chinese Asscn for Science and Tech. (USA) 2008, Int. Leader of the Year, World Trade Asscn of Utah 2008, Distinguished Service Award, LDS Int. Asscn 2011. *Publications:* Foreign Acquisitions in Japan: Hurdling the Ultimate Barrier (co-author) 1985, American Lawyers in Japan: Opportunities and Obstacles for Clients and Practitioners 1989, Ho wa Nichibei wo Hedateru Ka? (Does Law Create a Separation Between Japan and the United States?) 1990, Trilateral Perspectives on International Legal Issues: Relevance of Domestic Law & Policy (ed.) 1996, Japanese Law in Context: Readings in Society, The Economy, and Politics (co-author) 2002, International Environmental Law: Cases, Materials, Problems (co-author) (second edn) 2011, The Fundamentals of U.S. Trade Law and Policy (second edn) 2011; numerous articles in both English and Japanese in professional journals and in newspapers and popular journals. *Address:* Texas A&M University, 301 Tarrow St, College Station, Texas, TX 77840-7896, USA (office). *Telephone:* (979) 458-7700 (office). *E-mail:* chancellor@tamus.edu (office). *Website:* www.tamus.edu (office).

YOUNG, Michael W., BS, PhD; American geneticist, biologist and academic; *Richard and Jeanne Fisher Professor and Vice-President for Academic Affairs, The Rockefeller University;* b. 1949, Miami, Fla; m. Laurel Eckhardt; two d.; ed Univ. of Texas; Postdoctoral Researcher, Stanford Univ. School of Medicine 1975–78; Asst Prof., The Rockefeller Univ. 1978–84, Assoc. Prof. 1984–88, Prof. 1988–, Vice-Pres. for Academic Affairs and Richard and Jeanne Fisher Prof. 2004–; Investigator, Howard Hughes Medical Inst. 1987–96; Head of Rockefeller unit of NSF's Science and Tech. Center for Biological Timing 1991–2001; mem. NAS; Fellow, American Acad. of Microbiology; Neuroscience Prize, Peter and Patricia Gruber Foundation 2009, Louisa Gross Horwitz Prize, Columbia Univ. (co-recipient) 2011, Massry Prize 2012, Gairdner Int. Award 2012, Wiley Prize in Biomedical Science 2013, Shaw Prize in Life Science and Medicine (co-recipient) 2013, Nobel Prize in Physiology or Medicine (co-recipient with Michael Rosbash and Jeffrey C. Hall) 2017, GITAM Foundation Annual Award 2018. *Publications:* numerous papers in professional journals. *Address:* Young M Laboratory, The Rockefeller University, 1230 York Avenue, New York, NY 10065, USA (office). *E-mail:* michael.young@rockefeller.edu (office). *Website:* www.rockefeller.edu/research/faculty/labheads/MichaelYoung (office).

YOUNG, Neil, (Bernard Shakey); Canadian singer, songwriter and musician (guitar); b. 12 Nov. 1945, Toronto, Ont.; m. 1st Susan Acevedo 1968 (divorced 1970); m. 2nd Pegi Young 1978 (divorced 2014); m. 3rd Daryl Hannah 2018; one s. one d.; fmr lead singer, The Squires; with Buffalo Springfield 1966–69; with Crosby, Stills, Nash and Young 1969–74; solo artist with own backing group, Crazy Horse 1969–; Grammy Award for Best New Artist 1970, Melody Maker Poll Winner for Best Int. Group 1971, MTV Video Award 1989, Rolling Stone Critics' Award for Best Album 1989, Bay Area Music Award for Outstanding Album 1993, Q Award for Best Live Act 1993, Juno Award for Best Producer 2006, Americana Award for Artist of the Year 2006, Grammy Award for Best Rock Song (for Angry World) 2011, inducted into Rock and Roll Hall of fame 1995 (as solo artist) and 1997 (as mem. of Buffalo Springfield). *Films:* Journey Through the Past (dir) 1974, Rust Never Sleeps (dir) 1979, Human Highway (writer and dir) 1982, Made in Heaven (actor) 1987, '68 (actor) 1988, Freedom (actor) 1989, Love at Large (actor) 1990, Weld (actor) 1990, Year of the Horse (exec. producer) 1997, Greendale (writer, dir, actor, producer) 2003, Neil Young: Heart of Gold 2006, CSNY/Déjà Vu (writer, dir, score) 2008, Pearl Jam Twenty (actor) 2011, Sound City (actor) 2013, A MusiCares Tribute to Bruce Springsteen (actor) 2014, Paradox (actor) 2018. *Recordings include:* albums: with Buffalo Springfield: Buffalo Springfield 1967, Last Time Around 1968; with Crosby, Stills, Nash and Young: Déjà Vu 1970, Four Way Street 1971; solo: Neil Young 1969, Everybody Knows This Is Nowhere 1969, After The Goldrush 1970, Crazy Horse 1971, Harvest 1972, Journey Through The Past 1972, Time Fades Away 1973, On The Beach 1974, Tonight's The Night 1975, Zuma 1975, Long May You Run 1976, American Stars 'N' Bars 1977, Comes A Time 1978, Rust Never Sleeps 1979, Live Rust 1980, Where The Buffalo Roam (OST) 1980, Hawks & Doves 1980, Re-ac-tor 1981, Trans 1983, Everybody's Rockin' 1983, Old Ways 1985, Landing On Water 1986, Life 1987, This Note's For You 1988, Freedom 1989, Ragged Glory 1990, Arc 1991, Weld 1991, Harvest Moon 1992, Unplugged 1993, Sleeps With Angels 1994, Mirror Ball 1995, Dead Man (OST) 1996, Broken Arrow 1996, Year Of The Horse 1997, Silver & Gold 2000, Are You Passionate? 2002, Greendale (OST) 2003, Prairie Wind (Juno Award for Best Adult Alternative Album 2006) 2005, Living With War 2006, Chrome Dreams II 2007, Fork in the Road 2009, Le Noise 2010, Psychedelic Pill 2012, A Letter Home 2014, Storytone 2014, The Monsanto Years 2015, Earth 2016, Peace Trail 2016, The Visitor 2017. *Publication:* Waging Heavy Peace (memoir) 2012. *Address:* c/o Elliot Roberts, Lookout Management, 1460 Fourth Street, Santa Monica, CA 90401, USA (office). *Telephone:* (310) 393-5091 (office). *Fax:* (310) 319-533 (office). *E-mail:* webstar@lookoutmgmt.com (office). *Website:* lookoutmgmt.com (office); www.neilyoungarchives.com.

YOUNG, Richard Stuart; British photographer; b. 17 Sept. 1947, Welwyn Garden City, Herts., England; s. of David Young and Hilda Ellison; m. 1st Riita Sinikka Harju 1975 (died 1983); two s.; m. 2nd Susan Manije Walker 1985; one d.; photographer 1974–; opened Richard Young Gallery in West London with his wife, Susan Young 2008; lives and works in London and world-wide; Dr hc (Univ. of the

Arts London) 2013; Ischia Art Award 2012. *Television:* subject of a four-part Sky Arts documentary, Celebrity Exposed: The Photography of Richard Young 2012. *Publications:* By Invitation Only 1981, Paparazzo 1989, Shooting Stars 2004. *Leisure interests:* films, travel, books, music, good food. *Telephone:* (20) 7937-8911. *E-mail:* info@richardyounggallery.co.uk (office); office@richardyoungonline.com (office). *Website:* www.richardyounggallery.co.uk (office); www.richardyoungonline.com (office).

YOUNG, Robert (Bob), BA; Canadian software industry executive; *Chairman, Lulu Enterprises, Inc.;* b. 19 Jan. 1954, Ancaster, Ont.; three c.; ed Trinity Coll. School, Port Hope, Ont., Victoria Coll. at Univ. of Toronto; began career as sales and marketing exec. in computer industry 1976; f. Vernon Computer Rentals 1984, ACC Corp Inc. 1993, acquired Red Hat trademarks from Marc Ewing to develop and market Linux open-source operating software 1994, name changed to Red Hat Software 1995, subsequently changed to Red Hat, Inc., CEO 1995–99; co-f. Linux Journal 1994; Founder and Chair. Lulu Enterprises, Inc. 2002–, est. Lulu Blooker Prize 2006; f. Center for the Public Domain 1999; acquired Hamilton Tiger-Cats of Canadian Football League 2003. *Publication:* Under the Radar 1999. *Leisure interests:* family holidays, fly-fishing. *Address:* Lulu Enterprises, Inc., 3101 Hillsborough Street, Suite 210, Raleigh, NC 27607-5436, USA (office). *Telephone:* (919) 459-5858 (office). *Fax:* (919) 447-3198 (office). *Website:* www.lulu.com (office).

YOUNG, Rosie Margaret, CBE, MD, FRCP, FRCPE, FRCP (Glas), FRACP; British medical specialist and academic; *Honorary Consultant, Queen Mary Hospital;* b. (Yeung Tse Tse), 23 Oct. 1930, Hong Kong; d. of Yeung Shun Hang and Shiu Shui Ying; ed Univ. of Hong Kong; Dean, Faculty of Medicine, Univ. of Hong Kong 1983–85, Pro-Vice-Chancellor 1985–93, Hon. Prof. 2000–, fmr Prof. of Medicine; Chair. Medical Council of Hong Kong 1988–96; Chair. Hong Kong Educ. Comm. 1993–98; Overseas Adviser, Royal Coll. of Physicians of Edin. 1987–93; currently Hon. Consultant in Medicine, Queen Mary Hosp., Hong Kong Sanatorium & Hosp.; mem. Council Royal Australasian Coll. of Physicians 1993–96; JP in Hong Kong 1971; Hon. Fellow, Newnham Coll., Cambridge 1988, Hong Kong Acad. of Nursing Ltd; Gold Bauhinia Star (Hong Kong), Grand Bauhinia Medal (Hong Kong); Hon. DSc (Hong Kong Univ.) (Open Learning Inst. of Hong Kong) 1995, (City Univ. of Hong Kong) 2006. *Publications include:* more than 100 articles in int. medical journals, mostly on diabetes, CHO metabolism and endocrinology. *Address:* Room 413, Professorial Block, Queen Mary Hospital, 102 Pokfulam Road, Hong Kong Special Administrative Region, People's Republic of China (office). *Telephone:* (1) 22553838 (office). *Fax:* (1) 28175496 (office). *E-mail:* rttyoung@hkucc.hku.hk (office). *Website:* www.hku.hk (office).

YOUNG, Simone Margaret, AM; Australian conductor; b. 2 March 1961; m. Greg Condon; two d.; ed Sydney Conservatorium of Music; Conductor, Vienna Staatsoper, Bastille (Paris), Berlin Staatsoper, Cologne Opera, Royal Opera House (London), Metropolitan Opera (New York), Houston Grand Opera, Los Angeles Opera, New York Philharmonic Orchestra, Oslo Philharmonic Orchestra, Munich Philharmonic Orchestra, Maggio Musicale (Florence), ORF Radio Orchestra Vienna, NDR Hanover, NHK Symphony Orchestra (Japan), Hamburg Philharmonic Orchestra, Sydney, Melbourne and West Australian Symphony Orchestras; Chief Conductor, Bergen Philharmonic Orchestra 1999–2002; Music Dir Opera Australia 2001–05; Music Dir and Gen. Man. Hamburg State Opera 2005–15, Prin. Musical Dir Hamburg Philharmonic State Orchestra 2005–15; Prof. of Music and Theatre, Hamburg Univ. 2006–; First Guest Conductor, Gulbenkian Orchestra, Lisbon 2007–12; Chevalier, Ordre des Arts et des Lettres; Hon. DMus (Monash Univ.) 1998, (Univ. of New South Wales) 2001; Dr hc (Sydney), (Mebourne); Young Australian of the Year 1987, Goethe Medal, Goethe Inst. 2005, Conductor of the Year, Opernwelt magazine 2006, Schleswig-Holstein Brahms Prize 2009. *Recordings include:* numerous recordings, including Mathis der Mahler and Der Ring des Nibelungen (Hamburger Staats-opera), recordings with Hamburg Philharmonic Orchestra, including all Bruckner symphonies, all Johannes Brahms' Symphonies and Mahler's Second and Sixth Symphonies. *Repertoire includes:* opera: Rigoletto, Tosca, La Traviata, Oberto, Der fliegende Holländer, Der Rosenkavalier, Macbeth, Elektra, La Bohème, Cavalleria Rusticana, Pagliacci, Tales of Hoffmann, Il Trovatore, Lohengrin, Eugène Onegin, Salomé, Fidelio, Peter Grimes, Wozzeck, La Juive, Der Ring des Nibelungen, Die Meistersinger von Nürnberg, Die Fledermaus, Die Frau ohne Schatten, Faust, Ariadne auf Naxos, Simon Boccanegra, Tannhäuser, Falstaff, Don Carlos, Andrea Chenier, Tristan und Isolde, The Marriage of Figaro, Don Giovanni, Lulu, Otello; extensive symphonic repertoire, including works of Mahler, Strauss, Wagner, Brahms, Beethoven, Bruckner and Bartók. *Address:* c/o Judith Seidl, Michael Lewin International Artists' Management, Euroartists Künstlermanagement GmbH, Gluckgasse 1/1, 1010, Vienna, Austria (office). *E-mail:* judith.seidl@lewin-management.com (office). *Website:* www.simoneyoung.com.

YOUNG, Stuart Richard; Trinidad and Tobago lawyer and politician; *Minister of National Security;* b. 9 Feb. 1975; ed Univ. of Nottingham; admitted to the bar, Trinidad and Tobago, London (Gray's Inn), Commonwealth of Dominica and Antigua and Barbuda; practising attorney since 1998; has appeared as Counsel in numerous Comms of Enquiry, including Piarco Comm. of Enquiry, Comm. of Enquiry into the Construction Sector, Comm. of Enquiry into the Hindu Credit Union and CLF; Temporary Opposition Senator March–July 2014, Feb.–June 2015; mem. Parl. (PNM) for Port-of-Spain North/St Ann's West 2015–; Minister in the Ministry of Attorney-Gen. and Legal Affairs 2015–18, Minister of Communications and Minister in the Office of the Prime Minister June–Aug. 2018, Minister of Nat. Security 2018–; Founding mem. Synergy TV and WI Sports TV stations; mem. People's Nat. Movt (PNM). *Leisure interest:* karate. *Address:* Ministry of National Security, Temple Court, 31–33 Abercromby St, Port of Spain, Trinidad and Tobago (office). *Telephone:* 623-2441 (office). *Fax:* 627-8044 (office). *E-mail:* info@mns.gov.tt (office). *Website:* www.nationalsecurity.gov.tt (office).

YOUNG, Todd Christopher, BS, MBA, JD; American lawyer and politician; *Senator from Indiana;* b. 24 Aug. 1972, Lancaster, Pa; s. of Bruce Young and Nancy Young; m. Jenny Tucker 2005; four c.; ed US Naval Acad., Univ. of Chicago, Univ. of London Inst. of US Studies, UK; served in US Marine Corps 1995–2000, including as intelligence officer specializing in counter-narcotics and anti-terrorism, becoming Marine Corps Recruitment Officer, Chicago 1998, discharged from active duty 2000 (rank of Capt.); worked Heritage Foundation (think-tank), Washington, DC 2001; Legis. Asst to US Senator from Indiana Richard Lugar 2001–13; Man. Consultant, Crowe Chizek and Co., 2004; pvt. legal practice with Tucker and Tucker, PC 2006–; Deputy Prosecutor, Orange County 2007–10; mem. US House of Reps from Indiana 9th Dist 2011–17; Senator from Indiana 2017–; Pres. Orange County Bar Asscn 2008; Chair. Nat. Republican Senatorial Cttee 2018–; Republican. *Address:* 185 Dirksen Senate Office Building, Washington, DC 20510, USA (office). *Telephone:* (202) 224-5623 (office). *E-mail:* contact@toddyoung.org. *Website:* www.young.senate.gov (office); toddyoung.org.

YOUNG, William L., BSc, MBA; Canadian business executive; *Chairman, Magna International Inc.;* ed Queen's Univ., Kingston, Ont., Harvard Univ.; Partner in European practice of Bain & Co 1981–88; Founding Partner, Westbourne Management Group 1988–; Co-founder and Man. Partner, Monitor Clipper Partners (pvt. equity firm) 1998–; mem. Bd of Dirs Magna International Inc. 2011–, Chair. 2012–; Chair. Bd of Trustees, Queen's Univ., Kingston 2006–12, Chair. Emer. 2012–; mem. Bd of Dirs, Intact Financial Corpn, Monitor Co, Barnyard Industries Inc. and several other pvt. cos. *Address:* Magna International Inc., 337 Magna Drive, Aurora, ON L4G 7K1, Canada (office). *Telephone:* (905) 726-2462 (office). *E-mail:* info@magnaint.com (office). *Website:* www.magna.com (office).

YOUNG OF COOKHAM, Baron (Life Peer), cr. 2015, of Cookham in the Royal County of Berkshire; **Rt Hon. George Samuel Knatchbull Young,** 6th Bt, PC, CH, MA, MPhil; British politician; b. 16 July 1941, Oxford, England; s. of Sir George Peregrine 'Gerry' Young, 5th Bt and Elisabeth Knatchbull-Hugessen; m. Aurelia Nemon-Stuart 1964; two s. two d.; ed Eton Coll., Christ Church, Oxford, Univ. of Surrey; Economist, Nat. Econ. Devt Office 1966–67; Kobler Research Fellow, Univ. of Surrey 1967–69; Econ. Adviser, Post Office Corpn 1969–74; Councillor, London Borough of Lambeth 1968–71; mem. Greater London Council for London Borough of Ealing 1970–73; MP for Acton 1974–83, for Ealing Acton 1983–97, for NW Hampshire 1997–2015, mem. House of Commons Comm. 2009–12, Speaker's Cttee for the Ind. Parl. Standards Authority 2009–12, contested Speaker election 2009, mem. Public Accounts Comm. 2010–12, Parl. and Political Service Honours Cttee 2012–15; Opposition Whip 1976–79; Parl. Under-Sec. of State, Dept of Health and Social Security 1979–81, Dept of Environment 1981–86; Dir Lovell Partnerships 1987–90; Comptroller of HM Household 1990; Minister of State, Dept of Environment 1990–94; Financial Sec. to HM Treasury 1994–95; Sec. of State for Transport 1995–97; Opposition Front Bench Spokesman for Defence 1997–98; Shadow Leader of the House of Commons 1998–2000, 2009–10; Leader of the House of Commons and Lord Privy Seal 2010–12; Chief Whip in the House of Commons and Parl. Sec. to the Treasury 2012–14; mem. (Conservative), House of Lords 2015–; Patron, Tory Reform Group; Conservative. *Publications:* Accommodation Services in the UK 1970–80, Tourism, Blessing or Blight? 1973. *Leisure interests:* bicycling, Queens Park Rangers Footvall Club. *Address:* House of Lords, Westminster, London, SW1A 0PW, England (office). *Telephone:* (20) 7219-5353 (office). *E-mail:* sirgeorge@sirgeorgeyoung.org.uk. *Website:* sirgeorgeyoung.org.uk.

YOUNG OF GRAFFHAM, Baron (Life Peer), cr. 1984, of Graffham in the County of West Sussex; **David Ivor Young,** CH, PC, LLB, DL; British politician and business executive; *Chairman, Young Associates Limited;* b. 27 Feb. 1932, London, England; s. of Joseph Young and Rebecca Young; m. Lita Marianne Shaw 1956; two d.; ed Christ's Coll., Finchley and Univ. Coll. London; admitted solicitor 1955; solicitor, Malcolm Slowe, London 1955–56; Exec., Great Universal Stores 1956–61; Chair. Eldonwall Ltd 1961–74, Mfrs Hanover Property Services Ltd 1974–80; Chair. Greenwood Homes Ltd 1976–82; Dir Centre for Policy Studies 1979–82; Special Adviser, Dept of Industry 1979–82, of Educ. and Science 1981–82; Chair. Manpower Services Comm. 1982–84; mem. Chair. NEDC 1982–89; mem. (Conservative), House of Lords 1984–; Minister without Portfolio 1984–85, Sec. of State for Employment 1985–87, for Trade and Industry and Pres. Bd of Trade 1987–89; Deputy Chair. Conservative Party 1989–90; Head of Research Project on Tax Simplification, Centre for Policy Studies 2001; Chair. Camcon Ltd, Camcon Medical Ltd, Camcon Industrial Ltd, Camcon Auto Ltd, Camcon Oil Russia Ltd, Camcon Oil China Ltd, Young Associates Ltd, Newhaven Management Services Ltd, Deep Tek Offshore Ltd, Jewish Museum; Pres. Chai Cancer Care; Enterprise Adviser to the Prime Minister 2010– (resgnd, subsequently reappointed); Hon. FRPS 1981; Hon. Fellow, Univ. Coll., London 1988. *Publication:* The Enterprise Years: A Businessman in the Cabinet 1990, Common Sense Common Safety 2010, Make Business Your Business 2012, Growing Your Business 2013. *Leisure interests:* music, book collecting, photography. *Address:* Young Associates Ltd, Harcourt House, 19 Cavendish Square, London, W1G 0PL (office); House of Lords, Westminster, London, SW1A 0PW, England. *Telephone:* (20) 7447-8800 (office); (20) 7219-5353 (House of Lords). *Fax:* (20) 7447-8849 (office). *E-mail:* young@youngassoc.com (office).

YOUNG OF OLD SCONE, Baroness (Life Peer), cr. 1997, of Old Scone in the County of Perthshire; **Barbara Scott Young,** MA; British environmentalist and administrator; b. 8 April 1948, Scone; d. of George Young and Mary Young (née Scott); ed Perth Acad., Univ. of Edinburgh, Univ. of Strathclyde; Sector Admin. Greater Glasgow Health Bd 1973–78; Dir of Planning and Devt, St Thomas's Health Dist 1978–79; Dist Gen. Admin. NW Dist Kensington, Chelsea and Westminster Area Health Authority 1979–82; Dist Admin. Haringey Health Authority 1982–85; Dist Gen. Man. Paddington and N Kensington Health Authority 1985–88, Parkside Health Authority 1988–91; Chief Exec. Royal Soc. for the Protection of Birds 1991–98, Vice-Pres. 2000–; Chair. English Nature 1998–2000; Vice-Chair. of BBC 1998–2000; Chief Exec. Environment Agency 2000–08; Chair. Care Quality Comm. 2008–09; Pres. Inst. of Health Services Man. 1987–88, British Trust for Ornithology 2005–13; CEO Diabetes UK 2010–; mem. BBC Gen. Advisory Council 1985–88, UK Round Table on Sustainable Devt 1995, World Council Birdlife International 1994–98 (Vice-Pres.) 1999–; Trustee, Inst. of Public Policy Research 1999–; Patron Inst. of Ecology and Environmental Man. 1993–; Hon. Fellow, Sydney Sussex Coll., Cambridge 2003, Geologists Asscn, Linnean Soc., Inst. of Agricultural Eng; Hon. mem. Royal Inst. of Chartered Surveyors, Chartered Inst. of Water and Environmental Man.; CIWEM Chartered Environmentalist 2004; Eminent Fellow, Inst. of Agricultural Eng 2004; Hon. DUniv (Stirling) 1995, (Herts.) 1997, (Open Univ., Aberdeen, St Andrews, York) 2000; Hon. DSc (Cranfield) 1998; Green Ribbon Award 2000. *Publications:* What Women Want (contrib.) 1990, Medical Negligence (contrib.) 1990. *Leisure interests:*

cinema, gardening. *Address:* House of Lords, London, SW1A 0PW, England (office). *Telephone:* (20) 7219-5353 (office). *E-mail:* youngb@parliament.uk (office).

YOUSAFZAI, Malala; Pakistani education activist; b. 12 July 1997, Mingora, Swat Dist, North-West Frontier (now Khyber Pakhtunkhwa) Prov.; d. of Ziauddin Yousafzai and Tor Pekai Yousafzai; ed Edgbaston High School, Birmingham, UK, Lady Margaret Hall, Univ. of Oxford; wrote a blog under pen name Gul Makai for BBC Urdu detailing her life under Taliban occupation 2009; appeared on Pakistani talk show Capital Talk 2009; shot by a gunman as she was returning from school on a bus in the Swat Valley 9 Oct. 2012; sent to Queen Elizabeth Hosp., Birmingham, UK for intensive rehabilitation; lives in Birmingham, UK; gave speech to UN 2013; advocate for girls' education; Co-founder (with father) Malala Fund (charity); apptd UN Messenger of Peace 2017; Hon. Canadian citizenship 2013; Hon. Pres. Students' Union, Univ. of Sheffield 2016; Hon. MA (Edinburgh) 2013; Dr hc (Univ. of King's Coll., Canada) 2014, (Univ. of Ottawa) 2017; Nat. Youth Peace Prize 2011, Sitara-e-Shujaat (Pakistan) 2012, Mother Teresa Memorial Award for Social Justice 2012, Rome Prize for Peace and Humanitarian Action 2012, Simone de Beauvoir Prize 2013, Memminger Freiheitspreis 1525, Doughty Street Advocacy Award of Index on Censorship 2013, Fred and Anne Jarvis Award, UK Nat. Union of Teachers 2013, Global Trailblazer, Vital Voices Global Leadership Awards 2013, Premi Internacional Catalunya Award of Catalonia 2013, Annual Award for Devt, OPEC Fund for Int. Devt 2013, Int. Campaigner of the Year, Observer Ethical Awards 2013, Tipperary Int. Peace Award, Tipperary Peace Convention (Ireland) 2013, Int. Children's Peace Prize, KidsRights 2013, Amb. of Conscience Award, Amnesty International 2013, Clinton Global Citizen Award, Clinton Foundation 2013, Peter Gomes Humanitarian Award, Harvard Foundation of Harvard Univ. 2013, Anna Politkovskaya Award – Reach All Women In War 2013, Sakharov Prize for Freedom of Thought, European Parl. 2013, Pride of Britain Award 2013, Glamour magazine Woman of the Year 2013, GG2 Hammer Award, GG2 Leadership Awards 2013, Int. Prize for Equality and Non-Discrimination 2013, UN Human Rights Prize 2013, Liberty Medal, Nat. Constitution Center, Philadelphia 2014, Skoll Global Treasure Award 2014, Nat. Youth Peace Prize 2014, Nobel Peace Prize (shared with Kailash Satyarthi) 2014, World's Children's Prize 2014, Ellis Island Int. Medal of Honor 2017. *Publication:* I Am Malala: The Girl Who Stood Up for Education and Was Shot by the Taliban (with Christina Lamb) 2013, Malala's Magic Pencil (Jane Addams Children's Book Award 2018) 2017, We Are Displaced: My Journey and Stories From Refugee Girls Around the World 2019. *Website:* www.malala.org.

YOUSFI, Youcef, PhD; Algerian politician and diplomatist; *Minister of Industry and Mining;* b. 2 Oct. 1941, Batna; m. Rachida Bouaraara; three c.; ed Ecole Nationale Supérieure des Industries Chimiques, France, Université de Nancy, France; fmr Sr Lecturer, then Prof. of Chemical Eng Ecole Nationale Polytechnic d'Alger; fmr Prof. of Chemical Eng and Dir Chem. Inst., Houari Boumediene Univ. of Science and Tech., concurrently served as adviser on petroleum affairs to Ministry of Industry and Energy; fmr Vice-Pres. of Marketing, Sonatrach (nat. petroleum co.), CEO 1985; Chair. Bd, Mines, Petroleum and Hydraulics Participating Fund 1988; Chief of Staff to the Pres. Liamine Zéroual 1996–97; mem. Nat. Peoples's Ass. 1997; Minister of Energy and Mines 1997–99; Chair. OPEC 1998–99; Minister of Foreign Affairs 1999–2000, Minister-Del. to Chief of Govt 2000–01; Amb. to Canada 2001–06; Amb. and Perm. Rep. to UN, New York 2006–08; Amb. to Tunisia 2008–10; Minister of Energy 2010–15; Acting Prime Minister March–April 2014; Minister-Advisor to Pres. of Repub. (in-charge of energy issues) 2015–17; Minister of Industry and Mining 2017–. *Address:* Ministry of Industry and Mining, Immeuble de la Colisée, 2 rue Ahmed Bey, el-Biar, Algiers, Algeria (office). *Telephone:* (21) 23-91-43 (office). *Fax:* (21) 23-94-88 (office). *Website:* www.mipi.dz (office).

YOUSSOUF, Mahamoud Ali, MA, MiM; Djibouti politician; *Minister of Foreign Affairs and International Cooperation;* b. 2 Sept. 1965; m.; five c.; ed Lumière Univ. Lyon 2, France, Univ. of Liverpool, England, Univ. of Laval, Canada; joined Ministry of Foreign Affairs 1992, Head of Division Int. Org. 1993, Amb. to Egypt 1997–2001; Minister-Del. of Int. Cooperation 2001; Minister of Foreign Affairs and Int. Cooperation 2005–. *Address:* Ministry of Foreign Affairs, International Cooperation and Parliamentary Relations, Bd Cheick Osman, BP 1863, Djibouti (office). *Telephone:* 352471 (office). *Fax:* 353049 (office). *E-mail:* moussagora@yahoo.com (office). *Website:* www.djibdiplomatie.dj (office).

YOUSUF, Mohammad; Pakistani fmr professional cricketer; b. (Yousuf Youhana), 27 Aug. 1974, Lahore, Punjab; m. Tania (now Fatima) Yousuf; middle order right-handed batsman; right-arm off-break bowler; plays for Bahawalpur 1996–97, Water and Power Devt Authority 1997–98, Pakistan 1998–2010, Pakistan Int. Airlines 1999–2002, Lahore Blues 2000–01, ZTBL 2002–03, Lahore 2003–04, Lahore Badshahs 2004–07, Lancs. 2008, Islamabad Leopards 2010, Lahore Lions (Capt.) 2010, Warwicks. 2011, Asia XI; First-class debut 1996/97; Test debut: S Africa v Pakistan, Durban 26 Feb.–2 March 1998; One-Day Int. (ODI) debut: Zimbabwe v Pakistan, Harare 28 March 1998; T20I debut: England v Pakistan, Bristol 28 Aug. 2006; has played in 90 Tests and scored 7,530 runs (24 centuries, 33 half-centuries), highest score 223, average 52.29; ODIs: 288 matches, 9,720 runs (15 centuries, 64 half-centuries), average 41.71, strike rate 75.10), highest score 141 not out; Capt. of Test team for tour of NZ 2009; banned indefinitely from Test cricket by Pakistan Cricket Bd, along with Younus Khan, for "infighting" during tour of Australia March 2010, announced retirement from int. cricket 27 March 2010, ban later lifted, called back to squad for rest of Test series against England Aug. 2010; CNN-IBN Cricketer of the Year 2006, Wisden Cricketer of the Year 2007, ICC (Int. Cricket Council) Test Cricketer of the Year 2007, named in Test Team of the Year 2007, Sitara-i-Imtiaz 2011, Pride of Performance Award 2012. *Achievements include:* broke West Indian batsman Sir Vivian Richards' world record for the most Test runs (1,788) in a single calendar year 2006; third Pakistani batsmen to surpass 6,000 runs in Test cricket.

YOVCHEV, Tsvetlin, MA (Econ), PhD; Bulgarian politician and academic; *Scientific Secretary, Institute for Scientific Research and Doctoral Studies, State University of Library Studies and Information Technology;* b. 7 May 1964, Pleven; m. Milena Yovcheva; one c.; ed Nikola Vaptsarov Naval Acad., Varna, Erasmus Univ., Rotterdam, the Netherlands and St Clement of Ohrid Univ., Sofia (Jt Master Programme); Marine Engineer, Navigation Maritime Bulgare 1987–92; Chief Power Engineer, Gara Iztok Car Repair Factory 1992–93; consecutively

occupied all managerial positions in Nat. Security Service (NSS) 1993–2007, successively Head of Dept, Head of the Field and Deputy Dir NSS; Dir Gen. Counterintelligence Gen. Directorate, SANS 2008–09; Chair. State Agency for Nat. Security 2009–11 (resgnd); Lecturer, Univ. of Library Studies and Information Tech. 2011–13, Scientific Sec., Inst. for Scientific Research and Doctoral Studies March–May 2013, 2014–; Nat. Security Advisor to the Prime MInister 2011–12; Chief of the Cabinet to the Pres. of 2012–13; Deputy Prime Minister and Minister of the Interior 2013–14. *Address:* 1505 Sofia, 105 Oborishte Street, Bulgaria. *Telephone:* 88-9955930 (mobile). *E-mail:* 99tyovchev@gmail.com.

YSTAD, Vigdis, DPhil; Norwegian academic; *Professor Emeritus of Scandinavian Literature, University of Oslo;* b. 13 Jan. 1942, Verdal; d. of Ottar Ystad and Guri Todal; m. 1st Asbjørn Liland 1962; m. 2nd Daniel Haakonsen 1971; one s. one d.; ed Univs of Trondheim and Oslo; Lecturer, Univ. of Oslo 1974, apptd Prof. of Scandinavian Literature 1979, now Prof. Emer., mem. Univ. Bd 1990–92; Chair. Council for Research in the Humanities 1985; Chair. Bd Centre for Advanced Study, Norwegian Acad. of Science and Letters 1992–93; Vice-Chair. Nat. Acad. of Dramatic Art 1993–96; mem. Norwegian Research Council 1979–85, Norwegian Govt Research Cttee 1982–84; mem. Norwegian Acad. of Science and Letters, Norwegian Acad. for Language and Literature, Royal Swedish Acad. of Letters, History and Antiquities 2004, Kungliga Vetenskaps-Societeten 2004; mem. Bd Nat. Acad. of Art 2000–02, Oslo Acad. of Art 2000–02, Nansenskolen, Lillehammer 2001–; Gen. Ed. Henrik Ibsens skrifter 1998–2010; Kt of St Olav (First Class) 2012. *Publications include:* Kristofer Uppdals Lyrikk 1978, Henrik Ibsens Dikt 1991, Sigrid Undsel: Et kvinneliv-'livets endeløse gåde' 1993, Ibsens dikt og drama 1996, Contemporary Approaches to Ibsen, Ibsen studies (ed.), Henrik Ibsens skrifter 1–17 2005–10. *Address:* Thomas Heftyes gt. 56B, 0267 Oslo, Norway (home). *Telephone:* 22-55-94-66 (home); 90-14-37-43. *E-mail:* a.v.ystad@ibsen.uio.no (office).

YU, Darvish; Japanese professional baseball player; b. 16 Aug. 1986, Habikino, Osaka; s. of Farzad Darvishsefad and Ikuyo Darvishsefad; m. Saeko Darvish 2007; one s.; professional debut 2005; Japanese nat. team debut at Asian Baseball Championship, Taiwan 2007, also appeared for nat. team at 2008 Beijing Olympics and World Baseball Classic, Los Angeles 2009; pitcher for Hokkaido Nippon Ham Fighters 2005–11, Texas Rangers (Major League Baseball—MLB) 2012–; f. Yu Darvish Water Fund (charity) 2007; awards include Asia Series Most Valuable Player 2006, Eiji Sawamura Award 2007, MLB All-Star 2012–14. *Address:* Texas Rangers, Globe Life Park, 1000 Ballpark Way, Arlington, TX 76011, USA. *Website:* texas.rangers.mlb.com; darvish-yu.jp.

YU, Han, BA; Chinese business executive; *President and Chief Operating Officer, Maruhan Corporation;* ed Hosei Univ.; joined Chisan Co. Ltd 1988–90; joined Maruhan Co. Ltd 1990, Dir and Shizuoka Sales Div. Chief 1992–2001, Dir and Business Exec. Chief 2001–05, Man. Dir and Sales Div. Chief 2005–06, Vice-Pres. Maruhan Corpn 2006–08, Pres. and COO 2008–; mem. Bd of Dirs Sathapana Bank PLC. *Address:* Maruhan Corporation, 231 Seiryu-cho, Demachi, Imadegawa, Kamigyo-ku, Agaru, Kyoto 602-0822, Japan (office). *Telephone:* (75) 252-0011 (office). *Fax:* (75) 252-0018 (office). *E-mail:* info@maruhan.co.jp (office). *Website:* www.maruhan.co.jp (office).

YU, Hongyang, BA; Chinese diplomatist; b. Oct. 1957; m.; mem. staff, Embassy in Tehran 1981–86, mem. staff, Dept of West Asia and North Africa Affairs, Ministry of Foreign Affairs (MFA) 1986–90, Third, then Second Sec., Embassy in Tehran 1990–94, First Sec. and Dir, Dept of West Asia and North Africa Affairs, MFA 1994–98, Counsellor, Embassy in Tehran 1998–2001, Counsellor, Dept of West Asia and North Africa Affairs, MFA 2001–02, Visiting Scholar, Diplomatic Research Inst., Georgetown Univ., USA 2002–03, Consul-Gen. in Istanbul 2003–06, Counsellor, Dept of West Asia and North Africa Affairs, MFA 2006–07, Deputy Dir-Gen., Dept of West Asia and North Africa Affairs 2007–08, Amb. to Jordan 2008–10, to Iran 2010–14, to Turkey 2014–19.

YU, Hua, MA; Chinese writer; b. 3 April 1960, Gaotang, Shandong Prov.; m. Chen Hong; one s.; worked as a dentist for five years; writer 1983–; Ordre des Arts et des Lettres 2004; James Joyce Foundation Award 2002, Special Book Award of China 2005, Prix Courrier International 2008. *Publications include:* in trans.: Leaving Home at Eighteen 1984, To Live (Grinzane Cavour Award, Italy) 1992, Chronicle of a Blood Merchant 1995, The Past and the Punishments 1996, Shouting in the Drizzle, Events of the World Are Like Smoke, One Kind of Reality, An Incident, Mistake at Riverside, Brothers 2005, China in Ten Words (essays) 2011, Boy in the Twilight: Stories of the Hidden China 2014, Seventh Day 2015.

YU, Junbo; Chinese politician; b. Feb. 1941, Anshan, Liaoning Prov.; joined CCP 1977; mem. Standing Cttee CCP Haicheng Co. Cttee, Liaoning Prov., Deputy Sec. CCP Haicheng Co. Cttee; Vice-Magistrate of Haicheng Co. Liaoning Prov.; Deputy Sec., then Sec. Haicheng Cttee, Anshan Municipal Cttee; Vice-Mayor of Anshan City; Sec. Jinxi Municipal Cttee, Chair. Standing Cttee, Jinxi People's Congress; mem. Standing Cttee CCP Liaoning Prov. Cttee 1990, Dir Organizational Dept 1990; mem. Standing Cttee CCP Beijing Municipal Cttee 1996, Deputy Sec. 1997; Chair. Beijing Municipal People's Congress 2001–07; Del., 15th CCP Nat. Congress 1997–2002; Deputy, 9th NPC 1998–2003.

YU, Lu; Chinese theoretical physicist; *Research Professor, Institute of Physics, Chinese Academy of Sciences;* b. Zhenjiang, Jiangsu Prov.; ed Kharkov State Univ., USSR (now Ukraine); Research Assoc., Inst. of Physics, Chinese Acad. of Sciences 1961–65, Asst Research Prof. 1965–78, Assoc. Research Prof. 1978, Assoc. Research Prof., Inst. of Theoretical Physics 1978–82, Research Prof. 1983–2006, Dir Interdisciplinary Centre of Theoretical Studies 2002–06, Research Prof., Inst. of Physics 2006–; Head of Condensed Matter Physics Section, Int. Centre for Theoretical Physics, Trieste, Italy 1990–2002; Academician, Third World Acad. of Sciences 1990, Chinese Acad. of Sciences 1999; Fellow, American Physics Soc. 2005; Tate Medal for Leadership in Int. Physics 2007. *Publications:* three books and 200 papers in professional journals. *Address:* Institute of Physics, Chinese Academy of Sciences, PO Box 603, Beijing 100190, People's Republic of China (office). *Telephone:* (10) 82640073 (office). *E-mail:* lyu@iphy.ac.cn (office). *Website:* www.iop.cas.cn (office).

YU, Myeong-hee, PhD; South Korean microbiologist and academic; *Principal Research Scientist and Head, 21C Frontier R&D Program, Functional Proteomics*

Center, Korean Institute of Science and Technology; ed Univ. of California, Berkeley, USA; Post-doctoral research at MIT, Boston, USA; returned to South Korea in 1985; Investigator, Nat. Creative Research Initiatives, Korean Ministry of Science and Tech., Prin. Research Scientist, Korean Inst. of Science and Tech. 2000–, Head of 21C Frontier R&D Program, Functional Proteomics Center 2002–; Ed.-in-Chief Microbiological Soc. of Korea 2002; mem. Editorial Bd Molecules and Cells, 1993–, Journal of Biochemistry and Molecular Biology 1999–, On-line Journal; mem. Scientific Program, Korea UNESCO Cttee 1999–; Regional Sec. of Gender, Science and Tech., Asia and Pacific Rim, UNESCO 1999–2001; mem. Asia-Pacific Int. Molecular Biology Network 1998, Korean Acad. of Sciences 2002, Korean Soc. for Biochemistry and Molecular Biology, Korean Soc. of Molecular and Cellular Biology, American Soc. for Biochemistry and Molecular Biology 2002, Nat. Acad. of Science and Tech. 2002–; Distinguished Publication Award, Korean Fed. of Science and Eng Socs 1995, Mockam Award, First Korea Research Inst. of Bioscience and Biotechnology Award 1996, Korean Soc. of Molecular Biology 1996, L'Oréal-UNESCO Women in Science Award 1998, 50th Seoul City Cultural Award 2001, Order of Science and Tech., Ungbi Medal 2004. Publications: numerous articles in scientific journals on conformational transition process of proteins. Address: Korea Institute of Science and Technology, 39-1 Hawolgok-Dong, Seongbuk-gu, Seoul 136-791, Republic of Korea (office). Telephone: (2) 958-5114 (office). E-mail: mhyu@kist.re.kr (office). Website: www.kist.re.kr (office).

YU, Nick Rongjun; Chinese playwright and director; Deputy General Manager, Shanghai Dramatic Arts Centre; b. July 1971, Anhui Prov.; ed Shanghai Theatre Acad.; Dir Shanghai Dramatic Arts Centre, Shanghai Univ. Theatre Festival 2004–, Shanghai Int. Contemporary Theatre Festival; currently Deputy Gen. Man. Shanghai Dramatic Arts Centre; versions of his plays have been performed in Singapore, Japan, Turkey, UK, Canada, South Korea, Germany, Italy, Greek, Israel, Egypt, Denmark, Sweden, Austria, Poland and USA; has also translated several plays and musicals from English into Mandarin. Plays include: The Insane Asylum is Next Door to Heaven, Last Winter 2000, www.com 2001, A Very Serious Matter 2002, The Salty Taste of Cappuccino 2002, Behind the Lie 2003, Perfume 2003, Midnight at Havana Club 2004, Dog's Face 2004, Activated Charcoal 2004, Love in a Fallen City 2005, A Winter Tale of Two Cities 2005, A Man Among Women 2005, Sighing 2006, Cry to Heaven 2007, The Angel in Wheelchair 2007, Drift 2007, The Dream of the Red Chamber 2007, Street Angel 2008, Dust to Dust 2008, Heartquake 2008, 1977 2009, Das Kapital 2009, Boatmen 2010, Massage 2011, A Piano in the Factory 2011, Ballet Jane Eyre 2012; trans. into Mandarin include The Vagina Monologues (by Eve Ensler) 2006, I Love You, You're Perfect, Now Change (by Joe DiPietro and Jimmy Roberts) 2007, The Apocalypse 2012, Glorious Day 2012, Johann Strauss in 1872 2012, The Captain 2013. Television: Together For Life. Address: Shanghai Dramatic Arts Centre, 288 Anfu Lu, Xuhui, Shanghai 200031, People's Republic of China (office). Telephone: (21) 64738667 (office).

YU, Qiuyu; Chinese writer and critic; b. 23 Aug. 1946, Yuyao, Zhenjiang Prov.; ed Shanghai Acad. of Drama; fmrly Prof. and Pres. Shanghai Drama Acad.; Vice-Pres. Shanghai Dramatists Asscn; only Chinese scholar invited to attend UNESCO World Cultural Heritage Forum 2005; host, Qiuyu Moment talk show, Hong Kong Phoenix TV Station 2006–; guest lecturer on Chinese culture and world civilization at many prestigious insts including Harvard Univ., Yale Univ., Univ. of Madrid, US Library of Congress; numerous prizes, including Chinese Nat. Writers Lu Shun Prize, China Publisher Prize, Shanghai Outstanding Literary Work, Taiwan Reader Best Book (two consecutive years), Jin Shi Tong Most Influential Book Award, Taiwan Platinum Author Award, Most Popular Author Award in Malaysia. Publications include: A Bitter Journey Through Culture 1992, Notes From the Hills 1995, Cold River 1999, Draft History of Dramatic Theories, Dramatic Aesthetic-Psychology, A Narration of the History of Dramatic Culture in China, A Sigh of a Thousand Years 2000, Travel No End 2001, A Life Borrowed 2004.

YU, Shumin; Chinese business executive; President, Hisense Group; Pres. Hisense Group Co. Ltd 2001– (f. as Qingdao No. 2 Radio Factory in 1969, now has two listed cos, Hisense Electric Co. Ltd and Hisense Kelon Electrical Holdings Co. Ltd), Chair. Hisense Electric Appliance Co. Ltd; mem. CCP; Deputy to ninth and tenth People's Congress of Shandong Prov. Address: Hisense Group Co. Ltd, Hisense Tower, 17 Donghaixi Road, Qingdao 266071, Shandong Province, People's Republic of China (office). Telephone: (532) 83878888 (office). Fax: (532) 83872882 (office). E-mail: service@hisense.com (office); master@hisense.com (office). Website: www.hisense.com (office); www.hisense-transtech.com.cn (office).

YU, Shyi-kun, BA; Taiwanese politician; b. 25 April 1948, Yilan Co.; m. Yang Pao-yu 1978; two s.; ed Chih-Leei Coll. of Business, Tung-hai Univ. Dept of Political Science; elected mem. Seventh Taiwan Prov. Ass. 1981, Eighth 1985; co-f. Democratic Progressive Party (DPP) 1986, elected to First Cen. Standing Cttee 1986, Second 1987, Third 1988, Fourth 1989, Sec.-Gen. DPP HQ 1999–2000, Chair. 2006–07 (resgnd); Yilan Co. Magistrate 1990–97; Exec. Campaign Man. and Chief Spokesperson for DPP cand. Chen Shui-bian's Presidential Campaign 2000; Vice-Premier of Taiwan 2000, also Sec.-Gen., Office of the Pres. 2001–05; Premier of Taiwan 2002–05; Founder and Chair. Lan-yang Cultural and Educ. Foundation 1990–97, Chair. Taipei Rapid Transit Corpn 1998; Chair. Taiwan-India Co-operation Council 2006; indicted for embezzlement 2007; unsuccessful ccand. for Mayor of New Taipei City 2014. Publications: The Resignation of Tangwai Assemblymen 1985, The Road to Democracy: The Love for Native Land 1989.

YU, Xubo, EMBA; Chinese business executive; President, China National Cereals, Oils and Foodstuffs Corporation (COFCO); ed Univ. of Int. Business and Econs, China Europe Int. Business School; worked in USA for many years; joined China Nat. Cereals, Oils and Foodstuffs Corpn (COFCO, also known as China Agri-Industries Holdings Ltd) 1988, mem. Bd of Dirs and Pres. COFCO 2008–. Address: China National Cereals, Oils and Foodstuffs Corporation, 19F, COFCO Fortune Plaza No. 8, Chao Yang Men South Street, Chao Yang District, Beijing 100020, People's Republic of China (office). Telephone: (10) 85006637 (office). Fax: (10) 85006637 (office). E-mail: cofco-news@cofco.com (office). Website: www.cofco.com (office).

YU, Yong; Chinese steel industry executive; Chairman and General Manager, HeSteel Group; fmr Chair., Gen. Man., Vice-Chair. and Deputy Party Sec., Tangshan Iron & Steel Co. Ltd; Gen. Man., Vice-Chair. and Deputy Party Sec.,

Hebei Iron and Steel Group Co. Ltd (HeSteel Group Co. Ltd (HBIS), formed from merger of Tangsteel Co. Ltd and Hansteel Co. Ltd 2008) –2013, Chair., Gen. Man. and Deputy Party Sec. 2013–. Address: HeSteel Group Co. Ltd, 385 Sports South Avenue, Shijiazhuang 050023, Hebei Province, People's Republic of China (office). Telephone: (311) 66778886 (office). E-mail: info@hbisco.com (office). Website: www.hbisco.com (office).

YU, Zhen; Chinese politician; b. 1936, Haiyang, Shandong Prov.; ed Jilin Technological Univ.; joined CCP 1956; Dir Machinery Industry Bureau, Ministry of Light Industry mid-1980s, Vice-Minister of Light Industry 1985–93; Pres. China Nat. Light Industrial Machinery Corpn 1983–85, China Nat. Council of Light Industry 1993–98; Vice-Minister, State Econ. and Trade Comm. 1998–2003; Hon. Pres. China Machinery Industry Fed.; Del., 13th CCP Nat. Congress 1987–92, 14th CCP Nat. Congress 1992–97; Alt. mem. 15th CCP Cen. Cttee 1997–2002; mem. 10th CPPCC Nat. Cttee 2003.

YU, Zhengsheng; Chinese politician; Chairman, National Committee, Chinese People's Political Consultative Conference (CPPCC); b. April 1945, Shaoxin City, Zhejiang Prov.; ed Harbin Mil. Eng Inst.; joined CCP 1964; technician, No. 6 Radio Factory, Zhangjiakou City, Hebei Prov. 1967; Deputy Dir Electronics Application Research Inst., Ministry of Electronics Industry 1967, Deputy Dir-Gen. Planning and Construction Dept 1967; Vice-Chair. Exec. Council of Welfare Fund for the Handicapped 1984; Deputy Sec. CCP Yantai City Cttee and Vice-Mayor of Yantai City 1985, Mayor 1987; Sec. CCP Qingdao City Cttee and Mayor of Qingdao City 1993; Vice-Minister of Construction 1997–98, Minister 1998–2001; Sec. CCP Hubei Prov. Cttee 2001–02, Chair. Standing Cttee Hubei Provincial People's Congress 2002–07; Sec. CCP Shanghai Municipal Cttee 2007–12; Alt. mem. 14th CCP Cen. Cttee 1992; mem. 15th CCP Cen. Cttee 1997–2002, 16th CCP Cen. Cttee 2002–07, 17th CCP Cen. Cttee 2007–12, 17th CCP Politburo 2007–12; mem. 18th CCP Cen. Cttee 2012–17, 18th CCP Politburo 2012–17, 18th CCP Politburo Standing Cttee 2012–17; Chair. Nat. Cttee Chinese People's Political Consultative Conf. (CPPCC) 2013–; Chair. China Council for the Promotion of Peaceful Nat. Reunification 2015–. Address: Chinese Communist Party, Quanguo Renmin Diabiao Dahui, Zhongguo Gongchan Dang, 1 Zhongnanhai, Beijing, People's Republic of China. Website: cpc.people.com.cn (office).

YUAN, Changqing, MBA; Chinese economist and banking executive; Chairman of the Board of Supervisors, Agricultural Bank of China; b. Sept. 1961; ed Univ. of Hong Kong; Sec. Party Discipline Cttee, China Everbright (Group) Corpn 2008–12, Exec. Dir, Vice-Pres. and Sec. Party Discipline Cttee 2012–14, Chair. Everbright Securities Co. Ltd 2011–14, Vice-Gen. Man. and Sec. Party Discipline Cttee, China Everbright (Group) Corpn 2014–; Pres. Xinjiang Br. and Henan Br., Industrial and Commercial Bank of China (ICBC) and Gen. Man., Human Resources Dept, ICBC –2015; Chair. Bd of Supervisors, Agricultural Bank of China 2015–. Address: Agricultural Bank of China, 69 Jianguomen Nei Avenue, Dongcheng District, Beijing 100005, People's Republic of China (office). Telephone: (10) 85109619 (office). Fax: (10) 85108557 (office). E-mail: webmaster@intl.abocn.com (office); ir@abchina.com (office). Website: www.abchina.com (office).

YUAN, Guiren; Chinese academic and politician; b. Nov. 1950, Guzhen, Anhui Prov.; ed Beijing Normal Univ.; fmrly Prof. of Philosophy, Vice-Pres., Sec. CCP Cttee, Beijing Normal Univ.; Asst Mayor of Beijing and Dir Beijing Educational Comm. 1998–99; Pres. Beijing Normal Univ. 1999–2001; Vice-Minister of Educ. 2002–09, Minister of Educ. 2009–16; mem. CCP Central Comm. for Inspection 2007–12; mem. 17th CCP Cen. Cttee 2007–12, 18th CCP Cen. Cttee 2012–. Publications: Zhexue (Philosophy), Ren de Zhexue (The Philosophy of Man), Guanli Zhexue (The Philosophy of Management), Deng Xiaoping Lilun Gailun (Introduction to Deng Xiaoping's Theory).

YUAN, Li, PhD; Chinese insurance industry executive; b. 1962; ed China Insurance Man. Cadre Coll., Sun Yat-sen Univ., Peking Univ.; engaged in insurance sector from 1984; Dept Man., Peoples Insurance Co. of China, Hunan Changde Branch 1993–98; worked in China Insurance Regulatory Comm. 1998–2011, Chair. Asst and Spokesman 2006; Vice-Chair. China Life Insurance Co. Ltd –2011, Chair. 2011–12 (resgnd), Pres. China Life Insurance (Group) Co. 2011–12 (resgnd), Regional General Man., South China and Man., Guangdong Branch, New China Life Insurance Co. Ltd 2013–, Asst to Pres. 2013–. Address: New China Life Insurance Co. Ltd, Xinhua Insurance Building. A Jianguomenwai Avenue, Chaoyang District, Beijing 100022, People's Republic of China (office). E-mail: e@newchinalife.com (office). Website: www.newchinalife.com (office).

YUAN, Longping; Chinese agronomist; b. 7 Sept. 1930, De'an, Jiangxi Prov.; s. of Yuan Xin-Lie and Hua Jing; m. Deng Ze 1964; three s.; ed Southwest Agriculture Inst.; teacher, Hunan Prov. 1964–; Researcher, Hunan Acad. of Agricultural Sciences 1971; Technical Adviser, International Rice Institute 1980–81; Deputy, 5th NPC 1978–83; Sr Rice Breeder, Agric. Acad. of Hunan Prov. 1981; mem. Standing Cttee 6th CPPCC 1982–88; Deputy Leader, Nat. Hybrid Rice Experts Advisory Group 1982; Dir Hybrid Rice Research Centre under the Hunan Acad. of Agricultural Sciences 1985; Int. Chief Consultant, FAO 1991; Vice-Chair. CCP 7th Hunan Prov. Cttee; Fellow, Chinese Acad. of Eng; Gold Medal, UN World Property Org. 1985, Laureate of Science Prize, UNESCO 1987, Rank Prize for Food 1988, Magsaysay Prize 2001, Wolf Foundation Prize in Agriculture 2004, World Food Prize 2004, French Agriculture Achievement Medal 2010, Confucius Peace Prize 2012. Leisure interests: violin, swimming. Address: Hunan Academy of Agricultural Sciences, Mapoling, Furong District, Changsha 410125, Hunan Province, People's Republic of China (office). Telephone: (731) 4080755 (office). Fax: (731) 4691877 (office). E-mail: lpyuan@public.cs.hn.cn (office).

YUAN, Maozhen; Chinese energy industry executive; fmrly with State Power Corpn; Chair. China Southern Power Grid Co. Ltd 2003–10; mem. Bd of Dirs China Electricity Council; Hon. Vice-Chair. State Power Information Network.

YUAN, Gen. Shoufang; Chinese army officer; b. March 1939, Jilin City, Jilin Prov.; ed PLA Political Acad.; joined PLA 1958, CCP 1962; Deputy Regimental Political Commissar, later Regimental Political Commissar, PLA 1975–80; Dir Political Dept, Army (or Ground Force), PLA Services and Arms 1991; Deputy Dir Political Dept of Jinan Mil. Area Command 1991–95, Dir 1995–96; Asst Dir PLA Gen. Political Dept 1996, Deputy Dir 1996; mem. 14th CCP Cen. Comm. for

Discipline Inspection 1992–97, Alt. mem. 15th CCP Cen. Cttee 1997–2002, 16th CCP Cen. Cttee 2002–07; rank of Maj.-Gen. 1988, Gen. 2000.

YUAN, Weimin; Chinese sports administrator (retd) and civil servant; b. 8 July 1939, Suzhou, Jiangsu Prov.; ed Nanjing Sport Inst.; joined Jiangsu Prov. Men's Volleyball Team 1958; joined CCP 1962; joined Chinese Men's Volleyball Team 1962; Chief Coach, Chinese Women's Volleyball Team; Vice-Chair. All-China Sports Fed.; Vice-Chair. Chinese Olympic Cttee 1985–2000, Chair. 2000–05; Pres. Chinese Volleyball Asscn, Chinese Football Asscn 1992–2005, Asian Fed. for Wushu 1994–2000, Council of Physical Culture and Sports Science Soc. of China 1995; Exec. Vice-Chair. Asian Volleyball Fed. 1976–84, Chair. 1997–2001; Vice-Chair. State Comm. for Physical Culture and Sports 1984–98; Deputy Dir State Gen. Admin. for Sports 1998–2000, Dir 2000–04; Exec. Pres. Beijing Organizing Cttee for 2008 Summer Olympics; Alt. mem. CCP 12th Cen. Cttee 1982–87, mem. 13th CCP Cen. Cttee 1987–92, 14th CCP Cen. Cttee 1992–97, Alt. mem. CCP 15th Cen. Cttee 1997–2002, mem. 16th CCP Cen. Cttee 2002–07; introduced to Volleyball Hall of Fame 2007; Hon. Prof., Nanjing Inst. of Physical Culture 1992; China's Lifetime Achievement Award 2005. *Publication:* My Way of Coaching.

YUAN, Zhongyi, MA; Chinese archaeologist (retd); b. 1932, Jiangsu Prov.; m. Liu Yu; one d.; ed East China Teachers' Univ.; led excavations of Terracotta Warriors, Xian; fmr Vice-Dir Shaanxi Prov. Archaeological Research Inst. and Curator Qin Shi Huang's Terracotta Army Museum; Del. 5th People's Congress, Council of China; Outstanding Prof. of Shaanxi Prov., First Class of Nat. Excellence for book on Qin Dynasty Pottery Inscriptions and other book awards. *Publications:* Studies of the Terracotta Army at Qin Shi Huang's Mausoleum, Pottery Inscriptions of the Qin Dynasty, The Pits of Terracotta Warriors and Horses of Qin Shihuang Mausoleum – An Excavation of No. 1 Pit, An Excavation Report on the Bronze Chariots and Horses of Qin Shihuang Mausoleum. *Leisure interest:* handwriting.

YUASA, Joji; Japanese composer and professor of music; *Professor Emeritus of Music, University of California, San Diego;* b. 12 Aug. 1929, Koriyama City; s. of Daitaro Yuasa and Otoe Yuasa; Rena Yuasa (MDr), Ryuhei Yuasa (painter); m. Reiko Suzuki 1958; one s. one d.; ed Asaka High School, Keio Univ.; orchestral works commissioned by Kousevitzky Music Foundation 1974, Inst. for Research and Co-ordination in Acoustics and Music 1988, Suntory Music Foundation and by orchestras in Japan, Germany and Finland; resident on Berlin Artist Program (DAAD) 1976–77; Prof. of Music, Univ. of California, San Diego 1981–94, Prof. Emer. 1994–; Visiting Prof. of Music, Nihon Univ. 1994–; Visiting Prof., Tokyo Coll. of Music; mem. Experimental Workshop, Tokyo 1952; featured composer, Festival of the Arts of this Century, Hawaii 1970, Pacific Music Festival, Sapporo 1990, Music Today Festival, Tokyo 1992; mem. Int. Jury for World Music Days, Int. Soc. for Contemporary Music (ISCM) 1971, 1983, 1992, 2001; Composer-in-Residence, Centre for Music Experiment, Univ. of California at San Diego 1976, NSW Conservatorium of Music, Australia 1980, Univ. of Toronto, Canada 1981; resident at Institut Royal de la Culture Amazighe 1987, Civitella Ranieri Foundation 2002; a leader for Int. Composers' Workshops, Amsterdam 1984, 1992; Artistic Dir Int. Comm. Series for Orchestral Composition, Suntory Hall 1999–2011; Medal with Purple Ribbon 1997, Person of Culture Merit 2014; nine awards from ISCM 1971–2005, Odaka Prizes for Orchestra 1972, 1988, 1997, 2003, Kyoto Music Prize Grand Prix 1995, Suntory Music Prize 1996, Japan Acad. Prize 1999, Imperial Prize 1999. *Film scores include:* Osōshiki (The Funeral) (dir Yuzo Itami), Fukuro no Shiro (The Castle of Owls) (dir Mazathiro Shinoda). *Compositions include:* Projection for string quartet I & II 1971, 1985, Time of Orchestral Time 1976, Scenes from Basho (suite) 1980–89, Revealed Time for viola and orchestra 1986, Cosmos Haptic II for piano 1986, Nine Levels by Ze-Ami for chamber ensemble and quadraphonic tape 1988, Eye on Genesis II for orchestra 1992, Piano Concertino 1994, Symphonic Suite; The Narrow Road into the Deep North: Basho 1995, Libera me, in Requiem of Reconciliation 1995, Violin Concerto 1996, Cosmic Solitude 1997, Chronoplastic II for Orchestra 1999, Chronoplastic III for orchestra 2001, Projection for string trio 2002, Cosmos Haptic V for orchestra 2002, Eyes on Genesis III for orchestra 2005, Koto Uta (songs) from Buson's Five Haiku 2006, Projection for Chamber Orchestra 2008. *Radio includes:* Comet Ikeya (Prix Italia for stereophonic section) 1966, Ai to Shura (Prix Italia for stereophonic section) 1967 and others. *Television includes:* Yoshinobu Tokugawa (NHK) 1999 and others. *Publications include:* To the Cosmology of Music 1981, A Half of the Life – Towards the Open Horizon of Music 1999, The World of Joji Yuasa 2004. *Leisure interests:* skiing, reading. *Address:* Tokyo Concerts, 2–3–18 Nishiwaseda, Shinkjuku Ku, Tokyo 169-0051 (office); 7-16-21-101 Ikegami, Ohta-ku, Tokyo 146-0082, Japan (home). *Telephone:* (3) 3200-9755 (office); (3) 3754-8710 (home). *Fax:* (3) 3200-9882 (office); (3) 3754-8710 (home). *E-mail:* info@tokyo-concerts.co.jp (office). *Website:* www.tokyo-concerts.co.jp (office).

YUDASHKIN, Valentin Abramovich; Russian fashion designer; b. 14 Oct. 1963, Bakovka, Moscow Region; m. Marina Vladimirovna Yudashkina; one d.; ed Moscow Industrial Pedagogical Inst.; Founder and Artistic Dir Vali-Moda 1987, Founder and Dir Velentin Yudashkin Presents Co. 1989; has participated in numerous maj. fashion shows, including Paris 1990–92, Los Angeles, Israel, Egypt, Italy, etc.; costume designer for several Moscow Theatre New Opera productions; est. Valentin Yudashkin House of Fashion 1993; mem. Paris Haute Couture Syndicate 1996; Honoured mem. of Acad. of Arts of Russian Fed.; Chevalier, Ordre des Arts et des Lettres 2007, Hon. Order for contribution to Russian fashion 2008; Honoured Art Worker of Russian Fed. 1999, Nat. Painter of Russia 2005, People's Artist of Russia 2005. *Address:* Valentin Yudashkin Fashion House, Kutuzovsky pr. 19, 121151 Moscow, Russia (office). *Telephone:* (495) 240-11-89 (office). *Fax:* (495) 240-43-01 (office). *E-mail:* info@yudashkin.com (office). *Website:* www.yudashkin.com (office).

YUDHOYONO, Kristiani (Ani) Herrawati; Indonesian; b. 6 July 1952, Jogjakarta; d. of Sarwo Edhie Wibowo and Sunarti Sri Hadiyah; m. Susilo Bambang Yudhoyono (fmr Pres. of Indonesia) 1976; two s.; Nat. Amb. for HIV/AIDS, speaker at numerous events including UNESCO Regional Confs in Support of Global Literacy, Beijing, China 2007; Hon. Chair. Asscn for the Eradication of Tuberculosis Indonesia; Patron of numerous orgs including Indonesia Reading Foundation, White Ribbon Alliance for Safe Motherhood (Indonesia), Family Welfare Movt, Women's Int. Club, Jakarta, Nat. Crafts Agency; UN Environment Programme Global Leadership Award 2007, Golden Pin Award, Regional Microcredit Summit 2008.

YUDOF, Mark George, AB, LLB; American lawyer, academic and university administrator; *UC President Emeritus and Professor of Law (Emeritus), Berkeley Law, University of California, Berkeley;* b. 30 Oct. 1944, Philadelphia, Pa; m. Judith Lynn Yudof (née Gomel) 1965; one s. one d.; ed Univ. of Pennsylvania, Univ. of Pennsylvania Law School; law clerk to Judge Robert A. Ainsworth, US Court of Appeals Fifth Circuit 1968–69; Assoc. Gen. Counsel of the Comm. of ABA to Study the Fed. Trade Comm. 1969; Research Assoc. Harvard Center for Law and Educ. 1969–70, Sr Staff Attorney 1970–71; Asst Prof. of Law, Univ. of Texas at Austin 1971–74, Prof. 1974–97, Assoc. Dean of the Law School 1979–84, Dean 1984–94, James A. Elkins Centennial Chair in Law 1983–97, John Jeffers Research Chair in Law 1991–94, Exec. Vice Pres. and Provost, Univ. of Texas at Austin 1994–97; Pres. and Prof. (Law School), Univ. of Minnesota 1997–2002, Pres. Emer. and Prof. Emer. 2002–; Chancellor and Prof. (Law School), Univ. of Texas System 2002–08, Lee Hage and Joseph D. Jamail Regents Chair in Higher Educ. Leadership 2002–08, Charles Alan Wright Chair in Fed. Courts 2002–08; Pres. Univ. of California 2008–13, currently Pres. Emer.; Chair. Council of Public Univ. Pres. and Chancellors 2007; mem. Bd of Dirs World Council on Information Tech. 2004–07, HealthTronics 2005–08, Fellow, American Acad. of Arts and Sciences 2001–, American Bar Foundation, Texas Bar Foundation; Visiting Prof., Univ. of California, Berkeley Law 1977, currently Prof. of Law (Emer.), Univ. of Michigan Law School 1982; fmr Visiting Fellow, Univ. of Warwick, UK; mem. American Law Inst., Pres.' Council on Service and Civic Participation 2006–; Hon. Fellow, Queen Mary and Westfield Coll., Univ. of London 1990; Hon. Guest Prof., Fudan Univ. 2000, Peking Univ. Law School 2000; Hon. DHumLitt (Hebrew Union Coll.-Jewish Inst. of Religion) 2013; Jewish Nat. Fund Tree of Life Award (co-winner with wife) 1993, Univ. of Pennsylvania Law Alumni Award of Merit 1999, Odyssey Award, Big Brothers Big Sisters of Greater Minneapolis 2001, John R. Hogness Award, Asscn of Academic Health Center 2003, James Wilson Award, Univ. of Pennsylvania Law School 2004. *Publications include:* When Government Speaks 1983, Legal Deskbook for Administrators of Independent Colleges and Universities 1984, Gender Justice (jtly) 1987, Educational Policy and the Law (jtly) 2002; numerous book chapters and articles in professional journals. *Leisure interest:* collecting antique maps. *Address:* University of California, Berkeley, Room 788 Simon Hall, Berkeley, CA 94720, USA (office). *Telephone:* (510) 642-8531 (office). *E-mail:* yudof@law.berkeley.edu (office). *Website:* www.law.berkeley.edu (office).

YUE, Yi; Hong Kong banking executive; b. 1956; ed Wuhan Univ.; joined Bank of China (BOC) 1980, Vice-Pres. BOC Beijing 1993–2000, Gen. Man., Seoul Br. 2000–03, Retail Banking Dept 2003–05, Personal Banking Dept 2005–08, also mem. Group Exec. Cttee, Vice-Chair. Personal Banking Cttee and Global Head Personal Banking Business 2008–09, also mem. Group Exec. Cttee, Vice-Chair. Financial Markets Cttee and Global Head, Financial Markets Business 2009–10, Exec. Vice-Pres. BOC Ltd 2010–15, Chair. BOC (UK) Ltd 2010–15, BOC Int. Holdings Ltd 2011–15, BOC Luxembourg 2014–15, Vice-Chair., Exec. Dir and Chief Exec. Bank of China (Hong Kong) Ltd (BOCHK) 2015–18, Bank of China (Hong Kong) Holdings Ltd 2015–18, Chair. BOCHK Charitable Foundation, BOC Group Life Assurance Co. Ltd 2015–18, Designated Rep. of BOCHK to Hong Kong Asscn of Banks 2015–18; Chair. Bohai Industrial Investment Fund Man. Co. Ltd 2012–15, Vice-Chair. Bd of Trustee and Chair. of Investment Subcommittee, Ho Leung Ho Lee Foundation 2015–18; Vice-Pres. Hong Kong Inst. of Bankers 2015–18; Special Advisor, Maritime Silk Road Soc. 2015–18; mem. Exchange Fund Advisory Cttee 2015–18; mem. Bd of Dirs Hong Kong Interbank Clearing Ltd, Hong Kong Note Printing Ltd (Chair. 2018–); Hon. Pres. Hong Kong Chinese Enterprises Asscn 2015; Hon. mem. Hong Kong–Japan Business Co-operation Cttee 2016. *Address:* Hong Kong Interbank Clearing Ltd, Unit B, 25/F, MG Tower, 133 Hoi Bun Road, Kwun Tong, Kowloon, Hong Kong, People's Republic of China (office). *Telephone:* 25331111 (office). *Fax:* 25331122 (office). *E-mail:* hkicl@hkicl.com.hk (office). *Website:* www.hkicl.com.hk (office).

YUEN, Woo-Ping; Chinese film director, actor and choreographer; b. (Yuan He-Ping), 1 Jan. 1945, Guangzhou, Canton; s. of Yuen Hsiao-Tien; born into a family of Peking Opera artists, learned martial arts; worked with Jackie Chan (q.v.), Donnie Yen, Ng See Yuen. *Films include:* as director: Snake in the Eagle's Shadow 1978, Magnificent Butcher 1979, Drunken Master 1979, Dreadnaught 1981, Drunken Tai-Chi 1984, Mismatched Couples 1985, Tiger Cage 1988, In the Line of Duty 4 1989, Tiger Cage 2 1990, Tiger Cage 3 1991, The Wicked City 1992, Last Hero in China 1993, The Tai Chi Master 1993, The Iron Monkey 1993, Heroes Among Heroes 1993, Wing Chun 1994, Fist of Legend 1994, Fiery Dragon Kid 1995, Tai Chi 2 1996, True Legend 2010, Vigilante: The Lost Order 2013, Crouching Tiger, Hidden Dragon: Sword of Destiny 2016, The Thousand Faces of Dunjia 2017, Master Z: The Ip Man Legacy 2018; as actor: Miracle Fighters 1982, Mismatched Couples 1985, Eastern Condors 1986, Wicked City 1992, Cinema of Vengeance 1994, The Grandmaster 2013, Man of Tai Chi 2013; as choreographer: Fist of Legend 1994, Black Mask 1996, The Matrix 1999, Crouching Tiger, Hidden Dragon 2000, Kill Bill 2003, Kill Bill 2 2004, Kung Fu Hustle 2004, House of Fury 2005, Fearless 2006, The Forbidden Kingdom 2008, Ninja Assassin 2009, Man of Tai Chi 2013, I 2014, Ip Man 3 2015, Gong Shou Dao 2017. *Television:* produced TV Series The Practice 1976.

YUILL, Thomas M., BS, MS, PhD; American virologist and academic; *Professor Emeritus, School of Veterinary Medicine, University of Wisconsin;* b. 14 June 1937, Berkeley, Calif.; s. of Joseph Stuart Yuill and Louise Dunlop Yuill; m. Ann W Yuill; two c.; ed Univ. of Wisconsin, Utah State Univ.; Medical Biologist, SEATO Medical Research Lab., Thailand 1966–68; Prof., School of Veterinary Medicine, Univ. of Wisconsin 1968–2003, Prof. Emer. 2003–, also Dir Emer., Nelson Inst.; ProMED Viral Diseases Moderator, Int. Soc. for Infectious Diseases 2007–; Walter F. Rink Distinguished Prof. Award, School of Veterinary Medicine, Univ. of Wisconsin 1991, John Letty Phelan Distinguished Service Award, Univ. of Wisconsin, Distinguished Service and Emer. Awards, Wildlife Disease Asscn, Richard Moreland Trylor Award 2009. *Publications include:* over 120 published papers and book chapters. *Leisure interests:* music, hiking. *Address:* 2237 E 400 N, Mapleton, UT 84664, USA (office). *Telephone:* (801) 491-3226 (office). *Fax:* (801) 491-3226 (office). *E-mail:* tmyuill@wisc.edu (office). *Website:* www.vetmed.wisc.edu/departments/pathobiological-sciences (office).

YULDASHEV, Bekhzod, PhD; Uzbekistani nuclear physicist, politician and administrator; b. 9 May 1945, Tashkent; m.; two s.; ed Tashkent Univ., Moscow Univ., Joint Inst. of Nuclear Research, Russia; research in particle and nuclear physics, non-proliferation problems, Jt Inst. of Nuclear Research, Dubna, USSR 1968–71; Sr Researcher, Physical Tech. Inst., Tashkent 1972–83, Head of Lab. 1984–90; Dir-Gen. Inst. of Nuclear Physics 1990–2006; mem. Parl. 2000–05; Senator 2005–06; Adviser-Consultant, IAEA, Vienna 2006–07; Visiting Prof., Univ. of Washington, Seattle 1977–78, 1980–81, 1989–90, Stanford Univ., Calif. 2006–07; Visiting Fellow, Indiana Univ. 1997, Univ. of Cambridge, UK 2004; Visiting Scholar, Center for Int. Security and Cooperation, Stanford Univ. –2011, Consulting Prof. 2013–14; mem. Scientific Council Jt Inst. of Nuclear Research, Dubna 1992–2002, mem. Uzbekistan Acad. of Sciences (Pres. 2000–05), Kazakhstan Nat. Acad. of Sciences, American Physical Soc., Islamic Acad. of Sciences; Foreign mem. Nat. Acad. of Kazakhstan; Hon. Fellow, Indiana Univ. 1997; Hon. Prof., Samarkand Univ. 2005; Order 'For Glorious Work'; Dr hc (Jt Inst. of Nuclear Research, Dubna) 2004; State Prize in Science and Tech. 1983, ECO Prize in Science and Tech. 2004. *Publications:* more than 300 papers in int. physics journals; holds more than 20 patents.

YUMASHEV, Valentin Borisovich; Russian politician and journalist; b. 15 Dec. 1957, Perm; m. 1st; one d.; m. 2nd Tatiana Dyachenko (d. of fmr Pres. Yeltsin; ed Moscow State Univ.; errand boy for Komsomolskaya Pravda newspaper 1976, corresp., sr corresp. 1978–87; Moskovsky Komsomolets 1987–89; took part in election campaign of Boris Yeltsin to Supreme Soviet 1988, 1992, 1996; Head of Div., Ed., Deputy Ed.-in-Chief Ogonyok 1987–96; Adviser to Russian Press on mass media 1996–; Chair. Presidential Exec. Office of Pres. Yeltsin 1997–98 (dismissed); apptd Adviser to Boris Yeltsin 1998; helped Pres. Yeltsin in writing memoirs; now works in real estate devt; Austrian citizenship 2009–. *Leisure interest:* tennis. *Address:* c/o Presidential Executive Office, 103132 Moscow, Staraya Square 4, Russian Federation.

YUMKELLA, Kandeh K., BSc, MSc, PhD; Sierra Leonean politician and fmr UN official; b. 5 July 1959; m. Philomena Yumkella; several c.; ed Njala Univ. Coll., Univ. of Illinois, USA; held several academic and research positions in USA; Minister for Trade, Industry and State Enterprises, Sierra Leone 1994–95; Special Adviser to Dir-Gen., UNIDO 1996, Dir Africa and Least Developed Countries Regional Bureau 1996–2000, UNIDO Rep. and Dir Regional Industrial Devt Centre 2000–03, Sr Adviser to Dir-Gen. 2003–05, Dir-Gen. UNIDO 2005–13; Special Rep. of the Sec.-Gen. for Sustainable Energy for All, UN 2013–15; Chair. UN-Energy 2008–15; cand. in presidential election 2018; Dr hc (Univ. of Madras) 2008, (Njala Univ.) 2011, (Ekiti State Univ.) 2012; Lifetime Achievement Award, Green White and Blue Comm. 2013, Nayudamma Award for outstanding contributions to the energy sector 2014. *Publications include:* co-author of numerous books, articles and staff papers on int. trade and devt issues. *Address:* c/o Sustainable Energy for All Initiative, United Nations Headquarters, 760 United Nations Plaza, New York, NY 10017, USA.

YUN, Byung-se, MA; South Korean politician; b. 3 Aug. 1953, Seoul; m.; one d.; ed Seoul Nat. Univ., School of Advanced Int. Studies, Johns Hopkins Univ., USA; joined Ministry of Foreign Affairs (MOFA) 1977, Consul, Consulate-Gen. in Sydney 1984, Counsellor, Perm. Mission to UN, New York 1990, Dir, N America Div. I, MOFA 1994, Minister-Counsellor, Embassy in Singapore 1995, Deputy Dir-Gen., Asian and Pacific Affairs Bureau, Ministry of Foreign Affairs and Trade (MOFAT) Feb.–July 1999, Deputy Dir-Gen., N American Affairs Bureau, MOFAT July 1999, Minister, Perm. Mission to UN Secr. and Int. Orgs in Geneva 2000, Minister, Embassy in Washington, DC 2002, Sr Coordinator, Nat. Security Council 2004–06, Deputy Minister of Foreign Affairs 2006, Sr Presidential Sec. for Foreign, Security and Unification Policy 2006, Minister of Foreign Affairs and Trade 2013–17; Sr Adviser, Law Offices of Kim & Chang 2009; Visiting Prof., Grad. School of Int. Studies, Sogang Univ., Seoul 2009; mem. 18th Presidential Transition Cttee Sub-Cttee on Foreign Affairs, Nat. Defence and Unification 2013; Service Merit Medal 1992, Order of Service Merit (Yellow Stripes) 2005.

YUN, Gongmin; Chinese business executive; b. Sept. 1950, Inner Mongolia; ed Tsinghua Univ.; Chief of Yikezhao Banner of Inner Mongolia; Gen. Sec. Yikezhao Banner Cttee of CCP; Asst to the Pres. of Inner Mongolia Autonomous Region, Vice-Pres. Inner Mongolia Autonomous Region; Gen. Sec. Taiyuan Municipal Cttee of CCP; Vice-Gov. Shanxi Prov.; Vice-Gen. Sec. Shanxi Prov. Cttee of CCP; Deputy Chair. and Chair. Labour Union of Shenhua Group Corpn Ltd; Pres. and CEO China Huadian Corpn and Deputy Sec. Party Leadership Group 2008–16.

YUN, Jong-yong, BA; South Korean business executive; *Company Adviser, Samsung Electronics Company Limited;* b. 21 Jan. 1944, Youngchun, Kyoung-buk; m.; one s. one d.; ed Seoul Nat. Univ., MIT Sloan School, USA; joined Samsung Group 1966, with Samsung Electronics Co. Ltd 1969–, Head of Tokyo office 1977–80, Head of TV Business Div. 1980–81, Head of Video Business Div. 1981–85, Head of Research and Devt Div. 1985–88, Vice-Pres. Electronics Group 1988–90, Vice-Pres. and Rep. Dir Consumer Electronics Business Group 1990–92 (Pres. and Rep. Dir 1992–96), Pres. and CEO Samsung Electronics Co. Ltd 1996–99, Vice-Chair. and CEO 1999–2008, Co. Adviser 2008–; Pres. and CEO Samsung Electro-Mechanics Co. Ltd 1992, Samsung Display Devices Co. Ltd 1993, Samsung Japan HQ 1995; Chair. Nat. Acad. of Eng of Korea, Fed. of Korean Information Industries; Prize for Most Successful CEO in Korea (Korea Man. Asscn) 1999, Gold Medal for Contrib. to Industry 1992, Outstanding Achievement in Man. (Inst. of Inc. Engineers) 1998, Asia's Businessman of the Year (Fortune) 2000, CEO's Choice Award, Asia Business Leader Awards 2002. *Leisure interest:* golf. *Address:* Samsung Electronics Co. Ltd, 250 2-ga Taepyeong-no, jung-gu, Seoul 740-10 Hannam-dong, Yongsan-gu, Seoul 100-742, Republic of Korea (office). *Telephone:* (2) 727-7114 (office). *Fax:* (2) 727-7985 (office). *E-mail:* j-npr@samsung.co.kr (office). *Website:* www.samsung.com (office).

YUNIUPINGU, (James) Galarrwuy, AM; Australian community leader and business executive; *Chairman, Yothu Yindi Foundation;* b. 30 June 1948, Melville Bay, nr Yirrkala, Gove; s. of Mungurrawuy Yunupingu; ed Mission School, Yirrkala, Methodist Bible Coll., Brisbane; active in Gumatj Clan's land struggle in 1960s; joined Interim Northern Land Council 1975, Chair. 1977–80, 1983–2002; apptd Chair. Gumatj Asscn Inc. 1983; Public Officer/Dir Yunupingu Industries 1983; Chair. YBE Pty Ltd 1988–92; Chair. Yothu Yindi Foundation 1998–; Co-Chair. Aboriginal Devt Consultative Forum 2000; Dir Garrangali Crocodile Farm 1991, Gawpu Marine 1991; mem. Australian Crocodile Farmers Asscn 1990–, Council for Aboriginal Reconciliation 1991–96; Exec. Dir Yothu Yindi 1992; Gumatj Clan Leader 1979–; also singer and songwriter; Hon. LLD (Univ. of Melbourne) 2015; Australian of the Year 1978, honoured as one of Australia's Nat. Living Treasures 1998. *Publication:* Our Land Is Our Life. *Leisure interests:* fishing, hunting, songwriting, Australian Rules Football. *Address:* Yothu Yindi Foundation, PO Box 42119, Casuarina, NT 0811, Australia (office). *Website:* www.yyf.com.au (office).

YUNUS, Muhammad; Bangladeshi banker and academic; *Chairman, Yunus Centre;* b. 28 June 1940; m. Afrizi Yunus; one d.; ed Vanderbilt Univ., USA; Prof. of Econs, Chittagong Univ. 1976; f. Grameen Bank Project, pioneering microcredit loans to those in extreme poverty Dec. 1976, changed to ind. bank, Grameen Bank Sept. 1983, Man. Dir and CEO 1983–2011; Founder and Chair. Yunus Centre; f. Nagorik Shakti political party 2007; Chancellor Glasgow Caledonian Univ. UK 2012–; Dir UN Foundation; mem. Int. Advisory Group, Fourth World Conf. on Women, Beijing 1993–95, Advisory Council for Sustainable Econ. Devt 1993, UN Expert Group on Women and Finance, Prague Inst. for Global Urban Devt, UNESCO, Mahatma Gandhi Center for Global Nonviolence and numerous others; Sr Fellow, Inst. of Mediterranean Studies, Universita della Svizzera Italiana, Switzerland 2000–; numerous hon. degrees; Independence Day Award, Pres.'s Award and Cen. Bank Award (all Bangladesh), Ramon Magsaysay Award (Philippines), Aga Khan Award for Architecture, Mohamed Shabdeen Award for Science (Sri Lanka), World Food Prize (USA), Nobel Peace Prize (jtly with Grameen Bank) 2006, Presidential Medal of Freedom 2009, US Congressional Gold Medal 2010, St. Vincent de Paul Award 2011, Jean Mayer Global Citizen Award 2012, International Freedom Award 2012, Albert Schweitzer Humanitarian Award 2013, Congressional Gold Medal Award (US) 2013, Asian American/Asian Research Leadership Award 2013. *Publications include:* Creating a World Without Poverty: How Social Business Can Transform Our Lives 2008. *Address:* Yunus Centre, Grameen Bank Bhaban, Mirpur-2, Dhaka 1216, Bangladesh (office). *Telephone:* 2-801-1138 (office). *E-mail:* yunus@yunuscentre.org (office). *Website:* www.muhammadyunus.org.

YURKO, Allen, MBA; American business executive; *Partner, Avista Capital Partners;* b. 1951; ed Lehigh Univ., Baldwin-Wallace Coll.; early career in finance and accounting positions with Joy Manufacturing Co. and Eaton Corpn; Chief Financial Officer Mueller Holdings –1988; several management positions at Siebe including COO 1992–94, CEO 1994–98; CEO Invensys PLC (following merger of Siebe and BTR) 1998–2001; Operating Partner and Dir, Compass Partners International Ltd from 2001; European Industrial Partner, DLJ Merchant Banking Partners –2010; Partner, Avista Capital Partners 2010–; Dir, ArmoredAuto Group, Guala Closures, Telular Corpn, Top-Co. *Address:* Avista Capital Holdings, LP, 65 East 55th Street, 18th Floor, New York, NY 10022, USA (office). *Telephone:* (212) 593-6900 (office). *Fax:* (212) 593-6901 (office). *E-mail:* info@avistacap.com (office). *Website:* www.avistacap.com (office).

YUSGIANTORO, Purnomo, BSc, MS, PhD; Indonesian politician and international organization official; b. 16 June 1951, Semarang, Cen. Java; m.; three c.; ed Bandung Inst. of Tech., Univ. of Colorado, USA; worked with several int. think tanks during 1980s; energy consultant with World Bank (IBRD) and Asian Devt Bank 1988–2000; fmr Deputy Gov. Nat. Resilience Inst. (Lemhannas); adviser, Minister of Energy 1993–98; Minister for Energy and Mineral Resources 2000–09, Minister of Defence 2009–14; fmr Gov. OPEC, Vienna, Pres. OPEC Conf. and Acting Sec.-Gen. OPEC 2004; fmr Lecturer in Econs and Man., Atmajaya Univ., Jakarta and univs in USA; Co-founder Indonesian Inst. for Energy Econs.

YUSHCHENKO, Viktor Andriyovich, CandEconSc; Ukrainian economist, banker, politician and fmr head of state; b. 23 Feb. 1954, Khoruzhivka, Sumy Oblast; s. of Andriy Andriyovych Yushchenko and Varvara Tymofiyovna Yushchenko; m. Kateryna Mykhailivna Yushchenko; two s. three d.; ed Ternopil Inst. of Finance and Econ., Ukrainian Inst. of Econs and Agricultural Man.; economist, Br. Dir USSR State Bank, Ulianivskyi Dist, Sumy Oblast 1976–85, Deputy Dir of Agric. Credits, Ukrainian Br. of USSR State Bank 1985–87; Dept Dir Ukrainian Bank (fmrly Ukrainian Agro-Industrial Bank) 1987–91, First Deputy Chair. 1991–93; Gov. Nat. Bank of Ukraine 1993–99; Prime Minister of Ukraine 1999–2001; Founder and Chair. Nasha Ukraina (Our Ukraine) coalition 2002, mem. Parl. 2002–04; Pres. of Ukraine 2005–10; mem. Ukrainian Acad. of Econ. Sciences, Acad. of Econ. and Cybernetics; Order 'For Merits' of Class III 1996, Order of the White Eagle (Poland) 2005, Order of the White Rose of Finland 2006, Kt Grand Cross, Grand Order of King Tomislav (Croatia) 2007, Order of Heydar Aliyev (Azerbaijan) 2008, Royal Order of the Seraphim (Sweden) 2008, Order of Merit (Hungary) 2008, Order of the Golden Fleece (Georgia) 2009, Order of Victory St George (Georgia) 2009, Grand Cross, Order of Polonia Restituta 2009, Kt, Order of the Three Stars (First Class), Grand Collar of the Order of Vytautas the Great; Dr hc (Mohyla Acad.—Nat. Univ. of Kyiv, Ostroh Acad.), (Univ. of Maria Curie-Sklodowska) 2000, (Catholic Univ. of Lublin) 2009; Global Finance Award 1997, State Prize Laureate Science and Technology 1999, Man of the Year 'Wprost' 2004, Chatham House Prize, UK 2005. *Publications:* more than 250 articles and research papers in Ukrainian and int. journals. *Leisure interests:* painting, pottery, woodcarving, beekeeping.

YUSUF, Abdulqawi Ahmed, DrIur, DèsSc; Somali lawyer, academic and judge; *Judge and President, International Court of Justice;* b. 12 Sept. 1948, Eyl; ed Somali Nat. Univ., Centre for Studies and Research in Int. Law, Hague Academy of Int. Law, Netherlands, Grad. Inst. of Int. Studies, Univ. of Florence, Italy, Univ. of Geneva, Switzerland; barrister, Supreme Court of Somalia 1974–; Lecturer in Int. Law, Faculty of Law, Somali Nat. Univ. 1974–80, Chair. Public Law Dept 1976–78; adviser to Govt on int. legal matters; mem. various govt advisory bodies on legislation; Asst Prof., Faculty of Law, Univ. of Geneva 1981–83; Visiting Lecturer on public int. law and int. econ. law at univs and academic insts including Univ. of Siena, Italy 1984, Institut universitaire d'études du développement, Geneva 1984, Univ. of Florence 1985, Univ. of Milan-Bocconi, Italy 1990, Int. Devt Law Inst., Rome 1990, 1991, 1992, 1995, Univ. of Turin, Italy 1991, 1992, UNITAR Fellowship Programme in Int. Law, Hague Acad. of Int. Law, The Netherlands 1993, 1994, 1996, 1999, Thessaloniki Inst. of Public Int. Law and Int. Relations 2004; Rep. and Head, New York Office of UNCTAD 1992–94; Sr Liaison Officer,

UN Programme of Action for Least Developed Countries, New York 1992–94, Head of Legal Policies Section, Tech. Programme, Geneva June–July 1992, Legal Officer, Tech. Div., Geneva 1981–88; Legal Adviser and Dir Legal Service, UNIDO 1994–98, Acting Man. Dir Country Programmes and Funds Mobilization Div. 1997–98, Asst Dir-Gen. and Special Adviser on African Affairs 1998–2001; Legal Adviser and Dir Office of Int. Standards and Legal Affairs, UNESCO, Paris 2001–; *ad hoc* Judge, Int. Court of Justice in case concerning Certain Questions of Mutual Assistance in Criminal Matters (Djibouti v. France), Judge 2009–, Vice-Pres. 2015–18, Pres. 2018–; Rep. of Somalia to Third UN Conf. on the Law of the Sea 1975–81; Expert Adviser and UNCTAD Rep. at GATT Uruguay Round Trade Negotiations on TRIPS 1989–91; Legal Adviser to UNESCO 2001–; mem. Comm. on Environmental Law, Int. Union for Conservation of Nature (IUCN); mem. Academic Council Doctoral School of Int. Law, Univ. of Paris 1 (Sorbonne), France, Int. Curatorium of Thessaloniki Inst. of Public Int. Law and Int. Relations, Greece; Founder and Gen. Ed. African Yearbook of International Law/Annuaire Africain de droit international; mem. Editorial Advisory Bd Asian Yearbook of International Law; mem. Inst. of Int. Law (Institut de droit int.), Geneva, Soc. française de droit int.; Founding mem. African Asscn of Int. Law, African Foundation for Int. Law (Chair. Exec. Cttee). *Publications:* author or co-author of several books and numerous articles dealing with various aspects of int. law. *Address:* International Court of Justice, Peace Palace, Carnegieplein 2, 2517 KJ, The Hague, The Netherlands (office). *Telephone:* (70) 302-2323 (office). *Fax:* (70) 364-9928 (office). *E-mail:* info@icj-cij.org (office). *Website:* www.icj-cij.org (office).

YUSUF, Hamza; American theologian; *President, Zaytuna College;* b. (Mark Hanson), 1959, Walla Walla, Wash.; m.; five c.; ed Imperial Valley Coll., San Jose State Univ.; converted to Islam 1973 at age 17; moved to UAE to study Islam 1979–83; Co-founder and Exec. Dir Zaytuna Islamic Inst. (now Zaytuna Coll.), Calif. 1996, currently Pres. *Address:* Zaytuna College, 2515 Hillegass Ave, Berkeley, CA 94704, USA (office). *Telephone:* (510) 356-4760 (office). *Fax:* (510) 356-4768 (office). *E-mail:* info@zaytuna.org (office). *Website:* www.zaytunacollege .org (office).

YUSUF, Salim, OC, MD, MBBS, DPhil, FRSC, FRCPC; Canadian (b. Indian) physician and professor of medicine; *Director, Population Health Research Institute, McMaster University;* b. 26 Nov. 1952, Kottarakkara, Kerala, India; ed Bangalore Univ., St John's Medical Coll., Bangalore, Univ. of Oxford, UK; Registrar, Gen. Medicine and Cardiology, John Radcliffe Hosp., Oxford 1982; Registrar, Cardiology, Harefield Hosp. Regional Cardiac Centre, Middx 1982–84; Scientific Project Officer, NIH, Bethesda, Md, USA 1984, later Chair., working group for Women's Health clinical trial, Clinical Asst Prof., Uniformed Services Univ. Health Sciences 1987–88, Acting Chief of Clinical Trials Br., Nat. Heart, Lung and Blood Inst. 1991–92; Prof. of Medicine and Dir Div. of Cardiology, McMaster Univ. 1992–, also Dir, Population Health Research Inst. 2000–, concurrently Heart and Stroke Foundation of Ontario/Marion W. Burke Chair in Cardiovascular Disease, McMaster Univ.; Vice-Pres. of Research and Chief Scientific Officer, Hamilton Health Sciences 1998–2000; Visiting Prof., Univ. of Sydney, Australia 1998, Cleveland Clinic Foundation 2000, St John's Medical Coll., Bangalore; Ed. Journal of Evidence-Based Cardiology, Textbook of Evidence-Based Cardiovascular Medicine; mem. American Coll. of Cardiology, Canadian Cardiovascular Soc., American Heart Asscn, Canadian Inst. of Academic Medicine, Int. Acad. of Cardiovascular Sciences, American Soc. of Clinical Investigation; mem. World Heart Fed. (Pres.-elect 2013–); Fellow Int. Acad. of Cardiovascular Sciences; Hon. Fellow, Polish Cardiac Soc. 1995, Venezuelan Cardiac Soc. 1999; Sr Scientist, Canadian Insts of Health Research; over 20 nat. and int. awards for research including Durrer Lecturer 1988, NIH Group Award 1992, Indo-Canadian Chamber of Commerce Professional of the Year 1996, Int. Soc. of Thrombosis and Hemostasis Sol Sherry Lecturer Award 1999, Canadian Cardiovascular Soc. Lifetime Research Achievement Award 1999, Prix Galien Canada Research Award 2001, Lucian Award for Cardiovascular Research 2002, British Cardiac Soc. Paul Wood Silver Medal 2003, IACS Medal of Merit 2011, J. Allyn Taylor Int. Prize in Medicine 2013, Canada Gairdner Wightman Award 2014, inducted into Canadian Medical Hall of Fame 2014. *Publications:* more than 300 papers. *Address:*

McMaster University, Faculty of Health Sciences, Hamilton Health Sciences Corporation, 237 Barton Street East, Hamilton, ON L8L 2X2, Canada (office). *Telephone:* (905) 297-3781 (office). *Fax:* (905) 521-1166 (office). *E-mail:* yusufs@ mcmaster.ca (office). *Website:* fhs.mcmaster.ca (office).

YUTHASAK, Gen. (retd) Sasiprapha; Thai politician and fmr military officer; *President, National Olympic Committee of Thailand;* b. 8 Jan. 1937, Bangkok; s. of Lt-Gen. Att Sasiprapha and Jumroon Sasiprapha; m. Khunying Orapan Sasiprapha; three c.; ed St Gabriel's Coll., Chulachomklao, Royal Military Acad., Nat. Defence Coll. of Thailand; served in Royal Thai Army, Maj.-Gen. for Army Reserve Force Students Chief of Staff 1985–90, Lt-Gen. 1990–96, Gen. 1996; Dir-Gen. for Office of Policy and Planning, Ministry of Defence 1996, Perm. Sec. 1996–98; joined Thai Rak Thai Party, elected as party list MP; Deputy Defence Minister 2001–05, Minister of Defence 2011–12, Deputy Prime Minister Jan.–Oct. 2012; Pres. Nat. Olympic Cttee; Kt Grand Cross (First Class), Most Exalted Order of the White Elephant 1987, Kt Grand Cordon (Special Class), Most Noble Order of Crown of Thailand 1989, Kt Grand Cordon (Special Class) 1993, Grand Companion (Third Class, Higher Grade), Most Illustrious Order of Chula Chom Klao 1997. *Address:* Banampawan Sriayudhaya Road 226, Dusit, Bangkok 10300, Thailand (office). *Telephone:* (2) 281-1016 (office). *Fax:* (2) 280-3758 (office). *E-mail:* postmaster@olympicthai.or.th (office). *Website:* olympicthai.or.th (office).

YUZHANOV, Ilya Arturovich, CandEcon; Russian economist, politician and business executive; *Chairman, Polymetal Open Joint Stock Company;* b. 7 Feb. 1960, Leningrad (now St Petersburg); m.; three c.; ed Leningrad State Univ.; teacher, lecturer in Leningrad insts 1982–90; Chief Specialist, Leningrad Cttee on Econ. Reforms 1990–91; Head of Dept, First Deputy Chair. Cttee on Econ. Devt, St Petersburg 1991–94; Chair. Cttee on Land Resources of St Petersburg 1994–97; Chair. State Cttee on Land Resources of Russian Fed. 1997–98; Minister on Land Policy, Construction and Communal Econs May–Sept. 1998; Minister of Antimonopoly Policy and Support for Entrepreneurship 1999–2004; Chair. Supervisory Council NOMOS-Bank 2004–06, mem. Bd Dirs 2006–; Chair. Polymetal Open Jt Stock Co. 2008–; mem. Bd Dirs jt stock cos, including Unified Energy System of Russia 2000–08, NOVATEK 2006–09, Uralkalii 2006–, Kirovsky Zavod 2006–09, Alrosa 2009–; Medal in Commemoration of 850th Anniversary of Founding of Moscow 1997, Merited Economist of Russian Fed. 2000, Best Ind. Dir in Russia 2007. *Publications:* monographs and numerous articles in journals and newspapers on antimonopoly and other problems in econs. *Leisure interest:* sport. *Address:* NOMOS-Bank, Moscow 109240, Verkhnyaya Radishchevskaya str. 3, Russia (office). *Telephone:* (495) 725-32-30 (office). *Fax:* (495) 797-32-50 (office). *E-mail:* yuzhanov_ia@nomos.ru (office). *Website:* www.nomos.ru (office); www .polymetal.ru (office).

YZERMAN, Steve; Canadian sport organization executive and professional ice hockey player (retd); *Senior Advisor, Tampa Bay Lightning Hockey Club;* b. 9 May 1965, Cranbrook, BC; m.; three d.; ed Bell High School, Nepean, Ont.; played Jr hockey with Peterborough Petes of Ont. Hockey League 1981–83; drafted fourth overall in 1983 Nat. Hockey League (NHL) Entry Draft by Detroit Red Wings; named team capt. 1986, longest serving capt. in NHL history; won three Stanley Cup Championships with Red Wings 1997, 1998, 2002; became 11th player to score 600 goals in NHL 1999 (692 career goals); has scored 1,755 career points, finished second in Red Wings history and sixth in NHL history; played for Canada in World Championships 1989, 1990, World Cup 1996, Winter Olympics 1998, 2002 (winner Gold Medal); retd 2006; Vice-Pres. Detroit Red Wings 2006–10; Vice-Pres. and Gen. Man. Tampa Bay Lightning 2010–18, Sr Advisor 2018–; Gen. Man. for Hockey Canada at 2007 and 2008 IIHF World Championships, Exec. Dir for Hockey Canada for 2010, 2014 Winter Olympics; Lester B. Pearson Award 1989, Conn Smythe Trophy 1998, Frank J. Seike Trophy 2000, Bill Masterton Memorial Trophy 2003, Lester Patrick Award 2006; named to NHL All-Rookie Team 1984; named to 10 NHL All-Star Games, elected to Hockey Hall of Fame 2009. *Address:* Office of the Vice-President and General Manager, Tampa Bay Lightning Hockey Club, St. Pete Times Forum, 401 Channelside Drive, Tampa, FL 33602, USA (home). *Telephone:* (813) 301-6500 (office). *Website:* lightning.nhl.com (office).

Z

ZABALAGA ESTRADA, Marcelo, BEcons, MScS; Bolivian academic, economist and central banker; b. 1 Aug. 1953, Cochabamba; ed Univ. of Geneva, Switzerland; Deputy Dir DESAC (Center for Social and Econ. Devt) 1977–80; Man., ASAR, (Artisan and Rural Services Asscn) 1981–82; Project Dir CESAT (Center for Services and Support to the Wheat Production) 1985–87; Exec. Dir FADES (Foundation for Devt Alternatives) 1993–97; Gen. Man. AFP Futuro de Bolivia 1997–98; consultant on devt and microfinance in Spain, Honduras, Nicaragua and El Salvador and countries in South America 1999–2006; Int. Dir Argentaria 1999–2000; Research Dir CIREM Foundation 2000–02; Dir FINRURAL (Asscn of Financial Insts for Rural Devt); Supt of Banking and Finances Entities (now Financial System Authority) 2007–09; Pres. Banco Central de Bolivia 2010–17; Dir Fondo Latinoamericano De Reservas; has served as a Univ. Prof. since 2001.

ZABLUDOWICZ, Chaim 'Poju', BA; Finnish business executive and art collector; *Chairman and CEO, Tamares Investment Group;* b. 6 April 1953, Helsinki; s. of Shlomo Zabludowicz; m. Anita Zabludowicz; four c.; ed Svenska Samskolan i Tammerfors (Swedish-speaking school), Tel-Aviv Univ., Israel; raised in Tampere; trained with commercial bank in Frankfurt, Germany before joining Tamares Investment Group, Chair. and CEO 1990–; Chair. BICOM (Britain Israel Communications and Research Centre); mem. Jewish Leadership Council; holds Pocal Industries, Scranton, Pa, USA and br. in Gouldsboro, Pa; other business interests in the Middle East; exhibits pvt. art collection in Chalk Farm, N London 2007; has collected Young British Artists, including works by Tracy Emin; mem. Bd of Dirs GEMS (Asia Pacific pvt. equity fund), Mustavaara Kaivos Oy 2011–; Chair. Advisory Bd Synova Capital LLP 2007–; mem. European Advisory Bd of Citigroup, Advisory Bd Stratos Ventures (Finland-based early stage venture capital fund); Dir Tate Modern Int. 1999–, Outotec Oyj 2012–, Kiasma Museum of Contemporary Art 2009–; Trustee, Zabludowicz Collection 1994–; Co-founder (with wife) Zoo Art Fair; Patron, Finnish British Chamber of Commerce 2011–. *Address:* Tamares Investment Group, 41 Dover Street, London, W1S 4NS, England (office). *Telephone:* (20) 7629-6636 (office). *Fax:* (20) 7629-4244 (office). *E-mail:* poju@tamares.com (office). *Website:* www.tamares.com (office); www .zabludowiczcollection.com.

ZACKHEOS, Sotirios, MA; Cypriot diplomatist and business executive; *Executive Director, RCB Bank Ltd;* b. 24 Jan. 1950, Nicosia; m.; two c.; ed Univ. of Athens, Greece, Stanford Univ., USA; Counsellor, Embassy in Moscow 1979–85, Amb. to China (also accred to Japan, Pakistan, The Philippines and Mongolia) 1989–93, Dir of Econ. Affairs, Foreign Ministry 1993, of Political Affairs 1995, Perm. Rep. to UN, Geneva 1996–97, Amb. and Perm. Rep. to UN, New York 1997–2003, Chair. Fourth Cttee (Special Political and Decolonization) 1999, High Commr (non-resident) to St Lucia, Grenada and Trinidad & Tobago 1997–2003, Amb. (non-resident) to Suriname 1997–2003, Perm. Sec., Ministry of Foreign Affairs 2003–07; Chair. S. Zackheos & Assocs Ltd (consultancy); currently Exec. Dir RCB Bank Ltd; special envoy of Pres. of Cyprus to Russia; Chair. Bd of Dirs Cyprus Int. Inst. for the Environment and Public Health; Vice-Pres. Cyprus GCC Countries Business Asscn; Head of Greek-Cypriot del. for negotiations with Turkish-Cypriots on issue of Security and Guarantees 2008–12, currently Head of Greek-Cypriot del. on opening new crossing points; Co-Vice-Pres. Cyprus-Qatar Business Asscn; mem. Bd of Dirs Cyprus Inst. of Neurology & Genetics; mem. Advisory Bd, Diplomatic Acad., Univ. of Nicosia; mem. Bd of Trustees, Cyprus Inst.; Hon. mem. Cttee of Independent Social Support Body 2015–; Grand Cross, Order of the Phoenix (Greece), Golden Order for Services in Diplomacy (Slovenia); Man of the Year Award, Cyprus Hotel Asscn 2007, Lifetime Achievement Award, Cyprus Investment Promotion Agency 2014. *Publications:* Cyprus Diplomacy: A Personal Testimony (in Greek, English and Russian) 2010; contribs to Anthology of Young Cypriot Poets, Justice Pending: Indigenous Peoples and Other Good Causes; numerous articles in Cypriot newspapers. *Address:* RCB Bank Ltd, 2, Amathountos Street, POB 56868, 3310 Limassol, Cyprus (office). *Fax:* (22) 342192 (office). *E-mail:* rcb@rcbcy.com (office). *Website:* www.rcbcy.com (office).

ZACKIOS, Gerald M.; Marshall Islands/Palau politician and lawyer; *Ambassador to USA;* b. 1 April 1965; m. Viola Milne; nine c.; ed Univ. of Papua New Guinea, Int. Maritime Law Inst.; Attorney-Gen. 1995–2001; mem. Parl. for Arno Atoll 1999–2011; Minister of Foreign Affairs and Minister in Assistance to Pres., then Minister of Foreign Affairs 2001–08, also of Trade 2001–07, Amb. to USA 2016–; Dir North Pacific Regional Office, Secr. of the Pacific Community, Pohnpei, Federated States of Micronesia 2013–16; mem. Council and Bd of Regents, Univ. of the South Pacific; mem. Bd of Dirs Coll. of the Marshall Islands, Majuro Cooperative Schools, Assumption School System. *Address:* Embassy of the Republic of the Marshall Islands to the United States, 2433 Massachusetts Avenue NW, Washington DC 20008, USA (office). *Telephone:* (202) 234-5414 (office). *Fax:* (202) 232-3236 (office). *E-mail:* info@rmiembassyus.org (office). *Website:* www.rmiembassyus.org (office).

ZADORNOV, Mikhail Mikhailovich, Cand.Econ., PhD; Russian politician, economist and banker; b. 4 May 1963, Moscow; s. of Mikhail Zadornov and Raisa Zadornova; m. Natalya Zadornova 1982; one d.; ed G. Plekhanov Inst. of Nat. Econ.; mem. State Comm. on Econ. Reform, Russian Council of Ministers 1990–91; mem. State Duma (Parl.) (Yabloko faction) 1993–97, 1999–2003, re-elected as ind. 2003; Chair., Cttee on Budget, Taxation, Banks and Finances 1994–97; Minister of Finance 1997–99; Special Rep. of Pres. Boris Yeltsin, rank of First Deputy Prime Minister, in negotiations with int. financial orgs 1998–99; Deputy Chair. Cttee on Budget and Taxes, Chair. Sub-Cttee on Monetary Policy, Exchange and Capital Control and the Activities of the Cen. Bank of the Russian Fed. 1999–2003; apptd Pres. and Chair. VTB24 (jt stock bank) 2005–, Chair. VTB Insurance 2007–17, Council mem. VTB Bank (Armenia) 2016–18, mem. Supervisory Council (Georgia) 2016–18; Pres. and Chair. of Bd Otkritie FC Bank 2018–; Chair. JSC TransCreditBank 2011, Insurance Group MSK 2011–16, Transcapitalbank CJSC 2011–13; mem. Bd of Dirs Bank of Moscow 2011–16, OAO Svyazinvest; mem. Supervisory Council, Pochta Bank 2012–, Fed. State Autonomous Educational Inst. of Higher Professional Educ., Nat. Research Univ., Higher School of Econs 2014–; one of authors of Programme of Econ. Reforms 500 Days. *Publica-*

tions: more than 20 books; numerous articles on Russia's financial problems. *Leisure interest:* playing football.

ZAERA-POLO, Alejandro; Spanish architect; b. 17 Oct. 1963, Madrid; ed Escuela Técnica Superior de Arquitectura de Madrid, Harvard Univ. Grad. School of Design, USA; worked at Office for Metropolitan Architecture, Rotterdam 1991–93; moved to work in London, UK 1993; has worked for Rem Koolhaas, Rotterdam, Netherlands, Zaha Hadid, London, Renzo Piano, Genoa Italy; fmr Unit Master at Architectural Asscn School of Architecture; fmr Visiting Critic, UCLA, Columbia Univ., New York, Princeton Univ., School of Architecture, Madrid, Yokohama School of Architecture; co-f. Foreign Office Architects with ex-wife Farshid Moussavi (q.v.) 1992, later Dir, rep. Britain, Architecture Biennale, Venice 2002, co. dissolved 2011; est. Alejandro Zaera-Polo Architecture (AZPA), London 2011 (renamed Alejandro Zaera-Polo & Maider Llaguno Architecture (AZPML) 2013); holder of Berlage Chair, Delft Univ. for six years; Dean, Berlage Inst. 2002–06, School of Architecture at Princeton Univ. 2012–14 (Visiting Prof. 2008); first Norman Foster Visiting Prof., Yale Univ. 2009; fmr adviser, Quality Comm. for Architecture, Barcelona, Urban Age Think Tank of the LSE; contrib. El Croquis, Quaderns, A. D.; Enric Miralles Prize for Architecture 2003, Kanagawa Prize for Architecture in Japan 2003, RIBA Int. Award 2004, 2005, 2006, Lion Award for Topography, 9th Venice Architecture Biennale 2004, Charles Jencks Award for Architecture 2005, RIBA European Award 2008, European Business Award for the Environment 2008, Urban Land Inst. Award for Excellence 2008, RIBA Award 2009, Civic Trust Award 2010, Int. Council of Shopping Centres Award 2010, Int. Architecture Award 2010. *Works include:* Foreign Office Architects: Osanbashi Yokohama Int. Passenger Terminal, Japan 1995–2002, Bluemoon Hotel, Groningen, The Netherlands 1999–2000, Police HQ, La Villajoyosa, Spain 2000–03, Coastal park with outdoor auditoriums, Barcelona, Spain 2000–04, HQ for Dulnyouk Publrs, Paju, South Korea 2000–05, Municipal Theatre, Torrevieja, Spain 2000–06, John Lewis dept store and Cineplex and pedestrian bridges, Leicester, UK 2000–08, mixed-use extension of West Quay II retail centre, Southampton 2002–, La Rioja Tech. Transfer Centre, Logrono 2003–07, Trinity EC3 office complex, City of London 2003–, Bamboo Bldg, social housing in Madrid 2004–07, villa in Pedralbes, Barcelona 2004–08, D-38 Office Complex, Barcelona 2004–09, Spanish Pavilion at 2005 Int. Expo, Aichi 2004–05, Meydan Retail Complex and Multiplex, Istanbul 2005–07, Ravensbourne Coll., Greenwich Peninsula, London 2005–, Hadspen Gardens, Somerset, UK 2005–, The Palace Residential Towers, Busan, South Korea 2006–11, Museum of Contemporary Art, Cleveland, Ohio 2006–, KL Cen. Plot D Residential Towers, Kuala Lumpur 2006–, Sevenstone Quarter mixed-use complex, Sheffield, UK 2007–, Euston Station, London 2008–, Birmingham New Street Station 2008–; AZPML: Gapyong Community Centre, South Korea 2010–, 2014 ISAF Sailing World Championship Facilities, Santander, Spain 2011–, Hosp. Universitari Arnau de Vilanova, Lleida, Spain 2011–, BioPol Science Centre, Barcelona 2011–, Locarno Palazzo del Cinema, Switzerland 2013–. *Publications:* has published extensively as a critic in professional magazines world-wide; work featured in El Croquis, Quaderns, A+U, Arch+, Harvard Design Magazine; contribs to numerous publs. *Address:* AZPML, 55 Curtain Road, London EC2A 3PT, England (office). *Telephone:* (20) 7033-6480 (office). *Fax:* (20) 7033-6481 (office). *E-mail:* lon@ azpml.com (office). *Website:* azpml.com (office).

ZAEV, Zoran; Macedonian politician; *Prime Minister;* b. 8 Oct. 1974, Strumica, Socialist Repub. of Macedonia, Socialist Fed. Repub. of Yugoslavia; ed Univ. of Skopje; mem. Socijaldemokratski Sojuz na Makedonija (SDSM—Social Democratic Alliance of Macedonia) 1996–, Pres. regional admin of the party in Strumica region for two mandates, Deputy Chair. SDSM 2008–13, Chair. 2013–; mem. Macedonian Ass. 2003–05; Mayor of Strumica 2005–16; Leader of Opposition 2013–17; arrested along with five co-workers for alleged abuse of office and imprisoned July 2008, released by order of Pres. Branko Crvenkovski; charged with "conspiring with a foreign intelligence service to topple the government" Jan. 2015 (case dropped due to insufficient evidence); Prime Minister 2017–; Ewald von Kleist Prize 2019. *Address:* Office of the Prime Minister, 1000 Skopje, Ilindenska b.b. 2, North Macedonia (office). *Telephone:* (2) 3118022 (office). *Fax:* (2) 3112561 (office). *E-mail:* primeminister@primeminister.gov.mk (office). *Website:* www .vlada.mk (office).

ZAGAJEWSKI, Adam, MA; Polish writer, poet and academic; *Ferdinand Schevill Distinguished Service Professor, John U. Nef Committee on Social Thought, University of Chicago;* b. 21 June 1945, Lviv; s. of Tadeusz Zagajewski and Ludwika Zagajewska; m. Maria Zagajewska; ed Jagiellonian Univ., Kraków; taught at AGH Univ. of Science and Tech., Univ. of Houston, Univ. of Chicago; first published poetry and essays in literary reviews in 1960s; became known as leading poet of 'Generation of 1968'; first collection of poems 1972; lived in France and joined staff of Zeszyty Literackie 1982–2002; Assoc. Prof. of English, Creative Writing Program, Univ. of Houston, USA 1988–2007; Prof. of Social Thought, Univ. of Chicago 2007, currently Ferdinand Schevill Distinguished Service Prof.; mem. Polish Writers' Asscn, PEN Club; co-ed. Zeszyty Literackie; Order of Legion d'Honneur 2016, Bronze Cross of Merit, twice awarded Officer's Cross of the Order of Polonia Restituta; Dr hc (Jagiellonian Univ.) 2012; Koscielscy Foundation Award 1975, Andrzej Kijowski Award 1987, Alfred Jurzykowski Foundation Award 1989, Guggenheim Fellowship 1992, Int. Vilenica Prize (Slovenia) 1996, Tomas Transtromer Prize (Sweden) 2000, Neustadt Int. Prize for Fiction 2004, Zhongkun Int. Poetry Prize (China) 2013, Heinrich Mann Prize 2015, Griffin Poetry Prize Lifetime Recognition Award 2016, Dr. Leopold Lucas Prize, Univ. of Tübingen 2016. *Publications include:* collections of poetry: Komunikat (Communique) 1972, Sklepy miesne (Meat Shops) 1975, Letter: An Ode to Multiplicity 1983, Jechac do Lwowa (Travelling to Lvov) 1985, Plotno (The Canvas) 1990, Ziemia ognista (The Fiery Land) 1994, Pragnienie (Desire) 2000, Powrót (Without End) 2003, Anteny 2005, Unseen Hand 2009, Wiersze wybrane 2010; novels: Cieplo, zimno (Warm and Cold) 1975, Cienka kreska (The Thin Line) 1983, Absolute Pitch (in German); short stories: Two Cities 1991, Another Beauty 2002; essays: Swiat nie przedstawiony (The Unpresented World, with Julian Kornhauser) 1974, Drugi oddech (Second Wind) 1978, Solidarnosc i samotnosc (Solidarity and Solitude) 1986, W cudzym pieknie (In the Beauty of Others) 1998, Obrona żarliwości (In Defence of Fervour) 2002, Poeta rozmawia z filozofem 2007; trans.: Tremor 1987, Mysticism for Beginners: Poems 1999, Selected Poems 2004, Eternal Enemies: Poems 2014, A Defense of Ardor: Essays 2014. *Leisure interests:* walking, reading. *Address:* John U. Nef Committee on Social Thought, Division of the Social Sciences, University of Chicago, 1130 East 59th Street, Chicago, IL 60637, USA (office). *Telephone:* (773) 702-8408 (office). *E-mail:* adamz@uchicago.edu (office). *Website:* socialthought.uchicago.edu (office).

ZAGALLO, Mário Jorge Lobo; Brazilian professional football manager and fmr professional footballer; b. 9 Aug. 1931, Maceió; inside forward; began footballer career with América FC 1948–49; player for Fluminese, Flamengo 1950–58, Botafogo 1958–65; played for Brazil 1958–64 (33 appearances, five goals), played in World Cup Final 1958, 1962; Man. clubs: Botafogo 1966–70, Fluminense 1971–72, Flamengo 1972–74, 1984–85, 2000–01, Botafogo 1975, 1978–79, 1986–87, Al Hilal 1978–79, Vasco da Gama 1980–81, 1990–91, Bangu 1988–89, Portuguesa 1999–2000; first footballer to attain World Championship as player and then man.; coached Brazilian football team for 1970, 1974 and 1998 World Cups, adviser to nat. coach Brazil 1994–99, 2006; nat. coach Kuwait 1976–78, Saudi Arabia 1981–84, UAE 1989–90; brief return to manage Brazil nat. team for Nov. 2002 friendly against S Korea in Seoul while successor to outgoing man. was sought then Brazil coordinator 2003–06; Adviser, nat. football team of Lebanon 2011–; FIFA World Cup winning man. 1970, FIFA Confederations Cup winning man. 1997.

ZAGHEN, Paolo, PhD; Brazilian economist and banker; *Partner, Equitas Investimentos;* b. Crema, Italy; ed Univ. of São Paulo, Univ. of California, Berkeley, USA; Prof., FEA-USP for 22 years; Partner-Dir, Lucro DTVM Ltd 1988–91; Open Market Dir, Banespa Securities and Exchange Brokers; Chief Financial Officer and Public Relations Dir, Paranapanema Mining, Industry and Construction 1994–96; Dir, Cen. Bank 1996–99; Pres. Bank of Brazil SA 1999–2001, Chair. Bank of Brazil SA and Pres. BrasilCap 2001; mem. Bd of Dirs Visa Latin America 1999–2001; Chair. Brazil Bd of Health 1999–2001; currently Partner, Equitas Investimentos, mem. Asset Man. Investment Cttee 2006–07. *Address:* Equitas Investimentos, Rua Gomes de Carvalho, 1666 cj 162, Vila Olimpia, 04547-006 São Paulo, SP, Brazil. *Telephone:* (11) 3049-3300. *Fax:* (11) 3049-3305. *Website:* www.equitas.com.br.

ZAGLER, Wolfgang L., PhD; Austrian scientist, electrical engineer and academic; *Professor, Vienna University of Technology;* b. 1951, Vienna; ed Vienna Univ. of Technology; joined Institut für Industrielle Elektronik und Materialwissenschaften 1976; currently Prof., Vienna Univ. of Tech. and Head of fortec; Vice-Pres. AAL Austria—Innovationsplattform für intelligente Assistenz im Alltag 2012–16; mem. Scientific Advisory Bd Österreichische Plattform für Interdisziplinäre Alternsfragen 2010–16; mem. Int. Soc. for Gerontechnology 2008–16; Senator Holzer Prize 1986, Hans Lauda Innovation Award 1987, Victor Kaplan Medal 1992, Wilhelm Exner Medal, Austrian Asscn for SME (Oesterreichischer Gewerbeverein—OGV) (jtly) 2007, Wundsam-Hartig Prize 2006, European ICT Grand Prize, EU 2007. *Achievements include:* carried out research and devt of automatic seam following devices for precision welding equipment using optical pattern recognition; also developed a reading machine for assisting blind and visually impaired persons. *Publications:* Computers and Assistive Technology: ICCHP '98 Proceedings of the XV IFIP World Computer Congress (co-ed.) 1998, Computers Helping People with Special Needs: 10th International Conference, ICCHP 2006, Linz, Austria (Proceedings) 2006, Computers Helping People with Special Needs (with Joachim Klaus, Klaus Miesenberger and Dominique Burger), Strafvollzugsrecht. Österreichisches Recht; numerous papers in professional journals. *Address:* Institute of Design and Assessment of Technology, Centre for Applied Assistive Technologies, Favoritenstraße 11/187-2b, 1040 Vienna, Austria (office). *Telephone:* (1) 58801-187700 (office); 664-60588-4290 (mobile). *Fax:* (1) 58801-187799 (office). *E-mail:* zagler@fortec.tuwien.ac.at (office); zw@fortec .tuwien.ac.at (office). *Website:* www.aat.tuwien.ac.at (office).

ZAHAR, Mahmoud al-; Palestinian physician and government official; b. 1945, Zeitoun neighbourhood of Gaza City; m. Summaya az-Zahar; four c. (one s. deceased); ed Cairo Univ. and Ain Shams Univ., Egypt; spent much of his youth in Egypt; returned to occupied territories to lecture at Dept of Medicine of newly created Islamic Univ. of Gaza 1971; joined local offshoot of the Muslim Brotherhood; Co-founder (with Sheikh Ahmed Yassin), spokesperson and sr official, Islamic Resistance Movt (Hamas—Harakat al-Muqawama al-Islamiyya) 1987, unofficial rep. to Palestinian Liberation Org. 1990, deported to South Lebanon 1992, returned to Gaza 1993, arrested several times by Palestinian security forces and spent seven months in a Palestinian jail, his home in Gaza bombed and destroyed 2003, became a mem. of "collective leadership" of militant group after Sheikh Yassin and Abdel-Aziz Rantissi had been assassinated 2004; Minister of Foreign Affairs 2006–07 (resgnd). *Address:* c/o Harakat al-Muqawama al-Islamiyya, Gaza, Palestinian Territories.

ZAHARIEVA, Ekaterina, LLB, LLM; Bulgarian lawyer and politician; *Deputy Prime Minister, responsible for Justice Reforms, and Minister of Foreign Affairs;* b. 8 Aug. 1975, Pazardzhik; ed Paisii Hilendarski Univ. of Plovdiv, Ecole Nationale d'Admin, Paris, European Comm. for Democracy Through Law (Venice Commission) of the Council of Europe, Inst. of Public Admin, Dublin, Ireland, Bertholt Brecht Foreign Language School, Pazardjik; practised law 2001–03; legal adviser, Ministry of Environment and Water 2003–07, Dir of Legal, Admin. and Regulatory Services 2007–09; Deputy Minister of Regional Devt and Public Works 2009–12; Chief Sec. to Pres. 2012–13; Deputy Prime Minister and Minister of Regional Devt and Public Works in caretaker govt March–May 2013; Deputy Prime Minister for Econ. Policy, Minister of Regional Devt and Minister of Investment in caretaker govt Aug.–Nov. 2014; Minister of Justice 2015–17; mem. Grazhdani za Evropeysko Razvitie na Balgariya (GERB—Citizens for European Devt of Bulgaria); mem. Parl. (GERB) for Pazardzhik 2017–; Deputy Prime Minister, responsible for Justice Reforms, and Minister of Foreign Affairs 2017–; Commdr's Cross, Order of Merit of the Repub. of Poland; Honour Badge of the Union of Bulgarian Jurists. *Address:* Ministry of Foreign Affairs, 1113 Sofia, ul. Al. Zhendov 2, Bulgaria (office). *Telephone:* (2) 948-29-99 (office). *Fax:* (2) 971-36-20 (office). *E-mail:* crisis@ mfa.bg (office). *Website:* www.mfa.bg (office).

ZAHIR, Ahmed, BA; Maldivian politician and journalist; *Minister of Islamic Affairs;* b. 26 Sept. 1945; m.; one s. two d.; teacher until 1978; journalist for Reuters and Asia Week –1978; fmr Project Officer (Marubeni), Dept of Tourism and Foreign Investment, Asst Dir Tourism Section, then Dir, Dir-Gen. Dept of Tourism; Deputy Minister Ministry of Tourism, Attorney-Gen.'s Office; fmr Minister of Transport and Shipping, of Transport and Communications, of Justice, of Islamic Affairs 2018–; mem. People's Majlis (Parl.), Deputy Speaker –2004, Speaker 2004–08, chaired numerous standing cttees; mem. Bd of Dirs Maldives Nat. Ship Man. Ltd; mem. Maldives Press Council, Judicial Service Comm. 2008–; fmr Publr and Ed. Hafta weekly newspaper; led three parl. dels including the first Maldivian parl. del. to an int. conf.; Presidential Award for Meritorious Work in Journalism 1980, Golden Pen Award on 50th Anniversary of Maldivan Journalism 1993. *Publication:* A Guide Book on Saudi Arabia. *Address:* Ministry of Islamic Affairs, Islamic Centre, Blk 77, Medhuziyaaraimagu, Malé 20–156, The Maldives (office). *Telephone:* 3020200 (office). *Fax:* 3315161 (office). *E-mail:* info@ islamicaffairs.gov.mv (office). *Website:* islamicaffairs.gov.mv (office).

ZAHIR, Maj.-Gen. Mohamed; Maldivian army officer (retd); m. Fathimath Amira; four s. one d.; ed Hendon Police Coll., London, UK, Naval Postgraduate School, Monterey, Calif., USA, Sr Execs in Nat. and Int. Security Program, John F. Kennedy School of Govt, USA; joined civil service and worked in various Govt Depts before enlisting in Maldives Nat. Defence Force (MNDF—fmrly Nat. Security Service (NSS)) 1978, promoted to rank of Sergeant and commissioned as officer 1980, undertook various command positions within different units of MNDF, Deputy Chief of Staff, MNDF –1996, also commanded MNDF Defence Inst. for Training and Educ. (fmrly known as NSS Training Unit), promoted to rank of Brig., Chief of Staff, MNDF 1996–2008, promoted to rank of Maj.-Gen. 2004, Chair. MNDF Advisory Council; Nat. Security Adviser to Pres. Mohamed Nasheed 2008–10; Medal for Exceptional Bravery 1988, Presidential Medal, Distinguished Service Medal, Dedicated Service Medal, Medal of Honour 2008.

ZAHRA, Trevor; Maltese writer and illustrator; b. 16 Dec. 1947, Zejtun; m. Stella Zahra (deceased); one s. one d.; ed Teachers' Coll. of Educ.; mem. Maltese Acad. of Writers; Council mem. Nat. Book Council; Medal for Services to Repub. (Malta) in recognition for commitment to children's literature 2004; First Prize, Book Club, Malta 1974, Rothmas Award (co-winner) 1975, Nat. Literary Award (19 times). *Publications include:* Il-Pulena tad-Deheb (adventure story) 1971, Eden (poety) 1972, Il-Ghar tax-Xelter (adventure story) 1972, Dawra Durella (poetry for children) 1972, Dwal fil-Fortizza (adventure story) 1973, Is-Surmast (novel) 1973, Il-Praspar ta' Kuncett u Marinton (humorous short stories) 1974, Il-Kaxxa taz-Ziju (adventure story) 1974, Taht il-Weraq tal-Palm (novel) 1974, Praspar Ohra ta' Kuncett u Marinton (humorous short stories) 1975, Hdejn in-Nixxiegha (novel) 1975, Grajjiet in-Nannu Cens (humorous short stories) 1975, Qamar Ahdar (adventure story) 1976, Villa Siko-Sao 1977, Hmistax-il Numru 1977, Meta Jaqa' c-Cpar 1978, Il-Miraklu tal-Gizirana 1981, It-Tmien Kontinent 1981, Trid Kukkarda Hamra f'Gieh il-Biza'? 1982, Il-Praspar Kollha ta' Kuncett u Marinton 1983, Darba Kien Hemm Sultan 1984, LogHob Merill 1985, Qrempucu f'Belt il-Gobon 1985, Il-Ktieb tal-Fenek l-Ahmar 1986, Holm tal-Milied? 1987, Kliem ix-Xih 1988, Rigal tal-Milied 1989, Stella, Jien u HU 1990, Tlieta f'Wiehed 1994, Is-Surmast 1994, Fuklar Qadim u Bnadar Imcarrta 1995, Is-Seba' Trongiet Mewwija 1995, Hanut tal-Helu 1995, Lubien 1996, Taht Sema Kwiekeb 1997, Naqra Storja Zghra 1997, Sib it-Tezor 1999, Passiggata 1999, Mar id-Dawl 1999, Borma Minestra 1999, Koronata Traskurata 2000, Provenz 2000, Zvelajrin 2001, Mincott Hajt Iswed 2001, X'Tixtiequ Jaghmel il-Fenek? 2002, Din l-Art u Kull ma Fiha 2002, Il-Kotba ghat-Tfal 2002, Kieku Kieku 2005, Sfidi 2005, Kemm Naf Inpingi 2005, Ojnk Ojnk 2005, Krispella 2005, Il-Genn li jzommni f'Sikkti (autobiog.) 2008, Il-Hajja Sigrieta tan-Nanna Genoveffa (novel) 2008, Principessa 2009, Xi Jhobb jiekol id-Dragun 2009, 'Il Boghod mill-Habs 2009, Penumbra (short stories) 2010, Hadd Ma Jista' Jidhak (children's fiction trilogy) 2010, Penumbra (short stories) 2010, Vespri (short stories) 2015, The Secret Life of Nanna Genoveffa (novel). *Address:* 23 Qrempuc Street, Marsaskala MSK- 2205, Malta (home). *Telephone:* (356) 21632944 (home). *E-mail:* zahratrevor@gmail.com (home). *Website:* www .trevorzahra.com.

ZAHRADNÍK, Rudolf, DSc, DipEng; Czech physical chemist and academic; b. 20 Oct. 1928, Bratislava; s. of Rudolf Zahradník and Jindřiška Zahradníková; m. Milena Zahradníková; one d.; ed Czech Tech. Univ., Prague; scientific worker Inst. of Hygiene and Occupational Diseases, Prague 1952–61, Inst. of Physical Chem. and Electrochemistry, Acad. of Sciences, Prague 1961–93; Prof., Charles Univ., Prague 1967–; Guest Prof., Univs of Würzburg 1965, Darmstadt 1966, Groningen 1967, Osaka 1977, Basel 1981, Vanderbilt Univ. 1990; Dir Jaroslav Heyrovský Inst. of Physical Chem. and Electrochemistry Prague 1990–93; Pres. Czech Acad. of Sciences 1993–2001, apptd Hon. Pres. 2001; Pres. Czech Learned Soc. 1994–97; mem. many academic and scientific socs including Int. Acad. of Quantum Molecular Sciences 1982–, World Asscn of Theoretical Organic Chemists, European Acad. of Arts, Science and Literature, Ed. Council Special Journals; Hon. mem. Swiss and German Chemical Socs 1988, Hon. Pres. Acad. of Czech Repub. 2001; Cross of Honour (First Class) for Science and Arts (Austria) 1999, Chevalier dans l' Ordre des Palmes Académiques 2003; Dr hc (Dresden, Fribourg, Pardubice, Georgetown, Prague, Bratislava, Clarkson, Waterloo, Montreal); Jaroslav Heyrovský Golden Plaque Czech Acad. of Sciences 1990, Medal for Merit, Prague 1998, Emil Votočka Medal, Institute of Chemical Technology, Charles Univ. Gold Medal, Gold Medal, Slovak Chemical Soc., Heyrovský Medal 2013. *Publications include:* Organic Quantum Chemistry Problems (with P. Cársky) 1973, Elements of Quantum Chemistry (with R. Polák) 1976, Intermolecular Complexes (with P. Hobza) 1988, Thinking as Passion (with Lenka Jaklová) 1998, Rule of Sense 2002, Laboratory Diary 2008; author of 350 research papers and articles. *Leisure interests:* serious music and literature. *Address:* Dolejškova 3, 182 23, Prague 8, Czech Republic (home). *Telephone:* (2) 66052067 (home). *Fax:* (2) 86582307 (home).

ZAID, Yahya Abdul Kareem al-; Saudi Arabian diplomatist and fmr oil industry executive; ed Univ. of Colorado, USA; worked for Saudi Aramco (state-owned nat. oil co.) 1993–2006, roles included Man. Yanbu Petromin Refinery, Gen. Petroleum & Mineral Org. (PETROMIN), Sr Vice-Pres. Saudi Arabian Marketing & Refining Co. (SAMAREC), Vice-Pres. of Sales and Marketing, Aramco, Head of Jazan refinery initiative; Adviser to Minister of Petroleum and Mineral Resources 2006–08; Amb. to People's Repub. of China 2008–15; fmr Chair. Saudi Petroleum

Ltd, SASREF Saudi Petroleum Overseas Ltd; fmr Dir Petromin-Ashland JV, Petroserve, Yanbu Refinery Co.

ZAIDI, Syed Nasim Ahmed, PhD, MPA; Indian civil servant; b. 6 July 1952, Dehradun; s. of Aqil Ahmad and Hasnain Ahmad (née Fatima); m. Umm E. Rabab Zaidi; ed Indian Inst. of Finance, John F. Kennedy School of Govt, Harvard Univ., USA; joined Indian Admin. Service (IAS) from UP cadre 1976, first posting as Asst Collector of Unnao Dist, subsequent posts include Jt Sec. in Civil Aviation Ministry, Commr of Bareilly Devt Authority, Collector of Ghaziabad and Farukkhabad Dists in UP, Dir-Gen. of Civil Aviation (Perm. Rep. of India on Council of Int. Civil Aviation Org. 2005–08), retd from IAS as Sec. to Govt of India in Ministry of Civil Aviation 2012; Election Commr 2012–15, Chief Election Commr 2015–17; Mason Fellow for Public Policy, Harvard Inst. for Int. Devt. *Publications include:* Green Aviation 2013; several papers in scientific and admin. journals. *Telephone:* (11) 23014243 (home). *Fax:* (11) 23014343 (home).

ZAINUDDIN, Tun Daim, LLB; Malaysian business executive, lawyer, economist and fmr politician; b. 29 April 1938, Alor Star, Kedah State; ed Sultan Abdul Hamid Coll., St Xavier's Inst., Penang, Lincoln's Inn, London, UK; called to the Bar, Lincoln's Inn, London 1959; worked in chambers of Pillai & Co., later in chambers of Shearn Delamore; Pvt. legal practice, Kota Bharu, Kelantan 1960–62; joined Malaysian Civil Service as a Magistrate in Johor Baru, Johor 1962–63, Sessions Court Judge, Muar, Johor 1963–64, Deputy Public Prosecutor in Ipoh, Perak 1964–65; returned to Kuala Lumpur and joined law firm of Allen & Gledhill 1965–68; est. own law practice of Daim & Gamany 1968–69; first business venture in salt production 1969, then plastics production, later land and property devt with founding of Syarikat Maluri Sdn Bhd 1971; Owner Indo-Suez (renamed Malaysian-French Bank) 1981, exchanged majority stake for a smaller stake in the larger United Malayan Banking Corpn; Founder-Chair. Int. Commercial Banking Group 2001–; fmr Chair. Peremba, Fleet Holdings, Syarikat Televisyen Malaysia (TV3), Rakyat First Merchant Bankers; Visiting Scholar, Univ. of California, Berkeley, USA 1977–79, Harvard Inst. of Int. Devt 1991–92; Visiting Fellow, Univ. of Cambridge, UK 2002–03; mem. Dewan Negara (Senate) 1980–82; mem. Dewan Rakat (House of Reps) for Kuala Muda, Kedah 1982–86, for Merbok, Kedah 1986–2004; Minister of Finance 1984–91; Treas. of UMNO 1984, Barisan Nasional 1985; apptd Exec. Dir Nat. Econ. Action Council 1997; Econ. Adviser to Prime Minister Mahathir bin Mohammad; Minister of Finance Jan.–Nov. 1999, Minister of Finance and Minister of Special Functions Dec. 1999–2001; mem. Lembaga Pemegang Amanah Yayasan Pelaburan Bumiputra 1984–91; Chair. Northern Growth Triangle project (IMT-GT) between Thailand, Indonesia and Malaysia and Special Rep. for East Asean Growth (EAGA) between Philippines, Brunei, Indonesia and Malaysia 1992–2000, Labuan Devt Authority 1992–2000, Kumpulan Ladang-Ladang Perbadanan Kedah Sdn Bhd 1997–98, Internal Audit Cttee Asian Football, Kuala Lumpur; apptd Vice-Chair. Malaysian Business Council (Majlis Perdagangan Malaysia) 1991; Jt Chair. Langkawi Devt Authority; Founder-mem. Malaysian Wetlands Foundation 1997–99; mem. Bd of Govs, East-West Center, Hawaii, USA 2002, mem. East-West Center Audit Cttee, Bd of Trustees, Multimedia Univ., Malaysia, Coca-Cola's Malaysia Advisory Group 2009; Adjunct Prof., Univ. Utara Malaysia 1991–98; Pro-Chancellor, Univ. Sains Malaysia 1994–98; spends most of his time in Africa, engaging African govts on economy and planning; Grand Commdr of the Order of Loyalty to the Crown of Malaysia 1991; Highest Distinguished Award, Govt of Repub. of Benin 2006, Int. Business Leader Award, African Investor magazine 2006, Distinguished Assoc., Asia-Europe Inst., Univ. of Malaya 2011. *Publications:* Asian Economic Co-operation Agenda for the 1990's 1990, Managing Business: My Personal Experience 1995, Daim: The Man behind the Enigma 1995, Daim, Insan Di Sebalik Enigma 1996, Daim Speaks His Mind 1996, Daim Yang Diam, Sebuah Biografi 1997, War of Deception: The Facts and Fallacies about the War in Iraq 2004. *Leisure interests:* travelling, reading and writing on general global issue. *Address:* ICB Banking Group, Kuala Lumpur, Malaysia (office). *Telephone:* (3) 6201-6051 (office). *Fax:* (3) 6201-6053 (office). *E-mail:* kugan@icbglobal.com.my (office). *Website:* www.icbankingroup.com (office); daimzainuddin.com.

ZAITSEV, Vyacheslav Mikhailovich (Slava); Russian fashion designer and couturier; *President and Chief Designer, Slava Zaitsev Fashion House;* b. 2 March 1938, Ivanovo; s. of Mikhail Yakovlevich Zaitsev and Maria Ivanovna Zaitseva; one s.; ed Moscow Textile Inst.; chief designer, All-Union Fashion House 1965–78; chief designer, Moscow Fashion House 'Slava Zaitsev' 1982–, Pres. 1991–; participates in Paris fashion shows 1988–; Co-Chair. of Jury, Night of Fashion, Paris 1989; served as Pres. of numerous fashion festivals including "Velvet Seasons in Sochi"; shows collections world-wide; Prof., Moscow Textile Inst.; has exhibited paintings in USA, Belgium, UK and Germany; Pres. Nat. Acad. of Fashion Industry; elected Corresp. mem. Russian Acad. of Arts 2001, full mem. 2007; Hon. Citizen of Paris 1988, Ivanovo 1996; Hon. Academician, Russian Acad. of Jewellery 2002; Order of St Constantine the Great 1996; Order 'For Services to the Fatherland', IVth Degree 1998; Constantine Order of St George 2002, Zolotoj orden Za sluzhenie iskusstvu 2008, Order of the Glory of Russia 2008; Dr hc (Moscow State Technical Univ.) 2004; Medal 'For Labour Valour' 1974, 'Badge of Honour' 1980, Medal 'Veteran of Labour' 1987, The Five Best Fashion Designers of the World 1989; First Prize, 'Golden Mannequin' for Fashion Week in Moscow 1995, Silver Spindle with Gold Thread prize, Russian Fashion Week 1995, State Prize of Russian Fed. 1996, Medal 'For Merits in Development of Design' 2002, Medal 'Professional of Russia' 2004, Nat. Award 'Best of the Best' 2004, Large Silver Medal numbered outstanding figure of world culture of Sergei Diaghilev 2006, Medal 'Professional of Russia' 2006, Best Designer Award (Japan) 1989, Laureate of State Prize of Russian Fed. *Publications:* The Changing Fashion 1980, This Many-Faced World of Fashion 1980. *Leisure interest:* painting. *Address:* Moscow Fashion House, Prospekt Mira 21, 129110 Moscow, Russia (office). *Telephone:* (495) 971-11-22 (office). *Fax:* (495) 281-55-75 (office). *E-mail:* slava@zaitsev.info (office). *Website:* www.zaitsev.info (office).

ZAITSEV, Yury Vladimirovich, DTechSc; Russian engineer and diplomatist; b. 2 Aug. 1933, Moscow; m.; two d.; ed Kuibyshev Moscow Inst. of Construction Eng, Diplomatic Acad. Ministry of Foreign Affairs; Sr researcher Centre for Inst. of Scientific Information on Construction and Architecture, USSR Acad. of Construction and Architecture 1958–59, Research Inst. of Concrete and Reinforced Concrete 1959–64; Prof., Head of Chair., Pro-Rector All-Union Polytechnic Inst. by correspondence 1964–90; Chair. Comm. on Problems of Citizenship at Supreme Soviet, then with Russian Presidency 1990–92; mem. Supreme Soviet of Russian Fed. 1990–93; Perm. Rep. of Russia at int. orgs in Vienna 1992–97; First Deputy Head, Internal Policy Dept of Pres. Yeltsin's Admin 1997–98; mem. Acad. of Tech. Sciences, Acad. of Natural Sciences, Acad. of Eng. *Publications include:* 18 monographs, textbooks, over 200 articles in scientific journals.

ZAKAREISHVILI, Paata; Georgian politician and government official; b. 4 Aug. 1958, Tbilisi, Georgian SSR, USSR; m.; four c.; ed Kazan State Univ., Russian SFSR, Tbilisi Ecclesiastical Acad. and Seminary; Head of Div. of Religious Rights Protection, State Cttee on Human Rights and People-to-People Relations 1992–95; Head of Comm. for Protection of Civilians in Conflict Zone, Missing Persons and Prisoners of War during Georgian–Abkhazian conflict 1992–97; Adviser to Council of Ministers of Autonomous Repub. of Abkhazia on issues of Internally Displaced Persons and Refugees 1995; Forced Migration Project Coordinator, Open Soc. Foundation, New York 1995–97; Head of Staff, Cttee for Nat. Minority Issues and Human Rights Protection, Parl. of Georgia 1995–2000; Deputy Chair. Penitentiary Dept of Georgia 2000–01; mem. Exec. Bd Open Soc. Inst.—Georgia 2000–04; mem. Tbilisi Sakrebulo (City Council) 2002–06; Georgian Co-ordinator, California Univ. (Irvine) Georgian–Abkhazian Civil Dialogue project 1995–2012; Georgian Co-ordinator of Conciliation Resources (London), Georgian–Abkhazian projects and Georgian Co-ordinator of the 'Shlaining Process' 1998–2012; Chair. Inst. for Study of Nationalism and Conflict 2009–12; State Minister, responsible for Reintegration 2012–14, for Reconciliation and Civic Equality 2014–16 (resgnd).

ZAKARIA, Fareed, BA, PhD; American editor, academic, writer and television presenter; *Editor-at-Large, Time Magazine;* b. 20 Jan. 1964, India; m. Paula Throckmorton Zakaria; one s. two d.; ed Yale and Harvard Univs; Lecturer on Int. Politics and Econs, Harvard Univ., also Head of Project on the Changing Security Environment; Adjunct Prof., Columbia Univ., New York, Case Western Reserve Univ., Cleveland, OH; Man. Ed. Foreign Affairs journal 1992–2000; Ed. Newsweek Int. 2000–10, columnist, Newsweek (USA); Host and Man. Ed. Foreign Exchange with Fareed Zakaria (PBS Series) 2006–07; political commentator, ABC News 2006–07; host of Fareed Zakaria GPS, TV show on foreign affairs for CNN 2008–; Ed.-at-Large, Time Magazine 2010–; columnist, Washington Post 2001–; wine columnist for Slate (webzine); mem. Bd Trilateral Comm., IISS, Shakespeare and Co., The Century Asscn; Overseas Press Club Award, Deadline Club Award, Edwin Hood Award, India Abroad Person of the Year 2009, Padma Bhushan 2010, Ellis Island Medal of Honor 2017. *Publications include:* From Wealth to Power: The Unusual Origins of America's World Role, The American Encounter: The United States and the Making of the Modern World (co-ed.), The Future of Freedom 2003, The Post-American World 2008; contrib. to publs including The New York Times, The New Yorker and The Wall Street Journal. *Address:* CNN, 1 Constitution Avenue, NE, Washington, DC 20002-5618, USA (office). *Website:* globalpublicsquare.blogs.cnn.com (office); www.fareedzakaria.com (office).

ZAKAULLAH, Adm. Muhammad, MSc; Pakistani naval officer; b. 10 Jan. 1958; ed Royal Naval Staff Coll., UK, Nat. Defence Univ., Univ. of London, UK, Quaid-e-Azam Univ.; commissioned in Operations Branch, Pakistan Navy 1978, has held several command positions, including command of a destroyer and 25th Destroyer Squadron, Commdt, Pakistan Naval Acad., Commdr, Pakistan Fleet and Command of Multinational Maritime Task Force, staff appointments include Asst Chief of Naval Staff (Plans), Defence Attache, Embassy in Qatar, Dir-Gen. Nat. Accountability Bureau, Rawalpindi, Chief Inspector (Navy), Deputy Chief of Naval Staff (Training and Personnel), Naval Sec. and Deputy Chief of Naval Staff (Operations), Vice-Chief of Naval Staff, Naval Headquarters –2014, Chief of Naval Staff 2014–17; Gallant Commdr of Malaysian Armed Forces 2017; Sword of Honour and Chief of Naval Staff Gold Medal, Pakistan Naval Acad., Hilal-i-Imtiaz (Mil.), Sitara-i-Imtiaz (Military), Tamgha-i-Imtiaz (Mil.), Pres.'s Medal and Pres.'s Award for Pride of Performance. *Achievements include:* has represented Pakistan as yachtsman at numerous int. events, including 1984 Olympics, 1986 Asian Games, 1990 Asian Games; won Gold Medal at Asian Games twice and various awards at Int. Sailing Championships.

ZAKAYEV, Akhmed Khalidovich; Russian/Chechen rebel leader; b. 26 April 1956, Kirovskiy, Kazakh SSR, USSR; ed graduated from acting and choreography schools in Voronezh and Moscow; worked as actor at a Grozny theatre, specialized in Shakespearean roles; Chair. Chechen Union of Theatrical Actors 1991; field commdr, Chechen rebel movt 1994–96; 'Minister for Culture', 'Chechen Repub. of Ichkeriya' 1994; 'Deputy Prime Minister and Special Overseas Envoy' 1997–2002; 'Minister for Foreign Affairs' 1997–2007; 'Prime Minister of Chechen Repub. of Ichkeriya' Nov. 2007–09; living with immediate family in exile in London, UK since Jan. 2002, arrested in Poland Sept. 2010, but returned to London.

ZAKHARCHENKO, Maj.-Gen. Vitaliy Yuriyovych; Ukrainian police officer and politician; b. 20 Jan. 1963, Kostyantynivka, Donetsk Oblast; m. Lyudmyla Zakharchenko; two c.; ed Riga br. of Minsk Higher School of Interior of USSR; began career in police of Donetsk Oblast 1981; held leading positions in State Tax Admin in Poltava Oblast 2008–10, Head of State Tax Admin of Ukraine 2010–11; Minister of Internal Affairs 2011–14 (suspended by parl.).

ZAKHAROV, Aleksander Vladimirovich; Russian business executive; b. 3 Oct. 1955, Moscow; m.; three c.; ed G. Plekhanov Moscow Inst. of Nat. Econs, All-Union Acad. of Foreign Trade; expert, sr consultant, USSR Chamber of Industry and Commerce 1976–89; Deputy Rep., USSR Chamber of Industry and Commerce in Bulgaria 1989–91; Deputy Dir Centre on Interbank Currency Accounts USSR State Bank (Gosbank) Sept.–Dec. 1991; Dir, Moscow Interbank Currency Exchange (Micex) from 1992. *Leisure interests:* poetry, football. *Address:* c/o Moscow Interbank Currency Exchange (Micex), 125009 Moscow, Bolshoy Kislovskiy per. 13, Russian Federation. *E-mail:* globalexchange@moex.com.

ZAKHAROV, Mark Anatolievich; Russian theatre and film director and academic; *Artistic Director, Lenkom Theatre;* b. 13 Oct. 1933, Moscow; m. Nina Lapshinova; one d.; ed Lunacharsky Theatre Inst. (now Russian Acad. of Theatre Arts); actor since 1955; performed at Perm Regional Drama Theatre, Moscow Gogol Theatre; actor and Stage Dir, Moscow Theatre of Miniatures 1960–64, student theatre of Moscow State Univ. 1964–65; Stage Dir Moscow Satire Theatre 1965–73; Artistic Dir Lenkom Theatre (fmrly Moscow Theatre of Leninsky Komsomol) 1973–; teacher, Prof., Russian Acad. of Theatre Arts 1979–; mem.

Pres.'s Council 1996–98; Hon. mem. Russian Acad. of Arts; Order of Merit for the Fatherland 1997, 2003, 2008; People's Artist of the USSR 1988, State Prize of the USSR 1987, State Prizes of Russia 1992, 1997, 2003, Int. Stanislavsky Theatre Award 2010. *Plays directed include:* The Bankrupt by Alexander Ostrovsky 1967, Til by Grigory Gorin (after Charles de Koster) 1974, Juno and Avos by Andrey Voznesensky and Audrey Rybnikov 1981, Three Girls in Blue by Lyudmila Petrushevskaya 1985, Dictatorship of Conscience by Mikhail Shatrov 1986, The Commemorative Prayer by Grigory Gorin (after Sholom Aleihem) 1989, Wise Man by Alexander Ostrovsky 1989, The Marriage of Figaro by Beaumarchais 1993, The Seagull by Anton Chekhov 1994, Royal Games by Grigory Gorin 1995, Barbarian and Heretic (after Fyodor Dostoyevsky) 1997, The Mistification (after Dead Soles by Nickolay Gogol) 1998, The City of Millionaires by Eduardo de Philippo 2000, The Joker Balakirev by Grigory Gorin 2001, Va-Bank (after The Last Sacrifice by Alexander Ostrovsky) 2004. *Television films directed include:* Ordinary Wonder 1976, That Very Munchhausen 1979, The House That Swift Built 1983, The Formula of Love 1984, To Kill the Dragon 1989. *Film scripts:* author or co-author of scripts written for famous Russian films, including The Star of Fascinating Happiness, Sannikov's Land. *Publications include:* Contacts on Diverse Levels 1988, Super-Profession 2000; more than 100 articles on drama and on politics. *Address:* Lenkom Theatre, 127006 Moscow, 6 Malaya Dmitrova str., Russia (office). *Telephone:* (495) 699-96-68 (office). *Fax:* (495) 234-99-64 (office). *E-mail:* nimfa@lenkom.ru (office); lenkom1971@mail.ru (office). *Website:* lenkom.ru (office).

ZAKHAROVA, Svetlana; Ukrainian ballet dancer; *Principal Dancer, Bolshoi Ballet;* b. 10 June 1979, Lutsk; d. Yurii Zakharov and Halyna Zakharova; m. Vadim Repin; one c.; trained at Kiev Choreographic School for six years; obtained second prize for performance of Bluebird pas de deux, Int. Young Dancers Competition, St Petersburg 1995; admitted to Vaganova Ballet Acad. 1995–96; joined Mariinsky Ballet, St Petersburg 1996, promoted to soloist 1997, toured world-wide with Kirov in UK, USA, Germany, Austria, The Netherlands, Australia, Japan –2003; Prin. Dancer, Bolshoi Ballet, Moscow 2003–; an étoile, La Scala Theatre Ballet; Golden Mask Award (Best Female Role in Ballet) 1999, 2000, People of Our City Award of St Petersburg (for achievements in ballet) 2001, Honored Artist of Russia 2005, Benois de la Danse Int. Dance Asscn Prize 2005, People's Artist of Russia 2008. *Repertoire includes:* Princess Florentine in The Sleeping Beauty 1996, soloist in Tchaikovsky Pas de Deux 1996, The Dying Swan 1996, Maria in The Fountain of Bakhchisarai 1996, Masha in The Nutcracker 1996, Gulnara in Le Corsaire 1997, title role in Giselle 1997, the Bride in Les Noces 1997, Queen of the Dryads in Don Quixote 1997, Waltz and Mazurka Girl in Chopiniana 1997, friend of Juliet in Romeo and Juliet 1997, Aurora in The Sleeping Beauty 1998, Terpsichore in Apollo 1998, soloist in Serenade 1998, Odette-Odile in Swan Lake 1998, Poem of Ecstasy 1998, 1st Movt in Symphony in C 1999, Medora in Le Corsaire 1999, Nikiya in La Bayadère 1999, Diamonds in Jewels 2000, title role in Manon 2000, Kitri in Don Quixote 2000, soloist in Now and Then 2001, soloist in The Young Lady and The Hooligan 2001, Zobeide in Scheherazade 2001, Juliet in Romeo in Juliet 2002, soloist in Paquita Grand Pas 2003, soloist in Etudes 2003, A Legend of Love 2014, A Hero of Our Time 2015, Ivan the Terrible to music 2017. *Address:* Bolshoi Theatre, 103009 Moscow, 1, Teatralnaya Square, Russia. *E-mail:* mail@svetlana-zakharova.com. *Website:* www.svetlana-zakharova.com; www.bolshoi.ru.

ZAKHILWAL, Muhammad Omar, BA, MA, PhD; Afghan economist, academic, government official and diplomatist; *Ambassador to Pakistan;* ed Univ. of Winnipeg, Queen's Univ., Carleton Univ., Canada; fmr Prof. of Econs, Carleton Univ., Ottawa, Canada; fmr Sr Research Economist, Statistics Canada; fmr mem. Man. Bd Inst. for Afghan Studies, Ottawa; fmr Chief Policy Adviser, Afghan Ministry of Rural Rehabilitation and Devt; Acting Minister of Transport 2008; fmr Pres. and CEO Afghanistan Investment Support Agency; fmr mem. Supreme Council of da Afghanistan Bank (Afghanistan Cen. Bank); Acting Minister of Finance –2009, Minister of Finance 2010–14; Nat. Econ. Adviser to the Pres. 2014; Amb. to Pakistan 2016–, teacher of econs, Kabul Univ. *Publications include:* numerous articles and research papers on political, economic and social issues in newspapers and journals. *Address:* Embassy of Afghanistan, 8, St 90, G-6/3, Islamabad, 44000, Pakistan (office). *Telephone:* (51) 2824505 (office). *Fax:* (51) 2824504 (office). *E-mail:* contact@islamabad.mfa.gov.af (office).

ZAKI, Lt-Gen. Mohamed Ahmed, BSc, MS; Egyptian politician and army officer; *Minister of Defence;* b. 29 Jan. 1956; m.; three c.; Commdr of the Paratrooper Division 2008–12, Commdr of Presidential Guards 2012–18; apptd Lt-Gen. 2018; Minister of Defence 2018–; Medal of Military Duty, Medal of Long Service and Good Example, Medal of Excellent Service, Medal of Training, First Class, Medal of 25 January 2011, Medal of 30 June 2013. *Address:* Sharia 23 July, Kobri el-Kobba, Cairo, Egypt (office). *Telephone:* (2) 22602566 (office). *Fax:* (2) 22906004 (office). *E-mail:* mmc@afmic.gov.eg (office). *Website:* www.mod.gov.eg (office).

ZAKIS, Juris, DrSc; Latvian solid-state physicist, university administrator and politician; *Rector, Higher School of Social Technologies;* b. 4 Nov. 1936, Ogre; s. of Roderickh Zakis and Eugenia Zake; m. Anita Zake 1976; three s. two d.; ed Univ. of Latvia, Rīga; Researcher, Lecturer and Sr Researcher, Faculty of Physics and Math., Univ. of Latvia 1960–68, Head of Lab. of Semiconductor Physics 1968–78, Dir Inst. of Solid State Physics 1978–84, apptd Prof. 1978, Pro-rector 1984–87, Rector 1987–2000, Prof. Emer. 2000–; USSR People's Deputy 1989; Deputy of Saeima 1995–96; Rector, Higher School of Social Technologies (STA), Riga 2004–; mem. Riga City Council 2005–; mem. Council of Higher Educ. 2012–15; Visiting Researcher, Cornell Univ., USA 1969–70, Univ. of Chicago 1972–73; Pres. Rectors' Council of Latvia 1995–98; Corresp. mem. Latvian Acad. of Sciences 1982–90, Full mem. 1990–; mem. UNESCO Latvian Nat. Cttee 1990–2000; Latvian State Medal (Order) of Three Stars 2000, Lithuanian State Medal (Order) of Gedimino 2001; M.Keldish Prize, Latvian Acad. of Sciences 1986, Merited Scientist of Latvia 1986, S.Vavilov Medal, Russian Acad. of Sciences 1988, State Emer. Scientist 2002. *Publications:* Profesors ar novirzēm (novel) 2016; numerous articles on physics of disordered solids and on higher educ. policy. *Leisure interests:* skiing, linguistics. *Address:* Higher School of Social Technologies, 12 Bezdeligu Str., 1048 Riga, Latvia (office). *Telephone:* (2) 2929-9188 (home). *Fax:* (2) 6727-0228 (office). *E-mail:* Juris.Zakis@riga.lv (office). *Website:* www.sta-edu.lv (office).

ZAKRI, Tan Sri, Dato' Sri Abdul Hamid, BSc, MSc, PhD; Malaysian geneticist, academic, administrator and diplomatist; *Founding Chairman, Intergovernmental Platform on Biodiversity and Ecosystem Services;* b. 23 June 1948, Pahang; m.; five c.; ed Coll. of Agric., Malaya, Serdang, Louisiana State Univ. and Michigan State Univ., USA; began lecturing at Universiti Kebangsaan Malaysia (UKM—Nat. Univ. of Malaysia) late 1970s, Head of Dept of Genetics 1978–81, Assoc. Prof. 1980, Full Prof. 1986, Dean of Life Sciences Faculty 1987–92, Deputy Vice-Chancellor 1992–2000; Sec.-Gen. Soc. for the Advancement of Breeding Research in Asia and Oceania 1981–89; Founding Pres. Genetics Soc. of Malaysia 1994–2000; Founding Chair. Nat. Genetic Modification Advisory Cttee 1996–2000; Sr Malaysian del. during negotiation of UN Convention on Biological Diversity (CBD) 1990–92, later heading Malaysian del. to treaty's Conf. of the Parties 1993–2000; Dir UN Univ.'s Inst. of Advanced Studies (UNU-IAS), Yokohama, Japan 2001–08; Co-Chair. Millennium Ecosystem Assessment 2000–05; named the Tuanku Chancellor Chair at Universiti Sains Malaysia (USM) 2009, f. USM's Centre for Global Sustainability Studies 2009; apptd Science Adviser to the Prime Minister of Malaysia 2010; apptd Co-Chair. Secr. of Malaysia's Global Science and Innovation Advisory Council 2011; named Jt Chair. Malaysian Industry-Govt Group for High Tech. (MIGHT) 2011; co-chaired High-Level Int. Advisory Cttee of the World Conf. on Justice, Governance and Law on Environmental Sustainability 2012; apptd to UN Convention on Biological Diversity's High-level Panel on Global Assessment of Resources for implementing the Strategic Plan for Biodiversity 2011–2020 2012; Founding Chair. Intergovernmental Platform on Biodiversity and Ecosystem Services 2013; named to UN Sec.-Gen.'s Scientific Advisory Bd 2013; Chair. Nat. Professors Council, Malaysian Biotechnology Corpn; Foundation Fellow, Acad. of Sciences of Malaysia 1995; Fellow, Third World Acad. of Sciences (now The World Acad. of Sciences) 1996, World Acad. of Art and Science 2003, Islamic World Acad. of Sciences 2006; Kestria Mangku Negara, King of Malaysia 1993; Fulbright-Hays Malaysian Lecturer Award, Malaysian-America Comm. on Educational Exchange 1981, Excellent Service Award, Academic Asscn of UKM 1997, Langkawi Award 1998, Rotary Research Foundation Gold Medal (Agricultural and Biological Sciences) 1999, Excellence Award, Genetics Soc. of Malaysia 2011, Zayed Int. Prize (Category 2) (co-recipient) 2014. *Publications:* numerous papers in professional journals. *Address:* IPBES Secretariat, 10th Floor, Platz der Vereinten Nationen 1, 53113 Bonn, Germany (office). *Telephone:* (228) 8150570 (office). *E-mail:* secretariat@ipbes.net (office). *Website:* www.ipbes.net (office).

ZALAZNICK, Lauren, BA; American television executive and producer; *Executive Vice-President, NBCUniversal;* m.; three c.; ed Brown Univ.; Pres. Bravo Media, Oxygen Media 2004–08, has exec. responsibility for iVillage, also leads NBC Universal's environmental initiative, Green is Universal, oversaw launch of Bravo's suite of broadband services, including BravoTV.com, OUTzoneTV.com, BrilliantButCancelled.com and TelevisionWithoutPity.com, Pres. NBC Universal Women and Lifestyle Entertainment Networks 2008–10, Chair. Entertainment & Digital Networks and Integrated Media 2011–13, oversaw Bravo Media, Oxygen Media, Style Media, Telemundo Media, mun2, Sprout and TVOne, the digital properties DailyCandy, Fandango, Television Without Pity and iVillage, and the Integrated Strategic Marketing group, Exec. Vice-Pres., NBCUniversal 2013–, continues to oversee Fandango and DailyCandy; mem. NBCUniversal Foundation Bd, Chair. Women At NBCU Advisory Bd; mem. New York City Mayor Michael R. Bloomberg's MediaNYC2020, Brown Univ. Women's Leadership Council, Brown Univ. Creative; Trustee, Corpn of Brown Univ.; inducted into Broadcasting & Cable Hall of Fame 2012. *Films include:* Sublet (producer) 1991, Poison (actress and assoc. producer) 1991, Swoon (actress, exec. producer and line producer) 1992, Jumpin' at the Boneyard (line producer) 1992, Getting In (aka Student Body) (line producer) 1994, Safe (producer) 1995, Kids (co-producer) 1995, Girls Town (producer) 1996, Zoolander (exec. producer) 2001, Final Cut: The Making and Unmaking of Heaven's Gate (exec. producer) 2004. *Television includes:* Dottie Gets Spanked (producer) 1993, The RuPaul Show (series, exec. producer) 1996, 1996 VH1 Fashion Awards (exec. producer) 1996, 1998 VH1 Fashion Awards (exec. producer) 1998, Random Play (exec. producer, episode 1.2) 1999, 100 Greatest Women of Rock & Roll (exec. producer) 1999, Pop Up Video (series, exec. producer and supervising producer) 2000, Rock of Ages (series, exec. producer) 2000, It's Only Rock 'n' Roll (exec. producer) 2000, Sound Affects (exec. producer) 2000, Animal Trax (series, exec. producer) 2001, Name That Video (series, exec. producer) 2001, Bands on the Run (series, exec. producer) 2001, 100 Greatest Teen Stars (mini-series, exec. producer) 2006. *Address:* NBC Universal, 30 Rockefeller Plaza, New York, NY 10112, USA (office). *Telephone:* (212) 664-4444 (office). *Fax:* (212) 664-4085 (office). *E-mail:* info@nbcuni.com (office). *Website:* www.nbcuni.com (office).

ZALKALIANI, David; Georgian diplomatist and politician; *Minister of Foreign Affairs;* b. 27 Feb. 1968, Tbilisi, Georgian SSR, USSR; m.; two d.; ed Ivane Javakhishvili Tbilisi State Univ.; long career with Ministry of Foreign Affairs (MFA), including as Third Sec., later Second Sec., First Sec. and Deputy Head of Div., Dept of Int. Orgs 1992–95, Head of European Orgs Div. 1995–96, First Sec., Georgian Del. to Int. Orgs in Vienna and later Adviser, Embassy in Vienna 1996–2000, Adviser, First European Dept, MFA 2000–01, Adviser to Georgian Rep. to Int. Orgs in Vienna 2001–02, Deputy Perm. Rep. of Georgia to OSCE and other Int. Orgs in Vienna March–Sept. 2002, Sr Adviser, Embassy in USA, Canada and Mexico 2002–04, Amb. to Uzbekistan and Tajikistan 2004–07, Dir, MFA Global Relations Dept Jan.–Dec. 2007, Amb. for Extraordinary Assignments, MFA 2007–08, Amb. to Belarus 2008–09, First Deputy Minister of Foreign Affairs 2012–14, 2016–18, Minister of Foreign Affairs 2018–; Exec. Dir Levan Mikeladze Foundation 2015–16. *Address:* Ministry of Foreign Affairs, 0108 Tbilisi, Sh. Chitadze 4, Georgia (office). *Telephone:* (32) 294-50-00 (office). *Fax:* (32) 294-50-01 (office). *E-mail:* inform@mfa.gov.ge (office). *Website:* www.mfa.gov.ge (office).

ZALM, Gerrit; Dutch economist, politician, international organization official and business executive; *Chairman, Centraal Bureau voor de Statistiek;* b. 6 May 1952, Enkhuizen; ed Amsterdam Free Univ.; mem. staff, Econs Affairs section, Budget Preparation Div., Ministry of Finance 1975, Head of Section 1977, Head of Div. 1978, Head of Cen. Review Secr. 1980, Deputy Dir for Budgetary Affairs and Head of Budget Preparation Div. 1981; Deputy Dir for Gen. Econs Policy, Ministry of Econ. Affairs 1983–85, Dir 1985–88 (also mem. Econ. Policy Cttee of EC); Deputy Dir Cen. Planning Bureau 1988–89, Dir 1989; Prof. of Econs Policy, Amsterdam Free Univ. 1990; mem. Parl. and Chair. People's Party for Freedom and Democracy

(VVD) Parl. Group 2002–03; Minister of Finance 1994–2003, Minister of Finance and Deputy Prime Minister 2003–07; Sr Adviser, Permira 2007–08; Chief Economist DSB Bank NV June 2007–08, Chief Financial Officer Dec. 2007–08; Chair. of Trustees, Int. Accounting Standards Cttee Foundation 2008; Vice-Chair. RBS Holdings NV Jan.–Feb. 2009; CEO and Chair. ABN Amro 2009–17; CEO Royal Bank of Scotland NV 2009, Vice-Chair. 2012; Chair. Centraal Bureau voor de Statistiek (Statistics Netherlands) 2018–; mem. Bd of Dirs Royal Dutch Shell 2013– (also mem. Supervisory Bd –2016), Moody's Corp. 2018–; mem. Bd of Govs European Investment Bank; Hon. mem. VVD (liberal party); Hon. DEcon (Amsterdam Free Univ.) 2008. *Address:* Centraal Bureau voor de Statistiek, PO Box 24500, 2490 HA The Hague, Netherlands. *Website:* www.cbs.nl (office).

ZAMA, Francis; Solomon Islands politician; b. 3 July 1956, Hopongo Village, Rendova Island; fmrly with Solomon Islands Cen. Bank; fmr Prin. Tax Inspector, Ministry of Finance; mem. Parl. for South New Georgia/Rendova/Tetepare, Western Province constituency 2001–; Minister of Finance and Treasury 2003–06, of Educ. March–July 2003, Nov.–Dec. 2007, of Justice and Legal Affairs Oct.–Nov. 2007; Chair. Public Accounts Comm., Ministry of Finance, Nat. Reform and Planning 2007; mem. People's Alliance Party. *Address:* National Parliament of Solomon Islands, PO Box G19, Vavaya Ridge, Honiara, Solomon Islands (office). *Telephone:* 23424 (office). *Fax:* 24272 (office). *E-mail:* www.parliament.gov.sb (office).

ZAMACHOWSKI, Zbigniew; Polish actor; b. 17 July 1961, Brzeziny; m. 1st Anna Komornicka (divorced); two s. two d.; m. 2nd Aleksandra Justa (divorced 2012); partner Monika Richardson; ed State Higher Film, TV and Theatre School, Łódź; performed at The Studio Theatre 1985–97; actor at Nat. Theatre, Warsaw 1997–; best known as the voice of Shrek in the Polish version of Shrek (series); Aleksander Zelwerowicz Award 1993, Gdańsk Film Festival Prize for Best Actor, in Zawrócony 1994, Felix European Film Award, Wiktor Prize 1992, 1993, 1997. *Theatre includes:* Płatonow 1992, Amadeus 1993, Wujaszek Wania 1993, Don Juan 1996, Ildefonsjada 1996, Za i przeciw (Taking Sides) 1997, Slub 1998, Kartoteka (The Card Index) 1999, Wesele (The Wedding) 2000, A Midsummer Night's Dream 2000. *Films:* Wielka majówka 1981, Pierscien i róza 1987, Matka Królów 1987, Ucieczka 1987, Prywatne sledztwo 1987, Les possédés 1988, Zabij mnie, glino 1988, Niezwykla podróz Baltazara Kobera 1988, Sztuka kochania 1989, Bal na dworcu w Koluszkach 1990, Korczak 1990, Ucieczka z kina 'Wolnosc' 1990, Seszele 1991, 30 Door Key 1991, Three Colours: Blue 1993, Tak tak 1993, Naprawde krotki film o milosci, zabijaniu i jeszcze jednym przykazaniu 1993, Straszny sen Dzidziusia Górkiewicza 1994, Three Colours: White 1994, Three Colours: Red 1994, Pestka 1995, Pulkownik Kwiatkowski 1995, Odwiedz mnie we snie 1996, Taranthriller 1997, Szczesliwego Nowego Jorku 1997, Pulapka 1997, Demony wojny wedlug Goi 1998, Love Me and Do Whatever You Want 1998, Darmozjad polski 1998, 23 1998, With Fire and Sword 1999, Pierwszy milion 2000, Prymas – trzy lata z tysiaca 2000, Cabin Fever 2000, Proof of Life 2000, Weiser 2001, Lightmaker 2001, Hi, Tereska 2001, Station 2001, The Hexer 2001, The Pianist 2002, Squint Your Eyes 2002, Distant Lights 2003, The Birch-Tree Meadow 2003, Cialo 2003, Zhoorek 2003, Zróbmy sobie wnuka 2003, Skazany na bluesa 2005, Czas surferów 2005, Diabel (short) 2005, The Call of the Toad 2005, Dublerzy 2006, Nadzieja 2007, The Ballad of Piotrowski 2007, Janek (short) 2008, The Offsiders 2008, Luxury (short) 2008, Popieluszko. Wolnosc jest w nas 2009, Operation Dunaj 2009, Within the Whirlwind 2009, Fundacja Kultura (The Foundation) (short) 2009, Esterhazy (short) (voice) 2009, Randka w ciemno 2010, Projekt dziecko, czyli ojciec potrzebny od zaraz 2010, Objects in Mirror Are Closer Than They Appear (short) 2010, Father, Son & Holy Cow 2011, Aftermath 2012, Stacja Warszawa 2013, Walesa: Man of Hope 2013, Gabriel 2013, Lauf Junge lauf 2013, Jack Strong 2014. *Television:* Rycerze i rabusie (series) 1984, Zmiennicy (series) 1986, Ludozerca (short) 1987, Boczny tor (film) 1988, Zad wielkiego wieloryba (film) 1988, Dekalog: The Ten Commandments (mini-series) 1989, Sauna (film) 1992, Le clandestin (film) 1994, Reverted (film) 1994, Slawa i chwala (mini-series) 1998, 13 posterunek (series) 1998, Sto minut wakacji (film) 2001, Wiedzmin (mini-series) 2002, Inferno Below (film) 2003, Rodzinka (series) 2004, Niania (series) 2006, Przybyli ulani (film) 2006, Kryptonim Gracz (film) 2008, Naznaczony (series) 2009, Czarnobyl. Cztery Dni W Kwietniu (film) 2011, Do Dzwonka Cafe (series) 2012. *Address:* c/o Agata Domagata, ul. F. Schillera 6 m.12, 00-248 Warsaw, Poland. *Telephone:* (48) 501094390. *E-mail:* agat8@idea.net.pl.

ZAMAGNI, Stefano; Italian economist; *Professor of Economics, University of Bologna;* b. 4 Jan. 1943, Rimini; m. Vera Negri 1968; two d.; ed Univ. of Milan, Univ. of Oxford, UK; Assoc. Dir and Adjunct Prof., SAIS Europe, Johns Hopkins Univ. 1977–; Prof. of Econs, Univ. of Bologna 1985–, Chair. Dept of Econs 1985–88, 1991–94, Dean Faculty of Econs 1994–96, Co-ordinator PhD Programme in Econs 1989–93; Pres. Int. Catholic Migration Comm., Geneva 1999–, Fondazione Italia per il Dono 2014–; Vice-Pres. Italian Econ. Asscn 1989–92, State Vic. Bank Visiting Prof., Deakin Univ., Geelong, Australia; McDonnell Visiting Scholar, Wider, Helsinki, Finland; Co-Ed. Economia Politica (quarterly) 1983–, Italian Economic Papers 1990–, Journal of Int. and Comparative Economics, Ricerche Economiche; mem. Exec. Cttee Int. Econ. Asscn 1989–, Pontifical Council on Justice and Peace 1992–, Scientific Cttee, J. Maritain Int. Inst. 1995–, Bd of Dirs UNIBANCA 1999–2016, Scientific Cttee, Rosselli Foundation, Turin, Bd of Dirs Hosp. Bambino Gesù, Rome 2000–14; mem. Acad. of Sciences of Bologna and Milan; Paul Harris Fellow, Rotary Int. 1995; mem. Pontifical Acad. of Social Sciences 2014–; Hon. Citizen of Rosario and Mar del Plata, Argentina; Kt, Order of St Gregory the Great (Holy See); Hon. DEcon (Univ. F. de Vicoria, Madrid) 2010, (Universidad de Murcia, Spain) 2011, (Universitas Carolina, Prague) 2012, (Universidad Nacional de Cordoba, Argentina) 2014, (Universidad Catolica de Cordoba, Argentina) 2014; Accad. Lincei Award, St Vincent Prize in Econs, Capri Prize in Econs 1995, Golden Sigismondo Prize 1997, Gold Medal, Pio Manzu Int. Centre 1998, Gold Medal, Cooperative Credit 2005, Toniolo Prize for Economic Culture 2017. *Publications include:* Microeconomic Theory 1987, The Economic Theories of Production 1989, History of Economic Thought 1991, Value and Capital – Fifty Years Later (with L. McKenzie) 1991, Firms and Markets 1991, Man – Environment and Development: Toward a Global Approach 1991, The Economics of Crime and Illegal Markets 1993, The Economics of Altruism 1995, An Evolutionary Dynamic Approach to Altruism 1996, Technological Change: Time-Use Policies and Employment 1996, Globalization as Specificity of Post-Industrial Economy 1997, Civil Economy and Paradoxes of Growth in Post-Fordist Societies 1997, Civil Economy, Cultural Evolution and Participatory Development 1999, The Economics of Corruption and Illegal Markets (co-author) 1999, Financial Globalization and the Emerging Economies (co-author) 2000, Time in Economic Theory (with E. Agliardi) 2004, Toward a New Economic Theory of Cooperative Firm 2005, Economic Theory and Interpersonal Relations (with P. Sacco) 2006, Civil Economy (with L. Bruni) 2007, Markets, Money and History (co-ed. with Scazzieri and Sen) 2008, Avarice – The Passion of Having 2009, The Cooperative Enterprise (with Vera Zamagni) 2010, The Economics of Common Good 2010, Family and Work (with Vera Zamagni) 2012, Prudence 2012, Handbook on the Economics of Reciprocity and Social Enterprises 2013, Responsible Enterprise and Civil Market 2013, Civil Economy (with Luigino Bruni) 2016, Inclusive Solidarity and Integration of Marginalized People 2017. *Leisure interests:* sports, theatre, classical music. *Address:* Department of Economics, University of Bologna, Piazza Scaravilli 2, 40126 Bologna, Italy (office). *Telephone:* (051) 254395 (home). *Fax:* (051) 2098040 (office). *E-mail:* bruna.bordoni@unibo.it (office); stefano.zamagni@unibo.it (home).

ZAMBELLO, Francesca, BA; American opera and theatre director; *Artistic Director, Washington National Opera;* b. 24 Aug. 1956, New York; d. of Charles Carmine Zambello and Jean Sincere Zambello; ed American School of Paris, Moscow Univ., Colgate Univ.; Asst Dir, Lyric Opera of Chicago 1981–82, San Francisco Opera 1983–84, later Artistic Advisor; Artistic Dir, Skylight Music Theatre 1984–91; Gen. and Artistic Dir, Glimmerglass Opera, New York 2010–; fmr Artistic Advisor, Washington Nat. Opera, Artistic Dir 2013–; guest producer, Met, Chicago Lyric Opera, La Scala, ROH, Paris Opera, San Francisco Opera, Teatro La Fenice, Savonlinna Festival, Houston Grand Opera, Nat. Opera of Iceland, Seattle Opera, San Diego Opera, Opera Theatre of St Louis, Rome Opera, Théâtre Municipal de Lausanne, Teatro Regio, Greater Miami Opera, Pesaro Festival, Parma and Wexford Festival; has worked on theatre productions in London's West End and New York's Broadway; fmr Visiting Prof., Harvard Univ., Univ. of Calif., Berkeley; Dr hc (Colgate Univ.); Chevalier des Arts et des Lettres; Medal for Service to Culture, Russian Fed.; three Olivier Awards from London Soc. of Theatres and two Evening Standard Awards for Best Musical and Best Opera. *Works directed include:* The Makropolous Case (Skylight Opera Theater) 1984, Albert Herring (Savonlinna Opera Festival, Finland) 1984, Fidelio (Houston Grand Opera) 1984, (Washington Opera) 2003, The Mikado (Nat. Opera of Iceland) 1985, Tosca (Nat. Opera of Puerto Rico) 1985, 1986, (Earl's Court Arena, London) 1991, Carmen (Texas Opera Theater) 1986, (Skylight Opera Theater) 1988, (ROH) 2006, 2009, 2010, 2013, The Barber of Seville (Nat. Opera of Iceland) 1986, (Santa Fe Opera) 1994, Faust (Houston Grand Opera) 1986, (San Francisco Opera) 1987, (Seattle Opera and San Diego Opera) 1988, Beatrice di Tenda (Teatro La Fenice, Venice) 1987, L'Elisir d'Amore (Teatro Regio, Parma) 1988, 1992, The Devil and Kate (Wexford Festival) 1988, Salome (Houston Grand Opera) 1988, (Lyric Opera of Chicago) 2006, Don Giovanni (New Israeli Opera, Tel-Aviv) 1988, (ROH) 2002, 2003, 2012, La Bohème (San Francisco Opera) 1988, (Teatro Regio, Parma) 1991, (Royal Albert Hall) 2004, 2006, Idomeneo (Chicago Early Music Opera) 1989, Rigoletto (San Francisco Opera) 1989, War and Peace (Seattle Goodwill Festival) 1990, (Opéra Nat. de Paris) 2000, 2005, La Traviata (Skylight Opera Theater) 1990, (Roman Arena of the Orange Festival, France) 1993, (Bordeaux Opera) 1997, Les Troyens (Los Angeles Music Center Opera) 1991, (Met) 2003, 2012–13, Lucia di Lammermoor (Dublin Grand Opera) 1991, (Met) 1992, The Sorrows of Young Werther (Santa Fe Opera) 1992, Il Pirata (Zurich Opera) 1992, (Théâtre Municipal de Lausanne) 1993, Romulus Hunt (Met) 1993, Jenůfa (San Francisco Opera) 2001, (Dallas Opera) 1993, 2004, Khovanshchina (ENO) 1994, 2003, Blond Eckbert (Santa Fe Opera) 1994, Billy Budd (Grand Théâtre de Genève) 1994, (ROH) 1995, (Opéra Nat. de Paris) 1996, 2001, (Washington Opera and Teatro Regio, Parma) 2004, Street Scene (Houston Grand Opera) 1994, (Theater des Westens) 1995, Arianna (ROH) 1995, Tannhäuser (Royal Danish Opera, Copenhagen) 1995, Die Meistersinger von Nürnberg (Royal Danish Opera, Copenhagen) 1996, The Tales of Hoffmann (Staat Theater, Aalto) 1996, Emmeline (Santa Fe Opera) 1996, (New York City Opera) 1998, Paul Bunyan (Aldeburgh Festival) 1997, (ROH) 1999, Turandot (Opéra Nat. de Paris) 1997, 1999, Iphigénie en Tauride (Glimmerglass Opera) 1997, The Bartered Bride (ROH) 1998, 2001, Boris Godunov (ENO) 1998, (Canadian Opera Co.) 2002, (Paris Opera) 2005, Dialogues des Carmélites (Saito Kinen Festival, Japan) 1998, (Santa Fe Opera and Opéra Nat. de Paris) 1999, (Opéra Nat. de Paris) 2004, Tristan and Isolde (Seattle Opera) 1998, The Flying Dutchman (Bordeaux Opera) 1998, 2002, Madama Butterfly (Grand Théâtre de Genève) 1998, (Pittsburgh Opera) 2002, (San Diego Opera) 2003, (Houston Grand Opera) 2004, Aida (Grand Théâtre de Genève) 1999, Otello (Bayerisches Staatsoper) 1999, 2012, Peter Grimes (Netherlands Opera, Amsterdam) 2000, 2004, Luisa Miller (San Francisco Opera) 2000, (Dallas Opera) 2005, Thérèse Raquin (Dallas Opera) 2001, (L'Opéra de Montréal) 2002, (San Diego Opera) 2003, Of Mice and Men (Bregenz Festival and Washington Opera) 2001, (Houston Grand Opera) 2002, Florencia en el Amazons (Houston Grand Opera) 2001, (Seattle Opera) 2005, Die Walküre (Washington Opera) 2003, San Francisco) 2011, Alcina (New York City Opera) 2003, West Side Story (Bregenz Festival) 2003, 2004, The Little Prince (Houston Grand Opera) 2003, (Skylight Music Theater) 2004, (Boston Lyric Opera and New York City Opera) 2005, Queen of Spades (Grand Théâtre de Genève) 2003, (ROH) 2006, Guillaume Tell (Opéra Nat. de Paris) 2003, Fiery Angel (Bolshoi Theater) 2004, Der fliegende Holländer (Lithuanian Opera, Vilnius) 2004, Tibet Through the Red Box (Seattle Children's Theater) 2004, An American Tragedy (Met) 2005, Porgy and Bess (Washington Opera) 2005, Cyrano de Bergerac (Met) 2005, (ROH and Met) 2006, The Love for Three Oranges (Opera Australia) 2005, Das Rheingold (Washington Opera) 2006, The Little Mermaid (Broadway), Little House on the Prairie (Guthrie), First Wives Club (Old Globe), Cyrano (La Scala), Show Boat (Washington) 2013. *Leisure interests:* skiing, tennis, hiking. *Address:* c/o Caroline Woodfield, Opus Artists Ltd, 470 Park Avenue South, 9th Floor North, New York, NY 10016, USA (office); 257 West 52nd Street, 4th Floor, New York, NY 10019, USA (office). *Telephone:* (212) 584-7580 (office); (646) 736-2900 (office). *Fax:* (646) 300-8280 (office). *E-mail:* cwoodfield@opus3artists.com (office); francesca@francescazambello.com (office); fzambello@mac.com (home); Jtantleff@paradigmagency.com (office). *Website:* www.opus3artists.com (office); www.francescazambello.com.

ZAMFIR, Gheorghe; Romanian musician (pan-pipes); b. 6 April 1941, Găeşti, nr Bucharest; m. Marie-Noele Zamfir; ed self-taught and Bucharest Acad. of Music (studied under Fănică Luca); graduated in conducting at Ciprian Porumbescu

Conservatory, Bucharest 1968; toured numerous countries in Europe as student and won first prize in many int. competitions; conductor of 'Ciocirlia' Folk Ensemble in Bucharest 1969; Prof. of Pan-Pipes 1970; formed own orchestra 1970; numerous trips to Europe, Australia, S America, Canada and USA. *Recordings include:* Hora Romanilor & Tiganiada, Magic of the Panpipe, Legenda Romaneasca (muzica populara), Casa de discuri Media services, Romania, Gheorghe Zamfir en France (CD of popular music), Les Années 70, Mes Plus Belles Doina, Pan d'Amour – Kiss From a Rose, Recording with Gheorghe Zamfir – Archive, Music by Candlelight 1983, Romance 1984, Harmony 1987, The Lonely Shepherd 1988, A Return To Romance 1988, Doina din Arges 1990, Christmas at Notre Dame Basilica 1992, Panflute & Organ 1995, Harmony – Zauber der Panflöte (Beliebte Melodien) 1997, Magic of the Panpipes 2001, Like a Breeze 2008, Spirit of the Andes 2008, Vivaldi: The Four Seasons 2012. *Address:* c/o Michow Concerts and Management GmbH, Postfach 202364, 20216 Hamburg, Germany (office). *Telephone:* (40) 4800808 (office). *Fax:* (40) 484443 (office). *E-mail:* info@gheorghe-zamfir.com. *Website:* www.gheorghe-zamfir.com.

ZAMMAN, Muhammad Mansour; Yemeni central banker; *Governor, Central Bank of Yemen;* b. 1965; Minister of Finance 2014; Gov. Cen. Bank of Yemen 2018–. *Address:* Central Bank of Yemen, Aden, Yemen (office). *Telephone:* (1) 274314 (office). *Fax:* (1) 274360 (office). *E-mail:* cbyh@y.net.ye (office). *Website:* www.centralbank.gov.ye (office).

ZAMMIT DIMECH, Hon. Francis, MA, MBA, LLD; Maltese politician and lawyer; b. 23 Oct. 1954, St Julian's; s. of George Zammit and Anne Dimech; ed St Aloysius Coll. and Univ. of Malta; called to the Bar 1980; Pres. Students' Rep. Council of Univ. 1978–79; Vice-Pres. Democratic Youth Community of Europe 1981–83; Nationalist Party MP 1987–2017, Nationalist MEP (EPP Group) 2017–, Chair. Legislation Cttee 2008–10, Foreign and European Affairs 2010–12; Minister of Foreign Affairs Nov. 2012–March 2013; mem. Maltese Parl. Del. to Parl. Ass. of Council of Europe 1987–92; Parl. Sec., later Minister for Transport and Communications 1990–92, 1992–94; Minister for the Environment 1994–96, 1998–2002; Shadow Minister and Opposition Spokesman on Public Works and Environment 1996–98; Pres. Exec. Council Nationalist Party 1997–99; Minister for Resources and Infrastructure 2002–03, for Tourism 2003–04, for Tourism and Culture 2004–08; Chair. Editorial Bd Zaghzugh 1986–87; Ed. Il-Poplu Magazine 1988–90. *Publications include:* Poll of '76 1980, The Untruth Game 1986, Eddie – The People's Choice 1987. *Leisure interests:* reading, broadcasting, theatre, swimming. *Address:* 7 St Julian's Hill, St Julian's, STJ 1342, Malta (home). *Telephone:* 79497590 (home). *E-mail:* francis@fzdadvocates.com (office). *Website:* www.fzdassociates.com (office).

ZANATI, Zanati Muhammad az-; Libyan government official; Sec. of Gen. People's Congress (Mutamar Al Sha'ab Al Aam), Tripoli 1992–2008.

ZANDANSHATAR, Gombojav, MA; Mongolian politician; b. 6 March 1970, Baatsagaan sum, Bayankhongor Prov.; m.; two c.; ed State People's Econs Inst., Russia, Maastricht Univ., Netherlands; mem. research staff, Coll. of Market Study 1992–93, Lecturer 1993–95; Expert Economist, Bank of Agric. 1995–96, Head of Foreign Relations and Co-operation Dept 1996–98, Man. 1998–99; Man., Training Center, Bank of Mongolia 1999, Bank of Mongolia Rep. to Bank of Agric. 1999–2000, Deputy Dir Bank of Agric. 2000–03; Vice-Minister, Ministry of Agric. 2003–04; mem. Mongolian Great Khural (Parl.) 2004–12; Minister of External Relations 2009–12; Gen. Sec. Mongolian People's Party 2012–13; Visiting Scholar, Freeman Spogli Inst. for Int. Studies, Center on Democracy, Development, and the Rule of Law, Stanford Univ. 2014. *Address:* Mongolian People's Party, Palace of Independence, Ulan Bator.

ZANDER, Edward J., BS, MBA; American engineer and telecommunications industry executive; b. 12 Jan. 1947, Brooklyn, New York; m. Mona Zander; two c.; ed Rensselaer Polytechnic Inst., Boston Univ.; engineer with Raytheon Co. 1968–73; Sr Man. Data Gen. 1973–82; fmr Sr Man. Apollo Computer Co.; joined Sun Microsystems 1987, later becoming Pres. and COO –2002; Man. Dir Silver Lake Pnrs (Pvt. equity firm) 2002–03; CEO Motorola Inc. 2004–07, Chair. 2004–08; mem. Bd of Dirs Eagleview Technologies 2008–, Seagate Tech. 2002–04, Time Warner 2007; mem. Science Advisory Bd, Rensselaer Polytechnic Inst., Advisory Bd, Boston Univ. School of Man.; mem. Econs Club Chicago, Exec. Club Chicago, Commercial Club Chicago.

ZANDER, Michael, QC, FBA; British legal scholar and academic; *Professor Emeritus of Law, London School of Economics;* b. 16 Nov. 1932, Berlin, Germany; s. of Walter Zander and Margaret Zander; m. Elizabeth Treeger 1965; one s. one d.; ed Royal Grammar School, High Wycombe, Jesus Coll. Cambridge and Harvard Law School; Sullivan & Cromwell, New York 1958–59; admitted solicitor of Supreme Court 1962; Asst Lecturer, LSE 1963, Lecturer 1965, Sr Lecturer 1970, Reader 1970, Prof. of Law 1977–98, Prof. Emer. 1998–, also mem. of Staff Manheim Centre for Criminology; Convenor (Head) 1984–88, 1997–98; Legal Corresp., The (Manchester) Guardian 1963–88; mem. Royal Comm. on Criminal Justice 1991–93, Home Office's PACE Strategy Bd 2007–; Hon. LLD (King's Coll. London) 2010; Halsbury Legal Award for Lifetime Contribution 2015. *Publications include:* Lawyers and the Public Interest 1968, Cases and Materials on the English Legal System 1972, 2007, A Bill of Rights 1975, 1997, Legal Services for the Community 1978, The Law-Making Process 1980, 2004, The Police and Criminal Evidence Act 1984, 2018, A Matter of Justice 1989, The State of Justice 2000. *Leisure interests:* swimming (daily). *Address:* 12 Woodside Avenue, London, N6 4SS, England (home). *Telephone:* (20) 8883-6257 (home). *E-mail:* mandbzander@btinternet.com (office). *Website:* www.lse.ac.uk/collections/mannheim (office).

ZANE, William George (Billy); American actor and producer; b. 24 Feb. 1966, Chicago, Ill.; s. of William Zane, Sr and Thalia Zane; m. Lisa Collins 1989 (divorced 1995); two d. with Candice Neil; ed American School, Switzerland, Francis W. Parker School, Harand Camp of the Theater Arts, Evanston, Ill.; moved to Hollywood 1984; stage appearances in American Music, New York, The Boys in the Backroom (Actors' Gang, Chicago); Chair. Francesco Fucilla Film production co. 21st Century Filmworks; hon. degree from Lium Univ., Bellinzona, Switzerland 2010. *Achievement:* participated in first Gumball 3000 rally, driving a 1964 Aston Martin DB5 1999. *Films:* Back to the Future 1985, Critters 1986, Dead Calm 1989, Back to the Future Part II 1989, Megaville 1990, Memphis Belle 1990, Blood and Concrete: A Love Story 1991, Millions, Femme Fatale 1991, Posse 1993, Orlando 1993, Sniper 1993, Flashfire, Tombstone 1993, The Silence of the Hams 1994, Cyborg Agent, Only You 1994, Tales from the Crypt Presents: Demon Knight 1995, Reflections in the Dark, Danger Zone 1995, The Phantom 1996, This World – Then the Fireworks 1996, Head Above Water 1996, Titanic 1998, Taxman 1999, Morgan's Ferry 1999, Cleopatra 1999, Hendrix 2000, Invincible 2001, The Diamond of Jeru 2001, The Believer 2001, Sea Devils 2002, Vlad 2003, Imaginary Grace 2003, Silver City 2004, Three 2004, Dead Fish 2004, Big Kiss 2004, The Pleasure Drivers 2005, The Last Drop 2005, BloodRayne 2005, Mem-o-re 2005, Kurtlar vadisi: Irak 2006, Survival Island (aka Three) 2006, Valley of the Wolves: Iraq 2006, Memory 2006, The Mad 2007, Fishtales (also co-producer) 2007, Alien Agent 2007, Perfect Hideout 2008, The Man Who Came Back 2008, Love N' Dancing 2009, Surviving Evil 2009, Magic Man 2009, Blue Seduction 2009, Evil – In the Time of Heroes 2009, Darfur 2009, The Confidant 2010, Flutter 2010, Enemies Among Us 2010, Mama, I Want to Sing! 2011, The Roommate 2011, Sniper: Reloaded 2011, Mercenaries 2011, The Scorpion King 3: Battle for Redemption 2012, Chimera 2012, Electrick Children 2012, Two Jacks 2012, Border Run 2012, Dark Star Hollow 2012, The Employer 2013, The Kill Hole 2013, Blood of Redemption 2013, Scorned 2013, Come Find Me (short) 2013, The Ganzfeld Haunting 2014, Ghost of Goodnight Lane 2014, Mining for Ruby 2014, Zombie Killers: Elephant's Graveyard 2014, Beyond the Game 2014, Finding Harmony 2014. *Television includes:* (series): Heart of the City 1986, Matlock 1987, 21 Jump Street 1987, Crime Story 1988, Murder, She Wrote: A Very Good Year for Murder 1988, Twin Peaks 1991, Tales From the Crypt: Well-Cooked Ham 1993, The New Batman Adventures 1998, Boston Public 2001, Charmed 2005, Samantha Who? 2009, The Deep End 2010, Robot Chicken (series) 2012, Psych – The Break-Up 2014; (films): Brotherhood of Justice 1986, Lake Consequence 1993, Cleopatra 1999, Hendrix 2000, Sole Survivor 2000, Invincible 2001, Bet Your Life 2004, Journey to Promethea 2010, Barabbas 2012, Red Clover (originally released as Leprechaun's Revenge) 2012, Hannah's Law 2012. *Address:* c/o Creative Artists Agency, 2000 Avenue of the Stars, Los Angeles, CA 90067, USA (office). *Telephone:* (424) 288-2000 (office). *Fax:* (424) 288-2900 (office). *Website:* www.caa.com (office).

ZANGANEH, Bijam Namdar, MSc; Iranian civil engineer and politician; *Minister of Petroleum;* b. 1953, Kermanshah; ed Univ. of Tehran; fmr Lecturer, Dept of Eng, Khajeh Nasir Toosi Univ. of Tech.; Deputy Minister of Culture and Islamic Guidance 1980, Minister of Agric. 1983–88, of Energy 1988–97, of Petroleum 1997–2005, 2013–; fmr Chair. Heavy Equipment Production Co.; mem. Expediency Council 1996. *Address:* Ministry of Petroleum, Hafez Crossing, Taleghani Avenue, Tehran 15936-57919, Iran (office). *Telephone:* (21) 66152606 (office). *Fax:* (21) 66154977 (office). *E-mail:* public-relations@nioc.ir (office). *Website:* www.mop.ir (office).

ZANGPO, Jigme; Bhutanese politician; mem. Nat. Ass. from Monggar constituency 2013–18, also Speaker 2013–18; mem. People's Democratic Party (PDP). *Address:* Tshogdu Chenmo (National Assembly) Secretariat, Gyelyong Tshokhang, PO Box 139, Thimphu, Bhutan (office). *Telephone:* (2) 322729 (office). *Fax:* (2) 324210 (office). *E-mail:* jzangpo@nab.gov.bt (office). *Website:* www.nab.gov.bt (office).

ZANINI, Marco; Italian fashion designer; b. 10 Sept. 1971, Milan; ed Accademia di Belle Arti, Milan; began career as First Asst at Lawrence Steele; fmr First Asst to Domenico Dolce at Dolce & Gabbana; Founding mem. Memphis 1981; First Designer, Versace's Women's Wear, Ready to Wear and Haute Couture lines, where he worked with Donatella Versace –2007; Creative Dir, Halston 2007–09; Creative Dir, Rochas 2009–13; Creative Dir Schiaparelli 2013–14.

ZANKER, Paul, DPhil; German archaeologist and academic; *Professor Emeritus of Classical Archeology, Scuola Normale Superiore di Pisa;* b. 7 Feb. 1937, Konstanz; ed Univ. of Munich, Univ. of Freiburg, Univ. of Rome, Italy; with Deutsches Archäologisches Inst. Rome 1963, Dir 1996–; Asst, Univ. of Bonn 1964; Lecturer, Univ. of Freiburg 1967; Prof., Univ. of Göttingen 1972; Prof. of Classical Archaeology, Univ. of Munich 1976; Prof. of Classical Archeology, Scuola Normale Superiore, Pisa, Italy, now Prof. Emer.; mem. Inst. of Advanced Study, Princeton, NJ, USA; mem. Bayerische Akad. der Wissenschaften, British Acad., Academia Europaea (London), Deutsches Archäologisches Inst.; Bavarian Maximilian Order for Science and Art 2008; Reuchlin Prize 1999. *Publications:* Wandel der Hermesgestalt 1965, Forum Augustum 1968, Forum Romanum 1972, Porträts 1973, Studien zu den Augustus-Porträts, Band 1: Der Actium-Typus 1973, Klassizistiche Statuen. Studien zur Veränderung des Kunstgeschmacks in der römischen Kaiserzeit 1974, Provinzielle Kaiserporträts. Zur Rezeption der Selbstdarstellung des Princeps 1983, Augustus und die Macht der Bilder 1987, Die Trunkene Alte. Das Lachen der Verhöhnten 1988, The power of images in the age of Augustus (trans. by Alan Shapiro) 1988, Pompeji. Stadtbild und Wohngeschmack 1995, Stadtbild und Bürgerbild im Hellenismus (co-ed.) 1995, Die Maske des Sokrates. Das Bild des Intellektuellen in der Antiken Kunst 1995, Eine Kunst für die Sinne. Zur Bildwelt des Dionysos und der Aphrodite 1998, Mit Mythen leben. Die Bilderwelt der römischen Sarkophage (co-author) 2004, Die Apotheose der römischen Kaiser. Ritual und städtische Bühne 2004, Die Roemische Kunst 2007, Die römische Stadt. Eine kurze Geschichte 2014. *Address:* Scuola Normale Superiore di Pisa, Palazzo della Carovana, 4th Floor, Room 100, 7-56124 Pisa, Italy (office); Meiserstrasse 10, 80333 Munich, Germany (home). *Telephone:* (50) 509074 (office). *E-mail:* paul.zanker@sns.it (office).

ZANNA, Mark P., BA, PhD, FRSC; Canadian social psychologist and academic; *Distinguished Professor Emeritus, Department of Psychology, University of Waterloo;* ed Yale Univ.; Asst Prof., Princeton Univ. 1970–75; Assoc. Prof., Univ. of Waterloo 1975–79, Prof. 1979–2004, Prof. of Health Studies (cross-appointment) 1986, Inaugural Univ. Prof. 2004–15, now Distinguished Prof. Emer. Chair. Div. of Social Psychology 1978–79, 1989–91, 1992–93, 2002–03, Assoc. Chair./Undergraduate Affairs, Dept of Psychology 1983–86, Deputy Chair. Dept of Psychology 1986–88, 2008, Chair. 1997–2000, 2009, mem. Senate 2000–03, mem. Bd of Dirs Center for Applied Health Research 1984–88; Visiting Assoc. Prof., Stanford Univ. 1979; Visiting Prof., Princeton Univ. 1981, McGill Univ. 1986, Univ. of Minnesota 1995, Univ. of California, Santa Cruz 1996, Univ. of Exeter, UK 1998; collaborative work on Int. Tobacco Control Policy Survey; Consulting Ed. Social Psychology Quarterly 1977–79, Journal of Personality 1977–79, 1982–97, Journal of Personality and Social Psychology 1978–86, 1990–, Canadian Journal of Behavioural Science 1978–79, 1982–90, Journal of Experimental Social Psychology 1978–79,

1982–91, Review of Personality and Social Psychology 1983–93, Journal of Consumer Psychology 1991–2000, Personality and Social Psychology Bulletin 1994–97, Basic and Applied Social Psychology 1994–2010, Group Processes and Intergroup Relations 1997–, Political Psychology 2002–10; Assoc. Ed. Journal of Experimental Social Psychology 1980–81; Co-Ed. Ontario Symposium on Personality and Social Psychology 1981–; Ed. Advances in Experimental Social Psychology 1990–; President-Elect, President, Past President, SPSP, 1996–98; Pres. President, SESP, 1985, Soc. of Personality and Social Psychology (first Canadian), Int. Soc. of Experimental Social Psychology (first Canadian); mem. Canadian Psychological Asscn (mem. Bd of Dirs 1990–91), American Psychological Asscn (APA) Div. 8: Soc. of Personality and Social Psychology (mem. Exec. Cttee APA 1992–94), APA Div. 9: Soc. for the Psychological Study of Social Issues (SPSSI) (mem. Council SPSSI 1985–8), APA Div. 35: Soc. for the Psychology of Women, APA Div. 3: Div. of Experimental Psychology, Asscn for Psychological Science (fmrly American Psychological Soc.), American Asscn of Applied and Preventive Psychology, Eastern Psychological Asscn, Midwestern Psychological Asscn, Soc. of Experimental Social Psychology (mem. Exec. Cttee 1982–85); Fellow, Canadian Psychological Asscn 1978, American Psychological Asscn 1979 (Div. 8/SPSP 1980, Div. 9/SPSSI 1982, Div. 35/SPW 2002, Div. 3/DEP); Fellow-Elect, Center for Advanced Studies in the Behavioral Sciences 1982; Charter Fellow, Asscn for Psychological Science 1988, American Asscn of Applied and Preventive Psychology 1991; Departmental Honours with Exceptional Distinction, Yale Univ. 1966, NSF Grad. Fellow, Yale Univ. 1966–70, Otto Klineberg Intercultural and Int. Relations Prize, SPSSI 1992, Donald O. Hebb Award for Distinguished Contribs to Psychology as a Science, CPA 1993, Kurt Lewin Fellow, Univ. of Amsterdam 1994, Raymond D. Fowler Award for Professional Devt of Grad. Students, American Psychological Asscn of Grad. Students 1996, Donald T. Campbell Award for Distinguished Research in Social Psychology, Soc. of Personality and Social Psychology 1997, Inaugural Excellence in Research Award, Univ. of Waterloo 2000, Inaugural Outstanding Performance Award, Univ. of Waterloo 2004, 2008, 2011, Inaugural Award for Excellence in Grad. Supervision, Univ. of Waterloo 2005, Distinguished Scientist Award, Soc. of Experimental and Social Psychology 2007, Inaugural Fellow, Soc. of Experimental and Social Psychology 2009, Kurt Lewin Award for Distinguished Scientific Contributions, SPSSI 2010, Service Award for Contribs to the Field of Personality/Social Psychology, SPSP 2010, Killam Prize in the Social Sciences, Canada Council for the Arts 2011. *Publications:* numerous papers in professional journals on the psychology of attitudes. *Address:* PAS 3048, Department of Psychology, University of Waterloo, Waterloo, ON N2L 3G1, Canada (office). *Telephone:* (519) 888-4567 (ext. 35799) (office); (519) 747-9366 (home). *Fax:* (519) 746-8631 (office). *E-mail:* mzanna@uwaterloo.ca (office). *Website:* www.psychology.uwaterloo.ca (office).

ZANNIER, Lamberto, DIur; Italian lawyer, diplomatist and international organization official; *High Commissioner on National Minorities, Organization for Security and Co-operation in Europe;* b. 1954; m.; two s. two d.; ed Univ. of Trieste, Italian Diplomatic Inst.; served with FAO Legal Office, Rome 1976–78; joined Ministry of Foreign Affairs in 1978, worked on Multilateral Econ. Co-operation Desk, Second Sec., Embassy in Abu Dhabi 1979–82, First Sec. (for Multilateral Affairs), Embassy in Vienna 1982–87, with Political Affairs Div. then Office of Sec.-Gen., Ministry of Foreign Affairs 1987–91; seconded to NATO as Head of Disarmament, Arms Control and Cooperative Security Section 1991–97; Deputy Chief of Mission, Perm. Mission to OSCE, Vienna, Chair. for negotiations on Adaptation of the Treaty on Conventional Armed Forces in Europe 1997–2000; Rep. Exec. Council of Org. for Prohibition of Chemical Weapons 2000–02; Dir OSCE Conflict Prevention Centre 2002–06; worked on EU common foreign and security policy, Ministry of Foreign Affairs 2006–08; UN Sec.-Gen.'s Special Rep. for Kosovo and Head of Mission, UN Interim Admin. Mission in Kosovo (UNMIK) 2008–11; Sec.-Gen. OSCE 2011–17, High Commr on Nat. Minorities 2017–. *Publications include:* numerous publs and articles on arms control, peace-keeping and security co-operation. *Address:* Organization for Security and Co-operation in Europe (OSCE), Wallnerstrasse 6, 1010 Vienna, Austria (office). *Telephone:* (1) 514-36-0 (office). *Fax:* (1) 514-36-96 (office). *E-mail:* info@osce.org (office). *Website:* www.osce.org (office).

ZANOTTI, Guerrino; San Marino politician and fmr head of state; *Secretary of State for Internal Affairs, Public Administration, Relations with the Committees, Regulatory Simplification, Institutional Business and Peace Delegation;* b. 24 Oct. 1962; m.; two c.; Head of Econ. Performance, Inst. of Social Security; mem. Partito dei Socialisti e dei Democratici (Party of Socialists and Democrats) 2005–; mem. Consiglio Grande e Generale (Parl.) 2006–08, 2012–; mem. Perm. Council Comm. on Health and Natural Resources; Co-Capt. Regent (jt head of state) of San Marino Oct. 2014–April 2015; Sec. of State for Internal Affairs, Public Admin, Relations with the Cttees, Regulatory Simplification, Institutional Business and Peace Delegation 2016–. *Leisure interest:* racing. *Address:* Parva Domus, Piazza della Libertà 2, 47890 San Marino (office). *Telephone:* 0549 882425 (office). *Fax:* 0549 885080 (office). *E-mail:* segreteria.interni@gov.sm (office). *Website:* www.interni.segreteria.sm (office).

ŽANTOVSKÝ, Michael; Czech politician, scientist, translator, author and fmr diplomatist; *Director, Václav Havel Library;* b. 3 Jan. 1949, Prague; s. of Jiří Žantovský and Hana Žantovská; m. 1st Kristina Žantovská (divorced 2000); one s. one d.; m. 2nd Jana Žantovská; one s. one d.; ed Charles Univ., Prague, McGill Univ., Montreal; scientific worker in a research inst., Prague 1973–80; freelance translator and interpreter 1980–88; Prague Corresp., Reuters 1988–89; activist for ind. creative org. Open Dialogue 1988; Founder mem. restored PEN 1989; Press Spokesman for Centre of Civic Forum 1989–90; mem. Advisory Bd to Pres. Václav Havel 1990–91; Press Spokesman to Pres. 1991–92; with Ministry of Foreign Affairs Aug. 1992; Amb. of Czech and Slovak Fed. Repub. to USA 1992, Amb. of Czech Repub. to USA 1993–97; mem. Senate 1996–2002, Chair. Senate Comm. for Foreign Affairs, Defence and Security 1996–2002; Amb. to Israel 2003–09, to UK 2009–15; Dir Václav Havel Library 2015–; mem. Civic Democratic Alliance (ODA) 1997–, Chair. March–Nov. 1997, 2001, Vice-Chair. 1998–2001; mem. Bd of Supervisors OPS Prague—'European City of Culture 2000' 1999–2001. *Publications include:* papers in scientific journals on psychological motivation and sexual behaviour, author of lyrics and translator of numerous works of fiction, drama and poetry. *Leisure interest:* tennis. *Address:* Václav Havel Library, Ostrovní 13, 110 00 Prague 1, Czech Republic (office). *Telephone:* (222) 220-112 (office). *E-mail:* info@vaclavhavel-library.org (office). *Website:* www.vaclavhavel-library.org (office).

ZANUSSI, Krzysztof; Polish film director and scriptwriter; b. 17 June 1939, Warsaw; s. of Jerzy Zanussi and Jadwiga Zanussi; m. Elżbieta Grocholska; ed Jagiellonian Univ., Kraków Univ., Łódź Higher Film School; Dir TOR State Film Studio 1967–; Lecturer, Stage Dept of Higher State School of Film, TV and Drama, Łódź 1970–72; Prof. Univ. of Silesia; has directed numerous short feature films; Vice-Chair., Polish Film Asscn 1971–81; fmr Pres. EUROVISIONI Asscn; Pres. European Fed. of Film Dirs (FERA) 1990, European Fed. of Audiovisual Producers 1990–94; mem. Polish Acad. of Arts and Sciences, PEN Club, European Film Acad. 2012–, Polish Film Acad., Pontificia Accademia delle Arti e Lettere, Pontifical Comm. of Culture, Vatican, The Int. Fed. of Film Critics (Fipresci), Moscow, Polish Writers Asscn; Kt's Cross of Order of Polonia Restituta, Gold Cross of Merit 1981, Chevalier, Ordre des Sciences et Lettres 1986; Dr hc (Moscow WGIC) 1998, (Minsk European Univ. Acad. of Arts, Bucharest), (European Humanities Univ., Minsk) 2001, (All-Russian State Inst. of Cinematography VGIK, Moscow), (Nat. Univ. of Drama and Film, Bucharest), Yanka Kupala State Univ., Grodno), (Bulgarian Univ., Sophia), (Univ. of Film and TV, St Petersburg), (Catholic Univ. of Lublin), (Opole Univ.); Best Director Cannes Film Festival 1980, Special Jury Prize, Venice Film Festival 1982, Grand Prix Venice 1984, State Prize 1st Class 1984, Grand Prix Moscow 2000, Luka Brajnovic Award, Lifetime Achievement Award, Int. Film Festival of India 2012. *Films include:* Death of Provincial (awards in Venice, Mannheim, Valladolid and Moscow) 1966, Structure of Crystals (award in Mar del Plata) 1969, Family Life (awards in Chicago, Valladolid and Colombo) 1971, Illumination (Grand Prize in Locarno 1973) 1973, The Catamount Killing (USA) (OCIC Prize, West Berlin Int. Film Festival) 1974, Quarterly Balance 1975, Camouflage (special prize, Tehran Int. Film Festival 1977, Grand Prix, Polish Film Festival 1977) 1977, Spiral (Prize of Journalists, V Polish Film Festival 1978, Cannes 1978, OCIC Prize) 1978, Wege in der Nacht (FRG) 1979, Constant Factor (Best Dir Cannes, OCIC Prize) 1980, Contract (Distribution Prize, Venice Film Festival) 1980, From a Far Country (Donatello Prize, Florence) 1980, Versuchung 1981, Imperative (Special Prize and Passinetti Award, Venice), The Unapproachable 1982, Year of the Quiet Sun (Grand Prix Golden Lion, Venice) 1984, The Power of Evil (OCIC Prize, Montreal) 1985, Wherever You Are (Oecumenical Prize, Moscow, Best Script and Act. European Award, Viareggio) 1989, Life for Life 1990, At Full Gallop (Special Jury Prize, Tokyo) 1995, Our God's Brother 1997, Life as a Fatal, Sexually Transmitted Disease (Grand Prix, Moscow Int. Film Festival) 2000, Supplement 2002, Julie Walking Home (exec. producer) 2002, Pregi (producer) 2004, Csoda Krakkóban (producer) 2004, Persona non Grata 2005, The Black Sun 2006, With an Open Heart 2008, Revisited 2009, Venice 70: Future Reloaded 2013, Foreign Body 2014. *TV films:* Portrait of the Composer (prizes in Cracow, Leipzig), Face to Face 1967, Credit 1968, Pass Mark 1969, Mountains at Dark 1970, Role (FRG) 1971, Behind the Wall (Grand Prix, San Remo Int. Film Festival 1972) 1971, Hipotese (FRG) 1972, Nachtdienst (FRG) 1975, Penderecki Lutosławski Baird (documentary) 1976, Anatomiestunde (FRG) 1977, Haus der Frauen (FRG) 1978, Mein Krakau (documentary) 1979, Blaubart (FRG, Switzerland) (Prize, Venice Film Festival) 1984, Mia Varsavia 1987, Erloeschene Zeiten 1987, The Silent Touch 1993, Wrong Address (BBC) 1995, Don't Be Afraid (RAI) 1996, Weekend Stories 1995–2000. *Plays:* One Flew Over the Cuckoo's Nest 1977, Der König stirbt 1980, Mattatoiò 1982, Day and Night, Duo for One 1983, Hiòb, Les Jeux des Femmes (Paris) 1985, Alle Meine Sonne 1986, Giulio Cesare 1986, Alte Zeiten 1988, Koenig Roger 1988, Geburtstag der Infantin 1989, Regina dei Insort 1989, Death and the Maiden (Poznań and Berlin) 1994, Pl. Presidente (Rome, Florence) 1995, Re Pescatore (San Miniatò) 1996, L'uomo che vide (San Miniatò, Borgione) 1998, Herodias et Salomé (Rome) 1998, Amys Way (Essen) 1998, Parenti Terribili (Rome) 2002, Der Beweis (Cologne) 2002, Horrible Parents (Rome) 2002, Partners in Crime (Essen, Berlin) 2005 (Kiev) 2007, Duo (Novosibirsk) 2008, Medea (Syracuse) 2009, Rabbit Hole (Amberg) 2010. *Television:* Old Times (Harold Pinter) ARD 1988, L'Alouette (Jean Anouilh) TVP 2000, Casting Session 2003, Inner Voices 2008. *Publications:* Nowele Filmowe (short feature films) 1976, Scenariusze Filmowe (film scripts) 1978, Un rigorista nella fortezza assediata 1982, Scenariusze Filmowe (film scripts) II, III 1986, IV 1998, The Time to Die (autobiography) 1997, Weekend Stories 1997, Between Kermess and Salon 1999, Six Scripts (USA) 2001, Bigos Will Last in the European Family 2003, A Portrait of the Artist 2008. *Leisure interests:* travel, skiing, horse-riding. *Address:* Studio TOR, ul. Puławska 61, 02-595 Warsaw (office); ul. Kaniowska 114, 01-529 Warsaw, Poland (home). *Telephone:* (22) 8455303 (office); (22) 8392556 (home). *Fax:* (22) 8455303 (office). *E-mail:* tor@tor.com.pl (office). *Website:* www.tor.com.pl (office).

ZAORÁLEK, Lubomír, PhDr; Czech politician; b. 6 Sept. 1956; m. (divorced); three c.; ed Faculty of Philosophy, Jan Evangelista Purkyně Univ., Brno; script ed. Ostrava studio of Česká televize (Czech TV); worked for Československá Socialistická Strana (Czechoslovak Socialist Party) 1986–89; Founding mem. Občanské fórum (Civic Forum), Ostrava 1989, mem. Fed. Ass. as MP for Ostrava II Jan.–June 1990; mem. Ostrava Municipal Council 1990–96; Lecturer, Faculty of Philosophy, Univ. of Ostrava 1990–96; joined Česká Strana Sociálně Demokratická (ČSSD—Czech Social Democratic Party) 1994, Chair. Culture Cttee, Deputy Chair. ČSSD 2009–; mem. Chamber of Deputies for Moravskoslezský (ČSSD) 1996–2013, 2013–, Chair. 2002–06, served as Chair. Foreign Affairs Cttee; Minister of Foreign Affairs 2014–17. *Address:* Česká Strana Sociálně Demokratická, Lidový dům, Hybernská 7, 110 00 Prague 1, Czech Republic (office). *Telephone:* 296522111 (office). *Fax:* 224222190 (office). *E-mail:* info@socdem.cz (office). *Website:* www.cssd.cz (office).

ZAOURAR, Hocine; Algerian photographer; b. 18 Dec. 1952, Birmandreiss; s. of Mohamed Zaourar and Khedidja Bourahla; started as amateur photographer 1970; teacher of photography, Ecole des Beaux-Arts, Algiers 1983–93; joined Reuters as photojournalist 1989; photojournalist, Agence France-Presse, Algiers 1993–; World Press Photo People in the News, 1st Prize 1997, Prix Munn, Paris 1997, Prix Bayeux des correspondants de guerre 1998, Festival Int. du scoop et du journalisme, 1st Prize 1998. *Address:* 5 Lotissement Tardithe, Birmandreiss, Algiers, Algeria (home).

ZARB, Frank Gustav, MBA; American financial executive, insurance industry executive and fmr government official; *Senior Advisor, Hellman and Friedman LLC;* b. 17 Feb. 1935, New York; s. of Gustave Zarb and Rosemary Zarb (née

Antinora); m. Patricia Koster 1957; one s. one d.; ed Hofstra Univ.; Grad. trainee, Cities Service Oil Co. 1957–62; Gen. Partner, Goodbody & Co. 1962–69; Exec. Vice-Pres., CBWL-Hayden Stone 1969–71, Exec. Vice-Pres. Hayden Stone 1972–73, 1977; Asst Sec., US Dept of Labor 1971–72; Assoc. Dir Exec. Office of the Pres., Office of Man. and Budget 1973–74; Admin., Fed. Energy Admin. 1974–77; Asst to the Pres. for Energy Affairs 1976; Gen. Pnr Lazard Frères 1977–88; Chair. and CEO Smith Barney, Harris Upham 1988–93, Smith Barney Shearson 1993; Chair., CEO Nat. Asscn of Securities Dealers 1997–2001; apptd Sr Advisor and Man. Dir Hellman & Friedman LLC 2002, now Sr Advisor; Chair. Promontory Financial Group, Nassau County Interim Finance Authority; Chair. New York State Comm. on Educ. Reform 2003–; Dir Securities Investor Protection Corpn 1988; Vice-Chair. Group Chief Exec. Travelers Inc. 1993–94; Chair., Pres., CEO Alexander & Alexander Services Inc., New York 1994–97; mem. Bd of Dirs Kraft Foods, Inc.; fmr mem. Bd of Dirs American Int. Group (AIG) Inc. (Interim Chair. 2005), CS First Boston Inc., Council on Foreign Relations; Chair. Bd of Trustees, Hofstra Univ.; mem. US Presidential Advisory Cttee on Fed. Pay, US Investment Policy Advisory Cttee; Exec. in Residence, Columbia Univ.; Gerald R. Ford Foundation Distinguished Scholar Award, Hofstra Univ. *Publications include:* The Stock-market Handbook 1969, Handbook of Financial Markets 1981, The Municipal Bond Handbook. *Address:* Hellman and Friedman LLC, 390 Park Avenue, 21st Floor, New York, NY 10022, USA (office). *Telephone:* (212) 871-6680 (office). *Fax:* (212) 871-6688 (office). *Website:* www.hf.com (office).

ZARDARI, Asif Ali; Pakistani business executive, politician and fmr head of state; *President, Pakistan People's Party;* b. 26 July 1955, Karachi, Sindh; s. of Hakim Ali Zardari; m. Benazir Bhutto 1987 (died 2007); one s. two d.; ed Cadet Coll. Petaro, Karachi, studied business in London, UK; mem. Nat. Ass. for Nawabshah 1990–93, 1993–96; imprisoned on blackmail charges 1990–93 (charges dropped); Fed. Minister of the Environment 1993; Fed. Minister for Investment 1995–96; imprisoned on corruption charges 1996–2004 (charges dropped); elected Senator 1997–99 (Parl. dissolved); apptd Co-Chair. Pakistan People's Party (PPP) (following assassination of Benazir Bhutto) 2008–15, Pres. PPP Parliamentarians 2015–; Pres. of Pakistan 2008–13; Vice-Pres. Socialist Int. 2008–; Dir M/s Zardari Group (Pvt.) Ltd. *Leisure interest:* polo (fmr mem. Zardari Four polo team). *Address:* Pakistan Peoples Party, 8 Street 19, F-8/2, Islamabad, Pakistan (office). *Telephone:* (51) 2255264 (office). *Fax:* (51) 2282741 (office). *E-mail:* ppp@comsats .net.pk (office). *Website:* www.ppp.org.pk (office).

ZARE, Richard (Dick) Neil, BA, PhD, FRSC, FAAS, FMRS; American scientist and academic; *Marguerite Blake Wilbur Professor in Natural Science, Stanford University;* b. 19 Nov. 1939, Cleveland, Ohio; s. of Milton Zare and Dorothy Sylvia Zare (née Amdur); m. Susan Leigh Shively 1963; three d.; ed Harvard Univ., Univ. of California, Berkeley; Postdoctoral Research Assoc., Jt Inst. for Lab. Astrophysics, Univ. of Colorado 1964–65, Asst Prof., Dept of Physics and Astrophysics 1966–68, Assoc. Prof. 1968–69; Asst Prof., Dept of Chem., MIT 1965–66; Prof. of Chem., Columbia Univ. 1969–77, Higgins Prof. of Natural Science 1975–77; Prof. of Chem., Stanford Univ. 1977–, Marguerite Blake Wilbur Prof. in Natural Science 1987–, Shell Distinguished Prof. of Chem. 1980–85, Fellow 1984–86, Prof. of Physics 1992–, Chair. Dept of Chem. 2005–11; Prof., Howard Hughes Medical Inst.; Christensen Fellow, St Catherine's Coll., Oxford 1982; Chair. Nat. Science Foundation Advisory Panel (Chem. Div.) 1980–82, Div. of Chemical Physics, American Physical Soc. 1985–86, NAS Panel on Science and Tech. Centers 1987; Chair. Nat. Research Council's Comm. on Physical Sciences, Math. and Applications 1992–95, Nat. Science Bd 1992–98; mem. Nat. Research Council's Cttee on Atomic and Molecular Science 1983–85, Directed Energy Weapons Study Panel of American Physical Soc. 1985–87, Govt-Univ.-Ind. Roundtable of NAS 1989–, Nat. Science Bd 1992–2000; Chair. Bd of Dirs Annual Reviews Inc. 1995–; Ed. Chemical Physics Letters 1982–85; mem. Editorial Advisory Bd Chemical Physics, Journal of Molecular Spectroscopy, Annual Reviews, Molecular Physics, Cambridge Univ. Press; mem. NAS 1976– (mem. Council 1995–), ACS, American Acad. of Arts and Sciences, American Philosophical Soc.; Fellow, American Physical Soc., Int. Advisory Bd, Optical Soc. of America 1994–, Inst. of Physics 1999–; Foreign mem. Royal Soc. 1999, Royal Swedish Acad. of Eng Sciences 2005, Chinese Acad. of Sciences 2005, IVA, Indian Acad. of Sciences 2008, The Acad. of Sciences for the Developing World (TWAS) 2009; mem. Bd of Dirs Camille and Henry Dreyfus Foundation 2010–, Chair. Cttee, Science, Engineering, Medicine and Public Policy 2012–; more than 100 distinguished lecturerships; Hon. Fellow, Chinese Chemical Soc. 2010, Hon. mem. Japan Soc. for Analytical Chem. 2011; Hon. DSc (Arizona) 1990, (Columbia) 2000, (State Univ. of W Georgia) 2001, Dr hc (Northwestern Univ.) 1993, (ETH, Zurich) 1993, (Uppsala) 2000, (Univ. of York) 2001, (Hunan Univ.) 2002, (Université Paul Sabatier) 2003, (Chalmers Inst. of Tech.) 2007, (Univ. of South Florida) 2013, (Univ. of Edinburgh) 2016, Einstein Professorship, Chinese Acad. of Sciences 2011; numerous honours and awards, including Nat. Medal of Science 1983, Irving Langmuir Prize, American Physical Soc. 1985, Kirkwood Award Medal, Yale Univ. 1986, ACS Willard Gibbs Medal 1990, ACS Peter Debye Award 1991, NAS Award in Chemical Sciences 1991, Harvey Prize 1993, Dannie-Heineman Preis 1993, California Scientist of the Year 1997, Eastern Analytical Symposium Award 1997, NASA Exceptional Scientific Achievement Award 1997, ACS Award in Analytical Chem. 1998, Welch Award in Chem. 1999, ACS E. Bright Wilson Award in Spectroscopy 1999, ACS Nobel Laureate Signature Award for Grad. Educ. in Chem. 2000, Arthur L. Schawlow Prize in Laser Science, American Physical Soc. 2000, CaSSS Scientific Achievement Award 2000–01, ACS Charles Lathrop Parsons Award 2001, Madison Marshall Award 2001, Distinguished Chemist Award, ACS Sierra Nevada Section 2002, Wolf Prize in Chem. 2005, Chandler Medal, Columbia Univ. 2005, Pupin Medal "for service to the nation", Columbia Univ. School of Eng 2005, Oesper Award, Univ. of Cincinnati and Cincinnati Section of the ACS 2006, Dudley R. Herschbach Award for Excellence in Research in the field of Collision Dynamics, Dynamics of Molecular Collisions Meeting, Santa Fe 2007, James Flack Norris Award for Outstanding Achievement in the Teaching of Chem. 2004, ACS George C. Pimentel Award in Chemical Educ. 2008, F. Albert Cotton Award for Excellence in Chemical Research 2009, ACS Priestley Medal 2010, Pres.'s Award of Excellence in Science, Math., and Eng Mentoring 2010, R.B. Bernstein Award in Stereodynamics 2010, BBVA Foundation Frontiers of Knowledge Award in the Basic Sciences category 2010, ACS (Northeastern Section) Richards Medal 2010, King Faisal Int. Prize in Science (co-recipient) 2011, Torbern Bergman Medal 2012, Int. Science and Technology Cooperation Award, People's Republic of China 2012, Johannes Marcus Marci Medal 2016. *Publications include:* Angular Momentum 1988, Laser Experiments for Beginners 1995, Angular Momentum: Understanding Spatial Aspects in Chemistry and Physics and Companion to Angular Momentum (co-author) 1998, Annual Review of Analytical Chemistry, Vol. 1 (co-author) 2008, A Companion to Angular Momentum (co-author) 2009; more than 900 research articles. *Leisure interests:* chess, cooking, music, theatre. *Address:* Department of Chemistry, Stanford University, Room 133, Mudd Building, 333 Campus Drive, Stanford, CA 94305-5080 (office); 724 Santa Ynez Street, Stanford, CA 94305-8441, USA (home). *Telephone:* (650) 723-3062 (office); (650) 328-0890 (home). *Fax:* (650) 725-0259 (office). *E-mail:* zare@stanford.edu (office); rnz@stanford.edu (office). *Website:* www.stanford.edu/group/Zarelab (office).

ZARIF, Farid; Afghan diplomatist and UN official; b. 9 Jan. 1951; m. Alia Zarif; two s.; ed Faculty of Law and Political Science, Kabul Univ., Afghan Inst. of Diplomacy, Univ. of Oxford, UK; joined Ministry of Foreign Affairs 1974, First Sec., later Chargé d'affaires, Embassy in Havana 1979–80, Amb. and Perm. Rep. to UN, New York 1981–87, Deputy Foreign Minister 1987–89; Prin. Foreign Policy Adviser to Pres. 1989–91; Sec.-Gen. Economic Advisory Council, Chambers of Commerce and Industry 1991–92; joined UN 1993, Referendum/Elections Coordinator UN missions in Eritrea and South Africa 1993 and 1995, Chief Elections Officer, UN Mission in Liberia (UNMIL) 1994–96, UN Deputy Humanitarian Coordinator in Iraq 1997–2000, fmr Chief, then Dir Office of Iraq Programme, New York, Chief of Staff, UN Assistance Mission for Iraq (UNAMI) 2004, then Chief of Staff and Acting Deputy Special Rep. of Sec.-Gen., UN Mission in Sudan (UNMIS), Dir Europe and Latin America Div., Dept of Peace-keeping Operations (DPKO) 2010, Special Rep. of Sec.-Gen. for Kosovo and Head, UN Interim Admin Mission in Kosovo (UNMIK) 2011–15, Special Rep. of Sec.-Gen. and Head, UN Mission in Liberia (UNMIL) 2015–18.

ZARIF, Mohammad Javad, BA, MA, PhD; Iranian diplomatist and politician; *Minister of Foreign Affairs;* b. 7 Jan. 1960, Tehran; m. Maryam Imanieh 1979; two c.; ed San Francisco State Univ., Univ. of Denver, USA; served as Adviser, later Counsellor and Chargé d'affaires, Perm. Mission to UN, New York 1982–89, Deputy Perm. Rep. 1989–92, Chair. Sixth (Legal) Cttee, UN Gen. Ass. 1992–93, Perm. Rep. 2002–07, Vice-Pres. UN Gen. Ass. 2003–05, OIC Expert Cttee on Dialogue among Civilizations 2000–02, UN Disarmament Comm. 2000, UNESCO Culture Comm. 2007, mem. UN Group of Eminent Persons on Dialogue among Civilizations 2000–02; Adviser to Minister of Foreign Affairs, Tehran 1988–89, Deputy Minister of Foreign Affairs 1992–2002, Minister of Foreign Affairs 2013–; Visiting Prof., Coll. of Int. Relations, Tehran 1989–, Univ. of Tehran 1997–; Pres. Asian African Legal Consultative Cttee, New Delhi 1997–98; Order of Merit and Man., 1st Class 2016, Grand Cross of Order of the Condor of the Andes (Bolivia) 2016, Order of Friendship (Kazakhstan) 2018; Chatham House Prize (co-recipient) 2016. *Publications:* numerous articles on int. affairs in journals and newspapers; served as ed. in numerous scholarly journals. *Address:* Ministry of Foreign Affairs, 12, Imam Khomeini Sq., Tehran, Iran (office). *Telephone:* (21) 66739191 (office). *Fax:* (21) 66743149 (office). *E-mail:* info@mfa.gov.ir (office). *Website:* www.mfa.gov .ir (office).

ZARZALEJOS NIETO, José Antonio; Spanish newspaper editor; b. 1954, Bilbao; s. of José Antonio Zarzalejos Altares; ed Univ. of Deusto; joined El Correo de Bilbao 1989, Deputy Dir 1990, Dir and Chair. Group Editorial Bd 1993–, Owner, ABC as part of Vocento, Dir ABC 1998–2004, 2005–08; Exec. Vice-Pres. Llorente & Cuenca 2008–09, CEO 2009, currently Sr Expert; El Confidencial 2009–; Mariano Cavia Award, Javier Godó Journalism Award, Luca de Tena Award. *Address:* Llorente & Cuenca, Lagasca 88, Planta 3, 28001 Madrid, Spain (office). *Telephone:* (91) 5637722 (office). *Fax:* (91) 5632466 (office). *Website:* www.llorenteycuenca.com (office).

ZATLERS, Valdis; Latvian surgeon and fmr head of state; *Chairman, Reformu Partija (Reform Party);* b. 22 March 1955, Rīga; m. Lilita Zatlere; three c.; ed Rīga Secondary School No. 50, Rīga Inst. of Medicine, Yale Univ. and Syracuse Univ., USA; served in Latvian Nat. Front 1988–89; practised medicine at Yale Univ., Syracuse Univ. and Keggi Orthopaedic Foundation, USA 1990–91; traumatologist and orthopaedist, Rīga Hosp. No. 2 1979–85, Head of Traumatology Dept 1985–94; Dir Latvian Hosp. of Traumatology and Orthopaedics, Rīga 1994–2007, Chair. of Bd 1998–2007; mem. Bd Latvian Popular Front 1988–89; Pres. of Latvia 2007–11; Founder and Chair. Zatlers' Reform Party (renamed Reformu Partija (Reform Party) April 2012) 2011–; Chair. Latvian Asscn for Traumatology and Orthopaedics 2003–; f. Latvian Arthroscopy Asscn, Pres. 1990–93, Vice-Pres. 1994–98; mem. Int. Soc. of Arthroscopy, Knee Surgery and Orthopaedic Sports Medicine (ISACOS) 1993–; Patron European Acad. of Science and Art (Austria) 2009; Hon. mem. Georgian Asscn of Orthopaedics and Traumatology 1992, Univ. of Latvia 2009; Hon. Prof., Nat. Governance Acad. (Kazakhstan) 2008; Three-Star Order (Fourth Class) 2007, Stars, First Grade, with Chain (Latvia) 2007, Knightly Order Pro Merito Melitensi of the Sovereign Mil. Hosp. Order of St John of Jerusalem of Rhodes and of Malta 2008, Order of Special Service to the Fatherland (Uzbekistan) 2008, Order of Friendship, First Degree (Kazakhstan) 2008, Grand Order of King Tomislav, First Grade, with the Ribbon and Great Star (Croatia) 2008, Order of Yaroslav the Wise, First Grade (Ukraine) 2008, Order of the Three Stars, First Class 2008, Order of Viesturs, First Grade (Latvia) 2008, Cross of Recognition, First Grade (Latvia) 2008, Victory Order of St George (Georgia) 2009, Heydar Aliyev Order with Chain (Azerbaijan) 2009, Ismoili Samoni Order with Chain (Tajikistan) 2009, Order and Chain of Isabel the Catholic (Spain) 2009, Order of the Cross of St Mary's Land (Estonia) 2009, Order of the White Rose 2010, Order of Vytautas the Great 2011, Order of Liberty (Ukraine) 2011; Dr hc (Yerevan State Univ., Armenia) 2009, (John Paul II Catholic Univ. of Lublin, Poland) 2010, (Univ. Stradiņša, Rīga) 2010; Int. Arthroscopy Asscn Prize 1993, Medal of Honour, Local Govt of Miraflores, Lima, Peru 2008, Medal of Achievement, Baltic Defence Coll., Estonia 2009, Commemorative Medallion in honour of 90th anniversary of Latvian Border Guard 2009, Medal of Latvian Asscn of Reserve Officers 2010. *Address:* Reformu Partija (Reform Party), Vīlandes iela 14-1/6, Rīga 1050, Latvia (office). *Telephone:* 6728-3908 (office). *E-mail:* birojs@reformupartija.lv (office). *Website:* www.reformupartija.lv (office).

ZATULIN, Konstantin Fedorovich; Russian business executive and economist; *Director, Institute of CIS Countries;* b. 7 Sept. 1958, Batumi; s. of Zatulin Fedor

Ivanovich; m. 1979; one d.; ed Moscow State Univ.; functionary, Cen. Komsomol Cttee 1988–89; Dir-Gen. Int. Asscn of Heads of Enterprises 1989–; Co-founder Moscow Stock Exchange; Chair. Bd Co.-Rostok; Pres. Moscow Exchange Union 1992–; mem. Bd Russian Party of Unity and Consent 1993–94; Chair. Businessman for New Russia Union 1993–, Cttee on CIS affairs and connections with compatriots 1994–; mem. State Duma (Parl.) 1993–95; mem. Govt Comm. on Compatriots Abroad 1994–; Dir Inst. for Problems of Diaspora and Integration (now Inst. of CIS Countries), Moscow 1996–; Chair. Fund for Devt of Econ. Reforms; Adviser to Mayor of Moscow 1997, Bd Moscow Fund of Presidential Programmes 2000–, Derzhava Movt 1998–, Sochi Friends Club 1998–; mem. Bd Otechestvo political org. 1998; Deputy, State Duma 2003–11; presenter, Russian Question weekly TV 2012–; Adviser to Chair. of State Council of Repub. of Crimea 2014, to Head of Repub. of Crimea 2015; mem. Public Scientific and Methodological Advisory Council, Central Election Comm. 2013–, Public Chamber of Russian Fed. 2015–; Trustee, Admirals Club 2007–; Hon. mem. Russian Community of Crimea 2006, Hon. Citizen of Repub. of Abkhazia 2008; Order of Friendship 2006, Order of Merit 2014; Awards of Russian Govt, Medal of Honour (Armenia). *Address:* Institute of CIS Countries, 109180 Moscow, ul. B. Glade, d. 7/10 (office); 1st Truzhenikov per. 17, Apt 79, Moscow, Russia (home). *Telephone:* (495) 959-34-51 (office); (495) 248-05-79 (home). *Fax:* (495) 959-34-49 (office). *E-mail:* zatulin@zatulin.ru (office). *Website:* www.zatulin.ru (office).

ZATZ, Mayana, PhD; Israeli biologist and academic; *Professor of Genetics and Director, Centre for Studies of the Human Genome, University of São Paolo;* b. 1948; m.; two c.; ed Univ. of São Paolo and Univ. of California, Los Angeles, USA; moved with family to France where she lived until age seven, moved to Brazil 1955; post-doctoral work in Medical Genetics, UCLA; Prof. of Genetics, Dept of Biology, Inst. of Biosciences, Univ. of São Paulo and Dir Centre for Studies of the Human Genome 1969–, Rector of Research 2006–09; Founder and Pres. Brazilian Muscular Dystrophy Asscn; mem. Int. Human Genome Project; mem. Conselho Nacional de Desenvolvimento Científico e Tecnológico, Science Acad. of the State of São Paulo, Brazilian Science Acad.; Grã-Cruz da Ordem Nacional do Mérito Científico e Tecnológico 2000; Research Award, Muscular Dystrophy Asscn (USA) 1986, Medal of Scientific and Technological Merit, Govt of State of São Paulo 2000, Nat. Order of Scientific and Technological Merit, Presidency of Repub. of Brazil 2000, L'Oréal-UNESCO For Women in Science Award 2001, Premio Claudia 2001, Prize in Basic Medical Sciences, Third World Acad. of Sciences 2004, Prêmio Hospitalar 2005, Prêmio Scopus 2007, Premio da Maçonaria 2007, Mulher Cidadã Bertha Lutz, Senado Federal 2008. *Publications:* more than 170 papers in scientific journals and approx. 150 articles in foreign magazines on genetics of neuromuscular diseases. *Address:* Department of Biology, Institute of Biosciences, University of São Paulo, Rua do Matão, 277 Sala 211, Travessa 14, 321-Butantã, 05508-900 São Paulo SP, Brazil (office). *Telephone:* (11) 3091-7563 (office). *Fax:* (11) 3091-7419 (office). *E-mail:* mayazatz@usp.br (office); ib@edu.usp.br (office). *Website:* www.ib.usp.br (office).

ZAVALA LOMBARDI, Fernando Martin, MBA; Peruvian economist, business executive and government official; b. 16 Feb. 1971, Tacna; m. Marta González-Revilla; ed Universidad del Pacífico, Univ. of Piura, Univ. of Birmingham, UK; began career with Samtronics Peru; fmr Chief Financial Officer, Apoyo SA; CEO Instituto Nacional de Defensa de la Competencia y de la Protección de la Propiedad Intelectual 1995–2000; Deputy Minister of Economy and Finance 2004–05, Minister of Economy and Finance 2005–06, June–Sept. 2017; Gov. for Peru, IDB 2005–06; Vice-Pres. of Strategy and Corp. Relations, Backus & Johnston SA (subsidiary of SABMiller) 2006–09, Pres. Cervecería Nacional—SABMiller Panamá 2009–13, Gen. Man. Backus & Johnston SA 2013–16; Pres., Council of Ministers (Prime Minister) 2016–17; Dir-Gen. Indecopi; fmr Dir Corporación Andina de Fomento (CAF); fmr Dir Interbank, Alicorp, Inmobiliaria IDE, Cervecería San Juan, Banco Falabella, Enersur, Corporación Financiera de Desarrollo (Cofide); fmr mem. Comisión de Promoción del Perú para la Exportación y el Turismo (Promperú); mem. Global Agenda Council, World Econ. Forum in Latin America.

ZAVALETA LÓPEZ, Javier Eduardo; Bolivian architect and politician; *Minister of Defence;* b. 20 Aug. 1970, La Paz; ed Univ. of San Andres; worked in the field of design and construction 1994; Co-Founder and mem. Movimiento Sin Miedo (MSM) 2000; Dir Maintenance and Emergencies, Municipal Govt of La Paz 2001; mem. Chamber of Deputies 2006–, Pres. Parliamentary Network for Childhood and Adolescence 2011–13, Planning, Econ. Policy and Finance Comm. 2013–14, 2015–17, Vice-Pres. Chamber of Deputies 2014–18, Pres. CEMIPyC (Comisión especial mixta de Investigación de la privatización y capitalización) 2015; Uninominal Deputy Circumscription 8, Dept of La Paz 2006–09, 2014–18 (now called Circumscription 6), Pres. Comm. of Defence and Armed Forces 2006, Sec. Grupo Parlamentario Interamericano (GPI); Minister of Defence 2018–. *Address:* Ministry of Defence, Calle 20 de Octubre, esq. Pedro Salazar, Plaza Avaroa 2502, La Paz, Bolivia (office). *Telephone:* (2) 261-0548 (office). *E-mail:* utransparencia@mindef.gob.bo (office). *Website:* www.mindef.gob.bo (office).

ZAVARZIN, Col-Gen. Victor Mikhailovich; Russian army officer (retd) and politician; b. 28 Nov. 1948, Zaoleshenka, Kursk Region; m.; two d.; ed Ordzhonikidze Higher Gen. Army School, Frunze Mil. Acad., Acad. of Gen. Staff; posts in Middle Asia Command 1970–78, Head of Staff of Div. Far E Command 1981–85, Head of Staff, Deputy Commdr, Commdr of Div., Commdr Training Cen. Carpathian Command 1985–90, Commdr United Russian-Turkmen Armed Force in Turkmenistan 1993–94, Commdr United Peacekeeping Forces in Tajikistan 1996–97, Deputy, First Deputy Head of Staff Russian Army, responsible for co-operation with CIS countries April–Oct. 1997, Mil. Rep. of Russia to NATO HQ, Brussels 1997–99, led Russian mil. unit from Bosnia and Herzegovina to Kosovo, Yugoslavia 1999; mem. State Duma (Parl.) (Yedinaya Rossiya faction) 2003–, fmr Chair. Cttee on Defense, currently Chair. Ethics Cttee. *Address:* State Duma; 103265 Moscow, Okhotnyi ryad 1, Russia (office). *Telephone:* (495) 292-83-10 (office). *Fax:* (495) 292-94-64 (office). *Website:* www.duma.ru (office).

ZAVGAYEV, Doku Gapurovich, CandEcon; Russian/Chechen politician and diplomatist; *Ambassador to Slovenia;* b. 22 Dec. 1940; mem. CPSU 1966–91; teacher at elementary school, mechanic, engineer of sovkhoz, man. Regional Union Selkhoztechnika, Dir sovkhoz Znamensky, Chair. Nadterechny Regional Exec. Cttee 1971–72; Chief Repub. Union of Sovkhozes 1972–75; Minister of Agric. of Checheno-Ingush SSR 1975–77; head of div., Second Sec. Checheno-Ingush Regional CP Cttee 1977–89; First Sec. Repub. CP Cttee 1989–91; Chair. Supreme Soviet of Checheno-Ingush Autonomous SSR 1990–91, mem. Cen. CPSU Cttee 1990–91; People's Deputy of RSFSR 1990–93; in Admin. of Pres. of Russia 1994–95; Pres. of Chechen Repub. 1995–96; Deputy, Council of Russian Fed. 1995–97; Amb. to Tanzania 1997–2004, Deputy Minister of Foreign Affairs 2004, Dir-Gen. Ministry of Foreign Affairs 2004–09, Amb. to Slovenia 2009–; Order of Red Banner of Labour, Badge of Honour; awarded four medals. *Publication:* System of Agric. in Checheno-Ingush Republic. *Leisure interests:* walking, travelling. *Address:* Embassy of the Russian Federation, 1000 Ljubljana, Tomšičeva 9, Slovenia (office). *Telephone:* (1) 4256875 (office). *Fax:* (1) 4256878 (office). *E-mail:* ambrus.slo@siol.net (office). *Website:* www.rus-slo.mid.ru (office).

ZAVOS, Panayiotis Michael, BA, MS, EdS, PhD; American reproductive specialist and andrologist; *President, Zavos Organization;* b. 23 Feb. 1944, Trikomo, Cyprus; m. Dr Panayota N. Zavos; three c.; ed Emporia State Univ., Univ. of Minnesota; Dir of Laboratory Facilities and Visiting Scholar, OB/GYN Dept, Fertility Inst. of Chicago, Northwestern Univ. 1978–79; Founder, Dir and Chief Andrologist, Andrology Inst. of America 1990–, Andrology Inst. of America-Middle East 2010–; Co-Founder, Scientific Dir and Chief Embryologist, Kentucky Center for Reproductive Medicine; Founder and Pres. Zavos Org. 1995–; Pres. and CEO ZDL, Inc., Lexington, Ky; Prof., Univ. of Kentucky 1979, now Prof. Emer.; mem. Editorial Bd American Soc. for Reproductive Medicine, Infertility, and many others; mem. ASRM, American Soc. of Andrology, European Soc. for Human Reproduction and Embryology, M.E. Fertility Soc., Japanese Fertility Soc. and numerous other professional socs; Hon. Prof., Chinese Acad. of Science; Distinguished Alumnus Award, Emporia State Univ., Distinquished Research Award, Univ. of Minnesota Outstanding Teacher Award, Emporia State Univ., Paul Harris Fellow, Rotary Int. *Publications include:* more than 500 specialist articles on reproduction and infertility. *Leisure interests:* golf, running, fishing. *Address:* ZDL, Inc., 181 Southland Drive, Lexington, KY 40523, USA (office). *Telephone:* (859) 278-6806 (office). *Fax:* (859) 278-6906 (office). *E-mail:* zavos@zavos.org (office). *Website:* www.zavos.org (office); www.aia-zavos.com (office).

ZAWADZKI, Włodzimierz, PhD; Polish scientist; b. 4 Jan. 1939, Warsaw; ed Warsaw Univ.; Prof. 1985; scientific worker and Prof., Inst. of Physics, Polish Acad. of Sciences (PAN) 1961–; with MIT, Cambridge, Mass, USA 1965–67, Ecole Normale Supérieure, Paris, France 1974; Visiting Prof., Linz Univ., Austria 1978, North Texas State Univ. 1980, Tech. Univ., Munich, FRG 1981, Innsbruck Univ., Austria 1983, Université des Sciences et Techniques du Languedoc Montpellier 1984; analyst for Polish weekly, Polityka; mem. Polish Physical Soc.; Annual Prize of Polish Science 1973, Maria Sklodowska-Curie Award 1977, State Prize (1st degree, collective) 1978, Mich. Univ. Award 1995, Marian Smoluchowski Medal 1997. *Publications include:* more than 170 works on theory of semiconductors; also novels and collections of poetry, including Wanka-Wstanka 1990, Szekspir Socjalu 1991 and prose, including Wielki inkwizytor 1993. *Leisure interests:* literature, music, sports, skiing, tennis, basketball. *Address:* al. J. Ch. Szucha 11 m. 26, 00-580 Warsaw, Poland. *Telephone:* (22) 8410285. *E-mail:* zawad@ifpan.edu.pl.

ZAWAHIRI, Ayman Muhammad Rabi'-al, MS, DMed; Egyptian paediatrician, theologian and guerrilla leader; b. 19 June 1951, Maadi; grandson of Muhammad Rabi'a Zawahiri and Umayma Azzam; m. Azza Ahmed 1978 (died 2001); ed Cairo Univ.; mem. The Muslim Brotherhood (arrested for membership 1966); Founder Egyptian Islamic Jihad; imprisoned on firearms charge following Egyptian Pres. Sadat's assassination 1981–84; joined mujahidin troops fighting Soviet occupation forces in Afghanistan 1984; co-f. Int. Front for Fighting Jews and Crusaders (with Osama bin Laden) 1998; co-f. al-Qa'ida; personal physician and political adviser to Osama bin Laden; fmr Leader Vanguards of Conquest Movt; assumed to be the figurehead of al-Qa'ida following death of Osama bin Laden 2 May 2011, confirmed by press release from al-Qa'ida's general command on 16 June; under worldwide sanctions by UN Security Council Resolution 1267 as a mem. or affiliate of al-Qa'ida.

ZAYANI, Lt-Gen. (retd) Abdul Latif bin Rashid al-, PhD; Bahraini international organization official and fmr army officer; *Secretary-General, Gulf Co-operation Council;* b. Muharraq; ed Royal Mil. Acad. Sandhurst and Aeronautical Eng Programme, Perth, UK, Air Force Inst. of Tech., Dayton, Ohio, Naval Postgraduate School, Monterey, Calif., Command and Gen. Staff Course, Fort Leavenworth, Kan. and Leaders in Devt Program, Harvard Univ., USA; commissioned as officer, Bahrain Defence Force 1973, numerous positions including Officer, 1st Royal Mechanized Bn, Royal Air Defence, Royal Bahraini Air Force, Dir of Planning and Org., Dir of Jt Operations, Asst Chief of Staff for Operations; Chief of Public Security, Ministry of the Interior 2004; Adviser with rank of Minister, Gen. Court of Ministry of Foreign Affairs 2010; Sec.-Gen., Gulf Co-operation Council 2011–; Chair. Jt Steering Cttee between Bahrain and UK; Chair. Devt and Regulation Cttee, Ministry of Foreign Affairs; fmr Prof. of Quantitative Methods, Univ. of Bahrain; fmr Prof. of Math. and Statistics, Univ. of Maryland, Bahrain; Efficiency Medal 2nd Class, Mil. Assessment Medal 1st Class, Bahrain Medal 3rd Grade, Shaikh Isa Medal 3rd Grade, Bahrain Medal 2nd Grade, Mil. Duty Medal, Hawar Medal 1st Grade, Liberation of Kuwait Medal 2nd Grade, Liberation of Kuwait Medal, Security Medal for Devotion to Duty 1st Class, Bahrain Medal 1st Grade, Sword of Honor along with title of Master Logistician from USA Army, Int. Police Leadership Award NPIA, UK 2010. *Leisure interests:* travel, fitness, sports. *Address:* Gulf Co-operation Council Building, King Khaled Road Diplomatic Area, PO Box 7153, Riyadh 11462 (office); Secretariat-General, Gulf Cooperation Council for the Arab States of the Gulf, PO Box 7153, Riyadh 11466, Saudi Arabia (office). *Telephone:* (1) 4827777 (office); (1) 4829015 (office). *Fax:* (1) 4829089 (office); (1) 4828008 (office). *E-mail:* dr.alzayani.off@gmail.com (office); info@gcc-sg.org (office). *Website:* www.gcc-sg.org (office).

ZAYCHANKA, Mikalay Petrovich; Belarusian economist and politician; b. 1948, Pogranichnyi, Maritime (Primorskii) Krai, Russia; ed Belarusian Polytechnic Inst.; Engineer then Sr Engineer, Inst. of Machine Planning, Acad. of Sciences of Belarusian SSR; Sr Economist and Jr Scientific Colleague, Inst. of Econs, Acad. of Sciences of Belarusian SSR; Sr Scientific Colleague, responsible for methodology, Scientific Research Inst. of Gosplan (State Planning Cttee); First Deputy Minister of the Economy 1997–2003, Minister of the Economy 2003–09; Medal for Services to Labour.

ZBIDI, Abdelkarim, MD; Tunisian physician, academic and government official; *Minister of National Defence;* b. 25 June 1950, Réjiche, Mahdia; ed Univ. Claude Bernard, Lyon, France; Foreign Asst Dr, Univ. of Medicine Grange Blanche, Lyon 1976–78; Teaching Asst, Univ. of Medicine of Sousse 1978–81, Assoc. Lecturer 1982–86, Teaching Prof. 1987–, Coordinator of High Health Technicians Training 1981–88, Head of Basic Sciences Dept 1982–89; Head of Functional Investigation Dept, Farhat Hached Hosp. of Sousse 1990–99, Dean, Faculty of Medicine 2005–08; Exec. of expert missions to IAEA 1992–; Chair. Physiology and Functional Investigation Coll., Ministry of Public Health 1994–97, Centre Univ. (Sousse, Monastir, Mahdia and Kairouan), Ministry of Higher Educ. 1995–99; Sec. of State to the Prime Minister for Scientific Research and Tech. 1999–2000; Minister of Public Health 2001, of Scientific Research and Tech. 2002, of Nat. Defence 2011–13, 2017–; Chair. Public Health Hosp. 'RAZI' 2008–10, Scientific and Orientation Bd, Tech. Center of Sousse 2009–10; Founding mem. and Co-ordinator of Teaching, Medical School of Djibouti 2007–; mem. High-level Science and Technology Cttee to the Prime Minister 2009–10. *Publications:* 140 publs and 300 scientific papers. *Address:* Ministry of National Defence, boulevard Bab Menara, 1008 Tunis, Tunisia (office). *Telephone:* (71) 560-240 (office). *Fax:* (71) 561-804 (office). *E-mail:* defnat@defense.tn (office). *Website:* www.defense.tn (office).

ŽBOGAR, Samuel, BA; Slovenian diplomatist and politician; *Head of Delegation to North Macedonia, European Union;* b. 5 March 1962, Postojna; m. Maja Žbogar; three c.; ed Faculty of Social Sciences, Univ. of Ljubljana; Sec. Foreign Students' Club, Inst. for Int. Scientific, Tech. and Cultural Cooperation 1986, adviser Dept of Neighbouring Countries 1987–90; Third Sec. Dept of Neighbouring Countries, Ministry of Foreign Affairs 1990, Counsellor and Sec. to Slovenian Del. at Int. Conf. on Fmr Yugoslavia 1991; Sec. Slovenian Rep. Office, EC Monitoring Mission in Zagreb 1991; Counsellor to the Minister and Sec. in the Office of the Sec.-Gen., Ministry of Foreign Affairs 1992; Chargé d'affaires a.i. and First Sec., Embassy in Beijing 1993–95; Counsellor to Govt and State Under-Sec. and Dir Dept for Africa, Asia, Latin America and the Pacific, Ministry of Foreign Affairs 1995–97; Deputy Perm. Rep. to UN, New York 1997–2001, Deputy Perm. Rep. to UN Security Council 1998–99; State Sec., Ministry of Foreign Affairs 2001–04; Amb. to USA 2004–08; Dir Inst. for Strategic Studies Oct.–Nov. 2008; Minister of Foreign Affairs 2008–12; EU Special Rep. in Kosovo 2012–16; Head of Del. of the EU to North Macedonia, Skopje 2016–. *Leisure interest:* long distance running. *Address:* Delegation of the European Union to North Macedonia, Sv Kiril i Metodij, 52B, 1000 Skopje, Macedonia (office). *Telephone:* (2) 3248500 (office). *E-mail:* samuel.zbogar@eeas.europa.eu (office). *Website:* eeas.europa.eu/delegations/republic-north-macedonia_en (office).

ZBRUYEV, Alexander Victorovich; Russian actor; b. 31 March 1938, Moscow; s. of Viktor Alekseevich Zbruyev and Tatiana Aleksandrovna Fedorova; m. Ludmila Savelyeva; one d.; ed Shchukin Higher School of Theatre Art; actor, Moscow Theatre of Lininsky Comsomol 1961–; f. TRAM (Theatre Restaurant of Moscow Actors) 1998–; People's Artist of Russian Fed. 1989; numerous awards and decorations for his works in film and on stage. *Plays include:* Optimistic Tragedy, Hamlet, Goodbye, Boys, The Day of the Wedding, My Poor Marat, 104 Pages About Love, Wizard, Gambler, The Last Night of the Last Tsar, The Barbarian and Heretic. *Films include:* My Younger Brother 1962, Zdravstvuy, zhizn! 1963, Puteshestviye v aprel 1963, Chistye prudy 1965, Dva bileta na dnevnoy seans 1966, Ot snega do snega 1968, Sotvori boy 1969, Gde 042? 1969, Opekun 1970, Antratsit 1972, Povest o chelovecheskom serdtse 1974, Krug 1974, Romans o vlyublyonnykh 1974, Menya eto ne kasaetsya 1976, Melodii beloy nochi 1978, Vystrel v spinu 1980, Takiye zhe, kak my! 1980, Koltso iz Amsterdama 1981, Tayna zapisnoy knizhki 1982, Naslednitsa po pryamoy 1982, Predisloviye k bitve 1983, U opasnoy cherty 1983, Sem chasov do gibeli 1983, Tayna villy Greta 1984, Shyol chetvyortyy god voyny 1985, Odinokaya zhenshchina zhelayet poznakomitsya 1986, Khrani menya, moy talisman 1986, Zina-Zinulya 1986, Poputchik 1986, Uspekh 1987, Svobodnoye padeniye 1987, Filyor 1987, Ubit drakona 1988, Avtoportret neizvestnogo 1988, Chyornaya roza: emblema pechali, krasnaya roza—emblema lyubvi 1989, The Inner Circle 1991, Zoloto 1992, The House at Rozhdestvensky Boulevard 1992, Ty u menya odna (as A. Zbruyev) 1993, Maestro vor 1994, Kafe V'Limon 1994, Vsyo budet khorosho 1995, Bednaya Sasha 1997, Bremenskie muzykanty 2001, Shizofreniya 2001, Severnoye siyaniye 2001, Kozha salamandry 2004, O lyubvi 2004. *Television includes:* The Long Recess (mini-series) 1972, Manon Lesko (film) 1979, Dom, kotoryy postroil Svift (film) 1982, Batalyony prosyat ognya (mini-series) 1985. *Leisure interests:* sports, cars. *Address:* 103050 Moscow, Tverskaya str. 19, Apt 76, Russian Federation. *Telephone:* (495) 299-99-34.

ZECCHINI, Salvatore, MBA, PhD; Italian economist, government official and academic; *Vice-Chair, Committee on Economic Cooperation and Integration, United Nations Economic Commission for Europe;* b. 17 Nov. 1943, Palermo; m. Eliana de Leva 1971; one s. one d.; ed Columbia Univ. and Univ. of Pennsylvania, Wharton School of Finance, USA; economist, Research Dept, Banca d'Italia, Dir Research Dept 1972–81, Dir 1981–84; Adviser to Govt of Italy 1978–84; Exec. Dir IMF 1984–89; Special Counsellor, OECD 1989–90, Asst Sec.-Gen. 1990–96, then Deputy Sec.-Gen., Chair. Working Party on Small and Medium Sized Enterprises and Entrepreneurship 2011–; Dir Centre for Co-operation of Economies in Transition 1990–96; Prof. of Int. Econ. Policy, Univ. of Rome 1997–; Econ. Adviser to Minister of Finance 1997–2000, to Minister of Industry and Trade 2001–09; Dir Public Investment Evaluation Centre 1997–98, Chair. Advisory Council of ICE (External Trade Agency) 2002–05; Chair. Gestore del Mercato Elettrico 2006–09; Chair. Europex, IPI Inst. for Industrial Promotion; Vice-Chair. Cttee on Econ. Co-operation and Integration, UN Econ. Comm. for Europe 2011–. *Publications:* The Transition to a Market Economy (co-ed.) 1991, Lessons from The Economic Transition (ed.) 1996; articles in professional journals and books on econs and int. finance. *Leisure interests:* history, travel, hiking. *Address:* UN Economic Commission for Europe, Palais des Nations, 1211 Geneva 10, Switzerland (office). *Website:* www.unece.org/eci.html (office).

ZEDILLO PONCE de LEÓN, Ernesto, MA, MPhil, PhD, DEcon; Mexican economist, academic and fmr head of state; *Director, Center for the Study of Globalization, Yale University;* b. 27 Dec. 1951, Mexico City; s. of Rodolfo Zedillo Castillo and Martha Alicia Ponce de León; m. Nilda Patricia Velasco Núñez; five c.; ed Instituto Nacional Politécnico, Yale Univ., USA; joined Partido Revolucionario Institucional (PRI) 1971, with Instituto de Estudios Políticos, Económicos y Sociales (Iepes) (affil. to PRI); econ. researcher, Dirección Gen. de Programación Económica y Social; economist, Deputy Man. Econ. Research, Gen. Dir Trust Fund for the Renegotiation of Pvt. Firms' External Debt and Deputy Dir, Banco de Mexico (BANXICO) 1978–87; Prof. of Macroeconomics and Int. Econs, Instituto Nacional Politécnico and Colegio de México 1979–87; Under-Sec. of the Budget 1987–88, Sec. Budget and Econ. Planning 1988–92, Sec. of Educ. 1992–93; campaign man. for the late Luis Donaldo Colosio (fmr presidential cand.) 1993–94; Pres. of Mexico 1994–2000; Chair. UN High Level Panel on Financing for Devt 2000–01, Global Devt Network; Co-Chair. UN Comm. on Pvt. Sector and Devt 2004, Int. Task Force on Global Public Goods (sponsored by Govts of Sweden and France); Jt Coordinator UN Millennium Project's Task Force on Trade 2002–05; mem. Advisory Panel to Dir-Gen. WTO 2001–02, Trilateral Comm., Int. Advisory Bd of Council on Foreign Relations and Bd of Dirs Inst. for Int. Econs, Int. Crisis Group Bd, High-Level Panel on Legal Empowerment of the Poor, Foundation Bd of World Econ. Forum, Club de Madrid, Group of Thirty Consultative Group on Int. Econ. and Monetary Affairs, Inc. (G-30), Washington, DC 2005–; UN Special Envoy for 2005 World Summit; Distinguished Visiting Fellow, Centre for Global Governance, LSE 2001; Distinguished Lecturer, Univ. of Miami 2001; Distinguished Collins Fellow, John F. Kennedy School of Govt, Harvard Univ. 2001; Prof. in the Field of Int. Econs and Politics and Dir Yale Center for the Study of Globalization, Yale Univ., USA 2002–; mem. Bd of Dirs Procter and Gamble, ALCOA, Union Pacific Corpn, Citigroup 2010–, Inst. for Int. Economics; mem. Int. Advisory Bd Coca Cola Co., MAGNA; mem. Editorial Bd Americas Quarterly; Trustee, Fundacion Carolina, Madrid; decorations from govts of 32 countries; Hon. LLD (Yale) 2001, (Harvard) 2003; Hon. DHumLitt (Miami) 2002; Dr hc (Massachusetts, Amherst) 2003; Wilbur Cross Medal, Democracy and Peace Award, Inst. of the Americas, Univ. of California, San Diego 2001, Franklin D. Roosevelt Freedom from Fear Award 2002, Tribuna Americana Award, Casa de America, Madrid, Spain 2002, Commencement Speaker, Harvard Univ. 2003, Gold Insigne, The Americas Soc. 2003, Berkeley Medal, Univ. of California, Berkeley 2004, Sustainable Devt Leadership Award, The Energy Resources Inst. (TERI), India 2006. *Address:* Yale Center for the Study of Globalization, Betts House, 393 Prospect Street, New Haven, CT 06511, USA (office). *Telephone:* (203) 432-1900 (office). *Fax:* (203) 432-1200 (office). *E-mail:* ernesto.zedillo@yale.edu (office); globalization@yale.edu (office). *Website:* www.ycsg.yale.edu (office).

ZEFFIRELLI, Franco (Gian Franco Corsi); Italian theatre, opera and film director and set designer; b. 12 Feb. 1923, Florence; ed Liceo Artistico, Florence and Univ. of Florence School of Architecture; moved to Rome to debut as an actor in cinema and theatre 1946; met Luchino Visconti which proved crucial for his film and theatre training, hired as asst and later as set designer for productions of William Shakespeare's Troilus and Cressida 1949 and Tennessee Williams' A Streetcar Named Desire; worked as asst dir in various theatre productions and in films The Earth Trembles 1947, Bellissima 1951, Senso 1954; produced set designs for Romeo and Juliet, staged at the Old Vic Company, London 1960; staged, amongst others, productions of La Cenerentola by Gioachino Rossini 1953, La Traviata by Giuseppe Verdi with Maria Callas 1958; release of film The Taming of the Shrew 1967, Romeo and Juliet 1968; commissioned by leading opera houses world-wide, including Teatro alla Scala of Milan, The Met, New York, Covent Garden, London and Staatsoper, Vienna, to stage performances; numerous opera productions with artists including Maria Callas, Plácido Domingo, Luciano Pavarotti, Herbert Von Karajan, Leonard Bernstein, Carlos Kleiber; productions include Il Turco in Italia with Maria Callas, Aïda and La Bohéme at Teatro alla Scala, Milan, Carmen at the Staatsoper, Vienna, Tosca, Turandot, Falstaff and La Traviata at the Metropolitan, New York, Aïda, Il Trovatore, Carmen and Madama Butterfly in Verona, and two experiments in Busseto with small productions of Aïda and La Traviata; Aïda of Busseto brought to Moscow 2004, La Traviata of Busseto staged in Moscow and Tel-Aviv 2005 (also I Pagliacci); Teatro dell'Opera, Rome presented Don Giovanni 2006, followed by Aïda 2006; returned to Teatro dell'Opera, Rome for a new comeback of La Traviata 2007, Tosca 2008, I Pagliacci 2009, Falstaff 2010; production of Carmen at Arena of Verona 2009, Turandot 2010, also Aïda, Madama Butterfly, Carmen and Il Trovatore; new Turandot celebrated the opening of Royal Opera House of Muscat, Sultanate of Oman 2011; presented Mozart's Don Giovanni at Arena di Verona 2012; made film-opera of Cavalleria Rusticana by Pietro Mascagni and I Pagliacci by Ruggero Leoncavallo 1980; cr. film version of Verdi's La Traviata; also successful in prose theatre, both in Italy and abroad, with works by Shakespeare: Hamlet with Giorgio Albertazzi, also performed in London, and Romeo and Juliet; other works include La Lupa by Verga, starring Anna Magnani, and pieces by contemporary authors: Who's Afraid of Virginia Woolf by Edward Albee, After the Fall by Arthur Miller, Due più due non fa più quattro by Lina Wertmüller, Sabato, Domenica e Lunedì by Eduardo, at the Old Vic, London and featuring Sir Laurence Olivier; Hon. KBE 2005; Prix des Nations 1976, Premio Colosseo, City of Rome 2009 and numerous others. *Theatre includes:* Romeo and Juliet (Old Vic, London) 1960, Othello (Stratford) 1961, Hamlet (Nat. Theatre, London) 1964, After the Fall (Rome) 1964, Who's Afraid of Virginia Woolf (Paris) 1964, (Milan) 1965, La Lupa (Rome) 1965, Much Ado About Nothing (Nat. Theatre, London) 1966, Black Comedy (Rome) 1967, A Delicate Balance (Rome) 1967, Saturday, Sunday, Monday (Nat. Theatre, London) 1973, Filumena (Lyric, London) 1977, Six Characters in Search of an Author (London) 1992, Absolutely Perhaps! (London) 2003, Pagliacci (Teatro Carlo Felice, Genoa) 2011. *Operas include:* Lucia di Lammermoor, Cavalleria Rusticana, Pagliacci (Covent Garden) 1959, 1973, Falstaff (Covent Garden) 1961, L'Elisir d'amore (Glyndebourne) 1961, Don Giovanni, Alcina (Covent Garden) 1962, Tosca, Rigoletto (Covent Garden) 1964, 1966, 1973, (Metropolitan, New York) 1985, Don Giovanni (Staatsoper Wien) 1972, (Metropolitan, New York) 1990, Otello (Metropolitan, New York) 1972, Antony and Cleopatra (Metropolitan, New York) 1973, Otello (La Scala) 1976, La Bohème (Metropolitan, New York) 1981, Turandot (La Scala) 1983, 1985, (Metropolitan, New York) 1987, Don Carlos 1992, Carmen 1996, Aïda (New Theatre, Tokyo) 1997, (Busseto) 2000, La Traviata (Metropolitan, New York) 1998, Tosca (Rome) 2000, Il Trovatore (Arena di Verona) 2001, Aïda (Arena di Verona) 2002, La Bohème (La Scala) 2003, (Rome) 2003, Carmen (Arena di Verona) 2003, I Pagliacci (Covent Garden, London) 2003, (Tel-Aviv, Israel) 2005, Madama Butterfly (Arena Di Verona) 2004, Aïda (La Scala, Milan) 2006, La Traviata (Rome) 2007, I Pagliacci (Taormina) 2008, La Bohème (Tel-Aviv) 2008, Aïda (Tel-Aviv) 2009, I Pagliacci (Rome) 2009, Falstaff (Rome) 2010, Carmen

(Arena di Verona) 2009, Turandot (Arena di Verona) 2010, Aïda (Arena di Verona) 2010, Madama Butterfly (Arena di Verona) 2010, Il Trovatore (Arena di Verona) 2010, Turandot (Royal Opera House of Muscat, Sultanate of Oman) 2011, Don Giovanni and Pagliacci (Arena di Verona) 2012. *Ballet:* Swan Lake 1985; produced Beethoven's Missa Solemnis, San Pietro, Rome 1971. *Films include:* The Taming of the Shrew 1966, Romeo and Juliet (five Nastri d'argento Awards, Italian cinematographic journalists) 1967, Brother Sun and Sister Moon 1973, The Champ 1979, Endless Love 1981, La Traviata 1983, Cavalleria Rusticana 1983, Otello 1986, The Young Toscanini 1987, Hamlet 1990, Storia di una capinera (Sparrow) 1993, Jane Eyre 1995, Tea with Mussolini 1998, Callas Forever 2002, Omaggio a Roma (short) 2009. *Television includes:* Florence, Days of Destruction (film) 1966, Jesus of Nazareth (mini-series) 1977, celebrative concert of the second century of the birth of Ludwig van Beethoven (RAI) held in St Peter's Basilica in the presence of Pope Paul VI. *Publication:* Zeffirelli by Zeffirelli (autobiog.) 1986 (second edn 2006). *Address:* Via Lucio Volumnio 45, 00178 Rome, Italy. *Fax:* (06) 7184213. *E-mail:* fzeffirelli@tin.it.

ZEGLIS, John D., LLB, JD; American lawyer and telecommunications industry executive (retd); s. of Donald Zeglis; ed Univ. of Illinois Coll. of Business, Harvard Law School; began legal career as Assoc., Sidley & Austin 1973, later becoming Partner –1984; joined AT&T Wireless Services, Inc. 1984, Corp. Vice-Pres. of Law 1984–86, Gen. Counsel 1984–96, Vice-Chair. and Pres. 1997–99, Chair. and CEO AT&T Wireless 1999–2004 (retd after AT&T Wireless acquired by Cingular Wireless LLC); currently Co-owner, with his son-in-law, NBA D-League team Fort Wayne Mad Ants; mem. Bd of Dirs, Helmerich and Payne Corpn, AMX Corpn, State Farm Insurance; fmr mem. Bd of Dirs Dynergy Corpn, Sara Lee Corpn, Georgia Pacific; fmr Sr Ed. Harvard Law Review; Chair. Bd of Trustees, George Washington Univ.; Trustee, Culver Educ. Foundation, Marshall County Community Fund, St Joseph Medical Center of Plymouth, Ind.; mem. Bd, Rural School and Community Trust, Washington; mem. Kellogg Advisory Bd, J.L. Kellogg Grad. School of Man.; mem. Northwestern Univ., Univ. of Illinois Business Advisory Council.

ZEHRI, Nawab Sanaullah Khan, BA; Pakistani politician; b. 4 Aug. 1961, Anjeera, Khuzdar Dist; s. of Sardar Doda Khan Zehri; m.; ed Balochistan Univ.; Leader of Zehri tribe and Chief of Jhalawan; mem. Provincial Ass. of Balochistan 1990–93, Senator from Balochistan 1997–99, mem. Provincial Ass. of Balochistan 2002–07, re-elected 2008; Minister of Local Govt 1990–93, Minister of Prisons and Tribal Affairs 2002, Minister of Services and Gen. Admin 2008–13, Sr Minister with portfolios of communication, mines, minerals and industries 2013–15; Chief Minister of Balochistan 2015–18; mem. Nat. Party –2008, then joined Pakistan Muslim League—Nawaz (PML—N), Pres. PML-N Balochistan 2010–. *Address:* B-39 Jhalawan House, Chaman Housing Scheme, Quetta (home); c/o Pakistan Muslim League—Nawaz (PML—N), 20H Street 10, F-8/3, Islamabad, Pakistan.

ZEIBOTS, Vice-Adm. Gaidis Andrejs; Latvian naval officer and radio and electronics engineer; *Member of the Council, Rīga Shipyard;* b. 26 June 1945, Valka Dist; m. Dzintra Zeibots; one d.; ed Naval Acad. of Radioelectronics, Leningrad (now St Petersburg), Russia, Coll. of Strategic Studies, George C. Marshall Centre, Germany, US Army War Coll., USA; Chief of Radio Eng Service of destroyer, Tallinn Naval Base, Estonia 1969–70, Liepaja Naval Base 1970–72; Exec. Officer of destroyer, Liepaja 1975–76, Commdr of frigate 1976–78; Deputy Chief of Staff, Missile Carrier Div., Baltic Naval Base 1980–86; Deputy Commdr Naval Base 1986–88; Commdr Naval Div., Gdynia, Poland 1988–91; C-in-C Latvian Naval Forces 1991–99; Exec. Sec. for NATO Integration, Ministry of Defence 1999–2002; Deputy Commdr and Operational Commdr Latvian Nat. Armed Forces 2002–03, Chief of Defence 2003–06; Advisor to Minister of Defence 2007–09; mem. Council, Rīga Shipyard 2009–; Norwegian Order of Royal Kts, Order of King Gedimins (Fourth Class), Orders from Estonia, Italy, Netherlands; Medal of Order of Three Stars, two Ministry of Defence Awards, NAF Commdr Medal, Naval Commdr Medal. *Address:* Rīga Shipyard, Gales Street 2, Rīga 1015, Latvia (office). *Telephone:* 67046317 (office). *Fax:* 67353452 (office). *E-mail:* zeibots@riga-shipyard.com (office); office@eiroholdings.lv (office). *Website:* www.riga-shipyard.com (office).

ZEIDAN, Ali; Libyan politician and fmr diplomatist; b. 1950; served as Libyan diplomat during 1970s, including in India; defected 1980; est. Nat. Front for the Salvation of Libya, mem. –2011; served as Nat. Transitional Council's Europe envoy during uprising 2011; mem. Nat. Forces Alliance 2011–12; Ind. 2012–; elected for Jufra in Congressional election 2012; Prime Minister of Libya 2012–14.

ZEIDANE, Zeine Ould, DEA, PhD; Mauritanian economist, banker and politician; *Senior Adviser, Middle East and Central Asia Department, International Monetary Fund;* b. 1966, Tamchekett; ed Univ of Nice-Sophia Antipolis, France; taught math. at Univ of Nice 1995–96 and Univ of Nouakchott 1996–97; Head of Treasury Dept, Gen. Bank of Mauritania 1997–98; Co-ordinator of Analysis and Econ. Synthesis, Ministry of the Economy and Devt 1998–2000; Economist, World Bank, Nouakchott 2000–02; Co-ordinator, Mauritanian Centre for Political Analysis 2002–04; Econ. Adviser to the Pres. 2003–04; Gov., Cen. Bank of Maurtania 2004–06; Prime Minister 2007–08 (resgnd); unsuccessful cand. in presidential elections 2007; Sr Adviser, Middle East and Central Asia Dept, IMF 2012–. *Address:* International Monetary Fund, 700 19th Street, NW, Washington, DC 20431, USA (office). *Telephone:* (202) 623-7000 (office). *Website:* www.imf.org (office).

ZEIDLER, Eberhard Heinrich, OC, OOnt, PA, DEng, DArch, FRAIC, RCA, OAA, MAIBC, OAQ; Canadian architect; b. 11 Jan. 1926, Braunsdorf, Germany; s. of Paul Zeidler and Dorothea Dabbert; m. Phyllis Jane Abbott 1957; one s. three d.; ed Bauhaus Weimar and Univ. Fridericiana, Karlsruhe Technische Hochschule; designer, Prof. Egon Eiermann, Karlsruhe 1949–50; Assoc. with Prof. Emanuel Lindner, Osnabrück 1950–51; emigrated to Canada 1951; Assoc.-in-Charge of Design, W. & W. R. L. Blackwell & Craig, Peterborough 1951–54; Partner, Blackwell, Craig & Zeidler Architects, Peterborough and Toronto 1954–57, Craig & Zeidler Architects, Peterborough and Toronto 1957–61, Craig, Zeidler & Strong, Peterborough and Toronto 1961–75, Zeidler Partnership/Architects, Toronto 1975–80, Zeidler Roberts Partnership/Architects, Toronto 1980–2001, Zeidler Grinnell Partnership 2001–03, Zeidler Partnership Architects 2003–, now Sr Partner Emer.; Hon. FAIA 1981; Gold Medal, Royal Architectural Inst. of Canada 1986; more than 100 nat. and int. awards. *Projects include:* Beth Israel Synagogue, Peterborough 1964, McMaster Univ. Health Science Centre, Hamilton, Ont. 1972, Ontario Place theme park (including Cinesphere), Toronto 1967–71, Walter C. Mackenzie Health Sciences Centre, Toronto 1975–86, Eaton Centre shopping mall and offices, with Bregman & Hamann Architects, Edmonton, Alberta 1977–81, Yerba Buena Gardens, San Francisco 1980–84, redevelopment of the Queen's Quay Terminal, Toronto 1979–83, Canada Place for Expo '86, Vancouver 1986, MediaPark Cologne 1990–2004, Raymond F. Kravis Center for the Performing Arts, West Palm Beach, Fla 1992, Toronto Centre for the Arts 1993, Living Arts Centre, Mississauga, Ont. 1997, Hosp. for Sick Children Atrium, Toronto 1993, Rogers Office Campus, Toronto 1992, York Univ. Accolade Project, Toronto 2005–06, Sherway Gardens Phase IV, Toronto 1989–90, Royal Victoria Hosp. Atrium, Barrie, Queen's Quay Terminal restoration, Toronto 1983, Markham Stouffville Hosp., Ont. 1990, Gladstone Hotel restoration 2002–03, Toronto Trump Int. Hotel and Tower, Toronto 2012. *Publications include:* Healing the Hospital 1974, Multi-use Architecture in the Urban Context 1983, Zeidler Roberts Partnership: Ethics and Architecture 1999. *Leisure interests:* skiing, tennis. *Address:* Zeidler Partnership Architects, 315 Queen Street West, Toronto, ON M5V 2X2, Canada (office). *Telephone:* (416) 596-8300 (home). *Fax:* (416) 596-1408 (home). *E-mail:* eb@zeidler.com (office); info@zeidler.com (office). *Website:* www.zeidler.com (office).

ZEILER, Gerhard; Austrian media executive; *President, Turner Broadcasting System International;* b. 20 July 1955, Vienna; ed Univ. of Vienna; fmr freelance journalist; fmr press spokesman for Austrian Chancellors, Fred Sinowatz and Franz Vranitzky; Gen. Sec. ORF (broadcaster), Vienna 1986–90, CEO 1994–98; CEO Tele5, Munich 1991–92; CEO RTL 2, Munich 1992–94, CEO RTL Television 1998–05, CEO RTL Group 2003–11, also mem. Bd of Dirs Groupe M6; Pres. Turner Broadcasting System Int., London 2011–; mem. Exec. Bd Bertelsmann Group 2003–2012; mem. Bd of Dirs Cen. European Media Enterprises; mem. Supervisory Bd Vonovia 2015–. *Address:* Turner Broadcasting System International, 16 Great Marlborough Street, London, W1F 7HS, England (office). *Telephone:* (20) 7693-1000 (office). *E-mail:* anna.cheffins@turner.com (office). *Website:* www.turner.com (office).

ZEILINGER, Anton, PhD; Austrian physicist and academic; *President, Austrian Academy of Sciences;* b. 20 May 1945, Ried/Innkreis; ed Bundesgymnasium Wien 13, Univ. of Vienna, Tech. Univ. of Vienna; Research Asst, Atominstitut Vienna with Prof. Helmut Rauch 1972–79, Asst Prof. 1979–83; Research Assoc. (Fulbright Fellow), Neutron Diffraction Lab., MIT, USA 1977–78, Assoc. Prof. of Physics (Visiting) 1981–83; Assoc. Prof., Tech. Univ. of Vienna 1983–90; Prof. of Physics (Lehrstuhlvertretung), Tech. Univ. of Munich 1988–89; Prof. of Experimental Physics, Univ. of Innsbruck 1990–99; Prof. of Experimental Physics, Univ. of Vienna 1999–13, Dean of Faculty of Physics 2006–09, mem. Founding Convent, Univ. of Vienna 2002–03, Emer. Prof. 2013–; Scientific Dir IQOQI Inst. of Quantum Optics and Quantum Information, Austrian Acad. of Sciences, Vienna 2004–13, Sr Scientist 2004–; Guest Researcher (part-time), Institut Laue-Langevin, Grenoble, France 1974–89; regular summer research appointments at MIT 1983–90; Adjunct Full Prof. (part-time), Hampshire Coll., Amherst, USA 1986–89; Chaire Internationale, Collège de France, Paris 1995; Hon. Prof. Univ. of Science and Tech. of China 1996, Einstein Visiting Prof. 2016–; Visiting Research Fellow, Merton Coll., Oxford, UK 1998, (part-time) 2010; Sr Humboldt Fellow, Humboldt Univ., Berlin, Germany 2001–04; est. a new postgraduate research inst. implemented as Inst. of Science and Tech. of Austria 2002, mem. Exec. Bd, Inst. of Science and Tech. of Austria 2006–12, Vice-Chair. Bd of Trustees 2006–; mem. Editorial Bd Physical Review A 1994–2000, Foundations of Physics 1988–, New Journal of Physics 2006–08; Pres. Austrian Physical Soc. 1997–98, Int. Acad. Traunkirchen 2009–; Corresp. mem. Austrian Acad. of Sciences 1994, Full mem. 1998, mem. Planning and Strategy Cttee 2008–09, Pres. 2013–; mem. Quantum Electronics and Optics Div., European Physical Soc. 1996–98, Academia Scientiarum et Artium Europaea 2000, Berlin-Brandenburg Acad. of Sciences 2002, German Acad. of Sciences Leopoldina 2005, Academia Europaea 2011; Foreign mem. Serbian Acad. of Sciences and Arts 2006, Acad. des Sciences, Institut de France 2009, Russian Acad. of Sciences 2016; Foreign Assoc. NAS 2013, US Nat. Acad. of Sciences 2014; Fellow, American Physical Soc. 1999, AAAS 2012, The World Acad. of Sciences 2014; Hon. Prof., Nanjing Univ. 2016; Hon. mem. Slovak Acad. of Sciences 2005, Inst. of Electrical and Electronics Engineers (IEEE) 2018; Foreign Hon. mem. Romanian Acad. of Sciences 2016; Decoration of Sciences and Arts (Austrian equivalent to the Order of Merit) 2001, Order pour le Mérite for Sciences and Arts (Germany) 2001, Great Cross of Merit with Star (Germany) 2009, Großer Tiroler Adler Orden 2013; Dr hc (Humboldt Univ., Berlin) 2005, (Gdansk Univ., Poland) 2006, (Nat. Acad. of Sciences of Ukraine) 2015; numerous awards including Prize of the City of Vienna for the Encouragement of Young Scientists 1975, Prize for Jr Scientists, Kardinal Innitzer Foundation, Vienna 1979, Sir Thomas Lyle Lecturer, Univ. of Melbourne, Australia 1984, Prix Vinci d'Excellence, Fondation LVMH, Paris 1995, Colloquium Ehrenfestii, Univ. of Leiden, Netherlands 1996, 2004, Austrian Scientist of the Year 1996, European Lecturer, European Physical Soc. 1996, H.L. Welsh Lecture in Physics, Univ. of Toronto, Canada 1997, European Optics Prize, European Optical Soc. 1997, Schrödinger Lecturer, Trinity Coll., Dublin, Ireland 1999, Science Prize, City of Vienna 2000, Sr Humboldt Fellow Prize, Alexander von Humboldt Stiftung, Germany 2000, Johannes Kepler Prize, Science Prize of Upper Austria 2002, Niels Bohr Lecturer, Univ. of Copenhagen, Denmark 2003, Schrödinger Lecturer, Imperial Coll., London, UK 2003, Amos de-Shalit Memorial Lecturer, Weizmann Inst., Rehovot, Israel 2003, Sartorius Prize, Göttingen Acad. of Sciences, Germany 2003, Lorenz Oken Medal, Soc. of German Researchers and Physicians 2004, Descartes Prize, EC 2005, King Faisal Prize, Saudi Arabia 2005, Wilhelm Exner Medal, Austrian Asscn for SME (Oesterreichischer Gewerbeverein—OGV) (jtly) 2005, Rosenthal Lecturer, Yale Univ., USA 2006, Barut Memorial Lecturer, Bogazici Univ., Istanbul, Turkey 2006, Grand Gold Decoration, City of Vienna 2006, Quantum Electronics Prize, European Physical Soc. 2007, Asher Perez Memorial Lecturer, Technion, Haifa, Israel 2008, Newton Prize Lecture and Medal, Inst. of Physics, London 2008, Quantum Communication Award, Tamagawa Univ., Japan 2008, PITP Lecture on Quantum Phenomena, Pacific Inst. of Theoretical Physics, Vancouver, Canada 2009, Inaugural Kavli Colloquium, Kavli Inst. of Nanoscience, Delft Univ. of Tech., Netherlands 2009, Berlin

Brandenburg Acad. of Sciences, Humboldt Univ., Berlin 2009, Celsius Lecturer, Uppsala Univ. 2010, Dvorak Memorial Lecturer, Univ. of Prague 2010, Ockham Lecturer, Merton Coll., Oxford 2010, Frontiers in Physics Lecturer, City Coll., CUNY 2010, Wolf Prize in Physics 2010, Van Fleck Lecturer, Univ. of Minnesota, USA 2011, Mark W. Zemansky Lecturer, City Coll. of New York 2011 Cherwell-Simon Lecturer, Oxford Univ. 2012, Zhongshan Lecturer, Nanjing Univ., China 2016, Medal of the Senate of the Czech Repub. 2017, John Stewart Bell Prize for Research on Fundamental Issues in Quantum Mechanics and their Applications 2017. *Publications include:* Matter Wave Interferometry. On the occasion of the 100th anniversary of E. Schrödinger's birth (co-ed.) 1988, Fundamental Problems in Quantum Theory. In Honor of Professor John A. Wheeler, Annals of the New York Academy of Sciences, Vol. 755 (co-ed.) 1995, The Physics of Quantum Information – Quantum Cryptography, Quantum Teleportation, Quantum Computation (co-ed.) 2000, Quantum Information – An Introduction to Basic Theoretical Concepts and Experiments, Springer Tracts in Modern Physics, Vol. 173 (co-ed.) 2001, Quantum Computation and Quantum Information Theory (co-ed.) 2001, Quantum [Un]speakables – From Bell to Quantum Information (co-ed.) 2002; more than 450 scientific publs, including more than 350 in peer-reviewed, ISI-ranked journals; popular science books: Einsteins Schleier 2003, Einsteins Spuk 2005, Dance of the Photons 2010. *Address:* Institute for Quantum Optics and Quantum Information, Austrian Academy of Sciences, Boltzmanngasse 3, 1090 Vienna, Austria (office). *Telephone:* (1) 4277-29582 (office). *E-mail:* anton.zeilinger@univie.ac.at (office). *Website:* www.iqoqi-vienna.at/people/zeilinger-group/anton-zeilinger (office).

ZEITLIN, (Benjamin Harold) Benh; American filmmaker, composer and animator; *President of Board, Court 13;* b. 14 Oct. 1982, Queens, New York City, NY; s. of Steve Zeitlin and Amanda Dargan; ed Hastings-on-Hudson High School, Wesleyan Univ., Middletown, Conn.; began career as a filmmaker aged six when he and a friend made a Batman film; spent a summer in Prague working with a prominent animation artist; returned to USA to work in a pvt. Manhattan school helping elementary students create short films; co-f. Court 13 ind. collection of filmmakers 2004, mem. Bd, also Pres.; Breakthrough Dir Award, Gotham Ind. Film Awards 2012, also received the inaugural Bingham Ray Award 2012, Smithsonian American Ingenuity Award for the Visual Arts 2012. *Films include:* Egg (short) (writer and dir) 2005, The Origins of Electricity (short) (writer and dir) 2006, Death to the Tinman (short) (composer) 2007, Glory at Sea (short) (writer, composer and dir) 2008, Beasts of the Southern Wild (Caméra d'Or Award, Cannes Film Festival, Grand Jury Prize: Dramatic, Sundance Film Festival, Grand Jury Prize, Deauville American Film Festival, Los Angeles Film Festival Audience Award for Best Narrative Feature, Seattle Int. Film Festival Golden Space Needle Award for Best Dir, Humanitas Prize (Jtly)) 2012, Mediterranea (composer) 2015, Brimstone & Glory (documentary) (writer, composer and dir) (International Documentary Association Creative Recognition Award for Best Music (jtly) 2017) 2017. *E-mail:* josh@court13.com (office). *Website:* www.court13.com (office).

ZEKI, Semir, BSc, PhD, FRS, FMedSci; British neurobiologist and academic; *Professor, Laboratory of Neurobiology, University College, London;* m. Anne-Marie Claire; one s. one d.; ed Univ. Coll., London; joined teaching staff, Univ. Coll., London 1969, Prof., Dept of Anatomy and Embryology 1981, later Co-Head, Wellcome Lab. of Cognitive Neurology, Prof. of Neurobiology 1981–, Lab. of Neurobiology; Henry Head Research Fellow, Royal Soc., London 1980–85; fmr Visiting Prof., Univ. of Calif., Berkeley, USA; mem. Bd of Scientific Govs Scripps Scientific Research Inst., La Jolla, Calif., USA, Nat. Science Council of France; mem. Bd of Advisers Beit Memorial Trust; Ed. The Philosophical Transactions of the Royal Society; Foreign mem. American Philosophical Soc.; Fellow, Inst. for Neuroscience, New York, Academia Europea 1993, European Acad. of Sciences and Arts 1995; Trustee, Fight for Sight; Hon. DSc (Aston, Aberdeen); Hocart Prize, Royal Anthropological Inst. 1961, first Golden Brain Award, Minerva Foundation, Berkeley 1985, Science for Art Prize, LVMH 1991, Rank Prize in Optoelectronics 1992, Betty and David Koetser Foundation Prize 1997, King Faisal Int. Prize in Biology 2004, Erasmus Medal 2008. *Publications:* A Vision of the Brain 1993, La Quête de l'essentiel (co-author) 1995, Inner Vision – An Exploration of Art and the Brain 1999, Splendours and Miseries of the Brain 2008; numerous articles in scientific journals. *Address:* Department of Anatomy, University College, Darwin Building, Gower Street, London, WC1E 6BT, England (office). *Telephone:* (20) 7679-7316 (office). *E-mail:* zeki.pa@ucl.ac.uk (office). *Website:* www.vislab.ucl.ac.uk (office); www.neuroesthetics.org (office); profzeki.blogspot.in.

DÍAZ ZELAYA, Gen. Fredy Santiago; Honduran army officer and government official; *Minister of Defence Chief of Joint Staff of Armed Forces –2015;* apptd Deputy Minister of Defence 2017, Minister of Defence 2018–. *Address:* Secretariat of National Defence, Blvd Suyapa, Col. Florencia Sur, frente a Iglesia Colegio Episcopal, Tegucigalpa, Honduras (office). *Telephone:* 2239-2330 (office). *Fax:* 2235-8922 (office). *E-mail:* transparencia@sedena.gob.hn (office). *Website:* www.sedena.gob.hn.

ZELAYA ROSALES, José Manuel; Honduran politician and fmr head of state; b. 20 Sept. 1952, Catacamas, Olancho; s. of Jose Manuel Zelaya Ordoñez and Hortensia Esmeralda Rosales Sarmiento; m. Xiomara Castro Sarmiento; four c.; ed Nat. Honduran Univ.; trained as civil engineer; ranch owner; mem. Liberal Party of Honduras; Deputy in Nat. Congress 1985–, Chair. Natural Resources and Petroleum Cttee 1985–89; Minister for Investment, in charge of Honduran Investment Fund 1994–2002; Sec. Cen. Exec. Council for Advertising and Org. 1999–2004; Founder and Leader, Movimiento Esperanza Liberal (faction within Liberal Party) 2005–; Pres. of Honduras 2005–09; in exile in Dominican Republic 2010–11; Founder and Pres. Partido Libertad y Refundación (LIBRE) 2011–; Deputy, Central American Parliament (PARLACEN) 2010–; Chair. Bd of Dirs Asociación de Industriales de la Madera 1987–94; mem. Honduran Nat. Business Council (COEHP) 1987–94; fmr mem. Bd of Dirs Sogerin Bank. *Website:* libre.hn.

ZELENSKIY, Volodymyr Oleksandrovych; Ukrainian politician, producer, actor and screenwriter; b. 25 Jan. 1978, Krivoy Rog, Ukrainian SSR, USSR; s. Oleksandr Zelenskiy and Rimma Zelenska; m. Olena Zelenska 2003; one s. one d.; ed Kyiv Nat. Econ. Univ.; actor 2005–; owner, Kvartal 95 film studio mid-2000s–; mem. Sluha Narodu polical party 218–; cand. in Presidential election 2019; mem. Bd and gen. producer, Inter channel 2010–12. *Television includes:* The Three Musketeers (film) (actor, writer) 2005, Svaty (series) (producer) 2009–12, Legenda:

Lyudmila Gurchenko (writer) 2011, Skazochnaya Rus (series) (actor) 2012, Papashi (series) (producer) 2012, Lyubov v bolshom gorode 3 (series) (actor, producer) 2014, Sluha Narodu (Servant of the People) (series) 2015. *Films include:* Kushat podano! (writer) 2006, No Love in the City (actor) 2009, Sluzhebnyy roman: Nashe vremya (actor, producer, writer) 2011, Rzhevskiy protiv Napoleona (actor) 2012, I'll Be Around (producer) 2012, Love in Vegas (actor) 2014, 8 novykh svidaniy (actor) 2015, 8 luchshikh svidaniy (actor) 2016, Sluga naroda 2 (producer) 2016, Ya, Ty, Vin, Vona (actor, producer, writer) 2018. *Address:* Sluha Narodu, Velyka Vasylkivska 72, Kiev. *E-mail:* kievoffice@ze2019.com. *Website:* ze2019.com.

ZELENSKY, Igor Anatolyevich; Russian ballet dancer and artistic director; *Artistic Director, Moscow Stanislavsky Ballet Company;* b. 13 July 1969, Labinsk, Krasnodar Dist; ed Tbilisi School of Choreography, Leningrad Vaganova School of Choreography; with Tbilisi Opera and Ballet Theatre 1988–89, Mariinsky Opera and Ballet Theatre 1988–2013, Prin. 1991–2013; dancer with New York City Ballet 1992–97; Soloist, Royal Ballet, Covent Garden 1997–2001 (performed in Manon and Romeo and Juliet (choreography by Kenneth MacMillan), The Sleeping Beauty (Anthony Dowell version), La Bayadère (Natalia Makarova version), Giselle (Peter Wright version) and Apollo (choreography by George Balanchine); Prin. Guest Dancer, Bayerische Staatsoper 2000, Prin. Guest Soloist, Bolshoi Theatre 2000, performed lead roles in La Bayadère and Swan Lake; Prin. Guest Soloist, La Scala, Milan, the Colón, Buenos Aires, theatres in Boston, San Francisco and Rio de Janeiro; Asst Dir Athens Opera House 2001–06, choreographer and staging master of Don Quixote, Raymonda, Swan Lake, The Sleeping Beauty and La Bayadère; Artistic Dir Ballet Co. of the Novosibirsk State Academic Theatre of Opera and Ballet 2006–; Artistic Dir Moscow Stanislavsky Ballet Co. 2011–; Honoured Artist of Russia 2000, People's Artist of Russia 2008; Grand Prix and Gold Medal, Int. Competition of Ballet Artists, Paris 1990, Prix de Lumières of Italian Cinema, Baltika Prize 2001, Golden Mask Nat. Theatre Award 2009. *Ballets include:* Basil in Don Quixote, Siegfried in Swan Lake, Aki in Corsair, Solor in La Bayadère, Albert in Gisèle, leading roles in Romeo and Julliet, Apollo, Manon, Sleeping Beauty. *Address:* Moscow Stanislavsky Ballet Company, ul. Bolshaya Dmitrovka 17, Moscow, Russian Federation (office). *Telephone:* (495) 723-73-25 (office). *Website:* stanmus.com/person/827 (office).

ZELENYI, Lev Matveevich; Russian physicist; *Director, Space Research Institute, Russian Academy of Sciences;* b. 23 Aug. 1948, Moscow; m. Eugenia Zelenya; ed Faculty of Space Research and Aerophysics, Moscow Inst. of Physics and Tech.; joined Space Research Inst., Russian Acad. of Sciences 1972, Dir 2002–; Academician, Russian Acad. of Sciences 2008–, Vice-Pres. Russian Acad. of Sciences 2013–; mem. Bureau, Int. Council for Science Cttee on Space Research (COSPAR); Foreign mem., Bulgarian Acad. of Sciences 2008; mem. Editorial Bd of several journals including Earth and Universe, Flight, Geophysical Research Journal – Space Physics (USA), Nonlinear Processes in Geophysics (Germany); Russian Fed. Pres.'s Prize in Educ. 2003, Officer's Cross of Merit 2004. *Address:* Space Research Institute of the Russian Academy of Sciences, 117997 Moscow, 84/32 Profsoyuznaya Street, Russia (office). *Telephone:* (495) 334-266 (office). *Fax:* (495) 333-33-11 (office). *E-mail:* lzelenyi@iki.rssi.ru (office). *Website:* www.ras.ru (office).

ŽELEZNÝ, Jan; Czech fmr athlete; b. 16 June 1966, Mladá Boleslav; s. of Jaroslav Zelezny and Jana Zelezny; javelin thrower; fmr mechanic and army col; set five world javelin records; won 106 out of 135 competitions 1991–2001; current world record javelin throw (of 98.48m) at Jena 1996; World Champion 1993, 1995, 2001, bronze medal, Rome 1987, Seville 1999; silver medal, Olympic Games 1988, gold medal 1992, 1996, 2000; bronze medal, European Championships, Helsinki 1994, Gothenburg 2006; mem. IOC 2000–02, 2004–; Czech Athlete of the Year 1993, 1995, 2000, 2011, Men's European Athlete of the Year 1996, 2000, IAAF Athlete of the Year 2000, Medal of Merit, Czech Repub. 2001. *Leisure interests:* fishing, golf, tennis, fine wine. *Address:* c/o Czech Olympic Committee, Benešovská 6, 101 00 Prague 10, Czech Republic. *Telephone:* (2) 71730622. *Fax:* (2) 71731318. *E-mail:* info@olympic.cz. *Website:* www.olympic.org/czech-republic; www.iaaf.org/athletes/czech-republic/jan-zelezny-3207.

ŽELEZNÝ, Vladimír, PhDr; Czech politician, publicist, manager and entrepreneur; *CEO, TV Barrandov;* b. 3 March 1945, Samara, Russia; s. of Theodor Železný and Alexandra Železný; m. 1st (divorced); two s.; m. 2nd; one s. one d.; ed Charles Univ., Prague; producer, Czechoslovak TV; student leader 1964–68; worked in radio, TV and newspapers 1970–89; spokesman of Civic Forum during Velvet Revolution 1989–91; Adviser to Prime Minister 1991–92; Founder and Dir-Gen. TV Nova 1993–2003; CEO TV Barrandov 2013–; has written and co-written over 100 popular science programmes for radio and TV; Senator 2002–04; mem. European Parl. (Independence/Democracy Group) 2004–09, mem. Cttee on Regional Devt, Substitute mem. Cttee on Agric. and Rural Devt, mem. Del. to EU-Russia Parl. Co-operation Cttee, Substitute mem. Del. for Relations with Israel; Vice-Pres. Intergroup Viticulture-Tradition-Quality; Founder and Vice-Pres. Franz Kafka Soc. and Franz Kafka Foundation, Prague; Head, Bd of Trustees Galerie Foundation; Vice-Pres. B'nai B'rith Renaissance, Prague; mem. Bd KKL (Czech Repub.); Prize for the popularization of science, Czechoslovak Acad. of Science 1988. *Publications include:* screenplays, televised plays and books; several popular science studies, including Windows of the Universe Wide Open. *Leisure interests:* art collector, photographer, propagator of wineculture. *Address:* Dlouhá 12, 110 00 Prague 1, Czech Republic (office). *E-mail:* vladimir.zelezny@centrum.cz (office); v.zelezny@tanzberg.cz (office). *Website:* www.vladimirzelezny.cz (office).

ZELIANG, T. R., BA; Indian politician; b. 21 Feb. 1952, Peren Dist, Nagaland; s. of Rangleu Zeliang; m. Kevizenuo Rangkau; two s. one d.; ed Arts Coll., Kohima; mem. Nagaland Legis. Ass. for Tening 6 constituency 1989–2004, for Peren 7 constituency 2008–; Nagaland Minister of State for Information and Tourism 1989–90, for Relief and Rehabilitation 1994–98, Minister for Environment and Forests and Geology and Mining 1998–2003, for Planning, Animal Husbandry and Parl. Affairs 2008; mem. Rajya Sabha (upper house of Parl.) for Nagaland 2004–08; Chief Minister of Nagaland 2014–17 (resgnd), July 2017–March 2018; fmr mem. Indian Nat. Congress; mem. Nagaland People's Front, currently Leader.

ŻELICHOWSKI, Stanisław; Polish politician; b. 9 April 1944, Księżostany, Zamość Prov.; m.; one s. one d.; ed Dept of Forestry, Agric. Univ., Warsaw; began career in Presidium of Dist People's Council, Ostrołęka; Lecturer, Ciechanów Forest Inspectorate 1969; Forest Insp. Dwukoły Forest Inspectorate 1974; mem. Nat. Forestry Council; mem. United Peasants' Party (ZSL) 1970–89; mem. Tribunal of State 1989–91; mem. Main Exec. Cttee Polish Peasants' Party (PSL) and Pres. Prov. Bd of PSL, Ciechanów 1990–, mem. Comm. for Foreign Affairs; Deputy to Sejm (Parl.) 1985–89, 1991–, Vice-Chair. Parl. Cttee for Environmental Protection, Natural Resources and Forestry 1997–2001; Minister of Environmental Protection, Natural Resources and Forestry 1993–97, of the Environment 2001–03. *Leisure interests:* tourism, sports. *Address:* Kancelaria Sejmu, 00-902 Warsaw, ul. Wiejska 4/6/8, Poland (office). *E-mail:* stanislaw.zelichowski@sejm.pl (office). *Website:* www.sejm.gov.pl (office).

ZELLICK, Graham John, CBE, QC (Hon.), MA, PhD, FAcSS; British lawyer, academic, public servant and judge; b. 12 Aug. 1948, London, England; m. Jennifer Temkin 1975; one s. one d.; ed Christ's Coll., Finchley, London, Gonville & Caius Coll., Cambridge, Stanford Univ., USA; Lecturer in Laws, Queen Mary and Westfield Coll., Univ. of London 1971–78, Reader in Law 1978–82, Prof. of Public Law 1982–88, Dean Faculty of Laws 1984–88, Head, Dept of Law 1984–90, Drapers' Prof. of Law 1988–91, Sr Vice-Prin. and Acting Prin. 1990–91, Prin. 1991–98, Prof. of Law 1991–98, Prof. Emer. 1998–; Dean Faculty of Laws, Univ. of London 1986–88, Deputy Vice-Chancellor 1994–97, Vice-Chancellor and Pres. 1997–2003; Visiting Prof. of Law, Univ. of Toronto 1975, 1978–79; Visiting Scholar, St John's Coll. Oxford 1989; Visiting Prof., Queen Mary, Univ. of London 2007–12; barrister, Middle Temple 1992, Master of Bench 2001, Reader 2013; Chair. Criminal Cases Review Comm. 2003–08; mem. Competition Comm. Appeal Tribunals 2000–03, Competition Appeal Tribunal 2003, Criminal Injuries Compensation Appeals Panel 2000–03, Investigatory Powers Tribunal 2013–; Electoral Commr 2001–04; Ed. Public Law 1981–86; Founding Ed. European Human Rights Reports 1978–82; Gov. Tel-Aviv Univ.; Pres. W London (Reform) Synagogue 2000–06, Valuation Tribunal for England 2009–15; Ford Foundation Fellow in Criminal Law and Policy, Stanford Law School 1970–71; Chair. Bd of Govs Leo Baeck Coll. 2005–06, Bd of Trustees, Richmond The American Int. Univ. in London 2005–06; Fellow, Inst. of Continuing Professional Devt 1998; mem. Court, Drapers' Co. 2000–, Master 2009–10; Fellow, Acad. of Social Sciences 2000; Fellow, Heythrop Coll., Univ. of London 2005; Freeman, City of London 1992; Hon. Prof., School of Law, Univ. of Birmingham 2004–11; Hon. Fellow, Soc. of Advanced Legal Studies 1997–, Burgon Soc., Gonville and Caius Coll., Cambridge 2001, Leo Baeck Coll. 2007; Hon. FRAM 2003; Hon. LHD (New York) 2001; Hon. LLD (Richmond—The American Univ. in London) 2003, (Birmingham) 2006; Hon. DLit (Queen Mary, London) 2010.

ZELLWEGER, Renée, BA; American actress; b. 25 April 1969, Katy, Tex.; d. of Emil Zellweger and Kjellfrid Zellweger; m. Kenny Chesney 2005 (annulled); ed Katy High School, Univ. of Texas. *Films include:* Dazed and Confused 1993, Reality Bites 1994, Love and a .45 1994, 8 Seconds 1994, The Low Life 1995, Empire Records 1995, The Whole Wide World 1996, Jerry Maguire 1996, Texas Chainsaw Massacre: The Next Generation 1997, Deceiver 1997, One True Thing 1998, A Price Above Rubies 1998, The Bachelor 1999, Me, Myself and Irene 2000, Nurse Betty (Golden Globe Award, Best Actress in a Comedy 2001) 2000, Bridget Jones' Diary 2001, Chicago (Golden Globe Award, Best Actress in a Musical 2003, Screen Actors' Guild Award, Best Actress 2003) 2002, Down With Love 2003, Cold Mountain (Golden Globe Award, Best Supporting Actress 2004, Critics' Choice Award, Best Supporting Actress 2004, BAFTA Award, Best Actress in a Supporting Role, Screen Actors Guild Best Supporting Actress Award 2004, Acad. Award, Best Supporting Actress 2004) 2003, Bridget Jones: The Edge of Reason 2004, Cinderella Man 2005, Miss Potter 2006, Bee Movie (voice) 2007, Leatherheads 2008, Appaloosa 2008, New in Town 2009, My One and Only 2009, My Own Love Song 2010, The Whole Truth 2016, Bridget Jones's Baby 2016. *Television includes:* Shake, Rattle and Rock Movie 1993, Murder in the Heartland 1994. *Address:* c/o John Carrabino, John Carrabino Management, 100 North Crescent Drive, Beverly Hills, CA 90210, USA (office).

ZELMANOV, Efim Isaakovich, MSc, PhD; Russian mathematician and academic; *Rita L. Atkinson Professor of Mathematics, University of California, San Diego;* b. 7 Sept. 1955, Khabarovsk; ed Novosibirsk State Univ. and Leningrad State Univ.; apptd to staff, Novosibirsk State Univ.; Jr Researcher, Inst. of Math., USSR Acad. of Sciences, Novosibirsk 1980–85, Sr Researcher 1985–86, Leading Researcher 1986–87; left Soviet Union 1987; Prof., Univ. of Wisconsin-Madison, USA 1990–94; Prof., Univ. of Chicago 1994–95; Visiting Prof., Yale Univ. 1995–2002; Rita L. Atkinson Prof. of Math., Univ. of California, San Diego 2002–; Distinguished Prof., Korea Inst. for Advanced Study; has given invited talks at Int. Congress of Mathematicians, Warsaw 1983, Kyoto 1990, Zurich 1994; mem. American Acad. of Arts and Sciences 1996, NAS 2001; Foreign mem. Spanish Royal Acad. of Sciences 1997, Korean Acad. of Science and Eng 2000; Fellow, American Math. Soc. 2012; Dr hc (Hagen) 1997, (Oviedo) 2007; Medal of Collège de France 1992, Fields Medal, Int. Congress of Mathematicians, Zurich 1994, Andre Aizenstadt Prize 1996. *Publications:* numerous articles in math. journals on combinatorial problems in non-associative algebra and group theory. *Address:* Department of Mathematics, University of California, San Diego, Applied Physics & Mathematics Building 7260, 9500 Gilman Drive, Department 0112, La Jolla, CA 92093-0112, USA (office). *Telephone:* (858) 534-2647 (office). *Fax:* (858) 534-5273 (office). *E-mail:* ezelmanov@ucsd.edu (office); ezelmano@math.ucsd.edu (office). *Website:* www.math.ucsd.edu/people/faculty/Efim-Zelmanov (office).

ZELNICK, Strauss, BA, JD, MBA; American business executive; *Chairman, ZelnickMedia LLC;* b. 26 June 1957, Boston, Mass.; s. of Allan Zelnick and Elsa Lee Strauss; m. Wendy Belzberg 1990; two s.; ed Wesleyan and Harvard Univs; called to Bar NY 1984; Dir Int. TV Columbia Pictures Int. Corpn 1983–85, Vice-Pres. Int. TV 1985–86; Sr Vice-Pres. Corp. Devt Vestron Inc. 1986–87, Exec. Vice-Pres. 1987, Pres., COO 1988–89; Pres., COO Twentieth Century Fox 1989–93; Pres., CEO Crystal Dynamics 1993–95; Pres., CEO BMG Entertainment N America 1995–98, BMG Entertainment, New York 1998–2000 (resgnd); f. and Chair. ZelnickMedia LLC 2001–; Chair. (non-exec.) Take-Two Interactive Software 2007–; Trustee, Wesleyan Univ. 1992–; mem. Bd of Dirs Covenant House 1995–2000, Insignia Financial Group, Inc., Carver Bancorp, Inc., UGO Networks, Inc. *Leisure interests:* squash, sailing, skiing. *Address:* ZelnickMedia LLC, 19 West 44th Street, 18th Floor, New York, NY 10036, USA (office). *Telephone:* (212) 223-1383 (office). *Fax:* (212) 223-1384 (office). *Website:* www.zelnickmedia.com (office).

ZELNIK, Patrick; French music industry executive; *President, Naïve Records;* b. 10 Nov. 1946, Paris; began career at Polydor as Int. Marketing Dir 1973–80; met Richard Branson who offered to let him found Virgin France, Pres. and CEO Virgin France 1980–97, launched Virgin Retail, Pres. 1988–97, Pres. Champs Elysées Megastore 1988–2000; Co-Founder and Pres. label Naïve Records 1997–, acquired labels Opus 111 and Ambroisie; Pres. Syndicat national de l'édition phonographique (SNEP) 1990–92, 1994–97, UPFI 2000–04; Pres. Impala (ind. music cos asscn) 2006–08, Co-Pres. (with Michel Lambot and Horst Weidenmüller) 2008–12; Pres. Gaite Lyrique (cultural centre) 2008–; Head, French govt mission Création et internet 2009–10. *Address:* Naïve Records, 9 rue Victor Masse, 75009 Paris, France (office). *E-mail:* contact@naive.fr (office). *Website:* www.naive.fr (office); gaite-lyrique.net/en (office).

ZEMAN, Miloš; Czech politician and head of state; *President;* b. 29 Jan. 1944, Kolín, Czechoslovakia (now Czech Repub.); m. 1st Blanka Zemanová (divorced 1978) one s.; m. 2nd Ivana Bednarčíková 1993; one d.; ed School of Econs, Prague; teacher, School of Econs, Prague 1969–70; joined CP of Czechoslovakia 1968; expelled 1970; researcher Prognostic Inst., Prague 1971–89; Chair. Česká Strana Sociálně Demokratická (Czech Social Democratic Party) 1993–2001; Chair. Parl. of Czech Repub. 1996–98; mem. Cttee of Socialist International 1997–2002; Chair. Cttee for Protection of Econ. Interests of Czech Repub., Cttee for Handicapped People 1998–; Prime Minister of Czech Repub. 1998–2002; presidential cand. 2003; f. Party of Civic Rights 2009–; Pres. of Czech Repub. 2013–; Kt Grand Cross, Order of the White Lion 2013, Order of Tomáš Garrigue Masaryk 2013, Order of the White Double Cross, Order of Merit of the FRG. *Publications include:* Confession of a Former Prognosis Maker (with J. Bauer) 1995, Our Post-Totalitarian Crisis and Its Potential Cure 1992; many articles on econs in papers and magazines. *Leisure interests:* biking, cross-country skiing, science fiction, chess. *Address:* Office of the President, Pražský hrad, 119 08 Prague 1 (office); Strana Práv Občanů, Opletalova 1418/23, Prague 1, 11000 Czech Republic (office). *Telephone:* 224371111 (office); 296515321 (office). *Fax:* 224373300 (office). *E-mail:* ladislav.jakl@hrad.cz (office). *Website:* www.hrad.cz (office).

ZEMECKIS, Robert L.; American film director, film producer and screenwriter; b. 14 May 1951, Chicago, Ill.; s. of Alphonse Zemeckis and Rose Zemeckis (née Nespeca); m. 1st Mary Ellen Trainor 1980 (divorced 2000); one s.; m. 2nd Leslie Harter 2001; two s.; ed Univ. of Southern California. *Films directed include:* The Lift 1972, Field of Honor 1973, I Wanna Hold Your Hand 1978, Used Cars 1980, Romancing the Stone 1984, Back to the Future 1985, Who Framed Roger Rabbit 1988, Back to the Future II 1989, Back to the Future III 1990, Death Becomes Her 1992, Forrest Gump 1994, Contact (also producer) 1997, What Lies Beneath (also producer) 2000, Cast Away (also producer) 2000, The Polar Express (also writer and producer) 2004, Beowulf (also producer) 2007, A Christmas Carol (also writer and producer) 2009, Flight (also producer) 2012. *Films produced include:* The Public Eye 1992, Trespass 1992, Demon Knight 1995, The Frighteners 1996, Bordello of Blood 1996, House on Haunted Hill 1999, Ritual 2001, Thir13en Ghosts 2001, Ghost Ship 2002, Matchstick Men 2003, Gothika 2003, Clink Inc. 2003, House of Wax 2005, The Prize Winner of Defiance, Ohio 2005, Last Holiday 2006, Monster House 2006, The Reaping 2007, Behind the Burly Q (exec. producer) 2010, Mars Needs Moms 2011, Real Steel 2011, Back for the Future (short) (exec. producer) 2011, Bound by Flesh (documentary) (exec. producer) 2012. *Television includes:* Tales from the Crypt (several episodes) 1989–96, Two-Fisted Tales 1991, Johnny Bago (series) 1993, W.E.I.R.D. World 1995, Perversions of Science (series) 1997, The 20th Century: The Pursuit of Happiness 1999. *Address:* c/o Gelfand, Rennert & Feldman, 1880 Century Park East, Suite 1600, Los Angeles, CA 90067; South Side Amusement, Bldg 484, 100 Universal City Plaza, CA 91608, USA.

ZEMLIN, Jim; American technology executive; *Executive Director, Linux Foundation;* Brand Man., Western Wireless 1995–98; Co-founder and Dir of Marketing, Corio Inc. 1998–2000; Vice-Pres. of Marketing, Covalent Technologies 2000–04; Exec. Dir and Pres. Free Standards Group 2004–07 (group merged with Open Source Devt Labs (OSDL) to form Linux Foundation), Exec. Dir Linux Foundation 2007–; adviser on open source strategy to various cos and governmental groups, including Hyperic, Zmanda, Chinese Open Source Promotion Union. *Address:* The Linux Foundation, 210 Fell Street, Suite 16, San Francisco, CA 94102, USA (office). *Telephone:* (415) 723-9709 (office). *Fax:* (415) 723-9709 (office). *E-mail:* info@linuxfoundation.org (office). *Website:* www.linuxfoundation.org (office); www.linuxfoundation.org/blogs/jzemlin.

ZEN ZE-KIUN, HE Cardinal Joseph, PhD, STL; Hong Kong ecclesiastic; *Bishop Emeritus of Hong Kong (Xianggang);* b. 13 Jan. 1932, Shanghai; ed Salesian Pontifical Univ.; ordained priest, Salesians of St John Bosco 1961; Coadjutor Bishop of Hong Kong (Xianggang) 1996; Bishop of Hong Kong (Xianggang) 2002–09, Bishop Emer. 2009–; cr. Cardinal 2006. *Address:* Catholic Diocese Centre 12F, 16 Caine Road, Hong Kong Special Administrative Region, People's Republic of China (office). *Telephone:* 2522-3677 (office). *Fax:* 2522-3749 (office). *E-mail:* hkcsco@catholic.org.hk (office). *Website:* www.catholic.org.hk (office).

ZENG, Peiyan; Chinese politician and electronics engineer; *Chairman, China Center for International Economic Exchanges;* b. 1 Dec. 1938, Shanghai; ed Tsinghua Univ., Beijing, CCP Cen. Cttee Cen. Party School; technician, later Chief of Research Project Group, Shanghai Electrical Appliances Inst., First Ministry of Machine-Building Industry 1962–64; technician, later Group Leader, Rectifier Research Office, Xi'an Switch and Rectifier Factory, First Ministry of Machine-Building Industry 1964–65, Group Leader, later Deputy Head and Deputy Chief Engineer, Xi'an Rectifier Inst. 1965–82; joined CCP 1978; Second then First Sec. Science and Tech. Counsellor's Office, Embassy, USA 1982–84; Head, Gen. Office then Dir-Gen. Planning Dept, Ministry of Electronics Industry 1984–88; Vice-Minister, Ministry of Electronics Industry 1987–88, Ministry of Machinery-Building and Electronics Industry 1988–92; Deputy Sec.-Gen. and Dir of Office (Minister) Cen. Finance and Econ. Leading Group 1992–; Vice-Minister, State Devt and Reform Comm. 1992–94, Minister 1994 (Sec. Leading Party Group 1998–2002); Deputy Dir Three Gorges Project Construction Cttee 1998–2000; Chair. China Center for Int. Econ. Exchanges 2008–; Dir Western Region Devt Office, State Council 2000–01, Head 2001–02; Deputy Leader, State Leading

Group for Information 2001–02, Head, 2001–02; Vice-Premier, State Council 2003–08; Alt. mem. 14th CCP Cen. Cttee 1992–97, mem. 15th CCP Cen. Cttee 1997–2002, 16th CCP Cen. Cttee 2002–07, Political Bureau 2002–07. *Address:* China Center for International Economic Exchanges, 5 Yong Ding Men Nei Street, Xicheng District, Beijing 100050, People's Republic of China (office). *Fax:* (10) 83362199 (office). *Website:* www.cciee.org.cn (office).

ZENG, Qinghong; Chinese politician (retd); b. July 1939, Ji, Jiangxi Prov.; s. of Zeng Shan; ed Beijing Inst. of Tech.; joined CCP 1960; technician, No. 743 Army Unit, Group Army, PLA Services and Arms 1963–65; technician, No. 6 Office, No. 2 Dept, Second Acad., Seventh Ministry of Machine-Building Industry 1965–69, No. 2 Dept 1970–73; sent to do manual labour, Chikan Base, Army (or Ground Force), PLA Services and Arms 1969–70, Xihu Production Base, Hunan Prov. 1969–70; technician, Production Div., Comm. of Science, Tech. and Industry for Nat. Defence, Beijing 1973–79; Sec.-Gen. Office, State Devt and Reform Comm. 1979–81; Deputy Div. Dir-Gen. Office, State Energy Comm. 1981–82; worked in Liaison Dept, Foreign Affairs Bureau, Ministry of Petroleum Industry 1982–83; Deputy Man. Liaison Dept, China Nat. Offshore Oil Corpn 1983–84; Deputy Dir Foreign Affairs Bureau, Ministry of Petroleum Industry 1983–84; Sec. CCP Party Cttee, South and Yellow Seas Petroleum Corpn 1983–84; Deputy Head, later Head, Org. Dept, CCP Shanghai Municipal Cttee 1984–86, Sec.-Gen. Standing Cttee 1984–86, Deputy Sec. CCP Shanghai Municipal Cttee 1986–89; Deputy Dir, Gen. Office, 13th and 14th CCP Cen. Cttees 1989–93, Dir, Gen. Office, 14th CCP Cen. Cttee 1993–97, Sec. Work Cttee, Offices Under Cen. Cttee 1993–97, mem. 15th CCP Cen. Cttee 1992–97, Dir, Gen. Office, 15th CCP Cen. Cttee 1997–99, Dir Work Cttee, Offices Under Cen. Cttee 1997–99, Head, Org. Dept 1999–2002, Alt. mem. Politburo 1997–2002, mem. Politburo Secr. 1997, mem. 16th CCP Cen. Cttee 2002–07, Standing Cttee Politburo 2002–07, Sec.-Gen. 17th CCP Nat. Congress 2007–12; Chief Strategist to Pres. Jiang Zemin –2002; Vice-Pres. People's Repub. of China 2003–07 (retd).

ZENG, Xianlin; Chinese government official; b. 1929, Anyue, Sichuan Prov.; ed Moscow Stalin Machine Tools and Tools Inst.; joined CCP 1947; spent over a decade as Dir and Deputy Engineer at Dalian Machine Tools Plant; Vice-Minister for Science and Tech. 1985–87, for State Planning Comm. 1986–87; Minister for Light Industry 1987–93; Alt. mem. 13th CCP Cen. Cttee 1987–92, 14th CCP Cen. Cttee 1992–97; Vice-Chair. Finance and Econ. Cttee of 9th NPC 1998–2003.

ZENNSTRÖM, Niklas, MSc; Swedish internet industry executive; *CEO, Atomico;* b. 1966; m. Catherine Zennström; ed Uppsala Univ., Univ. of Michigan, USA; began career in business devt at Tele2 (telecom operator), launched (with Janus Friis) get2net (ISP) and everyday.com (also CEO); launched and served as CEO several cos including KaZaA (software co.), Joltid (software co.), Altnet (peer to peer network); Co-founder (with Janus Friis) and CEO Skype Technologies SA (internet telephony co.) 2003–07, mem. of group that reacquired Skype from eBay, currently mem. Bd of Dirs; Co-founder (with Janus Friis) and Co-Chair. Joost N.V. 2007; Founding Partner and CEO Atomico (venture capital group), London 2006–; mem. Bd of Dirs Fon, Jolicloud, Rdio; Co-founder (with Catherine Zennström) Zennström Philanthropies 2007; KTH Great Prize 2009, Lifetime Achievement Award, Oxford Internet Inst. 2011, Gold Medal, Royal Swedish Acad. of Eng Sciences 2013, HM The King's Medal (12:e storleken) 2013. *Leisure interests:* sailing, skiing, outdoor activities, travelling. *Address:* Atomico, 50 New Bond Street, London, W1S 1BJ, England (office). *E-mail:* contact@atomico.com (office). *Website:* www.atomico.com (office).

ZEPHANIAH, Benjamin Obadiah Iqbal; British poet, writer, dramatist, musician and singer and academic; *Professor of Poetry and Creative Writing, Brunel University;* b. 15 April 1958, Birmingham; ed Deykin Avenue Primary School, Birmingham Ward End Hall Comprehensive School, Birmingham Broadway Comprehensive School, Birmingham Boreatton Park Approved School, Baschurch; Writer-in-Residence, Africa Arts Collective, Liverpool 1989, Hay-on-Wye Literature Festival 1991, Memphis State Univ., USA 1991–95, Keats House, Hampstead 2011; currently Prof. of Poetry and Creative Writing, Brunel Univ.; numerous radio performances, acting roles, appearances; mem. Musicians' Union, Equity, Performing Rights Soc., Authors' Licensing and Collecting Soc.; Dr hc (Univ. of North London) 1998, (Univ. of West of England) 1999, (Staffordshire Univ.) 2001, (Oxford Brookes Univ.) 2002, (South Bank Univ., London) 2002, (Univ. of East London) 2003, (Univ. Coll. Northampton) 2003, (Open Univ.) 2004, (Univ. of Central England) 2005; Hon. DLitt (Westminster Univ.) 2006, (Univ. of Birmingham) 2008, (Univ. of Hull) 2010, (Univ. of Glamorgan) 2011, (De Montfort Univ.) 2015; BBC Young Playwrights Festival Award 1988. *Recordings include:* albums: Rasta 1983, Us and Dem 1990, Back To Our Roots 1995, Belly Of The Beast 1996, Heading For The Door 2000, Naked 2006; singles: Dub Ranting (EP) 1982, Big Boys Don't Make Girls Cry 1984, Free South Africa 1986, Crisis 1992, Naked 2004, Naked & Mixed-Up 2006. *Compositions include:* contrib. to Dancing Tribes (single, with Back To Base) 1999, Illegal (with Swayzak) 2000, What is In Between (with Mieko Shimizo) 2006, The Imagined Village 2007, The Police in Dub 2008, Skanny Skannky (Toddla T) 2009. *Plays include:* Playing the Right Tune 1985, Job Rocking 1987, Delirium 1987, Streetwise 1990, The Trial of Mickey Tekka 1991. *Radio plays include:* Hurricane Dub 1988, Our Teacher's Gone Crazy 1990, Listen To Your Parents 2000, Face 2002. *Television plays include:* Dread Poets Society 1991, Peaky Blinders 2013, 2014. *Publications include:* fiction: Face 1999, Refugee Boy 2001, Teacher's Dead 2007; poetry: Pen Rhythm 1980, The Dread Affair 1985, Inna Liverpool 1988, Rasta Time in Palestine 1990, City Psalms 1992, Talking Turkeys 1994, Funky Chickens 1996, Propa Propaganda 1996, School's Out 1997, We Are Britain 2002, Too Black, Too Strong 2002, The Little Book of Vegan Poems 2002, Gangsta Rap 2004, My Story 2011, When I Grow Up 2011, Kung Fu Trip 2011, Liam 2012, Terror Kid 2014; non fiction: The Life and Rhyme of Benjamin Zephaniah 2018; contrib. to periodicals, radio, TV. *Leisure interests:* kung fu, tai chi, collecting bank notes. *Address:* c/o United Agents, 12–26 Lexington Street, London, W1F 0LE, England (office). *Telephone:* (20) 3214-0800 (office). *Fax:* (20) 3214-0801 (office). *E-mail:* info@unitedagents.co.uk (office). *Website:* unitedagents.co.uk (office); www.benjaminzephaniah.com.

ZEPPOS, Nicholas S., BA, JD; American lawyer and university administrator; *Chancellor, Vanderbilt University;* b. 1954, Milwaukee, Wis.; m. Lydia Howarth; ed Univ. of Wisconsin, Madison; Practising Attorney, Wilmer, Cutler & Pickering, Washington, DC 1982–87; Prof., Vanderbilt Law School 1987, becoming Provost and Vice-Chancellor for Academic Affairs 2001, Chief Academic Officer 2002, Interim Chancellor 2007, Chancellor 2008–; fmr Chair. Scholars Cttee on Fed. Judiciary; fmr Chair. Rules Advisory Cttee US Court of Appeals for Sixth Circuit; Dir Nashville Area Chamber of Commerce, Nashville Alliance for Public Educ. *Address:* Office of the Chancellor, Vanderbilt University, 211 Kirkland Hall, Nashville, TN 37240, USA (office). *Telephone:* (615) 322-1813 (office). *Fax:* (615) 322-6060 (office). *E-mail:* chancellor@vanderbilt.edu (office). *Website:* www.vanderbilt.edu/chancellor (office).

ZERHOUNI, Elias Adam, MD; American (b. Algerian) physician, professor of radiology and fmr medical administrator; *Professor of Radiology and of Biomedical Engineering, School of Medicine, Johns Hopkins University;* b. 12 April 1951, Nedroma, Algeria; m. Nadia Azza; two s. one d.; ed Univ. of Algiers School of Medicine, Algeria, Johns Hopkins School of Medicine, USA; came to USA aged 24, naturalized US citizen 1990; Residency in Diagnostic Radiology, Johns Hopkins Univ. School of Medicine 1975–78, Chief Resident, Dept of Radiology 1977–78, Instructor 1978–79, Asst Prof. 1979–81, Assoc. Prof. 1985–92, Prof. of Radiology 1992– (Chair. of Dept 1996–2002), Prof. of Biomedical Eng (Secondary) 1995–2002, Exec. Vice-Dean, Vice-Dean for Clinical Affairs and Pres. Clinical Practice Asscn 1996–99, Vice-Dean for Research 1999–2000, Exec. Vice-Dean 2000–02, Martin Donner Prof. of Radiology and Prof. of Biomedical Eng (Secondary) 2000–02, 2009–, Chair. Russell H. Morgan Dept of Radiology and Radiological Science 2000–02; Asst Prof., Dept of Radiology, Eastern Va Medical School, Norfolk, Va 1981–83, Assoc. Prof. 1983–85; Dir Nat. Insts of Health (NIH) 2002–08; Asst Dir Body CT, The Johns Hopkins Hosp. 1978–81, Radiologist-in-Chief 1996–; Vice-Chair. and Dir Body Imaging Section, De Paul Hosp., Eastern Va Medical School 1982–85; Co-Dir, MRI and Body CT Coordinator of Clinical Research, The Johns Hopkins Medical Insts 1985–88, Dir Divs of Thoracic Imaging and MRI Dept of Radiology 1988–96, est. Inst. for Cell Eng; Dir Advanced Medical Imaging Inst., Norfolk 1991–92; Sr Fellow, Bill and Melinda Gates Foundation (Global Health) 2008–; Scientific Advisor to CEO Chris Viehbacher of Sanofi-Aventis 2009, apptd Head of Research and Development 2010; Chief Scientific Advisor, Science Translational Medicine (journal), AAAS 2009–; apptd US Special Envoy in Science and Technology 2009; f. Zerhouni Group, LLC 2010; Co-founder SurgiVision, Inc.; mem. NAS Inst. of Medicine, Bd of Scientific Advisors of the Nat. Cancer Inst. 1998–; Fellow, Int. Soc. of Magnetic Resonance Medicine 1998; Trustee, King Abdullah Univ. of Science and Technology 2009–; Légion d'honneur 2008; Dr hc (Univ. of Algiers) 2005; Hon. LHD (Johns Hopkins Univ.) 2010; American Roentgen Ray Soc. Gold Medal Award 1985, 1987, Paul Lauterbur Award for MRI Research 1989, 1993, Frank T. McClure Fellowship Award 1990–92, Royal Swedish Soc. of Radiology Centennial Speaker 1995, Fleischner Soc. Medal, London, UK 1997. *Publications include:* author or co-author of more than 200 publs and 11 book chapters; eight patents. *Leisure interests:* playing the lute and piano, opera, tennis, scuba diving. *Address:* Whitaker Biomedical Engineering Institute, Johns Hopkins University School of Medicine, 720 Rutland Avenue, Baltimore, MD 21205, USA (office). *Telephone:* (410) 955-3131 (office). *Fax:* (410) 502-9814 (office). *Website:* www.bme.jhu.edu (office).

ZERIHOUN, Tayé-Brook, MPhil; Ethiopian diplomatist and UN official; *Assistant Secretary-General for Political Affairs, United Nations;* b. 13 Dec. 1942; m.; one s. three d.; ed Columbia Univ., USA; joined UN 1981, worked on special assignments on decolonization, trusteeship, conflict prevention and resolution, peacemaking and peace-building, New York, Deputy Dir, then Dir Africa I Div., Dept of Political Affairs, with responsibility for countries of Horn of Africa, Great Lakes and Southern Africa regions and regional orgs including Inter-Governmental Authority on Devt and Southern African Devt Community 1995–2003, Chair. Inter-departmental Task Force for Sudan 2003–04, Sec.-Gen.'s Prin. Deputy Special Rep. in Sudan with rank of Asst Sec.-Gen. 2004–08, Special Rep. of Sec.-Gen. and Head of UN Peacekeeping Force in Cyprus (UNFICYP) 2008–10, Asst Sec.-Gen. for Political Affairs 2010–. *Address:* Department of Political Affairs, United Nations, New York, NY 10017, USA (office). *Telephone:* (212) 963-1234 (office). *Fax:* (212) 963-4879 (office). *Website:* www.un.org/Depts/dpa (office).

ZERPA DELGADO, Simón Alejandro; Venezuelan economist and politician; *Minister of Economy and Finance;* b. 28 Aug. 1983; s. of Ivan Zerpa Guerrero; Pres. Fondo Nacional de Desarrollo (Fonden) (govt investment agency) 2014; Chief Financial Officer PDVSA Petróleo SA (state oil co.) 2017; fmr Vice Minister of Investment and Devt, Minister of Economy and Finance 2017–; fmr Pres. Banco de Desarrollo Económico y Social de Venezuela (BANDES); Presidential Commr, China-Venezuela Jt Fund; mem. Bd of Dirs CA Nacional Teléfonos de Venezuela. *Address:* Ministry of Economy and Finance, Edif. Ministerio de Finanzas, esq. Carmelitas, Avda Urdaneta, Caracas, 1010, Venezuela (office). *Telephone:* (212) 802-1000 (office). *Website:* www.mppef.gob.ve (office).

ZERROUGUI, Leila; Algerian lawyer, judge and UN official; *Special Representative and Head, United Nations Stabilization Mission in Democratic Republic of Congo (MONUSCO);* b. 1956, Souk-Ahras; ed Ecole Nationale d'Administration; Juvenile Judge and Judge of First Instance 1980–86, Appeal Court Judge 1986–97; legal adviser to Cabinet, Ministry of Justice 1998–2000; apptd to Supreme Court 2000; Deputy Special Rep. of Sec.-Gen. and Deputy Head, UN Org. Stabilization Mission in Democratic Repub. of the Congo (MONUSCO) 2008–12, Special Rep. of Sec.-Gen. and Head 2017–, Special Rep. of UN Sec.-Gen. for Children and Armed Conflict 2012–17; mem. Working Group on Arbitrary Detention under UN Human Rights Council 2001, Chair.-Rapporteur Working Group 2003–08; Assoc. Prof., Ecole Supérieure de la Magistrature. *Address:* Department of Peacekeeping Operations, Room S-3727B, United Nations, New York, NY 10017, USA (office). *Telephone:* (212) 963-8077 (office). *Fax:* (212) 963-9222 (office). *Website:* peacekeeping.un.org (office).

ZETA-JONES, Catherine, CBE; British actress; b. 25 Sept. 1969, Swansea, Wales; d. of David James Jones; m. Michael Douglas (q.v.) 2000; one s. one d. *Stage appearances include:* The Pyjama Game, Annie, Bugsy Malone, 42nd Street, Street Scene, A Little Night Music, Broadway (Outer Critics Circle Award, Drama Desk Award, Tony Award for Best Leading Actress in a Musical 2010) 2009. *Television appearances include:* The Darling Buds of May (series) 1991, Out of the Blue 1991, The Cinder Path 1994, The Return of the Native 1995, Catherine the Great 1995, Titanic 1996, Feud 2017. *Films:* Les 1001 nuits 1990, The Adventures of Young

Indiana Jones: Daredevils of the Desert 1992, Christopher Columbus: The Discovery 1992, Splitting Heirs 1993, Blue Juice 1995, The Phantom 1996, The Mask of Zorro 1998, Entrapment 1999, The Haunting 1999, High Fidelity 2000, Traffic 2000, America's Sweethearts 2001, Chicago (BAFTA Award for Best Supporting Actress 2003, Screen Actors Guild Award for Best Supporting Actress 2003, Acad. Award for Best Supporting Actress 2003) 2002, Sinbad: Legend of the Seven Seas (voice) 2003, Intolerable Cruelty 2003, The Terminal 2004, Ocean's Twelve 2004, The Legend of Zorro 2005, No Reservations 2007, Death Defying Acts 2007, The Rebound 2009, Playing for Keeps 2012, Side Effects 2013, Red 2 2013, Dad's Army 2016. *Address:* c/o Sam Fischer, Ziffren, Brittenham, Branca, Fischer, Gilbert-Lurie, Stiffelman & Cook LLP, 1801 Century Park West, Los Angeles, CA 90067-6406; c/o William Morris Agency, Inc., 1 William Morris Place, Beverly Hills, CA 90212, USA.

ZETI, Tan Sri Dato' Sri Akhtar Aziz, BSc, PhD; Malaysian economist and fmr central banker; b. 27 Aug. 1947; d. of Diraja Tun Ungku Aziz and Sharifah Azah Mohamed Alsagoff; m. Dato' Dr Tawfiq Ayman; two c.; ed Univ. Malaya, Wharton School, Univ. of Pennsylvania, USA; served in the South-East Asian Research and Training Centre (SEACEN) 1979–84; joined Bank Negara Malaysia (Cen. bank) 1985, Rep. in London, UK 1989–94, Deputy Gov. 1995–98, Acting Gov. 1998–2000, Gov. 2000–16; Man. Dir Pengurusan Danaharta Nasional Bhd 1998–2000; mem. Bd of Dirs Khazanah Nasional Bhd 2000–08; apptd mem. UN task force to assess reform of global financial system 2008; Chair. Task Force for Islamic Finance and Global Financial Stability, Islamic Devt Bank 2009–; Chair. Inauguration Cttee, Islamic Financial Services Bd, Asian Inst. of Finance; headed launch of Malaysian global Islamic SUKUK; mem. Wharton Exec. Bd for Asia; Cen. Bank Gov. of the Year, Euromoney magazine 2003.

ZETSCHE, Dieter, DrIng; German automotive industry executive; *Chairman of the Board of Management, Daimler AG;* b. 5 May 1953, Istanbul, Turkey; ed Univs of Karlsruhe and Paderborn; joined Research Dept of Daimler-Benz AG 1976–81, Asst to Devt Man., Commercial Vehicles Business Unit 1981–84, Co-ordinator, Commercial Vehicle Devt Activities 1984–86, Sr Man. and Chief Engineer of Cross-Country Vehicle Unit 1986–87, Head of Devt Dept and Chief Engineer, Mercedes-Benz do Brasil 1987–89, mem. Man. Bd 1988–89, Pres. Mercedes-Benz Argentina 1989–91, Pres. Freightliner Corp., Portland, Ore., USA 1991–92, Deputy mem. Bd of Man., Mercedes-Benz AG and Chief Engineer, Devt Div., Passenger Cars Business Unit, 1992–95, mem. Bd of Man., Sales Div., Mercedes-Benz AG 1995–99, mem. Bd of Man., Sales Div., Daimler-Benz AG 1997–99, mem. Bd of Man., Sales Div., DaimlerChrysler AG 1998–99, mem. Bd of Man., Commercial Vehicle Div., DaimlerChrysler AG 1999, mem. Bd of Man., CEO and Pres. Chrysler Group 2000–05, Chair. Bd of Man. and Head, Mercedes Car Group, DaimlerChrysler AG (now Daimler AG after sale of Chrysler group to Cerberus Capital Management 2007), Stuttgart 2006–; Pres. European Automobile Manufacturers' Asscn 2016–17. *Address:* Daimler AG, 70546 Stuttgart, Germany (office). *Telephone:* (711) 170 (office). *Fax:* (711) 1722244 (office). *E-mail:* dialog@daimler.com (office). *Website:* www.daimler.com (office).

ZEWDE, Sahle-Work; Ethiopian diplomatist, UN official and head of state; *President;* b. 21 Feb. 1950; two s.; ed Univ. of Montpellier, France; Amb. to Senegal (also accred to Mali, Cape Verde, Guinea-Bissau, Gambia and Guinea) 1989–93, Amb. to Djibouti and Perm. Rep. to IGAD 1993–2002, Amb. to France and Perm. Rep. to UNESCO (also accred to Tunisia and Morocco) 2002–06, Perm. Rep. of Ethiopia to the African Union (AU) and UN ECA 2006–09, Dir-Gen. for African Affairs, Ministry of Foreign Affairs 2006–09, has represented Ethiopia in the Peace and Security Council of the AU 2006–; Special Rep. of the UN Sec.-Gen. and Head of UN Integrated Peacebuilding Office in the Cen. African Repub. (BINUCA) 2009–11, Dir-Gen. UN Office at Nairobi (UNON) 2011–18, Special Rep. to African Union and Head UN Office of African Union (UNOAU) June–Oct. 2018; Pres. of Ethiopia 2018–; Co-Chair. UN Security Council-AU Peace and Security Council jt meeting, New York April 2008; has attended most IGAD meetings, as well as OAU/AU summits and led the experts group in different partnership summits with Africa (China-India-EU-France-S America-Turkey), and has led OAU observer team in parl. and presidential elections in Mali 1991 and Niger 1993, 1996. *Address:* Office of the President, PO Box 1031, Addis Ababa, Ethiopia (office). *Telephone:* (11) 1551000 (office). *Fax:* (11) 1552030 (office).

ZGONEA, Valeriu Ştefan, BA, MA; Romanian politician; b. 3 Sept. 1967, Craiova, Dolj Co.; ed Fraţii Buzeşti Nat. Coll., Craiova, Univ. of Civil Eng, Bucharest, Nat. Inst. for Constructions, Univ. of Amsterdam, the Netherlands, American Council of Young Political Leaders, USA, Social Democrat Inst., Nat. Inst. of Admin, Nat. Defence Coll., Nat. Security Superior Coll.; employee at SC Construcţii Feroviare SA, Craiova 1985, 1990–93; with Incertrans, Bucharest 1985–90; engineer with Compania Naţională CFR SA 1994–2000; mem. Partidul Democraţiei Sociale din România (PDSR—Social Democratic Party of Romania) 1996–2001, Partidul Social Democrat (PSD—Social Democratic Party) 2001–, Pres. Youth Org. of PDSR, Dolj Co. 1999–2000, Vice-Pres. Exec. Cttee of Nat. Council of PDSR, mem. Exec. Bureau of PDSR, Dolj Co., Vice-Pres. Dolj Co. PSD Org. 2001, mem. Nat. Council of PSD 2001–, Exec. Sec., PSD Nat. Perm. Bureau 2007–, apptd Vice-Pres. PSD 2010, Exec. Chair. 2015–16; mem. Dolj Co. Council June–Nov. 2000; mem. Camera Deputaţilor (Chamber of Deputies) 2000–, mem. Cttee for Information, Tech. and Communications 2000–04, Exec. Cttee of Interparliamentary Union, Friendship Parl. Group with Armenia and Kuwait 2000–04, Vice-Leader of Parl. Group of PSD 2004–08, mem. Cttee for European Integration 2004–08, Exec. Cttee of Interparliamentary Union of GB and NI 2004–08, Cttee for Public Admin, Territorial Devt and Environmental Balance 2004–08, EU Observer in European Parl. on behalf of Romania (Socialist and Social-Democrat Group) 2004–08, mem. Budget Cttee 2005, Questor, Chamber of Deputies (Camera Deputaţilor) Feb.–Sept. 2006, Sec. 2006–10, Vice-Chair. 2010–12, Chair. Parl. Group of PSD May–July 2012, Chair. Chamber of Deputies July 2012–16. *E-mail:* webmaster@cdep.ro (office). *Website:* www.cdep.ro (office).

ZHADOBIN, Lt-Gen. Yuri; Belarusian army officer and government official; b. 14 Nov. 1954, Dnipropetrovsk, Ukraine; ed Kazan Armour Command School, Malinovsky Acad. of Armoured Forces, Moscow; began mil. service 1972, moved through ranks from platoon leader to regt commdr 1976–90, various command posts in Belarusian civil defence and internal security troops within Ministry of Internal Affairs 1990–99, Deputy Minister of Internal Affairs and Commdr, Internal Troops 1999–2003, in charge of Belarusian Pres.'s Security Service 2003–07, Chair. State Security Cttee 2007–08, State Sec., Nat. Security Council 2008–09, Minister of Defence 2009–14.

ZHAI, Jun; Chinese diplomatist; *Ambassador to France;* b. Dec. 1954, Hebei Prov.; Third Sec., West Asian and North African Affairs Dept, Ministry of Foreign Affairs (MFA) 1985–92, First Sec., Embassy in Riyadh 1992–96, Counsellor, West Asian and North African Affairs Dept, MFA 1996–97, Amb. to Libya 1997–2000, Deputy Dir-Gen., West Asian and North African Affairs Dept, MFA 2000, mem. City Cttee, CCP Standing Cttee, Zhenjiang City, Jiangsu Prov. 2000–01, Dir-Gen. Chinese Diplomatic Missions Abroad Dept, MFA 2001–03, Dir-Gen. West Asian and North African Affairs Dept 2003–06, Asst Minister of Foreign Affairs 2006–10, Vice-Minister of Foreign Affairs 2010–14, Amb. to France 2014–. *Address:* Embassy of the People's Republic of China, 11 avenue George V, 75008 Paris, France (office). *Telephone:* 1-49-52-19-50 (office). *Fax:* 1-47-20-24-22 (office). *E-mail:* chinaemb_fr@mfa.gov.cn (office). *Website:* www.amb-chine.fr (office).

ZHAI, Ruoyu; Chinese energy executive; b. 1947; ed Liaoning Univ.; joined Liaoning Power Plant 1966, becoming Deputy Dir, later Dir; Deputy Chief, Security and Environmental Protection Div., Ministry of Energy 1992, later Deputy Dir and Dir Supervisory Bureau, Ministry of Power Industry; fmr Head of Gen. Office, State Power Corpn; Gen. Man. Northeastern China br., Nat. Power Co. 1999, becoming Pres. North China Power Group 2000; Chair. and CEO Datang International Power Generation Co. Ltd 2004–10, also Gen. Man. China Datang Corpn 2002; mem. Bd of Dirs Buffalo Jayhawk China 2007–, China Nat. Nuclear Corpn 2013–; Del. 10th NPC 2003; Del. CPPCC 2008; China CEO of the Year 2005, Asia Business Leader Awards. *Address:* c/o Datang International Power Generation Co. Ltd, 9 Guangningbo Street, Xicheng District, Beijing 100140, People's Republic of China.

ZHAN, Tao, PhD; Chinese mathematician and academic; *Director, Ministry of Education Management Information Centre;* b. April 1963, Shandong; Prof. of Pure Math., Shandong Univ. 1987, fmr Dean Dept of Math. and Vice-Pres. Shandong Univ., Pres. Shandong Univ. 2000–08; Pres. Jilin Univ. 2008–11; Dir, Ministry of Educ. Man. Information Centre 2011–; has served as visiting prof. at univs in France, Netherlands and USA; fmr Vice-Pres. Shandong Youth Fed.; Deputy Dir Young Scientist Asscn of China; Standing mem. Chinese Asscn of Math., All China Youth Fed.; Chair. Shandong Asscn of Math.; numerous awards including Science and Tech. Prize for Young Scientists of China, Ministry of Educ., Science and Tech. Advancement Award, Univ. Science and Tech. Award of China, Nat. Award for Outstanding Teaching Achievement. *Address:* Management Information Centre, Ministry of Education, 37 Damucang Hutong, Xidan, Beijing 100816, People's Republic of China (office). *Telephone:* (10) 66096114 (office). *E-mail:* nglish@moe.edu.cn (office). *Website:* www.moe.edu.cn (office).

ZHANDOSOV, Oraz Aliyevich; Kazakhstani economist and politician; b. 26 Oct. 1961, Almaty; m.; one s. two d.; ed Moscow M. V. Lomonosov State Univ.; Jr Academic Assoc., Inst. of Econs of Kazakh SSR 1987–91; worked at Higher Econ. Council, office of Pres. of Kazakhstan, first as consultant then as Deputy Head, Council of Econ. Consultants 1991–92; First Deputy Minister and Chair. Nat. Agency for Foreign Investment, Ministry of Economy 1993–94; First Deputy Chair. then Chair. Nat. Bank of Kazakhstan 1994–98; First Deputy Prime Minister of Kazakhstan and Chair. State Cttee for Investment 1998–99; Deputy Prime Minister and Minister of Finance Jan.–Oct. 1999; Pres. Kazakhstani Co. for Man. of Electric Networks (KEGOS) 1999–2000; Deputy Prime Minister 2000–01; Chair. Asscn of Financiers of Repub. of Kazakhstan 2001–02; apptd Asst to Pres. of Kazakhstan on economic and financial issues 2003; Chair. Republican Agency for Regulation of Natural Monopolies and Protection of Competition 2003–04; Co-Chair. Real Bright Road—Democratic Party of Kazakhstan (Naghyz Ak Zhol) 2005–07; Advisor to Nat. Econ. Chamber of Kazakhstan (Atameken); Chair. Bd of Trustees Kazakhstan Asscn of Economists; mem. Presidium, Nat. Chamber of Entrepreneurs; mem. Political Council, Democratic Party of Kazakhstan Social Org. 2001–02; mem. Bd of Dirs Batys tranzit JSC, RAKURS Center for Economic Analysis 2008–, JSC Subsidiary Bank Punjab National Bank Kazakhstan –2011, DAMU Entrepreneurship Devt Fund JSC 2012–; Order of Kurmet. *Address:* c/o RAKURS Center for Economic Analysis, 136 Dostyk Avenue, Business Center RFCA, 8th Floor, Almaty 050059, Kazakhstan.

ZHANG, Baoming; Chinese government official and mining engineer; *President, China Occupational Safety and Health Association;* b. Nov. 1940, Qiqihar, Heilongjiang Prov.; ed Fuxin Mining Inst.; technician, later Deputy Dir Haizhou Open-Cut Coal Mine, Fuxin Mining Admin 1960s–70s, Deputy Dir Fuxin Mining Admin 1982, later Dir; Section Chief, Designing Inst., Changchun Open-Cut Coal Mine 1978–82; joined CCP 1974; Vice-Minister of Coal Industry 1986–88, 1993–98; Deputy Gen. Man. China Gen. Coal Corpn 1990–93; Dir State Admin of Coal Industry 1998–2000; Dir State Admin for Safe Production Supervision 2000–03; Pres. China Occupational Safety and Health Asscn 2002–; Alt. mem. 15th CCP Cen. Cttee 1997–2002. *Publications:* China Coal Industry Reform and Development. *Address:* China Occupational Safety and Health Association, No. 21 HePingLi North Street, Dong Cheng District, Beijing 100713, People's Republic of China (office). *E-mail:* cosha@cosha.org.cn (office).

ZHANG, Chaoyang, (Charles Zhang), PhD; Chinese business executive and inventor; *Chairman and CEO, Sohu.com;* b. 31 Oct. 1964, Xi'an, Shaanxi Prov.; ed Tsinghua Univ., Massachusetts Inst. of Tech., USA; Liaison Officer for MIT in Asia-Pacific Region 1993; Chief Rep. in China, Internet Securities 1995–; Founder of ITC and the inventor of the Chinese search engine Sohu; Chair. Bd and CEO Sohu.com 1998–; mem. All-China Fed. of Industry & Commerce 2003–; took part in Mount Everest expedition 2003 (reached height of 6,666m); Tsung-Dao Lee Scholarship, Acad. of Man. Distinguished Exec. of the Year 2004, Ernst &Young Entrepreneur of the Year 2007. *Address:* Sohu.com, Internet Plaza, No.1 Park, Zhongguancun East Road, Haidian District, Beijing 100084, People's Republic of China (office). *Telephone:* (10) 62726666 (office). *Website:* corp.sohu.com (office).

ZHANG, Chunxian; Chinese government official; b. 1953, Yuzhou City, Henan Prov.; ed Dongbei Heavy Machinery School, Harbin Inst. of Tech.; joined PLA 1970, soldier, Wuhan Mil. Dist 1970–75; joined CCP 1972; Dir Industrial Machinery Dept Supervision Bureau, Ministry of Supervision 1991–92; Deputy Man., China Nat. Packaging Corpn 1992–93, Man. 1993–95, also Sec., CCP Party

Cttee 1993–95; Asst Gov. Yunnan Prov. 1995–97; Vice-Minister of Transport 1998–2002, Minister of Transport 2002–05; Sec., CCP Provincial Cttee, Hunan Prov. 2005–10, also mem. CCP Provincial Cttee Standing Cttee 2005–10, Chair. 2006–10; Sec., CCP Autonomous Regional Cttee, Xinjiang Uygur Autonomous Region 2010–16; Deputy Leader, Leading Group for Party Building 2016–; mem. 16th CCP Cen. Cttee 2002–07, 17th CCP Cen. Cttee 2007–12, 18th CCP Cen. Cttee 2013–17, also mem. 18th CCP Cen. Cttee Politburo 2012–17. *Address:* c/o Autonomous Regional Committee, Xinjiang Uygur Autonomous Region, Ürümqi 830000, People's Republic of China (office). *Website:* www.urumqi.gov.cn (office).

ZHANG, Cunhao, MSc; Chinese physical chemist; *Professor, Dalian Institute of Chemical Physics, Chinese Academy of Sciences;* b. (Chang Tsun-Hao), 23 Feb. 1928, Wudi Co., Shandong Prov.; s. of Zhang Zhu and Long Wenyuan; m. Chi Yunxia 1954; two s.; ed Nanjing Cen. Univ., Nankai Univ., Univ. of Michigan, USA, Chinese Univ. of Hong Kong; joined China Democratic League 1952, CCP 1959; joined Dalian Inst. of Chemical Physics; Chinese Acad. of Sciences 1953, served in numerous positions including Assoc. Research Fellow, Research Fellow, Prof. 1962–, Vice-Dir 1979–83, Dir, 1986–90, Dir Chem. Div. 1994, mem. Praesidium of Gen. Ass. 1996; mem. Nat. Cttee China Asscn for Science and Tech. 1991–, Academic Degree Cttee of the State Council 1998, Nat. Natural Science Fund Cttee; Del., 13th CCP Nat. Congress 1987–92, 14th CCP Nat. Congress 1992–97; Deputy Ed.-in-Chief of several scientific journals; Fellow, Chinese Acad. of Sciences 1980–, Third World Acad. of Sciences (now Acad. of Sciences for the Developing World) 1992–, Royal Soc. of Chem. 2007–; Hon. Pres. Nat. Natural Science Foundation of China 1999–; Hon. DSc (Chinese Univ. of Hong Kong) 1998; Nat. Natural Sciences Award (2nd and 3rd Class) 1957, 1982, 1993, 1997, 1999; Chinese Acad. of Sciences Award 1980, 1985, 1989, 1991, 1996, 1997, Tan Kah-Kee Chem. Science Prize 2000; Ho Leung Ho Lee Prize for Science and Tech. Progress 2002, Highest Science and Technology Award 2013. *Achievement:* asteroid named in his honour 2016. *Publications:* more than 90 research papers. *Leisure interests:* mountaineering, music, art. *Address:* Dalian Institute of Chemical Physics, Chinese Academy of Sciences, 457 Zhongshan Road, Dalian 116023, Liaoning Province (office); Xinke Garden, Room 1-1306, Zhong Guan Cun, Beijing 100080, People's Republic of China (home). *Website:* dicp.cas.cn (office).

ZHANG, Daniel, (Zhang Yong), BA; Chinese accountant and business executive; *Director and CEO, Alibaba Group;* b. 1972; ed Shanghai Univ. of Finance and Econs; Accountant, Arthur Andersen LLP, Shanghai 1995–2002; Sr Man., Audit and Business Advisory Div., PricewaterhouseCoopers 2002–05; Chief Financial Officer, Shanda Interactive Entertainment Ltd (online game developer) 2005–07; joined Alibaba Group as Chief Financial Officer, Taobao Marketplace and Gen. Man., Taobao Mall 2007, Pres. Tmall.com 2011–14, COO Alibaba Group 2013–15, Dir and CEO 2015–, also Founding mem. Alibaba Partnership; mem. Bd of Dirs Alibaba Health, Haier, Intime Retail Group, Weibo; mem. Chinese Inst. of Certified Public Accountants. *Address:* Alibaba.com, 6th Floor Chuangye Mansion, East Software Park, No. 99 Huaxing Road, Hangzou, Zhejiang Province, 310012 (office); Alibaba.com Technology Corpn Ltd, Room 408, Fanli Building, 22 Chaoyangwai Street, Chaoyang District, Beijing, 100020, People's Republic of China (office). *Telephone:* (571) 85022088 (Hangzhou) (office); (10) 6588-9698 (office). *Fax:* (571) 88157866 (Hangzhou) (office); (10) 6588-9699 (office). *Website:* www.alibaba.com (office).

ZHANG, Dejiang; Chinese politician; b. Nov. 1946, Tai'an Co., Liaoning Prov.; ed Yanbian Univ., Kim Il Sung Comprehensive Univ., Pyongyang, N Korea; sent to countryside, Taiping Brigade, Luozigou Commune, Wangqing Co., Jilin Prov. 1968–70; Sec. Propaganda Dept, CCP Communist Youth League of China Wangqing Co. Cttee 1970–72; mem. CCP 1971–; mem. Standing Cttee, CCP Party Cttee, Yanbian Univ. 1975–78, 1980–83, Vice-Chair CCP Revolutionary Cttee 1975–78, Vice-Pres. Yanbian Univ. 1980–83; Deputy Sec. CCP Yanji City Cttee 1983–85; Deputy Sec. CCP Yanbian Korean Autonomous Prefectural Cttee 1985–86, Sec. 1990–95; Vice-Minister of Civil Affairs 1986–90; Deputy Sec. CCP Jilin Prov. Cttee 1990–95, Sec. 1995–98; Chair. Jilin Prov. People's Congress 1998; Alt. mem. 14th CCP Cen. Cttee 1992–97, mem. 15th CCP Cen. Cttee 1997–2002, 16th CCP Cen. Cttee 2002–07, Politburo 2002–07; Sec., CCP Zhejiang Prov. Cttee 1998–2002, Guandong Prov. 2002–07; mem. 17th CCP Cen. Cttee 2007–12, Politburo 2007–12; Vice-Premier 2008–13; mem. 18th CCP Cen. Cttee 2012–17, Politburo 2012–17, Politburo Standing Cttee 2012–17; Sec., Chongqing Municipal Cttee, CCP 2012; Chair. Standing Cttee 12th NPC 2013–18 (retd). *Address:* c/o Great Hall of the People, West Edge, Tiananmen Square, Beijing, People's Republic of China (office).

ZHANG, Dinghua; Chinese politician; b. June 1933, Shanxian Co., Henan Prov.; ed Northwest China Univ.; joined CCP 1956; worked for Qinghai Oil Prospecting Bureau; Deputy Head, Shengli Oilfield Prospecting Newspaper 1964; Dir Political Dept, CCP Cttee, Shengli Oilfield Command HQ 1970–79; Sec. CCP Dagang Petroleum Admin. Bureau Cttee; Dir Propaganda Dept CCP Tianjin Municipal Cttee, Sec. CCP Tianjin Mun. Comm. for Discipline Inspection; mem. 13th CCP Cen. Comm. for Discipline Inspection 1987; Vice-Sec. CCP Inner Mongolia Autonomous Regional Cttee 1988–91; apptd Vice-Pres. and First Sec. Secr. All-China Fed. of Trade Unions 1991–98; mem. Govt Del., Hong Kong Handover Ceremony 1997; Del., 13th CCP Nat. Congress 1987–92; mem. 14th CCP Cen. Cttee 1992–97, 15th CCP Cen. Cttee 1997–2002; Vice-Chair. Cttee for Internal and Judicial Affairs, NPC 1998–2003.

ZHANG, Fangyou, MBA; Chinese engineer and automotive industry executive; *Chairman, Guangzhou Automobile Industry Group;* b. Oct. 1956, Zengcheng, Guangdong Prov.; ed South China Normal Univ., Zhongshan Univ.; joined CCP 1975; fmr Gen. Man. China Lounge Investments; Sec., Guangdong Zengcheng Town (City) Govt 1991–95, Deputy Sec.-Gen. Guangzhou Municipal Govt and Office Dir of Automotive Industry Office 1996–97; joined Denway Motors Ltd 1997, Chair. 1998–99, Man. Dir 1999–2004; joined Guangzhou Automobile Group 1997, Chair. Guangzhou Automobile Industry Group 2000–, Exec. Dir Guangzhou Automobile Group Co. Ltd 2005–, Chair. Guangzhou Auto Group (Hong Kong) Ltd, China Lounge Investments Ltd, Ind. Dir, Guangzhou Dept Store Enterprises Group Co. Ltd, Dir, Guangzhou Honda Automobile Co. Ltd; mem. 6th and 9th Guangzhou Municipal Party Cttee; Del. to 8th and 10th Guangdong Party's Congress and to 11th Guangdong People's Congress; Figure of Chinese Economy 2007, Nat. Model Worker 2010. *Address:* Guangzhou Automobile Industry Group,

448–458 Dongfeng Middle Road, Guangzhou 510030, People's Republic of China (office). *Telephone:* (20) 83151380 (office). *Fax:* (20) 83150335 (office). *Website:* www .gaig.com.cn (office).

ZHANG, Furong, BA, MA, PhD; Chinese banking executive; ed Liaoning Finance and Econs Coll., Dongbei Univ. of Finance and Econs; joined People's Bank of China 1971; joined Industrial and Commercial Bank of China Ltd (ICBC) 1984, worked successively as Chief of Accounting Div. and Vice-Pres. ICBC Liaoning Br. 1986–94, concurrently served as Vice-Pres. ICBC Liaoning Br. and Pres. ICBC Dalian Br. 1994–97, Asst to the Pres. of ICBC and Gen. Man. of Human Resources Dept 1997–2000, Vice-Pres. ICBC 2000–05, Exec. Dir and Vice-Pres. ICBC 2005–10; Chair. Bd of Supervisors, China Construction Bank 2010–14; Exec. Dir Bank of Tianjin Co., Ltd 2014, Sec. of Bd of Dirs 2015, Vice-Pres. 2016–; Chair. and Dir (non-exec.) Industrial and Commercial Bank of China (Canada); Vice-Chair. Banking Accounting Soc. of China, Financial Planning Standards Council of China.

ZHANG, Fusen; Chinese politician; b. March 1940, Shunyi Dist, Beijing Municipality; ed Tsinghua Univ., Beijing; joined CCP 1958; Chair. Tsinghua Students' Fed.; Head, Student Dept, CCP Communist Youth League of China, Beijing Municipal Cttee, Deputy Sec. 1979; Exec. Deputy Sec. then Sec. CCP Haidian Dist Cttee of Beijing Municipality 1979–84; Sec. Commercial and Foreign Econ. Relations and Trade Work Cttee 1979; mem. Standing Cttee of CCP Beijing Mun. Cttee 1990; Deputy Sec., later Sec.-Gen. and Pres. Party School, CCP Xinjiang Uygur Autonomous Regional Cttee 1990; Vice-Minister of Justice 1995–97; Deputy Sec. CCP Beijing Municipal Cttee 1997–2001; Vice-Mayor of Beijing Municipality 1997–2000; Minister of Justice 2000–05; mem. 13th CCP Cen. Cttee 1987–92, 14th CCP Cen. Cttee 1992–97, 15th CCP Cen. Cttee 1997–2002, 16th CCP Cen. Cttee 2002–07; mem. 10th CPPCC Nat. Cttee Standing Cttee 2003–08, 11th CPPCC Nat. Cttee Standing Cttee 2008–13; Dir 11th CPPCC Cttee for Social and Legal Affairs 2008–13.

ZHANG, Gaoli; Chinese politician; b. Nov. 1946, Jinjiang, Fujian Prov.; m. Kang Jie; one s.; ed Xiamen Univ.; joined CCP 1973; Deputy Sec. CCP Maoming City Cttee, Guangdong Prov.; Chair. Guangdong Econ. Comm. 1985–88; Vice-Gov. Guangdong Prov. 1988–93, Vice-Gov. and Acting Gov. 2001, Gov. 2002–03; First Sec. Shenzhen Garrison, CCP Party Cttee PLA Guangzhou Mil. Region 1998–2000; Chair. Standing Cttee Shenzhen Municipal People's Congress 2000; Deputy Sec. CCP Guangdong Prov. Cttee 1998–2001; Chair. Standing Cttee of Prov. People's Congress, Shandong Prov. 2003–07; Sec. CCP Tianjin Municipal Cttee 2007–12; mem. State Council 2013–18, Vice-Premier 2013–18; Dir State Construction Comm. 2013–; Deputy Dir State Energy Comm. 2013–; Alt. mem. 15th CCP Cen. Cttee 1997–2002; mem. 16th CCP Cen. Cttee 2002–07, 17th CCP Cen. Cttee 2007–12, 17th CCP Politburo 2007–12, 18th CCP Cen. Cttee 2012–17, Politburo 2012–17, Politburo Standing Cttee 2012–17. *Address:* Chinese Communist Party, Quanguo Renmin Diabiao Dahui, Zhongguo Gongchan Dang, 1 Zhongnanhai, Beijing, People's Republic of China. *Website:* cpc.people.com.cn (office).

ZHANG, Guoli; Chinese actor and director; b. 17 Jan. 1955, Shaanxi; m. Deng Jie; one s. (from previous m.); with Sichuan People's Art Theatre 1983; with China Rail Arts Co. Drama Troupe, Beijing 1993; Chair. Cttee for Chinese Young Film Workers 2006–; host, CCTV New Year's Gala 2014; 4th Nat. Theatre Plum Blossom Award for Best Actor, MTV Grand Award for Best Dir 1995, Hundred-Flower Award for Best Actor 1996, 29th Golden Rooster Award for Best Actor 2013. *Films:* The Trouble-shooters 1988, The Strangers in Beijing 1996, A Long Sigh 2000, Cell Phone 2003, The 601st Phone Call 2006, Lady Cop & Papa Crook 2008, The Founding of a Republic 2009, The Monkey King: Uproar in Heaven 2012, Back to 1942 2012, Who Is Your Dish 2013, Bringing Joy Home 2014, Everybody's Fine 2016. *Television:* Hunchback Liu: The Prime Minister 1996, The Legend of Liulichang 1998, Emperor Kangxi Travelling Incognito 1999, Emperor Kangxi Travelling Incognito: A Sequel 2000, Golden Wedding (series) 2007 (14th Shanghai TV Festival Magnolia Best Actor Award 2008), Da Shenghuo 2008, Ganzou Nide Youyu 2008, The Bronze Teeth IV 2008, Better Dance 2010, 1942 2012, Tangshan Earthquake 2013, Spring Husband 2013, Win the World 2018.

ZHANG, Guoqing, PhD; Chinese engineer, business executive and government official; *Acting Mayor of Tianjin;* b. 1964, Luoshan Co., Henan Prov.; ed Econs Man. Inst., Tsinghua Univ., Beijing, Harvard Business School, USA; joined CCP 1984; Vice-Pres. China North Industries Group Corpn (NORINCO Group) 1996–2004, Sec., CCP Party Cttee 1998–2004, Deputy Gen. Man. 1999–2008, mem. CCP Leading Party Group 1999–2013, Pres. NORINCO 2004–08, Gen. Man., Pres. and Deputy Sec. Leading Party, NORINCO Group 2008–13; Alt. mem. 17th CCP Cen. Cttee 2007–12, mem. 18th Cen. Cttee 2012–17; Deputy Sec., Municipal Cttee, Chongqing Municipality, CCP 2013–17; Mayor of Chongqing 2017; apptd Acting Mayor of Tianjin 2018. *Address:* Office of the Mayor, Tianjin 300000, People's Republic of China (office). *E-mail:* www.tj.gov.cn.

ZHANG, Huan, BA, MA; Chinese artist; b. 23 Jan. 1965, An Yang City, He Nan Prov.; ed He Nan Univ., Kai Feng, Central Acad. of Fine Arts, Beijing; lives and works in Shanghai and New York; performance artist, sculptor and photographer; works held in numerous int. galleries including Museum of Modern Art, New York, Solomon R. Guggenheim Museum, New York, Museum of Fine Arts, Boston, Fukuoka Art Museum, Japan, Nat. Gallery of Australia, Centre Pompidou, Paris, Charles Saatchi Collection, London, Shanghai Art Museum, Museum of Contemporary Art, Barcelona, Israel Museum, Jerusalem. *E-mail:* zhanghuan@zhanghuan.com (home). *Website:* www.zhanghuan.com.

ZHANG, Jianguo, MEcons; Chinese banking executive and diplomatist; *Ambassador to Mauritania;* b. 1954; ed Tianjin Coll. of Finance and Econs; worked at Tianjin Br., People's Bank of China 1982–84; held several positions in Industrial and Commercial Bank of China 1984–2001, including Deputy Gen. Man. and Gen. Man. Int. Banking Dept, Deputy Gov. Tianjin Br., Deputy Gov. and Gov. Tianjin Econ. and Tech. Devt Area Br., and Deputy Man. Int. Banking Dept, Tianjin Br.; Vice-Pres. Bank of Communications Co. Ltd (BOCOM) 2001–04, Pres. and Vice-Chair. 2004–06; Pres. China Construction Bank 2006–15, Vice-Chair. and Exec. Dir Oct. 2006–15; Amb. to Mauritania 2017–. *Address:* Embassy of the People's Republic of China, rue 42–133, Tevragh Zeina, BP 257, Nouakchott, Mauritania (office). *Telephone:* 45-25-20-70 (office). *Fax:* 45-25-24-62 (office). *E-mail:* chinaemb_mr@mfa.gov.cn (office). *Website:* mr.chineseembassy.org (office).

ZHANG, Jie, PhD; Chinese physicist, university administrator and academic; b. 31 Jan. 1958; ed Inst. of Physics, Chinese Acad. of Sciences, Beijing; began career as research scientist at Inst. of Physics, Chinese Acad. of Sciences, becoming Deputy Dir Inst. of Physics 1998–2003, Dir Chinese Spallation Neutron Source 2002–06, Dir-Gen. Bureau of Basic Sciences 2003–06; Pres. Shanghai Jiaotong Univ. 2006–17; Alexander-von-Humboldt Research Fellow, Max-Planck-Institut für Quantenoptik, Germany 1989–90; Sr Research Scientist, Rutherford Appleton Lab., UK 1991–98; mem. Editorial Bd High Energy Density Physics, Chemical Physics Letters, Acta Physica Sinica; mem. Council and Co-Chair. Asscn of Asia Pacific Physical Socs, Asian Laser Network, Int. Workshop on Fast Ignition of Fusion Targets, OECD High Power Laser Cttee, and others; Academician Chinese Acad. of Sciences 2003, Vice-Pres. 2017; Alt. mem. 17th CCP Cen. Cttee 2007–12, 18th CCP Cen. Cttee 2012–17; Foreign Assoc. mem. American Nat. Acad. of Sciences; mem. Acad. of Sciences Leopoldina; Foreign mem. Royal Acad. of Eng; Fellow Third World Acad. of Sciences; Nat. Award for Outstanding Young Scientists 1998, Qiushi Award for Outstanding Young Scientists 1999, COS Wang Daheng Award in Optics 2002, CPS Rao Yutai Award in Physics, Chinese Physical Soc. 2003, Achievement in Asia Award, Overseas Chinese Physical Soc. 2004, State Natural Sciences Prize 2006, TWAS Prize in Physics 2007, Teller Medal Award, American Nuclear Soc. 2015. *Address:* Shanghai Jiaotong University, 800 Dongchuan Road, Minhang District, Shanghai 200240, People's Republic of China (office). *Website:* www.en.sjtu.edu.cn (office).

ZHANG, Jike; Chinese table tennis player; b. 16 Feb. 1988, Qingdao, Shandong; debut in Int. Tournament, Hungary 2002; silver medal (singles, doubles and mixed doubles), gold medal (team), Asian Championship, Lucknow 2009; gold medal (team), World Team Cup, Linz 2009; silver medal (mixed doubles), bronze medal (doubles), World Championship, Yokohama 2009; gold medal (team), World Team Cup, Dubai 2010; silver medal (singles), Men's World Cup, Magdeburg 2010; gold medal (team), World Championship, Moscow 2010; gold medal (mixed doubles and team), Asian Games, Guangzhou 2010; gold medal (singles), Men's World Cup, Paris 2011; gold medal (singles), bronze medal (doubles), World Championship, Rotterdam 2011; gold medal (mixed doubles), Int. Table Tennis Fed. (ITTF) Pro Tour Grand Finals, London 2011; silver medal (singles), gold medal (team), Asian Championship, Macau 2011; gold medal (team), World Championship, Dortmund 2012; gold medal (singles and team), Olympic Games, London 2012; winner (singles): China Open 2010, German Open 2011, Slovenian Open and Korea Open 2012, Kuwait Open 2013, winner (mixed doubles): Kuwait Open 2010, English Open, UAE Open, German Open, China Open, Slovenian Open 2011, Korea Open and Slovenian Open 2012; gold medal (team) Men's World Cup, Guangzhou 2013; gold medal (team) Asian Championship, Busan 2013; gold medal Men's World Cup (singles) Düsseldorf 2014; gold medal (team) World Championship, Tokyo 2014; gold medal (mixed doubles and team) Asian Games, Incheon 2014; gold medal (team) Men's World Cup, Dubai 2015; gold medal (team) Asian Championship, Pattaya 2015; gold medal (doubles), bronze medal (singles) World Championship, Suzhou 2015; gold medal (team) World Team Table Tennis Championships, Kuala Lumpur 2016; gold medal (team), silver medal (singles) Olympic Games, Rio de Janerio 2016. *Address:* c/o Chinese Table Tennis Association, C3 Longtan Road, Chongwen Qu, Beijing 100061, People's Republic of China. *Website:* tabletennis .sport.org.cn.

ZHANG, Junjiu; Chinese business executive; b. 1940, Funan, Anhui Prov.; Vice-Pres. China North Industries Group 1990–93; Deputy Gen. Man., later Gen. Man. China Nat. Ordnance Industry Corpn 1994; Pres. China N Industries Group; mem. China Council for the Promotion of International Trade 1994; Vice-Chair. and First Sec. Secr. All-China Fed. of Trade Unions 1998–2002, Vice-Pres. Exec. Cttee 2002–05; Vice-Minister, State Comm. of Science, Tech. and Industry for Nat. Defence 1998–2003; Chair. Bd of Trustees, Beijing Univ. of Science and Eng 1995; Alt. mem. 14th CCP Cen. Cttee 1992–97; mem. 15th CCP Cen. Cttee 1997–2002, 16th CCP Cen. Cttee 2002–07.

ZHANG, Li; Chinese real estate executive; *Co-Chairman and CEO, R&F Properties Group;* b. 1953, Guangdong; m.; one c.; ed Guangzhou Open Univ.; Chief Man. Garden Village Hotel 1986; f. property co. with Hong Kong-born pnr Li Sze Lim in 1994, set up R&F Properties Group in 1996, listed on Hong Kong Stock Exchange 2005, Co-Chair. and CEO 2005–; Exec. Dir Kinetic Mines and Energy Ltd 2010, Chair. 2012–; currently CEO Caifu Holdings Ltd; Vice Chair. China Real Estate Chamber of Commerce; Prof. (part-time) of Jinan Univ. *Address:* R&F Properties Group, 45th Floor, R&F Center, 10 Huaxia Road, Tianhe District, Guangzhou 510630, People's Republic of China (office). *Telephone:* (20) 38882777 (office). *Website:* www.rfchina.com (office).

ZHANG, Ligui; Chinese telecommunications executive; b. 1942; ed Beijing Univ. of Posts and Telecommunications; began career in telecommunications industry 1966; fmr Dir-Gen. Beijing Telecommunications Bureau; fmr Dir-Gen. Directorate-Gen. of Telecommunications, Ministry of Posts and Telecommunications; Dir-Gen. Gansu Posts and Telecommunications –2000; Pres. China Mobile Communications Corpn 2000–04 (retd).

ZHANG, Ning; Chinese badminton player; b. 19 May 1975, Shenyang, Liaoning Prov.; ed Jingzhou Municipal Sports School, Liaoning and Liaoning Prov. Sports School; left home aged 12 to train full-time; joined prov. badminton team in 1989, nat. children's team in 1990 and nat. team in 1991; World Grand Prix results: winner, Women's Singles, Singapore Open 2001, Noonnoppi Korea Open 2002, 2004, Hong Kong Open 2003, Yonex German Open 2003, Proton Eon Malaysia Open 2004, Yonex Japan Open 2006, Aviva Open Singapore 2007; runner-up, Women's Singles, China Open 2002, Indonesia Open 2002, Singapore Open 2002, China Open 2006; World Championship results: semi-finalist, Women's Singles, Seville, Spain 2001, Gold Medal, Women's Singles, Birmingham, UK 2003; Gold Medals, Women's Singles, Olympic Games, Athens, Greece 2004, Beijing 2008; represented China as flag bearer, 2008 Summer Olympics closing ceremony; mem. Liaoning Badminton Club. *Leisure interests:* drawing, travelling, reading.

ZHANG, Ping; Chinese politician; *President, China Consumers Association;* b. 1 Jan. 1946, Anhui Prov.; ed Anhui School of Banking; joined CCP 1979; accountant and Deputy Section Chief, People's Bank of China, Chaoxian Co., Anhui Prov. 1967–78; staff mem., Finance and Trade Office, Chaoxian Co. 1978–80; Sec., Research Office, Provincial People's Congress, Anhui Prov. 1981–85; Deputy Dir, later Dir, No. 2 Office, People's Govt, Anhui Prov. 1981–85; Deputy Dir, Provincial Planning Cttee, Anhui Prov. 1985–91, Dir 1991–92; Dir, Provincial Econ. Information Centre, Anhui Prov. 1988–92; Acting Mayor, Wuhu City, Anhui Prov. 1992–93, Mayor 1993–95; Asst Gov., Anhui Prov. 1995–96, Vice-Gov. 1996–99; Sec.-Gen., People's Govt, Anhui Prov. 1996–97; Deputy Sec., Anhui Prov., Leading Party Group, CCP Provincial Planning Cttee 1985–91, Sec. 1991–92, mem. Standing Cttee, Anhui Prov. CCP Provincial Cttee 1999–2005, Deputy Sec. 1999–2005; Deputy, 9th NPC 1998–2003, Chair. 12th Standing Cttee 2013–18; Sec.-Gen., State Council 2005–08; Deputy Minister of Nat. Devt and Reform Comm. 2005, Minister 2008–13; alt. mem. 16th CCP Cen. Cttee 2002–07, mem. 17th CCP Cen. Cttee 2007–12; Pres. China Consumers Asscn 2015–. *Website:* www.cca.cn.

ZHANG, Qingli; Chinese party official; *Director, Standing Committee, Provincial People's Congress, Hebei Province;* b. 1951, Dongping, Shandong Prov.; ed CCP Shandong Prov. Cttee Party School, Beijing Agricultural Univ.; began career as worker at fertilizer plant, Shandong Prov., Dongping Co. 1971–76; joined CCP 1973, mem. CCP Dongping Co. Cttee 1976–79, Standing Cttee Shandong Prov. 1976–79; Vice-Mayor, Dongyi City 1986–93, Mayor 1993–95; Chair., City People's Congress, Tai'an City 1997; sr positions in CCP regional cttees in Shandong Prov. 1997–98, Gansu Prov. 1998–99; Dir, City People's Congress, Lanzhou City 1999; mem. CCP Standing Cttee, Xinjiang Uygur Autonomous Region 1999–2004, Deputy Sec., CCP Regional Cttee 2004–06, Vice-Pres., People's Govt, Xinjiang Uygur 2005–; Gen. Man., Xinjian Group Co. of China 2002–05; Acting Sec., CCP Regional Cttee, Tibet Autonomous Region 2005–06, Sec. 2006–11; Dir, Standing Cttee, Provincial People's Congress, Hebei Prov. 2012–; mem. 16th CCP Central Cttee 2002–07, 17th CCP Cen. Cttee 2007–12, 18th CCP Cen. Cttee 2012–; Deputy, 10th NPC 2003–08. *Address:* Standing Committee, Provincial People's Congress, Shijiazhuang 05000, Hebei Province, People's Republic of China (office). *Website:* english.hebei.gov.cn/government.html (office).

ZHANG, Quanjing; Chinese politician; b. 1931, Pingyuan Co., Shandong Prov.; joined CCP 1949; Deputy Section Chief, CCP Dezhou Pref. Cttee; Deputy Sec. CCP Dezhou Municipal Cttee 1950–66; Div. Chief and Deputy Head, Org. Dept CCP Shandong Prov. Cttee 1971–86; mem. Standing Cttee and Head, Org. Dept CCP Shandong Prov. Cttee 1986–88; Sec. CCP Shandong Prov. Comm. for Inspecting Discipline 1988; Exec. Deputy Dir CCP Cen. Cttee Org. Dept 1991–94, Head 1994–99; Del., 13th, 14th and 15th CCP Nat. Congresses 1987–2002; mem. Standing Cttee 9th CPPCC Nat. Cttee 1998–2003; Deputy Head, CCP Cen. Cttee Party Building Directorate 1999–. *Address:* Party Building Directorate, Central Committee of Communist Party of China, Beijing, People's Republic of China (office).

ZHANG, Renzhi; Chinese landscape artist; b. 7 Dec. 1935, Hebei Prov.; s. of Zhang Pu and Zhang Chen; m. Lang Mei 1966; two s.; ed Cen. Art Inst.; joined Beijing Art Acad. as professional artist; jt exhbns, Xinxiang, Henan Prov., Macao, Beijing, Japan 1991, Exhbn of Buddhism 1991, Nat. Exhbn 1992, Beseto Arts Festival 1997, etc.; Wintertime Lotus and other works in collection of James Art Museum, Vermont State Univ., USA; Artist, Chinese Artists Asscn; mem. Chinese Calligraphers Asscn; Exec. Dir Oriental Inst. of Art Exchanges; Artist of the First Grade; Award of Excellence (for 'Quiet Valley'), Nat. Exhbn of Fine Arts 1991; prize for 'Lasting Forever' (burnt pine tree), Bronze Prize (for 'Mount Fanjing After Rain'), Nat. Exhbn of Fine Arts 1999. *Publications:* Zhang Renzhi's Album of Paintings, (Vol. 2) 1991, Collection of Landscape Paintings 2000. *Leisure interest:* travel. *Address:* Room 501, Building 2, Beijing Arts Institute, Chao Yang District, Beijing, People's Republic of China (office). *Telephone:* (10) 85973316 (office).

ZHANG, Ruimin, MBA; Chinese business executive and engineer; *Chairman and CEO, Haier Group;* b. 5 Jan. 1949, Laizhou, Shandong Prov.; m.; one s.; ed China Science and Tech. Univ., Beijing; worker, Qingdao Construction Plant, Shandong Prov. 1968–75; Deputy Man., Qingdao Appliance Industry Co. 1982–88; Dir Qingdao Refrigerator Factory 1984–91 (renamed Qingdao Haier Group 1991), Chair. and CEO Haier Group 1991–, Sec., Party Cttee; mem. 14th, 15th and 16th CCP Nat. Congresses 1992–; Alt. mem. 16th CCP Cen. Cttee 2002–07, 17th CCP Cen. Cttee 2007–12, 18th CCP Cen. Cttee 2012–; Dale Carnegie Leadership Award 2012, State Award for Excellent CCP Members 2001, Best Practices Award, American Best Practices Institute Legend in Leadership Award, Yale School of Man. 2016. *Address:* Haier Garden, Haier Industrial Park, Haier Lu, Haier Group, Qingdao 266101, Shandong Province, People's Republic of China (office). *Telephone:* (532) 8938888 (office). *Fax:* (532) 8938666 (office). *E-mail:* info@haier.com (office). *Website:* www.haier.com (office).

ZHANG, Shengman, MPA; Chinese banking executive; b. 1957, Shanghai; ed Fudan Univ., McGill Univ., Canada, Univ. of Washington, DC; Asst to Exec. Dir of World Bank (IBRD) 1983–87; Section Head then Vice-Dir, Dept of IBRD, Ministry of Finance 1987–92; Deputy Exec. Dir, then Exec. Dir World Bank 1992–95, Exec. Dir for China 1994–95, Vice-Pres. and Corp. Sec. 1995–97, directed Corp. and Support Functions, then Sectors and Regions 1997–2001, Man. Dir 2001–05; Vice-Chair. Global Banking, Citigroup Corp. and Investment Banking, New York 2006–09, also Chair. Citibank Public Sector Group, Chair. Asia Pacific Region 2009–16, Country Officer and CEO for Citi Hong Kong and Macau –2013; mem. Bd of Dirs Fosun International Ltd 2006–, Cabot Corp. 2006–10, China Guangfa Bank Co. Ltd 2007–, Seazen Holdings Co., Ltd 2016–18.

ZHANG, Shiping; Chinese economist and business executive; *Chairman, Shandong Weiqiao Pioneering Group;* ed Anhui Coll. of Finance and Trading; Gen. Man. Chuangye Group (including its predecessor) 1996–98; Chair. Weiqiao Textile Co. Ltd (including its predecessor) 1998–2000; Dir Binzhou Weiqiao Technology Industrial Park Co. Ltd 2001–10; Chair. Aluminum Technology 2002–07, Chuangye Group, Hongqiao Holdings, Profit Long Investment, Weiqiao Pioneering (Hong Kong) Import & Export Co. Ltd; Chair. Shandong Weiqiao Chuangye Group Co. Ltd; currently Chair. Shandong Weiqiao Pioneering Group; Dir Shandong Hongqiao 1994–, Exec. Chair. China Hongqiao Group Ltd 2011–; Dir (non-exec.) Weiqiao Textile Co. Ltd, Zouping Supply and Marketing Investment Co. Ltd; Party Sec. Zouping County Supply and Marketing Co-operation Union; Deputy to 9th and 10th NPC; selected by the State Council as Nat. Model

Worker 1995. *Address:* Shandong Weiqiao Pioneering Group, 1 Weifang Road, Zouping Economic Development Zone, Shandong 256200, People's Republic of China (office). *Telephone:* (543) 4161111 (office). *Fax:* (543) 4161188 (office). *E-mail:* wqcy@wqfz.com (office). *Website:* www.weiqiaocy.com (office).

ZHANG, Shuguang, BS, PhD; American (b. Chinese) biochemist, molecular biologist and academic; *Head, Molecular Architecture Group, Massachusetts Institute of Technology;* ed Sichuan Univ., Chengdu, Univ. of California, Santa Barbara (Regent Fellowship and a Grad. Mentor Fellowship); American Cancer Soc. Postdoctoral Fellow, Structural and Molecular Biology, MIT 1988–91, Research Scientist, Dept of Biology and Center for Biomedical Eng 1992–96, Prin. Research Scientist 1997–2012, Assoc. Dir Center for Biomedical Eng 1998–2012, apptd Prin. Investigator, Center for Bits and Atoms 2012, Head, Molecular Architecture Group 2012–; Visiting Prof., Tsinghua Univ., Beijing, Sichuan Univ., Chinese Acad. of Medical Science, Beijing, China Univ. of Petroleum, Qingdao; co-f. three startup cos, including 3DMatrix, Tokyo, Japan, Beaver Biosciences, Guanzhou, Beaver Nanotech, Suzhou, People's Repub. of China; mem. AAAS, American Soc. of Biochemistry and Molecular Biology, Human Genome Org. Americas, Protein Soc., New York Acad. of Sciences, Int. Soc. for the Study of Origin of Life; Foreign Corresp. mem. Austrian Acad. of Sciences; Fellow, Japan Soc. for Promotion of Science 2003, Japan Advancement for Medical Instrument 2005, American Inst. of Medical and Biological Eng; Hon. Prof. and Distinguished Changjiang Scholar, Sichuan Univ. 2004–; Hon. Prof., China Univ. of Petroleum 2010–, Shanghai Jiaotong Univ. 2014–; R&D100 Award 2004, his team's work on biosolar energy selected by Discover Magazine to be one of the Top 100 Science Stories in 2004, Guggenheim Fellow 2006, Wilhelm Exner Medal, Austrian Asscn for SME (Oesterreichischer Gewerbeverein—OGV) (jtly) 2006, numerous invited lectures. *Achievements include:* discovered a self-assembling peptide system. *Publications:* Self-Assembling Peptide Systems in Biology, Engineering and Medicine (with A. Aggeli and N. Boden) 2001; 170 scientific articles, ten issued patents and 20 pending patent applications on self-assembling peptide systems. *Address:* Media Lab Building, Massachusetts Institute of Technology, 20 Ames Street, Cambridge, MA 02138, USA (office). *Telephone:* (617) 258-7514 (office). *Fax:* (617) 253-7035 (office). *E-mail:* shuguang@mit.edu (office). *Website:* www.moleculararchitecture.org (office).

ZHANG, Weiqing; Chinese politician; b. 1944, Lintong Co., Shaanxi Prov.; ed Peking Univ.; joined CCP 1972; Sec. CCP Communist Youth League of China Baode Co. Cttee, Shanxi Prov., Sec. CCP Baode Co. Cttee; Sec. CCP Huguan Co. Cttee, Shanxi Prov. 1975–83; Sec. Communist Youth League Shanxi Provincial Cttee 1982–83, Vice-Gov. Shanxi Prov. 1983–84; mem. Standing Cttee and Head Propaganda Dept, CCP Shanxi Prov. Cttee 1985–93; Vice-Minister, State Population and Family Planning Comm. 1994–98, Minister 1998–2008; Del., 14th CCP Nat. Congress 1992–97; mem. 15th CCP Cen. Cttee 1997–2002, 16th CCP Cen. Cttee 2002–07.

ZHANG, Wenkang; Chinese politician; b. April 1940, Nanhui Co., Shanghai; ed Shanghai No. 1 Medical Coll.; joined PLA 1962, CCP 1966; Lecturer, later Chief of Diving Physiology Office, later Dir Training Dept, later Assoc. Prof., later Vice-Pres., No. 2 Medical Univ. of the Chinese PLA 1962–90; Deputy Dir Health Dept, PLA Gen. Logistics Dept 1990–93; Vice-Minister of Public Health 1993–98, Minister 1998–2003 (resgnd); Dir State Admin of Traditional Chinese Medicine 1993–98, Drugs Licensing Cttee 1994; Deputy Head, Nat. Group for Narcotics Control 1997; mem. State Academic Degrees Cttee 1999; Pres. Chinese Medical Asscn 1999; mem. 15th CCP Cen. Cttee 1997–2002, 16th CCP Cen. Cttee 2002–07, Deputy Dir CCP Cen. Cttee Cen. Health Cttee 1998; Hon. Chair. Council of China Pharmaceutical Univ. 1995; Hon. Vice-Pres. Red Cross Soc. of China 1999.

ZHANG, Wenyue; Chinese politician; b. Oct. 1944, Pucheng Co., Fujian Prov.; ed Beijing Inst. of Geology; joined CCP 1965; Dir Geology and Mineral Resources Bureau of Sichuan Prov.; Dir-Gen. Office of Ministry of Geology and Mineral Resources 1986; Dir State Admin. on Mineral Resources 1989; Vice-Minister of Land and Resources (fmrly Geology and Mineral Resources) 1990–95; Deputy Sec. CCP Xinjiang Uygur Autonomous Regional Cttee 1996–2001; Vice-Chair. Xinjiang Uygur Autonomous Regional People's Govt 1999–2001; Deputy Sec. CCP Liaoning Prov. Cttee 2001–07, Sec. 2007–09; Chair. CPPCC Liaoning Prov. Cttee 2003–04; mem. CCP Cen. Comm. for Discipline Inspection 1992, 15th CCP Cen. Cttee 1997–2002, Alt. mem. 16th CCP Cen. Cttee 2002–07, mem. 17th CCP Cen. Cttee 2007–12; Acting Gov. Liaoning Prov. 2004, Gov. 2004–07; Deputy, 11th NPC 2008–13, Deputy Dir NPC Environmental and Resources Protection Cttee 2009–13.

ZHANG, Xiang, BS, MS, PhD; American (b. Chinese) professor of engineering; *Ernest S. Kuh Endowed Chair and Professor of Mechanical Engineering, University of California, Berkeley;* ed Nanjing Univ., China, Univ. of Minnesota, Univ. of California, Berkeley; Asst Prof., Pennsylvania State Univ. 1996–99; Assoc. Prof., then Full Prof., UCLA 1999–2004; Prof. of Mechanical Eng, Univ. of California, Berkeley 2004–, Ernest S. Kuh Endowed Chair and LBNL Materials Sciences Div. Dir, Miller Professorship 2011; Co-Chair. NSF Nanoscale Science and Eng Annual Grantee Confs 2004–05, Tech. Program of IEEE Second Int. Conf. on Micro and Nano Engineered and Molecular Systems 2007, Academic Advisory Bd, Research Centre for Applied Science, Academia Sinica, Taiwan; Distinguished Visiting Scientist, Univ. of Toronto 2011; NSF Career Award 1997, SME Dell K. Allen Outstanding Young Manufacturing Engineer Award 1998, ONR Young Investigator Award 1999, Chancellor's Professorship, Univ. of California, Berkeley 2004–09, Distinguished Lecturer, Univ. of Texas, Austin 2004 and SEMETECH 2005, Rohsenow Lecturer, MIT 2009, Fred Kavli Distinguished Lectureship, Materials Research Soc. 2011, William Reynolds Lecturer, Stanford Univ. 2012, Fitzroy Medal 2014, Julius Springer Prize for Applied Physics (co-recipient) 2016. *Publications:* more than 240 papers in professional journals on nanoscale science and tech., materials physics, photonics and biotechnologies. *Address:* 5130 Etcheverry Hall, Mailstop 1740, University of California, Berkeley, CA 94720-1740, USA (office). *Telephone:* (510) 643-4978 (office). *E-mail:* xzhang@me.berkeley.edu (office). *Website:* www.me.berkeley.edu (office); xlab.me.berkeley.edu (office).

ZHANG, Xiaogang; Chinese steel industry executive; *President, Anshan Iron and Steel Group Corporation (Ansteel);* apptd Chair. and Gen. Man. Angang Steel Co. Ltd 2007, Sec. CPC Party Cttee 2007, currently Pres. and Chair. Anshan Iron and Steel Group Corpn (Ansteel); Vice-Chair. World Steel Asscn 2010–11, Chair. 2011–12; Pres. Int. Org. for Standardization (ISO) 2015–17; Del. 17th CPC Nat. Congress 2007–12, also Alt. mem. Cen. Cttee; Deputy, 11th CPC 2008–13; mem. 18th CPC, Cen. Cttee, Cen. Comm. for Discipline Inspection 2012–17. *Address:* Anshan Iron and Steel Group Corporation, Dong Shan Street 77, Anshan 114009, Liaoning Province, People's Republic of China (office). *Telephone:* (2) 6723090 (office). *Fax:* (2) 6723080 (office). *E-mail:* office@ansteel.com.cn (office). *Website:* www.ansteelgroup.com (office).

ZHANG, Xiwu, DEng; Chinese engineer and mining executive; ed Jixi Coll. of Tech., Liaoning Univ. of Eng and Tech.; worked as First Deputy Mine Head, later Mine Head, later Asst Bureau Chief, Dayan Coal Mining Bureau, Inner Mongolia; fmr mem. CCP Leadership Group and Deputy Chief of Bureau of Coal Industry, Jilin Prov. and Deputy Gen. Man. Northeast Inner Mongolia Coal Group Co.; served as mem. CCP Party Leadership Group, Pres. and Dir Shenhua Group 2004–08, Vice-Pres. Shenhua Group, Chair., mem. CCP Cttee and Gen. Man. Shenhua Shendong Coal Co., Chair. and Standing mem. CCP Cttee of Shenhua Dongsheng Coal Co., Gen. Man. Fine Coal Business Dept, Shenhua Group, Sec. CCP Leadership Group and Chair. Shenhua Group Corpn Ltd 2008–14, also Exec. Dir and Chair. China Shenhua 2010–14; currently Research Fellow.

ZHANG, Xuanlong; Chinese business executive; *Chairman, Founder Group;* b. 1956, Quanzhou, Fujian Prov.; ed First Jr School of Quanzhou, Fujian; Gen. Man. Hong Kong Kingsoft Co. 1980; Gen. Man. and Vice-Chair. Tianjin Stone, a jt venture with Stone Group; as Vice-Chair. Founder Group, set up Super Chinese Card Dept and brought Founder Golden WPS software into the market 1990, currently Chair. Founder Group; Pres. Founder (Hong Kong) Co. Ltd and Deputy Pres. Founder Group 1992, Chair. Founder Holdings Ltd; f. PUC Founder (MSC) Berhad, Malaysia, Founder Int. Inc., Japan. *Address:* Peking University Founder Group, Founder Tower, Zhong Guan Cun, Haidian District, Beijing, People's Republic of China (office). *Website:* www.founder.com/en (office).

ZHANG, Xuezhong; Chinese politician; b. Feb. 1943, Lanzhou, Gansu Prov.; ed Lanzhou Univ.; joined CCP 1960; primary school teacher, Lanzhou Teachers' School; Sec. CCP Longnan Pref. Cttee 1961–89; People's Air Defence Office, Gansu Prov.; Office Sec., PLA Lanzhou Mil. Region (HQ) 1990; Sec. of Secr., Gen. Office of CCP Gansu Provincial Cttee 1990; Sec. CCP Fafang Commune Cttee, Wuwei Co., Sec. CCP Yuzhong Co. Cttee 1990; Deputy Sec. CCP Lanzhou Municipal Cttee 1990; Vice-Gov. Gansu Prov. 1990; Deputy Sec. CCP Tibet Autonomous Region Cttee 1990–94; Vice-Minister of Personnel 1994–2000, Minister 2000–02; Sec. CCP Sichuan Prov. Cttee 2002–06; Chair. Standing Cttee Sichuan Prov. People's Congress 2003–06; Deputy Dir 10th NPC Internal and Judicial Affairs Cttee 2006; mem. 16th CCP Cen. Cttee 2002–07.

ZHANG, Yimou; Chinese film actor and director; b. 1951, Xian, Shanxi Prov.; m. Xiao Hua 1982 (divorced 1990); ed Xian Middle School, Beijing Film Acad.; directed opening and closing ceremonies, Summer Olympics, Beijing 2008; Dr hc (City Univ. of Hong Kong) 2005. *Opera productions as director:* Turandot (Beijing) 1998, The First Emperor (Metropolitan Opera, New York) 2006. *Films include:* The Old Well (8th Golden Rooster Best Actor Award 1988), Red Sorghum (Hong Gaoliang), Raise the Red Lantern 1991, The Story of Qiu Ju 1992, Keep Cool 1997, Not One Less (Golden Lion, Venice) 1999, The Road Home 1999 (Grand Jury Prize, Berlin 1999), Happy Times 2001, Hero 2003, House of Flying Daggers (Best Foreign Language Film, Los Angeles Film Critics' Asscn) 2004, Riding Alone for Thousands of Miles 2005, Curse of the Golden Flower 2006, The Flowers of War 2011.

ZHANG, Yin, (Cheung Yan); Chinese business executive; *Chairwoman, Nine Dragons Paper Industries Company Ltd;* b. Heilongjiang Prov.; d. of Cheung Deen; m. 2nd Ming Chung Liu; two c.; went to Hong Kong 1985, started career in waste paper trading with 30,000 yuan; moved to USA with husband 1990; f. America Chung Nam 1990; returned to Hong Kong 1995; Founder and Chair. Nine Dragons Paper Industries Co. Ltd, Dongguan, Guangdong Prov. 1996–; mem. CPPCC 2007; Vice-Chair. Women's Fed. of Commerce, All-China Fed. of Industry and Commerce; Hon. Citizen, City of Dongguan, Guangdong; Worldwide Chinese Amb. of Love 2006. *Address:* Nine Dragons Paper Industries Co. Ltd, Xinsha Port Industry Zone, Mayong Town, Dongguan 523147, Guangdong, People's Republic of China (office). *Telephone:* (769) 88234888 (office). *Fax:* (769) 88824198 (office). *E-mail:* info@ndpaper.com (office). *Website:* www.ndpaper.com (office).

ZHANG, Yitang (Tom), BSc, MSc, PhD; American (b. Chinese) mathematician and academic; *Professor, University of New Hampshire;* b. 1955, Shanghai, China; ed Peking Univ., Purdue Univ.; worked for several years in a variety of jobs, including accountant and delivery worker in New York and a motel in Kentucky; Lecturer, Univ. of New Hampshire 1999–2014, Full Prof. 2014–; Morningside Special Achievement Award in Math. 2013, Ostrowski Prize 2013, Frank Nelson Cole Prize in Number Theory 2014, Rolf Schock Prize, Royal Swedish Acad. of Sciences 2014, MacArthur 'Genius' Award 2014. *Achievements include:* est. the first finite bound on gaps between prime numbers, believed at the time to be unattainable by current methods. *Publications:* numerous papers in professional journals. *Address:* Department of Mathematics and Statistics, University of New Hampshire, W383 Kingsbury Hall, 33 Academic Way, Durham, NH 03824, USA (office). *Telephone:* (603) 862-4407 (office). *Fax:* (603) 862-4096 (office). *E-mail:* yitangz@unh.edu (office). *Website:* www.math.unh.edu (office).

ZHANG, Youfu; Chinese ecologist; b. 21 May 1940, Jiangsu Prov.; s. of Zhang Changsheng and Zhong Yinlan; m. Xu Chunlan 1968; two s.; ed Nanking Univ., Chendu Inst. of Geography, Chinese Acad. of Sciences; has been engaged in research work on biological prevention of mudflow damage, soil and water conservation and forest ecology for over 20 years. *Publications:* numerous papers on mudflow, erosion, debris flow, landslides, disaster prevention, measures against debris flow, remote sensing information, etc. *Leisure interest:* photography. *Address:* Institute of Mountain Hazards and Environment, Chinese Academy of Science, PO Box 417, Chengdu 610041, Sichuan Province, People's Republic of China (office). *Telephone:* (28) 85228816 (office). *E-mail:* sdb@imde.ac.cn (office). *Website:* www.imde.ac.cn (office).

ZHANG, Youxi; Chinese engineer and mining industry executive; *Chairman, Datong Coal Mine Group Company Ltd;* b. Dec. 1958; ed China Univ. of Mining and Tech., Cen. Party School; mine technician, tech. dir, production vice-mayor, gov., deputy chief engineer, Datong Mining Bureau, Baidong 1976–92, Deputy Dir, Jinwan Mine and mem. Party Cttee, Datong Mining Bureau 1992–97, Sec. of the Party Cttee and Deputy Dir, Yanya coal mine, Datong Mining Bureau 1997–98, Coal Mine Dir and Sec. of Party Cttee, Datong Mining Bureau 1998–2003, Deputy Gen. Man., Coal Mine Dir and Sec. of Party Cttee Datong Coal Ltd 2003–05, Vice-Chair. and Gen. Man. Datong Coal Industry Co. Ltd 2005–07, Deputy Gen. Man. Datong Coal Mine Group Co., Xuangang, Vice-Chair. and Gen. Man. coal company 2007–09, Chair. and Deputy Gen. Man. Datong Coal Mine Group gas and electric co. 2009–10, Deputy Gen. Man. Datong Coal Mine Group Co. Feb.–April 2010, Vice-Chair. and Gen. Man. Datong Coal Mine Group Co. Ltd 2010–11, Chair. and Party Sec. 2011–, Chair. Datong Coal Industry Ltd 2012–; Sec., Party Cttee, Zhangze Power Ltd 2013–; Vice-Pres. China Nat. Coal Asscn 2013–; sr expert, Shanxi Prov. Asscn; Deputy to NPC. *Address:* Datong Coal Mine Group Co. Ltd, 11 Dongmen Street, Datong 037003, People's Republic of China (office). *Telephone:* (352) 7868200 (office). *Fax:* (352) 7868201 (office). *E-mail:* dtmkjt@dtcoalmine.com (office). *Website:* www.dtcoalmine.com (office).

ZHANG, Yuan; Chinese film director; b. 1963; m. Ning Dai; ed Beijing Film Acad.; has directed music videos for leading Chinese rock singer Cui Jian; also producer and dir for MTV; has also made several documentaries. *Films:* Mama (Special Jury Prize, Nantes Film Festival 1991) 1990, Beijing Bastards 1992, The Square 1994, East Palace West Palace 1996, Seventeen Years (Best Dir, Venice Film Festival) 1999, Little Red Flowers 2006 (CICAE Award, Berlin Film Festival 2006) Dada's Dance 2008, Beijing Flickers 2013.

ZHANG, Yun, PhD; Chinese economist and business executive; *Executive Vice-Chairman and President, Agricultural Bank of China;* ed Wuhan Univ.; served successively as Deputy Pres. Shenzhen br., Agricultural Bank of China, Deputy Pres. Guangdong br., and Pres. Guangxi Autonomous Region br., Exec. Asst Pres. and Gen. Man. Personnel Dept, Agricultural Bank of China 2001, Exec. Vice-Pres. Agricultural Bank of China 2001–09, Exec. Vice-Chair. and Pres. Agricultural Bank of China 2009–. *Address:* Agricultural Bank of China, 69 Jianguomen Nei Avenue, Dongcheng District, Beijing 100005, People's Republic of China (office). *Telephone:* (10) 85109619 (office). *Fax:* (10) 85108557 (office). *E-mail:* webmaster@intl.abocn.com (office); ir@abchina.com (office). *Website:* www.abchina.com (office).

ZHANG, Yunchuan; Chinese politician; b. Oct. 1946, Dongyang, Zhejiang Prov.; ed Harbin Inst. of Mil. Eng; joined CCP 1973; fmr technician, Factory No. 6214, Ministry of Machine Industry No. 6; mem. Standing Cttee, CCP Jiujiang City Cttee Jiangxi Prov. 1985–86, Vice-Mayor of Jiujiang City 1985–86; Commr Admin. Office and Deputy Sec. CCP Ganzhou Prefectural Cttee, Jiangxi Prov. 1986–91; mem. Standing Cttee CCP Jiangxi Prov. Cttee 1991–93; Asst to Gov. Jiangxi Prov. 1991–93, Vice-Gov. 1993–95; mem. Standing Cttee and Exec. Vice-Chair. Xinjiang Uygur Autonomous Region 1995–99, Deputy Sec. 1998–2001; Sec. Changsha Municipal Cttee 1999–2001; Vice-Gov. Hunan Prov. 2001, Acting Gov. 2001–02, Gov. 2002–03; Minister-in-Charge, Comm. of Science, Tech. and Industry for Nat. Defence (COSTIND) 2003–07; mem. 16th CCP Cen. Cttee 2002–07, 17th CCP Cen. Cttee 2007–12; Sec. CCP Hebei Prov. Cttee 2007–11; Chair. Standing Cttee, Hebei Provincial People's Congress 2008–11. *Address:* Hebei CCP Provincial Committee, Shijiazhuang, People's Republic of China (office). *Website:* www.hebei.gov.cn (office).

ZHANG, Yuzhuo, BEng, MEng, PhD; Chinese engineer and mining executive; *Chairman, Shenhua Group Corporation;* b. Jan. 1962; ed Shandong Univ. of Science and Tech., China Coal Research Inst., Univ. of Science and Tech. of Beijing; worked as Deputy Dir Research Office, Beijing Mining Research Inst., China Coal Research Inst. (CCRI), later Asst Pres., Vice-Pres., Pres. and Deputy Party Sec. CCP Cttee of CCRI, later Deputy Dir Beijing Mining Research Inst.; conducted post-doctoral research in Dept of Mining and Environmental Eng., Southern Illinois Univ., Carbondale, USA and Univ. of Southampton, UK; served as Vice-Pres. Shenhua Group, Chair. China Shenhua Coal Liquefaction Chemical Co. 2002–10, Dir, Shenhua Group Corpn 2008–, Chair. Shenhua Int. (Hong Kong) Co. Ltd 2005–10, Gen. Man. Shenhua Group Corpn 2008–14, Vice-Chair. 2011–14, Chair. 2014–, mem. CCP Leadership Group and Dir Shenhua Group Corpn Ltd, Exec. Dir and Vice-Chair. China Shenhua; fmr Pres. of China Coal Research Inst.; mem. Advisory Bd Nat. Energy Comm., Exec. Cttee IEA Coal Industry Advisory Bd; Vice-Chair. China Coal Soc., China Energy Research Soc.; Fellow, Chinese Acad. of Eng. *Address:* Shenhua Group Corporation Ltd, Guohua Investment Plaza, 3 Dongzhimen South Street, Dongcheng District, Beijing 100007, People's Republic of China (office). *Telephone:* (10) 58133113 (office); (10) 58132001 (office); (10) 58132114 (office). *E-mail:* shjt@shenhuagroup.com.cn (office). *Website:* www.shenhuagroup.com.cn (office).

ZHANG, Zhongwei; Chinese politician (retd); b. Feb. 1942, Dujiangyan, Sichuan Prov.; one s.; ed CCP Cen. Cttee Cen. Party School; joined CCP 1960; Office Sec., CCP Zhongxing Dist Cttee, Sichuan Prov. 1958–64, Org. Dept, CCP Guanxian Co. Cttee, Sichuan Prov. 1959–64, CCP Wenjiang Prefectural Cttee, Sichuan Prov. 1962–74 (Deputy Sec., later Sec. CCP Communist Youth League of China Wenjiang Prefectural Cttee 1972–78); Sec. CCP Pengxian Co. Cttee, Sichuan Prov. 1978–82; Deputy Sec. CCP Wenjiang Prefectural Cttee 1982–83; mem. Standing Cttee CCP Chengdu City Cttee, Sichuan Prov. 1983–87, Sec. Rural Work Cttee 1983–87; Deputy Head, Org. Dept, CCP Sichuan Prov. Cttee 1987–88; Dir Agriculture and Animal Husbandry Dept, Sichuan Prov. 1988–93; Vice-Gov. of Sichuan Prov. 1993–94, Acting Gov. 1997–99, Gov. 2000–07; mem. Standing Cttee CCP Sichuan Prov. Cttee 1994–97, Deputy Sec. Sichuan Prov. Cttee; mem. 16th CCP Cen. Cttee 2002–07.

ZHANG, Ziyi; Chinese actress; b. 9 Feb. 1979, Beijing; partner Wang Feng; one d.; ed Beijing Dance Acad., Beijing Cen. Drama Coll. *Films include:* Wo de fu qin mu qin (The Road Home) 1999 (Hundred Flowers Best Actress Award 2000), Wo hu cang long (Crouching Tiger, Hidden Dragon) 2000 (Golden Bauhinia Best Supporting Actress Award 2001, Golden Horse Film Festival Best Actress Award 2000, BAFTA Best Performance by an Actress in a Supporting Role 2001), Rush Hour II 2001, Shu shan zheng zhuan (The Legend of Zu) 2001, Musa 2001, Ying xiong (Hero) 2002 (Hong Kong Film Awards Best Supporting Actress 2003), Zi hudie (Purple Butterfly) 2003, Jopog manura II: Dolaon jeonseol (My Wife is a Gangster II) 2003, Shi mian mai fu (House of Flying Daggers) 2004 (BAFTA Best Performance by an Actress in a Leading Role 2005), 2046 (Best Actress, Hong Kong

Film Critics' Soc. Awards 2005) 2004, Mo li hua kai (Jasmine) 2004 (Golden Rooster Best Actress Award 2004), Operetta tanuki goten 2005, Memoirs of a Geisha 2005 (BAFTA Best Performance by an Actress in a Leading Role 2006, Golden Globe Best Performance by an Actress 2006), The Banquet 2006, TMNT (voice) 2007, Mei Lanfang 2008, Horsemen 2009, Sophie's Revenge 2009, The Founding of a Republic 2009, Mo shu wai zhuan 2011, Dangerous Liaisons 2012, The Grandmaster 2013, Better and Better 2013, My Lucky Star 2013, The Crossing 2014, The Crossing 2 2015, Run for Love 2016. *Address:* c/o Nine Muses and Apollo Inc., 525 Broadway, Suite 201, New York, NY 10012, USA (office). *Telephone:* (212) 431-2665 (office). *Fax:* (212) 431-2667 (office). *E-mail:* linglucas@aol.com (office).

ZHANG, Zongyan, MBA; Chinese engineer and business executive; *President, China Railway Construction Corporation Ltd;* ed Guanghua School of Man. of Peking Univ.; joined CRCC Group 1981, Deputy Gen. Man. China Railway 12th Bureau Group Co. Ltd 2002–05, Chair. and Sec. to CCP Cttee 2005–08, Chair. and Deputy Sec. 2008–09, Vice-Pres. China Railway Construction Corpn Ltd 2009–13, Exec. Dir, Pres. and Deputy Sec. 2013–. *Address:* China Railway Construction Corporation Ltd, 40 Fuxing Road, Beijing 100855, People's Republic of China (office). *Telephone:* (10) 51888114 (office). *E-mail:* ir@crcc.cn (office). *Website:* www.crcc.cn (office).

ZHANG, Zuoji; Chinese politician; b. Jan. 1945, Bayan, Heilongjiang Prov.; ed Heilongjiang Univ.; joined CCP 1972; Vice-Pres. Party School, CCP State No. 123 Factory Cttee 1967–77; Sec. Political Dept, 5th Ministry of Machine-Building Industry 1977–87, Deputy Chief, Publicity Div. 1977–87; Deputy Sec. Org. Dept, Ministry of Ordnance Industry 1977–87; Deputy Dir Labour Bureau, Ministry of Labour and Personnel 1987–88, Dir Labour Force Admin. and Employment Dept 1988–91; Vice-Mayor of Xi'an City, Shaanxi Prov. 1991; Vice-Minister of Labour 1993–94; Deputy Sec.-Gen. State Council 1994–98; Minister of Labour and Social Security 1998–2003; Gov. Heilongjiang Prov. 2003–07; mem. Standing Cttee CCP Heilongjiang Prov. Cttee 2003–; mem. CCP Cen. Cttee Cen. Comm. for Discipline Inspection 1997, 16th CCP Cen. Cttee 2002–07, 17th CCP Cen. Cttee 2007–12; Dir 11th CPPCC Econ. Cttee 2008–12. *Publications:* A Review of Labor Systems in Three East European Countries, The Reality, Difficulties and Countermeasures, Chinese Labor System in Reform. *Address:* CCP Provincial Committee, Harbin, Heilongjiang Province, People's Republic of China (office).

ZHANGKE, Jia; Chinese film director; b. 24 May 1970, Fenyang; m. 1st Zhu Jiong 1999 (divorced 2006); m. 2nd Zhao Tao 2012; ed Shanxi Univ.; a leading figure of the 'Sixth Generation' of Chinese film directors; est. Xstream Pictures production Co. 2003; jury mem. BigScreen Italia Film Festival, Kunming 2006; f. Pingyao Int. Film Festival 2017. *Films include:* Xiaoshan huijia 1995, Xiao Wu (The Pickpocket) (Netpac Award, Berlin Int. Film Festival 1998, Golden Montgolfiere, Nantes Three Continents Festival 1998, New Currents Award, Pusan Int. Film Festival 1998, Dragons and Tigers Award, Vancouver Int. Film Festival 1998) 1997, Zhantai (Best Film, Buenos Aires Int. Festival of Independent Cinema 2001, Don Quixote Award and FIPRESCI Prize, Fribourg Int. Film Festival 2001, Golden Montgolfiere, Nantes Three Continents Festival, Young Cinema Award, Singapore Int. Film Festival 2001) 2000, Gong gong chang suo (In Public) (Grand Prix, Marseille Festival of Documentary Film 2002) 2001, Ren xiao yao (Unknown Pleasures) 2002, Shijie (The World) 2004. Sanxia haoren (Still Life) (Best Dir, Durban Int. Film Festival 2007, Golden Lion, Venice Film Festival 2006) 2006, Dong (Doc/It Award, Venice Film Festival) 2006, 24 City 2008, Cry Me a River 2008, Black Breakfast 2008, I Wish I Knew 2010, A Touch of Sin 2013, Mountains May Depart 2015, Ash Is Purest White 2018.

ZHAO, Bandi; Chinese artist; b. 1966, Beijing; ed Cen. Acad. of Fine Arts, Beijing; painting, photography and installation work; exhibitions worldwide; best known for satirical photographs featuring toy pandas. *Address:* c/o ShangHART Main Gallery, Bldg 16, 50 Moganshan Rd, Putuo District, Shanghai 200060, People's Republic of China. *Telephone:* (189) 30613031. *Fax:* (21) 63594570. *E-mail:* info@shanghartgallery.com. *Website:* www.shanghartgallery.com.

ZHAO, Gang; Chinese engineer and business executive; *Deputy General Manager and Vice-President, China North Industries Group Corporation (NORINCO Group);* b. June 1968, Shenyang City, Liaoning Prov.; ed Beijing Inst. of Tech.; Deputy Dir, China North Industries Group Corpn (NORINCO Group), Middle East Div. 1997–98, Rep., Iran Office Iran, Tehran 1998–2000, Dir, Human Resources Dept 2000–03, Asst Pres. NORINCO Group 2003–04, Vice-Pres. 2004–07, Pres. 2007–13, Deputy Sec. CCP Party Cttee 2010–13, Asst Gen. Man. 2010–13, mem. CCP Leading Party Group 2013–, Deputy Gen. Man. and Vice-Pres. NORINCO Group 2014–. *Address:* China North Industries Group Corporation (NORINCO Group), 46 Sanlihe Road, Beijing 100821, People's Republic of China (office). *Telephone:* (10) 68594210 (office); (10) 68787608 (office). *Fax:* (10) 68594232 (office); (10) 68594555 (office). *E-mail:* webmaster@norincogroup.com.cn (office). *Website:* www.norincogroup.com.cn (office).

ZHAO, Guangfa, MBA; Chinese engineer and business executive; b. Aug. 1952; ed Asia Int. Open Univ., Macao; joined China Railway Construction Corpn Ltd 1970, served as Deputy Chief, then Chief and Deputy Sec. CCP Cttee of 18th Eng Bureau, Ministry of Railways (predecessor of China Railway 18th Bureau Group Co. Ltd) 1994–99, Dir and Deputy Sec. CCP Cttee of China Railway 18th Eng Bureau 1999–2001, Chair. and Deputy Party Sec. China Railway 18th Bureau Group Co. Ltd 2001–04, Deputy Gen. Man. China Railway Construction Corpn Ltd 2004–07, Vice-Pres. 2007–09, Pres. and Exec. Dir 2009–13.

ZHAO, Houlin, MSc; Chinese engineer and international organization official; *Secretary-General, International Telecommunication Union;* b. 1950, Jiangsu; m.; one s.; ed Nanjing Univ. of Posts and Telecommunications, Univ. of Essex, UK; began career as engineer, Design Inst. of Ministry of Posts and Telecommunications; various sr positions with Int. Telegraph and Telephone Consultative Cttee 1986–92; with Telecommunication Standardization Bureau (TSB), ITU 1993–98, Dir TSB 1999–2006, Deputy Sec.-Gen., ITU 2007–14, Sec.-Gen. 2015–. *Address:* International Telecommunication Union, Place des Nations, 1211 Geneva 20, Switzerland (office). *Telephone:* 227305111 (office). *Fax:* 227337256 (office). *E-mail:* itumail@itu.int (office). *Website:* www.itu.int (office).

ZHAO, Jianguo; Chinese business executive; Vice-Pres. China Southern Power Grid Co. Ltd –2006, Pres. and CEO 2006–10, Chair. 2010–16; Dir (non-Exec.) Huadian Power Int. Corpn Ltd 2017–19, fmr Chair. Bd of Dirs Strategic Cttee. *Address:* c/o 2 Xuanwumennei Street Xicheng District, Beijing 100031, People's Republic of China (office).

ZHAO, Kezhi; Chinese politician; *Minister of Public Security;* b. Dec. 1953, Laixi, Shandong Prov.; began career as teacher, Laixi, Shandong Prov. 1973; joined CCP 1975; Mayor and Deputy CCP Chief, Laixi County 1984–87; Magistrate, County People's Court, Laixi County 1984–87; Mayor and Deputy CCP Sec., Jimo City 1987–89, CCP Sec., Jimo 1989–97; CCP Sec., Dezhou City 1997–2001; Vice-Gov., Shandong Prov. 2001–06; Exec. Vice-Gov., Jiangsu Prov. 2006–10; Gov., Guizhou Prov. 2010–12; CCP Sec., Guizhou Prov. 2012–15, Hebei Prov. 2015–17; Minister of Public Security 2017–; mem. State Council 2018–; mem. 18th CCP Cen. Cttee 2012–17, 19th CCP Cen. Cttee 2017–. *Address:* Ministry of Public Security, 14 Dongchangan Dajie, Dongcheng Qu, Beijing 100741, People's Republic of China (office). *Telephone:* (10) 66262114 (office). *E-mail:* gabzfwz@mps.gov.cn (office). *Website:* www.mps.gov.cn (office).

ZHAO, Leji; Chinese politician; *Secretary, Central Commission for Discipline Inspection;* b. March 1957, Xi'ning, Qinghai Prov.; ed Peking Univ., Beijing; joined CCP 1975; teacher, later Deputy Dir Dean's Office, Qinghai Prov. Commerce School 1980–83; Deputy Dir Political Div., Commerce Dept, Qinghai Prov. 1983–84, Deputy Dir, later Dir Commerce Dept 1986–93 (also Sec. CCP Party Cttee), Dir Financial Dept 1993–94; Sec. CCP Qinghai Prov. Cttee 1984–86, 2003–07, Deputy Sec. 2000–03; Asst Gov. of Qinghai Prov. 1993–94, Vice-Gov. 1994–99, Acting Gov. 1999–2000, Gov. 2000–03; Sec. CCP Xining City Cttee, Qinghai Prov. 1997–98; Chair. Standing Cttee Qinghai Prov. People's Congress 2004–07; Sec. CCP Shaanxi Prov. Cttee 2007–12, also mem. Standing Cttee 2007–12; mem. 16th CCP Cen. Cttee 2000–07, 17th CCP Cen. Cttee 2007–12, 18th CCP Cen. Cttee 2012–17, 18th CCP Cen. Cttee Politburo and Secr. 2012–17; mem. 19th CCP Cen. Cttee 2017–, also mem. 19th CCP Cen. Cttee Politburo 2017– and Politburo Standing Cttee 2017–; Head, CCP Cen. Cttee Organization Dept 2012–17; Sec., Central Comm. for Discipline Inspection 2017–. *Address:* CCP Central Commission for Discipline Inspection, Zhongnanhai, Beijing, People's Republic of China (office). *Website:* cpc.people.com.cn (office).

ZHAO, Qizheng; Chinese politician; *Chairman, Foreign Affairs Committee, CCP Central Committee;* b. Jan. 1940, Beijing; s. of Zhao Jingyuan and Wan Shuxian; m. Zheng Shiting; one d.; ed China Univ. of Science and Tech.; joined CCP 1979; technician, later Sr Engineer 1963–74; Deputy Dir Shanghai Broadcasting Materials Factory 1982–84; Deputy Sec. Industrial Work Cttee, CCP Shanghai Municipal Cttee 1984, Deputy Head, later Head, Org. Dept 1984–86, mem. Standing Cttee 1986–91, Dir Dist Admin. Cttee 1993; Sec. Work Cttee CCP Pudong Dist Cttee, Shanghai 1992; Vice-Mayor of Shanghai 1993–98; Deputy Dir then Dir CCP Cen. Cttee Int. Communications Office 1998–; Deputy Dir, then Dir Information Office of State Council 1998–2005; mem. 16th CCP Cen. Cttee 2002–07; Vice-Chair. Foreign Affairs Cttee, CCP Cen. Cttee 2005–08, Chair. 2008–; Dean, School of Journalism and Communication, Renmin Univ. of China 2005–. *Publications:* America and American People in Chinese People's Eyes 2005, Introducing China to the Rest of the World 2006, A Friendly Dialogue between an Atheist and a Christian (with Luis Palau) 2008. *Address:* c/o State Council Information Office, 225 Chaoyangmen Neidajie, Beijing 100010, People's Republic of China. *Telephone:* (10) 6559-2339 (office). *Fax:* (10) 6559-2364 (office). *E-mail:* xuying@scio.gov.cn (office).

ZHAO, Ruichun; Chinese artist; b. Nov. 1935, Wenzhou, Zhejiang; s. of Zhao Loshu and Huang Shenghong; m. 1st 1956; one d.; m. 2nd Yun Xiuying; one d.; ed Chinese Cen. Fine Arts Inst.; Lecturer, Guangzhou Inst. of Fine Arts 1959–71; teacher, Chinese Cen. Fine Arts Inst. 1980–82; painter, Guangzhou Art Acad. 1984–, now Sr Painter; first one-man exhbn 1962; mem. Chinese Artists' Asscn, Chinese Engraving Asscn; Sec.-Gen. Chinese Asscn of Copper-Plate, Lithographic and Silkscreen Engraving; Ed.-in-Chief Modern Engraving; works exhibited in USA, Japan, UK, Australia, New Zealand, Ireland, Singapore, Denmark, Switzerland, Korea, Sweden, Thailand, Canada, USSR, Algeria, Italy and Taiwan; exhbn'Vibrant Sincerity', Beijing Central Acad. of Fine Arts 2017. *Publications:* On Engraving Education 1981, Woodcut Techniques 1983, The Practice and Theory of Sketching 1986, Silk-screen Plate Techniques 1987. *Leisure interest:* Chinese cooking. *Address:* Guangzhou Academy of Fine Arts, 257 Changgang Donglu, Haizhu District, Guangzhou (office); 609 Dongnan Mansion, Gongyuan Road, Wenzhou 325000, Zhejiang, People's Republic of China (home).

ZHAO, Shiping, BA; Chinese engineer and business executive; *Chairman, Yangquan Coal Industry (Group) Company Ltd;* b. March 1955, Zuo Quan Co., Shanxi Prov.; mem. CCP 1985–; mem. Bd of Dirs and Gen. Man. Yangquan Coal Industry (Group) Co. Ltd 2006–12, Sec., Party Cttee and Chair. 2012–. *Address:* Yangquan Coal Industry (Group) Co. Ltd, 5 Beida Street, Yangquan 045000, Shanxi, People's Repub. of China (office). *Telephone:* (353) 7078728 (office). *Fax:* (353) 7078718 (office). *E-mail:* webmaster@ymjt.com.cn (office). *Website:* www.ymjt.com.cn (office).

ZHAO, Shuangliang; Chinese business executive; *Chairman, China National Cereals, Oils and Foodstuffs Corporation (COFCO);* ed Grad. School of the Party School of the Cen. Cttee of the Chinese Communist Party; successively held posts of Vice-Dir, Vice-Party Sec. and Dir of Suburban Dist of Baotou City, Deputy Mayor and mem. Standing Cttee of Baotou City, Deputy Party Sec., Chief of Jirem League, Deputy Party Sec., Mayor and Sec. of Municipal Party Cttee of Tongliao City, Vice-Pres. of Inner Mongolia Autonomous Region; Chair. China Grain Reserves Corpn (Sinograin) –2016; Chair. China Nat. Cereals, Oils and Foodstuffs Corpn (COFCO, also known as China Agri-Industries Holdings Ltd) 2016–. *Address:* China National Cereals, Oils and Foodstuffs Corporation, 19F, COFCO Fortune Plaza No. 8, Chao Yang Men South Street, Chao Yang District, Beijing 100020, People's Republic of China (office). *Telephone:* (10) 85006637 (office). *Fax:* (10) 85006637 (office). *E-mail:* cofco-news@cofco.com (office). *Website:* www.cofco.com.cn (office).

ZHAO, Xizheng; Chinese power industry executive; b. 1942; ed Tsingua Univ.; Dir-Gen. Northeast Electric Power Admin Bureau and Pres. Northeast Electric Power Group Corpn 1989–93; Deputy Minister of Electric Power 1993–98; Exec. Vice-Pres. State Power Corpn of China (also known as State Grid Corpn of China) 1993–2003, CEO 2003; apptd Pres. China Electricity Council 2004; Chair. Presidium, China Fed. of Industrial Econs (CFIE); mem. CPPCC 2007.

ZHAO, Zhongxian, DrSc; Chinese physicist; b. 30 Jan. 1941, Liaoning Prov.; s. of Zhao Desheng and Zhang Naibin; m. Zhou Yaqin 1967; two s.; ed Univ. of Science and Tech. of China; Researcher, Inst. of Physics, Acad. Sinica 1964–; Dir Nat. Lab. for Superconductivity 1991–2000; Chair. Scientific Council, Inst. of Physics 1999–; mem. CPPCC Nat. Cttee 1993–98, 2003–07, 2008–13; Vice-Pres. China Asscn for Science and Tech. 2001–; Dir Working Cttee on Consultation and Evaluation of Chinese Academia Sinica 2000–08; mem. Presidium Chinese Acad. of Sciences 1998–2008; Vice-Pres. Chinese Physical Soc. 1994–2003, China Innovation Asscn 1996–; Fellow, Third World Acad. of Sciences 1987, Acad. of Ceramics (Int.) 1989, Chinese Acad. of Sciences 1991; mem. Council of Asscn of Asia Pacific Physical Soc. 1990–97; Special mem. China Center of Advanced Sciences and Tech. 1987; Hon. Fellow, India Materials Research Soc. 1991, China Materials Research Soc. 1996; Hon. DSc (Chinese Univ. of Hong Kong) 1988; Hon. Physics Award, Third World Acad. of Sciences 1986, Tan Kah-Kee Material Science Prize 1988, Natural Sciences Prize of China (1st Class) 1990, 2013, (2nd Class) 2002, 2011, Wang Danping Science Prize 1992, Science and Tech. Progress Award, Ho Leung Ho Lee Foundation Physics Prize 1997, Award for Outstanding Achievement in Science and Tech., Chinese Acad. of Sciences 2005. *Leisure interests:* music, photography, calligraphy. *Address:* Institute of Physics, Chinese Academy of Sciences, Room D-420, Zhong Guan Cun, PO Box 603, Beijing 100080 (office); Building 17-105, Yan-Gui-Yuan, Zhong Guan Cun, Bei Er Tiao, Beijing 100080, People's Republic of China (home). *Telephone:* (10) 82649190 (office); (10) 82649361 (office); (10) 62564951 (home). *Fax:* (10) 82649486 (office); (10) 82649531 (office). *E-mail:* zhxzhao@aphy.iphy.ac.cn (office). *Website:* www.iphy.ac.cn (office).

ZHAPAROV, Akylbek Usenbekovich; Kyrgyzstani economist and politician; b. 14 Sept. 1964, Rybachye; ed Frunze (now Bishkek) Polytechnical Inst., Bishkek Financial-Econ. Acad.; worked in Automotive Highways and Roads Dept, Frunze Polytechnical Inst. 1986–91; Deputy Gen. Dir Tolkun org. 1991–92; Head, Youth Policy Dept, Office of the Pres. 1992–93; Head, Admin of Social Democratic Party of Kyrgyzstan 1993–95; Adviser to First Deputy Prime Minister 1995–96; Sec., Nat. Cttee for Securities, Office of the Pres. 1996–97; Chief Inspector, Ministry of Finance and Man. State Tax Inspectorate 1997–2000; Deputy, Zhogorku Kenesh (Parl.) 2000–05; Minister of Finance 2005–06 (resgnd), 2011–12, apptd Minister of Econ. Devt and Trade 2009, First Deputy Prime Minister 2009–10; Honoured Economist of the Kyrgyz Repub. 2002.

ZHARIKOV, Alexander Nikolayevich; Russian trade union official and engineer; b. 2 Jan. 1945, Arsenyevo; s. of Nicolai Philippovich Zharikov and Claudia Egorovna Gorodnicheva; m. 1st Olga Borisovna Suhova 1975 (deceased); one s.; m. 2nd Eva Shvachova; one s. one d.; ed Leningrad Shipbuilding Inst.; mil. service 1962–66; Sec. of Youth and Student Org. of Leningrad 1971–74; Chair. Student Council of USSR 1974–78; Vice-Pres. Int. Union of Students 1978–84; official, Int. Dept Cen. Cttee of CPSU 1984–88; Dir Int. Dept USSR All-Union Council 1988–90; Gen. Sec., World Fed. of Trade Unions (WFTU) 1990–2006; Hon. Prof. (Russian State Univ. of Humanitarian Science); Order of Honour (Russia) 1974. *Publications:* book on world student movt 1979; numerous articles on social issues, labour and trade union relations in newspapers and magazines. *Leisure interests:* swimming, collecting mushrooms, reading, skiing.

ZHENG, Silin; Chinese politician; *President, China Association of National Advertisers;* b. May 1940, Wu Co., Jiangsu Prov.; ed Taiyuan Science Univ.; joined CCP 1965; worked at Dandong Automobile Repair Plant, Liaoning Prov. 1965–81; Dir Dandong TV Parts Factory 1982–83; Vice-Mayor Dandong City 1983–85; Dir Comm. for Foreign Econ. Relations and Trade and Asst Gov., Liaoning Prov. 1985–89; Vice-Gov. Shaanxi Prov. People's Govt 1989–93; Vice-Minister of Foreign Trade and Econ. Co-operation 1993–94; Deputy Sec. 9th CCP Jiangsu Prov. Cttee 1994–98; Acting Gov. of Jiangsu Prov. 1994–95, Gov. 1995–98; Deputy Dir State Econ. and Trade Comm. 1998–2000; Minister of Labour and Social Security 2003–05; mem. ILO Social Protection Floor Advisory Group 2010–; Vice-Chair. NPC Foreign Affairs Cttee; Co-Chair. Canada-China Legislative Asscn; Exec. Vice-Pres. China Enterprise Confed., China Enterprise Dirs Asscn; Founder and Pres. China Asscn of Nat. Advertisers 2005–; Alt. mem. 13th Cen. Cttee CCP 1987–92, mem. 14th Cen. Cttee 1992–97, 15th CCP Cen. Cttee 1997–2002 (Deputy Dir Cen. Work Cttee of Large Enterprises 2000–03), 16th CCP Cen. Cttee 2002–07. *Address:* China Association of National Advertisers, No.10 Xisanhuan Zhonglu, Haidian District, Beijing 100036, People's Republic of China (office). *Telephone:* (10) 88028766/ (office). *Website:* www.cananet.org.cn (office).

ZHENG, Wanchun, PhD; Chinese economist and banking executive; *President, China Minsheng Banking Corporation Ltd;* b. Feb. 1964, Anhui Prov.; fmr Deputy Gen. Man. and Gen. Man. Creditors' Dept, Gen. Man. Business Man. Dept and Asst Pres. China Huarong Asset Man. Co. Ltd (China Huarong), fmr Vice-Pres. China Huaron, Chair. Huarong Securities and Chair. Rongde Asset Man. Co. Ltd (Sino-German jt venture co.) 2004–09, Vice-Pres. China Huaron, Chair. Huarong Securities and Chair. Huarong Futures 2009–11; Pres. China Great Wall Asset Man. Corpn 2011–13; fmr Deputy Gen. Man. Industrial and Commercial Credit Dept, Industrial and Commercial Bank of China Ltd (ICBC), fmr Asst Pres. Hainan Prov. Br., ICBC and fmr Gen. Man. Business Dept of the Br., Vice-Pres. Industrial and Commercial Bank of China Ltd 2013–15; Sec., CCP Party Cttee and Pres. China Minsheng Banking Corpn Ltd 2015–. *Address:* China Minsheng Banking Corporation Ltd, 2 Fuxingmennei Avenue, Beijing 100873, People's Republic of China (office). *Telephone:* (10) 68946790 (office). *E-mail:* webmaster@cmbc.com.cn (office). *Website:* www.cmbc.com.cn (office).

ZHENG, Wantong; Chinese politician; b. May 1941, Tianjin; ed Tianjin Teachers' Coll.; joined CCP 1960; high school teacher and cadre, Communist Youth League Hebei Dist Cttee, Tianjin 1961–68; cadre, CCP Hebei Dist Cttee, Tianjin 1974–78; cadre then Dir-Gen. Office of CCP Tianjin Municipal Cttee 1978–83; Sec.-Gen. CCP Tianjin Municipal Cttee 1983–88; Guest Research Fellow, Tianjin Acad. of Social Sciences; Vice-Chair. and mem. Secr. All-China Fed. of Trade Unions 1988–93; Deputy Head, United Front Work Dept of CCP Cen. Cttee 1993–; mem. CCP Cen. Comm. for Discipline Inspection 1997–; Vice-Chair. 8th Exec. Cttee All-China Fed. of Industry and Commerce 1997–; Vice-Pres. China Overseas

Friendship Asscn 1997–, First Council of Chinese Research Asscn for Economy and Soc. 2001–; Deputy Sec.-Gen. 8th CPPCC Nat. Cttee 1993–98, Sec.-Gen. 9th CPPCC Nat. Cttee 1998–2003, 10th CPPCC Nat. Cttee 2003–08, Vice-Chair. 11th CPPCC Nat. Cttee 2008–13; mem. 16th CCP Cen. Cttee 2002–07. *Address:* National Committee of Chinese People's Political Consultative Conference, 23 Taipingqiao Street, Beijing, People's Republic of China (office).

ZHENG, Wenxue; Chinese business executive; *CEO, Kailuan (Group) LLC;* CEO Kailuan (Group) LLC (coal mining co.) 2008–. *Address:* Kailuan (Group) Ltd Liability Corporation, 70 Xinhua Hua Dong Road, Tangshan 063018, People's Republic of China (office). *Telephone:* (31) 53022324. *Fax:* (31) 52827307. *E-mail:* info@kailuan.com (office). *Website:* www.kailuan.com.cn (office).

ZHENG, Xiaoying; Chinese conductor and professor of music; b. 27 Sept. 1929, Shanghai; d. of Zheng Wei and Wen Siying; m. Liu Enyü 1947; one d.; ed China Central Conservatory of Music (CCOM), Moscow P.I. Tchaikovsky State Conservatoire, USSR (now Russian Fed.); mem. song and dance troupe 1949; teacher and conductor, Cen. Conservatoire 1950–60, 1963–; Dean 1998; conducted Cen. Conservatoire Chorus and Symphony Orchestra, Radio Orchestra of USSR 1961–63, Cen. Philharmonic, China Broadcasting Orchestra, Canberra Orchestra, Hong Kong Philharmonic; Chief Conductor Cen. Opera Theatre 1978–88; Founder, Musical Dir and Conductor Women's Chamber Orchestra, Capital Opera Inst. 1988; Artistic Dir and Chief Conductor Xiamen Philharmonic Orchestra 1998–2013 (retd); Artistic Dir 4th World Choir Games 2006, Xiamen; appeared at Hong Kong Performing Arts Festival, Savonlinna Opera Festival, Finland, Singapore Inaugural, Macao Int. Music Festival, Chinese Arts Festival; mem. Exec. Council Chinese Musicians' Asscn; numerous recordings; took part as torch bearer, Olympic Flame Relay, Xiamen, May 2008; Special Honour for Outstanding Women 1979, 1983, Nat. First Prize for Conductors 1981, La Donna nel Mondo (Italy) 1983, Médaille d'honneur des arts et des lettres (France) 1985, Olay Women's World Excellence Awards 2006, Golden Melody Prize 2011. *Leisure interests:* travel, sports. *Address:* Central Conservatory, 43 Baojia Street, Beijing 100031 (office); Hai Tan Lu, Gulangyu, Xiamen 100031, People's Republic of China (home). *Telephone:* (592) 2061549 (Xiamen) (home); (610) 65520019 (Beijing) (home). *Fax:* (592) 2061549 (Xiamen) (home); (610) 65523164 (Beijing) (home). *E-mail:* ccom@ccom.edu.cn (office). *Website:* www.xiaoying.com.cn.

ZHENG, Zhijie, BSc, MMan; Chinese business executive; *Vice-Chairman and President, China Development Bank Corporation;* b. May 1958; ed Univ. of Nagasaki, Japan, Stanford Univ., USA; fmr Sr Man. Dir, CITIC Capital Partners; fmr CEO, Gen. Man. and Man. Partner, Kaixin Investment Co. Ltd; Man. Partner Walden Int. from 2001, mem. Advisory Bd Walden Int.; Exec. Vice-Pres. China Devt Bank Corpn –2008, Vice-Chair. and Exec. Dir 2008–14, Vice-Chair. and Pres. 2014–; Ind. Dir (non-exec.), Chinasoft Int. Ltd 2003–, AutoNavi Holdings Ltd 2006–, E-House (China) Holdings Ltd 2008–, Great Wall Technology Co. Ltd 2011–; Ind. Dir Vimicro I Int. Corpn 2009–, SMIT Corpn 2005–, China Great Wall Computer Shenzhen Co. Ltd 2004–, Gaga Holdings Ltd 2008; Exec. Dir China Br., Asia America MultiTechnology Asscn; mem. Bd China Western Returned Scholars Asscn. *Address:* China Development Bank Corporation, 29 Fuchengmenwai Street, Xicheng District, Beijing 100037, People's Republic of China (office). *Telephone:* (10) 6830-6688 (office). *Fax:* (10) 6830-6699 (office). *E-mail:* info@bcdb.com.cn (office). *Website:* www.cdb.com.cn (office).

ZHENOVACH, Sergey Vassilyevich; Russian theatre director; *Artistic Director, The Theatre Art Studio;* b. 15 May 1957, Potsdam, Germany; ed Krasnodar Inst. of Culture, Moscow Inst. of Theatre Arts; Dir Youth Theatre Studio Stroitel, Krasnodar 1979, 1982–83; army service 1979–82; teacher, Moscow Inst. of Theatre Arts (now Russian Acad. of Theatre Arts—GITIS) 1990–2001, Prof. and Artistic Dir, Dirs' Chair 2001–, Head of Dirs' Chair 2004–; Dir, Chelovek theatre-studio 1988–91; Dir Moscow Theatre on Malaya Bronnaya 1991–96, Chief Artistic Dir 1996–98; together with graduates from GITIS hosted a festival of graduation productions, Six Plays in Waiting for a Theatre, and f. The Theatre Art Studio 2005, Artistic Dir 2005–; Honoured Art Worker of the Russian Fed.; Mayor of Moscow Prize 1992, Golden Mask Prize 1996, Stanislavsky Prize 1997, Stanislavsky Award "For the studio-spirit revival" 2005, State Prize of the Russian Fed. *Stage productions include:* Chelovek theatre-studio: Pannochka (N. Sadur after N. Gogol's Viy 1988, Illusion (P. Corneille) 1989, The Truth is Good but Happiness is Better, The Imaginary Invalid; Malaya Bronnaya Theatre: King Lear (Shakespeare) 1992, The Idiot (trilogy after F. Dostoyevsky's novel) (Golden Mask for Best Dir) 1995; other productions: Vladimir, 3rd Class (after N. Gogol) 1991, The Sound and the Fury (after W. Faulkner) 1993, A Month in the Country (after play by Turgenev) 1997, participated in Avignon Theatre Festival 1997; productions in Norway of plays by Chekhov, Ibsen and Shakespeare 1994, 1996, 1997; Woe from Wit (A. Griboedov), Maly Theatre 2000, Truth is Good and Happiness is Better (after a play by Ostrovsky) (Golden Mask Nat. Theatrical Award Jury Special Prize for Best Ensemble, Union of Theatre Workers' Award 'Highlight of the Season') 2002, The White Guard (M. A. Bulgakov), Moscow Art Theatre 2004, The Imaginary Invalid (after Moliere's play) (Golden Mask for Best Large-Scale Performance) 2005, Boys (production after nine chapters from The Brothers Karamazov by Dostoyevsky) (included in out-of-competition programme of the Golden Mask Festival and programme of 6th Chekhov Int. Festival 2005) (Crystal Turandot Theatre Award) 2006; Theatre Art Studio: A Family in Decline (after N. Leskov) (Golden Mask for Best Dir, Best Small-scale Production, Best Actress) 2006, Gamblers (after N. Gogol) 2007, The Battle of Life (after Dickens) (Golden Mask for Best Small-scale Production) 2008, The River Potudan (after a short story by A. Platonov) (Golden Mask for Best Small-scale Production) 2009, Three Years (after a story by Chekhov) 2009, Notebooks (after Chekhov) 2010, Brother Ivan Fyodorovich (after Part 4, Vol. 11 of The Brothers Karamazov by F. Dostoevsky) 2011, Moscow to the End of the Line (after prose poem by V. Erofeev) (Golden Mask for Best Actor) 2012, A Dead Man's Memoir (after A Theatrical Novel by M. Bulgakov) 2014, The Suicide (after Erdman) 2015. *Address:* The Theatre Art Studio, 109004 Moscow, Stanislavsky str. 21, Building 7, Russian Federation (office). *Telephone:* (495) 646-74-55 (office). *Fax:* (495) 646-74-58 (office). *E-mail:* teatr@sti.ru (office). *Website:* www.sti.ru (office).

ZHEVAGO, Konstantin; Ukrainian business executive; m.; two c.; ed Kiev Inst. of Nat. Economy; Finance Dir Closed Jt Stock Co. Finance and Credit (bank) 1993, then Owner (bank declared insolvent 2015); Man., Poltava Ore Mining and Enrichment Works 1994 (now Ferrexpo Poltava Mining), now Owner and Deputy Chair. Supervisory Bd, also Dir (non-exec.) Ferrexpo plc; also owns other cos including AvtoKraz and Rosava with interests in vehicles, tires, pharmaceuticals, oil and gas; Deputy, Verkhovna Rada (Parl.) 1998–, mem. Yuliya Timoshenko Block political faction 2006–12, mem. Parl. Cttee on Law Policy and Co-Chair. Parl. Group for Inter-Parl. Relations with Japan. *Address:* c/o Supervisory Board, Ferrexpo Poltava Mining, Stroitelej Str., Komsomolsk 39802, Poltava region, Ukraine (office). *E-mail:* pgok@ferrexpo.com (office). *Website:* ferrexpo.ua (office); www.fc.kiev.ua.

ZHIGUNOV, Sergei Viktorovich; Russian actor and film producer and director; *Director-General, Shans Company Mosfilm Cinema Corporation;* b. 2 Jan. 1963, Rostov-Don; ed Shchukin Theatre School; Dir-Gen. Shans Co. Mosfilm Cinema Corpn; Producer State Cttee on Radio and TV 1997–; Pres. Guild of Russian Film Actors 2000–; Russian Artist of Merit; Guild of Russian Film Actors' Prize 1997. *Film roles include:* Priznat vinovnym (as S. Zhigunov) 1983, Shans 1984, Poruchit generalu Nesterovu 1984, Dva gusara 1984, Vnimaniye! Vsem postam... 1985, Pravo lyubit 1985, Poslednyaya doroga 1986, Zaveshchanie 1986, Po glavnoy ulitse s orkestrom 1987, Piloti 1988, A Tale of Adam Mickiewicz's 'Forefathers' Eve' 1989, Poyezdka v Visbaden 1989, Podzemelye vedm 1989, Sekskazka 1991, Vivat, gardemariny! 1991, Serdtsa tryokh 1992, Richard lvinoye serdtse 1992, Rytsar Kennet 1993, A vot i ya... (short) 1993, Istoriya pro Richarda, milorda i prekrasnuyu Zhar-ptitsu 1997, Printsessa na bobakh (also producer) 1997, Shekspiru i ne snilos (also producer) 2007, Terra Nova 2008, Ten Winters 2009, O nyom (also exec. producer) 2012. *Films produced:* Chyornyy kvadrat 1992, En un claroscuro de la luna 1999, The Garden Was Full of Moon 2000, Vovochka 2002, Tri mushketera 2013. *Film directed:* Tri mushketera (also writer) 2013. *Television includes:* Tsigni pitsisa (meore natsili) (film) 1983, Tsigni pitsisa (film) 1983, Naval Cadets, Charge! (mini-series) 1987, Koroleva Margo (series, also producer) 1996, Pan ili propal (series, also producer) 1998, Poka ya ne umer (film, also producer) 2001, Igra na vybyvanie (series) 2004, Moya prekrasnaya nyanya (series) 2004–08, Zvezda epokhi (mini-series) 2005, Sakvoyazh so svetlym budushchim (mini-series) 2006, Rita (film) 2010, Schaste po kontraktu (film) 2010, Veronika. Poteryannoye schastye (series) 2012, Torgovyy tsentr (series) 2013, Delo chesti (series) 2013. *Television productions:* Grafinya de Monsoro (series) (producer) 1998, Chto skazal pokoynik (series) 2000. *Address:* Bolshevo 141090, 3D Gorogok 12, Apt 106, Moscow Region, Russia. *Telephone:* (495) 515-30-06.

ZHIRINOVSKII, Col Vladimir Volfovich, DPhil; Russian lawyer, politician and army officer; *Chairman, Liberalno-Demokraticheskaya Partiya Rossii (LDPR—Liberal Democratic Party of Russia);* b. (Vladimir Eidelstein), 25 April 1946, Almatı, Kazakh SSR, USSR; m. Galina Aleksandrovna Lebedeva; one s.; ed Inst. of Eastern languages (now Inst. of Asian and African Countries) and Faculty of Law, Moscow M.V. Lomonosov State Univ. (MGU); officer, USSR Ministry of Defence, with Gen. Staff of Transcaucasian command 1970–72; with Int. Dept, Soviet Soc. of Friendship and Cultural Relations, Cttee for Peace 1973–75; with Office of Dean of Foreign Students, Higher School of Trade Union Movt 1975–77; legal consultant, Inyurcollegia 1977–83; Head of Legal Dept, Mir Publs 1983–90; f. Liberalno-Demokraticheskaya Partiya Sovetskogo Soyuza (LDPSS—Liberal-Democratic Party of the Soviet Union, now Liberalno-Demokraticheskaya Partiya Rossii—LDPR—Liberal Democratic Party of Russia) 1989, Chair. 1990–, Chair. State Duma Parl. Group 1993–2000; mem. State Duma (Parl.) 1993–, Deputy Chair. 2000–11; apptd Head of Russian del. to NATO Parl. Ass. 2002; unsuccessful cand. in Russian presidential elections 1991, 1996, 2000, 2008, 2012; attained rank of Col in Army Reserve 1995; Hon. Railwayman; Order of Merit for the Fatherland (4th Class), Order of Honour, Zhukov Medal, 850th Anniversary of Moscow Medal, Medal of Merit in the Russian Population Census, 300th Anniversary of St Petersburg Medal, Medal Anatoliya Koni, Order 'For Personal Courage' (DMR), Order of Honour and Glory (Abkhazia); Distinguished Lawyer of the Russian Fed., Diploma of the Pres. of the Russian Fed. *Publications:* The Last Leap South 1993, Political Landscape of Russia 1995, Economic Ideas of a Politician 1996, Geopolitics and the Russian Question 1997, The Zhirinovsky Phenomenon in Russia 1998 and more than 100 other books and publs. *Leisure interests:* volleyball, swimming. *Address:* State Duma, 103265 Moscow, Okhotnyi ryad 1 (office); Liberalno-Demokraticheskaya Partiya Rossii (Liberal Democratic Party of Russia), 103045 Moscow, Lukov per. 9, Russia (office). *Telephone:* (495) 692-62-66 (Duma) (office); (495) 623-02-44 (LDPR) (office). *Fax:* (495) 697-42-58 (Duma) (office); (495) 692-92-42 (LDPR) (office). *E-mail:* stateduma@duma.gov.ru (office); info@ldpr.ru (office). *Website:* www.duma.gov.ru (office); ldpr.ru (office).

ZHITINKIN, Andrei Albertovich; Russian theatre director; b. 18 Nov. 1960; ed Shchukin Theatre High School; Dir Mossoviet Theatre 1991–2001; Chief Artistic Dir Drama Theatre, Malaya Bronnaya 2001–03; Artistic Dir Author's Theatre Andrei Zhitinkin; People's Artist of the Russian Fed.; numerous Russian and Int. theatre awards. *Plays include:* Dog's Waltz 1992, Yellow Angel 1993, All of a Sudden Last Summer 1994, My Poor Marat 1995, He Has Come 1996, Mon Ami 1997, Merchant of Venice 1999, Anna Karenina 2001, Caligula 2001, Lulu 2002, Meteor 2002, Nijinsky 2003, Portrait of Dorian Gray 2003, Homo Erectus 2005. *Television:* Udachnyy obmen (film, actor and dir) 2007. *Publications:* several books. *Address:* Malaya Bronnaya Theatre, 103104 Moscow, Malaya Bronnaya str. 4, Russian Federation (office). *Telephone:* (495) 690-67-31 (office). *E-mail:* mbronnaya@theatre.ru (office). *Website:* mbronnaya.theatre.ru (office).

ZHONG, Jun; Chinese business executive; *President and CEO, China Southern Power Grid Company Ltd;* Pres. and CEO China Southern Power Grid Co. Ltd 2010–; mem. Nat. Cttee of the CPPCC. *Address:* China Southern Power Grid Co. Ltd, 6 Huasui Road, Zhujiang Xincheng, Tianhe District, Guangzhou 510623, People's Republic of China (office). *Telephone:* (20) 3812-1958 (office); (20) 3812-1080 (office). *Fax:* (20) 3886-5670 (office); (20) 3812-0189 (office). *E-mail:* international@csg.cn (office). *Website:* www.csg.cn (office); eng.csg.cn (office).

ZHONG, Ming, FRSA; Chinese artist; b. 1949, Beijing; elected to Chinese Artists' Asscn 1980; Founder mem. Beijing Oil Painting Research Asscn; achieved int. recognition with painting He is Himself—Sartre 1980; moved to UK 1984; exhibited at Open Exhbn of Royal Soc. of Painters in Watercolour, Bankside Gallery 1984; has also exhibited in Japan, Sweden, USA; speaker at int. symposium The Authentic Garden, Leiden, Netherlands 1990; returned to China 1998; worked as Dir, Shanghai TV and China Central TV. *Publications include:*

The Craft of Gardens (photographer) 1988; articles on art and cultural subjects in various periodicals. *Address:* Huanghua Road, Shanghai 201103, People's Republic of China.

ZHONG, Shan, PhD; Chinese economist and politician; *Minister of Commerce;* b. Oct. 1955, Shangyu County, Zhejiang Prov.; ed Zhejiang Univ.; joined CCP 1974; Chair. and Gen. Man., Zhejiang Zhongda Group Ltd 1987–97, also Sec. CCP Cttee 1987–94; Dir, Foreign Trade and Econs Dept, Zhejiang Prov. 1997–2003, also Sec., CCP Leading Party Group 1997–2003; Vice-Gov., Zhejiang Prov. 2003–08; Vice-Minister of Commerce 2008–17, Minister 2017–, also Ministry of Commerce Int. Trade Rep. 2013–; mem. 19th CCP Cen. Cttee 2017–. *Address:* Ministry of Commerce, 2 Dongchangan Dajie, Dongcheng Qu, Beijing 100731, People's Republic of China (office). *Telephone:* (10) 53771360 (office). *Fax:* (10) 53771311 (office). *E-mail:* webmaster@mofcom.gov.cn (office). *Website:* www.mofcom.gov.cn (office).

ZHONG, Shengjian; Chinese real estate executive; *Chairman and CEO, Yanlord Land Group Ltd;* b. 1958, Lufeng, Guangdong Prov.; moved to Singapore 1989; since 1980s has f. several trading, manufacturing, real estate and financial services cos spanning China, Singapore, Hong Kong, Indonesia, Malaysia and Australia; Founder, Chair. and CEO Yanlord Land Group Ltd early 1990s–; mem. Sichuan Singapore Trade and Investment Cttee, Network China; Hon. Citizen of Nanjing, Zhuhai and Shanwei; Hon. Business Adviser to Int. Enterprise Singapore (IE Singapore) for China 2004–07; White Magnolia Award for contribs to Municipal City of Shanghai 2005. *Address:* Yanlord Land Group Ltd, 9 Temasek Boulevard #36-02, Suntec City Tower Two, Singapore 038989 (office); Shanghai Yanlord Property Co. Ltd, 30F POS-Plaza No. 1600 Century Avenue, Pudong New Area, Shanghai 200122, People's Republic of China (office). *Telephone:* 63362922 (Singapore) (office); (21) 68768888 (Shanghai) (office). *Fax:* 62386256 (Singapore) (office); (21) 68765858 (Shanghai) (office). *Website:* www.yanlordland.com (office).

ZHOU, Chunya, BFA, MFA; Chinese painter; b. 1955, Chongqing; ed Sichuan Acad. of Fine Arts, Univ. of Kassel. *Address:* Zihua Road, Huangpu Qu, Shanghai Shi 200000, People's Republic of China.

ZHOU, Guangzhao, MS; Chinese nuclear physicist; b. 15 May 1929, Changsha City, Hunan Prov.; s. of Fengjiu Zhou and Zhen-zhao Tao; m. Zheng Aiqin 1955; one d.; ed Tsinghua Univ., Peking Univ.; joined CCP 1952; Lecturer, Physics Dept, Tsinghua Univ.; Researcher, Dubra Jt Nuclear Research Inst., Moscow, USSR 1957–60; Deputy Dir Theoretical Dept, later Dir and Chief Engineer, Nuclear Weapons Research Inst. 1961; Dir 9th Research Inst. of Second Ministry of Machine-Bldg Industry; Research Fellow and Dir Physics Research Inst. of Chinese Acad. of Sciences 1982, Vice-Pres. Chinese Acad. of Sciences 1984–87, Pres. 1987–97; Vice-Pres. China Physics Soc.; Vice-Chair. IUPAC 1993; mem. State Leading Group for Science and Tech. 1996; Chair. State Science and Tech. Comm. 1996; Alt. mem. 12th CCP Cen. Cttee 1982–85, mem. 1985–87, 13th CCP Cen. Cttee 1987–92, 14th CCP Cen. Cttee 1992–97, 15th CCP Cen. Cttee 1997–2002; Vice-Chair. Standing Cttee of 9th NPC 1998–2003; took part in making of China's first atomic bomb and hydrogen bomb; Hon. Pres. Chinese People's Asscn for Peace and Disarmament 1998; First Prize, State Award for Natural Sciences 1982, Meritorious Service Medal, CCP Cen. Cttee, State Council and Cen. Mil. Comm. 1999. *Achievements include:* Asteroid No. 3462, found in 1996 by Chinese astronomers, was named after Zhou Guangzhao 1996. *Publications:* Language Reform of China 1961, A Free Talk on Chinese Language 1992, Alphabets of the World 1993. *Leisure interests:* swimming, table tennis. *Address:* Chinese Academy of Sciences, 52 San Li He Road, 100864 Beijing, People's Republic of China (office). *Telephone:* (10) 68597521 (office).

ZHOU, Houjian; Chinese business executive; *Chairman, HiSense Group Corporation;* b. Aug. 1957, Qingdao, Shandong Prov.; ed Shandong Univ.; technician, Deputy Div. Head, Man.'s Asst, Vice-Man. then Man. Qingdao TV Plant 1982–94; Gen. Man. Qingdao HiSense Electric Co. 1994–95, Chair. 1995–, Chair. HiSense Group Corpn 1994–; Deputy 10th NPC 2003; awarded the Global Young Entrepreneurs Man. Talent Special Prize 1996, Nat. Wuyi Labour Medal 1998, Magnificent Ten Award 2005. *Leisure interests:* football, boxing. *Address:* HiSense Group Corporation, No. 17 Donghai West Road, Shinan District, Qingdao 266071, Shandong Province, People's Republic of China (office). *Telephone:* (532) 80873176 (office). *E-mail:* wlfw@hisense.com.cn (office). *Website:* www.hisense-transtech.com.cn (office).

ZHOU, Jichang, PhD; Chinese engineer and business executive; ed Tongji Univ., Beijing Jiaotong Univ.; joined China Communications Construction Co. Ltd 1977, Deputy Gen. Man. The First Highway Survey & Design Inst. of the fmr China Road and Bridge Corpn (a predecessor of the China Communications Construction Group Ltd) 1987–92 and Gen. Man. and Chair. China Road and Bridge Construction Co. (predecessor of China Road and Bridge Corpn) 1995–97, Gen. Man. China Road and Bridge Corpn 1997–2005, Chair. China Communications Construction Co. Ltd 2006–13, also Chair. ZPMC, CRBC International Co. Ltd (subsidiaries); Chair. Shanghai Zhenhua Heavy Industry (Group) Co. Ltd 2011–13.

ZHOU, Jiping, MSc; Chinese oil industry executive; b. 1952; ed China Univ. of Petroleum; has worked in oil and gas industry since 1970s; Vice-Pres. China Nat. Oil & Gas Exploration and Devt Corpn (CNODC) 1996–97, Pres. Greater Nile Petroleum Operating Co. (Sudan) 1996–97, Pres. CNODC 1997–2001, Asst Pres. China Nat. Petroleum Corpn (CNPC) 2001, Pres. CNODC 2001–03, Vice-Pres. CNPC 2003–08, Vice-Chair. and Pres. PetroChina 2008–11, Pres. CNPC 2011–13, Acting Chair. March–April 2013, Chair. and Pres. April–July 2013, Chair. July 2013–15.

ZHOU, Gen. Kunren; Chinese naval officer; b. Sept. 1937, Danyang Co., Jiangsu Prov.; ed PLA Political Acad. and PLA Univ. of Nat. Defence; joined PLA 1956; mem. CCP 1960–; Vice-Dir Political Dept of Navy; rank of Maj.-Gen. 1988; Political Commissar South Sea Fleet; Vice-Political Commissar, PLA Navy 1992, Political Commissar 1992; rank of Lt-Gen. 1993, Gen. 2000; Political Commissar, PLA Gen. Logistics Dept 1995–2002; Vice-Chair. 10th NPC Law Cttee 2003–; mem. 15th CCP Cen. Cttee 1997–2002.

ZHOU, Long, DMA; Chinese/American composer and academic; *Distinguished Professor of Music Composition, Conservatory of Music and Dance, University of Missouri-Kansas City;* b. 8 July 1953, Beijing; m. Chen Yi; ed Central Conservatory of Music, Beijing, Columbia Univ., USA; sent to rural state farm during Cultural Revolution; Composer-in-Residence, Nat. Broadcasting Symphony Orchestra of China 1983; moved to USA in 1985; Music Dir, Music from China, New York 1988–99; Music Alive! Composer-in-Residence, Seattle Symphony's Silk Road Project Festival with Yo-Yo Ma May 2002; commissions from Koussevitsky and Fromm Music Foundations, Chamber Music America and New York State Council on the Arts, and from ensembles including Bavarian Radio Symphony Orchestra, Tokyo and Brooklyn Philharmonics, New Music Consort, Pittsburgh New Music Ensemble, Peabody Trio and Kronos, Shanghai, Ciompi and Chester String Quartets and vocal ensemble Chanticleer; currently Distinguished Prof. of Music Composition, Univ. of Missouri-Kansas City Conservatory of Music and Dance, Tianjin Conservatory of Music; fellowships from American Acad. of Arts and Letters, Nat. Endowment for the Arts and Guggenheim and Rockefeller Foundations, ASCAP Adventurous Programming Award 1999, Lifetime Achievement Award, American Acad. of Arts and Letters 2003, CalArts/Alpert Award in the Arts 2009, Barlow Int. Composition Competition, Fifth Int. Composition Competition, d'Avray (France), Ensemblia Competition, Mönchengladbach (Germany). *Compositions include:* Poems from Tang, The Future of Fire, The Ineffable, Soul, Tian Ling, Spirit of Chimes, Dhyana, Ding, Madame White Snake (Pulitzer Prize for Music 2011), University Festival Overture 2012, Beijing Rhyme—A Symphonic Suite 2012, Nine Odes 2013, Tales from the Nine Bells 2014. *Address:* UMKC Conservatory of Music and Dance, Grant Hall, 5227 Holmes Street, Kansas City, MO 64110-2229, USA (office). *E-mail:* zhoul@umkc.edu (office). *Website:* conservatory.umkc.edu (office).

ZHOU, Mingchen; Chinese business executive; ed Beijing Inst. of Foreign Trade (now Univ. of Int. Trade and Econs); fmr Vice-Pres. China Nat. Metals & Minerals Import & Export Corpn; fmr Pres. China Nat. Instrument Import & Export Corpn; apptd Dir China Nat. Cereals, Oils and Foodstuffs Import & Export Co. (COFCO) 1992, Chair. 1993–2006; Dir Xingda Int. Holdings Ltd 2005–11; Partner Uni-Quantum Pvt. Equity Fund. *Address:* c/o Uni-Quantum Private Equity Fund, Room 906 Tower 3, China Central Place, No. 77 Jianguo Avenue, Chaoyang District, Beijing 100025, People's Republic of China (office).

ZHOU, Mubing, MA, PhD; Chinese business executive; *Executive Chairman, Agricultural Bank of China Ltd;* b. Sept. 1957, Chongqing Municipality; ed Jiangjin Normal School, Sichuan Finance and Econs Coll., Renmin Univ.; spent much of his career at Industrial and Commercial Bank of China; Deputy Sec., Dist Cttee of CCP, Chongqing Municipality, Yubei Dist 2000–01; Chief Exec. People's Gov., Chongqing Municipality 2001–01; Sec., Dist Cttee of CCP, Chongqing Municipality 2001–02; Sec., People's Gov., Gen. Office of CCP, Leading Party Group, Chongqing Municipality 2002–04, Dir 2002–04, Sec.-Gen. 2003–04, mem. People's Gov. CCP 2004–10; Deputy Mayor of Chongqing 2004–10; Student, Cen. Party School, CCP Cen. Cttee 2005–06; Vice-Chair. China Banking Regulatory Comm. 2010–16; Sec. CCP Cttee, Agricultural Bank of China Ltd May 2016–, Exec. Chair. June 2016–. *Address:* Agricultural Bank of China Ltd, 69 Jianguomen Nei Avenue, Dongcheng District, Beijing 100005, People's Republic of China (office). *Telephone:* (10) 85109619 (office). *Fax:* (10) 85108557 (office). *E-mail:* webmaster@intl.abocn.com (office); ir@abchina.com (office). *Website:* www.abchina.com (office).

ZHOU, Qiang, LLB, LLM; Chinese lawyer and government official; *President, Supreme People's Court;* b. 1960, Huangmei Co., Hubei Prov.; ed Southwest Univ. of Political Science and Law, Chongqing; began career with Ministry of Justice, several roles including Cadre, Policy Research Office 1985–89, Deputy Chief, Statute Bureau, Law and Statute Dept 1989–91, Chief, Statute Bureau 1991–93, Deputy Dir, Ministry of Justice Gen. Office 1993–95, Leader, Legal System Bureau 1995; mem. Communist Youth League of China Cen. Cttee Secr. 1995–97, co-Sec. 13th Cen. Cttee Secr. 1995, Exec. Sec. 1997–98, First Sec. 1998–2006; Deputy, 9th NPC 1998–2003, 10th NPC 2003–08, 11th NPC 2008–13, mem. NPC Internal and Judicial Affairs Cttee 1998–2003; Deputy Sec., Hunan CCP Prov. Cttee 2006–10, Sec. 2010–13; Acting Gov. Hunan Prov. 2006–07, Gov. 2007–10; Chair. Standing Cttee, Hunan Prov. People's Congress 2010–13; Pres. Supreme People's Court 2013–; mem. 16th CCP Cen. Cttee 2002–07, 17th CCP Cen. Cttee 2007–12, 18th CCP Cen. Cttee 2012–. *Address:* Supreme People's Court, Qianmen Dongdajie, Dongcheng District, Beijing, People's Republic of China (office). *Website:* en.chinacourt.org (office).

ZHOU, Qifeng; Chinese chemist, academic and university administrator; *President, International Union of Pure and Applied Chemistry (IUPAC);* b. Oct. 1947, Hunan; ed Peking Univ., Univ. of Massachusetts, USA; mem. of Faculty, Peking Univ. 1970–, Assoc. Prof. 1990, Prof. 1999, Pres. Peking Univ. 2008–13; Dir Grad. Student Affairs Office, Ministry of Educ. 2001–03; Dir State Academic Affairs Cttee 2001–03, Deputy Sec.-Gen. 2003–04; Pres. Jilin Univ. 2004–08; Pres. Int. Union of Pure and Applied Chem. (IUPAC) 2018–; mem. Jury of WISE Prize for Educ. 2014; mem. Chinese Acad. of Sciences 1999–; mem. Nat. Natural Science Foundation of China 2004–. *Address:* Peking University, College of Chemistry and Molecular Engineering, No. 5 Yiheyuan Road, Haidian District, Beijing 100871, People's Republic of China (office); IUPAC Secretariat, PO Box 13757, Research Triangle Park, NC 27709-3757, USA. *Telephone:* (919) 485-8700 (IUPAC Secretariat) (office). *E-mail:* qfzhou@pku.edu.cn (office); qfzhou@iupac.org (office). *Website:* www.chem.pku.edu.cn (office); iupac.org (office).

ZHOU, Shengxian; Chinese politician (retd); b. 30 Dec. 1949, Wuzhong, Ningxia Hui Autonomous Region; ed Wuzhong Teachers' Coll. and CCP Cen. Cttee Cen. Party School; teacher Weizhou Middle School, Tongxian Co. 1969–79; joined CCP 1972; Deputy Magistrate Tongxian Co. 1981–83; Sec. CCP Tongxian Co. Cttee 1983–86; Sec. CCP Xiji Co. Cttee 1986–89; Vice-Chair. People's Govt of Ningxia Hui Autonomous Region 1993–2003; Deputy Dir State Admin. for Forestry 1999–2000, Dir 2000–05 (also Sec. CCP Leading Party Group 2000–05); Minister, Environmental Protection Admin. 2005–08, Minister of Environmental Protection 2008–15; Alt. mem. 16th CCP Cen. Cttee 2002–07, mem. 17th CCP Cen. Cttee 2007–12, 18th CCP Cen. Cttee 2012–17, 18th CCP Cen. Cttee 2017–.

ZHOU, Shouwei; Chinese engineer and petroleum industry executive; b. 1950; ed Southwest Petroleum Inst.; joined China Nat. Offshore Oil Corpn (CNOOC) 1983, Deputy Gen. Man. China Offshore Oil Bohai Corpn (subsidiary co.), Gen. Man.

Tianjin Br., CNOOC China Ltd, Exec Dir 1999–, Exec. Vice-Pres. 1999–2002, Pres. 2002–09, Vice-Pres. CNOOC 2000–15, also Dir CNOOC Int. Ltd, Exec Dir CNOOC Engineering Co. Ltd (subsidiary co.) 1999–2015, Chair. 2003, Chair. CNOOC Southeast Asia Ltd (subsidiary co.) 2003–15, Chair. Offshore Oil Engineering Co. Ltd 2003–10, Exec. Dir CNOOC Ltd 1999–2009, Dir (non-exec.) 2009–14; Pres. 7th Council of China Petroleum & Petrochemical Equipment Industry Asscn 2010–; Academician, Chinese Acad. of Eng (Energy and Mining Div.) 2009.

ZHOU, Wenzhong; Chinese diplomatist; b. Aug. 1945, Jiangsu Prov.; m.; one d.; ed Univ. of Bath and London School of Econs, UK; staff mem., Beijing Diplomatic Service Bureau 1970–73, univ. studies 1973–75, staff mem., Dept of Trans. and Interpretation, Ministry of Foreign Affairs 1975–78, Attaché, then Third Sec., Washington, DC 1978–83, Second Sec., Deputy Div. Dir, then Div. Dir Dept of Translation and Interpretation, Ministry of Foreign Affairs 1983–87, Deputy Consul-Gen., San Francisco 1987–90, Amb. to Barbados and Antigua and Barbuda 1990–93, Deputy Dir-Gen. N American and Oceanic Affairs Dept, Ministry of Foreign Affairs 1993–94, Consul-Gen., Los Angeles 1994–95, Deputy Chief of Mission, Embassy in Washington, DC 1995–98, Amb. to Australia 1998–2001, Asst Minister of Foreign Affairs 2001–03, Vice-Minister of Foreign Affairs 2003–05, Amb. to USA 2005–10; apptd Sec.-Gen. Boao Forum for Asia 2010; Vice-Pres. China-US People's Friendship Asscn 2010–. *Address:* Secretariat of Boao Forum for Asia, Room 2210, China World Tower, 1 Jianguomenwai Avenue, Beijing 100004, People's Republic of China (office). *Telephone:* (10) 65057377 (office). *Fax:* (10) 65051833 (office). *E-mail:* bfa@boaoforum.org (office). *Website:* english .boaoforum.org (office).

ZHOU, Xiaochuan, PhD; Chinese economist and fmr central banker; *Chief Representative and Vice-Chairman, Boao Forum for Asia;* b. 29 Jan. 1948, Dongan, Heilongjiang Prov.; s. of Zhou Jiannan; ed Beijing Chemical Eng Inst., Tsinghua Univ.; worker, Beijing Inst. of Automation; Deputy Dir Inst. of Chinese Econ. Reform Research 1986–87; mem. State Council Econ. Policy Group 1986–87; Asst Minister of Foreign Trade and Econ. Co-operation 1986–89; mem. Nat. Cttee on Econ. Reform 1986–91; Deputy Gov. People's Bank of China (PBOC) 1991–95, 1996–98, Gov. 2002–18 (retd), mem. Policy Comm. 2000– (also CCP Sec.); Dir State Admin of Foreign Exchange 1995–98; Pres. China Construction Bank 1998–2000; Chair. China Securities Regulatory Comm. 2000–02; Prof., Tsinghua Univ. School of Man., Grad. School PBOC, Univ. of Science and Tech. of China Business School; mem. Group of Thirty Consultative Group on Int. Econ. and Monetary Affairs, Inc. (G-30), Washington, DC; mem. 16th CCP Cen. Cttee 2002–07, 17th CCP Cen. Cttee 2007–12; Vice-Chair. 12th CPPCC Nat. Cttee 2013–; Chief Rep. and Vice-Chair., Boao Forum for Asia 2018–; Hon. Pres. Univ. of Science and Tech. of China Business School. *Publications include:* more than 12 monographs and 100 journal articles on econ. reform including Rebuilding the Relationship Between the Enterprise and the Bank (Sun Zhifang Economics Thesis Prize 1994), Marching Toward an Open Economic System (An Zijie Int. Trade Publication Award 1994), Social Security: Reform and Policy Recommendations (Sun Zhifang Economics Thesis Prize 1997). *Leisure interest:* tennis. *Address:* Boao Forum of Asia, Room 2210,China World Tower A, No. 1 Jianguomenwai Avenue, Beijing 100004, People's Republic of China (office). *Telephone:* (10) 65057377 (office). *Fax:* (10) 65051833 (office). *E-mail:* bfa@boaoforum.org (office). *Website:* english.boaoforum .org.

ZHOU, Xuhong, PhD; Chinese engineer, academic and university administrator; *President, Chongqing University;* b. Oct. 1956, Hunan Prov.; ed Hunan Univ.; Asst Engineer, China State Construction Eng Corpn 1982–84; Assoc. Prof., Civil Eng Dept, Hunan Univ. 1986–94, Prof. 1994–96, also Vice-Dean, Civil Eng Dept 1994–96, Head, Civil Eng Grad. School 1996–99, Vice-Pres. Hunan Univ. 1999–2002; Pres. Chang'an Univ. 2002–06; Pres. Lanzhou Univ. 2006–13; Pres. Chongqing Univ. 2013–; Vice-Pres. China Steel Structure Asscn; mem. Chinese Acad. of Eng; Nat. Science Progress Award, Hubei Prov. Science Progress Award, Chinese Univs Science Progress Award, Hunan Prov. Teaching Achievements Prize. *Publications:* over 280 research papers in nat. and int. journals. *Address:* Office of the President, Chongqing University, 174 Shazhengjie, Shapingba, Chongqing 400044, People's Republic of China (office). *Website:* cqu.edu.cn (office).

ZHOU, Xun; Chinese actress and singer; b. 18 Oct. 1976, Quzhou, Zhejiang; d. of Zhou Tianning and Chen Yiqin; m. Archie Kao 2014; ed Zhejiang Arts Inst. *Films include:* Old Grave 1991, Nü'er Hong 1994, Temptress Moon 1995, The Pampered Wife 1995, My Rice Noodle Shop 1998, The Emperor and the Assassin 1999, Suzhou River 2000, Beijing Bicycle 2001, Hollywood Hong Kong 2001, A Pinwheel Without Wind 2002, Where Have All the Flowers Gone 2002, Balzac and the Little Chinese Seamstress (Paris Film Festival Best Actress Award 2002) 2002, A West Lake Moment 2004, Beauty Remains 2004, Baobei in Love (Chinese Director's Association Award for Best Actress 2004) 2004, Stolen Life 2005, Perhaps Love (Hong Kong Film Critics Society Award for Best Actress 2005, Hong Kong Film Award for Best Actress 2006, Golden Bauhinia Award for Best Actress 2006, Golden Horse Award for Best Actress 2006) 2005, The Banquet (Hong Kong Film Award for Best Supporting Actress 2007, Golden Bauhinia Award for Best Supporting Actress 2007) 2006, Ming Ming 2006, The Equation of Love and Death (Asian Film Award for Best Actress 2009) 2008, Painted Skin 2008, All About Women 2008, The Message 2009, Confucius 2010, True Legend 2010, The Founding of a Party 2011, The Flying Swords of Dragon Gate 2011, The Great Magician 2011, Painted Skin: The Resurrection 2012, The Silent War 2012, Cloud Atlas 2012, Women Who Flirt 2014, Overheard 3 2014, Meet Miss Anxiety 2014. *Television includes* Hongchufang 1997, Palace of Desire 1998, Taiping Tianguo 1998, Jingtan Fengyun 1998, Lüvi Hongniang 1999, April Rhapsody 1999, Kaixin Jiuhao 1999, Yuanlai Yijiaren 1999, Love Story in Shanghai 2000, Jinqian Bense 2000, Xin Wang 2000, Ripening Orange 2001, The Legend of the Condor Heroes 2002, Beach 2003, Business Family 2003, Red Sorghum 2015. *Recordings:* albums: Summer 2003, Come Across 2005. *Address:* c/o Huayi Brothers Artist Agency, Huayi Brothers Media Corporation, Shunyi, Tianzhu, Wenyu River, Lou Tai Duan, Beijing, 101312, People's Republic of China (office). *Telephone:* (86) 10-6457-9338 (office). *E-mail:* stars@huayimedia.com (office). *Website:* www.hbstars.com (office).

ZHOU, Yaohe, DrSciTech; Chinese metallurgist; *Professor, School of Material Science and Engineering, Shanghai Jiao Tong University;* b. 30 May 1927, Beijing; ed Yaohua High School, Tsinghua Univ., Beijing, Moscow Institute of Steel and

Iron, USSR; Asst Lecturer Dept of Mechanical Eng, Nankai Univ. 1950–52; Prof. School of Materials Science and Eng, Northwest Polytechnic Univ. 1957–; Prof. School of Materials Science and Eng, Shanghai Jiao Tong Univ. 1996–; Pres. Casting Soc. of China Machinery Eng Soc. and Chair. Int. Soc. of Casting; Fellow, Chinese Acad. of Sciences 1991–; Nat. Science and Tech. Advancement Award, Nat. Invention Award and five ministerial awards. *Publications:* more than 200 publs in scientific journals. *Address:* Shanghai Jiao Tong University, Shanghai, People's Republic of China (office). *Telephone:* (21) 62932026 (office). *E-mail:* yhzh@sjtu.edu.cn (office). *Website:* www2.sjtu.edu.cn (office).

ZHOU, Yiping; Chinese economist, diplomatist and UN official; b. 1955; ed Fudan Univ. of Shanghai, Canberra Coll. of Advanced Educ., Australia; served in Perm. Mission to UN, New York 1984–85, Policy Officer, Dept of Int. Relations, Ministry of Foreign Econ. Relations and Trade 1980–84, Project Man. Officer, Office for Project Services 1985–92; Regional Programme Officer, UNDP Regional Bureau for Asia and the Pacific 1992–97; Deputy Dir and Sr Policy Adviser, Special Unit for South-South Cooperation, UN 1997–2004, Envoy of Sec.-Gen. on South-South Cooperation 2014–16, Dir UN Unit for South-South Cooperation 2014–16; Ed.-in-Chief Cooperation South.

ZHOU, Yongkang; Chinese government official; b. Dec. 1942, Wuxi City, Jiangsu Prov.; ed Beijing Petroleum Inst.; joined CCP 1964; intern and technician, Geological Survey Team, No. 673 Factory, Daqing, Heilongjiang Inst. 1967–70; Brigade Leader, Regional Office and technician, Geological Survey Regt, Liaohe Oil Exploration Campaign HQ 1970–73 (also Sec. CCP Party Br.), Dir Geophysical Survey Div., Liaohe Oil Exploration Bureau 1973–76, Deputy Dir Political Dept 1976–79, Deputy Dir-Gen. Liaohe Petroleum Exploration Bureau 1979–83 (also Party Sec. Drilling HQ and Geophysical Survey Div., CCP Party Cttee), Commdr Geophysical Survey Div. 1979–83, Dir-Gen. Liaohe Petroleum Exploration Bureau 1983–85 (also Deputy Sec. CCP Party Cttee); Mayor of Panjin City, Liaoning Prov. 1983–85, Vice-Sec. CCP Panjin City Cttee 1983–85; Vice-Minister of Petroleum Industry 1985–88; Deputy Gen. Man. China Nat. Petroleum Corpn 1988–96, Gen. Man. 1996–98 (also Sec. CCP Leading Party Group); Gen. Man. Head Office of China Petroleum and Natural Gas Company 1996–98; Commdr Tarim Oil Exploration Campaign HQ 1988–96 (also Sec. CCP Party Cttee 1989–90); Sec. CCP Dongying City Cttee, Shandong Prov. 1988–96; Dir-Gen. Petroleum Admin, Shengli, Shandong Prov. 1988–96 (Sec. CCP Party Cttee); Minister of Land and Resources 1998–99 (also Sec. CCP Leading Party Group); Sec. CCP Sichuan Prov. Cttee 1999–2002; State Councillor 2003–08; Minister of Public Security 2002–07; Alt. mem. 14th CCP Cen. Cttee 1992–97, mem. 15th CCP Cen. Cttee 1997–2002, 16th CCP Cen. Cttee 2002–07, 16th CCP Politburo 2003–07, CCP Politburo Secr. 2002–07, 17th CCP Cen. Cttee 2007–12, 17th CCP Politburo Standing Cttee 2007–12, Sec. Political and Legis. Affairs Cttee, CCP Cen. Cttee 2007–12 (retd); accused of several crimes including bribery 2013, arrested and expelled from Party 2014, charged with bribery and abuse of power April 2015.

ZHOU, Zhongshu, BA; Chinese business executive; b. Nov. 1952, Xuzhou, Jiangsu Prov.; ed Shanghai Inst. of Foreign Languages; Deputy Dir 7th Dept, China Nat. Metals and Minerals Corpn (China Minmetals Corpn) 1985, successively promoted to Exec. Pres. Minmetals Brazil 1988, Gen. Man. Minmetals 1990, Asst to the Pres. 1993–94, Sr Vice-Pres. Minmetals 1994, Pres. 2004–14, Chair. Minmetals Devt Co.; Co-Chair. China Business Summit.

ZHOU, Zhuping, MEng; Chinese accountant and business executive; *Chairman of the Board of Supervisors, China Pacific Insurance (Group) Company Ltd;* ed Tianjin Univ.; began career at Baosteel 1994, served as Dir of Finance Dept and Vice-Pres. Baosteel Int. Economic & Trading Co. Ltd, Deputy Chief Financial Officer Baosteel Int. Trade Corpn, Deputy Gen. Man. Baoshan Iron & Steel Trading Co. Ltd, Dir of Operations, Baosteel Group Corpn, Gen. Man. Baosteel Group Enterprise Devt Corpn, Pres. Baosteel Devt Co. Ltd, Deputy Dir of Planning and Finance Dept, Shanghai Baosteel Group Corpn, Sec. to Bd of Dirs, Baoshan Iron & Steel Co. Ltd, Vice-Financial Pres. Shanghai Baosteel Int. Econs & Trading Co. Ltd, Vice-Pres. Trading Br. of Baoshan Iron & Steel Co. Ltd, currently Chair. Baosteel Group Finance Co. Ltd, Baosteel Finance Co. Ltd and Fortune Investment Co. Ltd, Supervisor of Bd of Supervisors, Baoshan Iron & Steel Co. Ltd 2006–, Deputy Gen. Man., Shanghai Baosteel Group Corpn 2008–, Vice-Pres. 2009–; fmr Deputy Dir Finance Dept, Luzhong Metallurgical Mining Co.; Chair. Bd of Supervisors, China Pacific Insurance (Group) Co. Ltd 2010–; mem. CCP. *Address:* China Pacific Insurance (Group) Co. Ltd, 190 Yincheng Zhong Road, Shanghai 200120, Shanghai Province, People's Republic of China (office). *Telephone:* (21) 58776688 (office). *Fax:* (21) 68870922 (office). *E-mail:* info@cpic .com.cn (office). *Website:* www.cpic.com.cn (office).

ZHOU, Gen. Ziyu; Chinese army officer; b. Nov. 1935, Wucheng, Shandong Prov.; joined PLA 1951, CCP 1955; political instructor, Air Force Aviation School, rose to rank of Political Commissar, Maj.-Gen. of PLA Air Force 1988, Gen. 1996; Deputy Dir PLA Gen. Political Dept 1993–2000; Deputy Sec. CCP Cen. Comm. for Discipline Inspection 1997–2002; Deputy, 8th NPC 1993–98; mem. 15th CCP Cen. Cttee 1997–2002; mem. CPPCC Nat. Cttee, Standing Cttee 2003.

ZHU, Fushou, BEng, MBA; Chinese automotive industry executive; b. Oct. 1962, Tongcheng, Anhui Prov.; ed Hefei Univ. of Tech., Zhongnan Univ. of Econs and Law; joined Dongfeng Motor Corpn 1984, Deputy Man. Dir Wheel Co. 1994–97, Deputy Gen. Man. Dongfeng Motor Wheel Co. Ltd 1997–99, Chair. and Gen. Man. 1999–2000, Gen. Man. and Sec. Party Cttee of Light Duty Vehicle Plant, Dongfeng Automobile Co. Ltd Feb.–Oct. 2000, Deputy Gen. Man. Dongfeng Motor Corpn, Gen. Man., Sec. Party Cttee of Automobiles Subsidiary Co. of Dongfeng Automobile Co. Ltd 2000–02, mem. Standing Cttee of Party Cttee of Dongfeng Motor Corpn and Gen. Man. Dongfeng Automobile Co. Ltd 2001–03, Gen. Man. 2003–05, Vice-Pres. Dongfeng Motor Corpn 2005–10, Dir (non-exec.) 2004–10, Pres. and Exec. Dir 2010–11, Gen. Man. and Pres. 2011–15; placed under investigation by CCP's Cen. Comm. for Discipline Inspection Nov. 2015, expelled from party and demoted Jan. 2016; honoured as a sr engineer 1997.

ZHU, Jimin; Chinese business executive; *Chairman and Party Secretary, Shougang Corporation;* served as Deputy Gen. Man. and Gen. Man. Shougang Gen. Co., currently Chair. and Party Sec. Shougang Corpn, Vice-Chair. Shougang Gen. Co. –2002, Chair. 2002–, Chair. Beijing Shougang Co. Ltd, Shougang Jingtang Iron & Steel United Co. Ltd 2011–. *Address:* Shougang Corporation, 68

Shijingshan Road, Beijing 100041, People's Republic of China (office). *Telephone:* (10) 88291114 (office). *Fax:* (10) 88294218 (office). *E-mail:* info@shougang.com.cn (office). *Website:* www.shougang.com.cn (office).

ZHU, Mengyi; Chinese real estate executive; *Chairman, Hopson Development Holding Ltd;* b. 1959, Fengshun, Guangdong Prov.; Chair. Hopson Devt Holding Ltd, Guangdong Zhujiang Investment, Tianjin Real Estate; mem. 11th CPPCC Nat. Cttee 2008–13. *Address:* Hopson Development Holding Ltd, 16/F Zhujiang Investment Building, 421 Zhujiang East Road, Zhujiang New City, Guangzhou 510623, Gaungdong, People's Republic of China (office). *E-mail:* info@hopson.com.cn (office). *Website:* www.hopson.com.cn (office).

ZHU, Mingshan; Chinese jurist; b. May 1937, Jiutai Co., Jilin Prov.; two s.; ed People's Univ., Beijing; joined CCP 1961; exiled to countryside during Cultural Revolution 1966–76; judge, Criminal Court, Supreme People's Court 1978–82, Vice-Pres. 1982–83, Vice-Pres. Supreme People's Court 1983–2003 (title of Grand Justice); apptd Vice-Chair. NPC Cttee for Internal and Judicial Affairs 2006.

ZHU, Qingshi, FRSC; Chinese physical chemist, university administrator and academic; b. 7 Feb. 1946, Chengdu, Sichuan Prov.; ed Univ. of Science and Tech. of China; workman, later planner, Xining Mountain-River Machine Tool Foundry, Qinghai Prov. 1968–74; trainee Research Fellow and Asst Research Fellow, Qinghai Salt Lake Inst., Chinese Acad. of Sciences (CAS) 1974–84, transferred to Dalian Inst. of Chemical Physics, CAS, working successively as leader of research group, dir of research lab., Assoc. Research Fellow and Research Fellow; teacher and researcher, Univ. of Science and Tech. of China (USTC) 1994–96, Vice-Pres. 1996–98, Pres. 1998–2008; Founding Pres. South Univ. of Science and Technology of China 2009–14; Visiting Scholar, Univ. of Calif., Santa Barbara, MIT; Guest Scientist, Brookhaven Nat. Lab., USA, Nat. Research Council of Canada; Guest Prof., Univ. of Grenoble, Univ. of Dijon, Univ. of Paris-Sud, France, Univ. of Helsinki, Finland; Guest Research Fellow, Royal Soc., worked at Univs of Cambridge, Oxford and Nottingham, UK; Exec. mem. Bd of Dirs China Soc. of Chem.; mem. Bd of Dirs Br. of Physical Chem., IUPAC; Vice-Chair. China Soc. of Scientific History, Asscn of East Asia Research Univs, China Soc. of Dialectics of Nature; Deputy to 8th and 9th NPC; Vice-Pres. Anhui Prov. Asscn of Science and Tech.; Academician, CAS 1991; Fellow, Third World Acad. of Sciences 2001; Hon. DrSc (Soka Univ., Nottingham Univ.); SOCP Award for Achievements in Asia 1994, Thompson Memorial Award, Spectrochimica Acta 1994. *Publications:* Green Chemistry 1998, The Collected Works of Qinghsi Zhu 2000, Dynamics of Quantum Transitions in Laser Field (co-author) 2000; more than 140 articles and papers.

ZHU, Senlin; Chinese politician; b. Oct. 1930, Chuansha Co., Shanghai; ed Qinghua Univ.; Deputy Sec.-Gen. and Dir-Gen. Gen. Office Guangzhou City Cttee of CCP 1981–83; later Deputy Sec. Guangzhou City Cttee of CCP and Mayor of Guangzhou City; mem. Guangdong Provincial Cttee of CCP and Sec. Guangzhou City Party Cttee; Deputy Sec. Guangzhou Provincial Party Cttee, Acting Gov. 1991–93, Gov. of Guangdong Prov. 1992–96; Chair. Guangdong Provincial People's Congress 1996–2001; Alt. mem. 13th CCP Cen. Cttee 1987–92, 14th CCP Cen. Cttee 1992–97; Deputy to 7th, 8th and 9th NPC 1988–2003.

ZHU, Shanzhong, BA, MA; Chinese international organization official; *Executive Director, World Tourism Organization;* b. 1953, Nantong City, Jiangsu; ed Nanjing Univ., The New School, New York; Dept Man., China Int. Travel Service 1985–89; Dir Sydney Office and New York Office, China Nat. Tourism Admin, Deputy Dir-Gen. Int. Marketing, Dir-Gen. Marketing and Communication Dept, Vice-Chair. 2008–13; Exec. Dir Tech. Cooperation and Services, World Tourism Org. 2013–2018, Exec. Dir 2018–; mem. China Nat. Tourism Admin, Communist Party of China. *Address:* World Tourism Organization, Calle Capitan Haya 42, 28020 Madrid, Spain (office). *Telephone:* (91) 5678100 (office). *Fax:* (91) 5678218 (office). *E-mail:* comm@unwto.org (office). *Website:* www2.unwto.org (office).

ZHU, Xiaohua, PhD; Chinese mathematician and academic; *Professor of Mathematics, Peking University;* b. 1968; ed Hangzhou Univ.; Post-doctor, Dept of Math., Zhejiang Univ. 1997–99; Post-doctor, School of Math. Sciences, Peking Univ. 1997–99, Assoc. Prof. of Math. 1999–2001, Prof. of Math. 2001–; Researcher, Australian Nat. Univ. Math. Center 2002–04; Visiting Prof., Univ. of Wisconsin-Madison 2006; Simons Visiting Prof., Stony-Brook Univ., New York 2009; Einsenbud Visiting Prof., Univ. of Calif., Berkeley 2016; Chair. Organizing Cttee, Pacific Rim Complex Geometry Conf. 2006, 2013; expert in studies on complex differential geometry; Qiu Shi Science and Tech. Prize 2001, Int. Centre for Theoretical Physics (ICTP) Prize 2005, Nat. Science and Tech. Award 2013, Chern Award, Chinese Math. Soc. 2017. *Publications:* numerous papers in professional journals. *Address:* School of Mathematical Sciences, 1375 E, Building 1, Peking University, No.5 Yiheyuan Road, Haidian District, Beijing 100871, People's Republic of China (office). *Fax:* (10) 62759408 (office). *E-mail:* xhzhu@math.pku.edu.cn (office). *Website:* www.math.pku.edu.cn (office).

ZHU, Xiaohua; Chinese government official; b. 23 Jan. 1940, Xi'an, Shanxi Prov.; m. Li Yazhi 1962; three s.; ed Shanghai Univ. of Finance and Econs; with People's Bank of China 1979–90, positions include Deputy Dir, Financial Research Division, Deputy Pres. Shanghai Office, Deputy Gov. People's Bank of China 1993–96; Special Appointee IMF 1991–92; apptd Deputy Dir Science and Tech. Dept, State Family Planning Comm. 1992; Deputy Dir Econs Dept, Xinhua News Agency, Hong Kong 1992–93; Dir-Gen. State Admin of Foreign Exchange Control 1993–96; Chair. and CEO China Everbright Holdings Co. Ltd, Hong Kong 1996–99; charged with corruption; expelled from CCP Aug. 2002; convicted of bribery and sentenced to 15 years' imprisonment Oct. 2002.

ZHU, Xiaohuang, PhD; Chinese economist and business executive; *Chairman of the Board of Supervisors, CITIC Group Corporation;* b. July 1956; positions held include Deputy Dir of Gen. Office, China Construction Bank, Deputy Dir of Credit Div. I, Deputy Dir-Gen. of Credit Man. Dept, Deputy Gen. Man. Liaoning Br., Dir-Gen. of Business Dept, Gen. Man. Guangdong Br., Dir-Gen. of Corp. Business Dept, Chief Risk Officer, Vice-Pres. and Exec. Dir; Vice-Pres. CITIC, Gov. of Citic Bank, Chair. Bd of Supervisors, CITIC Group Corpn 2014–. *Address:* CITIC Group Corporation, Capital Mansion, 6 Xinuan Nanlu, Beijing 10004, People's Republic of China (office). *Telephone:* (10) 64660088 (office). *Fax:* (10) 64661186 (office). *Website:* www.citic.com (office); www.citic.com.cn (office).

ZHU, Xun; Chinese state official; b. 1930, Funing Co., Jiangsu Prov.; ed China People's Univ. and in USSR; joined CCP 1946; Vice-Minister of Geology and Minerals 1982–85, Minister 1985–94; Alt. mem. 12th CCP Cen. Cttee 1982, mem. 1985–87, mem. 13th CCP Cen. Cttee 1987–92, 14th CCP Cen. Cttee 1992–97; Sec.-Gen. 8th Nat. Cttee CPPCC 1994–98; Chair. Cttee for Liaison with Hong Kong, Macao, Taiwan and Overseas Chinese Affairs, 9th CPPCC Nat. Cttee 1998–2003; Hon. mem. Int. Hydrogeologists' Asscn 1989; Hon. Academician, Russian Acad. of Natural Sciences 1996, Int. Euro-Asian Acad. of Sciences 1999; Boris Yeltsin Friendship Medal 1999. *Publications:* Introduction to Ore-Seeking Philosophy, Mineral Resources in China, Geo-science and Sustainable Development. *Leisure interests:* swimming, walking, music, film.

ZHU, Yanfeng; Chinese automobile industry executive and government official; *Executive Chairman, Dongfeng Motor Corporation;* b. 1961, Fenghua City, Zhejiang Prov.; ed Zhejiang Univ.; joined CCP 1982; joined China FAW Group Corpn as technician 1983, served as Deputy Dir Research Dept, Metering Div. 1986, Dir Foreign Econ. Div. 1994–97, Vice-Pres. China FAW Group Corpn 1997–98, Exec. Vice-Pres. 1998–99, Pres. 1999–2007, also Pres. FAW Sedan Co. 1997; Chair. Tianjin Automobile Group Corpn 2002–06; Vice-Gov. Jilin Prov. from 2007, also Deputy Sec. of Prov. CCP Cttee; Exec. Chair. Dongfeng Motor Corpn and Sec. DFM Party Cttee 2015–; Alt. mem. 16th CCP Cen. Cttee 2002–07, 17th CCP Cen. Cttee 2007–12, 18th CCP Cen. Cttee 2012–; Chair. CIFE Presidium. *Address:* Dongfeng Motor Corporation, 29 Baiye Road, Wuhan 430015, Hubei Province, People's Republic of China (office). *Telephone:* (719) 8226-962 (office). *Fax:* (719) 8226-845 (office). *E-mail:* info@dfmc.com.cn (office). *Website:* www.dfmc.com.cn (office).

ZHU, Yinghuang, MA; Chinese journalist, translator and academic; b. 28 Dec. 1943, Shanghai; m. Yao Xiang 1972; one d.; ed Fudan Univ., Stanford Univ., USA; mem. teaching faculty, Shangdong Normal Univ. 1977; Ed.-in-Chief, China Daily 1993–2004, Ed.-in-Chief Emer. 2004–; currently Sr Visiting Prof. of Journalism and Communications, Tsinghua Univ.; also Prof., China Communication Univ.; Doctoral tutor, China Communications Univ.; Vice-Chair. China Translation Asscn, China Pacific Econ. Cooperation Cttee; Special Adviser to China-US Exchange Foundation; mem. CPPCC 2003–08; mem. Foreign Policy Advisory Cttee of Chinese Foreign Ministry; took part in translation work of Basic Law of Hong Kong Special Admin. Region 1987–88; Outstanding Journalist of China 1984. *Publications include:* Translations: Inside Stories of Australia and New Zealand, The Memoirs of Dwight Whip, The Rich and Super Rich, Socialist Democratic Parties in Western Europe, Three Generations of a Newspaper Tycoon. *Address:* c/o China Daily, 15 Huixin Dongjie, Chao Yang Qu, Beijing 100029, People's Republic of China (office). *Telephone:* (10) 64995027 (office); (10) 64280990 (home). *Fax:* (10) 64918377 (office). *E-mail:* yhzhu@chinadaily.com.cn (office). *Website:* www.chinadaily.com.cn (office).

ZHU, Yongpeng, BEng; Chinese engineer and business executive; b. 1950, Shanghai; ed Electric Power Eng Dept, Northeast Dianli Univ.; began career in electric power industry 1968; joined CCP 1981; professor-level Sr Engineer with governmental special allowance issued by the State Council; served as Deputy Shift Supervisor, Heilongjiang Hulin Power Plant; successively, Technician, Asst Engineer, Engineer and Deputy Div. Chief in Tech. Div., Electric Power Production Dept, Ministry of Water Conservancy and Electric Power, as Div. Chief of Integrated Man. Div. of Electric Power Dept, Ministry of Energy, as Exec. Vice-Pres. and mem. Leading Party Group, later Pres. and Sec. Leading Party Group, China Longyuan Power Group Corpn, Ministry of Electric Power, as Vice-Chair., Pres. and Sec. Leading Party Group, GD Power Devt Co. Ltd, as Exec. Vice-Pres. and mem. Party Group, as Vice-Gen. Man. China Guodian Group 2002–08, as Pres. and Assoc. Sec. Leading Party Group, China Guodian Corpn, Chair. and Gen. Man. 2007–13, Chief Legal Advisor 2008–13; Dir (non-exec.) China Longyuan Power Group Corpn Ltd 2009–13. *Address:* c/o China Guodian Corporation, 6–8 Fuchengmen Bei Street, Beijing 100034, People's Republic of China. *E-mail:* cgdcb@cgdc.com.cn.

ZHUKOV, Aleksandr Dmitreyevich, MBA; Russian politician and economist; *First Deputy Chairman, State Duma (Parliament);* b. 1 June 1956, Moscow; s. of Dmitrii Anatolyevich Zhukov; m. Yekaterina Zhukova; one s.; ed Moscow State Univ., Harvard Univ., USA; mem. All-Union Research Inst. of Systems Studies and State Cttee on Science and Tech. –1980; mem. Chief Currency Econ. Dept, USSR Ministry of Finance 1980–91; Vice-Pres. Avtotractorexport Co., Ministry of Foreign Trade 1991–93; mem. State Duma (Parl.) 1993–2004, Chair. Cttee on Budget, Taxes, Banks and Finance 1997–2003, Deputy Chair. of Govt 2004–11, First Deputy Chair., State Duma 2012–; Pres. Russian Chess Fed. 2003–09, Russian Olympic Cttee 2010–; Order of Honour 2003, Order of Merit for the Fatherland (Fourth Class) 2006, (Third Class) 2011, Order of Friendship 2007; Diploma of the Pres. of Russia 2009. *Address:* Office of the State Duma (Parliament), 103265 Moscow, Okhotny Riad 1, Russia (office). *Telephone:* (495) 692-17-85 (office). *Fax:* (495) 692-86-00 (office). *Website:* www.duma.ru (office).

ZHUMALIYEV, Kubanychbek Myrzabekovich; Kyrgyzstani scientist and politician; b. 26 April 1956, Kichik-Ak-Zhol, Osh Oblast; ed Ryazan' Radio Tech. Inst.; worked as scientific researcher in Frunze Polytechnical Inst. 1978–86, Inst. of Physics Nat. Acad. of Sciences 1986–88; Exec. Dir Scientific Cen. Zhalyn Acad. of Sciences 1988–92; Chair. State Cttee of Science and New Tech. 1992–94; First Vice-Minister of Educ. and Science 1994–95; First Deputy to Sec. of State 1995–96; Head, Admin. of Pres. Akayev 1996–98; Prime Minister of Kyrgyzstan 1998–2001; Gov., Jalal-Abad Oblast 1998–2001; Minister of Transport and Communications 2001–02; Deputy Prime Minister 2002; mem. Nat. Acad. of Sciences.

ZHURKIN, Vitaliy Vladimirovich, DPhil, DHist; Russian political scientist; *Honorary Director, Institute of Europe, Russian Academy of Sciences;* b. 14 Jan. 1928, Moscow; m. Dina Zhurkina 1961 (died 1997); one s.; ed Moscow Inst. of Int. Relations; Ed. USA: Economics, Politics, Ideology (journal); Deputy Dir USA and Canada Inst. 1971–87; Founder and Dir Inst. of Europe, USSR (now Russian) Acad. of Sciences 1987–99, Hon. Dir 1999–, Sec., Dept of Int. Relations, Acad. of Sciences 1991–97, Corresp. mem. USSR (now Russian) Acad. of Sciences 1984, mem. 1990; mem. Academia Europaea 1990, World Acad. of Art and Science 1994; USSR State Prize 1980; ten govt decorations. *Publications include:* works on the political and mil. aspects of contemporary int. relations, International Conflicts

1972, UN Study on Deterrence 1985, Building Greater Europe 1990, EU: Foreign Policy, Security, Defence 1998, European Security and Defence 2005, European Army – Defeats and Victories: EU Common Security and Defence Policy 2012. *Leisure:* trekking, collecting books. *Address:* Institute of Europe, 125993 Moscow, 11-3, Mokhovaya Street, Russia (office). *Telephone:* (495) 203-73-43 (office). *Fax:* (495) 200-42-98 (office). *E-mail:* europe@ieras.ru (office).

ZHVANETSKY, Mikhail Mikhailovich; Russian satirist, writer and TV presenter; b. 6 March 1934, Odessa; s. of Emmanuil Moiseevich Zhvanetsky and Raisa Yakovlevna Zhvanetskaya; m.; two s. one d.; ed Odessa Inst. of Naval Eng; worked as technician and engineer, Prodmash factory, Odessa shipbuilding yard 1956–64; literary work 1964–; wrote short stories for Comedy Theatre of A. Raikin; f. Odessa Miniature Theatre (with R. Kartsev and V. Ilchenko) 1970; performed readings of short stories 1970–; stories banned because of criticism of state; Founder and Artistic Dir Moscow Theatre of Miniatures; Pres. Odessa Int. Film Festival; Founder and Ed. Magazin journal 1991; Hon. Citizen of Odessa 1994; Order of Friendship of the Peoples 1994, Order of Merit for the Fatherland 2009; Triumph Prize 1994, People's Artist of Ukraine 1999, Meritorious Artist of Russian Fed. 2001, Merited Artist of Autonomous Repub. of Crimea, Ukraine 2002, People's Artist of Russia 2012. *Publications include:* Meetings in the Streets 1977, A Year For Two (short stories) 1989, My Life, Stay with Me (novel) 1989, Wir brauchen Helden! (short stories) 1992, My Odessa 1993 (short stories), Complete Works 2001; also stories in newspapers and periodicals. *Address:* 125047 Moscow, Lesnaya Str. 4, Apt 63, Russia (home).

ZIA, Begum Khaleda; Bangladeshi politician; b. 15 Aug. 1945; d. of Iskander Majumder and of Begum Taiyaba Majumder; m. Capt. Ziaur Rahman (later Pres. of Bangladesh) 1960 (deceased); two s.; ed Surendranath Coll., Dinajpur; held captive during Bangladesh's war of independence; Vice-Chair. Bangladesh Jatiyatabadi Dal (Bangladesh Nationalist Party) (BNP) 1982–84, Chair. 1984–2018; helped to form seven-party alliance leading to ousting of Pres. Ershad from power 1990; Prime Minister of Bangladesh 1991–96, 2001–06, Minister in charge of Armed Forces Div., Cabinet Div., Chittagong Hill Tracts Affairs, Defences, Establishment, Power, Energy and Mineral Resources, Primary and Mass Educ. 2001–06; Chair. SAARC 1993–95, 2005; sentenced to five years' imprisonment for corruption Feb. 2018, four-month bail granted March 2018. *Publications:* Together for Better Tomorrow: Speeches of Begum Khaleda Zia 1992, Visions for the Future: Selected Speeches of Begum Khaleda Zia 2002. *Leisure interests:* reading, listening to music, gardening. *Address:* c/o Bangladesh Nationalist Party, Banani Office, House 23, Road 13, Dhaka, Bangladesh (office). *Telephone:* (2) 8819525 (office). *Fax:* (2) 8813063 (office). *E-mail:* bnpbd@e-fsbd.net (office). *Website:* www.bnpbd.com (office).

ZIAD, Abu Amr, BA, MA, PhD; Palestinian academic, politician and government official; *Deputy Prime Minister;* b. 1950, Gaza City; m.; four c.; ed Damascus Univ., Syria, Georgetown Univ., USA; early career as teacher, Bahrain, Oman, Syria; elected mem. Palestinian Legis. Council (PLC) 1996 (ind.), re-elected 2006, Chair. PLC Political Cttee, mem. PLO-CC; Minister of Culture 2003, of Foreign Affairs March–June 2007; Prof. of Political Science, Birzeit Univ., Ramallah, West Bank 1985–96; Deputy Prime Minister 2013–; has done work for Centre for Policy Analysis on Palestine, Washington, DC and Centre for Palestine Research and Studies, Nablus; Pres. Palestinian Council on Foreign Relations; organised talks between the 12 major Palestinian factions within West Bank and Gaza to determine direction of intifada 2002; frequently serves as mediator between Hamas and Fatah. *Publications:* several books on books on Islamist movts and politics in Gaza 1948–67 including Islamic Fundamentalism in the West Bank and Gaza: Muslim Brotherhood and Islamic Jihad, Civil Society and Democratization in Palestine, The Significance of Jerusalem: A Muslim's Perspective and Emerging Trends in Palestinian Strategic Thinking and Practice.

ZIANKAHN, Maj.-Gen. Daniel D., BBA, MSc; Liberian army officer and politician; *Minister of Defence;* b. 12 July 1971, River Cess County; m. Nathaline Ziankahn; one s. one d.; ed African Methodist Episcopal Zion Univ., Monrovia, Coll. of US Army Command and Gen. Staff Coll., Fort Leavenworth, USA; enlisted into new Armed Forces of Liberia (AFL) July 2006; rank of Sergeant 2006, 2nd Lt 2007, 1st Lt 2009, Capt. 2010, Maj. 2012, Lt-Col 2013, Maj.-Gen. 2016; roles include Platoon Leader and later Exec. Officer and Co. Commdr, Alpha Co., 1st Bn, 23rd Infantry Brigade, Mil. Asst to Minister of Defence, AFL Deputy Asst Chief of Staff for Operations, becoming Chief of Staff, Armed Forces of Liberia 2014–18; Head, Econ. Community of West African States (ECOWAS) Chiefs of Defence Staff 2016; Minister of Defence 2018–. *Address:* Ministry of Defence, Benson St, POB 10-9007, 1000 Monrovia 10, Liberia (office). *Website:* mod.gov.lr (office).

ZIBARI, Hoshyar az-, BA, MA; Iraqi politician; b. 1953, Aqra, Iraqi Kurdistan; four s. one d.; ed Univ. of Jordan, Univ. of Essex, UK; responsible for Kurdish Student Soc. in Europe, Chair. Overseas Student Cttee, UK 1978–80; participated in armed resistance campaign against regime of Saddam Hussein 1980–88; elected to Cen. Cttee, Kurdistan Democratic Party (KDP) 1979, Chief Foreign Rep. 1988–91 (acted as a spokesman during the 1991 Gulf War), mem. Political Bureau and Chief Rep. of Kurdistan Front in Europe 1989, liaised with coalitions' Operation Provide Comfort and Mil. Coordinating Centre, Zakho, Iraqi Kurdistan 1991–95, Head of KDP Int. Relations Bureau 1992–2003; mem. Kurdistani Nat. Ass. 1992–; elected to Exec. Council Iraqi Nat. Congress (INC) 1992, Head of Int. Relations of the Iraqi Opposition 1992, mem. INC Leadership Council 1999, mem. Iraqi Opposition Coordination and Follow-Up Cttee 2002; Prin. Negotiator in Kurdish peace talks that produced Washington Peace Agreement between KDP and Patriotic Union of Kurdistan 1998; Interim Minister of Foreign Affairs 2003–05, Minister of Foreign Affairs 2005–14, of Finance 2014–16.

ZICO; Brazilian professional football coach, fmr professional football player and fmr politician; b. (Arthur Antunes Coimbra), 3 March 1953, Rio de Janeiro; s. of José Antunes Coimbra and Matilde da Silva Coimbra; m. Sandra de Sá Coimbra; three s.; playmaker/attacking midfielder; youth player for Flamengo 1967–71; sr player for Flamengo 1971–83, 1985–89 (212 appearances, 123 goals, won Rio State Championship 1972, 1974, 1978, 1979, 1979 (special), 1981, 1986, Brazilian Championship 1980, 1982, 1983, 1987, Libertadores Cup 1981, Intercontinental Cup 1981), Udinese 1983–85, Sumitomo Metals, Japan 1991–92, Kashima Antlers, Japan 1992–94 (won J League 1st Stage Championship 1993); player, Brazilian nat. team 1976–88, played in World Cup 1978, 1982, 1986, 72 caps, 52 goals; won Beach Soccer World Championship 1995, 1996, American Cup Beach Soccer 1995, 1996; became a politician on retirement and apptd Minister of Sport; retd from politics and launched new J League, Japan; Asst Coach to Mário Zagallo (q.v.), World Cup 1998; Man. Kashima Antlers 1999, Japan nat. team 2002–06 (won Asian Cup 2004), Fenerbahçe, Turkey 2006–08 (won Turkcell Super League 2006/07, Turkish Super Cup 2007), FC Bunyodkor, Uzbekistan 2008–09 (won Uzbekistani Cup 2008, Uzbek League 2008), PFC CSKA Moscow, Russia 2009 (won Russian Super Cup 2009, Russian Cup 2008/09), Olympiacos FC, Greece 2009–10, Iraq Nat. Team 2011–12; 'Bola de Ouro' Brazilian Footballer of the Year, Placar Magazine (Brazil) 1974, 1982, Silver Ball, Placar Magazine (Brazil) 1974, 1975, 1977, 1982, 1987, set goal record in a single season as Flamengo player (49 goals) 1974 (56 goals) 1976, Rio State Championship Top Scorer (30 goals) 1975, (27 goals) 1977, (19 goals) 1978, (26 goals) 1979, (Special, 34 goals) 1979, (21 goals) 1982, South American Footballer of the Year, El Mundo (Venezuela) 1977, 1981, Brazilian Championship Top Scorer (21 goals) 1980, (21 goals) 1982, Libertadores Cup Best Player 1981, Libertadores Cup Top Scorer (11 goals) 1981, Intercontinental Cup Best Player 1981, World Footballer of the Year, Guerin Esportivo (Italy), El Mundo (Venezuela), El Balón (Spain), Placar Magazine (Brazil) 1981, Brazilian Top Scorer of the Year (59 goals) 1982, World Cup Bronze Shoe 1982, World Cup All-Star Team Player 1982, South American Footballer of the Year, El Mundo (Venezuela), El Gráfico (Argentina) 1982, Player of the Year, World Soccer 1983, Premier Player of the Year, Italian League 1983/84 1984, second highest scorer of Italian League (19 goals) 1984, Third Best Player of the Year, World Soccer Magazine 1984, Japan Soccer League record for goals scored in consecutive matches (11 goals in 10 straight matches) 1992, Top Scorer in Flamengo's history (568 goals), Top Scorer in Maracanã Stadium's history (333 goals), Beach Soccer World Championship Top Scorer (12 goals) 1995, Beach Soccer World Championship Best Player 1995, Third Best Brazilian Player of 20th Century 1999, IFFHS 7 Best Players in South America in 20th Century 1999, IFFHS Players of the 20th Century 1999, France Football Players of the 20th Century, World Soccer Players of the 20th Century, inducted into FIFA Hall of Fame 2000, named in FIFA 100 2004, Prize Golden Foot Award (Legend of Football) 2006. *Address:* Zico's Soccer Centre, Avenida Miguel Antônio Fernandes, nº 700 Recreio dos Bandeirantes, Rio de Janeiro RJ, Brazil (office). *Telephone:* (21) 24902431 (office). *E-mail:* centrodefutebolzico@hotmail.com (office). *Website:* www.ziconarede.com.br.

ZIDA, Lt-Col Yacouba Isaac; Burkinabè army officer and politician; b. 16 Nov. 1965, Passoré Prov.; m.; three c.; ed Univ. of Lyon, France; long career in army, including with Presidential Security Regt from 1996, becoming Deputy Commdr; Liaison Officer during Pres. Blaise Compaoré's mediation in Ivorian crisis 2002–11; with UN peacekeeping operation, Democratic Repub. of Congo 2008–09; took power following Burkinabé uprising and removal of Pres. Compaoré Oct. 2014, Head of State 1–12 Nov. 2014; Prime Minister 2014–15, also Minister of Defence 2014–15; removed from office and arrested following coup Sept. 2015; Acting Prime Minister Sept.–Dec. 2015.

ŽIDAN, Dejan; Slovenian veterinary physician and politician; *Deputy Prime Minister and Minister of Agriculture, Forestry and Food;* b. 16 Oct. 1967, Maribor, Socialist Repub. of Slovenia, Socialist Fed. Repub. of Yugoslavia; ed School for Animal Husbandry and Veterinary Technicians, Maribor, and later in Kamnik, Veterinary Faculty, Univ. of Ljubljana; completed traineeship at Reproduction Dept of Animal Husbandry and Veterinary Centre for Pomurje region, Murska Sobota; passed state examination at Ministry of Agric., Forestry and Food 1994; employed at Agromerkur, in the establishment's own veterinary clinic, and later at Nabergoj veterinary eng; began working at Reproduction Dept of regional unit, Animal Health Centre of Slovenia (AHCS), Murska Sobota 1995, Co-ordinator, later Head of AHCS regional unit, Murska Sobota 2000, in charge of regional unit of Nat. Veterinary Inst., Veterinary Faculty, Murska Sobota following reorganization of veterinary service; responsible for co-ordination of education of breeders and non-veterinary staff, Centre for Continuing Educ., Veterinary Faculty; Ed. Reja prašičev (Pig farming) magazine –2003; mem. Bd KG Rakičan d.d. 2003–13; Pres. Man. Bd, Panvita Group, KG Rakičan d.d. 2007–13; External Assoc., Veterinary Faculty, Ljubljana, elected as professional adviser for porcine health and reproduction 2003; reappointed mem. Animal Husbandry Council, Ministry of Agric., Forestry and Food 2007; Visiting Expert of Faculty of Agric., Univ. of Maribor 2007; Minister for Agric., Forestry and Food 2010–11, 2013–, also Deputy Prime Minister 2013–, Acting Minister of Defence 9–21 April 2015; mem. Nat. Ass. 2011–, Chair. Cttee for Agric., Forestry, Food and the Environment. *Address:* Ministry of Agriculture and the Environment, 1000 Ljubljana, Dunajska 22, Slovenia (office). *Telephone:* (1) 4789000 (office). *Fax:* (1) 4789021 (office). *E-mail:* gp.mkgp@gov.si (office). *Website:* www.mkgp.gov.si (office).

ZIDANE, Zinedine Yazid, (Zizou); French football coach, sports commentator and fmr professional footballer; *Manager, Real Madrid Club de Fútbol;* b. 23 June 1972, Marseille; s. of Ismail Zidane and Malika Zidane; m. Véronique Fernández 1994; four s.; ed Centre de Formation de l'Asscn Sportive, Cannes; attacking midfielder; youth player, US Saint-Henri 1982–83, SO Septèmes-les-Vallons 1983–87, Cannes 1987–88; sr player, AS Cannes 1988–92 (61 games, six goals), Bordeaux 1992–96 (139 games, 28 goals, won UEFA Intertoto Cup 1995), Juventus, Turin 1996–2001 (151 games, 24 goals, won Serie A 1996/97, 1997/98, Italian Super Cup 1997, European Super Cup 1996, Intercontinental Cup 1996, UEFA Intertoto Cup 1999), Real Madrid (transferred for record £45 million fee) 2001–06 (155 games, 37 goals, won La Liga 2002/03, Spanish Super Cup 2001, 2003, UEFA Champions League 2001/02 (scored winning goal), European Super Cup 2002, Intercontinental Cup 2002); mem. French nat. team 1994–2004, 2005–06 (108 games, 31 goals), in winning team FIFA World Cup 1998, UEFA European Championship 2000, Capt. 2005–06; announced retirement from int. football Aug. 2004, announced return to int. football Aug. 2005, announced retirement from football 2006; football commentator, Canal+ 2006–; Adviser to Pres. of Real Madrid Club de Fútbol 2010–11, Sporting Dir 2011–13, Asst Coach under Carlo Ancelotti 2013–14 (won UEFA Champions League and Copa del Rey), Coach of Real Madrid's B team, Real Madrid Castilla 2014–16, Man., Real Madrid 2016–18 (won three Champions League, one La Liga, two UEFA Super Cup, one FIFA Club World Cup), 2019–; Co-owner brasserie Nulle part ailleurs, Bordeaux; Chevalier, Légion d'honneur 1998, Officier 2009; Ordre Nat. du Mérite (Algeria) 2006; Ligue 1 Best Young Player 1994, Ligue 1 Best Player 1996, UEFA

Champions League Best Midfielder 1998, Ballon d'Or 1998, UEFA Euro Player of the Tournament 2000, Serie A Foreign Footballer of the Year 1997, 2001, Serie A Footballer of the Year 2001, Onze d'Or 1998, 2000, 2001, French Player of the Year 1998, 2002, FIFA World Cup All-Star Team 1998, 2006, UEFA Club Footballer of the Year 2002, Don Balón Award Foreign Player of the Year in La Liga 2002, UEFA Team of the Year 2001, 2002, 2003, FIFA World Player of the Year 1998, 2000, 2003, UEFA European Championship Team of the Tournament 2000, 2004, UEFA Golden Jubilee Poll 2004, named in FIFA 100 2004, FIFA World Cup Golden Ball 2006, FIFPro World XI All-Star Team 2005, 2006, IFFHS World's Best Playmaker 2006, FIFA World Cup Golden Ball 2006, FIFA World Player of the Year Second Place 2006, UNFP Hon. Award 2007, Marca Leyenda Award 2008, Goal.com Team of the Decade 2009, ESPN Team of the Decade 2009, ESPN Player of the Decade 2009, Sports Illustrated Player of the Decade 2009, Laureus Lifetime Achievement Award 2011, UEFA Champions League Best Player of the Past 20 Years 2011, World Soccer Greatest XI of All Time 2013, Best Manager, Globe Soccer 2017. *Film appearance:* Astérix at the Olympic Games 2008. *Leisure interests:* music, tennis, boating, cooking, Formula 1 racing. *Address:* c/o Alain Migliaccio, Calle 131, No 46, El Plantio Canada, 46182 Valencia, Spain (office); Real Madrid Club de Fútbol, Avda. de Concha Espina 1, 28036 Madrid, Spain (office). *E-mail:* publicite@sporever.fr (office). *Telephone:* (91) 3984300 (office). *Fax:* (91) 3984382 (office). *Website:* www.realmadrid.com (office).

ZIEDAN, Youssef, PhD; Egyptian academic, writer and novelist; *Director, Centre and Museum of Manuscripts, Bibliotheca Alexandrina;* b. 30 June 1958; one s. two d.; ed Univ. of Alexandria; Lecturer in Islamic Philosophy and History of Science, Damanhur Alexandria Univ. 1992–97; currently Dir Centre and Museum of Manuscripts, Bibliotheca Alexandrina; consultant to UNESCO, UN Econ. and Social Comm. for Western Asia (ESCWA), Arab League; Kuwait Foundation for the Advancement of Science Prize 1994, 2005. *Publications include:* ltiqa' al-Bahrin (essays in literary criticism), Zil al Af'a (novel), Azazel (novel) (Int. Prize for Arabic Fiction (Arabic Booker) 2009) 2008, Al-Nabati (The Nabataean) (novel) 2010, Arabic Theology 2010; more than 50 works of philosophy, history of medicine and information science. *Address:* Bibliotheca Alexandrina, PO Box 138, El Shatby, Alexandria 21526 (office); c/o Dar El Shorouk, 8 Sibaweh El Masry Street, Nasr City, Egypt. *Telephone:* (3) 4839999 (ext. 1300) (Alexandria) (office); (2) 24023399 (Dar El Shorouk). *Fax:* (3) 4820461 (Alexandria) (office); (2) 24037567 (Dar El Shorouk). *E-mail:* youssef.ziedan@bibalex.org (home); secretariat@bibalex.org (office); ziedan@ziedan.com (home); dar@shorouk.com. *Website:* www.shorouk.com (office); www.ziedan.com.

ZIEGLER, Jean, DenD, DenScPol; Swiss academic, writer and politician; *Vice-President, Advisory Committee, United Nations Human Rights Council;* b. 19 April 1934, Berne; s. of Hans Ziegler and Léa Ziegler; m.; one s.; ed Univs of Geneva, Berne, Paris-Sorbonne and Columbia Univ. New York; with Swiss American Corpn New York 1959; Jr lawyer in training with Theodor Haffner, New York; Asst to Sec.-Gen. of Int. Comm. of Jurists; UN expert, Léopoldville and Elisabethville, Congo 1961–62; Research Assoc., Faculté de Droit, Inst. Africain de Geneva 1963; Prof., Inst. d'Etudes Politiques, Univ. of Grenoble 1967; Faculty of Law and Social and Econ. Sciences, Univ. of Berne 1969; Prof., Faculty of Econ. and Social Sciences, Univ. of Geneva and Univ. Inst. of Devt Studies 1975; Prof., Univ. of Paris I—Sorbonne 1983; numerous research tours in Africa, Latin America and Asia since 1963; City Councillor, Geneva 1963; mem. Swiss Nat. Council 1967–83, 1987–99; mem. Fed. Parl. for Geneva; UN Special Rapporteur for the Right to Food 2000–08, Vice-Pres. Advisory Cttee of UN Human Rights Council 2009–; mem. Cen. Cttee Swiss Socialist Party; mem. Exec. Council, Socialist Int; Chevalier, Ordre des Arts et des Lettres 1994; Dr hc (Univ. Mons-Hainault, Univ. of Paris VIII, Univ. de Savoie); Adlai Stevenson Peace Award 1964, Bruno Kreisky Peace Prize 2000, Pres.'s Gold Medal (Italy). *Publications include:* La contre-révolution en Afrique 1963, Vive le pouvoir! ou les délices de la raison d'Etat 1985, Sankara. Un nouveau pouvoir africain (with J. P. Rapp) 1986, Dialogue Est-Ouest (with Y. Popov) 1987, La Suisse lave plus blanc 1990, La victoire des vaincus, oppression et résistance culturelle 1991, Le bonheur d'être Suisse 1993, Il s'agit de ne pas se rendre (with Régis Debray) 1994, L'or du Maniéma (novel) 1996, La Suisse, l'or et les morts 1997, Les seigneurs du crime, les nouvelles mafia contre la démocratie 1999, La faim dans le monde racontée à mon fils 2001, Les Nouveaux Maîtres du Monde 2003, L'Empire de la honte 2005, La Haine de l'Occident 2009, Der Aufstand des Gewissens: Die nicht-gehaltene Festspielrede 2011, Destruction massive: Géopolitique de la faim, 2011; numerous book chapters, articles in reviews, journals, newspapers etc. *Leisure interests:* skiing, tennis, mountaineering. *Address:* PO Box 136, 1211 Geneva 4, Switzerland (office). *Telephone:* (22) 908-44-33 (office). *Fax:* (22) 908-62-76 (office). *E-mail:* jeziegler@vtxnet.ch (home); jean.ziegler@unige.ch.

ZIEGLER, Philip Sandeman, CVO, MA, FRHistS, FRSL; British writer; b. 24 Dec. 1929, Ringwood, Hants.; s. of Colin Louis Ziegler and Dora Ziegler (née Barnwell); m. 1st Sarah Collins 1960 (deceased); one s. one d.; m. 2nd Mary Clare Charrington 1971; one s.; ed Eton Coll., New Coll. Oxford; joined Foreign Office 1952, served in Vientiane, Paris, Pretoria, Bogotá; Editorial Dir Collins Publishers 1972, Ed.-in-Chief 1979–80, resgnd when apptd to write official biog. of the late Earl Mountbatten; Chair. London Library 1979–85, Soc. of Authors 1988–90, Public Lending Right Advisory Cttee 1993–96; Hon. DLitt (Westminster Coll., Mo., USA) 1987, (Univ. of Buckingham) 2000; Chancellor's Essay Prize 1950, Heinemann Award 1976. *Publications include:* Duchess of Dino 1962, Addington 1965, The Black Death 1969, William IV 1971, Omdurman 1973, Melbourne 1976, Crown and People 1978, Diana Cooper 1981, Mountbatten 1985, Elizabeth's Britain 1926 to 1986 1986, The Sixth Great Power: Barings 1762–1929 1988, King Edward VIII, The Official Biography 1990, Wilson: The Authorized Life of Lord Wilson of Rievaulx 1993, London at War: 1939–45 1994, Osbert Sitwell 1998, Britain Then and Now 1999, Soldiers: Fighting Men's Lives 1901–2001 2001, Rupert Hart-Davis: Man of Letters 2004, Edward Heath: The Authorised Biography (Elizabeth Longford Prize 2011) 2010, Olivier 2013, George VI: The Dutiful King 2014, Between the Wars: 1919–1939 2016; ed.: The Diaries of Lord Louis Mountbatten 1920–1922 1987, Personal Diary of Admiral the Lord Louis Mountbatten 1943–1946 1988, From Shore to Shore: The Diaries of Earl Mountbatten of Burma 1953–1979 1989, Brooks's: A Social History (with Desmond Seward) 1991, Legacy: the Rhodes Trust and the Rhodes Scholarship 2008. *Address:* c/o Caroline Dawnay, United Agents LLP, 12-26 Lexington Street, London W1F 0LE, England (office); 22 Cottesmore Gardens, London, W8 5PR, England (home). *Telephone:* (20) 3214 0882 (office); (20) 7937-1903 (home). *Fax:* (20) 3214-0801 (office); (20) 7937-5458 (home). *E-mail:* info@unitedagents.co.uk (office). *Website:* www.unitedagents.co.uk/philip-ziegler (office).

ZIEJKA, Franciszek, PhD, DHabil; Polish philologist, writer, academic and fmr university rector; *Honorary Professor, Jagiellonian University;* b. 10 March 1940, Radłów; m. Maria Gluszek (deceased); two c.; ed Jagiellonian Univ., Kraków; mem. Faculty, Jagiellonian Univ. 1963–, Inst. of Polish Philology 1963–, Head of Chair of History of 19th century Polish Literature, Prof. 1998–, Vice-Dir 1988–89, Dean of Philological Faculty 1990–93, Vice-Rector 1993–99, Rector 1999–2005, held UNESCO Chair in Translation Studies and Intercultural Communication, apptd Hon. Prof. 2012; Visiting Prof., Provençal Univ., Aix-en-Provence 1970–73, Univ. of Lisbon 1979–80; Lecturer, Inst. des Langues et Civilisations Orientales, Paris 1984–88; Chair. Coll. of Kraków Univ. Rectors 1999–2005; Deputy Chair. Conf. of Academic Rectors of Polish Schools (KRASP) 1999–2002, Chair. 2002–05; mem. Social Cttee of the Restoration of Historical Monuments of Krakow 1996– (Chair. 2005–); Chair. National Museum in Krakow; mem. United Peasant Party (ZSL) 1962–89, Solidarity Trade Union 1989–93; mem. Editorial Bd Ruch Literacki, Regiony, Studia Academiae Scientiarum Hungaricae; mem. Polish Acad. of Arts and Sciences 2002–, PEN-Club 2002–, Nat. Council for European Integration 2002–05; Hon. Citizen of Tarnòw and Sanok; Chevalier des Palmes académiques 1994, Officier 2002, Kt's Cross of Order of the Rebirth of Poland 1997, Commdr, Cross of the Rebirth of Poland 2002, Order of Cross of the South (Brazil) 2002; Gold Rays with Neck Ribbon of the Order of the Rising Sun (Japan) 2002, Grand Golden Cross for Services Rendered to the Repub. of Austria 2002, Chevalier, Légion d'honneur 2006, Grand Officer, Order of Merit (Portugal) 2008; Dr hc (Pedagogical Univ. of Kraków, Pontifical Faculty of Theology, Wrocław) 2003, (Swietorzyska Acad.) 2004; awards from Minister of Nat. Educ., Tomasz Nocznicki Award, Miesięcznik Literacki Award, Zycie Literackie Award, Fundusz Literatury Award, Kazimierz Wyka Literary Award of the City of Kraków, Zygmunt Gloger Award and Medal, Wlodzimierz Tetmajer Award, Jan Stanislawski Award, Cracovian of the Year 2000, Scena Illustrata Premio Internazionale I migliore dell Anno 2000, Super Express Golden Wings Award 2000, Pro Meritis Medal, Int. Mauthausen Committee 2003, Gieysztora Award 2015. *TV screenplays include:* Origin of the Legend: The Panorama of Racławice 1981, Polish November 1983, Traugutt 1991. *Radio plays include:* It Happened During Carnival 1996, A Book of Stone About the Past 1996, You Will Be a Pearl for Poland... 1997. *Publications:* Polish and Provençal Studies 1977, The Panorama of Racławice 1984, The Golden Legend of Polish Peasants 1985, Paris and Young Poland 1993, Our Family in Europe 1995, Wyspiański's 'Wedding' in Polish Myths 1997, Poets—Missionaries—Scientists 1998, Mythes polonais. Autour de "La Noce" de Stanisław Wyspiański 2001, The City of Poets 2005, Gaudium veritatis 2005. *Address:* ul. Lipińskiego 9/9, 30-349 Kraków, Poland (home). *Telephone:* (12) 2662315 (home).

ŽIEMELIS, Vidmantas; Lithuanian lawyer and politician; b. 4 Dec. 1950, Gailiskiai, Moletai Region; one d.; ed Vilnius State Univ.; mem. CPSU –1989, voluntarily withdrew from CP; workman, later legal adviser Amalgamation of Chem. Consumer Products 1977–81; Asst to Prosecutor at Vilnius Prosecutor's Office 1981–84; Prosecutor-Gen. Supervision Dept Prosecutor's Office Repub. of Lithuania 1984–90; involved in Sajudis Movt from late 1980s; mem. Council of Sajudis, Vilnius City 1989–90; elected Deputy of Supreme Soviet Repub. of Lithuania Feb. 1990; signatory March 11th Act on Re-establishment of Independence; mem. Seimas (Parl.) Repub. of Lithuania (Homeland Union Group 2004–12) 1992–2012, Chair. Sub-cttee on the Evaluation of the Legal System and the Seimas Drafts 2005–12, mem. Cttee on State Issues and Legal Affairs 1989–96, Cttee on Legal Affairs 2004–12, Comm. on Drug Addiction Prevention 2004–12, Comm. for Parl. Scrutiny of Intelligence Operations 2005–12; Minister of Interior 1996–98.

ZIGUÉLÉ, Martin; Central African Republic politician and insurance company executive; b. 12 Feb. 1957, Paoua; m.; six c.; ed State Coll. of Bangui Rapids, Univ. of Bangui, Int. Inst. of Insurance, Yaoundé, Cameroon; mem. staff Insurance Dept, Ministry of Finance 1978; Asst Gen. Man., then Head various depts. state-owned insurance co. SIRIRI 1988–95; Prin. Insp. of Taxes, seconded to regional insurance co. CICARE; Dir for the Central African Republic, Banque des Etats de l'Afrique Centrale (BEAC); Prime Minister of the Central African Republic 2001–03.

ZIJLSTRA, Halbe, PhD; Dutch politician; b. 21 Jan. 1969, Oosterwolde; m. Ingrid de Bondt; one s.; ed Groningen Univ.; Account Man., Arval BV (car insurance co.) 1996–99; mem. Utrecht city council (VVD) 1998–2001, 2003–06; worked for Activity Project Man. Services, Driebergen 1999–2001; Owner Improvex (project man. co.) 2001–07; mem. States Gen. Second Chamber (lower house of parl.) (VVD) 2006–, VVD Leader in Second Chamber 2012–17; Sec. of State for Educ., Culture and Science 2010–12; Minister of Foreign Affairs 2017–18 (resgnd); mem. World Econ. Forum Young Political Leaders Cttee 2016–; mem. Volkspartij voor Vrijheid en Democratie (VVD) (People's Party for Freedom and Democracy) 1994–. *Address:* c/o Ministry of Foreign Affairs, Bezuidenhoutseweg 67, POB 20061, 2500 EB The Hague, Netherlands (office).

ŽIKEŠ, Ivan; Czech business executive; *Vice-President, Association of Czech, Moravian and Silesian Real Estate Agencies (ARKCR);* b. 27 April 1945, Šternov; s. of Josef Žikeš and Vera Žikeš; m. Vera Žikeš; two s.; ed Tech. Univ., Prague; mem. staff, Vodní stavby, Prague 1969–90; Acting Sec. and Owner Recom Reality 1990–; Vice-Pres. ARKCR. *Leisure interest:* golf. *Address:* Recom Reality s.r.o., Varšavská 13, 360 01 Karlovy Vary (office); ARKCR, Strašnická 3165/1b, 102 00, Prague 10, Czech Republic (office). *Telephone:* (3) 53228545 (Karlovy Vary) (office); (2) 72762953 (Prague) (office). *Fax:* (3) 53228546 (Karlovy Vary) (office); (2) 72771412 (Prague) (office). *E-mail:* zikes@recomreality.cz (office); arkcr@arkcr.cz (office). *Website:* www.recomreality.cz (office); www.arkcr.cz (office).

ZIKMUND, Miroslav; Czech writer and film producer; b. 14 Feb. 1919, Plzeň; s. of Antonín Zikmund and Magdalena Zikmund; m. Eva Mašková (divorced 1972); one s.; ed Univ. of Econs; Hon. Citizen Zlín 1994, Plzeň 1999, Koprivnice 2000; Dr hc (Tomas Bata Univ., Zlín) 2014; Order of the Repub. 1953; Golden Plaque Czech Acad. of Sciences 1965, Medal of Merit of Czech Repub. 1999, Gold Medal Silesian Univ. 1999, Gold Medal, Palacký's Univ. Olomouc 2009. *Films:* From Morocco to Kilimanjaro 1953, From the Equator to Table Mountain 1953, From Argentina to Mexico 1954, If There be Paradise on Earth 1962, Criss-cross Life 2002, Africa I, II.

Television: numerous documentaries. *Publications:* Africa, Dreams and Reality (with Jiří Hanzelka) 1952, With the Czech Flag to Kilimanjaro, Conquer the Desert 1954, Over There Behind the River is Argentina 1956, Over the Cordilleras 1957, Great Waters Iguazu 1957, Amazon Head Hunters 1958, Between Two Oceans 1959, Crescent Upside Down 1961, Kashmir 1962, Turkey 1962, 2010, Syria 1963, Kurdistan 1963, Thousand and Two Nights 1967, Continent under the Himalayas 1969, Political Analysis of the USSR 1989, Ceylon 1991, Life of Dreams and Reality 1997, Blue Mauritius 1999, Afrika um den Tatra 2002, Elephants Live up to Hundred Years (co-author) 2002, Tomtoms of Time: New Guinea (co-author) 2002, Das grosse Wasser Iguassu 2003, Die Wüste besiegt 2006, Trap on the Equator: Indonesia (co-author) 2008, Legend H+Z (Vol. 1) 2010, Legend Z+H (Vol. 2) 2011. *Leisure interests:* genealogy, travelling. *Address:* Pod Nivami 2894, 760 01 Zlín, Czech Republic.

ŽILINSKAS, Tomas, BA, MA; Lithuanian fmr police officer and politician; *Head, Corporate Security Unit, Prevention Department, Lithuanian Railways;* b. 27 June 1977, Vilnius; m.; one d.; ed Naujininkai High School (fmr Secondary School No. 39), Vilnius, Vilnius Police School of Ministry of the Interior, Vilnius Univ., Mykolas Romeris Univ.; police officer, Public Police Subdivision, Transport Police Airport Service of the Police Dept 1996–97, Jr Insp./Insp. of Man. Div., Sr Insp. of Personnel Div., Transport Police Service, Police Dept under Ministry of the Interior 1997–2001, Insp./Sr Insp./Commr Insp. of Int. Co-operation and European Integration Service 2001–03; Deputy Dir of Int. Relations and EU Affairs, Dept of Ministry of the Interior 2003–06; Home Affairs Attaché, Perm. Representation of Lithuania to EU, Brussels 2006–09; Advisor to Police Commr Gen. 2009; Dir of Public Security Policy Dept, Ministry of the Interior 2009–16; Minister of the Interior April–Dec. 2016; Deputy Head, Corp. Security Unit, Prevention Dept, Lithuanian Railways May–Aug. 2017, Head 2017–. *Leisure interests:* sports, photography of old Vilnius, travelling. *Address:* Lithuanian Railways, Mindaugo str. 12, Vilnius LT- 03603, Lithuania (office). *Telephone:* (5) 269-2038 (office); (5) 269-2820 (office). *Fax:* (5) 269-2128 (office). *Website:* www.litrail.lt (office).

ZILLE, Helen, BA; South African politician and fmr journalist; *Premier of the Western Cape;* b. 9 March 1951; m. Johann Maree; two s.; ed Univ. of Witwatersrand; Political Corresp., Rand Daily Mail 1974–82, oversaw investigation into death of Steve Biko; Sr Partner, Zille Shandler Assocs (public policy consultancy) 1989–93; Dir of Communications, Univ. of Cape Town 1993–99; joined Democratic Party (later Democratic Alliance) 1995, Caucus Chair., Western Cape Prov. 2002, Caucus Leader 2002–03, Nat. Spokesperson 2004–07, Educ. Spokesperson 2004–07, Leader 2007–15 (also mem. Exec. Cttee –2017); mem. Prov. Parl. 1999–2004; Minister of Educ. in Western Cape Prov. 1999–2001; mem. Nat. Parl. 2004–06; Mayor of Cape Town 2006–09; Premier of the Western Cape 2009–; fmr Bd mem. Open Soc. Foundation, Ind. Media Diversity Trust, Black Sash; Newsmaker of the Year, Nat. Press Club 2006, World Mayor of the Year 2008. *Publication:* Not Without a Fight 2016. *Address:* Office of the Premier, First Floor, 7 Wale Street, Cape Town 8001, South Africa (office). *E-mail:* Premier .Premier@westerncape.gov.za (office). *Website:* www.westerncape.gov.za (office); www.helenzille.co.za.

ZILLMAN, John W., AO, BSc, BA, MSc, DPhil, FAA; Australian meteorologist; b. 28 July 1939, Brisbane; ed Univ. of Queensland, Univ. of Melbourne, Univ. of Wisconsin, USA; joined Bureau of Meteorology 1957 as a cadet meteorologist in Brisbane, then served as forecaster in Sydney and Brisbane regional offices, then moved to Melbourne 1966; Dir Australian Bureau of Meteorology 1978–2003; Commonwealth Dir of Meteorology 1978–2003; Perm. Rep. of Australia to WMO 1978–2004, mem. WMO Exec. Council 1979–2004, First Vice-Pres. 1987–95, Pres. 1995–2003; Chair. Commonwealth Heads of Marine Agencies 1994–2003; Prin. Del. of Australia to Intergovernmental Panel on Climate Change 1994–2005; Fellow, Australian Acad. of Technological Sciences and Eng 1980–, Hon. Sec. 1990–94, Vice-Pres. 1995–98, Pres. 2003–06; Pres. Nat. Acads Forum 2005–06; Pres. Int. Council of Acads of Eng and Technological Sciences 2005; Chair. Australian Partnership for Advanced Computing 2005–07; Chair. Steering Cttee, Global Climate Observing System 2006–09; Chair. Steering Cttee, Victorian Life Sciences Computing Initiative, Victorian Centre for Climate Change Adaptation Research; fmr mem. Prime Minister's Science, Eng and Innovation Council; mem. Health and Climate Foundation; mem. Council, Monash Univ. 2005–; Vice-Chancellor's Fellow, School of Earth Sciences, Univ. of Melbourne; Hon. mem. American Meteorological Soc. 2009; Hon. DSc 1997; Centenary Medal 2003, Cleveland Abbe Award, American Meteorological Soc. 2004, Int. Meteorological Org. Prize 2005.

ZIMBA, Lyonpo Yeshey, MA (Econs); Bhutanese politician; b. 10 Oct. 1952, Omladama, Punakha Dist; m. Thuji Zangmo; one s. three d.; ed Univ. of Wisconsin, USA; joined civil service in the Royal Secr. 1974, planning officer, Ministry of Planning 1977, Jt Sec. 1991; apptd Chair. Royal Monetary Authority (Cen. Bank) 1986; Chair. Bank of Bhutan; Minister of Finance 1998–2003; Prime Minister and Chair. Council of Ministers 2000–01, 2004–05; Minister of Trade and Industry 2003–04, 2005–07 (resgnd), of Works and Human Settlements 2008–13; Silver Medal for Scholastic Achievement, Gold Medal for Best All-Round Coll. Student, Red Scarf 1991, Druk Thuksey and Coronation Medals 1999. *Leisure interests:* nature, walking.

ZIMERMAN, Krystian; Polish pianist and conductor; b. 5 Dec. 1956, Zabrze; m. Maria Drygajło; one s. one d.; ed State Higher Inst. of Music, Katowice, with Prof. Andrzej Jasiński; Lecturer, Acad. of Music, Basel, Switzerland 1996–; Founder and Conductor, Polish Festival Orchestra 1999–; world premier of Lutosławski's Piano Concerto, Salzburg Festival (with composer conducting) 1988; collaborated with conductors Abbado, Bernstein, von Karajan, Ozawa, Muti, Maazel, Previn, Boulez, Mehta, Haitink, Skrowaczewski, Rattle and others; has performed in numerous European countries and USA; numerous prizes in prin. pianist competitions in Poland and abroad including First Prize, Beethoven Competition, Hradec Kralové 1973, Grand Prix IX Chopin Int. Pianist Competition, Warsaw 1975, Chigiana's Acad. Award for Best Young Pianist of the Year, Siena 1985, Orfeusz (Critics' Award), Polish Artists of Music Asscn 1988, Grand Prix de Disque, French Acad. 1989, Int. Critics' Award 1989, Edison Classical Music Award for Best Concert 2007. *Recordings include:* works for piano and chamber music by Schumann, Grieg (with von Karajan), Mozart (with Danczowska), Schubert, Brahms, Chopin Piano Concertos (with Polish Festival Orchestra), Liszt, Debussy and others, Bartók Piano Concertos (with Andsnes and Grimaud) (Midem Classical Music Award for Concertos 2006), Lutosławski: Piano Concerto 2015, Schubert: Piano Sonatas D 959 & D 960 (ICMA Award for Best Solo Instrument Recording 2018) 2017. *Address:* HarrisonParrott Ltd, The Ark, 201 Talgarth Road, London, W6 8BJ, England (office); Kernmatterstrasse 8B, 4102 Binningen, Switzerland. *E-mail:* jasper.parrott@harrisonparrott.co.uk (office). *Website:* www.harrisonparrott.com/artist/profile/krystian-zimerman (office).

ZIMMER, Hans Florian; German film score composer; b. 12 Sept. 1957, Frankfurt am Main; m. 1st Vicki Carolyn 1982; one d.; m. 2nd Suzanne Zimmer; four c.; ed in England; mem. The Buggles (produced hit song Video Killed the Radio Star); pioneered use of digital synthesizers with computer tech. and traditional orchestras; mem. BMI; Lifetime Achievement Award in Film Composition, Nat. Board of Review' Frederick Loewe Award, Palm Springs Int. Film Festival 2003, ASCAP Henry Mancini Award for Lifetime Achievement. *Film scores include:* Moonlighting 1982, Histoire d'O: Chapitre 2 1984, Success is the Best Revenge 1984, Insignificance 1985, Separate Vacations 1986, The Wind 1987, Terminal Exposure 1987, Rain Man 1988, Twister 1988, Taffin 1988, Spies Inc 1988, The Fruit Machine 1988, Burning Secret 1988, A World Apart (with Stanley Myers) 1988, Wiezien Rio 1989, Paperhouse 1989, Dark Obsession 1989, Black Rain 1989, Driving Miss Daisy 1989, Green Card 1990, Pacific Heights 1990, Nightmare at Noon 1990, Fools of Fortune 1990, Chicago Joe and the Showgirl 1990, Bird on a Wire 1990, Days of Thunder 1990, K2 (European version) 1991, Backdraft 1991, Regarding Henry 1991, Thelma & Louise 1991, Where Sleeping Dogs Lie 1992, The Power of One 1992, A League of Their Own 1992, Radio Flyer 1992, Toys 1992, Cool Runnings 1993, Calendar Girl 1993, Point of No Return 1993, True Romance 1993, Younger and Younger 1993, The House of the Spirits 1993, The Lion King (Acad. Award, Golden Globe) 1994, Africa: The Serengeti 1994, I'll Do Anything 1994, Renaissance Man 1994, Drop Zone 1994, Two Deaths 1995, Crimson Tide (Grammy Award) 1995, Nine Months 1995, Something to Talk About 1995, Beyond Rangoon 1995, Muppet Treasure Island 1996, Broken Arrow 1996, The Preacher's Wife 1996, The Whole Wide World, 1996, The Fan 1996, The Peacemaker 1997, As Good As It Gets 1997, The Last Days 1998, The Thin Red Line 1998, The Prince of Egypt 1998, Chill Factor 1999, Gladiator (Golden Globe) 2000, The Road to El Dorado 2000, Mission: Impossible II 2000, An Everlasting Piece 2000, Hannibal 2001, Pearl Harbor 2001, Riding in Cars with Boys 2001, Invincible 2001, Black Hawk Down 2001, Spirit 2002, The Ring 2002, Tears of the Sun 2003, Matchstick Men 2003, The Last Samurai 2003, Something's Gotta Give 2003, King Arthur 2004, Thunderbirds 2004, Shark Tale 2004, Lauras Stern 2004, Spanglish 2004, The Ring Two 2005, Madagascar 2005, Batman Begins 2005, The Weather Man 2005, The Little Polar Bear: The Mysterious Island (with Nick Glennie-Smith) 2005, Pirates of the Caribbean: Dead Man's Chest 2006, The Holiday 2006, Pirates of the Caribbean: At World's End 2007, The Simpsons Movie 2007, Casi divas 2008, Kung Fu Panda 2008, The Dark Knight (Grammy Award for Best Score Soundtrack Album for Motion Picture 2009, Classical BRIT Award for Soundtrack of the Year 2009) 2008, The Burning Plain 2008, Frost/Nixon 2008, Madagascar: Escape 2 Africa 2008, The Dark Knight Rises 2012, Man of Steel 2013, 12 Years a Slave 2013, The Amazing Spider-Man 2 2014, Interstellar 2014, The Little Prince 2015, Boss Baby 2016, Dunkirk 2017, Dark Phoenix 2019. *Television scores include:* Wild Horses 1985, First Born 1989, Millennium 1992, Space Rangers 1993, The Critic (theme) 1994, High Incident (theme) 1996, Die Motorrad-Cops: Hart am Limit 1999, El Candidato 1999, Carnivàle (series) 2003, Threat Matrix (series title theme) 2003, The Contender (series) 2005, The Pacific (mini-series) 2010, Through the Wormhole 2011–14, The Crown (series) 2016. *Recordings include:* Wings of Film 2001, numerous soundtrack recordings. *Address:* c/o William Morris Endeavor Entertainment, LLC, 9601 Wilshire Blvd, Beverly Hills, CA 90210, USA (office). *Website:* www.hans-zimmer.com.

ZIMMER, Robert Jeffrey, AB, PhD; American mathematician, academic and university administrator; *President, University of Chicago;* b. 5 Nov. 1947, New York City, NY; ed Brandeis Univ., Harvard Univ.; Lecturer, US Naval Acad. 1975–77; L.E. Dickson Instructor of Math., Univ. of Chicago 1977–79, Assoc. Prof. 1979–80, Prof. 1980–, becoming Max Mason Distinguished Service Prof. of Math. –2002, Pres. Math. Dept 1991–95, Pres. Univ. of Chicago 2006–, Chair. Bd of Govs, Argonne Nat. Lab., Chair. Fermi Research Alliance LLC; Prof. of Math., Univ. of California, Berkeley 1981–83; Ford Foundation Prof. of Math. and Provost, Brown Univ. 2002–06; mem. Bd of Math. Sciences, Nat. Research Council 1992–95 (mem. Exec. Cttee 1993–95); mem. Bd of Dirs Chicago Council on Global Affairs; mem. Exec. Cttee Council on Competitiveness, Washington DC, Nat. Science Bd (governing body of NSF), Pres.'s Cttee on the Nat. Medal of Science 2008–10; Fellow, American Acad. of Arts and Sciences, AAAS. *Publications:* Ergodic Theory and Semisimple Groups 1984, Essential Results of Functional Analysis 1990; more than 80 math. research articles. *Address:* Office of the President, The University of Chicago, 5801 South Ellis Avenue, Suite 501, Chicago, IL 60637, USA (office). *Telephone:* (773) 702-8800 (office). *E-mail:* president@uchicago.edu (office). *Website:* president.uchicago.edu (office).

ZIMMERMAN, Jean, BA (Hons); American fashion industry executive; *Executive, Oscar de la Renta;* m.; several c.; ed Univ. of Florida; began career in sales promotion at Charles of the Ritz for four years; joined Bristol-Myers in new product marketing; later worked for Estée Lauder as Dir of Fragrance Marketing; joined Chanel as Dir of Beauté Marketing 1978, responsible for launching Chanel cosmetics in the US market, Exec. Vice-Pres., Chanel, Inc. –2005, mem. Operating Cttee, Global Coordinating Cttee, Strategic Advertising Cttee; f. own consulting firm, JHZ Creative Man., LLC; Man. Consultant, Fragrance Div., Oscar de la Renta, Exec. 2012–; mem. Bd of Dirs Cosmetic Exec. Women (Chair. and Pres. for eight years), Fragrance Foundation; mem. Advertising Women of New York, The Fashion Group, New York Cttee for United Cerebral Palsy; mem. Advisory Bd for Grad. Program and Adjunct Prof., Cosmetics and Fragrance Marketing and Man., Fashion Inst. of Tech., New York; mem. Auxiliary Bd Lenox Hill Hosp.; mem. Bd of Advisors, Kate Somerville Skin Care; Chair. Sprayology; The Cartier Scholarship Recognition Award, Fashion Inst. of Tech., The Cosmetic Executive Women Achiever Award, Alumni of Distinction Award, Univ. of Florida, Leah E. Harrison Humanitarian Award, Children Protection Center, Montefiore Hosp. 2003. *Address:* Oscar de la Renta Ltd, 11 West 42nd Street, 25th Floor, New York, NY 10036, USA (office). *Telephone:* (212) 288-5810. *E-mail:* info@oscardelarenta.com (office). *Website:* www.oscardelarenta.com (office).

ZIMMERMANN, Frank Peter; German violinist; b. 27 Feb. 1965, Duisburg; m. Young Joo Zimmermann; two s.; ed Folkwang Musikhochschule, Essen, Staatliche Hochschule der Künste, Berlin and with Herman Krebbers in Amsterdam; made debut aged 10 playing Mozart's violin concerto in G major, K216 in Duisburg; now performs with all major orchestras in world and has undertaken extensive tours in Europe, USA, Japan and Australia; also gives worldwide recitals, with pianists Alexander Lonquich –1994, Enrico Pace 1998–, Martin Helmchen 2018– and with Heinrich Schiff, Christian Zacharias, Piotr Anderszewski and Emanuel Ax; Founder, Trio Zimmerman with Antoine Tamestit and Christian Poltera; appeared with English Chamber Orchestra conducted by Sir Colin Davis at Buckingham Palace by special invitation of HRH The Prince of Wales 1991; soloist at Europa Concert given by Berlin Philharmonic under Bernard Haitink at Royal Albert Hall, London and televised live world-wide 1993; Bundesverdienstkreuz 1 Klasse; Premio Accad. Musicale Chigiana, Siena 1990, Rheinischer Kulturpreis 1994, Musikpreis, City of Duisburg 2002; Int. Classical Music Award for Chamber Music 2015, numerous awards and prizes for recordings. *Recordings include:* concertos of Tchaikovsky, Brahms, Beethoven, Mozart, Prokofiev, Sibelius, Mendelssohn, Dvořák, Glazunov, Berg, Britten, Hindemith, Dean, Bruch, Busoni, Saint-Saëns, Szymanowski, Weill, Ligeti, Lindberg and Stravinsky; with pianist Alexander Lonquich recorded all Mozart and Prokofiev sonatas and works by Ravel, Debussy, Janáček etc.; with pianist Enrico Pace, 6 Sonatas by J.S. Bach; with Heinrich Schiff, duo works for violin and cello by Honegger, Martinů, J.S. Bach, Ravel and Pintscher; with Trio Zimmermann, string trios by Beethoven, Mozart and Schubert, Hindemith: Violin Sonatas & Concerto (Echo Klassik Instrumentalist of the Year—Violin 2014, Int. Classical Music Award for Best Collection 2014) 2013. *Leisure interests:* gastronomy, sports, wine, arts, literature. *Address:* Nymus Artists, 34 Avenue du Beau Sejour, 1180 Brussels, Belgium (office). *Telephone:* (2) 372-30-05 (office). *E-mail:* jt@nymusartists.com (office). *Website:* www.nymusartists.com (office).

ZIMMERMANN, Reinhard, Dr iur; German legal scholar and academic; *Director, Max Planck Institute for Comparative and International Private Law;* b. 10 Oct. 1952, Hamburg; s. of Fritz Zimmermann and Inge Hansen; ed Univ. of Hamburg, Regional Appeal Court, Hamburg; W.P. Schreiner Chair of Roman and Comparative Law and Head of Dept Univ. of Cape Town 1981–88, Deputy Dean and Dean, Faculty of Law 1983–88; Vice-Pres. and Pres. Soc. of South African Teachers of Law 1984–86; Prof. of Roman Law, German Pvt. Law and Comparative Legal History, Univ. of Regensburg 1988–, Dean, Faculty of Law 1994–96; Visiting Prof., Univ. of Edinburgh, Tulane Univ., Univ. of Stellenbosch, Univ. of California, Berkeley, Cornell Univ., Yale Law School, Univ. of Auckland; Max Rheinstein Visiting Prof., Univ. of Chicago Law School 1993; A.L. Goodhart Prof. of Legal Science, Univ. of Cambridge, UK 1998–99; Visiting Fellow, All Souls Coll., Oxford, UK; Dir Max Planck Inst. for Comparative and Int. Pvt. Law 2002–; Affiliate Prof., Bucerius Law School 2008–; Pres. Studienstiftung des Deutschen Volkes 2011–; Chair. Zivilrechtslehrervereinigung 2011–15, Gesellschaft für Rechtsvergleichung 2014–; Co-Ed. Rabels Zeitschrift für ausländisches und internationales Privatrecht, Zeitschrift für Europäisches Privatrecht, Schriftenreihe zur Europäischen Rechtsgeschichte; mem. Acad. of Arts and Sciences Goettingen, Bavarian Acad. of Arts and Sciences; Foreign mem. Royal Netherlands Acad. of Arts and Science, Royal Soc. of Edin., Accad. delle Scienze Torino, British Acad., Austrian Acad. of Sciences; Hon. Dr iur (Chicago) 1997, (Aberdeen) 2002, (Maastricht) 2006, (Lund) 2006, (Cape Town) 2006, (Edinburgh) 2007, (Lleida) 2007, (Stellenbosch) 2009, (McGill Univ., Montreal) 2010; Leibniz Prize 1996. *Publications include:* Richterliches Moderationsrecht oder Totalnichtigkeit? 1979, Das römisch-holländische Recht in Südafrika 1983, The Law of Obligations: Roman Foundations of the Civilian Tradition 1993, Southern Cross (with D. Visser) 1996, Itinera Fiduciae (with R.H. Helmholz) 1998, Good Faith in European Contract Law (with S. Whittaker) 2000, A History of Private Law in Scotland (two vols) (with K. Reid) 2000, Roman Law, Contemporary Law, European Law: The Civilian Tradition Today 2001, Zivilrechtswissenschaft und Schuldrechtsreform (with W. Ernst) 2001, Comparative Foundations of a European Law of Set-Off and Prescription 2002, Jurists Uprooted (with J. Beatson) 2004, Mixed Systems in Comparative Perspective (with K. Reid and D. Visser) 2004, The New German Law of Obligations 2005, Die Europäisierung des Privatrechts und die Rechtsvergleichung 2006, Oxford Handbook of Comparative Law (with M. Reimann) 2006, Digest of European Tort Law (with H. Koziol *et al.*) 2007, Störungen der Willensbildung beim Vertragsschluss 2007, Historisch-kritischer Kommentar zum BGB Vol. II (Parts II/1 and II/2) (with M. Schmoeckel and J. Rückert) 2007, Exploring the Law of Succession: Studies National, Historical and Comparative (with K. Reid and M. de Waal) 2007, The Draft Civil Code for Israel in Comparative Perspective (with K. Siehr) 2008, Handwörterbuch des Europäischen Privatrechts (with J. Basedow and K. J. Hopt) 2009, Digest of European Tort Law Vol. II (with H. Koziol *et al.*) 2011, Revision des Verbraucheracquis (with H. Eidenmüller *et al.*) 2011, Comparative Succession Law: Testamentary Formalities (with K. Reid and M. de Waal) 2011, Max Planck Encyclopedia of European Private Law (with J. Basedow and K. J. Hopt) 2012, Freedom of Testation/Testierfreiheit 2012, Judge and Jurist (with A. Burrows and D. Johnston) 2013, Historisch-kritischer Kommentar zum BGB Vol. III (Parts III/1 and III/2) (with M. Schmoeckel and J. Rückert) 2013, Comparative Succession Law: Intestate Succession (with K. Reid and M. de Waal) 2015, Zivilrecht und Steuerrecht, Erwerb von Todes wegen und Schenkung (with K. Muscheler) 2015, Zukunftsperspektiven der Rechtsvergleichung 2016, Legislators, Judges, and Professors (with J. Basedow and H. Fleischer) 2016, European Union Law, National Private Law, European Private Law (with C. Sieburgh) 2016. *Leisure interests:* field hockey, tennis, running, classical music. *Address:* Max-Planck-Institut für ausländisches und internationales Privatrecht, Mittelweg 187, 20148 Hamburg, Germany (office). *Telephone:* (40) 41900401 (office). *Fax:* (40) 41900402 (office). *E-mail:* r.zimmermann@mpipriv.de (office). *Website:* www.mpipriv.de (office).

ZIMPHER, Nancy L., BS, MA, PhD; American university administrator; b. 29 Oct. 1946, Gallipolis, Ohio; d. of Aven Denzle Zimpher and Elsie Gordon Zimpher (née Hammond); m. 1st William Fletcher Zimpher; one s.; m. 2nd Kenneth R. Howey 1987; ed Ohio State Univ.; fmr Exec. Dean, Professional Colls and Dean, Coll. of Educ., Ohio State Univ.; Chancellor, Univ. of Wisconsin-Milwaukee and mem. Faculty, School of Educ. 1998–2003; Pres. Univ. of Cincinnati (first woman) 2003–09; Chancellor, State Univ. of New York (first woman) 2009–17; Pres. Holmes Partnership 1996–2001; fmr Co-Chair. Milwaukee Partnership Acad.; Co-Chair. Ohio Bd of Regents Articulation and Transfer Advisory Council; Chair. Urban Serving Univs 2005–; Chair. Nat. Asscn of State Univs and Land-Grant Colls 2007– (fmr Chair. Comm. on Int. Programs); fmr Project Dir, Teacher Quality Grant, Dept of Educ.; fmr mem. American Council on Educ. Leadership Comm., Nat. Council for Accreditation of Teacher Educ.; fmr mem. Exec. Bd of American Asscn of Colls for Teacher Educ., Bd of Nat. Collegiate Athletic Asscn Div. One Exec. Cttee; mem. Cincinnati Business Cttee, A Greater Cincinnati Initiative Advisory Cttee; mem. Bd Greater Cincinnati Chamber of Commerce, Cincinnati Center City Devt Corpn, Greater Cincinnati Convention and Visitors Bureau, United Way of Greater Cincinnati, Uptown Consortium, Hebrew Union Coll.-Univ. of Cincinnati Ethics Center; YWCA Women of Achievement Award 1997, Ohio Women's Hall of Fame 1998, Outstanding Women of Achievement Educ. Award 2000, US Postal Service Women Putting Their Stamp on Metro Milwaukee Award 2003, Council for the Advancement and Support of Educ. Chief Exec. Leadership Award 2003, Asscn of Teacher Educators Distinguished Research Award, Edward C. Pomeroy Award for Outstanding Contribs to Teacher Educ., Virginia Commonwealth Univ. Distinguished Woman Scholar Award, US Postal Service Women's History Month Award 2004, YWCA Career Women of Achievement Award 2004, Ohio State Univ. Alumni Asscn Professional Achievement Award 2004. *Publications include:* University Leadership in Urban School Renewal, A Time for Boldness: A Story of Institutional Change, Profiles of Preservice Teacher Education: Inquiry into the Nature of Programs, Creating a New Kind of University 2006, Recruiting, Preparing and Retaining Teachers for Urban Schools 2006, Boundary Spanners: A Key to Success in Urban P-16 University-School Partnerships; numerous chapters, articles and monographs.

ZINGRAFF, René; French business executive; b. 1936; ed Ecole Nationale Supérieure de Chimie et de Physique de Bordeaux; trained as chemical engineer; joined Michelin 1963, various man. positions including Dir of Quality, Mfg Plants in UK, Head of Sr Man. Personnel, Dir of Mfg Plants in N America 1983–86, Man. Pnr Compagnie Générale des Établissements Michelin (CGEM) 1986–2006 (retd); Vice-Pres. Siparex Associés 2006–12; Pres. Fondation Institut Français de Mécanique Avancée 2006–15.

ZINKE, Ryan, BS, MBA, MS; American government official and fmr naval officer; b. 1 Nov. 1961, Bozeman, Mont.; s. of Ray Dale Zinke and Jean Montana Petersen (née Harlow); m. Lolita Hand; three c.; ed Univ. of Oregon, Nat. Univ.; service as USN SEAL 1986–2008, becoming Deputy and Acting Commdr, Combined Jt Special Operations Task Force, Arabian Peninsula 2004, Dean, Naval Special Warfare Grad. School, Naval Special Warfare Advanced Training Command –2008 retd from navy with rank of Commdr); mem. Montana State Senate for Senate Dist 2 2009–11; CEO Continental Divide Int. 2008–14; mem. US House of Reps from Montana's at-large Dist 2015–; Sec. of the Interior 2017–18; Republican; Bronze Star Meritorious Service Ribbon, Meritorious Service Medal. *Address:* c/o Department of the Interior, 1849 C Street, NW, Washington, DC 20240, USA (office).

ZINKERNAGEL, Rolf Martin, PhD; Swiss professor of immunology; *Professor Emeritus, Institute of Experimental Immunology, University Hospital, University of Zurich;* b. 6 Jan. 1944, Basel; m.; three c.; ed Mathematisch-Naturwissenschaftliches Gymnasium, Basel, Univ. of Basel, Univ. of Zurich, ANU, Canberra, Australia; intern, Surgical Dept, Clara-Spital Hosp., affiliated to Faculty of Medicine, Univ. of Basel 1969; Postdoctoral Fellow, Lab. for Electron Microscopy, Inst. of Anatomy, Univ. of Basel 1969–70; Postdoctoral Fellow, Inst. of Biochemistry, Univ. of Lausanne 1971–73; Visiting Fellow, Dept of Microbiology, John Curtin School of Medical Research, ANU, Canberra 1973–75; Assoc. mem. (Asst Prof.) Dept of Immunopathology, Research Inst. of Scripps Clinic, La Jolla, Calif., USA 1976–79, Adjunct Assoc. Prof., Dept of Pathology 1977–79, Full Prof., Dept of Immunopathology, Scripps Clinic and Research Foundation 1979; Assoc. Prof., Dept of Pathology, Univ. Hosp., Univ. of Zurich 1979–88, Full Prof. 1988–92, Head, Inst. of Experimental Immunology 1992–2008, now Prof. Emer.; mem. numerous scientific advisory bodies including WHO Group of Experts in Vaccine Devt 1985–89, Advisory Council of Cancer Research Inst. 1988–; mem. editorial bds of immunology, pathology, microbiology and virology journals; mem. numerous professional orgs including Swiss Soc. of Allergy and Immunology 1971–76 (Pres. 1993–94, Hon. mem. 1996–), Academia Europaea 1989–, European Network of Immunological Insts 1990–, Int. Soc. for Antiviral Research 1990–; Fellow, American Acad. of Microbiology 1996; Foreign Fellow, NAS 1996, Australian Acad. of Sciences 1996, American Acad. of Arts and Sciences 1998, Royal Soc. 1998, Acad. Royale de Médicine, Belgium 1998, Berlin-Brandenburgische Akad. der Wissenschaften 1998; Dr hc (Liège, ANU) 1996, (Oslo, Québec, Genoa) 1997, (Latvian Univ., Riga, Agricultural Univ. of Warsaw) 1998; Cloëtta Prize 1981, Ernst Jung Prize 1982, Mack-Forster Prize 1985, Gairdner Foundation Int. Award 1986, Inst. for Cancer Research William B. Coley Award 1987, Christoforo Colombo Award 1992, Albert Lasker Medical Research Award 1995, Nobel Prize in Physiology or Medicine 1996. *Publications:* numerous articles in learned journals. *Address:* Department of Pathology, University Hospital, Institute of Experimental Immunology, Schmelzbergstrasse 12, 8091 Zürich, Switzerland (office). *Telephone:* (44) 2552989 (office). *Fax:* (44) 2554420 (office). *E-mail:* rolf.zinkernagel@usz.ch (office). *Website:* www.unizh.ch/pathol/experimentelle-immunologie/pti_rzi_cv_e.html (office).

ZINMAN, David Joel; American conductor; b. 9 July 1936, New York; s. of Samuel Zinman and Rachel Ilo Zinman (née Samuels); m. 1st Leslie Heyman (deceased); one s. one d.; m. 2nd Mary Ingham 1974; one s.; ed Oberlin Coll. Conservatory of Music, Univ. of Minnesota, Tanglewood Music Center; studied conducting at Berkshire Music Center, Tanglewood and with Pierre Monteux; Asst to Monteux 1961–64; Music Dir, Nederlands Kamerorkest 1964–77, Rochester Philharmonic Orchestra, New York 1974–85, Baltimore Symphony Orchestra 1985–98; Prin. Guest Conductor, Rotterdam Philharmonic Orchestra 1977–79, Chief Conductor 1979–82; Music Dir Minnesota Orchestra's Viennese Sommerfest 1994–96, Tonhalle Orchester Zürich 1995–2014; Music Dir, Aspen Music Festival and School 1997–2010; numerous recordings; Chevalier, Ordre des Arts et des Lettres 2000; three Grammy Awards, two Grand Prix du Disques, two Edison Awards, Gramophone Best Selling Record (for Górecki) 1993, Gramophone Award (for Jungle Book) 1994, Peabody Medal 1996, Ditson Award, Columbia Univ. 1997, Deutschen Schallplatten Prize 1999, Art Prize of the City of Zurich 2002, Theodore

Thomas Award, Conductors Guild 2006, MIDEM Classical Artist of the Year Award 2008. *Address:* HarrisonParrott, The Ark, 201 Talgarth Road, London, W6 8BJ, England (office). *Telephone:* (20) 7229-9166 (office). *Fax:* (20) 7221-5042 (office). *E-mail:* info@harrisonparrott.co.uk (office). *Website:* www.harrisonparrott.com/artist/profile/david-zinman (office).

ZINNI, Gen. (retd) Anthony, BA, MA; American diplomatist, academic, business executive and fmr military officer; b. 17 Sept. 1947, Philadelphia, Pa; m. Dale Elaine Bathke 1966; three c.; ed Vilanova Univ., Central Michigan Univ.; joined US Marine Corps 1961, infantry officer 1965, rising to rank of Gen.; active service in Viet Nam (injured 1970), Philippines, Mediterranean, Caribbean, Korea, Turkey, Iraq, Soviet Union, Kenya; Head Unified Task Force Somalia in Operation Restored Hope 1992–93, supervised withdrawal of US forces 1995, also Asst to Special Envoy to Somalia; Deputy Commanding Gen. US Marine Corps. Combat Devt Command, Quantico, Va 1992–94, Commanding Gen. 1st Marine Expeditionary Force 1994–96; Commdr US Cen. Command 1997–2000, in charge of mil. forces in 25 countries in Middle East, Africa and fmr USSR; Head of Persian Gulf forces 1997–2000, Commdr in charge of Operation Desert Fox, Iraq 1998; retd from mil. Aug. 2000; fmr academic positions include Stanley Chair in Ethics, Va Mil. Inst., Nimitz Chair, Univ. of Calif., Berkeley, Hofheimer Chair, Jt Forces Staff Coll., Weissberg Chair in Int. Studies, Beloit Coll., Harriman Prof. of Govt, Coll. of William and Mary; mem. Bd Reves Center for Int. Studies, Coll. of William and Mary, Center for Responsible Leadership and Governance, Villanova Univ.; has worked with Inst. on Global Conflict and Cooperation, Univ. of Calif., US Inst. of Peace and Henri Dunant Centre for Humanitarian Dialogue, Geneva; Pres. Center for Middle East Devt, UCLA; Distinguished Advisor, Center for Strategic and Int. Studies, Washington 2000–; US Envoy to Middle East 2001–03, also participated in diplomatic missions to Somalia, Pakistan, Ethiopia and Eritrea; mem. Council on Foreign Relations; mem. Bd of Dirs BAE Systems, Inc 2002–14, Chair. 2009–12; Exec. Vice-Pres. Dyncorp Int. 2007–08; Special Envoy working on Persian Gulf Disputes 2017–19; mem. Bd of Dirs Caliburn Int. Corpn 2018–; Defense Distinguished Service Medal, Defense Superior Service Medal (with two oak leaf clusters), Bronze Star Medal with Combat "V", Purple Heart; non-military awards include Papal Gold Cross of Honor, Union League's Abraham Lincoln Award, Italic Studies Inst.'s Global Peace Award, Distinguished Sea Service Award from Naval Order of US, Eisenhower Distinguished Service Award from Veterans of Foreign Wars, Chapman Award from Marine Corps Univ Foundation, Penn Club Award, St. Thomas of Villanova Alumni Medal, Grant Patriot Award. *Publications include:* Battle Ready (with Tom Clancy and Tony Koltz) 2004, The Battle for Peace (with Tony Koltz) 2006, Leading the Charge: Leadership Lessons from the Battlefield to the Boardroom (with Tony Koltz) 2009.

ZINOUSKY, Uladzimir Ivanovich; Belarusian engineer, civil servant and government official; b. 1955, Yelizovo, Asipovichy (Osipovichi) Dist, Mogilev (Mahiloŭ) Oblast, Belarusian SSR, USSR; ed Kuibyshev Belarusian State Inst. of Nat. Economy, Acad. of Public Admin under Council of Ministers; Sr Engineer, Main Computing Dept, Cen. Statistics Bureau (CSB), Belorusian Soviet Socialist Repub. (BSSR); Sr and Leading Economist, CSB Industry Statistics Dept, Asst Dir CSB and Asst Dir BSSR State Statistics Cttee 1981–86; Deputy Head, Statistics Dept, Minsk Oblast 1986–89; held various positions in Council of Ministers, including Sr Officer, Econ. Analysis and Planning Sector of Economy Div., Leading Specialist of Economy Div., Leading Specialist of Dept for Economy and Foreign Relations, Leading Specialist of Economy Dept, Main Specialist of Sector for Forecasting and Analysis of Social and Econ. Devt of Economy Dept of Admin of Council of Ministers 1989–92; First Deputy Chair. State Cttee on Statistics and Analysis, First Deputy Statistics and Analysis Minister 1992–98; Statistics and Analysis Minister 1998–2008; Chair. Nat. Statistics Cttee 2008–14; Minister of the Economy 2014–18. *Address:* c/o Ministry of the Economy, 220050 Minsk, vul. Bersona 14, Belarus (office). *Telephone:* (17) 222-60-48 (office). *Fax:* (17) 200-37-77 (office). *E-mail:* minec@economy.gov.by (office). *Website:* www.economy.gov.by (office).

ZINSOU, Lionel; French-Benin economist, banker and politician; *Prime Minister;* b. 23 Oct. 1954, Paris, France; s. of René Zinsou; nephew of Émile Zinsou (fmr Pres. of Dahomey, now Benin); m.; three d.; ed École Normale Supérieure, Paris, London School of Econs, UK; started as Lecturer and Prof. of Econs, Univ. of Paris; Head of Cabinet of Laurent Fabius (Prime Minister of France) 1984; with BSN (now Danone) 1986–97, various positions including Group Corp. Devt Dir, Man. Dir of HP and Lea & Perrins, mem. Group Exec. Cttee; joined Rothschild Bank as Gen. Partner 1997, becoming Head of Consumer Products Group, Head of Middle East and Africa and mem. Global Investment Bank Cttee –2008; joined Paribas Affaires Industrielles (PAI) Partners (investment fund) 2008, becoming Chair. and CEO 2009; Special Adviser to Pres. of Benin Yayi Boni 2006–11; Prime Minister, in charge of Econ. Devt, Evaluation of Public Policies and Promotion of Good Governance 2015–; cand. in presidential election March 2016; Pres. Fondation AfricaFrance 2015; f. Zinsou Foundation, Ouidah, Benin (first museum of contemporary art in sub-Saharan Africa outside South Africa) 2013; mem. Supervisory Bd Libération (French daily newspaper) 2005. *Publication:* Le Fer de lance: Essai sur les nationalisations industrielles 1985. *Address:* Office of the Prime Minister, Cotonou, Benin (office). *Website:* www.gouv.bj (office).

ZINZINDOHOUÉ, Armand; Benin politician; Cabinet Dir, Ministry of Transport and Public Works 2006–07, Del. Minister to the Pres. for Transport and Public Works 2007–08; Minister of the Interior and Public Security 2008–10; Pres. Friends of Radio Maranatha Asscn 2000.

ZIOBRO, Zbigniew Tadeusz; Polish lawyer and politician; *Minister of Justice;* b. 18 Aug. 1970, Kraków; m. Patrycja Kotecka; two s.; ed Jagiellonian Univ., Krakow; legal training at regional prosecutor's office in Katowice; worked for investigative bodies, including Gen. Customs Inspectorate, Kraków; f. Katon Asscn and Help Centre for Victims of Crime and Social Pathology 1999; wrote communal draft of penal code 2000; fmr Adviser to Minister of Internal Affairs and Admin; elected to Sejm; Deputy Minister of Justice 2001, fmr Vice-Chair., Legislative Comm. and Special Comm. for Changes to Codifications; Minister of Justice and Public Prosecutor Gen. 2005–07, Minister of Justice 2015–; mem. European Parl. for Lesser Poland and Świętokrzyskie 2009–14. *Address:* Ministry of Justice, 00-950 Warsaw, Al. Ujazdowskie 11 (office); Law and Justice Party, 02-018 Warsaw, ul. Nowogrodzka 84/86, Poland (office). *Telephone:* (22) 6215035 (office). *Fax:* (22) 6216767 (office). *E-mail:* biuro@pis.org.pl (office). *Website:* www.pis.org.pl (office).

ZIRINSKY, Susan; American journalist and producer; *President and Senior Executive Producer, CBS News;* b. 3 March 1952, New York; d. of Richard Zirinsky and Cynthia Zirinsky (née Finkelstein); one c.; ed Amercian Univ.; joined CBS News, Washington Bureau in 1972, covered the White House for more than 10 years, Sr Exec. Producer, 48 Hours (TV series) 1996–2019, Pres. and Sr Exec. Producer, CBS News 2019–; has worked with Dan Rather, Lesley Stahl, Ed Bradley, James L. Brooks; First Amendment Service Award, Radio TV and Digital News Foundation 2003, Lifetime Achievement Award, Int. TV & Film Awards 2013. *Television includes:* as assoc. producer: Broadcast News 1987; exec. producer: movie documentaries: 9/11 2002, Elvis by the Presleys 2005, That's the Way It Is: Celebrating Cronkite at 90 2007, In God's Name (Christopher Award for TV and Film (jtly) 2007) 2007, The Lord's Boot Camp 2008, That's the Way It Was: Remembering Walter Cronkite 2009, CBS 48 Hours Presents, Vanity Fair: Hollywood Scandal 2011, Vanity Fair's Hollywood 2013; movies: Ted Kennedy: The Last Brother 2009, Fashion's Night Out 2010, Person to Person (co-exec. producer) 2012, David Letterman: A Life on Television (sr exec. producer) 2015. *Address:* CBS Broadcast Center, 530 W,57th Street, New York, NY 10019, USA (office). *Website:* www.cbsnews.com/team/susan-zirinsky/ (office).

ZIRNBAUER, Martin, MSc, DPhil; German theoretical physicist and academic; *Professor, University of Cologne;* b. 25 April 1958, Moosburg, Bavaria; ed Technical Univ. of Munich, Univ. of Oxford, UK; mem. Balliol Coll., Oxford 1979–82; Research Assoc., Max Planck Inst. for Nuclear Physics, Heidelberg 1982–84; Research Assoc., California Inst. of Tech., USA, Weingart Prize Fellowship 1984–87, Asst Prof. 1988; Assoc. Prof. (C3) for Theoretical Physics, Univ. of Cologne 1987–95, Full Prof. (C4) for Theoretical Physics 1996–, Dean of Physics 2007–08, mem. Cttee Previewing Faculty Appointments (Beirat für Berufungsangelegenheiten) 2005–; Founding Dir Transregional Collaborative Research Centre 'Symmetries and Universality in Mesoscopic Systems' (SFB/TR 12, Cologne-Bochum-Essen-Warsaw) 2003–06; mem. Scientific Cttee, Max Planck Inst. for Math., Bonn 2004–14, Scientific Cttee, Mathematisches Forschungsinstitut Oberwolfach 2010–14, Chair. Max Planck Medal Cttee 2018–; Deputy Chair. Bonn-Cologne Grad. School of Physics and Astronomy 2007–12, Chair. 2012–14; mem. St John's Coll., Cambridge, UK 2008–; Assoc. Ed., Nuclear Physics B: Field Theory and Statistical Mechanics 2004–14; mem. German Nat. Science Acad. Leopoldina 2007; mem. Scientific Advisory Bd, Erwin Schrödinger Int. Inst. for Mathematics and Physics 2016–; ranked among the top ten high school graduates of the Fed. State of Bavaria 1976, gifted student scholarship, Bavarian State Govt (Bayerische Begabtenförderung) 1976–79, Scholar of the German Nat. Scholarship Foundation 1976–82, Gottfried Wilhelm Leibniz Prize, German Science Foundation 2009, Max Planck Medal, Deutsche Physikalische Gesellschaft 2012. *Publications:* numerous papers in professional journals. *Address:* Room 206, Institute for Theoretical Physics, Department of Physics, University of Cologne, Zülpicher Str. 77, 50937 Cologne, Germany (office). *Telephone:* (221) 4704302 (office). *Fax:* (221) 4702189 (office). *E-mail:* zirnbauer@uni-koeln.de (office). *Website:* www.thp.uni-koeln.de (office).

ŽITŇANSKÁ, Lucia, PhD, JUDr; Slovak government official, lawyer and politician; *Minister of Justice;* b. 3 June 1964, Bratislava; m.; three c.; ed Comenius Univ.; property rights lawyer 1987–89; business lawyer, Práca Publrs 1989–90; Expert Asst, Anti-Monopoly Office 1990–92, mem. Appeal Comm. 1993–99; Jr Asst, Dept of Commercial, Econ. and Financial Law, Faculty of Law, Comenius Univ. 1992–2002, Sr Asst 2002–; State Sec. of Justice 2002–06, Minister of Justice 2006, 2010–12; mem. Parl. (Slovenská Demokratická a Krestanská Únia-Demokratická Strana (SDKÚ-DS—Slovak Democratic and Christian Union-Democratic Party)) 2006–10, (Most/Híd—Bridge) 2012–16, mem. Parl. Constitutional Affairs Cttee; Minister of Justice 2016–; Nat. Consultant, PHARE project 2000; mem. Examination Comm. for collective investment exams 2000–, Ministry of Justice Working Group on EU and Co. Law 2000–01, Council of Govt Special Comm. on the financial market 2000–02, Advisory Comm. on the financial market 2002–; Guest Lecturer, Inst. for Econ. Law of Cen. and Eastern Europe, Vienna 1998, 2001; mem. Bd of Govs, Acad. of European Law. *Address:* Ministry of Justice, Župné nám. 13, 813 11 Bratislava (office); Gorkého 10, 811 10 Bratislava, Slovakia (home). *Telephone:* (2) 5935-3111 (office). *Fax:* (2) 5935-3602 (office). *E-mail:* tlacove@justice.sk (office). *Website:* www.justice.gov.sk (office).

ZIVA, Vladimir P.; Russian conductor; *Artistic Director and Principal Conductor, Moscow Symphony Orchestra;* b. 7 March 1957, Arkhangelsk; m. Anna Ziva; two s.; ed Leningrad State Conservatory, Moscow State Conservatory; asst to Prin. Conductor, Symphony Orchestra of Moscow Philharmonics 1984–87; teacher, Moscow State Conservatory 1988–89; Artistic Dir and Chief Conductor Nizhne-Novgorod Philharmonic Orchestra 1988–2000; Prin. Conductor, St Petersburg Mussorgsky Theatre of Opera and Ballet 1990–92; Prin. Conductor Moscow Symphony Orchestra 1997–, Artistic Dir 2000–; Co-founder Krasnodar Opera Co. 2003–; also currently Artistic Dir and Chief Conductor, South Jutland Symphony Orchestra; opera stage productions, in collaboration with B. Pokrovsky, include The Turn of the Screw, Albert Herring by B. Britten, Snow Maiden by P. Tchaikovsky; Honoured Artist of Russia 1994, State Prize of the Russian Federation 1995, Conductor of the Year 1996, 1997, Music Review; State Prize of Russian Federation 1995. *Address:* Moscow Symphony Orchestra, 191285 Moscow, Mosfilmovskaya 1, Russia (office). *Telephone:* (499) 143-97-13 (office). *E-mail:* info@moscowsymphony.ru (office). *Website:* www.moscowsymphony.ru (office).

ŽIVKOVIĆ, Zoran; Serbian politician; *Leader, New Party (Nova stranka);* b. 22 Dec. 1960, Niš; m. Biserka Živković; one s. one d.; ed Bora Stankovic Grammar School, Niš and Belgrade Two-Year College of Econs; set up pvt. co. 1988; Pres. City Cttee of Democratic Party, Niš 1993–95; Rep. to Nat. Ass. of Repub. of Serbia 1993–97; Mayor of Niš 1996–2003; Founding mem. Democratic Party 1992, Deputy Chair., First Vice-Pres. and Deputy Pres. –2012; Minister of the Interior, Fed. Govt of Yugoslavia 2000–03; Prime Minister of Serbia and Montenegro 2003–04; Founder and Leader New Party (Nova stranka) 2013–; Owner House of Wines Živković. *Address:* New Party (Nova stranka), 11000 Belgrade, Simina 9A, Serbia (office). *Telephone:* (11) 4066–541 (office). *E-mail:* infor@novastranka.rs (office). *Website:* www.novastranka.rs (office).

ŽIŽEK, Slavoj, PhD; Slovenian sociologist, philosopher, critic and academic; *Global Distinguished Professor of German,, New York University;* b. 21 March 1949, Ljubljana; m. 1st Renata Salecl; m. 2nd Analia Hounie 2004; ed Univ. of Ljubljana, Univ. Paris-VIII, France; moved to France early 1970s; prevented from gaining post at Univ. of Ljubljana after his degree thesis was deemed politically suspect 1975, spent next few years undertaking nat. service in Yugoslav army, eventually became involved with group of Slovenian scholars studying psychoanalytic theory of Jacques Lacan; apptd Researcher, Inst. for Sociology, Univ. of Ljubljana 1979–, now Sr Researcher; Prof. of Philosophy and Psychoanalysis European Graduate School, Saas-Fee, Switzerland; Int. Dir Birkbeck Inst. for the Humanities, Birkbeck, Univ. of London; currently Global Distinguished Prof. of German, New York Univ.; Visiting Prof., Univ. of Paris-VIII 1982–83, 1985–86, Centre for the Study of Psychoanalysis and Art, SUNY Buffalo 1991–92, Univ. of Minnesota 1992, Tulane Univ. 1993, Cardozo Law School, New York 1994, Columbia Univ. 1995, Princeton Univ. 1996, New School for Social Research 1997, Univ. of Michigan 1998, Georgetown Univ. 1999; cand. for Liberal Democracy of Slovenia in 1990 presidential elections; Founding Pres. Soc. for Theoretical Psychoanalysis, Ljubljana. *Television:* The Pervert's Guide to Cinema (three-part documentary, More 4 channel, UK) 2006. *Publications include:* The Sublime Object of Ideology 1989, For They Know Not What They Do: Enjoyment as a Political Factor 1991, Looking Awry: An Introduction to Jacques Lacan through Popular Culture 1991, Everything You Always Wanted to Know About Lacan (But Were Afraid to Ask Hitchcock) (ed) 1992, Enjoy Your Symptom! Jacques Lacan in Hollywood and Out 1992, Tarrying With the Negative: Kant, Hegel and the Critique of Ideology 1993, Mapping Ideology (ed) 1994, The Metastases of Enjoyment: Six Essays on Woman and Causality (Wo Es War) 1994, The Indivisible Remainder: An Essay on Schelling and Related Matters 1996, Gaze and Voice as Love Objects (co-ed.) 1996, The Plague of Fantasies 1997, The Abyss of Freedom: Ages of the World (co-ed) 1997, The Ticklish Subject: The Absent Centre of Political Ontology 1999, Contingency, Hegemony, Universality: Contemporary Dialogues on the Left (co-ed) 2000, The Art of the Ridiculous Sublime, On David Lynch's Lost Highway 2000, The Fragile Absolute or Why the Christian Legacy is Worth Fighting For 2000, On Belief 2001, The Fright of Real Tears: Kieslowski and the Future 2001, Did Somebody Say Totalitarianism? Five Essays on the (Mis)Use of a Notion 2001, Opera's Second Death 2001, Welcome to the Desert of the Real 2002, Revolution at the Gates: Žižek on Lenin, the 1917 Writings 2002, The Puppet and the Dwarf 2003, Organs Without Bodies: On Deleuze and Consequences 2003, Iraq: The Borrowed Kettle 2004, Interrogating the Real 2005, The Universal Exception 2006, Neighbors and Other Monsters (in The Neighbor: Three Inquiries in Political Theology) 2006, The Parallax View 2006, Living in the End Times 2010, The Year of Dreaming Dangerously 2012, God in Pain: Inversions of Apocalypse (with Boris Gunjević) 2012; series ed.: Analecta, Wo es war, SIC; contrib. articles to newspapers, journals and websites, including London Review of Books, Guardian Unlimited. *Address:* Department of German, New York University, 19 University Place, 3rd floor, New York, NY 10003, USA (office); Institute of Sociology, University of Ljubljana, Kardeljeva ploščad 5, 1000 Ljubljana, Slovenia (office). *Telephone:* (212) 998-8650 (NYU) (office); (1) 5805100 (office). *Fax:* (212) 995-4823 (NYU); (1) 5805101 (office). *E-mail:* sz21@nyu.edu; szizek@yahoo.com (home); slavoj.zizek@fdv.uni-lj.si (office). *Website:* german.as.nyu.edu/page/home (office); www.fdv.uni-lj.si (office).

ZLATANOVA, Zinaida Kamenova, LLM; Bulgarian politician; b. 24 July 1973, Sofia; ed German Language School and Sofia Univ. 'St Kliment Ohridski'; work experience includes, amongst others, Dir of Directorate for Coordination of EU Affairs and Int. Financial Insts of Council of Ministers; fmr Head of EU Integration Unit, Ministry of Environment and Water, fmr Sr Expert, EU Integration and Int. Cooperation Dept; Head of EC Representation in Bulgaria 2008–13; Deputy Prime Minister and Minister of Justice (also in charge of EU Funds Absorption) 2013–14.

ZLATEVA, Denitsa; Bulgarian politician; *Deputy Prime Minister for Bulgaria's Presidency of the Council of the European Union;* Admin. Man., Bayer Bulgaria EOOD 1995–2008; mem. Nat. Ass. (Narodno Sobraniye—Parl.) 2013–14, Chair. Cttee on European Affairs and Oversight of European Funds; mem. Exec. Bureau/Int. Sec., Balgarska Sotsialisticheska Partiya (BSP—Bulgarian Socialist Party) 2009–17; Sec. of the Pres. in charge of EU Presidency, Office of the Pres. of Bulgaria Jan. 2017–; Deputy Prime Minister for Bulgaria's Presidency of the Council of the EU 2018 in the Caretaker Govt of 2017–. *Address:* Office of the Council of Ministers, 1594 Sofia, bul. Dondukov 1, Bulgaria (office). *Telephone:* (2) 940-29-99 (office). *Fax:* (2) 980-21-01 (office). *E-mail:* gis@government.bg (office). *Website:* www.government.bg (office).

ŻMIJEWSKI, Artur; Polish artist, filmmaker and photographer; b. 26 May 1966, Warsaw; ed Warsaw Acad. of Fine Arts, diploma at studio of Prof. Grzegorz Kowalski; Bursar, Gerrit Rietveld Academie, Amsterdam 1995; Guarene Arte exhibition (Prize of the Fondazione Sandretto Re Rebaudengo Per L'Arte for his work 'An Eye for an Eye') 2000; his 'Repetition' was shown in Polish Pavilion at the Venice Biennale 2005; Bursar, DAAD Artists in Residence, Berlin 2007–08, prepared latest project 'Democracies'; creates installations, photographs of objects, video realizations and films; fmr Ed. Czereja magazine; art critic and curator; Dir Seventh Berlin Biennale; Ordway Prize, New Museum, New York and Creative Link for the Arts 2010. *Address:* c/o Fundacja Galerii Foksal, Górskiego 1A, 00-033 Warsaw, Poland. *Telephone:* (22) 8265081. *E-mail:* mail@fgf.com.pl. *Website:* www.fgf.com.pl.

ZOBEL DE AYALA, Jaime, BA; Philippine business executive and art photographer; *Chairman Emeritus, Ayala Corporation;* b. 18 July 1934; s. of Alfonson Zobel de Ayala and Carmen Pfitz y Henero; m. Beatriz Miranda 1985; two s. five d.; ed De La Salle Univ., Madrid, Harvard Univ.; with House of Ayala 1958– (renamed Ayala Corpn 1967), Pres. and Chair. 1983–2005, Chair. Emer. 2006–; Amb. to UK 1970–75; fmr Adviser to Pres. Aquino; fmr Chair. Bank of Philippines Islands; exhibits photography regularly in the Philippines and abroad and has produced several books; Chevalier des Arts et des Lettres 1980, Philippine Legion of Honour 2009; Hon. DBA (De La Salle Univ., Manila) 1985, Hon. LLD (Univ. of Philippines) 1991; Senator Award 1986. *Achievements include:* first Filipino amateur photographer to be confirmed Licentiate by Royal Photographic Soc. *Leisure interests:* photography, scuba diving. *Address:* c/o Ayala Corporation, 7/F Makati Stock Exchange Building, Ayala Avenue, 1254 Makati, Metro Manila 1200, Philippines. *Website:* www.jaimezobel.com.

ZOELLICK, Robert Bruce, BA, JD; American lawyer, business executive and fmr government official; *Chairman, International Advisory Board, Goldman Sachs;* b. 25 July 1953, Evergreen Park, Ill.; s. of William T. Zoellick and Gladys Zoellick; m. Sherry Lynn Ferguson 1980; ed Swarthmore Coll., Harvard Law School and Kennedy School of Govt, Harvard Univ.; Special Asst to Asst Attorney-Gen., Criminal Div., Dept of Justice 1978–79; fellowship to Hong Kong 1980; pvt. law practice 1981–82; Vice-Pres., Asst to Chair. and CEO Bd Fannie Mae 1983–85, Exec. Vice-Pres. Housing and Law 1993–97; Special Asst to Deputy Sec., Deputy Asst Sec. for Financial Insts Policy, Counsellor to Sec. and Exec. Sec. Treasury Dept 1985–88; Counsellor with rank of Under-Sec. Dept of State 1989–92, Under-Sec. for Econ. and Agricultural Affairs 1991–92; Deputy Chief of Staff, Asst to Pres. 1992–93; Olin Prof. of Nat. Security Affairs, US Naval Acad. 1997–98; Pres. and CEO Center for Strategic and Int. Studies 1998–99; US Trade Rep. 2001–05; Deputy Sec. of State and COO Dept of State 2005–06; Vice-Chair., Int., Goldman Sachs Group Inc., New York 2006–07, Chair. Int. Advisory Bd 2013–; Pres. World Bank Group, Washington, DC 2007–12; mem. Bd of Dirs Temasek Holdings (sovereign wealth fund of Singapore), Alliance Capital, Said Capital, German Marshall Fund US; Dir Aspen Inst. Strategy Group; mem. Int. Advisory Bd Rolls-Royce Group; Kt Commdr's Cross (Germany); Hon. DHumLitt (St Joseph's Coll., Rensselaer, Ind.); Distinguished Service Award, Treasury Dept, Alexander Hamilton Award, State Dept, Department of Defense Medal for Distinguished Public Service. *Address:* Goldman Sachs, 200 West Street, #200, New York, NY 10282, USA (office). *Telephone:* (212) 902-1000 (office). *Website:* www.goldmansachs.com (office).

ZOGBY, James, BA, PhD; American political analyst and international organization executive; *President, Arab American Institute;* b. 19 Nov. 1945, New York, NY; m. Eileen Patricia McMahon; five c.; ed Le Moyne Coll., Temple Univ.; Pres. Arab American Inst. 1985–; Co-Pres. Builders for Peace Cttee 1993; Chair. Forum on Palestinian Economy, Casablanca Econ. Summit 1994; Co-Convenor Nat. Democratic Ethnic Coordinating Cttee; elected to Democratic Nat. Cttee's Exec. Cttee as Rep. of Nat. Democratic Ethnic Coordinating Cttee 1999, Chair. Resolutions Cttee; mem. Bd American Civil Liberties Union, Nat. Immigration Forum, Council on Foreign Relations; mem. Human Rights Watch Middle East Advisory Cttee; currently Sr Analyst, Zogby Int.; lectured on Middle East Issues, US-Arab relations, and history of Arab American community; Co-founder Palestinian Human Rights Campaign; Co-founder and Exec. Dir American-Arab Anti-Discrimination Cttee; Co-founder and Nat. Endowment for the Humanities Post-doctoral Fellow, Princeton Univ. 1976; Hon. LLD (Le Moyne); Distinguished Public Service Award. *Television:* host of Viewpoint with James Zogby on Abu Dhabi TV and Link TV, USA. *Publications:* books include What Ethnic Americans Really Think, and What Arabs Think: Values, Beliefs and Concerns, Arab Voices: What They Are Saying to Us, and Why it Matters 2010; author of 'Washington Watch' newspaper column 1992–. *Address:* Arab American Institute, 1600 K Street NW, Suite 601, Washington, DC 20006, USA (office). *Telephone:* (202) 429-9210 (office). *Fax:* (202) 429-9214 (office). *E-mail:* jzogby@aaiusa.org (office). *Website:* www.aaiusa.org (office); www.zogby.com.

ZOGHBI, Huda Y., BSc, MD; American (b. Lebanese) neurologist, geneticist and academic; *Professor, Departments of Pediatrics, Molecular and Human Genetics, Neurology and Neuroscience, Baylor College of Medicine;* b. (Huda El-Hibri), 29 June 1955, Beirut, Lebanon; m. William Zoghbi; one s. one d.; ed American Univ. of Beirut, Meharry Medical Coll., Nashville, Tenn.; moved to Tex. at outbreak of Lebanese civil war 1975; Pediatrician, Texas Children's Hosp. and Ben Taub Gen. Hosp.; Prof., Depts of Pediatrics, Molecular and Human Genetics, Neurology and Neuroscience, Baylor Coll. of Medicine, Houston, Tex. 1994–; Investigator, Howard Hughes Medical Inst. 1996–; Dir Jan and Dan Duncan Neurological Research Inst., Texas Children's Hosp.; mem. NAS, Inst. of Medicine; Fellow, AAAS; Cátedra Laboris Prof., Univ. of Monterrey 2009; Hon. DMS (Yale Univ.); Hon. DSc (Meharry Medical School, Middlebury Coll.); Kilby Award for Extraordinary Contribs to Soc. 1995, E. Mead Johnson Award, Soc. of Pediatric Research 1996, Javits Award, NINDS Council, NIH 1998, Soriano Award, American Neurological Asscn 1998, Sidney Carter Award, American Acad. of Neurology 1998, Bernard Sachs Award, Child Neurology Soc. 2001, Raymond D. Adams Award, American Neurological Asscn 2002, Marta Philipson Award in Pediatrics, Philipson Foundation for Research 2004, Neuronal Plasticity Prize, IPSEN Foundation 2004, Bristol-Myers Squibb Neuroscience Distinguished Achievement Award 2006, Robert J. and Claire Pasarow Foundation Award in Neuropsychiatry 2007, Texas Women's Hall of Fame Award, Texas Gov.'s Comm. for Women 2008, Vilcek Prize for Biomedical Research 2009, Int. Rett Syndrome Foundation's Circle of Angels Research Award 2009, Marion Spencer Fay Award, Drexel Univ. Coll. of Medicine 2009, Vita and Lee Lyman Dewey Tuttle Brookwood Legacy Award for Excellence and Partnership in Medicine 2011, Gruber Prize in Neuroscience 2011, Dickson Prize in Medicine 2013, March of Dimes Prize in Developmental Biology 2014, Edward M. Scolnick Prize in Neuroscience 2014, Shaw Prize in Life Science and Medicine (co-recipient) 2016. *Publications:* numerous papers in professional journals. *Address:* Huda Zoghbi Lab, Jan and Dan Duncan Neurological Research Institute, Texas Children's Hospital 1250 Moursund Street, Suite 1350 Mail stop NR-1350, Houston, TX 77030, USA (office). *Telephone:* (713) 798-6558 (office). *Fax:* (713) 798-8728 (office). *E-mail:* hzoghbi@bcm.edu (office). *Website:* www.bcm.edu/research/labs/huda-zoghbi (office).

ZOHAR, Israel; Israeli artist; b. 7 Feb. 1945, Oktubinsk, Kazakh SSR, USSR; m. 1st Ruth Bregman 1966 (divorced 1974); m. 2nd Arna Meyuhas 1974 (divorced 1982); m. 3rd Wendy Caron 1984; m. 4th Layil Barr; five s. one d.; ed Bezalel Acad. of Art, Jerusalem and with artists A. Yaskil and Ernst Fuchs; lectured at Hebrew Univ. Jerusalem 1979; major works include portraits of HRH The Princess of Wales 1990, Henry Catto (fmr US Amb. to UK) 1990, 24ft×8ft painting of Jacob's Ladder for Music Festival, Exeter Cathedral, UK 1992, Anne Frank, Music Festival, Bad Kissingen 1992, Edith Sitwell for Hampstead Festival, London 1995, Judge Michael Sherrard for the Middle Temple, London, group portrait for the High Court of Justice at Hon. Soc. of the Middle Temple 2005, portrait of Wallace Browne, Lord Mayor of Belfast (now Lord Browne of Belmont) 2006; also writes, adapts and directs plays for theatre, including Thomas Mann's Death in Venice (Duke of Cambridge, London), Brecht's The Jewish Wife (Cockpit, London), works by Strindberg, Chekhov, Sartre, Dostoevsky for Café Theatre, London, etc. *Telephone:* (20) 8341-1754. *E-mail:* zohar.london@googlemail.com. *Website:* www.izohar.co.uk.

ZOLL, Andrzej, PhD, DHabil; Polish professor of law; b. 27 May 1942, Sieniawa; m.; one s.; ed Jagiellonian Univ., Kraków; Asst, Criminal Law Dept, Jagiellonian Univ., Kraków 1964–75, Asst Prof. of Criminal Law 1975–88, Extraordinary Prof. 1988–91, Ordinary Prof. from 1991; Judge, Constitutional Tribunal 1989–97, Pres. 1993–97; Vice-Chair. State Election Comm. 1989, Chair. 1990–93; Chair. Legislation Bd attached to the Prime Minister 1998–2000; Commr for Citizens' Rights 2000–06; currently Lecturer, School of Law and Public Admin in Przemysl; Commdr's Cross, Order of Polonia Restituta 1997, Great Cross of Merit with Star (Germany) 1997, Golden Star on Ribbon of Order of Merit (Austria) 1997, Great Duke Gedymin Order (Lithuania) 1997; Dr hc (Mainz) 1996, (Vilnius) 2003. *Publications:* more than 170 works on penal law, philosophy of law and constitutional law including Materialnoprawna problematyka warunkowego umorzenia postępowania karnego 1973, Okoliczności wyłączające bezprawność czynu 1982, O normie prawnej w prawie karnym 1990, Komentarz do kodeksu karnego (co-author) 1998. *Leisure interests:* mountaineering, classical music, books. *Address:* School of Law and Public Administration in Przemyśl, ul. Wybrzeże Ojca Świętego Jana Pawła II 2, 37-700 Przemyśl, Poland (office). *Telephone:* (16) 6779050 (office). *E-mail:* sekretariat.p@wspia.eu (office). *Website:* www.wspia.eu (office).

ZOLLER, Peter, PhD; Austrian theoretical physicist and academic; *Professor of Physics, University of Innsbruck;* b. 16 Sept. 1952; m. Johanna Zoller; two s. one d.; ed Gymnasium, Innsbruck, Univ. of Innsbruck; Max Kade Fellow, Univ. of Southern California, Los Angeles, USA 1978–79; Asst Prof., Univ. of Innsbruck 1977–90, Habilitation 1981, tenure 1981–, Prof. of Physics, Inst. for Theoretical Physics 1994–, Head of Inst. 1995–99, Vice-Dean of Studies 2001–04; Scientific Dir Inst. for Quantum Optics and Quantum Information, Austrian Acad. of Sciences, Innsbruck 2003–; Jt Inst. for Lab. Astrophysics (JILA) Visiting Fellow, Univ. of Colorado, USA 1981–82, 1988, Prof. of Physics and JILA Fellow, Jt Inst. for Lab. Astrophysics (JILA) 1991–94, JILA Adjoint Fellow 1994–; Guest Prof., Univ. Paris-Sud, Orsay, France 1986; Chair Prof., Tsinghua Univ., Beijing, People's Repub. of China; Yan Jici Chair Professorship, Univ. of Science and Tech. of China, Heifei 2004; Lorentz-Prof., Leiden Univ. March–June 2005; Guest Prof., Institut Henri Poincaré, Paris 2006; Distinguished Fellow, Max Planck Inst. of Quantum Optics, Garching, Germany 2012–13; Speaker, Sonderforschungsbereich Quantum Control and Measurement, Innsbruck 1999–; Jacques Solvay Int. Chair in Physics, Int. Solvay Insts 2015; Distinguished Visiting Scholar, KITP Simons 2016; mem. Advisory Bds ITAMP, Harvard Univ. 1996–99, Max Planck Inst. for Quantum Optics, Garching 2001–, BEC Inst., Trento, Italy 2003–, Perimeter Inst., Canada 2005, Chinese Nat. Lab., Univ. of Science and Tech. of China 2005–, Arnold Sommerfeld Centre, LMU, Munich 2005–; mem. Int. Advisory Cttee for Inst. of Theoretical Physics, Beijing, Chinese Acad. of Sciences 2005–; Div. Assoc. Ed. Physical Review Letters 1994–98; Ed. Reviews of Modern Physics (Atomic Physics, Quantum Optics and Quantum Information) 1999–2003; Corresp. mem. Austrian Acad. of Sciences 1999–2001, mem. 2001–; mem. Austrian Physical Soc., Optical Soc. of America, NAS 2008, Royal Netherlands Acad. of Arts and Sciences 2008, Spanish Royal Acad. of Sciences 2009, German Acad. of Sciences Leopoldina 2010, European Acad. of Sciences 2012, Academia Europaea 2013; Fellow, American Physical Soc. 1993; Dr hc (Free Univ. of Amsterdam) 2012; Award of the City of Innsbruck 1981, Ludwig-Boltzmann Award, Austrian Physical Soc. 1983, Wittgenstein Award, Austrian Fed. Ministry of Science and Austrian Science Foundation 1998, Max Born Award, Optical Soc. of America 1998, Schrödinger Prize, Austrian Acad. of Sciences 1998, Sr Humboldt Award 2000, K. Innitzer Award 2001, Loeb Lecturer, Harvard Univ. 2004, Max Planck Medal, German Physical Soc. 2005, Niels Bohr/UNESCO Gold Medal 2005, Sixth Int. Quantum Communication Award 2006, Dirac Medal 2006, Dirac Medal, ICTP Trieste 2006, BBVA Foundation Frontiers of Knowledge Award in Basic Sciences (Spain) 2008, Wissenschaftspreis der Stiftung Südtiroler Sparkasse 2009, Benjamin Franklin Medal, Franklin Inst. 2010, Blaise Pascal Medal, European Acad. of Sciences 2011, Hamburg Prize for Theoretical Physics 2011, ERC Synergy Grant (shared with I. Bloch, E. Altman and J. Dalibard) 2012, David Ben Gurion Medal 2013, Wolf Prize in Physics (co-recipient) 2013, Herbert-Walther-Preis 2016, Norman F. Ramsey Prize 2018. *Publications:* Quantum Noise, A Handbook of Markovian and Non-Markovian Quantum Stochastic Methods with Applications to Quantum Optics (co-author) 2004; numerous scientific papers in professional journals. *Address:* Institute for Theoretical Physics, University of Innsbruck, Technikerstraße 21a, 6020 Innsbruck, Austria (office). *Telephone:* (512) 507-4780 (office). *Fax:* (512) 507-9815 (office). *E-mail:* peter.zoller@uibk.ac.at (office). *Website:* www.uibk.ac.at/th-physik/people/staffdb/354190.xml (office); bozon.uibk.ac.at/qo/zoller (office).

ZOLOTOV, Yuri Alexandrovich, DrChem; Russian chemist; *Principal Researcher, Kurnakov Institute of General and Inorganic Chemistry;* b. 4 Oct. 1932, Vysokovskoe, Moscow Region; m.; one s.; ed Moscow State Univ.; researcher, Deputy Dir, Head of Lab., Inst. of Geochemistry and Analytical Chem. 1958–89; Dir N Kurnakov Inst. of Gen. and Inorganic Chem. 1989–99, Prin. Researcher 2005–; Distinguished Prof., Moscow Univ.; currently Prof. and Head Analytical, Chemistry Div. Devt of Chemistry, Lomonosov Moscow State Univ.; Corresp. mem., USSR (now Russian) Acad. of Sciences 1970, mem. 1987–; main research in analytical chem., extraction of inorganic compounds, ion chromatography; Hon. Mem. Japan Soc. of Analytical Chem. 1991, Göteborg Royal Soc. of Art and Sciences, Sweden 1999; Dr hc (Kiev) 1994, (Krasnodar) 2002, (Ufa) 2012; Prize of USSR Council of Ministers 1985, USSR State Prize 1972, State Prize of Russia 1991, 2000, Prize of Russian Govt 2010, Hanus Medal, Prague 2012. *Publications:* 52 books, 900 scientific papers. *Leisure interests:* fishing, writing. *Address:* N. Kurnakov Institute of General and Inorganic Chemistry, 31 Leninsky prosp., 119991 Moscow, Russia (office). *Telephone:* (495) 633-84-92 (office), (499) 132-20-10 (home). *Fax:* (495) 952-34-20 (office). *E-mail:* zolotov@igic.ras.ru (office); zolotov.32@mail.ru (office); zolotov@analyt.chem.msu.ru (office).

ZONG, Qinghou; Chinese food industry executive; *Chairman and CEO, Hangzhou Wahaha Group;* b. 1945, Hangzhou, Zhejiang Prov.; m. Shi Youzhen; one d.; spent 17 years on Zhejiang state farms; returned to Hangzhou to take marketing position; hired to run sales dept of school-run business in Shangcheng Dist, Hangzhou 1987; launched Wahaha Nutritional Food Factory with two retd teachers to produce children's nutritional drinks 1989, merged with Hangzhou Canning Food Factory to form Hangzhou Wahaha Group Corpn 1991, merged with three cos in Fulin to support construction of Three Gorges area and form Wahaha Fulin Co., entered jt venture with Danone Group to form five new subsidiaries 1996, CEO Wahaha Group (largest beverage co. in China) –2007 (resgnd as Chair. of the jt venture); Del. to NPC 2002–; State Spark Second Prize, State Science Comm. 1992, recognized as a China Man. Master 1994, State Award for Excellent Operation Mans, Wu-Yi Medal, China Fed. of Trade Unions, Award for Nat. Model Worker, Fed. of Trade Unions 1995, Honoured Shuangduikou Excellent Personnel, Zhejiang Prov. 1998, honorary titles include: Nat. Excellent Entrepreneur, Nat. Excellent Manager, Model of Patriotism to Support the Armed Forces, Outstanding Builder of Socialism with Chinese Characteristics, First Chinese Entrepreneurs Entrepreneurship Prize. *Address:* Hangzhou Wahaha Group, 160 Qingtai Street, Hangzhou 310009, Zhejiang, People's Republic of China (office). *Telephone:* (571) 86032866 (office). *Fax:* (571) 86846000 (office). *E-mail:* whh@wahaha.com.cn (office). *Website:* www.wahaha.com.cn (office).

ZONGO, Tertius, MEconSc; Burkinabè diplomatist, civil servant and academic; b. 18 May 1957, Kougoudgou, Boulkiemdé Prov.; m.; three c.; ed Inst. of Enterprises Admin., Nantes, France; Head of Accounts, Nat. Office of Crops 1983–85, Dir-Gen. 1985–88; Sec.-Gen. Chamber of Commerce, Industry and Crafts 1986; Prof. of Accounting, Business Economy and Financial Analysis, Univ. of Ouagadougou; Chief of Dept Multilateral Co-operation 1988–92; Dir-Gen. of Co-operation, Ministry of Finances and Planning 1992; Minister of Budget and Planning 1996–97, of Economy and Finance 1997–2000; Govt Spokesman 1996–2000; Amb. to USA 2002–07; Prime Minister of Burkina Faso 2007–11 (resgnd), reappointed 13 Jan.–18 April 2011; mem. Bd of Dirs SEMAFO Inc. (mining co.) 2012–; Kt and Officer of the Nat. Order. *Publications:* numerous contribs to papers on agric. and devt. *Leisure interests:* reading, sports.

ZÖPEL, Christoph, PhD; German politician, economist, publisher and academic; b. 4 July 1943, Gleiwitz; s. of Kurt Zöpel and Martha Zöpel (née Grohla); m. Barbara Rössler 1969; one s. two d.; ed Minden, Westphalia, Free Univ. Berlin, Ruhr Univ., Bochum; mem. SDP 1964–, Deputy Chair. SDP in Landtag 1975–78, mem. Exec. Cttee 1986–95, mem. Presidium 1992–95; City Councillor, Bochum 1969–72; mem. Landtag of Land North Rhine/Westphalia 1972–1990, Minister for Fed. Affairs 1978–80, for Rural and Urban Devt 1980–85, for Urban Devt, Housing and Transport 1985–90; mem. Bundestag 1990–2005, mem. Cttee on Foreign Affairs 1990–99, 2002–05, Deputy Chair. Cttee on the Affairs of the EU 1991–92, Minister of State, Fed. Foreign Office 1999–2005; mem. Parl. Ass. OSCE 1994–99; Deputy Mem. N Atlantic Ass. 1998–99; Chair. Cttee on the Economy, Social Cohesion and the Environment, Socialist Int. 2000–; Prof., German-Jordanian Univ., Amman; apptd Assoc. Prof., EBZ Business School, Univ. of Applied Sciences 2010; Special Adviser to Chair. of Social Democratic Party of Europe, Sergei Stanishev, for Central and Eastern Europe 2016–; Hon. Prof., Technische Universität Dortmund. *Publications include:* Weltstadt Ruhr, Essen 2005, Politik mit 9 Milliarden Menschen in einer Weltgesellschaft, Berlin 2008. *Address:* Kastanienweg 4, 44799 Bochum, Germany (home). *Telephone:* (30) 20654830 (office); (234) 30765798 (home). *E-mail:* christoph.zoepel@t-online.de (home). *Website:* www.christoph-zoepel.de.

ZORAMTHANGA, Shri Pu, BA; Indian politician; *Chief Minister of Mizoram;* b. 13 July 1944, Samthang village; s. of Darphunga Zoramthanga and Vanhnuaichhingi Zoramthanga; m. Roneihsangi Rohlira 1988; one s. one d.; ed Champhai Gandhi Memorial High School and Imphal D.M. Coll., Manipur; Sec. to Pres. Pu Laldenga, Leader of Mizo Nat. Front 1969–75, exiled with Pu Laldenga to Pakistan 1972–76, Foreign Rep. 1972–76; Minister of Finance and Educ., Mizoram State Govt 1987–90; Pres. Mizo Nat. Front 1990–; Chief Minister of Mizoram 1998–2008, 2018–; served as interlocutor for Home Ministry between Myanmar Cen. govt and various ethnic insurgents 2015. *Address:* Chief Minister's Office, McDonald Hill, Zarkawt, Aizawl 796 001, Mizoram (office); Mizo National Front, Aizawl 796 001, India (office). *Telephone:* (389) 2322150 (office). *Fax:* (389) 2322245 (office). *E-mail:* cm-mizoram@nic.com (office). *Website:* mizoram.nic.in (office).

ZORE, Edward J., BS, MS; American insurance industry executive; b. 5 July 1945, Milwaukee, Wis.; m. Diane Zore (neé Widemshek) 1967; two d.; ed Univ. of Wisconsin-Milwaukee; joined Investment Dept, Northwestern Mutual 1969, various positions 1969–90, Chief Investment Officer 1990–98, Chief Financial Officer 1995–98, elected Exec. Vice-Pres. 1995, apptd Head of Life and Disability Insurance Operations 1998, mem. Bd of Trustees 2000–, Pres. 2000–01, Chair. and CEO 2001–10 (retd), Dir, Northwestern Mutual Wealth Man. Co., Northwestern Investment Man. Co., Northwestern Long Term Care Insurance Co., Northwestern Int. Holdings, Inc., Northwestern Mutual Series Fund, Northwestern Mutual Foundation, Chair. Russell Investment Group, Tacoma, Wash. (subsidiary of Northwestern Mutual); mem. Bd of Dirs Frank Russell Co., Manpower Inc., American Council of Life Insurers; mem. The Business Roundtable and Conf. Bd; mem. Bd Children's Hosp. of Wis. Inc., Competitive Wis., Froedtert Health System, Greater Milwaukee Cttee, Medical Coll. of Wis., Metropolitan Milwaukee Asscn of Commerce, Susan G. Komen Breast Cancer Foundation Inc., United Performing Arts Fund, United Way, Wisconsin Policy Research Inst.; mem. Advisory Bd Zilber Neighborhood Initiative; Trustee, YMCA of Metropolitan Milwaukee; Hon. mem. Bd Million Dollar Round Table Foundation.

ZORIN, Leonid Genrikhovich; Russian playwright and writer; b. 3 Nov. 1924, Baku, Azerbaijan; s. of Genrikh Zorin and Polina Zorin; m. 1st 1951 (deceased); m. 2nd Tatjana Pospelova 1985; one s.; ed Azerbaijan State Univ., M. Gorky Inst. of Literature in Moscow; with Baku Russian Drama Theatre; later freelance, mem. USSR Union of Writers 1941–, Int. PEN Club, Russian PEN Centre, Russian Acad. of Cinema, Science and the Arts; Grand Prix for the best film script Grandmaster (Festival in Kranje, Yugoslavia), Golden Medal for film script Peace to the Newcomer, Venice Film Festival 1961, Prize of All-Union Contest of Playwrights Revival of Russia (for Moscow Nest) 1995, (for Lusgan) 1997, Laureate of Apollon Igoziev-Price 2003, Prize of the Russian Authors Org. 2006. *Plays include:* more than 50 produced in 16 countries, including Youth 1949, The Guests 1953, Alien Passport 1957, Kind Men 1959, The Deck 1963, The Decembrists 1967, Warsaw

Melody 1967, The Coronation 1969, Tsar's Hunt 1974, The Copper Grandmother 1975, The Invisibles 1999, Roman Comedy 2000, The Maniac 2000, The Misprint 2001, The Outcome 2002, The Detectives 2003, The Phantoms 2005, The Quotation, The Perished Plot, The Infidelity, The Carnival, The Moscow Nest, Lusgan. *Film scripts:* 15 including A Man from Nowhere 1961, The Law, Peace to the Newcomer 1961, The Friends and the Years 1966, Tsar's Hunt 1971, Grandmaster 1974, Pokrovskye Gates 1982, Hard Sand 2002. *Publications include:* novels and short stories: Old Manuscript 1983, Wanderer 1987, The Topic of the Day 1992, Proscenium 1997, The Plots 1998, The Teetotaller (Banner Prize, Apollon Grigorjev Prize) 2001, The Auction (collection) 2001, Whip (Banner Prize) 2002, Jupiter 2002, Oblivion 2004, The Prose (collection) in two vols; numerous essays; Theatre Fantasy (collection of plays) 1974, Selected Plays (2 vols) 1986, The Green Notebooks (collection of essays), The Curtain of the Millennium (collection of later plays) 2002, The Sansara (novel) 2004, The Will of Yzand (humorous book) 2005, The Parting March (humorous book) 2005, The National Idea 2006, The Letters from Petersburg 2006. *Leisure interests:* reading, chess. *Address:* Krasnoarmeyskaya str. 21, Apt. 73, 125319 Moscow, Russia (home). *Telephone:* (495) 151-43-33 (home).

ZORIN, Vladimir Yuryevich; Russian politician; b. 9 April 1948, Moscow; m.; three s. one d.; ed Tashkent Inst. of Nat. Econs, Acad. of Public Sciences at Cen. CP Cttee; fmr teacher; People's Deputy of Uzbekistan 1990, Deputy Perm. Rep., Cabinet of Ministers, Repub. of Uzbekistan to Govts of USSR and Russian Fed. 1991–93; fmr consultant on finance, regional policy and investments in various commercial cos; Deputy, then First Deputy Head Territorial Dept of Fed. Organs of Exec. Power, Chechen Repub.; Co-ordinator Exec. Cttee Int. Movt of Democratic Reforms on Relationship with CIS States 1991–93; mem. State Duma 1995–99; Deputy Head of Govt Del. on Peace Talks in Chechnya 1996; Chair. Perm. Cttee on Problems of Fed. and Regional Policy; Pres. Russian Asscn of Theory and Modelling of Int. Relations; mem. Political Council of Our Home is Russia Movt 1994–99; Deputy Rep. Plenipotentiary of Russian Pres. to Volga Fed. Dist 2000–01, Minister of Fed. Problems, Nat. and Migration Policy, then Minister without Portfolio, in charge of Nationalities Policy 2002–04. *Publications:* Chechen Conflict (1991–96): Estimate, Analysis and Ways of Solution, and numerous other publs on politics, history and sociology. *Leisure interests:* chess, painting, Russian folk and classical music, table tennis.

ZORKIN, Valerii Dmitriyevich, DJur; Russian lawyer, academic and judge; *Chairman, Constitutional Court;* b. 18 Feb. 1943, Konstantinovka, Oktyabrskii Dist, Maritime (Primorskii) Krai, Russian SFSR, USSR; widower; one d.; ed Faculty of Law, Moscow State Univ.; Sr Lecturer in Law, Moscow State Univ. 1964–67, Asst Prof. 1967–79; Prof. of Constitutional Law and Theory of State, Law Acad. of the USSR Ministry of Internal Affairs 1979–86, Prof. of Public Legal Disciplines 1986–; led group of experts on Constitutional Comm. 1990–91; Judge, Constitutional Court Oct. 1991, Chair. Nov. 1991–93 (resgnd), 2003–; Merited Lawyer of the Russian Fed. 2000; Order of Merit for the Fatherland (Third Class) 2008, (Second Class) 2011; Order of Friendship (Armenia) 2016; Diploma of the Pres. of the Russian Fed. 2008. *Publications include:* Positivist Theory of Law in Russia 1978, Russia and the Constitution in the 21st Century 2007, Constitution and Human Rights in 21st Century: to the 15th Anniversary of the Constitution of the Russian Federation and 60th Anniversary of the Universal Declaration on Human Rights 2008, Modern World, Law and Constitution 2010, Russia's Constitutional and Legal Development 2011, Law in the Context of Global Change 2013, Civilization of Law and Development of Russia 2015, Constitutional Court of Russia: Doctrine and Practice 2017. *Address:* Constitutional Court of the Russian Federation (Konstitutsionnyi Sud Rossiiskoi Federatsii), 190000 St Petersburg, pl. Senatskaya 1, Russia (office). *Telephone:* (812) 404-33-11 (office). *E-mail:* ksrf@ksrf .ru (office). *Website:* www.ksrf.ru/en/Info/Judges/Pages/judge.aspx?Param=2 (office).

ZOU'BI, Moneef Rafe', BEng, MSc, PhD; Jordanian engineer and scientific researcher; *Director-General, Islamic World Academy of Sciences;* b. 30 Dec. 1963, Amman; s. of Rafe' Abdul Hamid Zou'bi and Wadha Sharif Zou'bi; m. Dr Basma A. S. Dajani; two s. one d.; ed Bishop's School, Amman, Beeston Coll., Nottingham, UK, Univs of Brighton and Loughborough, UK, Univ. of Malaya, Kuala Lumpur, Malaysia; Resident Engineer, Jordan Royal Corps of Engineers 1988–90; Tech. Affairs Officer, Islamic World Acad. of Sciences 1990–91, Tech. Affairs Dir 1991–95, Deputy Exec. Dir 1995–98, Dir-Gen. 1998–, Chief Ed. Newsletter of the Islamic Acad. of Sciences; Grad. mem. ICE (UK), Inst. of Structural Engineers (UK); mem. Advisory Bd UNESCO Int. Centre for South-South Co-operation in Science, Tech. and Innovation, Malaysia, 2008, Muslim-Science.Com; mem. (Ex-Officio) Asscn of Engineers (Jordan), Licensing Execs Soc., Jordan Computer Soc., Jordanian Friends of Archaeology Asscn, Arab Youth Forum, Royal Automobile Club of Jordan, US-Islamic World Forum, Rosenberg Int. Water Forum, Council of Islamic World Acad. of Sciences 2009–, Canadian Soc. for the History and Philosophy of Science, Engineers Without Borders Canada, New York Acad. of Sciences, AAAS, European Asscn for Study of Science and Tech., mem. Int. Advisory Bd, Econ. Cooperation Org. Science Foundation, Bd of Judges, Templeton Prize 2018, 2019; Fellow, World Acad. of Art and Science, Acad. of Engineering and Tech. of the Developing World; Hon. Prof., East Kazakhstan State Univ. 2012, British Columbia Centennial Medal 2006, Tatarstan Acad. of Sciences Medal 2007, CICA Medal (Kazakhstan) 2012. *Publications include:* Health, Nutrition and Development in the Islamic World (co-author) 1995, Water in the Islamic World (co-author) 1995, An Overview of the Islamic Academy of Sciences 1999, Science Education and Technology Management in the Islamic World (co-author) 2000, Personalities Noble (ed.) 2000, Information Technology for Development in the Islamic World (co-author) 2001, Biotechnology and Genetic Engineering for Development in the Islamic World (co-author) 2004, Materials Science and Technology and Culture of Science (co-author) 2004, Islamic World Academy of Sciences Outreach 2005, Energy for Sustainable Development (co-ed.), Science and Technology for Socioeconomic Developemnt (co-ed.) 2006, Higher Education Excellence (co-ed.) 2009, Science, Technology and Innovation for Sustainable Development in the Islamic World: The Policies and Politics Rapprochement 2009, UNESCO Science Report 2010, UNESCO Science Report: Towards 2030 2015. *Leisure interests:* walking, photography, calligraphy, travel, cinema, reading. *Address:* Islamic World Academy of Sciences, PO Box 830036, Amman 11183 (office); 54 Oqba Bin Nafe' Street, Jabal Amman, Fourth Circle, Jordan (home).

Telephone: (6) 5522104 (office); (6) 5932043 (home). *Fax:* (6) 5511803 (office). *E-mail:* ias@go.com.jo (office); mrzoubi@yahoo.com (home). *Website:* iasworld.org (office).

ZOUIOUECHE, Nazim Charif Eddine; Algerian engineer and oil company executive; *Chairman, Medex Petroleum;* b. 19 Feb. 1940, Algiers; m. Fariel Essid 1971; two s.; ed Ecole Nat Supérieure des Télécommunications, Ecole Nat. Supérieure du Pétrole, Paris; telecommunications engineer, Ministry of Telecommunications 1965–68; production engineer, Elf/Aquitaine 1968–71; Man. Hassi-Messaoud Dist 1971–76; Dir Production Div. Sonatrach 1976–79, Exec. Vice-Pres. and Man. Dir Sonatrach, in charge of Hydrocarbons Div. 1979–85, CEO Transmediterranean Pipeline Co. 1985–93, Chief of Staff Sonatrach 1994–95, Dir-Gen. 1995–98; Chair. Observatoire Méditerranéen pour l'Energie 1995–97; currently Chair. Medex Petroleum; mem. Bd Alfor Drilling Co. (SEDCO/Sonatrach Jt co.) 1977–82. *Leisure interests:* bridge, tennis, horse riding, jogging. *Address:* Medex Petroleum Ltd, Tour de l'Horloge, 4 place Louis Armand, 75603 Paris Cedex 12, France. *Telephone:* 1-73-02-03-55. *Fax:* 1-72-76-25-99. *E-mail:* contact@ medexoil.com.

ZOUMBOULAKIS, Petros I.; Greek artist, stage designer and professor of plastic arts; b. 19 April 1937, Athens; ed Polytechnic School of Athens, Athens School of Fine Arts with Yannis Moralis; participant in numerous group exhbns in Greece, including Nat. Gallery; work also shown in group exhbns abroad including São Paulo Bienal 1969, Int. Exhbn of Visual Arts, Moscow 1988, 5th Int. Biennale, Cairo 1994, 1st Int. Biennale of Art (CIAC), Rome 1995, Plein Air, Varna 1999, 3ème Biennale Méditerranéene des Arts de la Ville de Tunis 2004; teacher in applied arts, drawing, colour and stage design, Doxiadis School of Interior Design 1964–86; works in Nat. Gallery, Ministry of Educ. Collection and many public and pvt. collections at home and abroad; Acad. Award, Acad. of Arts-Letters-Sciences of Greece 2011. *Address:* Tsimiski 2, 11471 Athens (Studio); Evrou 18-20, 15234 Athens, Greece (home). *Telephone:* (1) 3630028 (Studio); (1) 6842088 (home). *Fax:* (1) 3630028 (office). *E-mail:* zoubmar@yahoo.gr (home).

ZSÁMBÉKI, Gábor; Hungarian theatrical manager and director; b. 30 Dec. 1943, Pécs; s. of János Zsámbéki and Judit Almásy; two d.; ed Faculty of Directing, Budapest Acad. of Dramatic Art and Film Art; Gen. Man. Csiky Gergely Theatre, Kaposvár 1974–78; Prof., Faculty of Acting and Directing, Budapest Acad. of Dramatic Art and Film Art 1978–; Head Dir, Budapest Nat. Theatre 1978–82; Founding mem. Katona József Theatre, Budapest, Art Dir 1982–89, Gen. Man. and Stage Dir 1989, 2003–11; Stage Dir Theater Tribühne, Stuttgart 1988–2002; Pres. Union des Théâtres de l'Europe, Paris 1998–2002; mem. MITOS21; Chevalier, Ordre des Arts et des Lettres 2004; Jászai Mari Award 1973, Kossuth Prize 1988, BITEF Prize (for The Government Inspector) 1989, French Critics' Prize for Best Foreign Production (for Ubu Roi, Théâtre de l'Odéon, Paris) 1990, Best Foreign Production (for The Government Inspector), Caracas Int. Festival 1990, Merited Artist of the Hungarian Repub., Hedda Award 2004, Theatre Critics Award for Best Director (co-recipient) and Best Performance (for Médeia) 2004/2005, Metropolitan Municipality Theatre Award (for A Notorious Serial) 2008, Curtain Prize for Best Director (A Mizantróp) 2011, and other awards. *Productions:* about 150, including classics (Goldoni, Shakespeare, Gogol, Chekhov etc.), modern works (Jarry, Wesker, Gombrowicz) and world premières of contemporary Hungarian plays (Halleluyah by Kornis, The Imposter, Chickenhead, Bump by Spiró); productions in Cuba, Czechoslovakia, Finland, Germany, Israel, Norway.

ZU GUTTENBERG, Baron Karl-Theodor; German fmr politician; *Founder and Chairman, Spitzberg Partners LLC;* b. 5 Dec. 1971, Munich; m.; two d.; ed Univ. of Bayreuth; fmr freelance journalist for Die Welt; mem. Kulmbach Dist Council 2002; mem. Bundestag (Christian Social Union—CSU) 2002–11, served as spokesman on Foreign Affairs Cttee, also mem. Parl. Ass. of the Council of Europe; mem. CSU Gen. Secr. 2008–09; Fed. Minister of Econs and Tech. Feb.–Oct. 2009, of Defence 2009–11 (resgnd); fmr Man. Partner, Guttenberg GmbH, Munich; Owner, Guttenberg Ventures 2011–; Distinguished Statesman (non-resident), Center for Strategic and Int. Studies 2011–; Founder and Chair. Spitzberg Partners LLC (corp. advisory and investment firm), New York 2013–. *Address:* Spitzberg Partners LLC, 270 Lafayette Street, Suite 1005, New York, NY 10012, USA (office). *Telephone:* (212) 845-9569 (office). *E-mail:* info@spitzberg -partners.com (office). *Website:* spitzberg-partners.com (office).

ZUAITER, Abbas Farouq, BSBA; American/Palestinian business executive; *Co-founder and Managing Member, Zuaiter Capital Holdings, LLC;* m. Samar Zuaiter; three d.; ed Georgetown Univ., USA; Chief Financial Officer and Head of Fixed Income, Currency and Commodity Trading, AFN Associates, Inc. 1991–94; Assurance and Business Advisory Partner, PricewaterhouseCoopers LLP 1992–2002; COO and Chief Financial Officer, Soros Fund Management 2002–13; currently adviser to the Soros family; Co-founder and Man. mem. Zuaiter Capital Holdings, LLC 2013–; Chair. Bd of Dirs, Adecoagro, SA, RoC Capital Management, LLC; mem. Bd of Dirs, Arab Bank PLC, The Capital Holdings Funds PLC; mem. Bd of Advisors and Regents, McDonough School of Business, Georgetown Univ., USA; mem. Bd of Advisers iMENA Group, Ltd, Encore Realty, LLC; mem. Bd, Arab Fund for Arts and Culture, Arab Bankers Asscn of North America, Welfare Asscn, Middle East Inst. Int. Advisory Council. *Address:* Zuaiter Capital Holdings, LLC, 888 7th Avenue, New York, NY 10106, USA (office). *Telephone:* (212) 586-3800 (office).

ZUBAIR, Muhammad, MBA; Pakistani politician and government official; ed Inst. of Business Administration, Karachi; taught Financial Man. at the Inst. of Business Admin, Karachi 1981–86; Treasury and Investment Operations Man., IBM 1988–90, Accounting and Treasury Man. 1990–92, Financial Operations Officer 1993–95, Financial Controller and Chief Financial Officer 1995–97, Chief Financial Officer 1998–2007; mem. Pakistan Muslim League—N Economic, Tax Reforms Media Cttee 2012–13; Chair. Bd of Investment July–Dec. 2013; Minister of State/Chair. Privatization Comm. 2013–17; Gov. of Sindh 2017–18; mem. Overseas Investors, Chamber of Commerce and Industry 2004–07, Bd of financial advisers, American Business Council 2004–07; Administrative Achievement Award for best employee, IBM 1981, Pres.'s Award for best performance, IBM 1997. *Address:* Pakistan Muslim League, House Number 20, Street 10, F-8/3, Islamabad, Pakistan (office). *Telephone:* (51) 2852662 (office). *Fax:* (51) 2852663 (office). *E-mail:* info@pmln.org (office). *Website:* pmln.org (office).

ZUBAK, Krešimir; Bosnia and Herzegovina politician; b. 29 Nov. 1947, Doboj; m.; two c.; ed Sarajevo Univ.; worked in judicial bodies of Bosnia and Herzegovina; Pres. of Higher Court in Doboj; mem. del. of Croatian population to sign the Washington Agreement and Vienna Agreement; First Pres. of Fed. of Bosnia and Croatia 1994–97; fmr Croatian Co-Chair. of Bosnia and Herzegovina; Chair. New Croatian Initiative (Nova Hrvatska Inicijativa—NHI) following split from Croat Democratic Union of Bosnia and Herzegovina (HDZBiH) 1998–2007 (party merged into Croatian Peasant Party of Radić Stjepan).

ZUBEIR WAKO, HE Cardinal Gabriel; Sudanese ecclesiastic; *Archbishop Emeritus of Khartoum;* b. 27 Feb. 1941, Mboro; ed St Paul's Nat. Major Seminary, Tore River, Pontifical Urban Univ. and Pontifical Lateran Univ., Rome, Italy; ordained priest 1963; Bishop of Wau 1974–79; Coadjutor Archbishop of Khartoum 1979–81; Archbishop of Khartoum 1981–2016, Archbishop Emer. 2016–; cr. Cardinal (Cardinal Priest of Sant'Atanasio a Via Tiburtina) 2003; participated in Papal Conclave 2005, 2013. *Address:* Catholic Church, PO Box 49, 11111 Khartoum, Sudan. *Telephone:* (915) 716321 (office).

ZUBERBÜHLER, Daniel; Swiss lawyer and banking regulator; b. 5 Oct. 1948, Bern; m. Lorna Austin; one d., three s.; ed Univ. of Berne; Legal Officer, Eidgenössische Bankenkommission (Swiss Fed. Banking Comm.) 1976–77, Head of Legal Service 1977–86, Vice-Dir 1986–88, Deputy Dir 1988–96, CEO 1996–2008; mem. Group of Experts, Amendment of Swiss Penal Code on Money Laundering 1988–90, Financial Action Task Force on Money Laundering 1989–94, Tripartite Group of Banking, Securities and Insurance Supervisors 1993–95, Working Party 3 of Int. Org. of Securities Comm. (IOSCO) 1990–96, Basel Cttee on Banking Supervision, BIS 1996–2010, Tech. Cttee of IOSCO 2009–11, Financial Stability Bd Standing Cttee on Supervisory and Regulatory Co-operation; Vice-Chair. Swiss Financial Market Supervisory Authority (FINMA) 2009–11; Sr Financial Consultant, KPMG Switzerland 2012–13; mem. Bd of Dirs EFG Int. 2014–19, Banca Popolare di Sondrio (Suisse). *Leisure interests:* jogging, cycling, skiing, listening to modern jazz, political cabaret. *Address:* Sonnenbergstrasse 3, 3013 Berne, Switzerland (home). *Telephone:* (78) 7104874 (home). *E-mail:* d.zuberbuehler@hispeed.ch (home).

ZUBKO, Hennadiy Hryhorovych, PhD; Ukrainian engineer and politician; *Vice-Prime Minister, Minister of Regional Development, Construction and Communal Services;* b. 27 Sept. 1967, Mykolayiv, Ukrainian SSR, USSR; m. Lyudmila Mykolaivna; one s. one d.; ed V. Szymanowski Steel Structure Research and Design Inst., Kyiv; mil. service in USSR Armed Forces 1986–88; Software Engineer, Zhytomyr Region Tech. Connection Dept 1988–90; Software Engineer, PE Nyva, Zhytomyr 1991–92; Commercial Dir, SERGYI Production Co., Zhytomyr 1992–94; Dir, Mayak LLC, Zhytomyr 1994–97; Dir, Tantal, Zhytomyr 1997–2002; Project Man., JSC LYNOS, Lysychanskyi 2001; Deputy Chair., JSC Zhytomyr Construction Co. 2002–10, Chair. 2010–; Head, Coordination Dept, Ukrmontazhspetsstroy State Corpn, Kyiv 2003–07; mem. Zhytomyr City Council 2006–12; mem. Verkhovna Rada (parl.) (Batkivshchyna (Fatherland) party) for constituency no. 62 2012–; Acting Head, Admin of State Affairs May–June 2014, First Deputy Head, Presidential Admin June–Dec. 2014; Vice-Prime Minister, also Minister of Regional Devt, Construction and Communal Services 2014–; Order of Danylo Halytsky 2009; Medal for Distinction in Mil. Service (II degree) 1987, Medal of 70 Years of the USSR Armed Forces 1988. *Address:* Office of the Cabinet of Ministers, 01008 Kyiv, vul. M. Hrushevskoho 12/2, Ukraine (office). *Telephone:* (44) 256-63-33 (office). *E-mail:* stoliarchuk@kmu.gov.ua (office). *Website:* www.kmu.gov.ua (office).

ZUBKOV, Viktor Alekseyevich, PhD; Russian government official and business executive; *Chairman, OAO Gazprom;* b. 15 Sept. 1941, Arbat, Kushva Dist, Sverdlovsk Oblast, Russian SFSR, USSR; m.; one d.; ed Leningrad (now St Petersburg) Agricultural Inst.; began career in state farm network, Leningrad Oblast including Gen. Dir Pervomaiskoye Sovkhoz (State Farm) Union 1967–85; various roles within CP including First Sec. Priozersk Municipal Exec. Cttee and First Deputy Chair. Leningrad Oblast Exec. Cttee 1985–91; Deputy Chair. External Relations Cttee, St Petersburg City Council 1992–93; Deputy Chair. Fed. Tax Service and Head, State Tax Inspectorate, St Petersburg 1993–99; Deputy Minister for Tax 1999–2001; Deputy Minister of Finance 2001–04; Chair. Financial Monitoring Service, Ministry of Finance 2004–07; Chair. of the Govt 2007–08, (Acting) 7–8 May 2012, First Deputy Chair. of the Govt 2008–12; Russian Special Presidential Rep. for Co-operation with Gas Exporting Countries Forum 2012–; Chair. OAO Gazprom 2008–, Chair. Man. Cttee and Dir-Gen. Gazprom Gazomotornoye Toplivo 2012–14; Russian Special Presidential Rep. for Co-operation with Gas Exporting Countries Forum 2014–; Honoured Economist of the Russian Fed. 2001, Hon. Citizen of Leningrad Oblast 2009; Ceremonial dagger, Order of the Badge of Honour 1975, Order of the Red Banner of Labour 1981, Medal 'Veteran of Labour' 1986, Order of Merit for the Fatherland (Fourth Class) 2000, (Third Class) 2006, (Second Class) 2008, Order of Holy Prince Daniel of Moscow (First Class) (Russian Orthodox Church) 2011; Diploma of the Govt of the Russian Fed. 1998, ranked 84th in a survey of Russia's most influential politicians 2006. *Address:* OAO Gazprom, 117997 Moscow, ul. Nametkina 16, V-420, GSP-7, Russia (office). *Telephone:* (495) 719-30-01 (office). *Fax:* (495) 719-83-33 (office). *E-mail:* gazprom@gazprom.ru (office). *Website:* www.gazprom.com (office).

ZUCKER, Jeffrey (Jeff), BA; American television executive; *President, CNN Worldwide;* b. 9 April 1965, Homestead, Fla; s. of Arlene Zucker; m. Caryn Stephanie Zucker (née Nathanson) 1996; four c.; ed North Miami Sr High School, Harvard Coll.; became ed. school paper and teenage freelance reporter for The Miami Herald newspaper while a teenager attending N Miami Sr High School; participated in Northwestern Univ. Nat. High School Inst. Program for journalism; Pres. The Harvard Crimson 1985–86; hired by NBC to research material for coverage of Olympic Games in Seoul, S Korea 1988; field producer for The Today Show 1989, Exec. Producer 1992–93, 1994–2000; Pres. NBC Entertainment 2000–03, Pres. NBC Entertainment, News & Cable Group 2003–04, Pres. NBC Universal TV Group (following merger with Vivendi Universal) 2004–05, CEO NBC Universal TV Group 2005–07, CEO NBC Universal Inc. 2007–10; Pres. CNN Worldwide Jan. 2013–. *Address:* CNN Center, 190 Marietta Street NW, Atlanta, GA 30303, USA (office). *Telephone:* 404-827-2300 (office). *Website:* www.edition.cnn.com (office).

ZUCKERBERG, Mark Elliot; American computer scientist and business executive; *Co-Founder and CEO, Facebook, Inc.;* b. 14 May 1984, White Plains, NY; s. of Edward Zuckerberg and Karen Zuckerberg; m. Priscilla Chan 2012; one d.; ed Ardsley High School, Phillips Exeter Acad., Harvard Univ.; began programming in middle school; took Grad. course in programming at Mercy Coll. mid-1990s; co-f. Facebook (with Harvard classmates Dustin Moskovitz, Eduardo Saverin and Chris Hughes) 2004 and moved to Palo Alto, Calif.; f. Start-up: Education foundation 2010, Chan Zuckerberg Initiative 2015. *Address:* Facebook, Inc., 1601 South California Avenue, Palo Alto, CA 94304, USA (office). *Telephone:* (650) 543-4800 (office). *Fax:* (650) 543-4801 (office). *Website:* www.facebook.com/markzuckerberg (office).

ZUCKERMAN, Mortimer (Mort) Benjamin, BA, LLM, MBA; American (b. Canadian) real estate developer, publisher and editor; *Chairman and Editor-in-Chief, US News and World Report, L.P.;* b. 4 June 1937, Montreal, Québec; s. of Abraham Zuckerman and Esther Zuckerman; m. Marla Prather (divorced); two d.; ed McGill Univ., Univ. of Pennsylvania, Harvard Univ.; Sr Vice-Pres. Cabot, Cabot and Forbes 1965–69; Lecturer, then Assoc. Prof., Harvard Univ. Grad. School of Design 1966–74; Visiting Lecturer, Yale Univ. 1967–69; Chair. Boston Properties Co. 1970–2016; Dir RET Income Foundation 1976–79, Property Capital Trust Co. 1979–80; Pres., Chair. Atlantic Monthly Co., Boston 1980–; Chair. and Ed.-in-Chief US News and World Report 1984–; Propr, Chair. and Co-Publisher, New York Daily News 1993–2017; Vice Chair. Inst. Peace Inst.; mem. Global Wealth & Investment Man. Cttee, Bank of America; mem. Council on Foreign Relations, Washington Inst. for Near East Studies, Int. Inst. of Strategic Studies; Trustee, Memorial Sloan Kettering Cancer Center, Dana-Farber Cancer Inst.; Commandeur de l'Ordre des Arts et des Lettres; Dr hc (Colby Coll.), (Southampton Coll.), (Hebrew Coll.), (Berkeley Coll.), (Icahn School of Medicine, Mount Sinai), Hon. DIur (McGill Univ.); Sy Syms Humanitarian Award 2013, Yeshiva Univ., Lifetime Achievement Award, Guild Hall Acad. of the Arts, Gold Medal, American Inst. of Architecture, New York, Queen Elizabeth II Diamond Jubilee Medal (Canada). *Address:* US News and World Report L.P., 450 W 33rd Street, 11th Floor, New York, NY 10001 (office). *Telephone:* (212) 716-6800 (office). *Website:* www.usnews.com (office).

ZUGAZA MIRANDA, Miguel; Spanish museum director; *Director, Bilbao Fine Arts Museum;* b. 1964, Durango, Vizcaya; ed Universidad Complutense de Madrid; Deputy Dir Reina Sofía Museum of Contemporary Art, Madrid, then Dir 1994–96; Dir Bilbao Fine Arts Museum 1996–2002, 2017–; Dir Prado Museum, Madrid 2002–17. *Address:* Museo de Bellas Artes de Bilbao, Museo Plaza 2, 48009 Bilbao, Spain (office). *Telephone:* (94) 4396060 (office). *Fax:* (94) 4396145 (office). *E-mail:* info@museobilbao.com (office). *Website:* www.museobilbao.com (office).

ŽUGIĆ, Radoje, MEconSc, PhD; Montenegrin economist, politician and central banker; b. 3 April 1961, Novakovići, Žabljak; m.; three c.; ed Univ. of Podgorica, Univ. of Belgrade; Financial Dir Auto-Moto Asscn of Montenegro 1986; Sec., Directorate of Public Revenues 1992–96; Dir for payment system operations in Montenegro, Podgorica Br., ZOP (Clearing and Payments Agency) 1999–2001; Acting Dir Pension and Disability Insurance Fund 2004–05, Dir 2005; fmr Deputy Dir-Gen. for Payment System Operations, Cen. Bank of Montenegro, Gov. 2010–12; Minister of Finance 2012–16; Coordinator, Interbank Cttee for Payment System Reform; fmr mem. Parl. of Montenegro and Parl. of State Union of Serbia and Montenegro; fmr Dir Podgorička Banka, Prva Banka Crne Gore; fmr Chair. Servisimport, Cen. Depositary Agency, Lovćen Insurance.

ZUHUROV, Shukurjon; Tajikistani engineer and politician; *President, Assembly of Representatives (Majlisi Namoyandagon);* b. 16 April 1954, Kirovabod Dist (now Panj Dist), Khatlon Oblast, Tajik SSR, USSR; m.; five c.; ed Moscow Inst. of Land Use Planning Engineers, Russian Acad. of Public Admin; began career as engineer and geodesist, Khatlon Oblast; mem. Ass. of Reps (Majlisi Namoyandagon) for Qabodiyon Dist 2005–06, Pres. Ass. of Reps 2010–; Minister of Labour and Social Security 2006–10; mem. Hizbi Halki-demokratii Tojikiston (People's Democratic Party of Tajikistan); Award of Supreme Council of Tajikistan 1985, Order of Friendship 1998, Order of Honour. *Address:* Office of the President, Majlisi Namoyandagon (Assembly of Representatives), 734051 Dushanbe, Xiyoboni Rudaki 42, Tajikistan (office). *Telephone:* (372) 21-23-66 (office). *Fax:* (372) 21-92-81 (office). *E-mail:* mejparl@parliament.tojikiston.com (office). *Website:* parlament.tj (office).

ZUKERMAN, Pinchas; Israeli violinist, violist and conductor; b. 16 July 1948, Tel-Aviv; s. of Yehuda Zukerman and Miriam Zukerman; m. 1st Eugenia Rich 1968 (divorced); two d.; m. 2nd Tuesday Weld 1985 (divorced); m. 3rd Amanda Forsyth 2004; ed Israel Conservatory, Acad. of Music, Tel-Aviv, Juilliard School of Music, New York with Ivan Galamian; debut in New York with New York Philharmonic 1969, in UK at Brighton Festival 1969; concert and recital performances throughout USA and Europe; debut as conductor, London 1970; appearances as conductor with orchestras worldwide; has performed at Spoleto, Pablo Casals and Edinburgh Festivals; Dir South Bank Summer Music, London 1978–80; Musical Dir St Paul Chamber Orchestra 1980–87; Prin. Conductor Dallas Symphony Orch. 1993–95 (Prin. Guest Conductor Int. Summer Music Festival 1990–95); Music Dir Baltimore Symphony Orchestra Summer MusicFest 1997–99; Music Dir Nat. Arts Centre Orchestra, Canada 1998–2015; Prin. Guest Conductor, Royal Philharmonic Orchestra, London 2009–; Chair. Pinchas Zukerman Performance Program, Manhattan School of Music; Hon. DMus (Brown Univ.) 1989; winner, Leventritt Competition 1967, Isaac Stern Award for Artistic Excellence (Nat. Arts Awards) 2002, Grammy Award for Best Chamber Music Performance 1980, Grammy Award for Best Classical Performance, Instrumental Soloist without Orchestra 1981, ECHO Klassik Instrumentalist Award 2016. *Film soundtracks:* Prince of Tides, Critical Care. *Address:* Kirshbaum Demler & Associates, Inc., 711 West End Avenue, Suite 5KN, New York, NY 10025, USA (office). *E-mail:* info@kirshdem.com (office). *Website:* www.kirshdem.com (office).

ZULUAGA ESCOBAR, Oscar Iván, BA, MA; Colombian business executive and politician; b. 3 Feb. 1957, Pensilvania, Caldas; m. Martha Ligia Martínez Giraldo; three c.; ed Liceo de Cervantes, Universidad Javeriana, Univ. of Exeter, UK; elected Councillor in Pensilvania 1988–90, Mayor of Pensilvania 1990–92; Chair. ACESCO SA steel co. 1992–2001; launched campaign for Senate and won one of biggest votes in country 2001; supported candidacy of Alvaro Uribe Velez for Pres.

of Colombia, Presidential Sr Adviser 2006–07; Minister of Finance and Public Credit 2007–10; Democratic Centre cand. in presidential election 2014; fmr mem. several bds, including Nat. Fed. of Merchants (Federación Nacional de Comerciantes—FENALCO), Colombian Fed. of Metalworkers (Federación Colombiana de Industrias Metalúrgicas—Fedemetal), Colombo-Venezuelan Chamber of Commerce; fmr rep. of Colombian Iron and Steel Industry; fmr Nat. Pres. Asscn Internationale des Étudiants en Sciences Economiques et Commerciales (AIE-SEC)-COLOMBIA; winner, Concurso Nacional de Tesis Universitarias under the heading 'Portfolio Investment Actions', Nat. Asscn of Financial Insts 1983, honoured as one of "10 Best Young Executives of Colombia", Jr Chamber of Colombia (Bogotà Chapter) 1997, chosen by Congress as Best Minister of the Cabinet 2007, selected as one of five Best Finance Ministers of Latin America.

ZUMA, Jacob; South African politician and fmr head of state; b. 12 April 1942, Inkandla, KwaZulu-Natal; joined African Nat. Congress (ANC) 1959; mem. Umkhonto WeSizwe 1962 after ANC banned 1960, arrested 1963, sentenced to ten years' imprisonment; helped re-establish ANC underground structures, Natal Prov. 1973–75; left South Africa 1975; mem. ANC Nat. Exec. Cttee 1977, Deputy Chief Rep., Mozambique –1984, Chief Rep. 1984–87; Head of Underground Structures ANC Head Office, Lusaka, Zambia 1987, Chief Intelligence Dept, mem. political and mil. council mid-1980s; returned to S Africa after legalization of ANC 1990, Chair. South Natal Region 1990, Deputy Sec.-Gen. ANC 1991, Nat. Chair. 1994–97, Deputy Pres. 1997–2007, Pres. 2007–17; Deputy Pres. of South Africa 1999–2005, Pres. 2009–18; mem. Exec. Cttee Econ. Affairs and Tourism for KwaZulu Natal Gov. 1994–99, Chair. ANC in KwaZulu 1994–, est. and patron KwaZulu Reconstruction and Devt Project Bursary Fund; arrested and charged with rape Dec. 2005, found not guilty May 2006, charges of corruption dropped Sept. 2006, recharged by Nat. Prosecuting Authority, charges ruled invalid Sept. 2008, charges reinstated by court Jan. 2009, charges dropped April 2009; Co-Chair UN High-Level Comm. on Health Employment and Econ. Growth 2016–; Hon. Prof., Tsinghua Univ. 2014; Hon. DLitt (Fort Hare Univ.) 2001, Hon. DBA (Univ. of Zululand) 2001, Hon. DPhil (Medical Univ. of Southern Africa) 2001; Nelson Mandela Award for Outstanding Leadership (USA) 1998. *Address:* African National Congress of South Africa, PO Box 61884, Marshalltown 2107, South Africa (office). *Website:* www.anc.org.za (office).

ZUMBRUNNEN, Fabrice; Swiss business executive; *CEO, Migros Cooperatives;* b. 2 Dec. 1969, La Chaux; m.; two c.; ed Univ. of Neuenburg; Branch Man. Coop Neuenburg-Jura 1993–94; Private Sec. and Accountant, Claude Lebet, Luthier 1994–95; Sales Man., Obtech Medical AG 1995–96; Instructor and Project Man., Sales Directorate, Migros Neuenburg-Freiburg 1996–2000, then Sales Man. and Deputy Head 2000–01, Head of Marketing & Logistics and Deputy Man. Dir 2001–05 (also mem. Exec. Bd), Leader 2005–12; Head of Dept of Human Resources, Culture and Social Affairs, Leisure and mem. of Directorate-Gen., Migros Cooperatives 2012–, CEO 2017–; Chair. Bd of Dirs, Ferrovia Monte Generoso SA; Pres. Bd of Trustees, Eurocentres, Stiftung für Sprach - und Bildungszentren, Gottlieb Duttweiler Inst., Gurten-Park im Grünen, Münchenstein-Park im Grünen; mem. Fondation du Parc Pré Vert du Signal de Bougy. *Address:* Migros Cooperatives, Limmatstrasse 152, 8031 Zurich, Switzerland (office). *Telephone:* 442772111 (office). *Website:* www.migros.ch (office).

ZUMTHOR, Peter; Swiss architect; b. 26 April 1943, Basel; ed Schule für Gestaltung, Basel, Pratt Inst., USA; apprenticeship in cabinet-making; architect, Dept for the Care and Presentation of Monument, Canton Graubünden 1968; Tutor, Univ. of Zurich 1978; pvt. practice, Haldenstein, Graubünden 1979–; Visiting Prof., Southern Calif. Inst. of Architecture, USA 1988; workshop leader, Granz Summer School, Austria 1989; Davis Critic, Tulane Univ., USA 1992; Prof., Acad. of Architecture, Mendriso 1996; Fellow, Bayerische Akad. der Schönen Künste, Germany 2003; Hon. mem. Bund Deutscher Architekten, Germany; Hon. Fellow, American Inst. of Architects 2004; Foreign Hon. Fellow, American Acad. of Arts and Sciences 2009; Dr hc in Architettura (Univ. degli Studi di Ferrara, Italy) 2003; Auszeichnung guter Bauten im Kanton Graubünden 1987, 1994, Heinrich Tessenow Medal, Hanover Tech. Univ., Germany 1989, Gulam 1991, Int. Architecture Prize, Neues Bauen in den Alpen 1992, 1995, Best Building, 10 vor 10 1993, Int. Prize, Stone Architecture, Italy 1995, Erich-Schelling Architecture Prize, Germany 1996, Carlsberg Architecture Prize 1998, Praemium Imperiale 2008, Pritzker Prize 2009, RIBA Royal Gold Medal 2013. *Works include:* Churwalden Elementary School, Graubünden 1983, House Räth, Graubünden 1983, Atelier Zumthor, Graubünden 1986, St Benedict Chapel, Graubünden 1989, Chur Art Museum, Graubünden 1990, Gugalun House, Graubünden 1994, Thermal Baths Vals, Graubünden 1996, Bregenz Art Museum, Austria 1997, Topography of Terror, Int. Exhbn and Documentation Centre, Germany 1997, UK 1997, Swiss Pavilion, Expo 2000, Germany 1997–2000, Kolumba, Erzbischöfliches Diözesanmuseum, Germany 1997–2006, Field Chapel to St Nikolaus von der Flüe, Mechernich, Germany 2007, Kolumba Art Museum, Cologne, Germany 2007, Benedict Chapel, Sumvitg, Graubünden. *Publications include:* Three Concepts 1997, Peter Zumthor Works: Buildings and Projects 1979–1997 (with Helene Binet) 1998, Thinking Architecture 1998, Swiss Sound Box, Kunsthaus Bregenz 1999. *Address:* Süesswingel 20, 7023 Haldenstein, Switzerland (office). *Telephone:* (81) 3549292 (office). *Fax:* (81) 3539293 (office). *E-mail:* arch@zumthor.ch (office).

ZÚÑIGA CHAVES, Guillermo, BA, MBA; Costa Rican economist, academic and fmr politician; *Professor, National University of Costa Rica;* ed Univ. of Costa Rica, National Autonomous Univ. of Mexico; early position as Dir Fitch Cen. America (business ratings co.) and Man., Fitch Costa Rica Risk Rating SA; Deputy Minister of Finance 1986–90; Minister of Finance 2006–09, also mem. Bd of Dirs Banco Central de Costa Rica, and Chair. Budgetary Authority; served as Gov. for Costa Rica at IBRD and Inter-American Devt Bank; Deputy, Legis. Ass. 2010–11 (resgnd); Gen. Man. Banco Credito Agricola de Cartago 2011–13; currently Prof., Nat. Univ. of Costa Rica; Nat. Team Leader, UNDP Biodiversity Finance Initiative in Costa Rica; mem. Nat. Comm. on Prevention of Risks and Attention of Emergencies;. *Address:* National University of Costa Rica, Avenue 1 Calle 1, Heredia, Costa Rica (office). *Telephone:* 2277-3000 (office). *Website:* www.una.ac.cr (office).

ZUNZI; Chinese political cartoonist; b. (Wong Kei-kwan), 1955, Hong Kong; m. Chan Ya; ed Chinese Univ. of Hong Kong; comic artist 1980–; worked briefly as print journalist before concentrating on political cartoons; works appear in mass-circulation Chinese-language publs in Hong Kong including Ming Pao (daily), People's Monthly, Apple Daily, Next (weekly magazine). *Works include:* Black Material, Grandpa Deng (about Deng Xiao-ping), 100 Caricatures of China, Hong Kong and Taiwan Politicians, A Biography of Mr Legislator, The New Leader, V.I.P., Mickey in Hong Kong, Where the Heart Goes, Check, Ten Years' Memory, Law, Communication Between China and Hong Kong, The Judge Has Finished His Work, Awaiting Your Advice. *Address:* Ming Pao Daily News, 15/F, Block A, Ming Pao Industrial Centre, 18 Ka Yip Street, Chai Wan, Hong Kong Special Administrative Region, People's Republic of China (office). *Telephone:* (852) 25953111 (office). *Fax:* (852) 28983783 (office). *Website:* www.mingpao.com (office).

ZUR HAUSEN, Harald, DSc, MD; German virologist, medical scientist and academic; b. 11 March 1936, Gelsenkirchen, Westphalia; ed Gymnasium in Vechta, Univs of Bonn, Hamburg and Düsseldorf; Research Fellow, Univ. of Düsseldorf 1962–65, Children's Hosp. of Philadelphia, USA 1966–69; Sr Scientist, Inst. for Virology, Univ. of Wurzburg 1969–72; Chair. and Prof., Inst. of Clinical Virology, Univ. of Erlangen-Nurnberg 1972–77; Chair. and Prof., Inst. of Virology, Univ. of Freiburg 1977–83; Prof., Scientific Dir and Chair. Man. Bd, German Cancer Research Center 1983–2003, Prof. Emer. 2003–; Chair. Asscn of Nat. Research Centers 1989–81; Pres. Org. of European Cancer Insts. 1993–96; Ed.-in-Chief, Int. Journal of Cancer 2000–09; Vice-Pres. German Nat. Academy for Natural Sciences and Medicine (LEOPOLDINA) 2003–09; mem. Nat. Science Transfer and Devt Agency, Bangkok 2006–15, Heidelberg Acad. of Sciences, Polish Acad. of Sciences, Venezuela Nat. Acad. of Medicine, American Philosophical Soc., Inst. of Medicine, NAS; Great Cross of Merit 2004; hon. degrees from Univs of Chicago, Umeå, Prague, Salford, Helsinki, Erlangen-Nuremberg and Salerno; Robert Koch Prize and Medal 1975, Charles Mott Prize 1986, Paul Ehrlich-Ludwig Darmstatter Prize 1994, Virchow Medal 2000, San Marino Prize for Medicine 2002, William B. Coley Award 2006, Gairdner Foundation Int. Award 2008, Nobel Prize in Medicine (jtly) 2008. *Achievements include:* discovered how human papilloma virus (HPV) induces cervical cancer which led to devt of a vaccine that helps prevent the disease. *Publication:* Infections Causing Human Cancer 2006. *Address:* German Cancer Research Center, Im Neuenheimer Feld 280, 69120 Heidelberg, Germany (office). *Telephone:* (6221) 420 (office). *Fax:* (6221) 422995 (office). *Website:* www.dkfz.de (office).

ZURABISHVILI-KASHIA, Salomé; Georgian/French politician, head of state and fmr diplomatist; *President;* b. 18 March 1952, Paris; m. Janri Kashia (died 2012); two c.; ed Inst. of Political Sciences, Columbia Univ., USA; family fled Georgia following Soviet takeover in 1921; joined French Ministry of Foreign Affairs 1977, posted in Italy, USA, Chad, Perm. Mission to UN, New York; Amb. of France to Georgia 2003–04; Minister of Foreign Affairs of Georgia 2004–05; f. Salomé Zurabishvili Movt 2005; Founder and Leader Georgia's Way party 2006–10; Coordinator, Panel of Experts, UN Security Council's Iran Sanctions Cttee 2010–11; Pres. of Georgia 2018–; fmr Rep. to Euro Atlantic Council, Brussels. *Publication:* Une femme pour deux pays (A Woman for Two Countries) (autobiography). *Address:* Office of the President, 10103 Tbilisi, M. Abdushelishvili, Georgia (office). *Telephone:* (32) 228-27-12 (office). *E-mail:* info@president.gov.ge (office). *Website:* www.president.gov.ge (office).

ZURABOV, Aleksander Yuryevich, CEconSc; Russian banker; b. 1956, Leningrad (now St Petersburg); m.; two c.; ed Ordzhonekidze Moscow Inst. of Man., Acad. of Int. Trade; with Research Inst. of Marine Transport 1977–89; Lecturer, Acad. of Int. Trade 1989–91; Head of Div., Head of Dept, mem. Bd of Dirs Konversbank 1991–94; Chair. Trust and Investments Bank, also Deputy Chair. Bank Menatep 1994–95, Pres. and Chair. Bank Menatep 1996–99 (bought by man. and renamed Trust Nat. Bank); Chair. Russian Standard Bank 1999–2000; First Deputy Dir-Gen. for Financial, Econ. and Commercial Activities, Aeroflot 1999–2003, elected Chair. 2003; fmr Head of Working Group for Reorganization, Chair. Agroopttorgbank.

ZURABOV, Mikail Yuryevich; Russian engineer, government official and diplomatist; b. 3 Oct. 1953, Leningrad; m. Yuliya; one s. one d.; ed Moscow State Inst. of Man.; Lecturer, Moscow Inst. of Man. 1975–78; teacher, Moscow Higher School of Montage 1981–82; engineer, Moscow Research Inst. Orgtechstroi 1982–83; Sr Researcher and Head of Lab., All-Union Research Inst. of Montage Tech. 1983–88; Deputy Head of Montage Co. Mospromtechmontage 1988–92; Dir-Gen. Jt Stock Insurance Co. Max 1992, also Dir-Gen. Medical Insurance Co. Max-M 1994–98; First Deputy Minister of Public Health May–Sept. 1998, Minister of Public Health and Social Devt 2004–07; adviser on social problems to Pres. 1998–99; Amb. to Ukraine 2010–16; Chair. Bd of Dirs Konversbank; fmr Chair. Pension Fund of Russian Fed.

ZUROVCIK, Danielle Renee, MSc, PhD; American mechanical engineer, academic and entrepreneur; *CEO, Worldwide Innovative Healthcare, Inc. (WiCare);* d. of Andrew James Zurovcik and Patricia Zurovcik; ed Pennsylvania State Univ. (Schreyer Honors Coll.), Massachusetts Inst. of Tech.; Founder and CEO Worldwide Innovative Healthcare, Inc. (WiCare); Innovation Expo, Student Poster First Place Prize Award, Judges' Choice Award, MCC 2012, IEEE GHTC, First Place, Advamed MedTech Conf. Business Pitch Competition, MIT IDEAS Global Challenge Award Winner, Selected Program Participant, Founders' Skills Accelerator @ MIT Sloan, mem. of the Month, Engineering 4 Change, Invited Talk, CMU-UAEM Global Health Conf., Second Place, IEEE Pres.s' Change the World Competition, World Technology Network Award (Health and Medicine) 2010, Early Career Award, Penn State Mechanical Engineering Soc. 2015. *Publications include:* numerous papers in professional journals. *Leisure interests:* playing guitar, sketching, travelling, playing sports, mountaineering, dancing. *Telephone:* (617) 253-1000. *E-mail:* drz@mit.edu; drz@wicaresolutions.com (office). *Website:* www.wicaresolutions.com (office); web.mit.edu/drz/www/index.html.

ŽUŽUL, Miomir, PhD; Croatian politician, diplomatist and consultant; *Senior International Policy Advisor, Arnold & Porter Kaye Scholer LLP;* b. 1955, Split; m.; four c.; fmr Prof., Head of Dept on Developmental Psychology and Vice-Dean, Univ. of Zagreb; Nat. Security Advisor 1992–95; Special Envoy for peace talks apptd by Pres. of Croatia 1995–99, also served as head of Croatia's Cttee for Foreign Policy and Int. Relations; Visiting Prof., Woodrow Wilson School, Princeton Univ., USA 2000; fmr Amb. to USA; fmr mem. Parl.; Minister of Foreign Affairs 2003–05 (resgnd); has served as Pres. and Strategic Consultant to Four Corners Global

Consulting; fmr Dir European Business Devt, Livingston/Moffett Global Consultants; fmr Int. Affairs Advisor, Squire Patton Boggs, Washington, DC; Sr Int. Policy Advisor, Arnold & Porter Kaye Scholer LLP, Washington, DC 2018–; King Legacy Award for Outstanding Int. Service 2000. *Telephone:* (202) 942-6468 (office). *E-mail:* miomir.zuzul@arnoldporter.com (office). *Website:* www.arnoldporter.com (office).

ZVIZDIĆ, Denis, PhD; Bosnia and Herzegovina professor of architecture and politician; *Chairman of the Council of Ministers;* b. 9 June 1964, Sarajevo, Socialist Repub. of Bosnia and Herzegovina, Socialist Fed. Repub. of Yugoslavia; m.; one c.; ed Univ. of Sarajevo; fmr Prof. of Architecture, Univ. of Sarajevo; Premier, Sarajevo Canton 2003; fmr mem. Sarajevo Cantonal Ass., fmr Speaker; mem. Parl. of Fed. of Bosnia and Herzegovina 2010–14; Chair. Council of Ministers (Prime Minister) 2015–; mem. Stranka Demokratske Akcije (SDA—Party of Democratic Action) 1991–. *Address:* Office of the Chairman of the Council of Ministers, 71000 Sarajevo, trg Bosne i Hercegovine 1, Bosnia and Herzegovina (office). *Fax:* (33) 282613 (office). *E-mail:* kabinet@vm.gov.ba (office); predsjedatelj@vm.gov.ba (office). *Website:* predsjedavajuci.vijeceministara.gov.ba (office); www .vijeceministara.gov.ba (office).

ZVYAGINTSEV, Andrei; Russian actor, film director and screenwriter; b. 6 Feb. 1964, Moscow; ed Moscow State Inst. of Theatre Arts; actor, Epigone Theatre at Central House of Actors; Int. Venice Film Festival Golden Lion 2003. *Play:* A Month in the Country (actor). *Films include:* Reflection (actor), Genuine Threat (actor), Queen Margo (actor), The Return (dir) (Int. Venice Film Festival Best Debut Feature) 2003, The Banishment (dir) 2007, Elena (dir) 2011, Leviathan (Award for Best Screenplay, Cannes Film Festival 2014, Golden Globe Award for Best Foreign Language Film 2015) 2014. *Television:* episode of Chyornaya komnata, 'Obscure' (dir and producer) 2000. *Leisure interest:* swimming.

ZWAVELING, Albert, MD, PhD; Dutch professor of surgery (retd); b. 21 July 1927, Schoonebeek; s. of Jan H. Zwaveling and Engeline F. (née Hinnen) Zwaveling; m. 1st Susanna M. van Soest 1952 (died 1966); one s.; m. 2nd Anna M. F. Bloem 1969; two s.; ed State Univ. of Utrecht, University Hosp., Leiden; mil. doctor (rank of maj.) 1954–57; Gen. Practitioner in Indonesia 1957–58; surgical trainee, Leiden 1958–63; Fellow in Oncology, Univ. of Wis., USA 1963–64; Jr Consultant 1964–68; Assoc. Prof. of Surgical Oncology, Leiden Univ. 1968–72, Prof. of Surgery 1972; apptd Head, Dept of Surgery, Univ. Hosp., Leiden 1981; Chair. Concilium Chirurgicum Utrecht 1985, Medical Staff Univ. Hosp., Leiden 1986; mem. Royal Netherlands Acad. of Sciences 1979, Medical Adviser 1972–; Hon. mem. Dutch Soc. of Oncology 1986, Dutch Asscn of Surgery 1987, Dutch Asscn of Surgical Oncology 1991; Rotgans Medal of Nat. Cancer Inst. 1963, Zwanenberg Award 1969. *Publications:* Dutch Textbook of Oncology, Dutch Textbook of Surgery; 6 monographs on oncology, mainly cancer; more than 120 scientific papers. *Leisure interests:* collecting plastic art, gardening. *Address:* University Hospital, Leiden (office); Vlietpark 4, 2355 CT Hoogmade, Netherlands (home). *Telephone:* (71) 5018622 (home). *Fax:* (71) 5018622 (home). *E-mail:* a.zwaveling@inter.ne.net (home).

ZWICK, Edward, AB, MFA; American film director and producer; b. 8 Oct. 1952, Chicago, Ill.; m. Liberty Godshall; ed Harvard Univ.; Exec. Producer, The Bedford Falls Co. (film production co.). *Films include:* About Last Night 1986, Glory 1989, Leaving Normal 1992, Legends of the Fall 1994, Courage Under Fire 1996, The Siege 1998, The Last Samurai 2003, Blood Diamond 2006, Defiance 2008, Love and Other Drugs 2010, Pawn Sacrifice 2014. *Television includes:* thirtysomething (series) (exec. producer) 1987–91, Once and Again (writer and exec. producer) 1999–2002. *Address:* The Bedford Falls Company, 409 Santa Monica Blvd, Santa Monica, CA 90401, USA (office). *Telephone:* (310) 394-5022 (office).

ZWIRNER, David; American gallery owner and art dealer; *Director, David Zwirner Gallery;* b. 1974, Winnipeg, Canada; f. David Zwirner Gallery, Green Street, SoHo, New York City 1993 (relocated to Chelsea 2002); Co-founder and Partner (with Iwan Wirth), Zwirner & Wirth Gallery, New York City 2000–09; opened gallery in Mayfair, London 2012; mem. The Royal Art Lodge, Winnipeg. *Publications:* numerous catalogues and monographs. *Address:* David Zwirner Gallery, 525 West 19th Street, New York, NY 10011, USA (office). *Telephone:* (212) 727-2070 (office). *Fax:* (212) 727-2072 (office). *E-mail:* info@davidzwirner.com (office). *Website:* www.davidzwirner.com (office); www.zwirnerandwirth.com (office).

ZYAZIKOV, Murat Magometovich; Russian politician; b. 10 Sept. 1957, Osh, Kyrgyzstan; m.; three s.; ed Checheno-Ingush State Univ. (now Chechen State Univ.), KGB Acad.; worked in CP admin at local level 1980–81; served in army 1981–83; numerous positions in KGB 1984–92; Deputy Minister of Security for Ingushetiya 1992, Deputy Head of FSB Ingushetiya Office, then Head of Security Council 1992–96; Deputy Head of FSB Astrakhan Office, also mem. Comm. for Solution of Conflicts in Northern Caucasus 1996–2002; Deputy Presidential Envoy, South Russia Fed. Okrug Jan.–April 2002; elected Pres. Repub. of Ingushetiya 2002–05; apptd Pres. Repub. of Ingushetiya 2005–08 (resgnd); numerous civil and mil. awards and medals. *Address:* 366720 Ingushetiya, Magas, Dom Pravitelstva, Russia (office). *Telephone:* (8734) 55-11-55 (office). *Fax:* (8734) 55-11-55 (office). *E-mail:* murad@ingushetia.ru (office). *Website:* ingushetia.ru (office).

ŽYLIUS, Rimantas, MA; Lithuanian business executive and politician; b. 24 June 1973, Klaipėda; m.; ed Vilnius Univ.; Head of Travel Insurance Div., Preventa (insurance co.) 1994–96; Adviser to Prime Minister on Information Soc. Devt 1999–2000; Sr Adviser to Parl. Information Soc. Devt Cttee 2000–02; fmr Public and Research Sectors Man., Metasite (man. consultancy) 2002–03; Solution Architect, Hewlett-Packard 2003–09; Deputy Minister of the Economy 2009–11, Minister 2011–12; Man. Dir Norway Registers Devt 2013–18, mem. Bd 2018–; mem. Knowledge Economy Forum. *Address:* Norway Registers Development, Billingstadsletta 35, 1396 Billingstad, Norway (office). *E-mail:* rzy@nrd.no (office). *Website:* www.nrd.no (office).

ZYPRIES, Brigitte; German politician; b. 16 Nov. 1953, Kassel; in-service training, Giessen Land Court 1978–80; mem. academic staff, Univ. of Giessen 1980–1985; Deputy Head of Div., State Chancellery, Hessen 1985–88; mem. academic staff, Fed. Constitutional Court 1988–90; Head of Div., Lower Saxony State Chancellery 1991–95, Head of Dept 1995–97, State Ministry for Women, Labour and Social Affairs 1997–98; State Sec., Fed. Ministry of the Interior 1998–2002; Fed. Minister of Justice 2002–09; mem. Bundestag (parl.) for Darmstadt 2005–17; Parl. State Sec. for Aerospace Affairs 2017–18; Minister for Econ. Affairs and Energy 2017–18. *Address:* c/o Deutscher Bundestag, Platz der Republik 1, 11011 Berlin, Germany (office). *Website:* www.brigitte-zypries.de (office).

ZYUGANOV, Gennadii Andreyevich, DPhil; Russian politician; *Chairman, Central Committee, Kommunisticheskaya Partiya Rossiiskoi Federatsii (KPRF— Communist Party of the Russian Federation);* b. 26 June 1944, Mymrino, Khotynets Dist, Oryol Oblast, Russian SFSR, USSR; m. Nadezhda Zyuganova; ed Oryol Pedagogical Inst., Acad. of Social Sciences of Cen. CPSU Cttee; worked as secondary school teacher 1961–65; CP and trade union functionary 1967; First Sec., Regional Komsomol Cttee of Oryol 1971–74, Sec., Second Sec., Head of Propaganda Div. Oryol Oblast CPSU Cttee 1974–83; Instructor and Head of Propaganda Div. Cen. CPSU Cttee 1983–89; Deputy Head of Ideology Div., Cen. CPSU Cttee 1989–90; mem. Politburo, Sec., Cen. Cttee of CP of Russian Fed. 1990, Chair. Cen. Exec. Cttee CP of Russian Fed. 1993–; Co-Chair. Duma of Russian Nat. Sobor 1992–; Co-Chair. Political Council of the Front Natsionalnogo Spaseniya (Front of Nat. Salvation) 1992; Chair. Kommunisticheskaya Partiya Rossiiskoi Federatsii (KPRF—Communist Party of the Russian Fed.) 1993–; Chair. Soyuz Kommunisticheskikh Partii-Kommunisticheskaya Partiya Sovetskogo Soyuza (Union of Communist Parties-Communist Party of the Soviet Union) 2001–; mem. Gosudarstvennaya Duma (State Duma, Parl.) of Russia 1993–; KPRF presidential cand. 1996, 2000, 2008, 2012; mem. Parl. Ass. of the Council of Europe 1996–. *Publications:* Russia and the Contemporary World 1995, Russia, My Homeland (The Ideology of State Patriotism) 1997. *Address:* Kommunistechiskaya Partiya Rossiiskoi Federatsii (Communist Party of the Russian Federation), 127051 Moscow, per. M. Sukharevskii 3/1, Russia (office). *Telephone:* (495) 692-76-46 (office). *Fax:* (495) 692-68-54 (office). *E-mail:* inter@kprf.ru (office). *Website:* kprf .ru (office); www.zyuganov.kprf.ru.